CHILTON'S AUTO REPAIR MANUAL 1987-1991

Publisher	Kerry A. Freeman, S.A.E.
Editor-In-Chief	Dean F. Morgantini, S.A.E.
Managing Editor	David H. Lee, A.S.E., S.A.E.
Senior Editor	Richard J. Rivele, S.A.E.
Senior Editor	Nick D'Andrea
Senior Editor	Ron Webb
Project Manager	Peter M. Conti, Jr.
Project Manager	Ken Grabowski, A.S.E.
Project Manager	Richard T. Smith
Editorial Staff	Lawrence C. Braun, S.A.E., A.S.C.
	Robert E. Doughten
	Thomas G. Gaeta
	Jacques Gordon
	Michael Grady
	Martin J. Gunther
	Steven Horner
	Neil Leonard, A.S.E.
	Robert McAnally
	Steven Morgan
	James B. Steele
	Larry E. Stiles
	Jim Taylor
	Anthony Tortorici, A.S.E., S.A.E.
Manager of Manufacturing	John J. Cantwell
Production Manager	W. Calvin Settle, Jr., S.A.E.
Assistant Production Manager	Andrea M. Steiger
Mechanical Artist	Marsha Park Herman
Mechanical Artist	Lorraine Martinelli
Special Projects	Peter Kaprielyan

OFFICERS

President	Gary R. Ingersoll
Sr. Vice President, Book & Research	Ronald A. Hoxter

CHILTON BOOK COMPANY

ONE OF THE **ABC** PUBLISHING COMPANIES,
A PART OF **CAPITAL CITIES/ABC, INC.**

Manufactured in USA
© 1990 Chilton Book Company
Chilton Way Radnor, Pa. 19089
ISBN 0-8019-7903-X
ISSN 0069-3634

1234567890   9876543210

CAR MODELS

TABLE OF CONTENTS

Car Sections

Unit Repair Sections

HOW TO USE THIS MANUAL

This manual is arranged in two sections:

Car Section

Car sections are grouped by manufacturer and arranged in alphabetical order. The text and illustrations that comprise the service procedures in each Car Section are arranged in the following order of systems and components: Engine Electrical, Chassis Electrical, Engine Cooling, Fuel System, Emission Controls, Engine Mechanical, Engine Lubrication, Manual Transmission, Manual Transaxle, Clutch, Automatic Transmission, Automatic Transaxle, Transfer Case, Drive Axle, Steering, Brakes, Front Suspension and Rear Suspension.

Specification charts are always located at the front of each section. All illustrations are located as close as possible to the pertinent text. Procedures are for all models in the particular section unless specifically noted otherwise.

Unit Repair Section

The Unit Repair Section contains troubleshooting and overhaul procedures for the major components and systems of your car. This portion of the book is intended to be used in conjunction with the Car Sections.

Every major Unit Repair Section contains an Identification or Application chart to correlate the information contained in that section. The sections are usually arranged by brands, manufacturers or types of components rather than models of cars. All overhaul procedures in the Unit Repair Section begin with the component removed from the car. The reason for this division of material is an economic one. The steps involved in overhauling an engine are virtually the same for all engines. However, the operation of removing the engine from the car varies greatly from model to model. By combining where possible, and separating where necessary, we are able to publish the maximum amount of information.

Locating Information

The Table of Contents, at the front of the book, lists the beginning of each Car and Unit Repair Section in the manual.

To find where a particular Car Section is located in the book, you need only look in the Table of Contents. Once you have found the proper section, you may wish to find where specific procedures are located in that section. Turn to the Index at the front of the section. At the upper left-hand side is a listing of the main topics within the section and the page number they will be found on. Following the main topics is an alphabetical listing of all the procedures within the section and their page numbers.

Safety Notice

Proper service and repair procedures are vital to the safe, reliable operation of all motor vehicles, as well as the personal safety of those performing repairs. This manual outlines procedures for servicing and repairing vehicles using safe effective methods. The procedures contain many NOTES and CAUTIONS which should be followed along with standard safety procedures to eliminate the possibility of personal injury or improper service which could damage the vehicle or compromise its safety.

It is important to note that repair procedures and techniques, tools and parts for servicing motor vehicles, as well as the skill and experience of the individual performing the work vary widely. It is not possible to anticipate all of the conceivable ways or conditions under which vehicles may be serviced, or to provide cautions as to all of the possible hazards that may result. Standard and accepted safety precautions and equipment should be used when handling toxic or flammable fluids, and safety goggles or other protection should be used during cutting, grinding, chiseling, prying, or any other process that can cause material removal or projectiles.

Some procedures require the use of tools specially designed for a specific purpose. Before substituting another tool or procedure, you must be completely satisfied that neither your personal safety, nor the performance of the vehicle will be endangered.

Part Numbers

Part numbers listed in this book are not recommendations by Chilton for any product by brand name. They are references that can be used with interchange manuals and aftermarket supplier catalogs to locate each brand supplier's discrete part number.

Although information in this manual is based on industry sources and is as complete as possible at the time of publication, the possibility exists that some car manufacturers made later changes which could not be included here. Information on very late models may not be available in some circumstances. While striving for total accuracy, Chilton Book Company cannot assume responsibility for any errors, changes, or omissions that may occur in the compilation of this data.

Copyright Notice

AMC
Eagle

SPECIFICATIONS

VEHICLE IDENTIFICATION CHART

It is important for servicing and ordering parts to be certain of the vehicle and engine identification. The VIN (vehicle identification number) is a 17 digit number visible through the windshield on the driver's side of the dash and contains the vehicle and engine identification codes. The tenth digit indicates model year and the fourth digit indicates engine code. It can be interpreted as follows:

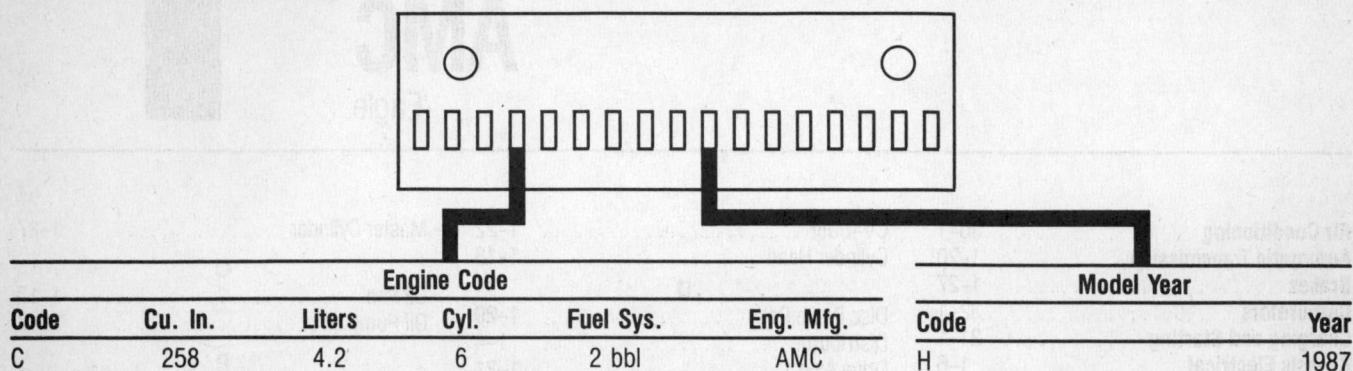

Engine Code						Model Year	
Code	Cu. In.	Liters	Cyl.	Fuel Sys.	Eng. Mfg.	Code	Year
C	258	4.2	6	2 bbl	AMC	H	1987

ENGINE IDENTIFICATION

Year	Model	Engine Displacement cu. in. (liter)	Engine Series Identification (VIN)	No. of Cylinders	Engine Type
1987	Eagle	6-258 (4.2)	C	6	OHV

GENERAL ENGINE SPECIFICATIONS

Year	VIN	No. Cylinder Displacement cu. in. (liter)	Fuel System Type	Net Horsepower @ rpm	Net Torque @ rpm (ft. lbs.)	Bore × Stroke (in.)	Compression Ratio	Oil Pressure @ rpm
1987	C	6-258 (4.2)	2 bbl	110 @ 3200	210 @ 1800	3.75 × 3.900	9.2:1	46 @ 2000

TUNE-UP SPECIFICATIONS

Year	VIN	No. Cylinder Displacement cu. in. (liter)	Spark Plugs Type	Gap (in.)	Ignition Timing (deg.) MT	AT	Compression Pressure (psi)	Fuel Pump (psi)	Idle Speed (rpm) MT	AT	Valve Clearance In.	Ex.
1987	C	6-258 (4.2)	RFN14LY	0.035	9B ①	9B ①	120–150	5–6½	900	800	Hyd.	Hyd.

① California—11B

FIRING ORDERS

NOTE: To avoid confusion, always replace spark plugs and wires one at a time.

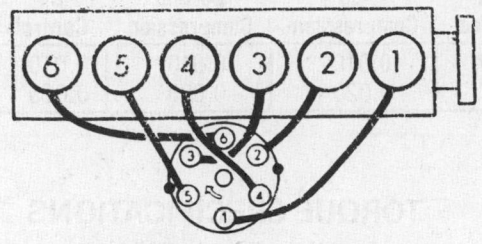

4.2L Engine
Engine Firing Order: 1-5-3-6-2-4
Distributor Rotation: Clockwise

CAPACITIES

Year	Model	VIN	No. Cylinder Displacement cu. in. (liter)	Engine Crankcase with Filter	Engine Crankcase without Filter	Transmission (pts.) 4-Spd	Transmission (pts.) 5-Spd	Transmission (pts.) Auto.	Drive Axle (pts.)	Fuel Tank (gal.)	Coolig System (qts.)
1987	Eagle	C	6-258 (4.2)	5.0	4.0	3.5	4.0	17	3 ①	22	14

① Front axle—2.5

CAMSHAFT SPECIFICATIONS

All measurements given in inches.

Year	VIN	No. Cylinder Displacement cu. in. (liter)	Journal Diameter 1	Journal Diameter 2	Journal Diameter 3	Journal Diameter 4	Journal Diameter 5	Lobe Lift In.	Lobe Lift Ex.	Bearing Clearance	Camshaft End Play
1987	C	6-258 (4.2)	2.0290–2.0300	2.0190–2.0200	2.0090–2.0100	1.9990–2.0000	—	0.248	0.248	0.001–0.003	0

CRANKSHAFT AND CONNECTING ROD SPECIFICATIONS

All measurements are given in inches.

Year	VIN	No. Cylinder Displacement cu. in. (liter)	Crankshaft Main Brg. Journal Dia.	Crankshaft Main Brg. Oil Clearance	Crankshaft Shaft End-play	Crankshaft Thrust on No.	Connecting Rod Journal Diameter	Connecting Rod Oil Clearance	Connecting Rod Side Clearance
1987	C	6-258 (4.2)	2.4996–2.5001	0.0010–0.0025	0.0015–0.0065	3	2.0934–2.0955	0.0010–0.0030	0.005–0.014

VALVE SPECIFICATIONS

Year	VIN	No. Cylinder Displacement cu. in. (liter)	Seat Angle (deg.)	Face Angle (deg.)	Spring Test Pressure (lbs.)	Spring Installed Height (in.)	Stem-to-Guide Clearance (in.) Intake	Stem-to-Guide Clearance (in.) Exhaust	Stem Diameter (in.) Intake	Stem Diameter (in.) Exhaust
1987	C	6-258 (4.2)	44.5	44	195 @ 1.411	1$\frac{13}{16}$	0.0010–0.0030	0.0010–0.0030	0.3720	0.3720

PISTON AND RING SPECIFICATIONS
All measurements are given in inches.

Year	VIN	No. Cylinder Displacement cu. in. (liter)	Piston Clearance	Ring Gap			Ring Side Clearance		
				Top Compression	Bottom Compression	Oil Control	Top Compression	Bottom Compression	Oil Control
1987	C	6-258 (4.2)	0.0009–0.0017	0.010–0.020	0.010–0.020	0.010–0.025	0.0017–0.0032	0.0017–0.0032	0.0010–0.0080

TORQUE SPECIFICATIONS
All readings in ft. lbs.

Year	VIN	No. Cylinder Displacement cu. in. (liter)	Cylinder Head Bolts	Main Bearing Bolts	Rod Bearing Bolts	Crankshaft Pulley Bolts	Flywheel Bolts	Manifold		Spark Plugs
								Intake	Exhaust	
1987	C	6-258 (4.2)	80–90	75–85	30–35	70–90	95–115	18–28	18–28	7–15

BRAKE SPECIFICATIONS
All measurements in inches unless noted.

Year	Model	Lug Nut Torque (ft. lbs.)	Master Cylinder Bore	Brake Disc		Standard Brake Drum Diameter	Minimum Lining Thickness	
				Minimum Thickness	Maximum Runout		Front	Rear
1987	Eagle	60–90	0.940	0.810	0.003	10.000	$1/32$	$1/32$

WHEEL ALIGNMENT

Year	Model	Caster		Camber		Toe-in (in.)	Steering Axis Inclination (deg.)
		Range (deg.)	Preferred Setting (deg.)	Range (deg.)	Preferred Setting (deg.)		
1987	Eagle	2P–3P	$2 1/2$P	$1/8$N–$5/8$P	$1/4$P	$1/16$–$3/16$ ②	$11 1/2$ ①

P Positive
N Negative
① Left—$3/4$P–$1/8$P; Right—$1/8$P
② Toe-out

ENGINE ELECTRICAL

NOTE: Disconnecting the negative battery cable on some vehicles may interfere with the functions of the on board computer systems and may require the computer to undergo a relearning process, once the negative battery cable is reconnected.

Distributor

REMOVAL

1. Disconnect the negative battery cable. Remove the distributor cap with the wires attached.
2. Matchmark the position of the rotor tip to the distributor housing and engine.
3. Disconnect and label the distributor wiring and vacuum hose(s).
4. Remove the distributor hold-down bolt and pull the distributor up out of the engine. Note the position of the rotor in relation to the engine as the rotor stops rotating.

INSTALLATION

Timing Not Disturbed

1. Install the distributor with the rotor pointing to the matchmark on the engine.
2. Rotate the housing and align the rotor-to-housing matchmark.

3. Install the distributor cap, hold-down clamp and nut. Tighten the nut hand tight.

4. Connect the distributor wiring and negative battery cable. Run the engine and adjust the ignition timing.

5. With the timing correct, tighten the hold-down nut and recheck the timing.

Timing Disturbed

1. Remove the spark plug from the No. 1 cylinder and position a compression gauge or a thumb over the spark plug hole.

2. Slowly crank the engine until compression pressure starts to build up.

3. Continue cranking the engine so the timing mark or pointer aligns with the TDC mark.

4. Install the distributor with its drive meshed, so the rotor points to the No. 1 terminal on the distributor cap with No. 1 cylinder piston at TDC.

5. Complete installation in the reverse order of removal and adjust the timing as required.

NOTE: Some engines may be sensitive to the routing of the distributor sensor wires. If routed near the high-voltage coil wire or spark plug wires, the electromagnetic field surrounding the high-voltage wires could generate an occasional disruption of the ignition system operation.

Ignition Timing

ADJUSTMENT

A scale is located on the timing chain cover and a notch milled into the vibration damper are used as references to set ignition timing. Do not use the timing probe socket as a reference point to check the ignition timing

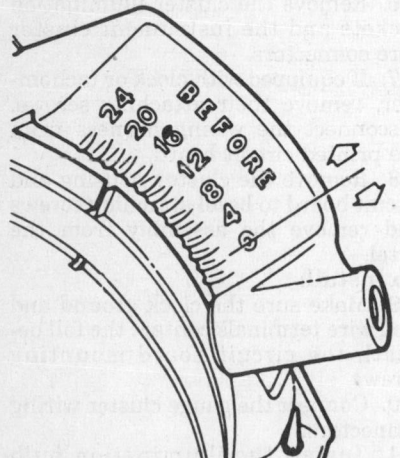

View of the ignition timing marks

when using a conventional timing light.

1. Operate the engine until normal operating temperatures are reached.

2. Disconnect the 3 wire connector from the vacuum input switch.

3. Disconnect and plug the distributor vacuum advance hose.

4. Attach a timing light according to the manufacturer's instructions. If the timing light has 3 wires, attach the pickup connector to the No. 1 spark plug with an adapter, the red lead to the positive battery terminal and the black lead to the negative battery terminal. Connect a tachometer lead to the negative terminal of the ignition coil.

5. Start the engine and increase the speed to 1600 rpm while observing the initial timing with the timing light.

6. If necessary, adjust the ignition timing to specifications.

NOTE: If the specifications listed in the charts differ from the specifications on the emission control label, use the specifications as listed on the label.

7. Remove the timing light and the tachometer from the engine wiring.

Alternator

For further information on the charging system, please refer to "Charging and Starting" in the Unit Repair section.

PRECAUTIONS

Several precautions must be observed with alternator equipped vehicles to avoid damage to the unit.

• If the battery is removed for any reason, make sure it is reconnected

with the correct polarity. Reversing the battery connections may result in damage to the one-way rectifiers.

• When utilizing a booster battery as a starting aid, always connect the positive to positive terminals and the negative terminal from the booster battery to a good engine ground on the vehicle being started.

• Never use a fast charger as a booster to start vehicles.

• Disconnect the battery cables when charging the battery with a fast charger.

• Never attempt to polarize the alternator.

• Do not use test lamps of more than 12 volts when checking diode continuity.

• Do not short across or ground any of the alternator terminals.

• The polarity of the battery, alternator and regulator must be matched and considered before making any electrical connections within the system.

• Never separate the alternator on an open circuit. Make sure all connections within the circuit are clean and tight.

• Disconnect the battery ground terminal when performing any service on electrical components.

• Disconnect the battery if arc welding is to be done on the vehicle.

BELT TENSION ADJUSTMENT

The serpentine drive belts are tensioned to a specific rating with the use of an appropriate belt tension gauge, placed on the belt midway between the pulleys. Install the gauge on the longest belt span possible. If the belt is notched on the inner surface, place the middle finger of the tensioner into 1 of

DRIVE BELT ADJUSTMENT TENSIONS

	New Belt		Used Belt	
	Ft. Lbs.	Newtons	Ft. Lbs.	Newtons
Serpentine Drive Belt	180–200	800–890	140–160	616–704
Alternator Drive Belt	125–155	556–689	90–115	400–512
Air Conditioning Compressor Belt	125–155	556–689	90–115	400–512
Air Pump Belt	125–155 ①	556–689 ①	90–115 ①	400–512 ①
	65–75 ②	289–334 ②	60–70 ②	267–311 ②
Power Steering Belt	125–155	556–689	90–115	400–512

① Without power steering
② With power steering

the notches. Correct belt tension is 140–160 lbs.

REMOVAL & INSTALLATION

1. Disconnect the negative battery cable.
2. Disconnect the terminal wire connector and output wire from the rear of the alternator.
3. Loosen the alternator adjustment and mounting bolts. Remove the drive belt.
4. Remove the mounting and adjustment bolts and the alternator.
5. To install, reverse the removal procedures.
6. Adjust the belt tension to specification.

Voltage Regulator

For further information on the charging system, please refer to "Charging and Starting" in the Unit Repair section.

Starter

For further information on the charging system, please refer to "Charging and Starting" in the Unit Repair section.

REMOVAL & INSTALLATION

1. Disconnect the negative battery cable.
2. Raise and safely support the vehicle.
3. Disconnect the starter motor wiring.
4. Remove the starter motor mounting bolts and remove the starter. Retain any shims which may have been used to align it with the ring gear.
To install:
5. Install the starter with any shims and tighten the mounting bolts to 18 ft. lbs.
6. Connect the starter motor wiring and lower the vehicle.
7. Connect the negative battery cable and check the starter motor operation.

CHASSIS ELECTRICAL

Heater Blower Motor

REMOVAL & INSTALLATION

1. Disconnect the negative battery cable.

2. Disconnect the wiring from the blower motor.
3. Remove the blower motor and fan assembly bolts or nuts. Remove the blower motor and fan assembly from the housing.
4. Squeeze and remove the blower fan retainer clip and slide the blower hub from the motor shaft; this will give access to the nuts attaching the motor to the mounting plate.
5. Remove the motor-to-mounting plate bolts and the motor.

To install:
6. Install the blower motor onto the mounting plate. Install the fan onto the motor shaft. Position the fan so a 0.350 in. clearance exists between the mounting plate and the end of the blower fan.
7. Position the ears of the spring clip retainer over the flat surface of the motor shaft; the edge of the clip must be flush with the edge of the fan hub.
8. Install the blower motor into the housing and the bolts or nuts.
9. Connect the negative battery cable and the wiring to the motor. Check operation of the motor and fan assembly.

Windshield Wiper Motor

REMOVAL & INSTALLATION

1. Disconnect the negative battery cable.
2. Remove the wiper arms and blades.
3. Remove the attaching screws, the wiring connector and pull the motor and linkage out of the dash panel opening.
4. Raise up the lock tab of the drive link-to-crank stud retaining clip and slide the clip from the stud.
5. Remove the wiper motor assembly.

To install:
6. Position the wiper motor and insert the crank stud into the drive link bushing.
7. Install the retaining clip onto the stud and slide it into position. Check for positive retention of the retaining clip on the crank stud.
8. Torque the wiper motor screws to 25 inch lbs. (3 Nm).
9. Connect the negative battery cable and operate the motor through several cycles and stop it in the park position.
10. Install the wiper arms and blades.

Windshield Wiper Switch

REMOVAL & INSTALLATION

1. Disconnect the negative battery cable.
2. Remove the control knob. A flat blade tool can be used to overcome the spring tension which holds the knob in place.
3. Separate switch from instrument panel and the wiring harness. Remove the switch.
To install:
4. Connect the switch to the wiring harness.
5. Install the switch into the instrument panel and tighten the nut.
6. Align the switch knob and push it onto the shaft.
7. Connect the negative battery cable.

Instrument Cluster

REMOVAL & INSTALLATION

1. Disconnect the negative battery cable.
2. Using a shop cloth, cover the steering column. Remove the lower steering column cover.
3. Remove the bezel retaining screws across top, over radio and behind the glove box door. Disconnect the glove box wire, if equipped. Tip bezel outward at top and disengage bottom tabs.
4. Disconnect the speedometer cable and push down on the 3 illumination lamp housings above the bezel to clear the instrument panel.
5. Disconnect the headlight switch, the wiper control connectors and the switch lamp. The headlight switch is disconnected by lifting the 2 locking tabs to disconnect its electrical connector.
6. Remove the cluster illumination sockets and the instrument cluster wire connectors.
7. If equipped with clock or tachometer, remove their attaching screws. Disconnect the wiring harness from the printed circuit board.
8. Remove the cluster housing and circuit board to bezel attaching screws and remove the assembly from the bezel.
To install:
9. Make sure the clock ground and feed wire terminals contact the foil beneath the circuit board mounting screws.
10. Connect the gauge cluster wiring connectors.
11. Install the illumination bulb sockets.

12. Connect the headlight and wiper switch wiring connectors and install the bulbs.

13. Align the bezel bottom tabs with the opening and tip it upward; it may be necessary to push the illumination bulb housing downward for clearance. Do not push the bezel into final position.

14. Connect the speedometer cable and the glove box lamp wire.

15. Push the bezel into position and install the retaining screws.

16. Install the lower steering column cover and connect the negative battery cable.

Speedometer

REMOVAL & INSTALLATION

1. Disconnect the negative battery cable.

2. Remove the instrument cluster.

3. Remove the cluster housing and the printed circuit board, exposing the speedometer and the gauges, mounted to the cluster case.

4. Remove the speedometer and/or gauges.

To install:

5. Install the speedometer and/or gauges.

6. Install the printed circuit board and the cluster housing.

7. Install the instrument cluster.

8. Connect the negative battery cable.

Radio

REMOVAL & INSTALLATION

1. Disconnect the negative battery cable. Remove the radio knobs and unfasten the control shafts retaining nuts.

2. Remove the bezel-to-dash screws and the bezel.

3. Loosen but do not remove the upper radio securing screw.

4. Raise the rear of the radio to separate its bracket from the upper securing screw.

5. Pull the radio forward, slightly, and disconnect all of the leads from it. Remove the radio.

6. To install, reverse the removal procedures. Adjust the antenna trimmer, if necessary.

Headlight Switch

REMOVAL & INSTALLATION

1. Disconnect the negative battery cable.

2. Relocate anything preventing full access to switch such as instrument cluster bezel, package tray, speedometer cable or switch overlay assembly.

3. Remove screws and tilt cluster assembly away from instrument panel.

4. Place switch in full **ON** position. Pull on knob and press shaft release button to release shaft and knob assembly.

5. Remove mounting sleeve nut, wiring connector, ground wire and the switch.

To install:

NOTE: When installing the headlight switch, position it properly before tightening

6. Install the switch into the instrument cluster assembly.

7. Connect the ground wire and the wiring connector.

8. Install the mounting sleeve nut and tighten.

9. Install the switch shaft and knob assembly.

10. Install the instrument cluster assembly.

11. Connect the speedometer cable and install the package tray, if equipped.

12. Connect the negative battery cable.

Dimmer Switch

REMOVAL & INSTALLATION

1. Disconnect the negative battery cable.

2. Remove the lower finish panel, tube cover and the package tray, if equipped.

3. Remove the wiring connector from the switch.

4. Tape the actuator rod to the column, remove the switch retaining screws and remove the switch by pulling it from the actuator rod.

To install:

5. Position the switch by pushing in onto the actuator rod and install the retaining screws.

6. Remove the tape holding the actuator rod to the column.

7. Adjust the switch by depressing it slightly and inserting a $\frac{3}{32}$ inch drill bit into the hole on the outer face of the switch; this prevents horizontal switch movement.

8. Move the switch towards the steering wheel to remove the lash from the actuator rod.

9. Torque the switch retaining screws to 35 inch lbs. (4 Nm).

10. Remove the drill bit and install the wiring connector.

11. Check the operation of the switch.

12. Install the finish panel, the tube cover and the package tray, if equipped.

13. Connect the negative battery cable.

Turn Signal Switch

REMOVAL & INSTALLATION

1. Disconnect the negative battery cable. If equipped with a tilt steering column, place the wheel in the straight ahead position. Remove the steering wheel.

2. Loosen the anti-theft cover attaching screws and remove the cover from the column.

NOTE: Do not hammer on the shaft. Do not move the screws from the cover; they are attached to it with plastic retainers.

3. Using a special compressor, depress the lockplate and pry the snapring from the steering shaft groove. Remove the tool, snapring, plate, turn signal cancelling cam, upper bearing preload spring and thrust washer from the shaft.

4. Place turn signal lever in right turn position and remove the lever.

5. Depress hazard warning light switch and remove button by turning counterclockwise.

6. Remove wire harness connector block. On column shift automatic transmission vehicles, use a stiff wire to depress the lock tab holding the shift quadrant light wire in the connector block.

7. To remove the harness from the steering column, perform the following procedures:

   a. Remove the steering tube cover.

   b. Remove the steering column bracket bolts and just loosen the column bracket nuts.

   c. Fold the wire harness connector over the harness and wrap it with tape to prevent snagging when it is removed.

8. Remove switch screws and pull the switch, with the wiring harness, from the column; if necessary, lift the column when pulling the switch and harness out. If equipped with a tilt column, remove the plastic harness protector when raising the column.

To install:

9. Install the turn signal switch and the wiring harness into the steering column.

NOTE: To install the wiring harness connector, fold the connector against the harness and feed it through the housing and shroud.

10. If equipped with a tilt column, in-

stall the plastic harness protector when lowering the column.

11. Align the turn signal switch in the housing, install the screws and torque to 35 inch lbs. (4 Nm).

12. If equipped with cruise control, install the lever and switch assembly.

13. Install the thrust washer, the upper bearing preload spring and cancelling cam onto the steering shaft.

14. Position the turn signal into the neutral position and install the hazard waring switch knob.

15. Using the compressor tool, install the depress the lockplate onto the steering shaft. Install the snapring and remove the compressor; be sure the snapring is fully seated.

16. Install the lockplate cover. If the column bolts have been loosened, torque the bracket bolts to 20 ft. lbs. (27 Nm) and the toe plate bolts to 10 ft. lbs. (14 Nm).

17. Align the matchmarks and install the steering wheel; torque the nut to 30 ft. lbs. (41 Nm).

18. To complete the installation, reverse the removal procedures. Connect the negative battery cable.

Ignition Lock

REMOVAL & INSTALLATION

1. Disconnect the negative battery cable. If equipped with a tilt steering column, place the wheel in the straight ahead position. Remove the steering wheel.

2. Loosen the anti-theft cover screws and remove the cover from the column.

NOTE: Do not hammer on the shaft. Do not move the screws from the cover; they are attached to it with plastic retainers.

3. Using a special compressor, depress the lockplate and pry the snapring from the groove in the steering shaft. Remove the tool, snapring, plate, turn signal cam, upper bearing preload spring and thrust washer from the shaft.

4. Place the turn signal lever in the right turn position and remove it.

5. Depress the hazard warning switch button and remove it by rotating it counterclockwise. Remove the package tray, if equipped, and the lower trim panel.

NOTE: In the next steps, provision is made for pulling the direction signal switch wiring harness entirely out of the steering column to replace the lock cylinder. Many times, this is not necessary. Follow the first part of the procedure in Step 7, pulling the wiring

upward using normal slack, in order to get the turn signal switch far enough away from the lock cylinder for clearance.

6. Disconnect the wire harness connector block from its mounting bracket, located on the right side of the lower column. Remove the steering column bracket bolts. Remove the turn signal switch wiring harness protector from the bottom of the column.

NOTE: To aid in the removal and replacement of the directional switch harness, tape the harness connector to the wire harness to prevent snagging when removing the wiring harness assembly through the steering column.

7. Remove the switch screws. Withdraw the switch and wire harness from the column.

8. Insert the key into the lock cylinder and turn to the **ON** position. Remove the warning buzzer switch and the contacts as an assembly using needle-nose pliers. Take care not to let the contacts fall into the column.

9. Turn the key to the **LOCK** position and compress the lock cylinder retaining tab. Remove the lock cylinder. If the tab is not visible through the slot, knock the casting flash out of the slot.

To install:

10. Hold the lock cylinder sleeve and turn the lock cylinder counterclockwise until it contacts the stop.

11. Align the lock cylinder key with the keyway in the housing and slip the cylinder into the housing.

12. Lightly depress the cylinder against the sector, while turning it counterclockwise, until the cylinder and sector are engaged.

13. Depress the cylinder until the retaining tab engages and the lock cylinder is secured.

14. Install the turn signal switch. Be sure the actuating lever pivot is properly seated and aligned in the top of the housing boss, before installing it with its screws.

15. Install the turn signal lever and check the operation of the switch.

16. Install the thrust washer, spring and turn signal cancelling cam on the steering shaft.

17. Align the lockplate and steering shaft splines and position the lockplate so the turn signal camshaft protrudes from the dogleg opening in the lockplate.

18. Using snapring pliers, install the snapring onto the steering shaft.

19. Secure the anti-theft cover with its screws.

20. Install the button on the hazard

warning switch. Install the steering wheel.

Ignition Switch

REMOVAL & INSTALLATION

The ignition switch is mounted on the lower steering column and is connected to the key lock by a remote lock rod.

1. Disconnect the negative battery cable.

2. With key in **OFF-LOCK** position, remove mounting screws, rod and wiring.

3. When installing, move slider to extreme left of switch pointing inward toward steering column. Put actuator rod in slider hole and install switch.

4. On tilt wheel columns, remove lash by pushing downward on switch before tightening the screws.

Stoplight Switch

ADJUSTMENT

1. Disconnect the negative battery cable.

2. Remove the package tray, if equipped.

3. Disconnect the electrical connector from the switch.

4. Loosen the locknut of the switch assembly and back off the switch.

5. Screw the switch in until it contacts the brake pedal stopper.

6. Depress the brake pedal several times to eliminate the vacuum in the power brake booster, then, depress the pedal by hand and observe the amount of pedal free-play. Free-play should be ½ in.

7. After adjustment, secure the switch by tightening locknut.

8. Connect the electrical wires to the switch. Connect the negative battery cable and check the operation of the brake lights.

REMOVAL & INSTALLATION

1. Disconnect the negative battery cable.

2. Remove the package tray, if equipped.

3. Disconnect the electrical connector from the switch.

4. Remove the locknut from the switch assembly and remove the switch.

To install:

5. Install the new switch in the mounting bracket until it contacts the brake pedal stopper.

6. Depress the brake pedal several times to eliminate the vacuum in the

power brake booster, then, depress the pedal by hand and observe the amount of pedal free-play. Free-play should be ½ in.

7. After adjustment, secure the switch by tightening locknut.

8. Connect the electrical wires to the switch. Connect the negative battery cable and check the operation of the brake lights.

Neutral Safety Switch

REMOVAL & INSTALLATION

1. Disconnect the negative battery cable.

2. Raise and safely support the vehicle.

3. Remove the 3 wire connector from the switch, located on the left side of the transmission.

4. Unscrew the switch from the case. Transmission fluid will drain from the case with the switch out.

5. Install the new switch and switch seal in the transmission case and torque to 24 ft. lbs.

6. Reconnect the 3 wire electrical connector.

7. Lower vehicle, test switch and correct the transmission fluid level.

Fuses, Circuit Breakers and Relays

LOCATION

Fuse Panel

The fuse panel is located under the left side of the instrument panel, adjacent to the parking brake mechanism.

Circuit Breakers

Circuit breakers are an integral part of the headlight switch and the wiper switch, as well as the air conditioning circuit. They are used to protect each circuit from an overload.

Circuit breakers for the power windows, power seats, door locks and rear wiper/washer are located on the fuse panel.

NOTE: When replacing a protective electrical relay, be very sure to install the same type of relay. Verify that the schematic imprinted on the original and replacement relays are identical. Do not rely on the relay part numbers for identification. Instead, use the schematic imprinted on the relay for positive identification.

Fusible Links

Fusible links are used to prevent ma-

jor wire harness damage in the event of a short circuit or an overload condition in the wiring circuits which are normally not fused, due to carrying high amperage loads or because of their locations within the wiring harness. Each fusible link is of a fixed value for a specific electrical load and should a link fail, the cause of the failure must be determined and repaired prior to installing a new fusible link of the same value.

Headlight circuit—Located at battery terminal of starter solenoid-to-main wiring harness.

Horn circuit—Located at battery terminal of horn relay-to-main wiring harness.

Ignition circuit—Located at battery terminal of starter solenoid-to-main wiring harness.

Alternator circuit—Located at alternator-to-battery terminal of starter solenoid.

Power option circuit—Located at battery terminal of starter solenoid-to-main wiring harness.

Computer

LOCATION

The Microcomputer Control Unit (MCU) is located behind the right-side kick panel in the passenger compartment.

Flashers

LOCATION

Turn Signal Flasher

The turn signal flasher, is located on the instrument panel behind the headlight switch.

Hazard Warning Flasher

The hazard warning flasher is plugged into the fuse panel.

Cruise Control

ADJUSTMENT

The cruise control regulator is mounted on a bracket which is located behind the headlight switch.

Centering

The centering adjustment screw on the regulator is used to balance the speed control to a specific road speed.

1. If the speed control engages at 2 or more mph than the selected speed, turn the centering adjusting screw counterclockwise a small amount.

2. If the speed control engages at 2 or less mph than the selected speed,

1. Centering adjustment
2. Low speed adjustment
3. Sensitivity adjustment

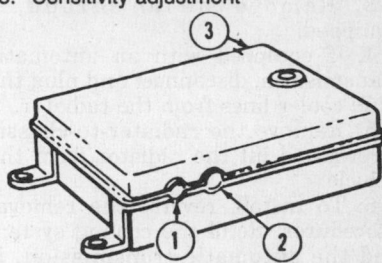

View of the cruise control regulator

turn the centering adjusting screw clockwise a small amount.

3. Check the adjustment on a level road.

Regulator

The regulator is a potentiometer which is a very delicate instrument and is preset by the manufacturer. If the other components of the system are functioning normally and the cruise control is inoperative, perform the following procedures:

1. Carefully, insert a screwdriver into the regulator slots and turn the screws.

NOTE: The screws have a maximum turning angle of ¾ turn.

2. Turn the sensitivity adjustment fully clockwise.

3. Turn the low speed and centering adjustment screws to the 10 o'clock position.

4. If the adjustments have no effect on the cruise control, replace the regulator.

Vacuum Dump Valve

1. Depress the brake pedal.

2. Force the dump valve, as far as possible, toward the brake pedal bracket.

3. Release the brake pedal.

ENGINE COOLING

Radiator

REMOVAL & INSTALLATION

1. Disconnect the negative battery cable and remove the radiator cap; be sure the engine is cold.

2. Drain the cooling system. Remove the upper/lower radiator hoses

and the coolant recovery hose, if equipped.

3. Remove the fan shroud, if equipped.

4. If equipped with an automatic transmission, disconnect and plug the fluid cooler lines from the radiator.

5. Remove the radiator-to-chassis screws and lift the radiator from the vehicle.

6. To install, reverse the removal procedures. Refill the cooling system and the automatic transmission, if equipped.

7. Connect the negative battery cable. Start the engine, allow it to reach normal operating temperatures and check for leaks.

Heater Core

REMOVAL & INSTALLATION

Without Air Conditioning

1. Disconnect the negative battery cable.

2. Drain the radiator.

3. Disconnect the heater hoses from the heater core tubes and plug the tubes to prevent coolant from draining during removal.

4. Disconnect the blower motor wires. Remove the blower motor and fan assembly.

5. Remove the housing nuts in the engine compartment near the blower motor position.

6. Remove the package tray, if equipped.

7. Disconnect the wiring connector from the blower motor resistor.

8. Snap the wiring harness cover open on the right side of the plenum chamber and remove the harness.

NOTE: Tape the harness to the plenum chamber.

9. Disconnect the heater, defroster and blend-air door cables at the housing.

10. Remove the right door sill plate and the right cowl trim kick panel.

11. Remove the right windshield pillar moulding, the instrument panel upper screws and the instrument panel-to-right door hinge post screw.

12. Remove the housing screws.

13. Pull the right side of the instrument panel slightly rearward and remove the housing.

14. Remove the cover, the heater core-to-housing screws and the heater core from the housing.

To install:

15. Install the heater core, the screws and the cover.

16. Install the housing and the screws. Ensure the heater core seals are properly installed to prevent air leakage around the perimeter of the heater core.

17. Install the instrument panel-to-right door hinge post screw, the instrument panel upper screws and the right windshield piller moulding.

18. Install the right cowl trim kick panel and sill plate.

19. Connect and adjust the control cables.

20. On the right side of the plenum, connect the wiring harness and install the wiring harness cover.

21. Connect the wiring connector to the blower motor resistor. Install the package tray, if equipped.

22. Install the housing nuts in the engine compartment near the blower motor position.

23. Install the blower motor and fan assembly. Connect the blower motor wires.

24. Connect the heater hoses to the heater core tubes.

25. Refill the cooling system and connect the negative battery cable.

26. Start the engine, allow it to reach normal operating temperatures and check for leaks. Bleed the cooling system.

With Air Conditioning

1. Disconnect the negative battery cable and drain the cooling system.

2. Disconnect heater hoses and plug hoses, cover fittings.

3. Disconnect blower wires and remove motor and fan assembly.

4. Remove the housing attaching nut from the stud in the engine compartment.

5. Remove package shelf, if equipped.

6. Disconnect wire at resistor, located below glove box.

7. Remove instrument panel center bezel, air outlet and duct.

8. Disconnect air and defroster cables from damper levers.

9. Remove right-side windshield pillar molding, the instrument panel upper sheet metal screws and the capscrew at the right door post.

10. Remove the right cowl trim panel and door sill plate.

11. Remove right kick panel and heater housing attaching screws.

12. Pull right side of instrument panel outward slightly and remove housing.

13. Remove core, defroster and blower housing.

14. Remove core from housing.

To install:

15. Install the heater core, the screws and the cover.

16. Install the housing and the screws. Ensure the heater core seals are properly installed to prevent air leakage around the perimeter of the heater core.

17. Install the instrument panel-to-right door hinge post screw, the instrument panel upper screws and the right windshield piller moulding.

18. Install the right cowl trim kick panel and sill plate.

19. Connect and adjust the control cables.

20. On the right side of the plenum, connect the wiring harness and install the wiring harness cover.

21. Connect the wiring connector to the blower motor resistor. Install the package tray, if equipped.

22. Install the housing nuts in the engine compartment near the blower motor position.

23. Install the blower motor and fan assembly. Connect the blower motor wires.

24. Connect the heater hoses to the heater core tubes.

25. Refill the cooling system and connect the negative battery cable.

26. Start the engine, allow it to reach normal operating temperatures and check for leaks. Bleed the cooling system.

Water Pump

REMOVAL & INSTALLATION

1. Disconnect the negative battery cable. Drain the cooling system.

2. Loosen the adjustment bolts from the alternator and the power steering pump, if equipped. Remove the drive belts.

3. Unfasten the fan ring. Remove the fan and pump pulley assembly. Withdraw the fan ring or shroud.

4. Remove the hoses at the pump.

5. Remove the water pump mounting bolts and withdraw the pump.

NOTE: Engines built for sale in California having a single, serpentine drive belt and viscous fan drive, have a reverse rotating pump and drive. These components are identified by the word REVERSE stamped on the drive cover and inner side of the fan and REV cast into the water pump body. Never interchange standard rotating parts with these.

To install:

6. Using a new gasket, install the water pump and torque the bolts to 13 ft. lbs.

7. Bleed the radiator by running the engine and opening the heater control valve. Run the engine long enough so the thermostat opens. Check the coolant level.

8. Torque the fan bolts to 18 ft. lbs. Adjust the drive belt(s).

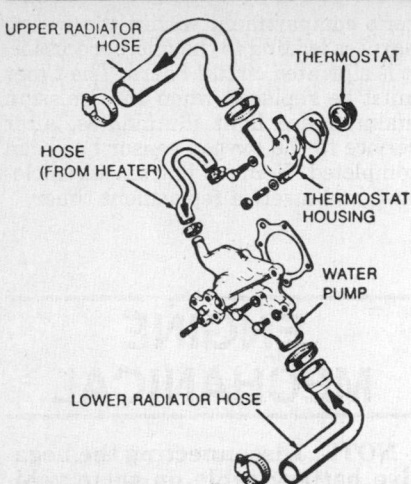

UPPER RADIATOR HOSE

THERMOSTAT

HOSE (FROM HEATER)

THERMOSTAT HOUSING

WATER PUMP

LOWER RADIATOR HOSE

Exploded view of the water pump and thermostat assemblies

9. Connect the negative battery cable.

Thermostat

REMOVAL & INSTALLATION

1. Disconnect the negative battery cable.
2. Drain the cooling system to a level below the thermostat; make sure the engine is cold.
3. If necessary, disconnect the upper radiator hose and heater hose from the thermostat housing.
4. Remove the thermostat housing-to-engine bolts, the housing and thermostat; discard the gasket.
5. To install, use a new gasket, a new thermostat, if necessary, and reverse the removal procedures.

FUEL SYSTEM

Fuel System Service Precautions

Safety is the most important factor when performing not only fuel system maintenance but any type of maintenance. Failure to conduct maintenance and repairs in a safe manner may result in serious personal injury or death. Maintenance and testing of the vehicle's fuel system components can be accomplished safely and effectively by adhering to the following rules and guidelines.

• To avoid the possibility of fire and personal injury, always disconnect the negative battery cable unless the repair or test procedure requires that battery voltage be applied.

• Always relieve the fuel system pressure prior to disconnecting any fuel system component, fitting or fuel line connection. Exercise extreme caution whenever relieving fuel system pressure to avoid exposing skin, face and eyes to fuel spray. Please be advised that fuel under pressure may penetrate the skin or any part of the body that it contacts.

• Always place a shop towel or cloth around the fitting or connection prior to loosening to absorb any excess fuel due to spillage. Ensure that all fuel spillage (should it occur) is quickly removed from engine surfaces. Ensure that all fuel soaked cloths or towels are deposited into a suitable waste container.

• Always keep a dry chemical (Class B) fire extinguisher near the work area.

• Do not allow fuel spray or fuel vapors to come into contact with a spark or open flame.

• Always use a backup wrench when loosening and tightening fuel line connection fittings. This will prevent unnecessary stress and torsion to fuel line piping. Always follow the proper torque specifications.

• Always replace worn fuel fitting O-rings with new. Do not substitute fuel hose or equivalent where fuel pipe is installed.

RELIEVING FUEL SYSTEM PRESSURE

1. Release the fuel vapor pressure in the fuel tank by removing the fuel tank cap and reinstalling it.
2. Cover the fuel line with an absorbent shop cloth and loosen the connection slowly to release the fuel pressure gradually.

Fuel Filter

The fuel filter is located between the fuel pump and the carburetor.

REMOVAL & INSTALLATION

1. Disconnect the negative battery cable. Relieve the fuel pressure.
2. Remove the air cleaner, if necessary.
3. Place an absorbent rag under the filter to catch the spillage.
4. Remove the hose clamps.
5. Remove the filter and short attaching hoses.
6. Remove the hoses if they are to be reused.
7. To install, use a new filter and reverse the removal procedures.

NOTE: Make sure the filter is installed in the correct direction of fuel flow.

8. Connect the negative battery cable. Start the engine and check for leaks.

Mechanical Fuel Pump

PRESSURE TESTING

1. Disconnect the negative battery cable. Relieve the fuel pressure.
2. Disconnect the fuel line from the carburetor.
3. Disconnect the fuel return line from the fuel filter, if equipped, and plug the nipple on the filter.
4. Install the T-fitting on the open end of the fuel line and refit the line to the carburetor.
5. Connect a pressure gauge into the opening of the T-fitting.
6. The hose leading to the pressure gauge should not be any longer than 6 in.
7. Start the engine and allow it to run at idle.
8. Bleed any air from the hose between the gauge and the T-fitting.
9. If the fuel pump is equipped with a fuel return line, plug the line.
10. Start the engine and check the fuel pressure; it should be 3–5 psi at idle.
11. Stop the engine and relieve the fuel pressure.
12. Remove the pressure gauge and the T-fitting and reconnect the fuel line.
13. Start the engine and check for leaks.

REMOVAL & INSTALLATION

1. Disconnect the negative battery cable.
2. Disconnect the fuel lines from the fuel pump.
3. Remove the fuel pump-to-engine bolts and the pump.
To install:
4. Using a new gasket, install the fuel pump and bolts.

NOTE: Be sure the actuating arm of the pump is positioned on the top of the camshaft eccentric.

5. Install the fuel inlet and outlet lines to the fuel pump.
6. Install the negative battery cable.
7. Start the engine and check for leakage.

Carburetor

REMOVAL & INSTALLATION

The vehicle is equipped with a BBD carburetor.

1. Allow the engine to cool. Disconnect the negative battery cable.

2. Remove the vacuum hoses, the air cleaner assembly and flange gasket. Mark the hoses to aid in assembly.

3. Disconnect the fuel line and vacuum hoses from the carburetor. Mark the hoses to aid in assembly.

4. Disconnect the throttle linkage and electrical wire connectors.

5. Remove the carburetor bolts/nuts and the carburetor from the intake manifold.

To install:

6. Clean the gasket mounting surfaces.

7. Using a new gasket, install the carburetor to the intake manifold.

8. Connect the throttle linkage and electrical wire connectors.

9. Connect the fuel line and vacuum hoses to the carburetor.

10. Install the air cleaner assembly and connect the vacuum hoses.

11. Connect the negative battery cable.

12. Start the engine and check the operation.

IDLE SPEED ADJUSTMENT

1. Connect a tachometer to the engine and run the engine until normal operating temperatures are reached. Block the drive wheels and apply the parking brake.

2. Position the transmission control lever according to the instruction on the underhood emission label.

3. Adjust the sol-vac vacuum actuator by removing the vacuum hose to the unit. Plug the hose.

4. Adjust the idle speed by using the vacuum actuator adjustment screw on the throttle lever. This adjustment is made with all accessories turned **OFF**.

5. Adjust the engine rpm to specifications.

6. After the vacuum actuator adjustment is completed, leave the vacuum hose plugged and disconnected.

7. Adjust the curb idle using the 1/4 in. hex-headed adjustment screw on the end of the sol-vac unit. Adjust to specifications.

NOTE: The engine speed will vary 10–30 rpm during this mode due to being in the closed loop fuel control.

8. Turn the engine **OFF** and remove the tachometer.

IDLE MIXTURE ADJUSTMENT

NOTE: If the carburetor is equipped with tamper proof caps, it will be necessary to first remove the carburetor from the vehicle and drill out the tamper proof caps before performing the idle mixture adjustment procedure.

1. Allow the engine to reach normal operating temperatures.

2. Block the drive wheels and apply the parking brake.

3. Connect a tachometer according to the manufacturer's instructions.

4. Set the idle speed to specifications.

5. Turn the mixture screws inward, in equal increments, until there is a noticable decrease in rpm. Then, slowly turn them out in equal increments until the highest rpm is 1st obtained. In other words, there will be a range in which the rpm remains constant even if the screws are turned outward. Set the screws as far in as they can be and still give the top rpm; this is referred to as lean best idle.

6. Adjust the idle drop to specifications. Carefully, watch the tachometer and turn the screws inward, in equal increments, slowly until the specified drop in rpm appears.

7. If this rpm is more than 30 rpm below the original curb idle rpm, adjust the curb idle to specification, then repeat Steps 3 and 4.

8. Install tamper proof caps or dowel pins to prevent future tampering.

9. Turn the engine **OFF** and remove the tachometer.

EMISSION CONTROLS

Please refer to "Emission Control" in the Unit Repair section for system maintenance procedures. Due to the complex nature of modern electronic engine control systems, comprehensive diagnosis and testing procedures fall outside the confines of this repair manual. For complete information on diagnosis, testing and repair procedures concerning all modern engine and emission control systems, please refer to "Chilton's Guide to Electronic Engine Controls".

Emission Warning Lamps

RESETTING

The 1000 hour emission maintenance E-Cell timer is located in the passenger's compartment within the wiring harness leading to the microprocessor; it is a printed circuit board. The timer must be replaced when the emission maintenance light illuminates, after service to the oxygen sensor has been completed. Remove it from its enclosure and insert a replacment timer.

ENGINE MECHANICAL

NOTE: Disconnecting the negative battery cable on some vehicles may interfere with the functions of the on board computer systems and may require the computer to undergo a relearning process, once the negative battery cable is reconnected.

Engine Assembly

REMOVAL & INSTALLATION

1. Drain the cooling system.

NOTE: Do not drain the cooling system until the coolant has cooled and the system pressure has been released.

2. Scribe the hood hinge locations and remove the hood.

3. Disconnect the battery cables and remove the battery.

4. Disconnect the wiring from the distributor, coil, distributor and the oil pressure sending switch.

5. Remove the vacuum switch assembly bracket from the cylinder head cover.

6. Disconnect the front fuel pipe from the fuel pump and insert a plug into the pipe.

7. Disconnect the right engine ground strap and remove the right front engine support cushion-to-bracket bolt.

8. If equipped with air conditioning, completely discharge the system and cap all openings. Disconnect the compressor clutch electrical connector.

9. Remove the electrical connectors from the starter motor.

10. Remove the air cleaner assembly. Label and disconnect the hoses, as necessary.

11. Disconnect the idle speed control solenoid wire connector, the fuel return hose from the fuel filter and the carburetor bowl vent hose from the canister.

12. Disconnect the throttle cable and remove from the bracket. Disconnect the throttle rod, if equipped. Discon-

nect the throttle rod from the bellcrank. Disconnect the stepper motor wire connector and oxygen sensor wire connector, if equipped.

13. If equipped, disconnect the heater control vacuum hose from the manifold and the temperature sending gauge wire connector.

14. Disconnect the upper/lower radiator hoses, the coolant hoses from the rear of the manifold and the thermostat housing.

15. Remove the fan shroud screws, disconnect the transmission oil cooler pipe fittings from the radiator, if equipped. Remove the radiator and the shroud.

16. Remove the fan assembly from the hub. Install a $^5/_{16}$ x ½ in. bolt through the fan pulley into the water pump flange to maintain alignment when the crankshaft is rotated.

17. Remove the power brake vacuum check valve, if equipped.

18. If equipped with power steering, disconnect the hoses from the steering gear fittings and drain the system.

19. Remove the transmission filler tube, if equipped.

20. Raise and safely support the vehicle. Remove the starter motor.

21. If equipped with an automatic transmission, remove the converter access plate, matchmark the converter to the drive plate and remove the converter-to-drive plate bolts. Remove the exhaust pipe support brace from the converter housing.

NOTE: This brace also supports the inner end of the transmission linkage.

22. If equipped with manual transmission, remove the flywheel access cover and the clutch release bellcrank inner support screws. Disconnect the springs and remove the clutch release bellcrank. Remove the outer bellcrank-to-throw-out lever rod bracket retainer. Disconnect the backup lamp switch wire harness under the hood at the firewall for access to the flywheel housing bolts.

23. Remove the engine mount cushion-to-bracket screws.

24. Disconnect both halfshafts and the front axle assembly.

25. Disconnect the exhaust pipe from the manifold, loosen the upper converter or flywheel housing-to-engine bolts and loosen the bottom bolts. Lower the vehicle.

26. If equipped with air conditioning, remove the compressor idler pulley and the mounting bracket.

27. Attach a lifting device to the engine and raise the engine off the front supports. Place a support stand under the converter or flywheel housing and remove the remaining bolts.

28. Remove the engine assembly from the engine compartment.

To install:

29. Install the engine assembly into the vehicle and install the upper engine-to-transmission bolts.

30. If equipped with air conditioning, install the mounting bracket and the compressor idler pulley.

31. Raise and safely support the vehicle. Connect the exhaust pipe to the manifold.

32. Connect the front axle assembly and both halfshafts. Torque the halfshafts-to-front axle to 45 ft. lbs.

33. Install the engine mount cushion-to-bracket screws.

34. Connect the backup lamp switch wire harness. Install the outer bellcrank-to-throw-out lever rod bracket retainer, the clutch release bellcrank and the springs. If equipped with a manual transmission, install the clutch release bellcrank inner support screws and the flywheel access cover.

35. Install the exhaust pipe support brace to the converter housing. If equipped with an automatic transmission, align and install the converter-to-drive plate bolts and the converter access plate. Torque the drive plate-to-converter bolts to 22 ft. lbs. and the converter housing-to-engine bolts to 54 ft. lbs.

36. Install the starter motor and lower the vehicle.

37. Install the transmission filler tube, if equipped.

38. If equipped with power steering, connect the hoses to the steering gear and refill the reservoir.

39. Install the power brake vacuum check valve, if equipped.

40. Remove the $^5/_{16}$ x ½ in. bolt from the fan pulley-to-the water pump flange. Install the fan assembly from the hub.

41. Install the shroud, the radiator and the transmission oil cooler pipe fittings to the radiator, if equipped.

42. Connect the upper/lower radiator hoses and the coolant hoses to the rear of the manifold and the thermostat housing.

43. If equipped, connect the heater control vacuum hose to the manifold and the temperature sending gauge wire connector.

44. Connect the stepper motor wire connector and oxygen sensor wire connector, if equipped. Install the bracket and the throttle cable.

45. Connect the idle speed control solenoid wire connector, the fuel return hose to the fuel filter and the carburetor bowl vent hose to the canister.

46. Install the air cleaner assembly and the hoses.

47. Connect the electrical connectors to the starter motor.

48. If equipped with air conditioning, connect the compressor clutch electrical connector and recharge the system.

49. Connect the right engine ground strap and the right front engine support cushion-to-bracket bolt.

50. Connect the front fuel pipe to the fuel pump.

51. Install the vacuum switch assembly bracket to the cylinder head cover.

52. Connect the wiring to the distributor, coil, distributor and the oil pressure sending switch.

53. Install the battery and connect the battery cables. Install the hood and refill the cooling system.

54. Start the engine, allow it to reach normal operating temperatures and check for leaks.

Engine Mounts

REMOVAL & INSTALLATION

1. Disconnect the negative battery cable.

2. Remove the heated air tube and engine mount bracket-to-axle housing attaching bolts, if required.

3. Remove the engine mount through bolts.

4. Raise the safely support the vehicle.

5. Disconnect the axle tube at right side and axle at pinion support, if required.

6. Position a jack under the engine and, carefully, raise the engine.

7. Remove the engine mount.

To install:

8. Install the replacement mount and torque the bolts to 33 ft. lbs. (45 Nm).

9. Install the engine mount support bracket. Lower the engine and remove the jack.

10. If required, raise the axle into position and install the bolts at pinion and at axle tube.

11. Install the engine mounts through bolts and torque to 45 ft. lbs. (60 Nm).

12. Lower the vehicle and reconnect the battery negative cable.

Cylinder Head

REMOVAL & INSTALLATION

1. Disconnect the negative battery cable.

2. Drain the cooling system. Disconnect the hoses from the thermostat housing.

3. Remove the air cleaner and its components.

4. Remove the air cleaner and the PCV valve moulded hose.

5. Disconnect the distributor vacuum advance hose from the CTO valve.

Disconnect the fuel line from the fuel pump.

6. Disconnect the PCV valve from the cover rubber grommet and the PCV shutoff valve vacuum hose.

7. Remove the vacuum switch and bracket assembly, the diverter valve with bracket and the necessary vacuum hoses and electrical connections to provide clearance for cover removal.

8. Remove the valve cover bolts and the cover.

9. Alternately, loosen the bridge and rocker arm pivot bolts, 1 turn at a time, to prevent damage to the bridges. Remove the pushrods.

NOTE: Keep the pushrods, bridges, pivots and rocker arms in their order of removal for ease of installation.

10. Without disconnecting the hoses, disconnect the power steering pump bracket and move the assembly aside.

11. Remove the intake and exhaust manifolds from the cylinder head.

12. If equipped with air conditioning, complete the following:

   a. Remove the air conditioning compressor drive belt.

   b. Loosen the alternator belt and remove the air conditioning compressor/alternator bracket-to-head mounting bolt.

   c. Remove the air compressor bolts and move it aside.

NOTE: The serpentine drive belt tension is released by loosening the alternator.

13. Remove the spark plugs. Disconnect the temperature sending wire connector and the negative battery cable. Remove the ignition coil and bracket.

14. Remove the cylinder head bolts and the cylinder head.
To install:
15. Clean the gasket mounting surfaces.

16. Apply an even coat of sealing compound, to both sides of the replacement head gasket. Position the gasket on the cylinder block with the word **TOP** facing upward.

NOTE: Do not apply sealing compound on the cylinder head or engine block gasket surfaces. Do not allow sealer to enter the cylinder bores.

17. Torque the cylinder head bolts, in the proper sequence, to 85 ft. lbs.

NOTE: The cylinder head gasket is made of an aluminum coated embossed steel and does not require re-torquing of the cylinder head bolts.

18. During the completion of the cylinder head installation, torque the bridge bolts to 19 ft. lbs., turning each, alternately, 1 turn at a time until the specified torque has been reached.

19. Install the cylinder head cover with a ⅛ inch bead of RTV sealer along the sealing surface of the head. Make sure not to delay more than 10 minutes in installing the cover onto the bead of sealer. Torque the cylinder head cover retaining bolts to 28 inch lbs.

20. To complete the installation, reverse the removal procedures. Refill the cooling system.

21. Start the engine, allow it to reach normal operating temperatures, check for leaks and operation.

Valve Lifters

REMOVAL & INSTALLATION

1. Remove the valve cover, the bridge and pivot assemblies and rocker arms.

NOTE: To avoid damaging the bridges, alternately loosen each bridge bolt a turn at a time.

2. Remove the pushrods, keeping them in their respective order.

3. Remove the cylinder head assembly and manifolds.

4. Using a lifter removal tool, remove the lifters through the pushrod openings; retain the lifters in their respective removed order.
To install:
5. Dip each lifter in clean engine oil and install them into their original bores.

6. Using a new head gasket, install the cylinder head assembly and torque the bolts in sequence to the proper torque specification. Install the manifolds, if removed separately.

7. Install the pushrods into their original positions. Install the rocker arms, bridges and the pivot assemblies. Torque the bridge bolts 1 turn at a time, alternately, to avoid damaging the bridges.

8. Pour the remaining oil supplement over the valve train.

9. Install the valve cover. To complete the installation, reverse the removal procedures.

10. Start the engine, allow it to reach normal operation, check for leaks and operation.

Valve Lash

ADJUSTMENT

The engine uses hydraulic valve tappets, eliminating the need for valve lash adjustment. The tappet plunger is positioned to a pre-set dimension when the valve train is bolted into place, allowing for noiseless operation of the valve system.

Rocker Arms

REMOVAL & INSTALLATION

1. Disconnect the negative battery cable.

2. Label and disconnect and all vacuum hoses and electrical connections as required.

3. Disconnect the fuel pipe from the fuel pump. Remove the vacuum switch and bracket assembly. Remove the diverter valve and bracket assembly.

4. Remove the valve cover.

5. Remove the bolts at each bridge and pivot assembly. Alternately, loosen each bolt, 1 turn at a time, to avoid damaging the bridges.

6. Remove the bridges, the pivots and the corresponding pairs of rocker arms; keep them in the order of removal.
To install:
7. Lubricate the components with oil and install them into their original positions.

8. At each bridge, torque the bolts

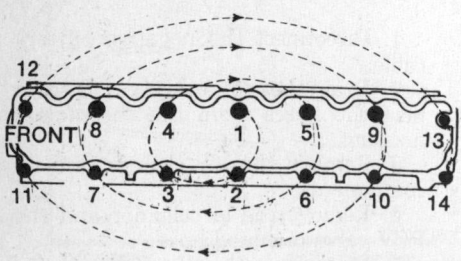

4.2L cylinder head torque sequence

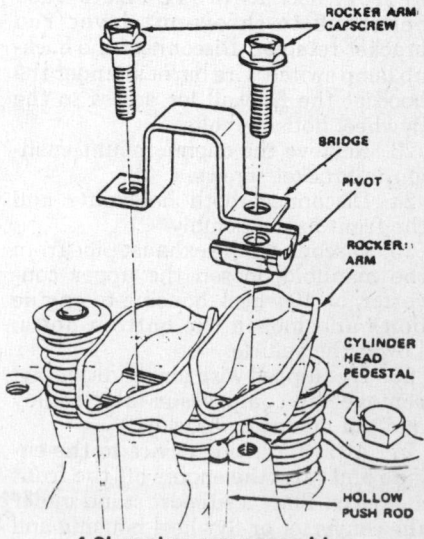

4.2L rocker arm assembly

alternately 1 turn at a time, to avoid damage to the bridge. Torque the bolts to 19 ft. lbs. and re-torque to 16–26 ft. lbs.

9. Using a new valve cover gasket, install the valve cover.

10. Connect the negative battery cable.

11. Start the engine, allow it to reach normal operating temperatures, check for leaks and operation.

Combination Manifold
REMOVAL & INSTALLATION

The intake manifold is mounted on the left-hand side of the engine and bolted to the cylinder head. A gasket is used between the intake manifold and the head; none is required for the exhaust manifold. Note that an improved clamp washer is supplied for this manifold and is used at bolt locations No. 3–10. Do not use these washers at positions 1, 2, 11 and 12, where smaller, chamfered washers are used.

1. Disconnect the negative battery cable.

2. Remove the air cleaner. Disconnect the fuel line, vent hose and solenoid wire, if equipped.

3. Disconnect the accelerator cable from the accelerator bellcrank.

4. Disconnect the PCV vacuum hose from the intake manifold and the TCS solenoid and bracket, if equipped.

5. Remove the spark CTO switch and EGR valve or exhaust back-pressure sensor vacuum lines from each of these components.

6. Disconnect the hoses from the air pump and the injection manifold check valve. Disconnect the vacuum line from the diverter valve and remove the diverter valve with hoses, if equipped.

7. Remove the air pump and power steering bracket, if equipped, and the air pump. Move the power steering pump aside, without disconnecting the hoses.

8. Remove the air conditioning drive belt idler assembly from the cylinder head, if equipped. It may be necessary to remove the air conditioning compressor. Do not discharge the air conditioning system; just move the compressor aside.

9. If equipped with automatic transmission, disconnect the throttle valve linkage.

10. Disconnect the exhaust pipe from the manifold.

11. On some vehicles, an oxygen sensor is screwed in the exhaust manifold just above the exhaust pipe connection. Disconnect the wire and remove the sensor, if equipped.

12. Remove the manifold bolts, nuts

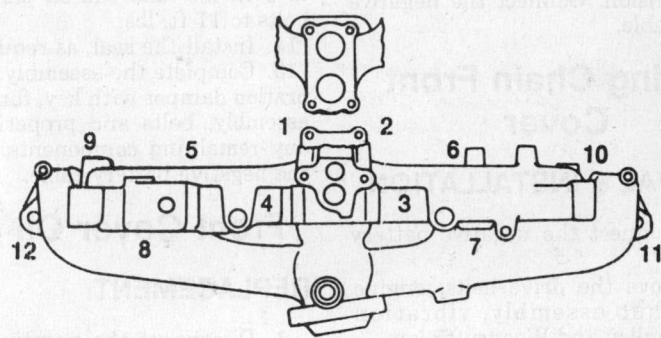
Intake and exhaust manifold torque sequence—6 cylinder

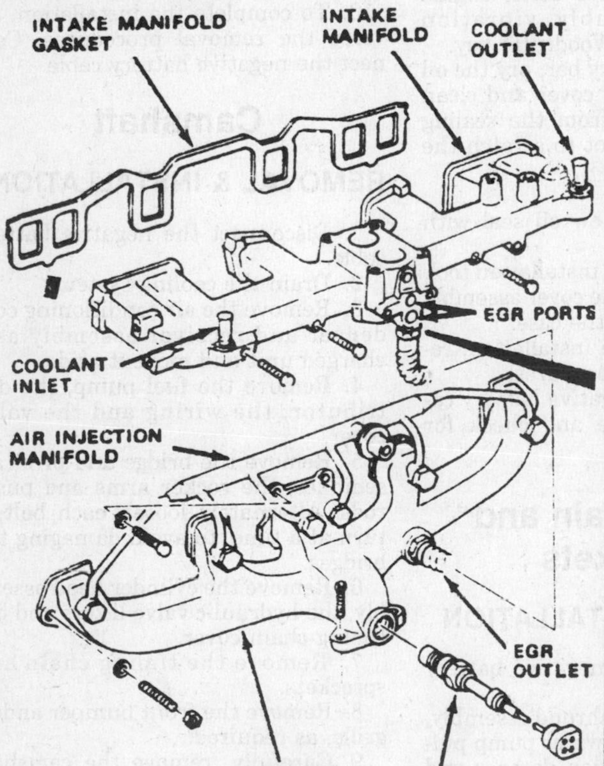

4.2L engine intake/exhaust manifold assembly

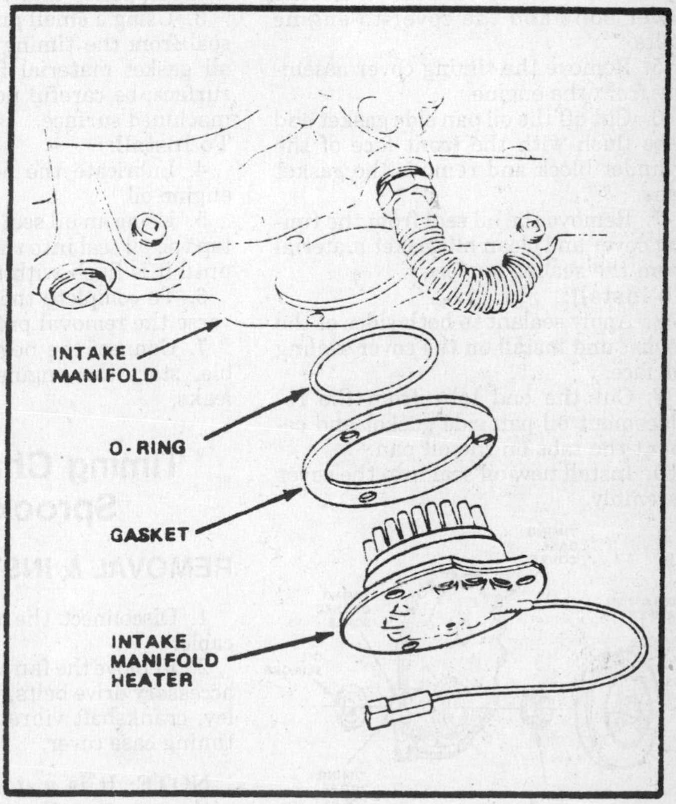

and clamps and the intake/exhaust manifolds as an assembly. Discard the gasket. Both manifolds are separated at the heat riser.

To install:

13. Clean the gasket mounting surfaces of the cylinder head and manifolds.

14. Assemble the manifolds and torque the heat riser retaining nuts to 5 ft. lbs.

15. Using a new gasket, install the manifold and torque the bolts and nuts in the proper sequence to the specified torque.

16. To complete the installation, reverse the removal procedures. Adjust the automatic transmission throttle linkage, if equipped. Adjust the drive belt(s) tension. Connect the negative battery cable.

Timing Chain Front Cover

REMOVAL & INSTALLATION

1. Disconnect the negative battery cable.

2. Remove the drive belts, engine fan and hub assembly, vibration damper, pulley and Woodruff® key.

3. Remove the air conditioning compressor and alternator bracket, if equipped.

4. Remove the oil pan-to-timing cover bolts and the cover-to-engine bolts.

5. Remove the timing cover assembly from the engine.

6. Cut off the oil pan side gasket end tabs flush with the front face of the cylinder block and remove the gasket tabs.

7. Remove the oil seal from the timing cover and clean all gasket material from the sealing surface.

To install:

8. Apply sealant to both sides of the gasket and install on the cover sealing surface.

9. Cut the end tabs from the replacement oil pan side gasket and cement the tabs on the oil pan.

10. Install new oil seal into the cover assembly.

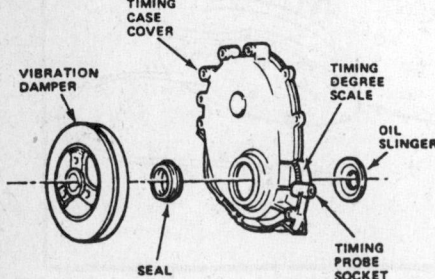

4.2L front cover assembly

(labels: TIMING CASE COVER / VIBRATION DAMPER / TIMING DEGREE SCALE / OIL SLINGER / SEAL / TIMING PROBE SOCKET)

NOTE: The oil seal can be installed after the cover has been installed on the engine block, depending upon the cover alignment tools available.

11. Coat the front cover seal end tab recesses with RTV sealant and position the seal on the cover bottom.

12. Position the cover on the engine block and with an alignment tool in the crankshaft opening.

NOTE: Two types of alignment tools are available, without seal in housing or with seal in housing.

13. Install the cover-to-engine block bolts and the oil pan-to-cover bolts. Torque the cover-to-engine block bolts to 5 ft. lbs. and the oil pan-to-cover bolts to 11 ft. lbs.

14. Install the seal, as required.

15. Complete the assembly of the vibration damper with key, fan and hub assembly, belts and properly adjust, any remaining components. Connect the negative battery cable.

Front Cover Oil Seal

REPLACEMENT

1. Disconnect the negative battery cable.

2. Remove the drive belts, engine fan and hub assembly, vibration damper, pulley and Woodruff® key.

3. Using a small pry bar, pry the oil seal from the timing cover and clean all gasket material from the sealing surface; be careful not to scratch the machined surface.

To install:

4. Lubricate the new oil seal with engine oil.

5. Using an oil seal installation tool, tap the oil seal into the cover assembly until it is flush with the case.

6. To complete the installation, reverse the removal procedures.

7. Connect the negative battery cable, start the engine and check for leaks.

Timing Chain and Sprockets

REMOVAL & INSTALLATION

1. Disconnect the negative battery cable.

2. Remove the fan shroud assembly, accessory drive belts, water pump pulley, crankshaft vibration damper and timing case cover.

NOTE: It is a good practice to either remove the radiator or cover the radiator core area when

working around the radiator, as damage can result to the radiator cores.

3. Rotate the crankshaft until the **0** timing mark, on the crankshaft sprocket, aligns with the timing mark on the camshaft sprocket.

4. Remove the oil slinger from the crankshaft.

5. Remove the camshaft retaining bolt, the sprocket and chain assembly.

To install:

6. Turn the tensioner lever to the unlocked position and pull the tensioner block toward the tensioner lever to compress the spring. Hold the block and turn the tensioner lever to the locked up position.

7. Install the crankshaft/camshaft sprockets and timing chain; make sure the timing marks are aligned.

8. Install the camshaft sprocket retaining bolt and washer; torque the bolt to 80 ft. lbs. (108 Nm).

NOTE: To verify correct installation of the timing chain, rotate the crankshaft until the camshaft sprocket timing mark is approximately at the 1 o'clock position; there should be 20 pins between the marks.

9. Using a new gasket, install the oil slinger and timing case cover.

10. To complete the installation, reverse the removal procedures. Connect the negative battery cable.

Camshaft

REMOVAL & INSTALLATION

1. Disconnect the negative battery cable.

2. Drain the cooling system.

3. Remove the air conditioning condenser and receiver assembly as a charged unit and move it aside.

4. Remove the fuel pump, the distributor, the wiring and the valve cover.

5. Remove the bridge and pivot assemblies, the rocker arms and pushrods. Alternately loosen each bolt, 1 turn at a time, to avoid damaging the bridges.

6. Remove the cylinder head assembly, the hydraulic valve lifters and the timing chain cover.

7. Remove the timing chain and sprockets.

8. Remove the front bumper and/or grille, as required.

9. Carefully, remove the camshaft from the engine block so as not to damage the camshaft bearings.

To install:

10. Lubricate the camshaft with engine oil supplement. Carefully, install

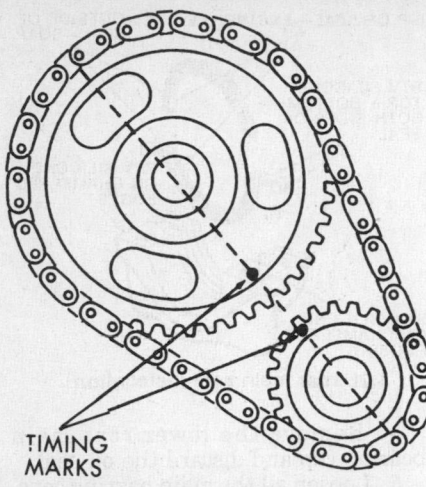

TIMING MARKS

Timing marks alignment—4.2L engines

the camshaft into the engine to avoid damage to the camshaft bearings.

11. With the timing marks aligned, install the timing chain and sprockets. Install the camshaft sprocket retaining bolt and torque to 50 ft. lbs.

12. Install the timing chain cover with the new seal and gasket. Install the vibration damper and pulley, the fan assembly, the shroud and the drive belts and torque to specifications. Install the fuel pump.

13. Rotate the crankshaft a full revolution to place the No. 1 cylinder piston on TDC of it's compression stroke. Install the distributor so the rotor is aligned with the No. 1 spark plug terminal of the distributor cap.

NOTE: If the crankshaft/camshaft remains in position with the timing marks aligned, the No. 6 cylinder will be on its compression stroke.

14. Install the lifters, the cylinder head and gasket, the pushrods, the rocker arms, the bridges and pivots. Torque both bolts for each bridge alternately, 1 turn at a time, to avoid damage to the bridges.

NOTE: Lubricate the hydraulic valve train with engine oil supplement and allow it to remain with the engine oil for at least 1000 miles.

15. Install the valve cover, the air compressor condenser and receiver assembly, the radiator and shroud. Refill the cooling system.

16. Install the front bumper/grille. Connect the negative battery cable.

17. Start the engine, allow it to reach normal operating temperatures and check for leaks. Check and/or adjust the ignition timing and idle.

Piston and Connecting Rod

POSITIONING

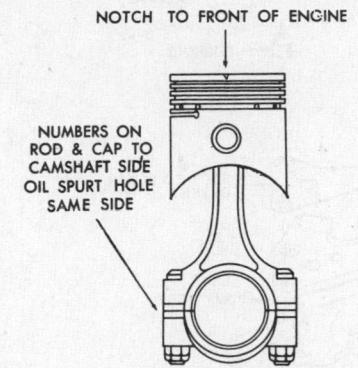

NOTCH TO FRONT OF ENGINE

NUMBERS ON ROD & CAP TO CAMSHAFT SIDE OIL SPURT HOLE SAME SIDE

4.2L piston positioning

ENGINE LUBRICATION

Oil Pan

REMOVAL & INSTALLATION

1. Disconnect the negative battery cable. Drain engine oil.
2. Lock the steering wheel. Remove the air cleaner.
3. Install the holding fixture and support engine.
4. Raise and safely support the vehicle.
5. Remove the front axle universal joint clamp strap bolts.
6. Remove the bolts from the engine cushions.
7. Remove the bolts from sill-to-crossmember brace bar at crossmember and rotate the bar aside.
8. Loosen the pitman arm at gear and the idler arm at steering linkage.
9. Remove the steering damper-to-crossmember bolt.
10. Loosen the sway bar bolts and lower sway bar.
11. Support the axle and crossmember assembly. Remove the bolt from right bracket at axle tube bolt bars.
12. Remove the bolts from left upper axle bracket at upper end. Remove the bolts from pinion end bracket at pinion.
13. Remove the crossmember nuts and bolts. Lower the crossmember and axle assembly.
14. Disconnect the electrical connectors and remove the starter motor.
15. Remove the torque converter inspection shield.

16. Remove the oil pan screws, pry it loose and slide it rearward.
To install:
17. Clean the gasket mounting surfaces.
18. Install the replacement oil pan front seal on timing case cover and apply sealant to tab ends.
19. Cement replacement oil pan side gaskets into position on engine block and apply sealant to ends of gaskets.
20. Coat inside curved surface of replacement oil pan rear seal with soap. Apply sealant to gasket contacting surface of seal end tabs.
21. Install the seal in recess of rear main bearing cap; make sure it is fully seated.
22. Apply engine oil to oil pan contacting surface of front and rear oil pan seals.
23. Install the oil pan and drain plug.
24. Install the starter motor and connect the electrical connectors.
25. Install the torque converter housing access cover.
26. Raise the crossmember assembly and install the nuts and bolts.
27. Install the engine cushion bolts and the sill-to-crossmember brace bolts.
28. Install the pitman arm-to-steering gear and torque the nut. Install the idler arm-to-steering linkage and torque the nut. Torque sway bar bolts to 25 ft. lbs. (34 Nm).
29. Install the steering damper-to-crossmember and torque the bolt to 50 ft. lbs. (68 Nm).
30. Raise and install front axle assembly. Connect at axle tube, upper left axle bracket and pinion bracket; torque all axle connections to 45 ft. lbs. (61 Nm).
31. Install the front universal clamp strap and torque the bolts to 14 ft. lbs. (19 Nm).
32. Connect both halfshafts-to-front axle and torque to 45 ft. lbs. (61 Nm).
33. Remove the engine holding fixture and install air cleaner.
34. Connect the negative battery cable. Start engine and check for leaks.

Oil Pump

REMOVAL & INSTALLATION

NOTE: Whenever the oil pump is disassembled or the cover removed, the gear cavity must be filled with petroleum jelly (vaseline) for priming purposes. Do not use grease.

1. Disconnect the negative battery cable.
2. Raise and safely support the vehicle. Drain the engine oil and remove the oil pan.

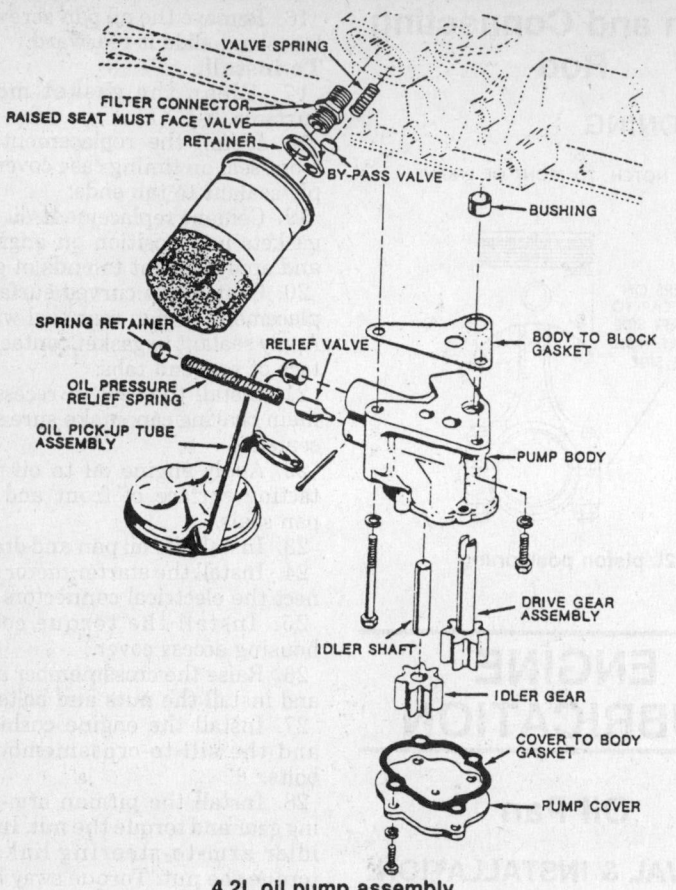

4.2L oil pump assembly

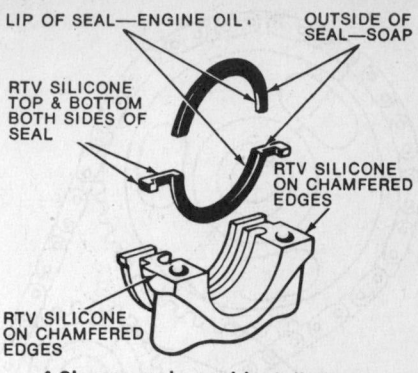

4.2L rear main seal installation

3. Remove the oil pump retaining bolts, the oil pump and gasket.

NOTE: The oil pump removal and installation will not affect the distributor timing because the distributor drive gear remains meshed with the camshaft. Do not disturb the position of the oil inlet tube and strainer assembly in the pump body. If the tube is moved in the body, a replacement tube and strainer must be installed to assure an airtight seal.

To install:

4. To insure self priming, fill the gear cavity with petroleum jelly before installing the cover.

5. Using a new gasket, install the pump and torque the short bolts to 10 ft. lbs. and the long bolts to 17 ft. lbs.

6. Using new gasket and seals, install the oil pan. Refill the oil pan.

7. Connect the negative battery cable.

8. Start the engine and check for leaks.

CHECKING

1. Using the Plastigage® method, measure the gear end clearance; it should be 0.002–0.006 in. (0.05–0.15mm) with 0.002 in. (0.05mm) perferred.

2. Using a feeler gauge, measure the gear-to-pump body clearance; it should be 0.002–0.004 in. (0.05–0.10mm). If the gear-to-body clearance is not within specifications, replace the idler gear, the idler shaft and/or drive gear assembly.

3. Remove the oil inlet tube/strainer assembly and cotter pin. Inspect for binding of the spring retainer, spring and relief valve plunder in the pump body; if necessary, replace the parts.

Rear Main Bearing Oil Seal

REMOVAL & INSTALLATION

This seal is a 2-piece neoprene type with a single lip.

1. Disconnect the negative battery cable.

2. The crankshaft rear main bearing seal consists of 2-pieces, an upper and a lower seal, each with a single lip.

3. Raise and safely support the vehicle. Drain the engine oil and remove the oil pan.

4. Remove the lower rear main bearing cap and discard the oil seal.

5. Loosen all the main bearing caps. Tap the upper seal with a brass drift and hammer until the seal protrudes enough to grasp it and pull it from the engine block.

To install:

6. Coat the lip of the new seal with engine oil and position the seal with the lip towards the front of the engine. Install the seal into the engine block.

7. Position the lower ½ of the seal into the rear main bearing cap, after coating both sides of the lower seal tabs with RTV sealant and the lip of the seal with engine oil. Coat the outer curved surface of the seal with soap. Seat the seal firmly into the rear main bearing cap.

8. Install the rear main bearing cap and torque the bolts to 80 ft. lbs.

9. Install the oil pan and its components. Refill the oil pan.

10. Connect the negative battery cable. Start the engine and check for leaks.

MANUAL TRANSMISSION

For further information on transmissions/transaxles, please refer to "Chilton's Guide to Transmission Repair".

Transmission Assembly

REMOVAL & INSTALLATION

1. Disconnect the negative battery cable.

2. Shift transmission into **N**.

3. Remove gearshift lever bezel and boot-to-floorpan screws.

4. Slide the bezel and boot upward on gearshift lever to provide access to lever bolts.

5. Remove gearshift lever-to-lever mounting cover bolts on the transmission adapter housing and remove gearshift lever.

6. Remove gearshift lever mounting cover-to-transmission adapter bolts and the cover to provide access to the transfer case upper mounting stud nut in transmission adapter housing.

7. Remove the nut from transfer case upper mounting stud located inside transmission adapter housing.

8. Raise and safely support the vehicle.

9. Remove the skid plate.

10. Remove the speedometer adapter retainer bolt, the retainer, adapter and cable. Discard the adapter O-ring and plug adapter opening in transfer case to prevent excessive oil spillage.

NOTE: Matchmark the position of the speedometer adapter for assembly alignment, before removing it.

11. Matchmark the driveshafts and axle yokes for assembly alignment and disconnect the propeller shafts from the transfer case.

12. Disconnect the backup lamp switch wire.

13. Place a support stand under the engine.

14. Using a transmission jack, support transmission and transfer case.

15. Remove the rear crossmember.

16. Remove the catalytic converter bracket from transfer case and the brace rod from bracket.

17. Remove transmission-to-clutch housing bolts.

18. Remove the transmission and transfer case as an assembly.

19. Remove transmission-to-transfer case nuts and transmission from transfer case.

To install:

20. Position the transmission onto transfer case and torque the nuts to 26 ft. lbs.

21. Using a transmission jack, support the transmission/transfer case assembly.

22. Align the transmission clutch shaft with throw-out bearing and clutch disc splines and seat transmission against clutch housing.

23. Install and torque transmission-to-clutch housing bolts to 55 ft. lbs.

24. Connect the propeller shafts-to-transfer case yokes and torque the clamp strap bolts to 15 ft. lbs.

25. Install the brace rod and rear crossmember and torque the bolts to 30 ft. lbs.

26. Connect the backup lamp switch wire.

27. Install a new O-ring on the speedometer adapter. Install the adapter, cable and retainer; torque the retainer bolt to 100 inch lbs.

NOTE: Do not attempt to reuse the original adapter O-ring. The ring is designed to swell in service to improve its sealing qualities and could be cut or torn during installation if reuse is attempted.

28. Attach the catalytic converter bracket-to-transfer case and torque the skid plate bolts to 30 ft. lbs. Check and correct lubricant levels in transmission and transfer case, if necessary.

29. Install the skid plate and torque the bolts to 30 ft. lbs.

30. Remove the engine support stand and transmission jack, if not removed previously.

31. Lower the vehicle.

32. Clean mating surfaces of gearshift lever mounting cover and transmission adapter housing.

33. Apply RTV-type sealant to gearshift lever mounting cover, install the cover and torque the bolts to 13 ft. lbs. torque.

34. Install the gearshift lever on the mounting cover. Before tightening lever bolts, make certain lever is engaged with the shift rail; torque lever bolts to 18 ft. lbs.

35. Position gearshift lever boot and bezel in floorpan and install bezel screws.

36. Connect the negative battery cable and check the transmission operation.

CLUTCH

Clutch Assembly

REMOVAL & INSTALLATION

1. Disconnect the negative battery cable.

2. Raise and safely support the vehicle.

3. Remove the transmission, starter motor and throw-out bearing.

4. Disconnect the clutch linkage from the housing and remove the housing.

5. Mark the clutch cover and flywheel for reassembly.

6. Remove the clutch cover and the driven plate by loosening the bolts alternately and in several stages. Remove the clutch assembly.

7. Remove the pilot bushing lubricating wick and soak the wick in engine oil.

To install:

8. Inspect the parts for signs of overheating (blue color), distortion, scoring or wear. Overheated or deeply scored or worn parts should be replaced. Light wear may be cleaned up by sanding or refacing.

9. Using an alignment tool, position the clutch and pressure plates onto the flywheel.

10. Align the matchmarks and tighten the pressure plate-to-flywheel bolts alternately and in several stages.

11. Install the housing-to-engine and torque the bolts.

12. Install the throw-out bearing, the clutch linkage, the starter and the transmission.

13. Connect the negative battery cable.

Clutch Master Cylinder

REMOVAL & INSTALLATION

1. Disconnect the negative battery cable.

2. Remove the brake master cylinder and power booster as an assembly; if possible, move the assembly aside, do not disconnect the brake lines from the master cylinder.

3. Disconnect and plug the hydraulic line from the clutch master cylinder.

4. Disconnect the cylinder-to-clutch pedal pushrod.

5. Remove the clutch master cylinder-to-dash nuts and the cylinder-to-bracket nuts.

6. Remove the clutch master cylinder from the vehicle.

To install:

7. Install the clutch master cylinder to the dash and torque the nuts.

8. Using a new cotter pin, connect the pushrod between the clutch master cylinder and the clutch pedal.

9. Connect the hydraulic line to the clutch master cylinder.

10. Refill the clutch master cylinder with clean brake fluid and bleed the system. Check and/or repair any leaks.

11. Install the brake master cylinder and power booster to the cowl and install the nuts.

12. Connect the negative battery cable.

Clutch Slave Cylinder

ADJUSTMENT

All vehicles have hydraulically actuated clutch systems with no provision for adjustment.

REMOVAL & INSTALLATION

1. Disconnect the negative battery cable.

2. Raise and safely support the vehicle.

3. Disconnect and plug the hydraulic line from the slave cylinder.

4. Remove the slave cylinder/heat shield-to-clutch housing bolts and the cylinder/heat shield from the vehicle.

To install:

5. Install the slave cylinder/heat shield-to-clutch housing, align the pushrod with the throw-out lever, install the bolts and torque them securely.

6. Connect the hydraulic line to the slave cylinder.

7. Lower the vehicle.

8. Refill the clutch master cylinder with clean brake fluid and bleed the system. Check and/or repair any leaks.

9. Connect the negative battery cable.

Hydraulic Clutch System Bleeding

1. Fill the reservoir with brake fluid.

2. Loosen the bleed screw and have an assistant depress the clutch pedal to the floor.

3. Tighten the bleed screw and release the clutch pedal.

4. Repeat the bleeding operation until the fluid is free of air bubbles.

NOTE: It is suggested to attach a hose to the bleeder and place the other end into a container at least ½ full of brake fluid during the bleeding operation. Do not allow the reservoir to run out of fluid during the bleeding operation.

AUTOMATIC TRANSMISSION

For further information on transmissions/transaxles, please refer to "Chilton's Guide to Transmission Repair".

Transmission Assembly

REMOVAL & INSTALLATION

1. Disconnect the negative battery cable.

2. Open the engine hood and disconnect the fan shroud. Remove the fill tube attaching bolt.

3. Raise and safely support the vehicle.

4. Remove the skid plate.

5. Matchmark and remove the driveshaft(s).

6. Remove or loosen the necessary exhaust system components and bracing brackets.

7. Remove the starter assembly and the stiffening braces.

8. Matchmark and remove speedometer adapter and cable assembly.

9. Disconnect the shift and throttle linkage. If equipped with column shift, remove the bellcrank bracket bolt from the converter housing.

10. Disconnect the neutral start and backup light switch connector. Remove the TCS switch oil line, if equipped.

11. Remove cover in front of the converter, if equipped.

12. Matchmark converter-to-converter drive plate and remove the converter-to-drive plate bolts.

13. Using a transmission jack, support the transmission/transfer assembly.

14. Remove bolt(s) at the rear support cushion.

15. Remove the rear crossmember and ground strap, if equipped with a strap.

16. Move the transmission, as necessary, to remove the oil cooler lines.

17. Place a support stand under the engine, as required.

18. Remove transmission fill tube, as required.

NOTE: Transmission fluid will drain out. Plug fill tube hole.

19. Remove the transmission-to-engine bolts. While holding the converter in position, move the transmission assembly rearward and lower the assembly from under the vehicle.

To install:

20. If the torque converter was removed or inadvertently separated from the transmission, a new pump seal should be installed and the pump rotor drive lugs re-aligned with an aligning tool, before the converter is re-installed.

21. Using a transmission jack, raise the transmission assembly and align the converter housing with the engine attaching flange dowel pins.

22. Align the matchmarks between the converter and the drive plate. Install the attaching bolts, seat the converter housing flush with the engine flange before tightening the bolts.

NOTE: Drive plate bolts must not be reused.

23. Install the oil cooler lines, the rear engine crossmember and the mount bolt(s).

24. Complete the assembly and check the fluid level of the transfer case lubricant.

25. Lower the vehicle and complete the assembly topside.

26. Fill the transmission with fluid and correct the level, as necessary.

27. Connect the negative battery cable. Road test the vehicle and check the transmission operation.

SHIFT LINKAGE ADJUSTMENT

1. Raise and safely support the vehicle.

2. Loosen the shift rod trunnion retaining setscrew.

3. Move the shift lever into the **P** position.

4. Move the valve body manual lever rearward to the **P** detent; be sure the lever is moved rearward as far as possible.

5. Try to rotate the driveshaft shaft; if the driveshaft will not rotate, the park lock pawl if fully engaged.

6. Tighten the shift rod trunnion retaining setscrew.

7. Move the shift lever to the **N** and the **P** positions and attempt to start the engine; it should only start in these position.

NOTE: If the engine starts in the R, D, 2 or 1 positions, the adjustment is incorrect or the neutral/safely switch is defective.

8. Lower the vehicle.

THROTTLE LINKAGE ADJUSTMENT

1. Disconnect the throttle control rod spring.

2. Using the throttle control rod spring, connect it to and hold the adjusting link in the forward position against the nylon washer.

3. Block the choke in the open position and set the carburetor throttle off the fast idle cam.

4. Raise and safely support the vehicle.

5. Loosen the throttle control adjusting link bolts; do not remove the spring clip and nylon washer.

6. Using a spare throttle return spring, connect it to the transmission throttle lever and hold it forward against the stop.

7. Push the end of the link to eliminate the lash and pull the clamp rearward so the rod bolt bottoms in the rear of the rod slot. Using the forward bolt, tighten the clamp to the link.

8. Pull the throttle control rod rearward so the rod bolt bottoms in the

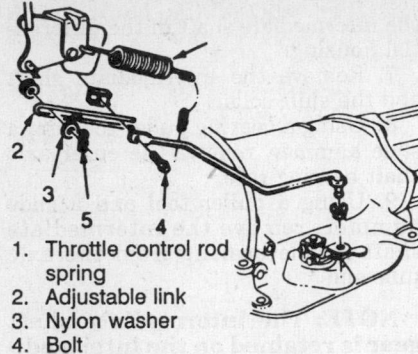

1. Throttle control rod spring
2. Adjustable link
3. Nylon washer
4. Bolt
5. Spring clip

Exploded view of the throttle control rod assembly

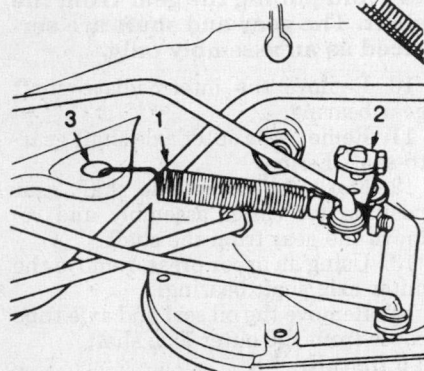

1. Spare throttle return spring
2. Transmission throttle lever
3. Torque converter casting boss

Using a spare throttle return spring to secure the transmission throttle lever

front of the rod slot and tighten the rear retaining bolt.

9. Remove the spare throttle return spring from the throttle lever.
10. Lower the vehicle.
11. Remove the throttle control rod spring form the adjusting link and install it onto the control rod.

TRANSFER CASE

Transfer Case Assembly

TORQUE BIAS TEST

This test may be performed to determine the condition of the viscous coupling, which is the "heart" of the AMC transfer case. Note that if a malfunction in the coupling is observed, the coupling cannot be repaired in any way but must be replaced.

1. Drive the vehicle onto a level surface, turn the engine **OFF** and place the transmission shift lever in **N**. Place the Select Drive lever in the **4WD** position.
2. Raise and safely support 1 of the front wheels and remove the wheel cover.
3. Attach a socket and torque wrench to any 1 of the lug nuts of the raised wheel.
4. Rotate the wheel with the torque wrench and note the amount of torque required to turn the wheel.
5. A reading of 45 ft. lbs. minimum should be obtained. If the reading is less than 45 ft. lbs., the transfer case must be disassembled and the bench test of the coupling should be performed. If the reading is 45 ft. lbs. or more, the coupling is operating properly.
6. Remove the torque wrench and socket, install the wheel cover and lower the vehicle.

REMOVAL & INSTALLATION

Manual Transmission

1. Disconnect the negative battery cable.
2. Raise and safely support the vehicle.
3. Remove the skid plate and rear brace rod at the transfer case. Support engine/transmission assembly.
4. Matchmark and remove the speedometer adapter and cable.
5. Matchmark the driveshafts and remove from the transfer case yokes.
6. Remove the vacuum shift motor harness.
7. Using a transmission jack, support the transfer case. Remove the transfer case nuts and the transfer case.
To install:
8. Using a transmission jack, install the transfer case assembly and torque the nuts.
9. Install the vacuum shift motor harness.
10. Install the transfer case yokes. Align the matchmarks and install the driveshafts.
11. Align the matchmark and install the speedometer cable and adapter housing.
12. Install the rear brace rod to the transfer case and the skid plate. Remove the support from under the engine/transmission assembly.
13. Lower the vehicle and connect the negative battery cable.
14. Check the fluid level in the transfer case and its operation.

Automatic Transmission

1. Disconnect the negative battery cable.

2. Raise and safely support the vehicle.
3. Support the engine/transmission assembly.
4. Disconnect catalytic converter support bracket at the adapter housing, if equipped.
5. Remove the skid plate and rear brace rod at the transfer case.
6. Matchmark and remove the speedometer adapter and the speedometer cable.
7. Matchmark the driveshafts and disconnect from the transfer case yokes.
8. Disconnect the gearshift and throttle linkage from the transmission.
9. Using a transmission jack, support the transfer case. Lower the rear crossmember.
10. Remove the retaining case-to-adapter housing stud nuts and remove the transfer case.
To install:
11. Install the transfer case and torque the nuts.
12. Install the rear crossmember and remove the transmission jack from the transfer case.
13. Connect the throttle and gearshift linkage to the transmission.
14. Install the transfer case yokes. Align the matchmarks and install the driveshafts.
15. Using a new O-ring, align the matchmark and install the speedometer cable and speedometer adapter.
16. Install the rear brace to the transfer case and the skid plate.
17. Connect the catalytic converter support bracket to the adapter housing, if equipped.
18. Remove the support from under the engine/transmission assembly.
19. Lower the vehicle and connect the negative battery cable.
20. Check the fluid levels of the transmission and transfer case.

NOTE: If the transfer case has been disassembled and repaired, fill the transfer case to the bottom edge of the filler hole with appropriate lubricant and install the plug. Drive the vehicle approximately 8–10 miles and recheck the lubricant level. Refill as necessary. This method results in a more accurate lubricant fill.

DRIVE AXLE

Halfshaft

REMOVAL & INSTALLATION

1. Raise and safely support the vehicle.

2. Remove wheel, caliper and rotor.

3. Remove the attaching axle shaft flange-to-halfshaft bolts.

4. Remove the cotter pin, nut lock and axle hub nut.

5. Remove the halfshaft.

To install:

6. Install the halfshaft, the axle flange-to-halfshaft bolts and the hub nut. Torque the halfshaft-to-flange bolts to 45 ft. lbs. (61 Nm) and the hub nut to 175 ft. lbs. (237 Nm).

7. Install nut lock and cotter pin. Install rotor, caliper and wheel.

CV-Boot

REMOVAL & INSTALLATION

Inner (Inboard)

1. Disconnect the negative battery cable.

2. Raise and safely support the vehicle. Remove the front wheels.

3. Remove the boot retaining clamps and the spacer ring.

4. Slide the halfshaft and the spider bearing assembly out of the tri-pot housing. Install the spider retainer onto the spider bearing assembly.

5. Remove the spider assembly and the boot from the halfshaft.

6. To install, pack the new boot with grease and reverse the removal procedures.

Outer (Outboard)

1. Disconnect the negative battery cable.

2. Raise and safely support the vehicle. Remove the front wheels.

3. Remove the brake caliper and support on a wire. Remove the rotor.

4. Slide the outer CV-joint assembly off the halfshaft.

5. Remove the bearing retaining ring, the boot retainer, the clamp and the outer boot.

6. To install, pack the new boot with grease and reverse the removal procedures.

Driveshaft and U-Joints

REMOVAL & INSTALLATION

Front Driveshaft

1. Disconnect the negative battery cable.

2. Place the transfer case in **2WD**.

3. Raise and safely support the vehicle.

4. Matchmark the axle and driveshaft yokes for assembly reference.

5. Disconnect the driveshaft at the axle yoke and from the transfer case.

NOTE: The axle yoke is attached to the drive pinion nut. Do not loosen this nut.

6. Remove the driveshaft.

To install:

7. Align the matchmarks and install the driveshaft; torque the clamp strap bolts to 17 ft. lbs. (23 Nm).

8. Lower the vehicle.

9. Connect the negative battery cable. Test drive the vehicle and check the operation.

Rear Driveshaft

1. Disconnect the negative battery cable.

2. Place the transmission in **N**.

3. Raise and safely support the vehicle.

4. Matchmark the axle and driveshaft yokes for assembly reference.

5. Disconnect the driveshaft at the axle yoke and from the transfer case.

NOTE: The axle yoke is attached to the drive pinion nut. Do not loosen this nut.

6. Remove the driveshaft.

To install:

7. Align the matchmarks and install the driveshaft; torque the clamp strap bolts to 17 ft. lbs. (23 Nm).

8. Lower the vehicle.

9. Connect the negative battery cable. Test drive the vehicle and check the operation.

Front Axle Shaft, Bearing and Seal

The front axle assembly consists of a shift housing, an intermediate shaft and 2 outer axle shafts.

REMOVAL & INSTALLATION

1. Remove the front axle assembly from the vehicle.

2. Remove the axle cover and drain the lubricant.

3. Remove the shift housing cover retaining bolts and cover. Remove the shift fork, housing and the shift motor as an assembly.

4. Remove the axle tube retaining bolts; the bolts are accessible through the access hole in the outer axle shaft flange.

5. Remove the outer axle shaft assembly by tapping the shaft flange with a rubber or plastic mallet.

6. Remove the snapring that retains the intermediate shaft in the differential housing.

7. Remove the intermediate shaft and the shift collar.

8. Using a bearing puller tool and a slide hammer, remove the outer axle shaft bearing race.

9. Using a puller tool and a slide hammer, remove the intermediate shaft needle bearing from the axle tube end.

NOTE: The intermediate shaft gear is retained on the intermediate shaft by an internal-type, expandable snapring. When removing the bearing from the gear, support the gear face on vise jaws to avoid pulling the gear from the shaft. The gear and shaft are serviced as an assembly only.

10. Remove the intermediate shaft gear bearing.

11. Remove the outer axle shaft gear-to-shaft E-ring.

12. Mark the outer axle shaft gear position for easier assembly and remove the gear from the shaft.

13. Using an arbor press, remove the outer axle shaft bearing.

14. Remove the oil seal and axle tube cover from the outer axle shaft.

To install:

15. Install the axle tube cover and the oil seal on the outer axle shaft.

16. Using an arbor press, install the outer axle shaft bearing and race onto the shaft.

17. With the gear splines facing outward, install the outer axle shaft gear onto the shaft with the arbor press. Install the E-ring onto the outer axle shaft.

18. Using a bearing installer, install the intermediate shaft needle bearing in the axle tube.

19. Using an arbor press, install the intermediate shaft gear needle bearing in the gear bore.

20. Install the intermediate shaft in the axle tube. Install the shift collar on the intermediate shaft and seat the shaft in the differential.

21. Install the intermediate shaft-to-differential lockring. Install the outer axle shaft assembly and install the axle tube cover bolts evenly and in a criss-cross pattern to seat the bearing race and seal. Torque the bolts to 144 inch lbs.

22. Install the gasket on the shift housing cover and install the gasket and axle shift housing. Torque the housing bolts to 108 inch lbs.

23. Using a new gasket, install the axle housing cover and torque the bolts to 20 ft. lbs. Fill the shift housing cavity and the gear housing with gear lubricant. Install the fill plugs and tighten securely.

Rear Axle Shaft, Bearing and Seal

REMOVAL & INSTALLATION

The hub and drum are separate units and are removed after the wheel is removed. The hub and axle shaft are serrated together on the taper. An axle shaft key assures proper alignment during assembly.

1. With the wheel on the ground and the parking brake applied, remove and discard the axle shaft nut cotter pin and remove the nut. Raise and safely support the vehicle. Remove the wheel, release the parking brakes and remove the drum.

2. Using a wheel puller, remove the hub.

NOTE: Use of a knock-out puller should be discouraged, since it may result in damage to the axle shaft, wheel bearings or differential thrust block.

3. Disconnect the parking brake cable from the equalizer.

4. Disconnect the brake tube from the wheel cylinder. Remove the brake support plate assembly, oil seal and axle shims; note that the axle shims are located on the left side only.

5. Using a screw type puller, remove the axle shaft and bearings from the axle housing.

NOTE: On twin-grip axles, rotating the differential with a shaft removed will misalign the side gear splines, preventing installation of the replacement shaft.

6. Remove the axle shaft inner oil seal and install new seals at assembly.

7. The bearing is a press fit and should be removed with an arbor press.

To install:

8. The axle shaft bearings have no provision for lubrication after assembly. Before installing the bearings, pack them with a good quality wheel bearing lubricant.

9. Press the axle shaft bearings onto the axle shaft with the small diameter of the cone facing the outer (tapered) end of the shaft.

10. Soak the inner axle shaft seal in light lubricating oil. Coat the outer surface of the seal retainer with sealant.

11. Install the inner oil seal.

12. Install the axle shafts, indexing the splined end with the differential side gears.

13. Install the outer bearing cup.

14. Install the brake support plate. Sealant should be applied to the axle housing flange and brake support mounting plate.

15. Install the original shims, oil seal and brake support plate. Torque the nuts to 30–35 ft. lbs.

NOTE: The oil seal and retainer go between the axle housing flange and the brake support plate.

16. To adjust the axle shaft endplay, strike the axle shafts with a lead mallet to seat the bearings. Install a dial indicator on the brake support plate and check the play while pushing and pulling the axle shaft; endplay should be 0.004–0.008 in.

NOTE: Add shims to the left side only to decrease the play and remove shims to increase the play.

17. Slide the hub onto the axle shafts aligning the serrations and the keyway on the hub with the axle shaft key.

18. Replace the hub and drum, install the wheel, lower the vehicle and torque the axle shaft nut to 250 ft. lbs. If the cotter pin hole is not aligned with a castellation on the nut, tighten the nut to the next castellation.

NOTE: A new hub must be installed whenever a new axle shaft is installed. Install 2 thrust washers on the shaft. Tighten the new hub onto the shaft until the hub is 1³⁄₁₆ inch (30.14mm) from the end of the shaft. Remove the nut and a thrust washer. Install the nut and torque to 250 ft. lbs. New hubs do not have serrations on the axle shaft mating surface. The serrations are cut when the hub is installed to the axle shaft.

19. Connect the parking brake cable to the equalizer.

20. Connect the brake tube at the wheel cylinder and bleed the brakes.

Front Wheel Hub, Knuckle and Bearings

REMOVAL & INSTALLATION

1. Raise and safely support the vehicle.

2. Remove wheel, caliper and rotor.

3. Remove the attaching axle shaft flange-to-halfshaft bolts.

4. Remove the cotter pin, nut lock and axle hub nut.

5. Remove the halfshaft.

6. Remove the steering arm from steering knuckle.

7. Remove the caliper anchor plate from steering knuckle.

8. Remove the 3 Torx® head bolts retaining hub assembly.

9. Remove the hub assembly from the steering knuckle.

10. Clean grease from steering knuckle cavity.

To install:

11. Partially fill the hub cavity of steering knuckle with chassis lubricant and install hub assembly.

12. Torque the hub Torx® head bolts to 75 ft. lbs. (102 Nm).

13. Install the caliper anchor plate and torque the bolts to 100 ft. lbs. (136 Nm).

14. Install the halfshaft, the axle flange-to-halfshaft bolts and the hub nut. Torque the halfshaft-to-flange bolts to 45 ft. lbs. (61 Nm) and the hub nut to 175 ft. lbs. (237 Nm).

15. Install nut lock and cotter pin. Install rotor, caliper and wheel.

Adjustment

The vehicle has a unique front axle hub and bearing assembly. The assembly is sealed and does not require lubrication, periodic maintenance or adjustment. The hub has tapered or ball bearings which seat in races machined directly into the hub. There are darkened areas surrounding the bearing race areas of the hub. These darkened areas, from a heat treatment process, are normal and should not be mistaken for a problem condition.

Pinion Seal

REMOVAL & INSTALLATION

1. Raise and safely support the vehicle.

2. Matchmark the driveshaft to the differential yoke and remove the driveshaft.

3. Using an inch lb. torque wrench, rotate the drive pinion several times to measure and record the turning torque.

4. Using a yoke holder tool, secure the yoke and remove the pinion nut.

5. Matchmark the yoke to the drive pinion.

6. Using a yoke puller and adapters, pull the yoke from the drive pinion; it may be necessary to place an catch pan under the differential to catch the oil.

7. Using a pry bar, pry the pinion seal from the differential housing; be careful not to scratch the drive pinion or the seal's seat.

To install:

8. Using a seal installer, lubricate the new seal with axle lubricant and install it into the housing until it is flush with the end of the housing.

9. Align the yoke and drive pinion matchmarks and install the yoke.

10. Using a new pinion nut, install and tighten it enough to remove the endplay.

11. Using an inch lb. torque wrench, check the torque required to turn the pinion.

12. Gradually, tighten the nut and recheck the preload; be sure to add 5 inch lbs. (0.6 Nm) to the recorded preload.

NOTE: Do not overtorque the pinion nut. If the desired preload is exceeded, a new crush sleeve must be installed and the drive pinion preload reset.

Differential Carrier

REMOVAL & INSTALLATION

Front

1. Remove the front axle assembly and support it in a vise.

2. Remove the cover-to-axle housing bolts and the cover. Drain the fluid from the housing.

3. Remove the axles from the housing.

4. Matchmark the bearing caps so they are reassembled in the same position and location. Loosen the bearing cap bolts.

5. Using an axle spreader tool and adapters, install them to the axle housing. Using a dial indicator, attach it to the axle housing and position the pointer on a side of the housing opening. Spread the axle housing a maximum of 0.020 in. (0.05mm) and remove the dial indicator.

6. Remove the bearing caps and pry the differential assembly from housing.

To install:

7. Install the differential assembly into the axle housing and tighten the bearing cap bolts securely, without applying full torque.

8. Adjust the differential bearing preload by performing the following procedures:

   a. Using a pry bar, pry the differential outer bearing races toward the center of the case.

   b. Using various feeler gauge thicknesses, insert them between both outer bearing races and the axle housing, until the ring gear backlash is 0.001–0.002 in. (0.025–0.051mm).

   c. Assemble identical shim packs that will provide the desired backlash and insert them between the outer bearing races and the housing.

   d. Recheck the backlash.

   e. With the backlash correct, remove the differential assembly from the housing and add an additional 0.015 in. (0.38mm) shim to the drive tooth side of the ring gear shim pack.

   f. Remove the differential bear-

ings and install the preselected shim packs to the appropriate side of the differential assembly.

   g. Install the differential assembly into the axle housing and mesh the ring gear with the pinion gear teeth.

   h. Install the bearing caps, apply sealant to the bolts and torque the bolts to 40 ft. lbs. (54 Nm).

9. Install the axle shafts.

10. Apply a thin coat of silicone sealant, to the housing cover, install the cover and torque the bolts to 20 ft. lbs. (27 Nm).

11. Refill the housing with clean lubricant.

12. Install the axle housing and lower the vehicle.

Rear

1. Remove the rear axle assembly and support it in a vise.

2. Remove the cover-to-axle housing bolts and the cover. Drain the fluid from the housing.

3. Matchmark the bearing caps so they are reassembled in the same position and location.

4. Remove the bearing caps and pry the differential assembly from the housing.

5. Remove the ring gear-to-differential assembly bolts and the ring gear.

To install:

6. Install the differential assembly into the axle housing, without the ring gear.

7. Adjust the differential bearing endplay by performing the following procedures:

   a. Install a 0.142 in. (3.6mm), on each side of the differential assembly, between the bearing race and the housing.

   b. Install the bearing caps and tighten the bolts finger-tight.

   c. Attach a dial indicator to the axle housing and position the pointer against the ring gear mounting surface of the differential assembly.

   d. Using 2 pry bars, pry between the shims and housing. Pry the assembly to a side and zero the dial indicator.

   e. Pry the assembly to the other side. Read and record the indicator reading; the amount is the shim thickness to be added for a no endplay condition.

NOTE: Shims are available in thicknesses of 0.142–0.174 in. (3.6–4.4mm) with increments of 0.002 in. (0.05mm).

8. Install the ring gear onto the differential case and torque the bolts, evenly, to 52 ft. lbs. (71 Nm).

9. Install the differential case into

the axle housing and torque the bearing cap bolts to 57 ft. lbs. (77 Nm).

10. Check and/or adjust the backlash by performing the following procedures:

   a. Using a dial indicator, attach it to the housing and position the pointer so it contacts the drive side of a ring gear tooth, at a right angle to it.

   b. Rock the ring gear and note the movement on the dial indicator; the backlash should be 0.005–0.009 in. (0.13–0.23mm).

   c. To increase the backlash, install a thinner shim on the drive gear side and a thicker shim on the opposite side. To decrease the backlash, install a thicker shim on the drive gear side and a thinner shim on the opposite side.

11. Adjust the differential bearing preload by performing the following procedures:

   a. Remove the differential assembly from the housing.

   b. Remove the differential bearings and install the 0.004 in. (0.10mm) shim thickness to each side of the differential assembly.

   c. Using a soft malled (sic) tap the differential assembly into the axle housing and mesh the ring gear with the pinion gear teeth.

   d. Install the bearing caps, apply sealant to the bolts and torque the bolts to 57 ft. lbs. (77 Nm).

12. Apply a thin coat of silicone sealant, to the housing cover, install the cover and torque the bolts to 15 ft. lbs. (20 Nm).

13. Refill the housing with clean lubricant.

14. Install the axle housing and lower the vehicle.

Axle Housing

REMOVAL & INSTALLATION

Front

1. Raise and safely support the vehicle. Remove the halfshaft-to-axle flange bolts. Secure the axle halfshafts to the underbody.

2. Compress and secure the halfshafts to prevent shaft separation.

3. Matchmark the driveshaft and axle yoke for ease of installation.

4. Using a floor jack, support the axle assembly, then remove the brace rod from the axle and the shift motor shield.

5. Remove the axle-to-chassis bolts; there are 5 on the left side and 1 on the right side.

6. Disconnect the vacuum harness from the axle shift motor and partially lower the axle assembly to allow access to the vent hose.

7. Remove the vent hose, lower the axle assembly and remove it from under the vehicle.
To install:
8. Raise the axle assembly and connect the vent hose.
9. Connect the vacuum harness to the axle shift motor and raise the axle assembly into position and torque the axle-to-chassis bolts to 50 ft. lbs.
10. Install the brace rod to the axle and the shift motor shield. Remove the floor jack.
11. Align the matchmarks and install the driveshaft.
12. Connect the halfshafts and torque the halfshaft-to-flange bolts to 45 ft. lbs.
13. Lower the vehicle.

Rear

1. Apply the parking brake to lock the rear wheels. Remove the axle shaft nuts.
2. Raise and safely support the vehicle. Remove the rear wheels.

NOTE: The brake drums and axle shafts can be removed at this time or can be removed after the axle assembly has been removed from the vehicle.

3. Disconnect the flexible brake line from the body floorpan bracket. Release and disconnect the parking brake cables from the equalizer.
4. Matchmark the driveshaft and yokes for assembly reference.
5. Remove the stabilizer bar, if equipped.
6. Disconnect the axle vent hose. Using a floor jack, support the rear axle.
7. Disconnect the shock absorbers from the spring tie plates.
8. Remove the spring U-bolts, spring plates and spring clip plate, if equipped with the stabilizer bar.
9. Lower the axle assembly and remove from under the vehicle.
To install:
10. Raise the axle assembly and install the spring plates, the spring U-bolts and the spring clip plate, if equipped with a stabilizer bar.
11. Torque the U-bolt nuts to 55 ft. lbs.

NOTE: The driveshaft is a balanced unit; care must be used in handling. Do not bend or distort the tube or yokes, or vibration will result.

12. Connect the shock absorbers to the spring tie plates.
13. Remove the floor jack and connect the axle vent hose.
14. Install the stabilizer bar, if equipped.

15. Align the matchmarks and install the yokes and driveshaft.
16. Connect the parking brake cables to the equalizer. Connect the flexible brake line to the body floorpan bracket.
17. Install the rear wheels and lower the vehicle.
18. Install the axle shaft nuts.
19. Check and/or refill the rear axle housing. Test drive the vehicle and check the operation.

STEERING

Steering Wheel

REMOVAL & INSTALLATION

1. Disconnect the negative battery cable.
2. Remove the horn button and disconnect the wires.
3. Remove the steering wheel center nut and washer. Before removing the wheel, note the position of the index marks on the wheel and the steering shaft. If none are present, paint an alignment mark on the shaft and wheel.
4. Remove the wheel with a puller.

NOTE: Do not hammer on the end of the steering shaft; the plastic retainers could shear, which maintain the rigidity of the energy-absorbing steering column.

To install:
5. Align the matchmarks and install the steering wheel. Torque the nut to 25 ft. lbs. (34 Nm).

NOTE: Some shafts have metric threads. These can be identified by a groove in the shaft splines. Metric nuts are coded blue.

6. Connect the horn wire and install the button.
7. Connect the negative battery cable.

Steering Column

REMOVAL & INSTALLATION

1. Disconnect battery negative cable.
2. Paint identifying marks on intermediate shaft and gear to aid assembly.
3. Remove flexible coupling nuts and disengage intermediate shaft from coupling.
4. If equipped with column shift,

disconnect shift rod from steering column shift lever.
5. Move the seat rearward, as far as possible.
6. Remove lower finish panel or tube cover.
7. Remove package tray, if equipped.
8. Lift locking tab on steering column harness connector and separate column harness from instrument panel harness connector.
9. Press locking tabs on ignition switch harness connectors and disconnect harness from switch; remove black connector first.
10. Disconnect the cruise command harness connector, if equipped.
11. Disconnect the shift quadrant pointer control cable from shift bowl.
12. Remove toe plate bolts from dash panel.
13. Remove the steering column mounting bracket-to-column bolts.

NOTE: The column mounting bracket bolts are metric and are color-coded blue for identification. Keep these bolts with the bracket for assembly.

14. Support the column assembly and remove the column mounting bracket-to-instrument panel nuts. Remove bracket and store in safe place to protect break-away capsules.
15. Remove column assembly from vehicle.

NOTE: Use only the specified screws, bolts and nuts during assembly and torque to maintain proper energy-absorbing action of the assembly. Over-length bolts must not be used as they may prevent a portion of the assembly from compressing under impact. The column mounting bracket-to-instrument panel nuts/bolts must be torqued so the column mounting bracket will break away under impact.

16. Remove the column holding fixture and install mounting bracket on column. Torque the bracket bolts to 20 ft. lbs.
To install:
17. If the intermediate steering shaft was removed, install shaft on column using alignment marks made during removal.
18. Install the column in vehicle.
19. Engage intermediate shaft flange with steering gear flexible coupling and loosely, install 2 column mounting bracket-to-instrument panel nuts, finger-tighten nuts only.
20. Install toe plate gasket, toe plate and toe plate bolts, finger-tighten bolts only.

21. Install the flexible coupling nuts and torque to 30 ft. lbs.

22. Install the remaining column mounting bracket-to-instrument panel nuts, finger-tighten nuts only.

23. Position the column so flexible coupling is flat and not distorted; torque column mounting bracket-to-instrument panel nuts to 10 ft. lbs.

24. Align toe plate, clamp and torque the bolts to 10 ft. lbs.

25. Connect shift linkage and check operation; adjust, if necessary.

26. Connect the quadrant cable-to-shift-bowl, if equipped.

27. Connect the ignition switch harness, steering column harness and cruise command connector, if equipped.

28. Install the lower finish panel, tube cover or package tray, if equipped.

29. Remove the protective covering from column painted areas.

30. Connect battery negative cable.

Manual Steering Gear

ADJUSTMENT

Worm Bearing Preload

1. Loosen the worm bearing adjuster locknut.

2. Carefully, tighten the worm bearing adjuster until it bottoms, then, back off adjuster ¼ turn.

3. Install a socket and torque wrench on the splined end of the wormshaft.

4. Rotate the wormshaft clockwise to its stop, noting the number of turns. Then, back off the shaft ½ the number of turns.

5. Tighten the worm bearing adjuster until the torque required to rotate the wormshaft is 5–8 inch lbs. (0.6–0.9 Nm).

6. Torque the worm bearing adjuster locknut to 90 ft. lbs.

Pitman Shaft Overcenter Drag Torque

1. Rotate the wormshaft from stop-to-stop and count the total number of turns.

2. Turn the wormshaft back ½ the total number of turns to place the ball nut and pitman shaft in centered position.

3. Install a socket and an torque wrench on the pitman shaft splines.

4. Tighten the pitman shaft adjuster screw while rotating the shaft back and forth overcenter until the torque required to rotate the shaft overcenter equals the worm bearing preload setting.

5. Rotate the shaft overcenter and continue tightening the adjuster screw

until the drag torque is increased by an additional 4–10 inch lbs. (0.5–1 Nm) but do not exceed the total of 16 inch lbs. (2 Nm).

6. Hold the adjuster screw in position and torque the adjuster screw locknut to 23 ft. lbs. (31 Nm). Do not allow the screw to turn while tightening the locknut.

REMOVAL & INSTALLATION

1. Disconnect the negative battery cable.

2. Place the wheels in a straight-ahead position.

3. Remove the flexible coupling-to-intermediate shaft attaching nuts.

4. Raise and safely support the vehicle.

5. Remove the following:
   a. Skid plate, if equipped
   b. Left side crossmember-to-sill support brace
   c. Stabilizer bar brackets from the frame

6. Mark the pitman arm for alignment and remove using special puller.

7. Remove the steering gear-to-chassis bolts and the steering gear assembly.

To install:

8. Install the steering gear-to-chassis and torque the bolts.

9. Check the steering gear worm bearing preload and pitman shaft overcenter drag torque adjustment.

NOTE: Always adjust the worm bearing preload first and the pitman shaft overcenter drag torque last.

10. Align the pitman arm-to-steering gear alignment mark, install the arm and torque the nut.

11. Install the following equipment:
    a. Stabilizer bar brackets to the frame
    b. Left side crossmember-to-sill support brace
    c. Skid plate, if equipped

12. Lower the vehicle. Install the flexible coupling-to-intermediate shaft nuts.

13. Connect the negative battery cable.

Power Steering Gear

ADJUSTMENT

Worm Bearing Preload

1. Using a spanner wrench, seat the adjuster plug firmly in the housing; approximately 20 ft. lbs. (27 Nm) is required to seat the housing.

2. Place an index mark on the gear housing opposite 1 of the holes in the adjuster plug.

3. Measure back counterclockwise $3/16$–¼ in. (4.7–6.3mm) from the index mark and remark the housing.

4. Turn the adjuster plug counterclockwise until the hole in the plug is aligned with the 2nd mark on the housing.

5. Install the adjuster plug locknut and torque to 85 ft. lbs. (115 Nm); be sure the adjuster plug does not turn when tightening the locknut.

6. Turn the stub shaft clockwise to stop, then, turn the shaft back ¼ turn.

7. Using a torque wrench and a socket, measure the torque required to turn the stub shaft. Take the reading with the torque wrench at vertical position while turning the stub shaft at an even rate. The torque required to turn the stub shaft should be 4–10 inch lbs. (0.45–1.13 Nm).

Pitman Shaft Overcenter Drag Torque

1. Turn the pitman shaft adjuster screw counterclockwise until fully extended, then, turn it back ½ turn clockwise.

2. Rotate the stub shaft from stop-to-stop and count the total number of turns.

3. Turn the stub shaft back ½ the total number of turns.

NOTE: When the gear is centered, the flat on the stub shaft should face upward and be parallel with the side cover; also, the master spline on the pitman shaft should be aligned with the adjuster screw.

4. Using a torque wrench and a socket, measure the torque required to turn the stub shaft. Take the reading with the torque wrench at vertical position. Rotate the torque wrench 45 degrees each side of the center and record the highest drag torque measured on or near center.

5. Adjust the overcenter drag torque by turning the pitman shaft adjusting screw clockwise until the desired drag torque is obtained. Adjust the drag torque to the following limits:
   a. On new steering gears, add 4–8 inch lbs. (0.45–0.90 Nm) to previously measured worm bearing preload torque but do not exceed a combined total of 18 inch lbs. (2 Nm) drag torque.
   b. On used steering gears, add 4–5 inch lbs. (0.5–0.6 Nm) to previously measured worm bearing preload torque but do not exceed a combined total of 14 inch lbs. (2 Nm) drag torque.

6. Torque the pitman shaft adjusting screw locknut to 35 ft. lbs. (47 Nm) after the adjusting overcenter drag torque.

REMOVAL & INSTALLATION

1. Disconnect the negative battery cable.

2. Place wheels in straight-ahead position.

3. Position drain pan under steering gear.

4. Disconnect hoses from the steering gear. Raise and secure hoses above pump fluid level to prevent excessive oil spillage and cap ends of hoses to keep out dirt.

5. Remove flexible coupling-to-intermediate shaft nuts.

6. Raise and safely support the vehicle. Remove the following items:

   a. Skid plate, if equipped

   b. Left side crossmember-to-sill support brace

   c. Stabilizer bar brackets from the frame

7. Paint alignment marks on pitman arm and pitman shaft for assembly reference.

8. Using a removal tool, press the pitman arm.

9. Remove the steering gear-to-chassis bolts and the steering gear.

To install:

10. Center the steering gear. Using the flexible coupling, turn the stub shaft from stop-to-stop and count total number of turns; then, turn back from either stop ½ total number of turns to center gear. At this point, flat on stub shaft should be facing upward.

11. Align the flexible coupling and intermediate shaft flange.

12. Install the gear bolts in gear, the spacer and the gear onto frame side-sill. Torque gear mounting bolts to 65 ft. lbs.

13. Install the flexible coupling nuts and torque to 25 ft. lbs.

14. Using the alignment marks, install the pitman arm to the shaft.

15. Install pitman arm nut and torque to 115 ft. lbs. Stake the nut to the pitman shaft.

NOTE: The pitman arm nut must be staked to the shaft to retain it properly.

16. Install the following items:

   a. Stabilizer bar brackets.

   b. Left side crossmember-to-sill support brace.

   c. Skid plate, if equipped.

17. Align flexible coupling, if necessary.

18. Connect hoses to gear and torque fittings to 25 ft. lbs.

19. Fill pump reservoir with power steering fluid.

20. Connect the negative battery cable. Start the engine and bleed air from system.

21. Lower the vehicle.

Power Steering Pump

REMOVAL & INSTALLATION

NOTE: The power steering pump on some California vehicles, is driven by a single serpentine belt. Do not attempt to move the pump to adjust the belt. Use the adjusting hole in the alternator bracket and adjust the tension to 140 lbs. force.

1. Disconnect the negative battery cable. Remove the fan belt.

2. Place a container under the pump to catch fluid. Remove the fuel vapor storage canister and air cleaner, if necessary.

3. Disconnect the hoses and cap the outlets, so the power steering unit does not lose fluid. Remove the air pump belt.

4. If equipped with air conditioning, loosen the idler pulley adjusting bolt and idler pulley, air pump adjusting strap mounting bolt and the compressor drive belt from the idler pulley. Loosen both upper leg of the aluminum idler pulley mounting bracket-to-cylinder head nuts and remove the lower leg of the mounting bracket-to-the engine front cover bolt.

5. Remove the air pump mounting stud nut, the power steering pump-to-engine front cover front adapter plate, do not unbolt the adapter plate from the pump, the long adjusting bolt that passes through the adapter plate and the bolt hidden behind the flange in the rear adapter plate. Remove the pump, adapter plate and mounting bracket together.

6. To install, reverse the removal procedures.

7. Refill and bleed the power steering system.

BELT ADJUSTMENT

1. Position a belt tension gauge on the longest accessible span of the belt.

2. Loosen the alternator adjustment and pivot bolts; do not loosen the bracket-to-engine bolts.

3. Using a ½ in. drive lug, insert it into the ½ in. sq. adjustment hole in the alternator mounting bracket and pivot the bracket to tighten the belt.

4. When the belt tension is 140–160 ft. lbs. (189–217 Nm) for a used belt or 180–200 ft. lbs. (244–271 Nm) for a new belt, torque the alternator adjustment and pivot bolts to 28 ft. lbs. (38 Nm).

5. Remove the belt tension gauge.

SYSTEM BLEEDING

1. Raise and safely support the vehicle.

2. With the wheels turned all the way to the left, add power steering fluid to the **COLD** mark on the fluid level indicator.

3. Start the engine and run at fast idle momentarily, turn **OFF** the engine and recheck fluid level. If necessary add fluid to to bring level to the **COLD** mark.

4. Start the engine and bleed the system by turning the wheels from side-to-side without hitting the stops.

NOTE: Fluid with air in it has a light tan or red bubbly appearance.

5. Return the wheels to the center position and keep the engine running for 2–3 minutes.

6. Lower the vehicle. Road test the vehicle and recheck the fluid level making sure it is at the **HOT** mark.

Tie Rod Ends

REMOVAL & INSTALLATION

1. Raise and safely support the vehicle.

2. Remove the cotter pin and the retaining nut from the tie rod end stud.

3. Matchmark the position of the tie rod end, the adjuster tube and the inner tie rod.

4. Loosen the adjuster tube clamps.

5. Using a tie rod end puller, disconnect the tie rod end from the steering arm.

6. Remove the tie rod end from the adjuster tube.

7. To install, reverse the removal procedures. Torque the tie rod end-to-steering arm nut to 35 ft. lbs. and install the new cotter pin.

8. Adjust the toe-in and tighten the clamps.

BRAKES

For all brake system repair and service procedures not detailed below, please refer to "Brakes" in the Unit Repair section.

Master Cylinder

REMOVAL & INSTALLATION

1. Disconnect the negative battery cable.

2. Disconnect the fluid sensor electrical connector, if equipped.

3. Disconnect the brake lines. Cover the master cylinder outlet ports and brake lines to prevent the entry of dirt.

4. If equipped with a manual brake,

disconnect the master cylinder push-rod from the brake pedal.

5. Remove the master cylinder-to-chassis nuts/bolts.

6. Remove the proportioning valve bracket, if necessary.

7. Remove the master cylinder from the vehicle.

To install:

8. Before installing the replacement master cylinder on the vehicle, bench bleed the master cylinder.

9. Install the master cylinder and torque the nuts/bolts. Install the proportioning valve bracket, if necessary.

10. If equipped with a manual brake, connect the master cylinder pushrod to the brake pedal.

11. Connect the brake lines to the master cylinder.

12. Connect the fluid sensor electrical connector, it equipped.

13. Connect the negative battery cable and bleed the brake system.

Combination Valve

The combination valve is a combination pressure differential/rear brake proportioning valve and is located on the right-side fender panel near the heater blower motor.

REMOVAL & INSTALLATION

1. Disconnect the negative battery cable.

2. Disconnect the electrical connector from the combination valve.

3. Disconnect and plug the brake fluid lines from the combination valve.

4. Remove the combination valve-to-fender screws, if equipped, and the valve.

NOTE: The combination valve is serviced as an assembly only.

To install:

5. Install the combination valve and secure with screws, if equipped.

6. Unplug and connect the brake fluid lines to the combination valve.

7. Connect the electrical connector to the combination valve.

8. Connect the negative battery cable and bleed the brake system.

Power Brake Booster

REMOVAL & INSTALLATION

1. Disconnect the negative battery cable.

2. Disconnect the booster unit pushrod and brake lamp switch from the brake pedal.

3. Remove the vacuum hose from the booster check valve.

4. Remove the master cylinder-to-booster nuts and lockwashers. Seperate the master cylinder from the

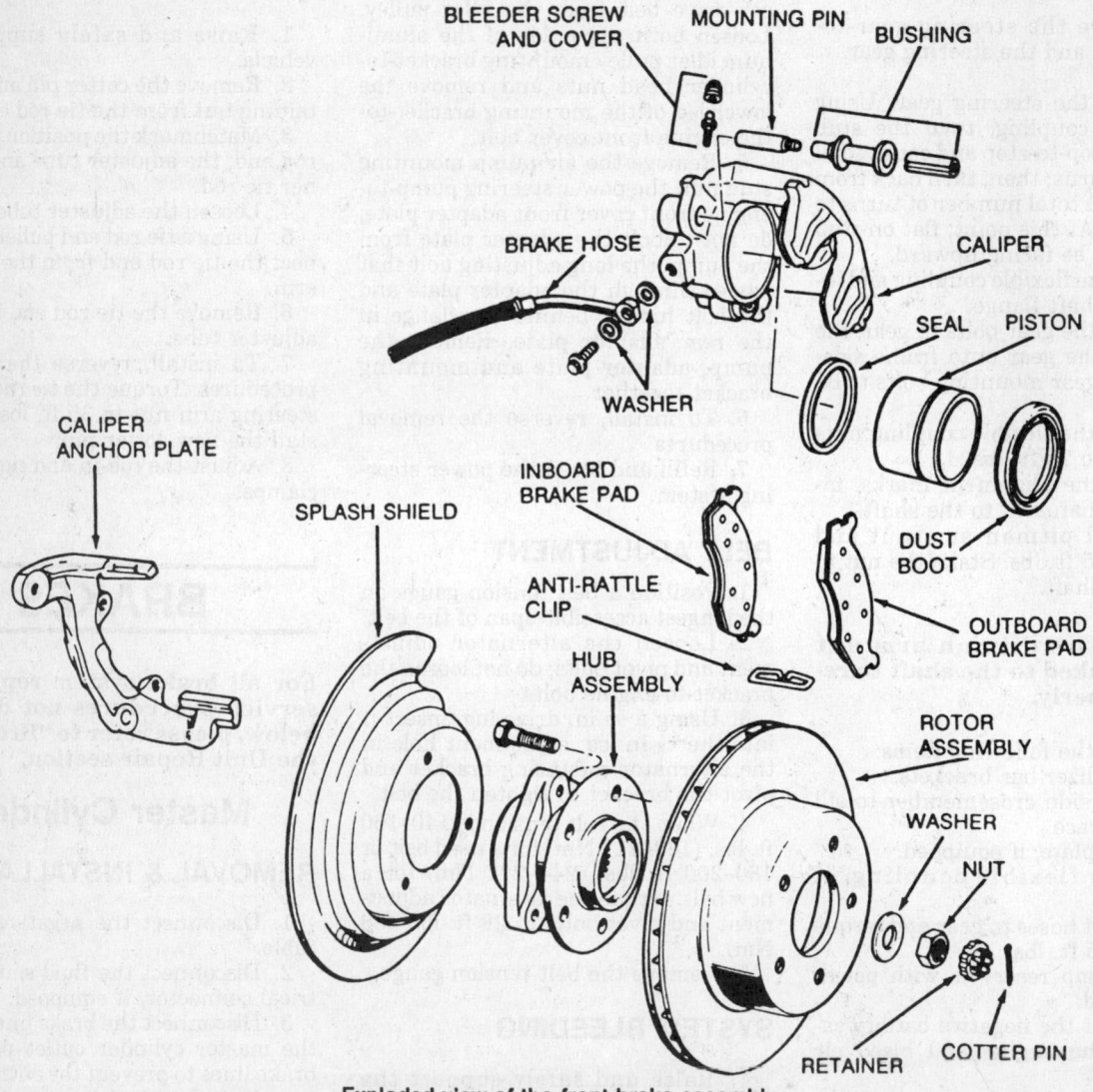

Exploded view of the front brake assembly

booster; do not disconnect the brake lines.

5. Remove the booster-to-dash panel nuts/lockwashers and the booster.

6. To install, reverse of the removal procedures. Connect the negative battery cable and check the booster operation.

Brake Caliper

Brake calipers are used on the front of the vehicle only.

REMOVAL & INSTALLATION

1. Drain and discard ⅔ of the brake fluid from the master cylinder reservoir serving the front disc brakes; do not drain the reservoir completely.

2. Remove the hub cap and loosen the wheel lug nuts.

3. Raise and safely support the vehicle.

4. Remove the front wheel(s).

5. Using a shop cloth, wipe all dirt and grease from the caliper brake hose fitting.

6. Disconnect and plug the brake line from the caliper and discard the hose fitting washer.

7. Using a C-clamp, press the caliper's piston into the bottom of it's bore.

8. Using an Allen wrench, remove the caliper-to-caliper support pins.

9. Lift the caliper from the anchor plate.

To install:

10. Using new disc pads, position them onto the caliper anchor plate.

NOTE: When installing the caliper, be careful not to tear the dust boot.

11. Position the brake caliper onto the caliper anchor plate, insert the pins and torque them to 26 ft. lbs.

12. Using a new brake hose washer, connect the brake hose to the caliper.

13. Install the front wheel(s), lower the vehicle and install the hub cap(s).

14. Refill the master cylinder reservoir, bleed the brake system and seat the brake pads.

Disc Brake Pads

REMOVAL & INSTALLATION

1. Drain and discard ⅔ of the brake fluid from the master cylinder reservoir serving the front disc brakes; do not drain the reservoir completely.

2. Remove the hub cap and loosen the wheel lug nuts.

3. Raise and safely support the vehicle.

4. Remove the front wheel(s).

5. Using a C-clamp, press the caliper's piston into the bottom of it's bore.

6. Using an Allen wrench, remove the caliper-to-caliper support pins.

7. Lift the caliper from the vehicle and suspend the assembly from the coil spring using a wire; do not allow the brake hose to support the weight of the caliper.

8. Remove the outboard brake pad from the anchor plate while holding the anti-rattle clip against the plate; note the position of the anti-rattle clip for reassembly purposes.

9. Remove the inboard brake pad and the anti-rattle clip.

To install:

10. Clean the anchor plate abutment surfaces and lightly lubricate with molybdenum disulfide grease.

11. Install the anti-rattle clip on the trailing end of the anchor plate being sure the split end of the clip faces away from the rotor.

12. While holding the anti-rattle clip in position, install the new inboard disc pad onto the anchor plate and install the outboard brake pad.

NOTE: When installing the caliper, be careful not to tear the dust boot.

13. Position the brake caliper onto the caliper anchor plate, insert the pins and torque them to 26 ft. lbs.

14. Install the front wheel(s), lower the vehicle and install the hub cap(s).

15. Refill the master cylinder reservoir, bleed the brake system and seat the brake pads.

Brake Rotor

REMOVAL & INSTALLATION

1. Loosen the wheel lug nuts.

2. Raise and safely support the vehicle.

3. Remove the front wheel(s).

4. Remove the brake caliper and support it from the coil spring on a wire; do not allow the brake hose to support the weight of the caliper.

5. Remove the rotor from the hub.

To install:

6. Install the rotor onto the hub.

7. Install the brake pads and caliper onto the anchor plate.

8. Install the wheel and torque the nuts to 75 ft. lbs.

9. Lower the vehicle.

NOTE: Be sure to check for a firm brake pedal and proper brake operation before moving the vehicle.

Brake Drums

REMOVAL & INSTALLATION

1. Release the parking brake.

2. Remove the wheel cover and loosen the lug nuts.

NOTE: If the vehicle is equipped with styled wheels, it will be necessary to raise the vehicle and remove the wheel first.

3. Raise and safely support the vehicle.

4. Remove the wheel and the brake drum.

5. To install, reverse the removal procedures and lower the vehicle.

Brake Shoes

REMOVAL & INSTALLATION

1. Release the parking brake.

2. Loosen the wheel lug nuts. Raise and safely support the vehicle.

3. From under the vehicle, loosen the parking brake adjusting nuts, at the equalizer, and disconnect the rear parking brake cables from the equalizer.

4. Remove the wheel and the brake drum.

5. Remove the adjusting lever tang from the hole in the secondary shoe.

6. Place a wheel cylinder clamp over the wheel cylinder to retain the pistons while the brake shoes are removed.

7. Using a brake spring removal tool, remove the return springs by twisting them off the anchor pin.

8. Carefully, remove the secondary shoe return spring, the adjusting cable, the primary shoe return spring, the cable guide, the adjusting lever and spring.

NOTE: Be careful that all the components do not fly out at once when the spring tension is being released.

9. Remove the hold-down springs and brake shoes.

10. Clean all of the dirt from the backing plate.

To install:

11. Clean the embossed, working surfaces of the support plate and coat them with molybdenum disulfide grease.

12. Position new brake shoes and retain them with the hold-down springs.

13. Install the adjusting lever/spring, the cable guide, the primary shoe return spring, the adjusting cable and the secondary return spring.

14. Using a brake spring installation tool, install the return springs onto the anchor pin.

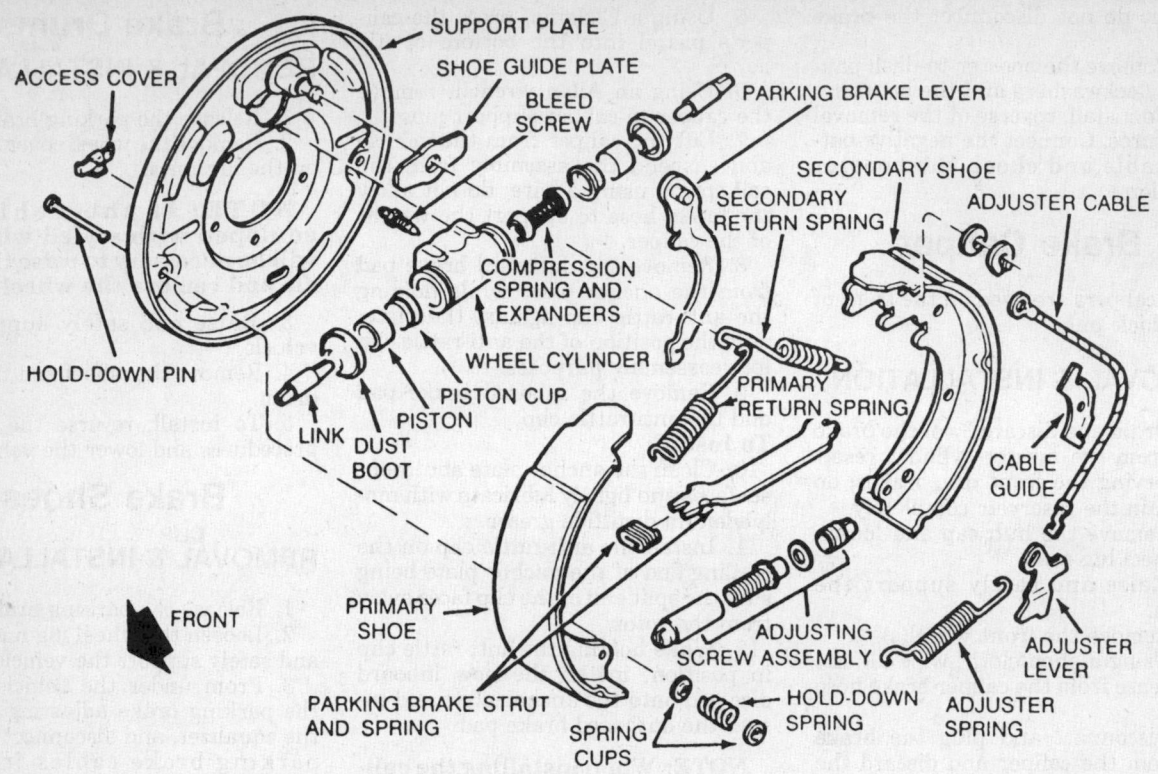

ACCESS COVER

SUPPORT PLATE

SHOE GUIDE PLATE

BLEED SCREW

PARKING BRAKE LEVER

SECONDARY SHOE

SECONDARY RETURN SPRING

ADJUSTER CABLE

COMPRESSION SPRING AND EXPANDERS

WHEEL CYLINDER

PISTON CUP

PRIMARY RETURN SPRING

CABLE GUIDE

HOLD-DOWN PIN

PISTON

DUST BOOT

LINK

FRONT

PRIMARY SHOE

ADJUSTING SCREW ASSEMBLY

ADJUSTER LEVER

PARKING BRAKE STRUT AND SPRING

SPRING CUPS

HOLD-DOWN SPRING

ADJUSTER SPRING

Exploded view of the rear drum brake assembly

15. Remove the wheel cylinder clamp from the wheel cylinder.

16. Install the adjusting lever tang into the hole in the secondary shoe.

17. Check and/or adjust the rear brake shoe-to-drum clearance.

18. Install the brake drum and the wheel. Connect the rear parking brake cables to the equalizer and adjust the parking brake.

19. Lower the vehicle.

Wheel Cylinder

REMOVAL & INSTALLATION

1. Raise and safely support the vehicle.

2. Remove the wheel, the brake drum and the brake shoes.

3. Disconnect and plug the brake line from the wheel cylinder.

4. Remove the wheel cylinder-to-backing plate bolts and the cylinder.

To install:

5. Insert the wheel cylinder into the backing and secure with bolts.

6. Connect the brake line to the wheel cylinder.

7. Install the brake shoes, the brake drum and the wheel.

8. Bleed the brake system and lower the vehicle.

Parking Brake Cable

ADJUSTMENT

1. Check the rear brake shoe-to-drum clearance and/or adjust, if necessary.

2. Apply the brakes several times while backing up to adjust the drum brakes. Make 1 forward application for each reverse application to equalize the adjustment.

3. Fully, apply and release the parking brake about 10 times. Set the pedal on the 1st notch from the released position.

4. Raise and safely support the vehicle.

5. Tighten the cable, at the equalizer, so the wheels can just barely be turned forward; be sure to hold the end of the cable screw to prevent the cable from turning.

6. Release the parking brake and check for rear brake drag; the wheels should rotate freely with the parking brake **OFF**.

REMOVAL & INSTALLATION

Front

1. Release the parking brake.

2. Raise and safely support the vehicle.

3. Disconnect the return spring and remove the cable adjuster nut at the equalizer.

4. Remove the cable-to-frame bracket clip and the cable-to-floorpan clips.

5. Remove the left side cowl trim panel and scuff plate.

6. Disconnect the return spring and remove the front cable clip at the lever assembly.

7. Pull back the carpet and disconnect the front cable at the lever assembly.

8. Pull the cable grommet from the floorpan and remove the front cable.

To install:

9. Install the cable and grommet into the floorpan.

10. Install the cable to the lever assembly. Install the clip and connect the lever assembly return spring.

11. Reposition the carpet and install the cowl panel and the scuff plate.

12. Install the cable into the frame bracket and secure with the clip.

13. Install the cable into the equalizer and secure with the cable adjusting nut.

14. Adjust the parking brake cable and lower the vehicle.

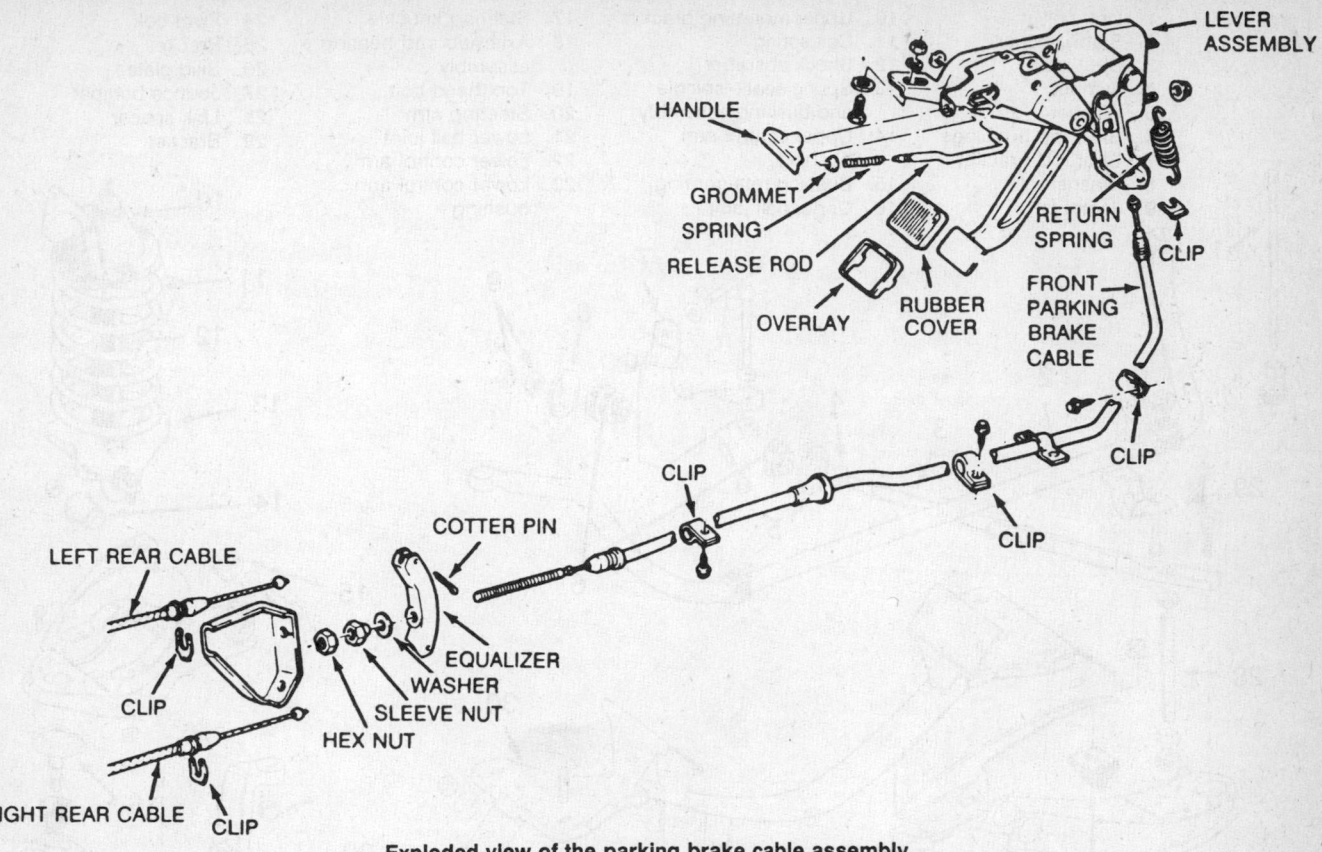

LEVER ASSEMBLY

HANDLE

GROMMET
SPRING
RELEASE ROD

RETURN SPRING

CLIP

OVERLAY

RUBBER COVER

FRONT PARKING BRAKE CABLE

CLIP

CLIP

CLIP

COTTER PIN

CLIP

LEFT REAR CABLE

EQUALIZER
WASHER
SLEEVE NUT
HEX NUT

CLIP

RIGHT REAR CABLE

CLIP

Exploded view of the parking brake cable assembly

Rear

The vehicle is equipped with dual rear cables.

1. Raise and safely support the vehicle.
2. Loosen the cable adjusting nut at the equalizer.
3. Remove the cotter pin from the equalizer.
4. Remove the cable-to-frame bracket clip and disconnect the cable, to be removed, at the frame bracket.
5. Remove the cable-to-rear axle bracket bolts.
6. Remove the brake shoes. Using a worm drive hose clamp, compress the cable lock tabs at the brake support plate and remove the cable.

To install:

7. Insert the cable into the brake support plate and pull the cable through the plate until the cable lock tabs engage the plate.
8. Insert the cable into the frame mounting bracket and install the clip.
9. Assemble the brake shoes, the brake drum and the wheel.
10. Install the cable-to-rear axle housing bolts.
11. Engage the cable in the equalizer and install the cotter pin.
12. Install the adjuster nut and connect the pull back spring, if equipped.
13. Adjust the parking brake and lower the vehicle.

Brake System Bleeding

1. Fill the master cylinder to within ¼ in. of the reservoir rim.
2. Raise and safely support the vehicle.
3. Bleed the system in the following sequence:
   a. Right rear
   b. Left rear
   c. Right front
   d. Left front
4. Bleed 1 wheel at a time.
5. Install a rubber hose on the bleeder screw of the caliper or wheel cylinder to be bled and place the opposite end of the hose in a container partially filled with brake fluid.
6. Open the bleeder screw ¾ turn. Have a helper depress the brake pedal to the floor, then tighten the bleeder screw. Have the helper slowly release the brake pedal.
7. Repeat the bleeding operation until clear brake fluid flows without air bubbles.

NOTE: Check the master cylinder fluid level frequently during the bleeding procedure and refill, if necessary.

8. After the bleeding operation is completed, discard the fluid in the container. Fill the master cylinder to ¼ in. from the reservoir rim and check the brake operation.

FRONT SUSPENSION

Shock Absorbers

REMOVAL & INSTALLATION

1. Remove both lower shock absorber attaching nuts, the washers and the grommets.
2. Remove the upper mounting bracket nuts and bolts.
3. Remove the bracket, complete with the shock.
4. Remove the upper attaching nut and separate the shock from the mounting bracket.
5. For adjustable shocks: To adjust the shock, compress the piston completely. Holding the upper part of the shock, turn the shock until the lower arrow is aligned with the desired setting. A click will be heard when the desired setting is reached.

To install:

6. Before installing a new shock ab-

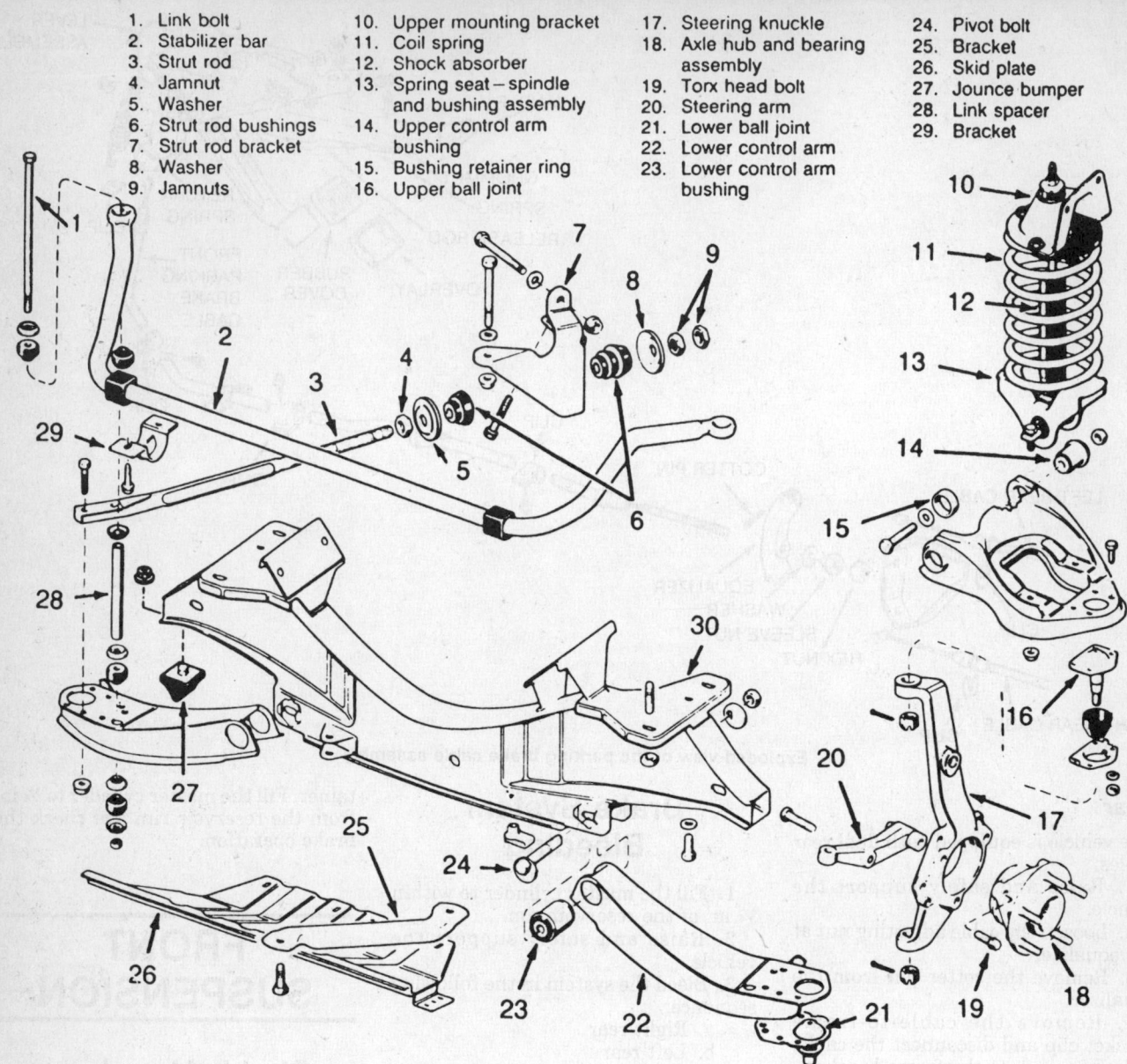

1. Link bolt
2. Stabilizer bar
3. Strut rod
4. Jamnut
5. Washer
6. Strut rod bushings
7. Strut rod bracket
8. Washer
9. Jamnuts
10. Upper mounting bracket
11. Coil spring
12. Shock absorber
13. Spring seat – spindle and bushing assembly
14. Upper control arm bushing
15. Bushing retainer ring
16. Upper ball joint
17. Steering knuckle
18. Axle hub and bearing assembly
19. Torx head bolt
20. Steering arm
21. Lower ball joint
22. Lower control arm
23. Lower control arm bushing
24. Pivot bolt
25. Bracket
26. Skid plate
27. Jounce bumper
28. Link spacer
29. Bracket

Exploded view of the front suspension assembly

sorber, purge it of air by extending it, in its normal position and compressing it while inverted. Do this several times. It is normal for there to be more resistance to extend than to compress.

7. Fit the grommets, washers, the upper mounting bracket and nut on the shock, in the reverse order of removal. Torque the nut to 8 ft. lbs.

8. Fully, extend the shock and install both grommets on the lower mounting studs.

9. Lower the shock through the hole in the wheel arch. Fit the lower attachment studs through the lower spring seat.

10. Install the grommets, washers and nuts; torque the nuts to 15 ft. lbs.

11. Secure the upper mounting bracket with its attachment nuts and bolts; Torque them to 20 ft. lbs.

Coil Springs

REMOVAL & INSTALLATION

1. Remove the shock absorber.
2. Install the spring compressor through the upper spring seat opening and bolt it to the lower spring seat using the lower shock absorber mounting holes.
3. Remove the lower spring seat pivot retaining nuts, then, tighten the compressor tool to compress the spring about 1 in. (25.4mm).
4. Raise and support the front of the vehicle; support the vehicle by the subframe, allowing the control arms to hang free.
5. Remove the front wheel and pull the lower spring seat outward, away

from the vehicle. Slowly, release the spring tension and remove the coil spring and lower spring seat.

To install:

6. Place the spring compressor through the coil spring and tape the rubber spring cushion to the small diameter end of the spring (upper).
7. Place the lower spring seat against the spring with the end of the coil against the formed shoulder in the seat. The shoulder and coil end face inwards, toward the engine, when the spring is installed.
8. Place the spring against the upper seat, then, align the lower spring seat pivot so the retaining studs will enter the holes in the upper control arm.
9. Compress the coil spring and install the spring.

10. Install the wheel and tire and lower the vehicle; place the weight on the suspension.

11. Install and torque the lower spring seat spindle retaining nuts to 35 ft. lbs.

12. Remove the spring compressor and install the shock absorber.

Strut Rods

REMOVAL & INSTALLATION

1. Raise and safely support the front of the vehicle.

2. Remove the jamnut and caster adjustment nut from the strut rod.

3. Disconnect the strut rod from the lower control arm and remove the rod, bushings and washers.

To install:

4. Assemble the strut rod, washer, bushings and nuts.

5. Install the assembly into the bracket.

6. Attach the strut rod to the control arm and torque the bolts to 75 ft. lbs. (102 Nm).

7. Torque the strut rod caster adjustment nuts to 65 ft. lbs. (88 Nm) and the jamnuts to 75 ft. lbs. (102 Nm).

8. Lower the vehicle. Check and/or adjust the front wheel alignment.

Upper Ball Joints

INSPECTION

1. Check and/or adjust the front wheel bearings.

2. Raise and safely support the front of the vehicle; support the vehicle by the subframe, allowing the control arms to hang free.

3. Place a dial indicator with it's plunger against the tire scrub bead; just outside the whitewall.

4. Move the upper portion of the wheel and tire toward the vehicle's center, while watching the dial indicator.

5. Move the wheel/tire back out while watching the indicator.

6. Replace the upper ball joint, if the movement is greater than 0.160 in. (4.06mm).

REMOVAL & INSTALLATION

1. Place a 2 × 4 × 5 in. block of wood on the side sill so it supports the control arm.

2. Raise and safely support the front of the vehicle; support the vehicle by the subframe, allowing the control arms to hang free.

3. Install 2 lug nuts to retain the rotor onto the wheel hub.

4. Remove the ball joint's cotter pin and retaining nut.

5. Place the jackstand under the lower control and support it.

6. Using a ball joint removal tool, separate the ball joint from the steering knuckle.

7. Chisel the heads from the upper ball joint-to-control arm rivets. Using a punch, drive the rivets from the control arm.

To install:

8. Position the new ball joint so it's rivet holes align the holes in the upper control arm.

9. Using hardened 5/16 in. bolts, torque the upper ball joint-to-control arm bolts to 25 ft. lbs.

10. Apply chassis grease to the steering stops and fit the knuckle pin and retaining nut onto the ball joint stud; torque the nut to 75 ft. lbs. and install a new cotter pin.

11. Lower the vehicle and check the front wheel alignment.

Lower Ball Joints

The lower ball joint and control arm must be replaced as an assembly.

INSPECTION

1. Raise and safely support the front of the vehicle; support the vehicle by the subframe, allowing the control arms to hang free.

2. Grasp the lower portion of the wheel and pull it in and out.

3. If there is noticeable lateral freeplay, the lower ball joint is worn and must be replaced.

Upper Control Arms

REMOVAL & INSTALLATION

1. Remove the shock absorber and the mounting bracket.

2. Using a spring compressor, secure the spring and compress it about 2 in.

3. Raise and safely support the vehicle. Remove the wheel and tire assembly.

4. Remove the upper ball joint stud cotter pin and nut. Using a ball joint removal tool, separate the ball joint from the steering knuckle.

5. Remove the upper control arm-to-chassis pivot bolts and the control arm from the vehicle.

To install:

6. Install the upper control arm to the chassis but do not tighten the pivot bolts.

7. Install the upper ball joint-to-steering knuckle and torque the nut to 75 ft. lbs. (102 Nm); install a new cotter pin.

8. Loosen the spring compressor; be sure to guide the spring onto it's seat.

9. Install the wheel/tire assembly and lower the vehicle.

10. Install the lower spring seat pivot nuts and torque to 35 ft. lbs. (47 Nm).

11. Torque the upper control arm-to-chassis pivot bolts to 80 ft. lbs. (108 Nm).

12. Remove the spring compressor. Install the shock absorber and bracket.

13. Check and/or adjust the front alignment.

Lower Control Arms

The lower ball joint and control arm must be replaced as an assembly.

REMOVAL & INSTALLATION

1. Remove the grease cup, the cotter pin, the locknut and hub nut.

2. Raise and safely support the front of the vehicle; support the vehicle by the subframe, allowing the control arms to hang free.

3. Remove the wheel/tire assembly, the brake caliper and rotor.

4. Remove the lower ball joint-to-steering knuckle cotter pin and nut.

5. Using a ball joint, separate the ball joint from the steering knuckle.

6. Remove the halfshaft flange bolts and the halfshaft.

7. Remove the strut-to-lower control arm bolts and separate the strut from the arm.

8. Remove the stabilizer bar-to-lower control arm bolts and separate the stabilizer bar from the arm.

9. Remove the lower control arm-to-crossmember pivot bolt and the control arm from the vehicle.

To install:

10. Install the new lower control arm/ball joint assembly onto the crossmember but do not tighten the pivot bolt.

11. Install the ball joint-to-steering knuckle and torque the nut to 75 ft. lbs. (102 Nm); install a new cotter pin.

12. Install the stabilizer bar-to-lower control arm and torque the locknut to 7 ft. lbs. (9 Nm).

13. Install the strut-to-lower control arm and torque the bolts to 75 ft. lbs. (102 Nm).

14. Install the halfshaft-to-axle flange and torque the bolts to 45 ft. lbs. (61 Nm).

15. Place a jack under the lower control arm, raise the jack to compress the spring and torque the lower control arm-to-crossmember pivot bolt to 110 ft. lbs. (149 Nm).

16. Install the rotor, the brake caliper and torque the hub nut to 180 ft. lbs. (240 Nm). Install a new cotter pin and the wheel/tire assembly.

17. Lower the vehicle. Check and/or adjust the front alignment.

Sway Bar

REMOVAL & INSTALLATION

1. Raise and safely support the vehicle.

2. Remove the wheel/tire from the right side.

3. Disconnect the idler arm from the chassis side sill; do not loose the bolt spacer.

4. Remove the stabilizer bar-to-chassis side sill clamps.

5. Remove the stabilizer bar-to-lower control arm link bolts, grommets, spacer and retainers.

6. Remove the stabilizer bar from the right side of the vehicle. If necessary, move the steering linkage and the left wheel to provide clearance.

To install:

7. Maneuver the stabilizer bar and steering linkage to position the bar onto the vehicle.

8. Install the stabilizer mounting clamps and bolts; do not tighten the clamp bolts completely.

9. Install the link bolts, grommets, spacer, retainers and link bolt nuts. Torque the clamp bolts to 35 ft. lbs. (47 Nm) and the link bolt nuts to 7 ft. lbs. (9 Nm).

10. Connect the idler arm-to-chassis sill and torque the bolts to 50 ft. lbs. (68 Nm).

11. Install the wheel/tire assembly and lower the vehicle.

REAR SUSPENSION

Shock Absorbers

REMOVAL & INSTALLATION

1. Raise and safely support the vehicle.

2. Remove the shock absorber-to-axle locknut, retainer and grommet.

3. Pull the shock absorber from the axle stud and compress it.

4. Remove the upper shock absorber bracket-to-body bolts and lockwashers. Remove the shock absorber/bracket assembly.

5. If necessary, remove the shock absorber-to-bracket locknut, retainer, grommet and bracket.

6. To install, reverse the removal procedures. Torque the shock absorber-to-bracket locknut to 8 ft. lbs. (11 Nm), the shock absorber bracket-to-body bolts to 15 ft. lbs. (20 Nm).

Leaf Springs

REMOVAL & INSTALLATION

1. Raise and safely support the vehicle.

2. Using a hydraulic jack, support the rear axle assembly.

3. Remove the shock absorber-to-rear axle locknut, retainer and grommet. Disengage the shock absorber and compress it.

4. Remove the spring-to-axle housing U-bolts and clamps bracket.

5. Remove the pivot nut/bolt from the spring's front eye.

6. Remove the shackle nuts, shackle plate and shackle from, the rear spring eye. Remove the spring.

To install:

7. Install the front spring eye into the front hanger and torque the pivot nut/bolt to 110 ft. lbs. (149 Nm).

8. Install the shackle plate and locknuts onto the shackle pins and torque the locknuts to 30 ft. lbs. (41 Nm).

9. Install the clamp bracket, spring plate and U-bolts. Install the U-bolt locknuts and torque to 50 ft. lbs. (56 Nm).

NOTE: When installing the springs on the axle, be sure the spring's center bolt is positioned in the clamp bracket and spring plate before tightening the U-bolt locknuts.

10. Install the shock absorber-to-axle and torque the locknut to 8 ft. lbs. (11 Nm).

11. Lower the vehicle.

Chrysler/Eagle
Front Wheel Drive
Eagle—Summit, Talon
Plymouth—Laser

SPECIFICATIONS

VEHICLE IDENTIFICATION CHART

It is important for servicing and ordering parts to be certain of the vehicle and engine identification. The VIN (vehicle identification number) is a 17 digit number visible through the windshield on the driver's side of the dash and contains the vehicle and engine identification codes. The tenth digit indicates model year and the eighth digit indicates engine code. It can be interpreted as follows:

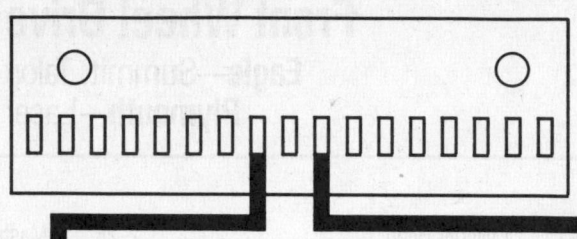

Engine Code						Model Year	
Code	Cu. In.	Liters	Cyl.	Fuel Sys.	Eng. Mfg.	Code	Year
T	107	1.8	4	MPI	Mitsubishi	K	1989
R	122	2.0	4	MPI	Mitsubishi	L	1990
U	122	2.0	4	MPI-Turbo	Mitsubishi	M	1991
X	92	1.5	4	MPI	Mitsubishi		
Y	98	1.6	4	MPI	Mitsubishi		

ENGINE IDENTIFICATION

Year	Model	Engine Displacement cu. in. (liter)	Engine Series Identification (VIN)	No. of Cylinders	Engine Type
1989	Eagle Summit	4-96 (1.5)	X	4	SOHC
	Eagle Summit	4-98 (1.6)	Y	4	DOHC
1990–91	Eagle Summit	4-96 (1.5)	X	4	SOHC
	Eagle Summit	4-98 (1.6)	Y	4	DOHC
	Plymouth Laser	4-107 (1.8)	T	4	SOHC
	Plymouth Laser	4-122 (2.0)	R	4	DOHC
	Plymouth Laser	4-122 (2.0)	U	4	DOHC w/Turbo
	Eagle Talon	4-122 (2.0)	R	4	DOHC
	Eagle Talon	4-122 (2.0)	U	4	DOHC w/Turbo

SOHC Single Overhead Cam Engine
DOHC Double Overhead Cam Engine

GENERAL ENGINE SPECIFICATIONS

Year	VIN	No. Cylinder Displacement cu. in. (liter)	Fuel System Type	Net Horsepower @ rpm	Net Torque @ rpm (ft. lbs.)	Bore × Stroke (in.)	Compression Ratio	Oil Pressure @ rpm
1989	X	4-96 (1.5)	MPI	81 @ 5500	91 @ 3000	2.972 × 3.228	9.4:1	54 @ 2000
	Y	4-98 (1.6)	MPI	113 @ 6500	99 @ 5000	3.243 × 2.955	9.2:1	54 @ 2000
	T	4-107 (1.8)	MPI	92 @ 5000	105 @ 3500	3.172 × 3.388	9.0:1	41 @ 2000
	R	4-122 (2.0)	MPI	135 @ 6000	125 @ 5000	3.349 × 3.467	9.0:1	41 @ 2000
	U	4-122 (2.0)	MPI-TC	190 @ 6000	203 @ 3000	3.349 × 3.467	7.8:1	41 @ 2000

GENERAL ENGINE SPECIFICATIONS

Year	VIN	No. Cylinder Displacement cu. in. (liter)	Fuel System Type	Net Horsepower @ rpm	Net Torque @ rpm (ft. lbs.)	Bore × Stroke (in.)	Compression Ratio	Oil Pressure @ rpm
1990–91	X	4-96 (1.5)	MPI	81 @ 5500	91 @ 3000	2.972 × 3.228	9.4:1	54 @ 2000
	Y	4-98 (1.6)	MPI	113 @ 6500	99 @ 5000	3.243 × 2.955	9.2:1	54 @ 2000
	T	4-107 (1.8)	MPI	92 @ 5000	105 @ 3500	3.172 × 3.388	9.0:1	41 @ 2000
	R	4-122 (2.0)	MPI	135 @ 6000	125 @ 5000	3.349 × 3.467	9.0:1	41 @ 2000
	U	4-122 (2.0)	MPI-TC	190 @ 6000	203 @ 3000	3.349 × 3.467	7.8:1	41 @ 2000

MPI Multipoint Injection
TC   Turbocharged

TUNE-UP SPECIFICATIONS

Year	VIN	No. Cylinder Displacement cu. in. (liter)	Spark Plugs Type	Spark Plugs Gap (in.)	Ignition Timing (deg.) MT	Ignition Timing (deg.) AT	Compression Pressure (psi)	Fuel Pump (psi)	Idle Speed (rpm) MT	Idle Speed (rpm) AT	Valve Clearance In.	Valve Clearance Ex.
1989	X	4-96 (1.5)	RN9YC4	0.040	5B ①	5B ①	137	48 ②	750	750	0.006	0.010 ③
	Y	4-98 (1.6)	RN9YC4	0.030	5B ①	5B ①	177	48 ②	750	750	Hyd.	Hyd.
1990	X	4-96 (1.5)	RN9YC4	0.040	5B ①	5B ①	137	48 ②	750	750	0.006	0.010 ③
	Y	4-98 (1.6)	RN9YC4	0.030	5B ①	5B ①	177	48 ②	750	750	Hyd.	Hyd.
	T	4-107 (1.8)	RN9YC4	0.040	5B ①	5B ①	131	48 ②	850 ④	650 ⑤	Hyd.	Hyd.
	R	4-122 (2.0)	RN9YC	0.030	5B ①	5B ①	137	48 ②	850 ④	650 ⑤	Hyd.	Hyd.
	U	4-122 (2.0)	RN9YC4	0.040	5B ①	5B ①	114	36 ②	850 ④	650 ⑤	Hyd.	Hyd.
1991		REFER TO UNDERHOOD SPECIFICATIONS										

① Advance controlled by Engine Control Unit
  Basic timing—5°BTDC—Actual ignition timing
  at curb idle speed = 1.5L Engine—10°BTDC
             1.6L Engine— 8°BTDC
             1.8L Engine— 8°BTDC
             2.0L Engine— 8°BTDC
② Regulated Pressure—Electric In-Tank Pump
③ Adjust engine hot
④ In Neutral—Air Conditioner-ON-Curb idle 600–800 rpm
⑤ In Drive—Air Conditioner-ON-Curb idle 600–800 rpm

FIRING ORDERS

NOTE: To avoid confusion, always replace spark plug wires one at a time.

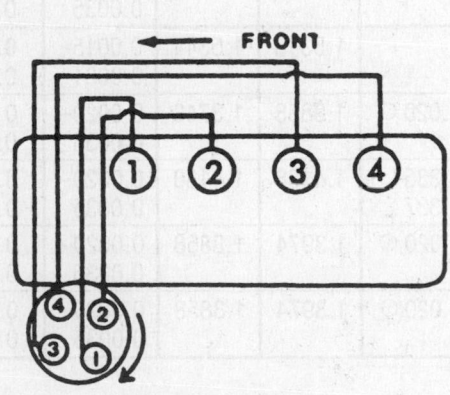

1.5L and 1.8L Engines
Engine Firing Order: 1–3–4–2
Distributor Rotation: Clockwise

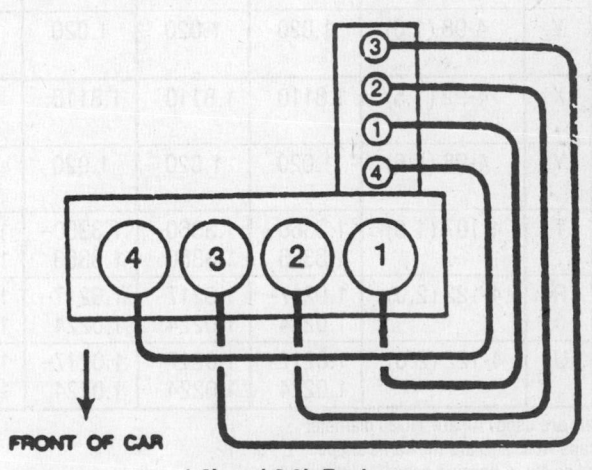

1.6L and 2.0L Engines
Engine Firing Order: 1–3–4–2
Distributorless Ignition

CAPACITIES

Year	Model	VIN	No. Cylinder Displacement cu. in. (liter)	Engine Crankcase (qts.) with Filter	Engine Crankcase (qts.) without Filter	Transmission (pts.) 4-Spd	Transmission (pts.) 5-Spd	Transmission (pts.) Auto.	Drive Axle (pts.)	Fuel Tank (gal.)	Cooling System (qts.)
1989	Summit	X	4-92 (1.5)	3.6 ①	3.0 ①	3.6	3.8 ②	13 ③	③	13.2	5.3
	Summit	Y	4-98 (1.6)	4.6 ①	4.1 ①	3.6	3.8	13 ③	③	13.2	5.3
1990–91	Summit	X	4-92 (1.5)	3.6 ①	3.0 ①	3.6	3.8 ②	13 ③	③	13.2	5.3
	Summit	Y	4-98 (1.6)	4.6 ①	4.2 ①	3.6	3.8	13 ③	③	13.2	5.3
	Laser and Talon	T	4-107 (1.8)	4.1 ①	3.6 ①	—	3.8	13 ③	③	16.0	6.6
	Laser and Talon	R	4-122 (2.0)	4.6 ①	4.1 ①	—	4.6 ⑤	13 ③	③	16.0	7.6
	Laser and Talon	U	4-122 (2.0)	4.6 ①	4.1 ①	—	4.8 ⑥	13 ③	⑦	16.0	7.6

① Use API class SF or SF/CC engine oil
② 3.8 pts. for transaxle models KM201, KM206
  4.4 pts. for transaxle model KM210
  See Vehicle Information Code Plate on firewall
  for transaxle number. Manual transaxles,
  use API class GL-4 or higher Hypoid Gear Oil
③ Automatic—Use Dexron II type fluid. Quantity
  shown includes converter. Check when hot.
④ Add 0.5 qt. for oil cooler on Turbo models
⑤ 2WD-Turbo
⑥ 4WD-Turbo
⑦ Rear axle—with 4WD, capacity 0.75 qt. plus 0.63 qt.
  in transfer case

CAMSHAFT SPECIFICATIONS
All measurements given in inches

Year	VIN	No. Cylinder Displacement cu. in. (liter)	Journal Diameter 1	2	3	4	5	Lobe Lift In.	Lobe Lift Ex.	Bearing Clearance	Camshaft End Play
1989	X	4-92 (1.5)	1.8110	1.8110	1.8110	—	—	1.5318	1.5344	0.0015–0.0031	0.002–0.008
	Y	4-98 (1.6)	1.020	1.020	1.020	1.020	1.020 ①	1.3858	1.3743	0.002–0.0035	0.004–0.008
1990–91	X	4-92 (1.5)	1.8110	1.8110	1.8110	—	—	1.5318	1.5344	0.0015–0.0031	0.002–0.008
	Y	4-98 (1.6)	1.020	1.020	1.020	1.020	1.020 ①	1.3858	1.3743	0.0020–0.0035	0.004–0.008
	T	4-107 (1.8)	1.3360–1.3366	1.3360–1.3366	1.3360–1.3366	1.3360–1.3366	1.336–1.337	1.4138	1.4138	0.0020–0.0035	0.004–0.008
	R	4-122 (2.0)	1.0217–1.0224	1.0217–1.0224	1.0217–1.0224	1.0217–1.0224	1.020 ①	1.3974	1.3858	0.0020–0.0035	0.040–0.008
	U	4-122 (2.0)	1.0217–1.0224	1.0217–1.0224	1.0217–1.0224	1.0217–1.0224	1.020 ①	1.3974	1.3858	0.0020–0.0035	0.004–0.008

① Six journals are used. All are 1.020 diameter
Bearing caps Nos. 2–5 are the same shape. "L" or "R"
is stamped on No. 1 bearing cap. L = intake side,
R = exhaust side. Bearing caps should be reinstalled
at their original locations

CRANKSHAFT AND CONNECTING ROD SPECIFICATIONS

All measurements are given in inches.

Year	VIN	No. Cylinder Displacement cu. in. (liter)	Crankshaft				Connecting Rod		
			Main Brg. Journal Dia.	Main Brg. Oil Clearance	Shaft End-play	Thrust on No.	Journal Diameter	Oil Clearance	Side Clearance
1989	X	4-92 (1.5)	1.890	0.0008–0.0018	0.0020–0.0071	3	1.6500	0.0006–0.0017	0.0039–0.0098
	Y	4-98 (1.6)	2.240	0.0008–0.0020	0.0020–0.0071	3	1.7700	0.0008–0.0020	0.0039–0.0098
1990-91	X	4-92 (1.5)	1.890	0.0008–0.0018	0.0020–0.0071	3	1.6500	0.0006–0.0017	0.0039–0.0098
	Y	4-98 (1.6)	2.240	0.0008–0.0020	0.0020–0.0071	3	1.7700	0.0008–0.0020	0.0039–0.0098
	T	4-107 (1.8)	2.240	0.0008–0.0020	0.0020–0.0070	3	1.7700	0.0008–0.0020	0.0039–0.0098
	R	4-122 (2.0)	2.243–2.244	0.0008–0.0020	0.0020–0.0070	3	1.7709–1.7715	0.0008–0.0020	0.0040–0.0098
	U	4-122 (2.0)	2.243–2.244	0.0008–0.0020	0.0020–0.0070	3	1.7709–1.7715	0.0008–0.0020	0.0040–0.0098

VALVE SPECIFICATIONS

Year	VIN	No. Cylinder Displacement cu. in. (liter)	Seat Angle (deg.)	Face Angle (deg.)	Spring Test Pressure (lbs.)	Spring Installed Height (in.)	Stem-to-Guide Clearance (in.)		Stem Diameter (in.)	
							Intake	Exhaust	Intake	Exhaust
1989	X	4-92 (1.5)	44–44.5	45–44.5	53 ②	1.756 ①	0.0008–0.0020	0.0020–0.0035	0.2600	0.2600
	Y	4-98 (1.6)	44–44.5	45–45.5	53 ②	1.803 ③	0.0008–0.0019	0.0020–0.0033	0.2585–0.2586	0.2571–0.2579
1990-91	X	4-92 (1.5)	44–44.5	45–44.5	53 ②	1.756 ①	0.0008–0.0020	0.0020–0.0035	0.2600	0.2600
	Y	4-98 (1.6)	44–44.5	45–45.5	66 ②	1.902 ④	0.0008–0.0019	0.0020–0.0033	0.2585–0.2586	0.2571–0.2579
	T	4-107 (1.8)	44–44.5	45–45.5	62 ②	1.937 ⑦	0.0012–0.0024 ⑤	0.0020–0.0035 ⑥	0.3100	0.3100
	R	4-122 (2.0)	44–44.5	45–45.5	66 ②	1.902 ⑧	0.0008–0.0019 ⑤	0.0020–0.0033 ⑥	0.2585–0.2591	0.2571–0.2579
	U	4-122 (2.0)	44–44.5	45–45.5	66 ②	1.902 ⑧	0.0008–0.0019 ⑤	0.0020–0.0033 ⑥	0.2585–0.2591	0.2571–0.2579

NA—Not Available
① Free length, not installed height
   Used limit = 1.717
② At installed height
③ Free length, not installed height
   Used limit = 1.768
④ Free length, not installed height
   Used limit = 1.862
⑤ Used limit = 0.004
⑥ Used limit = 0.006
⑦ Free length, not installed height
   Used limit = 1.898
⑧ Free length, not installed height
   Used limit = 1.862

PISTON AND RING SPECIFICATIONS

All measurements are given in inches.

Year	VIN	No. Cylinder Displacement cu. in. (liter)	Piston Clearance	Ring Gap			Ring Side Clearance		
				Top Compression	Bottom Compression	Oil Control	Top Compression	Bottom Compression	Oil Control
1989	X	4-92 (1.5)	0.0008–0.0016	0.0079–0.0138	0.0079–0.0138	0.0079–0.0276	0.0012–0.0028	0.0008–0.0024	NA
	Y	4-98 (1.6)	0.0008–0.0016	0.0098–0.0157	0.0138–0.0197	0.0079–0.0276	0.0012–0.0028	0.0012–0.0028	NA
1990-91	X	4-92 (1.5)	0.0008–0.0016	0.0079–0.0138	0.0079–0.0138	0.0079–0.0276	0.0012–0.0028	0.0008–0.0024	NA
	Y	4-98 (1.6)	0.0008–0.0016	0.0098–0.0157	0.0138–0.0197	0.0079–0.0276	0.0012–0.0028	0.0012–0.0028	NA
	T	4-107 (1.8)	0.0004–0.0012	0.0118–0.0177	0.0079–0.0138	0.0080–0.0280	0.0018–0.0033	0.0008–0.0024	NA
	R	4-122 (2.0)	0.0008–0.0016	0.0098–0.0177	0.0138–0.0197	0.0079–0.0276	0.0012–0.0028	0.0012–0.0028	NA
	U	4-122 (2.0)	0.0012–0.0020	0.0098–0.0177	0.0138–0.0197	0.0079–0.0276	0.0012–0.0028	0.0012–0.0028	NA

TORQUE SPECIFICATIONS

All readings in ft. lbs.

Year	VIN	No. Cylinder Displacement cu. in. (liter)	Cylinder Head Bolts	Main Bearing Bolts	Rod Bearing Bolts	Crankshaft Pulley Bolts	Flywheel Bolts	Manifold		Spark Plugs
								Intake	Exhaust	
1989	X	4-92 (1.5)	①	36–40	23–25	51–72 ②	94–101	13–18	11–14	15–21 ③
	Y	4-98 (1.6)	④	47–51	36–38	80–94 ⑤	94–101	18–22	18–22	15–21 ③
1990-91	X	4-92 (1.5)	①	36–40	⑥	51–72 ②	94–101	13–18	11–14	15–21 ③
	Y	4-98 (1.6)	④	47–51	36–38	80–94 ⑤	94–101	18–22	18–22	15–21 ③
	T	4-107 (1.8)	51–54	37–39	24–25	80–94	94–101	13–18	18–22	15–21 ③
	R	4-122 (2.0)	65–72	47–51	36–38	80–94	94–101	18–22	18–22	15–21 ③
	U	4-122 (2.0)	65–72	47–51	36–38	80–94	94–101	18–22	18–22	15–21 ③

① 51–54 COLD
　58–61 HOT
② Pulley to Crankshaft Sprocket—9–11
③ Spark plugs used in aluminum heads should always have lubricated threads
④ 65–72 COLD
　72–80 HOT
⑤ Pulley to crankshaft sprocket—14–22
⑥ Torque to 14.5 ft. lbs., back off, torque again to 14.5 ft. lbs., then turn additional 1/4 turn

BRAKE SPECIFICATIONS

All measurements in inches unless noted

Year	Model	Lug Nut Torque (ft. lbs.)	Master Cylinder Bore	Brake Disc		Standard Brake Drum Diameter	Minimum Lining Thickness	
				Minimum Thickness	Maximum Runout		Front	Rear
1989	Summit ⑤	65–80	13/16	0.449 ①	0.006	7.10 ②	0.080	0.040
	Summit ⑥	65–80	7/8	0.882 ①③	0.006	—	0.080	0.080
1990–91	Summit ⑤	65–80	13/16	0.449 ①	0.006	7.10 ②	0.080	0.040
	Summit ⑥	65–80	7/8	0.882 ①③	0.006	—	0.080	0.080
	Laser	65–80	④	0.882 ①③	0.003	—	0.080	0.080
	Talon	65–80	④	0.882 ①③	0.003	—	0.080	0.080

① Front discs
② Wear Limit—7.20
③ Vehicles with rear disc brakes—0.331 minimum thickness
④ Vehicles with 1.8L or 2.0 DOHC engine, Non-Turbo—7/8
  Vehicles with 2.0L DOHC engine, With-Turbo—15/16
⑤ 1.5L Engine
⑥ 1.6L Engine

WHEEL ALIGNMENT

Year	Model	Caster		Camber		Toe-in (in.)	Steering Axis Inclination (deg.)
		Range (deg.)	Preferred Setting (deg.)	Range (deg.)	Preferred Setting (deg.)		
1989	Summit	2°20′ ±30′	2°20′	0°00′ ±30′	0°00′	0 ±.12	NA
1990–91	Summit	①	20°21′	0°00′ ±30′ ①	0°00′	0 ±.12	NA
	Laser 1.8L	2°20′ ±30′	2°20′	14′ ±30′	14′	0 ±.12	NA
	Laser 2.0L	2°24′ ±30′	2°24′	5′ ±30′	5′	0 ±12	NA
	Talon 2.0L	2°24′ ±30′	2°24′	5′ ±30′	5′	0 ±.12	NA
	Talon 4WD 2.0L	2°18′ ±30′	2°18′	10′ ±30′	10′	0 ±.12	NA

NA—Not Available
① Camber and caster are pre-set
  at the factory and cannot be adjusted.
  If not within specification replace bent
  or damaged parts.

ENGINE ELECTRICAL

NOTE: Disconnecting the negative battery cable on some vehicles may interfere with the functions of the on board computer systems and may require the computer to undergo a relearning process, once the negative battery cable is reconnected.

Distributor
REMOVAL
1. Rotate the engine and bring No. 1 cylinder to top dead center of its compression stroke. Remove the distributor cap and see that the rotor lines up with No. 1 plug wire position. Check that the notch on the crankshaft pulley lines up with the timing mark.

2. Disconnect the negative battery cable.

3. Disconnect the wiring harness from the distributor lead wire. It may be helpful to matchmark the rotor position to the distributor housing.

4. Remove the distributor mounting nut and remove the distributor assembly from the engine cylinder head. Note that there should be a fine cut (groove or projection) on the distributor flange. This factory matchmark is used at installation.

INSTALLATION
Timing Not Disturbed
1. To install, double check that the crankshaft mark and timing mark are still aligned and that the engine has not been turned. Align the mating mark on the distributor housing described above with the mating mark (punch) on the distributor driven gear.

2. Install the distributor assembly while aligning the mating mark on the distributor attaching flange with the center of the hold-down stud.

3. Connect all wiring and reinstall distributor cap and seal.

4. Connect the negative battery cable. Start engine and set timing. Then tighten distributor mounting nut.

Timing Disturbed

1. Remove the spark plug from No. 1 cylinder and position a compression gauge or a thumb over the spark plug hole.

2. Slowly crank the engine until compression pressure starts to build up.

3. Continue cranking the engine so the timing marks align with the TDC mark.

4. Install the distributor assembly while aligning the mating mark on the distributor attaching flange with the center of the hold-down stud.

5. Connect all wiring and reinstall distributor cap and seal.

6. Connect the negative battery cable. Start engine and set timing. Then tighten distributor mounting nut.

NOTE: Some engines may be sensitive to the routing of the distributor sensor wires. If routed near the high-voltage coil wire or the spark plug wires, the electromagnetic field surrounding the high voltage wires could generate an occasional disruption of the ignition system operation.

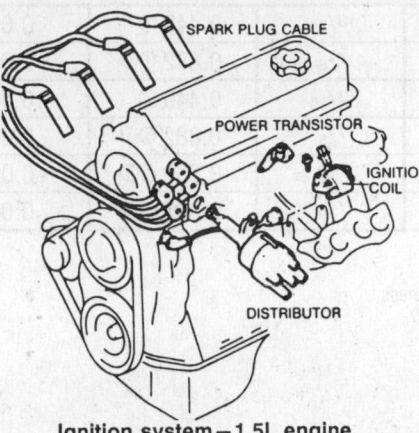

Ignition system—1.5L engine

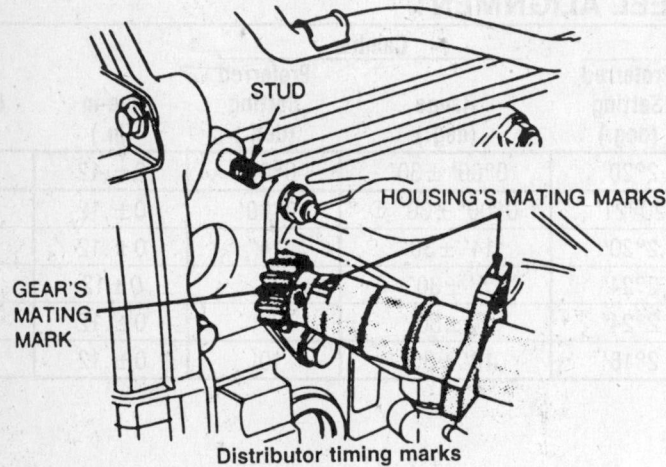

Distributor timing marks

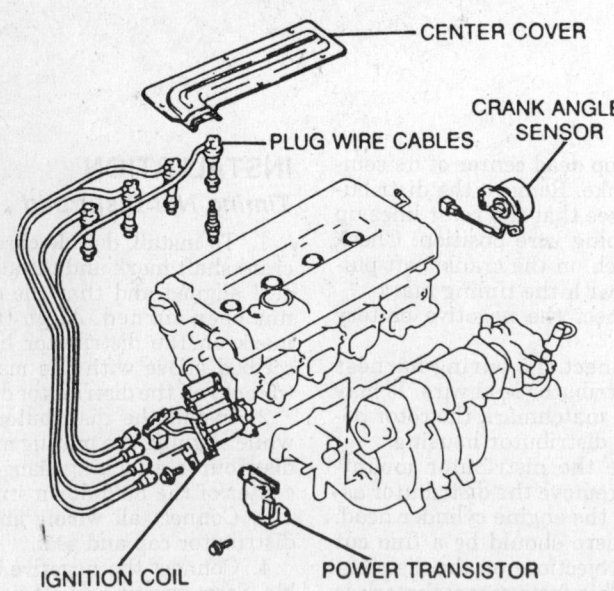

Distributorless ignition system—1.6L engine

Distributorless Ignition

REMOVAL & INSTALLATION

Crank Angle Sensor

1. Disconnect the battery negative cable.

2. The crank sensor is driven off the back of the intake camshaft. To remove, turn the crankshaft by hand so the No. 1 cylinder piston is at top dead center.

3. Disconnect the multi-wire connector.

4. Remove the retainer bolts and lift the sensor from the cylinder head.

To install:

5. At installation, align the punch mark on the crank angle sensor housing with the notch in the plate, then install the crank sensor. Make sure the flat drive tang registers into the slot in the camshaft.

6. Reconnect the multi-wire connector.

7. Reconnect the battery negative cable and check the timing.

Ignition Coil

1. Disconnect the battery negative cable.

2. The ignition coil is mounted on the front of the intake manifold. Remove and tag the spark plug cables.

3. Remove the mounting bolts and remove from engine.

To install:

4. Install coil to manifold. Install bolt and tighten to 15-19 ft. lbs.

5. Install spark plug cables in the correct locations.

6. Reconnect the battery negative cable.

Power Transistor

1. Disconnect the battery negative cable.

2. The power transistor is mounted on the front of the intake manifold. Remove and retaining screw and disconnect the wires to remove.

To install:

3. Install power transistor to manifold. Install screw and tighten.

4. Reconnect the battery negative cable.

Ignition Timing

ADJUSTMENT

1. Run engine until normal operating temperature is reached.

2. Turn all accessories **OFF**. Place transaxle in **P** for automatic transaxles or **N** for manual transaxles.

3. Connect a timing light.

4. Locate the wire connector on the

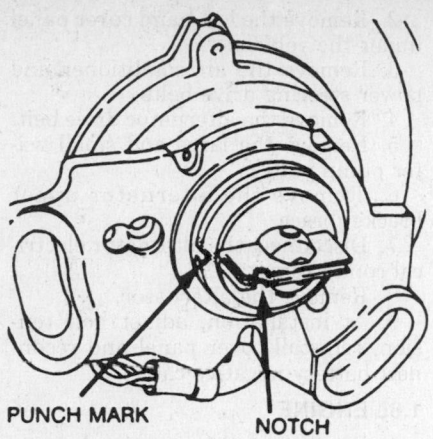

PUNCH MARK   NOTCH

Crank angle sensor alignment marks

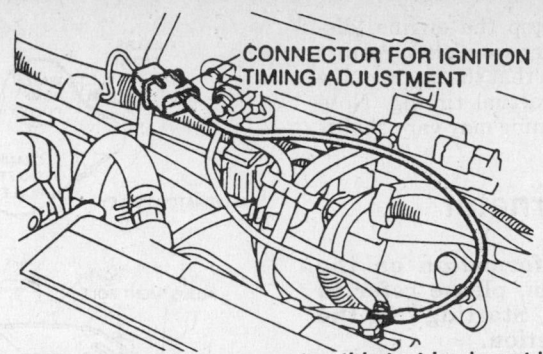

CONNECTOR FOR IGNITION TIMING ADJUSTMENT

Since timing is controlled by the computer, this test lead must be grounded to override the settings so adjustment can be made

ignition coil connector. Insert a paper clip behind the TACH terminal connector to act as a tach hookup adapter. Connect a tachometer to the paper clip.

NOTE: Do not separate the connector. The paper clip should be inserted along terminal surface.

5. Check and adjust curb idle speed.
6. Stop the engine. Disconnect the connector from the ignition timing adjusting connector, located in the engine compartment, and with a jumper wire, ground this wire.
7. Start the engine and run at curb idle speed. Check the ignition timing.
8. To adjust the ignition timing on

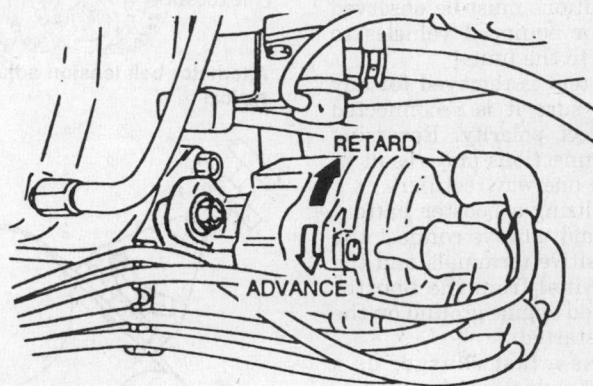

RETARD

ADVANCE

Turn the distributor to adjust timing—1.5L and 1.8L engines

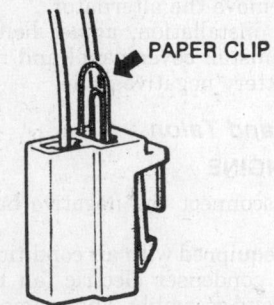

PAPER CLIP

Insert paper clip as shown

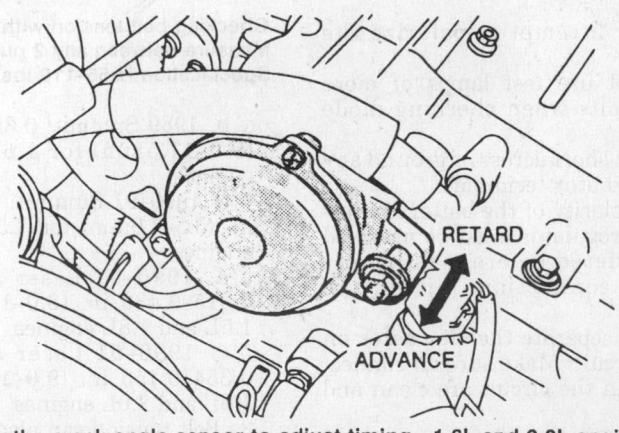

RETARD

ADVANCE

Turn the crank angle sensor to adjust timing—1.6L and 2.0L engines

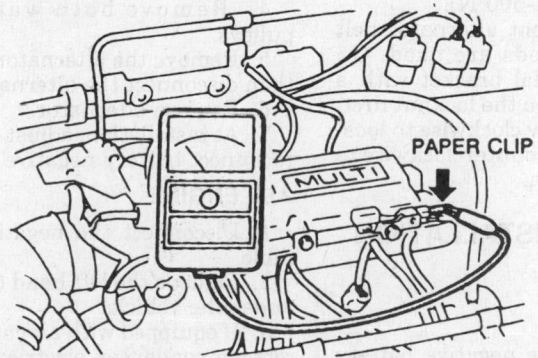

PAPER CLIP

MULTI

Tachometer hookup using paper clip adapter

1.5L and 1.8L engines, loosen the distributor and turn as required. Turning the distributor clockwise, viewed from the cap end, retards the spark, counterclockwise advances the timing.

9. To adjust the timing on 1.6L and 2.0L engines, loosen the crank angle sensor mounting nut and adjust by turning the crank angle sensor. The crank angle sensor is located and driven by the back of the intake camshaft. Turning the sensor to the right advances the timing, to the left retards it.

10. After adjustment, tighten the

mounting nut. Stop the engine, disconnect the jumper wire, then restart the engine. Check that the timing now advances to the actual timing. Note that the actual timing may vary slightly when running.

Alternator

For further information on the charging system, please refer to "Charging and Starting" in the Unit Repair section.

PRECAUTIONS

Several precautions must be observed with alternator equipped vehicles to avoid damage to the unit.
- If the battery is removed for any reason, make sure it is reconnected with the correct polarity. Reversing the battery connections may result in damage to the one-way rectifiers.
- When utilizing a booster battery as a starting aid, always connect the positive to positive terminals and the negative terminal from the booster battery to a good engine ground on the vehicle being started.
- Never use a fast charger as a booster to start vehicles.
- Disconnect the battery cables when charging the battery with a fast charger.
- Never attempt to polarize the alternator.
- Do not use test lamps of more than 12 volts when checking diode continuity.
- Do not short across or ground any of the alternator terminals.
- The polarity of the battery, alternator and regulator must be matched and considered before making any electrical connections within the system.
- Never separate the alternator on an open circuit. Make sure all connections within the circuit are clean and tight.
- Disconnect the battery ground terminal when performing any service on electrical components.
- Disconnect the battery if arc welding is to be done on the vehicle.

BELT TENSION ADJUSTMENT

1. Place a straight edge along the belt between 2 pulleys.
2. Measure the deflection with a force of about 22 lbs. applied midway between the 2 pulleys. Deflection should be:
   a. 1989 Summit: 0.276–0.354 in. (7.0–9.0mm) for 1.5L and 1.8L engines

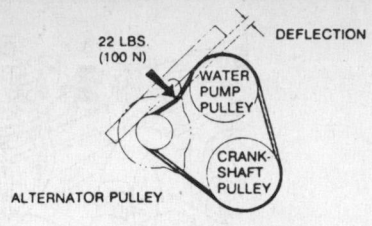

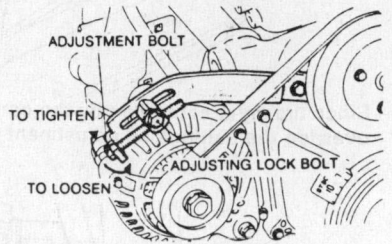

Alternator belt tension adjustment—typical

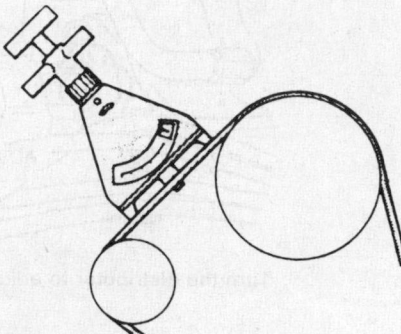

Checking belt tension with a gauge. Measure between any 2 pulleys. Specification is 55–110 lbs. tension.

   b. 1989 Summit: 0.354–0.453 in. (9.0–11.5mm) for 1.6L and 2.0L engines
   c. 1990–91 Summit: 0.217–0.276 in. (5.5–7.0mm) for 1.5L and 1.8L engines
   d. 1990–91 Laser and Talon: 0.315–0.433 in. (8.0–11.0mm) for 1.5L and 1.8L engines
   e. 1990–91 Laser and Talon: 0.354–0.453 in. (9.0–11.5mm) for 1.6L and 2.0L engines
3. Belt tension can also be checked with a tension gauge. Measure between any 2 pulleys. The value should be 55–110 lbs. (250–500 N).
4. Several different alternator belt adjustment methods are used. On units using a special bracket with a tension screw, loosen the locknut first. Then turn the screw clockwise to loosen the tension and counterclockwise to increase the tension.

REMOVAL & INSTALLATION

Summit

1.5L ENGINE

1. Disconnect the negative battery cable.
2. Remove the left hand cover panel under the vehicle.
3. Remove the air conditioner and power steering drive belts.
4. Remove the alternator drive belt.
5. Remove the large and small water pump pulleys.
6. Remove the alternator upper bracket/brace.
7. Disconnect the alternator electrical connectors.
8. Remove the alternator.
9. At installation, adjust belt tension, reinstall cover panel and reconnect battery negative cable.

1.6L ENGINE

1. Disconnect the negative battery cable.
2. Remove the left hand cover panel under the vehicle.
3. Remove the alternator and power steering drive belts.
4. Remove both water pump pulleys.
5. Remove the alternator adjuster brace.
6. Remove the alternator electrical connection.
7. Remove the flat strap-like battery hold-down and remove the battery.
8. Remove the windshield washer tank.
9. Remove the battery tray.
10. Remove the attaching bolts at the top of the radiator and lift up the radiator. Do not disconnect the radiator hoses.
11. Remove the alternator.
12. At installation, adjust belt tension, reinstall cover panel and reconnect battery negative cable.

Laser and Talon

1.8L ENGINE

1. Disconnect the negative battery cable.
2. If equipped with air conditioning, remove condenser electric fan motor and shroud assembly. Then remove air conditioner compressor drive belt.
3. Remove alternator and water pump belts.
4. Remove both water pump pulleys.
5. Remove the alternator top brace, then disconnect the alternator wiring.
6. Remove alternator.
7. At installation, adjust drive belts, reconnect battery negative cable.

2.0L ENGINE

1. Disconnect the negative battery cable.
2. Remove the left hand cover panel under the vehicle.
3. If equipped with air conditioning, remove condenser electric fan motor and shroud assembly.

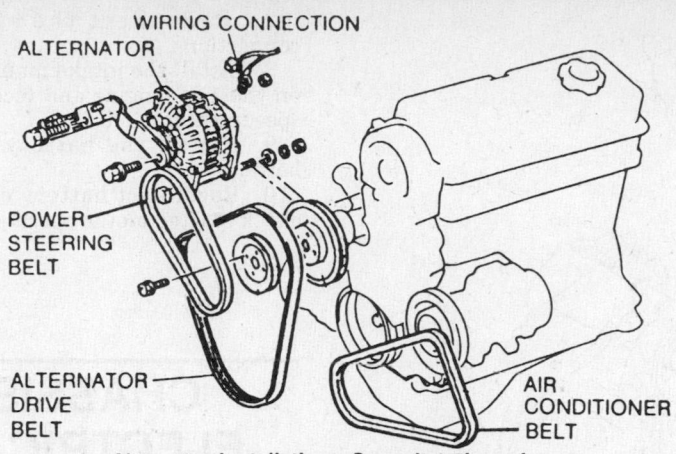

Alternator installation—Summit 1.5L engine

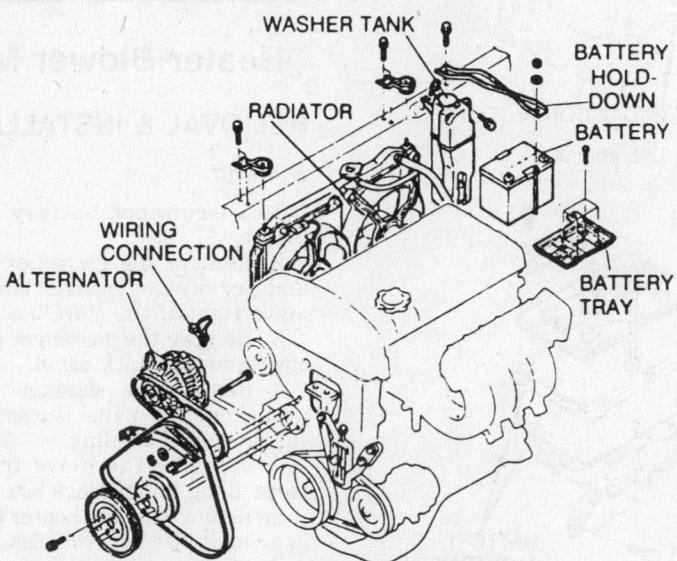

Alternator installation—Summit 1.6L engine

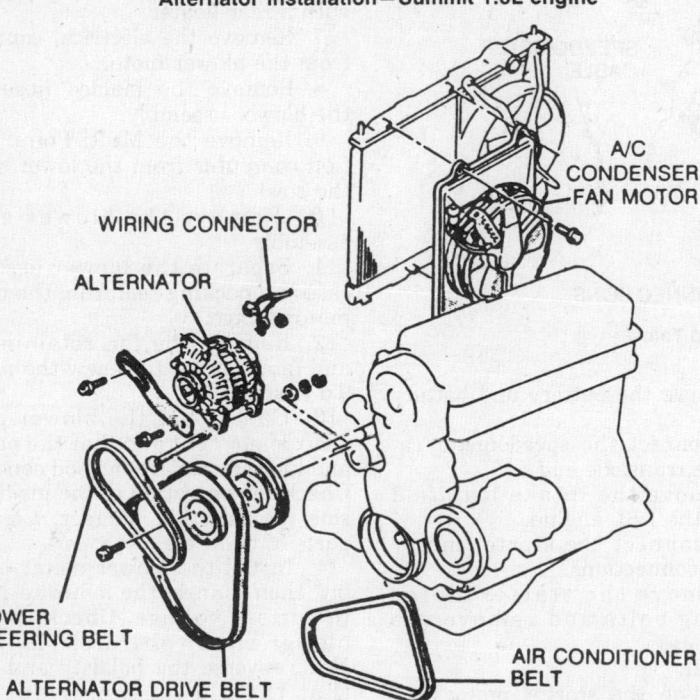

Alternator installation—Laser and Talon 1.8L engine

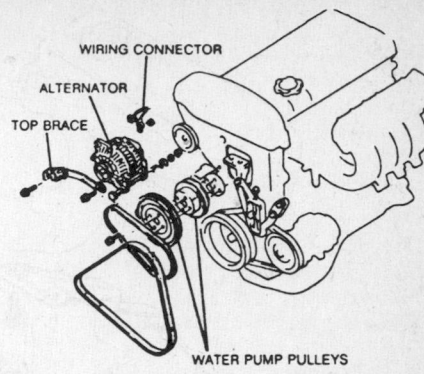

Alternator installation—Laser and Talon 2.0L engine

3. Remove alternator and water pump belts.

4. Remove both water pump pulleys.

5. Remove the alternator top brace, then disconnect the alternator wiring.

6. Remove alternator.

7. At installation, adjust belt tension, reinstall cover panel and reconnect battery negative cable.

Voltage Regulator

For further information on the charging system, please refer to "Charging and Starting" in the Unit Repair section.

Starter

For further information on the charging system, please refer to "Charging and Starting" in the Unit Repair section.

REMOVAL & INSTALLATION

Summit

1. Disconnect the negative battery cable.

2. Remove the air cleaner assembly. First disconnect the air-flow sensor connector and remove the breather hose. Remove the resonator retaining nuts and remove the air intake hose and resonator assembly.

NOTE: Use care when removing the air cleaner cover because the air-flow sensor is attached.

3. Remove the heat shield from beneath the intake manifold on the 1.5L engine.

4. Disconnect the starter motor electrical connections.

5. Remove the starter motor mounting bolts and remove the starter.

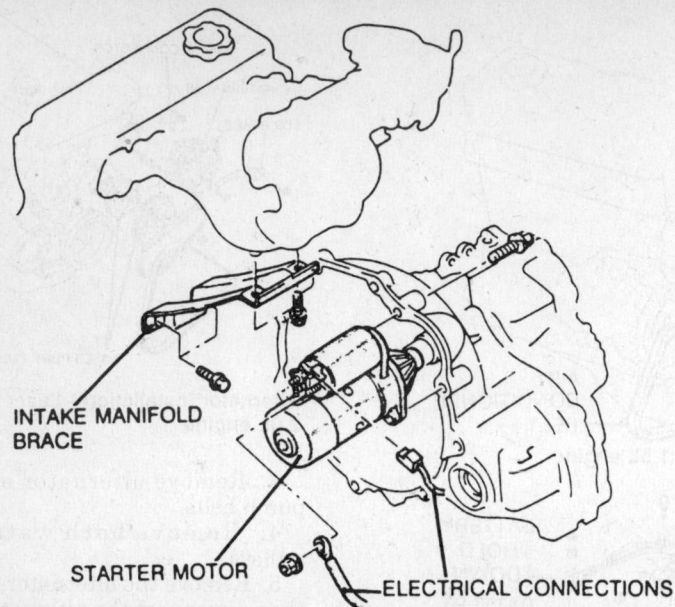

INTAKE MANIFOLD
BRACE

STARTER MOTOR

ELECTRICAL CONNECTIONS

Starter installation—Summit with 1.5L engine

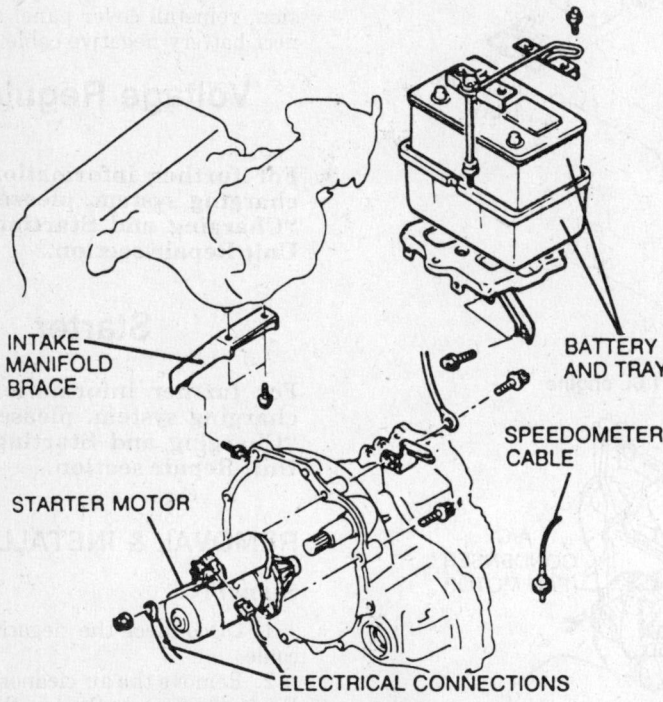

INTAKE
MANIFOLD
BRACE

BATTERY
AND TRAY

SPEEDOMETER
CABLE

STARTER MOTOR

ELECTRICAL CONNECTIONS

Starter installation—Laser and Talon

To install:

6. Position the starter motor and install the mounting bolts.

7. Reconnect the electrical connections.

8. Install the heat shield to intake manifold and install air cleaner assembly.

9. Reconnect battery negative cable and check starter motor operation.

Laser and Talon

1. Disconnect both battery cables.

2. Remove the battery and battery tray.

3. Disconnect the speedometer cable on the transaxle end.

4. Remove the intake manifold brace on the 1.8L engine.

5. Disconnect the starter motor electrical connections.

5. Remove the starter motor mounting bolts and remove the starter.

To install:

6. Position the starter motor and install the mounting bolts.

7. Reconnect the electrical connections.

8. Install the intake manifold brace on the 1.8L engine and reconnect the speedometer cable.

9. Install the battery tray and battery.

10. Reconnect battery cables and check starter motor operation.

CHASSIS ELECTRICAL

Heater Blower Motor

REMOVAL & INSTALLATION

Summit

1. Disconnect battery negative cable.

2. Remove the glove box assembly and pry off the speaker cover to the lower right of the glove box.

3. Remove the passenger side lower cowl side trim kick panel.

4. Remove the passenger side knee protector, the panel surrounding in the glove box opening.

5. Remove the glove frame, the piece along top of glove box opening.

6. Remove the lap heater duct. This is a small piece on vehicles without a rear heater, much larger on vehicles with a rear heater.

7. Remove the electrical connector from the blower motor.

8. Remove the molded hose from the blower assembly.

9. Remove the Multi-Point Injection computer from the lower side of the cowl.

10. Remove the blower motor assembly.

11. Separate the blower assembly case and packing seal from the blower motor flange.

12. Remove the fan retaining nut and fan in order to renew the motor.

To install:

13. Check that the blower motor shaft is not bent and that the packing and blower case are in good condition. Check the operation of the inside/outside air selection damper. Clean all parts of dust, etc.

14. Install the blower motor assembly, then connect the motor terminals to battery voltage. Check that the blower motor operates smoothly. Next, reverse the polarity and check that the blower motor operates smoothly in the reverse direction.

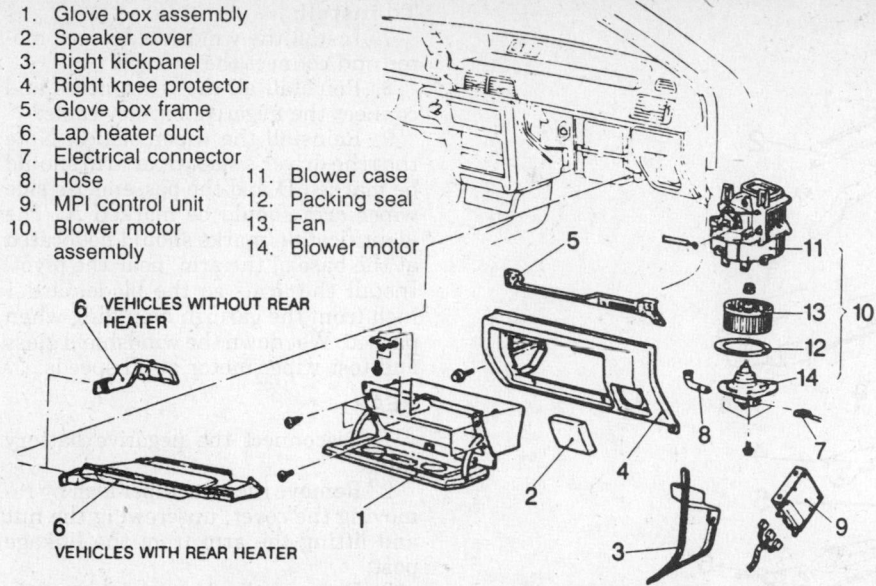

1. Glove box assembly
2. Speaker cover
3. Right kickpanel
4. Right knee protector
5. Glove box frame
6. Lap heater duct
7. Electrical connector
8. Hose
9. MPI control unit
10. Blower motor assembly
11. Blower case
12. Packing seal
13. Fan
14. Blower motor

Heater blower motor assembly — Summit

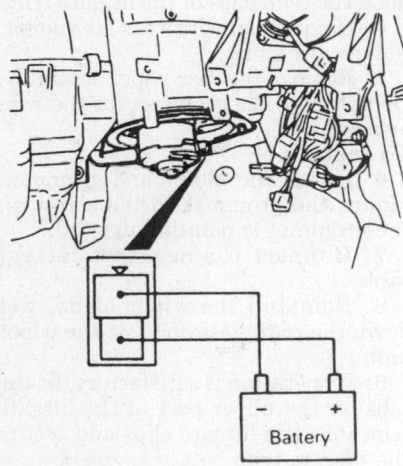

Hookup for testing blower motor

Laser and Talon

1. Disconnect battery negative cable.

2. Remove the right hand duct, if equipped.

3. Remove the molded hose from the blower assembly.

4. Remove the blower motor assembly.

5. Remove the packing seal.

6. Remove the fan retaining nut and fan in order to renew the motor.

To install:

7. Check that the blower motor shaft is not bent and that the packing is in good condition. Clean all parts of dust, etc.

8. Install the blower motor then connect the motor terminals to battery voltage. Check that the blower motor operates smoothly. Next, reverse the polarity and check that the blower motor operates smoothly in the reverse direction.

9. Install duct if removed. Connect battery negative cable.

Windshield Wiper Motor

REMOVAL & INSTALLATION

Summit
FRONT

1. Disconnect the negative battery cable.

2. Remove the windshield wiper arms by unscrewing the cap nuts and lifting the arms from the linkage posts.

3. Remove the front garnish panel.

4. Remove both windshield holders.

5. Remove the clips that hold the deck cover. If of the pin type, they may be removed using the following procedure:

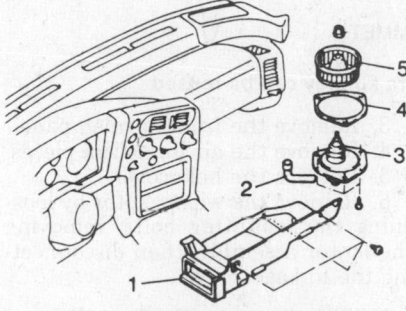

1. Duct, if so equipped
2. Molded hose
3. Blower motor assembly
4. Packing seal
5. Fan

Heater blower motor assembly — Laser and Talon

a. This type of clip is removed by pressing down on the center pin with a suitable blunt pointed tool. Press down a little more than $\frac{1}{16}$ in. (2mm). This releases the clip. Pull the clip outward to remove it.

b. Do not push the pin inward more than necessary because it may damage the grommet, or the pin may fall in, if pushed in too far. Once the clips are removed, use a plastic trim stick to pry the deck cover loose.

6. Remove the air intake screen.

7. Loosen the wiper motor assembly mounting bolts and remove the windshield wiper motor. Disconnect the linkage and the motor assembly. If necessary, remove the linkage.

NOTE: The installation angle of the crank arm and the motor has been factory set, do not remove them unless it is necessary to do so. If they must be removed, remove them only after marking their mounting positions.

To install:

8. Install the windshield wiper motor and connect the linkage.

9. When installing the trim and garnish pieces and reusing pin type clips, use the following procedure:

a. With the pin pulled out, insert the trim clip into the hole in the trim.

b. Push the pin inward until the pin's head is flush with the grommet.

c. Check that the trim is secure.

10. Connect the negative battery cable.

11. Reinstall the wiper blades, wet down the windshield glass and test wiper motor at all speeds.

REAR

1. Disconnect the negative battery cable.

2. Remove the hatchback wiper arm by removing the cap nut cover, unscrewing the cap nut and lifting the arm from the linkage post.

3. Remove the large interior trim panel. Use a plastic trim stick to unhook the trim clips of the liftgate trim. There will be a row of metal liftgate clips across the top. There will be 2 rows of trim clips that retain the rest of the panel.

4. Remove the rear wiper assembly. Do not loose the grommet for the wiper post.

To install:

5. Install the motor and grommet. Mount the grommet so the arrow on the grommet is pointing downward.

6. Connect the negative battery cable.

7. Reinstall the wiper blade, wet

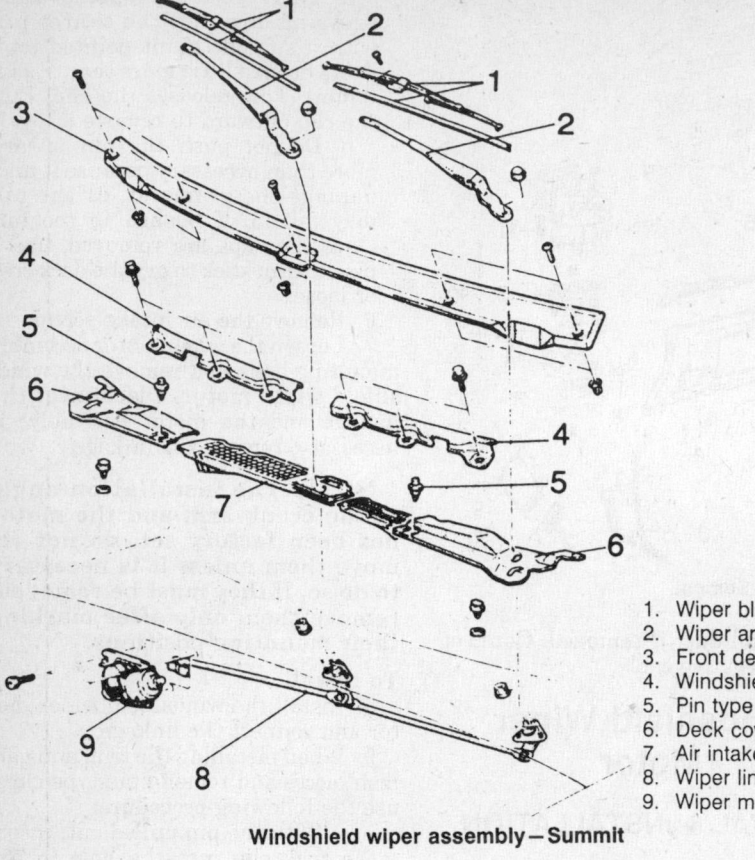

1. Wiper blades
2. Wiper arms
3. Front deck garnish
4. Windshield holder
5. Pin type trim clip
6. Deck cover
7. Air intake screen
8. Wiper linkage
9. Wiper motor

Windshield wiper assembly—Summit

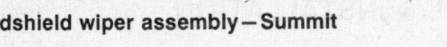

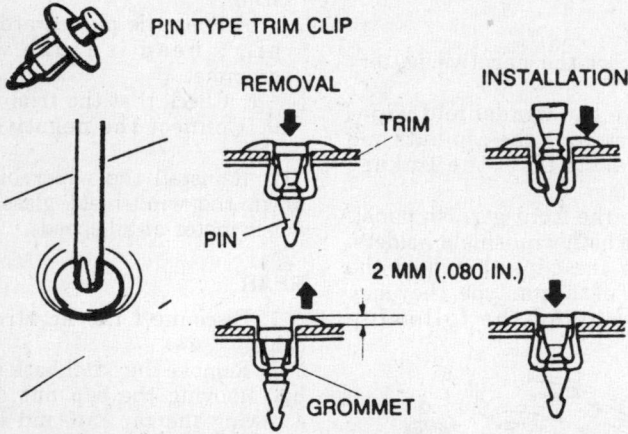

Remove the pin clips with care so they can be reused

down the liftgate glass and test the wiper motor.

8. If operation is satisfactory, fit the tabs on the upper part of the liftgate trim into the liftgate clips and secure the liftgate trim.

Laser and Talon

FRONT

1. Disconnect the negative battery cable.

2. Remove the windshield wiper arms by unscrewing the cap nuts and lifting the arms from the linkage posts.

3. Remove the front garnish panel.
4. Remove the air inlet trim pieces.
5. Remove the hole cover.
6. Remove the wiper motor by loosening the mounting bolts, removing the motor assembly, then disconnecting the linkage.

NOTE: Because the installation angle of the crank arm and the motor has been factory set, do not remove them unless it is necessary to do so. If they must be removed, remove them only after marking their mounting positions.

To install:

7. Install the windshield wiper motor and connect the linkage.

8. Reinstall all the trim pieces and connect the negative battery cable.

9. Reinstall the wiper blades. Note that the driver's side wiper arm should be marked **D** and the passenger's side wiper arm should be marked **A**. The identification marks should be located at the base of the arm, near the pivot. Install the arms so the blades are 1 inch from the garnish moulding when parked. Wet down the windshield glass and test wiper motor at all speeds.

REAR

1. Disconnect the negative battery cable.

2. Remove the rear wiper arm by removing the cover, unscrewing the nut and lifting the arm from the linkage post.

3. Remove the large interior trim panel. Use a plastic trim stick to unhook the trim clips of the liftgate trim.

4. If equipped with rear air spoiler, remove grommet.

5. Remove the rear wiper assembly. Do not loose the grommet for the wiper post.

To install:

6. Install the motor and grommet. Mount the grommet so the arrow on the grommet is pointing upward.

7. Connect the negative battery cable.

8. Reinstall the wiper blade, wet down the rear glass and test the wiper motor.

9. If operation is satisfactory, fit the tabs on the upper part of the liftgate trim into the liftgate clips and secure the liftgate trim.

Windshield Wiper Switch

REMOVAL & INSTALLATION

Summit

1. Disconnect the negative battery cable.

2. The windshield wiper switch is located on the steering column. Remove the knee protector panel under the steering column, then the upper and lower column covers.

3. Remove the horn pad by pulling the lower end.

4. Remove the steering wheel.

NOTE: Make mating marks on the steering wheel and the steering wheel shaft. Use a steering wheel puller to remove the steering wheel. Do not hammer on the steering wheel to remove it or the collapsible mechanism may be damaged.

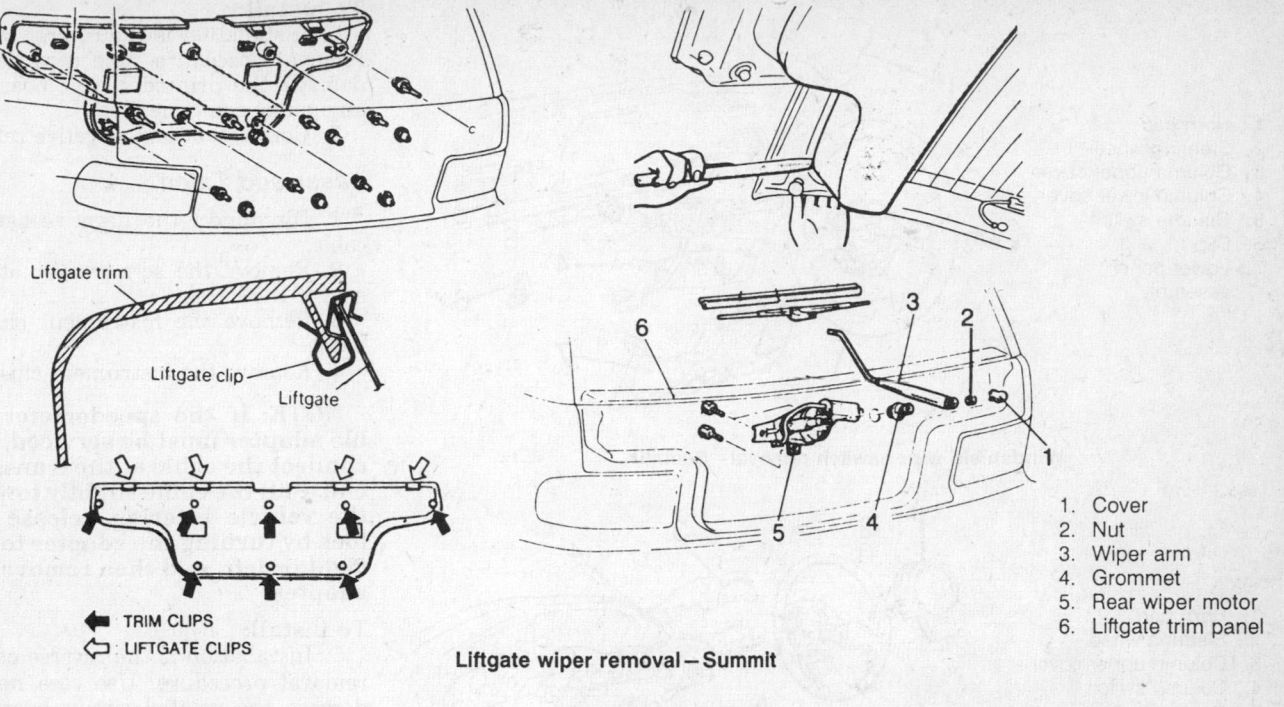

Liftgate trim
Liftgate clip
Liftgate

⬅ TRIM CLIPS
⬅ LIFTGATE CLIPS

Liftgate wiper removal—Summit

1. Cover
2. Nut
3. Wiper arm
4. Grommet
5. Rear wiper motor
6. Liftgate trim panel

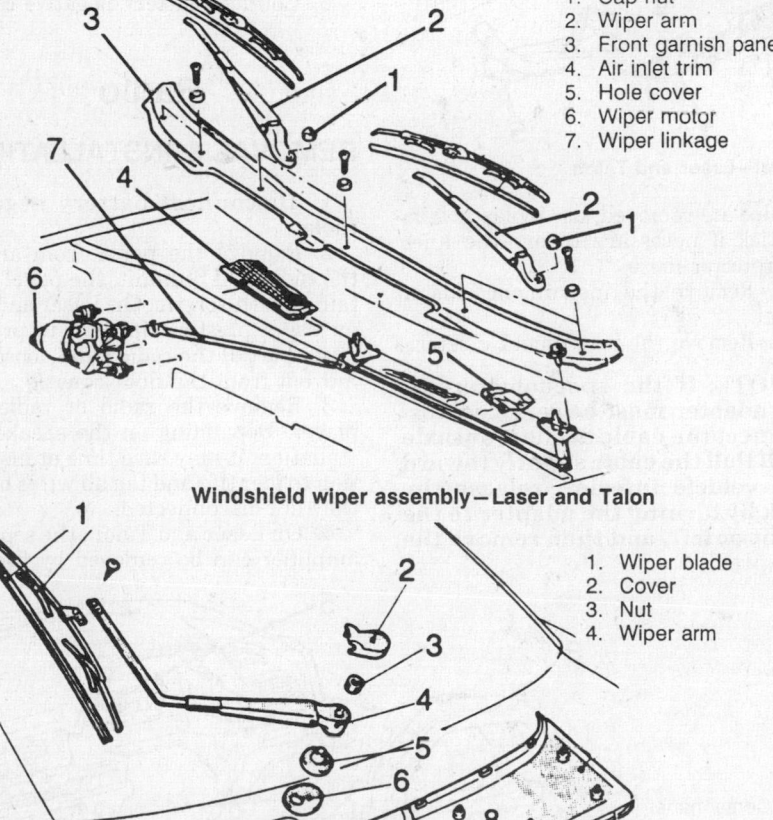

1. Cap nut
2. Wiper arm
3. Front garnish panel
4. Air inlet trim
5. Hole cover
6. Wiper motor
7. Wiper linkage

Windshield wiper assembly—Laser and Talon

1. Wiper blade
2. Cover
3. Nut
4. Wiper arm

5. Grommet
6. Air spoiler grommet (if equipped)
7. Wiper motor
8. Interior trim panel

Rear glass wiper removal—Laser and Talon

5. Remove the wiring clip and remove the column switch assembly.

To install:

6. At installation, take care that no wires are pinched or out of place.

7. Torque the steering wheel-to-column nut to 25–33 ft. lbs.

8. Check the steering wheel position with the wheels straight ahead.

9. Connect battery negative cable.

Laser and Talon

1. Disconnect the negative battery cable.

2. Remove the horn pad by removing the screw from behind the steering wheel and then pressing the pad upward.

3. Remove the steering wheel.

NOTE: Make mating marks on the steering wheel and the steering wheel shaft. Use a steering wheel puller to remove the steering wheel. Do not hammer on the steering wheel to remove it or the collapsible mechanism may be damaged.

4. Locate the rectangular plugs in the knee protector on either side of the steering column. Pry these plugs out, remove the screws. Remove the screws from the hood lock release lever and remove the knee protector.

5. Remove the upper and lower column covers.

6. Remove the lap cooler ducts.

7. Remove the band retaining the switch wiring.

8. Remove the column switch.

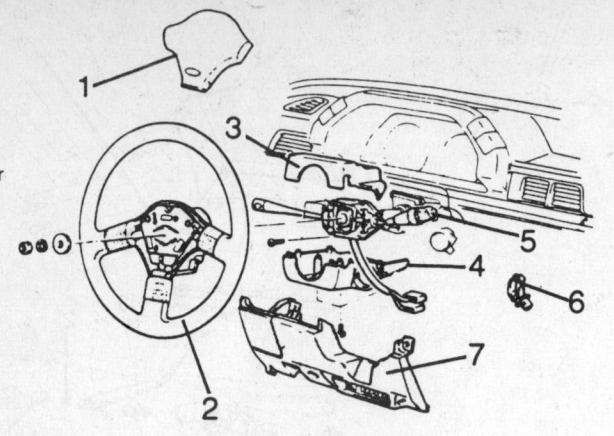

1. Horn pad
2. Steering wheel
3. Column upper cover
4. Column lower cover
5. Column switch
6. Clip
7. Lower panel assembly

Windshield wiper switch removal—Summit

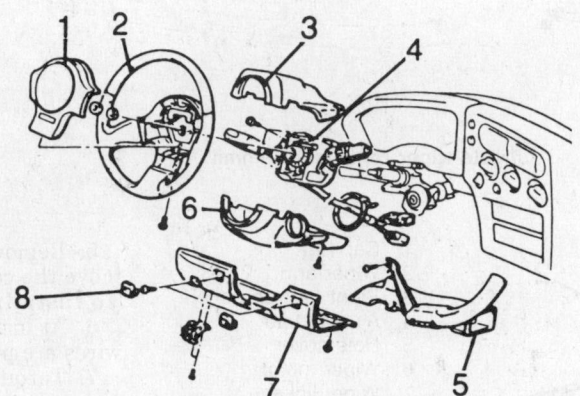

1. Horn pad
2. Steering wheel
3. Column upper cover
4. Column switch
5. Cooler duct
6. Column lower cover
7. Knee protector
8. Screw plugs

Windshield wiper switch removal—Laser and Talon

To install:

9. Installation is the reverse of the removal procedure. Take care that no wires are pinched or out of place.

10. Torque the steering wheel-to-column nut to 25–33 ft. lbs.

11. Check the steering wheel position with the wheels straight ahead.

12. Connect battery negative cable.

Instrument Cluster

REMOVAL & INSTALLATION

Summit

1. Disconnect the negative battery cable.

2. Remove the center panel.

3. Remove the knee protector. If pin type clips are used, they may be removed using the following procedure:

   a. This type of clip is removed by pressing down on the center pin with a suitable blunt pointed tool. Press down a little more than $1/16$ in. (2mm). This releases the clip. Pull the clip outward to remove it.

   b. Do not push the pin inward more than necessary because it may damage the grommet or the pin may fall in, if pushed in too far. Once the

clips are removed, use a plastic trim stick if necessary to pry the knee protector loose.

4. Remove the instrument cluster bezel.

5. Remove the instrument cluster.

NOTE: If the speedometer cable adapter must be serviced, disconnect the cable at the transaxle end. Pull the cable slightly toward the vehicle interior, release the lock by turning the adapter to the right or left, and then remove the adapter.

To install:

6. Installation is the reverse of the removal procedure. Use care not to damage the printed circuit board or any gauge components.

7. Connect battery negative cable.

Laser and Talon

1. Disconnect the negative battery cable.

2. Remove the screw cover at the side of the bezel.

3. Remove the instrument cluster bezel.

4. Remove the instrument cluster.

NOTE: If the speedometer cable adapter must be serviced, disconnect the cable at the transaxle end. Pull the cable slightly toward the vehicle interior, release the lock by turning the adapter to the right or left, and then remove the adapter.

To install:

5. Installation is the reverse of the removal procedure. Use care not to damage the printed circuit board or any gauge components.

6. Connect battery negative cable.

Radio

REMOVAL & INSTALLATION

1. Disconnect battery negative cable.

2. Remove the panel from around the radio. On Summit, the panel is retained with screws. On Laser and Talon use a plastic trim tool to pry the lower part of the radio panel loose. Remove it from the floor console.

3. Remove the radio or radio/tape player. Depending on the speaker installation, it may save time at installation to identify and tag all wires before they are disconnected.

4. On Laser and Talon, the separate amplifier can be removed by first re-

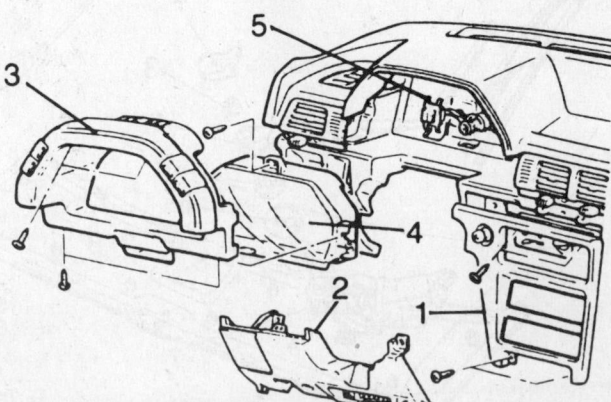

1. Center panel
2. Knee protector
3. Instrument cluster bezel
4. Instrument cluster
5. Speedometer adapter

Instrument cluster removal—Summit

1. Screw cover
2. Instrument cluster bezel
3. Instrument cluster
4. Speedometer adapter

Instrument cluster removal—Laser and Talon

moving the side cover of the console box. Then remove the amplifier.

5. Remove the mounting brackets from the radio.

To install:

6. Installation is the reverse of the removal procedure. Make all electrical and antenna connections before fastening the radio assembly in place.

7. Install the center panel.

8. Connect the battery negative cable.

Concealed Headlights

MANUAL OPERATION

Laser and Talon

To open the headlights manually, remove the boot on the rear area of the pop-up motor and turn the manual knob approximately 10 turns clockwise. Perform this procedure on both the left and right sides.

Combination Switch

REMOVAL & INSTALLATION

Summit

NOTE: The headlights, turn signals, dimmer switch, windshield/washer and, on some models, the cruise control function are all built into one multi-function combination switch that is mounted on the steering column.

1. Disconnect the negative battery cable.

2. Remove the knee protector panel under the steering column, then the upper and lower column covers.

3. Remove the horn pad by pulling the lower end.

4. Remove the steering wheel.

NOTE: Make mating marks on the steering wheel and the steering wheel shaft. Use a steering wheel puller to remove the steering wheel. Do not hammer on the steering wheel to remove it or the collapsible mechanism may be damaged.

5. Remove the wiring clip and remove the column switch assembly.

To install:

6. Installation is the reverse of the removal procedure. Take care that no wires are pinched or out of place.

7. Torque the steering wheel-to-column nut to 25-33 ft. lbs.

8. Check the steering wheel position with the wheels straight ahead.

9. Connect battery negative cable.

Laser and Talon

NOTE: The headlights, turn signals, dimmer switch, windshield/washer and, on some models, the cruise control function are all built into one multi-function combination switch that is mounted on the steering column.

1. Disconnect the negative battery cable.

2. Remove the horn pad by removing the screw from behind the steering wheel and then pressing the pad upward.

3. Remove the steering wheel.

NOTE: Make mating marks on the steering wheel and the steering wheel shaft. Use a steering wheel puller to remove the steering wheel. Do not hammer on the steering wheel to remove it or the collapsible mechanism may be damaged.

4. Locate the rectangular plugs in the knee protector on either side of the steering column. Pry these plugs out and remove the screws. Remove the screws from the hood lock release lever and remove the knee protector.

5. Remove the upper and lower column covers.

6. Remove the lap cooler ducts.

7. Remove the band retaining the switch wiring.

8. Remove the column switch.

To install:

9. At installation, take care that no wires are pinched or out of place.

10. Torque the steering wheel-to-column nut to 25-33 ft. lbs.

11. Check the steering wheel position with the wheels straight ahead.

12. Connect battery negative cable.

Ignition Lock/Switch

REMOVAL & INSTALLATION

1. Disconnect the negative battery cable.

2. Remove the lower instrument panel knee protector.

3. Remove the lower steering column cover.

4. Remove the clip that holds the wiring against the steering column.

5. Unplug the ignition switch from the steering lock cylinder.

6. Insert the key into the steering lock cylinder and turn to the **ACC** position.

7. With a small pointed tool, push the lock pin of the steering lock cylinder inward and pull the lock out.

NOTE: Laser and Talon models equipped with automatic transmission safety-lock systems will have a key interlock cable installed in a slide lever on the side of the key lock.

To install:

8. Installation is the reverse of the removal process. Make sure the lock pin snaps into place. Install the ignition switch plug carefully and make sure no wires are pinched.

9. Reconnect the negative battery cable.

Stoplight Switch

ADJUSTMENT

1. The stoplight switch works off the brake pedal lever. To adjust, disconnect the electrical connection and loosen the switch locknut.

2. Screw the switch inward until it

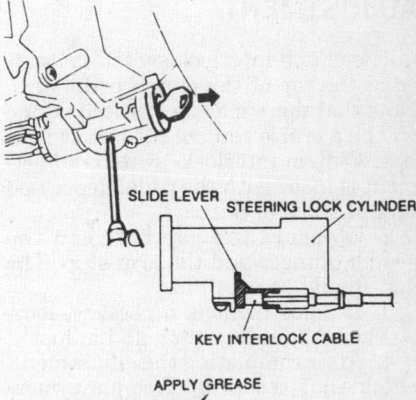
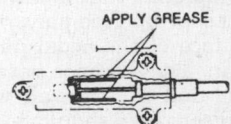

Ignition lock removal and optional automatic transmission safety interlock cable

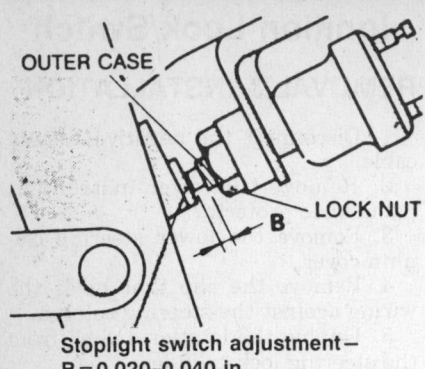

Stoplight switch adjustment—
B = 0.020–0.040 in.

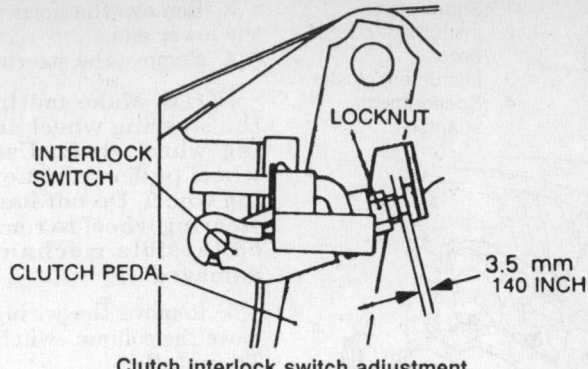

Clutch interlock switch adjustment

contacts the stop on the brake pedal arm. Back out the switch ½–1 full turn. The gap between the switch plunger and the brake lever stop should be 0.020–0.040 inch.

3. Tighten the locknut, connect the wires.

4. Check that the stoplights are not on unless the pedal is depressed.

REMOVAL & INSTALLATION

1. Disconnect the negative battery cable.

2. Locate the stoplight switch above the brake pedal lever.

3. Disconnect the wiring connectors from the switch and unscrew the switch.

4. Installation is the reverse of the removal process. Install the replacement switch and adjust to 0.020–0.040 in. clearance.

5. Reconnect the stoplight wires.

6. Reconnect the negative battery cable.

Clutch Switch

ADJUSTMENT

The clutch interlock switch is located at the top of the clutch pedal arm. Note that there may be 2 switches; one will be a cruise control cut-out switch.

1. Clutch interlock switch adjustment is made with the pedal depressed its full stock of 6 in.

2. Measure the gap between the switch plunger and the arm stop. The gap should be 0.140 in.

3. If adjustment is necessary, loosen the locknut and turn and adjust.

4. After completing the adjustment, check that the pedal free-play, measured at the face of the pedal pad, is 0.240–0.510 in. The distance between the pedal pad and the firewall when the clutch is disengaged should be 2.20 in. or more for Summit, 2.80 in. or more for Laser and Talon. If these dimensions are not right, the hydraulic

clutch system will probably need to be bled.

REMOVAL & INSTALLATION

1. Disconnect the negative battery cable.

2. Locate the interlock switch above the clutch pedal lever.

3. Disconnect the wiring connectors from the switch and unscrew the switch.

4. Installation is the reverse of the removal procedure. Install the replacement switch and adjust to 0.140 in. clearance.

5. Reconnect the interlock wires.

6. Reconnect the negative battery cable.

Neutral Safety Switch

ADJUSTMENT

1. Locate the neutral safety switch on the top of the transaxle. Note that several different cable attaching methods have been used. The procedure here can be used as a general guide for all.

2. Place the selector lever in N.

3. Loosen the 2 adjusting nuts to free up the cable and lever.

4. Place the safety switch manual control lever in N.

5. Note that one end of the safety switch manual control lever has a 12mm wide square end. There is also a 12mm wide tab on the switch body flange. Loosen both retaining bolts and turn the safety switch until these portions align. Tighten the bolts, making sure the switch doesn't move.

6. Loosen the adjuster nuts and gently pull the cable to remove any slack. Gently tighten adjusting nut until it just starts to contact the adjuster. Secure adjusting nut with its locknut then turn nut to lock.

7. Verify that the switch lever moves to positions corresponding to each position of the selector lever.

8. To test, apply the parking and

service brake securely. Place the selector in R. Turn the ignition key to the START position. Slowly move the selector lever upward until it clicks and fits in the notch of the P range. If the starter motor operates when the lever makes a click the P position is correct. Slowly move the lever to the N range. Using the same procedure, if the starter operates when the selctor fits in the N position, adjustment is correct. Also check that the vehicle doesn't begin to move and the lever doesn't stop between P-R-N-D.

REMOVAL & INSTALLATION

1. Disconnect the negative battery cable.

2. Remove the adjustment nuts from the switch lever.

3. Remove the 2 retaining screws and lift off the switch.

4. Installation is the reverse of the removal procedure. Install the replacement switch. Do not tighten the bolts until the switch is adjusted.

5. Test to verify correct adjustment.

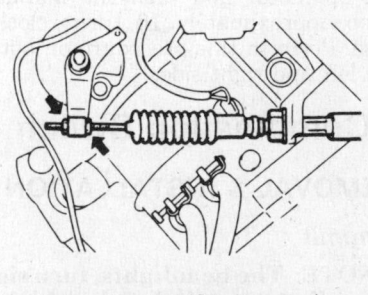

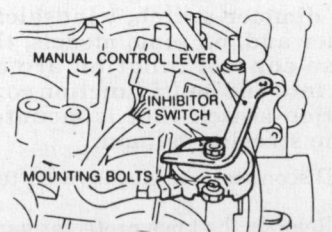

Automatic transmission neutral safety (inhibitor) switch and adjustment

Fuses and Relays

LOCATION

Summit

FUSES

The Summit has several fuse panels. One fuse panel is located on the passenger side, under the hood, just behind the battery. It shares the panel with a bank of relays. This panel also contains several fusible links. Another fuse panel is on the driver's side, under the hood, up front behind the headlight. It controls air conditioning functions. A third fuse panel is the multi-purpose fuse block located inside the car, on the left side behind the driver's knee protector.

RELAYS

The Summit uses a number of relays. The headlight relay, power window relay, radiator fan motor relay and alternator relay share a panel with fuses and fusible links. It is located on the passenger side, under the hood, just behind the battery. Another panel is on the driver's side, under the hood, up front behind the headlight. This panel also shares space with air conditioning system fuses. These relays are the air conditioner compressor relay, the condenser fan motor relay and the condenser fan motor control relay.

The intermittent wiper relay is incorporated into the column switch. The seat belt warning timer relay is located behind the instrument panel to the right of the center air conditioning outlets. The Multi-Point Injection control relay is mounted behind the forward part of the console, on the left side, while the starter relay is on the right side. The defogger relay is located under the driver's left side knee protector. The door lock relay is behind the driver's side kickpanel, at the bottom.

The multi-purpose fuse panel located under the driver's left side knee protector also contains the heater relay, the turn signal and hazard flasher unit and the defogger timer. The automatic seatbelt motor relay is located in the driver's side windshield post in Summit Hatchbacks, and inside the trim panel on the driver's side rear quarter panel, just behind the door post in Summit Sedans.

Laser and Talon

FUSES

The Laser and Talon has several fuse panels. There are 3 main fusible links the MPI circuit—20 amp, the radiator fan motor circuit—30 amp and the ignition switch circuit—30 amp. They are found under the hood in a centralized junction with the battery positive cable clamp. Another fuse panel is located on the passenger side, under the hood, just forward of the strut tower. It shares the panel with a bank of relays. This panel contains fuses and several fusible links. Another fuse panel is on the driver's side, under the hood, back against the firewall. A fourth fuse panel is the multi-purpose fuse block located inside the car, on the left side behind the driver's knee protector.

RELAYS

The Laser and Talon uses a number of relays. A centralized fuse/relay panel on the passenger side, under the hood, just forward of the strut tower contains the taillight relay, headlight relay, radiator fan motor relay, pop-up (retractable light) motor relay, power window relay, alternator relay and fog light relay. Also in the engine compartment on the driver's side a panel contains 2 air conditioning condenser fan relays and the air conditioning compressor clutch relay. Inside the vehicle, the interior relay box contains the door lock relay, starter relay, defogger timer and room of other relays as required (use in Canada, etc).

Computers

LOCATION

Summit

A number of computers or control units are used. The primary unit is the Multi-Point Injection (MPI) control unit located under the instrument panel at the top of the passenger side kick panel, next to the blower motor. Another unit is mounted behind the glove box to control the air conditioning compressor. The automatic transmission control unit is mounted on the floor at the very front of the console. The cruise control unit is under the instrument panel behind the driver's side knee protector. The electric door lock control unit is fastened to the body structure behind the driver's side kick panel. The automatic seat belt control unit is under the console next to hand brake handle.

Laser and Talon

A number of computers or control units are used. The primary unit is the Multi-Point Injection (MPI) control unit located under the instrument panel at the front of the center console. Another unit is mounted behind the glove box to control the A/C compressor. The automatic transmission control unit is mounted on the floor at the very front of the console. The cruise control unit is mounted at top of instrument panel structure near where the dash pad and windshield meet. The electric door lock control unit or theft-alarm control unit is fastened to the body structure behind the passenger's side kick panel. The automatic seat belt control unit is fastened to the body structure under the trim panel at the base of the driver's side door latch pillar.

Flashers

LOCATION

Turn Signal Flasher

The turn signal and hazard flasher unit is located in the multi-purpose fuse panel located under the driver's left side knee protector.

Cruise Control

ADJUSTMENT

Before starting adjustments, turn air conditioner and lights **OFF**. Warm engine until the idle is stable and the rpm is correct. Stop engine, ignition switch **OFF**. On Laser and Talon with the 1.5L and 1.8L engines, turn the ignition switch to the **ON** position, without starting the engine, and leave in the position for approximately 15 seconds. Confirm there are no sharp bends in the accelerator cables. Check the inner cables for correct slack. If too loose or too tight, adjust with the following procedure:

1. Remove the air cleaner. If vehicle is equipped with a protective cover over the actuator, remove it.

2. First, adjust accelerator cable **B**, throttle valve side. After loosening the adjustment bolts at the air intake plenum side and freeing the inner cable, use the adjusting bolts that secure the plate so the free-play of the inner cable becomes 0.040–0.080 in. (1–2mm). If there is excessive play of the accelerator cable, when climbing a hill the vehicle speed will drop substantially (undershoot). If there is no play, (excessive tension) the idling speed will increase.

3. After adjusting the accelerator cable **B**, confirm that the throttle lever touches the idle position switch.

4. Next, adjust accelerator cable **A** on the accelerator pedal side. Loosen the adjusting bolt or locknut. While keeping the intermediate link **A** of the actuator in close contact with the stop, adjust the inner cable play of accelerator cable **A** to 0–0.040 in. (0–1mm) for manual transmission vehicles and

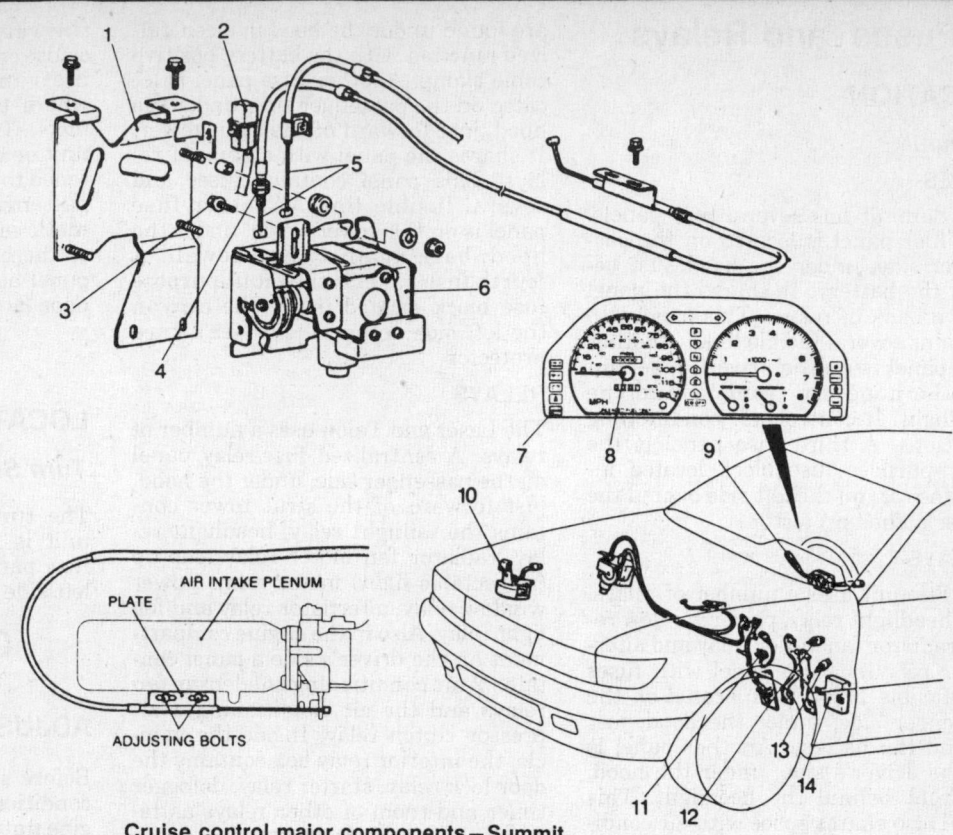

1. Bracket
2. Actuator connector
3. Cable A adjusting bolt
4. Cable B adjusting nut
5. Actuator inner cables
6. Actuator
7. Auto-cruise indicator
8. Vehicle speed sensor
9. Auto-cruise control switch
10. Transmission safety switch
11. Accelerator switch (A/T)
12. Clutch switch (M/T)
13. Stop light switch
14. Auto-cruise control unit

Cruise control major components—Summit

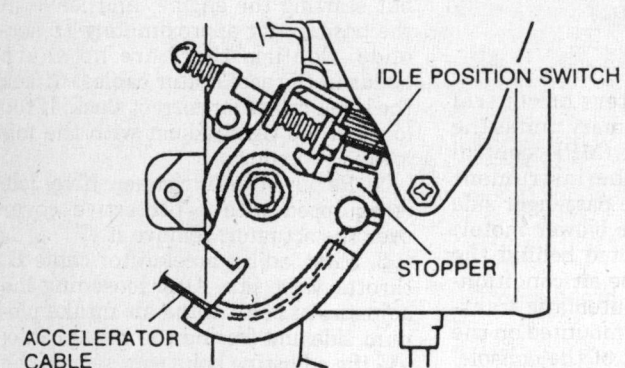

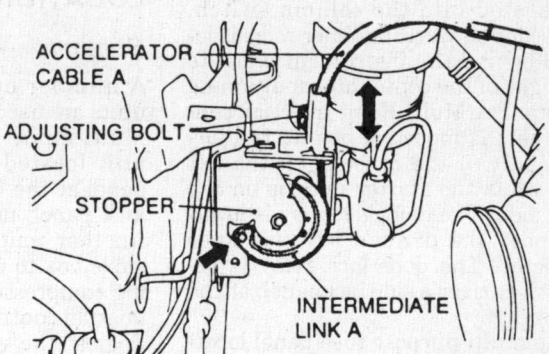

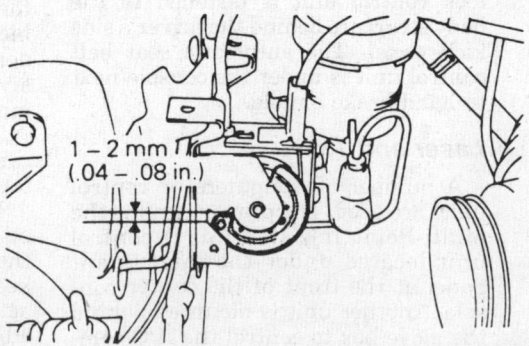

Cruise control adjusments—Summit

0.080–0.120 in. (2–3mm) for automatic transmission vehicles.

5. After making the adjustment of the cable check to be sure the throttle lever at the engine side moves 0.040–0.080 in. (1–2mm) when the actuator link is turned.

6. Confirm that the throttle valve fully opens and closes by operating the accelerator pedal.

7. Install the air cleaner.

ENGINE COOLING

Radiator

REMOVAL & INSTALLATION

1. Disconnect the negative battery cable.

2. Drain the cooling system.

3. Disconnect the overflow tube. Some vehicles may also require removal of the overflow tank.

4. Disconnect upper and lower radiator hoses.

5. Disconnect electrical connectors for cooling fan and air condtioning condenser fan, if so equipped.

6. Disconnect thermo sensor wires.

7. Disconnect and plug automatic transmission cooler lines, if used.

8. Remove the upper radiator mounts and lift out the radiator/fan assembly.

To install:

9. At installation, use proper mix of coolant suitable for use in engines with aluminum components.

10. Reconnect the negative battery cable.

11. Check automatic transaxle fluid level and refill as necessary.

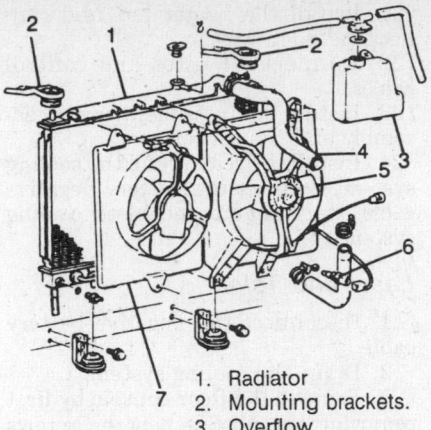

1. Radiator
2. Mounting brackets.
3. Overflow
4. Upper radiator hose
5. Cooling fan
6. Thermo switch
7. A/C condenser fan

Electric fan and radiator layout—typical

Electric Cooling Fan

TESTING

1. Disconnect the negative battery cable.

2. Disconnect the electrical plug from the fan motor harness.

3. On Summit the connector has 3 openings, on Laser and Talon models the connector has 4 openings. Apply battery voltage and make sure motor runs smoothly, without abnormal noise or vibration.

4. Reconnect the negative battery cable.

REMOVAL & INSTALLATION

1. Disconnect the negative battery cable.

2. Remove the radiator/fan assembly.

3. Remove the fan shroud assembly from the radiator.

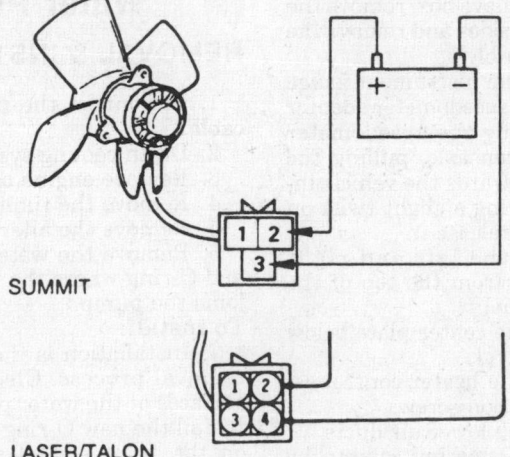

SUMMIT

LASER/TALON

Electric cooling fan test

4. Remove the fastener from the motor shaft and pull off the fan.

5. Remove the bolts that hold the motor to the shroud and remove the motor.

To install:

6. Installation is the reverse of the removal procedure. Use care to get the fan and shroud aligned properly.

7. Install the radiator/fan assembly.

8. Reconnect the negative battery cable.

Heater Core

REMOVAL & INSTALLATION

Summit

1. Disconnect the negative battery cable.

2. Drain the cooling system.

3. Remove the front seats by removing the covers over the anchor bolts, the underseat tray, the seat belt guide ring, the seat mounting nuts and bolts and disconnect the seat belt switch wiring harness from under the seat. Then lift out the seats.

4. Remove the floor console by first taking out the coin holder and the console box tray. Remove the remote control mirror switch, or cover if not equipped. All of these items require only a plastic trim tool to carefully pry them out.

5. Remove the rear half of the console.

6. Remove the shift lever knob on manual transmission vehicles.

7. Remove the front console box assembly.

8. A number of the instrument panel pieces may be retained by pin type fasteners. They may be removed using the following procedure:

  a. This type of clip is removed by pressing down on the center pin with a suitable blunt pointed tool. Press down a little more than $1/16$ in. (2mm). This releases the clip. Pull the clip outward to remove it.

  b. Do not push the pin inward more than necessary because it may damage the grommet, or the pin may fall in, if pushed in too far. Once the clips are removed, use a plastic trim stick to pry the piece loose.

9. Remove the instrument panel assembly. Use the following procedure:

  a. Remove both lower cowl trim panels (kick panels).

  b. Remove the ashtray and center panel around the radio.

  c. Remove the sunglass pocket at the upper left side of panel and the side panel into which it mounts.

  d. Remove the driver's side knee

protector and the hood release handle.

e. Remove the steering column top and bottom covers.

f. Remove the radio.

g. Remove the glove box striker and box assembly.

h. Remove the instrument panel lower cover, 2 small pieces in the center, by pulling forward.

i. Remove the heater control assembly screw.

j. Remove the instrument cluster bezel and pull out the gauge assembly.

k. Remove the speedometer adapter by disconnecting the speedometer cable at the transaxle pulling the cable sightly towards the vehicle interior, and giving a slight twist on the adapter to release it.

l. Insert a small flat-tip tool to open the tab on the gauge cluster connector, and remove the harness connectors.

m. Remove, by prying with a plastic trim tool, the right hand speaker cover and the speaker, the upper side defroster grills and the clock (or plug if not equipped) to gain access to some of the instrument panel mounting bolts.

n. Drop the steering column by removing the bolt and nut.

o. Remove the instrument panel bolts and the instrument panel.

9. Disconnect the heater hoses.

10. Disconnect the air selection, the temperature and mode selection control cables from the heater box and remove the heater control assembly.

11. Remove the connector for the ECI control relay (8 pin for 1.5L engine, 10 pin for 1.6L engine).

12. Remove both stamped steel instrument panel supports.

13. Remove the heater ductwork.

14. Remove the heater box mounting nuts.

15. Remove the automatic transmission ELC control box.

16. Remove the evaporator mounting nuts and clips.

17. With the evaporator pulled outward, toward the vehicle interior, remove the heater unit. Be careful not to damage the heater tubes or to spill coolant.

18. Remove the cover plate around the heater tubes and the core fastener clips. Pull the heater core from the heater box, being careful not to damage the fins or tank ends.

To install:

19. Installation is the reverse of the removal procedure. Install the heater core to the heater box. Install the clips and cover.

20. Install the evaporator and the automatic transmission ELC box.

21. Install the heater box and connect the duct work.

22. Connect all wires and control cables.

23. Install the instrument panel assembly and the console.

24. Install the seats, refill the cooling system. Connect the battery negative cable, start engine and bleed cooling system.

Laser and Talon

1. Disconnect the negative battery cable.

2. Drain the cooling system.

3. Remove the floor console by first removing the plugs, then the screws retaining the side covers and the small cover piece in front of the shifter. Remove the shifter knob, manual transmission, and the cup holder. Remove both small pieces of upholstery to gain access to retainer screws. Disconnect the two electrical connectors at the front of the console. Remove the shoulder harness guide plates and remove the console assembly.

4. Remove the instrument panel assembly. Use the following procedure:

a. Locate the rectangular plugs in the knee protector on either side of the steering column. Pry these plugs out, remove the screws. Remove the screws from the hood lock release lever and remove the knee protector.

b. Remove the upper and lower column covers.

c. Remove the narrow panel covering the instrument cluster cover screws, and take out the cover.

d. Remove the radio panel and take out the radio.

e. Remove the center air outlet assembly by reaching through the grill and pushing the side clips out with a small flat-tip tool while carefully prying the outlet free.

f. Pull the heater control knobs off and remove the heater control panel assembly.

g. Open the glove box, remove the plugs from the sides and remove the glove box assembly.

h. Remove the instrument gauge cluster and the speedometer adapter by disconnecting the speedometer cable at the transaxle, pulling the cable sightly towards the vehicle interior, then giving a slight twist on the adapter to release it.

i. Remove the left and right speaker covers from the top of the instrument panel.

j. Remove the center plate below the heater controls.

k. Remove the heater control assembly installation screws.

l. Remove the lower air ducts.

m. Drop the steering column by removing the bolts.

n. Remove the instrument panel mounting screws, bolts and the instrument panel assembly.

5. Remove both stamped steel reinforcement pieces.

6. Remove the lower ductwork from the heater box.

7. Remove the upper center duct.

8. Vehicles without air conditioning will have a square duct in place of the evaporator. Remove this duct if the vehicle does not have air conditioning. If the vehicle does have air conditioning, remove the evaporator assembly. Properly discharge the air conditioning system. Disconnect and cap the refrigerant lines at the evaporator. Remove the wiring harness connectors and the electronic control unit. Remove the drain hose and lift out the evaporator unit.

9. With the evaporator removed, take out the heater unit. To prevent bolts from falling inside the blower assembly, set the inside/outside air-selection damper to the position that permits outside air introduction.

10. Remove the cover plate around the heater tubes and remove the core fastener clips. Pull the heater core from the heater box, being careful not to damage the fins or tank ends.

To install:

11. Installation is the reverse of the removal procedure. Install the heater core to the heater box. Install the clips and cover.

12. Install the evaporator and the automatic transmission ELC box.

13. Install the heater box and connect the duct work.

14. Connect all wires and control cables.

15. Install the instrument panel assembly and the console.

16. Connect the battery negative cable, start engine and bleed cooling system. Recharge the air conditioning system.

Water Pump

REMOVAL & INSTALLATION

1. Disconnect the negative battery cable.

2. Drain cooling system.

3. Remove engine under cover.

4. Remove the timing belt.

5. Remove the alternator bracket.

6. Remove the water pump, gasket and O-ring where the water inlet pipe joins the pump.

To install:

7. Installation is the reverse of the removal process. Clean both gasket surfaces of the water pump and block. Install the new O-ring into the groove on the front end of the water inlet pipe. Do not apply oils or grease to the

O-ring. Wet with water only. Install the gasket and pump assembly and tighten the bolts. Note the marks on the bolt heads. Those marked **4** should be torqued to 9–11 ft. lbs. Those bolts marked **7** should be torqued from 14–20 ft. lbs.

8. Reinstall the alternator bracket.
9. Install the timing covers, drive pulleys and belts and the undercover.
10. Refill with coolant.
11. Reconnect the negative battery cable, start engine and bleed cooling system.

Thermostat

REMOVAL & INSTALLATION

1. Disconnect the negative battery cable.
2. Drain cooling system.
3. Remove the engine side of the upper radiator hose.
4. Remove the water outlet and gasket.
5. Remove the thermostat.
To install:
6. Installation is the reverse of the removal process. Make sure the thermostat is installed so its flange seats tightly in the machined groove in the intake manifold or thermostat case.
7. Use a new gasket and reinstall the water outlet, and connect the radiator hose.
8. Refill cooling system.
9. Reconnect the negative battery cable, start engine and bleed cooling system.

FUEL SYSTEM

Fuel System Service Precaution

Safety is the most important factor when performing not only fuel system maintenance but any type of maintenance. Failure to conduct maintenance and repairs in a safe manner may result in serious personal injury or death. Maintenance and testing of the vehicle's fuel system components can be accomplished safely and effectively by adhering to the following rules and guidelines.

• To avoid the possibility of fire and personal injury, always disconnect the negative battery cable unless the repair or test procedure requires that battery voltage be applied.
• Always relieve the fuel system pressure prior to disconnecting any fuel system component (injector, fuel

rail, pressure regulator, etc.), fitting or fuel line connection. Exercise extreme caution whenever relieving fuel system pressure to avoid exposing skin, face and eyes to fuel spray. Please be advised that fuel under pressure may penetrate the skin or any part of the body that it contacts.

• Always place a shop towel or cloth around the fitting or connection prior to loosening to absorb any excess fuel due to spillage. Ensure that all fuel spillage (should it occur) is quickly removed from engine surfaces. Ensure that all fuel soaked cloths or towels are deposited into a suitable waste container.
• Always keep a dry chemical (Class B) fire extinguisher near the work area.
• Do not allow fuel spray or fuel vapors to come into contact with a spark or open flame.
• Always use a backup wrench when loosening and tightening fuel line connection fittings. This will prevent unnecessary stress and torsion to fuel line piping. Always follow the proper torque specifications.
• Always replace worn fuel fitting O-rings with new. Do not substitute fuel hose or equivalent where fuel pipe is installed.

RELIEVING FUEL SYSTEM PRESSURE

1. On Summit, gain access to the fuel pump electrical connector by removing the rear seat by raising the front part of the lower cushion while pulling both levers at the lower front of the cushion. On Laser and Talon, the connector is at the fuel tank rear side.
2. Locate and disconnect the fuel pump harness connector.
3. Start the engine and after it stops by itself, turn the ignition switch to **OFF**.
4. Disconnect the battery negative terminal.
5. Connect the fuel pump harness connector.

Fuel Filter

REMOVAL & INSTALLATION

1. Remove the air cleaner. This involves removing the battery, the breather hoses, the connector for the air flow sensor, and depending on model and body style, whatever hoses or ducts are in the way to gaining access to the fuel filter.
2. Relieve fuel system pressure. Disconnect battery negative cable.
3. Remove the eyebolt while holding the fuel filter nut securely.

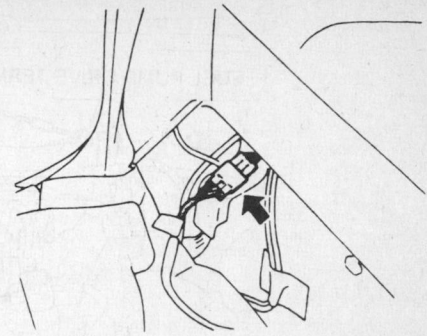

Fuel pump electrical connector behind rear seat

4. Remove the fuel filter.
To install:
5. Installation is the reverse of the removal procedure. Use new gaskets when the fuel filter is remounted. Tighten the eyebolts to 25 ft. lbs.
6. After installation, apply battery voltage to the terminal for fuel pump activation to run the fuel pump, and check for leaks. This terminal is in the engine compartment, close to the firewall.
7. Reinstall the air cleaner assembly, hoses, battery and cables.

Electric Fuel Pump

PRESSURE TESTING

1. Relieve fuel system pressure. Disconnect the battery negative cable.
2. Disconnect the fuel high pressure hose at the delivery pipe side.
3. Connect a fuel pressure gauge to a suitable adapter with appropriate seals or gaskets to prevent leaks during the test. Install the gauge and adapter between the delivery pipe and high pressure hose.

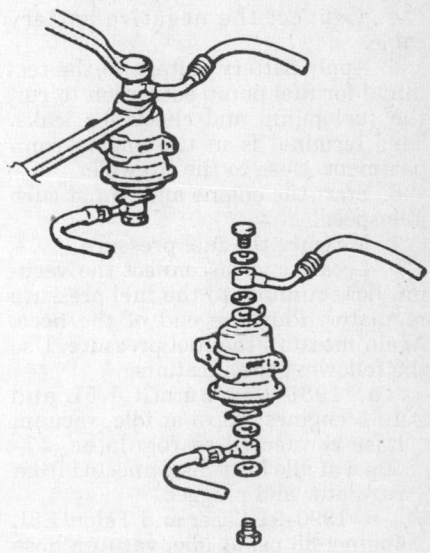

Removing fuel filter

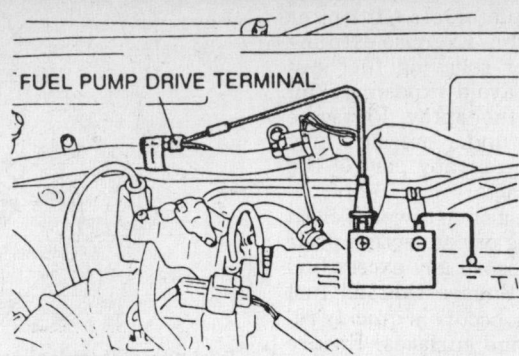

Typical underhood fuel pump test terminal

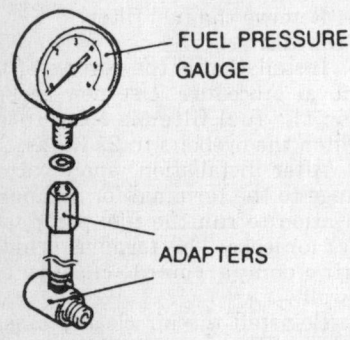

FUEL PRESSURE GAUGE

ADAPTERS

38 PSI AT IDLE

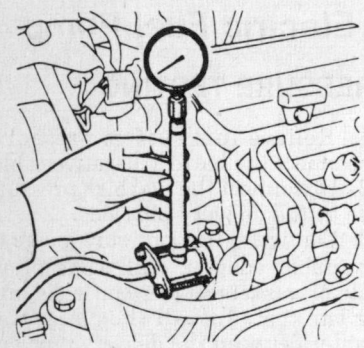

Fuel system pressure testing

4. Connect the negative battery cable.

5. Apply battery voltage to the terminal for fuel pump activation to run the fuel pump and check for leaks. This terminal is in the engine compartment, close to the firewall.

6. Start the engine and run at curb idle speed.

7. Measure the fuel pressure.

8. Locate and disconnect the vacuum hose running to the fuel pressure regulator. Plug the end of the hose. Again measure the fuel pressure. Use the following specifications:

   a. 1989–91 Summit 1.5L and 1.6L engines: 38psi at idle, vacuum hose connected to regulator, 47–50psi at idle hose disconnected from regulator and plugged.

   b. 1990–91 Laser and Talon 1.8L engine: 38 psi at idle, vacuum hose connected to regulator, 47–50psi at idle hose disconnected from regulator and plugged.

   c. 1990–91 Laser and Talon 2.0L engine normally aspirated: 38 psi at idle, vacuum hose connected to regulator, 47–50psi at idle hose disconnected from regulator and plugged.

   d. 1990–91 Laser and Talon 2.0L turbocharged: 27 psi at idle, vacuum hose connected to regulator, 36–38 psi at idle hose disconnected from regulator and plugged.

9. Race the engine 2–3 times and check that the fuel pressure does not fall when the engine is running at idle.

10. Check to be sure there is fuel pressure in the return hose by gently pressing the fuel return hose with fingers while racing the engine. There will be no fuel pressure in the return hose when the volume of fuel flow is low.

11. If fuel pressure is too low, check for a clogged fuel filter, a defective fuel pressure regulator or a defective fuel pump, any of which will require replacement. If fuel pressure is too high, the fuel pressure regulator is defective and will have to be replaced or the fuel return is bent of clogged. If the fuel pressure reading does not change when the vacuum hose is disconnected, the hose is clogged or the valve is stuck in the fuel pressure regulator and it will have to be replaced.

12. Stop the engine and check for changes in the fuel pressure gauge. It should not drop. If the gauge reading does drop, watch the rate of drop. If fuel pressure drops slowly, the likely cause is a leaking injector which will require replacement. If the fuel pressure drops immediately after the engine is stopped, the check valve in the fuel pump isn't closing and the fuel pump will have to be replaced.

13. Relieve fuel system pressure.

14. Disconnect the high pressure hose and remove the fuel pressure gauge from the delivery pipe.

15. Install a new O-ring in the groove of the high pressure hose. Connect the hose to the delivery pipe and tighten

the screws. After installation, apply battery voltage to the terminal for fuel pump activation to run the fuel pump, and check for leaks. This terminal is in the engine compartment, close to the firewall.

REMOVAL & INSTALLATION

1. Relieve fuel system pressure.
2. Disconnect the negative battery cable.
3. Drain the fuel from the fuel tank.
4. Raise and safely support the vehicle.
5. Disconnect the return hose, high pressure hose and whatever hose might keep the tank from being lowered to gain access to the in-tank pump. For example, some Talon models may require removing the rear lateral track rod.
6. Remove the filler hose, the breather hose and lower the fuel tank.
7. Remove the fuel pump assembly.

To install:

8. Installation is the reverse of the removal procedure. Inspect the tank for rust or contamination. If the tank must be cleaned, wipe out with kerosene. Inspect all hoses. Inspect the pump filter.
9. Install the replacement pump using a new gasket. Be certain the pump is installed in the same location, facing the same direction as before. Make all hose connections and raise the tank back in place.
10. Connect battery neagtive cable. Check operation.

Fuel Injection

IDLE SPEED ADJUSTMENT

1.5L Engine

The electronic system controls the idle speed and adjustment of the idling speed is usually unnecessary. The idle speed may be checked using the following procedure:

1. Warm the engine to operating temperature, and leave lights, electric cooling fan and accessories **OFF**. The transaxle should be in **N** or **P** for automatic transmission. The steering wheel in a neutral position for vehicles with power steering.
2. Check the ignition timing and adjust, if necessary.
3. Connect a tachometer to the special terminal under the hood.
4. Run the engine for more than 5 seconds at 2000–3000 rpm. Allow the engine to idle for 2 minutes. Check the idle rpm. Curb idle should be 750 ± 100 rpm.

1. Fuel pump
2. In-tank filter
3. Fuel gauge tank unit
4. Two-way valve
5. Vapor hose
6. Check valve
7. High pressure hose
8. Return hose
9. Tank drain plug

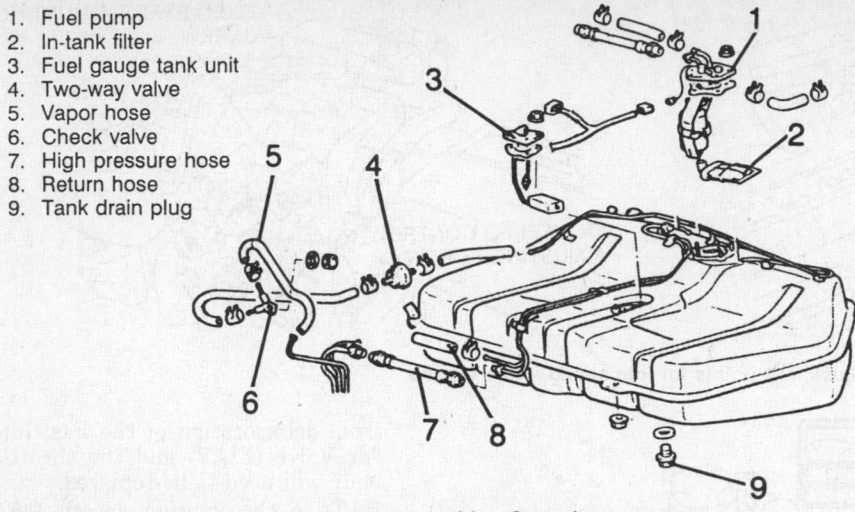

Fuel tank assembly—Summit

1.8L Engine

The electronic system controls the idle speed and adjustment of the idling speed is usually unnecessary. The idle speed may be checked using the following procedure:

1. Warm the engine to operating temperature, leave lights, electric cooling fan and accessories **OFF**. The transaxle should be in **N** or **P** for automatic transmission. The steering wheel in a neutral position for vehicles with power steering.

2. Check the ignition timing and adjust, if necessary.

3. Connect a tachometer to the CRC filter connector. Use a paper clip for a tach adapter.

4. Run the engine for more than 5 seconds at 2000–3000 rpm. Allow the engine to idle for 2 minutes. Check the idle rpm. Curb idle should be 700 ± 100 rpm.

5. If adjustment is required, slacken the accelerator cable.

6. Connect a digital voltmeter between terminal 19 throttle position sensor output voltage) of the engine control unit and terminal 24 (ground).

7. Set the ignition switch to **ON**, without starting the engine, and hold it in that position for 15 seconds or more. Turn the ignition switch **OFF**.

8. Disconnect the connectors of the idle speed control servo and lock the idle speed control plunger at the initial position. Back out the fixed Speed Adjusting Screw (SAS).

9. Start the engine and allow to idle. Basic idle speed should be 700 ± 50 rpm. A new engine may idle a little lower. If the vehicle stalls or has a very low idle speed, suspect a deposit build-up on the throttle valve which must be cleaned.

10. If the idle speed is wrong, adjust with the idle speed control adjusting screw. Use a hexagon wrench if possible. Turn in the fixed SAS until the engine speed rises. Then back out the fixed SAS until the Touch Point where the engine speed does not fall any longer, is found. Back out the fixed SAS an additional ½ turn from the touch point.

11. Stop the engine. Turn the ignition switch to **ON** but do not start engine. Check that the output voltage from the throttle position sensor is 0.48–0.52 volts. If it is out of specification, adjust by loosening the throttle position sensor mounting screws and rotating the throttle position sensor. Turning the throttle position sensor clockwise increases the output voltage. After adjustment, tighten screws firmly.

12. Turn the ignition switch **OFF**.

13. Adjust the free-play of the accelerator cable, reconnect the connectors of the idle speed control servo and remove the voltmeter.

14. Start the engine and check the curb idle. It should be 700 ± 100 rpm.

15. Turn the ignition switch to **OFF**, disconnect the negative battery cable for more than 10 seconds and reconnect. This clears any trouble codes introduced during testing.

16. Restart the engine, allow to run for 5 minutes and check for good idle quality.

2.0L Engine

The electronic system controls the idle speed and adjustment of the idling speed is usually unnecessary. The idle speed may be checked using the following procedure:

1. Warm the engine to operating temperature, leave lights, electric cooling fan and accessories **OFF**. The transaxle should be in **N**. The steering wheel in a neutral position for vehicles with power steering.

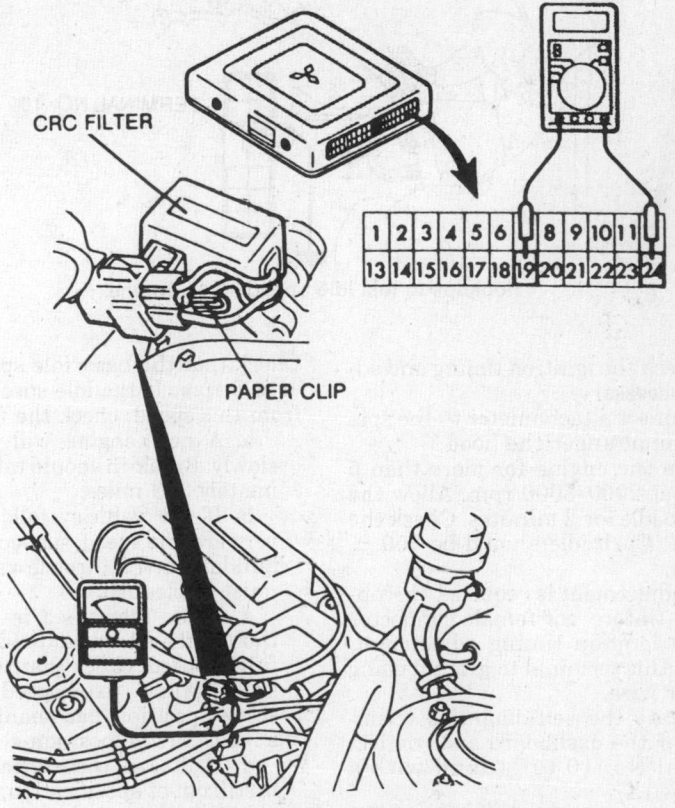

Hookups to test idle speed—1.8L engine

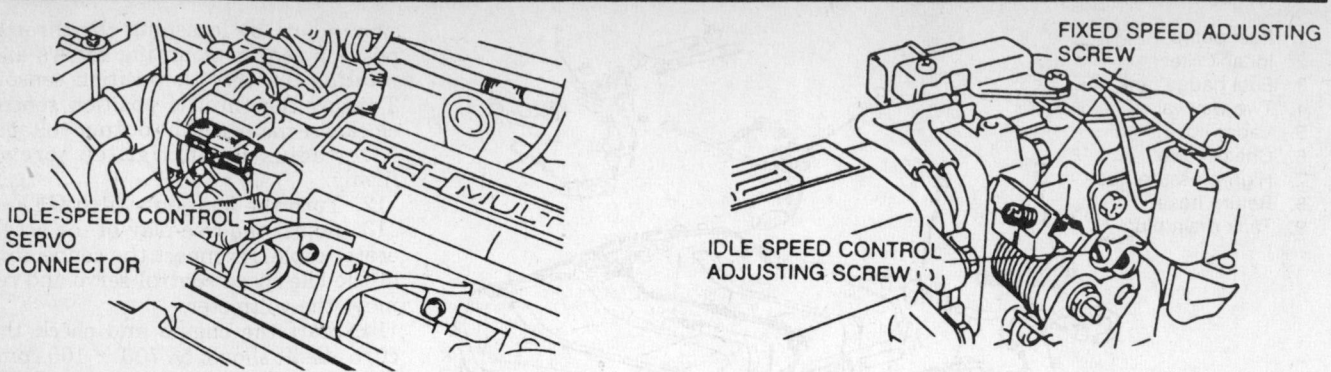

Adjustment points for idle speed—1.8L engine

IDLE-SPEED CONTROL SERVO CONNECTOR

FIXED SPEED ADJUSTING SCREW

IDLE SPEED CONTROL ADJUSTING SCREW

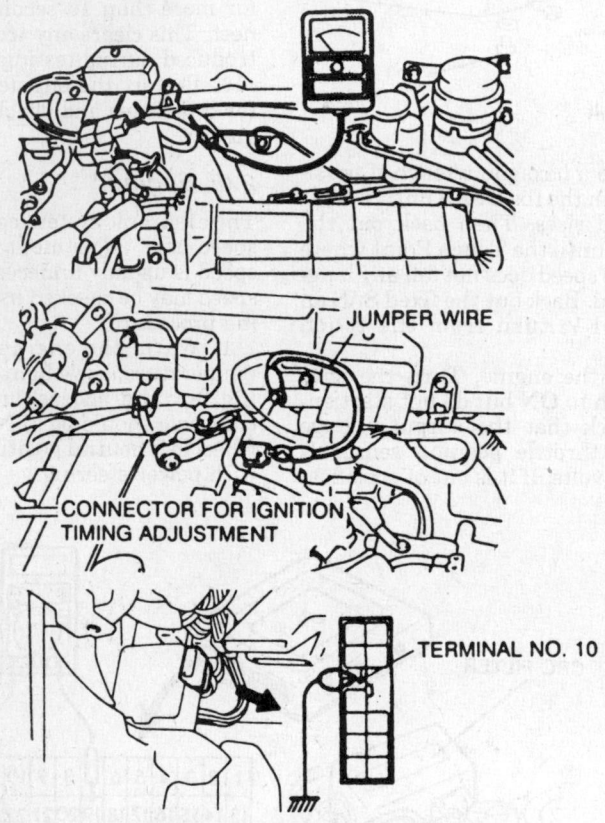

JUMPER WIRE

CONNECTOR FOR IGNITION TIMING ADJUSTMENT

TERMINAL NO. 10

Hookups to test idle speed—2.0L engine

2. Check the ignition timing and adjust, if necessary.

3. Connect a tachometer to the special terminal under the hood.

4. Run the engine for more than 5 seconds at 2000–3000 rpm. Allow the engine to idle for 2 minutes. Check the idle rpm. Curb idle should be 750 ± 100 rpm.

5. If adjustment is required, disconnect the waterproof female connector used for ignition timing adjustment. Connect this terminal to ground using a jumper wire.

6. Locate the self-diagnosis terminal under the dashboard and connect terminal No. 10 to ground with a jumper wire.

7. Start the engine and allow to idle.

Check that the basic idle speed is 750 ± 100 rpm. If the idle speed deviates from this speed, check the following:

a. A new engine will idle more slowly. Break-in should take approximately 300 miles.

b. If the vehicle stalls or has a very low idle speed, suspect a deposit buildup on the throttle valve which must be cleaned.

c. If the idle speed is high even though the speed adjusting screw is fulley closed, check that the idle position switch (fixed speed adjusting screw) position has changed. If so, adjust the idle position switch.

d. If after all these checks the idle is still out of specification, it is probable that there is leakage resulting

from deterioration of the Fast-Idle Air Valve (FIAV) and the throttle body will need to be replaced.

8. Turn the ignition switch **OFF** and stop the engine. Disconnect the jumper wire from the diagnosis connector, disconnect the jumper wire from from the ignition timing connector and reconnect the waterproof connector. Disconnect the tachometer.

9. Restart the engine, allow to run for 5 minutes and check for good idle quality.

Fuel Injector

REMOVAL & INSTALLATION

1. Relieve fuel system pressure.

2. Disconnect the negative battery cable.

3. Remove the high pressure line where it connects to the delivery pipe, or fuel rail. The O-ring must be replaced. Do not reuse.

4. Remove the return line from the pressure regulator. Also remove the vacuum line from the regulator.

5. Remove the fuel pressure regulator. The O-ring must be replaced. Do not reuse.

6. Remove the injector electrical connectors.

7. Remove the delivery pipe/injector assembly. Use care. Do not let the injectors drop.

8. Pull injectors from the delivery pipe for replacement.

To install:

9. Injectors can be checked for electrical resistance between the terminals. Resistance should be 13–16 ohms. If out of specification, replace injector.

10. Install the grommets on the injector first, then the O-ring. Apply light oil to lubricate the O-rings. Install the injector by pushing into the delivery pipe while turning back and forth. The injector should turn smoothly. If it does not, the O-ring may be trapped or dislodged. Remove the injector, check and insert injector again.

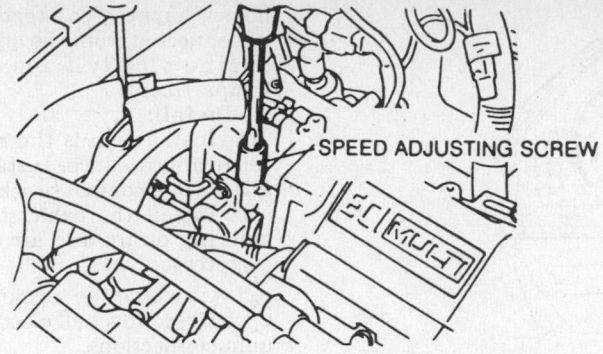

Adjustment point for idle speed – 2.0L engine

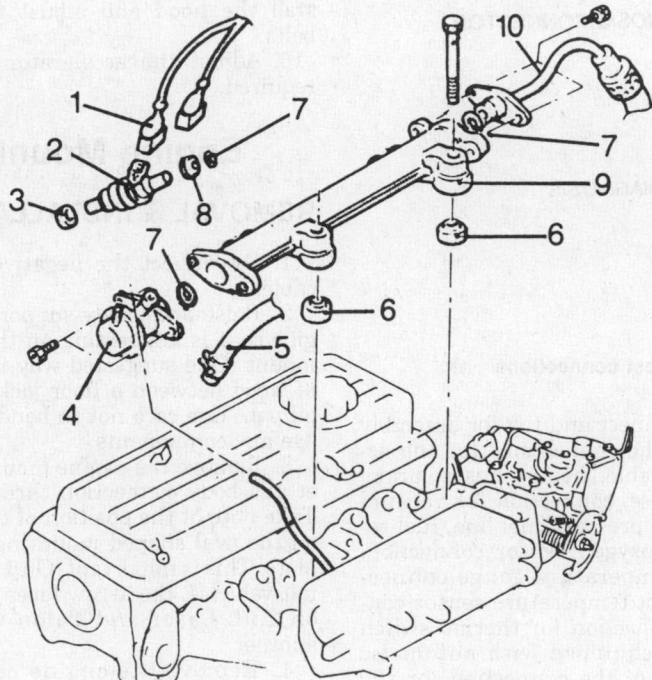

1. Injector Harness
2. Injector
3. Insulator
4. Pressure regulator
5. Return hose
6. Insulator
7. O-ring
8. Injector grommet
9. Delivery pipe
10. Pressure line

Injector layout – 1.5L engine

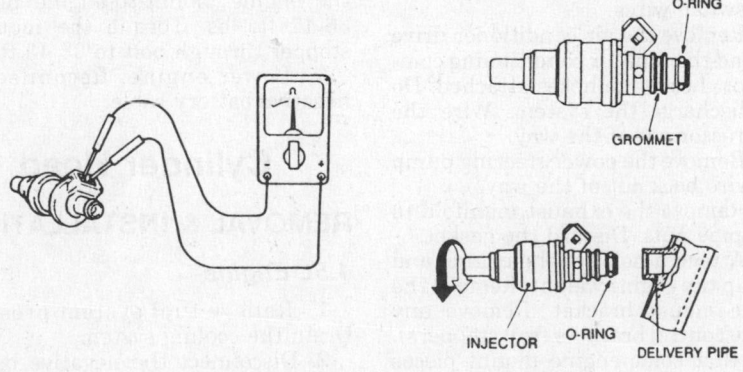

Injector testing, seals and installation

11. The O-ring for the pressure regulator and high pressure line should also be lubed with light oil or gasoline.

12. After assembly, the fuel pressure should be checked.

EMISSION CONTROLS

Please refer to "Emission Control" in the Unit Repair section for system maintenance procedures. Due to the complex nature of modern electronic engine control systems, comprehensive diagnosis and testing procedures fall outside the confines of this repair manual. For complete information on diagnosis, testing and repair procedures concerning all modern engine and emission control systems, please refer to "Chilton's Guide to Electronic Engine Controls".

Emission Warning Lamps

RESETTING

Among the self diagnosis items, a malfunction indicator light comes on to notify the driver of the emission control items when an irregularity is detected. However, when an irregular signal returns to normal and the engine control unit judges that it has returned to normal, the malfunction indicator light goes out. Moreover, when the ignition switch is turned **OFF**, the light goes out. If the ignition switch is turned on again, the light does not come on until the irregularity is detected.

Immediately after the ignition switch is turned **ON**, the malfunction indicator light is lit for 5 seconds to indicate that the malfunction indicator light operates normally. If the light does not come on, check the harness and bulb.

Items indicated by the lighted malfunction light: engine control unit, oxygen sensor, air flow sensor, intake air temperature sensor, throttle position sensor, motor position sensor, engine coolant temperature sensor, crank angle sensor, No. 1 cylinder TDC sensor, barometric pressure sensor, injector, fuel pump, EGR (California).

Trouble codes can be recalled with a voltmeter. After service is completed, make sure the ignition switch is **OFF**

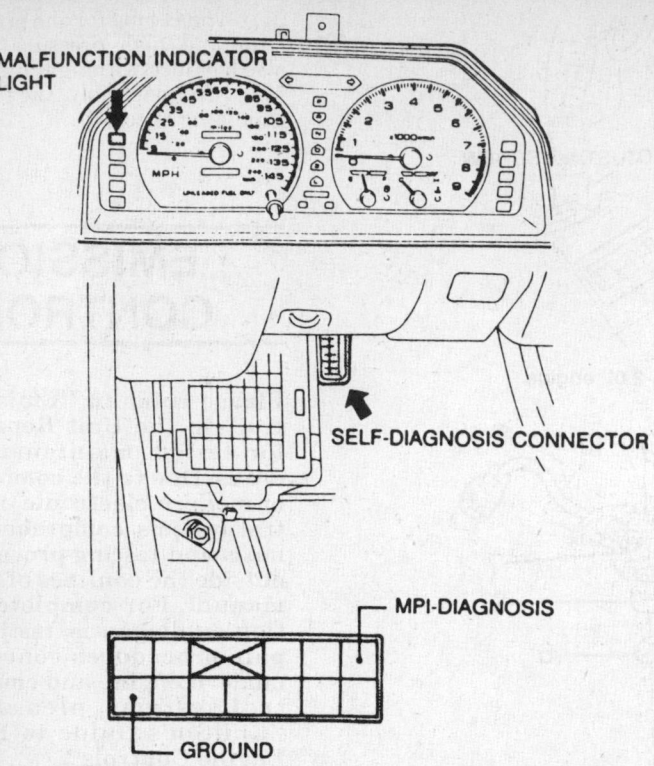

Typical malfunction indicator light and test connections

then disconnect the battery ground cable for 10 seconds or more to erase failure codes.

ENGINE MECHANICAL

NOTE: Disconnecting the negative battery cable on some vehicles may interfere with the functions of the on board computer systems and may require the computer to undergo a relearning process, once the negative battery cable is reconnected.

Engine Assembly

REMOVAL & INSTALLATION

The following procedure can be used on both Summit, Laser and Talon vehicles. Slight variations may occur due to extra connections, etc., but the basic procedure should cover all models.

1. Relieve fuel system pressure.
2. Disconnect the negative battery cable.
3. Matchmark hood and hinges and remove hood assembly.
4. Drain the engine coolant and remove the radiator assembly.
5. Remove the transaxle.

6. Disconnect and tag for assembly reference the connections for the accelerator cable, heater hoses, brake vacuum hose, connection for vacuum hoses, high pressure fuel line, fuel return line, oxygen sensor connection, coolant temperature gauge connection, coolant temperature sensor connector, connection for thermo switch sensor, if equipped with automatic transmission, the connection for the idle speed control, the motor position sensor connector, the throttle position sensor connector, the EGR temperature sensor connection (California vehicles), the fuel injector connectors, the power transistor connector, the ignition coil connector, the condenser and noise filter connector, the distributor and control harness, the connections for the alternator and oil pressure switch wires.
7. Remove the air conditioner drive belt and then the air conditioning compressor. Leave the hoses attached. Do not discharge the system. Wire the compressor out of the way.
8. Remove the power steering pump and wire back out of the way.
9. Remove the exhaust manifold to head pipe nuts. Discard the gasket.
10. Attach a hoist to the engine and take up the engine weight. Remove the engine mount bracket. Remove any torque control brackets (roll stoppers). Note that some engine mount pieces have arrows on them for proper assembly. Double check that all cables,

hoses, harness connectors, etc., are disconnected from the engine. Lift the engine slowly from the engine compartment.

To install:

11. Installation is the reverse of the removal procedure. Install the engine and torque control brackets.
12. Install the exhaust pipe, power steering pump and air conditioning compressor.
13. Checking the tags installed at removal, reconnect all electrical and vacuum connections.
14. Install the transaxle.
15. Refill with engine oil, coolant, install the hood and adjust the drive belts.
16. Adjust the accelerator cable as required.

Engine Mounts

REMOVAL & INSTALLATION

1. Disconnect the negative battery cable.
2. Raise and safely support the engine so it is not resting on the engine mount. One suggested way is a block of wood between a floor jack and the oil pan. Use care not to bend or damage any components.
3. Remove the engine mount bracket and body connection through bolt. Take note of the position of the arrow on the oval shaped mounting stopper plate. This is important. On 1.5L Summit vehicles, the arrow faces one way, on 2.0L Laser and Talon vehicles, another.
4. Remove the engine mounting bracket. Vehicles with the 1.6L and 2.0L engines will have an additional small strap that should be removed.
5. Remove the stopper plate.

To install:

6. Installation is the reverse of the removal procedure. Note the arrows on the stopper plates and make sure they are installed properly. Torque the engine mount-to-body bolts as well as the engine mount-to-engine nuts to 36-47 ft. lbs. Torque the mounting stopper through bolt to 33-43 ft. lbs.
7. Lower engine. Reconnect the negative battery cable.

Cylinder Head

REMOVAL & INSTALLATION

1.5L Engine

1. Relieve fuel system pressure. Drain the cooling system.
2. Disconnect the negative battery cable. Remove the upper radiator hose and heater hose.

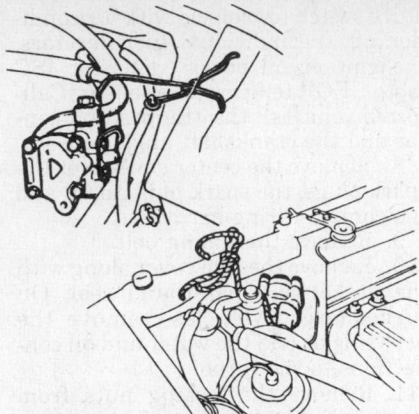

Tie back air conditioning compressor and power steering pump without disconnecting hoses

3. Remove the timing belt upper cover and rocker arm cover.

4. Rotate the crankshaft and align the timing marks.

5. Remove the camshaft sprocket together with the timing belt and support it with wire to prevent disturbing valve timing.

6. Remove the exhaust pipe self-locking nuts and separate the exhaust pipe from the exhaust manifold.

7. If necessary, remove the rocker arm/shaft assembly.

8. Loosen the cylinder head mounting bolts according to sequence in 2 or 3 steps. Clean all the gasket material from mating surfaces.

To install:

9. Installation is the reverse of the removal process. Check the cylinder head for cracks, damage or engine coolant leakage. Remove scale, sealing compound and carbon. Clean oil passages throughly. Check the head for flatness. End to end, the head should be within 0.002 in. normally with 0.008 in. the maximum allowed out of true. The total thickness allowed to be removed from the head and block is 0.008 in. maximum.

10. Place a new head gasket on the cylinder block with any identification marks facing upward.

11. Carefully install the cylinder head on the block. Tighten the mounting bolts in sequence and torque in 3 steps to 51–54 ft. lbs.

12. Complete installation by reversing the removal procedure.

1.6L Engine

1. Relieve fuel system pressure. Drain the cooling system.

2. Disconnect the negative battery cable.

3. Remove the connection for the accelerator cable and the electrical connection for the air flow sensor.

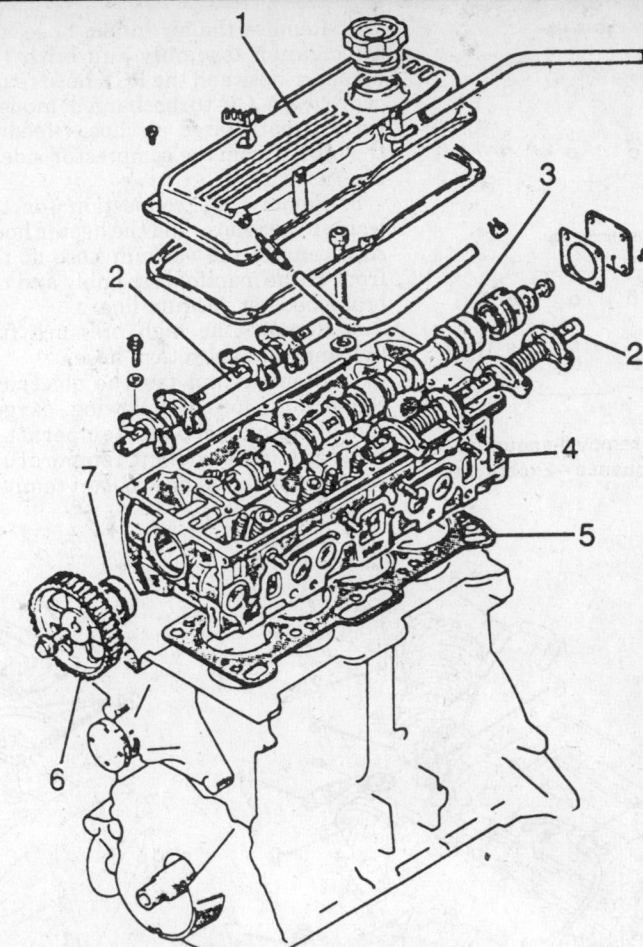

1. Cam cover
2. Rocker shaft assembly
3. Camshaft
4. Cylinder head
5. Head gasket
6. Cam sprocket
7. Cam seal

Head and valve train layout—1.5L engine

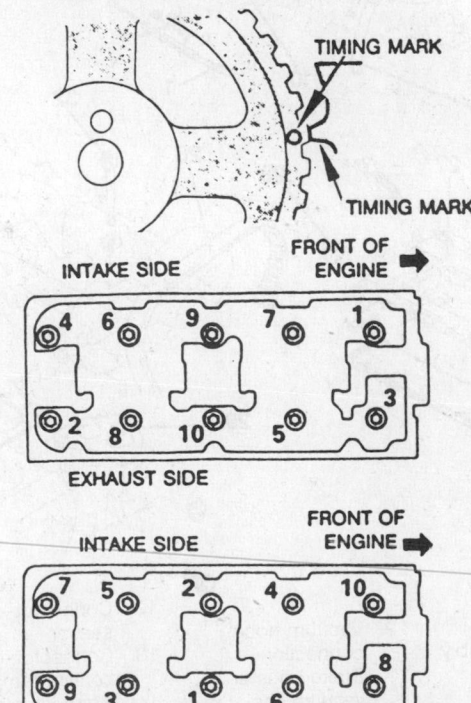

Cylinder head bolt removal sequence and installation sequence—1.5L engine

FRONT OF ENGINE ➡
INTAKE SIDE

4	6	9	7	1
2	8	10	5	3

EXHAUST SIDE

FRONT OF ENGINE ➡
INTAKE SIDE

7	5	2	4	10
9	3	1	6	8

EXHAUST SIDE

Cylinder head bolt removal sequence and installation sequence—Except 1.5L engine

4. Remove the air intake hose, the air cleaner assembly and both the breather hose and the PCV hose to the cam cover. On turbocharged models, remove both large air hoses feeding the intake from the compressor side of the turbo.

5. Remove the connection for the water bypass hose and the heater hose. Also remove the vacuum hose at the front of the manifold assembly and the brake booster vacuum line.

6. Remove the high pressure fuel line and the fuel return hose.

7. Remove and tag the electrical connections for the following: oxygen sensor, engine coolant temperature sensor, engine coolant temperature gauge unit, the engine coolant temper-ature switch for vehicle with air conditioning, the individual fuel injectors, the ignition coil, power transistor, ISC motor, EGR temperature sensor (California vehicles), throttle position sensor and the crankshaft angle sensor.

8. Remove the center cover over the spark plugs, the spark plug cables and the control wiring harness.

9. Remove the timing belt.

10. Remove the cam cover along with the gasket and half-round seal. On turbocharged vehicles, remove the heat shields and the water and oil connections to the turbo.

11. Remove the locking nuts from the exhaust pipe-to-manifold connection. Discard the gasket.

12. Remove the tension rod bolted to

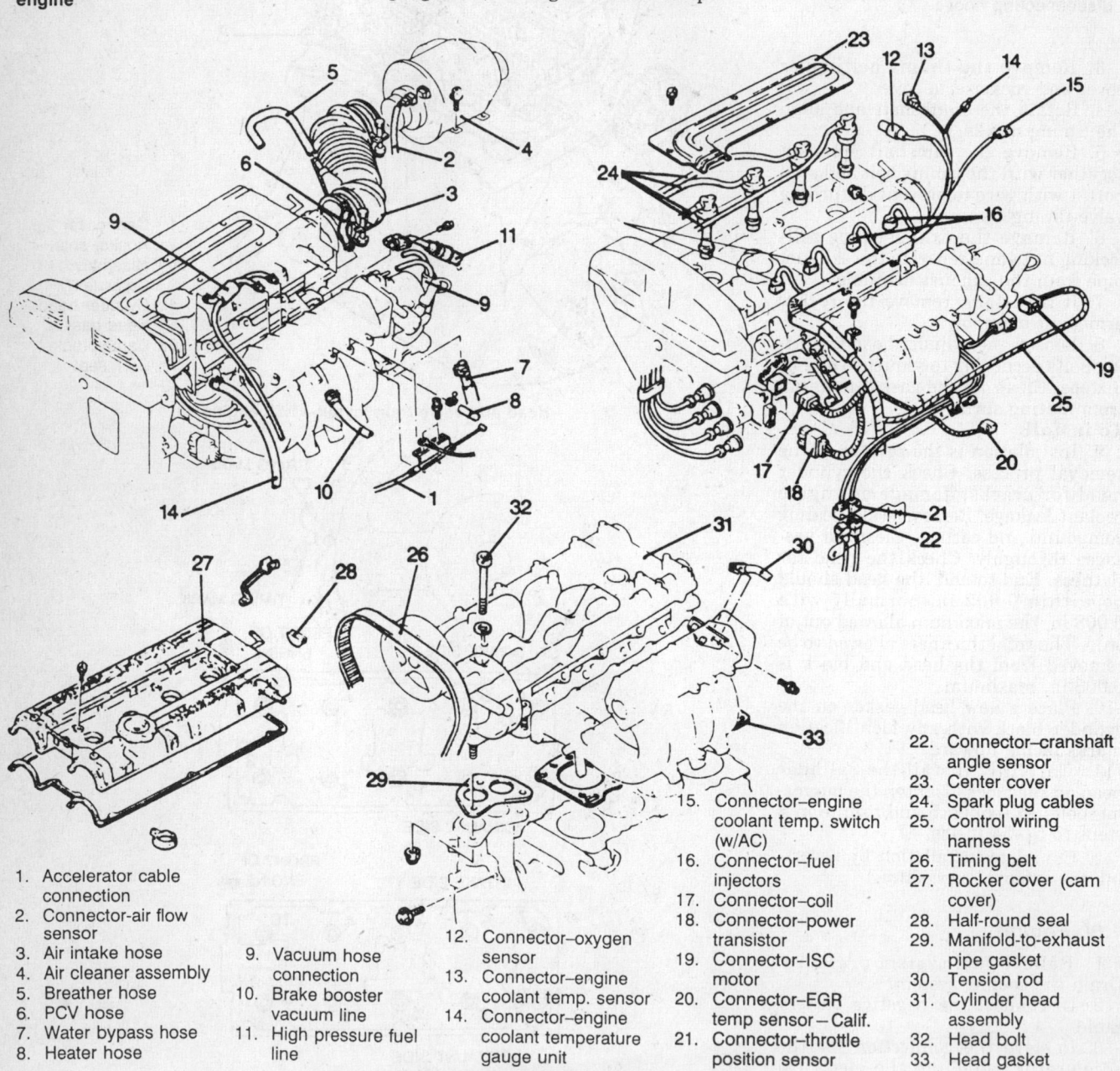

1. Accelerator cable connection
2. Connector-air flow sensor
3. Air intake hose
4. Air cleaner assembly
5. Breather hose
6. PCV hose
7. Water bypass hose
8. Heater hose
9. Vacuum hose connection
10. Brake booster vacuum line
11. High pressure fuel line
12. Connector-oxygen sensor
13. Connector-engine coolant temp. sensor
14. Connector-engine coolant temperature gauge unit
15. Connector-engine coolant temp. switch (w/AC)
16. Connector-fuel injectors
17. Connector-coil
18. Connector-power transistor
19. Connector-ISC motor
20. Connector-EGR temp sensor—Calif.
21. Connector-throttle position sensor
22. Connector-cranshaft angle sensor
23. Center cover
24. Spark plug cables
25. Control wiring harness
26. Timing belt
27. Rocker cover (cam cover)
28. Half-round seal
29. Manifold-to-exhaust pipe gasket
30. Tension rod
31. Cylinder head assembly
32. Head bolt
33. Head gasket

1.6L engine components, cylinder head removal

the backside of the engine, where the manifold meets the head.

13. Remove the head bolts by loosening the bolts in sequence in 2 or 3 steps and lift off the cylinder head. Discard the gasket.

To install:

14. Installation is the reverse of the removal process. Clean all the gasket material from mating surfaces. Check the cylinder head for cracks, damage or engine coolant leakage. Remove scale, sealing compound and carbon. Clean oil passages throughly. Check the head for flatness. End to end, the head should be within 0.002 in. normally with 0.008 in. the maximum allowed out of true. The total thickness allowed to be removed from the head and block is 0.008 in. maximum.

15. Place a new head gasket on the cylinder block with any identification marks facing upward.

16. Carefully install the cylinder

head on the block. Tighten the mounting bolts in sequence and torque in 3 steps to 65–72 ft. lbs.

17. Complete installation by reversing the removal procedure.

1.8L Engine

1. Relieve fuel system pressure. Drain the cooling system.

2. Disconnect the negative battery cable.

3. Remove the connections for the air intake hose and the breather hose.

4. Remove the connection for the accelerator cable. There will be 2 cables if the vehicle is equipped with cruise-control.

5. Remove the connection for the high pressure fuel line.

6. Remove the upper radiator hose, the water breather hose, the water bypass hose and the heater hose.

7. Remove the connector for the PCV hose.

8. Remove the spark plug cables.

9. Remove the fuel return line.

10. Remove the vacuum line for the brake booster.

11. Remove the electrical connections for the oxygen sensor, engine coolant temperature gauge unit and the water temperature sensor.

12. Remove the electrical connections for the ISC motor, throttle position sensor, distributor, MPS, fuel injectors, EGR temperature sensor (California vehicles), power transistor, condenser and ground cable.

13. Remove the engine control wiring harness.

14. Remove the clamp that holds the power steering pressure hose to the engine mounting bracket.

15. Place a jack and wood block under the oil pan and carefully lift just enough to take the weight off the engine mounting bracket and remove the bracket.

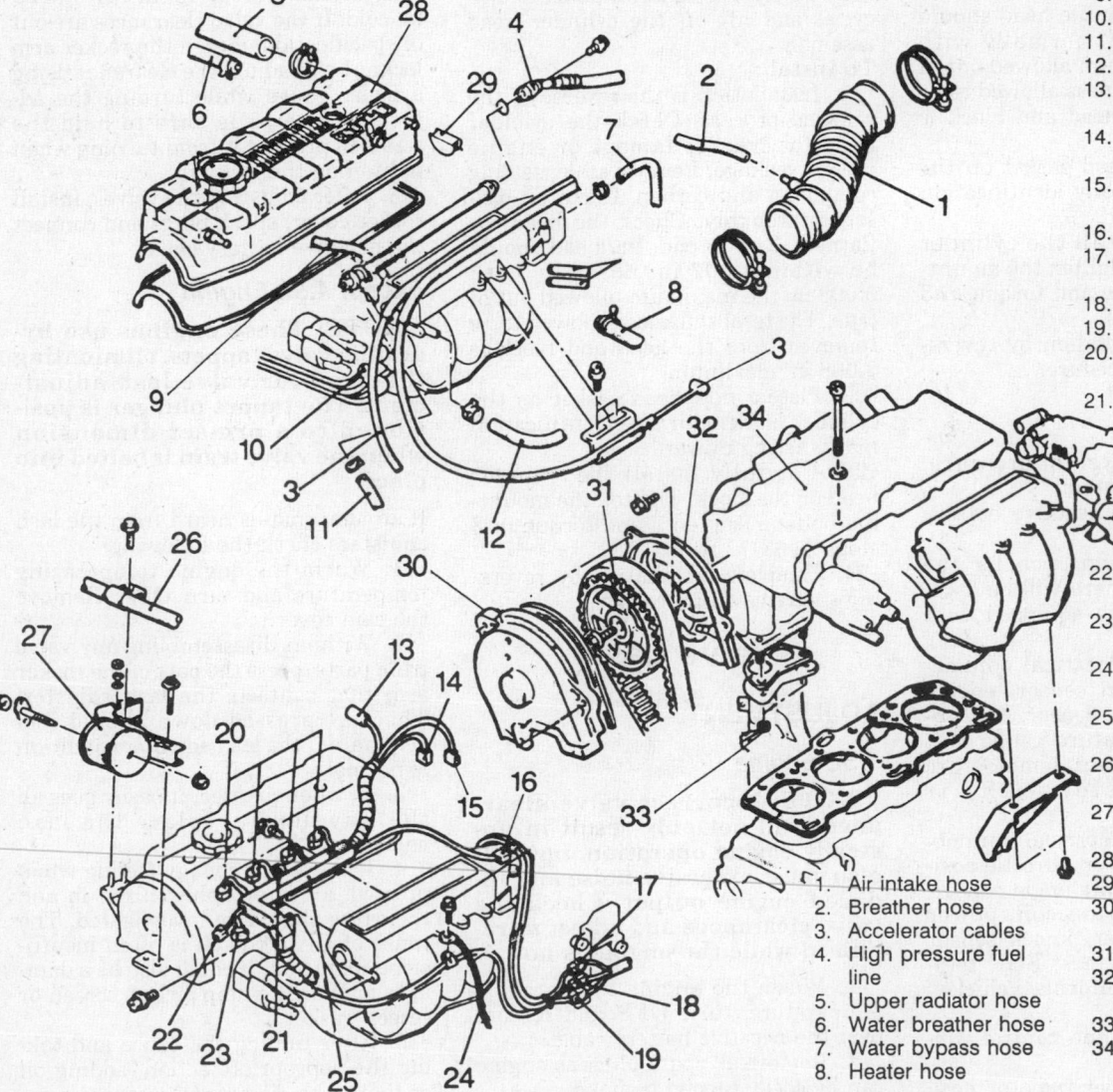

9. PCV hose
10. Spark plug cables
11. Fuel return line
12. Brake booster hose
13. Connector–oxygen sensor
14. Connector–coolant temp, gauge unit
15. Connector–water temp sensor
16. Connector–ISC
17. Connector–throttle position sensor
18. Connector–distributor
19. Connector–MPD
20. Connector–fuel injectors
21. Connector–EGR temp (Calif.)

22. Connector–power transistor
23. Connector–condenser
24. Connector–ground cable
25. Engine control wiring harness
26. Power steering pressure hose
27. Engine mounting bracket
28. Rocker cover
29. Half-round seal
30. Timing belt front upper cover
31. Camshaft sprocket
32. Timing belt rear upper cover
33. Exhaust locknuts
34. Cylinder head assembly

1. Air intake hose
2. Breather hose
3. Accelerator cables
4. High pressure fuel line
5. Upper radiator hose
6. Water breather hose
7. Water bypass hose
8. Heater hose

1.8L engine components, cylinder head removal

16. Remove the rocker cover, gasket and half-round seal.

17. Remove the timing belt front upper cover.

18. Remove the camshaft sprocket. First rotate the crankshaft clockwise until the timing marks on the sprocket align. Remove the sprocket with the timing belt attached and place on the timing belt front lower cover. Remove the timing belt rear upper cover.

19. Remove the exhaust pipe self-locking nuts and separate the exhaust pipe from the exhaust manifold. Discard the gasket.

20. Loosen the cylinder head mounting bolts according to sequence in 2–3 steps and lift off the cylinder head assembly.

To install:

21. Installation is the reverse of the removal process. Check the cylinder head for cracks, damage or engine coolant leakage. Remove scale, sealing compound and carbon. Clean oil passages throughly. Check the head for flatness. End to end, the head should be within 0.002 in. normally with 0.008 in. the maximum allowed out of true. The total thickness allowed to be removed from the head and block is 0.008 in. maximum.

22. Place a new head gasket on the cylinder block with any identification marks facing upward.

23. Carefully install the cylinder head on the block. Tighten the mounting bolts in sequence and torque in 3 steps to 51–54 ft. lbs.

24. Complete installation by reversing the removal procedure.

2.0L Engine

1. Relieve fuel system pressure. Drain the cooling system.

2. Disconnect the negative battery cable.

3. Remove the connection for the accelerator cable. There will be 2 cables if the vehicle is equipped with cruise-control.

4. Remove the electrical connections for the oxygen sensor, engine coolant temperature sensor, the engine coolant temperature gauge unit and the engine coolant temperature switch on vehicles with air conditioning.

5. Remove the electrical connections for the ISC motor, throttle position sensor, crankshaft angle sensor, fuel injectors, ignition coil, power transistor, noise filter, knock sensor on turbocharged engines, EGR temperature sensor (California vehicles) and ground cable.

6. Remove the engine control wiring harness.

7. Remove the upper radiator hose and the overflow tube.

8. Remove the connections for the air intake hose on turbocharged models, and the breather hose. Remove the large bellows-type air intake hose.

9. Remove the connection for the high pressure fuel line.

10. Remove the small vacuum hoses.

11. Remove the heater hose and water bypass hose.

12. Remove the PCV hose.

13. If turbocharged, remove the vacuum hoses, water line, eyebolt connection for the oil line for the turbo.

14. Remove the fuel return hose.

15. Remove the brake booster hose.

16. Remove the timing belt.

17. Remove the rocker cover and the half-round seal.

18. On non-turbo models, remove the exhaust pipe self-locking nuts and separate the exhaust pipe from the exhaust manifold. Discard the gasket.

19. On turbocharged engines, remove the sheetmetal heat protector.

20. Loosen the cylinder head mounting bolts according to sequence in 2–3 cycles and lift off the cylinder head assembly.

To install:

21. Installation is the reverse of the removal process. Check the cylinder head for cracks, damage or engine coolant leakage. Remove scale, sealing compound and carbon. Clean oil passages throughly. Check the head for flatness. End to end, the head should be within 0.002 in. normally with 0.008 in. the maximum allowed out of true. The total thickness allowed to be removed from the head and block is 0.008 in. maximum.

22. Place a new head gasket on the cylinder block with any identification marks facing upward.

23. Carefully install the cylinder head on the block. Tighten the mounting bolts in sequence and torque in 3 steps to 65–72 ft. lbs.

24. Complete installation by reversing the removal procedure.

Valve Lash

ADJUSTMENT

1.5L Engine

NOTE: Incorrect valve clearances will not only result in unsteady engine operation, but will also cause excessive noise and reduced engine output. Check the valve clearances and adjust as required while the engine is hot.

1. Warm the engine to operating temperature, turn **OFF** and disconnect the negative battery cable.

2. Remove all spark plugs so engine can be easily turned by hand.

3. Remove the rocker cover.

4. Turn the crankshaft clockwise until the notch on the pulley is lined up with the **T** mark on the timing belt lower cover. This brings both No. 1 and No. 4 cylinder pistons to Top Dead Center (TDC).

5. Wiggle the rocker arms on No. 1 and No. 4 cylinders up and down to determine which cylinder is at TDC on the compression stroke. Both rocker arms should move if the piston in that cylinder is at TDC on the compression stroke.

6. Measure the valve clearance with a feeler gauge. When the No. 1 piston is at TDC on the compression stroke, check No. 1 intake and exhaust, No. 2 intake and No. 3 exhaust. Then turn the crankshaft clockwise one turn to bring No. 4 to TDC on its compression stroke. With No. 4 on TDC, compression stroke, check No. 2 exhaust, No. 3 intake and No. 4 intake and exhaust.

7. Valve lash specifications are: Exhaust– 0.0098 in. hot or 0.0067 in. cold; Intake– 0.0059 in. hot or 0.0028 in. cold. If the valve clearances are out of specification, loosen the rocker arm locknut and adjust the clearance using a feeler gauge while turning the adjusting screw. Be sure to hold the screw to prevent it from turning when tightening the locknut.

8. After adjusting the valves, install rocker cover, spark plugs and connect the negative battery cable.

Except 1.5L Engine

NOTE: These engines use hydraulic valve tappets, eliminating the need for valve lash adjustment. The tappet plunger is positioned to a pre-set dimension when the valve train is bolted into place.

If an abnormal is heard from the lash adjusters check the following:

1. Warm the engine to operating temperature and turn **OFF**. Remove the cam cover.

2. Without disassembling any valve train parts, press the part of the rocker arm that contacts the lash adjuster. The part pressed down should feel very hard if the lash adjuster condition is normal.

3. If, when pressed, it easily goes all the way down, replace the lash adjuster.

4. If there is a spongy feeling when pressed, air is probably mixed in and the cause should be investigated. The cause of air in the oil is often insufficient engine oil. It could also be a damaged engine oil pump pickup screen or screen gasket.

5. After finding the cause and taking the appropriate action, adding oil or fixing the oil system, warm the engine and drive for a short time at low

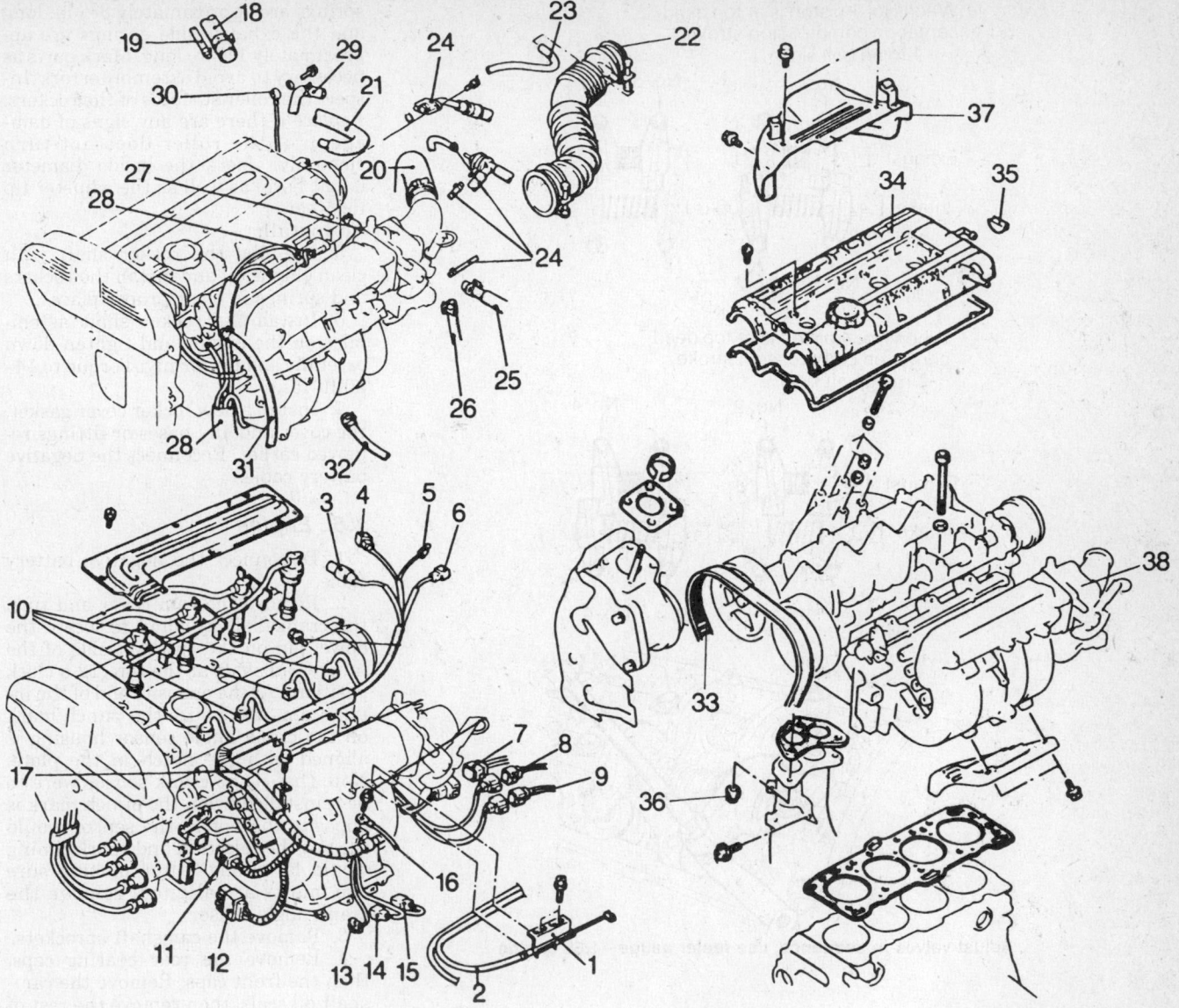

2.0L engine components, cylinder head removal

1. Accelerator cable
2. Cruise control cable
3. Connector–oxygen sensor
4. Connector–engine coolant temp sensor
5. Connector–engine coolant gauge unit
6. Connector–engine coolant temp switch (w/AC)
7. Connector–ISC
8. Connector–throttle position sensor
9. Connector–crankshaft angle sensor
10. Connector–fuel injectors
11. Connector–ignition coil
12. Connector–power transistor
13. onnector–noise filter
14. Connector–knock sensor turbo
15. Connector–EGR temp. sensor (Calif.)
16. Connector–ground cable
17. Engine control wiring harness
18. Upper radiator hose
19. Overflow tube
20. Air intake–turbo
21. Breather hose–turbo
22. Bellows type air intake
23. High pressure fuel line
24. Assorted vacuum hoses
25. Heater hose
26. Water by-pass hose
27. PCV hose
28. Vacuum hoses (turbo)
29. Water line (turbo)
30. Oil line (turbo)
31. Fuel return line
32. Brake booster hose
33. Timing belt
34. Rocker cover
35. Half-round seal
36. Exhaust locking nuts
37. Heat protector (turbo)
38. Cylinder head assembly

When No. 1 piston is at top dead
center on compression stroke
Timing belt side

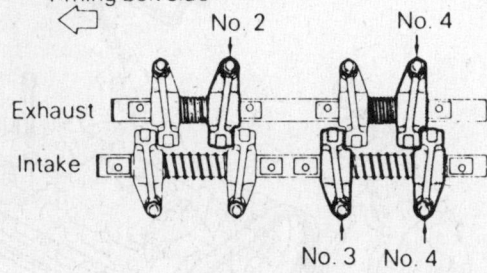

When No. 4 piston is at top dead
center on compression stroke
Timing belt side

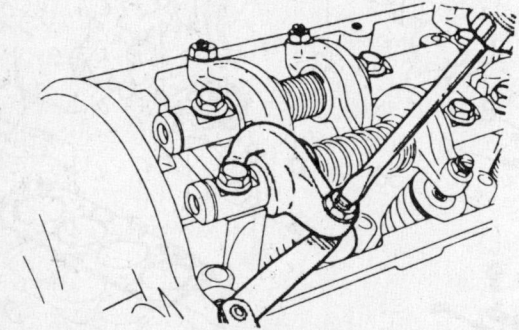

Adjust valves in sequence, use feeler gauge—1.5L engine

Rocker Arms/Shafts

REMOVAL & INSTALLATION

1.5L Engine

1. Disconnect the negative battery cable.
2. Pull the PCV valve from the rocker cover, disconnect any hoses or wires that will interfere with removing the rocker cover and remove the cover. Discard the gasket.
3. Remove the rocker shaft hold-down bolts uniformly, a little at a time and remove the rocker shaft/arm assemblies.
4. Note that the rocker arms are marked. Odd numbered cylinders are marked 1–3 and even number cylinder 2–4. In addition, there are 2 types of rocker arms. If the rocker shaft is to be disassembled, note the locations of the marks. The springs have different free lengths. The intake rocker shaft

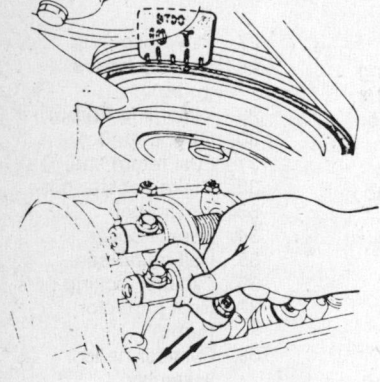

Set engine to TDC, check rockers for lash—1.5L engine

speed. Stop the engine and wait a few minutes. Then drive again at low speed. Repeat this procedure a few times to bleed out the air from the lash adjusters.

springs are approximately 3¼ in. long and the exhaust side springs are approximately 1¾ in. long. Mark parts as necessary to avoid assembly errors. Inspect the roller surfaces of the rockers. Replace if there are any signs of damage or if the roller does not turn smoothly. Check the inside diameter (shaft bore) as well as the adjuster tip for wear.

To install:

5. Pre-lube the rocker shaft with clean engine oil and install the rockers and springs in their proper places.
6. Install the rocker shaft assemblies on the engine and tighten down carefully and uniformly. Torque to 14–20 ft. lbs.
7. Install a new rocker cover gasket, the cover and any hoses or fittings removed earlier. Reconnect the negative battery cable.

1.6L Engine

1. Disconnect the negative battery cable.
2. Remove the cam cover and turn the crankshaft by hand to locate the dowel pin on the sprocket side of the intake camshaft at the top (12 o'clock position). At the opposite end of the intake cam, make sure the punch mark on the crank angle sensor housing is aligned with the notch in the plate. Note that if the crank sensor were to be reinstalled when the punch mark is opposite the notch, the sensor would fit, but the injection and spark timing would be wrong. After making sure the marks are aligned, remove the crank angle sensor.
3. Remove the camshaft sprockets.
4. Remove the rear bearing caps, then the front caps. Remove the camshaft oil seals, then remove the rest of the camshaft bearing caps. Note that bearing caps No. 2–5 are the same shape. At installation, check the markings on the cap to identify the cap number and the intake/exhaust identification symbol. L=intake camshaft side and R=exhaust camshaft side. Only **L** or **R** is stamped on the No. 1 bearing cap.
5. Remove the camshafts, then pull out the rocker arms. The lash adjusters can also be removed if necessary.
6. Inspect the rockers for wear. Replace if there are any signs of damage or if the roller does not turn smoothly.

To install:

7. Install the lash adjusters and rockers. Apply clean engine oil to the bearing journals and cams of the camshafts and install them into the engine. Use care not to confuse the intake and exhaust cams. The intake camshaft has a slit on its rear end for driving the crank angle sensor. Also make sure the dowel pins on the cam-

shaft sprocket end are located on the top.

8. Install the bearing caps and tighten from the center outwards tightening is several steps, finally torquing to 15 ft. lbs. Make sure rocker arm is correctly mounted on the lash adjuster and the valve stem end.

9. A driver is recommended for installing the camshaft end seals. Apply engine oil to the seals, guide onto the camshaft and gently drive the seal into the head.

10. Install the crank angle sensor onto the back of the intake camshaft, being careful to align the marks.

11. Install the cam sprockets, timing belt, cam cover and reinstall all hoses and wiring removed during disassembly.

12. Reconnect the negative battery cable.

Intake Manifold

REMOVAL & INSTALLATION

1. Relieve fuel system pressure.
2. Disconnect battery negative cable and drain the cooling system.
3. Remove the accelerator cable, breather hose and air intake hose.
4. Disconnect the upper radiator hose, heater hose and water bypass hose.
5. Remove all vacuum hoses and pipes as necessary, including the brake booster vaccum line.
6. Remove the high pressure fuel line, fuel return hose and throttle control cable brackets.
7. Remove and tag all electrical connectors that may interfere with the removal procedure, including spark plug wires.
8. Remove the delivery pipe, fuel injectors, pressure regulator and insulators as necessary.
9. On 1.5L engine, remove the intake manifold stay (brace) bracket and the distributor. On 1.6L and 2.0L engines, remove the throttle body stay bracket.
10. Remove the intake manifold mounting bolts and remove the intake manifold assembly.
To install:
11. Installation is the reverse of the removal proces. Clean all gasket material from the cylinder head intake mounting surface and intake manifold assembly. Check both surfaces for cracks or other damage. Check the intake manifold water passages and jet air passages for clogging. Clean if necessary.
12. Check the manifold for flatness with a straightedge and feeler gauge. It should be within 0.006 in. The limit is 0.012 in.

13. Torque the manifold in a criss-cross pattern. Torque all nuts and bolts to 14 ft. lbs.
14. Refill the cooling system and connect the battery negative cable.

Exhaust Manifold

REMOVAL & INSTALLATION

Except 1.6L and 2.0L Engines with Turbocharger

1. Disconnect battery negative cable.
2. Raise and safely support vehicle.
3. Remove the exhaust pipe to exhaust manifold nuts and separate exhaust pipe. Discard gasket.
4. Lower vehicle.
5. On 1.6L engines, remove electric cooling fan assembly.
6. Remove outer exhaust manifold heat shield, engine hanger and remove oxygen sensor.
7. Remove the exhaust manifold mounting bolts, the inner heat shield and remove the exhaust manifold.
To install:
8. Installation is the reverse of the removal procedure. Clean all gasket material from mating surfaces.
9. When installing, use new gaskets. Tighten from the center, outwards in a criss-cross pattern. Tighten the nuts to 18–22 ft. lbs.

1.6L and 2.0L Engines with Turbocharger

1. Disconnect battery negative cable. Drain the cooling system.
2. Raise and safely support vehicle.
3. Remove the exhaust pipe to turbocharger nuts and separate exhaust pipe. Discard gasket.
4. Lower vehicle. Remove air intake and vacuum hose connections.
5. Remove the upper exhaust manifold and turbocharger heat shields.
6. Remove the engine hanger, water and oil lines from the turbo.
7. Remove the exhaust manifold mounting bolts. Remove the exhaust manifold and gasket.
To install:
8. Installation is the reverse of removal. Clean all gasket material from mating surfaces.
9. When installing, use new gaskets. Tighten from the center, outwards in a criss-cross pattern. Tighten the nuts to 18–22 ft. lbs.

Turbocharger

REMOVAL & INSTALLATION

1. Disconnect negative battery cable.

2. Drain engine oil, cooling system and remove radiator. On Laser and Talon with air conditioning, remove the condenser fan assembly with the radiator.
3. Disconnect the oxygen sensor connector and remove sensor. Pull out oil dipstick and tube on Laser and Talon.
4. Remove the air intake bellows hose, the wastegate vacuum hose, the connections for the air outlet hose and the upper and lower heat shields. On Laser and Talon, unbolt the power steering pump and bracket assembly and leaving the hoses connected, wire it back out of the way.
5. Remove the self-locking exhaust manifold nuts, the triangular engine hanger bracket, the eyebolt and gaskets that connect the oil feed line to the turbo center section and the cooling water lines. The water line under the turbo has a threaded connection.
6. Remove the exhaust pipe nuts and gasket and lift off the exhaust manifold. Discard the gasket. Remove the 2 through bolts and 2 nuts that hold the exhaust manifold to the turbo.
7. Remove the 2 capscrews from the oil return line (under the turbo). Discard the gasket. Separate the turbo from the exhaust manifold. The 2 water pipes and oil feed line can still be attached.
To install:
8. Visually check the turbine wheel (hot side) and compressor wheel (cold side) for cracking or other damage. Check whether the turbine wheel and the compressor wheel can be easily turned by hand. Check for oil leakage. Check whether or not the wastegate valve remains open. If any problem is found, replace the part.

NOTE: Many turbocharger failures are due to oil supply problems. Heat soak after hot shutdown can cause the engine oil in the turbocharger and oil lines to 'coke.' Often the oil feed lines will become partially or completely blocked with hardened particles of carbon, blocking oil flow. Always check the oil feed pipe and oil return line for clogging. Clean these tubes well. Always use new gaskets above and below the oil feed eyebolt fitting. Use care that no particles of dirt of old gasket enter the oil passage hole and that no portion of the new gasket blocks the passage.

9. The wastegate can be checked with a pressure tester. Apply approximately 9 psi to the actuator and make sure the rod moves. Do not apply more than 10.3 psi or the diaphragm in the

wastegate may be damaged. Do not attempt to adjust the wastegate valve.

10. Installation is the reverse of the removal process. Note that the oil feed line should be primed with clean engine oil. None of the self-locking nuts should be reused. Replace all locking nuts. Before installing the threaded connection for the water inlet pipe, apply light oil to the inner surface of the pipe flange.

11. Fill the engine crankcase, cooling system and reconnect the battery negative cable.

Timing Belt Front Cover/Oil Seal

REMOVAL & INSTALLATION

1. Disconnect the negative battery cable.

2. Raise and safely support vehicle. Remove the under panel.

3. Place a wooden block between a jack and the oil pan. Slightly raise the engine and remove the engine mount bracket.

4. Remove all accessory drive belts, tension pulley bracket, water pump pulley, crankshaft compressor pulley and crankshaft pulley. The crankshaft pulley may be difficult to remove since the crankshaft will tend to turn when the center bolt is loosened. Use an old drive belt, wrap it around the pulley and draw it tight to hold the pulley.

5. Remove the upper and lower timing belt covers.

6. If removal of the front crank seal is necessary, pry the seal from the case cover.

To install:

7. Installation is the reverse of the removal process. Apply engine oil to the surface of the new seal. With a suitable pipe-like driver, tap the new seal into place.

8. Install the timing belt covers and

the pulleys and drive belts. Adjust accessory drive belt tension.

9. Install the engine mounting brackets, lower the engine connect the battery cable.

Timing Belt and Tensioner

ADJUSTMENT

1.5L Engine

1. Loosen the pivot side tensioner bolt and then the slot side bolt.

2. Tighten the slot side tensioner bolt and then the pivot side bolt.

NOTE: If the pivot side bolt is tightened first, the tensioner could turn with bolt, causing over tension.

3. Turn the crankshaft clockwise. Loosen the pivot side tensioner bolt and then the slot side bolt. Tighten the slot bolt and then the pivot side bolt.

4. Check the belt tension by holding the tensioner and timing belt together by hand and give the belt a slight thumb pressure at a point level with tensioner center. Make sure the belt cog crest comes as deep as about ¼ of the width of the slot side tensioner bolt head.

1.6L and 2.0L Engines

1. After turning the crankshaft ¼ turn counterclockwise, turn it clockwise to move No. 1 cylinder to TDC.

2. Loosen the center bolt. Using tool MD998738 or equivalent, and a torque wrench, apply a torque of 1.88–2.03 ft. lbs. (2.6–2.8 Nm). Tighten the center bolt.

3. Screw the special tool into the engine left support bracket until its end makes contact with the tensioner arm. At this point, screw the special tool in some more and remove the set wire attached to the auto tensioner, if wire was not previously removed. Then, remove the special tool.

4. Rotate the crankshaft 2 complete turns clockwise and let it sit for approximately 15 minutes. Then, measure the auto tensioner protrusion, the distance between the tensioner arm and auto tensioner body, to ensure that it is within 0.15–0.18 inches (3.8–4.5mm). If out of specification, repeat Step 1–4 until the specified value is obtained.

5. If the timing belt tension adjustment is being performed with the engine mounted in the vehicle, and clearance between the tensioner arm and the auto tensioner body cannot be measured, the following alternative method can be used:

1. Upper heat shield
2. Exhaust manifold
3. Air hose connector
4. Air inlet fitting
5. Oil feed pipe
6. Water line
7. Connection–air intake
8. Turbocharger assembly
9. Oil drainback line
10. Exhaust fitting
11. Exhaust pipe
12. Oxygen sensor
13. Lower heat shield
14. Water line
15. Gasket
16. Ring
17. Brace/bracket
18. Manifold gasket

Turbocharger installation

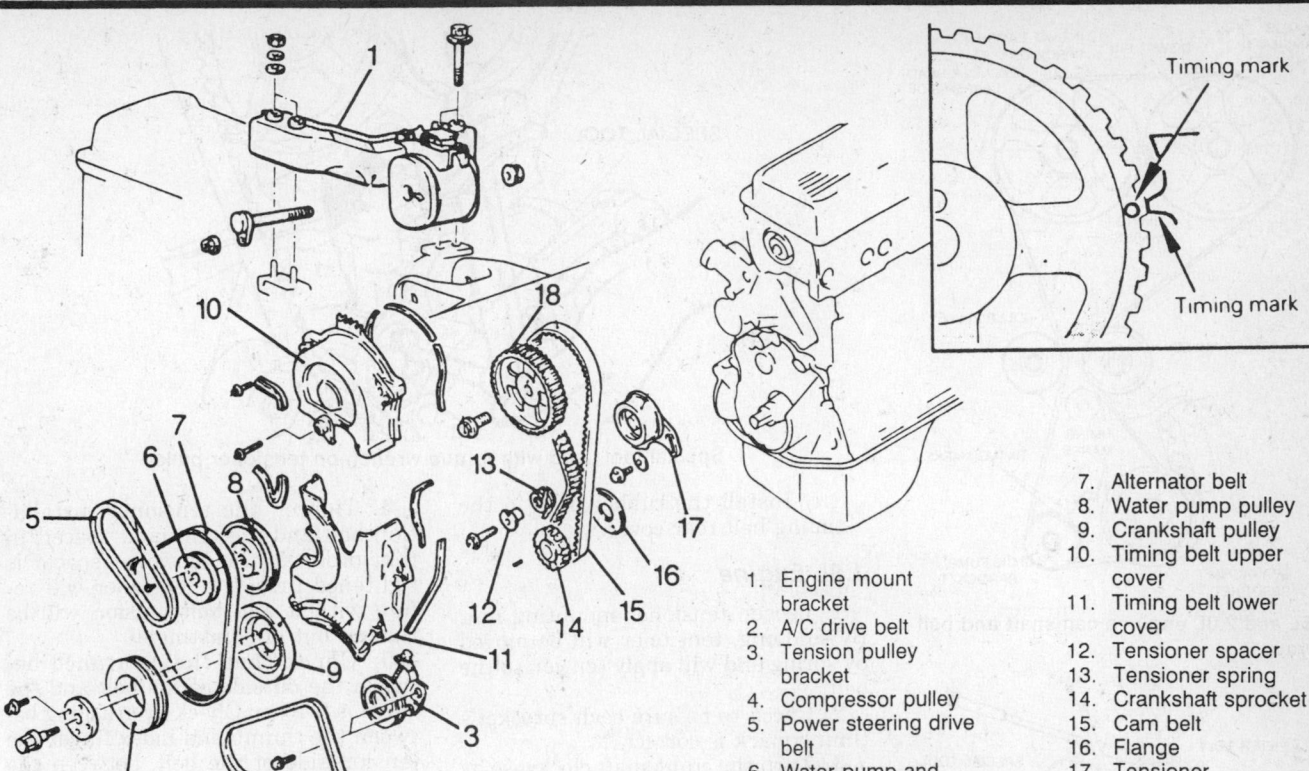

Camshaft belt layout—1.5L engine

1. Engine mount bracket
2. A/C drive belt
3. Tension pulley bracket
4. Compressor pulley
5. Power steering drive belt
6. Water pump and power steering pulley
7. Alternator belt
8. Water pump pulley
9. Crankshaft pulley
10. Timing belt upper cover
11. Timing belt lower cover
12. Tensioner spacer
13. Tensioner spring
14. Crankshaft sprocket
15. Cam belt
16. Flange
17. Tensioner
18. Cam sprocket

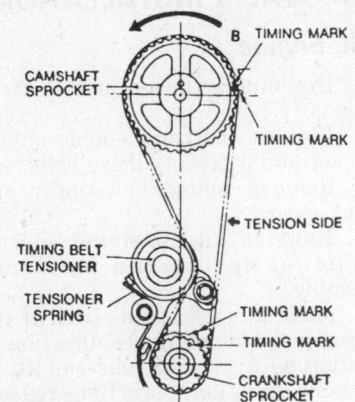

Timing marks alignment—1.5L engine

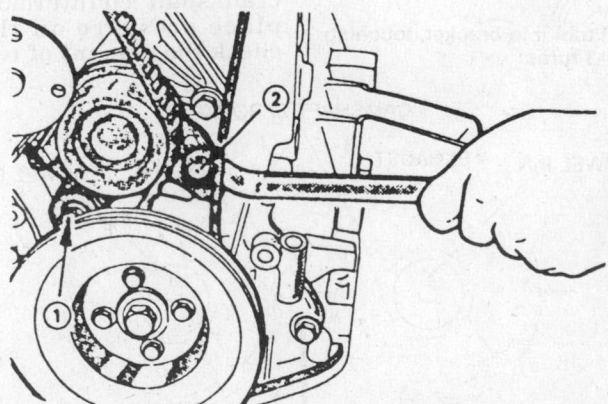

After loosening bolts, tighten slot side tensioner bolt first (2), then pivot side bolt (1)—1.5L engine

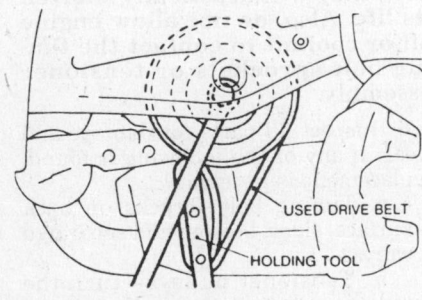

Holding crankshaft from turning with old belt and holding tool

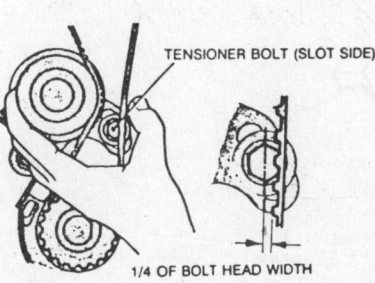

Checking belt tension—1.5L engine

a. Screw in special tool MD998738 or equivalent, until its end makes contact with the tensioner arm.

b. After the special tool makes contact with the arm, screw it in some more to retract the auto tensioner pushrod while counting the number of turns the tool makes until the tensioner arm is brought into contact with the auto tensioner body. Make sure the number of turns the special tool makes conforms with the standard value of 2½–3 turns.

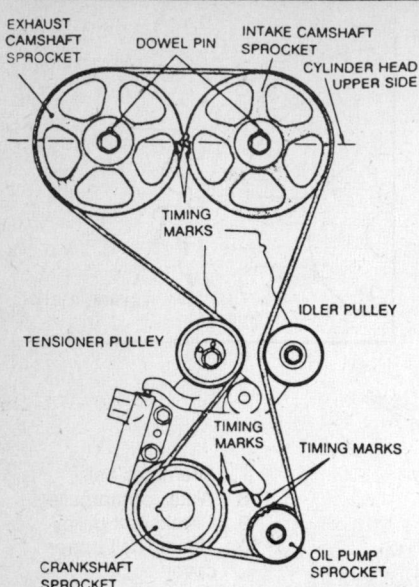

1.6L and 2.0L engines camshaft and belt layout

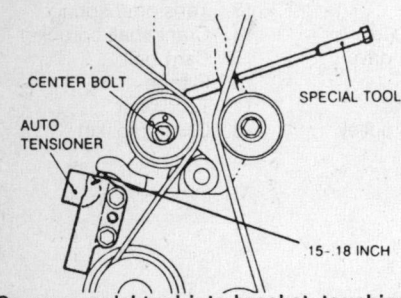

Screw special tool into bracket, touching belt, plus 2½–3 turns

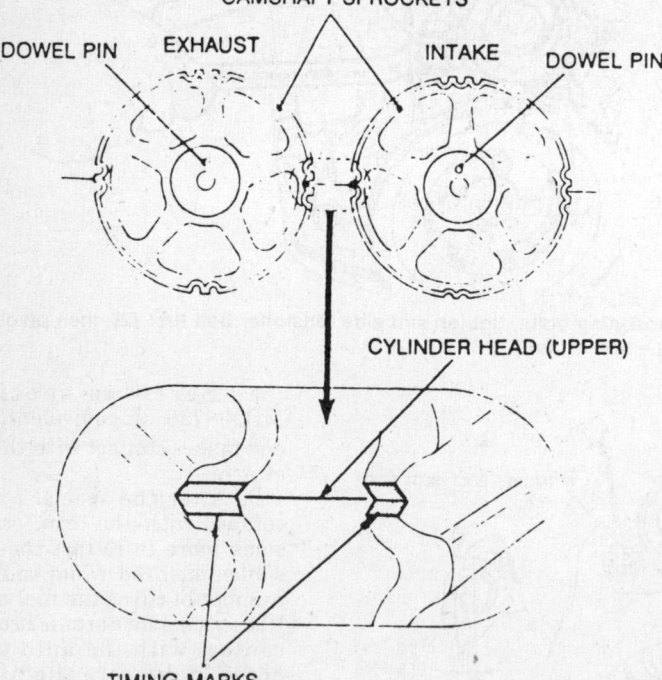

To time, align dowel pins at top, timing marks facing each other level with top surface of head—also align marks at crank and oil pump sprocket

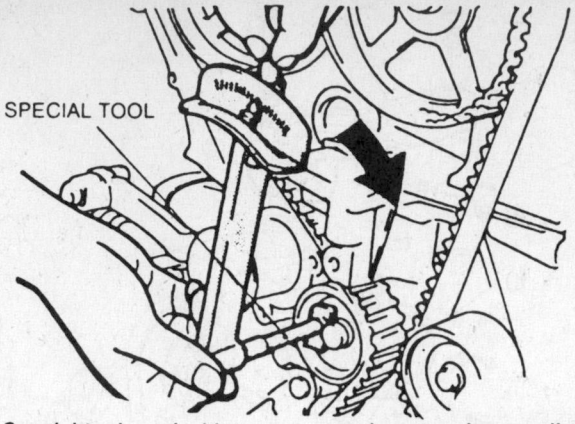

Special tool used with torque wrench on tensioner pulley

c. Install the rubber plug to the timing belt rear cover.

1.8L Engine

1. Loosen tensioner mounting nut. By so doing, tensioner will be moved by spring and will apply tension to the belt.

2. Check to be sure each sprocket's timing mark is correct.

3. Turn the crankshaft clockwise by 2 teeth of the camshaft sprocket.

NOTE: The purpose of this procedure is to apply the proper amount of tension on the timing belt. Be sure not to rotate the crankshaft counterclockwise or place pressure on the belt to check the amount of tension.

4. Tighten the tensioner installation bolt and the tensioner spacer, in that order. If the tensioner spacer is tightened first, the tensioner will rotate with it and belt tension will be thrown out of adjustment.

5. Check that the clearance between the outside of the belt and the cover is 0.40 in. Check by grasping between the thumb and index finger the tension side of the belt, between the camshaft sprocket and oil pump sprocket, and the center part of the belt.

REMOVAL & INSTALLATION

1.5L Engine

1. Disconnect the negative battery cable.

2. Remove the front engine mount bracket and accessory drive belts.

3. Remove timing belt upper and lower covers.

4. Remove the tensioner spacer, tensioner spring and tensioner assembly.

5. Make a mark on the back of the timing belt indicating the direction of rotation so it may be reassembled in the same direction if it is to be reused. Remove the timing belt.

NOTE: If coolant or engine oil comes in contact with the timing belt, they will drastically shorten its life. Also, do not allow engine oil or coolant to contact the timing belt sprockets or tensioner assembly.

6. Inspect all parts for damage and wear. If any of the following is found, replacement is necessary:

   a. Timing belt—cracks on back surface, sides, bottom and separated canvas.

   b. Tensioner pulleys—turn the pulleys and check for binding, excessive play, unusual noise or if there is a grease leak.

To install:

7. Installation is the reverse of the removal procedure. Position the tensioner, tensioner spring and tensioner spacer on engine block. Install the mounting bolt and torque to 14–20 ft. lbs. (20–27 Nm).

8. Align the timing marks on the camshaft sprocket and crankshaft sprocket. This will position No. 1 piston on TDC on the compression stroke.

9. Position the timing belt on the crankshaft sprocket and keeping the tension side of the belt tight, set it on the camshaft sprocket.

10. Apply counterclockwise force to the camshaft sprocket to give tension to the belt and make sure all timing marks are lined up.

11. Perform the belt tension adjustment and complete installation by reversing the removal procedure.

1.6L and 2.0L Engine

1. Disconnect the negative battery cable.

2. Raise the vehicle and support it safely. Remove the under cover.

3. Remove the front engine mount bracket.

4. Loosen the water pump pulley and remove all accessory drive belts, tensioner pulley, water pump pulley and crankshaft pulley.

5. Remove the timing belt upper and lower covers.

6. Rotate the crankshaft clockwise and align the timing marks so No. 1 piston will be at TDC of the compression stroke. At this time the timing marks on the camshaft sprocket and the upper surface of the cylinder head should coincide, and the dowel pin of the camshaft sprocket should be at the upper side.

NOTE: Always rotate the crankshaft in a clockwise direction. Make a mark on the back of the timing belt indicating the direction of rotation so it may be reassembled in the same direction if it is to be reused.

7. Hold the camshaft with a wrench at its hexagon (between No. 2 and 3 journals) and remove the camshaft sprocket bolt. Remove the camshaft sprocket and timing belt.

8. Remove the timing belt tensioner pulley, tensioner arm, idler pulley, oil pump sprocket, special washer, flange and spacer.

9. Remove the timing belt rear right cover, upper rear left cover and lower rear left cover.

10. Inspect all parts for damage and wear. If any of the following is found, replacement is necessary:

a. Timing belt – cracks on back

surface, sides, bottom and separated canvas.

b. Tensioner and idler pulleys – turn the pulleys and check for binding, excessive play, unusual noise or if there is a grease leak.

c. Auto tensioner – measure the tensioner rod. If the rod protrudes more than 0.47 in., replace the auto tensioner. Clamp the auto tensioner in a vise in a level position. Do not allow the plug at the bottom of the tensioner to come in direct contact with the vise. If the rod can be easily retracted, replace the auto tensioner. There should be a fair amount of resistance when pushing the rod in. If the auto tensioner leaks, replace it.

To install:

11. Installation is the reverse of the removal procedure. During assembly of the parts, the following should be observed:

a. Pay special attention to the direction of the flange and crankshaft sprocket. If these parts are installed in the wrong direction, the timing belt may be damaged.

b. Carefully push the auto tensioner rod in until the set hole in the rod aligned up with the hole in the cylinder. Place a wire into the hole to retain the rod.

c. Install the tensioner pulley onto the tensioner arm. Locate the pinhole in the tensioner pulley shaft to the left of the center bolt. Then, tighten the center bolt finger-tight.

12. When installing the timing belt, turn the 2 camshaft sprockets so their dowel pins are located on top. Align the timing marks facing each other with the top surface of the cylinder head. When you let go of the exhaust camshaft sprocket, it will rotate 1 tooth in the counter-clockwise direction. This should be taken into account when installing the timing belts on the sprocket.

NOTE: Both camshaft sprockets are used for the intake and exhaust camshafts and are provided with 2 timing marks. When the sprocket is mounted on the exhaust camshaft, use the timing mark on the right with the dowel pin hole on top. For the intake camshaft sprocket, use the one on the left with the dowel pin hole on top.

13. Align the crankshaft sprocket and oil pump sprocket timing marks. Install the timing belt as follows:

a. Install the timing belt around the intake camshaft sprocket and retain it with 2 spring clips or binder clips.

b. Install the timing belt around

the exhaust sprocket, aligning the timing marks with the cylinder head top surface using 2 wrenches. Retain the belt with 2 spring clips.

c. Install the timing belt around the idler pulley, oil pump sprocket, crankshaft sprocket and the tensioner pulley. Remove the 2 spring clips.

d. Lift upward on the tensioner pulley in a clockwise direction and tighten the center bolt. Make sure all timing marks are lined up.

e. Rotate the crankshaft a ¼ turn counterclockwise. Then, turn in clockwise until the timing marks are lined up again.

14. Perform the timing belt tension adjustment and remove the set wire attached to the auto tensioner.

15. Complete installation by reversing the removal procedure.

Camshaft

REMOVAL & INSTALLATION

1.5L and 1.8L Engines

1. Relieve the fuel system pressure.

2. Disconnect the battery negative cable.

3. Remove the distributor.

4. Remove the rocker cover, timing belt cover and timing belt.

5. Remove the camshaft sprocket and oil seal.

6. Loosen both rocker arms assembly uniformly and remove.

7. Remove the camshaft rear cover, rear cover gasket, thrust plate and camshaft thrust case. Remove the camshaft.

8. After the camshaft has been removed, check the following:

a. Check the camshaft journals for wear or damage.

b. Check the fuel pump drive eccentric cam and distributor drive gear tooth surfaces.

c. Check the cam lobes for damage. Also, check the cylinder head oil holes for clogging.

To install:

9. Lubricate the camshaft with heavy engine oil and slide it into the head.

10. Insert the camshaft thrust case in cylinder head with the threaded hole facing upward and align the threaded hole with the bolt hole in the cylinder head. Install and firmly tighten the attaching bolt.

11. Check the camshaft endplay between the thrust case and camshaft. The camshaft endplay should be 0.0020–0.0080 inches (0.5–0.20mm). If the endplay is not within specification, replace the camshaft thrust bearing.

12. When installing the oil seal, coat the external surface with engine oil. Position the seal on the camshaft end and drive into place using tool MD998306 or equivalent.

13. Complete installation by reversing the removal procedure.

1.6L and 2.0L Engines

1. Relieve the fuel system pressure.
2. Disconnect battery negative cable.
3. Remove the accelerator cable connection.
4. Remove the timing belt cover and timing belt.
5. Remove the center cover, breather and PCV hoses and spark plug cables.
6. Remove the rocker cover, semicircular packing, throttle body stay, crankshaft angle sensor, both camshaft sprockets and oil seals.
7. Loosen the bearing cap bolts in 2–3 steps. Label and remove both camshaft bearing caps.

NOTE: If the bearing caps are difficult to remove, use a plastic hammer to gently tap the rear part of the camshaft.

8. Remove the intake and exhaust camshafts.
9. After the camshaft has been removed, check the following:
   a. Check the camshaft journals for wear or damage.
   b. Check the cam lobes for damage. Also, check the cylinder head oil holes for clogging.

To install:

10. To install, lubricate the camshafts with heavy engine oil and position the camshafts on the cylinder head.

NOTE: Do not confuse the intake camshaft with the exhaust camshaft. The intake camshaft has a split on its rear end for driving the crank angle sensor.

11. Make sure the dowel pin on both camshaft sprocket ends are located on the top.
12. Install the bearing caps. Tighten the caps in sequence and in 2 or 3 steps. No. 2 and 5 caps are of the same shape. Check the markings on the caps to identify the cap number and intake/exhaust symbol. Only **L** (intake) or **R** (exhaust) is stamped on No.1 bearing cap. Also, make sure the rocker arm is correctly mounted on the lash adjuster and the valve stem end.
13. Apply a coating of engine oil to

the oil seal. Using tool MD998307 or equivalent, press-fit the seal into the cylinder head.

14. Align the punch mark on the crank angle sensor housing with the notch in the plate. With the dowel pin on the sprocket side of the intake camshaft at top, install the crank angle sensor on the cylinder head.

NOTE: The crank angle sensor can be installed with the punch mark positioned opposite the notch; however, that position will result in incorrect fuel injection and ignition timing.

15. Complete the installation by reversing the removal procedure.

Intermediate Shaft

REMOVAL & INSTALLATION

1.8L Engine

1. Disconnect the negative battery cable.
2. Remove the oil filter, oil pressure switch, oil gauge sending unit and oil filter mounting bracket and gasket.
3. Drain engine oil. Remove engine oil pan, oil screen and gasket.
4. Remove the front engine cover which is also the oil pump cover. Different length bolts are used. Take note of their locations. If the cover sticks to the block, look for a special slot provided and pry with a suitable tool. Discard the shaft seal and gasket.
5. Remove the oil pump driven gear flange bolt. When loosening this bolt, first insert a suitable tool approximately 3/8 in. diameter into the plug hole on the left side of the cylinder block to hold the silent shaft. Remove the oil pump gears and remove the front case assembly. Remove the threaded plug, the oil pressure relief spring and plunger.
6. Remove the silent shaft oil seals, the crankshaft oil seal and front case gasket.
7. Remove the silent shafts.

To install:

8. Installation is the reverse of the removal procedure. Use new gaskets and seals. Clean all mating surfaces well.
9. Use care to get the proper length bolt in the correct location on the timing cover as well as the oil pump cover.
10. Refill with engine oil. Install new filter. Check for leaks.

Piston and Connecting Rod

POSITIONING

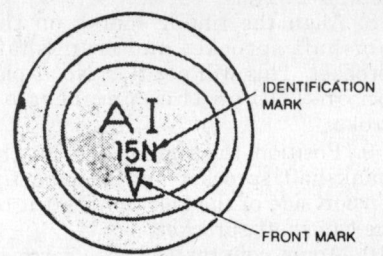

Piston identification marks, typical 1.5L engine

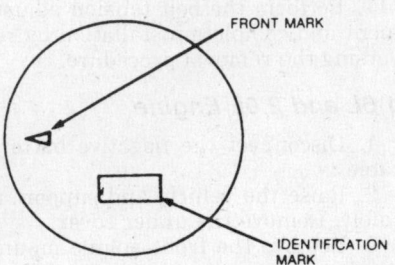

Piston identification marks, typical 1.6L, 1.8L, 2.0L engines

ENGINE LUBRICATION SYSTEM

Oil Pan

REMOVAL & INSTALLATION

1. Disconnect the negative battery cable.
2. Raise the vehicle and support it safely.
3. Remove the oil pan drain plug and drain the engine oil. On 1.6L engine equipped with turbocharger, remove the oil return pipe and gasket.
4. On 1.8L engines, disconnect and lower the exhaust pipe.
5. On 2.0L engine, remove the crossmember, discoonect and lower the exhaust pipe and on turbocharged engines, disconnect the return pipe for the turbocharger from the side of the oil pan.
6. Remove the oil pan mounting bolts, separate and remove the engine oil pan.

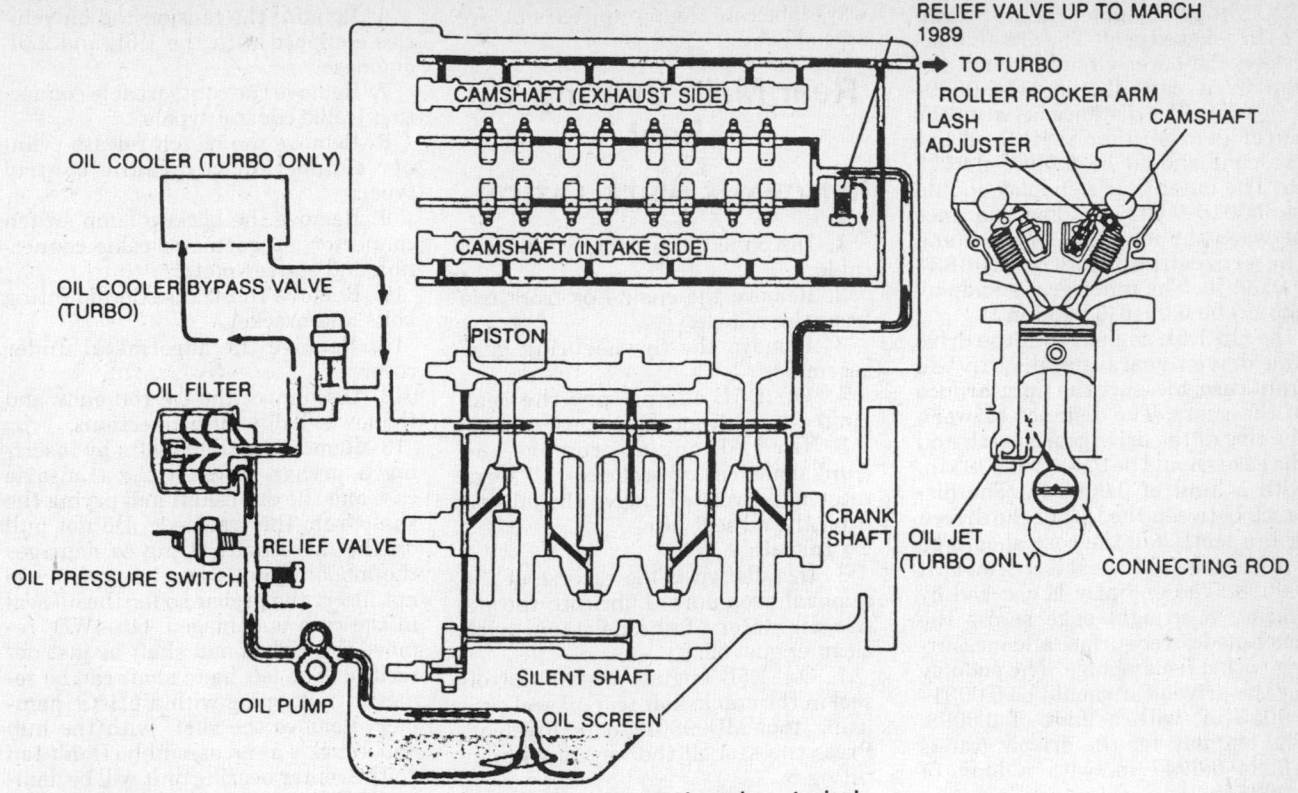

Oil system layout 2.0L engine—typical

To install:

7. Installation is the reverse of the removal process. Clean all sealant from the oil pan and cylinder block.

8. Apply a thin bead of sealer, around the surface of the oil pan.

9. Assemble the oil pan to the cylinder block within 15 minutes after applying the sealant.

10. Install the oil pan mounting bolts and torque to 4–6 ft. lbs. (6–8 Nm). On 1.6L engine equipped with turbocharger, install the oil return pipe using a new gasket.

11. Install the oil pan drain plug. Refill with oil, check for leaks.

Oil Pump

REMOVAL & INSTALLATION

NOTE: Whenever the oil pump is disassembled or the cover removed, the gear cavity must be filled with petroleum jelly (vaseline) for priming purposes. Do not use grease.

1. Disconnect the negative battery cable.

2. Remove the front engine mount bracket and accessory drive belts.

3. Remove timing belt upper and lower covers.

4. Remove the timing belt and crankshaft sprocket.

5. Remove the oil pan drain plug and drain the engine oil. On 1.6L en-gine equipped with turbocharger, remove the oil return pipe and gasket.

6. Remove the oil pan mounting bolts separate and remove the engine oil pan.

7. Remove the oil screen and gasket.

8. Remove and tag the front cover mounting bolts. All mounting bolts are of different length.

9. On 1.6L engine, remove the plug cap using tool MD998162 or equivalent and remove the oil pressure switch.

10. Remove the front case cover and oil pump assembly.

NOTE: On 1.5L engine, the outer gear does not have any marks indicating its installed direction. Make a mark on the reverse side of the outer gear so it can be reinstalled in its proper position.

11. Check the oil pump housing and gears for cracks, wear and other damage.

12. Remove the oil seal from the front cover.

13. Clean all gasket material from mounting surfaces.

14. To install, apply engine oil to the entire surface of the gears. On 1.5L engine, make sure the outer gear is installed in the same direction as before according to the mark made at the time of removal.

15. On 1.6L engine, install the drive/driven gears with the 2 timing marks aligned.

16. Assemble the front case cover and oil pump assembly to the engine block using a new gasket. On 1.6L engine, assemble the front case cover and oil pump assembly using tool MD998285 or equivalent on the front end of the crankshaft.

17. On 1.5L engine, apply engine oil to the surface of seal installer tool MD998305 or equivalent and slide the new seal along the tool until it touches the front case. Tap the oil seal into place.

18. On 1.6L engine, install the crankshaft oil seal using tool MD998375 or equivalent.

19. Complete installation by reversing the removal procedure. Connect battery, run engine and check for leaks.

CHECKING

1. After disassembling the oil pump, clean all parts.

2. Assemble the oil pump gear to the front case and rotate it to ensure smooth rotation and no looseness. Make sure there is no ridge wear on the contact surface between the front case and the gear surface of the oil pump front cover.

3. The gear clearance should be checked using the following procedure:

a. On 1.5L engine, check the outer ring shaped gear. The distance between the outer circumference and the front case should be 0.0039–0.0079 in. The distance between the outer gear's inner teeth and the crescent should be 0.0087–0.0173 in. The outer gear's endplay should be 0.0016–0.0039 in. The clearance between the inner gear's teeth and the crescent should be 0.0083–0.0134 in. The inner gear's endplay should be 0.0016–0.0039 in.

b. On 1.6L engine, with the drive and driven gears installed in the front case, measure the tip clearance of the gears. The distance between the tips of the drive gear's teeth and the case should be 0.0063–0.0083 in. with a limit of 0.0098 in. The distance between the tips of the driven gear's teeth and the case should be 0.0051–0.0071 with a limit of 0.0098. The end play is checked by placing a straight edge across the machined cover surface and measuring with a feeler gauge. The endplay for the drive gear should be 0.0031–0.0055 in. with a limit of 0.0098. The endplay for the driven gear is 0.0024–0.0047 in. with a limit of 0.0098 in.

c. On 1.8L engine, with the drive and driven gears installed in the front case, measure the tip clearance of the gears. The distance between the tips of the drive gear's teeth and the case should be 0.0024–0.0047 in. with a limit of 0.079 in. The distance between the tips of the driven gear's teeth and the case should be 0.0039–0.0079 with a limit of 0.071. The endplay is checked by placing a straight edge across the machined cover surface and measuring with a feeler gauge. The endplay for the drive gear should be 0.0039–0.0063 in. with a limit of 0.008. The endplay for the driven gear is 0.0008–0.0020 in. with a limit of 0.006 in.

d. On 2.0L engine, with the drive and driven gears installed in the front case, measure the tip clearance of the gears. The distance between the tips of the drive gear's teeth and the case should be 0.0063–0.0083 in. with a limit of 0.0098 in. The distance between the tips of the driven gear's teeth and the case should be 0.0051–0.0071 with a limit of 0.0098. The endplay is checked by placing a straight edge across the machined cover surface and measuring with a feeler gauge. The endplay for the drive gear should be 0.0031–0.0055 in. with a limit of 0.0098. The endplay for the driven gear is 0.0024–0.0047 in. with a limit of 0.0098 in.

4. If in doubt, replace the pump. Always lubricate the pump gears before assembly.

Rear Main Bearing Oil Seal

REMOVAL & INSTALLATION

1. Disconnect the negative battery cable.
2. Remove the engine or transaxle from the vehicle.
3. Remove the flywheel/ring gear assemble.
4. On 1.5L engine, pry the rear main oil seal from the oil seal case.
5. On 1.6L engine, remove the crankshaft rear oil seal case, oil separator and gasket. Remove the oil seal from the oil seal case.

To install:

6. Installation is the reverse of the removal procedure. Lubricate the inner diameter of the new seal with clean engine oil.
7. On 1.5L engine, install the oil seal in the crankshaft rear oil seal case using tool MD998011 or equivalent. Press the seal all the way in without tilting it.
8. On 1.6L engine, install the oil seal in the crankshaft rear oil seal case using tool MD998376 or equivalent. Press the seal all the way in without tilting it. Force the oil separator into the oil seal case so the oil hole in the separator is at 6 o'clock position.
9. Install the flywheel and transaxle. Check oil level.

MANUAL TRANSAXLE

For further information on transmissions/transaxles, please refer to ''Chilton's Guide to Transmission Repair''.

Transaxle Assembly

REMOVAL & INSTALLATION

Summit

1. Disconnect the negative battery cable.
2. Remove the battery and battery tray.
3. Remove the air cleaner assembly and air hoses.
4. Raise the vehicle and support it safely.
5. Drain the transaxle oil.

6. Remove the tension rod on vehicles equipped with the 1.6L and 2.0L engines.
7. Remove the control cable connection (cable control type).
8. Remove the clutch release cylinder connection (hydraulic control type).
9. Remove the backup lamp switch connector, speedometer cable connection and starter motor.
10. Remove the transaxle mounting bolts and bracket.
11. Remove the sheetmetal under cover.
12. Disconnect the tie rod ends and the lower ball joint connections.
13. Remove the halfshafts by inserting a prybar between the transaxle case and the driveshaft and prying the shaft from the transaxle. Do not pull on the driveshaft. Doing so damages the inboard joint. Use the prybar. Do not insert the prybar so far the oil seal in the case is damaged. On 4WD, remove the right hand shaft as just described. The left hand shaft can be removed by tapping with a plastic hammer. Remove the shaft with the hub and knuckle as an assembly. Don't tap on the center bearing or it will be damaged. Tie the shafts back out of the way. Note the circle clip on the end of the inboard shafts. These should not be reused.
14. Remove the bellhousing lower cover. Remove the transaxle to engine bolts and lower the transmission from the vehicle.

To install:

15. Installation is the reverse of the removal procedure, with the following points to watch. When installing the halfshafts, always use new circlips on the axle ends. Take care to get the inboard joint parts straight, not bent relative to the axle. Care must be taken to ensure that the oil seal lip of the transaxle is not damaged by the serrated part of the driveshaft.
16. When bolting up the starter, make sure the ground cable is securely fastened.
17. Note that the hydraulic system for the clutch should be bled after installation.
18. Make sure the vehicle is level when refilling the transaxle. Use Hypoid gear oil or equivalent, GL-4 or higher.

Laser and Talon

1. Disconnect the negative and positive battery cables and remove the battery.
2. Remove the Auto-Cruise Actuator and bracket underhood, on the passenger side inner fender wall.
3. Drain the transaxle oil. On 4WD the transfer case also has a drain plug.

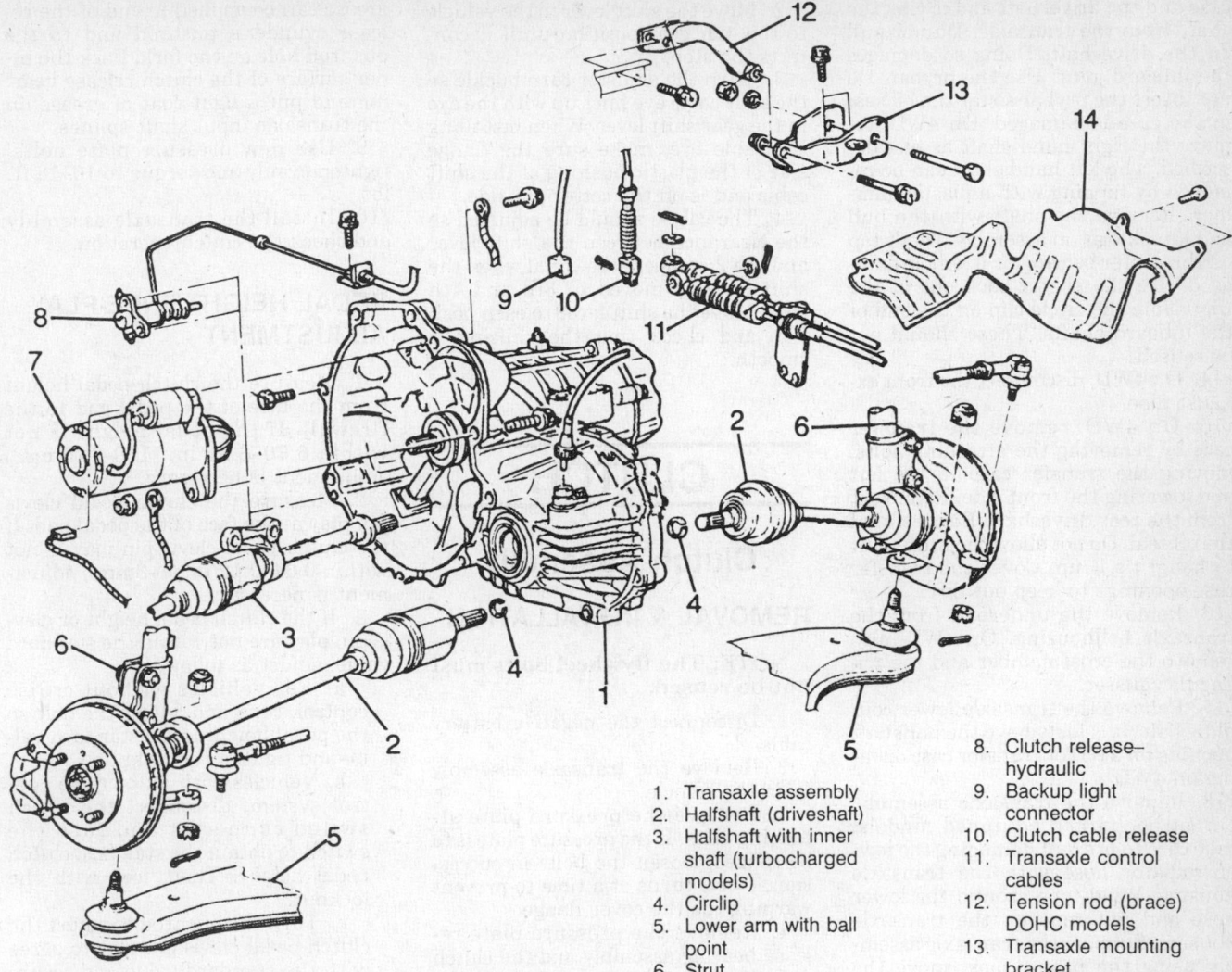

1. Transaxle assembly
2. Halfshaft (driveshaft)
3. Halfshaft with inner shaft (turbocharged models)
4. Circlip
5. Lower arm with ball point
6. Strut
7. Starter motor
8. Clutch release— hydraulic
9. Backup light connector
10. Clutch cable release
11. Transaxle control cables
12. Tension rod (brace) DOHC models
13. Transaxle mounting bracket
14. Under cover

Manual transaxle layout—typical

OIL SEAL

HALFSHAFT

LEVER

TRANSAXLE CASE

Pry halfshaft from transaxle case as shown and tie back out of the way

4. Remove the air intake hose.

5. Remove the cotter pin securing the select and shift cables and remove the cable ends from the transaxle.

6. Remove the connection for the clutch release cylinder and without disconnecting the hydraulic line, secure at the body side out of the way.

7. Disconnect the backup light switch and the speedometer cable.

8. Disconnect the starter electrical connections and remove the starter motor.

9. Remove the transaxle mount bracket.

10. Raise and safely support vehicle and remove the under cover.

11. Remove the cotter pin and disconnect the tie rod end from the steering knuckle.

12. Remove the self-locking nut and remove the lower arm ball joint.

13. Remove the halfshafts by inserting a prybar between the transaxle

case and the driveshaft and prying the shaft from the transaxle. Do not pull on the driveshaft. Doing so damages the inboard joint. Use the prybar. Do not insert the prybar so far the oil seal in the case is damaged. On 4WD, remove the right hand shaft as just described. The left hand shaft can be removed by tapping with a plastic hammer. Remove the shaft with the hub and knuckle as an assembly. Don't tap on the center bearing or it will be damaged. Tie the shafts back out of the way. Note the circle clip on the end of the inboard shafts. These should not be reused.

14. On 4WD, disconnect the front exhaust pipe.

15. On 4WD, remove the transfer case by removing the attaching bolts, moving the transfer case to the left and lowering the front side. Remove it from the rear driveshaft. Be careful of the oil seal. Do not allow the prop shaft to hang; tie it up. Cover the transfer case openings to keep out dirt.

16. Remove the underpan from the transaxle bellhousing. On 4WD, also remove the crossmember and the triangular gusset.

17. Remove the transaxle lower coupling bolt. It is just above the halfshaft opening on 2WD or transfer case opening on 4WD.

18. Remove the transaxle assembly. On turbocharged equipped models, take care to prevent damaging the lower radiator hose with the transaxle housing. Wind tape around the lower hose and put tape on the transaxle housing. Support the transaxle assembly using the proper jack, move the transaxle to the right and lower it.

To install:

19. Installation is the reverse of the removal procedure, with the following points to watch. When installing the halfshafts, always use new circlips on the axle ends. Take care to get the inboard joint parts straight, not bent relative to the axle. Care must be taken to ensure that the oil seal lip of the transaxle is not damaged by the serrated part of the driveshaft.

20. When bolting up the starter, make sure the ground cable is securely fastened.

21. Make sure the vehicle is level when refilling the transaxle. Use Hypoid gear oil or equivalent, GL-4 or higher. Check transaxle and transfer case on 4WD.

LINKAGE ADJUSTMENT

There are 2 cables, the select cable and the shift cable.

1. On the transaxle, put select lever in **N** and move the transaxle shift lever to put it in **4th** gear. Depress the clutch, if necessary, to shift.

2. Move the shift lever in the vehicle to the **4th** gear position until it contacts the stop.

3. Turn the adjuster turn buckle so the shift cable eye lines up with the eye in the gear shift lever. When installing the cable eye, make sure the flange side of the plastic bushing at the shift cable end is on the cotter pin side.

4. The cables should be adjusted so the clearance between the shift lever and the 2 stoppers are equal when the shift lever is moved to 3rd and 4th gear. Move the shift lever to each position and check that the shifting is smooth.

CLUTCH

Clutch Assembly

REMOVAL & INSTALLATION

NOTE: The flywheel bolts must not be reused.

1. Disconnect the negative battery cable.

2. Remove the transaxle assembly from the vehicle.

3. Remove the pressure plate attaching bolts. If the pressure plate is to be reused, loosen the bolts in succession, 1 or 2 turns at a time to prevent warping the the cover flange.

4. Remove the pressure plate release bearing assembly and the clutch disc. Do not use solvent to clean the bearing.

5. Inspect the condition of the clutch components and replace any worn parts.

NOTE: On some models, the release bearing and pressure plate are not serviced separately. The bearing is permanently attached to the pressure plate diaphragm fingers. The pressure plate and bearing must be serviced as an assembly.

To install:

6. Installation is the reverse of the removal process. Inspect the flywheel for heat damage or cracks. Replace if necessary.

7. Install the clutch disc to the flywheel. Use an alignment tool. Install the pressure plate assembly and tighten the pressure plate bolts evenly to 16–18 ft. lbs. Remove the alignment tool.

8. Apply a very light coat of high temperature grease to the clutch fork at the ball pivot and where the fork contacts the bearing. Also a little bit of grease can be applied to end of the release cylinder's pushrod and to the pushrod hole on the fork. Pack the inner surface of the clutch release bearing and put a light coat of grease on the transaxle input shaft splines.

9. Use new pressure plate bolts, tighten evenly and torque to 16–18 ft. lbs.

10. Install the transaxle assembly and check the clutch operation.

PEDAL HEIGHT/FREE-PLAY ADJUSTMENT

1. Measure the clutch pedal height from the face of the pedal pad to the firewall. If the pedal height is not within 6.70–6.89 in. (170–175mm), adjustment is necessary.

2. Measure the clutch pedal clevis pin play at the face of the pedal pad. If the clutch pedal clevis pin play is not within 0.04–0.12 in. (1–3mm), adjustment is necessary.

3. If the clutch pedal height or clevis pin play are not within the standard value, adjust as follows:

   a. For vehicles without cruise control, turn and adjust the bolt so the pedal height is the standard value and tighten the locknut.

   b. Vehicles with auto-cruise control system, disconnect the clutch switch connector and turn the switch to obtain the standard clutch pedal height. Then, lock with the locknut.

   c. Turn the pushrod to adjust the clutch pedal clevis pin play to agree with the standard value and secure the pushrod with the locknut.

NOTE: When adjusting the clutch pedal height or the clutch pedal clevis pin play, be careful not to push the pushrod toward the master cylinder.

   d. Check that when the clutch pedal is depressed all the way 5.9 in. (149mm), the interlock switch switches over from **ON** to **OFF**.

Clutch Master Cylinder

REMOVAL & INSTALLATION

1. Disconnect the negative battery cable.

2. Loosen the line at the cylinder and allow the fluid to drain. Use care. Brake fluid damages paint. On Laser and Talon, it may be necessary to remove the air filter for access.

3. Remove the cotter pin and the clutch pedal and remove the washer and clevis pin.

4. Remove the 2 nuts and pull the cylinder from the firewall. A seal

should be between the mounting flange and firewall. This seal should be replaced.

5. Reverse the removal procedure to install. A bit of grease should be applied to clevis pin and washer. The system should be refilled and bled.

Clutch Slave Cylinder

ADJUSTMENT

These models use hydraulic systems which are self-adjusting.

REMOVAL & INSTALLATION

1. Remove the hydraulic line and allow the system to drain.
2. Remove the bolts and pull the cylinder from the transaxle housing. On some 1.5L engines, instead of a pushrod bearing against the clutch arm, a clevis pin and yoke is used. Simply remove the circlip, pull out the clevis pin and remove the cylinder.
3. Reverse the removal procedure to install. Apply a bit of grease to the pivot points.
4. Bleed the system.

Hydraulic Clutch System Bleeding

1. Fill the reservoir with brake fluid.
2. Loosen the bleed screw, have the clutch pedal pressed to the floor.
3. Tighten the bleed screw and release the clutch pedal.
4. Repeat the bleeding operation until the fluid is free of air bubbles.

NOTE: It is suggested to attach a hose to the bleeder and place the other end into a container at least ½ full of brake fluid during the bleeding operation. Do not allow the reservoir to run out of fluid during the bleeding operation.

AUTOMATIC TRANSAXLE

For further information on transmissions/transaxles, please refer to "Chilton's Guide to Transmission Repair".

Transaxle Assembly

REMOVAL & INSTALLATION
Summit

1. Disconnect the negative battery cable.

2. Remove the battery and battery tray.
3. Remove the air pipe and air hose.
4. Raise the vehicle and support it safely.
5. Drain the transaxle oil.
6. Remove the tension rod on vehicle equipped with 1.6L and 2.0L engines.
7. Remove the control cable connection and cooler lines connections.
8. Remove the throttle control cable connection (3 Speed transaxle).
9. Remove the shift control solenoid valve connector connection (4 Speed transaxle).
10. Remove the inhibitor switch connector and kickdown servo switch connector (4 Speed transaxle).
11. Remove the pulse generator connector and oil temperature sensor connector (4 Speed transaxle).
12. Remove the speedometer cable connection and starter.
13. Remove the transaxle mounting bolts and bracket.
14. Remove the under guard pan.
15. Disconnect the steering tie rod end and the ball joint from the steering arm.
16. Remove the halfshafts at the inboard side from the transaxle. Tie the joint up out of the way.
17. Remove the bell housing cover and remove the drive plate bolts.
18. Remove the transaxle assembly lower connecting bolt, just over the halfshaft opening.
19. Properly support the transaxle assembly and lower it moving it to the right for clearance.
20. Installation is the reverse of the removal process. After the torque converter has been mounted on the transaxle, install the transaxle assembly on the engine. If the torque converter is first mounted on the engine, a damaged oil seal in the transaxle could result. Tighten the drive plate bolts to 34–38 ft. lbs. Install the bell housing cover.
21. Install the halfshafts to the transaxle and connect the tie rods and ball joint connections.
22. Install the underguard and the mounting bracket. Reconnect the cable controls, oil cooler lines and electrical connections.
23. Lower vehicle, refill with Dexron or Dexron II automatic transmission fluid. Start engine and allow to idle for 2 minutes. Apply parking brake and move selector through each gear position, ending in **N**. Recheck fluid level and add if necessary. Fluid level should be between the marks in the **HOT** range.

Laser and Talon

1. Disconnect the battery cables and remove the battery.

2. On vehicle equipped with Auto-cruise, remove the control actuator and bracket.
3. Drain the transaxle fluid.
4. Remove the air cleaner assembly.
5. Remove the adjusting nut and disconnect the shift cable.
6. Disconnect and tag as required the electrical connectors for the solenoid, neutral safety switch (inhibitor switch), the pulse generator kickdown servo switch and oil temperature sensor.
7. Disconnect the speedometer cable and oil cooler lines.
8. Disconnect the wires to the starter motor and remove the starter.
9. Remove the upper transaxle to engine bolts.
10. Remove the transaxle mounting bracket.
11. Raise and safely support vehicle and remove the sheetmetal under guard.
12. Remove the tie rod ends and the ball joints from the steering knuckle.
13. Remove the halfshafts by inserting a prybar between the transaxle case and the driveshaft and prying the shaft from the transaxle. Do not pull on the driveshaft. Doing so damages the inboard joint. Use the prybar. Do not insert the prybar so far the oil seal in the case is damaged. Tie the halfshafts out of the way.
14. Remove the lower bellhousing cover and remove the bolts holding the flexplate to the torque converter. These are special bolts. Do not loose. To remove, turn the engine crankshaft with a box wrench and bring the bolts into position one at a time. After removing the bolts, push the torque converter toward the transaxle so it doesn't stay on the engine side and allow oil to pour out the converter hub.
15. Remove the lower transaxle to engine bolts and remove the transaxle assembly.

To install:

16. Installation is the reverse of the removal process. After the torque converter has been mounted on the transaxle, install the transaxle assembly on the engine. If the torque converter is first mounted on the engine, a damaged oil seal in the transaxle could result. Tighten the drive plate bolts to 34–38 ft. lbs. Install the bell housing cover.
17. Install the halfshafts to the transaxle and connect the tie rods and ball joint connections.
18. Install the underguard and the mounting bracket. Reconnect the cable controls, oil cooler lines and electrical connections.
19. Lower vehicle, refill with Dexron or Dexron II automatic transmission fluid. Start engine and allow to idle for 2 minutes. Apply parking brake and

move selector through each gear position, ending in **N**. Recheck fluid level and add if necessary. Fluid level should be between the marks in the **HOT** range.

SHIFT LINKAGE ADJUSTMENT

1. The shifter cable adjustment is done at the neutral safety switch (inhibitor switch). Locate the switch on the transaxle and not the alignment hole in the arm and the body of the switch. Place the selector lever in **N**. Place the manual lever of the transaxle in **N**.

2. Align the holes on the switch.

3. If the cable needs to be adjusted, loosen the nut on the cable end and pull the cable end by hand until the alignment holes match. Tighten the nut. Check that the transaxle shifts and conforms to the positions of the selector lever.

THROTTLE LINKAGE ADJUSTMENT

1. Check that the throttle lever is in the curb idle position, with the engine **OFF** but at normal operating temperature.

2. At the lower cable bracket, raise the cone shaped cover to uncover a small fitting on the cable. By loosening the locknut and adjuster nut, make the distance between the fitting on the cable and the lower collar 0.040 in. ± 0.020 in.

3. With the throttle in the wide open position, check that the cable does not bind.

NOTE: Not all vehicles use a throttle linkage. The throttle position sensor on some models feeds an electric signal to the transaxle so no linkage adjustment is required. If the throttle position sensor itself needs to be adjusted, use the following procedure:

THROTTLE POSITION SENSOR ADJUSTMENT

1. Slacken the accelerator cable. Connect a digital voltmeter between terminal 19 (throttle position sensor output voltage) of the engine control unit and terminal 24 (ground).

2. Turn the ignition switch to **ON** but do not start engine. Check the output voltage. It should be 0.48–0.52 volts. If it is out of specification, loosen the mounting screws and turn the throttle position sensor. Turning clockwise increases the output voltage. Tighten screws.

3. Turn the ignition **OFF**. Remove voltmeter. Remove the battery negative cable for at least 10 seconds, then reconnect. This clears any trouble codes from the electronic system.

DETENT CABLE ADJUSTMENT

1. Several special factory tools may be required for this operation. Locate the detent switch on the transaxle. Remove the road dirt from around it. Remove the snapring and pull out the kickdown servo switch.

2. To keep the piston in the transaxle from turning, the special tool has fingers or pawls that engage the slots in the piston to hold it while adjustment is made. Do not press in on the piston with the special tool or its equal. With the piston restrained from turning, loosen the locknut. Using the special tool, tighten to 7.2 ft. lbs. (10 Nm) and return or back off the adjustment 2 times. Then tighten to 3.6 ft. lbs. (5 Nm). Finally back off the adjustment 2–2¼ turns and making sure the piston does not turn, tighten the locknut.

3. Install a new O-ring into the groove in the switch, install the switch and fit the snapring in place.

TRANSFER CASE

Transfer Case

REMOVAL & INSTALLATION

1. Disconnect the battery negative cable.
2. Raise and safely support vehicle.
3. Disconnect the front exhaust pipe.
4. Unbolt the transfer case assembly and remove by sliding it off the rear driveshaft. Be careful not to damage the oil seal in the transfer case output housing. Do not let the rear driveshaft hang. Tie up with wire. Cover the opening in the transaxle to keep oil from dripping and to keep dirt out.
To install:
5. Installation is the reverse of the removal procedure. Use care when installing the rear driveshaft to the transfer case output shaft. Tighten the transfer case to transaxle bolts to 40–43 ft. lbs.
6. Install the exhaust pipe using a new gasket.
7. Check oil levels in transaxle and transfer case.

LINKAGE ADJUSTMENT

There are 2 cables, the select cable and the shift cable.

1. On the transaxle, put select lever in **N** and move the transfer case shift lever to **N**.

2. Turn the adjuster turn buckle so the shift cable eye lines up with the eye in the select lever. When installing the cable eye, make sure the flange side of the plastic bushing at the shift cable end is on the cotter pin side.

3. The cables should be adjusted so the clearance between the shift lever and the 2 stoppers are equal when the shift lever is moved to 3rd and 4th gear. Move the shift and select levers to each position and check that the shifting is smooth.

DRIVE AXLE

Halfshaft

REMOVAL & INSTALLATION

1. Remove the cotter pin, front halfshaft nut and washer. It is recommended that the halfshaft nut be removed while the vehicle is on the floor with the brakes applied.

2. Raise and safely support vehicle. Remove lower ball joint and the tie rod end.

3. On vehicles with an inner shaft, remove the inner support bolts and spacers.

4. On vehicles with an inner shaft, remove the halfshaft by setting up a puller on the outside wheel hub and pushing the halfshaft from the front hub. Then tap the joint case with a plastic hammer to remove the halfshaft shaft and inner shaft from the transaxle.

5. On vehicles without an inner shaft, remove the halfshaft by setting up a puller on the outside wheel hub and pushing the halfshaft from the front hub. While pressing the outer shaft, insert a prybar between the transaxle case and the halfshaft and pry the shaft from the transaxle. Do not pull on the shaft. Doing so damages the inboard joint. Use the prybar. Do not insert the prybar so far the oil seal in the case is damaged.
To install:
6. Inspect the halfshaft boot for damage or deterioration. Check the ball joints and splines for wear.

7. Installation is the reverse of the removal process. When installing the wheel hub, be sure to install the washer and halfshaft nut in the proper di-

rection. After installing the wheel, lower the vehicle to the floor for final tightening. If the position of the cotter pin holes does not match up, tighten the nut up to 188 ft. lbs. maximum. Install the cotter pin and bend it securely.

CV-Boot

These vehicles used several different types of joints. Engine size, transmission type, whether the joint is an inboard or outboard joint, even which side of the vehicle is being serviced will make a difference in joint type. Proper identification is important when ordering parts. Be sure to properly identify the joint before attempting joint or boot replacement. Look for identification numbers at the big end of the boots and on the end of the metal retainer bands.

The 4 types of joints used are the Birfield Joint, (B.J.), the Tripod Joint (T.J.), the Double Offset Joint (D.O.J.) and the Rzeppa Joint (R.J.). In addition, some left hand shafts will have a round dynamic damper installed on the shaft. Special grease is generally used with these joints and is often supplied with the replacement joint and/or boot. Do not use regular chassis grease.

In most cases, a specification is called out for the distance between the

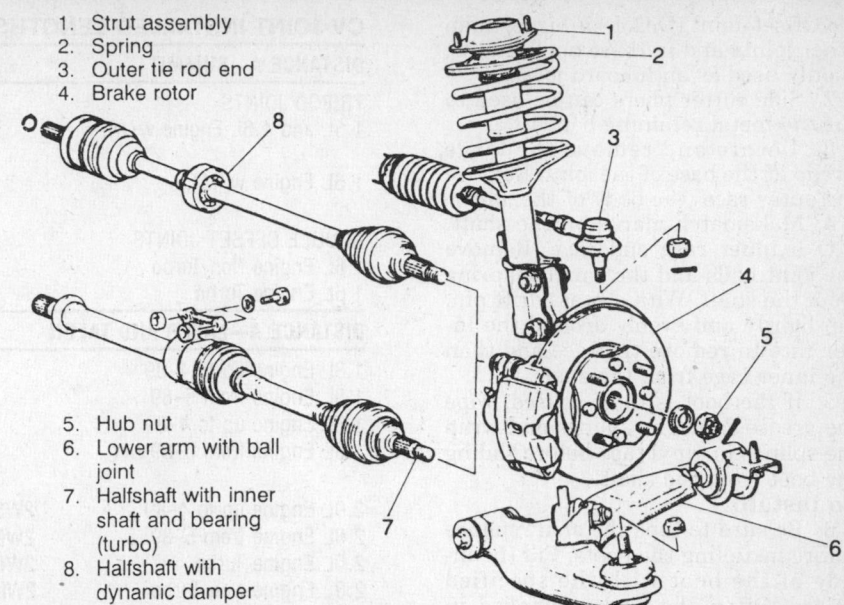

1. Strut assembly
2. Spring
3. Outer tie rod end
4. Brake rotor
5. Hub nut
6. Lower arm with ball joint
7. Halfshaft with inner shaft and bearing (turbo)
8. Halfshaft with dynamic damper

Halfshaft/CV joint removal—pry inboard joint from case, press outboard shaft from hub, tape splines to protect boot, matchmark joint parts

large and small boot bands. This is so the boot will not be installed either too loose or too tight which could cause early wear and cracking, allowing the grease to get out and water and dirt in, leading to early joint failure.

OIL SEAL

TRIPOD JOINT OR DOUBLE OFFSET JOINT

LEVER

TRANSAXLE

SCREW PRESS

MATCHMARKS

VINYL TAPE ON SPLINES

Front suspension and drive axle—typical

REMOVAL & INSTALLATION

Although joint types vary, the basic procedures are the same, with the exception of the Double Offset Joint. The following is a general procedure which should apply to most applications.

1. Remove the halfshaft.
2. Remove the snapring next to the tripod joint spider from the halfshaft with snapring pliers and remove the spider from the shaft. Do not disassemble the spider and use care in handling.
3. Side cutter pliers can be used to cut the metal retaining bands.
4. If the boot is be reused, wrap vinyl tape around the spline part of the shaft so the boot will not be damaged when removed. Remove the dynamic damper, if used, and boots from the shaft.

To install:

5. Double check that the correct replacement parts are being installed. Wrap vinyl tape around the splines to protect the boot and install the boots and damper, if used, in the correct order.
6. Fill the inside of the boot with the specified grease. Often the grease supplied in the replacement parts kit is meant to be divided in half, with half being used to lube the joint and half being used inside the boot. Keep grease off the rubber part of the dynamic damper (if used).
7. Secure the boot bands with the halfshaft horizontal.

Double Offset Joint

1. Remove the halfshaft. The Dou-

ble Offset Joint (D.O.J.) is bigger than other joints and in these applications, is only used as an inboard joint.

2. Side cutter pliers can be used to cut the metal retaining bands.

3. Locate and remove the large circlip at the base of the joint. Remove the outer race (the body of the joint).

4. Makematch marks on the shaft, D.O.J. inner race and cage. Remove the joint balls and the small snapring from the shaft. With a brass drift pin, tap lightly and evenly around the inner race to remove the race and then the inner cage from the shaft.

5. If the boot is to be reused, wipe the grease from the splines and wrap the splines in vinyl tape before sliding the boot from the shaft.

To install:

6. Be sure to tape the shaft splines before installing the boots. Fill the inside of the boot with the specified grease. Often the grease supplied in the replacement parts kit is meant to be divided in half, with half being used to lube the joint and half being used inside the boot.

7. Install the cage onto the halfshaft so the small diameter side of the cage is installed first. Align the matchmarks made at disassembly on the inner race and shaft. With a brass drift pin, tap lightly and evenly around the inner race to install the race until it comes into contact with the rib of the shaft. Apply the specified grease to the inner race and cage and fit them together aligning the matchmarks. Insert the balls into the cage.

8. Install the outer race (the body of the joint) after filling with the specified grease. The outer race should be filled with this grease.

9. Tighten the boot bands securely.

Driveshaft and U-Joints (4WD)
REMOVAL & INSTALLATION

1. Raise and safely support vehicle

2. The rear driveshaft is a 3 piece unit, with a front, center and rear propeller shaft. Remove the nuts and insulators from the support bearings. Work carefully. There will be a number of spacers which will differ from vehicle to vehicle. Check the number of spacers and write down their locations for reference during reassembly.

3. Make matchmarks on the rear differential companion flange and the rear driveshaft flange yoke. Remove the companion shaft bolts and remove the driveshaft, keeping it as straight as possible so as to ensure that the boot is not damaged or pinched. Use care to keep from damaging the oil seal in the output housing of the transfer case.

CV-JOINT INSTALLED LENGTHS
DISTANCE A—SUMMIT

TRIPOD JOINTS		
1.5L and 1.6L Engine w/AT,	LH Shaft—3.15 in.±.12 in. (80mm±3mm)	
	RH Shaft—3.35 in.±.12 in. (85mm±3mm)	
1.6L Engine w/MT,	—3.35 in.±.12 in. (80mm±3mm)	
DOUBLE OFFSET JOINTS		
1.6L Engine Non Turbo	—2.92 in.±.12 in. (75mm±3mm)	
1.6L Engine Turbo	—3.15 in.±.12 in. (80mm±3mm)	

DISTANCE A—LASER AND TALON

1.8L Engine up to 4-89	LH Shaft—3.15 in.±.12 in. (80mm±3mm)	
1.8L Engine from 5-89	LH Shaft—2.95 in.±.12 in. (75mm±3mm)	
1.8L Engine up to 4-89	RH Shaft—3.15 in.±.12 in. (80mm±3mm)	
1.8L Engine from 5-89	RH Shaft—3.35 in.±.12 in. (85mm±3mm)	
2.0L Engine up to 4-89	2WD-LH Shaft—2.95 in.±.12 in. (75mm±3mm)	
2.0L Engine from 5-89	2WD-LH Shaft—3.15 in.±.12 in. (80mm±3mm)	
2.0L Engine Turbo	2WD-LH Shaft—3.15 in.±.12 in. (80mm±3mm)	
2.0L Engine Non Turbo	2WD-RH Shaft—3.15 in.±.12 in. (80mm±3mm)	
2.0L Engine Turbo	2WD-RH Shaft—3.15 in.±.12 in. (80mm±3mm)	
2.0L Engine Non Turbo	4WD-LH Shaft—3.35 in.±.12 in. (85mm±3mm)	
2.0L Engine Non Turbo	4WD-RH Shaft—3.35 in.±.12 in. (85mm±3mm)	

① Automatic transaxle
② Manual transaxle

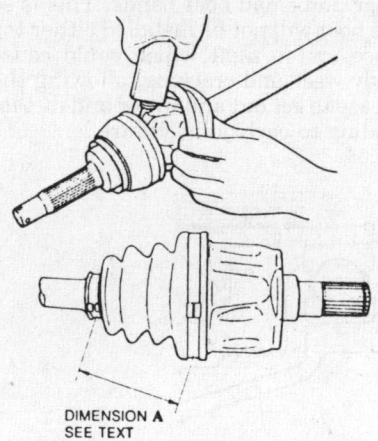

DIMENSION A
SEE TEXT

Pack with special grease, install boot and clamps, set distance A carefully

NOTE: Damage to the boot can be avoided and work will be easier, if a piece of cloth or similar material is inserted in the boot.

4. Do not lower the rear of the vehicle or oil will flow from the transfer case. Cover the opening to keep out dirt.

To install:

5. Installation is the reverse of the removal process. The shafts should be checked for staightness. A dial indicator and V-blocks set as much as possible to the end of the shaft can be used. The limit is 0.024 in. Check the bearing for smooth operation.

6. At installation, match up the companion shaft marks made at removal.

7. Install the spacers and insulators where they were before or use new spacers of equal thickness. Torque the mounting nuts to 22–29 ft. lbs.

8. Lower vehicle and test drive for signs of vibration.

Front Axle Shaft, Bearing and Seal
REMOVAL & INSTALLATION

1. Remove the hub cotter pin, axle nut and washer.

2. Raise and safely support vehicle. Remove front wheels. Remove the brake caliper and hang by a wire.

3. Remove the ball joint from the lower arm and disconnect the tie rod end.

4. Remove the halfshaft.

5. Unbolt the lower end of the strut and remove the hub and steering knuckle assembly.

6. Set up a puller with the knuckle/hub in a vise and pull the hub from the knuckle. If the hub and knuckle are disassembled by hitting them with a hammer, the bearing will be damaged.

7. Once the hub and outer bearing inner race are removed with a puller, the bearing outer races can be removed by tapping out with a brass drift pin and a hammer.

To install:

8. Apply a thin coat of grease to the outside of the outer races and install into the hub with a bearing driver.

9. Apply multi-purpose grease to

the bearings, inside surface of the hub and the lip of the grease seal. Place the outside bearing into the knuckle and install the seal with a driver.

10. The hub is assembled to the knuckle with a puller. Draw the parts together firmly to seat the bearings. Use a small torque wrench to check the bearing turning torque. It should be 11 in. lbs. or less. Check that the bearings feel smooth when rotated. A dial indicator is used to check endplay which should be 0.008 inch or less.

11. Apply a thin coat of grease to the lip of the halfshaft side axle seal and drive into place until it contacts the inner bearing outer race.

12. Installation of the hub assembly is the reverse of the removal procedure.

Pinion Seal

REMOVAL & INSTALLATION

Laser and Talon 4WD Rear Differential

1. Raise and safely support vehicle.
2. Make matchmarks on the rear driveshaft and companion flange and remove the shaft. Don't let it hang from the transaxle. Tie it up to the underbody.
3. Remove the large self-locking nut in the center of the companion flange.
4. With a suitable puller, remove the flange. Pry the old seal out.

To install:

5. Installation is the reverse of the removal process. Apply a thin coat of multi-purpose grease to the seal lip and the companion flange seal contacting surface.Install the new seal with a suitable driver. Install the companion flange. Torque the locknut to 116–160 ft. lbs.
6. Install the propeller shaft, matching up the marks made at disassembly. Torque the bolts to 40–47 ft. lbs.

Differential Carrier

REMOVAL & INSTALLATION

Laser and Talon 4WD Rear Differential

1. Raise and safely support vehicle.
2. Drain the differential gear oil and remove the center exhaust pipe.
3. Make matchmarks on the rear propeller shaft and companion flange and remove the rear driveshaft. Don't let it hang from the transaxle. Tie it up to the underbody.
4. Remove the halfshafts by unbolting the 3 bolts at the wheel hub and prying the inboard joint from the carrier housing.

5. The large mounting bolts that hold the differential carrier support plate to the underbody use self-locking nuts. Before removing them support the rear axle assembly in the middle with a suitable transaxle jack. Remove the locking nuts, then remove the support plate and the square dynamic damper from the rear of the carrier.
6. Remove the large mounting bolts and lower the differential carrier.

To install:

7. Installation is the reverse of the removal process. Clean all parts well. The large locknut that held the mounting plate to the underbody should not be reused. The replacements should be torqued to 80–94 ft. lbs.
8. Use new circlips on the inboard joints and snap into place.
9. Install the rear driveshaft, matching up the marks made at disassembly. Torque the bolts to 40–47 ft. lbs.

STEERING

Steering Wheel

REMOVAL & INSTALLATION

1. Disconnect battery negative cable.
2. Remove horn pad. Disconnect horn button connector.
3. Remove steering wheel attaching nut.
4. Make matchmarks on the steering wheel and shaft for proper installation position.
5. Using a suitable puller, remove the steering wheel.

NOTE: Do not hammer on steering wheel to remove it. The collapsible column mechanism may be damaged.

To install:

6. Position the steering wheel on shaft with mating marks aligned.
7. Install the steering wheel attaching nut and torque to 33 ft. lbs. (45 Nm).
8. Reconnect the horn button and connector. Install the horn pad.
9. Reconnect battery negative cable.

Steering Column

REMOVAL & INSTALLATION

1. Disconnect the negative battery cable.

2. Remove the instrument panel under cover.
3. Remove the trim clip, foot shower duct and lap shower duct.
4. Remove the horn pad, steering wheel and column upper and lower cover.
5. Remove the band from the steering joint cover and remove the joint assembly and gear box connecting bolt.
6. Remove the lower and upper column mounting brackets.
7. Remove the steering column assembly.
8. Installation is the reverse of the removal procedure.

Manual Steering Rack

ADJUSTMENT

1. Remove the rack and pinion asssembly.
2. Mount rack in a vise and with a small torque wrench and an adapter to connect to the input shaft, position the rack at its center. Tighten the rack support cover, the bottom plug, to 11 ft. lbs. In the neutral position, rotate the shaft clockwise 1 turn in 4–6 seconds. Return the rack support cover 30–60 degrees and adjust the torque from 0–90° – 5–11 inch lbs. and from 90–650 degrees – 2–9 inch lbs.
3. When adjusting, set to the high side of the specification. Make sure there is no ratcheting or catching when operating the rack. If the rack cannot be adjusted to spec, check the rack support cover components or replace. After adjusting, lock the rack support cover with the locking nut.

REMOVAL & INSTALLATION

Summit

1. Disconnect the battery negative cable. Raise and safely support vehicle.
2. Remove the bolt holding lower steering column joint to the rack and pinion input shaft.
3. Remove the cotter pins and disconnect the tie rod ends.
4. Remove the rack and pinion steering assembly and its rubber mounts.
5. Installation is the reverse of the removal procedure. Note that none of the self-locking should be reused. Replace with new parts. Check the steering wheel position with the front wheels straight ahead. Align the front end, if necessary.

Laser and Talon

1. Disconnect the negative battery cable. Raise and safely support vehicle.
2. Remove the bolt holding lower

steering column joint to the rack and pinion input shaft.

3. Remove the cotter pins and disconnect the tie rod ends.

4. Locate the triangular brace near the stabilizer bar brackets on the crossmember and remove both the brace and the stabilizer bar brackets.

5. Remove the through bolt from the round roll stopper and remove the rear bolts from the center crossmember.

6. Disconnect the front exhaust pipe.

7. Remove the rack and pinion steering assembly and its rubber mounts. Move the rack to the right to remove from the crossmember. Use caution to avoid damaging the boots.

8. Installation is the reverse of the removal procedure. Note that none of the self-locking should be reused. Replace with new parts. When installing the rubber rack mounts, align the projection of the mounting rubber with the indentation in the crossmember. Check the steering wheel position with the front wheels straight ahead. Align the front end, if necessary.

Power Steering Rack

ADJUSTMENT

1. Disconnect the negative battery cable.

2. Raise and support the vehicle safely.

3. Remove the steering rack assembly from the vehicle.

4. Secure the steering rack assembly in a vise. Do not clamp the vise jaws on the steering housing tubes. Clamp the vise jaws only on the housing cast metal.

5. Remove the steering gear housing end plug from the steering gear shaft bore using tool 6103 or equivalent.

6. Remove the preload adjustment cap locknut from the steering gear housing bore using tool 6097 or equivalent.

7. Loosen the preload adjustment cap. Retorque the preload adjustment cap to 45–50 inch lbs. (5–6 Nm), then back off the plug by turning it 45–50 degrees counterclockwise.

8. Secure the preload adjustment cap with a new locknut using tool 6097 or equivalent. Do not allow the adjustment cap to rotate when tightening the locknut.

9. Install the end plug using tool 6103 or equivalent. Complete installation by reversing the removal procedure.

REMOVAL & INSTALLATION

Summit

1. Disconnect the negative battery cable.

2. Raise the vehicle and support it safely.

3. Drain the power steering fluid.

4. Remove the band from the steering joint cover.

5. Remove the joint assembly and gear box connecting bolt.

6. Remove the pressure and return hoses.

7. Separate the tie rod ends from the steering knuckles.

8. Remove the gear box mounting clamps and remove the gear box assembly.

9. To install, reverse the removal procedure. Refill the system and bleed out the air. Check the steering wheel position with the front wheels straight ahead. Align the front end if necessary.

Laser and Talon

1. Disconnect the negative battery cable.

2. Raise the vehicle and support it safely.

3. Drain the power steering fluid.

4. Remove the bolt holding lower steering column joint to the rack and pinion input shaft.

5. Disconnect the return and high pressure lines from the rack assembly.

6. Remove the cotter pins and disconnect the tie rod ends.

7. Locate the triangular brace near the stabilizer bar brackets on the crossmember and remove both the brace and the stabilizer bar brackets.

8. Remove the through bolt from the round roll stopper and remove the rear bolts from the center crossmember.

9. Disconnect the front exhaust pipe.

10. Remove the rack and pinion steering assembly and its rubber mounts. Move the rack to the right to remove from the crossmember. Use caution to avoid damaging the boots.

11. Installation is the reverse of the removal procedure. Note that none of the self-locking nuts should be reused. Replace with new parts. When installing the rubber rack mounts, align the projection of the mounting rubber with the indentation in the crossmember.

12. Refill the system and bleed out the air. Check the steering wheel position with the front wheels straight ahead. Align the front end, if necessary.

Power Steering Pump

REMOVAL & INSTALLATION

1. Disconnect the battery negative cable.

2. Remove the pressure switch connector from the side of the pump.

3. Note that the alternator is located under the oil pump. Cover the alternator with a shop towel to protect it from oil. Disconnect the return fluid line. Remove the reservoir cap and allow the return line to drain the fluid from the reservoir. Disconnect the ignition high tension cable and crank the engine several times to drain the fluid from the gearbox. Disconnect the pressure line.

4. Remove the pump drive belt and unbolt the pump from its bracket.

To install:

5. Installation is the reverse of removal. Do not reuse the O-rings under the pressure line fitting. Note that when installing the high pressure line, connect the pressure line so the notch in the fitting aligns and contacts the pump's guide bracket. Refill with fluid, bleed the system.

BELT ADJUSTMENT

1. Press the belt in about the center between the power steering pump pulley and the pulley it shares, usually the water pump pulley. With reasonable pressure applied (about 22 lbs.) the belt should deflect about ¼–⅜ in.

2. Adjustment can be made by loosening the 3 bolts that hold the pump. Place a suitable bar or lever between the body of the pump and gently pry to get the desired tension.

3. Retighten the 3 bolts and check again.

SYSTEM BLEEDING

1. Raise and safely support the vehicle.

2. Manually turn the pump pulley a few times.

3. Turn the steering wheel all the way to the left and to the right 5 or 6 times.

4. Disconnect the ignition high tension cable and then, while operating the starter motor intermittently, turn the steering wheel all the way to the left and right 5–6 times for 15–20 seconds. During bleeding, make sure the fluid in the reservoir never falls below the lower position of the filter. If bleeding is attempted with the engine running, the air will be absorbed in the fluid. Bleed only while cranking.

5. Connect ignition high tension cable, start engine and allow to idle.

6. Turn the steering wheel left and

right until there are no air bubbles in the reservoir. Confirm that the fluid is not milky and the level is up to the specified position on the gauge. Confirm that there is is very little change in the fluid level when the steering wheel is turned. If the fluid level changes more than 0.2 in. the air has not been completely bled. Repeat the process.

Tie Rod Ends

REMOVAL & INSTALLATION

1. Disconnect the battery negative cable.
2. Raise and safely support vehicle.
3. Wire brush the threads on the tie rod shaft and lubricate with penetrating oil. Loosen the locknut.
4. Remove the cotter pin and nut and press the tie rod end from the steering knuckle. Hold the tie rod shaft in locking pliers and turn the tie rod end off. Counting the exact number of turns and installing the replacement tie rod end the same number of turns will put the toe-in alignment close to spec.
5. It is possible to drive the dust cover from the joint and replace the joint end. Use high quality chassis grease. Use sealer on the boot when installing.
6. Install the tie rod end. Measure from the end of the rack and pinion boot to the inner part of the tie rod end. This dimension should be:
   a. Summit with manual rack and pinion: 7.5–7.6 in. (192–194mm)
   b. Summit with power rack and pinion: 7.48–7.56 in. (190–192mm)
   c. Laser and Talon with manual rack and pinion: 7.24–7.32 in. (184–186mm)
   d. Laser and Talon 2WD with power rack and pinion: 7.22–7.30 in. (183.4–185.4mm)
   e. Lasdre and Talon 4WD with power rack and pinion: 7.07–7.15 in. (179.6–181.6mm).
7. When the tie rod is adjusted properly, lock with locking nut.
8. Reinstall tie rod ends in steering knuckle.

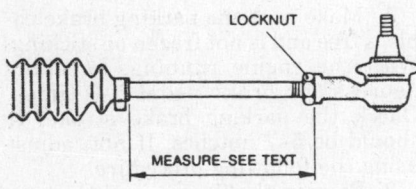

Measure this distance when installing steering rack boots

BRAKES

For all brake system repair and service procedures not detailed below, please refer to "Brakes" in the Unit Repair section.

Master Cylinder

REMOVAL & INSTALLATION

1. Disconnect battery negative cable.
2. Drain the brake fluid.
3. Disconnect the fluid level sensor connector.
4. Disconnect the brake lines. On Laser and Talon, a separate reservoir is used. Disconnect the lines from the reservoir.
5. Remove the 2 nuts securing the master cylinder and lift off.
To install:
6. Reverse the removal procedure to install. Add fluid and bleed brakes.

Proportioning Valve

REMOVAL & INSTALLATION

1. Disconnect battery negative cable.
2. On most models the proportioning valve is located on the body under the master cylinder. Disconnect and tag for proper reassembly the brake lines, disconnect the electrical connector and unbolt the valve from the body.
To install:
3. Reverse the removal procedure to install. Use care not to crossthread any connections. Tighten flared brake lines to 9–12 ft. lbs. Add fluid and bleed brakes.

Power Brake Booster

REMOVAL & INSTALLATION

1. Disconnect battery negative cable.
2. Remove master cylinder.
3. Disconnect vacuum line. Pull straight off. Prying off the vacuum hose could damage the check valve installed in the brake booster.
4. Inside the vehicle, locate and remove the cotter pin and clevis pin from the brake pedal. Then remove the nuts that secure the the booster to the bracket and remove the booster, spacer and firewall dust seals.
To install:
3. Reverse the removal procedure to install. Use a bit of grease on the clevis

pin. Refill brake fluid as required and bleed brakes if necessary.

Brake Caliper

REMOVAL & INSTALLATION

Front

1. Disconnect the battery negative cable. Raise and safely support vehicle, remove appropriate wheel assembly.
2. Drain the brake fluid.
3. Disconnect the front brake hose. Hold the nut on the brake hose side, loosen the flared brake line nut.
4. Remove the caliper lock pins and remove the caliper.
To install:
5. Reverse the removal procedure to install. Make sure the brake hose is not twisted after installation. Refill brake fluid as required and bleed brakes.

Rear

1. Disconnect battery negative cable. Raise and safely support vehicle, remove appropriate wheel assembly.
2. Drain the brake fluid.
3. Disconnect the parking brake cable and the rear brake hose. Hold the nut on the brake hose side, loosen the flared brake line nut.
4. Remove the rear caliper assembly.
To install:
5. Reverse the removal procedure to install. Make sure the brake hose is not twisted after installation. Refill brake fluid as required and bleed brakes. Adjust parking brake if required.

Disc Brake Pads

REMOVAL & INSTALLATION

1. Disconnect battery negative cable.
2. Raise and safely support vehicle.
3. Remove appropriate wheel assembly.
4. Remove the caliper from its bracket. Do not disconnect the brake line. Do not allow the caliper to hang by the brake line. Take note of the clips, pins, anti-squeak shims and other parts that are installed for assembly reference. These will vary from model to model.
5. On vehicles with rear disc brakes, loosen the parking brake cable from inside the car and disconnect the parking brake end from the rear caliper.
To install:
6. Reverse the removal procedure to install. Check for fluid contamination that might indicate leaking caliper seals.

7. Always replace disc brake pads in complete sets of 4. The limit for lining wear is 0.080 in. of lining remaining. On rear disc brake caliper, a special tool may be needed to retract the piston due to the parking brake mechanism. Note that these rear disc pads should have a projection on the back side of the shoe that fits into the rear caliper piston.

8. Make sure the brake hose is not twisted after installation.

9. Refill brake fluid as required and bleed brakes. Adjust parking brake, if required.

Brake Rotor

REMOVAL & INSTALLATION

Front

1. Loosen the large driveshaft nut while the vehicle is still on the ground with the brakes applied. Then raise and safely support vehicle. Remove appropriate wheel assembly.

2. Remove the caliper from its bracket. Do not disconnect the brake line. Do not allow the caliper to hang by the brake line.

3. Remove the lower ball joint connection and the tie rod end.

4. Remove the halfshaft.

5. Remove the bolts from the lower strut and separate the hub/rotor assembly.

6. A puller can be set up to separate the hub from the knuckle freeing the rotor.

To install:

7. Installation is the reverse of the removal process. When installing the wheel hub, be sure to install the washer and halfshaft nut in the proper direction. After installing the wheel, lower the vehicle to the floor for final tightening. If the position of the cotter pin holes does not match up, tighten the nut up to 188 ft. lbs. maximum. Install the cotter pin and bend it securely.

Rear

1. Raise and safely support vehicle, remove appropriate wheel assembly.

2. Disconnect the parking brake cable. Remove the caliper from its bracket. Do not disconnect the brake line. Do not allow the caliper to hang by the brake line.

3. The rotor is held to the hub by 2 small bolts. Remove the bolts and pull off the rotor.

To install:

4. Installation is the reverse of the removal process.

Brake Drums

REMOVAL & INSTALLATION

1. Raise and safely support vehicle, remove appropriate wheel assembly.

2. Remove the grease cap and remove the center wheel bearing nut.

3. Remove the outer bearing and brake drum assembly.

To install:

4. Installation is the reverse of the removal process. Check the drum inside diameter. The wear limit is 7.20 in. (182mm). Inspect the rear hub nut. Replace if unuseable.

Brake Shoes

REMOVAL & INSTALLATION

1. Raise and safely support vehicle, remove appropriate wheel assembly.

2. Remove the brake drum.

3. Take note of the springs and clips for proper reassembly. Remove the shoe hold-down clips and remove the shoes.

To install:

4. Installation is the reverse of the removal process. Whenever the brake shoes are serviced, always replace both left and right assemblies to prevent the car from pulling under braking.

5. Check the lining thickness. If there is a big difference in wear thickness, check for a sticking or siezed brake cylinder piston.

6. Apply a touch of multi-purpose grease to the shoe and backing plate contact surfaces, the brake adjuster, the shoe and anchor plate contact surfaces and the piston ends. A touch of sealer can be applied to the shoe hold-downpins on the back of the backing plate.

7. Inspect the rear hub nut. Replace if unuseable.

Wheel Cylinder

REMOVAL & INSTALLATION

1. Disconnect battery negative cable. Then raise and safely support vehicle, remove appropriate wheel assembly.

2. Remove the brake drum.

3. Take note of the springs and clips for proper reassembly. Remove the shoe hold-down clips and remove the shoes.

4. Remove the brake line and unbolt the wheel cylinder.

To install:

5. Installation is the reverse of the removal procedure. Apply some sealer to the back of the wheel cylinder before putting in place on the backing

plate. Inspect the rear hub nut. Replace if unuseable.

Parking Brake Cable

ADJUSTMENT

Rear Drum Brakes

1. Make sure the parking brake cable is free and is not frozen or sticking. With the engine running, forcefully depress the brake pedal 5–6 times. Check the parking brake stroke. It should be 5–7 notches. If not, adjust using the following procedure.

2. Remove the floor console by prying out the coin holder, box tray and remote mirror switch or if not so equipped, the cover. Remove the small cover around the seat belt from the console side. The console is in 2 pieces. Remove the screws from the center section and remove the rear part of the console.

3. Loosen the locknut then loosen the adjusting to the end of the cable and free the parking brake cable. Repeat the procedure to pull the parking brake lever back with a force of about 44 lbs. until the lever stoke ceases to change. If the lever stroke does not change, the automatic adjustment mechanism is functioning normally and the clearance between the shoe and drum is correct.

4. Rotate the adjusting nut to adjust the parking brake stroke to the 5–7 notch setting. After making the adjustment check there is no looseness between the adjusting nut and the parking brake lever, then tighten the locknut.

NOTE: Do not adjust the parking brake too tight. If the number of notches is less than specification, the cable has been pulled too much and the automatic adjuster will fail. Use the 5–7 notch specification.

5. After adjusting the lever stroke, jack up the rear of the vehicle. With the parking brake lever in the released position, turn the rear wheel to confirm that the rear brakes are not dragging.

Rear Disc Brakes

1. Make sure the parking brake cable is free and is not frozen or sticking. With the engine running, forcefully depress the brake pedal 5–6 times. Check the parking brake stroke. It should be 5–7 notches. If not, adjust using the following procedure.

2. Remove the floor console by prying out the coin holder, box tray, and remote mirror switch, or if not so equipped, the cover. Remove the small

cover around the seat belt from the console side. The console is in 2 pieces. Remove the screws from the center section and remove the rear part of the console.

3. Loosen the locknut then loosen the adjusting to the end of the cable and free the parking brake cable. Repeat the procedure to pull the parking brake lever back with a force of about 44 lbs. until the lever stoke ceases to change. If the lever stroke does not change, the automatic adjustment mechanism is functioning normally and the clearance between the shoe and drum is correct.

4. Check to be sure the distance between the stopper and the parking brake lever at the caliper side is 0.078 in. (2 mm) or less. If the clearance between the parking lever (on the caliper) and the stopper exceeds 0.078 in., the probable causes are brake cable sticking, improper cable installation or a malfunction of the automatic adjuster in the caliper which will require disassembling the caliper.

5. Turn the adjusting nut to get the brake lever stroke to spec, 5–7 notches.

NOTE: Do not adjust the parking brake too tight. If the number of notches is less than spec., the cable has been pulled too much and the automatic adjuster will fail. Use the 5–7 notch specification.

6. After making the adjustment, check to be sure there is no play between the adjusting nut and the parking brake lever, then tighten the locknut. After adjusting the lever stroke, jack up the rear of the vehicle. With the parking brake lever in the released position, turn the rear wheel to confirm that the rear brakes are not dragging.

REMOVAL & INSTALLATION

1. Remove the floor console by prying out the coin holder, box tray and remote mirror switch, if so equipped, or the cover. Remove the small cover around the seat belt from the console side. The console is in 2 pieces. Remove the screws from the center section and remove the rear part of the console.

2. Remove the rear seat cushion by pulling the 2 levers at floor level and removing the seat cushion.

3. Remove the center cable clamp and grommet.

4. Raise and safely support vehicle.

5. At the rear wheel, remove the brake drum and disconnect the cable end from the parking brake strut lever and the snap ring which retains the cable to the back plate (rear drum brakes) or cable end and clip (rear disc brakes). Unfasten any other frame retainers and remove the cables.

To install:

6. Installation is the reverse of the removal procedure. Check parking brake adjustment and adjust as required.

Brake System Bleeding

System Dry

1. If the master cylinder is dry, disconnect the brake tube from the master cylinder.

2. With an assistant, have one person slowly depressing the brake pedal and holding it down. The other person should use a finger to close the outlet port of the master cylinder and then the first person should release the pedal. Repeat these steps 3 or 4 times. Keep the cylinder full of brake fluid. This operation bleeds the master cylinder.

3. Connect the brake tube to the master cylinder.

4. Start the engine. Using the bleeder screws are the calipers and wheel cylinders, bleed the brakes at the wheels in the following sequence: Right Rear, Left Front, Left Rear, Right Front.

5. Do not allow the master cylinder reservoir to run out of fluid.

Normal Service Bleeding

1. Press the brake pedal several times until resistance is felt.

2. With the brake pedal depressed, loosen the bleeder screw ⅓–½ turn and then tighten it before the fluid pressure is gone.

3. Release the brake pedal. Repeat this procedure until there are no more air bubbles in the brake fluid.

FRONT SUSPENSION

MacPherson Strut

REMOVAL & INSTALLATION

1. Raise and safely support vehicle.

2. Remove the brake hose and tube bracket. Do not pry the brake hose and tube clamp away when removing it.

3. Remove the strut lower bolts. Support the lower arm with a jack. Use a piece of wire to suspend the knuckle to keep the weight off the brake hose.

4. Before removing the top bolts, make matchmarks on the body and the strut insulator for proper reassembly. If this plate is installed improperly, the wheel alignment will be wrong. Remove the strut upper bolts and pull the strut/spring from the vehicle.

To install:

5. Inspect the strut for signs of oil leakage or damage. Installation is the reverse of the removal process. Check that the top plate is properly installed or alignment will be affected. Torque the strut to knuckle bolts to 80–94 ft. lbs.

Lower Ball Joints

INSPECTION

The lower ball joints on these vehicles cannot be removed. If defective, the entire lower arm must be replaced. The ball joints can be checked using the following procedure:

1. Raise and safely support vehicle.

2. Remove the stabilizer link.

3. Remove the ball joint locknut.

4. Remove the lower arm front and rear bolts. Separate the lower arm from the steering knuckle.

5. If the ball joint boot is cracked, replace the cover, adding grease. Wiggle the ball joint a few times to make sure it is free. Double-nut the stud and use a torque wrench to measure how much torque is required to turn it. Starting torque should be 48 inch lbs. or less. If it takes more than this to turn the joint, replace the lower arm assembly. If the torque is substantially less, it may still be reused unless it has excessive play.

6. New covers can be installed using a large socket for a driver.

Sway Bar

REMOVAL & INSTALLATION

Two types of sway or stabilizer bars have been used: a conventional rubber bushing type and a ball stud type.

1. Raise and safely support vehicle.

2. Remove the tie rod end from the steering knuckle.

3. Remove the center crossmember rear bolts.

4. Remove the stabilizer link bolts. On the ball stud type, hold ball stud with a hex wrench and remove the self-locking nut with a box wrench.

5. Remove the stabilizer bar mounts and drop the bar from the vehicle. Note that some vehicles will have an access opening, the steering rack access opening, through which the bar can be removed.

To install:

6. Installation is the reverse of the removal process. Note that the bar brackets are left hand and right hand. Assemble properly.

Front Wheel Bearings

These vehicles are all front or all-wheel drive. Please refer to the Drive Axle section for bearing information.

REAR SUSPENSION

MacPherson Strut

REMOVAL & INSTALLATION

1. Remove the trim panel inside the trunk area for access to the top mounting nuts.
2. Remove the top cap and mounting nuts.
3. Raise and safely support vehicle.
4. On Laser and Talon, first remove the brake tube bracket bolt, then remove the shock absorber lower mounting bolt and remove the shock absorber/spring assembly from the vehicle.

To install:

5. Installation is the reverse of the removal procedure. It is recommended that the self-locking nuts used at the top and bottom mount not be reused, but replaced.

Rear Control Arms

REMOVAL & INSTALLATION

These vehicles use a rear beam axle with the exception of Laser and Talon 4WD models which use an independent rear suspension. These lower control arms can be removed with the following procedure:

1. Raise and safely support vehicle.
2. Remove the locknut for the lower arm ball joint.
3. Remove the rear stabilizer bar link to the lower arm.
4. Remove the inboard lower arm pivot bolt and separate the arm from the vehicle.

To install:

5. Installation is the reverse of the removal procedure. It is recommended that the self-locking nuts not be reused, but replaced. Torque the inboard pivot bolt and nut to 65–80 ft. lbs., and the ball joint stud nut to 43–52 ft. lbs.

Rear Wheel Bearing

REMOVAL & INSTALLATION

1. Raise and safely support vehicle.
2. Remove appropriate wheel and grease cap, if used. Remove the hub locking nut and remove the outer wheel bearing. Pull off the brake drum, or hub if rear disc, and remove the inner bearing.

To install:

3. Installation is the reverse of the removal procedure. Lube the wheel bearings with good quality wheel bearing grease. A new seal should be installed. It is recommended that the self-locking nut not be reused, but replaced. Fill the grease cap with wheel bearing grease.

ADJUSTMENT

1. Raise and safely support vehicle.
2. Remove appropriate wheel and grease cap, if used. Release the parking brake lever. On vehicles with disc brakes, remove the caliper assembly and brake rotor.
3. Set up a dial indicator and measure the endplay while moving the hub or drum in and out. If the endplay exceeds the limit of 0.004 inch for Laser and Talon, 0.008 inch for Summit, retighten the locknut. Torque should be 144–188 ft. lbs. for Laser and Talon, 108–145 ft. lbs. for Summit. Recheck. If the endplay is still beyond the limit, replace the wheel bearing.

Rear Axle Assembly

REMOVAL & INSTALLATION

Summit Torsion Axle and Arm Assembly

REAR DRUM BRAKES

1. Raise the vehicle and support it safely.
2. Remove the rear wheels.
3. Remove the hub cap, wheel bearing nut and outer wheel bearing inner race.
4. Remove the rear brake drum, parking brake cable, brake hose and tube bracket.
5. Remove the lateral rod mounting bolt and nut and secure the lateral rod to the axle beam with a piece of wire.
6. Place a wooden block on a jack and slightly raise the torsion axle and arm assembly. Remove the cap and upper mounting nuts from the shock absorber.
7. Remove the trailing arm bolts and remove the rear suspension assembly.

8. To install, reverse the removal procedure. Adjust the parking brake.

REAR DISC BRAKES

1. Raise the vehicle and support it safely.
2. Remove the parking brake cable, brake hose and tube bracket.
3. Remove the rear disc brake, hub cap and wheel bearing nut.
4. Remove the outer wheel bearing inner race, rear hub assembly, dust shield and brake adapter.
5. Remove the lateral rod mounting bolt and nut and secure the lateral rod to the axle beam with a piece of wire.
6. Place a wooden block on a jack and slightly raise the torsion axle and arm assembly. Remove the cap and upper mounting nuts from the shock absorber.
7. Remove the trailing arm bolts and remove the rear suspension assembly.
8. To install, reverse the removal procedure. Adjust the parking brake.

Laser and Talon 2WD

1. Raise the vehicle and support it safely.
2. Remove the parking brake hose and tube racket.
3. Remove the rear caliper and hang from piece of wire. Remove brake rotor.
4. Remove the dust cap, wheel bearing nut, washer, rear hub assembly and dust shield.
5. Remove the lateral rod mounting bolt and nut.
6. Place a wooden block on a jack and slightly raise the torsion axle and arm assembly. Jack in the center and make sure the jack doesn't contact the lateral rod. Remove the bolts from the shock absorber.
7. Remove the trailing arm bolts and lower the jack slowly. Remove the rear torsion axle and arm assembly.
8. To install, reverse the removal procedure. Torque the spindle nut to 144–188 ft. lbs., align with the spindle's indentation and crimp in place. Adjust the parking brake.

Laser and Talon 4WD

1. Remove the interior trim over the top of the shock absorber to gain access to the top shock absorber installation nuts. Remove these 2 nuts.
2. Raise the vehicle and support it safely.
3. Remove the parking brake cable, brake hose and tube bracket.
4. Remove the rear caliper and hang from piece of wire. Remove brake rotor. Note that the caliper lock pin has a special grease on it that should not be

wiped off. This grease helps the lock pin stay clean. After removing the caliper, cover the pin with a cloth.

5. Remove the center exhaust pipe and gaskets.

6. Place matchmarks on the rear driveshaft flange and the axle companion flange. Remove the driveshaft from the rear companion flange.

7. The large mounting bolts use self-locking nuts. Before removing them support the rear axle assembly in the middle with a suitable transaxle jack. Remove the locking nuts, then remove the support plate.

8. Remove the small brackets at the front of the crossmember assembly.

9. Remove the parking brake cable installation bolt. It will probably be necessary to lower the transaxle jack slightly. After this bolt is removed, lower the transaxle assembly.

CAUTION

The lowering of the rear suspension assembly and removing it from the transmission jack to the bench or floor requires 3 individuals due to the amount of weight being handled. One technician should hold the differential and one on either side of the lower arm. Use care. Should the assembly shift, personal injury could result. When lowering the assembly to the floor or bench, place wood blocks under the rear suspension as-

sembly ball joints to avoid damaging the brake dust shields.

10. Move the assembly toward the rear (in the direction of the fuel tank) and gradually lower the jack. Avoid hitting the stabilizer bar and the driveshaft.

To install:

10. Check the crossmember for crack or other damage.

11. Installation is the reverse of the removal procedure. Make sure to match the marks on the driveshaft and companion flange. When connecting the parking brake cable end to the parking brake lever prying up on the end will make installation easier.

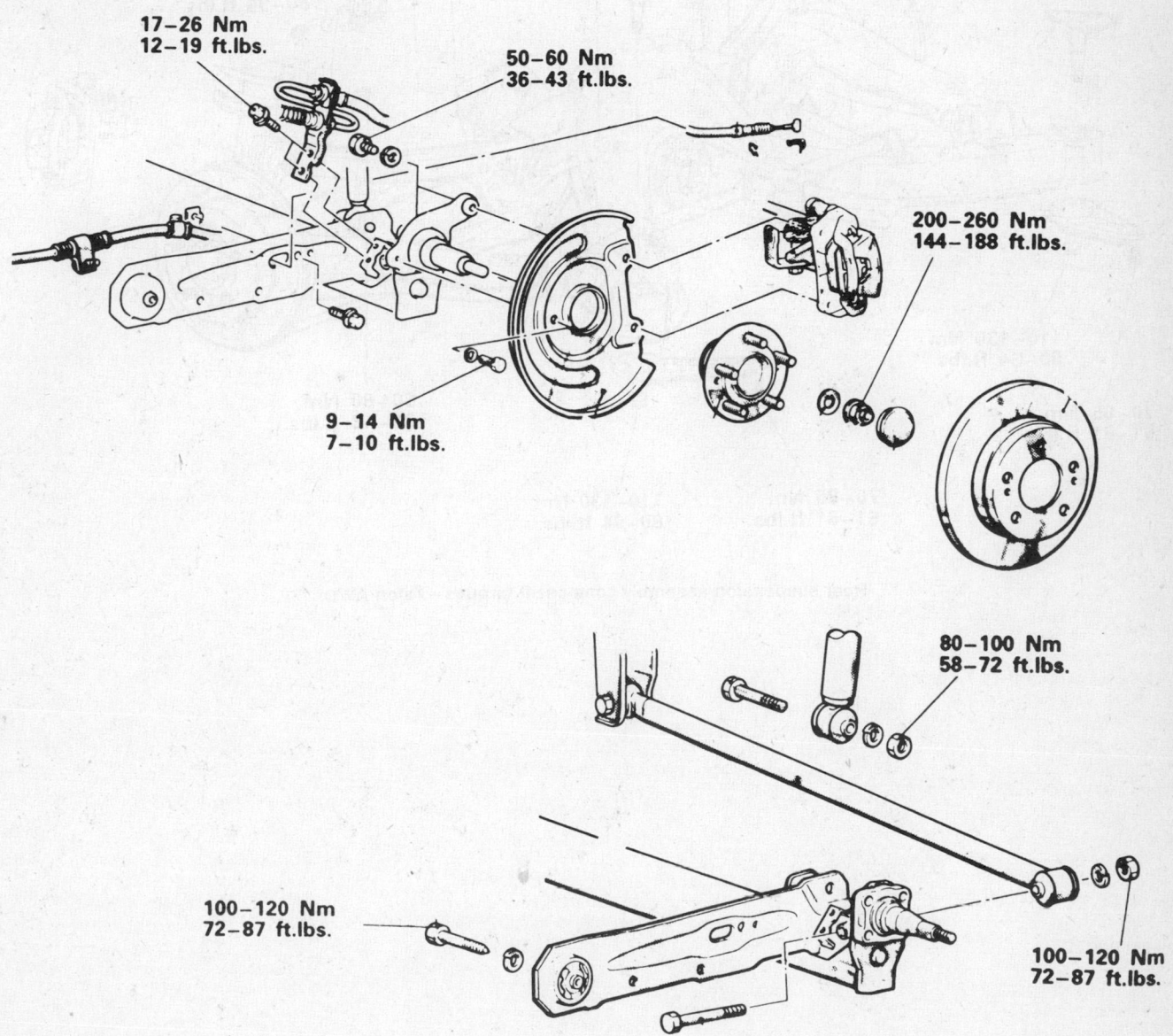

17–26 Nm
12–19 ft.lbs.

50–60 Nm
36–43 ft.lbs.

200–260 Nm
144–188 ft.lbs.

9–14 Nm
7–10 ft.lbs.

80–100 Nm
58–72 ft.lbs.

100–120 Nm
72–87 ft.lbs.

100–120 Nm
72–87 ft.lbs.

Rear suspension assembly component torques—Talon

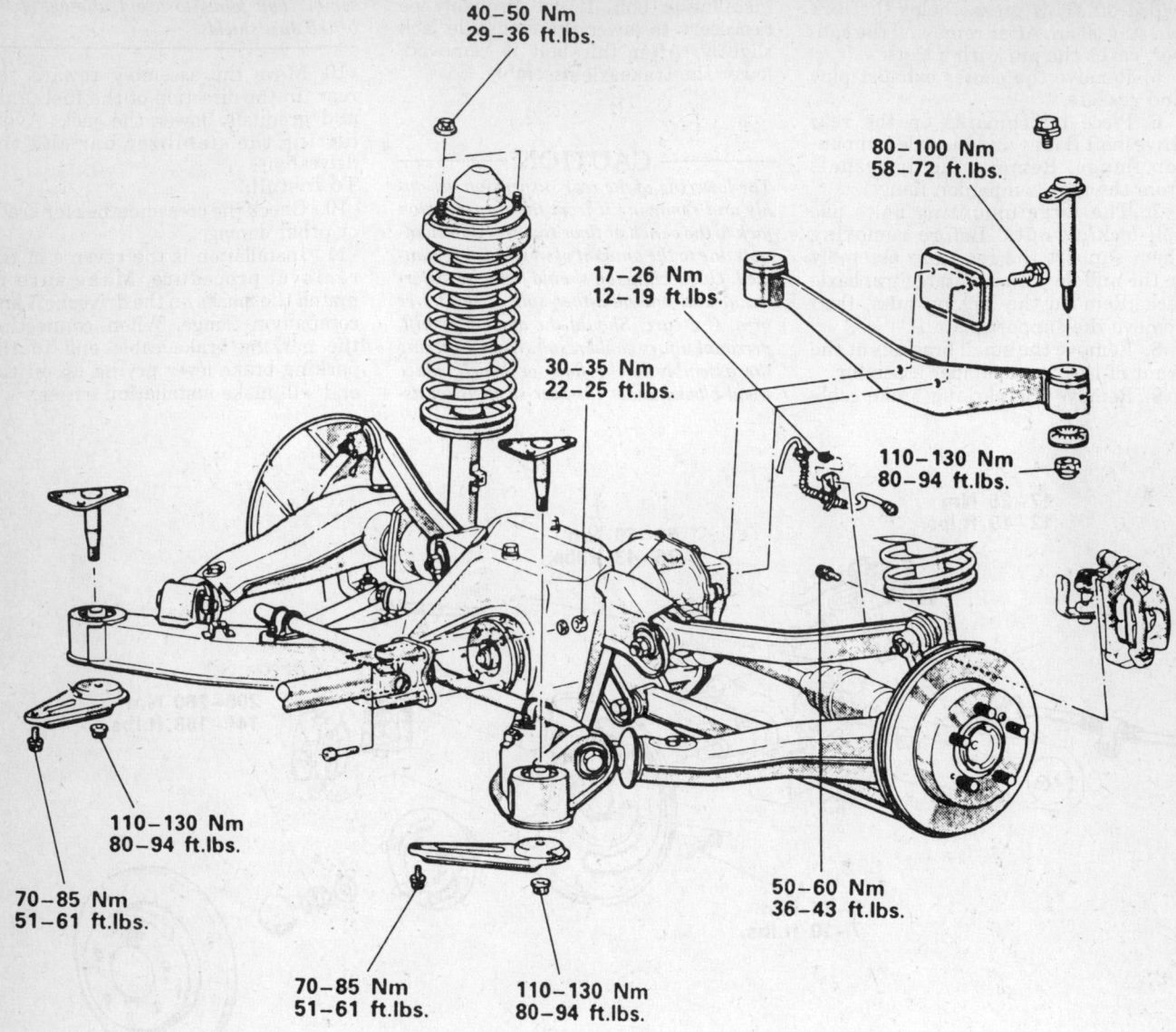

40–50 Nm
29–36 ft.lbs.

80–100 Nm
58–72 ft.lbs.

17–26 Nm
12–19 ft.lbs.

30–35 Nm
22–25 ft.lbs.

110–130 Nm
80–94 ft.lbs.

110–130 Nm
80–94 ft.lbs.

70–85 Nm
51–61 ft.lbs.

70–85 Nm
51–61 ft.lbs.

110–130 Nm
80–94 ft.lbs.

50–60 Nm
36–43 ft.lbs.

Rear suspension assembly component torques—Talon AWD

Chrysler/Eagle
Front Wheel Drive
Medallion/Monaco/Premier

SPECIFICATIONS

1988

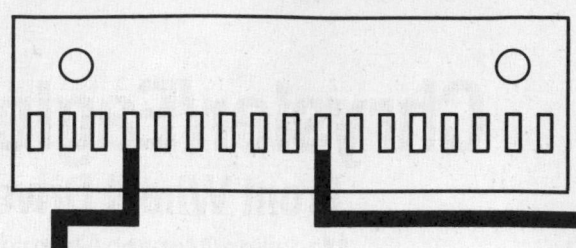

Engine Code					
Code	Cu. In.	Liters	Cyl.	Fuel Sys.	Eng. Mfg.
F	132	2.2	4	MPI	Renault
Z	150	2.5	4	TBI	AMC
J	182	3.0	6	MPI	Renault

Model Year	
Code	Year
J	1988

1989-91

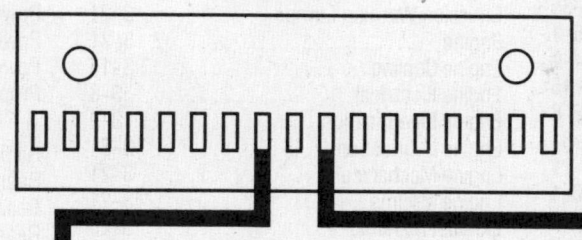

Engine Code					
Code	Cu. In.	Liters	Cyl.	Fuel Sys.	Eng. Mfg.
F	132	2.2	4	MPI	Renault
H	150	2.5	4	TBI	AMC
U	182	3.0	6	MPI	Renault

Model Year	
Code	Year
K	1989
L	1990
M	1991

ENGINE IDENTIFICATION

Year	Model	Engine Displacement cu. in. (liter)	Engine Series Identification (VIN)	No. of Cylinders	Engine Type
1988	Medallion	4-132 (2.2)	F	4	SOHC
	Premier	4-150 (2.5)	Z	4	OHV
	Premier	6-182 (3.0)	J	6	SOHC
1989	Medallion	4-132 (2.2)	F	4	SOHC
	Premier	4-150 (2.5)	H	4	OHV
	Premier	6-182 (3.0)	U	6	SOHC
1990-91	Premier	4-150 (2.5)	H	4	OHV
	Premier	6-182 (3.0)	U	6	SOHC
	Monaco	4-150 (2.5)	H	4	OHV
	Monaco	6-182 (3.0)	U	6	SOHC

OHV Overhead Valve Engine
SOHC Single Overhead Cam Engine

GENERAL ENGINE SPECIFICATIONS

Year	VIN	No. Cylinder Displacement cu. in. (liter)	Fuel System Type	Net Horsepower @ rpm	Net Torque @ rpm (ft. lbs.)	Bore × Stroke (in.)	Compression Ratio	Oil Pressure @ rpm
1988	F	4-132 (2.2)	MPI	103 @ 5000	124 @ 2500	3.46 × 3.50	9.2:1	44 @ 3000
	Z	4-150 (2.5)	TBI	111 @ 4750	142 @ 2500	3.87 × 3.18	9.2:1	55 @ 3500
	J	6-182 (3.0)	MPI	150 @ 5000	171 @ 3750	3.66 × 2.87	9.3:1	60 @ 4000
1989	F	4-132 (2.2)	MPI	103 @ 5000	124 @ 2500	3.46 × 3.50	9.2:1	44 @ 3000
	H	4-150 (2.5)	TBI	111 @ 4750	142 @ 2500	3.88 × 3.19	9.2:1	37–75 @ 1600
	U	6-182 (3.0)	MPI	150 @ 5000	171 @ 3750	3.66 × 2.87	9.3:1	60 @ 4000
1990–91	H	4-150 (2.5)	TBI	111 @ 4750	142 @ 2500	3.88 × 3.19	9.2:1	37–75 @ 1600
	U	6-182 (3.0)	MPI	150 @ 5000	171 @ 3750	3.66 × 2.87	9.3:1	60 @ 4000

MPI Multiport Injection
TBI Throttle Body Injection

GASOLINE ENGINE TUNE-UP SPECIFICATIONS

Year	VIN	No. Cylinder Displacement cu. in. (liter)	Spark Plugs Type	Gap (in.)	Ignition Timing (deg.) MT	AT	Compression Pressure (psi)	Fuel Pump (psi)	Idle Speed (rpm) MT	AT	Valve Clearance (in.) In.	Ex.
1988	F	4-132 (2.2)	RS9YC	0.035	①	①	②	34–36	800	700	0.006	0.008
	Z	4-150 (2.5)	RC12LYC	0.035	①	①	②	14–15	—	750	Hyd.	Hyd.
	J	6-182 (3.0)	RS9YC	0.035	①	①	②	36–37	—	800	Hyd.	Hyd.
1989	F	4-132 (2.2)	RS9YC	0.035	①	①	②	34–36	800	700	0.006	0.008
	H	4-150 (2.5)	RN12LYC	0.035	①	①	②	14–15	①	①	Hyd.	Hyd.
	U	6-182 (3.0)	RS9YC	0.035	①	①	②	28–30	①	①	Hyd.	Hyd.
1990–91	H	4-150 (2.5)	RC12LYC	0.035	①	①	②	14–15	①	①	Hyd.	Hyd.
	U	6-182 (3.0)	RS9YCX	0.035	①	①	②	28–30	①	①	Hyd.	Hyd.

① Refer to Underhood Sticker
② The lowest reading should be no less than 75% of the highest reading.

FIRING ORDERS

NOTE: To avoid confusion, always replace spark plugs and wires one at a time.

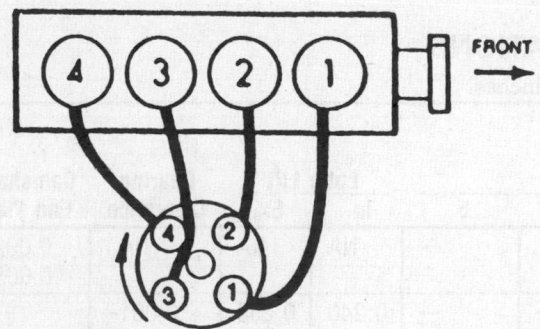

2.5L Engine
Engine Firing Order: 1–3–4–2
Distributor Rotation: Clockwise

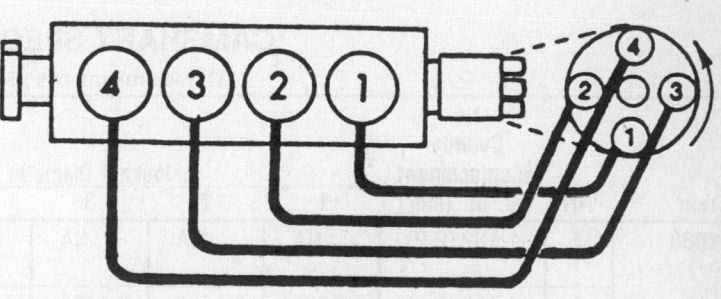

2.2L Engine
Engine Firing Order: 1–3–4–2
Distributor Rotation: Counterclockwise

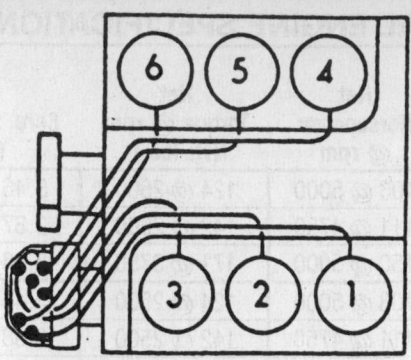

3.0L Engine
Engine Firing Order: 1–6–3–5–2–4
Distributor Rotation: Counterclockwise

CAPACITIES

Year	Model	VIN	No. Cylinder Displacement cu. in. (liter)	Engine Crankcase (qts.) with Filter	Engine Crankcase (qts.) without Filter	Transmission (pts.) 4-Spd	Transmission (pts.) 5-Spd	Transmission (pts.) Auto.	Drive Axle (pts.)	Fuel Tank (gal.)	Cooling System (qts.)
1988	Medallion	F	4-132 (2.2)	5.25	4.75	4.8	—	12.8 ②	—	17	7.0
	Premier	Z	4-150 (2.5)	5.0	4.5	—	—	14.8 ②	1.32 ①	17	8.6
	Premier	J	6-182 (3.0)	6.0	5.5	—	—	14.8 ②	1.32 ①	17	8.6
1989	Medallion	F	4-132 (2.2)	5.0	4.5	4.8	—	12.8 ②	—	17	7.0
	Premier	H	4-150 (2.5)	5.0	4.5	—	—	14.8 ②	1.32 ①	17	8.6
	Premier	U	6-182 (3.0)	6.0	5.5	—	—	14.8 ②	1.32 ①	17	8.6
1990–91	Premier	H	4-150 (2.5)	5.0	4.5	—	—	②③	1.32 ①	17	8.6
	Monaco	U	6-182 (3.0)	6.0	5.5	—	—	②③	1.32 ①	17	8.6

① Differential requires a synthetic-type SAE grade 75W-140 gear lubricant. It is the only lubricant recommended. It is factory filled and designed to last the life of the differential under normal conditions. Periodic lubricant changes are not required.

② Use Mopar Mercon automatic transmission fluid only. This is the only fluid to be used in the ZF-4 transmission. Do not substitute any other type of fluid.

③ 1990–91 ZF-4 four speed automatic: 14.75 pts. Refill 5.5 pts. after fluid/filter change

CAMSHAFT SPECIFICATIONS
All measurements given in inches.

Year	VIN	No. Cylinder Displacement cu. in. (liter)	Journal Diameter 1	Journal Diameter 2	Journal Diameter 3	Journal Diameter 4	Journal Diameter 5	Lobe Lift In.	Lobe Lift Ex.	Bearing Clearance	Camshaft End Play
1988	F	4-132 (2.2)	NA	NA	NA	NA	—	NA	NA	NA	0.002–0.005
	Z	4-150 (2.5)	2.0290–2.0300	2.0190–2.0200	2.0090–2.0100	1.9990–2.0000	—	0.240	0.250	0.001–0.003	—
	J	6-182 (3.0)	NA	NA	NA	NA	—	NA	NA	NA	0.003–0.0055

CAMSHAFT SPECIFICATIONS

All measurements given in inches.

Year	VIN	No. Cylinder Displacement cu. in. (liter)	Journal Diameter					Lobe Lift		Bearing Clearance	Camshaft End Play
			1	2	3	4	5	In.	Ex.		
1989	F	4-132 (2.2)	NA	NA	NA	NA	—	NA	NA	NA	0.002–0.005
	H	4-150 (2.5)	2.0290–2.0300	2.0190–2.0200	2.0090–2.0100	1.9990–2.0000	—	0.240	0.250	0.001–0.003	—
	U	6-182 (3.0)	NA	NA	NA	NA	—	NA	NA	NA	0.003–0.0055
1990–91	H	4-150 (2.5)	2.0290–2.0300	2.0190–2.0200	2.0090–2.0100	1.9990–2.0000	—	0.240	0.250	0.001–0.003	—
	U	6-182 (3.0)	NA	NA	NA	NA	—	NA	NA	NA	0.003–0.0055

NA Not Available

CRANKSHAFT AND CONNECTING ROD SPECIFICATIONS

All measurements are given in inches.

Year	VIN	No. Cylinder Displacement cu. in. (liter)	Crankshaft				Connecting Rod		
			Main Brg. Journal Dia.	Main Brg. Oil Clearance	Shaft End-play	Thrust on No.	Journal Diameter	Oil Clearance	Side Clearance
1988	F	4-132 (2.2)	2.4660–2.4760	0.0015–0.0035	0.002–0.009	1	2.206–2.216	0.0008–0.0030	0.012–0.022
	Z	4-150 (2.5)	2.4996–2.5001	0.0020	0.002–0.007	2	2.0934–2.0955	0.0015–0.0020	0.010–0.019
	J	6-182 (3.0)	2.7576–2.7583	0.0015–0.0035	0.003–0.010	1	2.3611–2.3618	0.0008–0.0030	0.008–0.015
1989	F	4-132 (2.2)	2.4760	0.0015–0.0035	0.005–0.011	1	2.206–2.216	0.0008–0.0030	0.012–0.022
	H	4-150 (2.5)	2.4996–2.5001	0.0020	0.002–0.007	2	2.0934–2.0955	0.0015–0.0020	0.010–0.019
	U	6-182 (3.0)	2.7576–2.7583	0.0015–0.0035	0.002–0.007	1	2.3611–2.3618	0.0008–0.0030	0.008–0.015
1990–91	H	4-150 (2.5)	2.4996–2.5001	0.0020	0.002–0.007	2	2.0934–2.0955	0.0015–0.0020	0.010–0.019
	U	6-182 (3.0)	2.7576–2.7583	0.0015–0.0035	0.002–0.007	1	2.3611–2.3618	0.0008–0.0030	0.008–0.015

VALVE SPECIFICATIONS

Year	VIN	No. Cylinder Displacement cu. in. (liter)	Seat Angle (deg.)	Face Angle (deg.)	Spring Test Pressure (lbs.)	Spring Installed Height (in.)	Stem-to-Guide Clearance (in.)		Stem Diameter (in.)	
							Intake	Exhaust	Intake	Exhaust
1988	F	4-132 (2.2)	②	②	NA	NA	0.004	0.004	0.315	0.315
	Z	4-150 (2.5)	45	45	200 @ 1.216	1¹¹/₁₆	0.001–0.003	0.001–0.003	0.312	0.312
	J	6-182 (3.0)	45	45	155 @ 1.220	1¹³/₁₆	NA	NA	0.315	0.315

VALVE SPECIFICATIONS

Year	VIN	No. Cylinder Displacement cu. in. (liter)	Seat Angle (deg.)	Face Angle (deg.)	Spring Test Pressure (lbs.)	Spring Installed Height (in.)	Stem-to-Guide Clearance (in.)		Stem Diameter (in.)	
							Intake	Exhaust	Intake	Exhaust
1989	F	4-132 (2.2)	②	②	NA	NA	0.004	0.004	0.315	0.315
	H	4-150 (2.5)	①	45	200 @ 1.21	1 11/16	0.001– 0.003	0.001– 0.003	0.311– 0.312	0.311– 0.312
	U	6-182 (3.0)	45	45	155 @ 1.220	1 13/16	NA	NA	0.315	0.315
1990–91	H	4-150 (2.5)	①	45	200 @ 1.21	1 11/16	0.001– 0.003	0.001– 0.003	0.311– 0.312	0.311– 0.312
	U	6-182 (3.0)	45	45	155 @ 1.220	1 13/16	NA	NA	0.315	0.315

NA Not Available
① Intake—44.5
　Exhaust—40.5
② Intake—60
　Exhaust—45

PISTON AND RING SPECIFICATIONS

All measurements are given in inches.

Year	VIN	No. Cylinder Displacement cu. in. (liter)	Piston Clearance	Ring Gap			Ring Side Clearance		
				Top Compression	Bottom Compression	Oil Control	Top Compression	Bottom Compression	Oil Control
1988	F	4-132 (2.2)	NA	①	①	①	NA	NA	NA
	Z	4-150 (2.5)	0.0013– 0.0021	0.0100– 0.0200	0.0100– 0.0200	0.0150– 0.0550	0.0010– 0.0032	0.0010– 0.0032	0.0010– 0.0095
	J	6-182 (3.0)	NA	0.0160– 0.0220	0.0160– 0.0220	—	0.0010– 0.0020	0.0010– 0.0020	0.0015– 0.0035
1989	F	4-132 (2.2)	NA	①	①	①	NA	NA	NA
	H	4-150 (2.5)	0.0013– 0.0021	0.0100– 0.0200	0.0100– 0.0200	0.0150– 0.0550	0.0010– 0.0032	0.0010– 0.0032	0.0010– 0.0085
1990–91	H	4-150 (2.5)	0.0013– 0.0021	0.0100– 0.0200	0.0100– 0.0200	0.0150– 0.0550	0.0010– 0.0032	0.0010– 0.0032	0.0010– 0.0085
	U	6-182 (3.0)	0.0013– 0.0021	0.0160– 0.0220	0.0160– 0.0220	NA	0.0010– 0.0020	0.0010– 0.0020	0.0015– 0.0035

NA—Not Available
① The factory specifies only 1 type of ring for this engine. The ring gap is pre-adjusted

TORQUE SPECIFICATIONS

All readings in ft. lbs.

Year	VIN	No. Cylinder Displacement cu. in. (liter)	Cylinder Head Bolts	Main Bearing Bolts	Rod Bearing Bolts	Crankshaft Pulley Bolts	Flywheel Bolts	Manifold		Spark Plugs
								Intake	Exhaust	
1988	F	4-132 (2.2)	①	69	46	96	44	11	13	11
	Z	4-150 (2.5)	100	80	33	80	48-54	23	23	28
	J	6-182 (3.0)	②	③	37	133	48-54	11	13	11
1989	F	4-132 (2.2)	①	69	46	96	44	11	13	11
	H	4-150 (2.5)	④	80	33	80	48-54	23	23	22
	U	6-182 (3.0)	52	80	35	125	48-54	11	13	11

TORQUE SPECIFICATIONS
All readings in ft. lbs.

Year	VIN	No. Cylinder Displacement cu. in. (liter)	Cylinder Head Bolts	Main Bearing Bolts	Rod Bearing Bolts	Crankshaft Pulley Bolts	Flywheel Bolts	Manifold Intake	Manifold Exhaust	Spark Plugs
1990–91	H	4-150 (2.5)	④	80	33	80	48-54	23	23	22
	U	6-182 (3.0)	52	80	35	125	48-54	11	13	11

① Torque in 3 steps, in sequence:
   1st—37 ft. lbs.
   2nd—59 ft. lbs.
   3rd—69 ft. lbs.
   Run engine for 15 minutes, shut off and allow to cool for 6 hours and recheck, should be 65–72 ft. lbs.
② Torque in 2 steps, in sequence:
   1st—45 ft. lbs.
   2nd—Angular tighten to 106 degrees
   Run engine for 15 minutes, shut off and allow to cool for 6 hours. Angular tighten to 45 degrees.
③ Tighten in 2 steps, in sequence:
   1st—20 ft. lbs.
   2nd—Angular torque 75 degrees
④ No. 1–7 and No. 9–10—110 ft. lbs.
   No. 8—100 ft. lbs.

BRAKE SPECIFICATIONS
All measurements in inches unless noted

Year	Model	Lug Nut Torque (ft. lbs.)	Master Cylinder Bore	Brake Disc Minimum Thickness	Brake Disc Maximum Runout	Standard Brake Drum Diameter	Minimum Lining Thickness Front	Minimum Lining Thickness Rear
1988	Medallion	66	.810	.697 ①	.002	9.000	1/32	1/32
	Premier	63	.945	.807	.003	8.197	1/32	1/32
1989	Medallion	66	.810	.697 ①	.002	9.000	1/32	1/32
	Premier	63	.945	.807	.003	8.197	1/32	1/32
1990–91	Premier	63	.945	.807	.003	8.197	1/32	1/32
	Monaco	63	.945	.807	.003	8.197	1/32	1/32

① Disc Rotor must not be machined. If excessive wear is evident, the rotor must be replaced

WHEEL ALIGNMENT

Year	Model	Caster Range (deg.)	Caster Preferred Setting (deg.)	Camber Range (deg.)	Camber Preferred Setting (deg.)	Toe-in (in.)	Steering Axis Inclination (deg.)
1988	Medallion	1 1/2 P–3 1/2 P	2 1/2 P	1/16 P–13/16 P	7/16 P	5/64 ①	12 3/4
	Premier	1 5/16 P–2 13/16 P	2 1/8 P	9/16 N–1/16 N	5/16 N	1/8 ①	NA
1989	Medallion	1 1/2 P–3 1/2 P	2 1/2 P	1/16 P–13/16 P	7/16 P	5/64 ①	12 3/4
	Premier	1 1/2 P–3 1/2 P	2 1/8 P	9/16 N–1/16 N	5/16 N	1/8 ①	NA
1990–91	Premier	1 1/2 P–2 1/2 P	2 P	9/16 N–1/16 N	5/16 N	0	NA
	Monaco	1 1/2 P–2 1/2 P	2 P	9/16 N–1/16 N	5/16 N	0	NA

P Positive
N Negative
NA Not Applicable
① Toe-out

ENGINE ELECTRICAL

NOTE: Disconnecting the negative battery cable on some vehicles may interfere with the functions of the on board computer systems and may require the computer to undergo a relearning proces, once the negative battery cable is reconnected.

Distributor

REMOVAL

2.2L and 2.5L Engines

1. Remove the negative battery cable. Remove the distributor cap with the wires attached.
2. Matchmark the position of the rotor tip to the distributor housing and engine.
3. Disconnect and tag the distributor wiring and vacuum hose(s).
4. Remove the distributor hold-down bolt and pull the distributor up out of the engine. Note the position of the rotor in relation to the engine as the rotor stops rotating.
5. Do not rotate the engine with the distributor removed.

3.0L Engine

1. Disconnect the battery negative cable.
2. Remove accessory drive belt, if required.
3. Remove the timing belt cover.
4. Remove the spark plug wires from the spark plugs.
5. Remove the screws retaining the distributor cap.
6. Remove the screw that attach the distributor drive to the rotor and remove the rotor. Remove the dust shield from inside the housing.
7. Separate the distributor drive front and rear sections. Remove the distributor housing attaching bolts and remove the housing and seal.

INSTALLATION

Timing Not Disturbed

2.2L AND 2.5L ENGINES

1. Install the distributor with the rotor pointing to the matchmark on the engine.
2. Rotate the housing and align the rotor-to-housing matchmark.
3. Install the distributor cap, hold-down clamp and nut. Tighten the nut hand tight.
4. Connect the distributor wiring

and negative battery cable. Run the engine and adjust the ignition timing.
5. With timing correct, tighten the hold-down nut and recheck the timing.

3.0L ENGINE

1. Lightly coat the seal lips with clean engine oil and install the seal and housing.
2. Install the distributor drive rear section through the back of the cover, past the seal and into the housing.
3. Align the dowel in the top of the rear section with the dowel hole in the bottom of the distributor drive front section and tap them together.
4. Place the dust shield inside the distributor housing and the rotor on the the distributor drive. Install the retaining screw and tighten to 26 inch lbs.
5. Install the distributor cap and tighten the cap retaining bolts to 35 inch lbs. Attach the spark plug wires.

Timing Disturbed

2.2L ENGINE

1. Remove the spark plug from the No. 1 cylinder and position a compression gauge or a thumb over the spark plug hole.
2. Slowly crank the engine until compression pressure starts to build up.
3. Continue cranking the engine so that the timing mark or pointer aligns with the TDC mark.
4. Install the distributor with its drive meshed, so that the rotor points to the No. 1 terminal on the distributor cap with No. 1 cylinder piston at TDC.
5. Complete installation in the reverse order of removal and adjust the timing as required.

NOTE: Some engines may be sensitive to the routing of the distributor sensor wires. If routed near the high-voltage coil wire or spark plug wires, the electromagnetic field surrounding the high-voltage wires could generate an occasional disruption of the ignition system operation.

2.5L ENGINE

1. Rotate the engine until the No. 1 piston is at TDC of the compression stroke.
2. Using an appropriate tool inserted in the distributor hole, rotate the oil pump gear so that the slot in the oil pump shaft is slightly past the 3 o'clock position, relative to the length of the engine block.
3. With the distributor cap removed, install the distributor with the rotor at the 5 o'clock position, relative to the oil pump gear shaft slot. When

the distributor is completely in place, the rotor should be at the 6 o'clock position. If not, remove the distributor and perform the entire procedure again.
4. Tighten the lock bolt.

3.0L ENGINE

1. Remove the spark plug from the No. 1 cylinder and position a compression gauge or a thumb over the spark plug hole.
2. Slowly crank the engine until compression pressure starts to build up.
3. Continue cranking the engine so that the timing mark or pointer aligns with the TDC mark.
4. Install the distributor drive rear section through the back of the cover, past the seal and into the housing.
5. Align the dowel in the top of the rear section with the dowel hole in the bottom of the distributor drive front section and tap them together.
6. Place the dust shield inside the distributor housing and the rotor on the the distributor drive. Install the retaining screw and tighten to 26 inch lbs.
7. Install the distributor cap and tighten the cap retaining bolts to 35 inch lbs. Attach the spark plug wires.

Ignition Timing

ADJUSTMENT

Ignition timing is adjusted by the vehicle's Electronic Control Unit (ECU). The ECU uses input from sensors in the engine to determine various conditions during operation such as, manifold pressure, engine speed, manifold air temperature and coolant temperature. These inputs allow the ECU to adjust the timing under a variety of engine conditions. Therefore no timing adjustment is needed for normal vehicle service.

Alternator

For further information on the charging system, please refer to "Charging and Starting" in the Unit Repair section.

PRECAUTIONS

Several precautions must be observed with alternator equipped vehicles to avoid damage to the unit.
 • If the battery is removed for any reason, make sure it is reconnected with the correct polarity. Reversing the battery connections may result in damage to the one-way rectifiers.
 • When utilizing a booster battery

as a starting aid, always connect the positive to positive terminals and the negative terminal from the booster battery to a good engine ground on the vehicle being started.

- Never use a fast charger as a booster to start vehicles.
- Disconnect the battery cables when charging the battery with a fast charger.
- Never attempt to polarize the alternator.
- Do not use test lamps of more than 12 volts when checking diode continuity.
- Do not short across or ground any of the alternator terminals.
- The polarity of the battery, alternator and regulator must be matched and considered before making any electrical connections within the system.
- Never separate the alternator on an open circuit. Make sure all connections within the circuit are clean and tight.
- Disconnect the battery ground terminal when performing any service on electrical components.
- Disconnect the battery if arc welding is to be done on the vehicle.

BELT TENSION ADJUSTMENT

A single serpentine belt is used to drive all engine accessories. On Premier with 2.5L engine, the drive belt tension is adjusted with the power steering pump. On Premier with 3.0L engine, the drive belt tension is adjusted with the alternator. On the Medallion, the drive belt tension is adjusted with the belt tension adjuster bolt, next to the alternator.

Place the tension gauge on the longest belt span between pulleys, when checking and adjusting belt tension. Specifications are: 180–200 lbs. for a new belt, 140–160 lbs. for a used belt.

REMOVAL & INSTALLATION

Premier and Monaco

1. Disconnect battery negative cable.
2. On 2.5L engine, perform the following procedures:
   a. Remove the power steering pump locking nut from mounting bracket.
   b. Loosen pivot bolt, adjusting bolt and 2 bolts located at rear of power steering pump.
   c. Remove alternator drive belt and disconnect electrical connectors from alternator.
   d. Remove pivot bolt, mounting bolts and alternator assembly.

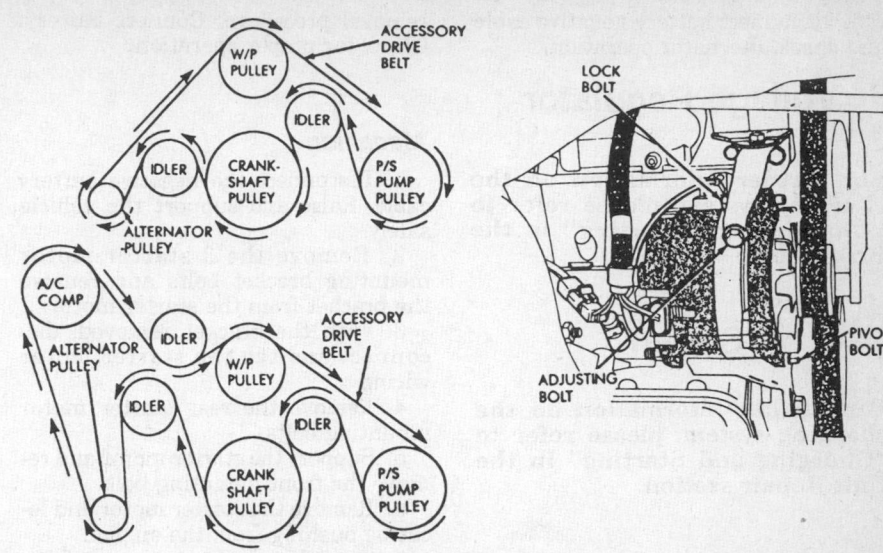

Serpentine belt and alternator adjust points—Premier

3. On 3.0L engine, perform the following procedure:
   a. Raise and safely support the vehicle.
   b. Remove the lower splash shield.
   c. Loosen alternator adjusting bolt to relieve the belt tension. Remove alternator drive belt, mounting bolt and pivot bolt.
   d. Disconnect electrical connectors from alternator and remove alternator assembly.

To install:
4. Position the alternator on engine and install pivot bolt and mounting bolts finger tight.
5. Reconnect electrical connectors and install the drive belt.
6. On 2.5L engine, perform the following procedure:
   a. Install a belt tension gauge and tighten adjusting bolt to obtain the proper belt tension.
   b. Torque pivot bolt to 30 ft. lbs. (40 Nm).
   c. Torque the 2 rear power steering mounting bolts to 20 ft. lbs. (27 Nm).
   d. Torque the locking nut to 20 ft. lbs. (27 Nm).
7. On 3.0L engine, perform the following procedure:
   a. Torque pivot bolt to 37 ft. lbs. (50 Nm).
   b. Tighten adjusting bolt to obtain the proper belt tension.
   c. Torque mounting bolt to 20 ft. lbs. (27 Nm).
   d. Install the lower splash shield and lower the vehicle.
8. Reconnect battery negative cable and check alternator operation.

Medallion

1. Disconnect the negative battery cable. Raise and support the vehicle safely.
2. Remove the lower splash shield.
3. Loosen but do not remove the locking bolt and adjusting nut from the drive belt tension adjuster.
4. Remove the lower alternator mounting nut. The nut is also used by the top tensioner mount.
5. Loosen the top alternator mounting bolt. Remove the tensioner from the alternator.

NOTE: Never use a sharp instrument to remove the drive belt from the pulley. The belt is made of synthetic material and may be damaged.

6. Remove the serpentine drive belt from the alternator pulley.
7. Disconnect and tag the alternator wiring. Remove the top alternator mounting bolt.
8. Remove the alternator from the engine.

To install:
9. Position alternator and install the top mounting bolt.
10. Install alternator lower mounting nut and tensioner. Tighten mounting nut finger tight.
11. Install electrical connectors. Install serpentine belt.
12. Tighten tensioner nut finger tight and tensioner adjuster nut to obtain proper belt tension.
13. Tighten all mounting bolts and nuts.
14. Install splash shield and lower vehicle.

15. Reconnect battery negative cable and check alternator operation.

Voltage Regulator

For further information on the charging system, please refer to "Charging and Starting" in the Unit Repair section.

Starter

For further information on the charging system, please refer to "Charging and Starting" in the Unit Repair section.

REMOVAL & INSTALLATION

Premier and Monaco

1. Disconnect the negative battery cable. Raise and support the vehicle safely.
2. Disconnect and tag the starter motor wiring.
3. On 2.5L engine, remove the starter motor mounting bolts. Remove the starter motor from the engine and remove the bushing in the starter motor mounting plate.
4. On 3.0L engine, remove the starter motor mounting bolts. Remove the starter motor and mounting plate from the engine.
5. Installation is the reverse of the

removal procedure. Connect battery. Check for proper operation.

Medallion

1. Disconnect the negative battery cable. Raise and support the vehicle safely.
2. Remove the 3 starter motor mounting bracket bolts and remove the bracket from the starter motor.
3. With the bracket removed, disconnect and tag the starter motor wiring.
4. Remove the rear starter motor mounting bolts.
5. Support the starter motor and remove the front mounting bolt.
6. Remove the starter motor and locating bushing from the engine.
7. Transfer the rear mount from the old starter motor to the new motor.

To install:

8. Place the bushing in the front starter motor mount on the engine.
9. Install the starter motor on the engine and tighten the mounting bolts.
10. Connect the starter motor wiring.
11. Install the starter motor mounting bracket and tighten the mounting bolts.
12. Lower the vehicle and connect the negative battery cable.
13. Check the starter motor operation when finished.

CHASSIS ELECTRICAL

Heater Blower Motor

REMOVAL & INSTALLATION

Without Air Conditioning

PREMIER AND MONACO

1. Disconnect the negative battery cable.
2. Disconnect the electrical connector from the coolant reservoir.
3. Remove the coolant reservoir retaining strap and move the reservoir aside.
4. Remove the coolant reservoir mounting bracket. Disconnect the electrical wires from the blower motor.
5. Remove the blower motor mounting bolts and remove the blower motor.
6. Install the blower and mounting bolts. Connect the electrical leads and install the coolant reservoir.
7. Connect the negative battery cable.

MEDALLION

1. Disconnect the negative battery cable.
2. Remove the glove box door straps

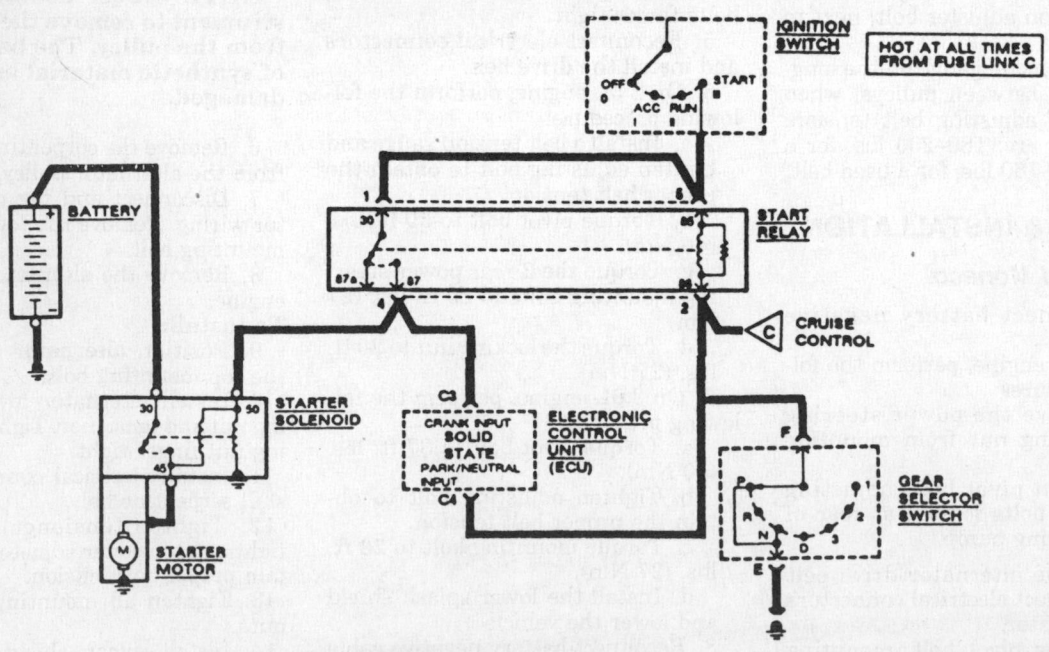

Ignition schematic—Premier

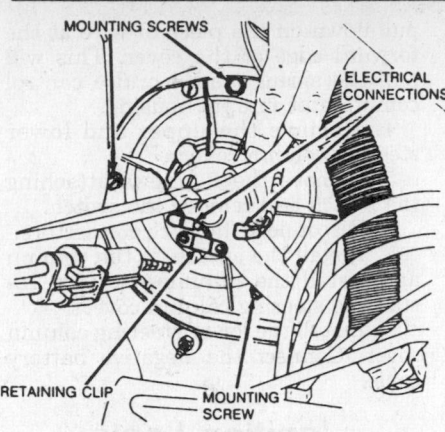

Heater blower motor mount and connections—Premier

and remove the glove box door. Remove the inner glove box.

3. Unclip the ventilator outlet from the right side of the blower housing. Disconnect the electrical connector from the blower motor.

4. Remove the blower housing retaining screws and remove the housing.

5. Remove the fan assembly from the blower housing.

6. Install the fan assembly into the blower housing and install the retaining screws. Connect the electrical connector and the ventilator outlet.

7. Install the inner glove box and the glove box door.

8. Connect the negative battery cable.

With Air Conditioning

1. Disconnect the negative battery cable. Drain the cooling system.

2. Remove the lower instrument panel trim cover and support rod. Disconnect the shift cable from the column lever. Pull the plastic sleeve down on the lower steering column and expose the intermediate shaft joint. Matchmark the intermediate and steering shafts. Remove the bolt from the intermediate shaft.

3. Remove the bolts that hold the steering column to the instrument panel and lower the column. Disconnect the column electrical connector. Remove the column from the vehicle.

4. Remove the windshield defroster grill. Remove the parking brake assembly mounting screws and lower the assembly. Remove the ashtray and cigarette lighter.

5. Disconnect all of the electrical connectors behind the instrument panel. Remove the bolts that hold the instrument panel to the center floor bracket.

6. Lift up and rearward on the instrument panel and remove it from the vehicle.

NOTE: The air conditioning system must be discharged before disconnecting the refrigerant lines. The refrigerant will freeze anything it contacts including skin and eyes.

7. Disconnect the heater hoses, vacuum lines and electrical connectors.

8. Remove the nuts retaining the heater case to the firewall and remove the case from the vehicle.

9. Remove the plastic tabs retaining the heater core and remove the heater core from the case.

To install:

10. Install the heater core in the heater housing and secure with retaining tabs. Verify that the housing seals are in place and in good condition.

11. Position the heater housing to the dash panel being certain that the drain tube extends through its opening in the floor and all electrical wiring and vacuum lines extends through the dash panel.

12. Complete installation by reversing the removal procedure.

13. Connect the negative battery cable, refill the cooling system and recharge the air conditioning system.

Windshield Wiper Motor

REMOVAL & INSTALLATION

Premier and Monaco

1. Disconnect the negative battery cable.

2. Remove the wiper arms. Remove the screws retaining the left and right cowl screens and remove both screens.

3. Remove the motor and linkage mounting screws.

4. Disconnect the electrical connector and remove the motor and linkage as an assembly.

5. Install the motor/linkage assembly and connect the electrical leads.

6. Install the cowl screens and the wiper arms. Connect the negative battery cable.

Medallion

1. Disconnect the negative battery cable.

2. Remove the wiper arms. Remove the screws retaining the cowl in front of the windhield and remove the cowl.

3. Disconnect the electrical plug at the wiper motor. Remove the screws retaining the wiper motor and transmission and remove the assembly.

4. Install the wiper and transmission assembly. Connect the electrical plug to the wiper motor.

5. Install the cowl and the wiper arms.

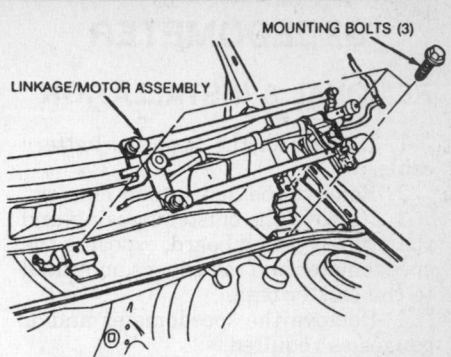

Wiper transmission and motor removal—Premier

6. Connect the negative battery cable.

Instrument Cluster

REMOVAL & INSTALLATION

Premier and Monaco

1. Disconnect the negative battery cable.

2. Remove the screws retaining the instrument cluster bezel and remove the bezel.

3. Remove the cluster retaining screws and tilt the cluster forward. Disconnect the electrical connectors.

4. If necessary, disconnect the speedometer cable.

5. Remove the lower instrument panel cover and remove the cluster.

6. Install the cluster and lower trim cover. Connect the electrical leads to the cluster.

7. Install the instrument panel bezel. Connect the negative battery cable.

Medallion

1. Disconnect the negative battery cable.

2. Remove the instrument glare shield retaining screws. Press the holding tabs in and remove the glare shield.

3. Open the fuse panel access door, reach through the fuse panel door and remove the speedometer cable from the rear of the instrument cluster.

4. Remove the instrument cluster mounting screws and pull the cluster forward. Disconnect the electrical wiring and remove the cluster from the vehicle.

5. Install the cluster and connect the electrical wiring. Install the glare shield. Connect the speedometer cable and connect the negative battery cable.

SPEEDOMETER

REMOVAL & INSTALLATION

1. Disconnect the negative battery cable.
2. Remove the instrument cluster.
3. Remove the cluster housing and the printed circuit board, exposing the speedometer and the gauges, mounted to the cluster case.
4. Remove the speedometer and/or gauges as required.
5. Installation is the reverse of the removal procedure.

Radio

REMOVAL & INSTALLATION

1. Disconnect the battery negative cable.
2. Remove the instrument cluster bezel by removing the screws.
3. Remove the radio mounting screws.
4. Disconnect the electrical connector, the ground wire and unplug the antenna.
To install:
5. Installation is the reverse of removal. Connect all electrical plugs, position the radio into the instrument panel and secure with the screws.
6. Install the instrument bezel and connect the battery negative cable.

Combination Switch

REMOVAL & INSTALLATION

Premier and Monaco

The 2-speed intermittent electric windshield wipers and electric washers are standard equipment. The controls for the windshield wipers are part of the control switch module, turn signals, wiper, lights combination switch, mounted on the left hand switch pod located on the left side of the steering column.

1. Disconnect the negative battery cable.
2. Remove the screws and instrument panel lower cover, if equipped.
3. Remove the screws and remove the support rod and pull the air duct out of the way.
4. Cut the plastic tie-wrap straps.
5. Loosen the hold-down nut in the center of the steering column electrical connector and separate the connector.
6. Separate the left hand pod switch connector from the steering column connector by placing a flat blade tool between the connectors to disengage the locking tab. Push on the wire side

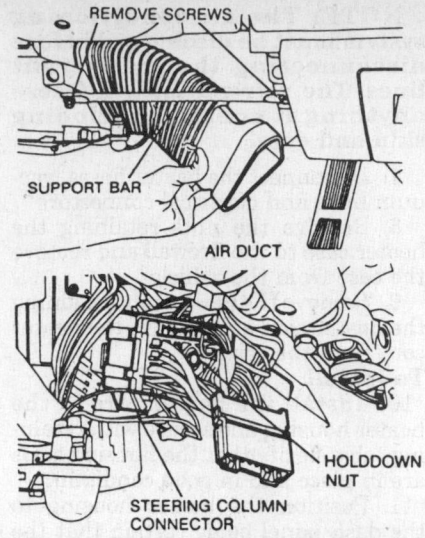

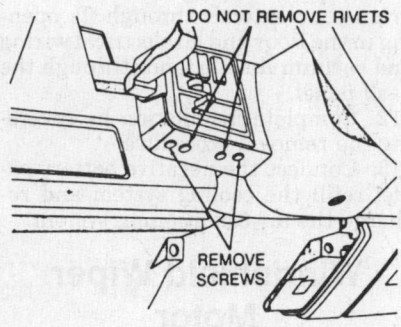

To remove combination switch, remove duct, electrical connection and pod screws

of the left hand pod switch connector and slide the connector out of the channels of the steering column connector.
7. Disconnect the electrical connector, remove the bottom 2 screws (not the rivets) from the pod assembly.
8. To gain access to the inside of the pod, remove the screws from the back of the left hand switch pod assembly and remove the switch pod housing back cover.

NOTE: There are small retaining clips on the left hand pod that may fall off when the switch is removed.

9. Carefully pull the switch pod far enough from the housing to expose the 2 screws, remove them and gently pull the switch forward and pull the harness out through the housing to remove the switch.

Medallion

1. Disconnect the negative battery cable.
2. Remove the screws from the lower steering column cover and remove the cover.
3. If equipped with cruise control,

pull down on the piece of wire at the forward edge of the cover. This will pull the spring loaded cruise control commutator into its housing.
4. Remove the upper and lower steering column covers.
5. Remove the 2 screws attaching the switch and remove the switch.
6. Disconnect the wire connectors.
7. Install the switch to the column and install the retaining screws. Install the steering column covers.
8. Install the lower steering column cover. Connect the negative battery cable.

Ignition Lock

REMOVAL & INSTALLATION

Premier and Monaco

1. Disconnect the negative battery cable. Remove the steering wheel.
2. Remove the turn signal cancelling cam, unlock the tabs and slide the canceler off the steering shaft.
3. If equipped with a tilt wheel, remove the tilt control lever.
4. Remove the screws retaining the right and left switch pods. Remove the ignition switch trim ring.
5. Remove the screws from the pod housing/column cover. Remove the pod housing/column cover by pulling it up, guide the pods through the cover and remove the cover.
6. Insert the key into the ignition and align the key with groove in the lock cylinder housing. Push in the locking tab on the bottom of the housing, with a punch and remove the cylinder. Separate the switch from the wires by removing the screw retaining the connector.
To install:
7. Insert the key into the ignition and align key with groove in lock cylinder housing.
8. Depress the tab and install the lock cylinder.
9. Install the pod housing/column cover and install the pods. Install the ignition switch trim ring.

NOTE: The retaining clips on the left and right switch pods must be in place when the switches are installed.

10. Install the tilt lever, if equipped. Install the turn signal cam with pin bore in the steering wheel. Reconnect electrical connector.
11. Align the reference mark on the steering shaft and install the steering wheel. Reconnect the negative battery cable.

MEDALLION

1. Disconnect the negative battery cable.

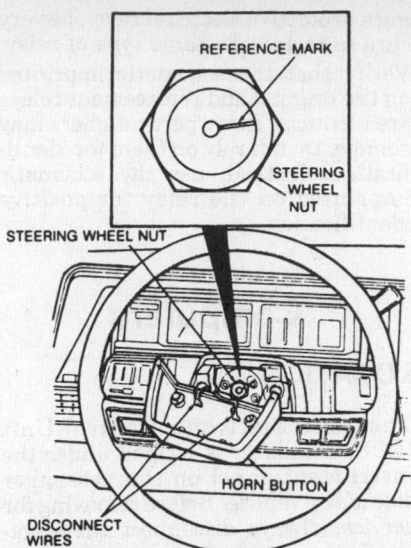

Matchmark nut at column before removal

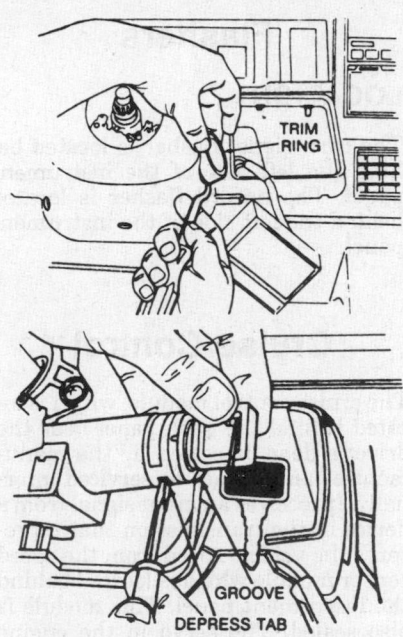

Ignition lock repair requires trim ring removal and pushing the lock tab

2. Remove the screws from the lower steering column cover and remove the cover.

3. If equipped with cruise control, pull down on the piece of wire at the forward edge of the cover. This will pull the spring loaded cruise control commutator into its housing.

4. Remove the upper and lower steering column covers. Remove the screws retaining the lower instrument panel and remove the panel.

5. Remove the ignition switch cover. Remove the ignition switch mounting screw.

6. Insert the key into the ignition and turn it to the unmarked arrow on the switch. Push in the locking tabs on

the side of the housing with a punch and remove the switch. Separate the switch from the wires by removing the screw retaining the connector.

To install:

7. Install the switch into the lock cylinder, push the wires through the cylinder hole. Push the locking tabs in and lock the switch in position.

8. Connect the electrical leads. Install the ignition switch cover. Install the trim covers.

9. Connect the negative battery cable.

Ignition Switch

REMOVAL & INSTALLATION

Premier and Monaco

1. Disconnect battery negative cable.

2. Remove instrument panel lower cover attaching screws and remove cover.

3. Remove the horn pad. Disconnect the wires and remove the horn button.

4. Remove the steering wheel and the turn signal cancel cam.

5. If equipped with tilt wheel, use a small wrench to unscrew the tilt lever.

6. Remove the screws retaining the right and left switch pods. Remove the ignition switch trim ring.

7. Remove the screws from the pod housing/column cover. Remove the pod housing/column cover by pulling it up, guide the pods through the cover and remove the cover.

8. Remove the lower column shroud attaching screws and remove lower shroud.

9. Remove the upper column shroud attaching screws and remove upper shroud.

10. Remove the ignition switch retaining screws and separate the switch from cylinder housing.

11. Cut the tie straps and remove the harness anchor.

12. Loosen the retaining nut in the center of the steering column connector and separate the switch pod connector by disengaging locking tabs.

13. Remove the electrical harness from the channels of steering column connector and remove the ignition switch assembly.

To install:

14. Slide the switch pod connectors into the ignition switch connector and install the nut.

15. Install the ignition switch and secure with retaining screws.

16. Route the wiring harness along the underside of steering column and secure with tie straps. Install the harness anchor and secure with retaining screw.

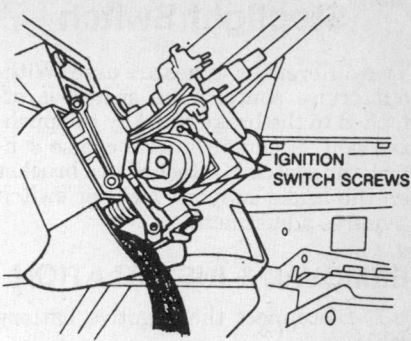

The ignition switch is retained by 2 screws—Premier

17. Follow the remaining removal procedure to complete installation.

18. When installing the steering wheel, align the pin on the turn signal cam with the pin bore on the steering wheel. Tighten the steering wheel nut to 52 ft. lbs. (70 Nm).

19. Reconnect battery negative cable.

Medallion

1. Disconnect battery negative cable.

2. Remove 4 screws from lower steering column cover.

3. On cruise control equipped vehicles, pull down on the wire at the forward edge of the lower cover. This allow the spring loaded commutator brush to be pull into its housing.

NOTE: If the lower steering cover is removed before the commutator brush is pulled into its housing, the brush will be broken off the cover.

4. Remove the upper steering column cover and ignition switch cover.

5. Remove the gray and black wire connectors and ignition switch mounting screw from beneath the key cylinder housing.

6. Turn the key to the unmarked arrow on cylinder lock. Push on both locking tabs on side of lock cylinder housing and remove the ignition switch. Feed wiring harness through the lock cylinder hole.

7. Separate the tumbler by removing the 2 attaching screws.

To install:

8. Guide the wire harness through the lock cylinder hole and slide the switch into the hole. Press both locking tabs inward and slide the switch into place until it locks.

9. Install the ignition switch mounting screw at the bottom of cylinder housing and reconnect electrical connectors.

10. Install the ignition switch cover and lower steering column cover.

11. Reconnect battery negative cable.

Stoplight Switch

Two different switches are used. Without cruise control, the switch is attached to the brake pedal by the pushrod bolt. If equipped with cruise control, the switch is attached to a bracket on the brake support. Neither switch requires adjustment.

REMOVAL & INSTALLATION

1. Disconnect the negative battery cable.
2. Remove the bolt retaining the master cylinder pushrod to the brake pedal.
3. Disconnect the electrical wires from the stoplight switch and remove the switch.
4. Install the switch and the master cylinder pushrod to the brake pedal and install the retaining bolt.
5. Connect the electrical wires to the switch. Connect the negative battery cable and check the operation of the brake lights.

Neutral Safety Switch

REMOVAL & INSTALLATION

Premier and Monaco

1. Disconnect battery negative cable.
2. Disconnect the neutral switch harness connector located in the engine compartment.
3. Raise and support the vehicle safely. Remove the splash shield.
4. Remove the bolt attaching the switch bracket to transaxle case and remove switch from case.

To install:

5. Place a new O-ring on the switch and reverse removal procedure.
6. Lower the vehicle, reconnect switch harness connector and battery negative cable.

Medallion

A Multi-function switch located on the transaxle assembly allows the vehicle to start only in **N** and **P** positions.

1. Disconnect the negative battery cable.
2. Remove the electrical connection from switch.
3. Remove the switch mounting screws and remove the switch.
4. Installation is the reverse of the removal procedure.

Fuses, Circuit Breakers and Relays

LOCATION

Fuses

The fuse panel is located above the

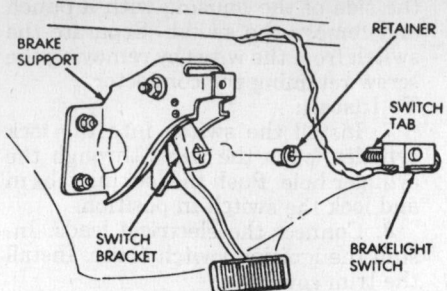

Brake light installation—Premier

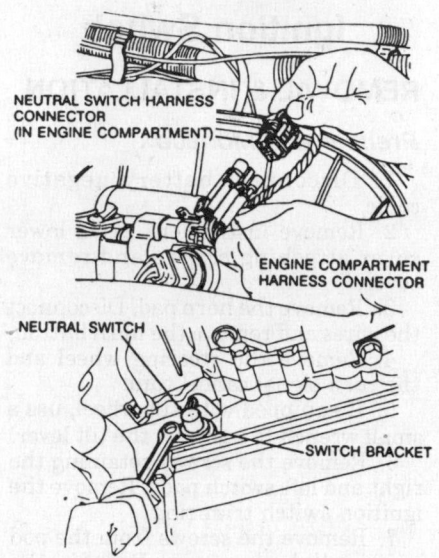

Disconnect wires, then remove neutral switch

parking brake release lever, under the instrument panel.

Fusible Links

Fusible links are used to prevent major wire harness damage in the event of a short circuit or an overload condition in the wiring circuits which are normally not fused, due to carrying high amperage loads or because of their locations within the wiring harness. Each fusible link is of a fixed value for a specific electrical load and should a link fail, the cause of the failure must be determined and repaired prior to installing a new fusible link of the same value.

Circuit Breakers

Circuit breakers are an integral part of the headlight switch, the wiper switch and the air conditioning circuit. They are used to protect each circuit from an overload.

Relays

Relays are used through out the system in various locations. When replac-

ing a protective electrical relay, be very sure to install the same type of relay. Verify that the schematic imprinted on the original and replacement relays are identical. Relay part numbers may change. Do not rely on them for identification. Instead, use the schematic imprinted on the relay for positive identification.

Computers

LOCATION

The main Electronic Control Unit (ECU) computer is located under the instrument panel on the passenger side of the vehicle. Before removing for service, always disconnect the negative battery cable first.

Flashers

LOCATION

The turn signal flasher is located behind the left side of the instrument panel. The hazard flasher is located behind the left side of the instrument panel.

Cruise Control

The cruise control module, which is located behind the dash panel near the driver's door, is sealed by the manufacturer and cannot be serviced internally. It receives an input signal from a device in the transmission that represents the vehicle speed from the speed sensor module which is located behind the instrument panel. This module is also sealed. The servo in the engine compartment is controlled by the cruise control module. A cable connects the servo to the throttle linkage.

REMOVAL & INSTALLATION

The cruise control switch on the Medallion and Premier is located in the steering wheel cover.

1. Disconnect the negative battery cable.
2. Remove the steering wheel center pad. Disconnect the electrical leads.
3. Pry up on the switch panel and remove it.
4. Install the switch panel to the steering wheel and connect the electrical leads.
5. Install the horn cover. Connect the negative battery cable.

ENGINE COOLING

Radiator

REMOVAL & INSTALLATION

NOTE: Try to keep coolant off of the accessory drive belt and pulleys. Cover the belt and pulley with shop cloths prior to woring on them. If coolant contacts the belts or pulleys, flush with water. Do not remove radiator cap or block drains when the system is hot.

1. Disconnect battery negative cable.
2. Remove electric cooling fan assembly.
3. Attach one end of a ¼ in. hose about 3 feet long to the end of the radiator drain, the other end in a clean container. Open drain and remove the radiator cap to drain the system.
4. Disconnect upper and lower hoses from the radiator.
5. Remove the front grill then disconnect the radiator from the air conditioning condenser by removing the top and bottom attaching screws. Lift out radiator.

To install:

6. Installation is the reverse of removal. Note that the radiator is equipped with alignment dowels on the bottom that fit into holes in the body crossmembers. Align these dowels at installation. Refill and bleed cooling system.

Electric Cooling Fan

TESTING

All vehicles are equipped with an electric cooling fan systems designed to operate automatically under different conditions. The system reacts with the changes in engine temperature. When the engine coolant temperature reaches 198°F for 1988–89 models or 188°F for 1990–91 models, but below 212°F, the cooling fan switch low speed contacts close. This activates the cooling fan in low speed operation. When the coolant temperature exceeds 212°F the fan switch activates the fan in high speed operation. If equipped with air conditioning, the coolant fan switch automatically turns the cooling fan **ON** while the air conditioning is activated.

If the cooling fan does not operate with the air conditioning on but the compressor operates, repair an open between terminal 5 of the cooling fan relay connector and the compressor clutch relay.

Cooling Fan Temperature Switch

1. Turn ignition switch to **RUN**. Connect a jumper wire between coolant temperature switch terminals **A** and **B**. The cooling fan should operate.
2. If the cooling fan operates, replace the cooling fan temperature switch.
3. If the cooling fan does not operate, check the cooling fan relay.

Cooling Fan Relay

1. Turn ignition switch to **RUN**, with the relay plugged in. Note that the cooling fan relay can be found in the relay panel in the engine compartment. Look for a panel on the driver's side fender wall area, with 4 relays. The front one should be the starter relay, next behind it is the ignition relay, then the radiator fan relay, with the back relay the air conditioning clutch relay. Connect a jumper wire between coolant temperature switch terminals **A** and **B**. Check for voltage at the cooling fan relay connector terminal 5. If battery voltage is not present, repair an open between terminal 5 and the ignition switch.
2. If battery voltage is present, test for voltage at the cooling fan relay connector terminal 4. If battery voltage is not present, repair an open between terminal 4 and fusible link **G**. The multiple fusible link connection is the main electrical feed near the battery positive cable.
3. If battery voltage is present at terminal 4, check for voltage at the cooling fan relay connector terminal 2. If zero voltage is not present, some power is getting through, repair an open to ground since the system is trying to ground through the test meter. If zero voltage is indicated, check for voltage at connector terminal 1.
4. If battery voltage is not present at connector terminal 1, replace the cooling fan relay. If battery voltage is present, check and clean the connections at the cooling fan motor. If connections are okay, replace the cooling fan.

REMOVAL & INSTALLATION

1. Disconnect the negative battery cable.
2. Remove the radiator support bracket screws. Remove the vibration cushion nuts.
3. Remove the upper radiator crossmember mounting screws and remove the crossmember.

4. Disconnect the electrical connectors from the fan. Remove the cooling fan and shroud mounting bolts and remove the fan by lifting upwards.
5. Install the fan into position and install the mounting bolts. Install the radiator crossmember and support bracket.
6. Connect the negative battery cable.

Heater Core

REMOVAL & INSTALLATION

1. Disconnect the negative battery cable. Drain the cooling system.
2. Remove the lower instrument panel trim cover and support rod. Disconnect the shift cable from the column lever. Pull the plastic sleeve down on the lower steering column and expose the intermediate shaft joint. Matchmark the intermediate and steering shafts. Remove the bolt from the intermediate shaft.
3. Remove the bolts that hold the steering column to the instrument panel and lower the column. Disconnect the column electrical connector. Remove the column from the vehicle.
4. Remove the windshield defroster grill. Remove the parking brake assembly mounting screws and lower the assembly. Remove the ashtray and cigarette lighter.
5. Disconnect all of the electrical connectors behind the instrument panel. Remove the bolts that hold the instrument panel to the center floor bracket.
6. Lift up and rearward on the instrument panel and remove it from the vehicle.

NOTE: The air conditioning system must be discharged before disconnecting the refrigerant lines. The refrigerant will freeze anything it contacts including skin and eyes.

7. Disconnect the heater hoses, vacuum lines and electrical connectors.
8. Remove the nuts retaining the heater case to the firewall and remove the case from the vehicle.
9. Remove the plastic tabs retaining the heater core and remove the heater core from the case.

To install:

10. Install the heater core in the heater housing and secure with retaining tabs. Verify that the housing seals are in place and in good condition.
11. Position the heater housing to the dash panel being certain that the drain tube extends through its opening in the floor and all electrical wiring and vacuum lines extends through the dash panel.

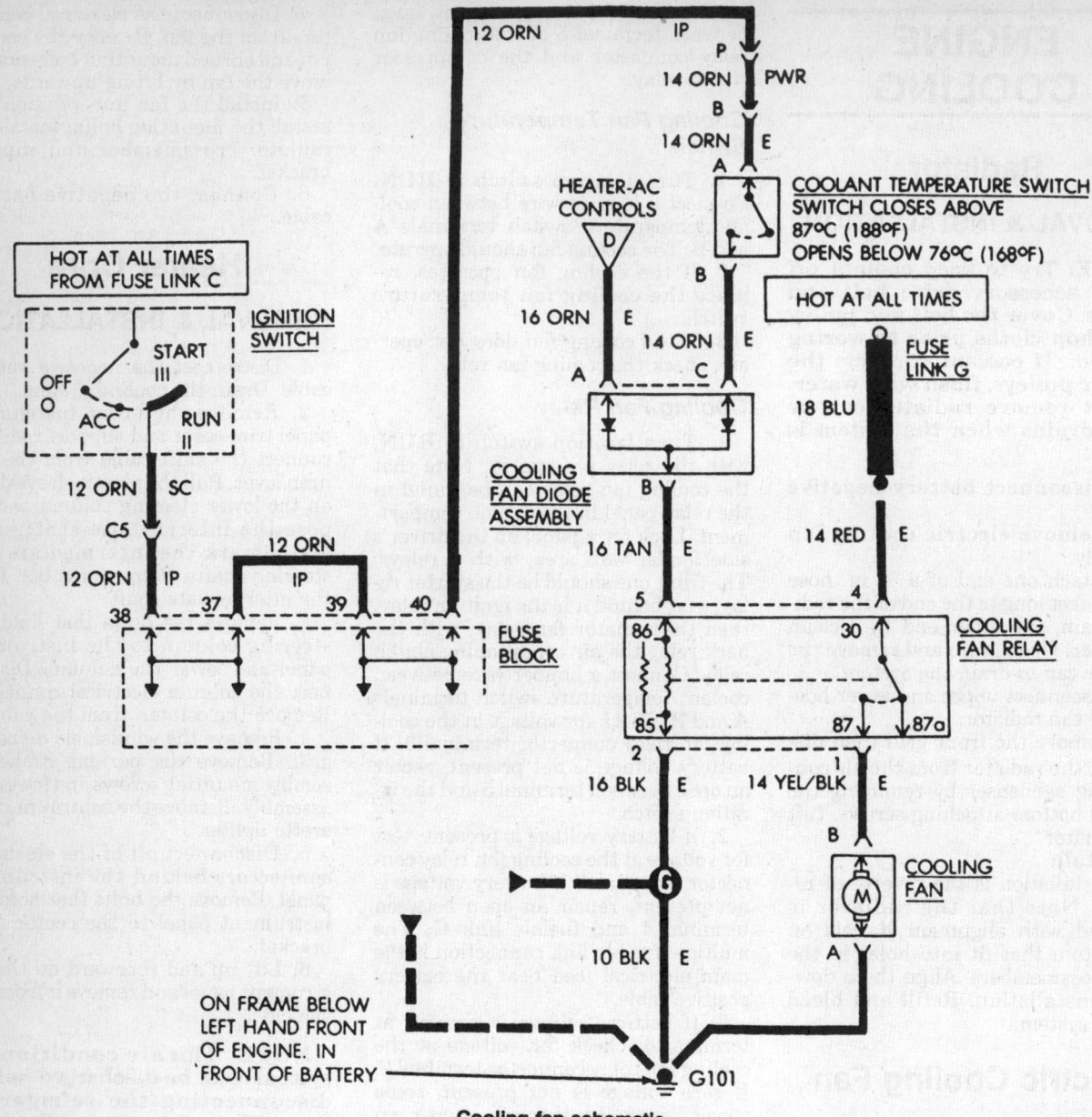

Cooling fan schematic

12. Complete installation by reversing the removal procedure.

13. Connect the negative battery cable, refill the cooling system and recharge the air conditioning system.

Water Pump

REMOVAL & INSTALLATION

2.2L Engine

1. Disconnect the negative battery cable.
2. Drain the cooling system.
3. Remove the accessory drive belts.
4. Remove the timing belt cover.
5. Remove the water pump pulley bolt and remove the pulley.

6. Remove the timing belt and tensioner. Remove the hoses from the pump.
7. Remove the water pump attaching bolts and remove the water pump.
8. Clean the gasket mating surfaces.

To install:
9. Position the pump on the engine block using a new gasket. Tighten the bolts to 20 ft. lbs.
10. Install the timing belt and tensioner. Adjust the timing belt tension.
11. Install the timing belt cover. Install the water pump pulley and the accessory drive belts. Install the hoses.
12. Fill the cooling system and connect the negative battery cable. Bleed the cooling system.

2.5L Engine

1. Disconnect the negative battery cable.
2. Drain the cooling system. Remove the serpentine drive belt.
3. Disconnect the hoses from the engine. Remove the water pump pulley mounting bolts and remove the pulley.
4. Remove the water pump mounting bolts and remove the pump.
5. Clean the gasket mating surfaces. Install the water pump using a new gasket. Tighten the bolts to 13 ft. lbs.
6. Install the hoses and the water pump pulley. Tighten the pulley retaining bolts to 20 ft. lbs.
7. Install the accessory drive belt.

NOTE: It is important that the serpentine belt is installed correctly. If it is incorrectly routed, the water pump could be rotated in the wrong direction, causing the engine to overheat.

8. Fill the cooling system. Connect the negative battery cable. Start the engine and bleed the cooling system.

3.0L Engine

1. Disconnect the negative battery cable.
2. Drain the cooling system.
3. Remove the spark plug wire holder from the top of the thermostat housing. Remove the nuts holding the engine damper to the engine.
4. Remove the accessory drive belt. Remove the upper and lower radiator hoses from the radiator.
5. Disconnect the electrical lead to the coolant temperature sensor.
6. At the back of the water pump disconnect the hoses to the cylinder heads and the heater hoses.
7. Remove the water pump mounting bolts and remove the water pump.
To install:
8. Position the water pump to the block and tighten the mounting bolts to 13 ft. lbs.
9. Connect all of the hoses to the water pump, making sure that they are not kinked. Connect the electrical lead to the coolant temperature sensor.
10. Install the accessory drive belt and the engine damper. Adjust the drive belt tension.
11. Install the spark plug wire holder to the thermostat housing.
12. Fill the cooling system. Connect the negative battery cable. Start the engine and bleed the cooling system, check for leaks.

Thermostat

REMOVAL & INSTALLATION

1. Disconnect negative battery cable.
2. Drain coolant until below level of thermostat housing. If good, save for reuse.
3. Disconnect the coolant temperature sensor wire connector from the sensor.
4. Some models have a spark plug wire holder on the top of the housing which should be moved.
5. Place shop towels on the serpentine belt. Chemicals deteriorate the synthetic materials in the belt. Always protect the belt and pulleys with clean shop towels.
6. Remove the thermostat housing and pull out thermostat. Leave the radiator hose connected.

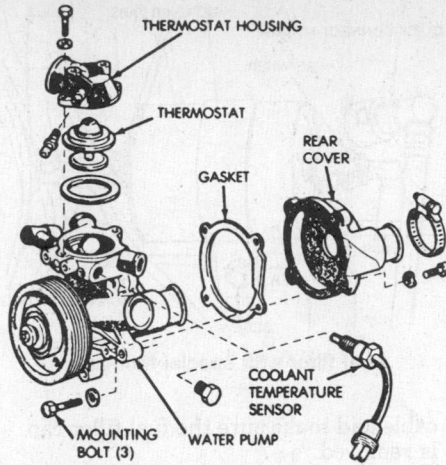

Water pump and thermostat assembly — 3.0L engine

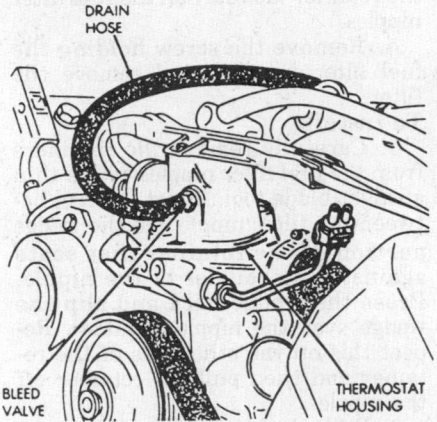

Cooling system bleed valve — 3.0L engine

To install:
7. Clean gasket surfaces well. Inspect housing ports for blockage. Install new thermostat and fresh gasket.
8. Reverse removal procedure to finish installation.

Cooling System Bleeding

3.0L Engine

NOTE: This procedure should be followed after any cooling system component has been replaced or removed and installed. It is essential that coolant does not contact the accessory drive belt or pulleys. Chemicals deteriorate the synthetic materials in the belt. Always protect the the serpentine belt and pulleys with clean shop towels. When installing the drain hose to the air bleed valve on the thermostat housing, route the hose away from the belt, pulleys and cooling fan.

1. Attach one end of a 4 foot long ¼

in. hose to the air bleed on the thermostat housing. Route the hose away from the drive belt and pulleys. Place the other end of the hose in a clean container. The purpose of this hose is to keep coolant away from the belt and pulleys.
2. Open the bleed valve.
3. Slowly fill the coolant pressure bottle until a steady stream of coolant flows from the hose attached to the bleed valve. Close the bleed valve and continue filling to the full mark on the bottle. The full mark is the top of the post inside the bottle. Install the cap tightly on the coolant pressure bottle.
4. Remove the hose from the bleed valve, start and run the engine until the upper radiator hose is warm to the touch.
5. Turn the engine **OFF**, reattach the drain hose to the bleed valve. Be sure to route the hose away from the belt and pulleys. Open the bleed valve until a steady stream of coolant flows from the hose. Close the bleed valve and remove the hose.
6. Check that the coolant pressure bottle is at or slightly above the full mark, at the top of the post inside the coolant pressure bottle. The full mark on the coolant pressure bottle is the correct coolant level for a cold engine. A hot engine will normally have a coolant level higher than the full mark.

FUEL SYSTEM

Fuel System Service Precautions

Safety is the most important factor when performing not only fuel system maintenance but any type of maintenance. Failure to conduct maintenance and repairs in a safe manner may result in serious personal injury or death. Maintenance and testing of the vehicle's fuel system components can be accomplished safely and effectively by adhering to the following rules and guidelines.

• To avoid the possibility of fire and personal injury, always disconnect the negative battery cable unless the repair or test procedure requires that battery voltage be applied.

• Always relieve the fuel system pressure prior to disconnecting any fuel system component (injector, fuel rail, pressure regulator, etc.), fitting or fuel line connection. Exercise extreme caution whenever relieving fuel system pressure to avoid exposing skin, face and eyes to fuel spray. Please be advised that fuel under pressure may penetrate the skin or any part of the body that it contacts.

• Always place a shop towel or cloth around the fitting or connection prior to loosening to absorb any excess fuel due to spillage. Ensure that all fuel spillage (should it occur) is quickly removed from engine surfaces. Ensure that all fuel soaked cloths or towels are deposited into a suitable waste container.

• Always keep a dry chemical (Class B) fire extinguisher near the work area.

• Do not allow fuel spray or fuel vapors to come into contact with a spark or open flame.

• Always use a backup wrench when loosening and tightening fuel line connection fittings. This will prevent unnecessary stress and torsion to fuel line piping. Always follow the proper torque specifications.

• Always replace worn fuel fitting O-rings with new. Do not substitute fuel hose or equivalent where fuel pipe is installed.

RELIEVING FUEL SYSTEM PRESSURE

NOTE: Always wear eye protection when servicing the fuel system. Do not smoke or allow open flame near the fuel system or components during fuel system service.

Modern fuel injection systems operate under high pressure, this makes it necessary to first relieve the system of pressure before servicing. The pressurized fuel when released may ignite or cause personal injury. The following outlined steps may be used for most fuel systems:

1. Remove the fuel tank filler cap to relieve fuel tank pressure.
2. Disconnect fuel pump electrical harness connector at the fuel tank side.
3. Start engine and let it run until it stops. Turn ignition OFF.
4. Disconnect battery negative cable and reconnect fuel pump electrical harness.

NOTE: Always wrap shop towels around the fuel lines before disconnecting them. The shop towels will absorb spilled fuel.

Fuel Filter

REMOVAL & INSTALLATION

1. Relieve fuel system pressure.
2. Disconnect the battery negative

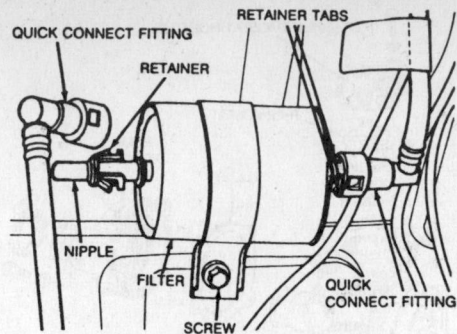

Fuel filter with special fittings

cable and make sure the fuel filler cap is removed.

3. Depress, or squeeze the retainer tabs together and slowly pull the connectors from the fuel filter. Note that the retainer tabs stay on the fuel filter nipples.
4. Remove the screw holding the fuel filter in place and remove the filter.

To install:
5. Carefully remove the retainers from the fuel filter nipples with a thin straight blade tool. Insert the tool between the filter nipple and the wedge portion of the retainer that seats against the shoulder of the nipple. Press the wedge back and slip the wedge over the nipple shoulder. Repeat this on the other side of the retainer and then pull the retainer off the nipple.
6. Push the retainers back into the fuel line quick-connect fittings. Ensure that the locking ears and the shoulder (stop bead) on the fuel tube are completely visible in the windows on the side of the quick-connect fitting.
7. The fuel filter may be marked IN and OUT at the nipple ends. The side marked IN is connected to the fuel line from the fuel tank. The side of the filter marked OUT is connected to the fuel line that runs to the engine. After determining the proper direction, install the fuel filter with the attaching screw.
8. Use a clean cloth to wipe the tube ends clean and lightly lubricate the fuel tube ends with clean 30 weight motor oil. The connectors contain O-rings which do not have to be replaced when the fittings are disconnected. Push the quick-connect fitting over the fuel tube until a click is heard. If the quick-connect fitting is type that has windows on the side, ensure that the locking ears on the retainer and the shoulder (stop bead) on the fuel tube are completely visible in the windows. Do not rely on the audible click to confirm that a secure connection has been made. Pull back on the quick-

connect fitting to further ensure that the connection is complete and the connector is locked in place.

9. Connect the negative battery cable, install the fuel filler cap, turn the key to ON to pressurize the fuel system and check for leaks.

Fuel Tubes and Quick-Connect Fittings

The fuel system in these vehicles utilize plastic fuel tubes with quick-connect fittings that have sealed O-rings. The O-rings of the quick-connect fittings do not have to be replaced when the fittings are disconnected.

The quick-connect fitting consists of the O-rings, retainer and casing. When the fuel tube nipple is inserted into the quick-connect fitting, the shoulder of the nipple is locked in place by the retainer and the O-rings seal the tube.

The fuel tube nipples must first be lubricated with clean 30 weight engine oil prior to reconnecting the quick-connect fitting.

When the fittings are disconnected the retainer will stay on the nipple of the component that the tube is being disconnected from. A fuel tube should never be inserted into a quick-connect fitting without the retainer being either on the tube or already in the quick-connect fitting. In either case, care must be taken to ensure that the retainer is locked securely into the quick-connect fitting.

If the quick-connect fitting has windows in the side of the casing, the retainer locking ears and the shoulder (stop bead) on the tube must be visible in the windows or the retainer is not properly installed. After connecting a quick-connect fitting, the connection should be verified by pulling on the lines to ensure that the lock is secure.

There is a factory tool that can be used at the 3.0L engine fuel rail and fuel pressure regulator to remove the quick-connect fitting and retainer as an assembly. The retainer will remain in the fitting in the correct position. To install the fuel tube, push it over the nipple until a click is heard. Pull back on the tube to ensure that the connector is locked in place.

Electric Fuel Pump

The fuel pump used on both the TBI and MPI system is a positive displacement, single speed type pump. The pump, except models equipped with a 2.2L engine, is integral with the fuel sender unit and is suspended in the fuel tank.

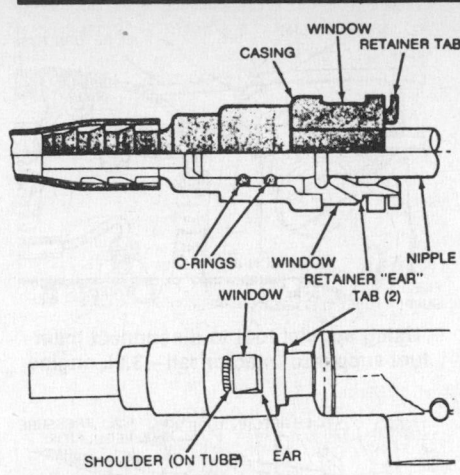

Special quick-connect fittings—use care removing and installing

PRESSURE TESTING

2.2L Engine

1. Relieve the fuel system pressure.
2. Disconnect the hose from the fuel pressure regulator to fuel rail.
3. Disconnect the vacuum hose from the pressure regulator and connect it to a vacuum pump.
4. Connect a fuel gauge to the fuel rail and start the engine.
5. Check the fuel pressure readings. It should be 36 ± 3 psi.
6. Apply 15 inches of vacuum to the pressure regulator. The pressure should drop to 29 ± 3 psi.
7. Turn the ignition **OFF**. Remove the fuel gauge from fuel rail.
8. Reconnect the vacuum hose to the pressure regulator and hose from the pressure regulator to the fuel rail.

2.5L Engine

NOTE: The throttle body has 2 port plugs on it. The test port is located on the side of the fuel pressure regulator next to the fuel return tube connection.

1. Allow the engine to cool down before removing the test port.
2. Relieve the fuel system pressure.
3. Placed a shop towel over test port to catch fuel and slowly remove the test port plug from the throttle body.
4. Install fuel pressure test adapter along with a 0–30 psi (0–207 kpa) gauge into test port.
5. Start the engine and let it idle. Check the fuel pressure reading. The fuel pressure should be 14–15 psi (97–103 kpa). If the pressure is not within specifications adjust the fuel pressure regulator as followed:
    a. Locate the fuel pressure regulator adjusting screw behind the aluminum plug in the nose of the fuel pressure regulator casing.

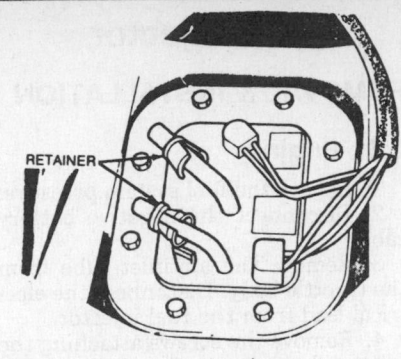

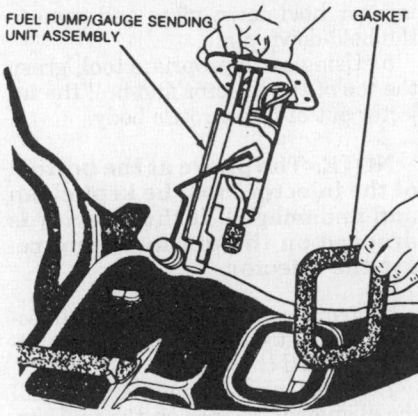

Removing fuel pump and gauge unit—note special connection fittings—Premier

    b. Lightly tap the plug with a small punch and hammer until it pops out.
    c. Run the engine at 750–800 rpm, then turn the adjustment screw until the fuel pressure is within specifications.
6. Turn the ignition switch **OFF**. Disconnect the fuel gauge and pressure test adapter.
7. Install the plug in test port. Install the aluminum plug in front of the regulator adjusting screw.
8. Replace the fuel tank filler cap.

3.0L Engine

1. Relieve the fuel system pressure.
2. Remove the black fuel supply tube from the fuel rail using tool 6182 or equivalent. Slide the tool over the nipple and up into the connector until the handle fits the connector. Pull the fuel supply tube off the fuel rail.
3. Install fuel tube adapter 6175 or equivalent and a 0–60 psi gauge. Push the adapter female end with the quick connect fitting over the fuel rail. Push the male end with the nipple into the black fuel supply tube.
4. Start the engine and check the fuel pressure. It should be 28–30 psi (193–207 kpa).

NOTE: The fuel pressure regulator used on this system is non-adjustable.

5. If the fuel pressure is not within specifications. Check items such as a restricted fuel return hose, pressure regulator vacuum hose for leaks, faulty fuel pump or a faulty pressure regulator.
6. Remove the fuel tube adapter 6175 or equivalent.
7. Lightly lubricate the ends of the fuel supply tube with clean engine oil. Install the black fuel supply tube to fuel rail and grey fuel return tube to the pressure regulator.

REMOVAL & INSTALLATION

2.5L and 3.0L Engines

1. Relieve the fuel system pressure.
2. Disconnect the negative battery cable.
3. Drain the fuel from the fuel tank.
4. Raise and safely support the vehicle. Remove the right rear wheel and inner fender splash shield.
5. Disconnect the fuel lines at the fuel filter and the electrical connectors from the tank. Disconnect the fuel tank vent tube from the filler neck. Disconnect the ground wire from the body.
6. Place a suitable support under the tank and remove the retaining straps. Lower the tank from the vehicle.
7. Remove the bolts holding the tank sending unit to the tank. Pull the sending unit/pump from the tank, note the position of the gasket.
8. Disconnect electrical connectors from the terminals on fuel pump and remove the pump holding bracket.
9. Disconnect hose clamp at inlet port. Unscrew hose clamp and remove fuel pump.

NOTE: There is a tray in the bottom of the fuel tank that is contoured to hold the fuel filter. Be certain when installing the pump/sending unit that the filter correctly fits into the tray.

To install:
10. Position the gasket so that the holes in the gasket line up with bolts holes in the fuel tank.
11. Install the sending unit/pump into the fuel tank and install the retaining bolts.
12. To complete installation, follow the removal procedure.

2.2L Engine

The fuel pump used on the 2.2L engine is mounted on a plate located under the vehicle in front of the rear axle assembly.

1. Release the fuel system pressure.
2. Disconnect battery negative cable.

3. Raise and support the vehicle safely.

4. Disconnect electrical connectors from pump.

5. Plug the pump inlet and outlet hoses to prevent fuel flow.

6. Disconnect fuel pump hoses. Wrap a shop towel around the hoses and remove hoses from fuel pump.

7. Remove the pump retaining strap and remove the fuel pump.

8. Installation is the reverse of the removal procedure.

NOTE: The pump terminals are different sizes to ensure the pump rotates in the correct direction.

Fuel Injection

IDLE SPEED ADJUSTMENT

The idle speed on fuel injected vehicles is controlled by the ECU through the use of an Idle Speed Control motor (ISC) or an idle speed regulator. The ISC motor does not require periodic adjustment. If the ISC is removed or replaced, it must be adjusted to establish the initial position of the plunger. To adjust the ISC, use the following procedure:

2.2L and 3.0L Engines

The idle speed on vehicles equipped with a 2.2L and 3.0L engines is controlled by an idle speed regulator. A permanent magnet motor inside the regulator regulates the valve between the fully open and fully closed positions. The ECU controls the idle speed regulator by alternately grounding its coils to adjust the air bypass flow rate to maintain proper idle speed.

The idle regulating valve cannot be adjusted. Idle mixture is adjusted at the factory and should not be attempted.

2.5L Engine

1. Start the engine and allow it to reach normal operating temperature.

2. Disconnect the ISC motor wire connector.

3. Locate the diagnostic terminals on the right side inner fender well. Connect a tachometer to terminals D1–1 and D1–3 of the diagnostic connector.

4. An adapter may be required to connect to the ISC motor. Fully extend the ISC motor plunger.

5. Adjust the plunger screw until the engine is running at 3500 rpm.

6. Remove adapter and reconnect the idle speed motor electrical connector. Idle speed should automatically return to normal.

Fuel Injector

REMOVAL & INSTALLATION

2.5L Engine

1. Relieve the fuel system pressure.

2. Disconnect the negative battery cable.

3. Remove the air inlet tube from the throttle body. Disconnect the electrical lead from the fuel injector.

4. Remove the screws attaching the injector hold-down plate and remove the hold-down plate.

5. Using an appropriate tool, grasp the top of the injector and pull the injector out of the throttle body.

NOTE: The pintle at the bottom of the injector must be kept clean and undamaged. If the injector is dropped on the pintle, do not re-use the injector.

6. Remove the upper O-ring, injector alignment washer and the lower O-ring. Discard the O-rings.

7. Install new O-rings and install the alignment washer on the injector. Install the injector into the throttle body by pushing down on the injector.

8. Install the injector hold-down plate. Connect the electrical connector.

9. Install the air inlet tube and connect the negative battery cable.

2.2L and 3.0L Engines

1. Relieve the fuel system pressure.

2. Disconnect the negative battery cable.

3. Disconnect the fuel lines from the fuel rail assembly.

4. Disconnect and tag the electrical leads from the fuel injectors and lay the harness aside.

5. Disconnect the accelerator cable from the the throttle body. On the 3.0L engine, remove the 4 screws attaching the engine cover and remove the cover.

6. Remove the fuel rail mounting bolts. Pull the fuel rail and injectors from the engine, using a back and forth twisting motion.

7. Install the fuel rail and injectors to the engine, be careful not to damage the O-rings on the injectors. Install the fuel rail hold-down bolts and connect the fuel lines.

8. Connect the electrical leads to the injectors. Connect the throttle cable. On the 3.0L engine install the engine cover plate.

9. Connect the negative battery cable. Turn the ignition to the **ON** position to pressurize the fuel system and check for leaks.

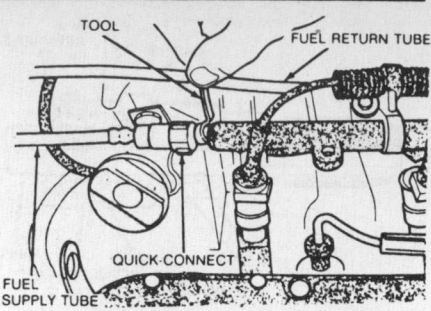

Using special tool to disconnect main fuel supply to injector rail—3.0L engine

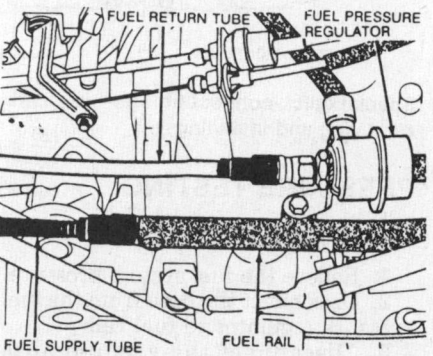

Return hose and regulator layout—3.0L engine

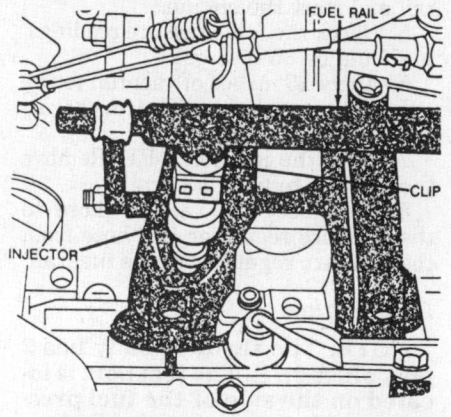

Fuel injector and rail, installed—3.0L engine

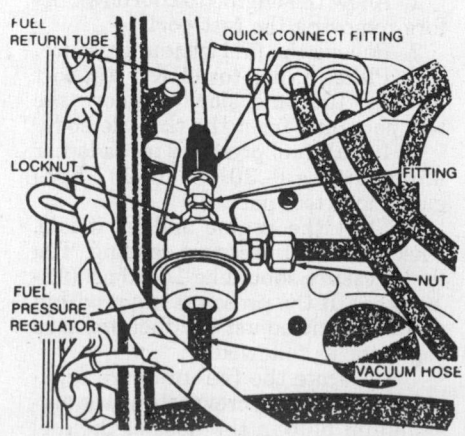

Fuel lines and routing—3.0L engine

EMISSION CONTROLS

Please refer to "Emission Control" in the Unit Repair section for system maintenance procedures. Due to the complex nature of modern electronic engine control systems, comprehensive diagnosis and testing procedures fall outside the confines of this repair manual. For complete information on diagnosis, testing and repair procedures concerning all modern engine and emission control systems, please refer to "Chilton's Guide to Electronic Engine Controls".

Emission Warning Lamps

RESETTING

These vehicles are equipped with a Vehicle Maintenance Monmitor (VMM). The dashboard display is activated at 7,500 mile intervals to remind the vehicle owner that regular service and maintenance is due. Perform the required service and then press the **RESET** button located on the left side of the instrument panel under the monitor display.

ENGINE MECHANICAL

NOTE: Disconnecting the negative battery cable on some vehicles may interfere with the functions of the on-board computer systems and may require the computer to undergo a relearning process, once the negative battery cable is reconnected.

Engine Assembly

REMOVAL & INSTALLATION

1. Matchmark the hood to the hinges and remove the hood.
2. Disconnect the negative battery cable, the coil wire, all vacuum and fuel lines.
3. Disconnect the lower radiator hose and drain the coolant. Remove the air cleaner.
4. Remove the grille. Remove the screws retaining the front facia panel and radiator support and remove the panel and support.
5. Remove the radiator and cooling fan. If equipped with air conditioning, remove the condensor and the radiator as an assembly.

NOTE: On vehicles equipped with air conditioning, the system will have to be discharged before the engine can be removed.

6. Remove the ECU cover and disconnect the electrical leads to the unit.
7. Remove the accelerator cable from the brackets on the valve cover.
8. Remove the bolts that attach the exhaust head pipes-to-the exhaust manifold. Remove the heater hoses and on automatic transaxle equipped vehicles, remove the cooler lines.
9. Raise the vehicle and safely support. Remove the underbody splash shield.
10. Remove the power steering pump mounting bolts and support the pump to the side. Remove the header pipe-to-converter bolts and remove the converter.
11. If equipped with automatic transaxle, disconnect the shifter linkages. On manual transaxle vehicles, disconnect the clutch cable at the transaxle.
12. Remove the wheel assemblies and remove the front stabilizer bar. Remove the brake calipers and support aside. Disconnect the tie rod ends from the steering knuckle. Remove the halfshaft retaining pin and remove the halfshaft assembly. Remove the strut-to-steering knuckle bolts.
13. Loosen the upper strut mounting bolts and swing the axle/strut assembly aside, support the axles safely.
14. Disconnect the speedometer cable. Disconnect the vapor canister and remove it.
15. Loosen the bolts attaching the transmission support to the engine cradle. Remove the bolts attaching the left and right halves of the crossmember to the transaxle. Lower the vehicle.
16. Attach a suitable lifting device to the engine lifting eyes and lift the engine slightly, remove the engine support bolts and remove the engine/transaxle assembly. Lift the engine out at an angle, make sure the transaxle clears the engine compartment. Separate the engine from the transaxle.

To Install:

17. Position the engine in vehicle and align the engine mounts with the engine cradle.
18. Install the engine mount bolts and remove the lifting device. Install

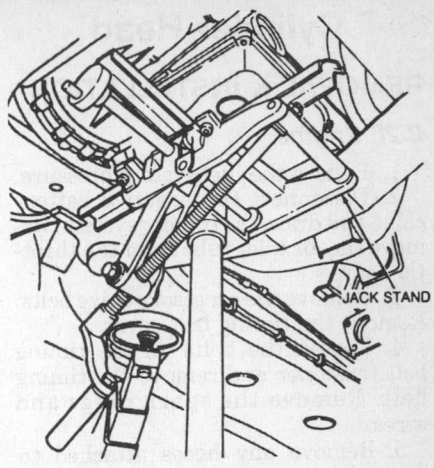

Use safety stand when removing engine/cradle assembly

the left and right sections of the crossmember.

19. Position and install the halfshafts to the transaxle, use new retaining pins. Install the shock absorber-to-steering knuckle bolts and attach the tie rod ends. Attach the front stabilizer bar.
20. Install the brake calipers on the rotors and tighten the retaining bolts to 73 ft. lbs. Install the front wheels.
21. Install the converter to the header pipe. Install the power steering pump and adjust the belt tension. Connect the shift linkage and throttle cables.
22. Reconnect all electrical and vacuum leads. Install the canister and the air cleaner assemblies. Reconnect the fuel lines and coolant hoses.
23. Install the radiator and fan assemblies. Attach the front facia and support assembly. Install the grill.
24. Attach the negative battery cable and install the hood.
25. Check all fluid levels. Fill and bleed the cooling system.

Engine Mounts

REMOVAL & INSTALLATION

1. Disconnect the negative battery cable.
2. Remove the engine mount upper attaching bolt.
3. Remove the engine pitch restrictor (dog bone).
4. Raise the vehicle and support it safely.
5. Remove the engine mount bottom attaching bolt.
6. Carefully raise the engine and remove the engine mount.
7. Installation is the reverse of the removal procedure.

Cylinder Head

REMOVAL & INSTALLATION

2.2L Engine

1. Relieve the fuel system pressure.
2. Disconnect the negative battery cable and drain the cooling system. Remove the air inlet tube from the throttle body.
3. Remove the accessory drive belts. Remove the timing belt cover.
4. Loosen the bolts on the timing belt tensioner and remove the timing belt. Remove the spark plugs and wires.
5. Remove any hoses attached to the rocker cover and remove the rocker arm cover. Remove the distributor from the rear of the head.
6. Remove all of the cylinder head bolts except for the bolt at position No. 10 in the tightening sequence. Loosen the bolt at position No. 10 and pivot the cylinder head on that bolt. This can be done by tapping the opposite end of the head with an block of wood. This is necessary to free the cylinder head from the cylinder liners.

NOTE: When the cylinder head has been removed it is recommended by the manufacturer that the cylinder liners in the block, be retained with a liner hold-down clamp. This tool is designed to prevent the cylinder liners from being knocked out of position.

7. Once the head is free, remove the last bolt and remove the cylinder head. Clean all gasket material from mating surfaces.

To install:

8. Place the new cylinder head gasket on the block using the alignment dowel, on the block, to hold it in place.
9. Position the cylinder head on the block and insert the cylinder head bolts. Tighten the bolts in sequence and in 3 steps to specification.
10. Install the distributor to the head. Install the rocker arm cover, using a new gasket. Tighten the rocker cover bolts to 35 inch lbs.
11. Install the timing belt and adjust the belt tension. Install the timing belt cover. Install the spark plugs and wires.
12. Install the accessory drive belts and reconnect all hoses that were disconnected.
13. Install the air inlet tube. Fill the cooling system.
14. Reconnect the negative battery cable. Run the engine and bleed the cooling system. Check for leaks.

2.5L Engine

1. Relieve the fuel system pressure.

2. Disconnect the negative battery cable and drain the cooling system.
3. Loosen the accessory drive belt and remove it.
4. Remove the bolts attaching the air conditioning compressor and without disconnecting the pressure lines, move the compressor aside.
5. Disconnect the upper radiator hose and the heater hoses.
6. Remove the rocker arm cover. Remove the rocker arms and assemblies, keep all of the valve train components in their original order, for installation.
7. Remove the intake and exhaust manifolds.
8. Remove the cylinder head bolts and remove the cylinder head.
9. Clean all gasket material from mating surfaces.

To install:

10. To install, place the new cylinder head gasket on the block with the numbers facing UP.

NOTE: The cylinder head gasket used on this engine is a composite gasket and does not require the use of any sealing compound.

11. Place the cylinder head on the block and install the bolts. Tighten the bolts in 3 steps and in sequence to the correct torque.
12. Install the valve train components in their original sequence. Place a new gasket on the cylinder head and install the rocker cover.
13. Connect all of the hoses removed and install the air conditioing compressor, tighten the mounting bolts to 20 ft. lbs. Route the accessory drive belt and adjust the tension.
14. Connect the battery cable and fill the cooling system. Run the engine and bleed the cooling system, check for leaks.

3.0L Engine

1. Relieve the fuel system pressure.
2. Disconnect the negative battery cable and drain the cooling system.
3. Remove the accessory drive belt and remove the air conditioning compressor from the cylinder head cover.
4. Remove the intake and exhaust manifolds.
5. Remove the spark plug wires. Remove the rocker arm cover.
6. Remove the alternator mounting bracket and remove the top timing case bolts that thread into the cylinder head.

NOTE: The timing sprocket and chain must be supported in place and not allowed to drop into the timing case. If the chain and sprocket slip into the case the

timing case will have to be removed.

7. Turn the crankshaft until the camshaft sprocket dowel is straight up. A special tool is available called a timing chain support bracket. This support bracket and dummy bearing attaches to the timing case cover. On the left cylinder head, remove the distributor assembly.
8. Remove the threaded plug on the front of the timing case cover to gain access to the camshaft sprocket bolt.
9. Remove the cylinder head bolts. Remove the rocker shaft assembly.
10. Remove the rear camshaft cover and gasket at the rear of the cylinder head.
11. Loosen the camshaft thrust plate screw, located behind the timing sprocket, and move the thrust plate up. This will allow the camshaft to move back in the head as the sprocket bolt is removed.
12. Loosen the camshaft sprocket bolt and pull the camshaft back until the bolt is free from the camshaft, the bolt will stay in the sprocket. Use an old pushrod or a long thin drift punch as a tool and insert it into the front and rear cylinder head bolt holes on the exhaust manifold side of the head. Tap the dowel down below the head gasket. The reason for this is that the cylinder head is not to be removed by pulling straight upward which would pull the cylinder liners loose from the block. It is to be bumped sideways to break the seal.

NOTE: Do not pull straight up on the cylinder head to remove it. This will cause the cylinder liners to come out of the block.

13. Position a block of wood on the intake manifold side of the head and strike it with a hammer, do the same on the exhaust manifold side of the head. Repeat this until the cylinder head is loose. Remove the cylinder head.

NOTE: When the cylinder head has been removed it is recommended by the manufacturer that the cylinder liners be retained with a liner hold-down clamp or equivalent. This tool is designed to prevent the cylinder liners from being knocked out of position.

14. Remove the cylinder head gasket and clean all gasket material from mating surfaces. Remove the cylinder head locating dowels. Check that the cylinder liners protrude between 0.002–0.005 in.

To install:

15. When installing, cut the gasket

flush with the cylinder head gasket face at the back of the timing case cover and remove the pieces. Clean the back of the timing cover. Cut sections of new gasket to replace the pieces removed and attach them with adhesive. Install a small punch into the hole in the block below the locating dowel bolt holes. This will act as a stop for the dowel. Push the dowel into the block until it contacts the punch. The dowel should not be at the proper height.

16. Install a new cylinder head gasket over the alignment dowels on the head. Place a small bead of RTV or equivalent, at the point where the head gasket meets the timing case cover.

17. Place the cylinder head on the block and install the top timing case cover to cylinder head bolts, finger tighten the bolts.

18. Remove the timing sprocket support tool. Position the camshaft into the sprocket and line up the dowel to the slot in the camshaft. Install the sprocket bolt and lightly tighten it. Slide the thrust plate into position and tighten the thrust plate bolt to 4 ft. lbs.

19. Install the rocker shaft assembly and install the head bolts. Tighten the cylinder head bolts, in sequence, in the following steps:

   a. Starting with bolt No. 1, pretighten all bolts to 44 ft. lbs.

   b. The following is performed on all bolts, one at a time. Starting with bolt No. 1, loosen the bolt completely, then tighten to 30 ft. lbs.

   c. Place an angle adapter on the torque wrench between the socket and wrench and angle tighten each bolt, in sequence another 180 degrees, ± 20 degrees.

20. Install the rocker covers, intake and exhaust manifold.

21. Install the timing case plug, spark plug wires and the air conditioning compressor. Reconnect all hoses and fill the cooling system.

22. Install the distributor assembly on the left cylinder head.

23. Install the accessory drive belt and adjust the tension. Connect the negative battery terminal. Start the engine and bleed the cooling system. Check for leaks.

Valve Lifters

REMOVAL & INSTALLATION

2.5L Engine

1. Disconnect the battery negative cable. Remove the valve cover, the bridge and pivot assemblies and rocker arms.

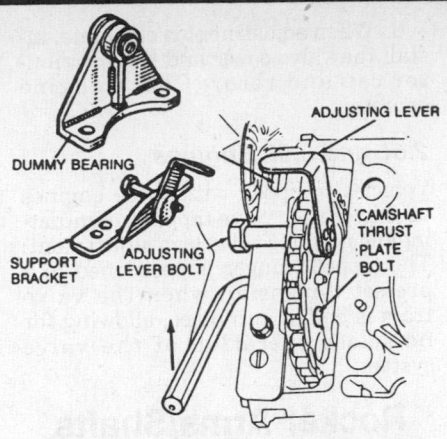

Special tools are recommended to retain cam drive when head is removed—3.0L engine

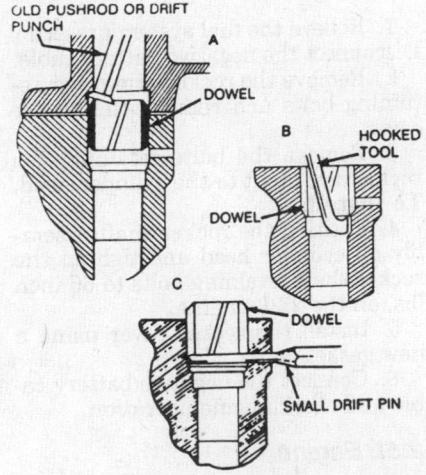

A—Push locating dowel below head gasket level so head can be bumped sideways to remove; B—Pull dowel out with hook shaped tool; C—Use pin punch to gauge depth of dowel at installation—3.0L engine

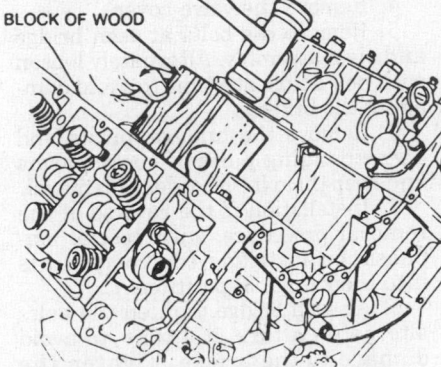

Lifting the head could dislodge the cylinder liner; instead, bump sideways as shown

NOTE: To avoid damaging the bridges, alternately loosen each bridge bolt a turn at a time.

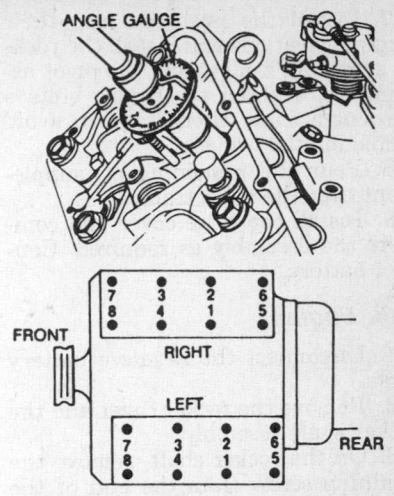

Head bolt torque sequence and angle gauge—3.0L engine

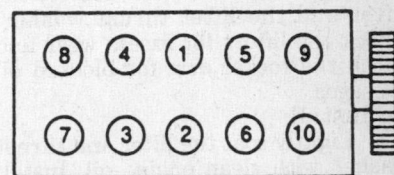

Head bolt torque sequence—2.2L engine

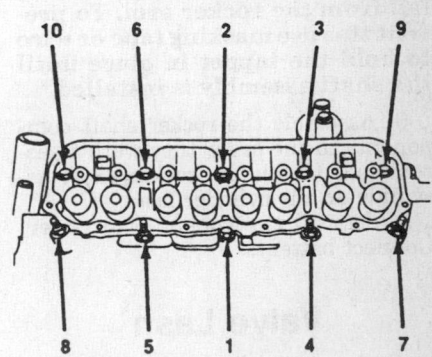

Head bolt torque sequence—2.5L engine

2. Remove the pushrods, keeping them in their respective order.

3. Remove the cylinder head assembly and manifolds.

4. Remove the lifters through the pushrod openings, with a lifter removal tool. Retain the lifters in their respective removed order.

To install:

5. Installation is the reverse of the removal procedure. Be sure to dip each lifters in clean engine oil before installation.

NOTE: Install the used lifters into their original bores.

6. Install the cylinder head assembly onto the engine block using a new head gasket. Tighten in sequence to the proper torque specification. Install the manifolds, if removed separately.

7. Install the pushrods into their original positions and install the rocker arms and bridges and the pivot assemblies. Tighten the bridge bolts a turn at a time, alternately, to avoid damaging the bridges.

8. Pour the remaining oil supplement over the valve train.

9. Install the valve cover and complete the assembly as required. Connect battery.

3.0L Engine

1. Disconnect the negative battery cable.

2. Remove the rocker cover and the rocker shaft assembly.

3. On the rocker shaft, remove the retaining screw from the end of the shaft and carefully disassemble the rocker shaft components.

4. From the rocker arm, remove the lifter and the lifter thrust washer. Check the lifters for excess wear and check the rocker arm for blocked oil passages.

To install:

5. Lightly coat the lifter and thrust washer with clean engine oil. Install the lifter in the rocker arm.

NOTE: **The lifter may tend to fall from the rocker arm. To prevent this use masking tape or wire to hold the tappet in place until the shaft assembly is installed.**

6. Assemble the rocker shaft components in the order they were disassembled. Install the rocker shaft assembly on the cylinder head.

7. Install the rocker arm cover. Connect battery.

Valve Lash

ADJUSTMENT

2.2L Engine

1. Warm engine to normal operating temperature.

2. Stop engine and remove the valve cover.

3. Remove the distributor cap and rotor. Place the No. 1 piston on the TDC of its compression stroke.

4. Using tool MOT-647 or equivalent, loosen the locknut on the adjuster and turn the adjuster to obtain the proper clearance.

NOTE: **Check the adjuster to be sure that it is aligned evenly with the valve stem. If it is not aligned, valve damage could occur.**

5. Rotate the crankshaft to bring each set of valves to the TDC of its compression stroke and adjust them in the same manner.

6. When adjustment is complete, install the valve cover and the distributor cap and rotor. Check engine operation.

2.5L and 3.0L Engines

Vehicles equipped with these engines uses hydraulic valve tappets, eliminating the need for valve lash adjustment. The tappet plunger is positioned to a pre-set dimension when the valve train is bolted into place, allowing for noiseless operation of the valve system.

Rocker Arms/Shafts

REMOVAL & INSTALLATION

2.2L Engine

1. Relieve the fuel system pressrue. Disconnect the negative battery cable.

2. Remove the rocker arm cover retaining bolts and remove the rocker cover.

3. Remove the bolts retaining the rocker arm shaft to the cylinder head.

To install:

4. Position the rocker shaft assembly on cylinder head and tighten the rocker shaft retaining bolts to 66 inch lbs. on the 2.2L engine.

5. Install the rocker cover using a new gasket.

6. Connect the negative battery cable and check engine operation.

2.5L Engine

1. Disconnect the negative battery cable.

2. Disconnect and mark all vacuum hoses and electrical connections as required.

3. Remove the vacuum switch and bracket assembly. Remove the diverter valve and bracket assembly.

4. Remove the valve cover.

5. Remove the bolts at each bridge and pivot assembly. Alternately loosen each bolt a turn at a time to avoid damaging the bridges.

6. Remove the bridges, pivots and corresponding pairs of rocker arms and keep them in the order of removal.

7. Installation is the reverse of the removal procedure, with special emphasis on installing the components into their original positions.

8. At each bridge, tighten the bolts alternately a turn at a time, to avoid damage to the bridge. Tighten the bolts to 19 ft. lbs. with a re-torque of 16–26 ft. lbs.

3.0L Engine

1. Relieve the fuel system pressure. Disconnect the negative battery cable.

2. Remove the engine cover mounting bolts and remove the engine cover.

3. Disconnect vacuum hoses and electrical connectors, as required.

4. Remove the spark plug wire holder and loosen the accessory drive belt.

5. Remove the air conditioning compressor mounting bolts and position the compressor out of the way, if required.

6. Remove the power steering reservoir, idle speed regulator bracket, accelerator cable and bracket, if required. Lay to the side.

7. Remove the rocker arm cover attaching bolts and remove the rocker cover.

8. Remove the rocker arm shaft attaching bolts and remove the shaft assembly.

NOTE: **Both left and right rocker shaft assemblies are identical and can be used on either cylinder head. Always install them on the same cylinder head that they were removed from.**

To install:

9. Lightly coat the rocker shaft assembly with clean engine oil and position on the cylinder head. Tighten the attaching bolts to 53 inch lbs. (6 Nm).

10. Before installing the rocker cover, apply a light coating of sealer to the top of the timing case cover at cylinder head joints area. Complete installation by reversing the removal procedure.

Intake Manifold

REMOVAL & INSTALLATION

2.2L Engine

1. Disconnect the negative battery cable.

2. Drain the cooling system.

3. Relieve the fuel system pressure.

4. Remove the air inlet/filter housing and tube.

5. Disconnect the fuel lines at the injector rail. Disconnect the vacuum lines at the intake manifold.

6. Disconnect the throttle linkage at the throttle body. Remove the electrical connectors from the injectors.

7. Remove the intake manifold retaining bolts and remove the intake manifold.

8. Clean gasket mating surfaces.

To install:

9. Position the intake manifold on the head using a new gasket and insert the bolts. Torque the manifold bolts to 11 ft. lbs. in the proper sequence.

10. Connect the electrical leads to the injectors and the fuel lines to the fuel rail.

11. Connect the vacuum lines at the manifold and the throttle linkage at the throttle body.

12. Attach the air inlet to the throttle

body. Fill the cooling system and connect the negative battery cable.

13. Run the engine, bleed the cooling system and check for leaks.

3.0L Engine

1. Relieve the fuel system pressure.
2. Disconnect the negative battery cable.
3. Remove the engine cover retaining bolts and remove the cover.
4. Remove the air inlet cover from the throttle body.
5. Disconnect the transaxle kickdown cable, accelerator cable and cruise control cable from the throttle body. Remove the vacuum hoses from the intake manifold.
6. Remove the electrical connector from the throttle position sensor. Disconnect and tag the electrical connectors from the fuel injectors and lay the harness aside.
7. Remove the EGR tube. Remove the wire from the air temperature sensor.
8. Remove the fuel lines from the injector rails.
9. Remove the 4 bolts retaining the intake manifold and remove the manifold. Remove and discard the O-rings, from the cylinder heads.

NOTE: When the intake manifold has been removed the O-rings in the cylinder heads must be replaced.

10. Clean all gasket mating surfaces.
To install:
11. Use new O-rings and install the intake manifold. Torque the retaining bolts to 11 ft. lbs. Tighten in an X pattern starting in the middle, working toward the ends.
12. Install the fuel lines to the fuel rail assembly. Connect the electrical connectors to the fuel injectors. Connect all of the elctrical connectors and vacuum hoses removed.
13. Connect the EGR tube. Connect the transaxle kickdown cable, accelerator and cruise control cables. Connect the negative battery cable.
14. Install the air inlet to the throttle body. Install the engine cover. Connect battery.
15. Run the engine and check for leaks.

Exhaust Manifold

REMOVAL & INSTALLATION

2.2L Engine

1. Disconnect the negative battery cable.
2. Remove the exhaust manifold heat shield and hot air tube.

3. Remove the EGR tube from the manifold.
4. Remove the bolts retaining the header pipe to the manifold.
5. Remove the manifold mounting nuts. Remove the manifold and gaskets.
6. To install, place the manifold gaskets and the manifold on the block and tighten the mounting nuts to 13 ft. lbs. Start at the center and work toward the manifold ends.
7. Install the heat shield and the EGR tube.
8. Connect the negative battery cable.

3.0L Engine

1. Disconnect the negative battery cable.
2. Disconnect the EGR tube from the right manifold.
3. Raise the vehicle and support it safely.
4. Remove the nuts retaining the header pipe to the manifolds.
5. On the right manifold, remove the nuts securing the dipstick tube to the manifold. On the left manifold remove the starter heat shield and the heat stove.
6. Lower the vehicle.
7. Remove the manifold mounting nuts and remove the manifolds.
8. Place new manifold gaskets over the mounting studs and install the manifolds. Tighten the nuts to 13 ft. lbs.
9. Complete installation by reversing the removal procedure.

Combination Manifold

REMOVAL & INSTALLATION

2.5L Engine

1. Relieve the fuel system pressure.
2. Disconnect the negative battery cable.
3. Remove the air inlet cover and hose from the throttle body.
4. Loosen the accessory drive belt and remove it. Remove the power steering pump and brackets. Support the pump to the side, do not disconnect the pressure lines.
5. Disconnect the fuel lines and the accelerator cable from the throttle body. Disconnect the electrical connectors for the idle speed sensor, throttle position sensor, coolant temperature sensor, air intake temperature sensor and the oxygen sensor.
6. Disconnect the electrical plug from the fuel injector. Disconnect the vacuum lines at the intake manifold.
7. Remove the bolts supporting the EGR tube to the exhaust manifold. Remove the heater hoses from the intake manifold.

8. Remove the intake/exhaust manifold mounting bolts and remove the manifolds from the engine.
To install:
9. Clean all of the gasket mounting surfaces.
10. To install, position the new intake manifold gasket and the new exhaust manifold spacers over the locating dowels and install the manifold to the head. Tighten the bolts in sequence and to the specified torque.
11. Install the EGR tube to the exhaust manifold. Connect the heater and vacuum hoses. Attach the fuel lines to the throttle body.
12. Reconnect all electrical connectors. Install the power steering pump and brackets.
13. Connect the accelerator cable. Install the accessory drive belt and adjust the tension. Install the air inlet tube and cover.
14. Connect the negative battery cable and fill the cooling system.
15. Run the engine and bleed the cooling system, check for leaks.

Timing Chain Front Cover

REMOVAL & INSTALLATION

2.5L Engine

1. Disconnect the negative battery cable.
2. Remove the drive belts, engine fan and hub assembly, vibration damper, pulley and key.
3. Remove the air conditioning compressor and alternator bracket, if equipped.
4. Remove the oil pan to cover bolts and the cover to engine block bolts.
5. Remove the front cover assembly from the engine.
6. Cut off the oil pan side gasket end tabs flush with the front face of the cylinder block and remove the gasket tabs.
7. Remove the oil seal from the timing cover and clean all gasket material from the sealing surface.
To install:
8. Apply sealant to both sides of the gasket and install on the cover sealing surface.
9. Cut the end tabs from the replacement oil pan side gasket and cement the tabs on the oil pan.
10. Install new oil seal into the cover assembly.

NOTE: The oil seal can be installed after the cover has been installed on the engine block, depending upon the cover aligning tools available.

11. Coat the front cover seal end tab

recesses with RTV sealant and position the seal on the cover bottom.

12. Position the cover on the engine block and position an alignment tool into the crankshaft opening.

NOTE: Two different types of alignment tools are available, without seal in housing or with seal in housing.

13. Install the cover-to-engine block bolts and the oil pan-to-cover bolts. Tighten the cover-to-engine block bolts to 5 ft. lbs. torque and the oil pan-to-cover bolts to 11 ft. lbs. torque.

14. Install the seal, as required.

15. Complete the assembly of the vibration damper with key, fan and hub assembly, belts and properly adjust, any remaining components.

3.0L Engine

1. Disconnect the negative battery cable.

2. Remove the rocker covers. Hold the camshaft sprocket in place and remove the distributor drive/camshaft sprocket bolt. Remove the distributor assembly.

3. Remove the accessory drive belt. Remove the nuts retaining the front engine vibration damper to the engine and move it toward the radiator.

4. Remove the crankshaft pulley nut and remove the crankshaft pulley.

NOTE: The crankshaft pulley nut is put on with a threaded lock installed with the nut. It may be necessary to strike the pulley with a brass hammer to loosen it.

5. Remove the timing cover mounting bolts. Place a suitable prying tool between the cylinder block and a special boss on the front cover and gently pry off the cover. Discard the gaskets.

6. Remove the oil seal from the cover.

To install:

7. To prevent the key from falling into the oil pan, rotate the crankshaft so that the keyway points upward.

8. Apply a bead of RTV sealer to the points where the cylinder heads meet the block and the lower case meets the block.

9. Install the cover with new gasket over the alignment dowels. Tighten the bolts to 9 ft. lbs.

10. Install the distributor assembly and install the rocker covers.

11. Install the crankshaft pulley, apply thread locking compound to the threads of the pulley nut and tighten to 133 ft. lbs.

12. Install the accessory drive belt and adjust the belt tension.

NOTE: It is very important the accessory drive belt is routed cor-

rectly. If it is incorrectly routed the water pump could be driven in the wrong direction, causing the engine to overheat.

13. Install the engine vibration damper. Connect the negative battery cable.

Timing Chain and Sprockets

REMOVAL & INSTALLATION

2.5L Engine

1. Disconnect the negative battery cable.

2. Remove the fan shroud assembly, accessory drive belts, water pump pulley, crankshaft vibration damper and timing case cover.

NOTE: It is a good practice to either remove the radiator or cover the radiator core area when working around the radiator, as damage can result to the radiator core.

3. Rotate the crankshaft until the **0** timing mark on the crankshaft sprocket aligns with the timing mark on the camshaft sprocket.

4. Remove the oil slinger from the crankshaft.

5. Remove the camshaft retaining bolt and remove the sprocket and chain assembly.

6. If the timing chain tensioner is to

be replaced, the oil pan must also be removed.

To install:

7. Turn the tensioner lever to the **UNLOCK** position and pull the tensioner block toward the tensioner lever to compress the spring. Hold the block and turn the tensioner lever to the lock **UP** position.

8. Install the crankshaft/camshaft sprockets and timing chain. Make sure

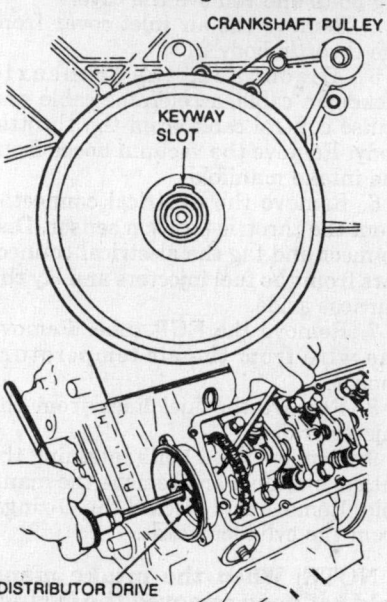

When removing crank pully, turn keyway to top keeping key from falling into engine; hold cam gear as shown—3.0L engine

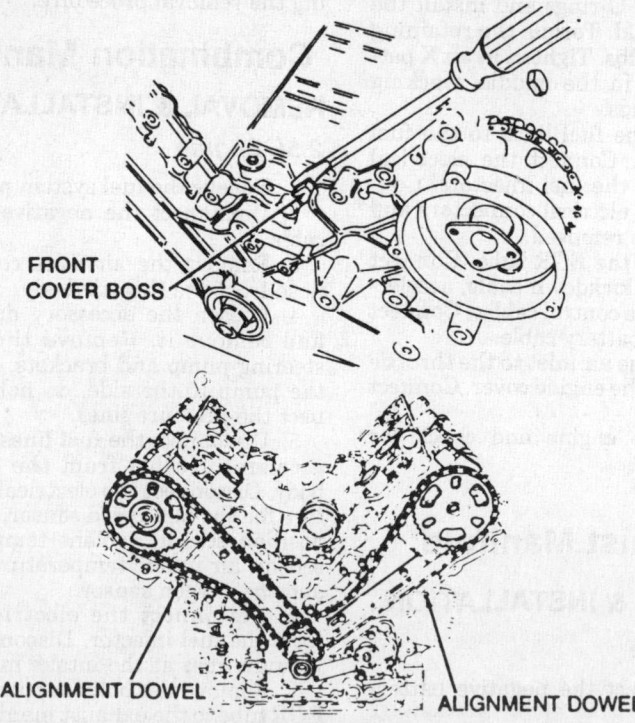

When prying loose front cover, note two alignment dowels—3.0L engine

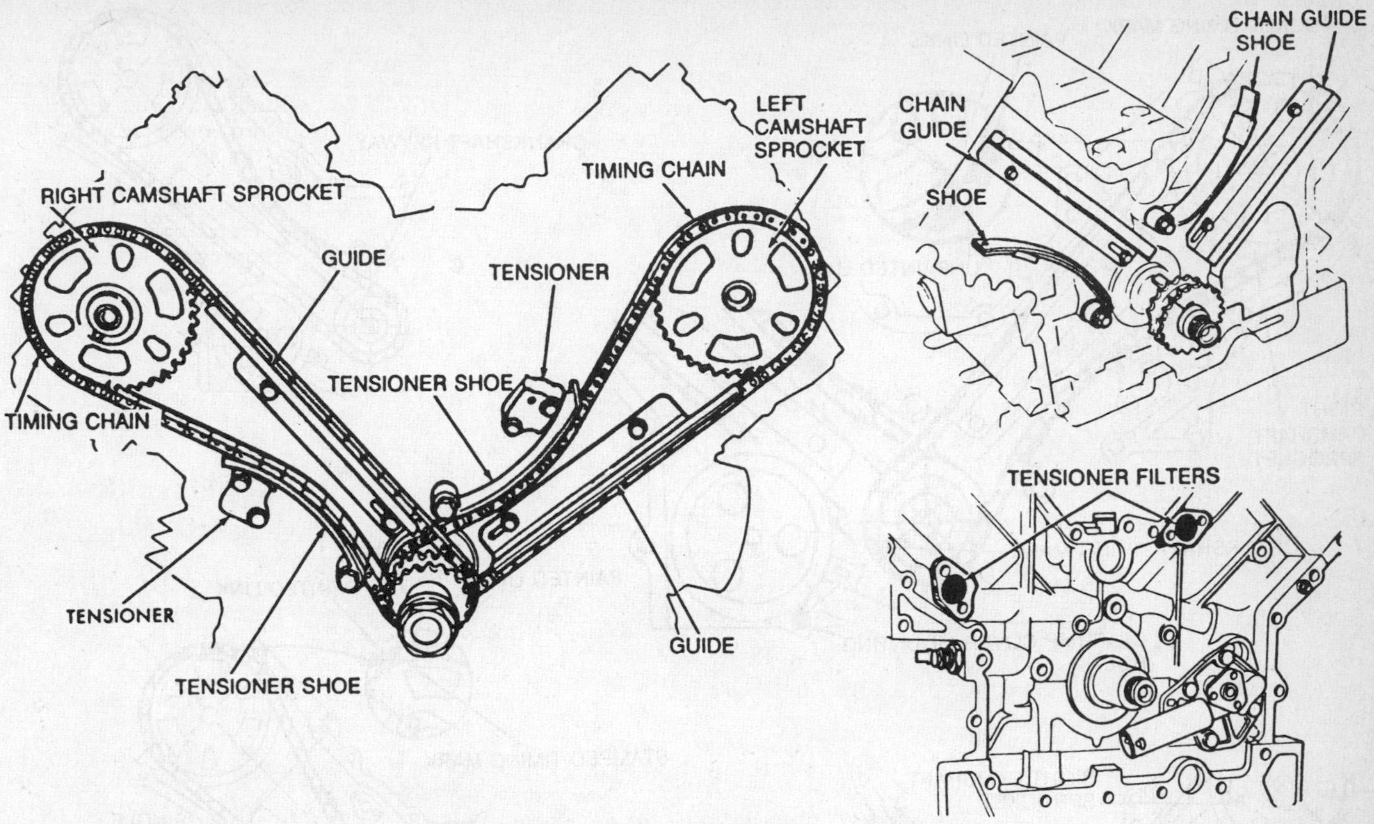

Timing chain and tensioner layout—3.0L engine

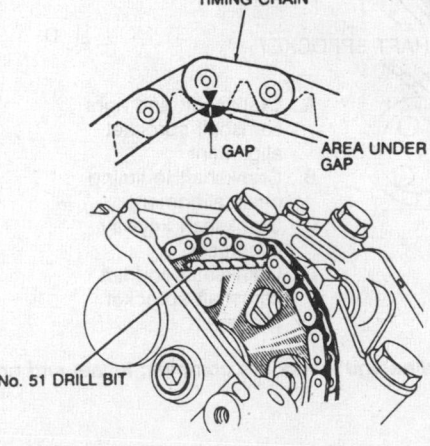

Measuring chain wear using a No. 51 drill as gauge—3.0L engine

the timing marks are lined up as indicated in Step 3.

9. Install the camshaft sprocket retaining bolt and washer. Torque the bolt to 80 ft. lbs. (108 Nm).

NOTE: To verify correct installation of the timing chain, rotate the crankshaft until the camshaft sprocket timing mark is approximately at the 1 o'clock position. There should be 20 pins between the marks.

10. Install the oil slinger and timing case cover using a new gasket.
11. Complete installation by reversing the removal procedure.

3.0L Engine

1. Remove the cylinder head cover.
2. Inspect the chain and sprocket for wear by pulling on the top of the chain. This will produce a gap between the bottom of the timing chain and the bottom of the area between the 2 sprocket teeth. The maximum gap is 0.067 in. This must not be exceeded. This gap corresponds to a travel of 0.866 in. by the timing chain tensioner plunger.
3. Use the solid end of a number 51 drill bit (0.067 in. dia.) to gauge the gap. If the solid end of the drill bit fits into the gap between the timing chain

and the 2 sprocket teeth, then the following parts must be replaced: timing chain shoes, tensioners, guides, sprockets, tensioner shoes. Use the following procedure.
4. Disconnect the negative battery cable.
5. Remove the front cover assembly. Turn the crankshaft until piston No. 1 is at TDC of the compression stroke.
6. Remove the oil pump sprocket re-

taining bolts and remove the sprocket/chain assembly.
7. Remove the bolt attaching the right side camshaft sprocket to the camshaft. Remove the right side tensioner and let the tensioner shoe hang down.
8. Remove the right side timing chain and sprocket. Remove the right side chain guide and tensioner shoe.

NOTE: Keep all of the components from each side together. This will aid in installation.

9. Remove the bolt attaching the left side camshaft sprocket to the camshaft. Remove the left side tensioner and let the tensioner shoe hang down.
10. Remove the left side timing chain and sprocket. Remove the left side chain guide and tensioner shoe.

To install:

NOTE: Inspect the timing chain tensioner. An opening shows the tensioner lock inside. This tensioner lock should not be removed. The lock is held in place by a spring that pushes a steel ball against the lock finger. If the lock is removed accidentally, replace the tensioner assembly because there is no way of checking the position of the lock finger in relation to the steel ball. When install-

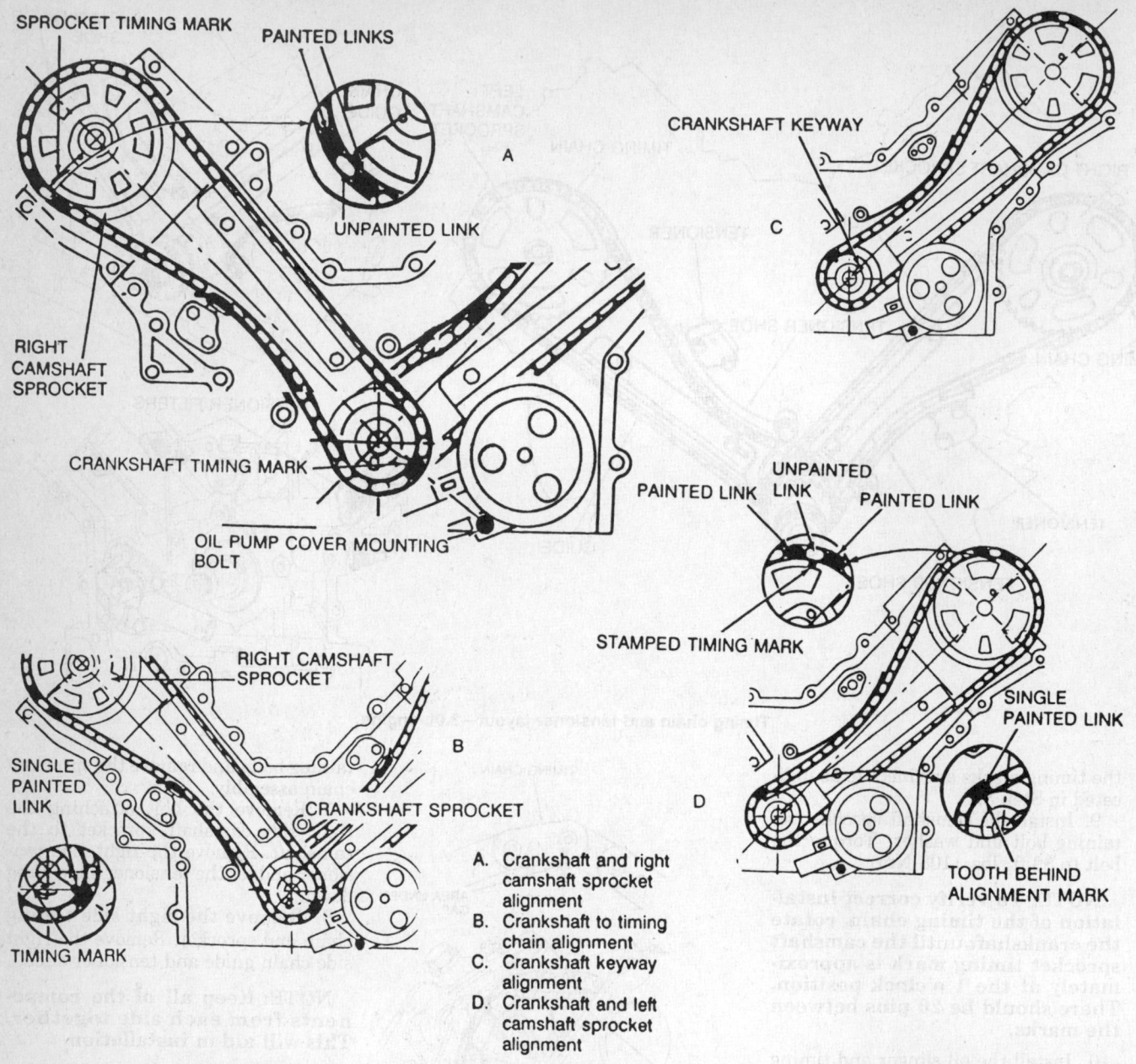

A. Crankshaft and right camshaft sprocket alignment
B. Crankshaft to timing chain alignment
C. Crankshaft keyway alignment
D. Crankshaft and left camshaft sprocket alignment

3.0L engine timing chains and marks are complex; locate and note marks before removal

ing a tensioner use a thin blade tool to turn the ratchet counterclockwise. Then push the tensioner arm in. Position the tensioner over the filter and the tensioner shoe into the arm.

11. To install, place the left and right chain guides into position and tighten the bolts to 48 inch lbs. Install the tensioner shoes and tighten the mounting bolts to 9 ft. lbs.

12. Turn the left camshaft until the keyway slot is in the 11 o'clock position. Turn the right camshaft so that the keyway is in the 8 o'clock position.

13. Turn the crankshaft until the keyway is aligned with the centerline of the left cylinder head.

NOTE: The crankshaft has 3 sprockets on it. A sprocket each for the left and right timing chains and 1 for the oil pump drive. The timing mark is located on the center sprocket.

14. Install the left camshaft sprocket. Install the left timing chain on the crankshaft. Position the single painted link of the timing chain, on the tooth of the rear sprocket, that is directly behind the timing mark of the center sprocket.

15. Install the left timing chain over the camshaft sprocket. The chain must be positioned with the unpainted link, that is between 2 painted links, aligned with the stamped timing mark on the camshaft sprocket.

16. Once the left chain is positioned, install the tensioner shoe and turn the tensioner arm inward. Tighten the mounting bolts to 48 inch lbs.

17. Turn the crankshaft until the timing mark on the center sprocket is aligned with the lower oil pump mounting bolt.

18. Install the right camshaft sprocket. Install the right timing chain over

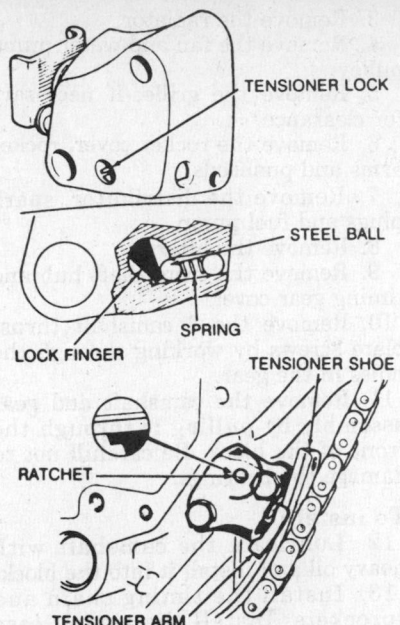

3.0L engine chain tensioner

the crankshaft sprocket. Position the single painted link over the timing mark on the crankshaft sprocket.

19. Position the right timing chain over the camshaft sprocket. The chain must be positioned with the unpainted link, that is between 2 painted links, aligned with the stamped timing mark on the camshaft sprocket.

20. Once the right chain is positioned, install the tensioner shoe and turn the tensioner arm inward. Tighten the mounting bolts to 48 inch lbs.

21. Install the right camshaft sprocket bolt and tighten to 59 ft. lbs. Push both of the chain tensioner shoes in to release them, this will adjust the chain tension.

NOTE: Once the crankshaft has been rotated the painted marks on the chain will no longer align with the timing marks. When checking valve timing it is the relation of the timing marks to each other that is used, not the position of the paint marks on the chains. To check, rotate the crankshaft 180 degrees. Check that the right camshaft sprocket timing mark and the crankshaft sprocket timing mark are aligned. Rotate the crankshaft another 90 degrees. Check that the left camshaft sprocket timing mark and the crankshaft sprocket timing mark are aligned.

22. Install the oil pump sprocket and chain, apply a suitable thread locking compound to the retaining bolts and tighten to 48 in. lbs.

23. Install the front cover assembly. Connect the negative battery cable. Check timing.

Timing Belt Front Cover

REMOVAL & INSTALLATION

2.2L Engine

1. Remove all V-belts, fan and pulley.
2. Remove vibration damper.
3. Remove oil pan to cover bolts and cover to block bolts.
4. Raise cover and pull oil pan front seal up far enough to extract the tabs from the holes in the cover.

NOTE: If this isn't done, the oil pan will have to be removed to get the seals into place.

5. Remove cover gasket from block. Cut off seal tab flush with the front face of the block.
To install:
6. Clean all mating surfaces and remove the oil seal.
7. Install a new front oil seal.
8. Install a new neoprene seal in the front of the oil pan, cutting off the protruding tabs to match original. Use sealer on the tab ends and the gasket surfaces.
9. Position cover on block and install bolts. Tighten cover bolts to 4–6 ft. lbs.; 4 lower bolts to 10–12 ft. lbs.
10. Install vibration damper, tightening the bolt to the specified torque. Install the accessory drive belt(s).

OIL SEAL REPLACEMENT

1. Remove the timing belt cover.
2. Clean cover well.
3. Drive out old seal. Install new seal with a round driver.
4. Reinstall timing belt cover.

NOTE: The front oil seal can be installed with the cover in place only if the proper tool or equivalant is available.

Timing Belt and Tensioner

ADJUSTMENT

1. Rotate the crankshaft clockwise 2 complete turns.
2. Loosen the tensioner bolts ¼ turn.
3. The spring loaded timing belt tensioner will automatically adjust to the correct position.
4. Tighten the bottom tensioner

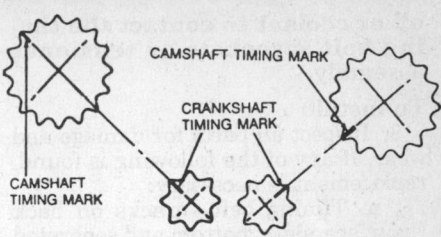

Align crank and right cam mark (A); turn crank 90° and check left cam mark (B)

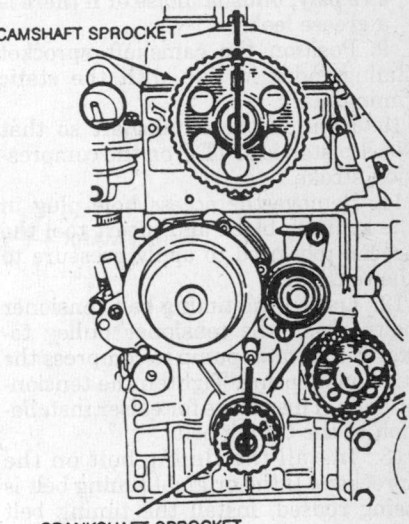

Camshaft sprocket timing marks alignment—2.2L engine Timing index and timing marks alignment—2.2L engine

bolt first, then the upper bolt. Torque both bolts to 18 ft. lbs.

5. Check timing belt deflection. It should be 0.216–0.276 in. (5.5–7.0mm).

REMOVAL & INSTALLATION

2.2L Engine

1. Disconnect the negative battery cable.
2. Remove the drive belts, vibration damper, pulley and key.
3. Remove the air conditioning compressor and alternator bracket, if equipped.
4. Remove the timing belt cover.
5. Make a mark on the back of the timing belt indicating the direction of rotation so it may be reassembled in the same direction if it is to be reused.
6. Loosen the timing belt tensioner pivot bolt and locking bolt.
7. Remove the timing belt.

NOTE: If coolant or engine oil comes in contact with the timing belt, they will drastically shorten its life. Also, do not allow engine

oil or coolant to contact the timing belt sprockets or tensioner assembly.

To install:

8. Inspect all parts for damage and wear. If any of the following is found, replacement is necessary:

a. Timing belt—cracks on back surface, sides, bottom and separated canvas.

b. Tensioner pulleys—turn the pulleys and check for binding, excessive play, unusual noise or if there is a grease leak.

9. Position the camshaft sprocket timing index in line with the static timing mark.

10. Position the crankshaft so that No. 1 piston is at TDC on the compression stroke.

11. Remove the access hole plug in the cylinder block and insert tool the special tool used to apply pressure to the tensioner.

12. Loosen the timing belt tensioner bolts. Push the tensioner pulley towards the water pump to compress the tensioner spring. Tighten the tensioner bolts. This allows for eaiser installation of the timing belt.

13. Install the timing belt on the sprockets. If the original timing belt is being reused, install the timing belt with the arrow previously made, pointing in the proper direction of rotation.

14. Loosen the tensioner bolts and allow the spring loaded tensioner to contact the belt. This will automatically tension the belt. Then, tighten the tensioner retaining bolts.

15. Position the timing belt cover over the sprockets and check the position of the camshaft sprocket timing mark with the index on the cover.

16. Install cylinder block plug, check the timing belt tension adjustment and complete installation by reversing the removal procedure.

Timing Sprockets

REMOVAL & INSTALLATION

1. Disconnect battery negative cable.

2. Turn crankshaft until piston No. 1 is at TDC of the compression stroke.

3. Remove the accessory drive belts.

4. Remove crankshaft vibration damper.

5. Remove the timing belt cover.

6. Remove the timing belt.

7. Make sure the camshaft sprocket has the rectangular hole upwards and

timing mark is at the 12 o'clock position.

8. Loosen the camshaft sprocket bolt and gently tap the sprocket from the rear to remove.

To install:

9. Installation is the reverse of the removal procedure. Make sure the timing marks are aligned.

10. Install and adjust the timing belt.

11. Install the timing cover using a new seal, if required.

12. Install accessory belts. Connect battery. Check timing.

Camshaft

REMOVAL & INSTALLATION

2.2L Engine

1. Relieve the fuel system pressure.

2. Disconnect the negative battery cable. Drain the cooling system.

3. Remove the intake and exhaust manifolds.

4. Remove the rocker cover and remove the rocker shaft assembly.

5. Remove the accessory drive belt. Remove the timing belt cover.

6. Remove the timing belt. Remove the cylinder head retaining bolts and remove the cylinder head.

7. Remove the camshaft sprocket and the bolts retaining the camshaft thrust plate.

8. Pry the oil seal out from around the camshaft and slide the camshaft from the head. Use care not to damage the camshaft lobes or the bearings.

To install:

9. Lubricate the camshaft with heavy oil and slide it into the head.

10. Install the camshaft thrust plate. Install a new camshaft oil seal using tool MOT–791–10 or equivalent. Install the camshaft sprocket and tighten the retaining bolt to 37 ft. lbs.

11. Install the cylinder head using a new gasket, tighten all bolts in sequence, to the specified torque.

12. Install the timing belt and adjust the tension. Install the timing belt cover.

13. Install the rocker shaft assembly. Install the rocker cover, intake and exhaust manifolds.

14. Install the accessory drive belt and fill the cooling system. Connect the negative battery cable. Run the engine and bleed the cooling system.

2.5L Engine

1. Relieve the fuel system pressure.

2. Disconnect the negative battery cable. Drain the cooling system.

3. Remove the radiator.

4. Remove the fan and water pump pulley.

5. Remove the grille, if necessary for clearance.

6. Remove the rocker cover, rocker arms and pushrods.

7. Remove the distributor, spark plugs and fuel pump.

8. Remove the lifters.

9. Remove the crankshaft hub and timing gear cover.

10. Remove the 2 camshaft thrust plate screws by working through the holes in the gear.

11. Remove the camshaft and gear assembly by pulling it through the front of the block. Be carefull not to damage the bearings.

To install:

12. Lubricate the camshaft with heavy oil and install it into the block.

13. Install the timing chain and sprockets. Install the timing case cover.

14. Install the valve lifters and related components. Install the rocker cover.

15. Install the crankshaft hub and the water pump pulley. Install the accessory drive belts.

16. Position the distributor and tighten the hold-down bolt, install the spark plugs.

17. Install the grille. Connect the negative battery cable.

3.0L Engine

The camshafts used in this engine are removed from the rear of the cylinder heads after the cylinder heads have been removed.

1. Relieve the fuel system pressure.

2. Disconnect the negative battery cable.

3. Drain the cooling system.

4. Remove the accessory drive belt. Remove the air inlet tube from the throttle body.

5. Remove the intake and exhaust manifolds.

6. Remove the front cover and remove the timing chains and sprockets.

7. Remove the rocker covers and the rocker shaft assemblies. Remove the cylinder head(s).

8. Remove the camshaft cover at the rear of the cylinder head. Loosen the camshaft retainer bolt and slide the retainer away from the camshaft.

9. Slide the camshaft out of the head, use care not to damage the camshaft lobes or bearings.

To install:

10. Coat the camshaft with heavy oil and slide it into the head. Position the

retainer in the grove of the camshaft and tighten the mounting bolt to 9 ft. lbs.

11. Push the camshaft to the front and check the camshaft endplay by inserting a feeler gauge between the retainer and the front of the camshaft.

12. Install the camshaft cover using a new gasket, tighten the bolts to 48 inch lbs.

13. Install the cylinder heads and tighten the bolts in the proper sequence, to the correct specification. Install the intake and exhaust manifolds.

14. Install the timing chains and sprockets.

15. Install the front cover assembly and the accessory drive belt.

16. Install the rocker shaft assemblies and the rocker covers.

17. Fill the cooling system and connect the negative battery cable. Install the air inlet tube.

18. Run the engine and bleed the cooling system, check for leaks.

Intermediate Shaft

REMOVAL & INSTALLATION

2.2L Engine

1. Disconnect the negative battery cable.

2. Remove the timing belt cover and the timing belt.

3. Remove the oil pump driveshaft cover, located on the side of the block.

4. Screw a piece of threaded rod into the top of oil pump driveshaft and remove it.

5. Remove the bolt retaining the intermediate shaft sprocket and remove the intermediate shaft sprocket.

6. Remove the bolts from the intermediate shaft cover. Remove the cover and gasket. Remove the bolt from the intermediate shaft retainer and pivot the retainer. Remove the intermediate shaft by pulling it from the block.

7. To Install, coat the shaft with heavy oil and slide it into the block. Pivot the retainer into position and tighten the bolt. Install the shaft cover and loosely install the retaining bolts.

8. Install the shaft oil seal and align the cover using tool MOT–790 or equivalent. Tighten the cover retaining bolts.

9. Install the sprocket and bolt, tighten the bolt to 37 ft. lbs.

10. Install the oil pump driveshaft and cover.

11. Install the timing belt and cover, check the belt tension.

12. Connect the negative battery cable.

Piston and Connecting Rod

POSITIONING

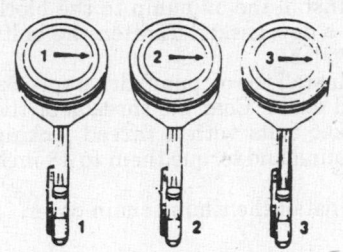

LEFT BANK

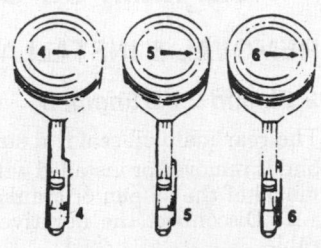

RIGHT BANK

Piston positioning—3.0L engine
Piston positioning—2.2L engine
2.5L engine—oil squirt holes face the camshaft and the arrow on the top of the piston must face the front of the engine

---

ENGINE LUBRICATION

Oil Pan

REMOVAL & INSTALLATION

2.2L Engine

1. Disconnect the negative battery cable.

2. Raise and safely support the vehicle.

3. Remove the underbody splash shield and drain the engine oil.

4. Remove the engine mount cushion nuts.

5. Lower the vehicle and position engine support tool MS–1900 or equivalent, on the inner fender flanges.

6. Tighten the support tool until the engine comes up enough to remove the oil pan.

7. Raise and safely support the vehicle. Remove the oil pan bolts and remove the oil pan.

To install:

8. Before installing, clean all the gasket mating surfaces with a suitable solvent and wipe dry.

9. Install the oil pan to the engine block using a new gasket. Do not use any sealer on the gasket, it must be installed dry.

NOTE: There are 3 sizes of bolts used to retain the oil pan on this engine. Note the location of each bolt when it is removed.

10. Tighten the oil pan bolts attaching the pan to the clutch/converter housing first, then tighten the remaining bolts. Tighten all of the bolts to 88 inch lbs.

11. Install the splash shield and lower the vehicle.

12. Remove the support tool and install the engine mount bolts.

13. Fill the engine with the required amount of oil.

2.5L and 3.0L Engines

1. Disconnect the negative battery cable.

2. Raise and safely support the vehicle. Drain the oil.

3. Remove the front anti-sway bar retaining bolts and remove the sway bar.

4. Loosen the engine mount stud and nut assemblies. Remove the front tires.

5. Remove the lower ball joint retaining bolts and disengage the lower ball joints from the steering knuckles.

6. Remove the nuts at the center of the transaxle crossmember securing the rear of the transaxle to the crossmember.

7. Lower the vehicle and attach engine support tool MS-1900 to the engine.

8. With the vehicle down, loosen the 4 sub-frame attaching nuts. Remove the front 2 first, allowing the sub-frame to pivot to the ground. Support the rear of the sub-frame and remove the 2 rear nuts. Lower the sub-frame away from the vehicle.

9. Raise and support the vehicle. Remove the oil pan retaining bolts and remove the oil pan.

To install:

10. Before installing, clean all of the gasket mating surfaces. Install the oil pan using a new gasket. Do not use any sealer, the gasket must be installed dry.

11. Tighten all of the retaining bolts to 9 ft. lbs.

12. Install the sub-frame assembly and tighten the mounting nuts to 92 ft. lbs.

13. Connect the lower ball joints and tighten the attaching nut to 77 ft. lbs. Tighten the transaxle-to-crossmember bolts to 20 ft. lbs.

14. Remove the engine support tool. Attach the anti-sway bar and install the front wheels.

15. Lower the vehicle. Fill the crankcase with the appropriate quantity and grade of oil.

Oil Pump

REMOVAL & INSTALLATION

2.2L Engine

1. Disconnect the negative battery cable.
2. Remove the oil pump drive cover plate bolts and remove the cover.
3. Using a threaded rod, thread it into the top of the pump driveshaft. Remove the pump driveshaft by pulling it out of the block.
4. Raise and safely support the vehicle. Drain the oil.
5. Remove the oil pan. Remove the oil pump mounting bolts and remove the pump.

To install:

6. Install the oil pump using a new gasket. Tighten the mounting bolts to 33 ft. lbs.
7. Install the oil pan. Fill the crankcase with the correct grade and quantity of oil.
8. Install the oil pump driveshaft and cover.
9. Start the vehicle and check for leaks.

2.5L Engine

1. Disconnect the negative battery cable.
2. Raise the vehicle and support safely. Drain the engine oil and remove the oil pan.
3. Remove the oil pump retaining bolts, the oil pump and gasket.

NOTE: **The oil pump removal and installation will not affect the distributor timing because the distributor drive gear remains meshed with the camshaft. Do not disturb the position of the oil inlet tube and strainer assembly in the pump body. If the tube is moved in the body, a replacement tube and strainer must be installed to assure an airtight seal.**

4. To insure self priming, fill the gear cavity with petroleum jelly before installing the cover.
5. Install the pump with a new gasket. Tighten the short bolts to 10 ft. lbs. and the long bolts to 17 ft. lbs.
6. Install the oil pan using new gaskets and seals. Complete the assembly as required.

3.0L Engine

1. Disconnect the negative battery cable.

2. Remove the timing chain cover assembly.
3. Remove the bolts retaining the oil pump drive sprocket. Remove the sprocket and the oil pump drive chain.
4. Remove the oil pump mounting bolts and remove the oil pump.
5. Install the oil pump to the block using a new gasket. Tighten the bolts to 9 ft. lbs.
6. Install the oil pump drive sprocket and chain. Coat the threads of the sprocket bolts with a thread locking compound and torque them to 48 inch lbs.
7. Install the timing chain cover.

Rear Main Oil Seal

REMOVAL & INSTALLATION

2.2L and 2.5L Engines

The rear main oil seal is a single unit and is removed or installed without removal of the oil pan or crankshaft.

1. Disconnect the negative battery cable.
2. Remove the transaxle, flywheel or torque converter bellhousing and the flywheel or flexplate.
3. Remove the rear main oil seal with a small prying tool. Be extremely careful not to scratch the crankshaft.

To install:

4. Oil the lips of the new seal with clean engine oil. Install the new seal by hand onto the rear crankshaft flange. The helical lip side of the seal should face the engine. Make sure the seal is firmly and evenly installed.
5. The new seal is installed with a special installer. Use the tool as follows:

   a. Back the plastic wing nut off until it contacts the cap nut on the end of the shaft.
   b. Lightly lubricate both the inside and outside edges of the seal.
   c. Install the seal on the tool with the dust shield facing toward the plastic wing nut.
   d. Fit the tool pilot in the center of the front surface of the installer into the pilot hole in the back of the crankshaft; the small dowel at the top of the front surface of the tool must fit into the corresponding small hole in the crankshaft at the same time. Hold the tool in this position and thread the 2 attaching screws into the crankshaft.
   e. Turn the plastic wing nut in until it bottoms out to fully seat the seal. Unscrew the attaching nuts and remove the seal installer.
   f. Inspect the dust shield all around to make sure it is not curled under. If it is, gently to pull the lip out.

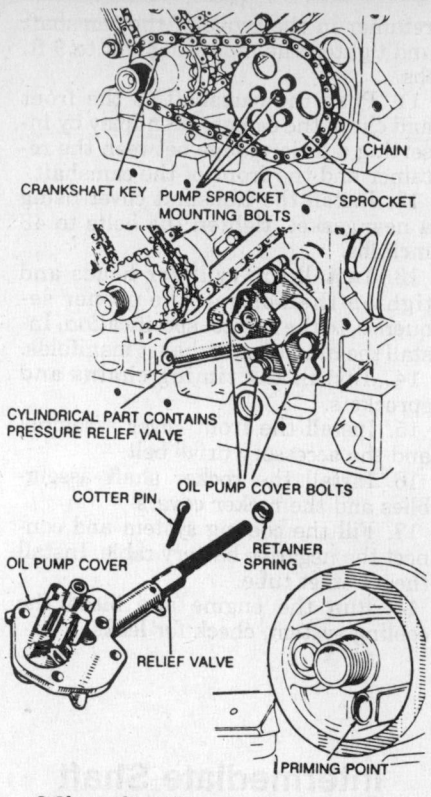

CYLINDRICAL PART CONTAINS PRESSURE RELIEF VALVE

COTTER PIN — OIL PUMP COVER BOLTS

OIL PUMP COVER — RETAINER SPRING

RELIEF VALVE — PRIMING POINT

CHAIN

CRANKSHAFT KEY — PUMP SPROCKET MOUNTING BOLTS — SPROCKET

3.0L engine oil pump drive, mount, components and priming point

g. Replace the flywheel or flexplate, bell housing and transaxle.

3.0L Engine

1. Disconnect the negative battery cable.
2. Remove the transaxle assembly.
3. Remove the bolts from the lower rear main seal housing.
4. Remove the rear main seal housing bolts and remove the housing.
5. Push the old rear main seal from the housing.
6. Clean the gasket mating surfaces.

To install:

7. Install the rear main seal housing on the block. Use a new housing gasket.
8. Tighten the seal housing-to-block bolts first, then tighten the lower bolts. Torque all bolts to 9 ft. lbs.
9. Install the new rear seal to tool MOT–259–01 or equivalent, lightly coat the inner edges of the seal with oil. Install the seal to the seal housing by lightly tapping on the installation tool.
10. Remove the installation tool. Install the transaxle assembly.
11. Connect the negative battery cable. Start the vehicle and check for leaks.

MANUAL TRANSAXLE

For further information on transmissions/transaxles, please refer to "Chilton's Guide to Transmission Repair".

REMOVAL & INSTALLATION

1. Disconnect the negative battery cable.
2. Disconnect and remove the flexible heat tube from the engine.
3. Remove the TDC sensor retaining bolt and remove the sensor.
4. Remove the bolts retaining the steering bracket and remove the bracket.
5. Remove the bolts attaching the crossmember to the side sill and body.
6. Raise and safely support the vehicle.
7. Remove the front wheels. Disconnect and remove the passenger side tie rod.
8. Loosen the bolt retaining the coolant expansion tank and move the tank aside.
9. Attach an engine support tool to the engine and take up the engine weight.
10. Remove the bolts attaching the exhaust head pipe to the manifold. Remove the bolts attaching the exhaust head pipe to the converter and remove the head pipe.
11. Remove the crossmember by turning it and taking out through the passenger side wheel well.
12. Disengage the clutch cable. Remove the upper steering knuckle mounting bolt and loosen the lower bolt.
13. Remove the halfshaft retaining pin. Swing each rotor and steering knuckle outward and slide the halfshafts from the transaxle.
14. Disconnect the reverse lockout cable and disconnect the shift rod from the lever. Disconnect the speedometer cable. Disconnect the ground strap at the transaxle.
15. Support the transaxle. Remove the transaxle support cushion nuts. Remove the bolts that attach the 2 transaxle mounting brackets to the transaxle.
16. Disconnect the wiring harness connector and remove the starter. Remove the bolts attaching the clutch housing to the engine.
17. Pull the transaxle straight back until the clutch shaft is clear of the engine and lower the transaxle.
To install:
18. Raise and position the transaxle

into the vehicle. Align the release bearing and the release fork.
19. Install the transaxle-to-engine mounting bolts. Tighten to 37 ft. lbs.
20. Install the starter and connect the electrical connectors. Slightly raise the transaxle and install the mounting brackets. Align the transaxle support cushion bolts and install the retaining nuts.
21. Connect the speedometer cable and the shift rods. Connect the clutch cable.
22. Install the halfshafts by tilting the steering knuckle in, install the upper bolt and tighten both bolts to 148 ft. lbs.
23. Install the axle retaining pins. Connect the ground strap to the case.
24. Install the crossmember through the wheel well opening and position it on the side sills. Install and tighten the bolts.
25. Connect the tie rods to the steering bracket and tighten the mounting bolts to 25 ft. lbs. Connect the steering gear bracket to the steering rack and tighten the bolts to 30 ft. lbs.
26. Install the front wheels. Install the TDC sensor and the heat tube. Connect the exhaust header pipe to the converter and manifold.
27. Check and fill the transaxle fluid. Remove the engine support tool and connect the battery.
28. Check the operation of the shift mechanism.

CLUTCH

Clutch Assembly

REMOVAL & INSTALLATION

1. Disconnect the negative battery cable.
2. Remove the transaxle assembly from the vehicle.
3. Remove the pressure plate attaching bolts.
4. Remove the pressure plate release bearing assembly and the clutch disc.
To install:
5. Inspect the condition of the clutch components and replace any worn parts.

NOTE: The release bearing and pressure plate are not serviced separately. The bearing is permanently attached to the pressure plate diaphragm fingers. The pressure plate and bearing must be serviced as an assembly.

6. Inspect the flywheel for heat

damage or cracks. Replace it if necessary.
7. Install the clutch disc to the flywheel. Install alignment tool EMB-786-01 or equivalent. Install the pressure plate assembly and tighten the pressure plate bolts evenly to 18 ft. lbs. Remove the alignment tool.
8. Install the transaxle assembly and check the clutch operation.

Clutch Cable

ADJUSTMENT

The Medallion uses a cable operated, self adjusting clutch mechanism. The adjustment is automatically set during operation by a quadrant mechanism on the clutch pedal assembly.

AUTOMATIC TRANSAXLE

For further information on transmissions/transaxles, please refer to "Chilton's Guide to Transmission Repair".

Transaxle Assembly

REMOVAL & INSTALLATION

Premier and Monaco

1. Disconnect the negative battery cable.
2. Loosen the throttle valve cable adjusting nut and remove the cable from the engine bracket.
3. Disengage the shift cable and support it to the side. Remove the upper steering knuckle mounting bolt and loosen the lower bolt.
4. Remove the halfshaft retaining pin. Swing each rotor and steering knuckle outward and slide the halfshafts from the transaxle.
5. Remove the underbody splash shield.
6. Remove the converter housing covers. Remove the converter-to-flexplate bolts. Support the transaxle.
7. Remove the nuts attaching the crossmember to the side sills. Remove the large bolt and nut that attach the rear cushion to the support bracket.
8. Remove the support bracket and rear cushion.
9. Disconnect the header pipes from the exhaust manifold and the catalytic converter.
10. Loosen the engine cradle bolts. Remove the starter, plate and dowel.

Disconnect the shift cable from the transaxle lever. Remove the cable bracket bolts and separate the bracket from the case.

11. Disconnect and remove the TDC sensor, disconnect the speedometer sensor. Disconnect the transaxle cooling lines.

12. Remove the transaxle-to-engine bolts, pull the transaxle back and away from the engine.

To install:

13. Position the transaxle to the engine. Install the transaxle-to-engine bolts and tighten to 31 ft. lbs.

14. Connect all electrical leads, install the TDC sensor. Connect the speedometer. Install the transaxle cooler lines.

15. Attach the shift bracket to the case and tighten the bolts to 125 inch lbs. Install the shift cable into the bracket.

16. Install the starter. Connect the exhaust head pipes to the manifolds and he converter.

17. Install the rear support and cushion, install the mounting bolts and tighten to 49 ft. lbs.

18. Tighten the engine cradle bolts to 92 ft. lbs. Connect the halfshafts.

19. Install the converter-to-flexplate bolts and tighten to 24 ft. lbs. Install the converter housing covers.

20. Tilt the steering knuckles in and install the top bolts, tighten all to 148 ft. lbs.

21. Install the front wheels. Install the under body splash shield. Attach the throttle valve cable.

22. Connect the negative battery cable. Check the fluid level.

Medallion

1. Disconnect the negative battery cable.

2. Disconnect and remove the flexible heat tube from the engine.

3. Remove the TDC sensor retaining bolt and remove the sensor.

4. Remove the bolts retaining the steering bracket and remove the bracket.

5. Remove the bolts attaching the crossmember to the side sill and body.

6. Raise and safely support the vehicle.

7. Remove the front wheels. Disconnect and remove the passenger side tie rod.

8. Loosen the bolt retaining the coolant expansion tank and move the tank aside.

9. Attach an engine support tool to take up the weight of the engine.

10. Remove the bolts attaching the exhaust head pipe to the manifold. Remove the bolts attaching the exhaust head pipe to the converter and remove

the head pipe. Disconnect the coolant lines to the heat exchanger.

11. Remove the crossmember by turning it and taking out through the passenger side wheel well.

12. Disengage the shift cable and support it to the side. Remove the upper steering knuckle mounting bolt and loosen the lower bolt.

13. Remove the halfshaft retaining pin. Swing each rotor and steering knuckle outward and slide the halfshafts from the transaxle.

14. Disconnect the speedometer cable. Disconnect the ground strap at the transaxle. Disconnect the BVA module harness.

15. Support the transaxle. Remove the transaxle support cushion nuts. Remove the bolts that attach the 2 transaxle mounting brackets to the transaxle.

16. Disconnect the wiring harness connector and remove the starter. Remove the converter-to-flywheel bolts. Remove the transaxle-to-engine bolts.

17. Pull the transaxle straight back until the converter is clear of the engine and lower the transaxle. Install converter retainer BVI–465 or equivalent, to keep the converter from falling out.

To install:

18. Raise and position the transaxle into the vehicle. Apply a small amount of grease to the torque converter pilot. Align the painted marks on the converter with the painted marks on the flywheel. Install the converter to flywheel bolts, tighten to 34 ft. lbs.

19. Install the transaxle-to-engine mounting bolts. Tighten to 37 ft. lbs.

20. Install the starter and connect the electrical connectors. Slightly raise the transaxle and install the mounting brackets. Align the transaxle support cushion bolts and install the retaining nuts.

21. Connect the speedometer cable and the shift cable.

22. Install the halfshafts by tilting the steering knuckle in, install the upper bolt and tighten both bolts to 148 ft. lbs.

23. Install the axle retaining pins. Connect the ground strap to the case.

24. Install the crossmember through the wheel well opening and position it on the side sills. Install and tighten the bolts.

25. Connect the tie rods to the steering bracket and tighten the mounting bolts to 25 ft. lbs. Connect the steering gear bracket to the steering rack and tighten the bolts to 30 ft. lbs. Connect the cooling lines.

26. Install the front wheels. Install the TDC sensor and the heat tube. Connect the exhaust header pipe to the converter and manifold. Connect the BVA wiring.

27. Check and fill the transaxle fluid. Remove the engine support tool and connect the battery.

SHIFT LINKAGE ADJUSTMENT

Premier and Monaco

1. Disconnect negative battery cable.

2. Shift into the **P** detent.

3. Remove the shifter cover and locate the shift cable cross-lock where the cable meets the shifter bracket. Release the shift cable cross-lock by pulling it upward.

4. Move the transaxle shift lever all the way rearward into the **P** detent. Be sure the lever is centered in the detent. Verify positive engagement of the park lock by attempting to rotate the halfshafts. The shafts cannot be turned if the park lock is properly engaged.

5. Verify that the cable is properly routed and secured and that the cable grommet is fully seated in the floor pan. Press the cable cross-lock downward until it snaps in place.

6. Position the cable self-adjusting unit in the fork of the lower cable mounting bracket at the transaxle. Use the index key to properly index and seat the cable within the bracket.

7. Seat the cable core end fitting onto the transaxle operating lever pin.

8. At the transaxle end fitting, push the core-adjust slider mechanism until it smaps into a locked position. This will properly adjust and lock the gearshift cable. No other adjustment is required.

9. Check the shift cable adjustment. Engine should start in **P** and **N** only.

THROTTLE VALVE CABLE ADJUSTMENT

1. Disconnect negative battery cable.

2. Loosen the cable locknuts and lift the threaded shank of the the cable out of the engine bracket.

3. Place the throttle lever in the curb idle position.

4. An accurate measurement must now be made. Vernier calipers are suggested. If accurate calipers are not available, fabricate a cable adjustment gauge from a small piece of sheet stock or other material that can be shipped over the throttle cable wire. The gauge must be 1.55 in. (39.5mm) long.

5. Pull the cable wire forward and position the vernier calipers or fabricated gauge on the wire between the cable connector and cable end.

6. Pull the cable shank rearward to the detent position but not to the wide

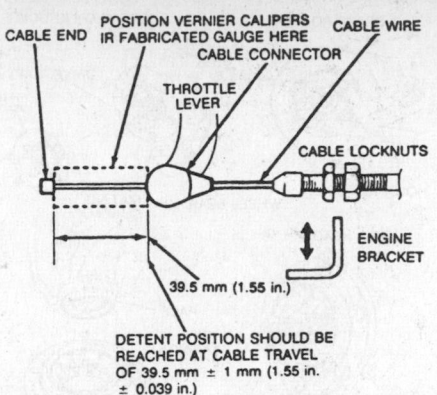

Throttle valve cable adjustment—Premier and Monaco

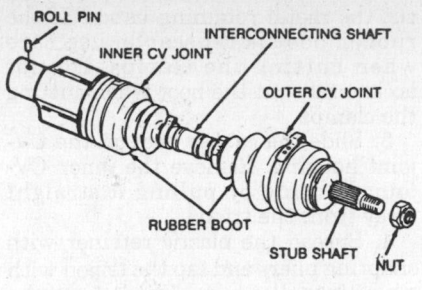

Halfshaft driveshaft—Premier

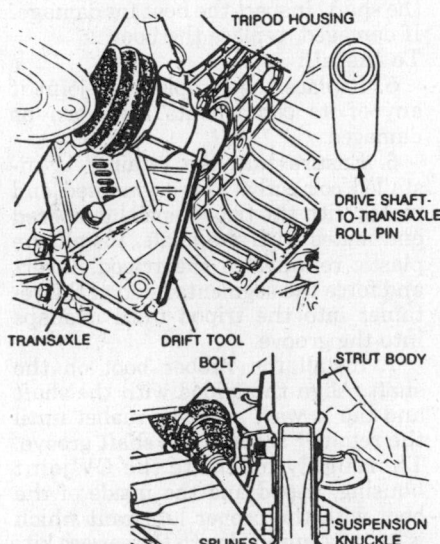

Remove halfshaft by driving out roll pin and removing joint from knuckle

open throttle position, detent position feels similar to a stop when reached.

7. Hold the cable shank at the detent position, then insert the cable shank into the cable bracket and tighten the cable locknuts.

8. Remove the vernier calipers or gauge and verify the adjustment. The cable detent position should be reached when the cable wire travels 1.55 in. ± 0.039 in. (39.5mm ± 1mm).

DRIVE AXLE

Halfshaft

REMOVAL & INSTALLATION

Premier and Monaco

The halfshafts are comprised of an inner CV-joint, an interconnecting shaft and an outer Rzeppa CV-joint with a stub shaft. The inner tripod CV-joint can be disassembled but must be replaced as a unit. The outer Rzeppa joint CV-joint cannot be disassembled and must be replaced as a unit. The protective rubber boots and clamps that cover each CV-joint are replaceable components.

1. Raise the vehicle and support it safely.

2. Remove the tires and wheels.

3. Remove the brake caliper. Do not disconnect the brake hose from the caliper. Wire it out of the way. Do not allow the brake hose to support the caliper weight.

4. Remove the halfshaft hub nut. A holding fixture may be required to hold the wheel hub/rotor when removing the nut.

5. A single, spiral wound roll pin is used to retain each halfshaft at the transaxle. Using a drift type tool, re-

move the halfshaft to transaxle roll pin.

NOTE: Before proceding to the next step, be certain the front suspension is hanging free. The strut body to suspension knuckle bolts are splined. Remove the bolts only as instructed in the following steps.

6. Remove the 2 splined bolts that attach the strut body to the suspension knuckle. Do this by the following: Loosen and turn the nuts until they are almost at the end of the bolt threads. Tap the nuts with a brass hammer to loosen the bolts and disengage the splines. Remove the nuts and slide the bolts out of the strut body and suspension knuckle.

7. Place a drain pan under the transaxle end of the halfshaft.

8. Wrap a shop towel around the halfshaft outer rubber boot to prevent damaging the boot.

9. Tilt the suspension knuckle out and away from the strut body and remove the halfshaft.

To install:

10. During installation, mate the

halfshaft with the transaxle shaft and align the roll pin holes in each shaft.

NOTE: One side of the roll pin hole in the transaxle shaft is beveled. Align the beveled side of that hole with the side of the hole in the CV-joint housing that is located in the housing "valley."

11. Insert the driveshaft to transaxle shaft roll pin and seat it with a hammer and a drift type tool.

12. Complete installation by reversing the removal procedure.

Medallion

1. Disconnect the negative battery cable.

2. Raise the vehicle and support it safely.

3. Remove the front wheels.

4. Remove the halfshaft nut.

5. Remove the double roll pins that attach the halfshaft to the side gear shaft.

6. Remove the tie rod end.

7. Remove the upper bolt that attaches the knuckle to the strut. Then, loosen but do not remove the lower bolt.

NOTE: The driveshaft splines are secured to the hub splines with Loctite. Set up a screw puller/press to push the shaft from the hub. Do not attempt to loosen the shaft with a hammer.

8. Tilt the rotor/knuckle outward and remove the driveshaft.

9. To install, reverse the removal procedure.

CV-Joint Boot

The protective rubber boots and clamps that cover each CV-joint are replaceable components. The applicable CV-joint must be removed from the interconnecting shaft to replace a rubber boot.

REPLACEMENT

Outer CV-Joint

1. Remove the halfshaft.

2. Side cutter pliers can be used to cut the metal retaining bands. If the rubber boot is reuseable, use care when cutting the clamps. Do not accidentally cut the boot when cutting the clamps.

3. Slide the rubber boot off the CV-joint housing for access to the plastic retainer.

4. Spread the plastic retainer at the seam with snapring pliers.

5. Tap the outer CV-joint with a plastic mallet to disengage the interconnecting shaft from the retainer.

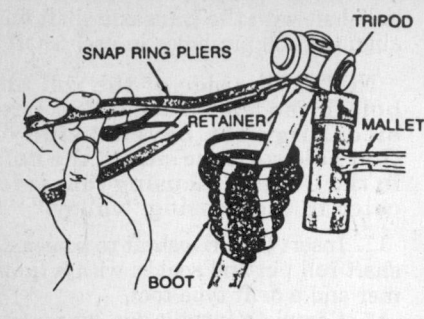

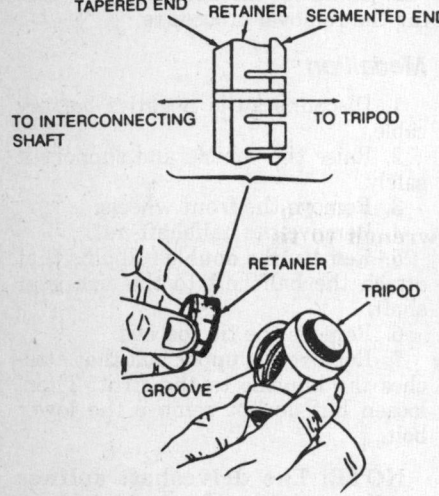

Typical joint removal and retainer orientation

6. Separate the outer CV-joint from the interconnecting shaft. Slide off the rubber boot. Inspect the boot for damage. If damaged, replace the boot.

To install:

7. Inspect the plastic retainer in the outer CV joint. Replace the retainer if it is damaged or defective. If a replacement retainer must be installed, ensure that it is installed correctly. The tapered end mates with the shaft and the segmented end mates with the CV-joint.

8. Install the rubber boot on the shaft. Thoroughly lubricate the CV-joint and the inside of the boot with the proper lubricant which is usually supplied with the service kit.

9. Align the shaft with the plastic retainer and the CV-joint, then tap the CV-joint onto the shaft with a plastic mallet. Continue tapping the CV-joint until the segmented end of the retainer snaps into position on the shaft.

10. Position the rubber boot on the clamp grooves machined in the CV-joint and in the shaft. Install the replacement clamps and crimp or otherwise tighten as required. Install the halfshaft in the vehicle.

Inner CV-Joint

1. Remove the halfshaft.
2. Side cutter pliers can be used to cut the metal retaining bands. If the rubber boot is reuseable, use care when cutting the clamps. Do not accidentaly cut the boot when cutting the clamps.

3. Slide the rubber boot off the CV-joint housing. Remove the inner CV-joint housing by pulling it straight away from the tripod.

4. Spread the plastic retainer with snapring pliers and tap the tripod with a plastic mallet to remove it from the shaft. If necessary, cut the retainer to remove it. Slide the rubber boot from the shaft. Inspect the boot for damage. If damaged, replace the boot.

To install:

5. Replace the complete CV-joint if any of its components are worn or damaged.

6. Ensure that the retainer is installed correctly. The segmented end mates with the tripod and the tapered end mates with the shaft. Install the plastic retainer in the tripod. Insert and force the segmented end of the retainer into the tripod until it snaps into the groove.

7. Install the rubber boot on the shaft. Align the tripod with the shaft and tap it with a plastic mallet until the retainer seats in the shaft groove. Thoroughly lubricate the CV-joint housing, tripod and the inside of the boot with the proper lubricant which is usually supplied with the service kit.

8. Position the CV-joint housing over the tripod/bearings. Position the seat of the rubber boot in the grooves in the housing and in the shaft.

9. Use caution in this step. The air must be allowed to vent from the boot. Insert a smooth rod between the rubber boot and the housing to allow the air pressure to equalize. Use care not to damage the rubber boot with the rod. Use a rod free from burrs or rough edges with the end chamfered. When the air pressure is equalized, remove the rod. Install the replacement clamps and crimp or otherwise tighten as required. Install the halfshaft in the vehicle.

Front Wheel Hub and Bearings

REMOVAL & INSTALLATION

The front wheel hub can be removed without removing the bearing from the suspension knuckle. However, the wheel hub must be removed before the bearing can be removed from the suspension knuckle. The wheel hub and bearing are independently replaceable.

When servicing the suspension knuckle, the wheel hub and bearing can and should be removed as a unit.

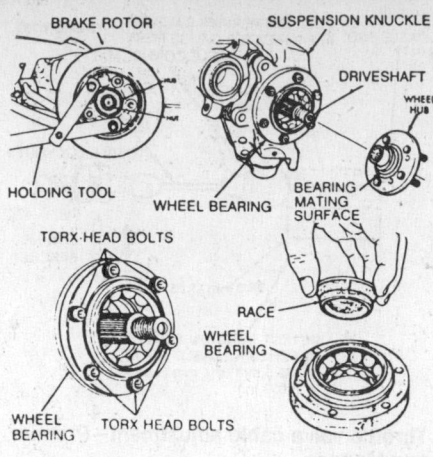

Front wheel bearing removal—Premier

Although the wheel bearing components can be disassembled for inspection, the bearing must be replaced as a unit only. If any of the bearing components are worn, damaged or defective, the complete bearing must be replaced.

1. Raise and safely support the vehicle.

2. Remove the tire and wheel assembly.

3. Remove the brake caliper. Do not disconnect the brake hose from the caliper. Wire it out of the way. Do not allow the brake hose to support the caliper weight.

4. Remove the halfshaft hub nut. A holding fixture may be required to hold the wheel hub/rotor when removing the nut.

5. Push the halfshaft inward, to disengage the shaft splines from the wheel hub splines. If it does not push out easily, use a screw type puller to press the shaft from the hub.

6. Install a puller plate that can be used with a slide hammer and pull the rotor/hub assembly from the suspension knuckle. Use care to keep dirt and debris from the bearing as the hub assembly is removed.

7. If necessary, the rotor and hub can be separated by removing the rotor safety nuts. If these safety nuts are damaged by removal, always replace with new ones.

8. If the wheel hub must be replaced, remove the outer race from the hub with a shop press and the appropriate adapters.

To install:

9. If a replacement wheel hub is being installed, force the original bearing outer race on the replacement hub with a shop press and a suitable length of steel pipe that has the correct inside diameter to fit around the hub.

10. Lubricate the bearing mating surface on the wheel hub bearing out-

er race with an EP (extreme pressure) type wheel bearing lubricant.

11. Position the wheel hub on the halfshaft and insert the hub into the wheel bearing. Tap the wheel hub with a brass hammer until 3 or 4 of the halfshaft threads extend beyond the hub.

12. If removed, install the brake rotor on the wheel hub, using new safety nuts if required.

13. Install the halfshaft-to-wheel hub nut. Use an appropriate holding tool to keep the hub from rotating while tightening the nut to 181 ft. lbs. (245 Nm) torque.

NOTE: Do not use an impact wrench to tighten the driveshaft-to-wheel hub nut. Use a torque wrench only to tighten the nut. It is also essential that the halfhaft-to-wheel hub nut be tighten to the specified torque. In addition to retaining the wheel hub on the halfshaft, the specified torque also establishes the wheel bearing preload.

14. Install the brake caliper, tire and wheel assembly and lower the vehicle. Depress the brake pedal several times to seat the brake pads before moving the vehicle.

Suspension Knuckle

REMOVAL & INSTALLATION

The front wheel hub and bearing must be removed as a unit before the suspension knuckle can be removed. This is the only service situation that requires that the wheel hub and bearing be removed together.

1. Raise and safely support the vehicle.

2. Remove the tire and wheel assembly. Wrap a heavy shop cloth or towel around the outer CV-joint boot to protect it.

3. Remove the brake caliper. Do not disconnect the brake hose from the caliper. Wire it out of the way. Do not allow the brake hose to support the caliper weight.

4. Remove the halfshaft hub nut. A holding fixture may be required to hold the wheel hub/rotor when removing the nut.

5. Push the halfshaft inward, to disengage the shaft splines from the wheel hub splines. If it does not push out easily, use a screw type puller to press the shaft from the hub.

6. Install a puller plate that can be used with a slide hammer and pull the rotor/hub assembly from the suspension knuckle. Use care to keep dirt and debris from the bearing as the hub assembly is removed.

7. Remove the rotor from the hub by removing the rotor safety nuts. If these safety nuts are damaged by removal, always replace with new ones.

8. Rotate the wheel hub as necessary and use the access hole in the hub to remove each wheel bearing-to-suspension knuckle Torx-head bolt. Reinstall the brake rotor, attach a puller plate to it that can be used with a slide hammer and pull the rotor/hub assembly from the suspension knuckle. Use care to keep dirt and debris from the bearing as the hub assembly is removed.

9. Loosen but do not remove the stabilizer bar inner bracket retaining bolts at the engine cradle. Remove the stabilizer bar outer bracket retaining nuts at the suspension arm and remove the bracket from the retaining bolts. Note that the stabilizer bar outer bracket retaining nuts also retain the ball joint to the suspension arm. Move the stabilizer bar away from the suspension arm and reinstall one of the nuts on either of the ball joint retaining bolts.

10. Loosen but do remove the nuts and bolts at the bushings that attach the suspension arm to the engine cradle.

11. Remove the ball joint stud pinch bolt and disengage the ball joint stud from the suspension knuckle.

12. Note that the 2 bolts that hold the bottom of the MacPherson strut to the suspension knuckle have splines under the bolt head. This keeps the bolt from rotating. Remove the bolts only as follows. Loosen the nuts, not the bolt heads. Turn the nuts until thay are almost at the end of the bolt threads. Tap the nuts with a brass hammer to loosen the bolts and disengage the splines. Remove the nuts and pull out the bolts. Remove the suspension knuckle from the driveshaft.

To install:

13. Position the suspension knuckle over the halfshaft and insert the ball joint stud into the knuckle. Install the pinch bolt. Note that there is a recess, groove or keyway machined into the ball joint stud. The pinch bolt must be seated in this groove. Torque to 77 ft. lbs.

14. Position the knuckle to the strut and install the through bolts. Note that the splines under the bolt heads must be properly aligned in the strut hole. Tap the bolts in place and install the nuts. Use a wrench on the bolt head to keep the bolt from turning and stripping the splines when the nut is tightened.

15. Remove the balljoint retaining nut and position the stabilizer bar at the suspension arm. Position the outer bracket on the stabilizer bar and install the nuts but do not tighten yet.

The ball joint nuts must not be tightened until the vehicle is lowered and the tire and wheel assembly is installed and supporting the weight of the vehicle.

16. Position the wheel bearing and hub over the halfshaft and insert into the knuckle with the hub splines mated with the halfshaft splines.

17. Remove the brake rotor from the hub. Rotate the hub, as necessary, and use the access hole in the hub to install each wheel bearing-to-knuckle Torx head bolt. Tighten each bolt to 11 ft. lbs. Install brake rotor.

18. Install the halfshaft-to-wheel hub nut. Use an appropriate holding tool to keep the hub from rotating while tightening the nut to 181 ft. lbs. (245 Nm) torque.

NOTE: Do not use an impact wrench to tighten the halfshaft-to-wheel hub nut. Use a torque wrench only to tighten the nut. It is also essential that the halfshaft-to-wheel hub nut be tighten to the specified torque. In addition to retaining the wheel hub on the halfshaft, the specified torque also establishes the wheel bearing preload.

19. Install the brake caliper, tire and wheel assembly and lower the vehicle.

20. With the vehicle weight being supported by the tire and wheels, torque the suspension arms-to-engine cradle nuts and bolts at the bushings to 103 ft. lbs., torque the stabilizer bar outer bracket retaining nuts to 60 ft. lbs. and tighten the stabilizer bar inner bracket retaining bolts to 21 ft. lbs. Depress the brake pedal several times to seat the brake pads before moving the vehicle.

Front Wheel Bearings

ADJUSTMENT

The wheel bearings are pre-set to specification by design and therefore cannot be adjusted. Bearing preload is set when the halfshaft nut is properly torqued.

REMOVAL & INSTALLATION

1. Raise and safely support the vehicle.

2. Remove the tire and wheel assembly. Wrap a heavy shop cloth or towel around the outer CV-joint boot to protect it.

3. Remove the brake caliper. Do not disconnect the brake hose from the caliper. Wire it out of the way. Do not allow the brake hose to support the caliper weight.

4. Remove the halfshaft hub nut. A

holding fixture may be required to hold the wheel hub/rotor when removing the nut.

5. Push the halfshaft inward, to disengage the shaft splines from the wheel hub splines. If it does not push out easily, use a screw type puller to press the shaft from the hub.

6. Install a puller plate that can be used with a slide hammer and pull the rotor/hub assembly from the suspension knuckle. Use care to keep dirt and debris from the bearing as the hub assembly is removed.

7. Remove the rotor from the hub by removing the rotor safety nuts. If these safety nuts are damaged by removal, always replace with new ones.

8. Rotate the wheel hub, as necessary, and use the access hole in the hub to remove each wheel bearing-to-suspension knuckle Torx-head bolt. These bolts hold the bearing to the knuckle. Remove the bearing assembly. If the bearing must be replaced, remove the bearing outer race from the wheel hub with a shop press and the apropriate adapter.

To install:

9. If the original wheel bearing is being installed, pack the bearing and lubricate both races (inner and outer) with an EP (extreme pressure) type wheel bearing lubricant.

10. If a replacement wheel bearing is being installed, prepare the bearing as follows: remove and discard the plastic protective covers. Locate, remove and discard the plastic protective sleeve from the replacement bearing bore. Remove the inner and outer bearing races from the bearing. Pack the bearing with lube which may be supplied with the replacement bearing. Insert the bearing inner race in the bearing and force the bearing outer race on the wheel hub with a press and suitable length of steel pipe.

11. Install the bearing in the suspension knuckle. Install the Torx head bolts and torque to 11 ft. lbs.

12. Position the wheel hub on the halfshaft and insert the hub into the wheel bearing. Tap the wheel hub with a brass hammer until three or four of the halfshaft threads extend beyond the hub.

13. If removed, install the brake rotor on the wheel hub, using new safety nuts, if required.

14. Install the halfshaft-to-wheel hub nut. Use an appropriate holding tool to keep the hub from rotating while tightening the nut to 181 ft. lbs. (245 Nm) torque.

NOTE: Do not use an impact wrench to tighten the halfshaft-to-wheel hub nut. Use a torque wrench only to tighten the nut. It is also essential that the halfshaft-to-wheel hub nut be tighten to the specified torque. In addition to retaining the wheel hub on the halfshaft, the specified torque also establishes the wheel bearing preload.

15. Install the brake caliper, tire and wheel assembly and lower the vehicle. Depress the brake pedal several times to seat the brake pads before moving the vehicle.

Transaxle Output Shaft Seal

REMOVAL & INSTALLATION

1. Raise the vehicle and support it safely.
2. Remove the tires and wheels.
3. Remove the transaxle drain plug and drain lube.
4. Remove the sprial roll pins attaching the halfshafts to the transaxle output shafts with a suitable pin punch.
5. Remove the differential fill plug.
6. With a suitable tool, pry out the dust cover from the output shaft.
7. Loosen the shaft bolt in the center of the output shaft and pull the short shaft and bearing out of the transaxle case. Pry out the shaft seal.

To install:

8. Installation is the reverse of removal. Torque the short output shaft center bolt to 18 ft. lbs. Install the seal with a suitable driver.
9. Refill the differential with synthetic-type 75W-140 hypoid gear lubricant. Add lube until it starts to flow out of the fill plug opening.

STEERING

Steering Wheel

REMOVAL & INSTALLATION

1. Disconnect the negative battery cable.
2. Unsnap the horn button and disconnect the wires. Remove the horn button.
3. Note the position of the reference mark on the end of the steering shaft. Remove the nut and slide the wheel off the shaft. If required, use a suitable steering wheel puller.
4. Install the electrical connector. Align the pin on the turn signal cam with the pin bore in the steering wheel and slide the wheel into place.
5. Align wheel with the reference mark on the steering shaft and install the nut. Tighten the nut to 52 ft. lbs.
6. Connect the negative battery cable.

Steering Column

REMOVAL & INSTALLATION

1. Disconnect battery negative cable.
2. Remove the screws that attach the instrument panel lower trim cover to the instrument panel and remove the cover.
3. Remove the screws that attach the instrument panel support rod to the instrument panel and remove the rod.
4. Disconnect the steering column wire harness connector.
5. Remove the screw that attaches the dash panel wire harness connector to the dash panel.
6. If equipped with a steering column gearshift mechanism, use the following procedure:
   a. Disconnect the automatic transaxle shift cable receptacle from the shift lever ball joint with a small, suitable pry bar.
   b. Disconnect the shift cable retainer from the steering coulmn bracket by depressing the cable retainer lock tabs with pliers.
   c. Slide the shift cable retainer out of the steering column bracket.
   d. Remove the screw that attaches the shift position indicator bracket to the steering column and remove the indicator wire from the pivot pin.
7. Detach the steering column boot from the steering column. Slide the upper half of the 2-piece boot downward over the lower half of the boot for access to the steering column shaft and intermediate shaft U-joint.
8. Score an alignment mark on the steering column shaft and on the intermediate shaft U-joint coupling for installation alignment reference.
9. Remove the bolt from the intermediate steering shaft U-joint coupling clamp.
10. Remove the bolts and nuts that attach the steering column to the instrument panel.
11. Carefully lower the steering column to the vehicle floor. Disconnect the steering shaft from the intermediate shaft and remove the column from the vehicle.

To install:

12. Installation is the reverse of the removal procedure. Align the reference marks and insert the steering shaft into the intermediate shaft U-joint coupling clamp.

13. Install but do not tighten the intermediate shaft U-joint clamp bolt.

14. Place the steering column into position, install the nuts and bolts and torque to 33 ft. lbs. Tighten the intermediate shaft U-bolt clamp bolt to 30 ft. lbs.

15. Reassemble the shift mechanism. Check shift indicator alignment. Place the gearshift in **N** and observe the position of the shift indicator pointer. If the pointer is not aligned, loosen the shift position indicator bracket screw and move the bracket forward or backward to correctly align the pointer with the **N** on the quadrant. Tighten the screw.

15. Align the 2 halves of the steering shaft boot. Rotate the upper half of the boot until the **X** mark on the lower half is centered in the oval alignment cutout, or window, in the upper half of the boot. Verify that the alignment mark on the metal boot flange is at the 6 o'clock position.

16. Finish instrument panel assembly and install battery cable.

Power Steering Rack and Pinion

The rack and pinion steering gear is not to be overhauled. A defective steering gear must be replaced. The steering tie rods are connected to the steering rack shaft via a spacer block located at the center of the steering rack body. The tie rods are connected to the strut body brackets.

ADJUSTMENT

1. Disconnect the negative battery cable.

2. Raise and support the vehicle safely.

3. Remove the steering rack assembly from the vehicle.

4. Secure the steering rack assembly in a vise. Do not clamp the vise jaws on the steering housing tubes. Clamp the vise jaws only on the housing cast metal.

5. Remove the steering gear housing end plug from the steering gear shaft bore using tool 6103 or equivalent.

6. Remove the preload adjustment cap locknut from the steering gear housing bore using tool 6097 or equivalent.

7. Loosen the preload adjustment cap. Retorque the preload adjustment cap to 45–50 inch lbs. (5–6 Nm), then back off the plug by turning it 45–50 degrees counterclockwise.

8. Secure the preload adjustment cap with a new locknut using tool 6097 or equivalent. Do not allow the adjust-

ment cap to rotate when tightening the locknut.

9. Install the endplug using tool 6103 or equivalent. Complete installation by reversing the removal procedure.

REMOVAL & INSTALLATION

1. Disconnect the negative battery cable.

2. Unsnap the steering shaft boot flange from the dash panel opening and slide the boot upward.

3. Remove the intermediate steering shaft bolt. Reference mark the intermediate shaft and the steering gear shaft, separate the shafts.

4. Raise and support the vehicle safely.

5. In the engine compartment, remove the splash shield from the steering gear.

6. Fold back the lock tabs on the inner tie rod retaining bolts. Loosen the bolts that hold the steering gear to the body and remove the steering gear through the left fender well.

To install:

7. Position the steering gear and install the mounting nuts. Connect the tie rods to the steering knuckles. Disconnect the power steering lines and plug them.

8. Remove the steering gear mounting nut.

9. Raise and safely support the vehicle. Remove the left front wheel. Remove the nuts retaining the outer tie rods to the steering knuckle.

10. Tighten the bolts to 35 ft. lbs.

11. Connect the power steering lines. Tighten the bolts attaching the tie rods to the steering gear to 55 ft. lbs. and bend the lock tabs over the bolts.

12. Install the splash shield over the steering gear.

13. Inside the vehicle, align the intermediate shaft with the steering shaft and connect the shafts. Install the retaining bolt and tighten it to 25 ft. lbs.

14. Reposition the shaft boot. Connect the negative battery cable.

15. Fill and bleed the power steering system.

Power Steering Pump

REMOVAL & INSTALLATION

1. Disconnect the negative battery cable.

2. Raise and safely support the vehicle.

3. Remove the underbody splash shield. Loosen the accessory drive belt.

4. Disconnect and plug the power steering fluid lines.

5. Remove the pump mounting bolts and remove the pump.

6. Install the pump to the engine and connect the pressure lines. Install the accessory drive belt and adjust the tension.

7. Lower the vehicle. Fill and bleed the system.

SYSTEM BLEEDING

1. With the wheels turned all the way to the left, add power steering fluid to the **COLD** mark on the fluid level indicator.

2. Start the engine and run at fast idle momentarily, shut engine **OFF** and recheck fluid level. If necessary, add fluid to bring level to the **COLD** mark.

3. Start the engine and bleed the system by turning the wheels from side to side without hitting the stops.

NOTE: Fluid with air in it has a light tan or red bubbly appearance.

4. Return the wheels to the center position and keep the engine running for 2–3 minutes.

5. Road test the car and recheck the fluid level making sure it is at the **HOT** mark.

Tie Rod Ends

The rack and pinion system is mounted high in the body. The steering tie rods are connected to the steering rack shaft via a spacer block located at the center of the steering rack body. The tie rods are connected to strut body brackets.

REMOVAL & INSTALLATION

1. Raise and safely support vehicle.

2. Remove the wheel and tire assemblies.

3. Remove the nuts attaching the tie rod end ball studs to the strut body brackets.

4. Loosen the locknuts that secure the tie rod ends to the tie rods. A wire brush and solvent will help clear the threads of road debris.

5. Disconnect the tie rod ends with an appropriate press type tool.

6. Unscrew the tie rod ends. Counting the turns will make installation easier and get the front end alignment close.

To install:

7. Installation is the reverse of removal. Because the tie rod ends were removed, the front wheel toe position should be measured and reset.

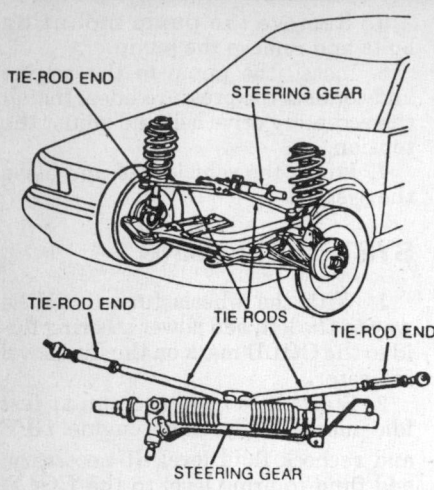

Rack and pinion steering assembly—Premier

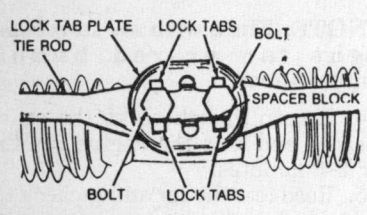

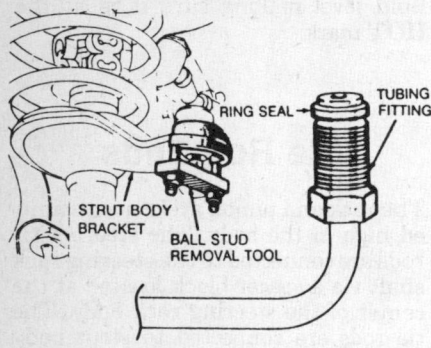

Inner tie rod end removal and special power steering fittings—Premier

BRAKES

For all brake system repair and service procedures not detailed below, please refer to "Brakes" in the Unit Repair section.

Master Cylinder

REMOVAL & INSTALLATION

1. Disconnect the negative battery cable.
2. Disconnect the fluid sensor electrical connector, if required.
3. Disconnect the brake lines. Cover the master cylinder outlet ports and brake lines to prevent the entry of dirt.

4. If equipped with manual brake, disconnect the master cylinder push-rod at the brake pedal.
5. Remove the master cylinder retaining bolts or nuts.
6. Remove the proportioning valve bracket, if required.
7. Remove the master cylinder from the vehicle.
8. Before installing the replacement master cylinder on the vehicle, bench bleed the master cylinder.
9. Installation is the reverse of the removal procedure.

Proportioning Valve

REMOVAL & INSTALLATION

1. Disconnect battery negative cable.
2. Loosen all brake lines attaching master cylinder to booster.
3. Remove the bolt and nut attaching the valve to the bracket.
4. Disconnect the brake lines from the valve and remove the valve.
To install:
5. Installation is the reverse of removal. Bleed brakes after installation.

Power Brake Booster

REMOVAL & INSTALLATION

1. Disconnect the negative battery cable.
2. Disconnect the vacuum line from the booster.
3. Remove the clip retaining the throttle cables to the bracket on the booster. Remove the master cylinder.
4. Inside the vehicle, disconnect the connector from the brake light switch. Remove the pushrod from the brake pedal.
5. Remove the booster retaining nuts and remove the booster.
6. Install the booster to the firewall and connect the pushrod to the brake pedal. Connect the brake light switch.
7. Install the master cylinder and clip the throttle cables in place.
8. Connect the negtive battery cable and bleed the brake system.

Brake Caliper

REMOVAL & INSTALLATION

Front

1. Raise and safely support vehicle.
2. Remove wheel and tire assemblies.
3. Remove fitting bolt and disconnect brake hose from caliper.
4. Remove caliper slide pins and lift caliper up and out of the bracket.

To install:
5. Installation is the reverse of removal. Bleed brakes after installation. Pump brake pedal to seat caliper pistons and brake shoes before moving vehicle.

Rear

The rear calipers are a unique, dual function design. They serve as the normal wheel brake units and as the vehicle parking brakes. The rear calipers are not serviceable and must be replaced if defective.

1. Raise and safely support vehicle.
2. Remove wheel and tire assemblies.
3. Disconnect the brake hose at the caliper. Retain the bolt but discard the two seal washers.
4. Unseat the operating lever return spring at the caliper.
5. Remove the operating lever attaching bolt and pry the lever off the drive disc.
6. Remove the lever return spring. Remove the operating lever from the parking brake cable.
7. Remove caliper slide pins and remove the caliper. Remove the brake shoe retaining pin and remove the brake shoes and anti-rattle spring.
To install:
8. Installation is the reverse of removal. A spanner tool may be required, along with an appropriate socket and extension to turn the piston **clockwise** until it is fulley seated in the bore. Lubricate the caliper slide pins and bushings with silicone lubricant. Use new seal washers on the brake line. Check that the return spring is properly assembled to the brake operating lever.
9. Bleed brakes after installation. Pump brake pedal to seat caliper pistons and brake shoes before moving vehicle.

Brake Rotor

REMOVAL & INSTALLATION

Front

1. Raise and safely support vehicle.
2. Remove wheel and tire assemblies.
3. Remove caliper and brake shoes. Tie the caliper up. Do not allow the brake hose to take the weight of the caliper.
4. Remove the bolts attaching the caliper bracket to the steering knuckle.
5. Remove the rotor retaining nuts and pull the rotor from the hub.
To install:
6. Installation is the reverse of re-

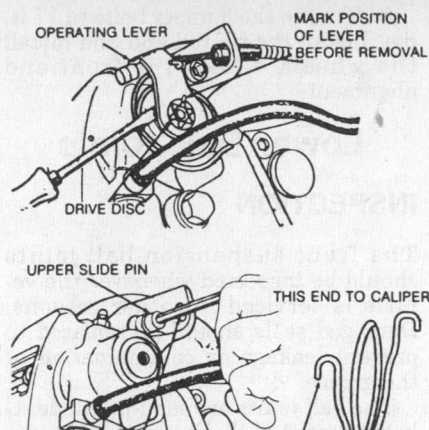

Rear disc brake caliper removal—Premier

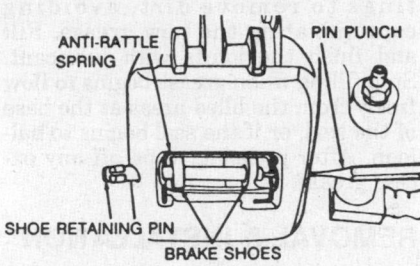

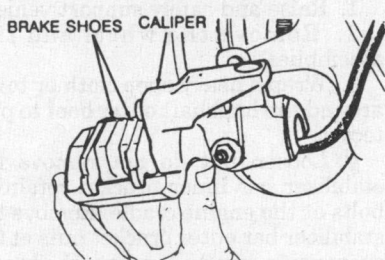

Drive pins from rear caliper and rotate downward—Premier

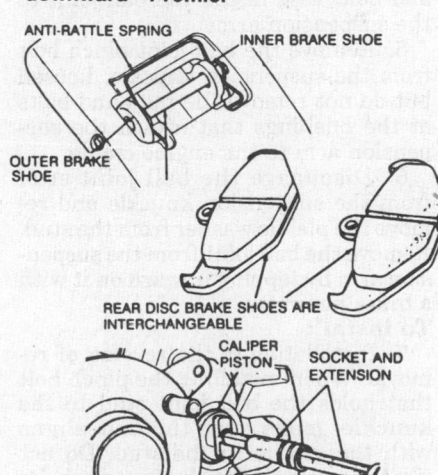

Cranking piston back into bore; spring, shoe and pin arrangement

moval. Pump brake pedal to seat caliper pistons and brake shoes before moving vehicle. Check master cylinder fluid level.

Rear

1. Raise and safely support vehicle.
2. Remove wheel and tire assemblies.
3. Remove the 2 slide pins attaching the caliper to the halfshaft, lift the caliper up and off the rotor. Tie the caliper up. Do not allow the brake hose to take the weight of the caliper.
4. Remove the rotor retainers and pull the rotor from the hub.

To install:

5. Installation is the reverse of removal. If a new rotor is installed, the caliper piston must be reseated (bottomed) in the bore to accomodate the thickness of the new rotor.
6. Pump brake pedal to seat caliper pistons and brake shoes before moving vehicle. Check master cylinder fluid level.

Brake Drums

REMOVAL & INSTALLATION

1. Raise and safely support vehicle.
2. Remove wheel and tire assemblies.
3. Remove drum retaining nuts and pull the drum from the hub.
4. If the drum is difficult to remove, the brake shoes are probably holding the drum in place and must be backed off. Remove the access plug from the backing plate. Unseat the adjuster lever with a small pointed tool and back off the adjuster screw with a brake tool.

To install:

5. Installation is the reverse of removal. Adjust the brake shoes, as necessary.

Brake Shoes

REMOVAL & INSTALLATION

1. Raise and safely support vehicle.
2. Remove wheel and tire assemblies.
3. Remove the brake drum and hub as an assembly. Do this by removing the hub cap but not the drum retaining nuts. Remove the large center hub nut and pull off the hub/drum.
4. If the drum is difficult to remove, the brake shoes are probably holding the drum in place and must be backed off. Remove the backing plate plug. Unseat the adjuster lever with a small pointed tool and back off the adjuster screw with a brake tool.
5. Remove the upper return spring

with brake pliers. Install a wheel cylinder clamp to hold the piston in place. Remove the lower return spring.

6. Remove the parking brake adjuster cross lever (strut). Disengage the parking brake cable by moving the end of the cable away from the lever with expanding type snapring pliers and disengage the cable from the lever.
7. Remove the adjuster screw. Remove the secondary hold-down springs and the secondary brake shoe. Remove the horseshoe clip and remove the parking brake lever from the brake shoe.
8. Remove the primary brake shoe hold-down spring and remove the shoe.

To install:

9. Installation is the reverse of removal. Clean and lubricate the shoe contact surfaces on the backing plate, the parking brake lever pivot and the adjuster screw threads with moly grease. When installing the adjuster screw, be sure the adjuster position is correct. The large notch in the adjuster screw goes to the brake shoe. The small notch goes to the adjuster lever. The long end goes to the secondary brake shoe.
10. Adjust the brake shoes as necessary.

Wheel Cylinder

REMOVAL & INSTALLATION

1. Raise and safely support vehicle.
2. Remove wheel and tire assemblies.
3. Remove drum retaining nuts and pull the drum from the hub.
4. Remove the brake shoe upper return spring and spread the shoes slightly to make room for cylinder removal.
5. Disconnect the brake line at the cylinder, remove the cylinder attaching bolts and remove the cylinder from the backing plate.

To install:

6. Installation is the reverse of removal. Bleed the brake system. Adjust the brake shoes and parking brake, if necessary.

Parking Brake Cable

ADJUSTMENT

1. Check the rear brake shoe to drum clearance, adjust if necessary.
2. If brake shoes have been replaced, apply and release the parking brake 5 times to center the shoes in the drums. Set the pedal on the first notch from the released position.
3. Raise and support the vehicle safely.

4. Tighten the cable at the equalizer so that the wheels can just barely be turned forward. Be sure to hold the end of the cable screw to prevent the cable from turning.

5. Release the parking brake and check for rear brake drag. The wheels should rotate freely with the parking brake OFF.

REMOVAL & INSTALLATION

1. Raise and safely support the vehicle.

2. Loosen the cable adjusting nut at the equalizer.

3. Remove the cotter pin for the cable to be replaced from the equalizer. Then remove the retaining clip attaching the cable to the frame.

4. If only replacing the right side, remove the bolts attaching the cable to the rear axle housing. Disconnect the cable at the frame bracket.

5. Remove the rear wheels and brake drum. Remove the shoes. Compress the locking tabs at the backing plate with a hose clamp or a suitably sized box wrench and remove the cable.

To install:

6. Installation is the reverse of the removal process. Use a new cotter pin for the connection to the equalizer. Adjust the brake mechanism.

Brake System Bleeding

1. Fill the master cylinder to within ¼ in. of the reservoir rim.

2. Raise and support the vehicle safely.

NOTE: The rear wheels must be at normal ride height for satisfactory bleeding. Do not allow the rear wheels to hang free.

3. Bleed the system in the following sequence: right rear, left rear, right front and left front.

4. Bleed 1 wheel at a time.

5. Install a rubber hose on the bleeder screw of the caliper or wheel cylinder to be bled and place the opposite end of the hose in a container partially fill with brake fluid.

6. Open the bleeder screw ¾ turn. Have a helper press the brake pedal to the floor, then tighten the bleeder screw. Have the helper slowly release the brake pedal.

7. Repeat the bleeding operation until clear brake fluid flows without air bubbles.

NOTE: Check the master cylinder fluid level frequently during the bleeding procedure and refill, if necessary.

8. After bleeding operation is completed, discard the fluid in the container. Fill the master cylinder to ¼ in. from the reservoir rim and check the brake operation.

FRONT SUSPENSION

MacPherson Strut

REMOVAL & INSTALLATION

1. Raise and safely support vehicle. Do not support vehicle by placing supports under the suspension arms.

2. Remove the wheel and tire assemblies.

3. Remove the outer tie rod ends with a screw type puller.

--- **CAUTION** ---

Do not remove the strut strut-to-tower cushion locknut (the center nut). The coil spring is compressed and has very strong tension. Bodily injury could result.

4. Remove the 3 strut tower cushion-to-tower attaching bolts.

NOTE: Before proceeding to the next step, make sure the suspension is hanging free. There must not be any pressure or tension on any front suspension components. Note too that the strut body-to-knuckle bolts are splined. Do not try to turn the bolt head. Turn the nuts only. Follow the procedure below.

5. Remove the splined bolts by loosening the nuts until they are almost at the end of the bolt threads. Tap the nuts with a brass hammer to loosen the bolts and disengage the splines. Remove the nuts, then the bolts.

6. For protection, wrap the halfshaft boot with heavy shop towels. Then press down on the suspension arm and guide the strut and spring past the halfshaft.

To install:

7. Installation is the reverse of removal. Carefully route the strut into place and install the 3 upper strut tower cushion-to-body bolts finger tight. Make sure the splines are lined up on the bolts and tap into place. Tighten the nuts only. Do not allow the bolt heads to turn or the splines will stip. Hold the bolt heads with a wrench while the nuts are tightened. Torque the nuts to 123 ft. lbs.

8. Torque the 3 upper bolts to 17 ft. lbs. Install the tie rod end and install the wheels. Check the front end alignment.

Lower Ball Joints

INSPECTION

The front suspension ball joints should be inspected whenever the vehicle is serviced for other reasons. Damaged seals should be replaced to prevent leakage or contamination of the grease.

The ball joints are semi-permanently lubricated at the factory with a special grease. When lubricating ball joints, use only a special long life lubricant. Before greasing clean the accumulated dirt and grease from the outside of the seal. Wipe the grease fittings to remove dirt, avoiding contaminating the new grease. Fill and flush the joints with lubricant. Stop filling when grease begins to flow freely from the blled areas at the base of the seal, or if the seal begins to balloon. After greasing, wipe off any excess grease.

REMOVAL & INSTALLATION

1. Raise and safely support vehicle.

2. Remove the wheel and tire assemblies.

3. Wrap a heavy shop cloth or towel around the halfshaft outer boot to protect it.

4. Loosen but do not remove the stabilizer bar inner bracket retaining bolts at the engine cradle. Remove the stabilizer bar outer bracket nuts at the suspension arm and remove the bracket. Note that the outer bracket nuts and bolts also fasten the ball joint to the suspension arm.

5. Remove the ball joint pinch bolt from the suspension knuckle. Loosen but do not remove the nuts and bolts at the bushings that attach the suspension arm to the engine cradle.

6. Disengage the ball joint stud from the suspension knuckle and remove the plastic washer from the stud. Remove the ball joint from the suspension arm by tapping upward on it with a brass hammer.

To install:

7. Installation is the reverse of removal. When installing the pinch bolt that holds the ball joint stud to the knuckle, make sure the bolt aligns with the groove in the stud. Do not tighten any stabilizer bar nuts or bolts until the vehicle is lowered and the wheel and tires are supporting the weight of the vehicle. At that time, torque the suspension arm-to-engine cradle nuts and bolts to 103 ft. lbs., the

stabilizer outer bracket nuts to 60 ft. lbs. and the stabilizer bar inner bracket nuts to 21 ft. lbs.

Lower Control Arms

REMOVAL & INSTALLATION

1. Raise and safely support vehicle.
2. Remove the wheel and tire assemblies.
3. Wrap a heavy shop cloth ot towel around the halfshaft outer boot to protect it.
4. Loosen but do not remove the stabilizer bar inner bracket retaining bolts at the engine cradle. Remove the stabilizer bar outer bracket nuts at the suspension arm and remove the bracket. Note that the outer bracket nuts and bolts also fasten the ball joint to the suspension arm. Reinstall a nut to keep the ball joint from separating from the arm.
5. Remove the ball joint pinch bolt from the suspension knuckle. Remove the nuts and bolts at the bushings that attach the suspension arm to the engine cradle.
6. Disengage the ball joint stud from the suspension knuckle, remove the plastic washer from the stud and remove the arm from the vehicle.
To install:
7. Installation is the reverse of removal. Inspect the suspension arm bushings and replace if necessary. When installing the pinch bolt that holds the ball joint stud to the knuckle, make sure the bolt aligns with the groove in the stud. Do not tighten any stabilizer bar nuts or bolts until the vehicle is lowered and the wheel and tires are supporting the weight of the vehicle. At that time, torque the suspension arm-to-engine cradle nuts and bolts to 103 ft. lbs., the stabilizer outer bracket nuts to 60 ft. lbs. and the stabilizer bar inner bracket nuts to 21 ft. lbs.

Sway Bar

REMOVAL & INSTALLATION

1. For ease of stabilizer bar (sway bar) removal and installation, do not raise the vehicle. Leave the vehicle's weight on the tires.

2. Remove the bolts that hold the stabilizer bar inner brackets to the engine cradle.
3. Remove the retaining nuts from the stabilizer bar outer bracket bolts at the suspension arms. Note that the outer bracket nuts and bolts also fasten the ball joint to the suspension arm. Remove the stabilizer bar and brackets from the vehicle. Reinstall a nut to keep the ball joint from separating from the arm.
To install:
4. Installation is the reverse of removal. Inspect the stabilizer bushings and replace, if necessary. Tighten stabilizer bar nuts or bolts only finger tight until all the fasteners are in place. Then tighten the stabilizer outer bracket nuts to 60 ft. lbs. and the stabilizer bar inner bracket nuts to 21 ft. lbs.

REAR SUSPENSION

Shock Absorbers

REMOVAL & INSTALLATION

Never raise an Eagle Premier or Monaco vehicle with a lift positioned under the V–shaped rear crossmember. Never let the hoist arms come into contact with the lower edge of the rocker panel. If necessary, place a small block of wood between the hoist pad and the body lifting points so that the vehicle does not rest on the rocker panels. The factory does not recommend use of a twin post under-the-vehicle hoist.

Eagle Premier and Monaco vehicles are equipped with conventional gas charged rear shock absorbers and torsion bars for rear springs.
1. Raise and safely support the rear of the vehicle.
2. Lift upward on the trailing arm to relieve the weight from the shock absorber.
3. Remove the top and bottom bolts and remove the shock absorber.
4. Installation is the reverse of re-

moval. Torque the top bolt to 60 ft. lbs., the bottom bolt to 85 ft. lbs.

Rear Wheel Bearings

REMOVAL & INSTALLATION

The rear wheel bearings and hubs are replaced as assemblies only. They are non-adjustable. The maximum allowable bearing endplay is 0.001 in. If the endplay exceeds this the bearing/hub assembly must be replaced.
1. Raise and safely support the rear of the vehicle. Remove the wheel.
2. Remove the brake drum from the axle shaft hub.
3. Remove the axle shaft hub nut and remove the hub/bearing assembly.
To install:
4. Installation is the reverse of removal. Lightly oil the axle shaft before installing the hub/bearing assembly. Install the hub to the axle shaft using a new nut. Tighten the nut to 123 ft. lbs.
5. Install the brake drum. Install the wheel and lower the vehicle.

Rear Axle Assembly

REMOVAL & INSTALLATION

1. Raise and safely support the vehicle.
2. Remove the rear wheels.
3. Remove the parking brake cables from the body support.
4. Disconnect and plug the brake hoses at the axle. Remove the shock absorbers.
5. Support the axle assembly and remove the support bracket bolts. Lower the axle assembly and remove.
To install:
6. Installation is the reverse of removal. Position the axle under the vehicle and raise it into place. Install and tighten the support bracket bolts, tighten to 68 ft. lbs.
7. Connect the brake hoses at the axle. Connect the parking brake cables. Install the shock absorbers, tighten the upper shock bolt to 60 ft. lbs. and the lower bolt to 85 ft. lbs.
8. Install the rear wheels, bleed the brake system and adjust the parking brake cable.

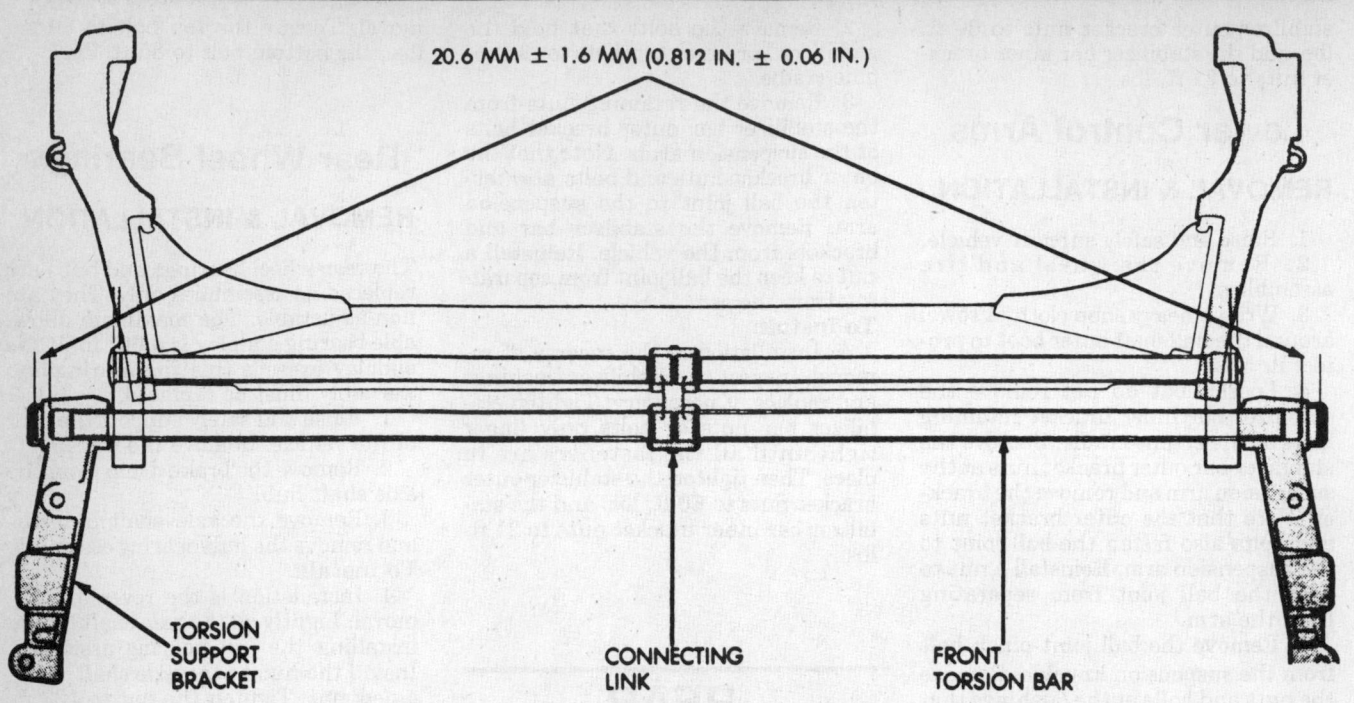

20.6 MM ± 1.6 MM (0.812 IN. ± 0.06 IN.)

TORSION
SUPPORT
BRACKET

CONNECTING
LINK

FRONT
TORSION BAR

Torsion bar centering adjustment points

Chrysler Corp.
Front Wheel Drive

"A" Body—Spirit, Acclaim, LeBaron Landau **"E" Body**—600, Caravelle, New Yorker **"G" Body**—Daytona **"H" Body**—Lancer, LeBaron GTS **"J" Body**—LeBaron **"K" Body**—Aries, Reliant, LeBaron **"P" Body**—Shadow, Sundance **TC** by Maserati

SPECIFICATIONS

VEHICLE IDENTIFICATION CHART
Except TC Maserati

It is important for servicing and ordering parts to be certain of the vehicle and engine identification. The VIN (vehicle identification number) is a 17 digit number visible through the windshield on the driver's side of the dash and contains the vehicle and engine identification codes. The tenth digit indicates model year and the eighth digit indicates engine code. It can be interpreted as follows:

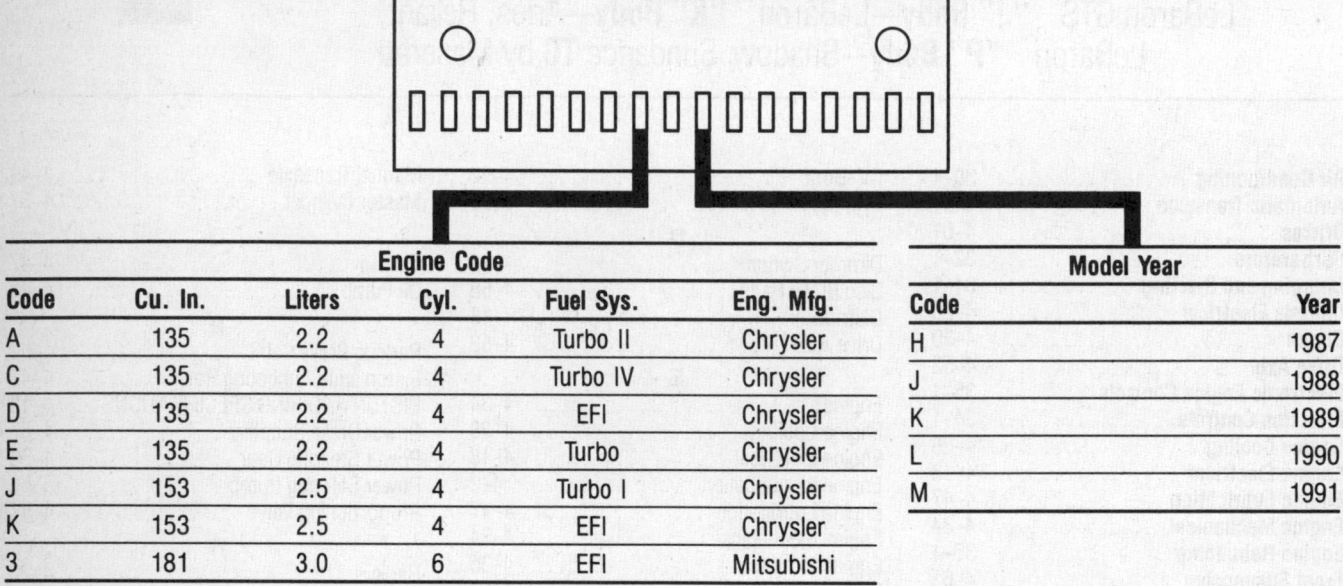

Engine Code						Model Year	
Code	Cu. In.	Liters	Cyl.	Fuel Sys.	Eng. Mfg.	Code	Year
A	135	2.2	4	Turbo II	Chrysler	H	1987
C	135	2.2	4	Turbo IV	Chrysler	J	1988
D	135	2.2	4	EFI	Chrysler	K	1989
E	135	2.2	4	Turbo	Chrysler	L	1990
J	153	2.5	4	Turbo I	Chrysler	M	1991
K	153	2.5	4	EFI	Chrysler		
3	181	3.0	6	EFI	Mitsubishi		

VEHICLE IDENTIFICATION CHART
TC Maserati

It is important for servicing and ordering parts to be certain of the vehicle and engine identification. The VIN (vehicle identification number) is a 17 digit number visible through the windshield on the driver's side of the dash and contains the vehicle and engine identification codes. The tenth digit indicates model year and the fifth digit indicates engine code. It can be interpreted as follows:

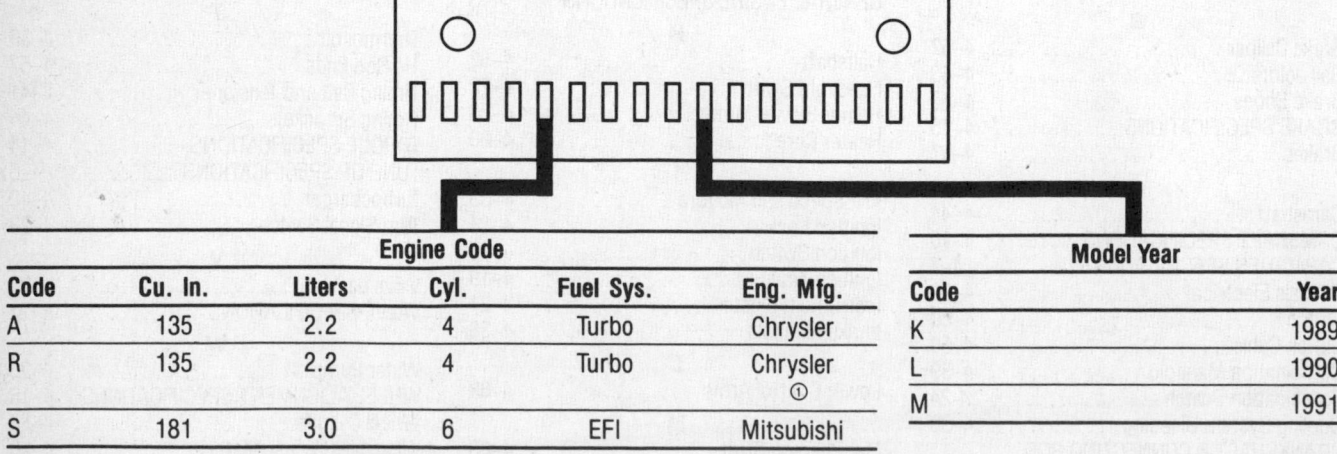

Engine Code						Model Year	
Code	Cu. In.	Liters	Cyl.	Fuel Sys.	Eng. Mfg.	Code	Year
A	135	2.2	4	Turbo	Chrysler	K	1989
R	135	2.2	4	Turbo	Chrysler ①	L	1990
S	181	3.0	6	EFI	Mitsubishi	M	1991

① Cylinder heads and related parts by Maserati

ENGINE IDENTIFICATION

Year	Model	Engine Displacement cu. in. (liter)	Engine Series Identification (VIN)	No. of Cylinders	Engine Type
1987	Aries	135 (2.2)	D	4	OHC
	Aries	153 (2.5)	K	4	OHC
	Reliant	135 (2.2)	D	4	OHC
	Reliant	153 (2.5)	K	4	OHC
	Daytona	135 (2.2)	D	4	OHC
	Daytona	135 (2.2)	E	4	OHC
	Daytona	153 (2.5)	K	4	OHC
	600	135 (2.2)	D	4	OHC
	600	135 (2.2)	E	4	OHC
	600	153 (2.5)	K	4	OHC
	Caravelle	135 (2.2)	D	4	OHC
	Caravelle	135 (2.2)	E	4	OHC
	Caravelle	153 (2.5)	K	4	OHC
	LeBaron	135 (2.2)	D	4	OHC
	LeBaron	135 (2.2)	E	4	OHC
	LeBaron	153 (2.5)	K	4	OHC
	LeBaron (J body)	135 (2.2)	E	4	OHC
	LeBaron (J body)	153 (2.5)	K	4	OHC
	Lancer	135 (2.2)	D	4	OHC
	Lancer	135 (2.2)	E	4	OHC
	Lancer	153 (2.5)	K	4	OHC
	LeBaron GTS	135 (2.2)	D	4	OHC
	LeBaron GTS	135 (2.2)	E	4	OHC
	LeBaron GTS	153 (2.5)	K	4	OHC
	New Yorker	135 (2.2)	E	4	OHC
	New Yorker	153 (2.5)	K	4	OHC
	Shadow	135 (2.2)	D	4	OHC
	Shadow	135 (2.2)	E	4	OHC
	Shadow	153 (2.5)	K	4	OHC
	Sundance	135 (2.2)	D	4	OHC
	Sundance	135 (2.2)	E	4	OHC
	Sundance	153 (2.5)	K	4	OHC
1988	Aries	135 (2.2)	D	4	OHV
	Aries	153 (2.5)	K	4	OHC
	Reliant	135 (2.2)	D	4	OHC
	Reliant	153 (2.5)	K	4	OHC
	Daytona	135 (2.2)	E	4	OHC
	Daytona	153 (2.5)	K	4	OHC
	600	135 (2.2)	D	4	OHC
	600	135 (2.2)	E	4	OHC
	600	153 (2.5)	K	4	OHC
	Caravelle	135 (2.2)	D	4	OHC
	Caravelle	135 (2.2)	E	4	OHC
	Caravelle	153 (2.5)	K	4	OHC

ENGINE IDENTIFICATION

Year	Model	Engine Displacement cu. in. (liter)	Engine Series Identification (VIN)	No. of Cylinders	Engine Type
1988	LeBaron	135 (2.2)	D	4	OHC
	LeBaron	135 (2.2)	E	4	OHC
	LeBaron	153 (2.5)	K	4	OHC
	LeBaron (J body)	135 (2.2)	E	4	OHC
	LeBaron (J body)	153 (2.5)	K	4	OHC
	Lancer	135 (2.2)	E	4	OHC
	Lancer	153 (2.5)	K	4	OHC
	LeBaron GTS	135 (2.2)	E	4	OHC
	LeBaron GTS	153 (2.5)	K	4	OHC
	New Yorker	135 (2.2)	E	4	OHC
	Shadow	135 (2.2)	D	4	OHC
	Shadow	135 (2.2)	E	4	OHC
	Shadow	153 (2.5)	K	4	OHC
	Sundance	135 (2.2)	D	4	OHC
	Sundance	135 (2.2)	E	4	OHC
	Sundance	153 (2.5)	K	4	OHC
1989	Aries	135 (2.2)	D	4	OHC
	Aries	153 (2.5)	K	4	OHC
	Reliant	135 (2.2)	D	4	OHC
	Reliant	153 (2.5)	K	4	OHC
	Daytona	135 (2.2)	A	4	OHC
	Daytona	153 (2.5)	J	4	OHC
	Daytona	153 (2.5)	K	4	OHC
	LeBaron (J body)	135 (2.2)	A	4	OHC
	LeBaron (J body)	153 (2.5)	J	4	OHC
	LeBaron (J body)	153 (2.5)	K	4	OHC
	Lancer	135 (2.2)	D	4	OHC
	Lancer	135 (2.2)	A	4	OHC
	Lancer	153 (2.5)	J	4	OHC
	Lancer	153 (2.5)	K	4	OHC
	LeBaron GTS	135 (2.2)	D	4	OHC
	LeBaron GTS	135 (2.2)	A	4	OHC
	LeBaron GTS	153 (2.5)	J	4	OHC
	LeBaron GTS	153 (2.5)	K	4	OHC
	Shadow	135 (2.2)	D	4	OHC
	Shadow	153 (2.5)	J	4	OHC
	Shadow	153 (2.5)	K	4	OHC
	Shadow	135 (2.2)	A	4	OHC
	Sundance	135 (2.2)	D	4	OHC
	Sundance	153 (2.5)	J	4	OHC
	Sundance	153 (2.5)	K	4	OHC
	Spirit	153 (2.5)	J	4	OHC
	Spirit	153 (2.5)	K	4	OHC
	Spirit	181 (3.0)	3	6	OHC

ENGINE IDENTIFICATION

Year	Model	Engine Displacement cu. in. (liter)	Engine Series Identification (VIN)	No. of Cylinders	Engine Type
1989	Acclaim	153 (2.5)	J	4	OHC
	Acclaim	153 (2.5)	K	4	OHC
	Acclaim	181 (3.0)	3	6	OHC
	TC	135 (2.2)	A	4	OHC
	TC	135 (2.2)	R	4	DOHC
1990–91	Daytona	153 (2.5)	J	4	OHC
	Daytona	135 (2.2)	C	4	OHC
	Daytona	181 (3.0)	3	6	OHC
	LeBaron	153 (2.5)	K	4	OHC
	LeBaron	153 (2.5)	J	4	OHC
	LeBaron	135 (2.2)	C	4	OHC
	LeBaron	181 (3.0)	3	6	OHC
	LeBaron Landau	181 (3.0)	3	6	OHC
	Shadow	135 (2.2)	D	4	OHC
	Shadow	135 (2.2)	C	4	OHC
	Shadow	153 (2.5)	K	4	OHC
	Shadow	153 (2.5)	J	4	OHC
	Sundance	135 (2.2)	D	4	OHC
	Sundance	153 (2.5)	K	4	OHC
	Sundance	153 (2.5)	J	4	OHC
	Spirit	153 (2.5)	K	4	OHC
	Spirit	153 (2.5)	J	4	OHC
	Spirit	181 (3.0)	3	6	OHC
	Acclaim	153 (2.5)	K	4	OHC
	Acclaim	153 (2.5)	J	4	OHC
	Acclaim	181 (3.0)	3	6	OHC
	TC	181 (3.0)	S	6	OHC
	TC	135 (2.2)	R	4	DOHC

GENERAL ENGINE SPECIFICATIONS

Year	VIN	No. Cylinder Displacement cu. in. (liter)	Fuel System Type	Net Horsepower @ rpm	Net Torque @ rpm (ft. lbs.)	Bore × Stroke (in.)	Compression Ratio	Oil Pressure @ rpm
1987	D	4-135 (2.2)	EFI	99 @ 5600	121 @ 3200	3.44 × 3.62	9.5:1	30–80 @ 3000
	E	4-135 (2.2)	Turbo	146 @ 5200	170 @ 3600	3.44 × 3.62	8.0:1	30–80 @ 3000
	K	4-153 (2.5)	EFI	100 @ 4800	133 @ 2800	3.44 × 4.09	9.0:1	30–80 @ 3000
1988	D	4-135 (2.2)	EFI	99 @ 5600	121 @ 3200	3.44 × 3.62	9.5:1	30–80 @ 3000
	E	4-135 (2.2)	Turbo	146 @ 5200	170 @ 3600	3.44 × 3.62	8.0:1	30–80 @ 3000
	K	4-153 (2.5)	EFI	100 @ 4800	133 @ 2800	3.44 × 4.09	9.0:1	30–80 @ 3000

GENERAL ENGINE SPECIFICATIONS

Year	VIN	No. Cylinder Displacement cu. in. (liter)	Fuel System Type	Net Horsepower @ rpm	Net Torque @ rpm (ft. lbs.)	Bore × Stroke (in.)	Compression Ratio	Oil Pressure @ rpm
1989	A	4-138 (2.2)	Turbo	174 @ 5200	170 @ 3600	3.44 × 3.62	8.1:1	30–80 @ 3000
	D	4-135 (2.2)	EFI	99 @ 5600	121 @ 3200	3.44 × 3.62	9.5:1	30–80 @ 3000
	K	4-153 (2.5)	EFI	100 @ 4800	135 @ 2800	3.44 × 4.09	8.9:1	30–80 @ 3000
	J	4-153 (2.5)	Turbo	150 @ 4800	180 @ 2000	3.44 × 4.09	7.8:1	30–80 @ 3000
	3	6-181 (3.0)	EFI	141 @ 5000	171 @ 2000	3.59 × 2.99	8.6:1	30–80 @ 3000
	R	4-135 (2.2)	Turbo	200 @ 5500	220 @ 3400	3.44 × 3.62	7.4:1	30–80 @ 3000
1990–91	C	4-135 (2.2)	Turbo	174 @ 5200	210 @ 2400	3.44 × 3.62	8.0:1	30–80 @ 3000
	D	4-135 (2.2)	EFI	99 @ 4800	122 @ 3200	3.44 × 3.62	9.5:1	30–80 @ 3000
	K	4-153 (2.5)	EFI	100 @ 4800	135 @ 2800	3.44 × 4.09	8.9:1	30–80 @ 3000
	J	4-153 (2.5)	Turbo	150 @ 4800	180 @ 2000	3.44 × 4.09	7.8:1	30–80 @ 3000
	3	6-181 (3.0)	EFI	141 @ 5000	171 @ 2800	3.59 × 2.99	8.9:1	30–80 @ 3000
	S	6-181 (3.0)	EFI	141 @ 5000	170 @ 2800	3.59 × 2.99	8.9:1	30–80 @ 3000
	R	4-135 (2.2)	Turbo	200 @ 5500	220 @ 3400	3.44 × 4.09	7.4:1	30–80 @ 3000

ENGINE TUNE-UP SPECIFICATIONS

Year	VIN	No. Cylinder Displacement cu. in. (liter)	Spark Plugs Type	Gap (in.)	Ignition Timing (deg.) MT	AT	Compression Pressure (psi)	Fuel Pump (psi)	Idle Speed (rpm) MT	AT	Valve Clearance In.	Ex.
1987	D	4-135 (2.2)	RN12YC	0.035	12B	12B	100 ①	15	900	700	Hyd.	Hyd.
	E	4-135 (2.2)	RN12YC	0.035	12B	12B	100 ①	55	900	800	Hyd.	Hyd.
	K	4-153 (2.5)	RN12YC	0.035	12B	12B	100 ①	15	900	900	Hyd.	Hyd.
1988	D	4-135 (2.2)	RN12YC	0.035	12B	12B	100 ①	15	850	850	Hyd.	Hyd.
	E	4-135 (2.2)	RN12YC	0.035	12B	12B	100 ①	55	900	900	Hyd.	Hyd.
	K	4-153 (2.5)	RN12YC	0.035	12B	12B	100 ①	15	850	850	Hyd.	Hyd.
1989	A	4-135 (2.2)	RN12YC	0.035	12B	—	100 ①	55	900	900	Hyd.	Hyd.
	D	4-135 (2.2)	RN12YC	0.035	12B	12B	100 ①	15	850	850	Hyd.	Hyd.
	J	4-153 (2.5)	RN12YC	0.035	12B	12B	100 ①	55	900	720	Hyd.	Hyd.
	K	4-153 (2.5)	RN12YC	0.035	12B	12B	100 ①	15	850	850	Hyd.	Hyd.
	3	6-181 (3.0)	RN11YC4	0.040	—	12B	178 ②	48	—	700	Hyd.	Hyd.
	R	4-135 (2.2)	DCPR-7E	0.030	12B	—	128	55	900	—	0.012	0.016
1990	C	4-135 (2.2)	RN12YC	0.035	12B	—	100 ①	55	900	—	Hyd.	Hyd.
	D	4-135 (2.2)	RN12YC	0.035	12B	12B	100 ①	15	850	850	Hyd.	Hyd.
	K	4-153 (2.5)	RN12YC	0.035	12B	12B	100 ①	15	850	850	Hyd.	Hyd.
	J	4-153 (2.5)	RN12YC	0.035	12B	12B	100 ①	55	900	850	Hyd.	Hyd.
	3	6-181 (3.0)	RN11YC4	0.040	—	12B	178 ②	48	—	700	Hyd.	Hyd.
	S	6-181 (3.0)	RN11YC4	0.040	—	12B	178 ②	48	—	700	Hyd.	Hyd.
	R	4-135 (2.2)	DCPR-7E	0.030	12B	—	128	55	900	—	0.012	0.016
1991		SEE UNDERHOOD SPECIFICATIONS STICKER										

① Minimum
② At 250 rpm

FIRING ORDERS

NOTE: To avoid confusion, always replace spark plug wires one at a time.

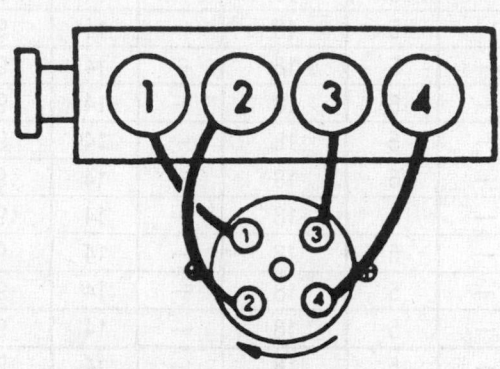

2.2L and 2.5L Engines
Engine Firing Order: 1–3–4–2
Distributor Rotation: Clockwise

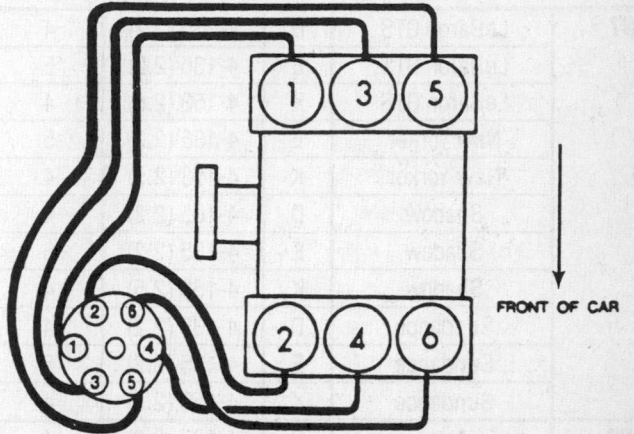

FRONT OF CAR

3.0L Engine
Engine Firing Order: 1–2–3–4–5–6
Distributor Rotation: Counterclockwise

CAPACITIES

Year	Model	VIN	No. Cylinder Displacement cu. in. (liter)	Engine Crankcase (qts.) with Filter	without Filter	Transmission (pts.) 4-Spd	5-Spd	Auto. ①	Drive Axle (pts.)	Fuel Tank (gal.)	Cooling System (qts.)
1987	Aries	D	4-135 (2.2)	4	4	—	5	18	—	14	9
	Aries	K	4-153 (2.5)	4	4	—	5	18	—	14	9
	Reliant	D	4-135 (2.2)	4	4	—	5	18	—	14	9
	Reliant	K	4-153 (2.5)	4	4	—	5	18	—	14	9
	Daytona	D	4-135 (2.2)	4	4	—	5	18	—	14	9
	Daytona	E	4-135 (2.2)	5	5	—	5	18	—	14	9
	Daytona	K	4-153 (2.5)	4	4	—	5	18	—	14	9
	600	D	4-135 (2.2)	4	4	—	5	18	—	14	9
	600	E	4-135 (2.2)	5	5	—	5	18	—	14	9
	600	K	4-153 (2.5)	4	4	—	5	18	—	14	9
	Caravelle	D	4-135 (2.2)	4	4	—	5	18	—	14	9
	Caravelle	E	4-135 (2.2)	5	5	—	5	18	—	14	9
	Caravelle	K	4-153 (2.5)	4	4	—	5	18	—	14	9
	LeBaron	D	4-135 (2.2)	4	4	—	5	18	—	14	9
	LeBaron	E	4-135 (2.2)	5	5	—	5	18	—	14	9
	LeBaron	K	4-153 (2.5)	4	4	—	5	18	—	14	9
	LeBaron (J body)	E	4-135 (2.2)	5	5	—	5	18	—	14	9
	LeBaron (J body)	K	4-153 (2.5)	4	4	—	5	18	—	14	9
	Lancer	D	4-135 (2.2)	4	4	—	5	18	—	14	9
	Lancer	E	4-135 (2.2)	5	5	—	5	18	—	14	9
	Lancer	K	4-153 (2.5)	4	4	—	5	18	—	14	9

CAPACITIES

Year	Model	VIN	No. Cylinder Displacement cu. in. (liter)	Engine Crankcase (qts.) with Filter	Engine Crankcase (qts.) without Filter	Transmission (pts.) 4-Spd	Transmission (pts.) 5-Spd	Transmission (pts.) Auto. ①	Drive Axle (pts.)	Fuel Tank (gal.)	Cooling System (qts.)
1987	LeBaron GTS	D	4-135 (2.2)	4	4	—	5	18	—	14	9
	LeBaron GTS	E	4-135 (2.2)	5	5	—	5	18	—	14	9
	LeBaron GTS	K	4-153 (2.5)	4	4	—	5	18	—	14	9
	New Yorker	E	4-135 (2.2)	5	5	—	5	18	—	14	9
	New Yorker	K	4-153 (2.5)	4	4	—	5	18	—	14	9
	Shadow	D	4-135 (2.2)	4	4	—	5	18	—	14	9
	Shadow	E	4-135 (2.2)	5	5	—	5	18	—	14	9
	Shadow	K	4-153 (2.5)	4	4	—	5	18	—	14	9
	Sundance	D	4-135 (2.2)	4	4	—	5	18	—	14	9
	Sundance	E	4-135 (2.2)	5	5	—	5	18	—	14	9
	Sundance	K	4-153 (2.5)	4	4	—	5	18	—	14	9
1988	Aries	D	4-135 (2.2)	4	4	—	5	18	—	14	9
	Aries	K	4-153 (2.5)	4	4	—	5	18	—	14	9
	Reliant	D	4-135 (2.2)	4	4	—	5	18	—	14	9
	Reliant	K	4-153 (2.5)	4	4	—	5	18	—	14	9
	Daytona	E	4-135 (2.2)	4	4	—	5	18	—	14	9
	Daytona	K	4-153 (2.5)	4	4	—	5	18	—	14	9
	600	D	4-135 (2.2)	4	4	—	5	18	—	14	9
	600	E	4-135 (2.2)	4	4	—	5	18	—	14	9
	600	K	4-153 (2.5)	4	4	—	5	18	—	14	9
	Caravelle	D	4-135 (2.2)	4	4	—	5	18	—	14	9
	Caravelle	E	4-135 (2.2)	4	4	—	5	18	—	14	9
	Caravelle	K	4-153 (2.5)	4	4	—	5	18	—	14	9
	LeBaron	D	4-135 (2.2)	4	4	—	5	18	—	14	9
	LeBaron	E	4-135 (2.2)	4	4	—	5	18	—	14	9
	LeBaron	K	4-153 (2.5)	4	4	—	5	18	—	14	9
	LeBaron (J body)	E	4-135 (2.2)	4	4	—	5	18	—	14	9
	LeBaron (J body)	K	4-153 (2.5)	4	4	—	5	18	—	14	9
	Lancer	E	4-135 (2.2)	4	4	—	5	18	—	14	9
	Lancer	K	4-153 (2.5)	4	4	—	5	18	—	14	9
	LeBaron GTS	E	4-135 (2.2)	4	4	—	5	18	—	14	9
	LeBaron GTS	K	4-153 (2.5)	4	4	—	5	18	—	14	9
	New Yorker	E	4-135 (2.2)	4	4	—	5	18	—	14	9
	Shadow	D	4-135 (2.2)	4	4	—	5	18	—	14	9
	Shadow	E	4-135 (2.2)	4	4	—	5	18	—	14	9
	Shadow	K	4-153 (2.5)	4	4	—	5	18	—	14	9
	Sundance	D	4-135 (2.2)	4	4	—	5	18	—	14	9
	Sundance	E	4-135 (2.2)	4	4	—	5	18	—	14	9
	Sundance	K	4-153 (2.5)	4	4	—	5	18	—	14	9

CAPACITIES

Year	Model	VIN	No. Cylinder Displacement cu. in. (liter)	Engine Crankcase (qts.) with Filter	without Filter	Transmission (pts.) 4-Spd	5-Spd	Auto. ①	Drive Axle (pts.)	Fuel Tank (gal.)	Cooling System (qts.)
1989	Aries	D	4-135 (2.2)	4	4	—	5	18	—	14	9
	Aries	K	4-153 (2.5)	4	4	—	5	18	—	14	9
	Reliant	D	4-135 (2.2)	4	4	—	5	18	—	14	9
	Reliant	K	4-153 (2.5)	4	4	—	5	18	—	14	9
	Daytona	A	4-135 (2.2)	4	4	—	5	—	—	14	9
	Daytona	J	4-153 (2.5)	4	4	—	5	18	—	14	9
	Daytona	K	4-153 (2.5)	4	4	—	5	18	—	14	9
	LeBaron (J body)	A	4-135 (2.2)	4	4	—	5	—	—	14	9
	LeBaron (J body)	J	4-153 (2.5)	4	4	—	5	18	—	14	9
	LeBaron (J body)	K	4-153 (2.5)	4	4	—	5	18	—	14	9
	Lancer	D	4-135 (2.2)	4	4	—	5	18	—	14	9
	Lancer	A	4-135 (2.2)	4	4	—	5	—	—	14	9
	Lancer	J	4-153 (2.5)	4	4	—	5	18	—	14	9
	Lancer	K	4-153 (2.5)	4	4	—	5	18	—	14	9
	LeBaron GTS	D	4-135 (2.2)	4	4	—	5	18	—	14	9
	LeBaron GTS	A	4-135 (2.2)	4	4	—	5	—	—	14	9
	LeBaron GTS	J	4-153 (2.5)	4	4	—	5	18	—	14	9
	LeBaron GTS	K	4-153 (2.5)	4	4	—	5	18	—	14	9
	Shadow	D	4-135 (2.2)	4	4	—	5	18	—	14	9
	Shadow	J	4-153 (2.5)	4	4	—	5	18	—	14	9
	Shadow	K	4-153 (2.5)	4	4	—	5	18	—	14	9
	Shadow	A	4-135 (2.2)	4	4	—	5	—	—	14	9
	Sundance	D	4-135 (2.2)	4	4	—	5	18	—	14	9
	Sundance	J	4-153 (2.5)	4	4	—	5	18	—	14	9
	Sundance	K	4-153 (2.5)	4	4	—	5	18	—	14	9
	Spirit	J	4-153 (2.5)	4	4	—	5	18	—	14	9
	Spirit	K	4-153 (2.5)	4	4	—	5	18	—	14	9
	Spirit	3	6-181 (3.0)	4	4	—	—	18	—	14	9.5
	Acclaim	J	4-153 (2.5)	4	4	—	5	18	—	14	9
	Acclaim	K	4-153 (2.5)	4	4	—	5	18	—	14	9
	Acclaim	3	6-181 (3.0)	4	4	—	—	18	—	14	9.5
	TC	A	4-135 (2.2)	4	4	—	5	—	—	14	9
	TC	R	4-135 (2.2)	4	4	—	5	18	—	14	9
1990-91	Daytona	J	4-153 (2.5)	4	4	—	5	18	—	14	9
	Daytona	C	4-135 (2.2)	4	4	—	5	—	—	14	9
	Daytona	3	6-181 (3.0)	4	4	—	—	18	—	14	9.5
	LeBaron	K	4-153 (2.5)	4	4	—	5	18	—	14	9
	LeBaron	J	4-153 (2.5)	4	4	—	5	18	—	14	9
	LeBaron	C	4-135 (2.2)	4	4	—	5	—	—	14	9
	LeBaron	3	6-181 (3.0)	4	4	—	—	18	—	14	9.5
	LeBaron Landau	3	6-181 (3.0)	4	4	—	—	18	—	14	9.5

CAPACITIES

Year	Model	VIN	No. Cylinder Displacement cu. in. (liter)	Engine Crankcase (qts.) with Filter	Engine Crankcase (qts.) without Filter	Transmission (pts.) 4-Spd	Transmission (pts.) 5-Spd	Transmission (pts.) Auto. ①	Drive Axle (pts.)	Fuel Tank (gal.)	Cooling System (qts.)
1990–91	Shadow	D	4-135 (2.2)	4	4	—	5	18	—	14	9
	Shadow	C	4-135 (2.2)	4	4	—	5	—	—	14	9
	Shadow	K	4-153 (2.5)	4	4	—	5	18	—	14	9
	Shadow	J	4-153 (2.5)	4	4	—	5	18	—	14	9
	Sundance	D	4-135 (2.2)	4	4	—	5	18	—	14	9
	Sundance	K	4-153 (2.5)	4	4	—	5	18	—	14	9
	Sundance	J	4-153 (2.5)	4	4	—	5	18	—	14	9
	Spirit	K	4-153 (2.5)	4	4	—	5	18	—	14	9
	Spirit	J	4-153 (2.5)	4	4	—	5	18	—	14	9
	Spirit	3	6-181 (3.0)	4	4	—	—	18	—	14	9.5
	Acclaim	K	4-153 (2.5)	4	4	—	5	18	—	14	9
	Acclaim	J	4-153 (2.5)	4	4	—	5	18	—	14	9
	Acclaim	3	6-181 (3.0)	4	4	—	—	18	—	14	9.5
	TC	S	6-181 (3.0)	4.5	4	—	—	18	—	14	9.5
	TC	R	4-135 (2.2)	4	4	—	5	18	—	14	9

① 1989–91 A413 transaxle lockup—17 pts.

CAMSHAFT SPECIFICATIONS

All measurements given in inches.

Year	VIN	No. Cylinder Displacement cu. in. (liter)	Journal Diameter 1	Journal Diameter 2	Journal Diameter 3	Journal Diameter 4	Journal Diameter 5	Lobe Lift In.	Lobe Lift Ex.	Bearing Clearance	Camshaft End Play
1987	D	4-135 (2.2)	1.375–1.376	1.375–1.376	1.375–1.376	1.375–1.376	1.375–1.376	NA	NA	—	0.005–0.020
	E	4-135 (2.2)	1.375–1.376	1.375–1.376	1.375–1.376	1.375–1.376	1.375–1.376	NA	NA	—	0.005–0.020
	K	4-153 (2.5)	1.375–1.376	1.375–1.376	1.375–1.376	1.375–1.376	1.375–1.376	NA	NA	—	0.005–0.020
1988	D	4-135 (2.2)	1.375–1.376	1.375–1.376	1.375–1.376	1.375–1.376	1.375–1.376	NA	NA	—	0.005–0.020
	E	4-135 (2.2)	1.375–1.376	1.375–1.376	1.375–1.376	1.375–1.376	1.375–1.376	NA	NA	—	0.005–0.020
	K	4-153 (2.5)	1.375–1.376	1.375–1.376	1.375–1.376	1.375–1.376	1.375–1.376	NA	NA	—	0.005–0.020
1989	A	4-135 (2.2)	1.375–1.376	1.375–1.376	1.375–1.376	1.375–1.376	1.375–1.376	NA	NA	—	0.005–0.020
	D	4-135 (2.2)	1.375–1.376	1.375–1.376	1.375–1.376	1.375–1.376	1.375–1.376	NA	NA	—	0.005–0.020
	J	4-153 (2.5)	1.375–1.376	1.375–1.376	1.375–1.376	1.375–1.376	1.375–1.376	NA	NA	—	0.005–0.020
	K	4-153 (2.5)	1.375–1.376	1.375–1.376	1.375–1.376	1.375–1.376	1.375–1.376	NA	NA	—	0.005–0.020
	3	6-181 (3.0)	NA	NA	NA	NA	NA	①	①	—	NA
	R	4-135 (2.2)	NA	NA	NA	NA	NA	NA	NA	—	NA

CAMSHAFT SPECIFICATIONS

All measurements given in inches.

Year	VIN	No. Cylinder Displacement cu. in. (liter)	Journal Diameter 1	2	3	4	5	Lobe Lift In.	Ex.	Bearing Clearance	Camshaft End Play
1990–91	C	4-135 (2.2)	1.375–1.376	1.375–1.376	1.375–1.376	1.375–1.376	1.375–1.376	NA	NA	—	0.005–0.020
	D	4-135 (2.2)	1.375–1.376	1.375–1.376	1.375–1.376	1.375–1.376	1.375–1.376	NA	NA	—	0.005–0.020
	J	4-153 (2.5)	1.375–1.376	1.375–1.376	1.375–1.376	1.375–1.376	1.375–1.376	NA	NA	—	0.005–0.020
	K	4-153 (2.5)	1.375–1.376	1.375–1.376	1.375–1.376	1.375–1.376	1.375–1.376	NA	NA	—	0.005–0.020
	3	6-181 (3.0)	NA	NA	NA	NA	NA	①	①	—	NA
	S	6-181 (3.0)	NA	NA	NA	NA	NA	①	①	—	NA
	R	4-135 (2.2)	NA	NA	NA	NA	NA	NA	NA	—	NA

① Height of cam lobe: 1.604–1.624 in.

CRANKSHAFT AND CONNECTING ROD SPECIFICATIONS

All measurements are given in inches.

Year	VIN	No. Cylinder Displacement cu. in. (liter)	Crankshaft Main Brg. Journal Dia.	Main Brg. Oil Clearance	Shaft End-play	Thrust on No.	Connecting Rod Journal Diameter	Oil Clearance	Side Clearance
1987	D	4-135 (2.2)	2.362–2.363	0.0003–0.0040	0.002–0.014	3	1.968–1.969	0.0008–0.0040	0.005–0.013
	E	4-135 (2.2)	2.362–2.363	0.0003–0.0040	0.002–0.014	3	1.968–1.969	0.0008–0.0040	0.005–0.013
	K	4-153 (2.5)	2.362–2.363	0.0003–0.0040	0.002–0.014	3	1.968–1.969	0.0008–0.0040	0.005–0.013
1988	D	4-135 (2.2)	2.362–2.363	0.0003–0.0040	0.002–0.014	3	1.968–1.969	0.0008–0.0040	0.005–0.013
	E	4-135 (2.2)	2.362–2.363	0.0003–0.0040	0.002–0.014	3	1.968–1.969	0.0008–0.0040	0.005–0.013
	K	4-153 (2.5)	2.362–2.363	0.0003–0.0040	0.002–0.014	3	1.968–1.969	0.0008–0.0040	0.005–0.013
1989	A	4-135 (2.2)	2.362–2.363	0.0003–0.0040	0.002–0.014	3	1.968–1.969	0.0008–0.0040	0.005–0.013
	D	4-135 (2.2)	2.362–2.363	0.0003–0.0040	0.002–0.014	3	1.968–1.969	0.0008–0.0040	0.005–0.013
	J	4-153 (2.5)	2.362–2.363	0.0003–0.0040	0.002–0.014	3	1.968–1.969	0.0008–0.0040	0.005–0.013
	K	4-153 (2.5)	2.362–2.363	0.0003–0.0040	0.002–0.014	3	1.968–1.969	0.0008–0.0040	0.005–0.013
	3	6-181 (3.0)	2.361–2.363	0.0006–0.0020	0.002–0.010	3	1.968–1.969	0.0008–0.0028	0.004–0.010
	R	4-135 (2.2)	2.362–2.363	0.0011–0.0031	0.002–0.007	3	1.9695–1.9705	0.0006–0.0016	0.006–0.009

CRANKSHAFT AND CONNECTING ROD SPECIFICATIONS

All measurements are given in inches.

Year	VIN	No. Cylinder Displacement cu. in. (liter)	Crankshaft				Connecting Rod		
			Main Brg. Journal Dia.	Main Brg. Oil Clearance	Shaft End-play	Thrust on No.	Journal Diameter	Oil Clearance	Side Clearance
1990–91	C	4-135 (2.2)	2.361–2.363	0.0003–0.0040	0.002–0.014	3	1.968–1.969	0.0008–0.0040	0.005–0.013
	D	4-135 (2.2)	2.361–2.363	0.0003–0.0040	0.002–0.014	3	1.968–1.969	0.0008–0.0040	0.005–0.013
	J	4-153 (2.5)	2.361–2.363	0.0003–0.0040	0.002–0.014	3	1.968–1.969	0.0008–0.0040	0.005–0.013
	K	4-153 (2.5)	2.361–2.363	0.0003–0.0040	0.002–0.014	3	1.968–1.969	0.0008–0.0040	0.005–0.013
	3	6-181 (3.0)	2.361–2.363	0.0006–0.0020	0.002–0.010	3	1.968–1.969	0.0008–0.0028	0.004–0.010
	S	6-181 (3.0)	2.361–2.363	0.0006–0.0020	0.002–0.010	3	1.968–1.969	0.0008–0.0028	0.004–0.010
	R	4-135 (2.2)	2.362–2.363	0.0011–0.0031	0.002–0.007	3	1.9695–1.9705	0.0008–0.0016	0.006–0.009

VALVE SPECIFICATIONS

Year	VIN	No. Cylinder Displacement cu. in. (liter)	Seat Angle (deg.)	Face Angle (deg.)	Spring Test Pressure (lbs.)	Spring Installed Height (in.)	Stem-to-Guide Clearance (in.)		Stem Diameter (in.)	
							Intake	Exhaust	Intake	Exhaust
1987	D	4-135 (2.2)	45	45	95	1.65	0.001–0.003	0.0030–0.0047	0.3124	0.3103
	E	4-135 (2.2)	45	45	104	1.65	0.001–0.003	0.0030–0.0047	0.3124	0.3103
	K	4-153 (2.5)	45	45	95	1.65	0.001–0.003	0.0030–0.0047	0.3124	0.3103
1988	D	4-135 (2.2)	45	45	114	1.65	0.001–0.003	0.0030–0.0047	0.3124	0.3103
	E	4-135 (2.2)	45	45	114	1.65	0.001–0.003	0.0030–0.0047	0.3124	0.3103
	K	4-153 (2.5)	45	45	114	1.65	0.001–0.003	0.0030–0.0047	0.3124	0.3103
1989	A	4-135 (2.2)	45	45	114	1.65	0.001–0.003	0.0030–0.0047	0.3124	0.3103
	D	4-135 (2.2)	45	45	114	1.65	0.001–0.003	0.0030–0.0047	0.3124	0.3103
	J	4-153 (2.5)	45	45	114	1.65	0.001–0.003	0.0030–0.0047	0.3124	0.3103
	K	4-153 (2.5)	45	45	114	1.65	0.001–0.003	0.0030–0.0047	0.3124	0.3103
	3	6-181 (3.0)	44.5	45.5	180	1.59	0.001–0.002	0.002–0.003	0.313–0.314	0.312–0.313
	R	4-135 (2.2)	NA	NA	NA	①	0.001–0.002	0.001–0.003	0.275–0.276	0.275–0.276

VALVE SPECIFICATIONS

Year	VIN	No. Cylinder Displacement cu. in. (liter)	Seat Angle (deg.)	Face Angle (deg.)	Spring Test Pressure (lbs.)	Spring Installed Height (in.)	Stem-to-Guide Clearance (in.) Intake	Stem-to-Guide Clearance (in.) Exhaust	Stem Diameter (in.) Intake	Stem Diameter (in.) Exhaust
1990–91	C	4-135 (2.2)	45	45	114	1.65	0.001–0.003	0.0030–0.0047	0.3124	0.3103
	D	4-135 (2.2)	45	45	114	1.65	0.001–0.003	0.0030–0.0047	0.3124	0.3103
	J	4-153 (2.5)	45	45	114	1.65	0.001–0.003	0.0030–0.0047	0.3124	0.3103
	K	4-153 (2.5)	45	45	114	1.65	0.001–0.003	0.0030–0.0047	0.3124	0.3103
	3	6-181 (3.0)	44.5	45.5	180	1.59	0.001–0.002	0.002–0.003	0.313–0.314	0.312–0.313
	S	6-181 (3.0)	44.5	45.5	180	1.59	0.001–0.002	0.002–0.003	0.313–0.314	0.312–0.313
	R	4-135 (2.2)	NA	NA	NA	①	0.001–0.002	0.001–0.003	0.275–0.276	0.275–0.276

① Freelength: 1.164 in.

PISTON AND RING SPECIFICATIONS

All measurements are given in inches.

Year	VIN	No. Cylinder Displacement cu. in. (liter)	Piston Clearance	Ring Gap Top Compression	Ring Gap Bottom Compression	Ring Gap Oil Control	Ring Side Clearance Top Compression	Ring Side Clearance Bottom Compression	Ring Side Clearance Oil Control
1987	D	4-135 (2.2)	0.0005–0.0015	0.010–0.039	0.011–0.039	0.015–0.074	0.0015–0.0040	0.0015–0.0040	0.0002–0.0080
	E	4-135 (2.2)	0.0005–0.0015	0.010–0.039	0.011–0.039	0.015–0.074	0.0015–0.0040	0.0015–0.0040	0.0002–0.0080
	K	4-153 (2.5)	0.0005–0.0015	0.010–0.039	0.011–0.039	0.015–0.074	0.0015–0.0040	0.0015–0.0040	0.0002–0.0080
1988	D	4-135 (2.2)	0.0005–0.0015	0.010–0.039	0.011–0.039	0.015–0.074	0.0015–0.0040	0.0015–0.0040	0.0002–0.0080
	E	4-135 (2.2)	0.0005–0.0015	0.010–0.039	0.011–0.039	0.015–0.074	0.0015–0.0040	0.0015–0.0040	0.0002–0.0080
	K	4-153 (2.5)	0.0005–0.0015	0.010–0.039	0.011–0.039	0.015–0.074	0.0015–0.0040	0.0015–0.0040	0.0002–0.0080
1989	A	4-135 (2.2)	0.0005–0.0015	0.010–0.039	0.009–0.037	0.015–0.074	0.0016–0.0030	0.0016–0.0035	0.0002–0.0080
	D	4-135 (2.2)	0.0005–0.0015	0.010–0.039	0.011–0.039	0.015–0.074	0.0015–0.0040	0.0015–0.0040	0.0002–0.0080
	J	4-153 (2.5)	0.0006–0.0018	0.010–0.039	0.009–0.037	0.015–0.074	0.0016–0.0030	0.0016–0.0035	0.0002–0.0080
	K	4-153 (2.5)	0.0006–0.0018	0.010–0.039	0.011–0.039	0.015–0.074	0.0015–0.0040	0.0015–0.0040	0.0002–0.0080
	3	6-181 (3.0)	0.0008–0.0015	0.012–0.018	0.010–0.016	0.012–0.035	0.0020–0.0035	0.0008–0.0020	NA
	R	4-135 (2.2)	0.0005–0.0015	0.010–0.039	0.010–0.039	0.015–0.074	0.0015–0.0031	0.0015–0.0016	0.0002–0.0080

PISTON AND RING SPECIFICATIONS
All measurements are given in inches.

Year	VIN	No. Cylinder Displacement cu. in. (liter)	Piston Clearance	Ring Gap			Ring Side Clearance		
				Top Compression	Bottom Compression	Oil Control	Top Compression	Bottom Compression	Oil Control
1990–91	C	4-135 (2.2)	0.0005–0.0015	0.010–0.039	0.009–0.037	0.015–0.074	0.0016–0.0030	0.0016–0.0035	0.0002–0.0080
	D	4-135 (2.2)	0.0005–0.0015	0.010–0.039	0.011–0.039	0.015–0.074	0.0015–0.0040	0.0015–0.0040	0.0002–0.0080
	J	4-153 (2.5)	0.0006–0.0018	0.010–0.039	0.009–0.037	0.015–0.074	0.0016–0.0030	0.0016–0.0035	0.0002–0.0080
	K	4-153 (2.5)	0.0006–0.0018	0.010–0.039	0.011–0.039	0.015–0.074	0.0015–0.0040	0.0015–0.0040	0.0002–0.0080
	3	6-181 (3.0)	0.0008–0.0015	0.012–0.018	0.010–0.016	0.012–0.035	0.0020–0.0035	0.0008–0.0020	NA
	S	6-181 (3.0)	0.0008–0.0015	0.012–0.018	0.010–0.016	0.012–0.035	0.0020–0.0035	0.0008–0.0020	NA
	R	4-135 (2.2)	0.0005–0.0015	0.010–0.039	0.010–0.039	0.012–0.035	0.0015–0.0031	0.0015–0.0016	0.0002–0.0080

TORQUE SPECIFICATIONS
All readings in ft. lbs.

Year	VIN	No. Cylinder Displacement cu. in. (liter)	Cylinder Head Bolts	Main Bearing Bolts	Rod Bearing Bolts	Crankshaft Pulley Bolts	Flywheel Bolts	Manifold		Spark Plugs
								Intake	Exhaust	
1987	D	4-135 (2.2)	①	30 ③	40 ③	50	70	17	17	26
	E	4-135 (2.2)	①	30 ③	40 ③	50	70	17	17	26
	K	4-153 (2.5)	①	30 ③	40 ③	50	70	17	17	26
1988	D	4-135 (2.2)	①	30 ③	40 ③	50	70	17	17	26
	E	4-135 (2.2)	①	30 ③	40 ③	50	70	17	17	26
	K	4-153 (2.5)	①	30 ③	40 ③	50	70	17	17	26
1989	A	4-135 (2.2)	①	30 ③	40 ③	50	70	17	17	26
	D	4-135 (2.2)	①	30 ③	40 ③	50	70	17	17	26
	J	4-153 (2.5)	①	30 ③	40 ③	50	70	17	17	26
	K	4-153 (2.5)	①	30 ③	40 ③	50	70	17	17	26
	3	6-181 (3.0)	70	60	38	110	70	17	17	20
	R	4-135 (2.2)	②	④	⑤	50	70	17	13	13
1990–91	C	4-135 (2.2)	①	30 ③	40 ③	50	70	17	17	26
	D	4-135 (2.2)	①	30 ③	40 ③	50	70	17	17	26
	J	4-153 (2.5)	①	30 ③	40 ③	50	70	17	17	26
	K	4-153 (2.5)	①	30 ③	40 ③	50	70	17	17	26
	3	6-181 (3.0)	70	60	38	110	70	17	17	20
	S	6-181 (3.0)	70	60	38	110	70	17	17	20
	R	4-135 (2.2)	②	④	⑤	50	70	17	13	13

① Sequence: 45, 65, 65 plus ¼ turn
② Sequence: 32, 50, 65 plus ¼ turn
③ Plus ¼ turn
④ Sequence: 32, 43, 76
⑤ Sequence: 32, 47

BRAKE SPECIFICATIONS

All measurements in inches unless noted.

Year	Model	Lug Nut Torque (ft. lbs.)	Master Cylinder Bore	Brake Disc		Standard Brake Drum Diameter	Minimum Lining Thickness	
				Minimum Thickness	Maximum Runout		Front	Rear
1987	Aries	95	0.827	0.882	0.005	7.87	0.06	0.06
	Reliant	95	0.827	0.882	0.005	7.87	0.06	0.06
	600	95	0.827	0.882	0.005	8.66	0.06	0.06
	Caravelle	95	0.827	0.882	0.005	8.66	0.06	0.06
	LeBaron	95	0.827	0.882	0.005	7.87	0.06	0.06
	LeBaron (J body)	95	0.827	0.882	0.005	7.87	0.06	0.06
	Lancer	95	0.827	0.882	0.005	7.87	0.06	0.06
	LeBaron GTS	95	0.827	0.882	0.005	7.87	0.06	0.06
	New Yorker	95	0.827	0.882	0.005	8.66	0.06	0.06
	Shadow	95	0.827	0.882	0.005	7.87	0.06	0.06
	Sundance	95	0.827	0.882	0.005	7.87	0.06	0.06
	Daytona	95	0.827	0.882	0.005	7.87	0.06	0.06
	rear disc	—	—	0.291	0.005	—	—	0.06
1988	Aries	95	0.827	0.882	0.005	7.87	0.06	0.06
	Reliant	95	0.827	0.882	0.005	7.87	0.06	0.06
	600	95	0.827	0.882	0.005	8.66	0.06	0.06
	Caravelle	95	0.827	0.882	0.005	8.66	0.06	0.06
	LeBaron	95	0.827	0.882	0.005	7.87	0.06	0.06
	LeBaron (J body)	95	0.827	0.882	0.005	7.87	0.06	0.06
	Lancer	95	0.827	0.882	0.005	7.87	0.06	0.06
	LeBaron GTS	95	0.827	0.882	0.005	7.87	0.06	0.06
	New Yorker	95	0.827	0.882	0.005	8.66	0.06	0.06
	Shadow	95	0.827	0.882	0.005	7.87	0.06	0.06
	Sundance	95	0.827	0.882	0.005	7.87	0.06	0.06
	Daytona	95	0.827	0.882	0.005	8.66	0.06	0.06
	rear disc	—	—	0.291	0.005	—	—	0.06
1989	Aries	95	0.827	0.882	0.005	7.87	0.06	0.06
	Reliant	95	0.827	0.882	0.005	7.87	0.06	0.06
	Lancer	95	0.827	0.882	0.005	7.87	0.06	0.06
	LeBaron GTS	95	0.827	0.882	0.005	7.87	0.06	0.06
	Shadow	95	0.827	0.882	0.005	7.87	0.06	0.06
	Sundance	95	0.827	0.882	0.005	7.87	0.06	0.06
	Spirit	95	0.827	0.882	0.005	8.66	0.06	0.06
	Acclaim	95	0.827	0.882	0.005	8.66	0.06	0.06
	Daytona	95	0.827	0.882	0.005	—	0.06	—
	solid rear disc	—	—	0.409	0.005	—	—	0.06
	vented rear disc	—	—	0.797	0.005	—	—	0.06
	LeBaron (J body)	95	0.827	0.882	0.005	—	0.06	—
	solid rear disc	—	—	0.409	0.005	—	—	0.06
	vented rear disc	—	—	0.797	0.005	—	—	0.06
	TC	95	NA	0.882	0.005	—	0.06	—
	rear disc	—	—	0.291	0.005	—	—	0.06

BRAKE SPECIFICATIONS

All measurements in inches unless noted.

Year	Model	Lug Nut Torque (ft. lbs.)	Master Cylinder Bore	Brake Disc Minimum Thickness	Brake Disc Maximum Runout	Standard Brake Drum Diameter	Minimum Lining Thickness Front	Minimum Lining Thickness Rear
1990-91	LeBaron Landau	95	0.827	0.882	0.005	8.66	0.06	0.06
	Shadow	95	0.827	0.882	0.005	7.87	0.06	0.06
	Sundance	95	0.827	0.882	0.005	7.87	0.06	0.06
	Spirit	95	0.827	0.882	0.005	8.66	0.06	0.06
	Acclaim	95	0.827	0.882	0.005	8.66	0.06	0.06
	Daytona	95	0.827	0.882	0.005	—	0.06	—
	solid rear disc	—	—	0.409	0.005	—	—	0.06
	vented rear disc	—	—	0.797	0.005	—	—	0.06
	LeBaron (J body)	95	0.827	0.882	0.005	—	0.06	—
	solid rear disc	—	—	0.409	0.005	—	—	0.06
	vented rear disc	—	—	0.797	0.005	—	—	0.06
	TC	95	NA	0.882	0.005	—	0.06	—
	rear disc	—	—	0.291	0.005	—	—	0.06

WHEEL ALIGNMENT

Year	Model		Caster Range (deg.)	Caster Preferred Setting (deg.)	Camber Range (deg.)	Camber Preferred Setting (deg.)	Toe-in (in.)	Steering Axis Inclination (deg.)
1987	Aries	front	①	$1^3/_{16}$	$1/_4$N-$3/_4$P	$5/_{16}$P	$1/_{16}$	$13^5/_{16}$
		rear	—	—	$1^1/_4$N-$1/_4$N	$1/_2$N	0	—
	Reliant	front	①	$1^3/_{16}$	$1/_4$N-$3/_4$P	$5/_{16}$P	$1/_{16}$	$13^5/_{16}$
		rear	—	—	$1^1/_4$N-$1/_4$N	$1/_2$N	0	—
	Daytona	front	①	$1^3/_{16}$	$1/_4$N-$3/_4$P	$5/_{16}$P	$1/_{16}$	$13^5/_{16}$
		rear	—	—	$1^1/_4$N-$1/_4$N	$1/_2$N	0	—
	600	front	①	$1^3/_{16}$	$1/_4$N-$3/_4$P	$5/_{16}$P	$1/_{16}$	$13^5/_{16}$
		rear	—	—	$1^1/_4$N-$1/_4$N	$1/_2$N	0	—
	Caravelle	front	①	$1^3/_{16}$	$1/_4$N-$3/_4$P	$5/_{16}$P	$1/_{16}$	$13^5/_{16}$
		rear	—	—	$1^1/_4$N-$1/_4$N	$1/_2$N	0	—
	LeBaron	front	①	$1^3/_{16}$	$1/_4$N-$3/_4$P	$5/_{16}$P	$1/_{16}$	$13^5/_{16}$
		rear	—	—	$1^1/_4$N-$1/_4$N	$1/_2$N	0	—
	LeBaron (J body)	front	①	$1^3/_{16}$	$1/_4$N-$3/_4$P	$5/_{16}$P	$1/_{16}$	$13^5/_{16}$
		rear	—	—	$1^1/_4$N-$1/_4$N	$1/_2$N	0	—
	Lancer	front	①	$1^3/_{16}$	$1/_4$N-$3/_4$P	$5/_{16}$P	$1/_{16}$	$13^5/_{16}$
		rear	—	—	$1^1/_4$N-$1/_4$N	$1/_2$N	0	—
	LeBaron GTS	front	①	$1^3/_{16}$	$1/_4$N-$3/_4$P	$5/_{16}$P	$1/_{16}$	$13^5/_{16}$
		rear	—	—	$1^1/_4$N-$1/_4$N	$1/_2$N	0	—
	New Yorker	front	①	$1^3/_{16}$	$1/_4$N-$3/_4$P	$5/_{16}$P	$1/_{16}$	$13^5/_{16}$
		rear	—	—	$1^1/_4$N-$1/_4$N	$1/_2$N	0	—
	Shadow	front	①	$1^3/_{16}$	$1/_4$N-$3/_4$P	$5/_{16}$P	$1/_{16}$	$13^5/_{16}$
		rear	—	—	$1^1/_4$N-$1/_4$N	$1/_2$N	0	—
	Sundance	front	①	$1^3/_{16}$	$1/_4$N-$3/_4$P	$5/_{16}$P	$1/_{16}$	$13^5/_{16}$
		rear	—	—	$1^1/_4$N-$1/_4$N	$1/_2$N	0	—

WHEEL ALIGNMENT

Year	Model		Caster Range (deg.)	Caster Preferred Setting (deg.)	Camber Range (deg.)	Camber Preferred Setting (deg.)	Toe-in (in.)	Steering Axis Inclination (deg.)
1988	Aries	front	①	$1^3/_{16}$	$^1/_4$N–$^3/_4$P	$^5/_{16}$P	$^1/_{16}$	$13^5/_{16}$
		rear	—	—	$1^1/_4$N–$^1/_4$N	$^1/_2$N	0	—
	Reliant	front	①	$1^3/_{16}$	$^1/_4$N–$^3/_4$P	$^5/_{16}$P	$^1/_{16}$	$13^5/_{16}$
		rear	—	—	$1^1/_4$N–$^1/_4$N	$^1/_2$N	0	—
	Daytona	front	①	$1^3/_{16}$	$^1/_4$N–$^3/_4$P	$^5/_{16}$P	$^1/_{16}$	$13^5/_{16}$
		rear	—	—	$1^1/_4$N–$^1/_4$N	$^1/_2$N	0	—
	600	front	①	$1^3/_{16}$	$^1/_4$N–$^3/_4$P	$^5/_{16}$P	$^1/_{16}$	$13^5/_{16}$
		rear	—	—	$1^1/_4$N–$^1/_4$N	$^1/_2$N	0	—
	Caravelle	front	①	$1^3/_{16}$	$^1/_4$N–$^3/_4$P	$^5/_{16}$P	$^1/_{16}$	$13^5/_{16}$
		rear	—	—	$1^1/_4$N–$^1/_4$N	$^1/_2$N	0	—
	LeBaron	front	①	$1^3/_{16}$	$^1/_4$N–$^3/_4$P	$^5/_{16}$P	$^1/_{16}$	$13^5/_{16}$
		rear	—	—	$1^1/_4$N–$^1/_4$N	$^1/_2$N	0	—
	LeBaron (J body)	front	①	$1^3/_{16}$	$^1/_4$N–$^3/_4$P	$^5/_{16}$P	$^1/_{16}$	$13^5/_{16}$
		rear	—	—	$1^1/_4$N–$^1/_4$N	$^1/_2$N	0	—
	Lancer	front	①	$1^3/_{16}$	$^1/_4$N–$^3/_4$P	$^5/_{16}$P	$^1/_{16}$	$13^5/_{16}$
		rear	—	—	$1^1/_4$N–$^1/_4$N	$^1/_2$N	0	—
	LeBaron GTS	front	①	$1^3/_{16}$	$^1/_4$N–$^3/_4$P	$^5/_{16}$P	$^1/_{16}$	$13^5/_{16}$
		rear	—	—	$1^1/_4$N–$^1/_4$N	$^1/_2$N	0	—
	New Yorker	front	①	$1^3/_{16}$	$^1/_4$N–$^3/_4$P	$^5/_{16}$P	$^1/_{16}$	$13^5/_{16}$
		rear	—	—	$1^1/_4$N–$^1/_4$N	$^1/_2$N	0	—
	Shadow	front	①	$1^3/_{16}$	$^1/_4$N–$^3/_4$P	$^5/_{16}$P	$^1/_{16}$	$13^5/_{16}$
		rear	—	—	$1^1/_4$N–$^1/_4$N	$^1/_2$N	0	—
	Sundance	front	①	$1^3/_{16}$	$^1/_4$N–$^3/_4$P	$^5/_{16}$P	$^1/_{16}$	$13^5/_{16}$
		rear	—	—	$1^1/_4$N–$^1/_4$N	$^1/_2$N	0	—
1989	Aries	front	①	$1^3/_{16}$	$^1/_4$N–$^3/_4$P	$^5/_{16}$P	$^1/_{16}$	$13^5/_{16}$
		rear	—	—	$1^1/_4$N–$^1/_4$N	$^1/_2$N	0	—
	Reliant	front	①	$1^3/_{16}$	$^1/_4$N–$^3/_4$P	$^5/_{16}$P	$^1/_{16}$	$13^5/_{16}$
		rear	—	—	$1^1/_4$N–$^1/_4$N	$^1/_2$N	0	—
	Daytona	front	①	$1^3/_{16}$	$^1/_4$N–$^3/_4$P	$^5/_{16}$P	$^1/_{16}$	$13^5/_{16}$
		rear	—	—	$1^1/_4$N–$^1/_4$N	$^1/_2$N	0	—
	LeBaron	front	①	$1^3/_{16}$	$^1/_4$N–$^3/_4$P	$^5/_{16}$P	$^1/_{16}$	$13^5/_{16}$
		rear	—	—	$1^1/_4$N–$^1/_4$N	$^1/_2$N	0	—
	Lancer	front	①	$1^3/_{16}$	$^1/_4$N–$^3/_4$P	$^5/_{16}$P	$^1/_{16}$	$13^5/_{16}$
		rear	—	—	$1^1/_4$N–$^1/_4$N	$^1/_2$N	0	—
	LeBaron GTS	front	①	$1^3/_{16}$	$^1/_4$N–$^3/_4$P	$^5/_{16}$P	$^1/_{16}$	$13^5/_{16}$
		rear	—	—	$1^1/_4$N–$^1/_4$N	$^1/_2$N	0	—
	Shadow	front	①	$1^3/_{16}$	$^1/_4$N–$^3/_4$P	$^5/_{16}$P	$^1/_{16}$	$13^5/_{16}$
		rear	—	—	$1^1/_4$N–$^1/_4$N	$^1/_2$N	0	—
	Sundance	front	①	$1^3/_{16}$	$^1/_4$N–$^3/_4$P	$^5/_{16}$P	$^1/_{16}$	$13^5/_{16}$
		rear	—	—	$1^1/_4$N–$^1/_4$N	$^1/_2$N	0	—
	Spirit	front	①	$1^3/_{16}$	$^1/_4$N–$^3/_4$P	$^5/_{16}$P	$^1/_{16}$	$13^5/_{16}$
		rear	—	—	$1^1/_4$N–$^1/_4$N	$^1/_2$N	0	—

WHEEL ALIGNMENT

Year	Model		Caster Range (deg.)	Caster Preferred Setting (deg.)	Camber Range (deg.)	Camber Preferred Setting (deg.)	Toe-in (in.)	Steering Axis Inclination (deg.)
1989	Acclaim	front	①	$1^3/_{16}$	$1/_4$N–$3/_4$P	$5/_{16}$P	$1/_{16}$	$13^5/_{16}$
		rear	—	—	$1^1/_4$N–$1/_4$N	$1/_2$N	0	—
	TC	front	①	$1^3/_{16}$	$1/_4$N–$3/_4$P	$5/_{16}$P	$1/_{16}$	$13^5/_{16}$
		rear	—	—	$1^1/_4$N–$1/_4$N	$1/_2$N	0	—
1990–91	Daytona	front	①	$1^3/_{16}$	$1/_4$N–$3/_4$P	$5/_{16}$P	$1/_{16}$	$13^5/_{16}$
		rear	—	—	$1^1/_4$N–$1/_4$N	$1/_2$N	0	—
	LeBaron	front	①	$1^3/_{16}$	$1/_4$N–$3/_4$P	$5/_{16}$P	$1/_{16}$	$13^5/_{16}$
		rear	—	—	$1^1/_4$N–$1/_4$N	$1/_2$N	0	—
	LeBaron Landau	front	①	$1^3/_{16}$	$1/_4$N–$3/_4$P	$5/_{16}$P	$1/_{16}$	$13^5/_{16}$
		rear	—	—	$1^1/_4$N–$1/_4$N	$1/_2$N	0	—
	Shadow	front	①	$1^3/_{16}$	$1/_4$N–$3/_4$P	$5/_{16}$P	$1/_{16}$	$13^5/_{16}$
		rear	—	—	$1^1/_4$N–$1/_4$N	$1/_2$N	0	—
	Sundance	front	①	$1^3/_{16}$	$1/_4$N–$3/_4$P	$5/_{16}$P	$1/_{16}$	$13^5/_{16}$
		rear	—	—	$1^1/_4$N–$1/_4$N	$1/_2$N	0	—
	Spirit	front	①	$1^3/_{16}$	$1/_4$N–$3/_4$P	$5/_{16}$P	$1/_{16}$	$13^5/_{16}$
		rear	—	—	$1^1/_4$N–$1/_4$N	$1/_2$N	0	—
	Acclaim	front	①	$1^3/_{16}$	$1/_4$N–$3/_4$P	$5/_{16}$P	$1/_{16}$	$13^5/_{16}$
		rear	—	—	$1^1/_4$N–$1/_4$N	$1/_2$N	0	—
	TC	front	①	$1^3/_{16}$	$1/_4$N–$3/_4$P	$5/_{16}$P	$1/_{16}$	$13^5/_{16}$
		rear	—	—	$1^1/_4$N–$1/_4$N	$1/_2$N	0	—

① Not adjustable; variation between sides should not exceed 1.5°

ENGINE ELECTRICAL

NOTE: Disconnecting the negative battery cable on some vehicles may interfere with the functions of the on board computer systems and may require the computers to undergo a relearning process, once the negative battery cable is reconnected.

Distributor

REMOVAL

1. Disconnect the negative battery cable.
2. Disconnect the distributor pick-up lead wires. Remove the splash shield, if equipped.
3. Unscrew the distributor cap hold-down screws and lift off the distributor cap with all ignition wires still connected. Remove the coil wire, if necessary.
4. Matchmark the rotor to the distributor housing and the distributor housing to the engine.

NOTE: Do not crank the engine during this procedure. If the engine is cranked, the matchmark must be disregarded.

5. Remove the hold-down bolt and clamp.
6. Remove the distributor from the engine.

INSTALLATION

Timing Not Disturbed

1. Install a new distributor housing O-ring.
2. Install the distributor in the engine so the rotor is aligned with the matchmark on the housing and the housing is aligned with the matchmark on the engine. Make sure the distributor is fully seated and the distributor shaft is fully engaged.
3. Install the hold-down clamp and snug the hold-down bolt.
4. Connect the distributor pickup lead wires. Install the splash shield, if equipped.

5. Install the distributor cap and snap the retaining clips into place or tighten the screws.
6. Connect the negative battery cable.
7. Adjust the ignition timing and tighten the hold-down bolt.

Timing Disturbed

1. Install a new distributor housing O-ring.
2. Position the engine so the No. 1 piston is at TDC of the compression stroke and the mark on the vibration damper is aligned with **0** on the timing indicator.
3. Install the distributor in the engine so the rotor is aligned with the position of the No. 1 ignition wire on the distributor cap and the housing is aligned with the matchmark on the engine. Make sure the distributor is fully seated and the distributor shaft is fully engaged.

NOTE: There are distributor cap runners inside the cap on 3.0L engine. Make sure the rotor is pointing to where the No. 1 runner originates inside the cap and

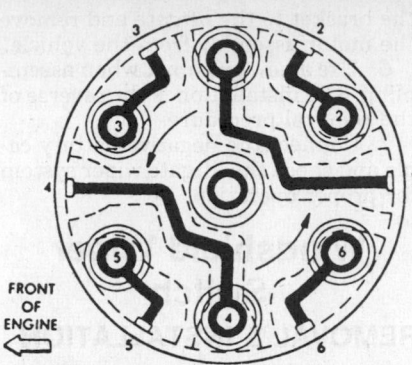

Distributor cap terminal routing—3.0L engine

FRONT
OF
ENGINE

not where the No. 1 ignition wire plugs into the cap.

4. Install the hold-down clamp and snug the hold-down bolt.

5. Connect the distributor pickup lead wires. Install the splash shield, if equipped.

6. Install the distributor cap and tighten the screws.

7. Connect the negative battery cable.

8. Adjust the ignition timing and tighten the hold-down bolt.

Ignition Timing

ADJUSTMENT

1. Start the engine, set the parking brake and run the engine until at normal operating temperature. Keep all lights and accessories **OFF**.

2. If a magnetic timing unit is available, insert the probe into the receptacle near the timing scale. The scale is located near the crankshaft pulley on the 3.0L engine and on the top of the bell housing on 2.2L and 2.5L engines.

3. If a magnetic timing unit is not available, connect a conventional power timing light to the No. 1 cylinder spark plug wire.

4. Connect the red lead of a tachometer to the negative primary terminal of the coil and connect the black lead to a good ground.

5. Set the idle speed according to the Vehicle Emission Control Information (VECI) label.

6. On 1989–91 vehicles, connect the Diagnostic Readout Box II (DRB II) and access the Basic Timing Mode. If the DRB II is not available, disconnect the coolant sensor located near the thermostat housing. The Check Engine lamp on the instrument panel must be **ON**.

7. Aim the timing light at the timing scale or read the magnetic timing unit.

8. Loosen the distributor hold-

down bolt enough so the disributor can be rotated.

9. Turn the distributor in the proper direction until the specified timing according to the VECI label is reached. Tighten the hold-down bolt and recheck the timing and idle speed.

10. Turn the engine **OFF**. Connect the coolant sensor and check to make sure the Check Engine lamp does not come on when the vehicle is restarted. Disconnect the timing apparatus and tachometer.

11. If the coolant temperature sensor was disconnected, erase the created fault code using the Erase Fault Code mode on the DRB II.

Alternator

For further information on the charging system, please refer to "Charging and Starting" in the Unit Repair section.

PRECAUTIONS

Several precautions must be observed when working with the alternator to avoid damage to the unit.

- If the battery is removed for any reason, make sure it is reconnected with the correct polarity. Reversing the battery connections may result in damage to the one-way rectifiers.

- When utilizing a booster battery as a starting aid, always connect the positive to positive terminals and the negative terminal from the booster battery to a good engine ground on the vehicle being started.

- Never use a fast charger as a booster to start vehicles.

- Disconnect the battery cables when charging the battery with a fast charger.

- Never attempt to polarize the alternator.

- Do not use test lamps of more than 12 volts when checking diode continuity.

- Do not short across or ground any of the alternator terminals.

- The polarity of the battery, alternator and regulator must be matched and considered before making any electrical connections within the system.

- Never separate the alternator on an open circuit. Make sure all connections within the circuit are clean and tight.

- Disconnect the battery ground terminal when performing any service on electrical components.

- Disconnect the battery if arc welding is to be done on the vehicle.

BELT TENSION ADJUSTMENT

NOTE: The belt tension is automatically adjusted by a dynamic tensioner on the 3.0L engine. Periodic adjustment is not necessary.

1. Loosen the pivot bolt slightly.

2. Raise the vehicle and support safely. Remove the splash shield. Loosen the adjuster slot bolt or "T" bolt locknut enough so the alternator can be moved. Loosen the adjusting bolt locknut, if equipped.

3. Tighten the adjusting bolt down until the belt deflects about ¼ in. under a 10 lb. load.

4. Tighten the "T" bolt locknut, adjusting bolt locknut and pivot bolt.

REMOVAL & INSTALLATION

1. Disconnect the negative battery cable.

2. On 2.2L and 2.5L engines, remove the air conditioning compressor and position it to the side, if equipped. Remove the oil filter to allow the alternator to be removed from above.

3. On the 3.0L engine, release the dynamic belt tensioner using a ½ in. breaker bar and remove the belt. On other engines, loosen the mounting bolts and remove the drive belt.

4. Remove all mounting bolts, spacers and adjuster bolt, if equipped, and remove the alternator from the brackets.

5. Remove the battery positive, field and ground terminals from the rear of the alternator. Remove the wire harness hold-down screw from the alternator, if equipped.

To install:

6. Connect all wiring to the proper terminals on the rear of the alternator and install the wire harness hold-down screw, if equipped.

7. Position the alternator in the mounting brackets.

8. Install the spacers, pivot bolt, adjuster slot bolt and adjuster bolt, if equipped. Install the belt.

9. Install the air conditioning compressor and oil filter, if they were removed.

10. Adjust the belt tension, if necessary.

11. Connect the negative battery cable.

Starter

For further information on the charging system, please refer to "Charging and Starting" in the Unit Repair section.

REMOVAL & INSTALLATION

1. Disconnect the negative battery cable.

2. On 2.2L and 2.5L engines, remove the attaching nut and bolt at the top of the bell housing. Raise the vehicle and support safely.

3. Remove the rear mount from the starter, if equipped. Remove the heat shield from the starter, if equipped.

4. Unbolt the starter and remove the starter from the vehicle.

5. Disconnect the solenoid lead wires from the starter.

To install:

6. Connect the solenoid lead wires and install the heat shield, if equipped.

7. On the 2.2L and 2.5L engines, install the lower bolt loosely, then lower the vehicle and install the nut and bolt from above and torque to 40 ft. lbs. (54 Nm).

8. Raise the vehicle again and torque the bottom bolt to the same value. Install the rear mount to the starter.

9. On the 3.0L engine, install all mounting bolts and torque to 40 ft. lbs. (54 Nm) evenly.

10. Connect the negative battery cable and check the starter for proper operation.

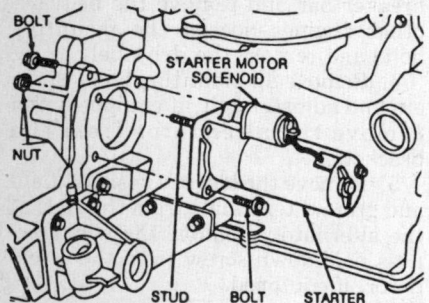

Removing or installing the starter—2.2L and 2.5L engines

CHASSIS ELECTRICAL

── CAUTION ──

On vehicles equipped with an air bag, the negative battery cable must be disconnected, before working on the system. Failure to do so may result in deployment of the air bag and possible personal injury.

Heater Blower Motor

REMOVAL & INSTALLATION

1. Disconnect the negative battery cable.

2. Remove the glove box assembly, lower right side instrument panel trim cover and right cowl trim panel, as required. Disconnect the blower lead wire connector.

3. If the vehicle is equipped with air conditioning, disconnect the 2 vacuum lines from the recirculating door actuator and position the actuator to the side.

4. Remove the 2 screws at the top of the blower housing that secure it to the unit cover.

5. Remove the 5 screws from around the blower housing and separate the blower housing from the unit.

6. Remove the 3 screws that secure the blower assembly to the heater or air conditioning housing and remove the assembly from the unit. Remove the fan from the blower motor.

7. The installation is the reverse of the removal procedure.

8. Connect the negative battery cable and check the blower motor for proper operation.

Windshield Wiper Motor

REMOVAL & INSTALLATION

1. Disconnect the negative battery cable.

2. If the cowl top plastic cover must be removed, remove the wiper arms and blades and remove the cover.

3. Remove the wiper motor cover and disconnect the motor wiring harness.

4. Disconnect the linkage drive crank from the motor crank arm.

5. Remove the motor mounting nuts and remove the wiper motor from the vehicle.

6. The installation is the reverse of the removal procedure.

7. Connect the negative battery cable and check the wiper motor for proper operation.

Liftgate Wiper Motor

REMOVAL & INSTALLATION

Daytona

1. Disconnect the negative battery cable.

2. To remove the wiper arm, lift the arm against its spring tension and release the latch. Lift the arm off of the motor shaft.

3. Open the liftgate and remove the trim panel. Disconnect the connector from the motor.

4. Remove the grommet from the liftgate glass.

5. Remove the screws that fasten the bracket to the liftgate and remove the motor assembly from the vehicle.

6. Use a new grommet when assembling. The installation is the reverse of the removal procedure.

7. Connect the negative battery cable and check the liftgate wiper system for proper operation.

Windshield Wiper Switch

REMOVAL & INSTALLATION

1987–89 Vehicles with Standard Column

1. Disconnect the negative battery cable.

2. Remove the lower steering column cover, if equipped.

3. Straighten the steering wheel so the tires are pointing straight ahead.

NOTE: For vehicles equipped with an airbag, it is imperative that the steering wheel removal and installation procedure under Steering is followed.

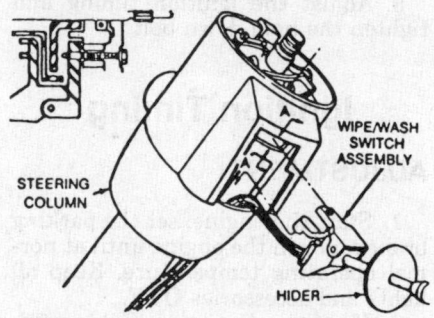

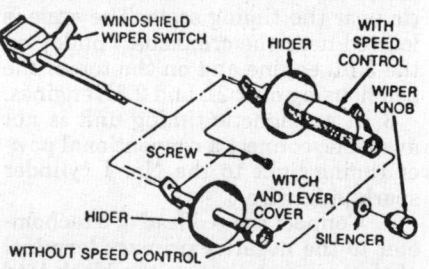

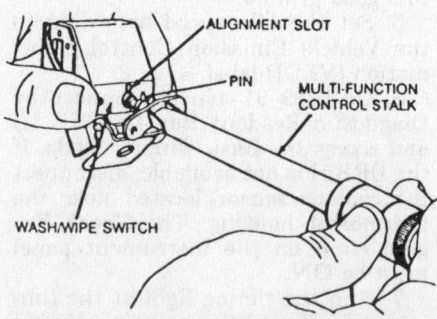

Removing the windshield wiper switch—standard column

4. Remove the steering wheel.

5. Remove the plastic wiring channel from the underside of the steering column.

6. Disconnect the wiper switch connector, intermittent wipe module connector and cruise control connector, if equipped.

7. Remove the side lock housing cover.

8. Remove the slotted hex-head screw that attaches the wiper switch to the turn signal switch and remove the switch.

9. Remove the control knob from the end of the stalk. Pull the round nylon hider up the control stalk and remove the revealed screws that attach the control stalk sleeve to the wiper switch.

10. Rotate the control stalk shaft to the full clockwise position and remove the shaft from the wiper switch by pulling it straight out.

To install:

11. Install the control shaft to the wiper switch, install the screws, the hider and the control knob.

12. Run the wiring through the opening and down the steering column, position the switch and install the hex-head screw. Make sure the dimmer switch rod is properly engaged.

13. Install the side lock housing cover.

14. Connect the wires and install the wiring channel.

15. Install the steering wheel torque the nut to 45 ft. lbs. (61 Nm).

16. Install the horn pad.

17. Connect the negative battery cable and check the wiper and washer, cruise control, turn signal switch and dimmer switch for proper operation.

18. Install the lower column cover, if equipped.

1987–89 Vehicles with Tilt Wheel and TC

1. Disconnect the negative battery cable.

2. Remove the lower steering column cover, if equipped and remove the plastic wiring channel from the underside of the steering column.

3. Straighten the steering wheel so the tires are pointing straight ahead.

NOTE: For vehicles equipped with an airbag, it is imperative that the steering wheel removal and installation procedure under Steering is followed.

4. Remove the steering wheel.

5. Depress the lockplate with the proper depressing tool, remove the retaining ring from its groove and remove the tool, ring, lockplate, cancelling cam and spring.

6. Remove the switch stalk actuator screw and arm.

7. Remove the hazard switch knob.

8. Disconnect the turn signal switch, wiper switch, intermittent module and cruise control connectors, if equipped.

9. Remove the 3 screws and remove the turn signal switch. Tape the connector to the wires to aid in removal.

10. Remove the ignition key lamp.

11. Place the key in the **LOCK** position and remove the key. Insert a thin tool into the slot next to the switch mounting screw boss, depress the spring latch at the bottom of the slot releasing the lock. Remove the lock cylinder.

12. Remove the buzzer switch and wedge spring.

13. Remove the 3 housing cover screws and remove the housing cover.

14. Remove the wiper switch pivot pin with a punch and remove the switch.

15. Remove the control knob from the end of the stalk. Pull the round nylon hider up the control stalk and remove the revealed screws that attach the control stalk sleeve to the wiper switch.

16. Rotate the control stalk shaft to the full clockwise position and remove the shaft from the wiper switch by pulling it straight out.

To install:

17. Install the control shaft to the wiper switch, install the screws, the hider and the control knob.

18. Run the wiring through the opening and down the steering column, position the switch and install the wiper switch pivot pin.

19. Install the housing cover.

20. Install the buzzer switch and wedge spring.

21. Install the lock cylinder.

22. Install the ignition key lamp.

23. Install the turn signal switch, switch stalk actuator arm and hazard switch knob.

24. Install the spring, cancelling cam, lockplate and ring on the steering shaft. Depress the plate with the depressing tool and install the ring securely in the groove. Remove the tool slowly.

25. Connect the turn signal switch, wiper switch, intermittent module and cruise control connectors, if equipped. Install the channel.

26. Install the steering wheel and torque the nut to 45 ft. lbs. (61 Nm).

27. Install the horn pad.

28. Connect the negative battery cable and check the wiper and washer, cruise control, turn signal switch and dimmer switch for proper operation.

29. Install the lower column cover, if equipped.

1990–91 Daytona and LeBaron

1. Disconnect the negative battery cable.

2. Remove the panel vent grille above the switch pod assembly and remove the 2 revealed pod mounting screws.

3. Remove the 2 remaining screws underneath the pod and pull the pod out to disconnect the wiring harnesses. Remove the pod from the instrument panel.

4. Remove the inner panel from the pod. Disconnect the switch linkage from the buttons.

5. Remove the windshield wiper switch mounting screws and remove the entire switch assembly.

6. The installation is the reverse of the removal procedure.

7. Connect the negative battery cable and check the entire wiper system for proper operation.

Instrument Cluster

REMOVAL & INSTALLATION

Except 1990–91 Daytona and LeBaron

1. Disconnect the negative battery cable.

2. Remove the instrument cluster bezel. Cluster removal is not necessary if just removing gauges.

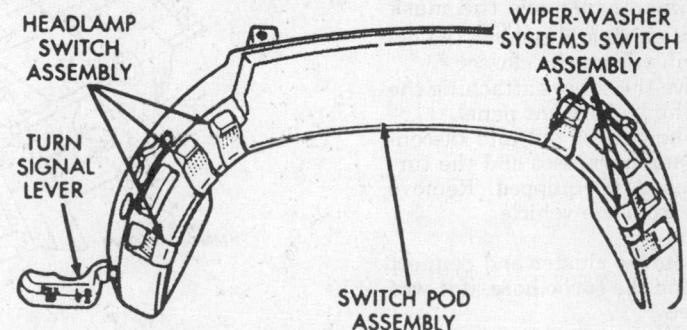

HEADLAMP SWITCH ASSEMBLY
TURN SIGNAL LEVER
WIPER-WASHER SYSTEMS SWITCH ASSEMBLY
SWITCH POD ASSEMBLY

Instrument panel switch pod assembly—1990–91 Daytona and LeBaron

3. When only removing gauge(s) or the speedometer, remove the trip odometer reset knob, if necessary, remove the mask and lens assembly and remove the desired gauge from the cluster. Disconnect the speedometer cable, if equipped, when removing the speedometer.

4. If equipped with automatic transaxle, remove the lower column cover and disconnect the gear indicator cable.

5. Remove the screws attaching the cluster to the instrument panel.

6. Pull the cluster out and disconnect all wiring harnesses and the speedometer cable, if equipped. Remove the cluster from the vehicle.

To install:

7. Position the cluster and feed the gear indicator cable through its slot.

8. Connect all wiring and install the speedometer cable to the speedometer, if removed; make sure the cable end is securely clicked in place.

9. Install the cluster retaining screws. Connect the gearshift indicator cable.

10. Install the cluster bezel.

11. Connect the negative battery cable, check all gauges and the speedometer for proper operation. Make sure the gearshift indicator is properly aligned.

1990–91 Daytona and LeBaron

1. Disconnect the negative battery cable.

2. Remove the panel vent grille above the switch pod assembly and remove the 2 revealed pod mounting screws.

3. Remove the 2 remaining screws underneath the pod and pull the pod out to disconnect the wiring harnesses. Remove the pod from the instrument panel.

4. Unscrew the tilt column lever, if equipped, remove the screws from underneath the upper steering column shrouds and remove the shrouds.

5. Pull rearward to disengage the cluster trim bezel retaining clips and remove the bezel.

6. When only removing gauges or the speedometer, remove the mask and lens assembly and remove the desired assembly from the cluster.

7. Remove the screws attaching the cluster to the instrument panel.

8. Pull the cluster out and disconnect all wiring harnesses and the turbo gauge hose, if equipped. Remove the cluster from the vehicle.

To install:

9. Position the cluster and connect all wiring and the turbo hose, if it was disconnected.

10. Install the cluster mounting screws.

11. Install the cluster trim bezel.

12. Install the steering column shrouds and the tilt lever, if equipped.

13. Install the switch pod assembly and panel vent grille.

14. Connect the negative battery cable and check all gauges, switches and the speedometer for proper operation.

Radio

REMOVAL & INSTALLATION

NOTE: On vehicles equipped with a compact disc player, removal and installation procedures are the same as for the radio.

1. Disconnect the negative battery cable.

2. Remove the console or cluster bezel, as required.

3. Remove the screws that attach the radio to the instrument panel.

4. Pull the radio out, disconnect the connectors, ground cable and antenna and remove the radio.

5. The installation is the reverse of the removal procedure.

6. Connect the negative battery cable and check the radio for proper operation.

Concealed Headlights

MANUAL OPERATION

1. Disconnect the negative battery cable.

2. Locate the manual override knob. On Daytona, they are located under access shields behind the bumper facia and under the center of the front bumper on LeBaron.

3. Remove the protective cover boot.

4. Rotate the manual override knob to raise the headlamp cover(s).

5. Connect the negative battery cable.

Headlight Switch

REMOVAL & INSTALLATION

Except 1990–91 Daytona and LeBaron

1. Disconnect the negative battery cable.

2. Remove the headlight switch bezel or cluster bezel, as required.

3. Remove the screws securing the headlight switch mounting plate to the instrument panel. Pull the assembly out to disconnect the connectors from the switch.

4. Depress the spring button and remove the headlight switch knob and stem.

5. Remove the escutcheon, if equipped, and remove the nut that attaches the switch to the mounting plate.

6. The installation is the reverse of the removal procedure.

7. Connect the negative battery cable and check the switch for proper operation.

1990–91 Daytona and LeBaron

1. Disconnect the negative battery cable.

2. Remove the panel vent grille

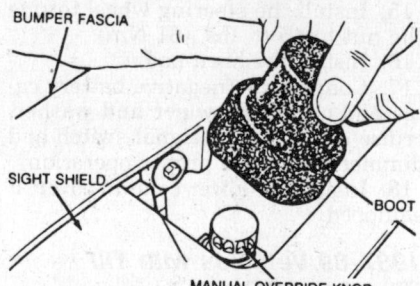

Manual override knob—Daytona

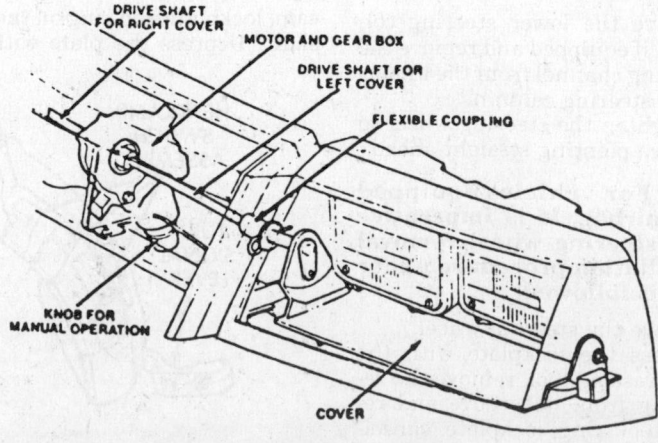

Manual override knob—LeBaron

above the switch pod assembly and remove the 2 revealed pod mounting screws.

3. Remove the 2 remaining screws underneath the pod and pull the pod out to disconnect the wiring harnesses. Remove the pod from the instrument panel.

4. Remove the turn signal switch lever by pulling it straight out of the pod.

5. Remove the inner panel from the pod. Remove the turn signal switch in order to gain access to the headlight switch.

6. Disconnect the switch linkage from the buttons.

7. Remove the switch mounting screws and remove the entire switch assembly.

8. The installation is the reverse of the removal procedure.

9. Connect the negative battery cable and check the system for proper operation.

Dimmer Switch

REMOVAL & INSTALLATION

NOTE: The dimmer switch is incorporated into the combination switch on 1990–91 LeBaron Landau, Shadow, Sundance, Spirit and Acclaim. On 1990–91 Daytona and LeBaron, it is incorporated with the remote turn signal switch.

1. Disconnect the negative battery cable.

2. Remove the lower steering column cover, if equipped.

3. Unplug the switch, located on the lower portion of the steering column.

4. Holding the actuating rod against its upper seat, remove the bolts that attach the switch to the column and remove the switch.

5. The installation is the reverse of the removal procedure. Adjust the switch as required.

6. Connect the negative battery cable and check the switch for proper operation.

Turn Signal Switch

REMOVAL & INSTALLATION

1987–89 Vehicles with Standard Column

1. Disconnect the negative battery cable.

2. Remove the lower steering column cover, if equipped.

3. Straighten the steering wheel so the tires are pointing straight ahead.

NOTE: For vehicles equipped with an airbag, it is imperative that the steering wheel removal and installation procedure under Steering is followed.

4. Remove the steering wheel.

5. Remove the plastic wiring channel from the underside of the steering column and disconnect the turn signal switch connector.

6. Remove the hazard switch knob. Remove the slotted hex-head screw that attaches the wiper switch to the turn signal switch.

7. Remove the 3 screws and pull the turn signal switch out of the column.

To install:

8. Run the wiring through the opening and down the steering column, position the switch and install the hex-head screw. Make sure the dimmer switch rod is properly engaged.

9. Install the 3 screws and the hazard switch knob.

10. Connect the wires and install the wiring channel.

11. Install the steering wheel and torque the nut to 45 ft. lbs. (61 Nm).

12. Install the horn pad.

13. Connect the negative battery cable and check the turn signal switch and dimmer switch for proper operation.

14. Install the lower column cover, if equipped.

1987–89 Vehicles with Tilt Wheel and TC

1. Disconnect the negative battery cable.

2. Remove the lower steering column cover, if equipped and remove the plastic wiring channel from the underside of the steering column.

3. Straighten the steering wheel so the tires are pointing straight ahead.

NOTE: For vehicles equipped with an airbag, it is imperative that the steering wheel removal and installation procedure under Steering is followed.

4. Remove the steering wheel.

5. Depress the lockplate with the proper depressing tool, remove the retaining ring from its groove and remove the tool, ring, lockplate, cancelling cam and spring.

6. Remove the stalk actuator screw and arm.

7. Remove the hazard switch knob.

8. Disconnect the turn signal switch connector.

9. Remove the 3 screws and remove the turn signal switch. Tape the connector to the wires to aid in removal.

To install:

10. Run the wiring through the opening and down the steering column, install the turn signal switch, switch stalk actuator arm and hazard switch knob.

11. Install the spring, cancelling cam, lockplate and ring on the steering shaft. Depress the plate with the depressing tool and install the ring securely in the groove. Remove the tool slowly.

12. Connect the turn signal switch connector and install the channel.

13. Install the steering wheel and

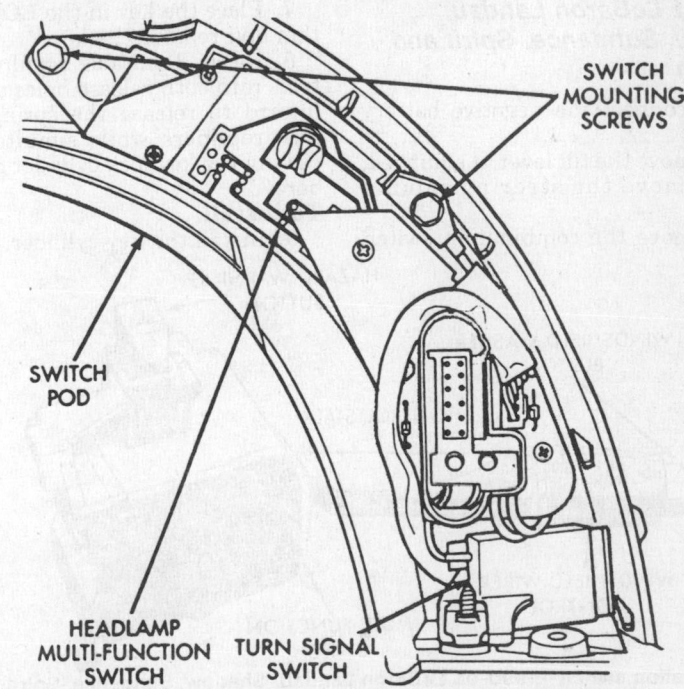

SWITCH
MOUNTING
SCREWS

SWITCH
POD

HEADLAMP
MULTI-FUNCTION
SWITCH

TURN SIGNAL
SWITCH

Turn signal switch location—1990-91 Daytona and LeBaron

torque the nut to 45 ft. lbs. (61 Nm).

14. Install the horn pad.

15. Connect the negative battery cable and check the turn signal switch and dimmer switch for proper operation.

16. Install the lower column cover, if equipped.

1990–91 Daytona and LeBaron

1. Disconnect the negative battery cable.

2. Remove the panel vent grille above the switch pod assembly and remove the 2 revealed pod mounting screws.

3. Remove the 2 remaining screws underneath the pod and pull the pod out to disconnect the wiring harnesses. Remove the pod from the instrument panel.

4. Remove the turn signal switch lever by pulling it straight out of the pod.

5. Remove the inner panel from the pod. Unplug the switch from the printed circuit board.

6. Remove the turn signal switch mounting screws and slide the switch out of the slot.

7. The installation is the reverse of the removal procedure.

8. Connect the negative battery cable and check the turn signal switch and dimmer function for proper operation.

Combination Switch

REMOVAL & INSTALLATION

1990–91 LeBaron Landau, Shadow, Sundance, Spirit and Acclaim

1. Disconnect the negative battery cable.

2. Remove the tilt lever, if equipped.

3. Remove the steering column covers.

4. Remove the combination switch

tamper-proof mounting screws and pull the switch away from the steering column.

5. Loosen the connector screw; the screw will remain in the connector. Disconnect the connector from the switch.

6. The installation is the reverse of the removal procedure.

7. Connect the negative battery cable and check all functions of the combination switch for proper operation.

Ignition Lock

REMOVAL & INSTALLATION

Vehicles with Standard Column Except 1990–91 Daytona and LeBaron

1. Disconnect the negative battery cable.

2. Straighten the steering wheel so the tires are pointing straight ahead.

NOTE: For vehicles equipped with an airbag, it is imperative that the steering wheel removal and installation procedure under Steering is followed.

3. Remove the steering wheel.

4. Remove the hazard switch knob. Remove the slotted hex-head screw that attaches the wiper switch to the turn signal switch.

5. Remove the 3 screws and pull the turn signal switch out of the column as far as it will go. Unplug it from below, if necessary.

6. Remove the ignition switch key lamp.

7. Place the key in the **LOCK** position and remove the key.

8. Insert 2 suitable small diameter tools into both release holes and push inward to release the spring loaded lock retainers while simultaneously pulling the key lock cylinder out of its bore.

To install:

9. Install the key cylinder.

10. Install the ignition switch key lamp.

11. Install the turn signal switch and hazard switch knob. Connect the wires, if they were disconnected.

12. Install the steering wheel and torque the nut to 45 ft. lbs. (61 Nm).

13. Install the horn pad.

14. Connect the negative battery cable and check the lock cylinder for proper operation.

15. Install the lower column cover, if equipped.

1987–89 Vehicles with Tilt Column and TC

1. Disconnect the negative battery cable.

2. Straighten the steering wheel so the tires are pointing straight ahead.

NOTE: For vehicles equipped with an airbag, it is imperative that the steering wheel removal and installation procedure under Steering is followed.

3. Remove the steering wheel.

4. Depress the lockplate, with the proper depressing tool, remove the retaining ring from its groove and remove the tool, ring, lockplate, cancelling cam and spring.

5. Remove the stalk actuator screw and arm.

6. Remove the hazard switch knob.

7. Remove the 3 screws and pull the turn signal switch out of the column as far as it will go. Unplug it below if necessary.

8. Remove the ignition key lamp.

9. Place the key in the **LOCK** position and remove the key. Insert a thin tool into the slot next to the switch mounting screw boss, depress the spring latch at the bottom of the slot releasing the lock and remove the lock cylinder.

To install:

10. Install the lock cylinder.

11. Install the ignition key lamp.

12. Install the turn signal switch, switch stalk actuator arm and hazard switch knob.

13. Install the spring, cancelling cam, lockplate and ring on the steering shaft. Depress the plate with the depressing tool and install the ring securely in the groove. Remove the tool slowly.

14. Connect the wires if they were disconnected.

15. Install the steering wheel and torque the nut to 45 ft. lbs. (61 Nm).

16. Install the horn pad.

17. Connect the negative battery cable and check the turn signal switch for proper operation.

18. Install the lower column cover, if removed.

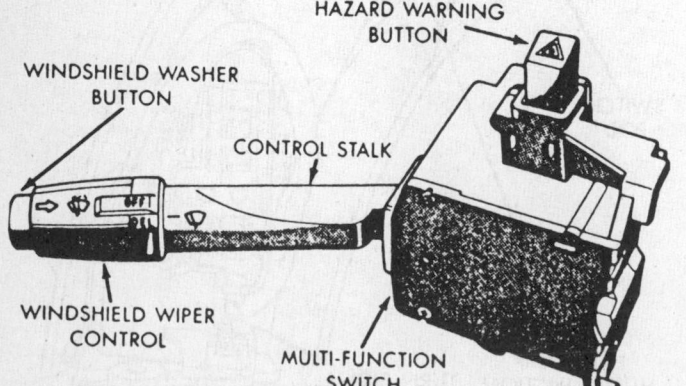

Combination switch – 1990–91 LeBaron Landau, Shadow, Sundance, Spirit and Acclaim

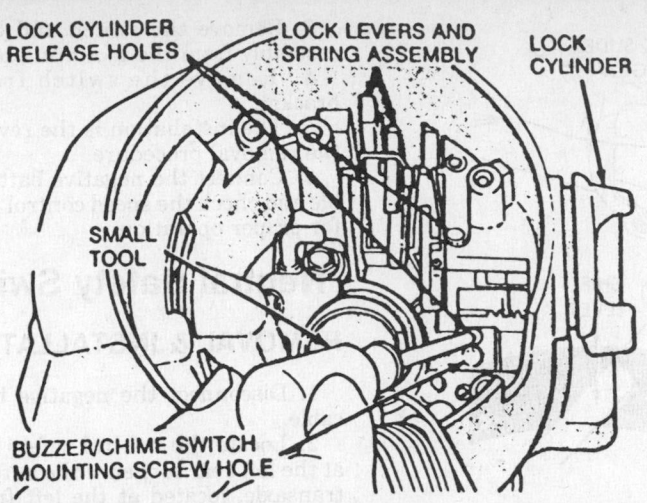

Removing the key lock cylinder—standard column, except 1990–91 Daytona and
LeBaron

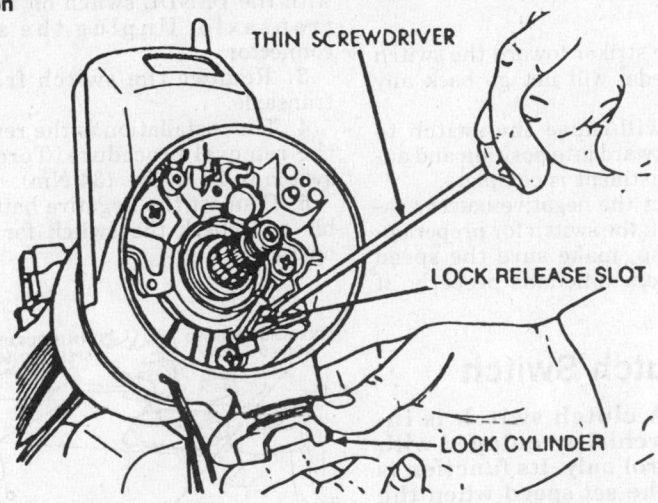

Removing the key lock cylinder—1987–89 tilt wheel and TC

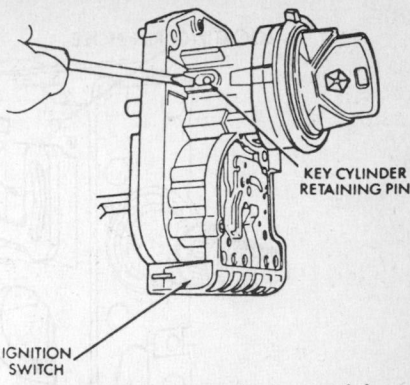

**Depressing the key cylinder retaining
pin—Acustar column**

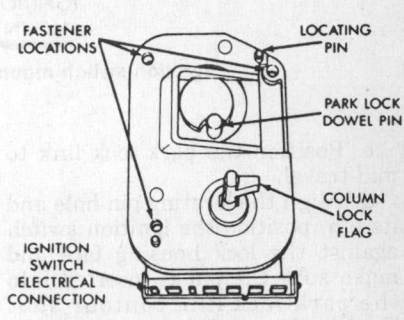

**Preparing the ignition switch for
installation—Acustar column**

Ignition Switch

REMOVAL & INSTALLATION

Except 1990–91 Vehicles with Acustar Steering Column

1. Disconnect the negative battery cable.
2. Remove the lower steering column cover.
3. Remove the steering column retaining nuts and allow the steering wheel to rest on the driver's seat.
4. Remove the 2 screws that attach the ignition switch to the column.
5. Rotate the switch 90 degrees and pull up to disengage it from the ignition switch rod.
To install:
6. Engage the switch with the rod, rotate the switch 90 degrees and push down until fully engaged.
7. Install the mounting screws finger tight.
8. Place the key in the **LOCK** posi-

tion and remove the key. Adjust the switch by pushing up gently on the switch to take up all slack in the rod.
9. Tighten the mounting screws and check the switch for proper operation in all positions.
10. Install the steering column and cover.

Ignition Lock/Switch

REMOVAL & INSTALLATION

1990–91 Vehicles with Acustar Steering Column

1. Disconnect the negative battery cable.
2. Remove the tilt lever, if equipped.
3. Remove the upper and lower column covers.
4. Remove the 3 ignition switch torx screws; APEX 440-TX20H or equivalent required.
5. Pull the switch away from the column. Release the connector locks

on the 2 wiring connectors and disconnect them from the switch.
6. Remove the key lock cylinder from the ignition switch:
   a. Insert the key and turn the switch to the **LOCK** position. Using a suitable small tool, depress the key cylinder retaining pin flush with the key cylinder surface.
   b. Rotate the key clockwise to the **OFF** position to unseat the key cylinder from the ignition switch assembly. The cylinder bezel should be about ⅛ in. above the ignition switch halo light ring. Do not attempt to remove the key cylinder.
   c. With the key cylinder in the unseated position, rotate the key counterclockwise to the **LOCK** position and remove the key.
   d. Remove the key cylinder from the ignition switch.
To install:
7. Connect the wiring connectors.
8. Mount ignition switch to the column:
   a. Position the shifter in **PARK** position. The park lock dowel pin on the ignition switch assembly must engage with the column park lock slider linkage.
   b. Verify that the ignition switch is in the **LOCK** position; the flag should be parallel to the ignition switch terminals. Apply a small amount of grease to the flag and pin.

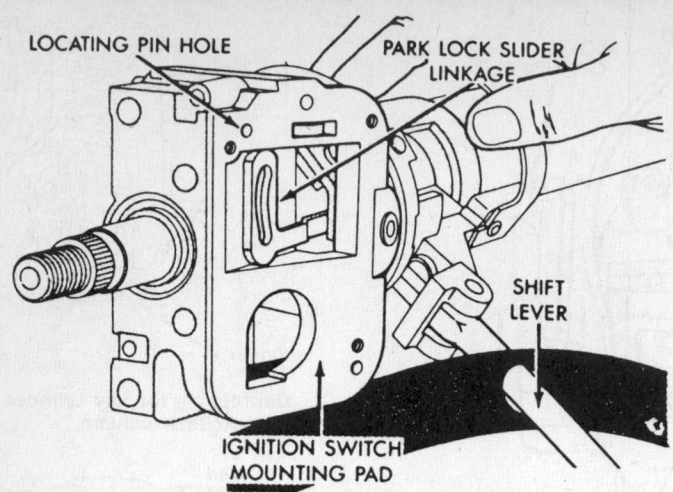

LOCATING PIN HOLE   PARK LOCK SLIDER LINKAGE

SHIFT LEVER

IGNITION SWITCH MOUNTING PAD

Ignition switch mounting pad—Acustar column

c. Position the park lock link to mid-travel.

d. Align the locating pin hole and its pin, position the ignition switch against the lock housing face and make sure the pin is inserted into the park lock link contour slot. Torque the retaining screws to 17 inch lbs.

9. With the key cylinder and ignition switch in the **LOCK** position, key not in cylinder, gently insert the key cylinder into the ignition switch until it bottoms.

10. Insert the key. Simultaneously, push in on the cylinder and rotate the key to the **RUN** position. This action should fully seat the cylinder in the ignition switch.

11. Install the column covers and the tilt lever, if equipped.

12. Connect the negative battery cable and check the push-to-lock and park lock functions, halo lighting and all ignition switch positions for proper operation.

Stoplight Switch

REMOVAL & INSTALLATION

1. Disconnect the negative battery cable.

2. Unplug the stoplight switch connectors near the brake pedal.

3. Remove the switch and bracket assembly from the brake pedal bracket.

4. Remove the switch from its bracket.

To install:

5. Install the switch and bracket assembly to the brake pedal bracket and push the switch forward as far as it will go; the brake pedal should move forward slightly.

6. Pull back on the brake pedal

bringing the striker toward the switch until the pedal will not go back any farther.

7. This will cause the switch to ratchet backward into position and automatic adjustment is complete.

8. Connect the negative battery cable and check the switch for proper operation. Also, make sure the speed control system functions properly, if equipped.

Clutch Switch

NOTE: A clutch switch is installed on vehicles equipped with speed control only. Its function is to cancel the set speed when the clutch is depressed.

REMOVAL & INSTALLATION

1. Disconnect the negative battery cable.

2. Unplug the switch connectors near the pedals.

3. Remove the switch and bracket assembly from the mounting bracket.

4. Remove the switch from its bracket.

5. The installation is the reverse of the removal procedure.

6. Connect the negative battery cable and check the speed control system for proper operation.

Neutral Safety Switch

REMOVAL & INSTALLATION

1. Disconnect the negative battery cable.

2. Locate the neutral safety switch at the left rear corner of the automatic transaxle, located at the left front of engine compartment. Do not confuse with the PRNDL switch on the A604 transaxle. Unplug the switch connector.

3. Remove the switch from the transaxle.

4. The installation is the reverse of the removal procedure. Torque the switch to 25 ft. lbs. (34 Nm).

5. Connect the negative battery cable and check the switch for proper operation.

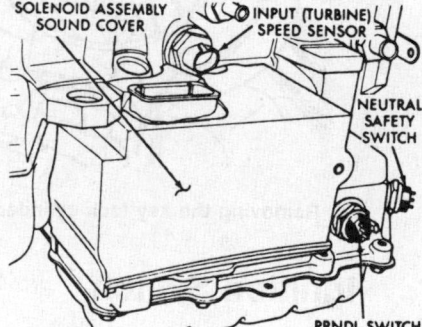

SOLENOID ASSEMBLY SOUND COVER   INPUT (TURBINE) SPEED SENSOR

NEUTRAL SAFETY SWITCH

PRNDL SWITCH

Neutral safety switch location—A604 automatic transaxle

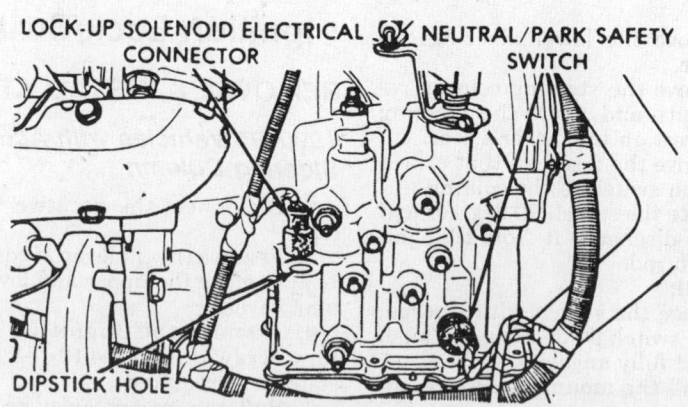

LOCK-UP SOLENOID ELECTRICAL CONNECTOR   NEUTRAL/PARK SAFETY SWITCH

DIPSTICK HOLE

Neutral safety switch location—A413 automatic transaxle

Fuses, Circuit Breakers and Relays

LOCATION

Aries, Reliant, 600, Caravelle, LeBaron (P Body) and New Yorker

The fuse block is located behind a removeable access panel, below the steering column. The hazard and turn signal flashers along with the time delay and horn relays are also located behind the panel.

Spirit, Acclaim, Shadow and Sundance

The fuse block is located behind the steering column cover, accessible by removing the fuse access panel above the hood latch release lever. The relay and flasher module is located behind an access panel in the glovebox. Included in the module are the hazard and turn signal flashers along with the time delay and horn relays.

Lancer and LeBaron GTS

The fuse block is located behind the glove box door, accessible by removing the fuse access panel. The relay and flasher module is located behind the cupholder in the center of the instrument panel. The entire module can be removed by pushing it up and off of its mounting bracket. Included in the module are the hazard and turn signal flashers along with the time delay and horn relays.

Daytona, LeBaron (J Body) and TC

The fuse block is located behind a removeable access panel to the left of the lower portion of the steering column. On TC and 1987–89 Daytona and LeBaron, the hazard and turn signal

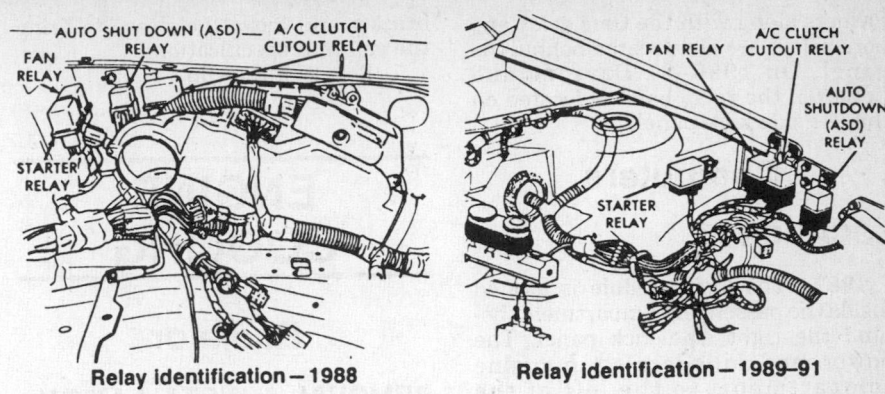

Relay identification — 1988

Relay identification — 1989-91

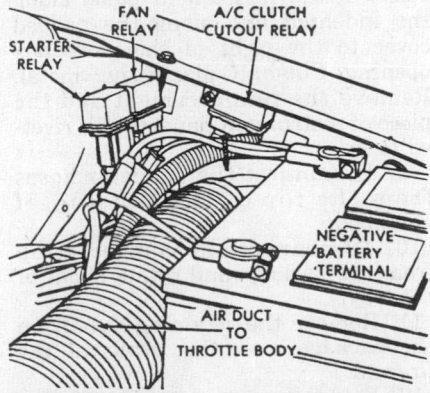

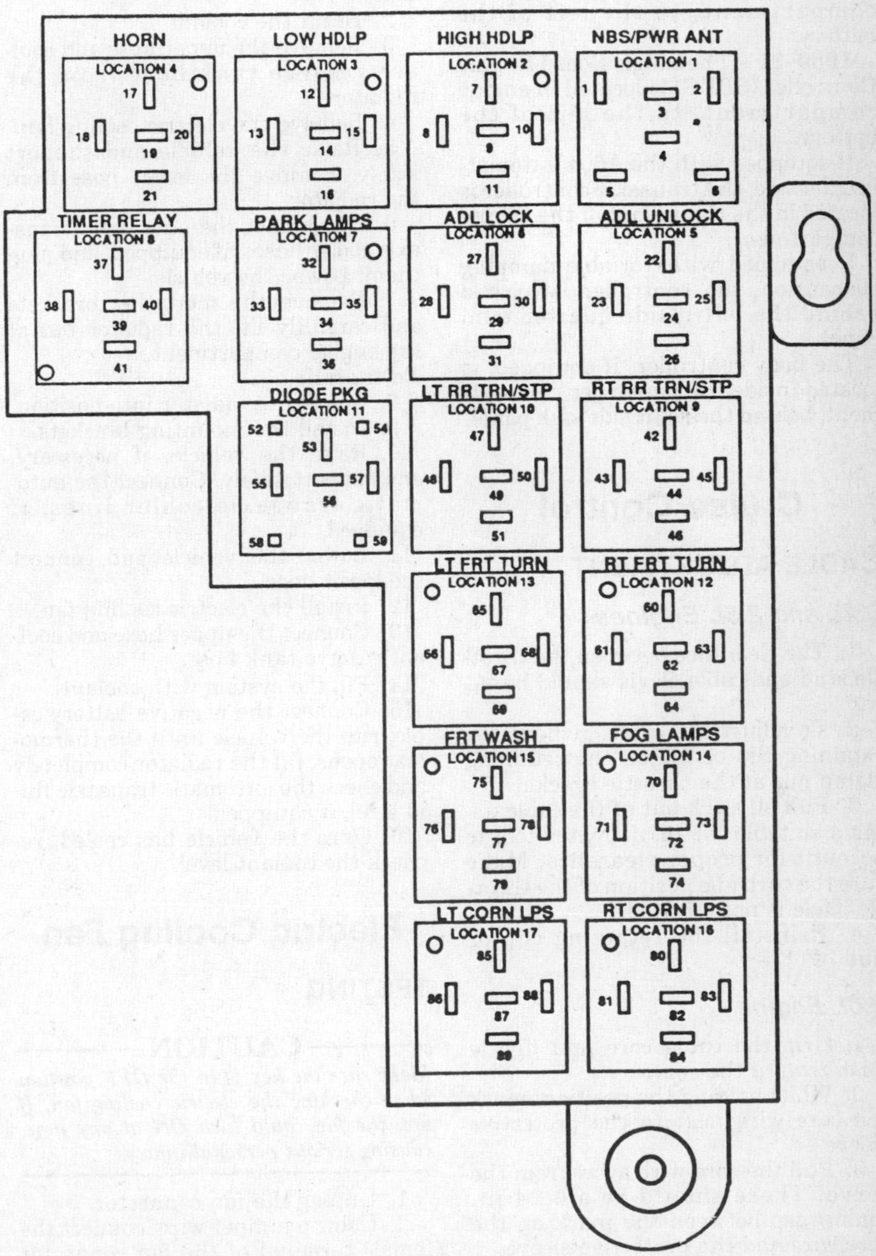

Relay identification — 1987. The Automatic Shutdown (ASD) relay is located inside the passenger compartment over the logic module.

Relay identification — view of wire end of relay bank on left side kick panel–1990–91 Daytona and LeBaron

flashers along with the time delay and horn relays are also located behind the panel. On 1990-91 Daytona and LeBaron, the relay bank is located on the left side kick panel.

Computers

LOCATION

1987—The logic module is located inside the passenger compartment, behind the right side kick panel. The power module is located in engine compartment, to the left of the battery.

1988—The Single Module Engine Controller (SMEC) is located in engine compartment, to the left of the battery.

1989-91—The Single Board Engine Controller (SBEC) is located in engine compartment, to the left of the battery.

If equipped with the A604 automatic transaxle, the transaxle controller is located in the right front of the engine compartment.

If equipped with variable damping suspension, the controller is located behind the left inside quarter trim panel.

The body controller, if equipped, is located inside the passenger compartment, behind the right side kick panel.

Cruise Control

CABLE ADJUSTMENT

2.2L and 2.5L Engines

1. The clearance between the throttle stud and cable clevis should be $1/16$ in.
2. To adjust the cable, remove the retaining clip or loosen the retaining clamp nut at the throttle bracket.
3. Pull all slack out of the cable using a suitable $1/16$ in. diameter tool to account for proper clearance. Make sure the curb idle position of the throttle blade is not affected.
4. Reinstall the retaining clip or nut.

3.0L Engine

1. Grip the cable core and lightly push toward the servo.
2. While holding the position, mark the core wire next to the protective sleeve.
3. Pull the core wire away from the servo. There should be a 0.24 in. (6mm) gap between the mark on the core wire and the protective sleeve.
4. If the gap is not correct, remove the adjustment clip from the throttle

bracket and move the sleeve to bring the gap into specification.
5. Reinstall the clip.

ENGINE COOLING

Radiator

REMOVAL & INSTALLATION

1. Disconnect the negative battery cable.
2. Drain the coolant.
3. Remove the upper hose and coolant reserve tank hose from the radiator.
4. Remove the electric cooling fan.
5. Raise the vehicle and support safely. Remove the lower hose from the radiator.
6. Disconnect the automatic transaxle cooler hoses, if equipped, and plug them. Lower the vehicle.
7. Remove the mounting brackets and carefully lift the radiator out of the engine compartment.
To install:
8. Lower the radiator into position.
9. Install the mounting brackets.
10. Raise the vehicle, if necessary, and support safely. Connect the automatic transaxle cooler lines, if equipped.
11. Lower the vehicle and connect the lower hose.
12. Install the electric cooling fan.
13. Connect the upper hose and coolant reserve tank hose.
14. Fill the system with coolant.
15. Connect the negative battery cable, run the vehicle until the thermostat opens, fill the radiator completely and check the automatic transaxle fluid level, if equipped.
16. Once the vehicle has cooled, recheck the coolant level.

Electric Cooling Fan

TESTING

—— **CAUTION** ——
Make sure the key is in the OFF position when checking the electric cooling fan. If not, the fan could turn ON at any time, causing serious personal injury.

1. Unplug the fan connector.
2. Using a jumper wire, connect the female terminal of the fan connector to the negative battery terminal.
3. The fan should come ON when

the male terminal is connected to the positive battery terminal.
4. If not, the fan is defective and should be replaced.

REMOVAL & INSTALLATION

1. Disconnect the negative battery cable.
2. Unplug the connector.
3. Remove the mounting screws.
4. Remove the fan assembly from the vehicle.
5. The installation is the reverse of the removal procedure.

Heater Core

REMOVAL & INSTALLATION

Without Air Conditioning

1. Disconnect the negative battery cable. Drain the cooling system.
2. Clamp off the heater hoses near the heater core and remove the hoses from the core tubes. Plug the hose ends and the core tubes to prevent spillage of coolant.
3. Remove the glove box, right side kick and sill panels and all modules, relay panels and computer components in the vacinity of the heater housing.
4. Remove the lower instrument panel silencers and reinforcements. Remove the radio and other dash-mounted optional equipment, as required.
5. Remove the floor console, if equipped. Remove the floor and defroster distribution ducts.
6. Remove the bolt holding the right side instrument panel to the right cowl.
7. Disconnect the blower motor wiring, antenna, resistor wiring and the temperature control cable.
8. On 1990-91 Daytona and LeBaron, using a suitable cutting device, cut the instrument panel along the indented line along the padded cover to the right of the glove box opening. Cut only plastic, not metal. Remove the reinforcement and the piece of instrument panel that is riveted to it.
9. Disconnect the demister hoses from the top of the housing, if equipped.
10. Disconnect the hanger strap from the package and rotate it out of the way.
11. Remove the retaining nuts from the package mounting studs at the firewall.
12. Fold the carpeting and insulation back to provide a little more working room and to prevent spillage from staining the carpeting. Pull the right

side of the instrument panel out as far as possible.

13. Remove the heater housing from the dash panel and remove it from the passenger compartment. Remove the passenger seat, if it is preventing removal.

14. To disassemble the housing assembly, remove the retaining screws from the cover and remove the cover.

15. Remove the retaining screw from the heater core and remove the core from the housing assembly.

To install:

16. Remove the temperature control door from the housing and clean the unit out with solvent. Lubricate the lower pivot rod and its well and install. Wrap the heater core with foam tape and place it in position. Secure it with its screw.

17. Assemble the housing, making sure all cover screws were used.

18. Connect the demister hoses. Install the nuts to the firewall and connect the hanger strap inside the passenger compartment.

19. Fold the carpeting back into position.

20. Install the bolt that attaches the right side of the instrument panel to the cowl.

21. Connect the blower motor wiring, antenna, resistor wiring and the temperature control cable.

22. Install the air distribution ducts.

23. Install the floor console, if equipped.

24. Install the radio and all other dash mounted items that were removed during the disassembly procedure.

25. Install the lower instrument panel reinforcements and silencers.

26. Install all modules, relay panels and computer components that were removed during the disassembly procedure.

27. Install the glove box and right side kick and sill panels. Install the passenger seat, if it was removed.

28. Connect the heater hoses.

29. Fill the cooling system.

30. Connect the negative battery cable and check the entire climate control system for proper operation and leakage.

With Air Conditioning

1. Disconnect the negative battery cable. Properly discharge the air conditioning system. Drain the cooling system.

2. Clamp off the heater hoses near the heater core and remove the hoses from the core tubes. Plug the hose ends and the core tubes to prevent spillage of coolant.

3. Disconnect the H-valve connection at the valve and remove the H-

valve. Remove the condensation tube.

4. Disconnect the vacuum lines at the brake booster and water valve.

5. Remove the glove box, right side kick and sill panels and all modules, relay panels and computer components in the vicinity of the housing.

6. Remove the lower instrument panel silencers and reinforcements. Remove the radio and other dash-mounted optional equipment, as required.

7. Remove the floor console, if equipped. Remove the floor and center distribution ducts.

8. Remove the bolt holding the right side instrument panel to the right cowl.

9. Disconnect the blower motor wiring, antenna, resistor wiring and the temperature control cable. Disconnect the vacuum harness at the connection at the top of the housing.

10. On 1990–91 Daytona and LeBaron, using a suitable cutting device, cut the instrument panel along the indented line along the padded cover to the right of the glove box opening. Cut only plastic, not metal. Remove the reinforcement and the piece of instrument panel that is riveted to it.

11. Disconnect the demister hoses from the top of the housing, if equipped.

12. Disconnect the hanger strap from the package and rotate it out of the way.

13. Remove the retaining nuts from the package mounting studs at the firewall.

14. Fold the carpeting and insulation back to provide a little more working room and to prevent spillage from staining the carpeting. Pull the right side of the instrument panel out as far as possible.

15. Remove the entire housing assembly from the dash panel and remove it from the passenger compartment. Remove the passenger seat, if it is preventing removal.

16. To disassemble the housing assembly, remove the vacuum diaphragm and retaining screws from the cover and remove the cover.

17. Remove the retaining screw from the heater core and remove the core from the housing assembly.

To install:

18. Remove the temperature control door from the housing and clean the unit out with solvent. Lubricate the lower pivot rod and its well and install. Wrap the heater core with foam tape and place it in position. Secure it with its screw.

19. Assemble the housing, making sure all vacuum tubing is properly routed.

20. Feed the vacuum lines through the hole in the firewall and install the assembly to the vehicle. Connect the vacuum harness and demister hoses. Install the nuts to the firewall and connect the hanger strap inside the passenger compartment.

21. Fold the carpeting back into position.

22. Install the bolt that attaches the right side of the instrument panel to the cowl.

23. Connect the blower motor wiring, antenna, resistor wiring and the temperature control cable.

24. Install the center and floor distribution ducts.

25. Install the floor console, if equipped.

26. Install the radio and all other dash mounted items that were removed during the disassembly procedure.

27. Install the lower instrument panel reinforcements and silencers.

28. Install all modules, relay panels and computer components that were removed during the disassembly procedure.

29. Install the glove box and right side kick and sill panels. Install the passenger seat, if removed.

30. Connect the vacuum lines at the brake booster and water valve.

31. Using new gaskets, install the H-valve and condensation tube.

32. Connect the heater hoses.

33. Using the proper equipment, evacuate and recharge the air conditioning system.

34. Fill the cooling system.

35. Connect the negative battery cable and check the entire climate control system for proper operation and leakage.

Water Pump

REMOVAL & INSTALLATION

2.2L and 2.5L Engines

1. Disconnect the negative battery cable.

2. Drain the cooling system.

3. If the vehicle is equipped with air conditioning, remove the compressor from the bracket and position it to the side.

4. Remove the alternator and bracket. Remove the pulley from the water pump.

5. Disconnect the lower radiator hose and heater hose from the water pump.

6. Remove the water pump housing attaching screws and remove the assembly from the vehicle. Discard the O-ring.

7. Remove the water pump from the housing.

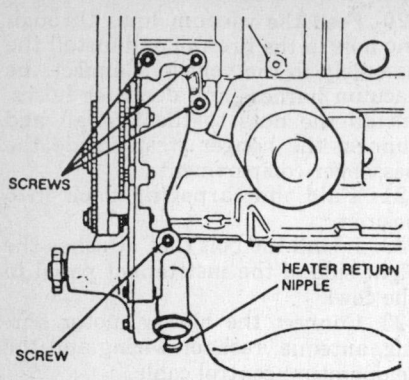

Water pump assembly—2.2L and 2.5L engines

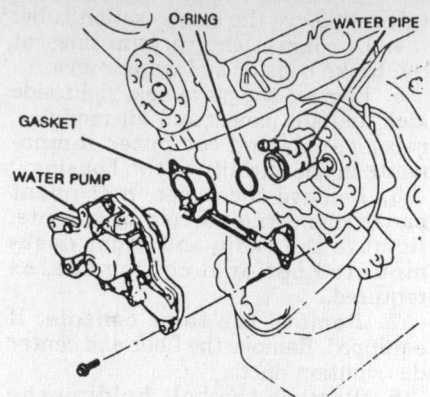

Water pump assembly—3.0L engine

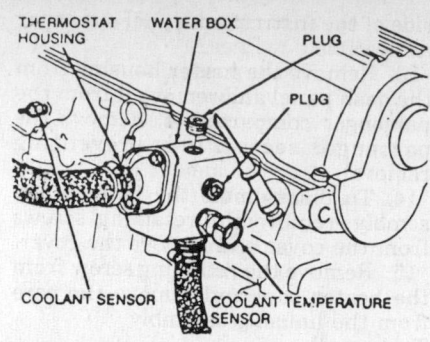

Cooling system bleed plug—2.2L and 2.5L engines

To install:

8. Using a new gasket or silicone sealer, install the water pump to the housing.

9. Install a new O-ring to the housing and install to the engine. Torque the bolts to 21 ft. lbs. (30 Nm).

10. Install the water pump pulley and torque the bolts to 21 ft. lbs. (30 Nm). Connect the radiator hose and heater hose to the water pump.

11. Install all items removed to gain access to the water pump, then adjust the belts.

12. Remove the hex-head plug on the top of the thermostat housing. Fill the radiator with coolant until the coolant comes out the plug hole. Install the plug and continue to fill the radiator.

13. Connect the negative battery cable, run the vehicle until the thermostat opens, fill the radiator completely and check for leaks.

14. Once the vehicle has cooled, recheck the coolant level.

3.0L Engine

1. Disconnect the negative battery cable.

2. Drain the cooling system.

3. Remove the timing cover. If the same timing belt will be reused, mark the direction of the timing belt's rotation, for installation in the same direction. Make sure the engine is positioned so the No. 1 cylinder is at the TDC of it's compression stroke and the sprockets timing marks are aligned with the engine's timing mark indicators.

4. Loosen the timing belt tensioner bolt and remove the belt. Position the tensioner as far away from the center of the engine as possible and tighten the bolt. Remove the water pump mounting bolts, separate the pump from the water inlet pipe and remove the pump from the engine.

To install:

5. Install the pump with a new gasket to the engine. Torque the water pump mounting bolts to 20 ft. lbs. (27 Nm).

6. If not already done, position both camshafts so the marks align with those on the alternator bracket (rear bank) and inner timing cover (front bank). Rotate the crankshaft so the timing mark aligns with the mark on the oil pump.

7. Install the timing belt on the crankshaft sprocket and while keeping the belt tight on the tension side (right side), install the belt on the front camshaft sprocket.

8. Install the belt on the water pump pulley, then the rear camshaft sprocket and the tensioner.

9. Rotate the front camshaft counterclockwise to tension the belt between the front camshaft and the crankshaft. If the timing marks are not aligned, repeat the procedure.

10. Install the crankshaft sprocket flange.

11. Loosen the tensioner bolt and allow the spring to tension the belt.

12. Turn the crankshaft 2 full turns in the clockwise direction only until the timing marks are aligned and torque the tensioner lock bolt to 21 ft. lbs. (29 Nm).

13. Refill the cooling system. This system uses a self-bleeding thermostat, so there is no need to bleed the system. Connect the negative battery cable, road test the vehicle and check for leaks.

Thermostat

REMOVAL & INSTALLATION

1. Disconnect the negative battery cable. Drain the coolant down to thermostat level or below.

2. Remove the thermostat housing.

3. Remove the thermostat and discard the gasket.

4. Clean the housing mating surfaces and use a new gasket.

5. The installation is the reverse of the removal procedure.

6. On 2.2L and 2.5L engines, remove the plug on top of the thermostat housing. Fill the radiator with coolant until the coolant comes out the plug hole. Install the plug or valve and continue to fill the radiator. The 3.0L engine thermostat is self-bleeding.

7. Connect the negative battery cable, run the vehicle until the thermostat opens, fill the radiator completely and check for leaks.

8. Once the vehicle has cooled, recheck the coolant level.

COOLING SYSTEM BLEEDING

To bleed air from the 2.2L and 2.5L engines, remove the plug on the top of the thermostat housing. Fill the radiator with coolant until the coolant comes out the hole. Install the plug and continue to fill the radiator. This will vent all trapped air from the engine.

The thermostat in the 3.0L engine is equipped with a small air vent valve that allows trapped air to bleed from the system during refilling. This valve negates the need for cooling system bleeding in those engines.

FUEL SYSTEM

Fuel System Service Precautions

Safety is the most important factor when performing not only fuel system maintenance but any type of maintenance. Failure to conduct maintenance and repairs in a safe manner may result in serious personal injury or death. Maintenance and testing of the vehicle's fuel system components can be accomplished safely and effectively by adhering to the following rules and guidelines.

• To avoid the possibility of fire and personal injury, always disconnect the negative battery cable unless the repair or test procedure requires that battery voltage be applied.

• Always relieve the fuel system pressure prior to disconnecting any fuel system component (injector, fuel rail, pressure regulator, etc.), fitting or fuel line connection. Exercise extreme caution whenever relieving fuel system pressure to avoid exposing skin, face and eyes to fuel spray. Please be advised that fuel under pressure may penetrate the skin or any part of the body that it contacts.

• Always place a shop towel or cloth around the fitting or connection prior to loosening to absorb any excess fuel due to spillage. Ensure that all fuel spillage (should it occur) is quickly removed from engine surfaces. Ensure that all fuel soaked cloths or towels are deposited into a suitable waste container.

• Always keep a dry chemical (Class B) fire extinguisher near the work area.

• Do not allow fuel spray or fuel vapors to come into contact with a spark or open flame.

• Always use a backup wrench when loosening and tightening fuel line connection fittings. This will prevent unnecessary stress and torsion to fuel line piping. Always follow the proper torque specifications.

• Always replace worn fuel fitting O-rings with new. Do not substitute fuel hose or equivalent where fuel pipe is installed.

RELIEVING FUEL SYSTEM PRESSURE

1987–88

1. Disconnect the negative battery cable.
2. Loosen the fuel filler cap to release fuel tank pressure.
3. Remove the wiring harness connector from the (any) injector.
4. Using a jumper wire, ground either injector terminal.
5. Being careful not to allow contact between the jumper leads, connect a second jumper wire to the other terminal and touch the other end to the positive battery post for no longer that 10 seconds. This will relieve fuel pressure.
6. Remove the jumper wires and continue with fuel system service.

1989–91

1. Loosen the fuel filler cap to release fuel tank pressure.

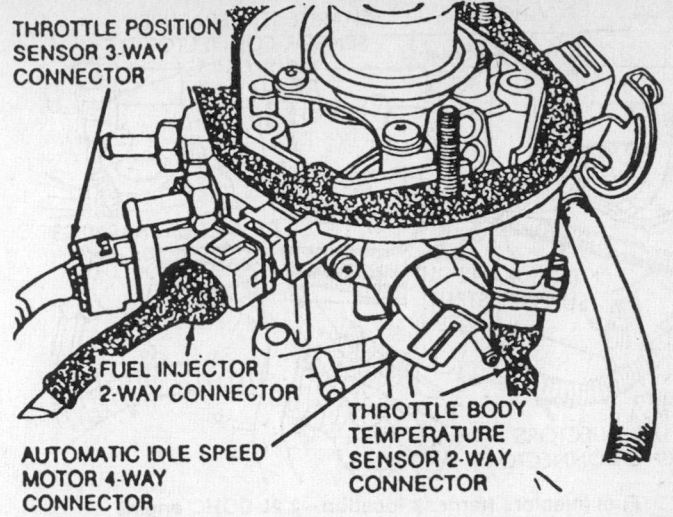

Fuel Injector harness location—2.2L and 2.5L non-turbocharged engine

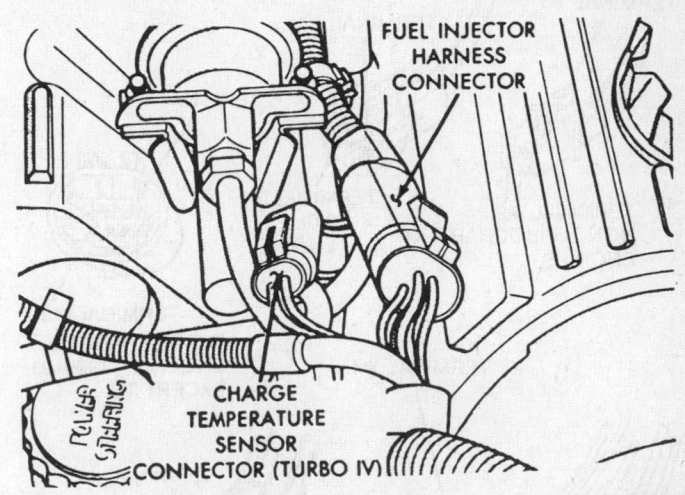

Fuel injectors harness location—turbocharged engine, except 2.2L DOHC. The connector may vary between vehicles

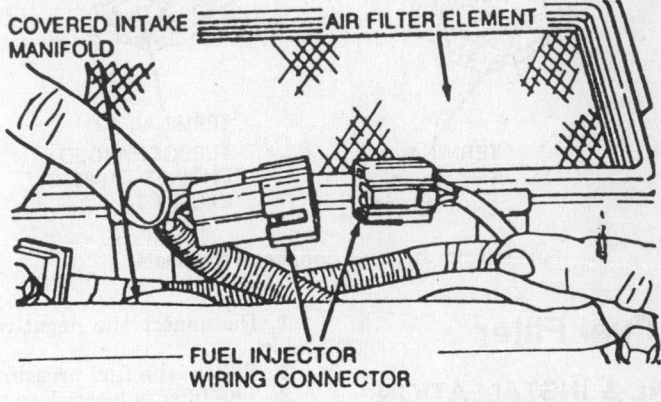

Fuel Injectors harness location—3.0L engine

2. Locate and disconnect the fuel injector harness connector.
3. Connect a jumper wire from terminal No. 1 of the appropriate connector to ground.
4. Being careful not to allow contact between the jumper leads, connect a jumper wire to terminal No. 2 of the connector and touch the other end of the jumper to the positive battery post for no longer than 5 seconds. This will relieve fuel pressure.
5. Remove the jumper wires and continue with fuel system service.

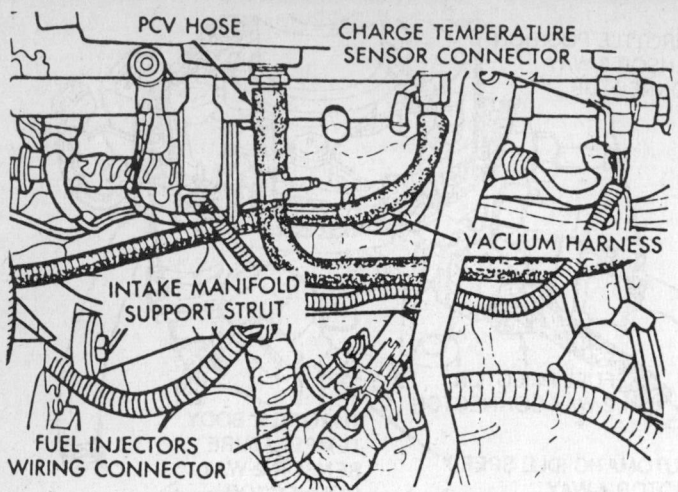

Fuel injectors harness location—2.2L DOHC engine

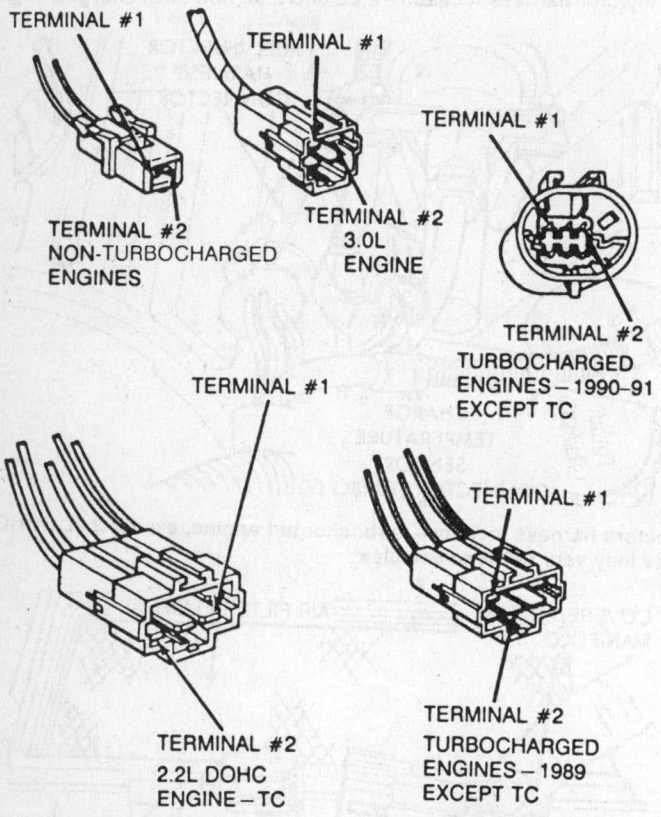

Fuel Injector harness connector terminals

Fuel Filter

REMOVAL & INSTALLATION

— CAUTION —

Do not use conventional fuel filters, hoses or clamps when servicing this fuel system. They are not compatible with the injection system and could fail, causing personal injury or damage to the vehicle. Use only hoses and clamps specifically designed for fuel injection.

1. Disconnect the negative battery cable.
2. Relieve the fuel pressure.
3. The filter is located on the frame rail toward the rear of the vehicle. Raise the vehicle and support safely. Remove the filter retaining screw and remove the filter assembly from the mounting plate.
4. Loosen the outlet hose clamp on the filter and inlet hose clamp on the rear fuel tube.
5. Wrap a shop towel around the hoses to absorb fuel. Remove the hoses from the filter and fuel tube and discard the clamps and the filter.

To install:

6. Install the inlet hose on the fuel tube and tighten the new clamp to 10 inch lbs.
7. Install the outlet hose on the filter outlet fitting and tighten the new clamp to 10 inch lbs.
8. Position the filter assembly on the mounting plate and tighten the mounting screw to 75 inch lbs. (8 Nm).
9. Connect the negative battery cable, start the engine and check for leaks.

Electric Fuel Pump

PRESSURE TESTING

1. Relieve the fuel pressure.
2. Properly connect the fuel system pressure tester:
   a. Non-turbocharged engines—special tool C–4799A, or equivalent is installed between the fuel supply hose and the engine fuel line assembly.
   b. Turbocharged engines—special tool C–4799A, or equivalent is installed to the fuel rail service valve.
3. With the key in the **RUN** position, put the DRB I or II in the activate auto shutdown relay mode; this will activate the fuel pump and pressurize the system.
4. If the pressure is within specifications, reinstall the fuel hose.
5. If fuel pressure is below specifications, install the tester in the fuel supply line between the tank and the filter and repeat the test.
6. If the pressure is 5 psi higher than in Step 5, replace the fuel filter. If no change is observed, squeeze the return hose. If pressure increases, replace the pressure regulator. If no change is observed, the problem is either a plugged in-tank sock filter or a defective pump.
7. If fuel pressure is above specifications, remove the fuel return line hose from the chassis line at the fuel tank and connect a 3 foot piece of fuel hose to the return line. Put the other end into a 2 gallon minimum capacity approved gasoline container. Repeat the test. If pressure is now correct, check the in-tank return hose for kinking. Replace the fuel pump assembly if the in-tank reservoir check valve or aspirator jet is obstructed.
8. If pressure is still above specifications, remove the fuel return hose from the throttle body. Connect a substitute hose to the throttle body return nipple and place the other end of the hose in a clean container. Repeat the

test. If pressure is now correct, check for a restricted fuel return line. If no change is observed, replace the fuel pressure regulator.

REMOVAL & INSTALLATION

1. Disconnect the negative battery cable.
2. Relieve the fuel pressure.
3. Raise the vehicle and support safely.
4. Using the proper equipment, drain the fuel tank.
5. Remove the screws that hold the filler neck to the quarter panel.
6. Disconnect the wiring and hoses from the tank.
7. Place a transmission jack or equivalent, under the center of the tank and apply slight pressure. Remove the tank straps.
8. Lower the tank and remove the filler tube from the tank.
9. Lower the tank and disconnect the vapor separator rollover valve hose and remove the fuel tank from the vehicle.
10. Using a hammer and a brass drift, tap the lock ring counterclockwise to release the pump.
11. Partially pull the pump assembly out of the tank until the return line hose connection is visible at the of the pump assembly.
12. Disconnect the fuel fitting by pressing in on the ears.
13. Remove the pump from the tank with the O-ring. Discard the O-ring, pump inlet filter and inlet seal. Disassemble as required.
To install:
14. Install a new inlet seal and filter on the end of the pump.
15. Install a new O-ring to the pump.
16. Connect the reservoir hose to the pump assembly at the suction end of the pump. Press the female fitting onto the pump assembly male end until the ears snap in place.
17. Install the pump into the tank so the fuel return hose is not kinked.
18. Install the lock ring with a hammer and brass punch turning the ring clockwise.
19. Install the fuel tank.
20. Connect the negative battery cable, start the engine and check for leaks.

Fuel Injection

IDLE SPEED ADJUSTMENT

The idle speed is controlled by the Automatic Idle Speed motor (AIS). The AIS is controlled by the logic module, SMEC or SBEC, which receives data from various sensors and switches in the system and adjusts the engine idle

to a predetermined speed. Idle speed specifications can be found on the Vehicle Emission Control Information (VECI) label located in the engine compartment. If the idle speed is not within specifications and there are no problems with the system, the throttle body should be replaced.

IDLE MIXTURE ADJUSTMENT

There is no idle mixture adjustment provided with any Chrysler fuel injection system.

Fuel Injector

REMOVAL & INSTALLATION

2.2L and 2.5L Non-Turbocharged Engines

1. Disconnect the negative battery cable.
2. Remove the air cleaner assembly.
3. Relieve the fuel pressure.
4. Remove the injector hold-down Torx® screw and the hold-down.
5. Using a small flat-tipped tool, lift the cap off of the injector.
6. Using the same tool, gently pry the injector from its pod.
7. Remove the lower O-ring from the pod.
To install:
8. Install the new lower O-ring on the injector.
9. Align the injector terminal housing with the locating socket in the injector cap.
10. Press the injector cap so the upper O-ring flange is flush with the lower surface of the cap.
11. Spray the inner surfaces of the injector pod with suitable carburetor parts cleaner to remove residual varnish and gasoline.
12. Lubricate the O-rings sparingly with unmedicated petroleum jelly.
13. Place the injector and cap into the injector pod and align the cap locating pin with the locating hole in the casting.
14. Press firmly on the injector cap

until it is flush with the casting surface.
15. Align the hole in the hold-down with the pin on the cap and install.
16. Push down on the cap, install the screw and torque to 35 inch lbs. (4 Nm).
17. Connect the negative battery cable and check for leaks using the DRB I or II to activate the fuel pump.
18. Install the air cleaner.

2.2L and 2.5L Turbocharged Engines

1. Disconnect the negative battery cable.
2. Relieve the fuel pressure.
3. Disconnect the injector wiring connector from the injector.
4. Unbolt the fuel rail from the rear of the engine. Position the fuel rail assembly so the fuel injectors are easily accessible. If necessary, disconnect the hoses from the fuel rail and remove it from the engine.
5. Remove the injector clip from the fuel rail and injector. Pull the injector straight out of the fuel rail receiver cup.
6. Check the injector O-ring for damage. If the O-ring is damaged, replace it. If the injector is being reused, install a protective cap on the injector tip to prevent damage.
7. Repeat the procedure for the remaining injectors.
To install:
8. Before installing an injector the rubber O-ring should be lubricated with a drop of clean engine oil to aid in installation.
9. Install injector top end into fuel rail receiver cup.
10. Install injector clip by sliding the open end into top slot of the injector and onto the receiver cup ridge into the side slots of clip.
11. Repeat the steps for the remaining injectors.
12. Install the fuel rail.
13. Connect the negative battery ca-

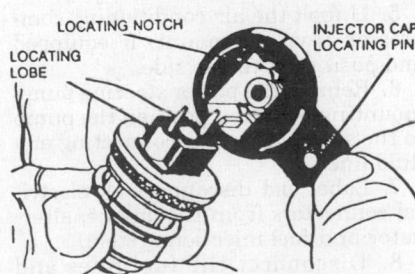

Installing the injector to the cap—2.2L and 2.5L non-turbocharged engines

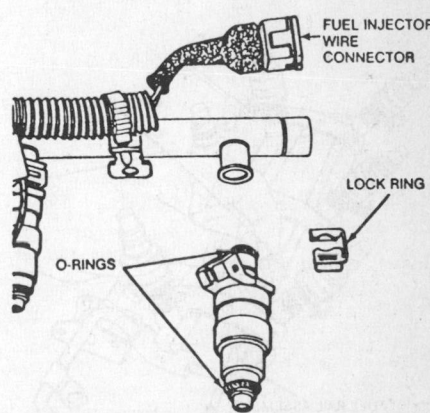

Fuel injector removal and installation—turbocharged engine

ble and check for leaks using the DRB I or II to activate the fuel pump.

3.0L Engine

1. Disconnect the negative battery cable.
2. Relieve the fuel pressure.
3. Remove the air cleaner to throttle body hose.
4. Disconnect the throttle cable from the throttle body and disconnect the kickdown linkage. Remove the throttle cable bracket attaching bolts.
5. Disconnect the connectors to the throttle body.
6. Matchmark and carefully remove the vacuum hoses from the throttle body.
7. Remove the PCV and brake booster hoses from the air intake plenum.
8. Remove the ignition coil from the intake plenum, if it is mounted there.
9. Remove the EGR tube flange from the intake plenum, if equipped.
10. Unplug the coolant temperature sensor and charge temperature sensor, if equipped.
11. Remove the vacuum connection from the air intake plenum vacuum connector.
12. Remove the fuel hoses from the fuel rail and plug them.
13. Remove the air intake plenum to intake manifold bolts and remove the plenum and gaskets. Cover the intake manifold openings.
14. Remove the vacuum hoses from the fuel rail.
15. Disconnect the fuel injector wiring harness.
16. Remove the fuel rail attaching bolts and remove the fuel rail with the wiring harness from the vehicle. Position the rail on the bench upside down so the injectors are easily accessible.
17. Remove the small connector retainer clip and unplug the injector. Remove the injector clip off the fuel rail and injector. Pull the injector straight out of the rail.

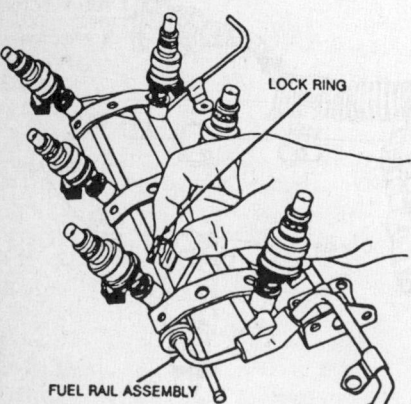

Fuel rail assembly—3.0L engine

To install:

18. Lubricate the rubber O-ring with clean oil and install to the rail receiver cap. Install the injector clip to the **TOP** slot of the injector, plug in the connector and install the connector clip.
19. Install the fuel rail to the vehicle and plug in the injector harness. Connect the vacuum hoses to the fuel rail.
20. Install new intake plenum gaskets with the beaded sealer side up and install the intake plenum. Torque the attaching bolts and nuts to 115 inch lbs. (13 Nm).
21. Install the fuel hoses to the fuel rail.
22. Install or connect all items that were removed or disconnected from the intake plenum and throttle body.
23. Connect the negative battery cable and check for leaks using the DRB I or II to activate the fuel pump.

ENGINE MECHANICAL

NOTE: Disconnecting the negative battery cable on some vehicles may interfere with the functions of the on board computer systems and may require the computers to undergo a relearning process, once the negative battery cable is reconnected.

Engine Assembly

REMOVAL & INSTALLATION

2.2L and 2.5L Engines

1. Disconnect the negative battery cable and all engine ground straps. Relieve the fuel pressure.
2. Mark the hood hinge outline on the hood and remove the hood.
3. Drain the cooling system. Remove the radiator hoses, fan assembly, radiator and intercooler, if equipped.
4. Remove the air cleaner, duct hoses and oil filter.
5. Unbolt the air conditioning compressor from its mount, if equipped and position it to the side.
6. Remove the power steering pump mounting bolts and position the pump to the side, without disconnecting any fluid lines.
7. Label and disconnect all electrical connectors from the engine, alternator and fuel injection system.
8. Disconnect the fuel lines and heater hoses.
9. Disconnect the throttle linkage.
10. Remove the alternator.

11. Raise the vehicle and support safely.
12. Disconnect the exhaust pipe from the manifold. Remove the right inner fender shield.
13. If equipped with a manual transaxle, remove the transaxle.
14. If equipped with an automatic transaxle, perform the following procedures:
    a. Remove the lower cover from the transaxle case.
    b. Remove the starter and set it aside.
    c. Matchmark the flexplate to the torque converter, for installation purposes.
    d. Remove the torque converter bolts. Separate the converter from the flexplate. Remove the lower bellhousing bolts.
15. Lower the vehicle and support the transaxle, if still in the vehicle, with a floor jack or equivalent. Attach an engine lifting device to the engine.
16. Remove the remaining bellhousing bolts.

NOTE: If removing the insulator-to-rail screws, first mark the position of the insulator on the side rail to insure proper alignment during reinstallation.

17. Remove the front engine mount nut/bolt and the left insulator through bolt or the insulator bracket to transaxle bolts.
18. Lift the engine from the vehicle and remove.

To install:

19. Lower the engine into the engine compartment. Loosely install all of the mounting bolts. With all bolts installed, torque the:
    Engine to mount bolts to 40 ft. lbs.
    Engine to transaxle bolts to 70 ft. lbs.
    Torque converter bolts to 40 ft. lbs.
20. Remove the lifting device.
21. Raise the vehicle and support safely.
22. If equipped with a manual transaxle, install the transaxle.
23. If equipped with an automatic transaxle, install the torque converter inspection plate and starter.
24. Connect the exhaust pipe. Lower the vehicle.
25. Install the alternator, power steering pump and air conditioning compressor, if equipped.
26. Connect the fuel lines and heater hoses.
27. Connect the throttle linkage.
28. Connect all remaining electrical connectors.
29. Install the air cleaner assembly and oil filter.
30. Install the radiator, fan assembly, hoses and intercooler, if equipped.

31. Fill the engine with the proper amount of engine oil. Connect the negative battery cable.

32. Refill the cooling system. Start the engine, allow it to reach normal operating temperature. Check for leaks.

33. Check the ignition timing and adjust, if necessary.

34. Install the hood.

3.0L Engine

1. Disconnect the negative battery cable. Relieve the fuel pressure.

2. Matchmark the hinge-to-hood position and remove the hood.

3. Drain the cooling system. Disconnect and label all engine electrical connections.

4. Remove the coolant hoses from the radiator and engine. Remove the radiator and cooling fan assembly.

5. Remove the air cleaner assembly. Disconnect the fuel lines from the engine. Disconnect the accelerator cable from the throttle body.

6. Raise the vehicle and support safely. Drain the engine oil.

7. Remove the air conditioning compressor mounting bolts, the drive belts and position the compressor to the side. Disconnect the exhaust pipe from the exhaust manifold.

8. Remove the transaxle inspection cover, matchmark the converter to the flexplate and remove the torque converter bolts.

9. Remove the power steering pump mounting bolts and set the pump aside, upright, with the fluid lines attached.

10. Remove the lower bellhousing bolts. Disconnect and label the starter motor wiring and remove the starter motor from the engine.

11. Lower the vehicle. Disconnect and label all electrical connectors from the engine, alternator and fuel injection system, vacuum hoses, and engine ground straps.

12. Support the transaxle with a floor jack or equivalent. Attach an engine lifting device to the engine.

13. Remove the upper transaxle-to-engine bolts.

14. To separate the engine mounts from the insulators, mark the right insulator-to-right frame support and remove the mounting bolts. Remove the front engine mount through bolt. Remove the left insulator through bolt, from inside the wheel housing. Remove the insulator bracket-to-transaxle bolts.

15. Lift and remove the engine from the vehicle.

To install:

16. Lower the engine into the engine compartment. Align the engine mounts and install the bolts; do not tighten the bolts until all bolts have been installed. Torque the through bolts to 75 ft. lbs.

17. Install the upper transaxle-to-engine mounting bolts and torque to 75 ft. lbs. Remove the engine lifting fixture from the engine.

18. Raise the vehicle and support safely.

19. Align the converter marks, install the torque converter bolts. Install the transaxle inspection cover.

20. Connect the exhaust pipe to the exhaust manifold. Install the starter motor and connect the wiring.

21. Install the power steering pump and air conditioning compressor. Adjust the drive belt tension, if necessary.

22. Lower the vehicle. Reconnect all vacuum hoses and electrical connections to the engine.

23. Connect the fuel lines and accelerator cable.

24. Install the radiator and fan assembly. Connect the fan motor wiring. Connect the radiator hoses and refill the cooling system.

25. Refill the engine with the proper oil to the correct level.

26. Connect the engine ground straps. Install the hood and align the matchmarks. Connect the battery.

27. Start and run the engine until it reaches normal operating temperatures and check for leaks. Adjust transaxle linkage, if necessary.

Engine Mounts

REMOVAL & INSTALLATION

1. Disconnect the negative battery cable.

2. Matchmark the engine mount to its frame mounting location.

3. Raise the vehicle and support safely, if necessary. Using the proper equipment, support the weight of the engine.

4. Remove all bolts and nuts that attach the mount to the engine strut, transaxle or body and remove the mount assembly from the vehicle.

5. Remove the through bolt and separate the insulator from the yoke bracket as required.

6. The installation is the reverse of the removal procedure. Make sure the matchmarks are aligned before tightening bolts.

Cylinder Head

REMOVAL & INSTALLATION

2.2L and 2.5L Engines Except DOHC

1. Disconnect the negative battery cable and unbolt it from the head. Relieve the fuel pressure. Drain the cooling system. Remove the dipstick bracket nut from the thermostat housing.

2. Remove the air cleaner assembly. Remove the upper radiator hose and disconnect the heater hoses.

3. Disconnect and label the vacuum lines, hoses and wiring connectors from the manifold(s), throttle body and from the cylinder head.

4. Disconnect the all linkages and the fuel line from the throttle body. Unbolt the cable bracket. Remove the ground strap attaching screw from the firewall.

5. If equipped with air conditioning, remove the upper compressor mounting bolts. The cylinder head can be remove with the compressor and bracket still mounted. Remove the upper timing belt cover.

6. Raise the vehicle and support safely. Disconnect the exhaust pipe from the exhaust manifold. Disconnect the water hose and oil drain from the turbocharger, if equipped.

7. Rotate the engine by hand until the timing marks align. The No. 1 piston should be at TDC of its compression stroke. Lower the vehicle.

8. With the timing marks aligned, remove the camshaft sprocket. The camshaft sprocket can be suspended to keep the timing intact. Remove the spark plug wires from the spark plugs.

9. Remove the valve cover and curtain. Remove the cylinder head bolts and washers, starting from the outside and working inward.

10. Remove the cylinder head from the engine.

11. Clean the cylinder head gasket mating surfaces.

To install:

12. Using new gaskets and seals, install the head to the engine. Using new head bolts assembled with the old washers, torque the cylinder head bolts in sequence, to 45 ft. lbs. (61 Nm). Repeating the sequence, torque the bolts to 65 ft. lbs. (88 Nm). With the bolts at 65 ft. lbs., turn each bolt an additional ¼ turn.

NOTE: Head bolt diameter is 11mm. These bolts are identified with the number 11 on the head of the bolt. The 10mm bolts used on previous vehicles will thread into an 11mm bolt hole, but will permanently damage the cylinder block. Make sure the correct bolts are being used when replacing head bolts.

13. Install the timing belt.

14. Install or connect all items that were removed or disconnected during the removal procedure.

15. Refill the cooling system. Con-

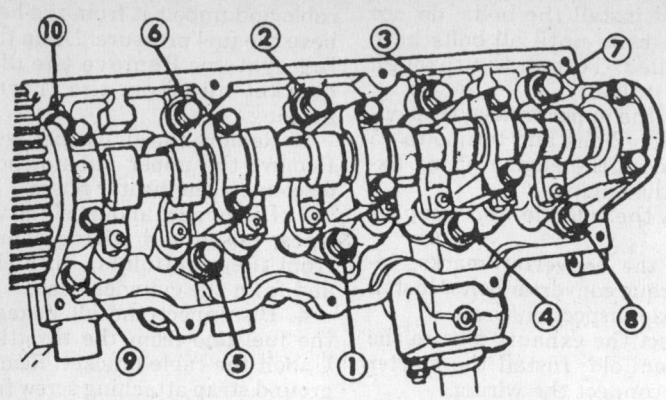

Cylinder head bolt torque sequence—2.2L and 2.5L engines, except 2.2L DOHC engine

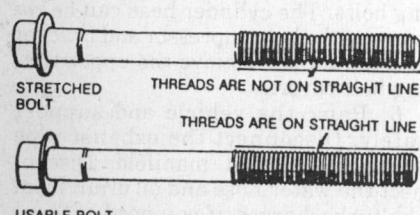

Checking the head bolt for stretching

nect the negative battery cable. Start the engine and check for leaks using the DRB I or II to activate the fuel pump. Adjust the timing, as required.

2.2L DOHC Engine

1. Disconnect the negative battery cable and unbolt it from the head. Relieve the fuel pressure. Drain the cooling system.

2. Remove the timing belt covers. Rotate the engine by hand until the timing marks align (No. 1 piston at TDC) and remove the timing belt.

3. Remove the air conditioning compressor and bracket from the cylinder head.

4. Disconnect the turbocharger coolant lines.

5. Remove the air cleaner assembly and separate the intake and exhaust manifolds from the cylinder head.

6. Disconnect and label all wiring connectors, hoses and ignition wires from the cylinder head.

6. Remove the cylinder head cover.

7. Remove both camshafts to expose cylinder head bolts.

8. Remove the cylinder head bolts and washers, starting from the outside and working inward.

9. Remove the cylinder head and gasket from the engine.

10. Clean the cylinder head gasket mating surfaces.

To install:

11. Using new gaskets and seals, install the head to the engine. Using new head bolts assembled with the old washers, torque the cylinder head

bolts in sequence, to 32 ft. lbs. (44 Nm). Repeating the sequence, torque the bolts to 50 ft. lbs. (69 Nm). Repeating the sequence a thirt time, torque the bolts to 65 ft. lbs. (88 Nm). With the bolts at 65 ft. lbs., turn each bolt an additional ¼ turn.

12. Install the camshafts and timing belt.

13. Install or connect all items that were removed or disconnected during the removal procedure.

14. Refill the cooling system. Connect the negative battery cable. Start the engine and check for leaks using the DRB I or II to activate the fuel pump. Adjust the timing as required.

3.0L Engine

1. Disconnect the negative battery cable. Relieve the fuel pressure. Drain the cooling system.

2. Remove the drive belt and the air conditioning compressor from its mount and support it aside. Using a ½ in. drive breaker bar, insert it into the square hole of the serpentine drive belt tensioner, rotate it counterclockwise to reduce the belt tension and remove the belt. Remove the alternator and power steering pump from the brackets and move them aside.

3. Raise the vehicle and support

safely. Remove the right front wheel assembly and the right inner splash shield.

4. Remove the crankshaft pulleys and the torsional damper.

5. Lower the vehicle. Using a floor jack and a block of wood positioned under the oil pan, raise the engine slightly. Remove the engine mount bracket from the timing cover end of the engine and the timing belt covers.

6. To remove the timing belt, perform the following procedures:

a. Rotate the crankshaft to position the No. 1 cylinder on the TDC of its compression stroke; the crankshaft sprocket timing mark should align with the oil pan timing indicator and the camshaft sprockets timing marks (triangles) should align with the rear timing belt covers timing marks.

b. Mark the timing belt in the direction of rotation for reinstallation purposes.

c. Loosen the timing belt tensioner and remove the timing belt.

NOTE: When removing the timing belt from the camshaft sprocket, make sure the belt does not slip off of the other camshaft sprocket. Support the belt so it can not slip off of the crankshaft sprocket and opposite side camshaft sprocket.

7. Remove the air cleaner assembly. Label and disconnect the spark plug wires and the vacuum hoses.

8. Remove the valve cover.

9. Install auto lash adjuster retainer tools MD998443 or equivalent, on the rocker arms.

10. If removing the front cylinder head, matchmark the distributor rotor-to-distributor housing and the housing-to-distributor extension locations. Remove the distributor and the distributor extension.

11. Remove the camshaft bearing assembly to cylinder head bolts (do not remove the bolts from the assembly). Remove the rocker arms, rocker shafts

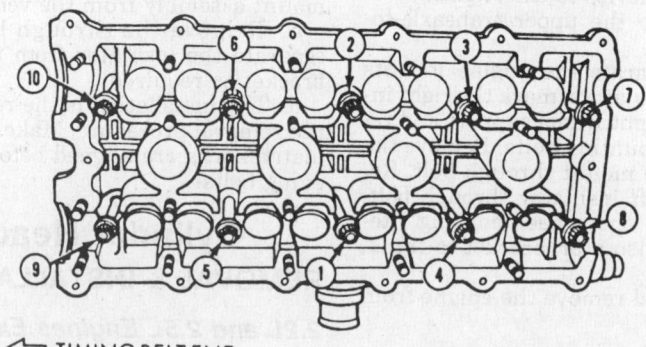

⇦ TIMING BELT END

Cylinder head bolt torque sequence—2.2L DOHC engine

and bearing caps as an assembly, as required. Remove the camshafts from the cylinder head and inspect them for damage, if necessary.

12. Remove the intake manifold assembly.

13. Remove the exhaust manifold.

14. Remove the cylinder head bolts, starting from the outside and working inward. Remove the cylinder head from the engine.

15. Clean the gasket mounting surfaces and check the heads for warpage; the maximum warpage allowed is 0.008 in. (0.20mm).

To install:

16. Install the new cylinder head gaskets over the dowels on the engine block.

17. Install the cylinder heads on the engine and torque the cylinder head bolts in sequence using 3 even steps, to 70 ft. lbs. (95 Nm).

18. Install or connect all items that were removed or disconnected during the removal procedure.

19. When installing the timing belt over the camshaft sprocket, use care not to allow the belt to slip off the opposite camshaft sprocket.

20. Make sure the timing belt is installed on the camshaft sprocket in the same position as when removed.

21. Refill the cooling system. Connect the negative battery cable. Start the engine and check for leaks using the DRB I or II to activate the fuel pump. Adjust the timing as required.

Valve Lifters

REMOVAL & INSTALLATION

2.2L and 2.5L Engines Except DOHC

1. Disconnect the negative battery cable.

2. Remove the valve cover and curtain. If removing all lifters, remove the camshaft and rocker arms.

3. If only removing 1 lifter, rotate the crankshaft until the low point of the desired cam lobe is contacting the rocker arm.

4. Using the special valve spring compressor tool 4682 or equivalent, depress the valve spring without dislodging the keepers and slide the rocker arm out.

5. Remove the valve lifter(s) from the bore(s).

6. Lubricate the lifter(s) and their bore(s) with clean engine oil.

7. The installation is the reverse of the removal procedure.

8. Connect the negative battery cable.

3.0L Engine

1. Disconnect the negative battery cable. Remove the air cleaner assembly.

2. Remove the valve cover.

3. Using the valve lifter retainer tools MD998443 or equivalent, install them on the rocker arms to keep the lifters from falling out.

4. On the right side cylinder head, remove the distributor extension.

5. Have a helper hold the rear end of the camshaft down. If the rear of the camshaft cannot be held down, the belt will dislodge and the valve timing will be lost. Loosen the camshaft cap bolts but do not remove them from the caps. Remove the caps, arms, shafts and bolts all as an assembly.

6. Remove the lifter(s) from the rocker arm(s).

7. Lubricate the lifter(s) and their bore(s) with clean engine oil.

8. The installation is the reverse of the removal procedure.

Valve Lash

ADJUSTMENT

2.2L DOHC Engine

1. Disconnect the negative battery cable.

2. Remove the valve cover.

3. Check the clearance of all valves by inserting a feeler gauge between the camshaft and adjusting disc when the cam lobe is pointing straight up. Record all measurements.

4. The specifications are:
Intake—0.012 in. (0.30mm)
Exhaust—0.016 in. (0.40mm)

5. If not at specifications, remove the camshaft(s) and use the appropriate adjusting discs to bring clearance to specification.

Rocker Arms/Shafts

REMOVAL & INSTALLATION

2.2L and 2.5L Engines Except DOHC

1. Disconnect the negative battery cable.

2. Remove the valve cover.

3. Rotate the crankshaft until the low point of the desired cam lobe is contacting the rocker arm.

4. Using the special valve spring compressor tool or equivalent, depress the valve spring without dislodging the keepers and slide the rocker arm out.

5. The installation is the reverse of the removal procedure.

3.0L Engine

1. Disconnect the negative battery cable. Remove the air cleaner assembly.

2. Remove the valve cover.

3. Using the auto lash adjuster retainer tools MD998443 or equivalent, install them on the rocker arms to keep the lash adjusters from falling out.

4. On the right side cylinder head, remove the distributor extension.

5. Have a helper hold the rear end of the camshaft down. If the rear of the camshaft cannot be held down, the belt will dislodge and the valve timing will be lost. Loosen the camshaft cap bolts but do not remove them from the caps. Remove the caps, arms, shafts and bolts all as an assembly.

6. Disassemble the unit keeping all parts in order and repair as required.

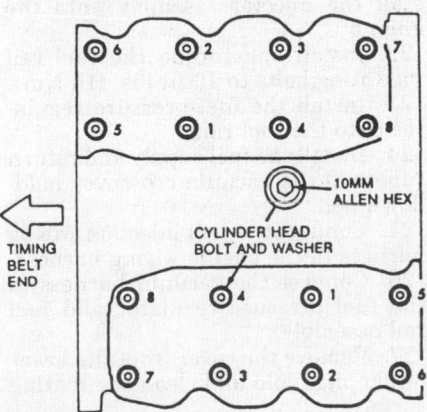

Cylinder head bolt torque sequence—3.0L engine

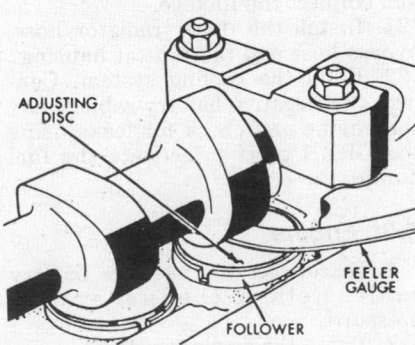

Checking valve clearance—2.2L DOHC engine

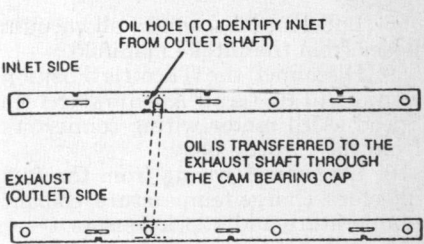

Identifying rocker shafts—3.0L engine

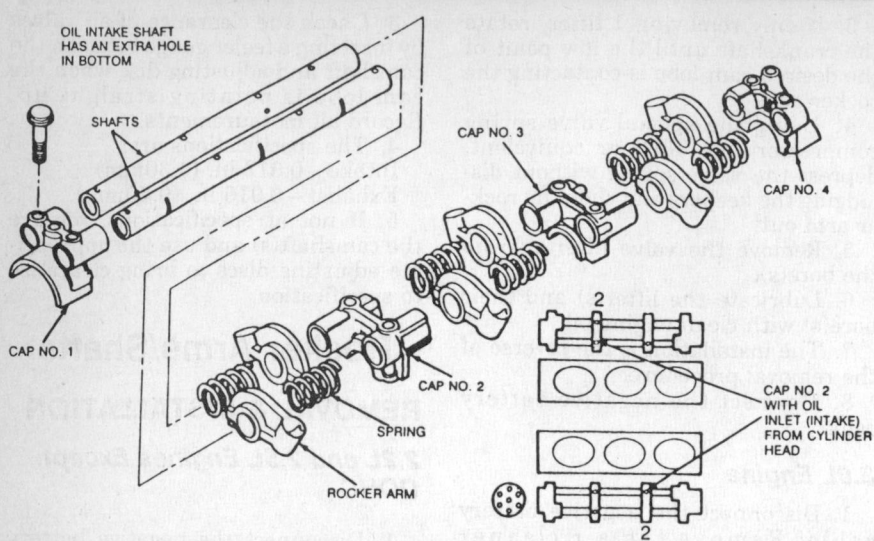

OIL INTAKE SHAFT HAS AN EXTRA HOLE IN BOTTOM

SHAFTS

CAP NO. 3

CAP NO. 4

CAP NO. 1

CAP NO. 2

SPRING

ROCKER ARM

CAP NO. 2 WITH OIL INLET (INTAKE) FROM CYLINDER HEAD

Rocker shafts/arms assembly—3.0L engine

7. When assembling, apply a drop of sealant to the rear edge of the rear cap.

8. The installation is the reverse of the removal procedure. Torque the cap bolts first to 85 inch lbs. (19 Nm), then to 180 inch lbs. (19 Nm) in the following order: No. 3 cap, No. 2 cap, No. 1 cap, No. 4 cap.

Intake Manifold

REMOVAL & INSTALLATION

2.2L DOHC Engine

1. Disconnect the negative battery cable. Relieve the fuel system pressure.

2. Drain the coolant system.

3. Using the proper equipment, support the weight of the engine. Remove the front engine mount through bolt and rotate the top of the engine away from the cowl.

4. Remove the upper radiator hose, bypass hose and thermostat housing.

5. Disconnect and plug the fuel hoses from the fuel tubes.

6. Remove the air cleaner assembly and all duct work.

7. Disconnect the linkage from the throttle body and disconnect the throttle body support bracket from the engine.

8. Label and disconnect all vacuum hoses from the intake manifold.

9. Disconnect the Throttle Position Sensor (TPS) and Automatic Idle Speed (AIS) motor wiring connectors from the throttle body.

10. Disconnect wiring from the fuel injectors, charge temperature, coolant temperature and knock sensors.

11. Remove the air conditioning compressor bracket to intake manifold attaching bolt.

12. Remove the intake manifold strut bolt.

13. Remove all 10 intake manifold attaching nuts and remove the manifold from the cylinder head.

14. Discard the intake manifold gasket. Clean the mating surfaces and inspect for damage and distortion. The mating surfaces must be flat within 0.006 in. (0.15mm) per foot of manifold length.

To install:

15. Install a new intake manifold gasket. Do not use sealer of any kind.

16. Position the manifold on the studs and install the retaining nuts. Starting at the center and working outwards, torque the nuts gradually and evenly to 17 ft. lbs. (23 Nm).

17. Install the strut bolt and torque to 21 ft. lbs. (29 Nm). Install the air conditioning compressor bracket bolt and torque to 21 ft. lbs. (29 Nm).

18. Install the front engine mount through bolt.

19. Connect all hoses and wiring that was disconnected during the removal procedure.

20. Install the throttle body bracket and connect the linkage.

21. Install the upper radiator hose, bypass hose and thermostat housing.

22. Refill the cooling system. Connect the negative battery cable. Start the engine and check for leaks using the DRB I or II to activate the fuel pump.

3.0L Engine

1. Disconnect the negative battery cable. Relieve the fuel system pressure.

2. Drain the cooling system.

3. Remove the throttle body to air cleaner hose.

4. Remove the throttle body and transaxle kickdown linkage.

5. Remove the AIS motor and TPS wiring connectors from the throttle body.

6. Remove and label the vacuum hose harness from the throttle body.

7. From the air intake plenum, remove the PCV and brake booster hoses and the EGR tube flange.

8. Disconnect and label the charge and temperature sensor wiring at the intake manifold.

9. Remove the vacuum connections from the air intake plenum vacuum connector.

10. Remove the fuel hoses from the fuel rail.

11. Remove the air intake plenum mounting bolts and remove the plenum.

12. Remove the vacuum hoses from the fuel rail and pressure regulator.

13. Disconnect the fuel injector wiring harness from the engine wiring harness.

14. Remove the fuel pressure regulator mounting bolts and remove the regulator from the fuel rail.

15. Remove the fuel rail mounting bolts and remove the fuel rail from the intake manifold.

16. Separate the radiator hose from the thermostat housing and heater hoses from the heater pipe.

17. Remove the intake manifold mounting bolts and remove the manifold from the engine.

18. Clean the gasket mounting surfaces on the engine and intake manifold.

To install:

19. Using new gaskets, position the intake manifold on the engine and install the mounting nuts and washers.

20. Torque the mounting nuts gradually and evenly, in sequence, to 15 ft. lbs. (20 Nm).

21. Make sure the injector holes are clean. Lubricate the injector O-rings with a drop of clean engine oil and install the injector assembly onto the engine.

22. Install and torque the fuel rail mounting bolts to 10 ft. lbs. (14 Nm).

23. Install the fuel pressure regulator onto the fuel rail.

24. Install the fuel supply and return tube and the vacuum crossover hold-down bolt.

25. Connect the fuel injection wiring harness to the engine wiring harness.

26. Connect the vacuum harness to the fuel pressure regulator and fuel rail assembly.

27. Remove the cover from the lower intake manifold and clean the mating surface.

28. Place the intake plenum gasket with the beaded sealant side up, on the

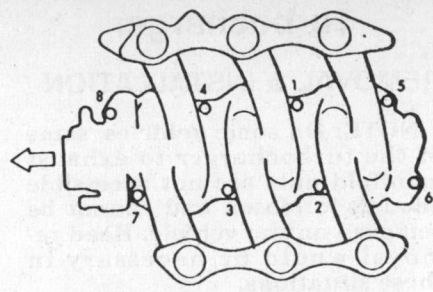

Intake manifold bolt torque sequence – 3.0L engine

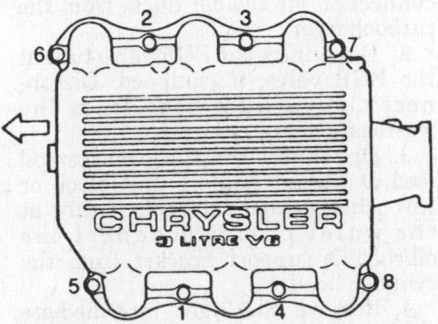

Air intake plenum bolt torque sequence – 3.0L engine

intake manifold. Install the air intake plenum and torque the mounting bolts gradually and evenly, in sequence, to 10 ft. lbs. (14 Nm).

29. Connect or install all remaining items that were disconnected or removed during the removal procedure.

30. Refill the cooling system. Connect the negative battery cable and check for leaks using the DRB I or II to activate the fuel pump.

Exhaust Manifold

REMOVAL & INSTALLATION

2.2L DOHC Engine

1. Disconnect the negative battery cable.
2. Remove the turbocharger assembly.
3. Remove the coolant tube from the cylinder head.
4. Remove the exhaust manifold retaining nuts and remove the manifold.
5. Clean the gasket mounting surfaces. Inspect the manifolds for cracks, flatness and/or damage.

To install:

5. Install a new exhaust manifold gasket. Do not use sealer of any kind.
6. Position the manifold on the studs and install the retaining nuts. Starting at the center and working outwards, torque the nuts gradually and evenly to 17 ft. lbs. (23 Nm).
6. Using a new gasket, connect the coolant tube to the cylinder head.

7. Install the turbocharger assembly.
8. Start the engine and check for exhaust leaks.

3.0L Engine

1. Disconnect the negative battery cable. Raise the vehicle and safely support.
2. Disconnect the exhaust pipe from the rear exhaust manifold, at the articulated joint.
3. Disconnect the EGR tube from the rear manifold and disconnect the oxygen sensor wire.
4. Remove the crossover pipe to manifold bolts.
5. Remove the rear manifold to cylinder head nuts and the manifold.
6. Lower the vehicle and remove the heat shield from the manifold.
7. Remove the front manifold to cylinder head nuts and remove the manifold.
8. Clean the gasket mounting surfaces. Inspect the manifolds for cracks, flatness and/or damage.

To install:

9. When installing, the numbers 1–3–5 on the gaskets are used with the rear cylinders and 2–4–6 are on the gasket for the front cylinders. Torque the manifold to cylinder head nuts to 14 ft. lbs. (19 Nm).
10. Install the crossover pipe to the manifold.
11. Connect the EGR tube and oxygen sensor wire.
12. Connect the exhaust pipe to the rear exhaust manifold, at the articulated joint.
13. Connect the negative battery cable and check the manifolds for leaks.

Combination Manifold

REMOVAL & INSTALLATION

2.2L and 2.5L Engines Except DOHC

WITHOUT TURBOCHARGER

NOTE: On some vehicles, some of the manifold attaching bolts are not accessible or too heavily sealed from the factory and cannot be removed on the vehicle. Head removal would be necessary in these situations.

1. Disconnect the negative battery cable.
2. Relieve the fuel system pressure.
3. Drain the cooling system.
4. Remove the air cleaner and disconnect all vacuum lines, electrical wiring and fuel lines from the throttle body.
5. Disconnect the throttle linkage.

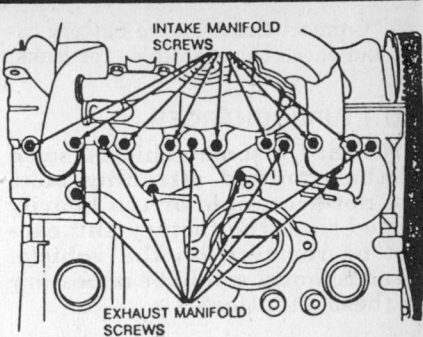

Combination manifold attaching nuts and bolts – 2.2L and 2.5L non-turbocharged engines

6. Loosen the power steering pump and remove the drive belt.
7. Remove the power brake vacuum hose from the intake manifold.
8. Remove the water hoses from the water crossover.
9. Raise and safely support the vehicle. Disconnect the exhaust pipe from the exhaust manifold.
10. Remove the power steering pump from its mounting bracket and set it aside.
11. Remove the intake manifold support bracket, if equipped.
12. Remove the EGR tube, if equipped.
13. Remove the intake manifold bolts.
14. Lower the vehicle.
15. Remove the intake manifold.
16. Remove the exhaust manifold nuts.
17. Remove the exhaust manifold.

To install:

18. Install a new combination manifold gasket.
19. Install the manifold assembly. Starting from the middle and working outwards, install the mounting nuts and torque to 13 ft. lbs. (18 Nm). Install the heat cowl to the exhaust manifold.
20. Install the intake manifold. Starting from the middle and working outward, torque the bolts to 17 ft. lbs. (23 Nm.) .
21. Install the EGR tube, if removed.
22. Install the intake support bracket, if equipped.
23. Install the power steering pump.
24. Raise the vehicle and support safely. Install the exhaust pipe to the exhaust manifold.
25. Install the water hoses to the water crossover.
26. Install the power brake vacuum hose to the intake manifold.
27. Connect the throttle linkage.
28. Install all vacuum lines, electrical wiring and fuel lines to the carburetor or throttle body.
29. Install the air cleaner assembly.
30. Refill the cooling system.

31. Connect the negative battery cable and check the manifolds for leaks.

WITH TURBOCHARGER

NOTE: On some vehicles, some of the manifold attaching bolts are not accessible or too heavily sealed from the factory and cannot be removed on the vehicle. Head removal would be necessary in these situations.

1. Disconnect the negative battery cable. Drain the cooling system. Raise and safely support the vehicle.
2. Disconnect the exhaust pipe at the articulated joint. Disconnect the oxygen sensor at the electrical connection.
3. Remove the turbocharger to engine support bracket.
4. Loosen the oil drain back tube connector hose clamps. Move the tube down on the engine block fitting.
5. Disconnect the turbocharger coolant inlet tube from the engine block and disconnect the tube support bracket.
6. Remove the air cleaner assembly, including the throttle body adaptor, hose and air cleaner box with support bracket.
7. Disconnect the accelerator linkage, throttle body electrical connector and vacuum hoses.
8. Relocate the fuel rail assembly. Remove the bracket to intake manifold screws and the bracket to heat shield clips. Lift and secure the fuel rail with injectors, wiring harness and fuel lines intact, up and out of the way.
9. Disconnect the turbocharger oil feed line at the oil sending unit tee fitting.
10. Disconnect the upper radiator hose from the thermostat housing.
11. Remove the cylinder head, manifolds and turbocharger as an assembly.
12. With the assembly on a workbench, loosen the upper turbocharger discharge hose end clamp.

NOTE: Do not disturb the center deswirler retaining clamp.

13. Remove the throttle body to intake manifold screws and throttle body assembly. Disconnect the turbocharger coolant return tube from the water box. Disconnect the retaining bracket on the cylinder head.
14. Remove the heat shield to intake manifold screws and the heat shield.
15. Remove the turbocharger to exhaust manifold nuts and the turbocharger assembly.
16. Remove the intake manifold bolts and the intake manifold.
17. Remove the exhaust manifold nuts and the exhaust manifold.

To install:

18. Place a new 2-sided Grafoil type intake/exhaust manifold gasket; do not use sealant.
19. Position the exhaust manifold on the cylinder head. Apply anti-seize compound to threads, install and torque the retaining nuts, starting at center and progressing outward in both directions, to 17 ft. lbs. (23 Nm). Repeat this procedure until all nuts are at 17 ft. lbs. (23 Nm).
20. Position the intake manifold on the cylinder head. Install and torque the retaining screws, starting at center and progressing outward in both directions, to 19 ft. lbs. (26 Nm). Repeat this procedure until all screws are at 19 ft. lbs. (26 Nm).
21. Connect the turbocharger outlet to the intake manifold inlet tube. Position the turbocharger on the exhaust manifold. Apply anti-seize compound to threads and torque the nuts to 30 ft. lbs. (41 Nm). Torque the connector tube clamps to 30 inch lbs. (41 Nm).
22. Install the tube support bracket to the cylinder head.
23. Install the heat shield on the intake manifold. Torque the screws to 105 inch lbs. (12 Nm).
24. Install the throttle body air horn into the turbocharger inlet tube. Install and torque the throttle body to intake manifold screws to 21 ft. lbs. (28 Nm). Torque the tube clamp to 30 inch lbs.
25. Install the cylinder head/manifolds/turbocharger assembly on the engine.
26. Reconnect the turbocharger oil feed line to the oil sending unit tee fitting and bearing housing, if disconnected. Torque the tube nuts to 10 ft. lbs. (14 Nm).
27. Install the air cleaner assembly. Connect the vacuum lines and accelerator cables.
28. Reposition the fuel rail. Install and torque the bracket screws to 21 ft. lbs. (28 Nm). Install the air shield to bracket clips.
29. Connect the turbocharger inlet coolant tube to the engine block. Torque the tube nut to 30 ft. lbs. (41 Nm). Install the tube support bracket.
30. Install the turbocharger housing-to-engine block support bracket and the screws hand tight. Torque the block screw 1st to 40 ft. lbs. (54 Nm). Torque the screw to the turbocharger housing to 20 ft. lbs. (27 Nm).
31. Reposition the drain back hose connector and tighten the hose clamps. Reconnect the exhaust pipe.
32. Connect the upper radiator hose to the thermostat housing.
33. Refill the cooling system.
34. Connect the negative battery cable and check the manifolds for leaks.

Turbocharger

REMOVAL & INSTALLATION

NOTE: On some vehicles, some of the turbocharger to exhaust manifold nuts are not accessible enough to loosen and cannot be removed on the vehicle. Head removal would be necessary in these situations.

1. Disconnect the negative battery cable. Drain the cooling system. Disconnect all air cleaner ducts from the turbocharger.
2. Disconnect the EGR valve tube at the EGR valve, if equipped. Disconnect the vacuum hose from the wastegate actuator.
3. Disconnect the turbocharger oil feed at the oil sending unit block or turbocharger and the coolant tube at the water box. Disconnect the oil/coolant support bracket from the cylinder head.
4. Remove the right intermediate shaft, bearing support bracket and outer driveshaft assemblies.
5. Remove the turbocharger to engine block support bracket.
6. Disconnect the exhaust pipe at the articulated joint. Disconnect the oxygen sensor at the electrical connection.
7. Loosen the oil drain-back tube connector clamps and move the tube hose down on the nipple.
8. Disconnect the coolant tube nut at the block outlet, below steering pump bracket, and the tube support bracket.
9. Remove the turbocharger to exhaust manifold nuts. Carefully routing the oil and coolant lines, move the assembly down and out of the vehicle.

To install:

NOTE: Before installing the turbocharger assembly, be sure it is first charged with oil. Failure to do this may cause damage to the assembly.

10. Position the turbocharger on the exhaust manifold. Apply an anti-seize compound, Loctite® 771-64 or equivalent, to the threads and torque the retaining nuts to 40 ft. lbs. (54 Nm). Connect the vacuum hose.
11. Connect the coolant tubes using new gaskets where necessary.
12. Position the oil drain-back hose and torque the clamps to 30 inch lbs.
13. Install and torque the:
   Turbocharger to engine support bracket block screw to 40 ft. lbs. (54 Nm).
   Turbocharger housing screw to 20 ft. lbs. (27 Nm).

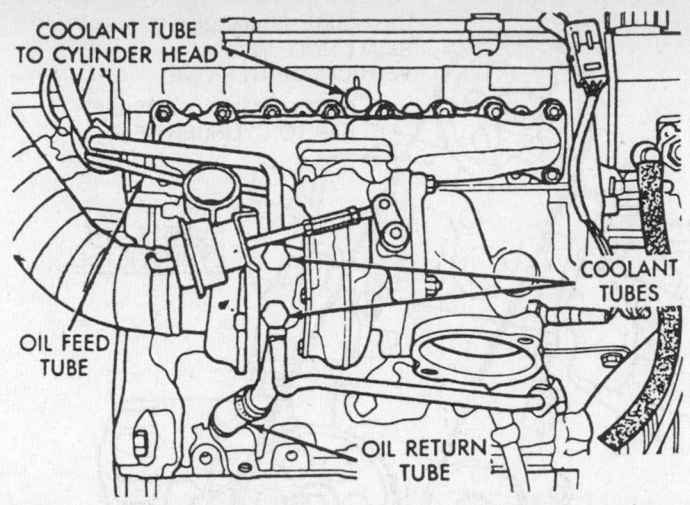

COOLANT TUBE TO CYLINDER HEAD

OIL FEED TUBE

COOLANT TUBES

OIL RETURN TUBE

Coolant and oil tube connections on turbo — 2.2L DOHC engine; others similar

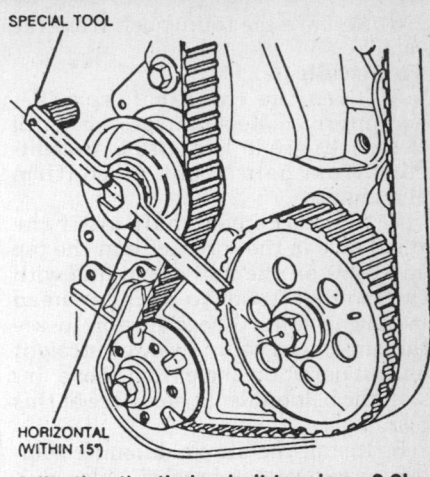

SPECIAL TOOL

HORIZONTAL (WITHIN 15°)

Adjusting the timing bolt tension — 2.2L and 2.5L engines

Articulated joint shoulder bolts to 21 ft. lbs. (28 Nm).

14. Install the right driveshaft assembly, the starter and the oil feed line.

15. Refill the cooling system. Connect the negative battery cable and check the turbocharger for proper operation.

Timing Belt Covers

REMOVAL & INSTALLATION

2.2L and 2.5L Engines

1. Disconnect the negative battery cable.

2. Remove the nuts and bolts that attach the upper cover to the valve cover, block or cylinder head.

3. Remove the bolt that attaches the upper cover to the lower cover.

4. Remove the upper cover.

5. Raise the vehicle and support safely. Remove the right side splash shield.

6. Remove the crankshaft pulley, water pump pulley and the belts.

7. Remove the lower cover attaching bolts.

8. Remove the lower cover.

9. The installation is the reverse of the removal procedure.

3.0L Engine

1. Disconnect the negative battery cable.

2. If equipped with air conditioning, loosen the adjustment pulley locknut, turn the screw counterclockwise to reduce the drive belt tension and remove the belt.

3. To remove the serpentine drive belt, insert a ½ in. breaker bar in to the square hole of the tensioner pulley, rotate it counterclockwise to reduce

the drive belt tension and remove the belt.

4. Remove the air conditioning compressor and the air compressor bracket, if equipped, power steering pump and alternator from the mounts; support them aside. Remove power steering pump/alternator automatic belt tensioner bolt and the tensioner.

5. Raise and safely support the vehicle. Remove the right inner fender splash shield.

6. Remove the crankshaft pulley bolt and the pulley/damper assembly from the crankshaft.

7. Lower the vehicle and place a floor jack under the engine to support it.

8. Separate the front engine mount insulator from the bracket. Raise the engine slightly and remove the mount bracket.

9. Remove the timing belt cover bolts and the upper and lower covers from the engine.

10. The installation is the reverse of the removal procedure.

Timing Belt and Tensioner

ADJUSTMENT

2.2L and 2.5L Engines

1. Disconnect the negative battery cable.

2. Raise the vehicle and support safely. Remove the right front inner splash shield.

3. Remove the tensioner cover.

4. Place the special tensioning tool C-4703 on the hex of the tensioner so the weight is at about the 10 o'clock position and loosen the bolt.

5. The tensioner should drop to the 9 o'clock position. Reposition the tool as required in order to have it end up at the 9 o'clock position (parallel to the ground, hanging toward the rear of the vehicle) plus or minus 15 degrees.

6. Hold the tool in position and tighten the bolt. Do not pull the tool past the 9 o'clock position or the belt will be too tight and will cause howling or possible breakage.

7. Install the cover and the splash shield.

3.0L Engine

1. Disconnect the negative battery cable.

2. Remove the timing belt covers.

3. Loosen the bolt that holds the timing belt tensioner in place.

4. Allow the spring only to pull the tensioner in automatically. Do not manualy move the tensioner or the belt will be too tight.

5. Tighten the tensioner locking bolt.

6. Install the timing belt covers and all related parts.

REMOVAL & INSTALLATION

2.2L and 2.5L Engines Except DOHC

1. If possible, position the engine so the No. 1 piston is at TDC of its compession stroke. Disconnect the negative battery cable.

2. Remove the timing belt covers. Remove the timing belt tensioner and allow the belt to hang free.

3. Place a floor jack under the engine and separate the right motor mount.

4. Remove the air conditioning compressor belt idler pulley, if equipped, and remove the mounting stud. Unbolt the compressor/alternator bracket and position it to the side.

5. Remove the timing belt from the vehicle.

To install:

6. Turn the crankshaft sprocket and intermediate shaft sprocket until the marks are in line. Use a straight-edge from bolt to bolt to confirm alignment.

7. Turn the camshaft until the small hole in the sprocket is at the top and rows on the hub are in line with the camshaft cap to cylinder head mounting lines. Use a mirror to see the alignment so it is viewed straight on and not at an angle from above. Install the belt but let at hang free at this point.

8. Install the air conditioning compressor/alternator bracket, idler pulley and motor mount. Remove the floor jack. Raise the vehicle and support safely. Have the tensioner at an arm's reach because the timing belt will have to be held in position with one hand.

9. To properly install the timing belt, reach up and engage it with the camshaft sprocket. Turn the intermediate shaft counterclockwise slightly, then engage the belt with the intermediate shaft sprocket. Hold the belt

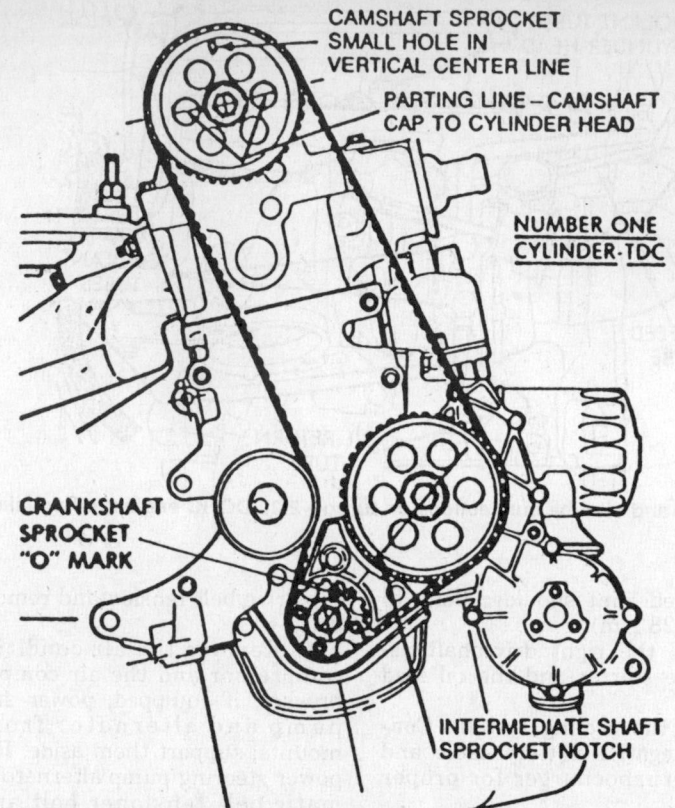

Timing belt installation—2.2L and 2.5L engines, except 2.2L DOHC

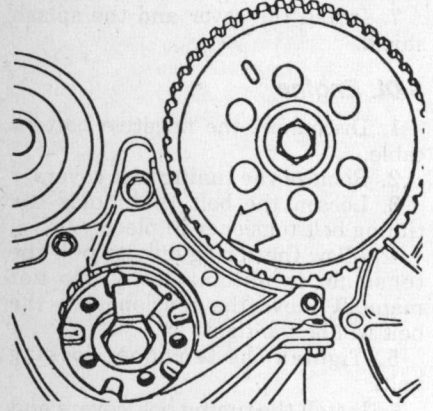

Alignment of the crankshaft sprocket and intermediate shaft sprocket—2.2L and 2.5L engines

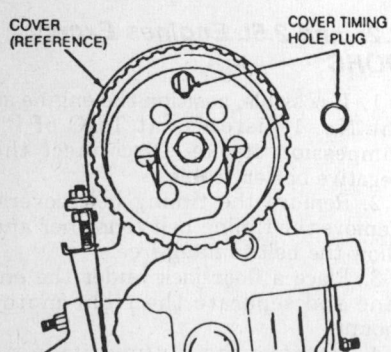

Alignment of arrows on the camshaft sprocket with the camshaft cap to cylinder head mounting line—2.2L and 2.5L engines, except 2.2L DOHC

against the intermediate shaft sprocket and turn clockwise to take up all tension; if the timing marks are out of alignment, repeat until alignment is correct.

10. Using a wrench, turn the crankshaft sprocket counterclockwise slightly and wrap the belt around it. Turn the sprocket clockwise so there is no slack in the belt between sprockets; if the timing marks are out of alignment, repeat until alignment is correct.

NOTE: If the timing marks are in line but slack exists in the belt between either the camshaft and intermediate shaft sprockets or the intermediate and crankshaft sprockets, the timing will be incorrect when the belt is tensioned. All slack must be only between the crankshaft and camshaft sprockets.

11. Install the tensioner and install the mounting bolt loosely. Place the special tensioning tool C–4703 on the hex of the tensioner so the weight is at about the 9 o'clock position (parallel to the ground, hanging toward the rear of the vehicle) plus or minus 15 degrees.

12. Hold the tool in position and tighten the bolt to 45 ft. lbs. (61 Nm). Do not pull the tool past the 9 o'clock position; this will make the belt too

tight and will cause it to howl or possibly break.

13. Lower the vehicle and recheck the camshaft sprocket positioning. If it is correct install the timing belt covers and all related parts.

14. Connect the negative battery cable and road test the vehicle.

2.2L DOHC Engine

1. If possible, position the engine so the No. 1 piston is at TDC of its compression stroke. Disconnect the negative battery cable.

2. Remove the timing belt covers.

3. Remove the timing belt tensioner and allow the belt to hang free.

4. Place a floor jack under the engine and separate the right motor mount.

5. Remove the timing belt from the vehicle.

To install:

6. Turn the crankshaft sprocket and intermediate shaft sprocket until the marks are in line. Use a straight-edge from bolt to bolt to confirm alignment.

7. Nos. 1 and 6 camshaft journals have aligning pin holes to index with the blind holes in the camshaft. Turn the camshafts until the pin holes in the journals align with the aligning holes in the corresponding bearing caps. Install pin punches to secure this timing position. At this position, the

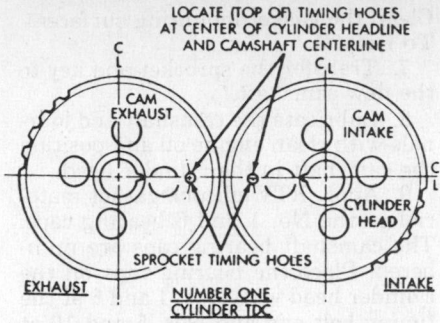

Camshaft sprocket timing—2.2L DOHC engine

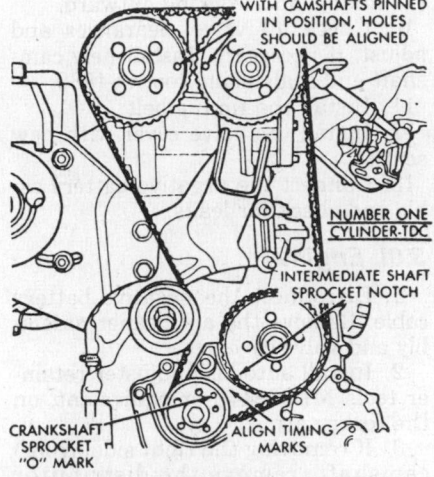

Timing belt installation—2.2L DOHC engine

sprocket timing holes on the camshaft sprockets should both be centered at the cylinder head mounting surface line.

8. Install the motor mount. Remove the floor jack. Raise the vehicle and support safely. Have the tensioner at an arm's reach because the timing belt will have to be held in position with one hand.

9. To properly install the timing belt, reach up and engage it with the camshaft sprockets, leaving no tension between sprockets. Turn the intermediate shaft counterclockwise slightly, then engage the belt with the intermediate shaft sprocket. Hold the belt against the intermediate shaft sprocket and turn clockwise to take up all tension; if the timing marks are out of alignment, repeat until alignment is correct.

10. Using a wrench, turn the crankshaft sprocket counterclockwise slightly and wrap the belt around it. Turn the sprocket clockwise so there is no slack in the belt between sprockets; if the timing marks are out of alignment, repeat until alignment is correct.

NOTE: If the timing marks are in line but slack exists in the belt anywhere except on the tensioner side, the timing will be incorrect when the belt is tensioned. All slack must be only between the crankshaft and exhaust camshaft sprockets.

11. Install the tensioner and install the mounting bolt loosely. Remove the pin punches from the camshafts. Place the special tensioning tool C–4703 on the hex of the tensioner so the weight is at about the 9 o'clock position (parallel to the ground, hanging toward the rear of the vehicle) plus or minus 15 degrees.

12. Hold the tool in position and tighten the bolt to 45 ft. lbs. (61 Nm). Do not pull the tool past the 9 o'clock position; this will make the belt too tight and will cause it to howl or possibly break.

13. Rotate the crankshaft 2 full revolutions. With the No. 1 cylinder at TDC, all timing marks must be in line. Repeat the procedure if the timing is not correct.

14. Install the timing belt covers and all related parts.

15. Connect the negative battery cable and road test the vehicle.

3.0L Engine

1. If possible, position the engine so the No. 1 cylinder is at TDC of its compression stroke. Disconnect the negative battery cable. Remove the timing covers from the engine.

2. If the same timing belt will be reused, mark the direction of the timing belt's rotation, for installation in the same direction. Make sure the engine is positioned so the No. 1 cylinder is at the TDC of it's compression stroke

and the sprockets timing marks are aligned with the engine's timing mark indicators.

3. Loosen the timing belt tensioner bolt and remove the belt. If not removing the tensioner, position it as far away from the center of the engine as possible and tighten the bolt.

4. If the tensioner is being removed, paint the outside of the spring to ensure it is not installed backwards. Unbolt the tensioner and remove it along with the spring.

To install:

5. Install the tensioner, if removed and hook the upper end of the spring to the water pump pin and the lower end to the tensioner in exactly the same position as originally installed. If not already done, position both camshafts so the marks align with those on the alternator bracket (rear bank) and inner timing cover (front bank). Rotate the crankshaft so the timing mark aligns with the mark on the oil pump.

6. Install the timing belt on the crankshaft sprocket and while keeping the belt tight on the tension side (right side), install the belt on the front camshaft sprocket.

7. Install the belt on the water pump pulley, then the rear camshaft sprocket and the tensioner.

8. Rotate the front camshaft counterclockwise to tension the belt between the front camshaft and the crankshaft. If the timing marks came out of line, repeat the procedure.

9. Install the crankshaft sprocket flange.

10. Loosen the tensioner bolt and allow the spring to tension the belt.

11. Turn the crankshaft 2 full turns in the clockwise direction only until the timing marks are aligned and

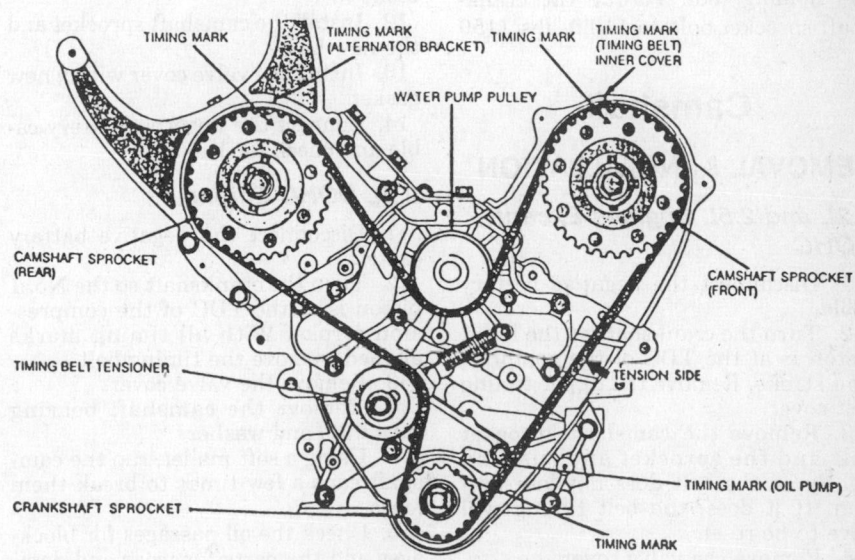

Timing belt installation—3.0L engine

torque the tensioner lock bolt to 21 ft. lbs. (29 Nm).

12. Install the timing belt covers and all related parts.

13. Connect the negative battery cable and road test the vehicle.

Timing Sprockets

REMOVAL & INSTALLATION

2.2L and 2.5L Engines

1. Disconnect the negative battery cable. Remove the timing belt.

2. Remove the crankshaft sprocket bolt. Using the puller tool C-4685 or equivalent and the button from tool L-4524 or equivalent, remove the crankshaft sprocket.

3. Using the tool C-4687 or equivalent, hold the camshaft and/or intermediate sprocket, remove the center bolt and the sprocket(s).

4. The installation is the reverse of the removal procedure. Torque the camshaft and intermediate sprocket bolts to 65 ft. lbs. (88 Nm) and the crankshaft sprocket bolt to 50 ft. lbs. (68 Nm).

3.0L Engine

1. Disconnect the negative battery cable.

2. Remove the timing belt.

3. To remove the camshaft sprocket, hold the sprocket with tool MB990775 or equivalent, and remove the retaining bolt and washer.

4. To remove the crankshaft sprocket, remove the bolt and remove the sprocket from the crankshaft.

5. The installation is the reverse of the removal procedure. Torque the camshaft sprocket bolt to 70 ft. lbs. (95 Nm) while holding the sprocket with the holding tool. Torque the crankshaft sprocket bolt. to 110 ft. lbs. (150 Nm).

Camshaft

REMOVAL & INSTALLATION

2.2L and 2.5L Engines Except DOHC

1. Disconnect the negative battery cable.

2. Turn the crankshaft so the No. 1 piston is at the TDC of the compression stroke. Remove the upper timing belt cover.

3. Remove the camshaft sprocket bolt and the sprocket and suspend tightly so the belt does not lose tension. If it does, the belt timing will have to be reset.

4. Remove the valve cover.

5. If the rocker arms are being re-used, mark them for installation identification and loosen the camshaft bearing bolts, evenly and gradually.

6. Using a soft mallet, tap the rear of the camshaft a few times to break the bearing caps loose.

7. Remove the bolts, bearing caps and the camshaft with seals.

NOTE: Take note of the color of the paint stripe on the rear camshaft seal. These stripes differentiate seal sizes. If a seal with a different color stripe is installed, a severe leak will develop if the seal is too small, or the cap will not be able to be fully installed if the seal is too big.

8. Check the oil passages for blockages and the parts for wear and damage and replace parts, as required. Clean the gasket mounting surfaces.

To install:

9. Transfer the sprocket key to the new camshaft. New rocker arms and a new camshaft sprocket bolt are normally included with the camshaft package. Install the rocker arms, lubricate the camshaft and install with end seals installed.

10. Place the bearing caps with No. 1 at the timing belt end and No. 5 at the transaxle end. The camshaft bearing caps are numbered and have arrows facing forward. Torque the camshaft bearing bolts evenly and gradually to 18 ft. lbs. (24 Nm).

NOTE: Apply RTV silicone gasket material to the No. 1 and 5 bearing caps. Install the bearing caps before the seals are installed.

11. Mount a dial indicator to the front of the engine and check the camshaft endplay. Play should not exceed 0.020 in.

12. Install the camshaft sprocket and the new bolt.

13. Install the valve cover with a new gasket.

14. Connect the negative battery cable and check for leaks.

2.2L DOHC Engine

1. Disconnect the negative battery cable.

2. Turn the crankshaft so the No. 1 piston is at the TDC of the compression stroke. With all timing marks aligned, remove the timing belt.

3. Remove the valve cover.

4. Remove the camshaft bearing caps nuts and washers.

5. Using a soft mallet, rap the camshaft caps a few times to break them loose.

6. Check the oil passages for blockages and the parts for wear and damage and replace parts, as required.

Clean the gasket mounting surfaces.

To install:

7. Transfer the sprocket and key to the new camshaft.

8. Lubricate the camshaft and journals with clean engine oil and position the camshaft in the cylinder head.

9. Apply RTV silicone gasket material to the No. 1 and 6 bearing caps. The camshaft bearing caps are numbered. Place the bearing caps on the cylinder head with Nos. 1 and 6 at the timing belt end and Nos. 5 and 10 at the transaxle end. Torque the camshaft bearing bolts evenly and gradually to 20 ft. lbs. (24 Nm) starting from the middle and working outward.

10. Check all valve clearances and adjust, if necessary. Install new camshaft end seals using tool C-4680.

11. Install the timing belt.

12. Install the valve cover with new seals.

13. Connect the negative battery cable and check for leaks.

3.0L Engine

1. Disconnect the negative battery cable. Remove the air cleaner assembly and valve covers.

2. Install auto lash adjuster retainer tools MD998443 or equivalent, on the rocker arms.

3. If removing the right side (front) camshaft, remove the distributor extension.

4. Remove the camshaft bearing caps but do not remove the bolts from the caps.

5. Remove the rocker arms, rocker shafts and bearing caps, as an assembly.

6. Remove the camshaft from the cylinder head.

7. Inspect the bearing journals on the camshaft, cylinder head and bearing caps.

To install:

8. Lubricate the camshaft journals and camshaft with clean engine oil and install the camshaft in the cylinder head.

9. Align the camshaft bearing caps with the arrow mark (depending on cylinder numbers) and in numerical order.

10. Apply sealer at the ends of the bearing caps and install the assembly.

11. Torque the bearing cap bolts, in the following sequence: No. 3, No. 2, No. 1 and No. 4 to 85 inch lbs. (10 Nm).

12. Repeat the sequence increasing the torque to 175 inch lbs. (18 Nm).

13. Install the distributor extension, if it was removed.

14. Install the valve cover and all related parts.

15. Connect the negative battery cable.

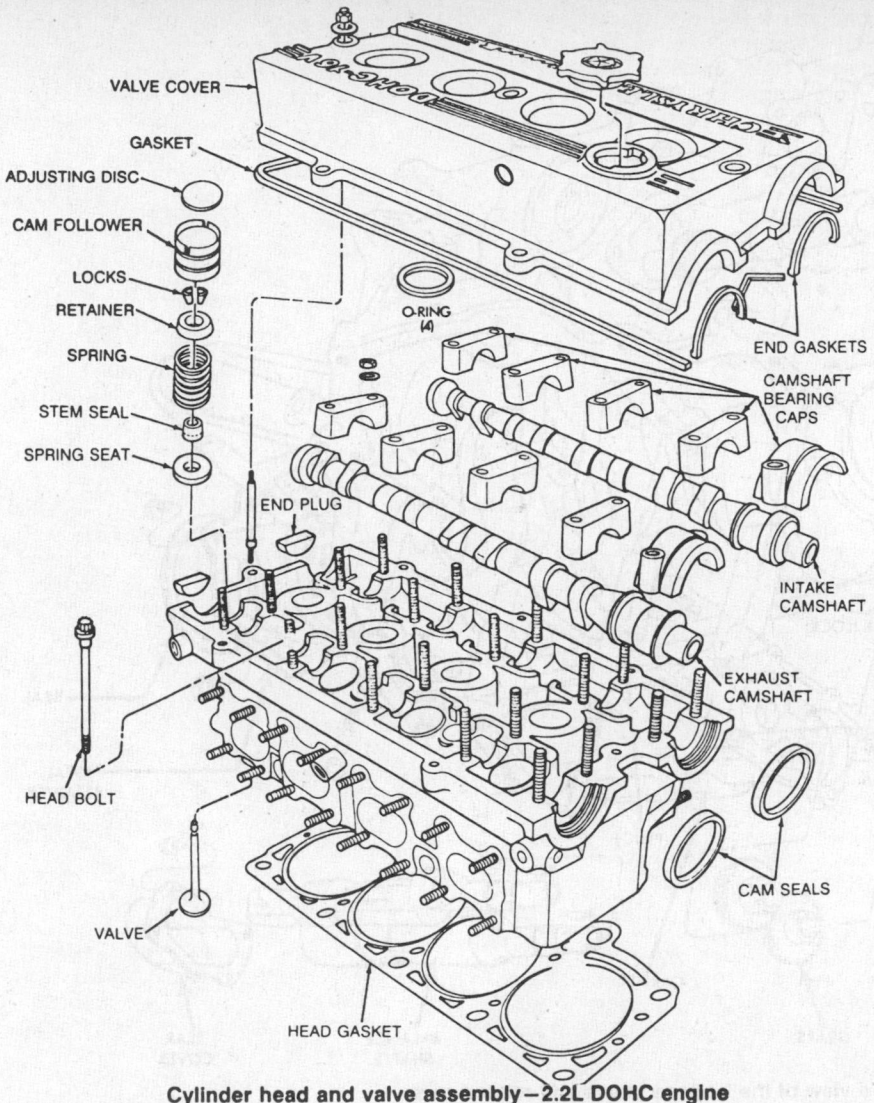

Cylinder head and valve assembly—2.2L DOHC engine

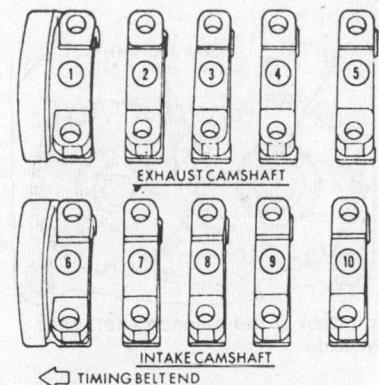

Camshaft bearing caps installation— 2.2L DOHC engine

Intermediate Shaft

REMOVAL & INSTALLATION

2.2L and 2.5L Engines

1. Disconnect the negative battery cable.

2. Crank the engine so the No. 1 piston is at TDC of its compression stroke. Remove the timing belt covers to confirm that all timing marks are aligned.

3. Remove the distributor. Looking down at the oil pump, the slot in the shaft must be parallel with the center line of the crankshaft. Remove the oil pump.

4. Remove the timing belt and the intermediate shaft sprocket.

5. Remove the shaft retainer bolts and remove the retainer from the block.

6. Remove the intermediate shaft from the engine.

7. If necessary, remove the front bushing using tool C–4697–2 and the rear bushing using tool C–4686–2.

To install:

8. Install the front bushing using tool C–4697–1 until the tool is flush with the block. Install the rear bushing using tool C–4686–1 until the tool is flush with the block.

9. Lubricate the distributor drive gear and install the intermediate shaft.

10. Replace the seal in the retainer and apply silicone sealer to the mating surface of the retainer. Install the retainer to the block and torque the bolts to 10 ft. lbs. (12 Nm).

11. Install the intermediate shaft sprocket and the timing belt.

12. With the timing belt properly installed, install the oil pump so the slot is parallel to the center line of the crankshaft. Install the distributor so the rotor is aligned with the No. 1 spark plug wire tower on the cap.

13. Connect the negative battery cable, check for leaks and adjust the ignition timing, as required.

Balance Shafts

REMOVAL & INSTALLATION

2.5L and 2.2L Engine with Turbo IV

1. Disconnect the negative battery cable. Raise the vehicle and support safely.

2. Remove the timing belt. Remove the oil pan, the oil pickup, the crankshaft belt sprocket and the front crankshaft oil seal retainer.

3. Remove the balance shaft chain cover, the guide and the tensioner.

4. Remove the balance shaft sprocket to shaft bolt, the gear cover to balance shaft bolt and the crankshaft sprocket to crankshaft bolts, then the sprockets with the balance shaft chain.

5. Remove the front gear cover to carrier housing stud, the gear cover and the balance shaft drive gears.

6. Remove the rear gear cover to carrier housing bolts, the rear cover and the balance shafts from the rear of the carrier.

7. If necessary, remove the carrier housing to crankcase bolts and the housing.

To install:

8. If the carrier housing is being installed, torque the carrier housing to crankcase bolts to 40 ft. lbs. (54 Nm).

9. Rotate the balance shafts until the keyways are facing upward, parallel to the vertical centerline of the engine.

10. Install the short hub gear on the sprocket driven shaft and the long hub gear on the gear driven shaft; make sure the gear timing marks are aligned (facing each other).

11. Install the front gear cover and torque the front gear cover to carrier housing stud bolt to 8.5 ft. lbs. (12 Nm).

12. Install the balance chain sprock-

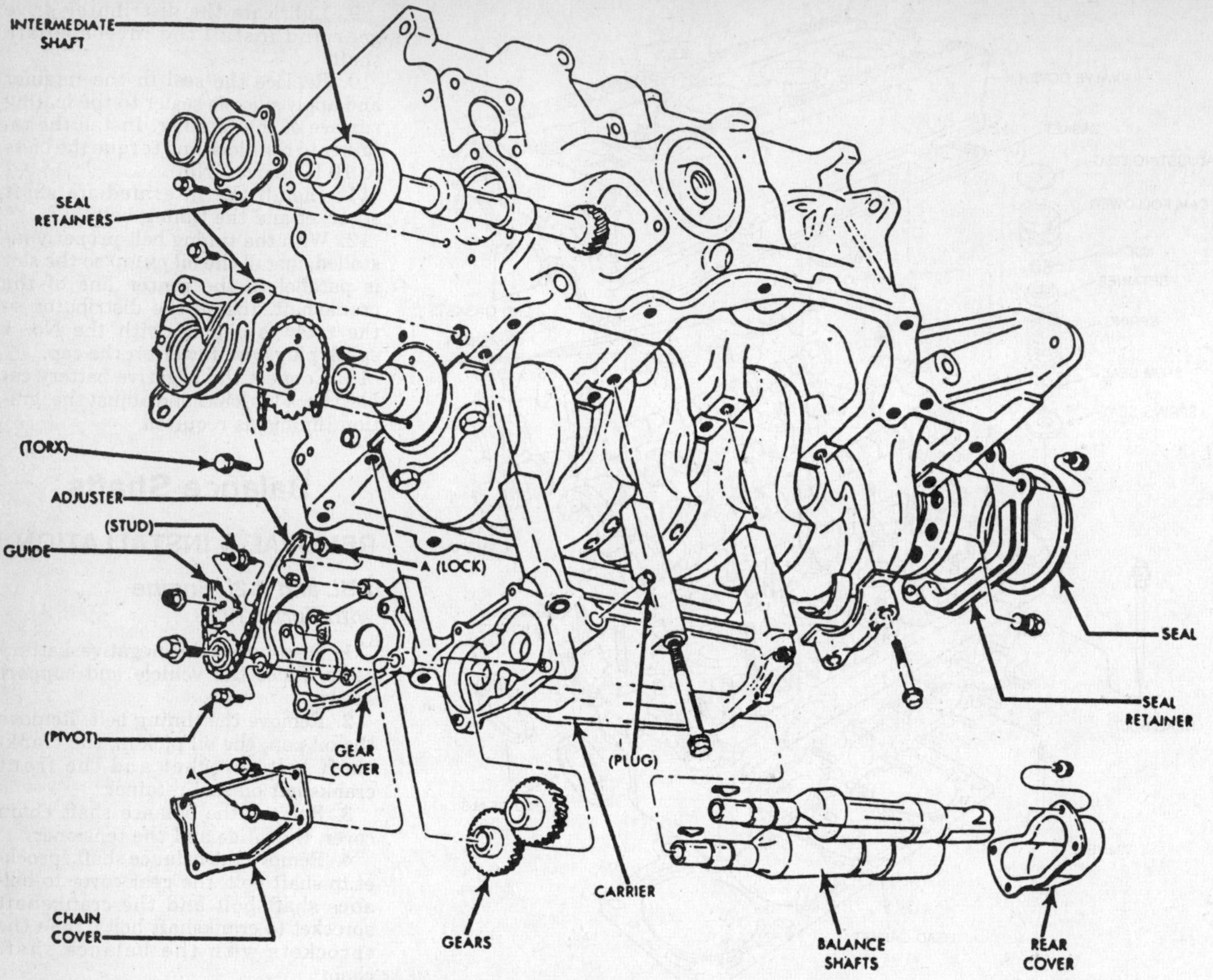

INTERMEDIATE SHAFT

SEAL RETAINERS

(TORX)

ADJUSTER

(STUD)

GUIDE

A (LOCK)

(PIVOT)

A

GEAR COVER

(PLUG)

CHAIN COVER

GEARS

CARRIER

BALANCE SHAFTS

REAR COVER

SEAL

SEAL RETAINER

Exploded view of the balance shafts and related parts

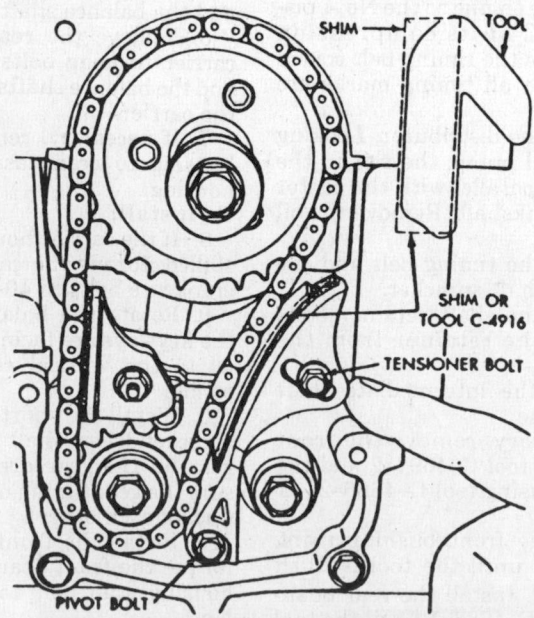

SHIM

TOOL

SHIM OR TOOL C-4916

TENSIONER BOLT

PIVOT BOLT

Adjusting the balance shaft chain tensioner

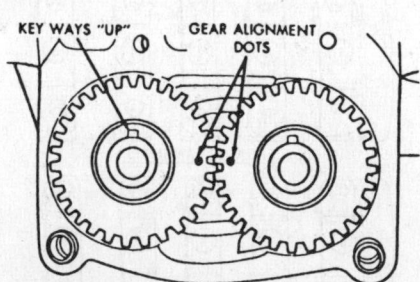

KEY WAYS "UP"

GEAR ALIGNMENT DOTS

Alignment of the balance shaft gear sprockets

et and torque the sprocket to crank-shaft bolts to 11 ft. lbs. (13 Nm).

13. Rotate the crankshaft to position the No. 1 cylinder on the TDC of the compression stroke; the timing marks on the chain sprocket should align with the parting line on the left side of the No. 1 main bearing cap.

14. Position the balance shaft sprocket into the balance chain so the sprocket (yellow dot) timing mark

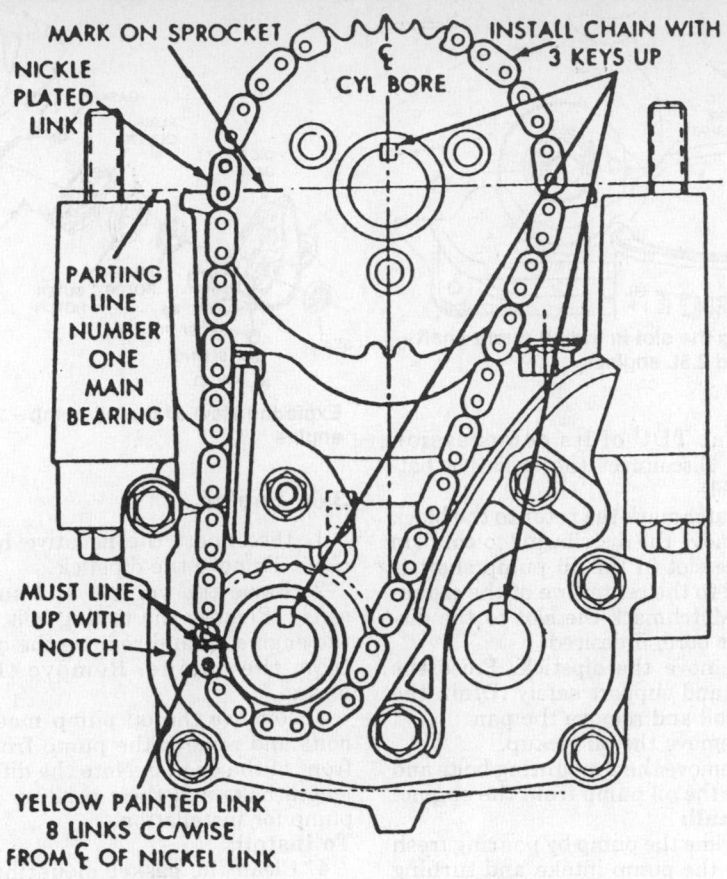

Balance shaft sprocket and crankshaft sprocket timing

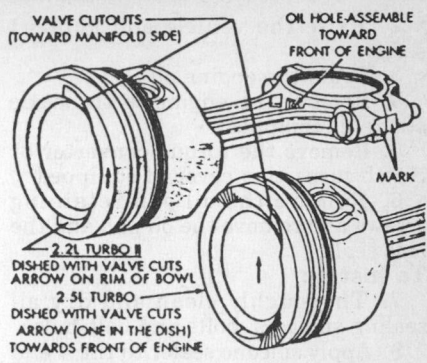

Piston and rod positioning—2.2L Turbo II and 1989 2.5L turbocharged engines

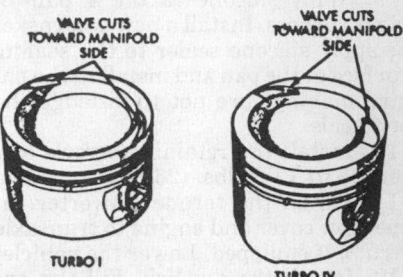

Piston and rod positioning—1990–91 2.5L turbocharged and 2.2L Turbo IV engines

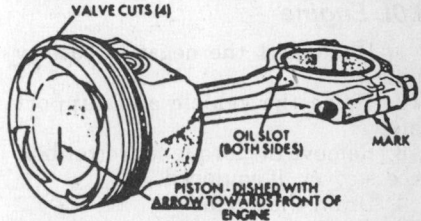

Piston and rod positioning—2.2L DOHC engine

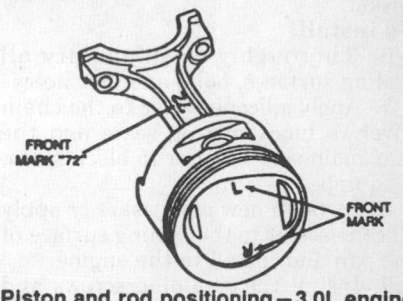

Piston and rod positioning—3.0L engine

mates with the yellow link on the chain.

15. Install the balance chain/sprocket assembly onto the crankshaft and the balance shaft. Torque the sprocket to shaft bolts to 21 ft. lbs. (28 Nm). If necessary to secure the crankshaft while tightening the bolts, place a block of wood between the crankcase and the crankshaft counterbalance.

16. Loosely, install the chain tensioners and place a shim (0.039 in. × 2.75 in.) between the chain and the tensioner. Apply firm pressure, to reduce the chain slack, to the tensioner shoe. Torque the tensioner to front gear cover bolts to 8.5 ft. lbs. (12 Nm).

17. Install the chain cover and the rear cover to the carrier housing and torque the bolts to 8.5 ft. lbs. (12 Nm).

18. Replace the crankshaft retainer seal, apply silicone sealer to the mating surface and install the retainer.

19. Install the oil pickup and oil pan.

20. Install the crankshaft sprocket and the timing belt.

21. Connect the negative battery cable and road test the vehicle.

Piston and Connecting Rod

POSITIONING

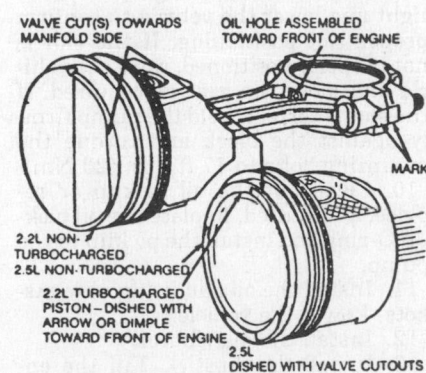

Piston and rod positioning—2.2L and 2.5L non-turbocharged engines and 1987–88 2.2L turbocharged engine

ENGINE LUBRICATION

Oil Pan

REMOVAL & INSTALLATION

2.2L and 2.5L Engines

1. Disconnect the negative battery cable. Remove the oil dipstick.

2. Raise the vehicle and support safely.

3. Drain the engine oil.

4. Remove the engine to transaxle struts, if equipped.

5. Remove the torque converter or clutch inspection cover, if equipped.

6. Remove the oil pan retaining screws and remove the oil pan and the side seals.

To install:

7. Thoroughly clean and dry all sealing surfaces, bolts and bolt holes.

8. Apply silicone sealer to the 4 end seal-to-block corners and install the end seals making sure the corners are not twisted.

9. Apply silicone to the 4 pan-to-block corners. Install a new pan gasket or apply silicone sealer to the sealing surface of the pan and install to the engine making sure not to dislodge the end seals.

10. Install the retaining screws and torque to 17 ft. lbs. (23 Nm).

11. Install the torque converter inspection cover and engine to transaxle struts, if equipped. Lower the vehicle.

12. Install the dipstick. Fill the engine with the proper amount of oil.

13. Connect the negative battery cable and check for leaks.

3.0L Engine

1. Disconnect the negative battery cable.

2. Raise the vehicle and support safely.

3. Remove the torque converter bolt access cover, if equipped.

4. Drain the engine oil.

5. Remove the oil pan retaining screws and remove the oil pan and gasket.

To install:

6. Thoroughly clean and dry all sealing surfaces, bolts and bolt holes.

7. Apply silicone sealer to the chain cover to block mating seam and the rear main seal retainer to block seam, if equipped.

8. Install a new pan gasket or apply silicone sealer to the sealing surface of the pan and install to the engine.

9. Install the retaining screws and torque to 50 inch lbs. (6 Nm).

10. Install the torque converter bolt access cover, if equipped. Lower the vehicle.

11. Install the dipstick. Fill the engine with the proper amount of oil.

12. Connect the negative battery cable and check for leaks.

Oil Pump

REMOVAL & INSTALLATION

2.2L and 2.5L Engines

1. Crank the engine so the No. 1 pis-

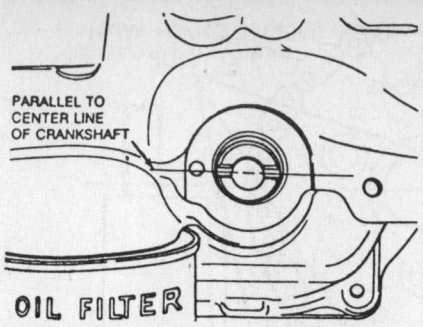

OIL FILTER

Aligning the slot in the oil pump shaft—2.2L and 2.5L engines

ton is at TDC of its compression stroke. Disconnect the negative battery cable.

2. Matchmark the rotor to the block and remove the distributor to confirm that the slot in the oil pump shaft is parallel to the centerline of the crankshaft. Matchmark the slot to the distributor bore, if desired.

3. Remove the dipstick. Raise the vehicle and support safely. Drain the engine oil and remove the pan.

4. Remove the oil pickup.

5. Remove the 2 mounting bolts and remove the oil pump from the engine.

To install:

6. Prime the pump by pouring fresh oil into the pump intake and turning the driveshaft until oil comes out the pressure port. Repeat a few times until no air bubbles are present.

7. Apply sealer (Loctite® 515, or equivalent) to the pump body to block machined surface interface. Lubricate the oil pump and distributor driveshaft.

8. Align the slot so it will be in the same position as when it was removed. If it is not, the distributor will not be timed correctly. Install the pump fully and rotate back and forth to ensure proper positioning between the pump mounting surface and the machined surface of the block.

9. Install the mounting bolts finger-tight and lower the vehicle to confirm proper slot positioning. If the slot is not properly positioned, raise the vehicle and move the gear as required. If the slot is correct, hold the pump firmly against the block and torque the mounting bolts to 17 ft. lbs. (23 Nm).

10. Clean out the oil pickup or replace, as required. Replace the oil pickup O-ring and install the pickup to the pump.

11. Install the oil pan using new gaskets. Lower the vehicle.

12. Install the distributor.

13. Install the dipstick. Fill the engine with the proper amount of oil.

14. Connect the negative battery cable, check the timing and check the oil pressure.

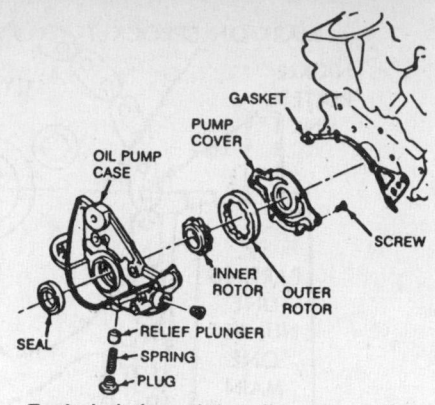

Exploded view of the oil pump—3.0L engine

3.0L Engine

1. Disconnect the negative battery cable. Remove the dipstick.

2. Raise the vehicle and support safely. Remove the timing belt, drain the engine oil and remove the oil pan from the engine. Remove the oil pickup.

3. Remove the oil pump mounting bolts and remove the pump from the front of the engine. Note the different length bolts and their position in the pump for installation.

To install:

4. Clean the gasket mounting surfaces of the pump and engine block.

5. Prime the pump by soaking its components with fresh oil and turning the rotors or, using petroleum jelly, pack the inside of the oil pump. Using a new gasket, install the oil pump on the engine and torque all bolts to 11 ft. lbs. (15 Nm).

6. Install the balancer and crankshaft sprocket to the end of the crankshaft.

7. Clean out the oil pickup or replace, as required. Replace the oil pickup gasket ring and install the pickup to the pump.

8. Install the timing belt, oil pan and all related parts.

9. Install the dipstick. Fill the engine with the proper amount of oil.

10. Connect the negative battery cable and check the oil pressure.

CHECKING

2.2L and 2.5L Engines

1. Remove the cover from the oil pump.

2. Check endplay of the inner rotor using a feeler gauge and a straight edge placed across the pump body. The specification is 0.001–0.004 in. (0.03–0.09mm).

3. Measure the clearance between the inner and outer rotors. The maximum clearance is 0.008 in. (0.20mm).

4. Measure the clearance between the outer rotor and the pump body. The maximum clearance is 0.014 in. (0.35mm).

5. The minimum thickness of the outer rotor is 0.944 in. (23.96mm). The minimum diameter of the outer rotor is 2.77 in. (62.70mm). The minimum thickness of the inner rotor is 0.943 in. (23.95mm).

6. Check the cover for warpage. The maximum allowable is 0.003 in. (0.076mm).

7. Check the pressure relief valve for damage. The spring's free length specification is 1.95 in. (49.50mm).

8. Assemble the outer rotor with the larger chamfered edge in the pump body. Torque the cover screws to 10 ft. lbs. (12 Nm).

3.0L Engine

1. Remove the rear cover.
2. Remove the pump rotors and inspect the case for excessive wear.
3. Measure the diameter of the inner rotor hub that sits in the case. Measure the inside diameter of the inner rotor hub bore. Subtract the first measurement from the second; if the result is over 0.006 in. (0.15mm), replace the oil pump assembly.
4. Measure the clearance between the outer rotor and the case. The specification is 0.004–0.007 in. (0.10–0.18mm).
5. Check the side clearance of the rotors using a feeler gauge and a straight-edge placed across the case. The specification is 0.0015–0.0035 in. (0.04–0.09mm).
6. Check the relief plunger and spring for damage and breakage.
7. Install the rear cover to the case.

Rear Main Bearing Oil Seal

REMOVAL & INSTALLATION

1. Disconnect the negative battery cable.
2. Remove the transaxle. Remove the flywheel or flexplate.
3. If there is any leakage coming from the rear seal retainer, drain the engine oil and remove the oil pan, if necessary. Remove the rear main oil seal retainer.
4. Remove the seal from the retainer.
To install:
5. Lightly coat the seal outer diameter with Loctite® Stud N' Bearing Mount or equivalent.
6. Install the seal to the retainer.
7. If the retainer was removed, thoroughly clean and dry the retainer to block sealing surfaces and install a

new gasket or apply silicone sealer and install the retainer. Install the pan, if it was removed.
8. Install the flywheel or flex plate and the transaxle.
9. Connect the negative battery cable and check for leaks.

MANUAL TRANSAXLE

For further information on transmissions/transaxles, please refer to "Chilton's Guide to Transmission Repair".

Transaxle Assembly

REMOVAL & INSTALLATION

NOTE: If the vehicle is going to be rolled while the transaxle is out of the vehicle, obtain 2 outer CV-joints to install to the hubs. If the vehicle is rolled without the proper torque applied to the front wheel bearings, the bearings will no longer be usable.

1. Disconnect the negative battery cable.
2. Remove the air cleaner assembly with all ducts. Remove the upper bell housing bolts. Disconnect the reverse light switch and the ground wire.
3. Remove the starter attaching nut and bolt at the top of the bell housing.
4. Raise the vehicle and support safely. Remove the tire and wheel assemblies. Remove the axle end cotter pins, nut locks, spring washers and axle nuts.
5. Remove the ball joint retaining bolts and pry the control arm from the steering knuckle. Position a drainpan under the transaxle where the axles enter the differential or extension housing. Remove the axles from the transaxle or center bearing. Unbolt the center bearing and remove the intermediate axle from the transaxle, if equipped.
6. Remove the anti-rotation link from the crossmember. Disconnect the shifter cables from the transaxle and unbolt the cable bracket.
7. Remove the speedometer gear adaptor bolt and remove the adaptor from the transaxle.
8. Remove the rear mount from the starter, unbolt the starter and position it to the side.
9. Using the proper equipment, support the weight of the engine.

10. Remove the front motor mount and bracket.
11. Position a suitable transaxle jack under the transaxle.
12. Remove the lower bell housing bolts.
13. Remove the left side splash shield. Remove the transaxle mount bolts.
14. Carefully pry the transaxle from the engine.
15. Slide the transaxle rearward until the input shaft clears the clutch disc.
16. Pull the transaxle completely away from the clutch housing and remove it from the vehicle.
17. To prepare the vehicle for rolling, support the engine with a suitable support or reinstall the front motor mount to the engine. Then reinstall the ball joints to the steering knuckle and install the retaining bolt. Install the obtained outer CV-joints to the hubs, install the washers and torque the axle nuts to 180 ft. lbs. (244 Nm). The vehicle may now be safely rolled.
To install:
18. Lubricate the pilot bushing and input shaft splines very lightly with high temperature lubricant.
19. Mount the transaxle securely on a suitable jack. Lift it in place until the input shaft is centered in the clutch housing opening. Roll the transaxle forward until the input shaft splines fully engage with the clutch disc and install the transaxle to clutch housing bolts.
20. Raise the transaxle and install the left side mount bolts.
21. Install the front motor mount and bracket.
22. Remove the engine and transaxle support fixtures.
23. Install the starter to the transaxle and install the lower bolt finger-tight.
24. Install a new O-ring to the speedometer cable adaptor and install to the extension housing; make sure it snaps in place. Install the retaining bolt.
25. Install the shift cable bracket and snap the cable ends in place. Install the anti-rotation link.
26. Install the axles and center bearing, if equipped. Install the ball joints to the steering knuckles. Torque the axle nuts to 180 ft. lbs. (244 Nm) and install new cotter pins. Fill the transaxle with SAE 5W-30 engine oil. Install the splash shield and install the wheels. Lower the vehicle.
27. Install the upper bell housing bolts.
28. Install the starter attaching nut and bolt at the top of the bell housing. Raise the vehicle and tighten the starter bolt from underneath the vehicle. Lower the vehicle.

29. Connect the reverse light switch and the ground wire.

30. Install the air cleaner assembly.

31. Connect the negative battery cable and check the transaxle for proper operation.

CABLE ADJUSTMENT

Except 1989–90 TC

1. Working over the left front fender, remove the lock pin from the transaxle selector shaft housing.

2. Reverse the lock pin so the long end is down and insert it into the same threaded hole while pushing the selector shaft into the selector housing. A hole in the selector shaft will align with the lock pin, allowing the lock pin to be screwed into the housing. This operation locks the selector shaft in the neutral position between 3rd and 4th gears.

3. Remove the gearshift knob, the retaining nut and the pull-up ring from the gearshift lever.

4. If necessary, remove the shift lever boot and console to expose the gearshift linkage.

5. Fabricate 2 cable adjusting pins: $^3/_{16}$ in. diameter × 5 in. long with a ½ in. 90 degree bend at one end.

6. Place a pin in the hole provided at the right side and the other in the hole provided at the rear side of the shifting mechanism; make sure the alignment holes match. Torque the selector (right side) and the crossover (left side) adjusting bolts to 4–5 ft. lbs.

7. Remove the lock pin from the selector shaft housing and reinstall the lock pin, with the long end up, in the selector shaft housing. Torque the lock pin to 10 ft. lbs. (12 Nm).

8. Check the first/reverse shifting and blockout into reverse.

9. Reinstall the console, boot, pull-up ring, retaining nut and knob.

1989–90 TC

1. Disconnect the negative battery cable.

2. Remove the console assembly to gain access to the cable ends.

3. Place the selector shaft in the neutral position.

4. Loosen the selector and crossover cables adjusting screws enough so the cables are free to move.

5. Install screw tool with tethered spacer block, which is taped to the shifter support bracket, to the support bracket.

6. Torque the cable adjusting screws to 70 inch lbs. (8 Nm).

7. Remove the tethered adjusting tool and attach it to the bracket for future use.

8. Install the console assembly.

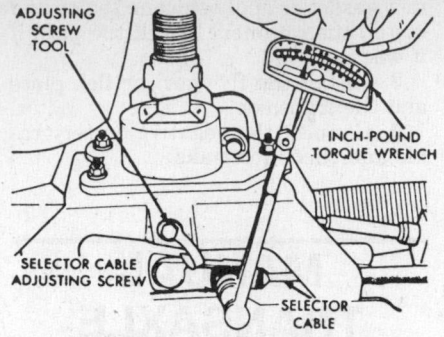

Adjusting the shifter cables—TC

9. Road test the vehicle and check for smooth shifting.

CLUTCH

Clutch Assembly

REMOVAL & INSTALLATION

1. Disconnect the negative battery cable. Remove the transaxle.

2. Matchmark the clutch/pressure plate cover and flywheel. Insert a suitable clutch plate alignment tool into the clutch disc hub.

3. Loosen the flywheel to pressure plate bolts gradually and evenly to avoid warpage.

4. Remove the pressure plate/clutch assembly from the flywheel.

5. Sand the flywheel or replace it if it is scored, cracked or heat damaged.

6. Sparingly apply anti-sieze compound to the input shaft and clutch disc splines. Install a new release bearing.

To install:

7. Using a suitable clutch disc alignment tool, tighten the pressure plate bolts to center the disc.

8. Torque the pressure plate/clutch assembly mounting bolts to the flywheel gradually and evenly to 21 ft. lbs. (28 Nm).

9. Install the transaxle.

10. Connect the negative battery cable and check the clutch and reverse lights for proper operation.

PEDAL FREE-PLAY ADJUSTMENT

All vehicles are equipped with a self-adjusting cable operated mechanism and no adjustment is provided. The mechanism is located above the clutch pedal, where the cable and pivot points may be lubricated.

Clutch Cable

REMOVAL & INSTALLATION

1. Disconnect the negative battery cable.

2. Remove the clip from the cable mounting bracket on the shock tower and remove the cable from the bracket.

3. Remove the retainer from the clutch release lever on the transaxle.

4. Pry out the ball end of the cable from the position adjuster inside the pedal.

5. The installation is the reverse of the removal procedure. After installing, push the clutch pedal 2 or 3 times to allow the self-adjuster mechanism to function.

6. Connect the negative battery ca-

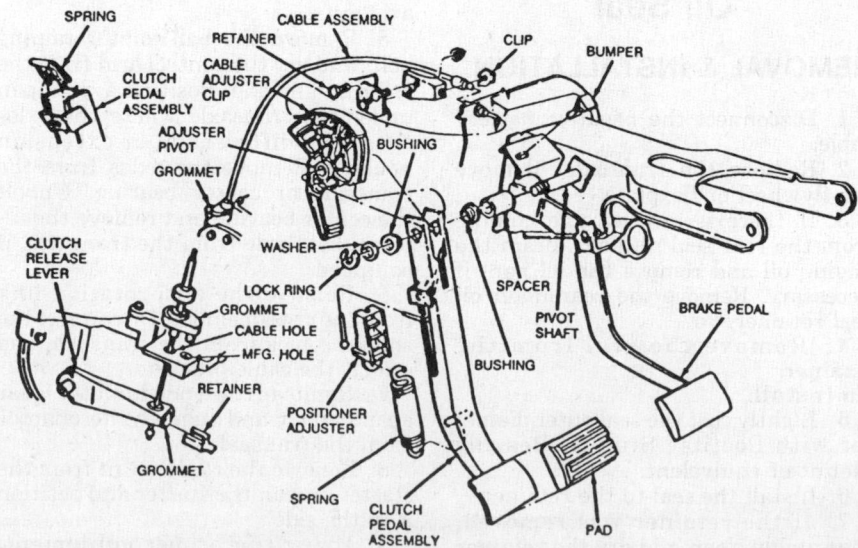

Clutch pedal, cable and related parts

ble and check the clutch for proper operation.

AUTOMATIC TRANSAXLE

For further information on transmissions/transaxles, please refer to "Chilton's Guide to Transmission Repair".

Transaxle Assembly

REMOVAL & INSTALLATION

NOTE: If the vehicle is going to be rolled while the transaxle is out of the vehicle, obtain 2 outer CV-joints to install to the hubs. If the vehicle is rolled without the proper torque applied to the front wheel bearings, the bearings will no longer be usable.

1. Disconnect the negative battery cable. If equipped with 3.0L engine, drain the coolant. Remove the dipstick.
2. Remove the air cleaner assembly if it is preventing access to the upper bell housing bolts. Remove the upper bell housing bolts and water tube, where applicable. Unplug all electrical connectors from the transaxle.
3. If equipped with a 2.2L or 2.5L engine, remove the starter attaching nut and bolt at the top of the bell housing.
4. Raise the vehicle and support safely. Remove the tire and wheel assemblies. Remove the axle end cotter pins, nut locks, spring washers and axle nuts.
5. Remove the ball joint retaining bolts and pry the control arm from the steering knuckle. Position a drainpan under the transaxle where the axles enter the differential or extension housing. Remove the axles from the transaxle or center bearing. Unbolt the center bearing and remove the intermediate axle from the transaxle, if equipped.
6. Drain the transaxle. Disconnect and plug the fluid cooler hoses. Disconnect the shifter and kickdown linkage from the transaxle, if equipped.
7. Remove the speedometer cable adaptor bolt and remove the adaptor from the transaxle.
8. Remove the starter. Remove the torque converter inspection cover, matchmark the torque converter to

the flexplate and remove the torque converter bolts.
9. Using the proper equipment, support the weight of the engine.
10. Remove the front motor mount and bracket.
11. Position a suitable transaxle jack under the transaxle.
12. Remove the lower bell housing bolts.
13. Remove the left side splash shield. Remove the transaxle mount bolts.
14. Carefully pry the transaxle from the engine.
15. Slide the transaxle rearward until dowels disengage from the mating holes in the transaxle case.
16. Pull the transaxle completely away from the engine and remove it from the vehicle.
17. To prepare the vehicle for rolling, support the engine with a suitable support or reinstall the front motor mount to the engine. Then reinstall the ball joints to the steering knuckle and install the retaining bolt. Install the obtained outer CV-joints to the hubs, install the washers and torque the axle nuts to 180 ft. lbs. (244 Nm). The vehicle may now be safely rolled.

To install:
18. Install the transmission securely on the transmission jack. Rotate the converter so it will align with the positioning of the flexplate.
19. Apply a coating of high temperature grease to the torque converter pilot hub.
20. Raise the transaxle into place and push it forward until the dowels engage and the bell housing is flush with the block. Install the transaxle to bell housing bolts.
21. Raise the transaxle and install the left side mount bolts. Install the torque converter bolts and torque to 55 ft. lbs. (74 Nm).
22. Install the front motor mount and bracket. Remove the engine and transaxle support fixtures.
23. Install the starter to the transaxle. Install the bolt finger-tight if equipped with a 2.2L or 2.5L engine.
24. Install a new O-ring to the speedometer cable adaptor and install to the extension housing; make sure it snaps in place. Install the retaining bolt.
25. Connect the shifter and kickdown linkage to the transaxle, if equipped.
26. Install the axles and center bearing, if equipped. Install the ball joints to the steering knuckles. Torque the axle nuts to 180 ft. lbs. (244 Nm) and install new cotter pins. Install the splash shield and install the wheels. Lower the vehicle. Install the dipstick.
27. Install the upper bell housing bolts and water pipe, if removed.

28. If equipped with 2.2L or 2.5L engine, install the starter attaching nut and bolt at the top of the bell housing. Raise the vehicle again and tighten the starter bolt from underneath the vehicle. Lower the vehicle.
29. Connect all electrical wiring to the transaxle.
30. Install the air cleaner assembly, if removed. Fill the transaxle with the proper amount of Mopar ATF Plus Type 7176 or conventional Dexron®II.
31. Connect the negative battery cable and check the transaxle for proper operation.

UPSHIFT AND KICKDOWN LEARNING PROCEDURE

A–604 Ultradrive Transaxle

In 1989, the A–604 4 speed, electronic transaxle was introduced; it is the first to use fully adaptive controls. The controls perform their functions based on real time feedback sensor information. Although, the transaxle is conventional in design, its functions are controlled by the ECM.

Since the A–604 is equipped with a learning function, each time the battery cable is disconnected, the ECM memory is lost. In operation, the transaxle must be shifted many times for the learned memory to be reinputed in the ECM; during this period, the vehicle will experience rough operation. The transaxle must be at normal operating temperature when learning occurs.

1. Maintain constant throttle opening during shifts. Do not move the accelerator pedal during upshifts.
2. Accelerate the vehicle with the throttle ⅛–½ open.
3. Make fifteen to twenty 1/2, 3/4 and 3/4 upshifts. Accelerating from a full stop to 50 mph each time at the aforementioned throttle opening is sufficient.
4. With the vehicle speed below 25 mph, make 5–8 wide open throttle kickdowns to 1st gear from either 2nd or 3rd gear. Allow at least 5 seconds of operation in 2nd or 3rd gear prior to each kickdown.
5. With the vehicle speed greater than 25 mph, make 5 part throttle to wide open throttle kickdowns to either 3rd or 2nd gear from 4th gear. Allow at least 5 seconds of operation in 4th gear, preferably at road load throttle prior to performing the kickdown.

SHIFT LINKAGE ADJUSTMENT

1. Place the shifter in the **P** detent.
2. Loosen the clamp bolt on the gearshift cable bracket.

3. Pull the shift lever all the way to the front detent position and tighten the lock screw.

4. Check for proper neutral safety switch operation.

THROTTLE PRESSURE CABLE ADJUSTMENT

1. Run the engine until it reaches normal operating temperature.

2. Loosen the cable mounting bracket lock screw.

3. Position the bracket so both alignment tabs are touching the transaxle case surface and tighten the lock screws.

4. Release the cross lock on the cable assembly by pulling the cross lock up.

5. To ensure proper adjustment, the cable must be free to slide all the way toward the engine against its stop after the cross lock is released.

6. Move the transaxle throttle control lever fully clockwise and press the cross lock down until it snaps into position.

7. Road test the vehicle and check the shift points.

THROTTLE PRESSURE ROD ADJUSTMENT

1. Run the engine until it reaches normal operating temperature.

2. Loosen the adjustment swivel lock screw.

3. To ensure proper adjustment, the swivel must be free to slide along the flat end of the throttle rod. Disassembly, clean and lubricate as required.

4. Hold the transaxle throttle control lever firmly toward the engine and tighten the swivel screw.

5. Road test the vehicle and check the shift points.

DRIVE AXLE

Halfshaft

REMOVAL & INSTALLATION

1. Disconnect the negative battery cable.

2. Raise the vehicle and support safely.

3. Remove the tire and wheel assembly.

4. Remove the cotter pin from the end of the halfshaft. Remove the nut lock, spring washer, axle nut and washer.

---

5. Remove the ball joint retaining bolt and pry the control arm down to release the ball stud from the steering knuckle.

6. Position a drainpan under the transaxle where the halfshaft enters the differential or extension housing. Remove the halfshaft from the transaxle or center bearing. Unbolt the center bearing from the block and remove the intermediate shaft from the transaxle, if equipped.

To install:

7. Install the halfshaft or intermediate shaft to the transaxle, being careful not to damage the side seals. Make sure the inner joint clicks into pace inside the differential. Install the center bearing retaining bolts, if equipped. Install the outer shaft to the center bearing, if equipped.

8. Pull the front strut out and insert the outer joint into the front hub.

9. If necessary, turn the ball joint stud to position the bolt retaining indent to the inside of the vehicle. Install the ball joint stud into the steering knuckle. Install the retaining bolt and nut.

10. Install the axle nut washer and nut and torque the nut to 180 ft. lbs. (244 Nm). Install the spring washer, nut lock and a new cotter pin.

---

11. Install the tire and wheel assembly.

CV-Boot

REMOVAL & INSTALLATION

NOTE: Use only clamps provided with the replacement package when servicing. Plastic wire ties and other straps will not clamp tightly enough and grease will sling out, causing costly damage to the joint.

Inner Joint

1. Remove the halfshaft from the vehicle.

2. If cutting the boot away, mark and note the boot positioning on the shaft relative to the raised shoulders. Remove the boot clamps to gain access to the tripod retention system.

3. Separate the housing from the tripod according to the following:

NOTE: Always hold the rollers in place when removing the housing from the tripod or the needle bearing may fall out.

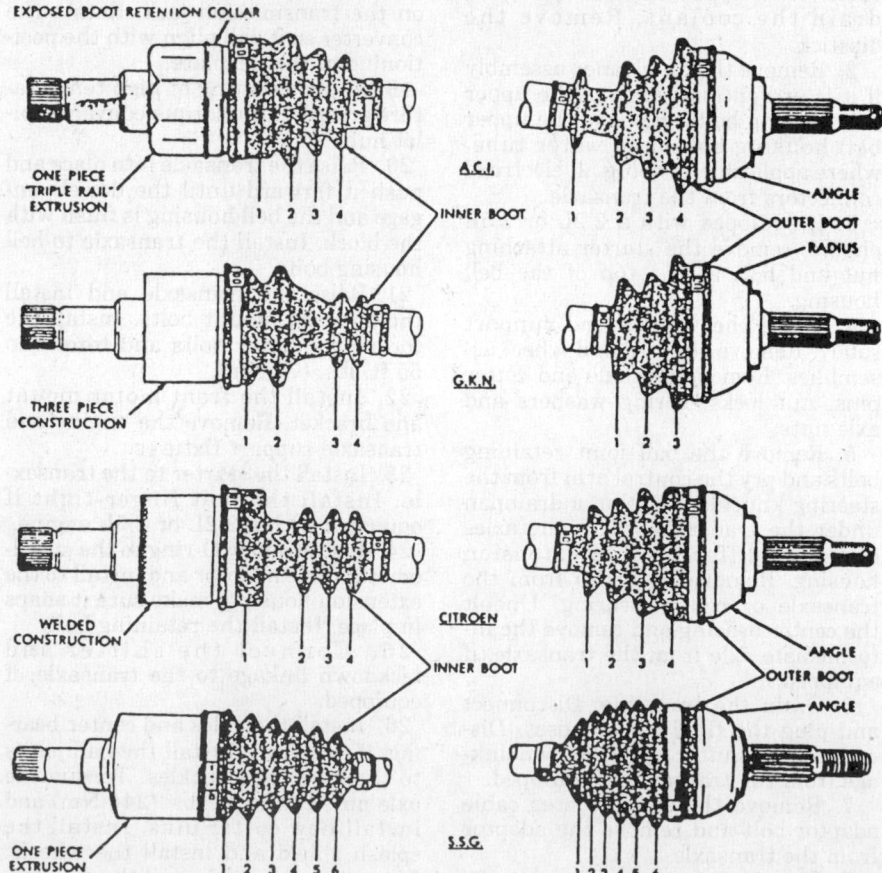

Halfshaft identification. Some S.S.G. inner boots may have 5 raised ridges instead of 6

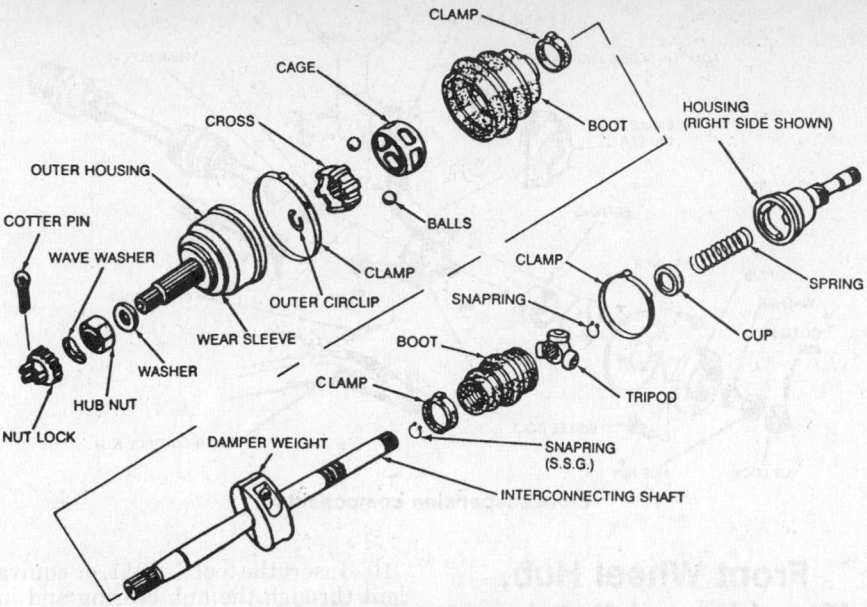

Typical driveshaft components

a. A.C.I.—Has retaining tabs integral with the staked boot retaining collar. Hold the housing and lightly compress the CV-joint retention spring while bending the tabs back. Support the housing as the retention spring pushes it from the housing.

b. G.K.N.—Has retaining tabs integral with the housing cover. Hold the housing and lightly compress the CV-joint retention spring while bending the tabs back. Support the housing as the retention spring pushes it from the housing.

c. Citroen—Uses a tripod retainer ring without tabs which is rolled into a groove in the housing. Slightly deform the retainer ring with a suitable tool in 3 evenly spaced locations. The retention spring will push the housing from the tripod. The retainer ring can also be cut and replaced, although it is acceptable to reshape he ring and reuse it.

d. S.S.G.—Uses a wire ring tripod retainer which expands into a groove around the top of the housing. Use a suitable tool to pry the wire ring, without damaging it, out of the groove and slide the tripod from the housing.

4. Remove the snapring ring from the end of the shaft and remove the tripod.

5. If not already done, mark the boot positioning on the shaft relative to the raised shoulders. Remove the boot from the shaft.

6. Remove as much old grease as possible from the joint. Inspect all parts for wear or damage.

NOTE: Do not use petroleum based solvents on the joints, shaft or boot to clean; it will ruin hidden rubber seals within the joint. Use only chlorine based cleaner or hot soapy water to clean the joint, if necessary. Make sure the joint is completely dry before assembling.

To install:

7. On right inner joint of shafts of turbocharged vehicles, slide a new rubber washer seal over the stub shaft and down into the groove provided.

8. If the clamping device is not a staight strap, install it on the shaft first, then install the boot to the shaft in the proper position. Using the proper tool, C-4975 for crimping with plastic boot, C-4124 for crimping with rubber boot or C-4653 for clamping a strap, secure the clamp.

9. Slide the tripod on the shaft:

a. A.C.I.—Slide the tripod on the shaft with the non-chamfered edge facing the tripod retainer ring groove.

b. G.K.N—Slide the tripod on the shaft with the non-chamfered edge facing the tripod retainer ring groove.

c. Citroen—The tripod may installed either way; both ends are the same.

d. S.S.G.Place the wire ring tripod retainer over the shaft, then slide the tripod. The tripod may installed either way; both ends are the same.

10. Install the snapring into its groove on the shaft to lock the tripod in position.

11. Distribute the grease provided in the grease package as follows, or according to the instructions in the package:

a. A.C.I.—Distribute 1 of the 2 packets of grease into the boot and the remaining packet into the housing.

b. G.K.N—Distribute 2 of the 3 packets of grease into the boot and the remaining packet into the housing.

c. Citroen—Distribute $2/3$ of the packet of grease into the boot and the remaining amount into the housing.

d. S.S.G.—Distribute $1/2$ of the packet of grease into the boot and the remaining amount into the housing.

12. Position the spring in the housing spring pocket with the spring cup attached to the exposed end of the spring. Place a dab of grease on the concave surface of the spring cup.

13. Keeping the spring centered, install the housing to the tripod as follows:

a. A.C.I.—Slip the housing onto the tripod. Do not bend the retaining tabs back into their original position. Instead, secure the boot to hold the housing. The tripod must be reengaged to the housing with the shaft installed on the vehicle.

b. G.K.N—Slip the housing onto the tripod. Bend the retaining tabs back into their original positions. Check for proper retention ability.

c. Citroen—Slip the housing onto the tripod. Reform the retainer ring or install a new one. Stake in place using a punch. Check for proper retention ability.

d. S.S.G.—Slip the housing onto the tripod and install the tripod wire retaining ring. Check for proper retention ability.

14. Position the larger end of the boot over the housing.

15. Using the proper tool, C-4975 for crimping with plastic boot, C-4124 for crimping with rubber boot or C-4653 for clamping a strap, secure the clamp.

16. Install the halfshaft to the vehicle. Fill the transaxle if fluid was lost when removing the halfshaft.

17. Road test the vehicle.

Outer Joint

1. Remove the halfshaft from the vehicle.

2. Mark and note the boot positioning on the shaft, relative to the raised shoulders, if cutting the boot away. Remove the boot clamps to gain access to the joint retention system.

3. Separate the housing from the tripod according to the following:

a. A.C.I.—Using a soft-jaw vise, support the halfshaft. Strike the joint assembly sharply with a soft-face hammer to dislodge the internal circlip and remove from the shaft.

b. G.K.N – Using a soft-jaw vise, support the halfshaft. Strike the joint assembly sharply with a soft-face hammer to dislodge the internal circlip and remove from the shaft.

c. Citroen – Using a soft-jaw vise, support the halfshaft. Strike the joint assembly sharply with a soft-face hammer to dislodge the internal circlip and remove from the shaft.

d. S.S.G. – Loosen the damper weight bolts and slide it and the boot toward the inner joint. Expand the snapring and slide the joint from the shaft. Reinstall the damper weight and torque the bolts to 21 ft. lbs. (28 Nm).

4. If damaged, remove the wear sleeve from the CV-joint machined ledge.

5. Remove the circlip from the groove.

6. If not already done, mark the boot positioning on the shaft relative to the raised shoulders and remove the boot from the shaft.

7. Remove as much old grease as possible from the joint. Inspect all parts for wear or damage.

NOTE: Do not use petroleum based solvents on the joints, shaft or boot to clean; it will ruin hidden rubber seals within the joint. Use only chlorine based cleaner or hot soapy water to clean the joint, if necessary. Make sure the joint it completely dry before assembling.

To install:

8. If the clamping device is not a staight strap, install it on the shaft first, then install the boot to the shaft in the proper position. Using the proper tool, C–4975 for crimping with plastic boot, C–4124 for crimping with rubber boot or C–4653 for clamping a strap, secure the clamp.

9. Install new circlip if provided in the replacement package.

10. Position the outer joint on the shaft with hub nut installed, engage the splines and strike sharply with a soft-face hammer to install. Make sure the circlip did not become dislodged.

11. Position the larger end of the boot over the housing.

12. Using the proper tool C–4975 for crimping with plastic boot, C–4124 for crimping with rubber boot or C–4653 for clamping a strap, secure the clamp.

13. Install the halfshaft to the vehicle. Fill the transaxle if fluid was lost when removing the halfshaft.

14. Road test the vehicle.

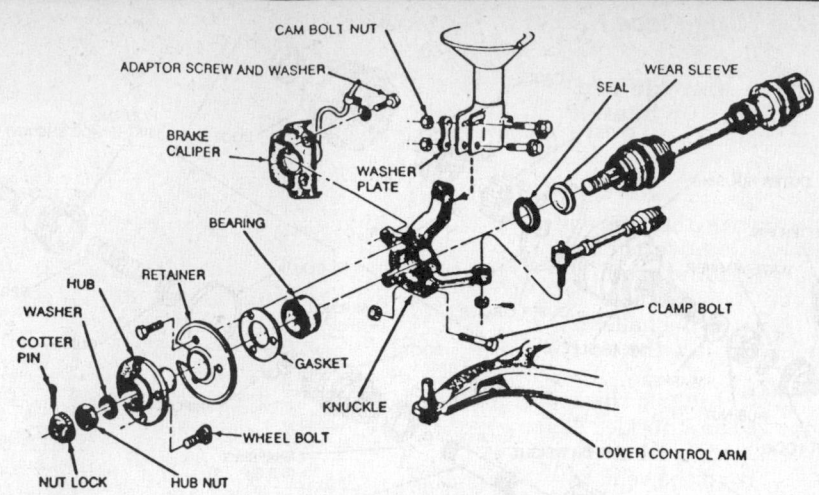

Front suspension components

Front Wheel Hub, Knuckle and Bearings

REMOVAL & INSTALLATION

Pressed in (Two-Piece Hub and Bearing)

NOTE: Some hub and bearing replacement packages include the one-piece unit described below. If this is the case, follow the installation steps for one-piece unit instead of for the two-piece unit described here.

1. Raise the vehicle and support safely.

2. Remove the tire and wheel assembly. Remove the brake caliper from the adaptor and remove the adaptor. Remove the brake disc.

3. Remove the halfshaft.

NOTE: Knuckle removal is not necessary for bearing and hub replacement.

4. Disconnect the tie rod from the knuckle.

5. Matchmark the lower strut mount to the knuckle. Remove the 2 strut clamp bolts and remove the knuckle from the vehicle.

6. Attach the hub removal tool C–4811 or equivalent, and the triangular adapter, to the 3 rear threaded holes of the steering knuckle housing with the thrust button inside the hub bore.

7. Tighten the bolt in the center of the tool, to press the hub from the steering knuckle. Remove the removal tools.

8. Remove the bolts and bearing retainer from the outside of the steering knuckle.

9. Carefully pry the bearing seal from the machined recess of the steering knuckle and clean the recess.

10. Insert the tool C–4811, or equivalent through the hub bearing and install bearing removal adapter to the outside of the steering knuckle. Tighten the tool to press the hub bearing from the steering knuckle. Discard the bearing and the seal.

To install:

11. Use tool C–4811 or equivalent, and the bearing installation adapter to press in the hub bearing into the steering knuckle.

12. Install a new seal, the bearing retainer and the bolts to the steering knuckle. Torque the bearing retainer bolts to 20 ft. lbs.

13. Use the tool C–4811 or equivalent, and the hub installation adapter, to press the hub into the hub bearing.

14. Using the bearing installation tool C–4698 or equivalent, drive the new dust seal into the rear of the steering the hub and bearing from the knuckle as required.

15. The installation of the knuckle and halfshaft is the reverse of the removal procedure. Torque the tie rod nut to 35 ft. lbs. (47 Nm).

16. Align the front end.

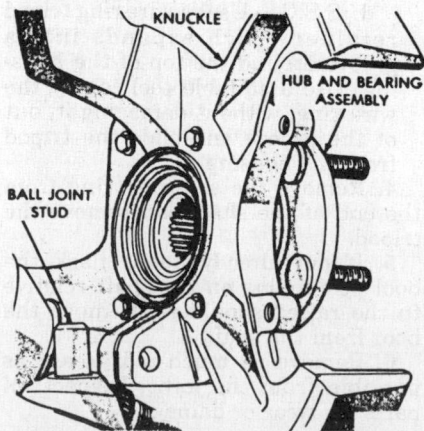

Bolt-in (one-piece) hub and bearing retaining bolts

Bolt In (One-Piece Hub and Bearing)

NOTE: Knuckle removal is not necessary for bearing and hub replacement.

1. Raise the vehicle and support safely.

2. Remove the tire and wheel assembly. Remove the brake caliper from the adaptor and remove the adaptor. Remove the brake disc.

3. Remove the halfshaft.

4. Disconnect the tie rod from the knuckle.

5. Matchmark the lower strut mount to the knuckle. Remove the 2 strut clamp bolts and remove the knuckle from the vehicle.

6. Remove the 4 hub and bearing assembly mounting bolts from the rear of the knuckle and remove the assembly from the knuckle.

7. Carefully pry the bearing seal from the machined recess of the steering knuckle and clean the recess.

8. Thoroughly clean and dry the knuckle and bearing mating surfaces and the seal installation area.

To install:

9. Install the hub and bearing assembly to the knuckle and torque the bolts in a criss-cross pattern to 45 ft. lbs. (65 Nm).

10. Install a new seal and wear sleeve. Lubricate the circumferences of the seal and sleeve liberally with grease.

11. The installation of the knuckle and halfshaft is the reverse of the removal procedure. Torque the tie rod nut to 35 ft. lbs. (47 Nm).

12. Align the front end.

Differential Case

REMOVAL & INSTALLATION

NOTE: The differential case can be removed from some vehicles with the transaxle installed. To do so, remove the halfshafts, remove the 2 K-frame mounting nuts and 2 bolts and lower the K-frame to provide enough room to pull the differential case out of its housing and over the lowered frame.

Individual parts in the TC-equipped Getrag manual transaxle are not serviceable; it must be replaced as an assembly.

1. Disconnect the negative battery cable. Raise the vehicle and support safely.

2. Remove the right side extension housing. Remove the differential cover.

3. Remove the bolts and remove the right side differential bearing retainer using tool L–4435, or equivalent.

4. Remove the differential case from the transaxle.

5. Use new seals and gasket material when assembling.

6. The installation is the reverse of the removal procedure. Torque the extension housing and bearing retainer bolts to 21 ft. lbs. (28 Nm).

7. Fill the transaxle with the proper oil.

STEERING

— CAUTION —

On vehicles equipped with an air bag, the negative battery cable must be disconnected, before working on the system. Failure to do so may result in deployment of the air bag and possible personal injury.

Steering Wheel

REMOVAL & INSTALLATION

Without Airbag

1. Disconnect the negative battery cable.

2. Straighten the steering wheel so the front tires are pointing straight forward.

2. Remove the horn pad.

3. Remove the steering wheel hold-down nut and remove the damper, if equipped. Matchmark the steering wheel to the shaft.

4. Using a suitable steering wheel puller, pull the steering wheel off of the shaft.

5. The installation is the reverse of the removal procedure. Torque the hold-down nut to 45 ft. lbs. (60 nm).

With Airbag

1. Disconnect the negative battery cable.

2. Straighten the steering wheel so the front tires are pointing straight forward.

3. Remove the 4 nuts located on the back side of the steering wheel that attach the airbag module to the steering wheel.

4. Lift the module and disconnect the connectors. Remove the speed control switch, if equipped.

NOTE: All columns except Acustar are equipped with a clock spring set screw held by a plastic tether on the steering wheel. Acustar mounted clock springs are auto-locking. If the steering column is not an Acustar and is

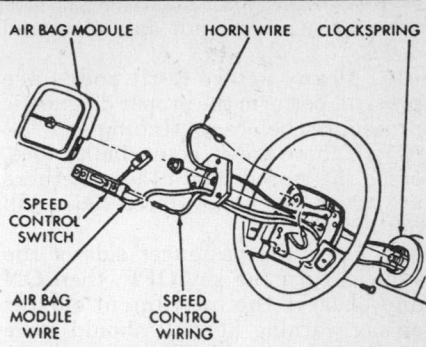

Wiring in a steering wheel with an airbag

lacking the set screw, obtain one before proceeding.

5. If equipped with the set screw, place it in the clock spring to ensure proper positioning when the steering wheel is removed.

6. Remove the steering wheel hold-down nut and remove the damper, if equipped. Matchmark the steering wheel to the shaft.

7. Using a suitable steering wheel puller, pull the steering wheel off of the shaft.

To install:

8. Position the steering wheel on the steering column. Make sure the flats on the hub of the steering wheel are aligned with the formations on the clock spring.

9. Pull the airbag and speed control connectors through the lower, larger hole in the steering wheel and pull the horn wire through the smaller hole at the top. Make sure the wires are not pinched anywhere.

10. Install the damper, if equipped.

11. Install the hold-down nut and torque to 45 ft. lbs. (60 nm).

12. If equipped with a clock spring set screw, remove the screw and place it in its storage location on the steering wheel.

13. Connect the horn wire.

14. Connect the speed control wire and install the speed control switch.

15. Connect the clock spring lead wire to the airbag module and install module to steering wheel.

NOTE: Do not allow anyone to enter the vehicle from this point on, until this procedure is completed.

16. Connect the DRB II to the Airbag System Diagnostic Module (ASDM) connector located to the right of the console.

17. From the passenger side of the vehicle, turn the key to the **ON** position.

18. Check to make sure nobody has entered the vehicle. Connect the negative battery cable.

19. Using the DRB II, read and

record any active fault data or stored codes.

20. If any active fault codes are present, perform the proper diagnostic procedures before continuing.

21. If there are no active fault codes, erase the stored fault codes. (If there are active codes, the stored codes will not erase).

22. From the passenger side of the vehicle, turn the key **OFF**, then **ON** and observe the instrument cluster airbag warning light. It should come on for 6–8 seconds, then go out, indicating the system is functioning normally. If the warning light either fails to come ON or stays lit, there is a system malfunction and the proper diagnostic procedures should be performed.

Steering Column

REMOVAL & INSTALLATION

1. Disconnect the negative battery cable.

2. Remove trim bezel, steering column cover and lower reinforcement, as required.

3. Disconnect all wiring connectors from below the instrument panel that lead up into the steering column.

4. Remove the nuts that attach the steering column assembly to the instrument panel support.

5. Firmly grasp the steering wheel and pull the steering column out, separating the stub shaft from the steering gear coupling.

6. The installation is the reverse of the removal procedure.

7. Connect the negative battery cable and check the steering column and all related components for proper operation.

Manual Rack and Pinion

REMOVAL & INSTALLATION

1. Disconnect the negative battery cable.

2. Raise the vehicle and support safely.

3. Remove front wheel assemblies.

4. Remove the cotter pins, castellated nuts and tie rod ends from the steering knuckles.

5. Remove the front suspension crossmember attaching bolts and nuts.

6. Lower the crossmember.

7. Remove the tie rod inner boot shields.

8. Remove the steering gear bolts from the front suspension crossmember.

9. Remove the steering gear from the left side of the vehicle.

To install:

10. Transfer the required parts to the new rack, if replacing it.

11. Place the rack on the crossmember and torque the steering gear attaching bolts to 21 ft. lbs. (29 Nm). Attach the boot shields.

12. Have a helper inside the vehicle remove the trim boot and align the stub shaft with the coupling while the crossmember is raised into position. If a helper is not available, the steering column will have to be unbolted so the steering shaft can be inserted into the coupling. The right rear crossmember bolt is a pilot bolt that correctly locates the crossmember; tighten it first. Torque the crossmember bolts to 90 ft. lbs.

13. Install the tie rod ends to the steering knuckle and torque the nut to 45 ft. lbs. (61 Nm). Install a new cotter pin.

14. Insert the stub shaft shim where the stub shaft goes into the coupling.

15. Connect the negative battery cable and check the gear for proper operation.

Power Rack and Pinion

REMOVAL & INSTALLATION

1. Disconnect the negative battery cable.

2. Raise the vehicle and support safely.

3. Remove front wheel assemblies.

4. Remove the cotter pins, castellated nuts and tie rod ends from the steering knuckles.

5. If equipped, remove the anti-ro-

tational link from the crossmember. The lower universal joint is removed with the steering gear.

6. Disconnect and plug the oil pressure line from the rack. Disconnect and plug the return hose from the line coming from the rack.

7. Remove the front suspension crossmember attaching bolts and nuts.

8. Lower the crossmember.

9. Remove the tie rod inner boot shields.

10. Remove the steering gear bolts from the front suspension crossmember.

11. Remove the steering gear from the left side of the vehicle.

To install:

12. Transfer the required parts to the new rack, if replacing it.

13. Place the rack on the crossmember and torque the steering gear attaching bolts to 21 ft. lbs. (29 Nm). Attach the fluid lines and the boot shields.

14. Have a helper inside the vehicle remove the trim boot and align the stub shaft with the coupling while the crossmember is raised into position. If a helper is not available, the steering column will have to be unbolted so the steering shaft can be inserted into the coupling. The right rear crossmember bolt is a pilot bolt that correctly locates the crossmember, tighten it first. Torque the crossmember bolts to 90 ft. lbs.

15. Install the anti-rotational link.

16. Install the tie rod ends to the steering knuckle and torque the nut to 45 ft. lbs. (61 Nm). Install a new cotter pin.

17. Insert the stub shaft shim where the stub shaft goes into the coupling.

18. Refill the power steering pump.

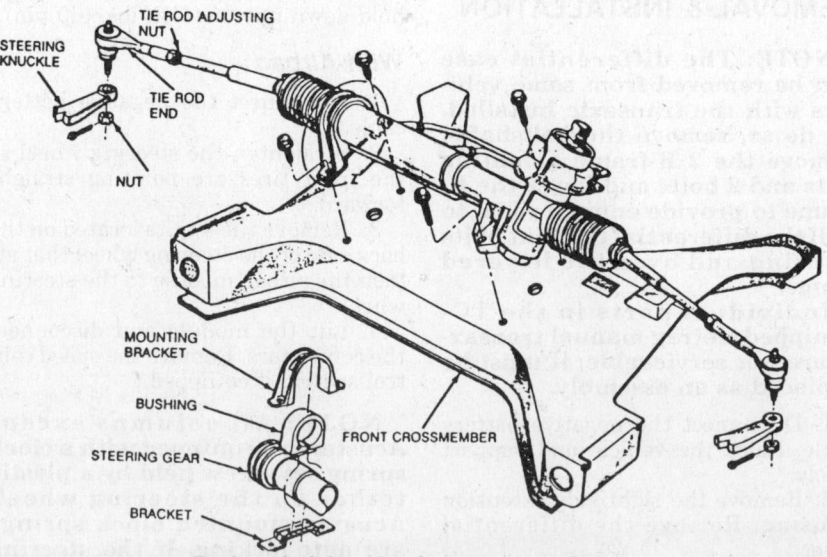

Rack and pinion steering gear mounting

19. Connect the negative battery cable and check the gear for proper operation.

Power Steering Pump

REMOVAL & INSTALLATION

1. Disconnect the negative battery cable.
2. Position a drain pan under the power steering pump.
3. Disconnect the fluid hoses from the pump and plug them.
4. Remove the front bracket attaching bolts and remove the belt from the pulley.
5. Remove the rear pump to bracket nut and remove the pump.
6. Remove the bracket from the pump.
7. Remove the pulley from the pump with the proper puller. Install the pulley on the new pump using the special installation tools.
8. The installation is the reverse of the removal procedure.

BELT ADJUSTMENT

NOTE: The belt tension is automatically adjusted by a dynamic tensioner on the 3.0L engine. Adjustment is not possible.

1. Loosen the bracket mounting bolts.
2. On 1987–89 vehicles, use a ½ in. drive breaker bar in the square hole provided in the bracket to move the pump away from the engine. On 1990–91 vehicles, tighten the adjusting nut until the pump is in the desired position. Do not pry against the fluid reservoir.
3. With the pump moved enough so the belt deflects about ¼–½ in. under a 10 lb. load, tighten the bolts.

SYSTEM BLEEDING

1. Fill the reservoir with power steering fluid.
2. Turn the wheels to the full left turn position and add fluid until the reservoir is full.
3. Start the engine and add fluid to bring the level to the correct level.
4. To purge the system of air, turn the steering wheel from side to side without contacting the stops.
5. Return the wheel to the straight ahead position and operate the engine for 2 minutes before road testing.

Tie Rod Ends

REMOVAL & INSTALLATION

1. Raise the vehicle and support safely.

2. Remove the cotter pin and nut from the tie rod end.
3. Using a suitable puller, remove the tie rod from the steering knuckle.
4. Loosen the sleeve clamp nut and bolt, if equipped, and unscrew the tie rod end from the sleeve or inner tie rod.
5. The installation is the reverse of the removal procedure. Torque the stud nuts to 45 ft. lbs. (61 Nm) and install a new cotter pin.
6. Perform a front end alignment as required.

BRAKES

For all brake system repair and service procedure not detained below, please refer to "Brakes" in the Unit Repair section.

Master Cylinder

REMOVAL & INSTALLATION

Except Anti-lock Brakes

1. Disconnect the negative battery cable.
2. Disconnect and plug the brake lines from the master cylinder.
3. Remove the nuts attaching the master cylinder to the power booster.
4. Remove the master cylinder from the mounting studs.
5. Remove the fluid reservoir from the cylinder.
To install:
6. Bench bleed the master cylinder.
7. Install to the studs and install the nuts.
8. Install the brake lines to the master cylinder.
9. Connect the negative battery cable and check the brakes for proper operation.

Combination Valve

REMOVAL & INSTALLATION

1. Disconnect the negative battery cable.
2. Raise the vehicle and support safely.
3. Tag and disconnect the brake lines from the valve.
4. Disconnect the wires to the pressure switch.
5. Remove the combination valve from the frame bracket.
6. The installation is the reverse of the removal procedure.
7. Bleed the brakes in the following order:

   a. Right rear wheel cylinder or caliper
   b. Left rear wheel cylinder or caliper
   c. Right front caliper
   d. Left front caliper
8. Connect the negative battery cable and check the brakes for proper operation.

Power Brake Booster

REMOVAL & INSTALLATION

1. Disconnect the negative battery cable. Disconnect the vacuum hose(s) from the booster.
2. Remove the nuts attaching the master cylinder to the booster and move the master cylinder to the side.
3. From inside of the vehicle, remove the clip that secures the booster pushrod to the brake pedal.
4. Remove the nuts that attach the booster to the dash panel and remove it from the vehicle.
5. Transfer the check valve to the new booster.
6. The installation is the reverse of the removal procedure.
7. Connect the negative battery cable and check the brakes for proper operation.

Brake Caliper

REMOVAL & INSTALLATION

Except Rear Disc Brakes—1988 Daytona and Anti-lock Brakes

1. Raise the vehicle and support safely.
2. Remove the tire and wheel assembly.
3. Remove the caliper mounting pin(s).
4. Lift the caliper off of the rotor. Remove the outer pad from the caliper.
5. Remove the brake hose retaining bolt from the caliper.
To install:
6. Install the brake hose to the caliper using new copper washers.
7. Position the caliper over the rotor so the caliper engages the adaptor correctly. Install the mounting pin(s). Install the hold-down spring, if equipped.
8. Fill the master cylinder and bleed the brakes.

1988 Daytona

1. Remove ⅔ of brake fluid from the master cylinder.
2. Remove access plug and insert a 4mm Allen wrench through hole.
3. Turn the retraction shaft coun-

terclockwise a few turns to increase clearance between pads and rotor.

4. Remove the anti-rattle spring from outboard pad taking care not to damage it.

5. Back the caliper guide pins out just enough to free caliper from adapter.

6. Lift the caliper off of rotor and carefully suspend with wire.

7. Remove the brake pads.

8. Insert the Allen wrench through access hole and turn clockwise, if necessary, to retract piston further to increase clearance.

To install:

9. Lower the caliper over rotor and pads.

10. Install the guide pins and tighten to proper torque.

11. Insert the Allen wrench through the access hole and turn clockwise until snug, no clearance between pads and rotors, and back off ⅓ turn to obtain proper clearance.

12. Check the brake fluid level and add if necessary.

Disc Brake Pads

REMOVAL & INSTALLATION

Except Rear Disc Brakes, 1988 Daytona and Anti-lock Brakes

1. Remove some of the fluid from the master cylinder.

2. Raise the vehicle and support safely. Remove the tire and wheel assemblies.

3. Remove the hold-down spring if necessary. Remove the caliper and remove the outer pad from the caliper.

4. Remove the inner pad from the adaptor.

To install:

5. Use a large C-clamp to compress the piston back into the caliper bore.

6. Install the inner pad to the adaptor.

7. Position the caliper over the rotor so the caliper engages the adaptor correctly and install the retainer pin(s).

8. Install the hold-down spring, if removed.

9. Refill the master cylinder.

1988 DAYTONA

1. Remove ⅔ of brake fluid from the master cylinder.

2. Remove access plug and insert a 4mm Allen wrench through hole.

3. Turn the retraction shaft counterclockwise a few turns to increase clearance between pads and rotor.

4. Remove the anti-rattle spring from outboard pad taking care not to damage it.

5. Back the caliper guide pins out

just enough to free caliper from adapter.

6. Lift the caliper off of rotor and carefully suspend with wire.

7. Remove the brake pads.

8. Insert the Allen wrench through access hole and turn clockwise, if necessary, to retract piston further to increase clearance for new pads.

To install:

9. Install new inner and outer pads.

NOTE: The outboard pads are marked for right and left hand sides and must be properly installed.

10. Lower the caliper over rotor and pads.

11. Install the guide pins and tighten to proper torque.

12. Insert the Allen wrench through the access hole and turn clockwise until snug, no clearance between pads and rotors, and back off ⅓ turn to obtain proper clearance.

13. Check the brake fluid level and add, if necessary.

Brake Rotor

REMOVAL & INSTALLATION

1. Raise the vehicle and support safely. Remove the tire and wheel assembly.

2. Remove the caliper and brake pads.

3. Remove the factory installed clips, if equipped. It is not necessary to reinstall these clips.

4. Remove the rotor from the hub.

5. The installation is the reverse of the removal procedure.

Brake Drum

REMOVAL & INSTALLATION

1. Raise the vehicle and support safely.

2. Remove the wheel and tire assembly.

3. Remove the dust cap.

4. Remove the cotter pin and nut lock.

5. Remove the wheel bearing nut and washer from the spindle.

6. Remove the outer wheel bearing.

7. Remove the drum with the inner wheel bearing from the spindle. If the drum is difficult to remove, remove the plug from the rear of the backing plate and push the self adjuster lever away from the star wheel. Rotate the star wheel to retract the shoes. Remove the grease seal.

To install:

8. Lubricate and install the inner wheel bearing. Install a new grease seal.

9. Install the drum to the spindle.

10. Lubricate and install the outer wheel bearing, washer and nut. When the bearing preload is properly set, install the nut lock and a new cotter pin.

11. Install the grease cap.

12. Install the wheel and tire assembly. Adjust the rear brakes as required.

Brake Shoes

REMOVAL & INSTALLATION

1. Raise the vehicle and support safely. Remove the wheel and tire assemblies and the drums.

2. Remove the automatic adjuster spring and lever.

3. Rotate the automatic adjuster star wheel enough so both shoes move out far enough to be free of the wheel cylinder boots.

4. Disconnect the parking brake cable from the actuating lever.

5. Remove the lower shoe to shoe or shoe to anchor spring(s).

6. With the shoes held together by the upper shoe to shoe spring, remove them from the backing plate.

To install:

7. Thoroughly clean and dry the backing plate. To prepare the backing plate, lubricate the bosses, anchor pin and parking brake actuating lever pivot surface lightly with lithium based grease.

8. Remove, clean and dry all parts still on the old shoes. Lubricate the star wheel shaft threads with antisieze lubricant and transfer all parts to their proper locations on the new shoes.

9. Install the lower spring(s).

10. Connect the parking brake cable.

11. Install the automatic adjuster lever and spring.

12. Adjust the star wheel.

13. Remove any grease from the linings and install the drum.

14. Complete the brake adjustment with the wheels installed.

Wheel Cylinder

REMOVAL & INSTALLATION

1. Raise the vehicle and support safely.

2. Remove the wheel, drum and brake shoes.

3. Remove and plug the brake line from the wheel cylinder.

4. Remove the wheel cylinder bolts and remove the cylinder from the backing plate.

To install:

5. Apply a very thin coating of silicone sealer to the cylinder mounting

surface, install the cylinder to the backing plate and install the retaining bolts.

6. Connect the brake line to the wheel cylinder.

7. Install all brake parts that were removed.

8. Install the tire and wheel assembly.

9. Bleed the brakes.

Parking Brake Cable

ADJUSTMENT

Except 1990–91 Daytona and LeBaron

1. Release the parking brakes fully.

2. Raise the vehicle and support safely.

3. Adjust the rear brakes.

4. Loosen the adjusting nut until there is slack in all the cables.

5. Rotate the rear wheels and tighten the cable adjusting nut until there is a slight drag at the wheels.

6. Continue to rotate the rear wheels and loosen the nut until all drag is eliminated.

7. Back off the nut an additional 2 turns.

8. Apply and release the parking brake several times. Upon the least release, verify there is no drag at the wheels.

9. To check the operation, make sure the parking brake holds on an incline.

1990–91 Daytona and LeBaron

The parking brake hand lever contains a self-adjusting loaded clockspring feature. Routine parking brake adjustment is not required.

REMOVAL & INSTALLATION

Front Cable

EXCEPT 1990–91 DAYTONA AND LEBARON

1. Disconnect the negative battery cable.

2. Loosen the adjusting nut and disengage the front cable from the equalizer bracket.

4. Lift the carpet and floor matting and remove the floor pan seal.

5. Pull the cable end forward and disconnect from the clevis.

6. Pull the cable through the hole and remove.

7. The installation is the reverse of the removal procedure.

8. Connect the negative battery cable and check the parking brakes for proper operation.

1990–91 DAYTONA AND LEBARON

— CAUTION —

The parking brake hand lever contains a self-adjusting loaded clockspring loaded to about 30 lbs. Care must be taken when handling components in the vicinity of the hand lever or serious personal injury may result.

1. Disconnect the negative battery cable.

2. Disengage the cable from the equalizer bracket in the console.

4. Lift the carpet and floor matting and remove the floor pan seal.

5. Separate the cable from the rear parking brake shoes lever.

6. Pull the cable through the hole and remove.

To install:

7. Install the cable and connect to the rear shoes and equalizer bracket. Install the floor pan seal and position the carpet.

8. To reload, lockout and adjust the system:

   a. Pull on the equalizer output cable with at least 30 lbs. pressure to wind up the spring. Continue until the self-adjuster lockout pawl is positioned about midway between the self-adjuster sector.

   b. Rotate the lockout pawl into the self-adjuster sector by turning the Allen screw clockwise. This action requires very little effort; do not force the screw.

   c. Adjust the rear drum-in-hat parking brake shoes.

   d. Turn the Allen screw counterclockwise about 15°. When turning the lockout device, self-adjuster release is a snapping noise followed by a detent that should be felt. Very light effort is required to seat the lockout device into the detent. Make sure to follow through into the detent.

   e. Cycle the lever a few times to complete the adjustment. Thwe wheels should rotate freely.

9. Connect the negative battery cable and check the parking brakes for proper operation.

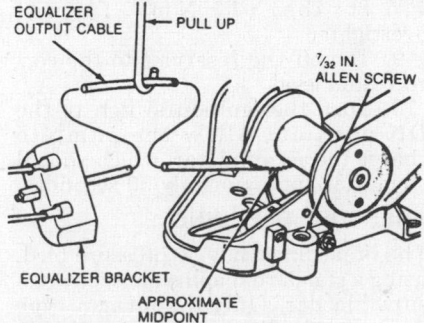

Self-adjusting parking brake lever assembly—1990–91 Daytona and LeBaron

Rear Parking Brake Cable

EXCEPT TC

1. Disconnect the negative battery cable. Loosen the adjusting nut.

2. Raise the vehicle and support safely. Remove the wheels and drums. Disconnect the cable from the actuating lever on the rear brake shoe assembly.

3. Remove the retaining clip from the cable at the support bracket and pull the cable from the trailing arm assembly.

4. The installation is the reverse of the removal procedure.

5. Connect the negative battery cable and check the parking brakes for proper operation.

TC

1. Raise the vehicle and support safely. Remove the wheels.

2. Loosen the adjusting nut and disconnect the rear cable from the connector.

3. Remove the brake cable retaining clips from the hanger bracket and caliper.

4. Disconnect the cable from the parking brake lever on the caliper. Remove the cable guide from the trailing arm.

5. Pull the cable assembly from the hanger bracket.

6. The installation is the reverse of the removal procedure.

7. Connect the negative battery cable and check the parking brakes for proper operation.

Brake System Bleeding

Except Anti-lock Brakes

NOTE: If using a pressure bleeder, follow the instructions furnished with the unit and choose the correct adaptor for the application. Do not substitute an adapter that "almost fits" as it will not work and could be dangerous.

MASTER CYLINDER

If the master cylinder is off the vehicle it can be bench bled.

1. Connect 2 short pieces of brake line to the outlet fittings, bend them until the free end is below the fluid level in the master cylinder reservoirs.

2. Fill the reservoir with fresh brake fluid. Pump the piston slowly until no more air bubbles appear in the reservoirs.

3. Disconnect the 2 short lines, refill the master cylinder and securely install the cylinder caps.

4. If the master cylinder is on the

vehicle, it can still be bled, using a flare nut wrench.

5. Open the brake lines slightly with the flare nut wrench while pressure is applied to the brake pedal by a helper inside the vehicle.

6. Be sure to tighten the line before the brake pedal is released.

7. Repeat the process with both lines until no air bubbles come out.

CALIPERS AND WHEEL CYLINDERS

1. Fill the master cylinder with fresh brake fluid. Check the level often during the procedure.

2. Starting with the right rear wheel, remove the protective cap from the bleeder, if equipped, and place where it will not be lost. Clean the bleed screw.

—— CAUTION ——
When bleeding the brakes, keep face away from the brake area. Spewing fluid may cause facial and/or visual damage. Do not allow brake fluid to spill on the car's finish; it will remove the paint.

3. If the system is empty, the most efficient way to get fluid down to the wheel is to loosen the bleeder about ½-¾ turn, place a finger firmly over the bleeder and have a helper pump the brakes slowly until fluid comes out the bleeder. Once fluid is at the bleeder, close it before the pedal is released inside the vehicle.

NOTE: If the pedal is pumped rapidly, the fluid will churn and create small air bubbles, which are almost impossible to remove from the system. These air bubbles will eventually congregate and a spongy pedal will result.

4. Once fluid has been pumped to the caliper or wheel cylinder, open the bleed screw again, have the helper press the brake pedal to the floor, lock the bleeder and have the helper slowly release the pedal. Wait 15 seconds and repeat the procedure (including the 15 second wait) until no more air comes out of the bleeder upon application of the brake pedal. Remember to close the bleeder before the pedal is released inside the vehicle each time the bleeder is opened. If not, air will be induced into the system.

5. If a helper is not available, connect a small hose to the bleeder, place the end in a container of brake fluid and proceed to pump the pedal from inside the vehicle until no more air comes out the bleeder. The hose will prevent air from entering the system.

6. Repeat the procedure on remaining wheel cylinders in order:
   a. left rear
   b. right front
   c. left front

7. Hydraulic brake systems must be totally flushed if the fluid becomes contaminated with water, dirt or other corrosive chemicals. To flush, bleed the entire system until all fluid has been replaced with the correct type of new fluid.

8. Install the bleeder cap(s), if equipped, on the bleeder to keep dirt out. Always road test the vehicle after brake work of any kind is done.

Anti-lock Brakes
BOOSTER BLEEDING

1. Depressurize the hydraulic accumulator.

2. Connect all pump/motor and hydraulic assembly electrical connections, if previously disconnected. Be sure that all brake lines and hose connections are tight.

3. Fill the reservoir to the full level.

4. Connect a transparent hose to the bleeder screw location on the right side of the hydraulic assembly. Place the other end of the hose into a clear container to receive brake fluid.

5. Open the bleeder screw ½-¾ of a turn.

6. Turn the ignition switch to the **ON** position. The pump/motor should run, discharging fluid into the container. After a good volume of fluid has been forced through the hose, an air-free flow in the plastic hose and container will indicate a good bleed.

7. Turn the ignition switch **OFF**.

NOTE: If the brake fluid does not flow, it may be due to a lack of prime to the pump/motor. Try shaking the return hose to break up air bubbles that may be present within the hose.

Should the brake fluid still not flow, turn the ignition switch OFF. Remove the return hose from the reservoir and cap nipple on the reservoir. Manually fill the return hose with brake fluid and connect to the reservoir. Repeat the bleeding process.

8. Remove the hose from the bleeder screw. Tighten the bleeder screw to 7.5 ft. lbs. (10 Nm). Do not overtighten.

9. Top off the reservoir to the correct fluid level.

10. Turn the ignition switch to the **ON** position. Allow the pump to charge the accumulator, which should stop after approximately 30 seconds.

PRESSURE BLEEDING

The brake lines may be pressure bled, using a standard diaphragm type pressure bleeder. Only diaphragm type pressure bleeding equipment should be used to bleed the system.

1. The ignition should be turned

OFF and remain **OFF** throughout this procedure.

2. Depressurize the hydraulic accumulator.

—— CAUTION ——
Failure to depressurize the hydraulic accumulator, prior to performing this operation may result in personal injury and/or damage to the painted surfaces.

3. Remove the electrical connector from fluid level sensor on the reservoir cap and remove the reservoir cap.

4. Install the pressure bleeder adapter.

5. Attach the bleeding equipment to the bleeder adapter. Charge the pressure bleeder to approximately 20 psi (138 kPa).

6. Connect a transparent hose to the caliper bleed screw. Submerge the free end of the hose in a clear glass container, which is partially filled with clean, fresh brake fluid.

7. With the pressure turned **ON**, open the caliper bleed screw ½–¾ turn and allow fluid to flow into the container. Leave the bleed screw open until clear, bubble-free fluid slows from the hose. If the reservoir has been drained or the hydraulic assembly removed from the car prior to the bleeding operation, slowly pump the brake pedal 1–2 times while the bleed screw is open and fluid is flowing. This will help purge air from the hydraulic assembly. Tighten the bleeder screw to 7.5 ft. lbs. (10 N).

8. Repeat Step 7 at all calipers. Calipers should be bled in the following order:
   a. Left rear
   b. Right rear
   c. Left front
   d. Right front

9. After bleeding all 4 calipers, remove the pressure bleeding equipment and bleeder adapter by closing the pressure bleeder valve and slowly unscrewing the bleeder adapter from the hydraulic assembly reservoir. Failure to release pressure in the reservoir will cause spillage of brake fluid and could result in injury or damage to painted surfaces.

10. Using a syringe or equivalent method, remove excess fluid from the reservoir to bring the fluid level to full level.

11. Install the reservoir cap and connect the fluid level sensor connector. Turn the ignition **ON** and allow the pump to charge the accumulator.

MANUAL BLEEDING

1. Depressurize the hydraulic accumulator.

—— CAUTION ——
Failure to depressurize the hydraulic accu-

mulator, prior to performing this operation may result in personal injury and/or damage to the painted surfaces.

2. Connect a transparent hose to the caliper bleed screw. Submerge the free end of the hose in a clear glass container, which is partially filled with clean, fresh brake fluid.

3. Slowly pump the brake pedal several times, using full strokes of the pedal and allowing approximately 5 seconds between pedal strokes. After 2–3 strokes, continue to hold pressure on the pedal, keeping it at the bottom of its travel.

4. With pressure on the pedal, open the bleed screw ½–¾ turn. Leave bleed screw open until fluid no longer flows from the hose. Tighten the bleed screw and release the pedal.

5. Repeat this procedure until clear, bubble-free fluid flows from the hose.

6. Repeat all steps at each of the calipers. Calipers should be bled in the following order:
   a. Left rear
   b. Right rear
   c. Left front
   d. Right front

Anti-Lock Brake System Service

PRECAUTIONS

Failure to observe the following precautions may result in system damage.
- Before performing electric arc welding on the vehicle, disconnect the Electronic Brake Control Module (EBCM) and the hydraulic modulator connectors.
- When performing painting work on the vehicle, do not expose the Electronic Brake Control Module (EBCM) to temperatures in excess of 185°F (85°C) for longer than 2 hrs. The system may be exposed to temperatures up to 200°F (95°C) for less than 15 min.
- Never disconnect or connect the Electronic Brake Control Module (EBCM) or hydraulic modulator connectors with the ignition switch ON.
- Never disassemble any component of the Anti-Lock Brake System (ABS) which is designated non-servicable; the component must be replaced as an assembly.
- When filling the master cylinder, always use brake fluid which meets DOT-3 specifications; petroleum base fluid will destroy the rubber parts.

DEPRESSURIZING THE HYDRAULIC ACCUMULATOR

1. With the ignition **OFF**, pump the brake pedal a minimum of 25 times, using approximately 50 lbs. (222 N) pedal force. A noticeable change in pedal feel will occur when the accumulator is discharged.

2. When a definite increase in pedal effort is felt, stroke the pedal a few additional times. This should remove all hydraulic pressure from the system.

Rear Disc Brake Caliper and Pads

REMOVAL & INSTALLATION

1. Depressurize the hydraulic accumulator. Remove ⅔ of brake fluid from the master cylinder.

2. Remove access plug and insert a 4mm Allen wrench through hole.

3. Turn the retraction shaft counterclockwise a few turns ro increase clearance between pads and rotor.

4. Remove the anti–rattle spring from outboard pad taking care not to damage it.

5. Back the caliper guide pins out just enough to free caliper from adapter.

6. Lift the caliper off of rotor and carefully suspend with wire.

7. Remove the brake pads.

8. Insert the Allen wrench through access hole and turn clockwise, if necessary to retract piston further to increase clearance for new pads.

To install:

9. Install new inner and outer pads.

NOTE: The outboard pads are marked for right and left hand sides and must be properly installed.

10. Lower the caliper over rotor and pads.

11. Install the guide pins and tighten to proper torque.

12. Insert the Allen wrench through the access hole and turn clockwise until snug, no clearance between pads and rotors, and back off ⅓ turn to obtain proper clearance.

13. Check the brake fluid level and add if necessary.

Pump/Motor Assembly

REMOVAL & INSTALLATION

1. Depressurize the hydraulic accumulator.

—————— **CAUTION** ——————

Failure to depressurize the hydraulic accumulator, prior to performing this operation may result in personal injury and/or damage to the painted surfaces.

2. Remove the fresh air intake ducts.

3. Disconnect all electrical connectors the pump motor.

4. Disconnect the high and low pressure hoses from the hydraulic assembly. Cap the spigot on the reservoir.

5. Disconnect the transmission shift selection cable bracket from the transaxle and move it aside.

6. Loosen the nuts on the 2 studs that position the pump/motor to the transaxle differential cover.

7. Remove the retainer bolts that are used to mount hose bracket and pump/motor. The engine inlet water extension pipe is also held in position by these bolts.

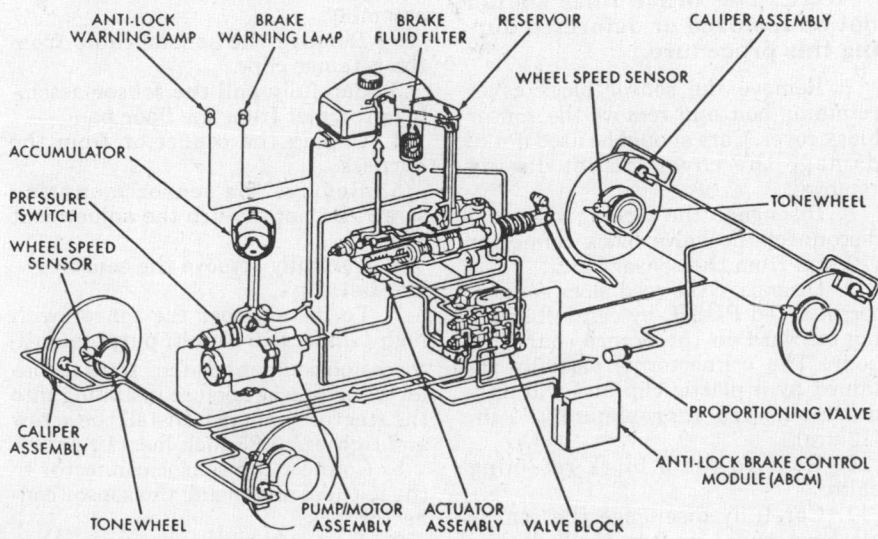

Anti-lock brake system components—TC

NOTE: Do not disturb the inlet water extension pipe, or engine coolant will leak out.

8. Disconnect the wiring harness retaining clip from the hose bracket.

9. Lift the pump/motor assembly off the studs and out of the vehicle.

10. Remove the heat shield from the pump/motor, if equipped, and discard.
To install:

11. Place a new heat shield to the pump/motor bracket, using fasteners provided.

12. Install the pump/motor assembly in the reverse order of the removal.

13. Readjust the gearshift linkage, if disturbed.

Hydraulic Assembly

REMOVAL & INSTALLATION

1. Depressurize the hydraulic accumulator.

------- CAUTION -------
Failure to depressurize the hydraulic accumulator, prior to performing this operation may result in personal injury and/or damage to the painted surfaces.

2. Remove the fresh air intake ducts.

3. Disconnect all electrical connectors from the hydraulic unit and pump/motor.

4. Remove as much of the fluid as possible from the reservoir on the hydraulic assembly.

5. Remove the pressure hose fitting (banjo bolt) from the hydraulic assembly. Use care not to drop the two washers used to seal the pressure hose fitting to the hydraulic assembly inlet.

6. Disconnect the return hose from the reservoir nipple. Cap the spigot on the reservoir.

7. Disconnect all brake tubes from the hydraulic assembly.

8. Remove the driver's side sound insulation panel.

9. Disconnect the pushrod from the brake pedal.

10. Remove the 4 underdash hydraulic assembly mounting nuts.

11. Remove the hydraulic assembly.
To install:

12. Position the hydraulic assembly on the vehicle.

13. Install and torque the mounting nuts to 21 ft. lbs. (28 Nm).

14. Using lubriplate or equivalent, coat the bearing surface of the pedal pin.

15. Connect the pushrod to the pedal and install a new retainer clip.

16. Install the brake tubes. If the proportioning valves were removed from the hydraulic assembly, reinstall

valves and tighten to 20 ft. lbs. (27 Nm).

17. Install the return hose to the nipple on the reservoir.

18. Install the pressure hose to the hydraulic assembly; be sure the 2 washers are in there proper position. Tighten the bango bolt to 13 ft. lbs. (18 Nm).

19. Fill the reservoir to the top of the screen.

20. Connect all electrical connectors to the hydraulic assembly.

21. Bleed the entire brake system.

22. Install the crosscar brace, if disturbed. Install the fresh air intake duct.

Sensor Block

REMOVAL & INSTALLATION

1. Depressurize the hydraulic accumulator.

------- CAUTION -------
Failure to depressurize the hydraulic accumulator, prior to performing this operation may result in personal injury and/or damage to the painted surfaces.

2. Disconnect all electrical connectors from the reservoir on the hydraulic assembly.

3. Working from under the dash, disconnect the pushrod from the brake pedal.

4. Remove the driver's side sound insulator panel.

5. Remove the 4 hydraulic assembly mounting nuts.

6. Working from under the hood, pull the hydraulic assembly away from the dash panel and rotate the assembly enough to gain access to the sensor block cover.

NOTE: The brake lines should not be removed or deformed during this procedure.

7. Remove the sensor block cover retaining bolt and remove the sensor block cover. Care should be used not to damage the cover gasket during removal.

8. Disengage the locking tabs and disconnect the valve block connector (12 pin) from the sensor block.

9. Disengage the reed block connector, marked PUSH, by carefully pulling outward on the orange connector body. The connector is partially retained by a plastic clip and will only move outward approximately ½ in. (13mm).

10. Remove the 3 block retaining bolts.

11. Carefully disengage the sensor block pressure port from the hydraulic assembly and remove the sensor block

from the vehicle. The sensor block pressure port is sealed with an O-ring and extra care should be taken to prevent damage to the seal.

12. Inspect the sensor block pressure port O-ring for damage. Replace the O-ring if cut or damaged. Check the sensor block wiring for any mispositioning or damage. Correct any damage or replace the sensor block if damage cannot be corrected.
To install:

13. Pull the reed block connector (2 pin) outward to the disengage position prior to installing the sensor block on the hydraulic unit.

14. Throughly lubricate the sensor block pressure port O-ring with fresh, clean brake fluid. Carefully insert the pressure port into the hydraulic assembly's orifice, taking care not to cut or damage the O-ring. Position the sensor block for installation of the mounting bolts.

15. Install the sensor block mounting bolts. Tighten to 11 ft. lbs. (15 Nm).

16. Engage the reed block connector by pressing on the orange connector body marked PUSH.

17. Connect the valve block connector (12 pin) to the sensor block.

18. Install the sensor block cover, gasket and mounting bolt.

19. Connect the sensor block and control pressure switch connectors.

20. Install the hydraulic assembly by reversing the removal procedure.

Speed Sensors

REMOVAL & INSTALLATION

1. Raise the vehicle and support safely. Remove the wheel and tire assembly.

2. Remove the sensor cable from the retainer clips.

3. Carefully pull the sensor assembly grommet from the floor pan.

4. Unplug the connector from the harness.

5. Remove the sensor mounting screw. Do not disturb the adjustment screw.

6. Carefully remove the sensor.
To install:

7. To install, coat the sensor with high temperature multi-purpose anti-corrosion compound at all areas it contacts the bracket before installing into the steering knuckle. Install the screw and tighten to 85 inch lbs. (10 Nm).

8. Connect the sensor connector to the harness and install the sensor connector lock.

9. Install the sensor assembly grommet.

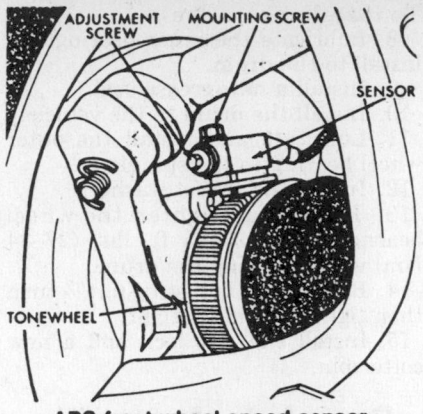

ABS front wheel speed sensor

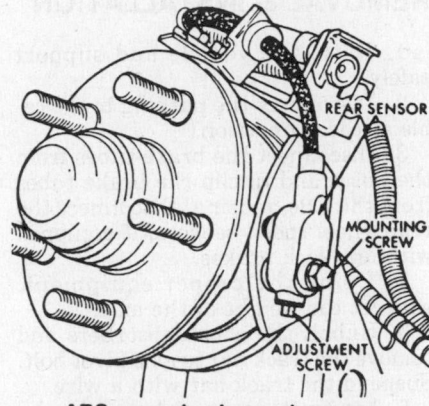

ABS rear wheel speed sensor

NOTE: Proper installation of the wheel speed sensor cables is critical to continued system operation. Be sure the cables are installed in retainers. Failure to install the cables in the retainers may result in contact with moving parts and/or over-extension of the cables, resulting in an open circuit.

FRONT SUSPENSION

MacPherson Strut

REMOVAL & INSTALLATION

1. Remove the 3 mounting nuts from the shock tower under the hood.
2. Raise the vehicle and support safely.
3. Remove the brake hose bracket screw from the strut.
4. Matchmark the lower strut mount to the knuckle and remove the strut to knuckle bolts, nuts and nut plate.

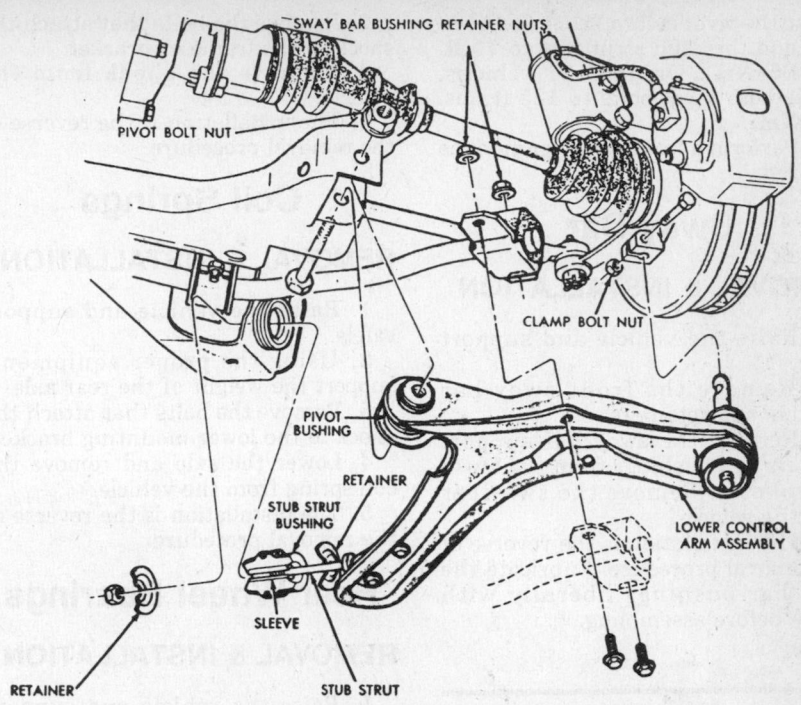

Lower control arm and related parts—1987–88 vehicles and TC

5. The installation is the reverse of the removal procedure. Torque the upper mounting nuts to 20 ft. lbs. (27 Nm). Do not tighten the lower mounting bolts until the front end alignment has been completed.
6. Perform a front end alignment. Torque the strut to knuckle nuts to 75 ft. lbs. (100 Nm) plus ¼ turn.

Lower Ball Joints

INSPECTION

To inspect the ball joints, grasp the grease fitting by hand with the vehicle on the ground. If the grease fitting can be moved at all by hand, the ball joint should be replaced.

REMOVAL & INSTALLATION

The ball joints are welded to the lower control arms. This necessitates replacement of the control arm assembly. Do not attempt to replace ball joints that are welded to the control arm; replacement control arms are equipped with a new ball joint.

Lower Control Arms

REMOVAL & INSTALLATION

1. Raise the vehicle and support safely. Remove the tire and wheel assembly.
2. Remove the sway bar.

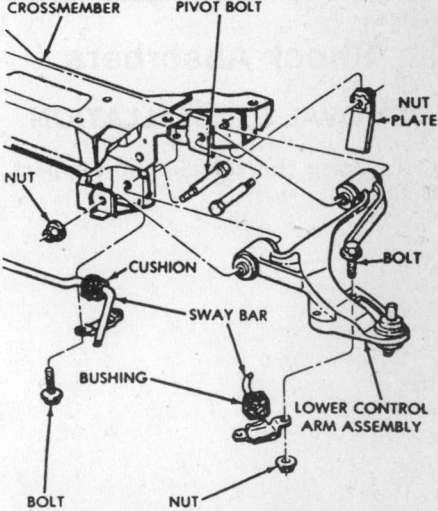

Lower control arm and related parts— 1989–91 vehicles, except TC

3. Remove the ball joint stud retaining bolt and nut.
4. Pry the lower control arm from the steering knuckle.
5. Remove the control arm to crossmember bolts, nuts bushings and retainers.
6. Remove the control arm from the vehicle.
7. Transfer all reusable parts to the new control arm and lubricate.
8. The installation is the reverse of the removal procedure.
9. Lower the vhicle so the full weight of the vehicle is on the ground.
10. On 1987–88 vehicles and TC,

torque the pivot bolt to 120 ft. lbs. (163 Nm) and the stub strut nut to 70 ft. lbs. (95 Nm). On 1989–91 vehicles, torque both pivot bolts to 125 ft. lbs. (169 Nm).

11. Perform a front end alignment as required.

Sway Bar

REMOVAL & INSTALLATION

1. Raise the vehicle and support safely.

2. Remove the front sway bar brackets and retainers.

3. Remove the sway bar support brackets and bushings from the lower control arm. Remove the sway bar from the vehicle.

4. The installation is the reverse of the removal procedure. Lubricate the sway bar bushings liberally with grease before assembling.

REAR SUSPENSION

Shock Absorbers

REMOVAL & INSTALLATION

1. Raise the vehicle and support safely.

2. Remove the bolts that attach the shock to the frame or bracket.

3. Remove the shock from the vehicle.

4. The installation is the reverse of the removal procedure.

Coil Springs

REMOVAL & INSTALLATION

1. Raise the vehicle and support safely.

2. Using the proper equipment, support the weight of the rear axle.

3. Remove the bolts that attach the shock to the lower mounting bracket.

4. Lower the axle and remove the coil spring from the vehicle.

5. The installation is the reverse of the removal procedure.

Rear Wheel Bearings

REMOVAL & INSTALLATION

1. Raise the vehicle and support safely.

2. Remove the tire and wheel assembly.

3. Remove the dust cap.

4. Remove the cotter pin, nut lock and nut.

5. Remove the thrust washer and the outer wheel bearing.

6. Remove the drum with the inner wheel bearing and the grease seal.

7. Remove the grease seal and remove the inner bearing.

To install:

8. Lubricate the inner bearing and install to the drum.

9. Install a new grease seal.

10. Install the drum to the vehicle.

11. Lubricate and install the outer wheel bearing to the spindle.

12. Install the thrust washer.

13. Install and tighten the wheel bearing nut to 20–25 ft. lbs. (27–34 Nm) while rotating the drum.

14. Back off the adjusting nut ¼ turn then tighten it finger-tight.

15. Install the nut lock and a new cotter pin.

Rear Axle Assembly

REMOVAL & INSTALLATION

1. Raise the vehicle and support safely.

2. Disconnect the parking brake cable at the connection.

3. Disconnect the brake tubes from the hoses and unclip the brake tubes from the axle housing. Disconnect the rear wheel speed sensors, if equipped with anti-lock brakes.

4. Using the proper equipment, support the weight of the axle.

5. Unbolt the shock absorbers and remove the track bar to axle pivot bolt. Suspend the track bar with a wire.

6. Lower the axle and remove the springs.

7. Remove the axle from the vehicle.

8. The installation is the reverse of the removal procedure.

Chrysler Corp.
Front Wheel Drive
Dynasty, Imperial, New Yorker

5

SPECIFICATIONS

VEHICLE IDENTIFICATION CHART

It is important for servicing and ordering parts to be certain of the vehicle and engine identification. The VIN (vehicle identification number) is a 17 digit number visible through the windshield on the driver's side of the dash and contains the vehicle and engine identification codes. The tenth digit indicates model year and the eighth digit indicates engine code. It can be interpreted as follows:

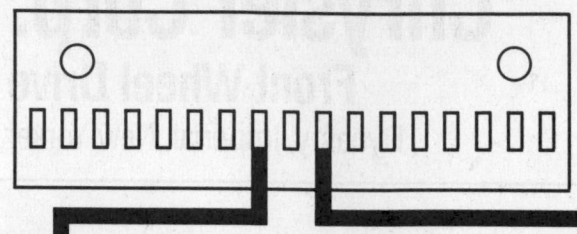

Engine Code						Model Year	
Code	Cu. In.	Liters	Cyl.	Fuel Sys.	Eng. Mfg.	Code	Year
K	153	2.5	4	EFI	Chrysler Corporation	J	1988
3	181	3.0	6	EFI	Mitsubishi	K	1989
R	201	3.3	6	EFI	Chrysler Corporation	L	1990
						M	1991

ENGINE IDENTIFICATION

Year	Model	Engine Displacement cu. in. (liter)	Engine Series Identification (VIN)	No. of Cylinders	Engine Type
1988	Dynasty	153 (2.5)	K	4	OHC
	Dynasty	181 (3.0)	3	6	OHC
	New Yorker Landau	181 (3.0)	3	6	OHC
1989	Dynasty	153 (2.5)	K	4	OHC
	Dynasty	181 (3.0)	3	6	OHC
	New Yorker Landau	181 (3.0)	3	6	OHC
1990–91	Dynasty	153 (2.5)	K	4	OHC
	Dynasty	181 (3.0)	3	6	OHC
	Dynasty	201 (3.3)	R	6	OHC
	New Yorker Landau	181 (3.0)	3	6	OHC
	New Yorker Landau	201 (3.3)	R	6	OHC
	New Yorker Salon	181 (3.0)	3	6	OHC
	New Yorker Salon	201 (3.3)	R	6	OHC
	New Yorker 5th Avenue	201 (3.3)	R	6	OHC
	Imperial	201 (3.3)	R	6	OHC

GENERAL ENGINE SPECIFICATIONS

Year	VIN	No. Cylinder Displacement cu. in. (liter)	Fuel System Type	Net Horsepower @ rpm	Net Torque @ rpm (ft. lbs.)	Bore × Stroke (in.)	Compression Ratio	Oil Pressure @ rpm
1988	K	4-153 (2.5)	EFI	100 @ 4800	135 @ 2800	3.44 × 4.09	8.9:1	30-80 @ 3000
	3	6-181 (3.0)	EFI	141 @ 5000	171 @ 2800	3.59 × 2.99	8.9:1	30-80 @ 3000
1989	K	4-153 (2.5)	EFI	100 @ 4800	135 @ 2800	3.44 × 4.09	8.9:1	30-80 @ 3000
	3	6-181 (3.0)	EFI	141 @ 5000	171 @ 2800	3.59 × 2.99	8.9:1	30-80 @ 3000
1990-91	K	4-153 (2.5)	EFI	100 @ 4800	135 @ 2800	3.44 × 4.09	8.9:1	30-80 @ 3000
	3	6-181 (3.0)	EFI	141 @ 5000	171 @ 2800	3.59 × 2.99	8.9:1	30-80 @ 3000
	R	6-201 (3.3)	EFI	183 @ 3600	183 @ 3600	3.66 × 3.19	8.9:1	30-80 @ 3000

GASOLINE ENGINE TUNE-UP SPECIFICATIONS

Year	VIN	No. Cylinder Displacement cu. in. (liter)	Spark Plugs Type	Spark Plugs Gap (in.)	Ignition Timing (deg.) MT	Ignition Timing (deg.) AT	Compression Pressure (psi)	Fuel Pump (psi)	Idle Speed (rpm) MT	Idle Speed (rpm) AT	Valve Clearance In.	Valve Clearance Ex.
1988	K	4-153 (2.5)	RN12YC	0.035	—	12B	100 ①	15	—	850	Hyd.	Hyd.
	3	6-181 (3.0)	RN11YC4	0.040	—	12B	178 ②	48	—	700	Hyd.	Hyd.
1989	K	4-153 (2.5)	RN12YC	0.035	—	12B	100 ①	15	—	850	Hyd.	Hyd.
	3	6-181 (3.0)	RN11YC4	0.040	—	12B	178 ②	48	—	700	Hyd.	Hyd.
1990-91	K	4-153 (2.5)	RN12YC	0.035	—	12B	100 ①	15	—	850	Hyd.	Hyd.
	3	6-181 (3.0)	RN11YC4	0.040	—	12B	178 ②	48	—	700	Hyd.	Hyd.
	R	6-201 (3.3)	RN16YC5	0.050	—	12B	100 ①	43-53	—	750	Hyd.	Hyd.

① Minimum
② At 250 rpm

FIRING ORDERS

NOTE: To avoid confusion, always replace spark plug wires one at a time.

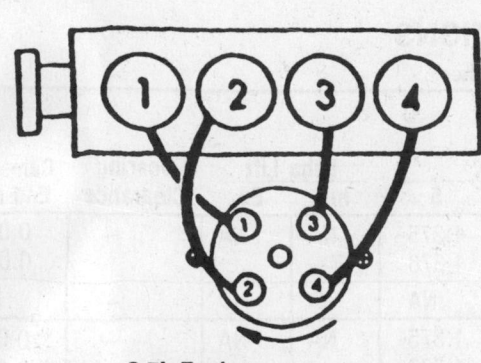

2.5L Engine
Engine Firing Order: 1-3-4-2
Distributor Rotation: Clockwise

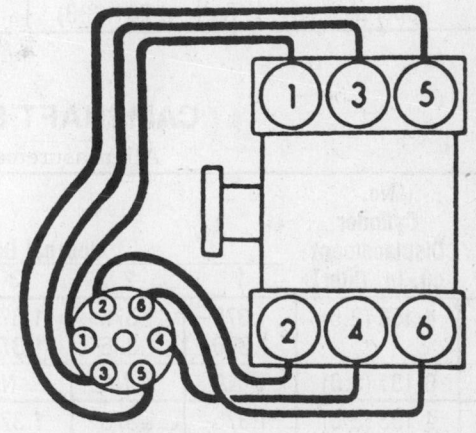

3.0L Engine
Engine Firing Order: 1-2-3-4-5-6
Distributor Rotation: Counterclockwise

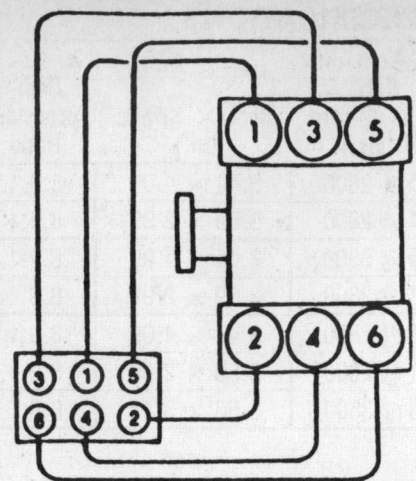

3.3L Engine
Engine Firing Order: 1–2–3–4–5–6
Distributorless Ignition System

CAPACITIES

Year	Model	VIN	No. Cylinder Displacement cu. in. (liter)	Engine Crankcase (qts.) with Filter	Engine Crankcase (qts.) without Filter	Transmission (pts.) 4-Spd.	Transmission (pts.) 5-Spd.	Transmission (pts.) Auto.	Drive Axle (pts.)	Fuel Tank (gal.)	Cooling System (qts.)
1988	Dynasty	K	4-153 (2.5)	4	4	—	—	18	—	16	9
	Dynasty	3	6-181 (3.0)	4	4	—	—	18	—	16	9.5
	New Yorker Landau	3	6-181 (3.0)	4	4	—	—	18	—	16	9.5
1989	Dynasty	K	4-153 (2.5)	4	4	—	—	17	—	16	9
	Dynasty	3	6-181 (3.0)	4	4	—	—	18	—	16	9.5
	New Yorker Landau	3	6-181 (3.0)	4	4	—	—	18	—	16	9.5
1990–91	Dynasty	K	4-153 (2.5)	4	4	—	—	17	—	16	9
	Dynasty	3	6-181 (3.0)	4	4	—	—	18	—	16	9.5
	Dynasty	R	6-201 (3.3)	4	4	—	—	18	—	16	9.5
	New Yorker Landau	3	6-181 (3.))	4	4	—	—	18	—	16	9.5
	New Yorker Landau	R	6-201 (3.3)	4	4	—	—	18	—	16	9.5
	New Yorker Salon	3	6-181 (3.0)	4	4	—	—	18	—	16	9.5
	New Yorker Salon	R	6-201 (3.3)	4	4	—	—	18	—	16	9.5
	New Yorker 5th Avenue	R	6-201 (3.3)	4	4	—	—	18	—	16	9.5
	Imperial	R	6-201 (3.3)	4	4	—	—	18	—	16	9.5

CAMSHAFT SPECIFICATIONS

All measurements given in inches.

Year	VIN	No. Cylinder Displacement cu. in. (liter)	Journal Diameter 1	Journal Diameter 2	Journal Diameter 3	Journal Diameter 4	Journal Diameter 5	Lobe Lift In.	Lobe Lift Ex.	Bearing Clearance	Camshaft End Play
1988	K	4-153 (2.5)	1.375–1.376	1.375–1.376	1.375–1.376	1.375–1.376	1.375–1.376	NA	NA	—	0.005–0.020
	3	6-181 (3.0)	NA	NA	NA	NA	NA	①	①	—	NA
1989	K	4-153 (2.5)	1.375–1.376	1.375–1.376	1.375–1.376	1.375–1.376	1.375–1.376	NA	NA	—	0.005–0.020
	3	6-181 (3.0)	NA	NA	NA	NA	NA	①	①	—	NA

CAMSHAFT SPECIFICATIONS

All measurements given in inches.

Year	VIN	No. Cylinder Displacement cu. in. (liter)	Journal Diameter					Lobe Lift		Bearing Clearance	Camshaft End Play
			1	2	3	4	5	In.	Ex.		
1990–91	K	4-153 (2.5)	1.375–1.376	1.375–1.376	1.375–1.376	1.375–1.376	1.375–1.376	NA	NA	—	0.005–0.020
	3	6-181 (3.0)	NA	NA	NA	NA	NA	①	①	—	NA
	R	6-201 (3.3)	1.997–1.999	1.980–1.982	1.965–1.967	1.949–1.952	—	0.400	0.400	0.001–0.005	0.005–0.012

NA Not Available
① Height of camshaft/lobe: 1.604–1.624 in.

CRANKSHAFT AND CONNECTING ROD SPECIFICATIONS

All measurements are given in inches.

Year	VIN	No. Cylinder Displacement cu. in. (liter)	Crankshaft				Connecting Rod		
			Main Brg. Journal Dia.	Main Brg. Oil Clearance	Shaft End-play	Thrust on No.	Journal Diameter	Oil Clearance	Side Clearance
1988	K	4-153 (2.5)	2.362–2.363	0.0002–0.0014	0.002–0.014	3	1.968–1.969	0.0008–0.0040	0.005–0.013
	3	6-181 (3.0)	2.361–2.362	0.0006–0.0020	0.002–0.010	3	1.968–1.969	0.0008–0.0028	0.004–0.010
1989	K	4-153 (2.5)	2.362–2.363	0.0002–0.0014	0.002–0.014	3	1.968–1.969	0.0008–0.0040	0.005–0.013
	3	6-181 (3.0)	2.361–2.362	0.0006–0.0020	0.002–0.010	3	1.968–1.969	0.0008–0.0028	0.004–0.010
1990–91	K	4-153 (2.5)	2.362–2.363	0.0002–0.0014	0.002–0.014	3	1.968–1.969	0.0008–0.0040	0.005–0.013
	3	6-181 (3.0)	2.361–2.362	0.0006–0.0020	0.002–0.010	3	1.968–1.969	0.0008–0.0028	0.004–0.010
	R	6-201 (3.3)	2.519	0.0007–0.0022	0.001–0.007	2	2.283	0.0008–0.0030	0.005–0.015

VALVE SPECIFICATIONS

Year	VIN	No. Cylinder Displacement cu. in. (liter)	Seat Angle (deg.)	Face Angle (deg.)	Spring Test Pressure (lbs.)	Spring Installed Height (in.)	Stem-to-Guide Clearance (in.)		Stem Diameter (in.)	
							Intake	Exhaust	Intake	Exhaust
1988	K	4-153 (2.5)	45	45	115	1.65	0.001–0.003	0.003–0.005	0.3124	0.3103
	3	6-181 (3.0)	44.5	45.5	73	1.59	0.001–0.002	0.002–0.003	0.3130–0.3140	0.3120–0.3130
1989	K	4-153 (2.5)	45	45	115	1.65	0.001–0.003	0.003–0.005	0.3124	0.3103
	3	6-181 (3.0)	44.5	45.5	73	1.59	0.001–0.002	0.002–0.003	0.3130–0.3140	0.3120–0.3130
1990–91	K	4-153 (2.5)	45	45	115	1.65	0.001–0.003	0.003–0.005	0.3124	0.3103
	3	6-181 (3.0)	44.5	45.5	73	1.59	0.001–0.002	0.002–0.003	0.3130–0.3140	0.3120–0.3130
	R	6-201 (3.3)	45	44.5	60	1.56	0.002–0.016	0.002–0.016	0.3110–0.3120	0.3110–0.3120

PISTON AND RING SPECIFICATIONS

All measurements are given in inches.

Year	VIN	No. Cylinder Displacement cu. in. (liter)	Piston Clearance	Ring Gap			Ring Side Clearance		
				Top Compression	Bottom Compression	Oil Control	Top Compression	Bottom Compression	Oil Control
1988	K	4-153 (2.5)	0.0006–0.0018	0.0010–0.0039	0.0011–0.0039	0.0015–0.0074	0.0015–0.0040	0.0015–0.0040	0.0002–0.0080
	3	6-181 (3.0)	0.0008–0.0015	0.0012–0.0018	0.0010–0.0016	0.0012–0.0035	0.0020–0.0035	0.0008–0.0020	NA
1989	K	4-153 (2.5)	0.0006–0.0018	0.0010–0.0039	0.0011–0.0039	0.0015–0.0074	0.0015–0.0040	0.0015–0.0040	0.0002–0.0080
	3	6-181 (3.0)	0.0008–0.0015	0.0012–0.0018	0.0010–0.0016	0.0012–0.0035	0.0020–0.0035	0.0008–0.0020	NA
1990–91	K	4-153 (2.5)	0.0006–0.0018	0.0010–0.0039	0.0011–0.0039	0.0015–0.0074	0.0015–0.0040	0.0015–0.0040	0.0002–0.0080
	3	6-181 (3.0)	0.0008–0.0015	0.0012–0.0018	0.0010–0.0016	0.0012–0.0035	0.0020–0.0035	0.0008–0.0020	NA
	R	6-201 (3.3)	0.0009–0.0022	0.0012–0.0022	0.0012–0.0022	0.0010–0.0040	0.0012–0.0037	0.0012–0.0037	0.0005–0.0089

TORQUE SPECIFICATIONS

All readings in ft. lbs.

Year	VIN	No. Cylinder Displacement cu. in. (liter)	Cylinder Head Bolts	Main Bearing Bolts	Rod Bearing Bolts	Crankshaft Pulley Bolts	Flywheel Bolts	Manifold		Spark Plugs
								Intake	Exhaust	
1988	K	4-153 (2.5)	①	30 ③	40 ③	50	70	17	17	26
	3	6-181 (3.0)	70	60	38	110	70	17	17	20
1989	K	4-153 (2.5)	①	30 ③	40 ③	50	70	17	17	26
	3	6-181 (3.0)	70	60	38	110	70	17	17	20
1990–91	K	4-153 (2.5)	①	30 ③	40 ③	50	70	17	17	26
	3	6-181 (3.0)	70	60	38	110	70	17	17	20
	R	6-201 (3.3)	②	30 ③	40 ③	40	70	17	17	30

① Sequence: 45, 65, 65, plus ¼ turn
② Sequence: 45, 65, 65, plus ¼ turn
Torque the small bolt in the rear of the head to 25 ft. lbs. last
③ Plus ¼ turn

BRAKE SPECIFICATIONS

All measurements in inches unless noted

Year	Model	Lug Nut Torque (ft. lbs.)	Master Cylinder Bore	Brake Disc		Standard Brake Drum Diameter	Minimum Lining Thickness	
				Minimum Thickness	Maximum Runout		Front	Rear
1988	Dynasty	95	0.827	②	0.005	8.66	0.06	0.06
	New Yorker Landau	95	0.827	②	0.005	8.66	0.06	0.06
1989	Dynasty	95	0.827 ①	②	0.005	8.66	0.06	0.06
	New Yorker Landau	95	0.827 ①	②	0.005	8.66	0.06	0.06

BRAKE SPECIFICATIONS

All measurements in inches unless noted

Year	Model	Lug Nut Torque (ft. lbs.)	Master Cylinder Bore	Brake Disc		Standard Brake Drum Diameter	Minimum Lining Thickness	
				Minimum Thickness	Maximum Runout		Front	Rear
1990–91	Dynasty	95	0.827 ①	②	0.005	8.66	0.06	0.06
	New Yorker Landau	95	0.827 ①	②	0.005	8.66	0.06	0.06
	New Yorker Salon	95	0.827 ①	②	0.005	8.66	0.06	0.06
	New Yorker 5th Ave.	95	0.827 ①	②	0.005	—	0.06	0.06
	Imperial	95	—	②	0.005	—	0.06	0.06

① Except ABS
② Front: 0.882 in.
   Rear: 0.339 in.

WHEEL ALIGNMENT

Year	Model		Caster		Camber		Toe-in (in.)	Steering Axis Inclination (deg.)
			Range (deg.)	Preferred Setting (deg.)	Range (deg.)	Preferred Setting (deg.)		
1988	Dynasty	front	①	1³/₁₆	¹/₄N–³/₄P	⁵/₁₆P	¹/₁₆	13⁵/₁₆
		rear	—	—	1¹/₄N–¹/₄N	¹/₂N	0	—
	New Yorker Landau	front	①	1³/₁₆	¹/₄N–³/₄P	⁵/₁₆P	¹/₁₆	13⁵/₁₆
		rear	—	—	1¹/₄N–¹/₄N	¹/₂N	0	—
1989	Dynasty	front	①	1³/₁₆	¹/₄N–³/₄P	⁵/₁₆P	¹/₁₆	13⁵/₁₆
		rear	—	—	1¹/₄N–¹/₄N	¹/₂N	0	—
	New Yorker Landau	front	①	1³/₁₆	¹/₄N–³/₄P	⁵/₁₆P	¹/₁₆	13⁵/₁₆
		rear	—	—	1¹/₄N–¹/₄N	¹/₂N	0	—
1990–91	Dynasty	front	①	1³/₁₆	¹/₄N–³/₄P	⁵/₁₆P	¹/₁₆	13⁵/₁₆
		rear	—	—	1¹/₄N–¹/₄N	¹/₂N	0	—
	New Yorker Landau	front	①	1³/₁₆	¹/₄N–³/₄P	⁵/₁₆P	¹/₁₆	13⁵/₁₆
		rear	—	—	1¹/₄N–¹/₄N	¹/₂N	0	—
	New Yorker Salon	front	①	1³/₁₆	¹/₄N–³/₄P	⁵/₁₆P	¹/₁₆	13⁵/₁₆
		rear	—	—	1¹/₄N–¹/₄N	¹/₂N	0	—
	New Yorker 5th Ave.	front	①	1³/₁₆	¹/₄N–³/₄P	⁵/₁₆P	¹/₁₆	13⁵/₁₆
		rear	—	—	1¹/₄N–¹/₄N	¹/₂N	0	—
	Imperial	front	①	1³/₁₆	¹/₄N–³/₄P	⁵/₁₆P	¹/₁₆	13⁵/₁₆
		rear	—	—	1¹/₄N–¹/₄N	¹/₂N	0	—

① Not adjustable—variation between sides should not exceed 1¹/₂°

ENGINE ELECTRICAL

NOTE: Disconnecting the negative battery cable on some vehicles may interfere with the functions of the on board computer systems and may require the computer to undergo a relearning process, once the negative battery cable is reconnected.

Distributor

REMOVAL

1. Disconnect the negative battery cable.
2. Disconnect the distributor pick-up lead wires. Remove the splash shield, if equipped.
3. Unscrew the distributor cap hold-down screws and lift off the distributor cap with all ignition wires still connected. Remove the coil wire, if necessary.

4. Matchmark the rotor to the distributor housing and the distributor housing to the engine.

NOTE: Do not crank the engine during this procedure. If the engine is cranked, the matchmark must be disregarded.

5. Remove the hold-down bolt and clamp.
6. Remove the distributor from the engine.

INSTALLATION

Timing Not Disturbed

1. Install a new distributor housing O-ring.
2. Install the distributor in the engine so the rotor is lined up with the matchmark on the housing and the housing is lined up with the matchmark on the engine. Make sure the distributor is fully seated and the distributor shaft is fully engaged.
3. Install the hold-down clamp and snug the hold-down bolt.
4. Connect the distributor pickup lead wires. Install the splash shield, if equipped.
5. Install the distributor cap and tighten the screws.
6. Connect the negative battery cable.
7. Adjust the ignition timing and tighten the hold-down bolt.

Timing Disturbed

1. Install a new distributor housing O-ring.
2. Position the engine so the No. 1 piston is at TDC of its compression stroke and the mark o003he vibration damper is lined up with **0** on the timing indicator.
3. Install the distributor in the engine so the rotor is aligned with the position of the No. 1 ignition wire on the distributor cap and the housing is lined up with the matchmark on the engine. Make sure the distributor is fully seated and that the distributor shaft is fully engaged.

NOTE: There are distributor cap runners inside the cap on 3.0L engines. Make sure the rotor is pointing to where the No. 1 runner originates inside the cap and not where the No. 1 ignition wire plugs into the cap.

4. Install the hold-down clamp and snug the hold-down bolt.
5. Connect the distributor pickup lead wires. Install the splash shield, if equipped.

6. Install the distributor cap and tighten the screws.
7. Connect the negative battery cable.
8. Adjust the ignition timing and tighten the hold-down bolt.

Ignition Coil

REMOVAL & INSTALLATION

1. Disconnect the negative battery cable.
2. Remove the spark plug wires from the coil.
3. Disconnect the electrical connector.
4. Remove the coil fasteners.
5. Remove the coil from the ignition module.
6. The installation is the reverse of the removal procedure.

Crank Position Sensor

REMOVAL & INSTALLATION

1. Disconnect the negative battery cable.
2. Disconnect the sensor lead at the harness connector.
3. Remove the sensor retaining bolt.
4. Pull the sensor straight up out the transaxle housing.
5. If the sensor is being reinstalled, remove any remains of the old spacer completely and attach a new spacer to the sensor. If a new spacer is not used, the sensor will not function properly. New sensors are packaged with a new spacer.

To install:

6. Install the sensor to the tranaxle housing and push the sensor down until it contacts the drive plate.
7. Hold in this position and install the retaining bolt. Torque to 9 ft. lbs. (12 Nm).
8. Connect the sensor lead wire.

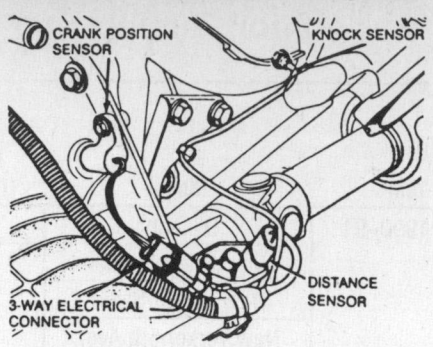

Crankshaft position sensor location—3.3L engine

Cam Position Sensor

REMOVAL & INSTALLATION

1. Disconnect the negative battery cable.
2. Disconnect the sensor lead at the harness connector.
3. Loosen the sensor retaining bolt sufficiently to allow the slotted mounting surface to slide past.
4. Pull the sensor straight up and out of the chain case cover. Resistance may be high due to the rubber O-ring.
5. If the sensor is being reinstalled, remove any remains of the old spacer completely and attach a new spacer to the sensor. If a new spacer is not used, the sensor will not function properly. New sensors are packaged with a new spacer.

To install:

6. Inspect the O-ring for damage and replace, if necessary.
7. Lubricate the O-ring with oil. Install the sensor to the chain case cover and push the sensor into its bore until contact is made with the cam timing gear.
8. Hold in this position and tighten the bolt to 9 ft. lbs. (12 Nm).
9. Connect the wire and rout it away from the accessory drive belt.

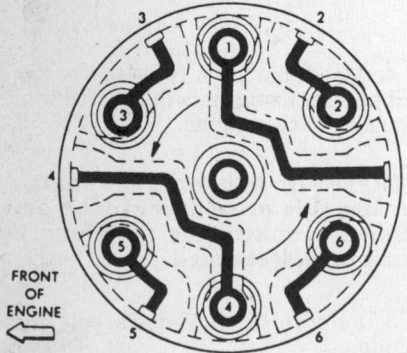

Distributor cap terminal routing—3.0L engine

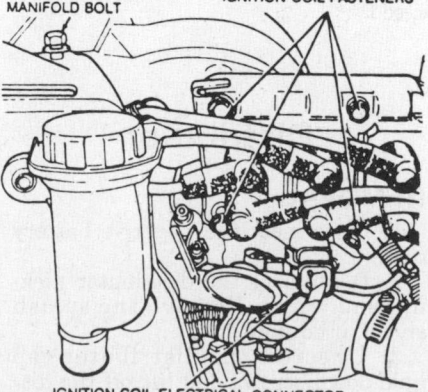

Ignition coil removal and installation—3.3L engine

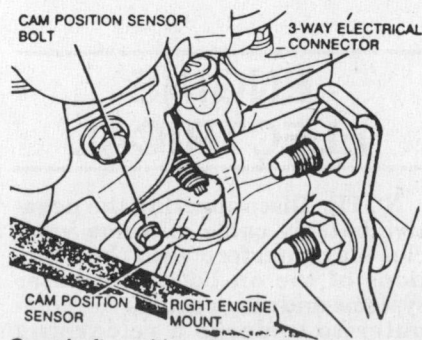

Camshaft position sensor location—3.3L engine

Ignition Timing

ADJUSTMENT

NOTE: The ignition timing on the distributorless 3.3L engine cannot be checked or changed.

1. Start the engine, set the parking brake and run the engine until at normal operating temperature. Keep all lights and accessories OFF.

2. If a magnetic timing unit is available, insert the probe into the receptacle near the timing scale. The scale is located on the top of the bell housing on the 2.5L engine and near the crankshaft pulley on the 3.0L engine.

3. If a magnetic timing unit is not available, connect a conventional power timing light to the No. 1 cylinder spark plug wire.

4. Connect the red lead of a tachometer to the negative primary terminal of the coil and connect the black lead to a good ground.

5. Set the idle speed according to the Vehicle Emission Control Information (VECI) label.

6. On 1988 vehicles, disconnect the coolant sensor wire. On 1989–91 vehicles, connect the Diagnostic Readout Box II (DRB II) and access the Basic Timing Mode. If the DRB II is not available, disconnect the coolant sensor located near the thermostat housing. The Check Engine lamp on the instrument panel must be on.

7. Aim the timing light at the timing scale or read the magnetic timing unit.

8. Loosen the distributor hold-down bolt just enough so the disributor can be rotated.

9. Turn the distributor in the proper direction until the specified timing according to the VECI label is reached. Tighten the hold-down bolt and recheck the timing and idle speed.

10. Turn the engine OFF. Connect the coolant sensor. Make sure the Check Engine lamp does not come ON when the vehicle is restarted. Disconnect the timing apparatus and tachometer.

11. If the coolant temperature sensor was disconnected, erase the created fault code using the Erase Fault Code mode on the DRB II.

Alternator

For further information on the charging system, please refer to "Charging and Starting" in the Unit Repair section.

PRECAUTIONS

Several precautions must be observed when working with the alternator to avoid damaging the unit.

- If the battery is removed for any reason, make sure it is reconnected with the correct polarity. Reversing the battery connections may result in damage to the one-way rectifiers.
- When utilizing a booster battery as a starting aid, always connect the positive to positive terminals and the negative terminal from the booster battery to a good engine ground on the vehicle being started.
- Never use a fast charger as a booster to start vehicles.
- Disconnect the battery cables when charging the battery with a fast charger.
- Never attempt to polarize the alternator.
- Do not use test lamps of more than 12 volts when checking diode continuity.
- Do not short across or ground any of the alternator terminals.
- The polarity of the battery, alternator and regulator must be matched and considered before making any electrical connections within the system.
- Never separate the alternator on an open circuit. Make sure all connections within the circuit are clean and tight.
- Disconnect the battery ground terminal when performing any service on electrical components.
- Disconnect the battery if arc welding is to be done on the vehicle.

BELT TENSION ADJUSTMENT

NOTE: The belt tension is automatically adjusted by a dynamic tensioner on the 3.0L and 3.3L engines. Periodic adjustment is not necessary.

1. Loosen the pivot bolt slightly.

2. Raise the vehicle and support safely. Remove the splash shield. Loosen the "T" bolt locknut enough so the alternator can be moved.

3. Tighten the adjusting bolt until the belt deflects about ¼ in. under a 10 lb. load.

4. Tighten the "T" bolt locknut and pivot bolt.

REMOVAL & INSTALLATION

1. Disconnect the negative battery cable.

2. On the 2.5L engine, remove the air conditioning compressor and position it to the side. Remove the oil filter to allow the alternator to be removed from above, if possible.

3. On 3.0L and 3.3L engines, re-lease the dynamic belt tensioner and remove the belt. On all other engines, loosen the mounting bolts, move the alternator toward the engine and remove the drive belt(s).

4. Remove the mounting bolts and spacers and remove the alternator from the brackets.

5. Remove the battery positive, field and ground terminals from the rear of the alternator. Remove the wire harness hold-down screw from the alternator, if equipped.

To install:

6. Connect all wiring to the proper terminals on the rear of the alternator and install the wire harness hold-down screw, if equipped.

7. Position the alternator in the mounting brackets.

8. Install the spacers, pivot bolt and adjuster bolt. Install the belt.

9. Install the air conditioning compressor and oil filter, if they were removed.

10. Adjust the belt tension, if necessary.

11. Connect the negative battery cable.

Starter

For further information on the charging system, please refer to "Charging and Starting" in the Unit Repair section.

REMOVAL & INSTALLATION

1. Disconnect the negative battery cable.

2. On the 2.5L engine, remove the attaching nut and bolt at the top of the bell housing. Raise the vehicle and support safely.

3. Remove the rear mount and heat shield from the starter, if equipped.

4. Unbolt the starter and remove from the vehicle.

5. Disconnect the solenoid lead wires from the starter.

To install:

6. Connect the solenoid lead wires and install the heat shield, if equipped.

7. On the the 2.5L engine, install

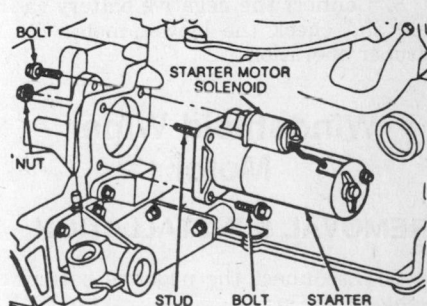

Starter mounting—2.5L engine

the lower bolt loosely, then lower the vehicle and install the nut and bolt from above and torque to 40 ft. lbs. (54 Nm).

8. Raise the vehicle and torque the bottom bolt to the same value. Install the rear mount to the starter.

9. On 3.0L and 3.3L engines, install all mounting bolts and torque to 40 ft. lbs. (54 Nm) evenly.

10. Connect the negative battery cable and check the starter for proper operation.

CHASSIS ELECTRICAL

— CAUTION —

On vehicles equipped with an air bag, the negative battery cable must be disconnected, before working on the system. Failure to do so may result in deployment of the air bag and possible personal injury.

Blower Motor

REMOVAL & INSTALLATION

1. Disconnect the negative battery cable.

2. Remove the glove box assembly, lower right side instrument panel trim cover and right cowl trim panel, as required. Disconnect the blower lead wire connector.

3. Disconnect the 2 vacuum lines from the recirculating door actuator and position the actuator to the side.

4. Remove the 2 screws at the top of the blower housing that secure it to the unit cover.

5. Remove the 5 screws from around the blower housing and separate the blower housing from the unit.

6. Remove the 3 screws that secure the blower assembly to the heater or air conditioning housing and remove the assembly from the unit. Remove the fan from the blower motor.

7. The installation is the reverse of the removal procedure.

8. Connect the negative battery cable and check the blower motor for proper operation.

Windshield Wiper Motor

REMOVAL & INSTALLATION

1. Disconnect the negative battery cable.

2. Remove the wiper arms and

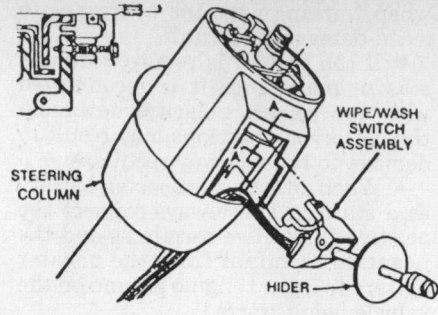

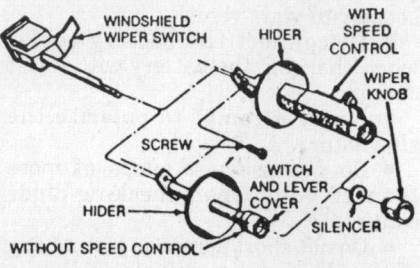

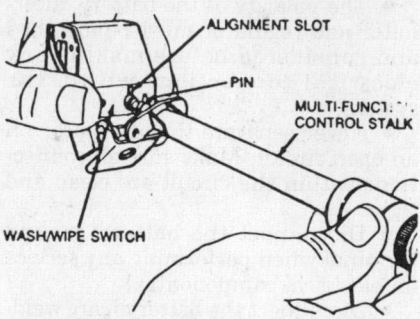

Removing the wiper switch—1988–89 standard column

blades and remove the plastic cowl top cover.

3. Remove the attaching screws from each pivot assembly.

4. Remove the motor mounting bolts.

5. Remove the nut and disconnect the wiper linkage drive from the motor shaft.

6. Remove the wiper motor from the vehicle.

7. The installation is the reverse of the removal procedure.

8. Connect the negative battery cable and check the wiper motor for proper operation.

Windshield Wiper Switch

REMOVAL & INSTALLATION

NOTE: On 1990–91 vehicles, the windshield wiper switch is part of the combination switch.

1988–89 Vehicles

STANDARD COLUMN

1. Disconnect the negative battery cable.

2. Remove the lower steering column cover.

3. Straighten the steering wheel so the tires are pointing straight ahead.

NOTE: For vehicles equipped with an airbag, it is imperative that the steering wheel removal and installation procedure under Steering is followed.

4. Remove the steering wheel.

5. Remove the plastic wiring channel from the underside of the steering column.

6. Disconnect the wiper switch connector, intermittent wipe module connector and cruise control connector, if equipped.

7. Remove the side lock housing cover.

8. Remove the slotted hex-head screw that attaches the wiper switch to the turn signal switch and remove the switch.

9. Remove the control knob from the end of the stalk. Pull the round nylon hider up the control stalk and remove the revealed screws that attach the control stalk sleeve to the wiper switch.

10. Rotate the control stalk shaft to the full clockwise position and remove the shaft from the wiper switch by pulling it straight out.

To install:

11. Install the control shaft to the wiper switch, install the screws, the hider and the control knob.

12. Run the wiring through the opening and down the steering column, position the switch and install the hex-head screw. Make sure the dimmer switch rod is properly engaged.

13. Install the side lock housing cover.

14. Connect the wires and install the wiring channel.

15. Install the steering wheel and torque the nut to 45 ft. lbs. (61 Nm).

16. Install the horn pad.

17. Connect the negative battery cable and check the wiper and washer, cruise control, turn signal switch and dimmer switch for proper operation.

18. Install the lower column cover.

TILT COLUMN

1. Disconnect the negative battery cable.

2. Remove the lower steering column cover and remove the plastic wiring channel from the underside of the steering column.

3. Straighten the steering wheel so the tires are pointing straight ahead.

NOTE: For vehicles equipped with an airbag, it is imperative that the steering wheel removal and installation procedure under Steering is followed.

4. Remove the steering wheel.

5. Depress the lock plate with the proper depressing tool, remove the retaining ring from its groove and remove the tool, ring, lock plate, cancelling cam and spring.

6. Remove the switch stalk actuator screw and arm.

7. Remove the hazard switch knob.

8. Disconnect the turn signal switch, wiper switch, intermittent module and cruise control connectors, if equipped.

9. Remove the 3 screws and remove the turn signal switch. Tape the connector to the wires to aid in removal.

10. Remove the ignition key lamp.

11. Place the key in the **LOCK** position and remove the key. Insert a thin tool into the slot next to the switch mounting screw boss, depress the spring latch at the bottom of the slot releasing the lock. Remove the lock cylinder.

12. Remove the buzzer switch and wedge spring.

13. Remove the 3 housing cover screws and remove the housing cover.

14. Remove the wiper switch pivot pin with a punch and remove the switch.

15. Remove the control knob from the end of the stalk. Pull the round nylon hider up the control stalk and remove the revealed screws that attach the control stalk sleeve to the wiper switch.

16. Rotate the control stalk shaft to the full clockwise position and remove the shaft from the wiper switch by pulling it straight out.

To install:

17. Install the control shaft to the wiper switch, install the screws, the hider and the control knob.

18. Run the wiring through the opening and down the steering column, position the switch and install the wiper switch pivot pin.

19. Install the housing cover.

20. Install the buzzer switch and wedge spring.

21. Install the lock cylinder.

22. Install the ignition key lamp.

23. Install the turn signal switch, switch stalk actuator arm and hazard switch knob.

24. Install the spring, cancelling cam, lock plate and ring on the steering shaft. Depress the plate with the depressing tool and install the ring securely in the groove. Remove the tool slowly.

25. Connect the turn signal switch, wiper switch, intermittent module and cruise control connectors, if equipped. Install the wiring channel.

26. Install the steering wheel and torque the nut to 45 ft. lbs. (61 Nm).

27. Install the horn pad.

28. Connect the negative battery cable and check the wiper and washer, cruise control, turn signal switch and dimmer switch for proper operation.

29. Install the lower column cover.

Instrument Cluster

REMOVAL & INSTALLATION

1. Disconnect the negative battery cable.

2. Remove the instrument cluster bezel. Cluster removal is not necessary if just removing gauges.

3. When only removing gauge(s) or the speedometer, remove the trip odometer reset knob, if necessary, remove the mask and lens assembly and remove the desired gauge from the cluster.

4. Remove the lower column cover and disconnect the gear indicator cable.

5. Remove the screws attaching the cluster to the instrument panel.

6. Pull the cluster out and disconnect all wiring harnesses. Remove the cluster from the vehicle.

To install:

7. Position the cluster and feed the gear indicator cable through its opening.

8. Connect all wiring in their proper positions.

9. Install the cluster retaining screws. Connect the gearshift indicator cable.

10. Install the cluster bezel.

11. Connect the negative battery cable and check all gauges and the speedometer for proper operation. Make sure the gearshift indicator is properly aligned.

Radio

REMOVAL & INSTALLATION

1. Disconnect the negative battery cable.

2. Remove the cluster bezel.

3. Remove the screws that attach the radio to the instrument panel.

4. Pull the radio out, disconnect the connectors, ground cable and antenna and remove the radio.

5. The installation is the reverse of the removal procedure.

6. Connect the negative battery cable and check the radio for proper operation.

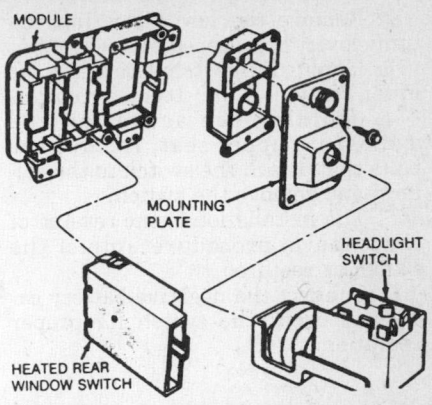

Headlight and heated rear window switches

Concealed Headlights

MANUAL OPERATION

1. Disconnect the negative battery cable.

2. Locate the manual override knob located under the center of the front bumper.

3. Rotate the manual override knob to raise the headlamp cover(s).

4. Connect the negative battery cable.

Headlight Switch

REMOVAL & INSTALLATION

1. Disconnect the negative battery cable.

2. Remove the headlight cluster bezel.

3. Remove the screws securing the headlight and heated rear window switch module to the instrument panel. Pull the assembly out to disconnect the connectors from the switch.

4. Depress the spring button and remove the headlight switch knob and stem.

5. Remove the escutcheon and remove the nut that attaches the switch to the mounting plate.

6. The installation is the reverse of the removal procedure.

7. Connect the negative battery cable and check the switch for proper operation.

Dimmer Switch

REMOVAL & INSTALLATION

NOTE: On 1990–91 vehicles, the dimmer switch is part of the combination switch.

1. Disconnect the negative battery cable.

2. Remove the lower steering column cover, if equipped.

3. Unplug the switch, located on the lower portion of the steering column.

4. Holding the actuating rod against its upper seat, remove the bolts that attach the switch to the column and remove the switch.

5. The installation is the reverse of the removal procedure. Adjust the switch as required.

6. Connect the negative battery cable and check the switch for proper operation.

Turn Signal Switch

NOTE: On 1990–91 vehicles, the turn signal switch is part of the combination switch.

REMOVAL & INSTALLATION

1988–89 Vehicles
STANDARD COLUMN

1. Disconnect the negative battery cable.

2. Remove the lower steering column cover.

3. Straighten the steering wheel so the tires are pointing straight ahead.

NOTE: For vehicles equipped with an airbag, it is imperative that the steering wheel removal and installation procedure under Steering is followed.

4. Remove the steering wheel.

5. Remove the plastic wiring channel from the underside of the steering column and disconnect the turn signal switch connector.

6. Remove the hazard switch knob. Remove the slotted hex-head screw that attaches the wiper switch to the turn signal switch.

7. Remove the 3 screws and pull the turn signal switch out of the column.
To install:
8. Run the wiring through the opening and down the steering column, position the switch and install the hex-head screw. Make sure the dimmer switch rod is properly engaged.

9. Install the 3 screws and the hazard switch knob.

10. Connect the wires and install the wiring channel.

11. Install the steering wheel and torque the nut to 45 ft. lbs. (61 Nm).

12. Install the horn pad.

13. Connect the negative battery cable and check the turn signal switch and dimmer switch for proper operation.

14. Install the lower column cover.

TILT COLUMN

1. Disconnect the negative battery cable.

2. Remove the lower steering column cover and remove the plastic wiring channel from the underside of the steering column.

3. Straighten the steering wheel so the tires are pointing straight ahead.

NOTE: For vehicles equipped with an airbag, it is imperative that the steering wheel removal and installation procedure under Steering is followed.

4. Remove the steering wheel.

5. Depress the lock plate with the proper depressing tool, remove the retaining ring from its groove and remove the tool, ring, lock plate, cancelling cam and spring.

6. Remove the stalk actuator screw and arm.

7. Remove the hazard switch knob.

8. Disconnect the turn signal switch connector.

9. Remove the 3 screws and remove the turn signal switch. Tape the connector to the wires to aid in removal.
To install:
10. Run the wiring through the opening and down the steering column, install the turn signal switch, switch stalk actuator arm and hazard switch knob.

11. Install the spring, cancelling cam, lock plate and ring on the steering shaft. Depress the plate with the depressing tool and install the ring securely in the groove. Remove the tool slowly.

12. Connect the turn signal switch connector and install the channel.

13. Install the steering wheel and torque the nut to 45 ft. lbs. (61 Nm).

14. Install the horn pad.

15. Connect the negative battery cable and check the turn signal switch and dimmer switch for proper operation.

16. Install the lower column cover.

Combination Switch

REMOVAL & INSTALLATION

1990–91 Vehicles

1. Disconnect the negative battery cable.

2. Remove the tilt lever, if equipped.

3. Remove the steering column covers.

4. Remove the combination switch tamper-proof mounting screws and pull the switch away from the steering column.

5. Loosen the connector screw; the screw will remain in the connector.

6. Disconnect the connector from the switch.

7. The installation is the reverse of the removal procedure.

8. Connect the negative battery cable and check all functions of the combination switch for proper operation.

Ignition Lock

REMOVAL & INSTALLATION

1988–89 Vehicles
STANDARD COLUMN

1. Disconnect the negative battery cable.

2. Straighten the steering wheel so the tires are pointing straight ahead.

NOTE: For vehicles equipped with an airbag, it is imperative that the steering wheel removal and installation procedure under Steering is followed.

3. Remove the steering wheel.

4. Remove the hazard switch knob. Remove the slotted hex-head screw that attaches the wiper switch to the turn signal switch.

5. Remove the 3 screws and pull the turn signal switch out of the column as far as it will go. Unplug it below if necessary.

6. Remove the ignition switch key lamp.

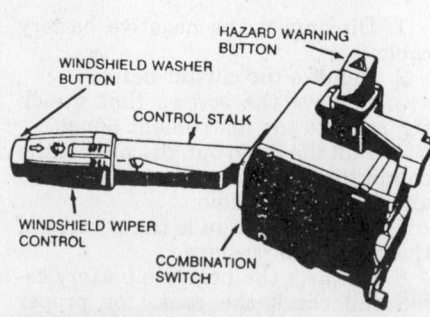

Combination switch—1990–91 vehicles

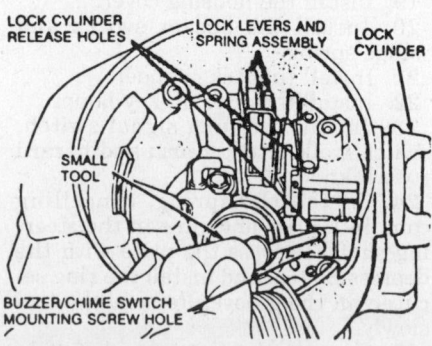

Removing the key lock cylinder—1988–89 standard column

7. Place the key in the **LOCK** position and remove the key.

8. Insert 2 suitable small diameter tools into both release holes and push inward to release the spring loaded lock retainers while simultaneously pulling the key lock cylinder out of its bore.

To install:

9. Install the key cylinder.

10. Install the ignition switch key lamp.

11. Install the turn signal switch and hazard switch knob. Connect the wires if they were disconnected.

12. Install the steering wheel and torque the nut to 45 ft. lbs. (61 Nm).

13. Install the horn pad.

14. Connect the negative battery cable and check the lock cylinder for proper operation.

15. Install the lower column cover, if equipped.

TILT COLUMN

1. Disconnect the negative battery cable.

2. Straighten the steering wheel so the tires are pointing straight ahead.

NOTE: For vehicles equipped with an airbag, it is imperative that the steering wheel removal and installation procedure under Steering is followed.

3. Remove the steering wheel.

4. Depress the lock plate with the proper depressing tool, remove the retaining ring from its groove and remove the tool, ring, lock plate, cancelling cam and spring.

5. Remove the stalk actuator screw and arm.

6. Remove the hazard switch knob.

7. Remove the 3 screws and pull the turn signal switch out of the column as far as it will go. Unplug it below if necessary.

8. Remove the ignition key lamp.

9. Place the key in the **LOCK** position and remove the key. Insert a thin tool into the slot next to the switch mounting screw boss, depress the spring latch at the bottom of the slot

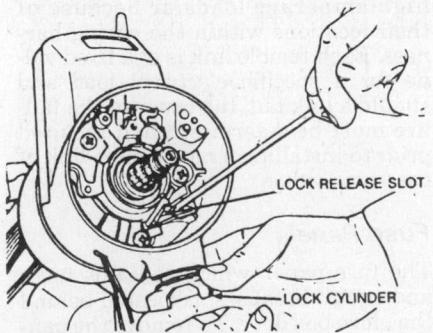

Removing the key lock cylinder—1988–89 tilt column

releasing the lock and remove the lock cylinder.

To install:

10. Install the lock cylinder.

11. Install the ignition key lamp.

12. Install the turn signal switch, switch stalk actuator arm and hazard switch knob.

13. Install the spring, cancelling cam, lock plate and ring on the steering shaft. Depress the plate with the depressing tool and install the ring securely in the groove. Remove the tool slowly.

14. Connect the wires if they were disconnected.

15. Install the steering wheel and torque the nut to 45 ft. lbs. (61 Nm).

16. Install the horn pad.

17. Connect the negative battery cable and check the turn signal switch for proper operation.

18. Install the lower column cover, if it was removed.

Ignition Switch

REMOVAL & INSTALLATION

1988–89 Vehicles

1. Disconnect the negative battery cable.

2. Remove the lower steering column cover.

3. Remove the steering column retaining nuts and allow the steering wheel to rest on the driver's seat.

4. Remove the 2 screws that attach the ignition switch to the column.

5. Rotate the switch 90 degrees and pull up to disengage it from the ignition switch rod.

To install:

6. Engage the switch with the rod, rotate the switch 90 degrees and push down until fully engaged.

7. Install the mounting screws finger tight.

8. Place the key in the **LOCK** position and remove the key. Adjust the switch by pushing up gently on the switch to take up all slack in the rod.

9. Tighten the mounting screws and check the switch for proper operation in all positions.

10. Install the steering column and cover.

Ignition Lock/Switch

REMOVAL & INSTALLATION

1990–91 Vehicles

1. Disconnect the negative battery cable.

2. Remove the tilt lever, if equipped.

3. Remove the upper and lower column covers.

4. Remove the 3 ignition switch tamper-proof torx screws (APEX 440–TX20H or equivalent required).

5. Pull the switch away from the column. Release the connector locks on the 2 wiring connectors and disconnect them from the switch.

6. Remove the key lock cylinder from the ignition switch by performing the following:

a. Insert the key and turn the switch in the **LOCK** position. Using a suitable small tool, depress the key cylinder retaining pin flush with the key cylinder surface.

b. Rotate the key clockwise to the **OFF** position to unseat the key cylinder from the ignition switch assembly. The cylinder bezel should be about ⅛ in. above the ignition switch halo light ring. Do not attempt to remove the key cylinder at this point.

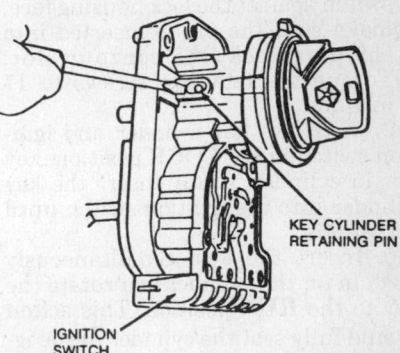

Depressing the key cylinder retaining pin

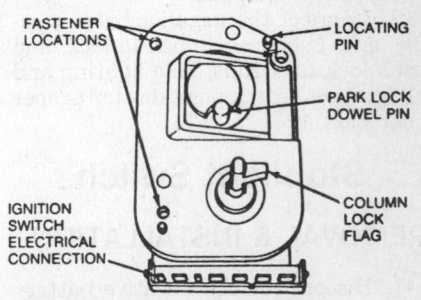

Preparing the ignition switch for installation

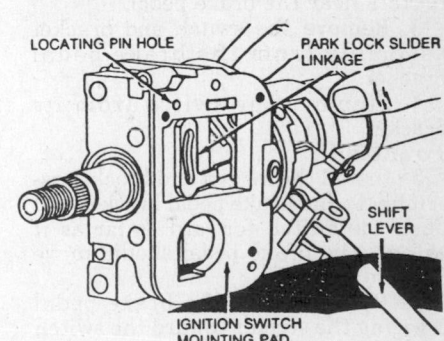

ignition switch mounting pad

c. With the key cylinder in the unseated position, rotate the key counterclockwise to the **LOCK** position and remove the key.

d. Remove the key cylinder from the ignition switch.

To install:

7. Connect the wiring connectors.

8. Mount ignition switch to the column by performing the following:

a. Position the shifter in **PARK** position. The park lock dowel pin on the ignition switch assembly must engage with the column park lock slider linkage.

b. Verify that the ignition switch is in the **LOCK** position. The flag should be parallel to the ignition switch terminals. Apply a small amount of grease to the flag and pin.

c. Position the park lock link to mid-travel.

d. Align the locating pin hole and its pin and position the ignition switch against the lock housing face, make sure the pin is inserted into the park lock link contour slot. Torque the retaining screws to 17 inch lbs.

9. With the key cylinder and ignition switch in the **LOCK** position, key not in cylinder, gently insert the key cylinder into the ignition switch until it bottoms.

10. Insert the key. Simultaneously push in on the cylinder and rotate the key to the **RUN** position. This action should fully seat the cylinder in the ignition switch.

11. Install the column covers and the tilt lever, if equipped.

12. Connect the negative battery cable and check the push-to-lock and park lock functions, halo lighting and all ignition switch positions for proper operation.

Stoplight Switch

REMOVAL & INSTALLATION

1. Disconnect the negative battery cable.

2. Unplug the stoplight switch connectors near the brake pedal.

3. Remove the switch and bracket assembly from the brake pedal bracket.

4. Remove the switch from its bracket.

To install:

5. Install the switch and bracket assembly to the brake pedal bracket and push the switch forward as far as it will go; the brake pedal should move forward slightly.

6. Pull back on the brake pedal bringing the striker toward the switch until the pedal will not go back any farther.

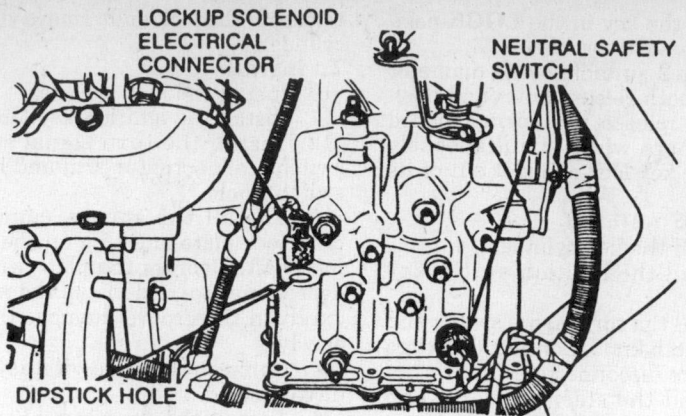

Neutral safety switch identification—A413 automatic transaxle

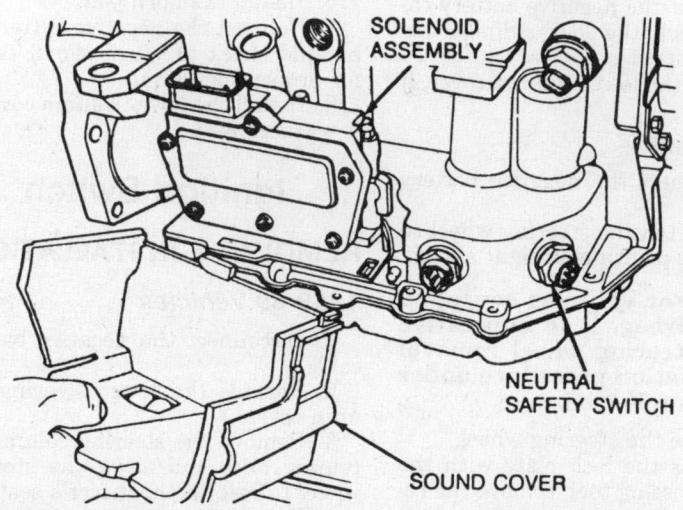

Neutral safety switch identification—A604 automatic transaxle

7. This will cause the switch to ratchet backward into position and automatic adjustment is complete.

8. Connect the negative battery cable and check the switch for proper operation. Also, make sure the speed control system functions properly, if equipped.

Neutral Safety Switch

REMOVAL & INSTALLATION

1. Disconnect the negative battery cable.

2. Locate the neutral safety switch at the left rear corner of the automatic transaxle, in the left front of engine compartment. Do not confuse with the white PRNDL switch on the A604 automatic transaxle. Unplug the switch connector.

3. Remove the switch from the transaxle.

4. The installation is the reverse of the removal procedure. Torque the switch to 25 ft. lbs. (34 Nm).

5. Connect the negative battery cable and check the switch for proper operation.

Fuses, Circuit Breakers, Relays and Flashers

LOCATION

Fusible Links

Fusible links are used to prevent major wire harness damage in the event of a short circuit or an overload condition in the wiring circuits which are normally not fused, due to carrying high amperage loads or because of their locations within the wiring harness. Each fusible link is of a fixed value for a specific electrical load and should a link fail, the cause of the failure must be determined and repaired prior to installing a new fusible link of the same value.

Fuse Panels

The fuse panel, which contains fuses and circuit breakers, is located behind the glove box door. To remove the panel, pull it out from the bottom and slide the tabs out from the top. Addi-

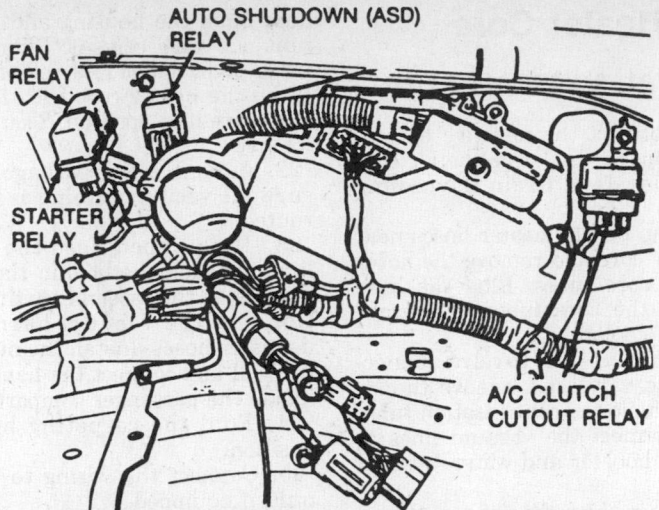

Engine compartment relay identification—1988 vehicles

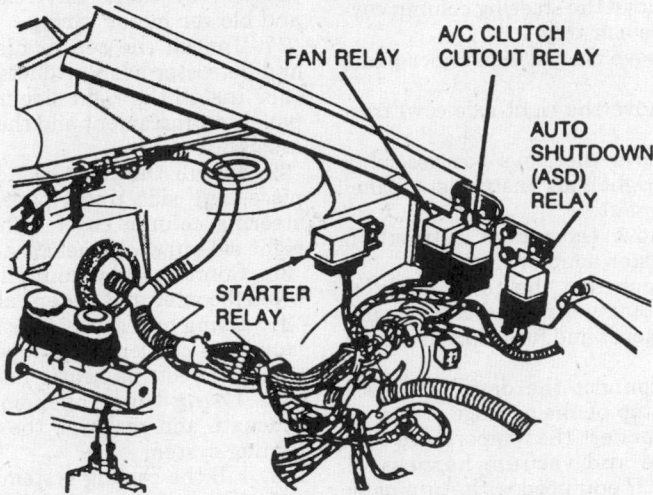

Engine compartment relay identification—1989 vehicles

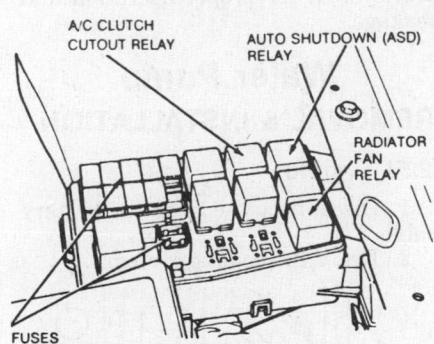

Relays and fuses in the Power Distribution Center—1990–91 vehicles

tional fuses are in the Power Distribution Center located near the left side strut tower in the engine compartment.

Relays and Flashers

The relay and flasher module is located behind the cupholder. The entire module can be removed by pushing it up and off of its mounting bracket. Additional relays are in the Power Distribution Center located near the left side strut tower in the engine compartment.

Computers

LOCATION

1988

The Single Module Engine Controller (SMEC) is located in engine compartment, to the left of the battery.

1989–91

SINGLE BOARD ENGINE CONTROLLER (SBEC)

Located in the engine compartment, to the left of the battery.

TRANSAXLE CONTROLLER

If equipped with the A604 automatic transaxle, the transaxle controller is located in the right front of the engine compartment.

ANTI-LOCK BRAKES CONTROLLER

If equipped with anti-lock brakes, the controller is located behind the rear seat bulkhead trim panel in the trunk.

AIR SUSPENSION CONTROLLER

If equipped with automatic load leveling or automatic air suspension, the controller is located behind the right side trunk trim panel.

BODY CONTROLLER

The body controller, if equipped, is located inside the passenger compartment, behind the right side kick panel.

Cruise Control

ADJUSTMENT

2.5L Engine

1. The clearance between the throttle stud and cable clevis should be $\frac{1}{16}$ in.
2. To adjust the cable, remove the retaining clip or loosen the retaining clamp nut at the throttle bracket.
3. Pull all slack out of the cable using a suitable $\frac{1}{16}$ in. diameter tool to account for proper clearance. Make sure the curb idle position of the throttle blade is not affected.
4. Reinstall the retaining clip or nut.

3.0L and 3.3L Engines

1. Grip the cable core and lightly push toward the servo.
2. While holding the position, mark the core wire next to the protective sleeve.
3. Pull the core wire away from the servo. There should be a 0.24 in. (6mm) gap between the mark on the core wire and the protective sleeve.
4. If the gap is not correct, remove the adjustment clip from the throttle bracket and move the sleeve to bring the gap into specification.
5. Reinstall the clip.

ENGINE COOLING

Radiator

REMOVAL & INSTALLATION

1. Disconnect the negative battery cable.
2. Drain the coolant.

3. Remove the upper hose and coolant reserve tank hose from the radiator.

4. Remove the electric cooling fan.

5. Raise the vehicle and support safely. Remove the lower hose from the radiator.

6. Disconnect and plug the automatic transaxle cooler hoses, if the cooler is in the radiator. Lower the vehicle.

7. Remove the mounting brackets and carefully lift the radiator out of the engine compartment.

To install:

8. Lower the radiator into position.

9. Install the mounting brackets.

10. Raise the vehicle and support safely. Connect the automatic transaxle cooler lines, if they were disconnected.

11. Connect the lower hose. Lower the vehicle.

12. Install the electric cooling fan.

13. Connect the upper hose and coolant reserve tank hose.

14. Fill the system with coolant and bleed the system.

15. Connect the negative battery cable, run the vehicle until the thermostat opens, fill the radiator completely and check the automatic transaxle fluid level.

16. Once the vehicle has cooled, recheck the coolant level.

Electric Cooling Fan
—— CAUTION ——

Make sure the key is in the OFF position when working the electric cooling fan. If not, the fan could turn ON at any time, causing serious personal injury.

TESTING

1. Unplug the fan connector.

2. Using a jumper wire, connect the female terminal of the fan connector to the negative battery terminal.

3. The fan should come ON when the male terminal is connected to the positive battery terminal.

4. If not, the fan is defective and should be replaced.

REMOVAL & INSTALLATION

1. Disconnect the negative battery cable.

2. Unplug the connector.

3. Remove the mounting screws.

4. Remove the fan assembly from the vehicle.

5. The installation is the reverse of the removal procedure.

Heater Core

REMOVAL & INSTALLATION

1. Disconnect the negative battery cable. Properly discharge the air conditioning system. Drain the cooling system.

2. Clamp off the heater hoses near the heater core and remove the hoses from the core tubes. Plug the hose ends and the core tubes to prevent spillage of coolant.

3. Disconnect the H-valve connection at the valve and remove the H-valve. Remove the condensation tube.

4. Disconnect the vacuum lines at the brake booster and water valve, if equipped.

5. Remove the right upper and lower under-panel silencers.

6. Remove the steering column cover and the ash tray.

7. Remove the left side under-panel silencer.

8. Remove the right side cowl trim piece.

9. Remove the glove box assembly and the right side instrument panel reinforcement.

10. Remove the center distribution and defroster adaptor ducts.

11. Disconnect the relay module, blower motor wiring and 25-way connector bracket and fuse block from the panel.

12. Disconnect the demister hoses from the top of the package.

13. Disconnect the temperature control cable and vacuum harness, if equipped. If equipped with Automatic Temperature Control (ATC), disconnect the instrument panel wiring from the rear of the ATC unit.

14. Disconnect the hanger strap from the package and rotate it out of the way.

15. Remove the retaining nuts from the package mounting studs at the firewall.

16. Fold the carpeting and insulation back to provide a little more working room and to prevent spillage from staining the carpeting.

17. Move the package rearward to clear the mounting studs and lower.

18. Pull the right side of the instrument panel out as far as possible. Rotate the package while removing it from under the instrument panel.

19. To disassemble the housing assembly, remove the vacuum diaphragm, if equipped. Then remove the retaining screws from the cover and remove the cover.

20. Remove the retaining screw from the heater core and remove the core from the housing assembly.

To install:

21. Remove the temperature control door from the housing and clean the unit out with solvent. Lubricate the lower pivot rod and its well and install. Wrap the heater core with foam tape and place it in position. Secure it with its screw.

22. Assemble the package, making sure all vacuum tubing is properly routed.

23. If equipped, feed the vacuum lines through the hole in the firewall and install the assembly to the vehicle. Connect the vacuum harness and demister hoses. Install the nuts to the firewall and connect the hanger strap inside the passenger compartment.

24. Fold the carpeting back into position.

25. Connect the wiring to the ATC unit, if equipped.

26. Install the fuse block. Connect the 25-way connector, relay module and blower motor wiring.

27. Install the center distribution and defroster adaptor ducts.

28. Install the right side instrument panel reinforcement and the glove box assembly.

29. Install the right side cowl trim piece, left side under-panel silencer, steering column cover, ash tray and right side under-panel silencers.

30. Connect the vacuum lines at the brake booster and water valve.

31. Using new gaskets, install the H-valve and condensation tube.

32. Connect the heater hoses.

33. Using the proper equipment, evacuate and recharge the air conditioning system.

34. Fill the cooling system.

35. Connect the negative battery cable and check the entire climate control system for proper operation and leakage.

Water Pump
REMOVAL & INSTALLATION

2.5L Engine

1. Disconnect the negative battery cable.

2. Drain the cooling system.

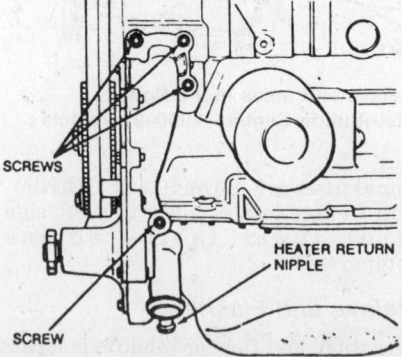

Water pump assembly—2.5L engine

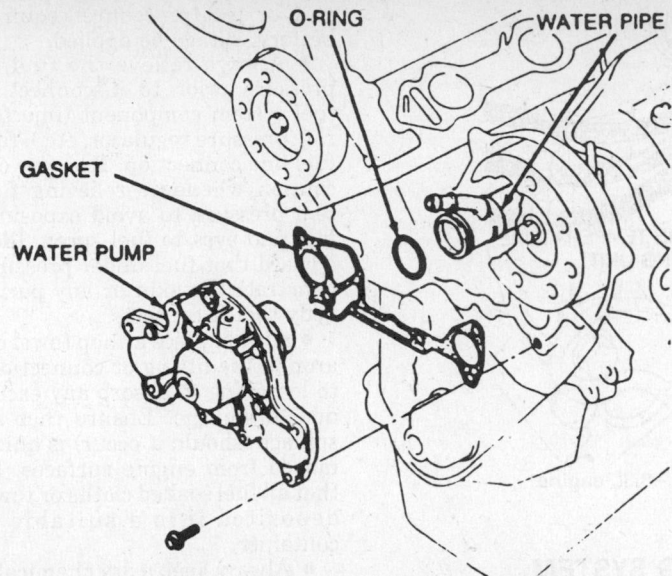

Water pump assembly—3.0L engine

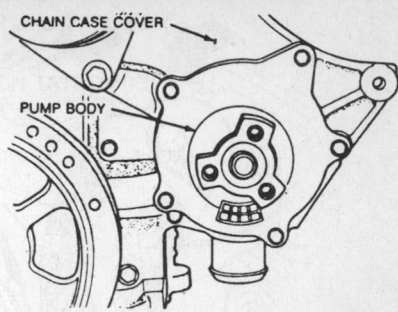

Water pump assembly—3.3L engine

3. Remove the air conditioning compressor from the bracket and position it to the side.

4. Remove the alternator and bracket. Remove the pulley from the water pump.

5. Disconnect the lower radiator hose and heater hose from the water pump.

6. Remove the water pump housing attaching screws and remove the assembly from the vehicle. Discard the O-ring.

7. Remove the water pump from the housing.

To install:

8. Using a new gasket or silicone sealer, install the water pump to the housing.

9. Install a new O-ring to the housing and install to the engine. Torque the bolts to 21 ft. lbs. (30 Nm).

10. Install the water pump pulley and torque the bolts to 21 ft. lbs. (30 Nm). Connect the radiator hose and heater hose to the water pump.

11. Install all items removed to gain access to the water pump, then adjust the belts.

12. Remove the hex-head plug on the top of the thermostat housing. Fill the radiator with coolant until the coolant comes out the plug hole. Install the plug and continue to fill the radiator.

13. Connect the negative battery cable, run the vehicle until the thermostat opens, fill the radiator completely and check for leaks.

14. Once the vehicle has cooled, recheck the coolant level.

3.0L Engine

1. Disconnect the negative battery cable.

2. Drain the cooling system.

3. Remove the timing cover. If the same timing belt will be reused, mark the direction of the timing belt's rotation, for installation in the same direction. Make sure the engine is positioned so the No. 1 cylinder is at the TDC of its compression stroke and the sprockets timing marks are aligned with the engine's timing mark indicators.

4. Loosen the timing belt tensioner bolt and remove the belt. Position the tensioner as far away from the center of the engine as possible and tighten the bolt. Remove the water pump mounting bolts, separate the pump from the water inlet pipe and remove the pump from the engine.

To install:

5. Install the pump with a new gasket to the engine. Torque the water pump mounting bolts to 20 ft. lbs. (27 Nm).

6. If not already done, position both camshafts so the marks line up with those on the alternator bracket (rear bank) and inner timing cover (front bank). Rotate the crankshaft so the timing mark aligns with the mark on the oil pump.

7. Install the timing belt on the crankshaft sprocket and while keeping the belt tight on the tension side (right side), install the belt on the front camshaft sprocket.

8. Install the belt on the water pump pulley, then the rear camshaft sprocket and the tensioner.

9. Rotate the front camshaft counterclockwise to tension the belt between the front camshaft and the crankshaft. If the timing marks became misaligned, repeat the procedure.

10. Install the crankshaft sprocket flange.

11. Loosen the tensioner bolt and allow the spring to tension the belt.

12. Turn the crankshaft 2 full turns in the clockwise direction only until the timing marks align again. Now that the belt is properly tensioned, torque the tensioner lock bolt to 21 ft. lbs. (29 Nm).

13. Refill the cooling system. This system uses a self-bleeding thermostat, so there is no need to bleed the system. Connect the negative battery cable and road test the vehicle.

3.3L Engine

1. Disconnect the negative battery cable.

2. Drain the cooling system.

3. Remove the serpentine belt.

4. Raise the vehicle and support safely. Remove the right front tire and wheel assembly and lower fender shield.

5. Remove the water pump pulley.

6. Remove the 5 mounting screws and remove the pump from the engine.

7. Discard the O-ring.

To install:

8. Using a new O-ring, install the pump to the engine. Torque the mounting bolts to 21 ft. lbs. (30 Nm).

9. Install the water pump pulley.

10. Install the fender shield and tire and wheel assembly. Lower the vehicle.

11. Install the serpentine belt.

12. Remove the engine temperature sending unit. Fill the radiator with coolant until the coolant comes out the sending unit hole. Install the sending unit and continue to fill the radiator.

13. Connect the negative battery cable, run the vehicle until the thermostat opens, fill the radiator completely and check for leaks.

14. Once the vehicle has cooled, recheck the coolant level.

Thermostat

REMOVAL & INSTALLATION

1. Disconnect the negative battery

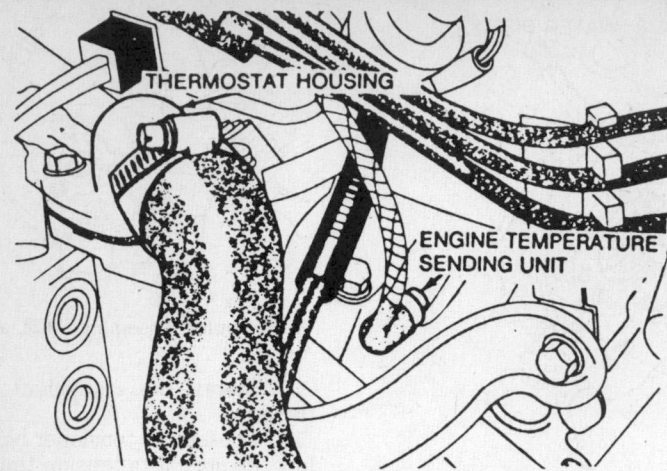

Coolant temperature sending unit location—3.3L engine

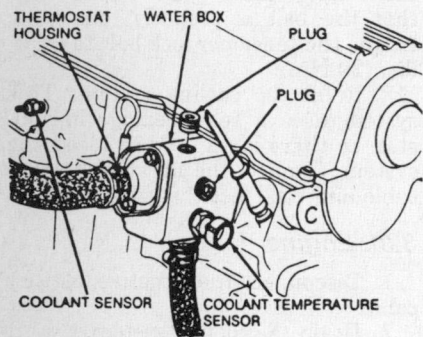

Cooling system bleed plug—2.5L engine

cable. Drain the coolant down to thermostat level or below.

2. Remove the thermostat housing.

3. Remove the thermostat and discard the gasket.

4. Clean the housing mating surfaces and use a new gasket.

5. The installation is the reverse of the removal procedure.

6. To properly fill the system with coolant:

  a. On the 2.5L engine, remove the hex-head plug on the thermostat housing. Fill the radiator with coolant until the coolant comes out the plug hole. Install the plug and continue to fill the radiator.

  b. The 3.0L engine is equipped with a self-bleeding thermostat; bleeding is not necessary.

  c. On the 3.3L engine, remove the engine temperature sending unit. Fill the radiator with coolant until the coolant comes out the sending unit hole. Install the sending unit and continue to fill the radiator.

7. Connect the negative battery cable, run the vehicle until the thermostat opens, fill the radiator completely and check for leaks.

8. Once the vehicle has cooled, recheck the coolant level.

COOLING SYSTEM BLEEDING

To bleed air from the 2.5L engine, remove the plug on the top of the thermostat housing. Fill the radiator with coolant until the coolant comes out the hole. Install the plug and continue to fill the radiator. This will vent all trapped air from the engine.

The thermostat in the 3.0L engine is equipped with a small air vent valve that allows trapped air to bleed from the system during refilling. This valve negates the need for cooling system bleeding in those engines.

On the 3.3L engine, remove the engine temperature sending unit. Fill the radiator with coolant until the coolant comes out the hole. Install the switch and continue to fill the radiator. This will vent all trapped air from the engine.

FUEL SYSTEM

Fuel System Service Precautions

Safety is the most important factor when performing not only fuel system maintenance but any type of maintenance. Failure to conduct maintenance and repairs in a safe manner may result in serious personal injury or death. Maintenance and testing of the vehicle's fuel system components can be accomplished safely and effectively by adhering to the following rules and guidelines.

• To avoid the possibility of fire and personal injury, always disconnect the negative battery cable unless the repair or test procedure requires that battery voltage be applied.

• Always relieve the fuel system pressure prior to disconnecting any fuel system component (injector, fuel rail, pressure regulator, etc.), fitting or fuel line connection. Exercise extreme caution whenever relieving fuel system pressure to avoid exposing skin, face and eyes to fuel spray. Please be advised that fuel under pressure may penetrate the skin or any part of the body that it contacts.

• Always place a shop towel or cloth around the fitting or connection prior to loosening to absorb any excess fuel due to spillage. Ensure that all fuel spillage (should it occur) is quickly removed from engine surfaces. Ensure that all fuel soaked cloths or towels are deposited into a suitable waste container.

• Always keep a dry chemical (Class B) fire extinguisher near the work area.

• Do not allow fuel spray or fuel vapors to come into contact with a spark or open flame.

• Always use a backup wrench when loosening and tightening fuel line connection fittings. This will prevent unnecessary stress and torsion to fuel line piping. Always follow the proper torque specifications.

• Always replace worn fuel fitting O-rings with new. Do not substitute fuel hose or equivalent where fuel pipe is installed.

RELIEVING FUEL SYSTEM PRESSURE

1988 Vehicles

1. Disconnect the negative battery cable.

2. Loosen the fuel filler cap to release fuel tank pressure.

3. Remove the wiring harness connector from the (any) injector.

4. Using a jumper wire, ground either injector terminal.

5. Being careful not to allow contact between the jumper leads, connect a second jumper wire to the other terminal and touch the other end to the positive battery post for no longer that 10 seconds. This will relieve fuel pressure.

6. Remove the jumper wires and continue with fuel system service.

1989–91 Vehicles

1. Loosen the fuel filler cap to release fuel tank pressure.

2. Locate and disconnect the fuel injector harness connector.

3. Connect a jumper wire from terminal No. 1 of the appropriate connector to ground.

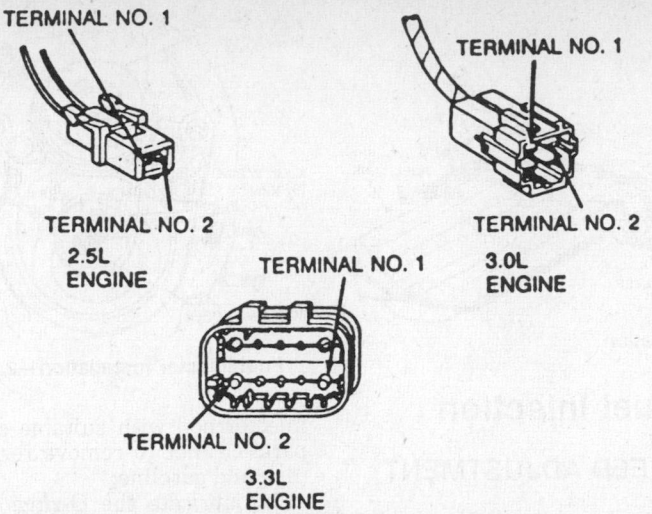

Fuel injector harness connector terminal identification

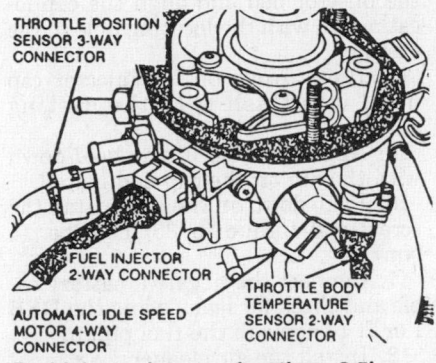

Fuel injector harness location — 2.5L engine

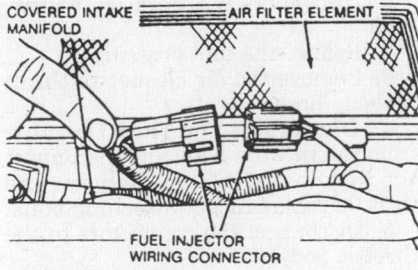

Fuel injector harness location — 3.0L engine

4. Being careful not to allow contact between the jumper leads, connect a jumper wire to terminal No. 2 of the connector and touch the other end of the jumper to the positive battery post for no longer than 5 seconds. This will relieve fuel pressure.

5. Remove the jumper wires and continue with fuel system service.

Fuel Filter

REMOVAL & INSTALLATION

—————— CAUTION ——————
Do not use conventional fuel filters, hoses

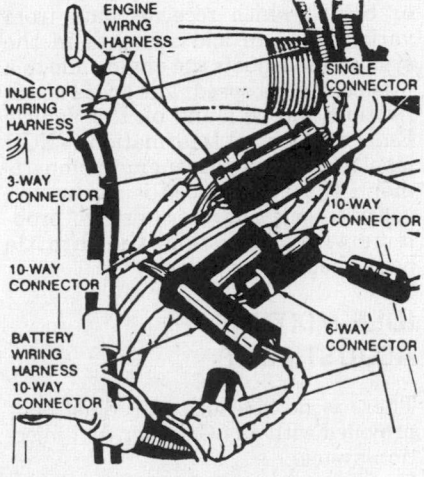

Fuel injector harness location — 3.3L engine

or clamps when servicing this fuel system. They are not compatible with the injection system and could fail, causing personal injury or damage to the vehicle. Use only hoses and clamps specifically designed for fuel injection.

1. Disconnect the negative battery cable.
2. Relieve the fuel pressure.
3. The filter is located on the frame rail toward the rear of the vehicle. Raise the vehicle and support safely. Remove the filter retaining screw and remove the filter assembly from the mounting plate.
4. Loosen the outlet hose clamp on the filter and inlet hose clamp on the rear fuel tube.
5. Wrap a shop towel around the hoses to absorb fuel. Remove the hoses from the filter and fuel tube and discard the clamps and the filter.
To install:
6. Install the inlet hose on the fuel

tube and tighten the new clamp to 10 inch lbs.
7. Install the outlet hose on the filter outlet fitting and tighten the new clamp to 10 inch lbs.
8. Position the filter assembly on the mounting plate and tighten the mounting screw to 75 inch lbs. (8 Nm).
9. Connect the negative battery cable, start the engine and check for leaks.

Electric Fuel Pump

PRESSURE TESTING

1. Relieve the fuel pressure.
2. Properly connect the fuel system pressure tester:
   a. 2.5L and 3.0L engines — special tool C–4799A or equivalent, is installed between the fuel supply hose and the engine fuel line assembly.
   b. 3.3L engine — special tool C–4799A or equivalent, is installed to the fuel rail service valve.
3. With the key in the **RUN** position, put the DRB I or II in the activate auto shutdown relay mode; this will activate the fuel pump and pressurize the system.
4. If the pressure is within specifications, reinstall the fuel hose.
5. If fuel pressure is below specifications, install the tester in the fuel supply line between the tank and the filter and repeat the test.
6. If the pressure is 5 psi higher than in Step 5, replace the fuel filter. If no change is observed, squeeze the return hose. If pressure increases, replace the pressure regulator. If no change is observed, the problem is either a plugged in-tank sock filter or a defective pump.
7. If fuel pressure is above specifications, remove the fuel return line hose from the chassis line at the fuel tank and connect a 3 foot piece of fuel hose to the return line. Put the other end into a 2 gallon minimum capacity approved gasoline container. Repeat the test. If pressure is now correct, check the in-tank return hose for kinking. Replace the fuel pump assembly if the in-tank reservoir check valve or aspirator jet is obstructed.
8. If pressure is still above specifications, remove the fuel return hose from the throttle body. Connect a substitute hose to the throttle body return nipple and place the other end of the hose in a clean container. Repeat the test. If pressure is now correct, check for a restricted fuel return line. If no change is observed, replace the fuel pressure regulator.

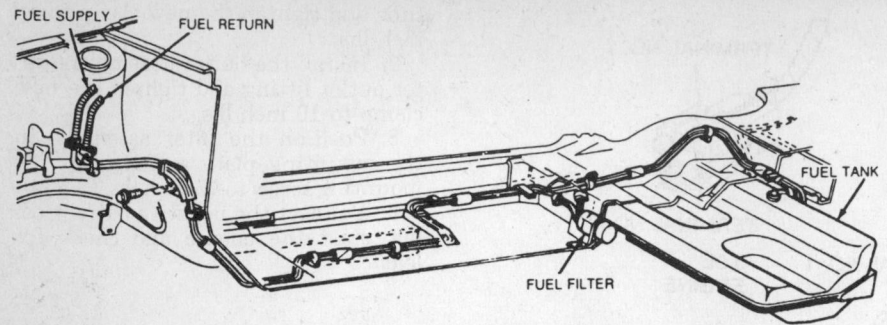

Fuel line layout and fuel filter location

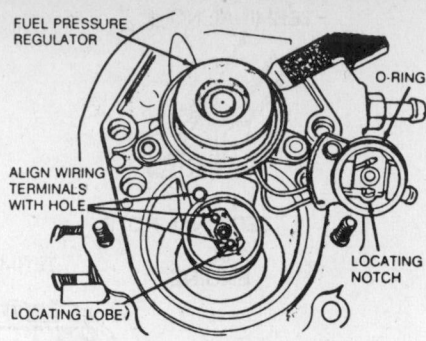

Fuel injector installation—2.5L engine

REMOVAL & INSTALLATION

1. Disconnect the negative battery cable.
2. Relieve the fuel pressure.
3. Raise the vehicle and support safely.
4. Using the proper equipment, drain the fuel tank.
5. Remove the screws that hold the filler neck to the quarter panel.
6. Disconnect the wiring and hoses from the tank.
7. Place a suitable transmission jack, or equivalent, under the center of the tank and apply slight pressure. Remove the tank straps.
8. Lower the tank and remove the filler tube from the tank.
9. Lower the tank and disconnect the vapor separator rollover valve hose and remove the fuel tank from the vehicle.
10. Using a hammer and a brass drift, tap the lock ring counterclockwise to release the pump.
11. Partially pull the pump assembly, only 1 hose goes to the pump, which is bigger than the sending unit, out of the tank until the return line hose connection is visible at the bottom of the pump assembly.
12. Disconnect the fuel fitting.
13. Remove the pump from the tank with the O-ring. Discard the O-ring, pump inlet filter and inlet seal. Disassemble as required.
To install:
14. Install a new inlet seal and filter on the end of the pump.
15. Install a new O-ring to the pump.
16. Connect the reservoir hose to the pump assembly at the suction end of the pump. Press the female fitting onto the pump assembly male end until the ears snap in place.
17. Install the pump into the tank so the fuel return hose is not kinked.
18. Install the lock ring with a hammer and brass punch turning the ring clockwise.
19. Install the fuel tank.
20. Connect the negative battery cable, start the engine and check for leaks.

Fuel Injection

IDLE SPEED ADJUSTMENT

The idle speed is controlled by the Automatic Idle Speed (AIS) motor. The AIS motor is controlled by the SMEC or SBEC, which receives data from various sensors and switches in the system and adjusts the engine idle to a predetermined speed. Idle speed specifications can be found on the Vehicle Emission Control Information (VECI) label located in the engine compartment. If the idle speed is not within specifications and there are no problems with the system, the throttle body should be replaced.

IDLE MIXTURE ADJUSTMENT

There is no idle mixture adjustment provided with any Chrysler fuel injection system.

Fuel Injector

REMOVAL & INSTALLATION

2.5L Engine

1. Disconnect the negative battery cable.
2. Remove the air cleaner assembly.
3. Relieve the fuel pressure.
4. Remove the injector hold-down Torx® screw and the hold-down.
5. Using a small flat-tipped tool, lift the cap off of the injector.
6. Using the same tool, gently pry the injector from its pod.
7. Remove the lower O-ring from the pod.
To install:
8. Install the new lower O-ring on the injector.
9. Align the injector terminal housing with the locating socket in the injector cap.
10. Press the injector cap so that the upper O-ring flange is flush with the lower surface of the cap.
11. Spray the inner surfaces of the

injector pod with suitable carburetor parts cleaner to remove residual varnish and gasoline.
12. Lubricate the O-rings sparingly with unmedicated petroleum jelly.
13. Place the injector and cap into the injector pod and align the cap locating pin with the locating hole in the casting.
14. Press firmly on the injector cap until it is flush with the casting surface.
15. Align the hole in the hold-down with the pin on the cap and install.
16. Push down on the cap, install the screw and torque to 35 inch lbs. (4 Nm).
17. Connect the negative battery cable and check for leaks using the DRB I or II to activate the fuel pump.
18. Install the air cleaner.

3.0L Engine

1. Disconnect the negative battery cable.
2. Relieve the fuel pressure.
3. Remove the air cleaner to throttle body hose.
4. Disconnect the throttle cable from the throttle body and disconnect the kickdown linkage. Remove the throttle cable bracket attaching bolts.
5. Disconnect the connectors to the throttle body.
6. Matchmark and carefully remove the vacuum hoses from the throttle body.
7. Remove the PCV and brake booster hoses from the air intake plenum.
8. Remove the ignition coil from the intake plenum, if it is mounted there.
9. Remove the EGR tube flange from the intake plenum, if equipped.
10. Unplug the coolant temperature sensor and charge temperature sensor, if equipped.
11. Remove the vacuum connection from the air intake plenum vacuum connector.
12. Remove the fuel hoses from the fuel rail and plug them.
13. Remove the air intake plenum to intake manifold bolts and remove the

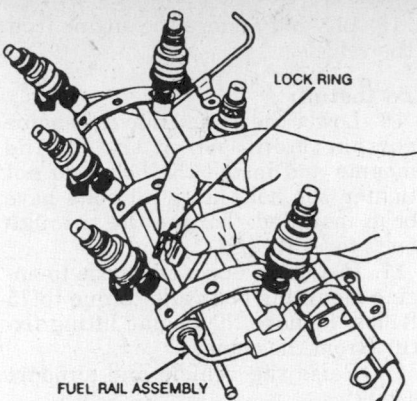

Fuel rail assembly—3.0L engine

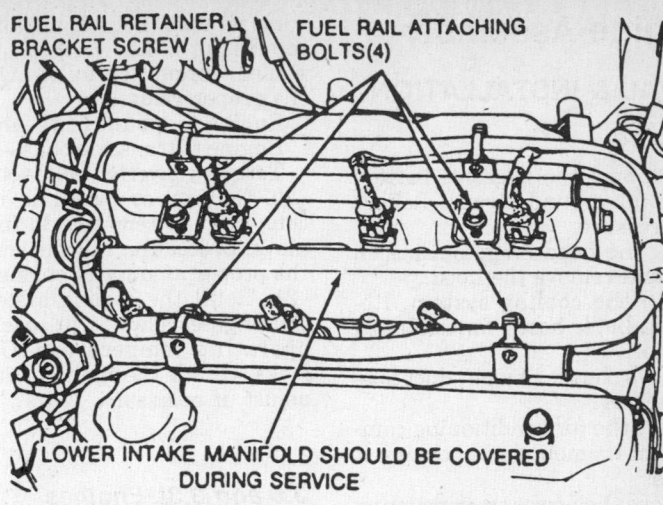

FUEL RAIL RETAINER BRACKET SCREW   FUEL RAIL ATTACHING BOLTS(4)

LOWER INTAKE MANIFOLD SHOULD BE COVERED DURING SERVICE

Fuel rail assembly—3.3L engine

plenum and gaskets. Cover the intake manifold openings.

14. Remove the vacuum hoses from the fuel rail.

15. Disconnect the fuel injector wiring harness.

16. Remove the fuel rail attaching bolts and remove the fuel rail with the wiring harness from the vehicle. Position the rail on the bench upside down so the injectors are easily accessible.

17. Remove the small connector retainer clip and unplug the injector. Remove the injector clip off the fuel rail and injector. Pull the injector straight out of the rail.

To install:

18. Lubricate the rubber O-ring with clean oil and install to the rail receiver cap. Install the injector clip to the **TOP** slot of the injector, plug in the connector and install the connector clip.

19. Install the fuel rail to the vehicle and plug in the injector harness. Connect the vacuum hoses to the fuel rail.

20. Install new intake plenum gaskets with the beaded sealer side up and install the intake plenum. Torque the attaching bolts and nuts to 115 inch lbs. (13 Nm).

21. Install the fuel hoses to the fuel rail.

22. Install or connect all items that were removed or disconnected from the intake plenum and throttle body.

23. Connect the negative battery cable and check for leaks using the DRB I or II to activate the fuel pump.

3.3L Engine

1. Disconnect the negative battery cable.

2. Relieve the fuel pressure.

3. Remove the air cleaner and hose assembly.

4. Disconnect the throttle cable. Remove the wiring harness from the throttle cable bracket and intake manifold water tube.

5. Remove the vacuum hose harness from the throttle body.

6. Remove the PCV and brake booster hoses from the air intake plenum.

7. Remove the EGR tube flange from the intake plenum, if equipped.

8. Unplug the charge temperature sensor and unplug all vacuum hoses from the intake plenum.

9. Remove the cylinder head to intake plenum strut.

10. Disconnect the MAP sensor and oxygen sensor connector. Remove the engine mounted ground strap.

11. Release the fuel hose quick disconnect fittings and remove the hoses from the fuel rail. Plug the hoses.

12. Remove the Direct Ignition System (DIS) coils and the alternator bracket to intake manifold bolt.

13. Remove the intake manifold bolts and rotate the manifold back over the rear valve cover. Cover the intake manifold.

14. Remove the vacuum harness from the pressure regulator.

15. Remove the fuel tube retainer bracket screw and fuel rail attaching bolts. Spread the retainer bracket to allow for clearance when removing the fuel tube.

16. Remove the fuel rail injector wiring clip from the alternator bracket.

17. Disconnect the cam sensor, coolant temperature sensor and engine temperature sensor.

18. Remove the fuel rail.

19. Position the rail on the bench so the injectors are easily accessible.

20. Remove the small connector retainer clip and unplug the injector. Remove the injector clip off the fuel rail and injector. Pull the injector straight out of the rail.

To install:

21. Lubricate the rubber O-ring with clean oil and install to the rail receiver cap. Install the injector clip to the slot in the injector, plug in the connector and install the connector clip.

22. Install the fuel rail.

23. Connect the cam sensor, coolant temperature sensor and engine temperature sensor.

24. Install the fuel rail injector wiring clip to the alternator bracket.

25. Install the fuel rail attaching bolts and fuel tube retainer bracket screw.

26. Install the vacuum harness to the pressure regulator.

27. Install the intake manifold with a new gasket. Install the bolts only fingertight. Install the alternator bracket to intake manifold bolt and the cylinder head to intake manifold strut and bolts. Torque the intake manifold mounting bolts to 21 ft. lbs. (28 Nm) starting from the middle and working outward. Torque the bracket and strut bolts to 40 ft. lbs. (54 Nm).

28. Install or connect all items that were removed or disconnected from the intake manifold and throttle body.

29. Connect the fuel hoses to the rail. Push the fittings in until they click in place.

30. Install the air cleaner assembly.

31. Connect the negative battery cable and check for leaks using the DRB I or II to activate the fuel pump.

ENGINE MECHANICAL

NOTE: Disconnecting the negative battery cable on some vehicles may interfere with the functions of the on board computer systems and may require the computer to undergo a relearning process, once the negative battery cable is reconnected.

Engine Assembly

REMOVAL & INSTALLATION

2.5L Engine

1. Disconnect the negative battery cable and all ground straps. Relieve the fuel pressure.
2. Mark the hood hinge outline on the hood and remove the hood.
3. Drain the cooling system. Remove the radiator hoses, fan assembly and radiator.
4. Remove the air cleaner, duct hoses and oil filter.
5. Unbolt the air conditioning compressor from its mount and position it to the side.
6. Remove the power steering pump mounting bolts and position the pump to the side, without disconnecting any fluid lines.
7. Label and disconnect all electrical connectors from the engine, alternator and fuel injection system.
8. Disconnect and plug the fuel lines and heater hoses.
9. Disconnect the throttle linkage.
10. Remove the alternator.
11. Raise the vehicle and support safely.
12. Disconnect the exhaust pipe from the manifold. Remove the right inner fender shield.
13. If equipped with an automatic transaxle, perform the following procedures:
   a. Remove the lower cover from the transaxle case.
   b. Remove the starter and set it aside.
   c. Matchmark the flexplate to the torque converter, for installation purposes.
   d. Remove the torque converter bolts. Separate the converter from the flexplate. Remove the lower bellhousing bolts.
14. Lower the vehicle and support the transaxle, if still in the vehicle, with a floor jack or equivalent.
15. Attach an engine lifting device to the engine.
16. Remove the remaining bellhousing bolts.

NOTE: If removing the insulator-to-rail screws, first mark the position of the insulator on the side rail to insure proper alignment during reinstallation.

17. Remove the front engine mount nut/bolt and the left insulator through bolt or the insulator bracket-to-transaxle bolts.
18. Lift the engine from the vehicle and remove.
To install:
19. Lower the engine into the engine compartment. Loosely install all of the mounting bolts. With all bolts installed, torque the following bollts to the proper values:
   Engine to mount bolts – 40 ft. lbs.
   Engine to transaxle bolts – 70 ft. lbs.
   Torque converter bolts – 40 ft. lbs.
20. Connect or install all items disconnected or removed during the removal procedure. Fill the engine with the proper amount of engine oil.
21. Refill the cooling system. Start the engine, allow it to reach normal operating temperature. Check for leaks. Check the ignition timing and adjust, if necessary.

3.0 and 3.3L Engines

1. Disconnect the negative battery cable. Relieve the fuel pressure.
2. Matchmark the hinge-to-hood position and remove the hood.
3. Drain the cooling system. Disconnect and label all engine electrical connections.
4. Remove the coolant hoses from the radiator and engine. Remove the radiator and cooling fan assembly.
5. Remove the air cleaner assembly. Disconnect the fuel lines from the engine. Disconnect the accelerator cable from the engine.
6. Raise the vehicle and support safely. Drain the engine oil.
7. Remove the air conditioning compressor mounting bolts, the drive belts and position the compressor to the side. Disconnect the exhaust pipe from the exhaust manifold.
8. Remove the transaxle inspection cover, matchmark the converter to the flexplate and remove the torque converter bolts.
9. Remove the power steering pump mounting bolts and set the pump aside, upright, with the fluid lines attached.
10. Remove the lower bellhousing bolts. Disconnect and label the starter motor wiring and remove the starter motor from the engine.
11. Lower the vehicle. Disconnect and label the vacuum hoses and engine ground straps.
12. Support the transaxle with a floor jack or equivalent. Attach an engine lifting device to the engine.
13. Remove the upper transaxle-to-engine bolts.
14. To separate the engine mounts from the insulators, mark the right insulator-to-right frame support and remove the mounting bolts. Remove the front engine mount through bolt. Remove the left insulator through bolt, from inside the wheel housing. Remove the insulator bracket-to-transaxle bolts.

15. Lift and remove the engine from the vehicle.

To Install:
16. Lower the engine into the engine compartment. Align the engine mounts and install the bolts; do not tighten the bolts until all bolts have been installed. Torque the through bolts to 75 ft. lbs.
17. Install the upper transaxle-to-engine mounting bolts and torque to 75 ft. lbs. Remove the engine lifting fixture from the engine.
18. Raise the vehicle and support safely.
19. Align the converter marks, install the torque converter bolts. Install the transaxle inspection cover.
20. Connect the exhaust pipe to the exhaust manifold. Install the starter motor and connect the wiring.
21. Install the power steering pump and air conditioning compressor. Adjust the drive belt tension, if necessary.
22. Lower the vehicle. Reconnect all vacuum hoses and electrical connections to the engine.
23. Connect the fuel lines and accelerator cable.
24. Install the radiator and fan assembly. Connect the fan motor wiring. Connect the radiator hoses and refill the cooling system.
25. Refill the engine with the proper oil to the correct level.
26. Connect the engine ground straps. Install the hood and align the matchmarks. Connect the battery.
27. Start and run the engine until it reaches normal operating temperatures and check for leaks. Adjust the transaxle linkage, if necessary.

Engine Mounts

REMOVAL & INSTALLATION

1. Disconnect the negative battery cable.
2. Matchmark the engine mount to its frame mounting location.
3. Raise the vehicle and support safely, if necessary. Using the proper equipment, support the weight of the engine.
4. Remove all bolts and nuts that attach the mount to the engine strut, transaxle or body and remove the mount assembly from the vehicle.
5. Remove the through bolt and separate the insulator from the yoke bracket, as required.
6. The installation is the reverse of the removal procedure. Make sure that matchmarks are aligned before tightening bolts.

Cylinder Head

REMOVAL & INSTALLATION

2.5L Engine

1. Relieve the fuel pressure. Disconnect the negative battery cable and unbolt it from the head. Drain the cooling system. Remove the dipstick bracket nut from the thermostat housing.

2. Remove the air cleaner assembly. Remove the upper radiator hose and disconnect the heater hoses.

3. Disconnect and label the vacuum lines, hoses and wiring connectors from the manifolds, throttle body and from the cylinder head.

4. Disconnect the all linkages and the fuel line from the throttle body. Unbolt the cable bracket. Remove the ground strap attaching screw from the firewall.

5. Remove the upper air conditioning compressor mounting bolts. The cylinder head can be remove with the compressor and bracket still mounted. Remove the upper timing belt cover.

6. Raise the vehicle and support safely. Disconnect the exhaust pipe from the exhaust manifold.

7. Rotate the engine by hand, until the timing marks align. The No. 1 piston should be at TDC of its compression stroke. Lower the vehicle.

8. With the timing marks aligned, remove the camshaft sprocket. The camshaft sprocket can be suspended to keep the timing intact. Remove the spark plug wires from the spark plugs.

9. Remove the valve cover and curtain. Remove the cylinder head bolts and washers, starting from the outside and working inward.

10. Remove the cylinder head from the engine.

11. Clean the cylinder head gasket mating surfaces.

To install:

12. Using new gaskets and seals, install the cylinder head to the engine block. Using new head bolts assembled with the old washers, torque the cylinder head bolts in sequence, to 45 ft. lbs. (61 Nm). Repeating the sequence, torque the bolts to 65 ft. lbs. (88 Nm). With the bolts at 65 ft. lbs., turn each bolt an additional ¼ turn.

13. Install the timing belt.

14. Install or connect all items that were removed or disconnected during the removal procedure.

15. Refill the cooling system. Connect the negative battery cable. Start the engine and check for leaks using the DRB I or II to activate the fuel pump.

16. Adjust the timing as required.

3.0L Engine

1. Relieve the fuel pressure. Disconnect the negative battery cable. Drain the cooling system.

2. Remove the compressor drive belt and the air conditioning compressor from its mount and support it aside. Using a ½ in. drive breaker bar, insert it into the square hole of the serpentine drive belt tensioner, rotate it counterclockwise to reduce the belt tension and remove the belt. Remove the alternator and power steering pump from the brackets and move them aside.

3. Raise the vehicle and support safely. Remove the right front wheel and the inner splash shield.

4. Remove the crankshaft pulleys and the torsional damper.

5. Lower the vehicle. Using a floor jack and a block of wood positioned under the oil pan, raise the engine slightly. Remove the engine mount bracket from the timing cover end of the engine and the timing belt covers.

6. To remove the timing belt, perform the following procedures:

   a. Rotate the crankshaft to position the No. 1 cylinder on the TDC of its compression stroke; the crankshaft sprocket timing mark should align with the oil pan timing indicator and the camshaft sprockets timing marks (triangles) should align with the rear timing belt covers timing marks.

   b. Mark the timing belt in the direction of rotation for reinstallation purposes.

   c. Loosen the timing belt tensioner and remove the timing belt.

NOTE: When removing the timing belt from the camshaft sprocket, make sure the belt does not slip off of the other camshaft sprocket. Support the belt so it can not slip off of the crankshaft sprocket and opposite side camshaft sprocket.

7. Remove the air cleaner assembly. Label and disconnect the spark plug wires and the vacuum hoses.

8. Remove the valve cover.

9. Install auto lash adjuster retainer tools MD998443 or equivalent, on the rocker arms.

10. If removing the front cylinder head, matchmark the distributor rotor to the distributor housing and the housing to distributor extension locations. Remove the distributor and the distributor extension.

11. Remove the camshaft bearing assembly to cylinder head bolts but do not remove the bolts from the assembly. Remove the rocker arms, rocker shafts and bearing caps as an assembly, as required. Remove the camshafts from the cylinder head and inspect them for damage.

12. Remove the intake manifold assembly.

13. Remove the exhaust manifold.

14. Remove the cylinder head bolts, starting from the outside and working inward. Remove the cylinder head from the engine.

15. Clean the gasket mounting surfaces and check the heads for warpage; maximum warpage is 0.008 in. (0.20mm).

To install:

16. Install the new cylinder head gasket(s) over the dowels on the engine block.

17. Install the cylinder head(s) on the engine and torque the cylinder head bolts in sequence using 3 even steps, to 70 ft. lbs. (95 Nm).

18. Install or connect all items that were removed or disconnected during the removal procedure.

19. When installing the timing belt over the camshaft sprocket, use care not to allow the belt to slip off the opposite camshaft sprocket.

20. Make sure the timing belt is installed on the camshaft sprocket in the same position as when removed.

21. Refill the cooling system. Connect the negative battery cable. Start the engine and check for leaks using

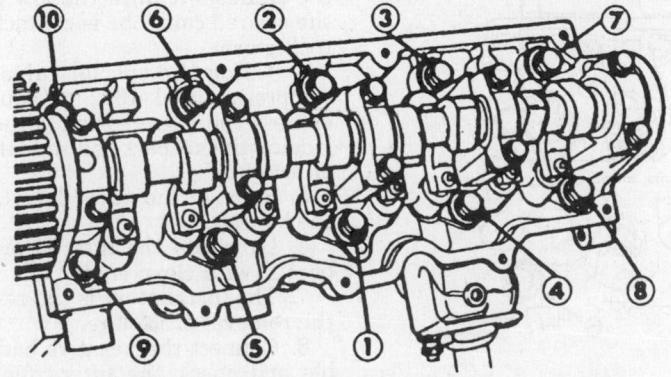

Cylinder head bolt torque sequence—2.5L engine

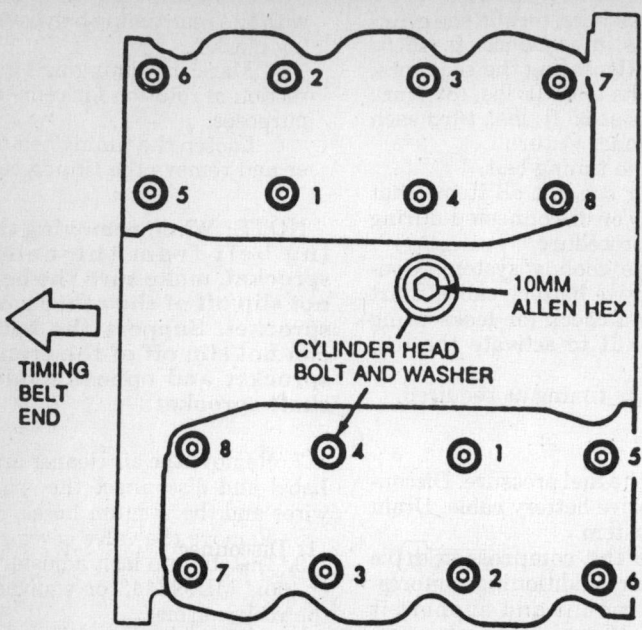

Cylinder head bolt torque sequence—3.0L engine

the DRB I or II to activate the fuel pump.

22. Adjust the timing as required.

3.3L Engine

1. Relieve the fuel pressure. Disconnect the negative battery cable. Drain the cooling system.

2. Remove the intake manifold with the throttle body.

3. Disconnect the coil wires, coolant temperature sending unit wire, heater hoses and bypass hose.

4. Remove the closed ventilation system hoses, evaporation control system hoses and valve cover.

5. Remove the exhaust manifold.

6. Remove the rocker arm and shaft assemblies. Remove the pushrods and identify them in ensure installation in their original positions.

7. Remove the head bolts and remove the cylinder head from the block.

To install:

8. Clean the gasket mounting surfaces and install a new head gasket to the block.

9. Install the head to the block. Before installing the head bolts, inspect them for stretching. Hold a straight edge up to the threads. If the threads are not all on line, the bolt is stretched and should be replaced.

10. Torque the bolts in sequence to 45 ft. lbs. (61 Nm). Repeat the sequence and torque the bolts to 65 ft. lbs. (88 Nm). With the bolts at 65 ft. lbs., turn each bolt an additional ¼ turn.

11. Torque the lone head bolt in the rear of the head to 25 ft. lbs. (33 Nm)

after the other 8 bolts have been properly torqued.

12. Install the pushrods, rocker arms and shafts and torque the bolts to 21 ft. lbs. (12 Nm).

13. Place a drop of silicone sealer onto each of the 4 manifold to cylinder head gasket corners.

CAUTION

The intake manifold gasket is composed of very thin and sharp metal. Handle this gasket with care or damage to the gasket or personal injury could result.

14. Install the intake manifold gasket and torque the end retainers to 105 inch lbs. (12 Nm).

15. Install the intake manifold and torque the bolts in sequence to 10 inch lbs. Repeat the sequence increasing the torque to 17 ft. lbs. (23 Nm) and recheck each bolt for 17 ft. lbs. After the bolts are torqued, inspect the seals to ensure that they have not become dislodged.

16. Lubricate the injector O-rings with clean oil and position the fuel rail in place. Install the rail mounting bolts.

17. Install the valve cover with a new gasket. Install the exhaust manifold.

18. Install or connect all remaining items that were removed or disconnected during the removal procedure.

19. Refill the cooling system. Connect the negative battery cable. Start the engine and check for leaks using the DRB I or II to activate the fuel pump.

Valve Lifters

REMOVAL & INSTALLATION

2.5L Engine

1. Disconnect the negative battery cable.

2. Remove the valve cover and curtain. If removing all lifters, remove the camshaft and rocker arms.

3. If only removing 1 lifter, rotate the crankshaft until the low point of the desired cam lobe is contacting the rocker arm.

4. Using the special valve spring compressor tool 4682 or equivalent, depress the valve spring without dislodging the keepers and slide the rocker arm out.

5. Remove the valve lifter(s) from the bore(s).

6. Lubricate the lifter(s) and their bore(s) with clean engine oil.

7. The installation is the reverse of the removal procedure.

8. Connect the negative battery cable and check the lifters for proper operation.

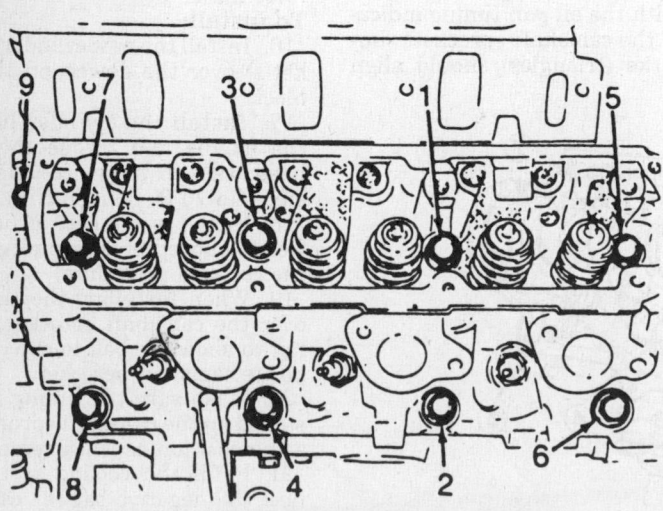

Cylinder head bolt torque sequence—3.3L engine

3.0L Engine

1. Disconnect the negative battery cable. Remove the air cleaner assembly.
2. Remove the valve cover.
3. Using the valve lifter retainer tools MD998443 or equivalent, install them on the rocker arms to keep the lifters from falling out.
4. On the right side cylinder head, remove the distributor extension.
5. Have a helper hold the rear end of the camshaft down. If the rear of the camshaft cannot be held down, the belt will dislodge and the valve timing will be lost. Loosen the camshaft cap bolts but do not remove them from the caps. Remove the caps, arms, shafts and bolts all as an assembly.
6. Remove the lifter(s) from the rocker arm(s).
7. Lubricate the lifter(s) and their bore(s) with clean engine oil.
8. The installation is the reverse of the removal procedure.
9. Connect the negative battery cable and check the lifters for proper operation.

3.3L Engine

1. Disconnect the negative battery cable. Relieve the fuel pressure.
2. Remove the cylinder head(s) to gain access to the valve lifter(s).

3. Remove the yoke retainer and aligning yoke(s).
4. Use an appropriate valve lifter removal tool to remove each lifter from its bore. If reinstalling the tappets, identify each upon removal to ensure installation in the original position.

To install:

5. Lubricate the lifter(s) and bore(s) and install.
6. Install aligning yoke(s).
7. Install the yoke retainer and torque the bolts to 105 inch lbs. (12 Nm).
8. Install the cylinder head(s) and all related components.
9. Connect the negative battery cable and check the lifters for proper operation.

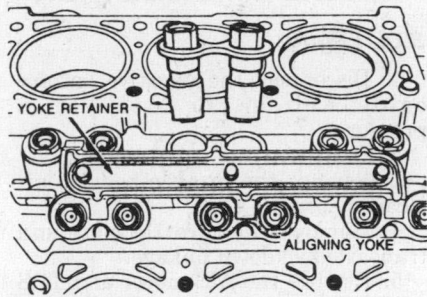

Aligning yoke and yoke retainer for roller lifters—3.3L engine

Rocker Arms/Shafts

REMOVAL & INSTALLATION

2.5L Engine

1. Disconnect the negative battery cable.
2. Remove the valve cover.
3. Rotate the crankshaft until the low point of the desired cam lobe is contacting the rocker arm.
4. Use the special valve spring compressor tool or equivalent, depress the valve spring without dislodging the keepers and slide the rocker arm out.
5. The installation is the reverse of the removal procedure.

3.0L Engine

1. Disconnect the negative battery cable. Remove the air cleaner assembly.
2. Remove the valve cover.
3. Using the auto lash adjuster retainer tools MD998443 or equivalent, install them on the rocker arms to keep the lash adjusters from falling out.
4. Remove the distributor extension, if necessary.
5. Have a helper hold the rear end of the camshaft down. If the rear of the camshaft cannot be held down, the

OIL INTAKE SHAFT HAS AN EXTRA HOLE IN BOTTOM

SHAFTS

CAP NO. 1

CAP NO. 3

CAP NO. 4

CAP NO. 2

SPRING

ROCKER ARM

2

2

CAP NO. 2 WITH OIL INLET (INTAKE) FROM CYLINDER HEAD

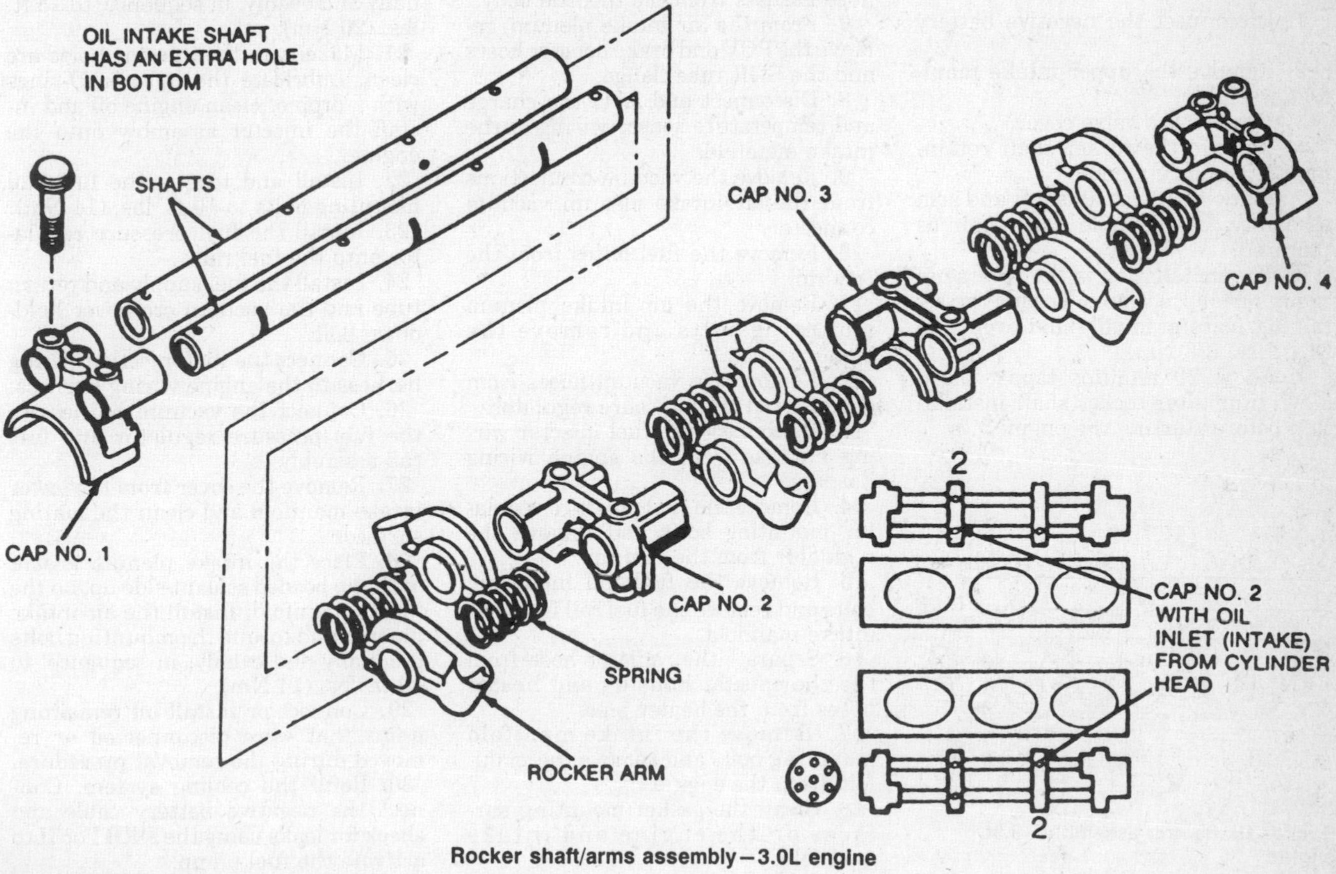

Rocker shaft/arms assembly—3.0L engine

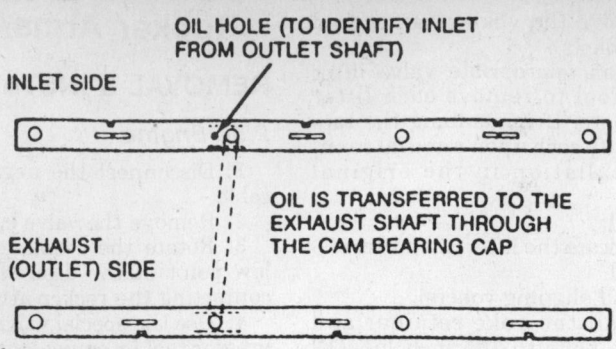

Identifying the rocker shafts—3.0L engine

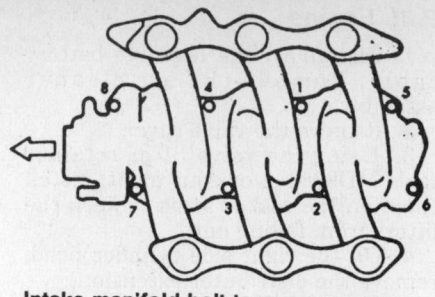

Intake manifold bolt torque sequence—3.0L engine

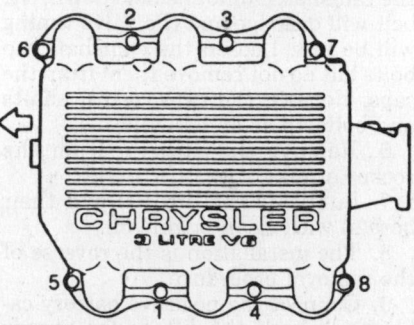

Air intake plenum bolt torque sequence—3.0L engine

belt will dislodge and the valve timing will be lost. Loosen the camshaft cap bolts but do not remove them from the caps. Remove the caps, arms, shafts and bolts all as an assembly.

6. Disassemble the unit keeping all parts in order and repair as required.

7. When assembling, apply a drop of sealant to the rear edge of the rear cap.

8. The installation is the reverse of the removal procedure. Torque the cap bolts first to 85 inch lbs. (19 Nm), then to 180 inch lbs. (19 Nm) in the following order: No. 3 cap, No. 2 cap, No. 1 cap and No. 4 cap.

3.3L Engine

1. Disconnect the negative battery cable.

2. Remove the upper intake manifold assembly.

3. Remove the valve cover.

4. Remove the rocker shaft retaining bolts and retainers.

5. Remove the rocker shaft and arm assembly. Disassemble and repair as required.

6. The installation is the reverse of the removal procedure. Torque the retaining bolts gradually and evenly to 21 ft. lbs. (28 Nm).

7. Allow 20 minutes tappet bleed down time after rocker shaft installation before starting the engine.

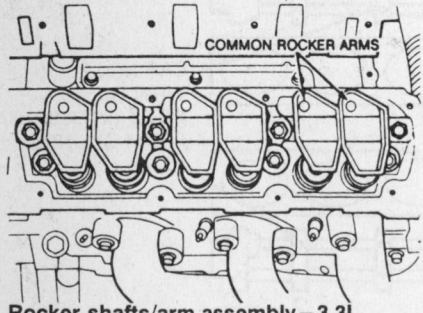

Rocker shafts/arm assembly—3.3L engine

Intake Manifold

REMOVAL & INSTALLATION

3.0L Engine

1. Disconnect the negative battery cable. Relieve the fuel system pressure.

2. Drain the cooling system.

3. Remove the throttle body to air cleaner hose.

4. Remove the throttle body and transaxle kickdown linkage.

5. Remove the AIS motor and TPS wiring connectors from the throttle body.

6. Remove and label the vacuum hose harness from the throttle body.

7. From the air intake plenum, remove the PCV and brake booster hoses and the EGR tube flange.

8. Disconnect and label the charge and temperature sensor wiring at the intake manifold.

9. Remove the vacuum connections from the air intake plenum vacuum connector.

10. Remove the fuel hoses from the fuel rail.

11. Remove the air intake plenum mounting bolts and remove the plenum.

12. Remove the vacuum hoses from the fuel rail and pressure regulator.

13. Disconnect the fuel injector wiring harness from the engine wiring harness.

14. Remove the fuel pressure regulator mounting bolts and remove the regulator from the fuel rail.

15. Remove the fuel rail mounting bolts and remove the fuel rail from the intake manifold.

16. Separate the radiator hose from the thermostat housing and heater hoses from the heater pipe.

17. Remove the intake manifold mounting bolts and remove the manifold from the engine.

18. Clean the gasket mounting surfaces on the engine and intake manifold.

To install:

19. Using new gaskets, position the intake manifold on the engine and install the mounting nuts and washers.

20. Torque the mounting nuts gradually and evenly, in sequence, to 15 ft. lbs. (20 Nm).

21. Make sure the injector holes are clean. Lubricate the injector O-rings with a drop of clean engine oil and install the injector assembly onto the engine.

22. Install and torque the fuel rail mounting bolts to 10 ft. lbs. (14 Nm).

23. Install the fuel pressure regulator onto the fuel rail.

24. Install the fuel supply and return tube and the vacuum crossover holddown bolt.

25. Connect the fuel injection wiring harness to the engine wiring harness.

26. Connect the vacuum harness to the fuel pressure regulator and fuel rail assembly.

27. Remove the cover from the lower intake manifold and clean the mating surface.

28. Place the intake plenum gasket with the beaded sealant side up, on the intake manifold. Install the air intake plenum and torque the mounting bolts gradually and evenly, in sequence, to 10 ft. lbs. (14 Nm).

29. Connect or install all remaining items that were disconnected or removed during the removal procedure.

30. Refill the cooling system. Connect the negative battery cable and check for leaks using the DRB I or II to activate the fuel pump.

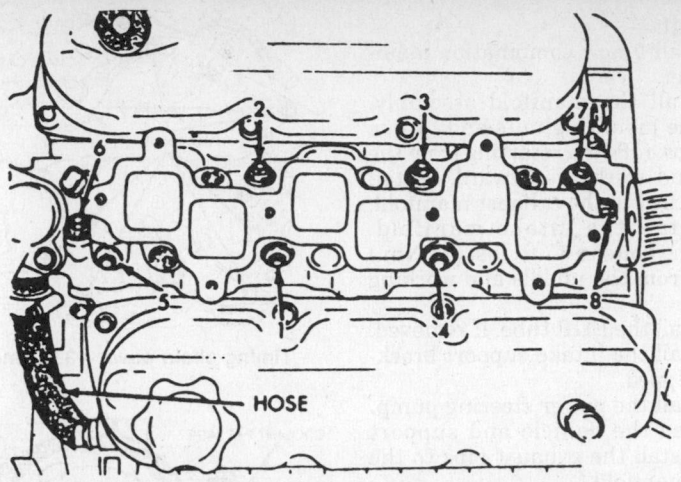

HOSE

Intake manifold bolt torque sequence—3.3L engine

3.3L Engine

1. Disconnect the negative battery cable. Relieve the fuel pressure. Drain the cooling system.
2. Remove the air cleaner to throttle body hose assembly.
3. Disconnect the throttle cable and remove the wiring harness from the bracket.
4. Remove AIS motor and TPS wiring connectors from the throttle body.
5. Remove the vacuum hose harness from the throttle body.
6. Remove the PCV and brake booster hoses from the air intake plenum.
7. Disconnect the charge temperature sensor electrical connector. Remove the vacuum harness connectors from the intake plenum.
8. Remove the cylinder head to the intake plenum strut.
9. Disconnect the MAP sensor and oxygen sensor connectors. Remove the engine mounted ground strap.
10. Remove the fuel hoses from the fuel rail and plug them.
11. Remove the DIS coils and the alternator bracket to intake manifold bolt.
12. Remove the upper intake manifold attaching bolts and remove the upper manifold.
13. Remove the vacuum harness connector from the fuel pressure regulator.
14. Remove the fuel tube retainer bracket screw and fuel rail attaching bolts. Spread the retainer bracket to allow for clearance when removing the fuel tube.
15. Remove the fuel rail injector wiring clip from the alternator bracket.
16. Disconnect the cam sensor, coolant temperature sensor and engine temperature sensor.
17. Remove the fuel rail.
18. Remove the upper radiator hose, bypass hose and rear intake manifold hose.
19. Remove the intake manifold bolts and remove the manifold from the engine.
20. Remove the intake manifold seal retaining screws and remove the manifold gasket.
21. Clean out clogged end water passages and fuel runners.

To install:

22. Clean and dry all gasket mating surfaces.
23. Place a drop of silicone sealer onto each of the 4 manifold to cylinder head gasket corners.

───────── **CAUTION** ─────────

The intake manifold gasket is composed of very thin and sharp metal. Handle this gasket with care or damage to the gasket or personal injury could result.

────────────────────

24. Install the intake manifold gasket and torque the end retainers to 10 ft. lbs. (12 Nm).
25. Install the intake manifold and torque the bolts in sequence to 10 inch lbs. Repeat the sequence increasing the torque to 17 ft. lbs. (23 Nm) and recheck each bolt for 17 ft. lbs. of torque. After the bolts are torqued, inspect the seals to ensure that they have not become dislodged.
26. Lubricate the injector O-rings with clean oil and position the fuel rail in place. Install the rail mounting bolts.
27. Connect the cam sensor, coolant temperature sensor and engine temperature sensor.
28. Install the fuel rail injector wiring clip to the alternator bracket.
29. Install the fuel rail attaching bolts and fuel tube retainer bracket screw.
30. Install the vacuum harness to the pressure regulator.
31. Install the upper intake manifold

with a new gasket. Install the bolts only fingertight. Install the alternator bracket to intake manifold bolt and the cylinder head to intake manifold strut and bolts. Torque the intake manifold mounting bolts to 21 ft. lbs. (28 Nm) starting from the middle and working outward. Torque the bracket and strut bolts to 40 ft. lbs. (54 Nm).
32. Install or connect all items that were removed or disconnected from the intake manifold and throttle body.
33. Connect the fuel hoses to the rail. Push the fittings in until they click in place.
34. Install the air cleaner assembly.
35. Connect the negative battery cable and check for leaks using the DRB I or II to activate the fuel pump.

Exhaust Manifold

REMOVAL & INSTALLATION

3.0L Engine

1. Disconnect the negative battery cable. Raise the vehicle and support safely.
2. Disconnect the exhaust pipe from the rear exhaust manifold at the articulated joint.
3. Disconnect the EGR tube from the rear manifold and unplug the oxygen sensor wire.
4. Remove the crossover pipe to manifold bolts.
5. Remove the rear manifold to cylinder head nuts and the manifold.
6. Lower the vehicle and remove the heat shield from the manifold.
7. Remove the front manifold to cylinder head nuts and the manifold.
8. Clean the gasket mounting surfaces. Inspect the manifolds for cracks, flatness and/or damage.

To install:

9. When installing, the numbers 1–3–5 on the gaskets are used with the rear cylinders and 2–4–6 are on the gasket for the front cylinders. Torque the manifold to cylinder head nuts to 14 ft. lbs. (19 Nm).
10. Install the crossover pipe to the manifold.
11. Connect the EGR tube and oxygen sensor wire.
12. Connect the exhaust pipe to the rear exhaust manifold, at the articulated joint.
13. Connect the negative battery cable and check the manifolds for leaks.

3.3L Engine

1. Disconnect the negative battery cable.
2. If removing the rear manifold, raise the vehicle and support safely. Disconnect the exhaust pipe at the ar-

ticulated joint from the rear exhaust manifold.

3. Separate the EGR tube from the rear manifold and disconnect the oxygen sensor wire.

4. Remove the alternator/power steering support strut.

5. Remove the bolts attaching the crossover pipe to the manifold.

6. Remove the bolts attaching the manifold to the head and remove the manifold.

7. If removing the front manifold, remove the heat shield, bolts attaching the crossover pipe to the manifold and the nuts attaching the manifold to the head.

8. Remove the manifold from the engine.

9. The installation is the reverse of the removal procedure. Torque all exhaust manifold attaching bolts to 17 ft. lbs. (23 Nm).

10. Start the engine and check for exhaust leaks.

Combination Manifold

REMOVAL & INSTALLATION

2.5L Engine

NOTE: On some cases, some of the manifold attaching bolts are not accessible or too heavily sealed from the factory and cannot be removed on the vehicle. Head removal would be necessary in these situations.

1. Disconnect the negative battery cable.

2. Relieve the fuel system pressure.

3. Drain the cooling system.

4. Remove the air cleaner and disconnect all vacuum lines, electrical wiring and fuel lines from the throttle body.

5. Disconnect the throttle linkage.

6. Loosen the power steering pump and remove the drive belt.

7. Remove the power brake vacuum hose from the intake manifold.

8. Remove the water hoses from the water crossover.

9. Raise the vehicle and support safely.

10. Disconnect the exhaust pipe from the exhaust manifold.

11. Remove the power steering pump from its mounting bracket and set it aside.

12. Remove the EGR tube.

13. Remove the intake manifold bolts.

14. Lower the vehicle.

15. Remove the intake manifold.

16. Remove the exhaust manifold nuts.

17. Remove the exhaust manifold.

To install:

18. Install a new combination manifold gasket.

19. Install the manifold assembly. Install the mounting nuts and torque to 13 ft. lbs. (18 Nm.) starting from the middle and working outward. Install the heat cowl to the exhaust manifold.

20. Install the intake manifold. Torque the bolts to 17 ft. lbs. (23 Nm.) starting from the middle and working outward.

21. Install the EGR tube, if removed.

22. Install the intake support bracket, if equipped.

23. Install the power steering pump.

24. Raise the vehicle and support safely. Install the exhaust pipe to the exhaust manifold.

25. Install the water hoses to the water crossover.

26. Install the power brake vacuum hose to the intake manifold.

27. Connect the throttle linkage.

28. Install all vacuum lines, electrical wiring and fuel lines to the throttle body.

29. Install the air cleaner assembly.

30. Refill the cooling system.

31. Connect the negative battery cable and check the manifolds for leaks.

Timing Chain Front Cover

REMOVAL & INSTALLATION

3.3L Engine

1. Disconnect the negative battery cable. Drain the cooling system.

2. Support the engine with a suitable engine support device and remove the right side motor mount.

3. Raise the vehicle and support safely. Drain the engine oil and remove the oil pan.

4. Remove the right wheel and splash shield.

5. Remove the drive belt.

6. Unbolt the air conditioning compressor and position it to the side. Remove the compressor mounting bracket.

7. Remove the crankshaft pulley bolt and remove the pulley using a suitable puller.

8. Remove the idler pulley from the engine bracket and remove the bracket.

9. Remove the cam sensor from the timing chain cover.

10. Remove the cover mounting bolts and the cover from the engine. Make sure the oil pump inner rotor does not fall out. Remove the 3 O-rings from the coolant passages and the oil pump outlet.

To install:

11. Thoroughly clean and dry the

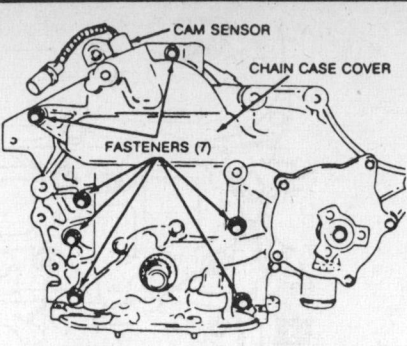

Timing chain cover—3.3L engine

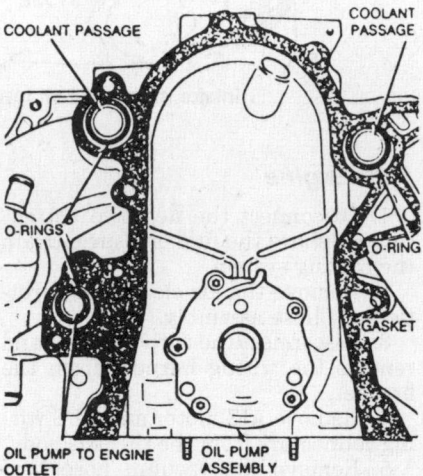

Timing cover removed—3.3L engine

gasket mating surfaces. Install new O-rings to the block.

12. Remove the crankshaft oil seal from the cover. The seal must be removed from the cover when installing to ensure proper oil pump engagement.

13. Using a new gasket, install the chain case cover to the engine.

14. Make certain that the oil pump is engaged onto the crankshaft before proceeding or severe engine damage will result. Install the attaching bolts and torque to 20 ft. lbs. (27 Nm).

15. Use tool C–4992 to install the crankshaft oil seal. Install the crankshaft pulley using a 5.9 in. suitable bolt used with thrust bearing and washer plate L–4524. Make sure the pulley bottoms out on the inner diameter of the crankshaft seal. Install the bolt and torque to 40 ft. lbs. (54 Nm).

16. Install the engine bracket and torque the bolts to 40 ft. lbs. (54 Nm). Install the idler pulley to the engine bracket.

17. To install the cam sensor, perform the following:

a. Clean off the old spacer from the sensor face completely. A new spacer must be attached to the cam sensor prior to installation; if a new spacer is not used, engine performance will be adversely affected.

b. Inspect the O-ring for damage and replace, if necessary. Lubricate the O-ring lightly with oil and push the sensor into its bore in the chain case cover until contact is made with the cam timing gear. Hold in this position and tighten the bolt to 9 ft. lbs. (12 Nm).

18. Install the air conditioning compressor and bracket.

19. Install the drive belt.

20. Install the inner splash shield and wheel.

21. Install the oil pan with a new gasket.

22. Install the motor mount.

23. Remove the engine temperature sensor and fill the cooling system until the level reaches the vacant sensor hole. Install the sensor and continue to fill the radiator. Fill the engine with the proper amount of oil.

24. Connect the negative battery cable and check for leaks.

Front Cover Oil Seal

REPLACEMENT

3.3L Engine

1. Disconnect the negative battery cable.

2. Raise the vehicle and support safely. Remove the right front wheel and the inner splash shield.

3. Remove the drive belt.

4. Remove the crankshaft bolt. Using a suitable puller, remove the crankshaft pulley.

5. Use tool C–4991 to remove the seal.

To install:

6. Clean out the bore. Place the seal with the spring toward the engine. Install the new seal using tool C–4992 until it is flush with the cover.

7. Install the crankshaft pulley using a suitable 5.9 in. bolt with thrust bearing and washer plate L-4524. Make sure the pulley bottoms out on the inner diameter of the crankshaft seal. Install the bolt and torque to 40 ft. lbs. (54 Nm).

8. Install the drive belt.

9. Install the splash shield and wheel.

10. Connect the negative battery cable and check for leaks.

Timing Chain and Gears

REMOVAL & INSTALLATION

3.3L Engine

1. If possible, position the engine so that the No. 1 piston is at TDC of its compression stroke. Disconnect the

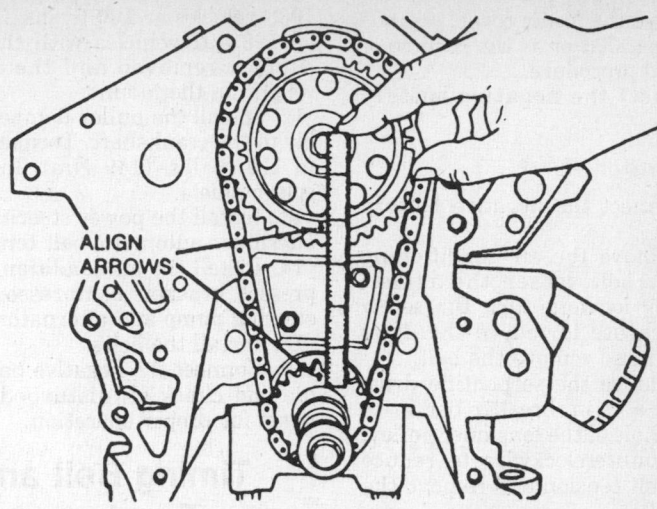

Aligning the timing marks—3.3L engine

negative battery cable. Drain the coolant.

2. Remove the timing chain case cover.

3. Remove the camshaft gear attaching cup washer and remove the timing chain with both gears attached. Remove the timing chain snubber.

To install:

4. Assemble the timing chain and gears.

5. Turn the crankshaft and camshaft to line up with the keyway locations of the gears.

6. Slide both gears over their respective shafts and use a straight edge to confirm alignment.

7. Install the cup washer and camshaft bolt. Torque the bolt to 35 ft. lbs. (47 Nm).

8. Check camshaft endplay. The specification with a new plate is 0.002–0.006 in. (0.051–0.052mm) and 0.002–0.010 in. (0.51–0.254mm) with a used plate. Replace the thrust plate if not within specifications.

9. Install the timing chain snubber.

10. Thoroughly clean and dry the gasket mating surfaces.

11. Install new O-rings to the block.

12. Remove the crankshaft oil seal from the cover. The seal must be removed from the cover when installing to ensure proper oil pump engagement.

13. Using a new gasket, install the chain case cover to the engine.

14. Make certain that the oil pump is engaged onto the crankshaft before proceeding or severe engine damage will result. Install the attaching bolts and torque to 20 ft. lbs. (27 Nm).

15. Use tool C-4992 to install the crankshaft oil seal. Install the crankshaft pulley using a 5.9 in. suitable bolt and thrust bearing and washer plate L-4524. Make sure the pulley bottoms out on the crankshaft seal di-

ameter. Install the bolt and torque to 40 ft. lbs. (54 Nm).

16. Install all other parts removed during the chain case cover removal procedure.

17. To install the cam sensor, first clean off the old spacer from the sensor face completely. Inspect the O-ring for damage and replace, if necessary. A new spacer must be attached to the cam sensor prior to installation; if a new spacer is not used, engine performance will be adversely affected. Oil the O-ring lightly and push the sensor into its bore in the chain case cover until contact is made with the cam timing gear. Hold in this position and tighten the bolt to 10 ft. lbs. (12 Nm).

18. Refill the cooling system and fill the engine with oil.

19. Connect the negative battery cable, road test the vehicle and check for leaks.

Timing Belt Front Cover

REMOVAL & INSTALLATION

2.5L Engine

1. Disconnect the negative battery cable.

2. Remove the nuts that attach the upper cover to the valve cover.

3. Remove the bolt that attaches the upper cover to the lower cover.

4. Remove the upper cover.

5. Raise the vehicle and support safely. Remove the right side splash shield.

6. Remove the crankshaft pulley, water pump pulley and the belts.

7. Remove the lower cover attaching bolts.

8. Remove the lower cover.

9. The installation is the reverse of the removal procedure.

10. Connect the negative battery cable.

3.0L Engine

1. Disconnect the negative battery cable.

2. To remove the air conditioning compressor belt, loosen the adjustment pulley locknut, turn the screw counterclockwise to reduce the drive belt tension and remove the belt.

3. To remove the serpentine drive belt, insert a ½ in. breaker bar in to the square hole of the tensioner pulley, rotate it counterclockwise to reduce the drive belt tension and remove the belt.

4. Remove the air conditioning compressor and the air compressor bracket, power steering pump and alternator from the mounts and support them to the side. Remove power steering pump/alternator automatic belt tensioner bolt and the tensioner.

5. Raise the vehicle and support safely. Remove the right inner fender splash shield.

6. Remove the crankshaft pulley bolt and the pulley/damper assembly from the crankshaft.

7. Lower the vehicle and place a floor jack under the engine to support it.

8. Separate the front engine mount insulator from the bracket. Raise the engine slightly and remove the mount bracket.

9. Remove the timing belt cover bolts and the upper and lower covers from the engine.

To install:

10. Install the timing covers and bolts.

11. Install the engine mount bracket. The engine mount through bolt must be torqued to 75 ft. lbs. (102 Nm) on

SPECIAL TOOL

HORIZONTAL
(WITHIN 15°)

Adjusting the timing belt—2.5L engine

1988 vehicles or 100 ft. lbs. (136 Nm) on 1989–91 vehicles with the engine support removed and the engine's weight on the mount.

12. Install the pulley damper assembly to the crankshaft. Torque the bolt to 110 ft. lbs. (149 Nm). Install the splash shield.

13. Install the power steering pump/alternator automatic belt tensioner.

14. Install the air conditioning compressor bracket, compressor, power steering pump and alternator.

15. Install the belts.

16. Connect the negative battery cable and check all disturbed components for proper operation.

Timing Belt and Tensioner

ADJUSTMENT

2.5L Engine

1. Disconnect the negative battery cable.

2. Raise the vehicle and support safely. Remove the right front inner splash shield.

3. Remove the tensioner cover.

4. Place the special tensioning tool C–4703 on the hex of the tensioner so the weight is at about the 10 o'clock position and loosen the bolt.

5. The tensioner should drop to the 9 o'clock position. Reposition the tool as required in order to have it end up at the 9 o'clock position, parallel to the ground, hanging toward the rear of the vehicle, ± 15 degrees.

6. Hold the tool in position and tighten the bolt. Do not pull the tool past the 9 o'clock position or the belt will be too tight and will cause howling or possible breakage.

7. Install the cover and the splash shield.

3.0L Engine

1. Disconnect the negative battery cable.

2. Remove the timing belt covers.

3. Loosen the bolt that holds the timing belt tensioner in place.

4. Allow the spring only to pull the tensioner in automatically. Do not manually move the tensioner or the belt will be too tight.

5. Tighten the tensioner locking bolt.

6. Install the timing belt covers and all related parts.

REMOVAL & INSTALLATION

2.5L Engine

1. If possible, position the engine so that the No. 1 piston is at TDC of its

compression stroke. Disconnect the negative battery cable.

2. Remove the timing belt covers. Remove the timing belt tensioner and allow the belt to hang free.

3. Place a floor jack under the engine and separate the right motor mount.

4. Remove the air conditioning compressor belt idler pulley, if equipped, and remove the mounting stud. Unbolt the compressor/alternator bracket and position it to the side.

5. Remove the timing belt from the vehicle.

To install:

6. Turn the crankshaft sprocket and intermediate shaft sprocket until the marks are in line. Position a straight edge from bolt to bolt to confirm alignment.

7. Turn the camshaft until the small hole in the sprocket is at the top and rows on the hub are in line with the camshaft cap to cylinder head mounting lines. Use a mirror to see the alignment so it is viewed straight on and not at an angle from above. Install the belt, but let at hang free at this point.

8. Install the air conditioning compressor/alternator bracket, idler pulley and motor mount. Remove the floor jack. Raise the vehicle and support safely. Have the tensioner at an arm's reach because the timing belt will have to be held in position with one hand.

9. To properly install the timing belt, reach up and engage it with the camshaft sprocket. Turn the intermediate shaft counterclockwise slightly, then engage the belt with the intermediate shaft sprocket. Hold the belt against the intermediate shaft sprocket and turn clockwise to take up all tension; if the timing marks are out of alignment, repeat until alignment is correct.

10. Using a wrench, turn the crankshaft sprocket counterclockwise slightly and wrap the belt around it. Turn the sprocket clockwise so there is no slack in the belt between sprockets; if the timing marks are out of alignment, repeat until alignment is correct.

NOTE: If the timing marks are in line but slack exists in the belt between either the camshaft and intermediate shaft sprockets or the intermediate and crankshaft sprockets, the timing will be incorrect when the belt is tensioned. All slack must be only between the crankshaft and camshaft sprockets.

11. Install the tensioner and install the mounting bolt loosely. Place the

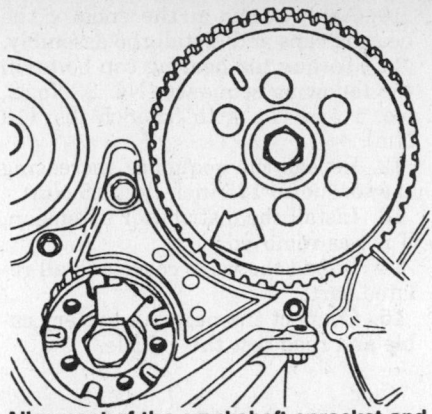

Alignment of the crankshaft sprocket and intermediate shaft sprocket — 2.5L engine

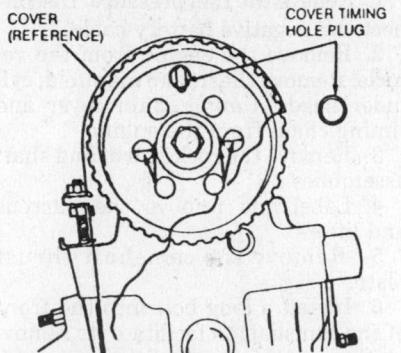

Alignment of the arrows on the camshaft sprocket with the camshaft cap- to-cylinder-mounting line — 2.5L engine

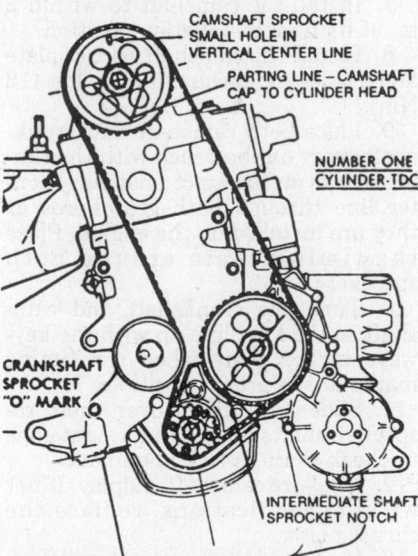

Proper timing belt positioning — 2.5L engine

special tensioning tool C–4703 on the hex of the tensioner so the weight is at about the 9 o'clock position, parallel to the ground, hanging toward the rear of the vehicle, ± 15 degrees.

12. Hold the tool in position and tighten the bolt to 45 ft. lbs. (61 Nm). Do not pull the tool past the 9 o'clock

position; this will make the belt too tight and will cause it to howl or possibly break.

13. Lower the vehicle and recheck the camshaft sprocket positioning. If it is correct install the timing belt covers and all related parts.

14. Connect the negative battery cable and road test the vehicle.

3.0L Engine

1. If possible, position the engine so that the No. 1 cylinder is at TDC of its compression stroke. Disconnect the negative battery cable. Remove the timing covers from the engine.

2. If the same timing belt will be reused, mark the direction of the timing belt's rotation, for installation in the same direction. Make sure the engine is positioned so the No. 1 cylinder is at the TDC of its compression stroke and the sprockets timing marks are aligned with the engine's timing mark indicators.

3. Loosen the timing belt tensioner bolt and remove the belt. If not removing the tensioner, position it as far away from the center of the engine as possible and tighten the bolt.

4. If the tensioner is being removed, paint the outside of the spring to ensure that it is not installed backwards. Unbolt the tensioner and remove it along with the spring.
To install:

5. Install the tensioner, if removed, and hook the upper end of the spring to the water pump pin and the lower end to the tensioner in exactly the same position as originally installed. If not already done, position both camshafts so the marks line up with those on the alternator bracket (rear bank)

and inner timing cover (front bank). Rotate the crankshaft so the timing mark aligns with the mark on the oil pump.

6. Install the timing belt on the crankshaft sprocket and while keeping the belt tight on the tension side (right side), install the belt on the front camshaft sprocket.

7. Install the belt on the water pump pulley, then the rear camshaft sprocket and the tensioner.

8. Rotate the front camshaft counterclockwise to tension the belt between the front camshaft and the crankshaft. If the timing marks became misaligned, repeat the procedure.

9. Install the crankshaft sprocket flange.

10. Loosen the tensioner bolt and allow the spring to tension the belt.

11. Turn the crankshaft 2 full turns in the clockwise direction only until the timing marks align again. Now that the belt is properly tensioned, torque the tensioner lock bolt to 21 ft. lbs. (29 Nm).

12. Install the timing belt covers and all related parts.

13. Connect the negative battery cable and road test the vehicle.

Timing Sprockets

REMOVAL & INSTALLATION

2.5L Engine

1. Disconnect the negative battery cable. Remove the timing belt.

2. Remove the crankshaft sprocket bolt. Using the puller tool C–4685 or equivalent, and the button from tool

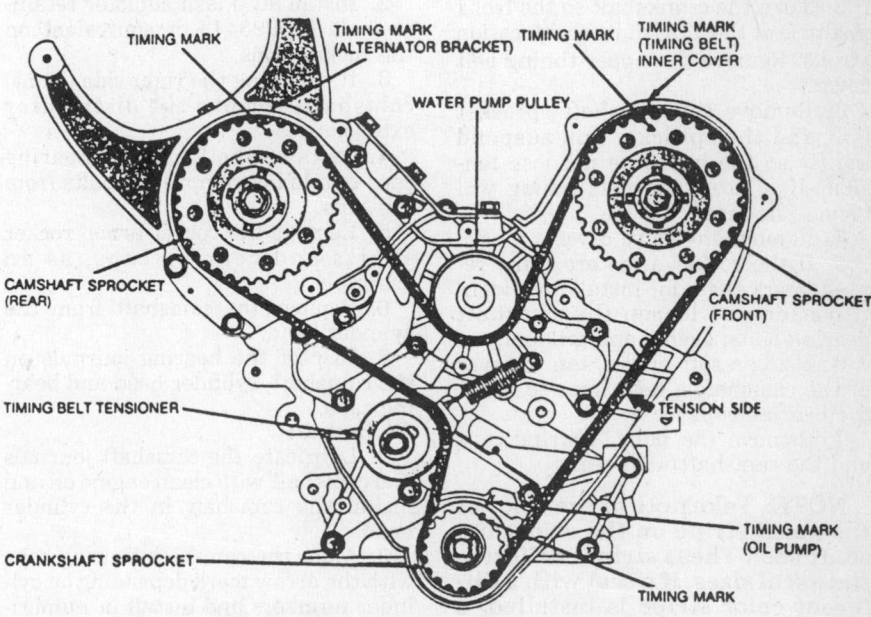

Proper timing belt positioning — 3.0L engine

L-4524 or equivalent, remove the crankshaft sprocket.

3. Using the tool C–4687 or equivalent, hold the camshaft and/or intermediate sprocket, remove the center bolt and the sprocket(s).

4. The installation is the reverse of the removal procedure. Torque the camshaft and intermediate sprocket bolts to 65 ft. lbs. (88 Nm) and the crankshaft sprocket bolt to 50 ft. lbs. (68 Nm).

5. Connect the negative battery cable and road test the vehicle.

3.0L Engine

1. Disconnect the negative battery cable.
2. Remove the timing belt.
3. To remove the camshaft sprocket, hold the sprocket with tool MB990775 or equivalent, and remove the retaining bolt and washer.
4. To remove the crankshaft sprocket, remove the bolt and remove the sprocket from the crankshaft.
5. The installation is the reverse of the removal procedure. Torque the camshaft sprocket bolt to 70 ft. lbs. (95 Nm) while holding the sprocket with the holding tool. Torque the crankshaft sprocket bolt. to 110 ft. lbs. (150 Nm).
6. Connect the negative battery cable and road test the vehicle.

Camshaft

REMOVAL & INSTALLATION

2.5L Engine

1. Disconnect the negative battery cable.
2. Turn the crankshaft so the No. 1 piston is at the TDC of its compression stroke. Remove the upper timing belt cover.
3. Remove the camshaft sprocket bolt and the sprocket and suspend tightly so the belt does not lose tension. If it does, the belt timing will have to be reset.
4. Remove the valve cover.
5. If the rocker arms are being re-used, mark them for installation identification and loosen the camshaft bearing bolts, evenly and gradually.
6. Using a soft mallet, tap the rear of the camshaft a few times to break the bearing caps loose.
7. Remove the bolts, bearing caps and the camshaft with seals.

NOTE: Take note of the color of the paint stripe on the rear camshaft seal. These stripes differentiate seal sizes. If a seal with a different color stripe is installed, a severe leak will develop if the seal

is too small or the cap will not be able to be fully installed if the seal is too big.

8. Check the oil passages for blockages and the parts for wear and damage and replace parts, as required. Clean the gasket mounting surfaces.
To install:
9. Transfer the sprocket key to the new camshaft. New rocker arms and a new camshaft sprocket bolt are normally included with the camshaft package. Install the rocker arms, lubricate the camshaft and install with end seals installed.

NOTE: Apply RTV silicone gasket material to the No. 1 and 5 bearing caps. Install the bearing caps before the seals are installed.

10. Place the bearing caps with No. 1 at the timing belt end and No. 5 at the transaxle end. The camshaft bearing caps are numbered and have arrows facing forward. Torque the camshaft bearing bolts evenly and gradually to 18 ft. lbs. (24 Nm).
11. Mount a dial indicator to the front of the engine and check the camshaft endplay. Play should not exceed 0.020 in.
12. Install the camshaft sprocket and the new bolt.
13. Install the valve cover with a new gasket.
14. Connect the negative battery cable and check for leaks.

3.0L Engine

1. Disconnect the negative battery cable. Remove the air cleaner assembly and valve covers.
2. Install auto lash adjuster retainer tools MD998443 or equivalent on the rocker arms.
3. If removing the right side (front) camshaft, remove the distributor extension.
4. Remove the camshaft bearing caps but do not remove the bolts from the caps.
5. Remove the rocker arms, rocker shafts and bearing caps, as an assembly.
6. Remove the camshaft from the cylinder head.
7. Inspect the bearing journals on the camshaft, cylinder head and bearing caps.
To install:
8. Lubricate the camshaft journals and camshaft with clean engine oil and install the camshaft in the cylinder head.
9. Align the camshaft bearing caps with the arrow mark depending on cylinder numbers and install in numerical order.

10. Apply sealer at the ends of the bearing caps and install the assembly.
11. Torque the bearing cap bolts, in the following sequence: No. 3, No. 2, No. 1 and No. 4 to 85 inch lbs. (10 Nm).
12. Repeat the sequence increasing the torque to 175 inch lbs. (18 Nm).
13. Install the distributor extension, if it was removed.
14. Install the valve cover and all related parts.
15. Connect the negative battery cable and road test the vehicle.

3.3L Engine

1. Relieve the fuel pressure. Disconnect the negative battery cable.
2. Remove the engine from the vehicle. Remove the intake manifold, cylinder heads, timing chain cover and timing chain from the engine.
3. Remove the rocker arm and shaft assemblies.
4. Label and remove the pusrods and lifters.
5. Remove the camshaft thrust plate.
6. Install a long bolt into the front of the camshaft to facilitate its removal. Remove the camshaft being careful not to damage the cam bearings with the cam lobes.
To install:
7. Install the camshaft to within 2 in. of its final installation position.
8. Install the camshaft thrust plate and 2 bolts and torque to 10 ft. lbs. (12 Nm).
9. Place both camshaft and crankshaft gears on the bench with the timing marks on the exact imaginary center line through both gear bores as they are installed on the engine. Place the timing chain around both sprockets.
10. Turn the crankshaft and camshaft so the keys line up with the keyways in the gears when the timing marks are in proper position.
11. Slide both gears over their respective shafts and use a straight edge to check timing mark alignment.
12. Measure camshaft endplay. If not within specifications, replace the thrust plate.
13. If the camshaft was not replaced, lubricate and install the lifters in their original locations. If the camshaft was replaced, new lifters must be used.
14. Install the pushrods and rocker shaft assemblies.
15. Install the timing chain cover, cylinder heads and intake manifold.
16. Install the engine in the vehicle.
17. When everything is bolted in place, change the engine oil and replace the oil filter.

NOTE: If the camshaft or lifters have been replaced, add 1 pint of Mopar crankcase conditioner or equivalent, when replenishing the oil to aid in break in. This mixture should be left in the engine for a minimum of 500 miles and drained at the next normal oil change.

18. Fill the radiator with coolant.

19. Connect the negative battery cable, set all adjustments to specifications and check for leaks.

Intermediate Shaft

REMOVAL & INSTALLATION

2.5L Engine

1. Disconnect the negative battery cable.

2. Crank the engine around until the No. 1 piston is at TDC of its compression stroke. Remove the timing belt covers to confirm that all timing marks are lined up.

3. Remove the fuel pump, if equipped. Remove the distributor. Looking down at the oil pump, the slot in the shaft must be parallel with the center line of the crankshaft. Remove the oil pump.

4. Remove the timing belt and the intermediate shaft sprocket.

5. Remove the shaft retainer bolts and remove the retainer from the block.

6. Remove the intermediate shaft from the engine.

7. If necessary, remove the front bushing using tool C–4697–2 and the rear bushing using tool C–4686–2.

To install:

8. Install the front bushing using tool C–4697–1 until the tool is flush with the block. Install the rear bushing using tool C–4686–1 until the tool is flush with the block.

9. Lubricate the distributor drive gear and install the intermediate shaft.

10. Replace the seal in the retainer and apply silicone sealer to the mating

surface of the retainer. Install the retainer to the block and torque the bolts to 10 ft. lbs. (12 Nm).

11. Install the intermediate shaft sprocket and the timing belt.

12. With the timing belt properly installed, install the oil pump so the slot is parallel to the center line of the crankshaft. Install the distributor so the rotor is aligned with the No. 1 spark plug wire tower on the cap.

13. Install the fuel pump, if equipped.

14. Connect the negative battery cable and road test the vehicle.

Balance Shafts

REMOVAL & INSTALLATION

2.5L Engine

1. Disconnect the negative battery cable. Raise the vehicle and support safely.

2. Remove the timing belt. Remove the oil pan, the oil pickup, the crank-

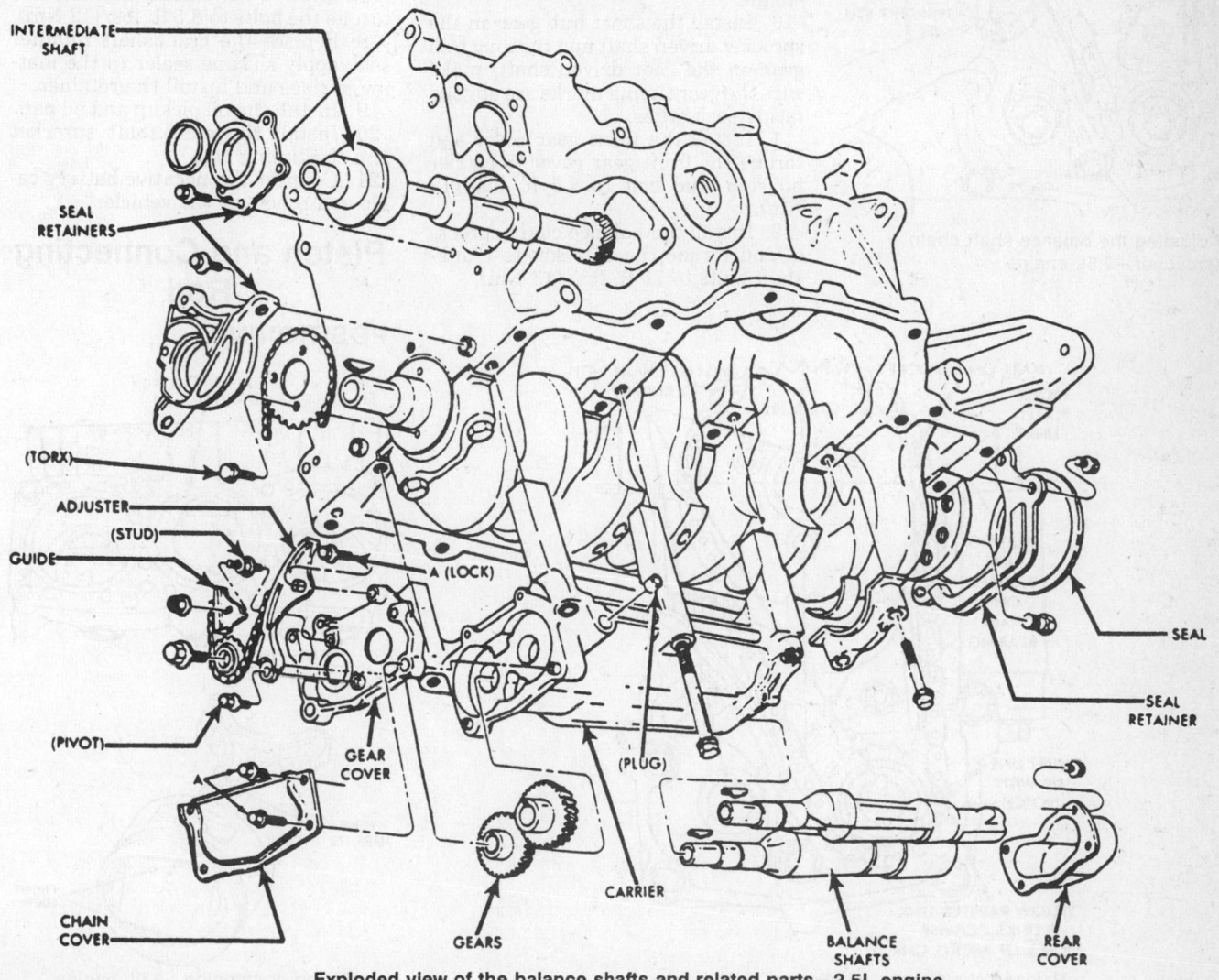

Exploded view of the balance shafts and related parts—2.5L engine

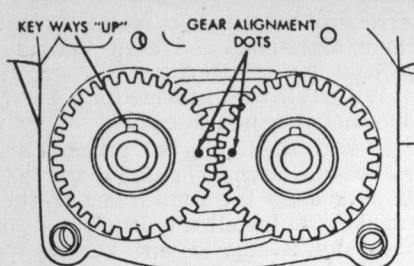

Aligning the balance shaft gear timing marks—2.5L engine

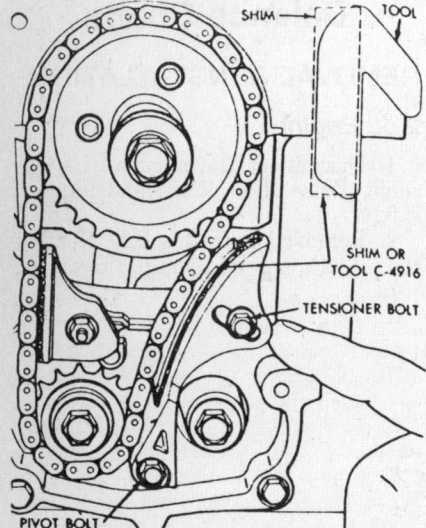

Adjusting the balance shaft chain tensioner—2.5L engine

shaft belt sprocket and the front crankshaft oil seal retainer.

3. Remove the balance shaft chain cover, the guide and the tensioner.

4. Remove the balance shaft sprocket to shaft bolt, the gear cover to balance shaft bolt and the crankshaft sprocket to crankshaft bolts, then the sprockets with the balance shaft chain.

5. Remove the front gear cover to carrier housing stud, the gear cover and the balance shaft drive gears.

6. Remove the rear gear cover to carrier housing bolts, the rear cover and the balance shafts from the rear of the carrier.

7. If necessary, remove the carrier housing to crankcase bolts and the housing.

To install:

8. If the carrier housing is being installed, torque the carrier housing to crankcase bolts to 40 ft. lbs. (54 Nm).

9. Rotate the balance shafts until the keyways are facing upward, parallel to the vertical centerline of the engine.

10. Install the short hub gear on the sprocket driven shaft and the long hub gear on the gear driven shaft; make sure the gear timing marks are aligned facing each other.

11. Install the front gear cover and torque the front gear cover to carrier housing stud bolt to 8.5 ft. lbs. (12 Nm).

12. Install the balance chain sprocket and torque the sprocket to crankshaft bolts to 11 ft. lbs. (13 Nm).

13. Rotate the crankshaft to position the No. 1 cylinder on the TDC of its compression stroke; the timing marks on the chain sprocket should align with the parting line on the left side of the No. 1 main bearing cap.

14. Position the balance shaft sprocket into the balance chain so the sprocket (yellow dot) timing mark mates with the yellow link on the chain.

15. Install the balance chain/sprocket assembly onto the crankshaft and the balance shaft. Torque the sprocket to shaft bolts to 21 ft. lbs. (28 Nm). If necessary to secure the crankshaft while tightening the bolts, place a block of wood between the crankcase and the crankshaft counterbalance.

16. Loosely install the chain tensioners and place a shim (0.039 in. × 2.75 in.) between the chain and the tensioner. Apply firm pressure, to reduce the chain slack, to the tensioner shoe. Torque the tensioner to front gear cover bolts to 8.5 ft. lbs. (12 Nm).

17. Install the chain cover and the rear cover to the carrier housing and torque the bolts to 8.5 ft. lbs. (12 Nm).

18. Replace the crankshaft retainer seal, apply silicone sealer to the mating surface and install the retainer.

19. Install the oil pickup and oil pan.

20. Install the crankshaft sprocket and the timing belt.

21. Connect the negative battery cable and road test the vehicle.

Piston and Connecting Rod

POSITIONING

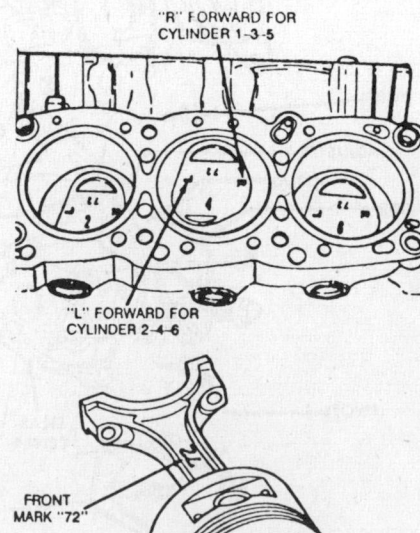

Piston positioning—3.0L engine

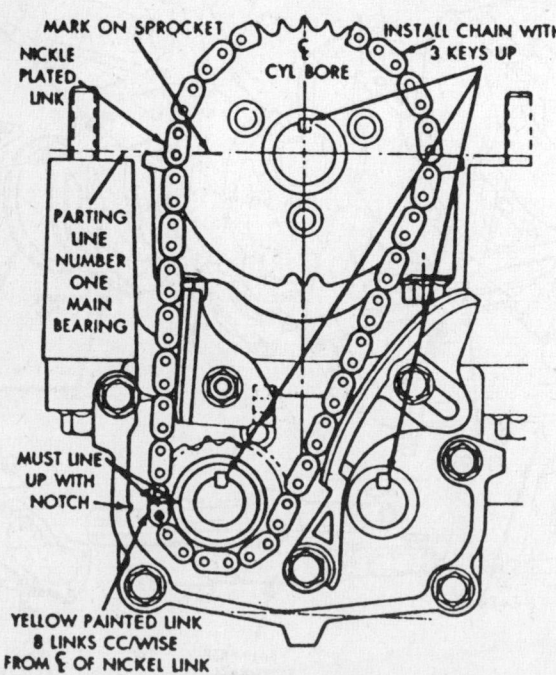

Balance shaft chain installation—2.5L engine

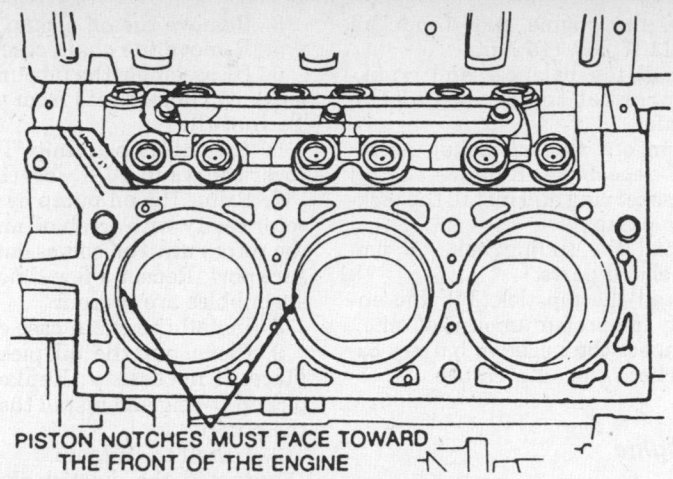

PISTON NOTCHES MUST FACE TOWARD
THE FRONT OF THE ENGINE

Piston positioning — 3.3L engine

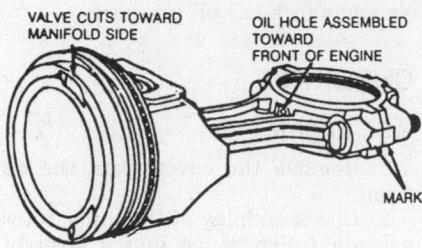

VALVE CUTS TOWARD
MANIFOLD SIDE

OIL HOLE ASSEMBLED
TOWARD
FRONT OF ENGINE

MARK

Piston positioning — 2.5L engine

ENGINE LUBRICATION

Oil Pan

REMOVAL & INSTALLATION

2.5L Engine

1. Disconnect the negative battery cable. Remove the oil dipstick.
2. Raise the vehicle and support safely.
3. Drain the engine oil.
4. Remove the engine to transaxle struts.
5. Remove the torque converter inspection cover.
6. Remove the oil pan retaining screws and remove the oil pan and the side seals.
To install:
7. Thoroughly clean and dry all sealing surfaces, bolts and bolt holes.
8. Apply silicone sealer to the 4 end seal to block corners and install the end seals making sure the corners are not twisted.
9. Apply silicone to the 4 pan to block corners. Install a new pan gasket or apply silicone sealer to the sealing

surface of the pan and install to the engine making sure not to dislodge the end seals.
10. Install the retaining screws and torque to 17 ft. lbs. (23 Nm).
11. Install the torque converter inspection cover and engine to transaxle struts. Lower the vehicle.
12. Install the dipstick. Fill the engine with the proper amount of oil.
13. Connect the negative battery cable and check for leaks.

3.0L and 3.3L Engines

1. Disconnect the negative battery cable.
2. Raise the vehicle and support safely.
3. Remove the torque converter bolt access cover.
4. Drain the engine oil.
5. Remove the oil pan retaining screws and remove the oil pan and gasket.
To install:
6. Thoroughly clean and dry all sealing surfaces, bolts and bolt holes.
7. Apply silicone sealer to the chain cover to block mating seam and the rear main seal retainer to block seam, if equipped.
8. Install a new pan gasket or apply

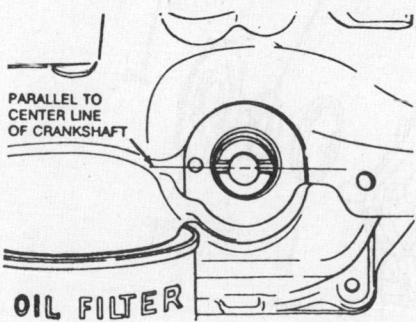

PARALLEL TO
CENTER LINE
OF CRANKSHAFT

OIL FILTER

Aligning the slot in the oil pump shaft — 2.5L engine

silicone sealer to the sealing surface of the pan and install to the engine.
9. Install the retaining screws and torque to 50 inch lbs. (6 Nm).
10. Install the torque converter bolt access cover, if equipped. Lower the vehicle.
11. Install the dipstick. Fill the engine with the proper amount of oil.
12. Connect the negative battery cable and check for leaks.

Oil Pump

REMOVAL & INSTALLATION

2.5L Engine

1. Crank the engine around so that the No. 1 piston is at TDC of its compression stroke. Disconnect the negative battery cable.
2. Matchmark the rotor to the block and remove the distributor to confirm that the slot in the oil pump shaft is parallel to the centerline of the crankshaft. Matchmark the slot to the distributor bore, if desired.
3. Remove the dipstick. Raise the vehicle and support safely. Drain the engine oil and remove the pan.
4. Remove the oil pickup.
5. Remove the 2 mounting bolts and remove the oil pump from the engine.
To install:
6. Prime the pump by pouring fresh oil into the pump intake and turning the driveshaft until oil comes out the pressure port. Repeat a few times until no air bubbles are present.
7. Apply Loctite® 515 or equivalent, to the pump body to block machined surface interface. Lubricate the oil pump and distributor driveshaft.
8. Align the slot so it will be in the same position as when it was removed. If it is not, the distributor will not be timed correctly. Install the pump fully and rotate back and forth to ensure proper positioning between the pump mounting surface and the machined surface of the block.
9. Install the mounting bolts fingertight and lower the vehicle to confirm proper slot positioning. If the slot is not properly positioned, raise the vehicle and move the gear, as required. If the slot is correct, hold the pump firmly against the block and torque the mounting bolts to 17 ft. lbs. (23 Nm).
10. Clean out the oil pickup or replace if necessary. Replace the oil pickup O-ring and install the pickup to the pump.
11. Install the oil pan using new gaskets. Lower the vehicle.
12. Install the distributor.
13. Install the dipstick. Fill the engine with the proper amount of oil.

14. Connect the negative battery cable, check the timing and check the oil pressure.

3.0L Engine

1. Disconnect the negative battery cable. Remove the dipstick.
2. Raise the vehicle and support safely. Remove the timing belt, drain the engine oil and remove the oil pan from the engine. Remove the oil pickup.
3. Remove the oil pump mounting bolts and remove the pump from the front of the engine. Note the different length bolts and their position in the pump for installation.
To install:
4. Clean the gasket mounting surfaces of the pump and engine block.
5. Prime the pump by pouring fresh oil into the pump and turning the rotors. Using a new gasket, install the oil

pump on the engine and torque all bolts to 11 ft. lbs. (15 Nm).
6. Install the balancer and crankshaft sprocket to the end of the crankshaft.
7. Clean out the oil pickup or replace, if necessary. Replace the oil pickup gasket ring and install the pickup to the pump.
8. Install the timing belt, oil pan and all related parts.
9. Install the dipstick. Fill the engine with the proper amount of oil.
10. Connect the negative battery cable and check the oil pressure.

3.3L Engine

1. Disconnect the negative battery cable. Remove the dipstick.
2. Raise the vehicle and support safely. Drain the oil and remove the oil pan.

3. Remove the oil pickup.
4. Remove the chain case cover.
5. Disassemble the oil pump and remove its components from the block.
To install:
6. Assemble the pump. Torque the cover screws to 10 ft. lbs. (12 Nm).
7. Prime the oil pump by filling the rotor cavity with fresh oil and turning the rotors until oil comes out the pressure port. Repeat a few times until no air bubbles are present.
8. Install the chain case cover.
9. Clean out the oil pickup or replace, if necessary. Replace the oil pickup O-ring and install the pickup to the pump.
10. Install the oil pan.
11. Install the dipstick. Fill the engine with the proper amount of oil.
12. Connect the negative battery cable and check the oil pressure.

CHECKING

2.5L Engine

1. Remove the cover from the oil pump.
2. Check endplay of the inner rotor using a feeler gauge and a straight edge placed across the pump body. The specification is 0.001–0.004 in. (0.03–0.09mm).
3. Measure the clearance between the inner and outer rotors. The maximum clearance is 0.008 in. (0.20mm).
4. Measure the clearance between the outer rotor and the pump body. The maximum clearance is 0.014 in. (0.35mm).
5. The minimum thickness of the outer rotor is 0.944 in. (23.96mm). The minimum diameter of the outer rotor is 2.77 in. (62.70mm). The minimum thickness of the inner rotor is 0.943 in. (23.95mm).
6. Check the cover for warpage. The maximum allowable is 0.003 in. (0.076mm).
7. Check the pressure relief valve for damage. The spring's free length specification is 1.95 in. (49.50mm).
8. Assemble the outer rotor with the larger chamfered edge in the pump body. Torque the cover screws to 10 ft. lbs. (12 Nm).

3.0L Engine

1. Remove the rear cover.
2. Remove the pump rotors and inspect the case for excessive wear.
3. Measure the diameter of the inner rotor hub that sits in the case. Measure the inside diameter of the inner rotor hub bore. Subtract the first measurement from the second; if the result is over 0.006 in. (0.15mm), replace the oil pump assembly.
4. Measure the clearance between

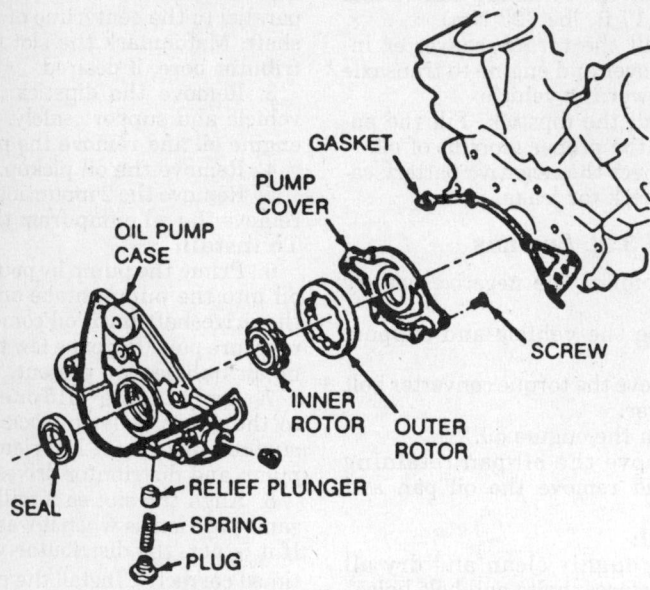

Exploded view of the oil pump—3.0L engine

GASKET
PUMP COVER
OIL PUMP CASE
INNER ROTOR
OUTER ROTOR
SCREW
SEAL
RELIEF PLUNGER
SPRING
PLUG

CHAIN CASE COVER
OIL PUMP INNER ROTOR
SCREW
OIL PUMP COVER
OIL PUMP OUTER ROTOR

Oil pump components—3.3L engine

the outer rotor and the case. The specification is 0.004–0.007 in. (0.10–0.18mm).

5. Check the side clearance of the rotors using a feeler gauge and a straight edge placed across the case. The specification is 0.0015–0.0035 in. (0.04–0.09mm).

6. Check the relief plunger and spring for damage and breakage.

7. Install the rear cover to the case.

3.3L Engine

1. Thoroughly clean and dry all parts. The mating surface of the chain case cover should be smooth. Replace the pump cover if it is scratched or grooved.

2. Lay a straight edge across the pump cover surface. If a 0.003 in. (0.076mm) feeler gauge can be inserted between the cover and straight edge, the cover should be replaced.

3. The minimum thickness of either rotor is 0.301 in. (7.63mm). The minimum diameter of the outer rotor is 3.14 in. (79.78mm).

4. Install the outer rotor onto the chain case cover, press to one side and measure the clearance between the rotor and case. If the measurement exceeds 0.022 in. (56mm) and the rotor is good, replace the chain case cover.

5. Install the inner rotor to the chain case cover and measure the clearance between the rotors. If the clearance exceeds 0.008 in. (0.203mm), replace both rotors.

6. Place a straight edge over the chain case cover between bolt holes. If a 0.004 in. (0.102mm) thick feeler gauge can be inserted under the straight edge, replace the pump assembly.

7. Inspect the relief valve plunger for scoring and freedom of movement. Small marks may be removed with 400 grit wet or dry sandpaper.

8. The relief valve spring should have a free length of 1.95 in.

9. Assemble the pump using new parts where necessary.

Rear Main Bearing Oil Seal

REMOVAL & INSTALLATION

1. Disconnect the negative battery cable.

2. Remove the transaxle. Remove the flexplate.

3. If there is any leakage coming from the rear seal retainer, drain the engine oil and remove the oil pan, if necessary. Remove the rear main oil seal retainer.

4. Remove the seal from the retainer.

To install:

5. Lightly coat the seal outer diameter with Loctite® Stud N' Bearing Mount or equivalent.

6. Install the seal to the retainer.

7. If the retainer was removed, thoroughly clean and dry the retainer to block sealing surfaces and install a new gasket or apply silicone sealer and install the retainer. Install the pan, if removed.

8. Install the flexplate and transaxle.

9. Connect the negative battery cable and check for leaks.

AUTOMATIC TRANSAXLE

For further information on transmissions/transaxles, please refer to "Chilton's Guide to Transmission Repair".

Transaxle Assembly

REMOVAL & INSTALLATION

NOTE: **If the vehicle is going to be rolled while the transaxle is out of the vehicle, obtain 2 outer CV-joints to install to the hubs. If the vehicle is rolled without the proper torque applied to the front wheel bearings, the bearings will no longer be usable.**

1. Disconnect the negative battery cable. If equipped with the 3.0L or 3.3L engine, drain the coolant. Remove the dipstick.

2. Remove the air cleaner assembly if it is preventing access to the upper bell housing bolts. Remove the upper bell housing bolts and water tube, where applicable. Unplug all electrical connectors from the transaxle.

3. If equipped with 2.5L engine, remove the starter attaching nut and bolt at the top of the bell housing.

4. Raise the vehicle and support safely. Remove the wheels. Remove the axle end cotter pins, nut locks, spring washers and axle nuts.

5. Remove the ball joint retaining bolts and pry the control arm from the steering knuckle. Position a drainpan under the transaxle where the axles enter the differential or extension housing. Remove the axles from the transaxle or center bearing. Unbolt the center bearing and remove the intermediate axle from the transaxle, if equipped.

6. Drain the transaxle. Disconnect and plug the fluid cooler hoses. Disconnect the shifter and kickdown linkage from the transaxle, if equipped.

7. Remove the speedometer cable adaptor bolt and remove the adaptor from the transaxle.

8. Remove the starter. Remove the torque converter inspection cover, matchmark the torque converter to the flexplate and remove the torque converter bolts.

9. Using the proper equipment, support the weight of the engine.

10. Remove the front motor mount and bracket.

11. Position a suitable transaxle jack under the transaxle.

12. Remove the lower bell housing bolts.

13. Remove the left side splash shield. Remove the transaxle mount bolts.

14. Carefully pry the transaxle from the engine.

15. Slide the transaxle rearward until the dowels disengage from the mating holes in the transaxle case.

16. Pull the transaxle completely away from the engine and remove it from the vehicle.

17. To prepare the vehicle for rolling, support the engine with a suitable support or reinstall the front motor mount to the engine. Then reinstall the ball joints to the steering knuckle and install the retaining bolt. Install the obtained outer CV-joints to the hubs, install the washers and torque the axle nuts to 180 ft. lbs. (244 Nm). The vehicle may now be safely rolled.

To install:

18. Install the transaxle securely on the jack. Rotate the converter so it will align with the positioning of the flexplate.

19. Apply a light coating of high temperature grease to the torque converter pilot hub.

20. Raise the transaxle into place and push it forward until the dowels engage and the bell housing is flush with the block. Install the transaxle to bell housing bolts.

21. Raise the transaxle and install the left side mount bolts. Install the torque converter bolts and torque to 55 ft. lbs. (74 Nm).

22. Install the front motor mount and bracket. Remove the engine and transaxle support fixtures.

23. Install the starter to the transaxle. Install the bolt finger tight, if equipped with 2.5L engine.

24. Install a new O-ring to the speedometer cable adaptor and install to the extension housing; make sure it snaps in place. Install the retaining bolt.

25. Connect the shifter and kickdown linkage to the transaxle, if equipped.

26. Install the axles and center bearing, if equipped. Install the ball joints to the steering knuckles. Torque the axle nuts to 180 ft. lbs. (244 Nm) and install new cotter pins. Install the splash shield and install the wheels. Lower the vehicle. Install the dipstick.

27. Install the upper bell housing bolts and water pipe, if removed.

28. If equipped with 2.5L engine, install the starter attaching nut and bolt at the top of the bell housing. Raise the vehicle again and tighten the starter bolt from underneath the vehicle. Lower the vehicle.

29. Connect all electrical wiring to the transaxle.

30. Install the air cleaner assembly, if it was removed. Fill the transaxle with the proper amount of Mopar ATF Plus Type 7176. Conventional Dexron®II may be used if Type 7176 is not available.

31. Connect the negative battery cable and check the transaxle for proper operation.

UPSHIFT AND KICKDOWN LEARNING PROCEDURE

A–604 Ultra-Drive Transaxle

In 1989, the A–604 4 speed, electronic transaxle was introduced; it is the first to use fully adaptive controls. The controls perform their functions based on real time feedback sensor information. Although, the transaxle is conventional in design, its functions are controlled by the ECM.

Since the A–604 is equipped with a learning function, each time the battery cable is disconnected, the ECM memory is lost. In operation, the transaxle must be shifted many times for the learned memory to be reinputed in the ECM; during this period, the vehicle will experience rough operation. The transaxle must be at normal operating temperature when learning occurs.

1. Maintain constant throttle opening during shifts. Do not move the accelerator pedal during upshifts.

2. Accelerate the vehicle with the throttle ⅛–½ open.

3. Make fifteen-to-twenty ½, ⅔ and ¾ upshifts. Accelerating from a full stop to 50 mph each time at the aforementioned throttle opening is sufficient.

4. With the vehicle speed below 25 mph, make 5–8 wide open throttle kickdowns to 1st gear from either 2nd or 3rd gear. Allow at least 5 seconds of operation in 2nd or 3rd gear prior to each kickdown.

5. With the vehicle speed greater than 25 mph, make 5 part throttle to wide open throttle kickdowns to either

3rd or 2nd gear from 4th gear. Allow at least 5 seconds of operation in 4th gear, preferably at road load throttle prior to performing the kickdown.

SHIFT LINKAGE ADJUSTMENT

1. Place the shifter in the **P** detent.
2. Loosen the clamp bolt on the gearshift cable bracket.
3. Pull the shift lever all the way to the front detent position and tighten the lock screw.
4. Check for proper neutral safety switch operation.

THROTTLE PRESSURE CABLE ADJUSTMENT

1. Run the engine until it reaches normal operating temperature.
2. Loosen the cable mounting bracket lock screw.
3. Position the bracket so that both alignment tabs are touching the transaxle case surface and tighten the lock screws.
4. Release the cross lock on the cable assembly by pulling the cross lock up.
5. To ensure proper adjustment, the cable must be free to slide all the way toward the engine against its stop after the cross lock is released.
6. Move the transaxle throttle control lever fully clockwise and press the cross lock down until it snaps into position.
7. Road test the vehicle and check the shift points.

DRIVE AXLE

Halfshaft

REMOVAL & INSTALLATION

1. Disconnect the negative battery cable.
2. Raise the vehicle and support safely.
3. Remove the tire and wheel assembly.
4. Remove the cotter pin from the end of the halfshaft. Remove the nut lock, spring washer, axle nut and washer.
5. Remove the ball joint retaining bolt and pry the control arm down to release the ball stud from the steering knuckle.
6. Position a drain pan under the transaxle where the halfshaft enters the differential or extension housing.

7. Pull the strut assembly out—be careful of air suspension components, if equipped—and remove the halfshaft from the hub and transaxle or center bearing. Unbolt the center bearing from the block and remove the intermediate shaft from the transaxle, if equipped.

To install:

7. Install the halfshaft or intermediate shaft to the transaxle, being careful not to damage the side seals. Make sure the inner joint clicks into pace inside the differential. Install the center bearing retaining bolts, if equipped. Install the outer shaft to the center bearing, if equipped.

8. Pull the front strut out—be careful of air suspension components, if equipped—and insert the outer joint into the front hub.

9. Turn the ball joint stud, if necessary, to position the bolt retaining indent to the inside of the vehicle. Install the ball joint stud into the steering knuckle. Install the retaining bolt and nut.

10. Install the axle nut washer and nut and torque the nut to 180 ft. lbs. (244 Nm). Install the spring washer, nut lock and a new cotter pin.

11. Install the tire and wheel assembly.

CV-Boot

REMOVAL & INSTALLATION

NOTE: Use only clamps provided with the replacement package when servicing. Plastic wire ties and other straps will not clamp tightly enough and grease will sling out, causing costly damage to the joint.

Inner Joint

1. Raise the vehicle and support safely. Remove the halfshaft from the vehicle.

2. If cutting the boot away, mark and note the boot positioning on the shaft relative to the raised shoulders. Remove the boot clamps to gain access to the tripod retention system.

3. Separate the housing from the tripod according to the following:

NOTE: Always hold the rollers in place when removing the housing from the tripod or the needle bearing may fall out.

  a. G.K.N.—Has retaining tabs integral with the housing cover. Hold the housing and lightly compress the CV-joint retention spring while bending the tabs back. Support the housing as the retention spring pushes it from the housing.

  b. S.S.G.—Uses a wire ring tripod

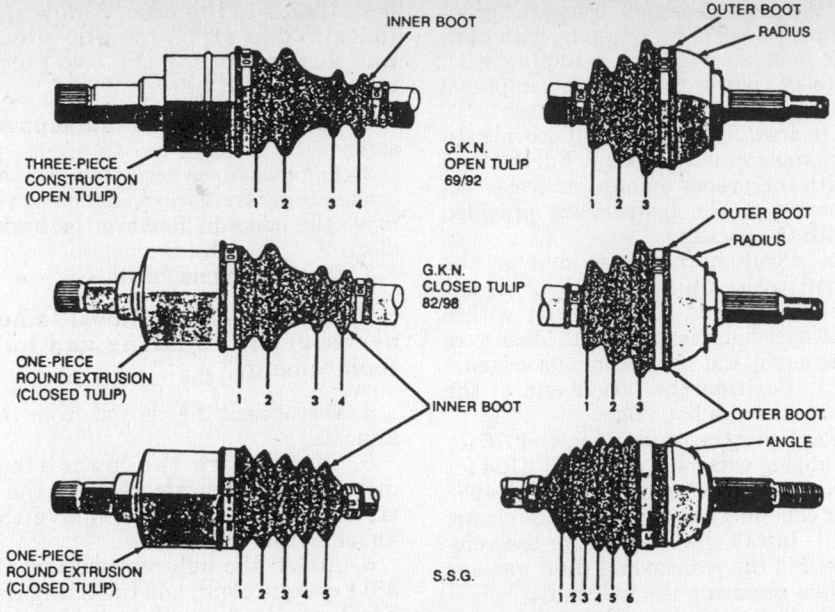

CV-joint boot identification

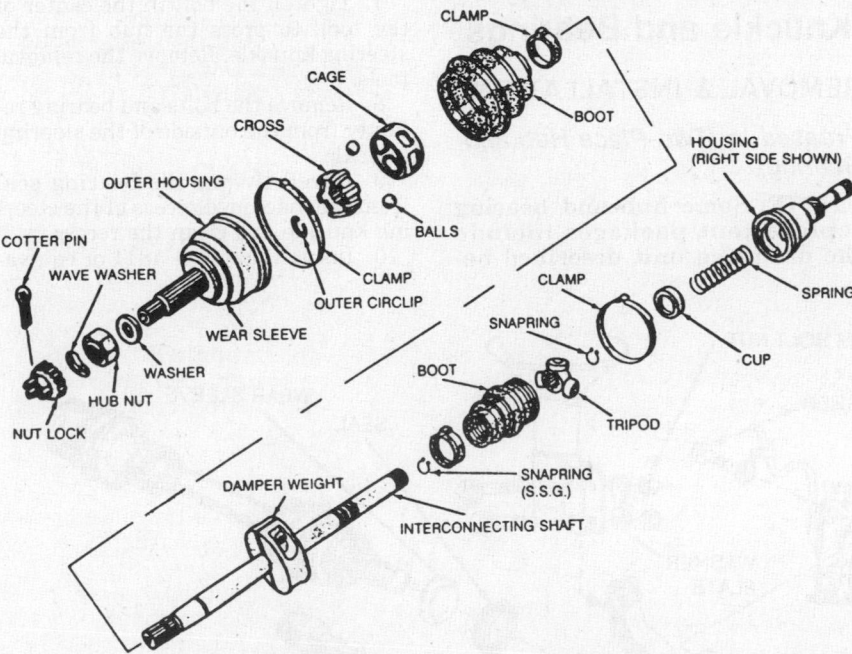

Exploded view of a typical halfshaft

retainer which expands into a groove around the top of the housing. Use a suitable tool to pry the wire ring, without damaging it, out of the groove and slide the tripod from the housing.

4. Remove the snapring from the end of the shaft and remove the tripod.

5. If not already done, mark the boot positioning on the shaft, relative to the raised shoulders and remove the boot from the shaft.

6. Remove as much old grease as possible from the joint. Inspect all parts for wear or damage.

NOTE: Do not use petroleum based solvents on the joints, shaft or boot to clean; it will ruin hidden rubber seals within the joint. Use only chlorine based cleaner or hot soapy water to clean the joint, if necessary. Make sure the joint it completely dry before assembling.

To install:

7. If equipped, slide a new rubber washer seal over the stub shaft and down into the groove provided.

8. If the clamping device is not a

staight strap, install it on the shaft first, then install the boot to the shaft in the proper position. Using the proper tool, C–4975 for crimping with plastic boot, C–4124 for crimping with rubber boot or C–4653 for clamping a strap, secure the clamp.

9. Slide the tripod onto the shaft:

a. G.K.N — Slide the tripod on the shaft with the non-chamfered edge facing the tripod retainer ring groove.

b. S.S.G. — Place the wire ring tripod retainer over the shaft, then slide the tripod. The tripod may installed either way; both ends are the same.

10. Install the snapring into its groove on the shaft to lock the tripod in position.

11. Distribute the grease provided in the grease package as follows, or according to the instructions in the package:

a. G.K.N — Distribute 2 of the 3 packets of grease into the boot and the remaining packet into the housing.

b. S.S.G. — Distribute ½ of the packet of grease into the boot and the remaining amount into the housing.

12. Position the spring in the housing spring pocket with the spring cup attached to the exposed end of the spring. Place a dab of grease on the concave surface of the spring cup.

13. Keeping the spring centered, install the housing to the tripod as follows:

a. G.K.N — Slip the housing onto the tripod. Bend the retaining tabs back into their original positions. Check for proper retention ability.

b. S.S.G. — Slip the housing onto the tripod and install the tripod wire retaining ring. Check for proper retention ability.

14. Position the larger end of the boot over the housing.

15. Using the proper tool, C–4975 for crimping with plastic boot, C–4124 for crimping with rubber boot or C–4653 for clamping a strap, secure the clamp.

16. Install the halfshaft to the vehicle. Fill the transaxle if fluid was lost when removing the halfshaft.

17. Road test the vehicle.

Outer Joint

1. Remove the halfshaft from the vehicle.

2. If cutting the boot away, mark and note the boot positioning on the shaft relative to the raised shoulders. Remove the boot clamps to gain access to the joint retention system.

3. Separate the housing from the tripod according to the following:

a. G.K.N — Using a soft-jaw vise,

support the halfshaft. Strike the joint assembly sharply with a soft-face hammer to dislodge the internal circlip and remove from the shaft.

b. S.S.G.—Loosen the damper weight bolts and slide it and the boot toward the inner joint. Expand the snapring and slide the joint from the shaft. Reinstall the damper weight and torque the bolts to 21 ft. lbs. (28 Nm).

4. If damaged, remove the wear sleeve from the CV-joint machined ledge.

5. Remove the circlip from the groove.

6. If not already done, mark the boot positioning on the shaft, relative to the raised shoulders and remove the boot from the shaft.

7. Remove as much old grease as possible from the joint. Inspect all parts for wear or damage.

NOTE: Do not use petroleum based solvents on the joints, shaft or boot to clean; it will ruin hidden rubber seals within the joint. Use only chlorine based cleaner or hot soapy water to clean the joint, if necessary. Make sure the joint it completely dry before assembling.

To install:

8. If the clamping device is not a straight strap, install it on the shaft first, then install the boot to the shaft in the proper position. Using the proper tool, C–4975 for crimping with plastic boot, C–4124 for crimping with rubber boot or C–4653 for clamping a strap, secure the clamp.

9. Install a new circlip if provided in the replacement package. Fill the boot with the proper amount of grease according to the instructions provided with the package.

10. Position the outer joint on the shaft with hub nut installed, engage the splines and strike sharply with a soft-face hammer to install. Make sure the circlip did not become dislodged.

11. Position the larger end of the boot over the housing.

12. Using the proper tool, C–4975 for crimping with plastic boot, C–4124 for crimping with rubber boot or C–4653 for clamping a strap, secure the clamp.

13. Install the halfshaft to the vehicle. Fill the transaxle if fluid was lost when removing the halfshaft.

14. Road test the vehicle.

Front Wheel Hub, Knuckle and Bearings

REMOVAL & INSTALLATION

Pressed In (Two-Piece Hub and Bearing)

NOTE: Some hub and bearing replacement packages include the one-piece unit described be- low. If this is the case, follow the installation steps for one-piece unit instead of for the two-piece unit described here.

1. Raise the vehicle and support safely.

2. Remove the wheel. Remove the brake caliper from the adaptor and remove the adaptor. Remove the brake disc.

3. Remove the halfshaft.

NOTE: Knuckle removal is not necessary for bearing and hub replacement.

4. Disconnect the tie rod from the knuckle.

5. Matchmark the lower strut mount to the knuckle. Remove the 2 strut clamp bolts and remove the knuckle from the vehicle.

6. Attach the hub removal tool C–4811 or equivalent, and the triangular adapter to the 3 rear threaded holes of the steering knuckle housing with the thrust button inside the hub bore.

7. Tighten the bolt in the center of the tool, to press the hub from the steering knuckle. Remove the removal tools.

8. Remove the bolts and bearing retainer from the outside of the steering knuckle.

9. Carefully pry the bearing seal from the machined recess of the steering knuckle and clean the recess.

10. Insert the tool C–4811 or equiva-

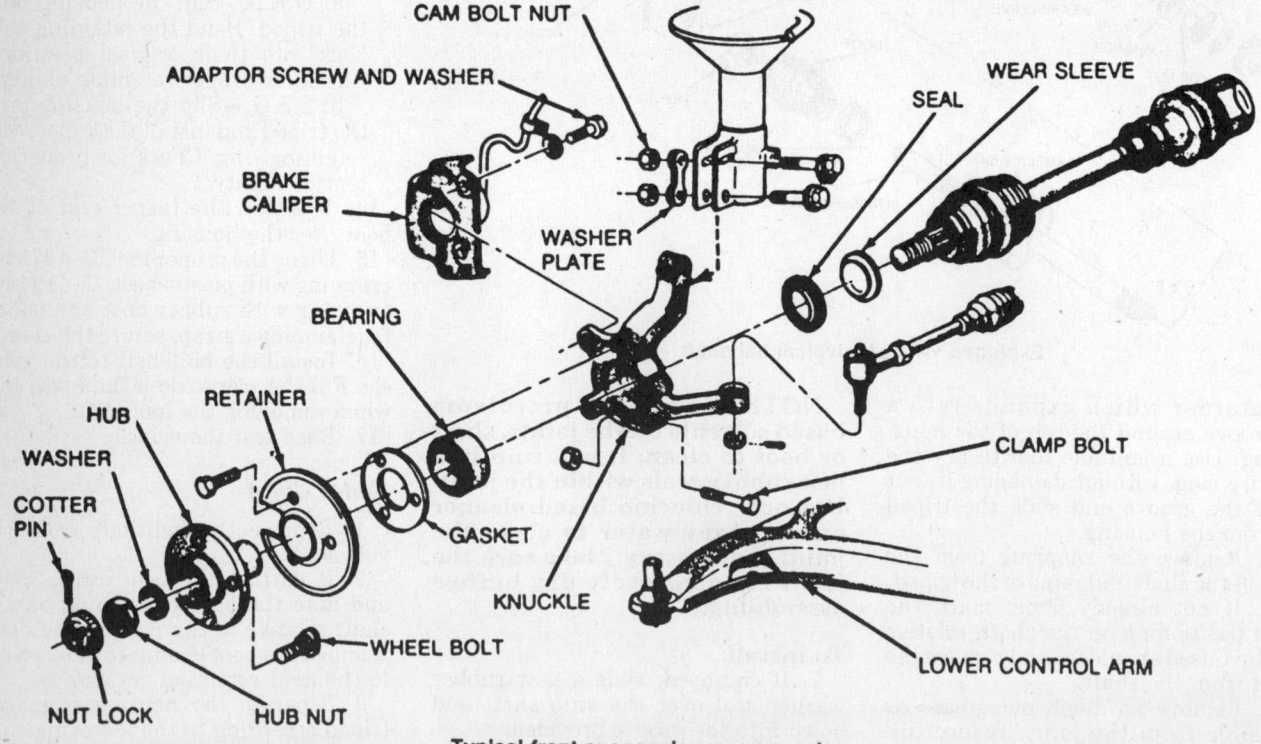

Typical front suspension components

lent, through the hub bearing and install bearing removal adapter to the outside of the steering knuckle. Tighten the tool to press the hub bearing from the steering knuckle. Discard the bearing and the seal.

To install:

11. Use tool C–4811 or equivalent and the bearing installation adapter to press the hub bearing into the steering knuckle.

12. Install a new seal, the bearing retainer and the bolts to the steering knuckle. Torque the bearing retainer bolts to 20 ft. lbs.

13. Use the tool C–4811 or equivalent and the hub installation adapter, to press the hub into the hub bearing.

14. Using the bearing installation tool C–4698 or equivalent, drive the new dust seal into the rear of the steering the hub and bearing from the knuckle, as required.

15. The installation of the knuckle and halfshaft is the reverse of the removal procedure. Torque the tie rod nut to 35 ft. lbs. (47 Nm).

16. Align the front end.

Bolt In (One-Piece Hub and Bearing)

NOTE: Knuckle removal is not necessary for bearing and hub replacement.

1. Raise the vehicle and support safely.

2. Remove the wheel. Remove the brake caliper from the adaptor and remove the adaptor. Remove the brake disc.

3. Remove the halfshaft.

4. Disconnect the tie rod from the knuckle.

5. Matchmark the lower strut mount to the knuckle. Remove the 2 strut clamp bolts and remove the knuckle from the vehicle.

6. Remove the 4 hub and bearing assembly mounting bolts from the rear of the knuckle and remove the assembly from the knuckle.

7. Carefully pry the bearing seal from the machined recess of the steering knuckle and clean the recess.

8. Thoroughly clean and dry the knuckle and bearing mating surfaces and the seal installation area.

To install:

9. Install the hub and bearing assembly to the knuckle and torque the bolts in a criss-cross pattern to 45 ft. lbs. (65 Nm).

10. Install a new seal and wear sleeve. Lubricate the circumferences of the seal and sleeve liberally with grease.

11. The installation of the knuckle and halfshaft is the reverse of the re-

moval procedure. Torque the tie rod nut to 35 ft. lbs. (47 Nm).

12. Align the front end.

Differential Case

REMOVAL & INSTALLATION

NOTE: The differential case can be removed from some vehicles with the transaxle installed. To do so, remove the halfshafts, remove the 2 K-frame mounting nuts and 2 bolts and lower the K-frame to provide enough room to pull the differential case out of its housing and over the lowered frame.

1. Disconnect the negative battery cable. Raise the vehicle and support safely.

2. Remove the right side extension housing. Remove the differential cover.

3. Remove the bolts and remove the right side differential bearing retainer using tool L–4435 or equivalent.

4. Remove the differential case from the transaxle.

5. Use new seals and gasket material when assembling.

6. The installation is the reverse of the removal procedure. Torque the extension housing and bearing retainer bolts to 21 ft. lbs. (28 Nm).

7. Fill the transaxle with the proper oil.

8. Connect the negative battery cable and check the differential for proper operation.

STEERING

Steering Wheel
—— CAUTION ——

On vehicles equipped with an air bag, the negative battery cable must be disconnected, before working on the system. Failure to do so may result in deployment of the air bag and possible personal injury.

REMOVAL & INSTALLATION

Without Airbag

1. Disconnect the negative battery cable.

2. Straighten the steering wheel so the front tires are pointing straight forward.

3. Remove the horn pad retaining screws, unplug the connector and remove the horn pad.

4. Remove the steering wheel hold-

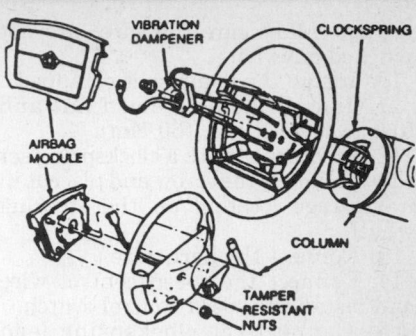

Air bag module and related components

down nut and remove the damper, if equipped. Matchmark the steering wheel to the shaft.

5. Using a suitable steering wheel puller, pull the steering wheel off of the shaft.

6. The installation is the reverse of the removal procedure. Torque the hold-down nut to 45 ft. lbs. (60 nm).

With Airbag

1. Disconnect the negative battery cable.

2. Straighten the steering wheel so the front tires are pointing straight forward.

3. Remove the 4 nuts located on the back side of the steering wheel that attach the airbag module to the steering wheel.

4. Lift the module and disconnect the connectors. Remove the speed control switch, if equipped.

NOTE: All columns except Acustar are equipped with a clockspring set screw held by a plastic tether on the steering wheel. Acustar mounted clocksprings are auto-locking. If the steering column is not an Acustar and is lacking the set screw, obtain one before proceeding.

5. If equipped with the set screw, place it in the clockspring to ensure proper positioning when the steering wheel is removed.

6. Remove the steering wheel hold-down nut and remove the damper, if equipped. Matchmark the steering wheel to the shaft.

7. Using a suitable steering wheel puller, pull the steering wheel off of the shaft.

To install:

8. Position the steering wheel on the steering column. Make sure the flats on the hub of the steering wheel are aligned with the formations on the clockspring.

9. Pull the airbag and speed control connectors through the lower, larger hole in the steering wheel and pull the horn wire through the smaller hole at

the top. Make sure the wires are not pinched anywhere.

10. Install the damper, if equipped.

11. Install the hold-down nut and torque to 45 ft. lbs. (60 Nm).

12. If equipped with a clockspring set screw, remove the screw and place it in its storage location on the steering wheel.

13. Connect the horn wire.

14. Connect the speed control wire and install the speed control switch.

15. Connect the clockspring lead wire to the airbag module and install module to steering wheel.

NOTE: Do not allow anyone to enter the vehicle from this point on, until this procedure is completed.

16. Connect the DRB II to the Airbag System Diagnostic Module (ASDM) connector located to the right of the console.

17. From the passenger side of the vehicle, turn the key to the **ON** position.

18. Check to make sure nobody has entered the vehicle. Connect the negative battery cable.

19. Using the DRB II, read and record any active fault data or stored codes.

20. If any active fault codes are present, perform the proper diagnostic procedures before continuing.

21. If there are no active fault codes, erase the stored fault codes. If there are active codes, the stored codes will not erase.

22. From the passenger side of the vehicle, turn the key **OFF**, then **ON** and observe the instrument cluster airbag warning light. It should come on for 6–8 seconds, then go out, indicating the system is functioning normally. If the warning light either fails to come **ON** or stays lit, there is a system malfunction and the proper diagnostic procedures should be performed.

Steering Column

REMOVAL & INSTALLATION

1. Disconnect the negative battery cable.

2. Remove trim bezel, steering column cover and lower reinforcement, as required.

3. Disconnect all wiring connectors from below the instrument panel that lead up into the steering column.

4. Remove the nuts that attach the steering column assembly to the instrument panel support.

5. Firmly grasp the steering wheel and pull the steering column out, separating the stub shaft from the steering gear coupling.

6. The installation is the reverse of the removal procedure.

7. Connect the negative battery cable and check the steering column and all related components for proper operation.

Power Rack and Pinion Steering Gear

REMOVAL & INSTALLATION

1. Disconnect the negative battery cable.

2. Raise the vehicle and support safely.

3. Remove the front wheels.

4. Remove the cotter pins, castellated nuts and tie rod ends from the steering knuckles.

5. The lower universal joint is removed with the steering gear.

6. Disconnect and plug the oil pressure line from the rack. Disconnect and plug the return hose from the line coming from the rack.

7. Remove the front suspension crossmember attaching bolts and nuts.

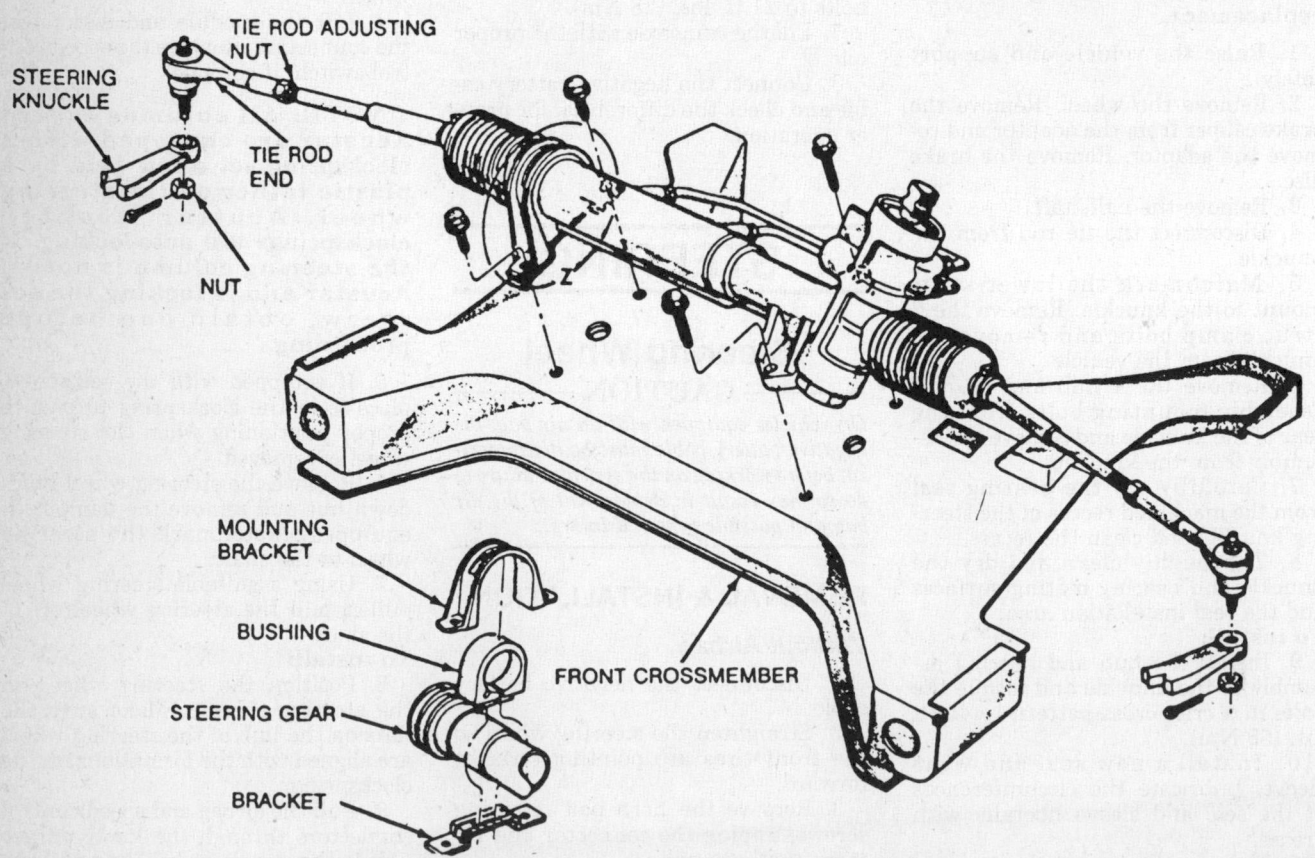

Rack and pinion steering gear mounting to the crossmember

8. Lower the crossmember.

9. Remove the tie rod inner boot shields.

10. Remove the steering gear bolts from the front suspension crossmember.

11. Remove the steering gear from the left side of the vehicle.

To install:

12. Transfer the required parts to the new rack, if replacing it.

13. Place the rack on the crossmember and torque the steering gear attaching bolts to 21 ft. lbs. (29 Nm). Attach the fluid lines and the boot shields.

14. Have a helper inside the vehicle remove the trim boot and align the stub shaft with the coupling while the crossmember is raised into position. If a helper is not available, the steering column will have to be unbolted so the steering shaft can be inserted into the coupling. The right rear crossmember bolt is a pilot bolt that correctly locates the crossmember; tighten it first. Torque the crossmember bolts to 90 ft. lbs.

15. Install the tie rod ends to the steering knuckle and torque the nut to 45 ft. lbs. (61 Nm). Install a new cotter pin.

16. Insert the stub shaft shim where the stub shaft goes into the coupling.

17. Refill the power steering pump.

18. Connect the negative battery cable and check the gear for proper operation.

Power Steering Pump

REMOVAL & INSTALLATION

1. Disconnect the negative battery cable.

2. Disconnect the vapor seperator hose from the throttle body.

3. Remove the drive belt from the pulley and remove bolts that are accessible from above.

4. Raise the vehicle and support safely. Remove the right front wheel and the splash shield, if necessary.

5. Position a drain pan under the return hose and disconnect the return hose from the line coming from the steering rack. Allow the fluid to drain and plug the hose.

6. Disconnect the pressure line from the pump.

7. Remove the lower mounting bolts and nuts.

8. Move the pump toward the firewall and remove the adjustment bracket.

9. Rotate the pump clockwise so the pump pulley faces the rear of the vehicle and pull the pump out of the engine compartment.

To install:

10. Position the pump and install the adjustment bracket.

11. Raise the vehicle and install the lower mounting bolts and nuts finger-tight.

12. Replace the O-rings on the pressure line and connect to the pump. Install the return hose and secure the clamps.

13. Wrap the drive belt around the pulley groove and adjust the belt tension, if possible. Tighten the mounting bolts to 30 ft. lbs. (41 Nm).

14. Install the splash shield, if removed.

15. Connect the vapor seperator to the throttle body.

16. Turn the wheels to the full left turn position and add fluid until the reservoir is full.

17. Start the engine and add fluid to bring the level to the correct level.

18. To purge the system of air, turn the steering wheel from side to side without contacting the stops.

19. Return the wheel to the straight ahead position and operate the engine for 2 minutes before road testing.

BELT ADJUSTMENT

NOTE: The belt tension is automatically adjusted by a dynamic tensioner on 3.0L and 3.3L engines. Adjustment is not possible.

1. Loosen the bracket mounting bolts.

2. On 1988–89 vehicles, use a ½ in. drive breaker bar in the square hole provided in the bracket to move the pump away from the engine. On 1990–91 vehicles, tighten the adjusting nut until the pump is in the desired position. Do not pry against the fluid reservoir.

3. With the pump moved enough so the belt deflects about ¼–½ in. under a 10 lb. load, tighten the bolts.

SYSTEM BLEEDING

1. Fill the reservoir with power steering fluid.

2. Turn the wheels to the full left turn position and add fluid until the reservoir is full.

3. Start the engine and add fluid to bring the level to the correct level.

4. To purge the system of air, turn the steering wheel from side to side without contacting the stops.

5. Return the wheel to the straight ahead position and operate the engine for 2 minutes before road testing.

Tie Rod Ends

REMOVAL & INSTALLATION

1. Raise the vehicle and support safely.

2. Remove the cotter pin and nut from the tie rod end.

3. Using a suitable puller, remove the tie rod from the steering knuckle.

4. Loosen the sleeve clamp nut and bolt, if equipped, and unscrew the tie rod end from the sleeve or inner tie rod.

5. The installation is the reverse of the removal procedure. Torque the stud nuts to 45 ft. lbs. (61 Nm) and install a new cotter pin.

6. Perform a front end alignment, as required.

BRAKES

For all brake system repair and service procedures not detailed below, please refer to "Brakes" in the Unit Repair section.

Master Cylinder

REMOVAL & INSTALLATION

Except Anti-Lock Brakes

1. Disconnect the negative battery cable.

2. Disconnect and plug the brake lines from the master cylinder.

3. Remove the nuts attaching the master cylinder to the power booster.

4. Remove the master cylinder from the mounting studs.

5. Remove the fluid reservoir from the cylinder.

To install:

6. Bench bleed the master cylinder.

7. Install to the studs and install the nuts.

8. Install the brake lines to the master cylinder.

9. Connect the negative battery cable and check the brakes for proper operation.

Combination Valve
REMOVAL & INSTALLATION

1. Disconnect the negative battery cable.

2. Raise the vehicle and support safely.

3. Tag and disconnect the brake lines from the valve.

4. Disconnect the wires to the pressure switch.

5. Remove the combination valve from the frame bracket.

6. The installation is the reverse of the removal procedure.

7. Bleed the brakes in the following order:

a. Right rear wheel cylinder or caliper

b. Left rear wheel cylinder or caliper

c. Right front caliper

d. Left front caliper

8. Connect the negative battery cable and check the brakes for proper operation.

Power Brake Booster

REMOVAL & INSTALLATION

1. Disconnect the negative battery cable. Disconnect the vacuum hose(s) from the booster.

2. Remove the nuts attaching the master cylinder to the booster and move the master cylinder to the side.

3. From inside the passenger compartment, remove the clip that secures the booster pushrod to the brake pedal.

4. Remove the nuts that attach the booster to the dash panel and remove it from the vehicle.

5. Transfer the check valve to the new booster.

6. The installation is the reverse of the removal procedure.

7. Connect the negative battery cable and check the brakes for proper operation.

Brake Caliper

REMOVAL & INSTALLATION

Front Brakes

1. Raise the vehicle and support safely.

2. Remove the tire and wheel assembly.

3. Remove the caliper mounting pin(s).

4. Lift the caliper off of the rotor. Remove the outer pad from the caliper.

5. Remove the brake hose retaining bolt from the caliper.

To install:

6. Install the brake hose to the caliper using new copper washers.

7. Position the caliper over the rotor so the caliper engages the adaptor correctly. Install the mounting pin(s). Install the hold-down spring, if equipped.

8. Fill the master cylinder and bleed the brakes.

Rear Brakes

1988 VEHICLES

1. Remove ⅔ of brake fluid from the master cylinder.

2. Remove access plug and insert a 4mm Allen wrench through hole.

3. Turn the retraction shaft counterclockwise a few turns to increase clearance between pads and rotor.

4. Remove the anti-rattle spring from the outboard pad taking care not to damage it.

5. Back the caliper guide pins out just enough to free caliper from adapter.

6. Lift the caliper off of rotor and remove the brake pads.

7. Disconnect the brake fluid hose from the caliper.

8. Insert the Allen wrench through access hole and turn clockwise, if necessary, to retract piston further to increase clearance.

To install:

9. Connect the hose. Lower the caliper over the rotor and pads.

10. Install the guide pins and tighten to the proper torque.

11. Insert the Allen wrench through the access hole and turn clockwise until snug, so there is no clearance between pads and rotors, then back off ⅓ turn to obtain proper clearance.

12. Check the brake fluid level and add, if necessary.

Disc Brake Pads

REMOVAL & INSTALLATION

Front Brakes

1. Remove some of the fluid from the master cylinder.

2. Raise the vehicle and support safely. Remove the tire and wheel assemblies.

3. Remove the hold-down spring, if necessary. Remove the caliper and remove the outer pad from the caliper.

4. Remove the inner pad from the adaptor.

To install:

5. Use a large C-clamp to compress the piston back into the caliper bore.

6. Install the inner pad to the adaptor.

7. Position the caliper over the rotor so the caliper engages the adaptor correctly and install the retainer pin(s).

8. Install the hold-down spring, if it was removed.

9. Refill the master cylinder.

Rear Brakes

1988 VEHICLES

1. Remove ⅔ of brake fluid from the master cylinder.

2. Remove access plug and insert a 4mm Allen wrench through hole.

3. Turn the retraction shaft counterclockwise a few turns to increase clearance between pads and rotor.

4. Remove the anti-rattle spring from outboard pad taking care not to damage it.

5. Back the caliper guide pins out just enough to free caliper from adapter.

6. Lift the caliper off of rotor and carefully suspend with wire.

7. Remove the brake pads.

8. Insert the Allen wrench through access hole and turn clockwise, if necessary to retract piston further to increase clearance for new pads.

To install:

9. Install new inner and outer pads.

NOTE: The outboard pads are marked for right and left hand sides and must be properly installed.

10. Lower the caliper over rotor and pads.

11. Install the guide pins and tighten to proper torque.

12. Insert the Allen wrench through the access hole and turn clockwise until snug, so that there is no clearance between pads and rotors, then back off ⅓ turn to obtain proper clearance.

13. Check the brake fluid level and add, if necessary.

Brake Rotor

REMOVAL & INSTALLATION

1. Raise the vehicle and support safely. Remove the tire and wheel assembly.

2. Remove the caliper and brake pads.

3. Remove the factory installed clips, if equipped. It is not necessary to reinstall these clips.

4. Remove the adaptor, if necessary. Remove the rotor from the hub.

5. The installation is the reverse of the removal procedure.

Brake Drum

REMOVAL & INSTALLATION

1. Raise the vehicle and support safely.

2. Remove the wheel and tire assembly.

3. Remove the dust cap.

4. Remove the cotter pin and nut lock.

5. Remove the wheel bearing nut and washer from the spindle.

6. Remove the outer wheel bearing.

7. Remove the drum with the inner

wheel bearing from the spindle. If the drum is difficult to remove, remove the plug from the rear of the backing plate and push the self adjuster lever away from the star wheel. Rotate the star wheel to retract the shoes. Remove the grease seal.

To install:

8. Lubricate and install the inner wheel bearing. Install a new grease seal.

9. Install the drum to the spindle.

10. Lubricate and install the outer wheel bearing, washer and nut. When the bearing preload is properly set, install the nut lock and a new cotter pin.

11. Install the grease cap.

12. Install the wheel and tire assembly. Adjust the rear brakes as required.

Brake Shoes

REMOVAL & INSTALLATION

1. Raise the vehicle and support safely. Remove the wheel and tire assemblies and the drums.

2. Remove the automatic adjuster spring and lever.

3. Rotate the automatic adjuster star wheel enough so both shoes move out far enough to be free of the wheel cylinder boots.

4. Disconnect the parking brake cable from the actuating lever.

5. Remove the lower shoe-to-shoe or shoe-to-anchor spring(s).

6. With the shoes held together by the upper shoe-to-shoe spring, remove them from the backing plate.

To install:

7. Thoroughly clean and dry the backing plate. To prepare the backing plate, lubricate the bosses, anchor pin and parking brake actuating lever pivot surface lightly with lithium based grease.

8. Remove, clean and dry all parts still on the old shoes. Lubricate the star wheel shaft threads with anti-sieze lubricant and transfer all parts to their proper locations on the new shoes.

9. Install the lower spring(s).

10. Connect the parking brake cable.

11. Install the automatic adjuster lever and spring.

12. Adjust the star wheel.

13. Remove any grease from the linings and install the drum.

14. Complete the brake adjustment with the wheels installed.

Wheel Cylinder

REMOVAL & INSTALLATION

1. Raise the vehicle and support safely.

2. Remove the wheel, drum and brake shoes.

3. Remove and plug the brake line from the wheel cylinder.

4. Remove the wheel cylinder bolts and remove the cylinder from the backing plate.

To install:

5. Apply a very thin coating of silicone sealer to the cylinder mounting surface, install the cylinder to the backing plate and install the retaining bolts.

6. Connect the brake line to the wheel cylinder.

7. Install all brake parts that were removed.

8. Install the tire and wheel assembly.

9. Bleed the brakes.

Parking Brake Cables

ADJUSTMENT

Except Anti-Lock Brakes

1. Release the parking brakes fully.

2. Raise the vehicle and support safely.

3. Adjust the rear brakes.

4. Loosen the adjusting nut until there is slack in all the cables.

5. Rotate the rear wheels and tighten the cable adjusting nut until there is a slight drag at the wheels.

6. Continue to rotate the rear wheels and loosen the nut until all drag is eliminated.

7. Back off the nut an additional 2 turns.

8. Apply and release the parking brake several times. Upon the least release, verify there is no drag at the wheels.

9. To check the operation, make sure the parking brake holds on an incline.

Anti-Lock Brakes

1. Fully release the parking brakes and pump the brakes several times. Raise the vehicle and support safely.

2. Tighten the cable adjusting nut until a very slight drag is felt at each rear wheel.

3. Loosen the adjusting nut 5 turns.

4. Actuate the parking brake lever on the rear calipers by manually pulling down and releasing each rear parking brake cable at the rear of the vehicle.

5. The parking brake lever should be touching the stop pin on both rear calipers. If not, loosen the adjusting nut 1 turn.

6. Repeat Steps 4 and 5 until the parking brake lever returns against the stop pin on both calipers.

7. When the adjustment is complete, the actuating levers on both calipers should return against the stop pins when the parking brakes are released and the wheels must rotate freely.

8. To confirm proper operation, make sure the parking brake holds on an incline.

REMOVAL & INSTALLATION

Front Cable

1. Disconnect the negative battery cable.

2. Loosen the adjusting nut and disengage the front cable from the equalizer bracket.

4. Lift the carpet and floor matting and remove the floor pan seal.

5. Pull the cable end forward and disconnect from the clevis.

6. Pull the cable through the hole and remove.

7. The installation is the reverse of the removal procedure.

8. Adjust the cables, connect the negative battery cable and check the parking brakes for proper operation.

Rear Cable

DRUM BRAKES

1. Disconnect the negative battery cable.

2. Raise the vehicle and support safely.

3. Remove the rear wheels.

4. Back off the adjusting nut enough to provide slack in all cables. Disconnect the cables from the cable connectors.

5. Remove the drums. Disconnect the cable from the brake shoe lever.

6. Compress the retaining clips on the end of the cable housing and pull the cable from the backing plate.

7. Remove the retaining clip at the support bracket and remove the cable from the trailing arm assembly.

8. The installation is the reverse of the removal procedure.

9. Adjust the cables, connect the negative battery cable and check the parking brakes for proper operation.

DISC BRAKES

1. Disconnect the negative battery cable.

2. Raise the vehicle and support safely.

3. Remove the rear wheels.

4. Remove the brake cable retaining clips from the hanger bracket and caliper.

5. Disconnect the cable from the parking brake lever on the caliper.

6. Remove the cable guide attaching nut and screw.

7. Pull the cable assembly out from the hanger bracket and caliper.

8. The installation is the reverse of the removal procedure.

9. Adjust the cables, connect the negative battery cable and check the parking brakes for proper operation.

Brake System Bleeding

Except Anti-Lock Brakes

NOTE: If using a pressure bleeder, follow the instructions furnished with the unit and choose the correct adaptor for the application. Do not substitute an adapter that "almost fits" as it will not work and could be dangerous.

MASTER CYLINDER

If the master cylinder is off the vehicle it can be bench bled.

1. Connect 2 short pieces of brake line to the outlet fittings, bend them until the free end is below the fluid level in the master cylinder reservoirs.

2. Fill the reservoir with fresh brake fluid. Pump the piston slowly until no more air bubbles appear in the reservoirs.

3. Disconnect the 2 short lines, refill the master cylinder and securely install the cylinder caps.

4. If the master cylinder is on the vehicle, it can still be bled, using a flare nut wrench.

5. Open the brake lines slightly with the flare nut wrench while pressure is applied to the brake pedal by a helper inside the vehicle.

6. Be sure to tighten the line before the brake pedal is released.

7. Repeat the process with both lines until no air bubbles come out.

CALIPERS AND WHEEL CYLINDERS

1. Fill the master cylinder with fresh brake fluid. Check the level often during the procedure.

2. Starting with the right rear wheel, remove the protective cap from the bleeder, if equipped, and place where it will not be lost. Clean the bleed screw.

─────── CAUTION ───────

When bleeding the brakes, keep face away from the brake area. Spewing fluid may cause facial and/or visual damage. Do not allow brake fluid to spill on the car's finish; it will remove the paint.

3. If the system is empty, the most effecient way to get fluid down to the wheel is to loosen the bleeder about ½–¾ turn, place a finger firmly over the bleeder and have a helper pump the brakes slowly until fluid comes out the bleeder. Once fluid is at the bleed-

er, close it before the pedal is released inside the vehicle.

NOTE: If the pedal is pumped rapidly, the fluid will churn and create small air bubbles, which are almost impossible to remove from the system. These air bubbles will eventually congregate and a spongy pedal will result.

4. Once fluid has been pumped to the caliper or wheel cylinder, open the bleed screw again, have the helper press the brake pedal to the floor, lock the bleeder and have the helper slowly release the pedal. Wait 15 seconds and repeat the procedure (including the 15 second wait) until no more air comes out of the bleeder upon application of the brake pedal. Remember to close the bleeder before the pedal is released inside the vehicle each time the bleeder is opened. If not, air will be induced into the system.

5. If a helper is not available, connect a small hose to the bleeder, place the end in a container of brake fluid and proceed to pump the pedal from inside the vehicle until no more air comes out the bleeder. The hose will prevent air from entering the system.

6. Repeat the procedure on remaining wheel cylinders in order:
    a. left rear
    b. right front
    c. left front

7. Hydraulic brake systems must be totally flushed, if the fluid becomes contaminated with water, dirt or other corrosive chemicals. To flush, bleed the entire system until all fluid has been replaced with the correct type of new fluid.

8. Install the bleeder cap(s) on the bleeder to keep dirt out. Always road test the vehicle after brake work of any kind is done.

Anti-Lock Brakes

BOOSTER BLEEDING

1. The hydraulic accumulator must be depressurized.

2. Connect all pump/motor and hydraulic assembly electrical connections, if previously disconnected. Be sure that all brake lines and hose connections are tight.

3. Fill the reservoir to the full level.

4. Connect a transparent hose to the bleeder screw location on the right side of the hydraulic assembly. Place the other end of the hose into a clear container to receive brake fluid.

5. Open the bleeder screw ½–¾ of a turn.

6. Turn the ignition switch to the ON position. The pump/motor should run, discharging fluid into the container. After a good volume of fluid has

been forced through the hose, an air-free flow in the plastic hose and container will indicate a good bleed.

7. Turn the ignition switch OFF.

NOTE: If the brake fluid does not flow, it may be due to a lack of prime to the pump/motor. Try shaking the return hose to break up air bubbles that may be present within the hose.
Should the brake fluid still not flow, turn the ignition switch to the OFF position. Remove the return hose from the reservoir and cap nipple on the reservoir. Manually fill the return hose with brake fluid and connect to the reservoir. Repeat the bleeding process.

8. Remove the hose from the bleeder screw. Tighten the bleeder screw to 7.5 ft. lbs. (10 Nm). Do not overtighten.

9. Top off the reservoir to the correct fluid level.

10. Turn the ignition switch to the ON position. Allow the pump to charge the accumulator, which should stop after approximately 30 seconds.

Pressure Bleeding

The brake lines may be pressure bled, using a standard diaphragm type pressure bleeder. Only diaphragm type pressure bleeding equipment should be used to bleed the system.

1. The ignition should be turned OFF and remain OFF throughout this procedure.

2. Depressurize the hydraulic accumulator.

─────── CAUTION ───────

Failure to depressurize the hydraulic accumulator, prior to performing this operation may result in personal injury and/or damage to the painted surfaces.

3. Remove the electrical connector from fluid level sensor on the reservoir cap and remove the reservoir cap.

4. Install the pressure bleeder adapter.

5. Attach the bleeding equipment to the bleeder adapter. Charge the pressure bleeder to approximately 20 psi (138 kPa).

6. Connect a transparent hose to the caliper bleed screw. Submerge the free end of the hose in a clear glass container, which is partially filled with clean, fresh brake fluid.

7. With the pressure turned ON, open the caliper bleed screw ½–¾ turn and allow fluid to flow into the container. Leave the bleed screw open until clear, bubble-free fluid slows from the hose. If the reservoir has been drained or the hydraulic assembly re-

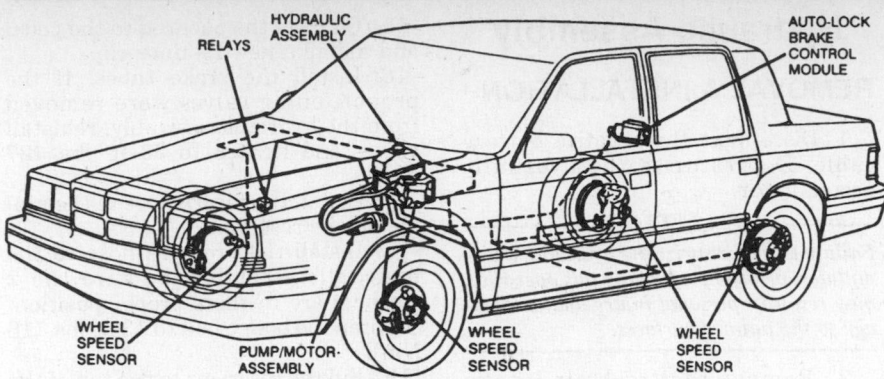

RELAYS
HYDRAULIC ASSEMBLY
AUTO-LOCK BRAKE CONTROL MODULE
WHEEL SPEED SENSOR
PUMP/MOTOR ASSEMBLY
WHEEL SPEED SENSOR
WHEEL SPEED SENSOR

Anti-lock brake system schematic

moved from the car prior to the bleeding operation, slowly pump the brake pedal 1–2 times while the bleed screw is open and fluid is flowing. This will help purge air from the hydraulic assembly. Tighten the bleeder screw to 7.5 ft. lbs. (10 N).

8. Repeat Step 7 at all calipers. Calipers should be bled in the following order:
   a. Left rear
   b. Right rear
   c. Left front
   d. Right front

9. After bleeding all 4 calipers, remove the pressure bleeding equipment and bleeder adapter by closing the pressure bleeder valve and slowly unscrewing the bleeder adapter from the hydraulic assembly reservoir. Failure to release pressure in the reservoir will cause spillage of brake fluid and could result in injury or damage to painted surfaces.

10. Using a syringe or equivalent method, remove excess fluid from the reservoir to bring the fluid level to full level.

11. Install the reservoir cap and connect the fluid level sensor connector. Turn the ignition **ON** and allow the pump to charge the accumulator.

Manual Bleeding

1. Depressurize the hydraulic accumulator.

─── **CAUTION** ───

Failure to depressurize the hydraulic accumulator, prior to performing this operation may result in personal injury and/or damage to the painted surfaces.

2. Connect a transparent hose to the caliper bleed screw. Submerge the free end of the hose in a clear glass container, which is partially filled with clean, fresh brake fluid.

3. Slowly pump the brake pedal several times, using full strokes of the pedal and allowing approximately 5 seconds between pedal strokes. After 2 or 3 strokes, continue to hold pressure

on the pedal, keeping it at the bottom of its travel.

4. With pressure on the pedal, open the bleed screw ½–¾ turn. Leave bleed screw open until fluid no longer flows from the hose. Tighten the bleed screw and release the pedal.

5. Repeat this procedure until clear, bubble-free fluid flows from the hose.

6. Repeat all steps at each of the calipers. Calipers should be bled in the following order:
   a. Left rear
   b. Right rear
   c. Left front
   d. Right front

Anti-Lock Brake System Service

PRECAUTIONS

Failure to observe the following precautions may result in system damage.
- Before performing electric arc welding on the vehicle, disconnect the Electronic Brake Control Module (EBCM) and the hydraulic modulator connectors.
- When performing painting work on the vehicle, do not expose the Electronic Brake Control Module (EBCM) to temperatures in excess of 185°F (85°C) for longer than 2 hrs. The system may be exposed to temperatures up to 200°F (95°C) for less than 15 min.
- Never disconnect or connect the Electronic Brake Control Module (EBCM) or hydraulic modulator connectors with the ignition switch ON.
- Never disassemble any component of the Anti-Lock Brake System (ABS) which is designated non-servicable; the component must be replaced as an assembly.
- When filling the master cylinder, always use brake fluid which meets DOT-3 specifications; petroleum base fluid will destroy the rubber parts.

DEPRESSURIZING THE HYDRAULIC ACCUMULATOR

1. With the ignition **OFF**, pump the brake pedal a minimum of 25 times, using approximately 50 lbs. (222 N) pedal force. A noticeable change in pedal feel will occur when the accumulator is discharged.

2. When a definite increase in pedal effort is felt, stroke the pedal a few additional times. This should remove all hydraulic pressure from the system.

Rear Disc Brake Caliper and Pads

REMOVAL & INSTALLATION

1. Depressurize the hydraulic accumulator. Remove ⅔ of brake fluid from the master cylinder.

2. Remove access plug and insert a 4mm Allen wrench through hole.

3. Turn the retraction shaft counterclockwise a few turns to increase clearance between pads and rotor.

4. Remove the anti-rattle spring from outboard pad taking care not to damage it.

5. Back the caliper guide pins out just enough to free caliper from adapter.

6. Lift the caliper off of rotor and carefully suspend with wire.

7. Remove the brake pads.

8. Insert the Allen wrench through access hole and turn clockwise, if necessary, to retract piston further to increase clearance for new pads.

To install:

9. Install new inner and outer pads.

NOTE: The outboard pads are marked for right and left hand sides and must be properly installed.

10. Lower the caliper over rotor and pads.

11. Install the guide pins and tighten to proper torque.

12. Insert the Allen wrench through the access hole and turn clockwise until snug, no clearance between pads and rotors, and back off ⅓ turn to obtain proper clearance.

13. Check the brake fluid level and add, if necessary.

Pump/Motor Assembly

REMOVAL & INSTALLATION

1. Disconnect the negative battery cable. Depressurize the hydraulic accumulator.

2. Remove the fresh air intake ducts.

3. Disconnect all electrical connectors the pump motor.

4. Disconnect the high and low pressure hoses from the hydraulic assembly. Cap the spigot on the reservoir.

5. Disconnect the shift selection cable bracket from the transaxle and move it aside.

6. Loosen the nuts on the 2 studs that position the pump/motor to the transaxle differential cover.

7. Remove the retainer bolts that are used to mount hose bracket and pump/motor. The engine inlet water extension pipe is also held in position by these bolts.

NOTE: Do not disturb the inlet water extension pipe, or engine coolant will leak out.

8. Disconnect the wiring harness retaining clip from the hose bracket.

9. Lift the pump/motor assembly off of the studs and out of the vehicle.

10. Remove the heat shield from the pump/motor, if equipped and discard.
To install:

11. Place a new heat shield to the pump/motor bracket, using fasteners provided.

12. Install the pump/motor assembly in the reverse order of the removal.

13. Readjust the gearshift linkage, if it was disturbed.

14. Connect the negative battery cable and check the assembly for proper operation.

Hydraulic Assembly

REMOVAL & INSTALLATION

1. Disconnect the negative battery cable. Depressurize the hydraulic accumulator.

2. Remove the fresh air intake ducts.

3. Disconnect all electrical connectors from the hydraulic unit and pump/motor.

4. Remove as much of the fluid as possible from the reservoir on the hydraulic assembly.

5. Remove the pressure hose fitting (banjo bolt) from the hydraulic assembly. Use care not to drop the two washers used to seal the pressure hose fitting to the hydraulic assembly inlet.

6. Disconnect the return hose from the reservoir nipple. Cap the spigot on the reservoir.

7. Disconnect all brake tubes from the hydraulic assembly.

8. Remove the driver's side sound insulation panel.

9. Disconnect the pushrod from the brake pedal.

10. Remove the 4 underdash hydraulic assembly mounting nuts.

11. Remove the hydraulic assembly.
To install:

12. Position the hydraulic assembly on the vehicle.

13. Install and torque the mounting nuts to 21 ft. lbs. (28 Nm).

14. Using Lubriplate® or equivalent, coat the bearing surface of the pedal pin.

15. Connect the pushrod to the pedal and install a new retainer clip.

16. Install the brake tubes. If the proportioning valves were removed from the hydraulic assembly, reinstall valves and tighten to 20 ft. lbs. (27 Nm).

17. Install the return hose to the nipple on the reservoir.

18. Install the pressure hose to the hydraulic assembly; be sure the 2 washers are in there proper position. Tighten the bango bolt to 13 ft. lbs. (18 Nm).

19. Fill the reservoir to the top of the screen.

20. Connect all electrical connectors to the hydraulic assembly.

21. Bleed the entire brake system.

22. Install the crosscar brace, if disturbed. Install the fresh air intake duct.

23. Connect the negative battery cable and check the assembly for proper operation.

Sensor Block

REMOVAL & INSTALLATION

1. Disconnect the negative battery cable. Depressurize the hydraulic accumulator.

2. Disconnect all electrical connectors from the reservoir on the hydraulic assembly.

3. Working from under the dash, disconnect the pushrod from the brake pedal.

4. Remove the driver's side sound insulator panel.

5. Remove the 4 hydraulic assembly mounting nuts.

6. Working from under the hood, pull the hydraulic assembly away from the dash panel and rotate the assembly enough to gain access to the sensor block cover.

NOTE: The brake lines should not be removed or deformed during this procedure.

7. Remove the sensor block cover retaining bolt and remove the sensor block cover. Care should be used not to damage the cover gasket during removal.

8. Disengage the locking tabs and disconnect the valve block connector (12 pin) from the sensor block.

9. Disengage the reed block connector, marked PUSH, by carefully pulling outward on the orange connector

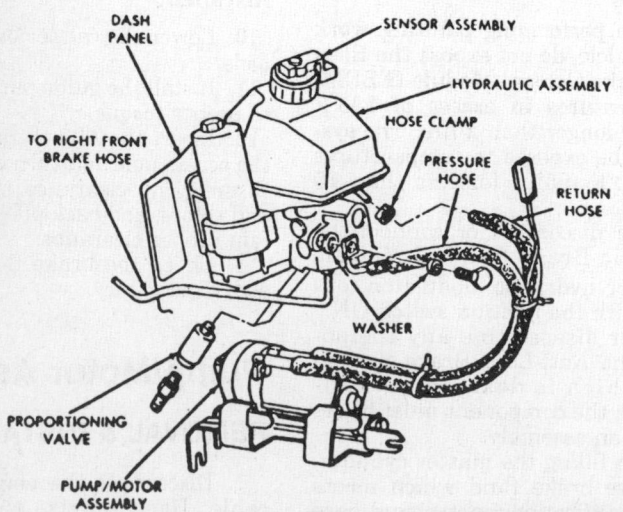

Hydraulic assembly, pump/motor assembly and related parts

body. The connector is partially retained by a plastic clip and will only move outward approximately ½ in. (13mm).

10. Remove the 3 block retaining bolts.

11. Carefully disengage the sensor block pressure port from the hydraulic assembly and remove the sensor block from the vehicle. The sensor block pressure port is sealed with an O-ring and extra care should be taken to prevent damage to the seal.

12. Inspect the sensor block pressure port O-ring for damage. Replace the O-ring if cut or damaged. Check the sensor block wiring for any mispositioning or damage. Correct any damage or replace the sensor block, if damage cannot be corrected.

To install:

13. Pull the reed block connector (2 pin) outward to the disengage position prior to installing the sensor block on the hydraulic unit.

14. Throughly lubricate the sensor block pressure port O-ring with fresh, clean brake fluid. Carefully insert the pressure port into the hydraulic assembly's orifice, taking care not to cut or damage the O-ring. Position the sensor block for installation of the mounting bolts.

15. Install the sensor block mounting bolts. Tighten to 11 ft. lbs. (15 Nm).

16. Engage the reed block connector by pressing on the orange connector body marked PUSH.

17. Connect the valve block connector (12 pin) to the sensor block.

18. Install the sensor block cover, gasket and mounting bolt.

19. Connect the sensor block and control pressure switch connectors.

20. Install the hydraulic assembly by reversing the removal procedure.

21. Connect the negative battery cable and check the sensor block for proper operation.

Speed Sensors

REMOVAL & INSTALLATION

Front Sensor

1. Raise the vehicle and support safely. Remove the wheel and tire assembly.

2. Remove the screw from the clip that holds the sensor to the fender shield.

3. Carefully pull the sensor assembly grommet from the fender shield.

4. Unplug the connector from the harness. Remove the retaininer clip from the strut damper bracket.

5. Remove the sensor mounting screw.

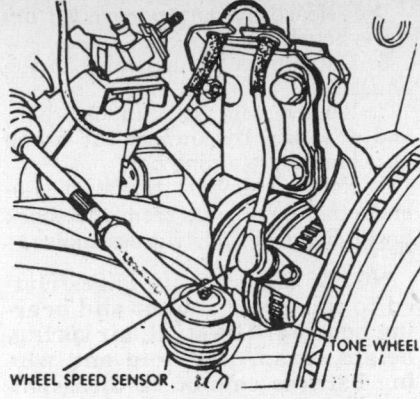

Front wheel speed sensor location

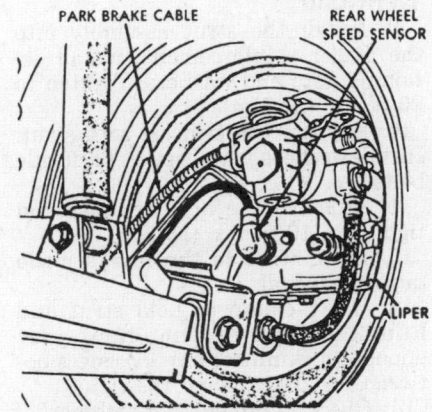

Rear wheel speed sensor location

6. Carefully remove the sensor.

To install:

7. Coat the sensor with high temperature multi-purpose anti-corrosion compound before installing into the steering knuckle. Install the screw and tighten to 60 inch lbs. (7 Nm).

8. Connect the sensor connector to the harness and install the sensor connector lock.

9. Install the sensor assembly grommet and attach the clip to the fender shield.

NOTE: Proper installation of the wheel speed sensor cables is critical to continued system operation. Be sure the cables are installed in retainers. Failure to install the cables in the retainers may result in contact with moving parts and/or over-extension of the cables, resulting in an open circuit.

10. Install the wheel.

Rear Sensor

1. Raise the vehicle and support safely. Remove the wheel and tire assembly.

2. Carefully pull the sensor assembly grommet from the underbody and pull the harness through the hole.

3. Unplug the connector from the harness. Remove the retaininer clip from the strut damper bracket.

4. Remove the sensor spool grommet clip retaining screw from the body hose bracket, located in front of the inside of the trailing arm.

5. Remove the outboard sensor assembly retaining nut and sensor mounting screw.

6. Carefully remove the sensor.

To install:

7. Coat the sensor with high temperature multi-purpose anti-corrosion compound before installing into the steering knuckle. Install the screw and tighten to 60 inch lbs. (7 Nm). Install the retaining nut.

8. Install the sensor spool grommet clip retaining screw

9. Feed the sensor connector wire through the grommet and connect to the harness.

10. Install the sensor assembly grommet.

11. Install the wheel.

FRONT SUSPENSION

MacPherson Strut

REMOVAL & INSTALLATION

Except with Automatic Air Suspension

1. Remove the 3 mounting nuts from the shock tower under the hood.

2. Raise the vehicle and support safely.

3. Remove the brake hose bracket screw from the strut.

4. Matchmark the lower strut mount to the knuckle and remove the strut to knuckle bolts, nuts and nut plate.

5. The installation is the reverse of the removal procedure. Torque the upper mounting nuts to 20 ft. lbs. (27 Nm). Do not tighten the lower mounting bolts until the front end alignment has been completed.

6. Perform a front end alignment. Torque the strut to knuckle nuts to 75 ft. lbs. (100 Nm) plus ¼ turn.

Air Suspension Strut

REMOVAL & INSTALLATION

1. Disconnect the negative battery cable.

2. Raise the vehicle and support

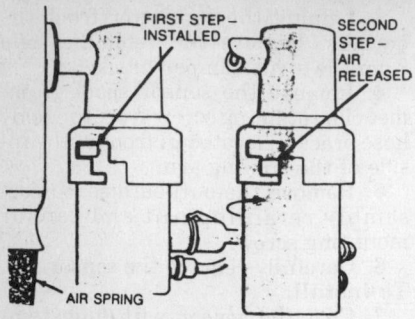

Air suspension spring solenoid positions

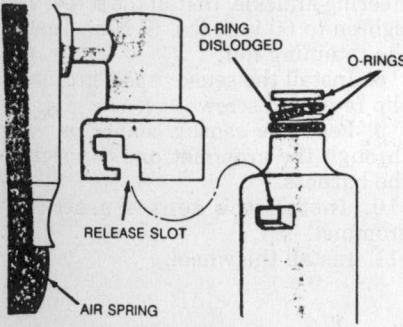

Air suspension solenoid removed

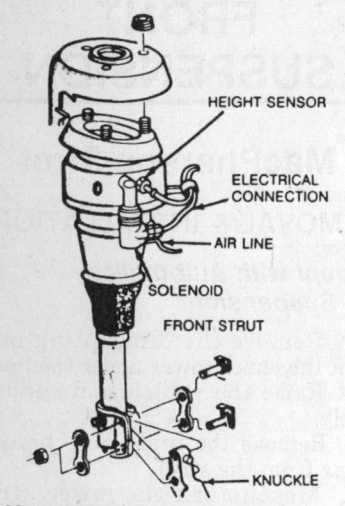

Air suspension strut assembly

safely. Remove the wheel and tire assembly.

3. To disconnect the air line, pull back on the plastic ring and pull the air line from the fitting.

4. Disconnect the electrical leads from the solenoid and the height sensor.

5. The solenoid has a molded square tang that fits into stepped notches in the air spring housing to provide for exhaust and a retaining positions. To vent the air spring:

a. Release the retaining clip.

b. Rotate the solenoid to the first step in the housing and allow the air presure to vent.

c. Rotate the solenoid farther to

the release slot and remove it from the housing.

6. Matchmark the assembly to the knuckle.

7. Remove cam bolt, knuckle bolt, and washers. Disconnect the brake hose bracket retaining bolt.

8. Hold or support the strut. Remove the upper nuts from the shock tower. Remove the strut assembly.

NOTE: Disassembly is restricted to the upper mount and bearing housing. The strut, air spring, height sensor, solenoid and wiring harness cannot be disassembled or serviced. They are replaced as a unit.

To install:

9. Install the strut assembly into the fender reinforcement; install retaining nuts and washers. Tighten to 20 ft. lbs. (27 Nm).

10. Position the knuckle into strut. Install washers with cam and knuckle bolts.

11. Attach brake hose retainer and tighten to 10 ft. lbs. (13 Nm).

12. Index strut to the marks made during removal.

13. Use C-clamp to hold strut and knuckle. Tighten the clamp just enough to eliminate any looseness between the knuckle and the strut.

14. Check alignment of matchmarks. Tighten the nuts on the cam and knuckle bolts to 75 ft. lbs. (100 Nm) plus ¼ turn.

15. Remove the C-clamp.

16. Install the solenoid to the top step in the housing.

17. Connect the electrical leads to the solenoid and height sensor.

18. Connect the air line by pushing it into place; it will lock in place.

19. Connect the negative battery cable.

20. To recharge the air spring, run the compressor for 60 seconds by jumping from pin No. 9 (black wire with red tracer) to pin No. 19 (gray wire with black tracer) of the controller connector. The air suspension controller is located behind the right side trunk trim panel.

21. Install the wheel and tire.

22. Check the system for proper operation.

Lower Ball Joints

INSPECTION

To inspect the ball joints, grasp the grease fitting by hand with the vehicle on the ground. If the grease fitting can be moved at all by hand, the ball joint should be replaced.

REMOVAL & INSTALLATION

The ball joints are welded to the lower control arms. This necessitates replacement of the control arm assembly. Do not attempt to replace ball

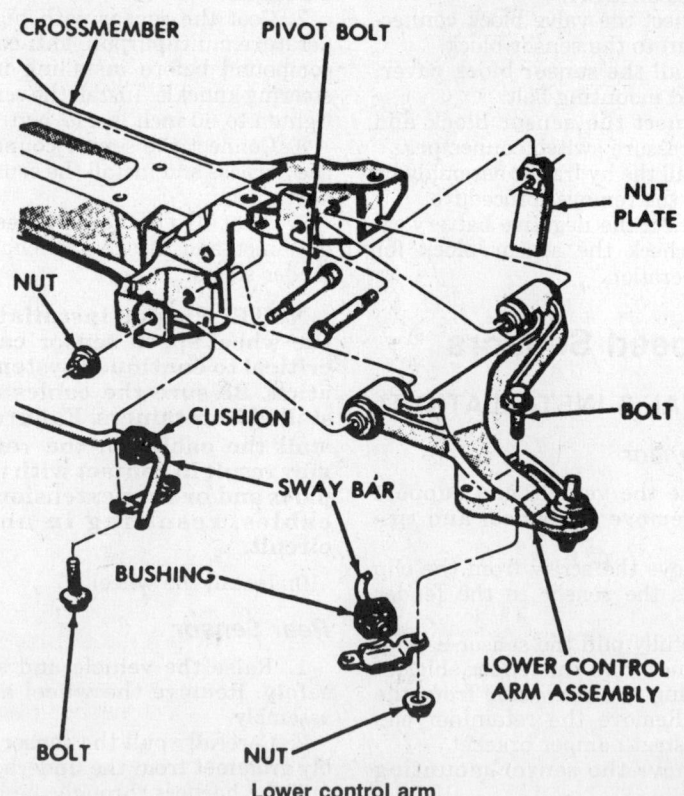

Lower control arm

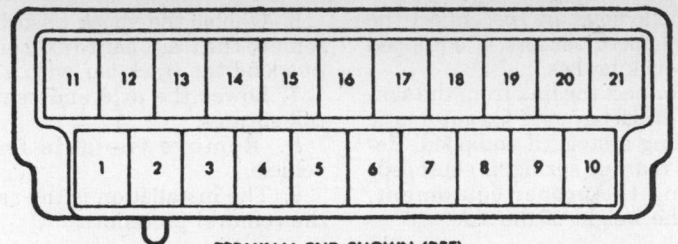

TERMINAL END SHOWN (REF)

Automatic air suspension controller connector terminals (terminal end)

joints that are welded to the control arm; replacement control arms are equipped with a new ball joint.

Lower Control Arms

REMOVAL & INSTALLATION

1. Raise the vehicle and support safely. Remove the tire and wheel assembly.
2. Remove the sway bar.
3. Remove the ball joint stud retaining bolt and nut.
4. Pry the lower control arm from the steering knuckle.
5. Remove the control arm to crossmember bolts and nuts.
6. Remove the control arm from the vehicle.
7. The installation is the reverse of the removal procedure.
8. Lower the vehicle so the full weight of the vehicle is on the ground.
9. Torque the pivot bolts to 124 ft. lbs. (169 Nm).
10. Perform a front end alignment as required.

Sway Bar

REMOVAL & INSTALLATION

1. Raise the vehicle and support safely.
2. Remove the front sway bar brackets and retainers.
3. Remove the sway bar support brackets and bushings from the lower control arm. Remove the sway bar from the vehicle.
4. The installation is the reverse of the removal procedure. Lubricate the sway bar bushings liberally with grease before assembling.

REAR SUSPENSION

Shock Absorbers

REMOVAL & INSTALLATION

1. Raise the vehicle and support

safely. Disconnect the height sensor and air line, if equipped. The air line is released by pulling back on the plastic retaining ring.
2. Remove the bolts that attach the shock to the frame or bracket.
3. Remove the shock from the vehicle.
4. The installation is the reverse of the removal procedure.

Coil Springs

REMOVAL & INSTALLATION

1. Raise the vehicle and support safely.
2. Using the proper equipment, support the weight of the rear axle.
3. Remove the bolts that attach the shock to the lower mounting bracket.
4. Lower the axle and remove the coil spring from the vehicle.
5. The installation is the reverse of the removal procedure.

Air Springs

REMOVAL & INSTALLATION

1. Disconnect the negative battery cable.
2. Raise the vehicle and support safely. Remove the wheel.
3. To disconnect the air line, pull back on the plastic ring and pull the air line from the fitting.
4. Disconnect the electrical leads from the solenoid and the height sensor.
5. The solenoid has a molded square tang that fits into stepped notches in the air spring housing to provide for exhaust and a retaining positions. To vent the air spring:
   a. Release the retaining clip.
   b. Rotate the solenoid to the first step in the housing and allow the air presure to vent.
   c. Rotate the solenoid farther to the release slot and remove it from the housing.
6. Release the upper air spring alignment/retaining clips.

7. Remove the nut that attaches the lower portion of the spring to the axle.
8. Pry the assembly down, pull the alignment studs through the retaining clips and remove the assembly from the vehicle.

To install:

9. Position the lower stud into its seat in the axle and the upper alignment pins through the frame rail adaptor. Install the retaining clips.
10. Loosely install the lower mounting nut.
11. Install the solenoid to the top step in the housing.
12. Connect the electrical lead to the solenoid.
13. Connect the air line by pushing it into place; it will lock in place.
14. Connect the negative battery cable.
15. To partially recharge the air spring, run the compressor for 60 seconds by jumping from pin No. 9 (black wire with red tracer) to pin No. 19 (gray wire with black tracer) of the controller connector. The air suspension controller is located behind the right side trunk trim panel.
15. When the air spring is properly inflated, torque the lower mouting nut to 50 ft. lbs. (68 Nm).
16. Install the wheel and tire.
17. Check the system for proper operation.

Rear Wheel Bearings

REMOVAL & INSTALLATION

1. Raise the vehicle and support safely.
2. Remove the tire and wheel assembly.
3. Remove the dust cap.
4. Remove the cotter pin, nut lock and nut.
5. Remove the thrust washer and the outer wheel bearing.
6. Remove the drum with the inner wheel bearing and the grease seal.
7. Remove the grease seal and remove the inner bearing.

To install:

8. Lubricate the inner bearing and install to the drum.
9. Install a new grease seal.
10. Install the drum to the vehicle.
11. Lubricate and install the outer wheel bearing to the spindle.
12. Install the thrust washer.
13. Install and tighten the wheel bearng nut to 20–25 ft. lbs. (27–34 Nm) while rotating the drum.
14. Back off the adjusting nut ¼ turn then tighten it finger-tight.
15. Install the nut lock and a new cotter pin.

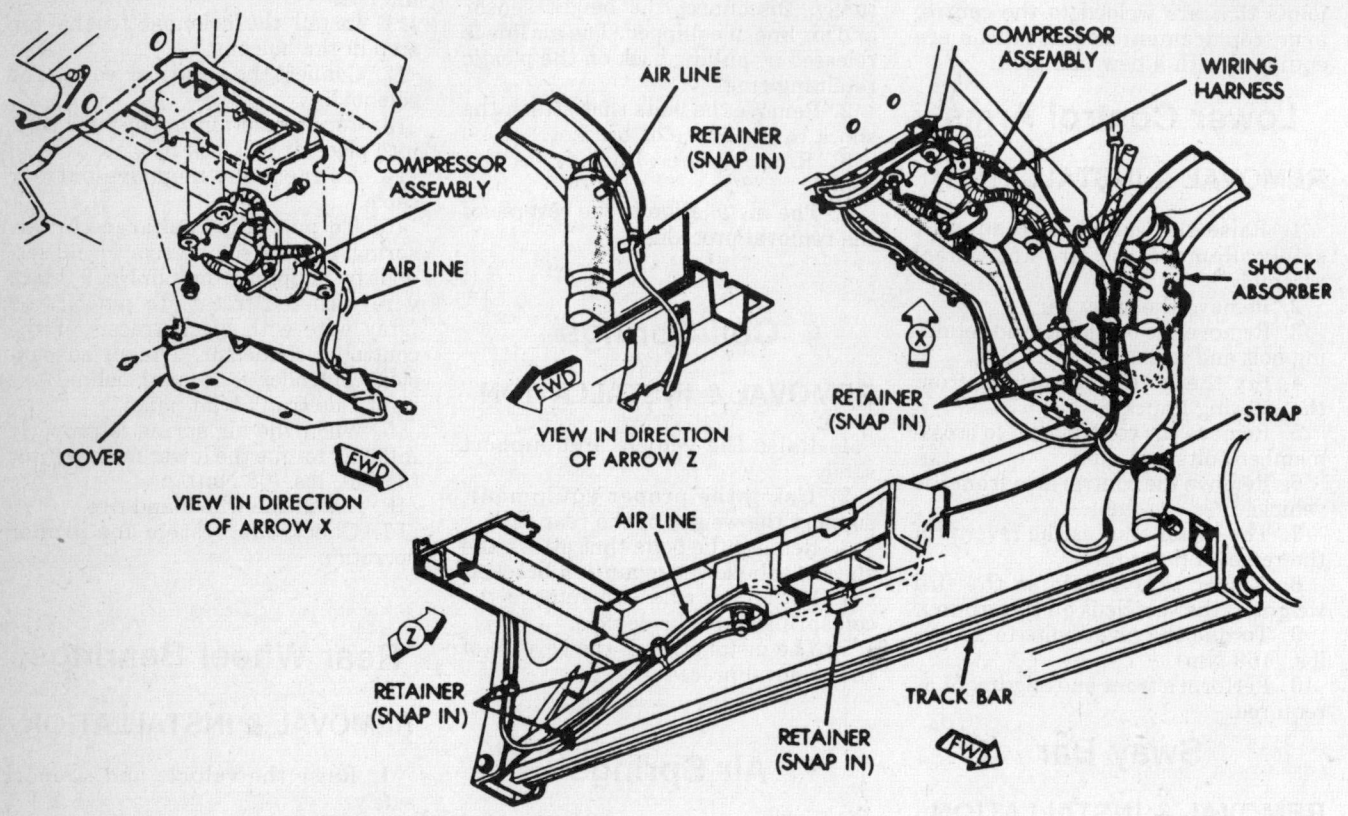

Rear Axle Assembly
REMOVAL & INSTALLATION

1. Raise the vehicle and support safely.

2. Disconnect the parking brake cable at the connection.

3. Disconnect the brake tubes from the hoses and unclip the brake tubes from the axle housing. Disconnect the rear wheel speed sensors, if equipped with anti-lock brakes.

4. Disconnect the link from the sensor to the track bar used for automatic load leveling system, if equipped. Remove the rear air spring, if equipped.

5. Using the proper equipment, support the weight of the axle.

6. Unbolt the shock absorbers and remove the track bar to axle pivot bolt. Suspend the track bar with a wire.

7. Lower the axle and remove the coil springs.

8. Remove the axle from the vehicle.

9. The installation is the reverse of the removal procedure.

Automatic air suspension

Chrysler Corp.
Front Wheel Drive
Dodge—Charger, Omni, Shelby Charger
Plymouth—Horizon

SPECIFICATIONS

VEHICLE IDENTIFICATION CHART

It is important for servicing and ordering parts to be certain of the vehicle and engine identification. The VIN (vehicle identification number) is a 17 digit number visible through the windshield on the driver's side of the dash and contains the vehicle and engine identification codes. The tenth digit indicates model year, and the eighth digit indicates engine code. It can be interpreted as follows:

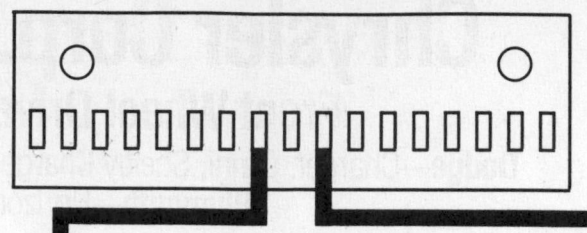

Engine Code

Code	Cu. In.	Liters	Cyl.	Fuel Sys.	Eng. Mfg.
C	135	2.2	4	2BBL	Chrysler
D	135	2.2	4	EFI	Chrysler
E	135	2.2	4	Turbo	Chrysler

Model Year

Code	Year
H	1987
J	1988
K	1989
L	1990
M	1991

ENGINE IDENTIFICATION

Year	Model	Engine Displacement cu. in. (liter)	Engine Series Identification (VIN)	No. of Cylinders	Engine Type
1987	Shelby Charger	135 (2.2)	E	4	OHC
	Charger	135 (2.2)	C	4	OHC
	Turismo	135 (2.2)	C	4	OHC
	Horizon	135 (2.2)	C	4	OHC
	Omni	135 (2.2)	C	4	OHC
1988	Horizon	135 (2.2)	D	4	OHC
	Omni	135 (2.2)	D	4	OHC
1989	Horizon	135 (2.2)	D	4	OHC
	Omni	135 (2.2)	D	4	OHC
1990–91	Horizon	135 (2.2)	D	4	OHC
	Omni	135 (2.2)	D	4	OHC

GENERAL ENGINE SPECIFICATIONS

Year	VIN	No. Cylinder Displacement cu. in. (liter)	Fuel System Type	Net Horsepower @ rpm	Net Torque @ rpm (ft. lbs.)	Bore × Stroke (in.)	Compression Ratio	Oil Pressure @ rpm
1987	C	4-135 (2.2)	2BBL	96 @ 5200	119 @ 3200	3.44 × 3.62	9.5:1	30–80 @ 3000
	E	4-135 (2.2)	Turbo	146 @ 5600	170 @ 3600	3.44 × 3.62	8.0:1	30–80 @ 3000
1988	D	4-135 (2.2)	EFI	99 @ 5600	121 @ 3200	3.44 × 3.62	9.5:1	30–80 @ 3000
1989	D	4-135 (2.2)	EFI	99 @ 5600	121 @ 3200	3.44 × 3.62	9.5:1	30–80 @ 3000
1990–91	D	4-135 (2.2)	EFI	99 @ 5600	121 @ 3200	3.44 × 3.62	9.5:1	30–80 @ 3000

EFI   Electronic Fuel Injection

GASOLINE ENGINE TUNE-UP SPECIFICATIONS

Year	VIN	No. Cylinder Displacement cu. in. (liter)	Spark Plugs Type	Spark Plugs Gap (in.)	Ignition Timing (deg.) MT	Ignition Timing (deg.) AT	Compression Pressure (psi)	Fuel Pump (psi)	Idle Speed (rpm) MT	Idle Speed (rpm) AT	Valve Clearance In.	Valve Clearance Ex.
1987	C	4-135 (2.2)	RN12YC	0.035	10B	10B	100 ①	4.5–6	800	900	Hyd.	Hyd.
	E	4-135 (2.2)	RN12YC	0.035	12B	12B	100 ①	55	850	850	Hyd.	Hyd.
1988	D	4-135 (2.2)	RN12YC	0.035	12B	12B	100 ①	15	850	850	Hyd.	Hyd.
1989	D	4-135 (2.2)	RN12YC	0.035	12B	12B	100 ①	15	850	850	Hyd.	Hyd.
1990-91	D	4-135 (2.2)	RN12YC	0.035	12B	12B	100 ①	15	850	850	Hyd.	Hyd.

① Minimum

FIRING ORDERS

NOTE: To avoid confusion, always replace spark plug wires one at a time.

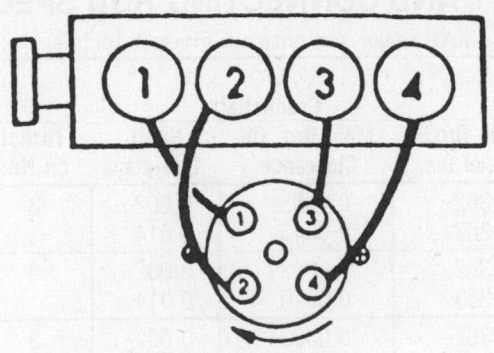

2.2L Engine
Engine Firing Order: 1–3–4–2
Distributor Rotation: Clockwise

CAPACITIES

Year	Model	VIN	No. Cylinder Displacement cu. in. (liter)	Engine Crankcase (qts.) with Filter	Engine Crankcase (qts.) without Filter	Transmission (pts.) 4-Spd	Transmission (pts.) 5-Spd	Transmission (pts.) Auto.	Drive Axle (pts.)	Fuel Tank (gal.)	Cooling System (qts.)
1987	Shelby Charger	E	4-135 (2.2)	4	4	—	4.8	—	—	13	9
	Charger	C	4-135 (2.2)	4	4	—	4.8	18	—	13	9
	Turismo	C	4-135 (2.2)	4	4	—	4.8	18	—	13	9
	Horizon	C	4-135 (2.2)	4	4	—	4.8	18	—	13	9
	Omni	C	4-135 (2.2)	4	4	—	4.8	18	—	13	9
1988	Horizon	D	4-135 (2.2)	4	4	—	4.8	18	—	13	9
	Omni	D	4-135 (2.2)	4	4	—	4.8	18	—	13	9
1989	Horizon	D	4-135 (2.2)	4	4	—	4.8	18	—	13	9
	Omni	D	4-135 (2.2)	4	4	—	4.8	18	—	13	9
1990-91	Horizon	D	4-135 (2.2)	4	4	—	4.8	18	—	13	9
	Omni	D	4-135 (2.2)	4	4	—	4.8	18	—	13	9

CAMSHAFT SPECIFICATIONS

All measurements given in inches.

Year	VIN	No. Cylinder Displacement cu. in. (liter)	Journal Diameter 1	2	3	4	5	Lobe Lift In.	Ex.	Bearing Clearance	Camshaft End Play
1987	C	4-135 (2.2)	1.375–1.376	1.375–1.376	1.375–1.376	1.375–1.376	1.375–1.376	NA NA	NA NA	—	0.005–0.020
	E	4-135 (2.2)	1.375–1.376	1.375–1.376	1.375–1.376	1.375–1.376	1.375–1.376	NA NA	NA NA	—	0.005–0.020
1988	D	4-135 (2.2)	1.375–1.376	1.375–1.376	1.375–1.376	1.375–1.376	1.375–1.376	NA NA	NA NA	—	0.005–0.020
1989	D	4-135 (2.2)	1.375–1.376	1.375–1.376	1.375–1.376	1.375–1.376	1.375–1.376	NA NA	NA NA	—	0.005–0.020
1990–91	D	4-135 (2.2)	1.375–1.376	1.375–1.376	1.375–1.376	1.375–1.376	1.375–1.376	NA NA	NA NA	—	0.005–0.020

CRANKSHAFT AND CONNECTING ROD SPECIFICATIONS

All measurements are given in inches.

Year	VIN	No. Cylinder Displacement cu. in. (liter)	Crankshaft Main Brg. Journal Dia.	Main Brg. Oil Clearance	Shaft End-play	Thrust on No.	Connecting Rod Journal Diameter	Oil Clearance	Side Clearance
1987	C	4-135 (2.2)	2.362–2.363	0.0003–0.0040	0.002–0.014	3	1.968–1.969	0.0008–0.0040	0.005–0.013
	E	4-135 (2.2)	2.362–2.363	0.0003–0.0040	0.002–0.014	3	1.968–1.969	0.0008–0.0040	0.005–0.013
1988	D	4-135 (2.2)	2.362–2.363	0.0003–0.0040	0.002–0.014	3	1.968–1.969	0.0008–0.0040	0.005–0.013
1989	D	4-135 (2.2)	2.362–2.363	0.0003–0.0040	0.002–0.014	3	1.968–1.969	0.0008–0.0040	0.005–0.013
1990–91	D	4-135 (2.2)	2.362–2.363	0.0003–0.0040	0.002–0.014	3	1.968–1.969	0.0008–0.0040	0.005–0.013

VALVE SPECIFICATIONS

Year	VIN	No. Cylinder Displacement cu. in. (liter)	Seat Angle (deg.)	Face Angle (deg.)	Spring Test Pressure (lbs.)	Spring Installed Height (in.)	Stem-to-Guide Clearance (in.) Intake	Exhaust	Stem Diameter (in.) Intake	Exhaust
1987	C	4-135 (2.2)	45	45	95	1.65	0.001–0.003	0.0030–0.0047	0.3124	0.3103
	E	4-135 (2.2)	45	45	95	1.65	0.001–0.003	0.0030–0.0047	0.3124	0.3103
1988	D	4-135 (2.2)	45	45	95	1.65	0.001–0.003	0.0030–0.0047	0.3124	0.3103
1989	D	4-135 (2.2)	45	45	95	1.65	0.001–0.003	0.0030–0.0047	0.3124	0.3103
1990–91	D	4-135 (2.2)	45	45	95	1.65	0.001–0.003	0.0030–0.0047	0.3124	0.3103

PISTON AND RING SPECIFICATIONS

All measurements are given in inches.

Year	VIN	No. Cylinder Displacement cu. in. (liter)	Piston Clearance	Ring Gap			Ring Side Clearance		
				Top Compression	Bottom Compression	Oil Control	Top Compression	Bottom Compression	Oil Control
1987	C	4-135 (2.2)	0.0005– 0.0015	0.0100– 0.0390	0.0110– 0.0390	0.0150– 0.0740	0.0015– 0.0040	0.0015– 0.0040	0.0002– 0.0080
	E	4-135 (2.2)	0.0005– 0.0015	0.0100– 0.0390	0.0110– 0.0390	0.0150– 0.0740	0.0015– 0.0040	0.0015– 0.0040	0.0002– 0.0080
1988	D	4-135 (2.2)	0.0005– 0.0015	0.0100– 0.0390	0.0110– 0.0390	0.0150– 0.0740	0.0015– 0.0040	0.0015– 0.0040	0.0002– 0.0080
1989	D	4-135 (2.2)	0.0005– 0.0015	0.0100– 0.0390	0.0110– 0.0390	0.0150– 0.0740	0.0015– 0.0040	0.0015– 0.0040	0.0002– 0.0080
1990–91	D	4-135 (2.2)	0.0005– 0.0015	0.0100– 0.0390	0.0110– 0.0390	0.0150– 0.0740	0.0015– 0.0040	0.0015– 0.0040	0.0002– 0.0080

TORQUE SPECIFICATIONS

All readings in ft. lbs.

Year	VIN	No. Cylinder Displacement cu. in. (liter)	Cylinder Head Bolts	Main Bearing Bolts	Rod Bearing Bolts	Crankshaft Pulley Bolts	Flywheel Bolts	Manifold		Spark Plugs
								Intake	Exhaust	
1987	C	4-135 (2.2)	①	30 ②	40 ②	50	70	17	17	26
	E	4-135 (2.2)	①	30 ②	40 ②	50	70	17	17	26
1988	D	4-135 (2.2)	①	30 ②	40 ②	50	70	17	17	26
1989	D	4-135 (2.2)	①	30 ②	40 ②	50	70	17	17	26
1990–91	D	4-135 (2.2)	①	30 ②	40 ②	50	70	17	17	26

① Sequence:
    1st step 45 ft. lbs.
    2nd step 65 ft. lbs.
    3rd step plus 1/4 turn
② Plus 1/4 turn

BRAKE SPECIFICATIONS

All measurements in inches unless noted.

Year	Model	Lug Nut Torque (ft. lbs.)	Master Cylinder Bore	Brake Disc		Standard Brake Drum Diameter	Minimum Lining Thickness	
				Minimum Thickness	Maximum Runout		Front	Rear
1987	Shelby Charger	95	0.827	0.431	0.005	7.87	0.06	0.06
	Charger	95	0.827	0.431	0.005	7.87	0.06	0.06
	Turismo	95	0.827	0.431	0.005	7.87	0.06	0.06
	Horizon	95	0.827	0.431	0.005	7.87	0.06	0.06
	Omni	95	0.827	0.431	0.005	7.87	0.06	0.06
1988	Horizon	95	0.827	0.431	0.005	7.87	0.06	0.06
	Omni	95	0.827	0.431	0.005	7.87	0.06	0.06

BRAKE SPECIFICATIONS
All measurements in inches unless noted.

Year	Model	Lug Nut Torque (ft. lbs.)	Master Cylinder Bore	Brake Disc Minimum Thickness	Maximum Runout	Standard Brake Drum Diameter	Minimum Lining Thickness Front	Rear
1989	Horizon	95	0.827	0.431	0.005	7.87	0.06	0.06
	Omni	95	0.827	0.431	0.005	7.87	0.06	0.06
1990-91	Horizon	95	0.827	0.431	0.005	7.87	0.06	0.06
	Omni	95	0.827	0.431	0.005	7.87	0.06	0.06

WHEEL ALIGNMENT

Year	Model		Caster Range (deg.)	Preferred Setting (deg.)	Camber Range (deg.)	Preferred Setting (deg.)	Toe-in (in.)	Steering Axis Inclination (deg.)
1987	Shelby Charger	Front	①	$19/10$P	$1/4$N–$3/4$P	$5/16$P	$1/16$	$13^3/8$
		Rear	—	—	$1^1/4$N–$1/4$N	$3/4$N	$3/32$	$13^3/8$
	Charger	Front	①	$19/10$P	$1/4$N–$3/4$P	$5/16$P	$1/16$	$13^3/8$
		Rear	—	—	$1^1/4$N–$1/4$N	$3/4$N	$3/32$	$13^3/8$
	Turismo	Front	①	$19/10$P	$1/4$N–$3/4$P	$5/16$P	$1/16$	$13^3/8$
		Rear	—	—	$1^1/4$N–$1/4$N	$3/4$N	$3/32$	$13^3/8$
	Horizon	Front	①	$19/10$P	$1/4$N–$3/4$P	$5/16$P	$1/16$	$13^3/8$
		Rear	—	—	$1^1/4$N–$1/4$N	$3/4$N	$3/32$	$13^3/8$
	Omni	Front	①	$19/10$P	$1/4$N–$3/4$P	$5/16$P	$1/16$	$13^3/8$
		Rear	—	—	$1^1/4$N–$1/4$N	$3/4$N	$3/32$	$13^3/8$
1988	Horizon	Front	①	$19/10$P	$1/4$N–$3/4$P	$5/16$P	$1/16$	$13^3/8$
		Rear	—	—	$1^1/4$N–$1/4$N	$3/4$N	$3/32$	$13^3/8$
	Omni	Front	①	$19/10$P	$1/4$N–$3/4$P	$5/16$P	$1/16$	$13^3/8$
		Rear	—	—	$1^1/4$N–$1/4$N	$3/4$N	$3/32$	$13^3/8$
1989	Horizon	Front	①	$19/10$P	$1/4$N–$3/4$P	$5/16$P	$1/16$	$13^3/8$
		Rear	—	—	$1^1/4$N–$1/4$N	$3/4$N	$3/32$	$13^3/8$
	Omni	Front	①	$19/10$P	$1/4$N–$3/4$P	$5/16$P	$1/16$	$13^3/8$
		Rear	—	—	$1^1/4$N–$1/4$N	$3/4$N	$3/32$	$13^3/8$
1990-91	Horizon	Front	①	$19/10$P	$1/4$N–$3/4$P	$5/16$P	$1/16$	$13^3/8$
		Rear	—	—	$1^1/4$N–$1/4$N	$3/4$N	$3/32$	$13^3/8$
	Omni	Front	①	$19/10$P	$1/4$N–$3/4$P	$5/16$P	$1/16$	$13^3/8$
		Rear	—	—	$1^1/4$N–$1/4$N	$3/4$N	$3/32$	$13^3/8$

① Variation between sides not to exceed $1^1/2$P

ENGINE ELECTRICAL

NOTE: Disconnecting the negative battery cable on some vehicles may interfere with the functions of the on board computer systems and may require the computer to undergo a relearning process, once the negative battery cable is reconnected.

Distributor

REMOVAL

1. Disconnect the negative battery cable.
2. Disconnect the distributor pickup lead wires. Remove the splash shield, if equipped.
3. Unscrew the distributor cap hold-down screws and lift off the distributor cap with all ignition wires still connected.
4. Matchmark the rotor to the distributor housing and the distributor housing to the engine.

NOTE: Do not crank the engine during this procedure. If the engine is cranked, the matchmark must be disregarded.

5. Remove the hold-down bolt and clamp.
6. Remove the distributor from the engine.

INSTALLATION

Timing Not Disturbed

1. Install a new distributor housing O-ring.
2. Install the distributor in the engine so the rotor is aligned with the matchmark on the housing and the housing is aligned with the matchmark on the engine. Make sure the distributor is fully seated and the distributor shaft is fully engaged.
3. Install the hold-down clamp and snug the hold-down bolt.
4. Connect the distributor pickup lead wires. Install the splash shield, if equipped.
5. Install the distributor cap and tighten the screws.
6. Connect the negative battery cable.
7. Adjust the ignition timing and tighten the hold-down bolt.

Timing Disturbed

1. Install a new distributor housing O-ring.
2. Position the engine so the No. 1

piston is at TDC of its compression stroke and the mark on the vibration damper is aligned with **0** on the timing indicator.

3. Install the distributor in the engine so the rotor is aligned with the position of the No. 1 ignition wire on the distributor cap and the housing is aligned with the matchmark on the engine. Make sure the distributor is fully seated and that the distributor shaft is fully engaged.
4. Install the hold-down clamp and snug the hold-down bolt.
5. Connect the distributor pickup lead wires. Install the splash shield, if equipped.
6. Install the distributor cap and tighten the screws.
7. Connect the negative battery cable.
8. Adjust the ignition timing and tighten the hold-down bolt.

Ignition Timing

ADJUSTMENT

1. Start the engine, set the parking brake and run the engine until at normal operating temperature. Keep all lights and accessories off.
2. If a magnetic timing unit is available, insert the probe into the receptacle near the timing scale. The scale is located on the top of the bell housing.
3. If a magnetic timing unit is not available, connect a conventional power timing light to the No. 1 cylinder spark plug wire.
4. Connect the red lead of a tachometer to the negative primary terminal of the coil and connect the black lead to a good ground.
5. On 1987 carbureted vehicles:
   a. Disconnect and plug the distributor vacuum advance hose, which is plugged into the advance diaphragm on the top of the computer, located next to the battery.
   b. Disconnect the carburetor 6-way electrical connector, remove the violet wire from the connector and reconnect the connector. This disables the electronic spark advance.
   c. Set the idle speed according to the Vehicle Emission Control Information (VECI) label.
6. If fuel injected, disconnect the coolant sensor located near the thermostat housing. The Check Engine lamp on the instrument panel must be on. On 1989–90 vehicles, the Diagnostic Readout Box II (DRB-II), if available, may be used in conjuction with the Basic Timing Mode.
7. Aim the timing light at the timing scale or read the magnetic timing unit.
8. Loosen the distributor hold-

down bolt just enough so the disributor can be rotated.

9. Turn the distributor in the proper direction until the specified timing according to the VECI label is reached. Tighten the hold-down bolt and re-check the timing and idle speed.
10. Turn the engine **OFF**. Connect the vacuum hose or coolant sensor. Make sure the Check Engine lamp does not come ON when restarted.
11. Disconnect the timing apparatus and tachometer. Reinstall the violet wire into the carburetor connector, if it was removed.
12. If the coolant temperature sensor was disconnected, erase the created fault code using the Erase Fault Code mode on the DRB-II. The code can also be erased by disconnecting the battery. If the coolant sensor code is not erased at this point, it will disappear after 50–100 vehicle key ON/OFF cycles, providing there is no problem with that circuit.

Alternator

For further information on the charging system, please refer to "Charging and Starting" in the Unit Repair section.

PRECAUTIONS

Several precautions must be observed when working with the alternator to avoid damaging the unit.

- If the battery is removed for any reason, make sure it is reconnected with the correct polarity. Reversing the battery connections may result in damage to the one-way rectifiers.
- When utilizing a booster battery as a starting aid, always connect the positive to positive terminals and the negative terminal from the booster battery to a good engine ground on the vehicle being started.
- Never use a fast charger as a booster to start vehicles.
- Disconnect the battery cables when charging the battery with a fast charger.
- Never attempt to polarize the alternator.
- Do not use test lamps of more than 12 volts when checking diode continuity.
- Do not short across or ground any of the alternator terminals.
- The polarity of the battery, alternator and regulator must be matched and considered before making any electrical connections within the system.
- Never separate the alternator on an open circuit. Make sure all connec-

tions within the circuit are clean and tight.

• Disconnect the battery ground terminal when performing any service on electrical components.

• Disconnect the battery if arc welding is to be done on the vehicle.

BELT TENSION ADJUSTMENT

1. Loosen the pivot bolt slightly.
2. Raise the vehicle and support safely. Remove the splash shield. Loosen the adjuster slot bolt or "T" bolt locknut enough so the alternator can be moved. Loosen the adjusting bolt locknut, if equipped.
3. Tighten the adjusting bolt until the belt deflects about ¼ in. under a 10 lb. load.
4. Tighten the "T" bolt locknut or adjusting bolt locknut.

REMOVAL & INSTALLATION

1. Disconnect the negative battery cable.
2. Remove the air conditioning compressor and position it to the side. Remove the oil filter to allow the alternator to be removed from above.
3. Loosen the mounting bolts, move the alternator toward the engine and remove the drive belts.
4. Remove the mounting bolts and spacers and remove the alternator from the brackets.
5. Remove the battery positive, field and ground terminals from the rear of the alternator. Remove the wire harness hold-down screw from the alternator, if equipped.

To install:
6. Connect all wiring to the proper terminals on the rear of the alternator and install the wire harness hold-down screw, if equipped.
7. Position the alternator in the mounting brackets.
8. Install the spacers, pivot bolt and adjuster bolt. Install the belt.
9. Install the air conditioning compressor and oil filter.
10. Adjust the belt tension.
11. Connect the negative battery cable and check the alternator for proper operation.

Starter

For further information on the charging system, please refer to "Charging and Starting" in the Unit Repair section.

REMOVAL & INSTALLATION

1. Disconnect the negative battery cable.

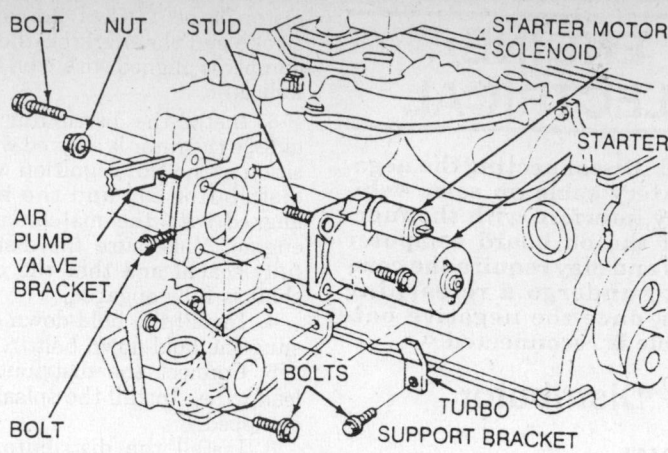

Starter motor mounting

2. Remove the attaching nut and bolt at the top of the bell housing. Raise the vehicle and support safely.
3. Remove the rear mount and heat shield from the starter.
4. Unbolt the starter and remove from the vehicle.
5. Disconnect the solenoid lead wires from the starter.

To install:
6. Connect the solenoid lead wires and install the heat shield.
7. Install the lower bolt loosely, then lower the vehicle and install the nut and bolt from above and torque to 40 ft. lbs. (54 Nm).
8. Raise the vehicle and torque the bottom bolt to the same value. Install the rear mount to the starter.
9. Connect the negative battery cable and check the starter for proper operation.

CHASSIS ELECTRICAL

—— CAUTION ——

On vehicles equipped with an air bag, the negative battery cable must be disconnected, before working on the system. Failure to do so may result in deployment of the air bag and possible personal injury.

Heater Blower Motor

REMOVAL & INSTALLATION

1. Disconnect the negative battery cable.
2. Remove the glove box assembly, lower right side instrument panel trim cover and right cowl trim panel, as required. Disconnect the blower lead wire connector.

3. If not equipped with air conditioning, remove the left side heater outlet duct. If equipped with air conditioning, disconnect the 2 vacuum lines from the recirculating door actuator and position the actuator to the side.
4. Remove the 2 screws at the top of the blower housing that secure it to the unit cover.
5. Remove the 5 screws from around the blower housing and separate the blower housing from the unit.
6. Remove the 3 screws that secure the blower assembly to the heater or air conditioning housing and remove the assembly from the unit. Remove the fan from the blower motor.
7. The installation is the reverse of the removal procedure.
8. Connect the negative battery cable and check the blower motor for proper operation.

Windshield Wiper Motor

REMOVAL & INSTALLATION

Front

1. Disconnect the negative battery cable. Open the hood.
2. Remove the plastic wiper motor cover and washer hose attaching clip.
3. Disconnect the motor connector.
4. Remove the 3 bolts that attach the motor mounting bracket to the firewall.
5. Pull the motor out of its cavity and remove the drive crank mounting nut.
6. The installation is the reverse of the removal procedure.
7. Connect the negative battery cable and check the wiper motor for proper operation.

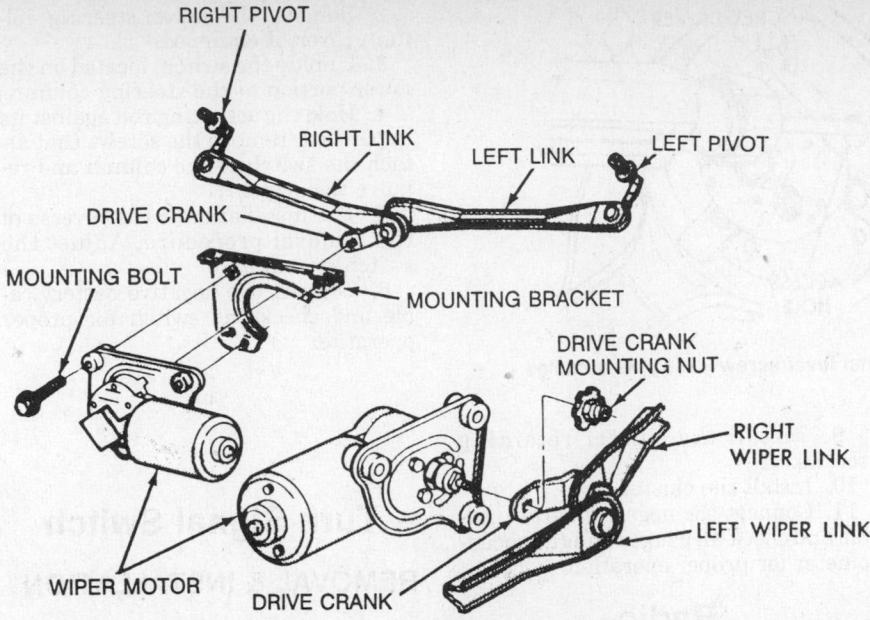

Wiper motor and linkage assembly

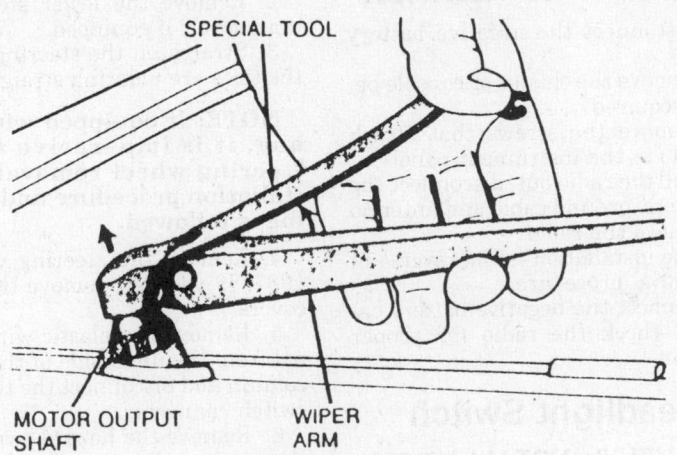

Removing the liftgate wiper arm

Rear

1. Disconnect the negative battery cable.

2. Remove the liftgate wiper using special tool C–3982.

NOTE: Prying the arm off of the shaft with a prying device could damage the arm permanently and possibly cause it to pop off of the shaft while in operation causing poor rear vision for the driver and a dangerous situation for the driver behind. Do not bend or push the spring clip at the base of the arm to release the arm; it is self-releasing. Use only the indicated tool.

3. Open the liftgate. Remove the plastic wiper motor cover.

4. Remove the pivot shaft nut, ring and seal assembly from the pivot shaft.

5. Disconnect the motor connector, remove the mounting screws and remove the wiper motor from the vehicle.
To install:

6. Install the motor to the liftgate and connect the connector.

7. Install the plastic cover.

8. Install the sealing washer about ½ in. down on the pivot shaft.

9. Install the seal, washer and nut on the pivot shaft and tighten the nut.

10. Install the wiper arm so that it is parallel to the lower edge of the liftgate glass in the park position.

11. Connect the negative battery cable and check the motor for proper operation.

Windshield Wiper Switch

REMOVAL & INSTALLATION

1987–89 Vehicles

1. Disconnect the negative battery cable.

2. Disconnect the electrical connectors to the wiper switch and the turn signal switch.

3. Remove the column covers, horn pad and felt switch hider disc.

4. Turn the steering wheel so the access hole in the hub area of the steering wheel is in the 9 o'clock position and loosen the turn signal pivot screw.

5. Disengage the dimmer switch pushrod from the wiper switch and remove the switch from the column.
To install:

6. Position the switch and engage the dimmer switch pushrod.

7. Secure the switch with the turn signal pivot screw.

8. Install the hider, column covers and horn pad.

9. Connect the connectors underneath the dash.

10. Connect the negative battery cable and check the switch for proper operation.

1990 Vehicles

1. Disconnect the negative battery cable.

2. Remove the lower steering column cover.

3. Straighten the steering wheel so the tires are pointing straight ahead.

NOTE: Since the vehicle is equipped with an air bag, it is imperative that the steering wheel removal and installation procedure under Steering is followed.

4. Remove the steering wheel.

5. Remove the plastic wiring channel from the underside of the steering column.

6. Disconnect the wiper switch connector, intermittent wipe module connector and cruise control connector, if equipped.

7. Remove the side lock housing cover.

8. Remove the slotted hex-head screw that attaches the wiper switch to the turn signal switch and remove the switch.

9. Remove the control knob from the end of the stalk. Pull the round nylon hider up the control stalk and remove the revealed screws that attach the control stalk sleeve to the wiper switch.

10. Rotate the control stalk shaft to

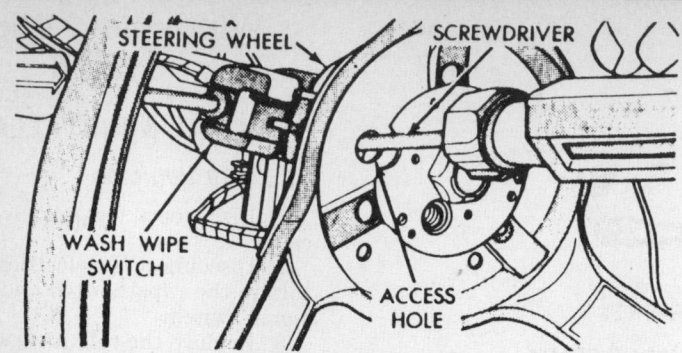

Access hole that reveals the turn signal lever screw—1987–89 vehicles

the full clockwise position and remove the shaft from the wiper switch by pulling it straight out.

To install:

11. Install the control shaft to the wiper switch, install the screws, the hider and the control knob.

12. Run the wiring through the opening and down the steering column, position the switch and install the hex-head screw. Make sure the dimmer switch rod is properly engaged.

13. Install the side lock housing cover.

14. Connect the wires and install the wiring channel and the column covers.

15. Install the steering wheel and torque the nut to 45 ft. lbs. (61 Nm).

16. Install the horn pad.

17. Connect the negative battery cable and check the wiper and washer, cruise control, turn signal switch and dimmer switch for proper operation.

18. Install the lower column cover.

Instrument Cluster

REMOVAL & INSTALLATION

1. Disconnect the negative battery cable.

2. Remove the instrument cluster bezel. Cluster removal is not necessary if just removing gauges.

3. When only removing gauges or the speedometer, remove the trip odometer reset knob, if necessary, remove the mask and lens assembly and remove the desired gauge from the cluster.

4. Remove the screws attaching the cluster to the instrument panel.

5. Pull the cluster out and disconnect the speedometer cable, if equipped, and all wiring harnesses.

6. Remove the cluster from the vehicle.

To install:

7. Position the cluster and connect the speedometer cable, if equipped.

8. Connect all wiring in their proper positions.

9. Install the cluster retaining screws.

10. Install the cluster bezel.

11. Connect the negative battery cable and check all gauges and the speedometer for proper operation.

Radio

REMOVAL & INSTALLATION

1. Disconnect the negative battery cable.

2. Remove the cluster or console bezel, as required.

3. Remove the screws that attach the radio to the instrument panel.

4. Pull the radio out, disconnect the connectors, ground cable and antenna and remove the radio.

5. The installation is the reverse of the removal procedure.

6. Connect the negative battery cable and check the radio for proper operation.

Headlight Switch

REMOVAL & INSTALLATION

1. Disconnect the negative battery cable.

2. Remove the left side trim bezel.

3. Remove the switch mounting screws, pull the switch assembly out and unplug the connector.

4. Remove the switch knob and shaft by depressing the release button on the switch.

5. Disengage the escutcheon from the mounting plate, unscrew the bracket retainer nut and remove the switch.

6. The installation is the reverse of the removal procedure.

7. Connect the negative battery cable and check the switch for proper operation.

Dimmer Switch

REMOVAL & INSTALLATION

1. Disconnect the negative battery cable.

2. Remove the lower steering column cover, if equipped.

3. Unplug the switch, located on the lower portion of the steering column.

4. Hold the actuating rod against its upper seat, remove the screws that attach the switch to the column and remove the switch.

5. The installation is the reverse of the removal procedure. Adjust the switch as required.

6. Connect the negative battery cable and check the switch for proper operation.

Turn Signal Switch

REMOVAL & INSTALLATION

1. Disconnect the negative battery cable.

2. Remove the lower steering column cover, if equipped.

3. Straighten the steering wheel so the tires are pointing straight ahead.

NOTE: If equipped with an air bag, it is imperative that the steering wheel removal and installation procedure under Steering is followed.

4. Remove the steering wheel. On 1987–89 vehicles, remove the column covers.

5. Remove the plastic wiring channel from the underside of the steering column and disconnect the turn signal switch connector.

6. Remove the hazard switch knob, if necessary. Remove the slotted hex-head screw that attaches the wiper switch to the turn signal switch.

7. Remove the 3 screws and pull the turn signal switch out of the column.

To install:

8. Run the wiring through the opening and down the steering column, position the switch and install the hex-head screw. Make sure the dimmer switch rod is properly engaged.

9. Install the 3 screws and the hazard switch knob.

10. Connect the wires and install the wiring channel.

11. Install the steering wheel and torque the nut to 45 ft. lbs. (61 Nm). Install the column covers, if they were removed.

12. Install the horn pad.

13. Connect the negative battery cable and check the turn signal switch and dimmer switch for proper operation.

14. Install the lower column cover.

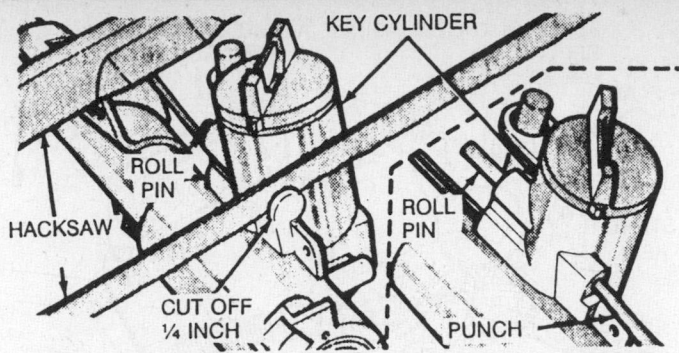

Cutting the key cylinder retainer pin boss—1987–89 vehicles

Ignition Lock

REMOVAL & INSTALLATION

1987–89 Vehicles

1. Disconnect the negative battery cable.
2. Place the key cylinder in the **LOCK** position and remove the key.
3. Remove the steering wheel, the column covers and the turn signal switch.
4. Using a hacksaw blade, cut the upper ¼ in. from the key cylinder retainer pin boss.
5. Using the proper size punch, drive the roll pin from the housing and remove the key cylinder.
To install:
6. Insert the cylinder into the housing, make sure it engages the lug on the ignition switch driver and install the roll pin.
7. Install the turn signal switch, column covers and the steering wheel.
8. Connect the negative battery cable and check the lock cylinder for proper operation in all positions.

1990 Vehicles

1. Disconnect the negative battery cable.
2. Straighten the steering wheel so the tires are pointing straight ahead.

NOTE: Since the vehicle is equipped with an air bag, it is imperative that the steering wheel removal and installation procedure under Steering is followed.

3. Remove the steering wheel.
4. Remove the hazard switch knob. Remove the slotted hex-head screw that attaches the wiper switch to the turn signal switch.
5. Remove the 3 screws and pull the turn signal switch out of the column as far as it will go. Unplug it below if necessary.
6. Remove the ignition switch key lamp.

7. Place the key in the **LOCK** position and remove the key.
8. Insert 2 suitable small diameter tools into both release holes and push inward to release the spring loaded lock retainers while simultaneously pulling the key lock cylinder out of its bore.
To install:
9. Install the key cylinder.
10. Install the ignition switch key lamp.
11. Install the turn signal switch and hazard switch knob. Connect the wires if they were disconnected.
12. Install the steering wheel and torque the nut to 45 ft. lbs. (61 Nm).
13. Install the horn pad.
14. Connect the negative battery cable and check the lock cylinder for proper operation in all positions.

Ignition Switch

REMOVAL & INSTALLATION

1. Disconnect the negative battery cable.
2. Remove the lower steering column cover, if equipped.
3. If necessary, remove the steering column retaining nuts and allow the steering wheel to rest on the driver's seat.
4. Remove the 2 screws that attach the ignition switch to the lower portion of the column.
5. Rotate the switch 90 degrees and pull up to disengage it from the ignition switch rod.
To install:
6. Engage the switch with the rod, rotate the switch 90 degrees and push down until fully engaged.
7. Install the mounting screws finger-tight.
8. Place the key in the **LOCK** position and remove the key. Adjust the switch by pushing up gently on the switch to take up all slack in the rod.
9. Tighten the mounting screws, connect the negative battery cable and check the switch for proper operation in all positions.

Stoplight Switch

REMOVAL & INSTALLATION

1. Disconnect the negative battery cable.
2. Unplug the stoplight switch connectors near the brake pedal.
3. Remove the switch and bracket assembly from the brake pedal bracket.
4. Remove the switch from its bracket.
To install:
5. Install the switch and bracket assembly to the brake pedal bracket and push the switch forward as far as it will go; the brake pedal should move forward slightly.
6. Pull back on the brake pedal, bringing the striker toward the switch, until the pedal will not go back any farther.
7. This will cause the switch to

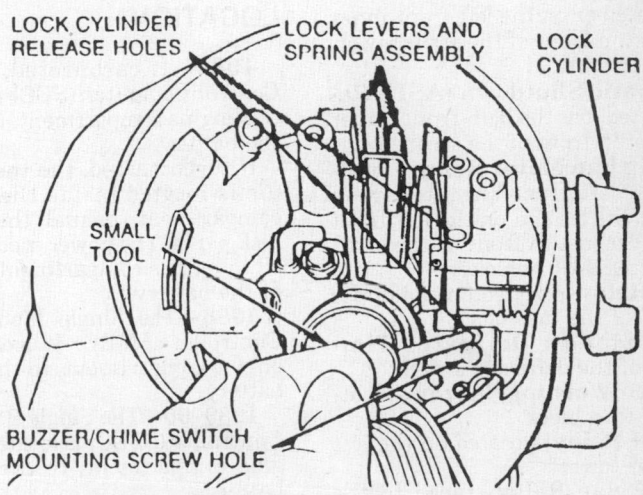

Removing the key lock cylinder—1990 vehicles

ratchet backward into position and automatic adjustment is complete.

8. Connect the negative battery cable and check the switch for proper operation. Also, make sure the speed control system functions properly, if equipped.

Neutral Safety Switch

REMOVAL & INSTALLATION

1. Disconnect the negative battery cable.

2. Locate the neutral safety switch at the left rear corner of the automatic transaxle, facing the front of the vehicle. Unplug the switch connector.

3. Remove the switch from the transaxle.

4. The installation is the reverse of the removal procedure. Torque the switch to 25 ft. lbs. (34 Nm).

5. Connect the negative battery cable and make sure the vehicle does not start in any gear except **P** and **N**. Also make sure the reverse lights come ON when the shifter is placed in R.

Fuses, Circuit Breaker, Relays and Flashers

LOCATION

Fuses, Circuit Breaker and Flashers

The fuse block, which contains the fuses, circuit breaker and flashers, is located on the left side kick panel, below the left side of the instrument panel.

Relays

A/C Clutch Cutout Relay—located on the right side of the carburetor, if carbureted or on the left front inner fender just in front of the strut tower, if fuel injected.

Automatic Shutdown (ASD) Relay—located on the left front inner fender just in front of the strut tower.

Cooling Fan Motor Relay—located on the left front strut tower on 1987–88 vehicles and on the left front inner fender just in front of the strut tower on 1989–90 vehicles.

Horn Relay—located on the upper right side of the fuse block.

Rear Window Defroster Timer—part of the defroster switch.

Seatbelt Warning Buzzer—located on the fuse block.

Starter Relay—located on the left front strut tower.

Time Delay Relay—taped to the wiring harness near the fuse block.

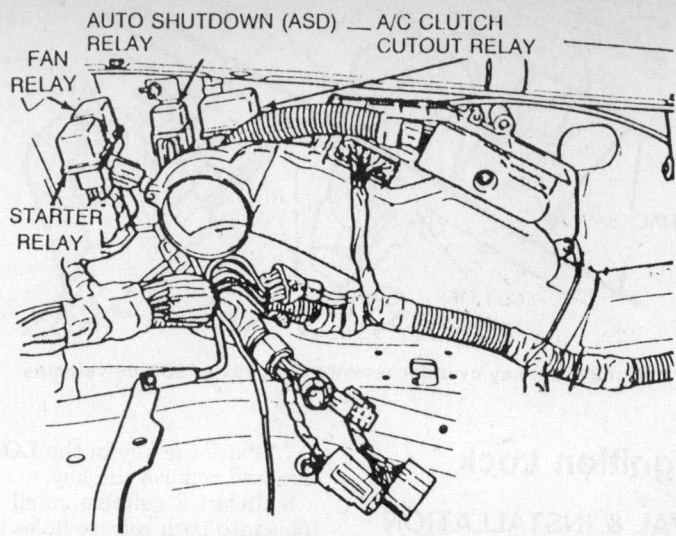

Underhood relay identification–1988 vehicles

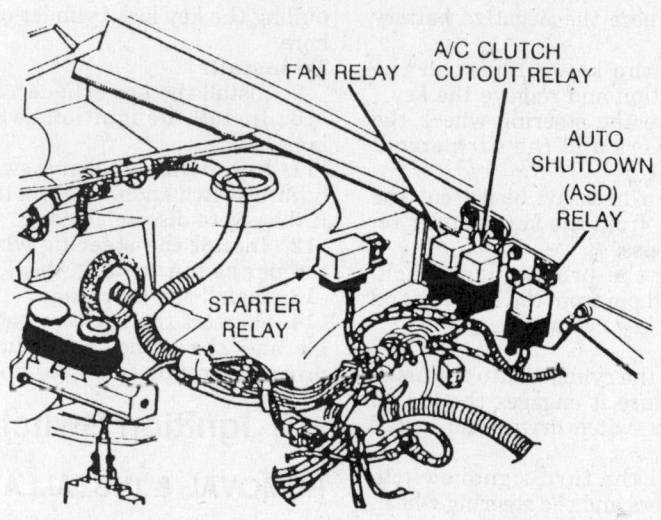

Underhood relay identification–1989–90 vehicles

Computers

LOCATION

1987—If carbureted, the Spark Control Computer (SCC) is located in the engine compartment, to the left of the battery.

If turbocharged, the the logic module is located inside the passenger compartment, behind the right side kick panel. The power module is located in engine compartment, to the left of the battery.

1988—The Single Module Engine Controller (SMEC) is located in the engine compartment, to the left of the battery.

1989–90—The Single Board Engine Controller (SBEC) is located in the engine compartment, to the left of the battery.

The Airbag System Diagnostic Module (ASDM), if equipped, is located under the instrument panel, to the right of the front of the console.

Cruise Control

ADJUSTMENT

1. The clearance between the throttle stud and cable clevis should be $\frac{1}{16}$ in.

2. To adjust the cable, remove the retaining clip or loosen the retaining clamp nut at the throttle bracket.

3. Pull all slack out of the cable using a suitable $\frac{1}{16}$ in. diameter tool to account for proper clearance. Make sure the curb idle position of the throttle blade is not affected.

4. Reinstall the retaining clip or nut.

ENGINE COOLING

Radiator

REMOVAL & INSTALLATION

1. Disconnect the negative battery cable.
2. Drain the coolant.
3. Remove the upper hose and coolant reserve tank hose from the radiator.
4. Remove the electric cooling fan.
5. Raise the vehicle and support safely. Remove the lower hose from the radiator.
6. Disconnect the automatic transaxle cooler hoses, if equipped, and plug them. Lower the vehicle.
7. Remove the mounting brackets and carefully lift the radiator out of the engine compartment.
To install:
8. Lower the radiator into position.
9. Install the mounting brackets.
10. Raise the vehicle and support safely. Connect the automatic transaxle cooler lines, if equipped.
11. Connect the lower hose. Lower the vehicle.
12. Install the electric cooling fan.
13. Connect the upper hose and coolant reserve tank hose.
14. Fill the system with coolant and bleed the system.
15. Connect the negative battery cable, run the vehicle until the thermostat opens, fill the radiator completely and check the automatic transaxle fluid level.
16. Once the vehicle has cooled, recheck the coolant level.

Electric Cooling Fan

——— CAUTION ———
Make sure the key is in the OFF position when working the electric cooling fan. If not, the fan could turn ON at any time, causing serious personal injury.

TESTING

1. Unplug the fan connector.
2. Using a jumper wire, connect the female terminal of the fan connector to the negative battery terminal.
3. The fan should come ON when the male terminal is connected to the positive battery terminal.
4. If not, the fan is defective and should be replaced.

REMOVAL & INSTALLATION

1. Disconnect the negative battery cable.
2. Unplug the connector.
3. Remove the mounting screws.
4. Remove the fan assembly from the vehicle.
5. The installation is the reverse of the removal procedure.

Heater Core

REMOVAL & INSTALLATION

Without Air Conditioning

1. Disconnect the negative battery cable.
2. Drain the coolant. Clamp off the heater hoses near the heater core and remove the hoses from the core tubes. Plug the hose ends and the core tubes to prevent spillage of coolant.
3. Disconnect the blower motor connector.
4. Remove the ash tray.
5. Depress the tab on the temperature control cable and pull the cable out of its housing on the heater assembly.
6. Remove the glove box assembly and unplug the resistor block.
7. Remove the 2 nuts fastening the heater assembly to the firewall and remove the screw attaching the heater support brace to the instrument panel.
8. Remove the heater support bracket nut. Disconnect the strap from the plenum stud and lower the assembly from under the instrument panel.
9. Depress the tab on the flag and pull the mode door control cable out of its housing on the heater assembly.
10. Move the assembly toward the right side of the vehicle and remove.
11. With the assembly on a workbench, remove the top cover and slide the heater out of its cavity in the assembly.
To install:
12. Clean the inside of the assembly and assemble.
13. Connect the mode control cable to the mode door crank and position the heater assembly under the instrument panel. Slide forward so that the mounting studs and heater core tubes project through their holes in the firewall. Install the support bracket and brace to hold the assembly in place.
14. From the engine compartment, install the 2 nuts on the firewall and connect the heater hoses.
15. Connect the temperature control cable, blower motor wiring and resistor block connector.
16. Install the defroster duct.

17. Install the ash tray and glove box.
18. Fill the cooling system.
19. Connect the negative battery cable and check the heater for proper operation and leaks.

With Air Conditioning

1. Disconnect the negative battery cable. Properly discharge the air conditioning system. Drain the cooling system.
2. Clamp off the heater hoses near the heater core and remove the hoses from the core tubes. Plug the hose ends and the core tubes to prevent spillage of coolant.
3. Disconnect the H-valve connection at the valve and remove the H-valve. Remove the condensation tube. Disconnect the vacuum lines at the brake booster and water valve.
4. Disconnect the temperature door cable from evaporator/heater assembly.
5. Remove the glove box assembly.
6. On 1990–90 vehicles, remove the Air Bag Diagnostic Module (ABDM) from its mount and position to the side. Remove the mounting bracket.
7. Disconnect the blower motor feed wire and vacuum harness.
8. Remove the central air duct cover from the central air distributor duct.
9. Remove the screws securing the central air conditioning air distributor duct. Remove the duct from under the dash panel.
10. From the engine compartment, remove the nuts that attach the unit to the firewall.
11. Remove the panel support bracket.
12. Remove the right side cowl lower panel and the top cover of the instrument panel.
13. Remove the instrument panel pivot bracket screw from the right side.
14. Remove the screws securing the lower instrument panel and steering column, if required.
15. Pull the carpet rearward as far as possible.
16. Remove the nut from the air conditioning to plenum mounting brace and blower motor ground cable. Support the unit and remove the brace from its stud.
17. Lift the unit and pull it rearward as far as possible to clear the dash panel and liner. Pull rearward on the lower instrument panel to gain enough clearance to remove the unit.
18. Slowly lower the unit to floor and slide out from the under dash panel.
19. With the unit on a workbench, remove the nut from the mode door actuator arm on the top cover. Remove the retaining clips from the front edge of the cover.

20. Remove the mode door actuator to cover screws and remove the actuator.

21. Remove the cover to heater evaporator assembly screws and remove the cover. Lift the mode door out of the unit.

22. Remove the heater core tube retaining bracket and screw. Lift the heater core out of the unit.

To install:

23. Remove the temperature control door from the housing and clean the unit out with solvent. Lubricate the lower pivot rod and its well and install. Wrap the heater core with foam tape and place it in position. Secure it with its screw.

24. Assemble the package, making sure all vacuum tubing is properly routed.

25. Feed the vacuum lines through the hole in the firewall and install the assembly to the vehicle. Connect the vacuum harness and defroster duct adaptor. Install the nuts to the firewall and connect the hanger strap inside the passenger compartment.

26. Fold the carpeting back into position. Connect the blower motor wiring and install the ABDM.

27. Install the center distribution and defroster adaptor ducts.

28. Secure the lower instrument panel and steering column, as required.

29. Install the instrument panel pivot bracket screw at the right side.

30. Install the right side cowl lower panel and the top cover of the instrument panel. Install the panel support bracket.

31. Connect the vacuum lines at the brake booster and water valve. Using new gaskets, install the H-valve and condensation tube.

32. Connect the heater hoses.

33. Using the proper equipment, evacuate and recharge the air conditioning system.

34. Fill the cooling system.

35. Connect the negative battery cable and check the entire climate control system for proper operation and leakage.

Water Pump

REMOVAL & INSTALLATION

1. Disconnect the negative battery cable.

2. Drain the cooling system.

3. If equipped with air conditioning, remove the compressor from the bracket and position it to the side.

4. Remove the alternator and bracket. Remove the pulley from the water pump.

5. Disconnect the lower radiator

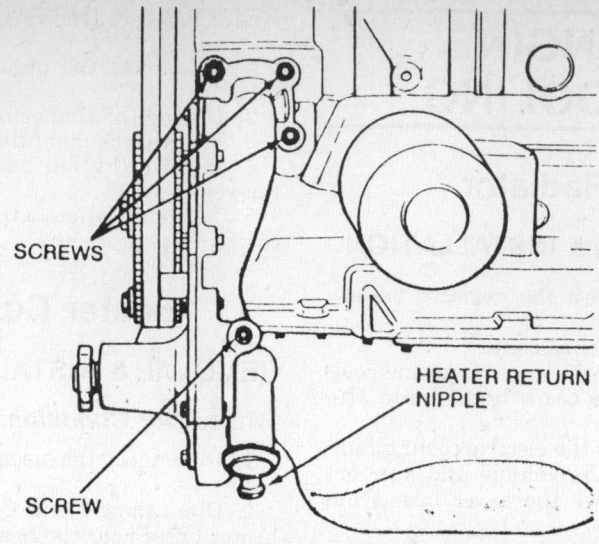

Water pump assembly

hose and heater hose from the water pump.

6. Remove the water pump housing attaching screws and remove the assembly from the vehicle. Discard the O-ring.

7. Remove the water pump from the housing.

To install:

8. Using a new gasket or silicone sealer, install the water pump to the housing.

9. Install a new O-ring to the housing and install to the engine. Torque the bolts to 21 ft. lbs. (30 Nm).

10. Install the water pump pulley and torque the bolts to 21 ft. lbs. (30 Nm). Connect the radiator hose and heater hose to the water pump.

11. Install all items removed to gain access to the water pump, then adjust the belts.

12. Remove the vacuum switch or hex-head plug on the top of the thermostat housing. Fill the radiator with coolant until the coolant comes out the plug hole. Install the plug and continue to fill the radiator.

13. Connect the negative battery cable, run the vehicle until the thermostat opens, fill the radiator completely and check for leaks.

14. Once the vehicle has cooled, recheck the coolant level.

Thermostat

REMOVAL & INSTALLATION

1. Disconnect the negative battery cable. Drain the coolant down to thermostat level or below.

2. Remove the thermostat housing.

3. Remove the thermostat and discard the gasket.

4. Clean the housing mating surfaces and use a new gasket.

5. The installation is the reverse of the removal procedure.

6. Remove the vacuum switch or hex-head plug on the thermostat housing. Fill the radiator with coolant until the coolant comes out the plug hole. Install the plug or valve and continue to fill the radiator.

7. Connect the negative battery cable, run the vehicle until the thermostat opens, fill the radiator completely and check for leaks.

8. Once the vehicle has cooled, recheck the coolant level.

COOLING SYSTEM BLEEDING

To bleed air from the engine, remove the vacuum switch or plug on the top of the thermostat housing. Fill the radiator with coolant until the coolant comes out the hole. Install the switch or plug and continue to fill the radiator.

FUEL SYSTEM

Fuel System Service Precautions

Safety is the most important factor when performing not only fuel system maintenance but any type of maintenance. Failure to conduct maintenance and repairs in a safe manner may result in serious personal injury or death. Maintenance and testing of the vehicle's fuel system components can be accomplished safely and effectively by adhering to the following rules and guidelines.

● To avoid the possibility of fire and personal injury, always disconnect the negative battery cable unless the repair or test procedure requires that battery voltage be applied.

● Always relieve the fuel system pressure prior to disconnecting any fuel system component (injector, fuel rail, pressure regulator, etc.), fitting or fuel line connection. Exercise extreme caution whenever relieving fuel system pressure to avoid exposing skin, face and eyes to fuel spray. Please be advised that fuel under pressure may penetrate the skin or any part of the body that it contacts.

● Always place a shop towel or cloth around the fitting or connection prior to loosening to absorb any excess fuel due to spillage. Ensure that all fuel spillage (should it occur) is quickly removed from engine surfaces. Ensure that all fuel soaked cloths or towels are deposited into a suitable waste container.

● Always keep a dry chemical (Class B) fire extinguisher near the work area.

● Do not allow fuel spray or fuel vapors to come into contact with a spark or open flame.

● Always use a backup wrench when loosening and tightening fuel line connection fittings. This will prevent unnecessary stress and torsion to fuel line piping. Always follow the proper torque specifications.

● Always replace worn fuel fitting O-rings with new. Do not substitute fuel hose or equivalent where fuel pipe is installed.

RELIEVING FUEL SYSTEM PRESSURE

1987–88 Vehicles

1. Disconnect the negative battery cable.
2. Loosen the fuel filler cap to release fuel tank pressure.
3. Remove the wiring harness connector from the (any) injector.
4. Using a jumper wire, ground either injector terminal.
5. Being careful not to allow contact between the jumper leads, connect a second jumper wire to the other terminal and touch the other end to the positive battery post for no longer that 10 seconds. This will relieve fuel pressure.
6. Remove the jumper wires and continue with fuel system service.

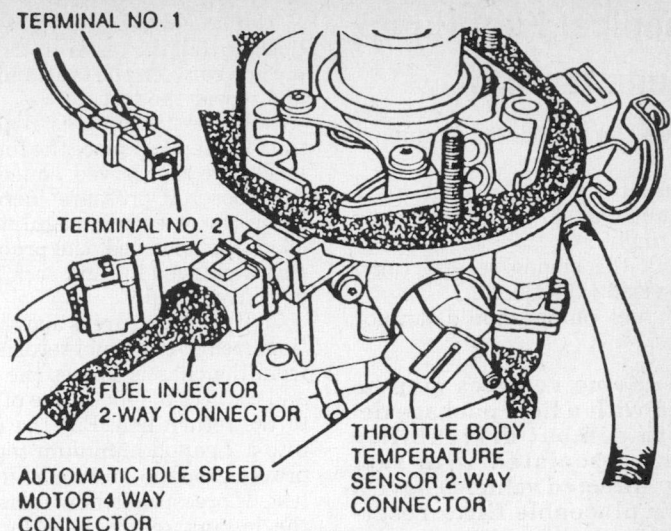

Throttle body fuel injector harness connector

1989–90 Vehicles

1. Loosen the fuel filler cap to release fuel tank pressure.
2. Locate and disconnect the fuel injector harness connector on the throttle body.
3. Connect a jumper wire from terminal No. 1 of the connector to ground.
4. Being careful not to allow contact between the jumper leads, connect a jumper wire to terminal No. 2 of the connector and touch the other end of the jumper to the positive battery post for no longer than 5 seconds. This will relieve fuel pressure.
5. Remove the jumper wires and continue with fuel system service.

Fuel Filter

REMOVAL & INSTALLATION

Carbureted Engine

1. Disconnect the negative battery cable.
2. Remove the fuel filter and any hoses that are included with the new filter kit.

NOTE: Some vehicles may be equipped with a field package designed to combat driveability problems associated with fuel foaming. Affected vehicles have a special replaceable filter/reservoir mounted on a plate on the carburetor. When the kit is installed, the conventional filter is discarded. Do not install a conventional filter or conventional clamps or hoses in place of the special replacement parts; they are not compatible with the electronic fuel pump installed with the kit.

3. Install the new filter, hoses and clamps.
4. Connect the negative battery cable, start the engine and check for leaks.

Fuel Injected Engine

— **CAUTION** —

Do not use conventional fuel filters, hoses or clamps when servicing this fuel system. They are not compatible with the injection system and could fail, causing personal injury or damage to the vehicle. Use only hoses and clamps specifically designed for fuel injection.

1. Disconnect the negative battery cable.
2. Relieve the fuel pressure.
3. The filter is located under the rear of the vehicle, in front of the fuel tank. Raise the vehicle and support safely. Remove the filter retaining screw and remove the filter assembly from the mounting plate.
4. Loosen the outlet hose clamp on the filter and inlet hose clamp on the rear fuel tube.
5. Wrap a shop towel around the hoses to absorb fuel. Remove the hoses from the filter and fuel tube and discard the clamps and the filter.

To install:

6. Install the inlet hose on the fuel tube and tighten the new clamp to 10 inch lbs.
7. Install the outlet hose on the filter outlet fitting and tighten the new clamp to 10 inch lbs.
8. Position the filter assembly on the mounting plate and tighten the mounting screw to 75 inch lbs. (8 Nm).
9. Connect the negative battery cable, start the engine and check for leaks.

Mechanical Fuel Pump

PRESSURE TESTING

1. Raise the vehicle and support safely.
2. Connect a pressure gauge (0–15 psi minimum range) to the fuel pump outlet fitting.
3. Crank the engine several times while observing the gauge.
4. The fuel pump should develop 4.5–6.0 psi.

NOTE: Some vehicles may be equipped with a field package designed to combat driveability problems associated with fuel foaming. Affected vehicles have a special replaceable filter/reservoir mounted on a plate on the carburetor, where the pressure testing equipment may be connected. If equipped with the field package, fuel pressure should be 13–15 psi.

REMOVAL & INSTALLATION

1. Disconnect the negative battery cable.
2. Raise the vehicle and support safely, if necessary.
3. Disconnect the fuel lines from the pump and plug them.
4. Remove the fuel pump retaining bolts and remove the pump from the engine.
5. Clean and dry the mounting surfaces and bolt holes and install a new gasket.
6. The installation is the reverse of the removal procedure.
7. Connect the negative battery cable, start the engine and check for leaks.

Electric Fuel Pump

PRESSURE TESTING

1. Disconnect the negative battery cable. Relieve the fuel pressure.
2. Properly connect the fuel system pressure tester:
   a. 2.2L EFI engine—special tool C-4799A or equivalent, is installed between the fuel supply hose and the engine fuel line assembly.
   b. 2.2L turbocharged engine—special tool C-4749 or equivalent, is installed to the fuel rail service valve.
3. With the key in the **RUN** position, put the DRB-I or II in the activate auto shutdown relay mode; this will activate the fuel pump and pressurize the system.
4. If the pressure is within specifications, reinstall the fuel hose.

5. If fuel pressure is below specifications, install the tester in the fuel supply line between the tank and the filter and repeat the test.
6. If the pressure is 5 psi higher than in Step 5, replace the fuel filter. If no change is observed, squeeze the return hose. If pressure increases, replace the pressure regulator. If no change is observed, the problem is either a plugged in-tank sock filter or a defective pump.
7. If fuel pressure is above specifications, remove the fuel return line hose from the chassis line at the fuel tank and connect a 3 foot piece of fuel hose to the return line. Put the other end into a 2 gallon minimum capacity approved gasoline container. Repeat the test. If pressure is now correct, check the in-tank return hose for kinking. Replace the fuel pump assembly if the in-tank reservoir check valve or aspirator jet is obstructed.
8. If pressure is still above specifications, remove the fuel return hose from the throttle body. Connect a substitute hose to the throttle body return nipple and place the other end of the hose in a clean container. Repeat the test. If pressure is now correct, check for a restricted fuel return line. If no change is observed, replace the fuel pressure regulator.

REMOVAL & INSTALLATION

1. Disconnect the negative battery cable.
2. Relieve the fuel pressure.
3. Raise the vehicle and support safely.
4. Using the proper equipment, drain the fuel tank.
5. Remove the screws that hold the filler neck to the quarter panel.
6. Disconnect the wiring and hoses from the tank.
7. Place a transmission jack or equivalent, under the center of the tank and apply slight pressure. Remove the tank straps.

8. Lower the tank and remove the filler tube from the tank.
9. Disconnect the vapor separator rollover valve hose and remove the fuel tank from the vehicle.
10. Using a hammer and a brass drift, tap the lock ring counterclockwise to release the pump.
11. Remove the pump from the tank with the O-ring. Discard the O-ring, pump inlet filter and inlet seal. Disassemble as required.

To install:

12. Install a new inlet seal and filter on the end of the pump.
13. Install a new O-ring to the pump.
14. Connect the reservoir hose to the pump assembly at the suction end of the pump. Press the female fitting onto the pump assembly male end until the ears snap in place.
15. Install the pump assembly into the tank.
16. Install the lock ring with a hammer and brass punch turning the ring clockwise.
17. Install the fuel tank.
18. Connect the negative battery cable, start the engine and check for leaks.

Carburetor

REMOVAL & INSTALLATION

1. Disconnect the negative battery cable.
2. Remove the air cleaner assembly.
3. Remove and install the fuel tank cap to relieve any pressure in the tank.
4. Matchmark all vacuum hoses and electrical connectors and remove them from the carburetor.
5. Disconnect the throttle, cruise control and kickdown cables and linkages, as required.
6. Disconnect and plug the fuel inlet line.
7. Remove the mounting nuts and remove the carburetor from the intake manifold.

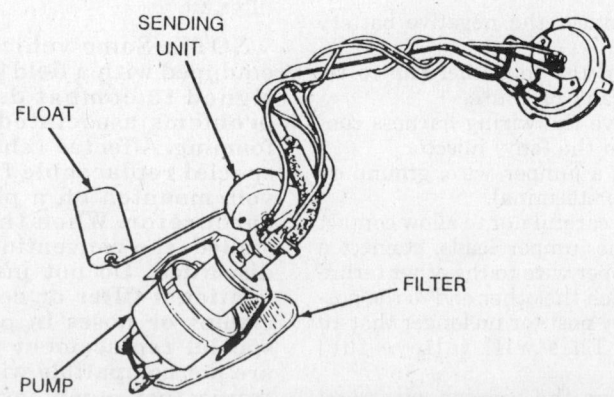

Electronic fuel pump assembly—non-turbocharged engine

To install:

8. Clean the mounting surface of the manifold and install a new base gasket.

9. Install the mounting nuts and tighten them alternately to compress the base gasket evenly.

10. Connect the fuel line.

11. Connect the throttle, cruise control and kickdown cables and linkages.

12. Install all vacuum hoses and electrical connectors in their proper locations.

13. Install the air cleaner.

14. Connect the negative battery cable, start the engine and perform all necessary adjustments.

IDLE SPEED ADJUSTMENT

1. Before checking or adjusting the idle speed, check ignition timing and adjust, if necessary.

2. Disconnect and plug the vacuum connector at the coolant vacuum switch cold closed valve.

3. Unplug the connector at the radiator fan and install a jumper wire so the fan will run continuously.

4. Remove the PCV valve and allow it to draw underhood air.

5. Connect a tachometer to engine.

6. Ground the carburetor switch with a jumper wire.

7. Disconnect the oxygen system test connector located on left fender shield, if equipped.

8. Start and run the engine until normal operating temperature is reached.

9. If tachometer indicates rpm is not at specifications, turn the idle speed screw until correct idle speed is obtained. The screw is located on top of the solenoid mounted on the back of the carburetor.

10. Reconnect the PCV valve, oxygen connector and vacuum connector.

11. Remove jumper wire and reconnect the radiator fan.

12. After Steps 9 and 10 are completed, the idle speed may change slightly. This is normal and engine speed should not be readjusted.

13. Make sure the solenoid kicker moves the throttle blade adequately so the idle does not change when the air conditioning is working.

IDLE MIXTURE ADJUSTMENT

1. Disconnect and plug the EGR hose. Disconnect the oxygen sensor, if equipped.

2. Disconnect and plug the $3/16$ in. hose at the canister.

3. Remove the PCV hose from the valve cover and allow it to draw underhood air.

4. Ground the carburetor switch with a jumper wire, if equipped.

5. Disconnect the vacuum hose from the computer, if equipped, and connect an auxiliary vacuum supply of 16 in. Hg.

6. Remove the concealment plug. Disconnect the vacuum supply hose to the tee and install a propane supply hose in its place.

7. Make sure all accessories are **OFF**. Install a tachometer and start the engine. Allow the engine to run for 2 minutes to stabilize.

8. Open the main propane valve. Slowly open the propane metering valve until the maximum engine rpm is reached. When too much propane is added, the engine will begin to stumble; at this point back off until the engine stabilizes.

9. Adjust the idle rpm to obtain the specified propane rpm. Fine tune the metering valve to obtain the highest rpm again. If there has been a change to the maximum rpm, readjust the idle screw to the specified propane rpm.

10. Turn the main propane valve off and allow the engine to run for 1 minute to stabilize.

11. Adjust the mixture screw to obtain the smoothest idle at the specified idle rpm.

12. Open the main propane valve. Fine tune the metering valve to obtain the highest rpm. If the maximum engine speed is more that 25 rpm different than the specified propane rpm, repeat the procedure.

13. Turn the propane valves off and remove the propane canister. Reinstall the vacuum supply hose to the tee.

14. Perform the idle speed adjustment procedure.

15. Connect all wires and hoses that were previously disconnected.

SERVICE ADJUSTMENTS

For all carburetor service adjustment procedures and Specifications, please refer to "Carburetor Service" in the Unit Repair section.

Fuel Injection

IDLE SPEED ADJUSTMENT

The idle speed is controlled by the Automatic Idle Speed (AIS) motor. The AIS motor is controlled by the SMEC or SBEC, which receives data from various sensors and switches in the system and adjusts the engine idle to a predetermined speed. Idle speed specifications can be found on the Vehicle Emission Control Information (VECI) label located in the engine compartment. If the idle speed is not within specifications and there are no problems with the system, the throttle body should be replaced.

IDLE MIXTURE ADJUSTMENT

There is no idle mixture adjustment provided with any Chrysler fuel injection system.

Fuel Injector

REMOVAL & INSTALLATION

Non-Turbocharged Engine

1. Disconnect the negative battery cable.

2. Remove the air cleaner assembly.

3. Relieve the fuel pressure.

4. Remove the injector hold-down Torx® screw and the hold-down.

5. Using a small flat-tipped tool, lift the cap off of the injector.

6. Using the same tool, gently pry the injector from its pod.

7. Remove the lower O-ring from the pod.

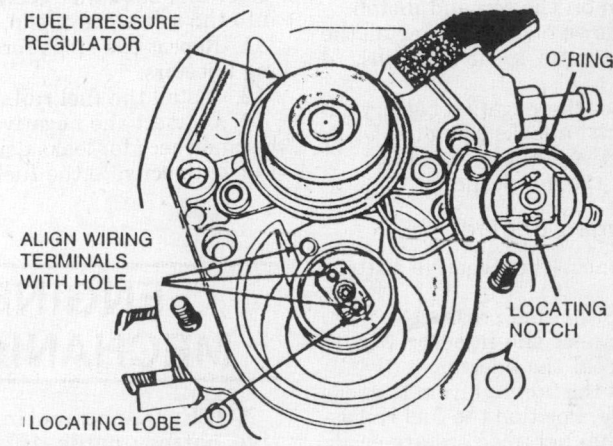

Fuel Injector installation—non-turbocharged engine

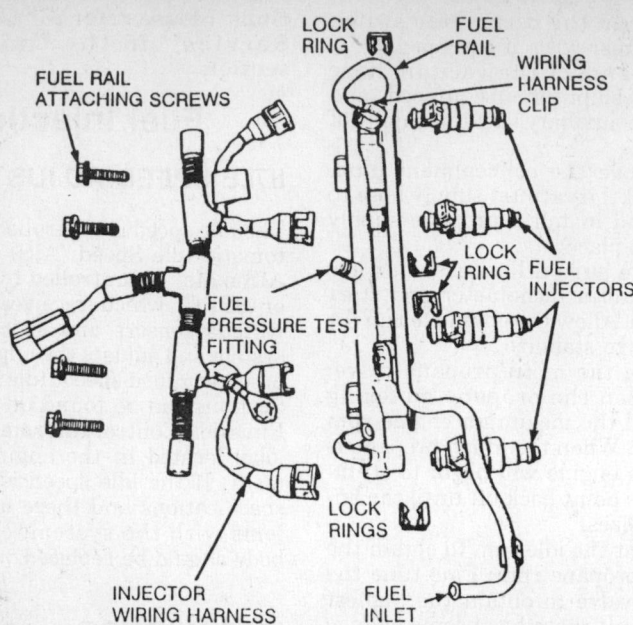

Fuel rail and injectors—turbocharged engine

tions of the on board computer systems and may require the computer to undergo a relearning process, once the negative battery cable is reconnected.

Engine Assembly

REMOVAL & INSTALLATION

1. Disconnect the negative battery cable and all engine ground straps. If equipped with fuel injection, relieve the fuel pressure.
2. Mark the hood hinge outline on the hood and remove the hood.
3. Drain the cooling system. Remove the radiator hoses, fan assembly and radiator.
4. Remove the air cleaner and air ducts.
5. Unbolt the air conditioning compressor from its mount, if equipped, and position it to the side.
6. Remove the power steering pump mounting bolts and position the pump to the side, without disconnecting any fluid lines.
7. Label and disconnect all electrical connectors and vacuum lines from the engine, alternator and carburetor or fuel injection system.
8. Disconnect the fuel lines and heater hoses.
9. Disconnect the throttle linkage.
10. Remove the alternator.
11. Raise the vehicle and support safely.
12. Disconnect the exhaust pipe from the manifold. Remove the right inner fender shield.
13. If equipped with a manual transaxle, remove the transaxle.
14. If equipped with an automatic transaxle, perform the following procedures:
    a. Remove the lower cover from the transaxle case.
    b. Remove the starter and set it aside.
    c. Matchmark the flexplate to the torque converter, for installation purposes.
    d. Remove the torque converter bolts. Separate the converter from the flexplate. Remove the lower bell housing bolts.
15. Lower the vehicle and support the transaxle, if still in the vehicle, with a floor jack or equivalent. Attach an engine lifting device to the engine.
16. Remove the remaining bell housing bolts.

NOTE: If removing the insulator-to-rail screws, first mark the position of the insulator on the side rail to insure proper alignment during reinstallation.

To install:

8. Install the new lower O-ring on the injector.
9. Align the injector terminal housing with the locating socket in the injector cap.
10. Press the injector cap so that the upper O-ring flange is flush with the lower surface of the cap.
11. Spray the inner surfaces of the injector pod with suitable carburetor parts cleaner to remove residual varnish and gasoline.
12. Lubricate the O-rings sparingly with unmedicated petroleum jelly.
13. Place the injector and cap into the injector pod and align the cap locating pin with the locating hole in the casting.
14. Press firmly on the injector cap until it is flush with the casting surface.
15. Align the hole in the hold-down with the pin on the cap and install.
16. Push down on the cap, install the screw and torque to 35 inch lbs. (4 Nm).
17. Connect the negative battery cable and check for leaks using the DRB-I or II to activate the fuel pump.
18. Install the air cleaner

Turbocharged Engine

1. Disconnect the negative battery cable.
2. Relieve the fuel pressure.
3. Disconnect the injector wiring connector from the injector.
4. Unbolt the fuel rail from the rear of the engine. Position the fuel rail assembly so the fuel injectors are easily accessible. If necessary, disconnect the

hoses from the fuel rail and remove it from the engine.
5. Remove the injector clip from the fuel rail and injector. Pull the injector straight out of the fuel rail receiver cup.
6. Check the injector O-ring for damage. If the O-ring is damaged, replace it. If the injector is being reused, install a protective cap on the injector tip to prevent damage.
7. Repeat the procedure for the remaining injectors.

To install:

8. Before installing an injector, the rubber O-ring should be lubricated with a drop of clean engine oil to aid in installation.
9. Install the top end of the injector into fuel rail receiver cup.
10. Install the injector clip by sliding the open end into the top slot of the injector and onto the receiver cup ridge into the side slots of clip.
11. Repeat the steps for the remaining injectors.
12. Install the fuel rail.
13. Connect the negative battery cable and check for leaks using the DRB-I or II to activate the fuel pump.

ENGINE MECHANICAL

NOTE: Disconnecting the negative battery cable on some vehicles may interfere with the func-

17. Remove the front engine mount nut/bolt and the left insulator through bolt or the insulator bracket to transaxle bolts.
18. Lift the engine from the vehicle and remove.
To install:
19. Lower the engine into the engine compartment. Loosely install all of the mounting bolts. With all bolts installed, torque the:
 Engine to mount bolts to 40 ft. lbs.
 Engine to transaxle bolts to 70 ft. lbs.
 Torque converter bolts, if equipped, to 40 ft. lbs.
20. Remove the lifting device.
21. Raise the vehicle and support safely.
22. If equipped with a manual transaxle, install the transaxle.
23. If equipped with an automatic transaxle, install the torque converter inspection plate and starter.
24. Connect the exhaust pipe. Lower the vehicle.
25. Install the alternator, power steering pump and air conditioning compressor, if equipped.
26. Connect the fuel lines and heater hoses.
27. Connect the throttle linkage.
28. Connect all remaining electrical connectors and vacuum lines.
29. Install the air cleaner assembly and oil filter.
30. Install the radiator, fan assembly and hoses.
31. Fill the engine with the proper amount of engine oil. Connect the negative battery cable.
32. Refill the cooling system. Start the engine, allow it to reach normal operating temperature and check for leaks.
33. Check the ignition timing and adjust, if necessary.
34. Install the hood.

Engine Mounts

REMOVAL & INSTALLATION

1. Disconnect the negative battery cable.
2. Matchmark the engine mount to its frame mounting location.
3. Raise the vehicle and support safely, if necessary. Using the proper equipment, support the weight of the engine.
4. Remove all bolts and nuts that attach the mount to the engine strut, transaxle or body and remove the mount assembly from the vehicle.
5. Remove the through bolt and separate the insulator from the yoke bracket, as required.
6. The installation is the reverse of the removal procedure. Make sure

that matchmarks are aligned before tightening bolts.

Cylinder Head

REMOVAL & INSTALLATION

1. Disconnect the negative battery cable and disconnect it from the head. Relieve the fuel pressure, if fuel injected. Drain the cooling system. Remove the dipstick bracket nut from the thermostat housing.
2. Remove the air cleaner assembly. Remove the upper radiator hose and disconnect the heater hoses.
3. Disconnect and label the vacuum lines, hoses and wiring connectors from the manifolds, carburetor or throttle body and cylinder head.
4. Disconnect the all linkages and fuel lines from the carburetor or throttle body. Unbolt the cable bracket. Remove the ground strap attaching screw from the firewall.
5. Remove the upper air conditioning compressor mounting bolts, if equipped. The cylinder head can be remove with the compressor and bracket still mounted. Remove the upper timing belt cover.
6. Raise the vehicle and support safely. Disconnect the exhaust pipe from the exhaust manifold.
7. Rotate the engine by hand, until the timing marks align. The No. 1 piston should be at TDC of its compression stroke. Lower the vehicle.
8. With the timing marks aligned, remove the camshaft sprocket. The camshaft sprocket can be suspended to keep the timing intact. Remove the spark plug wires from the spark plugs.
9. Remove the valve cover and curtain. Remove the cylinder head bolts and washers, starting from the outside and working inward.
10. Remove the cylinder head from the engine.
11. Clean the cylinder head gasket mating surfaces.
To install:
12. Using a new gasket and seals, in-

stall the cylinder head to the engine block. Using new head bolts assembled with the old washers, torque the cylinder head bolts in sequence, to 45 ft. lbs. (61 Nm). Repeating the sequence, torque the bolts to 65 ft. lbs. (88 Nm). With the bolts at 65 ft. lbs., turn each bolt an additional ¼ turn.

NOTE: Head bolt diameter is 11mm. These bolts are identified with the number 11 on the head of the bolt. The 10mm bolts used on previous vehicles will thread into an 11mm bolt hole, but will permanently damage the cylinder block. Make sure the correct bolts are being used when replacing head bolts.

13. Install the timing belt.
14. Install or connect all items that were removed or disconnected during the removal procedure.
15. Refill the cooling system. Connect the negative battery cable. Start the engine and check for leaks using the DRB-I or II to activate the fuel pump, if possible. Adjust the timing as required.

Valve Lifters

REMOVAL & INSTALLATION

1. Disconnect the negative battery cable.
2. Remove the valve cover and curtain. If removing all lifters, remove the camshaft and rocker arms.
3. If only removing 1 lifter, rotate the crankshaft until the low point of the desired cam lobe is contacting the rocker arm.
4. Using the special valve spring compressor tool 4682 or equivalent, depress the valve spring without dislodging the keepers and slide the rocker arm out.
5. Remove the valve lifter(s) from the bore(s).
6. Lubricate the lifter(s) and their bore(s) with clean engine oil.

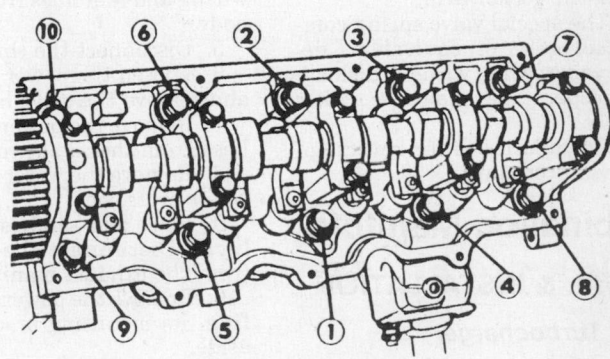

Cylinder head bolt torque sequence

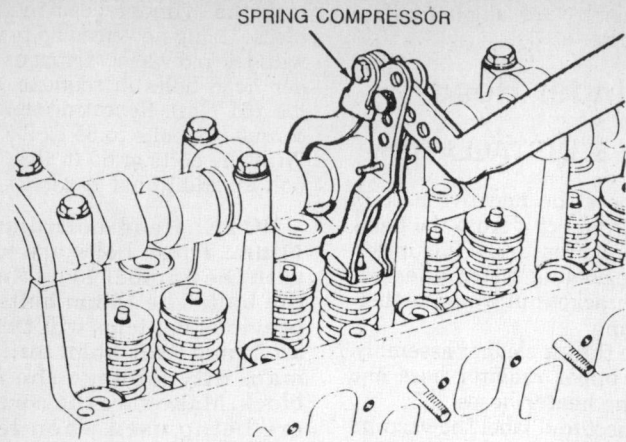

Using the special tool to compress the valve spring

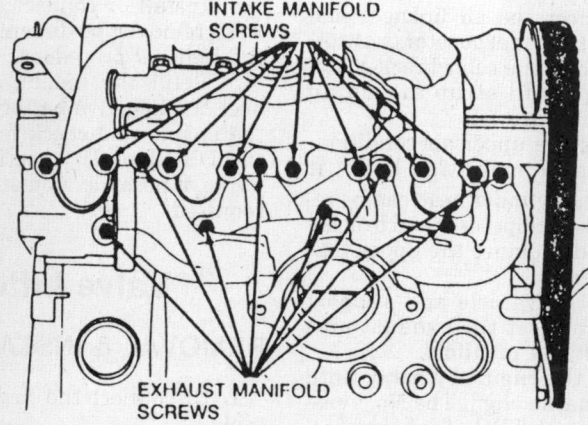

INTAKE MANIFOLD SCREWS

EXHAUST MANIFOLD SCREWS

Combination manifold attaching nuts and bolts—non-turbocharged engine

7. The installation is the reverse of the removal procedure.

Rocker Arms

REMOVAL & INSTALLATION

1. Disconnect the negative battery cable.
2. Remove the valve cover.
3. Rotate the crankshaft until the low point of the desired cam lobe is contacting the rocker arm.
4. Use the special valve spring compressor tool 4682 or equivalent, depress the valve spring without dislodging the keepers and slide the rocker arm out.
5. The installation is the reverse of the removal procedure.

Combination Manifold

REMOVAL & INSTALLATION

Without Turbocharger

NOTE: On some vehicles, some of the manifold attaching bolts are not accessible or too heavily sealed from the factory and cannot be removed on the vehicle. Head removal would be necessary in these situations.

1. Disconnect the negative battery cable.
2. Relieve the fuel system pressure, if fuel injected.
3. Drain the cooling system.
4. Remove the air cleaner and disconnect all vacuum lines, electrical wiring and fuel lines from the throttle body.
5. Disconnect the throttle linkage.
6. Loosen the power steering pump and remove the drive belt.
7. Remove the power brake vacuum hose from the intake manifold.
8. Remove the water hoses from the water crossover.
9. Raise and safely support the vehicle. Disconnect the exhaust pipe from the exhaust manifold.
10. Remove the power steering pump from its mounting bracket and set it aside.
11. Remove the intake manifold support bracket, if equipped.

12. Remove the EGR tube.
13. Remove the intake manifold bolts.
14. Lower the vehicle.
15. Remove the intake manifold.
16. Remove the exhaust manifold nuts.
17. Remove the exhaust manifold.
To install:
18. Install a new combination manifold gasket.
19. Install the manifold assembly. Starting from the middle and working outwards, install the mounting nuts and torque to 13 ft. lbs. (18 Nm). Install the heat cowl to the exhaust manifold.
20. Install the intake manifold. Starting from the middle and working outward, torque the bolts to 17 ft. lbs. (23 Nm).
21. Install the EGR tube.
22. Install the intake support bracket, if equipped.
23. Install the power steering pump.
24. Raise the vehicle and support safely. Install the exhaust pipe to the exhaust manifold.
25. Install the water hoses to the water crossover.
26. Install the power brake vacuum hose to the intake manifold.
27. Connect the throttle linkage.
28. Install all vacuum lines, electrical wiring and fuel lines to the carburetor or throttle body.
29. Install the air cleaner assembly.
30. Refill the cooling system.
31. Connect the negative battery cable and check the manifolds for leaks.

With Turbocharger

NOTE: On some vehicles, some of the manifold attaching bolts are not accessible or too heavily sealed from the factory and cannot be removed on the vehicle. Head removal would be necessary in these situations.

1. Disconnect the negative battery cable. Relieve the fuel pressure. Drain the cooling system. Raise the vehicle and safely support.
2. Disconnect the exhaust pipe at the articulated joint. Disconnect the oxygen sensor at the electrical connection.
3. Remove the turbocharger to engine support bracket.
4. Loosen the oil drain back tube connector hose clamps. Move the tube down on the engine block fitting.
5. Disconnect the turbocharger coolant inlet tube from the engine block and disconnect the tube support bracket.
6. Remove the air cleaner assembly, including the throttle body adaptor, hose and air cleaner box with support bracket.

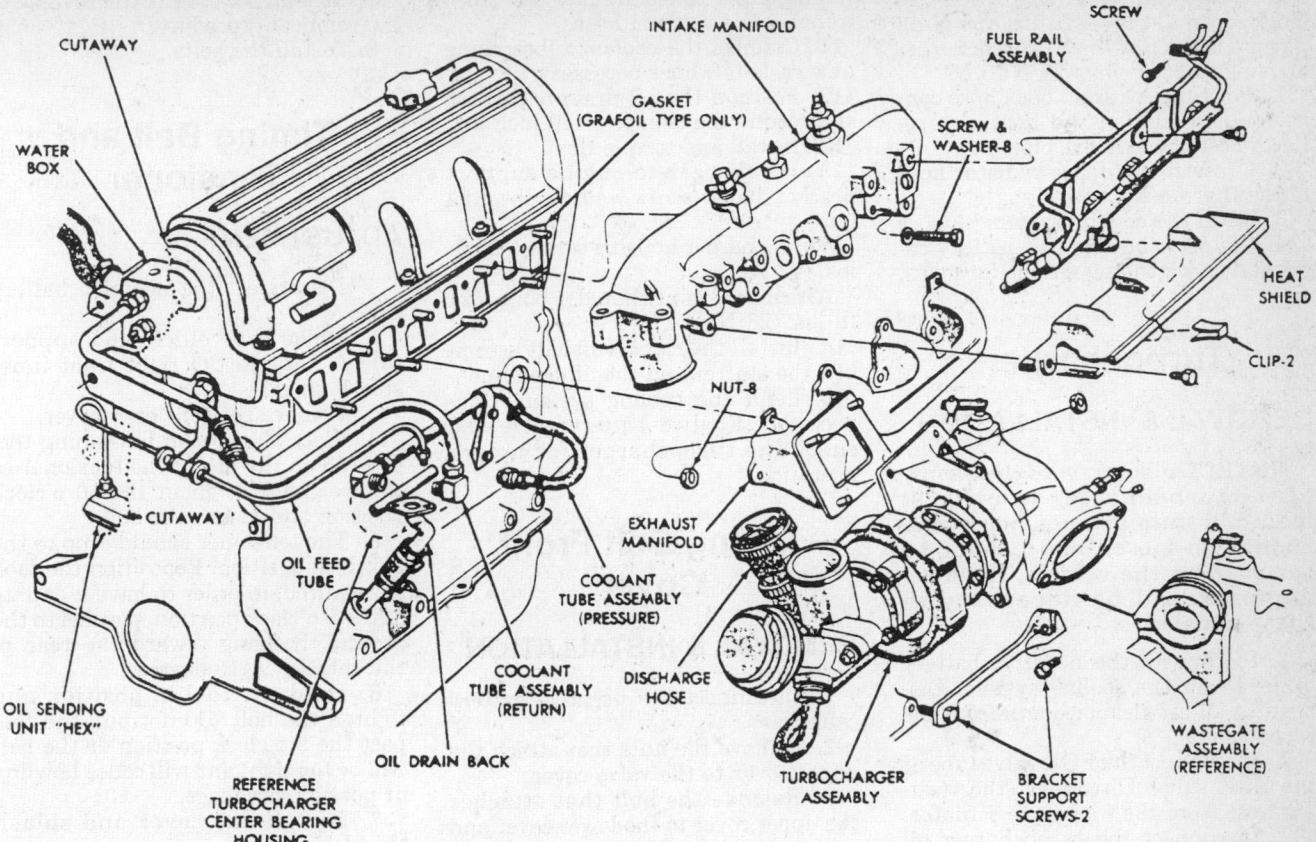

Intake and exhaust manifolds and related parts—turbocharged engine

7. Disconnect the accelerator linkage, throttle body electrical connector and vacuum hoses.

8. Relocate the fuel rail assembly. Remove the bracket to intake manifold screws and the bracket to heat shield clips. Lift and secure the fuel rail with injectors, wiring harness and fuel lines intact, up and out of the way.

9. Disconnect the turbocharger oil feed line at the oil sending unit tee fitting.

10. Disconnect the upper radiator hose from the thermostat housing.

11. Remove the cylinder head, manifolds and turbocharger as an assembly.

12. With the assembly on a work bench, loosen the upper turbocharger discharge hose end clamp.

NOTE: Do not disturb the center deswirler retaining clamp.

13. Remove the throttle body to intake manifold screws and throttle body assembly. Disconnect the turbocharger coolant return tube from the water box. Disconnect the retaining bracket on the cylinder head.

14. Remove the heat shield to intake manifold screws and the heat shield.

15. Remove the turbocharger to exhaust manifold nuts and the turbocharger assembly.

16. Remove the intake manifold bolts and the intake manifold.

17. Remove the exhaust manifold nuts and the exhaust manifold.

To install:

18. Place a new 2-sided Grafoil type intake/exhaust manifold gasket; do not use sealant.

19. Position the exhaust manifold on the cylinder head. Apply anti-seize compound to threads, install and torque the retaining nuts, starting at center and progressing outward in both directions, to 17 ft. lbs. (23 Nm). Repeat this procedure until all nuts are at 17 ft. lbs. (23 Nm).

20. Position the intake manifold on the cylinder head. Install and torque the retaining screws, starting at center and progressing outward in both directions, to 19 ft. lbs. (26 Nm). Repeat this procedure until all screws are at 19 ft. lbs. (26 Nm).

21. Connect the turbocharger outlet to the intake manifold inlet tube. Position the turbocharger on the exhaust manifold. Apply anti-seize compound to threads and torque the nuts to 30 ft. lbs. (41 Nm). Torque the connector tube clamps to 30 inch lbs.

22. Install the tube support bracket to the cylinder head.

23. Install the heat shield on the intake manifold. Torque the screws to 105 inch lbs. (12 Nm).

24. Install the throttle body air horn into the turbocharger inlet tube. Install and torque the throttle body to intake manifold screws to 21 ft. lbs. (28 Nm). Torque the tube clamp to 30 inch lbs.

25. Install the cylinder head/manifolds/turbocharger assembly on the engine.

26. Reconnect the turbocharger oil feed line to the oil sending unit tee fitting and bearing housing, if disconnected. Torque the tube nuts to 10 ft. lbs. (14 Nm).

27. Install the air cleaner assembly. Connect the vacuum lines and accelerator cables.

28. Position the fuel rail. Install and torque the bracket screws to 21 ft. lbs. (28 Nm). Install the air shield to bracket clips.

29. Connect the turbocharger inlet coolant tube to the engine block. Torque the tube nut to 30 ft. lbs. (41 Nm). Install the tube support bracket.

30. Install the turbocharger housing-to-engine block support bracket and

the screws hand tight. Torque the block screw 1st to 40 ft. lbs. (54 Nm). Torque the screw to the turbocharger housing to 20 ft. lbs. (27 Nm).

31. Position the drain back hose connector and tighten the hose clamps. Reconnect the exhaust pipe.

32. Connect the upper radiator hose to the thermostat housing.

33. Refill the cooling system.

34. Connect the negative battery cable and check the manifolds for leaks.

Turbocharger

REMOVAL & INSTALLATION

NOTE: On some vehicles, some of the turbocharger to exhaust manifold nuts are not accessible enough to loosen and cannot be removed on the vehicle. Head removal would be necessary in these situations.

1. Disconnect the negative battery cable. Drain the cooling system. Disconnect all air cleaner ducts from the turbocharger.

2. Disconnect the EGR valve tube at the EGR valve. Disconnect the vacuum hose from the wastegate actuator.

3. Disconnect the turbocharger oil feed at the oil sending unit block or turbocharger and the coolant tube at the water box. Disconnect the oil/coolant tube support bracket from the cylinder head.

4. Remove the right intermediate shaft, bearing support bracket and outer driveshaft assemblies.

5. Remove the turbocharger to engine block support bracket.

6. Disconnect the exhaust pipe at the articulated joint. Disconnect the oxygen sensor at the electrical connection.

7. Loosen the oil drain-back tube connector clamps and move the tube hose down on the nipple.

8. Disconnect the coolant tube nut at the block outlet, below the steering pump bracket and the tube support bracket.

9. Remove the turbocharger to exhaust manifold nuts. Carefully routing the oil and coolant lines, move the assembly down and out of the vehicle.
To install:

NOTE: Before installing the turbocharger assembly, be sure it is first charged with oil. Failure to do this may cause damage to the assembly.

10. Position the turbocharger on the exhaust manifold. Apply an anti-seize compound, Loctite® 771-64 or equivalent, to the threads and torque the re-

taining nuts to 40 ft. lbs. (54 Nm). Connect the vacuum hose.

11. Connect the coolant tubes using new gaskets where necessary.

12. Position the oil drain-back hose and torque the clamps to 30 inch lbs.

13. Install and torque the:
Turbocharger-to-engine support bracket block screw — 40 ft. lbs. (54 Nm)
Turbocharger housing screw — 20 ft. lbs. (27 Nm)
Articulated joint shoulder bolts — 21 ft. lbs. (28 Nm)

14. Install the right halfshaft assembly, the starter and the oil feed line.

15. Refill the cooling system. Connect the negative battery cable and check the turbocharger for proper operation.

Timing Belt Front Cover

REMOVAL & INSTALLATION

1. Disconnect the negative battery cable.

2. Remove the nuts that attach the upper cover to the valve cover.

3. Remove the bolt that attaches the upper cover to the lower cover and remove the upper cover.

4. Raise the vehicle and support safely. Remove the right side splash shield.

5. Remove the crankshaft pulley, water pump pulley and belts.

6. Remove the lower cover attaching bolts and remove the lower cover.

7. The installation is the reverse of the removal procedure.

8. Install the belts.

Timing Belt and Tensioner

ADJUSTMENT

1. Disconnect the negative battery cable.

2. Raise the vehicle and support safely. Remove the right front inner splash shield.

3. Remove the tensioner cover.

4. Place the special tensioning tool C-4703 on the hex of the tensioner so the weight is at about the 10 o'clock position and loosen the bolt.

5. The tensioner should drop to the 9 o'clock position. Reposition the tool, as required, in order to have it end up at the 9 o'clock position, parallel to the ground, hanging toward the rear of the vehicle, ± 15 degrees.

6. Hold the tool in position and tighten the bolt. Do not pull the tool past the 9 o'clock position or the belt will be too tight and will cause howling or possible breakage.

7. Install the cover and splash shield.

6. Install the timing belt covers and all related parts.

REMOVAL & INSTALLATION

1. If possible, position the engine so that the No. 1 piston is at TDC of its

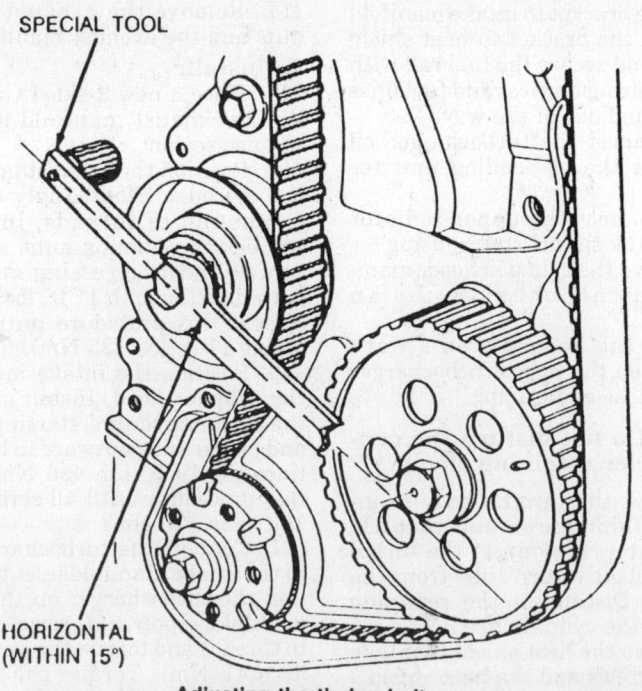

SPECIAL TOOL

HORIZONTAL
(WITHIN 15°)

Adjusting the timing belt

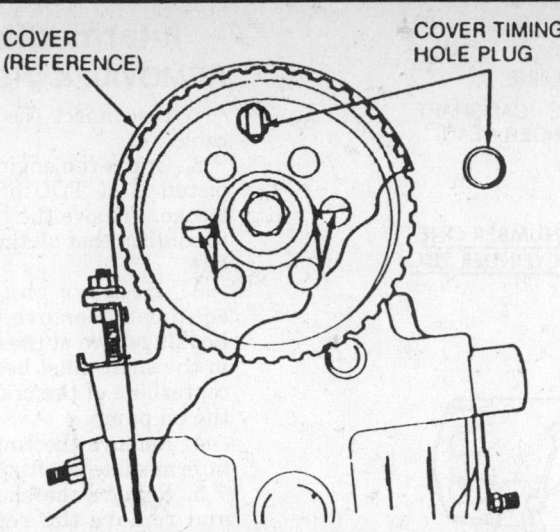

Alignment of the arrows on the camshaft sprocket with the camshaft cap to cylinder head mouting line

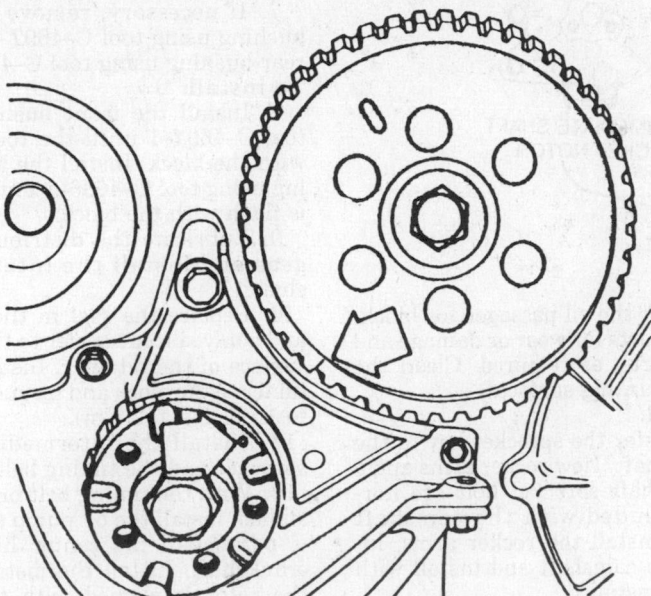

Allgnment of the crankshaft and intermediate shaft sprockets

compression stroke. Disconnect the negative battery cable.

2. Remove the timing belt covers. Remove the timing belt tensioner and allow the belt to hang free.

3. Place a floor jack under the engine and separate the right motor mount.

4. Remove the air conditioning compressor belt idler pulley, if equipped and remove the mounting stud. Unbolt the compressor/alternator bracket and position it to the side.

5. Remove the timing belt from the vehicle.

To install:

6. Turn the crankshaft sprocket and intermediate shaft sprocket until the marks are in line. Position a straight edge from bolt to bolt to confirm alignment.

7. Turn the camshaft until the small hole in the sprocket is at the top and rows on the hub are in line with the camshaft cap to cylinder head mounting lines. Use a mirror to see the alignment so it is viewed straight on and not at an angle from above. Install the belt but let it hang free at this point.

8. Install the air conditioning compressor/alternator brackct, idler pulley and motor mount. Remove the floor jack. Raise the vehicle and support safely. Have the tensioner at an arm's reach because the timing belt will have to be held in position with one hand.

9. To properly install the timing belt, reach up and engage it with the camshaft sprocket. Turn the intermediate shaft counterclockwise slightly, then engage the belt with the intermediate shaft sprocket. Hold the belt against the intermediate shaft sprocket and turn clockwise to take up all tension; if the timing marks are out of alignment, repeat until alignment is correct.

10. Using a wrench, turn the crankshaft sprocket counterclockwise slightly and wrap the belt around it. Turn the sprocket clockwise so there is no slack in the belt between sprockets; if the timing marks are out of alignment, repeat until alignment is correct.

NOTE: If the timing marks are in line but slack exists in the belt between either the camshaft and intermediate shaft sprockets or the intermediate and crankshaft sprockets, the timing will be incorrect when the belt is tensioned. All slack must be only between the crankshaft and camshaft sprockets.

11. Install the tensioner and install the mounting bolt loosely. Place the special tensioning tool C–4703 on the hex of the tensioner so the weight is at about the 9 o'clock position, parallel to the ground, hanging toward the rear of the vehicle, ± 15 degrees.

12. Hold the tool in position and tighten the bolt to 45 ft. lbs. (61 Nm). Do not pull the tool past the 9 o'clock position; this will make the belt too tight and will cause it to howl or possibly break.

13. Lower the vehicle and recheck the camshaft sprocket positioning. If it is correct install the timing belt covers and all related parts.

14. Connect the negative battery cable and road test the vehicle.

Timing Sprockets

REMOVAL & INSTALLATION

1. Disconnect the negative battery cable. Remove the timing belt.

2. Remove the crankshaft sprocket bolt. Using the puller tool C–4685 or equivalent, and the button from tool L–4524 or equivalent, remove the crankshaft sprocket.

3. Using the tool C–4687 or equivalent, hold the camshaft and/or intermediate sprocket, remove the center bolt and the sprocket(s).

4. The installation is the reverse of the removal procedure. Torque the camshaft and intermediate sprocket bolts to 65 ft. lbs. (88 Nm) and the crankshaft sprocket bolt to 50 ft. lbs. (68 Nm).

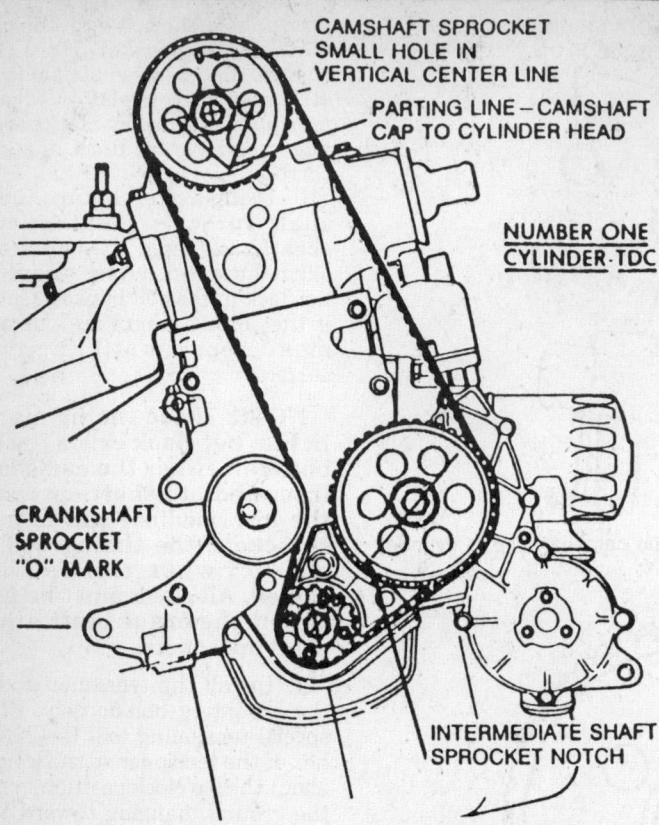

CAMSHAFT SPROCKET
SMALL HOLE IN
VERTICAL CENTER LINE

PARTING LINE – CAMSHAFT
CAP TO CYLINDER HEAD

NUMBER ONE
CYLINDER·TDC

CRANKSHAFT
SPROCKET
"O" MARK

INTERMEDIATE SHAFT
SPROCKET NOTCH

Timing belt properly installed

Camshaft

REMOVAL & INSTALLATION

1. Disconnect the negative battery cable.

2. Turn the crankshaft so the No. 1 piston is at the TDC of its compression stroke. Remove the upper timing belt cover.

3. Remove the camshaft sprocket bolt and the sprocket and suspend tightly so the belt does not lose tension. If it does, the belt timing will have to be reset.

4. Remove the valve cover.

5. If the rocker arms are being reused, mark them for installation identification and loosen the camshaft bearing bolts, evenly and gradually.

6. Using a soft mallet, tap the rear of the camshaft a few times to break the bearing caps loose.

7. Remove the bolts, bearing caps and the camshaft with seals.

NOTE: Take note of the color of the paint stripe on the rear camshaft seal. These stripes differentiate seal sizes. If a seal with a different color stripe is installed, a severe leak will develop if the seal is too small or the cap will not be able to be fully installed if the seal is too big.

8. Check the oil passages for blockages, the parts for wear or damage and replace parts, as required. Clean the gasket mounting surfaces.

To install:

9. Transfer the sprocket key to the new camshaft. New rocker arms and a new camshaft sprocket bolt are normally included with the camshaft package. Install the rocker arms, lubricate the camshaft and install with end seals installed.

10. Place the bearing caps with No. 1 at the timing belt end and No. 5 at the transaxle end. The camshaft bearing caps are numbered and have arrows facing forward. Torque the camshaft bearing bolts evenly and gradually to 18 ft. lbs. (24 Nm).

NOTE: Apply RTV silicone gasket material to the No. 1 and 5 bearing caps. Install the bearing caps before the seals are installed.

11. Mount a dial indicator to the front of the engine and check the camshaft endplay. Play should not exceed 0.020 in.

12. Install the camshaft sprocket and the new bolt.

13. Install the valve cover with a new gasket.

14. Connect the negative battery cable and check for leaks.

Intermediate Shaft
REMOVAL & INSTALLATION

1. Disconnect the negative battery cable.

2. Crank the engine until the No. 1 piston is at TDC of its compression stroke. Remove the timing belt covers to confirm that all timing marks are in line.

3. Remove the fuel pump, if equipped. Remove the distributor. Looking down at the oil pump, the slot in the shaft must be parallel with the center line of the crankshaft. Remove the oil pump.

4. Remove the timing belt and the intermediate shaft sprocket.

5. Remove the shaft retainer bolts and remove the retainer from the block.

6. Remove the intermediate shaft from the engine.

7. If necessary, remove the front bushing using tool C–4697–2 and the rear bushing using tool C–4686–2.

To install:

8. Install the front bushing using tool C–4697–1 until the tool is flush with the block. Install the rear bushing using tool C–4686–1 until the tool is flush with the block.

9. Lubricate the distributor drive gear and install the intermediate shaft.

10. Replace the seal in the retainer and apply silicone sealer to the mating surface of the retainer. Install the retainer to the block and torque the bolts to 10 ft. lbs. (12 Nm).

11. Install the intermediate shaft sprocket and the timing belt.

12. With the timing belt properly installed, install the oil pump so the slot is parallel to the center line of the crankshaft. Install the distributor so the rotor is aligned with the No. 1 spark plug wire tower on the cap.

13. Install the fuel pump, if equipped.

14. Connect the negative battery cable and road test the vehicle.

Piston and Connecting Rod
POSITIONING

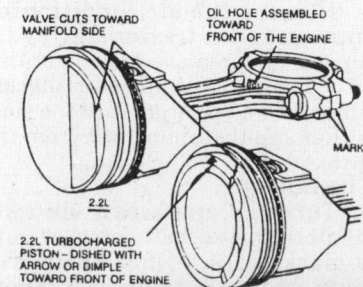

VALVE CUTS TOWARD
MANIFOLD SIDE

OIL HOLE ASSEMBLED
TOWARD
FRONT OF THE ENGINE

MARK

2.2L

2.2L TURBOCHARGED
PISTON – DISHED WITH
ARROW OR DIMPLE
TOWARD FRONT OF ENGINE

Piston and connecting rod positioning

ENGINE LUBRICATION

Oil Pan

REMOVAL & INSTALLATION

1. Disconnect the negative battery cable. Remove the oil dipstick.
2. Raise the vehicle and support safely.
3. Drain the engine oil.
4. Remove the engine to transaxle struts.
5. Remove the torque converter inspection cover.
6. Remove the oil pan retaining screws and remove the oil pan and the side seals.

To install:

7. Thoroughly, clean and dry all sealing surfaces, bolts and bolt holes.
8. Apply silicone sealer to the 4 end seal to block corners and install the end seals making sure the corners are not twisted.
9. Apply silicone to the 4 pan to block corners. Install a new pan gasket or apply silicone sealer to the sealing surface of the pan and install to the engine making sure not to dislodge the end seals.
10. Install the retaining screws and torque to 17 ft. lbs. (23 Nm).
11. Install the torque converter inspection cover and engine to transaxle struts. Lower the vehicle.
12. Install the dipstick. Fill the engine with the proper amount of oil.
13. Connect the negative battery cable and check for leaks.

Oil Pump

REMOVAL & INSTALLATION

1. Crank the engine so the No. 1 piston is at TDC of its compression stroke. Disconnect the negative battery cable.
2. Matchmark the rotor to the block and remove the distributor to confirm that the slot in the oil pump shaft is parallel to the centerline of the crankshaft. Matchmark the slot to the distributor bore, if desired.
3. Remove the dipstick. Raise the vehicle and support safely. Drain the engine oil and remove the pan.
4. Remove the oil pickup.
5. Remove the 2 mounting bolts and remove the oil pump from the engine.

To install:

6. Prime the pump by pouring fresh oil into the pump intake and turning the driveshaft until oil comes out the

PARALLEL TO CENTER LINE OF CRANKSHAFT

OIL FILTER

Aligning the slot in the oil pump shaft

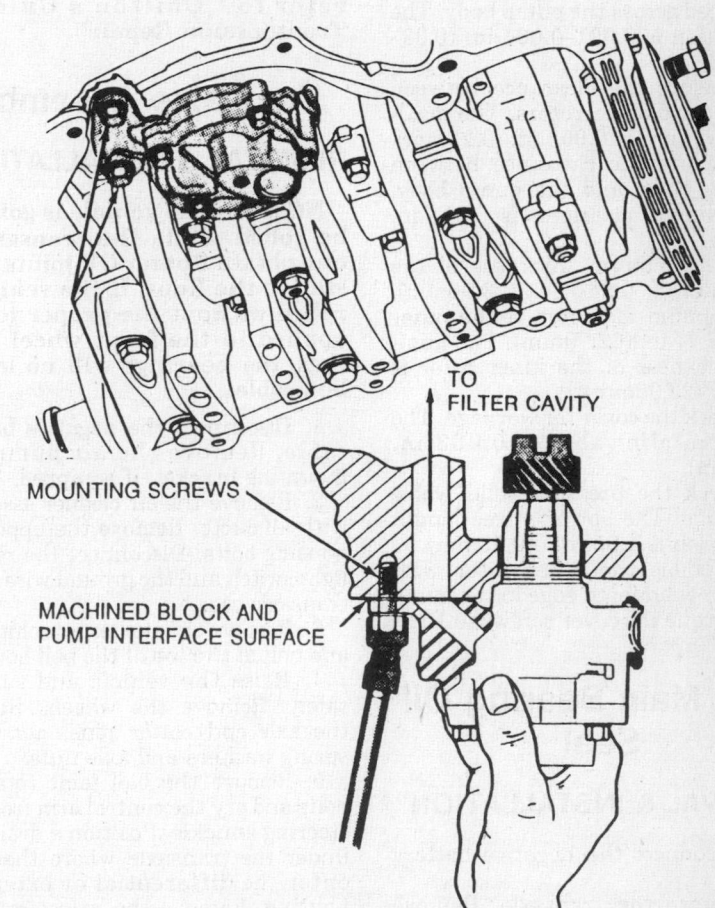

TO FILTER CAVITY

MOUNTING SCREWS

MACHINED BLOCK AND PUMP INTERFACE SURFACE

Oil pump assembly mounting

pressure port. Repeat a few times until no air bubbles are present.

7. Apply Loctite® 515 sealant or equivalent, to the pump body to block machined surface interface. Lubricate the oil pump and distributor driveshaft.

8. Align the slot so it will be in the same position as when it was removed. If it is not, the distributor will not be timed correctly. Install the pump fully

and rotate back and forth to ensure proper positioning between the pump mounting surface and the machined surface of the block.

9. Install the mounting bolts finger-tight and lower the vehicle to confirm proper slot positioning. If the slot is not properly positioned, raise the vehicle and move the gear, as required. If the slot is correct, hold the pump firmly against the block and torque the

mounting bolts to 17 ft. lbs. (23 Nm).

10. Clean out the oil pickup or replace, as required. Replace the oil pickup O-ring and install the pickup to the pump.

11. Install the oil pan using new gaskets. Lower the vehicle.

12. Install the distributor.

13. Install the dipstick. Fill the engine with the proper amount of oil.

14. Connect the negative battery cable, check the timing and check the oil pressure.

CHECKING

1. Remove the cover from the oil pump.

2. Check endplay of the inner rotor using a feeler gauge and a straight edge placed across the pump body. The specification is 0.001–0.004 in. (0.03–0.09mm).

3. Measure the clearance between the inner and outer rotors. The maximum clearance is 0.008 in. (0.20mm).

4. Measure the clearance between the outer rotor and the pump body. The maximum clearance is 0.014 in. (0.35mm).

5. The minimum thickness of the outer rotor is 0.944 in. (23.96mm). The minimum diameter of the outer rotor is 2.77 in. (62.70mm). The minimum thickness of the inner rotor is 0.943 in. (23.95mm).

6. Check the cover for warpage. The maximum allowable is 0.003 in. (0.076mm).

7. Check the pressure relief valve for damage. The spring's free length specification is 1.95 in. (49.50mm).

8. Assemble the outer rotor with the larger chamfered edge in the pump body. Torque the cover screws to 10 ft. lbs. (12 Nm).

Rear Main Bearing Oil Seal

REMOVAL & INSTALLATION

1. Disconnect the negative battery cable.

2. Remove the transaxle. Remove the flexplate or flywheel.

3. If there is any leakage coming from the rear seal retainer, drain the engine oil and remove the oil pan, if necessary. Remove the rear main oil seal retainer.

4. Remove the seal from the retainer.

To install:

5. Lightly coat the seal outer diameter with Loctite® Stud N' Bearing Mount or equivalent.

6. Install the seal to the retainer.

7. If the retainer was removed,

thoroughly clean and dry the retainer to block sealing surfaces and install a new gasket or apply silicone sealer and install the retainer. Install the pan, if it was removed.

8. Install the flexplate or flywheel and transaxle.

9. Connect the negative battery cable and check for leaks.

MANUAL TRANSAXLE

For further information on transmissions/transaxles, please refer to "Chilton's Guide to Transmission Repair".

Transaxle Assembly

REMOVAL & INSTALLATION

NOTE: If the vehicle is going to be rolled while the transaxle is out, obtain 2 outer CV-joints to install to the hubs. If the vehicle is rolled without the proper torque applied to the front wheel bearings, the bearings will no longer be usable.

1. Disconnect the negative battery cable. Remove the air pump and mounting bracket, if equipped.

2. Remove the air cleaner assembly with all ducts. Remove the upper bell housing bolts. Disconnect the reverse light switch and the ground wire to the transaxle case.

3. Remove the starter attaching nut and bolt at the top of the bell housing.

4. Raise the vehicle and support safely. Remove the wheels. Remove the axle end cotter pins, nut locks, spring washers and axle nuts.

5. Remove the ball joint retaining bolts and pry the control arm from the steering knuckle. Position a drain pan under the transaxle where the axles enter the differential or extension housing. Remove the axles from the transaxle or center bearing. Unbolt the center bearing and remove the intermediate axle from the transaxle, if equipped.

6. Remove the anti-rotation link from the crossmember, if equipped. Disconnect the shifter linkage from the transaxle.

7. Remove the speedometer gear adaptor bolt and remove the adaptor from the transaxle.

8. Remove the rear mount from the starter, unbolt the starter and position it to the side.

9. Using the proper equipment, support the weight of the engine.

10. Remove the front motor mount and bracket.

11. Position a suitable transmission jack under the transaxle.

12. Remove the lower bell housing bolts.

13. Remove the left side splash shield. Remove the transaxle mount bolts.

14. Carefully pry the transaxle from the engine.

15. Slide the transaxle rearward until the input shaft clears the clutch disc.

16. Pull the transaxle completely away from the clutch housing and remove it from the vehicle.

17. To prepare the vehicle for rolling, support the engine with a suitable support or reinstall the front motor mount to the engine. Then reinstall the ball joints to the steering knuckle and install the retaining bolt. Install the obtained outer CV-joints to the hubs, install the washers and torque the axle nuts to 180 ft. lbs. (244 Nm). The vehicle may now be safely rolled.

To install:

18. Lubricate the pilot bushing and input shaft splines very lightly with high temperature lubricant.

19. Mount the transaxle securely on a suitable jack. Lift it in place until the input shaft is centered in the clutch housing opening. Roll the transaxle forward until the input shaft splines fully engage with the clutch disc and install the transaxle to clutch housing bolts.

20. Raise the transaxle and install the left side mount bolts.

21. Install the front motor mount and bracket.

22. Remove the engine and transaxle support fixtures.

23. Install the starter to the transaxle and install the lower bolt finger-tight.

24. Install a new O-ring to the speedometer cable adaptor and install to the extension housing; make sure it snaps in place. Install the retaining bolt.

25. Install the shifter linkage and snap into place. Install the anti-rotation link, if equipped.

26. Install the axles and center bearing, if equipped. Install the ball joints to the steering knuckles. Torque the axle nuts to 180 ft. lbs. (244 Nm) and install new cotter pins. Fill the transaxle with SAE 5W-30 engine oil. Install the splash shield and install the wheels. Lower the vehicle.

27. Install the upper bell housing bolts.

28. Install the starter attaching nut and bolt at the top of the bell housing. Raise the vehicle and tighten the start-

er bolt from under the vehicle. Lower the vehicle.

29. Connect the reverse light switch and the ground wire.

30. Install the air cleaner assembly and air pump, if equipped.

31. Connect the negative battery cable and check the transaxle for proper operation.

LINKAGE ADJUSTMENT

1. Working over the left front fender, remove the lock pin from the transaxle selector shaft housing.

2. Reverse the lock pin so the long end is down and insert it into the same threaded hole while pushing the selector shaft into the selector housing. A hole in the selector shaft will align with the lock pin, allowing the lock pin to be screwed into the housing. This operation locks the selector shaft in the neutral position between 1st and 2nd gears.

3. Raise the vehicle and support safely.

4. Loosen the clamp bolt that secures the gear shift tube to the gear shift connector. Check to see that the connector slides and turns freely on the tube.

5. Position the shifter mechanism connector assembly so the isolator is just contacting the up standing flange and the rib on the isolator is pointing to the hole in the blockout bracket.

6. Hold the connector isolator in this position and tighten the clamp bolt on the gear shift tube to 14 ft. lbs. (19 Nm). Lower the vehicle.

7. Remove the lock pin from the selector shaft housing and reinstall the lock pin, with the long end up, in the selector shaft housing. Torque the lock pin to 10 ft. lbs. (12 Nm).

8. Check the first/reverse shifting and blockout into reverse.

CLUTCH

Clutch Assembly

REMOVAL & INSTALLATION

1. Disconnect the negative battery cable. Remove the transaxle.

2. Matchmark the clutch/pressure plate cover and flywheel. Insert a suitable clutch plate alignment tool into the clutch disc hub.

3. Loosen the flywheel to pressure plate bolts gradually and evenly to avoid warpage.

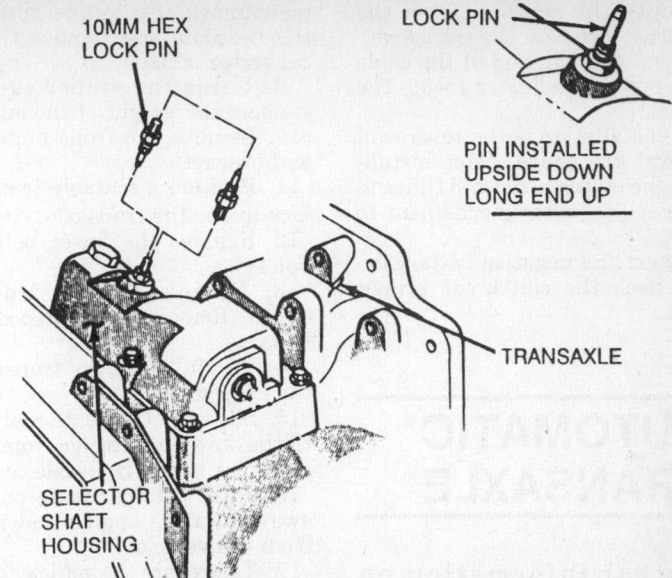

Manual transaxle pinned in the neutral position

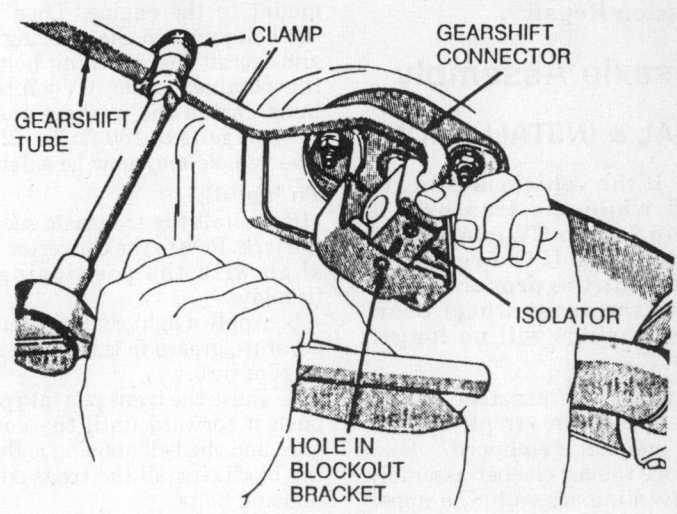

Adjusting the shifter linkage—manual transaxle

4. Remove the pressure plate/clutch assembly from the flywheel.

5. Sand the flywheel or replace it, if scored, cracked or heat damaged.

6. Sparingly apply anti-sieze compound to the input shaft and clutch disc splines. Install a new release bearing.

To install:

7. Using a suitable clutch disc alignment tool, tighten the pressure plate bolts to center the disc.

8. Torque the pressure plate/clutch assembly mounting bolts to the flywheel gradually and evenly to 21 ft. lbs. (28 Nm).

9. Install the transaxle.

10. Connect the negative battery cable and check the clutch and reverse lights for proper operation.

PEDAL FREE-PLAY ADJUSTMENT

All vehicles are equipped with a self-adjusting cable operated mechanism and no adjustment is provided. The mechanism is located above the clutch pedal, where the cable and pivot points may be lubricated.

Clutch Cable

REMOVAL & INSTALLATION

1. Disconnect the negative battery cable.

2. Remove the clip from the cable mounting bracket on the shock tower and remove the cable from the bracket.

3. Remove the retainer from the clutch release lever on the transaxle.

4. Pry out the ball end of the cable from the position adjuster inside the pedal.

5. The installation is the reverse of the removal procedure. After installing, push the clutch pedal 2–3 times to allow the self-adjuster mechanism to function.

6. Connect the negative battery cable and check the clutch for proper operation.

AUTOMATIC TRANSAXLE

For further information on transmissions/transaxles, please refer to ''Chilton's Guide to Transmission Repair''.

Transaxle Assembly

REMOVAL & INSTALLATION

NOTE: If the vehicle is going to be rolled while the transaxle is out, obtain 2 outer CV-joints to install to the hubs. If the vehicle is rolled without the proper torque applied to the front wheel bearings, the bearings will no longer be usable.

1. Disconnect the negative battery cable. Remove the air pump and mounting bracket, if equipped.

2. Remove the air cleaner assembly if it is preventing access to the upper bell housing bolts. Remove the upper bell housing bolts and unplug all electrical connectors from the transaxle.

3. Remove the starter attaching nut and bolt at the top of the bell housing.

4. Raise the vehicle and support safely. Remove the wheels. Remove the axle end cotter pins, nut locks, spring washers and axle nuts.

5. Remove the ball joint retaining bolts and pry the control arm from the steering knuckle. Position a drain pan under the transaxle where the axles enter the differential or extension housing. Remove the axles from the transaxle.

6. Drain the transaxle. Disconnect and plug the fluid cooler hoses. Disconnect the shifter and kickdown linkage from the transaxle.

7. Remove the speedometer cable adaptor bolt and remove the adaptor from the transaxle.

8. Remove the starter. Remove the torque converter inspection cover,

matchmark the torque converter to the flexplate and remove the torque converter bolts.

9. Using the proper equipment, support the weight of the engine.

10. Remove the front motor mount and bracket.

11. Position a suitable transmission jack under the transaxle.

12. Remove the lower bell housing bolts.

13. Remove the left side splash shield. Remove the transaxle mount bolts.

14. Carefully pry the transaxle from the engine.

15. Slide the transaxle rearward until the dowels disengage from the mating holes in the transaxle case.

16. Pull the transaxle completely away from the engine and remove it from the vehicle.

17. To prepare the vehicle for rolling, support the engine with a suitable support or reinstall the front motor mount to the engine. Then reinstall the ball joints to the steering knuckle and install the retaining bolt. Install the obtained outer CV-joints to the hubs, install the washers and torque the axle nuts to 180 ft. lbs. (244 Nm). The vehicle may now be safely rolled.

To install:

18. Install the transaxle securely on the jack. Rotate the converter so it will align with the positioning of the flexplate.

19. Apply a light coating of high temperature grease to the torque converter pilot hub.

20. Raise the transaxle into place and push it forward until the dowels engage and the bell housing is flush with the block. Install the transaxle to bell housing bolts.

21. Raise the transaxle and install the left side mount bolts. Install the torque converter bolts and torque to 55 ft. lbs. (74 Nm).

22. Install the front motor mount and bracket. Remove the engine and transaxle support fixtures.

23. Install the starter to the transaxle. Install the bolt finger-tight.

24. Install a new O-ring to the speedometer cable adaptor and install to the extension housing; make sure it snaps in place. Install the retaining bolt.

25. Connect the shifter and kickdown linkage to the transaxle.

26. Install the axles. Install the ball joints to the steering knuckles. Torque the axle nuts to 180 ft. lbs. (244 Nm) and install new cotter pins. Install the splash shield and install the wheels. Lower the vehicle.

27. Install the upper bell housing bolts.

28. Install the starter attaching nut and bolt at the top of the bell housing.

Raise the vehicle again and tighten the starter bolt from under the vehicle. Lower the vehicle.

29. Connect all electrical wiring to the transaxle. Install the air pump, if equipped.

30. Install the air cleaner assembly, if it was removed. Fill the transaxle with the proper amount of Mopar ATF Plus Type 7176. Conventional Dexron®II may be used if Type 7176 is not available.

31. Connect the negative battery cable and check the transaxle for proper operation.

SHIFT LINKAGE ADJUSTMENT

1. Place the shifter in the **P** detent.
2. Loosen the clamp bolt on the gear shift cable bracket.
3. Pull the shift lever all the way to the front detent position and tighten the lock screw.
4. Check for proper neutral safety switch operation.

THROTTLE PRESSURE CABLE ADJUSTMENT

1. Run the engine until it reaches normal operating temperature.
2. Loosen the cable mounting bracket lock screw.
3. Position the bracket so that both alignment tabs are touching the transaxle case surface and tighten the lock screws.
4. Release the cross lock on the cable assembly by pulling the cross lock up.
5. To ensure proper adjustment, the cable must be free to slide all the way toward the engine against its stop after the cross lock is released.
6. Move the transaxle throttle control lever fully clockwise and press the cross lock down until it snaps into position.
7. Road test the vehicle and check the shift points.

DRIVE AXLE

Halfshaft

REMOVAL & INSTALLATION

1. Disconnect the negative battery cable.
2. Raise the vehicle and support safely.
3. Remove the tire and wheel assembly.

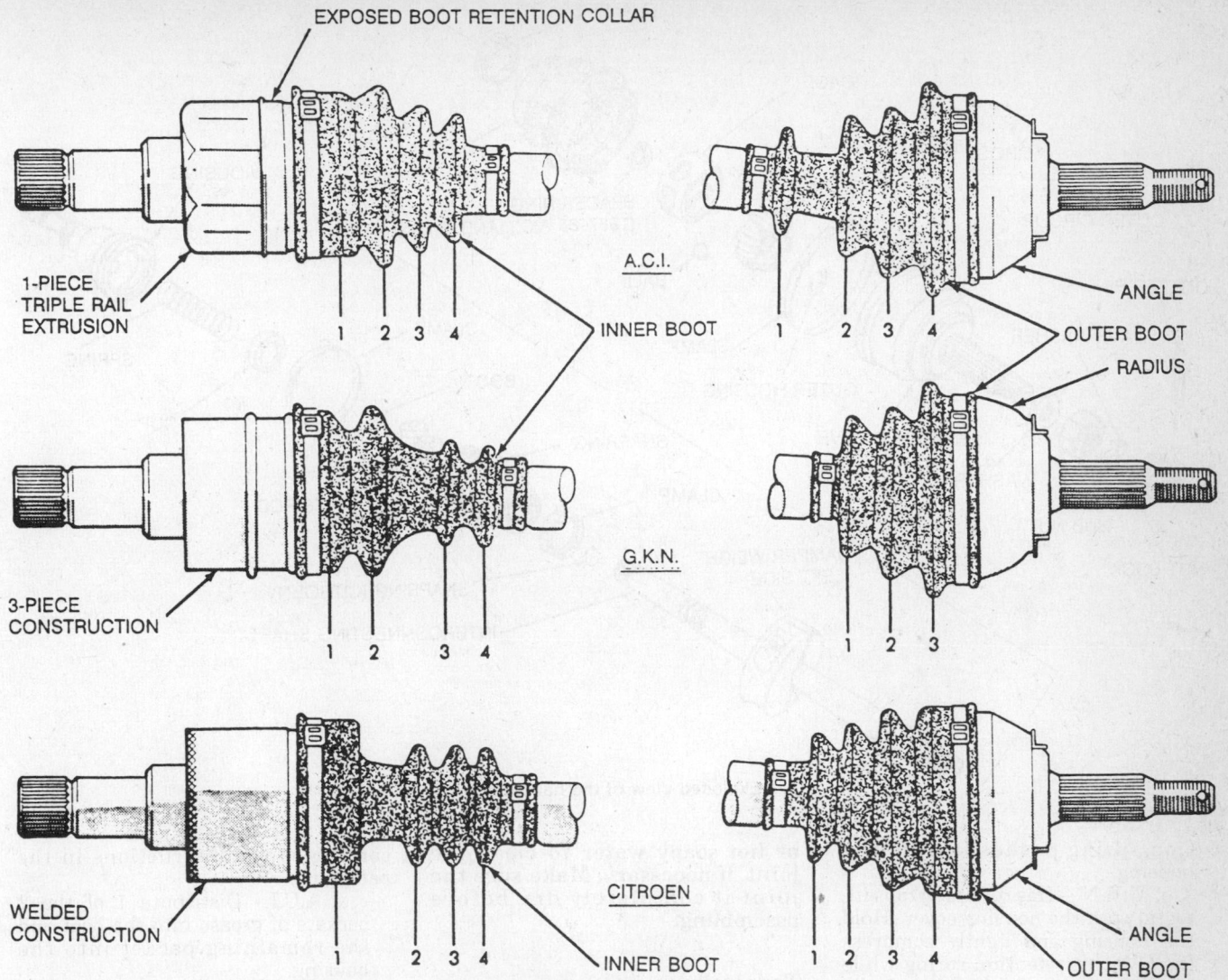

Halfshaft identification

4. Remove the cotter pin from the end of the halfshaft. Remove the nut lock, spring washer, axle nut and washer.

5. Remove the ball joint retaining bolt and pry the control arm down to release the ball stud from the steering knuckle.

6. Position a drain pan under the transaxle where the halfshaft enters the differential or extension housing. Remove the halfshaft from the transaxle or center bearing. Unbolt the center bearing from the block and remove the intermediate shaft from the transaxle, if equipped.

To install:

7. Install the halfshaft or intermediate shaft to the transaxle, being careful not to damage the side seals. Make sure the inner joint clicks into pace inside the differential. Install the center bearing retaining bolts, if equipped. Install the outer shaft to the center bearing, if equipped.

8. Pull the front strut out and insert the outer joint into the front hub.

9. If necessary, turn the ball joint stud to position the bolt retaining indent to the inside of the vehicle. Install the ball joint stud into the steering knuckle. Install the retaining bolt and nut.

10. Install the axle nut washer and nut and torque the nut to 180 ft. lbs. (244 Nm). Install the spring washer, nut lock and a new cotter pin.

11. Install the tire and wheel assembly.

CV-Boot

REMOVAL & INSTALLATION

NOTE: Use only clamps provided with the replacement package when servicing. Plastic wire ties and other straps will not clamp tightly enough and grease will sling out, causing damage to the joint.

Inner Joint

1. Remove the halfshaft from the vehicle.

2. If cutting the boot away, mark and note the boot positioning on the shaft relative to the raised shoulders. Remove the boot clamps to gain access to the tripod retention system.

3. Separate the housing from the tripod according to the following:

NOTE: Always hold the rollers in place when removing the housing from the tripod or the needle bearing may fall out.

a. A.C.I.—Has retaining tabs integral with the staked boot retaining collar. Hold the housing and lightly compress the CV-joint retention spring while bending the tabs back. Support the housing as the reten-

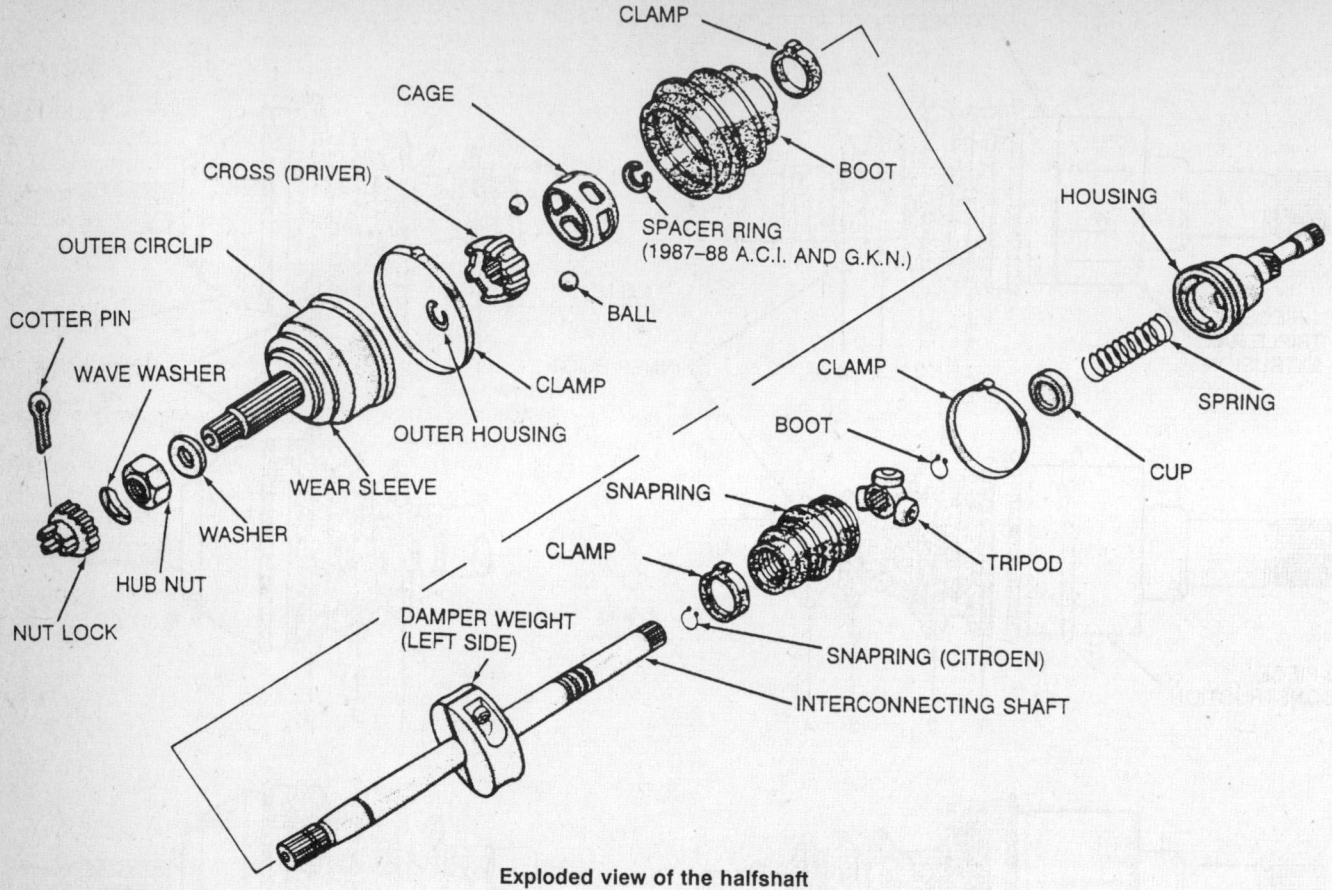

Exploded view of the halfshaft

tion spring pushes it from the housing.

b. G.K.N.—Has retaining tabs integral with the housing cover. Hold the housing and lightly compress the CV-joint retention spring while bending the tabs back. Support the housing as the retention spring pushes it from the housing.

c. Citroen—Uses a tripod retainer ring without tabs which is rolled into a groove in the housing. Slightly deform the retainer ring with a suitable tool in 3 evenly spaced locations. The retention spring will push the housing from the tripod. The retainer ring can also be cut and replaced, although it is acceptable to reshape the ring and reuse it.

4. Remove the snapring from the end of the shaft and remove the tripod.

5. If not already done, mark the boot positioning on the shaft, relative to the raised shoulders and remove the boot from the shaft.

6. Remove as much old grease as possible from the joint. Inspect all parts for wear or damage.

NOTE: Do not use petroleum based solvents on the joints, shaft or boot to clean; it will ruin hidden rubber seals within the joint. Use only chlorine based cleaner
or hot soapy water to clean the joint, if necessary. Make sure the joint it completely dry before assembling.

To install:

7. If equipped, slide a new rubber washer seal over the stub shaft and down into the groove provided.

8. If the clamping device is not a straight strap, install it on the shaft first, then install the boot to the shaft in the proper position. Using the proper tool, C–4124 for crimping with rubber boot or C–4653 for clamping a strap, secure the clamp.

9. Slide the tripod on the shaft:

a. A.C.I.—Slide the tripod on the shaft with the non-chamfered edge facing the tripod retainer ring groove.

b. G.K.N—Slide the tripod on the shaft with the non-chamfered edge facing the tripod retainer ring groove.

c. Citroen—The tripod may installed either way; both ends are the same.

10. Install the snapring into its groove on the shaft to lock the tripod in position.

11. Distribute the grease provided in the grease package as follows, or according to the instructions in the package:

a. A.C.I.—Distribute 1 of the 2 packets of grease into the boot and the remaining packet into the housing.

b. G.K.N—Distribute 2 of the 3 packets of grease into the boot and the remaining packet into the housing.

c. Citroen—Distribute ⅔ of the packet of grease into the boot and the remaining amount into the housing.

12. Position the spring in the housing spring pocket with the spring cup attached to the exposed end of the spring. Place a dab of grease on the concave surface of the spring cup.

13. Keeping the spring centered, install the housing to the tripod as follows:

a. A.C.I.—Slip the housing onto the tripod. Do not bend the retaining tabs back into their original position. Instead, secure the boot to hold the housing. The tripod must be reengaged to the housing with the shaft installed on the vehicle.

b. G.K.N—Slip the housing onto the tripod. Bend the retaining tabs back into their original positions. Check for proper retention ability.

c. Citroen—Slip the housing onto the tripod. Reform the retainer ring or install a new one. Stake in place using a punch. Check for proper retention ability.

14. Position the larger end of the boot over the housing.

15. Using the proper tool, C–4124 for crimping with rubber boot or C–4653 for clamping a strap, secure the clamp.

16. Install the halfshaft to the vehicle. Fill the transaxle if fluid was lost when removing the halfshaft.

17. Road test the vehicle.

Outer Joint

1. Remove the halfshaft from the vehicle.

2. If cutting the boot away, mark and note the boot positioning on the shaft relative to the raised shoulders. Remove the boot clamps to gain access to the joint retention system.

3. Separate the housing from the tripod according to the following:

a. A.C.I.—Using a soft-jaw vise, support the halfshaft. Strike the joint assembly sharply with a soft-face hammer to dislodge the internal circlip and remove from the shaft.

b. G.K.N—Using a soft-jaw vise, support the halfshaft. Strike the joint assembly sharply with a soft-face hammer to dislodge the internal circlip and remove from the shaft.

c. Citroen—Using a soft-jaw vise, support the halfshaft. Strike the joint assembly sharply with a soft-face hammer to dislodge the internal circlip and remove from the shaft.

4. If damaged, remove the wear sleeve from the CV-joint machined ledge.

5. Remove the circlip from the groove.

6. If not already done, mark the boot positioning on the shaft, relative to the raised shoulders and remove the boot from the shaft.

7. Remove as much old grease as possible from the joint. Inspect all parts for wear or damage.

NOTE: Do not use petroleum based solvents on the joints, shaft or boot to clean; it will ruin hidden rubber seals within the joint. Use only chlorine based cleaner or hot soapy water to clean the joint, if necessary. Make sure the joint it completely dry before assembling.

To install:

8. If the clamping device is not a straight strap, install it on the shaft first, then install the boot to the shaft in the proper position. Using the prop-er tool, C–4124 for crimping with rubber boot or C–4653 for clamping a strap, secure the clamp. Install a new circlip if provided in the replacement package.

9. Fill the boot with the proper amount of grease according to the instructions provided with the package.

10. Position the outer joint on the shaft with hub nut installed, engage the splines and strike sharply with a soft-face hammer to install. Make sure the circlip did not become dislodged.

11. Position the larger end of the boot over the housing.

12. Using the proper tool, C–4124 for crimping with rubber boot or C–4653 for clamping a strap, secure the clamp.

13. Install the halfshaft to the vehicle. Fill the transaxle if fluid was lost when removing the halfshaft.

14. Road test the vehicle.

Front Wheel Hub, Knuckle and Bearing

REMOVAL & INSTALLATION

Pressed In (Two-Piece Hub and Bearing)

NOTE: Some hub and bearing replacement packages include the one-piece unit described below. If this is the case, follow the installation steps for one-piece unit instead of for the two-piece unit described here.

1. Raise the vehicle and support safely.

2. Remove the wheel. Remove the brake caliper from the adaptor and remove the adaptor. Remove the brake disc.

3. Remove the halfshaft.

NOTE: Knuckle removal is not necessary for bearing and hub replacement.

4. Disconnect the tie rod from the knuckle.

5. Matchmark the lower strut mount to the knuckle. Remove the 2 strut clamp bolts and remove the knuckle from the vehicle.

6. Attach the hub removal tool C–4811 or equivalent, and the triangular adapter, to the 3 rear threaded holes of the steering knuckle housing with the thrust button inside the hub bore.

7. Tighten the bolt in the center of the tool, to press the hub from the steering knuckle. Remove the removal tools.

8. Remove the bolts and bearing retainer from the outside of the steering knuckle.

9. Carefully pry the bearing seal from the machined recess of the steering knuckle and clean the recess.

10. Insert the tool C–4811 or equivalent, through the hub bearing and install bearing removal adapter to the outside of the steering knuckle. Tighten the tool to press the hub bearing from the steering knuckle. Discard the bearing and the seal.

To install:

11. Use tool C–4811 or equivalent, and the bearing installation adapter to press in the hub bearing into the steering knuckle.

12. Install a new seal, the bearing retainer and the bolts to the steering knuckle. Torque the bearing retainer bolts to 20 ft. lbs.

13. Use the tool C–4811 or equivalent, and the hub installation adapter, to press the hub into the hub bearing.

14. Using the bearing installation tool C–4698 or equivalent, drive the new dust seal into the rear of the steering the hub and bearing from the knuckle, as required.

15. The installation of the knuckle and halfshaft is the reverse of the removal procedure. Torque the tie rod nut to 35 ft. lbs. (47 Nm).

16. Align the front end.

Bolt In (One-Piece Hub and Bearing)

NOTE: Knuckle removal is not necessary for bearing and hub replacement.

1. Raise the vehicle and support safely.

2. Remove the wheel. Remove the brake caliper from the adaptor and remove the adaptor. Remove the brake disc.

3. Remove the halfshaft.

4. Disconnect the tie rod from the knuckle.

5. Matchmark the lower strut mount to the knuckle. Remove the 2 strut clamp bolts and remove the knuckle from the vehicle.

6. Remove the 4 hub and bearing assembly mounting bolts from the rear of the knuckle and remove the assembly from the knuckle.

7. Carefully pry the bearing seal from the machined recess of the steering knuckle and clean the recess.

8. Thoroughly clean and dry the knuckle and bearing mating surfaces and the seal installation area.

To install:

9. Install the hub and bearing assembly to the knuckle and torque the bolts in a criss-cross pattern to 45 ft. lbs. (65 Nm).

10. Install a new seal and wear sleeve. Lubricate the circumferences of the seal and sleeve liberally with grease.

11. The installation of the knuckle and halfshaft is the reverse of the removal procedure. Torque the tie rod nut to 35 ft. lbs. (47 Nm).

12. Align the front end.

Differential Case

REMOVAL & INSTALLATION

NOTE: The differential case can be removed from some vehicles with the transaxle installed. To do so, remove the halfshafts, remove the 2 K-frame mounting nuts and 2 bolts and lower the K-frame to provide enough room to pull the differential case out of its housing and over the lowered frame.

1. Disconnect the negative battery cable. Raise the vehicle and support safely.

2. Remove the right side extension housing. Remove the differential cover.

3. Remove the bolts and remove the right side differential bearing retainer using tool L-4435, or equivalent.

4. Remove the differential case from the transaxle.

5. Use new seals and gasket material when assembling.

6. The installation is the reverse of the removal procedure. Torque the extension housing and bearing retainer bolts to 21 ft. lbs. (28 Nm).

7. Fill the transaxle with the proper oil.

STEERING

Steering Wheel
CAUTION

On vehicles equipped with an air bag, the negative battery cable must be disconnected, before working on the system. Failure to do so may result in deployment of the air bag and possible personal injury.

REMOVAL & INSTALLATION

Without Air Bag

1. Disconnect the negative battery cable.

2. Straighten the steering wheel so the front tires are pointing straight forward.

2. Remove the horn pad.

3. Remove the steering wheel hold-down nut. Matchmark the steering wheel to the shaft.

4. Using a suitable steering wheel

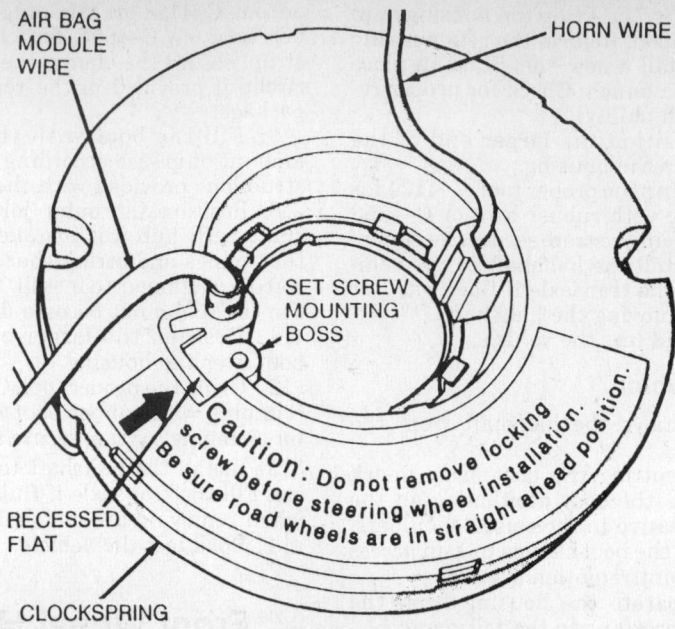

Air bag clockspring assembly

puller, pull the steering wheel off of the shaft.

5. The installation is the reverse of the removal procedure. Torque the hold-down nut to 45 ft. lbs. (60 Nm).

With Air Bag

1. Disconnect the negative battery cable.

2. Straighten the steering wheel so the front tires are pointing straight forward.

3. Remove the 4 nuts located on the back side of the steering wheel that attach the air bag module to the steering wheel.

4. Lift the module and disconnect the connectors. Remove the speed control switch, if equipped.

NOTE: The column should be equipped with a clockspring set screw held by a plastic tether on the steering wheel. If the steering column is lacking the set screw, obtain one before proceeding.

5. Place the set screw in the clockspring to ensure proper positioning when the steering wheel is removed.

6. Remove the steering wheel hold-down nut. Matchmark the steering wheel to the shaft.

7. Using a suitable steering wheel puller, pull the steering wheel off of the shaft.

To install:

8. Position the steering wheel on the steering column. Make sure the flats on the hub of the steering wheel are aligned with the formations on the clockspring.

9. Pull the air bag and speed control connectors through the lower, larger hole in the steering wheel and pull the horn wire through the smaller hole at the top. Make sure the wires are not pinched anywhere.

10. Install the hold-down nut and torque to 45 ft. lbs. (60 nm).

11. Remove the clockspring set screw and place it in its storage location on the steering wheel.

12. Connect the horn wire.

13. Connect the speed control wire and install the speed control switch, if equipped.

14. Connect the clockspring lead wire to the air bag module and install module to steering wheel.

NOTE: Do not allow anyone to enter the vehicle from this point on, until this procedure is completed.

15. Connect the DRB-II to the Airbag System Diagnostic Module (ASDM) connector located to the right of the console.

16. From the passenger side of the vehicle, turn the key to the ON position.

17. Check to make sure nobody has entered the vehicle. Connect the negative battery cable.

18. Using the DRB-II, read and record any active fault data or stored codes.

19. If any active fault codes are present, perform the proper diagnostic procedures before continuing.

20. If there are no active fault codes, erase the stored fault codes. If there

are active codes, the stored codes will not erase.

21. From the passenger side of the vehicle, turn the key **OFF**, then **ON** and observe the instrument cluster air bag warning light. It should come ON for 6–8 seconds, then go out, indicating the system is functioning normally. If the warning light either fails to come ON or stays lit, there is a system malfunction and the proper diagnostic procedures should be performed.

Steering Column

REMOVAL & INSTALLATION

1. Disconnect the negative battery cable.
2. Remove trim bezel, steering column cover and lower reinforcement, as required.
3. Disconnect all wiring connectors from below the instrument panel that lead up into the steering column.
4. Matchmark and remove the nuts that attach the steering column assembly to the instrument panel support.

NOTE: On 1987–89 vehicles, the upper coupling can be slipped out of the lower coupling without removing the roll pin. On 1990 vehicles, the stub shaft is separated from the steering gear coupling.

5. Firmly grasp the steering wheel and pull the steering column out.
6. The installation is the reverse of the removal procedure.
7. Connect the negative battery cable and check the steering column and all related components for proper operation.

Manual Rack and Pinion

REMOVAL & INSTALLATION

1. Disconnect the negative battery cable. On 1987–89 vehicles, drive out the upper roll pin, under the instrument panel, attaching the pinion shaft to the upper universal joint. Use a back-up device to steady the universal joint to prevent from damaging it.
2. Raise the vehicle and support safely.
3. Remove the front wheels.
4. Remove the cotter pins, castellated nuts and tie rod ends from the steering knuckles.
5. Remove the front suspension crossmember attaching bolts and nuts.
6. Lower the crossmember.
7. Remove the tie rod inner boot shields.

8. Remove the steering gear bolts from the front suspension crossmember.
9. Lower the rack to disengage it from the steering column stub shaft. Remove the steering gear from the left side of the vehicle.
To install:
10. Transfer the required parts to the new rack, if replacing it.
11. Place the rack on the crossmember and torque the steering gear attaching bolts to 21 ft. lbs. (29 Nm). Attach the boot shields.
12. Have a helper inside the vehicle remove the trim boot and align the stub shaft with the coupling while the crossmember is raised into position. If a helper is not available, the steering column will have to be unbolted so the steering shaft can be inserted into the coupling. Install the roll pin, if equipped.
13. The right rear crossmember bolt is a pilot bolt that correctly locates the crossmember; tighten it first. Torque the crossmember bolts to 90 ft. lbs.
14. Install the tie rod ends to the steering knuckle and torque the nut to 45 ft. lbs. (61 Nm). Install a new cotter pin.
15. Insert the stub shaft shim where the stub shaft goes into the coupling, if equipped.
16. Connect the negative battery cable and check the gear for proper operation.

Power Rack and Pinion Steering

REMOVAL & INSTALLATION

1. Disconnect the negative battery cable. On 1987–89 vehicles, drive out the upper roll pin, under the instrument panel, attaching the pinion shaft to the upper universal joint. Use a back-up device to steady the universal joint to prevent from damaging it.
2. Raise the vehicle and support safely.
3. Remove the front wheels.
4. Remove the cotter pins, castellated nuts and tie rod ends from the steering knuckles.
5. Disconnect and plug the oil pressure line from the rack.
6. Disconnect and plug the return hose from the line coming from the rack.
7. Remove the front suspension crossmember attaching bolts and nuts.
8. Lower the crossmember.
9. Remove the tie rod inner boot shields.
10. Remove the steering gear bolts

from the front suspension crossmember.
11. Lower the rack to disengage it from the steering column stub shaft. Remove the steering gear from the left side of the vehicle.
To install:
12. Transfer the required parts to the new rack, if replacing it.
13. Place the rack on the crossmember and torque the steering gear attaching bolts to 21 ft. lbs. (29 Nm). Attach the fluid lines and the boot shields.
14. Have a helper inside the vehicle remove the trim boot and align the stub shaft with the coupling while the crossmember is raised into position. If a helper is not available, the steering column will have to be unbolted so the steering shaft can be inserted into the coupling. Install the roll pin, if equipped.
15. Install the tie rod ends to the steering knuckle and torque the nut to 45 ft. lbs. (61 Nm). Install a new cotter pin.
16. Insert the stub shaft shim where the stub shaft goes into the coupling, if equipped.
17. Refill the power steering pump.
18. Connect the negative battery cable and check the gear for proper operation.

Power Steering Pump

REMOVAL & INSTALLATION

1. Disconnect the negative battery cable.
2. Remove the drive belt from the pulley and remove bolts that are accessible from above.
3. Raise the vehicle and safely support.
4. Remove the right front wheel and the splash shield.
5. Position a drain pan under the return hose and disconnect the return hose from the line coming from the steering rack. Allow the fluid to drain, then plug the hose.
6. Disconnect the pressure line from the pump.
7. Remove the lower mounting bolts and nuts.
8. Move the pump toward the firewall and remove the adjustment bracket.
9. Rotate the pump clockwise so the pump pulley faces the rear of the vehicle and pull the pump out of the engine compartment.
To install:
10. Position the pump and install the adjustment bracket.
11. Raise the vehicle and install the lower mounting bolts and nuts finger-tight.

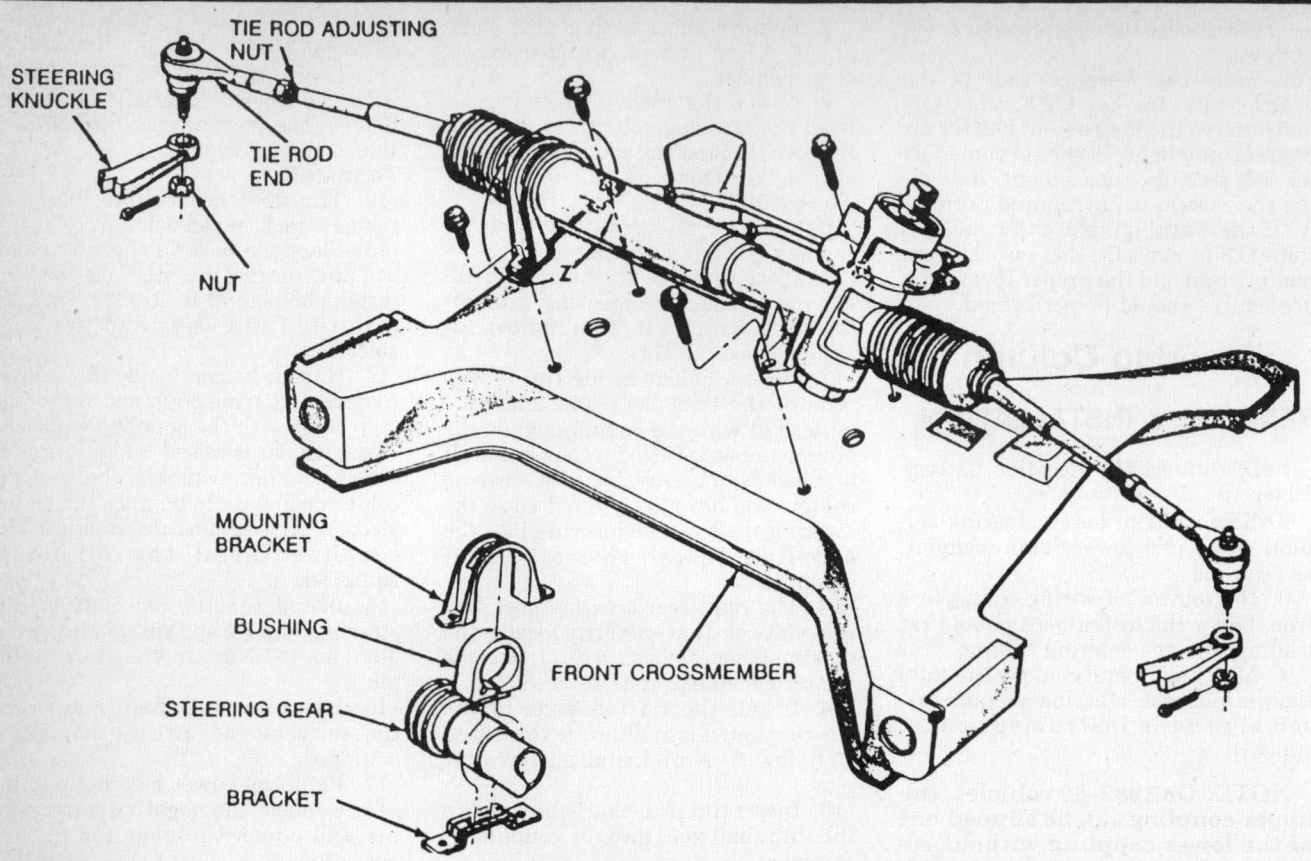

STEERING KNUCKLE

TIE ROD ADJUSTING NUT

TIE ROD END

NUT

MOUNTING BRACKET

BUSHING

STEERING GEAR

BRACKET

FRONT CROSSMEMBER

Rack and pinion steering gear mounting

12. Replace the O-rings on the pressure line and connect to the pump. Install the return hose and secure the clamps.

13. Wrap the drive belt around the pulley groove and adjust the belt tension. Tighten the mounting bolts to 30 ft. lbs. (41 Nm).

14. Install the splash shield.

15. Turn the wheels to the full left turn position and add fluid until the reservoir is full.

16. Start the engine and add fluid to bring the level to the correct level.

17. To purge the system of air, turn the steering wheel from side to side without contacting the stops.

18. Return the wheel to the straight ahead position and operate the engine for 2 minutes before road testing.

BELT ADJUSTMENT

1. Loosen the bracket mounting bolts.

2. Use a ½ in. drive breaker bar in the square hole provided in the bracket to move the pump away from the engine. Do not pry against the fluid reservoir.

3. With the pump moved enough so the belt deflects about ¼–½ in. under a 10 lb. load, tighten the bolts.

SYSTEM BLEEDING

1. Fill the reservoir with power steering fluid.

2. Turn the wheels to the full left turn position and add fluid until the reservoir is full.

3. Start the engine and add fluid to bring the level to the correct level.

4. To purge the system of air, turn the steering wheel from side to side without contacting the stops.

5. Return the wheel to the straight ahead position and operate the engine for 2 minutes before road testing.

Tie Rod Ends

REMOVAL & INSTALLATION

1. Raise the vehicle and support safely.

2. Remove the cotter pin and nut from the tie rod end.

3. Using a suitable puller, remove the tie rod from the steering knuckle.

4. Loosen the sleeve clamp nut and bolt, if equipped and unscrew the tie rod end from the sleeve or inner tie rod.

5. The installation is the reverse of the removal procedure. Torque the

stud nuts to 45 ft. lbs. (61 Nm) and install a new cotter pin.

6. Perform a front end alignment as required.

BRAKES

For all brake system repair and service procedures not detailed below, please refer to "Brakes" in the Unit Repair section.

Master Cylinder

REMOVAL & INSTALLATION

1. Disconnect the negative battery cable.

2. Disconnect and plug the brake lines from the master cylinder.

3. Remove the nuts attaching the master cylinder to the power booster.

4. Remove the master cylinder from the mounting studs.

5. Remove the fluid reservoir from the cylinder.

To install:

6. Bench bleed the master cylinder.

7. Install to the studs and install the nuts.

8. Install the brake lines to the master cylinder.

9. Connect the negative battery cable and check the brakes for proper operation.

Combination Valve

REMOVAL & INSTALLATION

1. Disconnect the negative battery cable.

2. Raise the vehicle and support safely.

3. Tag and disconnect the brake lines from the valve.

4. Disconnect the wires to the pressure switch.

5. Remove the combination valve from the frame bracket.

6. The installation is the reverse of the removal procedure.

7. Bleed the brakes in the following order:
   a. Right rear wheel cylinder
   b. Left rear wheel cylinder
   c. Right front caliper
   d. Left front caliper

8. Connect the negative battery cable and check the brakes for proper operation.

Power Brake Booster

REMOVAL & INSTALLATION

1. Disconnect the negative battery cable. Disconnect the vacuum hose(s) from the booster.

2. Remove the nuts attaching the master cylinder to the booster and move the master cylinder to the side.

3. From inside the passenger compartment, remove the clip that secures the booster pushrod to the brake pedal.

4. Remove the nuts that attach the booster to the dash panel and remove it from the vehicle.

5. Transfer the check valve to the new booster.

6. The installation is the reverse of the removal procedure.

7. Connect the negative battery cable and check the booster and brakes for proper operation.

Brake Caliper

REMOVAL & INSTALLATION

1. Raise the vehicle and support safely.

2. Remove the tire and wheel assembly.

3. Remove the caliper mounting pin.

4. Lift the caliper off of the pads, which should stay on the adaptor.

5. Remove the brake hose retaining bolt from the caliper.

To install:

6. Install the brake hose to the caliper using new copper washers.

7. Position the caliper over the rotor so the caliper engages the adaptor and pads correctly.

8. Install the caliper mounting pin.

9. Fill the master cylinder and bleed the brakes.

Disc Brake Pads

REMOVAL & INSTALLATION

1. Remove some of the fluid from the master cylinder.

2. Remove the wheels.

3. Remove the caliper and suspend securely.

4. Remove the inner and outer pads from the adaptor.

To install:

5. Use a large C-clamp to compress the piston back into the caliper bore.

6. Transfer the anti-rattle clips to the new brake pads, if necessary. Install the pads to the adaptor.

7. Position the caliper over the pads so the caliper engages the adaptor correctly.

8. Install the caliper mounting pin.

9. Refill the master cylinder.

Brake Rotor

REMOVAL & INSTALLATION

1. Raise the vehicle and support safely. Remove the tire and wheel assembly.

2. Remove the caliper and outer brake pad.

3. Remove the factory installed clips, if equipped. It is not necessary to reinstall these clips.

4. Remove the rotor from the hub.

5. The installation is the reverse of the removal procedure.

Brake Drums

REMOVAL & INSTALLATION

1. Raise the vehicle and support safely.

2. Remove the wheel and tire assembly.

3. Remove the dust cap.

4. Remove the cotter pin and nut lock.

5. Remove the wheel bearing nut and washer from the spindle.

6. Remove the outer wheel bearing.

7. Remove the drum with the inner wheel bearing from the spindle. If the drum is difficult to remove, remove the plug from the rear of the backing plate and push the self adjuster lever away from the star wheel. Rotate the star wheel to retract the shoes. Remove the grease seal.

To install:

8. Lubricate and install the inner wheel bearing. Install a new grease seal.

9. Install the drum to the spindle.

10. Lubricate and install the outer wheel bearing, washer and nut. When the bearing preload is properly set, install the nut lock and a new cotter pin.

11. Install the grease cap.

12. Install the wheel and tire assembly. Adjust the rear brakes as required.

Brake Shoes

REMOVAL & INSTALLATION

1. Raise the vehicle and support safely. Remove the wheels and the drums.

2. Remove the automatic adjuster spring and lever.

3. Rotate the automatic adjuster star wheel enough so both shoes move out far enough to be free of the wheel cylinder boots.

4. Disconnect the parking brake cable from the actuating lever.

5. Remove the lower shoe to shoe spring.

6. With the shoes held together by the upper shoe to shoe spring, remove them from the backing plate.

To install:

7. Thoroughly clean and dry the backing plate. To prepare the backing plate, lubricate the bosses, anchor pin and parking brake actuating lever pivot surface lightly with lithium based grease.

8. Remove, clean and dry all parts still on the old shoes. Lubricate the star wheel shaft threads with anti-sieze lubricant and transfer all parts to their proper locations on the new shoes.

9. Install the lower spring.

10. Connect the parking brake cable.

11. Install the automatic adjuster lever and spring.

12. Adjust the star wheel.

13. Remove any grease from the linings and install the drum.

14. Complete the brake adjustment with the wheels installed.

Wheel Cylinder

REMOVAL & INSTALLATION

1. Raise the vehicle and support safely.

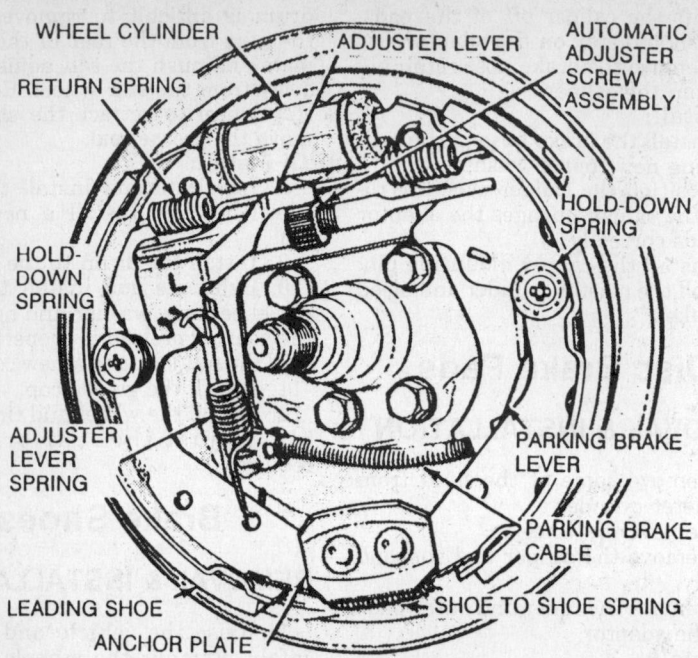

WHEEL CYLINDER
RETURN SPRING
ADJUSTER LEVER
AUTOMATIC ADJUSTER SCREW ASSEMBLY
HOLD-DOWN SPRING
HOLD-DOWN SPRING
ADJUSTER LEVER SPRING
PARKING BRAKE LEVER
PARKING BRAKE CABLE
LEADING SHOE
ANCHOR PLATE
SHOE TO SHOE SPRING

Rear drum brake components

2. Remove the wheel, drum and brake shoes.

3. Remove and plug the brake line from the wheel cylinder.

4. Remove the wheel cylinder bolts and remove the cylinder from the backing plate.

To install:

5. Apply a very thin coating of silicone sealer to the cylinder mounting surface, install the cylinder to the backing plate and install the retaining bolts.

6. Connect the brake line to the wheel cylinder.

7. Install all brake parts that were removed.

8. Install the tire and wheel assembly.

9. Bleed the rear brakes.

Parking Brake Cable

ADJUSTMENT

1. Release the parking brakes fully.

2. Raise the vehicle and support safely.

3. Adjust the rear brakes.

4. Loosen the adjusting nut until there is slack in all the cables.

5. Rotate the rear wheels and tighten the cable adjusting nut until there is a slight drag at the wheels.

6. Continue to rotate the rear wheels and loosen the nut until all drag is eliminated.

7. Back off the nut an additional 2 turns.

8. Apply and release the parking brake several times. Upon the least re-

lease, verify there is no drag at the wheels.

9. To check the operation, make sure the parking brake holds on an incline.

REMOVAL & INSTALLATION

Front Cable

1. Disconnect the negative battery cable.

2. Raise the vehicle and support safely.

3. Remove the cable adjusting nut and disengage the front cable from the connectors.

4. Loosen the heat shield for access and remove the cable housing to floor pan bracket and clips.

5. Remove the brake lever housing inside the passenger compartment and lift the floor mat for access to the floor pan. Pull the cable end forward and disconnect from the clevis.

6. Remove the floor seal panel.

7. Compress the cable housing retainer and push the cable out from the floor pan and remove from the vehicle.

To install:

8. Insert the cable housing retainer into the hole in the floor pan and install the seal panel.

9. Push the cable through the hole and engage the cable end to the clevis. Force the cable end retainer into the retainer until it is firmly seated.

10. Install the floor mat and brake lever housing.

11. Install the cable housing bracket and clips and install the heat shield.

12. Slide the adjuster end through the connectors and install the adjusting nut.

13. Adjust the cable, connect the negative battery cable and check the parking brakes for proper operation.

Rear Cable

1. Disconnect the negative battery cable.

2. Raise the vehicle and support safely.

3. Remove the rear wheels.

4. Remove the retaining clip from the brake cable bracket.

5. Remove the drums. Disconnect the cable from the brake shoe lever.

6. Compress the retaining clips on the end of the cable housing and pull the cable from the backing plate.

7. Remove the brake support plate from the axle.

8. The installation is the reverse of the removal procedure.

9. Adjust the cables, connect the negative battery cable and check the parking brakes for proper operation.

Brake System Bleeding

NOTE: If using a pressure bleeder, follow the instructions furnished with the unit and choose the correct adaptor for the application. Do not substitute an adapter that "almost fits" as it will not work and could be dangerous.

Master Cylinder

If the master cylinder is off the vehicle it can be bench bled.

1. Connect 2 short pieces of brake line to the outlet fittings, bend them until the free end is below the fluid level in the master cylinder reservoirs.

2. Fill the reservoir with fresh brake fluid. Pump the piston slowly until no more air bubbles appear in the reservoirs.

3. Disconnect the 2 short lines, refill the master cylinder and securely install the cylinder caps.

4. If the master cylinder is on the vehicle, it can still be bled, using a flare nut wrench.

5. Open the brake lines slightly with the flare nut wrench while pressure is applied to the brake pedal by a helper inside the vehicle.

6. Be sure to tighten the line before the brake pedal is released.

7. Repeat the process with both lines until no air bubbles come out.

Calipers and Wheel Cylinders

1. Fill the master cylinder with

fresh brake fluid. Check the level often during the procedure.

2. Starting with the right rear wheel, remove the protective cap from the bleeder, if equipped and place where it will not be lost. Clean the bleed screw.

———— **CAUTION** ————

When bleeding the brakes, keep face away from the brake area. Spewing fluid may cause facial and/or visual damage. Do not allow brake fluid to spill on the car's finish; it will remove the paint.

3. If the system is empty, the most effecient way to get fluid down to the wheel is to loosen the bleeder about ½-¾ turn, place a finger firmly over the bleeder and have a helper pump the brakes slowly until fluid comes out the bleeder. Once fluid is at the bleeder, close it before the pedal is released inside the vehicle.

NOTE: If the pedal is pumped rapidly, the fluid will churn and create small air bubbles, which are almost impossible to remove from the system. These air bubbles will eventually congregate and a spongy pedal will result.

4. Once fluid has been pumped to the caliper or wheel cylinder, open the bleed screw again, have the helper press the brake pedal to the floor, lock the bleeder and have the helper slowly release the pedal. Wait 15 seconds and repeat the procedure (including the 15 second wait) until no more air comes out of the bleeder upon application of the brake pedal. Remember to close the bleeder before the pedal is released inside the vehicle each time the bleeder is opened. If not, air will be induced into the system.

5. If a helper is not available, connect a small hose to the bleeder, place the end in a container of brake fluid and proceed to pump the pedal from inside the vehicle until no more air comes out the bleeder. The hose will prevent air from entering the system.

6. Repeat the procedure on remaining wheel cylinders in order:
   a. left rear
   b. right front
   c. left front

7. Hydraulic brake systems must be totally flushed if the fluid becomes contaminated with water, dirt or other corrosive chemicals. To flush, bleed the entire system until all fluid has been replaced with the correct type of new fluid.

8. Install the bleeder cap(s) on the bleeder to keep dirt out. Always road test the vehicle after brake work of any kind is done.

FRONT SUSPENSION

MacPherson Strut
REMOVAL & INSTALLATION

1. Remove the 3 mounting nuts from the strut tower under the hood.
2. Raise the vehicle and support safely.
3. Remove the brake hose bracket screw from the strut.
4. Matchmark the lower strut mount to the knuckle and remove the strut to knuckle bolts, nuts and nut plate.
5. The installation is the reverse of the removal procedure. Torque the upper mounting nuts to 20 ft. lbs. (27 Nm). Do not tighten the lower mounting bolts until the front end alignment has been completed.
6. Perform a front end alignment. Torque the strut to knuckle nuts to 75 ft. lbs. (100 Nm) plus ¼ turn.

Lower Ball Joints

INSPECTION
To inspect the ball joints, grasp the

grease fitting by hand with the vehicle on the ground. If the grease fitting can be moved at all by hand, the ball joint should be replaced.

REMOVAL & INSTALLATION

The ball joints are welded to the lower control arms, necessitating replacement of the control arm assembly. Do not attempt to replace ball joints that are welded to the control arm; replacement control arms are equipped with a new ball joint.

Lower Control Arms

REMOVAL & INSTALLATION

1. Raise the vehicle and support safely. Remove the tire and wheel assembly.
2. Remove the sway bar.
3. Remove the ball joint stud retaining bolt and nut.
4. Pry the lower control arm from the steering knuckle.
5. Remove the control arm to crossmember bolts, nuts bushings and retainers.
6. Remove the control arm from the vehicle.
7. Transfer all reusable parts to the new control arm and lubricate.

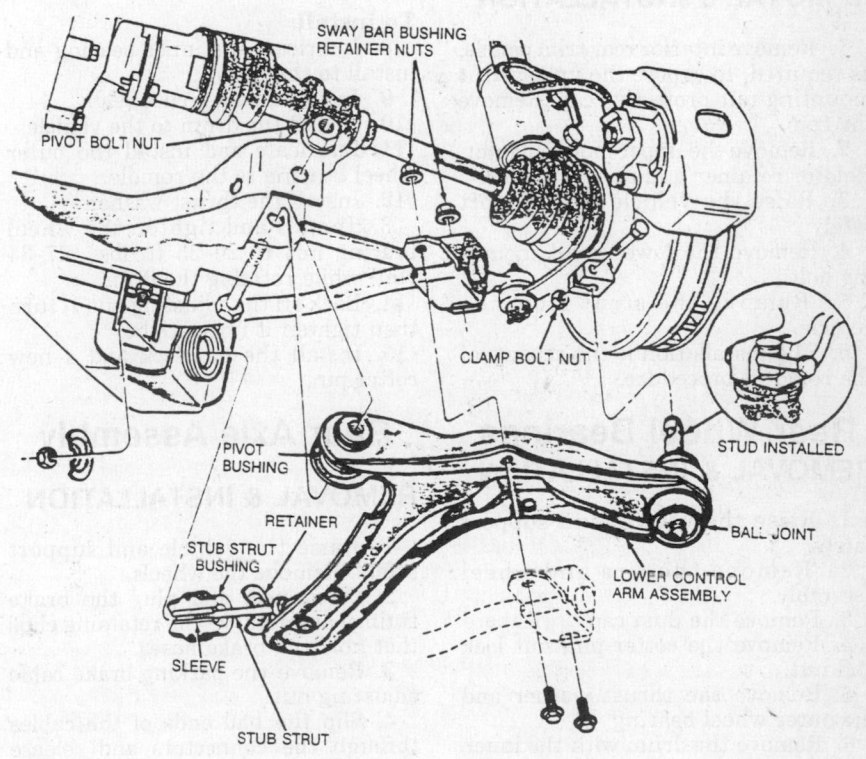

Lower control arm and related parts

8. The installation is the reverse of the removal procedure.

9. Lower the vehicle so it's full weight is on the ground.

10. Torque the pivot bolt to 120 ft. lbs. (163 Nm) and the stub strut nut to 70 ft. lbs. (95 Nm).

11. Perform a front end alignment, as required.

Sway Bar

REMOVAL & INSTALLATION

1. Raise the vehicle and support safely.

2. Remove the front sway bar brackets and retainers.

3. Remove the sway bar support brackets and bushings from the lower control arm. Remove the sway bar from the vehicle.

4. The installation is the reverse of the removal procedure. Lubricate the sway bar bushings liberally with grease before assembling.

REAR SUSPENSION

MacPherson Strut

REMOVAL & INSTALLATION

1. Remove interior rear trim panels, as required, to expose the upper strut mounting nut protective cap. Remove the cap.

2. Remove the upper mounting nut, isolator retainer and upper isolator.

3. Raise the vehicle and support safely.

4. Remove the lower strut mounting bolt.

5. Remove the strut from the vehicle.

6. The installation is the reverse of the removal procedure.

Rear Wheel Bearings
REMOVAL & INSTALLATION

1. Raise the vehicle and support safely.

2. Remove the tire and wheel assembly.

3. Remove the dust cap.

4. Remove the cotter pin, nut lock and nut.

5. Remove the thrust washer and the outer wheel bearing.

6. Remove the drum with the inner wheel bearing and the grease seal.

7. Remove the grease seal and remove the inner bearing.

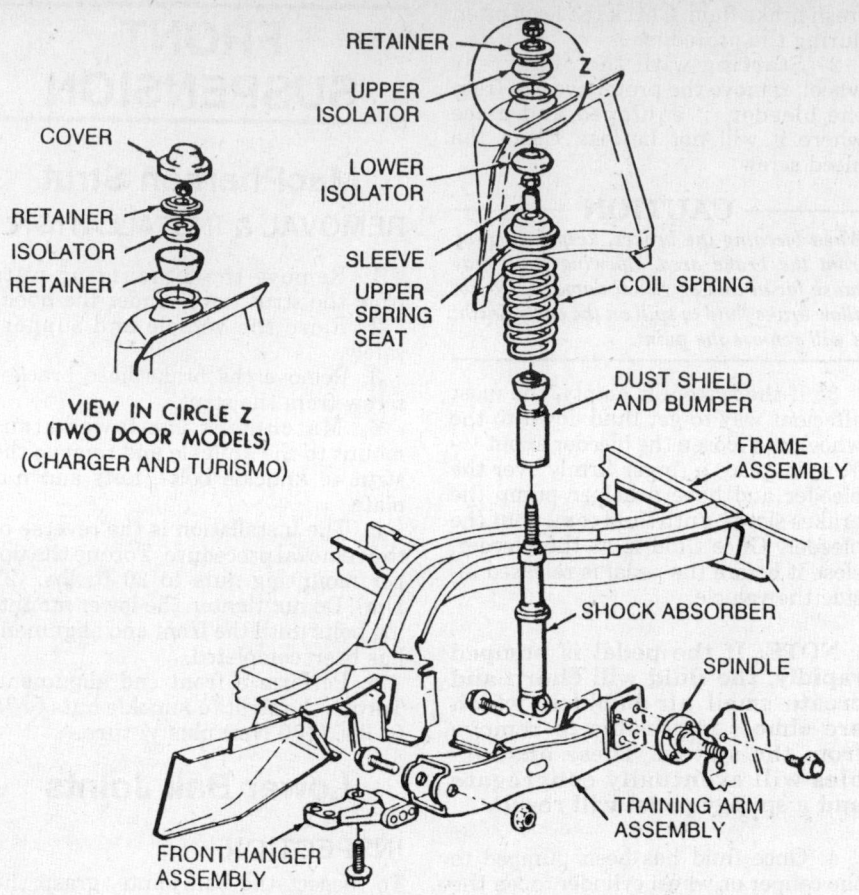

VIEW IN CIRCLE Z
(TWO DOOR MODELS)
(CHARGER AND TURISMO)

Rear suspension components

To install:

8. Lubricate the inner bearing and install to the drum.

9. Install a new grease seal.

10. Install the drum to the vehicle.

11. Lubricate and install the outer wheel bearing to the spindle.

12. Install the thrust washer.

13. Install and tighten the wheel bearing nut to 20–25 ft. lbs. (27–34 Nm) while rotating the drum.

14. Back off the adjusting nut ¼ turn then tighten it finger-tight.

15. Install the nut lock and a new cotter pin.

Rear Axle Assembly

REMOVAL & INSTALLATION

1. Raise the vehicle and support safely. Remove the wheels.

2. Disconnect and plug the brake fittings and remove the retaining clips that hold the brake hoses.

3. Remove the parking brake cable adjusting nut.

4. Slip the ball ends of the cables through the connectors and release both parking cables from their brackets. Pull the cable through the brackets.

5. Using the proper equipment, safely support the weight of the rear axle assembly at 2 points.

6. Remove the strut lower mounting bolts.

7. Remove the trailing arm to hanger bracket mounting bolts.

8. Lower the axle assembly and remove from the vehicle.

To install:

9. Raise the assembly into position under the vehicle.

10. Install the trailing arm to hanger mounting bracket loosely.

11. Feed the parking brake cable through the bracket and slip the ball end through the brake connectors on the cable bracket. Install both retaining clips.

12. Install the parking brake adjusting nut and tighten until all slack is removed from the cabels.

13. Install the wheels and lower the vehicle so that all of its weight is on the ground.

14. With the vehicle on the ground, torque the trailing arm to hanger bracket mounting bolts and the lower strut mounting bolts to 40 ft. lbs. (55 Nm).

15. Raise the vehicle and bleed the brakes. Adjust the parking brakes.

Chrysler Corp.
Rear Wheel Drive
Chrysler—Fifth Avenue, Newport
Dodge—Diplomat
Plymouth—Caravelle, Grand Fury

SPECIFICATIONS

VEHICLE IDENTIFICATION CHART

It is important for servicing and ordering parts to be certain of the vehicle and engine identification. The VIN (vehicle identification number) is a 17 digit number visible through the windshield on the driver's side of the dash and contains the vehicle and engine identification codes. The tenth digit indicates model year, and the eighth digit indicates engine code. It can be interpreted as follows:

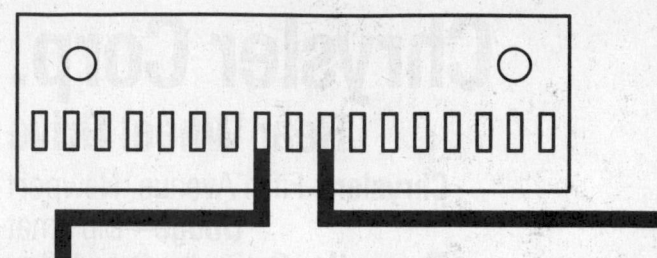

	Engine Code						Model Year	
Code	Cu. In.	Liters	Cyl.	Fuel Sys.	Eng. Mfg.		Code	Year
P	318	5.2	8	2 bbl	Chrysler		H	1987
R	318	5.2	8	4 bbl	Chrysler		J	1988
S	318 HD	5.2	8	4 bbl	Chrysler		K	1989
4	318	5.2	8	4 bbl	Chrysler			

ENGINE IDENTIFICATION

Year	Model	Engine Displacement cu. in. (liter)	Engine Series Identification (VIN)	No. of Cylinders	Engine Type
1987	Diplomat	318 (5.2)	P ③	8	OHV
	Grand Fury/Caravelle ①	318 (5.2)	P ③	8	OHV
	Grand Fury/Caravelle ①	318 (5.2)	R ④	8	OHV
	Grand Fury/Caravelle ①	318 (5.2)	S ②	8	OHV
	Fifth Avenue/Newport	318 (5.2)	P ③	8	OHV
	Fifth Avenue/Newport	318 (5.2)	R ④	8	OHV
	Fifth Avenue/Newport	318 (5.2)	S ②	8	OHV
1988	Diplomat	318 (5.2)	P ③	8	OHV
	Grand Fury/Caravelle ①	318 (5.2)	P ③	8	OHV
	Grand Fury/Caravelle ①	318 (5.2)	4 ④	8	OHV
	Grand Fury/Caravelle ①	318 (5.2)	S ②	8	OHV
	Fifth Avenue/Newport	318 (5.2)	P ③	8	OHV
	Fifth Avenue/Newport	318 (5.2)	4 ④	8	OHV
	Fifth Avenue/Newport	318 (5.2)	S ②	8	OHV
1989	Diplomat	318 (5.2)	P ③	8	OHV
	Grand Fury/Caravelle ①	318 (5.2)	P ③	8	OHV
	Grand Fury/Caravelle ①	318 (5.2)	4 ④	8	OHV
	Grand Fury/Caravelle ①	318 (5.2)	S ②	8	OHV
	Fifth Avenue/Newport	318 (5.2)	P ③	8	OHV
	Fifth Avenue/Newport	318 (5.2)	4 ④	8	OHV
	Fifth Avenue/Newport	318 (5.2)	S ②	8	OHV

① Caravelle—Canada
② 318 4 bbl Heavy Duty
③ 318 2 bbl
④ 318 4 bbl Standard

GENERAL ENGINE SPECIFICATIONS

Year	VIN	No. Cylinder Displacement cu. in. (liter)	Fuel System Type	Net Horsepower @ rpm	Net Torque @ rpm (ft. lbs.)	Bore × Stroke (in.)	Compression Ratio	Oil Pressure @ rpm
1987	P	8-318 (5.2)	2 bbl	140 @ 3600	265 @ 1600	3.910 × 3.310	9.0:1	80 @ 3000
	R	8-318 (5.2)	4 bbl	165 @ 4000	240 @ 2000	3.910 × 3.310	8.6:1	80 @ 3000
	S	8-318 (5.2)HD	4 bbl	175 @ 4000	250 @ 3200	3.910 × 3.310	8.0:1	80 @ 3000
1988	P	8-318 (5.2)	2 bbl	140 @ 3600	265 @ 1600	3.910 × 3.310	9.0:1	80 @ 3000
	4	8-318 (5.2)	4 bbl	165 @ 4000	240 @ 2000	3.910 × 3.310	8.6:1	80 @ 3000
	S	8-318 (5.2)HD	4 bbl	175 @ 4000	250 @ 3200	3.910 × 3.310	8.0:1	80 @ 3000
1989	P	8-318 (5.2)	2 bbl	140 @ 3600	265 @ 1600	3.910 × 3.310	9.0:1	80 @ 3000
	4	8-318 (5.2)	4 bbl	140 @ 3600	265 @ 2000	3.910 × 3.310	9.0:1	80 @ 3000
	S	8-318 (5.2)HD	4 bbl	175 @ 4000	250 @ 3200	3.910 × 3.310	8.0:1	80 @ 3000

HD Heavy Duty

TUNE-UP SPECIFICATIONS

Year	VIN	No. Cylinder Displacement cu. in. (liter)	Spark Plugs Type	Spark Plugs Gap (in.)	Ignition Timing (deg.) MT	Ignition Timing (deg.) AT	Compression Pressure (psi)	Fuel Pump (psi)	Idle Speed (rpm) MT	Idle Speed (rpm) AT	Valve Clearance In.	Valve Clearance Ex.
1987	P	8-318 (5.2)	RN12YC	0.035	—	7B	100	5.75–7.25	—	680	Hyd.	Hyd.
	R	8-318 (5.2)	RN12YC	0.035	—	16B	100	5.75–7.25	—	750	Hyd.	Hyd.
	S	8-318 (5.2)	RN12YC	0.035	—	16B	100	5.75–7.25	—	750	Hyd.	Hyd.
1988	P	8-318 (5.2)	RN12YC	0.035	—	7B	100	5.75–7.25	—	680	Hyd.	Hyd.
	4	8-318 (5.2)	RN12YC	0.035	—	16B	100	5.75–7.25	—	750	Hyd.	Hyd.
	S	8-318 (5.2)	RN12YC	0.035	—	16B	100	5.75–7.25	—	750	Hyd.	Hyd.
1989	P	8-318 (5.2)	RN12YC	0.035	—	7B	100	5.75–7.25	—	680	Hyd.	Hyd.
	4	8-318 (5.2)	RN12YC	0.035	—	16B	100	5.75–7.25	—	750	Hyd.	Hyd.
	S	8-318 (5.2)	RN12YC	0.035	—	16B	100	5.75–7.25	—	750	Hyd.	Hyd.

FIRING ORDERS

NOTE: To avoid confusion, always replace spark plug wires one at a time.

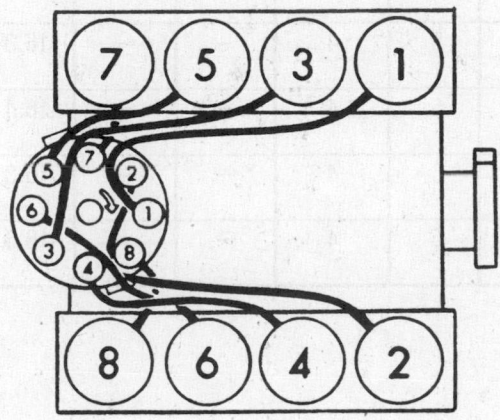

5.2L V8 Engine
Engine Firing Order: 1–8–4–3–6–5–7–2
Distributor Rotation: Clockwise

CAPACITIES

Year	Model	VIN	No. Cylinder Displacement cu. in. (liter)	Engine Crankcase with Filter	Engine Crankcase without Filter	Transmission (pts.) 4-Spd	Transmission (pts.) 5-Spd	Transmission (pts.) Auto.	Drive Axle (pts.)	Fuel Tank (gals.)	Cooling System (qts.)
1987	Diplomat	P	8-318 (5.2)	5	4	—	—	16.4	②	18	15.5 ③
	Grand Fury/ Caravelle ①	P	8-318 (5.2)	5	4	—	—	16.4	②	18	15.5 ③
	Grand Fury/ Caravelle ①	R	8-318 (5.2)	5	4	—	—	16.4	②	18	15.5 ③
	Grand Fury/ Caravelle ①	S	8-318 (5.2)	5	4	—	—	16.4	②	18	15.5 ③
	Fifth Avenue/ Newport	P	8-318 (5.2)	5	4	—	—	16.4	②	18	15.5 ③
	Fifth Avenue/ Newport	R	8-318 (5.2)	5	4	—	—	16.4	②	18	15.5 ③
	Fifth Avenue/ Newport	S	8-318 (5.2)	5	4	—	—	16.4	②	18	15.5 ③
1988	Diplomat	P	8-318 (5.2)	5	4	—	—	16.4	②	18	15.5 ③
	Diplomat	4	8-318 (5.2)	5	4	—	—	16.3	16.4	18	15.5 ③
	Diplomat	S	8-318 (5.2)	5	4	—	—	16.3	16.4	18	15.5 ③
	Grand Fury/ Caravelle ①	P	8-318 (5.2)	5	4	—	—	16.4	②	18	15.5 ③
	Grand Fury/ Caravelle ①	4	8-318 (5.2)	5	4	—	—	16.3	16.4	18	15.5 ③
	Grand Fury/ Caravelle ①	S	8-318 (5.2)	5	4	—	—	16.3	16.4	18	15.5 ③
	Fifth Avenue/ Newport	P	8-318 (5.2)	5	4	—	—	16.4	②	18	15.5 ③
	Fifth Avenue/ Newport	4	8-318 (5.2)	5	4	—	—	16.3	16.4	18	15.5 ③
	Fifth Avenue/ Newport	S	8-318 (5.2)	5	4	—	—	16.3	16.4	18	15.5 ③
1989	Diplomat	P	8-318 (5.2)	5	4	—	—	16.4	②	18	15.5 ③
	Diplomat	4	8-318 (5.2)	5	4	—	—	16.3	16.4	18	15.5 ③
	Diplomat	S	8-318 (5.2)	5	4	—	—	16.3	16.4	18	15.5 ③
	Grand Fury/ Caravelle ①	P	8-318 (5.2)	5	4	—	—	16.4	②	18	15.5 ③
	Grand Fury/ Caravelle ①	4	8-318 (5.2)	5	4	—	—	16.3	16.4	18	15.5 ③
	Grand Fury/ Caravelle ①	S	8-318 (5.2)	5	4	—	—	16.3	16.4	18	15.5 ③
	Fifth Avenue/ Newport	P	8-318 (5.2)	5	4	—	—	16.4	②	18	15.5 ③
	Fifth Avenue/ Newport	4	8-318 (5.2)	5	4	—	—	16.3	16.4	18	15.5 ③
	Fifth Avenue/ Newport	S	8-318 (5.2)	5	4	—	—	16.3	16.4	18	15.5 ③

① Caravelle-Canada only
② 7¼ in. axle—2.5 pts.
  8¼ in. axle—4.4 pts.
  9¼ in. axle—4.5 pts.
③ Add 1 qt. for models with air conditioning

CAMSHAFT SPECIFICATIONS

All measurements given in inches.

Year	VIN	No. Cylinder Displacement cu. in. (liter)	Journal Diameter					Lobe Lift		Bearing Clearance	Camshaft End Play
			1	2	3	4	5	In.	Ex.		
1987	P	8-318 (5.2)	1.998–1.999	1.982–1.983	1.967–1.968	1.951–1.952	1.5605–1.5615	0.373	0.400	0.001–0.003	0.002–0.010
	R	8-318 (5.2)	1.998–1.999	1.982–1.983	1.967–1.968	1.951–1.952	1.5605–1.5615	0.373	0.400	0.001–0.003	0.002–0.010
	S	8-318 (5.2)	1.998–1.999	1.982–1.983	1.967–1.968	1.951–1.952	1.5605–1.5615	0.373	0.400	0.001–0.003	0.002–0.010
1988	P	8-318 (5.2)	1.998–1.999	1.982–1.983	1.967–1.968	1.951–1.952	1.5605–1.5615	0.373	0.400	0.001–0.003	0.002–0.010
	4	8-318 (5.2)	1.998–1.999	1.982–1.983	1.967–1.968	1.951–1.952	1.5605–1.5615	0.373	0.400	0.001–0.003	0.002–0.010
	S	8-318 (5.2)	1.998–1.999	1.982–1.983	1.967–1.968	1.951–1.952	1.5605–1.5615	0.373	0.400	0.001–0.003	0.002–0.010
1989	P	8-318 (5.2)	1.998–1.999	1.982–1.983	1.967–1.968	1.951–1.952	1.5605–1.5615	0.373	0.400	0.001–0.003	0.002–0.010
	4	8-318 (5.2)	1.998–1.999	1.982–1.983	1.967–1.968	1.951–1.952	1.5605–1.5615	0.373	0.400	0.001–0.003	0.002–0.010
	S	8-318 (5.2)	1.998–1.999	1.982–1.983	1.967–1.968	1.951–1.952	1.5605–1.5615	0.373	0.400	0.001–0.003	0.002–0.010

CRANKSHAFT AND CONNECTING ROD SPECIFICATIONS

All measurements are given in inches.

Year	VIN	No. Cylinder Displacement cu. in. (liter)	Crankshaft				Connecting Rod		
			Main Brg. Journal Dia.	Main Brg. Oil Clearance	Shaft End-play	Thrust on No.	Journal Diameter	Oil Clearance	Side Clearance
1987	P	8-318 (5.2)	2.4995–2.5005	①	0.002–0.010	3	2.1240–2.1250	0.0005–0.0022	0.006–0.014
	R	8-318 (5.2)	2.4995–2.5005	①	0.002–0.010	3	2.1240–2.1250	0.0005–0.0022	0.006–0.014
	S	8-318 (5.2)	2.4995–2.5005	①	0.002–0.010	3	2.1240–2.1250	0.0005–0.0022	0.006–0.014
1988	P	8-318 (5.2)	2.4995–2.5005	①	0.002–0.010	3	2.1240–2.1250	0.0005–0.0022	0.006–0.014
	4	8-318 (5.2)	2.4995–2.5005	①	0.002–0.010	3	2.1240–2.1250	0.0005–0.0022	0.006–0.014
	S	8-318 (5.2)	2.4995–2.5005	①	0.002–0.010	3	2.1240–2.1250	0.0005–0.0022	0.006–0.014
1989	P	8-318 (5.2)	2.4995–2.5005	①	0.002–0.010	3	2.1240–2.1250	0.0005–0.0022	0.006–0.014
	4	8-318 (5.2)	2.4995–2.5005	①	0.002–0.010	3	2.1240–2.1250	0.0005–0.0022	0.006–0.014
	S	8-318 (5.2)	2.4995–2.5005	①	0.002–0.010	3	2.1240–2.1250	0.0005–0.0022	0.006–0.014

① No. 1—0.0005–0.0015;
No. 2-5—0.0005–0.0020

VALVE SPECIFICATIONS

Year	VIN	No. Cylinder Displacement cu. in. (liter)	Seat Angle (deg.)	Face Angle (deg.)	Spring Test Pressure (lbs.)	Spring Installed Height (in.)	Stem-to-Guide Clearance (in.)		Stem Diameter (in.)	
							Intake	Exhaust	Intake	Exhaust
1987	P	8-318 (5.2)	45	45	177 @ 1.31	1^{21}/$_{32}$	0.0010–0.0030	0.0020–0.0040	0.3725	0.3715
	R	8-318 (5.2)	45	45	177 @ 1.31	1^{21}/$_{32}$	0.0010–0.0030	0.0020–0.0040	0.3725	0.3715
	S	8-318 (5.2)	45	45	193 @ 1.25	1^{21}/$_{32}$	0.0015–0.0035	0.0025–0.0045	0.3720	0.3710
1988	P	8-318 (5.2)	45	45	177 @ 1.31	1^{21}/$_{32}$	0.0010–0.0030	0.0020–0.0040	0.3725	0.3715
	4	8-318 (5.2)	45	45	177 @ 1.31	1^{21}/$_{32}$	0.0010–0.0030	0.0020–0.0040	0.3725	0.3715
	S	8-318 (5.2)	45	45	193 @ 1.25	1^{21}/$_{32}$	0.0015–0.0035	0.0025–0.0045	0.3720	0.3710
1989	P	8-318 (5.2)	45	45	177 @ 1.31	1^{21}/$_{32}$	0.0010–0.0030	0.0020–0.0040	0.3725	0.3715
	4	8-318 (5.2)	45	45	177 @ 1.31	1^{21}/$_{32}$	0.0010–0.0030	0.0020–0.0040	0.3725	0.3715
	S	8-318 (5.2)	45	45	193 @ 1.25	1^{21}/$_{32}$	0.0015–0.0035	0.0025–0.0045	0.3720	0.3710

PISTON AND RING SPECIFICATIONS
All measurements are given in inches.

Year	VIN	No. Cylinder Displacement cu. in. (liter)	Piston Clearance	Ring Gap			Ring Side Clearance		
				Top Compression	Bottom Compression	Oil Control	Top Compression	Bottom Compression	Oil Control
1987	P	8-318 (5.2)	0.0005–0.0015 ①	0.0100–0.0200	0.0100–0.0200	0.0150–0.0550	0.0015–0.0030	0.0015–0.0030	0.0002–0.0050
	R	8-318 (5.2)	0.0005–0.0015 ①	0.0100–0.0200	0.0100–0.0200	0.0150–0.0550	0.0015–0.0030	0.0015–0.0030	0.0002–0.0050
	S	8-318 (5.2)	0.0005–0.0015 ①	0.0100–0.0200	0.0100–0.0200	0.0150–0.0550	0.0015–0.0030	0.0015–0.0030	0.0002–0.0050
1988	P	8-318 (5.2)	0.0005–0.0015 ①	0.0100–0.0200	0.0100–0.0200	0.0150–0.0550	0.0015–0.0030	0.0015–0.0030	0.0002–0.0050
	4	8-318 (5.2)	0.0005–0.0015 ①	0.0100–0.0200	0.0100–0.0200	0.0150–0.0550	0.0015–0.0030	0.0015–0.0030	0.0002–0.0050
	S	8-318 (5.2)	0.0005–0.0015 ①	0.0100–0.0200	0.0100–0.0200	0.0150–0.0550	0.0015–0.0030	0.0015–0.0030	0.0002–0.0050
1989	P	8-318 (5.2)	0.0005–0.0015 ①	0.0100–0.0200	0.0100–0.0200	0.0150–0.0550	0.0015–0.0030	0.0015–0.0030	0.0002–0.0050
	4	8-318 (5.2)	0.0005–0.0015 ①	0.0100–0.0200	0.0100–0.0200	0.0150–0.0550	0.0015–0.0030	0.0015–0.0030	0.0002–0.0050
	S	8-318 (5.2)	0.0005–0.0015 ①	0.0100–0.0200	0.0100–0.0200	0.0150–0.0550	0.0015–0.0030	0.0015–0.0030	0.0002–0.0050

① High Performance engines—0.001–0.002

TORQUE SPECIFICATIONS

All readings in ft. lbs.

Year	VIN	No. Cylinder Displacement cu. in. (liter)	Cylinder Head Bolts	Main Bearing Bolts	Rod Bearing Bolts	Crankshaft Pulley Bolts	Flywheel Bolts	Manifold Intake	Manifold Exhaust	Spark Plugs
1987	P	8-318 (5.2)	105	85	45	100	55	45	①	30
	R	8-318 (5.2)	105	85	45	100	55	45	①	30
	S	8-318 (5.2)	105	85	45	100	55	45	①	30
1988	P	8-318 (5.2)	105	85	45	100	55	45	①	30
	4	8-318 (5.2)	105	85	45	100	55	45	①	30
	S	8-318 (5.2)	105	85	45	100	55	45	①	30
1989	P	8-318 (5.2)	105	85	45	100	55	45	①	30
	4	8-318 (5.2)	105	85	45	100	55	45	①	30
	S	8-318 (5.2)	105	85	45	100	55	45	①	30

① Nuts—15 ft. lbs., bolts—20 ft. lb.

BRAKE SPECIFICATIONS

All measurements in inches unless noted.

Year	Model	Lug Nut Torque (ft. lbs.)	Master Cylinder Bore	Brake Disc Minimum Thickness	Brake Disc Maximum Runout	Standard Brake Drum Diameter	Minimum Lining Thickness Front	Minimum Lining Thickness Rear
1987	All Models	85	0.827 ①	0.940	.004	10.000 ②	1/8	1/8
1988	All Models	85	0.827 ①	0.940	.004	10.000 ②	1/8	1/8
1989	All Models	85	0.827 ①	0.940	.004	10.000 ②	1/8	1/8

① Heavy Duty—1.03
② Heavy Duty—11.000

WHEEL ALIGNMENT

Year	Model	Caster Range (deg.)	Caster Preferred Setting (deg.)	Camber Range (deg.)	Camber Preferred Setting (deg.)	Toe-in (in.)	Steering Axis Inclination (deg.)
1987	Fifth Avenue/Newport, Gran Fury/Caravelle ① Diplomat	1¼P–3¾P	2½P	¼N–1¼P	½P	1/8	8
1988	Fifth Avenue/Newport, Gran Fury/Caravelle ① Diplomat	1¼P–3¾P	2½P	¼N–1¼P	½P	1/8	8
1989	Fifth Avenue/Newport, Gran Fury/Caravelle ① Diplomat	1¼P–3¾P	2½P	¼N–1¼P	½P	1/8	8

① Caravelle—Canada only

ENGINE ELECTRICAL

NOTE: Disconnecting the negative battery cable on some vehicles may interfere with the functions of the on board computer systems and may require the computer to undergo a relearning process, once the negative battery cable is reconnected.

Distributor

REMOVAL

1. Disconnect the negative battery cable.
2. Remove the cap and wire assembly.
3. Disconnect the lead wire at the harness connector.
4. Mark the relative positions of the distributor and rotor on the engine block or distributor housing edge.
5. Loosen the distributor mounting and lift out the distributor. Should the distributor shaft rotate slightly during the removal, make a 2nd matchmark to indicated rotor positioning for installation.

INSTALLATION

Timing Not Disturbed

1. Align the distributor rotor-to-distributor housing matchmark, the distributor housing-to-engine matchmarks and the intermediate shaft with the oil pump drive.
2. Install the distributor into the engine until it seats.
3. Install the hold-down clamp and bolt; be sure to snug the hold-down bolt.
4. Connect the electrical harness connector.
5. Start the engine and check the ignition timing. Refer to the underhood vehicle emission information label for correct timing specifications.

Timing Disturbed

1. Rotate the crankshaft until No. 1 cylinder is at TDC.
2. The pointer on the timing chain case cover should be over the **0** mark on the crankshaft pulley.
3. The slot in the intermediate shaft which carries the gear that drives the oil pump and the distributor should be parallel to the crankshaft.
4. Hold the distributor over the mounting pad on the cylinder block so the distributor body flange coincides with the mounting pad and the rotor

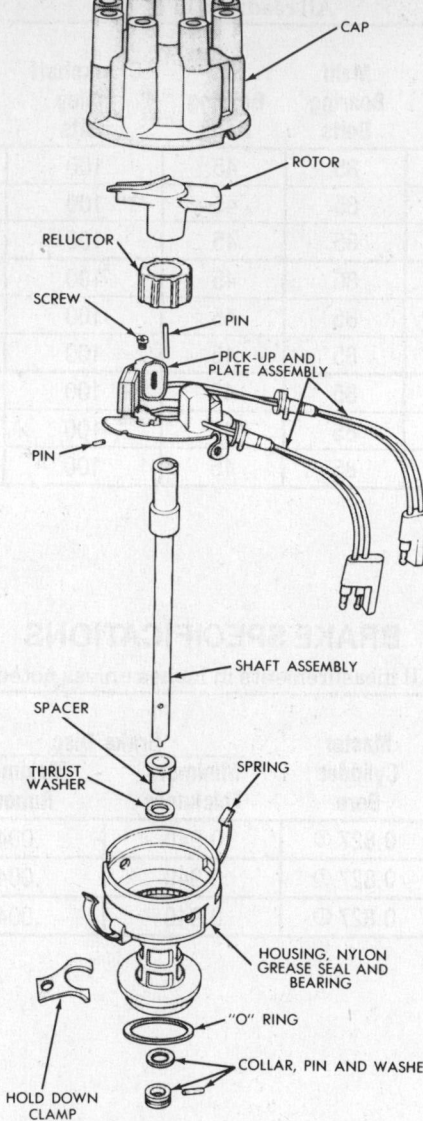

Exploded view of a V8 ESA dual pick-up distributor. Earlier models use single pick-up

points to the No. 1 cylinder firing position.
5. Install the distributor while holding the rotor in position, allowing it to move only enough to engage the slot in the drive gear.
6. Install the cap, snug down the retaining bolt and check the ignition timing. Refer to the underhood vehicle emission information label for correct timing specifications.

Ignition Timing

ADJUSTMENT

The ignition timing test indicates correct timing of the engine only at idle

and with the engine hot. Check timing as follows:
1. Connect tachometer and timing light. A magnetic timing probe receptacle is mounted to timing indicator and may be advisable to use.
2. Set parking brake and place transmission in **P** or **N** position. Start the engine and run until normal operating temperature is reached.
3. Connect jumper wire between carburetor switch and ground.
4. Adjust engine idle if necessary. Check ignition timing.
5. If timing is out of allowed specifications, loosen and rotate distributor housing.
6. Turn the distributor housing in the direction of rotor-rotation to retard the timing. Rotate the distributor housing against rotor rotation to advance the timing.
7. Tighten distributor hold-down bolt securely.
8. Recheck engine idle and remove test equipment.

Alternator

For further information on the charging system, please refer to "Charging and Starting" in the Unit Repair section.

PRECAUTIONS

Several precautions must be observed with alternator equipped vehicles to avoid damage to the unit.
- If the battery is removed for any reason, make sure it is reconnected with the correct polarity. Reversing the battery connections may result in damage to the one-way rectifiers.
- When utilizing a booster battery as a starting aid, always connect the positive to positive terminals and the negative terminal from the booster battery to a good engine ground on the vehicle being started.
- Never use a fast charger as a booster to start vehicles.
- Disconnect the battery cables when charging the battery with a fast charger.
- Never attempt to polarize the alternator.
- Do not use test lamps of more than 12 volts when checking diode continuity.
- Do not short across or ground any of the alternator terminals.
- The polarity of the battery, alternator and regulator must be matched and considered before making any electrical connections within the system.
- Never separate the alternator on an open circuit. Make sure all connections within the circuit are clean and tight.

- Disconnect the battery ground terminal when performing any service on electrical components.
- Disconnect the battery if arc welding is to be done on the vehicle.

BELT TENSION ADJUSTMENT

Satisfactory performance of the belt driven accessories depends on proper belt tension. The 2 tensioning methods are given in order of preference:
1. Belt tension gauge method
2. Torque equivalent method

Belt Tension Gauge Method

For this method, the belt is adjusted by measuring the tension of the belts with a belt tension gauge. Check belt tension in the middle of the span, between the 2 pulleys.

Torque Equivalent Method

Each adjustable accessory bracket is provided with a ½ in. (13mm) square hole for torque wrench use. Equivalent torque values for adjusting each accessory drive belt are specified.

REMOVAL & INSTALLATION

1. Disconnect the negative battery terminal.
2. Loosen the alternator mounting nut and bolt, the belt tensioner bracket bolt and remove the drive belt.
3. Remove the alternator mounting nut and bolt, the belt tensioner bracket bolt and spacer.
4. Disconnect the battery, field and ground leads from the alternator.
5. Disconnect the harness from the alternator and remove the alternator from the vehicle.
6. Position the harness to the alternator and reconnect the battery, field and ground leads to the alternator.
7. Position the alternator spacer between the end shields and install the mounting nut.
8. Install the adjustment bracket bolt and drive belt.
9. Adjust the drive belt tension.

Voltage Regulator

For further information on the charging system, please refer to "Charging and Starting" in the Unit Repair section.

REMOVAL & INSTALLATION

1. Disconnect the negative battery cable. Disconnect the wiring harness

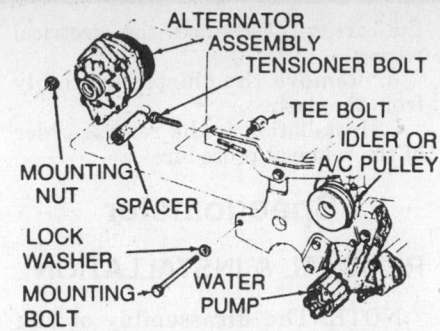

Alternator mounting – 8 clyinder engine

plug from the voltage regulator.
2. Remove the mounting screws from the voltage regulator base and remove the regulator.
3. Prior to installing the voltage regulator, clean the mounting surface of any dirt or corrosion build-up; the regulator must have a good ground contact.
4. Position the voltage regulator to the mounting surface and install the mounting screws.
5. Connect the wiring harness plug to the voltage regulator. Test the system for proper operation.

Starter

For further information on the charging system, please refer to "Charging and Starting" in the Unit Repair section.

REMOVAL & INSTALLATION

1. Disconnect the negative battery cable. Raise and support the vehicle safely.
2. Remove the cable from the starter and heat shield.
3. Disconnect the solenoid leads at the solenoid terminals.
4. Remove the starter securing bolts and remove the starter from the engine flywheel housing.
5. If fluid cooler tube bracket interferes with starter removal, remove the starter securing bolts, slide the cooler tube bracket off the stud and remove the starter.
To install:
6. Reverse order of the removal procedure. Be sure the starter and flywheel housing mating surfaces are free of dirt and oil.
7. When tightening the bolt and nut, hold the starter away from the engine to ensure proper alignment during its seating as the bolt is tightened. Do not damage the flywheel housing seal, if equipped.

CHASSIS ELECTRICAL

CAUTION

On vehicles equipped with an air bag, the negative battery cable must be disconnected, before working on the system. Failure to do so may result in deployment of the air bag and possible personal injury.

Heater Blower Motor

NOTE: Blower motor service is accomplished from inside the vehicle, under the right side of the instrument panel.

REMOVAL & INSTALLATION

1. Disconnect the battery ground cable.
2. Remove the blower motor feed and ground wires at the connector.
3. Remove the blower motor mounting nuts from the bottom of the recirculation housing or separate lower blower housing from upper housing.
4. Lower the blower motor assembly downward from under the instrument panel.
5. Remove the blower motor mounting plate screws.
6. Separate the blower motor housing from the blower motor and fan assembly housing.
To install:
7. Set the blower motor and fan assembly into the blower motor housing and install the housing to mounting plate screws.
8. Position the blower assembly into the recirculation housing and install the retaining nuts.
9. Install the blower motor feed and ground wire connector.
10. Install the battery ground cable.
11. Test the blower motor operation on all fan speeds.

Windshield Wiper Motor

REMOVAL & INSTALLATION

1. Disconnect the battery negative cable.
2. Remove the cowl screen.
3. Remove the crank-nut while holding the drive crank with a wrench to prevent overloading the gears.
4. Remove the drive crank from the motor and disconnect the electrical wiring connector.

5. Remove the nuts retaining the motor to the dash panel. Remove the motor carefully, so as not to lose the spacers and rubber grommet.

6. Installation is in the reverse order of the removal procedure. Be sure the wiper motor is correctly grounded by having the ground strap under 1 of the retaining nuts.

7. Tighten the crank nut to 95 inch lbs. (10.4mm).

Windshield Wiper Switch

REMOVAL & INSTALLATION

1. Disconnect the negative battery cable.
2. Remove the steering wheel.
3. If equipped with a tilt wheel, remove the lock plate cover and the lock plate.
4. Remove the lower instrument panel bezel.
5. If equipped with a tilt wheel, perform the following procedures:
   a. Remove the gear shift indicator.
   b. Remove the nuts retaining the column to the lower panel reinforcement.
   c. Remove the mounting bracket from the steering column after removing the retaining bolts.
6. Remove the wiring holder from the steering column by unsnapping the plastic retainers.
7. Remove the turn signal switch.
8. Remove the retaining screws and remove the lock housing cover.
9. Gently pull the wiper switch up from the column while guiding the wires through the column opening.
10. Installation is the reverse of the removal procedure.

Instrument Cluster

REMOVAL & INSTALLATION

1. Disconnect the negative battery cable.
2. Remove the instrument cluster bezel.
3. Loosen the shift pointer set screw and remove the pointer.
4. From under the dash, disconnect the speedometer cable.

NOTE: The speedometer cables are attached to the speedometer by a snap-on plastic ferrule, which attaches directly to the speedometer head and must be disconnected before the speedometer or cluster can be removed.

5. Remove the cluster retaining screws and pull the cluster away from

the carrier. Disconnect the electrical wiring.
6. Remove the cluster assembly from the dash.
7. Installation is the reverse order of the removal procedure.

Speedometer

REMOVAL & INSTALLATION

NOTE: The disassembly of the cluster and speedometer will vary to a small degree from each vehicle line to another. It is most important to mask surfaces which may become scratched or damaged during the disassembly or assembly procedures. Extreme care should be exercised when handling the internal components of the speedometer/cluster assembly. The electronic units cannot be repaired but must be replaced.

1. Disconnect the negative battery cable. Remove the instrument cluster.
2. Remove the cluster and the printed circuit board assembly from the carrier.
3. Remove the trip odometer knob from the shaft.
4. Remove the plastic pins and pull the lens and mask assembly away from the cluster housing.
5. Remove the screws retaining the speedometer to the cluster housing and the remove speedometer.
6. Disconnect the connector-to-odometer switch, if equipped.
7. Installation is the reverse order of the removal procedure.

Radio

REMOVAL & INSTALLATION

1. Disconnect the negative battery cable.
2. Remove the center bezel and the radio-to-panel mounting screws.
3. Pull the radio out through the front face of the panel. Detach the antenna lead, ground strap, power wire and speaker leads.
4. Installation is the reverse of the removal procedures.

Headlight Switch

REMOVAL & INSTALLATION

1. Disconnect negative battery cable.
2. Remove the instrument cluster bezel.
3. Remove the mounting screws

from switch module and pull assembly away from panel.
4. To remove the knob and stem assembly, depress the headlight switch stem release button and pull assembly from switch.
5. Disconnect electrical wiring.
6. Remove the switch from the vehicle.
7. Installation is the reverse of the removal procedure.

Dimmer Switch

REMOVAL & INSTALLATION

1. Disconnect the negative battery cable.
2. Remove the steering column lower cover.
3. Disconnect the electrical connector from the switch.
4. Remove the dimmer switch retaining nuts. Disengage the switch from the actuating rod. Remove the switch from the vehicle.
5. Install the switch to its proper mounting. Insert two $3/32$ in. drill shanks through the alignment holes.
6. Install the actuator rod into the washer/wiper switch pocket. Once the switch is installed, remove the drill shanks.

Turn Signal Switch

REMOVAL & INSTALLATION

Standard Column

1. Disconnect the negative battery cable. Remove the steering wheel and the steering column cover.
2. Remove sound deadening insulation panel and lower instrument panel bezel.
3. Loosen the Allen screw on the gear shift housing and remove the gearshift indicator.
4. Place the shift lever in full clockwise position.
5. Pry out the plastic buttons retaining wiring the harness holder to

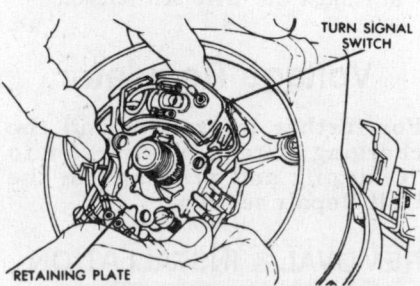

Removing turn signal switch from steering column

the column. Remove the harness holder.

6. Disconnect wiring connector from switch. Wrap the connector with tape to prevent snagging when removing the switch.

7. Remove the screw holding the turn signal lever assembly to the turn signal switch pivot. Leave the assembly in its installed location.

8. Remove the screws and bearing retainer fastening the turn signal switch to the upper bearing housing.

9. Remove the turn signal/hazard warning switch by gently pulling the switch up from the column while straightening and guiding wires up through column opening.

10. Installation is the reverse order of the removal procedure.

Tilt Column

1. Disconnect the negative battery cable. Remove the steering wheel and the steering column cover.

2. Remove the sound deadening insulation panel and lower instrument panel bezel.

3. Loosen the Allen screw on the gear shift housing and remove the gear shift indicator.

4. Place the gear shift lever in full clockwise position and tilt position at mid-point.

5. Remove the nuts retaining the column to the lower panel reinforcement.

6. Remove the steering column mounting bracket retaining bolts and remove the bracket from the column.

7. Pry out plastic buttons retaining wiring holder to the column and remove the holder.

8. Disconnect wiring connector from switch. Wrap the connector with tape to prevent snagging when removing the switch.

9. Remove the plastic cover from the lock plate. Depress the lock plate, using a lock plate depressing tool, and pry the retaining ring out of the groove. The full load of the upper bearing spring should not be relieved as the retaining ring will turn too easily, making removal more difficult.

10. Remove the lock plate, cancelling cam and cancelling cam spring. Place the turn signal switch in the right turn position.

11. Remove the screw attaching the hazard warning switch knob. Remove the screws attaching the turn signal switch to the steering column.

12. Remove the turn signal/hazard warning switch by gently pulling the switch up from the column while straightening and guiding wires up through column opening.

13. Installation is the reverse order of the removal procedure.

Combination Switch

REMOVAL & INSTALLATION

Standard Column

1. Disconnect the negative battery cable.

2. Remove the lower steering column cover.

3. Remove the wiring holder after unsnapping the plastic retainer clips.

4. Disconnect the speed control switch electrical connector from the instrument panel harness connector.

5. Remove the wiper control knob from the end of the lever.

6. Remove the screws attaching the speed control switch to the column.

7. Remove the upper steering column lock housing cover screws and remove the lock housing.

8. Remove the switch and harness from the column by pulling the switch up through the column.

9. Installation is the reverse order of the removal procedure.

Tilt Column

1. Disconnect the negative battery cable.

2. Remove the lower steering column cover.

3. Remove the steering column mounting nuts and lower the column down from the instrument panel taking care not to damage the gear indicator wire.

4. Remove the plastic screws attaching the support bracket to the column jacket.

5. Unsnap the plastic retainer clips and remove the wiring harness holder.

6. Disconnect the speed control switch electrical connector from the instrument panel harness connector.

7. Remove the wiper control knob from the end of the lever.

6. Remove the screws attaching the speed control switch to the column.

8. Remove the steering wheel and attach a flexible guide wire to the lower end of the speed control switch harness.

9. Pull the switch wires up through the lock housing between the lock plate and side of the housing.

10. Disconnect the guide wire from the harness and remove the switch.

11. Installation is the reverse order of the removal procedure.

Ignition Lock

REMOVAL & INSTALLATION

Standard Column

1. Disconnect the negative battery cable. Remove the steering wheel and turn signal lever. Pull the turn signal switch up out of the way.

2. Remove the retaining snapring and pry the upper bearing housing off the steering shaft.

3. Press out the pin attaching the lock plate to the steering shaft and remove the lock plate. Remove the lock lever guide plate. Remove the buzz/chime switch.

4. With the ignition lock cylinder in the **LOCK** position and the ignition key removed, insert 2 small diameter tools into the lock cylinder release openings to release the spring-loaded lock retainer. Pull the lock cylinder out of its housing.

5. To install, place the lock cylinder into the housing, positioning it in the **LOCK** position and remove the key. Insert the lock cylinder far enough into the housing to contact the switch actuator. Insert the key, press and turn until the retainer snaps into place.

6. Complete the reassembly in the reverse order of disassembly.

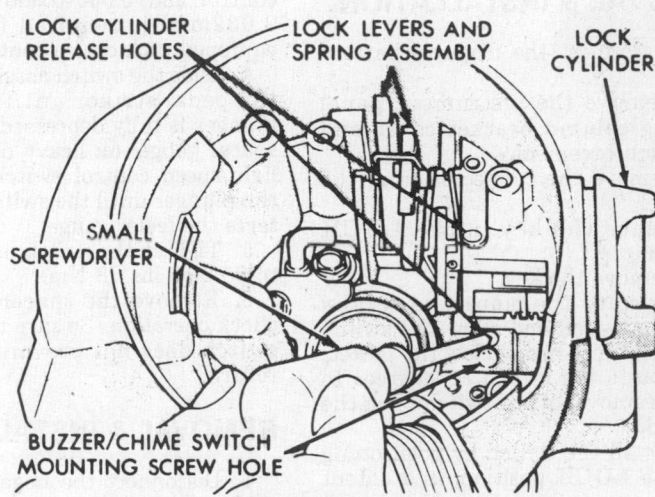

LOCK CYLINDER RELEASE HOLES LOCK LEVERS AND SPRING ASSEMBLY LOCK CYLINDER

SMALL SCREWDRIVER

BUZZER/CHIME SWITCH MOUNTING SCREW HOLE

Removal of lock cylinder from steering wheel

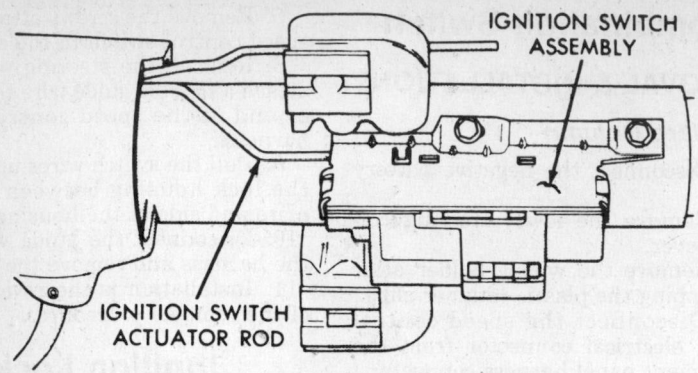

Ignition switch positioned on steering column

Tilt Column

1. Disconnect the negative battery cable. Remove the steering wheel, shaft lock cover, turn signal lever, tilt control lever and hazard warning knob.

2. Remove the lock plate, cancelling cam and spring, disconnect and pull the turn signal switch up out of the way. Remove key lamp.

3. With the ignition lock cylinder in the **LOCK** position and the key removed, insert a thin suitable tool into the lock cylinder release opening to release the spring-loaded lock retainer. Pull the lock cylinder out of its housing.

4. To install, place the lock cylinder in its housing, positioning it in the **LOCK** position and remove the key. Insert the cylinder into the housing until it contacts the switch actuator. Move the switch actuator rod up and down to align the parts. When aligned, move the lock cylinder inward and snap into place.

5. Complete the reassembly in the reverse order of disassembly.

Ignition Switch

REMOVAL & INSTALLATION

1. Disconnect the negative battery cable.

2. Remove the instrument panel steering column bracket cover and lower reinforcement.

3. Remove the connector from the switch.

4. Place the key in the **LOCK** position.

5. Remove the key.

6. Remove the mounting screws from the switch and allow the switch and pushrod to drop below the jacket.

7. Rotate the switch 90 degrees to permit removal of the switch from the pushrod.

8. Install the switch by positioning it in the **LOCK** position, 2nd detent from the top.

9. Place the switch at right angles to the column and insert the pushrod.

10. Rotate the switch 90 degrees to lock the actuator rod, align the switch on the bracket and install the screws.

11. With a light rearward load on the switch, tighten the screws. Check for proper operation.

Stoplight Switch

The stoplight switch or stoplight/speed control switch and mounting bracket, are attached to the brake pedal bracket. If equipped with speed control, the stoplight switch is a combined unit.

ADJUSTMENT

1. Loosen the switch assembly pedal-to-bracket screw and slide the assembly away from the pedal blade or striker plate.

2. Depress the brake pedal and allow it to return to free position, do not pull the brake pedal back at any time.

3. Position a spacer gauge on the pedal striker plate. A clearance of 0.130–0.150 in. (3.302–3.810mm) is required for vehicles without speed control and 0.060–0.080 in. (1.542–2.032mm) is required for vehicles equipped with cruise control.

4. Slide the switch assembly toward the pedal striker until the switch plunger is fully depressed against the spacer gauge; on heavy duty or stoplight/speed control switches, depress the plunger until the switch body contacts the feeler gauge.

5. Tighten the switch bracket screw to 75 inch lbs. (8 Nm).

6. Remove the spacer gauge and check operation. Be sure the stoplight switch does not prevent full pedal return.

REMOVAL & INSTALLATION

1. Disconnect the negative battery cable.

2. Remove the switch assembly pedal-to-bracket attaching screw and remove the switch and bracket as an assembly.

3. Remove the switch-to-bracket retaining nut and disassemble the switch from the bracket.

4. Installation is the reverse order of the removal procedure. Adjust the switch.

Neutral Safety Switch

REMOVAL & INSTALLATION

1. Disconnect the negative battery terminal.

2. Raise the vehicle and support it safely.

3. The neutral safety switch is located on the left side of the automatic transmission case. Fluid will drain from the transmission when the switch is unscrewed and removed.

4. Clean any dirt or grease from around the area of the switch.

NOTE: Care must be taken as not to allow dirt to enter the transmission.

5. Place a drain pan under the transmission, unscrew the neutral safety switch and allow the fluid drain out.

6. When installing the neutral safety switch, install a new seal and screw the neutral safety switch into the transmission. Torque the neutral safety switch to 25 ft. lbs. and replenish lost fluid.

Fuses, Circuit Breakers and Relays

LOCATION

Fusible Links

The fusible links are used to prevent major damage to wire harnesses in the event of a short circuit or an overload condition in the wiring circuits which normally are not fused, due to carrying high amperage loads or because of their locations within the wiring harness. Each fusible link is of a fixed value for a specific electrical load and should the link fail, the cause of the failure must be determined and repaired prior to installing a new fusible link of the same value.

When replacing fusible links connected to the battery terminal or starter relay, they should be serviced with the same type of prefabricated fusible link. All other fusible links can be replaced with fusible link wire cut from bulk rolls.

NOTE: When replacing fusible links, use only rosin core solder. Do not use acid core solder.

Circuit Breakers

Circuit breakers are used in varied circuits to control amperage surges and if the circuit is opened, to re-set themselves as the heat from the current flow load has diminished. Should a continual interruption of power be experienced when operation of a controlled electrical component is attempted, repairs to the circuits/components or replacement of the component must be accomplished. Circuit breakers are located in the fuse panel and, if necessary, can be changed quickly by pulling the assembly from the fuse panel and inserting a new one in its place.

Fuse Panel

The relays and circuit breakers are located on the fuse panel. The fuse panel is located on the left side of the passenger compartment, either mounted to the underside of the dash panel or to the inner side of the firewall panel.

Various Relays

ACCESSORY POWER RELAY — it supplies current to the dash bulk head and related accessories. It is located on the left side of the brake pedal support bracket.

STARTER RELAY — it supplies current directly from the battery to the starter solenoid. It is located in the upper left side of the firewall.

ILLUMINATED ENTRY RELAY — it supplies current to the illuminated entry switches, which ultimately directs current to the courtesy lamps whenever either front door handle is lifted for entry. It is located on the lower right side of the brake pedal support brace.

TIME DELAY RELAY — it supplies current to the ignition switch courtesy lamp. When either door is opened, the ignition switch lamp will illuminate until the ignition switch is either turned to the **ON** position or the engine is started. It is located in the fuse block, on the left side of the instrument panel.

HORN RELAY — it supplies current to the horn switch. The horn relay is located in the fuse block on the left side of the instrument panel.

Computer

LOCATION

The computer is located on the carburetor air cleaner. Should it become necessary to replace the computer, re-move the mounting screws from inside the air cleaner. Do not take the computer apart for any reason. It is not serviceable and must be replaced as an assembly.

Turn Signal and Hazard Flashers

LOCATION

Both the turn signal and hazard warning system flashers are mounted to the fuse panel. Both can be removed and replaced by simply pulling the flasher from the fuse panel and installing a new one in its place.

Cruise Control

ADJUSTMENT

Speed Control Cable

1. Have the engine at normal operating temperature with the choke off and the engine speed at curb idle.
2. Remove the spring clip from the lost motion link stud. The clearance between the stud and the cable clevis should be $1/16$ in.
3. Insert a gauge pin ($1/16$ in.) between the cable clevis and the stud. Loosen the clip at the cable support bracket.
4. Pull all the slack from the cable but do not pull the throttle away from the curb idle position.
5. Tighten the clip at the cable support bracket to 45 inch lbs. torque.
6. Remove the gauge pin and install the spring clip on the stud of the lost motion link.

Servo Lock-In Screw

1. If the set speed drops more than 2–3 mph or speed increase of more than 2–3 mph when the speed control is activated, the lock-in adjusting screw can be adjusted.
2. It must be remembered that lock-in accuracy will be affected by poor engine performance, power to weight ratio, loaded vehicle, empty vehicle or improper slack in the throttle control cable.
3. Adjust the lock-in screw counter-clockwise for an increase in speed correction of approximately 1 mph per ¼ turn of the lock-in screw.
4. Adjust the lock-in screw clockwise for a decrease in speed correction of approximately 1 mph per ¼ turn of the lock-in screw.

NOTE: This adjustment must not exceed 2 turns in either direction or damage to the servo unit may occur.

ENGINE COOLING

Radiator

REMOVAL & INSTALLATION

1. Disconnect the negative battery cable.
2. Place the heater temperature selector to FULL ON. Drain the cooling system by opening the drain cock at the bottom of the radiator. When the reserve tank is empty, remove the pressure cap.
3. Remove the oil cooler lines from the radiator.
4. Remove the upper and lower hose clamps and hoses. Remove the coolant reserve tank tube.
5. Remove the screws and position the shroud rearward to provide maximum clearance.
6. Loosen the retaining screws at the bottom of the radiator and remove the screws at the top.
7. Lift the radiator out of the engine compartment.

NOTE: Extreme care should be taken during removal not to damage the radiator cooling fins or water tubes.

8. Installation is the reverse order of the removal procedure. Fill the radiator to the top of neck and the reservoir tank to the MAX level. Warm the engine with the heater on and check the coolant level. Check the transmission fluid level after warm-up and add fluid, as necessary.

Heater Core

REMOVAL & INSTALLATION

Without Air Conditioning

1. Disconnect the negative battery cable.
2. Drain the radiator coolant.
3. Remove the air cleaner and disconnect the heater hoses. Plug the core tubes to prevent spillage.
4. Slide the front seat all the way back.
5. Remove the instrument cluster bezel assembly.
6. Remove the instrument panel upper cover by removing the mounting screws at the top inner surface of the glove box, above the instrument cluster, at the left end cap mounting, at the right side of the pad brow and in the defroster outlets.

7. Remove the steering column cover; it is the instrument panel piece under the column.

8. Remove the right intermediate side cowl trim panel. Remove the lower instrument panel; part with the glove box. Remove the instrument panel center to lower reinforcement.

9. Remove the floor console, if equipped.

10. Remove the right center air distribution duct. Detach the locking tab on the defroster duct.

11. Disconnect the temperature control cable from the housing. Disconnect the blower motor resistor block wiring.

12. Detach the vacuum lines from the water valve and tee in the engine compartment. Detach the wiring from the evaporator housing. Remove the vacuum lines from the inlet air housing and disconnect the vacuum harness coupling.

13. Remove the drain tube in the engine compartment. Remove the mounting nuts from the firewall.

14. Roll the heater unit back so the pipes clear and remove it.

15. Remove the blend air door lever from the shaft. Remove the screws and lift off the top cover. Lift the heater core out.

To install:

16. When installing the heater core, place the housing on the front floor under the instrument panel.

17. Tip the housing up under instrument panel and press mounting studs through the dash panel, making sure the defroster duct is properly seated on unit and gasket is installed properly. Connect the locking tab on the defroster duct.

18. While holding the housing in position, place the mounting bracket in position to the plenum stud and install the nut.

19. In engine compartment, install retaining nuts and tighten securely.

20. Connect electrical connectors to the resistor block and connect the control cable.

21. Connect vacuum lines in engine compartment, making sure the grommet is seated. Connect vacuum lines to inlet air housing and vacuum harness coupling.

22. Install right center air distribution duct.

23. Install instrument panel center to lower reinforcement.

24. Install lower instrument panel.

25. Install right intermediate side cowl trim panel.

26. Install steering column cover.

27. Install instrument panel upper cover.

28. Install cluster bezel assembly.

29. From engine compartment, re-

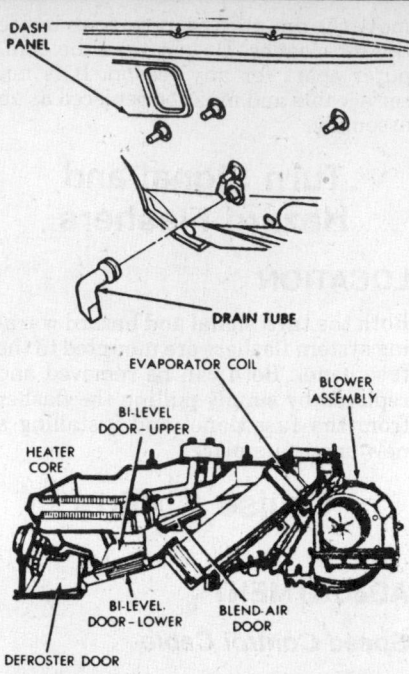

Evaporator/heater assembly, typical

move plugs from core tubes and connect hoses to heater. Install condensate tube and corbin clamp.

30. Fill cooling system and inspect for leaks.

31. Install air cleaner and connect battery negative cable.

With Air Conditioning

1. Disconnect the negative battery cable.

2. Discharge the air conditioning system.

3. Drain the radiator coolant.

4. Remove the air cleaner and disconnect the heater hoses. Plug the core tubes to prevent spillage.

5. Remove the H-type expansion valve.

6. Slide the front seat all the way back.

7. Remove the instrument cluster bezel assembly.

8. Remove the instrument panel upper cover by removing the mounting screws at the top inner surface of the glove box, above the instrument cluster, at the left end cap mounting, at the right side of the pad brow and in the defroster outlets.

9. Remove the steering column cover; it is the instrument panel piece under the column.

10. Remove the right intermediate side cowl trim panel. Remove the lower instrument panel; part with the glove box. Remove the instrument panel center to lower reinforcement.

11. Remove the floor console, if equipped.

12. Remove the right center air distribution duct. Detach the locking tab on the defroster duct.

13. Disconnect the temperature control cable from the housing. Disconnect the blower motor resistor block wiring.

14. Detach the vacuum lines from the water valve and tee in the engine compartment. Detach the wiring from the evaporator housing. Remove the vacuum lines from the inlet air housing and disconnect the vacuum harness coupling.

15. Remove the drain tube in the en-

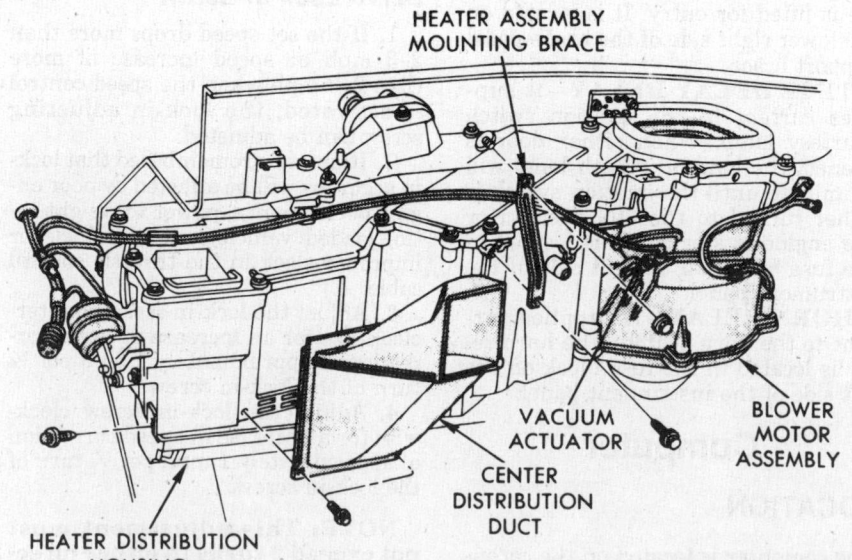

1983 Cordoba and Mirada heater assembly. Other models similar

gine compartment. Remove the mounting nuts from the firewall.

16. Remove the hanger strap from the rear of the evaporator and plenum stud.

17. Roll the heater/air conditioning unit back so the pipes clear and remove it.

18. Remove the blend air door lever from the shaft. Remove the screws and lift off the top cover. Lift the heater core out.

To install:

19. When installing the heater core, place the evaporator housing on the front floor under the instrument panel.

20. Tip the evaporator housing up under instrument panel and press mounting studs through the dash panel, making sure the defroster duct and air conditioning distribution duct is properly seated on unit and gasket is installed properly. Connect the locking tab on the defroster duct.

21. While holding the housing in position, place the mounting bracket in position to the plenum stud and install the nut.

22. In engine compartment, install retaining nuts and tighten securely. Install condensate drain tube.

23. Connect electrical connectors to the resistor block and connect the control cable.

24. Connect vacuum lines in engine compartment, making sure the grommet is seated. Connect vacuum lines to inlet air housing and vacuum harness coupling.

25. Install right center air distribution duct.

26. Install instrument panel center to lower reinforcement.

27. Install lower instrument panel.

28. Install right intermediate side cowl trim panel.

29. Install steering column cover.

30. Install instrument panel upper cover.

31. Install cluster bezel assembly.

32. From engine compartment, remove plugs from core tubes and connect hoses to heater. Install condensate tube and corbin clamp.

33. Install H-valve and install refrigerant lines to valve. Replace gaskets.

34. Fill cooling system and inspect for leaks.

35. After the evaporator heater housing assembly is installed in the vehicle, evacuate and recharge the system with the proper amount of refrigerant. It is recommended, operation of all controls be tested and an overall performance test be made after the repair or replacement of the evaporator assembly.

36. Install air cleaner and connect battery negative cable.

Water Pump

REMOVAL & INSTALLATION

1. Disconnect the negative battery cable. Drain the cooling system.

2. Remove the fan shroud screws and move the shroud out of the way.

3. It may be necessary to remove the radiator on some vehicles to obtain the working clearance necessary to remove the water pump.

4. Loosen the alternator mounting bolts. Loosen the mounting bolts for the power steering pump, idler pulley, air conditioning compressor and air pump, if equipped. Remove all the accessory belts.

5. Remove the fan, spacer or fluid drive and the pulley.

NOTE: For fluid-coupled fan drives, do not set the drive unit down with its shaft pointing downward. Keep the unit in a vertical position as installed on the engine. This will prevent the silicone fluid from leaking out.

6. If necessary, remove the alternator or compressor mounting bracket bolts from the water pump to swing the alternator or compressor out of the way; keep the compressor in an upright position.

7. If necessary, unbolt the power steering pump and set it aside; leave the hoses connected. Also remove the air pump and brackets, if equipped.

8. Detach the hoses from the water pump. Remove the bolts which secure the water pump body to its engine block housing. Remove the water pump and discard the gasket.

To install:

9. Install the bypass hose to the pump with the second clamp temporarily in the center of the hose. Install the water pump with a new gasket, using sealer. Torque the bolts to 30 ft. lbs. (40.7 Nm).

10. Rotate the pump shaft by hand to be sure it rotates freely. Install the alternator or compressor mounting bracket to the pump if either was removed. Install the pulley, spacer or fluid drive and the fan. Torque the nuts to 15 ft. lbs. (20.3 Nm).

11. Reinstall all accessory drive belts. Adjust them to get about ½ in. of play under moderate thumb pressure on the longest run of belt between pulleys.

12. Install the radiator, if removed.

13. Install the fan shroud. Fill the cooling system to 1¼ in. below the filler neck with correct water and antifreeze mixture, without a coolant reserve tank. With a reserve tank, fill the radiator and fill the tank to the indicated level. Warm up the engine with

the heater on and inspect the water pump for any leaks. Check the coolant level and add as required.

Thermostat

REMOVAL & INSTALLATION

1. Disconnect the negative battery cable.

2. Drain the cooling system to a level below the thermostat housing.

3. Remove the housing bolts and the thermostat housing and thermostat. Clean the gasket surfaces.

4. Installation is the reverse order of the removal procedure. Use a new gasket, dipped in water or sealant. Be sure the pellet end is facing the engine.

5. Refill the system, allow the engine to warm up with the heater on and check for leaks.

FUEL SYSTEM

Fuel System Service Precautions

Safety is the most important factor when performing not only fuel system maintenance but any type of maintenance. Failure to conduct maintenance and repairs in a safe manner may result in serious personal injury or death. Maintenance and testing of the vehicle's fuel system components can be accomplished safely and effectively by adhering to the following rules and guidelines.

• To avoid the possibility of fire and personal injury, always disconnect the negative battery cable unless the repair or test procedure requires that battery voltage be applied.

• Always relieve the fuel system pressure prior to disconnecting any fuel system component (injector, fuel rail, pressure regulator, etc.), fitting or fuel line connection. Exercise extreme caution whenever relieving fuel system pressure to avoid exposing skin, face and eyes to fuel spray. Please be advised that fuel under pressure may penetrate the skin or any part of the body that it contacts.

• Always place a shop towel or cloth around the fitting or connection prior to loosening to absorb any excess fuel due to spillage. Ensure that all fuel spillage (should it occur) is quickly removed from engine surfaces. Ensure that all fuel soaked cloths or towels are deposited into a suitable waste container.

• Always keep a dry chemical (Class

B) fire extinguisher near the work area.

• Do not allow fuel spray or fuel vapors to come into contact with a spark or open flame.

• Always use a backup wrench when loosening and tightening fuel line connection fittings. This will prevent unnecessary stress and torsion to fuel line piping. Always follow the proper torque specifications.

• Always replace worn fuel fitting O-rings with new. Do not substitute fuel hose or equivalent where fuel pipe is installed.

RELIEVING FUEL SYSTEM PRESSURE

1. Place a container under the fuel inlet fitting to catch any fuel that may be trapped in the fuel line.

2. Relieve the fuel pressure by slowly loosening the fuel inlet line, using 2 wrenches to avoid twisting the line.

3. Fuel will spray slightly from the line into the container. Wrap a shop towel around the connection to avoid the spray of fuel.

4. When repairs have been completed, tighten the fuel lines and inspect for fuel leaks.

Fuel Filter

REMOVAL & INSTALLATION

1. Locate the filter in the fuel line between the fuel pump and the carburetor.

2. Using hose-clamp pliers, remove the attaching clamps and pull the filter off.

3. Reverse this procedure for installation. Be sure the arrow on the filter is pointing toward the carburetor, direction of fuel flow.

NOTE: Some filters have a third line, the purpose of which is to prevent vapor lock by allowing fuel vapors to return to the tank.

Mechanical Fuel Pump

PRESSURE TESTING

1. Insert a tee fitting in fuel line at the carburetor.

2. Connect a 6 in. (152.4mm) piece of hose between the tee fitting and a fuel pressure gauge.

NOTE: The hose should not exceed 6 in. (152.4mm). The longer hose may collect fuel and additional weight of fuel would be added to pump pressure and result in an inaccurate reading.

3. Vent the pump for a few seconds to relieve air trapped in fuel chamber. If this is not done, pump will not operate at full capacity and low pressure reading will result.

4. Connect a tachometer, then start engine and run at idle. The reading should be as shown in specifications, depending on pump, and remain constant or return to **0** slowly, when engine is stopped. An instant drop to **0** indicates a leaky outlet valve. If pressure is too low, a weak diaphragm main spring or improper assembly of diaphragm may be the cause. If pressure is too high, main spring is too strong or the air vent is plugged.

REMOVAL & INSTALLATION

1. Disconnect the negative battery cable.

2. Remove the fuel lines from the fuel pump. It may be necessary to plug the line from the tank to prevent fuel from leaking out.

3. Remove the pump-to-block mounting bolts.

4. Remove the pump.

5. Remove the old gasket from the pump and replace with a new gasket during reinstallation.

6. Installation is the reverse order of removal procedure.

Carburetor

REMOVAL & INSTALLATION

1. Be sure the engine is cold before removing the carburetor from the engine. Disconnect the negative battery cable.

2. Remove the air cleaner.

3. Remove the fuel tank pressure vacuum filler cap.

4. Place a container under the fuel inlet fitting to catch any be remaining in the fuel line.

5. Disconnect fuel inlet line using a line wrench and a open end wrench to avoid twisting the line.

6. Disconnect the throttle linkage, choke linkage and all vacuum hoses.

7. Remove the carburetor mounting bolts or nuts and carefully remove the carburetor from the engine compartment. Hold the carburetor level to avoid spilling fuel from fuel bowl.

IDLE SPEED ADJUSTMENT

Holley 2280/6280 Electronic Feedback Carburetor

NOTE: Before checking or adjusting any idle speed, check ignition timing and adjust, if necessary.

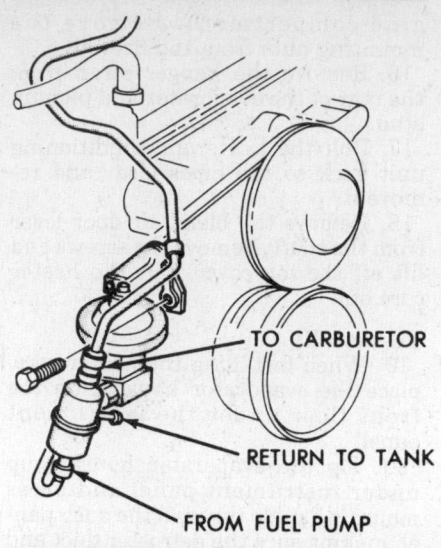

Fuel pump and filter location for V8

1. Disconnect and plug the vacuum hose at the EGR valve. Disconnect and plug the hose from the carburetor at the heated air temperature sensor. Remove air cleaner and disconnect and plug the canister purge hose at the canister and plug the vacuum hose at the ESA unit. Remove the PCV valve from the valve cover and allow the valve to draw underhood air. Install tachometer, start and run engine until normal operating temperature is reached. Turn **OFF** engine. Disconnect, then reconnect, fusible link at battery.

2. Ground the carburetor switch. Disconnect the engine harness lead from the oxygen sensor and ground the engine harness lead.

NOTE: Care should be exercised so no pulling force is put on the wire attached to the oxygen sensor. The bullet connector to be disconnected is approximately 4 in. from the sensor. Use care in working around the sensor as the exhaust manifold is extremely hot.

3. Start the engine and allow it to reach normal operating temperatures.

4. Connect a jumper wire between the positive battery terminal and the solenoid idle stop lead wire. Be sure to attach the wire to the right solenoid or damage to the wiring harness will occur.

5. Open throttle slightly to allow solenoid plunger to extend. Remove solenoid outer screw and spring. Insert a ⅛ in. Allen wrench into solenoid and adjust solenoid idle speed.

6. Install the screw and spring. Turn the screw in until it lightly bottoms out. Remove jumper wire. Set the idle speed by turning out solenoid screw.

7. The solenoid rpm is 900 and the idle rpm is 680.

8. Remove the tachometer. Unplug and reconnect all hoses. Reinstall the PCV valve and the air cleaner.

Rochester Quadrajet Electronic Feedback Carburetor

NOTE: Before checking or adjusting any idle speed, check ignition timing and adjust if necessary.

1. Disconnect and plug the vacuum hose at the EGR valve.

2. Disconnect and plug the hose from the carburetor at the heated air temperature sensor.

3. Remove air cleaner and disconnect and plug the canister purge hose at the canister.

4. Remove the PCV valve from the valve cover and allow the valve to draw underhood air.

5. Install tachometer and start and run engine until normal operating temperatures are reached.

6. Disconnect carburetor electrical connector. Attach a jumper wire between the ground switch terminal of the wiring harness connector (violet wire) and a good ground.

7. Attach a jumper wire between solenoid coil terminal of the carburetor connector (red wire) and battery positive post. Open throttle slightly to allow solenoid plunger to extend.

8. Remove outer screw and spring from solenoid. Insert a ⅛ in. Allen wrench into solenoid and adjust solenoid idle speed.

9. The solenoid rpm specification is 800. The idle rpm specification is 750.

10. Install screw and spring and turn in the outer screw until it lightly bottoms out. Remove jumper wire from carburetor connector and battery. Turn the outer solenoid screw until correct idle rpm is obtained.

11. Remove remaining jumper wire and reconnect carburetor connector. Remove tachometer, unplug and reconnect all hoses, reinstall the PCV valve and air cleaner.

IDLE MIXTURE ADJUSTMENT

Tampering with the carburetor is a violation of federal law. Adjustment of the carburetor idle air/fuel mixture can only be done under certain circumstances, as explained below. Upon completion of the carburetor adjustment, it is important to restore plugs and/or roll pins removed during the servicing of the carburetor.

This procedure should only be used if an idle defect still exists after normal diagnosis has revealed no other faulty condition, such as incorrect basic timing, incorrect idle speed, faulty wire or hose connections, etc. It is also important to make sure the combustion computer system is operating properly. Adjustment of the carburetor air/fuel mixture should be performed, if necessary, after a major carburetor overhaul.

Make all adjustments with engine fully warmed up, transmission in **N**, headlights OFF, air conditioning compressor not operating, idle stop carburetor switch, if equipped, grounded with a jumper wire and the vacuum hose at EGR valve, if equipped, and distributor or spark control unit disconnect and plugged. On ESC equipped vehicles, wait 1 minute after returning to idle before checking timing.

NOTE: Refer to the underhood emission control specification label for any further requirements or late changes in specifications before making carburetor or engine adjustments.

Holley 2280/6280 Electronic Feedback Carburetor

1. Disconnect the negative battery cable.

2. Remove the concealment plug as follows:

   a. Remove air cleaner.

   b. Disconnect all hoses from front of carburetor base.

   c. Remove the carburetor from the engine.

   d. Center punch at a point ¼ in. from end of mixture screw housing.

   e. Drill through outer housing at punch mark with a ³/₁₆ in. drill bit.

   f. Pry out and save concealment plug for reinstallation.

   g. Repeat operation on opposite side.

   h. Install the carburetor on the engine.

   i. Install all hoses to the carburetor and proceed to the idle mixture adjustment.

3. Set the parking brake and place the transmission in **N**. Reconnect the negative battery cable. Turn all lights and accessories OFF. Connect a tachometer to the engine.

4. Start the engine and allow it to warm up on the 2nd highest step of the fast idle cam until normal operating temperature is reached. Return the engine to idle and turn **OFF** engine.

5. Disconnect and plug the vacuum hoses at the EGR valve and ESA computer. No vacuum is to be applied to the computer. Disconnect and plug canister purge hose at canister.

6. Ground carburetor switch. Disconnect, then reconnect, battery fusible link.

7. Disconnect engine harness lead from sensor and ground engine harness lead.

NOTE: Care should be used so no pulling force is put on the wire attached to the sensor. The bullet connector to be disconnect is approximately 4 in. from the sensor. Use care in working around the sensor, as the exhaust manifold is extremely hot.

8. Start and run engine for at least 4 minutes.

9. Disconnect the vacuum supply hose from the choke diaphragm at the carburetor and install the propane supply hose in its place. Other connections at the tee must remain in place.

10. With the propane bottle upright and in a safe location, remove the PCV valve from the valve cover and allow the valve to draw underhood air.

11. Open the propane main valve. Slowly open the propane metering valve until the maximum engine rpm is reached. When too much propane is added, engine rpm will decrease. Fine tune the metering valve to obtain the highest engine rpm.

12. With the propane still flowing, adjust the idle speed screw on the solenoid to obtain the correct propane rpm. Again, Fine tune the metering valve to obtain the highest engine rpm. If there has been a change in the maximum rpm, readjust the idle speed screw to the specified propane rpm.

13. Turn off the propane main valve and allow the engine speed to stabilize. Slowly adjust the mixture screws by equal amounts, pausing between adjustments to allow engine speed to stabilize, to obtain the smoothest idle at the correct idle rpm.

14. The idle rpm specification is 680. The propane rpm is 740.

15. Turn ON the propane main valve and fine tune the metering valve to obtain the highest engine rpm. If the maximum engine speed is more than 25 rpm different than the specified propane rpm, repeat Steps 8–12.

16. Turn OFF propane main and metering valves. Remove the propane supply hose and reinstall the heated air sensor hose. Reinstall new concealment plugs. If installed, remove sensor ground wire and reconnect oxygen sensor. Reconnect vacuum line on ESA.

17. Perform all other carburetor adjustments.

Rochester Quadrajet Electronic Feedback Carburetor

1. Disconnect the negative battery cable.

2. Remove concealment plugs as follows:

a. Remove the carburetor from the engine.

b. Invert the carburetor and use a hacksaw to make 2 parallel cuts into the throttle body.

c. Make cuts on both sides of the locator points beneath the concealment plug. The cuts should reach down to the plug but should not extend more than ⅛ in. beyond the locater points.

d. The distance between the saw cuts will depend on the size of the punch to be used.

e. Place a flat punch at a point near the ends of the saw marks in throttle body.

f. Hold the punch at a 45 degree angel and drive it into the throttle body until the casting breaks away, exposing the steel plug.

g. Repeat the procedure for the other concealment plug.

h. Install the carburetor on the engine and proceed to the idle mixture adjustment.

3. Set the parking brake and place transmission in **N**. Turn OFF all lights and accessories, connect a tachometer to engine.

4. Start the engine and allow it to warm up on 2nd highest step of fast idle cam until normal operating temperatures are reached. Return engine to idle. Turn **OFF** engine.

5. Disconnect and plug vacuum hose at EGR valve and canister purge hose at canister. Disconnect idle solenoid connector. Ground carburetor switch (black wire).

6. Remove choke vacuum hose from carburetor nipple and install propane supply hose in its place.

7. With the bottle upright and in a safe location, remove the PCV valve from the valve cover and allow the valve to draw underhood air.

8. Disconnect the engine harness lead from the oxygen sensor and ground the engine harness lead.

NOTE: Care should be used so no pulling force is put on the wire attached to the oxygen sensor. The bullet connector to be disconnected is approximately 4 in. from the sensor. Use care in working around the sensor, as the exhaust manifold is extremely hot.

9. Reconnect the negative battery cable. Start and run engine for at least 2 minutes to allow effect of disconnecting the sensor to take place. Open propane main valve.

10. Slowly open propane metering valve until maximum engine rpm is reached. When too much propane is added, engine rpm will decrease. Fine tune the metering valve to obtain the highest rpm.

11. With propane still flowing, adjust the idle speed screw on the solenoid to achieve the specified propane rpm. Again, fine tune the metering valve to obtain the highest engine rpm. If there has been a change in the maximum rpm, readjust the idle speed screw on the solenoid to the specified propane rpm.

12. The rpm specification for propane is 800. The rpm specification for idle is 750.

13. Turn OFF propane main valve and allow engine speed to stabilize. Slowly adjust the idle mixture screws by equal amounts, pausing between adjustments to allow engine speed to stabilize, to achieve the smoothest idle at the specified rpm.

14. Turn ON propane main valve. Fine tune the metering valve to obtain the highest engine rpm. If the maximum speed is more than 25 rpm different than the specified rpm, repeat Steps 7–9.

15. Turn OFF propane main and metering valves. Remove the propane supply hose. Install the PCV valve. Unplug and reconnect all hoses. Remove the jumper wire and reconnect the oxygen sensor.

16. After adjustments are complete, seal the mixture screws in the throttle body using silicone sealant. The sealer is required to discourage unnecessary adjustments of the setting and to prevent fuel vapor loss in that area.

17. Perform all other carburetor adjustments.

SERVICE ADJUSTMENTS

For all carburetor service adjustment procedures and specifications, please refer to "Carburetor Service" in the Unit Repair section.

EMISSION CONTROLS

Please refer to "Emission Control" in the Unit Repair section for system maintenance procedures. Due to the complex nature of modern electronic engine control systems, comprehensive diagnosis and testing procedures fall outside the confines of this repair manual. For complete information on diagnosis, testing and repair procedures concerning all modern engine and emission control systems, please refer to "Chilton's Guide to Electronic Engine Controls".

ENGINE MECHANICAL

NOTE: Disconnecting the negative battery cable on some vehicles may interfere with the functions of the on board computer systems and may require the computer to undergo a relearning process, once the negative battery cable is reconnected.

Engine Assembly

REMOVAL & INSTALLATION

1. Scribe hood hinge positions and remove the hood.

2. Drain cooling system, remove the battery and carburetor air cleaner.

3. Remove the radiator/heater hoses and remove radiator. Set the fan shroud aside.

4. Remove the air conditioning compressor and set aside without removing lines.

5. Remove vacuum lines, distributor cap and wiring.

6. Remove the carburetor linkage, starter wires and oil pressure wire.

7. Remove the power steering hoses, if equipped.

8. Remove the starter motor, alternator, charcoal canister and horns.

9. Raise and support the vehicle safely.

10. Remove the exhaust pipe at the manifold.

11. Remove the bell housing bolts and inspection plate.

12. Remove the torque converter-to-flexplate bolts from torque converter flexplate. Mark the converter and flexplate to aid in re-assembly.

13. Support the transmission with a transmission stand tool. Attach a C-clamp on front bottom of transmission torque converter housing. This will assure that the torque converter will be retained in proper position in the transmission housing.

14. Disconnect the engine from the torque converter flexplate.

15. Install engine lifting fixture. Attach a chain hoist to fixture eyebolt.

16. Remove engine front mount bolts.

17. Remove engine from engine compartment and support it safely on a engine repair stand.

To install:

18. After all repairs have been made, remove engine from repair stand and install in engine compartment.

19. Install bell housing bolts and inspection plate. Remove stand from transmission.

20. Install torque converter-to-flexplate bolts and front end mounts. Remove C-clamp. Install inspection plate.

21. Remove engine lifting fixture and install carburetor and lines.

22. Install starter motor, alternator, charcoal canister and lines.

23. Install vacuum lines, distributor cap and wiring.

24. Install exhaust pipe. Torque to 24 ft. lbs. (33 Nm). Tighten nuts alternately so space between manifold flange and exhaust pipe flange is approximately equal.

25. Connect carburetor linkage and wiring to engine.

26. Install radiator, radiator hoses and heater hoses.

27. Install fan shroud. Fill cooling system.

28. Fill the engine crankcase with approved SAE rated oil.

29. Install the battery and carburetor air cleaner. Connect vacuum hose and power steering hoses, if equipped.

30. Install air conditioning equipment, if equipped.

31. Run engine until full operating temperature is reached and adjust carburetor, as necessary.

32. Install hood.

33. Road test vehicle.

Engine Mounts

REMOVAL & INSTALLATION

1. Disconnect the negative battery cable.

2. Position the fan to clear the radiator hose and radiator top tank.

3. Disconnect throttle linkage at transmission and at carburetor. Raise and support the vehicle safely.

4. Remove torque nuts from insulator studs.

5. Raise the engine just enough to remove the engine front mount assembly.

To install:

6. Before installing the engine mount, identify whether the mount is right or left hand.

7. Install the insulator to engine bracket and tighten.

8. Lower the engine and install washers and prevailing torque nuts to insulator studs; tighten the nuts.

9. Connect the throttle linkage at the transmission and carburetor.

Cylinder Head

REMOVAL & INSTALLATION

1. Disconnect the negative battery cable. Drain the cooling system.

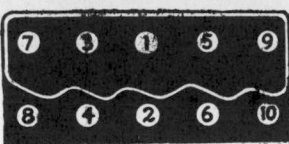

Tightening sequence for V8 engines

2. Remove alternator, carburetor air cleaner and fuel line.

3. Disconnect the accelerator linkage.

4. Remove the vacuum control hose between the carburetor and distributor.

5. Remove the distributor cap and wires.

6. Disconnect the coil wires, heat indicator sending unit wire, heater hoses and bypass hose.

7. Remove the closed ventilation system, evaporation control system and valve covers.

8. Remove the intake manifold, ignition coil and carburetor as an assembly.

9. Remove the exhaust manifolds.

10. Remove the rocker arm and shaft assemblies. Remove the pushrods and identify to insure installation in original location.

11. Remove the head bolts from each cylinder head and remove the cylinder heads.

To install:

12. Prior to installing the cylinder heads, clean all gasket surfaces of cylinder block and cylinder heads.

13. Inspect all surfaces with a straight edge if there is any reason to suspect leakage. If out of flatness exceeds 0.004 in., either machine or replace the head.

14. Remove cylinder heads from holding fixtures, install gaskets and place heads on engine.

15. Clean pipe sealant from bolt threads and bolt holes. Apply Mopar Lock N' Seal® or equivalent, to bolt threads. Install cylinder head bolts. Starting at top center, tighten all cylinder head bolts to 50 ft. lbs. (68 Nm) in sequence. Repeat procedure, retighten all cylinder head bolts to specified torque.

16. Inspect pushrods and replace worn or bent rods.

17. Install the pushrods, rocker arm and shaft assemblies with the notch on the end of rocker shaft pointing to centerline of engine and toward front of engine on the left bank and to the rear on right bank, making sure to install the long stamped steel retainers in the

No. 2 and No. 4 positions, tighten to 200 inch lbs. (23 Nm).

18. Do not use any sealer on side composition gaskets.

19. Install side gaskets to cylinder head.

20. Clean the cylinder block front and rear gasket surfaces using an approved solvent.

21. Apply a thin, uniform coating of a quick dry cement to the intake manifold front and rear gaskets and cylinder block gasket surface. Allow to dry 4–5 minutes or until tack free.

NOTE: When installing gaskets, the center hole in the gasket must engage the dowels in block. End holes in seals must be locked into tangs of head gasket.

22. Carefully install the front and rear intake manifold gaskets.

23. Place a drop, approximately ¼ in. diameter, of rubber sealer onto each of the 4 manifold to cylinder head gasket corners.

24. Carefully lower intake manifold into position on the cylinder block and cylinder heads. After the intake manifold is in place, inspect to make sure end seals are in place.

25. Install the finger tight. Tighten the intake manifold bolts, in 3 stages, in sequence. The 1st stage to 25 ft. lbs. (34 Nm), the 2nd stage to 40 ft. lbs. (54 Nm) and 3rd stage to 45 ft. lbs. (61 Nm).

26. Install exhaust manifolds and tighten screws to 20 ft. lbs. (27 Nm) and nuts to 15 ft. lbs. (20 Nm).

27. Adjust spark plug gap and install the plugs, tightening to 30 ft. lbs. (41 Nm).

28. Install the ignition wires, heat indicator sending unit wire, heater hoses and bypass hose.

29. Install the vacuum control hoses between carburetor and distributor.

30. Install the throttle linkage and adjust, as necessary.

31. Install the distributor cap and wires.

32. Install the fuel line, alternator and drive belt. Tighten the alternator mounting bolt to 30 ft. lbs. (41 Nm) and adjusting strap bolt to 200 inch lbs. (23 Nm).

33. Be certain the valve covers are not distorted at screw holes; flatten, if necessary.

34. Place the new valve cover gaskets in position and install valve covers. Tighten to 80 inch lbs. (9 Nm) using load spreader fasteners.

35. Install the closed crankcase ventilation system and evaporation control system.

36. Fill the cooling system and install battery ground cable.

Valve Lifters

REMOVAL & INSTALLATION

Except Roller Lifters

1. Disconnect the negative battery cable.
2. Remove valve cover, rocker assembly and pushrods; identify pushrods to insure installation in original location.
3. Slide a lifter extractor tool through the opening in the cylinder head and seat the tool firmly in the head of lifter.

NOTE: Although it is possible to remove the valve lifters without removing the intake manifold, it is recommended the manifold be removed.

4. Pull the lifter out of the bore with a twisting motion. If all liters are to be removed, identify lifters to insure installation in original locations.

NOTE: The plunger and lifter bodies are not interchangeable. The plunger and valve must always be installed to the original body. Work on 1 lifter at a time to avoid mixing of parts. Mixed parts are not compatible. Do not disassemble a lifter on a dirty work bench.

5. To install the lifters, lubricate lifters completely with engine oil.
6. Install lifters and pushrods in their original positions.
7. Install the rocker arm and shaft assembly.
8. Install the valve cover.
9. Start and operate engine. Warm up to normal operating temperature.

NOTE: To prevent damage to valve mechanism, engine must not be run above fast idle until all hydraulic lifters have filled with oil and have become quiet.

Roller Lifters

1. Disconnect the negative battery cable.
2. Remove the valve cover. Remove the rocker assembly and pushrods. Identify the pushrods to insure proper installation.
3. Remove the intake manifold. Remove the valve lifter yoke retainer and aligning yokes.
4. Remove the valve lifters using a valve lifter removal tool. Identify the lifters to insure proper installation.
5. Repair or replace the valve lifters, as required.
6. Installation is the reverse order of the removal procedure.
7. When installing the aligning yokes, make sure the arrow points toward the camshaft. Torque the retaining bolt to 200 inch lbs. (23 Nm).

Valve Lash

ADJUSTMENT

All engines use hydraulic lifters and non-adjustable rocker arms. The lifters take up lash automatically and no adjustment is possible. After engine re-assembly, these lifters adjust themselves shortly after oil pressure builds up.

Rocker Arms/Shafts

REMOVAL & INSTALLATION

1. Disconnect the negative battery cable.
2. Disconnect the spark plug wires by pulling on the boot straight out in line with the plug.
3. Disconnect closed crankcase ventilation system and evaporation control system from valve cover.
4. Remove the valve cover and gasket.
5. Remove rocker shaft bolts and retainers.
6. Remove rocker arms and shaft assembly.

To install:

7. Before installing the rocker arm assemblies, check the oil drain holes for blockage.
8. Install the rocker arm and shaft assemblies with the notch of rocker shaft pointing to centerline of engine and toward front of engine on the left bank and to the rear on right bank, making sure to install the long stamped steel retainers in the No. 2 and No. 4 positions. Tighten bolts to 200 inch lbs. (23 Nm).
9. Clean the valve cover gasket surface. Inspect cover for distortion and flatten, if necessary.
10. Clean the head rail, if necessary. Install the valve cover and tighten bolts to 80 inch lbs. (9 Nm).
11. Install closed crankcase ventilation system and evaporation control system.

Intake Manifold

REMOVAL & INSTALLATION

1. Drain the cooling system. Disconnect the negative battery cable.
2. Remove the alternator, the air cleaner and disconnect the fuel line from the carburetor.

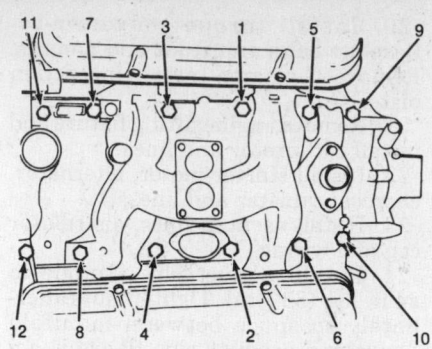

Intake manifold tightening sequence for V8 engines

3. Disconnect all vacuum lines and throttle linkage attached to the carburetor and intake manifold.
4. Disconnect the spark plug wires from the plugs and remove the distributor cap and wires as an assembly.
5. Disconnect the wires from the coil and the temperature sending unit.
6. Disconnect the heater hose and by pass hose from the intake manifold.
7. Remove the intake manifold attaching bolts and remove the manifold, carburetor and coil from the engine as an assembly.
8. Clean all gasket mounting surfaces and firmly cement new gaskets to the engine.
9. Installation is the reverse order of the removal procedure. Torque bolts to 45 ft. lbs. (61 Nm), in 3 passes, in sequence.

Exhaust Manifold

REMOVAL & INSTALLATION

1. Disconnect the negative battery cable.
2. Raise and support the vehicle safely.
3. Disconnect the exhaust manifold at the pipe flange. Access to these bolts is from underneath the vehicle.
4. If equipped, disconnect the air injection nozzles and carburetor heated air stove.
5. Disconnect any components of the EGR system which are in the way. Remove the exhaust manifold by removing the securing bolts and washers.
6. When the exhaust manifold is removed, sometimes the securing studs will come out with the nuts. If this occurs, studs must be replaced with the aid of sealing compound on the coarse thread ends. If this is not done, water leaks may develop at the studs.
7. Installation is the reverse order of the removal procedure. Torque the bolts to 20 ft. lbs. (27 Nm) and the nuts to 15 ft. lbs. (20 Nm).

NOTE: On the center branch of the manifold, no conical washers are used.

Timing Chain Front Cover

REMOVAL & INSTALLATION

1. Disconnect the negative battery cable.
2. Drain the cooling system.
3. Remove the water pump.
4. Remove the power steering pump.
5. Remove the pulley from the vibration damper and bolt and washer securing the vibration damper on the crankshaft.
6. Using a vibration damper pulling tool, remove the vibration damper from end of crankshaft.
7. Remove the fuel lines and fuel pump.
8. Loosen the oil pan bolts and remove the front bolt at each side.
9. Remove the chain case cover and gasket using extreme caution to avoid damaging the oil pan gasket.

To install:
10. Prior to installing the timing cover, be sure mating surfaces of chain case cover and cylinder block are clean and free from burrs.
11. Using a new cover gasket, carefully install the chain case cover to avoid damaging oil pan gasket. A 1/8 in. diameter bead of sealer is recommended on the oil pan gasket. Do not tighten the chain case cover bolts at this time.
12. Lubricate the seal lip with lubriplate, position vibration damper hub slot on crankshaft. Damper will act as a pilot for the crankshaft seal.
13. Press the vibration damper on the crankshaft.
14. Tighten the chain case cover screws to 30 ft. lbs. (41 Nm) first, tighten the oil pan screws to 200 inch lbs. (23 Nm).
15. Install the vibration damper bolt with the washer and tighten to 135 ft. lbs. (183 Nm).
16. Position the pulley on the vibration damper and attach with bolts and lock washers. Tighten to 200 inch lbs. (23 Nm).
17. Install the fuel pump and fuel lines.
18. Install the water pump and housing assembly, using new gaskets. Tighten bolts to 30 ft. lbs. (41 Nm).
19. Install the power steering pump.
20. Install the fan/belt assembly, hoses and close drains.
21. Fill the cooling system. Connect the negative battery cable.

Front Cover Oil Seal

REPLACEMENT

1. Disconnect the negative battery cable.
2. Loosen and remove the belts from the crankshaft pulley.
3. Remove the radiator shroud screws and set the shroud back over the engine.
4. Remove the fan and shroud from the engine.
5. Remove the crankshaft pulley and vibration dampener bolt and washer from the end of the crankshaft.
6. Pull the vibration dampener from the end of crankshaft.
7. Using a seal removing tool behind the lips of the oil seal, pry outward, being careful not to damage the crankshaft seal surface of cover.

To install:
8. Install the new seal by installing the threaded shaft part of the installing tool into the threads of the crankshaft.
9. Place the seal into the opening, with the seal spring toward the inside of the engine.
10. Place the installing tool with the thrust bearing and nut on the shaft. Tighten nut until tool is flush with the timing chain cover.
11. Lubricate the dampener hub and install the vibration dampener.
12. Install the vibration dampener bolt and washer and torque to 135 ft. lbs. (183 Nm).
13. Install the pulley on the vibration dampener and torque to 200 inch lbs. (23 Nm).
14. Set the radiator shroud back over engine and install the fan and belts.
15. Install the radiator shroud to the radiator.
16. Connect the negative battery cable.

Timing Chain and Sprockets

REMOVAL & INSTALLATION

1. Position the engine at TDC on the compression stroke.
2. Disconnect the negative battery cable.
3. Remove the front timing cover.
4. Remove the camshaft sprocket attaching cup washer, fuel pump eccentric and remove timing chain with crankshaft and camshaft sprockets.
5. Place both camshaft sprocket and crankshaft sprocket on the bench with timing marks on exact imaginary center line through both camshaft and crankshaft bores.

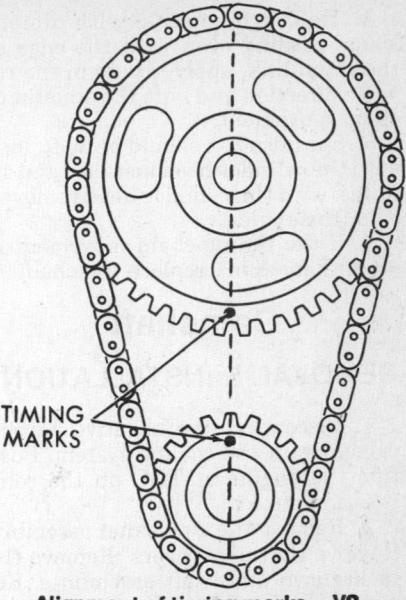

TIMING MARKS

Alignment of timing marks—V8

6. Place the timing chain around both sprockets.
7. Turn the crankshaft and camshaft to line up with keyway location in crankshaft sprocket and in camshaft sprocket.
8. Lift the sprockets and chain, keep the sprockets tight against the chain in position.
9. Slide both sprockets evenly over their respective shafts and use a straight edge to check alignment of the timing marks.
10. Install the fuel pump eccentric, cup washer and camshaft bolt. Tighten bolt to 35 ft. lbs. (47 Nm).
11. Check the camshaft for 0.002–0.006 in. (0.051–0.0152mm) endplay with a new thrust plate and up to 0.010 in. (0.254mm) endplay with a used thrust plate. If not within these limits, install a new thrust plate.
12. Continue the installation in the reverse order of the removal procedure.

Chain Slack Measurement
TIMING COVER REMOVED

1. Place a scale next to the timing chain so any movement of the chain can be measured.
2. Position a torque wrench and socket over the camshaft sprocket lock bolt, and apply torque in the direction of crankshaft rotation to take up the chain slack.
3. Specification should be 30 ft. lbs., with the cylinder head installed and 15 ft. lbs. with the cylinder head removed from the engine.

NOTE: When torque is applied to the camshaft sprocket bolt the crankshaft should not be permitted to move.

4. Holding the scale with dimensional reading even with the edge of the chain link, apply torque in the reverse direction and note the amount of chain movement.

5. Specification should be 30 ft. lbs., with the cylinder head installed and 15 ft. lbs. with the cylinder head removed from the engine.

6. If the timing chain movement is more than ⅛ in., replace the chain.

Camshaft

REMOVAL & INSTALLATION

1. Disconnect the negative battery cable. Drain the cooling system. Position the engine at TDC on the compression stroke.

2. Remove the air cleaner assembly. Remove the valve covers. Remove the rocker arm and shaft assemblies. Remove the distributor.

3. Remove the intake manifold assembly. Remove the pushrods and lifters. Be sure to identify the components, so each part will be replaced in its original location.

4. Remove the radiator assembly. Remove the front cover assembly. Remove the camshaft gear and timing chain.

5. As required, remove the air conditioning condenser. Before removing this component, properly discharge the system.

NOTE: If necessary, remove the grille assembly to allow enough room to remove the camshaft.

6. Install a long bolt into front of camshaft to facilitate removal of the camshaft. Remove the camshaft, being careful not to damage cam bearings with the cam lobes.

NOTE: To reduce internal leakage and help maintain higher oil pressure at idle, cup plugs have been pressed into the oil galleries behind the camshaft thrust plate.

To install:

7. Prior to installing the camshaft, lubricate the camshaft lobes and camshaft bearing journals and insert the camshaft to within 2 in. (50.8mm) of its final position in cylinder block.

8. When installing the camshaft thrust plate and chain oil tab. Make sure the tang enters the lower right hole in the thrust plate. Tighten to 210 inch lbs. (24 Nm). The top edge of the tab should be flat against the thrust plate in order to catch oil for chain lubrication.

9. Check the camshaft for 0.002–0.006 in. endplay with a new thrust plate and up to 0.010 in. endplay with a used thrust plate. If not within limits

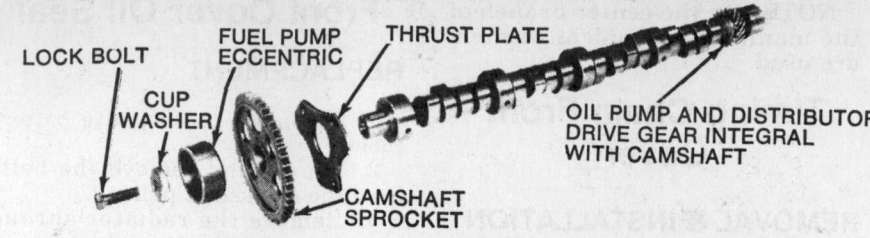

Camshaft and sprocket assembly—V8

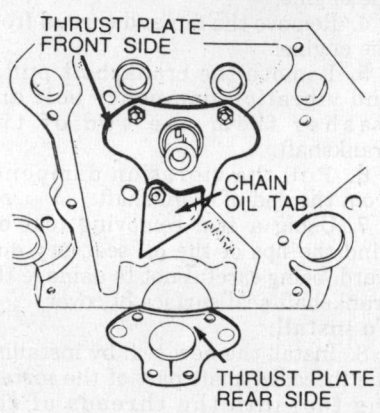

Timing chain oil tab installation, V8s

install a new thrust plate.

10. Reverse the removal procedures; be sure to torque the intake manifold bolts to specification and in the proper sequence.

11. Be sure to use new gaskets or RTV sealant, as required.

Piston and Connecting Rod

POSITIONING

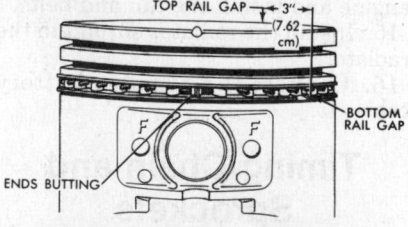

Proper oil ring installation

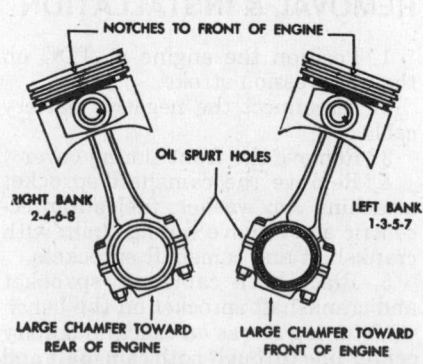

V8 piston and connecting rod assembly

ENGINE LUBRICATION

Oil Pan

REMOVAL & INSTALLATION

1. Disconnect the negative battery cable and remove dipstick.

2. Raise the vehicle, support it safely and drain the oil from the pan.

3. Remove the exhaust crossover pipe. Disconnect and lower center steering link.

4. Remove the starter nut and bolt and remove the starter.

5. Remove the torque converter inspection plate.

6. Remove the engine oil pan retaining bolts and remove the oil pan.

To install:

7. Inspect alignment of the oil strainer. The bottom of the strainer must be parallel with the machined surface of the cylinder block. The bottom of the strainer must touch the bottom of oil pan with $\frac{1}{16}$–⅛ in. (1.587–3.175mm) interference desirable.

8. Using a new pan gasket, add a drop of sealer at corners of rubber and cork.

9. Install the oil pan and torque the screws to 200 inch lbs. (23 Nm).

10. Install the torque converter inspection plate.

11. Install the starter and starter mounting nut and bolt.

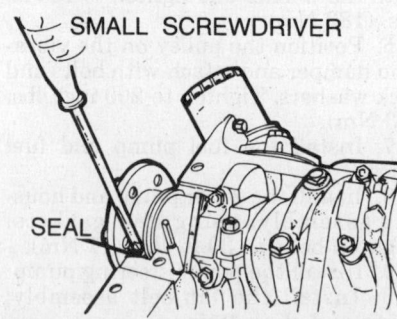

Removing upper main bearing oil seal with screwdriver. View showed with engine out of car.

12. Install the crossover pipe. Torque to 24 ft. lbs. (33 Nm).
13. Connect the center steering link.
14. Lower the vehicle, install dipstick and fill the engine with motor oil.
15. Connect the negative battery cable, start engine and check for leaks.

Oil Pump

REMOVAL & INSTALLATION

1. Disconnect the negative battery cable.
2. Raise the vehicle and support it safely.
3. Remove the oil pan.
4. Remove the oil pump from the rear main bearing cap.
5. Prime the oil pump before installation by filling the rotor cavity with engine oil and rotating the shaft.
6. Install the oil pump on the rear main bearing cap and tighten the retaining bolts to 30 ft. lbs. (41 Nm).

CHECKING

1. Throughly clean all of the parts. The mating surface of the oil pump cover should be smooth; if it is scratched or grooved, replace it.
2. Lay a straight edge across the pump cover surface. Using a 0.0015 in. (0.038mm) feeler gauge, check the cover for flatness; if the feeler gauge can be inserted between the pump cover and the straight edge, replace the cover.
3. Using a micrometer, measure the thickness and diameter of the outer rotor; if the thickness is 0.825 in. (20.9mm) or less or the diameter is 2.469 in. (62.7mm) or less, replace the outer rotor.
4. Using a micrometer, measure the thickness of the inner rotor; if the thickness is 0.825 in. (20.9mm) or less, replace the inner rotor.
5. Insert the outer rotor into the pump body with the large chamfered edge installed inside the pump body. Using a feeler gauge, measure the outer rotor-to-pump body clearance; if the measurement is 0.014 in. (0.356mm) or more, replace the oil pump assembly.
6. Install the inner rotor and shaft assembly into the pump body. Using a feeler gauge, measure the clearance between the inner and outer rotors; if the clearance is 0.010 in. (0.254mm) or more, replace the shaft and both rotors.
7. Place a straight edge across the face of the pump, between both bolt holes. If a 0.004 in. (0.102mm) or more feeler gauge can be inserted between the rotors and the straight edge, replace the pump assembly.

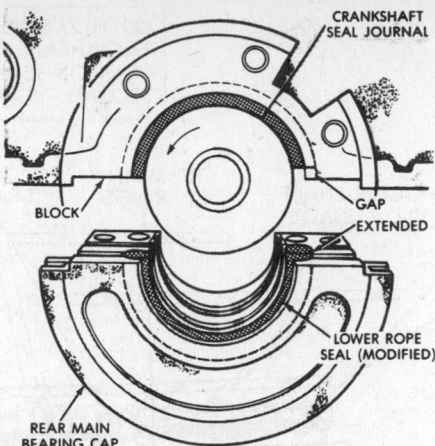

Exploded view of the rear main bearing oil seal

8. Inspect the oil pressure relief valve plunger for scoring and free operation in its bore; small marks can be removed with 400 grit sandpaper.
9. The relief valve spring has a free length of $2\frac{1}{32}$–$2\frac{3}{64}$ in. (51.6–52.0mm) and should test between 16.2–17.2 lbs. when compressed to $1\frac{11}{32}$ in. (32.1mm). Replace the spring if it does not meet specifications.
10. If the oil pressure is low and the pump is within specifications, inspect for worn engine bearings or other reasons for oil pressure loss.

Rear Main Bearing Oil Seal

REMOVAL & INSTALLATION

Rope Type

1. Disconnect the negative battery cable.
2. Raise the vehicle and support it safely.
3. Remove the oil pan.
4. Remove the rear main bearing cap.
5. Remove the lower rope oil seal by prying from the side of the bearing cap with a small pry tool.
6. Install a new lower seal half in the cap. Tap the seal down into position with a rope seal installing tool.
7. Cut the right bank seal end flush with the cap.
8. Remove the rope seal, rotate it end for end and re-install the seal back into the bearing cap with the cut end protruding above the surface so as to tightly fill the block half seal end compressed above the block/cap parting line.
9. Re-press the seal into the cap with the rope seal installing tool and cut the left bank side flush with the cap surface.

NOTE: This modification procedure insures the protruding end is properly formed without a frayed end.

10. Lightly oil the lower rope seal half with engine oil. Install the side seals in the bearing cap. Be sure the side seal identified with yellow paint is installed on the right side.
11. Remove the upper seal half with a rope seal remover tool.
12. Screw the tool into the seal, being careful not to damage the crankshaft. Pull the seal out with the tool while rotating the crankshaft.

To install:

13. Lightly lubricate the new seal before installing it.
14. Install the upper rope seal using a rope seal installer tool. Carefully trim the upper seal after installation.
15. Install the rear main bearing cap, being careful not to crimp the extended side of the oil seal between the cap and the block.
16. Install the main bearing bolts and torque to 85 ft. lbs. (115 Nm).
17. Complete the assembly of the oil pump and oil pan assembly. Add sealer at the bearing cap to block joint to provide oil pan end sealing.

AUTOMATIC TRANSMISSION

For further information on transmissions/transaxles, please refer to "Chilton's Guide to Transmission Repair".

Transmission Assembly

REMOVAL & INSTALLATION

1. The transmission and torque converter must be removed as an assembly; otherwise, the converter flexplate, pump bushing or oil seal may be damaged. The flexplate will not support a load; therefore, none of the weight of the transmission should be allowed to rest on the plate during removal.
2. Disconnect negative battery cable. Raise the vehicle and support it safely.
3. Some vehicles require the exhaust system be dropped for clearance.
4. Remove engine to transmission braces, if equipped.
5. Remove cooler lines at transmission.

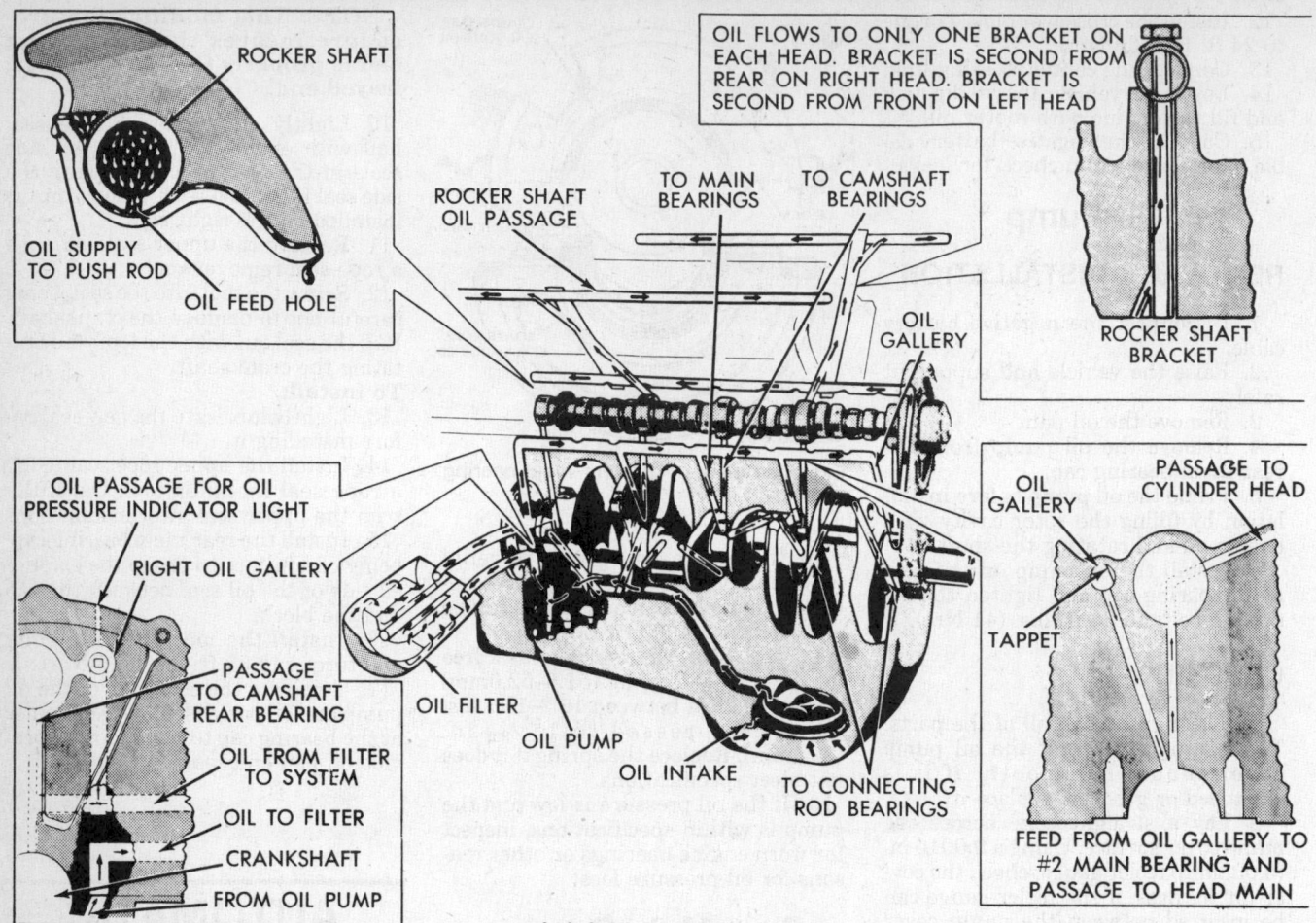

ROCKER SHAFT

OIL SUPPLY TO PUSH ROD

OIL FEED HOLE

OIL FLOWS TO ONLY ONE BRACKET ON EACH HEAD. BRACKET IS SECOND FROM REAR ON RIGHT HEAD. BRACKET IS SECOND FROM FRONT ON LEFT HEAD

ROCKER SHAFT OIL PASSAGE

TO MAIN BEARINGS

TO CAMSHAFT BEARINGS

OIL GALLERY

ROCKER SHAFT BRACKET

OIL PASSAGE FOR OIL PRESSURE INDICATOR LIGHT

RIGHT OIL GALLERY

PASSAGE TO CAMSHAFT REAR BEARING

OIL FROM FILTER TO SYSTEM

OIL TO FILTER

CRANKSHAFT

FROM OIL PUMP

OIL FILTER

OIL PUMP

OIL INTAKE

TO CONNECTING ROD BEARINGS

OIL GALLERY

PASSAGE TO CYLINDER HEAD

TAPPET

FEED FROM OIL GALLERY TO #2 MAIN BEARING AND PASSAGE TO HEAD MAIN

Lubrication system for V8

6. Remove starter motor and cooler line bracket.

7. Remove torque converter access cover.

8. Loosen oil pan bolts and tap the pan to break it loose, allowing fluid to drain.

9. Install the pan.

10. Mark torque converter and flexplate to aid in re-assembly. The crankshaft flange bolt circle, inner and outer circle of holes in the flexplate and the 4 tapped holes in front face of the torque converter all have 1 hole offset so these parts will be installed in the original position. This maintains balance of the engine and torque converter.

11. Rotate engine to position the bolts attaching torque converter to flexplate and remove bolts.

12. Mark parts for re-assembly, then disconnect propeller shaft at rear universal joint. Carefully pull shaft assembly out of the extension housing.

13. Disconnect wire connector from the back-up lamp and neutral safety switch.

14. Disconnect gearshift rod and torque shaft assembly from transmission.

NOTE: When it is necessary to disassemble linkage rods from levers using plastic grommets as retainers, the grommets should be replaced with new grommets. Use a prying tool to force rod from grommet in lever, then remove the old grommet. Use pliers to snap new grommet into lever and rod into grommet.

15. Disconnect throttle rod from lever at the left side of transmission. Remove linkage bellcrank from transmission, if equipped.

16. Remove oil filler tube and speedometer cable.

17. Install engine support fixture with frame hooks or a suitable substitute, that will support rear of the engine.

18. Raise the transmission slightly with service jack to relieve load on the supports.

19. Remove bolts securing transmis-

sion mount to crossmember and crossmember to frame, remove the crossmember.

20. Remove all bell housing bolts.

21. Carefully work the transmission and torque converter assembly rearward off engine block dowels and disengage converter hub from the end of the crankshaft. Attach a small C-clamp to the edge of the bell housing to hold the torque converter in place during transmission removal.

22. Lower the transmission and remove the assembly from under the vehicle.

23. To remove the torque converter assembly, remove the C-clamp from the edge of the bell housing, carefully slide the assembly out of the transmission.

To install:

NOTE: The transmission and torque converter must be installed as an assembly; otherwise, the torque converter flexplate, pump bushing and oil seal will be damaged. The flexplate will not

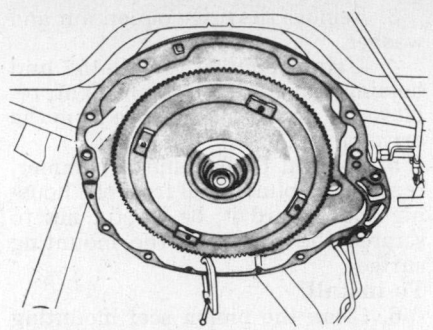

Attach a C-clamp to automatic transmission bell housing to keep torque converter in place when removing engine

support a load; therefore, none of the weight of transmission should be allowed to rest on the plate during installation.

24. Rotate the pump gears with an alignment tool until the 2 small holes in handle are vertical.

25. Carefully slide the torque converter assembly over the input shaft and reaction shaft. Make sure the torque converter hub slots are also vertical and fully engage the pump inner gear lugs.

NOTE: Test for full engagement by placing a straight edge on face of the case. The surface of torque converter front cover lug should be at least ½ in. to rear of straight edge when torque converter is pushed all the way into transmission.

26. Maintain the small C-clamp to edge of the torque converter housing to hold the torque converter in place during transmission installation.

27. Inspect the torque converter flexplate for distortion or cracks and replace, if necessary. Torque the flexplate to crankshaft bolts to 55 ft. lbs. (75 Nm). When the flexplate replacement has been necessary, make sure both transmission dowel pins are in the engine block and they are protruding far enough to hold the transmission in alignment.

28. Coat the converter hub hole in the crankshaft with multi-purpose grease. Place transmission and torque converter assembly on a service jack and position assembly under vehicle for installation. Raise or tilt, as necessary, until the transmission is aligned with the engine.

29. Rotate the torque converter so the mark on the torque converter, made during removal, will align with the mark on the flexplate. The offset holes in plate are located next to ⅛ in. hole in the inner circle of plate. Carefully work the transmission assembly forward over the engine block dowels

with the torque converter hub entering the crankshaft opening.

30. After the transmission is in position, install the converter housing bolts and tighten to 30 ft. lbs. (41 Nm). If equipped, install vibration damper weight on rear of the extension housing.

31. Install the crossmember to frame and lower transmission to install mount on extension to the crossmember. Tighten bolts.

32. The engine support fixture may now be removed.

33. Install the oil filler tube and speedometer cable.

34. Connect the throttle rod to the transmission lever.

35. Connect the gear shift rod and torque shaft assembly to the transmission lever and frame.

36. Place the wire connector on the combination back-up lamp and neutral/park starter switch.

37. Carefully guide the sliding yoke into the extension housing and on the output shaft splines. Align marks made at removal. Connect the propeller shaft to the rear axle pinion shaft yoke.

38. Rotate the crankshaft clockwise with socket wrench on the vibration dampener bolt, as needed to install the torque converter to flexplate bolts, matching marks made at removal. Tighten to 270 inch lbs. (31 Nm).

39. Install the torque converter access cover.

40. Install the starter motor and cooler line bracket.

41. Tighten the cooler lines to the transmission fittings.

42. Install the engine-to-transmission struts, if equipped. Tighten the bolts holding strut to transmission before the strut to engine bolts.

43. Replace the exhaust system, if it was disturbed and adjust for clearance.

44. Adjust the shift and throttle linkage.

45. Refill the transmission with Dexron®II type automatic transmission fluid.

SHIFT LINKAGE ADJUSTMENT

NOTE: Chrysler Corporation recommends, when it is necessary to disassemble linkage rods from their levers which use plastic grommets for retainers, the grommets should be replaced with new ones.

Column Shift

1. Make sure all linkage is free, especially the adjustable slide on the shift rod, so the pre-load spring action

is not reduced by friction. Disassemble, clean and lube, if necessary.

2. Put the shift lever in the **P** position.

3. With the adjustable swivel loose, move the shift lever all the way to the rear-most detent position, which is **P**.

4. Tighten swivel lock bolts to 90 inch lbs. (10 Nm).

5. Verify the vehicle will only start in **P** or **N**.

THROTTLE LINKAGE ADJUSTMENT

1. Perform transmission throttle rod adjustment while engine is at normal operating temperature. Otherwise, make sure carburetor is not on fast idle cam.

2. Raise the vehicle and support it safely.

3. Loosen adjustment swivel lock screw.

4. To insure proper adjustment, the swivel must be free to slide along the flat end of the throttle rod, this will insure the preload spring action is not restricted. Disassemble and clean or repair parts to assure free action, if necessary.

5. Hold transmission lever firmly forward against its internal stop and tighten swivel lock screw to 100 inch lbs. (11 Nm).

6. The adjustment is finished and linkage backlash was automatically removed by the preload spring.

7. Lower the vehicle, reconnect the choke, if disconnected, and test the linkage freedom of operation by moving the throttle rod rearward, slowly releasing it to confirm it will return fully forward.

DRIVE AXLE

Driveshaft and U-Joints

The driveshaft is a one-piece tubular shaft with 2 universal joints, one at each end. The front joint yoke serves as a slip yoke on the transmission output shaft. The rear universal joint is the type that must be disassembled to be removed.

REMOVAL & INSTALLATION

1. Raise and support the vehicle safely.

2. Matchmark the driveshaft, U-joint and pinion flange before disas-

sembly. These marks must be re-aligned during reassembly to maintain the balance of the driveline. Failure to align them may result in excessive vibration.

3. Remove both of the clamps from the differential pinion yoke and slide the driveshaft forward slightly to dis-engage the U-joint from the pinion yoke. Tape the 2 loose U-joint bearings together to prevent them from falling off.

NOTE: Do not disturb the bearing assembly retaining strap. Never allow the driveshaft to hang from either of the U-joints. Always support the unattached end of the shaft to prevent damage to the joints.

4. Lower the rear end of the driveshaft and gently slide the front yoke/driveshaft assembly rearward disengaging the assembly from the transmission output shaft. Be careful not to damage the splines or the surface with the output shaft seal rides on.
5. Check the transmission output shaft seal for sign of leakage.
6. Installation is the reverse order of the removal procedure. Be sure to align the matchmarks. The torque for the clamp bolts is 14 ft. lbs. (19 Nm).

Rear Axle Shaft, Bearing and Seal

REMOVAL & INSTALLATION

NOTE: Under no circumstances should rear axle bearing cones, cups, bores or journals be subjected to heating with a torch, hitting with a hammer or any other abnormal abuse, permanent damage may result.

1. Raise the vehicle and support it safely.
2. Remove the wheel cover and wheel and tire assembly. Remove the brake drum.
3. Loosen the housing cover and drain the lubricant from the rear axle. Remove the cover.
4. Turn the differential case to make the differential pinion shaft lock screw is accessible and remove the lock screw and pinion shaft.
5. Push the axle shafts toward the center of vehicle and remove the C-washers from the recessed groove of the axle shaft.
6. Remove the axle shaft from housing being careful not to damage the straight roller-type axle shaft bearing which will remain in the rear axle housing.

7. Inspect the axle shaft bearing surfaces for signs of imperfection, spalling or pitting. If any of these conditions are present both the shaft and the bearing should be replaced.
8. Remove the axle shaft seal from housing bore. Using a slide hammer motion, remove the axle shaft bearing. If the axle shaft and bearing show no signs of distress, they can be reinstalled along with a new axle shaft seal. Never reuse an axle shaft seal.
To install:

NOTE: Inspect housing bearing shoulder for burrs and remove any, if present.

9. Wipe the axle shaft bearing cavity of axle housing clean. The axle shaft oil seal bores at both ends of the housing should be smooth and free of rust and corrosion. This also applies to the brake support plate and housing flange face surface.
10. Insert the axle shaft bearing into cavity making sure it bottoms against the shoulder and it is not cocked in bore.

NOTE: Under no circumstances should the seal be used to position or bottom the bearing in its bore as this would damage the seal.

11. Install the axle shaft bearing seal using bearing installer tool, until the outer flange of tool bottoms against housing flange face. This positions the seal to the proper depth beyond the end of the flange face.
12. Lubricate the bearing and seal area of the axle shaft, slide the axle shaft into place being careful the splines of the shaft do not damage the oil seal and properly engage with the splines of differential side gears.
13. With the axle shaft in place, install the C-washers in recessed grooves of axle shaft and pull outward on the shaft so the C-washers seat in the counterbore of the differential side gear.
14. Install the differential pinion shaft through the case and pinions, aligning the hole in shaft with the lock screw hole. Install the lock screw and tighten to 100 inch lbs. (11 Nm).
15. Clean up the mating surfaces and apply a $1/16$–$3/32$ in. bead of silicone rubber sealant along the bolt circle of the cover. Allow sealant to cure.

Pinion Seal

REMOVAL & INSTALLATION

1. Raise and safely support the vehicle.
2. Remove the driveshaft from the differential pinion flange and support it aside.

3. Remove the drive pinion nut and washer.
4. Using removal tool C-452 and holding tool C-3281 or equivalent, remove the drive pinion flange from the drive pinion.
5. Using a prybar and a hammer, remove the pinion seal from the housing and discard it; be careful not to scratch the pinion or the mounting surface.
To install:
6. Clean the pinion seal mounting surface.
7. Using seal installer tool C-4002 for 7¼ in. axle or tool C-4076 for 8¼ in. axle, drive the new seal into the housing until it seats.
8. Using installer tool C-3718 and holding tool C-3281 or equivalent, press the drive pinion flange onto the drive pinion.
9. Install the drive pinion washer and nut. Torque the drive pinion nut to 210 ft. lbs. (284 Nm).
10. Using an inch lb. torque wrench, check the pinion bearing preload; the preload should be 15–30 inch lbs. (1–3 Nm) for 7¼ in. axle or 20–35 inch lbs. (2–4 Nm) for 8¼ in. axle.

NOTE: If the correct preload is not reached, continue tightening in small increments until it is reached.

11. Install the driveshaft to the drive pinion flange and torque the cap bolts to 10 ft. lbs. (14 Nm).
12. Check and/or refill the axle housing. Lower the vehicle.

Axle Housing

REMOVAL & INSTALLATION

1. Raise the vehicle and support it safely. Install suitable stands at the front of the rear springs.
2. Block the brake pedal in the UP position, using a wooden block or equivalent.
3. Drain the lubricant from differential housing.
4. Loosen and remove rear wheels. Do not removed drum retaining spring clips or brake drums.
5. Disconnect hydraulic brake lines at wheel cylinders and cap fittings to prevent loss of brake fluid.
6. Disconnect the parking brake cables.
7. Disconnect the driveshaft at differential pinion flange and secure in a near horizontal position to prevent damage to front universal joint.
8. Remove the shock absorbers from the spring plate studs and loosen rear spring U-bolt nuts and remove U-bolts.

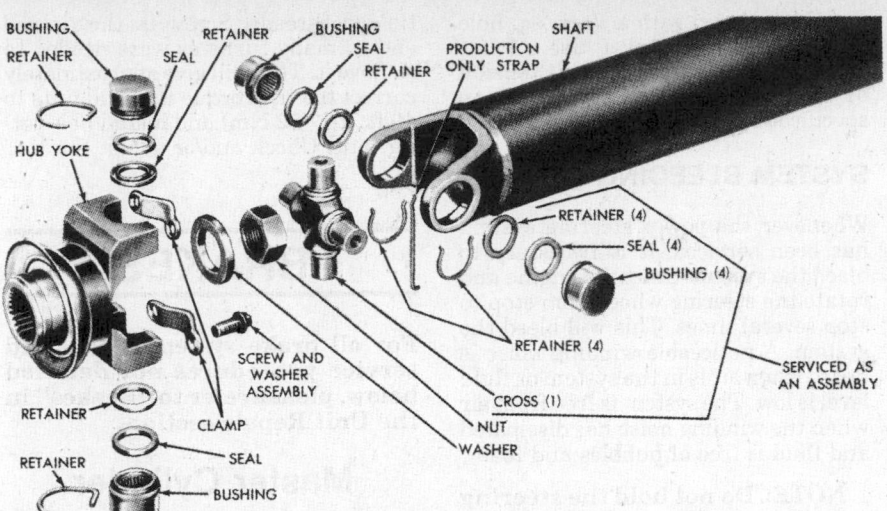

Rear driveshaft universal joint assembly—remove the two clamps to remove driveshaft

9. Remove the axle assembly from vehicle.
10. Installation is the reverse order of the removal procedure.

STEERING

Steering Wheel

— CAUTION —

On vehicles equipped with an air bag, the negative battery cable must be disconnected, before working on the system. Failure to do so may result in deployment of the air bag and possible personal injury.

REMOVAL & INSTALLATION

NOTE: All vehicles are equipped with collapsible steering columns. A sharp blow or excessive pressure on the column will cause it to collapse. Do not hammer on the steering wheel.

1. Disconnect the negative battery cable.
2. Remove the padded center assembly. This center assembly is often held on only by spring clips. There are usually holes in the back of the wheel so the pad can be pushed off. However, on some deluxe steering wheel pads, it is held on by screws behind the arms of the wheel. Remove the horn wire, if necessary.
3. On the tilt and telescoping steering column, remove the locking lever knob by releasing the clip on its underside. Remove the locking lever screws and the lever.

4. Remove the large center nut. Mark the steering wheel and steering shaft so the wheel may be replaced in its original position. In most cases, the wheel can only go on one way.
5. Using a puller, pull the steering wheel from the steering shaft.
6. Reverse the procedure to install the wheel. When placing the wheel on the shaft, make sure the front tires are in the straight ahead position and the steering wheel and shaft are properly aligned. Tighten the retaining nut to 45 ft. lbs.

Steering Column

REMOVAL & INSTALLATION

1. Disconnect the negative battery cable.
2. If equipped with column shift, disconnect the link by prying the shift rod out of the grommet in the shift lever.
3. Remove the steering shaft lower coupling to worm shaft roll pin.
4. Disconnect the wiring connectors at the steering column jacket.
5. Remove the steering wheel center pad assembly and disconnect the horn switch, if applicable.
6. Remove the steering wheel retaining nut and remove the steering wheel from the steering shaft.

NOTE: Do not bump or hammer on the steering shaft to remove the steering wheel.

7. Remove the floor plate to floor pan attaching screws.
8. To expose the steering column bracket retaining screws, remove in-

strument panel steering column cover and lower reinforcements.
9. Remove the nuts holding the steering column bracket to the instrument panel supports.
10. Carefully remove the lower coupler from the steering gear wormshaft, then remove the column assembly out through the passenger compartment.

NOTE: Do not damage the paint or trim during the removal procedure.

11. Should a new grommet be needed in the shift rod, install from the rod side of the lever.
12. The installation of the steering column is the reverse procedure of the removal.

Power Steering Gear

ADJUSTMENT

1. Disconnect the center link from the steering gear arm.
2. Start the engine and run at idle speed.
3. Turn the steering wheel gently from 1 stop to stop counting the number of turns. Then turn the wheel back exactly halfway, to center position.
4. Loosen the sector shaft adjusting screw until backlash is evident in steering gear arm. Feel backlash by holding the end of the steering gear arm between thumb and fore-finger with a light grip. Tighten the adjusting screw until backlash just disappears.
5. Continue to tighten to ⅜–½ turn from this position and tighten locknut to 28 ft. lbs. (38 Nm) to maintain this setting.

REMOVAL & INSTALLATION

1. Separate from the steering gear input shaft and remove the steering column.

NOTE: Chrysler Corporation recommends complete detachment from the floor and instrument panel of the steering column to avoid damage to the energy absorbing steering column components.

2. Remove the pressure and return fluid lines.
3. Raise the vehicle and support safely. Remove the retaining nut and washer from the steering gear arm sector shaft. With a puller tool, remove the steering gear arm.

NOTE: On some vehicles it may be necessary to remove the starter heat shield and drop the exhaust system.

4. Remove the steering gear assembly-to-frame bolts or nuts and remove the steering gear.

To install:

5. Center the sector shaft to its midpoint of travel.

6. Position the gear assembly on the frame and tighten the bolts or nuts.

7. Align the master serrations on the sector shaft to the splines in the steering arm, install and tighten the nut and washer.

8. Lower the vehicle and install the pressure and return fluid lines.

9. Install the steering column, fill the reservoir with fluid, start the engine and turn the steering wheel several times from stop to stop to bleed the system of air.

Power Steering Pump

REMOVAL & INSTALLATION

1. Back off the pump mounting and locking bolts. Remove the pump drive belt.

2. Disconnect all hoses at the pump.

3. Remove the pump bolts and pump with the bracket.

To install:

4. Place the pump in position and install the mounting bolts.

5. Install the pump drive belt and adjust. There should be no more than ½ in. of play, under moderate thumb pressure, on the longest run of belt. Some pump brackets have a ½ in. square hole for use in tensioning the belt. Torque the mounting bolts to 30 ft. lbs.

6. Connect the pressure and return hoses. Replace the pressure hose O-ring, if equipped.

7. Fill the pump with power steering fluid.

NOTE: Do not use transmission fluid, use only recommended power steering fluid.

8. Start the engine and rotate the steering wheel from stop to stop several times. This will bleed the system. Check the pump fluid level and fill as required.

9. Be certain the hoses are away from the exhaust manifolds and are not kinked or twisted.

BELT ADJUSTMENT

1. Disconnect the negative battery cable.

2. Install the pump drive belt and adjust.

3. There should be no more than ½ in. of play, under moderate thumb pressure, on the longest span of the belt.

4. If equipped with a ½ in. sq. hole on the adjusting bracket, use a ½ in. breaker bar to adjust the belt tension or torque wrench and adjust to specifications.

SYSTEM BLEEDING

Whenever the power steering system has been serviced, it is necessary to bleed the system. Start the engine and rotate the steering wheel from stop to stop several times. This will bleed the system. A noticeable winding noise is heard when air is in the system or fluid level is low. The system is free from air when the winding noise has dissipated and fluid is free of bubbles and foam.

NOTE: Do not hold the steering to either extreme for more than 5 seconds at a time. This can damage the pump and the gear seals by overheating the fluid.

Tie Rod Ends

REMOVAL & INSTALLATION

1. Loosen the tie rod adjuster sleeve clamp nuts.

2. Remove the tie rod end stud nut and cotter pin.

3. If the outer tie rod end is being removed, remove the stud from the steering knuckle. If the inner tie rod end is being removed, remove the stud from the center link. The studs on all the tie rod ends fit in a tapered hole, they can be removed with a ball joint removal tool.

NOTE: Use extreme care not to damage the rubber grease seals at the tie rod ends. If the seals become damaged they must be removed and the tie rod ends inspected.

4. Unscrew the tie rod end from the threaded sleeve and record the number of turns required to remove it; the threads may be left or right hand.

5. Installation is the reverse order of the removal procedure. Grease the

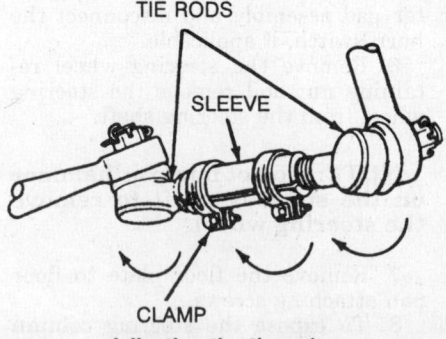

TIE RODS

SLEEVE

CLAMP

Adjusting the tie rods

tie rod threads. Screw in the tie rod end as many turns as were needed to remove it. This will give approximately correct toe-in. Torque the stud nuts to 40 ft. lbs. (52 Nm) and install new cotter pins. Check and/or adjust the toe.

BRAKES

For all brake system repair and service procedures not detailed below, please refer to "Brakes" in the Unit Repair section.

Master Cylinder

REMOVAL & INSTALLATION

1. Disconnect the negative battery cable.

2. Disconnect the brake lines from the master cylinder. Plug the brake line outlets to prevent fluid loss.

3. Remove the master cylinder-brake-booster nuts.

4. Slide the master cylinder straight out and off the brake booster.

5. Installation is the reverse order of the removal procedure. Refill the master cylinder and bleed the brake system.

Combination Valve

The combination valve is located below the master cylinder and attached to the fender splash shield. The valve assembly contains a warning switch, with a hold off valve and a proportioning valve.

REMOVAL & INSTALLATION

1. Disconnect the electrical connector from the combination valve.

2. Disconnect and plug the brake tubes at the combination valve.

3. Remove the valve-to-fender splash shield botls and the combination valve from the vehicle.

4. Installation is the reverse order of the removal procedure. Bleed the brake system.

Power Brake Booster

REMOVAL & INSTALLATION

1. Disconnect the negative battery cable.

2. Remove the master cylinder-to-brake booster nuts and position the master cylinder aside without disconnecting the lines. Use care not to kink the brake lines.

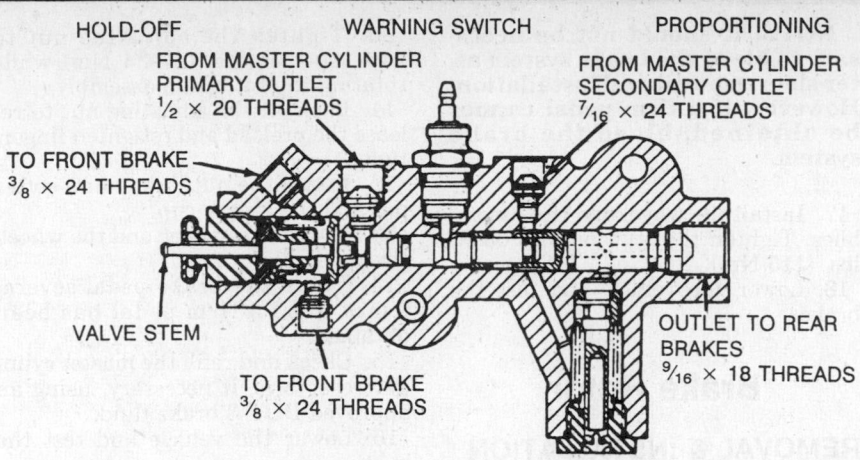

HOLD-OFF

WARNING SWITCH

PROPORTIONING

FROM MASTER CYLINDER
PRIMARY OUTLET
½ × 20 THREADS

FROM MASTER CYLINDER
SECONDARY OUTLET
7/16 × 24 THREADS

TO FRONT BRAKE
3/8 × 24 THREADS

VALVE STEM

TO FRONT BRAKE
3/8 × 24 THREADS

OUTLET TO REAR
BRAKES
9/16 × 18 THREADS

Exploded view of the combination valve

3. Disconnect the vacuum hose from the brake booster.

4. Working under the dash, remove the nut and bolt or retainer clip attaching the brake booster pushrod to the brake pedal.

5. Remove the brake booster attaching nuts and washers.

6. Remove booster assembly from the vehicle.

7. Installation is the reverse order of the removal. Torque mounting nuts to 200–250 inch lbs. (22–28 Nm) and pushrod nut/bolt to 30 ft. lbs. (41 Nm).

Brake Caliper

REMOVAL & INSTALLATION

1. Raise and safely support the vehicle.

2. Remove the front wheel and tire assembly.

3. Using a C-clamp, force the piston into the caliper.

4. Remove the caliper retaining screws, clips and anti-rattle springs.

5. Remove the caliper from the disc by slowly sliding the caliper assembly out and away from the disc.

6. Disconnect the brake hose from caliper.

7. Remove the caliper from the vehicle.

To install:

8. Connect the brake hose to the caliper.

9. Slowly slide the caliper assembly into position in the adapter and over the disc.

10. Align the caliper on the machined ways of the adapter. Be careful not to pull the dust boot from its groove as the piston and boot slide over the inboard shoe.

11. Tighten the retaining screws to 180 inch lbs. (20 Nm).

12. Bleed the brake system. Pump the brake pedal several times until a firm pedal has been obtained.

13. Check and refill the master cylinder reservoirs, if necessary, using an approved DOT 3 brake fluid.

14. Install the wheel and tire assemblies. Tighten the stud nuts to 85 ft. lbs. (115 Nm).

15. Lower the vehicle and test the brakes.

Disc Brake Pads

REMOVAL & INSTALLATION

1. Raise and safely support the vehicle.

2. Remove the front wheel and tire assemblies.

3. Remove the caliper retaining screws, clips and anti-rattle springs.

4. Remove the caliper from the disc by slowly sliding the caliper assembly out and away from the disc.

5. Remove the outboard shoe assembly, flanges on the outboard shoe will retain the shoe to the caliper, by prying between shoe and the caliper fingers.

6. Support the caliper to prevent damage to the flexible brake hose and remove the inboard shoe assembly. Do not allow the caliper to hang by the hose.

NOTE: Prior to installing the disc pads, check the caliper piston seal for leaks, evident by brake fluid in and around the boot area and inboard lining, and for ruptures of the piston dust boot. If the boot is damaged or fluid is evident, it will be necessary to disassemble the caliper assembly and overhaul or replace it. Check the mating surfaces of the abutments on the caliper and adapter. If corroded or rusty, clean surfaces with a wire brush.

To install:

7. Inspect the braking surfaces of the disc. Re-surface the disc, if heavy scoring or warping is evident.

8. Slowly and carefully, push the piston back into the bore until it is bottomed. Watch for possible master cylinder reservoir overflow.

9. Slide the new outboard shoe assembly into the recess of the caliper.

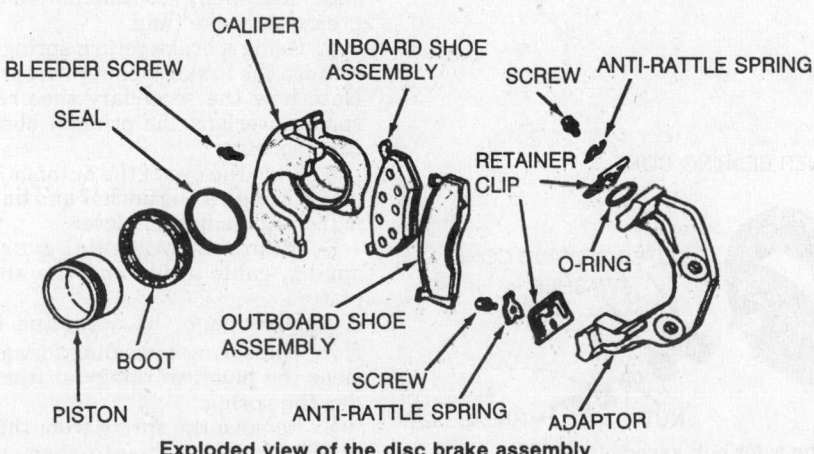

CALIPER

BLEEDER SCREW

INBOARD SHOE
ASSEMBLY

SCREW

ANTI-RATTLE SPRING

SEAL

RETAINER
CLIP

O-RING

BOOT

OUTBOARD SHOE
ASSEMBLY

SCREW

ANTI-RATTLE SPRING

ADAPTOR

PISTON

Exploded view of the disc brake assembly

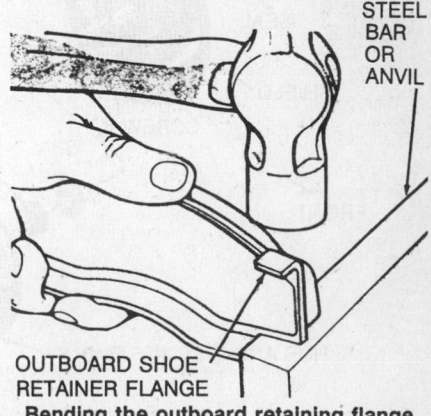

STEEL
BAR
OR
ANVIL

OUTBOARD SHOE
RETAINER FLANGE

Bending the outboard retaining flange

NOTE: There should be no free-play between the brake shoe flanges and the caliper fingers, this will cause disc brake rattle.

10. If free-play is evident by vertical shoe movement after installation, perform the following:

    a. Remove the shoe from the caliper and bend the flanges to create a slight interference fit to eliminate all vertical free-play when the shoe is installed.

    b. Install the shoe after the above modification, if necessary, by snapping the shoe into place.

11. Position the inboard shoe into position on the adapter with the shoe flanges in the adapter ways.

12. Slowly slide the caliper assembly into position in the adapter and over the disc.

13. Align the caliper on the machined ways of the adapter. Be careful not to pull the dust boot from its groove as the piston and boot slide over the inboard shoe.

14. Install the anti-rattle springs and retaining clips and tighten the retaining screws to 180 inch lbs. (20 Nm).

NOTE: The inboard shoe anti-rattle spring must be installed on top of the retainer spring plate.

15. Pump the brake pedal several times until a firm pedal has been obtained.

16. Check and refill the master cylinder reservoirs, if necessary, using an approved DOT 3 brake fluid.

NOTE: It should not be necessary to bleed the brake system after shoe removal and installation. However, if a firm pedal cannot be obtained, bleed the brake system.

17. Install the wheel and tire assemblies. Tighten the stud nuts to 85 ft. lbs. (115 Nm).

18. Lower the vehicle and test the brakes.

Brake Rotor

REMOVAL & INSTALLATION

1. Raise and safely support the vehicle.

2. Remove the front wheel and tire assemblies.

3. Remove the caliper retaining screws, clips and anti-rattle springs.

4. Remove the caliper from the rotor by slowly sliding the caliper assembly out and away from the rotor. Suspend the caliper on a wire.

5. Remove the grease cap, the cotter pin, the nut lock, the nut, the thrust washer and the outer wheel bearing.

6. Remove the rotor/hub assembly from the spindle.

To install:

7. Inspect the braking surfaces of the rotor. Re-surface the rotor, if heavy scoring or warping is evident.

8. Install the rotor/hub assembly onto the spindle.

9. Install the outer bearing, the thrust washer and the adjusting nut.

10. Tighten the adjusting nut to 240–300 inch lbs. (27–34 Nm) while rotating the rotor/hub assembly.

11. Back off the adjusting nut to release the preload and retighten finger-tight.

12. Install the nut lock, a new cotter pin and the grease cup.

13. Install the caliper and the wheel/tire assembly.

14. Pump the brake pedal several times until a firm pedal has been obtained.

15. Check and refill the master cylinder reservoirs, if necessary, using an approved DOT 3 brake fluid.

16. Lower the vehicle and test the brakes.

Brake Drums

REMOVAL & INSTALLATION

1. Raise and safely support the vehicle.

2. Remove the rear plug from the brake adjusting hole.

3. Insert a thin tool into the brake adjusting hole and hold the adjusting lever away from the notches of the adjusting screw.

4. Insert a brake adjusting tool into the brake adjusting hole and release the brake by adjusting the star adjuster downward.

5. Remove the rear wheels and the brake drums.

6. Install the brake drum and adjust the brakes. Install the wheel assemblies and lower the vehicle.

Brake Shoes

REMOVAL & INSTALLATION

1. Raise and safely support the vehicle.

2. Remove the rear wheels and the brake drums.

3. Inspect the brake lining for wear, shoe alignment, contamination from grease or brake fluid.

4. Using a brake return spring tool, remove the brake shoe return springs. Note how the secondary shoe return spring overlaps the primary shoe return spring.

5. Slide the eye of the automatic adjuster cable off the anchor and unhook it from the adjusting lever.

6. Remove the cable, overload spring, cable guide and the anchor plate.

7. Disengage the adjusting lever from the spring by sliding forward to clear the pivot, working out from under the spring.

8. Remove the spring from the pivot. Remove the shoe-to-shoe spring

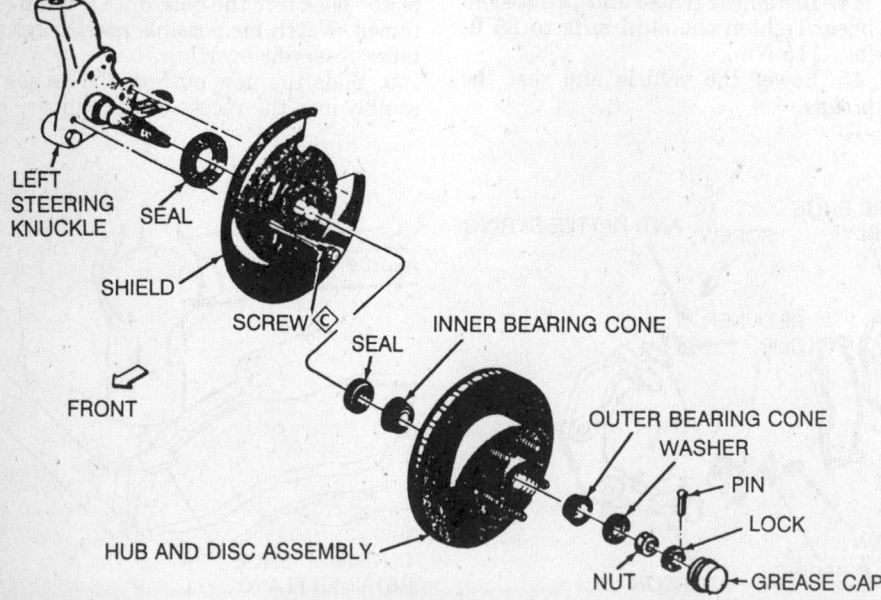

LEFT STEERING KNUCKLE — SEAL — SHIELD — SCREW — SEAL — INNER BEARING CONE — OUTER BEARING CONE — WASHER — PIN — LOCK — NUT — GREASE CAP — HUB AND DISC ASSEMBLY — FRONT

Exploded view of the rotor/hub assembly

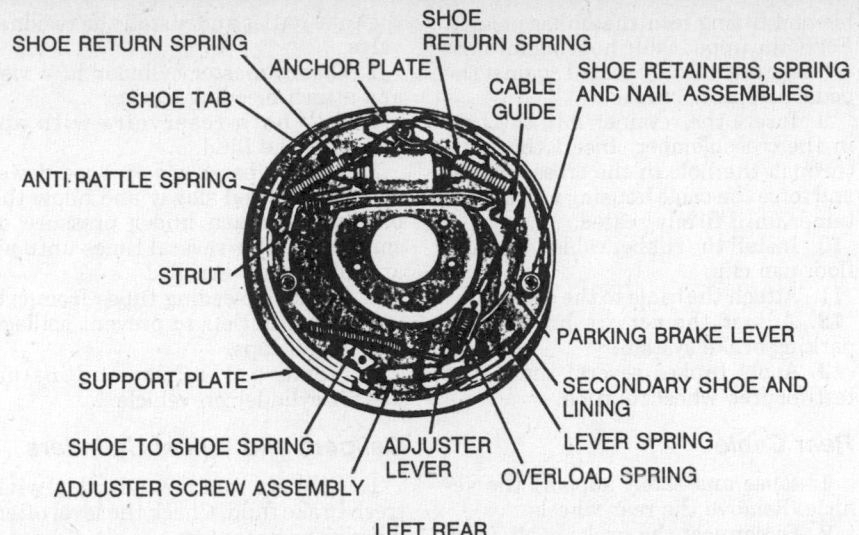

View of the 11 in. rear brake assembly—10 in. similar

from the secondary shoe web and disengage the front primary shoe web. Remove the spring.

9. Disengage the primary and secondary shoes and remove the adjusting star wheel assembly from the shoes.

10. Remove the brake lever from the secondary shoes. Remove the shoes.

11. Disengage the parking brake lever from the parking brake cable.

To install:

12. Clean the backing plate with a suitable solvent, inspect for rough or rusted shoe contact areas. Clean and inspect the adjusting screws for damaged threads. Apply a thin film of lubricant to the threads, socket and washer.

13. Replace the adjuster screw assembly if corrosion of any part inhibits free operation.

14. Install new brake shoe return springs and hold-down springs where the old springs have been overheated or their strength is questionable.

NOTE: Spring paint discoloration or distorted end coils indicate a spring has been overheated.

15. Examine the brake drum for cracks, excessive scoring or excessive run-out. If drum run-out exceeds 0.006 in., the drum must be resurfaced. Do not exceed the suggested resurfacing amount that is marked on the drum.

16. Lubricate the shoe tab contact pads on the support plate with a thin film of a multi-purpose lubricant.

17. Engage the parking brake lever with the cable. Install the parking brake lever into the rectangular hole of the secondary brake shoe.

18. Slide the secondary shoe against the support plate, at the same time engage the shoe web with the pushrod and against the anchor.

19. Slide the parking brake strut behind the axle flange and into the slot in the parking brake lever. Slide the anti-rattle spring over the free end of the strut.

20. Slide the primary shoe into position and engage it with the pushrod, if equipped, and free end of the strut.

21. Install the anchor plate over the anchor. Install the eye of the adjuster cable over the anchor.

22. Engage the primary shoe return spring into the web of the shoe and install the free end over the anchor using a brake return spring tool.

23. Insert the protruding hole rim of the cable guide into the hole in the secondary shoe web. Holding the guide in position, engage the secondary shoe return spring through both, hole in the guide and hole in the web.

24. Using a brake return spring tool, install the return spring over the anchor.

25. Using pliers, squeeze the ends of the spring loops, around the anchor, parallel.

26. Install the adjusting star wheel assembly between the primary and secondary shoes, with the star wheel next to the secondary shoe.

27. The left star wheel adjusting stud end is stamped **L**, indicating its position on the vehicle, and the star wheel is cadmium plated.

28. The right star wheel is black and the adjusting stud end is stamped **R**.

29. Install the shoe-to-shoe spring between the shoes. Engage the primary shoe first.

30. Vehicles with 11 in. brakes, install the shoe-to-shoe spring with the coil forward, opposite the adjuster lever.

31. Install the adjusting lever spring over the pivot pin on the shoe web. Install the adjusting lever slightly rearward to lock in position.

32. Using a brake spring hold-down tool, install the shoe retaining nails, retainers and springs.

33. Thread the adjuster cable over the guide and hook the end of the overload spring in the lever. Be sure the eye of the cable is pulled tight against the anchor and is in a straight line with the guide.

34. Install the brake drum and adjust the brakes. Install the wheel assemblies and lower the vehicle.

Wheel Cylinder

REMOVAL & INSTALLATION

1. Raise and safely support the vehicle.

2. Remove the wheel assembly and the brake drum.

3. Inspect the wheel cylinder for signs of leakage.

NOTE: If signs of leakage are present, the wheel cylinder must be replaced.

4. Remove the brake shoe assembly

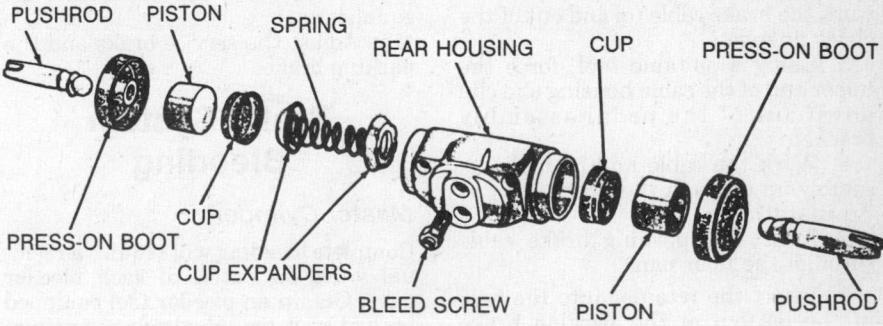

Exploded view of the wheel cylinder

form the backing plate.

5. Disconnect and plug the brake line at the wheel cylinder.

6. Remove the wheel cylinder-to-backing plate bolts and separate the wheel cylinder from the backing plate.

NOTE: It is recommended to replace the wheel cylinder instead of rebuilding it.

7. Install a new wheel cylinder. Installation is the reverse order of the removal procedure. Torque the wheel cylinder-to-backing plate bolts to 75 inch lbs. Bleed the brake system.

Parking Brake Cable

ADJUSTMENT

1. Raise the vehicle and support it safely.

2. Insert an adjusting tool through the rear brake adjusting hole and rotate the star wheel until a slight drag is felt while rotating the wheels. Back off the star wheel until no drag is felt with the aid of a welding rod type probe, to move the adjusting lever out of engagement with the star wheel.

3. Tighten the cable adjusting nut until a slight drag is felt in the rear wheels when the rear wheels are rotated. Loosen the cable adjusting nut until the rear wheels can be rotated freely. Back off the cable adjusting nut 2 additional turns.

4. Apply and release the parking brake several times and check to verify the rear wheels rotate freely, without any brake drag.

REMOVAL & INSTALLATION

Front Cable

1. Disengage the front parking brake cable from the left connector.

2. Using a suitable tool, force the cable housing and attaching clip forward out of the body crossmember.

3. Fold back the left front edge of the floor covering and remove the rubber cable cover from the floor pan.

4. Engage the parking brake and work the brake cable up and out of the clevis linkage.

5. Using a suitable tool, force the upper end of the cable housing and clip down out of the pedal assembly bracket.

6. Work the cable and housing assembly up through the floor pan.

To install:

7. Insert the parking brake cable through the floor pan.

8. Insert the retainer into the hole in the bottom of the parking brake pedal assembly bracket. Insert the cable through the hole and insert the ca-

ble end fitting into the linkage clevis. Force the upper cable housing into the retainer until firmly seated against the pedal assembly bracket.

9. Insert the retainer into the hole in the crossmember. Insert the cable through the hole in the crossmember and force the cable housing into the retainer until firmly seated.

10. Install the rubber cable cover and floor pan clip.

11. Attach the cable to the connector.

12. Adjust the service brakes and parking brake system.

13. Apply brakes several times and test for free wheel rotation.

Rear Cable

1. Raise and safely support the vehicle. Remove the rear wheels.

2. Disconnect the brake cable from the connector.

3. Remove the retaining clip from the brake cable bracket.

4. Remove the brake drum from the rear axle.

5. Remove the brake shoe return springs and adjuster mechanism.

6. Remove the brake shoe retaining springs.

7. Remove the brake shoe strut and spring and disconnect the brake cable from the operating arm.

8. Compress the retainers on the end of the brake cable housing and remove the cable from the support plate.

To install:

9. Insert the brake cable and housing into the brake support plate, making certain the housing retainers lock the housing firmly into place.

10. Holding the brake shoes in place on the support plate, engage the brake cable into the brake shoe operating lever. Install the parking brake strut and spring.

11. Install the brake shoe retaining springs, adjuster mechanism and brake shoe return springs.

12. Install the brake drum and wheel.

13. Insert the brake cable and housing into the cable bracket and install the retaining clip.

14. Insert the brake cable into the equalizer.

15. Adjust the service brake and the parking brake.

Brake System Bleeding

Master Cylinder

Complete bleeding will require a residual valve on outlet of each bleeder tube. Obtain an bleeder tool equipped with at least 1 residual valve on primary outlet tube. To modify secondary outlet tube use a flaring tool to flare

the tube outlet and install the residual valve.

1. Clamp master cylinder in a vise and attach bleeding tubes.

2. Fill both reservoirs with approved brake fluid.

3. Using a brass rod or wood dowel depress pushrod slowly and allow the pistons to return under pressure of springs. Do this several times until all air bubbles are expelled.

4. Remove bleeding tubes from cylinder, plug outlets to prevent spillage and install caps.

5. Remove from vise and install master cylinder on vehicle.

Calipers and Wheel Cylinders

1. Fill the master cylinder with fresh brake fluid. Check the level often during the procedure.

2. Start with the wheel farthest from the master cylinder. Pop the cap off of the bleeder screw, if equipped and place where it will not be lost. Clean the bleed screw.

─────── **CAUTION** ───────

When bleeding the brakes, keep face away from the brake area. Spewing fluid may cause facial and/or visual damage. Do not allow brake fluid to spill on the car's finish, it will remove the paint.

────────────────────────

3. If the system is empty, the most effecient way to get fluid down to the wheel is to loosen the bleeder about ½–¾ turn, place a finger firmly over the bleeder and have a helper pump the brakes slowly until fluid comes out the bleeder. Once fluid is at the bleeder, close it before the pedal is released inside the vehicle.

NOTE: If the pedal is pumped rapidly, the fluid will churn and create small air bubbles, which are almost impossible to remove from the system. These air bubbles will eventually congregate and a spongy pedal will result.

4. Once fluid has been pumped to the caliper or wheel cylinder, open the bleed screw again, have the helper press the brake pedal to the floor, lock the bleeder and have the helper slowly release the pedal. Wait 15 seconds and repeat the procedure, including the 15 second wait, until no more air comes out of the bleeder upon application of the brake pedal. Remember to close the bleeder before the pedal is released inside the vehicle each time the bleeder is opened. If not, air will be induced into the system.

5. If a helper is not available, connect a small hose to the bleeder, place the end in a container of brake fluid and proceed to pump the pedal from inside the vehicle until no more air

comes out the bleeder. The hose will prevent air from entering the system.

6. Repeat the procedure on remaining wheel cylinders and calipers still working from the wheel furthest away from the master cylinder. The bleeding sequence is as follows: right rear, left rear, right front and left front.

7. Hydraulic brake systems must be totally flushed if the fluid becomes contaminated with water, dirt or other corrosive chemicals. To flush, simply bleed the entire system until all fluid has been replaced with the correct type of new fluid.

8. Install the bleeder cap(s), if equipped, on the bleeder to keep dirt out.

9. Road test the vehicle after brake work of any kind is done.

FRONT SUSPENSION

Shock Absorbers

REMOVAL & INSTALLATION

1. Raise and safely support the vehicle.
2. Remove the front wheels.
3. Remove the nut and retainer from the shock absorber upper end.
4. Grip the shock absorber base, remove the lower attaching nut, retainer and bushing.
5. Fully compress the shock absorber by pushing it upward, disengaging it from the lower control arm. Pull the shock absorber down, firmly and remove it from the vehicle.
6. Check the shock absorber bushing, it they are worn, cracked or scored, replace them. Remove and install the bushings with a press or using a drift and a hammer. To ease installation, lubricate with soapy water.

NOTE: Do not use oil to ease the installation.

7. Purge the new shock absorber by repeatedly extending it in the upright position and compressing it in the inverted position. It is normal to have more resistance to extend than to compress.
To install:
8. Fully compress the new shock absorber, insert the top end through the upper bushing, install the retainer and nut. Torque the nut to 25 ft. lbs. (34 Nm).

NOTE: Be sure all the retainers are installed with the concave side in contact with the rubber.

9. Install the shock absorber to the lower control arm mount. Install the bolt, from the rear, or the retainer and nut finger tight.
10. Lower the vehicle and torque the nut to 35 ft. lbs. (47 Nm), with the full weight of the vehicle on the wheels.

Torsion Bars

REMOVAL & INSTALLATION

1. Raise the safely support the vehicle so the front suspension is in full rebound position.
2. Release load on both torsion bars by turning anchor adjusting bolts in frame crossmember counterclockwise. Remove anchor adjusting bolt on torsion bar to be removed.
3. Raise lower control arms until clearance between crossmember ledge, at jounce bumper, and torsion bar end bushing is 2⅞ in. (63.0mm). Support lower control arms at this design height, equal to 3 passenger position with vehicle on ground. This is necessary to align sway bar and lower control arm attaching points for disassembly and component re-alignment and attachment during reassembly.
4. Remove sway bar to control arm attaching bolt and retainers.
5. Remove bolts attaching torsion bar end bushing to lower control arm.
6. Remove bolts attaching torsion bar pivot cushion bushing to crossmember and remove torsion bar and anchor assembly from crossmember.
7. Carefully separate anchor from torsion bar.
To install:
8. Carefully slide balloon seal over end of torsion bar, cupped end toward hex.
9. Coat hex end of torsion bar with waterproof grease.
10. Install torsion bar hex end into anchor bracket. With torsion bar in a horizontal position, the ears of the anchor bracket should be positioned nearly straight up. Position swivel into anchor bracket ears.
11. Place bushing end of bar into position on top of lower control arm. Then install anchor bracket assembly into crossmember anchor retainer and install anchor adjusting bearing and bolt.
12. Attach pivot cushion bushing to crossmember with the bolt and washer assemblies. Leave bolt and washer assemblies loose enough to install friction plates.
13. With lower control arms at design height install the bolt and nut assemblies attaching torsion bar bushing to lower control arm. Torque to 70 ft. lbs. (95 Nm).

14. Ensure that torsion bar anchor bracket is fully seated in crossmember. Then install friction plates between crossmember and pivot cushion bushing with open end of slot to rear and bottomed out on mounting bolts. Tighten cushion bushing bolts to 85 ft. lbs. (115 Nm).
15. Position balloon seal over anchor bracket.
16. Reinstall bolt, through sway bar, retainer cushions and sleeve and attach to lower control arm end bushing. Torque bolt to 50 ft. lbs. (68 Nm).
17. Load torsion bar by turning anchor adjusting bolt clockwise.
18. Lower vehicle and adjust torsion bar height to specifications.
19. Road test vehicle make sure vehicle tracks straight. Set front end alignment adjustments, if necessary.

NOTE: Front vehicle height is measured from the head of the the front suspension front crossmember isolator bolt to the ground. To adjust turn torsion bar adjusting bolt clockwise to increase height and counterclockwise to reduce height.

Upper Ball Joints

INSPECTION

NOTE: Before making the inspection, verify that the wheel bearings are adjusted correctly and the control arm bushings are in good condition.

1. Place a jack under the lower control arm as close to the wheel as possible.
2. Raise the vehicle so the tire lightly contacts the floor.
3. Tighten the wheel bearing adjusting nut enough to remove all play.
4. Have an assistant try to move the top of the tire in and out while observing the upper ball joint. If there is any noticeable side play, replace the upper ball joint.
5. Correct the wheel bearing adjustment.

REMOVAL & INSTALLATION
——— CAUTION ———
The torsion bar remains under tension during this procedure.

NOTE: Turn the ignition key to the OFF or UNLOCKED position.

1. Raise and support the front of the vehicle. Place a jackstand under the lower control arm as close to the wheel as possible. Remove the wheel. The jackstand should not contact the brake splash shield and the rubber re-

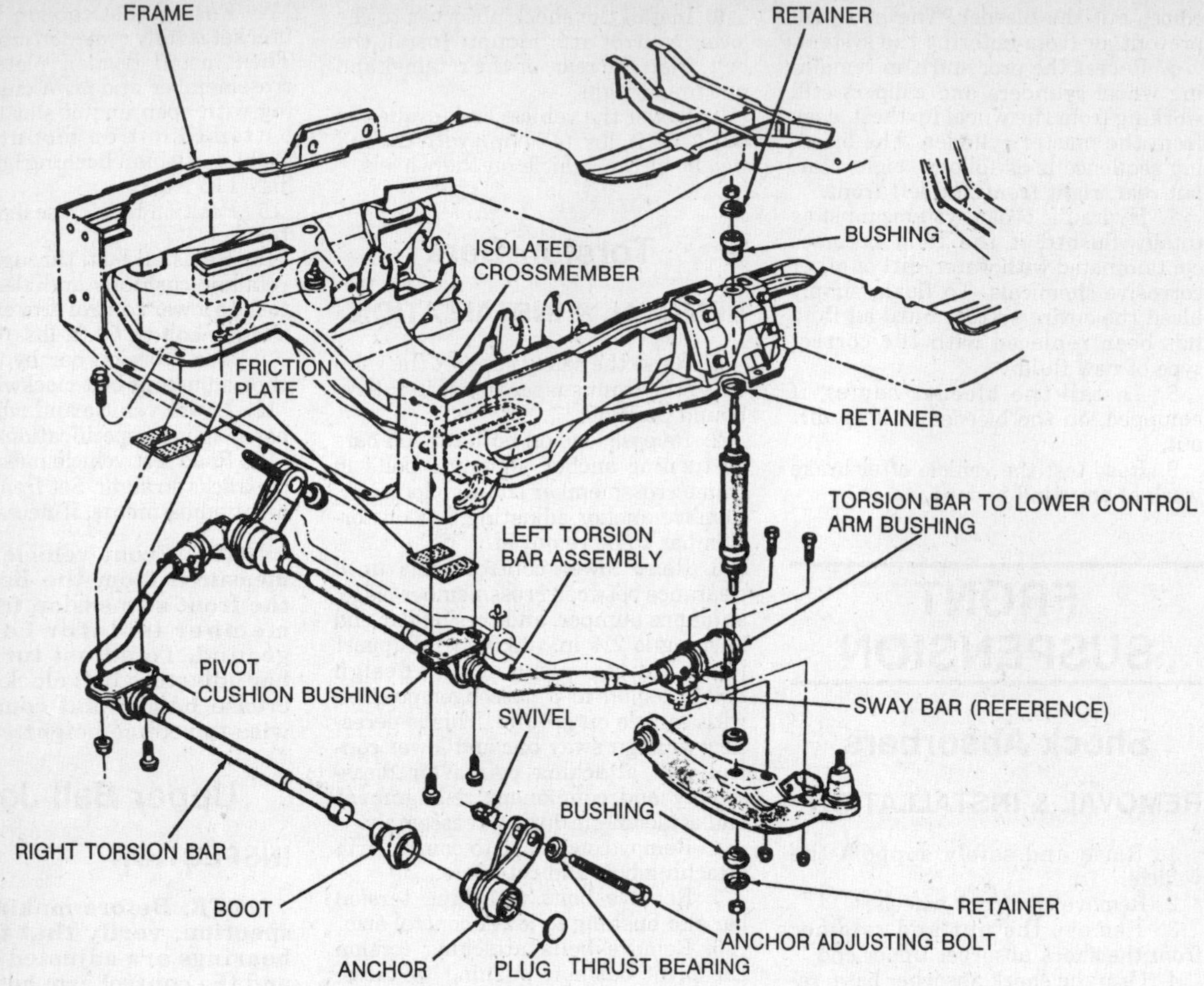

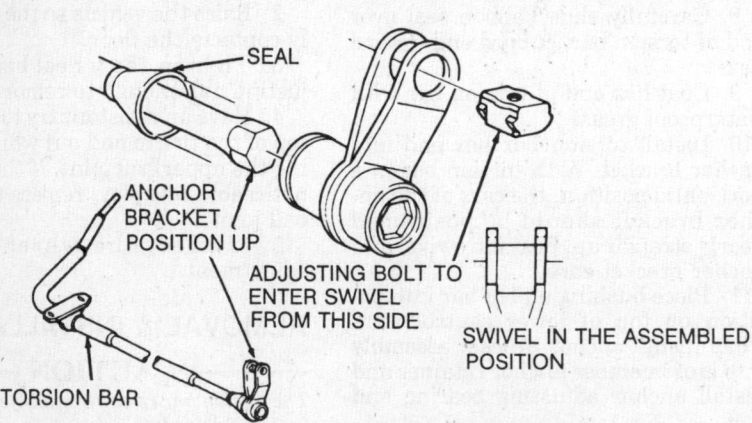

FRAME

RETAINER

BUSHING

ISOLATED
CROSSMEMBER

RETAINER

FRICTION
PLATE

TORSION BAR TO LOWER CONTROL
ARM BUSHING

LEFT TORSION
BAR ASSEMBLY

PIVOT
CUSHION BUSHING

SWIVEL

SWAY BAR (REFERENCE)

BUSHING

RIGHT TORSION BAR

BOOT

RETAINER

ANCHOR   PLUG   THRUST BEARING

ANCHOR ADJUSTING BOLT

Exploded view of the torsion bar assemblies

SEAL

ANCHOR
BRACKET
POSITION UP

ADJUSTING BOLT TO
ENTER SWIVEL
FROM THIS SIDE

SWIVEL IN THE ASSEMBLED
POSITION

TORSION BAR

Torsion bar anchor and swivel installation

bound bumper must not contact the frame.

2. Remove the cotter pin and nut that attaches the upper ball joint to the steering knuckle. Remove the cotter pin and nut from the lower ball

joint, to enable the removal tool to be used.

3. Slide the ball joint removal tool onto the lower ball joint stud, allowing the tool to rest on the knuckle arm. Set the tool securely against the upper

stud. Apply pressure to the upper stud by tightening the tool and strike the knuckle sharply to loosen the stud. Never strike the ball joint stud.

NOTE: The brake caliper may have to be removed for clearance.

4. After disengaging the ball joint, support the steering knuckle and brake assembly. Using tool, unscrew the upper ball joint from the upper control arm.

To install:

5. Position a new ball joint on the upper control arm and screw the joint into the arm. Be careful not to cross thread the joint in the arm. Torque it to 125 ft. lbs. (162.5 Nm).

6. Position a new seal on the ball joint stud and install the seal in the ball joint making sure the seal is fully seated on the ball joint housing.

7. Position the ball joint stud in the steering knuckle and install the retaining nut. Torque the nut to 100 ft.

lbs. (130 Nm). Install a new cotter pin.

8. To complete the installation, reverse the removal procedures. Lubricate the ball joint. Adjust the wheel alignment.

Lower Ball Joints

INSPECTION

NOTE: Before making the inspection, verify that the wheel bearings are adjusted correctly and the control arm bushings are in good condition.

1. Place a jack under the lower control arm as close to the wheel as possible.
2. Raise the vehicle until there is 1–2 in. (25.4–50.8mm) of clearance under the wheel.
3. Insert a bar under the wheel and pry upward. If the wheel raises noticeably the ball joint is worn.
4. Clamp a dial indicator to the lower control arm and measure the lower ball joint stud movement. The manufacturer's limit for lower ball joint play, measured at the joint and is 0.030 in. (0.76mm).
5. Correct the wheel bearing adjustment.

REMOVAL & INSTALLATION

NOTE: Turn the ignition key to the OFF or UNLOCKED position.

1. Raise the vehicle so the front suspension drops to the downward limit of its travel. Position jackstands beneath the front frame for extra support.
2. Remove the wheel and tire assembly.
3. Remove the brake caliper and tie it up out of the way, so there is no strain on the flexible brake hose.
4. Remove the hub/rotor assembly and splash shield. Disconnect shock absorber from the lower control arm.
5. Unload the torsion bar by rotating the adjusting bolt counterclockwise.
6. Remove the cotter pin and nut from the upper and lower ball joints. Slide the ball joint removal tool over the upper stud, so it rests on the steering knuckle. Tighten the tool to place the lower ball joint under pressure. Using a hammer, strike the steering knuckle to loosen the ball joint.
7. Use the ball joint pressing tool to press the ball joint out of the lower control arm.
To install:
8. When installing the new ball joint, use a ball joint pressing tool to press it into the lower control arm.

9. Place a new seal over the ball joint. Press the retainer portion of the seal down over the ball joint housing using a pressing tool until it locks into position.
10. Insert the ball joint stud through the opening in the steering knuckle and install the stud retaining nut. Torque to 100 ft. lbs. (130 Nm). Install the cotter pin and lubricate the ball joint.
11. Load the torsion bar by rotating the adjusting bolt clockwise.
12. Install the shock absorber, the splash shield, hub/rotor assembly and brake caliper. Install the wheel and tire assembly.
13. Adjust the front wheel bearings. Remove the jackstands and lower the vehicle. Adjust the front suspension height.

Upper Control Arms

REMOVAL & INSTALLATION

1. Raise and support the front of the vehicle. Place a jackstand under the lower control arm as close to the wheel as possible. Remove the wheel. The jackstand should not contact the brake splash shield and the rubber rebound bumper must not contact the frame.
2. Remove the cotter pin and nut that attaches the upper ball joint to the steering knuckle. Remove the cotter pin and nut from the lower ball joint, to enable the removal tool to be used.
3. Slide the ball joint removal tool onto the lower ball joint stud, allowing the tool to rest on the knuckle arm. Set the tool securely against the upper stud. Apply pressure to the upper stud by tightening the tool and strike the knuckle sharply to loosen the stud. Never strike the ball joint stud.
4. Remove the rubber engine splash shield and the upper control arm pivot shaft nuts. It will be easier to reset the alignment if you mark the original pivot bar location. Remove the control arm and pivot shaft assembly.
5. Installation is the reverse order of removal procedure.

Lower Control Arms

REMOVAL & INSTALLATION

1. Separate the lower ball joint from the steering knuckle.

NOTE: Unload both bars, even if removing only 1 control arm, to reduce the sway bar reaction.

2. Raise the lower control arm until there is 2⅞ in. clearance between the

crossmember ledge at the jounce bumper and the torsion bar bushing on the lower control arm. Unbolt the torsion bar busing from the control arm.
3. Remove the lower control arm pivot bolt and the control arm.

NOTE: If the control arm shaft bushings indicates wear or deterioration, replace them.

4. Installation is the reverse order of the removal procedure. Torque the control arm pivot bolt to 75 ft. lbs. (95.5 Nm) and the torsion bar end bushing-to-lower control arm to 50 ft. lbs. (65 Nm).

Sway Bar

REMOVAL & INSTALLATION

1. Raise the front of the vehicle and support it safely.
2. Release the load on both torsion bars by turning the anchor adjusting bolts counterclockwise.
3. Raise the lower control arms until there is 2⅞ in. clearance between the crossmember ledge, at the jounce bumper and the torsion bar bushing, on the lower control arm.
4. Support the lower control arms with a jackstands. Remove the sway bar-to-torsion bar bushing bolts, retainers, cushions and sleeves. Remove the retainer assembly strap and retainer bolts. Remove the sway bar.

NOTE: Inspect the cushions/bushings for wear or deterioration and replace, if necessary.

5. Installation is the reverse order of the removal procedure. Torque the sway bar-to-torsion bar to 50 ft. lbs. (65 Nm) and the sway bar retainer/strap bolts to 30 ft. lbs. (41 Nm). Load the torsion bar by turning the crossmember adjusting bolt clockwise. Lower the vehicle and adjust the torsion bar height.

Front Wheel Bearings

ADJUSTMENT

1. Raise the vehicle and support it safely.
2. Remove the grease cup, cotter pin and locknut.
3. Back off on the adjusting nut.
4. Check for free wheel rotation.
5. While rotating the wheel, tighten the wheel bearing adjustment nut to 240–300 inch lbs.
6. Loosen the nut ¼ turn (90 degrees). Retighten the nut so it is finger tight.
7. Position the nut lock so 1 pair of

the slots is in line with the cotter pin hole and install the cotter pin. This adjustment should give 0.001–0.003 in. endplay.

8. Install the rest of the components removed.

REMOVAL & INSTALLATION

1. Raise the vehicle and support it safely.

2. Remove the tire and wheel assembly.

3. Remove the brake caliper assembly and move to the side; do not disconnect the brake line.

NOTE: Avoid strain on the flexible brake hose.

4. Remove the grease cup, cotter pin and locknut.

5. Remove the adjusting nut and washer.

6. Remove the outer bearing and remove brake disc from spindle.

7. Remove the inner bearing by removing the bearing seal with a seal remover tool.

8. Installation is the reverse order of the removal procedure.

9. Adjust the wheel bearing and use a new cotter pin.

REAR SUSPENSION

Shock Absorbers

REMOVAL & INSTALLATION

1. Raise and safely support the vehicle under the axle assembly with jackstands, so as to relieve load from the shock absorbers.

2. Remove the nut, retainer and bushing, attaching the shock to the spring mounting plate. To avoid damage to the shock, grip the base of the shock below the base-to-reservoir weld while loosening the retaining nut.

3. At the upper mount, remove the shock attaching bolt/nut and the shock.

4. Purge the new shock of air by repeatedly extending it in its upright position and compressing it, in an inverted position. It is normal to have more resistance to extend than compress.

5. To install the shock, position it so the upper bolt or nut may be replaced, hand-tighten only. Align the shock with the spring mounting plate and install the bolt or nut, hand-tighten only.

6. Lower the vehicle and tighten the shock absorber mounting bolts. Torque the bottom bolt to 35 ft. lbs. (46 Nm) and the top bolt to 70 ft. lbs. (97.5 Nm).

Leaf Springs

REMOVAL & INSTALLATION

1. Raise and safely support the vehicle on jackstands; place the jackstands under the axle to relieve weight from the rear springs. Remove the wheels.

2. Disconnect the rear shock absorbers at the bottom. Lower the axle assembly to allow the rear springs to hang free. Disconnect the rear sway bar links, if equipped.

3. Remove the U-bolt nuts, bolts and spring plates. Remove the nuts securing the front spring hanger to the body mounting bracket.

4. Remove the rear spring hanger bolts and allow the spring to drop enough to allow the front spring hanger bolts to be removed.

5. Remove the front pivot bolt from the front spring hanger.

6. Remove the shackle nuts and shackle from the rear of the spring.

To install:

7. Assemble the shackle/bushings in the rear of the spring and hanger. Start the shackle bolt nut. Do not lubricate rubber bushings to ease installation or tighten the bolt nut.

8. Align the front spring hanger with the front spring eye and insert the pivot bolt and nut. Do not tighten.

9. Install the rear spring hanger-to-

body bracket and torque the bolts to 35 ft. lbs. (45.5 Nm).

10. With the aid of a helper, raise the spring and insert the bolts in the spring hanger mounting bracket holes. Install the nuts and torque them to 35 ft. lbs. (45.5 Nm).

11. Position the axle assembly so it is correctly aligned with the spring center bolt.

12. Position the center bolt over the lower spring plate. Insert the U-bolt and nut. Tighten the U-bolt to 45 ft. lbs. (58.5 Nm). Connect the rear shock absorbers.

13. Lower the vehicle. Torque the pivot bolts to 105 ft. lbs. (136.5 Nm). and the shackle nuts to 35 ft. lbs. (45.5 Nm).

NOTE: Road test the vehicle and re-check the front suspension heights and correct, if necessary.

Rear Control Arms

REMOVAL & INSTALLATION

1. Raise and safely support the vehicle.

2. Remove the sway bar link retaining nuts, retainers and insulators from the support.

3. Remove the nuts and retainer from each bracket fastened to each rail.

4. Remove the sway bar.

5. Installation is the reverse order of the removal procedure. Torque the retainer-to-bracket bolts to 17 ft. lbs. (23 Nm) and the link nuts to 8 ft. lbs. (11 Nm).

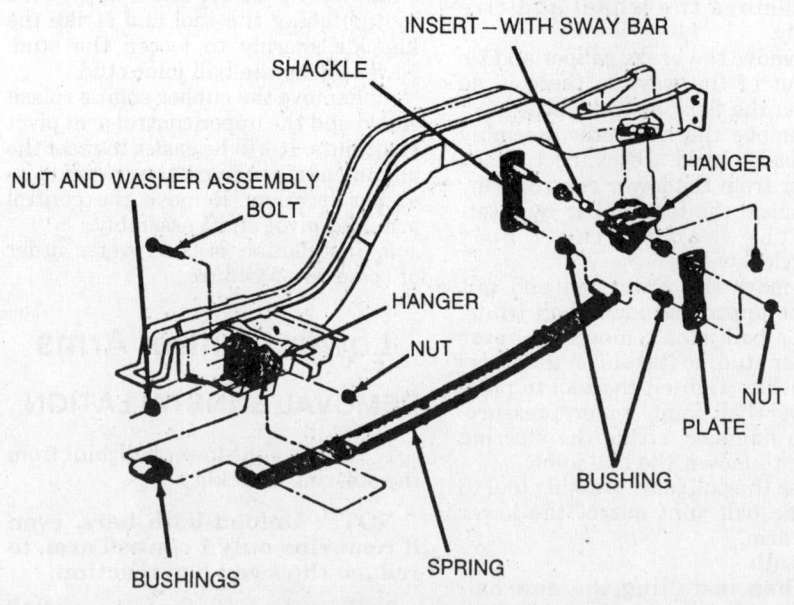

Exploded view of the rear spring assembly

Ford Motor Co.
Front Wheel Drive
Escort, Lynx, Tempo, Topaz

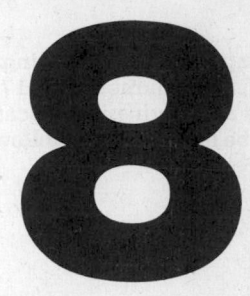

SPECIFICATIONS

VEHICLE IDENTIFICATION CHART

It is important for servicing and ordering parts to be certain of the vehicle and engine identification. The VIN (vehicle identification number) is a 17 digit number visible through the windshield on the driver's side of the dash and contains the vehicle and engine identification codes. The tenth digit indicates model year and the eighth digit indicates engine code. It can be interpreted as follows:

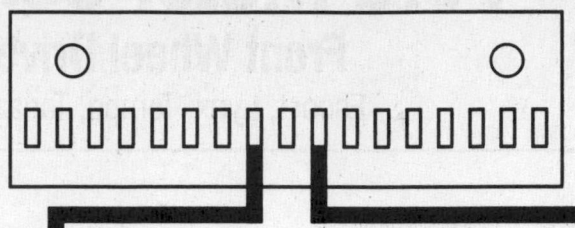

Engine Code

Code	Cu. In.	Liters	Cyl.	Fuel Sys.	Eng. Mfg.
9	116	1.9	4	CFI	Ford
J	116	1.9 HO	4	EFI	Ford
H	122	2.0	4	DIESEL	Toyo Kogyo
R ('87)	140	2.3 HSC	4	1bbl	Ford
R ('88–'91)	140	2.3 HSC	4	EFI	Ford
X ('87)	140	2.3	4	CFI	Ford
X ('88–'91)	140	2.3 HSC	4	EFI	Ford
S ('88)	140	2.3	4	EFI	Ford
S ('89–'91)	140	2.3 HSO	4	EFI	Ford

Model Year

Code	Year
H	1987
K	1988
K	1989
L	1990
M	1991

HSC High Swirl Combustion   CFI Central Fuel Injection
HO   High Output   EFI Electronic Fuel Injection
HSO High Specific Output

ENGINE IDENTIFICATION

Year	Model	Engine Displacement cu. in. (liter)	Engine Series Identification (VIN)	No. of Cylinders	Engine Type
1987	Escort	116 (1.9) CFI	9	4	OHC
	Escort	116 (1.9) EFI	J	4	OHC
	Escort	122 (2.0) D	H	4	OHC
	Lynx	116 (1.9) CFI	9	4	OHC
	Lynx	116 (1.9) EFI	J	4	OHC
	Lynx	122 (3.0) D	H	4	OHC
	Tempo	140 (2.3) HSC	R	4	OHV
	Tempo	140 (2.3) CFI	X	4	OHV
	Tempo	122 (2.0) D	H	4	OHC
	Topaz	140 (2.3) HSC	R	4	OHV
	Topaz	140 (2.3) CFI	X	4	OHV
	Topaz	122 (2.0) D	H	4	OHC
1988	Escort	116 (1.9) EFI	9	4	OHC
	Escort	116 (1.9) EFI HO	J	4	OHC
	Tempo	140 (2.3) HSC-EFI	X	4	OHV
	Tempo	140 (2.3) EFI	S	4	OHV
	Topaz	140 (2.3) HSC-EFI	X	4	OHV
	Topaz	140 (2.3) EFI	S	4	OHV

ENGINE IDENTIFICATION

Year	Model	Engine Displacement cu. in. (liter)	Engine Series Identification (VIN)	No. of Cylinders	Engine Type
1989	Escort	116 (1.9) EFI	9	4	OHC
	Escort	116 (1.9) EFI-HO	J	4	OHC
	Tempo	140 (2.3) HSC-EFI	X	4	OHV
	Tempo	140 (2.3) HSO-EFI	S	4	OHV
	Topaz	140 (2.3) HSC-EFI	X	4	OHV
	Topaz	140 (2.3) HSO-EFI	S	4	OHV
1990–91	Escort	116 (1.9) EFI	9	4	OHC
	Escort	116 (1.9) EFI-HO	J	4	OHC
	Tempo	140 (2.3) HSC-EFI	X	4	OHV
	Tempo	140 (2.3) HSO-EFI	S	4	OHV
	Topaz	140 (2.3) HSC-EFI	X	4	OHV
	Topaz	140 (2.3) HSO-EFI	S	4	OHV

HO High Output
HSC High Swirl Combustion
M-HO Methanol High Output
D Diesel
CFI Central Fuel Injection
EFI Electronic Fuel Injection
OHC Overhead Cam
OHV Overhead Valve

GENERAL ENGINE SPECIFICATIONS

Year	VIN	No. Cylinder Displacement cu. in. (liter)	Fuel System Type	Net Horsepower @ rpm	Net Torque @ rpm (ft. lbs.)	Bore × Stroke (in.)	Compression Ratio	Oil Pressure @ rpm
1987	9	4-116 (1.9)	2 bbl	86 @ 4800	100 @ 3000	3.23 × 3.46	9.0:1	35–65 @ 2000
	J	4-116 (1.9)	EFI	108 @ 5200	114 @ 4000	3.23 × 3.46	9.0:1	35–65 @ 2000
	H	4-122 (2.0)	Diesel	52 @ 4000	82 @ 2400	3.39 × 3.39	22.7:1	55–60 @ 2000
	R	4-140 (2.3)	1 bbl	84 @ 4600	118 @ 2600	3.70 × 3.30	9.0:1	35–65 @ 2000
	X	4-140 (2.3)	CFI	100 @ 4600	125 @ 3200	3.70 × 3.30	9.0:1	55–70 @ 2000
1988	9	4-116 (1.9)	CFI	90 @ 4600	106 @ 3400	3.23 × 3.46	9.0:1	35–65 @ 2000
	J	4-116 (1.9)	EFI	110 @ 5400	115 @ 4200	3.23 × 3.46	9.0:1	35–65 @ 2000
	X	4-140 (2.3)	EFI	98 @ 4400	124 @ 2200	3.70 × 3.30	9.0:1	55–70 @ 2000
	S	4-140 (2.3)	EFI	100 @ 4400	130 @ 2600	3.70 × 3.30	9.0:1	55–70 @ 2000
1989	9	4-116 (1.9)	EFI	90 @ 4600	106 @ 3400	3.23 × 3.46	9.0:1	35–65 @ 2000
	J	4-116 (1.9)	EFI-HO	110 @ 5400	115 @ 4200	3.23 × 3.46	9.0:1	35–65 @ 2000
	X	4-140 (2.3)	EFI	98 @ 4400	124 @ 2200	3.70 × 3.30	9.0:1	55–70 @ 2000
	S	4-140 (2.3)	EFI-HSO	100 @ 4400	130 @ 2600	3.70 × 3.30	9.0:1	55–70 @ 2000
1990–91	9	4-116 (1.9)	EFI	90 @ 4600	106 @ 3400	3.23 × 3.46	9.0:1	35–65 @ 2000
	J	4-116 (1.9)	EFI-HO	110 @ 5400	115 @ 4200	3.23 × 3.46	9.0:1	35–65 @ 2000
	X	4-140 (2.3)	EFI-HSC	98 @ 4400	124 @ 2200	3.70 × 3.30	9.0:1	55–70 @ 2000
	S	4-140 (2.3)	EFI-HSO	100 @ 4400	130 @ 2600	3.70 × 3.30	9.0:1	55–70 @ 2000

GASOLINE ENGINE TUNE-UP SPECIFICATIONS

Year	VIN	No. Cylinder Displacement cu. in. (liter)	Spark Plugs Type	Spark Plugs Gap (in.)	Ignition Timing (deg.) MT	Ignition Timing (deg.) AT	Compression Pressure (psi)	Fuel Pump (psi)	Idle Speed (rpm) MT	Idle Speed (rpm) AT	Valve Clearance In.	Valve Clearance Ex.
1987	9	4-116 (1.9)	AGSF-34C	0.044	10B	10B	—	13–17	750	750	Hyd.	Hyd.
	J	4-116 (1.9)	AGSF-24C	0.044	10B	10B	—	35–45	800	750	Hyd.	Hyd.
	R	4-140 (2.3)	AGSF-32C	0.044	10B	10B	—	4–6	800	750	Hyd.	Hyd.
	X	4-140 (2.3)	AWSF-52	0.044	10B	10B	—	35–45	750	650	Hyd.	Hyd.
1988	9	4-116 (1.9)	AGSF-34C	0.044	①	①	—	13–17	900 1000	900 1000	Hyd.	Hyd.
	J	4-116 (1.9)	AGSF-24C	0.044	①	①	—	30–45	900 1000	900 1000	Hyd.	Hyd.
	X	4-140 (2.3)	AWSF-42C	0.044	①	①	—	45–60	1500-1600	975-1075	Hyd.	Hyd.
	S	4-140 (2.3)	AWSF-42C	0.044	①	①	—	50–60	1500-1600	975-1075	Hyd.	Hyd.
1989	9	4-116 (1.9)	AGSF-34C	0.044	①	①	—	13–17	900 1000	900 1000	Hyd.	Hyd.
	J	4-116 (1.9)	AGSF-24C	0.044	①	①	—	30–45	900 1000	900 1000	Hyd.	Hyd.
	X	4-140 (2.3)	AWSF-42C	0.054	①	①	—	45–60	1500-1600	975-1075	Hyd.	Hyd.
	S	4-140 (2.3)	AWSF-42C	0.044	①	①	—	50–60	1500-1600	975-1075	Hyd.	Hyd.
1990	9	4-116 (1.9)	AGSF-34C	0.044	①	①	—	13–17	950	950	Hyd.	Hyd.
	J	4-116 (1.9)	AGSF-24C	0.044	①	①	—	35–45	950	950	Hyd.	Hyd.
	X	4-140 (2.3)	AWSF-42C	0.054	①	①	—	45–60	1500-1600	975-1075	Hyd.	Hyd.
	S	4-140 (2.3)	AWSF-42C	0.054	①	①	—	50–60	1500-1600	975-1075	Hyd.	Hyd.
1991		SEE UNDERHOOD SPECIFICATIONS STICKER										

B Before Top Dead Center
① Refer to the Vehicle Emission Control label

DIESEL ENGINE TUNE-UP SPECIFICATIONS

Year	VIN	No. Engine Displacement cu. in. (liter)	Valve Clearance Intake (in.)	Valve Clearance Exhaust (in.)	Intake Valve Opens (deg.)	Injection Pump Setting (deg.)	Injection Nozzle Pressure (psi) New	Injection Nozzle Pressure (psi) Used	Idle Speed (rpm)	Cranking Compression Pressure (psi)
1987	H	4-122 (2.0)	0.010	0.014	13	TDC Hot	1990–2105	1849–1900	725±50	384–427 @ 200

NOTE: See the Diesel Injection Timing Procedure text in this section.
TDC Top Dead Center

FIRING ORDERS

NOTE: To avoid confusion, always replace spark plug wires one at a time.

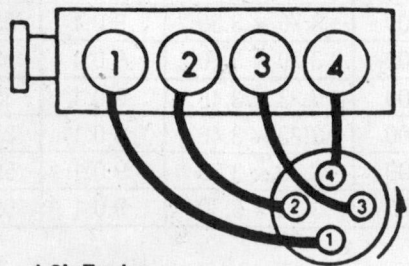

1.9L Engine
Engine Firing Order: 1–3–4–2
Distributor Rotation: Counterclockwise

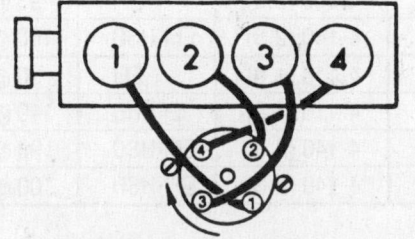

2.3L Engine
Engine Firing Order: 1–3–4–2
Distributor Rotation: Clockwise

CAPACITIES

Year	Model	VIN	No. Cylinder Displacement cu. in. (liter)	Engine Crankcase (qts.) with Filter	without Filter	Transmission (pts.) 4-Spd	5-Spd	Auto.	Drive Axle (pts.)	Fuel Tank (gal.)	Cooling System (qts.)
1987	Escort	9	4-116 (1.9)	4.0	3.5	5	6.2	16.6	①	13	③
	Escort	J	4-116 (1.9)	4.0	3.5	5	6.2	16.6	①	13	③
	Escort	H	4-122 (2.0)	7.2	7.0	5	6.2	16.6	①	13	③
	Lynx	9	4-116 (1.9)	4.0	3.5	5	6.2	16.6	①	13	③
	Lynx	J	4-116 (1.9)	4.0	3.5	5	6.2	16.6	①	13	③
	Lynx	H	4-122 (2.0)	7.2	7.0	5	6.2	16.6	①	13	③
	Tempo	R	4-140 (2.3)	5.0	4.0	—	6.2	②	⑥	④	③
	Tempo	X	4-140 (2.3)	5.0	4.0	—	6.2	②	⑥	④	③
	Tempo	H	4-122 (2.0)	7.2	7.0	—	6.2	②	⑥	④	③
	Topaz	R	4-140 (2.3)	5.0	4.0	—	6.2	②	⑥	④	③
	Topaz	X	4-140 (2.3)	5.0	4.0	—	6.2	②	⑥	④	③
	Topaz	H	4-122 (2.0)	7.2	7.0	—	6.2	②	⑥	④	③
1988	Escort	9	4-116 (1.9)	4.0	3.5	6.2	6.2	16.6	①	13	⑤
	Escort	J	4-116 (1.9)	4.0	3.5	6.2	6.2	16.6	①	13	⑤
	Tempo	S	4-140 (2.3)	5.0	4.0	—	6.2	②	⑥	④	⑦
	Tempo	X	4-140 (2.3)	5.0	4.0	—	6.2	②	⑥	④	⑦
	Topaz	S	4-140 (2.3)	5.0	4.0	—	6.2	②	⑥	④	⑦
	Topaz	X	4-140 (2.3)	5.0	4.0	—	6.2	②	⑥	④	⑦
1989	Escort	9	4-116 (1.9)	4.0	3.5	6.2	6.2	16.6	①	13	⑧
	Escort	J	4-116 (1.9)	4.0	3.5	6.2	6.2	16.6	①	13	⑧
	Tempo	S	4-140 (2.3)	5.0	4.0	—	6.2	②	⑥	④	⑦
	Tempo	X	4-140 (2.3)	5.0	4.0	—	6.2	②	⑥	④	⑦
	Topaz	S	4-140 (2.3)	5.0	4.0	—	6.2	②	⑥	④	⑦
	Topaz	X	4-140 (2.3)	5.0	4.0	—	6.2	②	⑥	④	⑦
1990–91	Escort	9	4-116 (1.9)	4.0	3.5	6.2	6.2	16.6	①	⑨	⑧
	Escort	J	4-116 (1.9)	4.0	3.5	6.2	6.2	16.6	①	⑨	⑧
	Tempo	S	4.140 (2.3)	5.0	4.0	—	6.2	16.6	①	④	⑦
	Tempo	X	4-140 (2.3)	5.0	4.0	—	6.2	16.6	①	④	⑦
	Topaz	S	4.140 (2.3)	5.0	4.0	—	6.2	16.6	①	④	⑦
	Topaz	X	4-140 (2.3)	5.0	4.0	—	6.2	16.6	①	④	⑦

① Included in transaxle capacity
② All models except the all wheel drive—16.6 pts.
All wheel drive models—20 pts.
③ All models without air conditioning—8.3 qts.
Manual transaxle with air conditioning—7.3 qts.
Automatic transaxle with air conditioning—7.8 qts.
④ All models except the all wheel drive—15.9
All all wheel drive models—14.2
⑤ All models without air conditioning—8.3 qts.
Manual transaxle with air conditioning—6.8 qts.
Automatic transaxle with air conditioning—7.3 qts.
⑥ Included in transaxle capacity. The all wheel drive model rear capacity is 1.3 pts.
⑦ Manual transaxle—7.3 qts.
Automatic transaxle—7.8 qts.
⑧ Manual transaxle without air conditioning—8.3 qts.
Automatic transaxle without air conditioning—8.3 qts.
Manual transaxle with air conditioning—6.8 qts.
Automatic transaxle with air conditioning—7.3 qts.

⑨ Standard—13.0 gal.
5 speed or automatic transaxle without air conditioning—11.5 gal.
Wagon, 5 speed—11.5 gal.
Manual transaxle with air conditioning
Fuel saver—11.5 gal.

CAMSHAFT SPECIFICATIONS

All measurements given in inches.

Year	VIN	No. Cylinder Displacement cu. in. (liter)	Journal Diameter					Lobe Lift	Bearing Clearance	Camshaft End Play
			1	2	3	4	5			
1987	9	4-116 (1.9)	1.8007–1.8017	1.8007–1.8017	1.8007–1.8017	1.8007–1.8017	1.8007–1.8017	0.240	0.001–0.003	0.002–0.006
	J	4-116 (1.9)	1.8007–1.8017	1.8007–1.8017	1.8007–1.8017	1.8007–1.8017	1.8007–1.8017	0.240	0.001–0.003	0.002–0.006
	H	4-122 (2.0)	1.2582–1.2589	1.2582–1.2589	1.2582–1.2589	1.2582–1.2589	1.2582–1.2589	NA	0.001–0.003	0.001–0.006
	R	4-140 (2.3)	2.006–2.009	2.006–2.009	2.006–2.009	2.006–2.009	—	①	0.001–0.003	0.009
	X	4-140 (2.3)	2.006–2.009	2.006–2.009	2.006–2.009	2.006–2.009	—	①②	0.001–0.003	.0.009
1988	9	4-116 (1.9)	1.8007–1.8017	1.8007–1.8017	1.8007–1.8017	1.8007–1.8017	1.8007–1.8017	0.240	0.001–0.003	0.002–0.006
	J	4-116 (1.9)	1.8007–1.8017	1.8007–1.8017	1.8007–1.8017	1.8007–1.8017	1.8007–1.8017	0.240	0.001–0.003	0.002–0.006
	X	4-140 (2.3)	2.006–2.009	2.006–2.009	2.006–2.009	2.006–2.009	—	①	0.001–0.003	0.009
	S	4-140 (2.3)	2.006–2.009	2.006–2.009	2.006–2.009	2.006–2.009	—	②	0.001–0.003	0.009
1989	9	4-116 (1.9)	1.8007–1.8017	1.8007–1.8017	1.8007–1.8017	1.8007–1.8017	1.8007–1.8017	0.240	0.001–0.003	0.002–0.006
	J	4-116 (1.9)	1.8007–1.8017	1.8007–1.8017	1.8007–1.8017	1.8007–1.8017	1.8007–1.8017	0.240	0.001–0.003	0.002–0.006
	X	4-140 (2.3)	2.006–2.009	2.006–2.009	2.006–2.009	2.006–2.009	—	①	0.001–0.003	0.009
	S	4-140 (2.3)	2.006–2.009	2.006–2.009	2.006–2.009	2.006–2.009	—	②	0.001–0.003	0.009
1990–91	9	4-116 (1.9)	1.8007–1.8017	1.8007–1.8017	1.8007–1.8017	1.8007–1.8017	1.8007–1.8017	0.240	0.001–0.003	0.002–0.006
	J	4-116 (1.9)	1.8007–1.8017	1.8007–1.8017	1.8007–1.8017	1.8007–1.8017	1.8007–1.8017	0.240	0.001–0.003	0.002–0.006
	X	4-140 (2.3)	2.006–2.009	2.006–2.009	2.006–2.009	2.006–2.009	—	①	0.001–0.003	0.009
	S	4-140 (2.3)	2.006–2.009	2.006–2.009	2.006–2.009	2.006–2.009	—	②	0.001–0.003	0.009

NA Not available

① Intake—0.249 in.
  Exhaust—0.239 in.
② 2.3L HO engine—0.2625 in.

CRANKSHAFT AND CONNECTING ROD SPECIFICATIONS

All measurements are given in inches.

Year	VIN	No. Cylinder Displacement cu. in. (liter)	Crankshaft				Connecting Rod		
			Main Brg. Journal Dia.	Main Brg. Oil Clearance	Shaft End-play	Thrust on No.	Journal Diameter	Oil Clearance	Side Clearance
1987	9	4-116 (1.9)	2.2827–2.2835	0.0008–0.0015	0.004–0.008	3	1.8854–1.8862	0.0008–0.0015	0.004–0.011
	J	4-116 (1.9)	2.2827–2.2835	0.0008–0.0015	0.004–0.008	3	1.8854–1.8862	0.0008–0.0015	0.004–0.011
	H	4-122 (2.0)	2.3598–2.3605	0.0012–0.0020	0.0016–0.0011	3	2.0055–2.0061	0.0010–0.0022	0.004–0.010
	R	4-140 (2.3)	2.2489–2.2490	0.0008–0.0015	0.004–0.008	3	2.1232–2.1240	0.0008–0.0015	0.004–0.011
	X	4-140 (2.3)	2.2489–2.2490	0.0008–0.0015	0.004–0.008	3	2.1232–2.1240	0.0008–0.0015	0.004–0.011
1988	9	4-116 (1.9)	2.2827–2.2835	0.0008–0.0015	0.004–0.008	3	1.7257–1.7279	0.0008–0.0015	0.004–0.011
	J	4-116 (1.9)	2.2827–2.2835	0.0008–0.0015	0.004–0.008	3	1.7257–1.7279	0.0008–0.0015	0.004–0.011
	X	4-140 (2.3)	2.2489–2.2490	0.0008–0.0015	0.004–0.008	3	2.1232–2.1240	0.0008–0.0015	0.004–0.011
	S	4-140 (2.3)	2.2489–2.2490	0.0008–0.0015	0.004–0.008	3	2.1232–2.1240	0.0008–0.0015	0.004–0.011
1989	9	4-116 (1.9)	2.2827–2.2835	0.0008–0.0015	0.004–0.008	3	1.7257–1.7279	0.0008–0.0015	0.004–0.011
	J	4-116 (1.9)	2.2827–2.2835	0.0008–0.0015	0.004–0.008	3	1.7257–1.7279	0.0008–0.0015	0.004–0.011
	X	4-140 (2.3)	2.2489–2.2490	0.0008–0.0015	0.004–0.008	3	2.1232–2.1240	0.0008–0.0015	0.004–0.011
	S	4-140 (2.3)	2.2489–2.2490	0.0008–0.0015	0.004–0.008	3	2.1232–2.1240	0.0008–0.0015	0.004–0.011
1990–91	9	4-116 (1.9)	2.2827–2.2835	0.0008–0.0015	0.004–0.008	3	1.7279–1.7287	0.0008–0.0015	0.004–0.011
	J	4-116 (1.9)	2.2827–2.2835	0.0008–0.0015	0.004–0.008	3	1.7279–1.7287	0.0008–0.0015	0.004–0.011
	X	4-140 (2.3)	2.2489–2.2490	0.0008–0.0015	0.004–0.008	3	2.1232–2.1240	0.0008–0.0015	0.004–0.011
	S	4-140 (2.3)	2.2489–2.2490	0.0008–0.0015	0.004–0.008	3	2.1232–2.1240	0.0008–0.0015	0.004–0.011

VALVE SPECIFICATIONS

Year	VIN	No. Cylinder Displacement cu. in. (liter)	Seat Angle (deg.)	Face Angle (deg.)	Spring Test Pressure (lbs.)	Spring Installed Height (in.)	Stem-to-Guide Clearance (in.)		Stem Diameter (in.)	
							Intake	Exhaust	Intake	Exhaust
1987	9	4-116 (1.9)	45	45.5	200 @ 1.09	1.44–1.48	0.0008–0.0027	0.0018–0.0037	0.3159–0.3167	0.3149–0.3156
	J	4-116 (1.9)	45	45.5	216 @ 1.016	1.44–1.48	0.0008–0.0027	0.0018–0.0037	0.3159–0.3167	0.3149–0.3156
	H	4-122 (2.0)	45	45	NA	NA	0.0016–0.0029	0.0018–0.0031	0.3138–0.3144	0.3138–0.3144
	R	4-140 (2.3)	44	44	181 @ 1.07	1.49	0.0018	0.0023	0.316	0.315
	X	4-140 (2.3)	44	44	181 @ 1.07	1.49	0.0018	0.0023	0.316	0.315

VALVE SPECIFICATIONS

Year	VIN	No. Cylinder Displacement cu. in. (liter)	Seat Angle (deg.)	Face Angle (deg.)	Spring Test Pressure (lbs.)	Spring Installed Height (in.)	Stem-to-Guide Clearance (in.) Intake	Stem-to-Guide Clearance (in.) Exhaust	Stem Diameter (in.) Intake	Stem Diameter (in.) Exhaust
1988	9	4-116 (1.9)	45	45.5	200 @ 1.09	1.44–1.48	0.0008–0.0027	0.0018–0.0037	0.3159–0.3167	0.3149–0.3156
	J	4-116 (1.9)	45	45.5	216 @ 1.016	1.44–1.48	0.0008–0.0027	0.0018–0.0037	0.3159–0.3167	0.3149–0.3156
	X	4-140 (2.3)	44	44	181 @ 1.07	1.49	0.0018	0.0023	0.3415–0.3422	0.3411–0.3418
	S	4-140 (2.3)	44	44	181 @ 1.07	1.49	0.0018–0.0028	0.0023	0.3415–0.3422	0.3411–0.3418
1989	9	4-116 (1.9)	45	45.5	200 @ 1.09	1.44–1.48	0.0008–0.0027	0.0018–0.0037	0.3159–0.3167	0.3149–0.3156
	J	4-116 (1.9)	45	45.5	216 @ 1.016	1.44–1.48	0.0008–0.0027	0.0018–0.0037	0.3159–0.3167	0.3149–0.3156
	X	4-140 (2.3)	44	44	181 @ 1.07	1.49	0.0018	0.0023	0.3415–0.3422	0.3411–0.3418
	S	4-140 (2.3)	44	44	181 @ 1.07	1.49	0.0018	0.0023	0.3415–0.3422	0.3411–0.3418
1990–91	9	4-116 (1.9)	45	45.5	200 @ 1.09	1.44–1.48	0.0008–0.0027	0.0018–0.0037	0.3159–0.3167	0.3149–0.3156
	J	4-116 (1.9)	45	45.5	216 @ 1.016	1.44–1.48	0.0008–0.0027	0.0018–0.0037	0.3159–0.3167	0.3149–0.3156
	X	4-140 (2.3)	44	44	181 @ 1.07	1.49	0.0018	0.0023	0.3415–0.3422	0.3411–0.3418
	S	4-140 (2.3)	44	44	181 @ 1.07	1.49	0.0018	0.0023	0.3415–0.3422	0.3411–0.3418

PISTON AND RING SPECIFICATIONS

All measurements are given in inches.

Year	VIN	No. Cylinder Displacement cu. in. (liter)	Piston Clearance	Ring Gap Top Compression	Ring Gap Bottom Compression	Ring Gap Oil Control	Ring Side Clearance Top Compression	Ring Side Clearance Bottom Compression	Ring Side Clearance Oil Control
1987	9	4-116 (1.9)	0.0016–0.0024	0.0010–0.0020	0.0010–0.0020	0.0016–0.0055	0.0015–0.0032	0.0015–0.0035	Snug
	J	4-116 (1.9)	0.0016–0.0024	0.0010–0.0020	0.0010–0.0020	0.0016–0.0055	0.0015–0.0032	0.0015–0.0035	Snug
	H	4-122 (2.0) Diesel	0.0013–0.0020	0.0079–0.0157	0.0079–0.0157	0.0079–0.0157	0.0020–0.0035	0.0016–0.0031	Snug
	R	4-140 (2.3)	0.0012–0.0022	0.0008–0.0016	0.0008–0.0016	0.0015–0.0055	0.0020–0.0040	0.0020–0.0040	Snug
	X	4-140 (2.3)	0.0012–0.0022	0.0008–0.0016	0.0008–0.0016	0.0015–0.0055	0.0020–0.0040	0.0020–0.0040	Snug
1988	9	4-116 (1.9)	0.0016–0.0024	0.0010–0.0020	0.0010–0.0020	0.0016–0.0055	0.0015–0.0032	0.0015–0.0035	Snug
	J	4-116 (1.9)	0.0016–0.0024	0.0010–0.0020	0.0010–0.0020	0.0016–0.0055	0.0015–0.0032	0.0015–0.0035	Snug
	X	4-140 (2.3)	0.0012–0.0022	0.0008–0.0016	0.0008–0.0016	0.0015–0.0055	0.0020–0.0040	0.0020–0.0040	Snug
	S	4-140 (2.3)	0.0012–0.0022	0.0008–0.0016	0.0008–0.0016	0.0015–0.0055	0.0020–0.0040	0.0020–0.0040	Snug

PISTON AND RING SPECIFICATIONS

All measurements are given in inches.

Year	VIN	No. Cylinder Displacement cu. in. (liter)	Piston Clearance	Ring Gap			Ring Side Clearance		
				Top Compression	Bottom Compression	Oil Control	Top Compression	Bottom Compression	Oil Control
1989	9	4-116 (1.9)	0.0016–0.0024	0.0010–0.0020	0.0010–0.0020	0.0016–0.0055	0.0015–0.0032	0.0015–0.0035	Snug
	J	4-116 (1.9)	0.0016–0.0024	0.0010–0.0020	0.0010–0.0020	0.0016–0.0055	0.0015–0.0032	0.0015–0.0035	Snug
	X	4-140 (2.3)	0.0012–0.0022	0.0008–0.0016	0.0008–0.0016	0.0015–0.0055	0.0020–0.0040	0.0020–0.0040	Snug
	S	4-140 (2.3)	0.0012–0.0022	0.0008–0.0016	0.0008–0.0016	0.0015–0.0055	0.0020–0.0040	0.0020–0.0040	Snug
	9	4-116 (1.9)	0.0016–0.0024	0.0010–0.0020	0.0010–0.0020	0.0016–0.0055	0.0015–0.0032	0.0015–0.0032	Snug
1990–91	J	4-116 (1.9)	0.0016–0.0024	0.0010–0.0020	0.0010–0.0020	0.0016–0.0055	0.0015–0.0032	0.0015–0.0032	Snug
	X	4-140 (2.3)	0.0012–0.0022	0.0008–0.0016	0.0008–0.0016	0.0015–0.0055	0.0020–0.0040	0.0020–0.0040	Snug
	S	4-140 (2.3)	0.0012–0.0022	0.0008–0.0016	0.0008–0.0016	0.0015–0.0055	0.0020–0.0040	0.0020–0.0040	Snug

TORQUE SPECIFICATIONS

All readings in ft. lbs.

Year	VIN	No. Cylinder Displacement cu. in. (liter)	Cylinder Head Bolts	Main Bearing Bolts	Rod Bearing Bolts	Crankshaft Pulley Bolts	Flywheel Bolts	Manifold		Spark Plugs
								Intake	Exhaust	
1987	9	4-116 (1.9)	①	67–80	19–25	74–90	59–69	12–15	15–20	8–15
	J	4-116 (1.9)	①	67–80	19–25	74–90	59–69	12–15	15–20	8–15
	H	4-122 (2.0)	①	61–65	51–54	115–123	130–137	12–16	16–20 ③	5–10
	R	4-140 (2.3)	④	51–66	21–26	140–170	54–64	15–23	③	5–10
	X	4-140 (2.3)	④	51–66	21–26	140–170	54–64	15–23	③	5–10
1988	9	4-116 (1.9)	①	67–80	19–25	74–90	54–64	12–15	15–20	8–15
	J	4-116 (1.9)	①	67–80	19–25	74–90	54–64	12–15	15–20	8–15
	X	4-140 (2.3)	④	51–66	21–26	140–170	54–64	15–23	③	5–10
	S	4-140 (2.3)	④	51–66	21–26	140–170	54–64	15–23	③	5–10
1989	9	4-116 (1.9)	①	67–80	26–30	81–96	54–64	12–15	15–20	8–15
	J	4-116 (1.9)	①	67–80	26–30	81–96	54–64	12–15	15–20	8–15
	X	4-140 (2.3)	④	51–66	21–26	140–170	54–64	15–23	③	5–10
	S	4-140 (2.3)	④	51–66	21–26	140–170	54–64	15–23	③	5–10
1990–91	9	4-116 (1.9)	①	67–80	26–30	81–96	54–64	12–15	15–20	8–15
	J	4-116 (1.9)	①	67–80	26–30	81–96	54–64	12–15	15–20	8–15
	X	4-140 (2.3)	④	51–66	21–26	130–160	54–64	15–22	③	5–10
	S	4-140 (2.3)	④	51–66	21–26	130–160	54–64	15–22	③	5–10

① Tighten in sequence to 44 ft. lbs.
   Loosen 2 turns
   Retighten in sequence to 44 ft. lbs.
   Turn all bolts 90 degrees
   Turn all bolts additional 90 degrees
② Manifold stud nuts—12–13 ft. lbs.
③ Tighten in 2 stages—5–7 ft. lbs. then 20–30 ft. lbs.
④ Tighten in 2 steps—52–59 ft. lbs. and then the final torque of 70–76 ft. lbs.

BRAKE SPECIFICATIONS

All measurements in inches unless noted

Year	Model	Lug Nut Torque (ft. lbs.)	Master Cylinder Bore	Brake Disc Minimum Thickness	Brake Disc Maximum Runout	Standard Brake Drum Diameter	Minimum Lining Thickness Front	Minimum Lining Thickness Rear
1987	Escort, Lynx	80–105	③	0.882	0.003	7.090 ①	0.48	②
	Tempo, Topaz	80–105	③	0.882	0.003	8.000	0.48	②
1988	Escort	80–105	③	0.882	0.003	7.090 ①	0.48	②
	Tempo, Topaz	80–105	③	0.882	0.003	8.000	0.48	②
1989	Escort	80–105	③	0.882	0.003	7.090 ①	0.125	②
	Tempo, Topaz	80–105	③	0.882	0.003	8.000	0.125	②
1990–91	Escort	85–105	③	0.882	0.003	7.146 ①	0.125	②
	Tempo, Topaz	85–105	③	0.882	0.003	8.059	0.125	②

① 4/5–door models—8.059
② 0.020 over rivet head; if bonded lining, use 0.062 in.
③ Primary bore—1.12
   Secondary bore—0.776

WHEEL ALIGNMENT

Year	Model	Caster Range (deg.)	Caster Preferred Setting (deg.)	Camber Range (deg.)	Camber Preferred Setting (deg.)	Toe-in (in.)	Wheel Turning Angle (deg.)
1987	Escort, Lynx	$1^5/_8$P–$3^1/_8$P	$2^3/_8$ ①	②	③	$^1/_4$N–0	Left 20.0 Right 18.2
	Tempo, Topaz Sport Coupe	$1^{11}/_{16}$P–$3^3/_{16}$P	$2^7/_{16}$ ①	④	⑤	$^1/_4$N–0	Left 20.0 Right 18.2
1988	Escort	$1^5/_8$P–$3^1/_8$P	$2^3/_8$	⑥	⑦	$^1/_4$N–0	Left 20.0 Right 18.2
	Tempo, Topaz	$1^{11}/_{16}$P–$3^3/_{16}$P	$2^7/_{16}$	⑧	⑨	$^1/_4$N–0	Left 20.0 Right 18.2
1989	Escort	$1^5/_8$P–$3/_{18}$P	$2^3/_8$	⑥	⑦	$^1/_4$N–0	Left 20.0 Right 18.2
	Tempo, Topaz	$1^{11}/_{16}$P–$3^3/_{16}$P	$2^7/_{16}$	⑧	⑨	$^1/_4$N–0	Left 20.0 Right 18.2
1990–91	Escort	$1^5/_8$P–$3^1/_8$P	$2^3/_8$	⑥	⑦	$^1/_4$N–0	Left 20.0 Right 18.2
	Tempo, Topaz	$1^{11}/_{16}$P–$3^3/_{16}$P	$2^7/_{16}$	⑧	⑨	$^1/_4$N–0	Left 20.0 Right 18.2

① Caster and camber are not adjustable. Measurements must be made by turning the wheel left and right through their respective sweep angles.
② Left—$^5/_{16}$P–$1^{13}/_{16}$P
   Right—0–$1^1/_2$P
③ Left—$1^1/_{16}$P
   Right—$^3/_4$P
④ Left—$^{21}/_{32}$P–$2^5/_{32}$P
   Right—$^7/_{32}$P–$1^{23}/_{32}$P
⑤ Left—$1^{13}/_{32}$P
   Right—$^{31}/_{32}$P
⑥ Left—$^3/_8$P–$1^7/_8$P
   Right—0–$1^1/_2$P
⑦ Left—$1^1/_8$P
   Right—$^3/_4$P
⑧ Left—$^{21}/_{32}$P–$2^5/_{32}$P
   Right—$^7/_{32}$P–$1^{23}/_{32}$P
⑨ Left—$1^{13}/_{32}$P
   Right—$^{31}/_{32}$P

ENGINE ELECTRICAL

NOTE: Disconnecting the negative battery cable on some vehicles may interfere with the functions of the on board computer systems and may require the computer to undergo a relearning process, once the negative battery cable is reconnected.

Distributor

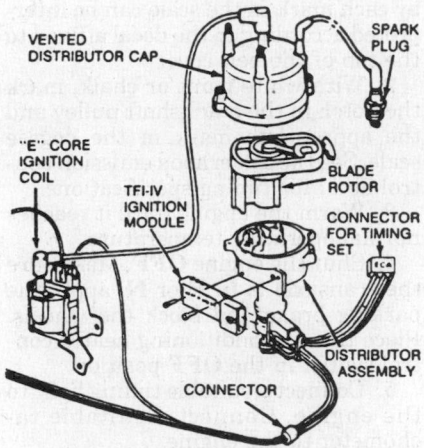

TFI-IV Ignition system—typical

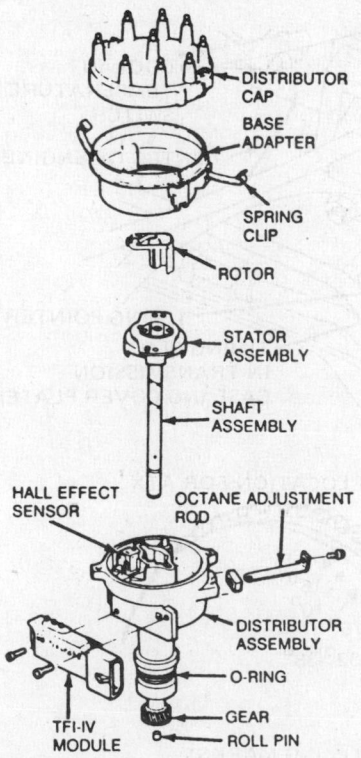

Universal distributor components—typical

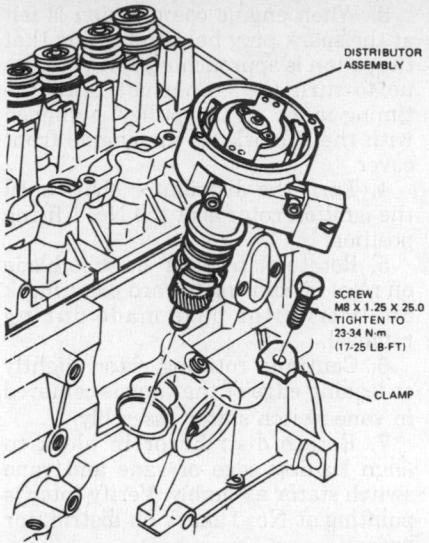

Distributor Installation on 2.3L HSC Engine

REMOVAL

1. Turn the engine over until No. 1 cylinder is at TDC of the compression stroke.
2. Mark the position of No. 1 cylinder wire on distributor base for reference when installing distributor.
3. Disconnect the negative battery cable.
4. Disconnect the primary wiring from the distributor.
5. Remove the cap screws and remove the distributor cap straight off to prevent damage to the rotor blade and spring. Remove rotor from distributor shaft and armature.
6. Scribe or paint an alignment mark on the distributor body, showing the position of the ignition rotor. Place another mark on the distributor body and cylinder head, showing the position of the body in relation to the head. These marks are used for reference when installing the distributor.
7. Remove the 2 distributor retaining bolts at the base of the distributor housing on 1.9L engine. Remove distributor hold-down bolt and clamp on 2.3L engine.
8. Pull the distributor out of the head.

NOTE: Some engines are equipped with security type distributor retaining bolts and special tool T82L–12270–A or equivalent, must be used to remove these bolts.

INSTALLATION

Timing Not Disturbed

1.9L ENGINE

1. Place the distributor in the cylin-

der head, seating the off-set tang of the drive coupling into the groove at the end of the camshaft.
2. Install the distributor retaining bolts and tighten them so that the distributor can just barely be moved.
3. Install the rotor, if removed, the distributor cap and all wiring. Tighten distributor cap to 18-23 inch lbs.
4. Set initial timing.
5. After timing has been set, tighten distributor hold-down bolts to 44-62 inch lbs.

2.3L ENGINE

1. Rotate distributor shaft so blade on rotor is pointing toward paint mark on distributor base made during removal.
2. Continue rotating rotor slightly so leading edge of the vane is centered in vane switch stator assembly.
3. Rotate distributor in block to align leading edge of vane and vane switch stator assembly. Verify rotor is pointing at No. 1 mark on distributor base.

NOTE: If vane and vane switch stator cannot be aligned by rotating distributor in cylinder block, remove distributor enough to just disengage distributor gear from camshaft gear. Rotate rotor enough to engage distributor gear on another tooth of camshaft gear.

4. Install the distributor retaining bolt and tighten so that the distributor can just barely be moved.
5. Install the rotor, if removed, the distributor cap and all wiring. Tighten distributor cap to 18-23 inch lbs.
6. Set initial timing according to procedures.
7. After timing has been set, tighten distributor hold-down bolt to 17-25 ft. lbs.

Timing Disturbed

1.9L ENGINE

1. If the crankshaft was rotated while the distributor was removed, the engine must be brought to TDC on the compression stroke of the No. 1 cylinder.
2. Remove the No. 1 spark plug. Place finger over the hole and rotate the crankshaft slowly in the direction of normal rotation, until engine compression is felt.

NOTE: Turn the engine only in the direction of normal rotation. Backward rotation may cause the cam belt to slip or lose teeth, altering engine timing.

3. When engine compression is felt at the spark plug hole, indicating that the piston is approaching TDC, contin-

ue to turn the crankshaft until the timing mark on the pulley is aligned with the **0** mark on the engine front cover.

4. Turn the distributor shaft until the ignition rotor is at the No. 1 firing position.

5. Place the distributor in the cylinder head, seating the off-set tang of the drive coupling into the groove at the end of the camshaft.

6. Install the distributor retaining bolts and tighten them so that the distributor can just barely be moved.

7. Install the rotor, if removed, the distributor cap and all wiring. Tighten distributor cap to 18-23 inch lbs.

8. Set initial timing.

9. After timing has been set, tighten distributor hold-down bolts to 44-62 inch lbs.

2.3L ENGINE

1. If the crankshaft was rotated while the distributor was removed, the engine must be brought to TDC on the compression stroke of the No. 1 cylinder.

2. Remove the No. 1 spark plug. Place finger over the hole and rotate the crankshaft slowly in the direction of normal rotation, until engine compression is felt.

NOTE: Turn the engine only in the direction of normal rotation. Backward rotation may cause the cam belt to slip or lose teeth, altering engine timing.

3. When engine compression is felt at the spark plug hole, indicating that the piston is approaching TDC, continue to turn the crankshaft until the timing mark on the pulley is aligned with the **0** mark on the engine front cover.

4. Turn the distributor shaft until the ignition rotor is at the No. 1 firing position.

5. Rotate distributor shaft so blade on rotor is pointing toward paint mark on distributor base made during removal.

6. Continue rotating rotor slightly so leading edge of the vane is centered in vane switch stator assembly.

7. Rotate distributor in block to align leading edge of vane and vane switch stator assembly. Verify rotor is pointing at No. 1 mark on distributor base.

NOTE: If vane and vane switch stator cannot be aligned by rotating distributor in cylinder block, remove distributor enough to just disengage distributor gear from camshaft gear. Rotate rotor enough to engage distributor gear on another tooth of camshaft gear.

8. Install the distributor retaining bolt and tighten so that the distributor can just barely be moved.

9. Install the rotor, if removed, the distributor cap and all wiring. Tighten distributor cap to 18-23 inch lbs.

10. Set initial timing according to procedures.

11. After timing has been set, tighten distributor hold-down bolt to 17-25 ft. lbs.

Ignition Timing

ADJUSTMENT

1.9L Engine

1. Ignition timing marks consist of a notch on the crankshaft pulley and a graduated scale molded into the camshaft belt cover. The number of degrees before or after TDC represented by each mark in the scale can be interpreted according to the decal affixed to the top of the belt cover.

2. With white paint or chalk, mark the notch in the crankshaft pulley and the appropriate mark in the degree scale. See the underhood emission control decal for timing specifications.

3. Warm the engine until it reaches normal operating temperature.

4. Shut the engine **OFF**. Make sure the transaxle is in **P** or **N**, apply the parking brake and block the wheels. Place the air conditioning/heater control switch in the **OFF** position.

5. Connect a suitable timing light to the engine. Connect a suitable tachometer to the engine.

6. Disconnect the single wire in-line spout connector or remove the shorting bar from the double wire spout

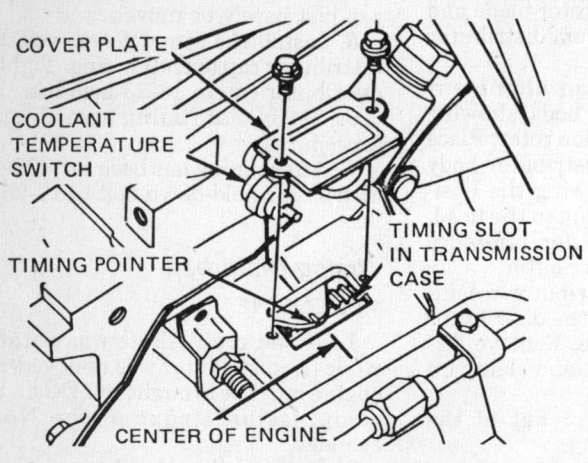

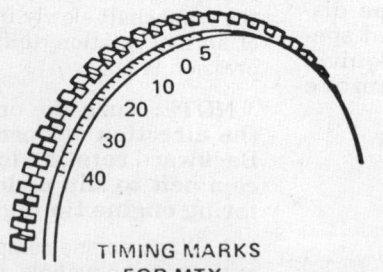

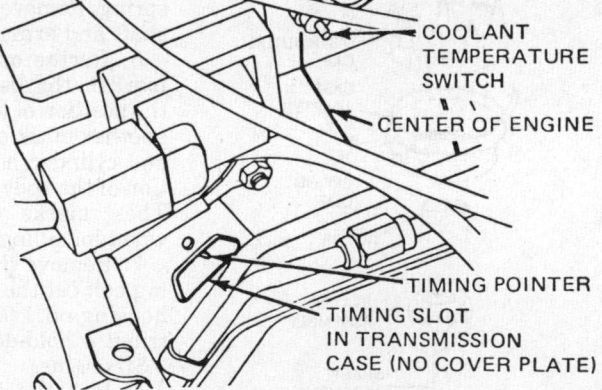

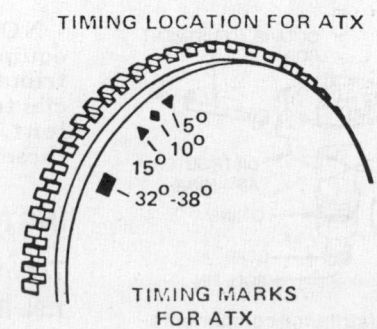

Tempo/Topaz timing marks

connector. The spout connector can be found in the distributor primary wiring harness near the distributor connector.

7. Start the engine and allow to reach normal operating temperature. Aim the light at the marks. If they are not aligned, loosen the distributor clamp bolts slightly and rotate the distributor body until the marks are aligned under timing light illumination.

8. Tighten the distributor clamp bolts. Connect the spout connector and check the timing to verify distributor advance beyond initial setting.

9. Shut the engine **OFF** and remove all test equipment.

2.3L HSC Engine

On engines equipped with a manual transaxle, the timing marks are located on the flywheel and visible through an access hole in the transaxle case. The timing cover plate must be removed in order to view the timing marks and adjust the timing.

NOTE: Some distributor retaining bolts have a security type head and cannot be loosened to adjust timing, unless special tool T82L–12270–A or equivalent, is available.

1. Place the transaxle in the **P** or **N** position. Firmly apply the parking brake and block the wheels.

2. Open the hood, locate the timing marks and clean with a stiff brush or solvent. On vehicles with manual transaxle, it will be necessary to remove the cover plate which allows access to to the timing marks.

3. Using white chalk or paint, mark the specified timing mark and pointer.

4. Remove the in-line spout connector or remove the shorting bar from the double wire spout connector. The spout connector is the center wire between the Electronic Control Assembly (ECA) connector and the Thick Film Ignition (TFI) module.

5. If the vehicle is equipped with a barometric pressure switch, disconnect it from the ignition module and place a jumper wire across the pins at the ignition module connector, yellow and black wire.

6. Connect a suitable inductive type timing light to the No. 1 spark plug wire. Do not, puncture and ignition wire with any type of probing device.

NOTE: The high ignition coil charging currents generated in the EEC-IV ignition system may falsely trigger timing lights with capacitive or direct connect pickups. It is necessary that an inductive type timing light be used in this procedure.

7. Connect a suitable tachometer to the engine. The ignition coil connector allows a test lead with an alligator clip to be connected to the Distributor Electronic Control (DEC) terminal without removing the connector.

8. Start the engine and let it run until it reaches normal operating temperature.

9. Check the engine idle rpm if it is not within specifications, adjust as necessary. After the rpm has been adjusted or checked, aim the timing light at the timing marks. If they are not aligned, loosen the distributor clamp bolts slightly and rotate the distributor body until the marks are aligned under timing light illumination.

10. Tighten the distributor clamp bolts and recheck the ignition timing. Readjust the idle speed. Shut the engine **OFF**, remove all test equipment, reconnect the in-line spout connector to the distributor and reinstall the cover plate on the manual transaxle vehicles.

Alternator

For further information on the charging system, please refer to "Charging and Starting" in the Unit Repair section.

PRECAUTIONS

Several precautions must be observed with alternator equipped vehicles to avoid damage to the unit.

• If the battery is removed for any reason, make sure it is reconnected with the correct polarity. Reversing the battery connections may result in damage to the one-way rectifiers.

• When utilizing a booster battery as a starting aid, always connect the positive to positive terminals and the negative terminal from the booster battery to a good engine ground on the vehicle being started.

• Never use a fast charger as a booster to start vehicles.

• Disconnect the battery cables when charging the battery with a fast charger.

• Never attempt to polarize the alternator.

• Do not use test lamps of more than 12 volts when checking diode continuity.

• Do not short across or ground any of the alternator terminals.

• The polarity of the battery, alternator and regulator must be matched and considered before making any electrical connections within the system.

• Never separate the alternator on an open circuit. Make sure all connections within the circuit are clean and tight.

• Disconnect the battery ground terminal when performing any service on electrical components.

• Disconnect the battery if arc welding is to be done on the vehicle.

BELT TENSION ADJUSTMENT

Conventional and Cogged Belts

1. Disconnect the negative battery cable.

2. Loosen the alternator adjustment and pivot bolts.

3. Using adjustable pliers or equivalent, to apply tension, position the bottom jaw of the pliers under the alternator adjustment boss and the top jaw in the notch at the top of the alternator adjustment bracket.

4. Squeeze the pliers together and using a belt tension gauge, set the belt to the proper tension. Tension should be 160 lbs. for a new belt and 140 lbs. for a used belt.

5. Maintaining proper belt tension, tighten the alternator adjustment bolt to 26 ft. lbs.

6. Remove the belt tension gauge and idle the engine for 5 minutes.

7. With the engine **OFF**, tension gauge in place and tension being applied to the adjustable pliers so that the existing tension is not lost, loosen the alternator adjustment bolt to allow the belt tension to increase to 160 lbs. for a new belt and 140 lbs. for a used belt.

8. Then tighten the adjustment bolt to 26 ft. lbs. Tighten the alternator pivot bolt to 52 ft. lbs.

9. Connect the negative battery cable.

Ribbed Belts

The V-ribbed belts used on some engines utilize an automatic belt tensioner whose function is to maintain the proper belt tension for the life of the belt.

NOTE: Movement of the automatic belt tensioner with engine idling is not an indication of malfunction. This movement is necessary to maintain constant belt tension with cyclical engine and accessory loads.

1. Disconnect the negative battery cable.

2. Loosen the alternator adjustment and pivot bolts.

3. Install a ½ in. breaker bar or equivalent, to the support bracket that is located behind the alternator.

4. Apply tension to the belt using the breaker bar. Using a belt tension gauge, set the belt to the proper tension. The tension should be 160 lbs.

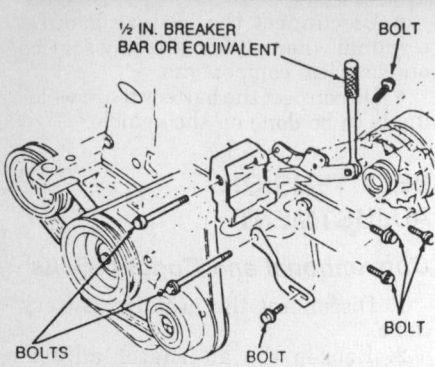

Alternator belt adjustment—1.9L engine

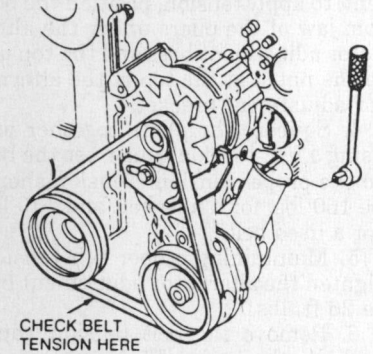

Alternator belt adjustment—2.0L Diesel engine

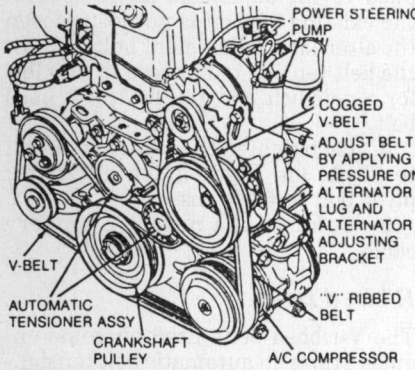

Drive belt arrangement—2.3L engine

for a new belt and 130 lbs. for a used belt.

5. While maintaining proper belt tension, tighten the alternator adjustment bolt to 30 ft. lbs.

6. Remove the belt tension gauge and breaker bar and idle the engine for 5 minutes.

7. With the engine **OFF**, check the belt tension. If the tension is below 120 lbs., retension the belt.

8. Tighten the adjustment bolt to 30 ft. lbs. Tighten the pivot bolt to 50 ft. lbs. and the support bracket bolt to 35 ft. lbs.

9. Connect negative battery cable.

REMOVAL & INSTALLATION

1. Disconnect battery ground cable.

2. Disconnect the wire harness attachments to the integral alternator/regulator assembly. Pull the 2 connectors straight out.

3. Loosen the alternator pivot bolt. Remove the adjustment arm bolt from the alternator.

4. Disengage the alternator drive belt from the alternator pulley.

5. Remove the alternator pivot bolt and alternator/regulator assembly.

6. Remove the alternator fan shield, if so equipped.
To install:

7. Position the integral alternator/regulator assembly on the engine.

8. Install the alternator pivot and adjuster arm bolts. Do not tighten the bolts until the belt is tensioned.

9. Install the drive belt over the alternator pulley.

NOTE: When adjusting belt tension, apply pressure only to alternator front housing.

10. If automatic belt tensioner is not used, adjust the belt tension, using belt tension gauge, to 160 lbs. for new belt, 140 lbs. for used belt. Tighten adjuster bolts to 30 ft. lbs. and pivot bolt to 50 ft. lbs.

11. Connect wiring harness to the alternator/regulator assembly. Push the two connectors straight in.

12. Attach the alternator fan shield to the alternator, if so equipped.

13. Connect battery ground cable.

Voltage Regulator

ADJUSTMENT

For further information on the charging system, please refer to "Charging and Starting" in the Unit Repair section.

NOTE: There are 2 types of regulators being used, depending on the vehicle, engine, alternator output and type of dash-mounted charging indicator used (light or ammeter). The regulators are 100% solid state and are calibrated and preset by the manufacturer. No adjustments are required or possible on these regulators.

REMOVAL & INSTALLATION

1. Disconnect the negative battery cable.

2. Disconnect the electrical connectors from the wiring harness.

3. Remove the regulator mounting screws and remove the regulator.

4. Installation is the reverse of the removal procedure.

5. Test the system for proper voltage regulation.

6. Connect negative battery cable.

Starter

For further information on the charging system, please refer to "Charging and Starting" in the Unit Repair section.

REMOVAL & INSTALLATION

Except Diesel Engine

1. Disconnect the negative battery cable.

2. Raise and safely support the vehicle.

3. Disconnect the starter cable at the starter terminal.

4. Remove the 2 bolts attaching the starter rear support bracket, remove the bracket.

5. On vehicles equipped with roll restrictor brace-to-starter studs on the transaxle housing, remove the nuts and remove the brace.

6. On Tempo and Topaz, remove the cable support.

7. For installation, reverse the removal procedure. Tighten the attaching studs or bolts to 30–40 ft. lbs. (41–54 Nm).

Diesel Engine

1. Remove the battery cover and disconnect the negative battery cable.

2. Disconnect the starter cable assembly from the starter relay and starter solenoid, located on the fender apron.

3. Remove the upper starter mounting stud bolt.

4. Raise and safely support the vehicle.

5. Disconnect the vacuum hose from the vacuum pump.

6. Remove the 3 starter support bracket screws and bracket. Remove the power steering hose bracket.

7. Remove the ground wire assembly and cable support on the starter bolt studs.

8. Remove the 2 starter mounting studs and position them away from the starter.

9. Remove the vacuum pump bracket. Remove the starter from the vehicle.
To install:

10. Position starter in place.

11. Install vacuum pump bracket.

12. Install two lower starter mounting studs.

13. Install starter support bracket.

14. Install cable support bracket and ground cable to starter stud bolts.

15. Install power steering hose bracket.

16. Connect vacuum hose to pump.
17. Safely lower vehicle.
18. Connect cable assembly to solenoid and relay.
19. Install upper starter mounting stud bolt.
20. Connect battery ground cable.
21. Check starter operation.

Diesel Glow Plugs

REMOVAL & INSTALLATION

1. Disconnect the negative battery cable, located in the luggage compartment.
2. Disconnect the glow plug harness from the glow plugs.
3. Using a 12mm deepwell socket, remove the glow plugs.
4. Install the glow plugs, using a 12mm deepwell socket. Tighten the glow plugs to 11–15 ft. lbs.
5. Connect the glow plug harness to the glow plugs. Tighten the nuts to 5–7 ft. lbs.
6. Connect the battery ground cable to the battery.
7. Check the glow plug system operation.

TESTING

1. Disconnect leads from each glow plug.
2. Connect one lead of ohmmeter to glow plug terminal and one lead to a good ground.
3. Set ohmmeter to **R × 1** ohm position.
4. Meter should read less than 1 ohm. If meter reads one ohm or more, replace glow plug.
5. Test each glow plug.
6. Reconnect leads to each glow plug.

CHASSIS ELECTRICAL

Heater Blower Motor

REMOVAL & INSTALLATION

Without Air Conditioning

1. Disconnect the negative battery cable.
2. On Escort and Lynx, remove the air inlet duct assembly. On Tempo and Topaz, remove the right ventilator assembly.
3. Remove the hub clamp spring from the blower wheel hub. Pull the blower wheel from the blower motor shaft.
4. Remove the blower motor flange attaching screws located inside the blower housing.
5. Pull the blower motor out from the blower housing (heater case) and disconnect the blower motor wires from the motor.
6. Connect the wires to the blower motor and position the motor in the blower housing.
7. Install the blower motor attaching screws.
8. Position the blower wheel on the motor shaft and install the hub clamp spring.
9. Install the air inlet duct assembly and the right ventilator assembly.
10. Connect negative battery cable.
11. Check the system for proper operation.

With Air Conditioning

1. Disconnect the negative battery cable.
2. Remove the glove compartment door and glove compartment.
3. Disconnect the blower motor wires from the blower motor resistor.
4. Loosen the instrument panel at the lower right hand side prior to removing the motor through the glove compartment opening.
5. Remove the blower motor and mounting plate from the evaporator case.
6. Rotate the motor until the mounting plate flat clears the edge of the glove compartment opening and remove the motor.
7. Remove the hub clamp spring from the blower wheel hub. Then, remove the blower wheel from the motor shaft.
8. Complete the installation of the blower motor by reversing the removal procedure.

Windshield Wiper Motor

REMOVAL & INSTALLATION

Front

1. Disconnect the negative battery cable.
2. Lift the water shield cover from the cowl on the passenger side.
3. Disconnect the power lead from the motor.
4. Remove the linkage retaining clip from the operating arm on the motor by lifting locking tab up and pulling clip away from pin.
5. Remove the attaching screws from the motor and bracket assembly and remove.

6. Remove the operating arm from the motor. Unscrew the 3 bolts and separate the motor from the mounting bracket.
7. Complete the installation of the wiper motor by reversing the removal procedures.

Rear

1. Remove wiper arm.
2. Remove pivot shaft attaching nut and spacers.
3. Hatchback: remove liftgate inner trim panel. Station Wagon: remove screws attaching license plate housing. Disconnect license plate lamp wiring and remove housing.
4. Disconnect electrical connector to wiper motor.
5. Remove three screws retaining bracket to door inner skin and remove complete motor, bracket and linkage assembly.
6. Complete the installation of the wiper motor by reversing the removal procedures.

Windshield Wiper Switch

The standard and interval front wiper and washer systems on 1987 Tempo and Topaz vehicles feature an instrument panel-mounted manual switch for wiper and washer control. Tempo and Topaz models, 1988–91, use a rotary switch mounted on the side of the instrument panel. On Escort vehicles, the wiper/washer control switch is column-mounted for both tilt and non-tilt models. The switch handle is an integral part of the switch and cannot be removed separately.

REMOVAL & INSTALLATION

Escort and Lynx

EXCEPT TILT STEERING WHEEL

1. Disconnect the negative battery cable.
2. Remove upper and lower trim shrouds.
3. Disconnect the quick connect electrical connector.
4. Peel back the foam sight shield. Remove the hex-head screws holding the switch and remove the wash/wiper switch.
5. Position the switch on the column and install the hex-head screws. Replace the foam sight shield over the switch.
6. Connect the quick connect electrical connector.
7. Install the upper and lower trim shrouds.
8. Connect the negative battery cable.

9. Check the steering column and wiper switch for proper operation.

TILT STEERING WHEEL

1. Disconnect the negative battery cable.

2. Remove the steering column shroud.

3. Peel back the side shield and disconnect the switch wiring connector.

4. Remove the screw attaching the wiring retainer to the steering column.

5. Grasp the switch handle and pull straight out to disengage the wiper switch from the turn signal switch.

6. Complete the installation of the switch by reversing the removal procedure.

Tempo and Topaz

DASH MOUNTED (FRONT)

1. Disconnect the negative battery cable.

2. Remove the instrument panel finish panel.

3. Remove the wiper switch housing retaining screws and remove the switch housing from the instrument panel.

4. Remove the wiper switch knob. Disconnect the electrical connectors from the switch assembly.

5. Remove the screws holding the wiper switch in the switch housing plate and remove the switch.

6. Complete the installation of the switch by reversing the removal procedure.

DASH MOUNTED (SIDE)

Rotary Switch

1. Disconnect the negative battery cable.

2. Insert a suitable prying tool into the small slots on top and bottom of the switch bezel.

3. Push down on the tool to work the top of the switch away from the instrument panel.

4. Work the bottom portion of the switch from the panel and completely remove the switch from the panel opening. Hold the switch and pull the wiring at the rear of the switch until the switch connector can be easily disconnected. Disconnect the connector and allow the wiring to hang from the switch mounting opening.

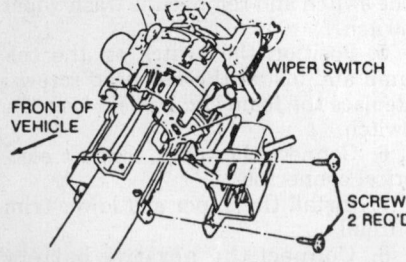

Wiper switch location—Escort and Lynx

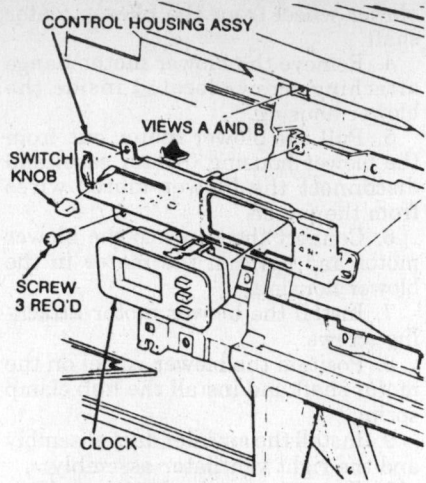

Wiper switch location—1987 Tempo and Topaz

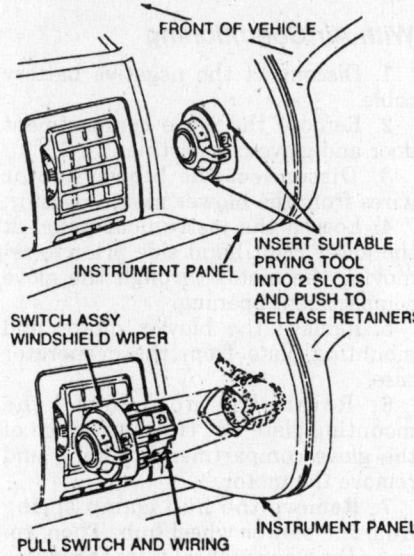

Wiper switch location—1988-91 Tempo and Topaz

5. Connect the wiring connector to the new switch and route the wiring back into the mounting opening. Insert the switch into the opening so that the graphics are properly aligned.

6. Push on the switch until the bezel seats against the instrument panel and the clips lock the switch into place.

7. Connect negative battery cable.

Instrument Cluster

REMOVAL & INSTALLATION

Tempo and Topaz

1987

1. Disconnect the negative battery cable.

2. Remove the 2 retaining screws at the bottom of the steering column and snap the steering column cover out.

3. Remove the steering column trim shroud and the snap-in lower cluster finish panels.

4. Remove the 8 instrument cluster finish panel screws, radio knobs as required and remove the finish panel.

5. Remove the 2 upper and lower screws retaining the instrument cluster to the instrument panel.

6. Disconnect the speedometer cable by reaching under the instrument panel and pressing on the flat surface of the speedometer cable quick connector.

7. Pull the cluster away from the instrument panel and disconnect the electrical feed plug to the cluster from its receptacle in the printed circuit.

8. Complete the installation of the instrument cluster by reversing the removal procedure.

1988-91

1. Disconnect the negative battery cable.

2. Remove two retaining screws at the bottom of the steering column and snap steering column cover out.

3. Remove snap-in lower cluster finish panels.

4. Remove four cluster opening finish panel retaining screws and pull panel forward.

5. Disconnect the speedometer cable by reaching under the instrument panel and pressing on the flat surface of the speedometer cable quick connector.

6. Remove four screws retaining instrument cluster to instrument panel and carefully pull rearward enough to disengage speedometer cable.

7. Carefully pull cluster away from instrument panel. Disconnect cluster feed plugs from printed circuit.

8. Complete installation of the instrument cluster by reversing the removal procedure.

Escort and Lynx

1. Disconnect the negative battery cable.

2. Remove 2 retaining screws at bottom of steering column opening and snap steering column cover out.

3. Remove 10 cluster opening finish panel retainer screws and remove finish panel.

4. Remove 2 upper and lower screws retaining cluster to instrument panel.

5. Reach under instrument panel and disconnect speedometer cable by pressing down on the flat surface of plastic connector (quick connect).

6. Pull cluster away from instrument panel. Disconnect cluster feed plug from its receptacle in printed circuit.

7. Complete installation of the instrument cluster by reversing the removal procedure.

Speedometer

REMOVAL & INSTALLATION

1. Disconnect the negative battery cable.
2. Remove instrument cluster.
3. Remove 7 screws that retain the lens and mask to the back plate.
4. Remove the nuts retaining the fuel gauge assembly to the back plate. Remove the fuel gauge assembly and then remove the speedometer assembly.

To install:

5. Apply a $^3/_{16}$ in. bead of silicone damping grease part number D7AZ–19A331–A or equivalent, in the drive hole of the speedometer head. Install speedometer head assembly into cluster.

NOTE: The speedometer is calibrated at the time of manufacture. Excessive rough handling of the speedometer may disturb the calibration.

6. Install retaining screws to retain the lens and mask to the back plate.
7. Install instrument cluster.
8. Connect battery ground and check operation of speedometer.

Radio

REMOVAL & INSTALLATION

Tempo and Topaz

EXCEPT 1988–91

1. Disconnect the negative battery cable.
2. Remove center instrument trim panel.
3. Remove 4 screws retaining radio and mounting bracket to instrument panel.
4. Pull radio to front and raise back end of radio slightly so rear support bracket clears clip in instrument panel.
5. Disconnect wiring connectors and antenna cable.
6. Transfer mounting brackets to new radio, if necessary.
7. Complete installation of radio by reversing the removal procedure.

NOTE: Amplifier for Premium Sound System, available on Tempo/Topaz (1987), is located on bottom of package shelf, accessible from luggage compartment.

1988–91

1. Disconnect the negative battery cable.

2. Insert radio removal tool T87P-19061-A or equivalent, into radio face plate. Press in 1 in. (25.4mm) to release radio retaining clips. Pull radio from instrument panel using tool as handles.

NOTE: Do not use excessive force when installing radio removal tools, as this will damage retaining clips, making radio removal difficult.

3. Disconnect wiring connectors and antenna cable.
4. Transfer rear mounting bracket to new radio, if necessary.
5. Complete installation of radio by reversing the removal procedure.

Headlight Switch

REMOVAL & INSTALLATION

1. Disconnect the negative battery cable.
2. On vehicles without air conditioning, remove the left hand side air vent control cable retaining screws and lower the cable to the floor.

3. Remove the fuse panel bracket retaining screws. Move the fuse panel assembly aside to gain access to the headlight switch.
4. Pull the headlight knob out to the **ON** position. Depress the headlight knob and shaft retainer button, which is located on the bottom of the headlight switch. Remove the knob and the shaft assembly from the switch.
5. Remove the headlight switch retaining bezel. Disconnect the multiple connector plug and remove the switch from the instrument panel.

To install:

6. Install the headlight switch into the instrument panel. Connect the multiple connector and install the headlight switch retaining bezel.
7. Install the knob and shaft assembly by inserting the shaft into the headlight switch gently pushing until the shaft is in the lock position.
8. Move the fuse panel back into position and install the fuse panel bracket with the two retaining screws.
9. On vehicles without air conditioning, install the left hand side air vent control cable and bracket. Install

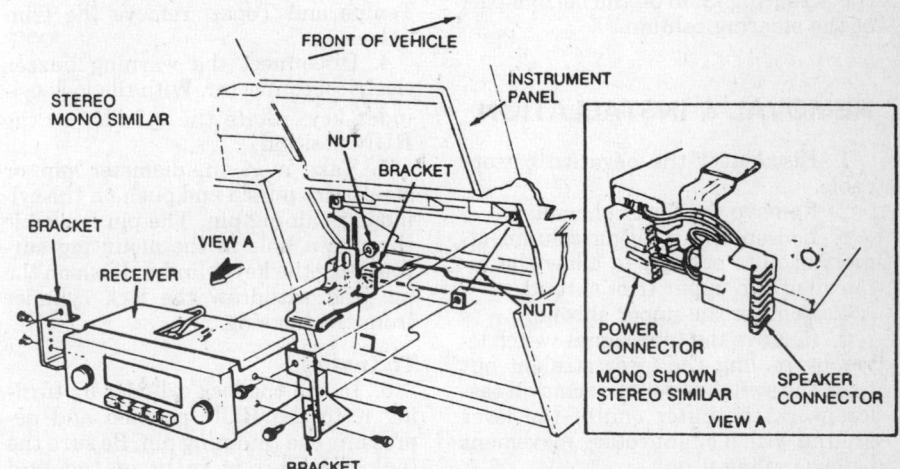

Radio mounting diagram—Except 1988–91 Tempo and Topaz

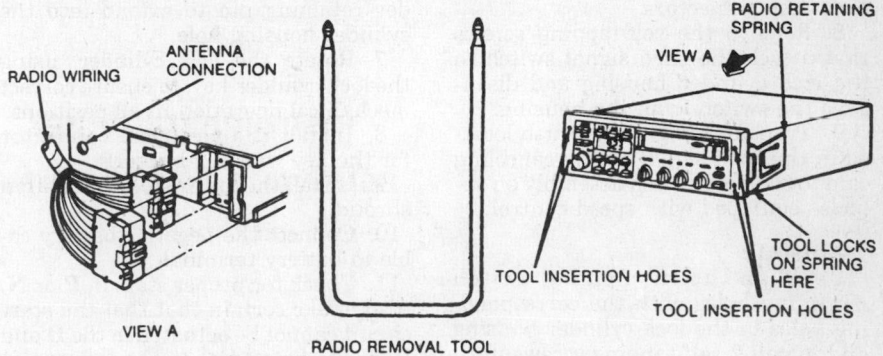

Radio removal—1988–91 Tempo and Topaz

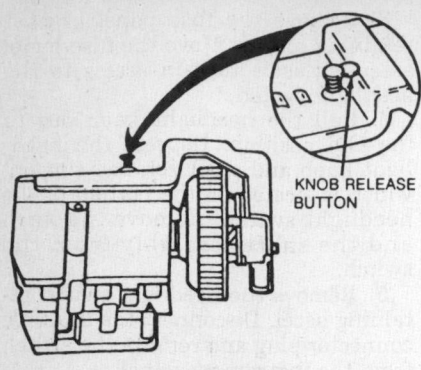

Headlight switch

the negative battery cable and check the headlight switch for the proper operation.

Combination Switch

The combination switch assembly is a multi-function switch comprising turn signal, hazard, headlight dimmer and flash-to-pass functions. The switch lever on the left side of the steering column, above the wiper switch lever, controls the turn signal, headlight dimmer and flash-to-pass functions. The hazard function is controlled by the actuating knob on the bottom part of the steering column.

REMOVAL & INSTALLATION

1. Disconnect the negative battery cable.
2. Remove the lower shroud.
3. Loosen the steering column attaching nuts enough to allow the removal of the upper trim shroud.
4. Remove the upper shroud.
5. Remove the turn signal switch lever by pulling the lever straight out from the switch. To make removal easier, work the outer end of the lever around with a slight rotary movement before pulling it out.
6. Peel back the foam sight shield from the turn signal switch.
7. Disconnect the turn signal switch electrical connectors.
8. Remove the self-tapping screws that attach the turn signal switch to the lock cylinder housing and disengage the switch from the housing.
9. Transfer the ground brush located in the turn signal switch canceling cam to the new switch assembly on vehicles equipped with speed control.

To install:

10. Align the turn signal switch mounting holes with the corresponding holes in the lock cylinder housing and install 2 self-tapping screws until tight.

11. Apply the foam sight shield to the turn signal switch.
12. Install the turn signal switch lever into the switch by aligning the key on the lever with the keyway in the switch and pushing the lever toward the switch to full engagement.
13. Install turn signal switch electrical connectors to full engagement.
14. Install the steering column trim shrouds.
15. Torque the steering column attaching nuts to 15–22 ft. lbs.
16. Connect the negative battery cable.
17. Check the steering column for proper operation.

Ignition Lock Cylinder

REMOVAL & INSTALLATION

1. Disconnect the negative battery cable.
2. If equipped with a tilt steering column, remove the upper extension shroud by unsnapping the shroud from the retaining clip at the 9 o'clock position.
3. Remove the steering column lower shroud on Escort and Lynx. On Tempo and Topaz, remove the trim halves.
4. Disconnect the warning buzzer electrical connector. With the lock cylinder key, rotate the cylinder to the **RUN** position.
5. Take a ⅛ in. diameter pin or small wire punch and push on the cylinder retaining pin. The pin is visible through a hole in the mounting surrounding the key cylinder. Push on the pin and withdraw the lock cylinder from the housing.

To install:

6. Install the lock cylinder by turning it to the **RUN** position and depressing the retaining pin. Be sure the lock cylinder is fully seated and aligned in the interlocking washer before turning the key to the **OFF** position. This action will permit the cylinder retaining pin to extend into the cylinder housing hole.
7. Rotate the lock cylinder, using the lock cylinder key, to ensure correct mechanical operation in all positions.
8. Install the electrical connector for the key warning buzzer.
9. Install the lower steering column shroud.
10. Connect the negative battery cable to battery terminal.
11. Check for proper start in **P** or **N**. Also, make certain that that the start circuit cannot be actuated in the **D** and **R** positions and that the column is locked in the **LOCK** position.

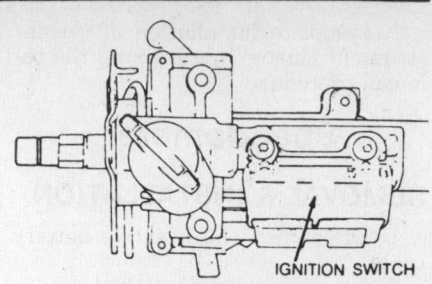

Ignition lock and switch assembly

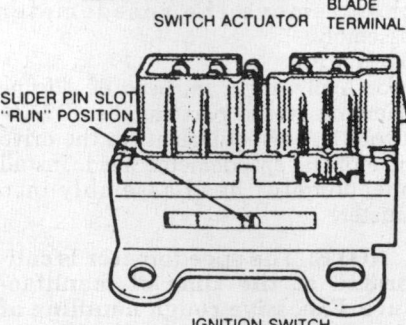

Ignition switch actuator position

Ignition Switch

REMOVAL & INSTALLATION

1. Disconnect the negative battery cable.
2. Remove the steering column upper and lower trim shroud by removing the self-tapping screws. The steering column attaching nuts may have to be loosened enough to allow removal of the upper shroud.
3. Remove 2 bolts and nuts holding steering column assembly to steering column bracket assembly and lower steering column to the seat.
4. Remove steering column shrouds.
5. Disconnect electrical connector from ignition switch.
6. Rotate ignition lock cylinder to the **RUN** position.
7. Remove 2 screws attaching switch to the lock cylinder housing.
8. Disengage the ignition switch from the actuator pin.

To install:

9. Check to see that the actuator pin slot in ignition switch is in the **RUN** position.

NOTE: A new switch assembly will be pre-set in the RUN position.

10. Make certain that the ignition key lock cylinder is in approximately the **RUN** position. The **RUN** position

is achieved by rotating the key lock cylinder approximately 90 degrees from the **LOCK** position.

11. Install the ignition switch onto the actuator pin. It may be necessary to move the switch slightly back and fourth to align the switch mounting holes with the column lock housing threaded holes.

12. Install the new screws and tighten to 50–70 inch lbs. (5.6–7.9 Nm).

13. Connect electrical connector to ignition switch.

14. Connect negative battery cable.

15. Check the ignition switch for proper function including **START** and **ACC** positions. Also make certain that the steering column is locked when in the **LOCK** position.

16. Position the top half of the shroud on the steering column.

17. Install the 2 bolts and nuts attaching the steering column assembly to the steering column bracket assembly.

18. Position lower shroud to upper shroud and install 5 self-tapping screws.

Stoplight Switch

The mechanical stoplight switch assembly is installed on the pin of the brake pedal arm, so that it straddles the master cylinder pushrod.

REMOVAL & INSTALLATION

1. Disconnect the negative battery cable.

2. Disconnect the wire harness at the connector from the switch.

NOTE: The locking tab must be lifted before the connector can be removed.

3. Remove the hairpin retainer and white nylon washer. Slide the stoplight switch and the pushrod away from the pedal. Remove the switch by sliding the switch up/down.

NOTE: Since the switch side plate nearest the brake pedal is slotted, it is not necessary to remove the brake master cylinder pushrod black bushing and 1 white spacer washer nearest the pedal arm from the brake pedal pin.

To install:

4. Position the switch so that the U-shaped side is nearest the pedal and directly over/under the pin. The black bushing must be in position in the push rod eyelet with the washer face on the side closest to the retaining pin.

5. Slide the switch up/down, trapping the master cylinder pushrod and black bushing between the switch side

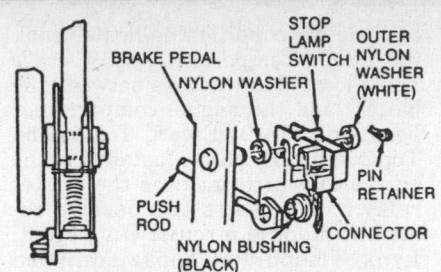

Stoplight switch assembly

plates. Push the switch and pushrod assembly firmly towards the brake pedal arm. Assemble the outside white plastic washer to pin and install the hairpin retainer to trap the whole assembly.

NOTE: Do not substitute other types of pin retainer. Replace only with production hairpin retainer.

6. Connect the wire harness connector to the switch.

7. Connect negative battery cable.

8. Check the stoplight switch for proper operation. Stoplights should illuminate with less than 6 lbs. applied to the brake pedal at the pad.

NOTE: The stoplight switch wire harness must have sufficient length to travel with the switch during full stroke at the pedal.

Clutch Switch

ADJUSTMENT

1. Remove panel above clutch pedal on the Tempo, Topaz vehicles.

2. Disengage the wiring connector by flexing the retaining tab on the switch and withdrawing the connector.

3. Using a test light, check to see that the switch is open with the clutch pedal up (engaged) and closed at approximately 1 in. from the clutch pedal full down position (disengaged).

4. If the switch does not operate as outlined in Step 3, check to see if the self-adjusting clip is out of position on the rod. It should be near the end of the rod.

5. If the self-adjusting clip is out of position, remove and reposition the clip approximately 1 in. from the end of the rod.

6. Reset the switch by pressing the clutch pedal to the floor. Repeat Step 3. If the switch is damaged or the clips do not remain in place replace the switch.

REMOVAL & INSTALLATION

1. Disconnect the negative battery cable.

2. Remove panel above clutch pedal, if equipped.

3. Disconnect the switch wiring connector.

4. Remove clutch interlock attaching screw and hairpin clip and remove switch.

NOTE: Always install the switch with the self-adjusting clip about 1 in. from the end of the rod. The clutch pedal must be fully up (clutch engaged). Otherwise, the switch may be misadjusted.

To install:

5. Insert eyelet end of rod over clutch pedal pin and secure with hairpin clip.

6. Swing switch around to line up hole in mounting boss with corresponding hole in bracket. Attach with screw.

7. Reset clutch interlock switch by pressing clutch pedal to floor.

8. Connect wiring connector.

9. Install the panel above clutch, if equipped.

10. Connect negative battery cable.

Neutral Safety Switch

ADJUSTMENT

The mounting location of the neutral safety switch does not provide for adjustment of the switch position when installed. If the engine will not start in **P** or **N** or if it will start in **R** or any of the **D** ranges, check the control linkage adjustment and/or replace with a known good switch.

REMOVAL & INSTALLATION

1. Set parking brake.

2. Disconnect the battery negative cable.

3. Disconnect the wire connector from the neutral safety switch.

4. Remove the 2 retaining screws from the neutral start switch and remove the switch.

To install:

5. Place the switch on the manual shift shaft and loosely install the retaining bolts.

6. Use a No. 43 drill (0.089 in.) and insert it into the switch to set the contacts.

7. Tighten the retaining screws of the switch, remove the drill and complete the assembly by reversing the removal procedure.

8. Connect negative battery cable.

9. Check the ignition switch for

proper starting in **P** or **N**. Also make certain that the start circuit cannot be actuated in the **D** or **R** position and that the column is locked in the **LOCK** position.

Fuses, Circuit Breakers and Relays

LOCATION

Fuses

Fuse panel is located under the instrument panel to the left of the steering column.

Fusible Links

Fusible links are used to prevent major wire harness damage in the event of a short circuit or an overload condition in the wiring circuits that are normally not fused, due to carrying high amperage loads or because of their locations within the wiring harness. Each fusible link is of a fixed value for a specific electrical load and should a fusible link fail, the cause of the failure must be determine and repaired prior to installing a new fusible link of the same value. Please be advised that the color coding of replacement fusible links may vary from the production color coding that is outlined in the text that follows.

Green 14 Gauge Wire—on Escort and Lynx equipped with diesel engine, there are 2 links (1 for Tempo and Topaz) located in the glow plug wiring to protect the glow plug control.

Black 16 Gauge Wire—on Escort and Lynx, there is 1 link located in the wiring for the rear window defogger. On Tempo and Topaz, there is 1 link located in the wiring for the anti-theft system.

Red 18 Gauge Wire—on Tempo and Topaz equipped with gasoline engines, there is 1 link used to protect the carburetor circuits. On the Escort and Lynx equipped with diesel engines, there is 1 link located in the heater fan wiring to protect the heater fan motor circuit.

Brown 18 Gauge Wire—on Tempo and Topaz, there is 1 link used to protect the rear window defogger and the fuel door release. On the Escort and Lynx, there is 1 link used to protect the heater fan motor circuit. There is 1 link used to protect the EEC module on Tempo, Topaz, Escort and Lynx with the 2.3L engine.

Blue 20 Gauge Wire—on Escort and Lynx with gasoline engines, there are 2 links in the wire between the starter relay and the EFE heater. On Tempo and Topaz there is link located in the wire between the ignition switch

and the air conditioning-heater cooling fan. On Tempo and Topaz, there is 1 link located in the wire between the battery and the engine compartment light. On 1988–91 Escort, Tempo and Topaz, a fusible link is installed in the engine compartment near the starter relay and protects the passive restraint module circuit. On Escort, Lynx, Tempo and Topaz equipped with diesel engine, there is 1 link used to protect the vacuum pump circuit. On the Tempo and Topaz, there is 1 link used to protect the heater fan motor circuit.

NOTE: Always disconnect the negative battery cable before servicing the high current fuses or serious personal injury may result.

Circuit Breakers

Circuit breakers are used to protect the various components of the electrical system, such as headlights and windshield wipers. The circuit breakers are located either in the control switch or mounted on or near the fuse panel.

TEMPO AND TOPAZ

Headlights and Highbeam Indicator—one 18 amp circuit breaker (22 amp in 1987 vehicles) incorporated in the lighting switch.

Front and Rear Marker, Side Parking, Rear and License Lamps—One 15 amp circuit breaker incorporated in the lighting switch.

Windshield Wiper and Rear Window Circuit—one 4½ amp circuit breaker located in the windshield wiper switch.

Power Windows—there are two 20 amp circuit breakers located in the starter relay and the fuse block.

Power Seats and Power Door Locks—one 20 amp circuit breaker located in the fuse block.

Station Wagon Power Back Window (Tail light switch)—one 20 amp circuit breaker located in the fuse block.

Intermittent 2-Speed Windshield Wiper—one 8¼ amp circuit breaker located in the fuse block.

Door Cigar Lighter—one 20 or 30 amp circuit breaker located in the fuse block.

Liftgate Wiper—one 4½ amp circuit breaker located in the instrument panel.

ESCORT AND LYNX

Headlights and High Beam Indicator—one 22 amp circuit breaker incorporated in the lighting switch.

Liftgate Wiper—one 4½ amp cir-

cuit breaker located in the instrument panel to the left of the radio.

Windshield Wiper and Wiper Pump Circuit—one 8¼ amp circuit breaker located in the fuse block.

Various Relays

TEMPO AND TOPAZ

Cooling Fan Controller—located behind the left side of the instrument panel.

Cooling Fan Controller Module—located behind the right side of the instrument panel.

Cooling Fan Relay—located in the air conditioning cooling fan control module.

Electronic Control Assembly—located under the left side of the instrument panel.

Electronic Engine Control Power Relay—located behind the glove box on the right side of the instrument panel.

Fuel Pump Relay—located behind the glove box.

Horn Relay—located in the fuse block.

Speed Sensor—located at the left rear side of the transaxle.

Speed Control Servo—located on the left front shock tower.

Speed Control Amplifier—located under the left side of the instrument panel.

Starter Relay—located on the left front fender apron in front of the shock tower.

ESCORT AND LYNX

Air Conditioning Fan Controller—located on the right side of the dash, behind the glove box.

Cold Start Module (Carbureted with automatic transaxle)—located at the left rear corner of the engine compartment.

Cooling Fan Relay—located on the left hand side of the instrument panel.

Electronic Control Assembly (ECA)—located at the front of the console.

Electronic Engine Control (EEC) Power Relay—located at the left hand side of the instrument panel.

EFE Heater Relay—mounted on the left hand side fender apron.

Fuel Pump Relay—located at the left hand side of the instrument panel.

Horn Relay—located behind the instrument panel on the left side of the radio.

RPM Module—located behind the glove box.

Starter Relay—located on the left hand side of the fender apron in front of the shock tower.

Computers

LOCATION

The Electronic Engine Control (EEC) module is located behind left hand side of instrument panel.

Turn Signal/Hazard Warning Flashers

LOCATION

The turn signal flasher is located on the front side of the fuse panel. The hazard flasher is located on the rear of the fuse panel behind the turn signal flasher.

Cruise Control

ADJUSTMENT

Actuator Cable

TEMPO AND TOPAZ

1. With engine **OFF**, set carburetor so that throttle plate is closed and choke linkage is off the fast idle cam.
2. Remove locking pin.
3. Pull bead chain through adjuster.
4. Insert locking pin in best hole of adjuster for tight bead chain without opening throttle plate.

ESCORT AND LYNX

1. Remove cable retaining clip.
2. Disengage throttle positioner (Escort and Lynx).
3. Set carburetor at hot idle (Escort and Lynx).
4. Pull or push on actuator cable end tube to take up any slack. Maintain a light tension on cable.
5. While holding cable, insert cable retaining clip and snap securely.

Vacuum Dump Valve

1. Firmly depress brake pedal and hold in position.
2. Push in dump valve until valve collar bottoms against retaining clip.
3. Place a 0.050–0.10 in. shim between white button of valve and pad on brake pedal.
4. Firmly pull brake pedal rearward to its normal position allowing dump valve to ratchet backwards in retaining clip.

ENGINE COOLING

Radiator

REMOVAL & INSTALLATION

1. Remove the negative battery cable.
2. Drain coolant from cooling system. Retain coolant in a suitable container for reuse.
3. On the Escort, remove air intake tube from radiator support.
4. Remove upper hose from radiator.
5. Remove 2 fasteners retaining upper end of fan shroud to radiator, and sight shield.

NOTE: If equipped with air conditioning, remove nut and screw retaining upper end of fan shroud to radiator at cross support, and nut and screw at inlet end of tank.

6. Disconnect electric cooling fan motor wires and air conditioning discharge line, if so equipped, from shroud and remove fan shroud from vehicle.
7. Loosen hose clamp and disconnect radiator lower hose from radiator.
8. Disconnect overflow hose from radiator filler neck.
9. If vehicle is equipped with an automatic transaxle, disconnect oil cooler hoses at transaxle using a quick-disconnect tool. Cap oil tubes and plug oil cooler hoses.
10. Remove 2 nuts retaining top of radiator to radiator support. If stud loosens, ensure it is tightened before radiator is installed. Tilt the top of radiator rearward to allow clearance with upper mounting stud and lift radiator from vehicle. Ensure mounts do not stick to radiator lower mounting brackets.

To install:

11. Ensure that lower radiator isomounts are installed over bolts on the radiator support.
12. Position radiator to radiator support making sure that radiator lower brackets are positioned properly on lower mounts.
13. Position top of radiator to mounting studs on radiator support and install 2 retaining nuts. Tighten to 5–7 ft. lbs. (7–9.5 Nm).
14. Connect radiator lower hose to engine water pump inlet tube. Install constant tension hose clamp between alignment marks on the hose.

15. Check to ensure radiator lower hose is properly positioned on outlet tank and install constant tension hose clamp. The stripe on lower hose should be indexed with rib on tank outlet.
16. Connect oil cooler hoses to automatic transaxle oil cooler lines, if so equipped. Use an appropriate oil resistant sealer.
17. Position fan shroud to radiator lower mounting bosses. On vehicles with air conditioning, insert lower edge of shroud into clip at lower center of radiator. Install 2 nuts and bolts retaining upper end of fan shroud to radiator. Tighten nuts on Tempo/Topaz to 35–41 inch lbs. (3.9–4.6 Nm). On Escort, tighten nut to 23–33 inch lbs. (2.6–3.7 Nm). Do not overtighten.
18. Connect electric cooling fan motor wires to wire harness.
19. Connect upper hose to radiator inlet tank fitting and install constant tension hose clamp.
20. Connect overflow hose to nipple just below radiator filler neck.
21. Install air intake tube or sight shield.
22. Connect negative battery cable.
23. Refill cooling system. Start engine and allow to come to normal operating temperature. Check for leaks. Confirm operation of electric cooling fan.

Electric Cooling Fan

TESTING

1. Check fuse or circuit breaker for power to cooling fan motor.
2. Remove connector(s) at cooling fan motor(s). Connect jumper wire and apply battery voltage to the positive terminal of the cooling fan motor.
3. Using an ohmmeter, check for continuity in cooling fan motor.

NOTE: Remove the cooling fan connector at the fan motor before performing continuity checks. Perform continuity check of the motor windings only. The cooling fan control circuit is connected

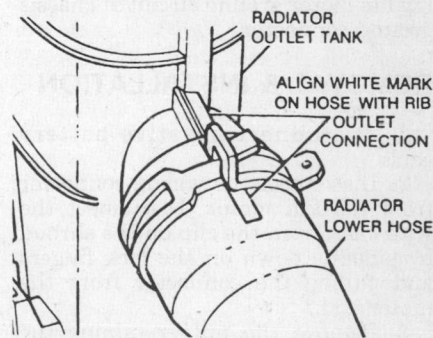

Radiator hose connection with alignment marks

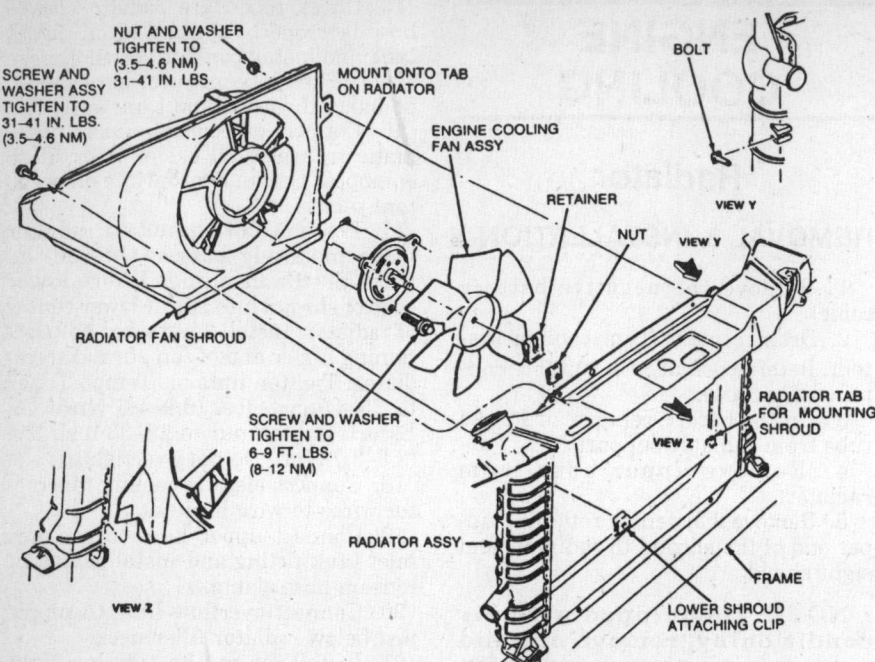

Tempo and Topaz radiator mounting diagram

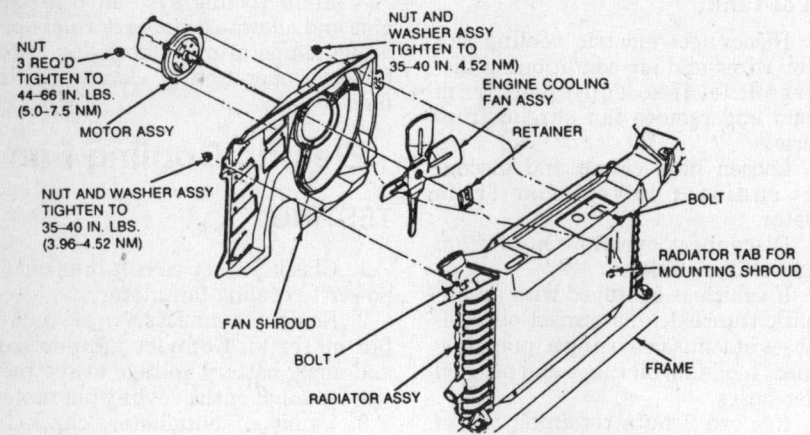

Escort and Lynx radiator mounting diagram

electrically to the ECM through the cooling fan relay center. Ohm-meter battery voltage must NOT be applied to the ECM.

4. Ensure proper continuity of cooling fan motor ground circuit at chassis ground connector.

REMOVAL & INSTALLATION

1. Disconnect negative battery cable.

2. Disconnect the wiring connector from the fan motor. Disconnect the wire loom from the clip on the shroud by pushing down on the lock fingers and pulling the connector from the motor end.

3. Remove the nuts retaining the fan motor and shroud assembly and remove the component.

4. Remove the retaining clip from the motor shaft and remove the fan.

NOTE: A metal burr may be present on the motor shaft after the retaining clip has been removed. If necessary, remove burr to facilitate fan removal.

5. Unbolt and withdraw the fan motor from the shroud.

To install:

6. Install the fan motor in position in the fan shroud. Install the retaining nuts and washers and tighten to 44–66 inch lbs.

7. Position the fan assembly on the motor shaft and install the retaining clip.

8. Position the fan, motor and shroud as an assembly in the vehicle. Install the retaining nuts and tighten

to 35–45 inch lbs. on Escort and Lynx models; 23–33 inch lbs. on Tempo and Topaz models.

9. Install the fan motor wire loom in the clip provided on the fan shroud. Connect the wiring connector to the fan motor. Be sure the lock fingers on the connector snap firmly into place.

10. Reconnect battery cable.

11. Check the fan for proper operation.

Heater Core

REMOVAL & INSTALLATION

Tempo and Topaz

1. Disconnect the negative battery cable.

2. Drain the cooling system.

3. Disconnect the heater hoses from the heater core.

4. From inside the vehicle, remove the 2 screws retaining floor duct to the plenum. Remove one screw retaining floor duct to instrument panel. Remove floor duct.

NOTE: Most vehicles are equipped with a removable heater core cover to provide access for servicing.

5. Remove the 4 screws attaching the heater core cover to the heater case assembly.

6. Remove the heater core and cover from the plenum.

7. Complete the installation of the heater core by reversing the removal procedure. Check the system for proper operation.

Escort and Lynx

1. Disconnect the negative battery cable.

2. Drain cooling system into clean container.

3. Loosen the heater hose clamps at the heater core tubes and disconnect the heater hoses from the heater core tubes.

4. Cap the heater core tubes to prevent spilling coolant into the passenger compartment.

5. Remove the glove compartment door, liner and lower reinforcement.

6. Move the temperature control lever to the **WARM** position.

7. Remove 4 screws attaching heater core cover to the heater assembly and remove the cover.

8. Working in the engine compartment, loosen the 2 nuts attaching the heater case assembly to the dash panel.

9. Push the heater core tubes to-

ward the passenger compartment to loosen the heater core from the heater case assembly.

10. Pull the heater core from the heater case assembly and remove the heater core through the glove compartment opening.

To install:

11. Position the heater core in the core opening in the case assembly with the heater core tubes on the top side of the end tank.

12. Slide the heater core into the opening of the heater case assembly.

13. Position the heater core acover to the heater case assembly. Install the 4 attaching screws. Tighten the cover attaching screws securely.

14. Tighten the 2 nuts attaching the heater case assembly to the dash panel.

15. Connect the heater hoses to the heater core tubes. Tighten the hose clamps.

16. Fill the cooling system to the proper level with the correct mixture of coolant and water.

17. Install the glove compartment door, liner and hinge bar.

18. Connect negative battery cable.

19. Start engine and check for coolant leaks. Allow engine to come to normal operating temperature. Recheck for coolant leaks.

Water Pump

REMOVAL & INSTALLATION

1.9L Engine

1. Disconnect the negative battery cable. Drain the cooling system.

2. Remove the alternator drive belt. If equipped with air conditioning or power steering, remove the drive belts.

3. Use a wrench on the crankshaft pulley to rotate the engine to TDC of the compression stroke on the No. 1 cylinder.

NOTE: Turn the engine only in the direction of normal rotation. Backward rotation will cause the camshaft belt to slip or lose teeth.

4. Remove the timing belt cover.

5. Loosen the belt tensioner attaching bolts, using torque wrench adapter T81P-6254-A or equivalent. Then secure the tensioner over as far as possible.

6. Pull the belt from the camshaft, tensioner and water pump sprockets. Do not remove it from or allow it to change its position on the crankshaft sprocket.

NOTE: Do not rotate the engine with the camshaft belt removed.

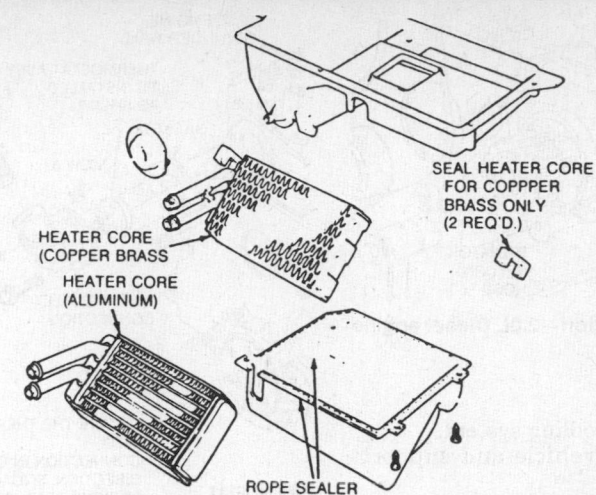

Heater core removal—Tempo and Topaz

7. Remove the camshaft sprocket.

8. Remove the rear timing cover stud. Remove the heater return tube hose connection at the water pump inlet tube.

9. Remove the water pump inlet tube fasteners and the inlet tube and gasket.

10. Remove the water pump to cylinder block bolts and remove the water pump and its gasket.

To install:

11. Make certain the mating surfaces on the pump and the block are clean.

12. Place the water pump assembly and new gasket to the cylinder block and apply pipe sealant with Teflon® D8AZ-19554-A or equivalent, to the water pump attaching bolts and tighten the bolts to 30–40 ft. lbs. on 1987 vehicles. On 1988–91 vehicles, torque the water pump retaining bolts to 6–9 ft. lbs. Make sure the pump impeller turns freely.

13. Complete the installation of the remaining components by reversing the removal procedures. Use new gaskets and sealer. Install the camshaft sprocket over the cam key.

14. Adjust the timing belt tension.

15. Fill the cooling system to the proper level.

2.0L Diesel Engine

1. Disconnect the negative battery cable.

2. Remove the front timing belt upper cover. Loosen and remove the front timing belt.

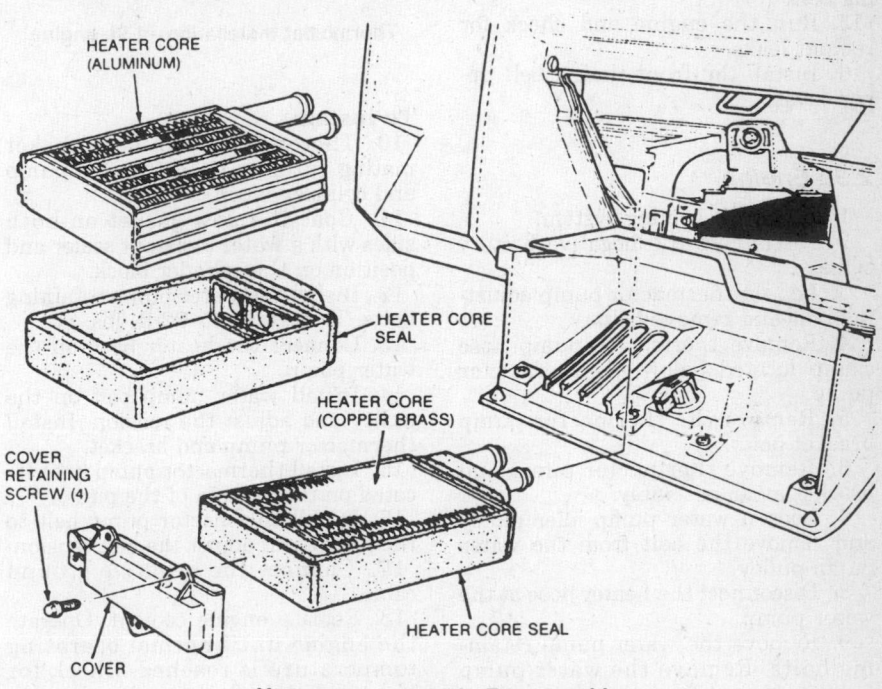

Heater core removal—Escort and Lynx

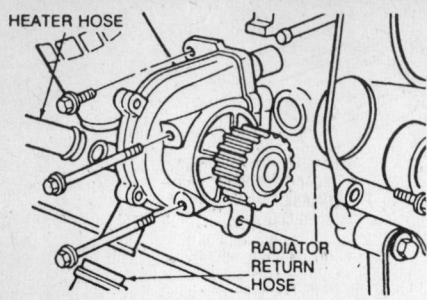

Water pump location—2.0L Diesel engine

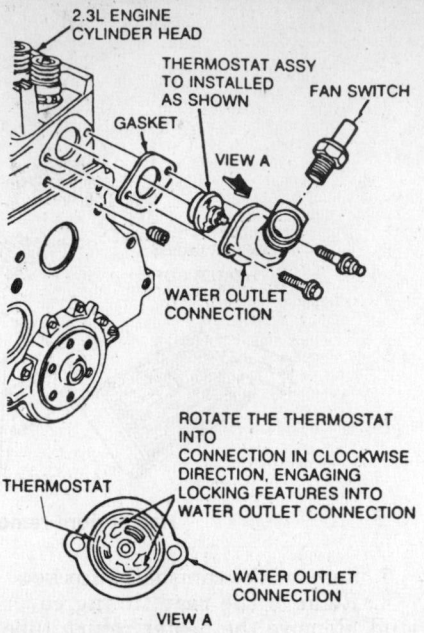

Thermostat installation—2.3L engine

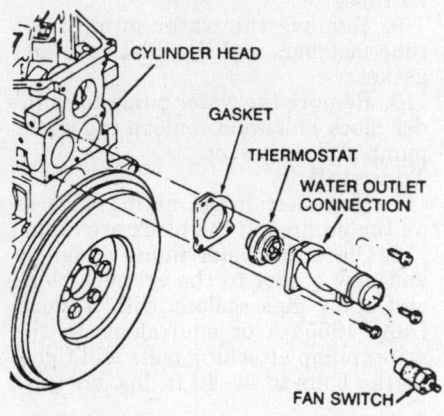

Thermostat installation—1.9L engine

3. Drain the cooling system.

4. Raise the vehicle and support safely.

5. Disconnect the lower radiator hose and heater hose from the water pump.

6. Disconnect the coolant tube from the thermostat housing and discard gasket.

7. Remove the 3 bolts attaching the water pump to the crankcase. Remove the water pump. Discard gasket.

8. Clean the water pump and crankshaft gasket mating surfaces.

9. Install the water pump, using a new gasket. Tighten bolts to 23–34 ft. lbs.

10. Connect the coolant tube from the thermostat housing on the water pump using a new gasket. Tighten bolts to 5–7 ft. lbs.

11. Connect the heater hose and lower radiator hose to the water pump.

12. Lower vehicle.

13. Fill and bleed the cooling system.

14. Install and adjust the front timing belt.

15. Run the engine and check for coolant leaks.

16. Install the front timing belt upper cover.

2.3L Engine

1. Drain the cooling system.

2. Disconnect the negative battery cable.

3. Loosen thermactor pump adjusting bolt and remove belt.

4. Remove thermactor pump hose clamp located below the thermactor pump.

5. Remove the thermactor pump bracket bolts.

6. Remove thermactor pump and bracket as an assembly.

7. Loosen water pump idler pulley and remove the belt from the water pump pulley.

8. Disconnect the heater hose at the water pump.

9. Remove the water pump retaining bolts. Remove the water pump from its mounting.

To install:

10. Thoroughly clean both gasket mating surfaces on the water pump and cylinder block.

11. Coat the new gasket on both sides with a water resistant sealer and position on the cylinder block.

12. Install the water pump retaining bolts. Tighten to 15–22 ft. lbs.

13. Connect the heater hose on the water pump.

14. Install water pump belt on the pulley and adjust the tension. Install thermactor pump and bracket.

15. Install thermactor pump hose located on the bottom of the pump.

16. Install thermactor pump belt to the pulley and adjust the belt tension.

17. Connect the negative ground cable.

18. Replace engine coolant. Operate the engine until normal operating temperature is reached. Check for leaks and recheck the coolant level.

Thermostat

REMOVAL & INSTALLATION

The thermostat is located on the front of the engine block on the 1.9L and 2.3L engines and at the rear of the engine, near the rear timing belt cover, on the 2.0L engine.

1. Disconnect the negative battery cable.

2. Disconnect wiring connector from thermal switch in thermostat housing.

3. Drain coolant system to a corresponding level just below water outlet connection. Drain coolant into a clean receptacle for reuse.

4. Loosen top hose clamp at radiator, remove water outlet connection retaining bolts, lift clear of engine and remove thermostat.

NOTE: Do not pry housing off.

To install:

5. Ensure that water outlet connection pocket and cylinder head mating surfaces are clean and free of gasket material.

6. Insert thermostat into position fully to compress gasket. Place water outlet connection to cylinder head and tighten bolts to 6–8.5 ft. lbs. (8–11.5 Nm). Position top hose to radiator and tighten clamps.

7. Refill cooling system with specified antifreeze solution.

8. Connect negative battery cable.

9. Start engine and bring to normal operating temperature. Check for leaks.

GASOLINE FUEL SYSTEM

Fuel System Service Precautions

Safety is the most important factor when performing not only fuel system maintenance but any type of maintenance. Failure to conduct maintenance and repairs in a safe manner may result in serious personal injury or death. Maintenance and testing of the vehicle's fuel system components can be accomplished safely and effectively by adhering to the following rules and guidelines.

• To avoid the possibility of fire and personal injury, always disconnect the negative battery cable unless the repair or test procedure requires that battery voltage be applied.

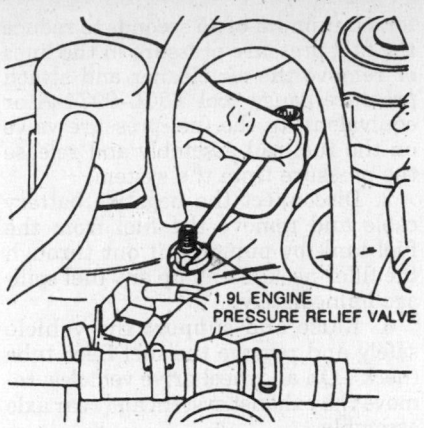

Pressure relief valve—1.9L EFI engine

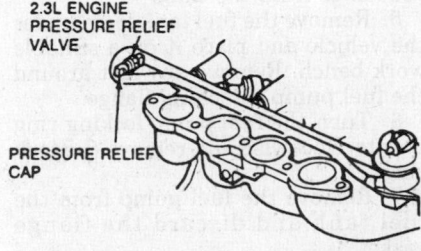

Pressure relief valve—2.3L HSC engine

- Always relieve the fuel system pressure prior to disconnecting any fuel system component (injector, fuel rail, pressure regulator, etc.), fitting or fuel line connection. Exercise extreme caution whenever relieving fuel system pressure to avoid exposing skin, face and eyes to fuel spray. Please be advised that fuel under pressure may penetrate the skin or any part of the body that it contacts.
- Always place a shop towel or cloth around the fitting or connection prior to loosening to absorb any excess fuel due to spillage. Ensure that all fuel spillage (should it occur) is quickly removed from engine surfaces. Ensure that all fuel soaked cloths or towels are deposited into a suitable waste container.
- Always keep a dry chemical (Class B) fire extinguisher near the work area.
- Do not allow fuel spray or fuel vapors to come into contact with a spark or open flame.
- Always use a backup wrench when loosing and tightening fuel line connection fittings. This will prevent unnecessary stress and torsion to fuel line piping. Always follow the proper torque specifications.
- Always replace worn fuel fitting O-rings with new. Do not substitute fuel hose or equivalent, where fuel pipe is installed.

RELIEVING FUEL SYSTEM PRESSURE

The pressure in the fuel system must be released before attempting to remove the fuel pump.

1. Disconnect the negative battery cable.
2. A special valve is incorporated in the fuel rail assembly for the purpose of relieving the pressure in the fuel system.
3. Remove the air cleaner.
4. Attach pressure gauge tool No. T80L-9974-A or equivalent, to the fuel pressure valve on the fuel rail assembly and release the pressure from the system.

Fuel Filter

REMOVAL & INSTALLATION

1. Disconnect the negative battery cable.

NOTE: Tempo and Topaz vehicles are not equipped with pressure relief valves. The fuel filter connection must be covered with a cloth to prevent fuel from spraying during disassembly.

2. With engine **OFF**, depressurize fuel system using an appropriate fuel pressure gauge.

NOTE: Nylon push connect fittings employ 2 different types of retaining clips. The fittings used with $5/16$ in. diameter tubing use a hairpin clip; removal outlined in Step 3. The fittings used with $1/4$ and $1/2$ in. diameter tubing use a duck bill clip; removal outlined in Step 4.

3. Remove the hairpin clips from the fuel fittings at both ends of the fuel filter.
   a. Remove the hairpin clip from the fitting by bending the shipping tab downward so that it will clear the body. Using hands only, spread 2 clip legs about $1/8$ in. each to disengage body and push legs into fitting. To completely remove clip, pull lightly from the triangular end of the clip to work it clear of the tube and fitting.
   b. Grasp fitting and hose assembly and pull in an axial direction to remove the fitting from the steel tube.
   c. Inspect tube end of fitting for damage.
4. Remove the duck bill clips from the fuel fittings at both ends of the fuel filter.

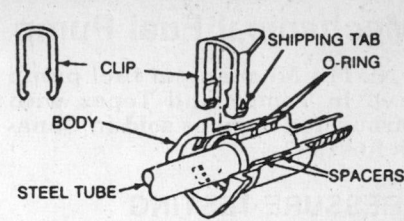

Hairpin clip fitting connector

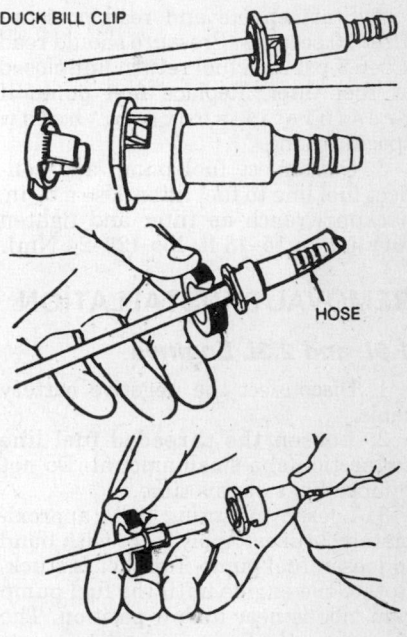

Duck Bill clip fitting connector

   a. Align the slot on quick connect/disconnect tool T82L-9500-AH or equivalent, with either tab on the clip and insert tool.
   b. Holding the tool and the tube with one hand, pull fitting away from the tube.
   c. Clean and inspect the tube sealing surface after disassembly.

To install:

5. Install retainer clips in each connect fitting.
6. Remove filter from bracket by loosening filter retaining clamp enough to allow filter to pass through.

NOTE: Observe flow direction arrow on replacement filter to ensure proper direction of fuel flow through the filter.

To install:

7. Install filter in bracket.
8. Install push connect fittings at both ends of the filter.
9. Connect negative battery cable.
10. Start engine and inspect for leaks.

Mechanical Fuel Pump

NOTE: Mechanical fuel pump used in Tempo and Topaz with carbureted engines sold in Canada for 1987.

PRESSURE TESTING

1. Connect a suitable pressure gauge, 0–15 psi (0–103 kPa), to fuel filter end of fuel line. No "T" is required.
2. Start engine and read pressure after 10 seconds. Pressure should read 4.5–6.5 psi with fuel return line closed at fuel filter. Replace fuel pump if pressure is above or below specification.
3. Disconnect fuel pump and connect fuel line to fuel filter. Use a 5/8 in. backup wrench on filter and tighten fuel line to 15–18 ft. lbs. (20–24 Nm).

REMOVAL & INSTALLATION

1.9L and 2.3L Engines

1. Disconnect the negative battery cable.
2. Loosen the threaded fuel line connection(s) a small amount. Do not remove lines at this time.
3. Loosen mounting bolts approximately 2 turns. Apply force with hand to loosen fuel pump if gasket is stuck. Rotate the engine until the fuel pump cam lobe is near its low position. The tension on the fuel pump will be greatly reduced at the low cam position.
4. Disconnect the fuel pump inlet and outlet lines.
5. Remove the fuel pump attaching bolts and remove the pump and gasket. Discard the old gasket and replace with new.
6. Measure the fuel pump pushrod length. It should be 2.34 in. (61.7mm) minimum. Replace if worn or out of specification.

To install:

7. Remove all fuel pump gasket material from the engine and the fuel pump if installing the original pump.
8. Install the attaching bolts into the fuel pump and install a new gasket. Position the fuel pump to the mounting pad. Tighten the attaching bolts alternately and evenly and tighten to 11–19 ft. lbs. (15–25 Nm).
9. Install fuel lines to fuel pump. Start the threaded fitting by hand to avoid cross threading. Tighten outlet nut to 15–18 ft. lbs. (20–24 Nm).
10. Start engine and inspect for fuel leaks.
11. Stop engine and check all fuel pump fuel line connections for fuel leaks by running a finger under the connections. Check for oil leaks at the fuel pump mounting gasket.

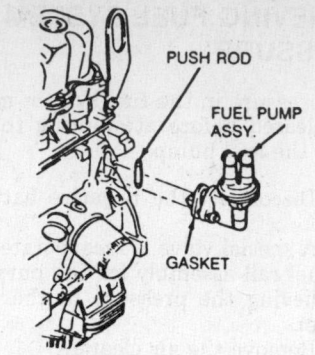

Mechanical fuel pump installation

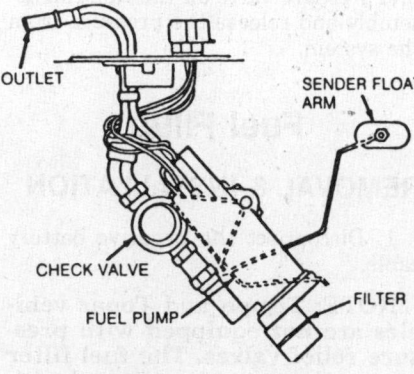

Electric fuel pump

Electric Fuel Pump

PRESSURE TESTING

NOTE: Fuel supply lines will remain pressurized for long periods of time after engine shut down. This pressure must be relieved before servicing of the fuel system is begun. Connect fuel pressure gauge T80L-9974-B or equivalent, to schrader valve on fuel rail assembly.

REMOVAL & INSTALLATION

—————— CAUTION ——————

Extreme caution should be taken when removing the fuel tank from the vehicle. Ensure that all removal procedures are conducted in a well ventilated area. Have a sufficient amount of absorbent material in the vicinity of the work area to quickly contain fuel spillages should they occur. Never store waste fuel in an open container as it presents a serious fire hazard.

NOTE: The fuel pump is mounted on the fuel sender assembly in the tank.

1. Depressurize the fuel system by disconnecting the electrical connector at the inertia switch. Crank the engine

for a minimum of 15 seconds to reduce the fuel pressure pressure in the lines or remove the air cleaner and attach pressure gauge tool T80L-9974-A or equivalent, to the fuel pressure valve on the fuel rail assembly and release the pressure from the system.
2. Disconnect the negative battery cable and remove the fuel from the fuel tank by pumping it out through the filler neck. Clean up any fuel spillage immediately.
3. Raise and support the vehicle safely and remove the fuel filler tube (neck). On all wheel drive vehicles, remove the exhaust system and rear axle assembly.
4. Support the fuel tank and remove the fuel tank straps, lower the fuel tank enough to be able to remove the fuel lines, electrical connectors and vent lines from the tank.
5. Remove the fuel tank from under the vehicle and place it on a suitable work bench. Remove any dirt around the fuel pump attaching flange.
6. Turn the fuel pump locking ring counterclockwise and remove the lock ring.
7. Remove the fuel pump from the fuel tank and discard the flange gasket.
8. On all wheel drive vehicles, partially raise the sender unit and disconnect the jet pump line and resistor electrical connector. Remove the fuel pump and bracket assembly with seal gasket. Remove the seal gasket and replace with new. Remove the jet pump assembly.

To install:

9. Clean fuel pump mounting flange and fuel tank mounting surface and seal ring groove.
10. Lightly coat the new seal ring gasket with a suitable lubricant compound part number C1AZ-19590-B or equivalent, to hold the gasket in place during installation.
11. All-wheel drive vehicles only: install jet pump assembly and retaining screw.
12. Install fuel pump and sender. Ensure that nylon filter is not damaged and that locating keys are in keyways and seal ring remains in place.
13. All-wheel drive vehicles only: connect jet pump line and electrical connector to resistor. Ensure locating keyways and seal ring remain in place.
14. Hold assembly in place and install locking ring finger-tight. Ensure that all locking tabs are under tank lock ring tabs.
15. Secure unit with locking ring by rotating ring clockwise using fuel sender wrench tool D84P-9275-A or equivalent, until ring stops against stops.
16. Remove tank from bench to vehicle and support tank while connecting

FUEL SYSTEM DIAGNOSIS

TEST STEP	RESULT	▶	ACTION TO TAKE
A1 INITIAL SYSTEM INSPECTION			
Check fuel system for adequate fuel supply.	Yes	▶	GO to **A2**.
Visually inspect the fuel delivery system including fuel tank lines, filter, injectors, pressure regulator, battery, electrical lines and connectors for leakage, looseness, cracks, pinching, kinking, corrosion, grounding, abrasion, or other damage caused by accident, collision, assembly or usage.	No	▶	SERVICE as required. GO to **A2**.
Verify that the battery is fully charged.			
Check fuse integrity.			
Is the system free of any evidence of leakage, damage, or any evident cause for concern?			
A2 CHECK STATIC FUEL PRESSURE			
Ground fuel pump lead of self-test connector using a jumper at the FP lead.	Yes	▶	GO to **A3**.
Install Fuel Pressure Gauge T80L-9974-B or equivalent.	No	▶	If pressure High, GO to **A5**.
Turn ignition key to the RUN position. Verify fuel pump runs.			If pressure is low, GO to **A6**.
Observe fuel pressure reading. Compare with specifications.			
Is the fuel pressure within specification?			

VIP SELF TEST CONNECTOR · SIGNAL RETURN

SELF TEST OUT · FP (FUEL PUMP) LEAD (SHORT END OF CONNECTOR)

TEST STEP	RESULT	▶	ACTION TO TAKE
A3 CHECK STATIC LEAKDOWN			
Run fuel pump for 10 seconds and note pressure (Ground FP lead of self test connector and turn ignition switch to the RUN position).	Yes	▶	GO to **A4**.
Turn off pump and monitor pressure for 60 seconds. (Disconnect ground or turn ignition switch to the OFF position).	No	▶	GO to **A10**.
Does fuel line pressure remain within 34 kPa (5 psi) of shut off pressure for 60 seconds?			
A4 CHECK VEHICLE UNDER LOAD CONDITIONS			
Remove and block vacuum line to pressure regulator.	Yes	▶	Fuel system is OK. DISCONNECT all test connections, RECONNECT vacuum line to regulator.
Run vehicle at idle and then increase engine speed to 2000 RPM or more in short bursts.			
Does fuel system pressure remain within chart limits?	No	▶	GO to **A12**.
NOTE: Operating vehicle under load (road test) should give same results.			

FUEL SYSTEM DIAGNOSIS CONT'D.

A5	CHECK FUEL PRESSURE		
	Disconnect return line at fuel pressure regulator. Connect outlet of regulator to appropriate receptacle to catch return fuel.	Yes ▶	CHECK return fuel line for restrictions. SERVICE as required. REPEAT A2. GO to A3.
	Turn on fuel pump (ground FP lead and turn ignition to the ON position) and monitor pressure.		
	Is fuel pressure within chart limits?	No ▶	SERVICE or REPLACE fuel regulator as required. REPEAT A2. GO to A3.

A6	CHECK FUEL PUMP OPERATION		
	Turn on fuel pump (ground FP lead and turn ignition to the RUN position).	Yes ▶	GO to A9.
	Raise vehicle on hoist and use stethoscope to listen at fuel tank to monitor fuel pump noise, or listen at filler neck for fuel pump sound.	No ▶	GO to A7.
	Is fuel pump running?		

A7	CHECK INERTIA SWITCH AND FUEL PUMP GROUND CONNECTOR		
	Check if inertia switch is tripped.	Yes ▶	GO to A8.
	Check fuel pump ground connection in vehicle.		
	Is inertia switch and ground connection OK?	No ▶	SERVICE switch or ground connection as required. REPEAT A2 and GO to A3.

A8	CHECK VOLTAGE AT FUEL PUMP		
	Check for continuity through fuel pump to ground by connecting meter to pump power wire lead as close to pump as possible.	Yes ▶	REPLACE fuel pump. REPEAT A2. If pressure OK GO to A3. If presure not OK CHECK fuel pump connector for oversize connectors or other sources of open electrical circuit. SERVICE as required. REPEAT A3.
	Check voltage as close to fuel pump as possible (turn on pump as outlined in A6).		
	Is voltage within 0.5 Volts of battery voltage and is there continuity through pump?	No ▶	If voltage not present, CHECK fuel pump relay, EEC relay, and wiring for problem. If no ground, CHECK connection at fuel tank, etc. SERVICE as required. REPEAT A2 and A3.

A9	CHECK FUEL PRESSURE REGULATOR		
	Replace fuel filter (if not replaced previously) and recheck pressure as in A2. If pressure not OK, continue. If pressure OK, go to A3.	Yes ▶	SERVICE or REPLACE regulator as required. REPEAT A2 and A3.
	Open return line at pressure regulator. Attach return fitting from regulator to suitable container to catch gasoline.		
	Turn on fuel pump as in A2.	No ▶	RECHECK systems for pressure restrictions. SERVICE as required. If no problem found, REPLACE fuel pump. GO to A2 and A3.
	Is fuel being returned from regulator with low pressure in system?		

FUEL SYSTEM DIAGNOSIS CONT'D.

A10	CHECK FUEL PRESSURE FOR LEAKS		
	Open return line at pressure regulator and attach suitable container to catch return fuel. Line should be clear to observe fuel flow.	Yes	▶ REPLACE regulator. REPEAT A2 and A3. If OK, GO to A4. If not OK, REPEAT A2 and follow procedure.
	Run fuel pump as in A2.		
	Turn off fuel pump by removing ground from self test connector or turning ignition to the OFF position.	No	▶ GO to A11.
	Observe fuel return flow from regulator and system pressure when pump is off.		
	Is there return flow when pump is turned off and system pressure is dropping?		
A11	CHECK FUEL PUMP CHECK VALVE		
	Open pressure line from fuel pump and attach pressure gauge to line and block line to allow pressure build up.	Yes	▶ CHECK injectors for leakage or regulator for internal leakage. SERVICE as required. Fuel pump check valve is OK. GO to A4.
	Operate pump momentarily as in A2 and bring pressure to about system pressure.		
	Observe fuel pressure for one minute.		
	Does pressure remain within 34 kPa (5 psi) of starting pressure over one minute period?	No	▶ CHECK lines and fittings from pump to rail for leakage, if none found REPLACE pump assembly. REPEAT A2. When OK GO to A4.
A12	CHECK FUEL FILTER FOR RESTRICTIONS		
	Replace fuel line filter (if not previously replaced during this procedure) and repeat test A5.	Yes	▶ System is OK. DISCONNECT all test connections and RECONNECT all loosened or removed parts and lines.
	Does system pressure remain within chart limits?	No	▶ CHECK pressure lines for kinks or restrictions. CHECK at fuel pump for low voltage. CHECK for wrong size injectors (too large). If no problem found, REPLACE pump and REPEAT A4. If problem found, SERVICE as required. REPEAT A4.

fuel lines, vent line and electrical connectors to appropriate places.

17. Install tank in vehicle and secure with retaining straps.

18. All-wheel drive vehicles only: install rear axle assembly and exhaust system.

19. Lower vehicle and install fuel in tank. Check for leaks.

20. Connect negative battery cable.

21. Check fuel pressure.

22. Remove the pressure gauge, start the engine and recheck for fuel leaks. Correct all fuel leaks immediately.

Carburetor

REMOVAL & INSTALLATION

1. Disconnect the negative battery cable. Remove the air cleaner assembly.

2. Disconnect the throttle cable from the throttle lever.

3. Disconnect the automatic transaxle TV rod from the throttle lever, if equipped.

4. Disconnect the distributor vacuum line, EGR vacuum line, venturi vacuum line, purge vacuum lines, PCV vacuum line, solenoid kicker vacuum line and fuel line. Use a back-up wrench on the fuel inlet fitting when removing the fuel line to avoid changing the float level.

NOTE: Identify all vacuum lines before removing, to aid in installation.

5. Disconnect the TSP electrical connection at the connector. Discon-

nect the electric choke wire at the connector.

6. Disconnect the canister vent hose at the bowl vent tube.

7. Remove the carburetor attaching nuts and remove the carburetor from the intake manifold. Remove carburetor mounting gasket.

To install:

8. Clean the gasket mounting surfaces of the intake manifold and the carburetor. Place a new gasket on the intake manifold. Position the carburetor on the gasket and install the attaching nuts. To prevent leakage, distortion, or damage to the carburetor body flange, snug the nuts and then tighten each nut to 20 ft. lbs.

9. Connect the canister vent hose at the bowl vent tube.

10. Connect the TSP electrical connection and the electric choke wire at the connector.

11. Connect the distributor vacuum line, EGR vacuum line, venturi vacuum line, purge vacuum line, solenoid kicker vacuum line and fuel line. Use a back-up wrench when installing the fuel line to avoid changing the float level.

12. Connect the automatic transaxle TV rod to the throttle lever.

13. Connect the throttle cable to the throttle lever.

14. Install the air cleaner assembly.

15. Check and adjust if necessary the curb idle speed, idle fuel mixture and fast idle speed.

IDLE SPEED ADJUSTMENT

Curb Idle Speed

NOTE: This adjustment is not required as part of a normal engine idle RPM check. It should only be performed on a customer complaint if engine continues to run after ignition key is turned to the OFF position.

1. Place transaxle in **N** or **P**, parking brake on.

2. Start engine and bring to normal operating temperature.

3. Disconnect throttle kicker vacuum line and plug.

4. Place air conditioner selector in the OFF position.

5. Disconnect the electrical lead to the Throttle Solenoid Positioner (TSP) and verify that the plunger collapses. Check and adjust the engine RPM to 600 RPM.

6. Shut engine OFF, reconnect TSP electrical lead and throttle kicker vacuum line.

Fast Idle Speed

1. Place the transaxle in **N** or **P**.

2. Bring the engine to normal oper-

ating temperature with the carburetor set on second step of fast idle cam.

3. Return the throttle to normal idle position.

4. Place the air conditioner selector in the OFF position.

5. Disconnect the vacuum hose at the EGR valve and plug.

6. Place the fast idle adjusting screw on the specified step of the fast idle cam.

7. Check and adjust the fast idle rpm to specification.

8. Increase the engine speed momentarily, allowing engine to return to idle. Stop the engine and turn ignition key to the OFF position.

9. Remove the plug from the EGR vacuum hose and reconnect.

IDLE MIXTURE ADJUSTMENT

Idle mixture adjustment is set at the factory and is not normally required. Adjustment should only be attempted during overhaul.

SERVICE ADJUSTMENTS

For all carburetor service adjustment procedures and specifications, please refer to "Carburetor Service" in the Unit Repair section.

Fuel Injection

DESCRIPTION

Electronic Fuel Injection (EFI)

The Electronic Fuel Injection (EFI) system is classified as a multi-point, pulse time, mass air flow fuel injection system. Fuel is metered into the intake air stream in accordance with engine demand through four injectors mounted on a tuned intake manifold.

An on board vehicle Electronic Engine Control (EEC) computer accepts input from various engine sensors to compute the required fuel flow rate necessary to maintain a prescribed air/fuel ratio throughout the entire engine operational range. The computer then outputs a command to the fuel injectors to meter the approximate quantity of fuel.

Central Fuel Injection (CFI)

The Central Fuel Injection (CFI) system is a single point, pulse time modulated injection system. Fuel is metered into the air intake stream according to engine demands by solenoid injection valves mounted in a throttle body on the intake manifold. Fuel is supplied from the fuel tank by a high pressure,

electric fuel pump alone or in conjunction with a low-pressure pump. The fuel is filtered and sent to the air throttle body where a regulator keeps the fuel delivery pressure at a constant 39 psi. Either one or two injector nozzles are mounted vertically above the throttle plates and connected in parallel (or in series if one injector nozzle is used) with the fuel pressure regulator. Excess fuel supplied by the pump but not needed by the engine, is returned to the fuel tank by a steel fuel return line.

IDLE SPEED ADJUSTMENT

1.9L CFI Engine

1. Engine OFF, remove air cleaner. Connect jumper wire between Self-Test Input (STI) and signal return pin on the self-test connector.

2. Turn ignition key ON but do not start engine. Wait for ISC plunger to retract approximately 10–15 seconds.

3. Disconnect vehicle harness from the ISC motor. Turn ignition key OFF and remove jumper wire.

4. Start engine, check idle rpm. If rpm is 600 ± 50, continue with Step 6. If not continue with Step 5.

5. Adjust throttle stop adjusting screw.

6. Shut engine OFF and reconnect vehicle harness to ISC motor. Reinstall air cleaner.

1.9L EFI Engine

1. Disconnect idle speed control-air bypass solenoid.

2. Start engine and run at 2000 rpm for 60 seconds.

3. Place transaxle in **N** or **P**.

4. Check/adjust idle rpm to 950 ± 50. Adjust by doing the following:

   a. Loosen the throttle camplate roller bolt.

   b. Turn the throttle plate stop screw to adjust rpm.

   c. Tighten the throttle camplate roller bolt.

5. Shut engine OFF, reconnect idle speed control-air bypass solenoid. Verify the throttle is not stuck in the bore and linkage is not preventing the throttle from closing.

6. Start engine and let stabilize for 2 minutes, then quickly open throttle and let return to idle, lightly depress and release accelerator. Check idle speed.

2.3L EFI ENGINE

1. Apply the parking brake, block the drive wheels and place the vehicle in **P** or **N**.

2. Start the engine and let it run until it reaches normal operating tem-

perature, then shut engine **OFF**.

3. Unplug spout line and verify that ignition timing is at base setting: ± 2 degrees BTDC. Refer to decal under hood.

4. Remove PCV hose at the PCV valve and install 0.200 in. diameter orifice, tool T86P-9600-A.

5. Start engine and run at 2500 rpm for 30 seconds.

6. Place automatic transaxle in **D** or manual transaxle in **N**.

7. Check/adjust idle rpm to 1025 ± 50 for automatic transaxle, 1550 ± 50 for manual transaxle. Adjust by doing the following:

   a. Loosen the throttle camplate roller bolt.

   b. Turn the throttle plate stop screw to adjust rpm.

   c. Tighten the throttle camplate roller bolt.

8. Engine **OFF**, reconnect spout line.

9. Remove orifice from PCV hose and reconnect to PCV valve.

10. Reconnect idle speed control-air bypass solenoid, verify that the throttle is not stuck in the bore and linkage is not preventing the throttle from closing.

11. Start engine and let stabilize for 2 minutes, then quickly open throttle and let return to idle, lightly depress and release accelerator. Check idle speed.

IDLE MIXTURE ADJUSTMENT

Idle mixture is controlled by the Electronic Control Unit.

Fuel Injector

REMOVAL & INSTALLATION

1.9L CFI Engine

1. Disconnect the negative battery cable.

2. Disconnect electrical connector from injector top.

3. Remove fuel injector retaining screw and retainer.

4. Remove injector and lower O-ring. Discard O-ring.

To install:

5. Lubricate a new lower O-ring and the injector seat area with clean engine oil. Do not use transmission fluid.

6. Install lower O-ring on injector.

7. Lubricate upper O-ring, clean and lubricate throttle body O-ring seat.

8. Install injector retainer and retaining screw.

9. Tighten retainer screws to 28–32 inch lbs. (3.2–3.6 Nm).

10. Connect electrical connector.

11. Connect negative battery cable.

1.9L EFI Engine

1. Disconnect the negative battery cable. Remove fuel tank cap and release pressure from the fuel system at the fuel pressure relief valve.

2. Remove spring-lock coupling retainer clips from fuel inlet and return fittings.

3. Disconnect fuel supply and return lines.

3. Remove vacuum line from fuel pressure regulator.

4. Disconnect the fuel injector wiring harness.

5. Remove the 2 bolts securing the injector manifold assembly and remove the assembly.

6. Carefully remove connectors from individual injectors(s) as required.

7. Grasping the injector's body, pull up while gently rocking the injector from side-to-side.

8. Inspect the injector O-rings (2 per injector) for signs of deterioration. Replace as required.

9. Inspect the injector "plastic hat" (covering the injector pintle) and washer for signs of deterioration. Replace as required. If that is missing, look for it in intake manifold.

To install:

10. Use a light grade oil to lubricate new O-rings and install 2 on each injector.

11. Install the injector(s). Use a light, twisting, pushing motion to install the injector(s).

12. Carefully seat the fuel injector manifold assembly on the injectors and secure the manifold with the attaching bolts. Tighten to 15–22 ft. lbs. (20–30 Nm).

13. Connect the vacuum line to the fuel pressure regulator.

14. Connect fuel injector wiring harness.

15. Connect fuel supply and fuel re-

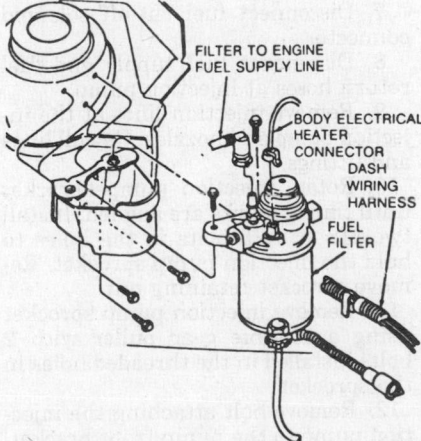

Fuel filter assembly—2.0L Diesel engine

turn lines. Tighten fuel return line to 15–18 ft. lbs.

16. Reconnect spring-lock coupling retaining clips on fuel inlet and return fittings.

17. Check entire assembly for proper alignment and seating.

18. Connect negative battery cable.

DIESEL FUEL SYSTEM

Fuel Filter

REPLACEMENT

1. Disconnect the negative battery cable.

2. Disconnect the module connector from the water level sensor probe pigtail located on the bottom of the fuel filter element.

NOTE: Failure to disconnect the water sensor connector/module will damage the water sensor probe.

3. Disconnect the heater power lead at the fuel heater connector.

4. Disconnect the the fuel line connections from the fuel inlet and outlet fittings of the fuel filler adapter.

5. Drain the fuel from the fuel condtioner assembly.

6. Remove the 2 bolts securing the filter adapter to the filter bracket and withdraw the fuel conditioner assembly consisting of the filter adapter and filter element.

7. Secure the filter adapter into a suitable vise. Using a suitable filter wrench, remove the filter element from the filter adapter.

NOTE: Position the filter adapter in the vise to prevent rotation during element disassembly. Do not position the filter adapter in such a manner as to cause stress to the fuel filter fittings or filter adapter flange, as damage to the filter adapter casting may occur.

8. Remove the water drain/valve sensor probe assembly from the bottom of the filter element by unscrewing the probe. Wipe the probe with a clean dry cloth.

9. Unsnap the sensor probe pigtail connector from the bottom of the filter element and wipe clean with a clean dry cloth.

To install:

10. Snap cleaned sensor probe pigtail connector on bottom of new element.

11. Lubricate two O-ring seals on water sensor probe with a light film of motor oil. Screw probe into bottom of new filter element and tighten securely.

12. Clean gasket sealing surface of filter element adapter.

13. Lubricate filter element seal with clean motor oil and screw filter element onto housing. Hand tighten filter, back off filter to the point where filter gasket just makes contact with adapter sealing surface.

14. Hand tighten filter element an additional ½ to ⅝ turn.

15. Position fuel conditioner assembly on filter bracket and secure with two attaching bolts. Tighten to 13–16 ft. lbs. (18–22 Nm).

16. Connect water level sensor module connector, heater lead connection, and inlet and outlet fuel line connections.

17. Prime fuel system by pressing by-pass button and holding tightly seated while pumping prime pump. Continue to pump until fuel is observed in clear fuel line connected between fuel filter/conditioner and high-pressure pump and there is an increased resistance to pumping, about 40–50 strokes.

18. Connect battery ground cable, start engine and inspect assembly for leaks.

DRAINING WATER FROM SYSTEM

NOTE: The fuel filter/conditioner must be purged of water at each engine oil change interval (7500 miles) as follows.

1. Make sure that the engine and the ignition switch are in the **OFF** position.

2. Place a suitable container under the fuel filter/conditioner water drain tube under the vehicle.

3. Open the water drain valve on the bottom of the filter.

4. Purge system by pressing in by-pass button and holding tightly seated, while pumping hand prime pump, located on top of fuel filter/conditioner, 10–14 strokes or until all water is purged from filter and clear diesel fuel is apparent.

5. Close the water vent valve.

6. Close the water vent valve.

7. Start engine and inspect assembly for leaks.

Diesel Injection Pump

REMOVAL & INSTALLATION

1. Disconnect battery ground cable

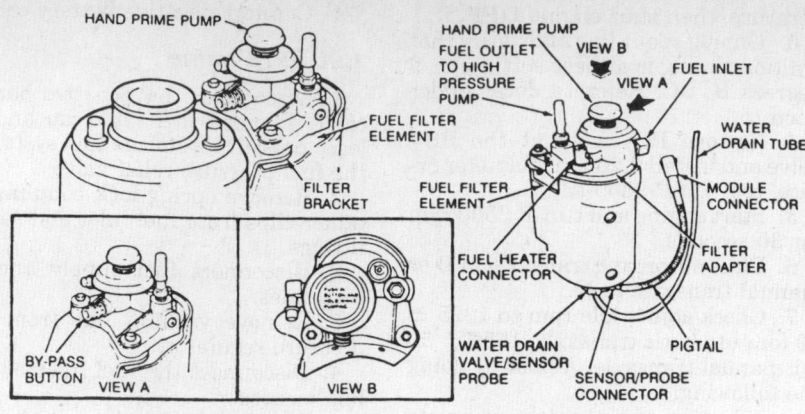

Water separator—2.0L Diesel engine

from the battery, located in the luggage compartment.

2. Properly relieve the fuel system pressure.

3. Disconnect the air inlet duct from the air cleaner and intake manifold. Install protective cap in intake manifold.

4. Remove rear timing belt cover and flywheel timing mark cover. Remove rear timing belt as follows:

  a. Remove rear timing belt cover.

  b. Remove flywheel timing mark cover from clutch housing.

  c. Rotate crankshaft until the flywheel timing mark is at TDC on No. 1 cylinder.

  d. Check that the injection pump and camshaft sprocket timing marks are aligned.

  e. Loosen tensioner locknut. With a prybar or equivalent tool, inserted in the slot provided, rotate the tensioner clockwise to relieve belt tension. Tighten locknut snug.

  f. Remove timing belt.

5. Disconnect throttle cable and speed cable, if so equipped.

6. Disconnect vacuum hoses at the air conditioner idle speed kicker and cold start diaphragm.

7. Disconnect fuel cut-off solenoid connector.

8. Disconnect fuel supply and fuel return hoses at injection pump.

9. Remove injection lines at the injection pump and nozzles. Cap all lines and fittings.

10. Rotate injection pump sprocket until timing marks are aligned. Install two M8 × 1.25 bolts in the holes to hold the injection pump sprocket. Remove sprocket retaining nut.

11. Remove injection pump sprocket using a suitable gear puller with 2 bolts installed in the threaded holes in the sprocket.

12. Remove bolt attaching the injection pump to the pump front bracket.

13. Remove the 2 nuts attaching the

injection pump to the pump rear bracket and remove the pump.

To install:

14. Install injection pump in position on the pump brackets.

15. Install 2 nuts attaching the pump to the rear bracket and tighten to 23–34 ft. lbs. (32–47 Nm).

16. Install bolt attaching the pump to the front bracket and tighten to 12–16 ft. lbs. (16–23 Nm).

17. Install injection pump sprocket. Hold the sprocket in place using the procedure described in Step 10. Install the sprocket retaining nut and tighten to 51–58 ft. lbs. (70–80 Nm).

18. Remove protective caps and install the fuel lines at the injection pump and nozzles. Tighten the fuel line capnuts to 18–22 ft. lbs. (25–29 Nm).

19. Connect fuel supply and fuel return hoses at the injection pump.

20. Connect fuel cut-off solenoid connector.

21. Connect vacuum lines to the cold start diaphragm and air conditioner idle speed kicker.

22. Connect throttle cable and speed control cable, if so equipped.

23. Install the rear timing belt. Loosen tensioner locknut and adjust timing belt using appropriate belt tension gauge. Belt tension should be 22–33 ft. lbs. (98–147 Nm). Install rear timing belt cover. Install flywheel timing mark cover.

24. Remove protective cap and install the air inlet duct to the intake manifold and air cleaner.

25. Connect battery ground cable to battery.

26. Air bleed fuel system.

27. Check and adjust the injection pump timing.

28. Run engine and check for fuel leaks.

29. Check and adjust engine idle.

IDLE SPEED ADJUSTMENT

1. Place the transaxle in **N**.
2. Bring the engine up to normal operating temperature. Stop engine.
3. Remove the timing hole cover. Clean the flywheel surface and install reflective tape.
4. Idle speed is measured with manual transaxle in **N**.
5. Check curb idle speed, using an appropriate hand-held tachometer. Curb idle speed is specified on the vehicle emissions control information decal. Adjust to specification by loosening the locknut on the idle speed adjusting bolt. Turn the idle speed adjusting bolt clockwise to increase or counterclockwise to decrease engine idle speed. Tighten the locknut.
6. Place transaxle in **N**. Increase the engine speed momentarily and re-check the curb idle rpm. Readjust if necessary.
7. Turn air conditioner **ON**. Check the idle speed. Adjust to specification by loosening nut on the air conditioner throttle kicker and rotating screw.

Diesel Injection Timing—Static

ADJUSTMENT

NOTE: Engine coolant temperature must be above 176°F (80°C) before the injection timing can be checked and/or adjusted.

1. Disconnect the battery ground cable from the battery located in luggage compartment.
2. Remove the injection pump distributor head plug bolt and sealing washer.
3. Install static timing gauge adapter, Rotunda tool 14-0303 or equivalent, with a metric dial indicator gauge tool, so that indicator pointer is in contact with injection pump plunger.
4. Remove timing mark cover from transaxle housing. Align timing mark (TDC) with pointer on the rear engine cover plate.
5. Rotate the crankshaft pulley slowly, counterclockwise until the dial indicator pointer stops moving, approximately 30–50 degrees BTDC.
6. Adjust dial indicator to zero.

NOTE: Confirm that dial indicator pointer does not move from zero by slightly rotating crankshaft left and right.

7. Turn crankshaft clockwise until crankshaft timing mark aligns with indicator pin. Dial indicator should read 0.04 ± 0.0008 in. (1 ± 0.02mm). If

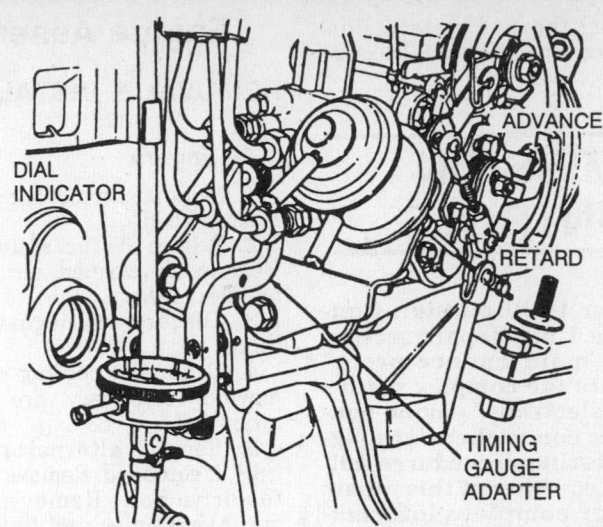

Engine injection timing—2.0L Diesel engine

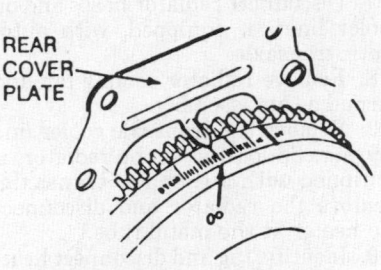

Flywheel timing mark—2.0L Diesel engine

reading is not within specification, adjust as follows:

a. Loosen injection pump attaching bolt and nuts.
b. Rotate the injection pump toward the engine to advance timing and away from the engine to retard timing.
c. Rotate the injection pump until the dial indicator reads 0.04 ± 0.0008 in. (1 ± 0.02mm).
d. Tighten the injection pump attaching nuts and bolt to 13–20 ft. lbs.
e. Repeat Steps 5–7 to check that timing is adjusted correctly.

8. Remove the dial indicator and adapter and install the injection pump distributor head plug and tighten to 10–14 ft. lbs.
9. Connect the battery ground cable to the battery.
10. Run the engine, check and adjust idle rpm, if necessary. Check for fuel leaks.

Fuel Injector

REMOVAL & INSTALLATION

1. Disconnect the negative battery cable.

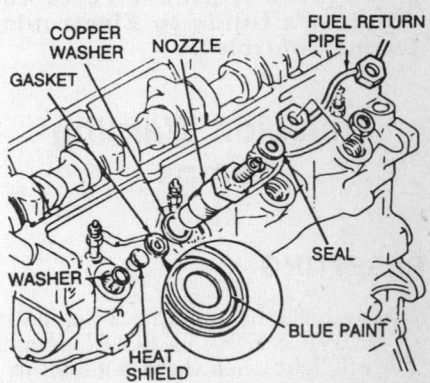

Injector installation—2.0L Diesel engine

2. Disconnect and remove the injection lines from the injection pump and nozzles. Cap all lines and fitting to prevent dirt contamination.
3. Remove the nuts attaching the fuel return line to the nozzles and remove the return line and seals.
4. Remove the injector nozzles using a 27mm socket. Remove the nozzle gaskets and washers from the nozzle seats using an O-ring pick tool.

To install:

5. Clean the outside of the nozzles with safety solvent and dry them thoroughly.
6. Position new sealing gaskets and heat shields in nozzle seats with the blue painted gasket surface facing up.
7. Position new copper gaskets in the nozzles bores. Install the nozzles and tighten to 44–51 ft. lbs. (60–70 Nm).
8. Position the fuel return line on the nozzles using new seals. Install the retaining nuts and tighten to 10 ft. lbs. (14 Nm).
9. Install the fuel lines on the injection pump and nozzles. Tighten to 18–22 ft. lbs. (25–29 Nm).

10. Air bleed the fuel system. Run the engine and check for fuel leaks.

EMISSION CONTROLS

Please refer to "Emission Control" in the Unit Repair section for system maintenance procedures. Due to the complex nature of modern electronic engine control systems, comprehensive diagnosis and testing procedures fall outside the confines of this repair manual. For complete information on diagnosis, testing and repair procedures concerning all modern engine and emission control systems, please refer to "Chilton's Guide to Electronic Engine Controls".

Emission Warning Lamps

RESETTING

These vehicles have a "Check Engine" or "SERVICE ENGINE SOON" lamp that will light when there is a fault in the engine control system. Depending upon the system or sensor involved, the light may go out if the fault is intermittent. However, the fault code will remain stored in the ECU until the system is serviced and the ECU memory cleared. When a fault is detected in certain systems or sensors, the light will remain lit until the system is serviced. When the system has been diagnosed, the problem corrected and the ECU memory cleared, the light will go out.

GASOLINE ENGINE MECHANICAL

NOTE: Disconnecting the negative battery cable on some vehicles may interfere with the functions of the on board computer systems and may require the computer to undergo a relearning process, once the negative battery cable is reconnected.

Engine Assembly

REMOVAL & INSTALLATION

1.9L Engine

1. Mark position of hood hinges and remove hood.
2. Relieve the fuel system pressure. Remove air cleaner, air intake duct and heat tube.
3. Disconnect negative battery cable.
4. Drain the cooling system. Remove the secondary wire from the ignition coil.
5. Remove alternator air intake tube, if equipped. Remove the alternator drive belt. Remove alternator mounting bolts and lay alternator aside.
6. Disconnect and remove thermactor air pump, if equipped.
7. Disconnect radiator hoses and oil cooler lines, if equipped, with automatic transaxle.
8. Remove radiator cooling fan and shroud as an assembly.
9. Remove the transaxle cooler line routing clip located at the radiator, if equipped with automatic transaxle. Remove the radiator and disconnect the heater at the metal tube.
10. Identify, tag and disconnect heater hoses, electrical connections and vacuum hoses as necessary. Disconnect the fuel pump supply and return lines. If equipped with power assist brakes, disconnect the power boost vacuum hose at the engine.
11. Disconnect kickdown rod at carburetor or fuel charging assembly, if equipped with automatic transaxle.
12. Disconnect accelerator cable at the fuel charging assembly and remove the cable routing bracket attaching screws. Disconnect the vapor hose at the carbon canister tube.
13. Raise and safely support the vehicle.
14. Remove the clamp from the heater supply and return hose. Remove knee brace at front of starter motor and remove battery cable from starter. Remove the starter motor.
15. Disconnect exhaust inlet pipe at manifold.
16. Remove support bracket in front of converter cover, if equipped with automatic transaxle and remove cover. Remove inspection cover from manual transaxle.
17. Remove crankshaft pulley and damper.
18. Remove torque converter to flywheel nuts, if equipped with automatic transaxle.
19. Remove timing belt cover lower attaching bolts, if equipped with manual transaxle.

20. Remove converter housing, if equipped with automatic transaxle, or flywheel housing, if equipped with manual transaxle.
21. Remove 2 oil pan-to-transaxle attaching bolts. Disconnect coolant bypass hose from intake manifold. If equipped, remove the bolt attaching the battery negative cable to the cylinder block.
22. Remove nut and bolt attaching insulator bracket to the engine bracket at front of engine.
23. Lower vehicle.
24. Install suitable lifting brackets on engine.

NOTE: The top rear bolt attaching the thermactor pump bracket to the engine can be removed and used as a lifting bracket attaching point.

25. Use a suitable lifting device connected to the engine lifting brackets and raise engine just enough to remove the through bolt from the front engine insulator and remove insulator.
26. Remove the remaining timing belt cover bolts and remove the cover, if equipped with manual transaxle.
27. Remove insulator attaching bracket from engine.
28. Position a jack under the transaxle. Raise jack just enough to support the weight of the transaxle.
29. Remove the converter housing, flywheel housing upper attaching bolts.
30. Remove engine assembly from vehicle.

To install:
31. Carefully lower engine into the vehicle using a suitable lifting device.
31. Join the engine and the transaxle, making sure the alignment dowels on the back of the engine engage the transaxle housing.

NOTE: If the vehicle is equipped with an manual transaxle, make sure the transaxle input shaft engages the clutch disc. If the vehicle is equipped with an automatic transaxle, make sure the torque converter studs engage the flywheel.

32. Install the converter housing if automatic transaxle, flywheel housing if manual transaxle, upper attaching bolts.
34. Install 2 oil pan to transaxle attaching bolts and tighten to 30–40 ft. lbs. (40–54 Nm). Then loosen bolts ½ turn.
35. Remove jack from under the transaxle.
36. Position engine insulator attaching casting on the engine and install the attaching bolt and nut.

37. Attach the nuts to the insulator to casting.
38. Remove lifting device and the lifting brackets.
39. Connect electrical connectors, vacuum hoses and carbon canister vapor hose.
40. If equipped with an automatic transaxle, connect the kickdown rod.
41. Connect the heater hoses.
42. Connect the fuel supply and return lines at the throttle body.
43. If equipped with power assist brakes, connect the vacuum hose to the power booster.
44. Position the accelerator cable routing bracket and install the attaching bolts.
45. Connect the accelerator cable to the fuel charging assembly.
46. Connect the coolant bypass hose, if equipped with an manual transaxle.
47. Install radiator.
48. Install battery negative cable to cylinder block attaching bolt.
49. Attach the lower cooler line, if equipped with an automatic transaxle.
50. Connect the radiator lower hose.
51. Attach the upper cooler line, if equipped with an automatic transaxle.
52. Install radiator cooling fan and shroud assembly.
53. Connect radiator upper hose.
54. Raise and safely support the vehicle.
55. Tighten the casting-to-insulator attaching nuts.
56. Install the torque converter-to-flywheel attaching bolts.
57. Install the crankshaft damper.
58. Install lower attaching bolts to converter housing, if equipped with automatic transaxle; flywheel housing if equipped with manual transaxle.
59. Install support bracket.
60. Install starter motor and connect battery cable.
61. Install starter brace at the front of the starter motor.
62. Connect the exhaust inlet pipe.
64. Install the cooler line routing bracket, if equipped with automatic transaxle.
65. Lower the vehicle.
66. Install the timing belt cover, if equipped with manual transaxle.
67. Install alternator and drive belt. Tighten the drive belt to specification.
68. Connect negative battery cable.
69. Install alternator air intake tube.
70. Fill cooling system, overflow bottle and bleed the cooling system.
71. Fill the crankcase to the proper level with the specified oil.
72. Install the hood.
73. Start engine and check for coolant, oil and fuel leaks.
74. Install air cleaner assembly with the intake duct and heat tube and connect remaining vacuum hoses.

2.3L Engine

NOTE: This procedure describes the removal and installation of the engine and transaxle as an assembly.

1. Mark position of hood hinges and remove hood.
2. Remove negative ground cable from battery.
3. Relieve the fuel system pressure. Remove air cleaner.
4. Remove lower radiator hose to drain engine coolant.
5. Remove upper radiator hose and disconnect transaxle cooler lines at rubber hoses below radiator, if equipped with automatic transaxle.
6. Remove coil and disconnect coolant fan at electrical connection.
7. Remove radiator shroud and cooling fan as an assembly. Remove radiator.
8. Discharge air conditioning system, if equipped and remove pressure and suction lines from compressor.

— CAUTION —

Use extreme care when discharging air conditioning system, as the refrigerant is under high pressure and may cause personal injury.

9. Identify, tag and disconnect all electrical and vacuum lines as necessary.
10. Disconnect TV linkage or clutch cable at transaxle.
11. Disconnect accelerator linkage and fuel lines.
12. Disconnect thermactor pump discharge hose at pump, if equipped.
13. Disconnect power steering lines at pump and bracket at the cylinder head, if equipped.
14. Install engine support tool to existing engine lifting eye.
15. Raise and safely support the vehicle.
16. Remove battery cable from starter and remove hose from catalytic converter.
17. Remove bolt attaching exhaust pipe bracket to oil pan and 2 exhaust pipe to manifold attaching nuts.
18. Pull exhaust system out of rubber insulating grommets and set aside.
19. Remove speedometer cable from transaxle.
20. Remove on heater hose from water pump inlet tube and the other from the steel tube on intake manifold.
21. Remove water pump inlet tube clamp bolt at engine block and clamp bolts at underside of oil pan. Remove inlet tube.
22. Remove bolts attaching control arms to body. Remove stabilizer bar brackets retaining bolts and remove brackets.

23. Halfshaft assemblies must be removed from transaxle at this time.
24. On manual transaxle equipped vehicles, remove roll restrictor nuts from transaxle. Pull roll restrictor from mounting bracket.
25. On manual transaxle equipped vehicles, remove shift stabilizer bar to transaxle attaching bolts. Remove shift mechanism to shift shaft attaching nut and bolt at transaxle.
26. On automatic transaxle equipped, disconnect manual shift cable clip from lever on transaxle. Remove manual shift linkage bracket bolts from transaxle and remove bracket.
27. Remove the left rear insulator mount bracket from body bracket.
28. Remove the left front insulator to transaxle mounting bolts.
29. Lower the vehicle. Install lifting equipment to the 2 existing lifting eyes on engine.

NOTE: Do not allow front wheels to touch floor.

30. Remove engine support tool.
31. Remove right No. 3A insulator intermediate bracket-to-engine bracket bolts, intermediate bracket-to-insulator attaching nuts and the nut on the bottom of the double ended stud which attaches the intermediate bracket-to-engine bracket. Remove bracket.
32. Carefully lower engine and transaxle assembly to the floor.
To install:
33. Raise and safely support the vehicle.
34. Position engine and transaxle assembly directly below engine compartment.
35. Slowly lower vehicle over engine and transaxle assembly.

NOTE: Do not allow the front wheels to touch the floor.

36. Install lifting equipment to both existing engine lifting eyes on engine.
37. Raise engine and transaxle assembly up through engine compartment and position accordingly.
38. Install right hand No. 3A insulator intermediate attaching nuts to intermediate bracket. Tighten to 55–75 ft. lbs. (75–100 Nm). Attach intermediate bracket to engine bracket bolts. Tighten to 52–70 ft. lbs. (70–95 Nm). Install nut on bottom of double-ended stud that attaches the intermediate bracket-to-engine bracket. Tighten to 60–90 ft. lbs. (80–120 Nm).
39. Install engine support tool to engine lifting eye.
40. Remove lifting equipment.
41. Raise and safely support the vehicle.
42. Position transaxle jack under engine. Raise engine and transaxle as-

sembly into mounted position.

43. Install insulator-to-bracket nut. Tighten to 45–65 ft. lbs. (61–68 Nm).

44. Vehicles equipped with manual transaxle, position roll restrictor onto starter studs. Install nuts attaching roll restrictor to transaxle. Tighten to 25-39 ft. lbs. (35–50 Nm).

45. Install starter cable to starter.

46. Install lower radiator hose and install retaining bracket and bolt.

47. Vehicles equipped with manual transaxle, install shift stabilizer bar-to-transaxle attaching bolt. Tighten to 23–35 ft. lbs. (31–47 Nm).

48. Vehicles equipped with manual transaxle, install shift mechanism-to-input shift shaft (on transaxle) bolt and nut. Tighten to 7–10 ft. lbs. (9–13 Nm).

49. Vehicles equipped with automatic transaxle, install manual shift linkage bracket bolts to transaxle. Install cable clip to lever on transaxle.

50. Install lower radiator hose to radiator.

51. Install speedometer cable to transaxle.

52. Position exhaust system up and into insulating rubber grommets located at rear of vehicle.

53. Install exhaust pipe-to-exhaust manifold studs.

54. Connect pulse air hose to catalytic converter.

55. Place stabilizer bar and control arm assembly into position. Install control arm-to-body attaching bolts. Install stabilizer bar brackets and tighten all fasteners.

56. Halfshaft assemblies must be installed at this time.

57. Lower vehicle.

58. Remove engine support tool.

59. Connect any remaining electrical and vacuum lines.

60. Install heater hose.

61. Install air conditioning discharge and suction lines to compressor, if equipped. Do not charge at this time.

62. Connect fuel supply and return lines to engine.

63. Connect accelerator cable.

64. Install power steering pressure and return lines.

65. Vehicles equipped with automatic transaxle, connect TV linkage at transaxle.

66. Vehicles equipped with manual transaxle, connect clutch cable to shift lever on transaxle. Check clutch adjustment.

67. Install radiator shroud and coolant fan assembly.

68. Vehicles equipped with automatic transaxle, connect transaxle cooler lines to rubber hoses below radiator.

69. Fill cooling system.

70. Connect battery ground cable.

71. Install air cleaner assembly.

72. Install hood.

73. Charge air conditioning system, if so equipped.

74. Check all fluid levels.

75. Start engine. Check for leaks.

Engine Mounts

REMOVAL & INSTALLATION

1.9L and 2.3L Engines

RIGHT ENGINE INSULATOR (NO. 3A)

1. Disconnect the negative battery cable. Place a floor jack and a block of wood under the engine oil pan. Raise the engine approximately ½ in. or enough to take the load off of the insulator.

2. Remove the lower support bracket attaching nut, bottom of the double ended stud. Remove the insulator-to-support bracket attaching nuts. Do not remove the nut on top of the double ended stud.

3. Remove the insulator support bracket from the vehicle. Remove the insulator attaching nuts through the right hand front wheel opening.

4. Remove the insulator attaching bolts through the engine compartment. Work the insulator out of the body and remove it from the vehicle.

To install:

5. Work insulator into the body opening.

6. Position the insulator and install the attaching nuts and bolts. Tighten the nuts to 75–100 ft. lbs. (100–135 Nm) and tighten the bolts to 37–55 ft. lbs. (50–75 Nm).

7. Install insulator support casting on top of the insulator and engine support bracket. Make sure the double-edged stud is through the hole in the engine bracket.

8. Tighten the insulator support casting-to-insulator attaching nuts to 55–75 ft. lbs. (75–100 Nm). Install and tighten lower support bracket nut to 60–90 ft. lbs. (80–120 Nm).

9. Install the insulator casting-to-engine bracket bolt and tighten to 60–90 ft. lbs. (80–120 Nm).

10. Lower engine. Connect negative battery cable.

LEFT REAR ENGINE INSULATOR (NO. 4)

1. Disconnect the negative battery cable. Raise the vehicle and support safely. Place a transaxle jack and a block of wood under the transaxle.

2. Raise the transaxle approximately ½ in. or enough to take the load off of the insulator.

3. Remove the insulator attaching nuts from the support bracket. Remove the 2 through bolts and remove the insulator from the transaxle.

To install:

4. Install the insulator over the left rear transaxle housing and support bracket studs.

5. Install the 2 insulator through bolts and tighten to 30–45 ft. lbs. (41–61 Nm).

6. Install 2 insulator-to-support bracket attaching nuts. Tighten to 80–100 ft. lbs. (108–136 Nm).

7. Lower vehicle and remove floor jack. Connect negative battery cable.

NOTE: To remove the left rear support bracket, remove the left rear engine insulator No. 4. Then remove the support bracket attaching bolts. When installing the support bracket, torque the attaching bolts to 45–65 ft. lbs. (61–88 Nm).

LEFT FRONT ENGINE INSULATOR (NO. 1)

1. Disconnect the negative battery cable. Raise and the vehicle and support safely. Place a transaxle jack and a block of wood under the transaxle. Raise the transaxle approximately ½ in. or enough to take the load off of the insulator.

2. Remove the insulator-to-support bracket attaching nut. Remove the insulators and transaxle attaching bolts and remove the insulator from the vehicle.

3. Complete the installation of the insulator by reversing the removal procedure. Torque the insulator to transaxle attaching bolts to 25–37 ft. lbs. (35–50 Nm). Torque the insulator-to-support bracket nut to 80–100 ft. lbs. (108–136 Nm).

Cylinder Head

REMOVAL & INSTALLATION

1.9L Engine

NOTE: The engine must be cold before removing the cylinder head, to reduce the possibility of warpage or distortion.

1. Disconnect the negative battery cable. Properly relieve the fuel system pressure.

2. Drain the cooling system and disconnect the heater hose at the fitting located under the intake manifold.

3. Disconnect the radiator upper hose at the cylinder head.

4. Disconnect the wiring terminal from the cooling fan switch.

5. Remove the air cleaner assembly.

6. Remove the PCV hose.

7. Identify, tag and disconnect the required vacuum hoses.

8. Remove the rocker arm cover.

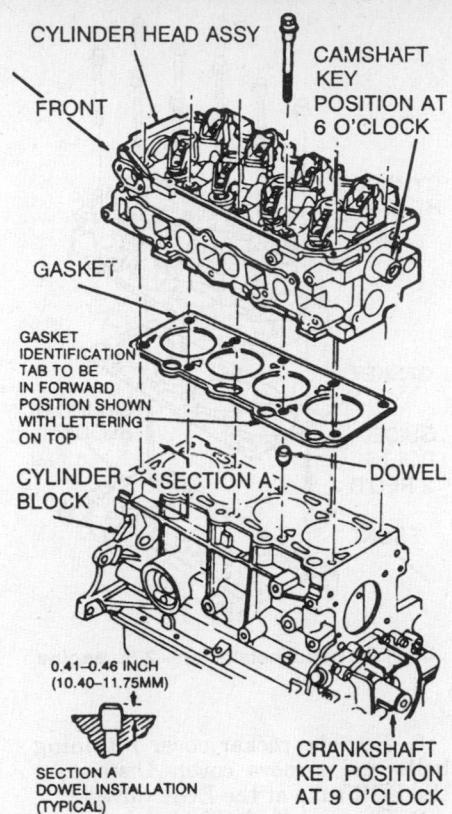

Cylinder head installation—1.9L engine

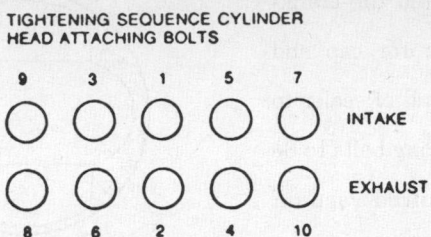

Cylinder head torque sequence—1.9L engine

9. Disconnect all accessory drive belts.

10. Remove the crankshaft pulley using the proper puller tool.

11. Remove the timing belt cover.

12. Set the engine No. 1 cylinder to TDC prior to removing the timing belt.

13. Remove the distributor cap and spark plug wires as an assembly.

14. Loosen both belt tensioner attaching bolts using torque wrench adapter tool T81P-6254-A or equivalent.

15. Secure the belt tensioner as far left as possible.

16. Remove the timing belt.

17. Disconnect the EGR tube at the EGR valve.

18. Disconnect the PVS hose connectors, as required, using tool T81P-8564-A or equivalent. Label the connectors and set aside.

19. Disconnect the choke cap wire.

20. Disconnect the fuel supply and return lines at the metal connectors, located on the right side of the engine, set rubber lines aside.

21. Disconnect the accelerator cable and, if equipped, the speed control cable.

22. Disconnect the altitude compensator, if equipped from the dash panel and place on the heater/air conditioner air intake.

NOTE: Caution should be taken not to damage the altitude compensator.

23. Disconnect the alternator air intake tube, if equipped, and the alternator wiring harness.

24. Remove the alternator and its mounting bracket.

25. If equipped with power steering, remove the thermactor pump drive belt, the pump and the pump mounting bracket.

26. Raise and safely support the vehicle.

27. Disconnect the exhaust system at the exhaust pipe.

28. Lower the vehicle.

29. Remove the cylinder head bolts and washers. Discard the bolts.

NOTE: Do not reuse the cylinder head retaining bolts. Use new bolts when installing head.

30. Remove the cylinder head with the exhaust and intake manifolds attached. Discard the cylinder head gasket.

NOTE: Do not lay the cylinder head flat. Damage to the spark plug or gasket contact surfaces may result.

To install:

31. Clean all gasket material from the mating surfaces on the cylinder head and block.

NOTE: Before installing cylinder head, check piston squish height. Procedure at the end of installation section.

32. If the camshaft has been turned or removed or if installing a replacement cylinder head, rotate the camshaft until the camshaft gear pointer is aligned with the timing mark on the cylinder head and the camshaft keyway is at the 6 o'clock.

33. Position the No. 1 piston 90 degrees BTDC, pulley keyway at 9 o'clock position, during the cylinder head installation.

34. Position the cylinder head gasket on the cylinder block.

35. Install the cylinder head and install new bolts and washers in the following order:

a. Apply a light coat of engine oil to the threads of the new cylinder head bolts and install the new bolts into the head.

b. Torque the cylinder head bolts in sequence to 44 ft. lbs. (60 Nm).

c. Loosen the cylinder head bolts approximately 2 turns and then torque again to 44 ft. lbs. (60 Nm) using the same torque sequence.

d. After setting the torque again, turn the head bolts 90 degrees in sequence and to complete the head bolt installation, turn the head bolts an additional 90 degrees in the same torque sequence.

NOTE: The cylinder head attaching bolts cannot be tightened to the specified torque more than once and must therefore be replaced when installing a cylinder head.

36. Raise and safely support the vehicle.

37. Connect the exhaust system at the exhaust pipe.

38. Lower the vehicle.

39. Install the thermactor pump mounting bracket, pump and drive belt, if removed.

40. Install the alternator mounting bracket and the alternator. Connect the alternator wiring harness and alternator air intake tube.

41. Connect the altitude compensator, if equipped.

42. Connect the accelerator cable and, if equipped, the speed control cable.

43. Connect the fuel supply and return lines at the metal connector, located on the right side of the engine.

44. Connect the choke cap wire. Connect the EGR tube to the EGR valve.

45. Rotate the crankshaft to bring No. 1 piston to TDC on its compression stroke. The crankshaft keyway should then be at the 12 o'clock position. The distributor rotor should be pointing toward the No. 1 spark plug firing position. Install the timing belt,

the timing belt cover and the crank-shaft pulley.

46. Install the distributor cap and spark plug wires.

47. Apply a $^3/_{16}$ in. bead of sealer to the valve cover flange.

48. Tighten the attaching bolts to 6–8 ft. lbs.

49. Connect the required vacuum hoses.

50. Connect the wiring terminal to the cooling fan switch.

51. Connect the radiator upper hose at the cylinder head.

52. Connect the heater hose to the fitting located below the intake manifold.

53. Fill the cooling system to the proper level and connnect the negative battery cable.

54. Start the engine and check for leaks.

55. After engine has reached operating temperature, check and, if necessary, add coolant.

56. Adjust the ignition timing.

57. Install the PVS hose, if equipped.

58. Install the air cleaner assembly.

Piston Squish Height

Before final installation of the cylinder head to the engine, piston "squish height" must be checked. Squish height is the clearance of the piston dome to the cylinder head dome at piston TDC. No rework of the head gasket surfaces (slabbing) or use of replacement parts (crankshaft, piston and connecting rod) causing the assembled squish height to be over or under the tolerance specification is permitted.

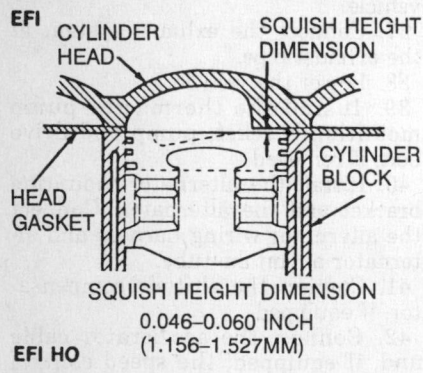

EFI

SQUISH HEIGHT DIMENSION
0.046–0.060 INCH
(1.156–1.527MM)

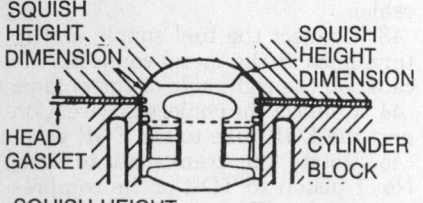

EFI HO

SQUISH HEIGHT DIMENSION
0.039–0.070 INCH (1.0–1.77MM)

Piston squish height—1.9L engine

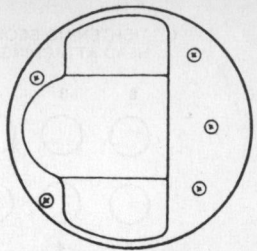

Solder locations to measure piston squish height

NOTE: If no parts other than the head gasket are replaced, the piston squish height should be within specification. If parts other than the head gasket or replaced, check the squish height. If the squish height is out of specification, replace the parts again and recheck the piston squish height.

1. Clean all gasket material from the mating surfaces on the cylinder head and engine block.

2. Place a small amount of soft lead solder or shot of an appropriate thickness on the piston spherical areas shown.

3. Rotate the crankshaft to lower the piston in the bore and install the head gasket and cylinder head.

NOTE: A compressed (used) head gasket is preferred.

4. Install used head bolts and tighten the head bolts to 30–44 ft. lbs. (40–60 Nm) following proper sequence.

5. Rotate the crankshaft to move the piston through its TDC position.

6. Remove the cylinder head and measure the thickness of the compressed solder to determine squish height at TDC. The solder should be 0.039–0.070 in. (1.0–1.77mm) for EFI HO engine and 0.046–0.060 in. (1.156–1.527mm) for EFI engine.

2.3L Engine

1. Disconnect the negative battery cable. Drain the cooling system.

2. Remove the air cleaner assembly. Properly relieve the fuel system pressure.

3. Disconnect the heater hose at the fitting located under the intake manifold. Disconnect the upper radiator hose at the cylinder head.

4. Disconnect distributor cap and spark plug wire and remove as an assembly.

5. Remove spark plugs, if necessary.

6. Disconnect and tag required vacuum hoses.

7. Remove dipstick. Disconnect the choke cap wire.

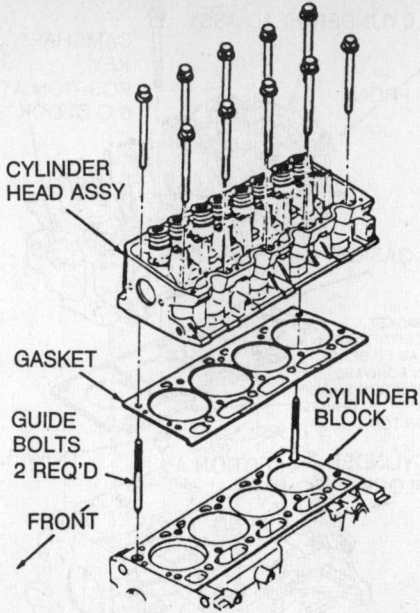

Cylinder head installation—2.3L engine

8. Remove rocker cover retaining bolts and remove cover. Disconnect the EGR tube at the EGR valve.

9. Disconnect the fuel supply and return lines at the rubber connections. Disconnect the accelerator cable and speed control cable, if equipped.

10. Loosen the thermactor pump belt pulley. Raise and support the vehicle safely.

11. Disconnect the exhaust system at the exhaust pipe, hose and tube. Lower the vehicle.

12. Remove thermactor pump. Remove the cylinder head bolts. Remove cylinder head and gasket with exhaust and intake manifolds attached.

To install:

NOTE: Do not lay the cylinder head flat. Damage to spark plugs or gasket surfaces may result.

13. Clean all gasket material from the mating surface of the cylinder head and block. Position the cylinder head gasket on the cylinder block, using a suitable sealer to retain the gasket.

14. Before installing the cylinder head, thread 2 cylinder head alignment studs, using exhaust manifold alignment studs T84P-6065-A or equivalent, through the head bolt holes in the gasket and into the block at opposite corners of the block.

15. Install the cylinder head and cylinder head bolts. Run down several head bolts until snug and remove the 2 guide bolts. Replace them with the remaining head bolts. Torque the cylinder head bolts to 52–59 ft. lbs. (70–80 Nm)and retorque the bolts to 70–76 ft.

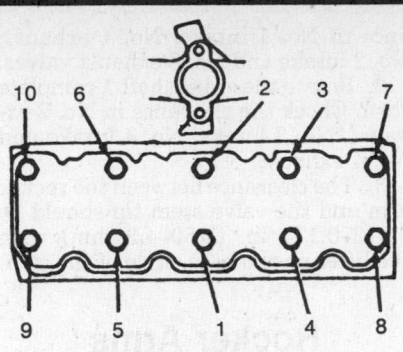

CYLINDER HEAD BOLT
TIGHTENING SEQUENCE

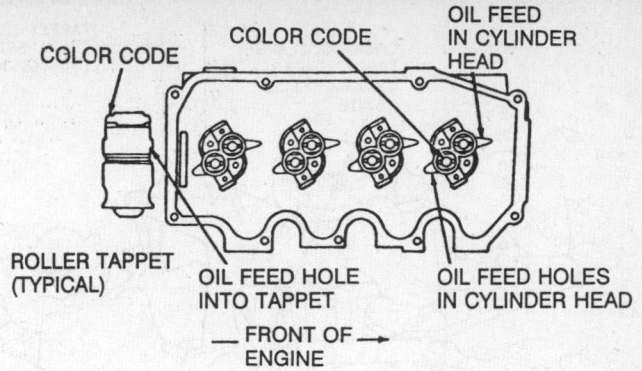

Roller tappet assemblies—installation

Cylinder head torque sequence—2.3L engine

lbs. (95–103 Nm) following the proper sequence.

16. Raise and safely support the vehicle. Connect the exhaust system at the exhaust pipe and hose to metal tube.

17. Lower the vehicle and install the thermactor pump and drive belt. Connect the accelerator cable and, if equipped, speed control cable.

18. Connect the fuel supply and return lines. Connect the choke cap wire.

19. Connect the EGR tube at the EGR valve. Install the distributor cap and spark plug wires as an assembly. Install the spark plugs, if removed.

20. Connect all accessory drive belts. Install the rocker arm cover.

21. Connect the required vacuum hoses. Install the air cleaner assembly. Connect the electric cooling fan switch at the connector.

22. Connect the upper radiator hose at the intake manifold. Fill the cooling system. Connect the negative battery cable.

23. Start the engine and check for leaks. After the engine has reached normal operating temperature, check and add coolant as necessary.

Valve Lifters

REMOVAL & INSTALLATION

1.9L Engine

1. Disconnect the negative battery cable.

2. Remove air cleaner assembly. Remove valve cover and gasket.

3. Remove rocker arms, lifter guides, lifter retainers and lifters.

NOTE: Always return lifters to the original bores unless they are being replaced.

To install:

4. Lubricate each lifter bore with

heavy SG engine oil.

5. If equipped with flat bottom lifters, install with oil hole in plunger upward. If equipped with roller lifters, install with plunger upward and position guide flats of lifters to be parallel with centerline of camshaft. Color orientation dots on lifters should be opposite the oil feed holes in cylinder head.

6. For roller lifters only, install lifter guide plates over tappet guide flats with notch toward exhaust side. For flat lifters, no guide plate is required.

7. Lubricate lifter plunger cap and valve tip with heavy SG engine oil.

8. Install lifter guide plate retainers into rocker arm fulcrum slots, in both intake and exhaust side. Notch to be with exhaust valve lifter.

9. Install 4 rocker arms in lifter position No's 3, 6, 7 and 8.

10. Lubricate rocker arm surface that will contact fulcrum surface with heavy SG engine oil.

11. Install 4 fulcrums. Fulcrums must be fully seated in slots of cylinder head.

12. Install 4 bolts. Tighten to 17–22 ft. lbs. (23–30 Nm).

13. Rotate the engine until the camshaft sprocket keyway is in the 6 o'clock position.

14. Repeat steps 9–12 in lifter position No's 1, 2, 4 and 5.

15. Install valve cover and gasket. Install air cleaner assembly.

16. Connect negative battery cable.

2.3L Engine

1. Disconnect the negative battery cable. Remove the cylinder head and related parts.

2. Using a magnet, remove the lifters. Identify, tag and place the lifters in a rack so they can be installed in the original positions.

3. If the lifters are stuck in their bores by excessive varnish or gum, it may be necessary to use a hydraulic lifter puller tool to remove the lifters. Rotate the lifters back and forth to loosen any gum and varnish which may have formed. Keep the assemblies

intact until they are to be cleaned.

To install:

4. Install new or cleaned hydraulic lifters through the pushrod openings with a magnet.

5. Install the cylinder head and related parts.

6. Connect negative battery cable.

Valve Lash

ADJUSTMENT

Collapsed Lifter Clearance

1.9L ENGINE

1. Connect an auxiliary starter switch in the starting circuit. Crank the engine with the ignition switch **OFF** until the No. 1 piston is on TDC of the compression stroke.

2. With the crankshaft in position, place the hydraulic lifter compressor tool on the rocker arm. Slowly apply pressure to bleed down the lifter until it completely bottoms. Hold the lifter in this position and check the available clearance between the rocker arm and the valve stem tip with a feeler gauge. The feeler gauge width must not exceed ⅜ in., in order to fit between the rails on the rocker arm. If the clearance is less than specifications, check the following for wear:

The fulcrum
The valve lifter
The camshaft lobe
The valve tip

3. With the No. 1 piston on TDC at the end of the compression stroke check the following valves:
   a. No. 1 intake, No. 1 exhaust
   b. No. 2 intake

4. Rotate the crankshaft 180 degrees and check the following valves: No. 3 intake, No. 3 exhaust.

5. Rotate the crankshaft another 180 degrees TDC and check the following valves:
   a. No. 4 intake, No. 4 exhaust.
   b. No. 2 exhaust

6. The collapsed lifter clearance

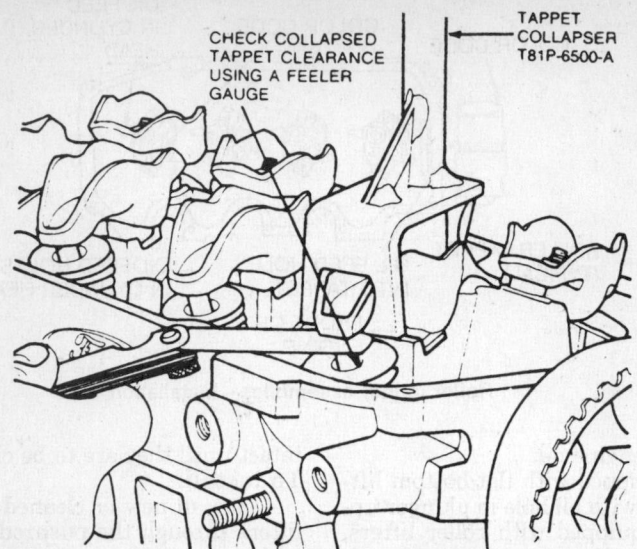

Checking the valve lifter clearance on 1.6L and 1.9L engines

Tappet Clearance Specifications

Engine	Tappet Type	Minimum Measurement	Normal Measurement	Maximum Measurement
1.9L ①	Roller	0.0mm	2.2mm	4.5mm
1.9L ①	Flat	0.7mm	2.9mm	4.2mm
1.9L ②	Roller	0.5mm	2.7mm	4.9mm
1.9L ②	Flat	1.2mm	3.4mm	5.6mm

① EFI
② EFI-HO

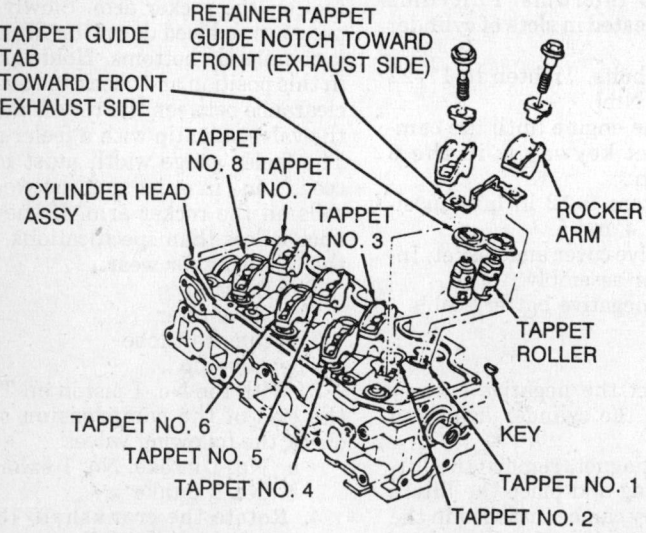

Rocker arm, fulcrum and tappet removal—1.9L engine

should be 0.059–0.194 in. On the 1.9L CFI engine, the collapsed lifter clearance should be 0.047–0.138. On the 1.9L EFI engine, the collapsed lifter clearance should be 0.059–0.150 in.

2.3L ENGINE

1. Set the No. 1 piston on TDC on the compression stroke. The timing marks on the camshaft and crankshaft gears will be together. Check the clear-

ance in No. 1 intake, No. 1 exhaust, No. 2 intake and No. 3 exhaust valves.

2. Rotate the crankshaft 1 complete turn. Check the clearance in No. 2 exhaust, No. 3 intake, No. 4 intake and No. 4 exhaust.

3. The clearance between the rocker arm and the valve stem tip should be 0.072–0.174 in. (1.80–4.34mm) with the lifter on the base circle of the cam.

Rocker Arms

REMOVAL & INSTALLATION

1.9L Engine

1. Disconnect the negative battery cable and remove the air cleaner assembly.

2. Remove and tag all necessary vacuum hoses from the rocker cover. Remove the rocker cover from the cylinder head.

3. Remove the rocker cover and gasket from the engine.

4. Remove the rocker arm nuts, fulcrums, rocker arms and fulcrum washers. Keep all parts in order so they can be reinstalled to their original position.

To install:

5. Before installation, coat the valve tips, rocker arm and fulcrum contact areas with Lubriplate® or equivalent.

6. Rotate the engine until the lifter is on the base circle of the cam (valve closed).

NOTE: Be sure to turn the engine only in the normal rotation. Backward rotation will cause the camshaft belt to slip or lose teeth, altering the valve timing and causing serious engine damage.

7. Install the rocker arm and components and torque the rocker arm bolts to 17–22 ft. lbs. (23–30 Nm). Be sure the lifter is on the base circle of the cam for each rocker arm as it is installed. Adjust the valves.

8. Install guide pins into the cylinder head and guide the gasket and rocker arm cover over the pins. Install the retaining screws and washer and torque the screws to 6–8 ft. lbs. (11.5 Nm).

9. Connect negative battery cable.

NOTE: Do not use any type of sealer with the rocker arm cover silicone gasket.

2.3L Engine

1. Disconnect the negative battery cable and remove the air cleaner assembly.

2. Remove and tag all necessary

vacuum hoses from the rocker cover. Remove the oil fill cap and set it aside. Disconnect the PCV hose and set it aside.

3. Disconnect the throttle linkage cable from the top of the rocker arm cover. Disconnect the speed control cable from the top of the rocker arm, if equipped.

4. Remove the rocker arm cover bolts. Remove the rocker cover and gasket from the engine.

5. Remove the rocker arm bolts, fulcrums, rocker arms and fulcrum washers. Keep all parts in order so they can be reinstalled to their original position.

To install:

6. Before installation, coat the valve tips, rocker arm and fulcrum contact areas with Lubriplate® or equivalent.

7. For each valve, rotate the engine until the lifter is on the base circle of the cam (valve closed).

8. Install the rocker arm and components and torque the rocker arm bolts in two steps: the first to 6–8 ft. lbs. (6–10 Nm) and the second torque to 20–26 ft. lbs. (26–38 Nm). Be sure the lifter is on the base circle of the cam for each rocker arm as it is installed. For the final tightening, the camshaft may be in any position. Adjust the valves.

9. Install guide pins into the cylinder head and guide the gasket and rocker arm cover over the pins. Install the retaining screws and washer and torque the screws to 7–10 ft. lbs. (10–13.5 Nm).

NOTE: Do not use any type of sealer with the rocker arm cover silicone gasket.

10. Install oil fill cap, all necessary vacuum hoses, PCV hose and air cleaner assembly.

11. Connect negative battery cable.

Intake Manifold

REMOVAL & INSTALLATION

1.9L EFI Engine

1. Raise and secure the hood in the open position.

2. Install protective fender covers.

3. Properly relieve the fuel system pressure. Disconnect the negative battery cable.

4. Partially drain the cooling system and disconnect the heater hose at the fitting located under the intake manifold.

5. Remove air cleaner assembly.

6. Identify, tag and disconnect the vacuum hoses.

7. Identify, tag and disconnect wiring connectors at the following points:

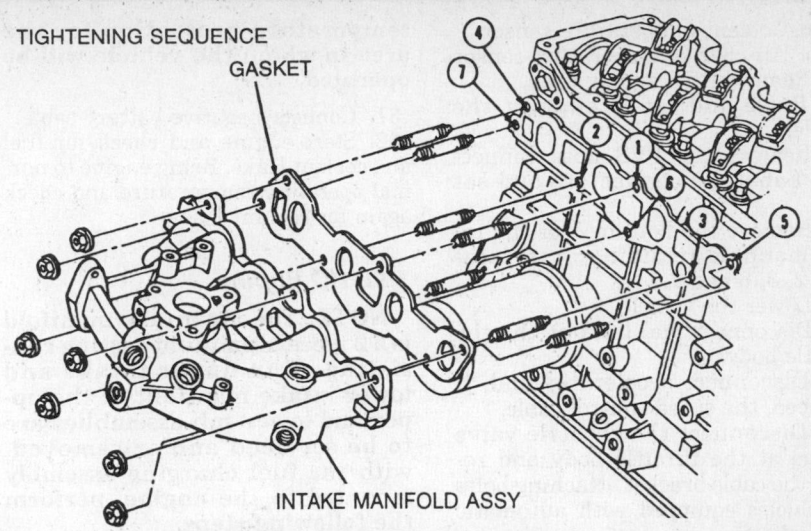

Intake manifold assembly and torque sequence—1.9L EFI engine

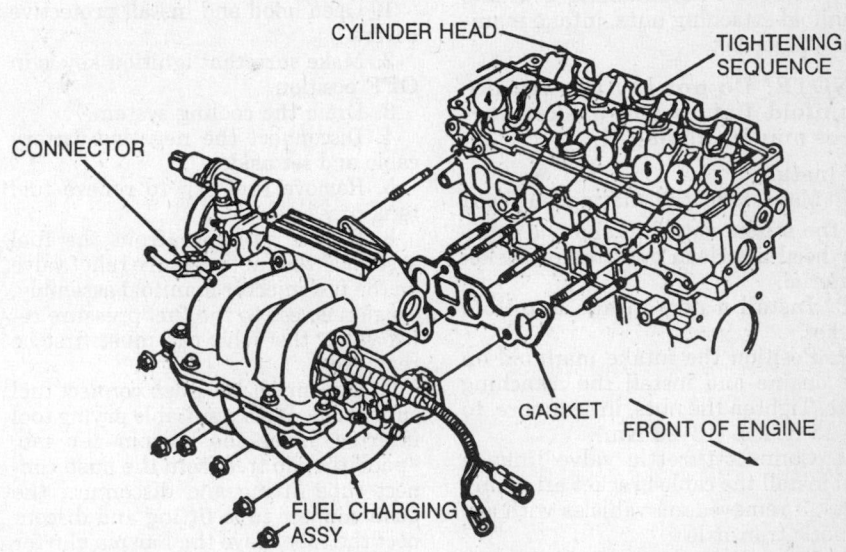

Intake manifold assembly and torque sequence—1.9L EFI HO engine

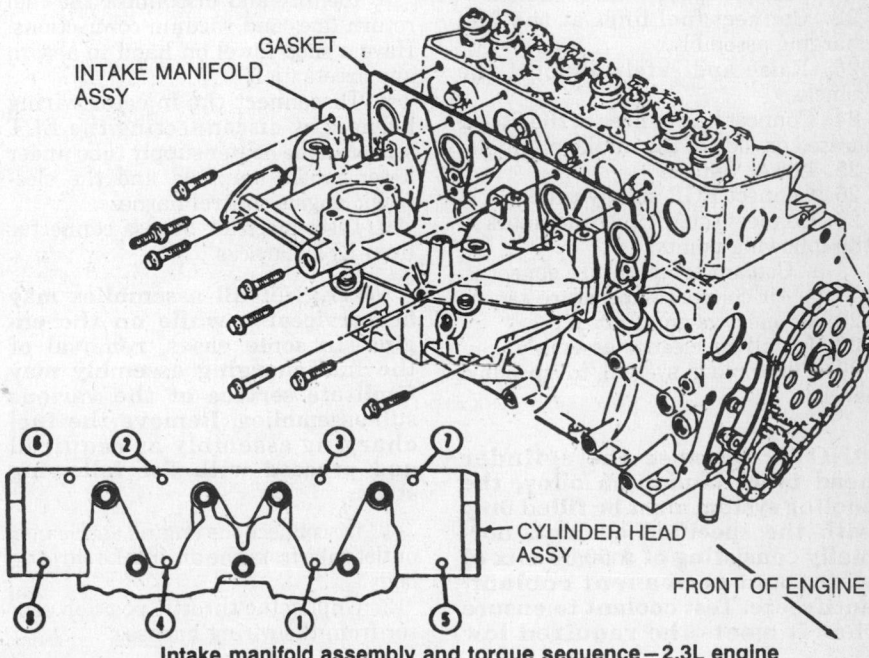

Intake manifold assembly and torque sequence—2.3L engine

   a. Coolant temperature sensor

   b. Air charge temperature sensor

8. Remove EGR supply tube.

9. Raise and safely support the vehicle.

10. Remove the PVS hose connectors. Label the connectors and set aside.

11. Remove the bottom 4 of the intake manifold retaining nuts, locations 2, 3, 6 and 7.

12. Lower the vehicle.

13. Disconnect fuel lines at the the throttle body.

14. Disconnect accelerator and, if equipped, the speed control cable.

15. Disconnect the throttle valve linkage at the throttle body and remove the cable bracket attaching bolts on vehicles equipped with automatic transaxle.

16. Remove the remaining 3 intake manifold attaching nuts, intake manifold and gasket.

NOTE: Do not lay the intake manifold flat as the gasket surfaces may be damaged.

To install:

17. Make sure the mating surfaces on the intake manifold and the cylinder head are clean and free of gasket material.

18. Install a new intake manifold gasket.

19. Position the intake manifold on the engine and install the attaching nuts. Tighten the nuts, in sequence, to 12–15 ft. lbs. (16–20 Nm).

20. Connect throttle valve linkage and install the cable bracket attaching bolts, if removed, on vehicles with automatic transaxle.

21. Connect accelerator cable and, if equipped, the speed control cable.

22. Connect fuel lines at the fuel charging assembly.

23. Raise and safely support the vehicle.

24. Connect heater hose to the fitting located on side of the intake manifold.

25. Lower vehicle.

26. Connect EGR supply tube.

27. Connect the wiring connectors at the following points:

   a. Coolant temperature sensor

   b. Air charge temperature sensor

28. Connect vacuum hoses.

29. Install air cleaner assembly.

30. Fill cooling system to specified level.

NOTE: Because the cylinder head is an aluminum alloy, the cooling system must be filled only with the specified coolant, normally consisting of a 50/50 mix of water and permanent coolant/antifreeze. Test coolant to ensure that it meets the required low

temperature protection for the area in which the vehicle will be operated.

31. Connect negative battery cable.

32. Start engine and check for fuel and coolant leaks. Bring engine to normal operating temperature and check again for coolant leaks.

1.9L HO Engine

NOTE: The air intake manifold is a 2 piece aluminum casting consisting of an upper intake and lower intake manifold. If the upper and lower sub-assemblies are to be serviced and/or removed, with the fuel charging assembly mounted to the engine, perform the following steps.

1. Open hood and install protective covers.

2. Make sure that ignition key is in **OFF** position.

3. Drain the cooling system.

4. Disconnect the negative battery cable and set aside.

5. Remove fuel cap to relieve fuel tank pressure.

6. Release pressure from the fuel system at the fuel pressure relief valve on the fuel injector manifold assembly. To gain access to the fuel pressure relief valve, the valve cap must first be removed.

7. Disconnect the push connect fuel supply line. With a suitable prying tool inserted under the hairpin clip tab, "pop" the clip free from the push connect tube fitting and disconnect the push connect tube fitting and disconnect the tube. Save the hairpin clip for use in reassembly.

8. Identify and disconnect the fuel return lines and vacuum connections. Have a shop towel on hand to absorb any excess fuel.

9. Disconnect the injector wiring harness by disconnecting the ECT sensor in the heater supply tube under lower intake manifold and the electronic engine control harness.

10. Disconnect air bypass connector from EEC harness.

NOTE: Not all assemblies may be serviceable while on the engine. In some cases, removal of the fuel charging assembly may facilitate service of the various sub-assemblies. Remove the fuel charging assembly as required and proceed with the following steps:

11. Disconnect the engine air cleaner outlet tube from the air intake throttle body.

12. Unplug the throttle position sensor from the wiring harness.

13. Unplug the air bypass valve connector.

14. Remove the upper manifold retaining bolts.

15. Remove upper manifold assembly and set it aside.

16. Remove and discard the gasket from the lower manifold assembly.

NOTE: If scraping is necessary, be careful not to damage the gasket surfaces of the upper and lower manifold assemblies, or allow material to drop into lower manifold.

To install:

17. Ensure that the gasket surfaces of the upper and lower intake manifolds are clean.

18. Place a new service gasket on the lower manifold assembly and mount the upper intake manifold to the lower, securing it with the retaining bolts. Torque the bolts to 15–22 ft. lbs.

19. Ensure the wiring harness is properly installed.

20. Connect electrical connectors to air bypass valve and throttle position sensor and the vacuum hose to the fuel pressure regulator.

21. Connect the engine air cleaner outlet tube to the throttle body intake securing it with a hose clamp tighten to 15–25 inch lbs.

22. Connect negative battery cable.

2.3L Engine

1. Open and secure the hood.

2. Disconnect the negative battery cable. Properly relieve the fuel system pressure.

3. Drain the cooling system.

4. Remove accelerator cable.

5. Remove air cleaner assembly and heat stove tube at heat shield.

6. Remove required vacuum lines and electrical connectors.

7. If equipped, remove thermactor belt from pulley. Remove hose below thermactor pump. Remove thermactor pump.

8. Disconnect the 3 exhaust pipe-to-exhaust manifold retaining nuts.

9. Remove exhaust manifold heat shield. Disconnect the oxygen sensor wire at the connector.

10. Disconnect EGR sensor wire at connector.

11. If equipped, disconnect thermactor check valve hose at tube assembly. Remove bracket-to-EGR valve attaching nuts.

12. Disconnect the water inlet tube at the intake manifold. Disconnect the fuel supply and return lines at the rubber connector.

13. Disconnect EGR tube at EGR valve.

14. Remove the intake manifold retaining bolts. Remove the intake man-

ifold. Remove the gasket and clean the gasket contact surfaces.

To install:

15. Install intake manifold with gasket and retaining bolts. Torque the retaining bolts, in the proper sequence to 15–22 ft. lbs. (20–30 Nm).

16. Connect water inlet tube at intake manifold.

17. Connect thermactor check valve hose at tube assembly. Install bracket to EGR valve attaching nuts.

18. Connect EGR sensor wire and the oxygen sensor wire at their proper connector.

19. Connect EGR tube to EGR valve.

20. Install exhaust manifold studs.

21. Connect exhaust pipe to exhaust manifold.

22. Install thermactor pump hose to pump. Install thermactor pump and thermactor pump drive belt.

23. Install vacuum lines.

24. Install air cleaner assembly and heat stove tube.

25. Install accelerator cable.

26. Connect negative ground cable and fill the cooling system.

27. Start engine and check for leaks.

Exhaust Manifold

REMOVAL & INSTALLATION

1.9L Engine

1. Disconnect the negative battery cable.

2. Remove the air cleaner assembly.

3. Disconnect the electric fan wire.

4. Remove the radiator shroud bolts and radiator shroud.

5. Disconnect the EGR tube at the exhaust manifold.

6. Disconnect thermactor tube at the exhaust manifold, if equipped. Remove the air conditioning hose bracket.

7. Remove exhaust manifold heat stove. Remove the oxygen sensor from the exhaust manifold.

8. Remove exhaust manifold retaining nuts.

9. Raise and safely support the vehicle.

10. Remove the anti-roll brace.

11. Disconnect the water tube brackets.

12. Disconnect the exhaust pipe at the catalytic converter.

13. Remove the exhaust manifold and gasket. Discard the gasket and replace with new.

To install:

14. Clean the exhaust manifold gasket contact areas.

15. Position the gasket and exhaust manifold.

16. Install exhaust pipe to the catalyst.

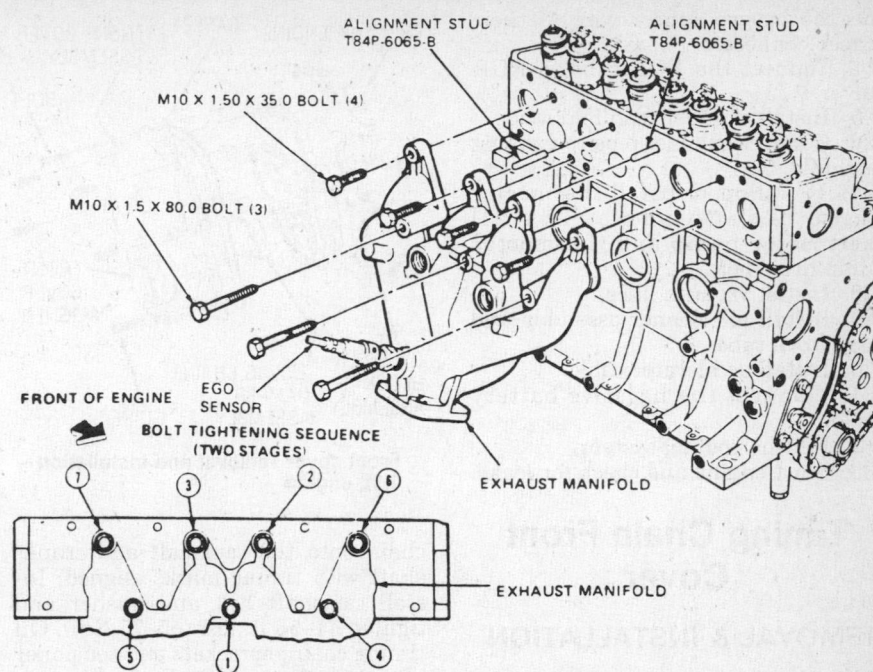

Exhaust manifold installation—2.3L HSC engine

17. Install anti-roll brace. Install water tube brackets.

18. Lower vehicle.

19. Install exhaust manifold retaining nuts. Tighten to 16–20 ft. lbs. (21–26 Nm).

20. Install exhaust manifold heat stove.

21. Install oxygen sensor in exhaust manifold. Tighten to 30–40 ft. lbs. (40–50 Nm).

22. Connect the EGR tube.

23. Install air conditioning hose brackets.

24. Position shroud and fan assembly on radiator and install bolts.

25. Connect electric fan wire.

26. Connect battery cable.

27. Install air cleaner assembly.

2.3L Engine

1. Open and secure the hood.

2. Disconnect the negative battery cable.

3. Drain the cooling system.

4. Remove the accelerator cable and position to the side.

5. Remove air cleaner assembly and heat stove tube at heat shield.

6. Identify, tag and disconnect all necessary vacuum lines.

7. If equipped, remove thermactor belt from pulley. Remove hose below thermactor pump. Remove thermactor pump.

8. Disconnect the exhaust pipe-to-exhaust manifold retaining nuts.

9. Remove exhaust manifold heat shield. Disconnect the oxygen sensor wire at the connector.

10. Disconnect EGR sensor wire at the connector.

11. Disconnect the thermactor check valve hose at tube assembly, if equipped. Remove bracket-to-EGR valve attaching nuts.

12. Disconnect water inlet tube at intake manifold.

13. Disconnect EGR tube from the EGR valve.

14. Remove the intake manifold.

15. Remove the exhaust manifold retaining nuts. Remove the exhaust manifold from the vehicle.

To install:

16. Position exhaust manifold to the cylinder head using guide bolts in holes 6 and 7.

17. Install the attaching bolts in holes 1 through 5.

18. Tighten the attaching bolts until snug, then remove guide bolts and install attaching bolts in holes 6 and 7.

19. Tighten all exhaust manifold bolts to specification using the following tightening procedure: torque retaining bolts in sequence to 5–7 ft. lbs. (7–10 Nm) then retorque in sequence to 20–30 ft. lbs. (27–41 Nm).

20. Install the intake manifold gasket and bolts. Torque the intake manifold retaining bolts, in the proper sequence to 15–22 ft. lbs. (20–30 Nm).

21. Connect the water inlet tube at intake manifold.

22. Connect thermactor check valve hose at tube assembly, if equipped. Install bracket to EGR valve attaching nuts.

23. Connect the EGR sensor wire

and the oxygen sensor wire at their proper connector.

24. Connect the EGR tube to EGR valve.

25. Install exhaust manifold studs.

26. Connect exhaust pipe to exhaust manifold.

27. If equipped install thermactor pump hose to pump. Install thermactor pump and thermactor pump drive belt.

28. Install vacuum lines.

29. Install air cleaner assembly and heat stove tube.

30. Install accelerator cable.

31. Connect the negative battery cable.

32. Fill the cooling system.

33. Start engine and check for leaks.

Timing Chain Front Cover

REMOVAL & INSTALLATION

2.3L Engine

1. Remove the engine and transaxle from the vehicle as an assembly and position in a suitable holding fixture. Remove the dipstick.

2. Remove accessory drive pulley, if equipped, Remove the crankshaft pulley attaching bolt and washer and remove pulley.

3. Remove front cover attaching bolts from front cover. Pry the top of the front cover away from the block.

4. Clean any gasket material from the surfaces.

5. Check timing chain and sprockets for excessive wear. If the timing chain and sprockets are worn, replace with new.

6. Check timing chain tensioner blade for wear depth. If the wear depth exceeds specification, replace tensioner.

7. Turn engine over until the timing marks are aligned. Remove camshaft sprocket attaching bolt and washer. Slide both sprockets and timing chain forward and remove as an assembly.

8. Check timing chain vibration damper for excessive wear and replace if necessary. The damper is located inside the front cover.

9. Remove the oil pan.

NOTE: Oil pan removal is recommended to ensure proper sealing to front cover.

To install:

10. Clean and inspect all parts before installation. Clean the oil pan, cylinder block and front cover of gasket material and dirt.

11. Slide both sprockets and timing

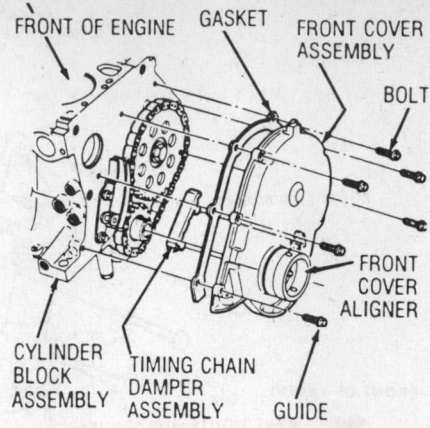

FRONT OF ENGINE   GASKET   FRONT COVER ASSEMBLY

BOLT

FRONT COVER ALIGNER

CYLINDER BLOCK ASSEMBLY   TIMING CHAIN DAMPER ASSEMBLY   GUIDE

Front cover removal and installation— 2.3L engine

chain onto the camshaft and crankshaft with timing marks aligned. Install camshaft bolt and washer and tighten 41–56 ft. lbs. (55–75 Nm). Oil timing chain, sprockets and tensioner after installation with clean engine oil.

12. Apply oil resistant sealer to a new front cover gasket and position gasket into front cover.

13. Remove the front cover oil seal and position the front cover on the engine.

14. Position front cover alignment tool T84P-6019-C or equivalent, onto the end of the crankshaft, ensuring the crank key is aligned with the keyway in the tool. Bolt the front cover to the engine and torque bolts to 6–9 ft. lbs. (8–12 Nm). Remove the front cover alignment tool.

15. If the front cover oil seal is damaged or worn, replace with new. Lubricate the hub of the crankshaft pulley with polyethylene grease to prevent damage to the seal during installation and initial engine start. Install crankshaft pulley.

16. Install the oil pan.

17. Install the accessory drive pulley, if equipped.

18. Install crankshaft pulley attaching bolt and washer. Tighten to 140–170 ft. lbs. (190–230 Nm).

19. Remove engine from work stand and install in vehicle.

Front Cover Oil Seal

REPLACEMENT

2.3L Engine

NOTE: The removal and installation of the front cover oil seal on these engines can only be accomplished with the engine removed from the vehicle.

1. Remove the engine from the ve-

hicle and position in a suitable holding fixture.

2. Remove bolt and washer at crankshaft pulley.

3. Remove the crankshaft pulley.

4. Remove the front cover oil seal.

5. Coat a new seal with grease. Install and drive the seal until it is fully seated. Check the seal after installation to be sure the spring is properly positioned in the seal.

6. Install crankshaft pulley, attaching bolt and washer. Torque the crankshaft pulley bolt to 140–170 ft. lbs. (190–230 Nm).

7. To complete the installation of the front cover oil seal, reverse the removal procedure.

Timing Chain and Sprockets

REMOVAL & INSTALLATION

2.3L Engine

1. Disconnect negative battery cable.

2. Remove engine and transaxle from vehicle as an assembly and position in a suitable holding fixture. Remove the dipstick.

3. Remove front cover from engine.

4. Check timing chain deflection as follows:

a. Rotate crankshaft counterclockwise, as viewed from the front of the engine, to take up slack on the left hand side of chain.

b. Make a reference mark on the block at approximately mid-point of chain. Measure from this point to chain.

c. Rotate crankshaft in opposite direction to take up slack on the right hand side of the chain. Force left hand side of chain out with fingers and measure distance between reference point and chain. The deflection is the difference between the 2 measurements.

d. If deflection measurement exceeds 0.5 in. (12.7mm), replace timing chain and sprockets. If wear on tensioner face exceeds 0.06 in. (1.5mm), replace tensioner.

5. Turn engine over until the timing marks are aligned. Remove camshaft sprocket attaching bolt and washer. Slide both sprockets and timing chain forward and remove as an assembly.

6. Check timing chain vibration damper for excessive wear and replace if necessary. The damper is located inside the front cover.

7. Remove the oil pan.

NOTE: Oil pan removal is recommended to ensure proper seal-

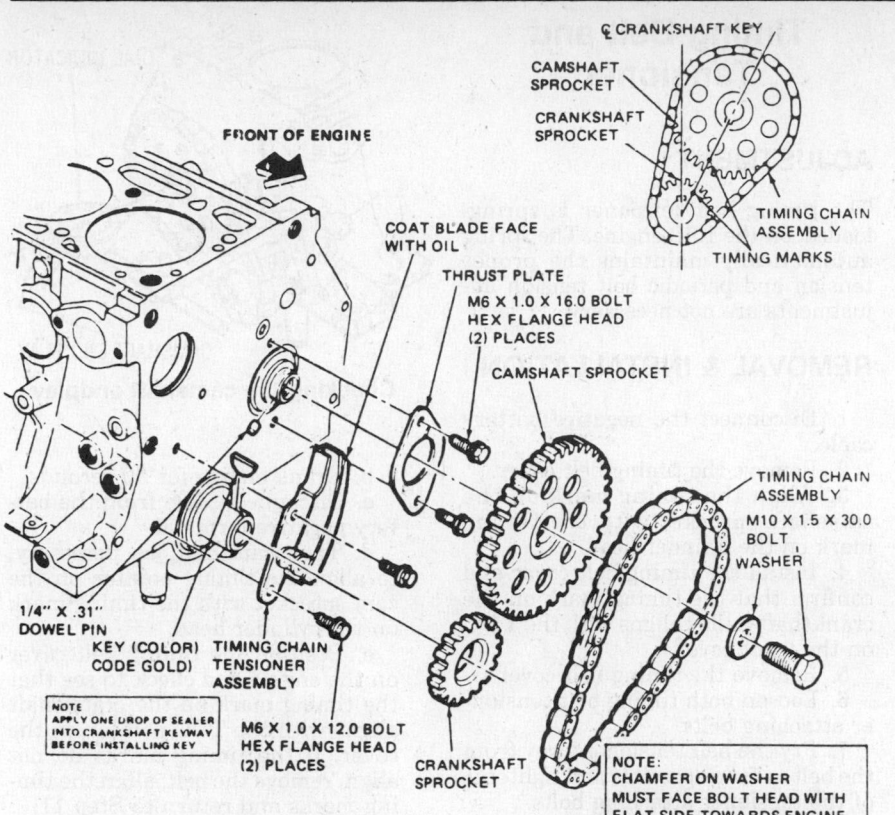

2.3 HSC engine timing chain and gear assembly

ing to front cover upon installation.

To install:

8. Clean and inspect all parts before installation. Clean the oil pan, cylinder block and front cover of gasket material and dirt.

9. Slide both sprockets and timing chain onto the camshaft and crankshaft with timing marks aligned. Install camshaft bolt and washer and tighten 41–56 ft. lbs. (55–75 Nm). Oil timing chain, sprockets and tensioner after installation with clean engine oil.

10. Apply oil resistant sealer to a new front cover gasket and position gasket into front cover.

11. Remove the front cover oil seal and position the front cover on the engine.

12. Position front cover alignment tool T84P–6019–C or equivalent, onto the end of the crankshaft, ensuring the crank key is aligned with the keyway in the tool. Bolt the front cover to the engine and torque bolts to 6–9 ft. lbs. (8–12 Nm). Remove the front cover alignment tool.

13. If the front cover oil seal is damaged or worn, replace with new. Lubricate the hub of the crankshaft pulley with polyethylene grease to prevent damage to the seal during installation and initial engine start. Install crankshaft pulley.

14. Install the oil pan.

15. Install the accessory drive pulley, if equipped.

16. Install crankshaft pulley attaching bolt and washer. Tighten to 140–170 ft. lbs. (190–230 Nm).

17. Remove engine from work stand and install in vehicle.

18. Connect negative battery cable.

Timing Belt Front Cover

REMOVAL & INSTALLATION

1. Disconnect the negative battery cable. Remove all the drive belts.

2. Remove the alternator, if necessary, to allow enough room to reach the top cover retaining bolts. Position the air conditioner compressor out of the way, if equipped to allow enough room to reach the bottom cover retainer bolts.

3. Remove the top 2 timing cover retaining nuts. Raise and safely support the vehicle.

4. Working from underneath the vehicle, remove the bottom 2 timing cover retaining cover screws. Lower the vehicle and remove the timing belt cover.

5. Complete the installation of the timing belt cover by reversing the removal procedure.

OIL SEAL REPLACEMENT

1. Disconnect the negative battery cable.

2. Remove the accessory drive belts.

3. Remove the timing belt cover.

4. Remove the timing belt.

NOTE: With the timing belt removed and pistons at TDC, do not rotate the engine. If the camshaft must be rotated, align the crankshaft pulley to 90 degrees BTDC.

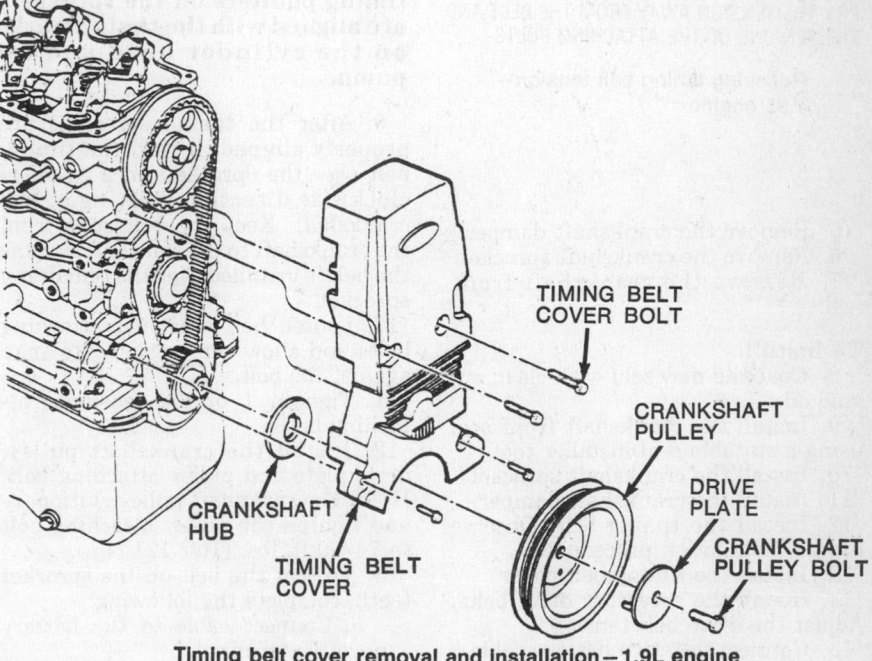

Timing belt cover removal and installation—1.9L engine

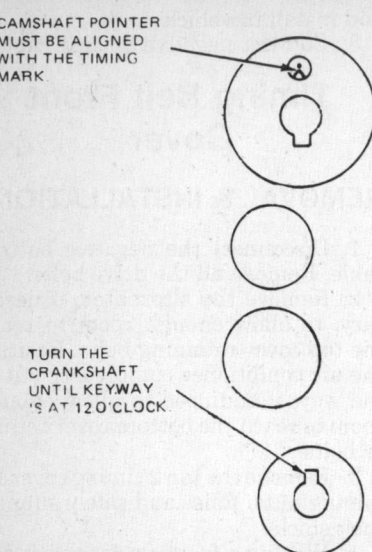

CAMSHAFT POINTER MUST BE ALIGNED WITH THE TIMING MARK

TURN THE CRANKSHAFT UNTIL KEYWAY IS AT 12 O'CLOCK

Aligning the timing marks on 1.6 and 1.9L engines

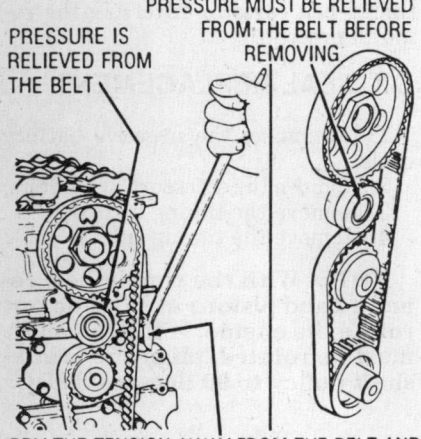

PRESSURE MUST BE RELIEVED FROM THE BELT BEFORE REMOVING

PRESSURE IS RELIEVED FROM THE BELT

PRY THE TENSION AWAY FROM THE BELT AND TIGHTEN ONE OF THE ATTACHING BOLTS

Relieving timing belt tension — 1.9L engine

5. Remove the crankshaft damper.
6. Remove the crankshaft sprocket.
7. Remove the crankshaft front seal.

To install:

8. Coat the new seal with clean engine oil.
9. Install the crankshaft front seal using a suitable seal installer tool.
10. Install the crankshaft sprocket.
11. Install the crankshaft damper.
12. Install the timing belt. Observe proper installation procedure.
13. Install the timing belt cover.
14. Install the accessory drive belts. Adjust the drive belt tension.
15. Connect negative battery cable.

Timing Belt and Tensioner

ADJUSTMENT

The timing belt tensioner is spring-loaded, on the 1.9L engine. The spring automatically maintains the proper tension and periodic belt tension adjustments are not necessary.

REMOVAL & INSTALLATION

1. Disconnect the negative battery cable.
2. Remove the timing belt cover.
3. Align the timing mark on the camshaft sprocket with the timing mark on the cylinder head.
4. Install the timing belt cover and confirm that the timing mark on the crankshaft pulley aligns with the **TDC** on the front cover.
5. Remove the timing belt cover.
6. Loosen both timing belt tensioner attaching bolts.
7. Pry the belt tensioner away from the belt as far as possible and tighten 1 of the tensioner attaching bolts.
8. Remove crankshaft pulley (damper) and remove the timing belt.

NOTE: With the timing belt removed and pistons at TDC, do not rotate the engine. If the camshaft must be rotated, align the crankshaft pulley to 90 degrees BTDC.

To install:

NOTE: Prior to installing the timing belt, make certain that the timing pointers on the sprockets are aligned with the timing marks on the cylinder head and oil pump.

9. After the timing sprockets are properly aligned, install the timing belt over the sprockets in a counterclockwise direction starting at the crankshaft. Keep the belt span from the crankshaft to the camshaft tight as the belt is installed over the remaining sprocket.
10. Loosen belt tensioner attaching bolts and allow the tensioner to snap against the belt.
11. Tighten 1 of the tensioner attaching bolts.
12. Install the crankshaft pulley, drive plate and pulley attaching bolt. Hold the crankshaft pulley stationary and tighten the pulley attaching bolt to 74–90 ft. lbs. (100–121 Nm).
13. To seat the belt on the sprocket teeth, complete the following:
    a. Connect cable to the battery negative terminal.

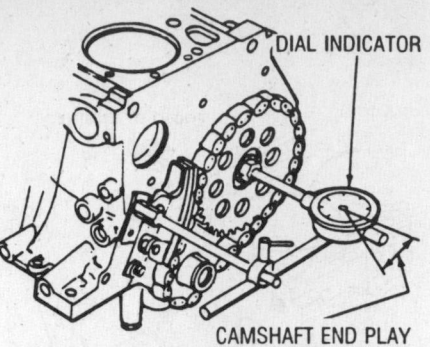

DIAL INDICATOR

CAMSHAFT END PLAY

Checking the camshaft endplay

b. Crank engine for 30 seconds.
c. Disconnect cable from the battery negative terminal.
d. Turn camshaft, as necessary, to align the timing pointer on the cam sprocket with the timing mark on the cylinder head.
e. Position the timing belt cover on the engine and check to see that the timing mark on the crankshaft aligns with the TDC pointer on the cover. If the timing marks do not align, remove the timing belt, align the timing marks and return to Step 11.
14. Loosen the belt tensioner attaching bolt tightened in Step 13.
15. Hold the crankshaft stationary and position a suitable torque wrench onto the camshaft sprocket bolt.
16. Turn the camshaft sprocket counterclockwise. Tighten the belt tensioner attaching bolt when the torque wrench reads as follows:
    a. New belt — 27–32 ft. lbs.
    b. Used belt (30 days or more in service) — 10 ft. lbs.

NOTE: The engine must be at room temperature. Do not set belt tension on a hot engine.

17. Install timing belt cover.
18. Install accessory drive belts and adjust the belt tension.
19. Connect negative battery cable.

Timing Sprockets

REMOVAL & INSTALLATION

1. Disconnect the negative battery cable.
2. Remove the timing belt cover and timing belt.

NOTE: With the timing belt removed and pistons at TDC, do not rotate the engine. If the camshaft must be rotated, align the crankshaft pulley to 90 degrees BTDC.

3. Remove the camshaft sprocket attaching bolt and washer and camshaft sprocket.

4. Remove the crankshaft sprocket attaching bolt and washer and crankshaft sprocket.

5. Install the camshaft sprocket and attaching bolt and washer. Tighten to 71–84 ft. lbs. (95–115 Nm).

6. Install the crankshaft sprocket.

7. Complete the installation of the timing sprockets by reversing the removal procedure. Observe proper installation of timing belt.

Camshaft

REMOVAL & INSTALLATION

1.9L Engine

1. Disconnect the negative battery cable.

2. Properly relieve the fuel system pressure. Remove the air cleaner and PCV hose.

3. Remove the accessory drive belts and crankshaft pulley.

4. Remove the timing belt cover and valve cover.

5. Set the engine No. 1 cylinder at TDC prior to removing timing belt.

NOTE: Make sure the crankshaft is positioned at TDC and do not turn the crankshaft until the timing belt is installed.

6. Remove rocker arms and lifters as follows:
   a. Remove hex flange bolts.
   b. Remove fulcrums.
   c. Remove rocker arms.
   d. Remove fulcrum washer.
   e. Remove tappets.

7. Remove the distributor assembly.

8. Loosen both timing belt tensioner attaching bolts using torque wrench adapter or equivalent.

9. Remove timing belt.

10. Remove the camshaft sprocket and key.

11. Remove the camshaft thrust plate.

12. Remove the ignition coil and coil bracket.

13. Remove the camshaft through the back of the head toward the transaxle.

14. Replace camshaft seal.

To install:

15. Thoroughly coat the camshaft bearing journals, cam lobe surfaces and thrust plate groove with a suitable lubricant.

16. Install camshaft through the rear of the cylinder head. Rotate camshaft during installation.

17. Install the camshaft thrust plate. Tighten attaching bolts to 7–11 ft. lbs. (10–15 Nm).

18. Align and install the cam sprocket over the cam key. Install attaching

washer and bolt. While holding camshaft stationary, tighten the bolt to 37–46 ft. lbs. (50–62.5 Nm).

19. Install the timing belt.

20. Install the timing belt cover.

21. Install the rocker arm assembly as follows:

NOTE: Replace used hex flange nuts with new ones. Lubricate all the parts with a heavy engine oil before installation.

   a. Install the lifters.
   b. Install the fulcrum washers.
   c. Install the rocker arms.
   d. Install the fulcrums.
   e. Install new rocker arm stud hex flange bolts. Tighten to 17–22 ft. lbs. (23–30 Nm).

22. Install the distributor assembly.

23. Install new valve cover gasket.

NOTE: Make sure the surfaces on the cylinder head and valve cover are clean and free of sealant material.

24. Install the rocker arm cover attaching bolts and studs. Tighten bolts and studs to 6–8 ft. lbs. (8–11.5 Nm).

25. Install PCV hose and the air cleaner assembly.

26. Connect negative battery cable.

27. Start engine and set the ignition timing.

2.3L Engine

1. Drain the cooling system, fuel system and crankcase.

2. Remove the engine from the vehicle and position in a suitable holding fixture. Remove the engine oil dipstick.

3. Remove necessary drive belts and pulleys.

4. Remove cylinder head. Remove the distributor.

5. Using a magnet, remove the hydraulic tappets and label them so that they can be installed in their original positions. If the tappets are stuck in the bores by excessive varnish, etc., use a suitable claw-type puller to remove the tappets.

6. Loosen and remove the drive belt, fan and pulley and crankshaft pulley.

7. Remove the oil pan.

8. Remove the cylinder front cover and gasket.

9. Check the camshaft endplay as follows:
   a. Push the camshaft toward the rear of the engine and install a dial indicator tool, so that the indicator point is on the camshaft sprocket attaching screw.

   b. Zero the dial indicator. Position a small pry bar or equivalent, between the camshaft sprocket or gear and block.

   c. Pull the camshaft forward and release it. Compare the dial indicator reading with the camshaft endplay specification of 0.009 in.

   d. If the camshaft endplay is over the amount specified, replace the thrust plate.

10. Remove fuel pump, gasket and fuel pump pushrod, if so equipped.

11. Remove the timing chain, sprockets and timing chain tensioner.

12. Remove camshaft thrust plate. Carefully remove the camshaft by pulling it toward the front of the engine. Use caution to avoid damaging bearings, journals and lobes.

To install:

13. Clean and inspect all parts before installation.

14. Lubricate camshaft lobes and journals with heavy engine oil. Carefully slide the camshaft through the bearings in the cylinder block.

15. Install the thrust plate. Tighten attaching bolts to 6–9 ft. lbs (8–12 Nm).

16. Install the timing chain, sprockets and timing chain tensioner. Check timing chain deflection.

17. Install the cylinder front cover and crankshaft pulley.

18. Clean the oil pump inlet tube screen, oil pan and cylinder block gasket surfaces. Prime oil pump by filling the inlet opening with oil and rotate the pump shaft until oil emerges from the outlet tube. Install oil pump, oil pump inlet tube screen and oil pan.

19. Install the accessory drive belts and pulleys.

20. Lubricate the tappets and tappets bores with heavy engine oil. Install tappets into their original bores.

21. Install cylinder head.

22. Install fuel pump, new gasket and fuel pump push rod, if so equipped. Tighten bolts to 15–21 ft. lbs. (20–28 Nm).

23. Position No. 1 piston at TDC after the compression stroke. Position distributor in the block with the rotor at the No. 1 firing position. Install distributor retaining clamp.

24. Connect engine temperature sending unit wire. Connect coil primary wire. Install distributor cap. Connect spark plug wires and the coil high tension lead.

25. Install engine in vehicle.

26. Fill the cooling system and crankcase to the proper levels.

27. Connect negative battery cable.

28. Start the engine. Check and adjust ignition timing. Connect distributor vacuum line to distributor. Check for leaks. Adjust engine idle speed.

Piston and Connecting Rod

POSITIONING

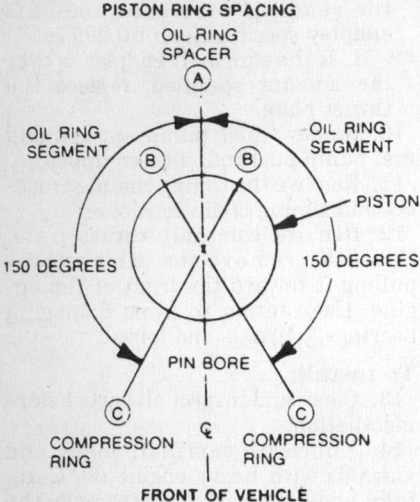

PISTON RING SPACING

OIL RING SPACER — A

OIL RING SEGMENT — B

OIL RING SEGMENT — B

PISTON

150 DEGREES

150 DEGREES

PIN BORE

COMPRESSION RING — C

COMPRESSION RING — C

FRONT OF VEHICLE

Piston ring positioning – 1.9L engine

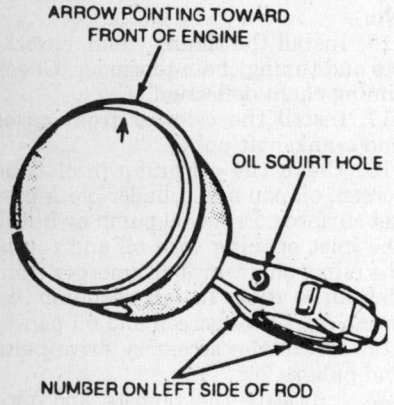

ARROW POINTING TOWARD FRONT OF ENGINE

OIL SQUIRT HOLE

NUMBER ON LEFT SIDE OF ROD

2.3L engine piston and rod assembly

DIESEL ENGINE MECHANICAL

Engine Assembly

REMOVAL & INSTALLATION

NOTE: Be sure to use the proper equipment when removing the engine and transaxle assembly, as the assembly is removed from underneath the vehicle.

1. Mark the position of the hood hinges and remove the hood.
2. Remove the negative ground cable from battery that is located in luggage compartment.
3. Properly relieve the fuel system pressure. Remove the air cleaner assembly.
4. Position a drain pan under the lower radiator hose. Remove the hose and drain the engine coolant.
5. Remove the upper radiator hose from the engine.
6. Disconnect the cooling fan at the electrical connector.
7. Remove the radiator shroud and cooling fan as an assembly. Remove the radiator.
8. Remove the starter cable from the starter.
9. Discharge air conditioning system, if equipped. Remove the pressure and suction lines from the air conditioning compressor. Cover or plug the line openings to prevent the entry of moisture and dirt.
10. Identify and disconnect all vacuum lines as necessary.
11. Disconnect the engine harness connectors (2) at the dash panel. Disconnect the glow plug relay connectors at the dash panel.

NOTE: Connectors are located under the plastic shield on the dash panel. Remove and save plastic retainer pins. Disconnect the alternator wiring connector on right hand fender apron.

12. Disconnect the clutch cable from the shift lever on transaxle.
13. Disconnect the injection pump throttle linkage.
14. Disconnect the fuel supply and return hoses on the engine.
15. Disconnect the power steering pressure and return lines at the power steering pump, if equipped. Remove the power steering lines bracket at the cylinder head.
16. Install engine support tool D79P-8000-A or equivalent, to existing engine lifting eye.
17. Raise the vehicle and support it safely.
18. Remove the bolt attaching the exhaust pipe bracket to the oil pan.
19. Remove the 2 exhaust pipes to exhaust manifold attaching nuts.
20. Pull the exhaust system out of rubber insulating grommets and set aside.
21. Remove the speedometer cable from the transaxle.
22. Position a drain pan under the heater hoses. Remove 1 heater hose from the water pump inlet tube. Remove the other heater hose from the oil cooler.
23. Remove the bolts attaching the control arms to the body. Remove the stabilizer bar bracket retaining bolts and remove the brackets.

24. Halfshaft assemblies must be removed from the transaxle at this time.
25. On manual transaxle equipped vehicles, remove the shift stabilizer bar-to-transaxle attaching bolts. Remove the shift mechanism to shift shaft attaching nut and bolt at the transaxle.
26. Remove the left rear insulator mount bracket from body bracket by removing the 2 nuts.
27. Remove the left front insulator to transaxle mounting bolts.
28. Lower the vehicle. Install lifting equipment to the 2 existing lifting eyes on engine.

NOTE: Do not allow front wheels to touch floor.

29. Remove engine support tool D79L-8000-A or equivalent.
30. Remove right insulator intermediate bracket to engine bracket bolts, intermediate bracket to insulator attaching nuts and the nut on the bottom of the double ended stud attaching the intermediate bracket to engine bracket. Remove the bracket.
31. Carefully lower the engine and transaxle assembly to the floor.

To install:

32. Raise the vehicle support safely.
33. Position the engine and transaxle assembly directly below the engine compartment.
34. Slowly lower the vehicle over the engine and transaxle assembly.

NOTE: Do not allow the front wheels to touch floor.

35. Install the lifting equipment to both existing engine lifting eyes on engine.
36. Raise the engine and transaxle assembly up through engine compartment and position accordingly.
37. Install right insulator intermediate attaching nuts and intermediate bracket to engine bracket bolts. Install nut on bottom of double ended stud attaching intermediate bracket to engine bracket. Tighten to 75–100 ft. lbs. (100–135 Nm).
38. Install engine support tool D79L-8000-A or equivalent, to the engine lifting eye.
39. Remove the lifting equipment.
40. Raise the vehicle.
41. Position a suitable floor or transaxle jack under engine. Raise the engine and transaxle assembly into mounted position.
42. Install insulator to bracket nut and tighten to 75–100 lbs. (100–135 Nm).
43. Tighten the left rear insulator bracket to body bracket nuts to 75–100 ft. lbs. (100–135 Nm).
44. Install the lower radiator hose and install retaining bracket and bolt.

45. Install the shift stabilizer bar to transaxle attaching bolt. Tighten to 23–35 ft. lbs. (31–47 Nm).

46. Install the shift mechanism to input shift shaft (on transaxle) bolt and nut. Tighten to 7–10 ft. lbs. (9–13 Nm).

47. Install the lower radiator hose to the radiator.

48. Install the speedometer cable to the transaxle.

49. Connect the heater hoses to the water pump and oil cooler.

50. Position the exhaust system up and into insulating rubber grommets located at the rear of the vehicle.

51. Install the exhaust pipe to exhaust manifold bolts.

52. Install the exhaust pipe bracket to the oil pan bolt.

53. Place the stabilizer bar and control arm assembly into position. Install control arm to body attaching bolts. Install the stabilizer bar brackets and tighten all fasteners.

54. Halfshaft assemblies must be installed at this time.

55. Lower the vehicle.

56. Remove the engine support tool D79L-6000-A or equivalent.

57. Connect the alternator wiring at the right fender apron.

58. Connect the engine harness to main harness and glow plug relays at dash panel. Reinstall the plastic shield.

59. Connect the vacuum lines.

60. Install the air conditioning discharge and suction lines to air conditioning compressor, if equipped. Do not charge system at this time.

61. Connect the fuel supply and return lines to the injection pump.

62. Connect the injection pump throttle cable.

63. Install the power steering pressure and return lines. Install bracket.

64. Connect the clutch cable to shift lever on transaxle.

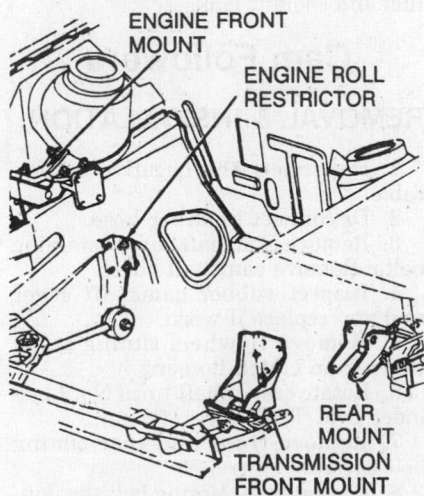

ENGINE FRONT MOUNT

ENGINE ROLL RESTRICTOR

REAR MOUNT

TRANSMISSION FRONT MOUNT

Engine/transmissions mounts – 2.0L Diesel engine

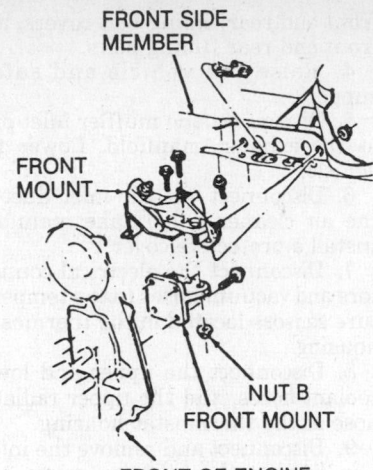

FRONT SIDE MEMBER

FRONT MOUNT

NUT B FRONT MOUNT

FRONT OF ENGINE

Front transmission mount – 2.0L Diesel engine

65. Connect the battery cable to starter.

66. Install the radiator shroud and coolant fan assembly. Tighten attaching bolts.

67. Connect the coolant fan electrical connector.

68. Install the upper radiator hose to engine.

69. Fill and bleed the cooling system.

70. Install the negative ground battery cable to battery.

71. Install the air cleaner assembly.

72. Install the hood.

73. Charge air conditioning system, if equipped.

74. Check and refill all fluid levels.

75. Start the engine. Check for leaks.

Engine Mounts

REMOVAL & INSTALLATION

Front Engine Mount

1. Disconnect the negative battery cable.

2. Support engine and transaxle using a floor jack and a wood block. Raise engine approximately ½ in. (12.7mm) to unload engine mount.

3. Remove nut B from engine mount. Nut B is removed from underneath the vehicle.

4. Remove top bolts from engine mount.

5. Lower engine assembly 1–2 in. (25–50mm) for clearance.

6. From inside right hand front wheel well, remove 2 nuts attaching engine mount to fender apron.

7. Remove 2 bolts attaching engine mount to right hand front rail.

8. Slide engine mount toward engine until studs clear fender apron. Remove mount.

To install:

9. Position engine mount on right hand front side members and loosely install 2 attaching bolts.

10. From inside right hand wheel well, install 2 attaching nuts and tighten to 75–100 ft. lbs. (100–135 Nm). Tighten 2 mount bolts on right front rail to 37–55 ft. lbs. (50-75 Nm).

11. Raise engine until engine bracket contacts engine mount.

12. Install nut B and top bolts. Tighten to 60-90 ft. lbs. (80–120 Nm).

13. Remove floor jack and wood block.

14. Connect negative battery cable.

Transaxle Mount

FRONT

1. Disconnect the negative battery cable.

2. Support transaxle with a floor jack and wood block.

3. Remove 3 bolts attaching mount to transaxle. Raise engine approximately ½ in. (12.7mm) to unload mount.

3. Remove nut attaching mount to left hand stabilizer bar bracket and remove mount.

To install:

4. Position mount on stabilizer bar bracket and install 3 bolts attaching mount to transaxle and tighten to 25–37 ft. lbs. (35–50 Nm).

5. Install attaching nut to stabilizer bar bracket and tigthen to 80–100 ft. lbs. (108–136 Nm).

6. Remove floor jack and wood block and connect battery ground cable.

REAR

1. Disconnect the negative battery cable.

2. Support with a floor jack and wood block. Raise engine approximately ½ in. (12.7mm) to unload mount.

3. Remove 2 nuts attaching mount to bracket.

4. Remove 2 bolts attaching mount to transaxle and remove mount.

To install:

5. Position mount on transaxle and install 2 attaching bolts. Tighten bolts to 30–45 ft. lbs. (41–61 Nm).

6. Install 2 nuts attaching engine mount to bracket and tighten to 80–100 ft. lbs. (108–136 Nm).

7. Remove floor jack and wood block and connect battery ground cable.

Cylinder Head

REMOVAL & INSTALLATION

1. Disconnect the battery ground cable from the battery, which is located in the luggage compartment.

2. Properly relieve the fuel system pressure. Drain the cooling system.

3. Remove the camshaft cover,

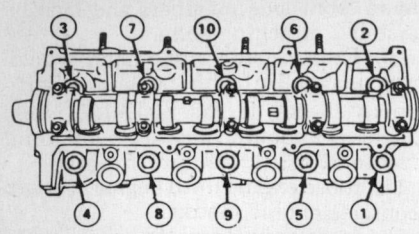

2.0L diesel cylinder head bolt removal

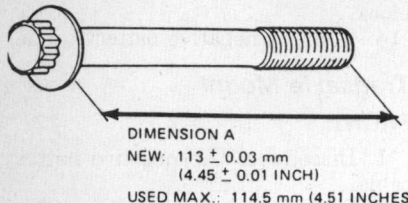

DIMENSION A
NEW: 113 ± 0.03 mm
(4.45 ± 0.01 INCH)
USED MAX.: 114.5 mm (4.51 INCHES)

2.0L diesel head bolt measurement

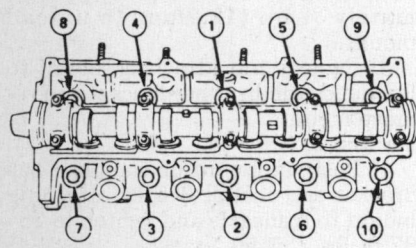

2.0L diesel head bolt tightening sequence

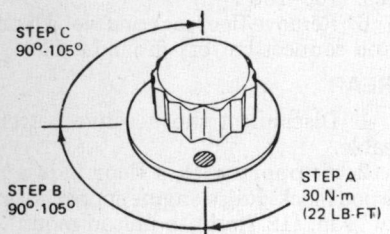

STEP C
90°-105°

STEP B
90°-105°

STEP A
30 N·m
(22 LB-FT)

2.0L diesel head bolt tightening steps

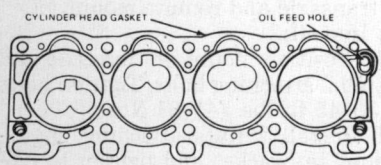

CYLINDER HEAD GASKET   OIL FEED HOLE

2.0L diesel head gasket identification

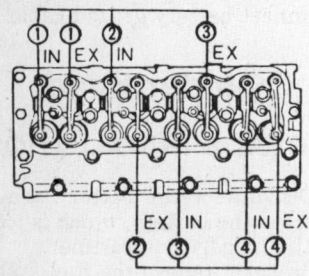

Diesel engine valve adjustment sequence

front and rear timing belt covers, and front and rear timing belts.

4. Raise the vehicle and safely support.

5. Disconnect the muffler inlet pipe at the exhaust manifold. Lower the vehicle.

6. Disconnect the air inlet duct at the air cleaner and intake manifold. Install a protective cover.

7. Disconnect the electrical connectors and vacuum hoses to the temperature sensors located in the thermostat housing.

8. Disconnect the upper and lower coolant hoses, and the upper radiator hose at the thermostat housing.

9. Disconnect and remove the injection lines at the injection pump and nozzles. Cap all lines and fittings.

10. Disconnect the glow plug harness from the main engine harness.

11. Remove the cylinder head bolts in the proper sequence. Remove the cylinder head.

12. Remove the glow plugs. Then remove pre-chamber cups from the cylinder head using a brass drift.

13. Clean the pre-chamber cups, pre-chambers in the cylinder heads and all gasket mounting surfaces on the cylinder head and engine block.

To install:

14. Install the pre-chambers in the cylinder heads making sure the locating pins are aligned with the slots provided.

15. Install the glow plugs and tighten to 11–15 ft. lbs. Connect glow plug harness to the glow plugs. Tighten the nuts to 5–7 ft. lbs.

NOTE: Carefully blow out the head bolt threads in the crankcase with compressed air. Failure to thoroughly clean the thread bores can result in incorrect cylinder head torque or possible cracking of the crankcase.

16. Position a new cylinder head gasket on the crankcase making sure the cylinder head oil feed hole is not blocked.

17. Measure each cylinder head bolt dimension A. If the measurement is more than 4.51 in. (114.5mm), replace the head bolt. Rotate the camshaft in the cylinder head until the cam lobes for No. 1 cylinder are at the base circle, both valves closed. Then, rotate the crankshaft clockwise until No. 1 piston is halfway up in the cylinder bore toward TDC. This is to prevent contact between the pistons and valves.

18. Install the cylinder head.

NOTE: Before installing the cylinder head bolts, paint a white reference dot on each one and apply a light coat of engine oil on the bolt threads.

19. Tighten cylinder head bolts as follows:

a. Tighten bolts in sequence to 22 ft. lbs.

b. Using the painted reference marks, tighten each bolt, in sequence, another 90–105 degrees.

c. Repeat Step b by turning the bolts another 90–105 degrees.

20. Connect the glow plug harness to main engine harness.

21. Remove the protective caps and install injection lines to the injection pump and nozzles. Tighten capnuts to 18–20 ft. lbs.

22. Air bleed the system.

23. Connect the upper and lower coolant hoses, and the upper radiator hose to the thermostat housing. Tighten upper coolant hose bolts to 5–7 ft. lbs.

24. Connect the electrical connectors and the vacuum hoses to the temperature sensors in the thermostat housing.

25. Remove the protective cover and install the air inlet duct to the intake manifold and air cleaner.

26. Raise the vehicle and support it safely. Connect the muffler inlet pipe to the exhaust manifold. Tighten nuts to 25–35 ft. lbs.

27. Lower the vehicle.

28. Install and adjust the front timing belt.

29. Install and adjust the rear timing belt.

30. Install the front upper timing belt cover and rear timing belt cover. Tighten the bolts to 5–7 ft. lbs.

31. Check and adjust the valves. Install the valve cover and tighten the bolts to 5–7 ft. lbs.

32. Fill and bleed the cooling system.

33. Check and adjust the injection pump timing.

34. Connect battery ground cable to battery. Run engine and check for oil, fuel and coolant leaks.

Cam Followers

REMOVAL & INSTALLATION

1. Disconnect the negative battery cable.

2. Disconnect breather hose.

3. Remove camshaft cover retaining bolts. Remove camshaft cover.

4. Inspect rubber camshaft cover seal and replace if worn.

5. Remove flywheel timing mark cover from clutch housing.

6. Rotate crankshaft until No. 1 cylinder is at TDC.

7. Remove front and rear timing belt covers.

8. Loosen front timing belt tensioner and remove from camshaft sprocket.

9. Using an adjustable wrench on boss provided on camshaft, loosen bolt attaching front camshaft sprocket to camshaft.

10. Hold camshaft with adjustable wrench and remove bolt retaining rear camshaft sprocket to camshaft.

11. Remove camshaft sprockets using puller T77F-4220-B1 and shaft protector D80L-625-4 or equivalent.

NOTE: Failure to follow procedures exactly as described in Steps 10 and 11 can result in damage to cylinder head and/or camshaft.

11. Remove No. 1, No. 3 and No. 5 camshaft bearing caps first.

12. For camshaft bearing caps No. 2 and No. 4, loosen as follows:

    a. Loosen one nut 2–3 turns.

    b. Loosen remaining nuts one at a time, 2–3 turns.

    c. Repeat this sequence, turning each nut 2–3 turns at a time, until all nuts are loose.

13. Remove camshaft and discard camshaft seals.

14. Remove cam followers and note their location so they can be returned to their original position.

To install:

NOTE: Camshaft bearings are to be installed with arrows pointing toward front of engine. No. 2, No. 3 and No. 4 bearing caps have their numbers cast in top surface. No. 1 and No. 5 bearings are not marked. However, No. 1 bearing cap has a slot to fit over camshaft thrust flange.

15. Install cam followers in their original positions.

NOTE: Follow Steps 15 through 17 exactly as described. Failure to do so may result in damage to the cylinder head and/or camshaft.

16. Position camshaft in cylinder head and install No. 2 and No. 4 bearing caps as follows:

    a. Tighten one nut 2–3 turns.

    b. Tighten remaining nuts, one at time, 2–3 turns.

    c. Repeat this sequence, turning each nut 2–3 turns, until bearing caps are seated.

17. Install No. 1 , No. 3 and No. 5 bearing caps. Tighten nuts for all 5 bearing caps to 15–19 ft. lbs. (20–27 Nm).

18. Install a new rear camshaft oil seal using a $1^{7}/_{16}$ in. (36.5mm) socket and a hammer.

19. Install a new front camshaft oil seal using valve stem seal installer T84P-6019-A or equivalent.

20. Install front and rear camshaft sprockets. While holding camshaft

with an adjustable wrench. Tighten camshaft sprocket bolts to 41–59 ft. lbs. (56–82 Nm).

21. Install and adjust front and rear timing belts.

22. Check and adjust valves, as necessary.

23. Install camshaft cover and tighten bolts to 5–7 ft. lbs. (7–10 Nm).

24. Connect breather hose.

25. Connect negative battery cable.

Valve Lash

ADJUSTMENT

1. Warm up the engine and allow to reach normal operating temperature.

2. Remove the valve cover.

3. Set No. 1 cylinder to TDC on the compression stroke and check the valve clearance of No. 1 and No. 2 intake and No. 1 and No. 3 exhaust valves.

4. Clearance for intake valves should be 0.008–0.011 in. (0.20–0.30mm). Exhaust valve clearance should be 0.011–0.015 in. (0.30–0.40mm).

5. Rotate the crankshaft 360 degrees and check the clearance of the No. 3 and No. 4 intake and No. 2 and No. 4 exhaust valves.

6. If adjustment is necessary, rotate the crankshaft until the cam lobe of the valve requiring adjustment is down against the cam follower.

7. Position the special cam follower retainer tool T84P-6513-B or equivalent, under the cam between the lobes so that the edge contacts the cam follower needing adjustment.

8. Rotate the camshaft until the cam lobe (of valve needing adjustment) is on its base circle (lobe pointing straight up).

9. Pry the adjusting shim out of the cam follower and replace with a new shim.

NOTE: Valve shims are available in thicknesses ranging from 0.13–0.18 in. (3.40–4.60mm). If the valve was too tight or loose, install a shim of the appropriate size. Shim thickness is stamped on the valve shim. Install the shim with the numbers down to avoid wearing the numbers off.

10. Rotate the camshaft until the lobe is down and remove the retainer tool.

11. Recheck the valve clearance by repeating the previous steps.

12. Install the valve cover using a new gasket. Tighten the retaining bolts to 5–7 ft. lbs. (7–10 Nm).

Intake Manifold

REMOVAL & INSTALLATION

1. Disconnect the negative battery cable. Disconnect the air inlet duct from the intake manifold and install a protective cap in the intake manifold.

2. Disconnect the glow plug resistor electrical connector.

3. Disconnect the breather hose.

4. Drain the cooling system.

5. Disconnect the upper radiator hose at the thermostat housing.

6. Disconnect the coolant hose at the thermostat housing.

7. Disconnect the connectors to the temperature sensors in the thermostat housing.

8. Remove the bolts attaching the intake manifold to the cylinder head and remove the intake manifold.

9. Clean the intake manifold and cylinder head gasket mating surfaces.

To install:

10. Install the intake manifold, using a new gasket, and tighten the bolts to 12–16 ft. lbs. (16–23 Nm).

11. Connect the temperature sensor connectors.

12. Connect the upper radiator hose to the thermostat housing and tighten the hose clamp.

13. Connect the coolant hose at the thermostat housing.

14. Connect the breather hose.

15. Connect the glow plug resistor electrical connector.

16. Remove the protective cap and install the air inlet duct.

17. Fill and bleed the cooling system.

18. Connect negative battery cable.

19. Run the engine and check for intake air leaks and coolant leaks.

Exhaust Manifold

REMOVAL & INSTALLATION

1. Disconnect the negative battery cable. Remove the nuts attaching the muffler inlet pipe to the exhaust manifold.

2. Remove the bolts attaching the heat shield to the exhaust manifold.

3. Remove the nuts attaching the exhaust manifold to cylinder head and remove the exhaust manifold.

To install:

4. Install the exhaust manifold, using new gaskets, and tighten nuts to 16–20 ft. lbs. (22–27 Nm).

5. Install the exhaust shield and tighten bolts to 12–16 ft. lbs. (16–23 Nm).

6. Connect the muffler inlet pipe to the exhaust manifold and tighten the nuts to 25–35 ft. lbs. (34–47 Nm).

7. Connect negative battery cable.

8. Run the engine and check for exhaust leaks.

Timing Belt Front Cover

REMOVAL & INSTALLATION

1. Disconnect the negative battery cable.

2. Remove front timing belt upper cover and flywheel timing mark cover.

3. Rotate engine clockwise until timing marks on flywheel and front camshaft sprocket are aligned with their pointers.

4. Connect a suitable engine support bar tool to existing engine lifting eyes.

5. With engine supported using the tool, remove right hand side engine mount and insulator assembly.

6. Remove accessory drive belts.

7. Lower engine until crankshaft pulley clears right hand side frame rail.

8. Install a suitable flywheel holding tool.

9. Remove 6 bolts attaching crankshaft pulley to crankshaft sprocket.

10. Install a suitable crankshaft pulley remover and remove crankshaft pulley.

11. Remove front timing belt lower cover.

To install:

12. Install front timing belt lower cover. Tighten bolts to 5–7 ft. lbs. (7–10 Nm).

13. Install crankshaft pulley. Tighten bolts to 17–24 ft. lbs. (23–32 Nm).

14. Remove flywheel holding tool.

15. Install flywheel timing mark cover.

16. Raise engine into position and install right hand engine mount.

17. Remove engine support bar tool.

18. Connect negative battery cable.

OIL SEAL REPLACEMENT

1. Disconnect the negative battery cable.

2. Remove crankshaft pulley and front timing belt.

3. Remove crankshaft timing sprocket bolt.

4. Remove crankshaft timing sprocket using an appropriate pulley remover and tip adapter.

5. Remove crankshaft front oil seal using carburetor jet plug remover T77L-9533-B or equivalent. Discard seal.

To install:

6. Coat sealing surface of new seal with engine oil.

7. Install seal using a suitable installer and the sprocket retaining bolt.

8. Remove the retaining bolt and seal installer, and install crankshaft timing sprocket. Tighten to 116–123 ft. lbs. (160–170 Nm).

9. Install and adjust front timing belt.

10. Install front timing belt lower cover.

11. Install crankshaft pulley. Tighten bolts to 17–24 ft. lbs. (23–33 Nm).

12. Install front timing belt upper cover.

13. Connect negative battery cable.

Timing Belt and Tensioner

ADJUSTMENT

Front

1. Disconnect the negative battery cable.

2. Remove front timing belt upper cover.

3. Remove flywheel timing mark cover.

4. Rotate crankshaft pulley 2 revolutions clockwise until flywheel TDC timing mark aligns with pointer on rear cover plate.

5. Check front camshaft sprocket to see that it is aligned with its timing mark.

6. Tighten tensioner lockbolt to 23–34 ft. lbs. (32–47 Nm).

7. Check belt tension using a suitable belt tension gauge. Belt tension should be 33–44 lbs. (147–196 N).

8. Install front cover. Tighten attaching bolts to 5–7 ft. lbs. (7–10 Nm).

9. Install flywheel timing mark cover.

10. Connect negative battery cable.

Rear

1. Disconnect the negative battery cable.

2. Remove the flywheel timing mark cover.

3. Remove rear timing belt cover.

4. Loosen tensioner pulley locknut.

5. Rotate crankshaft 2 revolutions until flywheel TDC timing mark aligns with pointer on rear cover plate.

6. Check that rear camshaft sprocket and injection pump sprocket are aligned with their timing marks.

7. Tighten tensioner locknut to 15–20 ft. lbs. (20–27 Nm).

8. Check belt tension using a suitable belt tension gauge. Belt tension should be 22–33 lbs. (98–147 N).

9. Install rear timing belt cover. Tighten 6mm bolts to 6–8 ft. lbs. (7–12 Nm) and 9mm bolts to 12–16 ft. lbs. (16–23 Nm).

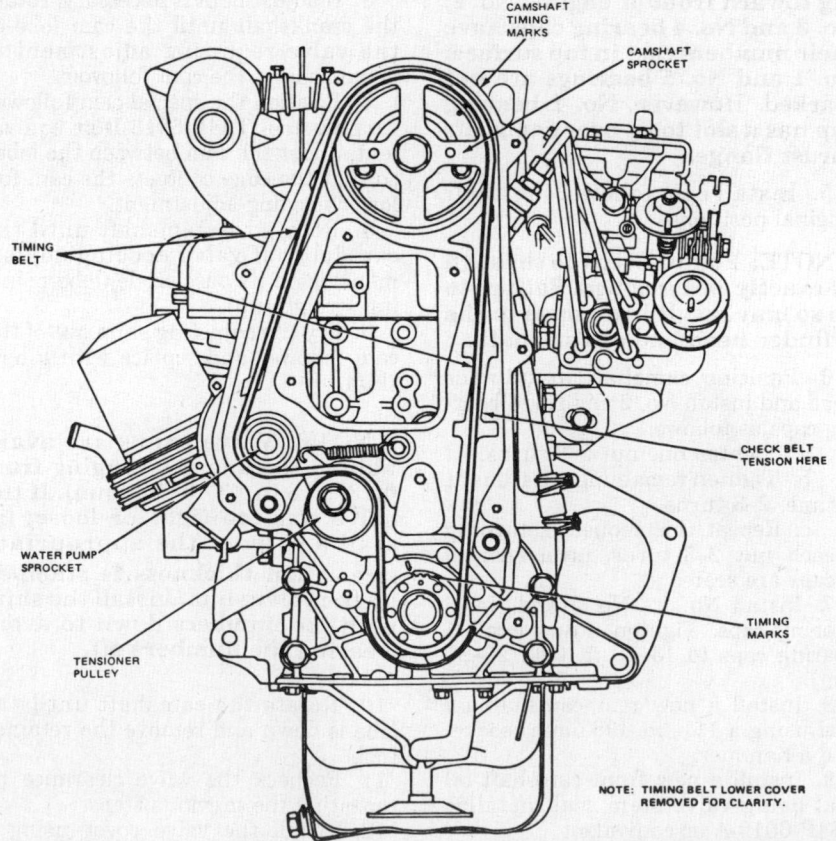

2.0L diesel timing belt installation

10. Install flywheel timing mark cover.

11. Connect negative battery cable.

REMOVAL & INSTALLATION

Front

1. Disconnect the negative battery cable.

2. Remove front timing belt upper cover and flywheel timing mark cover.

3. Rotate engine clockwise until timing marks on flywheel and front camshaft sprocket are aligned with their pointers.

4. Connect a suitable engine support bar tool to existing engine lifting eyes.

5. With engine supported using the tool, remove right hand side engine mount and insulator assembly.

6. Remove accessory drive belts.

7. Lower engine until crankshaft pulley clears right hand side frame rail.

8. Install a suitable flywheel holding tool.

9. Remove 6 bolts attaching crankshaft pulley to crankshaft sprocket.

10. Install a suitable crankshaft pulley remover and remove crankshaft pulley.

11. Remove front timing belt lower cover.

12. Loosen tensioning pulley and remove timing belt. Remove belt tensioner.

To install:

13. Push tensioner lever toward water pump as far as it will travel and tighten lockbolt snug.

14. With flywheel timing mark at TDC and camshaft aligned with its timing mark, install front timing belt.

NOTE: Check camshaft sprocket to ensure timing marks are aligned.

15. Adjust timing belt tension.

16. Install front timing belt lower cover. Tighten bolts to 5–7 ft. lbs. (7–10 Nm).

17. Install crankshaft pulley. Tighten bolts to 17–24 ft. lbs. (23–32 Nm).

18. Remove flywheel holding tool.

19. Install flywheel timing mark cover.

20. Raise engine into position and install right hand engine mount.

21. Remove engine support bar tool.

22. Connect negative battery cable.

Rear

1. Disconnect the negative battery cable.

2. Remove the rear timing belt cover.

3. Remove the flywheel timing mark cover from clutch housing.

4. Rotate the crankshaft until the flywheel timing mark is at TDC on No. 1 cylinder.

5. Check that the injection pump and camshaft sprocket timing marks are aligned.

6. Loosen the tensioner locknut. With a suitable tool inserted in the slot provided, rotate the tensioner clockwise to relieve belt tension. Tighten locknut snug.

7. Remove the timing belt. Remove the belt tensioner.

To install:

8. Install the belt tensioner. Install the belt.

9. Loosen the tensioner locknut and adjust timing belt.

10. Install rear timing belt cover and tighten bolts to 5–7 ft. lbs.

11. Connect negative battery cable.

Timing Sprockets

REMOVAL & INSTALLATION

Front

1. Disconnect the negative battery cable.

2. Remove front timing belt.

3. Remove crankshaft timing sprocet.

4. Remove cam cover.

5. With an adjustable wrench, hold camshaft on boss provided to prevent camshaft from turning.

6. Remove camshaft front timing sprocket.

To install:

7. Install crankshaft timing sprocket. Tighten attaching bolt to 116–123 ft. lbs. (160–170 Nm).

8. With an adjustable wrench, hold camshaft on boss provided to prevent camshaft from turning.

9. Install camshaft front timing sprocket. Tighten to 41–59 ft. lbs. (56–82 Nm).

10. Install and adjust front timing belt.

11. Install front timing belt cover.

12. Install cam cover, using new gasket.

13. Connect negative battery cable.

Rear

1. Disconnect the negative battery cable.

2. Remove rear timing belt cover.

3. Remove rear timing belt.

4. Remove cam cover.

5. With an adjustable wrench, hold camshaft on location provided to prevent camshaft from turning.

6. Remove camshaft rear timing sprocket.

7. Rotate injection pump sprocket until timing marks are aligned. Install 2 M8 × 1.25 bolts in the holes to hold

the injection pump sprocket. Remove sprocket retaining nut.

8. Remove injection timing pump sprocket using a suitable gear puller with 2 bolts installed in the threaded holes in the sprocket.

To install:

9. Install injection pump timing sprocket. Hold the sprocket in place using the procedure described in Step 5. Install the sprocket retaining nut and tighten to 51–58 ft. lbs. (70–80 Nm).

10. With an adjustable wrench, hold camshaft on boss provided to prevent camshaft from turning.

11. Install camshaft rear timing sprocket. Tighten to 41–59 ft. lbs. (56–82 Nm).

12. Install and adjust rear timing belt.

13. Install rear timing belt cover.

14. Connect negative battery cable.

Camshaft

REMOVAL & INSTALLATION

1. Disconnect the negative battery cable.

2. Disconnect breather hose.

3. Remove camshaft cover retaining bolts. Remove camshaft cover.

4. Inspect rubber camshaft cover seal and replace if worn.

5. Remove flywheel timing mark cover from clutch housing.

6. Rotate crankshaft until No. 1 cylinder is at TDC.

7. Remove front and rear timing belt covers.

8. Remove front and rear timing belts.

9. Using an adjustable wrench on boss provided on camshaft, loosen bolt attaching front camshaft sprocket to camshaft.

10. Hold camshaft with adjustable wrench and remove bolt retaining rear camshaft sprocket to camshaft.

11. Remove camshaft sprockets using puller T77F-4220-B1 and shaft protector D80L-625-4 or equivalent,.

NOTE: Failure to follow procedures exactly as described in Steps 12 and 13 can result in damage to cylinder head and/or camshaft.

12. Remove No. 1, No. 3 and No. 5 camshaft bearing caps first.

13. For camshaft bearing caps No. 2 and No. 4, loosen as follows:

    a. Loosen one nut 2–3 turns.

    b. Loosen remaining nuts one at a time, 2–3 turns.

    c. Repeat this sequence, turning each nut 2–3 turns at a time, until all nuts are loose.

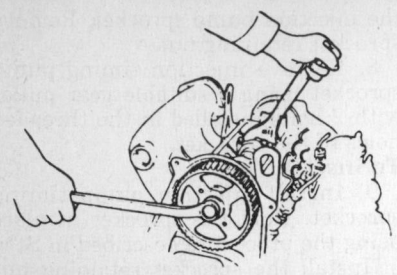

Removal of camshaft timing sprocket retaining bolt—2.0L Diesel engine

PULLER

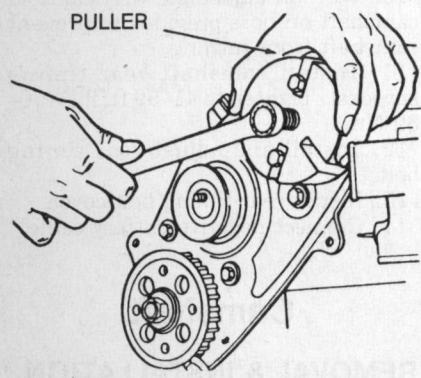

Removal of camshaft timing sprocket using puller—2.0L Diesel engine

14. Remove camshaft and discard camshaft seals.

To install:

NOTE: Camshaft bearings are to be installed with arrows pointing toward front of engine. No. 2, No. 3 and No. 4 bearing caps have their numbers cast in top surface. No. 1 and No. 5 bearings are not marked. However, No. 1 bearing cap has a slot to fit over camshaft thrust flange. Follow Steps 15 through 17 exactly as described. Failure to do so may result in damage to the cylinder head and/or camshaft.

15. Position camshaft in cylinder head and install No. 2 and No. 4 bearing caps as follows:

    a. Tighten one nut 2–3 turns.

    b. Tighten remaining nuts, one at time, 2–3 turns.

    c. Repeat this sequence, turning each nut 2–3 turns, until bearing caps are seated.

16. Install No. 1 , No. 3 and No. 5 bearing caps. Tighten nuts for all 5 bearing caps to 15–19 ft. lbs. (20–27 Nm).

17. Install a new rear camshaft oil seal using a 1 7/16 in. (36.5mm) socket and a hammer.

18. Install a new front camshaft oil seal using valve stem seal installer T84P-6019-A or equivalent.

19. Install front and rear camshaft sprockets. While holding camshaft

with an adjustable wrench. Tighten camshaft sprocket bolts to 41–59 ft. lbs. (56–82 Nm).

20. Install and adjust front and rear timing belts.

21. Check and adjust valves as necessary.

22. Install camshaft cover and tighten bolts to 5–7 ft. lbs. (7–10 Nm).

23. Connect breather hose.

25. Connect negative battery cable.

Piston and Connecting Rod

POSITIONING

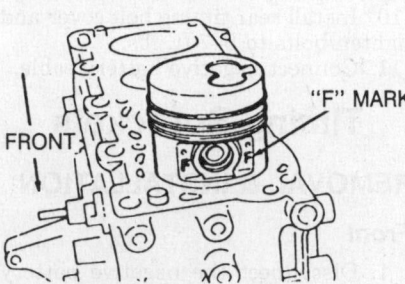

FRONT

"F" MARK

Piston alignment marks—2.0L Diesel engine

TOP RING
OIL RING
EXPANDER

SECOND RING

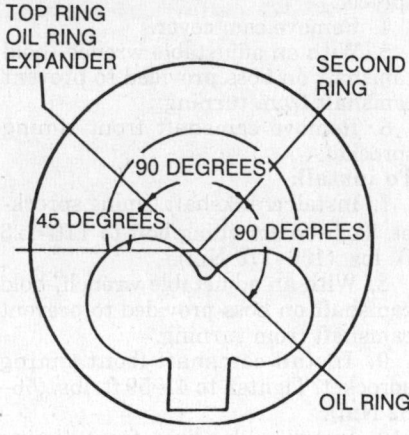

90 DEGREES

45 DEGREES   90 DEGREES

OIL RING

Piston ring gap position—2.0L Diesel engine

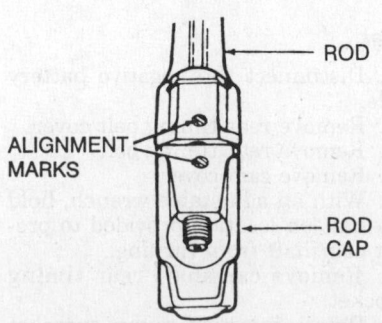

ROD

ALIGNMENT MARKS

ROD CAP

Connecting rod alignment marks—2.0L Diesel engine

ENGINE LUBRICATION

Oil Pan

REMOVAL & INSTALLATION

1.9L Engine

1. Disconnect negative cable at the battery.

2. Raise the vehicle and support safely.

3. Drain the crankcase.

4. Disconnect cable at the starter.

5. Remove knee-brace located at the front of the starter.

6. Remove starter attaching bolts and starter.

7. Remove knee-braces at the transaxle.

8. Disconnect the exhaust inlet pipe at the manifold and converter. Remove pipe.

9. Remove oil pan retaining bolts and oil pan.

10. Remove oil pan gasket and discard.

To install:

11. Clean the oil pan gasket surface and the mating surface on the cylinder block. Wipe the oil pan rail with a solvent-soaked cloth to remove oil traces.

12. Remove the clean the oil pump pick up tube and screen assembly. Install tube and screen assembly using a new gasket.

13. Apply a bead of suitable silicone rubber sealer at the corner of the oil pan front and rear seals and at the seating point of the oil pump to the block retainer joint.

14. Install the gasket in oil pan ensuring press fit tabs are fully engaged in oil pan gasket channel.

15. Install the oil pan attaching bolts. Tighten the bolts lightly until the 2 oil pan-to-transmission bolts can be installed.

NOTE: If the oil pan is installed on the engine outside of the vehi-

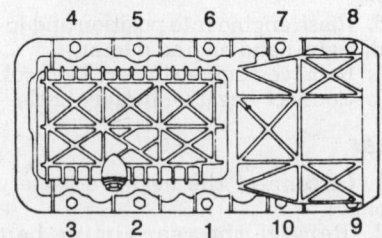

Oil pan attaching bolts torque sequence—1.9L engine

cle, a transaxle case or equivalent, fixture must be bolted to the block to line the oil pan up, flush with the rear face of the block.

16. Tighten the 2 pan-to-transmission bolts to 30–40 ft. lbs. (40–54 Nm).

17. Tighten the oil pan flange-to-cylinder block bolts to 15–22 ft. lbs. (20–30 Nm).

18. Install the transaxle inspection plate.

19. Install the starter, knee brace at the starter and connect the starter cable.

20. Install the exhaust inlet pipe. Lower the vehicle and fill the crankcase.

21. Connect negative battery cable.

23. Start the engine and check for oil leaks.

2.0L Engine

1. Disconnect the negative battery cable.

2. Raise and safely support the vehicle.

3. Drain engine oil.

4. Remove bolts attaching oil pan to crankcase, and remove pan.

5. Clean oil pan and crankcase gasket mating surfaces.

To install:

6. Apply a 1/8 in. (3.18mm) bead of silicone sealer or equivalent, to oil pan-to-crankcase mating surface.

7. Install oil pan. Tighten bolts to 5–7 ft. lbs. (7–10 Nm).

8. Lower vehicle.

9. Fill crankcase with specified quantity and quality of engine oil.

10. Connect negative battery cable.

11. Run engine and check for oil leaks.

2.3L Engine

1. Disconnect the negative battery cable. Raise the vehicle and support safely.

2. Drain the crankcase and drain the cooling system by removing the lower radiator hose.

3. Remove the roll restrictor on manual transaxle equipped vehicles.

4. Disconnect the starter cable.

5. Remove the starter.

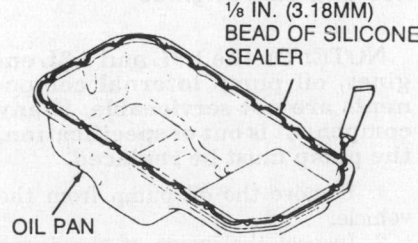

1/8 IN. (3.18MM) BEAD OF SILICONE SEALER

OIL PAN

Applying bead of silicone sealer – 2.0L Diesel engine

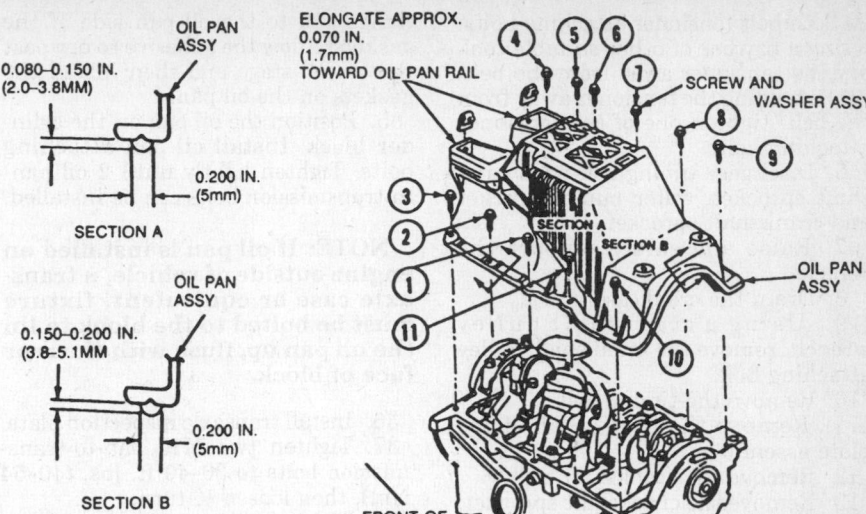

OIL PAN ASSY

ELONGATE APPROX. 0.070 IN. (1.7mm) TOWARD OIL PAN RAIL

0.080–0.150 IN. (2.0–3.8MM)

0.200 IN. (5mm)

SECTION A

OIL PAN ASSY

0.150–0.200 IN. (3.8–5.1MM)

0.200 IN. (5mm)

SECTION B

SCREW AND WASHER ASSY

SECTION A   SECTION B

OIL PAN ASSY

FRONT OF ENGINE

Oil pan installation – 2.3L engine

6. Disconnect the exhaust pipe from oil pan.

7. Remove the engine coolant tube from the lower radiator hose, water pump and at the tabs on the oil pan. Position air conditioner line off to the side. Remove the retaining bolts and remove the oil pan.

To install:

8. Clean both mating surfaces of oil pan and cylinder block making certain that all traces of RTV sealant are removed. Ensure that the block rails, front cover and rear cover retainer are also clean.

9. Remove and clean oil pump pick-up tube and screen assembly. After cleaning, install tube and screen assembly.

10. Apply RTV E8AZ-19562-A Sealer or equivalent, in oil pan groove. Completely fill oil pan groove with sealer. Sealer bead should be 0.200 in. (5mm) wide and 0.080–0.150 in. (2.0–3.8mm) high (above oil pan surface) in all areas except the half-rounds. The half-rounds should have a bead 0.200 in. (5mm) wide and 0.150–0.200 in. (3.8–5.1mm) high, above the oil pan surface.

NOTE: Applying RTV in excess of the specified amount will not improve the sealing of the oil pan, and could cause the oil pickup screen to become clogged with sealer. Use adequate ventilation when applying sealer.

11. Install oil pan to cylinder block within 5 minutes to prevent skinning over. RTV needs to cure completely before coming in contact with any engine oil, about 1 hour at ambient temperature between 65–75°F.

12. Install oil pan bolts lightly until the 2 oil pan-to-transmission bolts can be installed.

NOTE: If oil pan is installed on engine outside of vehicle, a transaxle case or equivalent, fixture must be bolted to the block to line the oil pan up, flush with the rear face of block.

13. Install 2 oil pan-to-transaxle bolts. Tighten to 30–39 ft. lbs. (40–54 Nm) to align oil pan with transaxle. Loosen bolts 1/2 turn.

14. Tighten all oil pan flange bolts to 15–22 ft. lbs. (20–30 Nm).

15. Tighten 2 oil pan-to-transmission bolts to 30–39 ft. lbs. (40–54 Nm).

16. If required, rework exhaust bracket to fit to oil pan.

17. Replace water inlet tube O-ring and install tube.

18. Install roll restrictor.

19. Lower vehicle.

20. Install engine oil and coolant.

21. Connect negative battery cable.

22. Start engine and check for coolant and oil leaks.

Oil Pump

REMOVAL & INSTALLATION

1.9L Engine

1. Disconnect the negative cable at the battery.

2. Loosen the alternator bolt on the alternator adjusting arm.

3. Lower the alternator to remove the accessory drive belt from the crankshaft pulley.

4. Remove the timing belt cover.

5. Set No. 1 cylinder at TDC. Loos-

en both belt tensioner attaching bolts. Using a pry bar of other suitable tool, pry the tensioner away from the belt. While holding the tensioner away from the belt, tighten one of the tensioner attaching bolts.

6. Disengage timing belt from camshaft sprocket, water pump sprocket and crankshaft sprocket.

7. Raise and safely support the vehicle.

8. Drain the crankcase.

9. Using a crankshaft pulley wrench, remove the crankshaft pulley attaching bolt.

10. Remove the timing belt.

11. Remove the crankshaft drive plate assembly.

12. Remove the crankshaft pulley.

13. Remove the crankshaft sprocket.

14. Disconnect the starter cable at the starter.

15. Remove the knee-brace from the engine.

16. Remove the starter.

17. Remove rear section of the knee-brace and inspection plate at the transaxle.

18. Remove oil pan retaining bolts and oil pan.

19. Remove 1 piece oil pan gasket.

20. Remove oil pump attaching bolts.

21. Remove oil pump and gasket.

22. Remove oil pump seal.

To install:

23. Make sure the mating surfaces on the cylinder block and the oil pump are clean and free of gasket material.

24. Remove the oil pick-up tube and screen assembly from the pump for cleaning.

25. Lubricate the outside diameter of the oil pump seal with clean engine oil.

26. Install the oil pump seal using a suitable seal installer tool.

27. Install pick-up tube and screen assembly on the oil pump. Tighten attaching bolts to 6–9 ft. lbs (8–12 Nm).

28. Lubricate the oil pump seal lip with light engine oil.

29. Position the oil pump gasket over the locating dowels.

30. Position the oil pump. Install attaching bolts and tighten to 5–7 ft. lbs (7–9 Nm).

31. Apply a bead of sealer approximately 1/8 in. (3.0mm) wide at the corner of the front and ear oil pan seals and at the seating point of the oil pump to the block retainer joint.

32. Install front oil pan by pressing firmly into the slot cut into the bottom of the pump.

33. Install the rear oil seal by pressing firmly into the slot cut into rear retainer assembly.

NOTE: Install the seal before the sealer has cured.

34. Apply adhesive evenly to oil pan flange and to the oil pan side of the gaskets. Allow the adhesive to dry past the "wet" stage and then install the gaskets on the oil pan.

35. Position the oil pan on the cylinder block. Install oil pan attaching bolts. Tighten lightly until 2 oil pan-to-transmission bolts can be installed.

NOTE: If oil pan is installed on engine outside of vehicle, a transaxle case or equivalent, fixture must be bolted to the block to lin the oil pan up, flush with the rear face of block.

36. Install transaxle inspection plate.

37. Tighten two M10 pan-to-transmission bolts to 30–40 ft. lbs. (40–54 Nm), then loosen 1/2 turn.

38. Tighten oil pan flange-to-cylinder M8 bolts to 15–22 ft. lbs. (20–30 Nm).

39. Tighten two M10 pan-to-transmission bolts to 30–40 ft. lbs. (40–54 Nm).

40. Install starter, knee-brace and connect the starter cable.

41. Install crankshaft gear and crankshaft pulley. Install the crankshaft drive plate assembly.

42. Install timing belt over the crankshaft pulley.

43. Using the crankshaft pulley wrench, install the crankshaft pulley attaching bolt.

44. Lower the vehicle and install the engine front timing cover.

45. Position the accessory drive belts over the alternator and crankshaft pulleys and tighten.

46. Connect the negative battery cable and fill the crankcase.

47. Start the engine and check for oil leaks.

2.0L Engine

1. Disconnect the negative battery cable.

2. Drain engine oil.

3. Remove oil pan.

4. Remove front timing belt.

5. Remove bolts attaching oil pump to crankcase and remove pump. Remove crankshaft front oil seal.

To install:

6. Clean oil pump and crankcase gasket mating surfaces.

7. Apply a 1/8 in. (3.18mm) bead of silicone sealer or equivalent, on oil pump-to-crankcase mating surface.

8. Install new O-ring.

9. Install oil pump, ensuring that oil pump inner gear engages with splines on crankshaft. Tighten 10mm bolts to 23–34 ft. lbs. (32–47 Nm) and 8mm bolts to 12–16 ft. lbs. (16–23 Nm).

10. Install a new crankshaft front oil seal.

11. Clean oil pan-to-crankcase mating surfaces.

12. Apply a 1/8 in. (3.18mm) bead of silicone sealer or equivalent, to oil pan-to-crankcase mating surface.

13. Install oil pan. Tighten bolts to 5–7 ft. lbs. (7–10 Nm).

14. Install and adjust, as necessary, crankshaft sprocket, front timing belt tensioner and front timing belt.

15. Fill crankcase with specified quantity and quality of oil.

16. Connect negative battery cable.

17. Start engine and check for oil, fuel and coolant leaks.

2.3L Engine

1. Disconnect the negative battery cable.

2. Raise and safely support the vehicle.

3. Remove oil pan.

4. Remove oil pump attaching bolts and remove oil pump and intermediate driveshaft.

To install:

5. Prime oil pump by filling inlet port with engine oil. Rotate pump shaft until oil flows from outlet port.

6. If screen and cover assembly have been removed, replace gasket. Clean screen and reinstall screen and cover assembly and tighten attaching bolts and nut.

7. Position intermediate driveshaft into distributor socket.

8. Insert intermediate driveshaft into oil pump. Install pump and shaft as an assembly.

NOTE: Do not attempt to force the pump into position if it will not seat. The shaft hex may be mis-aligned with the distributor shaft. To align, remove the oil pump and rotate the intermediate driveshaft into a new position.

9. Tighten the oil pump attaching bolts to 15–23 ft. lbs. (20–30 Nm).

10. Install oil pan with new gasket.

11. Connect negative battery cable.

12. Fill the crankcase. Start engine and check for leaks.

CHECKING

1.9L and 2.3L Engines

NOTE: On the 1.9L and 2.3L engines, oil pump internal components are not serviceable. If any component is out of specification, the pump must be replaced.

1. Remove the oil pump from the vehicle.

2. Inspect the inside of the pump housing for damage or excessive wear.

3. Check the mating surface for wear. Minor scuff marks are normal,

but if the cover, gears or housing are excessively worn, scored or grooved, replace the pump.

4. Inspect the rotor for nicks, burrs or score marks. Remove minor imperfections with an oil stone.

5. Measure the inner-to-outer rotor tip clearance. On 1.9L engine, the clearance should be 0.002–0.007 in. (0.05–0.18mm). On 2.3L engine, the clearance must not exceed 0.012 in. (0.30mm) with a feeler gauge inserted ½ in. minimum with the rotors removed from the pump housing.

6. With the rotor assembly installed in the housing, place a straight edge across the rotor assembly and housing. Measure the rotor endplay or clearance, between the the inner and outer rotors. On 1.9L engine, this clearance should be 0.0005–0.0035 in. (0.013–0.0089mm). On 2.3L engine, the clearance is 0.004 in. (0.101mm).

7. Check the relief valve spring tension. If the spring is worn or damaged, replace the pump. Check the relief valve piston for freedom of movement in the bore.

2.0L Engine

1. Disconnect the negative battery cable.

2. Remove the oil pump from the vehicle.

3. Inspect the inside of the pump housing for damage or excessive wear.

4. Check the mating surface for wear. Minor scuff marks are normal. If the cover, gears or housing are excessively worn, scored or grooved, replace the pump.

5. Inspect the rotor for nicks, burrs or score marks. Remove minor imperfections with an oil stone.

6. Measure the clearance between outer gear and crescent. Service limit: 0.0138 in. (0.35mm).

7. Measure the clearance between inner gear and crescent. Service limit: 0.0138 in. (0.35mm).

8. Measure the clearance between outer gear and pump body. Service limit: 0.0079 in. (0.20mm).

9. Measure the side clearance. Service limit: 0.0059 in. (0.15mm).

10. Check the relief valve spring tension. If the spring is worn or damaged, replace the pump. Check the relief valve piston for freedom of movement in the bore.

Rear Main Bearing Oil Seal

REMOVAL & INSTALLATION

1.9L Engine

1. Disconnect the negative battery cable.

2. Raise the vehicle and support it safely. Remove the transaxle.

3. Remove flywheel.

4. With a suitable tool, remove the oil seal.

NOTE: Use caution to avoid damaging the oil seal surface.

To install:

5. Inspect the crankshaft seal area for any damage which may cause the seal to leak. If damage is evident, service or replace the crankshaft, as necessary.

6. Coat the crankshaft seal area and the seal lip with engine oil.

7. Using a suitable seal installer tool, install the seal. Tighten the 2 bolts of the seal installer tool evenly so that the seal is straight and seats without mis-alignment.

8. Install the flywheel. Tighten attaching bolts to 54–64 ft. lbs. (73–87 Nm).

9. Install rear cover plate.

10. Complete the installation of the transaxle by reversing the removal procedure.

2.0L Engine

1. Disconnect the negative battery cable.

2. Remove transaxle and clutch.

3. Install flywheel holding tool and remove flywheel bolts and flywheel.

4. Remove oil seal.

To install:

5. Lubricate oil seal sealing lips with engine oil.

6. Install oil seal using seal installer and two flywheel retaining bolts.

NOTE: Flat on edge of seal installer must be parallel to oil pan or damage to seal retainer and/or oil pan may result.

7. Install flywheel and flywheel holding tool. Tighten flywheel retaining bolts to 131–137 ft. lbs. (180–190 Nm). Remove flywheel holding tool.

8. Install clutch and transaxle.

9. Connect negative battery cable.

10. Start engine and check for oil leaks.

2.3L Engine

1. Disconnect the negative battery cable.

2. Remove transaxle.

3. Remove flywheel.

4. Remove rear cover plate.

5. Insert a suitable tool into seal cavity and pry out old seal.

NOTE: Use caution to avoid damaging the oil seal surface.

To install:

5. Inspect the crankshaft seal area for any damage which may cause the

seal to leak. If damage is evident, service or replace the crankshaft, as necessary.

6. Coat the crankshaft seal area and the seal lip with engine oil.

7. Using a suitable seal installer tool, install the seal. Tighten the 2 bolts of the seal installer tool evenly so that the seal is straight and seats without mis-alignment.

8. Install the flywheel. Tighten attaching bolts to 54–64 ft. lbs. (73–87 Nm).

9. Install rear cover plate and 2 dowels.

10. Complete the installation of the transaxle by reversing the removal procedure.

MANUAL TRANSAXLE

For further information on transmissions/transaxles, please refer to "Chilton's Guide to Transmission Repair".

Transaxle Assembly

REMOVAL & INSTALLATION

1. Disconnect the negative battery cable. Wedge a 7 in. wooden block under the clutch pedal to hold the pedal up slightly beyond its normal position. Grasp the clutch cable, pull it forward and disconnect it from the clutch release shaft assembly. Remove the clutch casing from the rib on the top surface of the transaxle case.

2. Remove the upper 2 transaxle-to-engine bolts. Remove the air cleaner, if necessary, and the air management valve bracket-to-transaxle upper bolt, if equipped.

3. Raise and safely support the vehicle.

4. If equipped with a 5-speed, remove the front stabilizer bar-to-control arm nut and washer, on the driver's side and discard the nut. Remove both front stabilizer bar mounting brackets and discard the bolts.

5. Remove the lower control arm ball joint-to-steering knuckle nut/bolt and discard the nut/bolt; repeat this procedure on the opposite side.

6. Using a large pry bar, pry the lower control arm from the steering knuckle; repeat this procedure on the opposite side.

NOTE: Be careful not to damage or cut the ball joint boot and do not contact the lower arm.

7. Using a large pry bar, pry the left-side inboard CV-joint assembly from the transaxle.

NOTE: Plug the seal opening to prevent lubricant leakage.

8. Grasp the left-hand steering knuckle and swing it and the halfshaft outward from the transaxle; this will disconnect the inboard CV-joint from the transaxle.

NOTE: If the CV-joint assembly cannot be pried from the transaxle, insert a differential rotator tool through the left-side and tap the joint out; the tool can be used from either side of transaxle.

9. Using a wire, support the halfshaft in a near level position to prevent damage to the assembly during the remaining operations; repeat this procedure on the opposite side.

10. Disengage the locking tabs and remove the backup lamp switch connector from the transaxle backup lamp switch.

11. If equipped with a 5-speed, remove the starter studs-to-engine roll restrictor bracket nuts and the engine roll restrictor. Remove the starter stud bolts.

12. If equipped with a 4-speed, remove the starter bolts and the starter.

13. Remove the shift mechanism-to-shift shaft nut/bolt, the control selector indicator switch arm and the shift shaft.

14. Remove the shift mechanism stabilizer bar-to-transaxle bolt, control selector indicator switch and bracket assembly.

15. Using a crowfoot wrench, remove the speedometer cable from the transaxle.

16. Remove both oil pan-to-clutch housing bolts.

17. Using a floor jack and a transaxle support, position it under the transaxle and secure the transaxle to it.

18. If equipped with a 5-speed, remove the both left-hand rear No. 4 insulator-to-body bracket nuts and the left-hand front No.1 insulator-to-body bracket bolts.

19. If equipped with a 4-speed, remove both rear mount-to-floorpan bolts, loosen the nut at the bottom of the front mount and remove the front mount-to-transaxle bolts.

20. Lower the floor jack, until the transaxle clears the rear insulator. Support the engine by placing wood under the oil pan.

21. Remove the engine-to-transaxle bolts and lower the transaxle from the vehicle.

NOTE: One of the engine-to-transaxle bolts attaches the

ground strap and wiring loom stand off bracket.

To install:

22. Raise the transaxle into position and engage the input shaft with the clutch plate. Install the lower engine-to-transaxle bolts and torque to 28–31 ft. lbs. (38–42 Nm).

NOTE: Never attempt to start the engine prior to installing the CV-joints or differential side gear for dislocation and/or damage may occur.

23. Install the front mount-to-transaxle bolts and torque to 25–35 ft. lbs. (34–47 Nm); also, tighten the nut on the bottom of the front transaxle mount.

24. Install the air management valve-to-transaxle upper bolt, finger-tight and the bottom bracket bolt to 28–31 ft. lbs. (38–42 Nm).

25. Install both rear mount-to-floorpan brace bolts to 40–51 ft. lbs. (55–70 Nm). Remove the floor jack and adapter.

26. Using a crowfoot wrench, install the speedometer cable; be careful not to cross-thread the cable nut.

27. Install the shifter stabilizer bar/control selector indicator switch-to-transaxle bolt and torque to 23–35 ft. lbs. (31–47 Nm).

28. Install the shift mechanism-to-shift shaft, the switch actuator bracket clamp and torque the bolt to 7–10 ft. lbs. (9–13 Nm); be sure to shift the transaxle into **4th** for 4-speed or **5th** for 5-speed and align the actuator.

29. Install the stiffener brace-to-clutch housing and torque the bolts to 15–21 ft. lbs. (21–28 Nm). Install the starter-to-engine and torque the bolts to 30–40 ft. lbs. (41–54 Nm).

30. Install the backup light switch connector to the transaxle switch.

31. Install the new circlip onto both inner joints of the halfshafts, insert the inner CV-joints into the transaxle and fully seat them; lightly, pry outward to confirm that the retaining rings are seated.

NOTE: When installing the halfshafts, be careful not to tear the oil seals.

32. Connect the lower ball joint to the steering knuckle, insert a new pinch bolt and torque the new nut to 37–44 ft. lbs.; be careful not to damage the boot.

33. Refill the transaxle and lower the vehicle.

34. Install the upper air management valve bracket-to-transaxle bolt and torque to 28–31 ft. lbs. (38–42 Nm).

35. Install the both upper transaxle-

to-engine bolts and torque to 28–31 ft. lbs. (38–42 Nm).

36. Connect the clutch cable to the clutch release shaft assembly and remove the wooden block from under the clutch pedal. Connect the negative battery cable.

NOTE: Prior to starting the engine, set the hand brake and pump the clutch pedal several times to ensure proper clutch adjustment.

CLUTCH

Clutch Assembly

REMOVAL & INSTALLATION

1. Disconnect the negative battery cable. Raise and safely support the vehicle. Remove the transaxle.

2. Matchmark the pressure plate assembly and the flywheel so they can be assembled in the same position.

3. Loosen the pressure plate-to-flywheel bolts 1 turn at a time, in sequence, until spring tension is relieved to prevent pressure plate cover distortion.

4. Support the pressure plate and remove the bolts. Remove the pressure plate and clutch disc from the flywheel.

5. Inspect the flywheel, clutch disc, pressure plate, throwout bearing and the clutch fork for wear; replace parts, as required.

NOTE: If the flywheel shows any signs of overheating (blue discoloration) or if it is badly grooved or scored, it should be refaced or replaced.

To install:

6. Clean the pressure plate and flywheel surfaces thoroughly. Position the clutch disc and pressure plate into the installed position, aligning the matchmarks made previously; support them with a dummy shaft or clutch aligning tool.

7. Install the pressure plate-to-flywheel bolts. Tighten them gradually in a criss-cross pattern to 12–24 ft. lbs. (17–32 Nm). Remove the alignment tool.

8. Lubricate the release bearing and install it in the fork.

9. To complete the installation, reverse the removal procedures. Lower the vehicle and connect the negative battery cable.

Pedal Height/Free-Play Adjustment

The pedal height and free-play are controlled by a self-adjusting feature.

Clutch Cable

ADJUSTMENT

The free-play in the clutch is adjusted by a built in mechanism that allows the clutch controls to be self-adjusted during normal operation. The self-adjusting feature should be checked every 5000 miles. This is accomplished by insuring that the clutch pedal travels to the top of its upward position. Grasp the clutch pedal with hand or put foot under the clutch pedal, pull up on the pedal until it stops. Very little effort is required (about 10 lbs.). During the application of upward pressure, a click may be heard which means an adjustment was necessary and has been accomplished.

REMOVAL & INSTALLATION

1. Disconnect the negative battery cable.
2. Wedge a 7 in. wooden block under the clutch pedal to hold the pedal up slightly beyond its normal position.
3. Remove the air cleaner to gain access to the clutch cable.
4. Using a pair of pliers, grasp the clutch cable, pull it forward and disconnect it from the clutch release shaft assembly.

NOTE: Do not grasp the wire strand portion of the inner cable since it may cut the wires and cause cable failure.

5. Remove the clutch casing from the insulator which is located on the rib on the top of the transaxle case.
6. On the Tempo or Topaz, remove the panel from above the clutch pedal pad.
7. Remove the rear screw and move the clutch shield away from the brake pedal support bracket. Loosen the front retaining screw, located near the toe board, rotate the shield aside and snug the screw to retain the shield.
8. With the clutch pedal raised to release the pawl, rotate the gear quadrant forward, unhook the clutch cable and allow the quadrant to swing rearward; do not allow the quadrant to snap back.
9. Pull the cable through the recess between the clutch pedal and the gear quadrant and from the insulator of the pedal assembly.
10. Remove the cable from the engine compartment.

To install:

11. Lift the clutch pedal to disengage the adjusting mechanism.
12. Insert the clutch cable through the dash panel and the dash panel grommet.

NOTE: Be sure the clutch cable is routed under the brake lines and not trapped at the spring tower by the brake lines. If equipped with power steering, rout the cable inboard of the power steering hose.

13. Push the clutch cable through the insulator on the stop bracket and through the recess between the pedal and the gear quadrant.
14. Lift the clutch pedal to release the pawl, rotate the gear quadrant forward and hook the cable into the gear quadrant.
15. On the Tempo or Topaz, install the panel above the clutch pedal.
16. Using a piece of wire or tape, secure the pedal in the upmost position.
17. Insert the clutch cable through the insulator and connect the cable to the clutch release lever in the engine compartment.
18. Remove the wooden block from under the clutch pedal.
19. Depress the clutch pedal several times. Install the air cleaner and connect the negative battery cable.

AUTOMATIC TRANSAXLE

For further information on transmissions/transaxles, please refer to "Chilton's Guide to Transmission Repair".

Transaxle Assembly

REMOVAL & INSTALLATION

1. Disconnect the negative battery cable.

NOTE: Due to automatic transaxle case configuration, the right-side halfshaft assembly must be removed first. The differential rotator tool or equivalent, is inserted into the transaxle to drive the left-side inboard CV-joint assembly from the transaxle.

2. If necessary, remove the managed air valve-to-transaxle valve body cover bolts. Remove the air cleaner assembly, as required.
3. Disconnect the electrical harness connector from the neutral safety switch.
4. Disconnect the throttle valve linkage and the manual lever cable from their levers.

NOTE: Failure to disconnect the linkage and allowing the transaxle to hang, will fracture the throttle valve cam shaft joint, which is located under the transaxle cover.

5. To prevent contamination, cover the timing window in the converter housing. If equipped, remove the bolts retaining the thermactor hoses.
6. If equipped, remove the ground strap, located above the upper engine mount, the coil and bracket assembly.
7. Remove both upper transaxle-to-upper engine bolts; the bolts are located below and on both ides of the distributor. Raise and safely support the vehicle. Remove the front wheels.
8. Remove the control arm-to-steering knuckle nut, at the ball joint.
9. Using a hammer and a punch, drive the bolt from the steering knuckle; repeat this step on the other side. Discard the nut and bolt.

NOTE: Be careful not to damage or cut ball joint boot. The pry bar must not contact lower arm.

10. Using a pry bar, disengage the control arm from the steering knuckle; repeat this step on the other side.

NOTE: Do not hammer on the knuckle to remove the ball joints. The plastic shield installed behind the rotor contains a molded pocket into which the lower control arm ball joint fits. When disengaging the control arm from the knuckle, clearance for the ball joint can be provided by bending the shield back toward the rotor. Failure to provide clearance for the ball joint can result in damage to the shield.

11. Remove the stabilizer bar bracket-to-frame rail bolts and discard the bolts; repeat this step on the other side.
12. Remove the stabilizer bar-to-control arm nut/washer and discard the nut; repeat this step on the other side.
13. Pull the stabilizer bar from of the control arms.
14. Remove the brake hose routing clip-to-suspension strut bracket bolt; repeat this step on the other side.
15. Remove the steering gear tie rod-to-steering knuckle nut and disengage the tie rod from the steering knuckle; repeat this step on the other side.
16. Using a halfshaft removal tool, pry the halfshaft from the right side of the transaxle and support the end of the shaft with a wire.

NOTE: It is normal for some fluid to leak from the transaxle when the halfshaft is removed.

17. Using a differential rotator tool or equivalent, drive the left-side halfshaft from the differential side gear.

18. Pull the halfshaft from the transaxle and support the end of the shaft with a wire.

NOTE: Do not allow the shaft to hang unsupported, as damage to the outboard CV-joint may result.

19. Install seal plugs into the differential seals.

20. Remove the starter support bracket and disconnect the starter cable. Remove the starter bolts and the starter. If equipped with a throttle body, remove the hose and bracket bolts on the starter and a bolt at the converter and disconnect the hoses.

21. Remove the transaxle support bracket and the dust cover from the torque converter housing.

22. Remove the torque converter-to-flywheel nuts by turning the crankshaft pulley bolt to bring the nuts into position.

23. Remove the left front insulator-to-body bracket nuts, the bracket-to-body bolts and the bracket. Remove the left rear insulator bracket nut.

24. Disconnect the transaxle cooler lines.

25. Remove the manual lever bracket-to-transaxle case bolts.

26. Support the engine. Position a transaxle jack under the transaxle and remove the remaining transaxle-to-engine bolts.

27. Make sure the torque converter studs will be clear the flywheel. Insert a pry bar between the flywheel and the converter, then, pry the transaxle and converter away from the engine. When the converter studs are clear of the flywheel, lower the transaxle about 2–3 in. (51–76mm).

28. Disconnect the speedometer cable and lower the transaxle.

NOTE: When moving the transaxle away from the engine, watch the No. 1 insulator. If it contacts the body before the converter studs clear the flywheel, remove the insulator.

To install:
29. Raise the transaxle and align it with the engine and flywheel. Install the No. 1 insulator, if it was removed. Torque the transaxle-to-engine bolts to 25–33 ft. lbs. (34–45 Nm) and the torque converter-to-flywheel bolts to 23–39 ft. lbs. (31–53 Nm).

30. Install the manual lever bracket-to-transaxle case bolts and connect the transaxle cooler lines.

31. Install the left front insulator-to-body bracket nuts and torque the nuts to 40–50 ft. lbs. (55–70 Nm). Install the bracket-to-body and torque the bolts to 55–70 ft. lbs. (75–90 Nm).

32. Install the transaxle support bracket and the dust cover to the torque converter housing.

33. If equipped with a throttle body, install the hose and bracket bolts on the starter and a bolt to the converter and connect the hoses. Install the starter and the support bracket; torque the bolts starter-to-engine bolts to 30–40 ft. lbs. (41–54 Nm). Connect the starter cable.

34. Remove the seal plugs from the differential seals and install the halfshaft by performing the following procedures:

   a. Prior to installing the halfshaft in the transaxle, install a new circlip onto the CV-joint stub.

   b. Install the halfshaft in the transaxle by carefully aligning the CV-joint splines with the differential side gears. Be sure to push the CV-joint into the differential until the circlip is felt to seat in the differential side gear. Use care to prevent damage to the differential oil seal.

   c. Attach the lower ball joint to the steering knuckle, taking care not to damage or cut the ball joint boot. Insert a new pinch bolt and a new nut. While holding the bolt with a 2nd wrench, torque the nut to 37–44 ft. lbs.

35. Engage the tie rod with the steering knuckle and torque the nut to 23–35 ft. lbs. (31–47 Nm).

36. Install the brake hose routing clip-to-suspension strut bracket and torque the bolt to 8 ft. lbs. (11 Nm).

37. Install the stabilizer bar to control arm and using a new nut, torque it to 98–125 ft. lbs. (133–169 Nm).

38. Install the stabilizer bar bracket-to-frame rail bolts and using new bolts, torque them to 60–70 ft. lbs. (81–95 Nm).

39. Install the wheels and lower the vehicle. Install the upper transaxle-to-engine bolts and torque to 25–33 ft. lbs. (34–45 Nm).

40. If equipped, install the ground strap, located above the upper engine mount, the coil and bracket assembly.

41. If equipped, install the bolts retaining the thermactor hoses. Uncover the timing window in the converter housing.

42. Connect the throttle valve linkage and the manual lever cable to their levers.

43. Connect the electrical harness connector from the neutral safety switch.

44. Install the managed air valve-to-transaxle valve body cover bolts and

the air cleaner assembly, as required.

45. Connect the negative battery cable and road test the vehicle.

SHIFT LINKAGE ADJUSTMENT

1. Place the gear shift selector into **D**.

NOTE: Be sure to hold the gear selector lever in the rearward position during linkage adjustment.

2. Working at the transaxle, loosen the transaxle lever-to-control cable nut.

3. Move the transaxle lever to the **D** position or **2nd** detent from the rear.

4. Torque the adjusting nut to 10–15 ft. lbs. (14–20 Nm).

5. Make sure all gears engage correctly and the vehicle will only start in **P** or **D**.

THROTTLE LINKAGE ADJUSTMENT

Except 1.9L Engine

1. Disconnect the negative battery cable.

2. Remove the splash shield from the cable retainer bracket.

3. Loosen the trunnion bolt at the throttle valve rod.

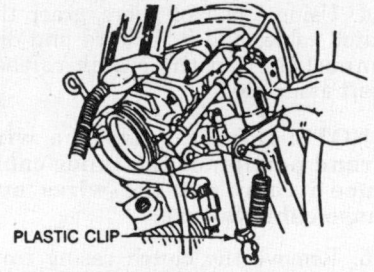

PLASTIC CLIP

Adjusting the throttle valve—except 1.9L engine

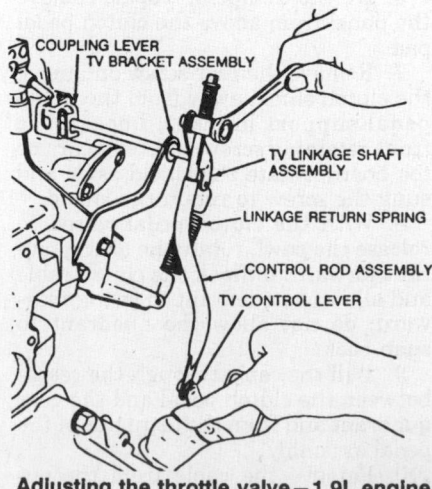

COUPLING LEVER

TV BRACKET ASSEMBLY

TV LINKAGE SHAFT ASSEMBLY

LINKAGE RETURN SPRING

CONTROL ROD ASSEMBLY

TV CONTROL LEVER

Adjusting the throttle valve—1.9L engine

4. Install a plastic clip to bottom the throttle valve rod; be sure the clip does not telescope.

5. Be sure the return spring is connected between the throttle valve rod and the retaining bracket to hold the transaxle throttle valve lever at it's idle position.

6. Make sure the throttle lever is resting on the throttle return control screw.

7. Tighten the throttle valve rod trunnion bolt and remove the plastic clip.

8. Install the splash shield. Connect the negative battery cable and check the vehicle's operation.

1.9L Engine

1. Disconnect the negative battery cable.

2. Set the parking brake and place the transaxle shift lever into **P**.

3. Loosen the sliding trunnion block bolt, located on the throttle valve control rod assembly, a minimum of 1 turn.

4. Make sure the trunnion block slides freely on the control rod.

5. Using a jumper wire, connect it between the STI connector and the signal return ground on the self-test connector.

6. Turn the ignition switch to the **RUN** position but do not start the engine. The Idle Speed Control (ISC) plunger should retract; wait until the plunger is fully retracted, about 10 seconds.

7. Turn the ignition switch **OFF** and remove the jumper wire.

8. Using light force, pull the throttle valve rod upward to ensure the control lever is against the internal stop.

9. Allow the trunnion to slide on the rod to it's normal position.

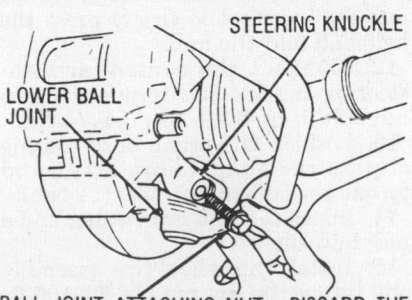

NOTE: TIGHTEN BOLTS IN THE NUMERICAL SEQUENCE SHOWN

Transfer case retaining bolts - installation and torque sequence

10. Without relaxing the pressure on the throttle valve control lever, tighten the trunnion block bolt.

11. Connect negative battery cable.

Transfer Case Assembly

REMOVAL & INSTALLATION

1. Disconnect the negative battery cable.

2. Raise and safely support the vehicle.

3. Using a light hammer and a dull chisel, remove the cup plug from the transfer case and drain the oil.

4. Remove the vacuum line retaining bracket bolt.

5. Remove the driveshaft front retaining bolts and caps; disengage the front driveshaft from the drive yoke.

6. If the transfer case is to be disassembled, check the backlash through the cup plug opening before removal in order to reset to existing backlash at installation. The backlash should be 0.012–0.024 in. on a 3 in. radius.

7. Remove the vacuum motor shield bolts and the shield.

8. Remove the vacuum lines from the vacuum servo.

9. Remove the transfer case-to-transaxle bolts; note and record the length and locations of the bolts.

10. Remove the the transfer case from the vehicle.

To install:

11. Position the transfer case to the transaxle.

12. Install the transfer case bolts in the proper positions and torque the bolts, in sequence, to 23–38 ft. lbs. (31–38 Nm) for 1987, 15–19 ft. lbs. (21–25 Nm) for 1988–89 or 12–15 ft. lbs. (16–20 Nm) for 1990–91.

13. Install the vacuum motor supply hose connector, vacuum motor shield and torque the bolts to 7–12 ft. lbs. (9–16 Nm).

14. Install the driveshaft-to-drive yoke, lubricate the bolts with Loctite® and torque the bolts to 15–17 ft. lbs. (21–23 Nm). Install the vacuum line retaining bracket and torque the bolt to 7–12 ft. lbs. (9–16 Nm).

15. Refill the transaxle and lower the vehicle. Road test the vehicle and check the performance of the transfer case.

DRIVE AXLE

Halfshaft

REMOVAL & INSTALLATION

Without All Wheel Drive (AWD)

1. Remove the cap from the hub and loosen the hub nut. Set the parking brake. The nut must be loosened without unstaking; the use of a chisel or similar tool may damage the spindle thread.

2. Raise and safely support the vehicle. Remove the wheel and tire assembly. Remove the hub nut/washer and discard the nut.

3. Remove the brake hose routing clip-to-strut bolt.

4. Remove the ball joint-to-steering

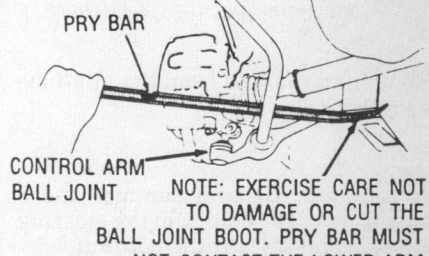

DO NOT ALLOW THE PRY BAR TO DAMAGE THE BALL JOINT BOOT

PRY BAR

CONTROL ARM BALL JOINT

NOTE: EXERCISE CARE NOT TO DAMAGE OR CUT THE BALL JOINT BOOT. PRY BAR MUST NOT CONTACT THE LOWER ARM

Rocker arm, fulcrum and pushrod removal – 2.3L engine

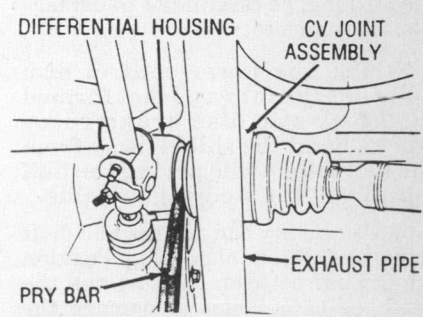

DIFFERENTIAL HOUSING

CV JOINT ASSEMBLY

EXHAUST PIPE

PRY BAR

Exhaust manifold bolt torque sequence – 2.3L engine

STEERING KNUCKLE

LOWER BALL JOINT

BALL JOINT ATTACHING NUT - DISCARD THE BOLT AND NUT AFTER REMOVAL

Removing the lower ball joint pinch bolt

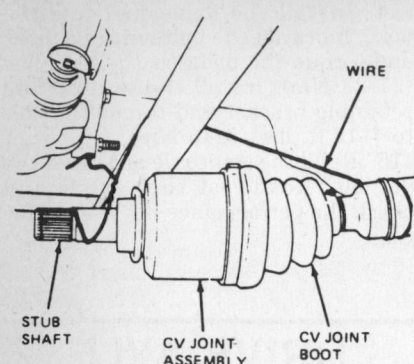

Support the halfshaft by wiring it to the body

METRIC ADAPTERS T81P-1104-B MAKE SURE THE ADAPTER S ARE FULLY THREADED ONTO THE HUB STUDS AND THAT THEY ARE POSITIONED OPPOSITE ONE ANOTHER

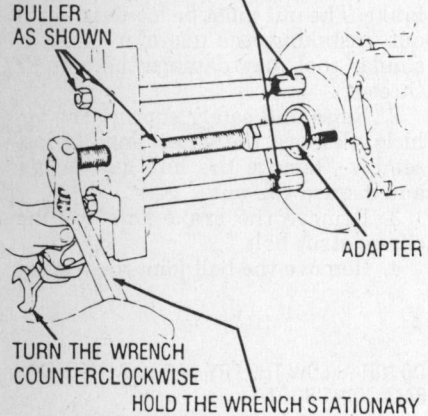

PULLER AS SHOWN

ADAPTER

TURN THE WRENCH COUNTERCLOCKWISE

HOLD THE WRENCH STATIONARY WHILE TURNING THE OTHER WRENCH

Removing the hub from the shaft assembly

knuckle nut. Using a hammer and a punch, drive the bolt from the steering knuckle and discard the bolt/nut.

5. Using a pry bar, separate the ball joint from the steering knuckle. Position the end of the pry bar outside of the bushing pocket to avoid damage to the bushing; be careful not to damage the ball joint boot.

NOTE: The lower control arm ball joint fits into a pocket formed in the plastic disc brake rotor shield; bend the shield away from the ball joint while prying the ball joint from the steering knuckle.

6. Using a pry bar, pry the halfshaft from the differential housing. Position the pry bar between the case and the shaft; be careful not to damage the dust deflector located between the shaft and the case.

NOTE: If extreme resistance is encountered when prying the halfshafts from the differential, remove the oil pan and use a large pry bar to dislodge the circlip from between the pinion shaft and the inboard CV-joint; this will free the haftshaft from the differential.

7. Using a piece of wire, support the end of the shaft from a convenient underbody component.

NOTE: Do not allow the shaft to hang unsupported, as damage to the outboard CV-joint may result.

8. Using a front hub removal tool, press the halfshaft's outboard CV-joint from the hub.

NOTE: Never use a hammer or separate the outboard CV-joint stub shaft from the hub. Damage to the CV-joint internal components may result.

To install:

9. Install a new circlip onto the inboard CV-joint stub shaft; the outboard CV-joint stub shaft does not have a circlip. To install the circlip properly, start one end in the groove and work the circlip over the stub shaft end and into the groove; this will avoid over expanding the circlip.

10. Carefully, align the splines of the inboard CV-joint stub shaft with the splines in the differential. Push the CV-joint into the differential until the circlip is seated in the differential side gear. Use care to prevent damage to the differential oil seal.

NOTE: A non-metallic mallet may be used to aid in seating the circlip into the differential side gear groove; if a mallet is necessary, tap only on the outboard CV-joint stub shaft.

11. Carefully, align the outboard CV-joint stub shaft splines with the hub splines and push the shaft into the hub, as far as possible; use the front hub replacer tool to firmly press the halfshaft into the hub.

12. Connect the control arm-to-steering knuckle and torque the new nut/bolt to 40–54 ft. lbs. (54–74 Nm).

13. Position the brake hose routing clip on the suspension strut and torque the bolt to 8 ft. lbs. (11 Nm).

14. Install the hub nut washer and a new hub nut.

15. Install the wheel/tire assembly and torque the lug nuts to 80–105 ft. lbs. (108–144 Nm). Lower the vehicle and torque the hub nut to 180–200 ft. lbs. (244–271 Nm).

16. Refill the transaxle and road test.

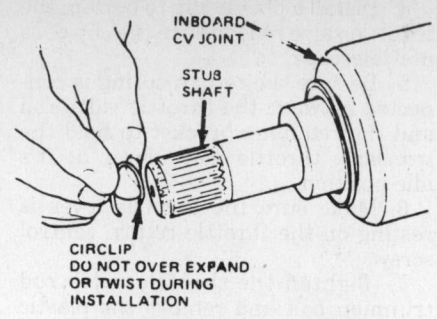

INBOARD CV JOINT

STUB SHAFT

CIRCLIP DO NOT OVER EXPAND OR TWIST DURING INSTALLATION

Stub shaft circlip installation

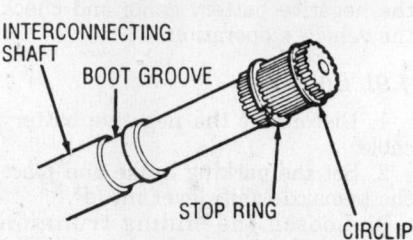

INTERCONNECTING SHAFT

BOOT GROOVE

STOP RING

CIRCLIP

Circlip and stop ring used on the inter connecting shafts

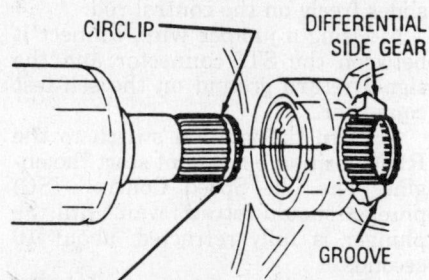

CIRCLIP

DIFFERENTIAL SIDE GEAR

GROOVE

SHAFT IS FULLY INSTALLED WHEN THE CIRCLIP IS FELT TO SEAT IN THE DIFFERENTIAL SIDE GEAR

Seating the circlip in the transaxle differential side gear

With All Wheel Drive (AWD)

1. Raise and safely support the vehicle. Remove the rear suspension control arm bolt.

2. Remove the outboard U-joint retaining bolts and straps. Remove the inboard U-joint retaining bolts and straps.

3. Slide the shaft together; do not allow the splined shafts to contact with excessive force. Remove the halfshafts; do not drop the halfshafts as the impact may cause damage to the U-joint bearing cups.

4. Retain the bearing cups. Inspect the U-joint assemblies for wear or damage, replace the U-joint if necessary.

To install:

5. Install the halfshaft at the inboard U-joint; the inboard shaft has a larger diameter than the outboard shaft. Install the U-joint retaining

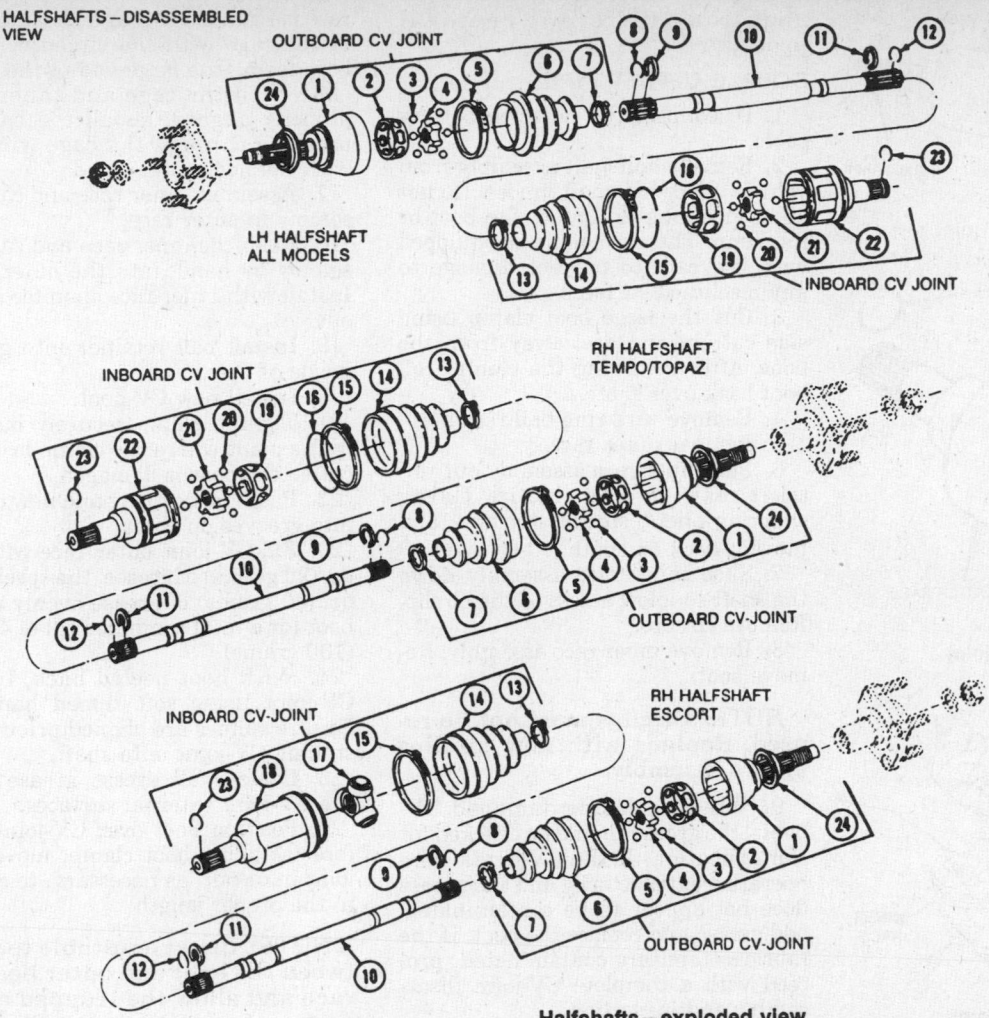

HALFSHAFTS – DISASSEMBLED VIEW

OUTBOARD CV JOINT

LH HALFSHAFT ALL MODELS

INBOARD CV JOINT

INBOARD CV JOINT

RH HALFSHAFT TEMPO/TOPAZ

OUTBOARD CV-JOINT

INBOARD CV-JOINT

RH HALFSHAFT ESCORT

OUTBOARD CV-JOINT

1. Outboard joint outer race and stub shaft
2. Ball cage
3. Balls (6)
4. Outboard joint inner race
5. Boot clamp (large)
6. Boot
7. Boot clamp (small)
8. Circlip
9. Stop ring
10. Interconnecting shaft
11. Stop ring
12. Circlip
13. Boot clamp (small)
14. Boot
15. Boot clamp (large)
16. Wire ring ball retainer
17. Tripod assy
18. Tripod outer race
19. Ball cage
20. Balls (6)
21. Inboard joint inner race
22. Inboard joint outer race and stub shaft
23. Circlip
24. Dust seal

Halfshafts – exploded view

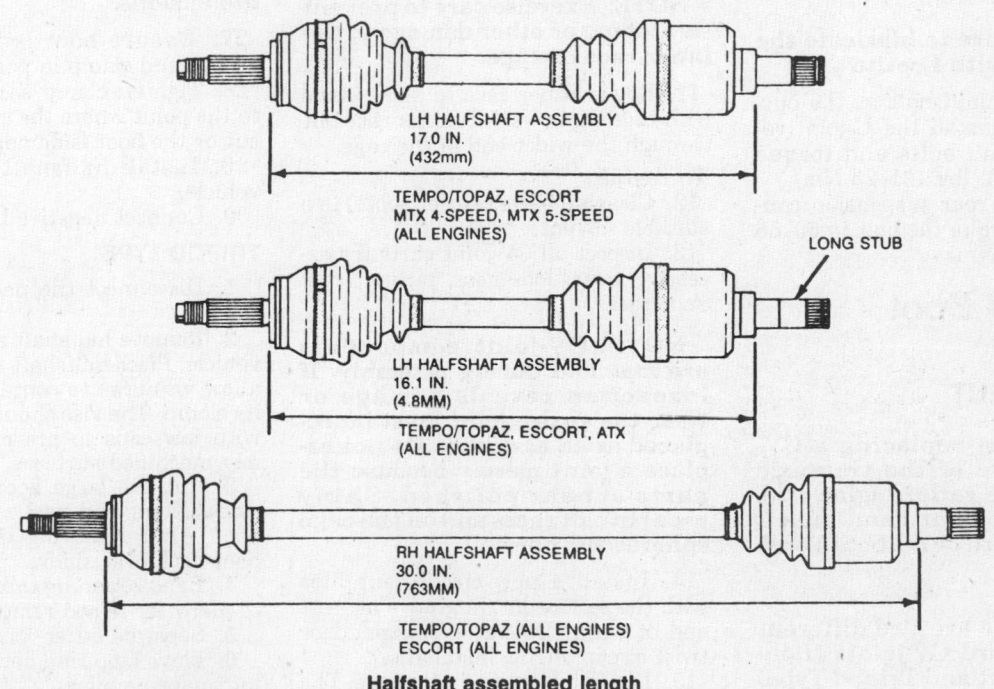

LH HALFSHAFT ASSEMBLY 17.0 IN. (432mm)

TEMPO/TOPAZ, ESCORT MTX 4-SPEED, MTX 5-SPEED (ALL ENGINES)

LONG STUB

LH HALFSHAFT ASSEMBLY 16.1 IN. (4.8MM)

TEMPO/TOPAZ, ESCORT, ATX (ALL ENGINES)

RH HALFSHAFT ASSEMBLY 30.0 IN. (763MM)

TEMPO/TOPAZ (ALL ENGINES) ESCORT (ALL ENGINES)

Halfshaft assembled length

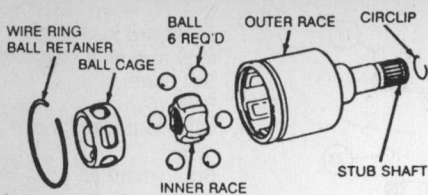

Double offset CV-joint

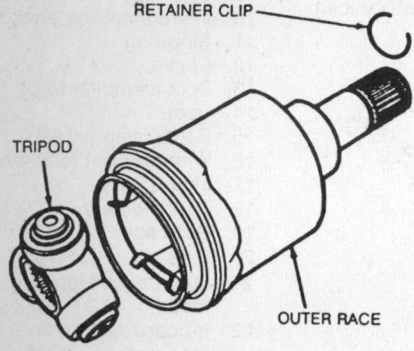

Tripod-type CV-joint

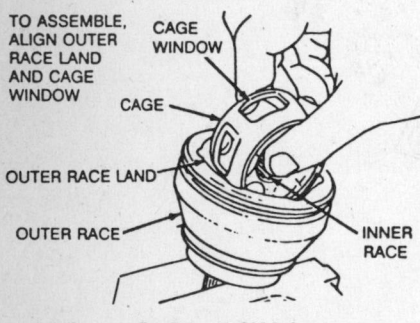

Outboard CV-joint

caps and bolts and torque them to 15–17 ft. lbs. (21–23 Nm).

NOTE: Be sure to lubricate the U-joint bolts with Loctite®.

6. Install the halfshaft at the outboard U-joint. Install the U-joint retaining caps and bolts and torque them to 15–17 ft. lbs. (21–23 Nm).
7. Install the rear suspension control arm and torque the bolt to 60–86 ft. lbs. (82–116 Nm).

CV-Boot

REPLACEMENT

NOTE: When replacing a CV-boot, be aware of the transaxle type, transaxle ratio, engine size, CV-joint type, right hand or left side and inboard or outboard end.

Inner Boot

NOTE: There are two different types of inboard CV-joints (Double Offset Joint and Tripod-Type)

requiring different removal procedures.

DOUBLE OFFSET TYPE

1. Disconnect the negative battery cable.
2. Remove halfshaft assembly from vehicle. Place halfshaft in vise. Do not allow vice jaws to contact the boot or its clamp. The vise should be equipped with jaw caps to prevent damage to any machined surfaces.
3. Cut the large boot clamp using side cutters and peel away from the boot. After removing the clamp, roll boot back over shaft.
4. Remove wire ring ball retainer.
5. Remove outer race.
6. Pull inner race assembly out until it rests on the circlip. Using snapring pliers, spread stop ring and move it back on shaft.
7. Slide inner race assembly down the shaft to allow access to the circlip. Remove circlip.
8. Remove inner race assembly. Remove boot.

NOTE: Circlips must not be reused. Replace with new circlips before assembly.

9. When replacing damaged CV-boots, the grease should be checked for contamination. If the CV-joints were operating satisfactorily and the grease does not appear to be contaminated, add grease and replace the boot. If the lubricant appears contaminated, proceed with a complete CV-joint disassembly and inspection.
10. Remove balls by prying from cage.

NOTE: Exercise care to prevent scratching or other damage to the inner race or cage.

11. Rotate inner race to align lands with cage windows. Lift inner race out through the wider end of the cage.

To install:
12. Clean all parts (except boots) in a suitable solvent.
13. Inspect all CV-joint parts for excessive wear, looseness, pitting, rust and cracks.

NOTE: CV-joint components are matched during assembly. If inspection reveals damage or wear the entire joint must be replaced as an assembly. Do not replace a joint merely because the parts appear polished. Shiny areas in ball races and on the cage spheres are normal.

14. Install a new circlip, supplies with the service kit, in groove nearest end of shaft. Do not over-expand or twist circlip during installation.
15. Install inner race in the cage. The

race is installed through the large end of the cage with the circlip counterbore facing the large end of the cage.
16. With the cage and inner race properly aligned, install the balls by pressing through the cage windows with the heel of the hand.
17. Assemble inner race and cage assembly in outer race.
18. Push the inner race and cage assembly by hand, into the outer race. Install with inner race chamfer facing out.
19. Install ball retainer into groove inside of outer race.
20. Install new CV-boot.
21. Tighten clamp securely but not to the point where the clamp bridge is cut or the boot is damaged.
22. Position stop ring and new circlip into grooves on shaft.
23. Fill CV-joint outer race with 3.2 oz. (90 grams) of grease, the spread 1.4 oz. (40 grams) of grease evenly inside boot for a total combined fill of 4.6 oz. (130 grams).
24. With boot peeled back, install CV-joint using soft tipped hammer. Ensure splines are aligned prior to installing CV-joint onto shaft.
25. Remove all excess grease from the CV-joint external surfaces.
26. Position boot over CV-joint. Before installing boot clamp, move CV-joint in or out, as necessary, to adjust to the proper length.

NOTE: Insert a suitable tool between the boot and outer bearing race and allow the trapped air to escape from the boot. The air should be released from the boot only after adjusting to the proper dimensions.

27. Ensure boot is seated in its groove and clamp in position.
28. Tighten clamp securely but not to the point where the clamp bridge is cut or the boot is damaged.
29. Install halfshaft assembly in vehicle.
30. Connect negative battery cable.

TRIPOD TYPE

1. Disconnect the negative battery cable.
2. Remove halfshaft assembly from vehicle. Place halfshaft in vice. Do not allow vise jaws to contact the boot or its clamp. The vise should be equipped with jaw caps to prevent damage to any machined surfaces.
3. Cut the large boot clamp using side cutters and peel away from the boot. After removing the clamp, roll boot back over shaft.
4. Bend retaining tabs back slightly to allow for tripod removal.
5. Separate outer race from tripod.
6. Move stop ring back on shaft using snapring pliers.

7. Move tripod assembly back on shaft to allow access to circlip.

8. Remove circlip from shaft.

9. Remove tripod assembly from shaft. Remove boot.

10. When replacing damaged CV-boots, the grease should be checked for contamination. If the CV-joints were operating satisfactorily and the grease does not appear to be contaminated, add grease and replace the boot. If the lubricant appears contaminated, proceed with a complete CV-joint disassembly and inspection.

To install:

11. Clean all parts (except boots) in a suitable solvent.

12. Inspect all CV-joint parts for excessive wear, looseness, pitting, rust and cracks.

NOTE: CV-joint components are matched during assembly. If inspection reveals damage or wear the entire joint must be replaced as an assembly. Do not replace a joint merely because the parts appear polished. Shiny areas in ball races and on the cage spheres are normal.

13. Install new CV-boot.

14. Tighten clamp securely but not to the point where the clamp bridge is cut or the boot is damaged.

15. Install tripod assembly on shaft with chamfered side toward stop ring.

16. Install new circlip.

17. Compress circlip and slide tripod assembly forward over circlip to expose stop ring groove.

18. Move stop ring into groove using snapring pliers. Ensure it is fully seated in groove.

19. Fill CV-joint outer race with 3.5 oz. (100 grams) of grease and fill CV boot with 2.1 oz. (60 grams) of grease.

20. Install outer race over tripod assembly and bend 6 retaining tabs back into their original position.

21. Remove all excess grease from CV-joint external surfaces. Position boot over CV-joint. Move CV-joint in and out as necessary, to adjust to proper length.

NOTE: Insert a suitable tool between the boot and outer bearing race and allow the trapped air to escape from the boot. The air should be released from the boot only after adjusting to the proper dimensions.

27. Ensure boot is seated in its groove and clamp in position.

28. Tighten clamp securely but not to the point where the clamp bridge is cut or the boot is damaged.

29. Install a new circlip, supplied with service kit, in groove nearest end of shaft by starting one end in the

groove and working clip over stub shaft end and into groove.

30. Install halfshaft assembly in vehicle.

31. Connect negative battery cable.

Outer Boot

1. Disconnect the negative battery cable.

2. Remove halfshaft assembly from vehicle.

3. Place halfshaft in vice. Do not allow vise jaws to contact the boot or its clamp. The vise should be equipped with jaw caps to prevent damage to any machined surfaces.

4. Cut the large boot clamp using side cutters and peel away from the boot. After removing the clamp, roll boot back over shaft.

5. Support the interconnecting shaft in a soft jaw vise and angle the CV-joint to expose inner bearing race.

6. Using a brass drift and hammer, give a sharp tap to the inner bearing race to dislodge the internal circlip and separate the CV-joint from the interconnecting shaft. Take care not to drop the CV-joint at separation.

7. Remove the boot.

8. When replacing damaged CV-boots, the grease should be checked for contamination. If the CV-joints were operating satisfactorily and the grease does not appear to be contaminated, add grease and replace the boot. If the lubricant appears contaminated, proceed with a complete CV-joint disassembly and inspection.

9. Remove circlip located near the end of the shaft. Discard the circlip. Use new clip supplied with boot replacement kit and CV-joint overhaul kit.

10. Clamp CV-joint stub shaft in a vise with the outer face facing up. Care should be taken not to damage dust seal. The vise must be equipped with jaw caps to prevent damage to the shaft splines.

11. Press down on inner race until it tilts enough to allow removal of ball. A tight assembly can be tilted by tapping the inner race with wooden dowel and hammer. Do not hit the cage.

12. With cage sufficiently tilted, remove ball from cage. Remove all 6 balls in this manner.

13. Pivot cage and inner race assembly until it is straight up and down in outer race. Align cage windows with outer race lands while pivoting the bearing cage. With the cage pivoted and aligned, lift assembly from the outer race.

14. Rotate inner race up and out of the cage.

To install:

15. Clean all parts (except boots) in a suitable solvent.

16. Inspect all CV-joint parts for excessive wear, looseness, pitting, rust and cracks.

NOTE: CV-joint components are matched during assembly. If inspection reveals damage or wear the entire joint must be replaced as an assembly. Do not replace a joint merely because the parts appear polished. Shiny areas in ball races and on the cage spheres are normal.

17. Apply a light coating of grease on inner and outer ball races. Install the inner race in cage.

18. Install inner race and cage assembly in the outer race.

19. Install the assembly vertically and pivot 90 degrees into position.

20. Align cage and inner race with outer race. Tilt inner race and cage and install one of the 6 balls. Repeat this process until the remaining balls are installed.

21. Install new CV-joint boot.

22. Tighten clamp securely but not to the point where the clamp bridge is cut or the boot is damaged.

23. Install the stop ring, if removed.

24. Install a new circlip, supplied with the service kit, in groove nearest the end of the shaft.

25. Pack CV-joint with grease. Any grease remaining in tube should be spread evenly inside boot.

26. With the boot "peeled" back, position CV-joint on shaft and tap into position using a plastic tipped hammer.

27. Remove all excess grease from the CV-joint external surfaces.

28. Position boot over CV-joint.

29. Ensure boot is seated in its groove and clamp into position.

30. Tighten clamp securely but not to the point where the clamp bridge is cut or the boot is damaged.

31. Install halfshaft assembly in vehicle.

32. Connect negative battery cable.

Driveshaft and U-Joints
REMOVAL & INSTALLATION

Tempo and Topaz with AWD

1. Raise the vehicle and support safely. Be sure to support the driveshaft using a suitable jack or hoist under the center bearing during removal and installation.

2. To maintain the driveshaft balance, mark the U-joints so they may be installed in their original position.

3. Remove the U-joint retaining bolts and straps. Slide the driveshaft toward the rear of the vehicle to disengage it.

4. Remove the rear U-joint bolts and retaining the driveshaft, from the torque tube yoke flange.

5. Slide the driveshaft toward the front of the vehicle to disengage. Do [not al]low the splined shafts to contact [with] excessive force.

[6.] Remove the center bearing retaining bolts. Remove the driveshaft and retain the bearing cups with tape, if necessary.

7. Inspect the U-joint assemblies for wear and or damage, replace the U-joint, if necessary.

To install:

8. Install the driveshaft at the rear torque yoke flange. Ensure that the U-joint is in its original position.

9. Install the U-joint retaining bolts and caps. Torque them to 15–17 ft. lbs. (21–23 Nm). Position the front U-joint. Install the U-joint retaining caps and bolts. Torque them to 15–17 ft. lbs. (21–23 Nm).

10. Install the center bearing and retaining bolts. Torque to 23–30 ft. lbs. (31–41 Nm). Do not drop the assembled driveshafts as the impact may cause damage to the U-joint bearing cups.

Front Wheel Hub, Knuckle and Bearings

REMOVAL & INSTALLATION

1. Remove wheel cover/hub cover from wheel and tire assembly and loosen wheel nuts.

2. Remove hub nut retainer and washer by applying sufficient torque to nut to break locking tab and remove hub nut retainer. The hub nut retainer must be discarded after removal.

3. Raise and safely support the vehicle. Remove wheel and tire assembly.

4. Remove brake caliper by loosening caliper locating pins and rotating caliper off rotor starting from lower end of caliper and lifting upward. Do not remove caliper pins from caliper assembly. Lift caliper off rotor and hang it free of rotor. Do not allow caliper assembly to hang from brake hose. Support caliper assembly with a length of wire.

5. Remove rotor from hub by pulling it off hub bolts. If rotor is difficult to remove from hub, strike rotor sharply between studs with a rubber or plastic hammer. If rotor will not pull off, apply rust penetrator to inboard and outboard rotor hub mating surfaces. Install a 3 jaw puller and remove rotor by pulling on rotor outside diameter and pushing on hub center. If excessive force is required for removal, check rotor for lateral runout.

6. Later runout must be checked with nuts clamping hat section of rotor.

7. Remove rotor splash shield.

8. Disconnect lower control arm and tie rod from knuckle (leave strut attached.).

9. Loosen the 2 strut top mount-to-apron nuts.

10. Install a suitable hub removal tool and remove hub/bearing/knuckle assembly by pushing out CV-joint outer shaft until it is free of assembly.

11. Support knuckle with a length of wire, remove strut bolt and slide hub/knuckle assembly off strut.

12. Carefully remove support wire and transfer hub/bearing assembly to bench.

13. Install a suitable front hub puller with jaws of puller on the knuckle bosses and remove hub.

NOTE: Ensure the shaft protector is centered, clears the bearing inside diameter and rests on the end face of the hub journal.

14. Remove snapring which retains bearing knuckle assembly and discard.

15. Using a hydraulic press, place a suitable front bearing spacer step side up on press plate and position knuckle on spacer with outboard side up. Install bearing removal tool on bearing inner race and press bearing out of knuckle.

16. Discard bearing.

17. Remove halfshaft.

18. Place halfshaft in vise. Remove bearing dust seal by uniformly tapping on outer edge with a light-duty hammer and screwdriver. Discard dust seal.

To install:

19. Place halfshaft in vise. Install a new dust seal using a suitable seal installer. Seal flange must face outboard.

20. Install halfshaft.

21. On bench, remove all foreign material from knuckle bearing bore and hub bearing journal to ensure correct seating of new bearing.

NOTE: If hub bearing journal is scored or damaged, replace hub. Do not attempt to service. The

front wheel bearings are of a cartridge design and are pregreased, sealed and require no scheduled maintenance. The bearings are preset and cannot be adjusted. If a bearing is disassembled for any reason, it must be replaced as a unit. No individual service seals, rollers or races are available.

22. Place suitable bearing spacer step side down on hydraulic press plate and position knuckle on spacer with outboard side down. Position a new bearing in inboard side of knuckle. Install a suitable front bearing installer on bearing outer race face with undercut side facing bearing and press bearing into knuckle. Ensure that bearing seats completely against shoulder of knuckle bore.

NOTE: Ensure proper positioning of bearing installer during installation to prevent bearing damage.

23. Install a new snapring in knuckle groove using snapring pliers.

24. Place suitable front bearing spacer on arbor press plate and position hub on tool with lugs facing downward. Position knuckle assembly on hub barrel with outboard side down. Place a suitable front bearing remover on inner race of bearing and press down on tool until bearing is freely in knuckle after installation.

25. Suspend hub/knuckle/bearing assembly on vehicle with wire and attach strut loosely to knuckle. Lubricate CV-joint stub shaft splines with SAE 30 weight motor oil and insert shaft into hub splines as far as possible using hand pressure only. Check that spline are properly engaged.

26. Install suitable front hub installer and wheel bolt adapter to hub and stub shaft. Tighten hub installer tool to 120 ft. lbs. (162 Nm) to ensure that hub is fully seated.

27. Remove tool and install washer and new hub nut retainer. Tighten hub nut retainer finger-tight.

28. Complete installation of front suspension components.

29. Install disc brake rotor to hub assembly.

30. Install disc brake caliper over rotor.

31. Ensure outer brake shoe spring end is seated under upper arm of knuckle.

32. Install wheel and tire assembly, tightening wheel nuts finger-tight.

33. Lower vehicle and block wheels to prevent vehicle from rolling.

34. Tighten wheel nuts to 85–105 ft. lbs. (115–142 Nm).

35. Manually thread hub nut retainer assembly on constant velocity output shaft as far as possible using a

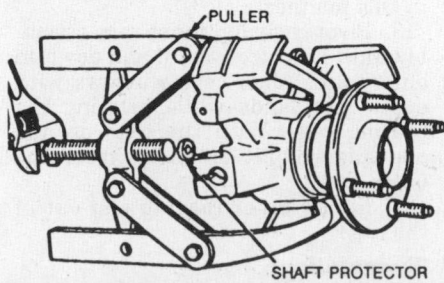

Front hub puller

30mm or 1³⁄₁₆ in. socket, tighten retainer assembly to 180–200 ft. lbs. (245–270 Nm).

NOTE: Do not use power or impact tools to tighten the hub nut. Do not move the vehicle before retainer is tightened.

36. During tightening, an audible click sound will indicate proper ratchet function of the hub nut retainer. As the hub nut retainer tightens, ensure that one of the 3 locking tabs is in the slot of the CV-joint shaft. If the hub nut retainer is damaged, or more than 1 locking tab is broken, replace the hub nut retainer.

37. Install wheelcover or hub cover and lower vehicle completely to ground.

38. Remove wheel blocks.

Axle Housing

REMOVAL & INSTALLATION

1. Disconnect the negative battery cable.

2. Raise and safely support the vehicle.

NOTE: Anytime a U-joint retaining bolt is removed, Loctite® or equivalent, must be applied to the retaining bolts prior to installation.

3. Position a hoist or jack under rear axle housing.

4. Remove muffler and exhaust system from catalytic converter back.

5. Remove rear U-joint retaining bolts and straps retaining driveshaft, from torque tube yoke flange. Remove driveshaft center bearing bolts. Disengage driveshaft from axle yoke and position driveshaft off to 1 side.

6. Remove 4 retaining bolts from torque tube support bracket. Remove damper.

7. Disconnect axle vent hose clip form body.

8. Remove axle retaining bolt from left hand differential support bracket.

9. Remove axle retaining bolt from center differential support bracket.

10. Lower axle assembly and remove inboard U-joint retaining bolts and straps from each halfshaft. Remove and wire halfshaft assemblies out of the way.

11. Remove rear axle assembly.

To install:

12. Position rear axle assembly under vehicle. Raise axle far enough for U-joint and halfshaft assemblies to be installed.

13. Position each inboard U-joint to rear axle. Install U-joint straps and retaining bolts.Using a T-30 Torx® bit,

tighten bolts to 15–17 ft. lbs. (21–23 Nm).

14. Raise into position being careful not to trap or pinch axle vent hose. Install bolts attaching differential housig to left hand and center differential support bracket. Tighten to 70–80 ft. lbs. (95–108 Nm).

15. Attach axle vent hose clip to body.

16. Position torque tube and mounting bracket and damper to crossmember.Install 4 attaching bolts. Tighten to 28–35 ft. lbs. (38–47 Nm). Install driveshaft and retaining bolts to torque tube yoke flange. Using a T-30 Torx® bit, tighten to 15–17 ft. lbs. (21–23 Nm).

17. Install exhaust from catalytic converter back.

18. Check lubricant level in axle.

19. Lower vehicle.

STEERING

Steering Wheel

CAUTION

On vehicles equipped with an air bag, the negative battery cable must be disconnected, before working on the system. Failure to do so may result in deployment of the air bag and possible personal injury.

REMOVAL & INSTALLATION

1. Disconnect the negative battery cable. Remove the steering wheel center horn pad cover by removing the retaining screws from the steering wheel assembly.

NOTE: The emblem assembly is removed after the horn pad cover is removed, by pushing it out from the backside of the emblem.

2. Remove the energy absorbing foam from the wheel assembly, if equipped. Remember the energy absorbing foam must be installed when the steering wheel is assembled. Disconnect the horn pad wiring connector.

3. On vehicles equipped with air bag restraint system, remove the 4 nuts located on the back of the steering wheel holding the air bag module to the steering wheel.

4. Lift the air bag module from the wheel and disconnect the air bag module to slip-ring clock spring connector.

5. On all vehicles, loosen and remove the center mounting nut and on the vehicles equipped with speed control system, remove the electrical con-

nectors. Discard the center nut and replace with new.

6. Remove the steering wheel with a suitable puller. Do not use a knock-off type puller, because it will cause damage to the collapsible steering column. Grasp the rim of the steering wheel and pull the steering wheel from the upper shaft.

NOTE: The multi-switch lever switch must be in the neutral position before installing the steering wheel or damage to the switch cam may result.

7. Position the steering wheel on the end of the steering wheel shaft. Align the mark on the steering wheel with the mark on the shaft to assure the straight-ahead steering wheel position corresponds to the straight-ahead position of the front wheels.

8. Install a new service wheel locknut or bolt. Torque the nut to 50–60 ft. lbs. and the bolt to 23–33 ft. lbs. Connect all the electrical connectors on the vehicles equipped with speed control.

9. If equipped with air bag, connect the air bag module wire to slip ring connector and place the module on the steering wheel with the 4 attaching nuts, torque the nuts to 35–33 inch lbs.

10. On the other vehicles, install the steering wheel hub cover and torque the nuts to 13–20 inch lbs.

11. Reconnect the negative battery cable and check the steering wheel for proper operation.

Steering Column
REMOVAL & INSTALLATION

NOTE: On air bag equipped vehicles, whenever the steering column is separated from the steering gear for any reason, the steering column must be locked to prevent the steering wheel from being rotated, which in turn will prevent damage to the air bag clockspring.

1. Disconnect the negative battery cable.

NOTE: Before disconnecting cable on air bag equipped vehicles, ensure wheels are in straight ahead position. Turn ignition switch to LOCK position and rotate steering wheel about 16 degrees counterclockwise until locked into position.

2. Remove steering column cover on lower portion of instrument panel (2 screws).

3. Remove speed control module, if so equipped (2 screws).

4. Remove lower steering column shroud (5 screws).

5. Loosen, but do not remove, 2 nuts and 2 bolts retaining steering column to support bracket and remove upper shroud.

6. Disconnect all steering column electrical connections: ignition, wash/wipe, turn signal, key warning buzzer, speed control. On console shift automatic transaxle, remove interlock cable retaining screw and disconnect cable from steering column.

7. Loosen steering column to intermediate shaft clamp connection and remove bolt or nut.

8. Remove 2 nuts and 2 bolts retaining steering column to support bracket.

9. Pry open steering column shaft in area of clamp on each side of bolt groove with steering column locked. Open enough to disengage shafts with minimal effort. Do not use excessive force.

10. Inspect 2 steering column bracket clips for damage. If clips have been bent or excessively distorted, they must be replaced.

To install:

11. Engage lower steering shaft to intermediate shaft and hand start clamp bolt and nut.

12. Align 2 bolts on steering column support bracket assembly with outer tube mounting holes and hand start 2 nuts. Check for presence of 2 clips on outer bracket. The clips must be present to ensure adequate performance of vital parts and systems. Hand start 2 bolts through outer tube upper bracket and clip and into support bracket nuts. On console shift automatic transaxles, install interlock cable and retaining screw.

13. Connect all quick-connect electrical connections: turn signal, wash/wipe, key warning buzzer, ignition, speed control and air bag clockspring connector, if equipped.

14. Install upper shroud.

15. Tighten steering column mounting nuts and bolts to 15–25 ft. lbs. (20–34 Nm).

16. On air bag equipped vehicles, unlock steering column and cycle steering wheel 1 turn left and 1 turn right to align intermediate shaft into column shaft. Power steering vehicles must have engine running.

17. Tighten steering shaft clamp nut to 20–30 ft. lbs. (27–40 Nm).

18. Install lower trim shroud with 5 screws.

19. Install speed control module, if equipped, with 2 screws.

20. Install steering column cover on instrument panel with 2 screws.

21. Connect battery ground cable.

22. Check steering column for proper operation.

Manual Steering Rack

ADJUSTMENT

Tie Rod Articulation Effort

1. With outer tie rod end removed from steering knuckle, loop a piece of wire through the hole in the tie rod end stud. Insert hook of spring scale through wire loop. Effort to move the tie rod after initial breakaway should be 0.7–5 ft. (3.1–22.2 N).

NOTE: Do not damage rod neck.

2. Replace ball joint/tie rod assembly if effort falls outside this range. Save tie rod end for use on new tie rod assembly.

REMOVAL & INSTALLATION

1. Disconnect the negative battery cable.

2. Turn the ignition key to the RUN position.

3. Remove the access trim panel from below the steering column.

4. Remove the intermediate shaft bolts at the rack and pinion input shaft and the steering column shaft.

5. Spread the slots enough to loosen the intermediate shaft at both ends. They cannot be separated at this time.

6. Raise the vehicle and support it safely. Separate the tie rod ends from the steering knuckles, using tool 3290-C or equivalent. Turn the steering wheel a full left turn so that the tie rod will clear the shift linkage for removal.

7. Separate the tie rod ends from the steering knuckles. Turn the right wheel to the full left turn position.

8. Remove the left tie rod end from the left tie rod and disconnect the speedometer cable at the transaxle on automatic transaxles only.

9. Disconnect the secondary air tube at the check valve. Disconnect the exhaust system at the manifold and support the exhaust system to allow clearance for the gear removal.

NOTE: Do not allow the exhaust system to hang by the rear support hangers. The system could fall to the floor.

10. Remove the exhaust hanger bracket from below the steering gear.

11. Remove the gear mounting brackets and insulators. Keep separated as they are not interchangeable.

12. Separate the gear assembly from the intermediate shaft, with an assistant pulling upward on the shaft from the inside of the vehicle.

NOTE: Care should be taken during steering gear removal and

installation to prevent tearing or damaging the steering gear bellows.

13. Rotate the gear forward and down to clear the input shaft through the dash panel opening.

14. With the gear in the full left turn position, move the gear through the right (passenger side) apron opening until the left tie rod clears the shift linkage and other parts so it may be lowered.

15. Lower the left side of the gear assembly and remove from the vehicle.

To install:

16. Rotate the input shaft to a full left turn stop. Position the right wheel to a full left turn.

17. Start the right side of the gear through the opening in the right apron. Move the gear in until the left tie rod clears all parts so that it may be raised up to the left apron opening.

18. Raise the gear and insert the left hand side through the apron opening. Rotate the gear so that the joint shaft enters the dash panel opening.

19. With an assistant guiding the intermediate shaft from the inside of the vehicle, insert the input shaft into the intermediate shaft coupling. Insert the intermediate shaft clamp bolts finger tight. Do not tighten at this time.

20. Install the gear mounting insulators and brackets in their proper places. Ensure the flat in the left mounting area is parallel to the dash panel. Tighten the bracket bolts in the sequence as described below:

   a. Tighten the left (driver's side) upper bolt halfway.

   b. Tighten the left hand lower bolt.

   c. Tighten the left hand upper bolt.

   d. Tighten the right hand bolts.

   e. Do not forget that the right hand and left hand insulators and brackets are not interchangeable side to side.

21. Attach the tie rod ends to the steering knuckles. Tighten the castellated nuts to minimum specifications, then tighten the nuts until the slot aligns with the cotter pin hole. Insert a new cotter pin.

22. Install the exhaust system. Install the speedometer cable, if removed.

23. Tighten the gear input shaft to intermediate shaft coupling clamp bolt first. Then, tighten the upper intermediate shaft clamp bolt.

24. Install the access panel below the steering column. Turn the ignition key to the OFF position.

25. Check and adjust the toe. Tighten the tie rod end jam nuts, check for twisted bellows.

Power Steering Rack

ADJUSTMENT

Rack Yoke Plug Preload

NOTE: This adjustment can be performed only with the gear out of the vehicle.

1. Disconnect the negative battery cable.
2. Raise and safely support the vehicle.
3. Remove power rack assembly from vehicle.
4. Clean exterior of steering gear thoroughly.
5. Mount steering gear in a suitable rack housing holding fixture.

NOTE: Do not mount gear in vice.

6. Do not remove external pressure lines, unless they are leaking or damaged. If these lines are removed, they must be replaced with new lines.
7. Drain power steering fluid by rotating unput shaft lock-to-lock twice using input shaft torque adapter T81P-3504-R or equivalent. Position adapter and wrench on input shaft.
8. Loosen yoke plug locknut with yoke locknut wrench T81P-3504-G or equivalent.
9. Loosen yoke plug using yoke plug adapter T87P-3504-G or equivalent.
10. With rack at center of travel, tighten yoke plug to 44–50 inch lbs. (5.0–5.7 Nm). Clean threads of yoke plug prior to tightening to prevent a false reading.
11. install yoke plug adapter T87P-3504-G or equivalent. Mark location of zero degree mark on housing. Back off adjuster so 48 degree mark lines up with zero degree mark.
12. Place yoke locknut wrench T81P-3504-G or equivalent, on yoke plug locknut. While holding yoke plug, tighten locknut to 40–50 ft. lbs. (54–68 Nm). Do not allow yoke plug to move while tightening or preload will be affected. Check input shaft torque after tightening locknut.
13. If external pressure lines were removed, the Teflon® seal rings must be replaced. Clean out Teflon® seal shreds from housing ports prior to installation of new lines.
14. Install power rack assembly in vehicle.
15. Lower vehicle.
16. Connect negative battery cable.

REMOVAL & INSTALLATION

1. Disconnect the negative battery cable.
2. Turn the ignition key to the **RUN** position.
3. Remove access panel from dash below the steering column.
4. Remove screws from steering column boot at the dash panel and slide boot up intermediate shaft.
5. Remove intermediate shaft bolt at gear input shaft and loosen the bolt at the steering column shaft joint.
6. With a suitable tool, spread the slots enough to loosen intermediates shaft at both ends. The intermediate shaft and gear input shaft cannot be separated at this time.
7. Remove the air cleaner.
8. On Escort and Lynx with air conditioning, wire the air conditioner liquid line above the dash panel opening. Doing so provides clearance for gear input shaft removal and installation.
9. Separate pressure and return lines at intermediate connections and drain fluid.
10. On Tempo and Topaz without diesel engine, remove the pressure switch.
11. Disconnect the exhaust secondary air tube at check valve. Raise the vehicle and support it safely. Disconnect exhaust system at exhaust manifold and remove exhaust system.
12. Separate tie rod ends from steering knuckles.
13. Remove left tie rod end from tie rod on manual transaxle vehicles. This will allow tie rod to clear the shift linkage.

NOTE: Mark location of rod end prior to removal.

14. Disconnect speedometer cable at transaxle on vehicles equipped with automatic transaxle. Remove the vehicle speed sensor.
15. Remove transaxle shift cable assembly at transaxle on vehicles equipped with automatic transaxle.
16. Turn steering wheel to full left turn stop for easier gear removal.
17. On Escort and Lynx, remove screws holding the heater water tube to shake brace below the oil pan.
18. On Escort and Lynx, remove nut from the lower of 2 bolts holding engine mount support bracket to transaxle housing. Tap bolt out as far as it will go.
19. Remove the gear mounting brackets and insulators.
20. Drape cloth towel over both apron opening edges to protect bellows during gear removal.
21. Separate gear from intermediate shaft by either pushing up on shaft with a bar from underneath the vehicle while pulling the gear down or with an assistant removing the shaft from inside the vehicle.
22. Rotate gear forward and down to clear the input shaft through the dash panel opening.
23. Make sure input shaft is in full left turn position. Move gear through the right (passenger) side apron opening until left tie rod clears left apron opening and other parts so it may be lowered. Guide the power steering hoses around the nearby components as the gear is being removed.
24. Lower the left hand side of the gear and remove the gear out of the vehicle. Use care not to tear the bellows.
To install:
25. Rotate the input shaft to a full left turn stop. Position the right road wheel to a full left turn.
26. Start the right side of the gear through the opening in the right apron. Move the gear in until the left tie rod clears all parts so that it may be raised up to the left apron opening.
27. Raise the gear and insert the left hand side through the apron opening. Move the power steering hoses into their proper position at the same time. Rotate the gear so that the joint shaft enters the dash panel opening.
28. With an assistant guiding the intermediate shaft from the inside of the vehicle, insert the input shaft into the intermediate shaft coupling. Insert the intermediate shaft clamp bolts finger tight. Do not tighten at this time.
29. Install the gear mounting insulators and brackets in their proper places. Ensure the flat in the left mounting area is parallel to the dash panel. Tighten the bracket bolts in the sequence as described below:
   a. Tighten the left (driver's side) upper bolt halfway.
   b. Tighten the left hand lower bolts.
   c. Tighten the left hand upper bolts.
   d. Tighten the right hand bolts.
   e. Do not forget that the right hand and left hand insulators and brackets are not interchangeable side to side.
30. Attach the tie rod ends to the steering knuckles. Tighten the castellated nuts to minimum specification, then tighten the nuts until the slot aligns with the cotter pin hole. Insert a new cotter pin.
31. On the Escort and Lynx, install the engine mount nut.
32. On the Escort and Lynx, install the heater water tube to the shake brace.
33. Install the exhaust system. Install the speedometer cable, if removed. Install the vehicle speed sensor and the transaxle shift cable.
34. Connect the secondary air tube at the check valve. Connect the pressure and return lines at the steering gear. Install the pressure switch, if removed.
35. Tighten the gear input shaft to intermediate shaft coupling clamp bolt

first. Then, tighten the upper intermediate shaft clamp bolt.

36. Install the access panel below the steering column. Turn the ignition key to the **OFF** position.

37. Fill the system. Check and adjust the toe. Tighten the tie rod end jam nuts, check for twisted bellows.

38. Connect negative battery cable.

Power Steering Pump

REMOVAL & INSTALLATION

Tempo and Topaz

1. Disconnect the negative battery cable. Loosen the alternator and remove the drive belt. Pivot the alternator to it most upright position.

2. Remove the radiator overflow bottle. Loosen and remove the power steering pump drive belt. Mark the pulley and pump drive hub with paint or grease pencil for location reference.

3. Remove the pulleys from the pump shaft.

4. Remove the return line from the pump. Be prepared to catch any spilled fluid in a suitable container.

5. Back off the pressure line attaching nut completely. The line will separate from the pump connection when the pump is removed.

6. Remove the pump mounting bolts and remove the pump.

7. Complete the installation of the pump by reversing the removal procedure. Fill the pump with fluid and check the system for proper opreation.

Escort and Lynx

1. Disconnect the negative battery cable. Remove the air cleaner, thermactor air pump and belt. Remove the reservoir filler extension and cover the hole to prevent dirt from entering.

2. On vehicles equipped with EFI and remote reservoir, remove the reservoir supply hose at the pump, drain the fluid and plug or cap the opening at the pump to prevent entry of contaminants during removal.

3. From under the vehicle, loosen 1 pump adjusting bolt. Remove 1 pump to bracket mounting bolt and disconnect the fluid return line.

4. From above the vehicle, loosen 1 adjusting bolt and the pivot bolt. Remove the drive belt and the 2 remaining pump to bracket mounting bolts.

5. Remove the pump by passing the pulley through the adjusting bracket opening. Remove the pressure hose from the pump assembly.

6. Complete the installation of the pump assembly by reversing the removal procedure. Fill the pump with fluid and check the system for proper operation.

BELT ADJUSTMENT

1.9L and 2.0L Engines

1. From engine compartment, loosen pivot bolt and upper adjustment bolt.

2. Raise and safely support the vehicle. From below vehicle:

   a. Loosen lower adjustment bolt.

   b. Apply pressure with ½ drive breaker bar.

   c. Tighten lower adjustment bolt to 38 ft. lbs. (52 Nm).

3. Lower vehicle. From engine compartment, tighten pivot bolt and upper adjustment bolt to 38 ft. lbs. (52 Nm).

2.3L Engine

The power steering belt on the 2.3L engine is drive by the accessory V-ribbed belt. Belt tension is maintained by the automatic belt tensioner and does not require adjustment.

SYSTEM BLEEDING

If air bubbles are present in the power steering fluid, bleed the system by performing the following:

1. Fill the reservoir to the proper level.

2. Operate the engine until the fluid reaches normal operating temperature (165–175°F).

3. Turn the steering wheel all the way to the left then all the way to the right several times. Do not hold the steering wheel in the far left or far right position stops.

4. Check the fluid level and recheck the fluid for the presence of trapped air. If apparent that air is still in the system, fabricate or obtain a vacuum tester and purge the system as follows:

   a. Remove the pump dipstick cap assembly.

   b. Check and fill the pump reservoir with fluid to the **COLD FULL** mark on the dipstick.

   c. Disconnect the ignition wire and raise the front of the vehicle and support safely.

   d. Crank the engine with the starter and check the fluid level. Do not turn the steering wheel at this time.

   e. Fill the pump reservoir to the **COLD FULL** mark on the dipstick. Crank the engine with the starter while cycling the steering wheel lock-to-lock. Check the fluid level.

   f. Tightly insert a suitable size rubber stopper and air evacuator pump into the reservoir fill neck. Connect the ignition coil wire.

   g. With the engine idling, apply a 15 in. Hg vacuum to the reservoir for 3 minutes. As air is purged from the system, the vacuum will drop off. Maintain the vacuum on the sys-

tem as required throughout the 3 minutes.

   h. Remove the vacuum source. Fill the reservoir to the **COLD FULL** mark on the dipstick.

   i. With the engine idling, re-apply 15 in. Hg vacuum source to the reservoir. Slowly cycle the steering wheel to lock-to-lock stops for approximately 5 minutes. Do not hold the steering wheel on the stops during cycling. Maintain the vacuum as required.

   j. Release the vacuum and disconnect the vacuum source. Add fluid, as required.

   k. Start the engine and cycle the wheel slowly and check for leaks at all connections.

   l. Lower the front wheels.

5. In cases of severe aeration, repeat the procedure.

Tie Rod Ends

REMOVAL & INSTALLATION

1. Remove and discard cotter pin and nut from worn tie rod end ball stud.

2. Disconnect tie rod end from spindle, using tie rod end remover tool 3290-D and adapter T81P-3504-W or equivalent.

3. Holding tie rod end with a wrench, loosen tie rod jam nut.

4. Grip tie rod hex flats with a pair of suitable locking pliers, and remove tie rod end assembly from tie rod. Note depth to which tie rod was located, using jam nut as a marker.

To install:

5. Clean tie rod threads. Apply a light coating of disc brake caliper slide grease D7AZ-19590-A or equivalent, to tie rod threads. Thread new tie rod end on tie rod to same depth as removed tie rod end. Tighten jam nut.

6. Place tie rod end stud into steering spindle.

7. Install a new nut on tie rod end stud. Tighten nut to minimum specification, and continue tightening nut to align next castellation with cotter pin hole in stud. Install a new cotter pin.

8. Set toe to specification and tighten jam nuts to specification. Do not twist bellows.

BRAKES

For all brake system repair and service procedures not detailed below, please refer to "Brakes" in the Unit Repair Section.

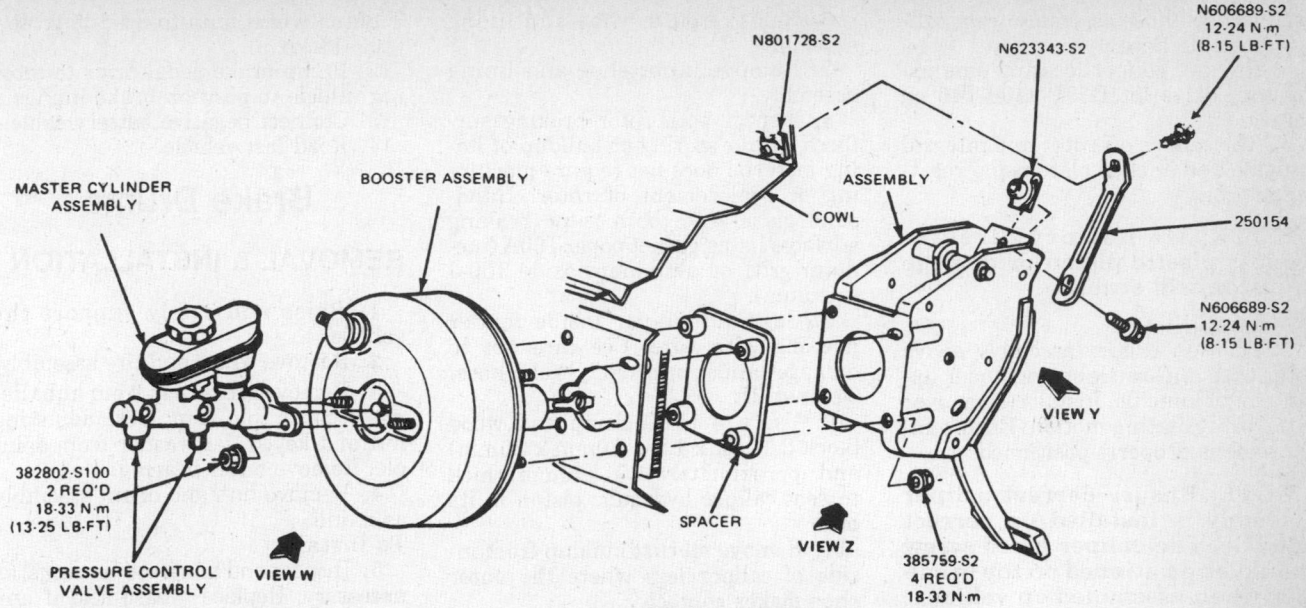

Typical master cylinder and power brake booster mounting

Master Cylinder

REMOVAL & INSTALLATION

1. Disconnect the negative battery cable.
2. Disconnect and plug the brake lines from the primary and secondary outlet ports of the master cylinder and the pressure control valve.
3. Remove the nuts attaching the master cylinder to the brake booster assembly. Disconnect the brake warning lamp wire.
4. Slide the master cylinder forward and upward from the vehicle.

To install:

5. Mount the master cylinder on the booster. Attach the brake fluid lines to the master cylinder but leave the fittings slightly loose.
6. Install the brake warning lamp wire.
7. Fill the reservoirs with fresh brake fluid. Use the foot pedal to bleed the master cylinder. Tighten the brake line fittings. Bleed the system.
8. Connect negative battery cable.

Pressure Control Valves

These valves are housed in the master cylinder assembly. One valve controls each rear wheel brake cylinder. They are designed to reduce the hydraulic pressure to the rear wheel brake cylinders when the pressure exceeds a pre-set value. The hydraulic pressure is limited in order to prevent rear wheel skidding during hard braking.

REMOVAL & INSTALLATION

1. Disconnect and plug primary and secondary brake tubes from master cylinder, as necessary.
2. Loosen and remove pressure control valve from the master cylinder housing.

To install:

3. Install pressure control valve in master cylinder housing port and tighten to 10–18 ft. lbs. (13–24 Nm).
4. Install the brake tube and tighten to 10–18 ft. lbs. (13–24 Nm).
5. Fill and bleed hydraulic system as outlined.

Power Brake Booster

REMOVAL & INSTALLATION

1. Disconnect the battery ground cable and remove the brake lines from the master cylinder.
2. Remove the retaining nuts and remove the master cylinder.
3. From under the instrument panel, remove the stoplight switch wiring connector from the switch. Remove the pushrod retainer and outer nylon washer from the brake pin, slide the stoplight switch along the brake pedal pin, far enough for the outer hole to clear the pin.
4. Remove the switch by sliding it upward. Remove the booster to dash panel retaining nuts. Slide the booster pushrod and pushrod bushing off the brake pedal pin.
5. Position the wire harness out of the way. Remove the transaxle shift cable and bracket.
6. Disconnect the manifold vacuum hose from the booster check valve and move the booster forward until the booster studs clear the dash panel and remove the booster.
7. Complete the installation of the power booster assembly by reversing the removal procedure. Bleed the brake system.

NOTE: On vehicles equipped with speed control, the vacuum dump valve must be adjusted if the brake booster has been removed.

8. To adjust the vacuum dump valve, complete the following:
    a. Firmly depress and hold the brake pedal.
    b. Push in the dump valve until the valve collar bottoms against the retaining clip.
    c. Place a 0.050–0.10 in. shim between the white button of the valve and the pad on the brake pedal.
    d. Firmly pull the brake pedal rearward to its normal position, allowing the dump valve to ratchet backward in the retaining clip.

Brake Caliper

REMOVAL & INSTALLATION

1. Disconnect the negative battery cable.
2. Raise and safely support the vehicle.
3. Remove wheel and tire assembly from rotor mounting face.
4. Disconnect flexible brake hose from caliper. Remove hollow retaining bolt that connects hose fitting to cali-

per. Remove hose assembly from caliper and plug hose.

5. Remove caliper locating pins using torx drive bit D79P-2100-T40 or equivalent.

6. Lift caliper off rotor and integral knuckle and anchor plate using rotating motion.

NOTE: Do not pry directly against plastic piston or damage to piston will occur.

To install:

7. Position caliper assembly above rotor with anti-rattle spring under upper arm of knuckle. Install caliper over rotor with rotating motion. Ensure inner shoe is properly positioned.

NOTE: Ensure correct caliper assembly is installed on correct knuckle. The caliper bleed screw should be positioned on top of caliper when assembled on vehicle.

8. Lubricate locating pins and inside of insulators with silicone grease. Install locating pins through caliper insulators and into knuckle attaching holes. The caliper locating pins must be inserted and threads started by hand.

9. Using torx drive bit D79P-2100-T40 or equivalent, tighten caliper locating pins to 18–25 ft. lbs. (24–34 Nm).

10. Remove plug and install brake hose on caliper with new gasket on each side of fitting outlet. Insert attaching bolt through washers and fittings. Tighten bolts to 30–40 ft. lbs. (40–54 Nm).

11. Bleed brake system. Always replace rubber bleed screw cap after bleeding.

12. Fill master cylinder as required.

13. Install wheel and tire assembly. Tighten wheel nuts to 80–105 ft. lbs. (109–142 Nm).

14. Connect negative battery cable.

15. Pump brake pedal prior to moving vehicle to position brake linings.

16. Road test vehicle.

Disc Brake Pads

REMOVAL & INSTALLATION

1. Remove master cylinder cap and check fluid level in reservoir. Remove brake fluid until reservoir is ½ full. Discard removed fluid.

2. Raise and safely support the vehicle.

3. Remove wheel and tire assembly.

4. Remove caliper locating pins.

5. Lift caliper assembly from integral knuckle and anchor plate and rotor using rotating motion. Do not pry directly against plastic piston or damage will occur.

6. Remove outer shoe and lining assembly.

7. Remove inner shoe and lining assembly.

8. Inspect both rotor braking surfaces. Minor scoring or buildup of lining material does not require machining or replacement of rotor. Hand-sand glaze from both rotor braking surfaces using garnet paper 100A (medium grit) or aluminum oxide 150-J (medium).

9. Suspend caliper inside fender housing with wire. Use care not to damage caliper or stretch brake hose.

To install:

10. Use a 4 in. C-clamp and wood block 2 ¾ in. x 1 in. (70mm x 25mm) and approximately ¾ in. (19mm) thick to seat caliper hydraulic piston in its bore.

11. Remove all rust buildup from inside of caliper legs where the outer shoe makes contact.

12. Install inner shoe and lining assembly in caliper piston(s). Do not bend shoe clips during installation in piston.

13. Install correct outer shoe and lining assembly. Ensure clips are properly seated.

14. Install caliper over rotor.

15. Install wheel and tire assembly. Tighten wheel nuts to 80–105 ft. lbs. (109–142 Nm).

16. Pump brake pedal prior to moving vehicle to position brake linings.

17. Connect negative battery cable.

18. Road test vehicle.

Brake Rotor

REMOVAL & INSTALLATION

1. Disconnect the negative battery cable.

2. Raise and safely support the vehicle.

3. Remove wheel and tire assembly.

4. Remove caliper locating pins.

5. Lift caliper assembly from integral knuckle and anchor plate and rotor using rotating motion. Do not pry directly against plastic piston or damage will occur.

6. Position caliper out of the way and support it with a length of wire to avoid damaging caliper.

7. Remove rotor from hub assembly by pulling it off the hub studs.

To install:

8. If rotor is being replaced, remove protective coating from new rotor with carburetor degreaser. If original rotor is being installed, make sure rotor braking and mounting surfaces are clean.

9. Install rotor on hub assembly.

10. Install caliper assembly on rotor.

11. Install wheel and tire assembly.

Tighten wheel nuts to 80–105 ft. lbs. (109–142 Nm).

12. Pump brake pedal prior to moving vehicle to position brake linings.

13. Connect negative battery cable.

14. Road test vehicle.

Brake Drums

REMOVAL & INSTALLATION

1. Raise and safely support the vehicle.

2. Remove wheel and tire assembly.

3. Remove grease cap from hub. Remove cotter pin, nut lock, adjusting nut and keyed flat washer from spindle. Remove outer bearing.

4. Remove hub and drum assembly as a unit.

To install:

5. Inspect and lubricate bearings, as necessary. Replace grease seal if any damage is visible.

6. Clean spindle stem and apply a thin coat of wheel bearing grease.

7. Install hub and drum assembly on spindle.

8. Install outer bearing into hub on spindle.

9. Install keyed flat washer and adjusting nut. Tighten nut finger-tight.

10. Adjust wheel bearing. Install nut retainer and a new cotter pin.

11. Install grease cap.

12. Install wheel and tire assembly. Tighten wheel nuts to 80–105 ft. lbs. (109–142 Nm).

13. Pump brake pedal prior to moving vehicle to position brake linings.

14. Connect negative battery cable.

15. Road test vehicle.

Brake Shoes

REMOVAL & INSTALLATION

1. Raise and safely support the vehicle.

2. Remove wheel and tire assembly.

3. Remove hub and drum assembly.

4. Remove hold-down spring and pins.

5. Lift brake shoe and adjuster assembly up and away from anchor block and shoe guide. Do not damage the boots when rotating shoes off the wheel cylinder.

6. Remove lower shoe-to-shoe spring from leading and trailing shoe slots.

7. Hold brake shoe/adjuster assembly, remove leading shoe-to-adjuster strut retracting spring.

8. Remove trailing shoe-to-parking brake strut retracting spring by pivoting strut downward until it disengages from trailing shoe.

9. Disassemble adjuster, if neces-

sary, by pulling quadrant away from knurled pin in strut and rotating quadrant in either direction until quadrant teeth are no longer meshed with pin. Remove spring and slide quadrant out of slot. Do not overstress spring during disassembly.

10. Remove parking brake lever from trailing shoe and lining assembly by removing horeshoe retaining clip and spring washer, and lifting lever off pin on brake shoe.

To install:

11. Apply light coating of high temperature grease at points where brake shoes contact the backing plate.

12. Apply light uniform coating of multi-purpose lubricant to strut at contact surface between strut and adjuster quadrant.

13. Install adjuster quadrant pin into slot in strut and install adjuster spring. Pivot quadrant until it meshes with knurled pin in third and fourth notch of outboard end of quadrant.

14. Assemble parking brake lever to trailing shoe. Install spring washer and new horseshoe clip. Crimp clip until lever is securely fastened.

15. Install trailing shoe-to-parking brake strut retracting spring by attaching spring to slots in each part and pivoting strut into position to tension spring.

16. Install lower shoe-to-shoe retracting spring between leading and trailing shoes. The spring hook with the longest straight section fits into hole in trailing shoe.

17. Install leading shoe-to-adjuster/strut retracting spring by installing spring to both parts and pivoting leading shoe over quadrant into position to tension spring.

18. Expand shoe and strut assembly to fit over anchor plate and wheel cylinder piston inserts.

19. Attach parking brake cable to parking brake lever.

20. Install hold-down pins and springs on each shoe and lining assembly.

21. Set brake shoe diameter.

22. Install hub/drum and wheel and tire assemblies.

23. Adjust wheel bearings.

24. Lower vehicle.

Wheel Cylinder

REMOVAL & INSTALLATION

1. Remove wheel/tire and hub/drum assemblies.

2. Remove brake shoe assembly.

3. Disconnect brake tube from wheel cylinder.

4. Remove wheel cylinder attaching bolts and remove wheel cylinder.

NOTE: Use caution to prevent brake fluid from contacting brake linings and drum braking surface. Contaminated linings must be replaced.

To install:

5. Ensure ends of hydraulic fittings are free of foreign matter before making connections.

6. Position wheel cylinder and foam seal on backing plate and finger-tighten brake tube to cylinder.

7. Secure cylinder to backing plate by installing attaching bolts. Tighten bolts to 8–10 ft. lbs. (10–14 Nm).

8. Tighten tube nut fitting.

9. Install and adjust brakes.

10. Install hub/drum and wheel assembly.

11. Bleed brake system before driving vehicle.

Parking Brake Cable

ADJUSTMENT

1. Apply the service brake approximately 3 times before adjusting the parking brake. On vehicles equipped with power brakes, the engine must be running.

2. Place the parking brake control assembly in the 12th notch position, 2 notches from full application. Tighten the adjusting nut until the rear wheel brakes drag slightly when the control assembly is fully released. Repeat as necessary.

3. Reposition the control assembly in the 12th notch. Loosen the adjusting nut just enough to eliminate rear brake drag when the control assembly is fully released.

REMOVAL & INSTALLATION

1. Place control assembly in seventh notch position and loosen adjusting nut. Completely release control assembly.

2. Raise vehicle. Remove rear parking brake cable from equalizer.

3. Remove hairpin clip holding cable to floor pan tunnel bracket.

4. Remove wire retainer holding cable to fuel tank mounting bracket. Remove cable from wire retainer. Remove cable and clip from the fuel pump bracket (EFI only).

5. Remove screw holding cable retaining clip to rear sidemember. Remove cable from clip.

6. Remove wheelcover, wheel and tire assembly and rear brake drum.

7. Disengage cable end from brake assembly parking brake lever. Depress cable prongs holding cable to backing plate. Remove cable through hole in backing plate.

To install:

8. Insert cable through hole in backing plate. Attach cable end to rear brake assembly parking brake lever.

9. Insert conduit end fitting into backing plate. Ensure retention prongs are locked into place.

10. Insert cable into rear attaching clip and attach clip to rear sidemember with screw.

11. Route cable through bracket in floorpan tunnel and install hairpin retaining clip.

12. Install cable end into equalizer.

13. Insert cable into wire retainer and snap retainer into hole in fuel tank mounting bracket. On vehicles equipped with EFI, insert cable and install clip into fuel pump bracket.

14. Install rear drum, wheel and tire assembly and wheelcover.

15. Lower vehicle.

16. Adjust parking brake.

Brake System Bleeding

1. Clean all the dirt from around the master cylinder filler cap. If the master cylinder is known or suspected to have air in bore, it must be bled before any wheel cylinders or calipers.

2. To bleed the master cylinder, loosen the upper secondary left front outlet fitting aproximately ¾ turn. Have an assistant push the brake pedal down slowly through full travel. Close the outlet fitting, then return the pedal slowly to the full released position. Wait 5 seconds, then repeat the operation until the air bubbles cease to appear.

3. Loosen the upper primary right front outlet fitting approximately ¾ turn and repeat Step 2.

4. To continue to bleed the system, remove the rubber cap dust cap from the wheel cylinder bleeder fitting or caliper fitting. Check to make sure the bleeder fitting is positioned at the upper half on the front of the caliper, if not the caliper is located on the wrong side.

5. Attach a suitable length of rubber hose to the fitting. Submerge the free end of the hose in a container partially filled with clean brake fluid and loosen the bleeder fitting approximately ¾ of a turn.

6. Have the assistant push brake pedal down slowly through full travel. Close the bleeder fitting, then return the pedal to the full release position. Wait 5 seconds, then repeat this operation until the air bubbles cease to appear at the submerged end of the bleeder hose.

7. When the fluid is completely free of air bubbles, properly tighten the bleeder fitting and reinstall the rubber

dust cap. Repeat this process on the opposite diagonal system. Refill the master cylinder reservoir after each wheel cylinder or caliper is bled and re-install the master cylinder cap.

NOTE: If all wheels are to be bled, proceed as follows: right hand rear, left hand front, left hand rear and right hand front.

8. When the bleeding operation is completed, the fluid level should be filled to the maximum fill level indicated on the reservoir. Always ensure the disc brake pistons are returned to their normal positions by depressing the brake pedal several times until the normal pedal travel is established. Check the pedal feel. If the pedal feels spongy, repeat the bleeding procedure.

FRONT SUSPENSION

MacPherson Strut

REMOVAL & INSTALLATION

NOTE: All vehicles except Tempo with base suspension are equipped with gas pressurized shock absorbers which will extend unassisted. Do not apply heat or flame to the shock strut tube during removal.

1. Loosen but do not remove, 2 top mount-to-shock tower nuts.
2. Raise and safely support the vehicle. Raise vehicle to a point where it is possible to reach the 2 top mount-to-shock tower nuts and the strut-to-knuckle pinch bolt.
3. Remove wheel and tire assembly.
4. Remove brake flex line-to-strut bolt.
5. Remove strut-to-knuckle pinch bolt.
6. Using a suitable tool, spread knuckle-to-strut pinch joint slightly.
7. Using a suitable bar, place top of bar under fender apron and pry down on knuckle until strut separates from knuckle.
8. Remove 2 top mount-to-shock tower nuts and remove strut from vehicle.
9. Install spring compressor in bench mount, install strut in compressor and compress spring.
10. Place deep 18mm socket on strut shaft nut. Insert an 8mm deep socket with ¼ in. drive socket with a suitable extension.

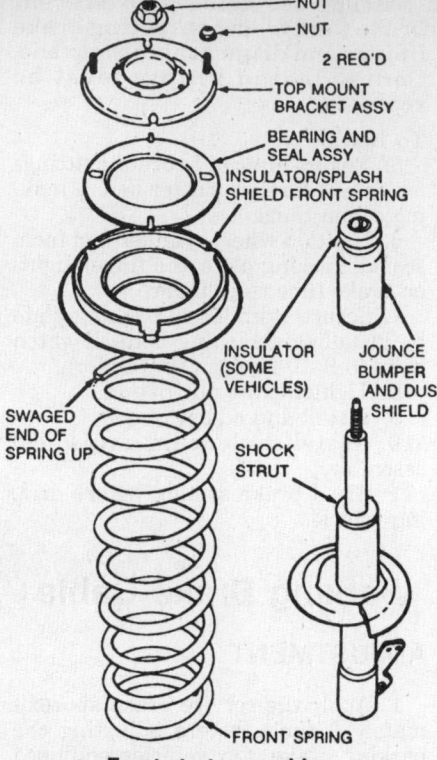

NUT
NUT
2 REQ'D
TOP MOUNT BRACKET ASSY
BEARING AND SEAL ASSY
INSULATOR/SPLASH SHIELD FRONT SPRING
INSULATOR (SOME VEHICLES)
JOUNCE BUMPER AND DUST SHIELD
SWAGED END OF SPRING UP
SHOCK STRUT
FRONT SPRING

Front strut assembly

NOTE: Do not attempt to remove shaft nut by turning shaft and holding nut. The nut must be turned and the shaft held to avoid possible damage to the shaft.

11. Loosen spring compressor tool and remove top mount bracket assembly, bearing, insulator and spring.
To install:
12. Install replacement strut in spring compressor.

NOTE: During reassembly of strut/spring assembly, be certain to follow correct sequence and proper positioning of bearing plate and seal assembly. If bearing and seal assembly are out of position, damage to the bearing will result.

13. Install spring, insulator, bearing and top mount bracket assembly.
14. Install top shaft mounting nut while holding shaft with ¼ drive 8mm deep socket and extension. Tighten nut to 35–50 ft. lbs. (48–68 Nm).
15. Install strut assembly in vehicle. Install 2 top mount-to-shock tower nuts. Tighten to 25–30 ft. lbs. (37–41 Nm).
16. Slide strut mounting flange onto knuckle.
17. Install strut-to-knuckle pinch bolt. Tighten to 68–81 ft. lbs. (92–110 Nm).
18. Install brake flex line-to-strut bolt.

19. Install wheel and tire assembly.
20. Lower vehicle.
21. Check alignment.

Lower Ball Joints

INSPECTION

1. Raise and safely support the vehicle so that wheels are in the full-down position.
2. Have an assistant grasp lower edge of the tire and move wheel and tire assembly in and out.
3. As wheel is being moved in and out, observe lower end of knuckle and lower control arm. Any movement indicates abnormal ball joint wear.
4. If any movement is observed, install new lower control arm assembly.

REMOVAL & INSTALLATION

The lower ball joint is integral to the lower control assembly and cannot be serviced individually. Any movement of the lower ball joint detected as a result of inspection requires replacement of the lower control arm assembly.

Lower Control Arms

REMOVAL & INSTALLATION

1. Raise and safely support the vehicle.
2. Remove nut from stabilizer bar end. Pull off large dished washer.
3. Remove lower control arm inner pivot nut and bolt.
4. Remove lower control arm ball joint pinch bolt. Using a suitable tool, slightly spread knuckle pinch joint and separate control arm from steering knuckle. A drift punch may be used to remove bolt.
5. Remove stabilizer bar spacer from the arm bushing.

NOTE: Ensure steering column is in unlocked position. Do not use a hammer to separate ball joint from knuckle.

To install:
6. Assemble lower control arm ball joint stud to the steering knuckle, ensuring that the ball stud groove is properly positioned.
7. Insert a new pinch bolt and nut. Tighten to 38–45 ft. lbs. (52–60 Nm).
8. Insert stabilizer bar spacer into arm bushing.
9. Clean stabilizer bar threads to remove dirt and contamination.
10. Position lower control arm onto stabilizer bar and position lower control arm to the inner underbody mounting. Install a new nut and bolt.

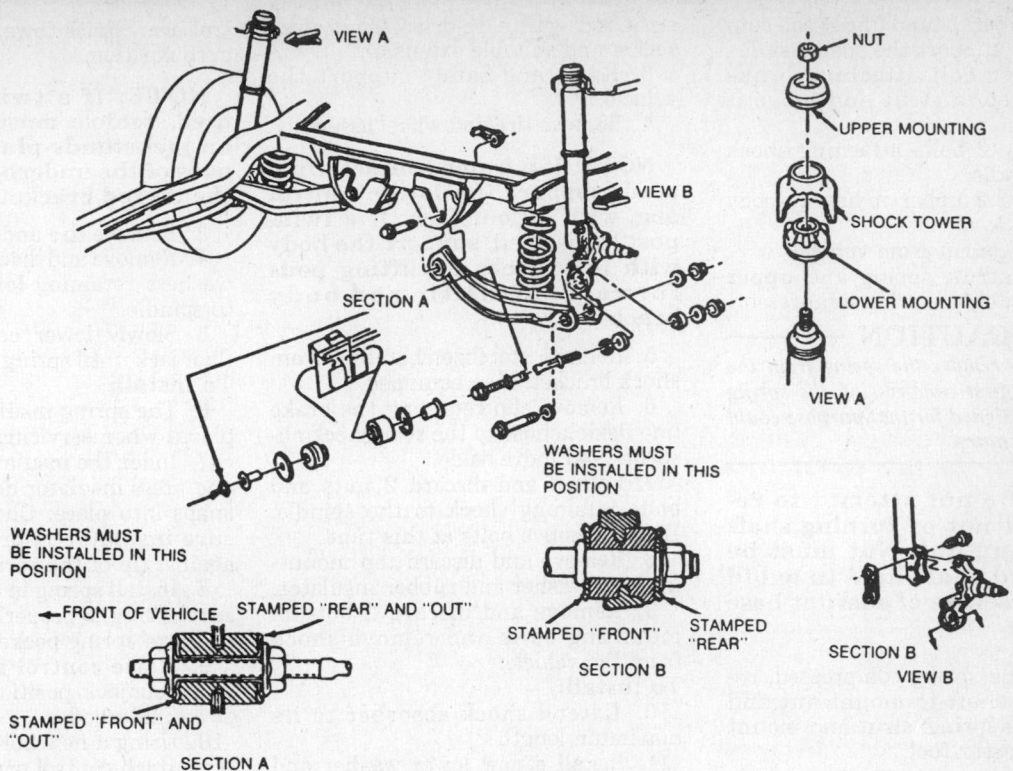

WASHERS MUST BE INSTALLED IN THIS POSITION

← FRONT OF VEHICLE   STAMPED "REAR" AND "OUT"

STAMPED "FRONT" AND "OUT"

SECTION A

WASHERS MUST BE INSTALLED IN THIS POSITION

STAMPED "FRONT"   STAMPED "REAR"

SECTION B

SECTION B VIEW B

Rear suspension—Escort and Lynx

Tighten to 48–55 ft. lbs. (65–74 Nm).

11. Assemble stabilizer bar, dished washer and a new nut to stabilizer. Tighten nut to 98–115 ft. lbs. (132–156 Nm).

12. Lower vehicle.

Stabilizer Bar

REMOVAL & INSTALLATION

1. Raise and safely support the vehicle.

2. Remove nut from stalizer bar at each lower control arm and pull off large dished washer. Discard nuts.

3. Remove stabilizer bar insulator U-bracket bolts and U-brackets and remove stabilizer bar assembly. Discard bolts.

NOTE: Stabilizer bar U-bracket insulators can be serviced without removing the stabilizer bar assembly.

To install:

4. Slide new insulators onto the stabilizer bar and position them in the approximate location.

5. Clean stabilizer bar threads to remove dirt and contamination.

6. Install spacers into the control arm bushings from forward side of control arm so that washer end of spacer will seat against stabilizer bar machined shoulder and push mounting brackets over insulators.

7. Insert end of stabilizer bar into the lower control arms. Using new bolts, attach the stabilizer bar and the insulator U-brackets to the bracket assemblies. Hand start all 4 U-bracket bolts. Tighten all bolts halfway, then tighten bolts to 59–68 ft. lbs. (80–92 Nm) on Tempo/Topaz, 85–100 ft. lbs. (115–135 Nm) on Escort/Lynx.

8. Using new nuts and the original dished washers (dished side away from bushing), attach the stabilizer bar to the lower control arm. Tighten nuts to 98–115 ft. lbs. (132–156 Nm).

9. Lower vehicle.

REAR SUSPENSION

MacPherson Strut

REMOVAL & INSTALLATION

Tempo and Topaz

NOTE: All Tempo and Topaz vehicles except Tempo with base suspension are equipped with gas-pressurized shock absorbers which will extend unassisted. Do not apply heat or flame to the shock strut during removal.

1. Open luggage compartment and loosen but do not remove, 2 nuts retaining the upper strut mount to body.

2. Raise and safely support the vehicle.

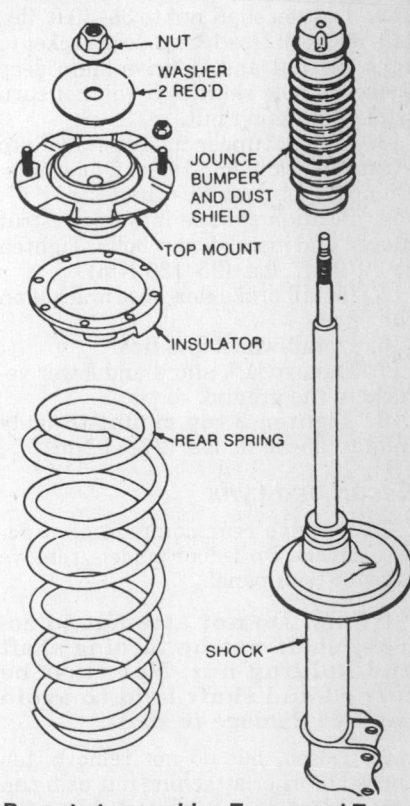

Rear strut assembly—Tempo and Topaz

3. Place a jack stand under the control arms to support the suspension.

4. Remove bolt attaching brake hose bracket to strut and move it aside.

5. Remove 2 bolts attaching shock strut to spindle.

6. Remove 2 upper mount-to-body nuts.

7. Remove strut from vehicle.

8. Place strut, spring and upper mount assembly in spring compressor.

————— CAUTION —————

Attempting to remove the spring from the strut without first compressing the spring with a tool designed for that purpose could cause bodily injury.

———————————————

NOTE: Do not attempt to remove shaft nut by turning shaft and holding nut. Nut must be turned and shaft held to avoid possible fracture of shaft at base of hex.

9. With the spring compressed, remove strut shaft-to-mount nut and then remove spring, strut and mount from compressor tool.

To install:

10. With spring compressed, install spring, spring insulator, top mount and upper washer on strut shaft.

11. Ensure spring is properly located in upper and lower spring seats. The dust shield must be within 0.39 in. (10mm) of the rod shoulder.

12. Tighten shaft nut to 35–50 ft. lbs. (48–68 Nm). Use 18mm deep socket to turn the nut and ¼ drive 8mm deep socket to hold shaft so it will not turn while tightening nut.

13. Insert 2 upper mount studs into strut tower and hand start 2 new nuts. Do not tighten at this time.

14. Position spindle into lower strut mount and install 2 new bolts. Tighten to 70–96 ft. lbs. (95–130 Nm).

15. Install brake flex-hose bracket on the strut.

16. Install wheel and tire.

17. Remove jack stand and lower vehicle to the ground.

18. Tighten 2 top mount-to-body nuts to 25–30 ft. lbs. (27–41 Nm).

Escort and Lynx

1. Remove rear compartment access panels. On 4-door models, remove quarter trim panel.

NOTE: Do not attempt to remove shaft nut by turning shaft and holding nut. Nut must be turned and shaft held to avoid possible damage to shaft.

2. Loosen, but do not remove, top shock absorber attaching nut using an 18mm deep socket while holding the strut rod with a ¼ drive, 8mm deep socket and suitable extension.

3. Raise and safely support the vehicle.

4. Remove tire and wheel assembly.

NOTE: If a frame contact lift is used, support the lower control arm with a floor jack. If a twin-post lift is used, support the body with floor jacks on lifting pads forward of the tie rod body bracket.

5. Remove stabilizer bar link from shock bracket, if so equipped.

6. Remove clip retaining the brake line flexible hose to the rear shock absorber and move aside.

7. Loosen and discard 2 nuts and bolts retaining shock to the spindle. Do not remove bolts at this time.

8. Remove and discard top mounting nut, washer and rubber insulator.

9. Remove and discard 2 bottom mounting bolts and remove shock from the vehicle.

To install:

10. Extend shock absorber to its maximum length.

11. Install a new lower washer and insulator assembly, using tire lubricant to ease insertion into the quarter panel shock tower.

12. Position upper part of shock absorber shaft into shock tower opening in the body and push slowly on lower part of the shock until mounting holes are lined up with mounting holes in the spindle.

13. Install new lower mounting bolts and nuts. Do not tighten at this time.

NOTE: The heads of both bolts must be to the rear of the vehicle.

14. Place a new upper insulator and washer assembly and nut on the upper shock absorber shaft. Tighten nut to 35–55 ft. lbs. (48–75 Nm), using the 18mm deep socket and ¼ drive, 8mm deep socket with extension. Do not grip the shaft with pliers or vise grips.

15. Tighten 2 lower mounting bolts to 70–100 ft. lbs. (95–135 Nm).

16. Install stabilizer bar link to bracket on shock, if so equipped. Tighten bolts to 40–55 ft. lbs. (55–75 Nm).

17. Install brake line flex hose and retaining clip.

18. Install wheel and tire assembly.

19. Install quarter trim and access panels, if removed.

Coil Springs

REMOVAL & INSTALLATION

1. Raise and safely support the vehicle.

2. Place floor jack under lower control arm. Raise lower control arm to curb position.

NOTE: If a twin-post lift is used, vehicle must be supported on jackstands place under jack pads of the underbody forward of the tie rod bracket.

3. Remove tire and wheel assembly.

4. Remove and discard nut, bolt and washers retaining lower control arm to spindle.

5. Slowly lower control arm with floor jack until spring can be removed.

To install:

6. The spring insulator must be replaced when servicing spring.

7. Index the insulator on the spring and press insulator downward until it snaps into place. Check again to ensure insulator is properly indexed against tip of the spring.

8. Install spring in control arm. Ensure spring is properly seated in control arm spring pocket.

9. Raise control arm and spring with floor jack. position spring in pocket on underbody.

10. Using a new bolt, nut and washers, attach control arm to spindle. Install bolt with the head toward front of the vehicle. Tighten to 70–96 ft. lbs. (95–130 Nm).

11. Install tire and wheel.

13. Remove floor jack and lower vehicle.

Rear Control Arms

REMOVAL & INSTALLATION

Tempo and Topaz

1. Raise and safely support the vehicle.

2. Remove and discard arm-to-spindle bolt and nut.

3. Remove and discard center mounting bolt and nut.

4. Remove arm from vehicle.

To install:

NOTE: When installing new control arms, the bushing with the 0.39 in. (10mm) hole is installed to the center of the vehicle and the bushing with the 0.48 in. (12mm) hole is installed to the spindle. The offset on the arm must face up on the right hand side of the vehicle and down on the left hand side of the vehicle. The flange edge of the arm stamping must also face the rear of the vehicle.

5. Position arm at center of vehicle and insert new bolt and nut. Do not tighten at this time.

6. Move arm end up to spindle and insert new bolt, washer and nut. En-

sure bolt engages both arms and spindle.

7. Tighten arm-to-body bolt to 30–40 ft. lbs. (40–54 Nm).
8. Tighten arm-to-spindle nut to 60–80 ft. lbs. (81–109 Nm).
9. Lower vehicle.

Escort and Lynx

1. Raise and safely support the vehicle.
2. Place floor jack under lower control arm. Raise lower control arm to curb position.

NOTE: If a twin-post lift is used, vehicle must be supported on jackstands place under jack pads of the underbody forward of the tie rod bracket.

3. Remove tire and wheel assembly.
4. Remove and discard nut, bolt and washers retaining lower control arm to spindle.
5. Slowly lower control arm with floor jack until spring can be removed.
6. Remove and discard bolt from the body end and remove control arm from vehicle.

To install:
7. Attach lower control arm-to-body bracket using a new bolt and nut. Head of the bolt should face the front of the vehicle. Do not tighten at this time.
8. The spring insulator must be replaced when servicing spring.
9. Index the insulator on the spring and press insulator downward until it snaps into place. Check again to ensure insulator is properly indexed against tip of the spring.
10. Using a floor jack, raise lower control arm until it is in line with mounting hole in the spindle.
11. Install lower control arm to spindle using a new bolt, nut and washers. Do not tighten at this time. Bolt head should face the front of the vehicle.
12. Using the floor jack, raise lower control arm to curb height.
13. Tighten control arm-to-spindle bolt to 70–96 ft. lbs. (95–130 Nm).
14. Tighten control arm-to-body bolt to 52–74 ft. lbs. (70-100 Nm).
15. Install tire and wheel.
16. Remove floor jack and lower vehicle.

Rear Wheel Bearings

ADJUSTMENT

Except Tempo and Topaz with AWD

1. Raise and safely support the vehicle.
2. Remove wheel cover or ornament and nut covers. Remove grease cap from hub.
3. Remove cotter pin and nut retainer. Discard cotter pin.
4. Back-off adjusting nut 1 full turn. Ensure nut turns freely on spindle threads. Correct any binding condition.
5. Tighten adjusting nut to 17–25 ft. lbs. (23–34 Nm) while rotating hub and drum assembly to seat bearings. Loosen adjusting nut ½ turn and tighten adjusting nut to 24–28 inch lbs. (2.7–3.2 Nm) using inch lb. torque wrench.
6. Position adjusting nut retainer over adjusting nut so slots in nut retainer flange are in line with cotter pin hole in spline.
7. Install a new cotter pin and bend ends around retainer flange.
8. Check hub rotation. If hub rotates freely, install grease cap. If not, check bearings for damage and replace as necessary.
9. Install wheel and tire assembly, wheel cover or ornaments, and nut covers as required.
10. Lower vehicle.

Tempo and Topaz with AWD

NOTE: Bearings on 4WD vehicles are not adjustable.

1. Raise the vehicle and support it safely.
2. Remove the wheel covers. Remove the grease cap from the hub being careful not to damage the cap.

NOTE: Styled steel wheels and aluminum wheels require removal of the wheel assembly to remove the dust cover.

3. Remove the cotter pin and nut retainer. Discard the cotter pin and replace with new.
4. Back-off the adjusting nut a full turn making certain that the nut rotates freely on the spindle thread. Correct any binding condition that may exist.
5. Tighten the adjusting nut to 17–25 ft. lbs. while rotating the hub and drum assembly to seat the bearings. Back-off the adjusting nut ½ turn. Then retighten it to between 10–15 inch lbs.
6. Position the nut retainer on the nut and install the cotter pin so tha the slots in the ntu retainer flange are aligned with the cotter pin hole in the spindle.
7. Spread the ends of the cotter pin and bend then around the nut retainer.
8. Check the hub rotation. If the hub rotates freely, install the grease cap. If binding occurs, check the bearing for damage and replace as necessary.

9. Install the wheels and lower the vehicle.

REMOVAL & INSTALLATION

Except Tempo and Topaz with AWD

1. Raise and safely support the vehicle.
2. Remove wheelcover or ornament and nut covers. Remove grease cap from hub.
3. Remove cotter pin and nut retainer. Discard cotter pin.
4. Pull hub and drum assembly off spindle being careful not to drop outer bearing assembly.
5. Remove outer bearing assembly.
6. Using seal remover, remove and discard grease seal. Remove inner bearing assembly from hub.
7. Wipe all lubricant from spindle and inside of hub. Cover spindle with a clean cloth and vacuum all loose dust and dirt from brake assembly. Carefully remove cloth to prevent dirt from falling on spindle.
8. Clean both bearing assemblies and cups using solvent. inspect bearing assemblies and cups for excessive wear, scratches, pits or other damage. Replace all worn or damaged parts as required.

NOTE: Allow solvent to dry before repacking bearings. Do not spin-dry bearings with air pressure.

9. If cups are replaced, remove them with wheel hub cup remover D80L-927-A and bearing cup puller T77F-1102-A or equivalent.

To install:
10. If inner or outer bearing cups were removed, install replacement cups using driver handle T80T-4000-W and bearing cup replacers T77F-1202-A and T73T-1217-A or equivalent. Support drum hub on wood block to prevent damage. Insure cups are properly seated in hub.

NOTE: Do not use cone and roller assembly to install cup as this will cause damage to bearing cup and cone and roller assembly.

11. Ensure all spindle and bearing surfaces are clean.
12. Using a bearing packer, pack bearing assemblies with a suitable wheel bearing grease.
13. Place inner bearing cone and roller assembly in inner cup. Apply light film of grease to lips of a new grease seal and install seal with rear hub seal replacer T81P-1249-A or equivalent. Ensure retainer flange is seated all around.

14. Apply light film of grease on spindle shaft bearing surfaces.

15. Install hub and drum assembly on spindle. Keep hub centered on spindle to prevent damage to grease seal and spindle threads.

16. Install outer bearing assembly and keyed flat washer on spindle. Install adjusting nut finger-tight. Adjust wheel bearings. Install a new cotter pin.

17. Install wheel and tire on drum.

18. Lower vehicle.

Tempo and Topaz with AWD

1. Raise and support the vehicle safely. Remove the tire and wheel assembly.

2. Remove the brake drum. Remove the parking brake cable from the brake backing plate.

3. Remove the brake line from the wheel cylinder. Remove the outboard U-joint retaining bolts. Remove the outboard end of the halfshaft from the wheel stub shaft yoke and wire it to the control arm.

4. Remove and discard the control arm to spindle bolt, washer and nut. Remove the tie rod nut, bushing and washer and discard the nut.

5. Remove and discard the 2 bolts retaining the spindle to the strut. Remove the spindle from the vehicle. Mount the spindle and backing plate assembly in a suitable vise.

6. Remove the cotter pin and nut attaching the stub shaft yoke to the stub shaft. Discard the cotter pin.

7. Remove the spindle and backing plate assembly from the vise. Remove the stub shaft yoke using a 2 jaw puller and shaft protector.

8. Position the spindle and backing plate assembly into a vise and remove the wheel stub shaft.

9. Remove the snapring retaining the bearing. Remove the bolts retaining the spindle to the backing plate and remove the backing plate.

10. Remove the spindle from the vise and mount it into a suitable press. With the spindle side facing upward, carefully press out the bearing from the spindle, using a driver handle and

bearing cup driver. Discard the bearing after removal.

To install:

11. Mount the spindle in a press, spindle side facing down. Position a new bearing in the outboard side of the spindle and carefully press in the new bearing using a driver handle and bearing installer.

12. Remove the spindle from the press and mount it in a vise. Install the snapring retaining the bearing. Position the backing plate to the spindle and install the retaining bolts.

13. Install the wheel stub shaft. Install the stub shaft yoke and attaching nut. Torque the nut to 120–150 ft. lbs. install a new cotter pin.

14. Remove the spindle and backing plate assembly from the vise. Position the spindle onto the tie rod and then into the strut lower bracket. Insert 2 new strut-to-spindle bolts. Do not tighten at this time.

15. Install the tie rod bushing washer and new nut. Install the new control arm to spindle bolt, washers and nut. Do not tighten them at this time.

16. Install a jack stand to support the suspension at the normal curb height before tightening the fasteners.

17. Torque the spindle to strut bolts to 70–96 ft. lbs. Torque the tie rod nut to 52–74 ft. lbs. Torque the control arm to spindle nut to 60–86 ft. lbs.

18. Position the outboard end of the halfshaft to the wheel stub shaft yoke. Install the retaining caps and bolts and torque them to 15–17 ft. lbs.

19. Install the brake line to wheel cylinder. Install the parking brake cable and brake drum. Install the wheel assembly, torque the lugs nuts to 80–105 ft. lbs.

20. Lower the vehicle and bleed the brake system. Check and adjust the toe, if necessary.

Rear Axle Assembly

REMOVAL & INSTALLATION

Tempo and Topaz with AWD

1. Raise the vehicle and support

safely. Position a hoist or a suitable transaxle jack under the rear axle housing.

2. Remove the exhaust system.

3. Remove the rear U-joint bolts and straps retaining the driveshaft, from the torque tube yoke flange. Lower and support the driveshaft.

4. Remove the retaining bolts from the torque tube support bracket. Remove the axle retaining bolt from the left hand differential support bracket.

5. Remove the axle retaining bolt from the center differential support bracket.

6. Lower the axle assembly and remove the inboard U-joint retaining bolts and straps from each of the halfshaft. Remove and wire the halfshaft assemblies out of the way.

7. Lower the jack and remove the rear axle from the vehicle.

To install:

8. Position the rear axle assembly under the vehicle. Raise the rear axle far enough for the U-joint and halfshaft assemblies to be installed.

9. Position each inboard U-joint to the rear axle. Install the U-joint straps and retaining bolts. Using a T-30 Torx® bit, torque the bolts to 15–17 ft. lbs. (21–23 Nm) to each halfshaft.

10. Raise the rear axle into position and install the bolts attaching the differential housing to the left hand center differential support bracket. Torque to 70–80 ft. lbs. (95–108 Nm).

11. Position the torque tube and mounting bracket to the crossmember. Install the attaching bolts and torque to 28–35 ft. lbs. (38–47 Nm). Install the driveshaft and retaining bolts to the torque tube yoke flange. Using a T-30 Torx® bit, torque the bolts to 15–17 ft. lbs. (21–23 Nm).

NOTE: Whenever a U-joint retaining bolt is removed, apply Loctite® or equivalent, to the bolt threads prior to installation.

12. Install the exhaust system.

13. Check the lubricant level in the rear axle and add, if necessary. Lower the vehicle and road test to check the rear axle for proper operation.

Ford Motor Co.
Rear Wheel Drive
Continental, Cougar, Crown Victoria, Grand Marquis,
Mark VII, Mustang, Thunderbird, Town Car

SPECIFICATIONS

VEHICLE IDENTIFICATION CHART

It is important for servicing and ordering parts to be certain of the vehicle and engine identification. The VIN (vehicle identification number) is a 17 digit number visible through the windshield on the driver's side of the dash and contains the vehicle and engine identification codes. The tenth digit indicates model year and the eighth digit indicates engine code. It can be interpreted as follows:

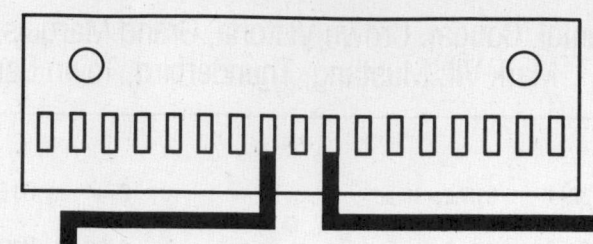

Engine Code

Code	Cu. In.	Liters	Cyl.	Fuel Sys.	Eng. Mfg.
A	140	2.3	4	EFI	Ford
T	140	2.3	4 (Turbo)	EFI	Ford
W	140	2.3	4 (Turbo)	EFI	Ford
3	232	3.8	6	EFI	Ford
4	232	3.8	6	EFI	Ford
R	232 (SC)	3.8	6	EFI	Ford
C	232 (SC)	3.8	6	EFI	Ford
F	302	5.0	8	EFI	Ford
M	302 (HO)	5.0	8	EFI	Ford
E	302 (HO)	5.0	8	EFI	Ford
G	351 (HO)	5.8	8	VV	Ford

Model Year

Code	Year
H	1987
J	1988
K	1989
L	1990
M	1991

EFI Electronic Fuel Injection
CFI Central Fuel Injection
HO High Output
SC Supercharged
VV Variable Venturi

ENGINE IDENTIFICATION

Year	Model	Engine Displacement cu. in. (liter)	Engine Series Identification (VIN)	No. of Cylinders	Engine Type
1987	Mustang	140 (2.3)	A	4	OHC
	Mustang	302 (5.0) HO	M	8	OHV
	Thunderbird	140 (2.3)	W	4	OHC-Turbo
	Thunderbird	232 (3.8)	3	6	OHV
	Thunderbird	302 (5.0)	F	8	OHV
	Cougar	232 (3.8)	3	6	OHV
	Cougar	302 (5.0)	F	8	OHV
	Crown Victoria	302 (5.0)	F	8	OHV
	Crown Victoria	351 (5.8)	G	8	OHV
	Grand Marquis	302 (5.0)	F	8	OHV
	Grand Marquis	351 (5.8)	G	8	OHV
	Continental	302 (5.0)	F	8	OHV

ENGINE IDENTIFICATION

Year	Model	Engine Displacement cu. in. (liter)	Engine Series Identification (VIN)	No. of Cylinders	Engine Type
1987	Continental	302 (5.0) HO	M	8	OHV
	Mark VII	302 (5.0)	F	8	OHV
	Mark VII	302 (5.0) HO	M	8	OHV
	Town Car	302 (5.0)	F	8	OHV
1988	Mustang	140 (2.3)	A	4	OHC
	Mustang	302 (5.0)	F	8	OHV
	Mustang	302 (5.0) HO	M	8	OHV
	Thunderbird	140 (2.3)	W	4	OHC-Turbo
	Thunderbird	232 (3.8)	3	6	OHV
	Thunderbird	302 (5.0)	F	8	OHV
	Cougar	232 (3.8)	3	6	OHV
	Cougar	302 (5.0)	F	8	OHV
	Crown Victoria	302 (5.0)	F	8	OHV
	Crown Victoria	351 (5.8)	G	8	OHV
	Grand Marquis	302 (5.0)	F	8	OHV
	Grand Marquis	351 (5.8)	G	8	OHV
	Mark VII	302 (5.0)	F	8	OHV
	Mark VII	302 (5.0) HO	M	8	OHV
	Town Car	302 (5.0)	F	8	OHV
1989	Mustang	140 (2.3)	A	4	OHC
	Mustang	302 (5.0) HO	M	8	OHV
	Thunderbird	232 (3.8)	3	6	OHV
	Thunderbird	232 (3.8) SC	R	6	OHV
	Cougar	232 (3.8)	3	6	OHV
	Cougar	232 (3.8) SC	R	6	OHV
	Crown Victoria	302 (5.0)	F	8	OHV
	Crown Victoria	351 (5.8)	G	8	OHV
	Grand Marquis	302 (5.0)	F	8	OHV
	Grand Marquis	351 (5.8)	G	8	OHV
	Mark VII	302 (5.0) HO	M	8	OHV
	Town Car	302 (5.0)	F	8	OHV
1990-91	Mustang	140 (2.3)	A	4	OHC
	Mustang	302 (5.0) HO	E	8	OHV
	Thunderbird	232 (3.8)	4	6	OHV
	Thunderbird	232 (3.8) SC	R ①	6	OHV
	Cougar	232 (3.8)	4	6	OHV
	Cougar	232 (3.8) SC	R ①	6	OHV
	Crown Victoria	302 (5.0)	F	8	OHV
	Crown Victoria	351 (5.8)	G	8	OHV
	Grand Marquis	302 (5.0)	F	8	OHV
	Grand Marquis	351 (5.8)	G	8	OHV
	Mark VII	302 (5.0) HO	E	8	OHV
	Town Car	302 (5.0)	F	8	OHV

OHC Overhead Camshaft
OHV Overhead Valve
HO High Output
SC Supercharged

① Early Production could be Code C

GENERAL ENGINE SPECIFICATIONS

Year	VIN	No. Cylinder Displacement cu. in. (liter)	Fuel System Type	Net Horsepower @ rpm	Net Torque @ rpm (ft. lbs.)	Bore × Stroke (in.)	Compression Ratio	Oil Pressure @ 2000 rpm
1987	A	4-140 (2.3) OHC	EFI	88 @ 4200	122 @ 2600	3.781 × 3.126	9.0:1	40–60
	W	4-140 (2.3) T	EFI	155 @ 4600	190 @ 2800	3.781 × 3.126	8.0:1	40–60
	3	6-232 (3.8)	EFI	120 @ 3600	205 @ 1600	3.810 × 3.390	8.7:1	40–60
	E	8-302 (5.0)	EFI	150 @ 3200	270 @ 2000	4.000 × 3.000	8.9:1	40–60
	F	8-302 (5.0)	EFI	150 @ 3200	270 @ 2000	4.000 × 3.000	8.9:1	40–60
	M	8-302 (5.0) HO	EFI	210 @ 4400	265 @ 3200	4.000 × 3.000	8.3:1	40–60
	G	8-351 (5.8) HO ①	VV	180 @ 3600	285 @ 2400	4.000 × 3.500	8.3:1	40–60
1988	A	4-140 (2.3)	EFI	88 @ 4200	122 @ 2600	3.780 × 3.126	9.0:1	40–60
	T	4-140 (2.3) T	EFI	155 @ 4600	190 @ 2800	3.780 × 3.126	8.0:1	40–60
	4	6-232 (3.8)	EFI	120 @ 3600	205 @ 1600	3.810 × 3.390	8.7:1	40–60
	F	8-302 (5.0)	EFI	150 @ 3200	270 @ 2000	4.000 × 3.000	8.9:1	40–60
	E	8-302 (5.0) HO	EFI	220 @ 4400	265 @ 3200	4.000 × 3.000	8.3:1	40–60
	G	8-351 (5.8) HO	VV	180 @ 3600	285 @ 2400	4.000 × 3.500	8.3:1	40–60
1989	A	4-140 (2.3)	EFI	88 @ 4200	122 @ 2600	3.780 × 3.126	9.0:1	40–60
	T	4-140 (2.3) T	EFI	155 @ 4600	190 @ 2800	3.780 × 3.126	8.0:1	40–60
	4	6-232 (3.8)	EFI	120 @ 3600	205 @ 1600	3.810 × 3.390	8.7:1	40–60
	R	6-232 (3.8) SC	EFI	210 @ 2000	315 @ 2600	3.810 × 3.390	8.2:1	40–60
	C	6-232 (3.8) SC	EFI	210 @ 2000	315 @ 2600	3.810 × 3.390	8.2:1	40–60
	F	8-302 (5.0)	EFI	150 @ 3200	270 @ 2000	4.000 × 3.000	8.9:1	40–60
	E	8-302 (5.0) HO	EFI	220 @ 4400	265 @ 3200	4.000 × 3.000	8.3:1	40–60
	G	8-351 (5.8) HO	VV	180 @ 3600	285 @ 2400	4.000 × 3.500	8.3:1	40–60
1990–91	A	4-140 (2.3)	EFI	88 @ 4000	132 @ 2600	3.780 × 3.126	9.0:1	40–60
	4	6-232 (3.8)	EFI	140 @ 3800	215 @ 2400	3.810 × 3.390	9.0:1	40–60
	R	6-232 (3.8) SC	EFI	210 @ 4000	315 @ 2600	3.810 × 3.390	8.2:1	40–60
	C	6-232 (3.8) SC	EFI	210 @ 4000	315 @ 2600	3.810 × 3.390	8.2:1	40–60
	F	8-302 (5.0)	EFI	150 @ 3200 ②	270 @ 2000 ③	4.000 × 3.000	8.9:1	40–60
	E	8-302 (5.0) HO	EFI	225 @ 4200	300 @ 3200	4.000 × 3.000	9.0:1	40–60
	G	8-351 (5.8) HO	VV	180 @ 3600	285 @ 2400	4.000 × 3.500	8.3:1	40–60

■ Horsepower and torque are SAE net figures. They are measured at the rear of the transmission with all accessories installed and operating. Since the figures vary when a given engine is installed in different models, some are representative rather than exact.

T Turbocharger
EFI Electronic Fuel Injection
HO High Output
HSC High Swirl Combustion
CFI Central Fuel Injection
VV Variable Venturi carburetor
SC Supercharged

① Canada and police only
② 160 @ 3400 with dual exhaust
③ 280 @ 2200 with dual exhaust

GASOLINE ENGINE TUNE-UP SPECIFICATIONS

Year	VIN	No. Cylinder Displacement cu. in. (liter)	Spark Plugs Type	Gap (in.)	Ignition Timing (deg.) MT	AT	Compression Pressure (psi)	Fuel Pump (psi)	Idle Speed (rpm) MT	AT	Valve Clearance In.	Ex.
1987	A	4-140 (2.3)	AWSF-44C	0.044	①	①	NA	35	750	750	Hyd.	Hyd.
	W	4-140 (2.3) T	AWSF-320	0.034	①	①	NA	35	825–975	825–975	Hyd.	Hyd.
	3	6-232 (3.8)	AWSF-54	0.044	①	①	NA	35	—	550	Hyd.	Hyd.
	E	8-302 (5.0)	ASF-32C	0.044	①	①	NA	39	①②	①②	Hyd.	Hyd.
	F	8-302 (5.0)	ASF-32C	0.044	①	①	NA	35	①	①	Hyd.	Hyd.
	M	8-302 (5.0) HO	ASF42	0.044	①	①	NA	35	700	700	Hyd.	Hyd.
	G	8-351 (5.8)	ASF-32C	0.044	①	①	NA	6–8	650	650	Hyd.	Hyd.
1988	A	4-140 (2.3)	AWSF-44C	0.044	①	①	NA	35	750	750	Hyd.	Hyd.
	T	4-140 (2.3)	AWSF-32C	0.034	①	①	NA	35	825–975	825–975	Hyd.	Hyd.
	4	6-232 (3.8)	AWSF-54	0.044	①	①	NA	39	—	550	Hyd.	Hyd.
	F	8-302 (5.0)	ASF-32C	0.044	①	①	NA	39	①	①	Hyd.	Hyd.
	E	8-302 (5.0) HO	ASF42	0.044	①	①	NA	39	700	700	Hyd.	Hyd.
	G	8-351 (5.8)	ASF-32C	0.044	①	①	NA	6–8	650	650	Hyd.	Hyd.
1989	A	4-140 (2.3)	AWSF-44C	0.044	①	①	NA	35	750	750	Hyd.	Hyd.
	T	4-140 (2.3)	AWSF-32C	0.034	①	①	NA	35	825–975	825–975	Hyd.	Hyd.
	4	6-232 (3.8)	AWSF-54	0.044	①	①	NA	39	—	550	Hyd.	Hyd.
	R	6-232 (3.8) SC	AWSF-54	0.044	①	①	NA	39	650	550	Hyd.	Hyd.
	C	6-232 (3.8) SC	AWSF-54	0.044	①	①	NA	39	650	550	Hyd.	Hyd.
	F	8-302 (5.0)	ASF-32C	0.044	①	①	NA	39	①	①	Hyd.	Hyd.
	E	8-302 (5.0) HO	ASF42	0.044	①	①	NA	39	700	700	Hyd.	Hyd.
	G	8-351 (5.8)	ASF-32C	0.044	①	①	NA	6–8	650	650	Hyd.	Hyd.
	G	8-351 (5.8)	ASF-32C	0.044	①	①	NA	6–8	650	650	Hyd.	Hyd.
1990	A	4-140 (2.3)	AWSF-44C	0.044	①	①	NA	35	750	750	Hyd.	Hyd.
	4	6-232 (3.8)	AWSF-44C	0.054	①	①	NA	39	—	550	Hyd.	Hyd.
	R	6-232 (3.8) SC	AWSF-34PP	0.054	①	①	NA	39	650	550	Hyd.	Hyd.
	C	6-232 (3.8) SC	AWSF-34PP	0.054	①	①	NA	39	650	550	Hyd.	Hyd.
	F	8-302 (5.0)	AWSF-44C	0.054	①	①	NA	39	①	①	Hyd.	Hyd.
	E	8-302 (5.0) HO	ASF-42C	0.054	①	①	NA	39	700	700	Hyd.	Hyd.
	G	8-351 (5.8)	AWSF-44C	0.054	①	①	NA	6–8	650	650	Hyd.	Hyd.
1991					SEE UNDERHOOD SPECIFICATIONS STICKER							

NOTE: The underhood specifications sticker often reflects tune-up specifications changes made in production. Sticker figures must be used if they disagree with those in this chart.

T Turbocharger
B Before top dead center
HO High output
— Not applicable
HSC High Swirl Combustion

① Calibrations vary depending upon the model; refer to the underhood sticker
② The carbureted models use spark plug ASF-42 (.044) and the idle speed is 700 rpm

FIRING ORDERS

NOTE: To avoid confusion, always replace spark plug wires one at a time.

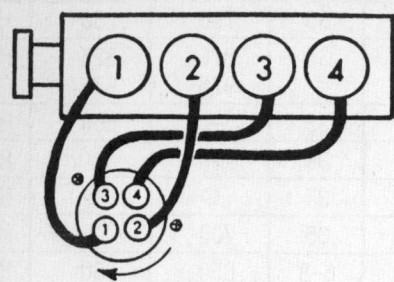

2.3L Engine
Engine Firing Order: 1–3–4–2
Distributor Rotation: Clockwise

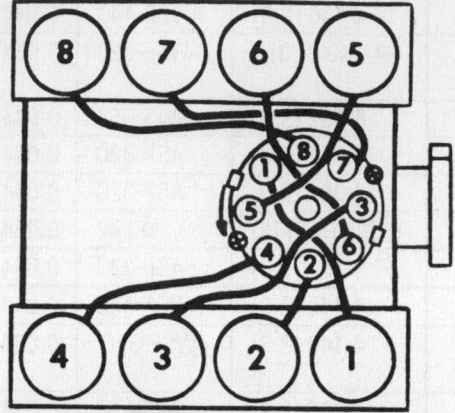

5.0L (except HO) Engine
Engine Firing Order: 1–5–4–2–6–3–7–8
Distributor Rotation: Counterclockwise

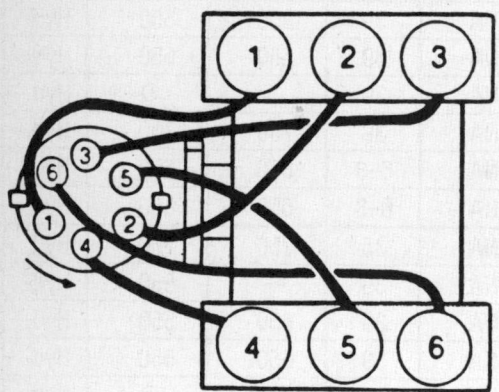

3.8L Engine
Engine Firing Order: 1–4–2–5–3–6
Distributor Rotation: Counterclockwise

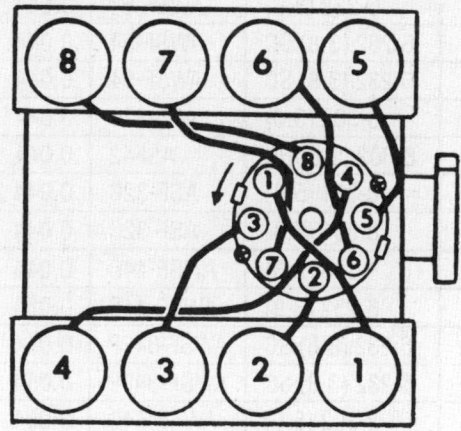

5.0L HO and 5.8L Engines
Engine Firing Order: 1–3–7–2–6–5–4–8
Distributor Rotation: Counterclockwise

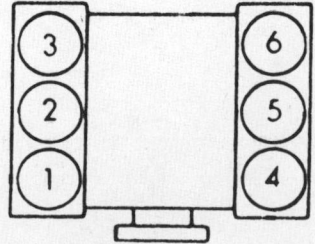

3.8L Engine
Engine Firing Order: 1–4–2–5–3–6
Distributorless Ignition System

CAPACITIES

Year	Model	VIN	No. Cylinder Displacement cu. in. (liter)	Engine Crankcase (qts.) with Filter	Engine Crankcase (qts.) without Filter	Transmission (pts.) 4-Spd	Transmission (pts.) 5-Spd	Transmission (pts.) Auto.	Drive Axle (pts.)	Fuel Tank (gal.)	Cooling System (qts.)
1987	Mustang	A	4-140 (2.3)	5	4 ③	2.8	4.75	16	3.25 ⑥	15.4	9.4
	Mustang	M	8-302 (5.0)	5	4	4.5	4.5	—	3.25	15.4	13.4
	T-bird	W	4-140 (2.3)	5	4.5 ③	4.75	4.75	—	3.25 ⑥	18	8.7
	T-bird	3	6-232 (3.8)	5	4	—	—	22	3.25 ⑥	21	10.7
	T-bird	F	8-302 (5.0)	5	4	—	—	22	3.25	20	13.4
	Cougar	W	4-140 (2.3)	5	4.5 ③	4.75	4.75	—	3.25 ⑥	18	8.7
	Cougar	3	6-232 (3.8)	5	4	—	—	22	3.25 ⑥	21	10.7
	Cougar	F	8-302 (5.0)	5	4	—	—	22	3.25	20	13.4
	Mark VII	E	8-302 (5.0)	5	4	—	—	22	3.25 ⑥	20.7	13.4
	Mark VII	M	8-302 (5.0)HO	5	4	—	—	22	3.25 ⑥	20.7	13.4
	Continental	E	8-302 (5.0)	5	4	—	—	22	3.25 ⑥	20.7	13.4
	Continental	M	8-302 (5.0)HO	5	4	—	—	22	3.25 ⑥	20.7	13.4
	Crown Victoria	F	8-302 (5.0)	5	4	—	—	24	①	20	15
	Crown Victoria	G	8-351 (5.8)	5	4	—	—	24	①	20	16
	Grand Marquis	F	8-302 (5.0)	5	4	—	—	24	①	20	15
	Grand Marquis	G	8-351 (5.8)	5	4	—	—	24	①	20	16
	Town Car	E	8-302 (5.0)	5	4	—	—	24	①	20	10
1988	Mustang	A	4-140 (2.3)	5	4	3.7	3.7	22	4.5	15.4	10
	Mustang	M	8-302 (5.0)	5	4	3.7	3.7	22	3.25	15.4	14.1
	T-bird	T	4-140 (2.3)	5	4.5 ③	4.75	4.75	16	3.25 ②	18	10
	T-bird	4	6-232 (3.8)	5	4	—	—	22	3.25 ②	21	11.8
	T-bird	F	8-302 (5.0)	5	4	—	—	22	3.25 ②	20.7	14.1
	Cougar	T	4-140 (2.3)	5	4.5 ③	4.75	4.75	16	3.25 ②	18	10
	Cougar	4	6-232 (3.8)	5	4	—	—	22	3.25 ②	21	11.8
	Cougar	F	8-302 (5.0)	5	4	—	—	22	3.25 ②	20.7	14.1
	Mark VII	E	8-302 (5.0)	5	4	—	—	22	3.25	20.7	14.1
	Crown Victoria	F	8-302 (5.0)	5	4	—	—	24	①	20	15
	Crown Victoria	G	8-351 (5.8)	5	4	—	—	24	①	20	16
	Grand Marquis	F	8-302 (5.0)	5	4	—	—	24	①	20	15
	Grand Marquis	G	8-351 (5.8)	5	4	—	—	24	①	20	16
	Town Car	F	8-302 (5.0)	5	4	—	—	24	①	20	16
1989	Mustang	A	4-140 (2.3)	5	4	3.7	3.7	22	4.5	15.4	10
	Mustang	E	8-302 (5.0)	5	4	3.7	3.7	22	3.25	15.4	14.1
	T-bird	4	6-232 (3.8)	5	4	—	—	22	3.25 ②	21	11.8
	T-bird	R	8-232 (3.8)SC	5	4	—	6.3	24	3.25 ②	18.8	11.8
	T-bird	C	8-232 (3.8)SC	5	4	—	6.3	24	3.25 ②	18.8	11.8

CAPACITIES

Year	Model	VIN	No. Cylinder Displacement cu. in. (liter)	Engine Crankcase (qts.) with Filter	without Filter	Transmission (pts.) 4-Spd	5-Spd	Auto.	Drive Axle (pts.)	Fuel Tank (gal.)	Cooling System (qts.)
1989	Cougar	4	6-232 (3.8)	5	4	—	—	22	3.25 ②	21	11.8
	Cougar	R	8-232 (3.8)SC	5	4	—	6.3	24	3.25 ②	18.8	11.8
	Mark VII	E	8-302 (5.0)	5	4	—	—	22	3.25	20.7	14.1
	Crown Victoria	F	8-302 (5.0)	5	4	—	—	24	①	20	15
	Crown Victoria	G	8-351 (5.8)	5	4	—	—	24	①	20	16
	Grand Marquis	F	8-302 (5.0)	5	4	—	—	24	①	20	15
	Grand Marquis	G	8-351 (5.8)	5	4	—	—	24	①	20	16
	Town Car	F	8-302 (5.0)	5	4	—	—	24	①	20	16
1990-91	Mustang	A	4-140 (2.3)	5.0	4.0	—	5.6	19	⑤	15.4	9.9
	Mustang	E	8-302 (5.0)	5.0	4.0	—	5.6	24	⑤	15.4	14.1
	T-bird	4	6-232 (3.8)	5.0	4.0	—	6.2	24	⑥	19.0	11.6
	T-bird	R ④	6-232 (3.8)	5.0	4.0	—	6.2	24	⑥	19.0	12.0
	Cougar	4	6-232 (3.8)	5.0	4.0	—	6.2	24	⑥	19.0	11.6
	Cougar	R ④	6-232 (3.8)	5.0	4.0	—	6.2	24	⑥	19.0	12.0
	Crown Victoria	F	8-302 (5.0)	5.0	4.0	—	—	24	3.75	18.0	14.1
	Crown Victoria	G	8-351 (5.8)	5.0	4.0	—	—	24	3.75	20.0	14.1
	Grand Marquis	F	8-302 (5.0)	5.0	4.0	—	—	24	3.75	18.0	14.1
	Grand Marquis	G	8-351 (5.8)	5.0	4.0	—	—	24	3.75	20.0	14.1
	Mark VII	E	8-302 (5.0)	5.0	4.0	—	—	24	3.75	22.1	14.1
	Town Car	F	8-302 (5.0)	5.0	4.0	—	—	24	3.75	18.0	14.1

① 6.75 in. axle—2.5 pts.
　7.5 in. axle—3.5 pts.
　8.5 in. axle—4.0 pts.
② Traction-lok—3.55 pts.
③ Turbo 4.5—add .5 with filter
④ Early Production could be Code C
⑤ 7.5 in. axle—3.25 pts.
　8.8 in. axle—3.75 pts.
⑥ 7.5 in. conventional axle—3.0 pts.
　7.5 in. Traction-lok axle—2.75 pts.
　8.8 in. Traction-lok axle—3.25 pts.

CAMSHAFT SPECIFICATIONS

All measurements given in inches

Year	VIN	No. Cylinder Displacement cu. in. (liter)	Journal Diameter 1	2	3	4	5	Lobe Lift In.	Ex.	Bearing Clearance	Camshaft End Play
1987	A	4-140 (2.3)	1.7713-1.7720	1.7713-1.7720	1.7713-1.7720	1.7713-1.7720	—	0.400	0.400	0.001-0.003	0.001-0.007
	W	4-140 (2.3)	1.7713-1.7720	1.7713-1.7720	1.7713-1.7720	1.7713-1.7720	—	0.400	0.400	0.001-0.003	0.001-0.007
	3	6-232 (3.8)	2.0515-2.0505	2.0515-2.0505	2.0515-2.0505	2.0515-2.0505	—	0.240	0.241	0.001-0.003	①
	E	8-302 (5.0)	2.0805-2.0815	2.0655-2.0665	2.0505-2.0515	2.0355-2.0365	2.0205-2.0215	0.2375 ②	0.2474 ②	0.001-0.003	0.001-0.007
	F	8-302 (5.0)	2.0805-2.0815	2.0655-2.0665	2.0505-2.0515	2.0355-2.0365	2.0205-2.0215	0.2375 ②	0.2474 ②	0.001-0.003	0.001-0.007
	M	8-302 (5.0)	2.0805-2.0815	2.0655-2.0665	2.0505-2.0515	2.0355-2.0365	2.0205-2.0215	0.2375 ②	0.2474 ②	0.001-0.003	0.001-0.007
	G	8-351 (5.8)	2.0805-2.0815	2.0655-2.0665	2.0505-2.0515	2.0355-2.0365	2.0205-2.0215	0.2780	0.2830	0.001-0.003	0.001-0.007
1988	A	4-140 (2.3)	1.7713-1.7720	1.7713-1.7720	1.7713-1.7720	1.7713-1.7720	—	0.400	0.400	0.001-0.003	0.001-0.007
	T	4-140 (2.3)	1.7713-1.7720	1.7713-1.7720	1.7713-1.7720	1.7713-1.7720	—	0.400	0.400	0.001-0.003	0.001-0.007
	4	6-232 (3.8)	2.0515-2.0505	2.0515-2.0505	2.0515-2.0505	2.0515-2.0505	—	0.240	0.241	0.001-0.003	①
	F	8-302 (5.0)	2.0805-2.0815	2.0655-2.0665	2.0505-2.0515	2.0355-2.0365	2.0205-2.0215	0.2375 ②	0.2474 ②	0.001-0.003	0.001-0.007
	E	8-302 (5.0)	2.0805-2.0815	2.0655-2.0665	2.0505-2.0515	2.0355-2.0365	2.0205-2.0215	0.2375 ②	0.2474 ②	0.001-0.003	0.001-0.007
	G	8-351 (5.8)	2.0805-2.0815	2.0655-2.0665	2.0505-2.0515	2.0355-2.0365	2.0205-2.0215	0.2375 ②	0.2474 ②	0.001-0.003	0.001-0.007
1989	A	4-140 (2.3)	1.7713-1.7720	1.7713-1.7720	1.7713-1.7720	1.7713-1.7720	—	0.400	0.400	0.001-0.003	0.001-0.007
	T	4-140 (2.3)	1.7713-1.7720	1.7713-1.7720	1.7713-1.7720	1.7713-1.7720	—	0.400	0.400	0.001-0.003	0.001-0.007
	4	6-232 (3.8)	2.0515-2.0505	2.0515-2.0505	2.0515-2.0505	2.0515-2.0505	—	0.240	0.241	0.001-0.003	①
	R	6-232 (3.8)SC	2.0515-2.0505	2.0515-2.0505	2.0515-2.0505	2.0515-2.0505	—	0.245	0.259	0.001-0.003	①
	C	6-232 (3.8)SC	2.0515-2.0505	2.0515-2.0505	2.0515-2.0505	2.0515-2.0505	—	0.245	0.259	0.001-0.003	①
	F	8-302 (5.0)	2.0805-2.0815	2.0655-2.0665	2.0505-2.0515	2.0355-2.0365	2.0205-2.0215	0.2375 ②	0.2474 ②	0.001-0.003	0.001-0.007
	E	8-302 (5.0)	2.0805-2.0815	2.0655-2.0665	2.0505-2.0515	2.0355-2.0365	2.0205-2.0215	0.2375 ②	0.2474 ②	0.001-0.003	0.001-0.007
	G	8-351 (5.8)	2.0805-2.0815	2.0655-2.0665	2.0505-2.0515	2.0355-2.0365	2.0205-2.0215	0.2375 ②	0.2474 ②	0.001-0.003	0.001-0.007
1990-91	A	4-140 (2.3)	1.7713-1.7720	1.7713-1.7720	1.7713-1.7720	1.7713-1.7720	—	0.400	0.400	0.001-0.003	0.001-0.007
	4	6-232 (3.8)	2.0515-2.0505	2.0515-2.0505	2.0515-2.0505	2.0515-2.0505	—	0.240	0.241	0.001-0.003	①

CAMSHAFT SPECIFICATIONS

All measurements given in inches

| Year | VIN | No. Cylinder Displacement cu. in. (liter) | Journal Diameter | | | | | Lobe Lift | | Bearing Clearance | Camshaft End Play |
			1	2	3	4	5	In.	Ex.		
1990-91	R	6-232 (3.8)SC	2.0515-2.0505	2.0515-2.0505	2.0515-2.0505	2.0515-2.0505	—	0.245	0.259	0.001-0.003	①
	C	6-232 (3.8)SC	2.0515-2.0505	2.0515-2.0505	2.0515-2.0505	2.0515-2.0505	—	0.245	0.259	0.001-0.003	①
	F	8-302 (5.0)	2.0805-2.0815	2.0655-2.0665	2.0505-2.0515	2.0355-2.0365	2.0205-2.0215	0.2375	0.2474	0.001-0.003	0.009 0.007
	E	8-302 (5.0)HO	2.0805-2.0815	2.0655-2.0665	2.0505-2.0515	2.0355-2.0365	2.0205-2.0215	0.2780	0.2780	0.001-0.003	0.009
	G	8-351 (5.8)	2.0805-	2.0655-	2.0505-	2.0355-	2.0205-	0.2780	0.2830	0.001-	0.001-

① The endplay is controlled by the button and spring on the camshaft end
② On the H.O. engine, intake lobe lift is 0.2780, exhaust is 0.2780

CRANKSHAFT AND CONNECTING ROD SPECIFICATIONS

All measurements are given in inches.

| Year | VIN | No. Cylinder Displacement cu. in. (liter) | Crankshaft | | | | Connecting Rod | | |
			Main Brg. Journal Dia.	Main Brg. Oil Clearance	Shaft End-play	Thrust on .No.	Journal Diameter	Oil Clearance	Side Clearance
1987	A	4-140 (2.3)	2.3990-2.3982	0.0008-0.0015	0.004-0.008	3	2.0464-2.0472	0.0008-0.0015	0.0035-0.0105
	W	4-140 (2.3)	2.3990-2.3982	0.0008-0.0015	0.004-0.008	3	2.0464-2.0472	0.0008-0.0015	0.0035-0.0105
	3	6-232 (3.8)	2.5190	0.0001-0.0010	0.004-0.008	3	2.3103-2.3111	0.0008-0.0026	0.0047-0.0114
	F	8-302 (5.0)	2.2482-2.2490	0.0004 0.0015	0.004-0.008	3	2.1228-2.1236	0.0008-0.0015	0.010-0.020
	M	8-302 (5.0)	2.2482-2.2490	0.0004-0.0015	0.004-0.008	3	2.1228-2.1236	0.0008-0.0015	0.010-0.020
	E	8-302 (5.0)	2.2482-2.2490	0.0004-0.0015	0.004-0.008	3	2.1228-2.1236	0.0008-0.0015	0.010-0.020
	G	8-351 (5.8)	2.2994-3.0002	0.0008-0.0015 ②	0.004-0.008	3	2.3103-2.3111	0.0008-0.0015	0.010-0.020
1988	A	4-140 (2.3)	2.3990-2.3982	0.0008-0.0015	0.004-0.008	3	2.0464-2.0472	0.0008-0.0015	0.0035-0.0105
	T	4-140 (2.3)	2.3990-2.3982	0.0008-0.0015	0.004-0.008	3	2.0464-2.0472	0.0008-0.0015	0.0035-0.0105
	4	6-232 (3.8)	2.5190	0.0001-0.0010	0.004-0.008	3	2.3103-2.3111	0.0008-0.0026	0.0047-0.0114
	F	8-302 (5.0)	2.2482-2.2490	0.0004-0.0015	0.004-0.008	3	2.1228-2.1236	0.0008-0.0015	0.010-0.020
	E	8-302 (5.0)HO	2.2482-2.2490	0.0004-0.0015	0.004-0.008	3	2.1228-2.1236	0.0008-0.0015	0.010-0.020
	G	8-351 (5.8)	2.2994-3.0002	0.0008-0.0015	0.004-0.008	3	2.3103-2.3111	0.0008-0.0015	0.010-0.020

CRANKSHAFT AND CONNECTING ROD SPECIFICATIONS

All measurements are given in inches.

Year	VIN	No. Cylinder Displacement cu. in. (liter)	Crankshaft Main Brg. Journal Dia.	Crankshaft Main Brg. Oil Clearance	Crankshaft Shaft End-play	Thrust on No.	Connecting Rod Journal Diameter	Connecting Rod Oil Clearance	Connecting Rod Side Clearance
1989	A	4-140 (2.3)	2.3990–2.3982	0.0008–0.0015	0.004–0.008	3	2.0464–2.0472	0.0008–0.0015	0.0035–0.0105
	T	4-140 (2.3)	2.3990–2.3982	0.0008–0.0015	0.004–0.008	3	2.0464–2.0472	0.0008–0.0015	0.0035–0.0105
	4	6-232 (3.8)	2.5190	0.0001–0.0010	0.004–0.008	3	2.3103–2.3111	0.0008–0.0026	0.0047–0.0114
	R	6-232 (3.8)SC	2.5194–2.5186	0.0009–0.0026	0.004–0.008	3	2.3103–2.3111	0.0008–0.0026	0.0047–0.0114
	C	6-232 (3.8)SC	2.5194–2.5186	0.0009–0.0026	0.004–0.008	3	2.3103–2.3111	0.0008–0.0026	0.0047–0.0114
	F	8-302 (5.0)	2.2482–2.2490	0.0004–0.0015	0.004–0.008	3	2.1228–2.1236	0.0008–0.0015	0.010–0.020
	E	8-302 (5.0)HO	2.2482–2.2490	0.0004–0.0015	0.004–0.008	3	2.1228–2.1236	0.0008–0.0015	0.010–0.020
	G	8-351 (5.8)	2.2994–3.0002	0.0008–0.0015	0.004–0.008	3	2.3103–2.3111	0.0008–0.0015	0.010–0.020
1990-91	A	4-140 (2.3)	2.3990–2.3982	0.0008–0.0015	0.004–0.008	3	2.0465–2.0472	0.0008–0.0015	0.0035–0.0105
	4	6-232 (3.8)	2.5190–2.5198	0.0001–0.0010	0.004–0.008	3	2.3103–2.3111	0.00086–0.0027	0.0047–0.0114
	R	6-232 (3.8)SC	①	0.0009–0.0026	0.004–0.008	3	2.3103–2.3111	0.00086–0.0027	0.0047–0.0114
	C	6-232 (3.8)SC	①	0.0009–0.0026	0.004–0.008	3	2.3103–2.3111	0.0086–0.0027	0.0047–0.0114
	F	8-302 (5.0)	2.2482–2.2490	0.0004–0.0015	0.004–0.008	3	2.1228–2.1236	0.0008–0.0015	0.010–0.020
	E	8-302 (5.0)HO	2.2482–2.2490	0.0004–0.0015	0.004–0.008	3	2.1228–2.1236	0.0008–0.0015	0.010–0.020
	G	8-351 (5.8)	2.2994–3.0002	0.0008–0.0015	0.004–0.008	3	2.3103–2.3111	0.0008–0.0015	0.010–0.020

① No. 1, 2, 3: 2.5194–2.5186 in.
  No. 4: 2.5100–2.5092 in.
② No. 1: 0.0001–0.0005

VALVE SPECIFICATIONS

Year	VIN	No. Cylinder Displacement cu. in. (liter)	Seat Angle (deg.)	Face Angle (deg.)	Spring Test Pressure (lbs. @ in.)	Spring Installed Height (in.)	Stem-to-Guide Clearance (in.) Intake	Stem-to-Guide Clearance (in.) Exhaust	Stem Diameter (in.) Intake	Stem Diameter (in.) Exhaust
1987	A	4-140 (2.3)	45	44	154 @ 1.12	1⁹/₁₆	0.0010–0.0027	0.0015–0.0032	0.3420	0.3415
	T	4-140 (2.3)	45	44	154 @ 1.12	1⁹/₁₆	0.0010–0.0027	0.0015–0.0032	0.3420	0.3415
	3	6-232 (3.8)	44.5	45.8	215 @ 1.79	1³/₄	0.0010–0.0027	0.0015–0.0032	0.3420	0.3415
	E	8-302 (5.0)	45	45	205 @ 1.36	1³/₄	0.0010–0.0027	0.0015–0.0032	0.3420	0.3420

VALVE SPECIFICATIONS

Year	VIN	No. Cylinder Displacement cu. in. (liter)	Seat Angle (deg.)	Face Angle (deg.)	Spring Test Pressure (lbs. @ in.)	Spring Installed Height (in.)	Stem-to-Guide Clearance (in.)		Stem Diameter (in.)	
							Intake	Exhaust	Intake	Exhaust
1987	F	8-302 (5.0)	45	45	205 @ 1.36	1³/₄	0.0010–0.0027	0.0015–0.0032	0.3420	0.3420
	M	8-302 (5.0)	45	45	205 @ 1.36	1³/₄	0.0010–0.0027	0.0015–0.0032	0.3420	0.3420
	G	8-351 (5.8)	45	45	204 @ 1.33	1⁴⁹/₆₄ ①	0.0010–0.0027	0.0015–0.0027	0.3416–0.3423	0.3411–0.3418
1988	A	4-140 (2.3)	45	44	154 @ 1.12	1⁹/₁₆	0.0010–0.0027	0.0015–0.0032	0.3420	0.3415
	T	4-140 (2.3)	45	44	154 @ 1.12	1⁹/₁₆	0.0010–0.0027	0.0015–0.0032	0.3420	0.3415
	4	6-232 (3.8)	44.5	45.8	215 @ 1.79	1³/₄	0.0010–0.0027	0.0015–0.0032	0.3420	0.3415
	F	8-302 (5.0)	45	45	205 @ 1.36	1³/₄	0.0010–0.0027	0.0015–0.0032	0.3420	0.3420
	E	8-302 (5.0)HO	45	45	205 @ 1.36	1³/₄	0.0010–0.0027	0.0015–0.0032	0.3420	0.3420
	G	8-351 (5.8)	45	45	204 @ 1.33	1⁴⁹/₆₄ ①	0.0010–0.0027	0.0015–0.0027	0.3416–0.3423	0.3411–0.3418
1989	A	4-140 (2.3)	45	44	154 @ 1.12	1⁹/₁₆	0.0010–0.0027	0.0015–0.0032	0.3420	0.3415
	T	4-140 (2.3)	45	44	154 @ 1.12	1⁹/₁₆	0.0010–0.0027	0.0015–0.0032	0.3420	0.3415
	4	6-232 (3.8)	44.5	45.8	215 @ 1.79	1³/₄	0.0010–0.0027	0.0015–0.0032	0.3420	0.3415
	R	6-232 (3.8)SC	45.8	45.8	220 @ 1.18	1³/₄	0.0010–0.0028	0.0015–0.0033	0.3423	0.3418–0.3418
	C	6-232 (3.8)SC	45.8	45.8	220 @ 1.18	1³/₄	0.0010–0.0028	0.0015–0.0033	0.3423	0.3418–0.3418
	F	8-302 (5.0)	45	45	205 @ 1.36	1³/₄	0.0010–0.0027	0.0015–0.0032	0.3420	0.3420
	E	8-302 (5.0)HO	45	45	205 @ 1.36	1³/₄	0.0010–0.0027	0.0015–0.0032	0.3420	0.3420
	G	8-351 (5.8)	45	45	204 @ 1.33	1⁴⁹/₆₄ ①	0.0010–0.0027	0.0015–0.0027	0.3416–0.3423	0.3411–0.3418
1990-91	A	4-140 (2.3)	45	44	128–141 @ 1.12	1¹⁸/₃₂	0.0010–0.0027	0.0015–0.0032	0.3416–0.3423	0.3411–0.3418
	4	6-232 (3.8)	44.5	45.8	220 @ 1.18	1³/₄	0.0010–0.0028	0.0015–0.0033	0.3423–0.3415	0.3418–0.3410
	R	6-232 (3.8)SC	45.8	45.8	220 @ 1.18	1³/₄	0.0010–0.0028	0.0015–0.0033	0.3423–0.3415	0.3418–0.3410
	C	6-232 (3.8)SC	45.8	45.8	220 @ 1.18	1³/₄	0.0010–0.0028	0.0015–0.0033	0.3423–0.3415	0.3418–0.3410
	F	8-302 (5.0)	45	44	205 @ 1.36	1³/₄	0.0010–0.0027	0.0015–0.0032	0.3416–0.3423	0.3416–0.3423
	E	8-302 (5.0)HO	45	44	211–230 @ 1.33	1³/₄	0.0010–0.0027	0.0015–0.0032	0.3416–0.3423	0.3416–0.3423
	G	8-351 (5.8)	45	44	205 @ 1.05	1⁴⁹/₆₄ ①	0.0010–0.0027	0.0015–0.0032	0.3416–0.3423	0.3411–0.3418

① Exhaust—1³⁷/₆₄

PISTON AND RING SPECIFICATIONS

All measurements are given in inches.

Year	VIN	No. Cylinder Displacement cu. in. (liter)	Piston Clearance	Ring Gap Top Compression	Ring Gap Bottom Compression	Ring Gap Oil Control	Ring Side Clearance Top Compression	Ring Side Clearance Bottom Compression	Ring Side Clearance Oil Control
1987	A	4-140 (2.3)	0.0030–0.0038	0.0100–0.0200	0.0100–0.0200	0.0150–0.0550	0.0020–0.0040	0.0020–0.0040	Snug
	W	4-140 (2.3)	0.0030–0.0038	0.0100–0.0200	0.0100–0.0200	0.0150–0.0550	0.0020–0.0040	0.0020–0.0040	Snug
	3	6-232 (3.8)	0.0014–0.0032	0.0100–0.0220	0.0100–0.0220	0.0150–0.0550	0.0020–0.0040	0.0020–0.0040	Snug
	F	8-302 (5.0)	0.0018–0.0026	0.0100–0.0200	0.0100–0.0200	0.0150–0.0550	0.0020–0.0040	0.0020–0.0040	Snug
	E	8-302 (5.0)	0.0018–0.0026	0.0100–0.0200	0.0100–0.0200	0.0150–0.0550	0.0020–0.0040	0.0020–0.0040	Snug
	M	8-302 (5.0)	0.0018–0.0026	0.0100–0.0220	0.0100–0.0220	0.0150–0.0550	0.0020–0.0040	0.0020–0.0040	Snug
	G	8-351 (5.8)	0.0022–0.0030	0.0100–0.0200	0.0100–0.0200	0.0150–0.0550	0.0020–0.0040	0.0020–0.0040	Snug
1988	A	4-140 (2.3)	0.0030–0.0038	0.0100–0.0200	0.0100–0.0200	0.0150–0.0550	0.0020–0.0040	0.0020–0.0040	Snug
	T	4-140 (2.3)	0.0030–0.0038	0.0100–0.0200	0.0100–0.0200	0.0150–0.0550	0.0020–0.0040	0.0020–0.0040	Snug
	4	6-232 (3.8)	0.0014–0.0032	0.0100–0.0220	0.0100–0.0220	0.0150–0.0550	0.0020–0.0040	0.0020–0.0040	Snug
	F	8-302 (5.0)	0.0018–0.0026	0.0100–0.0200	0.0100–0.0200	0.0150–0.0550	0.0020–0.0040	0.0020–0.0040	Snug
	E	8-302 (5.0)HO	0.0018–0.0026	0.0100–0.0200	0.0100–0.0200	0.0150–0.0550	0.0020–0.0040	0.0020–0.0040	Snug
	G	8-351 (5.8)	0.0022–0.0030	0.0100–0.0220	0.0100–0.0220	0.0150–0.0550	0.0020–0.0040	0.0020–0.0040	Snug
1989	A	4-140 (2.3)	0.0030–0.0038	0.0100–0.0200	0.0100–0.0200	0.0150–0.0550	0.0020–0.0040	0.0020–0.0040	Snug
	T	4-140 (2.3)	0.0030–0.0038	0.0100–0.0200	0.0100–0.0200	0.0150–0.0550	0.0020–0.0040	0.0020–0.0040	Snug
	4	6-232 (3.8)	0.0014–0.0032	0.0100–0.0220	0.0100–0.0220	0.0150–0.0550	0.0020–0.0040	0.0020–0.0040	Snug
	R	6-232 (3.8)SC	0.0040–0.0045	0.0100–0.0200	0.0100–0.0200	0.0150–0.0580	0.0016–0.0034	0.0016–0.0034	Snug
	C	6-232 (3.8)SC	0.0040–0.0045	0.0100–0.0200	0.0100–0.0200	0.0150–0.0580	0.0016–0.0034	0.0016–0.0034	Snug
	F	8-302 (5.0)	0.0018–0.0026	0.0100–0.0200	0.0100–0.0200	0.0150–0.0550	0.0020–0.0040	0.0020–0.0040	Snug
	E	8-302 (5.0)HO	0.0018–0.0026	0.0100–0.0200	0.0100–0.0200	0.0150–0.0550	0.0020–0.0040	0.0020–0.0040	Snug
	G	8-351 (5.8)	0.0022–0.0030	0.0100–0.0220	0.0100–0.0220	0.0150–0.0550	0.0020–0.0040	0.0020–0.0040	Snug
1990–91	A	4-140 (2.3)	0.0030–0.0038	0.0100–0.0200	0.0100–0.0200	0.0150–0.0550	0.0020–0.0040	0.0020–0.0040	Snug
	4	6-232 (3.8)	0.0014–0.0032	0.0100–0.0220	0.0100–0.0220	0.0150–0.0550	0.0020–0.0040	0.0020–0.0040	Snug

PISTON AND RING SPECIFICATIONS

All measurements are given in inches.

Year	VIN	No. Cylinder Displacement cu. in. (liter)	Piston Clearance	Ring Gap			Ring Side Clearance		
				Top Compression	Bottom Compression	Oil Control	Top Compression	Bottom Compression	Oil Control
1990–91	R	6-232 (3.8)SC	0.0040–0.0045	0.0100–0.0200	0.0100–0.0200	0.0150–0.0580	0.0016–0.0034	0.0016–0.0034	Snug
	C	6-232 (3.8)SC	0.0040–0.0045	0.0100–0.0200	0.0100–0.0200	0.0150–0.0580	0.0016–0.0034	0.0016–0.0034	Snug
	F	8-302 (5.0)	0.0018–0.0026	0.0100–0.0200	0.0100–0.0200	0.0150–0.0550	0.0020–0.0040	0.0020–0.0040	Snug
	E	8-302 (5.0)HO	0.0018–0.0026	0.0100–0.0200	0.0100–0.0200	0.0150–0.0550	0.0020–0.0040	0.0020–0.0040	Snug
	G	8-351 (5.8)	0.0022–0.0030	0.0100–0.0200	0.0100–0.0200	0.0150–0.0550	0.0020–0.0040	0.0020–0.0040	Snug

TORQUE SPECIFICATIONS

All readings in ft. lbs.

Year	VIN	No. Cylinder Displacement cu. in. (liter)	Cylinder Head Bolts	Main Bearing Bolts	Rod Bearing Bolts	Crankshaft Pulley Bolts	Flywheel Bolts	Manifold		Spark Plugs
								Intake	Exhaust	
1987	A	4-140 (2.3)	④	⑥	⑦	103–133	54–64	14–21 ③	20–30	5–10
	3	6-232 (3.8)	②	65–81	31–36	20–28	54–64	⑤	15–22	5–11
	E	8-302 (5.0)	⑩	60–70	19–24	70–90	75–85	23–25 ①	18–24	10–15
	F	8-302 (5.0)	⑩	60–70	19–24	70–90	75–85	23–25 ①	18–24	10–15
	G	8-351 (5.8)	⑪	95–105	40–45	70–90	75–85	23–25 ①	18–24	10–15
1988	A	4-140 (2.3)	④	⑥	⑦	103–133	54–64	14–21 ③	20–30	5–10
	T	4-140 (2.3)	④	⑥	⑦	103–133	54–64	13–18	20–30	5–10
	4	6-232 (3.8)	②	65–81	31–36	20–28	54–64	⑤	15–22	5–11
	R	6-232 (3.8)	⑧	65–81	31–36	20–28	54–64	⑨	15–22	5–11
	C	6-232 (3.8)	⑧	65–81	31–36	20–28	54–64	⑨	15–22	5–11
	F	8-302 (5.0)	⑩	60–70	19–24	70–90	75–85	23–25 ①	18–24	10–15
	E	8-302 (5.0)HO	⑩	60–70	19–24	70–90	75–85	23–25 ①	18–24	10–15
	G	8-351 (5.8)	⑪	95–105	40–45	70–90	75–85	23–25 ①	18–24	10–15
1989	A	4-140 (2.3)	④	⑥	⑦	103–133	54–64	20–29 ③	20–30	5–10
	R	6-232 (3.8)	⑧	65–81	31–36	20–28	54–64	⑨	15–22	5–11
	C	6-232 (3.8)	⑧	65–81	31–36	20–28	54–64	⑨	15–22	5–11
1990–91	A	4-140 (2.3)	④	⑥	⑦	103–133	54–64	20–29	20–30	5–10
	4	6-232 (3.8)	⑫	65–81	31–36	20–28	54–64	⑤	15–22	5–11
	R	6-232 (3.8)	⑬	65–81	31–36	20–28	54–64	⑨–⑪	15–22	5–11
	C	6-232 (3.8)	⑬	65–81	31–36	20–28	54–64	⑨–⑪	15–22	5–11

TORQUE SPECIFICATIONS

All readings in ft. lbs.

Year	VIN	No. Cylinder Displacement cu. in. (liter)	Cylinder Head Bolts	Main Bearing Bolts	Rod Bearing Bolts	Crankshaft Pulley Bolts	Flywheel Bolts	Manifold Intake	Manifold Exhaust	Spark Plugs
1990–91	F	8-302 (5.0)	⑩	60–70	19–24	70–90	75–85	23–25 ①	18–24	10–15
	E	8-302 (5.0)HO	⑩	60–70	19–24	70–90	75–85	23–25 ①	18–24	10–15
	G	8-351 (5.8)	⑪	95–105	19–24	70–90	75–85	23–25 ①	18–24	10–15

① Retorque with engine hot
② a. Tighten in 4 steps:
  37 ft. lbs. (50 Nm)
  45 ft. lbs. (60 Nm)
  52 ft. lbs. (70 Nm)
  59 ft. lbs. (80 Nm)
  b. Back-off all bolts 2–3 revolutions
  c. Repeat Step a (above)
③ Turbo: 5–7 ft. lbs., then 13–18 ft. lbs.
④ Tighten in 2 steps: 50–60 ft. lbs. and then 80–90 ft. lbs.
⑤ Tighten in 3 steps:
  7 ft. lbs. (10 Nm)
  15 ft. lbs. (20 Nm)
  24 ft. lbs. (32 Nm)
⑥ Tighten in 2 steps: 50–60 ft. lbs. and then 75–85 ft. lbs.
⑦ Tighten in 2 steps: 25–30 ft. lbs. and then 30–36 ft. lbs.

⑧ a. Tighten in 4 steps:
  32 ft. lbs. (50 Nm)
  45 ft. lbs. (60 Nm)
  52 ft. lbs. (70 Nm)
  59 ft. lbs. (80 Nm)
  b. Back-off all bolts 2–3 revolutions
  c. Repeat Step a (above) to 52 ft. lbs.
  d. In sequential order, rotate bolts an additional 90–110 degrees
⑨ Tighten in 2 steps:
  8 ft. lbs. and then
  11 ft. lbs.
⑩ Tighten in 2 steps:
  55–65 ft. lbs. and then 65–72 ft. lbs.
⑪ Tighten in 3 steps:
  85 ft. lbs.
  95 ft. lbs.
  105–112 ft. lbs.

⑫ a. Tighten in 4 steps:
  32 ft. lbs. (50 Nm)
  45 ft. lbs. (60 Nm)
  52 ft. lbs. (70 Nm)
  59 ft. lbs. (80 Nm)
  b. Back off all bolts 2–3 revolutions
  c. Tighten the long bolts in sequence to 11–18 ft. lbs. and rotate an additional 85–105 degrees.
  d. Tighten the short bolts in sequence to 11–18 ft. lbs. and rotate an additional 65–85 degrees
⑬ a. Tighten in 4 steps:
  32 ft. lbs. (50 Nm)
  45 ft. lbs. (60 Nm)
  52 ft. lbs. (70 Nm)
  59 ft. lbs. (80 Nm)
  b. Back off all bolts 2–3 revolutions
  c. Tighten the long and short bolts in numerical sequence to 48–55 ft. lbs. (65–75 Nm)
  d. Rotate an additional 9–110 degrees

BRAKE SPECIFICATIONS

All measurements in inches unless noted

Year	Model	Lug Nut Torque (ft. lbs.)	Master Cylinder Bore	Brake Disc Minimum Thickness	Brake Disc Maximum Runout	Standard Brake Drum Diameter	Minimum Lining Thickness Front	Minimum Lining Thickness Rear
1987	Mustang	80–105	0.872	0.9720 ③	0.003 ④	9.00 ①	0.125	0.030 ⑤
	Thunderbird Cougar	80–105	0.872	0.9720 ③	0.003 ④	9.00 ①	0.125	0.030 ⑤
	Crown Victoria, Grand Marquis	80–105	1.0	0.9720	0.003	10.00 ②	0.125	0.030
	Town Car	80–105	1.0	0.9720	0.003	10.00 ②	0.125	0.030
	Continental Mark VII	80–105	1.125	0.9720 ③	0.003 ④	—	0.125	0.125
1988	Mustang	80–105	0.872	0.9720 ③	0.003 ④	9.00 ①	0.125	0.030 ⑤
	Thunderbird Cougar	80–105	0.872	0.9720 ③	0.003 ④	9.00 ①	0.125	0.030 ⑤
	Crown Victoria, Grand Marquis	80–105	1.0	0.9720	0.003	10.00 ②	0.125	0.030
	Town Car	80–105	1.0	0.9720	0.003	10.00 ②	0.125	0.030
	Continental Mark VII	80–105	1.125	0.9720 ③	0.003 ④	—	0.125	0.125

BRAKE SPECIFICATIONS

All measurements in inches unless noted

Year	Model	Lug Nut Torque (ft. lbs.)	Master Cylinder Bore	Brake Disc		Standard Brake Drum Diameter	Minimum Lining Thickness	
				Minimum Thickness	Maximum Runout		Front	Rear
1989	Mustang	80–105	0.872	0.9720 ③	0.003 ④	9.00 ①	0.125	0.030 ⑤
	Thunderbird Cougar	80–105	0.872	0.9720 ③⑥	0.003 ④	9.00 ①	0.125	0.030 ⑤
	Crown Victoria, Grand Marquis	80–105	1.0	0.9720	0.003	10.00 ②	0.125	0.030
	Town Car	80–105	1.0	0.9720	0.003	10.00 ②	0.125	0.030
	Continental Mark VII	80–105	1.125	0.9720 ③	0.003 ④	—	0.125	0.125
1990–91	Mustang	80–105	0.872	0.9720 ⑦	0.003	9.00	0.125	0.030
	Thunderbird Cougar	80–105	0.872	0.9350 ⑧	0.003	9.8	0.125	0.030 ⑤
	Crown Victoria, Grand Marquis	80–105	1.0	0.9720	0.003	10.00 ⑨	0.125	0.030
	Town Car	80–105	1.0	0.9720	0.003	10.00	0.125	0.030
	Mark VII	80–105	1.125	0.9720 ⑩	0.003 ④	—	0.125	0.125

① 10.00 optional
② 11.00 optional
③ With rear disc brake—0.945
④ With rear disc brake—0.004
⑤ With rear disc brake—0.125
⑥ Thunderbird SC and Cougar XR7—0.872
⑦ Mustang with 2.3L engine—0.810
⑧ Thunderbird SC—0.895
⑨ Station Wagon, Police, Taxi—11.030
⑩ With rear disc brake—0.895

WHEEL ALIGNMENT

Year	Model	Caster		Camber		Toe-in (in.)	Steering Axis Inclination (deg.)
		Range (deg.)	Preferred Setting (deg.)	Range (deg.)	Preferred Setting (deg.)		
1987	Mustang with 5.0L without 5.0L	1/2P–2P 3/32P–1 9/16	1 1/4P 13/16P	3/4N–3/4P 3/4N–3/4P	0 0	1/16–5/16 1/16–5/16	—
	Thunderbird Cougar	1/2P–2	1 1/4P	1/2N–1P	1/4P	1/16–5/16	—
	Crown Victoria Grand Marquis	2 1/4P–3 3/4P	3P	1/4N–1 1/4P	1/2N	1/16–3/16	10 31/32
	Town Car	2 1/4P–4P	3P	1/4N–1 1/4P	1/2P	1/16–3/16	11
	Continental Mark VII	5/8P–2 3/4P	1 1/2P	3/4N–3/4P	0	0–1/4	11
	Thunderbird Turbo	13/32P–1 29/32P	1 5/32P	9/16N–31/32P	1 5/32P	3/16	—
1988	Mustang with 5.0L without 5.0L	1/2P–2P 13/32P–1 29/32	1 1/4P 1 13/32P	3/4N–3/4P 27/32N–21/32P	0 3/32N	1/16–5/16 1/16–5/16	—
	Thunderbird Cougar	1/2P–2	1 1/4P	1/2N–1P	1/4P	1/16–5/16	—

WHEEL ALIGNMENT

Year	Model	Caster Range (deg.)	Caster Preferred Setting (deg.)	Camber Range (deg.)	Camber Preferred Setting (deg.)	Toe-in (in.)	Steering Axis Inclination (deg.)
1988	Crown Victoria Grand Marquis	2 1/4P–3 3/4P	3P	1/4N–1 1/4P	1/2N	1/16–3/16	10 31/32
	Town Car	2 1/4P–4P	3P	1/4N–1 1/4P	1/2P	1/16–3/16	11
	Continental Mark VII	5/8P–2 3/4P	1 1/2P	3/4N–3/4P	0	0–1/4	11
	Thunderbird Turbo	13/32P–1 29/32P	1 5/32P	9/16N–31/32P	1 5/32P	3/16	—
1989	Mustang with 5.0L	1/2P–2P	1 1/4P	3/4N–3/4P	0	1/16–5/16	—
	without 5.0L	13/32P–1 29/32	1 13/32P	27/32N–21/32P	3/32N	1/16–5/16	—
	Thunderbird Cougar	1/2P–2	1 1/4P	1/2N–1P	1/4P	1/16–5/16	—
	Crown Victoria Grand Marquis	2 1/4P–3 3/4P	3P	1/4N–1 1/4P	1/2N	1/16–3/16	10 31/32
	Town Car	2 1/4P–4P	3P	1/4N–1 1/4P	1/2P	1/16–3/16	11
	Continental Mark VII	5/8P–2 3/4P	1 1/2P	3/4N–3/4P	0	0–1/4	11
	Thunderbird Turbo	13/32P–1 29/32P	1 5/32P	9/16N–31/32P	1 5/32P	3/16	—
1990–91	Mustang with 5.0L	1 5/32P–2 5/8P	1 29/32P	1 3/8N–1/8P	5/8N	(out) 1/4–0	15 23/32
	without 5.0L	1 5/32P–2 5/8P	1 29/32P	1 1/4N–1/4P	1/2N	(out) 1/4–0	15 23/32
	Thunderbird Cougar	1/8P–1/4P	1/8P	3/4N–3/4P	0	1/8–1/4	—
	Thunderbird Turbo	13/32P–1 29/32P	1 5/32P	9/16N–31/32P	1 5/32P	3/16	—
	Crown Victoria Grand Marquis	2 1/4P–3 3/4P	3P	1/4N–1 1/4P	1/2N	1/16–3/16	10 31/32
	Town Car Continental	2 1/4P–4P	3P	1/4N–1 1/4P	1/2P	1/16–3/16	11
	Mark VII	5/8P–2 3/4P	1 1/2P	3/4N–3/4P	0	0–1/4	11

P Positive
N Negative

ENGINE ELECTRICAL

NOTE: Disconnecting the negative battery cable on some vehicles may interfere with the functions of the on board computer systems and may require the computer to undergo a relearning process, once the negative battery cable is reconnected.

Distributor

REMOVAL

1. Disconnect the negative battery cable. Remove the air cleaner on V6 and V8 engines.
2. Remove the distributor cap and position the cap and ignition wires to the side.
3. Disconnect the wiring harness plug from the distributor connector. Disconnect and plug the vacuum hoses from the vacuum diaphragm assembly, if equipped.
4. Rotate the engine, in normal direction of rotation, until No. 1 piston is on Top Dead Center (TDC) of the compression stroke. The TDC mark on the crankshaft pulley and the pointer should align. Rotor tip pointing at the No. 1 spark plug wire position on the distributor cap.
5. On Dura Spark I or II equipped engines, turn the engine slightly past the No. 1 spark plug position to align the stator (pick-up coil) assembly pole

with an armature pole (the closest one). On Dura Spark III, the distributor sleeve groove, when looking down from the top, and the cap adaptor alignment slot should align. If equipped with EEC-IV, remove the rotor (2 screws) and note the position of the "polarizing square" and shaft plate for reinstallation reference.

6. Scribe a mark on the distributor body and the engine block to indicate the position of the rotor tip and the position of the distributor in the engine. Dura Spark III and some EEC-IV system distributors are equipped with a notched base and will only locate at 1 position on the engine.

7. Remove the hold-down bolt and clamp located at the base of the distributor. Some Dura Spark III and EEC-IV system distributors are equipped with a special hold-down bolt that requires a Torx® head wrench for removal. Remove the distributor from the engine. Pay attention to the direction the rotor tip points if it moves from the No. 1 position when the drive gear disengages. For reinstallation purposes, the rotor should be at this point to insure proper gear mesh and timing.

8. Avoid turning the engine, if possible, while the distributor is removed. If the engine is turned from TDC position, TDC timing marks will have to be reset before the distributor is installed.

INSTALLATION

Timing Not Disturbed

1. Position the distributor in the engine with the rotor aligned to the marks made on the distributor or at the position the rotor pointed when the distributor was removed. The stator and armature or "polarizing square" and shaft plate should also be aligned. Engage the oil pump intermediate shaft and insert the distributor until fully seated on the engine. If the distributor does not fully seat, turn the engine slightly to fully engage the intermediate shaft.

2. If equipped with an indexed distributor base, make sure when positioning the distributor that the slot in the distributor base will engage the block tab and the sleeve/adaptor slots are aligned.

3. After the distributor has been fully seated into the block, recheck the timing mark and rotor alignment. Install the hold-down bracket and bolt. If equipped with an indexed base, tighten the mounting bolt. On other engines, snug the mounting bolt so the distributor can be turned for ignition timing purposes.

4. On 4 cylinder engines, reinstall the thermactor pump belt and adjust the tension. On V6 and V8 engines, install the air cleaner assembly. Connect all electrical and vacuum leads. Connect the negative battery cable. Check and reset the ignition timing.

NOTE: A silicone compound is used on rotor tips, distributor cap contacts and on the inside of the connectors on the spark plugs cable and module couplers. Always apply silicone dielectric compound after servicing any component of the ignition system.

Timing Disturbed

If the engine was cranked with the distributor removed, it will have to be put into its compression stroke with the No. 1 cylinder at TDC. The following procedure will enable the proper setting of the timing.

1. Remove the No. 1 spark plug.
2. Place a finger over the spark plug hole and crank the engine slowly until compression is felt.
3. Align the timing mark on the crankshaft pulley with the **0** degree mark on the timing scale. This places the No. 1 cylinder at the TDC of its compression stroke.
4. Turn the distributor shaft until the rotor points to the No. 1 spark plug tower on the cap.
5. Install the distributor into the engine, aligning the marks made on the block and the distributor housing.
6. Tighten the distributor hold-down bolt and connect all trical wires and vacuum lines. Connect the negative battery cable. Check and adjust the timing.

Distributorless Ignition System (DIS)

The 3.8L supercharged engine, used in 1989–91 Thunderbird SC and Cougar XR7, uses an distributorless ignition system.

The DIS system uses various electronic sensors in place of the distributor and uses an coil that fires 2 cylinders at the same time. The various components in the system are as follows:

Crankshaft Timing Sensor—The crankshaft timing sensor is a single Hall effect magnetic switch. It is activated by 3 vanes on the crankshaft damper and pulley assembly. The signal provided by this sensor feeds base timing and rpm information to the DIS module and EEC-IV module. Base

timing is set at 10 degrees BTDC and is not adjustable.

Camshaft Sensor—This sensor is driven by the camshaft and provides cylinder position information for the ignition coil and fuel system

DIS Ignition Module—This module receives the signal from the crankshaft sensor, the camshaft sensor and spark signal from the EEC-IV module. The main purpose of this module is to take the information supplied to it and control the ignition coils so that they fire at the correct sequence. The DIS module also controls the engine dwell.

Ignition Coil Pack—The ignition coil pack contains 3 separate ignition coils which are controlled by the DIS module, through 3 coil leads. Each ignition coils fires 2 spark plugs at the same time, 1 on the compression stroke and 1 on the exhaust stroke.

REMOVAL & INSTALLATION

Crankshaft Timing Sensor

1. Disconnect the negative battery cable.
2. Loosen the accessory drive belt tensioners for both the air conditioning compressor and the supercharger. Remove the belts from the crankshaft pulley.
3. Disconnect the electrical connector from the sensor wiring.
4. Raise and safely support the front of the vehicle. Remove the upper and lower crankshaft damper covers.
5. Remove the crankshaft pulley and damper using a suitable puller.
6. Remove the 2 sensors mounting bolts and remove the sensor.
To install:
7. To install the sensor, position it on its mount and install the retaining bolts. Torque the retaining bolts to 31 inch lbs.
8. Install the crankshaft damper and pulley, tightening the pulley bolt to 103–132 ft. lbs.
9. Install the upper and lower damper covers and lower the vehicle.
10. Reconnect the sensor wiring and install the accessory drive belts. Connect the battery.

Camshaft Sensor

1. Disconnect the negative battery cable.
2. Disconnect the electrical leads from the camshaft sensor.
3. Remove the sensor mounting screws and remove the sensor.
4. Install the sensor in position and install the mounting screws, tightening to 31 inch. lbs.
5. Reconnect the electrical leads and connect the negative battery cable.

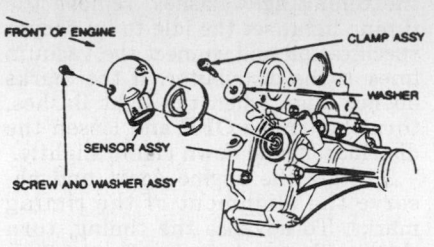

Removing the camshaft sensor assembly 3.8L SC

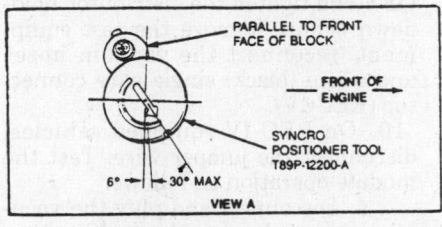

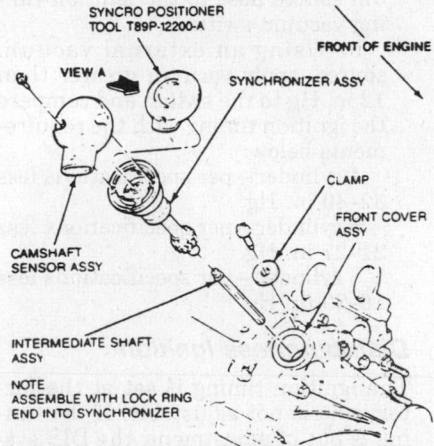

Installing the synchronizer assembly 3.8L SC

Synchronizer Assembly

NOTE: Before starting this procedure, set the No. 1 cylinder to 26 degrees after TDC of the compression stroke. Then note the position of the camshaft sensor electrical connector. The installation procedure requires that the connector be located in the same position.

1. Disconnect the negative battery cable.
2. Remove the camshaft sensor assembly.
3. Remove the synchronizer clamp, bolt and washer.
4. Remove the synchronizer from the front engine cover, by pulling it out. The oil pump intermediate shaft will come out with the assembly.

NOTE: If the replacement synchronizer does not contain a plastic locator cover tool, a special service tool such as the synchro positioner T89P-12200-A or

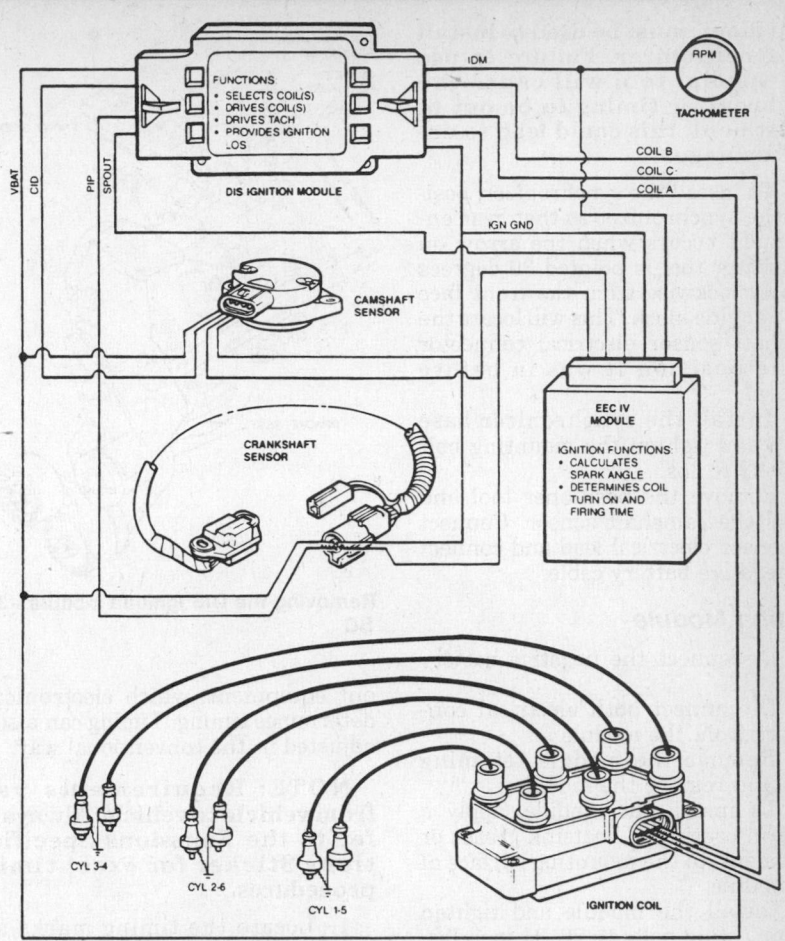

Distributorless ignition system (DIS) components

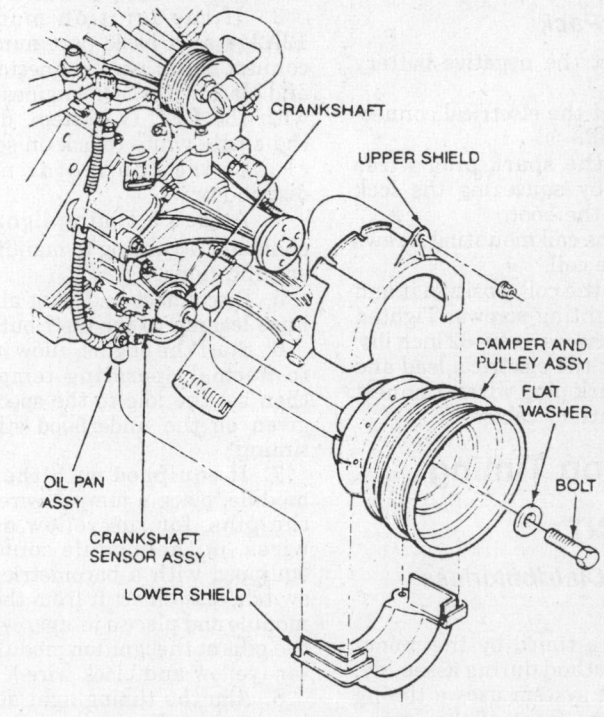

Removing the crankshaft timing sensor—3.8L SC

equivalent, must be used to install the synchronizer. Failure to use this special tool will cause the synchronizer timing to be out of adjustment, this could lead to engine damage.

5. To install the synchronizer, position the synchronizer so that gear engagement occurs when the arrow on the locator tool is pointed 30 degrees counterclockwise from the front face of the engine block. This will locate the camshaft sensor electrical connector to the position it was in before removal.

6. Install the synchronizer base clamp and tighten the mounting bolt to 15–22 ft. lbs.

7. Remove the positioner tool and install the camshaft sensor. Connect the sensor electrical lead and connect the negative battery cable.

Ignition Module

1. Disconnect the negative battery cable.

2. Disconnect both electrical connectors from the module.

3. Remove the module retaining bolts and remove the module.

4. To install the module, apply a uniform coating of heatsink grease or equivalent, to the mounting surface of the module.

5. Install the module and tighten the mounting bolts to 22–31 inch lbs.

6. Reconnect the electrical connectors and connect the negative battery cable.

Ignition Coil Pack

1. Disconnect the negative battery cable.

2. Disconnect the electrical connector from the coil.

3. Remove the spark plug wires from the coil by squeezing the lock tabs to release the boot.

4. Remove the coil mounting screws and remove the coil.

5. To install the coil, position it and install the mounting screws. Tighten the mounting screws to 40–62 inch lbs.

6. Reconnect the electrical lead and connect the spark plug wires. Connect the negative battery cable.

Ignition Timing

ADJUSTMENT

Except With Distributorless Ignition

The engines are timed by the monolithic timing method during assembly. The monolithic system uses a timing receptacle on the front of the engine which can be connected to digital read-

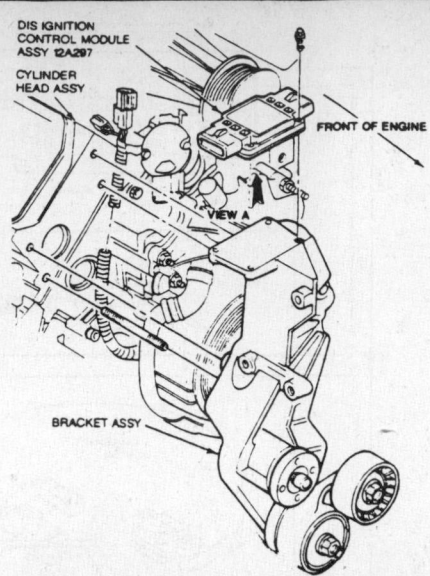

Removing the DIS ignition module – 3.8L SC

out equipment, which electronically determines timing. Timing can also be adjusted in the conventional way.

NOTE: Requirements vary from vehicle to vehicle. Always refer to the Emissions Specifications Sticker for exact timing procedures.

1. Locate the timing marks and pointer on the lower engine pulley and engine's front cover.

2. Clean the marks and apply chalk or bright-colored paint to the pointer.

3. If the ignition module has 12A244 as a basic part number, disconnect the 2 wire connector (yellow and black wires). On engines equipped with the EEC-IV system, disconnect the single white (black on some vehicles) wire connector near the distributor.

4. Attach a timing light and tachometer according to manufacturer's specifications.

5. Disconnect and plug all vacuum lines leading to the distributor.

6. Start the engine, allow it to warm to normal operating temperature, then set the idle to the specifications given on the underhood sticker (for timing).

7. If equipped with the ignition module, place a jumper wire between the pins, for the yellow and black wires, in the module connector. If equipped with a barometric pressure switch, disconnect it from the ignition module and place a jumper wire across the pins at the ignition module connector (yellow and black wire.)

8. Aim the timing light at the timing mark and pointer on the front of the engine. If the marks align when

the timing light flashes, remove the timing light, set the idle to its proper specification and connect the vacuum lines at the distributor. If the marks do not align when the light flashes, turn the engine OFF and loosen the distributor hold-down clamp slightly.

9. Start the engine again and observe the alignment of the timing marks. To advance the timing, turn the distributor clockwise, for the 3.8L and all V8 engines. When the timing marks are aligned, turn the engine OFF and tighten the distributor hold-down clamp. Remove the test equipment, reconnect the vacuum hoses and white (black) single wire connector (EEC-IV).

10. On EEC-IV equipped vehicles, disconnect the jumper wire. Test the module operation as follows:

   a. Disconnect and plug the vacuum source hose to the ignition timing vacuum switch.

   b. Using an external vacuum source, apply vacuum greater than 12 in. Hg to the switch and compare the ignition timing with the requirements below:

   4 cylinder – per specifications less 32–40 in. Hg.

   6 cylinder – per specifications less 21–27 in. Hg.

   8 cylinder – per specifications less 16–20 in. Hg.

Distributorless Ignition

The ignition timing is set at the factory and is not adjustable. If the timing is out of adjustment, the DIS system will have to be checked for proper operation.

Alternator

For further information on the charging system, please refer to "Charging and Starting" in the Unit Repair section.

PRECAUTIONS

Several precautions must be observed with alternator equipped vehicles to avoid damage to the unit.

• If the battery is removed for any reason, make sure it is reconnected with the correct polarity. Reversing the battery connections may result in damage to the one-way rectifiers.

• When utilizing a booster battery as a starting aid, always connect the positive to positive terminals and the negative terminal from the booster battery to a good engine ground on the vehicle being started.

• Never use a fast charger as a booster to start vehicles.

• Disconnect the battery cables

when charging the battery with a fast charger.
- Never attempt to polarize the alternator.
- Do not use test lamps of more than 12V when checking diode continuity.
- Do not short across or ground any of the alternator terminals.
- The polarity of the battery, alternator and regulator must be matched and considered before making any electrical connections within the system.
- Never separate the alternator on an open circuit. Make sure all connections within the circuit are clean and tight.
- Disconnect the battery ground terminal when performing any service on electrical components.
- Disconnect the battery if arc welding is to be done on the vehicle.

BELT TENSION ADJUSTMENT

Gauge Method

EXCEPT SERPENTINE BELT

Using belt tension gauge tool T63l–8620–A or equivalent, adjust the alternator belt if the tension is below new or used specifications, as indicated on the gauge.

SERPENTINE BELT

The correct belt tension is indicated on the indicator mark of the belt tensioner. If the indicator mark is not within specification, replace the belt or the tensioner.

Voltage Regulator

For further information on the charging system, please refer to "Charging and Starting" in the Unit Repair section.

REMOVAL & INSTALLATION

1. Disconnect the negative battery cable. The regulator is located behind the battery on some models and it is necessary to remove the battery to remove the regulator.
2. Remove the regulator mounting screws, unlock the wire connectors and remove the regulator.

NOTE: Always disconnect the connector plug from the regulator before removing the mounting screws.

3. Reverse the procedure to reinstall. On electro-mechanical regulators, the radio suppression condenser mounts under 1 screw.

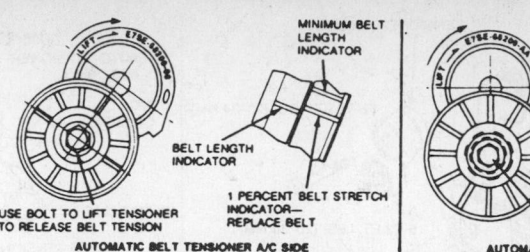
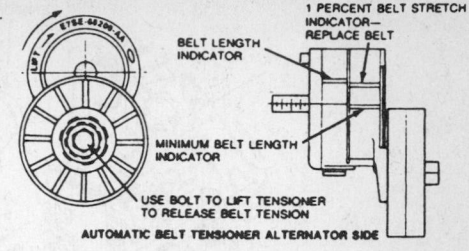

Belt wear indicator marks—Mustang with 2.3L engine

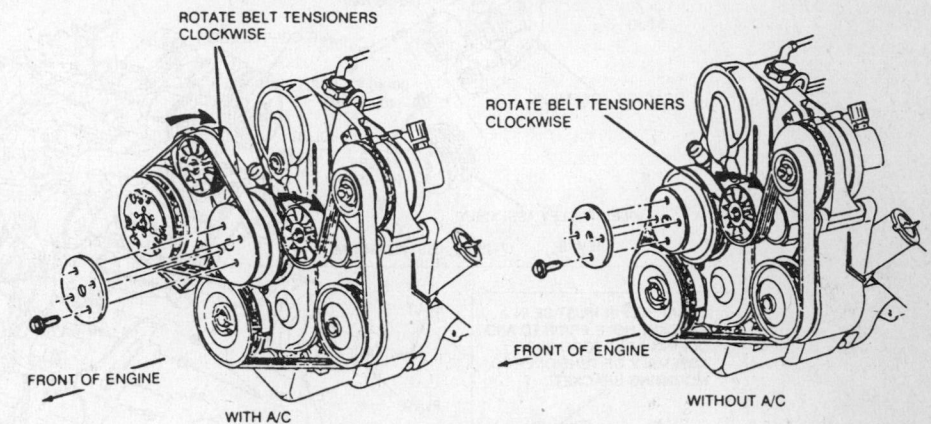

Belt installation—Mustang with 2.3L engine

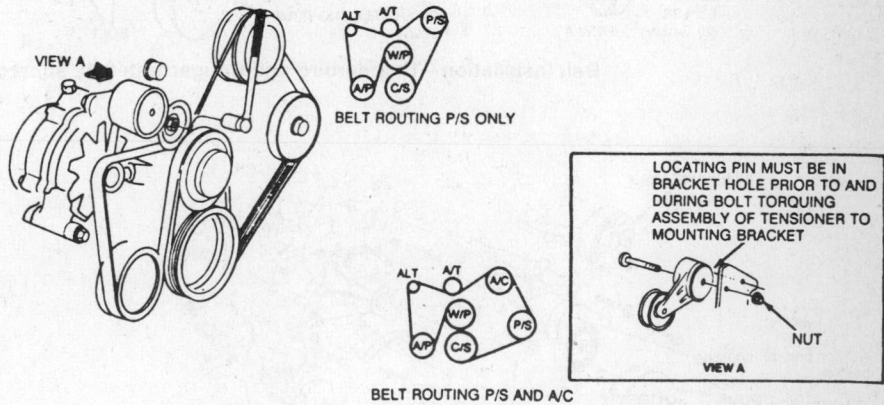

Belt installation—Mustang and Mark VII with 5.0L engine

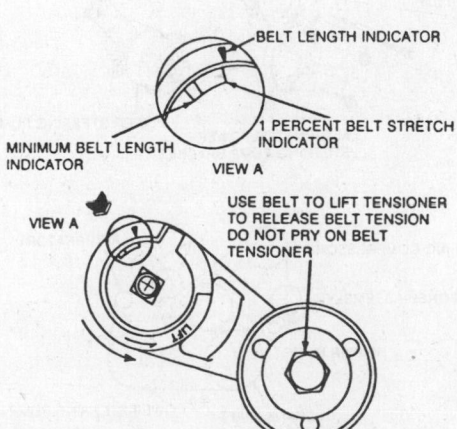

Belt tensioner—Mustang and Mark VII

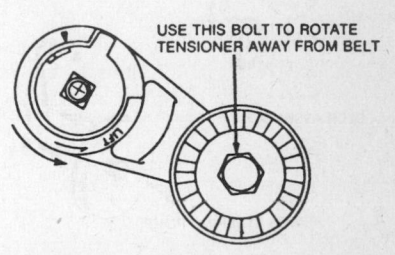

Belt tensioner—Thunderbird and Cougar with 3.8L engine

Starter

For further information on the charging system, please refer to "Charging and Starting" in the Unit Repair section.

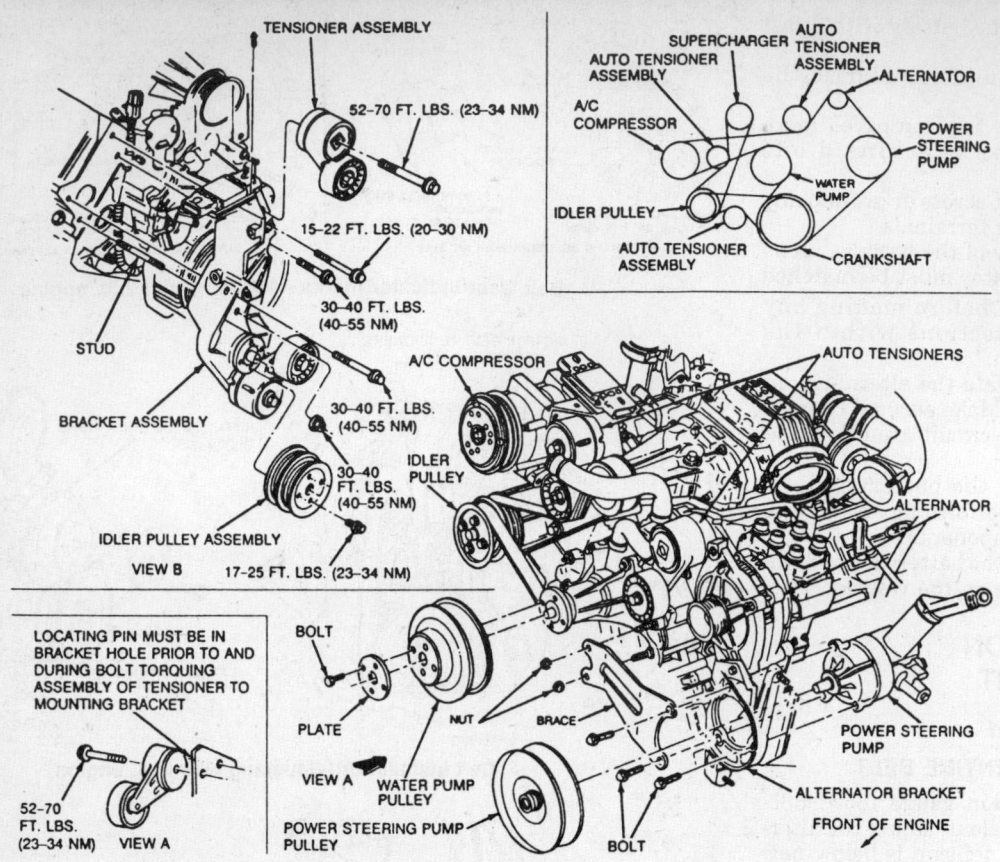

TENSIONER ASSEMBLY

52–70 FT. LBS. (23–34 NM)

SUPERCHARGER

AUTO TENSIONER ASSEMBLY

AUTO TENSIONER ASSEMBLY

ALTERNATOR

A/C COMPRESSOR

POWER STEERING PUMP

15–22 FT. LBS. (20–30 NM)

WATER PUMP

IDLER PULLEY

AUTO TENSIONER ASSEMBLY

CRANKSHAFT

30–40 FT. LBS. (40–55 NM)

STUD

A/C COMPRESSOR

AUTO TENSIONERS

BRACKET ASSEMBLY

30–40 FT. LBS. (40–55 NM)

30–40 FT. LBS. (40–55 NM)

IDLER PULLEY

ALTERNATOR

IDLER PULLEY ASSEMBLY

VIEW B   17–25 FT. LBS. (23–34 NM)

LOCATING PIN MUST BE IN BRACKET HOLE PRIOR TO AND DURING BOLT TORQUING ASSEMBLY OF TENSIONER TO MOUNTING BRACKET

BOLT

PLATE

NUT

BRACE

POWER STEERING PUMP

52–70 FT. LBS. (23–34 NM)   VIEW A

VIEW A   WATER PUMP PULLEY

POWER STEERING PUMP PULLEY

ALTERNATOR BRACKET

BOLT

FRONT OF ENGINE

Belt installation—Thunderbird and Cougar with 3.8L supercharged engine

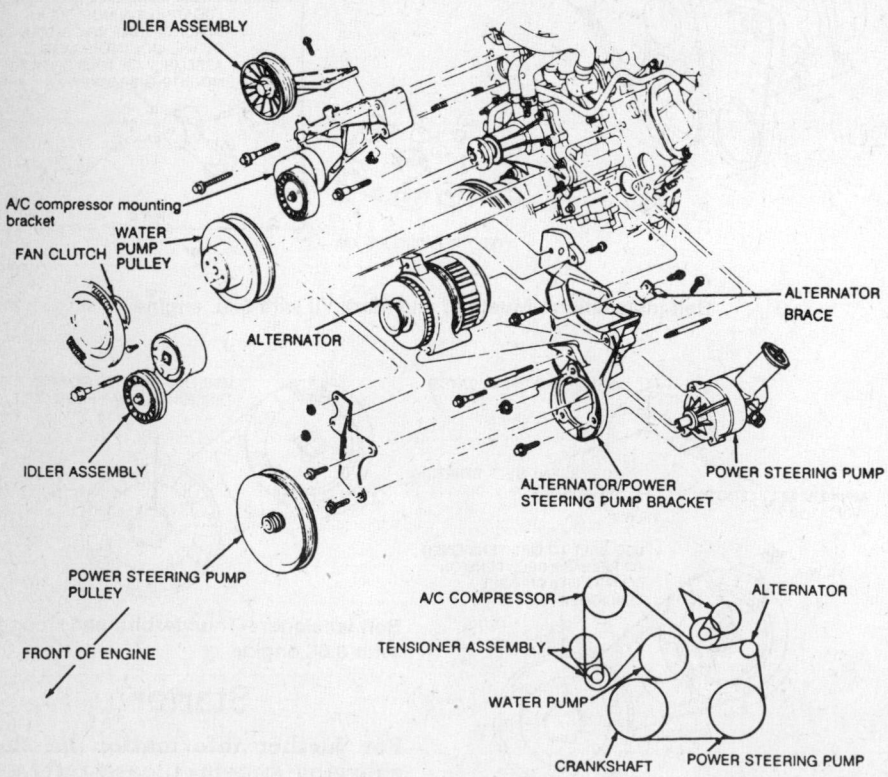

IDLER ASSEMBLY

A/C compressor mounting bracket

WATER PUMP PULLEY

FAN CLUTCH

ALTERNATOR

ALTERNATOR BRACE

IDLER ASSEMBLY

POWER STEERING PUMP PULLEY

ALTERNATOR/POWER STEERING PUMP BRACKET

POWER STEERING PUMP

FRONT OF ENGINE

A/C COMPRESSOR

ALTERNATOR

TENSIONER ASSEMBLY

WATER PUMP

CRANKSHAFT   POWER STEERING PUMP

Belt installation—Thunderbird and Cougar with 3.8L except supercharged engine

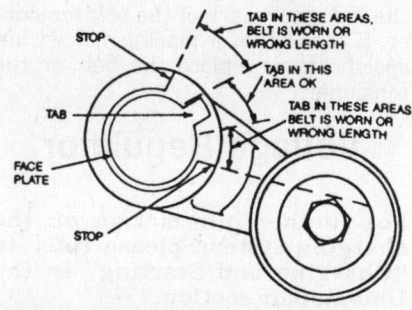

STOP

TAB IN THESE AREAS, BELT IS WORN OR WRONG LENGTH

TAB IN THIS AREA OK

TAB

TAB IN THESE AREAS, BELT IS WORN OR WRONG LENGTH

FACE PLATE

STOP

STOP

Belt adjustment—Thunderbird and Cougar with 3.8L engine

REMOVAL & INSTALLATION

1. Disconnect the negative battery cable.
2. Raise the vehicle and support it safely.
3. Disconnect the starter cable from the starter.
4. Remove the starter bolts and the starter.
5. Reposition the starter to the engine and tighten the mounting bolts to 15–20 ft. lbs.
6. Reconnect the electrical leads. Connect the negative battery cable.

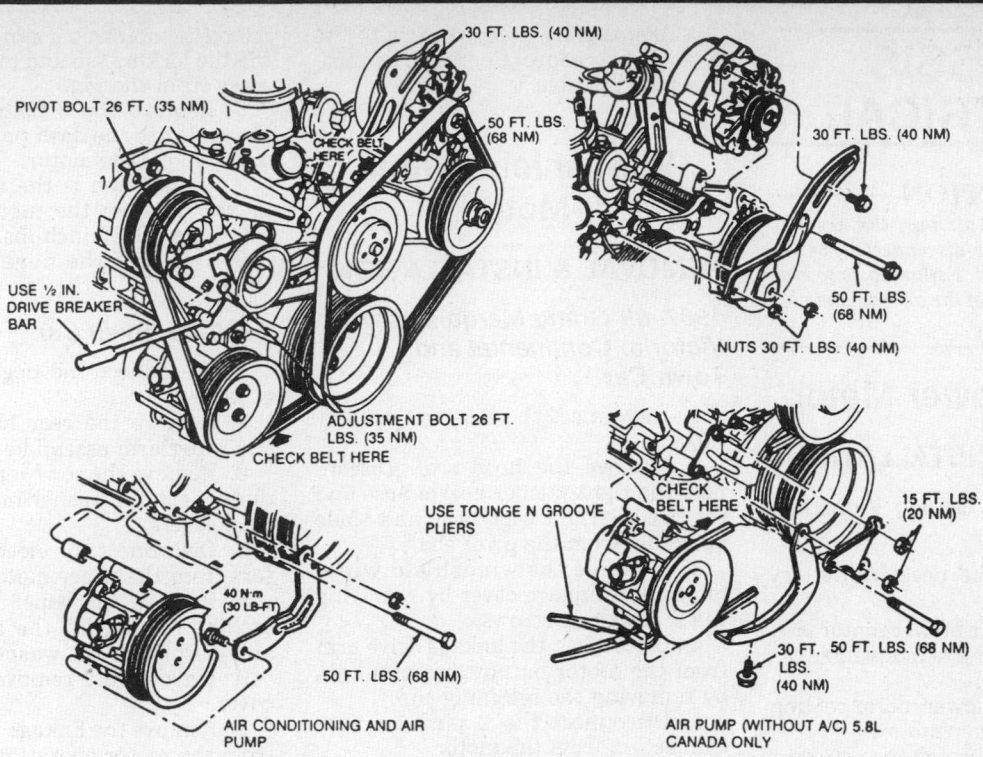

Belt installation—Town Car, Crown Victoria and Grand Marquis

BELT TENSION

BELT TENSION

Model/Engine	Belt Type	Belt Condition	lbs.
All except below	1/4 in. V-belt	New	50–90
		Used Reset	40–60
		Used Min.	40
	3/8 in. V-belt or 4000	New	90–130
		Used Reset	80–100
		Used Min.	60
	5 rib	New	120–160
		Used Reset	110–130
		Used Min.	70
	6 rib	New	150–190
		Used Reset	140–160
		Used Min.	90
Thunderbird & Cougar 5.0L	—	—	①
Mustang	—	—	①

① Mark on automatic tensioner must be between Min. and Max. marks

CHASSIS ELECTRICAL

——— CAUTION ———

If equipped with an air bag, the negative battery cable must be disconnected, before working on the system. Failure to do so may result in deployment of the air bag and possible personal injury.

Heater Blower Motor

REMOVAL & INSTALLATION

Grand Marquis, Crown Victoria and Town Car

1. Disconnect the negative battery cable.
2. Disconnect the blower motor lead connector from the wiring harness connector.
3. Remove the blower motor cooling tube from the blower motor.
4. Remove the 4 retaining screws.
5. Turn the motor and wheel assembly slightly to the right so that the bottom edge of the mounting plate follows the contour of the wheel well splash panel. Lift up on the blower and remove it from the blower housing.
6. Installation is the reverse of removal. Connect the negative battery cable.

Mark VII, Thunderbird and Cougar

1. Disconnect the negative battery cable.
2. Remove the air inlet duct and blower housing assembly from the vehicle.
3. Remove the 4 retaining screws.
4. Turn the motor and wheel assembly slightly to the right so that the bottom edge of the mounting plate follows the contour of the wheel well splash panel. Lift up on the blower and remove it from the blower housing.
5. Installation is the reverse of removal. Connect the negative battery cable.

Mustang

1. Disconnect the negative battery cable. Loosen glove compartment assembly by squeezing the sides together to disengage the retainer tabs.
2. Let the glove compartment and door hang down in front of instrument panel and remove blower motor cooling hose.
3. Disconnect electrical wiring harness. Remove 4 screws attaching motor to housing. Pull motor and wheel out of housing.

4. Installation is the reverse of the removal procedure. Connect the negative battery cable.

Windshield Wiper Motor

REMOVAL & INSTALLATION

1987–89 Grand Marquis, Crown Victoria, Continental and Town Car

1. Disconnect the negative battery cable.
2. Remove the hood seal. Disconnect the right washer nozzle hose and remove the right wiper arm and blade assembly from the pivot shaft.
3. Remove the windshield wiper motor and linkage cover by removing the 2 attaching screws.
4. Disconnect the linkage drive arm from the motor output arm crankpin by removing the retaining clip.
5. Disconnect the 2 push-on wire connectors from the motor.
6. Remove the 3 bolts that retain the motor to the dash panel extension and remove the motor.
7. To install, be sure the output arm is in the park position and reverse the removal procedure. Connect the negative battery cable.

1987–89 Thunderbird, Cougar, Mustang and Mark VII

1. Disconnect the battery ground cable.
2. Remove the right and left wiper blade assemblies.
3. Remove the grille on the top of the cowl.
4. Disconnect the linkage drive arm from the motor crankpin after removing the clip.
5. Disconnect the wiper motor electrical connector and remove the 3 attaching screws from the motor. Pull the motor from the opening.
6. Be sure the motor crank arm is in the park position and reverse the removal procedure to install. Connect the negative battery cable.

1990–91 Grand Marquis and Crown Victoria

1. Disconnect the negative battery cable.
2. Remove the rear hood seal and the right hand wiper arm assembly.
3. Disconnect the 2 push on wire connectors from the motor.
4. Remove the windshield wiper linkage cover by removing the 2 retaining screws and hose clip.
5. Remove the linkage retaining clip

from the motor operating arm by lifting the locking tab and pulling the clip away from the pin.
6. Remove the 3 bolts that retain the motor to the dash panel extension and remove the motor.
7. Installation is the reverse of removal. Tighten the motor mounting screws to 60–85 inch lbs.
8. Connect the negative battery cable.

1990–91 Town Car

1. Disconnect the negative battery cable.
2. Remove the rear hood seal and the wiper arm assemblies.
3. Remove the cowl vent screws and disconnect the washer hoses from the washer jets.
4. Disconnect the electrical connectors from the wiper motor.
5. Remove the wiper assembly attaching screws, lift the assembly out and disconnect the washer hose.
6. Unsnap and remove the linkage cover.
7. Remove the linkage retaining clip from the motor operating arm by lifting the locking tab and pulling the clip away from the pin.
8. Remove the motor retaining screws and remove the motor from the vehicle.
9. Installation is the reverse of removal. Connect the negative battery cable.

1990–91 Mark VII

1. Turn the wipers on until they reach full travel on the windshield then turn the key **OFF**.
2. Disconnect the negative battery cable and remove the arm and blade assemblies.
3. Remove the left hand cowl vent screen.
4. Disconnect the linkage drive arm from the motor crankpin after removing the clip.
5. Disconnect the electrical connector from the wiper motor, remove the 3 retaining bolts and remove the motor from the vehicle.
6. Installation is the reverse of removal. Tighten the motor mounting screws to 60–85 inch lbs.
7. Connect the negative battery cable. Cycle the motor, turn **OFF** the switch, then install the arm and blade assemblies.

NOTE: When installing the drive arm to the new motor, follow the instructions included in the new motor kit.

1987–91 Thunderbird and Cougar

1. Disconnect the negative battery cable.

2. With the wipers in the park position remove the arm and blade assemblies.

3. Remove the left hand cowl vent screen.

4. Remove the vacuum manifolds from the wiper module.

5. Remove the 5 screws and 1 nut from the wiper module and remove the wiper module.

6. Disconnect the linkage drive arm from the motor crankpin after removing the clip.

7. Disconnect the electrical connector from the wiper motor, remove the 3 retaining bolts and remove the motor from the vehicle.

8. Installation is the reverse of removal. Connect the negative battery cable. Cycle the motor, turn **OFF** the switch, then install the arm and blade assemblies.

NOTE: When installing the drive arm to the new motor, follow the instructions included in the new motor kit.

1987–91 Mustang

1. Disconnect the negative battery cable.

2. Remove the right hand wiper arm assembly.

3. Remove the cowl top retaining screws and grille.

4. Disconnect the linkage drive arm from the motor crankpin after removing the clip.

5. Disconnect the electrical connector from the wiper motor, remove the 3 retaining botls and remove the motor from the vehicle.

6. Installation is the reverse of removal. Connect the negative battery cable. Cycle the motor, turn **OFF** the switch, then install the arm and blade assemblies.

NOTE: When installing the drive arm to the new motor, follow the instructions included in the new motor kit.

Wiper Switch

REMOVAL & INSTALLATION

1. Disconnect the negative battery cable.

2. Remove the split steering column cover retaining screws.

3. Separate the halves and remove the wiper switch retaining screws.

4. Disconnect the wire connector and remove the wiper switch.

5. The installation of the wiper switch is the reverse of the removal procedure.

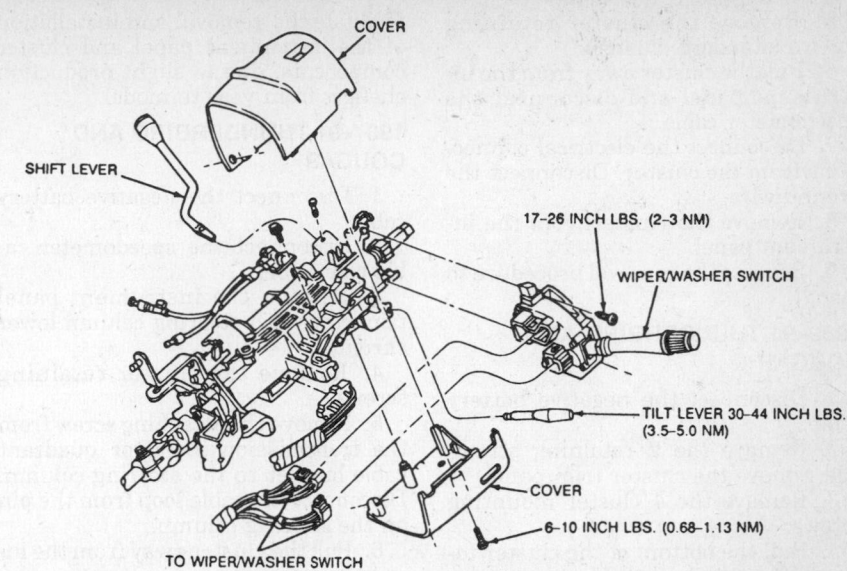

Wiper switch Installation—Town Car, Crown Victoria and Grand Marquis

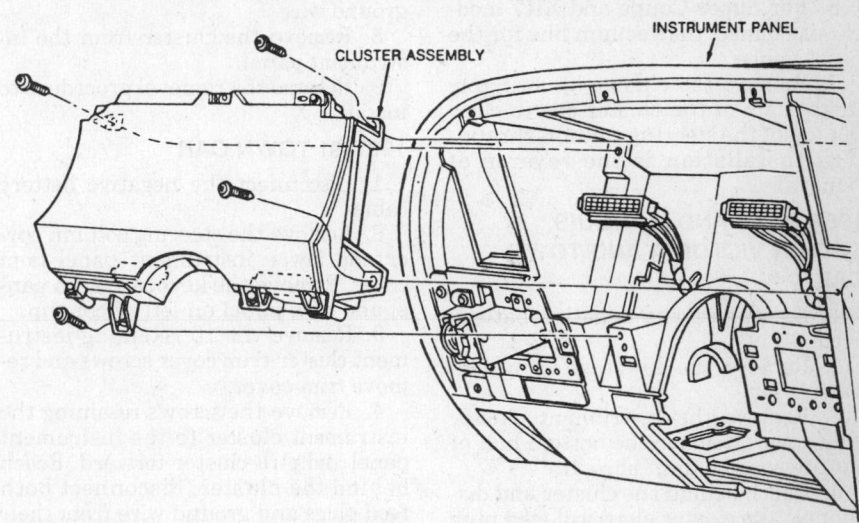

Standard instrument cluster installation—1987–88 Thunderbird and Cougar

Instrument Cluster

REMOVAL & INSTALLATION

Standard Cluster

1987–91 MUSTANG

1. Disconnect the negative battery cable.

2. Remove the upper retaining screws from the instrument cluster trim cover and remove the trim cover.

3. Pull the cluster away from the instrument panel and reach behind the instrument cluster to disconnect the speedometer cable by pressing on the flat surface of the plastic connector (quick disconnect).

4. Pull the cluster further away from the instrument panel and disconnect the cluster printed circuit connectors from their receptacles in the cluster backplate.

5. Remove cluster.

6. Installation is the reverse order of the removal procedure.

1987–88 THUNDERBIRD AND COUGAR

1. Disconnect the negative battery cable.

2. Disconnect the speedometer cable (standard cluster).

3. Remove the instrument panel trim cover and steering column lower shroud.

4. Remove the attaching screw from the transmission indicator quadrant cable bracket to the steering column. Disconnect the cable loop from the pin on the steering column.

5. Remove the cluster retaining screws (standard cluster).

6. Pull the cluster away from the instrument panel and disconnect the speedometer cable.

7. Disconnect the electrical connections from the cluster. Disconnect the ground wire.

8. Remove the cluster from the instrument panel.

9. Reverse the removal procedure to install.

1989–91 THUNDERBIRD AND COUGAR

1. Disconnect the negative battery cable.

2. Remove the 2 retaining screws and remove the cluster trim panel.

3. Remove the 4 cluster mounting screws.

4. Pull the bottom of the cluster towards the steering wheel.

5. Reach behind and under the cluster and unplug the 2 connectors.

6. For Super Coupe and XR7 models, disconnect the vacuum line for the boost gauge.

7. Remove the cluster by swinging the bottom of the cluster out to clear the top of the steering column shroud.

8. Installation is the reverse of removal.

1987–91 GRAND MARQUIS, CROWN VICTORIA AND TOWN CAR

1. Disconnect the negative battery cable.

2. Remove the lower steering column cover.

3. Remove the instrument cluster trim cover. Remove the bottom half of the steering column shroud.

4. Reach behind the cluster and disconnect the cluster electrical feed plug and the speedometer cable.

5. On the 1988–89 Crown Victoria and Grand Marquis, remove the headlamp switch and knob assembly.

6. Unsnap and remove the steering column shroud cover, if not previously done. Disconnect the transmission indicator cable from the tab in the shroud retainer.

7. Remove the attaching screw for the transmission indicator cable bracket to steering column. disconnect the cable loop from the pin on the steering column.

8. Remove the cluster retaining screws and remove the cluster assembly.

9. The installation is the reverse of the removal procedure.

Electronic Cluster

During the removal and installation procedures, slight variations may be required from the general outline, to facilitate the removal and installation of the instrument panel and cluster components, due to slight production changes from year to model.

1987–91 THUNDERBIRD AND COUGAR

1. Disconnect the negative battery cable.

2. Disconnect the speedometer cable connector.

3. Remove the instrument panel trim cover and steering column lower shroud.

4. Remove the cluster retaining screws.

5. Remove the attaching screw from the transmission indicator quadrant cable bracket to the steering column. Disconnect the cable loop from the pin on the steering column.

6. Pull the cluster away from the instrument panel.

7. Disconnect the electrical connections from the cluster. Disconnect the ground wire.

8. Remove the cluster from the instrument panel.

9. Reverse the removal procedure to install.

1987–91 TOWN CAR

1. Disconnect the negative battery cable.

2. Remove the steering column cover and lower instrument panel trim cover. Remove the keyboard trim panel and trim panel on left of column.

3. Remove the 10 retaining instrument cluster trim cover screws and remove trim cover.

4. Remove the screws retaining the instrument cluster to the instrument panel and pull cluster forward. Reach behind the cluster, disconnect both feed plugs and ground wire from their receptacles in the cluster back plate.

5. Disconnect the speedometer cable by pressing on the flat surface of the plastic connector (quick disconnect).

6. Remove the attaching screw from the transmission indicator cable bracket to the steering column. Detach the cable loop from the pin on the shift cane lever of the steering column.

7. Remove the plastic clamp from around steering column. Remove the cluster.

8. Installation is the reverse of the removal procedure.

1987–91 MARK VII

1. Disconnect the negative battery cable. Remove the screws retaining instrument finish panel and rotate top of panel toward steering wheel. Disconnect electrical and air sensor connectors at right hand portion of finish panel. Remove panel.

2. Remove 6 screws retaining instrument panel pad and rotate pad toward steering wheel and remove it.

3. Remove 4 screws retaining instrument cluster to instrument panel and remove it.

4. Disconnect electrical connector at lower left rear corner of cluster.

5. Installation is the reverse order of the removal procedure.

1987 CONTINENTAL

1. Disconnect the negative battery cable. Remove the steering column shroud.

2. Remove left and right instrument panel mouldings. Mouldings are held in with retaining clips.

3. Remove the 2 center moulding retaining screws and remove moulding above climate control head.

4. Remove the ash tray.

5. Remove the 2 remaining screws and take out the center moulding.

6. Remove the screws retaining the instrument cluster finish panel and remove the panel.

7. Disconnect the transmission indicator cable at the steering column.

8. Remove the 4 screws retaining the cluster to the instrument panel and disconnect the electrical connector at the lower left corner of the cluster.

9. Remove the instrument cluster from the vehicle.

10. Installation is the reverse order of the removal procedure.

Speedometer

REMOVAL & INSTALLATION

Except Electronic Cluster

1. Disconnect the negative battery cable.

2. Remove instrument cluster.

3. Disconnect speedometer cable by pressing flat surface and pulling cable away from head (quick connect).

4. Remove screws which attach the lens and mask to the cluster and remove lens and mask.

5. Remove 2 screws attaching speedometer head to cluster and remove speedometer.

6. On Town Car and Mark VII, remove 2 screws holding trip odometer reset assembly to the cluster and remove speedometer. Remove the screw from back of the trip odometer mechanism and unhook trip odometer reset assembly cable from the slot in the trip odometer.

7. Installation is the reverse order of removal procedure.

Electronic Cluster

The electronic instrument speedometer, if equipped, is removed with the electronic instrument cluster. The speedometer is an integral part of the cluster assembly.

Radio

REMOVAL & INSTALLATION

Continental

1. Disconnect the negative battery cable.
2. Remove the 4 radio plate to panel screws. Pull the radio with the front plate attached rearward until the rear bracket is clear.
3. Disconnect the wires from the chassis. If equipped with premium sound, remove the control assembly attaching nut and washer, remove the switch and remove the illumination lamp socket from the front bracket.
4. Remove the radio with the front plate attached. Remove the 4 screws and remove the plate.
5. Install the radio in the instrument panel and connect the electrical leads.
6. Install the radio trim panel. Connect the negative battery cable.

Crown Victoria and Grand Marquis

1. Disconnect the battery ground cable.
2. On all electronic radios, remove the radio to mounting plate screws and remove the mounting plate.
3. Remove the radio knobs, the screws that attach the bezel to the instrument panel and remove the bezel.
4. Remove the radio mounting plate attaching screws (standard radios) and disengage the radio by pulling it from the lower rear support bracket.
5. Disconnect all the leads from the radio.
6. Remove the radio mounting plate and the rear upper support; remove the radio from the instrument panel.
7. Install the radio in the instrument panel and connect the electrical leads.
8. Install the radio trim plate and connect the negative battery cable. Check the operation of the radio.

Mustang

1. Disconnect the negative battery cable.
2. Disconnect the electrical, speaker and antenna leads from the radio.
3. Remove the knobs, discs and control shaft nuts and washers from the radio shafts.
4. Remove the ash tray receptacle and bracket.
5. Remove the rear support nut from the radio.
6. Remove the instrument panel

lower reinforcement and the heater or air conditioning floor ducts.
7. Remove the radio from the rear support and drop the radio down and out from behind the instrument panel.
8. Install the radio in the instrument panel and connect the electrical leads.
9. Install the radio trim plate and connect the negative battery cable. Check the operation of the radio.

Thunderbird and Cougar

1. Disconnect the negative battery cable.
2. Remove the radio knobs. Remove the center trim panel.
3. Remove the radio mounting plate screws. Pull the radio towards the front seat to disengage it from the lower bracket.
4. Disconnect the radio and antenna connections.
5. Remove the radio. Remove the nuts and washers (conventional radios) as necessary.
6. On electronic radios, install the mounting plates before installing the retaining nuts and washers or screws. The rest of installation is the reverse of removal.

Headlight Switch

REMOVAL & INSTALLATION

1987–89 Grand Marquis and Crown Victoria

1. Disconnect the negative battery cable.
2. Underneath the instrument panel, depress the shaft retaining knob and pull the knob straight out.
3. Unscrew the trim bezel and remove the locknut.
4. Underneath the instrument panel, move the switch toward the front of the vehicle while tilting it downward.
5. Disconnect the wiring from the switch and remove the switch from the vehicle.
6. Installation is the reverse of removal.

1990–91 Grand Marquis and Crown Victoria

1. Disconnect the negative battery cable.
2. Remove the right hand and left hand moulding from the instrument panel by pulling up and snapping out of the retainers.
3. Remove the 4 top and 4 bottom screws retaining the finish panel to the instrument panel.
4. Remove the headlight switch knob from the shaft and remove the finish panel.

5. Remove the 2 headlight bracket retaining screws and pull the bracket and switch from from the instrument panel.
6. Remove the nut retaining the switch to the bracket.
7. Disconnect the electrical connector and remove the switch.
8. Installation is the reverse of removal.

1987–89 Town Car

1. Disconnect the ground cable from the battery.
2. Remove the headlight switch knob.
3. Remove the auto dimmer bezel and the autolamp delay bezel, if so equipped.
4. Remove the steering column lower shroud.
5. Remove the lower left instrument panel trim bezel.
6. Remove the 5 screws that retain the headlight switch mounting bracket to the instrument panel.
7. Carefully pull the switch and bracket from the instrument panel and disconnect the wiring connector(s) from the headlamp switch.
8. Remove the locknut and screw that retain the headlight switch to the switch bracket.
9. Installation is the reverse order of the removal procedure.

1990–91 Town Car

1. Disconnect the ground cable from the battery.
2. Remove the headlight switch knob.
3. Remove the auto dimmer bezel and the autolamp delay bezel, if so equipped.
4. Remove the right hand and left hand moulding from the instrument panel by pulling up and snapping out of the retainers.
3. Remove the 6 top and 6 bottom screws retaining the finish panel to the instrument panel.
4. Remove the headlight switch knob from the shaft and remove the finish panel.
5. Remove the 2 headlight bracket retaining screws and pull the bracket and switch from from the instrument panel.
6. Remove the nut retaining the switch to the bracket.
7. Disconnect the electrical connector and remove the switch.
8. Installation is the reverse of removal.

1987–91 Mark VII and Continental, 1987–88 Thunderbird and Cougar

1. Disconnect the negative battery

cable. Remove the lens assembly attaching screws and then the lens assembly.

2. Remove the screws securing the switch to the instrument panel and pull the switch out from the panel.

3. Disconnect the electrical connector and remove the switch from the vehicle.

4. Installation is the reverse order of the removal procedure.

1989–91 Thunderbird and Cougar

1. Disconnect the negative battery cable.

2. Remove the 2 cluster finish panel retaining screws.

3. Pull the headlight switch knob off.

4. Unsnap the cluster finish panel.

5. Disconnect the electrical connector to the headlight dimmer sensor assembly.

6. Through the opening in the instrument panel, depress the shaft release button on the switch and remove the shaft.

7. Remove the headlight switch retaining nut, pull the switch through the opening and disconnect the wiring connector.

8. Installation is the reverse of removal.

1987–91 Mustang

1. Disconnect the negative battery cable.

2. Disengage the 2 locking tabs on the left hand side of the switch by pushing the tabs in using a suitable tool and pulling the the left hand side of the switch.

3. Using a suitable tool, pry the right hand side of the switch out of the instrument panel.

4. Pull the entire switch out of the opening and disconnect the 2 connectors.

5. To install, install the connectors, insert the switch into the panel opening and push until the locking tabs on both sides of the switch slide in place.

Headlight Delay System

REMOVAL & INSTALLATION

NOTE: The delay system has an additional feature which is the potentiometer, which can be removed from the headlight switch. Both the headlight switch and the potentiometer can be replaced separately.

1. Disconnect the negative battery cable and remove the headlight switch.

2. Remove the headlight switch shaft and knob.

3. Remove the plastic spacer at the rear of the potentiometer by pushing out with a suitable tool.

4. Remove the strap securing the wiring harness to the switch.

5. Loosen the potentiometer retaining nut, washer and slide it out of the headlight switch.

6. Installation is the reverse order of the removal procedure.

Dimmer Switch

REMOVAL & INSTALLATION

1. Disconnect the negative battery cable. Remove the shroud from the steering column.

2. Disconnect the steering column wiring connector plug from the bracket and remove the screws that secure the switch to the column.

3. Installation is the reverse of removal procedure.

Automatic Headlight Dimmer Sensor

Vehicles equipped with the automatic headlight dimmer system use a sensor to control the high/low beam operation. This system can also be operated manually with a conventional dimmer lever on the steering column. The sensor is located in the vehicle attached to the rear view mirror. The mirror mounted sensor can be removed by taking out the retaining screw and disconnecting the electrical connector.

REMOVAL & INSTALLATION

1. Disconnect the negative battery cable.

2. Disconnect wire harness at rear of the sensor-amplifier unit. Do not pull on the cable sheathing as this could damage the leads.

3. Remove the sensor-amplifier and bracket mounting screws and remove the unit from vehicle.

4. Be certain that headlight system is properly aimed. Look through the front chamber to see that at least 50% of the sensor lens can be seen and is clean.

5. Installation is the reverse of removal procedures.

6. Test unit for proper operation and if necessary, adjust the vertical aiming.

Turn Signal Switch

REMOVAL & INSTALLATION

1987–88 Continental, Thunderbird and Cougar, 1987–89 Town Car, Grand Marquis, Crown Victoria and Mark VII

1. Disconnect the negative battery cable.

2. Use a pulling and twisting motion, while pulling straight out, to remove the turn signal switch lever.

3. Remove the steering column cover retaining screws and remove the cover.

4. Carefully lift the wiring connector retaining tabs and disconnect the connectors.

5. Remove the switch retaining screws and lift up the switch assembly.

6. To install, align the switch mounting holes and install the retaining screws.

7. Install the wiring connectors and the column cover.

8. Align the key on the turn signal lever with the keyway in the switch and push the lever into place.

9. Install the battery cable.

Combination Switch

REMOVAL & INSTALLATION

1990–91 Town Car, Grand Marquis, Crown Victoria and Mark VII

1. Disconnect the negative battery cable.

2. On the Town Car, Grand Marquis and Crown Victoria, position the tilt column to the lowest position and remove the tilt lever, if equipped.

3. Remove the ignition lock cylinder.

4. Remove the upper and lower shroud retaining screws.

5. Remove the 2 self-tapping screws which secure the switch to the steering column casting and disengage the switch from the housing.

6. Disconnect the 2 wiring connectors.

7. Installation is the reverse of removal.

1987–91 Mustang

1. Disconnect the negative battery cable.

2. Remove the upper and lower shroud retaining screws.

3. Remove the 2 self-tapping screws which secure the switch to the steering column casting and disengage the switch from the housing.

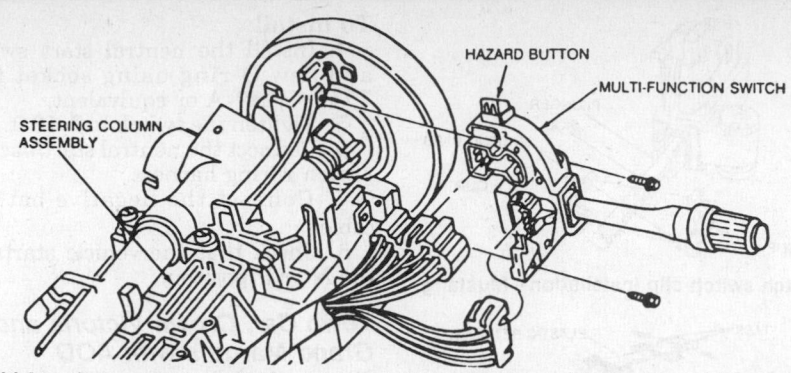

Multi-function switch installation–1990–91 Town Car, Grand Marquis and Crown Victoria, Mark VII

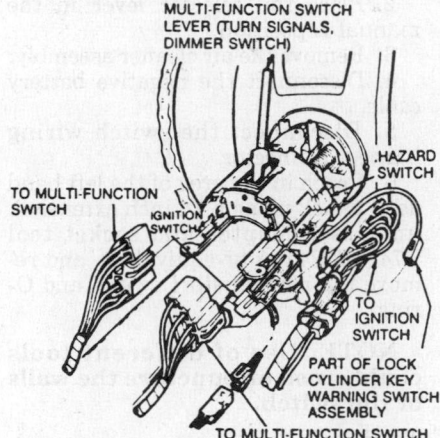

Turn signal switch installation – 1987 Mark VII, 1987–88 Continental, 1987–91 Thunderbird and Cougar, 1987–89 Town Car, Grand Marquis and Crown Victoria

4. Disconnect the 2 wiring connectors.

5. Installation is the reverse of removal.

1989–91 Thunderbird and Cougar

1. Disconnect the negative battery cable.

2. Remove the upper and lower shroud retaining screws.

3. Carefully lift the wiring connector retaining tabs and disconnect the connectors.

4. Remove the switch retaining screws and lift up the switch assembly.

5. Installation is the reverse of removal.

Ignition Lock

REMOVAL & INSTALLATION

1. Disconnect the negative battery cable.

2. On the tilt column models only, remove the upper extension shroud by

unsnapping the shroud retaining clip at the 9 o'clock position.

3. Remove the trim shroud halves by removing the attaching screws. Remove the electrical connector from the key warning switch.

4. Place the gear shift lever in **P**, for column shift only, and turn the ignition to the **RUN** position.

5. Place a ⅛ in. diameter wire pin or small drift punch in the hole in the casting surrounding the lock cylinder and depress the retaining pin while pulling out on the lock cylinder to remove it from the column housing.

To install:

6. To install the lock cylinder, turn it to the **RUN** position and depress the retaining pin. Insert the lock cylinder into its housing in the lock cylinder casting.

7. Make sure that the cylinder is fully seated and aligned in the interlocking washer before turning the key to the **OFF** position. This action will permit the cylinder retaining pin to extend into the hole in the lock cylinder housing.

8. Using the ignition key, rotate the cylinder to ensure the correct mechanical operation in all positions. Install the electrical connector onto the key warning switch.

9. Check for proper start in **P** or **N**. Also make sure that the start circuit cannot be actuated in **D** or **R** positions and that the column is locked in the **LOCK** position.

10. Install the trim shroud onto the steering column and install the negative battery cable.

Ignition Switch

REMOVAL & INSTALLATION

1. Disconnect the negative battery cable.

2. Remove the upper shroud below the steering wheel by unsnapping the retaining clips. On the tilt column, it will be necessary to remove the 5 attaching screws. Remove the upper ex-

tension shroud by unsnapping the shroud from the retaining clips at the 9 o'clock position.

3. Disconnect the electrical connector from the ignition switch.

4. Rotate the ignition key lock cylinder to the **RUN** position.

5. Remove the 2 screws attaching the ignition switch.

6. Disengage the ignition switch from the actuator pin and remove the switch.

To install:

7. Adjust the new ignition switch by sliding the carrier to the **RUN** position.

8. Check to ensure that the ignition key lock cylinder is in the **RUN** position. The **RUN** position is achieved by rotating the key lock cylinder approximately 90 degrees from the **LOCK** position.

9. Install the ignition switch onto the actuator pin.

10. Align the switch mounting holes and install the attaching screws.

11. Connect the electrical connector to the ignition switch.

12. Install the instrument panel lower steering column cover.

13. Install the steering column trim shrouds and tilt lever, if equipped.

Stoplight Switch

REMOVAL & INSTALLATION

1. Disconnect the negative battery cable. Disconnect the wire harness at the connector from the switch.

2. Remove the hairpin retainer, slide the stoplight switch, the pushrod and the nylon washers and bushings away from the pedal and remove the switch.

NOTE: Since the switch side plate nearest the brake pedal is slotted, it is not necessary to remove the brake master cylinder pushrod and 1 washer from the brake pedal pin.

3. Position the switch, pushrod, bushing and washers on the brake pedal pin and install the hairpin retainer.

4. Assemble the wire harness connector to the switch and install the wires in the retaining clip.

Clutch Switch

REMOVAL & INSTALLATION

Mustang

1. Disconnect the negative battery cable. Disconnect wiring connector.

2. Remove retaining pin from clutch pedal.

3. Remove switch bracket attaching screw.

4. Lift switch and bracket assembly upward to disengage tab from pedal support.

5. Move the switch outward to disengage actuating rod eyelet from clutch pedal pin and remove switch from vehicle.

NOTE: Always install the switch with the self-adjusting clip about 1.0 in. from the end of the rod. The clutch pedal must be fully up (clutch engaged). Otherwise, the switch may be misadjusted.

6. Place eyelet end of rod onto pivot pin.

7. Swing switch assembly around to line up hole in mounting boss with hole in bracket.

8. Install attaching screw.

9. Replace retaining pin in pivot pin.

10. Connect wiring connector.

Thunderbird and Cougar

1. Disconnect the negative battery cable.

2. Disconnect wiring connector from the switch.

3. Remove the C-clip from the clutch pedal switch pin and slide the pushrod off the pin.

4. Remove the switch pushrod from the switch.

5. Disconnect the switch from the plastic bracket.

6. Installation is the reverse of removal.

Neutral Safety Switch

ADJUSTMENT

1987 Thunderbird and Cougar with C5 Transmission

1. Loosen the neutral start switch attaching bolts.

2. Position the manual lever in neutral.

3. Insert a No. 43 drill end shank fully into the switch. Move the switch, as necessary, to allow the drill to rest against the case.

4. Tighten the switch attaching bolts to 55–75 inch lbs. and remove the drill.

REMOVAL & INSTALLATION

1987 Thunderbird and Cougar with C5 Transmission

1. Disconnect the negative battery cable.

2. Disconnect the switch wiring harness connector.

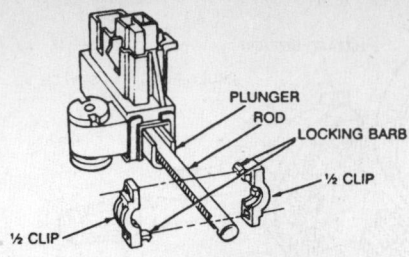

Clutch switch clip installation—Mustang

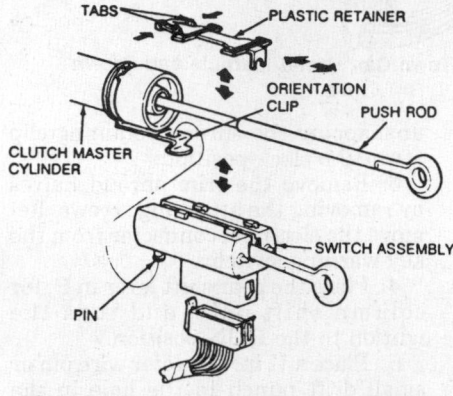

Clutch switch installation—Thunderbird and Cougar

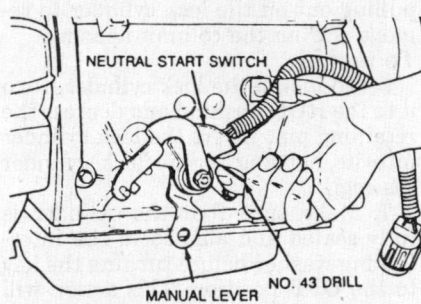

Neutral safety switch adjustment—1987 Thunderbird and Cougar with C5 transmission

3. Remove the outer throttle lever attaching nut and lock washer and remove the throttle lever from the throttle lever shaft.

4. Remove the neutral start/backup lamp switch attaching screws and slide the switch off the outer manual lever.

5. Installation is the reverse of removal.

All with A4LD Transmission

1. Disconnect the negative battery cable.

2. Disconnect the switch wiring harness connector.

3. Remove the neutral start switch and O-ring using socket tool T74P–77247–A or equivalent.

NOTE: Use of different tools could crush or puncture the walls of the switch.

To install:

4. Install the neutral start switch and new O-ring using socket tool T74P–77247–A or equivalent.

5. Tighten the switch to 7–10 ft. lbs.

6. Connect the neutral start/backup switch wiring harness.

7. Connect the negative battery cable.

8. Check that the vehicle starts in the **N** or **P** position.

Town Car, Crown Victoria and Grand Marquis with AOD Transmission

1. Set the parking brake.

2. Place the selector lever in the manual **L** position.

3. Remove the air cleaner assembly.

4. Disconnect the negative battery cable.

5. Disconnect the switch wiring harness connector.

6. Reach in the area of the left hand dash panel, using a 24 inch extension, universal adapter and socket tool T74P–77247–A or equivalent, and remove the neutral start switch and O-ring.

NOTE: Use of different tools could crush or puncture the walls of the switch.

To install:

7. Install the neutral start switch and new O-ring using socket tool T74P–77247–A or equivalent.

8. Tighten the switch to 8–11 ft. lbs.

9. Connect the neutral start/backup switch wiring harness.

10. Connect the negative battery cable.

11. Check that the vehicle starts in the **N** or **P** position.

Mark VII, Thunderbird, Cougar and Mustang with AOD Transmission

1. Place the selector lever in the manual **L** position.

2. Disconnect the negative battery cable.

3. Raise and support the vehicle safely.

4. Disconnect the switch wiring harness connector by inserting a long thin blade tool under the rubber plug section of the harness.

5. Install socket tool T74P–77247–A or equivalent and rachet on the neutral start switch. Once the ratchet and socket tool are over the switch, reach from the rear of the transmission over the extension housing area and remove the neutral start switch and O-ring.

NOTE: Use of different tools could crush or puncture the walls of the switch.

6. Install the neutral start switch and new O-ring using socket tool T74P-77247-A or equivalent.

7. Tighten the switch to 8–11 ft. lbs.

8. Connect the neutral start/backup switch wiring harness.

9. Connect the negative battery cable.

10. Check that the vehicle starts in the **N** or **P** position.

Fuses, Circuit Breakers and Relays

LOCATION

Fuses

A fuse panel is used to house the numerous fuses protecting the various branches of the electrical system and is normally the most accessible. The mounting of the fuse panel is usually on the left side of the passenger compartment, under the dash, either on the side kick panel or on the firewall to the left of the steering column. Certain models will have the fuse panel exposed while other models will have it covered with a removable trim cover.

Fusible Links

Fusible links are used to protect the main wiring harness and selected branches from complete burn-out, should a short circuit or electrical overload occur.

Circuit Breakers

Circuit breakers are used on certain electrical components requiring high amperage, such as the headlight circuit, electrical seats and/or windows to name a few. The advantage of the circuit breaker is its ability to open and close the electrical circuit as the load demands, rather than the necessity of a part replacement, should the circuit be opened with another protective device in line.

A list of some of the circuit breakers used, follows:

Headlight and High Beam—one 22 amp circuit breaker incorporated in the lighting switch.

Front and Rear Marker, Side Parking, Rear and License Lamps—one 15 amp circuit breaker incorporated in the lighting switch.

Windshield Wiper Circuit and Rear Window—one 4.5 amp circuit breaker located in the windshield wiper switch.

Power Windows—two 20 amp circuit breakers located in the starter relay and the fuse block. On the 1986 Continental and Mark VII there is a 30 amp circuit breaker used inplace of the 20 amp breaker.

Power Seats and Power Door Locks—a 20 amp circuit breaker located in the fuse block is used on all models except, Crown Victoria, Grand Marquis. These models use a 30 amp circuit breaker, which is also located in the fuse block.

Station Wagon Power Back Window—a 20 amp circuit breaker (or 30 amp depending on the size of the vehicle) located in the fuse block.

Intermitent 2-speed Windshield Wiper—a 8.25 amp circuit breaker located in the fuse block.

Door Cigar Lighter—A 20 or 30 amp circuit breaker located in the fuse block.

Liftgate Wiper—a 4.5 amp circuit breaker located in the instrument panel.

Relays

MUSTANG

Choke Relay—located on the right hand side fender apron near the voltage regulator.

Dimmer Relay—located behind the instrument panel, to the right of the steering column support.

Electronic Control Assembly (ECA)—attached to the lower left side of the cowl.

Electronic Engine Control (EEC) Power Relay—attached to the lower right side cowl near the electronic control assembly.

Fuel Pump Relay—located under the driver's seat.

Fuel Relays—at the center of the instrument panel behind the dash panel.

Horn Relay—located on right side of the instrument panel.

Low Oil Level Relay—located in the center of the dash panel.

Starter Relay—located on the right hand side fender apron in front of the wheel well or left side on Turbo models.

Thermactor Dump Control Relay—located under the instrument panel on the right side of the steering.

Timer Relay—located on the right side of the steering column support.

Wide Open A/C Cutout Relay—located under the instrument panel on the left side of the steering column brace.

THUNDERBIRD AND COUGAR

A/C Cutout Relay—on the left front fender apron.

Alarm Relay—located in the upper right side of the trunk.

Anti-Dieseling Time Relay—located on the right side front fender apron.

Auto-Lamp Relay No. 1—attached to the top rear of steering column support brace.

Auto-Lamp Relay No. 2—attached to the top rear of steering column support brace.

Cooling Fan Relay—located behind the strut tower on the right front fender apron.

Cornering Light Relays—in the center of the dash panel on the left side of the dash panel bracket.

Dis-Arm Relay—located in the upper right side of the trunk.

Electronic Control Assembly (ECA)—located at the access hole on the right side of the cowl.

Electronic Engine Control (EEC) Power Relay—under the right side of the instrument panel on the cowl.

Flash to Pass Relay—located behind the center of the instrument panel.

Fuel Pump Relay—located above right rear wheel well.

Headlight Dimmer Relay—attached to the top rear of steering column support brace.

Hi-Lo Beam Relay—located behind the left side of the instrument panel.

Horn Relay—located on right side of the instrument panel.

Power Door Lock Relay—on the crossbar under the passengers seat.

Power Window Safety Relay—Attached to the bottom of the shake brace.

Start Interrupt Relay—under the left side of the instrument panel.

Starter Relay—located on the right hand side fender apron.

Wide-Open-Throttle A/C Cutout Relay—located on the right front fender apron.

CROWN VICTORIA AND GRAND MARQUIS

Auto-Lamp Relay—attached to the left side of the steering column support brace.

Compressor Relay (Load Leveling) Sedan—located on a bracket on the right rear quarter panel.

Compressor Relay (Load Leveling) Wagon—located on a bracket on the right rear quarter panel.

Cornering Light Relays—in the center of the dash panel on the left side of the dash panel bracket.

Electronic Control Assembly (ECA)—under the left side of the instrument panel.

Electronic Engine Control (EEC) Power Relay—located on the left front fender apron.

Fuel Pump Relay—located on the left front fender apron.

Horn Relay—located in the center of the instrument panel.

Power Door Lock Relay—inside the upper right hand cowl access hole.

Power Door Un-Lock Relay—inside the upper right hand cowl access hole.

Power Window Safety Relay—Attached to the bottom of a shake brace under the left side of the instrument panel.

Starter Relay—located on the right hand side fender apron in front of the shock tower.

Thermactor Control Relay—on the left side of the instrument panel attached to a shake brace.

Throttle Kicker Control Relay—located on the right front fender apron.

CONTINENTAL, MARK VII AND TOWN CAR

A/C Cut-Out Relay—located on the left front fender apron.

Air Suspension Relay (Load Leveling)—located on the left front fender apron.

Alarm Relay—located under the right side of the package tray in the trunk.

Anti-Theft Starter Interrupt Relay—located under the instrument panel on the left side support brace.

Auto-Lamp Relay—attached to the left side of the steering column support brace.

Cooling Fan Relay—located on the right front fender apron.

Cornering Light Relays—in the center of the dash panel on the left side of the dash panel bracket.

Defrost Switch/Relay—located in the center of the instrument panel.

Disarm Relay—located under the right side of the package tray in the trunk.

Electronic Control Assembly (ECA)—located on the right side of the cowl.

Electronic Engine Control (EEC) Relay—located on the right side of the cowl.

Flash to Pass Relay—attached to the instrument panel brace.

Fuel Pump Relay—located on the left hand deck-lid hinge support.

Heated Seat Relays—located under the driver's or the passenger's seat.

Hi-Lo Beam Relay—attached to the instrument panel brace or above the fuse block on the 1985–87 Continental.

Horn Relay—located in the center of the instrument panel.

Interior Light Relay—in the center of the dash panel on the left side of the dash panel bracket.

Inverter Relay—located under the right side of the package tray in the trunk.

Power Antenna Relay—located in the right side of the trunk.

Power Mirror Relays—located in the left side of the trunk.

Power Window Safety Relay—attached to the bottom of a shake brace under the left side of the instrument panel.

Starter Relay—located on the left hand side fender apron.

Computers

LOCATION

Town Car—located on the left of the firewall below the wiper motor

Continental—located on the right side of the firewall next to the accumulator.

Thunderbird and Cougar—located behind the right side kick panel.

Mark VII—located behind the right side kick panel.

Mustang—located behind the right side kick panel.

Grand Marquis and Crown Victoria—located on the passenger's side of the firewall near the master cylinder.

Turn Signal and Hazard Flashers

LOCATION

The turn signal and hazard flashers are located in the fuse box.

Cruise Control

ADJUSTMENT

Actuator Cable

1. If equipped with a carburetor, set stroke on hot idle condition with the throttle positioner solenoid disengaged.
2. Remove the speed control cable retaining clip.
3. Push speed control cable through adjuster until a slight tension is felt.
4. Insert the cable retaining clip and snap into place.

Vacuum Pump

The vacuum dump valve is movable in its mounting bracket. It should be adjusted so that it is closed, no vacuum leaks, when the brake pedal is in its normal release position, not depressed, and open when the pedal is depressed. Use a hand vacuum pump to make this adjustment.

ENGINE COOLING

Radiator

REMOVAL & INSTALLATION

1. Disconnect the negative battery cable. Drain the cooling system.
2. Disconnect the upper, lower and overflow hoses at the radiator.
3. On automatic transmission equipped cars, disconnect the fluid cooler lines at radiator.
4. Depending on model; remove the 2 top mounting bolts and remove radiator and shroud assembly or remove the shroud mounting bolts and position the shroud out of the way. If the air conditioner condenser is attached to the radiator, remove the retaining bolts and position the condenser out of the way. Do not disconnect the refrigerant lines.
5. Remove the radiator attaching bolts or top brackets and lift out the radiator.

To install:

6. If a new radiator is to be installed, transfer the petcock from the old radiator to the new one. If equipped with automatic transmission, transfer the fluid cooler line fittings from the old radiator.
7. Position the radiator and install, do not tighten the radiator support bolts. If equipped with automatic transmission, connect the fluid cooler lines. Then tighten the radiator support bolts or shroud and mounting bolts.
8. Connect the radiator hoses. Close the radiator petcock. Fill and bleed the cooling system.
9. Start the engine and bring to operating temperature. Check for leaks.
10. If equpped with automatic transmission, check the cooler lines for leaks and interference. Check the transmission fluid level.

Electric Cooling Fan

SYSTEM OPERATION

The electric cooling fan system on 2.3L equipped Thunderbird and Mustang, is designed to provide engine cooling whenever the air conditioner is turned ON or when the coolant temperature exceeds 221°F. This is accomplished with a cooling fan controller, the controller consists of 2 relays mounted a printed circuit board. One relay powers the cooling fan and the other powers the air conditioner compressor coil, solid state circuitry controls the timing for the relays. The cooling fan controller is located under the left side of the instrument panel near the steering column.

When the engine coolant temperature reaches 221°F the cooling fan temperature switch, located in the heater hose tube, will close to complete the ground circuit to the to the fan relay coil in the controller. This will activate the fan which will operate until the coolant temperature is decreased to approximately 201°F. During air conditioner operation, the air conditioner clutch cycling pressure switch controls the evaporater temperature by controlling the compressor operation. The pressure switch will cause the fan relay to operate first, then the air conditioner relay will operate if voltage is available at the fan motor terminal. The air conditioner compressor will cycle with the pressure switch.

The electric cooling fan on the Thuderbird and Cougar with the 3.8L supercharged engine is controlled during vehicle operation by the integrated relay control assembly and the EEC-IV module, which will energize the cooling fan.

The cooling fan will run at low speed if the engine temperature reaches 222°F and stops running at 214°F. It will also run at low speed if the air conditioner is on and the vehicle speed does not provide enough natural air flow. The fan starts running at speeds at or below 43 mph and stops running at 48 mph.

The cooling fan will run at high speed if the engine temperature reaches 230°F and stops running at 224°F.

NOTE: The cooling fan will not cycle with the air conditioner.

REMOVAL & INSTALLATION

Mustang and Thunderbird with 2.3L Engine

1. Disconnect the negative battery cable and remove the fan wiring harness from the routing clip.
2. Disconnect the wiring harness from the fan motor connector and pull up on the single lock finger to separate the connectors.
3. Remove the 4 mounting bracket attaching screws and remove the fan assembly from the vehicle.
4. Remove the retaining clip from the end of the motor shaft and remove the fan.

5. Remove the nuts attaching the fan motor to the mounting bracket.

NOTE: After the retaining clip has been removed there may be a small burr left on the shaft, this burr must be removed in order to remove the fan from the motor shaft.

To install:

6. Position the fan motor on the mounting bracket and torque the attaching nuts to 70–95 inch lbs.
7. Install the fan and retaining clip on the motor shaft and position the fan assembly in the vehicle with the mounting bracket attaching screws.
8. Connect the motor wiring connector to the wiring harness and be sure that the lock finger on the connector snaps firmly into place.
9. Connect the negative battery cable and check the fan for proper operation.

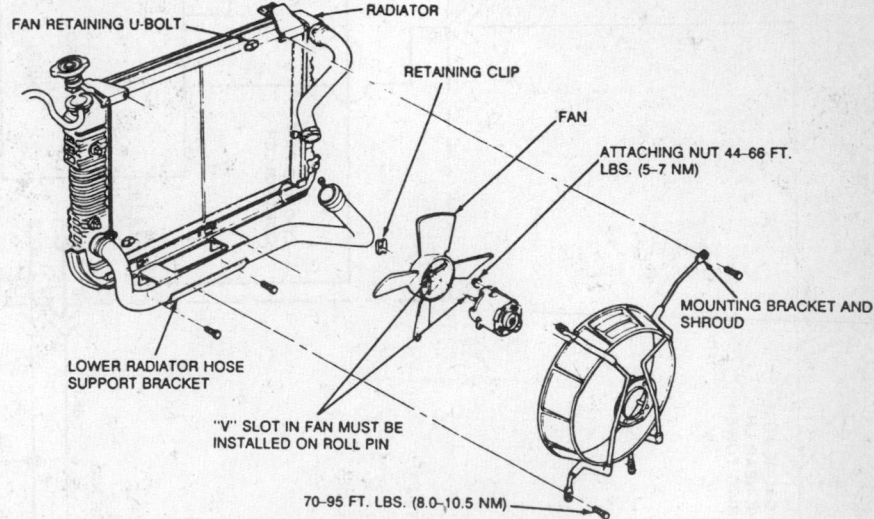

Electric cooling fan installation—Mustang and Thunderbird with 2.3L engine

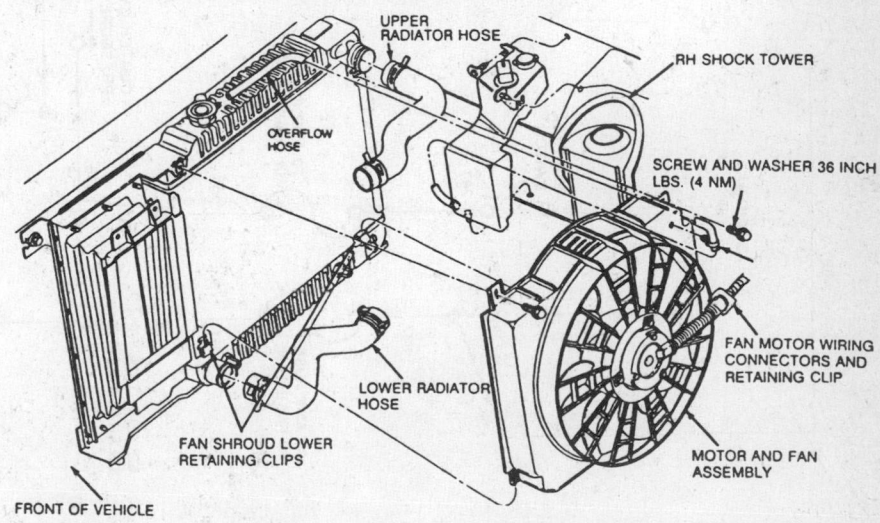

Electric cooling fan installation—Thunderbird and Cougar with 3.8L supercharged engine

Thunderbird and Cougar with 3.8L Supercharged Engine

1. Disconnect the negative battery cable and remove the fan wiring harness from the routing clip.
2. Remove the overflow hose from the fan shroud retaining clip.
3. Remove the 2 shroud upper retaining bolts at the radiator support.
4. Lift the cooling fan module past the radiator, disengaging the shroud from the lower retaining clips.
5. Installation is the reverse of removal.

Heater Core

REMOVAL & INSTALLATION
Without Air Conditioning
MUSTANG, THUNDERBIRD AND COUGAR

1. Disconnect the negative battery cable. Drain radiator coolant.

~~RD MOTOR CO.~~ REAR WHEEL DRIVE

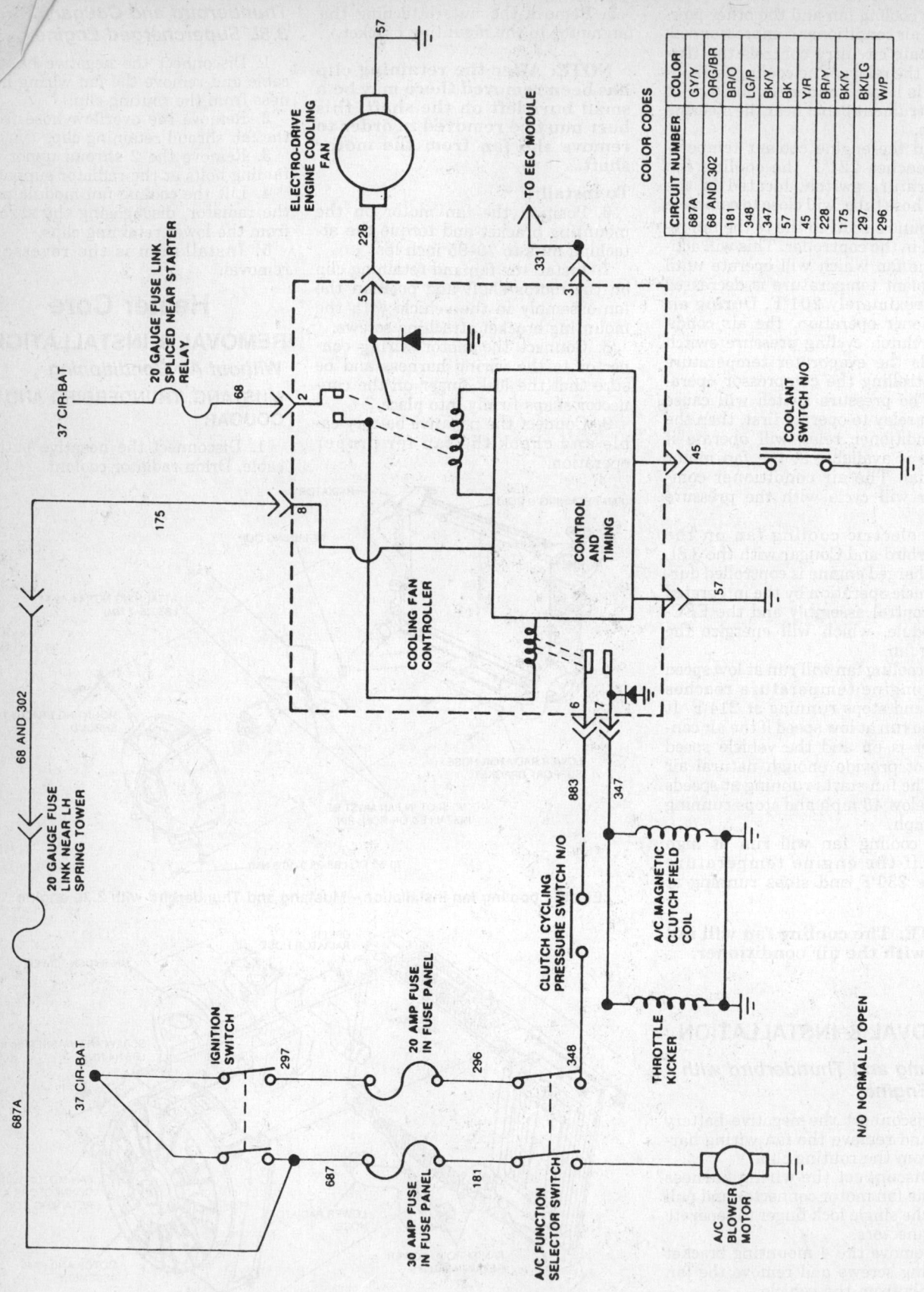

COLOR CODES	
CIRCUIT NUMBER	COLOR
687A	GY/Y
68 AND 302	ORG/BR
181	BR/O
348	LG/P
347	BK/Y
57	BK
45	Y/R
228	BR/Y
175	BK/Y
297	BK/LG
296	W/P

Cooling fan wiring schematic—1987 Mustang and Thunderbird with 2.3L engine

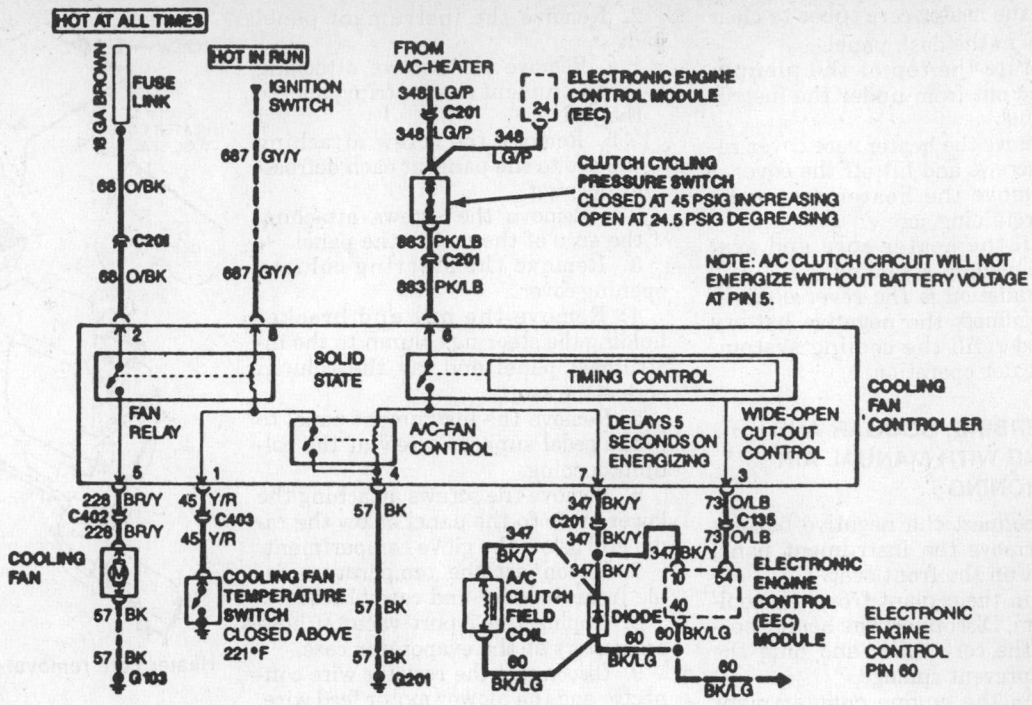

Cooling fan wiring schematic—1989 Mustang with 2.3L engine

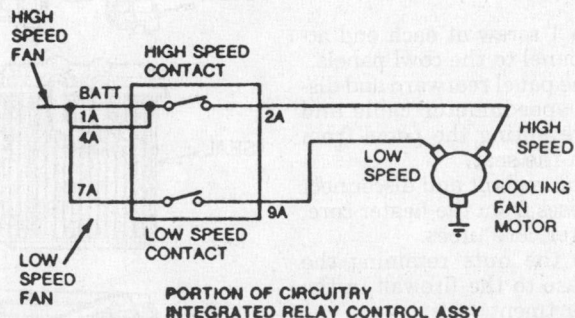

Cooling fan wiring schematic—Thunderbird and Cougar with 3.8L supercharged engine

2. Disconnect heater hoses at core connections.

3. Remove glove box.

4. Remove instrument panel to cowl brace retaining screws and brace.

5. Move temperature control lever to warm position.

6. Remove the heater core cover retaining screws.

7. Remove heater core cover through glove box opening.

8. In engine compartment, loosen heater case assembly mounting stud nuts.

9. Push heater core tubes and seal toward passenger compartment to loosen heater core assembly from heater case assembly.

10. Remove heater core from heater case assembly through the glove box opening.

11. Installation is the reverse of removal.

With Air Conditioning

GRAND MARQUIS, CROWN VICTORIA AND TOWN CAR

1. Drain the coolant.

2. Disconnect the negative battery cable.

3. Remove the heater hoses from the heater core.

4. Plug the heater core tubes to prevent coolant from spilling under the dash during plenum removal.

5. Remove the plenum to dash bolt, located under the windshield wiper motor at the left end of the plenum.

6. Remove the retaining nut from the heater case, engine side.

7. Disconnect the vacuum supply hose from the vacuum fitting and push the grommet and hose into the passenger compartment.

8. Remove the glove box assembly.

9. Loosen the right door sill plate

and remove the right side cowl trim panel.

10. Remove the lower right instrument panel to side cowl bolt.

11. Remove the instrument panel pad.

12. Remove the temperature control cable from the top of the plenum. Then, disconnect the temperature control cable from the blend door crank arm.

13. Remove the push clip attaching the center register duct bracket to the plenum and rotate the bracket up to the right.

14. Disconnect the vacuum jumper harness at the multiple vacuum connector near the floor air distribution duct.

15. Disconnect the white vacuum hose from the outside air door vacuum motor.

16. Remove the 2 screws attaching the seat side of the floor air distribution duct to the plenum.

NOTE: It may be necessary to remove the 2 screws attaching the lower panel door vacuum motor to the mounting bracket to gain access to the floor air distribution duct screw.

17. Remove the plastic pushpin fastener from the floor air distribution duct and remove the duct.

18. Remove the remaining plenum retaining nuts from the lower flange of the plenum.

19. Move the plenum toward the seat

the heater core tubes to clear __les in the dash panel.
__ Rotate the top of the plenum __own and out from under the instrument panel.

21. Remove the heater core cover retaining screws and lift off the cover.

22. Remove the heater core tube bracket retaining screw.

23. Pull the heater core and seal from the plenum assembly.

24. Installation is the reverse of removal. Connect the negative battery cable and refill the cooling system. Check heater operation.

THUNDERBIRD, COUGAR AND MUSTANG WITH MANUAL AIR CONDITIONING

1. Disconnect the negative battery cable. Remove the instrument panel and lay it on the front seat.

2. Drain the coolant from the cooling system. Disconnect the heater hoses from the core tubes and plug the tubes to prevent spillage.

3. From the engine compartment side remove the nuts attaching the evaporator case to the dash panel.

4. Under the dash, remove the screws attaching the evaporator case support bracket and the air inlet duct support bracket to the cowl top panel.

5. Remove the retaining nut from the bracket at the left end of the evaporator case and the nut attaching the heater core access cover to the evaporator case.

6. Carefully pull the evaporator case assembly away from the dash panel to gain access to the screws retaining the heater core access cover to the evaporator case.

7. Remove the heater core cover attaching screws and remove the cover.

8. Lift the heater core and seals from the evaporator case. Remove the seals from the core tubes.

9. Installation is the reverse of removal. Refill the cooling system and check heater operation.

CONTINENTAL, THUNDERBIRD, COUGAR AND MARK VII WITH AUTOMATIC TEMPERATURE CONTROL

NOTE: The instrument panel must be removed for access to the heater core. The air conditioning system must be discharged in order to remove the dash panel and gain access to the heater core. It is advisable to remove and replace the air conditioning receiver drier when the system has been evacuated.

1. Disconnect the negative battery cable.

2. Remove the instrument panel pad:

   a. Remove the screws attaching the instrument cluster trim panel to the pad.

   b. Remove the screw attaching the pad to the panel at each defroster opening.

   c. Remove the screws attaching the edge of the pad to the panel.

3. Remove the steering column opening cover.

4. Remove the nut and bracket holding the steering column to the instrument panel and lay the column across the seat.

5. Remove the instrument panel to brake pedal support screw at the column opening.

6. Remove the screws attaching the lower brace to the panel below the radio and below the glove compartment.

7. Disconnect the temperature cable from the door and case bracket.

8. Unplug the 7 port vacuum hose connectors at the evaporator case.

9. Disconnect the resistor wire connector and the blower motor feed wire.

10. Remove the screws attaching the top of the panel to the cowl and support the panel while removing the screws.

11. Remove 1 screw at each end attaching the panel to the cowl panels.

12. Move the panel rearward and disconnect the speedometer cable and any wires preventing the panel from laying flat on the seat.

13. Drain the coolant and disconnect the heater hoses from the heater core, plug the heater core tubes.

14. Remove the nuts retaining the evaporator case to the firewall in the engine compartment.

15. Remove the case support bracket screws and air inlet duct support bracket.

16. Remove the nut retaining the bracket to the dash panel at the left side of the evaporator case and the nut retaining the bracket below the case to dash panel.

17. Pull the case assembly away from the panel to get to the screws retaining the heater core cover to the case.

18. Remove the cover screws and cover, lift the heater core and seals out of the case assembly.

19. Installation is the reverse order of the removal procedure.

Water Pump

REMOVAL & INSTALLATION

1. Disconnect the negative battery cable.

2. Drain the cooling system.

3. If with power steering, remove the drive belt.

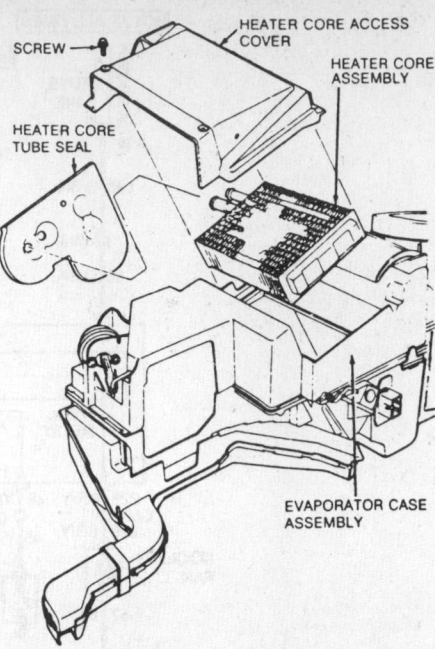

Heater core removal—1987-91 Mustang

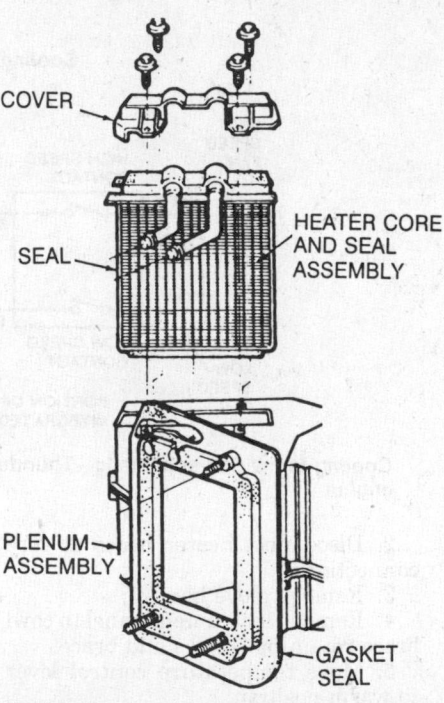

Heater core removal—1988-91 Town Car, Grand Marquis and Crown Victoria

4. If the vehicle is equipped with air conditioning, remove the idler pulley bracket and air conditioner drive belt. On supercharged engines, relieve the tension from the automatic tension adjuster and remove the belt.

5. On engines with a thermactor pump, remove the belt.

6. Disconnect the lower radiator hose and heater hose from the water pump.

7. Remove the retaining screws and position the fan shroud rearward.

8. Remove the fan and spacer from the engine, if equipped with a fan shroud, remove the fan and shroud from the engine as an assembly.

9. On 4 cylinder engines, remove the cam belt outer cover.

10. If equipped with water pump mounted alternators, loosen alternator mounting bolts, remove the alternator belt and remove the alternator adjusting arm bracket from the water pump.

11. Loosen bypass hose at water pump, if equipped.

12. Remove water pump retaining screws and remove pump from engine. On 3.8L engines, the 2 bolts through the thermostat housing must also be removed; they retain the lower portion of the pump housing.

13. Clean any gasket material from the pump mounting surface.

14. Remove the heater hose fitting from the old pump and install it on the new pump.

15. Coat both sides of the new gasket with a water-resistant sealer, then install the pump reversing the procedure.

Thermostat

REMOVAL & INSTALLATION

1. Disconnect the negative battery cable. Open the drain cock and drain the radiator so the coolant level is below the coolant outlet elbow which houses the thermostat.

NOTE: On some models it will be necessary to remove the distributor cap, rotor and vacuum diaphragm in order to gain access to the thermostat housing mounting bolts.

2. Remove the outlet elbow retaining bolts and position the elbow sufficiently clear of the intake manifold or cylinder head to provide access to the thermostat.

3. Remove the thermostat and the gasket.

To install:

4. Clean the mating surfaces of the outlet elbow and the engine to remove all old gasket material and sealer. Coat the new gasket with water-resistant sealer. Install the thermostat in the coolant elbow. The thermostat must be rotated clockwise to lock it in position, on all 8 cylinder engines. On 4 cylinder engines, be sure the full width of the heater outlet tube is visible within the thermostat port.

5. Install the outlet elbow and retaining bolts on the engine. Torque the bolts to 12–15 ft. lbs.

6. Refill the radiator. Connect the battery cable, run the engine to normal operating temperature and check for leaks. Recheck the coolant level.

FUEL SYSTEM

Fuel System Service Precautions

Safety is the most important factor when performing not only fuel system maintenance but any type of maintenance. Failure to conduct maintenance and repairs in a safe manner may result in serious personal injury or death. Maintenance and testing of the vehicle's fuel system components can be accomplished safely and effectively by adhering to the following rules and guidelines.

• To avoid the possibility of fire and personal injury, always disconnect the negative battery cable unless the repair or test procedure requires that battery voltage be applied.

• Always relieve the fuel system pressure prior to disconnecting any fuel system component (injector, fuel rail, pressure regulator, etc.), fitting or fuel line connection. Exercise extreme caution whenever relieving fuel system pressure to avoid exposing skin, face and eyes to fuel spray. Please be advised that fuel under pressure may penetrate the skin or any part of the body that it contacts.

• Always place a shop towel or cloth around the fitting or connection prior

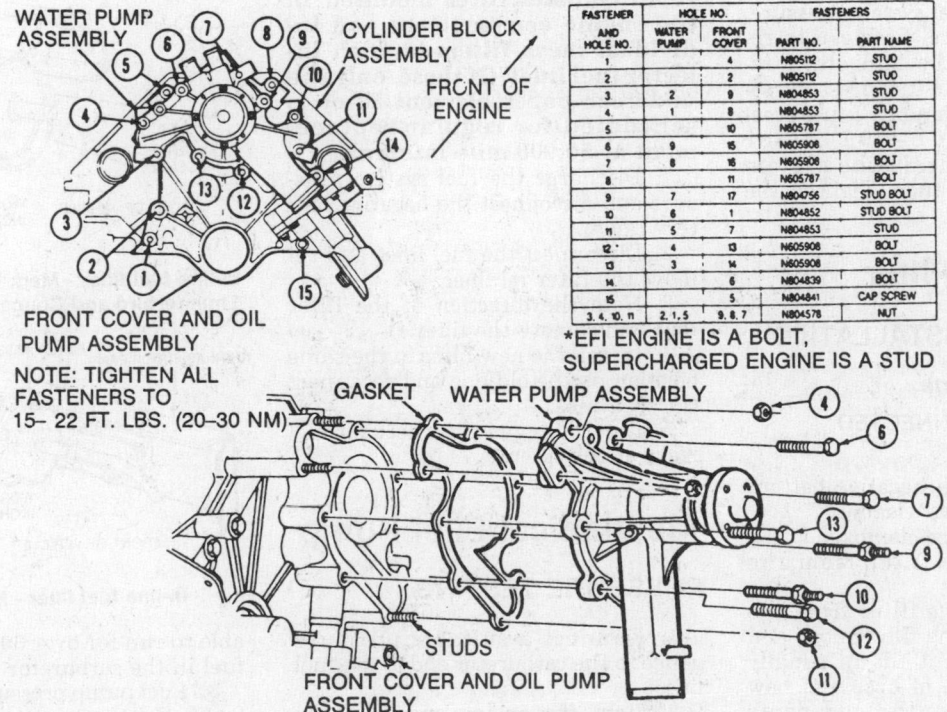

FASTENER AND HOLE NO.	HOLE NO. WATER PUMP	HOLE NO. FRONT COVER	FASTENERS PART NO.	PART NAME
1		4	N805112	STUD
2		2	N805112	STUD
3	2	9	N604853	STUD
4	1	8	N604853	STUD
5		10	N805787	BOLT
6	9	15	N605908	BOLT
7	8	16	N605908	BOLT
8		11	N605787	BOLT
9	7	17	N804756	STUD BOLT
10	6	1	N804852	STUD BOLT
11	5	7	N804853	STUD
12*	4	13	N605908	BOLT
13	3	14	N605908	BOLT
14		6	N804839	BOLT
15		5	N804841	CAP SCREW
3, 4, 10, 11	2, 1, 5	9, 8, 7	N804578	NUT

WATER PUMP ASSEMBLY

CYLINDER BLOCK ASSEMBLY

FRONT OF ENGINE

FRONT COVER AND OIL PUMP ASSEMBLY

NOTE: TIGHTEN ALL FASTENERS TO 15– 22 FT. LBS. (20–30 NM)

*EFI ENGINE IS A BOLT, SUPERCHARGED ENGINE IS A STUD

GASKET   WATER PUMP ASSEMBLY

STUDS
FRONT COVER AND OIL PUMP ASSEMBLY

Water pump fastener and hole location—3.8L engine (EFI)

to loosening to absorb any excess fuel due to spillage. Ensure that all fuel spillage (should it occur) is quickly removed from engine surfaces. Ensure that all fuel soaked cloths or towels are deposited into a suitable waste container.

• Always keep a dry chemical (Class B) fire extinguisher near the work area.

• Do not allow fuel spray or fuel vapors to come into contact with a spark or open flame.

• Always use a backup wrench when loosening and tightening fuel line connection fittings. This will prevent unnecessary stress and torsion to fuel line piping. Always follow the proper torque specifications.

• Always replace worn fuel fitting O-rings with new. Do not substitute fuel hose or equivalent where fuel pipe is installed.

RELIEVING FUEL SYSTEM PRESSURE

Fuel supply lines on all fuel injected engines will remain pressurized for some period of time after the engine is shut OFF. This pressure must be relieved before servicing the fuel system.

On the 2.3L turbocharged EFI engine this valve is located in the flexible fuel supply tube approximately 12 inches back from where it connects to the engine fuel rail. On the 5.0L EFI engines, the valve is located in the metal engine fuel line at the left hand front corner of the engine.

To relieve the fuel system pressure, first remove the fuel tank cap to relieve pressure in the tank, then remove the cap on the fuel pressure relief valve and attach an EFI fuel pressure gauge T80L-9974-A or equivalent, and drain the system through the drain tube. Tighten the cap to 4–6 inch lbs.

Fuel Filter

REMOVAL & INSTALLATION

Carbureted Engine

IN-LINE HOSE CONNECTED FILTERS

1. Disconnect the negative battery cable. Remove the air cleaner.
2. Loosen the hose clamps.
3. Unscrew the filter from the carburetor.
4. Disconnect the filter from the hose and discard the filter, hose and clamps. Replacement filters usually come with a length of hose and new clamps, always use the new parts when filter replacement is necessary.

5. Reverse the procedure to install the fuel filter. After installation, start the engine and check for fuel leakage.

INVERTED NUT (STEEL LINE) CONNECTED FILTERS

1. Disconnect the negative battery cable. Remove the air cleaner assembly.
2. Position an $^{11}/_{16}$ in. open end wrench on the filter hex nut to hold the filler in position and remove the steel fuel line from the filter using a suitable wrench.
3. Unscrew the filter from the carburetor.
4. Install the new filter in reverse order of removal.

IN CARBURETOR FILTERS

1. Disconnect the negative battery cable. Remove the air cleaner.
2. Disconnect the fuel line from the carburetor inlet fitting, while holding the inlet fitting with a suitable wrench.
3. Remove inlet fitting and fuel filter.
4. Install the spring, filter, gasket and fitting.
5. Connect the fuel line, start engine and check for leaks.

Fuel Injected Engine

NOTE: Models equipped with fuel injection actually have 4 fuel filters; a nylon mesh "sock" at the fuel pump inlet in the fuel tank; a large paper element filter mounted in the fuel line under the car; a small canister filter mounted in the engine compartment and individual mesh filters at each injector fuel inlet. Of these, only the undercar paper element filter is scheduled for regular replacement at 50,000 mile intervals.

1. Discharge the fuel system pressure and disconnect the negative battery cable.
2. Disconnect the fuel lines and remove the filter retainer.
3. Note the direction of the filter flow and remove the filter.
4. Install the new filter in the same position as the old one and reconnect the fuel lines.
5. Run the engine and check for fuel leaks at the filter.

Mechanical Fuel Pump

PRESSURE TESTING

1. Connect a suitable pressure gauge to the carburetor end of the fuel line.
2. Start the engine and read the pressure after 10 seconds. It should be

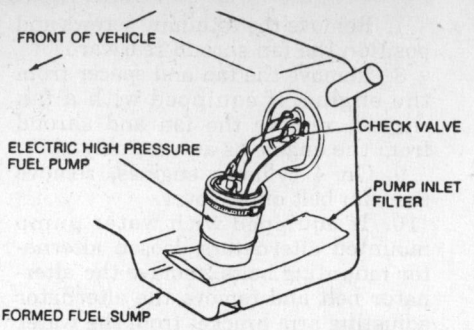

Fuel tank pump and filter assembly

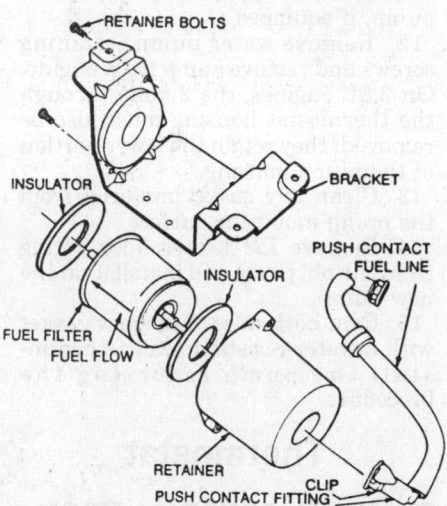

In-line fuel filter—Town Car, Crown Victoria and Grand Marquis

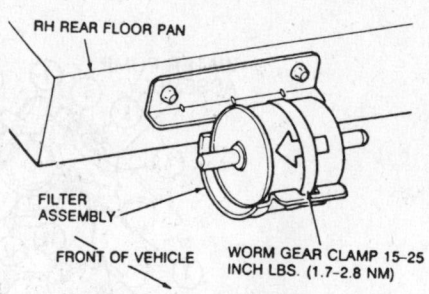

In-line fuel filter—Mark VII, Continental, Thunderbird and Cougar

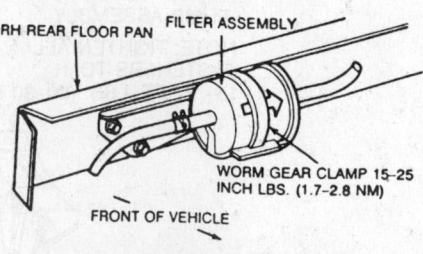

In-line fuel filter—Mustang

able to run for over 30 seconds on the fuel in the carburetor bowl.

3. Fuel pump pressure should be 6–8 psi. If pump pressure is too low or too high, install a new fuel pump.

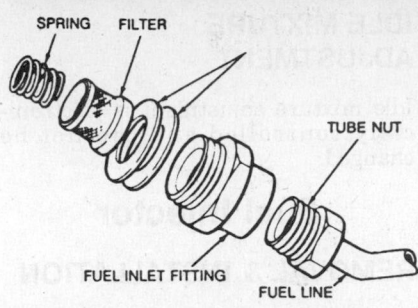

Typical carburetor fuel filter—Model 7200VV carburetor

REMOVAL & INSTALLATION

NOTE: Before removing the pump, rotate the engine so that the low point of the cam lobe is against the pump arm. This can be determined by rotating the engine with a fuel pump mounting bolts loosened slightly; when tension (resistance) is removed from the arm, proceed with removal.

1. Disconnect the negative battery cable. Remove the inlet, outlet and return vapor, if equipped, lines from the pump.
2. Remove the fuel pump mounting bolts and remove the pump and gasket.
To install:
3. Clean all gasket material from the pump mounting surface on the engine and apply a coat of oil-resistant sealer to the new gasket.
4. Position pump on engine and install retaining screws.
5. Reinstall lines, start engine and check for leaks.

NOTE: If resistance is felt while positioning the fuel pump on the block, the camshaft eccentric is in the high position. To ease installation, rotate the engine until the camshaft eccentric is in the low position.

Electric Fuel Pump

PRESSURE TESTING

Connect fuel pressure gauge T80L–9974–A or equivalent, to the Schrader valve on the fuel rail assembly. Turn the key to the **ON** position and check the gauge reading. The fuel pressure should be between 35–45 psi. If the pressure is not in this range check the system for blockage, damaged lines, faulty electrical connections or clogged fuel filters.

REMOVAL & INSTALLATION

NOTE: A single internally fuel tank mounted pump is used on fuel injected models.

1. Disconnect the negative battery cable.
2. Relieve the fuel system pressure and drain as much gas as possible from the tank by pumping out through the filler neck.
3. Raise and safely support the vehicle.
4. Disconnect the fuel supply, return and vent lines at the right and left side of the frame.
5. Disconnect the wiring harness to the fuel pump.
6. Support the gas tank, loosen and remove the mounting straps. Remove the gas tank.
7. Disconnect the lines and harness at the pump flange.
8. Clean the outside of the mounting flange and retaining ring. Turn the fuel pump lock ring counterclockwise and remove.
9. Remove the fuel pump.
To install:
10. Clean the mounting surfaces. Put a light coat of grease on the mounting surfaces and on the new sealing ring. Install the new fuel pump.
11. Installation is in the reverse order of removal. If single high pressure pump system, fill the tank with at least 10 gals. of gas.
12. Turn the ignition key **ON** for 3 seconds. Repeat 6–7 times until the fuel system is pressurized. Check for any fitting leaks.
13. Start the engine and check for leaks.

Carburetor

REMOVAL & INSTALLATION

7200VV Carburetor

1. Disconnect the negative battery cable. Remove the air cleaner. Relieve the fuel pressure.
2. Remove the throttle cable and transmission kickdown levers from the throttle lever. Disconnect and mark all vacuum lines, emission hoses, the fuel line and electrical connections to ease installation.
3. Remove the carburetor retaining nuts; then remove the carburetor. Remove the carburetor mounting gasket spacer, if equipped, and lower gasket from the intake manifold.
4. Installation is the reverse of removal procedure.
5. To prevent leakage, distortion or damage to the carburetor body flange, snug the nuts; then, alternately tight-

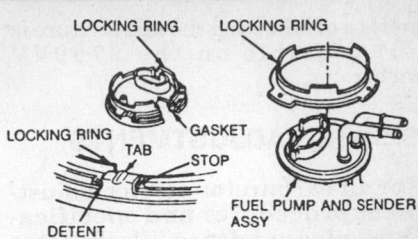

Typical in-tank fuel pump installation

en each nut in a criss-cross pattern to 12–15 ft. lbs.
6. Adjust engine idle speed.

IDLE SPEED ADJUSTMENT

7200VV Carburetor

1. Place the transmission in **N** or **P**. Apply the emergency brake and block the wheels. Bring the engine to normal operating temperature. Disconnect the vacuum hose at the EGR valve and plug.
2. Place the fast idle adjustment on the second step of the fast idle cam. Check and/or adjust fast idle rpm to specification. Rev engine momentarily and recheck. Remove plug from EGR vacuum hose and reconnect.
3. Place air conditioner selector in the OFF position. Disconnect and plug the vacuum hose at the throttle kicker and place the transmission in the specified position; check the underhood sticker. If adjustment is required, turn the curb idle speed screw. Put the transmission in **N**, increase the engine speed momentarily and recheck.
4. Apply a slight pressure on top of the nylon nut located on the accelerator pump to take up the linkage clearance. Turn the nut on the accelerator pump rod clockwise until a clearance of 0.010–0.005 in. is obtained between the top of the accelerator pump and the pump lever.
5. Turn the accelerator pump rod 1 turn counterclockwise to set the lever lash preload. Remove the plug from the throttle kicker vacuum hose and reconnect.
6. Disconnect and plug the vacuum hose at the Vacuum Operated Throttle Modulator (VOTM) kicker. Connect an external vacuum source providing a minimum of 4.88 in. Hg. to the VOTM kicker. With the transmission in the specified position, check/adjust the VOTM kicker speed.
7. If adjustment is required, turn the saddle bracket adjusting screw. Remove external vacuum source and reconnect VOTM kicker hose.

IDLE MIXTURE ADJUSTMENT

The normal propane enrichment

method of adjusting the idle mixture is not possible on the 2700VV carburetor.

SERVICE ADJUSTMENTS

For all carburetor service adjustment procedures and specifications, please refer to "Carburetor Service" in the Unit Repair section.

Fuel Injection

IDLE SPEED ADJUSTMENT

NOTE: Curb idle speed (rpm) is controlled by the EEC-IV processor, if equipped, and the idle speed control device. If the control system is operating properly, these speeds are self compensating and cannot be changed by traditional adjustment techniques.

2.3L and 3.8L Engines with EFI

1. Remove the air cleaner.
2. Locate the self-test connector and self-test input connector in the engine compartment.
3. Connect a jumper wire between the self-test input connector and the signal return pin, the top right terminal, on the self-test connector.
4. Place the ignition key in the RUN position and be careful not to start the engine. Wait approximately 10–15 seconds until the ISC plunger is fully retracted. Turn the ignition key OFF and wait an additional 10–15 seconds.
5. Remove the jumper wire from the diagnostic connector and disconnect the electrical connector from the ISC motor. Now perform the throttle stop adjustment as follows:
   a. Remove the EFI assembly from the vehicle.
   b. Use a small punch or equivalent to punch through and remove the aluminum plug which covers the throttle stop adjusting screw.
   c. Remove the throttle stop screw and install a new one.
6. Reinstall the EFI assembly on the vehicle, start engine and allow to stabilize. Check and adjust the idle speed, to specifiction, by turning the throttle stop screw. Cover throttle stop screw hole with a new cover.
7. Shut OFF the engine and reconnect the electrical connector to the ISC motor. Remove all test equipment and reinstall the air cleaner assembly.

2.3L Turbo Engine with EFI

1. Apply the parking brake and

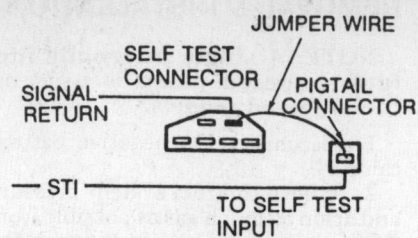

Jumping the self test connector on EEC-IV vehicles

block the drive wheels. Place the transmission in N.
2. Start the engine and let it run until it reaches normal operating temperature. Once the engine is hot, connect a suitable tachometer.
3. Disconnect the electrical connector to the air bypass valve—idle speed control motor. Start the engine and run it at 1500 rpm for 20 seconds.

NOTE: If the electric cooling fan comes ON during the idle speed adjusting procedures, wait for the fan to turn OFF before proceeding.

4. Let the engine return to idle and check the base idle speed.
5. The idle speed should be 700–800 rpm. If adjustment is necessary, turn the throttle stop adjusting screw to reach the specified rpm.
6. Shut the engine off and reconnect the power lead to the idle speed control air bypass valve. Disconnect all test equipment.

5.0L Engine with EFI

1. Apply the parking brake, block the drive wheels and place the vehicle in N.
2. Start the engine and let it run until it reaches normal operating temperature, then turn the engine OFF. Connect a tachometer to the engine.
3. Turn OFF all accessories and place the transmission in P for automatic transmission or N for manual transmission.
4. Run the engine at 1800 rpm for at least 30 seconds.
5. Place the transmission in D (automatic) or N (manual). Check the idle speed.
6. Check the vehicle emission information label for the correct idle speed specifications.
7. If the idle speed is not within specifications adjust it by turning the throttle plate stop screw.
8. After the correct rpm is reached, turn the throttle plate stop screw out an additional 1 turn to bring the ISC motor into its operating range.

IDLE MIXTURE ADJUSTMENT

Idle mixture adjustment is electronically controlled and can not be changed.

Fuel Injector

REMOVAL & INSTALLATION

1. Disconnect the negative battery cable. Remove the fuel cap from the fuel tank.
2. Relieve the fuel system pressure.
3. Remove the upper intake manifold.
4. Remove the electrical connectors to the fuel injectors and remove the bolts retaining the fuel rail.
5. Remove the fuel rail, with the injectors attached, from the engine.
6. To ease removal of the injector assembly, use a slight back and forth rocking motion to pull the injectors from the engine.
7. Replace the injector O-rings, 2 per injector. Inspect the injector plastic hat which covers the injector pintle, and washer for signs of deterioration. Replace as necessary. If the plastic hat is missing, look for it in the intake manifold.
To install:
8. Installation is the reverse order of the removal procedure.
9. Install the fuel cap on the fuel tank. Connect the negative battery cable.
10. Add engine coolant if required. Turn the ignition key ON and OFF several times without starting the engine to check for fuel leaks. Check all connections at the fuel rail and all push connections.

NOTE: The fuel system is normally pressurized to 39 psi.

11. Start the engine and let it reach normal operating temperature. Check for coolant and fuel leaks

EMISSION CONTROLS

Please refer to "Emission Control" in the Unit Repair section for system maintenance procedures. Due to the complex nature of modern electronic engine control systems, comprehensive diagnosis and testing procedures fall outside the confines of this repair manual. For complete information on diagnosis, testing and repair procedures concerning all modern engine and emission control systems, please refer to "Chilton's Guide to Electronic Engine Controls".

Emission Warning Lamps

RESETTING

These vehicles have an CHECK ENGINE lamp that will light when there is a fault in the engine control system.

This light can not be reset without diagnosing the fault in the system. When the system has been diagnosed and the problem corrected, the light will go out.

Service Lamp

1987–89 Cougar and Thunderbird

The SERVICE light will light after 5000–7500 miles depending on engine operation. To reset the interval light, depress both the TRIP and TRIP RESET buttons on the instrument cluster. The light will go out and 3 beeps will be heard.

ENGINE MECHANICAL

NOTE: Disconnecting the negative battery cable on some vehicles may interfere with the functions of the on board computer systems and may require the computer to undergo a relearning process, once the negative battery cable is reconnected.

Engine Assembly

REMOVAL & INSTALLATION

2.3L Engine

1. Raise the hood and secure it in the vertical position.
2. Drain coolant from the radiator and the oil from the crankcase.
3. On non-turbocharged engines, remove air cleaner and exhaust manifold shroud. On the turbocharged engine, disconnect the zip tube from the turbocharger inlet. Remove the ground strap on the turbocharger inlet elbow.

4. Disconnect the negative battery cable.
5. Remove the radiator upper and lower hoses.
6. Remove the radiator and fan. If equipped with an electric cooling fan, disconnect power lead to fan motor, then remove fan and shroud assembly.
7. Disconnect the heater hose from the water pump and carburetor choke fitting.
8. Disconnect the wires from the alternator and starter. Disconnect the accelerator cable from the carburetor or throttle body (EFI). On a vehicle with air conditioning, remove the compressor from the mounting bracket and position it out of the way, leaving the refrigerant lines attached.
9. Disconnect the flexible fuel line at the fuel pump line or at the fuel rail (EFI) and plug the fuel line.
10. Disconnect the coil primary wire at the coil. Disconnect the oil pressure and the water temperature sending unit wires from the sending units.
11. Remove the starter.
12. Raise and safely support the vehicle. Remove the flywheel or converter housing upper attaching bolts.
13. Disconnect the muffler inlet pipe at the exhaust manifold or turbocharger outlet.
14. Disconnect the engine right and left mounts at the No. 2 crossmember pedestals.
15. Remove the flywheel or converter housing. If equipped with a manual transmission, remove the flywheel housing lower attaching bolts.
16. If equipped with an automatic transmission, disconnect the converter from the flywheel. Disconnect transmission oil cooler lines, if attached to engine at pan rail. Remove the converter housing lower attaching bolts.
17. Lower the vehicle. Support the transmission and flywheel or converter housing with a jack.
18. Attach the engine lifting hooks to the existing lifting brackets. Carefully lift the engine out of the engine compartment. Install the engine on a work stand.
19. Installation is the reverse of removal procedure.

3.8L Engine Except Supercharged

1. Relieve the fuel system pressure. Drain engine cooling system.
2. Disconnect the negative battery cable.
3. If equipped with an underhood lamp, disconnect the wiring connector.
4. Mark position of the hood hinges and remove the hood.
5. Remove air cleaner assembly in-

cluding the air intake duct and heat tube.
6. Remove fan shroud attaching screws. Remove the fan/clutch assembly attaching bolts.
7. Remove fan/clutch assembly and shroud.
8. Loosen accessory drive belt idler. Remove the drive belt and the water pump pulley.
9. Disconnect radiator upper and lower hoses at radiator.
10. Disconnect thermactor hose from the downstream air tube check valve, if equipped.
11. Remove downstream air tube bracket attaching bolt at the rear of the right cylinder head.
12. Remove coil secondary wire from the coil.
13. If equipped with power steering, remove the pump mounting bracket attaching bolts. Leaving the hoses connected, place the pump and bracket assembly aside in a position to prevent the fluid from leaking out.
14. If equipped with air conditioning, remove the mounting bracket attaching bolts. Leaving hoses connected, secure the compressor to the right shock tower.
15. Remove alternator mounting bolts and set alternator aside.
16. Disconnect heater hoses from heater tube and water pump.
17. If equipped with speed control, disconnect the cable at the throttle body or fuel charging assembly.
18. Disconnect necessary vacuum hoses.
19. Remove screw attaching engine ground strap to dash panel.
20. Disconnect transmission linkage at the throttle body or fuel charging assembly.
21. Disconnect accelerator cable at the throttle body and remove cable routing bracket attaching bolts from the intake manifold (two places).
22. Disconnect necessary electrical connectors.
23. Disconnect fuel line and PCV hose at the throttle body, if equipped. Disconnect flexible fuel lines from steel lines over the rocker arm cover if equipped.
24. Disconnect flexible fuel inlet line at the throttle body. Plug the lines to prevent fuel leakage. Remove throttle body.
25. Leaving the EGR spacer and phenolic gasket in place, install Engine Lifting Plate T75T–6000–A or equivalent over the throttle body hold-down studs. Tighten nuts securely.

NOTE: Because the intake manifold is aluminum and of light weight design, all studs must be used to secure the lifting plate. Do not remove engine with the trans-

mission attached when using lifting plate.

26. Raise vehicle and support safely.

27. Drain crankcase.

28. Remove dust shield from the transmission converter housing.

29. Remove flexplate to torque converter attaching nuts.

30. Disconnect battery cable from the starter motor. Remove starter motor attaching bolts and starter.

31. Remove transmission oil cooler line routing clip.

32. Remove exhaust inlet pipe to exhaust manifold attaching nuts.

33. Disconnect exhaust heat control valve vacuum line and remove valve from exhaust manifold studs, if equipped.

34. Remove the 4 transmission to engine lower attaching bolts.

35. Remove engine mount to crossmember attaching nuts.

36. Lower vehicle.

37. Position a jack under the transmission. Raise the jack just enough to support the weight of the transmission.

38. Remove the 2 transmission to engine upper attaching bolts.

39. Position a protective cover, such as ¼ in. plywood, between the engine and the radiator to prevent damage to the radiator.

40. Raise the engine slightly and carefully pull it away from the transmission. Carefully lift the engine out of the engine compartment. Avoid bending or damaging the rear cover plate or other components. Install engine on a work stand.

To install:

41. Installation is the reverse of removal procedure.

42. Install engine mount to crossmember attaching nuts and tighten to 70–90 ft. lbs. (95–122 Nm).

43. Install flexplate to torque converter attaching nuts and tighten to 20–30 ft. lbs. (28–40 Nm).

44. Install exhaust inlet pipe to exhaust manifold attaching nuts. Tighten nuts to 16–24 ft. lbs. (21–32 Nm).

45. Position starter motor, install attaching bolts and tighten to 15–20 ft. lbs. (20–27 Nm).

46. Install the fuel charging assembly and tighten hold-down nuts to 12–15 ft. lbs. (16–20 Nm).

3.8L Supercharged Engine

1. Relieve the fuel system pressure. Drain the cooling system.

2. Disconnect the negative battery cable.

3. Disconnect the wiring for the underhood light. Mark the location of the hood hinges, for proper alignment during installation.

4. Remove the wiper module and left hand cowl vent screen.

5. Disconnect the alternator wiring.

6. Remove the upper intercooler tube at the supercharger and cooler assemblies. Remove the retaining bolt from the cooler tube at the power steering bracket and remove the tube.

7. Remove the upper radiator shield. Release the tension from the accessory drive belt and the supercharger drive belt, remove the belts.

8. Remove the air cleaner-to-throttle body tube assembly.

9. Disconnect the electric cooling fan and remove the assembly. Remove the radiator shroud and fan assembly.

10. Remove the upper radiator hose and disconnect the transmission cooler lines, if equipped with automatic transmission. Disconnect the lower radiator and heater hoses.

11. Remove the 2 push pins that retain the intercooler and remove it from the radiator bracket. Remove the radiator assembly.

12. Disconnect the power steering hoses and remove the pump assembly from its mounting bracket.

13. Discharge the air conditioning system and disconnect the refrigerant lines. Remove the air conditioning compressor from its mounting bracket and remove it from the vehicle.

14. Remove the coolant recovery bottle. Disconnect the accelerator cable mounting bracket and position it to the side.

15. With the fuel system pressure relieved, disconnect the fuel inlet hose and return hose.

16. Disconnect the engine control wiring harness from the multi-connector. Disconnect the the vacuum hoses.

17. Disconnect the DIS module wiring. Remove the coil pack retaining bolts and position the coil pack to the side.

18. Remove the nuts attaching the lower intercooler tube to the supercharger and remove the tube.

19. Remove the alternator bracket bolts, disconnect the alternator wiring and remove the alternator.

20. Disconnect the canister purge line and disconnect one end of the TV cable.

21. Raise and safely support the vehicle. Drain the engine oil and remove the oil filter.

22. Remove the exhaust pipe to manifold nuts and remove the the left exhaust shield. Disconnect the heated oxygen sensor.

23. Remove the inspection plug and remove the torque converter-to-flywheel bolts.

24. Remove the engine-to-transmission bolts. Remove the engine mount through bolts and the left mount retaining strap.

25. Remove the crankshaft pulley and damper assembly. Remove the starter.

26. Disconnect the oil level sender and the sending unit gauge wiring.

27. Lower the vehicle. Position a suitable jack under the transmission and install a suitable engine lifting device.

28. Remove the engine from the vehicle.

To install:

29. With an suitable lifting device installed, install the engine into the engine compartment.

30. Install 2 of the engine-to-transmission bolts and remove the lifting device.

31. Connect the oil pressure switch and level indicator. Install the remaining engine-to-transmission bolts, tighten to 40–50 ft. lbs.

32. Install the torque converter-to-flywheel bolts and tighten to 20–34 ft. lbs. Install the inspection cover. Install the starter.

33. Install the engine mount through bolts and retaining strap, tighten the bolts to 35–50 ft. lbs.

34. Install the oxygen sensor, exhaust pipe-to-manifold and heat shield. Install the crankshaft pulley and damper, tighten the bolt to 93–121 ft. lbs.

35. Install the oil filter and lower the vehicle. Connect the throttle cable bracket and all vacuum lines. Connect the canister purge line.

36. Install the alternator, power steering pump and brackets. Reconnect the power steering lines. Install the air conditioning compressor and lines.

37. Install the radiator and intercooler assemblies. Install the radiator shields and fan assembly.

38. Reconnect the radiator and heater hoses. Connect the intercooler tubes and the transmission oil cooler lines.

39. Install the ignition coil pack and reconnect the engine control harness.

40. Reconnect the fuel lines. Install the accessory and supercharger drive belts and adjust the tension. Install the remaining components.

41. Install the wiper module and cowl vent. Install the hood, aligning the marks during disassembly.

42. Connect the negative battery cable. Refill the cooling system and the engine crankcase to the proper levels. Check the power steering fluid level. Recharge the air conditioning system.

43. Run the engine and check for oil and coolant leaks. Bleed the cooling system and the power steering system.

5.0L and 5.8L Engines

1. Disconnect the negative battery cable. Relieve the fuel system pressure. Drain the cooling system and the crankcase.

2. Remove the hood. Disconnect the battery ground cables from the cylinder block.

3. Remove the air cleaner and intake duct assembly.

4. Disconnect the radiator upper hose from the coolant outlet housing and the radiator lower hose at the water pump. Disconnect the transmission oil cooler lines from the radiator. Remove the bolts attaching the fan shroud to the radiator.

5. Remove the radiator. Remove the fan, spacer, belt pulley and shroud.

6. Remove the alternator bolts and position the alternator out of the way.

7. Disconnect the oil pressure sending unit wire from the sending unit, disconnect low oil level sensor wire, if so equipped, at the middle of the rear oil sump on left hand side of oil pan and the flexible fuel line at the fuel tank line. Plug the fuel tank line.

8. Disconnect the accelerator cable from the carburetor. Disconnect the speed control cable, if so equipped. Disconnect the throttle valve vacuum line from the intake manifold, if so equipped. Disconnect the transmission filler tube bracket from the cylinder block. Disconnect the TV rod on the automatic overdrive transmission models.

9. If equipped with air conditioning, isolate and remove the compressor. If equipped with power steering, disconnect the power steering pump bracket from the cylinder head. Remove the drive belt. Position the power steering pump out of the way and in a position that will prevent the fluid from draining out. If equipped with vacuum boosted power brakes, disconnect the brake vacuum line from the intake manifold.

10. Disconnect the heater hoses from the water pump and intake the manifold. Disconnect the coolant temperature sending unit wire from the sending unit.

11. Remove the flywheel or converter housing to engine upper bolts.

12. Disconnect the primary wire connector from the ignition coil, except on Continental, the coil is located on right shock tower. Disconnect wiring to ECT, ACT and EGO sensors on EEC-IV equipped vehicles. Disconnect wiring to solenoids on left hand rocker cover. Remove the wire harness from the left rocker arm cover and position the wires out of the way. Disconnect the ground strap from the block.

13. Raise and safely support the front of the vehicle. Disconnect the starter cable from the starter. Remove the starter.

14. Disconnect the muffler inlet pipes from the exhaust manifolds. Disconnect the engine support insulators from the chassis. Disconnect the down stream Thermactor tubing and check valve from the right exhaust manifold stud, if so equipped. Disconnect transmission cooler lines from retainer and remove the converter housing inspection cover. Disconnect the flywheel from the converter. Secure the converter assembly in the housing. Remove the remaining converter housing to engine bolts.

15. Lower the vehicle and support the transmission. Attach the engine lifting sling and hoist to lifting brackets on intake manifolds.

16. Raise the engine slightly and carefully pull it from the transmission. Carefully lift the engine out of the engine compartment and avoid bending or damaging the rear cover plate or other components. Install the engine on a work stand.

17. Installation is the reverse of removal.

18. Tighten all the bolts to specifications.

Engine Mounts

REMOVAL & INSTALLATION

2.3L Engine

1. Disconnect the negative battery cable. Support the engine using a wood block and jack placed under the engine.

2. Remove the through bolts attaching both insulators to the No. 2 crossmember pedestal bracket. On turbocharged engine, remove nuts.

3. Disconnect shift linkage.

4. Raise the engine sufficiently to disengage the insulator studs from the crossmember pedestal bracket.

5. Remove the bolts attaching the insulator and bracket assembly to the engine. Remove the insulator and bracket assembly.

To install:

6. Position the insulator and bracket assembly to the engine. Install the attaching bolts. Tighten to 33–45 ft. lbs. (45–61 Nm).

7. Lower the engine into position making sure that the insulators are seated flat on the No. 2 crossmember and the insulator studs are at the bottom of the slots.

8. On 2.3L turbocharged engine, install engine bracket to the No. 2 crossmember. Lower engine into position until the through bolts line up. Hand start, then tighten nuts to 65–85 ft. lbs. (88–119 Nm).

9. Install fuel pump shield attaching screw to left engine support, if so equipped.

10. Install shift linkage.

3.8L Engine

1987–88

1. Disconnect the negative battery cable. Remove fan shroud attaching screws. On supercharged engine, disconnect the inlet and outlet tubes from the intercooler.

2. Support engine using a jack and wood block placed under the engine.

3. Remove through bolt or nuts attaching insulators to the No. 2 crossmember.

4. Remove shift linkage.

5. Raise engine high enough to clear clevis brackets or insulator studs from crossmember.

6. Remove fuel pump shield, if equipped, from right side of the engine.

7. Remove starter ground cable and oil cooler line attaching clips from right hand engine support bracket.

8. Remove bolts attaching insulator and bracket assembly to engine. Remove insulator and bracket assembly.

9. Installation is the reverse of the removal procedure.

1989–91

1. Disconnect the negative battery cable.

2. Remove fan shroud retaining screws.

3. Support engine using a jack and wood block placed under the engine.

4. Remove the through-bolts and

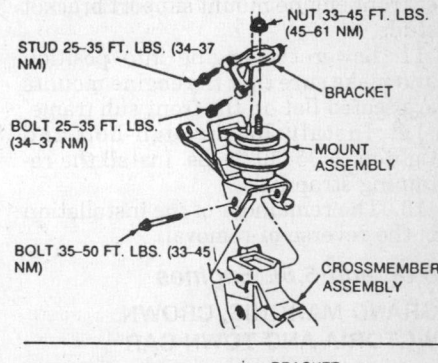

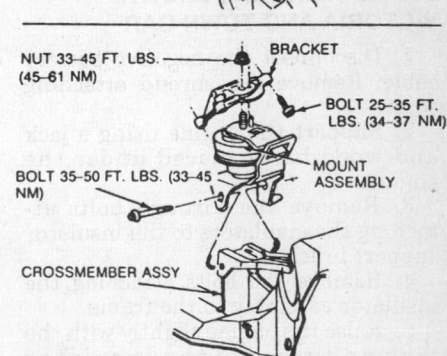

Front engine mounts—1987-88 with 3.8L engine

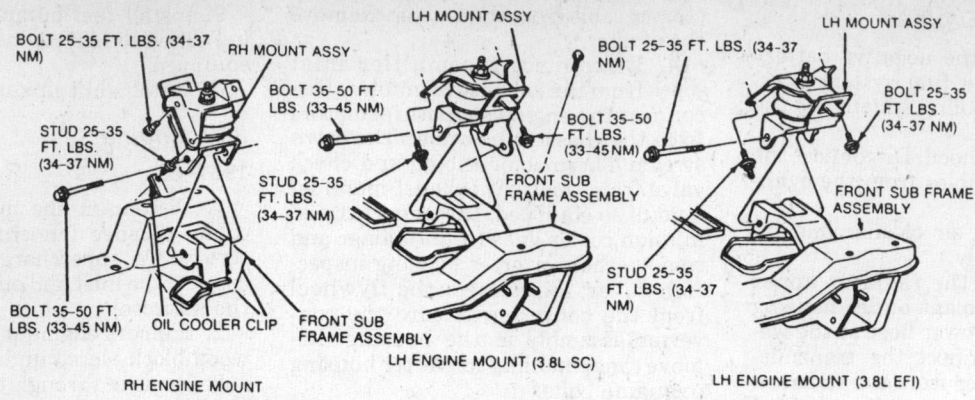

Front engine mounts—1989–91 with 3.8L engine

retaining strap bolt to the front sub frame.

5. Remove shift linkage.

6. Raise engine high enough to clear clevis brackets.

7. Remove the accessories and oil cooler line retaining clips from the engine support brackets.

8. Remove bolts attaching insulator and bracket assembly to engine. Remove insulator and bracket assembly.

NOTE: The left hand front engine mount removal on the supercharged engine may require lowering the front sub frame.

To install:

9. Position the engine mount and bracket assembly to the engine, install the retaining bolts and tighten to 25–35 ft. lbs.

10. Install the accessories to the lower front engine mount support bracket studs.

11. Lower the engine into position and make sure that the engine mounts are seated flat on the front sub frame.

12. Install the through-bolt and tighten to 35–50 ft. lbs. Install the retaining strap bolt.

13. The remainder of the installation is the reverse of removal.

5.0L and 5.8L Engines

GRAND MARQUIS, CROWN VICTORIA AND TOWN CAR

1. Disconnect the negative battery cable. Remove fan shroud attaching screw.

2. Support the engine using a jack and wood block placed under the engine.

3. Remove the through bolts attaching the insulators to the insulator support bracket.

4. Remove the bolts attaching the insulator assembly to the frame.

5. Raise the engine slightly with the jack and remove the insulator assembly.

To install:

6. Position the engine insulator assembly to the frame and install the attaching bolts. Tighten the bolts to 26–38 ft. lbs. (35–52 Nm).

7. Lower the engine into position and install the engine insulator assembly to insulator support bracket through bolts. Tighten the through bolts to 33–46 ft. lbs. (45–62 Nm).

8. Install fan shroud attaching screws and tighten to 24–48 inch lbs. (3–5 Nm).

5.0L Engine

MUSTANG, COUGAR, THUNDERBIRD, CONTINENTAL AND MARK VII

1. Disconnect the negative battery cable. Remove fan shroud attaching screws.

2. Support the engine using a jack and wood block placed under the engine.

3. Remove the nuts attaching insulators to the No. 2 crossmember.

4. Disconnect shift linkage.

5. Raise the engine sufficiently with the jack to disengage the insulator studs from the crossmember.

6. Remove the engine insulator and bracket assembly to cylinder block attaching bolts. Remove the engine insulator assembly.

To install:

7. Position the insulator assembly on the engine and install the attaching bolts. Tighten the bolts to 35–60 ft. lbs. (48–81 Nm).

8. Lower the engine into position making sure that the insulators are seated flat on the No. 2 crossmember and the insulator studs are at the bottom of the slots.

9. Install the insulator to the No. 2 crossmember and start the nut assemblies on the insulator studs and tighten to specification.

10. Install the fan shroud attaching

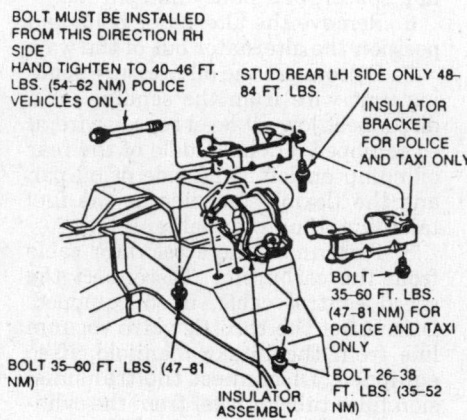

Front engine mounts, right side—Town Car, Crown Victoria and Grand Marquis

screws and tighten to 24–48 inch lbs. (3–5 Nm).

11. Connect shift linkage.

Cylinder Head

REMOVAL & INSTALLATION

2.3L Engine

1. Relieve the fuel system pressure. Disconnect the negative battery cable. Drain the cooling system.

2. Remove the air cleaner and the valve rocker cover. On turbocharged vehicles remove the inlet tube between the turbocharger and the throttle body.

3. Remove the intake and exhaust manifolds. The intake manifold, installed valves and sensors, if equipped and carburetor can be removed as an assembly.

4. Remove the camshaft drive belt cover.

5. Loosen the drive belt tensioner and remove the drive belt.

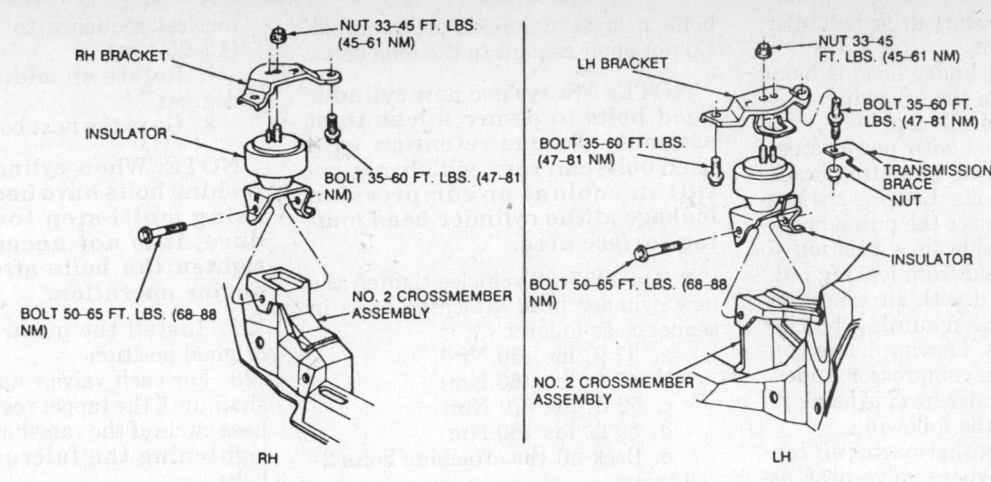

NUT 33-45 FT. LBS. (45-61 NM)
RH BRACKET
INSULATOR
BOLT 35-60 FT. LBS. (47-81 NM)
BOLT 50-65 FT. LBS. (68-88 NM)
NO. 2 CROSSMEMBER ASSEMBLY
RH

NUT 33-45 FT. LBS. (45-61 NM)
LH BRACKET
BOLT 35-60 FT. LBS. (47-81 NM)
TRANSMISSION BRACE NUT
INSULATOR
BOLT 50-65 FT. LBS. (68-88 NM)
NO. 2 CROSSMEMBER ASSEMBLY
LH

Front engine mounts—Thunderbird and Cougar with 5.0L engine

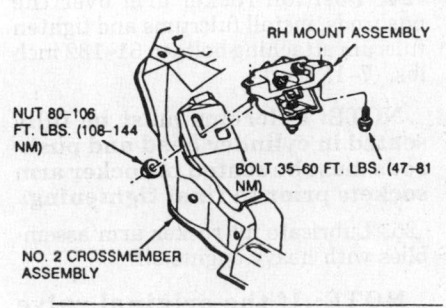

RH MOUNT ASSEMBLY
NUT 80-106 FT. LBS. (108-144 NM)
BOLT 35-60 FT. LBS. (47-81 NM)
NO. 2 CROSSMEMBER ASSEMBLY

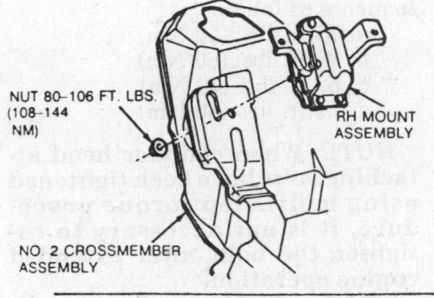

NUT 80-106 FT. LBS. (108-144 NM)
RH MOUNT ASSEMBLY
NO. 2 CROSSMEMBER ASSEMBLY

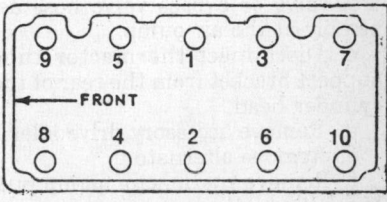

Cylinder head bolt torque sequence— 2.3L engine

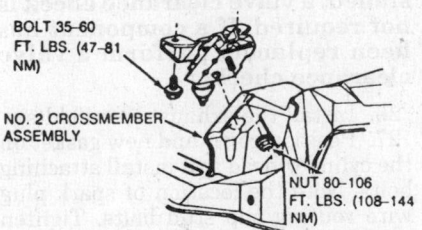

BOLT 35-60 FT. LBS. (47-81 NM)
NO. 2 CROSSMEMBER ASSEMBLY
NUT 80-106 FT. LBS. (108-144 NM)

Front engine mounts—Mustang with 5.0L engine except convertible

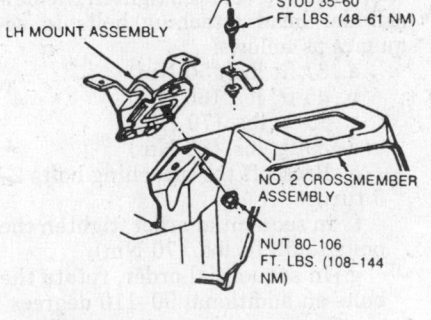

STUD 35-60 FT. LBS. (48-61 NM)
LH MOUNT ASSEMBLY
NO. 2 CROSSMEMBER ASSEMBLY
NUT 80-106 FT. LBS. (108-144 NM)

Front engine mounts—Mark VII and Continental

6. Remove the water outlet from the cylinder head.

7. Remove the cylinder head bolts evenly and remove the cylinder head.

To install:

8. Position a new cylinder head gasket on the block. Rotate the camshaft so that the locating pin is at the 5 o'clock position, to avoid valve damage.

9. Position the cylinder head on the block. Install the bolts finger tight and torque in sequence to specifications in 2 stages.

NOTE: If difficulty in positioning the head on the block is encountered, guide pins may be fabricated by cutting the heads off 2 extra cylinder head bolts.

10. Set the crankshaft at TDC and be sure that the camshaft drive gear and distributor are positioned correctly.

11. Install the camshaft drive belt and release the tensioner. Rotate the crankshaft 2 full turns clockwise, facing the engine, to remove all slack from the belt. The timing marks should again be aligned. Tighten the tensioner lockbolt and pivot bolts.

12. Install the camshaft drive belt cover.

13. Apply sealer to the water outlet and new gasket and install.

14. Install the intake and exhaust manifolds.

15. Adjust the valve clearance.

16. Install a new valve cover gasket and install the valve cover.

17. Install the air cleaner and crankcase ventilation hose. On turbo models install the inlet tube between the turbocharger and the throttle body.

18. Refill the cooling system. Run the engine and check for leaks.

3.8L Engine Except Supercharged

1. Relieve the fuel system pressure. Drain the cooling system.

2. Disconnect the negative battery cable.

3. Remove air cleaner assembly including the air intake duct and heat tube.

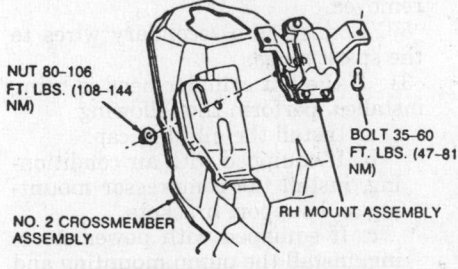

NUT 80-106 FT. LBS. (108-144 NM)
BOLT 35-60 FT. LBS. (47-81 NM)
RH MOUNT ASSEMBLY
NO. 2 CROSSMEMBER ASSEMBLY

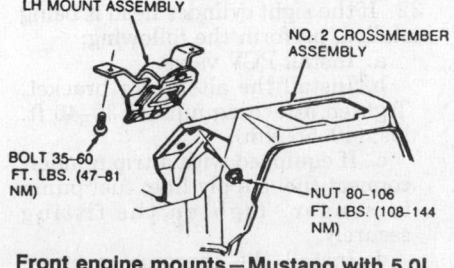

LH MOUNT ASSEMBLY
NO. 2 CROSSMEMBER ASSEMBLY
BOLT 35-60 FT. LBS. (47-81 NM)
NUT 80-106 FT. LBS. (108-144 NM)

Front engine mounts—Mustang with 5.0L engine

4. Loosen accessory drive belt idler. Remove drive belt.

5. If the left cylinder head is being removed, perform the following:

a. Remove oil fill cap.

b. If equipped with power steering, remove pump mounting brackets attaching bolts. Leaving the hoses connected, place the pump/bracket assembly aside in a position to prevent the fluid from leaking out.

c. If equipped with air conditioning, remove the mounting bracket attaching bolts. Leaving hoses connected, position compressor aside.

6. If right cylinder head is being removed, perform the following:

a. Disconnect thermactor air control valve or bypass valve hose assembly at the air pump.

b. Disconnect thermactor air control valve or bypass valve hose assembly at the air pump.

c. Disconnect thermactor tube support bracket from the rear of the cylinder head.

d. Remove accessory drive idler.

e. Remove alternator.

f. Remove thermactor pump pulley. Remove thermactor pump.

g. Remove alternator bracket.

NOTE: If equipped with trip minder, the fuel supply tube, fuel pump to sensor, must be disconnected to gain access to the alternator bracket upper attaching bolt.

h. Remove PCV valve.

7. Remove intake manifold.

8. Remove valve rocker arm cover attaching screws.

9. Remove exhaust manifold(s).

10. Loosen rocker arm fulcrum attaching bolts enough to allow the rocker arm to be lifted off the pushrod and rotated to 1 side.

11. Remove pushrods. Identify the position of each rod. The rods should be installed in their original position during assembly.

12. Remove cylinder head attaching bolts and discard.

13. Remove cylinder head(s).

To install:

NOTE: Lightly oil all bolt and stud bolt threads before installation except those specifying special sealant.

14. Clean all mating surfaces.

15. Position new head gasket(s) on the cylinder block using the dowels for alignment.

16. Position cylinder head(s) on block.

17. Install new cylinder head bolts. Apply a thin coating of pipe sealant to the threads of the short cylinder head bolts, nearest to the exhaust manifold. Do not apply sealant to the long bolts.

NOTE: Always use new cylinder head bolts to assure a leak-tight assembly. Torque retention with used bolts can vary, which may result in coolant or compression leakage at the cylinder head mating surface area.

18. On 1987–88 vehicles tighten the new cylinder head attaching bolts in sequence as follows:

a. 37 ft. lbs. (50 Nm)

b. 45 ft. lbs. (60 Nm)

c. 52 ft. lbs. (70 Nm)

d. 59 ft. lbs. (80 Nm)

e. Back-off the attaching bolts 2–3 turns

19. After backing off the head bolts 2–3 turns, retorque in 4 steps and in sequence as follows:

a. 37 ft. lbs. (50 Nm)

b. 45 ft. lbs. (60 Nm)

c. 52 ft. lbs. (70 Nm)

d. 59 ft. lbs. (80 Nm)

NOTE: When cylinder head attaching bolts have been tightened using multi-step torque procedure, it is not necessary to retighten the bolts after extended engine operation.

20. On 1989 vehicles tighten the new cylinder head attaching bolts in sequence as follows:

a. 37 ft. lbs. (50 Nm)

b. 45 ft. lbs. (60 Nm)

c. 52 ft. lbs. (70 Nm)

d. 59 ft. lbs. (80 Nm)

e. Back-off the attaching bolts 2–3 turns

f. In sequential order, tighten the bolts to 52 ft. lbs. (70 Nm)

g. In sequential order, rotate the bolts an additional 90–110 degrees

NOTE: When cylinder head attaching bolts have been tightened using multi-step torque procedure, it is not necessary to retighten the bolts after extended engine operation.

21. On 1990–91 vehicles tighten the new cylinder head attaching bolts in numerical sequence as follows:

a. 37 ft. lbs. (50 Nm)

b. 45 ft. lbs. (60 Nm)

c. 52 ft. lbs. (70 Nm)

d. 59 ft. lbs. (80 Nm)

e. Back-off the attaching bolts 2–3 turns

f. Tighten the long bolts in numerical sequence to 11–18 ft. lbs. (15–25 Nm)

g. Rotate an additional 85–105 degrees

h. Go to the next bolt in sequence

i. Tighten the short bolts in numerical sequence to 11–18 ft. lbs. (15–25 Nm)

j. Rotate an additional 65–85 degrees

k. Go to the next bolt in sequence

NOTE: When cylinder head attaching bolts have been tightened using multi-step torque procedure, it is not necessary to retighten the bolts after extended engine operation.

22. Install the pushrods, in their original position.

23. For each valve rotate the crankshaft until the tappet rests on the heel, base circle of the camshaft lobe, before tightening the fulcrum attaching bolts.

24. Position rocker arm over the pushrods, install fulcrums and tighten fulcrum attaching bolts to 61–132 inch lbs. (7–15 Nm).

NOTE: Fulcrums must be fully seated in cylinder head and pushrods must be seated in rocker arm sockets prior to final tightening.

25. Lubricate all rocker arm assemblies with heavy engine oil.

NOTE: If the original valve train components are being installed, a valve clearance check is not required. If a component has been replaced, perform a valve clearance check.

26. Install the exhaust manifold(s).

27. Position cover and new gasket on the cylinder head and install attaching bolts. Note the location of spark plug wire routing clip stud bolts. Tighten attaching bolts to 80–106 inch lbs. (9–12 Nm).

28. Install the intake manifold.

29. Install the spark plugs, if removed.

30. Connect the secondary wires to the spark plugs.

31. If the left cylinder head is being installed, perform the following:

a. Install the oil filler cap.

b. If equipped with air conditioning, install the compressor mounting and support brackets.

c. If equipped with power steering, install the pump mounting and support brackets.

32. If the right cylinder head is being installed, perform the following:

a. Install PCV valve.

b. Install the alternator bracket. Tighten attaching nuts to 30–40 ft. lbs. (40–55 Nm).

c. If equipped with a trip minder, connect fuel supply line, fuel pump to sensor. Tighten the fitting securely.

d. Install the thermactor pump and pump pulley.

e. Install the alternator.

f. Install the accessory drive belt idler pulley.

g. Install the thermactor air control valve or air bypass valve hose. Tighten the clamps securely to the air pump assembly.

33. Install the accessory drive belt and tighten to specification. Attach the thermactor tube(s) support bracket to the rear of the cylinder head. Tighten attaching bolts to 30–40 ft. lbs. (40–55 Nm).

34. Connect cable to the battery negative terminal.

35. Fill cooling system with the specified coolant.

36. Start engine and check for coolant, fuel and oil leaks.

37. Check and, if necessary, adjust the curb idle speed.

38. Install the air cleaner assembly including the air intake duct and heat tube.

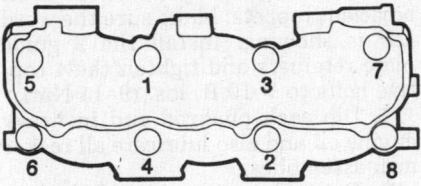

Cylinder head bolt torque sequence—3.8L engine

3.8L Supercharged Engine

1. Relieve the fuel system pressure. Drain the cooling system and disconnect the negative battery cable.

2. Remove the air cleaner assembly, air intake duct.

3. Remove the accessory and supercharger drive belts.

4. If the left cylinder head is being removed, remove the following components:

   a. Oil filler cap

   b. Power steering pump front bracket mounting bolts

   c. Alternator assembly and main belt tensioner

   d. Power steering pump/alternator bracket mounting bolts, lay pump and bracket aside

5. When removing the power steering pump and bracket, leave the hoses attached.

6. If the right cylinder head is being removed, remove the following components:

   a. Thermactor tube support bracket

   b. Air conditioner compressor drive belt and main drive belt

   c. Thermactor pump pulley and thermactor

   d. Air conditioning compressor, lay it aside

   e. PCV valve

7. When removing the air conditioning compressor, leave the refrigerant lines attached.

8. Remove the upper intake manifold assembly. Remove the valve cover.

9. Remove the the lower intake manifold and remove the exhaust manifold.

10. Loosen the rocker arm fulcrum attaching bolts enough to allow the rocker arm to be lifted off the pushrod an turn the rocker arms to the side.

11. Remove the pushrods, noting the position of each for installation.

12. Remove the head bolts and throw them away, new bolts must be used for reassembly.

13. Remove the head and discard the gasket. Check all head surfaces for warping or signs of water leakage.

To install:

14. Clean all gasket mating surfaces for assembly.

15. Position new cylinder head bolts on the cylinder block using dowel pins to keep them properly lined up.

16. Position the heads on the block. Apply a thin coating of pipe sealant with Teflon® or equivalent, to the threads of the short cylinder head bolts, the bolts nearest to the exhaust manifold. Do not apply sealant to the long bolts, instead, dip them in clean oil.

17. On 1987–88 vehicles tighten the new cylinder head attaching bolts in sequence as follows:

   a. 37 ft. lbs. (50 Nm)

   b. 45 ft. lbs. (60 Nm)

   c. 52 ft. lbs. (70 Nm)

   d. 59 ft. lbs. (80 Nm)

   e. Back-off the attaching bolts 2–3 turns

18. After backing off the head bolts 2–3 turns, retorque in 4 steps and in sequence as follows:

   a. 37 ft. lbs. (50 Nm)

   b. 45 ft. lbs. (60 Nm)

   c. 52 ft. lbs. (70 Nm)

   d. 59 ft. lbs. (80 Nm)

NOTE: When cylinder head attaching bolts have been tightened using multi-step torque procedure, it is not necessary to retighten the bolts after extended engine operation.

19. On 1989 vehicles tighten the new cylinder head attaching bolts in sequence as follows:

   a. 37 ft. lbs. (50 Nm)

   b. 45 ft. lbs. (60 Nm)

   c. 52 ft. lbs. (70 Nm)

   d. 59 ft. lbs. (80 Nm)

   e. Back-off the attaching bolts 2–3 turns

   f. In sequential order, tighten the bolts to 52 ft. lbs. (70 Nm)

   g. In sequential order, rotate the bolts an additional 90–110 degrees

NOTE: When cylinder head attaching bolts have been tightened using multi-step torque procedure, it is not necessary to retighten the bolts after extended engine operation.

20. On 1990–91 vehicles tighten the new cylinder head attaching bolts in sequence as follows:

   a. 37 ft. lbs. (50 Nm)

   b. 45 ft. lbs. (60 Nm)

   c. 52 ft. lbs. (70 Nm)

   d. 59 ft. lbs. (80 Nm)

   e. Back-off the attaching bolts 2–3 turns

   f. Tighten the long and short bolts in numerical sequence to 48–55 ft. lbs. (65–75 Nm)

   g. Rotate an additional 90–110 degrees

   h. Go to the next bolt in sequence

NOTE: When cylinder head attaching bolts have been tightened using multi-step torque procedure, it is not necessary to retighten the bolts after extended engine operation.

21. Dip each pushrod in heavy engine oil and install them in their original position in the heads.

22. For each valve, rotate the crankshaft until the tappet rests on the base circle of the camshaft lobe. Then tighten the rocker arm bolts to 43 inch. lbs. Do this for each tappet.

23. Final tighten the fulcrum bolts to 19–25 ft. lbs., after the intial tightening is complete. The camshaft can be in any position.

24. Install the exhaust and lower intake manifolds. Install the valve cover.

25. Install the upper intake manifold. Install each of the components removed, depending on the cylinder head removed.

26. Install the accessory drive belts and check the tension.

27. Fill the cooling system to the correct level and connect the negative battery cable.

28. Run the engine to normal operating temperature and check for coolant leaks.

5.0L and 5.8L Engines

1. Relieve the fuel system pressure. Disconnect the negative battery cable. Remove the intake manifold.

2. Remove the rocker arm cover(s). If the left cylinder head is to be removed on a vehicle with air conditioning, remove the mounting brackets and move the compressor aside. If the left cylinder head is to be removed, on vehicles with power steering, disconnect the power steering pump bracket from the left cylinder head and remove the drive belt from the pump pulley.

Position the power steering pump out of the way and in a position that will prevent the oil from draining out. Remove thermactor crossover tube from the rear of cylinder heads.

3. If the right cylinder head is to be removed, remove the alternator mounting bracket bolts and spacer from the right cylinder head assembly.

4. Disconnect the exhaust manifold(s) from the muffler inlet pipe(s).

5. Loosen the rocker arm fulcrum bolts so that the rocker arms can be rotated to the side. Remove the pushrods in sequence so that they may be installed in their original positions. Remove valve stem caps.

6. Remove the cylinder head attaching bolts and lift the cylinder head off the block. If required, remove the exhaust manifolds to gain access to the lower attaching bolts. Remove and discard the cylinder head gasket.

To install:

7. Clean all of the gasket mating surfaces. If the cylinder head was removed for a cylinder head gasket replacement, check the flatness of the cylinder head and block gasket surfaces.

8. Position the new cylinder head gasket over the cylinder dowels on the block. Position the cylinder head on the block and install the attaching bolts.

9. The cylinder head bolts are tightened in 2 progressive steps on the 5.0L engine and in 3 progressive steps on the 5.8L engine. Tighten all the bolts in sequence to specifications. When the cylinder head bolts have been tightened to specification, it is not necessary to retorque the bolts after extended operation. However, the bolts may be checked and retightened, if desired. If removed, install the exhaust manifolds and tighten the attaching bolts to specification.

10. Install the pushrods, making sure that they are in their original positions in the cylinder head.

11. Install the exhaust valve stem caps.

12. Install the rocker arms. If all original components are being installed, a valve clearance adjustment is not necessary. If any valve train components are replaced, perform a valve clearance adjustment.

13. Connect the exhaust manifold(s) at the muffler inlet pipe(s). Tighten nuts to specification.

14. If the right cylinder head was removed, install the alternator attaching bracket on the right cylinder head assembly. Install the alternator. Adjust the drive belt tension to specifications.

15. Clean the valve rocker arm cover(s). Position the valve rocker cover gasket in each cover, making sure that

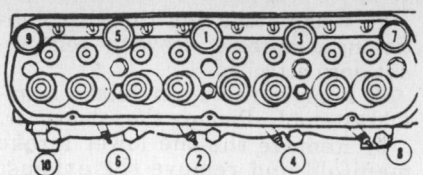

Cylinder head bolt torque sequence— 5.0L and 5.8L engines

the tabs engage the notches in the cover, making sure that the tabs engage the notches in the cover. Install valve rocker arm cover(s). The valve rocker cover is tightened in 2 steps. Tighten the bolts to specifications. After the engine reaches operating temperature, retighten bolts to the same specifications.

16. Install the air conditioner compressor, if equipped. Install the power steering drive belt and power steering pump bracket. Install the bracket attaching bolts. Adjust the drive belt to specifications. Install the thermactor crossover tube at rear of cylinder heads.

17. Install the intake manifolds.

Valve Lifters

REMOVAL & INSTALLATION

3.8L Engine

NOTE: Before replacing a tappet for noisy operation, be sure the noise is not caused by improper valve to rocker arm clearance or by worn rocker arms or pushrods.

1. Disconnect the negative battery cable. Disconnect secondary ignition wires at the spark plugs.

2. Remove plug wire routing clips from the studs on the rocker arm cover attaching bolts. Lay the plug wires, with the routing clips toward the front of the engine.

3. Remove intake manifold and supercharger assembly, if equipped.

4. Remove rocker arm covers.

5. Sufficiently loosen each rocker arm fulcrum attaching bolt to allow the rocker arm to be lifted off the pushrod and rotate to 1 side.

6. Remove pushrods. The location of each pushrod should be identified. When the engine is assembled each rod should be installed in its original position.

7. Remove the lifters using a magnet. The location of each tappet should be identified. When the engine is assembled, each tappet should be installed in its original position.

8. On 1989–91 vehicles, remove the 4 bolts holding the 2 guide plate retainers in place. The bolts are held secure in the retainers. Remove the 6 guide plates from the adjacent tappets.

To install:

9. Installation is the reverse of removal procedure.

10. On 1989–91 vehicles, align the flates on the side of the tappets and install the 6 guide plates between adjacent tappets. Make sure the word **UP** is showing. Install the 2 guide plate retainers and tighten the 4 captive bolts to 7–10 ft. lbs. (9–14 Nm).

11. Dip each pushrod end in heavy engine oil and also lubricate all rocker arm assemblies.

12. For each valve rotate the crankshaft until the tappet rests on the heel (base circle) of the camshaft lobe. Position rocker arm over the pushrods. Install fulcrums and tighten fulcrum attaching bolt to 7–15 Nm (62–132 inch lb.) for 1987 or 44 inch lbs. (5 Nm) for 1988–91.

13. Final tightening fulcrum bolts to 25–35 Nm (19–25 ft. lbs.). For final tightening, the camshaft may be in any position.

NOTE: Fulcrums must be fully seated in the cylinder head and pushrods must be seated in the rocker arm sockets before final tightening.

5.0L and 5.8L Engines

1. Disconnect the negative battery

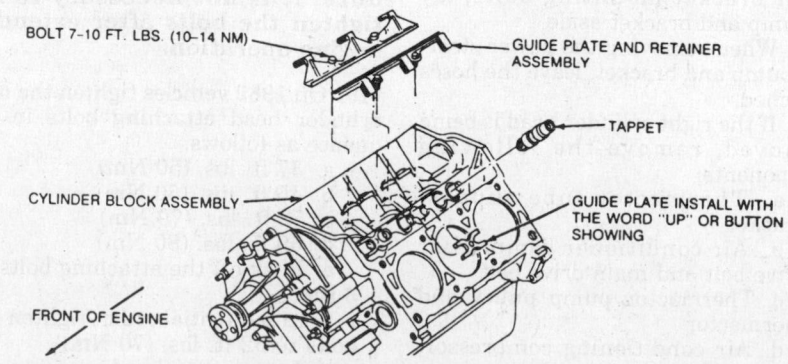

BOLT 7–10 FT. LBS. (10–14 NM)
GUIDE PLATE AND RETAINER ASSEMBLY
TAPPET
CYLINDER BLOCK ASSEMBLY
GUIDE PLATE INSTALL WITH THE WORD "UP" OR BUTTON SHOWING
FRONT OF ENGINE

Valve lifter installation—1989–91 3.8L engine

cable. Remove the intake manifold and related parts.

2. Remove the crankcase ventilation hoses, PCV valve and elbows from the valve rocker arm covers.

3. Remove the valve rocker arm covers. Loosen the valve rocker arm fulcrum bolts and rotate the rocker arms to the side.

4. Remove the valve pushrods and identify them so that they can be installed in their original position.

5. Using a magnet, remove the lifters and place them in a rack so that they can be installed in their original bores.

NOTE: 5.0L engines are equipped with roller type hydraulic lifters.

6. Lifters and bores are to be lubricated with engine oil, classification SF, before installation. Installation is the reverse of the removal procedure.

Valve Lash

ADJUSTMENT

2.3L Engine

1. Disconnect the negative battery cable.

2. Remove the air cleaner. Remove the valve cover assembly.

3. Turn the engine until the No. 1 piston is at TDC of it's compression stroke, then position the camshaft so that the base circle of the lobe is facing the cam follower of the valve to be checked.

4. Using follower compressing tool T745-6565-A or equivalent, slowly apply pressure to the cam follower until the the lash adjuster is completely collapsed.

5. With follower collapsed, insert a feeler gauge between the base circle of the camshaft and follower. The clearance should not be more than 0.040–0.050 in.

6. If the clearance is excessive, remove the camshaft and inspect the follower and camshaft for excessive wear or damage.

7. Replace any worn or damaged components and recheck the clearance.

8. Install the valve cover, air cleaner and any other removed components.

3.8L Engine

On V6 engines the valve arrangement is I-E-I-E-I-E on the right bank and E-I-E-I-E-I on the left bank.

The valve lash is not truly adjustable. If the clearance is found to be excessive, there are replacement push-

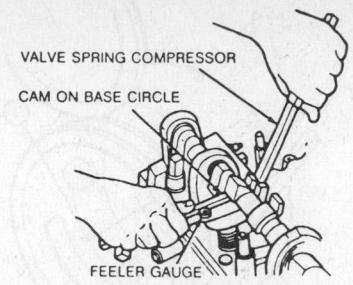

Valve lash adjustment—2.3L engine

rods available to compensate for some excess clearance.

NOTE: Valve stem to rocker clearance should be within specification with the tappet completely collapsed.

1. Disconnect the negative battery cable.

2. Remove the valve cover assembly on the side to be checked.

3. Turn the engine until the No. 1 piston is at TDC of it's compression stroke.

4. The following valves can be checked with the engine in this position:
    a. No. 1 intake—No. 1 exhaust
    b. No. 3 intake—No. 2 exhaust
    c. No. 6 intake—No. 4 exhaust

5. Rotate the engine 360 degrees and check the following valves:
    a. No. 2 intake—No. 3 exhaust
    b. No. 4 intake—No. 5 exhaust
    c. No. 5 intake—No. 6 exhaust

6. Check each of the lifters by placing the hydraulic lifter compressing tool on the rocker arm and slowly applying pressure to the tappet, until the tappet bottoms.

7. Hold the tappet in this position and check the clearance between the rocker arm and the and the valve stem tip. Clearance should not exceed ⅜ in.

8. Repeat this operation for each valve to be checked.

9. If the clearance is greater than specification, replace the pushrod with a longer one.

5.0L and 5.8L Engines

On V8 engines the valve arrangement is I-E-I-E-I-E on the right bank and E-I-E-I-E-I-E-I on the left bank.

The valve lash is not truly adjustable. If the clearance is found to be excessive, there are replacement pushrods available to compensate for some excess clearance.

Valve stem to rocker clearance should be within specification with the tappet completely collapsed.

To determine whether a shorter or a longer pushrod is necessary make the following check:

1987-88 5.0L Except HO Engine

1. Install an auxiliary starter switch. Crank the engine with the ignition switch off until the No. 1 piston is on TDC of it's compression stroke.

2. Position a tappet bleed down wrench tool No. T71P-6513-A or equivalent, on the rocker arm. Slowly apply pressure to bleed down the tappet until the plunger is completely bottomed. Hold the tappet in this position and check the available clearance between the rocker arm and the valve stem tip with a feeler gauge.

NOTE: If the clearance is less than specification, install a shorter pushrod.

If the clearance is greater than specification, install a longer pushrod.

3. Turn the engine until the No. 1 piston is at TDC of it's compression stroke.

4. The following valves can be checked with the engine in this 1st position:
    a. No. 1 intake—No. 1 exhaust
    b. No. 7 intake—No. 5 exhaust
    c. No. 8 intake—No. 4 exhaust

5. Rotate the engine 360 degrees (1 revolution) from the 1st position and check the following valves:
    a. No. 5 intake—No. 2 exhaust
    b. No. 4 intake—No. 6 exhaust

6. Rotate the engine 90 degrees (¼ revolution) from the 2nd position and check the following valves:
    a. No. 2 intake—No. 7 exhaust
    b. No. 3 intake—No. 3 exhaust
    c. No. 6 intake—No. 8 exhaust

1987–88 5.0L With HO Engine
1989–91 5.0L Engine
1987–91 5.8L Engine

1. Disconnect the brown lead (I terminal) and the red and blue lead (S terminal) at the starter relay.

2. Install an auxilary starter switch between the battery S terminals of the starter relay. Crank the engine with the ignition switch **OFF** until the No. 1 piston is on the TDC on the compression stroke.

3. Position a tappet bleed down wrench tool No. T71P-6513-A or equivalent, on the rocker arm. Slowley apply pressure to bleed down the tappet until the plunger is completely bottomed. Hold the tappet in this position and check the available clearance between the rocker arm and the valve stem tip with a feeler gauge.

NOTE: If the clearance is less than specification, install a shorter pushrod. If the clearance is greater than specification, install a longer pushrod.

4. Turn the engine until the No. 1 piston is at TDC of it's compression stroke. The following valves can be checked with the engine in this 1st position:

    a. No. 1 intake—No. 1 exhaust
    b. No. 4 intake—No. 3 exhaust
    c. No. 8 intake—No. 7 exhaust

5. Rotate the engine 360 degrees (1 revolution) from the 1st position and check the following valves:

    a. No. 3 intake—No. 2 exhaust
    b. No. 7 intake—No. 6 exhaust

6. Rotate the engine 90 degrees (¼ revolution) from the 2nd position and check the following valves:

    a. No. 2 intake—No. 4 exhaust
    b. No. 5 intake—No. 5 exhaust
    c. No. 6 intake—No. 8 exhaust

Rocker Arms

REMOVAL & INSTALLATION

2.3L Engine

1. Disconnect the negative battery cable. Remove the valve rocker arm cover and associated parts, as required.

2. Rotate the camshaft so that the base circle of the cam is facing the cam follower of the cylinder to be worked on.

3. Using valve spring compressor, collapse the lash adjuster and/or depress the valve spring, if necessary, and slide the cam follower over the lash adjuster and out.

4. Lift the hydraulic lash adjuster.

5. Place the hydraulic lash adjuster in position in the bore.

6. Using valve spring compressor, collapse the lash adjuster as necessary, to position the cam follower over the lash adjuster, and the valve stem. It may also be necessary to compress the valve spring.

7. Before rotating the camshaft to the next position, be sure the lash adjuster just installed is fully compressed and released.

8. Clean the gasket surfaces of the valve cover and cylinder head adhesive. Allow to dry past the "wet" stage and then install gasket in valve cover. Coat cylinder head contact surfaces with the same adhesive, allowing the adhesive to dry past the "wet" stage. Install the valve cover and gasket, making sure locating tabs are properly positioned in slots in cover.

9. Install 8 screws and tighten to 62–97 inch lbs. (7–11 Nm).

3.8L Engine

1987–88

1. Disconnect the negative battery cable.

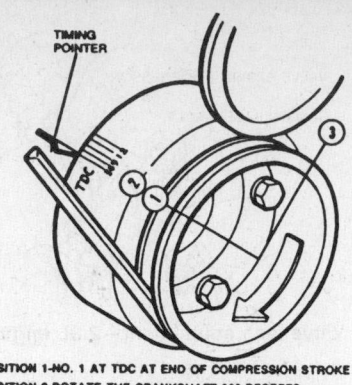

POSITION 1–NO. 1 AT TDC AT END OF COMPRESSION STROKE
POSITION 2–ROTATE THE CRANKSHAFT 360 DEGREES (ONE REVOLUTION) CLOCKWISE FROM POSITION 1
POSITION 3–ROTATE THE CRANKSHAFT 90 DEGREES (1/4 REVOLUTION) CLOCKWISE FROM POSITION 2

Valve adjustment—5.0L and 5.8L engines

2. Remove the spark plug wire routing clips from the rocker arm cover attaching studs.

3. To remove the left hand cover, remove the oil fill cap and disconnect and reposition the exhaust heat control valve vacuum tube.

4. To remove the right hand cover, reposition the air cleaner assembly and heat tube and remove the PCV valve.

5. Remove the cover attaching screws.

6. Remove the rocker arm fulcrum bolt and rocker arm.

7. Lubricate all parts with heavy SF oil before installation. When installing, rotate the crankshaft until the lifter is on the base of the cam circle (low point, no lift) and assemble the rocker arm and fulcrums. Torque the fulcrum bolts to 19–25 ft. lbs.

8. Clean the gasket surfaces and install a new cover gasket.

9. Tighten the cover bolts to 80–106 inch lbs.

10. The remainder of the installation is the reverse of removal.

1989–91

1. Disconnect the negative battery cable.

2. Remove the spark plug wire routing clips from the rocker arm cover attaching studs.

3. To remove the left hand cover:

    a. Remove the oil fill cap.
    b. On the supercharged engines, remove the intercooler tubes and the oil cooler inlet tubes.
    c. Remove the crankcase vent tube.

4. To remove the right hand cover:

    a. Reposition the air cleaner.
    b. Remove the PCV valve.
    c. On supercharged engines, remove the air inlet tube and remove the throttle body assembly.

5. Lubricate all parts with heavy SF oil before installation. When install-

ing, rotate the crankshaft until the lifter is on the base of the cam circle (low point, no lift) and assemble the rocker arm and fulcrums. Torque the fulcrum bolts to 19–25 ft. lbs.

6. Clean the gasket surfaces and install a new cover gasket.

7. Tighten the cover bolts to 80–106 inch lbs.

8. The remainder of the installation is the reverse of removal.

5.0L and 5.8L Engines

1. Disconnect the negative battery cable.

2. To remove the right hand cover, disconnect the PCV closure tube from the oil fill stand pipe at the rocker cover.

3. Remove the thermactor by-pass valve and air supply hoses as necessary to provide access.

4. Disconnect the spark plug wires from the spark plugs and move out of the way.

5. To remove the left hand rocker cover, disconnect the wires at the solenoid mounted on the cover, if so equipped, then remove the cover attaching bolts and remove the cover.

6. Remove the rocker arm fulcrum bolt, fulcrum seat and rocker arm.

7. Lubricate all parts with heavy SF oil before installation. When installing, rotate the crankshaft until the lifter is on the base of the cam circle (low point, no lift) and assemble the rocker arm. Torque the bolts to 18–25 ft. lbs.

8. Clean the gasket surfaces and install a new cover gasket.

9. Tighten the cover in 2 steps. Tighten the bolts to 3–5 ft. lbs. (1987), 6–9 ft. lbs. (1988 5.0L engine), 3.5 ft; lbs. (1988 5.8L engine), 10–13 ft. lbs. (1989–91 5.0L engine), 34–42 ft. lbs. (1989–91 5.8L engine) and 2 minutes later tighten the bolts to the same specification.

10. The remainder of the installation is the reverse of removal.

Intake Manifold

REMOVAL & INSTALLATION

2.3L Engine

1. Disconnect the negative battery cable.

2. Release the fuel system pressure.

3. Disconnect and label the electrical connectors at:

    a. the air bypass valve
    b. the throttle positioning sensor
    c. injector wiring harness
    d. knock sensor
    e. fan temperature sensor and coolant temperature sensor

2. Disconnect the upper intake

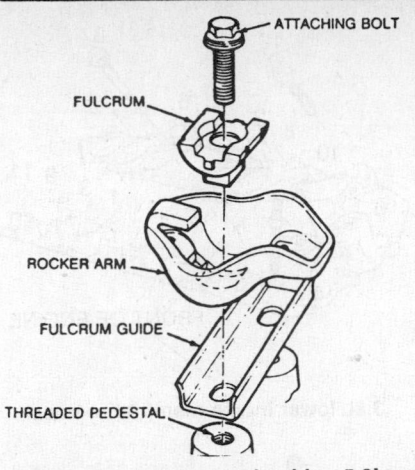

Rocker arm, fulcrum and guide—5.0L and 5.8L engines

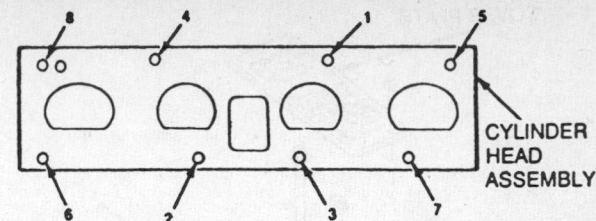

Manifold to cylinder head torque sequence—2.3L engine

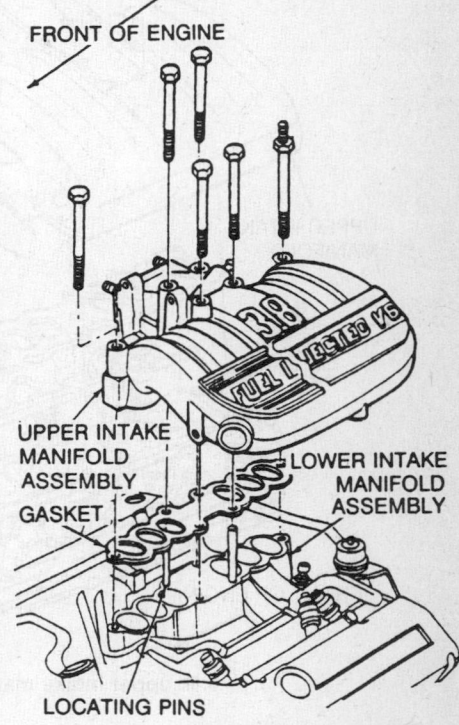

3.8L upper intake manifold removal

manifold vacuum fitting connections by disconnecting the vacuum line fitting at the cast air tube. Disconnect the rear vacuum line at the dash panel tree. Remove the vacuum line to the EGR valve and the vacuum line to the fuel pressure regulator. Label all lines for reinstallation identification.

3. Disconnect the throttle linkage. Unbolt the accelerator cable from the bracket and position the cable out of the way.

4. Remove the bolts that attach the cast air tube/intercooler assembly to the turbocharger.

5. Remove the nuts that attach the air throttle body to the fuel charging assembly.

6. Separate the cast air tube/intercooler from the turbocharger.

7. Remove and discard the mounting gasket between the cast tube and the turbocharger. Remove the throttle body and cast tube.

8. Disconnect the PCV system hose from the fitting on the underside of the upper intake manifold.

9. Disconnect the water bypass hose at the lower intake manifold.

10. Loosen the EGR flange nut and disconnect the EGR tube.

11. Remove the fuel injector wiring harness bracket retaining nuts and the bracket after separating the dipstick bracket.

12. Remove the upper intake manifold retaining bolts and/or studs and remove the upper intake manifold assembly.

13. Relieve the fuel system pressure and disconnect the push-connect fuel supply line.

14. Disconnect the fuel return line from the fuel supply manifold.

15. Disconnect the electrical connectors from the fuel injectors and move the harness aside.

16. Remove the fuel supply manifold retaining bolts and remove the mani-

fold carefully. Injectors can be removed at this time by exerting a slight twisting/pulling motion.

17. Remove the bottom and the top retaining bolts from the lower manifold. Remove the manifold.

To install:

18. Clean and inspect all mounting surfaces of the fuel charge manifolds and cylinder head.

19. Clean and oil all stud threads. Install a new mounting gasket over the studs.

20. Install the lower manifold to the cylinder head with lift bracket in position. Install the 4 upper manifold bolts finger tight. Install the 4 remaining bolts. Tighten all bolts on 1987–88 vehicles to 12–15 ft. lbs. in the proper torque sequence. Tighten all bolts on 1989–91 vehicles to 5–7 ft. lbs., then to 20–29 ft. lbs. in the proper torque sequence.

21. Install the remaining components in the reverse order of removal. Fuel supply manifold bolts are tighten to 12–15 ft. lbs. Upper manifold mounting bolts 15–22 ft. lbs. Dipstick and injector wiring harness bolts 15–22 ft. lbs. Cast air tube to turbocharger 14–21 ft. lbs. Air throttle body mounting 12–15 ft. lbs.

3.8L and 5.0L Engines with EFI—Except 3.8L Supercharged

UPPER INTAKE MANIFOLD

1. Disconnect the negative battery cable.

2. Relieve the fuel system pressure.

3. Disconnect the electrical connectors at the air bypass valve, throttle position sensor and EGR position sensor.

4. Disconnect the throttle linkage at the throttle ball and the transmission linkage from the throttle body. Remove the 2 bolts securing the cable bracket to the intake manifold and position out of the way.

5. Disconnect and tag the upper intake manifold vacuum lines. Disconnect the vacuum line to the EGR valve and the fuel pressure regulator.

6. Disconnect the vacuum connection to the canister purge line.

7. Remove the PCV vent closure tube at the throttle body and discon-

nect the hose at the rear of the manifold.

8. Remove the EGR coolant lines from the fittings on the EGR spacer.

9. Remove the 6 upper intake manifold retaining bolts. Remove the manifold and the throttle body as an assembly.

To install:

10. Clean and inspect the mounting surfaces.

11. Install the upper manifold and throttle body assembly and install the 6 mounting bolts. Torque the mounting bolts to 12–18 ft. lbs.

12. Reconnect all vacuum lines and electrical connections.

13. Connect the throttle linkage and bracket to the manifold.

LOWER INTAKE MANIFOLD

1. Disconnect the negative battery cable and relieve fuel system pressure.

2. Remove the upper intake manifold.

3. Disconnect the crossover fuel line from the fuel rail assembly. Remove

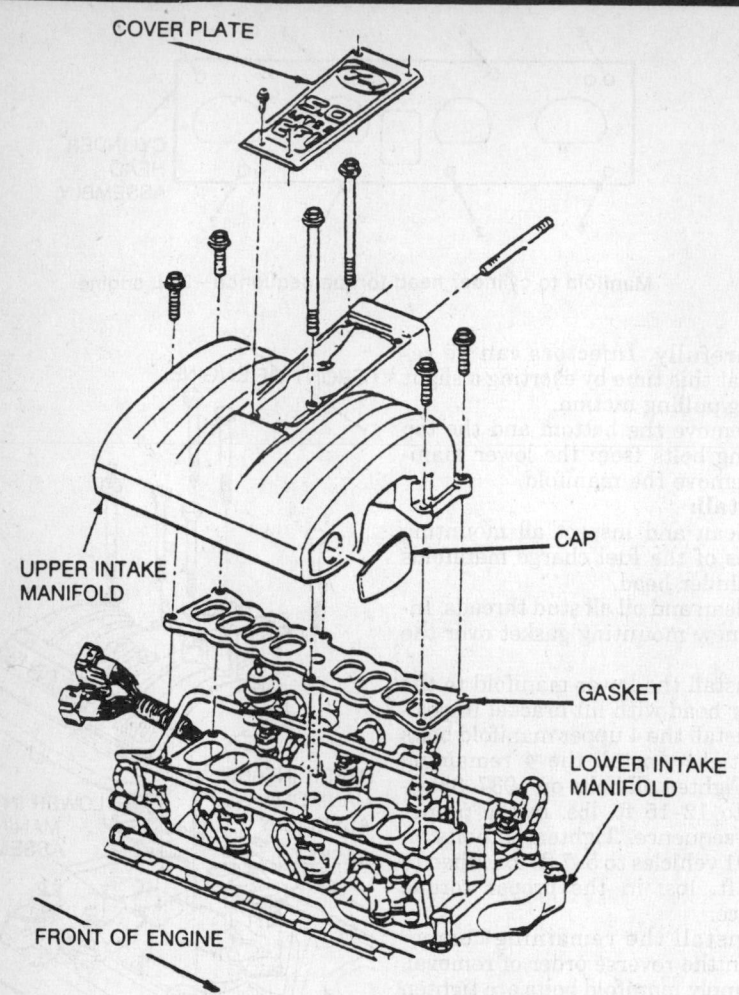

5.0L upper intake manifold removal

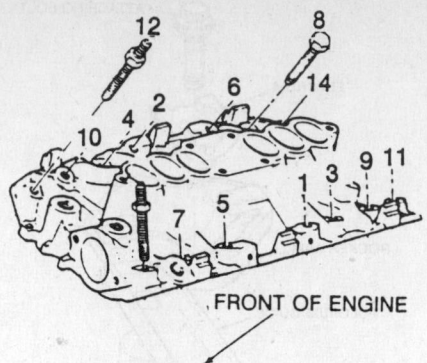

3.8L lower intake manifold removal

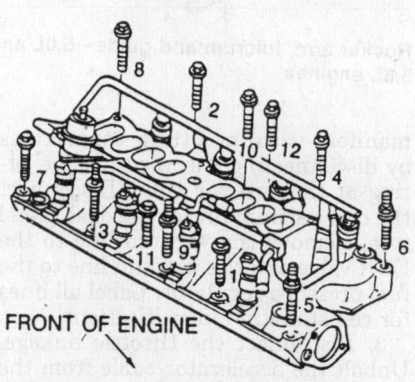

5.0L lower intake manifold removal

the injector electrical harness connector.

4. Remove the 4 fuel rail retaining bolts. Remove the fuel rail and the injectors as an assembly.

NOTE: To remove the fuel injectors from the manifold, use a back and forth twisting motion while pulling upward.

5. Disconnect the coolant bypass hose at the manifold. Disconnect the upper radiator hose at the thermostat housing.

6. Remove the heater tube, elbow and attaching bracket from the manifold. Lay the heater tube and bracket aside.

7. If equipped with air conditioning, remove the compressor support bracket.

8. Remove the lower intake manifold mounting bolts and remove the manifold.

NOTE: The front and rear of the manifold are sealed with RTV type sealer. It may be necessary to pry the manifold from the block

to break the seal. Use care not to damage the machined surface of the manifold or engine.

To install:

9. Clean all mating surfaces. Use new gaskets, apply a continuous ⅛ in. bead of RTV silicone sealer or equivalent at each corner where the cylinder and manifold meet. Apply a $^{1}/_{16}$ in. bead of RTV sealer or equivalent along the outer edge of the gaskets.

10. Carefully lower the intake manifold into position. Check the outer edge of the manifold to make sure that the gaskets stayed in place.

11. Install the manifold bolts and tighten in sequence to 23–25 ft. lbs.

NOTE: On 3.8L engines torque the manifold in 3 steps: first to 8 ft. lbs., then to 15 ft. lbs. and finally to 24 ft. lbs.

12. Install the coolant lines and hoses. Install the fuel rail assembly and the heater tube. If equipped with air conditioning, install the compressor support bracket.

13. Install the upper intake manifold

and throttle body assembly. Connect all electrical leads. Reconnect the fuel lines and the vacuum lines.

14. Check the coolant level and fill. Run the engine and check for fluid leaks.

3.8L Supercharged Engine

1. Disconnect the negative battery cable.

2. Relieve the fuel system pressure.

3. Remove the supercharger assembly.

4. Remove the thermostat housing and the thermostat.

5. Remove the temperature sending unit.

6. Remove the heater elbow and the vacuum hoses.

7. Remove the intake manifold retaining bolts and remove the manifold. If the manifold will not pull off easily, pry up on the edge to break the seal.

To install:

8. Clean all gasket mating surfaces. Check for nicked or burred edges on the sealing surfaces.

9. To install the intake manifold, lightly oil all attaching bolts and studs.

10. Apply a dab of gasket and trim adhesive or equivalent, to the cylinder head mating surfaces and install new intake manifold gaskets.

11. Apply a thin bead of silicone sealant to the points where the block and the cylinder head meet.

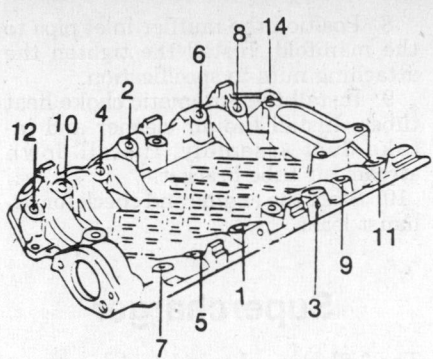

Intake manifold torque sequence—3.8L SC

12. Install new intake manifold seal end gaskets. Lower the intake manifold into position on the block.

13. Install the retaining bolts and tighten in numerical sequence to the correct torque.

14. Install the temperature sending unit, thermostat and housing.

15. Install the heater elbow and the vacuum hoses.

16. Install the supercharger assembly. Run the engine to normal operating temperature and check for leaks.

5.8L Engine

1. Disconnect the negative battery cable. Drain the cooling system, disconnect the upper radiator hose from the thermostat housing and the bypass hose from the manifold.

2. On all engines, remove the air cleaner and intake duct.

3. Disconnect the high tension lead and wires from the coil. Disconnect the engine wiring loom and position out of the way.

4. Disconnect the spark plug wires at the plugs by twisting and pulling on the molded plug cap only. Remove the distributor cap and wires as an assembly. Disconnect the vacuum hose(s) from the distributor. Disconnect the temperature sending unit wire.

5. Mark the position of the rotor and distributor body in relation to the manifold, remove the distributor holddown bolt and remove the distributor.

6. Remove the thermactor by pass valve and air supply hoses, if equipped.

7. Remove all vacuum lines from the manifold.

8. Disconnect the fuel line and vacuum hoses at the carburetor. Disconnect the accelerator linkage and downshift linkage, if so equipped and position out of the way.

9. Disconnect the crankcase vent hose at the rocker cover.

10. If equipped with air conditioning, remove the compressor mounting brackets from the manifold and posi-

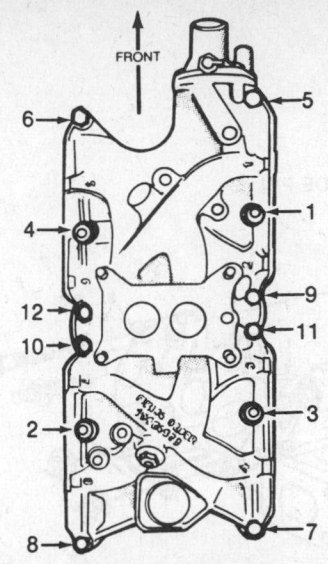

Intake manifold tightening sequence— 5.8L carbureted engine

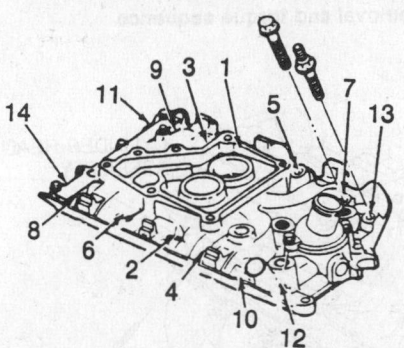

3.8L intake manifold torque sequence— CFI

tion the compressor out of the way. Do not disconnect any air conditioning. Also, remove the coil.

11. Remove the intake manifold and carburetor as an assembly. Be careful not to damage any gasket sealing surfaces.

To install:

12. Clean the mating surfaces of the manifold, block and heads. Apply a ⅛ in. bead of silicone sealer to the engine block to cylinder head mating surfaces.

13. Position the new end seals into place on the block, pressing the locating tabs into place. Position new manifold gaskets into place on the heads and apply a ⅛ in. bead of silicone sealer to the end seal to manifold gasket joints.

14. Carefully, lower the manifold into place. After it is positioned, check the seal area to be sure the seals are properly positioned. If they are not, remove the manifold and reposition the seals.

15. Torque the manifold to specification and in sequence in 3 stages. The

rest of installation is the reverse of removal. After installation, run the engine to operating temperature and retorque the manifold bolts.

Exhaust Manifold

REMOVAL & INSTALLATION

2.3L Engine

1. Disconnect the negative battery cable.

2. Disconnect the exhaust header pipe at the manifold.

3. Remove the heat shield. Remove the turbocharger, if equipped.

4. Disconnect any brackets from the manifold. Remove the manifold retaining bolts and remove the manifold.

5. Clean and check all gasket surfaces.

6. Installation is the reverse of the removal procedure.

3.8L Engine

LEFT SIDE

1. Disconnect the negative battery cable. Remove oil level dipstick tube support bracket.

2. Disconnect EGO sensor at the wiring connector, if equipped.

3. Disconnect wires from spark plugs.

4. Raise and safely support the vehicle.

5. Remove manifold to exhaust pipe attaching nuts.

6. Disconnect exhaust heat control valve vacuum line, if equipped.

7. Lower vehicle.

8. Remove exhaust manifold attaching bolts and manifold.

9. If a new exhaust manifold is being installed, remove EGO sensor, if equipped, and exhaust heat control valve, if equipped.

To install:

10. Installation is the reverse of removal procedure.

11. If equipped with an EGO sensor, coat the threads with high temperature anti-seize compound. Install the sensor into the exhaust manifold and tighten to 27–33 ft. lbs. (37–45 Nm).

12. Install the remaining manifold attaching bolts and tighten to 15–22 ft. lbs. (20–30 Nm).

RIGHT SIDE

1. Disconnect the negative battery cable. Remove air cleaner assembly and heat tube.

2. Disconnect thermactor hose from the downstream air tube check valve, if equipped.

3. Remove EGO sensor at the wiring connector, if equipped.

4. Disconnect coil secondary wire from the coil and the wires from the spark plugs.

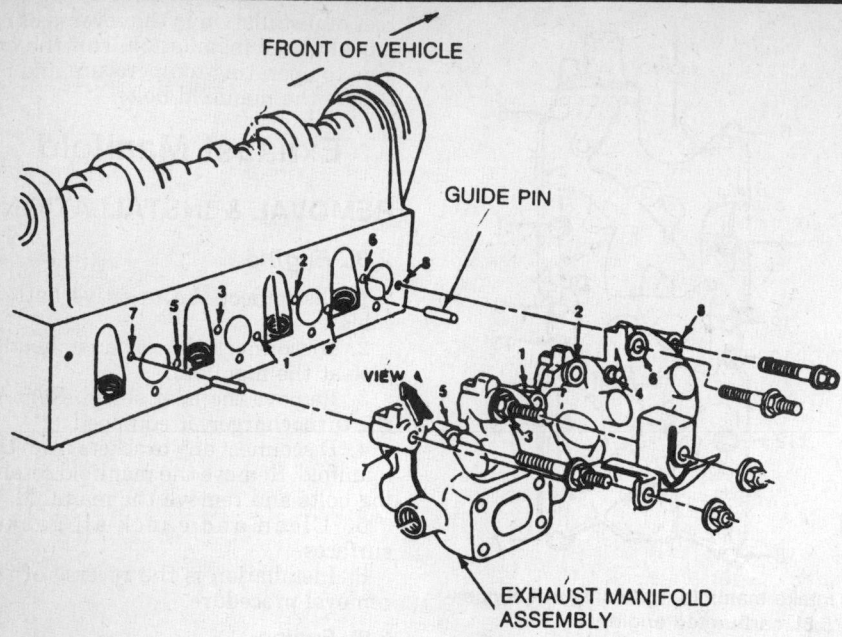

FRONT OF VEHICLE

GUIDE PIN

VIEW A

EXHAUST MANIFOLD ASSEMBLY

2.3L OHC/TURBO exhaust manifold removal and torque sequence

5. Remove spark plugs. Remove outer heat shroud.
6. Raise and safely support the vehicle.
7. Remove transmission dipstick tube.
8. Remove thermactor downstream air tube. Use an EGR clamp cutter and crimping tool to cut the tube clamp at the underbody catalyst, if equipped.
9. Remove manifold to exhaust pipe attaching nuts.
10. Lower the vehicle.
11. Remove exhaust manifold attaching bolts. Remove manifold and inner heat shroud as an assembly.
To install:
12. Installation is the reverse of removal procedures.
13. Install manifold attaching bolts and tighten to 15–25 ft. lbs. (20–30 Nm).
14. Connect exhaust pipe to the manifold and tighten the attaching nuts to 16–24 ft. lbs. (21–32 Nm).

5.0L and 5.8L Engines

1. Disconnect the negative battery cable. On a right exhaust manifold, remove the air cleaner and intake duct assembly and down stream air tube bracket, except Crown Victoria, Grand Marquis, Town Car, Mark VII and Continental.
2. Disconnect the automatic choke heat tubes. On left exhaust manifolds, remove the oil dipstick and tube assembly, air cleaner and inlet duct assembly for Crown Victoria, Grand Marquis, Town Car, Mark VII and Continental.

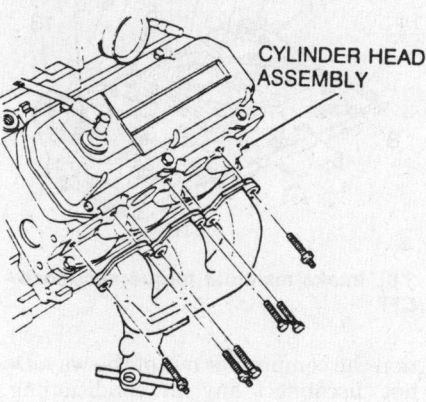

CYLINDER HEAD ASSEMBLY

3.8L exhaust manifold mounting

3. Remove speed control bracket, if equipped.
4. Disconnect the exhaust manifold from the muffler inlet pipe. Remove the attaching nuts and then remove the spark plug wires and spark plugs. Disconnect the exhaust gas oxygen (EGO) sensor, if equipped.
5. Remove the attaching bolts and washers and remove the exhaust manifold.
6. Clean the mating surfaces of the exhaust manifold and cylinder head. Clean the mounting flange of the exhaust manifold and muffler inlet pipe.
7. Position the exhaust manifold on the cylinder head and install the attaching bolts and washers. Working from the center to the ends, tighten the bolts to specifications. Install spark plugs and spark plug wires. Connect the Exhaust Gas Oxygen sensor (EGO), if equipped.

8. Position the muffler inlet pipe to the manifold. Install the tighten the attaching nuts to specification.
9. Install the automatic choke heat tubes. Install the air cleaner and intake duct assembly. Install down stream air tube bracket.
10. Start the engine and check for exhaust leaks.

Supercharger

The 3.8L supercharged engine uses a 2 rotor supercharger. The supercharger is a positive displacement pump that forces an increased volume of intake air into the engine. This causes an increase in air pressure and more power to the engine.

The supercharger is serviceable only by replacement. Disassembly of the supercharger unit may void any manufacturers warranty.

REMOVAL & INSTALLATION

1. Disconnect the negative battery cable. Drain the cooling system. Relieve the fuel system pressure.
2. Remove the air cleaner assembly, including air intake duct and heater tube.
3. Disconnect the accelerator cable at the throttle body and disconnect the speed control cable, if equipped.
4. Disconnect the TV cable at the throttle body. Remove the accelerator cable bracket and place it to the side.
5. Disconnect the thermactor hose at the check valve. Disconnect the flexible fuel lines over the valve covers and at the fuel injector rail.
6. Disconnect the upper radiator hose and the coolant bypass hose, at the manifold.
7. Disconnect the heater tube at the intake manifold and remove the tube support bracket, with the fuel lines attached and set it aside.
8. Disconnect vacuum lines at the fuel rail and the supercharger. Disconnect and tag all of the electrical connectors.
9. Remove the air conditioning compressor support bracket. Disconnect the PCV hose from the supercharger and the valve cover.
10. Remove the bolts that retain the supercharger-to-intercooler tube and disconnect the supercharger-to-lower intake manifold inlet tube.
11. Relieve the accessory drive belt tension and remove the supercharger drive belt from the super charger pulley.
12. Remove the supercharger retaining bolts and remove the supercharger from the lower intake manifold.
13. Remove the fuel rail assembly

from the lower intake manifold. Remove the heater water outlet hose.

To install:

14. Install the fuel injectors and fuel rail assembly. Install a new supercharger-to-intake manifold gasket and install the supercharger in position.

15. Install the mounting bolts, tighten the bolts on the supercharger first, to 52–70 ft. lbs. Tighten the air inlet-to-lower manifold bolts to 20–28 ft. lbs.

16. Install the air conditioning compressor bracket. Reconnect all of the electrical connectors and vacuum hoses.

17. Connect the heater tube to the heater elbow. Reconnect the supercharger-to-intercooler tube.

18. Install the heater tube support bracket. Connect the coolant bypass hose and the upper radiator hose.

19. Reconnect the fuel lines to the fuel rail assembly. Connect the flexible fuel lines over the valve covers.

20. Install the accelerator cable bracket. Reconnect the accelerator cable and the TV cable.

21. Fill the cooling system to the correct level with the correct coolant and run the engine to normal operating temperature.

22. Bleed the cooling system. Check for leaks.

Turbocharger

REMOVAL & INSTALLATION

NOTE: The turbocharger is serviced by replacement only.

1. Remove negative cable from the battery.

2. Drain the coolant from the radiator. Loosen upper and lower clamps securing hoses to intercooler.

3. Disconnect aspirator hoses at intercooler and loosen nut securing bracket to engine. Remove intercooler by first lifting and then pulling out.

4. Remove the hex head bolts retaining the throttle body discharge tube to the turbocharger. Also, loosen upper clamp on inlet hose.

5. Identify and disconnect vacuum hose tubes.

6. Disconnect PCV tube from the turbocharger air inlet elbow.

7. Remove throttle body discharge tube and hose as an assembly.

8. Disconnect electrical ground wire from turbocharger air inlet elbow.

9. Remove turbocharger oil supply line.

10. Disconnect oxygen sensor connector at turbocharger.

11. Raise and safely support the vehicle.

12. Disconnect exhaust pipe by re-

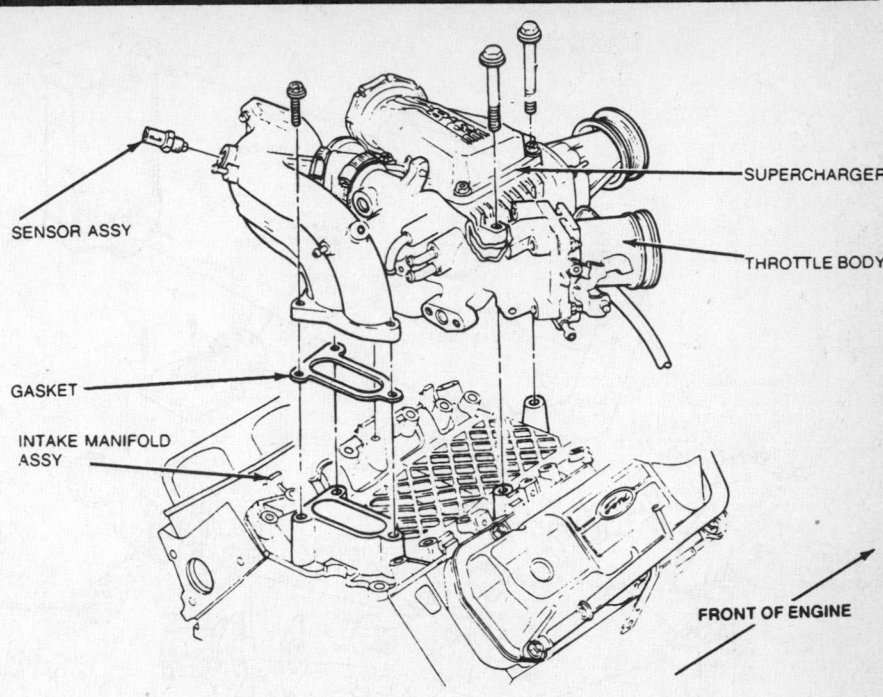

Removing the supercharger assembly – 3.8L SC

moving the exhaust pipe to turbocharger bolts.

13. Remove the bolts from oil return line located below the turbocharger. Do not kink or damage line as it is removed.

14. Remove the lower turbocharger bracket to block bolt.

15. Lower the vehicle.

16. Remove the front lower turbocharger retaining bolt.

17. Simultaneously, remove the remaining nuts as turbocharger is slid off studs.

18. Remove turbocharger assembly from vehicle.

To install:

19. Position a new turbocharger gasket on mounting studs. Be sure the bead faces outward.

20. Install the turbocharger assembly on the mounting studs.

21. Install turbocharger bracket on the 2 lower studs. Start the lower retaining nuts followed by the upper retaining nuts.

22. Raise and safely support the vehicle.

23. Install lower bracket to block bolt and tighten to 28–40 ft. lbs. (38–54 Nm).

24. Install a new oil return line gasket. Bolt oil return line to turbocharger. Tighten bolts to 12–21 ft. lbs. (19–29 Nm).

25. Install exhaust pipe. Tighten retaining nuts to 25–35 ft. lbs. (34–47 Nm).

26. Lower vehicle.

27. Using 4 new nuts, tighten the

turbocharger to exhaust manifold nuts to 28–40 ft. lbs. (38–54 Nm).

28. Install air inlet tube to turbocharger inlet elbow. Tighten bolts to 15–22 ft. lbs. (20–30 Nm). Tighten hose clamp to 15–22 inch lbs. (1.7–2.5 Nm).

29. Install PCV tube fitting and tighten clamp to 15–22 inch lbs. (1.7–2.5 Nm).

30. Connect all vacuum lines.

31. Connect oxygen sensor.

32. Connect electrical ground wire to air inlet elbow.

33. Install turbocharger oil supply line. Tighten fitting to 9–16 ft. lbs. (12–22 Nm).

34. Install air intake tube and clamp between turbocharger outlet and air intake throttle body. Tighten clamp to 15–20 ft. lbs. (20–27 Nm).

35. Connect ground cable to battery.

36. Start engine and check for leaks.

Timing Chain Front Cover

REMOVAL & INSTALLATION

3.8L, 5.0L and 5.8L Engines

1. Drain cooling system.

2. Disconnect the negative battery cable.

3. Remove air cleaner assembly and air intake duct. On supercharged engines remove the intercooler intake and outlet tubes.

4. Remove fan/clutch assembly and shroud.

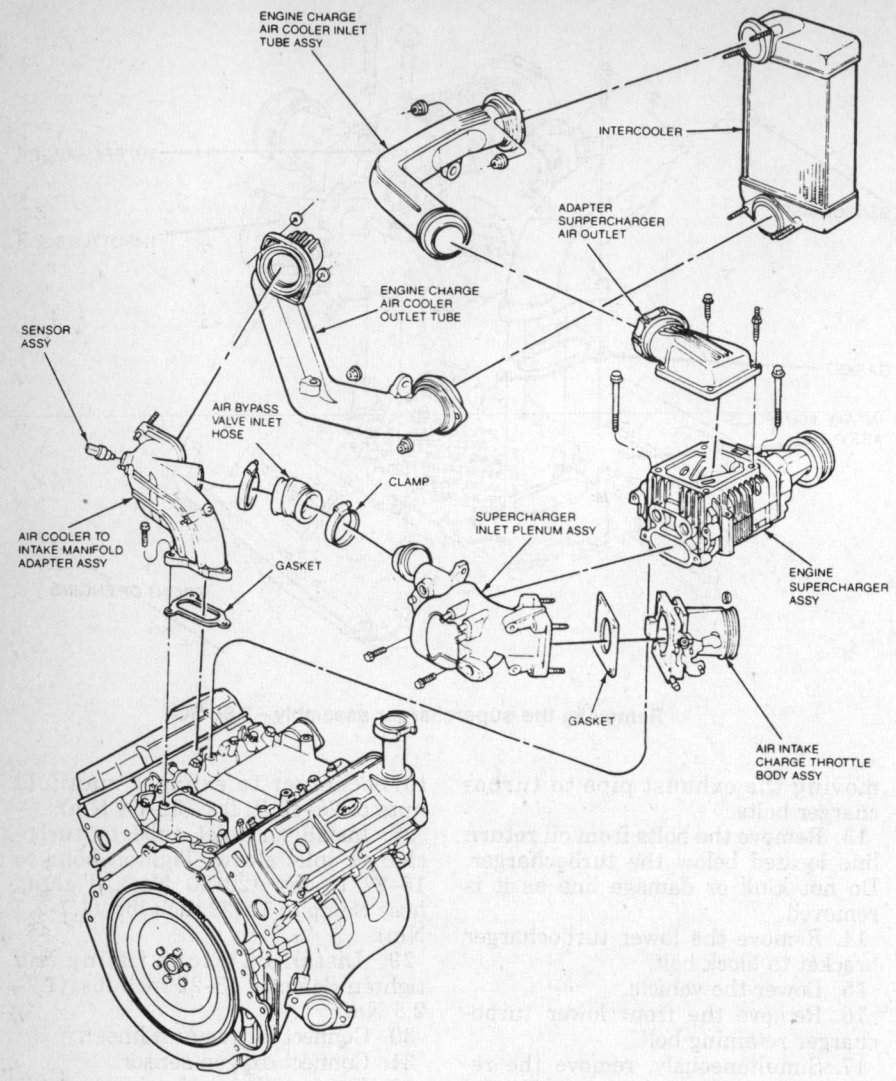

necessary to remove the oil pan, however, the oil pan should be covered to prevent debris from entering..

NOTE: On the 3.8L engine, the front cover cannot be removed without removing the oil pan.

17. Lower vehicle.
18. Remove front cover attaching bolts. It is not necessary to remove water pump.

NOTE: Do not overlook the cover attaching bolt located behind the oil filter adapter. The front cover will break if pried upon when all attaching bolts are not removed.

19. Remove ignition timing indicator.
20. Remove front cover and water pump as an assembly.

NOTE: On the 3.8L engine, the front cover contains the oil pump and intermediate shaft. If a new front cover is to be installed, remove the water pump, oil pump, oil filter adapter and intermediate shaft from the old front cover.

To install:
21. Installation is the reverse of the removal procedure. Lubricate crankshaft front oil seal with clean engine oil. Tighten all bolts to specifications.

Front Cover Oil Seal
REPLACEMENT

3.8L, 5.0L and 5.8L Engines

1. Disconnect the negative battery cable.
2. Remove the fan shroud assembly. Remove the cooling fan and pulley.
3. Remove the accessory drive belts.
4. Remove the crankshaft pulley, install puller on crankshaft damper and remove the damper.
5. Place front cover seal remover T70P–6B070–B or equivalent, onto the front cover plate over the front seal. Tighten the 2 through bolts to force the puller under the seal flange. Alternately tighten the puller bolts 1 turn at a time to remove the seal.
6. To install, use a new oil seal and coat with oil. Install the seal into tool T70P–6B070–A or equivalent. Install the tool on the front of the crankshaft and tighten adjuster screw to force the seal into the front cover.
7. Coat the outside of the seal and install the damper and pulley to the crankshaft.
8. Install the cooling fan and pulley. Install the accessory drive belts and adjust the belt tension. Attach the fan shroud to the radiator and run the engine to check for leaks.

Supercharger system components–3.8L SC

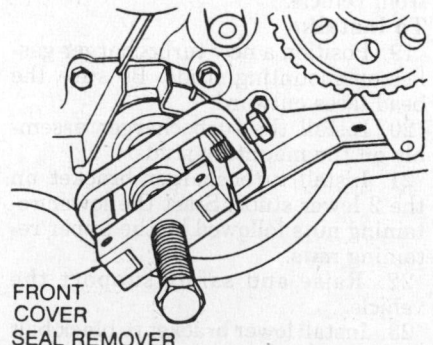

FRONT COVER SEAL REMOVER

2.3L front cover seal removal

5. Loosen accessory drive belt idler. Remove drive belt and water pump pulley.
6. If equipped with power steering, remove pump mounting brackets attaching bolts. Leaving the hoses connected, place the pump/bracket assembly aside in a position to prevent the fluid from leaking out.
7. If equipped with air conditioning, remove compressor front support bracket. Leave compressor in place.
8. Disconnect hoses at water pump.
9. Disconnect radiator upper hose at thermostat housing.
10. Disconnect coil wire from distributor cap and remove cap with the secondary wires attached. Remove distributor assembly.
11. If equipped with trip minder, remove the fuel flow meter support bracket. The fuel lines will support the flow meter.
12. Raise vehicle and safely support.

13. Remove crankshaft damper using puller.
14. Remove oil filter.
15. Disconnect radiator lower hose at the water pump.
16. On the 3.8L engine, remove the oil pan. On all other engines, it is not

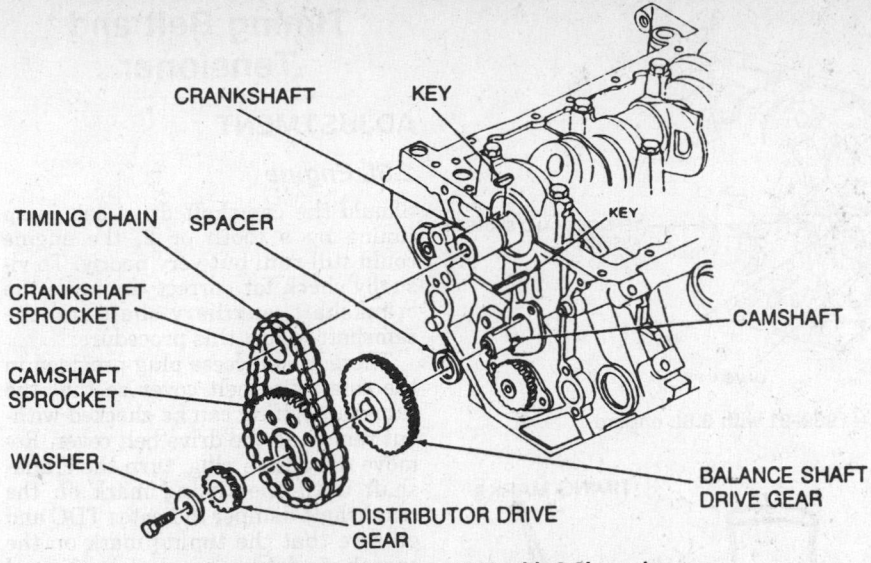

CRANKSHAFT KEY

TIMING CHAIN SPACER

CRANKSHAFT SPROCKET

CAMSHAFT SPROCKET

WASHER

KEY

CAMSHAFT

BALANCE SHAFT DRIVE GEAR

DISTRIBUTOR DRIVE GEAR

Timing chain and gears—1988 with 3.8L engine

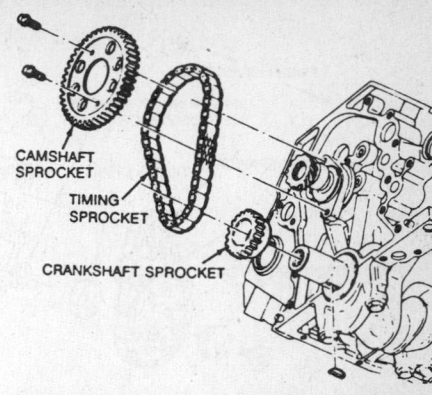

CAMSHAFT SPROCKET

TIMING SPROCKET

CRANKSHAFT SPROCKET

Timing chain and sprockets—1987 with 3.8L engine

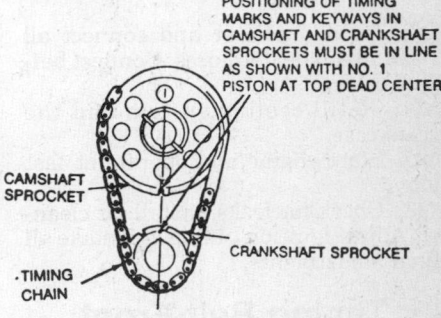

POSITIONING OF TIMING MARKS AND KEYWAYS IN CAMSHAFT AND CRANKSHAFT SPROCKETS MUST BE IN LINE AS SHOWN WITH NO. 1 PISTON AT TOP DEAD CENTER

CAMSHAFT SPROCKET

CRANKSHAFT SPROCKET

TIMING CHAIN

Timing chain and sprockets alignment 3.8L engine

Timing Chain and Sprockets

REMOVAL & INSTALLATION

3.8L, 5.0L and 5.8L Engines

1. Drain cooling system, remove air cleaner and disconnect the negative battery cable.

2. Disconnect the radiator hoses and remove the radiator.

3. Disconnect heater hose at water pump. Slide water pump by pass hose clamp toward the pump.

4. Loosen alternator mounting bolts at the alternator. Remove the alternator support bolt at the water pump. Remove thermactor (air) pump on all engines equipped. If equipped with power steering or air conditioning, unbolt the component, remove the belt and lay the pump aside with the lines attached. On supercharged models, disconnect the supercharger inlet and outlet tubes.

5. Remove the fan, spacer, pulley and drive belt.

6. Drain the crankcase.

7. Remove pulley from crankshaft pulley adapter. Remove cap screw and washer from front end of crankshaft. Remove crankshaft pulley adapter with a puller.

8. On models equipped with fuel injection, relieve the fuel system pressure. Disconnect fuel pump outlet line at the pump. Remove fuel pump retaining bolts and lay the pump to the side. Remove the engine oil dipstick. Remove the distributor on 3.8L engine.

NOTE: On the 3.8L engine, it is necessary to drop the oil pan be-fore the front cover cam be removed.**

9. Remove the front cover attaching bolts. On the 3.8L engine, remove the water pump and front cover as an assembly.

10. Remove the crankshaft oil slinger, if so equipped. On 1987 3.8L engine, remove the camshaft thrust button and spring.

NOTE: 1988 3.8L engine is equipped with an internal balance shaft. The balance shaft is driven off of the camshaft, by a gear positioned behind the camshaft timing sprocket. When removing the timing chain and sprockets, care should be taken to keep this gear in its proper position.

11. Check the timing chain deflection.

12. Crank engine until the timing sprocket timing marks are aligned at their closest together position.

13. Remove crankshaft sprocket cap screw, washers and fuel pump eccentric. Slide both sprockets and chain forward and off as an assembly.

To install:

14. Position sprockets and chain on the camshaft and crankshaft with both of the timing marks aligned at their closest together position. Install the fuel pump eccentric, washers and sprocket attaching bolt. Torque the sprocket attaching bolt to 40–45 ft. lbs.

15. Install the crankshaft front oil slinger.

NOTE: When replacing the front cover on the 1987 3.8L engine, RTV sealer is used. Apply an even ⅛ in. bead on the cover mating surface. 1988–91 3.8L engine uses a gasket.**

16. Clean all gasket mating surfaces and install a new front cover seal.

17. Coat a new cover gasket with sealer and position it on the block.

NOTE: On all engines, trim away the exposed portion of the oil pan gasket flush with the cylinder block. Cut and position the required portion of a new gasket to the oil pan, applying sealer to both sides of it. On 3.8L engines, after installing the cylinder front cover, install the oil pan using a new gasket.

18. Install front cover, using a crankshaft to cover alignment tool. Coat the threads of the attaching bolts with sealer. Torque attaching bolts to 12–15 ft. lbs.

19. Install the fuel pump, connect fuel pump outlet tube.

20. Install the crankshaft pulley adapter and torque attaching bolt. Install crankshaft pulley.

21. Install the water pump pulley, drive belt, spacer and fan.

22. Install the alternator support bolt at the water pump. Tighten the alternator mounting bolts. Adjust drive belt tension. Install the thermactor pump, if so equipped.

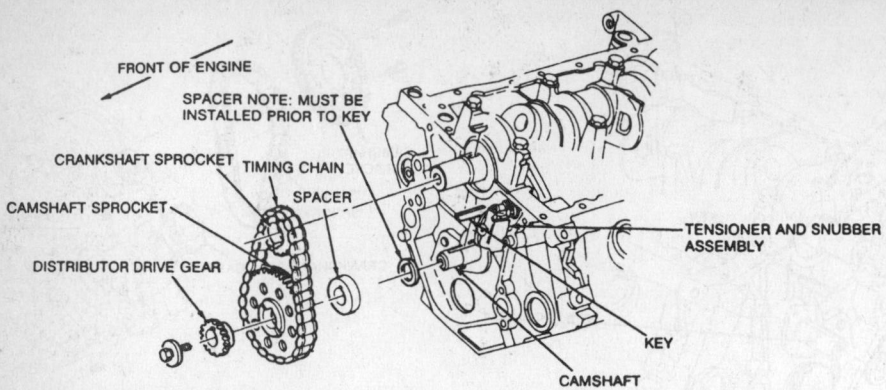

FRONT OF ENGINE

SPACER NOTE: MUST BE
INSTALLED PRIOR TO KEY

CRANKSHAFT SPROCKET   TIMING CHAIN

CAMSHAFT SPROCKET   SPACER

DISTRIBUTOR DRIVE GEAR

TENSIONER AND SNUBBER
ASSEMBLY

KEY

CAMSHAFT

Timing chain and sprockets—1989–91 with 3.8L engine

23. Install radiator and connect all coolant and heater hoses. Connect battery cables.

24. Refill cooling system and the crankcase.

25. Start engine and operate at fast idle.

26. Check for leaks, install air cleaner. Adjust ignition timing and make all final adjustments.

Timing Belt Front Cover

REMOVAL & INSTALLATION

2.3L Engine

1. Disconnect the negative battery cable and raise and support the vehicle safely, as necessary.

2. The front seal has been designed so that it is not necessary to remove the cylinder front cover with the engine in the chassis.

3. When disassembling the engine, first remove the front seal from the cover while the cover is still on the engine.

4. When assembling the engine, install the cover on the engine without the seal and then use tool to press the seal into place. This will avoid damage to the seal.

5. Before finally adjusting the cover into position and tightening the attaching bolts, use tool to position the cover in relation to the crankshaft. Tighten the bolts to 8–12 Nm (6–9 ft. lbs.) with this tool in place. This will assure that the timing belt does not interfere with the front cover when operating.

OIL SEAL REPLACEMENT

1. Disconnect the negative battery cable. Remove the front timing belt cover.

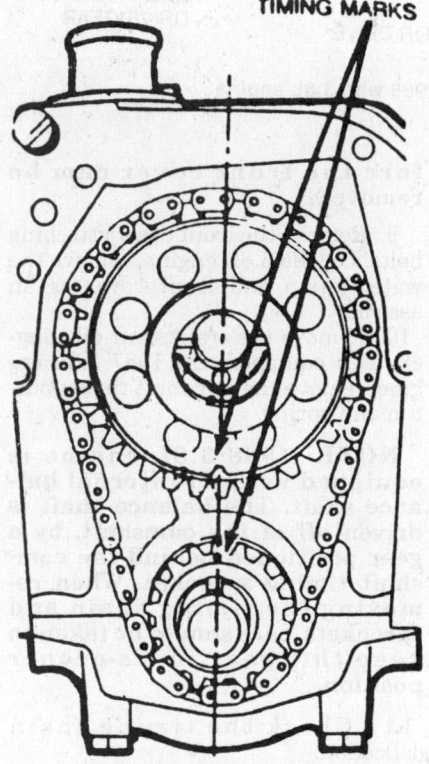

TIMING MARKS

5.0L and 5.8L timing mark alignment

2. Relieve the tension on the timing belt and remove it.

3. Remove the crankshaft sprocket using tool T74P–6306–A crankshaft sprocket remover or equivalent.

4. Using front seal removing tool T74P–6700–B or equivalent, place the jaws of the tool on the thin edge of the seal and remove the seal.

5. To install, lubricate the outer edge of the seal with light grease. Using front seal installer T74P–6150–A, place the seal on the tool and install the seal/tool into place.

6. Install the crankshaft sprocket and install the timing belt on to the timing gear.

7. Install the front cover. Run the engine and check for leaks.

Timing Belt and Tensioner

ADJUSTMENT

2.3L Engine

Should the camshaft drive belt jump timing by a tooth or 2, the engine could still run; but very poorly. To visually check for correct timing of the crankshaft, auxiliary shaft and the camshaft follow this procedure:

There is an access plug provided in the cam drive belt cover so that the camshaft timing can be checked without removing the drive belt cover. Remove the access plug, turn the crankshaft until the timing mark on the crankshaft damper indicates TDC and observe that the timing mark on the camshaft drive sprocket is aligned with the pointer on the inner belt cover. Also, the rotor of the distributor must align with the No. 1 cylinder firing position.

REMOVAL & INSTALLATION

1. Disconnect the negative battery cable. Set the engine with the No. 1 cylinder at TDC of it's compression stroke. The crankshaft and camshaft timing marks should align with their respective pointers and the distributor rotor should point to the No. 1 plug tower.

2. Loosen the adjustment bolts on the alternator and accessories and remove the drive belts. To provide clearance for removing the camshaft belt, remove the fan and pulley.

3. Remove the timing belt front cover.

4. Remove the distributor cap from

TIMING POINTER
MUST INDEX WITH
TIMING MARK
ON SPROCKET

ACCESS
PLUG

DISTRIBUTOR ROTOR
MUST ALIGN WITH
NO. 1 FIRING POSITION

TDC MARK ON COVER MUST
ALIGN
WITH MARK ON PULLEY

2.3L timing belt alignment check

the distributor and position it out of the way.

5. Loosen the belt tensioner adjustment and pivot bolts. Lever the tensioner away from the belt and retighten the adjustment bolt to hold it away.

6. Remove the crankshaft bolt and pulley. Remove the belt guide behind the pulley.

7. Remove the timing belt by sliding it off the camshaft pulley and off the engine.

To install:

8. Install the new belt over the crankshaft pulley first, then in an counterclockwise direction install it over the auxiliary shaft sprocket and the camshaft sprocket. Adjust the belt fore and aft so that it is centered on the sprockets.

9. Loosen the tensioner adjustment bolt, allowing it to spring back against the belt.

10. Rotate the crankshaft 2 complete turns in the normal rotation direction to remove any belt slack. Turn the crankshaft until the timing check marks are lined up. If the timing has slipped, remove the belt and repeat the procedure.

11. Tighten the tensioner adjustment bolt to 14–21 ft. lbs. and the pivot bolt to 28–40 ft. lbs.

12. Replace the belt guide and crankshaft pulley, distributor cap, belt outer cover, fan and pulley, drive belts and accessories. Adjust the accessory drive belt tension. Start the engine and check the ignition timing.

NOTE: Never turn the crankshaft in the opposite direction of normal rotation. Backward rotation of the crankshaft may cause the timing belt to slip and alter the timing.

Camshaft

REMOVAL & INSTALLATION

2.3L Engine

NOTE: The camshaft can be replaced with the cylinder head still mounted on the engine in the vehicle or with the cylinder head removed from the vehicle.

1. Disconnect the negative battery cable. Drain the cooling system. Remove the air cleaner assembly. On turbocharged engines, remove the intercooler to throttle body tube and the intercooler inlet tube. Remove the intercooler mounting bolts and remove the intercooler.

2. Label and remove all wires, electrical harnesses, vacuum lines and cables that will interfere with valve cover removal.

3. On fuel injected engines, relieve the fuel system pressure.

4. Remove the alternator and mounting brackets as an assembly and position to the side.

5. Remove the upper and lower radiator hoses. Remove the fan, motor and mounting shroud as an assembly.

6. Remove the valve cover.

7. Set the engine at No. 1 cylinder TDC on the compression stroke. Remove the timing belt.

8. Raise and safely support the front of the vehicle. Remove the right and left engine mount through bolts and joint to bracket retaining bolts.

9. Place a block of wood on a floor jack and raise the engine, carefully, as high as it will go. Place blocks of wood between the engine mounts. Lower the engine and lower the vehicle to the ground.

10. Remove the rocker arms.

11. Remove the camshaft drive gear attaching bolt and washer and remove the gear and belt guide plate.

12. The camshaft is removed through the front of the cylinder head after removing the front cam bearing seal. Use a new seal during assembly.

To install:

13. Reverse the removal procedure to install the camshaft and cylinder head, if removed.

NOTE: After any procedure requiring removal of the rocker arms, each lash adjuster must be fully collapsed after assembly, then released. This must be done before the camshaft is turned.

3.8L, 5.0L and 5.8L Engines

1. Disconnect the negative battery cable. Remove the intake manifold.

2. Remove the cylinder front cover, timing chain and sprockets.

3. Remove the grille and radiator. On vehicles with air conditioning, remove the condenser retaining bolts and position it out of the way. Do not disconnect refrigerant lines.

4. Remove the rocker arm covers.

5. Remove the pushrods and lifters and keep them in order so that they can be installed in their original positions.

6. Remove the camshaft thrust plate and washer, if so equipped. Remove the camshaft from the front of the engine. Use care not to damage camshaft lobes or journals while removing the cam from the engine.

7. Before installing the camshaft, coat the lobes with engine assembly lubricant, the journals and valve parts with heavy oil.

8. Reverse the procedure to install.

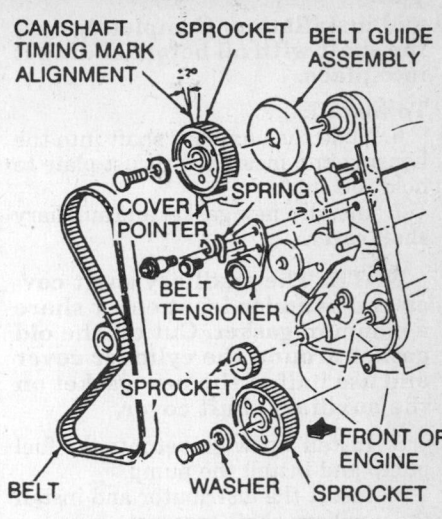

2.3L timing belt and sprockets

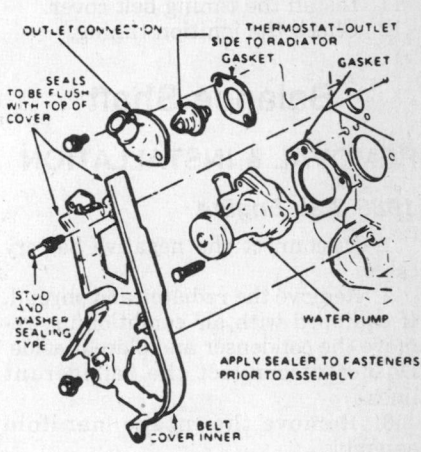

Water pump, thermostat and inner timing belt cover—2.3L engine

Auxiliary Shaft

REMOVAL & INSTALLATION

2.3L Engine

1. Disconnect the negative battery cable. Remove the front timing belt cover.

2. Remove the drive belt. Remove the auxiliary shaft sprocket. A puller may be necessary to remove the sprocket.

3. Remove the distributor and fuel pump.

4. Remove the auxiliary shaft cover and thrust plate.

5. Withdraw the auxiliary shaft from the block.

NOTE: The distributor drive gear and the fuel pump eccentric on the auxiliary shaft must not be allowed to touch the auxiliary shaft bearings during removal

and installation. Completely coat the shaft with oil before sliding it into place.

To install:

6. Slide the auxiliary shaft into the housing and insert the thrust plate to hold the shaft.

7. Install a new gasket and auxiliary shaft cover.

NOTE: The auxiliary shaft cover and cylinder front cover share a common gasket. Cut off the old gasket around the cylinder cover and use half of the new gasket on the auxiliary shaft cover.

8. Install a new gasket into the fuel pump and install the pump.

9. Insert the distributor and install the auxiliary shaft sprocket.

10. Align the timing marks and install the timing belt.

11. Install the timing belt cover.

12. Check the ignition timing.

Balance Shaft

REMOVAL & INSTALLATION

1988 3.8L Engine

1. Disconnect the negative battery cable.

2. Remove the radiator and shroud. If equipped with air conditioning, remove the condenser and place it aside. Do not disconnect the refrigerant lines.

3. Remove the intake manifold assembly.

4. Remove the cylinder front cover assembly.

5. Remove the camshaft timing sprocket and the timing chain. Remove the balance shaft drive gear from the camshaft end. Mark the relationship of the balance shaft with the driven gear.

6. Remove the balance shaft gear from the end of the balance shaft. Remove the balance shaft thrust plate and remove the shaft.

To install:

7. To install, lubricate the bearing lobes of the balance shaft with assembly lubricant and install the balance shaft into the block. Install the shaft thrust plate and the driven gear.

8. Install the balance shaft drive gear, aligning the keyway, on the end of the camshaft.

9. Install the timing belt and gear, the front cover assembly and the intake manifold. Install the radiator and air conditioning condenser. Install the grille.

10. Fill all fluids and run the engine to check for leaks. Correct all fluid levels, as necessary.

Piston and Connecting Rod

POSITIONING

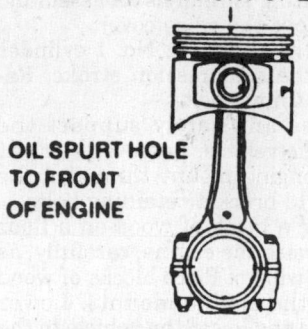

V6 piston and rod assembly

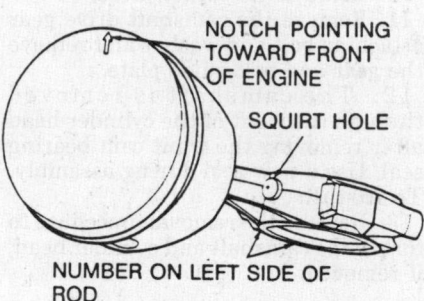

2.3L piston positioning

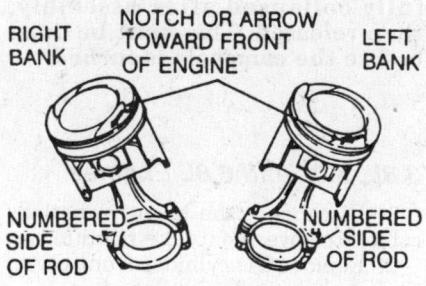

5.0L and 5.8L piston positioning

ENGINE LUBRICATION

Oil Pan

REMOVAL & INSTALLATION

2.3L Engine

1. Disconnect the negative battery cable.

2. Remove the fan shroud or fan shroud and electric fan assembly.

3. Raise and safely support the vehicle. Drain the crankcase.

4. Remove the right and left engine support bolts and nuts.

5. Using a jack with a piece of wood between the raising point and jack contact points, raise the engine as high as it will go. Place blocks of wood between the mounts and chassis brackets. Lower the engine. Remove shake brace.

6. Remove the sway bar retaining bolts and lower the sway bar.

7. Remove the starter motor.

8. Remove steering gear retaining bolts and lower the gear.

9. Remove the oil pan retaining bolts. Pivot the oil pan forward over the crossmember and remove.

To install:

10. Install new oil pan gasket and end seals.

11. Position the oil pan to the cylinder block and install retaining bolts and tighten to 20 inch lbs..

12. Reposition the steering gear and install bolts and nuts.

13. Install starter.

14. Raise the engine enough to remove the wood blocks, lower the engine. Install shake brace.

15. Install the right and left engine mount bolts and nuts, tighten to 33–45 ft. lbs..

16. Install the sway bar.

17. Install the fan shroud.

18. Fill the crankcase with oil.

19. Connect battery cable, run engine and check for leaks.

3.8L Engine

1987

1. Disconnect the negative battery cable.

2. Remove the air cleaner assembly including the air intake duct.

3. Remove the fan shroud attaching bolts and position the shroud back over the fan.

4. Remove the oil level dipstick.

5. Remove the screws attaching the vacuum solenoids to the dash panel. Lay the solenoids to the dash panel. Lay the solenoids on the engine without disconnecting the vacuum hoses or electrical connectors.

6. Raise and safely support the vehicle. Remove the exhaust manifold to exhaust pipe attaching nuts.

7. Drain the crankcase.

8. Remove the oil filter.

9. Remove the bolts attaching the shift linkage bracket to the transmission bell housing. Remove the starter motor for more clearance, if necessary.

10. Disconnect the transmission cooler lines at the radiator. Remove

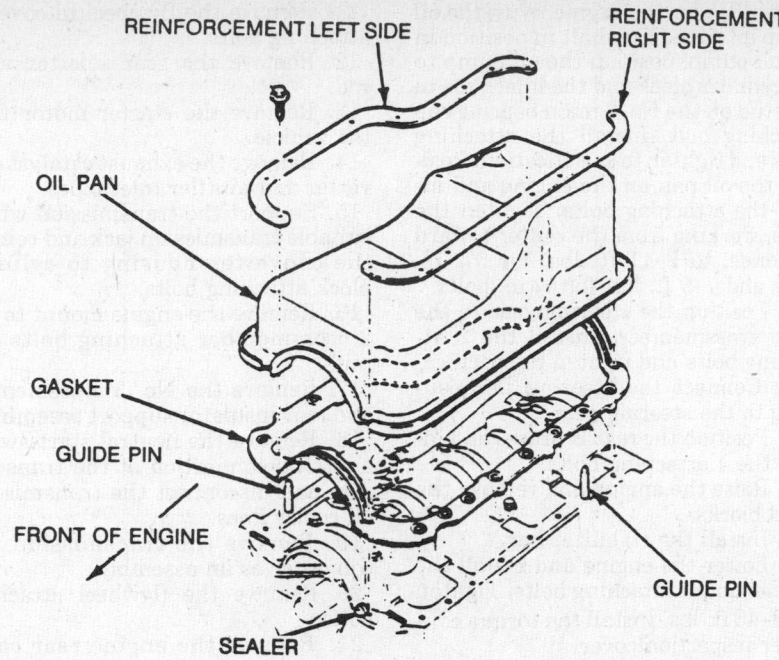

2.3L – oil pan installation

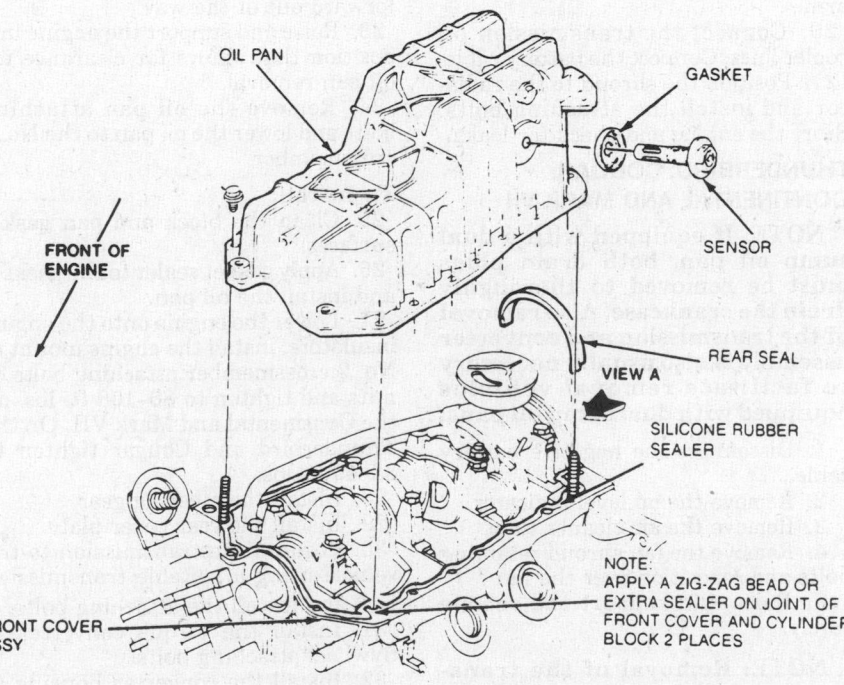

Removing the oil pan—3.8L SC

power steering hose retaining clamp from frame.
11. Remove the converter cover.
12. Remove the engine damper to No. 2 crossmember bracket attaching bolt. The damper must be disconnected from the crossmember.
13. Disconnect steering flex coupling. Remove the 2 bolts attaching the steering gear to main crossmember and let the steering gear rest on the frame away from oil pan.

14. Remove the front engine insulator attaching nut and washer.
15. Raise the engine 2–3 in. and insert wood blocks between the engine mounts and the vehicle frame.

NOTE: On some vehicles, it may be necessary to raise the engine as much as 5 in. to provide adequate pan to crossmember clearance. Watch the clearance between the transmission dipstick

tube and the thermactor downstream air tube. If the tubes contact before adequate pan to crossmember clearance is provided, lower the engine and remove the transmission dipstick tube and the downstream air tube.

16. Remove the oil pan attaching bolts. Work the oil pan loose and remove.
17. If with limited clearance, lower the oil pan onto the crossmember. Remove the oil pickup tube attaching nut. Lower the pick up tube/screen assembly into the pan and remove the oil pan through the front of the vehicle.
18. Remove the oil pan seal from the main bearing cap and discard.
To install:
19. Clean the gasket surfaces on the cylinder block, oil pan and oil pick-up tube.
20. Apply ⅛ in. bead of RTV sealer to all gasket mating surfaces of the oil pan and the engine front cover.
21. Install the oil pan. Torque the pan bolts to 80–106 inch. lbs.

NOTE: On models with limited clearance place the oil pick-up tube/screen assembly in the oil pan.

22. The balance of installation is the reverse of the removal procedure.
23. Fill the crankcase to the correct level with the oil.
24. Start the engine and check the fluid levels in the transmission.
25. Check for engine oil and transmission fluid leaks.

1988–91
1. Disconnect the negative battery cable.
2. Raise and safely support the vehicle. Drain the oil and remove the oil filter.
3. Remove the catalytic converter assembly from the exhaust manifold.
4. Remove the starter and remove the torque converter cover.
5. Remove the oil pan retaining bolts and remove the oil pan.
6. Clean all gasket mating surfaces.
7. Using a new gasket, apply a ⅛ in. bead of sealer to all gasket mating surfaces.
8. Install oil pan and tighten the retaining bolts to 80–106 inch lbs.
9. Install the starter and torque converter cover.
10. Install the catalytic converter assembly.
11. Fill the crankcase with oil and connect the negative battery cable.
12. Run the engine and check for leaks.

5.0L and 5.8L Engines

CROWN VICTORIA, GRAND MARQUIS, TOWN CAR AND MUSTANG

NOTE: If equipped with a dual sump oil pan, both drain plugs must be removed to thoroughly drain the crankcase. When raising the engine for oil pan removal clearance; drain cooling system, disconnect hoses, check fan to radiator clearance when jacking. Remove the radiator, if clearance is inadequate.

1. Disconnect the negative battery cable. Remove the fan shroud attaching bolts, positioning the fan shroud back over the fan. Remove the dipstick and tube assembly. Disconnect negative battery cable.
2. Drain the crankcase.
3. Remove the stabilizer bar from the chassis. Disconnect the engine stabilizer, if equipped.
4. On rack and pinion models, disconnect steering flex coupling. Remove the bolts attaching steering gear to main crossmember and let steering gear rest on frame away from oil pan. Disconnect power steering hose retaining clamp from frame. Remove the starter motor.
5. Remove the idler arm bracket retaining bolts, if equipped and pull the linkage down and out of the way.
6. Disconnect and plug the fuel line from the gas tank at the fuel pump.
7. Disconnect and lower the exhaust pipe/converter assemblies if they will interfere with pan removal/installation. Raise the engine and place 2 wood blocks between the engine mounts and the vehicle frame. Remove converter inspection cover.

NOTE: On fuel injected engines, relieve the fuel system pressure.

8. Remove the K braces (4 bolts).
9. Remove the oil pan attaching bolts and lower oil pan to the frame.
10. Remove oil pump attaching bolts and the inset tube attaching nut from the No. 3 main bearing cap stud and lower the oil pump into the oil pan.
11. Remove the oil pan, rotating the crankshaft, as necessary, to clear the counterweights.

To install:

12. Clean the gasket mounting surfaces thoroughly. Coat the surfaces on the block and pan with sealer. Position the pan side gaskets on the engine block. Install the rear main cap seal with the tabs over the pan side gaskets.
13. Position oil pump and inlet tube into the oil pan. Slide the oil pan into position under the engine. With the oil pump intermediate shaft in position in the oil pump, position the oil pump to the cylinder block and the inlet tube to the stud on the No. 3 main bearing cap attaching bolt. Install the attaching bolts and tighten to specification. Position the oil pan on the engine and install the attaching bolts. Tighten the bolts, working from the center toward the ends, to 9–11 ft. lbs. for $5/16$ in. bolts and 7–9 ft. lbs. for ¼ in. bolts.
14. Position the steering gear to the main crossmember. Install the 2 attaching bolts and tighten to specification. Connect the steering flex coupling to the steering gear.
15. Position the rear K braces and install the 4 attaching bolts.
16. Raise the engine and remove the wood blocks.
17. Install the stabilizer bar.
18. Lower the engine and install the engine mount attaching bolts. Tighten to 33–46 ft. lbs. Install the torque converter inspection cover.
19. Install the oil dipstick, tube assembly and fill crankcase with the specified engine oil. Install the idler arm.
20. Connect the transmission oil cooler lines. Connect the battery cable.
21. Position the shroud to the radiator and install the attaching bolts. Start the engine and check for leaks.

THUNDERBIRD, COUGAR, CONTINENTAL AND MARK VII

NOTE: If equipped with a dual sump oil pan, both drain plugs must be removed to thoroughly drain the crankcase. Also removal of the transmission and converter assembly is also usually necessary to facilitate removal vehicles equipped with dual sump oil pans.

1. Disconnect the negative battery cable.
2. Remove the oil level indicator.
3. Remove the air cleaner tube.
4. Remove the fan shroud retaining bolts and reposition over the fan.
5. Raise and support the vehicle safely.

NOTE: Removal of the transmission and converter assembly is usually necessary to facilitate removal of vehicles equipped with dual sump oil pans.

6. Drain the crankscase and transmission.
7. Remove the driveshaft assembly.
8. Disconnect the speedometer cable from the transmission.
9. Remove the gearshift bellcrank lever from the transmission.
10. Remove the flywheel housing cover retaining bolts and remove the cover.
11. Remove the flywheel to coverter attaching bolts.
12. Remove the gear selector valve rod.
13. Remove the starter motor from the vehicle.
14. Remove the exhaust catalyst converter and muffler inlet pipes.
15. Support the transmission with a suitable transmission jack and remove the converter housing to cylinder block attaching bolts.
16. Remove the engine mount to No. 2 crossmember attaching bolts and nuts.
17. Remove the No. 3 crossmember and rear insulator support assemblies.
18. Remove the neutral start switch electrical connection at the transmission and disconnect the transmission oil cooler lines.
19. Remove the transmission and converter as an assembly.
20. Remove the flywheel attaching bolts.
21. Remove the engine rear cover plate.
22. Remove the steering gear attaching bolts and position the steering gear forward out of the way.
23. Raise and support the engine in a position that allows for clearance for oil pan removal.
24. Remove the oil pan attaching bolts and lower the oil pan to the No. 2 crossmember.

To install:

25. Clean the block and pan gasket surfaces.
26. Apply gasket sealer to the gaskets and install the oil pan.
27. Lower the engine onto the engine insulators, install the engine mount to No. 2 crossmember attaching bolts or nuts and tighten to 80–106 ft. lbs. on the Continental and Mark VII. On the Thunderbird and Cougar tighten to 33–45 ft. lbs.
28. Install the steering gear.
29. Install the rear cover plate.
30. Position the transmission to the vehicle using a suitable transmission jack and install the attaching bolts.
31. Install the torque converter to flywheel attaching bolts.
32. Install the converter housing to the engine.
33. Install the starter motor and transmission cooler lines.
34. Connect the neutral start switch wire and speedometer cable to the transmission.
35. Position the transmission case brace to the left hand cylinder block and install the attaching bolts.
36. Connect the gearshift bellcrank lever, transmission control shaft and the flywheel housing cover.
37. Install the rear insulator and the No. 3 crossmember.

38. Install the gear selector valve rod.

39. Install the exhaust catalyst converter and muffler inlet pipes.

40. Install the driveshaft, then partially lower the vehicle.

41. Install the fan shroud, oil level indicator and air cleaner assembly.

42. Fill the engine and transmission with the proper type of lubricant and to the coreect level.

43. Connect the negative battery cable.

Oil Pump

REMOVAL & INSTALLATION

2.3L, 5.0L and 5.8L Engines

1. Disconnect the negative battery cable. Remove the oil pan.

2. Remove the oil pump inlet tube and screen assembly.

3. Remove the oil pump attaching bolts and gasket. Remove the oil pump intermediate shaft.

To install:

4. To install, prime the oil pump by filling the inlet and outlet ports with engine oil and rotating the shaft of pump to distribute the oil.

5. Position the intermediate driveshaft into the distributor socket.

6. Position a new gasket on the pump body and insert the intermediate driveshaft into pump body.

7. Install the pump and intermediate shaft as an assembly.

NOTE: Do not force the pump if it does not seat. The driveshaft may be misaligned with the distributor shaft. To align, rotate the intermediate driveshaft into a new position.

8. Install and torque the oil pump attaching screws to 12–15 ft. lbs. on the 2.3L engine, 20–25 ft. lbs. on 5.0L and 5.8L engines.

9. Install oil pan.

3.8L Engine

NOTE: The oil pump is mounted in the front cover assembly. Oil pan removal is necessary for pickup tube/screen replacement or service only.

1. Disconnect the negative battery cable. Raise and safely support the vehicle.

2. Remove the oil filter.

3. Remove the cover/filter mount assembly. On supercharged engines, remove the oil cooler assembly.

4. Lift the pump gears from their mounting pocket in the front cover.

To install:

5. Clean all gasket mounting surfaces.

6. Inspect the mounting pocket for wear. If excessive wear is present, complete timing cover assembly replacement is necessary.

7. Inspect the cover/filter mount gasket to timing cover surface for flatness. Place a straight edge across the flat and check clearance with a feeler gauge. If the measured clearance exceeds 0.004 in., replace the cover/filter mount.

8. Replace the pump gears if wear is excessive.

9. Remove the plug from the end of the pressure relief valve passage using a small drill and slide hammer. Use caution when drilling.

10. Remove the spring and valve from the bore. Clean all dirt, gum and metal chips from the bore and valve. Inspect all parts for wear. Replace as necessary.

NOTE: It is necessary to prime the oil pump after it has been disassembled to prevent it from failing on initial startup. This can be done by lightly packing the oil pump gear cavity with petroleum jelly before final assembly.

11. Install the valve and spring after lubricating them with engine oil. Install cover/filter mount using a new mounting gasket. Tighten the mounting bolts to 18–22 ft. lbs. Install the oil filter, add necessary oil for correct level.

Rear Main Bearing Oil Seal

REMOVAL & INSTALLATION

Split Seal

1. Disconnect the negative battery cable. Remove the oil pan.

2. Loosen all the main bearing caps, allowing the crankshaft to lower slightly.

NOTE: The crankshaft should not be allowed to drop more than $1/32$ in.

3. Remove the rear main bearing cap and remove the seal from the cap and block.

NOTE: Be very careful not to scratch the sealing surface. Remove the oil seal retaining pin from the cap, if equipped. It is not used with the replacement seal.

4. Carefully, clean the seal grooves in the cap and block with solvent.

5. Soak the new seal halves in clean engine oil.

6. Install the upper half of the seal in the block with the undercut side of

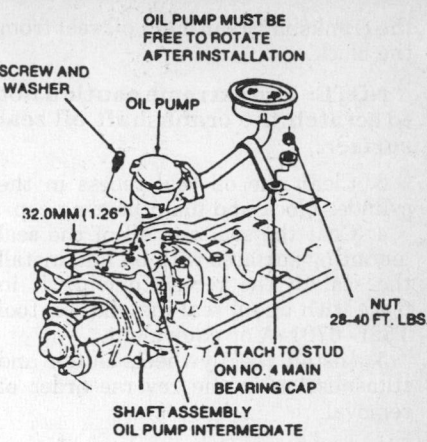

4 Cyl oil pump installation

the seal toward the front of the engine. Slide the seal around the crankshaft journal until $3/8$ in. protrudes beyond the base of the block.

7. Tighten all the main bearing caps, except the rear main, to specifications.

8. Install the lower seal into the rear cap, with the undercut side facing the front of the engine. Allow $3/8$ in. of the seal to protrude above the surface, at the opposite end from the block seal.

9. Squeeze a $1/16$ in. bead of silicone sealant onto the outer center edges of the bearing cap.

10. Install the rear cap and torque to specifications.

11. Install the oil pump and pan. Fill the crankcase with oil, start the engine and check for leaks.

Single Seal

1. Disconnect the negative battery cable. Remove the transmission and on manual transmission equipped vehicles, remove the clutch and flywheel.

2. Punch 2 holes in the crankshaft rear oil seal on opposite sides of the crankshaft, just above the bearing cap to cylinder block split line. Install a sheet metal screw in each of the holes or use a small slide hammer and pry

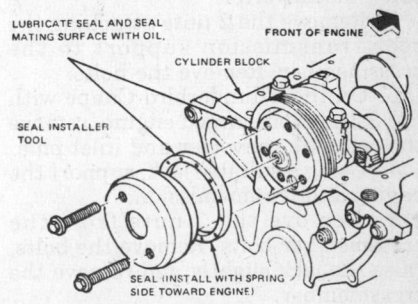

One piece rear main bearing oil seal installation

the crankshaft rear main oil seal from the block.

NOTE: Use extreme caution not to scratch the crankshaft oil seal surface.

3. Clean the oil seal recess in the cylinder block and main bearing cap.

4. Coat the seal and all of the seal mounting surfaces with oil and install the seal in the recess, driving it in place with an oil seal installation tool T82L–6701–A or equivalent.

5. Install the flywheel, clutch and transmission in the reverse order of removal.

MANUAL TRANSMISSION

For further information on transmissions/transaxles, please refer to "Chilton's Guide to Transmission Repair".

Transmission Assembly

REMOVAL & INSTALLATION

Except Thunderbird and Cougar with 3.8L EFI Supercharged Engine

1. Disconnect the negative battery cable.

2. Raise and support the vehicle safely.

3. Matchmark the driveshaft for reasembly. Disconnect the driveshaft from the rear U-joint flange. Slide the driveshaft off the transmission output shaft and install an extension housing seal installation tool into the extension housing to prevent lubricant from leaking.

4. Remove the bolts and remove the catalytic converter.

5. Remove the 2 nuts attaching the rear transmission support to the crossmember. Remove the bolts.

6. On the Thunderbird Coupe with the 2.3L turbocharged engine, remove the catalytic converter and inlet pipe.

7. Using a suitable jack, support the engine and tranmsmission.

8. Remove the 2 nuts from the crossmember bolts. Remove the bolts, raise the jack slightly and remove the crossmember.

9. Lower the transmission exposing the 2 bolts securing the shift handle to the shift tower and remove the shift handle.

10. Disconnect the wiring harness from the backup lamp switch. On the 5.0L engine, disconnect the neutral sensing switch.

11. Remove the bolt from the speedometer cable retainer and remove the speedometer driven gear from the transmission.

12. Remove the 4 bolts that secure the transmission to the flywheel housing.

13. Remove the transmission and jack rearward until the transmission input shaft clears the flywheel housing. If necessary lower the engine enough to obtain clearance for removing the transmission.

NOTE: Do not depress the clutch while the transmission is removed.

To install:

14. Installation is the reverse of removal. Observe the following torque values:

   a. Tighten the shift handle to shift tower attaching bolts to 23–32 ft. lbs. (31–43 Nm).

   b. Tighten the speedometer cable to extension housing attaching screw to 36–54 inch lbs. (4–6 Nm)

   c. Tighten the rear transmission support to 36–50 ft. lbs. (48–68 Nm).

   d. Tighten the rear transmission extension housing to support bolts to 25–35 ft. lbs. (38–48 Nm).

   e. Catalytic converter attaching bolts to 20–30 ft. lbs. (27–41 Nm).

   f. Align index marks and tighten U-bolt nuts to 42–57 ft. lbs. (56–77 Nm).

Thunderbird and Cougar with 3.8L EFI Supercharged Engine

1. Disconnect the negative battery cable.

2. Shift the transmission into the **N** position.

3. Remove the shift knob and the console top cover.

4. Remove the 2 shifter retaining bolts and remove the shifter.

5. Raise and support the vehicle safely.

6. Remove the drain plug and drain the oil from the transmission.

7. Remove the body reinforcement in front of the axle.

8. Disconnect the rear exhaust assembly from the resonator.

9. Remove the 4 bolts retaining the driveshaft to the companion flange. The rear driveshaft yoke and companion flange are marked for reassembly.

10. Position an axle stand under the front axle housing and remove the forward and rear retaining nuts and bolt plate.

11. Pull the vent tube from the hole in the sub-frame.

12. Lower the front of the axle housing with the axle stand and slide the driveshaft out of the transmission above the axle housing. Let the driveshaft rest on the front driveshaft support and axle assembly.

13. Remove the catalytic converter assembly.

14. Disconnect the hydraulic clutch line.

15. Disconnect the electrical connectors and remove the starter.

16. Position a transmission jack under the transmission. and remove the crossmember and bellhousing to engine bolts.

17. Move the transmission to the rear until the input shaft clears the engine flywheel and lower the transmission from the vehicle.

To install:

18. Installation is the reverse of removal. Observe the following torques:

   a. Tighten the bellhousing to engine retaining bolts to 40–50 ft. lbs. (54–67 Nm).

   b. Tighten the crossmember bolts to 35–50 ft. lbs. (47–68 Nm).

   c. Axle housing bushings and retaining nuts to 68–100 ft. lbs. (92–136 Nm).

CLUTCH

Clutch Assembly

REMOVAL & INSTALLATION

Except 1989–91 Thunderbird and Cougar

1. Disconnect the negative battery cable. Lift the clutch pedal to its uppermost position to disengage the pawl and quadrant. Push quadrant forward, unhook cable from quadrant and allow quadrant to slowly swing rearward.

2. Raise and safely support the vehicle and remove the dust shield.

3. Disconnect cable from the release lever. Remove the retaining clip and remove the clutch cable from the flywheel housing. On turbocharged engines, remove the clutch slave cylinder.

4. Remove starter and bolts that secure engine rear plate to front lower part of flywheel housing.

5. Remove the transmission, then the flywheel housing.

6. Remove clutch release lever from housing by pulling it through the window in housing until retainer spring is

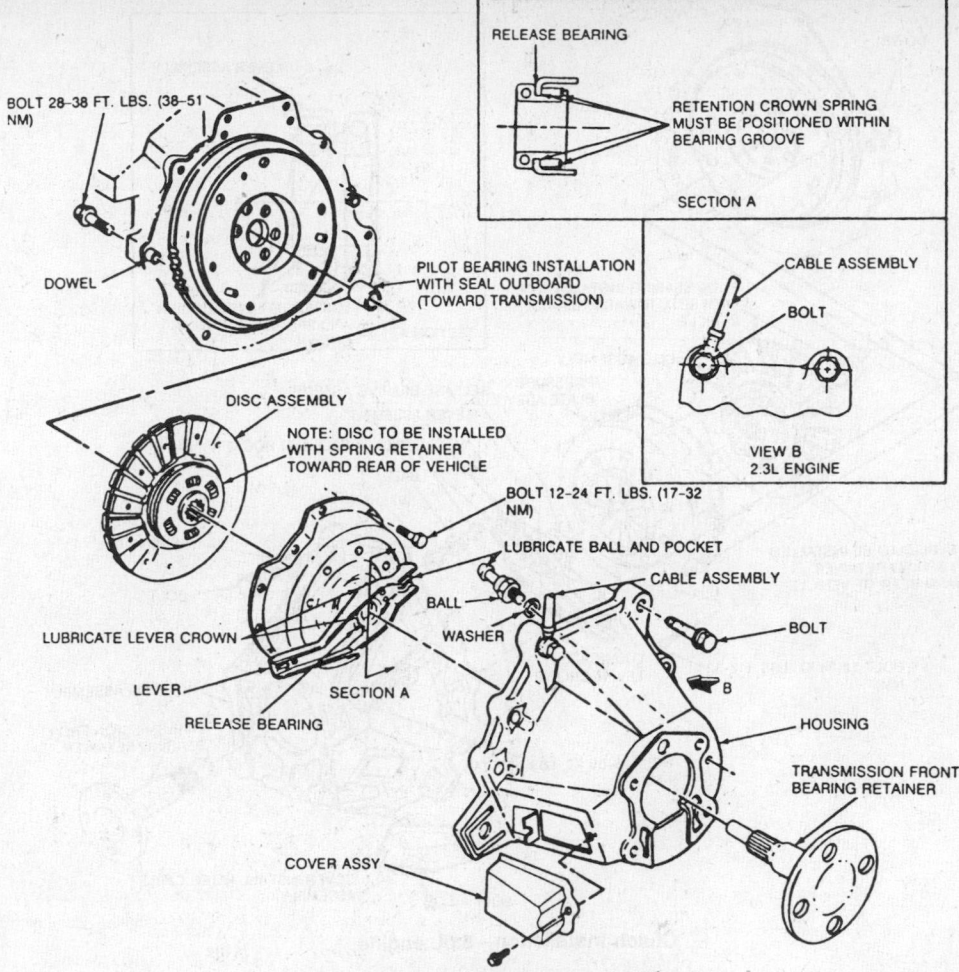

BOLT 28–38 FT. LBS. (38–51 NM)

DOWEL

PILOT BEARING INSTALLATION WITH SEAL OUTBOARD (TOWARD TRANSMISSION)

RELEASE BEARING

RETENTION CROWN SPRING MUST BE POSITIONED WITHIN BEARING GROOVE

SECTION A

CABLE ASSEMBLY

BOLT

VIEW B
2.3L ENGINE

DISC ASSEMBLY

NOTE: DISC TO BE INSTALLED WITH SPRING RETAINER TOWARD REAR OF VEHICLE

BOLT 12–24 FT. LBS. (17–32 NM)

LUBRICATE BALL AND POCKET

CABLE ASSEMBLY

BALL

WASHER

BOLT

LUBRICATE LEVER CROWN

LEVER

SECTION A

RELEASE BEARING

B

HOUSING

TRANSMISSION FRONT BEARING RETAINER

COVER ASSY

Clutch installation—2.3L engine

disengaged from pivot. Remove release bearing from release lever.

7. Loosen the pressure plate cover attaching bolts evenly to release spring tension gradually and avoid distorting cover. If same pressure plate and cover are to be installed, mark cover and flywheel so that pressure plate can be installed in its original position.

To install:

8. Installation is the reverse of the removal procedure. Align clutch disc using proper alignment tool inserted in pilot bearing. Tighten bolts to specifications.

1989–91 Thunderbird and Cougar

1. Disconnect the negative battery cable.

2. Disconnet the clutch hydraulic system master cylinder from the clutch pedal and dash panel.

3. Raise and support the vehicle safely.

4. Remove the starter.

5. Disconnect the hydraulic coupling at the transmission with tool

T88T–70522–A or equivalent, by sliding the white plastic sleeve toward the slave cylinder and applying a slight tug on the tube.

6. Remove the transmission.

7. Matchmark the assembled position of the pressure plate to the flywheel.

8. Loosen the pressure plate and cover attaching bolts evenly until the pressure plate springs are expanded, and remove the bolts.

9. Remove the pressure plate/cover assembly and the clutch disc from the flywheel.

To install:

10. Installation is the reverse of the removal procedure. Align clutch disc using proper alignment tool inserted in pilot bearing. Tighten the pressure plate to disc bolts in sequence to 15–25 ft. lbs. (21–32 Nm). Bleed the hydraulic system.

NOTE: Reuse the aluminum washers under the attaching bolts to prevent galvanic corrosion.

Clutch Cable

REMOVAL & INSTALLATION

Except 1989–91 Thunderbird and Cougar

1. Lift the clutch pedal to its upward most position to disengage the pawl and quadrant. Push the quadrant forward, unhook the cable from the quadrant and allow it to swing rearward.

2. Remove the screw that holds the cable insulator to the dash panel and pull the cable through the dash panel and into the engine compartment.

3. On 2.3L EFI and 5.0L engines, remove the cable bracket from the fender apron.

4. Raise and support the vehicle safely.

5. Remove the dust cover from the bell housing.

6. Remove the clip retainer holding the cable to the bell housing.

7. On the 5.0L engine, slide the ball on the end of the cable through the

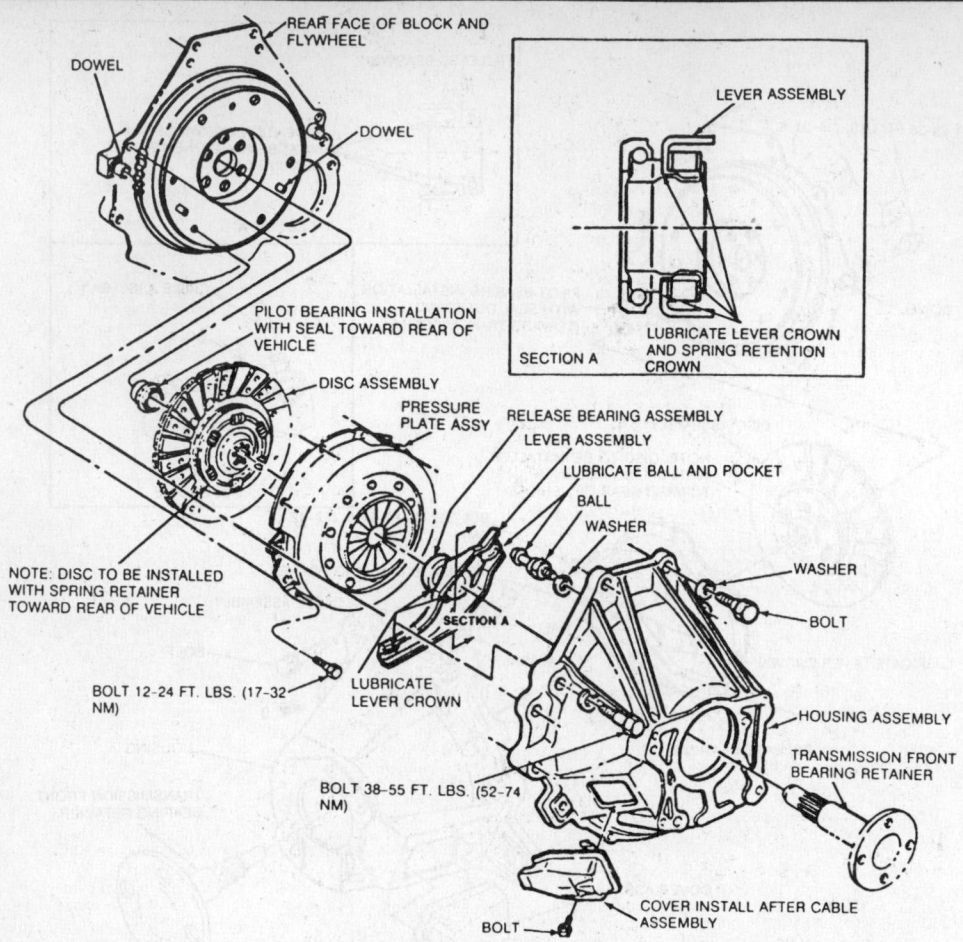

DOWEL

REAR FACE OF BLOCK AND FLYWHEEL

DOWEL

LEVER ASSEMBLY

SECTION A

LUBRICATE LEVER CROWN AND SPRING RETENTION CROWN

PILOT BEARING INSTALLATION WITH SEAL TOWARD REAR OF VEHICLE

DISC ASSEMBLY

PRESSURE PLATE ASSY

RELEASE BEARING ASSEMBLY

LEVER ASSEMBLY

LUBRICATE BALL AND POCKET

BALL

WASHER

WASHER

BOLT

NOTE: DISC TO BE INSTALLED WITH SPRING RETAINER TOWARD REAR OF VEHICLE

SECTION A

HOUSING ASSEMBLY

TRANSMISSION FRONT BEARING RETAINER

BOLT 12-24 FT. LBS. (17-32 NM)

LUBRICATE LEVER CROWN

BOLT 38-55 FT. LBS. (52-74 NM)

COVER INSTALL AFTER CABLE ASSEMBLY

BOLT

Clutch installation—5.0L engine

hole in the clutch release lever and remove the cable.

8. On the 2.3L engine, remove the hairpin clip, clevis pin and clevis from the end of the cable.

To install:

9. Slide the cable through the hole in the bell housing and through the hole in the the release lever. On the 5.0L engines, slide the ball on the end of the cable assembly into the cable ball pocket on the clutch release lever. On the 2.3L engines, place the cable ball into the clevis. Install the clevis and clevis pin onto the clutch release lever and into the clevis pin.

10. Install the clutch cable retaining clip on the bell housing.

11. Install the dust shield on the bell housing, if so equipped.

12. Push the cable assembly into the engine compartment and lower the vehicle.

13. Install the cable bracket to the fender apron, if equipped and slide the cable through the firewall.

14. Install the cable assembly by lifting the clutch pedal to disengage the pawl and quadrant. Then pushing the quadrant forward, hook the end of the cable over the rear of the quadrant.

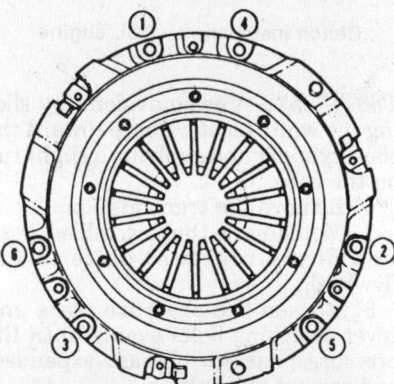

Pressure plate and disc to flywheel torque sequence—Thunderbird and Cougar with 3.8L EFI supercharged engine

15. Depress the clutch pedal several times to adjust the cable.

Clutch Master Cylinder

REMOVAL & INSTALLATION

Thunderbird and Cougar

1987–88

1. Disconnect the negative battery cable.

2. Remove the clutch slave cylinder.

3. Remove master cylinder reservoir by removing 2 self-tapping screws.

4. Remove the clutch pedal pushrod from the clutch master cylinder.

5. Remove master cylinder by turning it 45 degrees clockwise, pull the master cylinder out from the pedal mounting bracket, through the firewall.

6. Remove the pressure line.

To install:

7. Connect the pressure line and slide the clutch master cylinder into place.

8. Insert the clutch pedal pushrod and attach the fluid reservoir.

9. Fill the reservoir to the correct level with fluid and bleed the system.

1989–91

1. Disconnect the negative battery cable.

2. Disconnect the hydraulic line using tool T88T–70522–A or equivalent by sliding the white plastic sleeve toward the slave cylinder and applying a slight tug on the tube.

3. Remove the 2 push pins retaining the clutch master cylinder reservoir to the left hand shock tower.

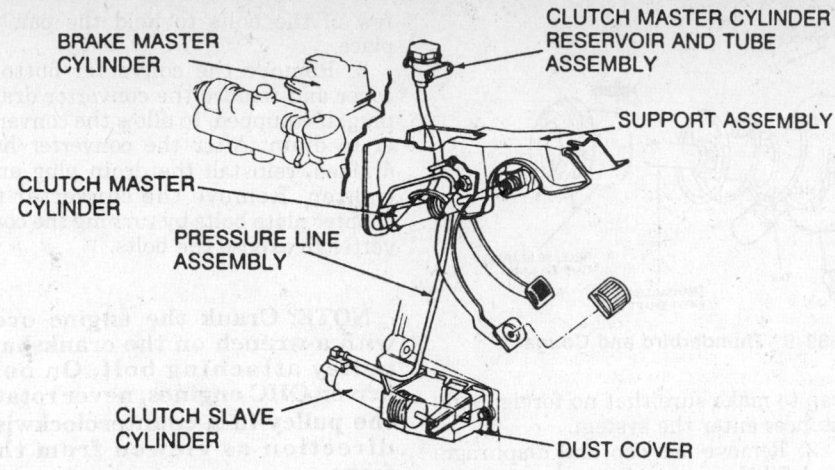

Hydraulic clutch components—1987–88 Thunderbird and Cougar

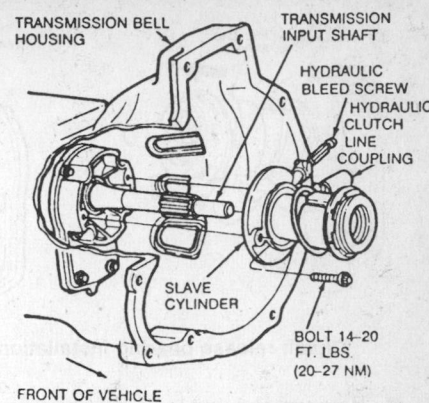

FRONT OF VEHICLE

Slave cylinder installation—1989–91 Thunderbird and Cougar

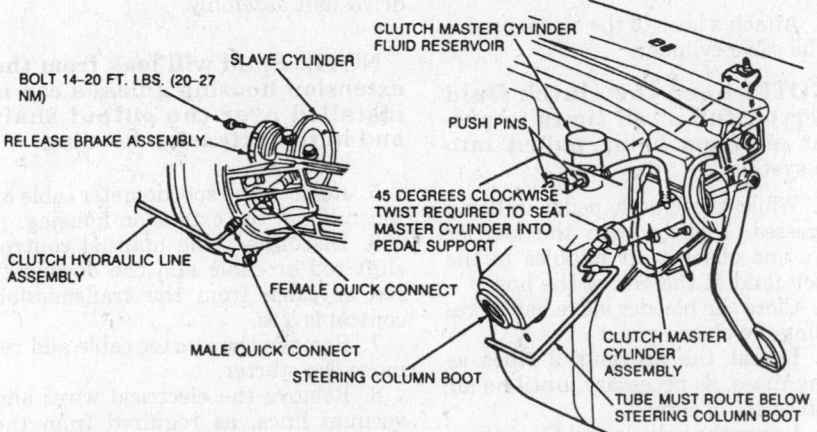

Clutch master cylinder installation—1989–91 Thunderbird and Cougar

4. Disconnect the clutch pedal from the pushrod.

5. Rotate the master cylinder 45 degrees counterclockwise, then carefully pull the master cylinder through the dash panel, noting the routing of the hydraulic line to the slave cylinder.

To install:

6. Position the clutch master cylinder in the engine compartment and route the hydraulic line to the slave cylinder.

7. Install the master cylinder to the dash panel, turn back 45 degrees clockwise, and attach the clutch pedal to the pushrod.

8. Install the clutch master cylinder fluid reservoir.

9. Install the hydraulic line to the slave cylinder, fill the reservor and bleed the system.

Clutch Slave Cylinder
REMOVAL & INSTALLATION
Thunderbird and Cougar
1987–88

1. Remove dust cover by removing self tapping screw.

2. Unlatch slave cylinder from the transmission housing bracket.

3. Remove pressure line if necessary.

4. Install the slave cylinder to the transmission. Install the dust cover and connect the pressure line.

5. Fill the reservoir to the correct level with fluid and bleed the system.

1989–91

1. Disconnect the negative battery cable.

2. Raise and support the vehicle safely.

3. Disconnect the hydraulic line, using tool T88T–70522–A or equivalent, by sliding the white plastic sleeve toward the slave cylinder and applying a slight tug on the tube.

4. Remove the transmission.

5. Remove the clutch release bearing.

6. Remove the clutch slave cylinder retaining bolts and remove the slave cylinder.

To install:

7. Position the slave cylinder over the input shaft aligning the bleeder

screw and line coupling with holes in the transmission housing.

8. Install the slave cylinder attaching screws and tighten to 15–20 ft. lbs. (20–27 Nm).

9. Install the relaese bearing and transmission.

10. Connect the hydraulic cylinder to the slave cylinder and bleed the system.

Clutch Release Bearing
REMOVAL & INSTALLATION
Thunderbird and Cougar
1989–91

1. Disconnect the negative battery cable.

2. Raise and support the vehicle safely.

3. Disconnect the hydraulic line using tool T88T–70522–A or equivalent by sliding the white plastic sleeve toward the slave cylinder and applying a slight tug on the tube.

4. Remove the transmission.

5. Rotate the release bearing assembly against the spring tension until the spring pushes the bearing off of the slave cylinder.

To install:

6. Lubricate the new release bearing and install it to the slave cylinder by pushing it into position.

7. Install the transmission, connect the hydraulic line and bleed the system.

Hydraulic Clutch System Bleeding
Thunderbird and Cougar
1987–88

1. Clean all dirt and grease from the cap to make sure that no foreign substances enter the system.

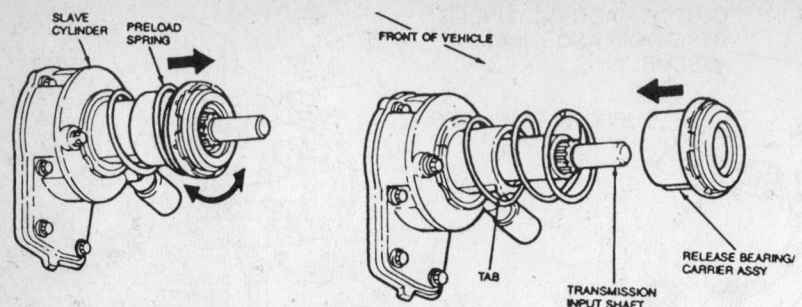

Clutch release bearing installation—1989–91 Thunderbird and Cougar

2. Remove the cap and diaphragm and fill the reservoir to the top with the approved DOT 3 brake fluid. Fully loosen the bleed screw which is in the slave cylinder body next to the inlet connection.

3. At this point bubbles of air will appear at the bleed screw outlet. When the slave cylinder is full and a steady stream of fluid comes out of the slave cylinder bleeder, tighten the bleed screw.

4. Assemble the diaphragm and cap to the reservoir, fluid in the reservoir should be level with the step. Exert a light load of about 20 lbs. to the slave cylinder piston by pushing the release lever towards the cylinder and loosen the bleed screw. Maintain a constant light load, fluid and any air that is left will be expelled through the bleed port. Tighten the bleed screw when a steady flow of fluid and no air is being expelled.

5. Fill the reservoir fluid level back to normal capacity and if necessary repeat Step 4.

6. Exert a light load to the release lever but do not open the bleeder screw as the piston in the slave cylinder will move slowly down the bore. Repeat this operation 2–3 times, the fluid movement will force any air left in the system into the reservoir. The hydraulic system should now be fully bled.

7. Check the the operation of the clutch hydraulic system and repeat this procedure, if neccessary. Check the pushrod travel at the slave cylinder to insure the minimum travel 0.57 in.

1989–91

NOTE: Be sure to pump the clutch at least 30 times to make sure that air is in the system. If the slave cylinder is pushed off the clutch plate, a similar pedal feel may occur. Pumping the clutch pushes fluid from the clutch reservoir into the slave cylinder, pushing it out to meet the clutch plate.

1. Clean all dirt and grease from the cap to make sure that no foreign substances enter the system.

2. Remove the cap and diaphragm and fill the reservoir to the top with the approved fluid.

3. Raise and support the vehicle safely.

4. Attach a hose to the bleeder valve at the slave cylinder.

NOTE: Keep the clutch fluid reservoir full at all times to prevent air from being pulled into the system.

5. While the clutch pedal is being depressed, slightly open the bleeder valve and observe air bubbles in the clutch fluid at the end of the hose.

6. Close the bleeder valve before releasing the clutch pedal.

7. Repeat the previous 2 steps as many times, as necessary, until no air bubbles are observed.

8. Lower the vehicle and fill the reservoir. Road test the vehicle.

AUTOMATIC TRANSMISSION

For further information on transmissions/transaxles, please refer to "Chilton's Guide to Transmission Repair".

Transmission Assembly

REMOVAL & INSTALLATION

1. Disconnect the negative battery cable. Raise the vehicle and support safely.

2. Drain the fluid from the transmission by removing all oil pan bolts except the 2 at the front. Loosen the 2 at the front and drop the oil pan at the rear to allow the fluid to drain into a container. When drained, reinstall a few of the bolts to hold the pan in place.

3. Remove the converter bottom cover and remove the converter drain plug, if equipped, to allow the converter to drain. After the converter has drained, reinstall the drain plug and tighten. Remove the converter to adapter plate bolts by turning the converter to expose the bolts.

NOTE: Crank the engine over with a wrench on the crankshaft pulley attaching bolt. On belt driven OHC engines, never rotate the pulley in a counterclockwise direction as viewed from the front.

4. Matchmark and disconnect the driveshaft assembly.

NOTE: Fluid will leak from the extension housing unless a cap is installed over the output shaft and in the extension housing.

5. Remove the speedometer cable or sensor from the extension housing.

6. Disconnect the manual control shift rod or cable and the downshift rod or cable from the transmission control levers.

7. Remove the starter cable and remove the starter.

8. Remove the electrical wires and vacuum lines, as required from the transmission assembly. Remove the bellcrank bracket, if equipped, from the converter housing.

9. Place a support under the transmission and slightly raise it. It may be necessary to raise the engine hood and loosen the fan shroud.

10. Remove the rear crossmember and engine rear support. Disconnect the necessary exhaust components.

11. Lower the transmission to expose the oil cooler line fittings. Disconnect the lines from the transmission.

12. Support the engine and remove the dipstick tube and all the bell housing retaining bolts except for the top 2.

13. Chain the transmission to the jack or support unit for safety.

14. Remove the 2 top bolts from the converter housing and move the transmission rearward and down from under the vehicle. Hold the converter in place to avoid having it drop from the transmission.

To install:

15. Tighten the converter drain plug.

16. Position the converter to the transmission and rotate into position. Align the orange balancing marks, if present.

17. Move the converter and trans-

mission assembly forward into position and make sure the converter is properly seated and moves freely.

18. Torque the transmission-to-engine bolts to:
    AOD – 40–50 ft. lbs.
    A4LD – 28 – 88 ft. lbs.

19. Remove the safety chain from around the transmission.

20. Install a new O-ring on the lower end of the transmission filler tube and install the tube to the transmission case.

21. Connect the speedometer cable to the transmission case.

22. Connect the oil cooler lines to the right side of the transmission case.

23. On all except the Thunderbird and Cougar, position the crossmember on the side supports. Position the rear mount on the crossmember and install the attaching bolt and nut.

24. Secure the engine rear support to the extension housing and tighten the bolts to 70–100 ft. lbs.

25. Install any exhaust system components., if removed.

26. Lower the transmission and remove the jack.

27. Secure the crossmember to the side supports with the attaching bolts and tighten to 70–100 ft. lbs.

28. Connect the TV linkage and the manual linkage rod.

29. Install the converter to flywheel attaching nuts and converter housing cover.

30. Secure the starter motor in place and connect all electrical connections.

31. Install the driveshaft, while making sure the index marks are aligned.

32. Fill the unit with correct fluid to its proper level, start the engine and check the transmission for leakage. Adjust the linkage as required.

THROTTLE VALVE CABLE ADJUSTMENT

AOD Transmission

1. Remove the air cleaner cover and inlet tube from the throttle body inlet to access the throttle lever and cable.

2. Using a small pry bar, pry the grooved pin on the cable assembly out of the grommet on the throttle body. Then push out the white locking tab.

3. Check the plastic block and pin, it should slide freely on the notched rod.

4. While holding the throttle lever firmly against the idle stop, push the grooved pin in as far as it will go.

5. Make sure that the throttle lever does not move while pushing the grooved pin in.

6. Install the air cleaner and inlet tube.

DRIVE AXLE

Rear Halfshaft
REMOVAL & INSTALLATION

Thunderbird and Cougar

1989–91

NOTE: Before removing the rear halfshafts, new inboard CV-joint stub shaft circlips and 2 new differential oil seals must be used for assembly.

1. Remove the right side wheel cover and wheel lug nuts.

2. Raise and support the vehicle safely by the frame only.

3. If equipped with drum brakes, remove the brake drum.

4. If equipped with disc brakes, perform the following:

   a. Remove the upper and lower caliper retaining bolts and remove the caliper. Support the caliper out of the way with a wire, do not support the caliper with the brake lines.

   b. Remove the brake rotor.

   c. On vehicles with anti-lock brakes, remove the anti-lock sensor bolts and remove the sensors.

   d. Pull back on the parking brake cable release lever and on the cable, this will release the tension.

5. Remove the upper control arm nut and bolt and wire the upper control arm, up and out of the way.

6. Using a paint marker, mark the position of the lower control arm in relation to the knuckle with the arms in the relaxed position.

NOTE: Failure to mark this relationship will cause axle bind up and incorrect ride height, causing tire wear and misalignment.

7. Remove the lower control arm to knuckle bolt. Remove the right halfshaft, inboard CV-joint, from the differential housing using halfshaft remover tool T89-3514–A or equivalent.

8. Remove the halfshaft and knuckle assembly from the vehicle. Insert a plug of some sort into the differential housing to prevent fluid loss.

To Install:

9. Install new circlips on the halfshaft, by sliding it into the groove on the splined end of the shaft.

10. Remove the plug from the differential housing. Lightly lubricate the stub shaft splines and carefully align the splines on the shaft with the splines in the differential.

11. Push the knuckle inward to seat the circlip in the differential side gear groove. Use care not to damage the seal.

12. Install the lower control arm bolt and nut, tighten to 118–148 ft. lbs.

13. Install the upper arm retaining bolt and tighten to 118–148 ft. bs.

14. Install the brake rotor. Install the brake caliper and tighten the retaining bolts to 80–100 ft. lbs.

15. Install the parking brake cable and the anti-lock sensor.

16. Install the tire and wheel assembly. Some vehicles have unidirectional tires, note the direction before installation.

CV-Boot

REMOVAL & INSTALLATION

1989–91 Thunderbird and Cougar

1. With the halfshaft assembly removed from the vehicle and placed in a soft jawed vice, use a light hammer and a suitable tool and carefully tap uniformly around the seal until it becomes unseated.

2. Cut and remove both boot clamps and slide the boot back on the shaft.

3. Slide the outer race off the tripod.

NOTE: When replacing damaged CV-joint boots, the grease should be checked for contamination, gritty feeling. If the CV-joints are operating satisfactory and the grease does not feel contaminated, add grease and replace the boot. If the grease appears contaminated the CV-joint should be disassembled and inspected.

4. Move the stop ring back on the shaft using snaping pliers.

5. Move the tripod back on the shaft to allow access to the circlip.

6. Remove the circlip from the shaft and remove the tripod from the shaft.

7. Remove the stop ring and remove the inboard CV-joint boot.

8. Reposition the halfshaft in a vice and remove the outboard CV-joint boot.

NOTE: The outboard CV-joint is permanently retained to the inter-connecting shaft and cannot be disassembled. Outboard CV-joints are serviced as an assembly, including the inter-connecting shaft, boot, clamps grease and circlips.

To install:

9. Before positioning the boot over the CV-joint, pack the CV-joint and boot with grease. The total amount of grease required is is 7.05 ounces (200 grams) for vehicles without anti-lock brakes and 8.82 ounces (250 grams)

for vehicles equipped with anti-lock brakes.

10. Position the boot on the CV-joint and install the boot clamps.

11. Slide the inboard CV-joint boot on the shaft.

12. With the stop ring installed past the splines, install the tripod assembly with the camfered side toward the stop ring.

13. Install the new circlip without over expanding or twisting it.

14. Compress the circlip and slide the tripod assembly forward over the circlip to expose the stop ring groove.

15. Move the stop ring into the groove using snapring pliers and make sure it is fully seated in the groove.

16. Fill the CV-joint outer race and boot with grease. The total amount of grease required is is 9 ounces (250 grams) for vehicles without anti-lock brakes and 10.58 ounces (300 grams) for vehicles equipped with anti-lock brakes.

17. Install the outer race on the tripod assembly.

18. Position the boot over the CV-joint. Move the CV-joint in and out, as necessary, to adjust to the proper length.

19. Release any air pressure by inserting a dulled tool between the boot and the outer bearing race.

20. Seat the boot in the groove and clamp in position without cutting the boot.

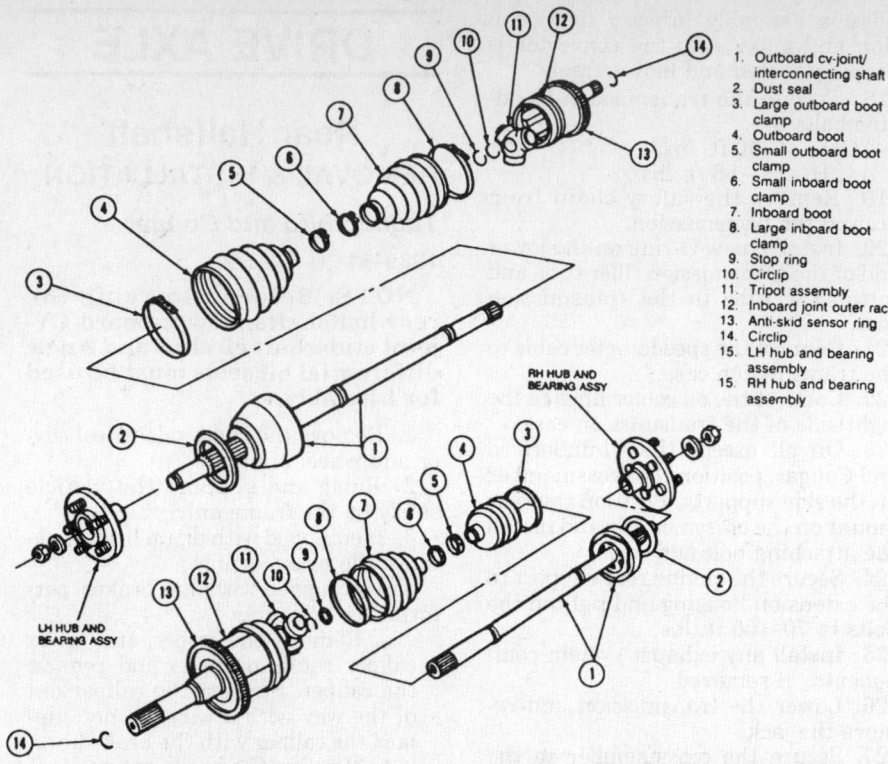

1. Outboard cv-joint/interconnecting shaft
2. Dust seal
3. Large outboard boot clamp
4. Outboard boot
5. Small outboard boot clamp
6. Small inboard boot clamp
7. Inboard boot
8. Large inboard boot clamp
9. Stop ring
10. Circlip
11. Tripot assembly
12. Inboard joint outer race
13. Anti-skid sensor ring
14. Circlip
15. LH hub and bearing assembly
15. RH hub and bearing assembly

Disassembled view of the halfshafts—1989–91 Thunderbird and Cougar

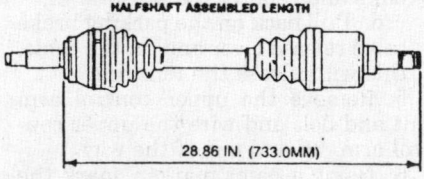

Halfshaft assembled length—1989–91 Thunderbird and Cougar

Driveshafts and U-Joints

REMOVAL & INSTALLATION

Except 1989–91 Thunderbird and Cougar

1. Raise and safely support the vehicle. Matchmark the rear driveshaft yoke and the companion flange so that the parts may be reassembled in the same way to maintain balance.

2. Remove the U-bolts and straps or coupling flange nuts and bolts at the rear of the driveshaft and tape the loose bearing caps to the spider.

3. Allow the rear of the driveshaft to drop down slightly. Pull the driveshaft and slip yoke out of the transmission extension housing.

4. Plug the transmission to prevent fluid leakage.

5. To install, lubricate the yoke splines and install the yoke into the transmission extension housing, aligning the splines. Be careful not to bottom the slip yoke hard against the transmission seal.

6. Rotate the pinion flange, as necessary, to align the matchmarks made earlier. New bolts should be used and torque the attaching bolts to 70–95 ft. lbs.

1989–91 Thunderbird and Cougar

1. Drain the fuel tank.
2. Raise and safely support the vehicle by the frame.
3. Remove the crossmember on the forward side of the fuel tank.
4. Remove the exhaust pipe insulator from the left hand rocker panel hanger stud.
5. Remove the exhaust pipe rear insulator from the exhaust pipe hanger stud.
6. Remove the exhaust pipe at the muffler and lower and support with a wire.
7. Remove the exhaust pipe heat shield.
8. Remove the driveshaft hoop on the rear side of the tank.
9. Remove the fuel tank filler tube

retaining bolt from the right hand frame rail.

10. Carefully place a transmission jack under the fuel tank and remove the front heat shield.

11. Remove the support on the forward side of the fuel tank.

12. Remove the fuel tank support straps and lower the tank approximatelt 6 in.

13. Locate the original paint mark on the axle companion flange and mark the driveshaft flange in the same location. If the original mark is not visible matchmark both flanges.

14. Remove the driveshaft retaining bolts and separate the driveshaft from the axle companion flange and pull the driveshaft rearward to remove. Install a plug in the extension housing to prevent fluid loss.

To install:

15. Lubricate the slip yoke splines and remove the plug from the extension.

16. Align the marks on the driveshaft with the axle companion flange. Install and tighten the bolts to 70–95 ft. lbs. (95–130 Nm).

17. Raise the tank and install the support straps. Tighten the retaining bolts to 36–48 inch lbs.

18. Install the driveshaft hoop and tighten the retaining bolts to 30–45 ft. lbs.

19. Install the exhaust heat shield.

20. Install the support on the for-

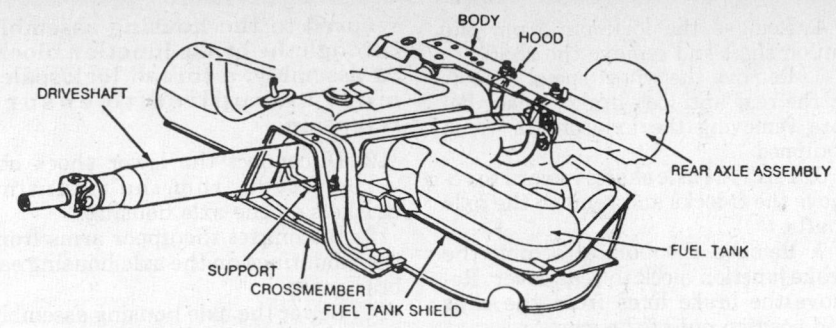

Driveshaft Installation—1989–91 Thunderbird and Cougar

ward side of the fuel tank and tighten the bolts to 30–45 ft. lbs.

21. Install the front heat shield.
22. Install the exhaust pipe to the muffler and tighten the bolts to 21–29 ft. lbs.
23. Install the front and rear exhaust pipe insulator on the hanger stud.
24. Install the crossmember on the forward side of the fuel tank and tighten the bolts to 12–17 ft. lbs.

Rear Axle Shaft, Bearing and Seal

REMOVAL & INSTALLATION

Except 1989–91 Thunderbird and Cougar

1. Raise vehicle and support safely. Remove wheel assembly and remove brake drums.
2. Drain the axle lubricant by removing the housing cover.
3. Remove differential pinion shaft lock bolt and pinion shaft. Remove wheel speed sensor, if so equipped.
4. Push flanged end of axle shafts toward center of vehicle and remove the C-lock from button end of the axle shaft. Remove axle shaft from housing.
5. Insert wheel bearing and seal replacer tool in bore and position it behind bearing so tangs on tool engage bearing outer race. Remove bearing and seal as a unit using an impact slide hammer.
6. Installation is the reverse of the removal procedure. Lubricate new bearing with rear axle lubricant.

Pinion Seal

REMOVAL & INSTALLATION

Except 1989–91 Thunderbird and Cougar

1. Raise and safely support the vehicle. Matchmark the rear driveshaft yoke and the companion flange so that

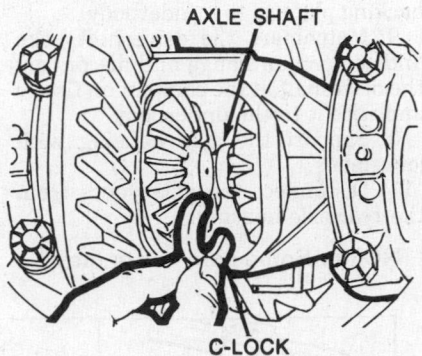

Removing the axle shaft C-locks

the parts may be reassembled in the same way to maintain balance.
2. Disconnect the driveshaft from the rear axle companion flange and remove the driveshaft and remove the driveshaft from the extension housing. Plug the extension housing to prevent leakage.
3. Install a torque wrench on the pinion nut and record the torque required to to maintain rotation of the pinion through several revolutions.
4. While holding the companion flange with a holder tool No. T78P–4851–A or equivalent, remove the pinion nut.
5. Clean the area around the oil seal and place a pan under the seal.
6. Mark the companion flange in relation to the pinion shaft so the flange can be installed in the same position.
7. Remove the rear axle companion flange using tool No. T65L–4851–B or equivalent.
8. Pry the seal out of the housing using a suitable tool.
9. Clean the oil seal seat surface and install the seal in the carrier using a seal replacer tool No. T79P–4676–A or equivalent. Apply a lubricant to the seal between the lips of the seal.
To install:
10. Apply a small amount of lubricant to the companion flange splines, align the marks on the flange and and the pinion shaft and install the flange.
11. Install a new nut on the pinion shaft and apply lubricant on the wash-

er side of the nut. Hold the flange with the holder tool while tightening the nut.
12. Rotate the pinion to ensure proper seating and take frequent pinion bearing torque preload readings until the original recorded preload reading is obtained.
13. If the original recorded preload is less than the minimum specification of 170 ft. lbs., tighten to specification. If the preload is higher than specification tighten to the original reading as recorded.

NOTE: Under no circumstances should the pinion nut be backed off to reduce preload. If reduced preload is required, a new collapsible pinion spacer and pinion nut should be installed.

14. Remove the seal replacer tool and install the front end of the driveshaft on the on the transmission output shaft.
15. Connect the rear end of the driveshaft to the axle companion flange, aligning the scribe marks and tighten the 4 bolts to 70–95 ft. lbs. (95–128 Nm).
16. Add lubricant until it is ¼–⁹⁄₁₆ in. below the bottom of the fill hole with the axle in operating position.

1989–91 Thunderbird and Cougar

1. Raise and safely support the vehicle.
2. Place a screw type jackstand under the rear axle pinion nose and remove the rear axle mount to axle cover retaining bolts and nuts.
3. Install the rear axle mount bolt in the lower bolt hole to allow the axle to pivot forward.
4. Mark the driveshaft in relation to the companion flange and remove the driveshaft retaining bolts.
5. Slide the driveshaft forward and rest on the driveshaft hoop.
6. Slowly lower the axle to gain access to the companion flange.

NOTE: The axle must always be supported.

7. Install an inch lb. torque wrench on the pinion nut and record the torque required to maintain rotation of the pinion through several revolutions.
8. While holding the companion flange with a holder tool T78P–4851–A or equivalent, remove the pinion nut.
9. Clean the area around the oil seal and place a pan under the seal.
10. Mark the companion flange in relation to the pinion shaft so the flange can be installed in the same position.

11. Remove the rear axle companion flange using tool T65L–4851–B or equivalent.

12. Pry the seal out of the housing using a suitable tool.

To install:

13. Clean the oil seal seat surface and install the seal in the carrier using a seal replacer tool T79P–4676–A or equivalent. Apply a lubricant to the seal between the lips of the seal.

14. Apply a small amount of lubricant to the companion flange splines, align the marks on the flange and and the pinion shaft and install the flange.

15. Install a new nut on the pinion shaft and apply lubricant on the washer side of the nut. Hold the flange with the holder tool while tightening the nut.

16. Rotate the pinion to ensure proper seating and take frequent pinion bearing torque preload readings until the original recorded preload reading is obtained.

17. If the original recorded preload is less than the minimum specification of 170 ft. lbs., tighten to specification. If the preload is higher than specification tighten to the original reading as recorded.

NOTE: Under no circumstances should the pinion nut be backed off to reduce preload. If reduced preload is required, a new collapsible pinion spacer and pinion nut should be installed.

18. Using a jack stand, raise and locate the axle on the front mounting bolts.

19. Install the front mounting nuts and tighten to 68–100 ft. lbs.

20. Remove the rear mount bolt from the pivot position.

21. Install the rear mount bolts in the axle cover mount and tighten to 80–100 ft. lbs. (108–136 Nm).

22. Align the marks on the driveshaft and the companion flange, install the retaining bolts and tighten to 70–95 ft. lbs. (95–129 Nm).

23. Fill the rear axle with lubricant to ¼ in. below bottom of filler hole.

Axle Housing

REMOVAL & INSTALLATION

Except 1989–91 Thunderbird and Cougar

1. Raise and safely support the vehicle. Position saftey stands under the rear crossmembers.

2. Remove the cover and drain the axle lubricant.

3. Remove the wheel and brake drums.

4. Remove the lock pin from the pinion shaft and remove the shaft.

5. Remove the wheel speed sensor, or the rear anti-lock brake sensor before removing the axle shafts, if so equipped.

6. Push the axle shafts inward to remove the C-locks and remove the axle shafts.

7. Remove the bolt attaching the brake junction block to rear cover. Remove the brake lines from the clips and position out of the way.

8. Remove the 4 retaining nuts from each backing plate and wire the backing plate to the underbody.

9. Matchmark the driveshaft yoke and companion flange and disconnect the driveshaft at the companion flange and wire it to the underbody.

10. Support the axle housing with jackstands.

11. Disconnect the axle vents from the rear axle housing.

NOTE: Some axle vents may be secured to the housing assembly through the brake junction block. At assembly, a thread lock/sealer must be applied to ensure retension.

12. Disconnect the lower shock absorber studs from the mounting brackets on the axle housing.

13. Disconnect the upper arms from the mountings on the axle housing ear brackets.

14. Lower the axle housing assembly until the coil springs are released and lift out the coil springs.

15. Disconnect the suspension lower arms to the axle housing. Disconnect both arms from the axle housing.

16. Lower the axle housing and remove it from the vehicle.

To install:

17. Position the axle housing under the vehicle and raise the axle with a hoist or jack. Conect the lower suspension arms to their mounting brackets on the axle housing. Do not tighten the bolts and nuts at this time.

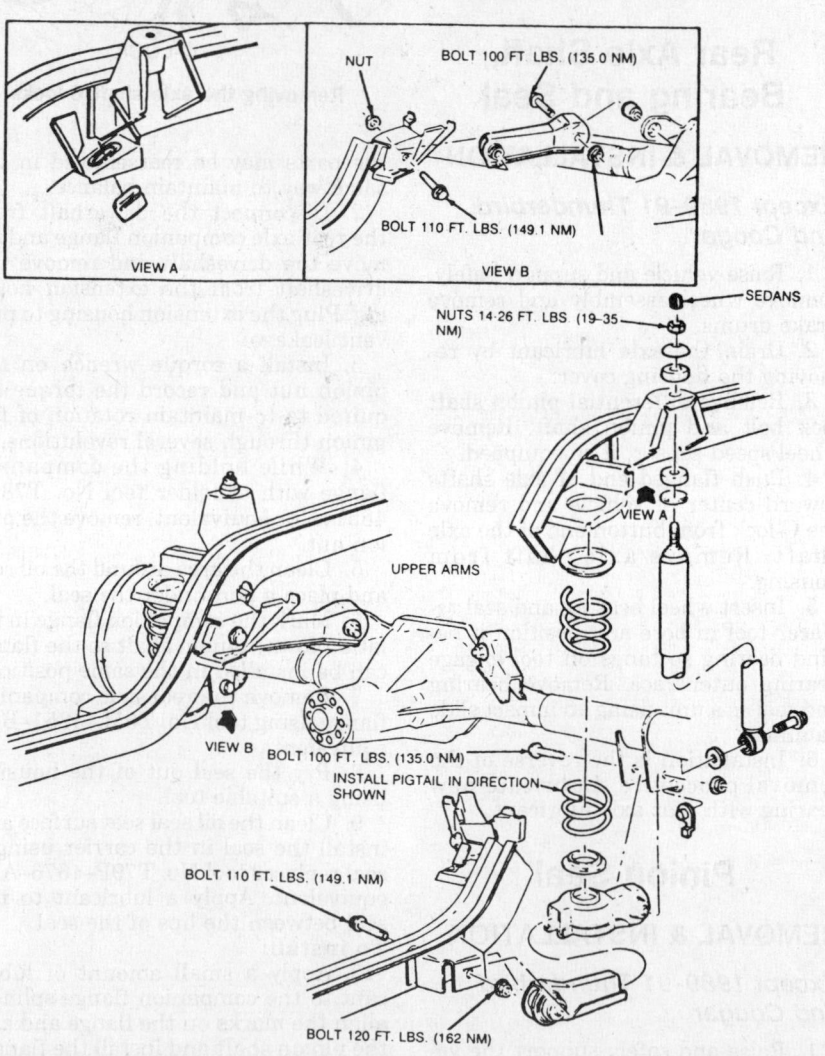

Installation of integral carrier axle with 7.5 inch ring gear—except 1989–91 Thunderbird and Cougar

18. Reposition the rear coil springs.
19. Raise the housing into position.
20. Connect the uppper arms to the mounting ears on the housing and tighten the nuts and bolts to 100 ft. lbs. (135 Nm). Tighten all bolts at this time. Tighten the lower arm bolts and nuts to 110 ft. lbs. (149 Nm).
21. Install the axle vent and the the brake line to the clips that retain the line to the axle housing.
22. Install the brake backing plates on the axle housing flanges. No gaskets required.
23. Connect the lower shock absorber studs to the mouning bracket on the axle housing and tighten to 12–18 ft. lbs.
24. Connect the driveshaft to the companion flange and tighten the bolts and nuts to 70–95 ft. lbs. (95–130 Nm).
25. Slide the rear axle shafts into the housing until the splines enter the side gear. Push the axle shafts inward and install the C-lock at the end of each shaft spline. Pull the shafts outboard until the C-lock enters the recess in the side gears.
26. Install the pinion shaft and the pinion shaft lock bolt. Tighten to 15–30 ft. lbs. (20–41 Nm).
27. Install the wheel speed sensor or anti-lock sensor ring on the axle shaft, if so equipped.
28. Install the rear brake drums and wheels.
29. Install the rear carrier cover using new silcone sealant gasket material. tighten to 25–35 ft. lbs. (34–47 Nm).
30. Install the brake junction block on the carrier cover and tighten to 10–18 ft. lbs. (14–24 Nm). Install the brake lines in the retaining clips.
31. Fill the axle with lubricant to the bottom of the filler hole. Install the filler plug and and tighten to 15–30 ft. lbs. (20-41 Nm).

1989–91 Thunderbird and Cougar

WITH DISC BRAKES

NOTE: Before removing the axle assembly on these vehicles be sure to to have available a new circlip on the inboard CV-joint stub shaft, new differential seals.

1. Loosen the wheel lug nuts.
2. Raise and safely support the vehicle under the frame.
3. Remove the wheel lug nuts and remove the wheel.

NOTE: If equipped with directional tires, note arrows on tires, and must be installed in their original position.

4. If equipped with anti-lock brakes,

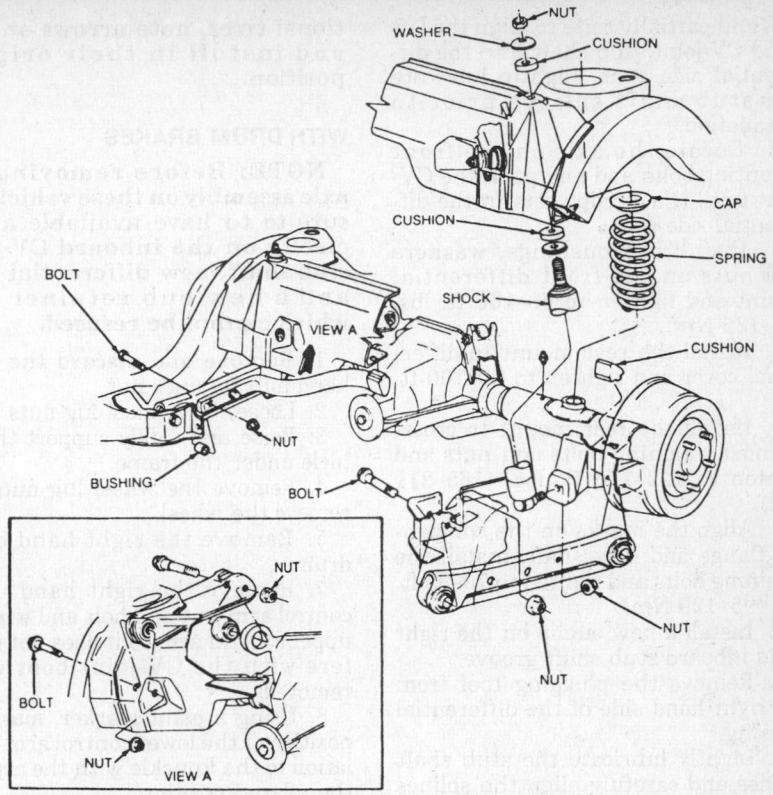

Installation of integral carrier axle with 8.8 inch ring gear—except 1989–91 Thunderbird and Cougar

remove the right hand and left hand anti-lock brake sensors.
5. Pull back on the parking brake cable release lever and at the same time pull back on the cable. This wiil release the tension so that it may be released and removed from the right hand brake caliper.
6. Remove the upper and lower caliper attaching attaching bolts from the right hand caliper and remove the caliper from the rotor. Carefully wire the caliper to to the brake junction bracket.
7. Remove the rotor.
8. Remove the right hand upper control arm nut/bolt and wire the upper control arm so it does not interfere with the CV-joint boot when removed.
9. Using a paint marker, mark the position of the lower control arm in relation to the knuckle with the arms in the relaxed position.

NOTE: Failure to mark this relationship will cause axle bind up and incorrect ride height, causing tire wear and misalignment.

10. Remove the lower control arm to knuckle bolt. Remove the right halfshaft, inboard CV-joint, from the differential housing using halfshaft remover tool T89–3514–A or equivalent. Push the tool inward toward the carrier.
11. Remove the halfshaft and knuckle assembly from the vehicle. Insert a plug of some sort into the differential housing to prevent fluid loss.
12. Mark the driveshaft in relation to the companion flange and remove the driveshaft retaining bolts.
13. Slide the driveshaft forward and rest on the driveshaft hoop.
14. With a suitable jack supporting the rear axle, remove the rear axle mount retaining bolts.
15. Remove the rear mount from the axle cover.
16. Remove the axle front retaining bolts, nuts, bushings and washers.
17. Remove the left halfshaft, inboard CV-joint, from the differential housing using halfshaft remover tool T89–3514–A or equivalent. Push the tool inward toward the carrier.
18. Partially lower the axle assembly. While lowering the axle, move to the right and disengage the axle from the left hand stub shaft.
19. Install a differential plug in the left hand side of the housing and lower the axle from the vehicle.
To install:
20. Replace the differential oil seals.
21. With the left hand halfshaft in the vehicle, install a new circlip on the left hand inboard stub shaft by pushing it into the stub shaft groove.
22. Position the axle on a suitable

jack and partially raise to align the left hand CV-joint stub shaft into the differential side gear. Lightly lubricate the stub shaft splines prior to installation.

23. Locate the axle on the front mounting bolts and and push the CV-joint until the circlip saets in the differential side gear.

24. Install the bushings, washers and nuts on the front differential mount and tighten to 68–100 ft. lbs. (92–136 Nm).

25. Install the rear mount to differential cover and tighten to 80–100 ft. lbs.

26. Install the rear mount to cross-member retaining bolts and nuts and tighten to 122–156 ft. lbs. (165–211 Nm).

27. Align the marks on the companion flange and driveshaft, install the retaining bolts and tighten to 70–95 ft. lbs. (95–129 Nm).

28. Install a new circlip on the right hand inboard stub shaft groove.

29. Remove the plugging tool from the right hand side of the differential housing.

30. Lightly lubricate the stub shaft splines and carefully align the splines of the inboard CV-joint stub shaft with the splines in the differential.

31. With the CV-joint splines engaged with the side gear, push the knuckle inward to seat the inboard CV-joint circlip in the differential side gear. Use a non-metallic mallet if necessary, to seat the circlip. Tap only on the outboard CV-joint stub shaft.

32. Install the lower control arm bolts and nuts, align the paint marks on the control arm and knuckle bushing and tighten the bolts to 118–148 ft. lbs. (160–200 Nm).

33. Install the upper control arm bolts and nuts and tighten to 118–148 ft. lbs. (160–200 Nm).

34. Install the brake rotor and new push nuts.

35. Install the caliper assembly over the rotor with the outer brake pad against the rotor's braking surface.

36. Install the upper and lower caliper retaining bolts and tighten to 80–100 ft. lbs. (105–135 Nm).

37. Install the parking brake cable in the caliper and reset the cable release lever to remove the slack in the cable.

38. Install the anti-lock brake sensors on each side of the differential and tighten to 14–20 ft. lbs. (19–27 Nm).

39. Fill the axle with lubricant and tighten the filler plug to 20–30 ft. lbs. (28–40 Nm).

40. Install the wheel and tighten the lug nuts to 80–105 ft. lbs. (108–144 Nm).

NOTE: If equipped with directional tires, note arrows on tires and install in their original position.

WITH DRUM BRAKES

NOTE: Before removing the axle assembly on these vehicles be sure to to have available a new circlip on the inboard CV-joint stub shaft, new differential seals and a new hub retainer nut, which cannot be resused.

1. Remove and discard the right hand hub retainer nut.
2. Loosen the wheel lug nuts.
3. Raise and safely support the vehicle under the frame.
4. Remove the wheel lug nuts and remove the wheel.
5. Remove the right hand brake drum.
6. Remove the right hand upper control arm nut and bolt and wire the upper control arm so it does not interfere with the CV-joint boot when removed.
7. Remove the right hand upper control arm nut and bolt and wire the upper control arm so it does not interfere with the CV-joint boot when removed.
8. Using a paint marker, mark the position of the lower control arm in relation to the knuckle with the arms in the relaxed position.

NOTE: Failure to mark this relationship will cause axle bind up and incorrect ride height, causing tire wear and misalignment.

9. Install tool T81P-1104-C or equivalent, to the right hand wheel studs and turn the wrench counterclockwise until the halfshaft is free in the hub.
10. Remove the lower control arm to knuckle retaining bolts and remove the knuckle assembly from the halfshaft.
11. Carefully rest the haslfshaft on the lower arm and the wire the knuckle assembly to the top of the shock.
12. Remove the right hand halfshaft from the differential housing using halfshaft remover tool T89-3514-A or equivalent.
13. Insert a plug of some sort into the differential housing to prevent fluid loss.
14. Mark the driveshaft in relation to the companion flange and remove the driveshaft retaining bolts.
15. Slide the driveshaft forward and rest on the driveshaft hoop.
16. With a suitable jack supporting the rear axle, remove the rear axle mount retaining bolts.
17. Remove the rear mount from the axle cover.
18. Remove the axle front retaining bolts, nuts, bushings and washers.
19. Remove the left halfshaft (inboard CV-joint) from the differential housing using halfshaft remover tool T89-3514-A or equivalent. Push the tool inward toward the carrier.
20. Partially lower the axle assembly. While lowering the axle, move to the right and disengage the axle from the left hand stub shaft.
21. Install a differential plug in the left hand side of the housing and lower the axle from the vehicle.

To install:

22. Replace the differential oil seals.
23. With the left hand halfshaft in the vehicle, install a new circlip on the left hand inboard stub shaft by pushing it into the stub shaft groove.
24. Position the axle on a suitable jack and partially raise to align the left hand CV-joint stub shaft into the differential side gear. Lightly lubricate the stub shaft splines prior to installation.
25. Locate the axle on the front mounting bolts and and push the CV-joint until the circlip seats in the differential side gear.
26. Install the bushings, washers and nuts on the front differential mount and tighten to 68–100 ft. lbs. (92–136 Nm).
27. Install the rear mount to differential cover and tighten to 80–100 ft. lbs.
28. Install the rear mount to cross-member retaining bolts and nuts and tighten to 122–156 ft. lbs. (165–211 Nm).
29. Align the marks on the companion flange and driveshaft, install the retaining bolts and tighten to 70–95 ft. lbs. (95–129 Nm).
30. Install a new circlip on the right hand inboard stub shaft groove.
31. Remove the plugging tool from the right hand side of the differential housing.
32. Push the halfshaft into the differential until the circlip engages into the differential side gear. Use a non-metallic mallet, if necessary, to seat the circlip. Tap only on the outboard CV-joint stub shaft.
33. Install the lower control arm bolts and nuts, align the paint marks on the control arm and knuckle bushing and tighten the bolts to 118–148 ft. lbs. (160–200 Nm).
34. Install a new hub retaining nut and pull the CV-joint into the hub as far as possible by hand.
35. Install the upper control arm bolts and nuts and tighten to 118–148 ft. lbs. (160–200 Nm).
36. Install the brake drum and new pushnuts and tighten to 14–20 ft. lbs. (19–27 Nm).
37. Fill the axle with lubricant and tighten the filler plug to 20–30 ft. lbs. (28–40 Nm).
38. Install the wheel and tighten the

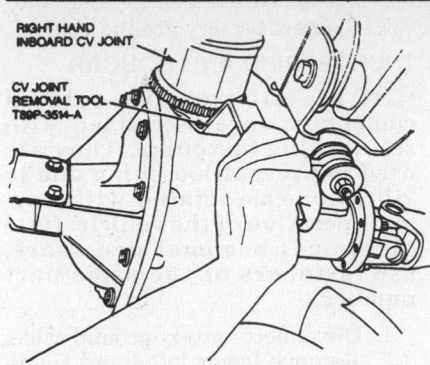

Removing the inboard CV-joint from the differential — 1989–91 Thunderbird and Cougar

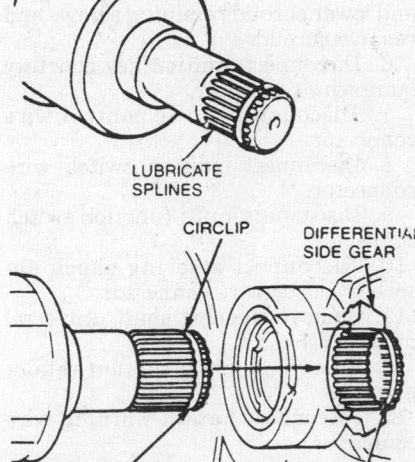

Installing the axle shaft in the differential — 1989–91 Thunderbird and Cougar

lug nuts to 80–105 ft. lbs. (108–144 Nm).

39. Tighten the hub nut to 250 ft. lbs. (340 Nm).

STEERING

Steering Wheel

— **CAUTION** —

If equipped with an air bag, the negative battery cable must be disconnected, before working on the system. Failure to do so may result in deployment of the air bag and possible personal injury.

REMOVAL & INSTALLATION

1. Disconnect the negative battery cable.

2. If equipped with air bag, remove the 4 air bag module retaining nuts and lift the module off the steering wheel. Disconnect the air bag wire harness and remove the module from the wheel.

3. If equipped with a horn ring, remove it by rotating it counterclockwise. If equipped with a steering wheel crash pad, remove the retaining screws from the underside of the steering wheel and then remove the crash pad. Disconnect the horn wires. If equipped with speed control, disconnect the wires from the inside of the steering wheel center. Matchmark the steering wheel to the column.

4. Remove and discard the steering wheel bolt, install a steering wheel puller on the end of the shaft and remove the steering wheel.

5. Installation is the reverse of the removal procedure. Be sure that the front wheels are positioned straight ahead before lining up the marks on the steering wheel and column. Use a new bolt and tighten to 23–33 ft. lbs. (31–48 Nm).

Steering Column

REMOVAL & INSTALLATION

1987–89

1. Disconnect the battery negative cable.

2. Remove the retaining nuts from the flexible coupling to the flange on the steering input shaft. Separate the safety strap and bolt assembly from the flexible coupling and disconnect the transmission shift rod from the control shift lever.

3. Remove the steering wheel assembly and the steering column trim shrouds.

4. Remove the steering column cover and hood release mechanism.

5. Disconnect all electrical connections to the steering column switches.

NOTE: To gain access to various nuts and bolts, the instrument cluster may have to be removed on certain models.

6. Loosen the nuts holding the column to the brake pedal support, allowing the column to be lowered enough to gain access to the shift quadrant indicator cable.

NOTE: Do not lower the column to the point where excessive weight is on the cable or plastic lever. Damage can result.

7. Disconnect the shift quadrant indicator cable from the cleat on the shift indicator lever. Remove the cable from the steering column tube.

8. Remove the screws holding the dust shield boot to the dash panel.

9. Remove the attaching bolts holding the column to the brake pedal support and lower the column to clear the mounting bolts.

10. Pull the column out so that the U-joint assembly will pass through the clearance hole in the dash panel.

11. With the column assembly out of the vehicle, the shift lever grommet should be replaced before installing the unit into the vehicle.

To install:

12. Install the steering column assembly into the dash opening so that the U-joint and lower shift cane clears the opening.

13. Align the 4 bolts on the brake pedal support with the mounting holes on the column collar and bracket. Attach the nuts loosely and allow the column to hang with a clearance between the column and the instrument panel.

14. Loosely assemble the shift selector cable clamp to the steering column outer tube.

15. Attach the cable to the shift lever cleat.

16. Tighten the nuts that hold the column to the brake pedal support to 20–37 ft. lbs.

17. Move the shift selector to the **D** position against the drive stop on the insert plate. Rotate the indicator bracket back and forth until the pointer in the instrument cluster points to the center of the letter **D**. Tighten the adjusting nut on the bracket.

18. Connect the electrical connectors to the wiring harness.

19. Engage the safety strap and bolt assembly to the flange on the steering gear input shaft. Tighten the nuts to a torque of 20–37 ft. lbs.

NOTE: The safety strap must be properly positioned to prevent metal to metal contact after tightening the nuts. The flexible coupling must not be distorted when the nuts are tightened. The flexible coupling must have a ⅛ in. coupling insulator flatness.

20. Connect the shift rod to the shift lever. Adjust the linkage as follows:

a. Raise the vehicle so that the transmission shift rod adjustment nut can be loosened and the transmission shift lever is in the **D** position.

b. Lower the vehicle, as necessary, to place the column shift lever in the **D** position.

c. Hang a weight on the gear shift lever on the column, to assure the lever is located firmly against the **D** detent in the steering column. The weight should be: all models, without automatic overdrive transmission, 8 lbs; or all models with automatic overdrive transmission, 12 lbs.

d. Make necessary adjustments on the shift rod adjustment nut and tighten the locking nut. Lower the vehicle.

21. Engage the dust boot at the base of the steering column to the dash panel opening. Install the retaining screws.

22. Attach the trim shrouds to the steering column upper end, the hood release mechanism and the steering column cover under the column assembly.

23. Install the steering wheel and remaining components.

24. Connect the negative battery cable.

25. Check the operation of the steering column and operating components.

NOTE: The steering column used with floorshift equipped vehicles is removed and installed in the same basic manner, except for the removal and installation of the shift mechanism.

1990–91

CROWN VICTORIA, GRAND MARQUIS AND TOWN CAR

NOTE: All steering column components are assembled with fasteners. They are designed with a thread locking system to prevent loosening due to vibrations associated with normal vehicle operation. Ensure that vehicle's front wheels are in the straight-ahead position.

1. Disconnect battery ground cable.
2. Remove steering wheel.
3. Remove air bag clockspring contact assembly.
4. Remove instrument panel lower trim cover.
5. Remove right hand and left hand lower mouldings from instrument panel by pulling up and snapping out of retainers.
6. Remove tilt lever by unscrewing it from column.
7. Rotate ignition lock cylinder to **RUN** position. Using a ⅛ in. drift, depress lock cylinder retaining pin through access hole and remove lock cylinder.
8. Remove 4 retaining screws from lower shroud and remove column shrouds.
9. Remove 2 instrument panel rein-

forcement brace bolts. Remove reinforcement.

10. Remove steering column to parking brake control shake brace.
11. Disconnect **PRND21** cable from lock cylinder housing by removing one screw.
12. Disconnect electrical connectors from multi-function switch and ignition switch.
13. Remove 2 multi-function switch retaining screws and remove multi-function switch.
14. Remove parking brake vacuum release assembly or disconnect vacuum hoses at switch.
15. Remove pinch bolt from steering column to extension shaft. Compress extension shaft toward engine and separate it from the column U-joint.
16. Disconnect shift cable from selector lever pivot.
17. Remove shift cable and bracket from lower column mounting.
18. While supporting column assembly, remove 4 column assembly retaining nuts. Remove column from vehicle.

To install:

19. Align the column lower universal joint to lower shaft and install the 1 bolt.
20. Support the column assembly to column support bracket and install the 4 retaining nuts.
21. Position shift cable bracket, with shift cable attached, to lower 2 screws of column.
22. Snap shift onto shift selector pivot ball.
23. Connect parking brake release vacuum hoses.
24. Position multi-function switch and install the 2 retaining screws.
25. Connect all electrical connectors.
26. Attach **PRNDL** cable loop on shift selector hook, and install **PRNDL** cable bracket to lock cylinder housing and install retaining screw.
27. Install steering column to parking brake control shake brace.
28. Install instrument panel reinforcement brace and secure with 2 retaining bolts.
29. Install lower instrument panel cover.
30. Snap right hand and left hand lower instrument panel mouldings into place.
31. Install upper and lower column shrouds.
32. Install lock cylinder assembly.
33. Install tilt lever onto column.
34. Install air bag contact assembly screw.
35. Install steering wheel onto column shaft and install a new retaining bolt.
36. Position air bag module to wheel and install the 4 retaining nuts.

37. Connect battery ground cable.

THUNDERBIRD AND COUGAR

NOTE: All steering column components are assembled with self-locking fasteners. They are used to prevent loosening due to vibrations associated with normal operation of the vehicle. If replacement becomes necessary, use fasteners of the same part number.

1. Disconnect battery ground cable.
2. Remove lower left hand finish panel retaining bolts.
3. Carefully pull lower left hand finish panel to disengage retaining clips.
4. Remove lower left hand reinforcement panel retaining bolts and remove reinforcement panel.
5. Remove steering column upper and lower shroud retaining screws and remove shroud.
6. Disconnect ignition key courtesy lamp wire connector.
7. Disconnect cruise control wire connector.
8. Disconnect ignition switch wire connector.
9. Disconnect multi-function switch connector.
10. Disconnect steering shock absorber sensor wire connector.
11. Remove steering shaft universal pinch bolt.
12. Remove steering column retaining nuts.
13. Disconnect hazard warning wire connector.
14. Remove starter interlock switch retaining screw and remove switch.
15. Remove steering column from vehicle.

To install

16. Position steering column and loosely install the retaining nut.
17. Install starter interlock switch.
18. Connect hazard warning wire connector.
19. Install steering column upper shroud.
20. Align steering column universal.
21. Install steering column retaining nuts.
22. Install universal pinch bolt and tighten to 30–42 ft. lbs. (41–57 Nm).
23. Connect steering shock absorber sensor wire connector.
24. Connect multi-function switch wiring connector.
25. Connect ignition switch wiring connector.
26. Connect cruise control wire connector.
27. Disconnect ignition key courtesy lamp wire connector.
28. Position steering column harness wiring and secure in place.
29. Install lower steering column shroud and retaining screws.

30. Position lower left hand reinforcement panel and install retaining bolts.

31. Position lower left hand finish panel and install retaining bolts.

32. Connect battery ground cable.

33. Check operation.

MUSTANG

1. Disconnect the negative battery cable.

2. Remove the 2 nuts retaining flexible coupling to the flange on the steering input shaft. Disengage the safety strap and bolt assembly from the flexible coupling.

3. Remove the steering column trim shrouds, fastened by self-tapping screws.

4. Remove the steering column cover and hood release mechanism directly under the column.

5. Disconnect all electrical connections (quick-couplers) from the steering column the turn signal, wash/wipe, ignition switches and key warning buzzer connecting wire.

6. Remove the 4 screws retaining dust boot to the dash panel.

7. Remove 4 nuts retaining column to brake pedal support. Lower column to clear the 4 mounting bolts and pull column out, so that U-joint assembly passes through clearance hole in the dash panel.

To install:

8. Install steering column by inserting U-joint assembly through opening in the dash panel. Use care not to damage column during installation.

9. Under instrument panel, align the 4 bolts on brake pedal support with the mounting holes on the column collar and bracket. Attach nuts and tighten to 20–37 ft. lbs. (27–50 Nm).

10. Connect the ignition switch, turn signal, key warning buzzer connector wire and wash/wipe switch connectors.

11. Engage safety strap and bolt assembly to flange on steering gear input shaft. Install the 2 nuts retaining steering column lower shaft and U-joint assembly to the flange on the steering gear input shaft. Tighten nuts to 20–37 ft. lbs. (27–50 Nm). The safety strap must be properly positioned to prevent metal-to-metal contact after tightening nuts. The flexible coupling must not be distorted when the nuts are tightened. Pry steering shaft up or down with a suitable pry bar to achieve plus or minus ⅛ in. coupling insulator flatness.

12. Engage the dust boot at the base of the steering column to the dash panel opening. Install the 4 screws retaining dust boot to the dash panel.

13. Install steering wheel.

14. Attach the steering column trim shrouds by installing self-tapping screws.

15. Install hood release mechanism and steering column cover beneath steering column.

16. Connect battery ground cable.

17. Check steering column for proper operation.

MARK VII

NOTE: All steering column components are assembled with fasteners. They are designed with a thread locking system to prevent loosening due to vibrations associated with normal vehicle operation.

Ensure that vehicle front wheels are in the straight-ahead position.

1. Disconnect the negative battery cable.

2. Remove steering wheel.

3. Remove air bag clockspring contact assembly.

4. Remove instrument panel lower trim cover.

5. Remove right hand and left hand lower mouldings from instrument panel by pulling up and snapping out of retainers.

6. Remove tilt lever by unscrewing it from column.

7. Rotate ignition lock cylinder to **RUN** position. Using a ⅛ in. drift, depress lock cylinder retaining pin through access hole and remove lock cylinder.

8. Remove 4 retaining screws from lower shroud and remove column shrouds.

9. Remove instrument panel reinforcement.

10. Remove 2 interlock cable retaining screws and remove cable.

11. Disconnect electrical connectors from multi-function switch and ignition switch.

12. Remove 2 multi-function switch retaining screws and remove multi-function switch.

13. Remove parking brake vacuum release assembly or disconnect vacuum hoses at switch.

14. Remove pinch bolt from steering shaft flex coupling.

15. Remove interlock cable retaining screws and cable end assembly.

16. While supporting column assembly, remove 4 column assembly retaining nuts. Remove column from vehicle.

To install:

17. Align the column lower universal joint to the lower shaft and install the one retaining bolt.

18. Support the column assembly to the column support bracket and install the 4 retaining nuts.

19. Connect parking brake release vacuum hoses and install interlock cable.

20. Install multi-function switch and secure with 2 retaining screws.

21. Connect all electrical connectors.

22. Install instrument panel reinforcement brace and secure with the 2 bolts.

23. Install lower instrument panel cover.

24. Snap right hand and left hand lower instrument panel mouldings into place.

25. Install upper and lower column shrouds.

26. Install lock cylinder assembly.

27. Install tilt lever on to column.

28. Install air bag clockspring contact assembly.

29. Install steering wheel onto column shaft and install a new bolt.

30. Position air bag module to wheel and install the 4 retaining nuts.

31. Connect battery ground cable.

Power Steering Rack and Pinion

ADJUSTMENT

The rack and pinion gear provides 2 means of service adjustment. The gear must be removed from the vehicle to perform both adjustments.

Support Yoke-to-Rack

1. Mount the steering gear on a bench mounted holding fixture tool T57L-500-B or equivalent. Rotate the pinion to set gear on center.

2. Remove yoke cover, gasket, shims and yoke spring. Clean cover and housing flange areas thoroughly. Reinstall cover, omitting the gasket, shims and the spring.

3. Tighten the bolts lightly until the cover just touches the yoke. Measure the gap between the cover and the housing flange. With the gasket, add selected shims to give a combined pack thickness 0.005–0.006 in. (0.13–0.15mm) greater than the measured gap.

4. Tighten cover bolts to 15–21 ft. lbs. (21–29 Nm).

Pinion Bearing Preload

1. Mount the steering gear on a bench mounted holding fixture tool T57L-500-B or equivalent. Loosen the bolts of the yoke cover to relieve spring pressure on the rack.

2. Remove pinion cover and gasket. Remove the spacer and shims. Install a new gasket.

3. Fit shims between the upper bearing and the spacer until the top of the spacer is flush with the gasket.

Check with a straight edge using light pressure.

4. Add an 0.0025 in. (0.06mm) shim to the pack in order to preload the bearings. The spacer must be assembled next to the pinion cover.

5. Remove oil seal from cover using centering tool T81P-350-Y or equivalent. Tighten bolts to 15–21 ft. lbs. (21–29 Nm). Install pinion shaft oil seal.

REMOVAL & INSTALLATION

Except Continental and Mark VII

1. Disconnect the negative battery cable.

2. Remove the bolt retaining the flexible coupling to the steering input shaft.

3. Place the ignition key in the **ON** position and raise the vehicle and support safely.

4. Remove the 2 tie rod end retaining nuts and cotter pins. Separate the tie rod stud from the spindle arms with the use of a separator tool.

5. Support the rack and pinion and remove the retaining nuts, washers and bolts from the rack and pinion to the crossmember.

6. Lower the gear assembly slightly to gain access to the pressure and return line fittings. Disconnect the fittings and plug the openings to prevent the entry of dirt.

7. Remove the rack and pinion gear assembly from the vehicle.

8. The installation of the rack and pinion assembly is the reverse of the removal procedure. On all except the 1989–91 Thunderbird and Cougar torque the mounting nuts to 30–40 ft. lbs. (41–54 Nm). On the 1989–91 Thunderbird and Cougar torque the steering rack retaining nuts to 175–230 ft. lbs. (237–312 Nm). Fill with fluid and bleed the system.

Continental and Mark VII

1. Turn **OFF** the air suspension switch, which is located in the trunk of the vehicle.

2. Disconnect the negative battery cable and turn the ignition switch to the **RUN** position.

3. Raise and support the vehicle safely and position a drain pan under the power steering lines in order to catch the fluid when the lines are removed.

4. Remove the bolt retaining the flexible coupling to the intake shaft.

5. Remove the 2 tie rod end retaining cotter pins and nuts. Separate the studs from the spindle arms, using ball joint spindle press T57P-3006-B or equivalent.

6. Remove the 2 nuts, insulator

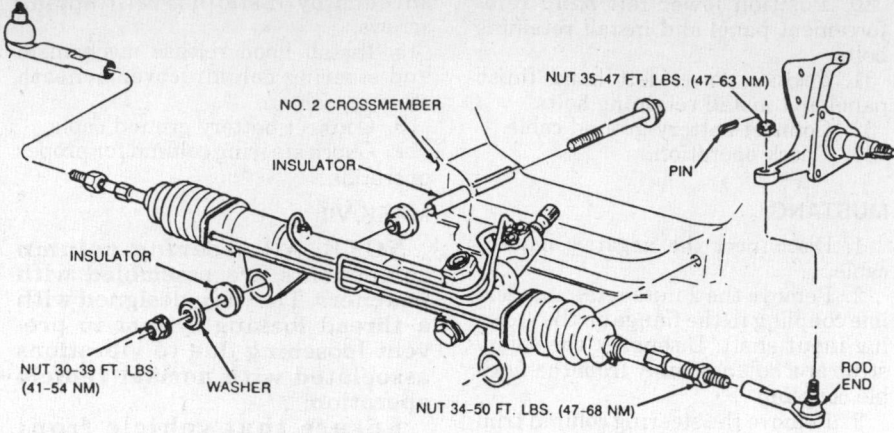

Integral power rack and pinion steering gear installation

washers and bolts retaining the steering gear to the No. 2 crossmember.

7. Remove the front rubber insulators and move the gear assembly forward so as to be able to remove the rear rubber insulators.

8. Position the gear to allow access to the hydraulic lines and disconnect the lines.

9. Pull the left hand side of the steering gear forward to clear the mounting spike and allow it to drop as far as possible without forcing it. Rotate the top of the gear assembly forward to clear the engine oil filter and remove the steering gear.

10. Installation is the reverse order of the removal procedure. Be sure to install a new rubber insulators and also new plastic seals on the hydraulic line fittings. Torque the lines to 10–15 ft. lbs. (14–20 Nm). Torque the flexible coupling bolt to 20–30 ft. lbs. (28–40 Nm). Torque the mounting nuts to 30–40 ft. lbs. (41–54 Nm).

11. Refill the system with power steering fluid and bleed the system.

Power Steering Gear

REMOVAL & INSTALLATION

1. Disconnect the negative battery cable. Remove the stone shield. Tag the fluid lines and disconnect them from the steering gear. Plug the lines and ports in the gear to prevent entry of dirt.

2. Remove the clamp bolts that hold the flexible coupling to the steering gear.

3. Raise the vehicle and remove the sector shaft attaching nut. Remove the pitman arm with a special pulling tool.

4. Support the steering gear and remove the attaching bolts.

5. Work the gear free of the flex coupling. Remove the gear and flex coupling.

6. Installation is the reverse of removal procedure. Fill with fluid and bleed the system.

Power Steering Pump

REMOVAL & INSTALLATION

1. Disconnect the negative battery cable. Disconnect the return and pressure lines from the power steering pump and allow to drain into a container. When the system is drained of fluid, plug the openings to avoid entry of dirt into the system. On supercharged models, remove the supercharger drive belt and the inlet tube.

NOTE: The Ford model CII power steering pump has a fiberglass nylon reservoir, incorporating a pump pressure fitting that allows the pump pressure line to swivel. This is normal and does not indicate a loose fitting. Do not remove the base fitting from the pump reservoir.

2. Loosen the drive belt tensioning nuts or bolts to facilitate the removal of the belt.

NOTE: On the fixed pump system, the alternator must be loosened to remove the pump drive belt.

3. On the fixed pump system, the pump pulley must be removed from the pump shaft with a puller tool, before the pump can be removed from the brackets.

NOTE: Do not hammer on the end of the pump shaft. Internal pump damage can be done.

4. Remove the pump retaining bolts and/or nuts from the brackets to pump. Remove the pump from the engine.

5. Installation is the reverse of removal.

SYSTEM BLEEDING

1. With the wheels turned all the way to the left, add power steering fluid to the **COLD** mark on the fluid level indicator.

2. Start the engine and run at fast idle momentarily, shut engine **OFF** and recheck fluid level. If necessary add fluid to to bring level to the **COLD** mark.

3. Start the engine and bleed the system by turning the wheels from side to side without hitting the stops.

NOTE: Fluid with air in it has a light tan or red appearance.

4. Return the wheels to the center position and keep the engine running for 2–3 minutes.

5. Road test the vehicle and recheck the fluid level making sure it is at the **HOT** mark. Refill as necessary.

Tie Rod Ends

REMOVAL & INSTALLATION

Except Rack and Pinion Steering Gear

1. Raise and support the vehicle safely.

2. Remove the cotter pin and nut from the rod end ball stud.

3. Loosen the sleeve clamp bolts and remove the rod end from the spindle arm center link using a ball joint separator.

4. Remove the rod end from the sleeve, counting the exact number of turns required.

5. Install the new end using the exact number of turns it took to remove the old one.

6. Install all parts. Torque the stud to 40–43 ft. lbs. and the clamp to 20–22 ft. lbs.

7. Check the toe-in.

With Rack and Pinion Steering Gear

1. Remove the cotter pin and nut at the spindle. Separate the tie rod end stud from the spindle with a puller.

2. Matchmark the position of the locknut with paint on the tie rod. Unscrew the locknut. Unscrew the tie rod end, counting the number of turns required to remove.

3. Install the new end the same number of turns. Attach the tie rod end stud to the spindle. Install the nut and torque to 35 ft. lbs., then continue to tighten until the cotter pin holes align. Install a new cotter pin. Check

the toe and adjust, if necessary, then torque the tie rod end locknut to 35 ft. lbs.

BRAKES

For all brake system repair and service procedures not detailed below, please refer to "Brakes" in the Unit Repair section.

Master Cylinder

REMOVAL & INSTALLATION

NOTE: If equipped with the anti-lock braking system, it is necessary to relieve the brake system pressure before performing any type of service. The pressure can be relieved by, placing the key in the OFF position and pumping the brake pedal at least 20 times or until increased pedal effort is felt.

1. Disconnect the negative battery cable.

2. Remove the brake tubes from the primary and secondary outlet ports of the master cylinder and pressure control valves.

3. Remove the nuts attaching master cylinder to the brake booster assembly. Disconnect brake warning lamp connector.

4. Slide the master cylinder forward and upward from vehicle.

5. Installation is the reverse of the removal procedure. Fill master cylinder to **MAX** line on side of reservoir with heavy duty brake fluid. Bleed brake system.

Proportioning Valve

REMOVAL & INSTALLATION

1. Disconnect the negative battery cable. Disconnect the brake warning lamp switch wire harness connector from the warning lamp switch.

2. Disconnect the front brake system inlet tube and rear system inlet tube from the brake control valve assembly.

3. Disconnect the left and right front brake outlet tubes from the brake control valve assembly.

4. Disconnect the rear system outlet tube from the brake control valve assembly.

5. Remove the screw that retains the brake control valve assembly on the frame. Remove the assembly from the vehicle.

NOTE: The brake control valve assembly is serviced only as an assembly.

6. Position the brake valve assembly on the frame. Install the mounting screw for frame mounting and tighten to 7–11 ft. lbs.

7. Install the inlet and outlet tubes in the reverse order of the removal procedure and torque tube nuts to 10–18 ft. lbs.

8. Connect the brake warning lamp switch wiring harness connector to the brake warning lamp switch. Verify the connection by turning the ignition switch to the **ON** position; lamp must turn ON. Also confirm that the locking fingers on the connector are locked into the switch.

9. Bleed the brake system and centralize the pressure differential valve by:

a. Turn the ignition switch to the **ON** or **ACC** position.

b. Depress the brake pedal and the piston will center itself, causing the brake warning lamp to turn OFF, if it was illuminated.

c. Turn the ignition switch to the **OFF** position.

d. Before driving the vehicle, check the operation of the brakes and be sure that a firm pedal is obtained.

NOTE: During the brake system bleeding operation, if equipped with a metering valve, the metering valve bleeder rod must be pushed in (pressure bleeding).

Power Brake Booster

REMOVAL & INSTALLATION

1. Disconnect the negative battery cable. Working inside the vehicle below the instrument panel, disconnect booster valve operating rod from the brake pedal assembly. To do this, disconnect the stoplight switch wires at the connector. Remove the hairpin retainer and nylon washer from the pedal pin. Slide the switch off just enough for the outer arm to clear the pin. Remove the switch.

2. Slide the boost pushrod, bushing and inner nylon washer off the pedal pin.

3. Remove the air cleaner for working clearance, if necessary.

4. If equipped with the 2.3L engine, disconnect the accelerator cable at the throttle body.

5. Remove the securing screw from the accelerator shaft bracket and remove the cable from the bracket. Remove the 2 screws attaching the brack-

et to the manifold; rotate the bracket toward the engine.

6. Disconnect the brake lines at the master cylinder outlet fittings.

7. Disconnect manifold vacuum hose from the booster unit. If equipped with speed control, remove the left cowl screen in the engine compartment. Remove the 3 nuts retaining the speed control servo to the firewall and move the servo out of the way.

8. Remove the 4 bracket to firewall attaching bolts.

9. Remove the booster and bracket assembly from the firewall, sliding the valve operating rod out from the engine side.

10. Install the booster assembly and the master cylinder. Reconnect the fluid lines. Reconnect the brake pedal arm to the booster. Bleed the brakes after installation is complete.

Hydro-Boost Power Unit

REMOVAL & INSTALLATION

1. Disconnect the negative battery cable. Open the hood and remove the 2 nuts attaching the master cylinder to the brake booster.

2. Remove the master cylinder from the hydro-boost accumulator.

3. Set the master cylinder aside without disturbing the hydraulic lines.

4. Disconnect the pressure, steering and return lines from the accumulator.

5. Plug the lines and ports.

6. Working below the instrument panel, disconnect the hydro-boost pushrod from the brake pedal. To do this, disconnect the stoplight switch at the connector. Remove the hairpin retainer. Slide the stoplight switch from the brake pedal pin far enough to clear the switch outer pin hole. Remove the switch from the pin.

7. Loosen the hydro-boost attaching nuts and remove the pushrod, washers and bushings from the brake pedal pin.

8. Remove the accumulator.

To install:

9. Install the unit in the vehicle. Leave the hydro-boost mounting nuts loose until the pushrod and stoplight switch are connected to the brake pedal. After installation, remove the coil wire from the distributor.

10. Fill the power steering reservoir and while cranking the engine, pump the brake pedal. Do not move the steering wheel until all the air has been pumped out of the system.

11. Check the power steering fluid level, install the coil wire, start the engine and pump the brakes while steering from lock to lock. Check for leaks.

Brake Caliper
REMOVAL & INSTALLATION

1. Raise and safely support vehicle.

2. Remove the wheel and tire. On models with anti-lock brakes, relieve the system of pressure.

3. Disconnect the hose from the caliper.

4. Remove the caliper locating pins using the appropriate Torx® bit.

NOTE: The base Thunderbird, Cougar and Mustang with the 2.3L non-turbocharged engine require the use of tool D79P–2100–T50 or equivalent, to remove the caliper pin.

5. Lift the caliper from the integral spindle/anchor plate or knuckle/anchor plate.

To install:

6. Install the caliper over the rotor with the outer brake shoe against the rotors braking surface. On the 1989–91 Thunderbird and Cougar make sure the anti-rattle spring is under the arm of the knuckle.

7. Make sure the locating pins are free of grease, oil or dirt and then hand start them into the caliper with a coating of silicone grease.

NOTE: Install new locating pins on the base Thunderbird, Cougar and Mustang models with the 2.3L non-turbocharged engine.

8. Tighten the locating pins to 45–65 ft. lbs. (61–88 Nm) on all models except the 1989–91 Thunderbird and Cougar. On the 1989–91 Thunderbird and Cougar tighten to 18–25 ft. lbs. (25–34 Nm).

9. Install the flexible brake hose to the caliper. Some models use a hose that threads into a self sealing fitting (no gasket) which is tightened to 20–30 ft. lbs. (28–63 Nm). When the hose is correctly tightened there should be 1 or 2 threads of of the fitting showing at the caliper. Other models use a hollow bolt with 2 new sealing washers to connect the hose to the caliper which is tightened to 17–25 ft. lbs. (23–34 Nm).

10. Bleed the brake system and fill the reservoir.

11. The remainder of the installation is the reverse of removal.

Disc Brake Pads
REMOVAL & INSTALLATION
Front

1. Raise and safely support vehicle.

2. Remove the wheel and tire. On models with anti-lock brakes, relieve the system of pressure.

3. Remove the caliper locating pins using the appropriate Torx® bit. Do not disconnect the brake lines and do not hang the caliper by the brake lines.

4. Lift the caliper from the rotor and mounting plate by using a slight turning motion.

5. Remove the brake pads by pulling them out of the caliper assembly.

To install:

6. Use a large C-clamp to push the caliper piston in. This must be done to give the caliper clearance on the rotor.

7. Install the inner pad, then the outer pad, making sure the clips are engaged in the caliper piston.

8. Install the caliper, by tilting it in over the rotor. Install and tighten the locating pins to 45–65 ft. lbs. (61–88 Nm) on all models except the 1989–91 Thunderbird and Cougar. On the 1989–91 Thunderbird and Cougar tighten to 18–25 ft. lbs. (25–34 Nm).

9. Install the wheel and tire and lower the vehicle. Pump the brakes a few times to ensure that the brake pads are seated. If the pedal is spongy or very low, the brake system may need to be bleed.

Rear

1. Raise and safely support vehicle.

2. Remove the wheel and tire.

3. Remove the screw retaining the brake hose bracket to the shock absorber bracket.

4. Remove the parking brake cable from the caliper. Hold the slider pin hex heads with an appropriate wrench. Remove the upper pinch bolt and loosen, but do not remove, the lower pinch bolt.

5. Tilt the caliper back from the rotor and remove the brake pads and anti-rattle clips from the anchor plate.

To install:

6. Using piston turning tool T87P–2588–A or equivalent, turn in the caliper piston until it is fully seated.

7. Install the inner and outer pads on the anchor plate. Tilt the caliper assembly over the pads and check to be sure the pads are correctly installed.

8. Apply threadlock sealer to the upper pinch bolt and install it, tightening to 23–26 ft. lbs. Tighten the lower pinch bolt to 23–26 ft. lbs.

9. Attach the parking brake cable. Install the wheel and tire, lower the vehicle.

Brake Rotor
REMOVAL & INSTALLATION

1. Raise and support the vehicle safely.

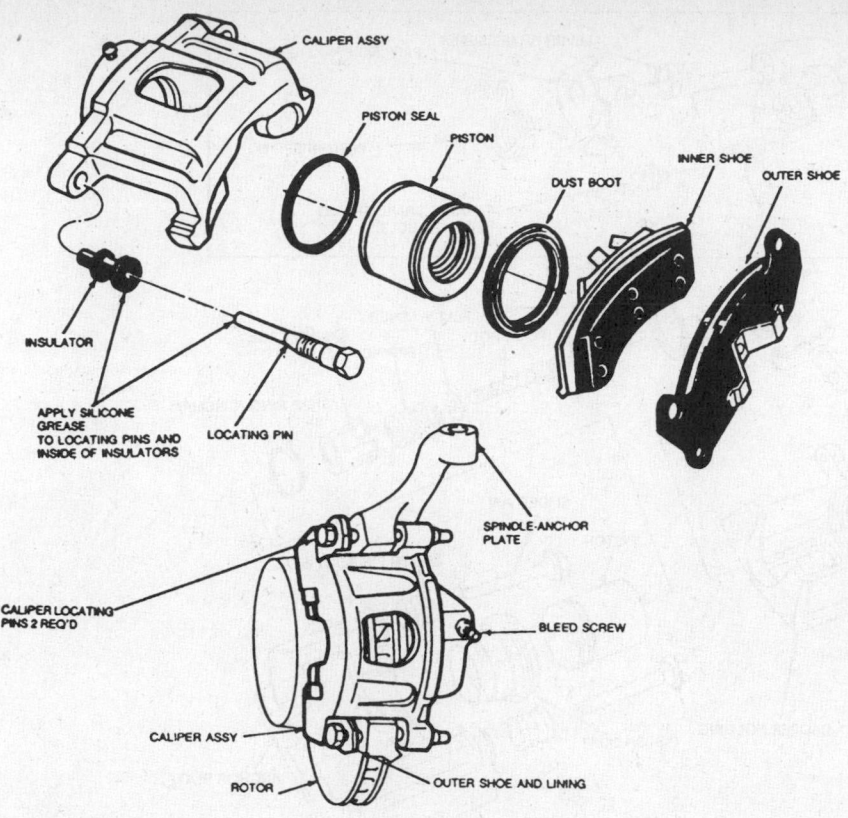

Exploded view of the front disc brakes—except 1989–91 Thunderbird and Cougar

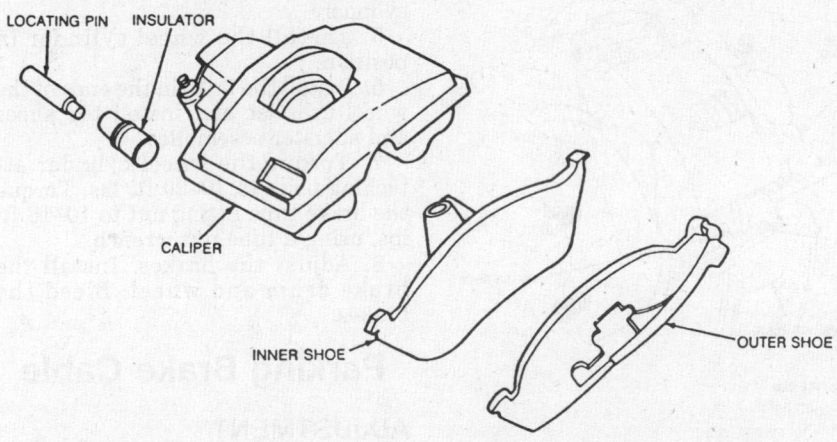

Exploded view of the front disc brakes—1989–91 Thunderbird and Cougar

2. Remove the caliper assembly.

3. Remove the gerease cap from the hub and remove the cotter pin, nut lock and adjusting nut.

4. Remove the outer bearing cone and roller assembly and remove the hub and rotor assembly.

5. Installation is the reverse of removal. Make sure the grease in the rotor is clean and adequate. Adjust the bearings.

Rear Brake Drum

REMOVAL & INSTALLATION

1. Raise and safely support the vehicle.

2. Remove the wheel and tire assembly.

3. Remove the drum retaining nuts and remove the brake drum.

4. Installation is the reverse of removal.

Rear Brake Shoes

REMOVAL & INSTALLATION

1. Raise and safely support the vehicle.

2. Remove the wheel and tire assembly. Remove the brake drum.

3. Disconnect the parking brake cable from the brake lever.

4. Remove the 2 brake shoe hold-down retainers, springs and pins.

5. Spread the brake shoes over the piston shoe guide slots. Lift the brake shoes, springs and adjusters off as an assembly. Be careful not to bend the adjuster.

6. Remove the adjuster spring. To separate the shoes, remove the retracting springs. Remove the parking brake lever retaining clip and spring washer, Remove lever from pin.

To install:

7. Apply a light coating of brake caliper slide grease or equivalent, to the backing plate where the brake shoes contact it.

8. Assemble brake adjuster with stainless steel washer. Turn the socket all the way down on the screw, then back off ½ turn.

9. Install parking brake lever to trailing shoe with the spring washer and new retaining clip. Crimp the clip to securely retain the lever.

10. Position the trailing shoe or backing plate and attach the hand brake cable.

11. Postion the leading shoe on the backing plate and attach lower retracting spring to the brake shoe.

12. Install the adjuster assembly to the slots in the brake shoes. The socket end must fit into the leading shoe. The slots in the adjuster nut must fit in the trailing shoe and parking brake lever.

13. Install the adjuster lever on the pin on the leading shoe and to the slot in the adjuster.

14. Install the upper retracting spring in the slot on the trailing shoe and in the slot in the adjuster lever. The adjuster lever should contact the star and adjuster assembly.

15. Install the brake shoe anchor pins, springs and retainers.

16. Install the brake drum, wheel and tire. Lower the vehicle.

Wheel Cylinder

REMOVAL & INSTALLATION

1. Remove the wheel and brake drum.

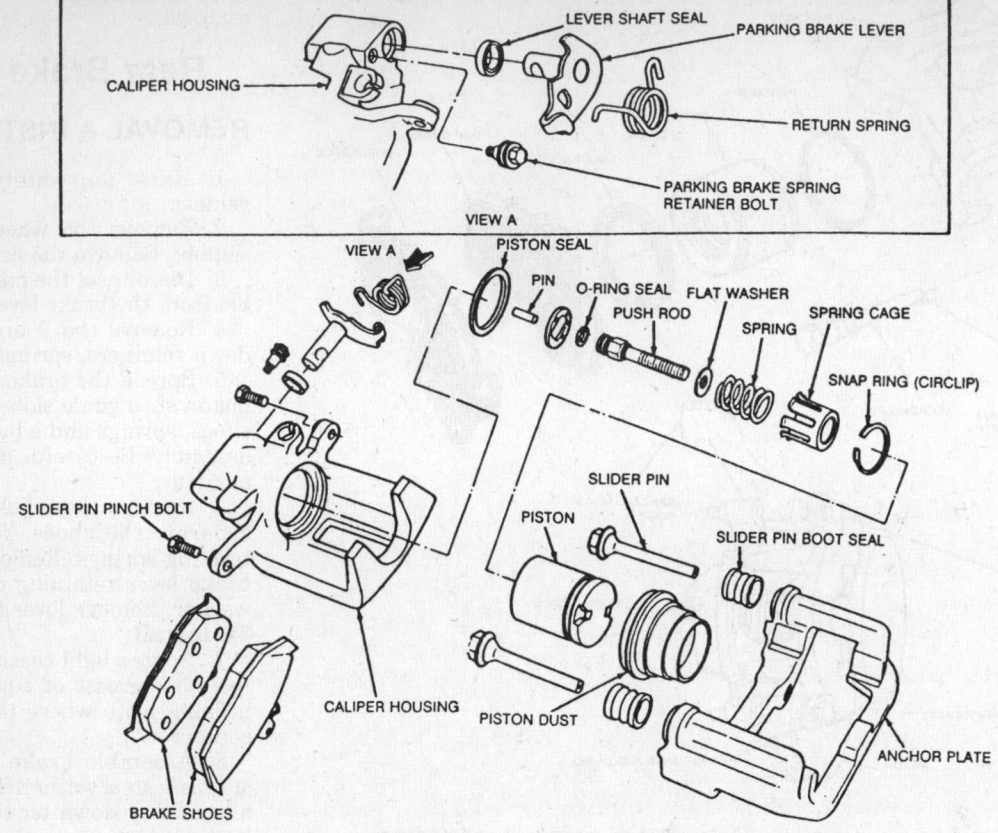

Exploded view of the rear disc brakes—1989–91 Thunderbird and Cougar

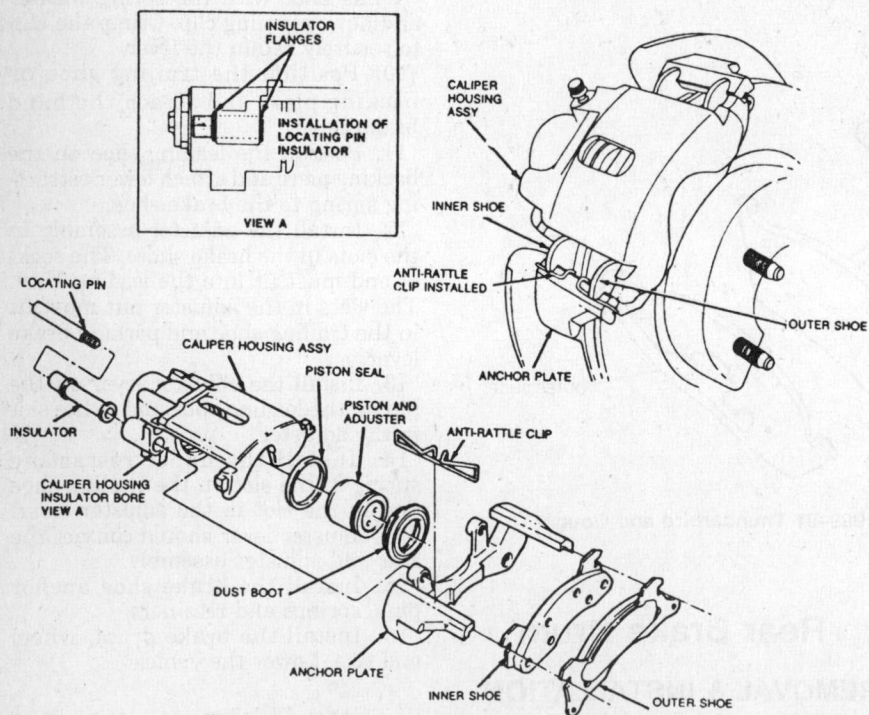

Exploded view of the rear disc brakes—Mark VII

2. Remove the brake shoe assemblies.

3. Disconnect the brake tube from the brake cylinder at the backing plate.

4. Remove the wheel cylinder at-

taching bolts and remove the wheel cylinder.

5. Install the wheel cylinder in position.

6. Install the links in the ends of the wheel cylinder and install the shoes and adjuster assemblies.

7. Torque the wheel cylinder attaching bolts to 10–20 ft. lbs. Torque the brake tube fitting nut to 10–18 ft. lbs. using a tube nut wrench.

8. Adjust the brakes. Install the brake drum and wheel. Bleed the brakes.

Parking Brake Cable

ADJUSTMENT

NOTE: If a new cable is installed, pre-stretch it by applying and releasing 5 times before making any adjustments.

Rear Drum Brakes

In most cases, a rear brake shoe adjustment will provide satisfactory parking brake action. However, if parking brake cables are excessively loose after releasing the hand brake, proceed as follows:

1. Fully release the parking brake.

2. Loosen locknut on equalizer rod

under the car. Then loosen the nut in front of the equalizer, several turns.

3. Turn the locknut forward against the equalizer until the cables are tight enough so that the rear wheels cannot be turned by hand. Then, back off the adjustment until the rear wheels turn freely.

4. When cables are properly adjusted, tighten both nuts against the equalizer.

5. Apply and release the brake and check the rear wheels. They should rotate freely.

Rear Disc Brakes

NOTE: **Parking brake adjustment is critical on 4 wheel disc brake equipped models. If the caliper has been overhauled or pads changed, be sure to pump pedal lightly approximately 30 times, before adjusting parking brake.**

1. Fully release the parking brake.

2. Locate the adjusting nut beneath the car on the driver's side. While observing the parking brake actuating levers on the rear calipers, tighten the adjusting nut until the levers just begin to move.

3. Apply and release parking brake control. Check the parking brake levers on the calipers to determine if they are fully returned to the stop position by attempting to pull them rearward.

4. If lever does not contact caliper lever stop, the cable adjustment is to tight. Repeat adjustment procedure.

REMOVAL & INSTALLATION

Front Cable

CROWN VICTORIA, GRAND MARQUIS AND TOWN CAR

1. Raise vehicle and loosen adjusting nut at adjuster.

2. Disconnect cable from intermediate cable connector located along left hand frame side rail.

3. Remove conduit retainer from frame. Remove screw holding the plastic inner fender apron to the frame, at the rear of the fender panel.

4. Pull back the fender apron and remove the spring clip retainer that holds the parking brake cable to the frame.

5. Pull the cable through the frame and let it hang in wheel housing. Lower the vehicle.

6. Inside the passenger compartment, remove the sound deadener cover from the cable at the dash panel.

7. Remove the spring retainer and cable end from the clevis at the parking brake control.

8. Remove conduit from the cable

assembly. Push the cable down through the dash panel and remove cable from inside the wheel housing.

9. Install the cable in position, slide the conduit down through the dash panel.

10. Install the inside sound deadener cover. Pull the cable through the frame and install the retaining clips.

11. Adjust the cable.

THUNDERBIRD, COUGAR, MUSTANG, MARK VII AND CONTINENTAL

1. Raise vehicle and loosen adjusting nut at adjuster.

2. Disconnect the front cable from the equalizer lever assembly and remove cable from the body bracket. Lower the vehicle.

3. Inside the passenger compartment, remove the retainer holding the cable conduit to the parking brake control and remove the cable.

4. Install the cable to the parking brake control.

5. Connect the cable to the equalizer lever assembly. Adjust the brake and lower the vehicle.

Intermediate Cable

CROWN VICTORIA, GRAND MARQUIS AND TOWN CAR

1. Raise vehicle and loosen the cable adjusting nut.

2. Disconnect parking brake release spring at frame.

3. Disconnect the cable from the cable connectors and remove it from the vehicle.

4. Connect the cable to the brake release spring. Adjust the brake and lower the vehicle.

THUNDERBIRD, COUGAR, MUSTANG, MARK VII AND CONTINENTAL

1. Raise vehicle and remove cable adjusting nut.

2. Disconnect the cable ends from the left hand rear and the transverse cable.

3. Remove the cotter pin, washer and spring from the pin protruding through the equalizer lever assembly and remove the lever.

4. Install the lever assembly and install the cotter pin and spring. Connect the cable ends to the left hand rear and transverse cables.

NOTE: **The intermediate cable cannot be separated from the lever assembly.**

5. Adjust the parking brake and lower the vehicle.

Transverse Cable

THUNDERBIRD, COUGAR, MUSTANG, MARK VII AND CONTINENTAL

1. Raise vehicle and loosen the adjusting nut on the rod until it is off rod.

2. Remove the cable ends from the right hand rear and intermediate cables.

3. Remove hairpin clips or conduit bracket as required to remove cable from vehicle.

4. Install the cable in the vehicle and attach the hairpin clips. Connect the cable ends to the right hand rear and intermediate cables.

5. Adjust the parking brake and lower the vehicle.

Rear Cables

1. Raise vehicle and remove adjuster nut at adjuster.

2. Disconnect parking the brake release spring at frame. Disconnect left hand cable from the intermediate cable connector.

3. Remove left hand conduit retainer from rod adjuster and remove the cable retainer from the left hand lower arm.

4. Release right hand conduit retainer from the frame and remove clip retaining right hand cable to the frame crossmember.

5. Remove cable retainer from right hand lower arm and disconnect cable from the retainer on right hand lower arm.

6. Remove rear wheels and brake drums. Remove brake automatic adjuster spring.

7. Compress the prongs on the parking brake cable retainer and pull cable retainer through backing plate hole.

8. With the tension off the cable spring at the parking brake lever, lift the cable end out of the slot in the lever. Remove the cable through backing plate hole.

9. Install the cable in through the backing plate and connect it to the lever.

10. Install the automatic brake adjuster spring and the brake drum. Complete the installation and adjust the brake.

11. Install the wheel and lower the vehicle.

Brake System Bleeding

WITHOUT ANTI-LOCK BRAKES

1. Clean all dirt from around the

master cylinder filler cap. If the master cylinder is known or suspected to have air in the bore, it must be bled before any wheel cylinders or calipers.

2. To bleed the master cylinder, loosen the upper secondary left front outlet fitting approximately ¾ turn. Have an assistant push the brake pedal down slowly through full travel. Close the outlet fitting, then return the pedal slowly to the full released position. Wait 5 seconds, then repeat the operation until the air bubbles cease to appear.

3. Loosen the upper primary right front outlet fitting approximately ¾ turn. and repeat Step 3.

4. To continue to bleed the system, remove the rubber cap dust cap from the wheel cylinder bleeder fitting or caliper fitting. Check to make sure the bleeder fitting is positioned at the upper half on the front of the caliper, if not the caliper is located on the wrong side.

5. Place a suitable box wrench on the bleeder fitting and attach the rubber drain tube to the fitting. Submerge the free end of the tube in a container partially filled with clean brake fluid and loosen the bleeder fitting approitmately ¾ of a turn.

6. Have the assisant push brake pedal down slowly through full travel. Close the bleeder fitting, then return the pedal to the full release position. Wait 5 seconds, then repeat this operation until the air bubbles cease to appear at the submerged end of the bleeder tube.

7. When the fluid is completely free of air bubbles, secure the bleeder tube and install the rubber dust cap on the bleeder fitting. Repeat this process on the opposite diagonal system. Refill the master cylinder reservoir after each wheel cylinder or caliper id bled and reinstall the master cylinder cap.

8. When the bleeding operation is completed, the fluid level should be filled to the maximum fill level indicated on the reservoir. Always ensure the disc brake pistons are returned to their normal positions by depressing the brake pedal several times until the normal pedal travel is established. Check the pedal feel. If the pedal feels spongy repeat the bleed procedure.

NOTE: 1988–91 Crown Victoria and Grand Marquis vehicles also have a bleeder fitting on the master cylinder. Follow steps 5 thru 7 to bleed the master cylinder.

WITH ANTI-LOCK BRAKES
—— CAUTION ——

Before servicing any component which contains high pressure, it is mandatory that the hydraulic pressure in the system be discharged or personal injury could result.

To discharge the system, turn the ignition **OFF** and pump the brake pedal a minimum of 20 times until an increase in pedal force is clearly felt. Read the service instructions carefully before servicing any component of the anti-lock brake system.

Town Car

NOTE: The anti-lock brake system on these vehicles must be bled in 2 steps.

1. The master cylinder and the hydraulic control unit must be bled using a Rotunda anti-lock brake breakout box/bleeding adapter tool T90P-50-ALA or equivalent. If this procedure is not followed air will be trapped in the Hydraulic Control Unit (HCU) which will lead to a spongy brake pedal.

a. To bleed the master cylinder and the HCU, disconnect the 55 pin plug from the HCU and install the anti-lock brake breakout box/bleeding adapter T90P-50-ALA, or equivalent to the wire harness 55 pin plug.

b. Place the bleed/harness switch in the **BLEED** position.

c. Turn the ignition to the **ON** position. At this point the red **OFF** light should turn ON.

d. Push the motor button adapter down to start the pump motor. The red **OFF** light will turn OFF and the green **ON** light will turn ON. The pump motor will run for 60 seconds once the motor is pushed. If the pump motor is to be turned OFF for any reason before this 60 seconds has elapsed, push the abort button and the pump motor will turn OFF.

e. After 20 seconds of pump motor operation, push and hold the valve button down. Hold the valve button for 20 seconds then release.

f. The pump motor will continue to run for an additional 20 seconds after the valve button is released.

2. The brake system can now be bled in the conventional manner as outlined in the previous procedure. Bleed in the following sequence. right hand rear, left hand front, left hand rear, right hand front.

Thunderbird, Cougar and Mark VII
FRONT

The front brakes can be bled in the conventional manner or with Rotunda Brake Bleeder 104-00064 or equivalent with or without the accumulator being charged.

Conventional Method

1. Remove dust cap from right hand front caliper bleeder fitting. Attach a rubber drain tube to fitting. Ensure

that the end of the tube fits snugly around the fitting.

2. Submerge free end of tube in a container partially filled with clean brake fluid.

3. Loosen bleeder fitting approximately ¾ turn. Have assistant push brake pedal down slowly through full travel and hold at that position.

4. Close bleeder fitting, then return pedal to full release position.

5. Wait 5 seconds, then repeat operation until air bubbles cease to appear at submerged end of the bleeder tube.

6. Repeat operation at left hand front caliper.

7. Proceed with rear brake bleeding procedures.

Pressure Bleeder Method

1. Clean all dirt from the reservoir filler cap area. Attach pressure bleeder Rotunda 104-00064 or equivalent, to reservoir cap opening.

2. Maintain 35 psi (240 kPa) pressure on the system.

3. Remove dust cap from right hand front caliper bleeder fitting. Attach a rubber drain tube to the fitting, making sure that the end of the tube fits snugly around the fitting.

4. With ignition switch in the **OFF** position, and the brake pedal in the fully released position, open the right hand front caliper bleeder fitting for 10 seconds at a time until an air-free stream of brake fluid flow is observed.

5. Repeat procedure at left hand front caliper.

6. Proceed with rear brake bleeding procedures.

REAR BRAKES

The rear brakes can be pressure bled using Rotunda brake bleeder 104-00064 or equivalent, or with a fully charged accumulator.

Pressure Bleeding Method

1. Clean all dirt from reservoir filler cap area. Attach pressure bleeder, Rotunda 04-00064 or Equivalent, to reservoir cap opening.

2. Maintain 35 psi (240 kPa) pressure on the system.

3. Remove dust cap from right hand caliper bleeder fitting. Attach a rubber drain tube to fitting, making sure that end of tube fits snugly around fitting.

4. With ignition switch in the **OFF** position, and brake pedal in the fully released position, open right hand rear caliper bleeder fitting for 10 seconds at a time until an air-free stream of brake fluid flow is observed.

5. Repeat procedure at left hand rear caliper.

6. Place ignition switch in the **RUN** position and pump brake pedal several times to complete the bleeding procedure and to fully charge accumulator.

7. Siphon off excess fluid in reservoir to adjust level to the **MAX** mark with a fully charged accumulator.

Bleeding System with a Fully Charged Accumulator

1. Remove dust cap from right hand rear caliper bleeder fitting. Attach a rubber drain tube to the fitting, making sure that end of tube fits snugly around fitting.
2. Turn ignition switch to the **RUN** position. This will turn on the electric pump to charge the accumulator as required.
3. Hold brake pedal in the applied position. Open the right hand rear caliper bleeder fitting for 10 seconds at a time until an air-free stream of brake fluid flow is observed.

——— **CAUTION** ———

Care must be used when opening the bleeder screws due to the high pressures available from a fully charged accumulator or personal injury may result.

4. Repeat procedure at left hand rear caliper.
5. Pump brake pedal several times to complete bleeding procedure and to fully charge accumulator.
6. Adjust fluid level in reservoir to **MAX** mark with a fully charged accumulator.

NOTE: If the pump motor is allowed to run continuously for approximately 20 minutes, a thermal safety switch inside the motor may shut the motor off to prevent it from overheating. If that happens, a 2-10 minute cool down period is typically required before normal operation can resume.

HYDRAULIC PUMP PRIMING

1. Remove dust cap from right hand rear caliper bleeder fitting. Attach a rubber drain tube to fitting making sure that end of tube fits snugly around fitting.
2. Turn ignition switch to the **RUN** position. This will turn on the electric pump.
3. Hold brake pedal in the applied position, and open the right hand rear caliper bleeder fitting for 10 seconds at a time until a steady stream of brake fluid flow is observed.
4. Repeat above procedures with left hand rear caliper.

Anti-Lock Brake System Service

PRECAUTIONS

- Before servicing any high pres-

sure component, discharge the hydraulic pressure from the system.
- Do not allow brake fluid to contact any electrical connections.
- Use care when opening the bleeder screws due to the high system pressure from the accumulator.

RELIEVING ANTI-LOCK BRAKE SYSTEM PRESSURE

——— **CAUTION** ———

Before servicing any component which contains high pressure, it is mandatory that the hydraulic pressure in the system be discharged or personal injury could result.

To discharge the system, turn the ignition **OFF** and pump the brake pedal a minimum of 20 times until an increase in pedal force is clearly felt. Read the service instructions carefully before servicing any component of the anti-lock brake system.

Front Wheel Speed Sensor

REMOVAL & INSTALLATION

Mark VII

1. Disconnect the negative battery cable.
2. From inside engine compartment, disconnect sensor electrical connector for right hand or left hand front sensor.
3. Raise vehicle and disengage wire grommet at right hand or left hand shock tower and pull sensor cable connector through hole. Use care not to damage connector.
4. Remove sensor wire from bracket on shock strut and side rail.
5. Remove tire.
6. Loosen 5mm setscrew holding sensor to sensor bracket post. Remove sensor through hole in disc brake splash shield.
7. To remove sensor bracket or sensor bracket post in case of damage, the caliper and hub and rotor assembly must be removed. After removing the hub and rotor assembly, remove 2 brake splash shield attaching bolts which attach sensor bracket.

NOTE: Replace the toothed sensor ring, if damaged.

To Install:
8. Install sensor bracket with sensor bracket post, if removed. Tighten post retaining bolt to 40–60 inch lb. (4.5–6.8 Nm) and splash shield attaching bolts to 10–15 ft. lbs. (13–20 Nm). Install hub and rotor assembly and caliper.

9. If a sensor is to be reused or adjusted, pole face must be clean of all foreign material. Carefully scrape pole face with a dull knife or similar tool, to ensure that sensor slides freely on the post. Glue a new front paper spacer on pole face, front paper spacer is marked with a **F** and is 0.051 in. (1.3mm) thick. Also, the steel sleeve around post bolt must be rotated to provide a new surface for setscrew to indent and lock into.
10. Install sensor through brake shield onto sensor bracket post. Ensure paper spacer on sensor is intact and does not come off during installation.
11. Push sensor toward toothed sensor ring until new paper sensor contacts the ring. Hold sensor against sensor ring and tighten the 5mm setscrew to 21–26 ft. lbs. (2.4–3.0 Nm).
12. Insert sensor cable into bracket on shock strut, rail bracket; then through inner fender apron to engine compartment and seat grommet.
13. Lower vehicle and from inside engine compartment, connect sensor electrical connection.

Town Car

1. Disconnect the negative battery cable.
2. From inside engine compartment, disconnect sensor assembly two-pin connector from wiring harness.
3. Remove steel routing clip attaching sensor wire to tube bundle on left hand sensor or remove plastic routing clip attaching sensor wire to frame on right hand sensor.
4. Remove rubber coated spring steel clip holding sensor wire to frame.
5. Remove sensor wire from steel routing clip on frame and from dust shield.
6. Remove sensor attaching bolt from front spindle and slide sensor out of mounting hole.

To install:
7. Install sensor into mounting hole in front spindle and attach with mounting bolt. Tighten to 40–60 inch lbs. (4.5-6.8 Nm).
8. Insert sensor routing grommets into dust shield and steel bracket on frame. Route wire into engine compartment.
9. Install rubber coated steel clip that holds sensor wire to frame into hole in frame.
10. Install steel clip that holds sensor wire to tube bundle on left hand side, or plastic clip that holds sensor to frame on right hand side.
11. Connect 2-pin connector to wire harness.

Thunderbird and Cougar

1. Disconnect the negative battery cable.

2. From underside of vehicle, up front near radiator support, disconnect sensor electrical connector for right hand or left hand front sensor.

3. Remove routing clips along wiring harness.

4. Remove Torx® head screw securing sensor to front spindle.

NOTE: If the toothed speed indicator ring is damaged, replace as outlined.

To install:

5. Install sensor into hole in spindle. No adjustment is necessary. Install Torx® head screw and tighten to 40–60 inch lbs. (4.5–6.8 Nm).

6. Route wiring using clips previously removed. Ensure wiring is routed properly as shown.

7. Connect sensor wiring connector to harness connector.

Rear Wheel Speed Sensor

REMOVAL & INSTALLATION

Mark VII

1. Disconnect the negative battery cable.

2. From inside the luggage compartment, disconnect the wheel sensor electrical connector located behind the forward luggage compartment trim panel.

3. Lift the luggage compartment carpet and push the sensor wire grommet through the hole in the luggage compartment floor.

4. Raise the vehicle and remove the appropriate wheel and tire assembly.

5. Carefully remove the wheel sensor wiring from the axle shaft housing. The wiring harness has 3 different types of retainers. The inboard retainer is a clip located on top of the differential housing. Bend the clip out of the way enough to remove the wiring harness. The second retainer is a C-clip located in the center of the axle shaft housing. Pull rearward on the clip to disengage the clip from the axle housing.

NOTE: Do not bend the clip open beyond the amount necessary to remove the clip from the axle housing. The third clip is at the connection between the rear wheel brake tube and the flexible hose. Remove the hold-down bolt and open the clip to remove the wiring harness.

6. Remove the rear wheel caliper and rotor assemblies.

7. Remove the wheel sensor E8 Torx® head retaining bolt. Slip the grommet out of the rear brake splash shield and pull the sensor wire outward through the hole.

8. Inspect the sensor bracket for possible damage. If damaged, remove the two 6mm self-tapping screws attaching the bracket to the axle adapter and remove the bracket.

NOTE: Replace the toothed sensor ring, if damaged.

To install:

9. Install the sensor bracket, if removed. Tighten the screws to 11–15 ft. lbs. (15–20 Nm)

10. Loosen the 5mm setscrew on the sensor and ensure that the sensor slides freely on the sensor bracket post.

11. If a sensor is to be reused or adjusted, the pole face must be clean of all foreign material. Carefully scrape the pole face with a dull knife or similar tool. Glue a new rear paper spacer on the pole face. Rear paper spacer is marked with a **R** and is 0.043-inch thick. If desired, a feeler gauge may be used instead of a paper spacer. If used, remove paper spacer prior to adjusting. Also, the steel sleeve around the post bolt must be rotated to provide a new surface for the setscrew to indent and lock into.

12. Insert the snesor into large hole in the sensor bracket and install the E8 Torx® head retaining bolt into the snesor bracket post. Tighten the bolt to 40–60 inch lbs. (4.5–6.8 Nm).

13. Push the snesor toward the toothed ring until the new paper sensor makes contact with the sensor ring. Hold the sensor against the toothed ring and tighten the 5mm setscrew to 21–26 inch lbs. (2.4–3.0 Nm).

14. Install the caliper and rotor.

15. Push the wire and connector through the splash shield hole and engage the grommet into the shield eyelet. Install the sensor wire in the retainers along the axle housing.

16. Push the connector through the hole in the luggage compartment and seat the grommet in the luggage compartment floorpan.

17. From inside the luggage compartment, connect the cable electrical connector. Install the carpet as necessary.

18. Check the function of the sensor by driving the vehicle and observing the "Check Anti-Lock Brakes" lamp in the overhead console.

Town Car

1. Disconnect the negative battery cable.

2. From inside luggage compartment disconnect two-pin sensor connector from wiring harness and push sensor wire through hole in floor.

3. From below vehicle, remove sensor wire from routing bracket located on top of rear axle carrier housing, and remove steel clip holding sensor wire and brake tube against axle housing.

4. Remove screw from clip holding sensor wire and brake tube to bracket on axle.

5. Remove sensor from bracket in rear brake backing plate by spreading open steel split ring with a small screwdriver or similar tool, and pulling sensor out of bracket.

To install:

6. Ensure that steel split ring is located in groove properly. Opening in ring must not line up with notch in tube shaped sensor retainer.

7. Insert sensor into bracket with notch correctly aligned with bracket. Push sensor in until split ring locks sensor into place.

8. Attach clip holding sensor and brake tube to bracket on axle housing and secure with screw.

9. Install steel clip around axle tube that holds sensor wire and brake tube against axle tube and push spool-shaped grommet into clip located on top of axle carrier housing.

10. Push sensor wire connector up through hole in floor and seat large round grommet into hole.

11. Connect sensor two-pin connector to wiring harness inside luggage compartment.

Thunderbird and Cougar

1. Disconnect the negative battery cable.

2. From inside luggage compartment, disconnect wheel sensor electrical connector located rearward of wheel well, behind carpeting on sides of luggage compartment.

3. Lift luggage compartment carpet and push sensor wire grommet through hole in luggage compartment floor.

4. Remove plastic clip holding sensor wire to axle carrier housing.

5. Remove wheel sensor retaining bolt using a ½ in. socket.

To install:

6. Align sensor locating tab and bolt hole with axle housing and push into position.

7. Install sensor retaining bolt and tighten to 14–20 ft. lbs. (19–27 Nm).

8. Install plastic clip retaining sensor wire to axle carrier housing and push electrical connector through hole in floor into luggage compartment. Ensure that rubber grommet is properly seated in hole in floor.

9. Connect sensor electrical connector to connector on harness.

FRONT SUSPENSION

NOTE: If equipped with the level ride air suspension power to the air system must be shut OFF before servicing the suspension. The switch is located in the luggage compartment, on the drivers side rear fender well.

Shock Absorbers

REMOVAL & INSTALLATION

NOTE: Purge a new shock of air by repeatedly extending it in its normal position and compressing it while inverted.

1. Remove the nut, washer and bushing from the upper end of the shock absorber.
2. Raise and safely support the vehicle by the frame rails allowing the front wheels to hang.
3. Remove the 2 bolts securing the shock absorber to the lower control arm and remove the shock absorber.
To install:
4. Install a new bushing and washer on the top of the shock absorber and position the unit inside the front spring. Install the 2 lower attaching bolts and torque them to 8–15 ft. lbs.
5. Lower the vehicle.
6. Place a new bushing and washer on the shock absorber top stud and install a new attaching nut. Torque to 22–30 ft. lbs.

MacPherson Strut

REMOVAL & INSTALLATION

Except 1989–91 Thunderbird and Cougar

1. Raise and safely support the front of the vehicle allowing the suspension to hang freely.
2. Remove the wheel and tire. Remove the brake caliper and position out of the way, do not allow the caliper to hang from the brake hose. Raise the lower control arm with a floor jack to compress the spring.
3. Remove the 3 upper strut mounting nuts from the top of the shock tower. If the upper mount is to be replaced on Thunderbird and Cougar models, loosen the 16mm strut rod nut at this time.
4. Remove the 2 lower strut nuts that attach the strut to the spindle bracket. Leave the bolts in place.
5. Compress the strut to clear the

upper mount. With the strut compressed, remove the lower strut thru-bolts. Push the mounting bracket free of the spindle and remove the strut.

NOTE: If equipped with gas pressurized struts, the strut will remain fully extended. Carefully remove both lower strut to spindle bolts, push the bracket free of the spindle and remove the strut.

To install:
6. Place the upper mount in position on the shock tower. Loosely install new upper mounting nuts. Extend the strut and position in the spindle bracket. Install the 2 lower mounting bolts and nuts. Tighten the nuts to 140–170 ft. lbs.
7. Raise the control arm with a floorjack and tighten the upper mount nuts to 50–70 ft. lbs.
8. Install the remaining parts in the reverse order of removal.

1989–91 Thunderbird and Cougar

1. Remove the plastic cover at the upper strut mount. If equipped with automatic ride control, remove the actuator assembly.
2. Remove the 3 upper strut retaining bolts. Raise and safely support the vehicle.
3. Remove the wheel and tire assembly. Remove the upper stabilizer link mounting stud.
4. Separate the link from the spindle using a joint separator, D88L-3006–A or equivalent.
5. Raise the control arm and spindle using a jack, until the stabilizer link can be completely separated from the spindle.
6. Remove the spindle to upper control arm attaching bolt and discard it. Lower the jack to separate the spindle and control arm. Do not allow the spindle to hang, wire it up.
7. Remove the support from the lower control arm and remove the strut assembly.
To Install:
8. Install the shock in position and install the lower strut bolt. Using a jack, raise the control arm and strut into position.
9. Connect the spindle and upper control arm, install a new bolt and tighten to 50–60 ft. lbs.
10. Position the stabilizer link and lower spindle assembly until the link can be installed. Install the nut on the link stud and tighten to 40–55 ft. lbs.
11. Remove the jack and tighten the lower strut bolt to 103–144 ft. lbs.
12. Install the tire and wheel and lower the vehicle. Install the collar plate and the 3 retaining nuts at the

top of the strut. Tighten the nuts to 16–23 ft. lbs.
13. Install the ride height actuator, if equipped. Install the plastic cover.

Coil Springs

REMOVAL & INSTALLATION

NOTE: The coil spring on the 1989–91 Thunderbird and Cougar, is removed with the strut assembly.

1. Raise and safely support the vehicle. Remove the tire and wheel.
2. Disconnect the stabilizer link from the lower arm.
3. Remove the lower shock absorber attaching bolts.
4. Remove the shock absorber upper nut and remove the shock.
5. Remove the steering center link from the pitman arm.
6. Install a spring compressor tool. Insert the securing pin through the upper ball nut and the compression rod. This pin can only be inserted 1 way. With the upper ball nut secured, turn the upper plate so it walks up the coil and contacts the upper spring seat. Back the nut off ½ turn.
7. Install the lower ball nut and the thrust washer on the compression rod and tighten the forcing nut until the spring is free in the seat.
8. Remove the 2 lower control arm pivot bolts.
9. Disengage the arm from the frame and remove the spring assembly.
10. If a new spring is being installed, mark the position of the upper and lower plates on the old spring. Also, measure the length of the spring and the amount of curvature in order to simplify the compressing and installation of the new spring.
11. Loosen the forcing nut and remove the spring from the tool.
To install:
12. Assemble the spring compressor tool on the new spring in the same position as the old spring was removed.
13. Position the spring in the lower arm.
14. Install the lower plate, ball nut, thrust washer and bearing. Install the lower arm into the crossmember and install new lower control arm bolts, tighten to 110–150 ft. lbs.
15. Connect the stabilizer bar link to the to the lower suspension arm and tighten the bolts to 90–100 ft. lbs.
16. Install the tie rod assembly and tighten the retaining nut to 35 ft. lbs. Install the brake caliper, tire and wheel assembly. Lower the vehicle.

Torsion Bars

REMOVAL & INSTALLATION

1. Turn the air suspension switch **OFF**, if equipped.
2. Raise the vehicle and safely support.
3. Disconnect the stabilizer bar from each link and bushing U-clamps. Remove the stabilizer bar assembly.
4. Remove the adapter brackets and U-clamps.
5. Cut the worn bushings from the stabilizer bar.

To install:

6. Coat the necessary parts of the stabilizer bar with Ford rubber suspension insulator lubricant E25Y–19533–A or equivalent, and slide the new bushings onto the stabilizer bar. Reinstall the U-clamps.
7. Reinstall the adapter brackets on the U-clamps.
8. Using a new nut and bolt, secure each end of the stabilizer bar to the lower suspension arm.
9. Using new bolts, clamp the stabilizer bar to the attaching brackets on the side rail.
10. Lower the vehicle. Turn air suspension switch **ON**, on vehicles equipped.

Upper Ball Joints

INSPECTION

1. Raise and safely support the vehicle allowing the front wheels to hang.
2. Have an assistant grasp the bottom of the tire and move the wheel in and out.
3. As the wheel is being moved, observe the upper control arm where the spindle attaches to it. Any movement between the upper part of the spindle and the upper ball joint indicates a bad ball joint which must be replaced.

NOTE: During this check the lower ball joint will be unloaded and may move; this is normal and not an indication of a bad ball joint. Also, do not mistake a loose wheel bearing for a defective ball joint. Ford Motor Company recommends replacement of the control arm and ball joint as an assembly. However, aftermarket replacement parts are available, which can be installed using the following procedure.

REMOVAL & INSTALLATION

1. Raise the vehicle and support on frame points so that the front wheels fall to their full down position.

2. Drill a 1/8 in. hole completely through each ball joint attaching rivet.
3. Using a large chisel, cut off the head of each rivet and drive them from the arm.
4. Place a jack under the lower arm and raise to compress the coil spring.
5. Remove the cotter pin and attaching nut from the ball joint stud.
6. Using a ball joint removal tool, loosen the ball joint stud from the spindle and remove the ball joint from the arm.
7. Clean all metal burrs from the arm and install the new ball joint, using the service part nuts and bolts to attach the ball joint. Do not attempt to rivet the ball joint once it has been removed. Tighten the ball joint-to-upper spindle to 75–90 ft. lbs.
8. Check front end alignment.

Lower Ball Joints

INSPECTION

1. Support the vehicle in normal driving position with ball joints loaded.
2. Wipe the wear indicator and ball joint cover checking surface clean.
3. The checking surface should project outside the cover. If the checking surface is inside the cover, replace the lower arm assembly.

REMOVAL & INSTALLATION

1. Raise and safely support the front of the vehicle allowing the front wheels to hang.
2. Have an assistant grasp the wheel top and bottom and apply alternate in and out pressure to the top and bottom of the wheel.
3. Radial play of 1/4 in. is acceptable measured at the inside of the wheel adjacent to the lower arm.
4. Drill a 1/8 in. hole completely through each ball joint attaching rivet.
5. Using a large chisel, cut off the head of each rivet and drive them from the arm.
6. Place a jack under the lower arm and raise it to compress the coil spring.
7. Remove the cotter pin and attaching nut from the ball joint stud.
8. Using a ball joint removal tool, loosen the ball joint stud from the spindle and remove the ball joint from the arm.
9. Clean all metal burrs from the arm and install the new ball joint, using the service part nuts and bolts to attach the ball joint. Do not attempt to rivet the ball joint once it has been removed. Tighten the ball joint-to-lower spindle bolt to 100–120 ft. lbs.
10. Check the front wheel alignment.

Upper Control Arms

REMOVAL & INSTALLATION

1. Raise and safely support the vehicle allowing the suspension to hang. Remove the wheel.
2. Remove the cotter pin from the upper ball joint stud nut. Loosen the nut a few turns but do not remove.
3. Install a ball joint removal tool between the upper and lower ball joint studs. Expand the tool until it places the upper stud under compression. Tap the spindle near the stud with a hammer to loosen the stud.
4. Remove the tool. Raise the lower arm with a jack until pressure is relieved from the upper stud. Remove the upper stud nut.
5. Remove the upper shaft attaching bolts and the upper arm.

To install:

6. Position the arm to the frame, install the attaching nuts and torque to 120–140 ft. lbs.
7. Connect the upper stud to the spindle. Install the attaching nuts and tighten to 75 ft. lbs., then continue to tighten until the cotter pin holes align.
8. Install a new cotter pin. Install the wheel, adjust the wheel bearings and lower the car.
9. Caster, camber and toe must be adjusted after installation.

Lower Control Arms

REMOVAL & INSTALLATION

Except 1989–91 Thunderbird and Cougar

1. Raise and safely support the front of the vehicle. Remove the wheel and brake caliper. Suspend the caliper with hose connected, out of the way.
2. Disconnect the tie rod end from the steering spindle.
3. Disconnect the stabilizer bar from the arm. Remove the steering gear bolts and lower the gear out of the way to provide clearance, if necessary, for suspension arm bolt removal.
4. Install a spring compressor. Turn the tightening nut on the tool so the spring is free in the seat.
5. Remove the 2 lower control arm pivot bolts and disengage the arm from the frame. Remove the spring.

To install:

6. Install the arm to the frame and install the lower pivot bolts.
7. Reconnect the stabilizer bar. Position the steering gear and install the mounting bolts.
8. Be sure the lower end of the spring is properly positioned between the 2 holes in the lower arm spring pocket.

9. Install the brake caliper and wheel.

1989–91 Thunderbird and Cougar

1. Raise and safely support the vehicle. Remove the tire and wheel.
2. Loosen the lower ball joint nut and separate the ball joint, leave it attached.
3. Support the spindle with a wire. Mark the position of the camber adjusting cam. Remove the nut attaching the tension strut to the control arm.
4. Remove the lower strut bolt and remove the pivot bolt.
5. Remove the ball joint nut and remove the arm.

To install:

6. Position the control arm in the vehicle and loosely install the pivot bolt.
7. Loosely install the ball joint nut. Install the tension strut insulators and install the tension strut to the control arm.
8. Tighten the lower strut bolt to 103–144 ft. lbs., the ball joint nut to 80–120 ft. lbs. and the tension strut-to-control arm to 90–120 ft. lbs.
9. Align the camber marks at the pivot bolt and tighten to 92–125 ft. lbs. Install the tire and wheel, lower the vehicle. Check the wheel alignment.

Front Wheel Bearings

ADJUSTMENT

1. Raise and safely support the front of the vehicle.
2. Remove the wheel cover and grease cap.
3. Remove the cotter pin and nut lock.
4. Loosen the adjusting nut 3 turns and rock the wheel back and forth a few times to release the brake pads from the rotor.
5. While rotating the wheel and hub assembly, tighten the adjusting nut to 17–25 ft. lbs. (23–34 Nm).
6. Back off the adjusting nut ½ turn, then retighten to 10–12 inch lbs. (1.1–1.7 Nm).
7. Install the locknut and a new cotter pin. Check the wheel rotation. If it is noisy or rough, the bearings either need to be cleaned, repacked or readjusted. After adjustments are complete, replace the grease cap.

REMOVAL & INSTALLATION

1. Raise and support the vehicle safely. Remove the wheel assembly. Remove the caliper.
2. Pry off the dust cap. Tap out and discard the cotter pin. Remove the locknut.

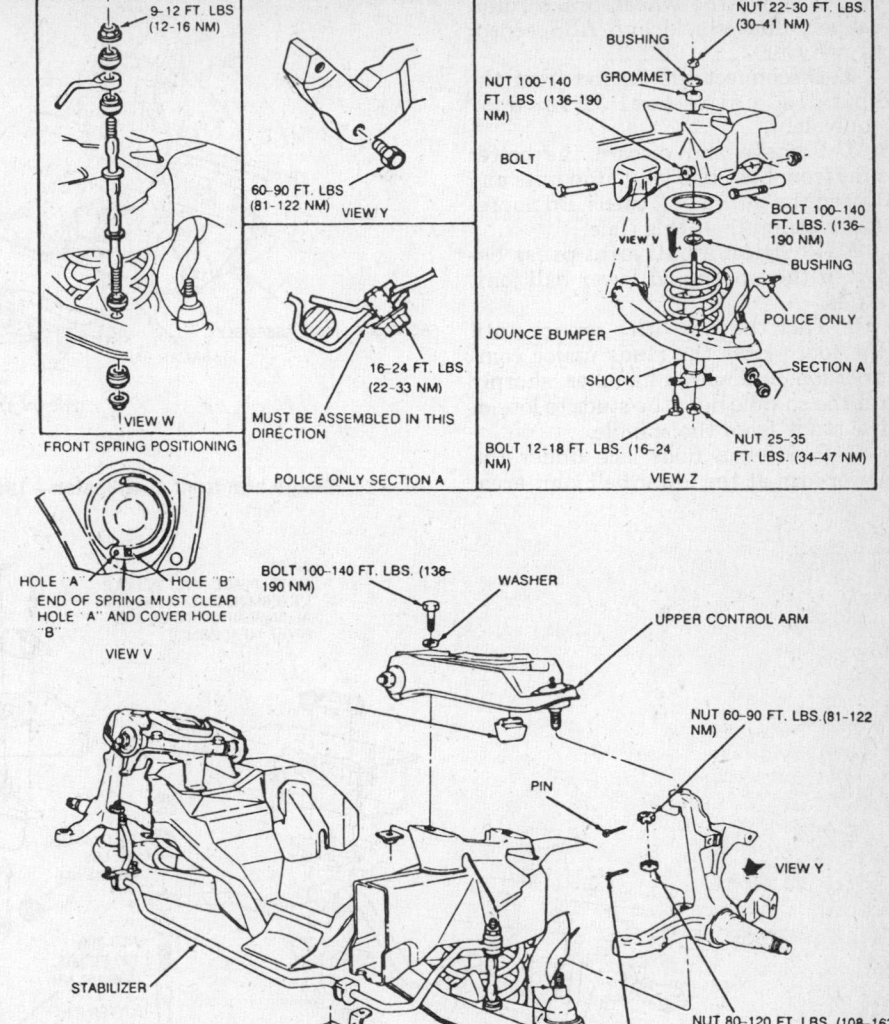

Spring on lower arm front suspension—Town Car, Crown Victoria and Grand Marquis

3. Being careful not to drop the outer bearing, pull off the brake disc and wheel hub.
4. Remove the grease inside the wheel hub.
5. Using a brass drift, carefully drive the outer bearing race out of the hub.
6. Remove the inner grease seal and bearing.
7. Check the bearings for wear or damage and replace them, if necessary.

To install:

8. Coat the inner surface of the hub with grease.
9. Grease the outer surface of the bearing race and drift it into place in the hub.
10. Pack the inner and outer wheel bearings with grease. If the brake disc has been removed and/or replaced,

tighten the retaining bolts to specification.

11. Install the inner bearing in the hub. Being careful not to distort it, install the oil seal with its lip facing the bearing. Drive the seal on until its outer edge is even with the edge of the hub.
12. Install the hub/disc assembly on the spindle, being careful not to damage the oil seal.
13. Install the outer bearing, washer and spindle nut. Adjust the bearing.

Front Spindle

REMOVAL & INSTALLATION

Crown Victoria, Grand Marquis and Town Car

1. Raise and support the vehicle safely.

2. Remove the wheel, brake rotor, caliper, dust shield and ABS sensor (Town Car).

3. Disconnect the tie rod from the spindle, using tool 3290-D or equivalent.

4. Remove and discard the cotter pins from both ball joint stud nuts and loosen the nuts 1 or 2 turns. Do not remove the nuts at this time.

5. Position a ball joint press between the upper and lower ball joint studs.

6. Turn the tool with a wrench until the tool places the studs under compression, and with a hammer, sharply hit the spindle near the studs to loosen the studs from the spindle.

7. Position a floor jack under the lower arm at the lower ball joint area.

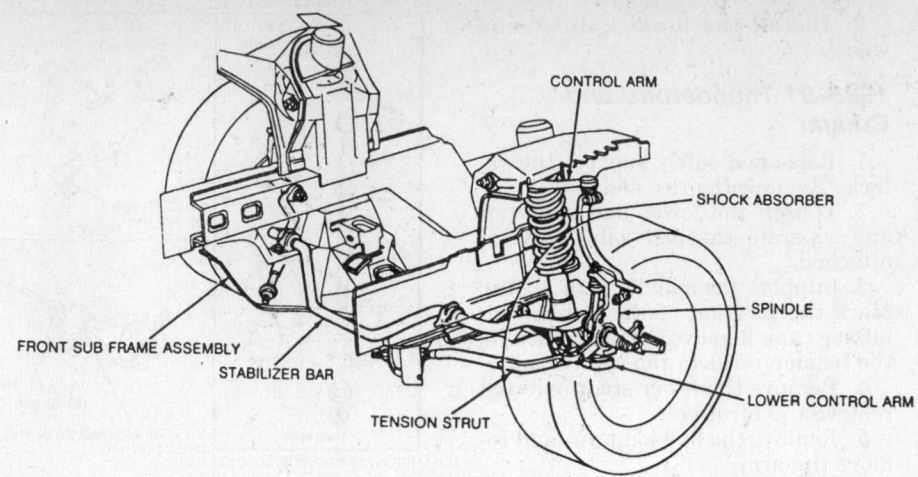

Single arm front suspension—1989–91 Thunderbird and Cougar

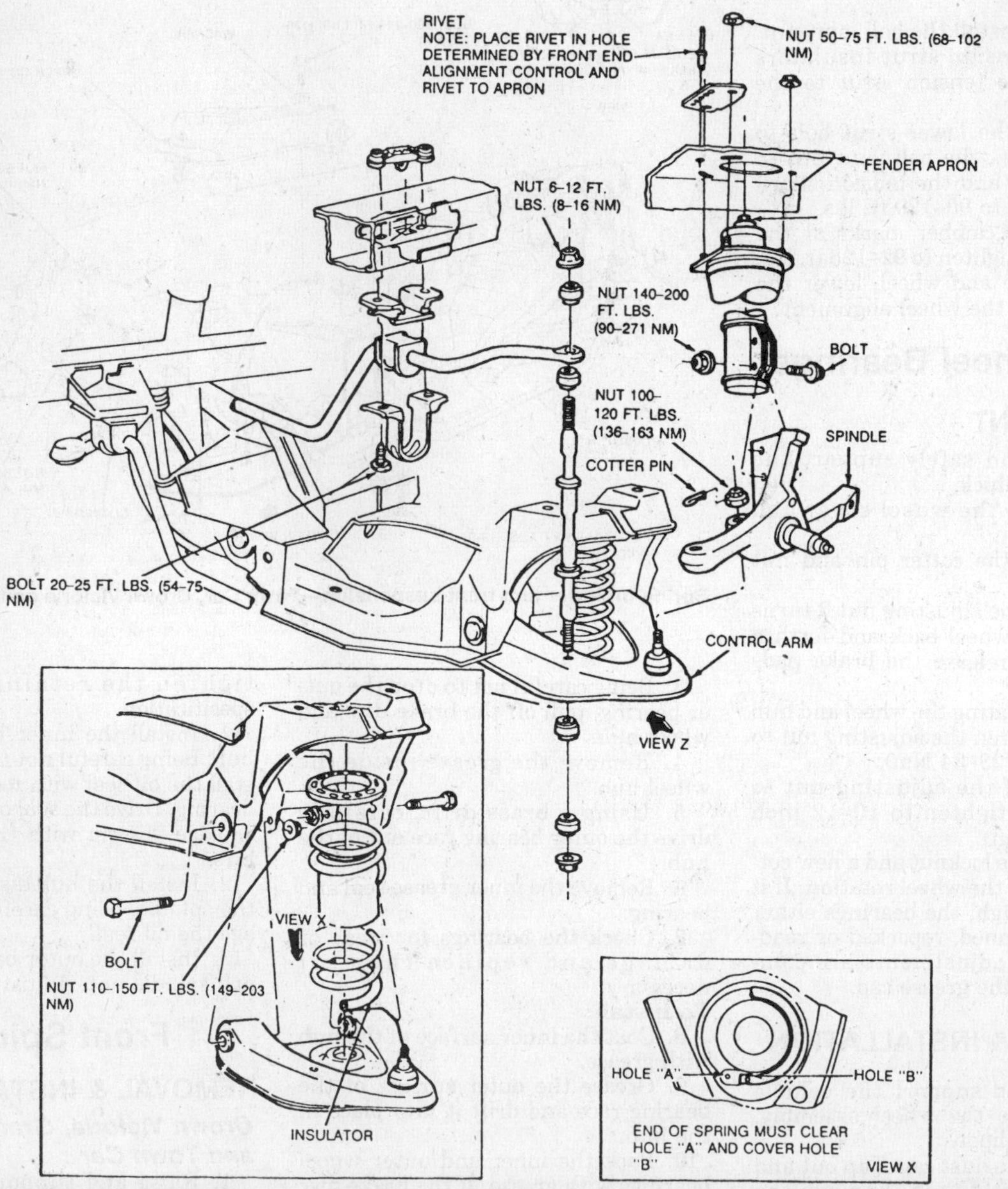

Single arm front suspension—Continental, Mark VII, Mustang and 1987–88 Thunderbird and Cougar

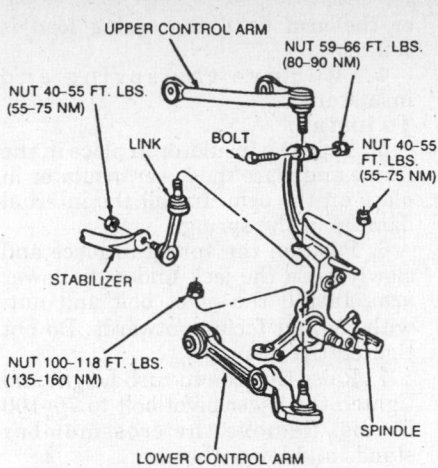

Single arm front suspension — 1989–91 Thunderbird and Cougar

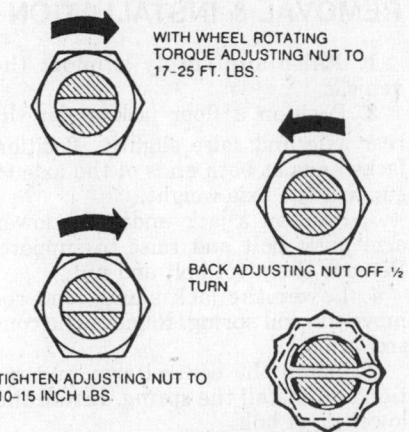

WITH WHEEL ROTATING TORQUE ADJUSTING NUT TO 17-25 FT. LBS.

BACK ADJUSTING NUT OFF ½ TURN

TIGHTEN ADJUSTING NUT TO 10-15 INCH LBS.

INSTALL THE LOCK AND NEW COTTER PIN

Wheel bearing adjustment

—— CAUTION ——

To avoid personal injury, use care as the jack will support the spring load on the lower arm.

8. Remove the upper and lower ball joint stud nuts.

To install:

9. Position the spindle on the lower ball joint stud and install and tighten the nut to 80–120 ft. lbs. (108–163 Nm). Continue to tighten until the slot for the cotter pin is aligned. Install a new cotter pin.

10. Raise the lower arm and guide the upper ball joint stud into the spindle. Install the stud nut and tighten the nut to 60–90 ft. lbs. (81–122 Nm). Continue to tighten until the slot for the cotter pin is aligned. Install a new cotter pin and remove the floor jack.

11. Connect the tie rod to the spindle and install and tighten the nut to 35–47 ft. lbs. (47–63 Nm). Continue to tighten for cotter pin alignment.

12. Install the brake dust shield, caliper, rotor and ABS sensor (Town Car) and wheel.

13. Check caster, camber and toe.

Continental, Mark VII, Mustang and 1987–88 Thunderbird and Cougar

1. Raise and support the vehicle safely.

2. Remove the wheel, brake rotor, caliper and dust shield.

3. Remove the stabilizer link from the lower arm assembly.

4. Remove the tie rod end from the spindle with tool 3290–C or equivalent.

5. Remove and discard the cotter pin from the ball joint stud nut and loosen the ball joint nut 1 or 2 turns. Do not remove the nut at this time.

6. Tap the spindle boss sharply to relieve the stud pressure.

7. Place a floor jack under the lower arm, compress the coil spring and remove the stud nut.

8. Remove and discard the 2 bolts and nuts attaching the spindle to the shock strut. Compress the shock strut until the working clearance is obtained.

9. Remove the spindle assembly.

To install:

10. Position the spindle on the ball joint stud and install the stud nut but do not tighten at this time.

11. Lower the shock strut until the until the attaching holes are in line with the holes in the spindle. Install 2 new bolts and nuts.

12. Tighten the ball stud nut to 100–120 ft. lbs. (136–163 Nm). Continue to tighten until the slot for the cotter pin is aligned. Install a new cotter pin.

13. Tighten the shock strut to spindle attaching nuts to 140–200 ft. lbs. (190–271 Nm).

14. Lower the floor jack from under the suspension arm and remove the jack.

15. Install the stabilizer link and tighten the attaching bolt and nut to 9–12 ft. lbs. (12–16 Nm).

16. Attach the tie rod end and tighten the retaining nut to 35–47 ft. lbs. (47–64 Nm).

17. Install the brake dust shield, caliper, rotor and wheel.

13. Check front end alignment.

1989–91 Thunderbird and Cougar

1. Raise and support the vehicle safely.

2. Remove the wheel, brake rotor and caliper.

3. Remove the hub and bearing assembly.

4. Remove the brake anti-lock sensor and move out of the way.

5. Remove the tie rod end from the spindle with tool 3290–C or equivalent.

6. Remove the stabilizer bar link at the spindle using joint separator D88L–3006–A or equivalent.

7. Separate the lower ball joint from the spindle. Loosen the nut and rap the spindle with a hammer and remove the nut.

8. Remove and discard the upper spindle to upper control arm bolt and nut. Spread the slot slightly and remove the spindle from the control arm and the vehicle.

To install:

9. Position the spindle on the lower ball joint and attach the upper control arm to the spindle.

10. Working from the front of the vehicle install a new bolt nut at the upper control arm and tighten to 50–65 ft. lbs. (70–90 Nm).

11. Install a new nut on the lower ball joint and tighten to 100–118 ft. lbs. (135–160 Nm).

12. Install the hub and bearing assembly.

13. Install the brake rotor and caliper.

14. Install and adjust the brake anti-lock sensor.

15. Install the stabilizer bar link to the spindle and tighten the retaining nut to 48–55 ft. lbs. (65–75 Nm).

16. Attach the tie rod end and tighten the retaining nut to 39 ft. lbs. (53 Nm) and continue to tighten until the slot for the cotter pin is aligned. Install a new cotter pin.

17. Install the wheel.

REAR SUSPENSION

Shock Absorbers

REMOVAL & INSTALLATION

NOTE: Purge a new shock of air by repeatedly extending it in its normal position and compressing it while inverted. Models equipped with axle dampers are serviced by supporting the rear of the vehicle, removing the wheel and disconnecting the front and rear mounting nuts and removing the damper.

Spring Between Axle Housing and Frame

1. Raise the vehicle and install jackstands.

2. Remove the shock absorber outer attaching nut, washer and insulator from the stud at the top side of the spring upper seat. Compress the shock sufficiently to clear the spring seat hole and remove the inner insulator and washer from the upper attaching stud.

3. Remove the locknut and disconnect the shock absorber lower stud at the mounting bracket on the axle housing. Remove the shock absorber.

To install:

4. Position a new inner washer and insulator on the upper spring seat. While maintaining the shock in this position, install a new outer insulator, washer and nut on the stud from the top side of the spring upper seat.

5. Extend the shock absorber. Locate the lower stud in the mounting bracket hole on the axle housing and install the locknut.

Spring Between Lower Control Arm and Frame

1. Remove the upper attaching nut, washer and insulator. Access is through the trunk on sedans or side panel trim covers on station wagons and hatchbacks. Sedan studs have rubber caps.

2. Raise and support the vehicle safely. Compress the shock to clear the upper tower. Remove the lower nut and washer; remove the shock.

To install:

3. Purge the shock of air and compress. Place the lower mounting eye over the lower stud and install the washer and a new locking nut. Do not tighten the nut yet.

4. Place the insulator and washer on the upper stud. Extend the shock, installing the stud through the upper mounting hole.

5. Torque the lower mounting nut to 40–55 ft. lbs.

6. Lower the car. Install the outer insulator and washer on the upper stud and install a new nut. Tighten to 14–26 ft. lbs. Install the trim panel on station wagons and hatchbacks or the rubber cap on sedans.

Coil Springs

REMOVAL & INSTALLATION

Spring Between Axle Housing and Frame

1. Raise and safely support the rear of the vehicle. Place a floor jack under the rear axle and lift the rear axle enough to take the tension off the springs.

2. Disconnect the lower studs of the shock absorbers from the mounting brackets on the axle housing.

3. Lower the axle housing until the springs are fully released.

4. Remove the springs and insulators from the vehicle.

To install:

5. Place the insulators in each upper seat and position the springs between the upper and lower seats.

6. With the springs in position, raise the axle housing until the lower studs of the rear shock absorbers reach the mounting brackets on the axle housing. Connect the lower studs and install the attaching nuts.

7. Remove the jack and lower the vehicle.

Spring Between Lower Control Arm and Frame

NOTE: If a spring must be replaced, the other should be replaced also. If the car has a stabilizer bar, the bar must be removed first.

1. Raise and support the car at the rear crossmember, while supporting the axle with a jack.

2. Lower the axle until the shocks are fully extended.

3. Place a jack under the lower control arm pivot bolt. Remove the pivot bolt and nut. Carefully and slowly lower the arm until the spring load is relieved.

4. Remove the spring and insulators.

To install:

5. Tape the insulator in place in the frame and place the lower insulator in place on the arm. Install the internal damper in the spring.

6. Position the spring in place and slowly raise the jack under the lower arm. Install the pivot bolt and nut, with the nut facing outwards. Do not tighten the nut.

7. Raise the axle to curb height and tighten the lower pivot bolt to 70–100 ft. lbs. Remove the crossmember stands and lower the car.

Rear Control Arms

REMOVAL & INSTALLATION

1. Raise and safely support the vehicle.

2. Position a floor jack under the rear axle and raise slightly. Position jackstands at both ends of the axle to support the axle weight.

3. Position a jack under the lower arm pivot bolt and raise to support. Remove the pivot bolt and nut.

4. Lower the jack slowly and remove the coil spring. Remove the control arm.

5. Install the control arm in position and install the spring. Install the lower pivot bolt.

6. Lower the vehicle.

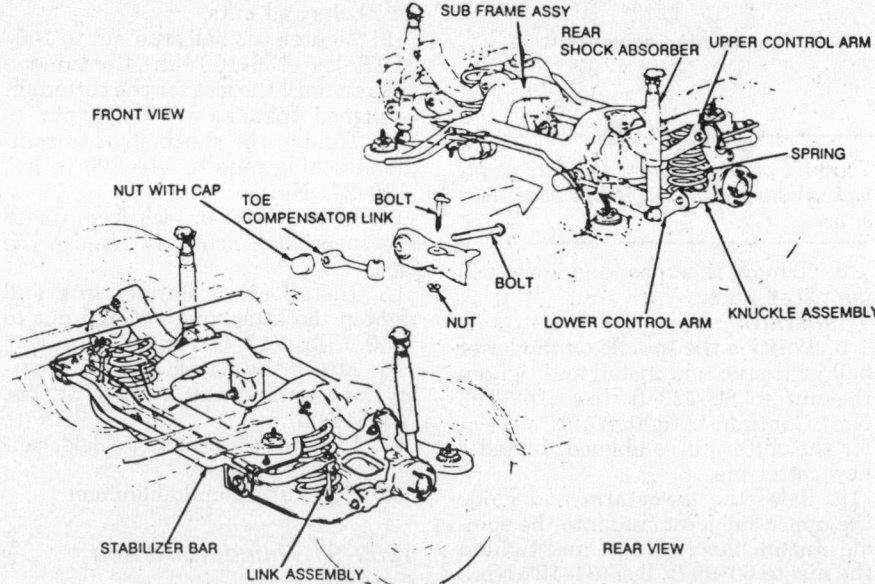

Exploded view of the rear suspension—1989–91 Thunderbird and Cougar

Ford Motor Co.
Front Wheel Drive
Festiva

SPECIFICATIONS

VEHICLE IDENTIFICATION CHART

It is important for servicing and ordering parts to be certain of the vehicle and engine identification. The VIN (vehicle identification number) is a 20 digit number visible through the windshield on the driver's side of the dash and contains the vehicle and engine identification codes. The tenth digit indicates model year and the eighth digit indicates engine code. It can be interpreted as follows:

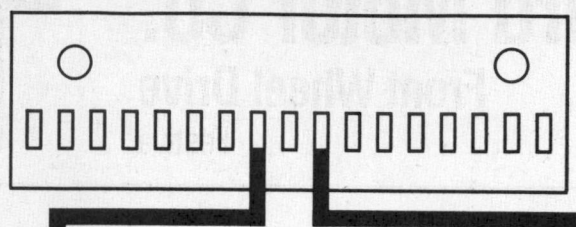

		Engine Code						Model Year	
Code	Cu. In.	Liters	Cyl.	Fuel Sys.	Eng. Mfg.		Code	Year
K	81	1.3	4	2 bbl	Kia Motors		J	1988
H	81	1.3	4	EFI	Kia Motors		K	1989
							L	1990
							M	1991

ENGINE IDENTIFICATION

Year	Model	Engine Displacement cu. in. (liter)	Engine Series Identification (VIN)	No. of Cylinders	Engine Type
1988	Festiva	81 (1.3)	K	4	OHC
1989	Festiva	81 (1.3)	K	4	OHC
	Festiva	81 (1.3)	H	4	OHC
1990–91	Festiva	81 (1.3)	H	4	OHC

GENERAL ENGINE SPECIFICATIONS

Year	VIN	No. Cylinder Displacement cu. in. (liter)	Fuel System Type	Net Horsepower @ rpm	Net Torque @ rpm (ft. lbs.)	Bore × Stroke (in.)	Compression Ratio	Oil Pressure @ rpm
1988	K	4-81 (1.3)	2 bbl	58 @ 5000	73 @ 3500	2.78 × 3.29	9.7:1	50–64 @ 3000
1989	K	4-81 (1.3)	2 bbl	58 @ 5000	73 @ 3500	2.78 × 3.29	9.7:1	50–64 @ 3000
	H	4-81 (1.3)	EFI	58 @ 5000	73 @ 3500	2.78 × 3.29	9.7:1	50–64 @ 3000
1990–91	H	4-81 (1.3)	EFI	63 @ 5000	73 @ 3000	2.79 × 3.29	9.7:1	50–64 @ 3000

GASOLINE ENGINE TUNE-UP SPECIFICATIONS

Year	VIN	No. Cylinder Displacement cu. in. (liter)	Spark Plugs Type	Gap (in.)	Ignition Timing (deg.) MT	AT	Compression Pressure (psi)	Fuel Pump (psi)	Idle Speed (rpm) MT	AT	Valve Clearance In.	Ex.
1988	K	4-81 (1.3)	AGS32C	0.040	TDC	—	①	3–6	700–750	–	0.012	0.012
1989	K	4-81 (1.3)	AGS32C	0.040	TDC ②	TDC ②	①	3–6	700–750	700–750	0.012	0.012
	H	4-81 (1.3)	AGS32C	0.040	2BTDC ②	2BTDC ②	①	③	800–900	800–900	Hyd.	Hyd.
1990	H	4-81 (1.3)	AGS32C	0.040	2BTDC ②	2BTDC ②	①	③	800–900	800–900	Hyd.	Hydr.
1991		SEE UNDERHOOD SPECIFICATIONS										

① The lowest cylinder pressure should be within 75% of the highest cylinder pressure reading. For example, if the highest cylinder is 134 psi, the lowest cylinder should be 101 psi. Engine should be at normal operating temperature with throttle body valve in the wide open position
② ± 1 degree
③ Fuel pressure is maintained at a constant 36.3 psi above manifold pressure.

FIRING ORDERS

NOTE: To avoid confusion, always replace spark plug wires one at a time.

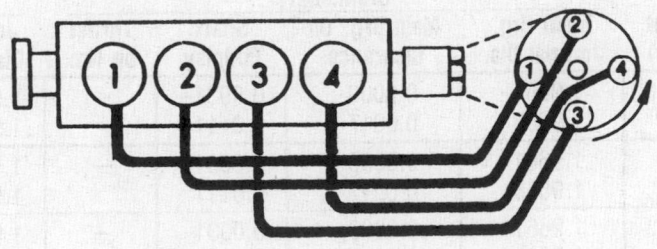

1.3L Engine
Engine Firing Order: 1–3–4–2
Distributor Rotation: Counterclockwise

CAPACITIES

Year	Model	No. Cylinder Displacement cu. in. (liter)	Engine Crankcase (qts.) with Filter	without Filter	Transmission (pts.) 4-Spd	5-Spd	Auto.	Drive Axle (pts.)	Fuel Tank (gal.)	Cooling System (qts.)
1988	Festiva	4-81 (1.3)	3.9	3.6	5.2	5.2	—	—	10	5.3
1989	Festiva	4-81 (1.3) ①	3.9	3.6	5.2	5.2	11.0	—	10	5.3
	Festiva	4-81 (1.3) ②	3.9	3.6	5.2	5.2	11.0	—	10	5.3
1990–91	Festiva	4-81 (1.3)	3.9	3.6	5.2	5.2	11.0	—	10	5.3

① Carbureted enginge
② Fuel injected engine

CAMSHAFT SPECIFICATIONS

All measurements given in inches.

Year	VIN	No. Cylinder Displacement cu. in. (liter)	Journal Diameter 1	2	3	4	5	Lobe Lift In.	Ex.	Bearing Clearance	Camshaft End Play
1988	K	4-81 (1.3)	1.7103–1.7112	1.7091–1.7100	1.7103–1.7112	—	—	1.4188–1.4224	1.4185–1.4224	0.0026–0.0045 ①	0.002–0.007 ②
1989	K	4-81 (1.3)	1.7103–1.7112	1.7091–1.7100	1.7103–1.7112	—	—	1.4188–1.4224	1.4185–1.4224	0.0026–0.0045 ①	0.002–0.007 ②
	H	4-81 (1.3)	1.7103–1.7112	1.7091–1.7100	1.7103–1.7112	—	—	1.4188–1.4224	1.4331–1.4371	0.0026–0.0045 ①	0.002–0.007 ②
1990–91	H	4-81 (1.3)	1.7103–1.7112	1.7091–1.7100	1.7103–1.7112	—	—	1.4188–1.4224	1.4331–1.4371	0.0026–0.0045 ①	0.002–0.007 ②

① Center bearing oil clearance shown.
 Front and rear bearing oil clearance—
 0.0014–0.0033
② In service limit—0.008

CRANKSHAFT AND CONNECTING ROD SPECIFICATIONS

All measurements are given in inches.

Year	VIN	No. Cylinder Displacement cu. in. (liter)	Crankshaft Main Brg. Journal Dia.	Main Brg. Oil Clearance	Shaft Endplay	Thrust on No.	Connecting Rod Journal Diameter	Oil Clearance	Side Clearance
1988	K	4-81 (1.3)	1.9661–1.9668	0.0009–0.0017	0.0031–0.0111	—	1.5724–1.5731	0.0009–0.0017	0.012
1989	K	4-81 (1.3)	1.9661–1.9668	0.0009–0.0017	0.0031–0.0111	—	1.5724–1.5731	0.0009–0.0017	0.012
	H	4-81 (1.3)	1.9661–1.9668	0.0009–0.0017	0.0031–0.0111	—	1.5724–1.5731	0.0009–0.0017	0.012
1990–91	H	4-81 (1.3)	1.9661–1.9668	0.0009–0.0017	0.0031–0.0111	—	1.5724–1.5731	0.0009–0.0017	0.012

VALVE SPECIFICATIONS

Year	VIN	No. Cylinder Displacement cu. in. (liter)	Seat Angle (deg.)	Face Angle (deg.)	Spring Test Pressure (lbs.)	Spring Installed Height (in.)	Stem-to-Guide Clearance (in.) Intake	Exhaust	Stem Diameter (in.) Intake	Exhaust
1988	K	4-81 (1.3)	45	45	—	1.717	0.008	0.008	0.2744–0.2750	0.2742–0.2748
1989	K	4-81 (1.3)	45	45	—	1.717	0.008	0.008	0.2744–0.2750	0.2742–0.2748
	H	4-81 (1.3)	45	45	—	1.717	0.008	0.008	0.2744–0.2750	0.2742–0.2748
1990–91	H	4-81 (1.3)	45	45	—	1.717	0.008	0.008	0.2744–0.2750	0.2742–0.2748

PISTON AND RING SPECIFICATIONS
All measurements are given in inches.

Year	VIN	No. Cylinder Displacement cu. in. (liter)	Piston Clearance	Ring Gap			Ring Side Clearance		
				Top Compression	Bottom Compression	Oil Control	Top Compression	Bottom Compression	Oil Control
1988	K	4-81 (1.3)	0.006	0.006–0.012	0.006–0.012	0.008–0.028	0.001–0.003	0.001–0.003	snug
1989	K	4-81 (1.3)	0.006	0.006–0.012	0.006–0.012	0.008–0.028	0.001–0.003	0.001–0.003	snug
	H	4-81 (1.3)	0.006	0.006–0.012	0.006–0.012	0.008–0.028	0.001–0.003	0.001–0.003	snug
1990–91	H	4-81 (1.3)	0.006	0.006–0.012	0.006–0.012	0.008–0.028	0.001–0.003	0.001–0.003	snug

TORQUE SPECIFICATIONS
All readings in ft. lbs.

Year	VIN	No. Cylinder Displacement cu. in. (liter)	Cylinder Head Bolts	Main Bearing Bolts	Rod Bearing Bolts	Crankshaft Pulley Bolts	Flywheel Bolts	Manifold		Spark Plugs
								Intake	Exhaust	
1988	K	4-81 (1.3)	①	②	③	11–15	71–76	14–19	12–17	11–17
1989	K	4-81 (1.3)	①	②	③	11–15	71–76	14–19	12–17	11–17
	H	4-81 (1.3)	①	②	③	11–15	71–76	14–19	12–17	11–17
1990–91	H	4-81 (1.3)	①	②	③	11–15	71–76	14–19	12–17	11–17

① Torque cylinder head bolts in sequence as follows:
  Step 1: 35–40 ft. lbs.
  Step 2: 56–60 ft. lbs.
② Torque main bearing cup bolts in sequence as follows:
  Step 1: 22–27 ft. lbs.
  Step 2: 40–43 ft. lbs.

③ Torque rod bearing nuts in sequence as follows:
  Step 1: 11–13 ft. lbs.
  Step 2: 22–25 ft. lbs.

BRAKE SPECIFICATIONS
All measurements in inches unless noted

Year	Model	Lug Nut Torque (ft. lbs.)	Master Cylinder Bore	Brake Disc		Standard Brake Drum Diameter	Minimum Lining Thickness	
				Minimum Thickness	Maximum Runout		Front	Rear
1988	Festiva	65–87	—	0.463	0.003	6.69	0.120	0.040
1989	Festiva	65–87	—	0.463	0.003	6.69	0.120	0.040
1990–91	Festiva	65–87	—	0.463	0.003	6.69	0.120	0.040

WHEEL ALIGNMENT

Year	Model	Caster		Camber		Toe-in (in.)	Steering Axis Inclination (deg.)
		Range (deg.)	Preferred Setting (deg.)	Range (deg.)	Preferred Setting (deg.)		
1988	Festiva	$1^5/_{16}$P–$1^{11}/_{16}$P	$1^9/_{16}$	$1/_4$N–$1^9/_{16}$P	$^{11}/_{16}$P	$1/_{32}$–$1/_2$ ①	$14^3/_{16}$P
1989	Festiva	$1^5/_{16}$P–$1^{11}/_{16}$P	$1^9/_{16}$	$1/_4$N–$1^9/_{16}$P	$^{11}/_{16}$P	$1/_{32}$–$1/_2$ ①	$14^3/_{16}$P
1990–91	Festiva	$1^5/_{16}$P–$1^{11}/_{16}$P	$1^9/_{16}$	$1/_4$N–$1^9/_{16}$P	$^{11}/_{16}$P	$1/_{32}$–$1/_2$ ①	$14^3/_{16}$P

P Positive
N Negative
① Preferred setting—$^5/_{16}$

ENGINE ELECTRICAL

NOTE: Disconnecting the negative battery cable on some vehicles may interfere with the functions of the on board computer systems and may require the computer to undergo a relearning process, once the negative battery cable is reconnected.

Distributor

REMOVAL

NOTE: If the distributor cap is being replaced, identify the spark plug wires and the cap towers with their respective cylinder numbers to ensure that the correct firing order will be retained when the new cap is installed.

1. Disconnect the negative battery cable.
2. Disconnect the spark plug wires from the distributor cap by gently twisting and pulling on the rubber boots.
3. Remove the cap to housing attaching screws and remove the cap.
4. Disconnect the vacuum hose connecting the carburetor spark port to the lower chamber nipple on the vacuum advance and the hose from the intake manifold to the upper chamber nipple.
5. Disconnect the ECM connector from the distributor wiring harness.
6. Remove the coil positive terminal nut and disconnect the distributor harness connector and suppression capacitor wire. Pull the distributor connector off the coil ground terminal post. Separate the harness routing clip tabs and free the coil primary wiring harness.
7. Scribe a timing reference mark across the distributor mounting flange and cylinder head surface to ensure

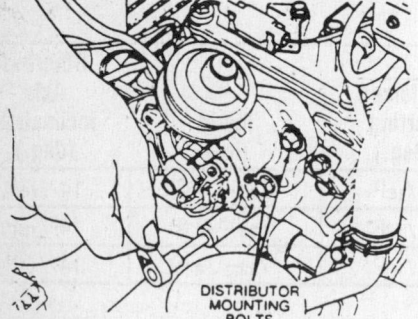

Distributor mounting bolt location

that the distributor will be installed without altering the timing.
8. Loosen the base flange mounting bolts and remove the distributor assembly from its mounting bore.
9. Remove the flange base O-ring and inspect for damage. Replace the O-ring as required. Coat the O-ring with clean engine oil and install into the flange base.

INSTALLATION

Timing Not Disturbed

1. Insert the distributor assembly into the cylinder head mounting bore. Rotate the distributor until the offset drive tang aligns and engages with the camshaft slot.
2. After the distributor is engaged with the camshaft, align the timing reference marks scribed across the flange base and cylinder head. When the timing marks are aligned, install and tighten the mounting bolts.
3. Position the distributor-to-coil primary harness and the supression capacitor lead in the harness routing clip and close the clip. Connect the harness to the coil primary terminals. Connect the supression capacitor and battery leads to the positive terminal. Connect the ECM connector to the distributor wiring harness.
4. Install the distributor cap, spark plug wires and reconnect the vacuum hoses to the vacuum advance unit.
5. Connect the negative battery cable.

Timing Disturbed

1. If the engine has been rotated while the distributor was removed, rotate the crankshaft until the No. 1 cylinder is at TDC, on the compression stroke.
2. The engine will be at TDC, when the **TC** mark on the belt cover is in alignment with the notch on the crankshaft pulley.
3. Insert the distributor assembly into the cylinder head mounting bore. Rotate the distributor until the offset drive tang aligns and engages with the camshaft slot.
4. Continue the installation in the reverse order of the removal procedure. Check the ignition timing.

Ignition Timing

ADJUSTMENT

1. Start the engine and allow to reach normal operating temperature.
2. Stop the engine and connect a tachometer. Start the engine and check

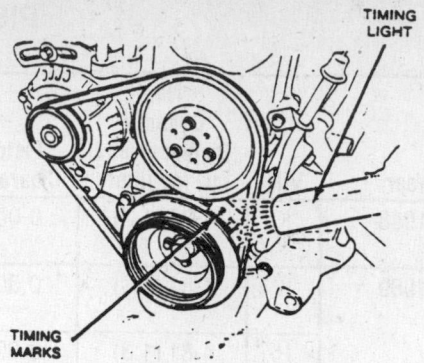

Ignition timing mark location

the idle speed. Adjust the idle speed, if necessary.
3. Disconnect the vacuum hoses from the vacuum advance unit and plug the hose openings. As required, disconnect the white altitude connector at the distributor.
4. Turn off all electrical accessories. As required, disconnect the barometric pressure switch, mounted high on the firewall on the right side of the engine.
5. Connect the timing light to the No. 1 spark plug wire. Start the engine.
6. With the timing light, observe the timing marks on the crankshaft pulley and timing case.
7. If the timing is not as specified, loosen the distributor mounting bolts and rotate the distributor clockwise to advance the timing and counterclockwise to retard the timing.
8. When the timing is adjusted to specification, tighten the distributor mounting bolts.
9. Stop the engine. Remove the timing light. Unplug the vacuum hoses and connect them to the vacuum advance unit. Connect the barometric pressure switch, if removed.
10. Start the engine and check the idle speed. Adjust the idle speed as required.

Alternator

For further information on the charging system, please refer to "Charging and Starting" in the Unit Repair section.

PRECAUTIONS

Several precautions must be observed with to avoid damage to the alternator.
If the battery is removed for any reason, make sure it is reconnected with the correct polarity. Reversing the battery connections may result in damage to the one-way rectifiers.

When utilizing a booster battery as a starting aid, always connect the positive to positive terminals and the negative terminal from the booster battery to a good engine ground on the vehicle being started.

Never use a fast charger as a booster to start vehicles.

Disconnect the battery cables when charging the battery with a fast charger.

Never attempt to polarize the alternator.

Do not use test lamps of more than 12 volts when checking diode continuity.

Do not short across or ground any of the alternator terminals.

The polarity of the battery, alternator and regulator must be matched and considered before making any electrical connections within the system.

Never separate the alternator on an open circuit. Make sure all connections within the circuit are clean and tight.

Disconnect the battery ground terminal when performing any service on electrical components.

Disconnect the battery if arc welding is to be done on the vehicle.

BELT TENSION ADJUSTMENT

1. Inspect the condition of the drive belt prior to adjustment. If the inspection reveals a severely glazed, frayed, oil contaminated or cracked belt, the belt must be replaced.
2. Raise the vehicle and support it safely.
3. Loosen the alternator mounting bolt and pivot bolt enough to allow for alternator movement.
4. Lower the vehicle.
5. Position a suitable pry bar between the alternator and an area in the vicinity of the through bolt, and apply moderate pressure to the bar. Do not pry against the stator frame.
6. Position a ruler perpendicular to center of the belt span between the alternator pulley and water pulley. The belt deflection may be determined through visual approximation by depressing the center of the belt with the thumb and observing the amount of deflection on the ruler.
7. For a used belt, belt deflection should be adjusted to 0.35–0.39 in. New belts require no engine run time and belt deflection should be within 0.31–0.35 in.
8. When the correct belt deflection is obtained, torque the adjusting bolt to 14–19 ft. lbs. and the pivot bolt to 27–46 ft. lbs.

REMOVAL & INSTALLATION

1. Disconnect the negative battery cable.
2. Pull the rubber boot away from the **B** terminal to expose the terminal nut. Remove the nut and electrical lead from the terminal post.
3. Remove the alternator adjusting bracket bolt.
4. Disconnect the electrical connectors from the rear of the alternator housing.
5. Loosen the alternator pivot bolt enough to allow for alternator movement. It may be necessary to raise the vehicle in order to gain access to the retaining bolts.
6. Move the alternator toward the engine enough to raise the drive belt from the alternator pulley. Allow the drive belt to remain suspended from the water pump and crankshaft pulleys.
7. Support the alternator by hand and remove the pivot bolt. Remove the alternator from the engine.
8. Installation is the reverse of the removal procedure. Torque the pivot bolt to 27–46 ft. lbs. Torque the adjusting bolt to 14–19 ft. lbs.

Starter

For further information on the charging system, please refer to "Charging and Starting" in the Unit Repair section.

REMOVAL & INSTALLATION

1. Disconnect the negative battery cable. Raise and support the vehicle safely.
2. Disconnect the wires from the starter terminals and position the wires off to the side.
3. Unbolt the starter motor bracket from the transaxle.
4. Support the starter by hand and remove the bolts attaching the starter motor to the transaxle clutch housing.
5. Remove the starter with support bracket from the engine.
To install:
6. Position the starter against the transaxle housing and install the mounting bolts. Torque the mounting bolts to 23–34 ft. lbs.
7. Align the support bracket and transaxle mounting holes and install the attaching bolts. Torque the attaching bolts to 23–34 ft. lbs.
8. Reconnect the wires to their respective terminal posts.
9. Reconnect the negative battery cable.

CHASSIS ELECTRICAL

Heater Blower Motor
REMOVAL & INSTALLATION

1. Disconnect the negative battery cable.
2. Locate the instrument panel spacer brace below the steering column and remove it.
3. Disconnect and lower the length of flexible air discharge hose from below the steering column.
4. Disconnect the blower motor wiring.
5. Remove the blower motor-to-air distribution plenum attaching screws and pull the blower motor with blower wheel away from the heater housing.
6. Remove the blower wheel retaining nut from the motor shaft and remove the blower wheel. Remove the washer from the motor shaft.
To install:
7. Assemble the blower wheel to the new blower motor by reversing the removal procedure.
8. Position the blower assembly onto the air distribution plenum and install the attaching screws. Connect the blower wiring.
9. Raise and connect the length of flexible hose. Install the support brace.
10. Connect the negative battery cable. Check the blower operation.

Windshield Wiper Motor
REMOVAL & INSTALLATION

1. Disconnect the negative battery cable. Disconnect the wiring at the wiper motor.
2. Remove the wiper motor attaching bolts. Remove the wiper motor ground wire attaching bolt and remove the wire from the bolt.
3. Remove the mounting plate attaching screws and pull the plate away from the dash panel.
4. With the proper tool, disengage the linkage pivot from the output arm. Remove the wiper motor from the vehicle.
To install:
5. Position the motor on the mounting plate and connect the output arm to the linkage pivot.
6. Position the mounting plate and install the attaching screws.
7. Install the wiper motor attaching

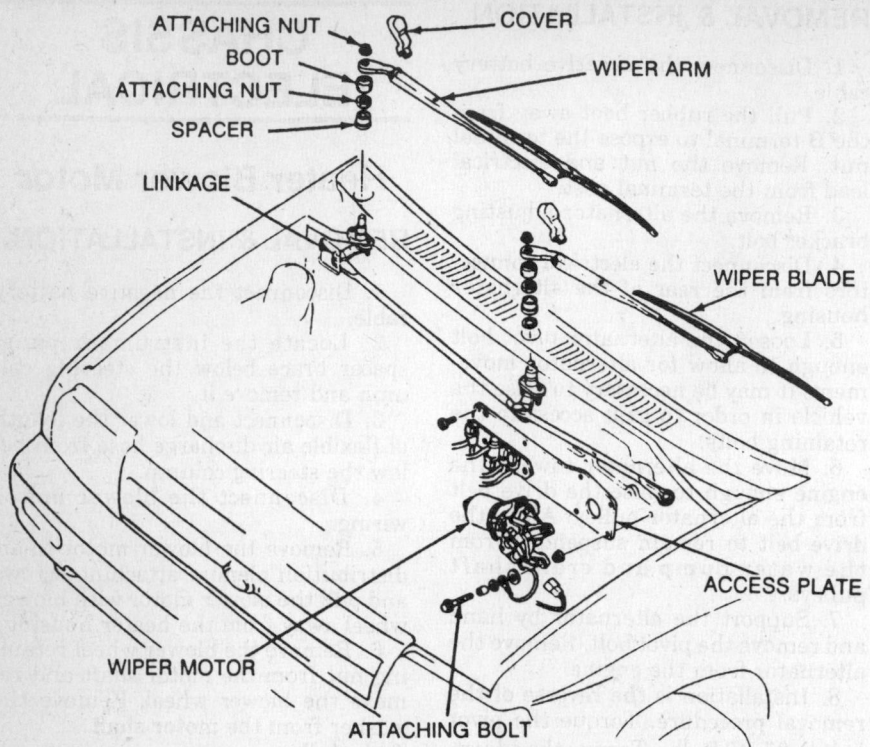

ATTACHING NUT
BOOT
ATTACHING NUT
SPACER
LINKAGE
COVER
WIPER ARM
WIPER BLADE
ACCESS PLATE
WIPER MOTOR
ATTACHING BOLT

Wiper motor, wiper arm and linkage assembly

bolts. Connect the ground wire to the top right attaching bolt and install.

8. Connect the wiper motor wiring connector. Check the wiper motor for proper operation and linkage movement.

Instrument Cluster

REMOVAL & INSTALLATION

1. Disconnect the battery negative cable.

2. If equipped with tilt wheel, release the tilt lock and lower the steering column. If not equipped with tilt wheel, remove the steering column upper and lower covers.

3. Remove the screws securing the instrument cluster bezel to the instrument cluster.

4. Pull the instrument cluster bezel away from the instrument cluster.

5. If equipped with rear window defogger, disconnect the wiring from the switch.

6. If equipped with rear window wiper, disconnect the wiring from the switch.

7. Remove the screws securing the instrument cluster in the instrument panel.

8. Pull the cluster away from the instrument panel.

9. Reach behind the cluster, lift the lock tab and disconnect the speedometer cable.

10. Lift the lock tab and disconnect the electrical connectors from the back of the instrument cluster.

11. Remove the instrument cluster from the vehicle.

To install:

12. Position the instrument cluster in the instrument panel opening.

13. Connect the electrical connectors to the back of the instrument cluster.

14. Slide the instrument cluster into the instrument panel.

15. Connect the speedometer cable.

16. Install and tighten the instrument cluster attaching screws.

17. Position the instrument cluster bezel on the instrument cluster. If necessary, connect the rear defogger and rear wiper switch wiring.

18. Install and tighten the instrument cluster bezel attaching screws.

19. If equipped with tilt wheel, raise the steering column and lock in desired position.

20. Connect the battery negative cable.

21. Check the operation of all instruments, gauges, and indicator lights.

Speedometer

REMOVAL & INSTALLATION

1. Disconnect the negative battery cable. Remove the instrument cluster from the vehicle.

2. Remove the odometer reset button, as required. Remove the speedometer from the instrument cluster.

NOTE: On vehicles equipped with a tachometer cluster, the speedometer and gauge face are removed as an assembly. If the speedometer is being replaced on these type clusters, transfer the tachometer and gauges to the new gauge face. On vehicles without a tachometer, the speedometer cluster is a separate module that can be removed and installed without removing the gauges.

3. Installation is the reverse of the removal procedure. Check the speedometer for proper operation.

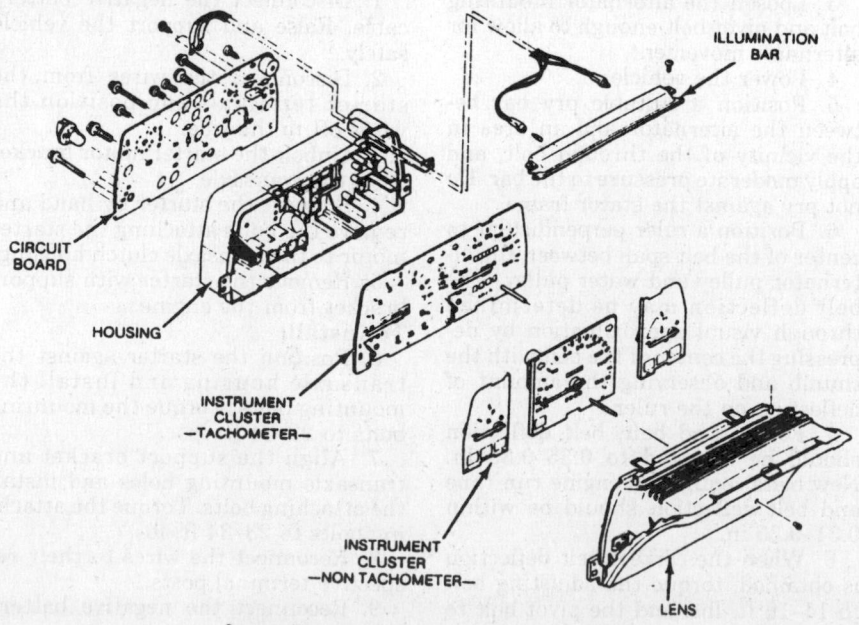

ILLUMINATION BAR
CIRCUIT BOARD
HOUSING
INSTRUMENT CLUSTER —TACHOMETER
INSTRUMENT CLUSTER —NON TACHOMETER
LENS

Assembly view of the instrument panel

Radio

REMOVAL & INSTALLATION

1. Disconnect the negative battery cable.
2. Remove the trim bezel attaching screws from beneath the radio. Remove the trim bezel.
3. Remove the screws retaining the radio in the console. Pull the radio out of the console.
4. Disconnect the electrical connector and antenna wire from the radio.
5. Remove the ground wire from the radio.
6. Installtion is the reverse of the removal procedure. Check the radio for proper operation.

Combination Switch

The combination switch controls the windshield wiper, turn signal and headlight operation.

REMOVAL & INSTALLATION

1. Disconnect the negative battery cable.

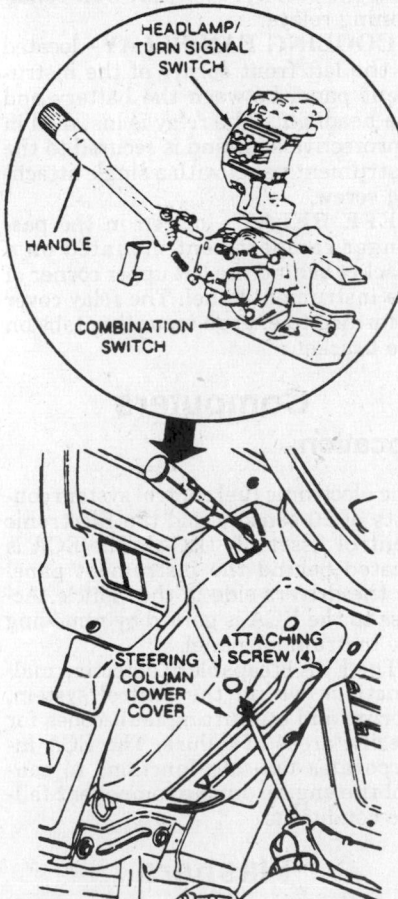

Combination switch assembly

2. Remove the steering wheel.
3. Remove the steering column lower cover attaching screws. Separate and remove the upper and lower steering column covers.
4. Compress the locking tabs and release the wiring harness clip. Unplug the 4 wiring harness connectors from the rear of the combination switch. From underneath the steering column, loosen the band clamp securing the switch hub to the steering column jacket.
5. Pull the switch assembly with the switch handle from the steering column.
To install:
6. Slide the combination switch assembly onto the steering column seating the switch against the column jacket. Make certain that the switch is level, then, tighten the band clamp on the switch hub to hold the switch assembly in place.
7. Plug the 4 wiring harness connectors back into the rear of the switch install the wiring harness clip.
8. Position the upper and lower steering column covers together and secure with the attaching screws.
9. Install the steering wheel. Connect the negative battery cable.

Ignition Lock
REMOVAL & INSTALLATION

1. Disconnect the negative battery cable. Remove the steering wheel, combination switch and ignition switch.
2. Using a needle nose pliers, grip and remove the round head mounting screws securing the steering lock housing and cap to the steering column jacket. Remove the lock housing. Discard the screws.
3. Position the steering lock housing onto the steering column jacket and install new mounting screws. Tighten the screws enough to hold the lock in postion.
4. Using the ignition key, verify that the mechanism locks and unlocks positively and without binding. If necessary, reposition the lock housing until proper operation is obtained. Tighten the mounting screws until the heads break off.
5. Complete the assembly of the ignition switch, combination switch and steering wheel by reversing the removal procedures. Connect the negative battery cable.

Ignition Switch
REMOVAL & INSTALLATION

1. Disconnect the battery negative cable.

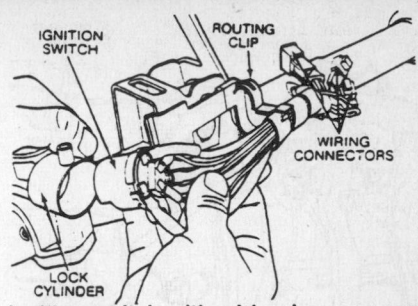

Ignition switch with wiring harness connections

2. Remove the upper and lower steering column covers by removing the attaching screws from the lower cover.
3. Remove the instrument panel spacer brace.
4. Remove the air discharge duct located below the steering column.
5. Remove the steering column attaching nuts and lower the steering column from its normal operating position.
6. Remove the tie strap securing the key warning buzzer switch wires to lock the cylinder housing. Discard the tie strap.
7. Remove the ignition switch retaining screw to release the switch from the steering column lock housing.
8. Remove the switch harness from the routing clip.
9. Separate the ignition switch wiring connectors and remove the ignition switch from the cylinder lock housing.
10. Installation is the reverse of the removal procedure.

Stoplight Switch

ADJUSTMENT

1. Disconnect the negative battery cable. Disconnect the switch wiring connector.
2. Loosen the upper and lower attaching nuts enough to allow for rotation of the switch.
3. Connect an ohmmeter across the switch terminals.
4. Rotate the switch until the ohmmeter indicates continuity.
5. Slowly rotate the switch toward the brake pedal until the ohmmeter indicates that the switch is open (infinite resistance).
6. Rotate the switch toward the brake pedal ½ additional turn and tighten the attaching nuts to retain the adjustment.
7. Connect the switch wiring connector and check the switch for proper operation.

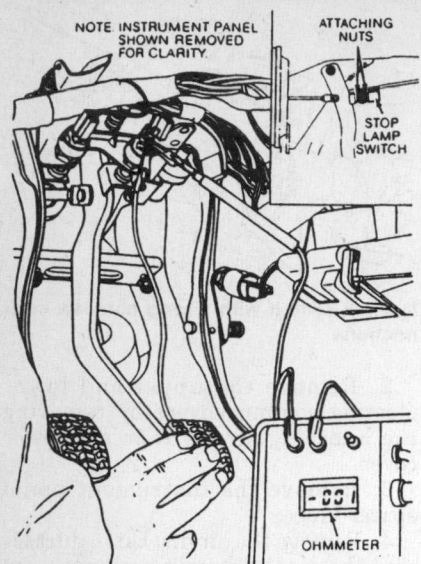

NOTE INSTRUMENT PANEL SHOWN REMOVED FOR CLARITY.

ATTACHING NUTS

STOP LAMP SWITCH

OHMMETER

Adjusting the stoplamp switch

REMOVAL & INSTALLATION

1. Disconnect the negative battery cable. Disconnect the stop lamp switch wiring connector.
2. Remove the upper attaching nut and lower the switch from the bracket.
3. Remove the lower attaching nut from the switch. Replace the switch, as required.
4. Transfer the lower attaching nut onto the new switch and install the switch into the mounting bracket. Install the upper attaching nut. Do not tighten the nuts or reconnnect the wiring connector at this time.
5. Adjust the switch.
6. Connect the switch wiring connector.
7. Check the switch for proper operation. Connect the negative battery cable.

Clutch Switch

ADJUSTMENT

1. To eliminate the possibility that the clutch cable is affecting the pedal height, loosen the cable adjusting nut and disengage the cable pin from the transaxle release lever.
2. Move the floor carpet and insulation out of the way of the dash panel to gain sufficient room for an accurate measurement.
3. Wit. a machinist's ruler, measure the distance from the upper center of the pedal to the dash panel. The pedal height should be 8.209–8.304 in.
4. If the pedal height is within this range, no adjustment is necessary. If the pedal height is not within specification, it must be adjusted.
5. Remove the instrument panel

bracket and air duct from under the instrument panel.
6. Locate the clutch switch and loosen the attaching nuts. Turn the switch in or out until the pedal height is within specification. Tighten the attaching nuts.
7. Connect the clutch cable to the transaxle release lever and adjust the pedal free play.
8. Measure the clutch pedal height. If the pedal height has changed after connecting the clutch cable, check for binding along the cable route.
9. Install the air inlet duct and instrument panel bracket. Place the insulation and floor carpet in their original positions.

REMOVAL & INSTALLATION

1. Disconnect the negative battery cable. Move the floor carpet out of the way.
2. Remove the instrument panel bracket, located under the steering column and remove the air duct.
3. Disconnect the clutch switch wiring connector.
4. Loosen the switch upper attaching nut and lower the switch from the mounting bracket. Remove the lower attaching nut from the switch and transfer to the new switch.
5. Position the switch into the mounting bracket and install the upper attaching nut. Connect the negative battery cable.

Neutral Safety Switch

The neutral safety switch is located in the lower right side of the transaxle.

REMOVAL & INSTALLATION

1. Disconnect the negative battery cable. Raise and support the vehicle safely.
2. Disconnect the neutral safety switch electrical wires.
3. Place a drain pan under the transaxle, to catch any excess transaxle fluid.
4. Remove the neutral safety switch from its mounting.
5. Installation is the reverse of the removal procedure. Be sure to replace any lost fluid.

Fuses, Circuit Breakers and Relays

LOCATION

Fusible Links

The main fuses are actually fusible links and are located in the engine

compartment in the front of the engine compartment. The main fuse panel contains 3 fusible links—**PTC**, **MAIN**, and **HEAD**. The ends of the fusible links are connected to the main fuse panel through standard push-on connectors. To remove a damaged link, grasp the insulator and pull until the connector separates from the panel. Install the new link by reversing the removal procedure.

Circuit Breakers

The branch circuit fuse panel is located in the passenger compartment to the left of the steering column. The fuse panel is concealed behind an access panel that clips into position on the instrument panel. The fuses are the cartridge type that must be removed for inspection. When making replacements, install only cartridge type fuses with the same amperage rating as the fuse that was removed.

Relays

HORN RELAY—mounted on a bracket in the upper left hand of the instrument panel.
A/C RELAYS—located in the left corner of the engine compartment, near the battery. There are 3 air conditioning relays.
COOLING FAN RELAY—located in the left front corner of the instrument panel between the battery and the headlight. The relay is installed in a protective boot and is secured to the instrument panel with a single attaching screw.
EFE RELAY—located in the passenger compartment mounted on a bracket behind the left upper corner of the instrument panel. The relay cover is formed to engage mounting tabs on the bracket.

Computers

Location

The electronic fuel control system consists of 10 sensors and the Electronic Control Assembly (ECA). The ECA is located behind the instrument panel on the drivers side of the vehicle. Access to the ECA is gained by removing the instrument panel.

The ECA is capable of detecting malfunctions within the control system, storing and outputting fault codes for specific areas of failure. The ECA incorporates fail-safe functions to control the engine during component failure conditions.

Flashers

Location

The turn signal and hazard flashers

are controlled by a single flasher unit. The flasher unit is located under the instrument panel, above the Electronic Control Assembly (ECA).

ENGINE COOLING

Radiator

REMOVAL & INSTALLATION

1. Disconnect the negative battery cable.
2. Disconnect the coolant recovery hose from the filler neck.
3. Loosen the retaining clamp and disconnect the upper radiator hose from the radiator.
4. Disconnect the cooling fan wiring harness connector. Disengage the wiring harness from the routing clamp on the cooling fan shroud.
5. Remove the radiator cap from the filler neck. Raise the vehicle and support safely.
6. Position a fluid catch pan under the radiator. Open the drain valve and drain the cooling system.
7. Disconnect the radiator temperature switch wires.
8. Loosen the retaining clamp and disconnect the lower radiator hose.
9. Lower the vehicle.
10. Support the radiator by hand and remove the 4 bolts attaching the radiator support brackets to the vehicle body. Raise the radiator/cooling fan/shroud assembly from the crossmember mounting insulator supports and remove from vehicle. Disconnect the cooling fan and shroud from the radiator as required.

To install:

11. Lower the radiator into the normal operating position making certain the mounting insualators engage with their supports. Attach the radiator to the support brackets with the 4 bolts.
12. Connect the upper radiator hose. Raise the vehicle and connect the lower radiator hose and temperature switch wires.
13. Close the drain valve and lower the vehicle. Connect the negative battery cable. Fill the cooling system to the proper level.
14. Start the engine and allow to reach normal operating temperature. Inspect for coolant leaks and correct as required.

Electric Cooling Fan

TESTING

Radiator Fan Switch

The cooling fan temperature switch is threaded into the front side of the thermostat housing. The themoswitch continuity test should be conducted when the coolant temperature is above and below the normal cut-in point of the switch (207°F).

--------- CAUTION ---------
To avoid the possibly of personal injury or damage to the vehicle, make certain that the ignition switch is in the OFF position before disconnecting the wire from the cooling fan temperature switch. If the wire is disconnected from the switch with the ignition switch in the ON position, the cooling fan may turn on. The maximum amount of time the engine is allowed to operate with the thermo switch disconnected is 2 minutes.

1. Turn the ignition switch to the **OFF** position. With the engine coolant below 207°F, disconnect the thermoswitch connector.
2. Using a test meter, check for continuity across the green wire terminal of the switch and ground. At this temperature, continuity should be read across the switch.
3. Connect the thermoswitch connector. Start the engine and allow the coolant to reach normal operating temperature (above 207°F).
4. Disconnnect the thermoswitch connector and check for continuity across the switch as described in Step 2. At this temperature, there should be no continuity across the switch.
5. Secure the engine and connect the thermoswitch connector. Replace the thermoswitch as required.

Cooling Fan Relay

The cooling fan relay is located in the left front corner of the engine compartment between the battery and the headlight. The relay is surrounded by a protective boot and is secured to the inner fender panel.

1. Turn the ignition switch to the **OFF** position.
2. Using a test meter, check for continuity across the green/yellow and black/red wire terminals. If continuity is not present, replace the cooling fan relay.

REMOVAL & INSTALLATION

1. Disconnect the negative battery cable.
2. Loosen the retaining clamp and

disconnect the upper radiator hose at the radiator.
3. Disconnect the cooling fan wiring harness connector and disengage the wiring harness from the routing clamp on the cooling fan shroud.
4. Remove the bolts attaching the top of the fan shroud to the radiator.
5. Support the fan shroud assembly and remove the bolts attaching the bottom of the fan shroud to the radiator. Remove the fan shroud assembly from the vehicle.
6. Complete the assembly by reversing the removal procedure.
7. Reconnect the negative battery cable and fill the cooling system to the proper level.
8. Start the engine and allow it to reach normal operating temperature. Check for cooling leaks.

Heater Core

REMOVAL & INSTALLATION

1. Disconnect the negative battery cable. Drain the cooling system.
2. Remove the instrument panel.
3. Remove the air distribution plenum by performing the following steps:
   a. Disconnect the heater hoses from inside the engine compartment.
   b. Disconnect the blower motor and blower resistor wiring.
   c. Disengage the wiring harness and antenna lead from the routing bracket on the front of the air distribution housing.
   d. Loosen the clamp screw securing the connector duct to the air inlet housing.
   e. Remove the upper and lower plenum attaching nuts. Disengage the plenum from the defroster ducts and remove from the vehicle.
4. Disconnect the link from the 2 defroster doors.
5. Locate and remove the screws just above and to the right of the blower resistor. Turn the plenum around and remove the screw located to the left of the blower motor opening.
6. Remove the retaining clips that

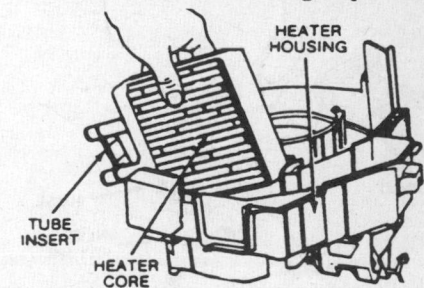

Heater core and tube insert removal

secure the the plenum halves. Separate the plenum halves.

7. Remove the heater core and tube insert/stiffener. Remove the tube insert/stiffener from the heater core and transfer to the new unit. Install the new heater core.

8. Complete the assembly and installation of the heater core and distribution plenum by reversing the disassembly and removal procedures.

9. Install the instrument panel.

10. Connect the negative battery cable. Refill and bleed the cooling system.

Water Pump

REMOVAL & INSTALLATION

1. Disconnect the negative battery cable.

2. Remove the timing belt.

3. Drain the cooling system.

4. Remove the radiator lower hose and heater return hose from the water pump inlet fitting.

5. Remove the bolts attaching the inlet fitting to the water pump housing. Remove the inlet fitting and gasket.

6. Remove the water pump-to-cylinder block attaching bolts. Remove the water pump and gasket from the cylinder block surface.

7. Remove all existing gasket material from the cylinder block and inlet fitting gasket surfaces.

To install:

8. Coat both sides of the new water pump and inlet fitting gaskets with a suitable water resistant sealer. Apply the gaskets to the engine and inlet fitting surfaces. Make certain the gasket holes are aligned with the bolt holes.

9. Position the water pump against

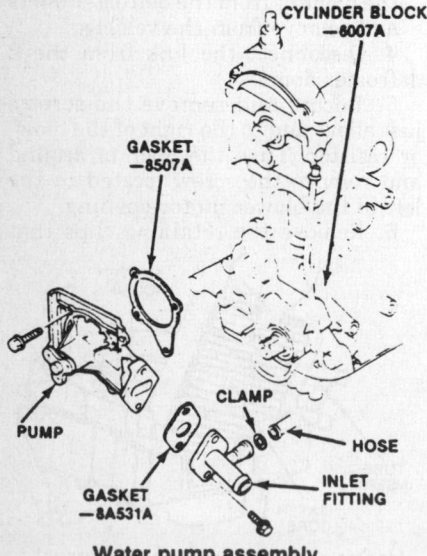

CYLINDER BLOCK
—6007A

GASKET
—8507A

PUMP

CLAMP

HOSE

GASKET
—8A531A

INLET
FITTING

Water pump assembly

the gasket. Make certain that the holes in the water pump are aligned with the gasket holes and that the pump does not shift the position of the gasket.

10. Install the water pump-to-cylinder block attaching bolts and torque to 14–19 ft. lbs. Position the inlet fitting and gasket against the water pump housing and install the attaching bolts. Torque the bolts to 14–19 ft. lbs.

11. Connect the inlet fitting hoses and install the timing belt.

12. Fill the cooling system to the proper level and tighten the expansion tank cap. Connect the negative battery cable.

13. Start the engine and allow to reach normal operating temperature. Check for coolant leaks.

Thermostat

REMOVAL & INSTALLATION

1. Disconnect the negative battery cable.

2. Disconnect the cooling fan temperature switch wire.

3. Remove the radiator cap and drain the cooling system to a level below the radiator upper hose. Disconnect the radiator inlet hose from the thermostat.

4. Remove the thermostat housing-to-cylinder head attaching bolts. Remove the thermostat housing and housing gasket. Withdraw the thermostat from the cylinder head.

5. Remove all gasket material from the thermostat housing and cylinder block surfaces.

To install:

6. Coat both sides of the new housing gasket with a suitable water resistant sealer.

7. Install the new thermostat into the cylinder head opening with the valve end first and the jiggle valve at the top. Apply the gasket to the cylinder block surface making certain that the gasket and cylinder block holes are evenly aligned.

8. Position the thermostat housing onto the cylinder head making certain that the bolt holes are aligned and the gasket does not shift. Install the housing attaching bolts but do not tighten at this time. Before tightening the bolts, ensure that the thermostat flange is properly seated against the recess of the housing. Torque the bolts to 14–19 ft. lbs.

9. Connect the radiator inlet hose to the thermostat housing. Fill the cooling system to the proper level and install the radiator cap. Connect the cooling fan temperature switch wire and the negative battery cable.

10. Start the engine and allow to reach normal operating temperature. Inspect for leaks.

Cooling System Bleeding

After working on the cooling system, even to replace the thermostat, the system must have the air bled from it. Air trapped in the system will prevent proper system filling and leave the coolant level low, risking possible overheating.

1. Fill the radiator to about 1 in. below the filler neck.

2. Start the engine and run it at slightly above normal idle speed. If air bubbles appear and the coolant level drops, fill the system with the correct anti-freeze/water mixture to bring the level to normal.

3. Run the engine until the thermostat opens and the water begins to move abruptly in the radiator.

4. Check the level of the coolant again, top it off if needed. Stop the engine.

5. Put the radiator cap on and check the coolant level in the overflow tank. Bring the overflow tank up to the correct level.

FUEL SYSTEM

Fuel System Service Precautions

Safety is the most important factor when performing not only fuel system maintenance but any type of maintenance. Failure to conduct maintenance and repairs in a safe manner may result in serious personal injury. Maintenance and testing of the vehicle's fuel system components can be accomplished safely and effectively by adhering to the following rules and guidelines.

To avoid the possibility of fire and personal injury, always disconnect the negative battery cable unless the repair or test procedure requires that battery voltage be applied.

Always relieve the fuel system pressure prior to disconnecting any fuel system component (injector, fuel rail, pressure regulator, etc.), fitting or fuel line connection. Exercise extreme caution whenever relieving fuel system pressure to avoid exposing skin, face and eyes to fuel spray. Please be advised that fuel under pressure may penetrate the skin or any part of the body that it contacts.

Always place a shop towel or cloth around the fitting or connection prior to loosening to absorb any excess fuel.

Ensure that all fuel spillage (should it occur) is quickly removed from engine surfaces. Ensure that all fuel soaked cloths or towels are deposited into a suitable waste container.

Always keep a dry chemical (Class B) fire extinguisher near the work area.

Do not allow fuel spray or fuel vapors to come into contact with a spark or open flame.

Always use a backup wrench when loosening and tightening fuel line connection fittings. Always follow the proper torque specifications.

Always replace worn fuel fitting O-rings with new. Do not substitute fuel hose or equivalent where fuel pipe is installed.

RELIEVING FUEL SYSTEM PRESSURE

1. Remove the rear seat cushion.
2. Disconnect the electrical connector from the fuel sending unit.
3. Start the engine and let it run until it stalls. Turn the ignition key **OFF**
4. Reconnect the electrical lead.

Fuel Filter
REMOVAL & INSTALLATION

The fuel filter is located in the rear left corner of the engine compartment next to the carbon canister.

1. Disconnect the negative battery cable. Properly relieve the fuel system pressure.
2. Disengage the filter from the mounting bracket.
3. Loosen the hose clamps and disconnect the filter inlet and outlet hoses. Discard the filter.
4. Connect the inlet and outlet hoses to the new fuel filter making certain that the flow arrow on top of the filter is pointing toward the fuel pump hose.
5. Secure the hoses with the clips and place the filter into the mounting bracket.
6. Connect the negative battery cable. Start the engine and inspect for leaks. Correct all fuel leaks immediately.

Mechanical Fuel Pump

The fuel pump is located on the firewall side of the cylinder head, near the distributor.

PRESSURE TESTING

1. Disconnect the negative battery cable. Relieve the fuel system pressure.
2. Connect a suitable pressure gauge to the end of the fuel pump discharge hose. Secure the gauge to the hose with a small hose clamp.
3. Locate the fuel return hose and disconnect the hose from the fuel

pump. Plug or cap the return port to prevent fuel leakage.
4. Connect the negative battery cable.
5. Crank the engine several revolutions and observe the reading on the gauge. The fuel pump pressure should be 3–6 psi. If the fuel pump pressure is not correct, the pump must be replaced.
6. Disconnect the pressure gauge. Connect and secure the fuel pump discharge and return lines.
7. Start the engine and inspect for fuel leaks. Correct all fuel leaks immediately.

REMOVAL & INSTALLATION

1. Relieve the fuel system pressure.
2. Disconnect the negative battery cable. Remove the air cleaner assembly. Identify and tag all vacuum hoses as required.
3. Tag and disconnect the fuel pump inlet, outlet and return hoses.
4. Loosen the fuel pump retaining bolts to allow for movement of the pump on the cylinder head mounting. Place the fuel pump arm on the low side of the cam circle.
5. Remove the pump retaining bolts.
6. Remove the pump from the mounting pad with insulator and gaskets. Replace the gaskets as required.
7. Clean the cylinder head and insulator gasket contact surfaces.
To install:
8. Install the pump, insulator and gaskets. Install the retaining bolts and torque to 17–22 ft. lbs.
9. Connect and secure the inlet, outlet and fuel return hoses to the fuel pump.
10. Complete the assembly of the air cleaner by reversing the removal procedure. Connect the ngeatrive battery cable.
11. Start the engine and inspect for fuel leaks. Correct all fuel leaks immediately.

Electric Fuel Pump

PRESSURE TESTING

Testing the fuel system pressure requires the use of a special fuel pressure gauge, the will connect to the diagnostic tap of the fuel rail.

1. Relieve the fuel system pressure. Disconnect the fuel return line at the fuel rail. Insert the end of the fuel return line into a calibrated container.
2. Remove the rear seat and disconnect the fuel pump connector from the fuel pump.
3. Connect the fuel pressure gauge to the fuel rail test tap.

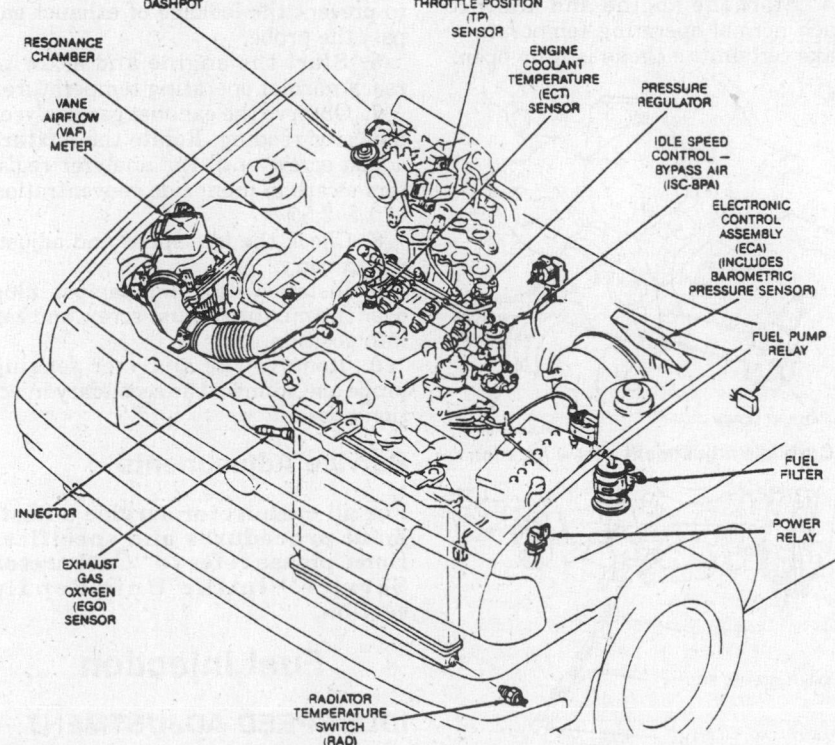

Fuel injection system component location

4. Energize the pump and check the pressure reading. The correct pressure should be approximately 36.5 psi.

5. Check the fuel volume after energizing the pump, the correct volume should be approximately 1 oz. per second.

REMOVAL & INSTALLATION

The fuel pump is located in the fuel tank as part of the sending unit assembly.

1. Relieve the fuel system pressure. Disconnect the negative battery cable.

2. Remove the rear seat. Remove the rear carpet hold-down pins.

3. Remove the fuel tank sending unit access cover.

4. Lift the plate and disconnect the sending unit electrical wiring.

5. Disconnect and plug the fuel line from the sending unit.

6. Remove the sending unit retaining screws. Remove the sending unit. Discard the gasket.

7. Remove the fuel filter from the pump. Remove the fuel pump wires from the sending unit.

8. Remove the retaining clamp screw. Remove the pump outlet hose clamp. Remove the fuel pump from the sending unit.

9. Installation is the reverse of the removal procedure.

Carburetor

REMOVAL & INSTALLATION

1. Relieve the fuel system pressure. Disconnect the negative battery cable.

2. Remove the air cleaner assembly.

3. Remove the retaining clip and disconnect the fuel supply line. Plug the hose opening to prevent contamination and the entry of foreign matter.

4. Disconnect the vacuum hoses from the carburetor. Identify each hose with its respective opening to ensure proper installation.

5. Disconnect the carburetor wiring connectors.

6. Disconnect the choke heater wire at the choke cap.

7. Move the throttle to the wide open position and disengage the throttle cable from the throttle lever.

8. Remove the carburetor retaining nuts and washers. Lift the carburetor upward from the intake manifold studs. Disconnect the idle up diaphragm link from the carburetor linkage. If the EFE heater sticks to the carburetor base, gently remove it. Discard the carburetor flange gaskets and replace with new.

To install:

9. Thoroughly clean the carburetor,

EFE heater and intake manifold gasket contact surfaces and install new gaskets.

10. Position the carburetor over the intake manifold mounting studs and support by hand. While supporting the carburetor, connect the idle up diaphragm link to the carburetor linkage. Install and tighten the mounting nuts and washers.

11. Move the throttle to the wide open position and connect the throttle cable to the throttle lever.

12. Connect the choke heater wire.

13. Connect the carburetor wires to their respective connectors.

14. Connect the vacuum hoses to their original openings.

15. Connect the the fuel supply line and install the retaining clip.

16. Install the air cleaner assembly and connect the negative battery cable.

17. Start the engine and adjust the idle speed, if necessary.

IDLE SPEED ADJUSTMENT

1. Disconnect the cooling fan electrical connector. Check the ignition timing and adjust, if necessary. Adjust the idle mixture, as required.

2. Place the transmission selector lever in **N** and firmly apply the parking brake. Make certain the air conditioning system is **OFF**. Be sure that all electrical accessories are **OFF**.

3. Connect a tachometer to the engine.

4. Start the engine and allow to reach normal operating temperature. Make certain the choke is fully open.

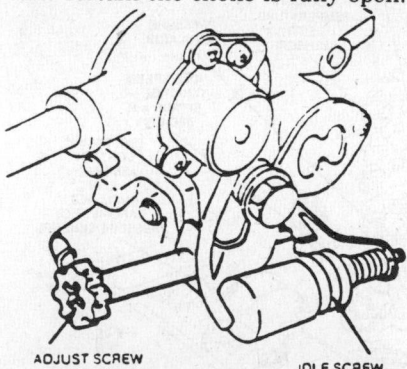

Curb idle adjustment screw location

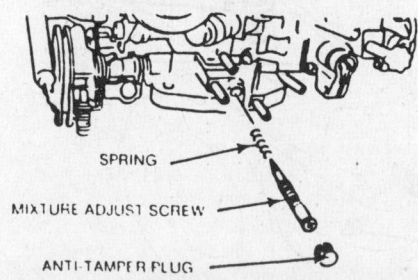

Idle mixture adjustment screw location

5. Allow the engine to remain at idle and observe the idle speed reading. The idle speed should be 700–750 rpm.

6. If the idle speed is not within specifications, rotate the idle speed adjusting screw, located on the right side of the carburetor, as required until the correct idle speed is obtained.

IDLE MIXTURE ADJUSTMENT

Adjustment of the idle mixture screw is normally unnecessary due to the fact that the adjustment has been made at the factory. The mixture adjusting screw is sealed with an anti-tamper plug and roll pin to discourage adjustment. If the adjustment is required, proceed as follows with the use of an exhaust gas analyzer.

1. Disconnect the negative battery cable.

2. Remove the carburetor from the engine and position in a suitable holding fixture.

3. Remove the anti-tamper plug from the mixture adjust screw bore and discard the plug. Gently tap the roll pin from the mixture adjusting screw bore.

4. Install the carburetor and connect the negative battery cable. Leave the secondary injection hose disconnected at this time.

5. Insert the sensing probe of an exhaust gas analyzer in the secondary injection hose elbow opening. Plug the hose around the area of the probe lead to prevent the leakage of exhaust gas past the probe.

6. Start the engine and allow to reach normal operating temperature.

7. Observe the exhaust gas analyzer indicator reading. Rotate the mixture adjust screw until the analyzer registers a carbon monoxide concentration of 1.5–2.5%.

8. Check the idle speed and adjust, if necessary.

9. Install a new anti-tamper plug over the mixture adjust screw and tap into position.

10. Remove the analyzer sensing probe and connect the secondary injection hose.

Service Adjustments

For all carburetor service adjustment procedures and specifications, please refer to "Carburetor Service" in the Unit Repair section.

Fuel Injection

IDLE SPEED ADJUSTMENT

NOTE: The test connector is located on the passenger side of the engine compartment, near the shock tower.

1. Disconnect the cooling fan electrical connector. Check the ignition timing and adjust if necessary. Adjust the idle mixture, as required.

2. Apply the parking brake. Make certain the air conditioning system is **OFF**. Be sure that all electrical accessories are **OFF**.

3. Connect a tachometer to the test connector (clear pin No. 1). Check the idle speed.

4. If adjustment is required, connect a jumper wire between the test connector (black pin No. 1) and ground and turn the air adjustment screw to obtain the correct specification. Specification should be 800–900 rpm.

5. After adjustment is made, remove the jumper wire.

IDLE MIXTURE ADJUSTMENT

Adjustment of the idle mixture screw is normally unnecessary due to the fact that the adjustment has been made at the factory. The idle mixture can not be adjusted.

Fuel Injector

REMOVAL & INSTALLATION

1. Relieve the fuel system pressure. Disconnect the negative battery cable.

2. Remove the intake plenum. Remove the fuel inlet line from the fuel rail.

3. Disconnect the fuel return line from the fuel rail. Disconnect the electrical connections at the injectors.

4. Remove the pressure regulator. Remove the fuel rail retaining bolts. Remove the fuel rail.

5. Remove the fuel injectors. Discard the O-rings.

6. Installation is the reverse of the removal procedure. Be sure to lubricate the new O-rings with clean gasoline.

EMISSION CONTROLS

Please refer to "Emission Control" in the Unit Repair section for system maintenance procedures. Due to the complex nature of modern electronic engine con-trol systems, comprehensive diagnosis and testing procedures fall outside the confines of this repair manual. For complete information on diagnosis, testing and repair procedures concerning all modern engine and emission control systems, please refer to "Chilton's Guide to Electronic Engine Controls".

Emission Warning Lamps

RESETTING

The malfunction indicator lamp (MIL) is a dual function lamp that informs the driver of possible engine malfunctions and emission system failure. The MIL is controlled by the ECA. The ECA functions to monitor engine, ignition, and emission related components and signals the driver when the engine is running improperly or emissions are unsatisfactory. If the MIL illuminates during vehicle operation, the cause of the fault or malfunction must be determined and corrected.

ENGINE MECHANICAL

NOTE: Disconnecting the negative battery cable on some vehicles may interfere with the functions of the on board computer systems and may require the computer to undergo a relearning process, once the negative battery cable is reconnected.

Engine Assembly

REMOVAL & INSTALLATION

NOTE: The engine and transaxle are removed as an assembly.

1. Disconnect the battery cables. Remove the battery and battery tray.

2. Mark the hinge location and remove the hood.

3. Drain the radiator coolant.

4. Drain the engine oil. drain the transaxle fluid. If equipped with automatic transaxle, disconnect and plug the fluid cooler lines.

5. Remove the air cleaner assembly and oil level dipstick. Remove the cooling fan and radiator as an assembly. Disconnect the accelerator cable and routing bracket, if equipped.

6. Disconnect the speedometer ca-ble. Disconnect and remove all fuel hoses. Plug or cover the hose openings to prevent contamination from entering the system.

7. On fuel injected engines disconnect the transaxle vacuum hoes. On automatic transaxles, remove the nut that connects the shift lever to the manual shaft assembly. Remove the shift cable from the transaxle.

8. Disconnect the heater hoses, brake booster vacuum hose, carburetor to chassis or body hoses and canister hoses.

9. Remove the engine harness connectors coil, distributor, fan temperature switch, temperature sending unit, starter, backup lamp, neutral start, alternator, carburetor, EGO sensor and EGR position sensor. Identify and tag all electrical wiring connectors to ensure proper installation.

10. Disconnect and remove the engine ground. Disconnect the upper and lower radiator hoses.

11. Raise the vehicle and support safely.

12. Remove the catalytic converter.

13. If equipped, loosen the air conditioning compressor from its mounting and position to the side. Do not disconnect refrigeration hoses.

14. Disconnect lower control arms from the steering knuckles. Separate the transaxle halfshafts and install the differential side gear holding tools.

15. Remove the clutch control cable and shift control cable rod.

16. Remove the stabilizer bar from the transaxle, as necessary.

17. Properly support the engine.

18. Remove the rear crossmember mount bolts at the chassis.

19. Remove the front engine mount nut through the hole in the crossmember. Remove the rear engine mount nuts at the crossmember. Remove the crossmember.

20. Lower the vehicle and attach engine lifter hooks. Remove right engine mount bolt.

21. Carefully remove the engine and transaxle as an assembly through the bottom of the vehicle.

To install:

22. Attach a lifting sling to the engine and transaxle assembly. Connect the sling to a suitable engine lift.

23. Raise the engine assembly into place in the vehicle engine compartment and install the engine mount bolts through the mounts.

24. Support the engine in the chassis. Raise and support the vehicle safely.

25. Install the front engine mount nut and torque to 27–46 ft. lbs.

26. Position the crossmember onto the mounts and chassis. Attach the rear nut and torque 27–46 ft. lbs. In-

stall the mount to crossmember nuts and torque to 27–46 ft. lbs.

27. Remove the differential side gear holding tools and install the halfshafts into the transaxle.

28. Connect the lower control arms to the steering knuckles. Attach the shift control rod and stabilizer bar to the transaxle. Attach the clutch cable, if equipped.

29. Attach the the air conditioning compressor to its mounting, if removed.

30. Connect the catalytic converter.

31. Lower the vehicle.

32. Install the radiator upper and lower hoses. Attach the engine ground wire.

33. Connect the engine electrical harness connectors coil, distributor, fan, temperature switch, starter, back-up light, neutral start switch, alternator, carburetor, EGO sensor, EGR position sensor, and the carburetor heater, if equipped.

34. Connect the carbon canister hoses, carburetor hoses, brake booster vacuum hose, heater hoses and fuel hoses.

35. Attach the speedometer cable. Connect the accelerator cable brackets, as required. If equipped with automatic transaxle, install the shift cable.

36. Install the cooling fan and radiator assembly. If equipped with automatic transaxle, install the fluid cooler lines. Install the air cleaner assembly.

37. Install the battery and tray.

38. Fill the engine with the proper weight and grade of engine oil to the proper level.

39. Fill the transaxle with the proper grade of fluid to the specified level.

40. Fill the cooling system with the proper coolant mixture to the correct level.

41. Install the hood. Connect the battery cable. Start the engine, check for leaks and proper fluid levels.

Engine Mounts

REMOVAL & INSTALLATION

Front Mount

1. Disconnect the negative battery cable. Remove the front mount through bolt attaching nut.

2. Properly support the engine.

3. Raise and support the vehicle safely.

4. Remove the front mount to crossmember attaching nuts.

5. Raise the vehicle, as required, to gain sufficient clearance to remove the front mount. Remove the front mount from the crossmember. Note and record the position of the mount to ensure proper installation.

To install:

6. Install the engine mount onto the crossmember in the original installation position.

7. Secure the mount to the crossmember with the attaching nuts. Torque the attaching nuts to 27–46 ft. lbs.

8. Lower the vehicle.

9. Move the engine as necessary until the holes in the mount align with the holes in the engine bracket. Install the through bolt and attaching nut. Torque the nut to 27–46 ft. lbs.

10. Remove the engine support.

Rear Mount

1. Disconnect the negative battery cable. Raise the vehicle and support safely.

2. Properly support the engine.

3. Remove the mount-to-crossmember attaching nut.

4. Remove the mount-to-engine attaching bolts.

5. If necessary, raise the engine to gain access to the rear mount. Remove the mount from the crossmember.

To install:

6. Position the mount onto the rear engine bracket.

7. Install the mount to engine bracket bolts. Torque the bolts to 27–46 ft. lbs.

8. Lower the engine and mount onto the crossmember.

9. Install the attaching nut and torque to 27–46 ft. lbs.

10. Remove the engine support.

Side Mount

1. Disconnect the negative battery cable. Properly support the engine.

2. Remove the through bolt, nut and washer.

3. Remove the bracket-to-engine attaching nuts.

4. Remove the side mount and bracket as an assembly.

To install:

5. Position the engine mount and bracket onto the engine.

6. Install the engine-to-bracket attaching nuts. Torque the nuts to 27–46 ft. lbs.

7. Position the washer against the mount. Install the through bolt and nut. Torque the nut and bolt to 27–46 ft. lbs.

8. Remove the engine support.

Cylinder Head

REMOVAL & INSTALLATION

1. Disconnect the negative battery cable. Drain the cooling system.

2. Position the engine at TDC on the compression stroke.

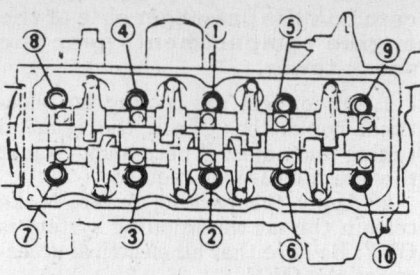

Cylinder head bolt torque sequence

3. Remove the valve cover. Remove the timing belt cover.

4. Remove the exhaust manifold. Remove the intake manifold.

5. Remove the spark plug wires and spark plugs. Remove the distributor.

6. Remove the front and rear engine lift hangers. Remove the engine ground wire.

7. Remove the wiring harness connector. Remove the upper radiator hose. Remove the bypass hose and bracket.

8. Remove the cylinder head retaining bolts. Remove the cylinder head from the engine. Discard the gasket.

To install:

9. Install the cylinder head gasket in position on the engine block.

10. Install the cylinder head in position on the block and tighten the bolts in the correct sequence, to the proper torque.

11. Connect the radiator hose, bypass hose and the the wiring harness connector.

12. Install the distributor, spark plugs and wires.

13. Install the intake and exhaust manifolds. Install the timing belt and cover.

14. Install the valve cover. Install the remaining components in position.

15. Connect the negative battery cable.

Valve Lash

ADJUSTMENT

Carbureted Engine

1. Start the engine and allow to reach normal operating temperature.

2. Set the No. 1 piston to **TDC** by rotating the crankshaft until the **TC** mark on the belt cover aligns with the notch on the crankshaft pulley.

3. Remove the valve cover.

4. Adjust the No. 1 and No. 2 intake valves to specification. Adjust the No. 1 and No. 3 exhaust valves to specification.

5. Rotate the crankshaft 360 degrees so that the No. 4 piston is at TDC of the compression stroke. Adjust the remaining valves to specification.

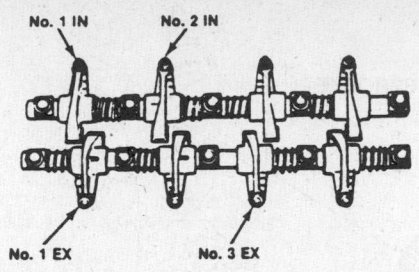

Intake and exhaust valve arrangement

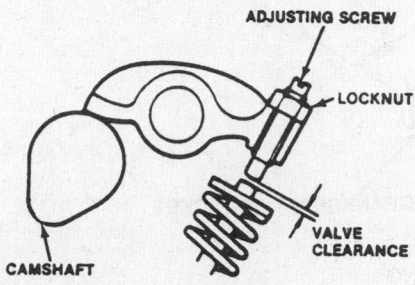

Adjusting valve clearance

6. Install the valve cover. Be sure to use a new gasket or RTV sealant, as required.

Fuel Injected Engine

1. Disconnect the negative battery cable. Remove the valve cover.
2. Inspect the lash adjuster operation by pushing down on each rocker arm. If the rocker arm moves down, replace the lash adjuster.
3. Remove the rocker arm shaft assemblies.
4. Remove the hydraulic lash adjuster from the rocker arm.
5. Installation is the reverse of the removal procedure.
6. Be sure to coat the new lash adjuster with clean engine oil. Fill the oil reservoir in the rocker arm with clean engine oil.
7. Be careful not to damage the O-ring when installing the lash adjuster.
8. When installing the valve cover be sure to use new gaskets or RTV sealant, as required.

Rocker Arms/Shafts

REMOVAL & INSTALLATION

1. Disconnect the negative battery cable.
2. Remove the air cleaner assembly, as required. If equipped with fuel injection, remove the air hose and the resonance chamber.
3. Disconnect the accelerator cable from the throttle lever bracket. Remove the PCV valve.
4. Remove the spark plug wires

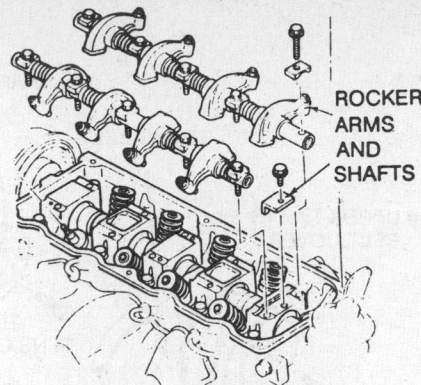

Rocker arm/shaft assembly

from the routing clips. Remove the upper timing belt cover.
5. Remove the valve cover retaining bolts. Remove the valve cover. Discard the gasket.
6. Remove the rocker arm assembly retaining bolts. Remove the rocker arm assemblies from the engine.
7. Installation is the reverse of the removal procedure. Be sure to use new gaskets or RTV sealant, as required. Torque the rocker arm bolts in sequence to 16–21 ft. lbs. Adjust the valves.

Intake Manifold

REMOVAL & INSTALLATION

1. Disconnect the negative battery cable. Drain the cooling system.
2. Remove the air cleaner assembly, on vehicles equipped with a carburetor. On vehicles equipped with fuel injection, remove the intake manifold bracket.
3. Disconnect the accelerator cable.
4. Identify, tag and disconnect all vacuum hoses and electrical wiring required to provide sufficient clearance to remove the intake manifold.
5. Support the intake manifold by hand and remove the retaining bolts. Remove the intake manifold from the cylinder head.
6. Remove the old gasket material and thoroughly clean the intake manifold and cylinder head surfaces.

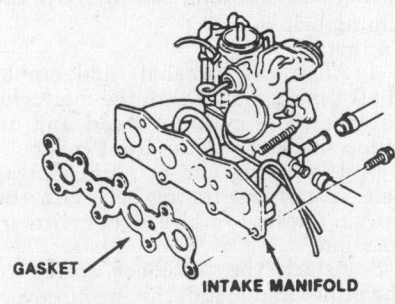

Assembly view of the intake manifold

To install:

7. Apply a new gasket to the cylinder head surface and hold in place.
8. Position the intake manifold onto the new gasket and install the retaining bolts. Make the bolts hand tight. Torque the retaining bolts to specification in a criss-cross pattern, from the inside out.
9. Connect the vacuum hoses and electrical wiring to their respective connections. Install the accelerator cable.
10. Install the air cleaner assembly, as required. Install the intake manifold bracket, as required.
11. Refill the cooling system to the proper level. Install the radiator cap. Connect the negative battery cable.

Exhaust Manifold

REMOVAL & INSTALLATION

1. Disconnect the negative battery cable.
2. Raise and safely support the vehicle.
3. Disconnect the catalytic converter inlet pipe from the exhaust manifold by removing the 3 attaching nuts.
4. Disconnect the pulse air tube from the air inlet pipe flange by removing the attaching nuts.
5. Unbolt the catalytic converter support bracket.
6. Lower the vehicle.
7. Remove the air cleaner assembly, as required. On fuel injected vehicles remove the air hose.
8. Remove the exhaust manifold heat shroud.
9. Separate the EGO sensor from the routing bracket and disconnect the electrical connector.
10. Unbolt the pulse air routing bracket clamp.
11. Remove the pulse air tube and gaskets. Discard the gaskets.
12. Support the exhaust manifold by hand and remove the attaching nuts. Separate the exhaust manifold from the cylinder head and inlet pipe. Re-

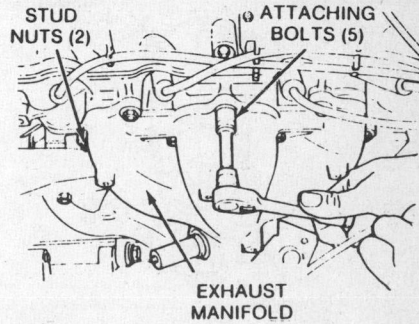

Exhaust manifold-to-cylinder head mounting

move the inlet pipe and exhaust manifold gaskets and discard.

13. With an oxygen sensor removal tool, remove the exhaust gas oxygen (EGO) sensor. Inspect the sensor gasket for damage and replace if necessary.

To install:

14. Remove all existing gasket material from the exhaust manifold, cylinder head inlet pipe and pulse air tube flange surfaces. Clean all threaded surfaces.

15. Position the gasket onto the EGO sensor and install into the exhaust manifold connection using the removal tool.

16. Apply a new gasket onto the cylinder head studs and position the exhaust manifold onto the gasket. Install the attaching nuts and torque to 12–17 ft. lbs.

17. Install the heat shroud.

18. Install the pulse air tube and mounting bracket clamp. On fuel injected vehicles, install the air hose.

19. Connect the EGO sensor electrical connector and secure the connector in the routing bracket. Install the air cleaner assembly, as required.

20. Raise the vehicle and support it safely.

21. Position a new gasket over the exhaust manifold studs and 2 new gaskets onto the pulse air tube studs.

22. Raise the catalytic converter inlet pipe into position on the exhaust manifold and pulse air tube studs and support by hand. Install the attaching nuts and torque to 23–34 ft. lbs.

23. Install the catalytic converter inlet pipe support bracket.

24. Lower the vehicle and connect the negative battery cable.

25. Start the engine and inspect for exhaust gas leaks.

Timing Belt Front Cover

REMOVAL & INSTALLATION

1. Disconnect the negative battery cable. Remove the drive belts.

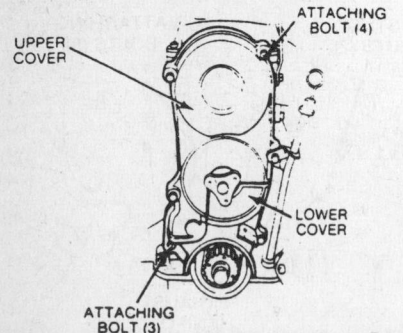

Upper and lower timing belt covers with attaching bolts

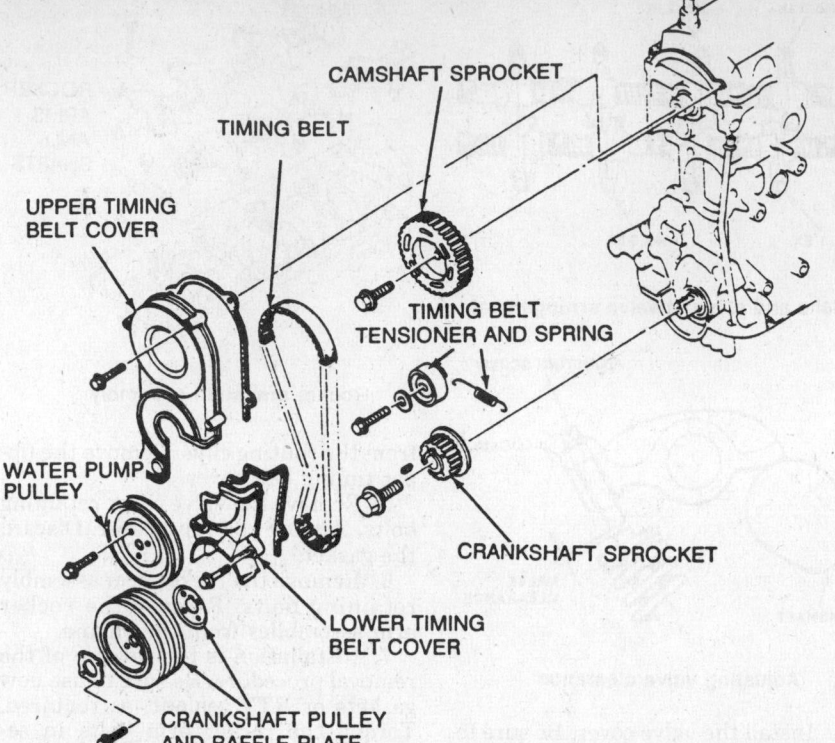

Assembly view of the crankshaft and camshaft sprockets and related components

2. Remove the water pump pulley.

3. Remove the crankshaft pulley retaining bolt. Remove the crankshaft pulley.

4. Remove the upper and lower cover retaining bolts. Remove the timing belt covers from the engine.

5. Installation is the reverse of the removal procedure.

Timing Belt and Tensioner

REMOVAL & INSTALLATION

1. Disconnect the negative battery cable. Position the engine at TDC on the compression stroke.

2. Remove the timing belt covers. Mark the direction of rotation of the timing belt.

3. Remove the timing belt tensioner spring and retaining bolt. Remove the timing belt.

To install:

4. Align the camshaft and crankshaft timing marks with the marks located on the cylinder head and oil pump housing (engine front cover).

5. If reusing the original timing belt, install the timing belt with the mark made for the direction of rotation.

6. Attach the tensioner spring to the pulley and install the spring cover. Position the tensioner assembly onto

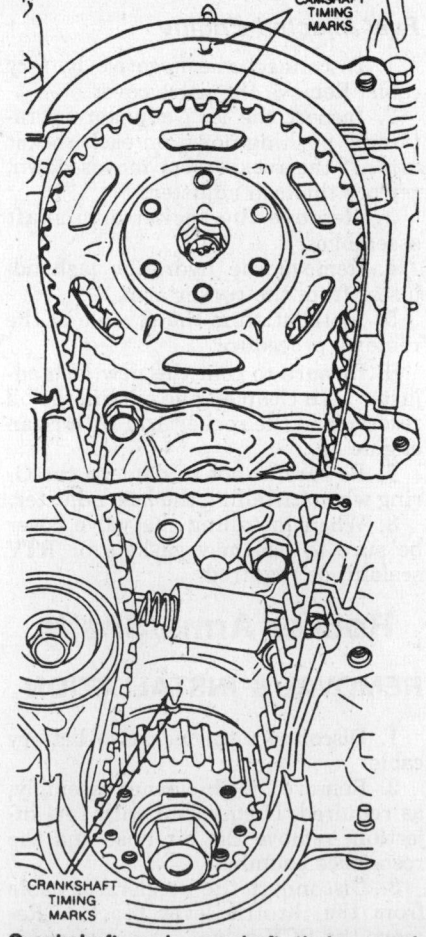

Crankshaft and camshaft timing mark alignment

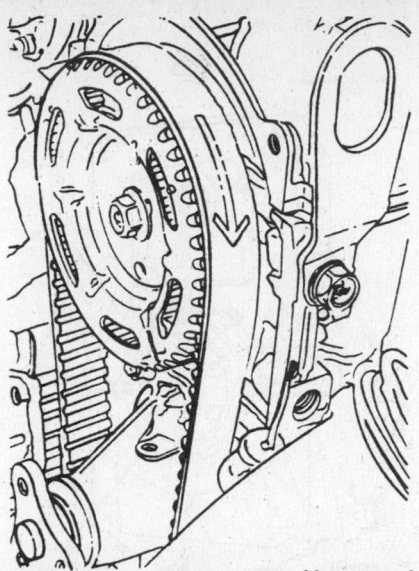

Timing belt rotation arrow. Always note arrow rotation before removal. Normal direction of rotation is clockwise

the engine and install the tensioner bolt, but do not tighten the bolt at this time.

7. Reconnect the free end of the spring to the spring anchor. Torque the tensioner bolt to 14–19 ft. lbs.

8. Install the timing belt covers and connect the negative battery cable.

Timing Sprockets

REMOVAL & INSTALLATION

Camshaft Sprocket

1. Disconnect the negative battery cable.

2. Remove the timing belt and timing belt tensioner.

3. With the appropriate size open end wrench or medium pry bar, hold the camshaft stationary and remove the camshaft sprocket retaining bolt.

4. Pull the camshaft sprocket with dowel pin from the camshaft. Take care not to lose the dowel pin.

5. With the proper tool, pry the camshaft front oil seal from the cylinder head bore. Discard the seal and replace with new.

To install:

6. Make certain that all seal seating surfaces are clean and install a new seal into the seal bore.

7. Install the camshaft sprocket, dowel pin and retaining bolt.

8. Hold the camshaft stationary and torque the retaining bolt to 36–45 ft. lbs.

9. Complete the installation of the timing belt by reversing the removal procedure.

10. Connect the negative battery cable.

Crankshaft Sprocket

1. Disconnect the negative battery cable.

2. Remove the timing belt and timing belt tensioner.

3. Remove the crankshaft sprocket retaining bolt.

4. Pull the crankshaft sprocket and alignment key from the crankshaft. Make certain not to lose the key when removing the crankshaft sprocket. Replace the key if worn or damaged.

To install:

5. Position the crankshaft sprocket onto the crankshaft and align the keyways. Install the key.

6. Coat the threads of the retaining bolt with a suitable non-hardening compound. Install the retaining bolt and torque to 80–94 ft. lbs.

7. Return the shift lever to the neutral position.

8. Complete the installation of the timing belt by reversing the removal procedure.

9. Connect the negative battery cable.

Camshaft

REMOVAL & INSTALLATION

1. Disconnect the negative battery cable. Drain the cooling system.

2. Remove the cylinder head from the engine.

3. Position the cylinder head in a suitable holding fixture. Remove the camshaft gear. Remove the rocker shaft assemblies.

4. Remove the camshaft from the cylinder head.

5. Installation is the reverse of the removal procedure.

6. Be sure to use new gaskets or RTV sealant, as required. Torque the cylinder head to specification and in

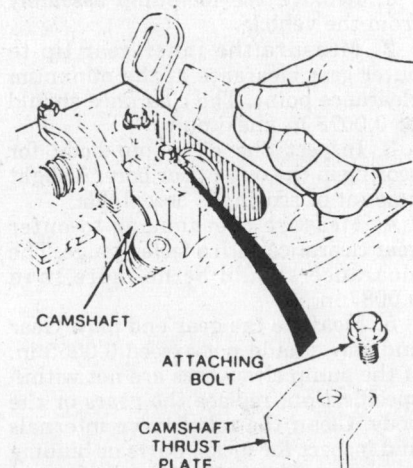

Removal and installation of the camshaft thrust plate

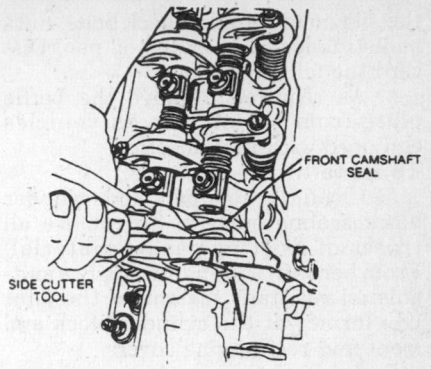

Removing the camshaft sprocket seal

the proper sequence. Check the engine timing after belt installation.

Piston and Connecting Rod

POSITIONING

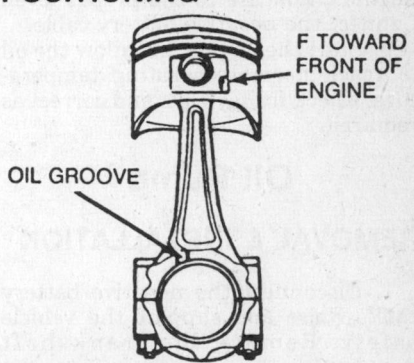

Crankshaft and connecting rod positioning

ENGINE LUBRICATION

Oil Pan

REMOVAL & INSTALLATION

1. Disconnect the negative battery cable. Raise and support the vehicle safely. Drain the engine oil.

2. Remove the flywheel dust cover retaining bolts and remove the cover.

NOTE: Depending on the position of the crankshaft, the oil pan may encounter interference during removal due to protruding crankshaft throws. If necessary, rotate the crankshaft retaining bolt until the oil pan can be removed without crankshaft interference.

3. Support the oil pan and remove

the oil pan to cylinder block bolts, nuts and stiffeners. Lower the oil pan. Discard the oil pan gasket.

4. As required, remove the baffle plate from the oil pan on vehicles equipped with fuel injection.

To install:

5. Clean the oil pan and cylinder block sealing surfaces to remove all traces of existing gasket material. From beneath the engine, apply a suitable oil resistant sealant to the joint line formed at the cylinder block and front and rear engine covers.

6. Apply the new rubber gasket to the oil pan.

7. Raise the oil pan and gasket against the cylinder block. Install the stiffeners, bolts and nuts. Torque the oil pan bolts in an alternate pattern to 5–7 ft. lbs.

8. Install the flywheel dust cover and attaching bolts. Torque the bolts to 13–20 ft. lbs.

9. Install the oil pan drain plug and fill the crankcase to the proper level. Connect the negative battery cable.

10. Start the engine and allow the oil to reach normal operating temperature. Check for oil leaks and correct as required.

Oil Pump

REMOVAL & INSTALLATION

1. Disconnect the negative battery cable. Raise and support the vehicle safely. Remove the crankshaft sprocket.

2. Drain the engine oil. Remove the oil pan.

3. Remove the oil pump assembly retaining bolts. Remove the oil pump assembly and gasket from the engine. Discard the gasket.

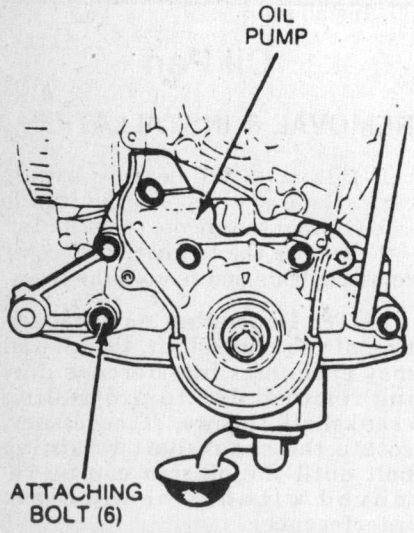

Oil pump assembly

4. As required, remove the pickup tube and screen.

5. Remove the screws from the oil pump cover. Remove the cover. Remove the oil pump gears.

6. Remove the front seal from the pump assembly. Remove the cotter pin, spring and relief valve from the oil pump body.

To install:

7. Clean the oil pump and cylinder block contact surfaces to remove the old gasket material and sealant. Thoroughly coat both sides of the new oil pump gasket with a suitable sealant compound. Apply the gasket to the oil pump and remove any excess sealant. Pack the pump cavity with petroleum jelly.

NOTE: Do not allow the sealant compound to enter the oil pump discharge opening once the gasket is in place. This opening must be free and clear before the oil pump is installed onto the cylinder block.

8. Position the oil pump against the cylinder block surface and install the retaining bolts. Torque the bolts to 14–19 ft. lbs.

9. Install a new gasket onto the oil pump inlet and bolt the pickup tube to the oil pump. Torque the bolts to 6–8 ft. lbs.

10. Complete the assembly of the remaining components by reversing the removal procedure. Fill the crankcase to the proper level with engine oil. Connect the negative battery cable.

11. Start the engine and allow the oil to reach normal operating temperature. Check for leaks and correct as required.

CHECKING

1. Remove the oil pump assembly from the vehicle.

2. Measure the inner gear tip to outer gear clearance at the minimum clearance point. The clearance should be 0.0078 in. maximum.

3. Inspect the oil pump body for scoring in the outer gear bore. A slight amount of scoring is acceptable.

4. Measure the housing-to-outer gear clearance with a feeler gauge. The clearance should be no more than 0.0087 in.

5. Measure the gear end play. Gear end play should not exceed 0.0055 in. If the pump clearances are not within specification, replace the gears or the body. Clean the relief valve internals and inspect for nicks, burrs or binding operation. Clean the pickup tube and screen.

6. Assemble the oil pump relief

N·m (69–95 in-lb).

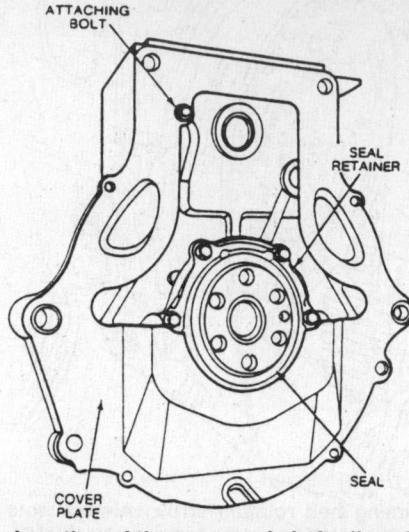

Location of the rear crankshaft oil seal

valve into the bore. Install the spring, retainer and cotter pin.

7. Press or drive a new oil seal into the oil pump body bore.

8. Coat the cover attaching screws with a suitable thread locking compound and install the cover.

9. Install the oil pump assembly in the vehicle.

Rear Main Bearing Oil Seal

REMOVAL & INSTALLATION

1. Disconnect the negative battery cable.

2. Remove the transaxle from the vehicle.

3. Remove the flywheel. If necessary, remove the cover plate.

4. Remove the seal retainer. Remove the crankshaft seal.

To install:

5. Install the gasket onto the retainer and position the retainer against the engine surface. Install the attaching bolts and torque to 6–8 ft. lbs. Trim the excess gasket material (if any) from the edge of the retainer after it has been fastened to the engine.

6. With a wire brush, remove all the old sealer from the flywheel bolts. Coat the threads of the bolts with stud and bearing mounting sealer.

7. Position the flywheel against the crankshaft and support by hand. Install the flywheel-to-crankshaft retaining bolts and tighten so that the flywheel no longer requires support. Install the flywheel locking tool to prevent the flywheel from turning.

8. Torque the flywheel retaining

bolts in an alternate pattern to 71–76 ft. lbs.

9. Continue the installation in the reverse order of the removal procedure.

MANUAL TRANSAXLE

For further information on transmissions/transaxles, please refer to "Chilton's Guide to Transmission Repair".

Transaxle Assembly

REMOVAL & INSTALLATION

1. Disconnect the negative battery cable.

2. Disconnect the back-up switch wiring connector.

3. Disconnect the neutral safety switch wiring connector.

4. Loosen the clutch cable adjusting nut and disengage the clutch cable pin from the release lever. Remove the cable routing bracket attaching bolts and position the cable and bracket to the side.

5. Remove the starter.

6. Remove the protective boot from the speedometer gear sleeve and slide the boot up onto the cable. Disconnect the speedometer cable.

7. Remove the 2 bolts from the top of the clutch housing.

8. Install an engine support bar tool. Raise and support the vehicle safely.

9. Remove the nut and bolt attaching the shift rod to the input shift rail.

10. Remove the nuts and bolts attaching the lower control arms to the steering knuckles.

11. Disengage the halfshafts from the differential side gears.

12. Install a differential side gear plug tool to prevent the side gears from moving.

13. Remove the noise vibration harness brackets.

14. Remove the crossmember.

15. Position a suitable transmission jack under the transaxle and secure the jack with a safety chain.

16. Remove the remaining lower transaxle attaching bolts and pull the transaxle away from the engine. Lower the transaxle from the vehicle and position the assembly in a suitable mounting fixture.

17. Clean the transaxle housing and

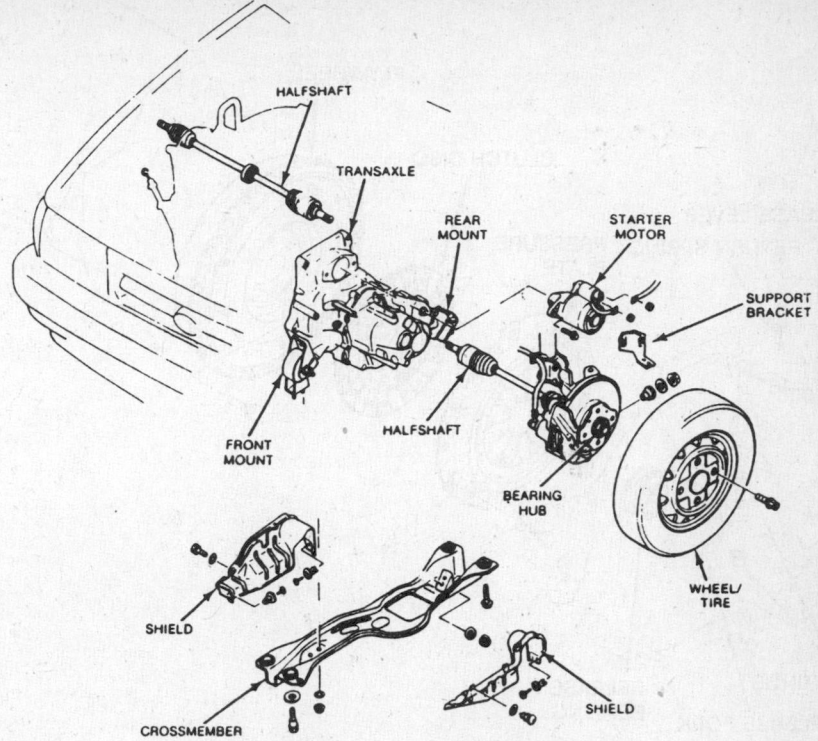

Manual transaxle and related components

rear engine contact surfaces. Apply about a $1/16$ in. bead of gasket eliminator sealing compound to the transaxle housing. To ensure proper sealing, make certain the sealant encircles the bolt holes during application.

To install:

18. Raise the transaxle into position and seat against the rear of the engine.

19. Install the lower transaxle attaching bolts. Torque the bolts to 47–66 ft. lbs.

20. Install the noise vibration harness brackets and remove the transmission jack.

21. Install the crossmember and remove the differential plugs. Torque the crossmember to chassis and engine mount nuts to 27–46 ft. lbs.

22. Remove and discard the old halfshaft circlips. Replace the circlips with new ones. Engage the halfshafts with the differential side gears.

23. Connect the lower control arms to the steering knuckles. Install the lower control arm attaching clamp bolts and nuts. Hold the clamp bolt stationary and torque the nut to 32–40 ft. lbs.

24. Position the shift rod on the input shift rail and install the attaching bolt and nut.

25. Lower the vehicle and remove the engine support bar.

26. Install the 2 bolts at the top of the clutch housing. Torque the bolts 47–66 ft. lbs.

27. Install the starter.

28. Install the clutch cable bracket and engage the clutch cable with the release lever. Connect the neutral and back-up switch wiring connectors.

29. Remove the speedometer driven gear from the transaxle case bore. With a clean rag, wipe the driven gear and reinsert into the transaxle case. Visually inspect the the oil level on the driven gear. The oil level should be between the **F** and **L** marks on the gear sleeve. If the level is not within the normal operating range, add oil through the speedometer bore as required.

30. Install the speedometer gear and connect the speedometer cable. Replace the rubber boot.

31. Connect the negative battery cable.

32. Adjust the clutch pedal free-play.

CLUTCH

Clutch Assembly

REMOVAL & INSTALLATION

1. Disconnect the negative battery cable.

2. Remove the transaxle assembly.

NOTE: During the removal procedure, do not allow oil or grease

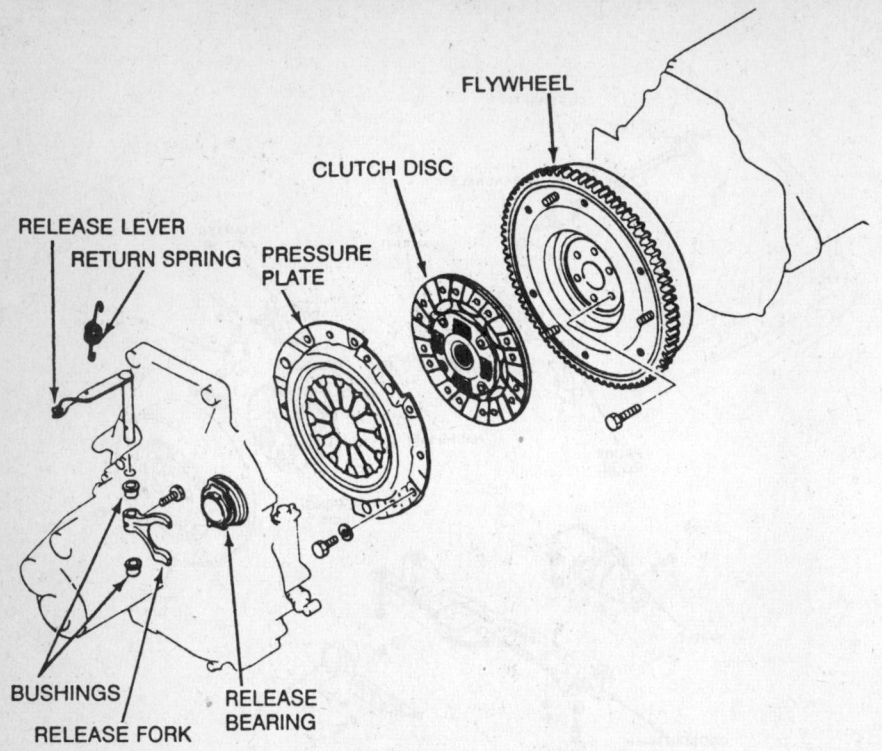

Assembly view of the clutch

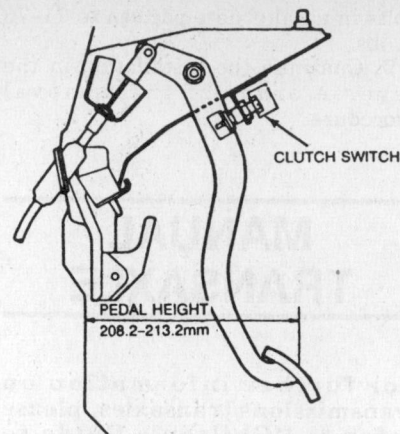

Clutch pedal height adjustment

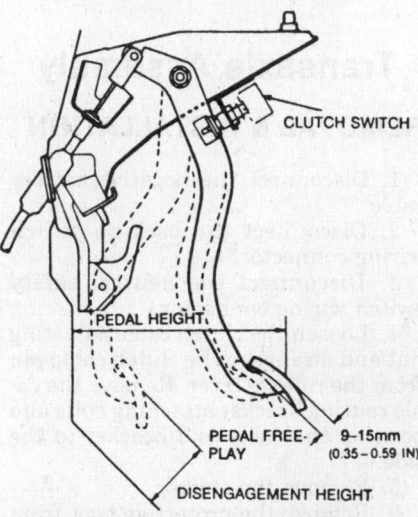

Clutch pedal free play adjustment

to come in contact with the clutch disc facing if the disc is to be reused. Handle the disc with clean rags wrapped around the edges and do not touch the disc facing. Even a small amount of dirt or grease may cause the clutch to grab or slip.

3. If the pressure plate is to be reused, paint or scribe alignment marks on the pressure plate and flywheel for assembly reference.

4. Install an appropriate locking tool to prevent the flywheel from turning.

5. Loosen the pressure plate attaching bolts in an alternate pattern 1 turn at a time. This will relieve the pressure plate spring tension evenly and prevent distortion of the pressure plate. Remove the pressure plate and clutch disc after the bolts are removed. Replace all clutch components as required.

To install:

6. Position the clutch disc on the flywheel and install a clutch alignment tool to hold the disc in place.

NOTE: When installing the clutch disc, make certain that the disc dampener springs are facing away from the flywheel. A new disc will be stamped FLYWHEEL to indicate the correct installation postion.

7. Align the reference marks, if present, and position the pressure plate on the flywheel and install the attaching bolts. Torque the bolts evenly, in an alternate pattern, to 13–20 ft. lbs. The bolts must be tightened in this manner to prevent distortion of the pressure plate.

8. Remove the clutch alignment tool.

9. Clean the clutch disc splines on the input shaft with a dry rag and coat the spline surfaces with clutch grease.

10. Complete the assembly of the transaxle by reversing the removal procedure.

11. Connect the negative battery cable.

12. Adjust the clutch pedal free-play.

PEDAL HEIGHT ADJUSTMENT

NOTE: The clutch pedal height is controlled by the clutch switch stop bolt.

1. To eliminate the possibility that the clutch cable is affecting the pedal height, loosen the cable adjusting nut and disengage the cable pin from the transaxle release lever. Move the floor carpet and insulation out of the way of the dash panel to ensure an accurate measurement.

2. With a ruler, measure the distance from the upper center of the pedal to the dash panel. The pedal height should be from 8.209–8.304 in. If the pedal height is within this range, no adjustment is necessary. If the pedal height is not within specification, inspect the clutch pedal mounting for damaged, worn or missing parts. If the mounting appears to be satisfactory, proceed as follows:

a. Remove the instrument panel bracket and air duct from under the instrument panel.

b. Locate the clutch switch and loosen the attaching nuts. Thread the switch in or out until the pedal height is within specification. Tighten the attaching nuts when the correct height is obtained.

c. Connect the clutch cable to the transaxle release lever and adjust the pedal free-play.

d. Measure the clutch pedal height. If the pedal height has changed after connecting the clutch cable, check for binding along the cable route.

e. Install the air inlet duct and instrument panel bracket. Place the insulation and floor carpet in their original positions.

Clutch Cable

FREE-PLAY ADJUSTMENT

1. Carefully move the clutch pedal back and forth and measure the amount of travel by visual approximation. If the clutch pedal free play is from 0.160–0.280 in., no adjustment is necessary.

2. If the free-play is not within specification, proceed as follows. Pull back the transaxle release lever and measure the clearance between the lever and the cable pin. The clearance should be from 0.060–0.100 in. Loosen and rotate the cable adjuster nut until the clearance between the pin and the lever is within specification.

3. When the proper clearance is obtained, tighten the adjuster nut.

4. Repeat the procedure described in Step 1 to ensure that the free-play travel is correct.

REMOVAL & INSTALLATION

1. Loosen the clutch cable adjusting nut and disengage the cable pin from the release lever. When the cable is free from the lever, completely remove the cable pin and adjusting nut.

2. Unbolt the cable routing bracket from the transaxle housing.

3. Remove the instrument panel bracket located under the steering column.

4. Remove the air inlet duct located under the steering column.

5. Remove the clip securing the cable casing to the pedal support bracket.

6. Pull upward on the cable to disengage the cable from the pedal extension.

7. Loosen the attaching nut and remove the routing bracket from the cable. Withdraw the cable from the dash panel grommet.

NOTE: Make certain that the dash panel grommet is properly seated before installing and routing the new clutch cable.

8. Route the new cable through the dash grommet and connect the routing bracket to the cable. Secure the cable to the routing bracket by tightening the attaching nuts and attach the bracket to the transaxle housing.

9. Pull upward on the cable and connect the cable the clutch pedal extension.

10. Install the cable casing retaining clip.

11. Install the air duct and instrument panel bracket.

12. Connect the cable pin to the release lever. Check the cable free-play and adjust if necessary.

AUTOMATIC TRANSAXLE

For further information on transmissions/transaxles, please refer to "Chilton's Guide to Transmission Repair".

Transaxle Assembly

REMOVAL & INSTALLATION

1. Disconnect the negative battery cable. Loosen the front wheel lug nuts.

2. Drain the transaxle fluid. Disconnect the speedometer cable from the transaxle.

3. Disconnect the transaxle electrical connectors, which are located next to the governor.

4. Disconnect the transaxle ground wire. Disconnect the transaxle vacuum hose.

5. Remove the nut which connects the shift lever to the manual shaft assembly.

6. Remove the shift cable from the transaxle. Support the engine using an appropriate engine support bar.

7. Raise and support the vehicle safely. Remove the tire and wheel assemblies.

8. Remove the left splash shield. Remove the stabilizer mounting nuts and brackets. Remove the left stabilizer body bracket.

9. Remove the lower arm clamp bolts and nuts. Pull the lower arms downward, separating the lower arms from the knuckles.

10. Remove the cotter pin and nut. Disconnect the tie rod end from the knuckle.

11. Remove the halfshafts. Install a differential plug tool between the differential side gears.

12. Disconnect and plug the oil cooler lines. Remove the crossmember. Remove the gusset plate to transaxle bolts.

13. Remove the flywheel cover. Remove the torque converter retaining bolts. Remove the starter.

14. Properly support the transaxle assembly.

15. Remove the engine-to-transaxle retaining bolts. Carefully remove the transaxle from the vehicle.

To install:

16. Position the transaxle under the vehicle. Install the engine-to-transaxle bolts. Tighten to 41–59 ft. lbs.

17. Install the starter. Install the torque converter bolts and tighten to 26–36 ft. lbs.

18. Install the flywheel cover and tighten the bolts to 61–87 inch lbs.

19. Install the crossmember and tighten the bolts to 47–66 ft. lbs. Install the front engine mount to the crossmember and tighten the bolts to 32–38 ft. lbs.

20. Install the halfshafts. Attach the tie rod ends and the stabilizer.

21. Install the splash shield and the front wheels.

22. Lower the vehicle. Remove the engine support tool.

23. Reconnect the hoses and electrical leads. Connect the shift linkage.

24. Connect the speedometer cable. Install the negative battery cable. Fill the transaxle to the proper level.

SHIFT LINKAGE ADJUSTMENT

1. Disconnect the negative battery cable.

2. Remove the shift console retaining screws and remove the shift console.

3. Shift the selector lever to **P**. Remove the selector lever knob and locknut.

4. Remove the shift quadrant attaching screws and remove the shift quadrant.

NOTE: Make sure that the detent spring roller is in the P detent.

5. Loosen the adjustment nuts until they reach the ends of the cable thread.

6. Shift the transaxle shift lever

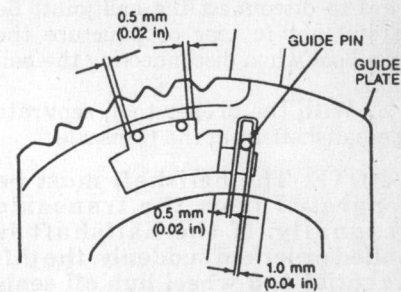

Shift linkage adjustment

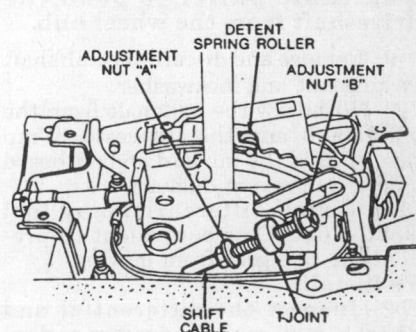

Shift linkage adjustment points

into the **P** position. Tighten the **A** adjusting nut until it lightly contacts the "T" joint. Tighten the **B** adjusting nut to 80–97 inch lbs. (9–11 Nm).

7. Check the guide plate and guide pin clearance, the correct clearance should be 0.5mm. The clearance should be the same in **N** and **D**.

8. Install the shift quadrant and install the remaining components in reverse order. Tighten the selector lever locknut to 11–15 ft. lbs. (15–20 Nm).

DRIVE AXLE

Halfshaft

REMOVAL & INSTALLATION

1. Disconnect the negative battery cable.

2. Raise the vehicle and support it safely.

3. Drain the transaxle fluid.

4. Remove the front tire and wheel assemblies. Remove the splash shields.

5. Bend back the lockwasher tab on the halfshaft locknut slot. Lock the brakes and loosen, but do not remove, the halfshaft locknut.

6. Remove the stabilizer bar control link from the lower suspension control arm.

7. Remove the clamp bolt and nut from the lower suspension control arm. With a suitable pry bar, pry the lower suspension control arm downward to disconnect the ball joint. Be careful not to tear or puncture the dust boot when disconnecting the ball joint.

8. With the proper tool, separate the halfshaft from the transaxle.

NOTE: The halfshaft must be separated from the transaxle gradually. If the halfshaft is pulled or jerked suddenly, the differential and wheel hub oil seals may be damaged. If necessary, use a suitable puller to push the driveshaft from the wheel hub.

9. Remove and discard the halfshaft locking nut and lockwasher.

10. Withdraw the halfshaft from the wheel hub and the transaxle. Wrap tape around the inboard and outboard splines to prevent damage.

11. Install differential plug tool T87C-7025-C or equivalent to prevent the side gear from moving.

To install:

12. Inspect the differential and wheel hub oil seals for damage and replace the seals as required.

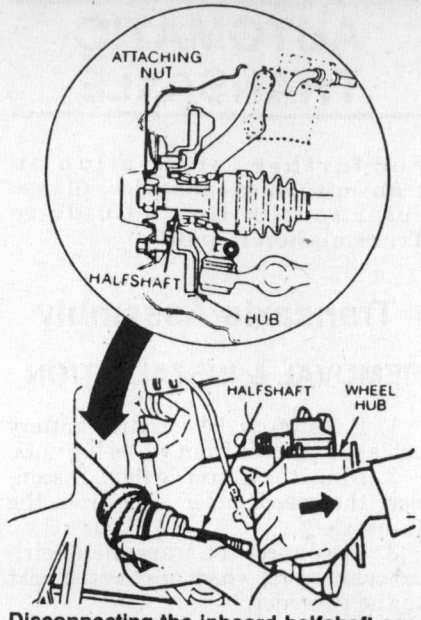

Disconnecting the inboard halfshaft section from the transaxle (section view of the Rzeppa type CV joint also shown)

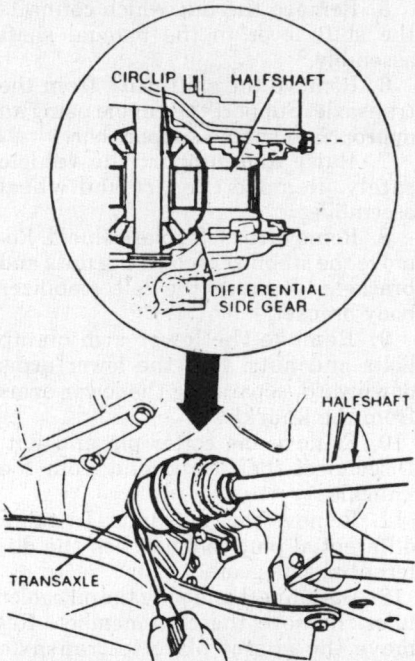

Disconnecting the outboard halfshaft section from the wheel hub (section veiw of the Birfield type CV joint also shown)

13. Remove the protective tape. Remove the circlips from the inboard halfshaft spline gear ends and replace with new. Coat the inboard and outboard halfshaft spline ends with grease.

14. Remove the differential gear holding plugs.

NOTE: If the right halfshaft is being installed at this point, the position of the dynamic damper

assembly must be checked. Push the outboard end of the halfshaft fully into the outboard CV-joint and measure the distance from the end of the shaft to the edge of the damper. The correct distance is 19.27–19.99 in. Adjust the position of the damper on the shaft as required to obtain the proper orientation. The left halfshaft does not incorporate a dynamic damper.

15. Position and install the inboard end of the halfshaft into the differential side gear. Take care not to damage the differential oil seal.

16. Position and install the outboard end of the halfshaft into the wheel hub. Take care not to damage the wheel hub oil seal.

17. Install the halfshaft lockwasher and locknut onto the halfshaft and tighten by hand.

18. Raise the lower suspension control arm and connect the arm to the ball joint. Take care not to damage the ball joint dust boot.

19. Install the lower suspension arm clamp nut and bolt. Hold the bolt stationary and torque the nut to 33–40 ft. lbs.

20. Make certain the brakes are still locked and torque the outboard halfshaft locknut to 116–174 ft. lbs. Bend a tab of the the lockwasher into a slot in the locknut with the proper tool.

NOTE: Do not stake the locking tab with a pointed tool. Make certain that the locking tab is depressed at least 0.16 in. into the locknut slot to ensure proper locking capabilty. After the lockwasher is locked into place, grasp the wheel hub and pull to ensure that the halfshaft is installed properly. Rotate the wheel hub by hand to ensure that the wheel hub turns smoothly.

21. Install the splash shields. Install the tire and wheel assemblies. Install and tighten the transaxle drain plug.

22. Fill the transaxle with the proper grade and type fluid to specification. Lower the vehicle.

CV-Boot

REMOVAL & INSTALLATION

1. Disconnect the negative battery cable. Raise and support the vehicle safely.

2. Remove the halfshaft from the vehicle. Support the assembly in a vise with protective jaws.

NOTE: During disassembly and assembly, do not allow dust or similar foreign matter to enter the halfshaft joints.

3. Remove the large boot clamp. Roll the boot back over the shaft. Remove the wire ring bearing retainer. Remove the outer race.

NOTE: Before removing the outer race, matchmark the outer race and tripot bearing for reassembly.

4. Matchmark the tripot bearing and the shaft. Remove the tripot bearing snapring.

5. As required, remove the small clamp and the CV joint boot from the halfshaft.

6. Installation is the reverse of the removal procedure.

Front Wheel Hub and Knuckle

REMOVAL & INSTALLATION

1. Disconnect the negative battery cable.

2. Raise the vehicle and support it safely.

3. Unbolt and remove front wheel from the hub assembly.

4. With a small cold chisel, straighten the staked edge of the halfshaft at-taching nut. Take care not to damage the halfshaft threads.

5. Remove and discard the halfshaft attaching nut.

6. Remove the retaining clip securing the caliper hose to the strut bracket.

7. Remove the cotter pin and tie rod end attaching nut. Discard the cotter pin and set the nut aside. Inspect the nut for damage and replace as required.

8. Using a tie rod end separator tool, release the tie rod end from the steering knuckle arm. If the tie rod appears to be siezed, strike the knuckle sharply with a soft-tipped hammer to acheive separation.

9. Support the brake caliper and remove the brake caliper attaching bolts. Lift the caliper assembly from the steering knuckle.

NOTE: After the caliper assembly is lifted from the steering knuckle, do not allow it to be suspended by the brake hose. Support the caliper by a length of rope or wire attached to the Mac-Pherson strut.

10. Remove the clamp bolt and nut at the point where the lower control arm ball joint connects to the steering knuckle. With a medium pry bar, release the lower ball joint from the steering knuckle by prying downward on the lower control arm.

11. Remove the 2 bolts that position the steering knuckle between the MacPherson strut bracket flanges.

12. Slide the rotor assembly from the end of the halfshaft. If binding occurs, tap the end of the shaft with a soft-tipped hammer. If the wheel hub is rusted to the halfshaft, use either a 2 jaw or a hub puller to achieve separation.

To install:

13. Clean the spline end and lubricate with a coating of wheel bearing grease. Apply a thin film of clean SAE 30 weight oil to the steering knuckle/rotor hub assembly up to the point where the uppermost arm of the steering knuckle seats into the MacPherson strut bracket.

14. Guide the steering knuckle/bearing hub assembly onto the halfshaft over the spline.

15. Install the strut to steering knuckle bolts. Torque the bolts to 69–86 ft. lbs.

16. Position the lower control arm ball joint in the steering knuckle. Install the lower control arm bolt and attaching nut. Torque the nut 32–40 ft. lbs.

17. Position the caliper assembly onto the steering knuckle and install the attaching bolts. Torque the bolts to 29–36 ft. lbs.

18. Position the hose into the strut routing bracket and install the retaining clip.

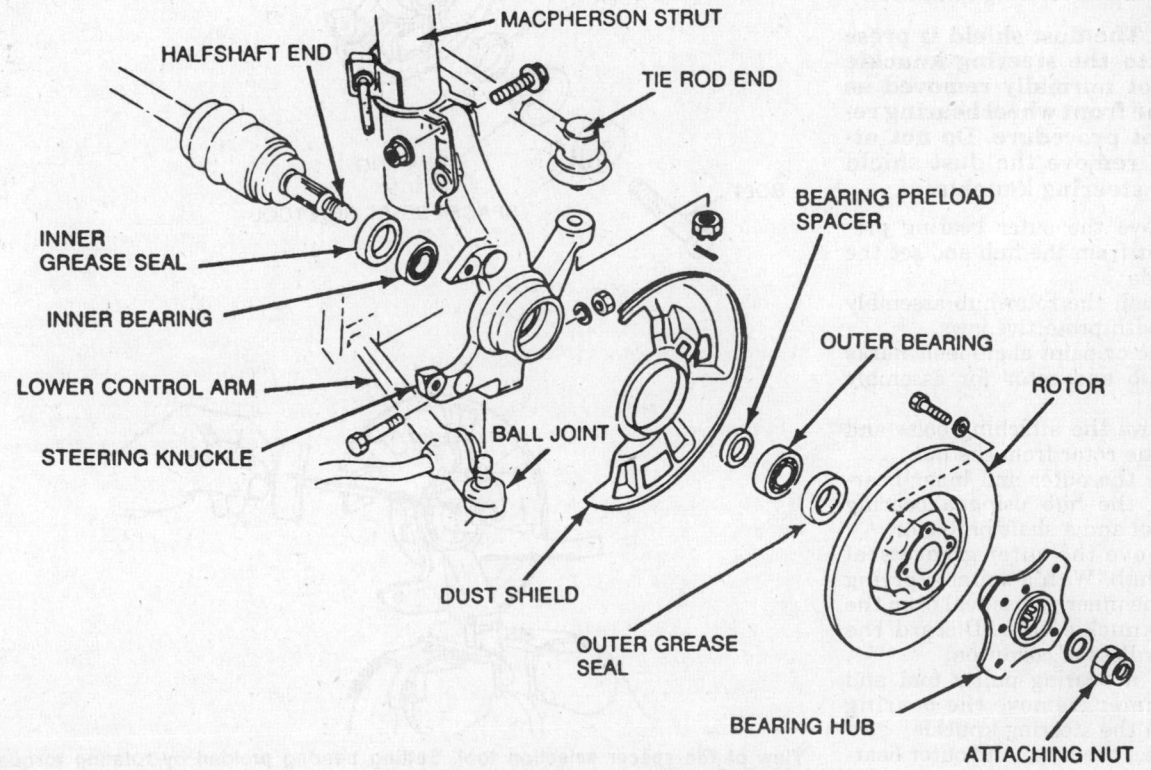

Front hub, knuckle and bearing assembly

19. Install a new halfshaft attaching nut. Torque the nut to 116–174 ft. lbs. Rotate the wheel hub assembly by hand to ensure that it turns freely.

20. With a small cold chisel, stake the halfshaft attaching nut into the halfshaft groove. Take care not to damage the nut when using the chisel. If the nut is damaged, it must be replaced.

21. Connect the tie rod end to the steering knuckle and install the attaching nut. Torque the nut to 22–33 ft. lbs.

22. Install and secure a new cotter pin through the tie rod end attaching nut and ball stud. If the openings in the nut do not align with the the rod end opening, tighten the nut until the holes align. Do not loosen the nut to achieve alignment.

23. Install the front wheel.

24. Lower the vehicle and torque the wheel bolts to 65-87 ft. lbs. Connect the negative battery cable.

Front Wheel Bearings

REMOVAL & INSTALLATION

1. Disconnect the negative battery cable.

2. Raise the vehicle and support it safely.

3. Remove the front wheel hub and knuckle assembly from the vehicle.

4. Remove the wheel hub/rotor assembly from the steering knuckle.

NOTE: The dust shield is press fitted onto the steering knuckle and is not normally removed as part of the front wheel bearing replacement procedure. Do not attempt to remove the dust shield from the steering knuckle.

5. Remove the outer bearing preload spacer from the hub and set the spacer aside.

6. Position the rotor/hub assembly in a vise with protective jaws.

7. Scribe or paint alignment marks on the hub and rotor for assembly reference.

8. Remove the attaching bolts and separate the rotor from the hub.

9. Press the outer and inner bearings from the hub using a bearing splitter tool and a shaft protector.

10. Remove the outer grease seal from the hub. With a suitable prying tool, pry the inner grease seal from the steering knuckle bore. Discard the seals regardless of condition.

11. With a bearing puller tool and slide hammer, remove the bearing races from the steering knuckle.

12. Inspect the inner and outer bearings for abnormal wear patterns. In-

Stamped Mark	Thickness In. (mm)
1	0.2474 (6.285)
2	0.2490 (6.325)
3	0.2506 (6.365)
4	0.2522 (6.405)
5	0.2538 (6.445)
6	0.2554 (6.485)
7	0.2570 (6.525)
8	0.2586 (6.565)
9	0.2602 (6.605)
10	0.2618 (6.645)
11	0.2634 (6.685)
12	0.2650 (6.725)
13	0.2666 (6.765)
14	0.2682 (6.805)
15	0.2698 (6.845)
16	0.2714 (6.885)
17	0.2730 (6.925)
18	0.2746 (6.965)
19	0.2762 (7.005)
20	0.2778 (7.045)
21	0.2794 (7.085)

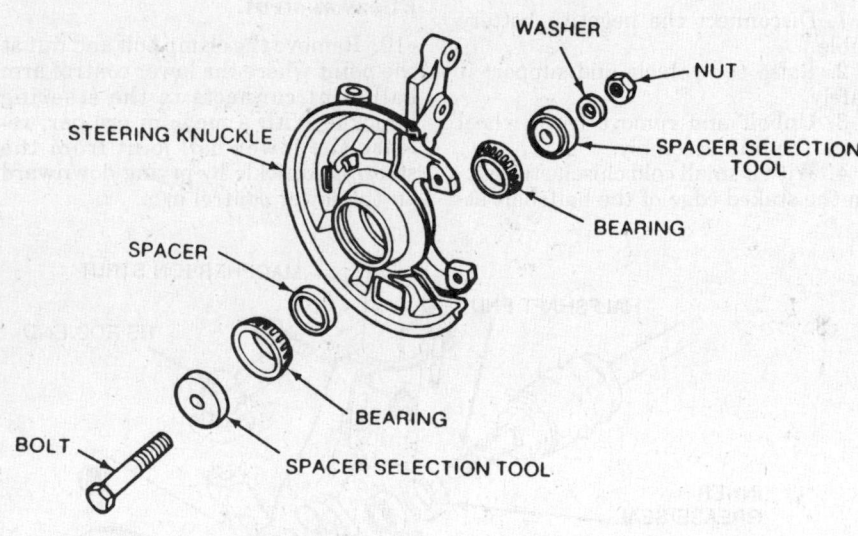

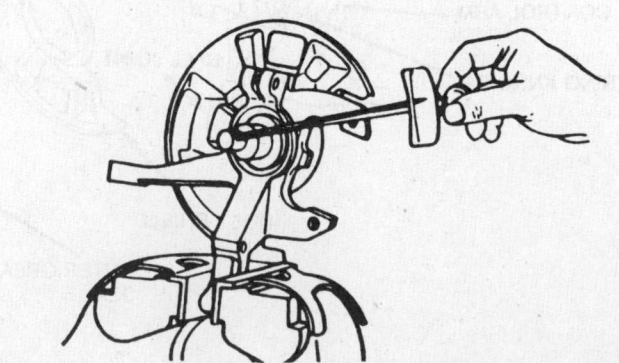

View of the spacer selection tool. Setting bearing preload by rotating torque also shown

spect the rotor hub for cracks, damage to the casting, abnormal wear at the oil seal contact surface, and scoring or rusting of the bearing bore. Inspect the steering knuckle for cracks and scoring or rusting of the bearing bore. Check the rotor dust shield for a loose or improper fit. Replace all damaged components as required.

To install:

13. Coat the bearing races with a light film of clean engine oil. With bearing cup replacer tool and universal drive handle tool, seat the bearing races in the steering knuckle bore.

14. Pack the inner and outer bearings with wheel bearing grease.

15. Place the inner bearing into the steering knuckle bore so that it rests in a level position. Lubricate the lip of the new inner grease seal with wheel bearing grease. Drive the inner grease seal and inner bearing into the bore of the steering wheel spokes. This will free the steering wheel cover assembly, cover bracket and horn buttons. Disconnect the horn wire from the horn button leads and remove the cover assembly.

4. Matchmark the steering wheel and steering column shaft for assembly reference. Using a steering wheel puller tool, remove the steering wheel.

5. Installation is the reverse of the removal procedure. Position the steering wheel onto the steering column shaft and align the matchmarks. Tighten the nut to 29–36 ft. lbs.

NOTE: When installing the steering wheel, make certain that the cutouts in the rear cover engage the turn signal cancelling cam. If necessary, use the steering wheel nut to seat the steering wheel onto the cancelling cam cutouts, then remove the nut.

Steering Column

REMOVAL & INSTALLATION

1. Disconnect the negative battery cable.

2. Remove the instrument panel brace below the steering column and remove the air duct.

3. Remove the combination switch upper and lower covers by removing the lower cover attaching screws.

4. Release the combination switch wiring harness clip and unplug the 4 connectors from the rear of the switch.

5. Remove the ignition switch.

6. Disconnect the steering column mounting bracket from the instrument panel crossmember by removing the retaining nuts. When the column is free from the instrument panel, it may be lowered as required to gain access to the intermediate shaft universal joint at the lower end.

7. With a white crayon or suitable marker, mark the point where the steering column shaft engages with the universal joint. Remove the universal joint clamp screw.

8. Loosen the 2 nuts securing the steering column hinge bracket to the clutch/brake pedal support.

9. Disengage the steering column from the universal joint by pulling to the rear. Remove the steering column from the vehicle. Remove the shim clips from the upper mounting bracket.

To install:

10. Install the joint clamp screw. Do not tighten the screw at this time as the clamp may need to shifted up or down on the shaft to align the steering column.

11. Install the steering column by aligning the index marks on the steering column shaft and universal joint. Engage the column hinge bracket with the pedal support studs and install the bracket nuts. Tighten the bracket nuts and raise the upper end of the column to seat under the instrument panel.

12. Install the shim clips onto the upper column mounting bracket flanges.

13. Install the steering column upper retaining nuts.

14. Turn the steering wheel from lock-to-lock several times to align the universal joints, then, tighten the universal clamp bolts.

15. Install the ignition switch. Connect the combination switch wiring harness connectors and secure the harness in its mounting clip.

16. Install the combination switch upper and lower covers.

17. Install the air duct and the instrument panel brace under the steering column. Connect the negative battery cable.

Manual Steering Rack and Pinion

ADJUSTMENT

Only the rack preload is adjustable, and only to a limited degree, since it is primarily determined by the yoke spring. Since adjustment requires removal of the attaching gear, it should only be undertaken after a thorough inspection of front suspension and steering column components fails to reveal damage or binding elsewhere. If necessary, adjust the rack yoke preload as follows:

1. Remove the steering rack from the vehicle.

2. Center the steering rack in a protected jaw vise, make sure there is equal left and right tie rod extension.

3. Measure the pinion operating torque with an inch lb. torque wrench and pinion torque adapter tool T87C–3504–C, or equivalent. Within 90 degrees of the centered rack position, pinion torque should be 8–11 inch lbs. Beyond 90 degrees, left or right, pinion torque should not exceed 13.3 inch lbs.

4. If the pinion torque is not within the specified limits, tighten or loosen the rack adjusting screw to increase or decrease the rack preload.

NOTE: Do not loosen the adjusting screw so that it no longer makes contact with the yoke spacer. Any clearance at this point will allow the rack to deflect under load, resulting in reduced tooth engagement with the pinion.

5. When the pinion operating torque is within specification, tighten the jam nut on the adjusting screw. With a suitable adapter, torque the jam nut to 7–11 ft. lbs. to retain the adjustment.

6. Complete the assembly of the steering gear by reversing the removal procedure.

REMOVAL & INSTALLATION

1. Disconnect the negative and positive battery cables and remove the battery from the vehicle.

2. Matchmark the steering column lower universal joint and steering rack pinion for assembly reference. Remove the steering column and intermediate shaft assembly from the vehicle.

3. Cut the plastic tie wrap securing the steering column boot to the steering rack.

4. Raise the vehicle and support safely. Remove the front tire and wheel assemblies.

5. Using the proper tool, separate both tie rod ends from the steering knuckles.

6. Remove the catalytic converter.

7. Cut and remove the plastic tie rod splash shield from the right inner fender.

8. Remove the steering rack mounting bolts and lower the steering rack until it is free of the steering column boot. Slide the rack to the right, through the inner fender tie rod opening, until the left tie rod is clear of the left inner fender, then lower the left end until the steering rack assembly can be withdrawn from the left side of the vehicle.

NOTE: While maneuvering the tie rod boots in and out of the inner fender openings, guide the steering rack assembly carefully to avoid cutting or nicking the boots.

To install:

9. From under the vehicle, insert the right side tie rod through the right inner tie rod opening, far enough to allow raising the left end of the assembly to enter the left fender opening. Shift the assembly to the left taking care not to catch the boots.

10.. Align the steering rack pinion shaft housing with the steering column boot. Raise the steering rack into the boot.

11. Install the steering rack mounting bolts from left to right. Torque the bolts to 23–34 ft. lbs.

12. Connect the tie rod ends to the steering knuckles. If the tie rod ends are not properly aligned with the knuckle ends during installation, release the small end boot clips before rotating the tie rods. This is done to avoid twisting the boots.

13. Attach the right side tie rod splash shield on the right inner fender panel.

14. Install the catalytic converter.

15. Install the tire and wheel assemblies and lower the vehicle.

16. Secure the steering column boot to the steering rack housing with a new tie wrap.

17. Align the matchmarks made on the steering column lower universal joint and the steering rack pinion shaft. Install the steering column when the proper alignment is acheived.

18. Install the battery.

Power Steering Rack and Pinion

REMOVAL & INSTALLATION

1. Disconnect the negative and positive battery cables and remove the battery from the vehicle.

2. Matchmark the steering column lower universal joint and steering rack pinion for assembly reference. Remove the steering column and intermediate shaft assembly from the vehicle.

3. Cut the plastic tie wrap securing the steering column boot to the steering rack.

4. Raise the vehicle and support safely. Remove the front tire and wheel assemblies.

5. Using the proper tool, separate both tie rod ends from the steering knuckles. Disconnect and plug the pressure lines.

6. Remove the catalytic converter.

7. Cut and remove the plastic tie rod splash shield from the right inner fender.

8. Remove the steering rack mounting bolts and lower the steering rack until it is free of the steering column boot. Slide the rack to the right, through the inner fender tie rod opening, until the left tie rod is clear of the left inner fender, then lower the left end until the steering rack assembly can be withdrawn from the left side of the vehicle.

NOTE: While maneuvering the tie rod boots in and out of the inner fender openings, guide the steering rack assembly carefully to avoid cutting or nicking the boots.

To install:

9. From under the vehicle, insert the right side tie rod through the right inner tie rod opening, far enough to allow raising the left end of the assembly to enter the left fender opening. Shift the assembly to the left taking care not to catch the boots.

10. Align the steering rack pinion shaft housing with the steering column boot. Raise the steering rack into the boot.

11. Install the steering rack mounting bolts from left to right. Torque the bolts to 23–34 ft. lbs.

12. Connect the tie rod ends to the steering knuckles. If the tie rod ends are not properly aligned with the knuckle ends during installation, release the small end boot clips before rotating the tie rods. This is done to avoid twisting the boots.

13. Attach the right side tie rod splash shield on the right inner fender panel.

14. Install the catalytic converter.

15. Install the tire and wheel assemblies and lower the vehicle.

16. Secure the steering column boot to the steering rack housing with a new tie wrap.

17. Align the matchmarks made on

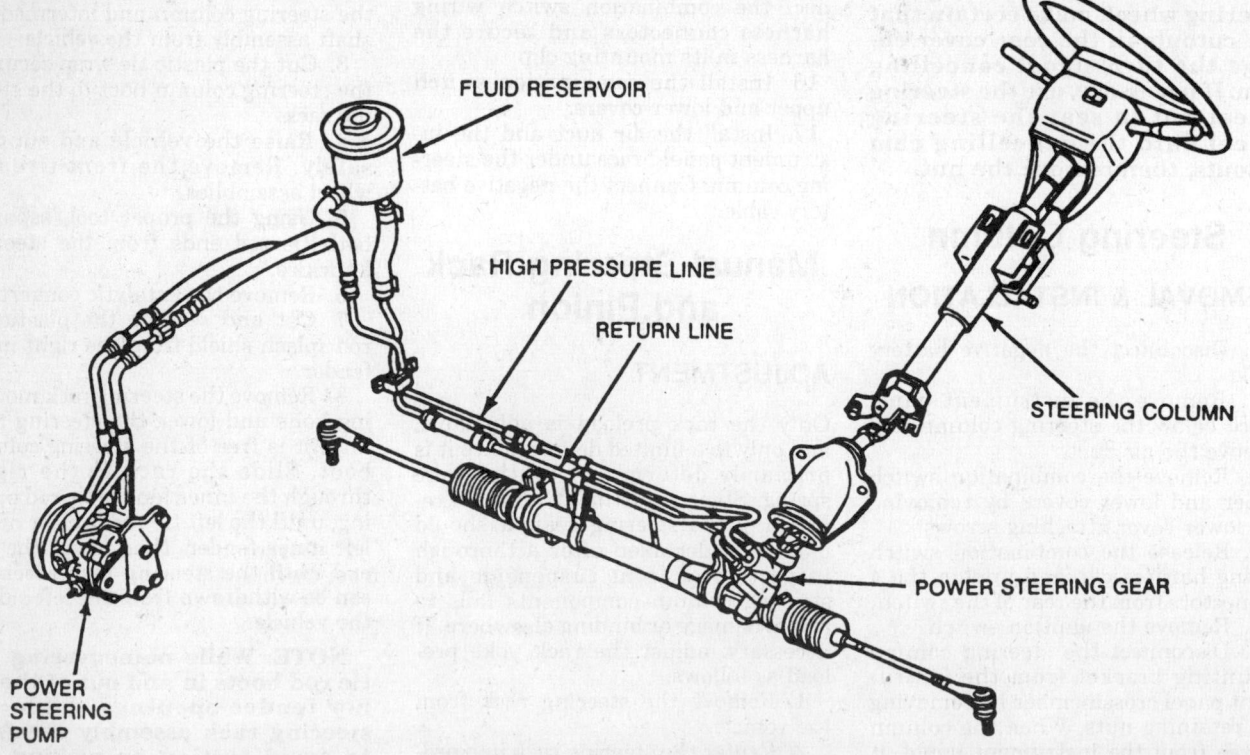

Power steering assembly components

FLUID RESERVOIR

HIGH PRESSURE LINE

RETURN LINE

STEERING COLUMN

POWER STEERING GEAR

POWER STEERING PUMP

the steering column lower universal joint and the steering rack pinion shaft. Install the steering column when the proper alignment is acheived.

18. Install the battery.

Power Steering Pump

REMOVAL & INSTALLATION

1. Disconnect the negative battery cable.
2. Remove the air duct and air cleaner unit.
3. Disconnect the electrical connector from the fluid pressure switch.
4. Disconnect and plug the fluid lines.
5. Remove the adjustment bolt and the bracket bolt.
6. Remove the accesory drive belt. Remove the pump from the bracket.
7. Installation is the reverse of the removal procedure. Torque the pressure lines to 29–36 ft. lbs. (39–49 Nm).

BELT TESNION ADJUSTMENT

1. Remove the air duct and air cleaner.
2. Loosen the pump mounting bolt. Loosen the adjusting locknut.
3. Using a belt tension gauge, adjust the tension at the adjusing bolt.
4. The coorect tension for a new belt is 110–132 lbs. and 95–110 lbs. for a used belt.
5. Tighten the pump mounting bolt to 27–40 ft. lbs. and the adjustment locknut to 27–38 ft. lbs.

SYSTEM BLEEDING

1. Add power steering fluid to the **L** mark on the reservoir.
2. Run the engine until it reaches normal operating temperature.
3. Turn the steering wheel lock to lock approximately 10 times.
4. Shut the engine off with the wheels in the straight ahead position.
5. Check the fluid level, the level should be between the **L** and **H** marks on the reservoir. Repeat the procedure if needed.

Tie Rod Ends

REMOVAL & INSTALLATION

1. Disconnect the negative battery cable.
2. Raise the vehicle and support it safely. Remove the wheel and tire assembly.
3. Remove the cotter pin and nut from the tie rod end stud. Discard the

cotter pin. Examine the nut for damage and replace as required.
4. Separate the tie rod end from the steering knuckle.
5. With a white crayon or suitable marker, place alignment marks across the jam nut and tie rod to the toe-in angle adjustment.
6. Loosen the jam nut and unscrew the tie rod end counting the number of turns required for removal. Replace the tie rod end as required.

NOTE: If new tie rod ends are being installed, place the old and new ends side-by-side and place alignment marks in the new end that match as closely as possible to the marks on the old end. Please be advised that the existing jam nut may not seat in exactly the same position on the new end and the toe-in angle may have to be checked and/or readjusted as a precaution.

7. When replacing a tie rod end, install a new dust boot over the stud with a suitable adapter. A ¾ in. socket will accomplish the task simply and effectively.
8. Thread the jam nut and tie rod end onto the tie rod observing the alignment marks and the number of turns required for installation.
9. Install the tie rod end into the steering knuckle. If the tie rod is correctly aligned, the taper should seat without twisting the tie rod or boot. Torque the stud nut to 26–30 ft. lbs. and install a new cotter pin. If the cotter pin does not align with stud bore, tighten (do not loosen) the nut until the castellations align with the pin bore.
10. Install the wheel and tire assembly. Lower the vehicle and connect the negative battery cable.

BRAKES

For all brake system repair and service procedures not detailed below, please refer to "Brakes" in the Unit Repair section.

Master Cylinder

REMOVAL & INSTALLATION

1. Disconnect the negative battery cable. Disconnect the low fluid level sensor connector.
2. Disconnect the brake tubes from the master cylinder connections. Plug or cover the tube openings to prevent the entry of dirt and contamination.

3. Remove the attaching nuts and washers and separate the master cylinder from the power booster mounting studs. Clean the master cylinder and power booster contact surfaces with a clean shop towel.
4. Position the master cylinder onto the power booster mounting studs.
5. Install the attaching washers and nuts. Torque the nuts to 7–12 ft. lbs.
6. Connect and properly tighten the brake tubes to master cylinder connections.
7. Connect the low fluid level sensor.
8. Fill the master cylinder to the proper level with brake fluid and bleed the brake system.

Proportioning Valve

The proportioning valve is located in the engine compartment. It is mounted to the dash panel below and to the right of the brake booster. The valve is not repairable and must be replaced if determined to be faulty.

REMOVAL & INSTALLATION

1. Disconnect the negative battery cable. Loosen the connector nuts and disconnect the brake tubes from the proportioning valve. Plug or cover the tube openings to prevent the entry of dirt and grease.
2. Loosen the valve attaching bolts and remove the valve from the dash panel.
3. Complete the installation of the proportioning valve by reversing the removal procedure.
4. Bleed the brake system.
5. Inspect for proper brake operation and inspect for leaks around the valve connections.

Power Brake Booster

REMOVAL & INSTALLATION

1. Disconnect the negative battery cable. Remove the master cylinder.

NOTE: It may be necessary to remove the master cylinder from the booster assembly without disconnecting the brake lines from the cylinder. If possible, position the master cylinder to the side.

2. Disconnect the vacuum hose from the brake booster unit.
3. From inside the vehicle, remove and discard the cotter pin securing the clevis pin. Remove the clevis pin from the clevis and disconnect the clevis from the brake pedal.
4. Support the power booster unit in the engine compartment.
5. From inside the vehicle, remove

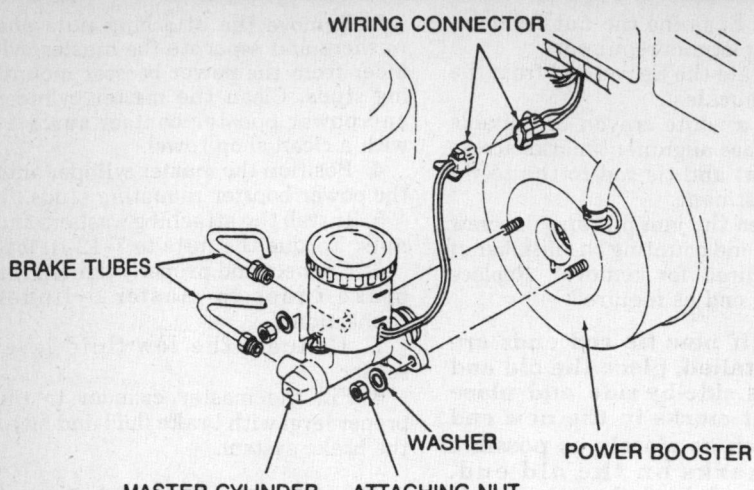

WIRING CONNECTOR

BRAKE TUBES

WASHER · POWER BOOSTER

MASTER CYLINDER · ATTACHING NUT

Master cylinder assembly

the nuts securing the unit to the bulk-head. Remove the unit from the engine compartment.

6. Remove the gasket between the power booster unit and the bulkhead. Replace the gasket, as required.

7. Position the gasket onto the power brake booster studs and have a second technician postion the unit against the bulkhead.

8. From inside the vehicle, secure the power booster to the bulkhead with the 4 retaining nuts. Torque the retaining nuts to 12–17 ft. lbs.

9. Lubricate the clevis with a coating of white lithium grease or equivalent. From inside the vehicle, attach the clevis to the brake pedal with the clevis pin. Secure the clevis pin with a new cotter pin.

10. Connect the vacuum to the power brake booster.

11. Complete the assembly of the master cylinder by reversing the removal procedure.

12. Bleed the brake system.

Brake Caliper

REMOVAL & INSTALLATION

1. Raise and safely support the vehicle.

2. Remove the wheel and tire assembly.

3. Remove the brake pads. Remove the brake hose attaching bolt, plug the hose end. Discard the O-rings.

4. Remove the caliper attaching bolts and the anit-squeak caps.

5. Remove the caliper from the vehicle.

6. Installation is the reverse of the removal procedure.

7. Use new O-rings on the brake hose and bleed the brake system. Tighten the caliper mounting bolts to 29–36 ft. lbs.

Disc Brake Pads

REMOVAL & INSTALLATION

1. Remove some of the brake fluid from the master cylinder. Raise and support the vehicle safely.

2. Remove the tire and wheel assembly.

3. Remove the brake pad pin retainer. Disengage the anti-rattle spring from the brake pads.

4. Remove the brake pad pins and the anti-rattle spring.

5. Remove the brake pads and shims. Do not discard the shims that are located behind the inner brake pad.

6. Installation is the reverse of the removal procedure. Be sure to refill the brake fluid resivior, as required.

Brake Rotor

REMOVAL & INSTALLATION

1. Raise and safely support the vehicle.

2. Remove the wheel and tire assembly.

3. Remove the brake pads and remove the brake caliper from the rotor, do not disconnect the brake hose from the rotor. Support the caliper aside.

4. Bend back the staked edge of the halfshaft retaining nut washer.

5. Remove the halfshaft attaching nut. Discard the nut.

6. Remove the rotor and bearing hub from the halfshaft end, using a suitable puller.

7. Remove the rotor-to-bearing hub retaining bolts. Tighten to 33–40 ft. lbs.

8. Installation is the reverse of the removal procedure. Replace the halfshaft retaining nut.

Brake Drums

REMOVAL & INSTALLATION

1. Raise and safely support the vehicle.

2. Remove the tire and wheel assembly.

3. Remove the grease cap from the brake drum. Bend back the flat washer on the retaining nut.

4. Remove and discard the retaining nut.

5. Remove the brake drum and bearings as an assembly.

6. Installation is the reverse of the removal procedure. Use a new retain-

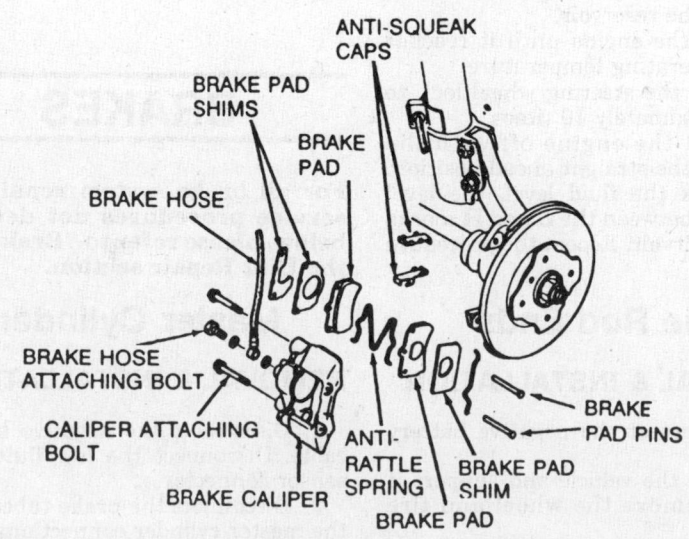

ANTI-SQUEAK CAPS

BRAKE PAD SHIMS

BRAKE PAD

BRAKE HOSE

BRAKE HOSE ATTACHING BOLT

CALIPER ATTACHING BOLT

BRAKE CALIPER

ANTI-RATTLE SPRING

BRAKE PAD SHIM

BRAKE PAD

BRAKE PAD PINS

Front disc brake assembly—exploded view

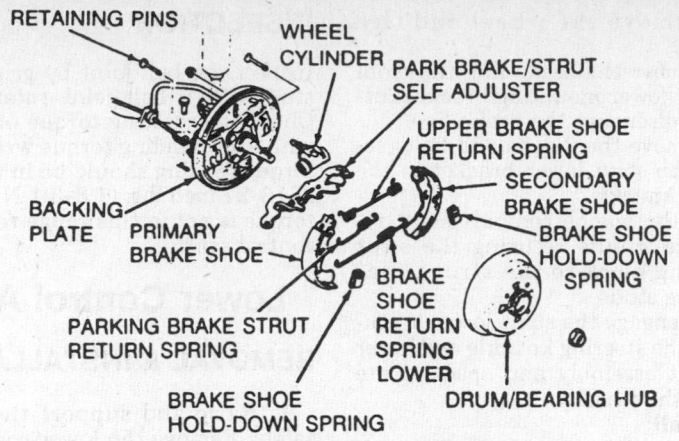

RETAINING PINS
WHEEL CYLINDER
PARK BRAKE/STRUT SELF ADJUSTER
UPPER BRAKE SHOE RETURN SPRING
SECONDARY BRAKE SHOE
BRAKE SHOE HOLD-DOWN SPRING
BACKING PLATE
PRIMARY BRAKE SHOE
BRAKE SHOE RETURN SPRING LOWER
PARKING BRAKE STRUT RETURN SPRING
BRAKE SHOE HOLD-DOWN SPRING
DRUM/BEARING HUB

Rear drum brake assembly—exploded view

ing nut for the drum and bearing assembly.

Brake Shoes

REMOVAL & INSTALLATION

1. Raise and support the vehicle safely.
2. Remove the tire and wheel assembly. Remove the brake drum.
3. Remove the brake shoe hold-down springs and pins.
4. Remove the brake shoe return springs. Pull the brake shoes away from the backing plate. Remove the brake shoes from their mounting.
5. Installation is the reverse of the removal procedure. Lubricate the brake shoe contact points before assembly.
6. Check the brake adjustemnt, the brake drum should turn with a little resistance. If it is too tight, back off the adjuster.

Wheel Cylinder

REMOVAL & INSTALLATION

1. Raise and support the vehicle safely.
2. Remove the rear brake shoes.
3. Disconnect the brake line from the wheel cylinder. Plug or cover the brake line opening to prevent the entry of dirt or grease.
4. Remove the 2 wheel cylinder attaching bolts and remove the wheel cylinder from the backing plate.
5. Position the wheel cylinder onto the backing plate and install the retaining bolts. Torque the retaining bolts to 7–9 ft. lbs.
6. Connect the brake line to the wheel cylinder.
7. Install the rear brake shoes.
8. Bleed the brake system.

Parking Brake Cable

ADJUSTMENT

1. Make certain that the parking brake is fully released.
2. Remove the parking brake console insert.
3. Remove the locking clip from the cable adjuster nut located at the base of the parking brake handle.
4. Raise and support the vehicle safely.
5. Tighten the cable adjuster nut until there is a slight brake drag when the rear wheels are rotated.
6. Back off on the adjuster nut until the brake drag disappears.
7. Check the operation of the parking brake. The rear brakes should be fully applied when the brake lever is pulled upward 11–16 notches.

REMOVAL & INSTALLATION

1. Remove the parking brake lever.
2. Remove the attaching screws and parking brake console mounting bracket.
3. Remove the attaching bolts and the front seat belt buckle assembly.
4. Remove the bolts attaching the lower half of the rear seat hinge to the floor pan.
5. Fold the rear seat forward and remove the bolts attaching the upper half of the rear seat hinge to the floor pan.
6. Remove the rear seat.
7. Remove the rear carpet push retainers and carefully pull the carpeting forward to expose the park brake cable guide.
8. Disconnect the park brake cable guide by removing the attaching screws.
9. Loosen the wheel bolts. Raise and support the vehicle safely.

10. Remove the rear wheels.
11. Remove the cotter pin and clevis pin attaching the park brake cable ends to the rear brake levers.
12. Remove the routing bracket retaining clips.
13. Disengage the park brake routing sleeves from the torsion beam routing brackets.
14. Remove the nut and bolt attaching the park brake to the fuel tank.
15. Remove the park brake cable equalizer attaching bolts.
16. Withdraw the lever end of the cable through the body opening and remove from the vehicle.

To install:

17. Position the lever end of the cable through the body opening.
18. Position the cable routing bracket on the fuel tank and install the attaching bolt.
19. Make certain that the cable seal is properly positioned in the floor pan.
20. Position the cable equalizer and install the attaching bolts. Make certain that the equalizer spacers are in position before tightening the attaching bolts.
21. Route the cable ends through the body brackets and install the retaining clips.
22. Seat the cable sleeves in the torsion beam routing brackets.
23. Attach the cable ends to the brake levers using the clevis pins and new cotter pins.
24. Install the rear wheels and lower the vehicle.
25. Route the end of the cable through the park brake lever.
26. Position the cable guide and secure with the attaching screws.
27. Position the carpet and install the push retainers. Install the rear seat and torque the retaining bolts to 28–38 ft. lbs.
28. Postion the seat belt assembly and install the attaching bolts and bolt spacers. Torque the bolts to 28–58 ft. lbs. The spacers must be installed on the bolts.
29. Position the console mounting bracket and install the attaching screws.
30. Install the parking brake adjuster nut and adjust the parking brake. Install the adjuster nut locking clip.
31. Raise the park brake handle and align with the parking brake console. Install the parking brake console.
32. Install the front push retainer and push insert. Install the park brake console insert.
33. Slide the front seats to their most forward postion. Install the park brake console attaching screws.
34. Position the front seats in their adjusted position.

Brake System Bleeding

If the master cylinder is known or suspected to contain air, the air must be removed.

1. Raise and safely support the vehicle. Remove the tire and wheel assemblies.
2. Loosen the front brake tube fitting and push the brake pedal slowly through its full travel. While the pedal is down, tighten the brake tube fitting. After the fitting is tight, release the brake pedal.
3. Repeat the procedure for the rear brake tube. Repeat the entire process several times to ensure all air is removed from the master cylinder.
4. Add brake fluid as required. Do not allow the brake fluid to spill on the vehicle painted surface, or damage to the paint will occur.

FRONT SUSPENSION

MacPherson Strut

REMOVAL & INSTALLATION

1. Disconnect the negative battery cable.
2. Raise the vehicle and support it safely.

3. Remove the wheel and tire assembly.
4. Remove the brake line clip from the strut lower mounting bracket cutout and disengage the brake line.
5. Remove the 2 nuts and bolts securing the strut lower bracket to the steering knuckle.
6. In the engine compartment, remove the 2 nuts securing the strut mounting block to the strut tower mounting studs.
7. Disengage the strut lower bracket from the steering knuckle and lower the strut assembly and spacer plate clear of the wheel well.

To install:

8. Place the strut assembly with spacer plate onto the strut tower with the white alignment mark facing outward.
9. Install the upper mounting block stud nuts and torque to 32–45 ft. lbs.
10. Engage the steering knuckle in the strut tower lower bracket and install the mounting bolts. Torque the bolts to 69–86 ft. lbs.
11. Postion the brake line into the strut lower mounting bracket cutout and install the retaining clip.
12. Install the wheel and tire assembly.
13. Connect the negative battery cable.

Ball Joints

NOTE: The ball joint is an integral part of the control arm. If inspection proves the ball joint to be bad, the entire lower control arm must be replaced.

INSPECTION

Inspect the ball joint by gripping the stud with a ball joint rotating tool. Check the rotating torque of the stud with a low reading torque wrench. The torque reading should be in the range of 16–27 inch lbs. (1.8–3.1 Nm). If the torque is not in this range replace the control arm.

Lower Control Arms

REMOVAL & INSTALLATION

1. Raise and support the vehicle safely. Remove the lower control arm pivot bolt at the frame bracket.
2. Remove the ball joint clamp bolt and and nut from the steering knuckle assembly.
3. Remove the stabilizer bar bushing retaining nut from the rear of the control arm and remove the rear bushing washer and bushing.
4. Lower the control arm, prying the ball joint stud out of the steering knuckle, if necessary. Disengage and remove the control arm from the stabilizer end.
5. Inspect the control arm for deformation or cracks, and check the pivot bushing for deterioration. Verify that the ball joint swivels freely but is not loose. If the control arm pivot bushing is to be replaced, remove the old bushing with C-frame tool T74P-3044-A1, bushing tool T81P-5493-B2 and receiver cup tool T88C-5493E or equivalents. Center the new bushing in the center of the control arm eye and in-

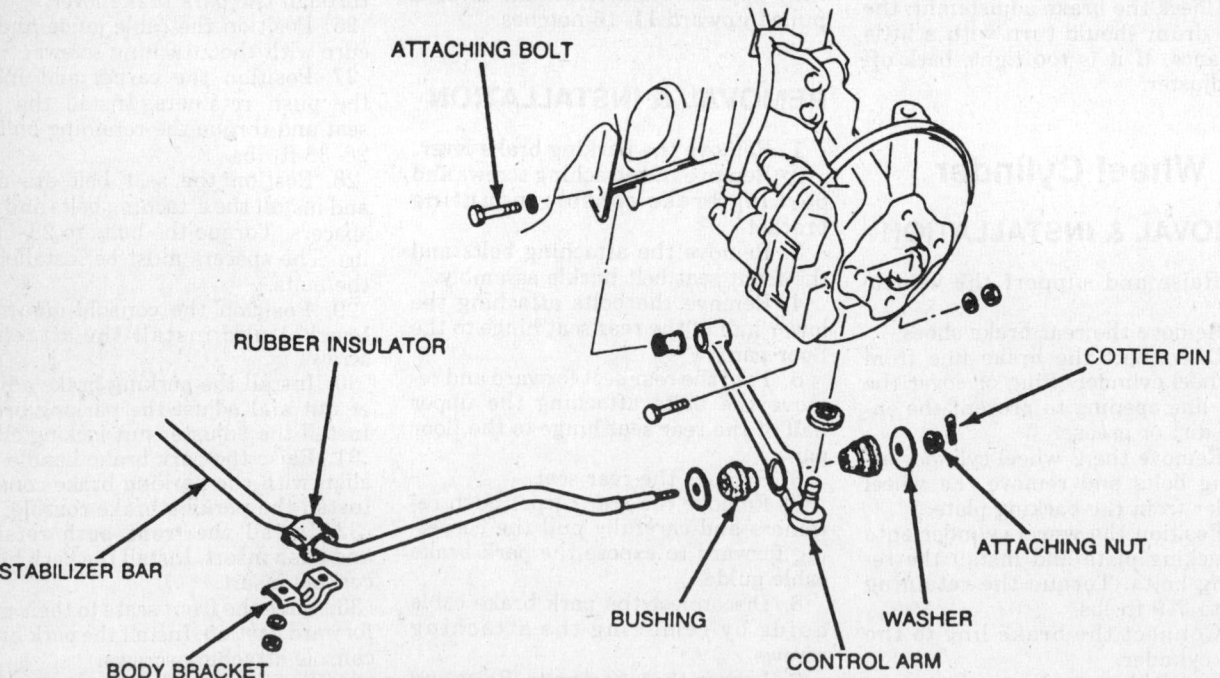

ATTACHING BOLT

RUBBER INSULATOR

COTTER PIN

STABILIZER BAR

ATTACHING NUT

BODY BRACKET

BUSHING

WASHER

CONTROL ARM

Lower control arm and stabilizer assembly

stall using the removal tools. Replace the lower control arm/ball joint assembly as required.

6. If the ball joint boot is damaged or deteriorated, pry the boot off with a small cold chisel. Install the new boot onto the ball joint using a suitable adapter such as a ¾ in. socket to properly seat the boot.

To install:

7. Position the front bushing washer (with "dished" side forward) and bushing onto the stabilizer end. Engage the control arm with the stabilizer.

8. Raise the control arm inner end onto the pivot bracket on the frame and start the pivot bolt to hold the control arm in place. Do not completely tighten the bolt at this time.

9. Engage the control arm ball joint stud with the clamp bore in the steering knuckle and install the clamp bolt and nut.

10. Install the stabilizer rear bushing and washer (with "dished" side forward) onto the stabilizer end with the retaining nut. Torque the retaining nut to 43–52 ft. lbs.

11. Torque the pivot bolt at the control arm frame bracket to 32–40 ft. lbs.

12. Hold the steering clamp bolt stationary and torque the clamp nut to 32–40 ft. lbs.

Stabilizer Bar

REMOVAL & INSTALLATION

1. Disconnect the negative battery cable.

2. Remove the stabilizer mounting bracket nuts and mounting brackets.

3. Remove the split bushings from the stabilizer bar. Replace deteriorated or worn bushings as required.

4. Remove the stabilizer bushing nuts at the lower control arms and remove the rear dished washers and bushings.

5. Pull the stabilizer bar forward to disengage it from both lower control arms. Remove the bushings and washers. Replace deteriorated or worn bushings as required.

To install:

6. Install the control arm bushing washers on the ends of the stabilizer bar and install the control arm front bushings.

7. Support the stabilizer bar by hand and insert the ends of the bar into the lower control arms. Install the control arm bushings and washers with the retaining nuts. Make the retaining nuts finger tight.

8. Install the split bushings on the the stabilizer bar cross bar with the split side forward and position them

next to the white alignment marks next to the bar.

9. Install the stabilizer bar mounting brackets. Torque the bracket retaining nuts to 32–38 ft. lbs.

10. Torque the control arm bushing retaining nuts to 43–52 ft. lbs.

11. Connect the negative battery cable.

REAR SUSPENSION

MacPherson Strut

REMOVAL & INSTALLATION

1. Raise the vehicle and support it safely.

2. Remove the rear wheel and tire assembly.

3. Install a spring compressor tool and release the strut spring tension.

4. From the cargo compartment, remove the rear quarter panel trim.

5. Remove the jam nut and flanged nut from the strut rod and remove the bushing washer and upper bushing.

6. Remove the strut lower end mounting bolt from the wheel support arm.

7. Withdraw the strut assembly downward from the wheel well and separate it from the spring and seat insulator. Remove the spring compressor.

8. Remove the lower grommet and jounce the bumper seat from the strut rod. Slide the jounce bumper and shield off the strut.

9. Inspect the material condition of the jounce bumper, spring seat insulator and strut rod bushings. Inspect the strut for leakage, endplay or erratic action. Inspect the strut lower end bushing for damage or deterioration. Replace any damaged or deteriorated components, as required.

To install:

10. Slide the jounce bumper and shield onto the strut rod. Install the bumper seat and and lower grommet on the strut rod.

11. Position the coil spring on the strut, making certain that the end of the coil seats against the end of the step in the strut spring seat. When the spring is properly seated, reinstall the spring compressor.

12. Guide the strut tower into the strut mounting hole through the wheel well.

13. Align the strut lower end with the mounting hole in the wheel support arm. Start the mounting bolt in by hand to hold the strut in position.

14. From the cargo compartment, install the rod upper end bushing, bushing washer and flanged nut. Torque the flanged nut to 12–18 ft. lbs. Hold the flanged nut stationary and tighten the locknut.

15. Torque the lower strut mounting bolt to 40–50 ft. lbs.

16. Back off on the spring compressor slowly to release the spring tension. Remove the spring compressor.

17. Install the wheel and tire assembly. Lower the vehicle.

Rear Wheel Bearings

REMOVAL & INSTALLATION

1. Raise the vehicle and support it

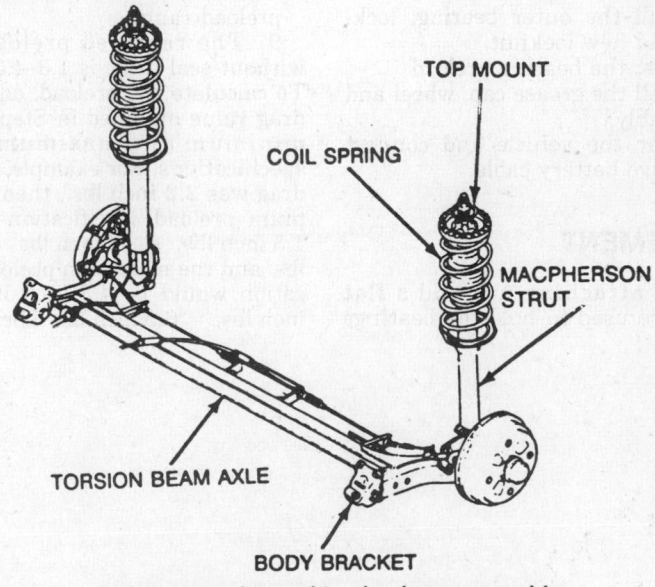

Rear suspension and torsion beam assembly

safely. Make certain that the parking brake is fully released.

2. Remove the wheel and tire assembly.

3. Remove the grease/dust cap.

4. With a small cape chisel, carefully raise the staked portion of the locknut to release the locknut from the spindle shaft.

NOTE: The drum/hub locknuts are threaded left and right. The left hand threaded locknut is located on the right hand side of the vehicle. Turn this locknut clockwise to loosen. The right hand threaded locknut is turned counterclockwise to loosen.

5. Remove the locknut and washer. Discard the locknut.

6. Pull the brake drum bearings and hub assembly away from the spindle shaft. Take care not to damage the spindle shaft threads.

7. With a small roll head pry bar or equivalent, remove the bearing grease seal from the bearing hub. Discard the seal regardless of condition.

8. Remove the inner and outer bearings from the bearing hub. If the bearings are to be reused, identify and tag each bearing for installation reference. Replace worn or damaged bearings as required. Wipe all bearing hub surfaces with a clean shop towel.

9. Pack the bearings with an ample amount of wheel bearing grease.

To install:

10. Position the inner bearing in the hub. Install and seat a new grease seal with a suitable driving tool.

11. Position the brake drum and hub assembly on the spindle. Keep the hub centered during positioning to prevent damage to the new grease seal and spindle threads.

12. Install the outer bearing, lockwasher and new locknut.

13. Adjust the bearing preload.

14. Install the grease cap, wheel and tire assembly.

15. Lower the vehicle and connect the negative battery cable.

ADJUSTMENT

A staked attaching nut and a flat washer are used to hold the bearings and hub in position on the spindle shaft. The attaching nuts are left and right hand thread. The right hand threaded nut (located on the left side of the vehicle) must be turned clockwise to tighten and the left hand threaded nut must be turned counterclockwise to tighten.

1. Make certain that the parking brake is fully released.

2. Raise the vehicle and support it safely. Remove the wheel and tire assembly.

3. Remove the grease cap. Rotate the brake drum to ensure freedom of rotation.

4. With a small cape chisel, carefully raise the staked portion of the locknut to release the locknut from the spindle shaft.

5. Remove the locknut and discard. Install the new locknut.

6. To seat the bearings, place torque wrench onto the locknut and torque the locknut (in the proper rotation) to 18–22 ft. lbs. Rotate the break drum by hand while tightening the locknut.

7. Loosen the locknut until it can be turned by hand.

8. Before the bearing preload can be set, the amount of seal drag must be measured and added to the the required preload. To measure the seal drag proceed as follows:

a. Install the proper size nut onto a wheel stud and rotate the brake drum until the stud is in the 12 o'clock position.

b. Place an inch lb. torque wrench onto the nut to measure the amount of force required to rotate the break drum.

c. Pull the torque wrench and note and record the torque reading at which rotation begins. This value will be used to calculate the bearing preload range.

9. The required preload range, without seal drag, is 1.3–4.3 inch lbs. To calculate the preload, add the seal drag value obtained in Step 8c to the minimum and maximum preload specifications. For example, if the seal drag was 2.2 inch lbs., then the minimum preload specification would be 1.3 inch lbs. + 2.2 inch lbs. = 3.5 inch lbs. and the maximum preload specification would be 4.3 inch lbs. + 2.2 inch lbs. = 6.5 inch lbs. Therefore, for a seal drag of 2.2 inch lbs. the bearing preload should be within the range of 3.5–6.5 inch lbs.

10. After the preload range is determined, tighten the locknut a slightly.

11. Rotate the brake drum until the nut and wheel are returned to the 12 o'clock position. Position the inch lb. torque wrench onto the nut and measure the amount of pull required to rotate the brake drum. Tighten the locknut until the torque shown on the torque wrench is within the range that was calculated in Step 9.

12. With the proper tool, stake the locknut in place. Take care not to damage the nut during staking.

13. Install the grease cap.

14. Install the wheel and tire assembly. Connect the negative battery cable.

Torsion Beam

REMOVAL & INSTALLATION

1. Raise and safely support the vehicle.

2. Remove the wheel and tire assemblies.

3. Remove the rear struts and disconnect the brake lines.

4. Disconnect the parking brake at the equalizer.

5. Remove the torsion beam pivot bolts from the body brackets and carefully lower the torsion beam from the vehicle.

6. If the torsion beam is being replaced, transfer any necessary components.

To install:

7. Install the torsion beam in position, in the body brackets and install the pivot bolts, do not tighten the nuts.

8. Reconnect the brake cables and lines.

9. Install the struts. Install the wheel and tire assemblies.

10. Lower the vehicle enough to load the suspension to normal ride height.

11. Tighten the torsion beam pivot bolts to 69–87 ft. lbs. (93–118 Nm).

12. Check the suspension for side-to-side equality in the distance between the struts.

13. Bleed the braking system. Lower the vehicle.

Ford Motor Co.
Front Wheel Drive
Probe

SPECIFICATIONS

VEHICLE IDENTIFICATION CHART

It is important for servicing and ordering parts to be certain of the vehicle and engine identification. The VIN (vehicle identification number) is a 17 digit number visible through the windshield on the driver's side of the dash and contains the vehicle and engine identification codes. The tenth digit indicates model year and the eighth digit indicates engine code. It can be interpreted as follows:

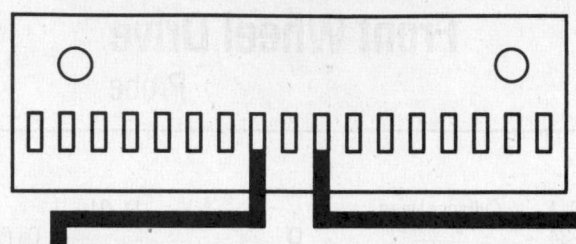

Engine Code

Code	Cu. In.	Liters	Cyl.	Fuel Sys.	Eng. Mfg.
C	133	2.2	4	MPFI	Mazda
L	133	2.2	4	MPFI ①	Mazda
U	182	3.0	6	MPFI	Mazda

MPFI—Multiport Fuel Injection
① Turbocharged

Model Year

Code	Year
K	1989
L	1990
M	1991

ENGINE IDENTIFICATION

Year	Model	Engine Displacement cu. in. (liter)	Engine Series Identification (VIN)	No. of Cylinders	Engine Type
1989	Probe GL	133 (2.2)	C	4	OHC
	Probe LX	133 (2.2)	C	4	OHC
	Probe GT	133 (2.2)	L ①	4	OHC
1990–91	Probe GL	133 (2.2)	C	4	OHC
	Probe LX	182 (3.0)	U	6	OHC
	Probe GT	133 (2.2)	L ①	4	OHC

OHC—Overhead Cam
① Turbocharged

GENERAL ENGINE SPECIFICATIONS

Year	VIN	No. Cylinder Displacement cu. in. (liter)	Fuel System Type	Net Horsepower @ rpm	Net Torque @ rpm (ft. lbs.)	Bore × Stroke (in.)	Compression Ratio	Oil Pressure @ rpm
1989	C	4-133 (2.2)	MPFI	110 @ 4700	130 @ 3000	3.39 × 3.70	8.5:1	57 @ 3000
	L	4-133 (2.2)	MPFI	145 @ 4300	190 @ 3500	3.39 × 3.70	7.8:1	57 @ 3000
1990–91	C	4-133 (2.2)	MPFI	110 @ 4700	130 @ 3000	3.39 × 3.70	8.5:1	57 @ 3000
	L	4-133 (2.2) ①	MPFI	145 @ 4500	190 @ 3500	3.39 × 3.70	7.8:1	57 @ 3000
	U	6-182 (3.0)	MPFI	140 @ 4300	160 @ 3000	3.50 × 3.14	9.3:1	60 @ 2500

MPFI—Multiport Fuel Injection
① Turbocharged

GASOLINE ENGINE TUNE-UP SPECIFICATIONS

Year	VIN	No. Cylinder Displacement cu. in. (liter)	Spark Plugs Type	Gap (in.)	Ignition Timing (deg.) MT	AT	Compression Pressure (psi)	Fuel Pump (psi)	Idle Speed (rpm) MT	AT	Valve Clearance In.	Ex.
1989	C	4-133 (2.2)	AGSP-33C	0.040	5–7 ①	5–7 ①②	—	36	725–775	725–775	Hyd.	Hyd.
	L	4-133 (2.2)	AGSP-33C	0.040	8–10	—	—	36	725–775	725–775	Hyd.	Hyd.
1990–91	C	4-133 (2.2)	AGSP-33C	0.040	5–7 ①	5–7 ①②	—	36	725–775	725–775	Hyd.	Hyd.
	L	4-133 (2.2)	AGSP-33C	0.040	5–7 ①	5–7 ①②	—	36	725–775	725–775	Hyd.	Hyd.
	U	6-182 (3.0)	AWSF-32P	0.044	③	③	—	39	725–775	725–775	Hyd.	Hyd.

① Distributor vacuum hoses disconnected and plugged
② Transaxle in Park
③ Refer to vehicle information label

FIRING ORDERS

NOTE: To avoid confusion, always replace spark plug wires one at a time.

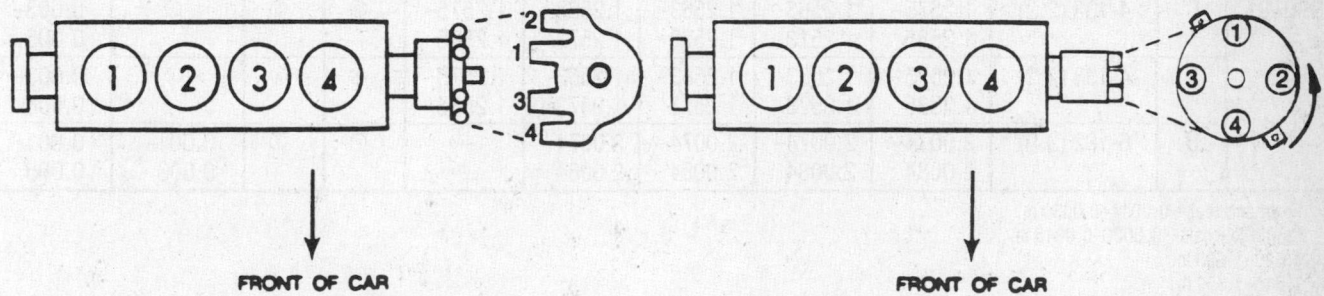

FRONT OF CAR   FRONT OF CAR

Ford Motor Co. (Mazda) 2.2L OHC engine
Firing Order: 1-3-4-2
Non-Turbo Type C

Ford Motor Co. (Mazda) 2.2L OHC engine
Firing Order: 1-3-4-2
Turbo Type L

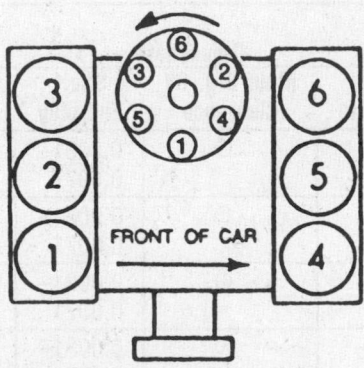

FRONT OF CAR

3.0L OHC ENGINE
ENGINE FIRING ORDER: 1–4–2–5–3–6
DISTRIBUTOR ROTATION: Counter-clockwise

CAPACITIES

Year	Model	VIN	No. Cylinder Displacement cu. in. (liter)	Engine Crankcase (qts.) with Filter	Engine Crankcase (qts.) without Filter	Transmission (pts.) 4-Spd	Transmission (pts.) 5-Spd	Transmission (pts.) Auto.	Drive Axle (pts.)	Fuel Tank (gal.)	Cooling System (qts.)
1989	Probe	C	4-133 (2.2)	4.4	4.1	—	7.2	14.4	—	15.1	7.9
	Probe	L	4-133 (2.2)	4.4	4.1	—	7.8	—	—	15.1	7.9
1990-91	Probe	C	4-133 (2.2)	4.4	4.1	—	7.2	14.4	—	15.1	7.9
	Probe	L	4-133 (2.2)	4.4	4.1	—	7.8	14.4	—	15.1	7.9
	Probe	U	6-182 (3.0)	4.5	4.0	—	7.8	14.4	—	15.1	11.0

CAMSHAFT SPECIFICATIONS

All measurements given in inches.

Year	VIN	No. Cylinder Displacement cu. in. (liter)	Journal Diameter 1	2	3	4	5	Lobe Lift In.	Lobe Lift Ex.	Bearing Clearance	Camshaft End Play
1989	C	4-133 (2.2)	1.2575-1.2585	1.2563-1.2573	1.2563-1.2573	1.2563-1.2573	1.2575-1.3585	②	③	①	0.003-0.006
	L	4-133 (2.2)	1.2575-1.2585	1.2563-1.2573	1.2563-1.2573	1.2563-1.2573	1.2575-1.2585	②	③	①	0.003-0.006
1990-91	C	4-133 (2.2)	1.2575-1.2585	1.2563-1.2573	1.2563-1.2573	1.2563-1.2573	1.2575-1.2585	②	③	①	0.003-0.006
	L	4-133 (2.2)	1.2575-1.2585	1.2563-1.2573	1.2563-1.2573	1.2563-1.2573	1.2575-1.2585	②	③	①	0.003-0.006
	U	6-182 (3.0)	2.0074-2.0084	2.0074-2.0084	2.0074-2.0084	2.0074-2.0084	—	④	④	0.001-0.003	0.001-0.005

① Front and rear—0.0014-0.0030 in.
  Center journals—0.0026-0.0045 in.
② 1.620-1.630 in.
③ 1.640-1.650 in.
④ 0.260 in.

CRANKSHAFT AND CONNECTING ROD SPECIFICATIONS

All measurements are given in inches.

Year	VIN	No. Cylinder Displacement cu. in. (liter)	Crankshaft Main Brg. Journal Dia.	Crankshaft Main Brg. Oil Clearance	Crankshaft Shaft End-play	Crankshaft Thrust on No.	Connecting Rod Journal Diameter	Connecting Rod Oil Clearance	Connecting Rod Side Clearance
1989	C	4-133 (2.2)	2.3597-2.3604	①	0.0031-0.0071	3	2.0055-2.0061	0.0011-0.0026	0.0004-0.0103
	L	4-133 (2.2)	2.3597-2.3604	①	0.0031-0.0071	3	2.0055-2.0061	0.0011-0.0026	0.0004-0.0103
1990-91	C	4-133 (2.2)	2.3597-2.3604	①	0.0031-0.0071	3	2.0055-2.0061	0.0011-0.0026	0.0004-0.0103
	L	4-133 (2.2)	2.3597-2.3604	①	0.0031-0.0071	3	2.0055-2.0061	0.0011-0.0026	0.0004-0.0103
	U	4-133 (2.2)	2.5190-2.5198	0.0001-0.0014	0.004-0.008	3	2.1253-2.1261	0.0001-0.0014	0.0006-0.0014

① No. 1, 2, 4 and 5—0.0010-0.0017 in.
  No. 3—0.0012-0.0019 in.

VALVE SPECIFICATIONS

Year	VIN	No. Cylinder Displacement cu. in. (liter)	Seat Angle (deg.)	Face Angle (deg.)	Spring Test Pressure (lbs.)	Spring Installed Height (in.)	Stem-to-Guide Clearance (in.)		Stem Diameter (in.)	
							Intake	Exhaust	Intake	Exhaust
1989	C	4-133 (2.2)	45	45	—	—	0.008	0.008	0.2744–0.2750	0.2742–0.2748
	L	4-133 (2.2)	45	45	—	—	0.008	0.008	0.2744–0.2750	0.2742–0.2748
1990–91	C	4-133 (2.2)	45	45	—	—	0.008	0.008	0.2744–0.2750	0.2742–0.2748
	L	4-133 (2.2)	45	45	—	—	0.008	0.008	0.2744–0.2750	0.2742–0.2748
	U	6-182 (3.0)	45	44	65 ①	1.58	0.0001–0.0028	0.0015–0.0033	0.3134–0.3126	0.3129–0.3121

① Loaded 180 @ 1.16 in.

PISTON AND RING SPECIFICATIONS

All measurements are given in inches.

Year	VIN	No. Cylinder Displacement cu. in. (liter)	Piston Clearance	Ring Gap			Ring Side Clearance		
				Top Compression	Bottom Compression	Oil Control	Top Compression	Bottom Compression	Oil Control
1989	C	4-133 (2.2)	0.0014–0.0030	0.008–0.014	0.006–0.012	0.012–0.035	0.001–0.003	0.001–0.003	—
	L	4-133 (2.2)	0.0014–0.0030	0.008–0.014	0.006–0.012	0.006–0.014	0.001–0.003	0.001–0.003	—
1990–91	C	4-133 (2.2)	0.0014–0.0030	0.008–0.014	0.006–0.012	0.012–0.035	0.001–0.003	0.001–0.003	—
	L	4-133 (2.2)	0.0014–0.0030	0.008–0.014	0.006–0.012	0.006–0.014	0.001–0.003	0.001–0.003	—
	U	6-182 (3.0)	0.0014–0.0022	0.010–0.020	0.010–0.020	0.010–0.049	0.001–0.003	0.001–0.003	—

TORQUE SPECIFICATIONS

All readings in ft. lbs.

Year	VIN	No. Cylinder Displacement cu. in. (liter)	Cylinder Head Bolts	Main Bearing Bolts	Rod Bearing Bolts	Crankshaft Sprocket Bolts	Flywheel Bolts	Manifold		Spark Plugs
								Intake	Exhaust	
1989	C	4-133 (2.2)	59–64	61–65	48–51	108–116	71–76	14–22	16–21	11–17
	L	4-133 (2.2)	59–64	61–65	48–51	108–116	71–76	14–22	16–21	11–17
1990–91	C	4-133 (2.2)	59–64	61–65	48–51	108–116	71–76	16–21	16–21	11–17
	L	4-133 (2.2)	59–64	61–65	48–51	108–116	71–76	16–21	16–21	11–17
	U	6-182 (3.0)	①	63–69	23–39	107	54–64	②	20–30	5–11

① Tighten in 2 steps
  A. 33–41 ft. lbs.
  B. 63–73 ft. lbs.
② Tighten in 3 steps
  A. 11 ft. lbs.
  B. 18 ft. lbs.
  C. 24 ft. lbs.

BRAKE SPECIFICATIONS

All measurements in inches unless noted

Year	Model	Lug Nut Torque (ft. lbs.)	Master Cylinder Bore	Brake Disc		Standard Brake Drum Diameter	Minimum Lining Thickness	
				Minimum Thickness	Maximum Runout		Front	Rear
1989	Probe GL	65–87	0.875	0.860 ①	0.003	9.0	0.120	0.040
	Probe LX	65–87	0.875	0.860 ①	0.003	9.0	0.120	0.040
	Probe GT	65–87	0.875	0.860 ①	0.003	10.0	0.120	0.040
1990–91	Probe GL	65–87	0.875	0.860 ①	0.003	9.0	0.120	0.040
	Probe LX	65–87	0.875	0.860 ①	0.003	9.0	0.120	0.040
	Probe GT	65–87	0.875	0.860 ①	0.003	9.0	0.120	0.040

① Rear disc—0.350 in.

WHEEL ALIGNMENT

Year	Model		Caster		Camber		Toe-in (in.)	Steering Axis Inclination (deg.)
			Range (deg.)	Preferred Setting (deg.)	Range (deg.)	Preferred Setting (deg.)		
1989	Probe GL	Front	0.47P–1.97P	1.22P	0.47N–1.03P	0.28P	0–0.24	12.78
		Rear	—	—	0.25N–1.25P	0.50P ①	0.12N–0.12P	—
	Probe LX	Front	0.47P–1.97P	1.22P	0.47N–1.03P	0.28P	0–0.24	12.78
		Rear	—	—	0.25N–1.25P	0.50P ①	0.12N–0.12P	—
	Probe GT	Front	0.47P–1.97P	1.22P	0.47N–1.03P	0.28P	0–0.24	12.78
		Rear	—	—	0.25N–1.25P	0.50P ①	0.12N–0.12P	—
1990–91	Probe GL	Front	0.47P–1.97P	1.22P	0.47N–1.03P	0.28P	0–0.24	12.78
		Rear	—	—	0.25N–1.25P	0.50P ①	0.12N–0.12P	—
	Probe LX	Front	0.47P–1.97P	1.22P	0.47N–1.03P	0.28P	0–0.24	12.78
		Rear	—	—	0.25N–1.25P	0.50P ①	0.12N–0.12P	—
	Probe GT	Front	0.47P–1.97P	1.22P	0.47N–1.03P	0.28P	0–0.24	12.78
		Rear	—	—	0.25N–1.25P	0.50P ①	0.12N–0.12P	—

① Not Adjustable

ENGINE ELECTRICAL

NOTE: Disconnecting the negative battery cable on some vehicles may interfere with the functions of the on board computer systems and may require the computer to undergo a relearning process, once the negative battery cable is reconnected.

Distributor

REMOVAL

1. Disconnect the negative battery cable.
2. Remove the distributor cap screws and cap, position the cap aside.
3. If not equipped with a turbocharger, perform the following procedures:
    a. Disconnect and label the vacuum lines from the distributor vacuum diaphragm.
    b. Disconnect the distributor electrical connectors from the ignition coil. On 3.0L engine disconnect the TFI-1V harness connector.
4. If equipped with a turbocharger, disconnect the distributor wiring harness connector located near the upper side of the distributor.
5. Using a wrench on the crankshaft pulley, rotate the crankshaft to position the No. 1 piston on the TDC of it's compression stroke; the crankshaft pulley notch should align with the timing plate indicator.
6. Using chalk or paint, mark the relationship of the distributor housing-to-cylinder head and the rotor-to-distributor housing; this will assist in installation.
7. Remove the distributor hold-down bolts and the distributor.

Note: Some 3.0L engines may be equipped with a security type distributor hold-down bolt, use the proper tool to remove.

8. Inspect the O-ring and replace it, if necessary, on 2.2L engine.

INSTALLATION

Timing Not Disturbed

1. Using engine oil, lubricate the O-ring on 2.2L engine.
2. Align the rotor-to-distributor housing and the distributor housing-to-cylinder head.
3. Install the distributor and make sure to engage the drive dog with the camshaft slot. Tighten the distributor

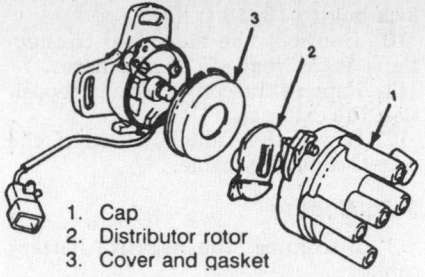

1. Cap
2. Distributor rotor
3. Cover and gasket

Exploded view of the distributor assembly—2.2L turbocharged engine

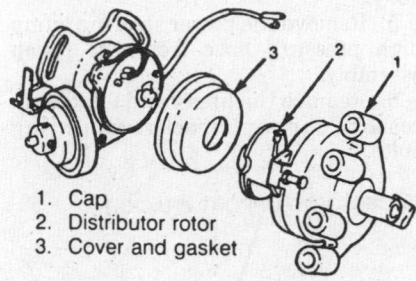

1. Cap
2. Distributor rotor
3. Cover and gasket

Exploded view of the distributor assembly—2.2L non-turbocharged engine

hold-down bolts finger tight.
4. Connect the electrical and the vacuum connections. Replace the distributor cap.
5. Start the engine and check or adjust the ignition base timing.
6. Tighten the hold-down bolts and recheck the timing, adjust if neccessary.

Timing Disturbed

1. Using engine oil, lubricate the O-ring on 2.2L engine.
2. Remove the spark plug from the No. 1 cylinder and press a thumb over the spark plug hole.
3. Using a wrench on the crankshaft pulley, rotate the crankshaft to position the No. 1 piston on the TDC of it's compression stroke; pressure will be felt at the spark plug hole and the crankshaft pulley notch should align with the timing plate indicator.
4. Align the rotor to the No. 1 spark plug wire terminal of the distributor cap.
5. Install the distributor and make sure to engage the drive dog with the camshaft slot. Tighten the distributor hold-down bolts finger tight.
6. Connect the electrical and vacuum connections. Replace the distributor cap.
7. Start the engine and check or adjust the ignition base timing.
8. Tighten the hold-down bolts and recheck the timing.

Ignition Timing

ADJUSTMENT

1. Turn **OFF** all of the accessories. Set the idle to specifications.
2. Firmly set the parking brake and position the gear shift selector in **P** for automatic transaxle or **N** for manual transaxle.
3. Start and operate the engine until normal operating temperatures are reached.
4. If not equipped with a turbocharger, disconnect and plug both vacuum hoses from the distributor vacuum diaphragm. If equipped with a turbocharger, connect a jumper wire between the test connector pin No. 1 and ground.
5. Using a timing light, point it at the timing plate which is located at the crankshaft pulley, connect it to the engine and check the ignition timing; the timing should be 5–7 degrees BTDC for 2.2L non-turbocharged engine or 8–10 degrees BTDC for 2.2L turbocharged engine and 10 degrees BTDC on the 3.0L engine.
6. If the ignition timing is not within specifications, loosen the distributor hold-down bolts, rotate the distributor to align the timing marks and tighten the hold-down bolts.

Alternator

For further information on the charging system, please refer to "Charging and Starting" in the Unit Repair section.

PRECAUTIONS

Several precautions must be observed with alternator equipped vehicles to avoid damage to the unit.

If the battery is removed for any reason, make sure it is reconnected with the correct polarity. Reversing the battery connections may result in damage to the one-way rectifiers.

When utilizing a booster battery as a starting aid, always connect the positive to positive terminals and the negative terminal from the booster battery to a good engine ground on the vehicle being started.

Never use a fast charger as a booster to start vehicles.

Disconnect the battery cables when charging the battery with a fast charger.

Never attempt to polarize the alternator.

Do not use test lamps of more than 12 volts when checking diode continuity.

Do not short across or ground any of the alternator terminals.

The polarity of the battery, alternator and regulator must be matched and considered before making any electrical connections within the system.

Never separate the alternator on an open circuit. Make sure all connections within the circuit are clean and tight.

Disconnect the battery ground terminal when performing any service on electrical components.

Disconnect the battery if arc welding is to be done on the vehicle.

BELT TENSION ADJUSTMENT

1. Disconnect the negative battery cable.
2. Loosen the alternator adjustment bolt and the through bolt.
3. Tighten the alternator adjustment screw to adjust the belt tension. The belt deflection should be 0.24–0.31 inch.
4. After adjustment, tighten the through bolt to 27–38 ft. lbs. and the lock bolt to 13–18 ft. lbs.

REMOVAL & INSTALLATION

2.2L Engine

1. Disconnect the negative battery cable. Raise and support the vehicle, safely.
2. Remove the catalytic converter by performing the following procedures:
   a. From both ends of the converter, remove the flange nuts and washers.
   b. Remove the resonator pipe-to-body insulators.
   c. Push the rear exhaust assembly rearward and remove the converter with the gaskets.
3. From the rear of the alternator, depress the lock tab(s) and disconnect the electrical connectors.
4. Loosen the alternator's adjusting and through bolts, tilt it and remove the drive belt.
5. Remove the alternator's adjusting bracket lock bolt and through bolt.
6. While supporting the alternator, slide (lower) it between the steering gear and the right halfshaft.
To install:
7. Reposition the alternator and install the mounting bolts finger tight.
8. Install the drive belt, turn the alternator bracket's jack screw to adjust the drive belt tension; the belt deflection should be 0.24–0.31 in.
9. After adjustment, tighten the through bolt to 27–38 ft. lbs. and the

lock bolt to 13–18 ft. lbs.
10. Connect the electrical connections at the rear of the alternator.
11. Replace the converter and reposition the exhaust.
12. Lower the vehicle. Connect the negative battery cable.

3.0L Engine

1. Disconnect the negative battery cable.
2. Remove the accessory drive belt.
3. Remove and set aside the windshield washer reservoir.
4. Remove the power steering pump reservoir return hose from the pump body.
5. Remove the power steering pump high pressure hose from the pump assembly.
6. Remove the upper and middle accessory support bracket mounting bolts.

ACCESSORY SUPPORT BRACKET

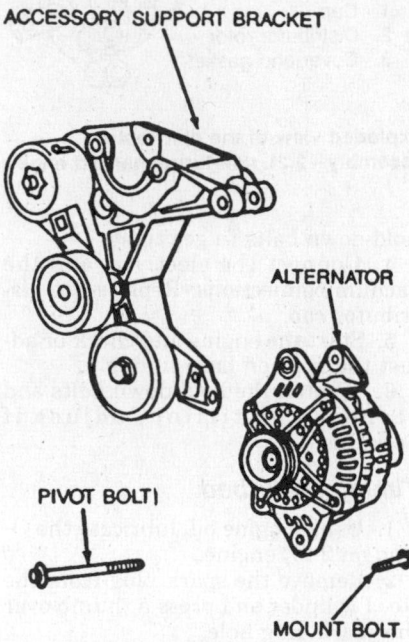

ALTERNATOR

PIVOT BOLT)

MOUNT BOLT

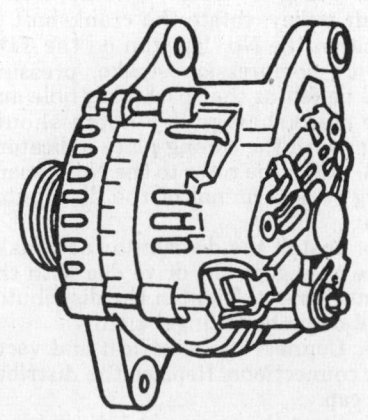

Alternator removal – 3.0L engine

7. Pull back on the idler tensioner, using the proper tool and remove the lower accessory support bracket mounting bolt.
8. Remove the mounting bolt from the side of the accessory bracket at the air conditioning compressor brace.
9. Raise the alternator/accessory support to clear the engine and set aside to remove the electrical connectors.
10. Remove the electrical connectors from the alternator and the alternator pivot bolt.
11. Remove the alternator mounting bolt from the back side of the alternator. Remove the alternator from the accessory support bracket.
To install:
12. Position the alternator on the accessory support bracket and install the alternator pivot bolt.
13. Install the alternator mounting bolt at the rear of the alternator.
14. Position the alternator/accessory support bracket in the proper position and install the electrical connectors on the back side of the alternator.
15. Install the mounting bolt through the air conditioning compressor brace into the support bracket.
16. Install the middle accessory support bracket mounting bolt.
17. Pull back on the idler tensioner, using the proper tool and install the lower accessory support bracket mounting bolt.
18. Connect the power steering pressure and return hoses.
19. Install the accessory drive belt and tighten.
20. Install the negative battery cable and replace the windshield washer resevoir.
21. Fill and bleed the power steering reservoir with the proper fluid.

Voltage Regulator

For further information on the charging system, please refer to "Charging and Starting" in the Unit Repair section.

Starter

For further information on the charging system, please refer to "Charging and Starting" in the Unit Repair section.

REMOVAL & INSTALLATION

2.2L Engine

1. Disconnect the negative battery cable. Raise and support the vehicle, safely.

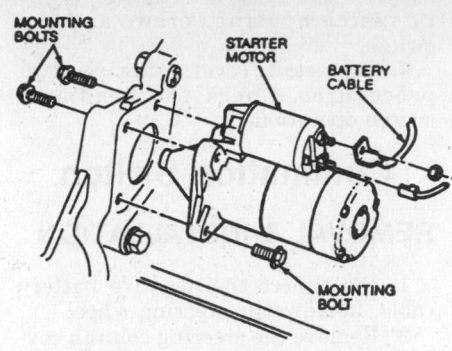

MOUNTING BOLTS · STARTER MOTOR · BATTERY CABLE · MOUNTING BOLT

Starter mounting—2.2L engine

2. If equipped with a manual transaxle, remove the exhaust pipe bracket.

3. Remove the transaxle-to-engine bracket and intake manifold-to-engine bracket.

4. Disconnect the electrical connectors from the starter.

5. Remove the starter mounting bolts and the starter.

To install:

6. Install the starter and torque the bolts to 23–34 ft. lbs.

7. Connect the electrical connectors to the starter and torque the battery cable-to-starter nut to 90–110 inch lbs.

8. Install the intake manifold-to-engine bracket bolts to 14–22 ft. lbs.

9. If equipped with an automatic transaxle, torque the transaxle-to-engine bracket bellhousing bolt to 66–86 ft. lbs. and all other mounting bolts to 27–38 ft. lbs.

10. If equipped with a manual transaxle, torque the:

transaxle-to-engine bracket bolts to 32–45 ft. lbs.

transaxle-to-exhaust pipe bracket bolts to 32–45 ft. lbs.

11. Safely, lower the vehicle.

12. Connect the negative battery cable and check the starter for proper operation.

3.0L Engine

1. Disconnect the negative battery cable.

2. Raise and safely support the vehicle.

3. Disconnect the electrical connections at the starter motor.

4. Remove the starter mounting bolts and remove the starter.

To install:

5. Position the starter and install the mounting bolts.

6. Connect the electrical connections at the starter motor.

7. Safely, lower the vehicle. Connect the negative battery cable.

8. Check the starter for proper operation.

CHASSIS ELECTRICAL

Heater Blower Motor

REMOVAL & INSTALLATION

1. Disconnect the negative battery cable.

2. Remove the sound deadening panel from the passenger side.

3. Remove the glove box assembly and the brace.

4. Remove the cooling hose from the blower motor assembly.

5. Disconnect the electrical connector from the blower motor.

6. Remove the blower motor-to-blower motor housing screws and blower motor.

7. If necessary, remove the blower wheel-to-blower motor clip and the wheel.

8. To install, reverse the removal procedures and check the blower motor operation.

Windshield Wiper Motor

REMOVAL & INSTALLATION

Front

1. Disconnect the negative battery cable.

2. Unscrew the retaining cap and remove the wiper blade/arm assemblies.

3. Disconnect the hose from the washer jets.

4. Remove the lower moulding and wiper linkage cover.

5. Pull the wiper linkage off the wiper motor output arm.

6. Disconnect the electrical connectors from the wiper motor.

7. Remove the wiper motor-to-chassis bolts and the motor from the vehicle.

8. To install, reverse the removal procedures. Check the wiper motor operation.

Rear

1. Disconnect the negative battery cable.

2. Lift the cover and remove the wiper blade/arm assembly-to-pivot arm nut and the assembly.

3. From the pivot arm, remove the boot, the retaining nut and the mount.

4. From the inner side of the tailgate, pry off the trim panel.

5. Disconnect the electrical connector from the wiper motor.

6. Remove the wiper motor-to-chassis bolts and the motor from the vehicle.

7. To install, reverse the removal procedures. Check the wiper motor operation.

Windshield Wiper Switch

REMOVAL & INSTALLATION

Front

1. Disconnect the negative battery cable. Remove the instrument cluster module cover.

2. Gently, pull the front washer/interval rate control switch knob and the front wiper control switch knob from the windshield wiper switch.

3. From the rear of the instrument cluster module cover, remove the windshield wiper switch housing screws and the switch.

4. To install, reverse the removal procedures. Check the windshield wiper switch operation.

Rear

1. Disconnect the negative battery cable. Remove the instrument cluster module cover.

2. Gently, pull the front washer/interval rate control switch knob and the front wiper control switch knob from the windshield wiper switch.

3. From the rear of the instrument cluster module cover, remove the windshield wiper switch housing screws and the switch.

4. Remove the rear wiper/washer switch-to-instrument cluster module cover screws.

5. While depressing the control button switch tangs (at the rear), remove the switch cover from the front of the instrument cover. Remove the rear wiper/washer switch from the rear of the instrument cover.

6. To install, reverse the removal procedures. Check the windshield wiper/washer switch and the rear wiper/washer switch operation.

Instrument Cluster

REMOVAL & INSTALLATION

1. Disconnect the negative battery cable. Remove the steering wheel.

2. Remove the steering column cover-to-instrument cover screws and the cover.

3. Remove the instrument cover-to-instrument cluster module cover screws, pull the module cover forward, disconnect the electrical connectors from the rear and remove the cover.

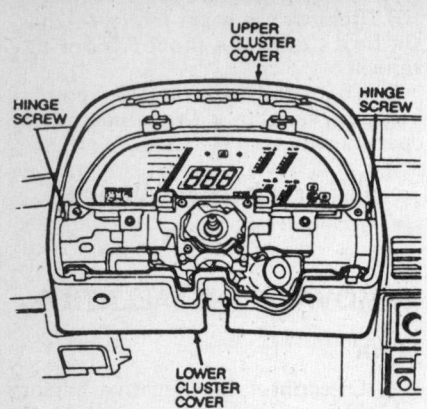

Instrument cluster removal

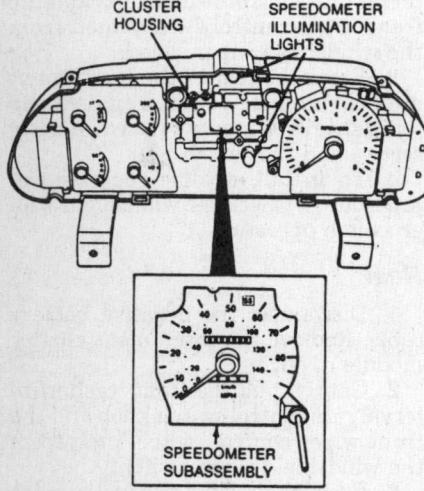

View of the electro-mechanical speedometer sub-assembly

4. Remove the instrument cluster cover-to-dash screws and the cover.

5. Remove the lower cluster panel screws and the panel.

6. Remove the instrument cluster-to-dash screws, pull the cluster forward, disconnect the electrical connectors from the rear of the cluster and remove the cluster.

NOTE: If equipped with an electro-mechanical cluster, disconnect the speedometer cable from the rear of the cluster.

7. To install, reverse the removal procedures. Check all gauges, speedometer and tachometer for proper operation.

Speedometer

REMOVAL & INSTALLATION

Electronic

The electronic speedometer is not serviceable. If a problem is detected within the speedometer circuitry or sup-

porting logic circuitry, replace the electronic instrument cluster.

Electro-mechanical

The electro-mechanical speedometer subassembly is not serviceable. If a problem is detected within the speedometer or supporting logic circuitry, replace the subassembly.

A speed sensor is used by the anti-lock brake system 4EAT on automatic transaxle. The speed sensor, the electronically controlled power steering and the programmed ride control system are located in the speedometer subassembly.

1. Disconnect the negative battery cable. Remove the instrument cluster.

2. Remove the lens assembly from the instrument cluster.

3. Remove the speedometer subassembly-to-instrument cluster screws and the subassembly from the cluster.

4. To install, reverse the removal procedures.

Radio

REMOVAL & INSTALLATION

1. Disconnect the negative battery cable.

2. Remove the ash tray receptacle.

3. Remove the selector trim panel on vehicles equipped with an automatic transaxle. Remove the gear shift and trim panel on vehicles equipped with a manual transaxle.

4. Remove the cigar lighter assembly and disconnect the cigar lighter connector.

5. Disconnect the cigar lighter lamp by twisting the socket and removing.

6. Remove the 2 radio mounting screws. Disconnect the electrical connections and the radio antenna.

7. Remove the radio.

Concealed Headlights

MANUAL OPERATION

A manual control knob is located under each headlamp retractor motor and is accessible from under the front fasica. The retractor motor is mounted on a bracket which is attached to the radiator support.

Headlight Switch

REMOVAL & INSTALLATION

1. Disconnect the negative battery cable. Remove the turn signal switch.

2. Gently, pull the rotary knob from the headlamp switch.

3. From the rear of the instrument cluster module cover, remove the rota-

ry switch housing screws and the switch.

4. To install, reverse the removal procedures. Check the headlamp switch operation.

Comination Switch

REMOVAL & INSTALLATION

1. Disconnect the negative battery cable. Remove the steering wheel.

2. Remove the steering column cover-to-instrument cover screws and the cover.

3. Remove the instrument cover-to-instrument cluster cover screws, pull the cover forward, disconnect the electrical connectors from the rear and remove the cover.

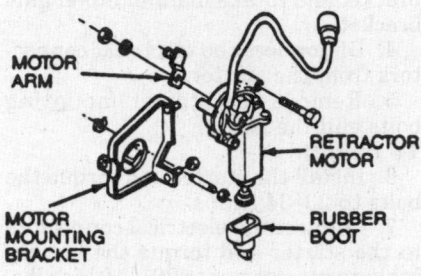

Exploded view of the headlamp retractor motor

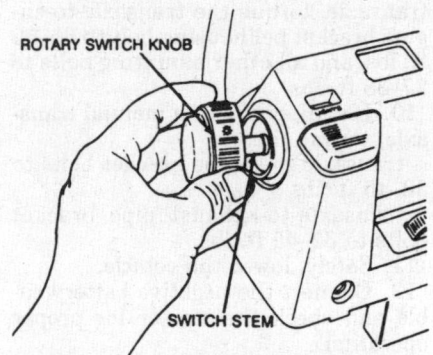

Removing the headlight switch from the instrument cluster module cover

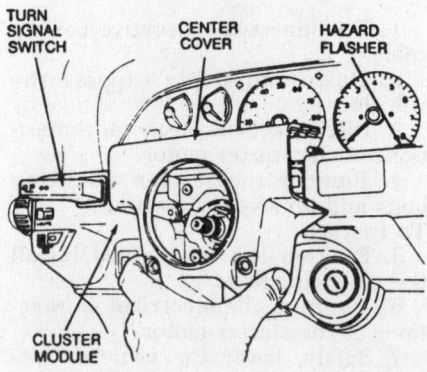

View of the turn signal switch location

4. Remove the turn signal lever-to-turn signal switch screw and the lever.

5. From the rear of the instrument cluster module cover, remove the turn signal switch-to-cover screws and the switch.

6. To install, reverse the removal procedures. Check the turn signal switch and the horn operation.

Ignition Lock/Switch

REMOVAL & INSTALLATION

1989 Vehicles

1. Disconnect the negative battery cable. Remove the steering wheel.

2. Remove the steering column cover-to-instrument cover screws and the cover.

3. Remove the instrument cover-to-instrument cluster cover screws, pull the cover forward, disconnect the electrical connectors from the rear and remove the cover.

4. Remove the instrument cluster cover-to-dash screws and the cover.

5. Remove the lower panel, the lap duct and the defrost duct.

6. Remove the lower hinge bracket support nuts.

7. Remove the upper steering column-to-support bracket nuts/bolts and lower the steering column.

8. Remove the ignition switch-to-ignition switch housing screw.

9. At the left side of the steering column, disconnect the ignition switch snap connectors and the protective looming from the ignition switch wires.

10. Note the position of each wire in the 4-wire terminal connector. From the 4-wire connector, disconnect the key-in warning buzzer wires: green wire and the red wire/orange tracer.

NOTE: Use a paper clip or equivalent, to disengage the wire tangs from the 4-wire connector.

11. To install, reverse the removal procedures. Check the ignition switch's operation.

1990–91 Vehicles

1. Disconnect the negative battery cable and remove the lower instrument cluster cover.

2. Loosen the shift cable nut retaining nut and allow the cable to hang down.

3. Remove the ignition switch mounting screw.

4. Disconnect the ignition switch wire connectors located to the left of the steering column.

4. Remove the protective looming from the ignition wires, note the position of each wire in the 4 terminal pro-

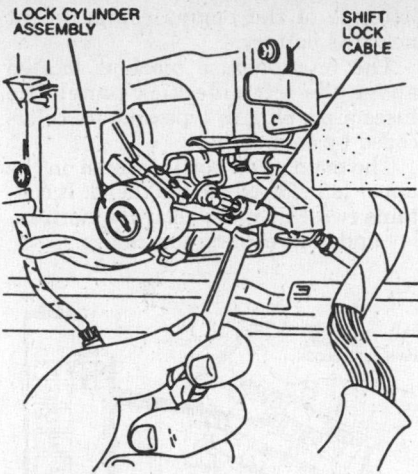

Ignition switch lock cylinder removal— 1990 Probe

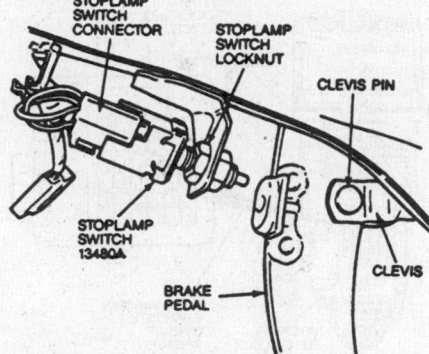

Stoplamp switch location

tector for replacing.

5. Disconnect the key in warning buzzer wires (green wire and red wire/orange tracer) by disengaging the tang with a paper clip or suitable tool.

6. Remove the ignition switch. Remove the lock cylinder mounting screws and the lock cylinder.

7. To install, reverse the removal procedure. Check the operation of the ignition switch.

Stoplight Switch

The stoplight switch is located at the top of the brake pedal and is used to adjust the brake pedal height.

ADJUSTMENT

1. If necessary, remove the lower steering column cover and ducts.

2. Disconnect the electrical connector from the stoplight switch.

3. Loosen the stoplight switch locknut.

4. Turn the stoplight switch until the brake pedal height is 8.54–8.74 inch from the center of the pedal pad to the firewall.

5. Tighten the stoplight switch locknut, reconnect the electrical connector and check the stoplight operation.

REMOVAL & INSTALLATION

1. Disconnect the negative battery cable. If necessary, remove the lower steering column cover and ducts.

2. Disconnect the electrical connector from the stoplight switch.

3. Remove the stoplight switch locknut and the switch.

4. To install, turn the stoplight switch until the brake pedal height is 8.54–8.74 inch from the center of the pedal pad to the firewall.

5. Tighten the stoplight switch locknut, reconnect the electrical connector and check the stoplight operation.

Clutch Switch

The clutch engage switch is located next to the clutch pedal.

REMOVAL & INSTALLATION

1. Disconnect the negative battery cable.

2. If necessary, remove the lower steering column cover and ducts.

3. Using an ohmmeter, inspect the switch operation. When the switch rod is pushed in, the ohmmeter should show continuity; when the switch rod is released, the ohmmeter should show no continuity.

4. If neccessary, replace the switch.

5. To install, reverse the removal procedures.

Neutral Safety Switch

The neutral safety switch is located on the top left side of the transaxle.

ADJUSTMENT

1. Raise and safely support the vehicle.

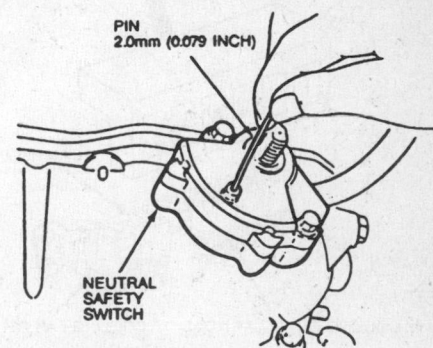

Neutral safety switch adjustment

2. Turn the manual shaft to the neutral position and loosen the mounting bolts.

3. Remove the screw and insert a 0.079 inch pin.

4. Move the neutral safety switch until the pin engages the switch in the alignment hole.

5. Tighten the mounting bolts and lower the vehicle.

REMOVAL & INSTALLATION

1. Disconnect the negative battery cable.

2. Raise and safely support the vehicle.

3. Remove the shift lever-to-neutral safety switch nut and lever.

4. Remove the neutral safety switch-to-transaxle bolts and the switch.

5. Disconnect the neutral safety switch electrical connector and the remove the switch from the vehicle.

6. To install, place a small drill bit in the switch alignment hole and reverse the removal procedures. Torque the shift lever-to-neutral safety switch nut to 22–29 ft. lbs. and remove the drill bit.

7. Safely, lower the vehicle.

Fuses, Circuit Breakers and Relays

LOCATION

Fuse Panel

The main fuse block is located in the left side of the engine compartment near the battery.

The interior fuse block is located above the left side kick panel. The fuses are a plug in type and are color-coded by amp rating.

The main relay box is located on the upper left side of the bulkhead. It contains two EFI main relays, a horn relay and both cooling fan relays.

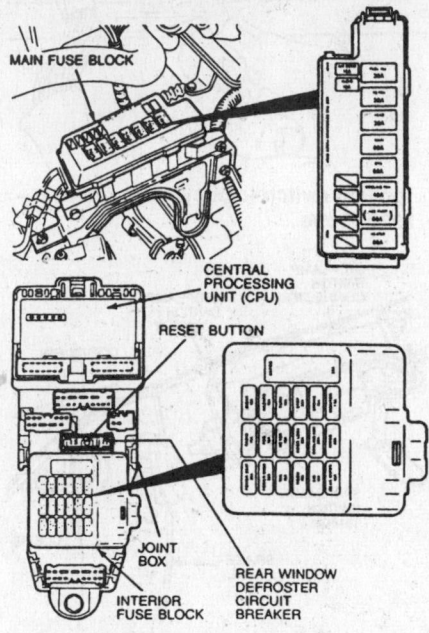

View of the Central Processing Unit (CPU), the interior fuse block, the rear window defroster circuit breaker and the main fuse panel

NOTE: The cooling fan relay No. 1 is used only on vehicles equipped an electronically controlled automatic transaxle (4EAT).

Relays

The relay box is mounted inside the vehicle, under the left side of the instrument panel on the bulkhead. It contains the turn signal/hazard flasher, fuel pump relay, the rear window defroster relay, the intermittent wiper relay, the stoplight/tail-light checker relay and the fog light relay.

EFI Main Relays (2)—located on the main relay box

Horn Relay—located on the main relay box

Cooling Fan Relay No. 1—located on the main relay box

Cooling Fan Relay No. 2—located on the main relay box

Turn Signal/Hazard Flasher Relay—located on the relay box

Fuel pump Relay—located on the relay box

Rear Window Defroster Relay—located on the relay box

Intermittent Wiper Relay—located on the relay box

Stoplight/Tail Light Checker Relay—located on the relay box

Fog Light Relay—located on the relay box

Computers

LOCATION

The Central Processing Unit (CPU) is located above the left side kick panel.

The trip computer is optional on the LX and GT models. The trip computer keyboard is located above the center register assembly. It is covered by a protective lid which must be lifted to gain access to the system.

Flashers

LOCATION

The turn/signal flasher relay is located on the relay box under the dash panel.

Cruise Control

ADJUSTMENT

1. If the vehicle is equipped with a turbocharger, remove the plastic cover from the electric actuator.

2. Loosen the locknut and adjusting nuts.

3. Pull on the cable without moving the actuator rod.

4. Position adjusting nut until

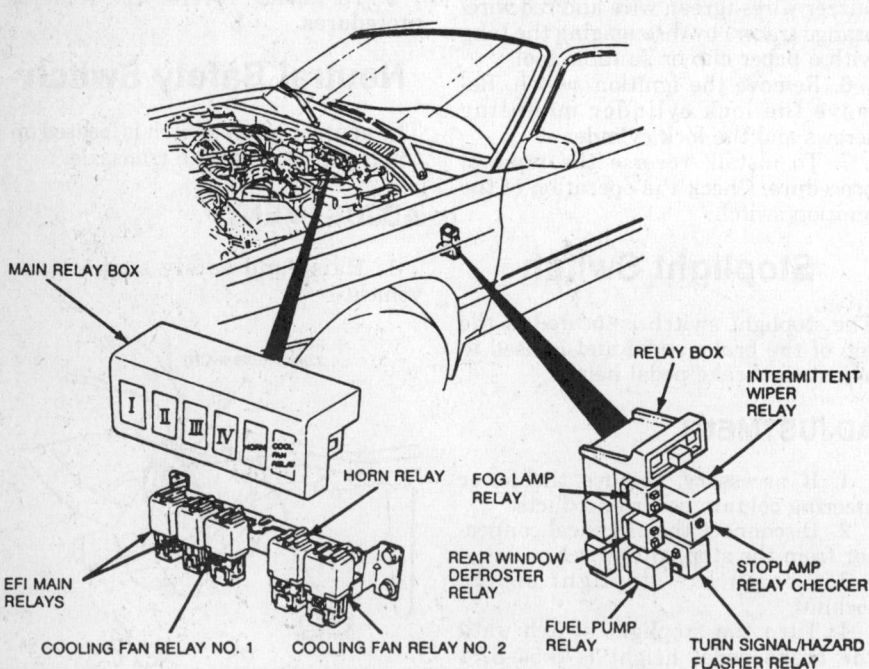

View of the main relay box and the relay box

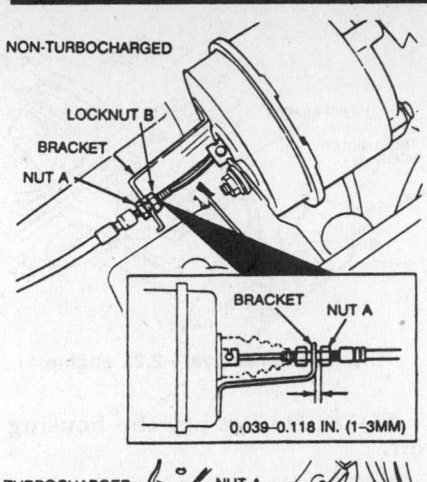

NON-TURBOCHARGED

LOCKNUT B
BRACKET
NUT A

BRACKET   NUT A

0.039–0.118 IN. (1–3MM)

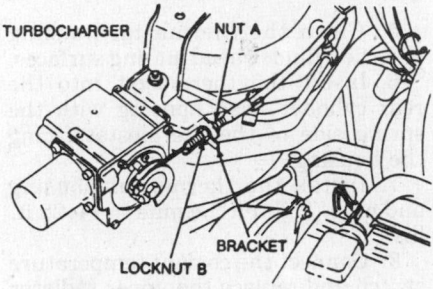

TURBOCHARGER   NUT A

BRACKET
LOCKNUT B

Adjusting the speed control actuators

there is 0.039–0.118 inch clearance between nut and the bracket.

5. Tighten the locknut securely. Replace the electric actuator plastic cover, if equipped.

ENGINE COOLING

Radiator

REMOVAL & INSTALLATION

1. Disconnect the negative battery cable and the cooling fan wiring harness connectors.

2. Remove the radiator pressure cap from the filler neck.

NOTE. If the system is hot and pressurized, be careful to release the pressure before removing the cap fully.

3. Disconnect the overflow tube from the filler neck.

4. Drain the cooling system. The drain valve is located at the bottom of the radiator on the right side.

5. Disconnect the upper and lower radiator hoses.

6. Disconnect and plug the cooler lines, if equipped with an automatic transaxle.

7. Disconnect the coolant temperature sensor wires on the 2.2L engine.

8. Remove the radiator mounting bolts.

9. Remove the radiator and the cooling fan as a complete assembly.

10. Remove the fan shroud mounting bolts.

11. Remove the fan and shroud assembly from the radiator.

To install:

12. Install the fan and shroud assembly. Tighten the mounting bolts to 61–87 ft. lbs.

13. Install the radiator, making sure the lower tank engages the insulators.

14. Install the upper radiator insulators and tighten the retaining bolts to 69–95 ft. lbs.

15. Unplug and connect the cooler lines, if required.

16. Reattach the wiring harness and install the upper and lower radiator hoses to the radiator.

17. Connect the overflow tube to the radiator and connect the cooling fan wiring connectors.

18. Close the radiator drain valve and fill the system with coolant.

19. Warm the engine to pressurize the system and check for leaks.

20. Recheck the coolant level and refill if neccessary.

Electric Cooling Fan

TESTING

With the key **ON** and the engine warmed up, disconnect the coolant temperature switch and ground the connector BK/GRN terminal. The fan should operate, if not, check the motor.

REMOVAL & INSTALLATION

1. Disconnect the negative battery cable.

2. Disconnect the cooling fan electrical connectors.

3. Remove the fan shroud-to-radiator screws and the fan/shroud assembly.

4. If removing the fan motor from the shroud, perform the following:

   a. Remove the fan blade-to-motor nut and washer.

   b. Remove the fan motor-to-shroud bolts and the motor.

5. To install, reverse the removal procedures.

Heater Core

REMOVAL & INSTALLATION

Without Air Conditioning

1. Disconnect the negative battery cable. Remove the instrument panel.

2. Drain the cooling system to a level below the heater core.

3. Disconnect and plug the hoses from the heater core.

4. Remove the main air duct from the heater case.

5. Remove the heater case-to-chassis screws and pull the heater case straight out; be careful not to damage the heater core extension tubes.

6. Remove the heater core tube braces-to-heater case screws and the tube braces.

7. Lift the heater core straight up and out of the heater case.

8. To install, reverse the removal procedures. Refill the cooling system. Start the engine, allow it to reach normal operating temperatures and check the heater operation and leaks.

With Air Conditioning

1. Disconnect the negative battery cable. Remove the instrument panel.

2. Drain the cooling system to a level below the heater core.

3. Discharge the air conditioning system. Disconnect and plug the refrigerant lines from the evaporator case.

4. Disconnect the electrical connectors from the air conditioning relays at the top of the evaporator case.

5. Remove the charcoal canister from the vehicle.

6. From both ends of the evaporator case, remove the air duct bands. Remove the drain hose from the evaporator case.

7. Remove the evaporator case-to-chassis nuts and the case from the vehicle.

8. Disconnect and plug the hoses from the heater core.

9. Remove the heater case-to-chassis bolts and pull the heater case straight; be careful not to damage the heater core extension tubes.

10. Remove the heater core tube braces-to-heater case screws and the tube braces.

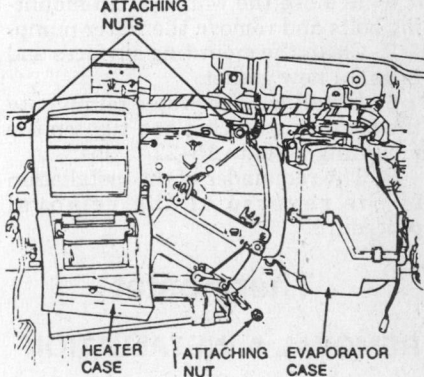

ATTACHING NUTS

HEATER CASE   ATTACHING NUT   EVAPORATOR CASE

View of the heater case assembly with air conditioning

11. Lift the heater core straight up and out of the heater case.

12. To install, reverse the removal procedures. Refill the cooling system and charge the air conditioning system.

13. Start the engine, allow it to reach normal operating temperatures and check the heater/air conditioning system operation and leaks.

Water Pump

REMOVAL & INSTALLATION

2.2L Engine

1. Disconnect the negative battery cable. Remove the timing belt.

2. Remove the timing belt tensioner pulley spring and the tensioner pulley.

3. Drain the cooling system to a level below the water pump.

4. Remove the water pump-to-engine bolts, the water pump and the O-ring and discard it.

5. Clean the gasket mounting surfaces.

To install:

6. Using a new water pump O-ring, install it onto the water pump.

7. Install the water pump and torque the bolts 14–19 ft. lbs.

8. To complete the installation, reverse the removal procedures. Refill the cooling system. Start the engine, allow it to reach normal operating temperatures and check for leaks. Check the timing.

3.0L Engine

1. Disconnect the negative battery cable. Raise and safely support the vehicle.

2. Drain the cooling system and remove the water pump belt.

3. Remove the water pump and heater hoses from the water pump.

4. Remove the lower radiator hose from the water pump steel tube.

5. Remove the steel brace bolt from the water pump mounting bracket.

6. Remove the water pump mounting bolts and remove the water pump.

7. Clean the mounting surfaces and install a new gasket.

8. Install the the water pump onto the mounting bracket and tighten the mounting bolts to 15–22 ft. lbs.

9. The remainder of the installation is the reverse of the removal procedure.

Thermostat

REMOVAL & INSTALLATION

2.2L Engine

1. Disconnect the negative battery

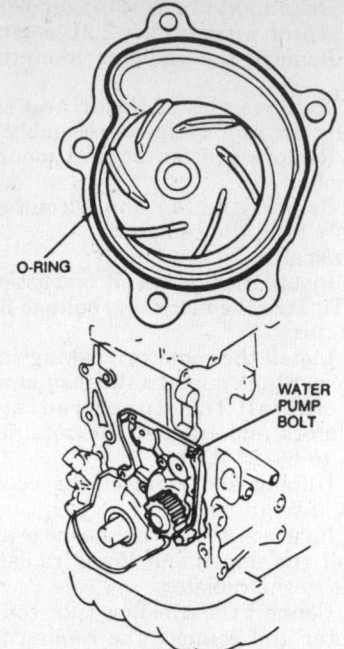

O-RING

View of the water pump

WATER PUMP BOLT

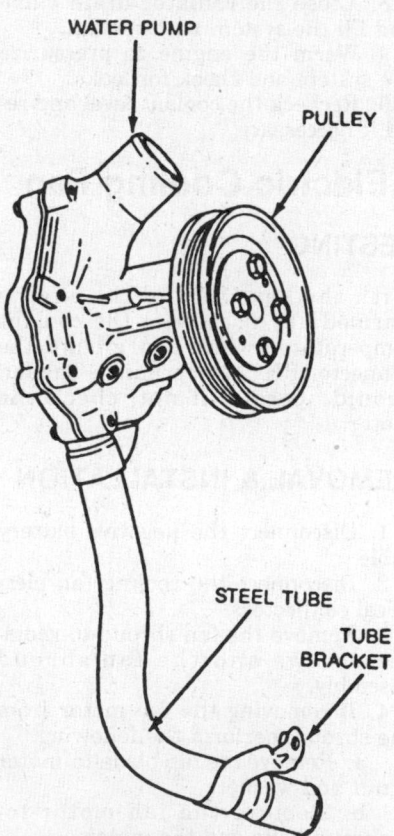

WATER PUMP

PULLEY

STEEL TUBE

TUBE BRACKET

Water pump removal – 3.0L engine

cable. Drain the radiator to below the level of the thermostat.

2. Disconnect the coolant temperature switch at the thermostat housing.

3. Remove the upper radiator hose.

4. Remove the mounting nuts, thermostat housing, thermostat and gasket.

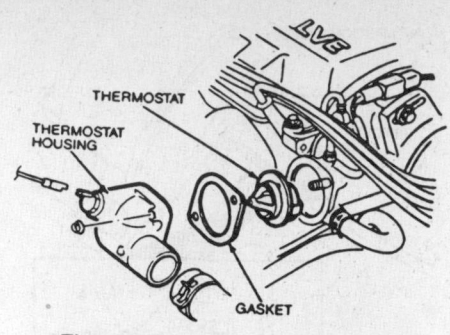

THERMOSTAT

THERMOSTAT HOUSING

GASKET

Thermostat removal – 2.2L engine

NOTE: Do not pry the housing off.

5. Clean the thermostat housing and the cylinder head mating surfaces.

6. Insert the thermostat into the rear cylinder head housing with the spring side of the thermostat facing the housing.

7. Install the thermostat housing and nuts. Tighten the nuts to 14–22 ft. lbs.

8. Connect the coolant temperature switch and replace the upper radiator hose.

9. Fill the cooling system and check for leaks.

3.0L Engine

1. Disconnect the negative battery cable. Drain the cooling system.

2. Remove the radiator hose from the thermosat housing.

3. Disconnect the wiring harness bracket and remove the ground wire.

4. Remove the thermostat housing mounting bolts and remove the thermostat.

5. Remove the gasket and clean the surface area.

6. The installation is the reverse of the removal procedure.

FUEL SYSTEM

Fuel System Service Precautions

Safety is the most important factor when performing not only fuel system maintenance but any type of maintenance. Failure to conduct maintenance and repairs in a safe manner may result in serious personal injury or death. Maintenance and testing of the vehicle's fuel system components can be accomplished safely and effectively by adhering to the following rules and guidelines.

To avoid the possibility of fire and

personal injury, always disconnect the negative battery cable unless the repair or test procedure requires that battery voltage be applied.

Always relieve the fuel system pressure prior to disconnecting any fuel system component (injector, fuel rail, pressure regulator, etc.), fitting or fuel line connection. Exercise extreme caution whenever relieving fuel system pressure to avoid exposing skin, face and eyes to fuel spray. Please be advised that fuel under pressure may penetrate the skin or any part of the body that it contacts.

Always place a shop towel or cloth around the fitting or connection prior to loosening to absorb any excess fuel due to spillage. Ensure that all fuel spillage, should it occur, is quickly removed from engine surfaces. Ensure that all fuel soaked cloths or towels are deposited into a suitable waste container.

Always keep a dry chemical (Class B) fire extinguisher near the work area.

Do not allow fuel spray or fuel vapors to come into contact with a spark or open flame.

Always use a backup wrench when loosening and tightening fuel line connection fittings. This will prevent unnecessary stress and torsion to fuel line piping. Always follow the proper torque specifications.

Always replace worn fuel fitting O-rings with new. Do not substitute fuel hose or equivalent where fuel pipe is installed.

RELIEVING FUEL SYSTEM PRESSURE

1. Start the engine.
2. From under the instrument panel, disconnect the fuel pump relay from the junction block.
3. After the engine stalls, turn the ignition switch **OFF** and reconnect the fuel pump relay to the junction block.
4. Disconnect the negative battery cable.

Fuel Filter

REMOVAL & INSTALLATION

1. Relieve the fuel pressure in the fuel system.
2. Disconnect the supply lines from both ends of the fuel filter. Plug the lines to prevent leakage.
3. Remove the in-line fuel filter from the engine mounting bracket.
4. Installation is the reverse of the removal procedure.
5. Check for any fuel leaks.

6. There is also a filter located inside the fuel tank at the end of the fuel pump.

Electric Fuel Pump

PRESSURE TESTING

1. Relieve the pressure in the fuel system.
2. Using a shop towel, place it under the fuel filter.
3. Install a fuel pressure guage between the fuel filter and the fuel line.
4. Start the engine and run at various speeds, the pressure should read between 35–45 psi.
5. After testing relieve the fuel pressure and remove the test equipment. Check for any leaks.

REMOVAL & INSTALLATION

The fuel pump is mounted on the fuel sending unit assembly in the fuel tank.

1. Relieve the fuel pressure and disconnect the negative battery cable.
2. Remove the rear seat and disconnect the electrical connector from the fuel tank sending unit.
3. Remove the sending unit cover-to-chassis screws and the cover.
4. Disconnect and plug the fuel hoses from the sending unit.
5. Remove the sending unit-to-fuel tank screws and the sending unit from the fuel tank.
6. To install, reverse the removal procedures. Start the engine and check the engine operation.

Fuel Injection

IDLE SPEED ADJUSTMENT

1. Turn **OFF** all of the accessories.
2. Firmly set the parking brake and position the gear shift selector in **P** if equipped with an automatic transaxle or **N** if equipped with a manual transaxle.
3. Start and operate the engine at 2500–3000 rpm for at least 3 minutes.

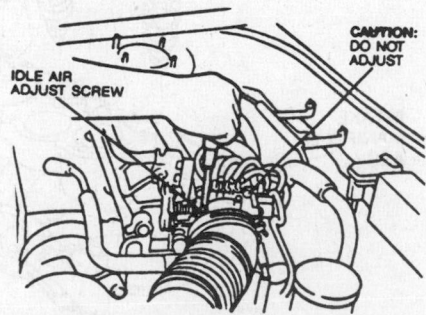

Idle speed adjustment–2.2L engine

4. Using a jumper wire, ground the test connector pin No. 1.
5. Using a tachometer, connect it to the engine and check the idle speed; the idle speed should be 725–775 rpm.
6. If the idle speed is not within specifications, adjust the air adjusting screw located on the throttle body.
7. After the idle speed is adjusted, remove the test equipment and the jumper wire.

NOTE: Do not tamper with the adjustment screw located just to the left of the idle air adjustment screw. Doing so may result in damage to the throttle body.

IDLE MIXTURE ADJUSTMENT

The air/fuel mixture is a function of the ECA and not adjustable.

Fuel Injector

REMOVAL & INSTALLATION

2.2L Engine

1. Relieve the fuel pressure and disconnect the negative battery cable.
2. Drain the cooling system.
3. Disconnect the accelerator cables from the throttle body.
4. Remove the air duct from the throttle body.
5. Label and disconnect the vacuum lines and coolant hoses from the throttle body.
6. Disconnect the electrical connectors from the TPS, the idle switch and the bypass air control valve.
7. Remove the engine lifting bracket mounting bolts from the throttle body and the engine block.
8. Disconnect the coolant line/EGR hose bracket from the throttle body and the throttle cable brackets from the intake plenum.
9. Remove the wire loom bracket and the EGR back-pressure transducer bracket from the right side of the plenum.
10. Remove the PCV hose and the vacuum line assembly bracket from the intake plenum.
11. Label and disconnect the vacuum lines from the intake plenum.
12. Remove the plenum-to-intake manifold nuts/bolts, the plenum and the gasket.
13. Disconnect the electrical connectors from the fuel injectors.
14. Carefully, bend the wire harness retainer brackets away from the wire harness and move the harness assembly away from the intake manifold.
15. Remove the fuel supply tube from the pulsation damper.

16. Remove the fuel return line bracket from the intake manifold, the clamp and the fuel return line from the bracket.

17. Remove the fuel rail-to-intake manifold bolts and the fuel rail with the pressure regulator and the pulsation damper attached.

18. Remove the fuel injectors, the grommet and the O-rings from the fuel rail. Remove the O-rings from the fuel injectors and discard it.

To install:

19. Using new O-rings, lubricate them with engine oil and install the fuel injectors into the fuel rail.

20. Install the fuel injector/rail assembly into the intake manifold and torque the bolts to 14–19 ft. lbs. Connect the electrical connectors to the fuel injectors.

21. Install the fuel return line bracket onto the intake manifold and the return line at the bracket.

22. Install the fuel supply line onto the pulsation damper and secure with a clamp.

23. Using a new gasket, install the intake plenum onto the intake manifold and torque the nuts/bolts to 14–19 ft. lbs.

24. Install with the wiring harness onto the retainer brackets and carefully bend the brackets toward the wire harness.

25. To complete the installation, reverse the removal procedures. Refill the cooling system. Start the engine, allow it to reach normal operating temperatures and check for leaks and engine operation.

3.0L Engine

1. Relieve the fuel pressure in the fuel system.

2. Disconnect the negative battery cable.

3. Remove the air cleaner tube and plastic shield from the throttle body.

4. Remove the EGR supply tube and disconnect all the vacuum hoses from the air intake throttle body.

5. Disconnect the ACT sensor, ISC servo and TPS solenoid.

6. Remove the MAP sensor from the throttle body.

7. Disconnect the throttle cable and the throttle valve control cable if equipped with an automatic transaxle from the throttle lever.

8. Remove the fuel rail bracket bolt from the throttle body.

9. Remove the air intake throttle body mounting bolts and lift off the throttle body.

10. Disconnect the fuel supply and return lines.

11. Remove the fuel injector wiring harness.

12. Disconnect the vacuum line from the fuel pressure regulator.

13. Remove the fuel injector manifold mounting bolts.

14. Disengage the fuel rail assembly by carefully, lifting and rocking the rail.

15. Remove the injectors by lifting while gently rocking side to side.

NOTE: Handle the injectors and rail assembly with extreme care to prevent damage to the sealing areas and metering orifices.

To install:

16. Inspect the injector O-rings for wear or damage.

17. Lubricate the new O-rings with a lightweight grade oil and install 2 on each injector.

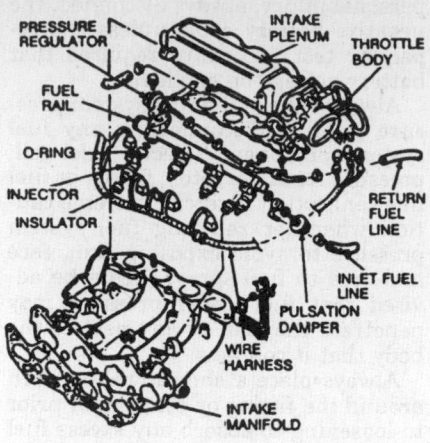

Exploded view of the air intake system and fuel rail assembly—2.2L engine

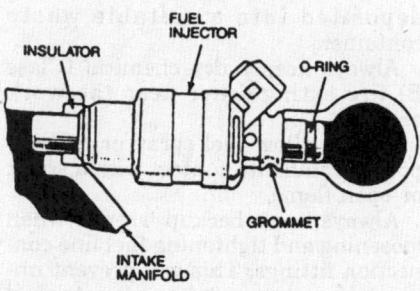

Exploded view of the fuel injector assembly—2.2L engine

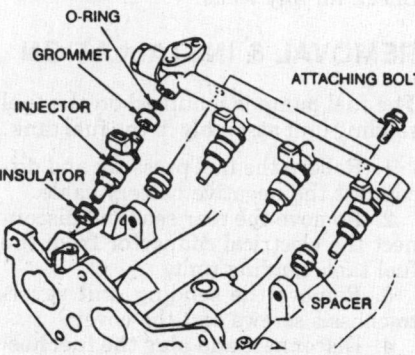

Exploded view of the fuel rail and fuel injectors—2.2L engine

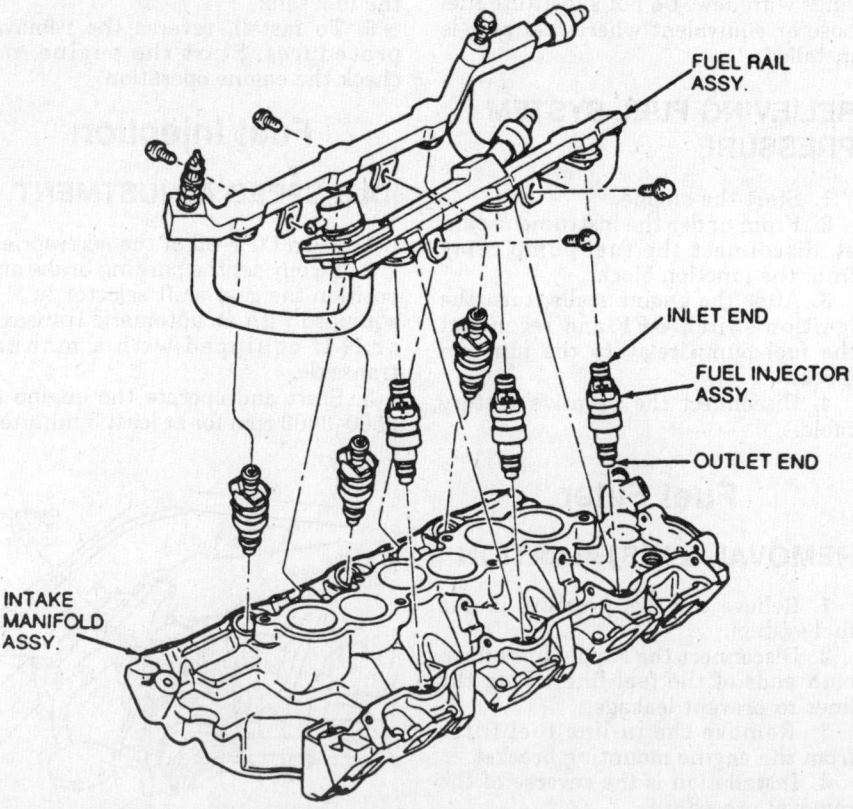

Exploded view of the fuel rail and the fuel injectors—3.0L engine

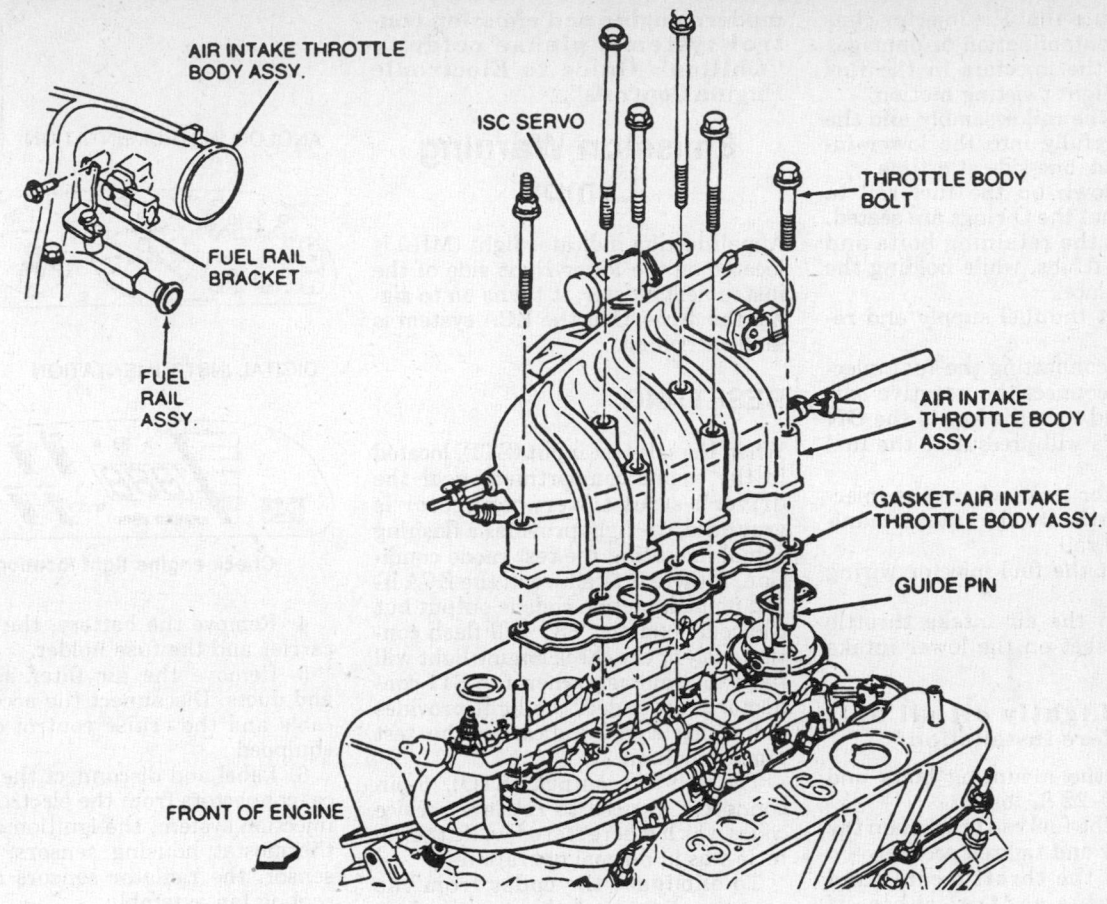

AIR INTAKE THROTTLE
BODY ASSY.

FUEL RAIL
BRACKET

FUEL
RAIL
ASSY.

ISC SERVO

THROTTLE BODY
BOLT

AIR INTAKE
THROTTLE BODY
ASSY.

GASKET-AIR INTAKE
THROTTLE BODY ASSY.

GUIDE PIN

FRONT OF ENGINE

3.0-V6

Exploded view of the air intake throttle body—3.0L engine

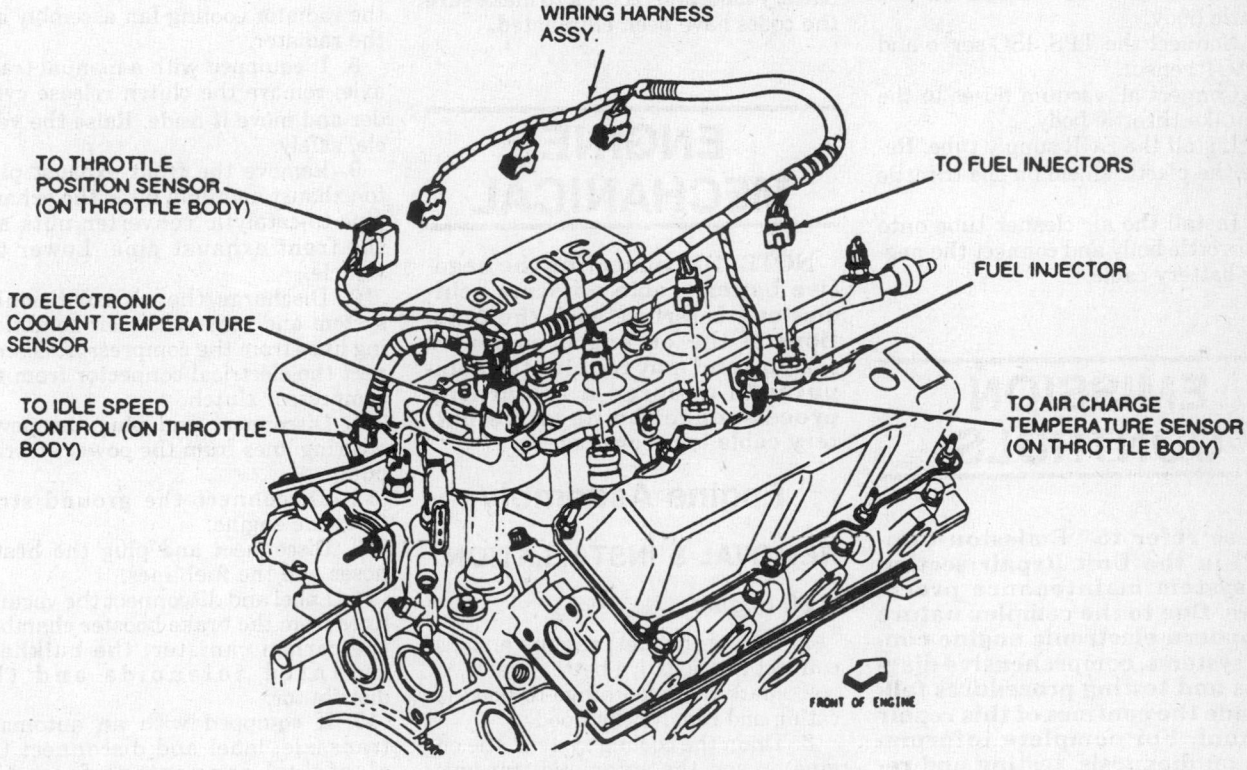

WIRING HARNESS
ASSY.

TO THROTTLE
POSITION SENSOR
(ON THROTTLE BODY)

TO ELECTRONIC
COOLANT TEMPERATURE
SENSOR

TO IDLE SPEED
CONTROL (ON THROTTLE
BODY)

TO FUEL INJECTORS

FUEL INJECTOR

TO AIR CHARGE
TEMPERATURE SENSOR
(ON THROTTLE BODY)

3.0-V6

FRONT OF ENGINE

Wiring harness connections—3.0L engine

18. Make sure that the injector cups are free of contamination or damage.

19. Install the injectors in the fuel rail using a light twisting motion.

20. Install the rail assembly and the injectors carefully into the lower intake manifold, one side at a time.

21. Push down on the fuel rail to make sure that the O-rings are seated.

22. Install the retaining bolts and tighten to 7 ft. lbs. while holding the fuel rail in place.

23. Connect the fuel supply and return lines.

24. Before connecting the fuel injector harness connect the negative battery cable and turn the key to the **ON** position. This will pressurize the fuel system.

25. Check for leaks where the injector is installed into the intake manifold and fuel rail.

26. Connect the fuel injector wiring harness.

27. Position the air intake throttle body and gasket on the lower intake manifold.

NOTE: Lightly oil all bolt threads before installation.

28. Install the mounting bolts and tighten to 15–22 ft. lbs.

29. Install the fuel rail bracket on the throttle body and tighten securely.

30. Install the throttle cable and throttle valve control cable, if equipped with an autmatic transaxle, on the throttle lever.

31. Install the MAP sensor on the throttle body.

32. Connect the TPS, ISC servo and the ACT sensor.

33. Connect all vacuum hoses to the air intake throttle body.

34. Install the EGR supply tube. Replace the plastic shield on the throttle body.

35. Install the air cleaner tube onto the throttle body and connect the negative battery cable.

EMISSION CONTROLS

Please refer to "Emission Control" in the Unit Repair section for system maintenance procedures. Due to the complex nature of modern electronic engine control systems, comprehensive diagnosis and testing procedures fall outside the confines of this repair manual. For complete information on diagnosis, testing and repair procedures concerning all modern engine and emission control systems, please refer to "Chilton's Guide to Electronic Engine Controls".

Emission Warning Lamps

A malfunction indicator light (MIL) is located on the lower right side of the instrument cluster; it turns on to signal the driver that the ECA system is malfunctioning.

RESETTING

When the self-test input (STI), located in the engine compartment near the driver's strut tower, connector is grounded, the light provides a flashing signal indicating the test mode condition. If there is a failure in the ECA itself no malfunction code is output but the code number "88" will flash continuously or the check engine light will flash continuously when the STI connector is grounded, the light provides a flashing signal indicating the test mode condition.

The self-test output (STO), 6-pin connector, is used to retrieve service codes which where stored while the vehicle was in normal operation.

To eliminate the codes from the memory, disconnect the negative battery cable, depress the brake pedal for 5–10 seconds, reconnect the negative battery cable and recheck to make sure the codes have been eliminated.

ENGINE MECHANICAL

NOTE: Disconnecting the negative battery cable on some vehicles may interfere with the functions of the on board computer systems and may require the computer to undergo a relearning process, once the negative battery cable is reconnected.

Engine Assembly

REMOVAL & INSTALLATION

2.2L Engine

1. Relieve the fuel pressure and disconnect the negative battery cable.

2. Mark the hood hinge-to-hood location and remove the hood.

3. Drain the cooling system, the engine oil and the automatic transmission fluid.

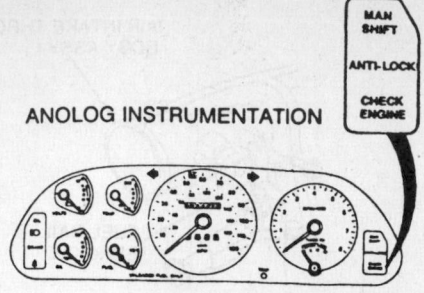

ANOLOG INSTRUMENTATION

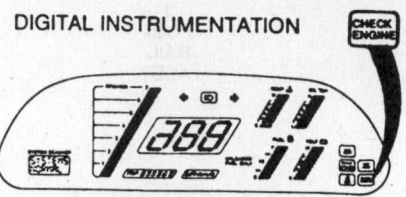

DIGITAL INSTRUMENTATION

Check engine light location

4. Remove the battery, the battery carrier and the fuse holder.

5. Remove the air filter assembly and ducts. Disconnect the accelerator cable and the cruise control cable, if equipped.

6. Label and disconnect the electrical connectors from the electronic fuel injection system, the ignition coil, the thermostat housing sensors, the O₂ sensor, the radiator sensors and the cooling fan assembly.

7. If equipped with an automatic transaxle, disconnect and plug the cooler lines from the radiator. Remove the radiator cooling fan assembly and the radiator.

8. If equipped with a manual transaxle, remove the clutch release cylinder and move it aside. Raise the vehicle, safely.

9. Remove the front exhaust pipe-to-exhaust manifold nuts, the exhaust pipe-to-catalytic converter nuts and the front exhaust pipe. Lower the vehicle.

10. Discharge the air conditioning system and remove the air conditioning lines from the compressor. Disconnect the electrical connector from the compressor clutch.

11. Disconnect and plug the power steering lines from the power steering pump.

12. Disconnect the ground strap from the engine.

13. Disconnect and plug the heater hoses and the fuel lines.

14. Label and disconnect the vacuum lines from the brake booster chamber, the carbon canister, the bulkhead mounted solenoids and the distributor.

15. If equipped with an automatic transaxle, label and disconnect the electrical connectors from the transaxle.

16. Disconnect the speedometer cable from the transaxle.

17. If equipped with a turbocharger, disconnect the hoses/pipes and cover it with a clean rag.

18. Raise and safely support the vehicle. Remove the halfshafts from the transaxle.

19. Disconnect the shift control cable, if equipped with an automatic transaxle or rod, if equipped with a manual transaxle from the transaxle. Lower the vehicle.

20. Using an engine lifting device, attach it to the engine and support it's weight.

21. Disconnect the engine mount bolts and remove the engine/transaxle assembly from the vehicle.

22. If neccessary, remove the transaxle-to-engine bolts and support the engine on an engine stand.

To install:

23. If the transaxle was removed from the engine, install it and torque the bolts to 66–86 ft. lbs.

24. Lower the engine/transaxle assembly into the vehicle and secure the engine mount bolts.

25. Install the halfshafts.

NOTE: When installing the halfshafts, hold the shafts to prevent damage to the seals, boots and joints caused by moving the joints through angles greater than 20 degrees.

26. Depending on which transaxle the vehicle is equipped with, connect the shift cable control or rod. If equipped with a manual transaxle, install the clutch release cylinder. If equipped with an automatic transaxle, connect the electrical connectors to the transaxle.

27. Connect the speedometer cable to the transaxle and the power steering lines to the power steering pump.

28. If equipped with air conditioning, use new O-rings and connect the high pressure and suction lines to the compressor. Reconnect the electrical connector to the compressor clutch.

29. Connect the engine ground strap. On a non-turbocharged vehicle, install the front exhaust pipe. If equipped with a turbocharger, connect the oil pipe and hoses to the turbocharger.

30. Install the radiator and the cooling fan assembly and reconnect the electrical connectors. If equipped with an automatic transaxle, reconnect the oil cooler lines to the radiator.

31. Connect the vacuum lines to the carbon canister, the bulkhead mounted solenoids, distributor and the brake booster.

32. Connect the heater hoses to the engine and the fuel lines to the fuel system. Connect the electrical connectors to the thermostat housing sensors, the coil and the electronic fuel injection assembly.

33. Install the accelerator cable and the cruise control cable (if equipped). Install the air filter and ducts.

34. Refill the cooling system, the crankcase and the automatic transaxle. Charge the air conditioning system. Refill the power steering reservoir and bleed the system.

35. Start the engine, allow it to reach normal operating temperatures and check for leaks.

3.0L Engine

1. Disconnect the battery cables. Remove and set aside the hood assembly.

2. Drain the cooling system and discharge the air conditioning system.

3. Remove the air cleaner assembly from the engine compartment and the vacuum valve assembly from the right hand shock tower.

4. Relieve the fuel pressure. Disconnect and plug the fuel lines.

5. Remove the upper radiator hose.

6. Disconnect the alternator, air conditioning compressor clutch, ignition coil and the Engine Coolant Temperature Sensor (ECTS).

7. Disconnect and tag the TFI module connector, injector wiring harness, Air Charge Temperature Sensor (ACTS) and the Throttle Position Sensor (TPS).

8. Disconnect the oil pressure sending switch, ground straps on both sides of the engine and the block heater, if equipped.

9. Disconnect the knock sensor on the back side of engine, EGR sensor and the oil level sensor on the back side of the oil pan.

10. Disconnect and tag all vacuum lines, heater hoses and crankcase ventilation hoses.

11. Remove the high pressure and return lines from the power steering pump.

12. Discharge the air conditioning system and disconnect the air conditioning lines from the condenser and chassis, leaving the manifold lines attached to the compressor.

13. Disconnect the accelerator linkage, transmission throttle valve linkage and the speed control cable, if equipped.

14. Remove the battery, battery tray and the fuse box assembly.

15. Disconnect and set aside the speed control servo assembly and the transmission shift cable, if equipped with an automatic transaxle.

16. Disconnect all automatic transmission wiring connectors and the speedometer cable on conventional (analog) cluster vehicles.

17. Disconnect the Vehicle Speed Sensor (VSS) on electronic cluster vehicles.

18. Disconnect and plug the cooler lines at the transmission, if equipped.

19. Remove the clutch release cylinder with the hose attached, if equipped with a manual transaxle.

20. Remove the radiator, cooling fan and shroud.

21. Raise and safely support the vehicle. Remove the front tires and wheels.

22. Remove the lower radiator hose, the front exhaust pipe and the starter motor.

NOTE: On vehicles with an automatic transaxle, it is advised that the torque converter nuts be removed at this time to facilitate the removal of the transaxle asembly from the engine after the engine/transaxle assembly is removed from the vehicle.

23. Remove the shift control rod and the extension bar on a manual transaxle.

24. Remove the stabilizer links, tie rod ends and disconnect the lower ball joints to disengage the control arms from the spindle.

25. Remove the dynamic damper mounting bolts on the right halfshaft assembly.

26. Disengage both halfshafts by pulling outward on both side brake and spindle assemblies.

27. Install 2 transaxle plugs or the equivalent into the differential side gears.

NOTE: Failure to install the transaxle plugs may allow the differential side gears to become misaligned.

28. Disconnect the lower transmission mount and safely, lower the vehicle.

29. Install and position the lifting devices. Disconnect the lower front engine mount.

TRANSAXLE PLUG

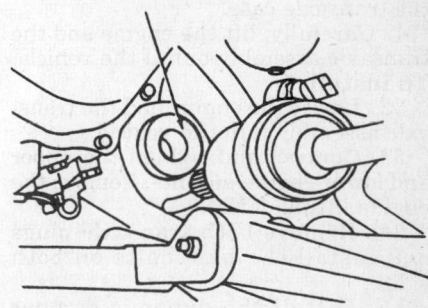

Installation of the transaxle plugs in the side gears

1. Ignition coil
2. Cooling fan voltage resistor
3. Engine coolant temperature sensor
4. TFI module
5. Injector wiring harness
6. Oil pressure sending switch
7. Ground wire
8. Block heater (if equipped)
9. Oil level sensor
10. Wiring harness

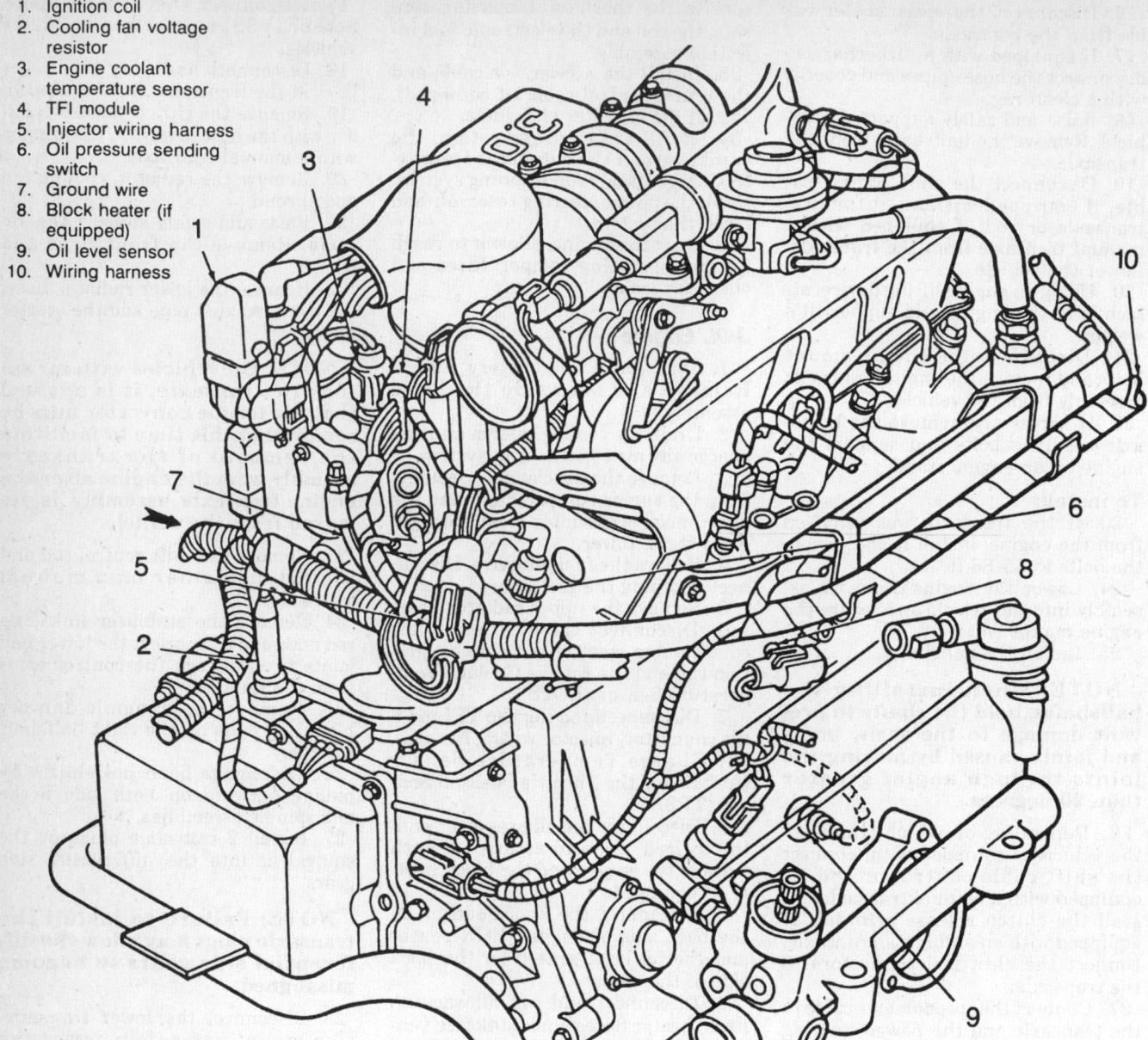

Engine assembly – 3.0L engine

30. Disconnect the right hand upper engine mount at the timing cover and the left hand upper engine mount at the transaxle case.
31. Carefully, lift the engine and the transaxle assembly out of the vehicle.
To install:
32. Lower the engine and the transaxle assembly into the vehicle.
33. Connect and tighten the upper and lower engine mounts. Remove the engine lifting devices.
34. Remove both transaxle plugs and install the halfshafts on both sides.
35. Install the dynamic damper mounting bolts on the right side halfshaft.
36. Engage the control arms and in-

stall the lower ball joints, tie rod ends and the stabilizer links.
37. Install the shift control rod and extension bar, if equipped with a manual transaxle.
38. Replace the torque converter nuts, if equipped with an automatic transaxle.
39. Install the starter, front exhaust pipe and the lower radiator hose.
40. Replace the front tires and wheels. Safely, lower the vehicle.
41. Install the cooling fan, shroud and the radiator.
42. Install the clutch release cable with the hose attached, if equipped.
43. Reconnect the cooler lines at the transmission, if equipped.

44. Connect the Vehicle Speed Sensor (VSS) on electronic cluster vehicles.
45. Connect all automatic transmission wiring connectors and the speedometer cable on conventional (analog) cluster vehicles.
46. Install the speed control servo assembly and the transmission shift cable, if equipped.
47. Replace the battery, battery tray and the fuse box assembly.
48. Connect the accelerator linkage, transmission throttle valve linkage and the speed control cable, if equipped.
49. Connect the air conditioning lines from the condensor and chassis and recharge the air conditioning

system.

50. Install the high pressure and return lines to the power steering pump.

51. Reconnect all vacuum lines, heater hoses and crankcase ventilation hoses.

52. Reconnect the knock sensor on the back side of engine, EGR sensor and the oil level sensor on the back side of the oil pan.

53. Replace the oil pressure sending switch, ground straps on both sides of the engine and the block heater, if equipped.

54. Reconnect the TFI module connector, injector wiring harness, Air Charge Temperature Sensor (ACTS) and the Throttle Position Sensor (TPS).

55. Install the alternator, air conditioning compressor clutch, ignition coil and the Engine Coolant Temperature Sensor (ECTS).

56. Connect the fuel lines and replace the upper radiator hose.

57. Replace the air cleaner assembly to the engine compartment and the vacuum valve assembly on the right hand shock tower.

58. Refill the cooling system.

59. Reconnect the battery cables and install the hood assembly.

60. Check all fluid levels and refill if needed. Check for any leaks.

30. Check the timing, adjust if neccessary.

Engine Mounts

REMOVAL & INSTALLATION

1. Disconnect the negative battery cable.

2. If necessary, raise and support the vehicle safely.

3. Using an engine lifting device, attach it to the engine and support it's weight.

4. Remove the engine mount(s)-to-engine bolts, the engine mount(s)-to-chassis bolts and the mounts.

5. To install, reverse the removal procedures. Remove the engine lift.

Cylinder Head

REMOVAL & INSTALLATION

2.2L Engine

1. Disconnect the negative battery cable. Remove the drive belts and the cranshaft pulley.

2. Remove the timing belt cover, timing belt and tensioner, if neccessary.

3. Remove the exhaust manifold, intake manifold and the distributor.

4. Remove rocker arm/shaft assemblies.

5. Drain the cooling system.

6. Remove the spark plug wires and the spark plugs.

7. Disconnect the electrical connectors from the thermostat housing sensors. Remove the upper radiator hose and the water bypass hose.

8. Remove the front and rear engine lifting eyes and the engine ground wire.

9. Remove the cylinder head bolts, a little at a time, in the reverse order of installation. Remove the cylinder head and discard the gasket.

10. Clean the gasket mounting surfaces. Check the cylinder head for warpage, cracks and/or damage; replace it, if necessary.

To install:

11. Using a new cylinder head gasket, position it on the engine block, install the cylinder head and torque the bolts to 59–64 ft. lbs., using 2 steps, in sequence.

12. Using new gaskets, install and torque the rear timing belt cover-to-cylinder head nut/bolt to 14–19 ft. lbs. and the rear housing-to-cylinder head nut/bolts to 14–19 ft. lbs.

13. Install the distributor and the front and rear engine lifting eyes.

14. Using a new gasket, torque the thermostat housing-to-rear cylinder head housing nuts to 14–22 ft. lbs.

15. Install the spark plugs and spark plug wires.

16. Install the intake and exhaust manifolds.

17. Install the rocker arm/shaft assemblies.

18. Install and adjust the timing belt. Replace the timing covers.

19. Install the crankshaft pulley and the drive belts.

20. Fill the cooling system and replace the negative battery cable.

21. Run the engine and check for any leaks. It may be necessary to adjust the ignition base timing.

3.0L Engine

1. Disconnect the negative battery cable and drain the cooling system.

2. Remove the air cleaner duct tube and the intake manifold.

3. Remove the accessory drive belts.

4. Remove the power steering pump assembly, if removing the front cylinder head.

5. Remove the alternator support bracket. Remove the oil level dipstick and tube.

6. Remove the ignition coil and bracket. Remove the exhaust manifolds.

7. Loosen the rocker arm fulcrum mounting bolts enough to allow the rocker arm to be lifted off the pushrod and rotated to one side.

8. Remove the pushrods, mark the position of each rod. This ensures the proper sequence if reused.

9. Remove the cylinder head mounting bolts and cylinder head.

10. Remove and discard the old cylinder head gasket(s).

11. Clean the cylinder head, intake manifold mounting surfaces.

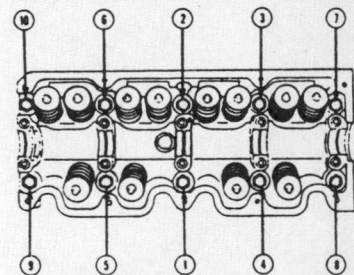

View of the cylinder head bolt torquing sequence—2.2L engine

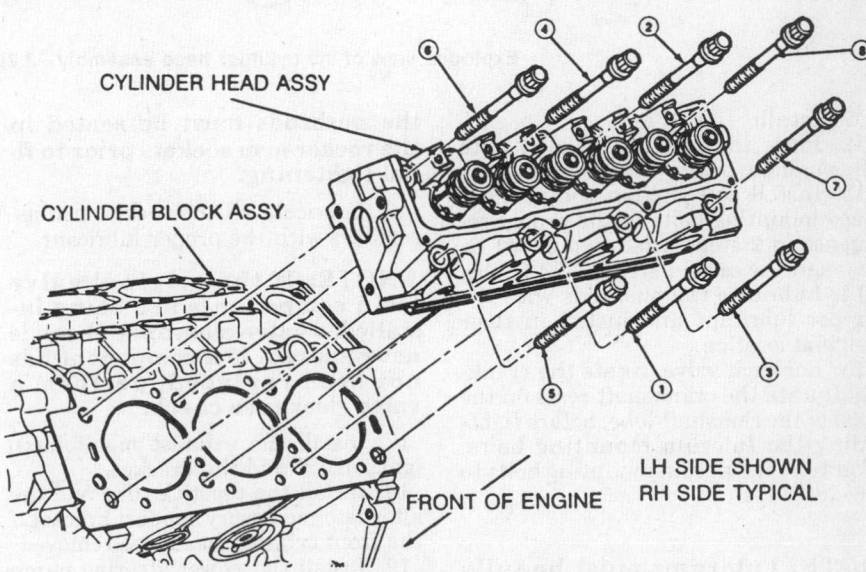

CYLINDER HEAD ASSY

CYLINDER BLOCK ASSY

FRONT OF ENGINE

LH SIDE SHOWN
RH SIDE TYPICAL

Cylinder head bolt tightening sequence—3.0L engine

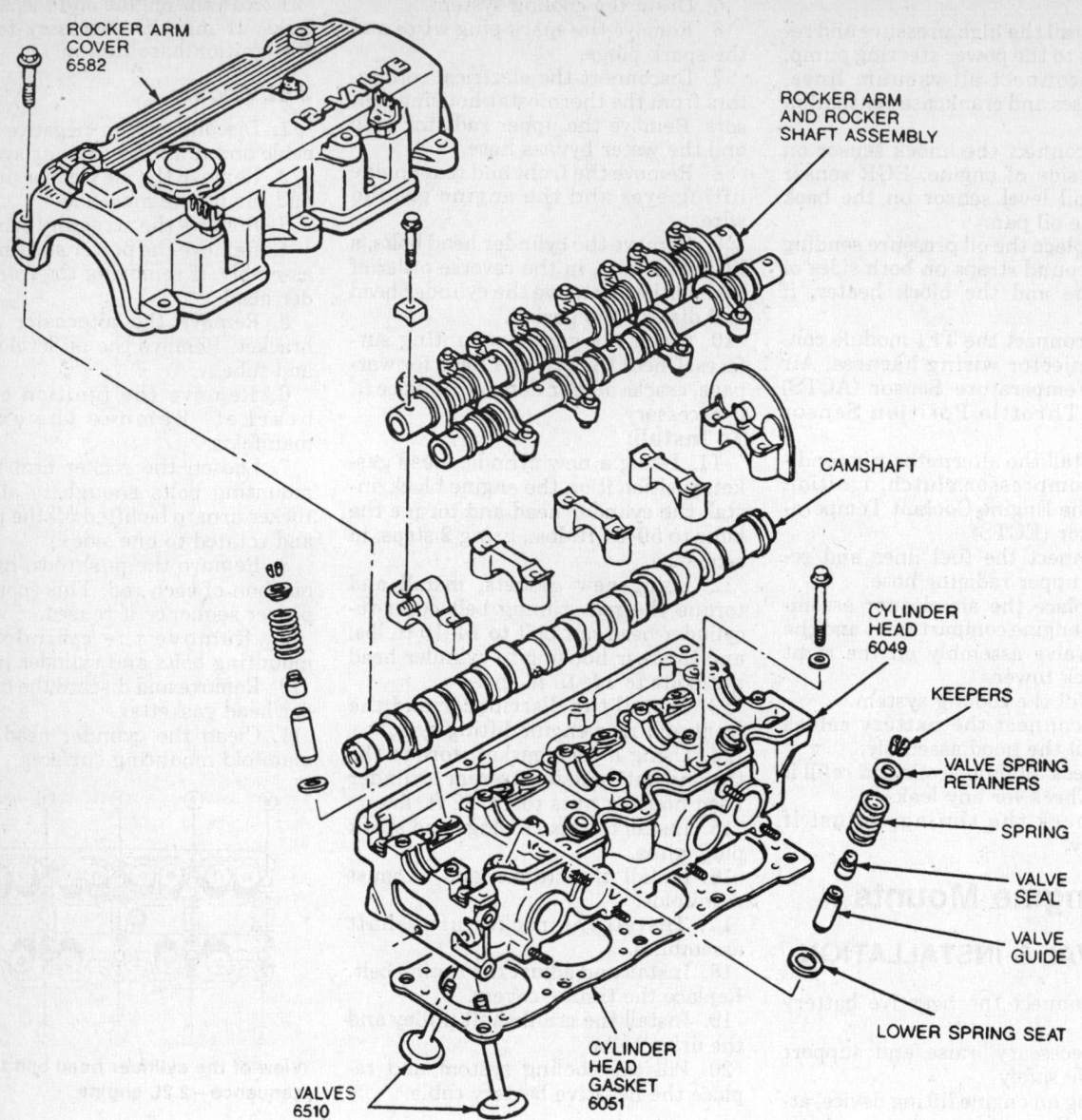

ROCKER ARM COVER 6582

ROCKER ARM AND ROCKER SHAFT ASSEMBLY

CAMSHAFT

CYLINDER HEAD 6049

KEEPERS

VALVE SPRING RETAINERS

SPRING

VALVE SEAL

VALVE GUIDE

LOWER SPRING SEAT

VALVES 6510

CYLINDER HEAD GASKET 6051

Exploded view of the cylinder head assembly—2.2L engine

To install:

12. Place the cylinder head(s) onto the engine block.

13. Install and tighten the cylinder head mounting bolts in the proper sequence in 2 steps: first step 33–41 ft. lbs. and the second step 63–73 ft. lbs.

14. Lubricate the pushrods with the proper lubricant and install in their original location.

15. For each valve, rotate the crankshaft until the crankshaft rests on the heel of the camshaft lobe, before tightening the fulcrum mounting bolts. Tighten the fulcrum mounting bolts to 20–28 ft. lbs.

NOTE: Fulcrums must be fully seated in the cylinder head and

the pushrods must be seated in the rocker arm sockets prior to final tightening.

16. Lubricate all the rocker arm assemblies with the proper lubricant.

NOTE: If the original valve train components are being installed, a valve clearance check is not required. If a component has not been replaced, perform a valve clearance check.

17. Install the exhaust manifold(s), ignition coil and the bracket.

18. Install the dipstick tube and the alternator/accessory support bracket if the front cylinder head was removed.

19. Install the power steering pump if the front cylinder head was

removed.

20. Install the accessary drive belts and the intake manifold.

21. Install the rocker arms and the air intake throttle body.

22. Install the air cleaner duct and replace the negative battery cable.

23. Refill the cooling system.

24. Adjust the throttle cable, speed control cable and the throttle valve control cable, if equipped with a automatic transaxle.

Valve Lifters

REMOVAL & INSTALLATION

2.2L Engine

The rocker arms ride directly on the

camshaft and are equipped with hydraulic lash adjusters.

3.0L Engine

NOTE: Before replacing a lifter for noisy operation, ensure that the noise is not caused by improper valve-to-rocker arm clearance, worn rocker arms or pushrods.

1. Disconnect the negative battery cable.
2. Drain the cooling system and remove the air intake throttle body.
3. Remove the rocker arm covers and the intake manifold assembly.
4. Loosen each rocker arm fulcrum mounting bolt to allow the rocker arm to be lifted off the pushrod and rotated to one side.
5. Remove the pushrods, marking the location of each pushrod to ensure the proper replacement in the original position.
6. Remove the lifter(s), using a magnet. Mark the location of each lifter to ensure the proper replacement in the original position.

NOTE: If the lifters are stuck in the bores, it may be neccessary to use a hydraulic lifter puller or equivalent.

7. Lubricate each lifter and the bore with the proper oil and install the lifters into the bore.
To install:
8. Lubricate each pushrod with the proper oil and insert in their original position.
9. For each valve, rotate the crankshaft until the lifter rests on the heel of the camshaft lobe.
10. Place the rocker arms over the pushrods. Position the fulcrums and tighten the mounting bolts to 20–28 ft. lbs.
11. Lubricate all the rocker arm assemblies.

NOTE: Fulcrums must be fully seated in the cylinder head and the pushrods must be seated in the rocker arm sockets prior to final tightening.

12. Install the intake manifold and the rocker arm covers.
13. Install the air intake throttle body and connect the negative battery cable.
14. Refill the cooling system and check for leaks.

Valve Lash

The valve lifters are hydraulic and no valve adjustment is needed.

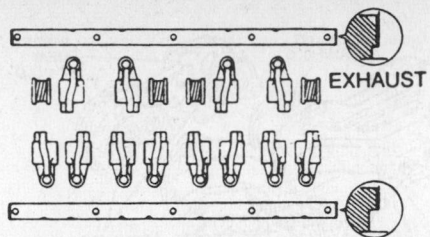

Exploded view of the rocker arm/shaft assemblies—2.2L engine

Rocker Arms/Shafts

REMOVAL & INSTALLATION

2.2L Engine

1. Disconnect the negative battery cable. Remove the vent hose and the PCV valve from the rocker arm cover.
2. Remove the spark plug wire clips and move the wires aside.
3. Remove the rocker arm cover-to-cylinder head bolts, the rocker arm cover and the gasket.
4. Remove the rocker arm shaft assemblies-to-cylinder head bolts and the assemblies from the cylinder head.
5. If neccessary, separate the rocker arms and springs from the shafts; be sure to keep the parts in order for reinstallation purposes.
6. Clean the gasket mounting surfaces. Inspect the parts for wear and/or damage; replace the parts, if necessary.
To install:
7. Assemble the rocker arms and springs onto the shafts.

NOTE: When installing the rocker arm shafts onto the cylinder head, pay attention to the notches at the ends of the shafts, they are different and cannot be interchanged.

8. Install the rocker arm/shaft assemblies onto the cylinder head and torque the rocker arm shaft-to-cylinder head bolts to 13–20 ft. lbs., using 2 steps.
9. Using a new gasket, position it onto the cylinder head, apply silicone sealant to the shaded areas at both ends of the cylinder head and install the rocker arm cover. Torque the rocker arm cover-to-cylinder head bolts to 52–69 inch lbs.
10. Install the spark plug retaining clips. Install the vent hose and the PCV valve onto the rocker arm cover.
11. Connect the negative battery cable.
12. Start the engine and check for leaks.

3.0L Engine

1. Disconnect the negative battery cable.

2. Remove the air cleaner tube and the plastic shield from the throttle body.
3. Remove the EGR supply tube, if equipped.
4. Disconnect all the vacuum hoses from the throttle body.
5. Disconnect the spark plug wires and the spark plugs.
6. Remove the plug wire loom brackets from the rocker cover stud/bolts. Remove the crankcase hose from the rocker cover.
7. Remove the alternator harness loom retainers and pull the injector harness out of the way.
8. Disconnect the ACT sensor, ISC servo, TPS and the EVP sensor, if equipped.
9. Disconnect the throttle cable and the throttle valve control cable, if equipped, from the throttle assembly.
10. Remove the fuel rail bracket from the throttle body. Remove the throttle body.
11. Remove the rocker cover mounting bolts/studs and remove the rocker cover(s) and gasket(s).
12. Remove the rocker fulcrum mounting bolts and remove the rocker arm/shaft assemblies.
To install:
13. Clean the mounting surfaces. Apply a proper sealer to intake manifold rail step and install a new gasket.
14. Position the cover on the cylinder head and tighten the mounting bolts/studs to 88–124 inch lbs.
15. Install the spark plug wires and connect the wiring harness.
16. Install the air intake throttle body onto the intake manifold and tighten the mounting bolts to 15–22 ft. lbs.
17. Install the fuel rail bracket onto the throttle body and tighten to 7 ft. lbs.
18. Install the throttle cable and the throttle valve control cable, if equipped.
19. Connect the EVP sensor, ISC servo, TPS and ACT sensor.
20. Connect all the vacuum hoses to the throttle body.
21. Install the EGR supply tube, if equipped.
22. Install the plastic shield on the throttle body. Connect the negative battery cable.
23. Run the engine and check for leaks.

Intake Manifold

REMOVAL & INSTALLATION

2.2L Engine

1. Relieve the fuel pressure and disconnect the negative battery cable.
2. Drain the cooling system.

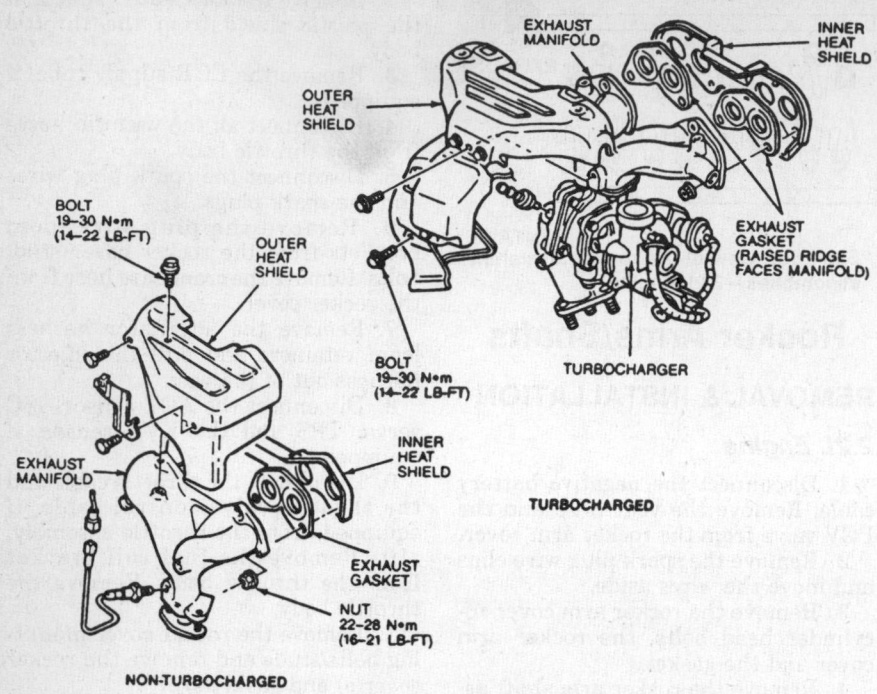

EXHAUST MANIFOLD

INNER HEAT SHIELD

OUTER HEAT SHIELD

EXHAUST GASKET (RAISED RIDGE FACES MANIFOLD)

TURBOCHARGER

TURBOCHARGED

BOLT 19–30 N•m (14–22 LB-FT)

OUTER HEAT SHIELD

BOLT 19–30 N•m (14–22 LB-FT)

INNER HEAT SHIELD

EXHAUST MANIFOLD

EXHAUST GASKET

NUT 22–28 N•m (16–21 LB-FT)

NON-TURBOCHARGED

Exploded view of the intake manifold—2.2L engine

3. From the bottom of the intake manifold, remove the water hose.

4. Disconnect the accelerator cables from the throttle body.

5. Remove the air duct from the throttle body.

6. Label and disconnect the vacuum lines and coolant hoses from the throttle body.

7. Disconnect the electrical connectors from the TPS, the idle switch and the bypass air control valve.

8. Remove the engine lifting bracket mounting bolts from the throttle body and the engine block.

9. Disconnect the coolant line/EGR hose bracket from the throttle body and the throttle cable brackets from the intake plenum.

10. Remove the wire loom bracket and the EGR back-pressure transducer bracket from the right side of the plenum.

11. Remove the PCV hose and the vacuum line assembly bracket from the intake plenum.

12. Label and disconnect the vacuum lines from the intake plenum.

13. Remove the plenum-to-intake manifold nuts/bolts, the plenum and the gasket.

14. Disconnect the electrical connectors from the fuel injectors.

15. Carefully, bend the wire harness retainer brackets away from the wire harness and move the harness assembly away from the intake manifold.

16. Disconnect the EGR pipe from the intake manifold. Label and disconnect any electrical connectors and hoses from the intake manifold.

17. Remove the intake manifold bracket-to-manifold nuts and the bracket. Remove the intake manifold-to-cylinder head nuts/bolts, the manifold and gasket.

18. Clean the gasket mounting surfaces.

To install:

19. Using a new gasket, position the intake manifold on the cylinder head studs and torque the nuts/bolts to 14–22 ft. lbs.

20. Install the intake manifold bracket-to-manifold nuts to 14–22 ft. lbs.

21. Install the fuel injector/rail assembly into the intake manifold and torque the bolts to 14–19 ft. lbs. Connect the electrical connectors to the fuel injectors.

22. Install the fuel return line bracket onto the intake manifold and the return line at the bracket, secure with a clamp.

23. Using a new gasket, install the intake plenum onto the intake manifold and torque the nuts/bolts to 14–19 ft. lbs.

24. Install with the wiring harness onto the retainer brackets and carefully bend the brackets toward the wire harness.

25. Install the water hose at the bottom of the intake manifold.

26. Connect the accelerator cable and install the air cleaner assembly.

27. Fill the cooling system and connect the negative battery cable.

28. Connect the fuel pump relay connector. Start the engine, allow it to reach normal operating temperatures and check for leaks and engine operation when finished.

3.0L Engine

1. Disconnect the negative battery cable and drain the cooling system.

2. Remove the air cleaner outlet hose to the throttle body.

3. Remove and mark the vacuum lines to the throttle body.

4. Remove the spark plug wires and the harnesses from the rocker cover retaining studs.

5. Remove the throttle body and release the fuel pressure.

6. Remove the fuel line safety clips and disconnect the fuel lines from the manifold.

7. Remove the fuel supply manifold and the fuel injectors.

NOTE: The injectors and the fuel supply manifold may be removed with the intake manifold as an assembly.

8. Remove the ignition coil and the rocker arm covers.

9. Disconnect the upper radiator hoses and the heater hoses.

10. Disconnect the EGR tube, if equipped. Mark and remove the distributor assembly.

11. Disconnect the engine coolant temperature sensor and remove the intake manifold retaining bolts.

12. Carefully, pry upward to loosen the intake manifold and remove by lifting up.

To install:

13. Clean the mating surfaces using care not to damage the aluminum. Lightly oil retaining bolts and stud threads.

14. Apply the proper sealant to the intersection of the cylinder block end rails and cylinder head.

15. Install the front and rear manifold end seals. Position the manifold gaskets into place.

NOTE: The gaskets are marked TO INTAKE MANIFOLD which faces the intake manifold sealing surfaces. Insert the locking tabs over the cylinder head gasket.

16. Carefully, lower the intake manifold into position to prevent smearing the silicone sealer.

17. Install the retaining bolts and tighten in numerical sequence in 2 steps; first step 11 ft. lbs. and second step 18 ft. lbs.

18. Install the fuel supply manifold and injectors, if removed. Install the fuel supply manifold retaining bolts and tighten to 7 ft. lbs.

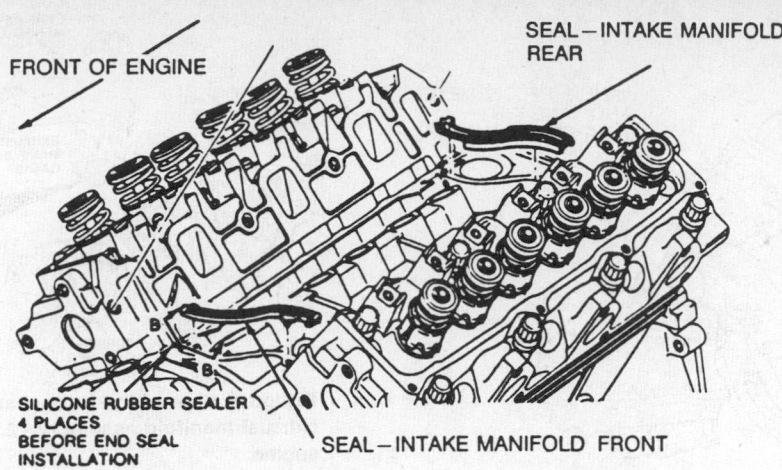

FRONT OF ENGINE

SEAL—INTAKE MANIFOLD REAR

SILICONE RUBBER SEALER
4 PLACES
BEFORE END SEAL
INSTALLATION

SEAL—INTAKE MANIFOLD FRONT

Front and rear intake manifold seal location—3.0L engine

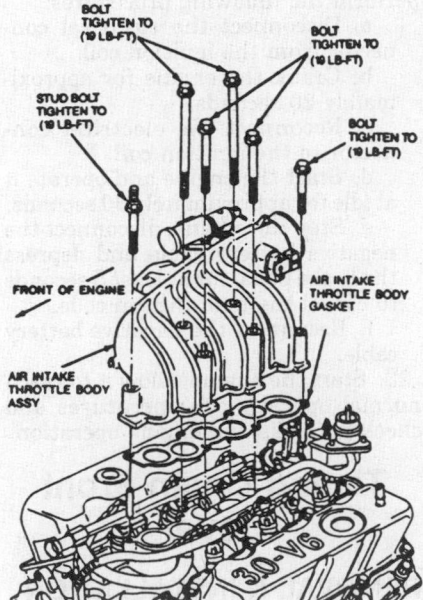

BOLT TIGHTEN TO (19 LB-FT)

BOLT TIGHTEN TO (19 LB-FT)

STUD BOLT TIGHTEN TO (19 LB-FT)

BOLT TIGHTEN TO (19 LB-FT)

FRONT OF ENGINE

AIR INTAKE THROTTLE BODY GASKET

AIR INTAKE THROTTLE BODY ASSY

3.0-V6

Air intake throttle body mounting— 3.0L engine

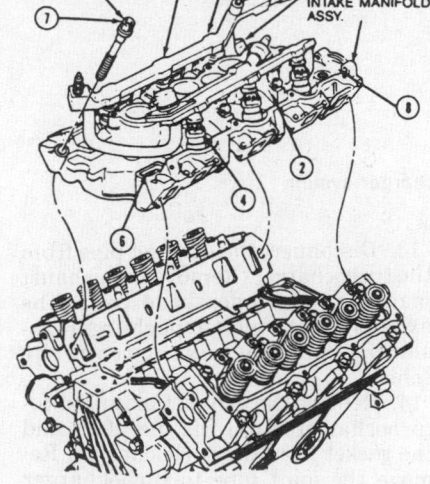

INTAKE MANIFOLD ATTACHING BOLT

INTAKE MANIFOLD ASSY.

Intake manifold bolt tightening sequence —3.0L engine

19. Install the thermostat housing and gasket, if removed.
20. Install the rocker arm covers and new gaskets.
21. Align the mark and install the distributor. Install the fuel injector harness.
22. Replace the spark plug wires, install the radiator hoses and heater hoses.
23. Install the throttle body and EGR tube and nut, if equipped.
24. Install the fuel line and the fuel line safety clips.
25. Install all the vacuum lines, ignition coil and the bracket.
26. Install the air cleaner outlet flex hose to the throttle body and connect all the electrical connections.
27. Fill and bleed the cooling system with the specified coolant.

NOTE: This engine has aluminum components and requires a special corrosion inhibited coolant.

28. Connect the negative battery terminal and check all fluid levels.
29. Start the engine and check for any leaks. Check timing and engine idle.

Exhaust Manifold

REMOVAL & INSTALLATION

2.2L Engine

1. Disconnect the negative battery cable.
2. Remove the turbocharger assembly, if equipped.
3. Remove the oxygen sensor from

the exhaust manifold on non-turbocharged vehicles.
4. Disconnect the exhaust pipe from the exhaust manifold and remove the heat shield.
5. Remove the exhaust manifold-to-cylinder head bolts and the exhaust manifold.
6. Remove the inner heat shield and the gaskets.
7. Clean the mating surfaces on the exhaust manifold and the cylinder head.

To install:
8. Position the inner heat shield on the studs
9. Install the exhaust manifold gaskets with the raise edge of the gasket facing the exhaust manifold.
10. Install the exhaust manifold and tighten the bolts to 16–21 ft. lbs.
11. Install the outer heat shield and tighten the bolts to 14–22 ft. lbs.
12. Install the exhaust gas oxygen sensor on non-turbocharged vehicles.
13. Install the turbocharger assembly, if equipped.
14. Connect the exhaust pipe to the exhaust manifold, using a new gasket. Tighten the bolts to 23–34 ft. lbs.
15. Connect the exhaust oxygen sensor wire and replace the negative battery cable.

3.0L Engine

1. Disconnect the negative battery cable. Raise and safely support the vehicle.
2. Remove the oil dipstick tube, support bracket and the heat shield retaining nuts.
3. Remove the exhaust manifold to front exhaust pipe mounting bolts.
4. Remove the EGR supply tube from the exhaust manifold, if equipped.
5. Remove the spark plugs and the heat shield retaining nuts on the right hand manifold.
6. Lower the vehicle. Remove the exhaust manifold mounting bolts and the exhaust manifold.
7. Installation is the reverse of the removal procedure. Tighten the following to the proper torque:
   a. Tighten the exhaust manifold mounting bolts to 15–22 ft. lbs.
   b. Tighten the exhaust pipe to manifold mounting bolts to 16–24 ft. lbs.
   c. Tighten the heat shield retaining nuts to 11–15 ft. lbs.

Turbocharger

REMOVAL & INSTALLATION

1. Disconnect the negative battery cable.
2. Drain the cooling system to a lev-

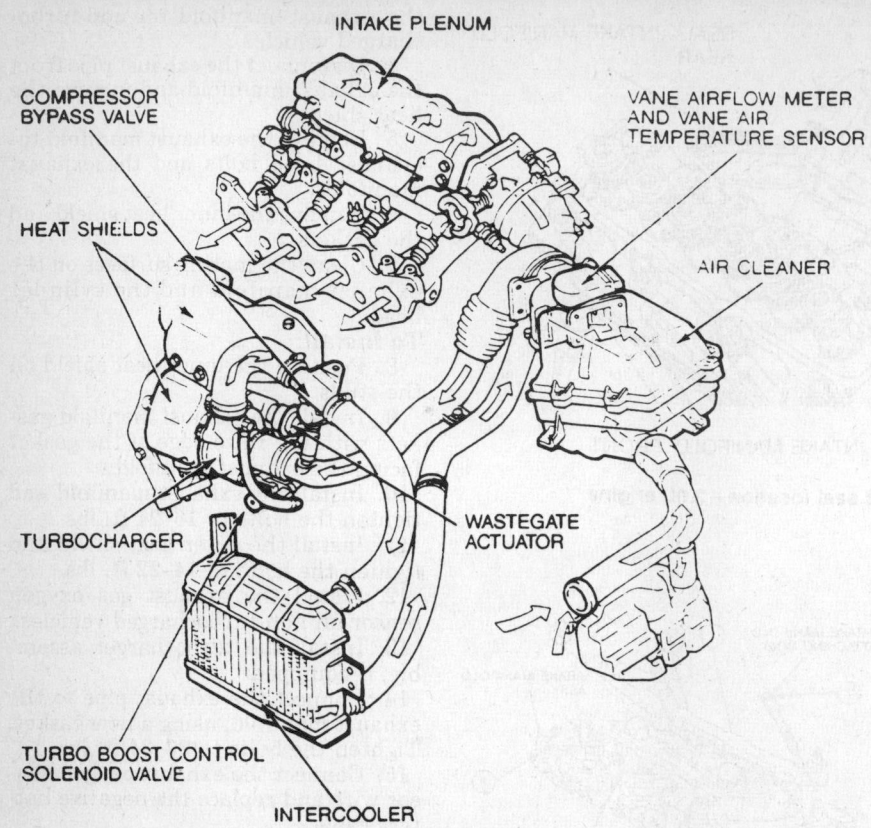

View of the turbocharger system

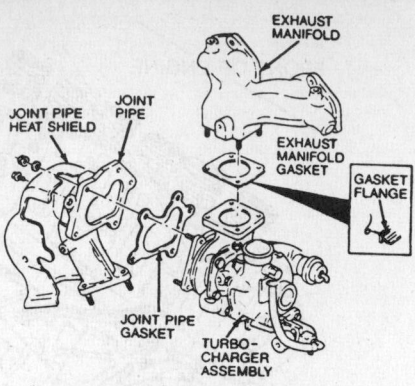

Exploded view of the turbocharger/exhaust manifold assembly—2.2L engine

el below the turbocharger.

3. Remove the air inlet and outlet hoses from the turbocharger's compressor.

4. Remove the heat shields from the exhaust manifold and turbocharger.

5. From above the distributor, disconnect the Exhaust Gas Oxygen sensor (EGO) electrical connector and place the wire over the front of the vehicle (away from the heat shield).

6. From the top of the turbocharger, remove the oil feed line. From the lower portion of the turbocharger, remove oil return line and gasket.

7. Label and disconnect the coolant inlet and outlet hoses from the turbocharger.

8. From the exhaust manifold, remove the EGR tube. From the air bypass valve joint pipe area, disconnect the turbo boost control solenoid valve electrical connector.

9. From the turbo boost control solenoid valve at the turbocharger outlet air hose, remove the air tube.

10. From under the turbocharger, remove the retaining bracket-to-turbocharger bolt.

11. Discharge the air conditioning system and remove the refrigerant line from the head of the compressor.

12. Remove the Exhaust Gas Oxygen sensor (EGO) from the exhaust manifold.

13. Disconnect the exhaust pipe from the turbocharger. Remove the exhaust manifold-to-cylinder head bolts, the exhaust manifold/turbocharger assembly and the gasket from the vehicle.

14. Remove the exhaust manifold-to-turbocharger nuts, the manifold and the gasket from the turbocharger. Remove the joint pipe-to-turbocharger nuts, the pipe and the gasket from the turbocharger.

15. Clean the gasket mounting surfaces.

To install:

16. Using a new gasket, install the joint pipe on the turbocharger and torque the nuts to 27–46 ft. lbs.

17. Using a new gasket, install exhaust manifold on the turbocharger and torque the nuts to 20–29 ft. lbs.

18. Using a new gasket, position the exhaust manifold/turbocharger assembly onto the cylinder head and torque the nuts to 16–21 ft. lbs.

19. Using a new gasket, install the exhaust pipe to the turbocharger and torque the nuts to 23–34 ft. lbs.

20. Install the coolant lines and oil return line to the turbocharger. Using 0.85 oz. of engine oil, insert it through the turbocharger oil feed passage.

21. To complete the installation, reverse the removal procedures. Refill the cooling system. Recharge the air

conditioning system.

22. After replacing the turbocharger, perform the following procedures:

a. Disconnect the electrical connector from the ignition coil.

b. Crank the engine for approximately 20 seconds.

c. Reconnect the electrical connector to the ignition coil.

d. Start the engine and operate it at idle for approximately 30 seconds.

e. Stop the engine, disconnect the negative battery cable and depress the brake pedal for at least 5 seconds to cancel the malfunction code.

f. Reconnect the negative battery cable.

23. Start the engine, allow it to reach normal operating temperatures and check for leaks and engine operation.

Timing Chain Front Cover

REMOVAL & INSTALLATION

3.0L Engine

1. Disconnect the negative battery cable.

2. Remove the drive belts. Raise and safely support the vehicle.

3. Remove the right front tire and wheel assembly and the plastic inner fender shield.

4. Lower the vehicle and support the engine with a suitable jack.

5. Remove the right front engine mount, if equipped with manual transaxle, or spacer, if equipped with an automatic transaxle, from the water pump bracket.

6. Remove the right hand upper engine mount to timing cover mounting bolts.

7. Lower the floor jack, carefully, allowing the engine to rest on the remaining mounts.

8. Raise the vehicle and remove the crankshaft damper bolt.

9. Remove the damper from the

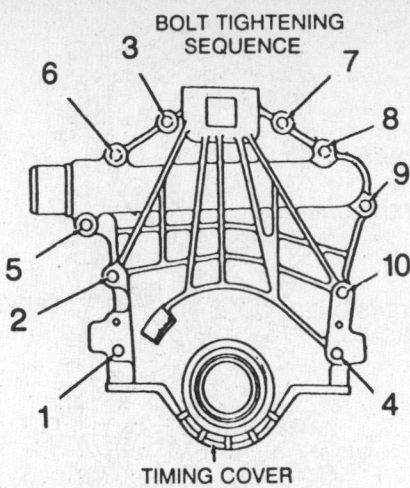

Timing cover bolt tightening sequence—3.0L engine

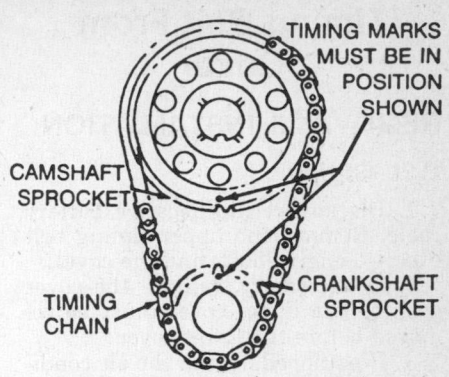

Timing mark locations—3.0L engine

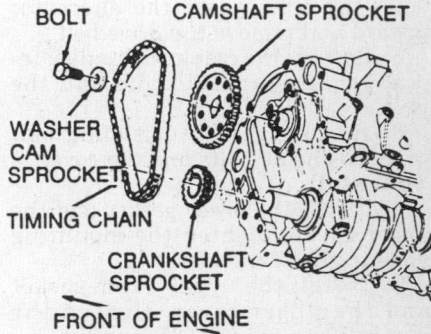

Exploded view of the timing chain assembly—3.0L engine

crankshaft using the proper tool.

10. Remove the nuts and bolt that mount the right side of the subframe to the body. This provides clearance to remove the damper.

NOTE: The damper must be carefully tipped down to clear the right hand inner fender.

11. Drain the engine oil and remove the oil pan. Remove the lowest timing cover bolts.

12. Lower the vehicle and remove the remaining timing cover bolts.

13. Carefully, pry the timing cover away from the block.

14. Remove the timing cover by pulling the cover over the end of the crankshaft and lower it through the engine compartment.

To install:

15. Clean the gasket mating surfaces on the timing cover and the cylinder block.

16. Install a new timing cover gasket over the cover locating dowels on the block.

17. Lift the cover into the engine compartment and install it on the cylinder block.

18. Install the upper mounting bolts, do not tighten. Bolt location 5 requires the application of pipe sealant on the threads of the bolt.

19. Raise and safely support the vehicle.

20. Install the lower cover bolts, do not tighten. Bolt location 2 requires the application of pipe sealant on the threads of the bolt.

21. Install the oil pan with a new gasket and tighten the bolts to 88–124 inch lbs.

22. Tighten the timing cover mounting bolts to 15–22 ft. lbs.

23. Coat the crankshaft damper sealing surface with clean engine oil. Ap-

ply proper sealant to the keyway of the damper prior to installation.

24. Install the damper with the proper tool. Replace the damper bolt with the flat washer and tighten to 92–122 ft. lbs.

25. Lower the vehicle.

26. Raise the engine, using a proper jack. Install the right hand engine mount and tighten the bolts to 55–76 ft. lbs.

27. Install the subframe nuts and bolt. Tighten the bolt to 26–40 ft. lbs. and the nuts to 68–97 ft. lbs.

28. Lower the engine and remove the jack assembly.

29. Install the spacer, if equipped with an automatic transaxle or the right engine mount, if equipped with a manual transaxle. Safely, raise the vehicle.

30. Install the water pump belt and the plastic splash shield.

31. Install the right wheel and tire assembly. Safely, lower the vehicle.

32. Install the other drive belt and the power steering pulley shield.

33. Connect the negative battery cable.

Front Cover Oil Seal

REPLACEMENT

3.0L Engine

1. Disconnect the negative battery cable.

2. Remove the crankshaft damper, using the proper tool.

3. Remove the oil seal using a suitable seal remover tool.

4. Inspect the timing cover and shaft seal for any damage.

5. Lubricate the seal lip with a suitable engine oil and install, using the proper tool.

6. Installation is the reverse of the removal procedure.

Timing Chain and Sprockets

REMOVAL & INSTALLATION

3.0L Engine

1. Disconnect the negative battery cable and drain the cooling system.

2. Remove the crankshaft pulley and damper. Remove the timing cover.

3. Rotate the crankshaft until the No.1 piston is at the Top Dead Center (TDC) and the timing marks are aligned.

4. Remove the camshaft sprocket retaining bolt and washer.

5. Slide the sprockets and the chain

forward and remove as an assembly.

6. Clean and inspect all the parts prior to installation.

To install:

7. Slide the sprockets and the chain on as as assembly with the timing marks aligned.

8. Install the camshaft retaining bolt and washer. Tighten the retaining bolt to 46 ft. lbs. and lubricate the chain and sprockets with a suitable engine oil.

NOTE: The camshaft retaining bolt has a drilled passage for timing chain lubrication. If damaged, do not replace with a standard bolt.

9. Position the timing cover gasket onto the cylinder block alignment dowels.

10. Install the timing cover onto the cylinder block. Do not damage the seal.

11. Install the oil pan using a new gasket.

12. Install the cranshaft damper and pulley.

13. Refill the crankcase and the cooling system. Connect the negative battery cable.

14. Start the engine and check for any leaks. Recheck the timimg.

Timing Belt Front Cover

REMOVAL & INSTALLATION

2.2L Engine

1. Disconnect the negative battery cable. Remove the upper timing belt cover-to-engine bolts and the cover.

2. If neccessary, remove the cover gasket. The upper cover must be removed before the lower cover.

3. If equipped, loosen the air conditioning compressor drive belt adjusting bolt, rotate the compressor inward and remove the drive belt.

4. Loosen the alternator drive belt adjusting bolt, rotate the alternator inward and remove the drive belt.

5. Remove the crankshaft pulley-to-crankshaft sprocket bolts and the pulley.

6. Remove the lower timing belt cover-to-engine bolts and the cover.

To install:

8. Install the lower gasket and the lower cover. Tighten the mounting bolts to 61–87 inch lbs.

9. Install the upper cover gasket and the upper cover. tighten the mounting bolts to 61–87 inch lbs.

10. Install the engine mount and the nuts and dowels on the engine mount.

11. Install the crankshaft pulley and tighten the pulley-to-crankshaft sprocket bolts to 109–152 inch lbs.

12. Install the drive belts and tighten the alternator bracket bolts.

13. Reposition the air conditioning compressor and tighten the bracket bolts, if equipped.

14. Connect the negative battery cable. Run the engine and check for leaks.

OIL SEAL REPLACEMENT

1 Disconnect the negative battery cable. Remove the timing belt.

2. If equipped with a manual transaxle, place the shift lever in the **4TH** gear and firmly apply the parking brake.

3. If equipped with an automatic transaxle, remove the lower flywheel cover and install the flywheel locking tool, onto the flywheel ring.

4. Remove the crankshaft sprocket-to-crankshaft bolt, the sprocket and the key.

5. Using a small pry bar, pry the oil seal from the engine block; be careful not to score the crankshaft or the seal seat.

6. Using an oil seal installation tool or equivalent, lubricate the seal lip with engine oil and drive the new into the engine until it seats.

7. Install the crankshaft key and sprocket. Torque the crankshaft sprocket-to-crankshaft bolt to 108–116 ft. lbs.

8. To complete the installation reverse the removal procedure.

Timing Belt and Tensioner

ADJUSTMENT

2.2L Engine

1. Disconnect the negative battery cable and remove the drive belts.

2. Remove the right inner fender panel and the crankshaft pulley.

3. Remove the nuts and the dowels from the right front engine mount and safely, support the engine.

4. Remove the engine mount and the timing belt covers from the engine.

5. Remove the timing belt tensioner and the idler pulley retaining bolt.

6. Mark the direction of the rotation of the timing belt and remove the belt. Remove the spark plugs.

7. Align the camshaft and the crankshaft sprockets with the marks on the cylinder head and the oil pump housing.

8. Install the timing belt with the direction of rotation facing the same way as marked before the belt removal.

9. Install the timing belt tensioner and the idler pulley.

10. Install the engine mount on the engine and tighten the nuts.

11. Install the timing belt covers and the crankshaft pulley. Replace the spark plugs.

12. Install the right hand inner fender panel and the drive belts.

13. Connect the negative battery cable and check the timing.

REMOVAL & INSTALLATION

1. Disconnect the negative battery cable. Remove the timing belt covers.

2. Rotate the crankshaft to align the notch on the crankshaft pulley with the TDC mark on the timing cover. Make sure the No. 1 arrow mark, on the camshaft sprocket, is aligned with the pointer at the top of the rear timing belt cover; if not aligned, rotate the crankshaft 180 degrees.

NOTE: With the timing marks aligned, the No. 1 cylinder will be on the TDC of it's compression stroke.

3. Remove the timing belt tensioner spring, the tensioner pulley bolt and the pulley.

4. On the timing belt, mark an ar-

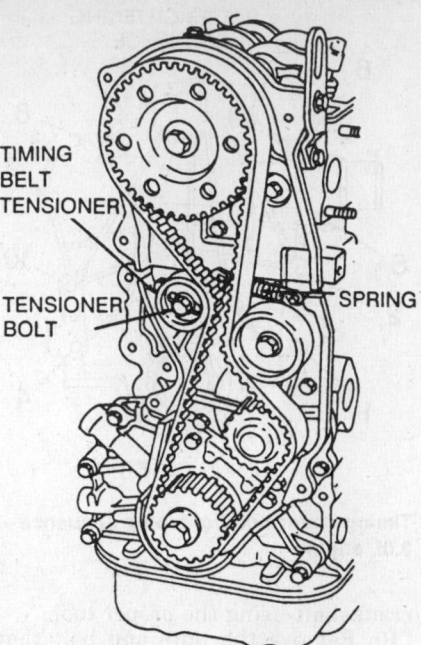

Timing belt installation—2.2L engine

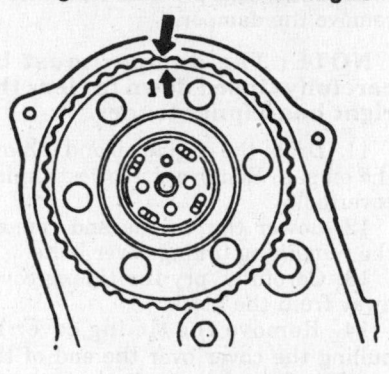

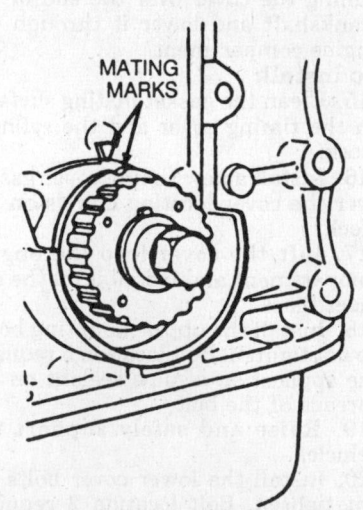

Timing mark locations—2.2L engine

row to indicate the direction of rotation. Remove the timing belt.

To install:

5. With the timing marks aligned, install the timing belt onto the sprockets.

6. Install the tensioner pulley and torque the bolt to 27–38 ft. lbs.; attach the spring. Make sure the timing belt is not loose at the water pump and idler pulley side.

7. Rotate the crankshaft 2 revolutions and realign the timing marks; if not aligned, re-perform the installation procedures.

8. Measure the timing belt deflection between the camshaft and crankshaft sprockets; if it is not 0.30–0.33 in. at 22 lbs.,
loosen the tensioner pulley bolt and repeat the adjustment or replace the tensioner.

9. Install the timing belt covers. Connect the negative battery cable.

10. Adjust the drive belt tension. Start the engine and check/adjust the engine timing.

Timing Sprockets

REMOVAL & INSTALLATION

2.2L Engine

1. Disconnect the negative battery cable. Remove the timing belt.

2. Insert a proper tool through one of the camshaft sprocket holes to lock it.

3. Remove the sprocket bolt and the sprocket from the camshaft.

4. If equipped with a manual transaxle, place the shift lever in **4th** gear and apply the parking brake. If equipped with an automatic transaxle remove the flywheel dust cover and hold the flywheel.

5. Remove the crankshaft sprocket bolt, sprocket and key.

6. Align the keyway on the sprocket with the mark on the oil pump housing.

7. Reverse the removal procedure for installation.

Camshaft

REMOVAL & INSTALLATION

2.2L Engine

1. Disconnect the negative battery cable. Remove the timing belt.

2. Remove rocker arm/shaft assemblies and the distributor.

3. Remove the camshaft sprocket by performing the following procedures:

   a. Using a small pry bar, insert it through the a hole in the camshaft sprocket (to lock it).

   b. Remove the camshaft sprocket-to-camshaft bolt and the sprocket.

4. Disconnect the electrical connectors from the thermostat housing sensors. Remove the upper radiator hose and the water bypass hose.

5. Remove the rear housing-to-cylinder head nut/bolts, the housing and gasket.

6. Remove the camshaft bearing caps and the camshaft.

7. Clean the gasket mounting surfaces. Check the camshaft for warpage, scoring and/or damage; replace it, if necessary.

To install:

8. Install the camshaft by performing the following procedures:

   a. Using new camshaft oil seals, install the camshaft and the bearing caps.

NOTE: The camshaft bearing caps and rocker arm/shaft share the same mounting bolts.

   b. Install the rocker arm/shaft assemblies onto the cylinder head and torque the rocker arm shaft-to-cylinder head bolts to 13–20 ft. lbs., using 2 steps.

NOTE: When installing the rocker arm shafts onto the cylinder head, pay attention to the notches at the ends of the shafts, they are different and cannot be interchanged.

9. Using a new rocker arm cover gasket, position it onto the cylinder head, apply silicone sealant to the shaded areas at both ends of the cylinder head and install the rocker arm cover. Torque the rocker arm cover-to-cylinder head bolts to 52–69 inch lbs.

10. Using a new gasket, install and torque the rear housing-to-cylinder head nut/bolts to 14–19 ft. lbs.

11. Install and torque the camshaft sprocket-to-camshaft bolt to 35–48 ft. lbs.

12. Install the distributor by performing the following procedures:

   a. Using engine oil, lubricate the O-ring.

   b. Align the rotor-to-distributor housing and the distributor housing-to-cylinder head.

   c. Install the distributor and make sure to engage the drive dog with the camshaft slot. Tighten the distributor hold-down bolts finger tight.

13. Using a new gasket, torque the thermostat housing-to-rear cylinder head housing nuts to 14–22 ft. lbs.

14. Connect the electrical connectors to the thermostat housing sensors.

15. Install the upper radiator hose and the bypass hose.

16. Install the timing belt.

17. Connect the negative battery cable. Refill the cooling system.

18. Start the engine and check for leak. It may be necessary to adjust the ignition base timing.

3.0L Engine

1. Disconnect the negative battery cable. Remove the engine assembly from the vehicle.

2. Remove the timing covers, rocker arm covers and the intake manifold.

3. Remove the hydraulic lifters using a magnet and keep them in order.

4. Check the camshaft endplay. If the endplay is excessive replace the thrust plate.

5. Remove the timing chain and sprockets.

6. Remove the camshaft thrust plate. Remove the camshaft by pulling it toward the front of the engine.

NOTE: Use caution to avoid damaging the bearings, journals and lobes.

7. Clean and inspect all the parts prior to installation.

To install:

8. Lubricate the camshaft lobes and the journals with a SAE 50 engine oil. Slide the camshaft through the bearings in the cylinder block.

9. Install the thrust plate and tighten the bolts to 6–8 ft. lbs.

10. Install the timing chain and sprockets. Check the camshaft sprocket bolt for blockage of drilled oil passages.

11. Install the timing cover and the crankshaft damper.

12. Lubricate the lifters and lifter bores with SAE 50 engine oil and install the lifters into their original bores.

13. Install the engine assembly and replace the negative battery cable.

14. Fill the cooling system and the crankcase with the proper fluids. Run the engine and check for leaks.

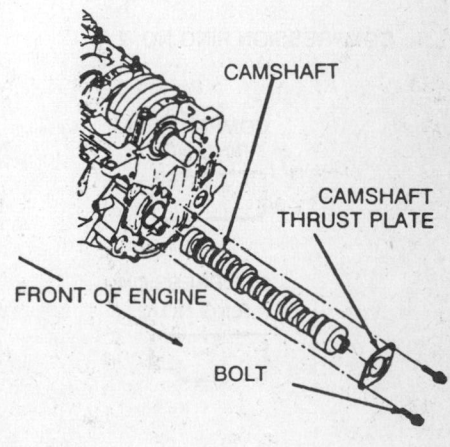

Camshaft removal—3.0L engine

Piston and Connecting Rod

POSITIONING

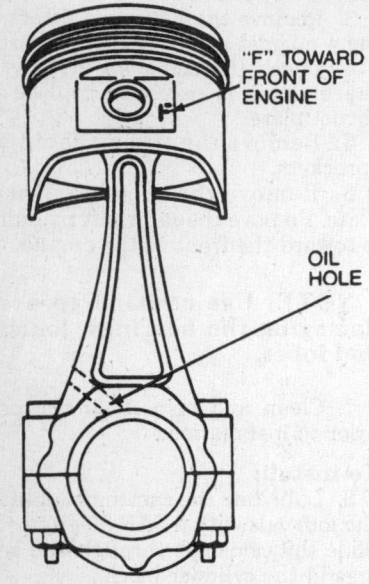

Determining the forward direction the piston and connecting rod—2.2L engine

COMPRESSION RING NO. 1

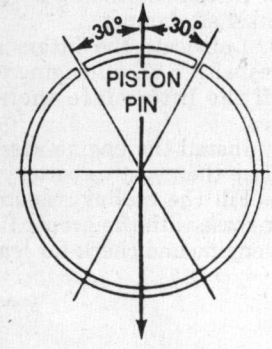

COMPRESSION RING NO. 2

COMPRESSION RING NO. 1

COMPRESSION RING NO. 2

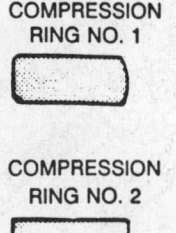

View of the compression rings positioning—2.2L engine

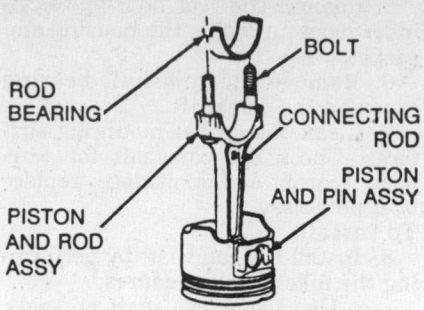

Exploded view of the piston and connecting rod—3.0L engine

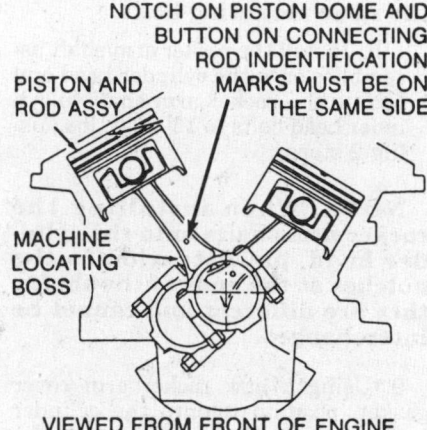

Piston location—3.0L engine

ENGINE LUBRICATION

Oil Pan

REMOVAL & INSTALLATION

2.2L Engine

1. Disconnect the negative battery cable.
2. Raise and support the vehicle, safely.
3. Remove the right wheel and the right inner splash shield.
4. Drain the crankcase.
5. Remove the engine-to-flywheel housing support bracket, the flywheel housing dust cover bolts and cover.
6. Remove the front exhaust pipe and the exhaust pipe support bracket.
7. Remove the oil pan-to-engine bolts, the oil pan, the oil pickup tube and the stiffener.
8. Clean the gasket mounting surfaces.

To install:

9. Using silicone sealant, apply a continuous bead on both sides of the stiffener, along the inside of the bolt holes.
10. Install the oil pan and tighten the mounting bolts to 69–104 inch lbs.
11. Install the flywheel housing dust cover and tighten the bolts to 49–95 inch lbs.
12. Install the flywheel housing support bracket-to-flywheel housing and tighten the bolts to 27–38 ft. lbs.
13. Tighten the flywheel housing-to-engine support bracket bolts to 27–38 ft. lbs.
14. Refill the crankcase. Start the engine and check for leaks.

3.0L Engine

1. Disconnect the negative battery cable. Raise and safely support the vehicle.
2. Drain the engine oil and remove the starter motor.
3. Remove the front and rear transaxle-to-engine braces.
4. Disconnect the low oil level sensor connector from the dash panel side of the oil pan.
5. Remove the exhaust inlet pipe from the manifolds and position it out of the way.
6. Drain the cooling system and remove the water pump.
7. Remove the water pump bracket and idler pulley tensioner.
8. Remove the mounting bolts and nuts from the front end of the right hand crossmember.
9. Loosen, but do not remove the bolts and nut from the rear end of the right hand crossmember.

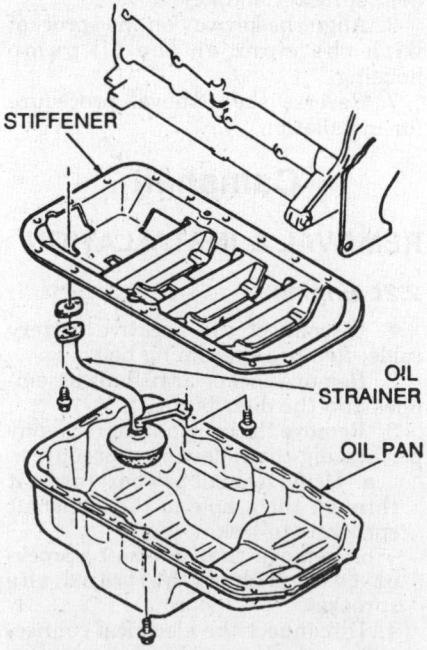

Exploded view of the oil pan, pickup tube and stiffener—2.2L engine

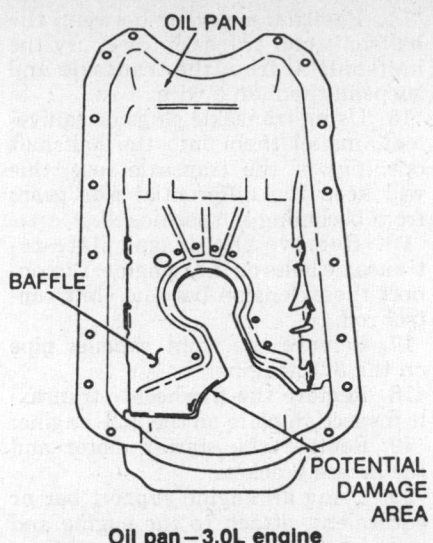

Oil pan—3.0L engine

NOTE: Allow the crossmember to drop as low as possible to allow the removal of the oil pan. If any attempt is made to remove the oil pan without lowering the cross-member first, damage to the baffle may occur. The oil pan must be pulled straight down without turning or prying it out.

10. Remove the oil pan mounting bolts and the oil pan.

To install:

11. Apply a bead of silicone sealer, or the equivalent, to the junction of the rear main bearing cap and the cylinder block and the junction of the front cover assembly and the cylinder block.

12. Position the oil pan gasket on the oil pan with the bend against the pan surface.

13. Place the oil pan on the cylinder block and tighten the mounting bolts to 71–106 ft. lbs.

14. Lift the right hand crossmember into place and tighten all the nuts and bolts.

15. Install the water pump mounting bracket and the idler pulley tensioner.

16. Install the water pump and the exhaust inlet pipe.

17. Connect the oil level sensor and install the tranaxle-to-engine braces.

18. Install the starter motor.

19. Lower the vehicle. Refill the crankcase and the cooling system.

20. Connect the negative battery cable. Run the engine and check for leaks.

Oil Pump

REMOVAL & INSTALLATION

2.2L ENGINE

1. Disconnect the negative battery cable. Raise and safely support the vehicle.

2. Remove the crankshaft sprocket. Drain the engine oil and remove the oil pan.

3. Remove the oil pump pickup tube-to-oil pump bolts, the tube and gasket.

4. Remove the oil pump-to-cylinder block bolts, the pump and gasket.

5. Using a small pry bar, pry the oil seal from the pump and clean the seal bore.

6. Clean the gasket mounting surfaces. Inspect the pump and gears for wear; if necessary, replace the parts.

To install:

7. Using a new oil seal, press it into the oil pump until it seats and lubricate the seal lip with engine oil. Install a new O-ring into the oil pump.

8. Apply a continuous bead to the oil pump gasket surface.

NOTE: When using sealant, do not allow the sealant to squeeze into the pump's outlet hole in the pump or cylinder block.

9. Install the oil pump to the cylinder block; be careful not to cut the oil seal lip. Tighten the upper oil pump-to-cylinder block bolts to 14–19 ft. lbs. and the lower oil pump-to-cylinder block bolts to 27–38 ft. lbs.

10. Using silicone sealant, apply a continuous bead on both sides of the stiffener, along the inside of the bolt holes.

11. Install the oil pan and tighten the mounting bolts to 69–104 inch lbs.

12. Install the flywheel housing dust cover and tighten the bolts to 49–95 inch lbs.

13. Install the flywheel housing support bracket-to-flywheel housing and tighten the bolts to 27–38 ft. lbs.

14. Tighten the flywheel housing-to-engine support bracket bolts to 27–38 ft. lbs.

15. Refill the crankcase. Start the engine and check for leaks.

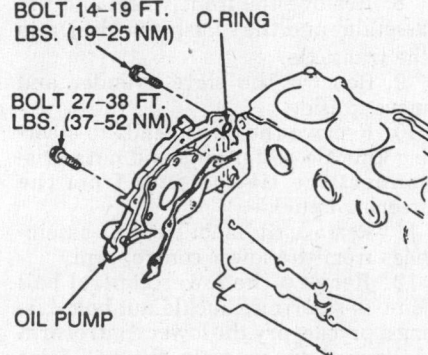

BOLT 14–19 FT. LBS. (19–25 NM)   O-RING

BOLT 27–38 FT. LBS. (37–52 NM)

OIL PUMP

Exploded view of the oil pump assembly—2.2L engine

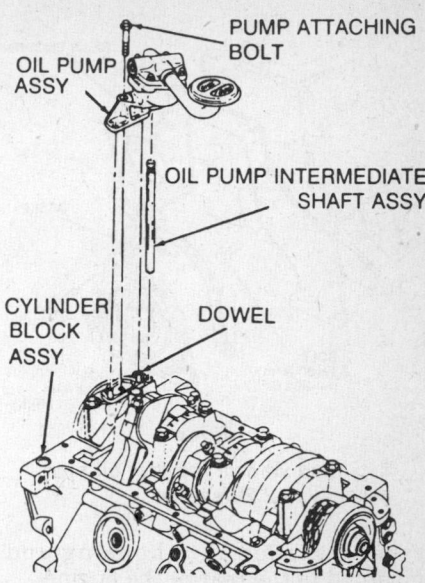

Oil pump location—3.0L engine

3.0L Engine

1. Raise and support the vehicle, safely. Drain the engine oil.

2. Remove the oil pan and the oil pump mounting bolt.

3. Remove the oil pump and the intermediate shaft from the rear main bearing cap.

4. Pull the intermediate shaft out of the oil pump.

5. Insert the pump intermediate shaft into the drive hole in the pump assembly until it clicks into place.

6. Pour a small amount of clean oil into the outlet hole in the body of the oil pump.

7. Lift the oil pump assembly into place guiding the intermediate shaft through the hole in the rear of the main bearing cap. Seat the pump securely on the locating dowels.

8. Install the pump mounting bolt and tighten to 30–41 ft. lbs.

9. Install the oil pan.

10. Lower the vehicle and refill the crankcase. Run the engine and check for leaks.

CHECKING

3.0L Engine

Measure the inner rotor tip clearance. Inner to outer rotor tip clearance must not exceed 0.010 inch with the feeler gauge inserted ½ inch minimum and the rotors removed from the pump housing.

Rear Main Bearing Oil Seal

The rear main oil seal is a solid ring

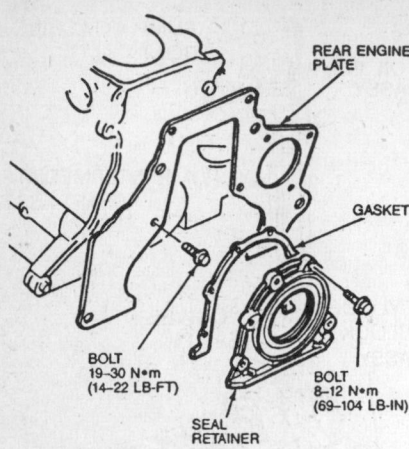

BOLT
19–30 N•m
(14–22 LB-FT)

SEAL
RETAINER

REAR ENGINE
PLATE

GASKET

BOLT
8–12 N•m
(69–104 LB-IN)

Exploded view of the rear oil seal assembly—2.2L engine

type, installed in a housing and mounted to the rear of the engine.

REMOVAL & INSTALLATION

1. Disconnect the negative battery cable.
2. Raise and support the vehicle, safely. Remove the transaxle assembly.
3. If equipped with a manual transaxle assembly, perform the following procedures:
   a. Matchmark the pressure plate to the flywheel.
   b. Remove the pressure plate-to-flywheel bolts, a little at a time to release the spring pressure at the pressure plate and the clutch plate.
   c. Remove the flywheel-to-crankshaft bolts and the flywheel.
4. If equipped with a flexplate, remove the flexplate-to-crankshaft bolts, the flexplate and shim plates.
5. Remove the rear oil seal housing-to-engine bolts, the rear oil seal-to-oil pan bolts, the housing and the gasket.
6. Using a small prybar, pry the oil seal from the oil seal housing. Clean the gasket mounting surfaces.
To install:
7. Using a new oil seal, face the seal's hollow side toward the engine and press it into the oil seal housing until it seats. Lubricate the seal lip with engine oil.
8. Apply sealant to the rear oil seal housing-to-oil pan surface.
9. Using a new gasket, install the rear oil seal housing and torque the seal housing-to-engine bolts to 69–104 inch lbs. on the 2.2L engine.
10. Install the flywheel, if equipped with a manual transaxle or flexplate, if equipped with an automatic transaxle to crankshaft bolts to 71–76 ft. lbs. on the 2.2L engine and 54–64 ft. lbs. on the 3.0L engine.
11. If equipped with a clutch plate,

perform the following procedures:
   a. Insert a clutch plate alignment tool into the pilot bearing.
   b. Position the clutch plate onto the alignment tool.
   c. Install the pressure plate, align the matchmark and torque the pressure plate-to-flywheel bolts to 16–24 ft. lbs. on the 2.2L engine and 12–24 ft. lbs. on the 3.0L engine.
12. Install the transaxle assembly. Lower the vehicle.

MANUAL TRANSAXLE

For further information on transmissions/transaxles, please refer to "Chilton's Guide to Transmission Repair".

Transaxle Assembly

REMOVAL & INSTALLATION

1. Disconnect the battery cables, negative cable first. Remove the battery and the battery tray.
2. Disconnect the main fuel block and coil wire from the distributor.
3. Disconnect the electrical connector from the air flow meter and remove the air cleaner assembly.
4. On 2.2L EFI engine, remove the resonance chamber and bracket. On 2.2L turbocharged engine, remove the throttle body-to-intercooler air hose and the air cleaner-to-turbocharger air hose.
5. Disconnect the speedometer cable (analog) or harness (digital).
6. Drain the engine coolant and close the drain valve. Remove the upper radiator hoses on 3.0L engine.
7. Disconnect both ground wires from the transaxle. Raise and safely support the vehicle.
8. Remove the front wheel and tire assembly and the splash shields. Drain the transaxle.
9. Remove the slave cylinder and move it aside.
10. Remove the tie rod ends-to-steering knuckle cotter pins and nuts. Disconnect the tie rod ends from the steering knuckle.
11. Remove the stabilizer link assemblies from the lower control arm.
12. Remove the lower control ball joint-to-steering knuckle nut/bolt. Using a prybar, pry the lower control arm downward to separate the ball joint from the steering knuckle.
13. At the right halfshaft, remove the halfshaft-to-engine bracket.

14. Position a prybar between the halfshaft and transaxle case; pry the halfshaft(s) from the transaxle and suspend them on a wire.
15. Using transaxle plugs or equivalent, install them into the halfshaft openings of the transaxle case; this will keep the differential side gears from becoming mispositioned.
16. Remove the gusset plate-to-transaxle bolts on 2.2L engine. Disconnect the extension bar and shift control rod.
17. Remove the front exhaust pipe on the 3.0L engine.
18. Remove the flywheel-to-transaxle inspection plate on the 2.2L engine.
19. Remove the starter motor and the access brackets.
20. Using an engine support bar or equivalent, attach to the engine and support it's weight.
21. Remove the center transaxle mount/bracket, the left transaxle mount and the right transaxle mount-to-frame nut/bolt.
21. Remove the crossmember and the left lower arm as an assembly.
22. Using a transmission jack or equivalent, attach it to the transaxle.
23. Remove the transaxle-to-engine bolts, lower the transaxle and remove it from the vehicle.
To install:
24. Using clutch grease, apply a small amount to the input shaft splines.
25. Raise and position the transaxle. Install the transaxle-to-engine bolts and torque to 66–86 ft. lbs.
26. Install the center transaxle mount/bracket and torque the bolts to 27–40 ft. lbs. and the nuts to 47–66 ft. lbs.; do not install the throttle air hose bracket nut.
27. Install the left transaxle mount and torque the left transaxle-to-mount bolts on the 2.2L EFI engine to 27–38 ft. lbs. and on the 2.2L turbocharged engine and 3.0L engine to 49–69 ft. lbs. Torque the mount-to-bracket nut and bolt to 49–69 ft. lbs.
28. Install the crossmember and the left side arm as an assembly. Tighten the bolts to 27–40 ft. lbs. and the nuts to 55–69 ft. lbs.
29. Install the right transaxle mount bolt and nut and tighten to 63–86 ft. lbs.
30. Install the starter motor and access brackets.
31. Install the flywheel inspection cover on 2.2L engine only. Tighten the bolts to 69–95 ft. lbs.
32. Connect the extension rod and control rod. Replace the front exhaust pipe on 3.0L engine.
33. Install the slave cylinder and tighten the bolts to 14–19 ft. lbs.
34. Install the gusset plate-to-transaxle bolts and tighten to 27–38 ft. lbs.

on the 2.2L engine.

35. On the end of each halfshaft, install a new retaining clip.

36. Remove the transaxle plugs and install the halfshaft until the retaining clips snap into place.

37. Install and torque the tie rod end-to-steering knuckle nut to 22–33 ft. lbs. and the lower control arm ball joint-to-steering knuckle nut and bolt to 32–40 ft. lbs.

38. Install the stabilizer link assembly-to-lower control arm. Turn the upper nuts (on each assembly) until 1.0 inch of the bolt can be measured above the nuts. When the length is reached, secure the upper nut and torque the lower nut to 12–17 ft. lbs.

39. Install the splash shields and the front wheels; torque the lug nuts to 65–87 ft. lbs. Lower the vehicle.

40. On 2.2L engine, install the resonance chamber and bracket; torque to 69–95 inch lbs. On turbocharged engines, install the throttle body-to-intercooler air hose and torque the bracket-to-mount bolt to 47–66 ft. lbs.

41. Connect the electrical connector to the air flow meter and install the air cleaner assembly.

42. Reconnect the main fuel block and the coil wire to the distributor.

43. Install the battery tray, battery and connect the battery cables.

44. Refill the transaxle assembly. Start the engine and check for leaks.

CLUTCH

Clutch Assembly

REMOVAL & INSTALLATION

1. Disconnect the negative battery cable. Raise and support the vehicle, safely. Remove the transaxle.

2. Using a clutch alignment tool or equivalent, position it through the pressure plate, clutch plate and into the pilot bushing; this will keep the assembly from dropping.

3. Using paint or chalk, matchmark the pressure plate-to-flywheel position.

4. Remove the pressure plate-to-flywheel bolts, a little at a time, evenly, to relieve the spring pressure.

5. Remove the pressure plate, clutch disc and alignment tool from the engine.

6. Inspect the parts for wear, damage and/or cracks; replace the parts, if necessary.

To install:

7. Using clutch grease, apply a small amount to the clutch disc and in-

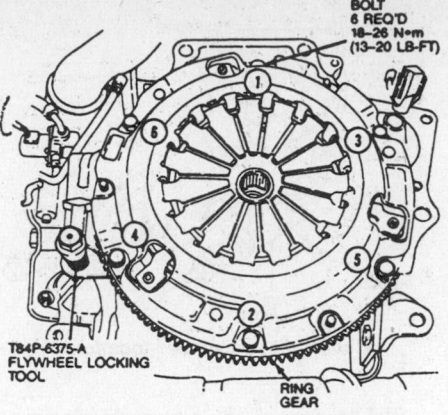

Clutch and flywheel assembly

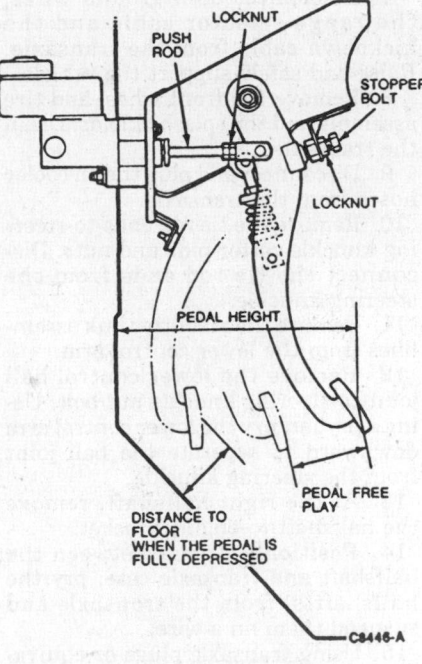

Clutch pedal adjustment

put shaft splines.

8. Install the clutch plate and alignment tool.

9. Align the pressure plate to the flywheel matchmark. Install the pressure plate-to-flywheel bolts and torque, evenly, a little at a time, to 13–20 ft. lbs.

10. Install the transaxle assembly and lower the vehicle.

11. Connect the negative battery cable. Check fluid levels .

PEDAL HEIGHT/FREE-PLAY ADJUSTMENT

Pedal height

1. To determine if the pedal height requires an adjustment, measure the distance from the bulkhead to the up-

per center of the pedal pad. The distance should be 8.524–8.720 inch.

2. To adjust, remove the lower dash panel and the air ducts.

3. Loosen the locknut and turn the stopper bolt until the desired pedal height is reached.

4. Tighten the locknut.

5. Install the ducts and the lower dash panel.

Pedal Free-play

1. To determine if the pedal free-play needs adjustment, measure the free-play. The free-play should be 0.20–0.51 inch.

2. To adjust, remove the lower dash panel and the air ducts.

3. Loosen the locknut and turn the pushrod until the pedal play is within specifications.

4. Measure the distance from the floor to the center of the pedal pad when the pedal is fully depressed. The distance should be 2.7 inch or more.

5. Tighten the locknut and replace the lower dash panel and the air ducts.

Clutch Master Cylinder

REMOVAL & INSTALLATION

1. Disconnect the negative battery cable. Remove the ABS relay box, if equipped.

2. Disconnect the pressure line to the cylinder, using the proper wrench.

3. Remove the mounting nuts and remove the clutch master cylinder.

4. Install the clutch master cylinder and tighten the mounting nuts to 14–19 ft. lbs.

5. Connect the pressure line and tighten the nut securely.

6. Install the ABS relay box, if equipped.

7. Bleed the air from the clutch system and road test the vehicle.

8. Connect the negative battery cable.

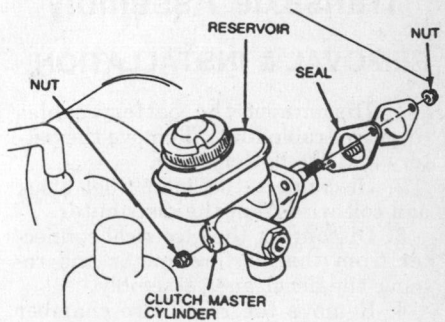

Exploded view of clutch master cylinder

Clutch Slave Cylinder

REMOVAL & INSTALLATION

1. Disconnect the negative battery cable.
2. Disconnect the pressure line at the slave cylinder. Plug the pressure line to prevent leaking.
3. Remove the slave cylinder mounting bolts and remove the slave cylinder.
4. Install the slave cylinder and tighten the mounting bolts to 10–16 ft. lbs.
5. Connect the negative battery cable. Refill before bleeding.
6. Bleed the air from the clutch system and road test the vehicle.

Hydraulic Clutch System Bleeding

1. Remove the bleeder cap from the slave cylinder and attach a vinyl hose to the bleeder screw.
2. Place the other end of the hose in a container.
3. Slowly, pump the clutch pedal a couple times. Refill before bleeding.
4. With the clutch pedal depressed, loosen the bleeder screw to release the fluid and air.
5. Tighten the bleeder screw. Repeat this procedure until there are no air bubbles in the fluid in the container.

AUTOMATIC TRANSAXLE

For further information on transmissions/transaxles, please refer to "Chilton's Guide to Transmission Repair".

Transaxle Assembly

REMOVAL & INSTALLATION

1. Disconnect the battery cables (negative cable first). Remove the battery and the battery tray.
2. Disconnect the main fuel block and coil wire from the distributor.
3. Disconnect the electrical connector from the air flow meter and remove the air cleaner assembly.
4. Remove the resonance chamber and bracket.
5. Disconnect the speedometer cable (analog) or harness (digital).

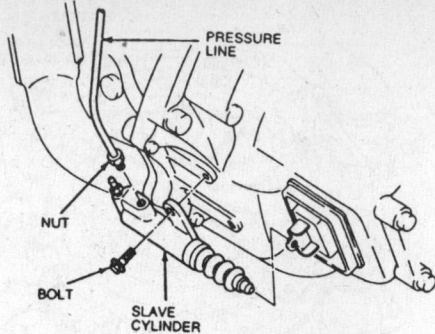

Clutch slave cylinder location

6. Disconnect the transaxle electrical connectors and separate the harness from the transaxle clips.
7. Disconnect both ground wires, the range selector cable and the kickdown cable from the transaxle. Raise and safely support the vehicle.
8. Remove the front wheel and tire assembly and the splash shields. Drain the transaxle.
9. Disconnect and plug the oil cooler hoses from the transaxle.
10. Remove the tie rod ends-to-steering knuckle cotter pins and nuts. Disconnect the tie rod ends from the steering knuckle.
11. Remove the stabilizer link assemblies from the lower control arm.
12. Remove the lower control ball joint-to-steering knuckle nut/bolt. Using a prybar, pry the lower control arm downward to separate the ball joint from the steering knuckle.
13. At the right halfshaft, remove the halfshaft-to-engine bracket.
14. Position a prybar between the halfshaft and transaxle case; pry the halfshaft(s) from the transaxle and suspend them on a wire.
15. Using transaxle plugs or equivalent, install them into the halfshaft openings of the transaxle case; this will keep the differential side gears from becoming mispositioned.
16. Remove the gusset plate-to-transaxle bolts.
17. Remove the torque converter-to-transaxle cover, the starter and the access brackets.
18. Using paint or chalk, matchmark the torque converter-to-flexplate position.
19. Using an engine support bar or equivalent, attach to the engine and support it's weight.
20. Remove the center transaxle mount/bracket, the left transaxle mount and the right transaxle mount-to-frame nut/bolt.
21. Remove the crossmember and the left lower arm as an assembly.
22. Using a transmission jack or equivalent, attach it to the transaxle.
23. Using a prybar, position it be-

tween the torque converter and flexplate; pry the torque converter off the studs and move it into the transaxle.
24. Remove the transaxle-to-engine bolts, lower the transaxle and remove it from the vehicle.

To install:

25. Raise and position the transaxle, align the torque converter-to-flexplate matchmark and studs. Install the transaxle-to-engine bolts and torque to 66–86 ft. lbs.
26. Install the center transaxle mount/bracket and torque the bolts to 27–40 ft. lbs. and the nuts to 47–66 ft. lbs.; do not install the throttle air hose bracket nut.
27. Install the left transaxle mount. Tighten the transaxle-to-mount nut to 63–86 ft. lbs. Tighten the mount-to-bracket bolt and nut to 49–69 ft. lbs.
28. Install the crossmember and left lower arm as an assembly. Tighten the bolts to 27–40 ft. lbs. and the nuts to 55–69 ft. lbs.
29. Install the right transaxle mount bolt and nut. Tighten to 63–86 ft. lbs.
30. Install the starter motor and access brackets.
31. Install the torque converter nuts and tighten to 32–45 ft. lbs.
32. Install the torque converter cover and tighten the bolts to 69–95 inch lbs.
33. Install the gusset plate-to-tranaxle bolts and tighten to 27–38 ft. lbs.
34. On the end of each halfshaft, install a new retaining clip.
35. Remove the transaxle plugs and install the halfshaft until the retaining clips snap into place.
36. Attach the lower ball joints to the steering knuckle.
37. Install the tie rods and tighten to 22–33 ft. lbs.
38. Install the bolts and nuts to the lower arm ball joints and tighten to 32–40 ft. lbs.
39. Install the stabilizer link assembly-to-lower control arm. Turn the upper nuts (on each assembly) until 1.0 inch (25.4mm) of the bolt can be measured above the nuts. When the length is reached, secure the upper nut and torque the lower nut to 12–17 ft. lbs.
40. Install the oil cooler hoses to the transaxle.
41. Install the splash shields and the front wheels; torque the lug nuts to 65–87 ft. lbs.
42. Connect and adjust the kickdown cable. Connect the range selector cable and torque the bolt to 22–29 ft. lbs.
43. Install the resonance chamber and bracket; torque to 69–95 inch lbs.
44. Connect the electrical connectors and attach the harness to the transaxle clips
45. Connect the speedometer or har-

ness, if equipped.

46. Install the air filter assemby and connect the air flow meter connector

47. Connect the center distributor terminal lead and main fuse block.

48. Install the battery carrier and the battery. Connect the battery cables.

49. Install the engine support bracket.

50. Refill the transaxle and check for leaks.

SHIFT CABLE ADJUSTMENT

1. Disconnect the negative battery cable. Shift the gear selector to the **P** detent.

2. Remove the selector lever mounting screws and remove the selector knob.

3. Remove the selector trim piece and the indicator mounting screws.

4. Disconnect the shift control switch and programmed ride control switch wiring harnesses.

5. Remove the position indicator.

NOTE: Make sure that the detent spring roller is in the P detent.

6. Loosen the nuts and the trunnion bolt.

7. Turn the transaxle-mounted shift lever clockwise to put the transaxle in the **P** position.

8. Tighten the rear nut (A) by hand until it contacts the spacer, then an additional ½ turn.

9. Tighten the trunnion bolt to 67–96 inch lbs. Tighten the front nut (B) to 67–96 inch lbs.

10. Lightly, press the selector pushrod and make sure that the guide plate and guide pin clearances are within specifications.

11. Check that the guide pin clearances are within the specifications when the selector lever is shifted to **N** and **D**.

12. Connect the illumination bulb.

13. Connect the shift control switch and the programmed ride control switch wiring harnesses.

14. Install the position indicator and tighten the mounting screws.

15. Install the selector trim piece and position the selector knob. Tighten the knob screws.

16. Connect the negative battery cable.

THROTTLE LINKAGE ADJUSTMENT

1. Warm the engine to operating temperature and confirm that the engine is running within idle specifications.

2. Measure the free-play at the ac-celerator pedal. The free-play should be 0.04–0.12 inch.

3. To adjust, loosen the locknut and adjust at the cable housing bracket located near the throttle body.

4. Tighten the locknut and adjust the wide open throttle position.

DETENT CABLE ADJUSTMENT

1. From the left front wheel well, remove the splash shield.

2. At the transaxle, remove the square head plug, marked **L**, and install an adapter and a pressure gauge in the hole.

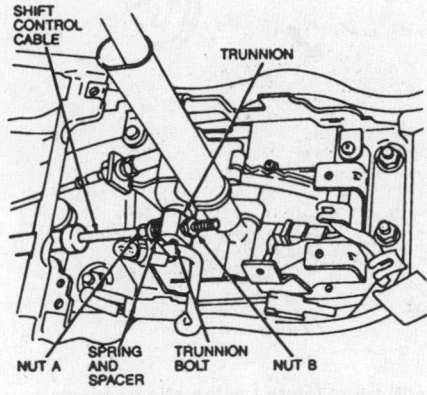

Shift cable adjustment

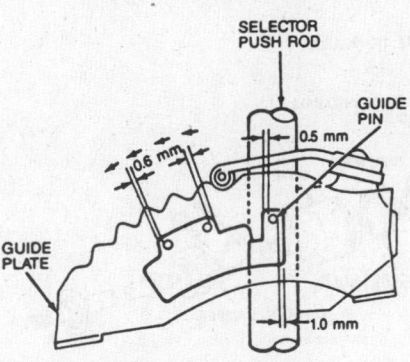

Guide pin clearances

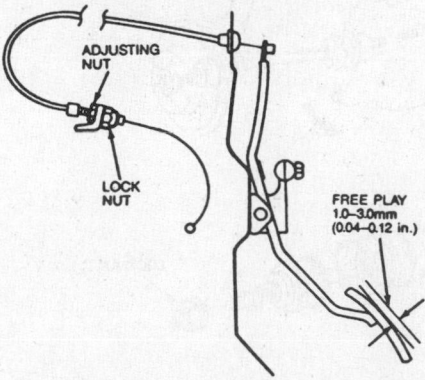

Throttle cable adjustment—2.2L engine

3. Rotate the kickdown cable locknuts to the furthest point from the throttle cam to loosen the cable all the way.

4. Place the transaxle into the **P** position and warm the engine; the idle speed should be 700–800 rpm.

5. Rotate the locknuts toward the throttle cam until the line pressure exceeds 63–66 psi, rotate the locknuts away from the throttle cam until the line pressure is 63–66 ft. lbs. and tighten the locknuts.

6. Turn the engine **OFF**, install the square head plug and torque to 43–87 inch lbs.

NOTE: If installing a new detent cable, fully open the throttle valve, crimp the pin with the protector installed and remove the protector.

DRIVE AXLE

Halfshaft

REMOVAL & INSTALLATION

1. Disconnect the negative battery cable. Raise and safely support the vehicle.

2. Remove the left front wheel and tire assembly, the hub grease cup and the left splash shield.

3. Remove the stabilizer link assembly from the lower control arm.

4. Using a cape chisel and a hammer, raise the staked portion of the hub nut.

5. Using an assistant to depress the brake pedal, loosen, do not remove, the hub nut.

6. Remove the lower control ball joint-to-steering knuckle nut/bolt. Using a prybar, pry the lower control arm downward to separate the ball joint from the steering knuckle.

7. Pull the steering knuckle outward.

8. Position a prybar between the halfshaft and transaxle case; pry the halfshaft from the transaxle and support it.

9. Remove and discard the hub nut. Slide the halfshaft from the steering knuckle.

NOTE: If the halfshaft binds in the hub splines, use a plastic hammer to bump it out or a wheel puller to press it out.

10. Using transaxle plugs or equivalent, install them into the halfshaft openings of the transaxle case; this will keep the differential side gears

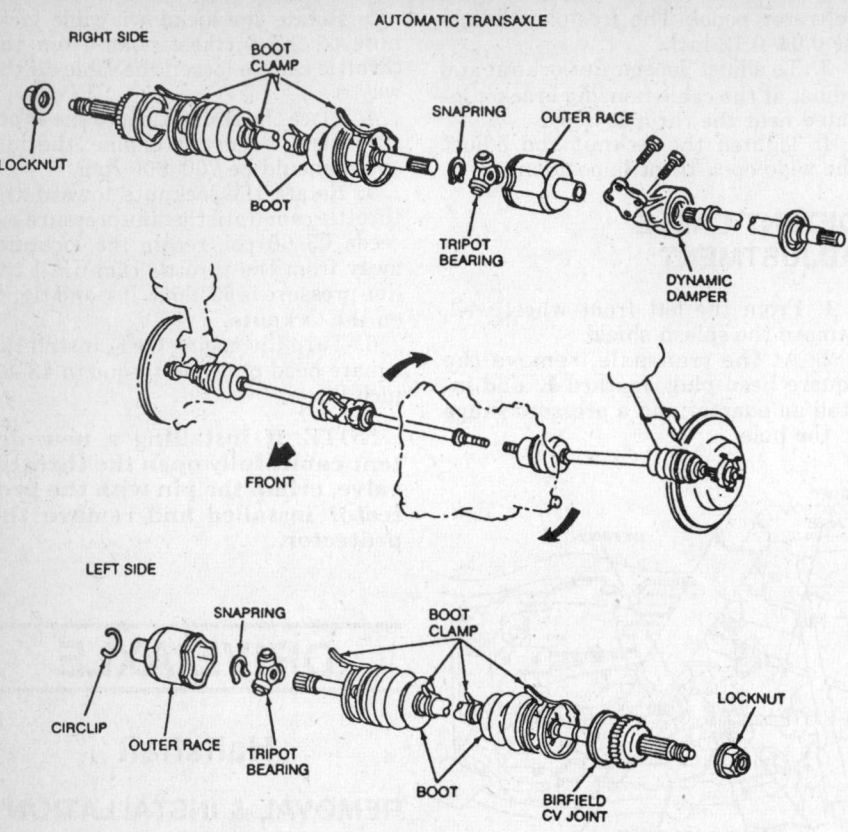

AUTOMATIC TRANSAXLE

RIGHT SIDE

LOCKNUT
BOOT CLAMP
BOOT
SNAPRING
OUTER RACE
TRIPOT BEARING
DYNAMIC DAMPER

FRONT

LEFT SIDE

SNAPRING
BOOT CLAMP
CIRCLIP
OUTER RACE
TRIPOT BEARING
BOOT
BIRFIELD CV JOINT
LOCKNUT

Exploded view of the of the halfshafts with tripot joints – automatic transaxle

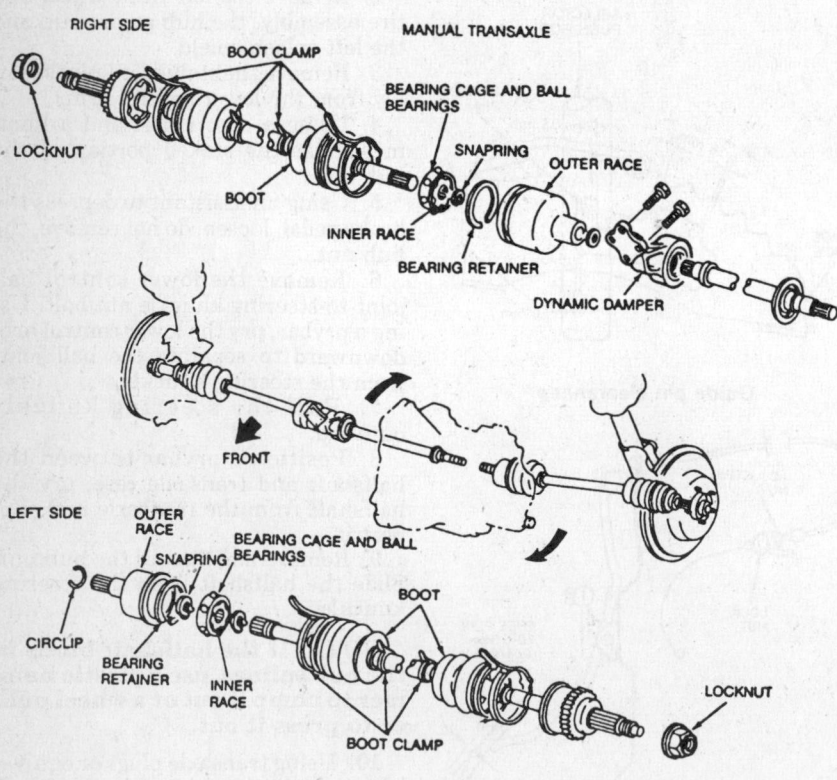

MANUAL TRANSAXLE

RIGHT SIDE

LOCKNUT
BOOT CLAMP
BOOT
BEARING CAGE AND BALL BEARINGS
SNAPRING
OUTER RACE
INNER RACE
BEARING RETAINER
DYNAMIC DAMPER

FRONT

LEFT SIDE
OUTER RACE
BEARING CAGE AND BALL BEARINGS
SNAPRING
CIRCLIP
BEARING RETAINER
INNER RACE
BOOT
LOCKNUT
BOOT CLAMP

Exploded view of the of the halfshafts with rzeppa joints – manual transaxle

from becoming mispositioned.

To install:

11. On the end of each halfshaft, install a new retaining clip.

12. Slide the halfshaft into the steering knuckle assembly.

13. Remove the transaxle plugs and install the halfshaft into the transaxle until the retaining clips snap into place.

14. Install and torque the lower control arm ball joint-to-steering knuckle nut and bolt to 32–40 ft. lbs.

15. Install the stabilizer link assembly-to-lower control arm. Turn the upper nuts (on each assembly) until 1.0 inch of the bolt can be measured above the nuts. When the length is reached, secure the upper nut and torque the lower nut to 12–17 ft. lbs.

16. Install the splash shields and the front wheels; torque the lug nuts to 65–87 ft. lbs.

17. Lower the vehicle and torque the new hub nut to 116–174 ft. lbs. Using a dull chisel, stake the hub nut.

CV-Boot

REMOVAL & INSTALLATION

Inner Boot

RZEPPA

1. Disconnect the negative battery cable. Raise and safely support the vehicle.

2. Remove the halfshaft and place it in a soft jawed vise, do not allow the vise to contact the boot.

3. Cut the inner joint boot clamps with the proper tool and move the boot rearward.

4. Using paint or chalk, matchmark the outer race to the halfshaft.

5. Using a small pry bar, pry the wire ring bearing retainer from the joint and remove the outer race.

6. Using paint or chalk, matchmark the bearing assembly to the halfshaft. Using a pair of snapring pliers, remove the outer snapring. Remove the inner race, cage and the ball bearings as an assembly.

7. Remove the boot.

8. Check the grease for grit; if necessary, clean the parts and regrease the assembly.

To install:

8. Install the new boot on the shaft; be careful not to cut the boot on the shaft splines.

9. Align the matchmarks and install the inner race, cage and ball bearings as an assembly. Install the snapring.

10. Align the matchmarks and install the outer race and the large wire snapring.

11. Position the boot over the outer race so it is extended to 3.5 in. between

the clamps. Using a dull blade prybar, lift the boot end to expell the trapped air.

12. Using new boot clamps, wrap them around the boots in a clockwise direction, pull them tight using a pair of pliers and bend the locking tabs to secure them in place.

13. Work the CV-joint through it's full range of travel at various angles; it should flex, extend and compress smoothly.

14. Install the halfshaft into the vehicle.

TRIPOT

1. Remove the halfshaft from the vehicle and position it in a soft jawed vise, do not allow the vise to contact the boot.

2. Using a pair of side cutters, cut inner joint boot clamps and move the boot rearward.

3. Using paint or chalk, matchmark the outer race to the halfshaft.

4. Using a small pry bar, pry the wire ring bearing retainer from the joint and remove the outer race.

5. Using paint or chalk, matchmark the tripot bearing to the halfshaft. Using a pair of snapring pliers, remove the outer snapring.

6. Using a brass drift and a hammer, drive the tripot bearing assembly from the halfshaft.

7. Wrap tape around the shaft splines and remove the boot.

8. Check the grease for grit; if necessary, clean the parts and regrease the assembly.

To install:

9. Install the new boot on the shaft; be careful not to cut the boot on the shaft splines.

10. Align the tripot bearing-to-halfshaft matchmarks. Using a brass drift and a hammer, drive the bearing assembly onto the halfshaft. Install the snapring.

11. Fill the CV-joint outer race with 3.5 oz. of grease.

12. Align the matchmarks and install the outer race and the large wire snapring.

13. Position the boot over the outer race so it is extended to 3.5 in. between the clamps. Using a dull blade prybar, lift the boot end to expell the trapped air.

14. Using new boot clamps, wrap them around the boots in a clockwise direction, pull them tight using a pair of pliers and bend the locking tabs to secure them in place.

15. Work the CV-joint through it's full range of travel at various angles; it should flex, extend and compress smoothly.

16. Install the halfshaft into the vehicle.

Outer Boot

The outer joint is not serviceable and must be replaced with the shaft as an assembly.

1. Remove the inner joint and boot assembly from the halfshaft.

2. Using a pair of side cutters, cut outer joint the boot clamps and remove the boot from the halfshaft.

3. Position the outer boot over the outer race so it is extended to 3.5 in. between the clamps. Using a dull blade prybar, lift the boot end to expell the trapped air.

4. Using new boot clamps, wrap them around the boots in a clockwise direction, pull them tight using a pair of pliers and bend the locking tabs to secure them in place.

5. To complete the installation, reverse the removal procedures. Install the halfshaft into the vehicle.

Rear Axle Shaft, Bearing and Seal

REMOVAL & INSTALLATION

1. Raise and support the vehicle, safely.

2. Remove the wheel and tire assembly and the grease cup.

3. Using a cape chisel and a hammer, raise the staked portion of the hub nut.

4. Remove and discard the hub nut.

5. Pull the brake drum assembly from the spindle.

6. Using a small prybar, pry the grease seal from the brake drum and discard it.

7. Remove the snapring. Using a shop press, press the wheel bearing from the brake drum.

To install:

8. Using a shop press, press the new wheel bearing into the brake drum until it seats and install the snapring.

9. Using a grease seal installation tool or equivalent, lubricate the seal lip with grease and drive it into the brake drum until it seats.

10. Position the brake drum assembly onto the wheel spindle.

11. Using a new locknut, torque it to 73–131 ft. lbs.

12. Check the wheel bearing freeplay.

13. Using a dull cold chisel, stake the locknut.

14. Install the grease cap.

15. Install the wheel and tire assembly. Lower the vehicle.

ADJUSTMENT

1. Raise and support the vehicle, safely.

2. Remove the wheel and tire as-

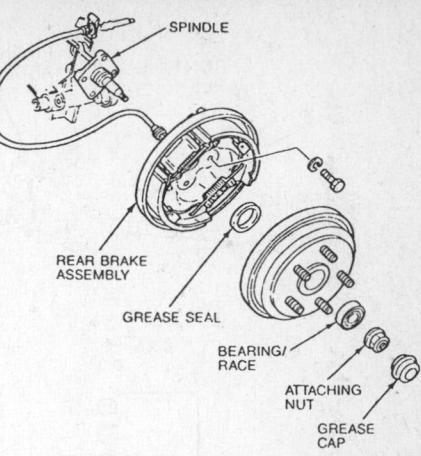

Exploded view of the rear wheel assembly

sembly and the grease cup.

3. Rotate the brake drum to make sure there is no brake drag.

4. Check the wheel bearing endplay. Endplay should not exceed 0.008 inch.

5. If the endplay exceeds the specifications, replace the wheel bearing.

Front Wheel Hub, Knuckle/Spindle and Bearings

REMOVAL & INSTALLATION

1. Raise and safely support the vehicle. Remove the front wheel and tire assembly and the grease cap.

2. Using a small cape chisel and a hammer, raise the staked portion of the hub nut.

3. Have an assistant apply the brakes and remove the hub nut (discard it).

4. Remove the stabilizer bar-to-control arm, bolt, nut, washers and bushings.

5. At the tie rod end, remove the cotter pin and nut. Using a tie rod end separator tool or equivalent, separate the tie rod end from the steering knuckle.

6. Remove the caliper support-to-steering knuckle bolts and support the caliper assembly on a wire.

7. Remove the rotor-to-hub screws and the rotor.

8. Remove the lower control arm ball joint clamp nut/bolt. Using a prybar, pry the lower control arm downward and separate the ball joint from the steering knuckle.

9. Remove the steering knuckle-to-strut nuts/bolts and slide the steering knuckle assembly from the strut bracket.

10. Slide the steering knuckle assembly from the halfshaft and support the

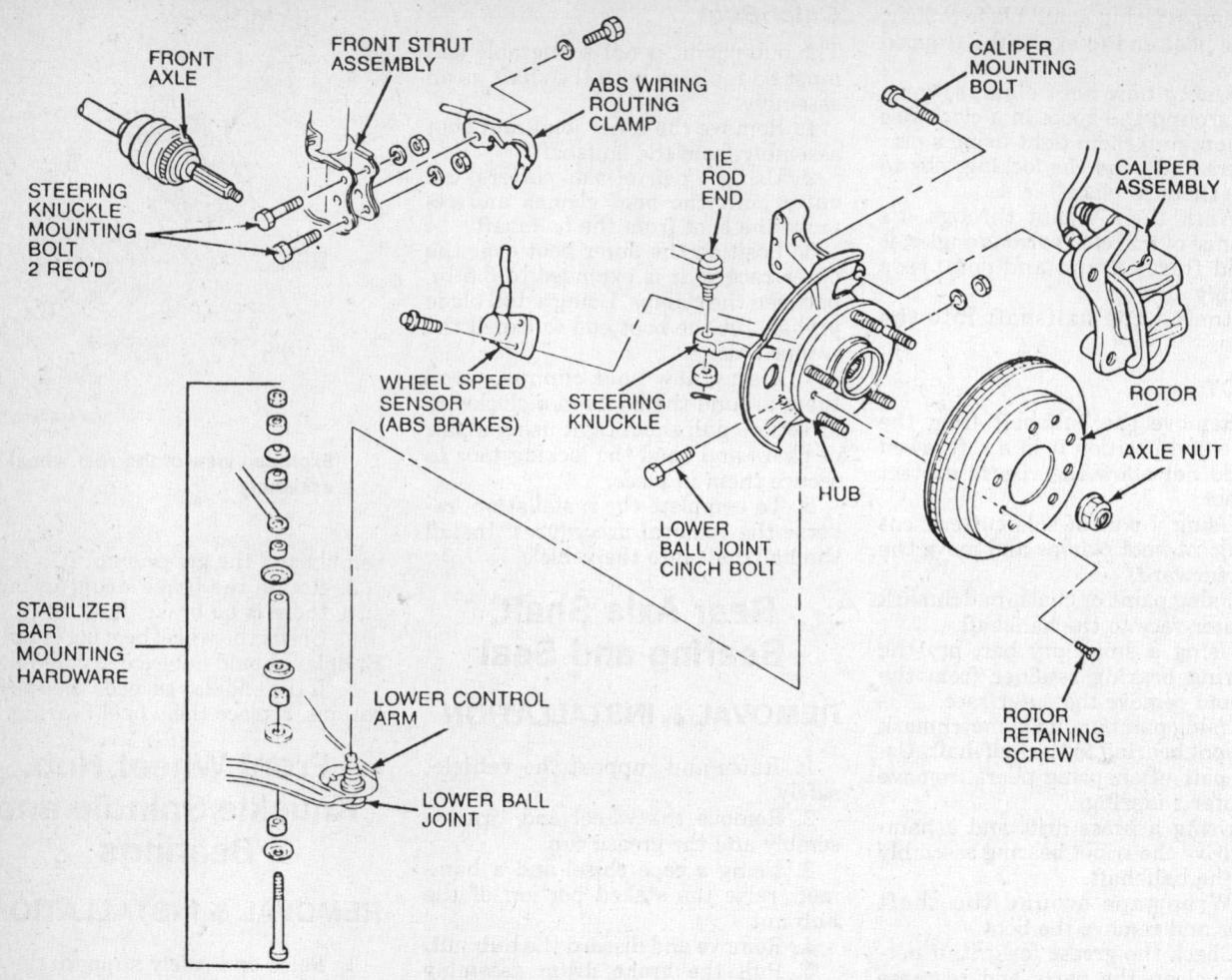

FRONT AXLE

FRONT STRUT ASSEMBLY

ABS WIRING ROUTING CLAMP

CALIPER MOUNTING BOLT

STEERING KNUCKLE MOUNTING BOLT 2 REQ'D

TIE ROD END

CALIPER ASSEMBLY

WHEEL SPEED SENSOR (ABS BRAKES)

STEERING KNUCKLE

ROTOR

AXLE NUT

HUB

LOWER BALL JOINT CINCH BOLT

STABILIZER BAR MOUNTING HARDWARE

LOWER CONTROL ARM

LOWER BALL JOINT

ROTOR RETAINING SCREW

Exploded view of the front wheel hub assembly

halfshaft on a wire; be careful not to damage the seals. Should the wheel hub bind on the halfshaft, use a plastic hammer to jar it free.

NOTE: If the halfshaft splines bind in the hub, it may be necessary to use a 2-jawed wheel puller to separate them.

11. Remove the wheel bearing by performing the following procedures:
    a. Using a prybar, pry the grease seal from the hub/steering knuckle assembly.
    b. Using a shop press, press the hub from the steering knuckle.

NOTE: If the inner race remains on the hub, grind the inner race to approximately 0.020 in. (0.5mm) and use a chisel to remove it.

    c. Remove the snapring from the steering knuckle.
    d. Using a shop press, press the wheel bearing from the steering knuckle.

NOTE: Unless the disc brake dust shield is damaged, it should be left on the steering knuckle; it is pressed on and is hard to get off without damaging.

To install:
12. Install the wheel bearing by performing the following procedures:
    a. Using a shop press, press the wheel bearing into the steering knuckle.
    b. Install the snapring to secure the wheel bearing.
    c. Using a new grease seal, lubricate the lip with grease. Using a seal installer tool or equivalent, drive the new seal into the steering knuckle until it seats.
    d. Using a shop press, press the hub into the steering knuckle until it seats.
13. Grease the halfshaft splines, slide the hub/steering knuckle onto the halfshaft and position it into the strut bracket. Torque the strut-to-steering knuckle nuts/bolts to 69–86 ft. lbs.

14. Push the lower control arm ball joint into the steering knuckle and torque the clamp bolt to 32–40 ft. lbs.
15. Install the brake rotor and secure with the retaining screw.
16. Install the caliper anchor bracket-to-steering knuckle bolts and torque to 58–72 ft. lbs.
17. Using a new hub nut, have an assistant apply the brakes and torque the nut to 116–174 ft. lbs. Using a rounded edge cold chisel, stake the hub nut.
18. Connect the tie rod end to the steering knuckle, torque the nut to 22–33 ft. lbs. and install a new cotter pin.

NOTE: Should the slots of the nut not align with the cotter pin hole, tighten the nut; never loosen it.

19. Connect the stabilizer bar to the lower control arm and tighten the nut until 0.79 in. (20mm) of the bolt threads are exposed beyond the nut.
20. Install the wheel and torque the lug nuts to 65–87 ft. lbs.

STEERING

Steering Wheel

REMOVAL & INSTALLATION

1. Disconnect the negative battery cable.

2. Remove the steering wheel horn pad mounting screws from the back side of the steering wheel.

3. Remove the steering wheel cover pad and disconnect the horn wire from the cover pad.

4. Matchmark the steering wheel to the steering shaft.

5. Remove the steering wheel, using a steering wheel puller.

6. Install the steering wheel over the steering shaft making sure the matchmarks are aligned.

7. Install the steering wheel mounting nut and tighten to 29–36 ft. lbs.

8. Connect the horn wire. Replace the cover pad and replace the mounting screws.

9. Connect the negative battery cable.

Steering Column

REMOVAL & INSTALLATION

1. Disconnect the negative battery cable.

2. Remove the steering wheel.

3. Remove the column cover screws and the cover.

4. Remove the instrument cover-to-instrument cluster cover screws. Carefully, pull the cover outward and disconnect the electrical connectors from the cover. Remove the ignition illumination bulb and the instrument cover.

5. Loosen the instrument cluster cover-to-hinge screws, remove the instrument cluster-to-dash screws and the instrument cluster cover.

6. Remove the lower panel, the lap duct and the defrost duct.

7. Disconnect the electrical connectors from the turn signal switch assembly.

8. Remove the U-joint cinch bolt from the lower end of the steering shaft.

9. Remove the mounting nuts and the hinge bracket.

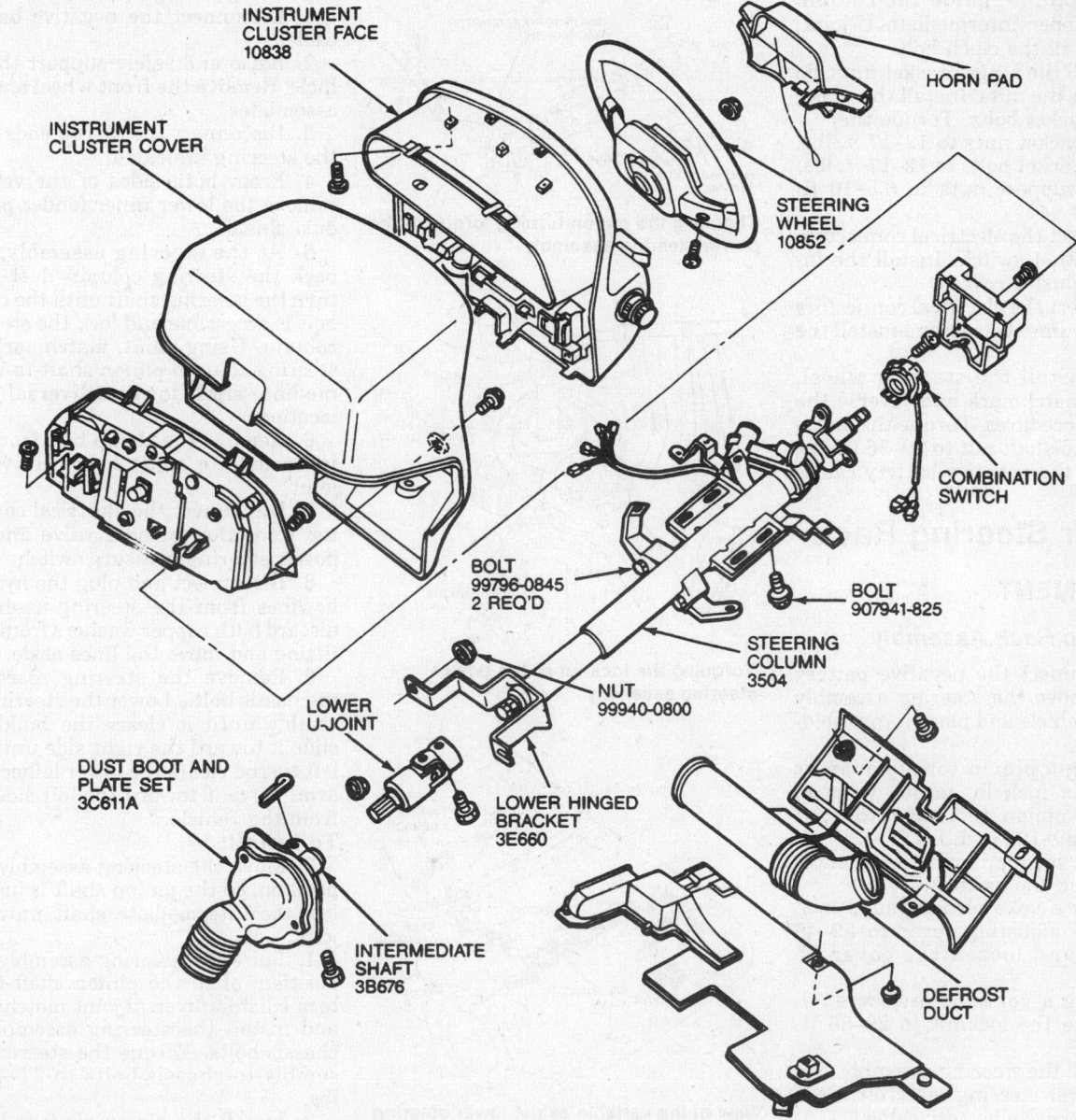

Exploded view of the steering column assembly

11 FORD MOTOR CO. PROBE

10. Remove the cluster support nuts and the upper steering column brackets nuts/bolts and the steering shaft assembly.

11. At the steering rack, lift the boot from the intermediate shaft U-joint and remove the U-joint cinch bolt.

12. Remove the intermediate shaft dust cover assembly nut, the intermediate shaft, the dust cover assembly and the steering column.

To install:

13. Using an assistant to support the intermediate shaft and dust cover assembly, guide the lower U-joint onto the steering rack pinion.

14. Install the lower intermediate shaft U-joint cinch bolt and torque it to 13–20 ft. lbs. Install the dust cover nut.

15. Using an assistant to support the steering column, guide the column into the upper intermediate U-joint; do not install the cinch bolt.

16. Install the hinge bracket nuts; do not tighten the nuts. Install the upper column bracket bolts. Torque the:

Hinge bracket nuts to 12–17 ft. lbs.
Upper bracket bolts to 12–17 ft. lbs.
Cluster support nuts to 6.5–10 ft. lbs.

17. Connect the electrical connectors at the ignition switch. Install the instrument cluster cover.

18. Connect the electrical connectors to the instrument cover and install the cover.

19. To install the steering wheel, align the matchmark and reverse the removal procedures. Torque the steering wheel-to-shaft nut to 29–36 ft. lbs. Reconnect the negative battery cable.

Power Steering Rack

ADJUSTMENT

Electronic Rack Assembly

1. Disconnect the negative battery cable. Remove the steering assembly from the vehicle and place it in a holding fixture.

2. Using a pinion torque adapter tool and an inch lb. torque wrench, check the pinion turning torque; it should be 89–124 inch lbs.

3. If the torque is not to specifications, loosen the locknut.

4. Using a yoke torque gauge tool, torque the adjusting cover to 39–48 inch lbs. and loosen the cover 35 degrees.

5. Using a yoke locknut wrench tool, torque the locknut to 29–36 ft. lbs.

6. Install the steering assembly. Refill the power steering reservoir. Connect the negative battery cable.

7. Start the engine and bleed the system. Test drive and check the steering operation.

Standard Rack Assembly

1. Disconnect the negative battery cable. Remove the steering assembly from the vehicle and place it in a holding fixture.

2. Using a pinion torque adapter tool and an inch lb. torque wrench, check the pinion turning torque; it should be 89–124 inch lbs.

3. If the torque is not to specifications, loosen the locknut.

4. Using a yoke torque gauge tool, torque the adjusting cover to 7.2 ft. lbs., loosen the cover, retorque to 3.6 ft. lbs. and loosen the cover 45 degrees.

5. Using a yoke locknut wrench tool, torque the locknut to 36–43 ft. lbs.

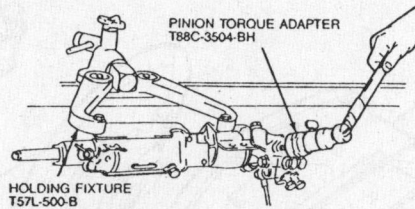

Checking the pinion turning torque of the power steering assembly

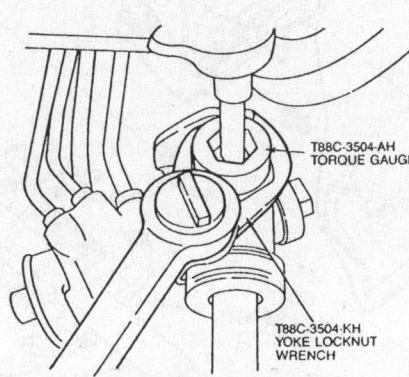

Torquing the locknut of the power steering assembly

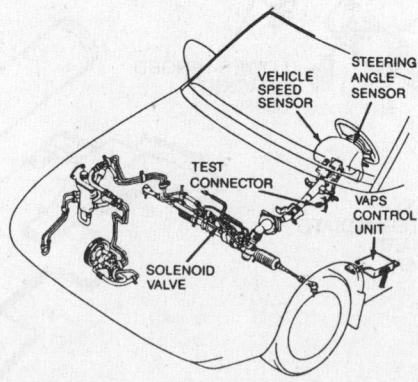

View of the variable assist lower steering (VAPS) system

6. Install the steering assembly. Refill the power steering reservoir. Start the engine and bleed the system. Test drive and check the steering operation.

REMOVAL & INSTALLATION

Electronic Rack Assembly

The variable assist power steering (VAPS) system automatically adjusts the power steering pressure. It provides light steering effort during low speed and parking maneuvers and higher steering effort at higher speeds for improved road feel.

The completely automatic system (no driver controls) consists of: a VAPS control unit, a steering angle sensor, a vehicle speed sensor, a solenoid valve, a test connector and interconnecting wiring.

1. Disconnect the negative battery cable.

2. Raise and safely support the vehicle. Remove the front wheel and tire assemblies.

3. Disconnect the tie rod ends from the steering knuckles.

4. From both sides of the vehicle, remove the lower inner fender plastic dust shield.

5. At the steering assembly, pull back the steering column dust boot, turn the steering shaft until the clamp bolt is accessible and lock the steering column. Using paint, matchmark the steering column pinion shaft-to-intermediate shaft lower universal joint location.

6. Remove the clamp bolt from the intermediate shaft lower universal joint.

7. Disconnect the electrical connector from the solenoid valve and the power steering pressure switch.

8. Disconnect and plug the hydraulic lines from the steering assembly; discard both copper washers from each fitting and move the lines aside.

9. Remove the steering assembly-to-chassis bolts. Lower the steering assembly until it clears the bulkhead, slide it toward the right side until the left tie rod clears the lower left control arm, move it toward the left side and from the vehicle.

To install:

10. Move the steering assembly into position, so the pinion shaft is just below the intermediate shaft universal joint.

11. Raise the steering assembly into position, align the pinion shaft-to-intermediate universal joint matchmark and install the steering assembly-to-chassis bolts. Torque the steering assembly-to-chassis bolts to 27–40 ft. lbs.

12. Install the pinion shaft-to-intermediate universal joint clamp bolt and

torque to 13–20 ft. lbs.

13. Using new copper washers, connect the hydraulic lines to the steering assembly.

14. Connect the tie rod ends to the steering knuckles.

15. Install the front wheel and tire assemblies. Lower the vehicle.

16. Refill the power steering reservoir. Start the engine, bleed the power steering system and check for leaks.

Standard Rack Assembly

The non-electronically controlled power rack and pinion steering gear has an integral valve and power assist system.

1. Disconnect the negative battery cable.

2. Raise and safely support the vehicle. Remove the front wheel and tire assemblies.

3. Disconnect the tie rod ends from the steering knuckles.

4. From both sides of the vehicle, remove the lower inner fender plastic dust shield.

5. At the steering assembly, pull back the steering column dust boot, turn the steering shaft until the clamp bolt is accessible and lock the steering column. Using paint, matchmark the steering column pinion shaft-to-intermediate shaft lower universal joint location.

6. Remove the clamp bolt from the intermediate shaft lower universal joint.

7. Disconnect and plug both hydraulic lines from the steering assembly; discard both copper washers from each fitting and move the lines aside.

8. Remove the steering assembly-to-chassis bolts. Lower the steering assembly until it clears the bulkhead, slide it toward the right side until the left tie rod clears the lower left control arm, move it toward the left side and from the vehicle.

To install:

9. Move the steering assembly into position, so the pinion shaft is just below the intermediate shaft universal joint.

10. Raise the steering assembly into position, align the pinion shaft-to-intermediate universal joint matchmark and install the steering assembly-to-chassis bolts. Torque the steering assembly-to-chassis bolts to 27–40 ft. lbs.

11. Install the pinion shaft-to-intermediate universal joint clamp bolt and torque to 13–20 ft. lbs.

12. Using new copper washers, connect the hydraulic lines to the steering assembly.

13. Connect the tie rod ends to the steering knuckles. Install the front wheel and tire assembly.

14. Lower the vehicle. Refill the power steering reservoir. Start the engine, bleed the power steering system and check for leaks.

Power Steering Pump

REMOVAL & INSTALLATION

2.2L Engine

1. Disconnect the negative battery cable.

2. At the right fender, remove the inner fender splash shield.

3. Loosen the power steering pump and remove the drive belt.

4. Disconnect and plug the pressure and return hoses from the pump

5. Remove the pump-to-bracket bolts and the pump; if necessary, remove the drive pulley from the pump.

To install:

6. Position the pump on the bracket and torque the bolts to 27–34 ft. lbs.

7. Connect the pressure and return hoses to the pump. Connect the negative battery cable.

8. Install the drive belt. Refill the power steering reservoir. Start the engine and bleed the system.

3.0L Engine

1. Disconnect the negative battery cable.

2. Remove the washer reservoir and place out of the way.

3. Remove the plastic shield and the accessory drive belt.

4. Remove the drive pulley from the pump.

5. Disconnect both power steering hoses from the pump.

6. Remove the pump mounting bolts and lift the pump from the accessory support bracket.

To install:

7. Position the pump on the accessory bracket.

8. Install the pump mounting bolts and tighten to 15–22 ft. lbs.

9. Install the drive pulley and replace both power steering hoses.

10. Install the drive belt and the plastic shield. Connect the negative battery cable.

BELT ADJUSTMENT

NOTE: There is no adjustment needed. The tensioner pulley provides the required pressure on the belt

SYSTEM BLEEDING

1. Raise and support the vehicle, safely.

2. Disconnect the coil wire. Refill the power steering pump reservoir to the specified level.

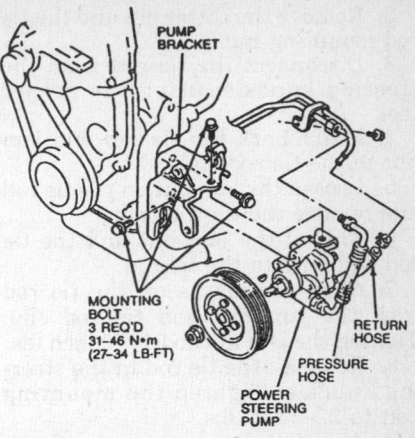

Mounting location of the power steering pump

Pump Assembly—3.0L EFI

Removal

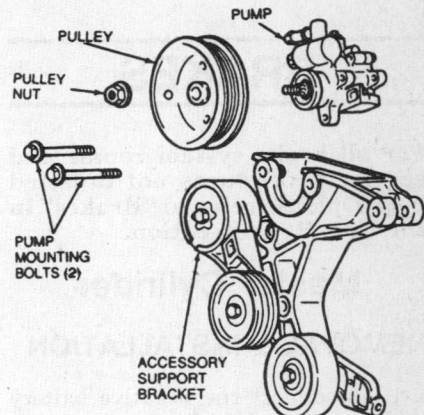

Power steering pump assembly—3.0L engine

3. Crank the engine. Check and refill the reservoir.

4. Crank the engine and rotate the steering wheel from lock-to-lock. Check and refill the power steering pump reservoir.

5. Connect the coil wire, start the engine and allow it to run for several minutes.

6. Rotate the steering wheel from lock-to-lock several times, until the air bubbles are eliminated from the fluid.

7. Turn the engine **OFF**. Check and/or refill the reservoir.

8. Disconnect the negative battery cable, depress the brake pedal for at least 5 seconds and reconnect the negative battery cable.

Tie Rod Ends

REMOVAL & INSTALLATION

1. Raise and support the vehicle, safely. Remove the tire and the wheel assembly.

2. Remove the cotter pin and the tie rod mounting nut.

3. Disconnect the tie rod from the steering knuckle, using the proper tool.

4. Matchmark the tie rod end jam nut to the tie rod end.

5. Loosen the jam nut on the tie rod and remove the tie rod end.

6. Thread the jam nut and the tie rod end onto to the tie rod.

7. Align the marks on the tie rod with the jam nut and tie rod end. Tighten the jam nut to 51–72 inch lbs.

8. Reinstall the tie rod in the steering knuckle. Tighten the mounting bolt to 22–33 ft. lbs.

9. Align the slots in the nut with the hole in the ball joint stud and install the cotter pin.

10. Install the tire and wheel assembly.

BRAKES

For all brake system repair and service procedures not detailed below, please refer to "Brakes" in the Unit Repair section.

Master Cylinder

REMOVAL & INSTALLATION

1. Disconnect the negative battery cable and low fluid level sensor connector from the master cylinder.

2. Disconnect and plug the fluid lines from the master cylinder.

3. Remove the master cylinder-to-power booster nuts and the cylinder.

4. To install, reverse the removal procedures. Refill the master cylinder reservoir. Bleed the brake system.

Proportioning Valve

REMOVAL & INSTALLATION

1. Disconnect the fuel filter bracket and position the fuel filter out of the way.

2. Remove the brake lines between the proportioning valve and the master cylinder, using the proper tool.

3. Remove the proportioning valve mounting bolts and the proportioning valve.

4. Install the proportioning valve on the bulkhead and install the mounting bolts, loosely.

5. Loosely, install the brake lines between the valve and the master cylinder.

6. Tighten the mounting bolts and

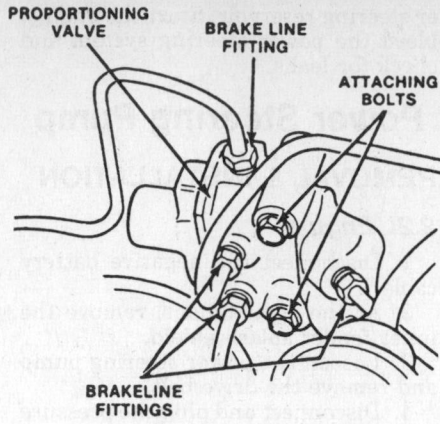

Proportioning valve location

all the brake lines, using the proper tool.

7. Reposition the fuel filter and connect the fuel filter bracket.

8. Bleed the brake system.

Power Brake Booster

REMOVAL & INSTALLATION

1. Disconnect the negative battery cable.

2. Remove the master cylinder and move it aside; it may not be necessary to disconnect the brake lines from the master cylinder.

3. Disconnect the intake manifold-to-power brake booster rubber hose.

4. From under the instrument panel, remove the spring clip from the brake pedal clevis pin and the clevis pin.

5. Remove the power brake booster-to-firewall nuts and the booster.

6. To install, reverse the removal procedures. If the brake tubes were disconnected from the master cylinder, bleed the brake system.

Brake Caliper

REMOVAL & INSTALLATION

Front

1. Raise and support the vehicle, safely. Remove the front wheel and tire assemblies.

2. Remove the banjo bolt mounting the brake flex hose to the caliper.

3. Remove the copper washers that seal the flex hose fitting.

4. Remove the caliper mounting bolts.

5. Pivot the caliper off the brake pads and slide the caliper off the guide pin.

6. Remove the guide pin dust boots and push out the caliper guide pin bushing.

To install:

7. Lubricate the guide pin bushings with a high temperature grease or the equivalent and install them in the caliper.

8. Install the guide pin bushing dust boots.

9. Position the caliper onto the guide pin. Pivot the caliper onto the brake pads. It may be neccessary to pull outward slightly, on the caliper to provide the neccessary clearance.

10. Install the caliper mounting bolts

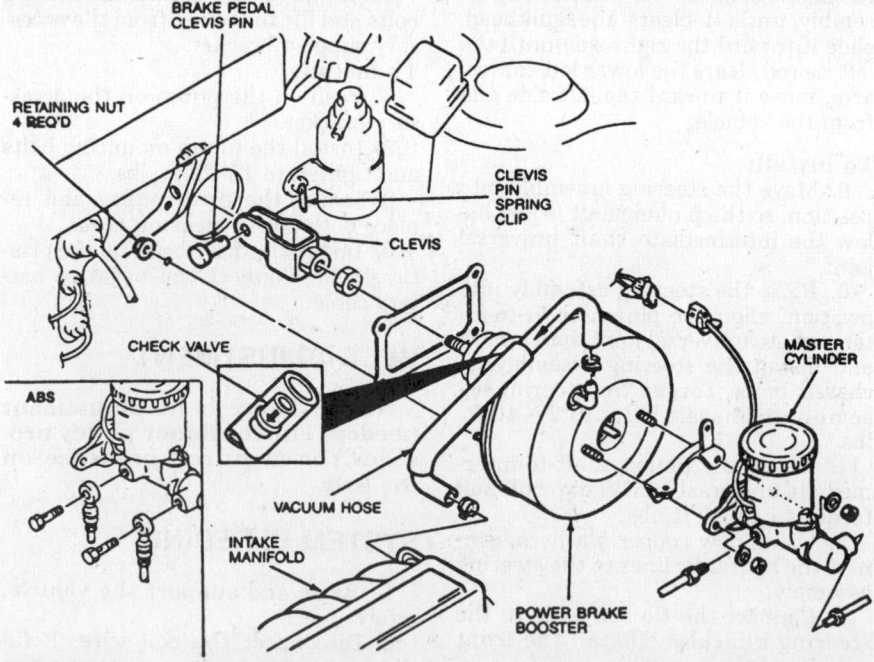

Exploded view of the power brake booster

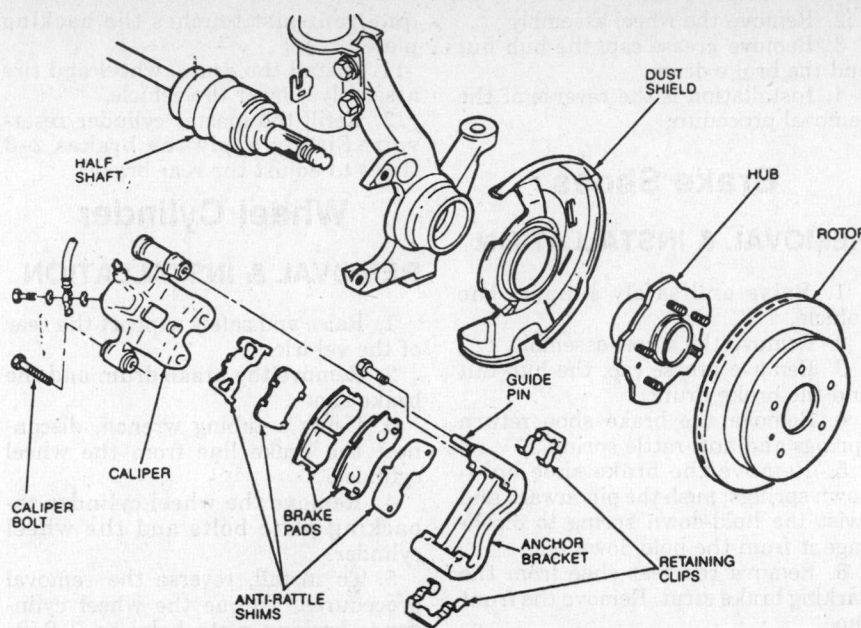

Exploded view of the front disc brake assembly

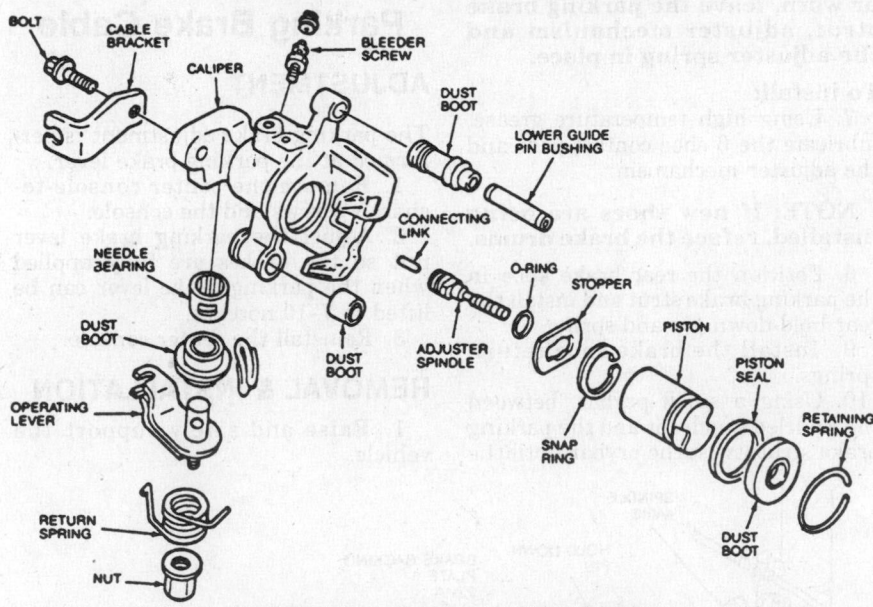

Exploded view of the rear caliper assembly

and tighten to 23–30 ft. lbs.

11. Install the copper washers and the banjo bolt on the flex hose fitting.

12. Position the flex hose on the caliper and replace the banjo bolt. Tighten the bolt to 16–22 ft. lbs.

13. Bleed the front brakes and replace the wheel assemblies.

14. Lower the vehicle.

Rear

1. Raise and safely support the vehicle. Remove the wheel and tire assembly.

2. Loosen the park brake adjusting nut. Remove the cable housing from the bracket and the park brake lever.

3. Remove the banjo bolt mounting the brake flex hose to the caliper.

4. Remove the copper washers that seal the flex hose fitting.

5. Remove the caliper mounting bolts.

6. Pivot the caliper off the brake pads and slide the caliper off the guide pin.

7. Remove the disc pads and the caliper guide pin from the anchor bracket.

8. Remove the bolts from the anchor bracket and the anchor bracket.

To install:

9. Install the anchor bracket and tighten the mounting bolts.

10. Install the disc pads and the caliper guide pin to the anchor bracket.

11. Install the caliper and tighten the mounting bolts to 12–17 ft. lbs.

12. Install new copper washers and replace the banjo bolt mounting the flex hose to the caliper.

13. Position the parking brake cable into the parking brake lever and bracket.

14. Adjust the parking brake cable. Replace the wheel and tire assembly.

15. Lower the vehicle.

Disc Brake Pads

REMOVAL & INSTALLATION

Front

1. Raise and support the vehicle, safely.

2. Remove the wheel and tire assembly.

3. Syphon 2/3 of the brake fluid from the master cylinder.

4. Using a prybar, insert it through the caliper opening and pry the brake pads to drive the piston back into the caliper.

5. Remove the lower caliper-to-bracket bolt and rotate the caliper upward.

6. Label the anti-rattle shims so they can be reinstalled in their original positions.

7. Remove the brake pads from the caliper anchor.

To install:

8. Install the brake pads into the caliper anchor; the pad with the wear indicator equipped pad is the inboard pad.

9. Rotate the caliper downward, install the caliper-to-anchor bolt and torque to 23–30 ft. lbs.

10. Install the wheel and tire assembly. Lower the vehicle.

11. Pump the brake pedal several times to seat the pads. Check and/or add fluid to the brake master cylinder reservoir.

Rear

1. Raise and support the vehicle, safely.

2. Remove the wheel and tire assembly.

3. Syphon 2/3 of the brake fluid from the master cylinder.

4. Loosen the parking brake cable housing adjusting nut. Remove the cable housing from the bracket and the parking brake lever.

5. Remove the caliper-to-bracket bolts, the caliper and suspend it on a wire.

6. Remove the **V** spring from the disc pads. Remove the disc pads, the anti-rattle shims and retaining clips.

NOTE: If the anti-rattle shims are to be reused, they must be installed in their original positions.

To install:

7. Install the retaining clips, the anti-rattle shims, the disc pads and the **V** spring.

8. Using high temperature grease, lubricate the guide pin busings.

9. Install the caliper and torque the bolts to 12–17 ft. lbs.

10. Install the parking brake cable, adjust the cable so there is no clearance between the cable end and the parking brake lever. Torque the parking brake cable locknut to 14–21 ft. lbs.

11. Install the wheel and tire assembly. Lower the vehicle.

12. Pump the brake pedal several times to seat the pads. Check and/or add fluid to the brake master cylinder reservoir.

Brake Rotor

REMOVAL & INSTALLATION

Front

1. Raise and support the vehicle, safely.

2. Remove the wheel and tire assembly.

3. Remove the caliper and the anchor bracket, position it out of the way.

4. Remove the rotor retaining screw and the rotor from the drive hub.

5. Inspect the rotor. Resurface or replace as neccessary.

6. Replace the rotor on the drive hub and install the retaining screw.

7. Replace the caliper and anchor assembly.

8. Install the wheel assembly and lower the vehicle.

Rear

1. Raise and support the vehicle, safely.

2. Remove the wheel and tire assembly.

3. Remove the caliper and the anchor bracket, position it out of the way.

4. Unstake the retaining nut, using a chisel.

5. Remove the nut and the washer. Remove the rotor.

6. Installation is the reverse of the removal procedure.

Brake Drums

REMOVAL & INSTALLATION

1. Raise and safely support the vehicle.

2. Remove the wheel assembly.

3. Remove grease cap, the hub nut and the brake drum.

4. Installation is the reverse of the removal procedure.

Brake Shoes

REMOVAL & INSTALLATION

1. Raise and safely support the vehicle.

2. Remove the wheel assembly.

3. Remove grease cap, the hub nut and the brake drum.

4. Remove the brake shoe return springs and anti-rattle spring.

5. Remove the brake shoe hold-down springs; push the pin inward and twist the hold-down spring to disengage it from the hold-down pin.

6. Remove the rear shoe from the parking brake strut. Remove the front shoe.

NOTE: Unless they are broken or worn, leave the parking brake strut, adjuster mechanism and the adjuster spring in place.

To install:

7. Using high temperature grease, lubricate the 6 shoe contact pads and the adjuster mechanism.

NOTE: If new shoes are being installed, reface the brake drums.

8. Position the rear brake shoe in the parking brake strut and install the rear hold-down pin and spring.

9. Install the brake shoe return springs.

10. Using a small prybar, between the knurled quadrant and the parking brake strut, twist the prybar until the quadrant just touches the backing plate.

11. Install the drum, wheel and tire assembly. Lower the vehicle.

12. Refill the master cylinder reservoir. Firmly apply the brakes 2–3 times to adjust the rear brakes.

Wheel Cylinder

REMOVAL & INSTALLATION

1. Raise and safely support the rear of the vehicle.

2. Remove the brake drum and the brake shoes.

3. Using a tubing wrench, disconnect the brake line from the wheel cylinder.

4. Remove the wheel cylinder-to-backing plate bolts and the wheel cylinder.

5. To install, reverse the removal procedures. Torque the wheel cylinder-to-backing plate bolts to 7–9 ft. lbs. Bleed the brake system.

Parking Brake Cable

ADJUSTMENT

The parking brake adjustment is performed at the parking brake lever.

1. Remove the center console-to-chassis screws and the console.

2. Adjust the parking brake lever nut so the brakes are fully applied when the parking brake lever can be lifted to 7–10 notches.

3. Reinstall the center console.

REMOVAL & INSTALLATION

1. Raise and safely support the vehicle.

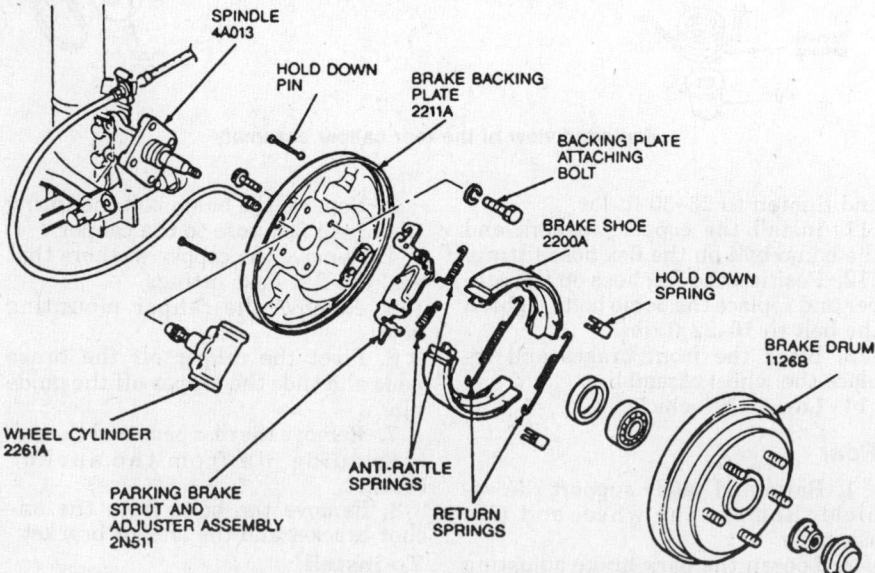

Exploded view of the rear drum brake assembly

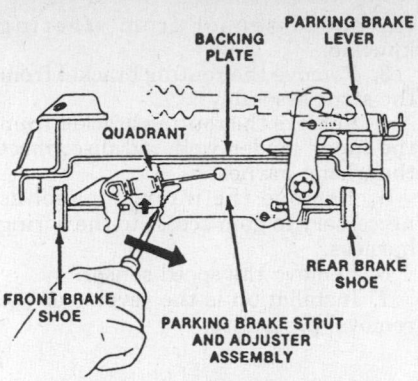

Park brake adjustment mechanism

2. Using a pair of needle-nose pliers, remove the parking brake return spring from each backing plate; be careful not to stretch the spring.

3. Remove the parking brake cable housing-to-backng plate bolts and pull it away from the backing plate.

4. Disconnect the parking brake cables from the parking brake levers at the backing plates.

5. From the rear of each trailing arm and frame, remove the parking brake housing clamp.

6. From near the equalizer, remove the parking brake cable housing-to-body bolt and clamp.

7. Disconnect the parking brake return spring from the parking brake equalizer.

8. Disconnect the parking brake cable from the equalizer and the cable from the vehicle.

9. Inspect the parking brake cable for free movement in the sheath; if necessary, lubricate it with grease.

To install:

10. Install the parking brake cable to the equalizer and connect the return spring to the equalizer.

11. Install the parking brake cable housing bolt and clamp.

12. Install the parking brake housing clamp at the rear of each trailing arm.

13. Connect the parking brake cables to the parking brake levers at the backing plates. Tighten the housing-to-backing plate bolts.

14. Install the brake return spring to each backing plate.

15. Adjust the parking brake. Lower the vehicle.

Brake System Bleeding

1. To bleed the calipers and the wheel cylinders, begin at the rear bleeder screw.

2. Attach a rubber drain hose to the bleeder screw. Place the free end of the hose in a container, partially filled with brake fluid.

3. Have an assistant pump the brake pedal 5–10 times and maintain pressure on the brake pedal.

4. Loosen the bleeder screw approximately ¾ turn. It is very important that constant pressure is maintained on the brake pedal until the brake pedal drops all the way down and the bleeder screw is closed. If the pedal pressure is released, air will be drawn back into the system.

5. Tighten the bleeder screw. Repeat this operation until the fluid is clear and air bubbles no longer appear.

6. Repeat these steps at the other wheel cylinders and calipers. Never re-use brake fluid.

Anti-Lock Brake System Service Precaution

Failure to observe the following precautions may result in system damage.

Before servicing any high pressure component, be sure to discharge the hydraulic pressure from the system.

Do not allow the brake fluid to contact any of the electrical connectors.

Use care when opening the bleeder screws due to the high system pressure from the accumulator.

Hydraulic Actuation Unit

REMOVAL & INSTALLATION

1. Disconnect the negative battery cable.

2. Remove the fuel filter and air filter assemblies.

3. Remove the coil and disconnect the wiring harness from the bottom of the coil and the fuel filter mounting bracket.

4. Remove the coil and fuel filter mounting bracket. Disconnect the electrical connectors.

5. Remove the banjo bolts and the copper washers from the brake lines at the actuation unit. Disconnect the brake lines, using the proper tool.

6. Remove the mounting bolts, lockwashers and washers. Lift the hydraulic actuation unit from the mounting bracket.

7. Remove the mounting bushings from the actuation assembly. If neccessary, remove the mounting bracket.

To install:

8. Install the mounting bushings and the actuation unit.

9. Insert new copper washers and connect the brake lines. Replace the banjo bolts.

10. Connect the electrical connec-

tors. Replace the fuel filter and coil mounting bracket.

11. Install the coil and connect the wiring connector.

12. Replace the fuel filter and air filter assemblies.

13. Connect the negative battery cable. Bleed the brake system.

Wheel Sensor Rotor

REMOVAL & INSTALLATION

Front

1. Raise and support the vehicle, safely. Remove the tire and wheel assembly.

2. Remove the halfshaft assembly.

3. Tap the sensor rotor from the outboard CV-joint.

4. Position the sensor rotor on the CV-joint with the chamfered edge facing the halfshaft.

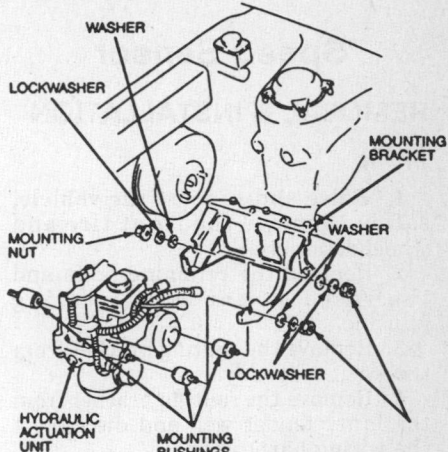

Exploded view of the hydraulic actuation unit

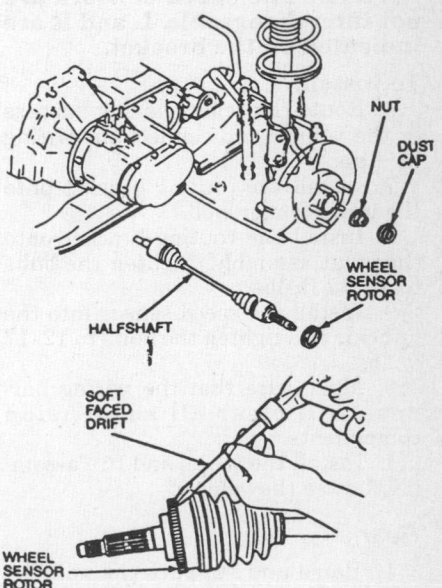

Exploded view of the front wheel sensor rotor

5. Tap the sensor rotor onto the outboard CV-joint and install the halfshaft.

6. Lower the vehicle.

Rear

1. Raise and support the vehicle, safely.

2. Remove the tire and wheel assembly.

3. Remove the caliper and anchor bracket. Remove the rotor assembly.

4. Remove the sensor rotor from the rotor, using the proper puller.

5. Positon the rotor in a suitable press with the wheel studs facing down.

6. Press the sensor onto the rotor, using the proper tool.

7. Install the caliper and anchor bracket.

8. Install the tire and wheel assembly. Lower the vehicle.

Speed Sensor

REMOVAL & INSTALLATION

Front

1. Raise and support the vehicle, safely. Remove the front tire and wheel assembly.

2. Remove the retaining bolts and the speed sensor from steering knuckle.

3. Remove the routing bracket from the strut assembly.

4. Remove the routing bracket from the inner fender well and disconnect the wiring harness.

5. Remove the speed sensor.

NOTE: The speed sensors are not interchangeable. L and R are indicated on the bracket.

To install:

6. Route the sensor wiring harness in the vehicle and connect the wiring harness.

7. Install the routing bracket onto the inner fender well.

8. Install the routing bracket onto the strut assembly. Tighten the bolts to 12–17 ft. lbs.

9. Install the speed sensor into the knuckle and tighten the bolts to 12–17 ft. lbs.

10. Make sure that the wiring harness will clear all suspension components.

11. Install the wheel and tire assembly. Lower the vehicle.

Rear

1. Raise and support the vehicle, safely. Remove the front tire and wheel assembly.

2. Remove the retaining bolts and

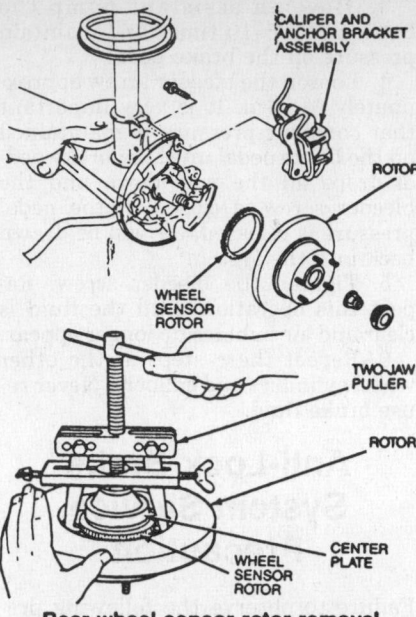

Rear wheel sensor rotor removal

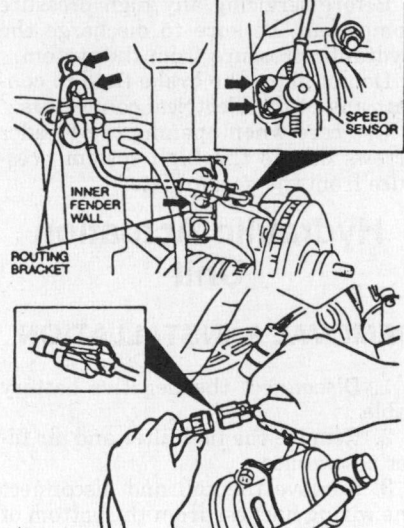

Location of the front speed sensor

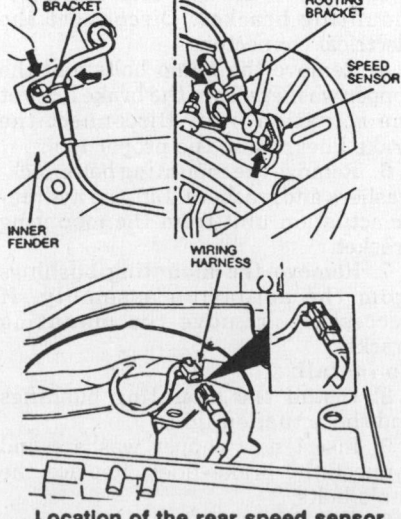

Location of the rear speed sensor

the speed sensor from steering knuckle.

3. Remove the routing bracket from the strut assembly.

4. Remove the routing bracket from the inner fender well and disconnect the wiring harness.

5. Remove the interior panel as neccessary to gain access to the wiring harness.

6. Remove the speed sensor.

7. Installation is the reverse of the removal procedure.

FRONT SUSPENSION

MacPherson Strut

REMOVAL & INSTALLATION

1. Raise and support the vehicle, safely.

2. Remove the wheel and tire assembly.

3. Remove the rubber cap from the strut mounting block. If equipped, disconnect the programmed ride control module connector.

4. At the inside of the strut mounting block and chassis strut tower, place an alignment mark.

5. If equipped with a programmed ride control module, remove it.

6. If equipped with an anti-lock brake system, disconnect the electrical harness and remove the bracket.

7. Remove the brake caliper-to-steering knuckle bolts and suspend the caliper on a wire; do not disconnect the pressure hose.

8. Remove the U-clip from the brake line hose and slide it out of the strut bracket.

9. Remove the strut-to-steering knuckle bolts.

10. If equipped, at the left strut, remove the vane airflow meter assembly and the ignition coil bracket.

11. Remove the strut-to-chassis nuts and the strut from the vehicle.

12. Place the strut assembly in a suitable holding fixture. Using a proper spring compressor, remove the upper strut nut and gradually release the spring compressor.

13. Remove the strut mounting block, dust boot, bump stopper and the coil spring from the strut assembly.

To install:

12. Align the strut-to-chassis matchmark and torque the strut-to-chassis nuts to 34–46 ft. lbs.

13. If equipped, at the left strut, install the vane airflow meter assembly

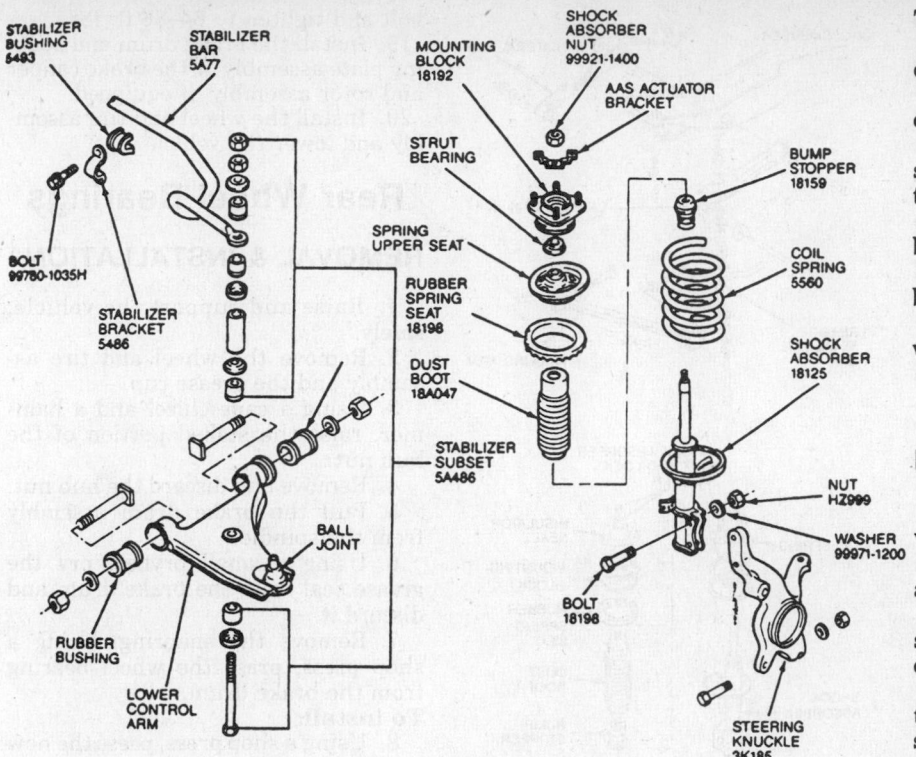

STABILIZER BUSHING 5493

STABILIZER BAR 5A77

BOLT 99780-1035H

STABILIZER BRACKET 5486

MOUNTING BLOCK 18192

SHOCK ABSORBER NUT 99921-1400

AAS ACTUATOR BRACKET

STRUT BEARING

SPRING UPPER SEAT

RUBBER SPRING SEAT 18198

DUST BOOT 18A047

STABILIZER SUBSET 5A486

BUMP STOPPER 18159

COIL SPRING 5560

SHOCK ABSORBER 18125

NUT HZ999

WASHER 99971-1200

BOLT 18198

STEERING KNUCKLE 3K185

BALL JOINT

RUBBER BUSHING

LOWER CONTROL ARM

Exploded view of the front suspension

and the ignition coil bracket.

14. If equipped with a programmed ride control module, install it and the control module connector.

15. Install the rubber cap on the strut tower.

16. Align the strut-to-steering knuckle and torque the nuts/bolts to 69–86 ft. lbs.

17. To complete the installation, reverse the removal procedures and torque the wheel lug nuts to 65–87 ft. lbs. Check and/or adjust the front wheel alignment.

Lower Ball Joints

The ball joints are not serviceable parts; they are serviced by replacing the lower control arms.

Lower Control Arms

REMOVAL & INSTALLATION

1. Raise and safely support the vehicle under the frame away from the lower control arm. Remove the wheel and tire assembly.

2. Remove the brake caliper-to-steering knuckle bolts and support it on a wire.

3. Remove the stabilizer link assembly from the lower control arm.

4. Remove the lower ball joint-to-steering knuckle nut and bolt. Using a prybar, pry downward to separate the

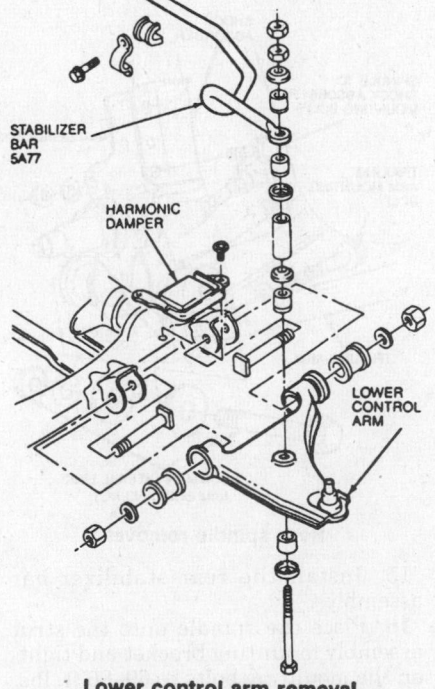

STABILIZER BAR 5A77

HARMONIC DAMPER

LOWER CONTROL ARM

Lower control arm removal

ball joint from the steering knuckle.

5. If equipped with an automatic transaxle, remove the harmonic damper from the chassis sub-frame; the damper is located on the left side near the lower control arm.

6. Remove the lower control arm-to-chassis nuts/bolts and the lower control arm.

To install:

7. Install the control arm and tighten the mounting bolts to 69–93 ft. lbs.

8. Install the harmonic damper, if equipped.

9. Install the ball joint stud into the steering knuckle and tighten the bolt to 32–40 ft. lbs.

10. Install the stabilizer link and bolt. Replace the brake caliper.

11. Install the wheel and tire assembly. Lower the vehicle.

12. Check and/or adjust the front wheel alignment.

Sway Bar

REMOVAL & INSTALLATION

1. Raise and safely support the vehicle.

2. Remove the tire and wheel assemblies.

3. Remove the stabilizer bar link assembly mounting bolts from the lower control arm.

4. Remove the mounting bolt from the stabilizer bar bushing. Remove the stabilizer bar.

5. Install the stabilizer bar link assembly mounting bolts at the control arm. Do not tighten.

6. Install the stabilizer bar bushing. Tighten the bushing bolt to 27–40 ft. lbs.

7. Tighten the link nut until 0.79 inch thread remains above the nut.

8. Install the tire and wheel assemblies. Lower the vehicle.

REAR SUSPENSION

MacPherson Strut

REMOVAL & INSTALLATION

1. Raise and support the vehicle, safely. Remove the wheel and tire assembly.

2. Remove the upper trunk garnish and lower trunk trim.

3. If equipped with programmed ride control, disconnect the programmed ride control module connector and removed the module.

4. If equipped with an anti-lock braking system, disconnect the anti-lock brake harness connector and remove the bracket.

5. If equipped with drum brakes, remove the drum and backing plate assembly. If equipped with rear disc brakes, remove the rear disc brake caliper and rotor assembly.

6. Remove the brake line U-clip from the strut housing.

7. Loosen the trailing arm bolt and remove the spindle-to-strut bolts.

8. From inside the vehicle, remove the strut-to-chassis nuts and the strut.

To install:

9. Position the strut into the vehicle and torque the strut-to-chassis nuts to 34–46 ft. lbs.

10. If equipped with programmed ride control, install the module and reconnect the connector.

11. To complete the installation, reverse the removal procedures and torque the:

Spindle-to-strut nuts and bolts to 69–86 ft. lbs.

Trailing arm-to-spindle bolt to 64–86 ft. lbs.

Wheel lug nuts to 65–87 ft. lbs.

Rear Trailing Arms

REMOVAL & INSTALLATION

1. Raise and support the vehicle, safely.

2. Remove the tire and wheel assembly.

3. Remove the brake drum and the backing plate assembly or the rear brake caliper and rotor assembly, if equipped.

4. Loosen, do not remove the spindle to strut assembly mounting bolts.

5. Remove the common lateral link arm bolt and nut from the spindle.

6. Remove the trailing arm mounting bolt at the spindle and the spindle to strut assembly mounting bolts.

7. Remove the spindle from the strut assembly.

8. Remove the rear stabilize bar.

9. Remove the nut from the common lateral link mounting bolt at the rear crossmember and remove the rear lateral link.

10. Remove the parking brake mounting bolts from the trailing arm assembly.

11. Remove the trailing arm mounting bolt and the trailing arm.

To install:

12. Position the trailing arm into the body mounting bracket and tighten the mounting bolt to 49–69 ft. lbs.

13. Install the parking brake mounting bolts to the trailing arm.

14. Position the rear lateral link onto the common lateral link mounting bolt at the rear crossmember. Tighten the mounting bolt and nut at the rear crossmember to 64–86 ft. lbs.

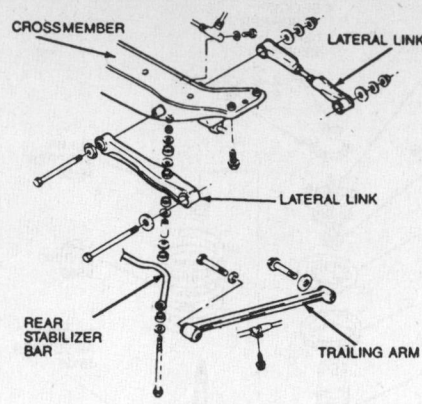

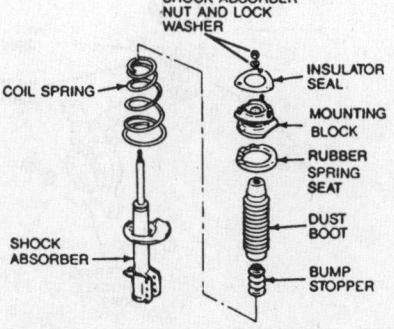

Exploded view of the rear suspension

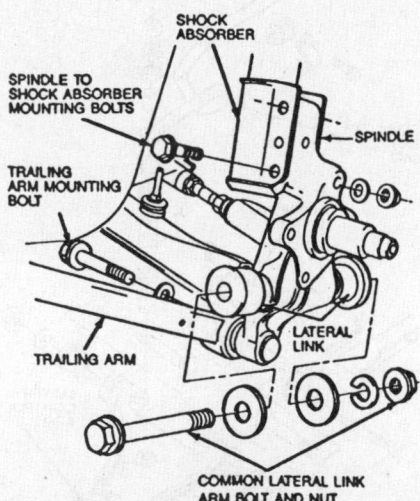

Rear spindle removal

15. Install the rear stabilizer bar assembly.

16. Place the spindle onto the strut assembly mounting bracket and tighten the mounting bolts to 69–86 ft. lbs.

17. Install the common lateral link arm and bolt through the spindle and tighten to 64–86 ft. lbs.

18. Install the trailing arm mounting

bolt and tighten to 64–86 ft. lbs.

19. Install the brake drum and backing plate assembly or the brake caliper and rotor assembly, if equipped.

20. Install the wheel and tire assembly and lower the vehicle.

Rear Wheel Bearings

REMOVAL & INSTALLATION

1. Raise and support the vehicle, safely.

2. Remove the wheel and tire assembly and the grease cup.

3. Using a cape chisel and a hammer, raise the staked portion of the hub nut.

4. Remove and discard the hub nut.

5. Pull the brake drum assembly from the spindle.

6. Using a small prybar, pry the grease seal from the brake drum and discard it.

7. Remove the snapring. Using a shop press, press the wheel bearing from the brake drum.

To install:

8. Using a shop press, press the new wheel bearing into the brake drum until it seats and install the snapring.

9. Using a grease seal installation tool or equivalent, lubricate the seal lip with grease and drive it into the brake drum until it seats.

10. Position the brake drum assembly onto the wheel spindle.

11. Using a new locknut, torque it to 73–101 ft. lbs.

12. Check the wheel bearing freeplay.

13. Using a dull cold chisel, stake the locknut.

14. To complete the installation, reverse the removal procedures.

ADJUSTMENT

1. Raise and support the vehicle, safely.

2. Remove the wheel and tire assembly and the grease cup.

3. Using a cape chisel and a hammer, raise the staked portion of the hub nut.

4. Remove and discard the hub nut.

5. Using a new locknut, torque it to 73–101 ft. lbs.

6. Check the wheel bearing freeplay.

7. Using a cold chisel, stake the locknut.

8. To complete the installation, reverse the removal procedures.

Ford Motor Co.
Front Wheel Drive
Ford—Taurus, Taurus SHO
Lincoln—Continental
Mercury—Sable

SPECIFICATIONS

VEHICLE IDENTIFICATION CHART

It is important for servicing and ordering parts to be certain of the vehicle and engine identification. The VIN (vehicle identification number) is a 17 digit number visible through the windshield on the driver's side of the dash and contains the vehicle and engine identification codes. The tenth digit indicates model year and the eighth digit indicates engine code. It can be interpreted as follows:

Engine Code

Code	Cu. In.	Liters	Cyl.	Fuel Sys.	Eng. Mfg.
D	153	2.5 HSC	4	CFI	Ford
U	182	3.0	6	EFI	Ford
Y	182	3.0 SHO	6	SEFI	Yamaha
4	232	3.8	6	EFI	Ford

Model Year

Code	Year
H	1987
J	1988
K	1989
L	1990
M	1991

CFI   Central Fuel Injection
EFI   Electronic Fuel Injection
SEFI Sequential Electronic Fuel Injection
HSC   High Swirl Combustion
SHO   Super High Output

ENGINE IDENTIFICATION

Year	Model	Engine Displacement cu. in. (liter)	Engine Series Identification (VIN)	No. of Cylinders	Engine Type
1987	Taurus	153 (2.5) HSC-CFI	D	4	OHV
	Taurus	182 (3.0) EFI	U	6	OHV
	Sable	153 (2.5) HSC-CFI	D	4	OHV
	Sable	182 (3.0) EFI	U	6	OHV
1988	Taurus	153 (2.5) HSC-CFI	D	4	OHV
	Taurus	182 (3.0) EFI	U	6	OHV
	Taurus	232 (3.8) EFI	4	6	OHV
	Sable	153 (2.5) HSC-CFI	D	4	OHV
	Sable	182 (3.0) EFI	U	6	OHV
	Sable	232 (3.8) EFI	4	6	OHV
	Continental	232 (3.8) EFI	4	6	OHV
1989	Taurus	153 (2.5) HSC-CFI	D	4	OHV
	Taurus	182 (3.0) EFI	U	6	OHV
	Taurus SHO	182 (3.0) EFI	Y	6	DOHC
	Taurus	232 (3.8) EFI	4	6	OHV
	Sable	153 (2.5) HSC-CFI	D	4	OHV
	Sable	182 (3.0) EFI	U	6	OHV
	Sable	232 (3.8) EFI	4	6	OHV
	Continental	232 (3.8) EFI	4	6	OHV

ENGINE IDENTIFICATION

Year	Model	Engine Displacement cu. in. (liter)	Engine Series Identification (VIN)	No. of Cylinders	Engine Type
1990–91	Taurus	153 (2.5) HSC-CFI	D	4	OHV
	Taurus	182 (3.0) EFI	U	6	OHV
	Taurus SHO	182 (3.0) EFI	Y	6	DOHC
	Taurus	232 (3.8) EFI	4	6	OHV
	Sable	182 (3.0) EFI	U	6	OHV
	Sable	232 (3.8) EFI	4	6	OHV
	Continental	232 (3.8) EFI	4	6	OHV

HSC High Swirl Combustion
EFI Electronic Fuel Injection
CFI Central Fuel Injection
SHO Super High Output
OHV Overhead Valve
DOHC Double Overhead Camshaft

GENERAL ENGINE SPECIFICATIONS

Year	VIN	No. Cylinder Displacement cu. in. (liter)	Fuel System Type	Net Horsepower @ rpm	Net Torque @ rpm (ft. lbs.)	Bore × Stroke (in.)	Compression Ratio	Oil Pressure @ rpm
1987	D	4-153 (2.5)	CFI	88 @ 4600	130 @ 2800	3.70 × 3.60	9.7:1	55–70 @ 2000
	U	6-182 (3.0)	EFI	140 @ 4800	160 @ 3000	3.50 × 3.10	9.3:1	55–70 @ 2000
1988	D	4-153 (2.5)	CFI	88 @ 4600	130 @ 2800	3.70 × 3.60	9.7:1	55–70 @ 2000
	U	6-182 (3.0)	EFI	140 @ 4800	160 @ 3000	3.50 × 3.10	9.3:1	55–70 @ 2000
	4	6-232 (3.8)	EFI	140 @ 3800	215 @ 2200	3.81 × 3.39	9.0:1	40–60 @ 2000
1989	D	4-153 (2.5)	CFI	88 @ 4600	130 @ 2800	3.70 × 3.60	9.7:1	55–70 @ 2000
	U	6-182 (3.0)	EFI	140 @ 4800	160 @ 3000	3.50 × 3.10	9.3:1	55–70 @ 2000
	Y	6-182 (3.0)	SEFI	220 @ 6200	200 @ 4800	3.50 × 3.15	NA	13 @ 800
	4	6-232 (3.8)	EFI	140 @ 3800	215 @ 2200	3.81 × 3.39	9.0:1	40–60 @ 2000
1990–91	D	4-153 (2.5)	CFI	90 @ 4400	130 @ 2600	3.70 × 3.60	9.0:1	55–70 @ 2000
	U	6-182 (3.0)	EFI	140 @ 4800	160 @ 3000	3.50 × 3.10	9.3:1	40–60 @ 2500
	Y	6-182 (3.0)	SEFI	220 @ 6200	200 @ 4800	3.50 × 3.15	9.8:1	13 @ 800
	4	6-232 (3.8)	EFI	140 @ 3800	215 @ 2200	3.81 × 3.39	9.0:1	40–60 @ 2500

NA Not available
CFI Central Fuel Injection
EFI Electronic Fuel Injection
SEFI Sequential Fuel Injection

12 FORD MOTOR CO. TAURUS/SABLE/CONTINENTAL (FWD)

ENGINE TUNE-UP SPECIFICATIONS

Year	VIN	No. Cylinder Displacement cu. in. (liter)	Spark Plugs Type	Gap (in.)	Ignition Timing (deg.) MT	AT	Compression Pressure (psi)	Fuel Pump (psi)	Idle Speed (rpm) ① MT	AT	Valve Clearance In.	Ex.
1987	D	4-153 (2.5)	AWSF-32C	0.044	10B	10B	NA	35–45	725	650	Hyd.	Hyd.
	U	6-182 (3.0)	AWSF-32C	0.044	—	10B	NA	35–45	—	625	Hyd.	Hyd.
1988	D	4-153 (2.5)	AWSF-32C	0.044	10B	10B	NA	35–45	725	650	Hyd.	Hyd.
	U	6-182 (3.0)	AWSF-32C	0.044	—	10B	NA	35–45	—	625	Hyd.	Hyd.
	4	6-232 (3.8)	AWSF-44C	0.056	①	①	NA	35–45	①	①	Hyd.	Hyd.
1989	D	4-153 (2.5)	AWSF-32C	0.044	10B	10B	NA	35–45	725	650	Hyd.	Hyd.
	U	6-182 (3.0)	AWSF-32C	0.044	—	10B	NA	35–45	—	625	Hyd.	Hyd.
	Y	6-182 (3.0)	AGSP-32P	0.044	10B	—	NA	36–39	800	—	0.008 ②	0.012 ②
	4	6-232 (3.8)	AWSF-44C	0.054	①	①	NA	35–45	①	①	Hyd.	Hyd.
1990	D	4-153 (2.5)	AWSF-32C	0.044	—	①	NA	35–45	—	①	Hyd.	Hyd.
	U	6-182 (3.0)	AWSF-32C	0.044	—	①	NA	35–45	—	①	Hyd.	Hyd.
	Y	6-182 (3.0)	AGSP-32P	0.044	①	—	NA	35–45	①	—	0.008 ②	0.012 ②
	4	6-232 (3.8)	AWSF-44C	0.054		①	NA	35–45	—	①	Hyd.	Hyd.
1991		SEE UNDERHOOD SPECIFICATIONS STICKER										

NA Not available
B Before top dead center
Hyd. Hydraulic valve lash lifters.
① The Calibration levels vary from vehicle to vehicle. Refer to the Vehicle Emission Control Information label for ignition timing and idle speed specifications.
② Shim set bucket type valve lifter is used.

FIRING ORDERS

NOTE: To avoid confusion, always replace spark plug wires one at a time.

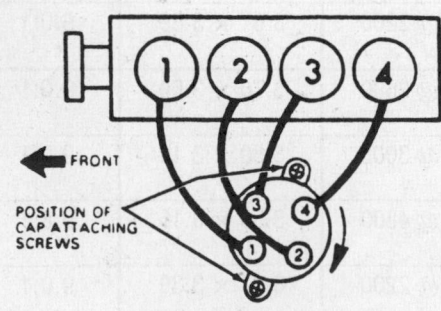

2.5L Engine
Engine Firing Order: 1–3–4–2
Distributor Rotation: Clockwise

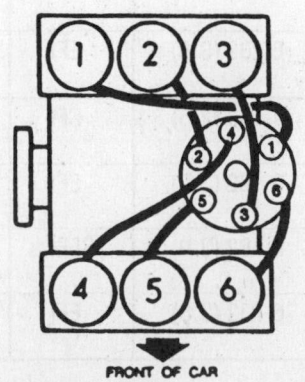

3.0L Engine
Engine Firing Order: 1–4–2–5–3–6
Distributor Rotation: Clockwise

FIRING ORDERS

NOTE: To avoid confusion, always replace spark plug wires one at a time.

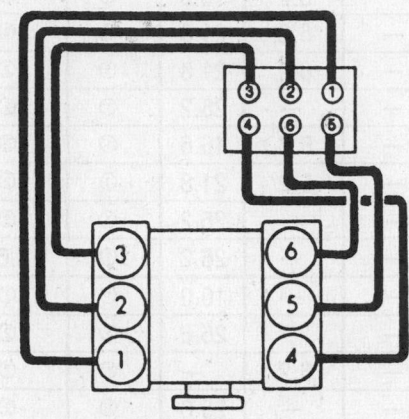

3.0L SHO Engine
Engine Firing Order: 1–4–2–5–3–6
Distributorless Ignition System

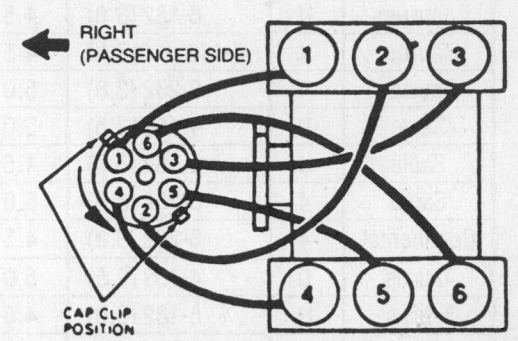

RIGHT
(PASSENGER SIDE)

CAP CLIP
POSITION

Ford 3800 cc (3.8L)
Firing order: 1–4–2–5–3–6
Distributor rotation: counterclockwise

CAPACITIES

Year	Model	VIN	No. Cylinder Displacement cu. in. (liter)	Engine Crankcase (qts.) with Filter	Engine Crankcase (qts.) without Filter	Transmission (pts.) 4-Spd	Transmission (pts.) 5-Spd	Transmission (pts.) Auto.	Drive Axle (pts.)	Fuel Tank (gal.)	Cooling System (qts.)
1987	Taurus	D	4-153 (2.5)	5.0	4.5	—	6.2	16.6	①	②	8.3
	Taurus	U	6-182 (3.0)	4.5	4.0	—	6.2	21.8	①	②	③
	Sable	D	4-153 (2.5)	5.0	4.5	—	6.2	16.6	①	②	8.3
	Sable	U	6-182 (3.0)	4.5	4.0	—	6.2	21.8	①	②	③
1988	Taurus	D	4-153 (2.5)	5.0	4.5	—	6.2	16.6	①	②	8.3
	Taurus	U	6-182 (3.0)	4.5	4.0	—	6.2	21.8	①	②	③
	Taurus	4	6-232 (3.8)	5.0	4.5	—	—	26.2	①	②	12.1
	Sable	D	4-153 (2.5)	5.0	4.5	—	6.2	16.6	①	②	8.3
	Sable	U	6-182 (3.0)	4.5	4.0	—	6.2	21.8	①	②	③
	Sable	4	6-232 (3.8)	5.0	4.5	—	—	26.2	①	②	12.1
	Continental	4	6-232 (3.8)	4.5	—	—	—	26.2	①	18.6	11.1

CAPACITIES

Year	Model	VIN	No. Cylinder Displacement cu. in. (liter)	Engine Crankcase (qts.) with Filter	without Filter	Transmission (pts.) 4-Spd	5-Spd	Auto.	Drive Axle (pts.)	Fuel Tank (gal.)	Cooling System (qts.)
1989	Taurus	D	4-153 (2.5)	5.0	4.5	—	6.2	16.6	①	②	8.3
	Taurus	U	6-182 (3.0)	4.5	4.0	—	6.2	21.8	①	②	③
	Taurus	Y	6-182 (3.0)SHO	4.5	4.0	—	6.2	21.8	①	②	11.6
	Taurus	4	6-232 (3.8)	5.0	4.5	—	—	26.2	①	②	12.1
	Sable	D	4-153 (2.5)	5.0	4.5	—	6.2	16.6	①	②	8.3
	Sable	U	6-182 (3.0)	4.5	4.0	—	6.2	21.8	①	②	③
	Sable	4	6-232 (3.8)	5.0	4.5	—	—	26.2	①	②	12.1
	Continental	4	6-232 (3.8)	4.5	4.0	—	—	26.2	①	18.6	12.1
1990-91	Taurus	D	4-153 (2.5)	5.0	4.5	—	—	16.0	①	②	8.3
	Taurus	U	6-182 (3.0)	4.5	4.0	—	—	25.6	①	②	③
	Taurus	Y	6-182 (3.0)SHO	5.0	4.5	—	6.2	—	①	②	11.6
	Taurus	4	6-232 (3.8)	4.5	4.0	—	—	25.6	①	②	12.1
	Sable	U	6-182 (3.0)	4.5	4.0	—	—	25.6	①	②	③
	Sable	4	6-232 (3.8)	4.5	4.0	—	—	25.6	①	②	12.1
	Continental	4	6-232 (3.8)	4.5	4.0	—	—	25.6	①	18.6	12.1

SHO Super High Output
① Included in the transaxle capacity
② Standard—16.0 gals.
  Optiononl extended range—18.6 gals.
③ All models except station wagon with air conditioning—11 qts.
  Station Wagon with air conditioning—11.8 qts.

CAMSHAFT SPECIFICATIONS

All measurements given in inches

Year	VIN	No. Cylinder Displacement cu. in. (liter)	Journal Diameter 1	2	3	4	5	Lobe Lift In.	Ex.	Bearing Clearance	Camshaft End Play
1987	D	4-153 (2.5)	2.006– 2.008	2.006– 2.008	2.006– 2.008	2.006– 2.008	2.006– 2.008	0.249	0.239	0.001– 0.003	0.009
	U	6-182 (3.0)	2.007– 2.008	2.007– 2.008	2.007– 2.008	2.007– 2.008	—	0.260	0.260	0.001– 0.003	0.005
1988	D	4-153 (2.5)	2.006– 2.008	2.006– 2.008	2.006– 2.008	2.006– 2.008	2.006– 2.008	0.249	0.239	0.001– 0.003	0.009
	U	6-182 (3.0)	2.007– 2.008	2.007– 2.008	2.007– 2.008	2.007– 2.008	—	0.260	0.260	0.001– 0.003	0.005
	4	6-232 (3.8)	2.050– 2.052	2.050– 2.052	2.050– 2.052	2.050– 2.052	—	0.240	0.241	0.001– 0.003	①

CAMSHAFT SPECIFICATIONS

All measurements given in inches

Year	VIN	No. Cylinder Displacement cu. in. (liter)	Journal Diameter					Lobe Lift		Bearing Clearance	Camshaft End Play
			1	2	3	4	5	In.	Ex.		
1989	D	4-153 (2.5)	2.006–2.008	2.006–2.008	2.006–2.008	2.006–2.008	2.006–2.008	0.249	0.239	0.001–0.003	0.009
	U	6-182 (3.0)	2.007–2.008	2.007–2.008	2.007–2.008	2.007–2.008	—	0.260	0.260	0.001–0.003	0.001–0.005
	Y	6-182 (3.0)	1.2189–1.2195	1.2189–1.2195	1.2189–1.2195	1.2189–1.2195	1.2189–1.2195	0.335	0.315	0.001–0.003	0.012
	4	6-232 (3.8)	2.050–2.052	2.050–2.052	2.050–2.052	2.050–2.052	—	0.240	0.241	0.001–0.003	①
1990-91	D	4-153 (2.5)	2.006–2.008	2.006–2.008	2.006–2.008	2.006–2.008	2.006–2.008	0.249	0.239	0.001–0.003	0.009
	U	6-182 (3.0)	2.007–2.008	2.007–2.008	2.007–2.008	2.007–2.008	—	0.260	0.260	0.001–0.003	0.001–0.005
	Y	6-182 (3.0)	1.2189–1.2195	1.2189–1.2195	1.2189–1.2195	1.2189–1.2195	1.2189–1.2195	0.335	0.315	0.001–0.003	0.012
	4	6-232 (3.8)	2.050–2.052	2.050–2.052	2.050–2.052	2.050–2.052	—	0.245	0.259	0.001–0.003	①

① The camshaft is retained by a spring; there is no endplay.

CRANKSHAFT AND CONNECTING ROD SPECIFICATIONS

All measurements are given in inches.

Year	VIN	No. Cylinder Displacement cu. in. (liter)	Crankshaft				Connecting Rod		
			Main Brg. Journal Dia.	Main Brg. Oil Clearance	Shaft End-play	Thrust on No.	Journal Diameter	Oil Clearance	Side Clearance
1987	D	4-153 (2.5)	2.2489–2.2490	0.0008–0.0015	0.004–0.008	3	2.1232–2.1240	0.0008–0.0014	0.0035–0.0105
	U	6-182 (3.0)	2.5190–2.5198	0.0010–0.0014	0.004–0.008	3	2.1253–2.1261	0.0010–0.0014	0.006–0.014
1988	D	4-153 (2.5)	2.2489–2.2490	0.0008–0.0015	0.004–0.008	3	2.1232–2.1240	0.0008–0.0014	0.0035–0.0105
	U	6-182 (3.0)	2.5190–2.5198	0.0010–0.0014	0.004–0.008	3	2.1253–2.1261	0.0010–0.0014	0.006–0.014
	4	6-232 (3.8)	2.5190–2.5198	0.0010–0.0014	0.004–0.008	3	2.3103–2.3111	0.0010–0.0014	0.0047–0.0114
1989	D	4-153 (2.5)	2.2489–2.2490	0.0008–0.0015	0.004–0.008	3	2.1232–2.1240	0.0008–0.0014	0.0035–0.0105
	U	6-182 (3.0)	2.5190–2.5198	0.0010–0.0014	0.004–0.008	3	2.1253–2.1261	0.0010–0.0014	0.006–0.014

CRANKSHAFT AND CONNECTING ROD SPECIFICATIONS

All measurements are given in inches.

Year	VIN	No. Cylinder Displacement cu. in. (liter)	Crankshaft				Connecting Rod		
			Main Brg. Journal Dia.	Main Brg. Oil Clearance	Shaft End-play	Thrust on No.	Journal Diameter	Oil Clearance	Side Clearance
1989	Y	6-182 (3.0)	2.5187–2.5197	0.0011–0.0022	0.0008–0.0087	3	2.0463–2.0472	0.0009–0.0022	0.0063–0.0123
	4	6-232 (3.8)	2.5190–2.5198	0.0010–0.0014	0.004–0.008	3	2.3103–2.3111	0.0010–0.0014	0.0047–0.0114
1990-91	D	4-153 (2.5)	2.2489–2.2490	0.0008–0.0015	0.004–0.008	3	2.1232–2.1240	0.0008–0.0015	0.0035–0.0105
	U	6-182 (3.0)	2.5190–2.5198	0.0010–0.0014	0.004–0.008	3	2.1253–2.1261	0.0010–0.0014	0.006–0.014
	Y	6-182 (3.0)	2.5187–2.5197	0.0011–0.0022	0.0008–0.0087	3	2.0463–2.0472	0.0009–0.0022	0.0063–0.0123
	4	6-232 (3.8)	2.5190–2.5198	0.0010–0.0014	0.004–0.008	3	2.3103–2.3111	0.0010–0.0014	0.0047–0.0114

VALVE SPECIFICATIONS

Year	VIN	No. Cylinder Displacement cu. in. (liter)	Seat Angle (deg.)	Face Angle (deg.)	Spring Test Pressure (lbs.)	Spring Installed Height (in.)	Stem-to-Guide Clearance (in.)		Stem Diameter (in.)	
							Intake	Exhaust	Intake	Exhaust
1987	D	4-153 (2.5)	45	44	182 @ 1.13	1.49	0.0018	0.0023	0.3422	0.3418
	U	6-182 (3.0)	45	44	185 @ 1.11	1.58	0.0010–0.0028	0.0015–0.0032	0.3126	0.3121
1988	D	4-153 (2.5)	45	44	182 @ 1.13	1.49	0.0018	0.0023	0.3422	0.3418
	U	6-182 (3.0)	45	44	185 @ 1.11	1.58	0.0010–0.0028	0.0015–0.0032	0.3126	0.3121
	4	6-232 (3.8)	46	46	190 @ 1.28	2.02	0.0010–0.0028	0.0015–0.0033	0.3423–0.0033	0.3418–0.3410
1989	D	4-153 (2.5)	45	44	182 @ 1.13	1.49	0.0018	0.0023	0.3422	0.3418
	U	6-182 (3.0)	45	44	185 @ 1.11	1.58	0.0010–0.0028	0.0015–0.0032	0.3126	0.3121
	Y	6-182 (3.0)	45	45.5	120.8 @ 1.19	1.52	0.0010–0.0023	0.0012–0.0025	0.2346–0.2352	0.2344–0.2350
	4	6-232 (3.8)	46	46	190 @ 1.28	2.02	0.0010–0.0028	0.0015–0.0033	0.3423–0.3415	0.3418–0.3410
1990-91	D	4-153 (2.5)	45	44	182 @ 1.13	1.49	0.0018	0.0023	0.3415–0.3422	0.3411–0.3418
	U	6-182 (3.0)	45	44	180 @ 1.16	1.58	0.0010–0.0028	0.0015–0.0033	0.3134–0.3126	0.3129–0.3121
	Y	6-182 (3.0)	45	45.5	120.8 @ 1.19	1.52	0.0010–0.0023	0.0012–0.0025	0.2346–0.2352	0.2344–0.2350
	4	6-232 (3.8)	44.5	45.8	220 @ 1.18	1.97	0.0010–0.0028	0.0015–0.0033	0.3423–0.3415	0.3418–0.3410

PISTON AND RING SPECIFICATIONS
All measurements are given in inches.

| Year | VIN | No. Cylinder Displacement cu. in. (liter) | Piston Clearance | Ring Gap | | | Ring Side Clearance | | |
				Top Compression	Bottom Compression	Oil Control	Top Compression	Bottom Compression	Oil Control
1987	D	4-153 (2.5)	0.0012–0.0022	0.0080–0.0160	0.0080–0.0160	0.0150–0.0550	0.0020–0.0040	0.0020–0.0040	Snug
	U	6-182 (3.0)	0.0012–0.0023	0.0100–0.0200	0.0100–0.0200	0.0100–0.0490	0.0016–0.0037	0.0016–0.0037	Snug
1988	D	4-153 (2.5)	0.0012–0.0022	0.0080–0.0160	0.0080–0.0160	0.0150–0.0550	0.0020–0.0040	0.0020–0.0040	Snug
	U	6-182 (3.0)	0.0014–0.0022	0.0100–0.0200	0.0100–0.0200	0.0100–0.0490	0.0016–0.0037	0.0016–0.0037	Snug
	4	6-232 (3.8)	0.0014–0.0032	0.0100–0.0200	0.0100–0.0200	0.0150–0.0583	0.0016–0.0037	0.0016–0.0037	Snug
1989	D	4-153 (2.5)	0.0012–0.0022	0.0080–0.0160	0.0080–0.0160	0.0150–0.0550	0.0020–0.0040	0.0020–0.0040	Snug
	U	6-182 (3.0)	0.0014–0.0022	0.0100–0.0200	0.0100–0.0200	0.0100–0.0490	0.0016–0.0037	0.0016–0.0037	Snug
	Y	6-182 (3.0)	0.0012–0.0020	0.0120–0.0180	0.0120–0.0180	0.0080–0.0200	0.0080–0.0024	0.0006–0.0022	0.0024–0.0050
	4	6-232 (3.8)	0.0014–0.0032	0.0100–0.0200	0.0100–0.0200	0.0150–0.0583	0.0016–0.0037	0.0016–0.0037	Snug
1990–91	D	4-153 (2.5)	0.0012–0.0022	0.0080–0.0160	0.0080–0.0160	0.0150–0.0550	0.0020–0.0040	0.0020–0.0040	Snug
	U	6-182 (3.0)	0.0014–0.0022	0.0100–0.0200	0.0100–0.0200	0.0100–0.0490	0.0012–0.0031	0.0012–0.0031	Snug
	Y	6-182 (3.0)	0.0012–0.0020	0.0120–0.0180	0.0120–0.0180	0.0080–0.0200	0.0080–0.0024	0.0006–0.0022	0.0024–0.0059
	4	6-232 (3.8)	0.0014–0.0032	0.0100–0.0200	0.0100–0.0200	0.0150–0.0583	0.0016–0.0034	0.0016–0.0034	Snug

TORQUE SPECIFICATIONS
All readings in ft. lbs.

| Year | VIN | No. Cylinder Displacement cu. in. (liter) | Cylinder Head Bolts | Main Bearing Bolts | Rod Bearing Bolts | Crankshaft Pulley Bolts | Flywheel Bolts | Manifold | | Spark Plugs |
								Intake	Exhaust	
1987	D	4-153 (2.5)	①	51–66	21–26	140–170	54–64	15–23	③	5–10
	U	6-182 (3.0)	③	65–81	④	141–169	54–64	⑤	②	5–10
1988	D	4-153 (2.5)	①	51–66	21–26	140–170	54–64	15–23	③	5–10
	U	6-182 (3.0)	③	65–81	④	141–169	54–64	⑤	②	5–10
	4	6-232 (3.8)	⑥	65–81	31–36	93–121	54–64	⑦	16–24	5–11
1989	D	4-153 (2.5)	①	51–66	21–26	140–170	54–64	15–23	②	5–10
	U	6-182 (3.0)	⑧	65–81	④	141–169	54–64	⑤	②	5–10
	Y	6-182 (3.0)	61–69	58–65	33–36	112–127	51–58	12–17	26–38	16–20
	4	6-232 (3.8)	⑥	65–81	31–36	93–121	54–64	⑦	16–24	5–11

TORQUE SPECIFICATIONS
All readings in ft. lbs.

Year	VIN	No. Cylinder Displacement cu. in. (liter)	Cylinder Head Bolts	Main Bearing Bolts	Rod Bearing Bolts	Crankshaft Pulley Bolts	Flywheel Bolts	Manifold Intake	Manifold Exhaust	Spark Plugs
1990-91	D	4-153 (2.5)	①	51-66	21-26	140-170	54-64	15-23	②	5-10
	U	6-182 (3.0)	⑧	63-69	23-29	107	54-64	⑤	19	5-11
	Y	6-182 (3.0)	61-69	58-65	33-36	112-127	51-58	12-17	26-38	16-20
	4	6-232 (3.8)	⑥	65-81	31-36	93-121	54-64	⑦	15-22	5-11

① Tighten in 2 steps: 52-59 ft. lbs. and then the final torque of 70-76 ft. lbs.
② Tighten in 2 steps
  Step 1: 5-7 ft. lbs.
  Step 2: 20-30 ft. lbs.
③ Tighten in 2 steps: 48-54 ft. lbs. and then the final torque of 63-80 ft. lbs.

④ Tighten to 20-28 ft. lbs. and then back off the nuts a minimum of 2 revolutions; then apply the final torque of 20-25 ft. lbs.
⑤ Tighten in 3 steps: 11, 18 and the final torque of 24 ft. lbs.

⑥ Tighten in 4 steps:
  Step 1: 37 ft. lbs.
  Step 2: 45 ft. lbs.
  Step 3: 52 ft. lbs.
  Step 4: 59 ft. lbs.

⑦ Tighten in 3 steps:
  Step 1: 7 ft. lbs.
  Step 2: 15 ft. lbs.
  Step 3: 24 ft. lbs.
⑧ Tighten in 2 steps:
  Step 1: 33-41 ft. lbs.
  Step 2: 63-73 ft. lbs.

BRAKE SPECIFICATIONS
All measurements in inches unless noted

Year	Model	Lug Nut Torque (ft. lbs.)	Master Cylinder Bore	Brake Disc Minimum Thickness	Brake Disc Maximum Runout	Standard Brake Drum Diameter	Minimum Lining Thickness Front	Minimum Lining Thickness Rear
1987	Taurus	80-105	0.875	0.896	0.003	8.86	0.125	0.030
	Sable	80-105	0.875	0.896	0.003	8.86	0.125	0.030
1988	Taurus	80-105	0.875	0.896	0.003	8.86	0.125	0.030
	Sable	80-105	0.875	0.896	0.003	8.86	0.125	0.030
	Continental	80-105	—	①	0.002	—	0.125	0.123
1989	Taurus	80-105	0.875	0.896	0.003	8.86	0.125	0.030
	Taurus SHO	80-105	0.875	②	③	—	0.125	0.123
	Sable	80-105	0.875	0.896	0.003	8.86	0.125	0.030
	Continental	80-105	—	①	0.002	—	0.125	0.123
1990-91	Taurus	80-105	0.875	0.974	0.003	④	0.125	0.030
	Taurus SHO	80-105	0.875	0.974	③	—	0.125	0.123
	Sable	80-105	0.875	0.974	0.003	④	0.125	0.030
	Continental	80-105	0.940	0.974	0.002	—	0.125	0.123

① Front—0.097 in.
  Rear—0.974 in.
② Front & rear—0.097 in.
③ Front—0.003 in.
  Rear—0.002 in.
④ Sedan—8.85
  Wagon—9.84

WHEEL ALIGNMENT

Year	Model		Caster Range (deg.)	Caster Preferred Setting (deg.)	Camber Range (deg.)	Camber Preferred Setting (deg.)	Toe-in (in.)	Steering Axis Inclination (deg.)
1987	Taurus	Front	3P-6P ①	4P	1³/₃₂N-³/₃₂P	¹/₂N	⁷/₃₂-¹/₆₄	15³/₈
		Rear	—	—	1⁵/₈N-¹/₄N	—	¹³/₆₄N-¹⁹/₆₄P ②	—
	Sable	Front	3P-6P ①	4P	1³/₃₂N-³/₃₂P	¹/₂N	⁷/₃₂-¹/₆₄	15³/₈
		Rear	—	—	1⁵/₈N-¹/₄N	—	¹³/₆₄N-¹⁹/₆₄P ②	—

WHEEL ALIGNMENT

Year	Model		Caster Range (deg.)	Caster Preferred Setting (deg.)	Camber Range (deg.)	Camber Preferred Setting (deg.)	Toe-in (in.)	Steering Axis Inclination (deg.)
1988	Taurus	Front	3P–6P	4P	$1^{3}/_{32}$N–$^{3}/_{32}$P	$^{1}/_{2}$N	$^{7}/_{32}$–$^{1}/_{64}$	$15^{3}/_{8}$
		Rear	—	—	$1^{5}/_{8}$N–$^{1}/_{4}$N	—	$^{13}/_{64}$N–$^{19}/_{64}$P ②	—
	Sable	Front	3P–6P ①	4P	$1^{3}/_{32}$N–$^{3}/_{32}$P	$^{1}/_{2}$N	$^{7}/_{32}$–$^{1}/_{64}$	$15^{3}/_{8}$
		Rear	—	—	$1^{5}/_{8}$N–$^{1}/_{4}$N	—	$^{13}/_{64}$N–$^{19}/_{64}$P ②	—
	Continental	Front	4P–6P ①	5P	$1^{3}/_{32}$N–$^{3}/_{32}$P	$^{1}/_{2}$N	$^{7}/_{32}$–$^{1}/_{64}$	$15^{3}/_{8}$
		Rear	—	—	$1^{5}/_{8}$N–$^{1}/_{4}$N	—	$^{13}/_{64}$N–$^{19}/_{64}$P ②	—
1989	Taurus	Front	3P–6P ①	4P	$1^{3}/_{32}$N–$^{3}/_{32}$P	$^{1}/_{2}$N	$^{7}/_{32}$–$^{1}/_{64}$	$15^{3}/_{8}$
		Rear	—	—	$1^{5}/_{8}$N–$^{1}/_{4}$N	—	$^{13}/_{64}$N–$^{19}/_{64}$P ②	—
	Sable	Front	3P–6P ①	4P	$1^{3}/_{32}$N–$^{3}/_{32}$P	$^{1}/_{2}$N	$^{7}/_{32}$–$^{1}/_{64}$	$15^{3}/_{8}$
		Rear	—	—	$1^{5}/_{8}$N–$^{1}/_{4}$N	—	$^{13}/_{64}$N–$^{19}/_{64}$P ②	—
	Continental	Front	4P–6P	5P	$1^{3}/_{32}$N–$^{3}/_{32}$P	$^{1}/_{2}$N	$^{7}/_{32}$–$^{1}/_{64}$	$15^{3}/_{8}$
		Rear	—	—	$1^{5}/_{8}$N–$^{1}/_{4}$N	$1^{15}/_{16}$	$^{13}/_{64}$N–$^{19}/_{64}$P ②	$15^{1}/_{2}$
1990–91	Taurus Sedan	Front	$2^{13}/_{16}$P–$5^{13}/_{16}$P ①	$3^{13}/_{16}$P	$1^{3}/_{32}$N–$^{3}/_{32}$P	$^{1}/_{2}$N	$^{7}/_{32}$N–$^{1}/_{64}$P	$15^{1}/_{2}$
		Rear	—	—	$1^{5}/_{8}$N–$^{1}/_{4}$N	$^{7}/_{8}$N	$^{1}/_{32}$N–$^{3}/_{32}$P ②	—
	Sable	Front	$2^{11}/_{16}$P–$5^{11}/_{16}$P ①	$3^{11}/_{16}$P	$1^{3}/_{32}$N–$^{3}/_{32}$P	$^{1}/_{2}$N	$^{7}/_{32}$N–$^{1}/_{64}$P	$15^{1}/_{2}$
		Rear	—	—	$1^{5}/_{8}$N–$^{1}/_{4}$N	$^{7}/_{8}$N	$^{1}/_{32}$N–$^{3}/_{32}$P ②	—
	Taurus-Sable Wagon	Front	$2^{11}/_{16}$P–$5^{11}/_{16}$P ①	$3^{11}/_{16}$P	$1^{3}/_{64}$N–$^{3}/_{32}$P	$^{1}/_{2}$N	$^{7}/_{32}$N–$^{1}/_{64}$P	$15^{1}/_{2}$
		Rear	—	—	$1^{5}/_{8}$N–$^{1}/_{4}$N	$^{7}/_{8}$N	$^{1}/_{32}$N–$^{3}/_{32}$P ②	—
	Continental	Front	$3^{5}/_{8}$P–$5^{1}/_{8}$P ①	$4^{3}/_{8}$P	$1^{11}/_{16}$N–$^{1}/_{2}$N	$1^{1}/_{8}$N	$^{7}/_{32}$N–$^{1}/_{32}$P	$15^{1}/_{2}$
		Rear	—	—	2N–$^{5}/_{8}$N	$1^{5}/_{16}$N	$^{1}/_{32}$N–$^{7}/_{32}$P ②	—

① The caster measurements are made by turning each individual wheel through the prescribed angle of sweep
② Individual sides

ENGINE ELECTRICAL

NOTE: Disconnecting the negative battery cable on some vehicles may interfere with the functions of the on board computer systems and may require the computer to undergo a relearning process, once the negative battery cable is reconnected.

Distributor

REMOVAL

Except 3.0L SHO Engine

The distributor used with these engines is a universal design which is gear driven and has a die cast base that incorporates in integrally mounted TFI-IV (Thick Film Ignition) ignition module, a Hall Effect vane switch stator assembly and provision for fixed octane adjustment. The design deletes the conventional centrifugal and vacuum advance mechanisms.

NOTE: No distributor calibration is required. Initial timing is a normal adjustment.

REMOVAL

1. Disconnect the negative battery cable.
2. Disconnect the primary wiring connector from distributor.

NOTE: Before removing the distributor cap, mark the position of the No. 1 wire tower on the distributor base for assembly reference.

3. Remove distributor cap and position it and the attached wires aside, so as not to interfere with removing the distributor.
4. Remove the rotor.

5. Remove the TFI-IV harness connector.
6. Remove the distributor hold-down bolt and clamp. Remove the distributor. Be careful not to disturb the intermediate driveshaft.

INSTALLATION

Timing Not Disturbed

1. Install the distributor in the same position it was when it was removed.
2. Install the distributor hold-down bolt and clamp but do not tighten at this time.
3. Connect the distributor to the wiring harness.
4. Install the rotor, distributor cap and spark plug wires. Make sure that the ignition wires are securely connected to the distributor cap and spark plugs. Tighten the distributor cap screws to 18–23 inch lbs. (2.0–2.6 Nm).
5. Connect a suitable timing light

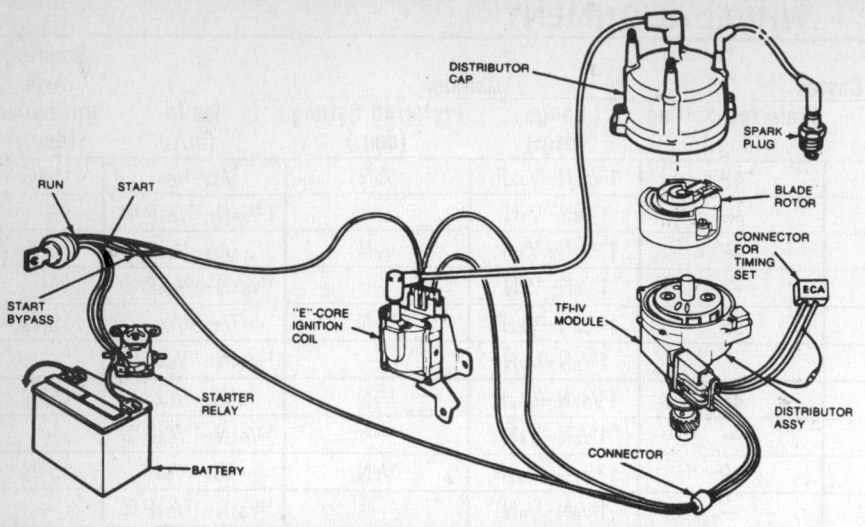

Exploded view of the distributor and ignition system

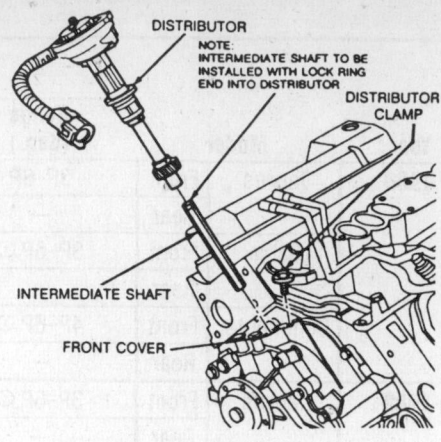

Distributor mounting—3.8L engine

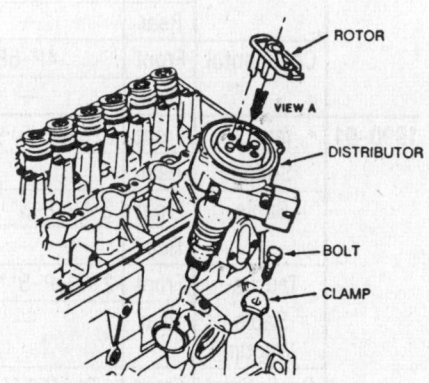

Distributor mounting—2.5L engine

and set the initial timing.

6. Tighten the distributor retaining bolt to 17–25 ft. lbs. (23–34 Nm) on 2.5L and 3.0L engines and 40 ft. lbs. (55 Nm) on 3.8L engines.

7. Recheck the initial timing and adjust if necessary.

Timing Disturbed

1. Rotate the engine until No. 1 piston is at TDC of the compression stroke and complete the following:

a. Align the timing marks for correct initial timing.

b. Rotate the distributor shaft so the center rod on the multi-point rotor (or rotor blade) is pointing toward the alignment mark previously made on the distributor base.

c. Continue rotating slightly so the leading edge of the vane is centered in the vane switch stator assembly.

d. Rotate the distributor in the block to align the leading edge of the vane and vane switch stator assembly and verify that the rotor is pointing at No. 1 cap terminal.

e. Install distributor retaining bolt and clamp. Do not tighten at this time.

2. If the vane and vane switch stator cannot be aligned by rotating the distributor in the block, pull the distributor out of the block enough to disengage the distributor gear and rotate the distributor shaft to engage a different distributor gear tooth. Repeat Step 1 as necessary.

3. Connect the distributor to the wiring harness.

4. Install the distributor cap, rotor and ignition wires. Check that the ignition wires are securely connected to the distributor cap and spark plugs. Tighten the distributor cap screws to 18–35 inch lbs. (2.0–2.6 Nm).

5. Set the initial timing with a suitable timing light.

6. Tighten the distributor retaining bolt to 17–25 ft. lbs. (23–34 Nm) on 2.5L and 3.0L engines and 40 ft. lbs. (55 Nm) on 3.8L engines.

7. Recheck the initial timing. Adjust if necessary.

Distributorless Ignition

3.0L SHO Engine

The 3.0L SHO engine is equipped with a distributorless ignition system (DIS) which consists of the following components:

Crankshaft timing sensor
Camshaft sensor
DIS ignition module
Ignition coil pack
The spark angle portion of the EEC-IV module

REMOVAL & INSTALLATION

Crankshaft Timing Sensor

1. Disconnect the negative battery cable.

2. Loosen the tensioner pulleys for the air conditioning compressor and the power steering pump belts.

3. Remove the belts from the crankshaft pulley.

4. Remove the upper timing belt cover.

5. Disconnect the sensor wiring harness at the connector and route the wiring harness through the belt cover.

6. Raise the vehicle and support it safely.

7. Remove the right front wheel and tire assembly.

8. Remove the crankshaft pulley using universal puller T67L-3600-A or equivalent.

9. Remove the lower timing belt cover.

10. Rotate the crankshaft by hand, to position the metal vane of the shutter outside of the sensor air gap.

11. Remove the crankshaft sensor mounting screws and remove the sensor.

To install:

12. Route the sensor wiring harness through the belt cover. Install the sensor assembly on the mounting pad and install but do not tighten, the retaining screws.

13. Use a 0.03 in. (0.8mm) feeler gauge to set the clearance between the crankshaft sensor assembly and 1 vane on the crankshaft timing pulley and vane assembly. Tighten the screws to 22–31 inch lbs. (2.5–3.5 Nm).

14. Install the lower timing belt cover. Install the crankshaft pulley using a suitable tool. Tighten the pulley bolt to 112–127 ft. lbs. (152–172 Nm).

15. Install the right front wheel and tire assembly. Lower the vehicle.

16. Route and connect the sensor wiring harness.

17. Install the upper timing belt cover.

18. Install the air conditioning and power steering belts and adjust them

to the proper tension.

19. Connect the negative battery cable.

Camshaft Sensor Assembly

1. Disconnect the negative battery cable.
2. Remove the engine torque strut.
3. Disconnect the camshaft sensor wiring connector.
4. Remove the mounting bolts and remove the sensor.
5. To install, reverse the removal procedure. Tighten the mounting bolts to 22–31 inch lbs. (2.5–3.5 Nm).

DIS Ignition Module

1. Disconnect the negative battery cable.
2. Disconnect the wiring connectors at the module.
3. Remove the module mounting bolts and remove the module.
4. To install, reverse the removal procedure. Apply a uniform coating of heat sink grease to the mounting surface of the DIS module before it is installed. Tighten the mounting bolts to 22–31 inch lbs. (2.5–3.5 Nm).

Ignition Coil Pack

1. Disconnect the negative battery cable.
2. Remove the cover from the coil pack and disconnect the electrical connector.
3. Remove the spark plug wires by squeezing the locking tabs to release the coil boot retainers.
4. Remove the coil pack mounting screws and remove the coil pack.
5. To install, reverse the removal procedure. Tighten the mounting screws to 40–62 inch lbs. (4.5–7 Nm).

Ignition Timing

ADJUSTMENT

The timing marks on the 2.5L engine are visible through a hole in the top of the transaxle case. The 3.0L, 3.0L SHO and 3.8L engines have the timing marks on the crankshaft pulley and a timing pointer near the pulley.

1. Place the transaxle in the **P** or **N** position. Firmly apply the parking brake and block the wheels.
2. Open the hood, locate the timing marks and clean with a stiff brush or solvent. On vehicles with manual transaxle, it will be necessary to remove the cover plate which allows access to to the timing marks.
3. Using white chalk or paint, mark the specified timing mark and pointer.
4. Remove the in-line spout connector or remove the shorting bar from the double wire spout connector. The spout connector is the center wire between the electronic control assembly (ECA) connector and the thick film ignition (TFI) module.
5. Connect a suitable inductive type timing light to the No. 1 spark plug wire. Do not, puncture and ignition wire with any type of probing device.

NOTE: The high ignition coil charging currents generated in the EEC-IV ignition system may falsely trigger timing lights with capacitive or direct connect pick-ups. It is necessary that an inductive type timing light be used in this procedure.

6. Connect a suitable tachometer to the engine. The ignition coil connector allows a test lead with an alligator clip to be connected to the Distributor Electronic Control (DEC) terminal without removing the connector.
7. Start the engine and let it run until it reaches normal operating temperature.
8. Check the engine idle rpm, if it is not within specifications, adjust as necessary. After the rpm has been adjusted or checked, aim the timing light at the timing marks. If they are not aligned, loosen the distributor clamp bolts slightly and rotate the distributor body until the marks are aligned under timing light illumination.
9. Tighten the distributor clamp bolts and recheck the ignition timing. Readjust the idle speed. Shut the engine off, remove all test equipment, reconnect the in-line spout connector to the distributor and reinstall the cover plate on the manual transaxle vehicles.

Alternator

For further information on the charging system, please refer to "Charging and Starting" in the Unit Repair section.

PRECAUTIONS

Several precautions must be observed with alternator equipped vehicles to avoid damage to the unit.

- If the battery is removed for any reason, make sure it is reconnected with the correct polarity. Reversing the battery connections may result in damage to the one-way rectifiers.
- When utilizing a booster battery as a starting aid, always connect the positive to positive terminals and the negative terminal from the booster battery to a good engine ground on the vehicle being started.
- Never use a fast charger as a booster to start vehicles.

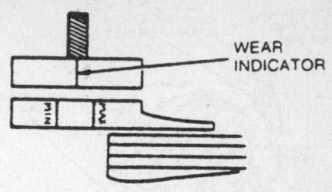

Automatic tensioner drive belt wear indicator used on some 3.0L engines and all 2.5 and 3.8L engines

- Disconnect the battery cables when charging the battery with a fast charger.
- Never attempt to polarize the alternator.
- Do not use test lamps of more than 12 volts when checking diode continuity.
- Do not short across or ground any of the alternator terminals.
- The polarity of the battery, alternator and regulator must be matched and considered before making any electrical connections within the system.
- Never separate the alternator on an open circuit. Make sure all connections within the circuit are clean and tight.
- Disconnect the battery ground terminal when performing any service on electrical components.
- Disconnect the battery if arc welding is to be done on the vehicle.

BELT TENSION ADJUSTMENT

2.5L and 3.8L Engines

The V-ribbed belts used on some engines utilize an automatic belt tensioner whose function is to maintain the proper belt tension for the life of the belt. The automatic belt tensioners used on the 2.5L and 3.8L engines incorporate wear indicator **MINIMUM** and **MAXIMUM** marks.

1. Inspect the wear indicator marks with the engine **OFF** (not running).
2. If the indicator mark is not within the 2 marks, the belt is worn or an improper belt is installed.
3. A loose or improper belt will result in slippage which will in turn cause a noise complaint or improper accessory operation.
4. Automatic tensioners do not require removal when making a drive belt replacement.
5. When removing a drive belt, rotate the tensioner away from the belt.

3.0L Engine

1. Disconnect the negative battery cable.
2. Loosen the alternator adjustment and pivot bolts.

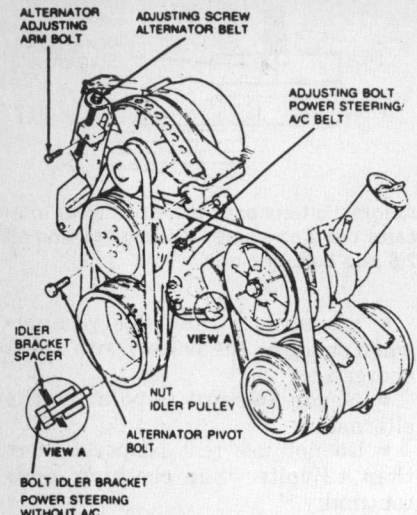

View of the drive belts—3.0L engine

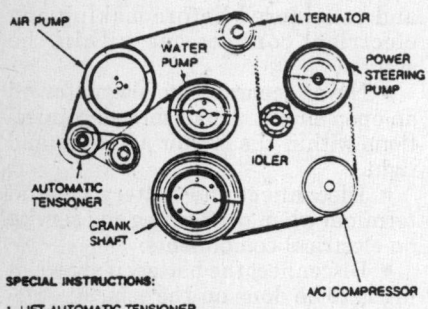

SPECIAL INSTRUCTIONS:

1. LIFT AUTOMATIC TENSIONER
   USING A 1/2-INCH DRIVE BREAKER BAR
   IN DIRECTION OF ARROW
2. INSTALL DRIVE BELT OVER PULLEYS
   PER APPROPRIATE BELT ROUTING

Drive belt arrangement—3.8L engines

3. Apply tension to the belt using the adjusting screw.

4. Using a belt tension gauge, set the belt to the proper tension. The tension should be 150 lbs. for a new belt and 120 lbs. for a used belt.

5. When the belt is properly tensioned, tighten the alternator adjustment bolt to 27 ft. lbs. (37 Nm).

6. Remove the tension gauge and run the engine for 5 minutes.

7. With the engine **OFF** and the belt tension gauge in place, check that the adjusting screw is in contact with the bracket before loosening the alternator adjustment bolt. Rotate the adjustment screw until the belt is tensioned to 120 lbs.

8. Tighten the alternator adjustment bolt to 27 ft. lbs. (37 Nm) and the pivot bolt to 51 ft. lbs. (69 Nm).

3.0L SHO Engine

1. Disconnect the negative battery cable.
2. Loosen the idler pulley nut.
3. Turn the adjusting bolt until the belt is adjusted properly.

NOTE: Turning the wrench to the right tightens the belt adjustment and turning the wrench to the left loosens the belt tension.

4. Tighten the idler pulley nut to 25–37 ft. lbs. (34–50 Nm) and check the belt tension.

REMOVAL & INSTALLATION

1. Disconnect the negative battery cable and remove the pulley cover shield, if equipped.

NOTE: Disconnecting the negative battery cable on some vehicles may interfere with the functions of the on board computer systems and may require the computer to undergo a relearning process, once the negative battery cable is reconnected.

2. Loosen the alternator pivot bolt and remove the adjustment bracket-to-alternator bolt. Slide the alternator downward and remove the drive belt.

3. Identify, tag and disconnect the alternator wiring.

NOTE: Some vehicles use a push-on wiring connector on the field and stator connections. Pull or push straight when removing or installing the connector. Be careful not to damage the connector.

4. Remove the pivot bolt and the alternator.

To install:

5. Position the alternator assembly on the engine and install the pivot bolt, but do not tighten until the belt is tensioned.

6. Install the drive belt over the alternator pulley.

7. Adjust the belt tension and tighten the adjuster and pivot bolts.

8. Connect the wiring to the alternator.

9. Install the pulley cover shield, if equipped. Connect the negative battery cable.

Voltage Regulator

For further information on the charging system, please refer to "Charging and Starting" in the Unit Repair section.

REMOVAL & INSTALLATION

NOTE: There are 3 types of regulators being used, depending on the vehicle, engine, alternator output and type of dash mounted charging indicator used (light or ammeter). The regulators are 100% solid state and are calibrated and preset by the manufacturer. No adjustments are required or possible on these regulators.

1. Disconnect the negative battery cable.

2. Disconnect the electrical connectors from the wiring harness.

3. Remove the regulator mounting screws and the regulator.

4. Installation is the reverse of the removal procedure.

5. Connect the negative battery cable. Test the system for proper voltage regulation.

Starter

For further information on the charging system, please refer to "Charging and Starting" in the Unit Repair section.

REMOVAL & INSTALLATION

1. Disconnect the negative battery cable and the cable connection at the starter.

2. Raise and support the vehicle safely.

3. Remove the cable support and ground cable connection from the upper starter stud bolt.

4. Remove the starter brace from the cylinder block and the starter.

5. Remove the starter-to-bell housing bolts.

6. Remove the starter between the sub-frame and radiator on the automatic transaxle vehicles. Remove the starter between the sub-frame and the engine on the manual transaxle vehicles.

7. For installation, reverse the removal procedures. Tighten the starter mounting bolts to 30–40 ft. lbs (41–54 Nm).

CHASSIS ELECTRICAL

——— CAUTION ———

On vehicles equipped with an air bag, the negative battery cable must be disconnected, before working on the system. Failure to do so may result in deployment of the air bag and possible personal injury.

Heater Blower Motor

REMOVAL & INSTALLATION

1. Disconnect the negative battery cable.

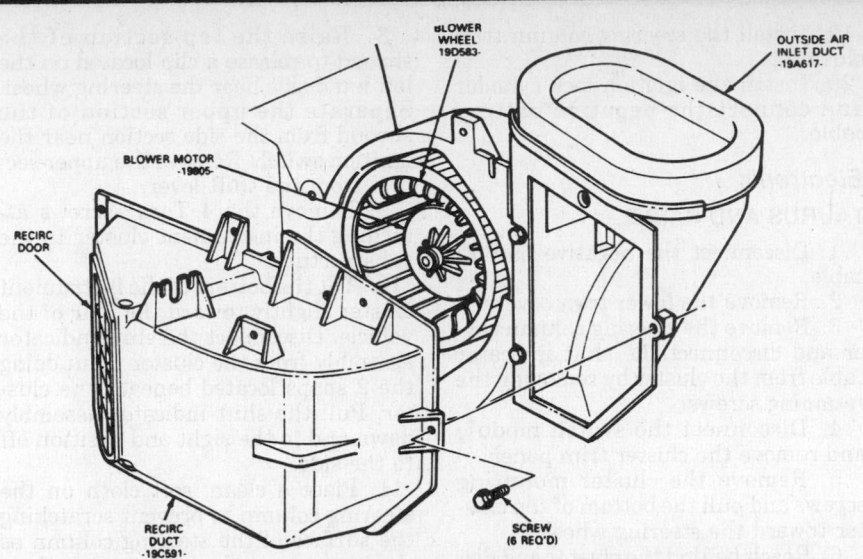

Exploded view of the heater motor and duct assembly

Windshield Wiper Motor

REMOVAL & INSTALLATION

Front

1. Disconnect the negative battery cable.
2. Disconnect the power lead from the motor.
3. Remove the left hand wiper arm.
4. On Continental, lift the water shield cover from the cowl on the passenger side. Remove the left hand cowl screen on Taurus and Sable.
5. Remove the linkage retaining clip from the operating arm on the motor.
6. Remove the attaching screws from the motor and bracket assembly and remove.
7. Complete the installation of the wiper motor by reversing the removal procedures.

Rear—Station Wagon

1. Remove the wiper arm and blade.
2. Remove the pivot shaft retaining nut and spacers.
3. Disconnect the electrical connector to the wiper motor.
4. Remove the nut retaining the motor to the handle and remove the motor.
5. Install in the reverse order of the removal procedure.

2. Open the glove compartment door, release the door retainers and lower the door.
3. Remove the screw attaching the recirculation duct support bracket to the instrument panel cowl.
4. Remove the vacuum connection to the recirculation door vacuum motor. Remove the screws attaching the recirculation duct to the heater assembly.
5. Remove the recirculation duct from the heater assembly, lowering

the duct from between the instrument panel and the heater case.
6. Disconnect the blower motor electrical lead. Remove the blower motor wheel clip and remove the blower motor wheel.
7. Remove the blower motor mounting plate screws and remove the blower motor from the evaporator case.
8. Complete the installation of the blower motor by reversing the removal procedure.

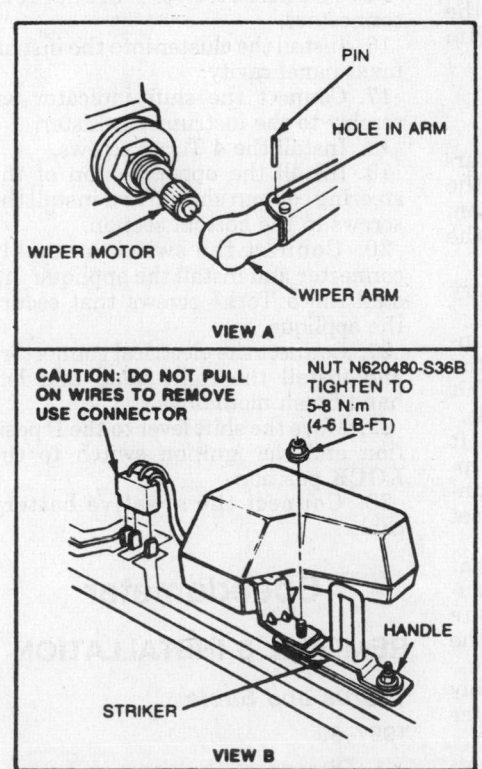

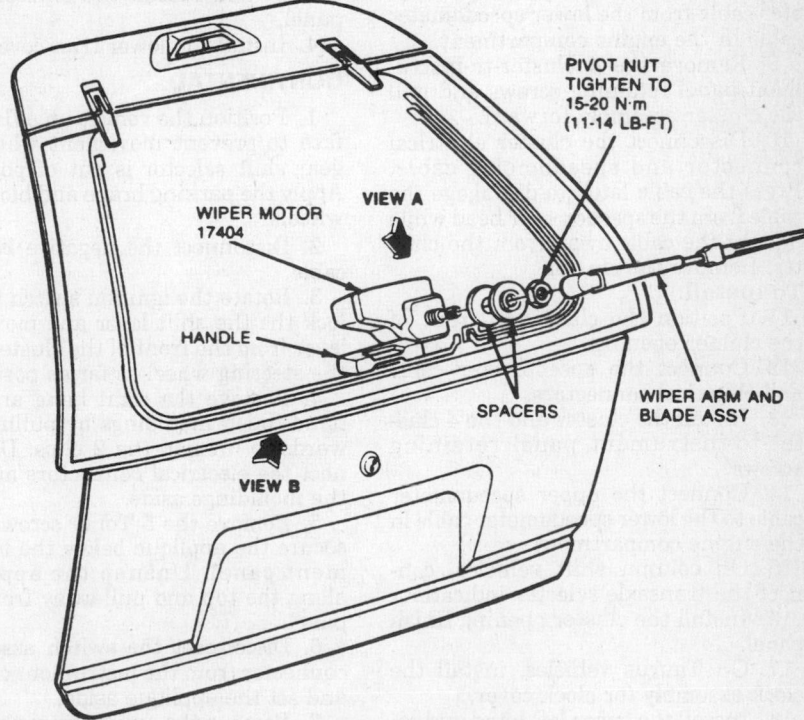

Exploded view of the rear wiper motor assembly—Station Wagon model

Windshield Wiper Switch

The standard and interval wiper systems feature a rotary actuated switch which is part of the turn signal lever of the multi-function switch.

Instrument Cluster

REMOVAL & INSTALLATION

Conventional

1. Disconnect the negative battery cable.

2. Remove the ignition lock cylinder to allow removal of the steering column shrouds.

3. Remove the steering column trim shrouds.

4. Remove the lower left hand and radio finish panel screws and snap the panels out.

5. On Taurus, remove the clock assembly (or clock cover) to gain access to the finish panel screw behind the clock.

6. Remove the cluster opening finish panel retaining screws and jam nut behind the headlamp switch. Remove the finish panel by rocking the edge upward and outward.

7. On column shift vehicles, disconnect the transaxle selector indicator from the column by removing the retaining screw.

8. Disconnect the upper speedometer cable from the lower speedometer cable in the engine compartment.

9. Remove the 4 cluster-to-instrument panel retaining screws and pull the cluster assembly forward.

10. Disconnect the cluster electrical connector and speedometer cable. Press the cable latch to disengage the cable from the speedometer head while pulling the cable away from the cluster. Remove the cluster.

To install:

11. Position the cluster in front of the cluster opening.

12. Connect the speedometer cable and electrical connectors.

13. Install the cluster and the 4 cluster-to-instrument panel retaining screws.

14. Connect the upper speedometer cable to the lower speedometer cable in the engine compartment.

15. On column shift vehicles, connect the transaxle selector indicator.

16. Install the cluster opening finish panel.

17. On Taurus vehicles, install the clock assembly (or clock cover).

18. Install the lower left hand and radio finish panels.

19. Install the steering column trim shrouds.

20. Install the ignition lock cylinder and connect the negative battery cable.

Electronic

TAURUS AND SABLE

1. Disconnect the negative battery cable.

2. Remove the lower trim covers.

3. Remove the steering column cover and disconnect the shift indicator cable from the cluster by removing the retaining screws.

4. Disconnect the switch module and remove the cluster trim panel.

5. Remove the cluster mounting screws and pull the bottom of the cluster toward the steering wheel.

6. Reach behind the cluster and disconnect the 3 electrical connectors.

7. Swing the bottom of the cluster out to clear the top of the cluster from the crash pad and remove.

To install:

8. Insert the top of the cluster under the crash pad leaving the bottom out.

9. Connect the 3 connectors.

10. Properly seat the cluster and install the retaining screws.

11. Connect the battery ground cable and check the cluster for proper operation.

12. Connect the shift indicator assembly to the cluster and secure with the retaining screw.

13. Connect the switch module to the cluster and install the cluster trim panel.

14. Install the lower trim covers.

CONTINENTAL

1. Position the vehicle on a flat surface to prevent movement when the gear shift selector is out of position. Apply the parking brake and block the wheels.

2. Disconnect the negative battery cable.

3. Rotate the ignition switch to unlock the the shift lever and move the lever from the front of the cluster. Tilt the steering wheel as far as possible.

4. Remove the right hand and left hand finish mouldings by pulling upwards to unsnap the 2 clips. Disconnect the electrical connectors and set the mouldings aside.

5. Remove the 5 Torx® screws that secure the applique below the instrument panel. Unsnap the applique along the top and pull away from the panel.

6. Disconnect the switch assembly connector from the instrument cluster and set the applique aside.

7. Remove the screws from the bottom of the steering column shroud.

8. Raise the top section of the shroud to release a clip located on the left hand side near the steering wheel. Separate the upper section of the shroud from the side section near the ignition switch. Remove the upper section from the shift lever.

9. Remove the 4 Torx® screws attaching the instrument cluster to the substructure.

10. Tilt the bottom of the instrument cluster slightly toward the rear of the vehicle. Disconnect the shift indicator assembly from the cluster by undoing the 2 snaps located beneath the cluster. Pull the shift indicator assembly down and to the right and position off to the side.

11. Place a clean, soft cloth on the steering column to prevent scratching the surface of the steering column as the instrument cluster is removed.

12. Push the bottom of the instrument cluster into the instrument panel cavity. Tilt the top of the instrument cluster toward the rear of the vehicle. Push the cluster up and out of the cavity.

13. Reach around the back of the instrument cluster to disconnect the 4 connectors; 2 on the right side, 1 in the middle and 1 on the left. The connectors have locking tabs that must be pressed in to release.

To install:

14. Position the instrument cluster in front of the instrument panel cavity.

15. Connect the 4 electrical connectors.

16. Install the cluster into the instrument panel cavity.

17. Connect the shift indicator assembly to the instrument cluster.

18. Install the 4 Torx® screws.

19. Install the upper section of the steering column shroud and install the screws in the bottom section.

20. Connect the switch assembly connector and install the applique. Install the 5 Torx® screws that secure the applique.

21. Connect the electrical connectors and install the right hand and left hand finish mouldings.

22. Move the shift lever to the **P** position and the ignition switch to the **LOCK** position.

23. Connect the negative battery cable.

Speedometer

REMOVAL & INSTALLATION

Taurus and Sable

1987–89

1. Disconnect the negative battery cable.

2. Remove the instrument cluster finish panel retaining screws and remove the finish panel.

3. Remove the mask-and-lens mounting screws and remove the mask and lens. On Sable, remove the lower floodlamp bulb and socket assemblies.

4. Remove the entire dial assembly from the instrument cluster by carefully pulling it away from the cluster backplate.

NOTE: The speedometer, tachometer and gauges are mounted to the main dial and some effort may be required to pull the quick-connect electrical terminals from the clip.

5. On column shift vehicles, remove the screws attaching the transaxle selector indicator to the main dial. Remove the transaxle selector indicator from the main dial/instrument cluster. On Sable, remove the odometer drive jack shaft and remove the attachment clip at the odometer, slip the jack shaft out of the odometer bracket and speedometer bridge.

6. Pull the reset knob from the trip odometer, if equipped. To remove the speedometer from the main dial, manually rotate the speedometer pointer to align it with the slot in the dial. Remove the mounting screws and carefully pull the speedometer away from the dial, making sure to guide the pointer through the slot.

7. Complete the installation of the speedometer by reversing the removal procedure. Connect the negative battery cable.

1990–91

1. Remove the instrument cluster.

2. Remove the 8 mask and lens mounting screws. Remove the mask and lens.

3. Remove the 2 screws attaching the transmission selector indicator or the filler bezel to the speedometer and remove the indicator or filler bezel from the cluster.

4. Pull the speedometer from the electrical clips and remove the speedometer.

5. Install in the reverse order of removal. Connect the negative battery cable.

Continental

The display of speedometer/odometer and fuel/multigauge information is accomplished by a remote Cluster Control Assembly (CCA) module that is integral with the electronic instrument cluster assembly.

1. Disconnect the negative battery cable.

2. Remove the electronic instrument cluster.

3. Locate and undo the Message Center Control Assembly (MCCA) module retaining snap and lift the module enough to clear the snap. Undo the bottom snap and remove the module.

4. Remove the CCA button assembly connector from the mask.

5. Undo the CCA housing snap on the left hand side of the module. Lift the end a small amount to clear the snap.

6. Remove the remaining snap and remove the module from the cluster assembly.

7. Complete the installation of the new CCA module with the cluster assembly by reversing the removal procedure. Connect the negative battery cable.

Radio

REMOVAL & INSTALLATION

1. Disconnect the negative battery cable.

2. On Continental, remove the center instrument trim panel.

3. Install radio removal tools T87P-19061-A or equivalent into the radio face plate. Push the tools in approximately 1 in. to release the retaining clips.

4. Apply a light spreading force on the tools and pull the radio out of the dash. On Continental, raise the back end of the radio slightly to allow the rear support bracket to clear the track in the instrument panel.

5. Disconnect the wiring connectors and the antenna cable. Remove the rear support bracket on Continental.

6. Installation is the reverse of the removal procedure.

Headlight Switch

REMOVAL & INSTALLATION

1. Disconnect the negative battery cable. On the Taurus, Continental and 1990–91 Sable, remove the headlamp switch knob.

2. On the Taurus, remove the bezel retaining nut and remove the bezel. On the 1987–89 Sable, remove the lower left finish panel. On the Continental, remove the right hand and left hand mouldings.

3. On the Taurus, remove the instrument cluster finish panel through the following procedure:
   a. Apply the parking brake.
   b. Remove the ignition lock cylinder.
   c. If equipped with a tilt column,

tilt the column to the most downward position and remove the tilt lever.
   d. Remove the 4 bolts and cover and the reinforcement assembly from under the steering column.
   e. Remove the steering column trim shrouds. Disconnect all electrical connections from the steering column multi-function switch.
   f. Remove the 2 screws retaining the multi-function switch and remove the switch.
   g. Pull the gear shift lever to the full down position.
   h. Remove the 4 cluster opening finish panel retaining screws. Remove the finish panel by pulling it toward the driver to unsnap the snap-in retainers and disconnect the wiring from the switches, clock and warning lamps.

4. On Continental, remove the 5 cluster opening finish panel retaining screws and remove the panel.

5. Remove the 2 screws retaining the headlight switch. Disconnect the electrical connector and remove the switch.

6. Complete the installation of the headlight switch by reversing the removal procedure.

Combination Switch

REMOVAL & INSTALLATION

1. Disconnect the negative battery cable. If equipped with a tilt steering column, set the tilt column to its lowest position and remove the tilt lever by removing the Allen head retaining screw.

2. Remove the ignition lock cylinder. Remove the steering column shroud screws and remove the upper and lower shrouds.

3. Remove the wiring harness retainer and disconnect the 3 electrical connectors.

4. Remove the self tapping screws attaching the switch to the steering column and disengage the switch from the steering column casting.

To install:

5. Align the turn signal switch mounting holes with the corresponding holes in the steering column and install self-tapping screws. Torque the screws to 18–27 inch lbs. (2–3 Nm).

6. Install the electrical connectors and install the wiring harness retainer.

7. Install the upper and lower steering column shroud and shroud retaining screws, torque the screws to 6–10 inch lbs. (0.7–1.1 Nm).

8. Install the ignition lock cylinder. Attach the tilt lever, if removed and torque the tilt lever Allen head retain-

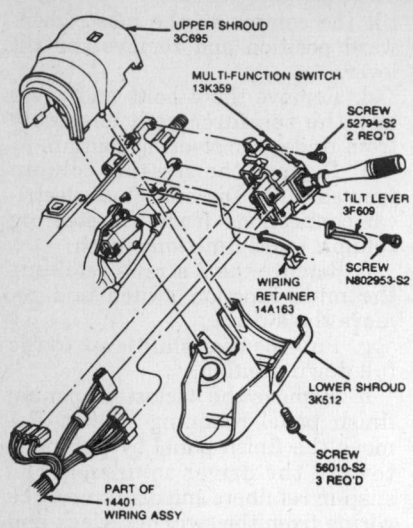

UPPER SHROUD
3C695

MULTI-FUNCTION SWITCH
13K359

SCREW
52794-S2
2 REQ'D

TILT LEVER
3F609

SCREW
N802953-S2

WIRING
RETAINER
14A163

LOWER SHROUD
3K512

SCREW
56010-S2
3 REQ'D

PART OF
14401
WIRING ASSY

Exploded view of the upper steering column—combination switch

ing screw to 6–9 inch lbs. (0.7–1.0 Nm).

9. Connect the negative battery cable. Check the switch and the steering column for proper operation.

Ignition Lock Cylinder

REMOVAL & INSTALLATION

Functional Lock

EXCEPT 1990–91 TAURUS AND SABLE

The following procedure applies to vehicles that have functional lock cylinders. Lock cylinder keys are available for these vehicles or the lock cylinder key numbers are known and the proper key can be made.

1. Disconnect the negative battery cable.
2. Turn the lock cylinder key to the **RUN** position.
3. Using an ⅛ in. diameter wire pin or a small drift, depress the lock cylinder retaining pin through the access hole, while pulling out on the lock cylinder to remove it from the column.

To install:

4. Install the lock cylinder by turning it to the **RUN** position and depressing the retaining pin. Insert the lock cylinder into it's housing. Make sure the cylinder is fully seated and aligned in the interlocking washer before turning the key to the **OFF** position. This will permit the cylinder retaining pin to extend into the cylinder housing.
5. Rotate the lock cylinder using the lock cylinder key, to ensure correct mechanical operation in all positions.
6. Connect the negative battery cable.

1990–91 TAURUS AND SABLE

1. Rotate the ignition lock cylinder to the **RUN** position. Using a ⅛ in. drift, depress the lock cylinder retaining pin through the access hole and remove the lock cylinder.
2. Remove the blue plastic bearing retainer by inserting a suitable prying tool with a 90 degree bend at the tip, between the bearing retainer and the bearing and by prying upward.

NOTE: Carefully note the position of the bearing retainer prior to removal.

3. Insert the tip of a suitable tool into the Double-D slot of the bearing, then rotate 90 degrees. Remove the bearing.
4. Remove the lock drive gear. Carefully note the relationship of the lock drive gear to the position of the rack teeth.

To install:

5. Position the lock drive gear in the base of the lock cylinder housing in the same position as that noted during the removal procedure. The position of the lock drive gear is correct if the last tooth on the drive gear is meshed with the last tooth on the rack.
6. Position the bearing retainer in the lock cylinder housing. Insert the tip of a suitable tool into the Double-D slot of the bearing, then rotate 90 degrees.
7. Press the blue plastic bearing retainer into the lock cylinder housing. Make sure the retainer is in it's original position.
8. Line up the flats of the drive gear with the flats of the washer by pulling down on the column lock actuator.
9. Install the lock cylinder assembly.
10. Connect the negative battery cable and check that the vehicle will start with the lock cylinder in the **P** and **N** positions. Also make sure the starter cannot be engaged in the **D** or **R** positions and the column is locked in the **LOCK** position.

Non-Functional Lock

The following procedure applies to vehicles in which the ignition lock is inoperative and the lock cylinder cannot be rotated due to a lost or broken lock cylinder key, unknown key number or a lock cylinder cap that has been damaged and/or broken to the extent that the lock cylinder cannot be rotated.

1. Disconnect the negative battery cable.
2. Remove the steering wheel.
3. Remove the 2 trim shroud halves by removing the 3 attaching screws.
4. Remove the electrical connector from the key warning switch.
5. Using an ⅛ in. diameter drill,

drill out the retaining pin, being careful not to drill deeper than ½ in.

6. Place a suitable chisel at the base of the ignition lock cylinder cap and using a suitable hammer, strike the chisel with sharp blows to break the cap away from the lock cylinder.
7. Using a ⅜ in. diameter drill, drill down the middle of the ignition key slot approximately 1¾ in. until the lock cylinder breaks loose from the breakaway base of the lock cylinder. Remove the lock cylinder and drill shavings from the lock cylinder housing.
8. Remove the retainer, washer, ignition switch and actuator. Thoroughly clean all the drill shavings from the casting.
9. Inspect the lock cylinder housing for damage from the removal operation.

To install:

10. Replace the lock cylinder housing if it was damaged.
11. Install the actuator and ignition switch.
12. Install the trim and electrical parts.
13. Install a new ignition lock cylinder.
14. Install the steering wheel.
15. Connect the negative battery cable.
16. Check the lock cylinder operation.

Ignition Switch

REMOVAL & INSTALLATION

Taurus and Sable

1987–89

1. Disconnect the negative battery cable.
2. Turn the ignition lock cylinder to the **RUN** position and depress the lock cylinder retaining pin through the access hole in the shroud with a ⅛ diameter punch.
3. Remove the lock cylinder. On vehicles equipped with tilt columns, remove the tilt release lever.
4. Remove the instrument panel lower cover and the steering column shroud.
5. Remove the 4 nuts attaching the steering column to the support bracket and lower the column.
6. Disconnect the ignition switch electrical connector.
7. Remove the lock actuator cover plate. The lock actuator assembly will slide freely out of the lock cylinder housing when the ignition switch is removed.
8. Remove the ignition switch and cover.

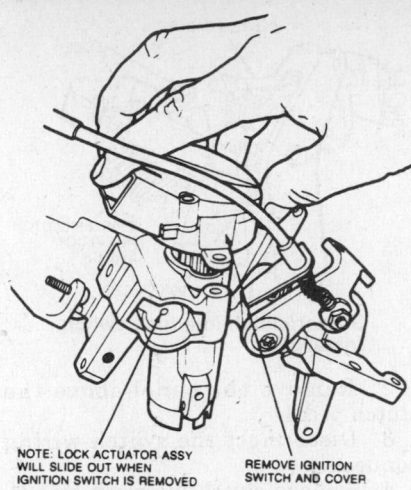

NOTE: LOCK ACTUATOR ASSY WILL SLIDE OUT WHEN IGNITION SWITCH IS REMOVED

REMOVE IGNITION SWITCH AND COVER

Removing the ignition switch from the lock actuator assembly

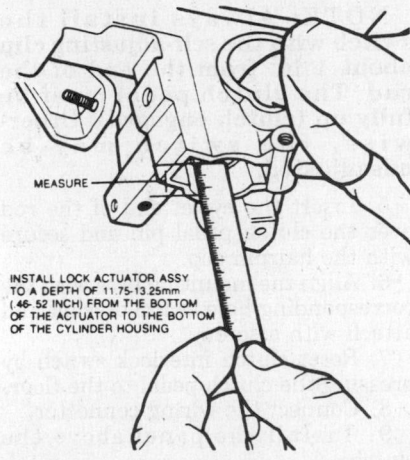

MEASURE

INSTALL LOCK ACTUATOR ASSY TO A DEPTH OF 11.75-13.25mm (.46-.52 INCH) FROM THE BOTTOM OF THE ACTUATOR TO THE BOTTOM OF THE CYLINDER HOUSING

Installing the lock actuator into the actuator housing

To install:

9. Make sure the ignition switch is in the **RUN** position by rotating the driveshaft fully clockwise to the **START** position and releasing.

10. Install the lock actuator assembly to a depth of 0.46–0.52 in. (11.75–13.25mm) from the bottom of the actuator assembly to the bottom of the lock cylinder housing.

11. While holding the actuator assembly at the proper depth, install the ignition switch. Install the ignition switch cover and tighten the retaining bolts to 30–48 inch lbs. (3.4–5.4 Nm).

12. Install the lock cylinder. Rotate the ignition lock cylinder to the **LOCK** position and measure the depth of the actuator assembly as in Step 10. The actuator assembly must be 0.92–1.00 in. (23.5–25.5mm) inside the lock cylinder housing. If the depth measured does not meet specification, the actuator assembly must be removed and installed again.

13. Install the lock actuator cover

plate and tighten the bolts to 30–48 inch lbs. (3.4–5.4 Nm).

14. Install the ignition switch electrical connector.

15. Connect the negative battery cable. Check the ignition switch for proper function in all positions, including **START** and **ACC**.

16. Check the column function as follows:

a. With the column shift lever in the **P** position or with the floor shift key release button depressed and with the ignition lock cylinder in the **LOCK** position, make certain that the steering column locks.

b. Position the column shift lever in the **D** position or the floor shift key release button fully extended and rotate the cylinder lock to the **RUN** position. Continue to rotate the cylinder toward the **LOCK** position until it stops. In this position make certain that the engine and all electrical accessories are **OFF** and that the steering shaft does not lock.

c. Turn the radio power button **ON**. Rotate the cylinder counterclockwise to the **ACC** position to verify that the radio is energized.

d. Place the shift lever in **P** and rotate the cylinder clockwise to the **START** position to verify that the starter energizes.

1990–91

1. Disconnect the negative battery cable.

2. Remove the steering column shroud by removing the self-tapping screws. Remove the tilt lever, if so equipped.

3. Remove the instrument panel lower steering column cover.

4. Disconnect the ignition switch electrical connector.

5. Turn the ignition key lock cylinder to the **RUN** position.

6. Remove the 2 screws attaching the ignition switch and disengage the switch from the actuator pin.

To install:

7. Adjust the ignition switch by sliding the carrier to the switch **RUN** position. A new replacement switch assembly will already be set in the **RUN** position.

8. Make sure the ignition key lock cylinder is in the **RUN** position. The **RUN** position is achieved by rotating the key lock cylinder approximately 90 degrees from the lock position.

9. Install the ignition switch into the actuator pin. It may be necessary to move the switch slightly back and forth to align the switch mounting holes with the column lock housing threaded holes.

10. Install the attaching screws and tighten to 50–70 inch lbs. (5.6–7.9 Nm).

11. Connect the electrical connector to the ignition switch.

12. Connect the negative battery cable.

13. Check the ignition switch for proper function, including **START** and **ACC** positions. Make sure the column is locked with the switch in the **LOCK** position.

14. Install the instrument panel lower steering column cover, the steering column trim shrouds and the tilt lever, if so equipped.

Continental

1. Disconnect the negative battery cable.

2. Rotate the ignition lock cylinder to the **RUN** position and depress the lock cylinder retaining pin through the access hole in the shroud with a ⅛ in. drift punch or wire pin. Push on the pin and pull out on the lock cylinder.

3. Remove the lock cylinder.

4. On vehicles equipped with tilt steering columns, remove the tilt release lever by removing the Allen head cap screw that holds the tilt lever to the steering column.

5. Remove the lower steering column/instrument panel cover by removing the 4 Torx® head sheet metal screws.

6. Remove the steering column shroud.

7. Remove the bolts and nuts that attach the steering column to the support bracket and lower the column.

8. Remove the 3 screws from the diverter plate and remove it from the column.

9. Disconnect the ignition switch electrical connector.

10. Remove the ignition switch and cover by removing the 2 tamper-resistant Torx® head bolts.

To install:

11. Make sure the ignition switch is in the **RUN** position by rotating the steering column shaft fully clockwise to the **START** position and releasing it.

12. Install the ignition switch and cover. Torque the cover retaining screws to 30–48 inch lbs. (3.4–5.4 Nm).

13. Install the ignition switch electrical connector.

14. Position the diverter plate on the column and secure it with 3 screws. Tighten to 30–48 inch lbs. (3.4–5.4 Nm).

15. Align the steering column mounting holes with the support bracket, center the steering column in the instrument panel opening and install the 4 nuts. Tighten to 15–25 ft. lbs. (20–34 Nm).

16. Install the 3 self-tapping screws and install the column trim shrouds.

Tighten to 6–10 inch lbs. (0.7–1.1 Nm).

17. Install the instrument panel lower cover.

18. On tilt columns, install the tilt release lever. Tighten the retaining screw to 6.5–8.5 ft. lbs. (9–11 Nm). Check the column tilt travel through it's entire range to make sure there is no interference between the column and the instrument panel.

19. Connect the negative battery cable.

20. Check the column function as follows:

a. With the column shift lever in the **P** position or with the floor shift key release button depressed and with the ignition lock cylinder in the **LOCK** position, make certain that the steering column locks.

b. Position the column shift lever in the **D** position or the floor shift key release button fully extended and rotate the cylinder lock to the **RUN** position. Continue to rotate the cylinder toward the **LOCK** position until it stops. In this position make certain that the engine and all electrical accessories are **OFF** and that the steering shaft does not lock.

c. Turn the radio power button **ON**. Rotate the cylinder counterclockwise to the **ACC** position to verify that the radio is energized.

d. Place the shift lever in **P** and rotate the cylinder clockwise to the **START** position to verify that the starter energizes.

Stoplight Switch

The mechanical stoplight switch assembly is installed on the pin of the brake pedal arm, so it straddles the master cylinder pushrod.

REMOVAL & INSTALLATION

1. Disconnect the negative battery cable.

2. Disconnect the wire harness at the connector from the switch.

NOTE: The locking tab must be lifted before the connector can be removed.

3. Remove the hairpin retainer. Slide the stoplight switch, the pushrod and the white nylon washer and black bushing away from the pedal. Remove the switch by sliding the switch up/down.

NOTE: Since the switch side plate nearest the brake pedal is slotted, it is not necessary to remove the brake master cylinder pushrod black bushing and 1 white spacer washer nearest the

pedal arm from the brake pedal pin.

To install:

4. Position the switch so the U-shaped side is nearest the pedal and directly over/under the pin. The black bushing must be in position in the push rod eyelet with the washer face on the side closest to the retaining pin.

5. Slide the switch up/down, trapping the master cylinder pushrod and black bushing between the switch side plates. Push the switch and pushrod assembly firmly towards the brake pedal arm. Assemble the outside white plastic washer to pin and install the hairpin retainer to trap the whole assembly.

NOTE: Do not substitute other types of pin retainer. Replace only with production hairpin retainer.

6. Connect the wire harness connector to the switch.

7. Check the stoplight switch for proper operation. stoplights should illuminate with less than 6 lbs. applied to the brake pedal at the pad.

NOTE: The stoplight switch wire harness must have sufficient length to travel with the switch during full stroke at the pedal.

Starter/Clutch Interlock Switch

ADJUSTMENT

1. Remove the panel above clutch pedal.

2. Disengage the wiring connector by flexing the retaining tab on the switch and withdrawing the connector.

3. Using a test light, check to see that the switch is open with the clutch pedal up (engaged) and closed at approximately 1 in. from the clutch pedal full down position (disengaged).

4. If the switch does not operate as outlined in Step 3, check to see if the self-adjusting clip is out of position on the rod. It should be near the end of the rod.

5. If the self-adjusting clip is out of position, remove and reposition the clip approximately 1 in. from the end of the rod.

6. Reset the switch by pressing the clutch pedal to the floor. Repeat Step 3. If the switch is damaged or the clips do not remain in place replace the switch.

REMOVAL & INSTALLATION

1. Disconnect the negative battery cable.

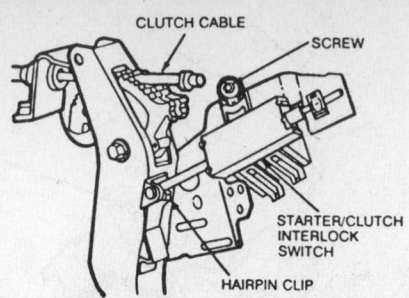

Starter/clutch interlock switch installation

2. Remove the panel above the clutch pedal.

3. Disconnect the switch wiring connector.

4. Remove clutch interlock attaching screw and hairpin clip and then remove the switch.

To install:

NOTE: Always install the switch with the self-adjusting clip about 1 in. from the end of the rod. The clutch pedal must be fully up (clutch engaged). Otherwise, the switch may be misadjusted.

5. Insert the eyelet end of the rod over the clutch pedal pin and secure with the hairpin clip.

6. Align the mounting boss with the corresponding hole in the bracket and attach with a screw.

7. Reset clutch interlock switch by pressing the clutch pedal to the floor.

8. Connect the wiring connector.

9. Install the panel above the clutch.

Neutral Safety Switch

REMOVAL & INSTALLATION

1. Disconnect the negative battery cable and set the parking brake.

2. Disconnect the wire connector from the neutral safety switch.

3. Remove the nut and washer holding the throttle valve (TV) lever. Hold the lever stationary while loosening to prevent internal damage. Remove the lever from the TV shaft.

4. Remove the 2 neutral safety switch attaching bolts and remove the neutral safety switch.

To install:

5. Place the manual lever in **N**.

6. Install the neutral safety switch on the manual shaft.

7. Loosely install the 2 neutral safety switch attaching bolts, lockwashers and flatwashers.

8. Insert a No. 43 (0.089) drill bit through the hole provided in the switch. Tighten the attaching bolts to 7–9 ft. lbs. (9–12 Nm) and remove the drill bit.

9. Connect the neutral safety switch connector.

10. Install the TV lever, lockwasher and nut. Hold the lever stationary while tightening to prevent internal damage. Tighten to 7.5–9.5 ft. lbs. (10–13 Nm).

11. Connect the negative battery cable.

12. Check the ignition switch for proper starting in **P** or **N**. Also make certain that the start circuit can not be actuated in the **D** or **R** position and that the column is locked in the **LOCK** position.

Fuses, Circuit Breakers and Relays

LOCATION

Fuses

The fuse panel is located under the left hand side of the instrument panel on all vehicles.

Fusible Links

Fusible links are used to prevent major wire harness damage in the event of a short circuit or an overload condition in the wiring circuits that are normally not fused, due to carrying high amperage loads or because of their locations within the wiring harness. Each fusible link is of a fixed value for a specific electrical load and should a fusible link fail, the cause of the failure must be determine and repaired prior to installing a new fusible link of the same value. Please be advised that the color coding of replacement fusible links may vary from the production color coding that is outlined in the text that follows.

TAURUS AND SABLE

Green 14 Gauge Wire—This fusible link is located in the wiring going to the starter relay and it protects the starter circuit.

Black 16 Gauge Wire—This fusible link is located in the wiring going to the starter relay and it protects the rear window defrost circuit.

Black 16 Gauge Wire—This fusible link is located on the left front inner fender panel, near the voltage regulator and is used to protect the voltage regulator and alternator circuit.

Black 16 Gauge Wire—On 1987 vehicles, this fusible link is located in the wiring going to the starter relay and it protects the starter and alternator circuit. On the 1988–91 vehicles this fusible link is located in the vicinity of the left hand shock tower and protects the battery feed to headlamp switch and fuse panel circuits.

Orange 16 Gauge Wire—This fusible link used on the 1988–91 vehicles is located in the vicinity of the left hand shock tower and functions to protect the battery feed to ignition switch and fuse panel circuits.

Blue 20 Gauge Wire—On 1987 vehicles, this fusible link is located on the starter relay and protects the electrical system in general. On the 1988–91 vehicles this fusible link is located on the left hand shock tower and protects the ignition coil, ignition module and cooling fan controller.

CONTINENTAL

The Continental does not use fusible links. The fusible links have been replaced by a high current fuse panel. The high current fuse panel is located in the engine compartment on the left hand fender apron.

NOTE: Always disconnect the negative battery cable before servicing the high current fuses or serious personal injury may result.

Circuit Breakers

Circuit breakers are used to protect the various components of the electrical system, such as headlights and windshield wipers. The circuit breakers are located either in the control switch or mounted on or near the fuse panel.

TAURUS AND SABLE

Headlights and High Beam Indicator—One 22 amp circuit breaker incorporated in the lighting switch.

Liftgate Wiper—One 4.5 amp circuit breaker located in the instrument panel to the left of the radio.

Windshield Wiper and Wiper Pump Circuit—One 6 amp circuit breaker located in the in the fuse block.

There are 3 circuit breakers all located in the fuse block. The 6 amp circuit breaker is used for the windshield wiper circuit and one 20 amp circuit breaker is used for the instrument illumination. There is also an in-line 30 amp circuit breaker for the power windows.

CONTINENTAL

Windshield Wiper Circuit—One 6 amp circuit breaker is located in the fuse panel and protects the windshield wiper governor, switch, motor, washer motor and fluid level switch.

Relays

Alternator Output Control Relay (3.0L and 3.8L engines with heated windshield)—is located between the right front inner fender panel and splash shield.

Alternator Output Control Relay—is located between the right front inner fender and the fender splash shield.

ATC Blower Motor Speed Controller—is located in the evaporator case, upstream of the evaporator core.

ATC High Blower Relay—is located on the upper half of the evaporator case.

Electronic Control Assembly—is located under the right side of the instrument panel.

Electronic Automatic Temperature Control Unit—is located behind the instrument panel.

Horn Relay—is located under the left side of the instrument panel.

Idle Speed Controller (3.0L engine)—is located on the left hand side of the engine.

Self-Test Connector—is located in the wiring harness behind the alternator.

Speed Control Servo—is attached to the electronic control assembly.

Speed Control Switch—is located in the steering wheel.

Starter Relay—is located on the left front fender apron in front of the shock tower.

Upshift Relay (Manual transaxle)—is located on the support brace under the instrument panel.

Vehicle Speed Sensor—is located near the electronic control assembly.

Heated Rear Window Defroster System Relay—is mounted to the instrument panel.

Speed Control Switch—is located in the steering wheel.

Computers

LOCATION

Taurus and Sable

The electronic engine control module is located on the passenger side of the firewall. The anti-lock brake control module is located at the front of the engine compartment next to the passenger side fender, except on Taurus SHO where it is located at the front of the engine compartment on the drivers side.

Continental

The electronic engine control module is located on the passenger side of the firewall. The anti-lock brake control module is located in the trunk on the passenger side under the package tray.

Flashers

LOCATION

Taurus and Sable

The turn signal flasher is located on the front side of the fuse panel. The hazard flasher is located on the rear of the fuse panel behind the turn signal flasher.

Continental

An electronic combination turn signal and emergency warning flasher is attached by a bracket to the lower left hand instrument panel reinforcement above the fuse panel.

Cruise Control

ADJUSTMENT

Actuator Cable

2.5L ENGINE

1. Remove locking pin.
2. Pull bead chain through adjuster.
3. Insert locking pin in best hole of adjuster for tight bead chain without opening throttle plate.

3.0L AND 3.8L ENGINE

1. Remove cable retaining clip.
2. Pull or push on actuator cable end tube to take up any slack. Maintain a light tension on cable.
3. While holding cable, insert cable retaining clip and snap securely.

Vacuum Dump Valve

The vacuum dump valve is adjustable in its mounting bracket. It should be adjusted so it is closed (no vacuum leak) when the brake pedal is in the normal release position (not depressed) and open when the pedal is depressed. Use a hand vacuum pump or equivalent to make this adjustment.

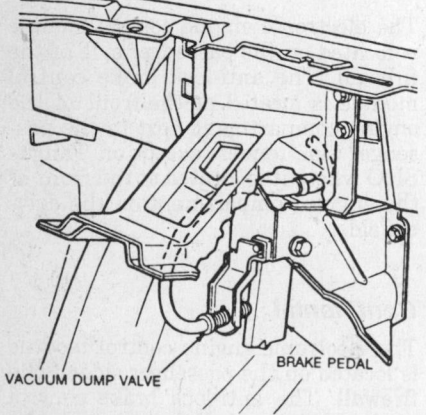

VACUUM DUMP VALVE   BRAKE PEDAL

Vacuum dump valve

ENGINE COOLING

Radiator

REMOVAL & INSTALLATION

1. Disconnect the negative battery cable.
2. Drain the cooling system by removing the radiator cap and opening the draincock located at the lower rear corner of the radiator inlet tank.
3. Remove the rubber overflow tube from the coolant recovery bottle and detach it from the radiator. On Taurus SHO, disconnect the tube from the radiator and remove the recovery bottle.
4. Remove 2 upper shroud retaining screws and lift the shroud out of the lower retaining clips.
5. Disconnect the electric cooling fan motor wires and remove the fan and shroud assembly.
6. Loosen the upper and lower hose clamps at the radiator and remove the hoses from the radiator connectors.
7. If equipped with an automatic transaxle, disconnect the transmission oil cooling lines from the radiator fittings using disconnect tool T82L-9500-AH or equivalent.
8. On vehicles equipped with 3.0L and SHO engines, remove 2 radiator upper retaining screws. On vehicles equipped with the 3.8L engine, remove 2 hex nuts from the right radiator support bracket and 2 screws from the left radiator support bracket and remove the brackets.
9. Tilt the radiator rearward approximately 1 in. and lift it directly upward, clear of the radiator support.
10. Remove the radiator lower support rubber pads, if pad replacement is necessary.

To install:
11. Position the radiator lower support rubber pads to the lower support, if previously removed.
12. Position the radiator into the engine compartment and to the radiator support. Insert the moulded pins at the bottom of each tank through the slotted holes in the lower support rubber pads.
13. Make sure the plastic pads on the bottom of the radiator tanks are resting on the rubber pads. Install 2 upper retaining bolts to attach the radiator to the radiator support. Tighten the bolts to 46–60 inch lbs. (5–7 Nm). On vehicles equipped with the 3.8L engine, tighten the bolts to 13–20 ft. lbs. (17–27 Nm).
14. On vehicles equipped with the

3.8L engine, fasten the left radiator support bracket to the radiator support with 2 screws. Tighten the screws to 8.7–17.7 ft. lbs. (11.8–24 Nm). Attach the right support bracket to the radiator support with 2 hex nuts. Tighten the nuts to 8.7–17.7 ft. lbs. (11.8–24 Nm).
15. Attach the radiator upper and lower hoses to the radiator. Position the hose on the radiator connector so the index arrow on the hose is in line with the mark on the connector. Tighten the clamps to 20–30 inch lbs. (2.3–3.4 Nm) on vehicles equipped with the 2.5L engine. On vehicles equipped with the 3.8L engine, install constant tension hose clamps between the alignment marks on the hoses.
16. On vehicles equipped with automatic transaxles, connect the transmission cooler lines using oil resistant pipe sealer.
17. Install the fan and shroud assembly by connecting the fan motor wiring and positioning the assembly on the lower retainer clips. Attach the top of the shroud to the radiator with 2 screw, nut and washer assemblies. Tighten to 35 inch lbs. (4 Nm).
18. Attach the rubber overflow tube to the radiator filler neck overflow nipple and coolant recovery bottle. On Taurus SHO, install the coolant recovery bottle and connect the overflow hose.
19. Refill the cooling system. If the coolant is being replaced, refill with a 50/50 mixture of water and antifreeze. Connect the negative battery cable. Operate the engine for 15 minutes and check for leaks. Check the coolant level and add, as required.

Electric Cooling Fan

The low and high speed electro-drive cooling fan is wired to operate only when the ignition switch is in the **RUN** position, thus preventing cycling of the fan after the engine is shut **OFF**. The cooling fan low speed is controlled during vehicle operation by the integrated relay control assembly and the EEC-IV module which will energize the cooling fan if the following conditions are met: engine temperature exceeds 215°F (102°C) or air conditioner is in use and the vehicle speed does not provide sufficient airflow. An engine temperature above 230°F (110°C) will cause the fan to operate in the high speed mode.

TESTING

1. Disconnect the wiring connector from the fan motor.
2. Connect a jumper wire from the positive terminal of the battery to one

of the terminals in the cooling fan electrical connector.

3. Ground the other connector terminal.

4. If the cooling fan does not function, it must be replaced.

5. If the cooling fan functions but does not run during normal engine operation, check the cooling fan temperature sensor and the integrated relay control assembly.

REMOVAL & INSTALLATION

1. Disconnect negative battery cable.

2. Disconnect the wiring connector from the fan motor. Remove the integrated relay control assembly from the radiator support.

3. Remove the nuts retaining the fan motor and shroud assembly and remove the component. Rotate the fan and shroud assembly and remove upwards past the radiator.

4. Remove the retaining clip from the motor shaft and remove the fan.

NOTE: A metal burr may be present on the motor shaft after the retaining clip has been removed. If necessary, remove the burr to facilitate fan removal.

5. Unbolt and withdraw the fan motor from the shroud.

6. Install in the reverse order of removal.

Heater Core

REMOVAL & INSTALLATION

1. Disconnect the negative battery cable.

2. Drain the cooling system.

3. Disconnect the heater hoses from the heater core.

4. Remove the instrument panel assembly and lay it on the front seat.

5. Remove the evaporator case.

6. Remove the vacuum source line from the heater core tube seal.

7. Remove the seal from the heater core tubes.

8. On Continental, remove the screws attaching the blend door actuator to the door shaft on the evaporator case. Remove the actuator from the case.

9. Remove the heater core access cover and foam seal from the evaporator case.

10. Lift the heater core with 3 foam seals from the evaporator case. Transfer the foam seals to the new heater core.

11. Installation is the reverse of the removal procedure.

Water Pump

REMOVAL & INSTALLATION

2.5L Engine

1. Disconnect the negative battery cable.

2. Remove the radiator cap and position a drain pan under the bottom radiator hose.

3. Raise and support the vehicle safely. Remove the lower radiator hose from the radiator and drain the coolant into the drain pan.

4. Remove the water pump inlet tube. Loosen the belt tensioner by inserting a ½ in. flex handle in the square hole of the tensioner and rotate the tensioner counterclockwise and remove the the belt from the pulleys.

5. Disconnect the heater hose from the water pump. Remove the water pump retaining bolts and remove the pump from the engine.

6. Installation is the reverse of the removal procedure. Torque the water pump-to-engine block retaining bolts to 15–23 ft. lbs. (20–30 Nm).

7. Refill the cooling system to the proper level. Start the engine and allow to reach normal operating temperature and check for leaks.

3.0L Engine Except SHO

1. Disconnect the negative battery cable and place a suitable drain pan under the radiator drain cock.

2. Remove the radiator cap, open the drain cock on the radiator and drain the cooling system.

3. Loosen the 4 water pump pulley retaining bolts while the accessory drive belts are still tight.

4. Loosen the alternator belt adjuster jack screw to provide enough clearance for removal of the alternator belt.

5. Using a ½ in. breaker bar, rotate the automatic tensioner down and to the left. Remove the power steering/air conditioner belt.

6. Remove the 2 nuts and 1 bolt retaining the automatic tensioner to the engine.

7. Disconnect and remove the lower radiator and heater hose from the water pump.

8. Remove the water pump to engine retaining bolts and lift the water pump and pulley up and out of the vehicle.

To install:

9. Clean the gasket surfaces on the water pump and front cover.

10. Install the water pump with the pulley loosely positioned on the hub, using a new gasket.

11. Install and tighten the retaining bolts as indicated. Apply a suitable pipe sealant prior to installation.

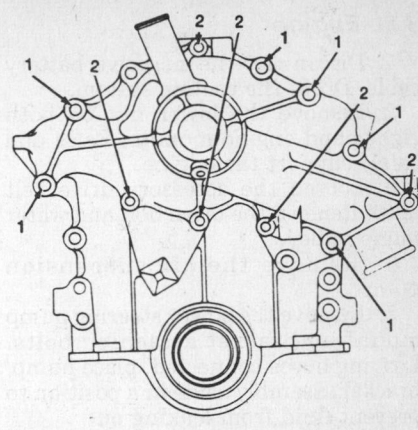

Water pump bolt torque specifications—3.0L engine

12. Hand tighten the water pump pulley retaining bolts.

13. Install the automatic belt tensioner assembly. Tighten the 2 retaining nuts and bolt to 35 ft. lbs. (48 Nm).

14. Install the alternator and power steering belts. Final tighten the water pump pulley retaining bolts to 16 ft. lbs. (21 Nm).

15. Install the lower radiator and heater hoses. Fill and bleed the cooling system with the appropriate quantity and coolant type.

16. Connect the negative battery cable. Start the engine and check for leaks.

3.0L SHO Engine

1. Disconnect the battery cables and remove the battery and the battery tray.

2. Drain the cooling system and remove the accessory drive belts.

3. Remove the bolts retaining the air conditioning and alternator idler pulley and bracket assembly.

4. Disconnect the electrical connector from the ignition module and ground strap.

5. Loosen the clamps on the upper intake connector tube, remove the retaining bolts and remove the connector tube.

6. Raise and safely support the vehicle. Remove the right hand wheel and tire assembly.

7. Remove the splash shield.

8. Remove the upper timing belt cover, crankshaft pulley and lower timing belt cover. 9. Remove the bolts from the center timing belt cover and position it out of the way.

10. Remove the water pump attaching bolts and remove the water pump.

11. To install, reverse the removal procedure. Tighten the water pump bolts to 12–16 ft. lbs. (15–23 Nm). Tighten the crankshaft pulley bolt to 113–126 ft. lbs. (152–172 Nm).

3.8L Engine

1. Disconnect the negative battery cable. Drain the cooling system.
2. Remove the lower nut on both right hand engine mounts. Raise and safely support the engine.
3. Loosen the accessory drive belt idler. Remove the drive belt and water pump pulley.
4. Remove the air suspension pump.
5. Remove the power steering pump mounting bracket attaching bolts. Leaving hoses connected, place pump/bracket assembly aside in a position to prevent fluid from leaking out.
6. If equipped with air conditioning, remove the compressor front support bracket.
7. Leave the compressor in place, if removed.
8. Disconnect coolant bypass and heater hoses at the water pump.
9. Remove the water pump-to-engine block attaching bolts and remove the pump from the vehicle. Discard the gasket and replace with new.

To install:
10. Lightly oil all bolt and stud threads before installation except those that require sealant. Thoroughly clean the water pump and front cover gasket contact surfaces.
11. Apply a coating of contact adhesive to both surfaces of the new gasket. Position a new gasket on water pump sealing surface.
12. Position water pump on the front cover and install attaching bolts.
13. Tighten the attaching bolts to 15–22 ft. lbs.
14. Connect the cooling bypass hose, heater hose and radiator lower hose to water pump and tighten the clamps.
15. If equipped with air conditioning, install compressor front support bracket.
16. Install the air suspension pump.
17. Position the accessory drive belt over the pulleys.
18. Install the water pump pulley, fan/clutch assembly and fan shroud. Cross-tighten fan/clutch assembly attaching bolts to 12-18 ft. lbs.

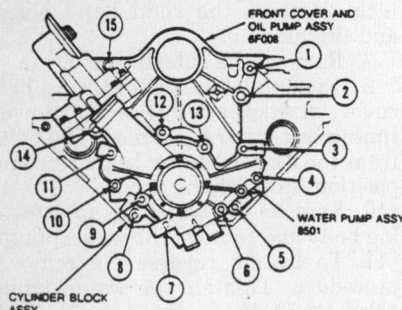

3.8L engine front cover assembly with attaching bolt locations.

19. Position accessory drive belt over pump pulley and adjust drive belt tension.
20. Lower the engine.
21. Install and tighten the lower right hand engine mount nuts.
22. Fill cooling system to the proper level.
23. Start engine and check for coolant leaks.

Thermostat

REMOVAL & INSTALLATION

2.5L Engine

1. Disconnect the negative battery cable.
2. Position a suitable drain pan below the radiator. Remove the radiator cap and open the draincock. Drain the radiator to a corresponding level below the water outlet connection. Close the draincock.
3. Remove the vent plug from the water outlet connection.
4. Loosen the top hose clamp at the radiator, remove the water outlet connection retaining bolts, lift clear of the engine and remove the thermostat by pulling it out of the water outlet connection.

NOTE: Do not pry the housing off.

To install:
5. Make sure the water outlet connection and cylinder head mating surfaces are clean and free from gasket material. Make sure the water outlet connection pocket and air vent passage are clean and free from rust. Clean the vent plug and gasket.
6. Place the thermostat in position, fully inserted to compress the gasket and pressed into the water outlet connection to secure. Install the water outlet connection to the cylinder head using a new gasket. Tighten the bolts to 12–18 ft. lbs. (16–24 Nm). Position the top hose to the radiator and tighten the clamps.
7. Refill the cooling system. Connect the negative battery cable. Start the engine and check for leaks. Check the coolant level and add as required.

3.0L Engine

1. Disconnect the negative battery cable.
2. Place a suitable drain pan beneath the radiator.
3. Remove the radiator cap and open the draincock. Drain the cooling system.
4. Remove the upper radiator hose from the thermostat housing.
5. Remove the 3 retaining bolts from the thermostat housing.

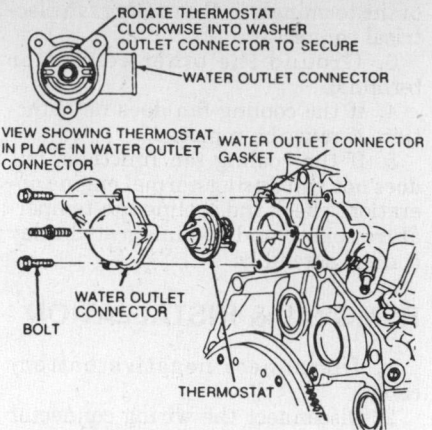

Thermostat installation—3.0L engine

6. Remove the housing and the thermostat as an assembly.

To install:
7. Make sure all sealing surfaces are free of old gasket material.
8. Install the thermostat into the housing as shown.
9. Position a new gasket onto the housing using the bolts as a holding device. Install the thermostat assembly and tighten the bolts to 9 ft. lbs. (12 Nm).
10. Install the upper radiator hose and tighten the clamp.
11. Fill and bleed the cooling system. Connect the negative battery cable, start the engine and check for coolant leaks. Check the coolant level and add as required.

3.0L SHO Engine

1. Disconnect the negative battery cable.
2. Place a suitable drain pan below the radiator. Remove the radiator cap and open the draincock. Partially drain the cooling system and then close the draincock.
3. Remove the air cleaner tube.
4. Disconnect the hose from the water outlet tube.
5. Remove the 2 retaining nuts and remove the water outlet tube.
6. Remove the thermostat and seal from the water outlet housing.

To install:
7. Install the seal around the outer rim of the thermostat and install the thermostat into the water outlet housing. Align the jiggle valve of the thermostat with the upper bolt on the water outlet housing.
8. Install the water outlet tube. Tighten the 2 retaining nuts to 5–8 ft. lbs. (7–11 Nm).
9. Install the air cleaner tube.
10. Refill the cooling system. Connect the negative battery cable. Start the engine and check for leaks. Check the coolant level and add as necessary.

3.8L Engine

1. Disconnect the negative battery cable.

2. Place a suitable drain pan below the radiator.

3. Remove the radiator cap and open the draincock. Drain the radiator to a level below the water outlet connection and then close the draincock.

4. Loosen the top hose clamp at the radiator, remove the water outlet connection retaining bolts and lift the water outlet clear of the engine. Remove the thermostat by rotating it counterclockwise in the water outlet connection until the thermostat becomes free to remove.

NOTE: Do not pry the housing off.

To install:

5. Make sure the water outlet connection pocket and all mating surfaces are clean.

6. Install the thermostat into the water outlet connection by rotating it clockwise until the engaging ramps on the thermostat are secure. Install the water outlet connection on the intake manifold with a new gasket and tighten the mounting bolts to 15–22 ft. lbs. (20–30 Nm). Position the top hose to the radiator and tighten the clamps.

7. Refill the cooling system. Connect the negative battery cable. Start the engine and check for leaks. Check the coolant level and add as required.

Cooling System Bleeding

When the entire cooling system is drained, the following procedure should be used to ensure a complete fill.

1. Install the block drain plug, if removed and close the draincock. With the engine off, add anti-freeze to the radiator to a level of 50% of the total cooling system capacity. Then add water until it reaches the radiator filler neck seat.

NOTE: On 2.5L engine, remove the vent plug on the water connection outlet. The vent plug must be removed before the radiator is filled or the engine may not fill completely. Do not turn the plastic cap under the vent plug or the gasket may be damaged. Do not try to add coolant through the vent plug hole. Install the vent plug after filling the radiator and before starting the engine.

2. Install the radiator cap to the first notch to keep spillage to a minimum.

3. Start the engine and let it idle until the upper radiator hose is warm. This indicates that the thermostat is open and coolant is flowing through the entire system.

4. Carefully remove the radiator cap and top off the radiator with water. Install the cap on the radiator securely.

5. Fill the coolant recovery reservoir to the FULL COLD mark with anti-freeze, then add water to the FULL HOT mark. This will ensure that a proper mixture is in the coolant recovery bottle.

6. Check for leaks at the draincock, block plug and at the vent plug on 2.5L engines.

FUEL SYSTEM

Fuel System Service Precautions

Safety is the most important factor when performing not only fuel system maintenance but any type of maintenance. Failure to conduct maintenance and repairs in a safe manner may result in serious personal injury or death. Maintenance and testing of the vehicle's fuel system components can be accomplished safely and effectively by adhering to the following rules and guidelines.

● To avoid the possibility of fire and personal injury, always disconnect the negative battery cable unless the repair or test procedure requires that battery voltage be applied.

● Always relieve the fuel system pressure prior to disconnecting any fuel system component (injector, fuel rail, pressure regulator, etc.), fitting or fuel line connection. Exercise extreme caution whenever relieving fuel system pressure to avoid exposing skin, face and eyes to fuel spray. Please be advised that fuel under pressure may penetrate the skin or any part of the body that it contacts.

● Always place a shop towel or cloth around the fitting or connection prior to loosening to absorb any excess fuel due to spillage. Ensure that all fuel spillage (should it occur) is quickly removed from engine surfaces. Ensure that all fuel soaked cloths or towels are deposited into a suitable waste container.

● Always keep a dry chemical (Class B) fire extinguisher near the work area.

● Do not allow fuel spray or fuel vapors to come into contact with a spark or open flame.

● Always use a backup wrench when loosening and tightening fuel line connection fittings. This will prevent unnecessary stress and torsion to fuel line piping. Always follow the proper torque specifications.

● Always replace worn fuel fitting O-rings with new. Do not substitute fuel hose or equivalent where fuel pipe is installed.

RELIEVING FUEL SYSTEM PRESSURE

1. The pressure in the fuel system must be released before attempting to disconnect any fuel lines.

2. A special valve is incorporated in the fuel rail assembly for the purpose of relieving the pressure in the fuel system.

3. Attach pressure gauge tool T80L–9974–A or equivalent to the fuel pressure valve on the fuel rail assembly and release the pressure from the system.

Fuel Filter

REMOVAL & INSTALLATION

1. Disconnect the negative battery cable. Relieve the fuel system pressure.

2. Remove the push connect fittings at both ends of the fuel filter. This is accomplished by removing the hairpin clips from the fittings. Remove the hairpin clips by first bending and then breaking the shipping tabs on the clips. Then spread the 2 clip legs approximately ⅛ in. to disengage the body and push the legs into the fitting. Pull on the triangular end of the clip and work it clear of the fitting.

3. Remove the filter from the mounting bracket by loosening the worm gear mounting clamp enough to allow the filter to pass through.

To install:

4. Install the filter in the mounting bracket, ensuring that the flow direction arrow is pointing forward. Locate the fuel filter against the tab at the lower end of the bracket.

5. Insert a new hairpin clip into any 2 adjacent openings on each push connect fitting, with the triangular portion of the clip pointing away from the

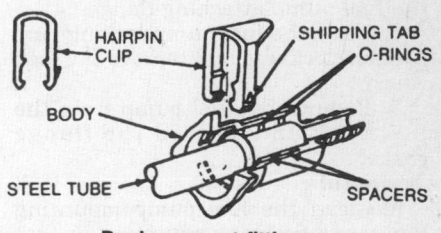

Push connect fittings

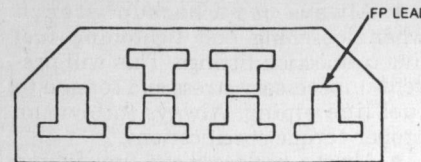

Self test connector

fitting opening. Install the clip to fully engage the body of the fitting. This is indicated by the legs of the hairpin clip being locked on the outside of the fitting body. Apply a light coat of engine oil to the ends of the fuel filter and then push the fittings onto the ends of the fuel filter. When the fittings are engaged, a definite click will be heard. Pull on the fittings to ensure that they are fully engaged.

6. Tighten the worm gear mounting clamp to 15–25 inch lbs. (1.7–2.8 Nm).

7. Start the engine and check for leaks.

Electric Fuel Pump

PRESSURE TESTING

1. Ground the fuel pump lead of the self-test connector through a jumper wire at the FP lead.

2. Connect a suitable fuel pressure tester to the fuel pump outlet.

3. Turn the ignition key to the **RUN** position to operate the fuel pump.

4. The fuel pressure should be 35–45 psi.

REMOVAL & INSTALLATION

1. Disconnect the negative battery cable.

2. Relieve the fuel system pressure and remove the fuel from the fuel tank by pumping it out through the filler neck. Use care to prevent combustion from any fuel spillage.

3. Raise and support the vehicle safely and remove the fuel filler tube (neck).

4. Support the fuel tank and remove the fuel tank straps, lower the fuel tank enough to be able to remove the fuel lines, electrical connectors and vent lines from the tank.

5. Remove the fuel tank from under the vehicle and place it on a suitable work bench. Remove any dirt around the fuel pump attaching flange.

6. Turn the fuel pump locking ring counterclockwise and remove the lock ring.

7. Remove the fuel pump from the fuel tank and discard the flange gasket.

To install:

8. Clean the fuel pump mounting flange and fuel tank mounting surface

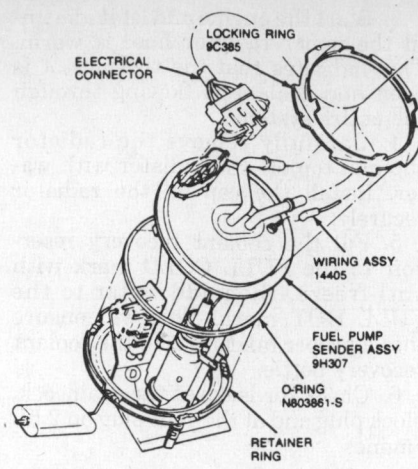

Electric fuel pump assembly

and seal ring groove.

9. Put a light coating of grease on the new seal gasket to hold it in place during assembly and install it in the fuel ring groove.

10. Install the fuel pump and sender assembly. Make sure the locating keys are in the keyways and the seal gasket remains in place.

11. Hold the assembly in place and install the lock ring making sure all locking tabs are under the tank lock ring tabs. Tighten the lock ring by turning it clockwise until it is up against the stops.

12. Remove the fuel tank from the bench to the vehicle and support the tank while connecting the fuel lines, vent line and electrical connectors.

13. Install the tank and secure it with the retaining straps. Lower the vehicle.

14. Install the filler tube and retaining screws.

15. Fill the tank with a minimum of 10 gallons of fuel and check for leaks.

16. Connect a suitable fuel pressure gauge. Turn the ignition switch to the **ON** position 5–10 times, leaving it on for 3 seconds at a time, until the pressure gauge reads at least 30 psi. Check for leaks at the fittings.

17. Remove the pressure gauge, start the engine and recheck for leaks.

Fuel Injection

IDLE SPEED ADJUSTMENT

2.5L Engine

NOTE: If for any reason the battery is disconnected or the vehicle has to be jump started, it may be necessary to perform the following procedure.

1. Apply the parking brake, block the drive wheels and place the vehicle in **P** or **N**.

2. Start the engine and let it run until it reaches normal operating temperature, then turn the engine **OFF**. Connect a suitable tachometer.

3. Start the engine and place the transaxle in **P** or **N**, let the engine run at idle for 2 minutes. The idle rpm should now return to the specified idle speed. The idle specifications can be found on the calibration sticker located under the hood.

4. Place the transaxle in **N** or **P** and the engine rpm should increase by approximately 100 rpm. Now lightly step on and off the accelerator. The engine rpm should return to the specified idle speed. If the rpm remains high, repeat the sequence. Remember it may take the the system approximately 2 minutes to adjust. If the vehicle does not respond as previously described, perform the following adjustment.

a. Shut the engine **OFF** and remove the air cleaner. Locate the self-test connector and self-test input connector in the engine compartment.

b. Connect a jumper wire between the self-test input connector and the signal return pin, the top right terminal on the self-test connector.

c. Place the ignition key in the **RUN** position and be careful not to start the engine. The ISC plunger will retract, so wait approximately 10–15 seconds until the ISC plunger is fully retracted. Turn the ignition key to the **OFF** position and wait 10–15 seconds.

d. Remove the jumper wire and unplug the ISC motor from the wire harness. Now perform the throttle stop adjustment as follows:

e. Remove the CFI assembly from the vehicle.

f. Use a small punch or equivalent to punch through and remove the aluminum plug which covers the throttle stop adjusting screw.

g. Remove and replace the throttle stop screw. Reinstall the CFI assembly onto the vehicle.

5. Start the engine and allow to the idle to stabilize. Set the idle rpm to the specifications listed on the calibration decal located under the hood on the throttle stop adjusting screw.

6. Turn **OFF** the engine. Reconnect the ISC motor wire harness, remove all test equipment and reinstall the air cleaner assembly.

3.0L Engine

NOTE: The curb idle speed rpm is controlled by the EEC-IV computer (ECM) and the idle speed control (ISC) air bypass valve assembly. The throttle stop screw is factory set and does not directly

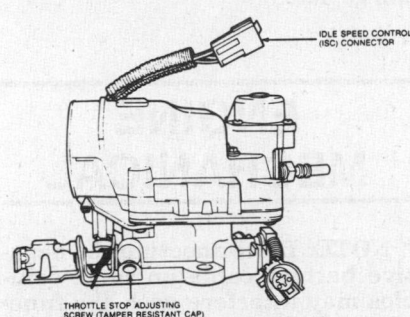

Connecting a jumper wire between the self-test and the self-test input connectors

View of the throttle body—2.5L CFI engine

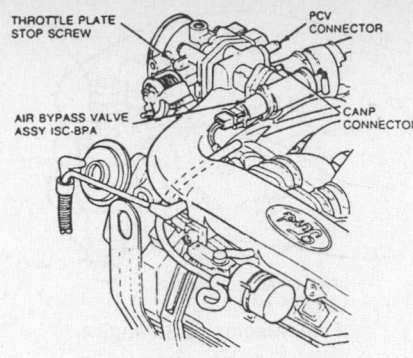

3.0L SEFI engine.

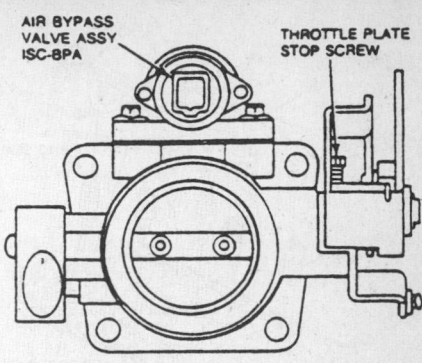

View of the throttle body—3.8L EFI engine

control the idle speed. Adjustment to this setting should be performed only as part of a full EEC-IV diagnosis of irregular idle conditions or idle speeds. Failure to accurately set the throttle plate stop position as described in the following procedure could result in false idle speed control.

1. Apply the parking brake, turn the air conditioning control selector **OFF** and block the wheels.

2. Connect a tachometer and an inductive timing light to the engine. Start the engine and allow it to reach normal operating temperatures.

3. Unplug the spout line at the distributor, then check and/or adjust the ignition timing to 8–12 degrees BTDC.

4. On the 3.0L EFI engine, remove the PCV entry line from the PCV valve. Using the orifice (0.200 in. dia.) tool, install it in the PCV entry line.

5. On the 3.0L SEFI engine, remove the PCV hose from the throttle body and plug it. Remove the CANP hose from the throttle body and connect it to the PCV connector of the throttle body.

6. Stop the engine and disconnect the electrical connector from the air bypass valve assembly.

7. Start the engine. Place the transaxle in **P** or **N**. Disconnect the electrical connector from the electric cooling fan.

8. Check and/or adjust, if necessary, the idle speed to 740–780 rpm on the 3.0L EFI engine and 770–830 rpm on the 3.0L SEFI engine by turning the throttle plate stop screw.

9. After adjusting the idle speed,

stop the engine and disconnect the battery for 3 minutes minimum.

10. Reconnect all hoses and electrical connections with the engine **OFF**.

11. Make sure the throttle plate is not stuck in the bore and that the throttle plate stop screw is setting on the rest pad with the throttle closed. Correct any condition that will not allow the throttle to close to the stop set position.

12. Start the engine and confirm that the idle speed is now adjusted to specifications, if not, readjust as necessary.

3.8L Engine

1. Apply the parking brake, block the drive wheels and place the vehicle in **P** or **N**.

2. Start the engine and let it run until it reaches normal operating temperature, then turn the engine **OFF**. Connect a suitable tachometer.

3. Start the engine and run the engine at 2500 rpm for 30 seconds.

4. Allow the engine idle to stabilize.

5. Adjust the engine idle rpm to the specification shown on the vehicle emission control label by adjusting the throttle stop screw.

6. After the idle speed is within specification, repeat Steps 3–5 to ensure that the adjustment is correct.

7. Stop the engine and reconnect the power lead to the idle speed control air bypass valve. Disconnect all test equipment.

Fuel Injector

REMOVAL & INSTALLATION

2.5L CFI Engine

1. Disconnect the negative battery cable.

2. Relieve the fuel system pressure.

3. Remove the fuel injector retaining screw and retainer.

4. Remove the injector and lower O-ring. Discard the O-ring.

To install:

5. Lubricate a new lower O-ring and

the injector seat area with clean engine oil (do not use transmission fluid). Install the lower O-ring on the injector.

6. Lubricate the upper O-ring and install the injector by centering and applying a steady downward pressure with a slight rotational force.

7. Install the injector retainer and retaining screw. Tighten the screw to 18–22 inch lbs. (2.0–2.5 Nm).

3.0L EFI Engine

1. Disconnect the negative battery cable.

2. Relieve the fuel system pressure.

3. Remove the air intake throttle body.

4. Disconnect the fuel supply and fuel return lines.

5. Disconnect the wiring harness from the injectors.

6. Disconnect the vacuum line from the fuel pressure regulator valve.

7. Remove the 4 fuel injector manifold retaining bolts.

8. Carefully disengage the fuel rail assembly from the fuel injectors by lifting and gently rocking the rail.

9. Remove the injectors by lifting while gently rocking from side to side.

To install:

10. Lubricate new O-rings with engine oil and install 2 on each injector.

11. Make sure the injector cups are clean and undamaged.

12. Install the injectors in the fuel rail using a light twisting-pushing motion.

13. Carefully install the rail assembly and injectors into the lower intake manifold, 1 side at a time. Make sure the O-rings are seated by pushing down on the fuel rail.

14. While holding the fuel rail assembly in place, install the 2 retaining bolts and tighten to 7 ft. lbs. (10 Nm).

15. Connect the fule supply and fuel return lines.

16. Before connecting the fuel injector harness, turn the ignition switch to the **ON** position. This will pressurize the fuel system.

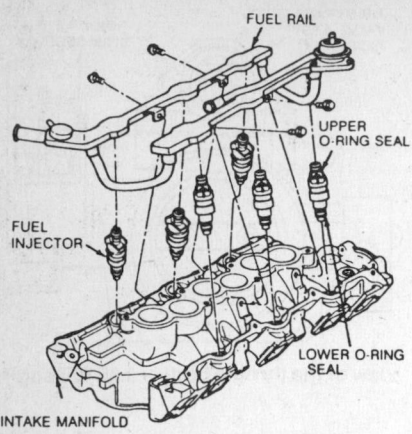

Injector removal—3.0L EFI engine

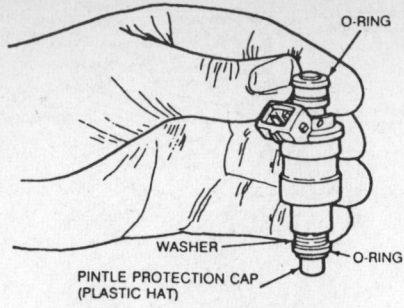

Fuel injector—3.8L engine

17. Using a clean paper towel. check for leaks where the injector connects to the fuel rail.

18. Install the air intake throttle body and connect the vacuum line to the fuel pressure regulator valve.

19. Connect the fuel injector harness, start the engine and let it idle for 2 minutes.

20. Using a clean paper towel, check for leaks where the injector is installed into the intake manifold.

3.0L SHO Engine

1. Disconnect the negative battery cable.
2. Relieve the fuel system pressure.
3. Remove the intake manifold.
4. Disconnect the electrical connectors at the fuel injectors.
5. Remove the fuel rail retaining bolts.
6. Raise and slightly rotate the fuel rail assembly and remove the injectors.

To install:

7. Lubricate new O-rings with engine oil and install them on the fuel injectors.
8. Install the injectors in the fuel rail by lightly twisting and pushing the injectors into position.
9. Install the fuel rail, making sure the injectors seat properly in the cylinder head.
10. Install the fuel rail retaining bolts and tighten to 11–17 ft. lbs. (15–23 Nm).
11. Connect the electrical connectors at the injectors. Install the intake manifold.
12. Run the engine and check for leaks.

3.8L Engine

1. Disconnect the negative battery cable.
2. Remove the fuel cap at the tank and release the pressure.
3. Relieve the pressure from the fuel system.

4. Remove the upper intake manifold and the fuel supply manifold.
5. Remove the injector retaining clips.
6. Remove the electrical connectors from the fuel injectors.
7. To remove the injector, pull it up while gently rocking it from side to side.
8. Inspect the injector pintle protection cap (plastic hat) and washer for deterioration and replace as required.

To install:

9. Lubricate new engine O-rings with engine oil and install 2 on each injector.
10. Install the injectors, using a light, twisting, pushing motion to install them.
11. Reconnect the injector retaining clips.
12. Install the fuel rail assembly.
13. Install the electrical harness connectors to the injectors.
14. Install the upper intake manifold.
15. Install the fuel cap at the tank.
16. Connect the negative battery cable.
17. Turn the ignition switch from **ON** to **OFF** position several times without starting the engine to check for fuel leaks.

EMISSION CONTROLS

Please refer to "Emission Control" in the Unit Repair section for system maintenance procedures. Due to the complex nature of modern electronic engine control systems, comprehensive diagnosis and testing procedures fall outside the confines of this repair manual. For complete information on diagnosis, testing and repair procedures concerning all modern engine and emission control systems, please refer to "Chilton's Guide to Electronic Engine Controls".

Emission Warning Lamps

These vehicles have a "Check Engine" lamp that will light when there is a fault in the engine control system. This light cannot be reset without diagnosing the fault in the system. When the system has been diagnosed and the problem corrected, the light will go out.

ENGINE MECHANICAL

NOTE: Disconnecting the negative battery cable on some vehicles may interfere with the functions of the on board computer systems and may require the computer to undergo a relearning process, once the negative battery cable is reconnected.

Engine Assembly

REMOVAL & INSTALLATION

2.5L Engine

1. Disconnect the negative battery cable and relieve the fuel system pressure.
2. On vehicles equipped with automatic transaxle, remove the transaxle timing window cover and rotate the engine until the flywheeel timing marker is aligned with the timing pointer.
3. Place a reference mark on the crankshaft pulley at the 12 o'clock position (TDC) then rotate the crankshaft pulley mark to the 6 o'clock position (BTDC).
4. Disconnect the negative battery cable and mark the position of the hood hinges and remove the hood.
5. Remove the air cleaner assembly and drain the cooling system.
6. Disconnect the upper radiator hose at the engine.
7. Identify, tag and disconnect all electrical wiring and vacuum hoses as required.
8. Disconnect the crankcase ventilation hose at the valve cover and intake manifold.
9. Disconnect the fuel lines and heater hoses at the throttle body.
10. Disconnect the engine ground wire.
11. Disconnect the accelerator and throttle valve control cables at the throttle body.

12. Evacuate the air conditioning system and remove the suction and discharge lines from the compressor, if equipped.

13. On manual transaxle equipped vehicles, remove the engine damper brace.

14. Remove the driver belt and water pump pulley.

15. Remove the air cleaner-to-canister hose.

16. Raise the vehicle and support safely.

17. Drain the engine oil and remove the oil filter.

18. Disconnect the starter cable and remove the starter motor.

19. On automatic transaxle equipped vehicles, remove the converter nuts and align the previously made reference mark as close to the 6 o'clock (BTDC) position as possible with the converter stud visible.

NOTE: The flywheel timing marker must be in the 6 o'clock (BDC) position for proper engine removal and installation.

20. Remove the engine insulator nuts.

21. Disconnect the exhaust pipe from the manifold.

22. Disconnect the canister and halfshaft brackets from the engine.

23. Remove the lower engine-to-transaxle retaining bolts.

24. Disconnect the lower radiator hose.

25. Lower the vehicle and position a suitable floor jack under the transaxle.

26. Disconnect the power steering lines from the pump.

27. Install engine lifting eyes tool D81L–6001–D or equivalent and engine support tool No. T79P–6000–A or equivalent.

28. Connect suitable lifting equipment to support the engine and remove the upper engine-to-transaxle retaining bolts.

29. Remove the engine from the vehicle and support on a suitable holding fixture.

To install:

30. Make sure the timing marker is in the 6 o'clock (BDC) position.

31. Remove the engine from the stand and position it in the vehicle. Remove the lifting equipment.

32. Install the upper engine-to-transaxle bolts and tighten. Use a floor jack under the transaxle to aid alignment.

33. Connect the power steering lines to the pump.

34. Raise the vehicle and support it safely.

35. Connect the lower radiator hose to the tube.

36. Install the lower engine-to-transaxle attaching bolts and tighten.

37. Connect the halfshaft bracket to the engine and the exhaust pipe to the manifold.

38. Install the engine insulator nuts and tighten.

39. Position the marks on the crankshaft pulley as close to 6 o'clock position (BDC) as possible and install the converter nuts.

40. Install the starter and connect the starter cable.

41. Install the oil filter and make sure the oil drain plug is tight.

42. Lower the vehicle.

43. Install the air cleaner-to-canister hose and the water pump pulley and drive belt.

44. Connect the air conditioning lines to the compressor, if so equipped.

45. Connect the accelerator cable and throttle valve control cable at the throttle body.

46. Connect the negative battery cable at the engine and the heater hoses at the throttle body.

47. Connect the crankcase ventilation hose at the valve cover and the intake manifold.

48. Connect the engine control sensor wiring assembly and vacuum lines.

49. Connect the upper radiator hose at the engine and install the air cleaner assembly.

50. Connect the negative battery cable.

51. Rotate the engine until the flywheel timing marker is aligned with the timing pointer. Install the timing window cover.

52. Connect the electrical connector at the inertia switch.

53. Fill the cooling system with the proper amount and type of coolant and fill the crankcase with the proper engine oil to the required level.

54. Install the hood.

55. Charge the air conditioning system, if equipped.

56. Check all fluid levels and start the vehicle. Check for leaks.

3.0L Engine

1. Disconnect the battery cables and drain the cooling system. Remove the engine hood.

2. Evacuate the air conditioning system safely and properly. Relieve the fuel system pressure. Remove the air cleaner assembly. Remove the battery and the battery tray.

3. Remove the integrated relay controller, cooling fan and radiator with fan shroud. Remove the engine bounce damper bracket on the shock tower.

4. Remove the evaporative emission line, upper radiator hose, starter brace and lower radiator hose.

5. Remove the exhaust pipes from both exhaust manifolds. Remove and plug the power steering pump lines.

6. Remove the fuel lines and remove and tag all necessary vacuum lines.

7. Disconnect the ground strap, heater lines, accelerator cable linkage, throttle valve linkage and speed control cable.

8. Disconnect and label the following wiring connectors; alternator, air conditioning clutch, oxygen sensor, ignition coil, radio frequency supressor, cooling fan voltage resistor, engine coolant temperature sensor, Thick film ignition module, injector wiring harness, ISC motor wire, throttle position sensor, oil pressure sending switch, ground wire, block heater, if equipped, knock sensor, EGR sensor and oil level sensor.

9. Raise the vehicle and support it safely. Remove the engine mount bolts and engine mounts. Remove the transaxle to engine mounting bolts and transaxle brace assembly.

10. Lower the vehicle. Install a suitable engine lifting plate onto the engine and use a suitable engine hoist to remove the engine from the vehicle. Remove the main wiring harness from the engine.

To install:

11. Install the main wiring harness on the engine. Position the engine in the vehicle and remove the engine lifting plate.

12. Raise the vehicle and support it safely. Install the engine mounts and bolts and tighten to 40–55 ft. lbs. (54–75 Nm). Install the transaxle brace assembly and tighten the bolts to 40–55 ft. lbs. (54–75 Nm).

13. Connect all wiring connectors according to their labels.

14. Connect the ground strap, heater lines, accelerator cable linkage, throttle valve linkage and speed control cables.

15. Connect the power steering pump lines.

16. Connect the exhaust pipes to the exhaust manifolds.

17. Connect the fuel lines and vacuum lines.

18. Install the evaporative emission line, upper radiator hose, starter brace and lower radiator hose.

19. Install the integrated relay controller, cooling fan and radiator with fan shroud. Install the engine bounce damper bracket on the shock tower.

20. Install the battery tray and the battery.

21. Install the air cleaner assembly and charge the air conditioning system.

22. Fill the cooling system with the proper type and quantity of coolant. Fill the crankcase with the correct type of motor oil to the required level.

23. Install the hood.

24. Connect the negative battery cable. Start the engine and check for leaks.

3.0L SHO Engine

1. Disconnect the battery cables and remove the battery and battery tray.

2. Drain the cooling system and relieve the fuel system pressure.

3. Disconnect the wiring connector retaining the under hood lamp, if equipped, mark the position of the hood hinges and remove the hood.

4. Remove the oil level indicator.

5. Disconnect the alternator and voltage regulator wiring assembly.

6. Remove the radiator upper sight shield.

7. Discharge the air conditioning system.

8. Remove the radiator coolant recovery reservoir assembly.

9. Remove the integrated relay controller, air cleaner hose assembly, upper radiator hose, electric fan and shroud assembly.

10. Remove the lower radiator hose and the radiator.

11. Disconnect the fuel inlet and return hose.

12. Remove the Barometric Air Pressure (BAP) sensor.

13. Remove the engine vibration damper and bracket assembly from the right hand side of the engine.

14. Remove the engine to damper bracket.

15. Remove the retaining bolt from the power steering reservoir and place the reservoir out of the way. Disconnect the hose to the power steering cooler at the pump.

16. Disconnect the throttle linkage and disconnect and tag the vacuum hoses.

17. Disconnect the heater hoses at the heater core.

18. Disconnect the electrical connectors from the harness on the rear of the engine.

19. Loosen the belt tensioner pulleys and remove the air conditioning compressor/alternator belt and the steering pump belt. Remove the lower tensioner pulley.

20. Disconnect the cycling switch on the top of the suction accumulator/drier.

21. Disconnect the air conditioning line at the dash panel and remove the accumulator and bracket assembly.

22. Remove the alternator assembly.

23. Disconnect the air conditioning discharge hose and remove the air conditioning compressor and bracket assembly.

24. Raise the vehicle and support it safely.

25. Place a drain pan beneath the oil pan and drain the motor oil and remove the filter element.

26. Remove the wheel and tire assemblies. Disconnect the oil level sensor switch.

27. Disconnect the right hand lower ball joint, tie rod end and stabilizer bar.

28. Disconnect the center support bearing bracket and right-hand CV-joint from the transaxle.

29. Disconnect the oxygen sensor assembly and the 4 exhaust catalyst to engine retaining bolts.

30. Remove the starter motor assembly.

31. Remove the lower transaxle to engine retaining bolts.

32. Remove the engine mount to subframe nuts.

33. Remove the crankshaft pulley assembly.

34. Lower the vehicle and remove the upper transaxle to engine retaining bolts.

35. Install engine lifting eyes.

36. Position a floor jack under the transaxle.

37. Position suitable engine lifting equipment, raise the transaxle assembly slightly and remove the engine from the vehicle.

To install:

38. Position the engine assembly in the vehicle.

39. Install the upper transaxle to engine bolts and remove the floor jack and engine lifting equipment. Remove the engine lifting eyes.

40. Raise the vehicle and support it safely.

41. Install the crankshaft pulley assembly. Tighten the retaining bolt to 113–126 ft. lbs. (152–172 Nm).

42. Install the engine mount to subframe nuts and the lower transaxle to engine retaining bolts. Tighten the bolts to 25–35 ft. lbs. (34–47 Nm).

43. Install the starter motor assembly.

44. Install the 4 exhaust catalyst to engine retaining nuts and tighten them to 19–34 ft. lbs. (27–47 Nm). Install the oxygen sensor assembly.

45. Connect the center support bearing bracket and install the right-hand CV-joint.

46. Connect the right hand lower ball joint, tie rod end and stabilizer bar.

47. Connect the oil level sensor and install the wheel and tire assemblies.

48. Install the oil filter. Install the oil drain plug and tighten to 15–24 ft. lbs. (20–33 Nm).

49. Lower the vehicle.

50. Install the air conditioning compressor and bracket assembly, tighten to 27–40 ft. lbs. (36–55 Nm) and connect the air conditioning discharge hose.

51. Install the alternator assembly and tighten to 36–53 ft. lbs. (48–72 Nm).

52. Install the accumulator and bracket assembly and connect the cycling switch to the top of the accumulator.

53. Install the lower belt tensioner. Install the power steering and air conditioning compressor/alternator belts and tighten the tensioner pulleys.

54. Connect the electrical connectors from the harness on the rear of the engine.

55. Connect the heater hoses, vacuum hoses and throttle linkage.

56. Connect the hose from the power steering cooler at the pump and install the power steering reservoir.

57. Install the damper bracket to the engine and install the engine vibration damper and bracket assembly to the right hand side of the engine.

58. Install the BAP sensor.

59. Connect the fuel inlet and return hoses.

60. Install the radiator assembly and the lower radiator hose.

61. Install the electric fan and shroud assembly, upper radiator hose, air cleaner hose, integrated relay controller, radiator coolant recovery reservoir and radiator upper sight shield.

62. Connect the alternator and voltage regulator wiring.

63. Install the oil level indicator tube.

64. Install the hood and connect the under hood lamp wiring, if so equipped.

65. Install the battery tray and the battery.

66. Install the negative battery cable.

67. Fill the cooling system with the proper type and quantity of coolant and fill the crankcase with the proper type of motor oil to the required level.

68. Drain, evacuate, pressure test and recharge the air conditioning system.

69. Start the engine and check for leaks.

3.8L Engine

1. Drain the cooling system and disconnect the battery ground cable. Properly relieve the fuel system pressure.

2. Disconnect the underhood lamp wiring connector. Mark position of hood hinges and remove hood.

3. Remove the oil level indicator tube.

4. Disconnect alternator to voltage regulator wiring assembly.

5. Remove the radiator upper sight shield. Remove the engine cooling fan motor relay retaining bolts and position cooling fan motor relay out of the way.

6. Remove the air cleaner assembly.

7. Disconnect the radiator electric fan and motor assembly. Remove fan shroud.

8. Remove upper radiator hose.

9. Disconnect the transaxle oil cooler inlet and outlet tubes and cover the openings to prevent the entry of dirt and grease. Disconnect the heater hoses.

10. Disconnect the power steering pressure hose assembly.

11. Disconnect the air conditioner compressor clutch wire assembly. Discharge the air conditioning system and disconnect the compressor-to-condenser line.

12. Remove the radiator coolant recovery reservoir assembly. Remove the wiring shield.

13. Remove accelerator cable mounting bracket.

14. Disconnect fuel inlet and return hoses.

15. Disconnect power steering pump pressure and return tube brackets.

16. Disconnect the engine control sensor wiring assembly.

17. Identify, tag and disconnect all necessary vacuum hoses.

18. Disconnect the ground wire assembly. Remove the duct assembly.

19. Disconnect one end of the throttle control valve cable. Disconnect the bulkhead electrical connector and transaxle pressure switches.

20. Remove transaxle support assembly retaining bolts and remove transaxle and support assembly from vehicle.

21. Raise the vehicle and support safely. Remove the wheel and tire assemblies. Drain the engine oil and remove the filter.

22. Disconnect the heated exhaust gas oxygen sensor assembly.

23. Loosen and remove drive belt assembly. Remove the crankshaft pulley and drive belt tensioner assemblies.

24. Remove the starter motor assembly. Remove the converter housing assembly and remove the inlet pipe converter assembly.

25. Remove the engine left and right front support insulator retaining nuts.

26. Remove the converter-to-flywheel nuts.

27. Disconnect the oil level indicator sensor. Remove crankshaft pulley assembly.

28. Disconnect the lower radiator hose.

29. Remove the engine-to-transaxle bolts and partially lower engine. Remove the wheel assemblies.

30. Remove the water pump pulley retaining bolts and the water pump pulley.

31. Remove the distributor cap and position out of the way. Remove distributor rotor.

32. Remove the exhaust manifold bolt lock retaining bolts. Remove the thermactor air pump retaining bolts and the thermactor air pump.

33. Disconnect the oil pressure engine unit gauge assembly.

34. Install engine lifting eyes and connect suitable lifting equipment to the lifting eyes.

35. Position a suitable jack under the transaxle and raise the transaxle a small amount.

36. Remove the engine from the vehicle and position in a suitable holding fixture.

To install:

NOTE: Lightly oil all bolt and stud threads before installation except those specifying special sealant.

37. Remove the engine assembly from the work stand and position it in the vehicle.

38. Install the engine to transaxle bolts and remove the jack from under the transaxle and the engine lifting equipment. Remove the engine lifting eyes.

39. Tighten the engine to transaxle bolts to 41–50 ft. lbs. (55–68 Nm).

40. Connect the oil pressure engine unit gauge assembly.

41. Install the air conditioning compressor and tighten the retaining bolts to 30–45 ft. lbs. (41–61 Nm). Connect the compressor to condenser discharge line and the compressor clutch wire assembly.

42. Connect the heater hoses, vacuum hoses and the fuel tube hose and return line hose.

43. Connect the engine control module wiring assembly.

44. Connect the transaxle oil cooler inlet and outlet tubes.

45. Install the radiator assembly.

46. Partially raise the vehicle and support it safely.

47. Install the converter to flywheel bolts and tighten to 20–34 ft. lbs. (27–46 Nm).

48. Install the left hand and right hand transaxle and engine mount retaining nuts and install the converter housing cover.

49. Install the starter motor.

50. Connect the lower radiator hose.

51. Install the drive belt tensioner assembly and the crankshaft pulley assembly. Tighten the crankshaft pulley retaining bolts to 20–28 ft. lbs. (26–38 Nm).

52. Install the catalytic converter assembly and connect the heated exhaust gas oxygen sensor.

53. Install the oil filter and connect the oil level indicator sensor.

54. Lower the vehicle.

55. Position the thermactor air sup-

ply pump and install the retaining bolts.

56. Connect the vacuum pump and install the exhaust air supply pump pulley assembly.

57. Install the wiring shield.

58. Install the distributor cap and rotor.

59. Install the radiator coolant recovery reservoir assembly, upper radiator hose and water pump pulley.

60. Connect the alternator-to-voltage regulator wiring assembly and the engine control module wiring assembly.

61. Connect the wiring assembly ground.

62. Install the accelerator cable mounting bracket.

63. Connect the power steering pressure hose assembly and the power steering line.

64. Install the fan shroud.

65. Connect the radiator electric motor assembly and install the engine cooling fan motor relay assembly.

66. Install the drive belts.

67. Position and install the transaxle support assembly.

68. Install the radiator upper sight shield.

69. Partially raise the vehicle and support it safely. Install the wheel and tire assemblies.

70. Install the hood and connect the negative battery cable.

71. Fill the cooling system with the proper type and quantity of coolant and fill the crankcase with the proper type of motor oil to the required level.

72. Drain, evacuate, pressure test and recharge the air conditioning system.

73. Start the engine and check for leaks.

Engine Mounts

REMOVAL & INSTALLATION

2.5L and 3.0L Engines

RIGHT REAR ENGINE INSULATOR (NO. 3)

1. Disconnect the negative battery cable. Remove the lower damper nut from the right side of the engine on manual transaxle equipped vehicles. Raise and support the vehicle safely.

2. Place a suitable jack and a block of wood the engine block.

3. Remove the nut attaching the right hand front and rear insulators to the frame.

4. Raise the engine with the jack until enough of a load is taken off of the insulator.

5. Remove the insulator retaining bolts and remove the insulator from the engine support bracket.

6. Installation is the reverse of the removal procedure. Tighten the insulator to engine support bracket to 40–55 ft. lbs. Tighten the nut attaching the right, front and rear insulators to frame to 55–75 ft. lbs.

LEFT ENGINE INSULATOR AND SUPPORT ASSEMBLY— AUTOMATIC TRANSAXLE

1. Disconnect the negative battery cable. Raise and support the vehicle safely. Remove the wheel assemblies.
2. Place a suitable jack and a block of wood under the tranmission and support the transaxle.
3. Remove the nuts attaching the insulator to the support assembly. Remove the through bolts attaching the insulator to the frame.
4. Raise the transaxle with the jack enough to relieve the weight on the insulator.
5. Remove the bolts attaching the support assembly to the transaxle. Remove the insulator and/or transaxle support assembly.
6. .Installation is the reverse of the removal procedure. Tighten the support assembly retaining bolts to 40–55 ft. lbs. (54–75 Nm). Tighten the insulator-to-frame bolts to 60–86 ft. lbs. (81–116 Nm). Tighten the insulator to support assembly nuts to 55–75 ft. lbs. (74–102 Nm).

LEFT ENGINE INSULATOR AND SUPPORT ASSEMBLY—MANUAL TRANSAXLE

1. Disconnect the negative battery cable. Raise and support the vehicle safely. Remove the wheel assemblies.
2. Place a suitable jack and a block of wood under the tranmission and support the transaxle.
3. Remove the bolts attaching the insulator to the frame.
4. Raise the transaxle with the jack enough to relieve the weight on the insulator.
5. Remove the bolts attaching the insulator to the transaxle. Remove the insulator and or transaxle support assembly.
6. Installation is the reverse of the removal procedure. Tighten the support assembly retaining bolts to 70–96 ft. lbs. Tighten the insulator-to-frame nuts and bolts to 70–96 ft. lbs.

RIGHT FRONT ENGINE INSULATOR (NO. 2)

1. Disconnect the negative battery cable. Remove the lower damper nut or bolt from the right side of the engine. Raise and support the vehicle safely.
2. Place a suitable jack and a block of wood the engine block.
3. Remove the nuts attaching the

right hand front and rear insulators to the frame.
4. Raise the engine with the jack until enough of a load is taken off of the insulator.
5. Remove the bolts and the insulator from the engine air conditioning bracket.
6. Installation is the reverse of the removal procedure. Tighten the insulator-to-engine air conditioning bracket to 40–55 ft. lbs. Tighten the nut attaching the right hand front and right hand rear insulators to frame to 55–75 ft. lbs.

3.0L SHO Engine
RIGHT FRONT (NO. 2) AND RIGHT REAR (NO. 3)

1. Remove the lower damper bolt from the right hand side of the engine.
2. Raise the vehicle and support it safely.
3. Place a jack and a wood block in a suitable place under the engine.
4. Remove the roll damper to engine retaining nuts and remove the roll damper.
5. Raise the engine enough to unload the insulator.
6. Remove the 2 through bolts and remove the insulators from the engine bracket.
7. Installation is the reverse of the removal procedure. Tighten the insulator-to-engine bracket bolts to 40–55 ft. lbs. (54–75 Nm). Tighten the insulator to frame nuts to 50–70 ft. lbs. (68–95 Nm). Tighten the roll damper retaining nuts to 40–55 ft. lbs. (54–75 Nm). Tighten the engine damper to engine bolt to 40–55 ft. lbs. (54–75 Nm).

LEFT ENGINE INSULATOR AND SUPPORT ASSEMBLY

1. Remove the bolt retaining the roll damper to the lower damper bracket and place the damper shaft out of the way.
2. Remove the backup lamp switch and the energy management bracket.
3. Raise the vehicle and support it with jackstands under the vehicle body, allowing the sub-frame to hang.
4. Remove the left hand tire and wheel assembly.
5. Place a jack and wood block in a suitable place under the transaxle.
6. Remove the nuts retaining the lower damper bracket to engine mount and the bolts retaining the insulator to the transaxle and sub-frame.
7. Raise the transaxle with the jack enough to unload the insulator.
8. Remove the insulator and lower damper bracket.
9. Installation is the reverse of the removal procedure. Tighten the damper bracket to insulator nuts to 40–55

ft. lbs. (54–75 Nm). Tighten the insulator to transaxle bolts to 70–95 ft. lbs. (95–130 Nm). Tighten the insulator to frame bolts to 60–85 ft. lbs. (81–116 Nm). Tighten the damper to damper bracket bolt to 40–55 ft. lbs. (54–75 Nm).

3.8L Engine
RIGHT FRONT ENGINE INSULATOR

1. Disconnect the negative battery cable. Remove the compressor-to-engine mounting bracket mounting bolts and position the compressor to the side. Do not discharge the air conditioning system.
2. Raise the vehicle and support safely.
3. Remove nut attaching engine mount to air conditioning compressor bracket.
4. Temporarily attach the air conditioning compressor to the mounting bracket with the 2 lower bolts.
5. Position a jack and wood block in a convenient location under the engine block.
6. Remove the upper and lower nuts attaching the right front and left rear insulators to the frame.
7. Raise the engine with the jack enough to relieve the load on the insulator.
8. Remove insulator assembly. Remove heat shield from insulator.
9. Installation is the reverse of the removal procedure. Tighten the upper insulator stud retaining nut to 40–55 ft. lbs. (54–75 Nm) and the lower retaining nut to 50–70 ft. lbs. (68–95 Nm).

RIGHT REAR ENGINE INSULATOR (NO. 3)

1. Disconnect the negative battery cable and raise and support the vehicle safely.
2. Remove the nuts retaining the right hand front and right hand rear engine mounts to the frame.
3. Lower the vehicle.
4. Using suitable engine lifting equipment, raise the engine approximately 1 in.
5. Loosen the retaining nut on the right hand rear (No. 3) mount and shiels assembly.
6. Raise and support the vehicle safely.
7. Remove the insulator retaining nut and the insulator and heat shield assembly.
8. Installation is the reverse of the removal procedure. Tighten the top retaining nut on the insulator to 40–55 ft. lbs. (54–75 Nm). Tighten the retaining nuts on the right hand front and right hand rear engine mounts to 55–75 ft. lbs. (68–95 Nm).

LEFT ENGINE MOUNT AND SUPPORT ASSEMBLY

1. Raise the vehicle and support it safely.

2. Remove the tire and wheel assembly.

3. Place a jack and wood block in a suitable place under the transaxle and support the transaxle.

4. Remove the 2 bolts retaining the vertical restrictor assembly.

5. Remove the nut retaining the transaxle mount to the support assembly.

6. Remove the 2 through bolts retaining the transaxle mount to the frame.

7. Raise the transaxle with the jack enough to unload the mount.

8. Remove the bolts retaining the support assembly to the transaxle and remove the mount and/or transaxle support assembly.

9. Installation is the reverse of the removal procedure. Tighten the support assembly to transaxle bolts to 35 ft. lbs. (48 Nm). Tighten the mount to frame bolts to 60–86 ft. lbs. (81–116 Nm). Tighten the transaxle mount to support nut to 55–75 ft. lbs. (74–102 Nm). Tighten the 2 bolts retaining the vertical restrictor assembly to 40–55 ft. lbs. (54–75 Nm).

Cylinder Head

REMOVAL & INSTALLATION

2.5L Engine

1. Disconnect the negative battery cable. Drain the cooling system.

2. Remove the air cleaner assembly. Properly relieve the fuel system pressure.

3. Disconnect the heater hose at the fitting located under the intake manifold. Disconnect the upper radiator hose at the cylinder head and the electric cooling fan switch at the plastic connector.

4. Disconnect distributor cap and spark plug wire and remove as an assembly.

5. Remove spark plugs, if necessary.

6. Disconnect and tag required vacuum hoses.

7. Remove dipstick. Disconnect the choke cap wire.

8. Remove rocker cover retaining bolts and remove cover. Disconnect the EGR tube at the EGR valve.

9. Disconnect the fuel supply and return lines at the rubber connections. Disconnect the accelerator cable and speed control cable, if equipped.

10. Raise the vehicle and support it safely. Disconnect the exhaust system at the exhaust pipe, hose and tube. Lower the vehicle.

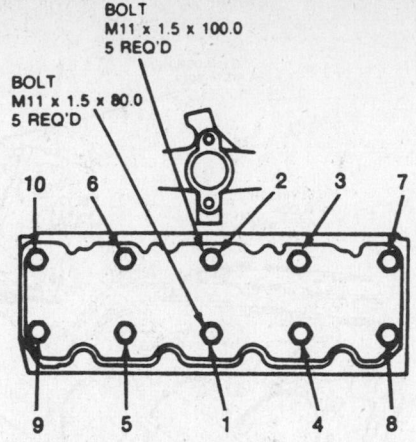

Cylinder head bolt torquing sequence— 2.5L engine

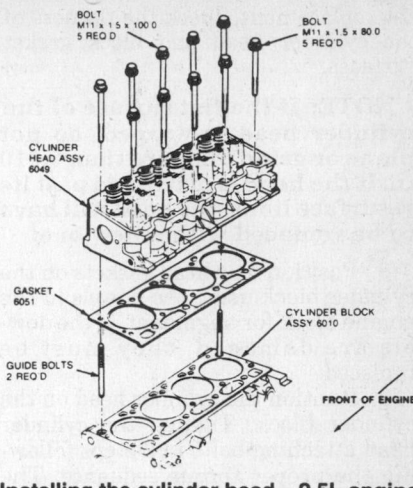

Installing the cylinder head—2.5L engine

11. Remove the cylinder head bolts. Remove the cylinder head and gasket with the exhaust manifold and intake manifold.

To install:

12. Clean all gasket material from the mating surface of the cylinder head and block. Position the cylinder head gasket on the cylinder block, using a suitable sealer to retain the gasket.

13. Before installing the cylinder head, thread 2 cylinder head alignment studs through the head bolt holes in the gasket and into the block at opposite corners of the block.

14. Install the cylinder head and cylinder head bolts. Run down several head bolts and remove the 2 guide bolts. Replace them with the remaining head bolts. Torque the cylinder head bolts in 2 steps, first to 52–59 ft. lbs. (70–80 Nm) and then to 70–76 ft. lbs. (95–103 Nm).

15. Raise and support the vehicle safely. Connect the exhaust system at the exhaust pipe and hose to metal tube.

16. Lower the vehicle and install the thermactor pump drive belt. Connect the accelerator cable and speed control cable, if equipped.

17. Connect the fuel supply and return lines. Connect the choke cap wire.

18. Connect the EGR tube at the EGR valve. Install the distributor cap and spark plug wires as an assembly. Install the spark plugs, if removed.

19. Connect all accessory drive belts. Install the rocker arm cover.

20. Connect the required vacuum hoses. Install the air cleaner assembly. Connect the electric cooling fan switch at the connector.

21. Connect the upper radiator hose at the intake manifold. Fill the cooling system. Connect the negative battery cable.

22. Start the engine and check for leaks. After the engine has reached normal operating temperature, check and if necessary add coolant.

3.0L Except SHO Engine

1. Disconnect the negative battery cable. Properly relieve the fuel system pressure. Drain the cooling system. Remove the air cleaner assembly.

2. Remove the intake manifold. Loosen the accessory drive belt idle pulley, remove the drive belt.

3. If the left hand cylinder head is being removed, remove the power steering automatic belt tensioner and mounting bracket retaining bolts. Leave the hoses connected and place the pump aside in a position to prevent fluid from leaking out.

4. If the right hand head is being removed, remove the alternator belt tensioner bracket, grounding straps and throttle cable support bracket.

5. Remove the exhaust manifolds from both heads. Remove the PCV and the rocker arm covers. Loosen the rocker arm fulcrum attaching bolts enough to allow the rocker arm to be lifted off the pushrod and rotated to one side.

6. Remove the pushrods. Be sure to identify and label the position of each pushrod. The rods should be installed in their original position during reassembly.

7. Remove the cylinder head attaching bolts and remove the cylinder heads from the engine. Remove and discard the old cylinder head gaskets.

To install:

8. Lightly oil all bolt and stud bolt threads before installation. Clean the cylinder head, intake manifold, rocker arm cover and cylinder head gasket contact surfaces. If the cylinder head was removed for a cylinder head gas-

ket replacement, check the flatness of the cylinder head and block gasket surfaces.

NOTE: If the flat surface of the cylinder head is warped, do not plane or grind off more than 0.010 in. If the head is machined past its resurface limit, the head will have to be replaced with a new one.

9. Position new head gaskets on the cylinder block using the dowels in the engine block for alignment. If the dowels are damaged, they must be replaced.

10. Position the cylinder head on the cylinder block. Tighten the cylinder head attaching bolts in 2 steps following the proper torque sequence. The first step is 37 ft. lbs. (50 Nm) and the second step is 68 ft. lbs. (92 Nm).

NOTE: When cylinder head attaching bolts have been tightened using the above procedure, it is not necessary to retighten the bolts after extended engine operation. The bolts can be rechecked for tightness if so desired.

11. Dip each pushrod end in oil conditioner or heavy engine oil. Install the pushrods in their original position.

12. Before installation, coat the valve tips, rocker arm and fulcrum contact areas with Lubriplate® or equivalent. Lightly oil all the bolt and stud threads before installation.

13. Rotate the engine until the lifter is on the base circle of the cam (valve closed).

14. Install the rocker arm and components and torque the rocker arm fulcrum bolts to 24 ft. lbs. (32 Nm). Be sure the lifter is on the base circle of the cam for each rocker arm as it is installed.

NOTE: The fulcrums must be fully seated in the cylinder head and the pushrods must be seated in the rocker arm sockets prior to the final tightening.

15. Install the exhaust manifolds, the oil dipstick tube. Install the intake manifold. Complete the installation of the remaining components by reversing the removal procedure.

16. Start the engine and check for leaks.

17. Check and if necessary, adjust the transaxle throttle linkage and speed control. Install the air cleaner outlet tube duct.

3.0L SHO Engine

1. Disconnect the negative battery cable.

2. Drain the cooling system. Properly relieve the fuel system pressure.

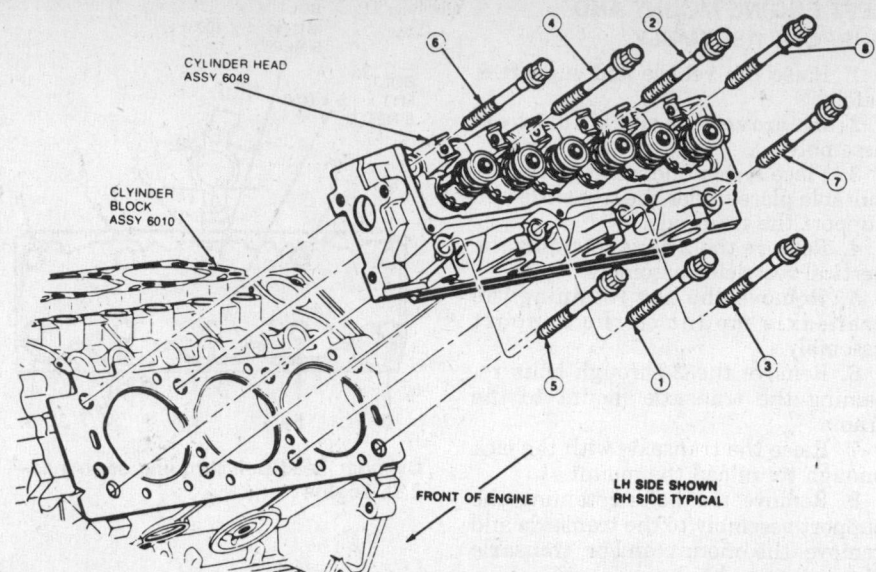

Cylinder head bolt torquing sequence— 3.0L engine

3. Remove the air cleaner outlet tube.

4. Remove the intake manifold.

5. Loosen the accessory drive belt idlers and remove the drive belts.

6. Remove the upper timing belt cover.

7. Remove the left idler pulley and bracket assembly.

8. Raise the vehicle and support it safely.

9. Remove the right wheel and inner fender splash shield.

10. Remove the crankshaft damper pulley.

11. Remove the lower timing belt cover.

12. Align both camshaft pulley timing marks with the index marks on the upper steel belt cover.

13. Release the tension on the belt by loosening the tensioner nut and rotating the tensioner with a hex head wrench. When tension is released, tighten the nut.

14. Disconnect the crankshaft sensor wiring assembly.

15. Remove the center cover assembly.

16. Remove the timing belt noting the location of the letters **KOA** on the belt. The belt must be installed in the same direction.

17. Remove the cylinder head covers.

18. Remove the camshaft timing pulleys.

19. Remove the upper rear and the center rear timing belt covers.

20. If the left cylinder head is being removed, remove the DIS coil bracket and the oil dipstick tube. If the right cylinder head is being removed, remove the coolant outlet hose.

21. Remove the exhaust manifold on the left cylinder head. On the right cylinder head the exhaust manifold must be removed with the head.

22. Remove the cylinder head to block retaining bolts.

23. Remove the cylinder head.

To install:

NOTE: Lightly oil all bolt and stud bolt threads before installation except those specifying special sealant.

24. Clean the cylinder head and engine block mating surfaces of all gasket material.

25. Position the cylinder head and

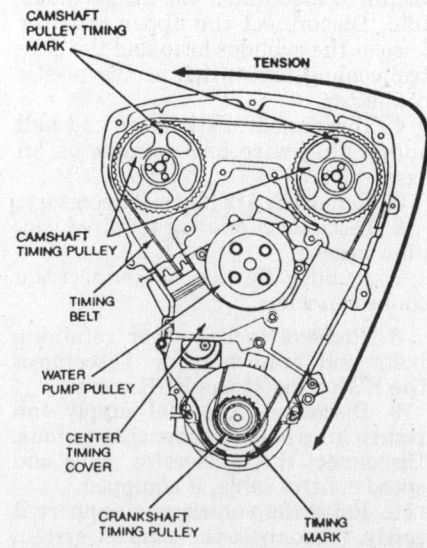

Camshaft pulley timing marks 3.0L SHO engine.

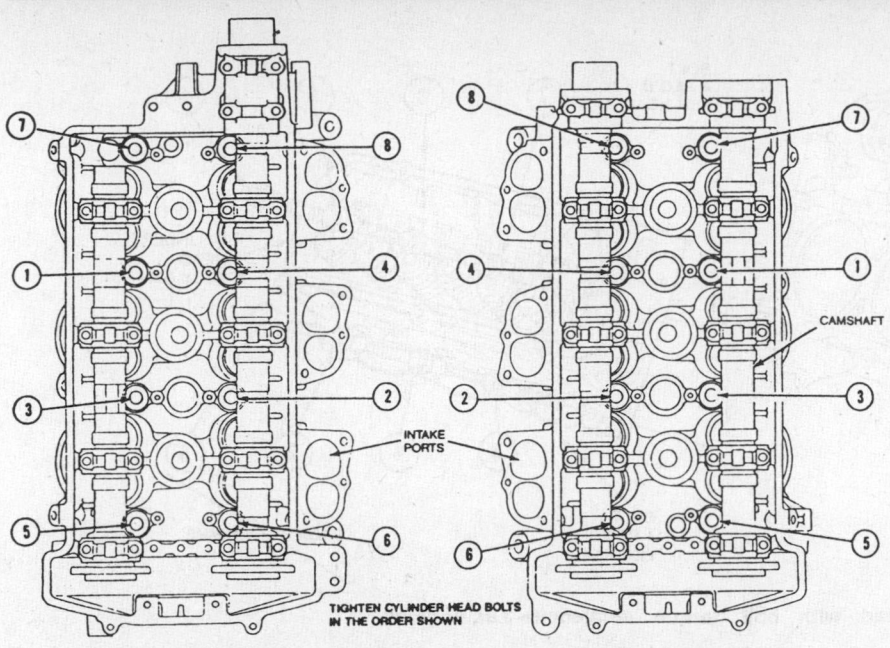

Cylinder head bolt tightening sequence 3.0L SHO engine.

TIGHTEN CYLINDER HEAD BOLTS IN THE ORDER SHOWN

gasket on the engine block and align with the dowel pins.

26. Install the cylinder head bolts and tighten in 2 steps, the first to 37–50 ft. lbs. (49–69 Nm) and finally to 62–68 ft. lbs. (83–93 Nm).

27. When installing the left hand cylinder head, install the exhaust manifold, DIS coil bracket and oil dipstick tube. When installing the right hand cylinder head, install the coolant outlet hose and connect the exhaust catalyst.

28. Install the upper rear and center rear timing belt covers.

29. Install the camshaft pulleys in the timed position.

30. Install the cylinder head covers.

31. Install and adjust the timing belt.

32. Install the center timing belt cover.

33. Connect the crankshaft sensor wiring assembly and install the lower timing belt cover.

34. Raise the vehicle and support it safely.

35. Install the inner fender splash shield and RH wheel and tire assembly.

36. Install the left hand idler pulley and bracket.

37. Install the upper timing belt cover.

38. Install the accessory drive belts.

39. Install the intake manifold.

40. Install the air cleaner oulet tube.

41. Connect the negative battery cable.

42. Fill the engine cooling system with the proper type and quantity of coolant.

43. Start the engine and check for coolant, fuel or oil leaks.

3.8L Engine

1. Drain the cooling system and disconnect the negative battery cable.

2. Properly relieve the fuel system pressure. Remove the air cleaner assembly including air intake duct and heat tube.

3. Loosen the accessory drive belt idler and remove the drive belt.

4. If the right head is being removed, proceed to Step 5. If the left cylinder head is being removed, perform the following to gain access to the upper intake manifold:

   a. Remove the oil fill cap.

   b. Remove the power steering pump. Leave the hoses connected and place the pump/bracket assembly aside in a position to prevent fluid from leaking out.

   c. If equipped with air conditioning, remove mounting bracket attaching bolts. Leaving the hoses connected, position the compressor aside.

   d. Remove the alternator and bracket.

5. If the right cylinder head is being removed, perform the following to gain access to the upper intake manifold:

   a. Disconnect the thermactor air control valve or bypass valve hose assembly at the air pump.

   b. Disconnect the thermactor tube support bracket from the rear of cylinder head.

   c. Remove accessory drive idler.

   d. Remove the thermactor pump pulley and thermactor pump.

   e. Remove the PCV valve.

6. Remove the upper intake manifold.

7. Remove the valve rocker arm cover attaching screws.

8. Remove the injector fuel rail assembly.

9. Remove the lower intake manifold and the exhaust manifold(s).

10. Loosen the rocker arm fulcrum attaching bolts enough to allow rocker arm to be lifted off the pushrod and rotate to one side. Remove the pushrods. Identify and label the position of each pushrod. Pushrods should be installed in their original position during assembly.

11. Remove the cylinder head attaching bolts and discard. Do not re-use the old bolts.

12. Remove the cylinder head(s). Remove and discard old cylinder head gasket(s).

To install:

13. Lightly oil all bolt threads before installation.

14. Clean cylinder head, intake manifold, valve rocker arm cover and cylinder head gasket contact surfaces. If cylinder head was removed for a cylinder head gasket replacement, check flatness of cylinder head and block gasket surfaces.

15. Position the new head gasket(s) onto cylinder block using dowels for alignment. Position cylinder head(s) onto block.

16. Apply a thin coating of pipe sealant with Teflon® to the threads of the short cylinder head bolts, nearest to the exhaust manifold. Do not apply sealant to the long bolts. Install the cylinder head bolts.

NOTE: Always use new cylinder head bolts to ensure a leak-tight assembly. Torque retention with used bolts can vary, which may result in coolant or compression leakage at the cylinder head mating surface area.

17. Tighten the cylinder head attaching bolts in the following sequence:

   Step 1–37 ft. lbs. (50 Nm)
   Step 2–45 ft. lbs. (60 Nm)
   Step 3–52 ft. lbs. (70 Nm)
   Step 4–59 ft. lbs. (80 Nm)

18. In sequence, retighten the cylinder head bolts 1 at a time in the following manner:

   a. Long cylinder head bolts: Loosen the bolts and back them out 2 or 3 turns. Retighten to 11–18 ft. lbs. (15–25 Nm). Then tighten the bolt an additional 85–105 degrees and go to the next bolt in sequence.

   b. Short cylinder head bolts: Loosen the bolts and back them out 2 or 3 turns. Retighten to 11–18 ft. lbs. (15–25 Nm). Then tighten the bolt an additional 65–85 degrees.

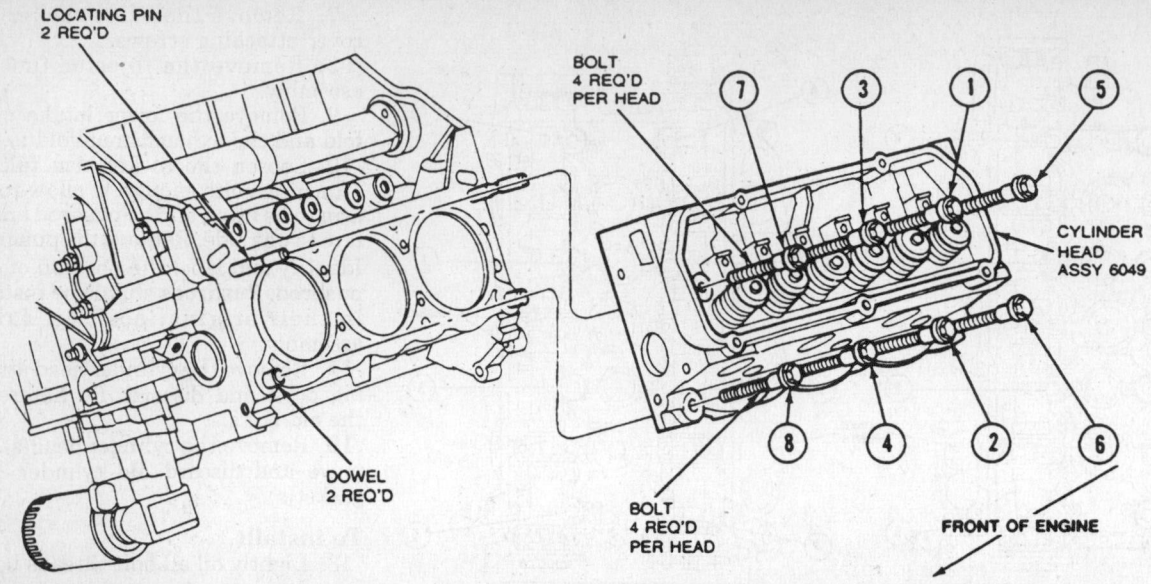

Cylinder head with bolt torque sequence—3.8L engines

NOTE: When cylinder head attaching bolts have been tightened using the above procedure, it is not necessary to retighten bolts after extended engine operation. However, bolts can be checked for tightness if desired.

19. Dip each pushrod end in oil conditioner or heavy engine oil. Install pushrods in their original position.

20. For each valve, rotate crankshaft until the tappet rests on the heel (base circle) of the camshaft lobe. Torque the fulcrum attaching bolts to 43 inch lbs. maximum.

21. Lubricate all rocker arm assemblies with oil conditioner or heavy engine oil.

22. Tighten the fulcrum bolts a second time to 19–25 ft. lbs. (25–35 Nm). For final tightening, camshaft may be in any position.

NOTE: If original valve train components are being installed, a valve clearance check is not required. If a component has been replaced, perform a valve clearance check.

23. Install the exhaust manifold(s), lower intake manifold and injector fuel rail assembly.

24. Position the cover(s) and new gasket on cylinder head and install attaching bolts. Note location of spark plug wire routing clip stud bolts. Tighten attaching bolts to 6–8 ft. lbs.

25. Install the upper intake manifold and connect the secondary wires to the spark plugs.

26. If the left cylinder head is being installed, perform the following: install oil fill cap, compressor mounting and support brackets, power steering

pump mounting and support brackets and the alternator/support bracket.

27. If the right cylinder head is being installed, perform the following: install the PCV valve, alternator bracket, thermactor pump and pump pulley, accessory drive idler, thermactor air control valve or air bypass valve hose.

28. Install the accessory drive belt. Attach the thermactor tube(s) support bracket to the rear of the cylinder head. Tighten the attaching bolts to 30–40 ft. lbs.

29. Connect the negative battery cable and fill the cooling system.

30. Start the engine and check for leaks.

31. Check and, if necessary, adjust curb idle speed.

32. Install the air cleaner assembly including air intake duct and heat tube.

Valve Lifters

REMOVAL & INSTALLATION

2.5L and 3.0L Engines

1. Disconnect the negative battery cable. Remove the cylinder head and related parts.

2. Using a magnet, remove the lifters. Identify, tag and place the tappets in a rack so they can be installed in the original positions.

3. If the lifters are stuck in their bores by excessive varnish or gum, it may be necessary to use a hydraulic lifter puller tool to remove the lifters. Rotate the lifters back and forth to loosen any gum and varnish which may have formed. Keep the assemblies intact until the are to be cleaned.

4. Install the lifters through the pushrod openings with a magnet.

5. Install the cylinder head and related parts.

3.8L Engine

1. Disconnect the negative battery cable. Disconnect the secondary ignition wires at the spark plugs.

2. Remove the plug wire routing clips from mounting studs on the rocker arm cover attaching bolts. Lay plug wires with routing clips toward the front of engine.

3. Remove the upper intake manifold, rocker arm covers and lower intake manifold.

4. Sufficiently loosen each rocker arm fulcrum attaching bolt to allow the rocker arm to be lifted off the pushrod and rotated to one side.

5. Remove the pushrods. The location of each pushrod should be identified and labeled. When engine is assembled, each rod should be installed in its original position.

6. Remove the 2 tappet guide plate retainers and 6 guide plates.

7. Remove the lifters using a magnet. The location of each lifters should be identified and labeled. When engine is assembled, each lifter should be installed in its original position.

NOTE: If lifters are stuck in bores due to excessive varnish or gum deposits, it may be necessary to use a hydraulic lifter puller tool to aid removal. When using a remover tool, rotate lifter back and forth to loosen it from gum or varnish that may have formed on the tappet.

To install:

8. Lightly oil all bolt and stud threads before installation. Using solvent, clean the cylinder head and valve rocker arm cover sealing surfaces.

9. Lubricate each lifter and bore with oil conditioner or heavy engine oil.

10. Install each lifter in bore from which it was removed. If a new tappet(s) is being installed, check new lifter for a free fit in bore.

11. Dip each pushrod end in oil conditioner or heavy engine oil. Install pushrods in their orignial positions.

12. For each valve, rotate crankshaft until lifter rests onto heel (base circle) of camshaft lobe. Position rocker arms over pushrods and install the fulcrums. Initially tighten the fulcrum attaching bolts to 44 inch lbs. maximum.

13. Lubricate all rocker arm assemblies with suitable heavy engine oil.

14. Finally tighten the fulcrum bolts to 19–25 ft. lbs. For the final tightening, the camshaft may be in any position.

NOTE: Fulcrums must be fully seated in the cylinder head and pushrods must be seated in rocker arm sockets prior to the final tightening.

15. Complete the installation of the lower intake manifold, valve rocker arm covers and the upper intake manifold by reversing the removal procedure.

16. Install the plug wire routing clips and connect wires to the spark plugs.

17. Start the engine and check for oil or coolant leaks.

Valve Lash

CHECKING

The valve stem-to-rocker arm clearance for all engines except the 3.0L SHO should be within specification with the valve lifter completely collapsed. To determine the rocker arm to valve lifter clearance, make the following checks.

2.5L Engine

1. Set the No. 1 piston on TDC on the compression stroke. The timing marks on the camshaft and crankshaft gears will be together. Check the clearance in No. 1 intake, No. 1 exhaust, No. 2 intake and No. 3 exhaust valves.

2. Rotate the crankshaft 1 complete turn, 180 degrees for the camshaft gear. Check the clearance in No. 2 exhaust, No. 3 intake, No. 4 intake and No. 4 exhaust.

3. The clearance between the rocker arm and the valve stem tip should be

0.072–0.174 in. (1.80–4.34mm) with the lifter on the base circle of the cam.

3.0L and 3.8L Engines, Except SHO

1. Rotate the engine until the No. 1 cylinder is at TDC of its compression stroke and check the clearance between the rocker arm and the following valves.
   a. No. 1 intake and No. 1 exhaust
   b. No. 3 intake and No. 2 exhaust
   c. No. 6 intake and No. 4 exhaust
2. Rotate the crankshaft 360 degrees and check the clearance between the rocker arm and the following valves.
   a. No. 2 intake and No. 3 exhaust
   b. No. 4 intake and No. 5 exhaust
   c. No. 5 intake and No. 6 exhaust
3. The clearance should be 0.09–0.19 in. (2.25–4.79mm).

3.0L SHO Engine

1. Remove the valve cover.
2. Remove the intake manifold assembly.
3. Insert a feeler gauge under the cam lobe at a 90 degree angle to the camshaft. Clearance for the intake valves should be 0.006–0.010 in. (0.15–0.25mm). Clearance for the exhaust valves should be 0.010–0.014 in. (0.25–0.35mm).

NOTE: The cam lobes must be directed 90 degrees or more away from the valve lifters.

ADJUSTMENT

3.0L SHO Engine

1. Disconnect the negative battery cable.
2. Remove the valve cover.
3. Remove the intake manifold assembly.
4. Install lifter compressor tool T89P–6500–A or equivalent, under the camshaft next to the lobe and rotate it downward to depress the valve lifter.
5. Install valve lifter holding tool T89P–6500–B or equivalent, and remove the compressor tool.
6. Using pick tool T71P–19703–C or equivalent, lift the adjusting shim and remove the shim with a magnet.
7. Determine the size of the shim by the numbers on the bottom face of the shim or by measuring with a micrometer.
8. Install the replacement shim with the numbers down. Make sure the shim is properly seated.
9. Release the lifter holder tool by installing the compressor tool.
10. Repeat the procedure for each valve by rotating the crankshaft as necessary.

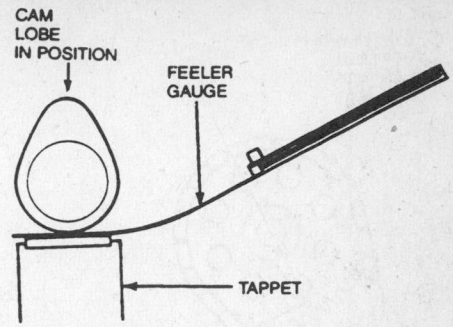

Checking valve clearance on the 3.0L SHO engine.

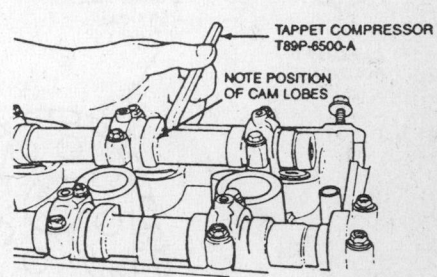

Valve lifter compressor tool.

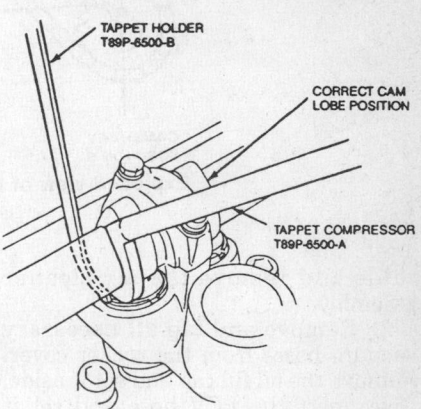

Valve lifter holding tool.

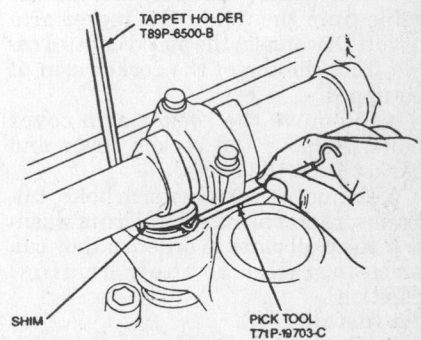

Removing the shim from the valve lifter.

Rocker Arms

REMOVAL & INSTALLATION

2.5L and 3.8L Engines

1. Disconnect the negative battery

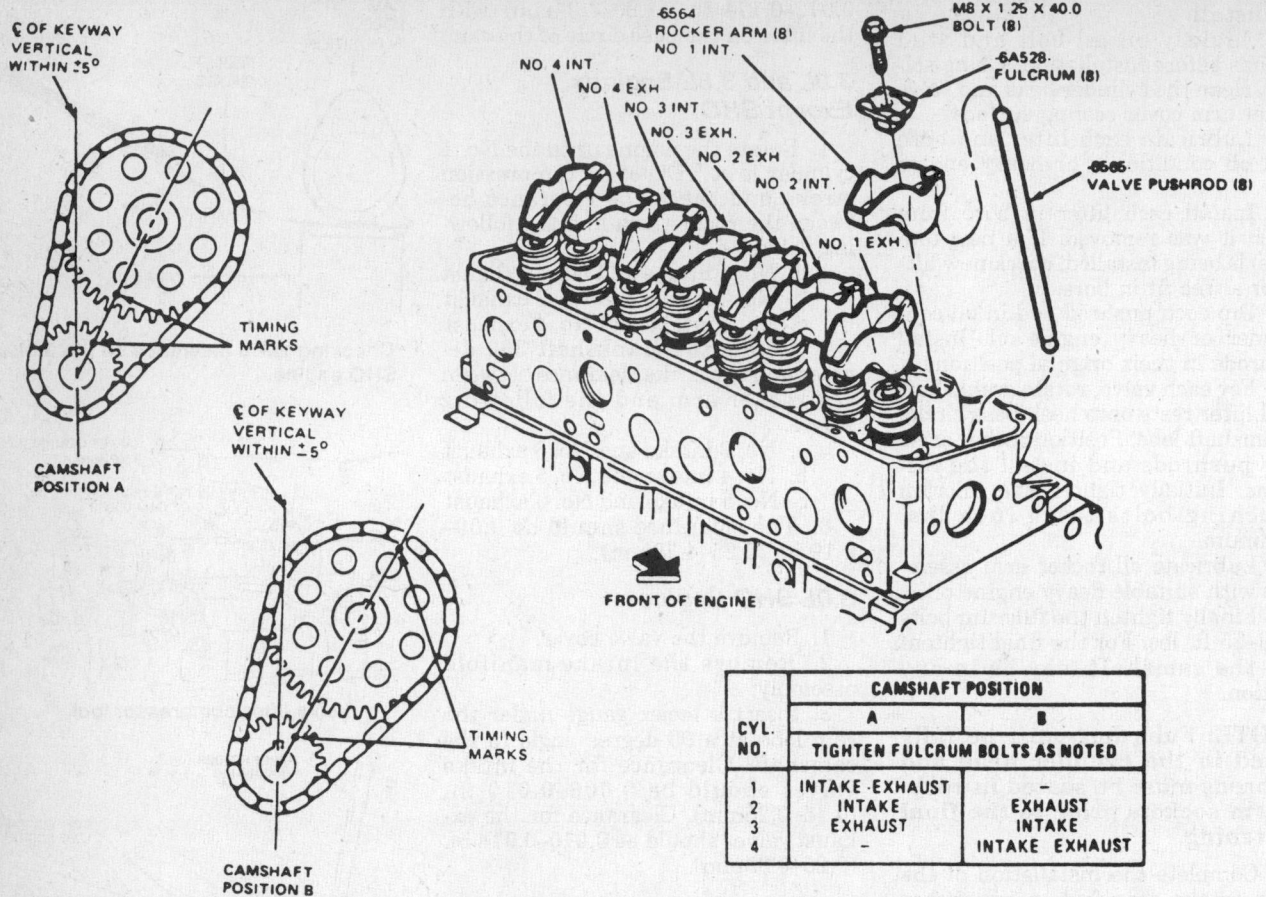

CYL. NO.	CAMSHAFT POSITION	
	A	B
	TIGHTEN FULCRUM BOLTS AS NOTED	
1	INTAKE · EXHAUST	—
2	INTAKE	EXHAUST
3	EXHAUST	INTAKE
4	—	INTAKE · EXHAUST

Exploded view of the rocker arm assemblies and valve procedures—2.5L engine

cable and remove the air cleaner assembly.

2. Remove and tag all necessary vacuum hoses from the rocker cover. Remove the oil fill cap and set it aside. Disconnect the PCV hose and set it aside.

3. Disconnect the throttle linkage cable from the top of the rocker arm cover. Disconnect the speed control cable from the top of the rocker arm, if equipped.

4. Remove the rocker arm cover bolts. Remove the rocker cover and gasket from the engine.

5. Remove the rocker arm bolts, fulcrums, rocker arms and fulcrum washers. Keep all parts in order so they can be reinstalled to their original position.

To install:

6. Coat the valve tips, rocker arm and fulcrum contact areas with Lubriplate® or equivalent.

7. For each valve, rotate the engine until the lifter is on the base circle of the cam (valve closed).

8. Install the rocker arm and components and tighten the rocker arm bolts in 2 steps, the first to 6–8 ft. lbs (8–12 Nm) and the second torque to 20–26 ft. lbs. (28–35 Nm). Be sure the lifter is on the base circle of the cam for each rocker arm as it is installed. For the final tightening, the camshaft may be in any position. Check the valve lash.

9. Install guide pins into the cylinder head and guide the gasket and rocker arm cover over the pins. Install the retaining screws and washer and tighten the screws to 7–10 ft. lbs. (9–13 Nm).

NOTE: Do not use any type of sealer with the rocker arm cover silicone gasket.

3.0L Engine

1. Disconnect the negative battery cable. Disconnect and tag the spark plug wires.

2. Remove the ignition wire separators from the rocker arm attaching bolt studs. If the left rocker arm cover is being removed, remove the oil fill cap, disconnect the air cleaner closure system hose and remove the fuel injector harness from the inboard rocker arm cover studs.

3. If the right rocker arm cover is being removed, remove the PCV valve, loosen the lower EGR tube, if equipped, retaining nut and rotate the tube out of the way, remove the throttle body and move the fuel injection harness out of the way.

4. Remove the rocker arm cover attaching screws and the covers and gaskets from the vehicle.

5. Remove the rocker arm bolts, fulcrums, rocker arms and fulcrum washers. Keep all parts in order so they can be reinstalled to their original position.

To install:

6. Coat the valve tips, rocker arm and fulcrum contact areas with Lubriplate® or equivalent. Lightly oil all the bolt and stud threads before installation.

7. Rotate the engine until the lifter is on the base circle of the cam (valve closed).

8. Install the rocker arm and components and torque the rocker arm fulcrum bolts in 2 steps: the first to 8 ft. lbs. (11 Nm) and the final to 24 ft. lbs. (32 Nm). Be sure the lifter is on the base circle of the cam for each rocker arm as it is installed. Adjust the valves.

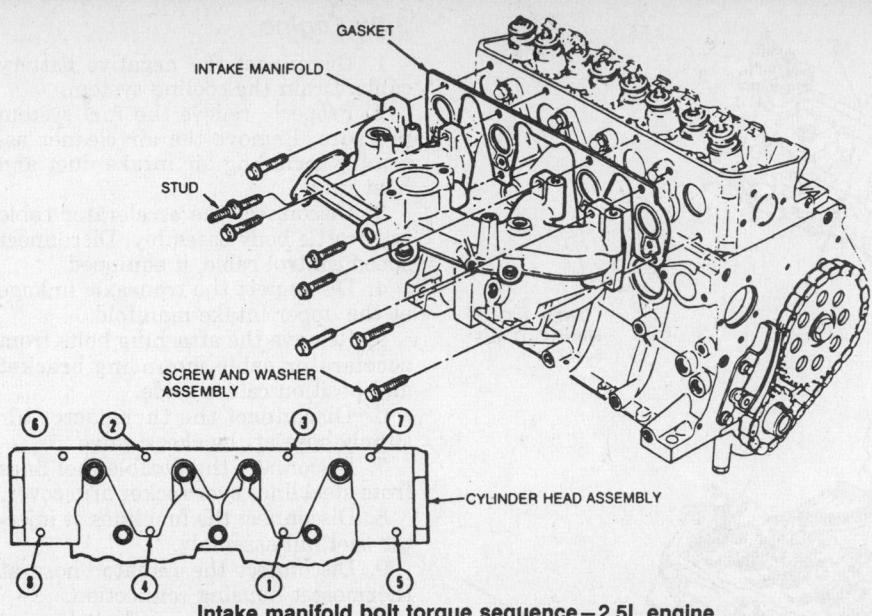

GASKET

INTAKE MANIFOLD

STUD

SCREW AND WASHER ASSEMBLY

CYLINDER HEAD ASSEMBLY

Intake manifold bolt torque sequence—2.5L engine

rocker arm covers. It will be necessary to remove the heater hoses in order to remove the right hand side rocker cover.

8. Disconnect the upper radiator hose, the water outlet heater hose and the thermostat housing. Mark and remove the distributor assembly.

9. Remove the intake manifold attaching bolts and studs. Remove the manifold assembly with the fuel rails and injectors in place. Remove the manifold side gaskets and end seals. Discard the gaskets and seals and replace with new.

To install:

NOTE: **Lightly oil all the attaching bolts and stud threads before installation. When using a silcone rubber sealer, assembly must occur within 15 minutes after the sealer has been applied. After this time, the sealer may start to set-up and its sealing quality may be reduced. In high temperature/humidty conditions, the sealant will start to set up in approximately 5 minutes.**

10. The intake manifold, cylinder head and cylinder block mating surfaces should be clean and free of old silicone rubber sealer. Use a suitable solvent to clean these surfaces.

11. Apply a suitable silicone rubber sealer to the intersection of the cylinder block assembly and head assembly on the each corner of the 2 manifold end seals.

12. Install the front intake manifold gaskets in place and insert the locking tabs over the tabs on the cylinder head gaskets. Apply a suitable silicone sealer on gasket in the same places as before on the manifold end seals.

13. Carefully lower the intake manifold into position on the cylinder block and cylinder heads to prevent smearing the silicone sealer and causing gasket voids.

14. Install the retaining bolts and tighten the bolts to 11 ft. lbs. (15 Nm), then retorque to 18 ft. lbs. (24 Nm).

15. Install the thermostat housing with a new thermostat and gasket, tighten the attaching bolts to 6–8 ft. lbs. (8–12 Nm).

16. Connect the PCV line at the PCV valve and exhaust manifold. Connect all necessary electrical connections. Connect the EGR valve assembly and all necessary vacuum lines. Apply a suitable silicone sealer to split between the head and the intake manifold (4 places).

17. Install the rocker arm covers with new gaskets, heater hoses and radiator hose.

18. Connect the fuel lines and fuel injector harness.

9. Install guide pins into the cylinder head and guide the gaskets and rocker arm covers over the pins. Install the attaching screws and washer and torque the screws to 7–10 ft. lbs. (9–13 Nm). Torque the EGR tube to 37 ft. lbs. (50 Nm).

NOTE: **Apply a bead of RTV silicone sealer or equivalent at the cylinder head to intake manifold rail step (two places per rail) before installing the gasket. Do not use any type of sealer with the silicone (rubber) gasket.**

Intake Manifold

REMOVAL & INSTALLATION

2.5L Engine

1. Open and secure the hood.
2. Disconnect the negative battery cable. Properly relieve the fuel system pressure.
3. Drain the cooling system.
4. Remove accelerator cable.
5. Remove air cleaner assembly and heat stove tube at heat shield.
6. Remove required vacuum lines.
7. Disconnect the thermactor check valve hose at the tube assembly. Remove the bracket to EGR valve attaching nuts.
8. Disconnect the water inlet tube at the intake manifold.
9. Disconnect EGR tube at EGR valve.
10. Remove the intake manifold retaining bolts. Remove the intake manifold. Remove the gasket and clean the gasket contact surfaces.

To install:

11. Install intake manifold with gasket and retaining bolts. Tighten the retaining bolts to 15–22 ft. lbs. (20–30 Nm).
12. Connect water inlet tube at intake manifold.
13. Connect thermactor check valve hose at tube assembly. Install bracket to EGR valve attaching nuts.
14. Connect EGR tube to EGR valve.
15. Install vacuum lines.
16. Install air cleaner assembly and heat stove tube.
17. Install accelerator cable.
18. Connect negative ground cable and fill the cooling system.
19. Start engine and check for leaks.

3.0L Except SHO Engine

1. Disconnect the negative battery cable and drain the engine cooling system.
2. Loosen the hose clamp attaching the flex hose to the throttle body. Remove the air cleaner flex hose. Remove the air intake throttle body assembly with gasket. Discard the gasket and replace with new.
3. Identify, tag and disconnect and all vacuum connections to the throttle body.
4. Disconnect the EGR valve assembly. Disconnect the throttle linkage, throttle position sensor, air charge temperature sensor and idle speed control.
5. Disconnect the PCV hose and disconnect the alternator support brace.
6. Mark and remove the distributor assembly.
7. Disconnect the fuel lines. Remove the fuel injection wiring harness from the engine. Disconnect and tag the spark plug wires and remove the

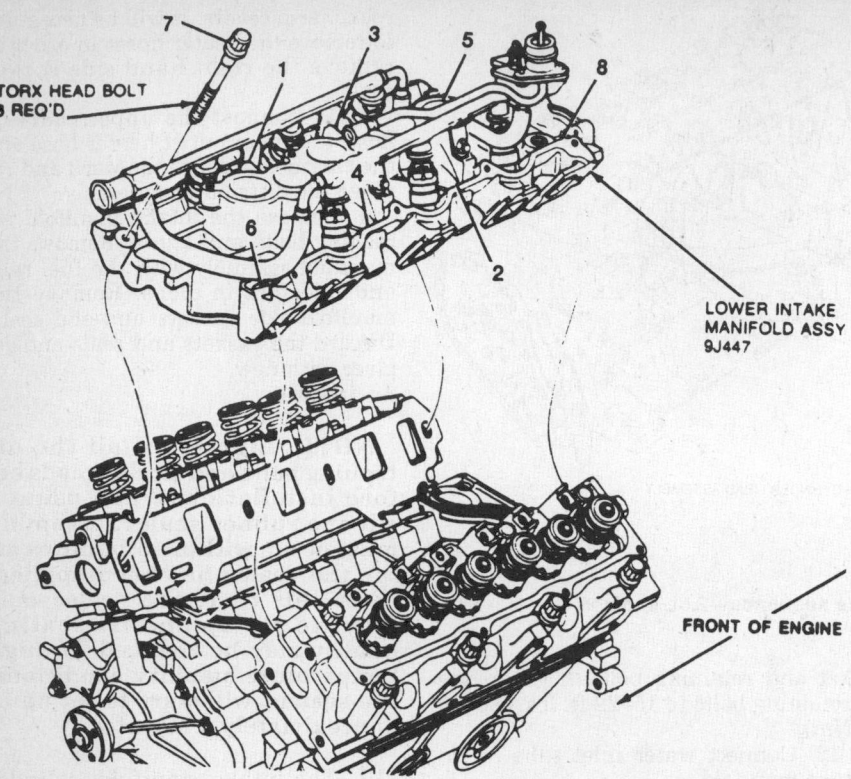

TORX HEAD BOLT
8 REQ'D

LOWER INTAKE
MANIFOLD ASSY
9J447

FRONT OF ENGINE

Exploded view and torque sequence of the intake manifold—3.0L engine

19. Install the distributor assembly and align to the mark.
20. Install the throttle body with a new gasket.
21. Install the coil and bracket.
22. Install and connect the air cleaner assembly and outlet tube. Fill the cooling system.
23. Reconnect the negative battery cable, start the engine and check for coolant, fuel and oil leaks.
24. Check and if necessary, adjust the engine idle speed, transaxle throttle linkage and speed control.

3.0L SHO Engine

1. Disconnect the negative battery cable. Properly relieve the fuel system pressure.
2. Partially drain the engine cooling system.
3. Disconnect all electrical connectors and vacuum lines from the intake assembly.
4. Remove the air cleaner tube.
5. Disconnect the coolant lines and cables from the throttle body.
6. Remove the bolts retaining the upper intake brackets.
7. Loosen the lower bolts and remove the brackets.
8. Remove the bolts retaining the intake to the cylinder heads.
9. Remove the intake assembly and the gaskets.

10. Installation is the reverse of the removal procedure.
11. Lightly oil the attaching bolts and stud threads before installation.

NOTE: The intake gasket is reuseable.

12. Install the retaining bolts and tighten to 11–17 ft. lbs. (15–23 Nm).

3.8L Engine

1. Disconnect the negative battery cable. Drain the cooling system.
2. Properly relieve the fuel system pressure. Remove the air cleaner assembly including air intake duct and heat tube.
3. Disconnect the accelerator cable at throttle body assembly. Disconnect speed control cable, if equipped.
4. Disconnect the transaxle linkage at the upper intake manifold.
5. Remove the attaching bolts from accelerator cable mounting bracket and position cables aside.
6. Disconnect the thermactor air supply hose at the check valve.
7. Disconnect the flexible fuel lines from steel lines over rocker arm cover.
8. Disconnect the fuel lines at injector fuel rail assembly.
9. Disconnect the radiator hose at thermostat housing connection.
10. Disconnect the coolant bypass hose at manifold connection.
11. Disconnect the heater tube at the intake manifold. Remove the heater tube support bracket attaching nut. Remove the heater hose at rear of heater tube. Loosen hose clamp at heater elbow and remove heater tube with hose attached. Remove heater tube with fuel lines attached and set the assembly aside.
12. Disconnect vacuum lines at fuel rail assembly and intake manifold.
13. Identify, tag and disconnect all necessary electrical connectors.
14. If equipped with air conditioning, remove the air compressor support bracket.
15. Disconnect the PCV lines. One is located on upper intake manifold. The

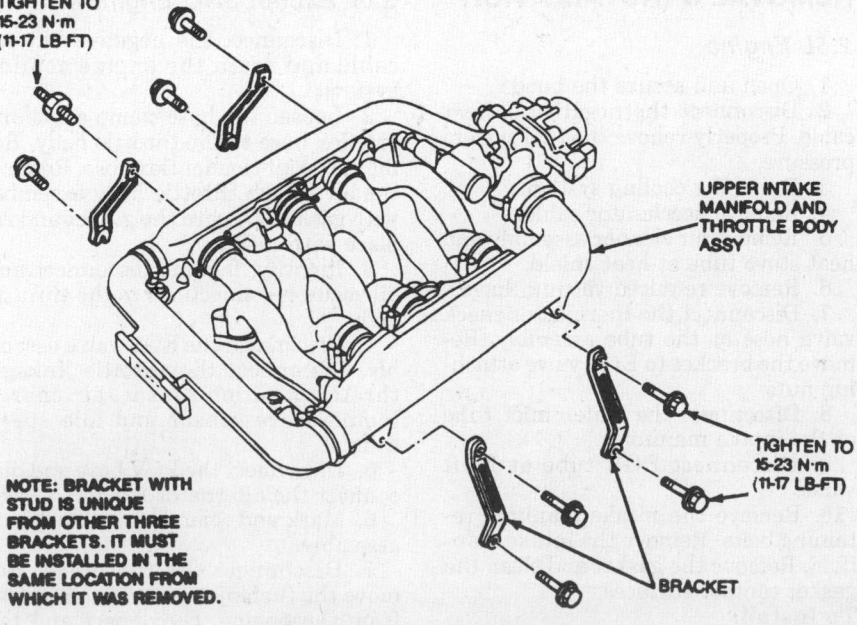

TIGHTEN TO
15-23 N·m
(11-17 LB-FT)

UPPER INTAKE
MANIFOLD AND
THROTTLE BODY
ASSY

TIGHTEN TO
15-23 N·m
(11-17 LB-FT)

NOTE: BRACKET WITH
STUD IS UNIQUE
FROM OTHER THREE
BRACKETS. IT MUST
BE INSTALLED IN THE
SAME LOCATION FROM
WHICH IT WAS REMOVED.

BRACKET

Intake manifold 3.0L SHO engine.

second is located at the left rocker cover and the lower intake stud.

16. Remove the throttle body assembly and remove the EGR valve assembly from the upper manifold.

17. Remove the attaching nut and remove wiring retainer bracket located at the left front of the intake manifold and set aside with the spark plug wires.

18. Remove the upper intake manifold attaching bolts/studs. Remove the upper intake manifold.

19. Remove the injectors with fuel rail assembly.

20. Remove the heater water outlet hose.

21. Remove the lower intake manifold attaching bolts/stud and remove the lower intake manifold. Remove the manifold side gaskets and end seals. Discard and replace with new.

NOTE: The manifold is sealed at each end with RTV-type sealer. To break the seal, it may be necessary to pry on the front of the manifold with a small or medium pry bar. If it is necessary to pry on the manifold, use care to prevent damage to the machined surfaces.

To install:

22. Lightly oil all attaching bolt and stud threads before installation.

NOTE: When using silicone rubber sealer, assembly must occur within 15 minutes after sealer application. After this time, the sealer may start to set-up and its sealing effectiveness may be reduced. The lower intake manifold, cylinder head and cylinder block mating surfaces should be clean and free of oil gasketing material. Use a suitable solvent to clean these surfaces.

23. Apply a bead of contact adhesive to each cylinder head mating surface. Press the new intake manifold gaskets into place, using locating pins as necessary to aid in assembly alignment.

24. Apply a 1/8 in. bead of silicone sealer at each corner where the cylinder head joins the cylinder block.

25. Install the front and rear intake manifold end seals.

26. Carefully lower the intake manifold into position on cylinder block and cylinder heads. Use locating pins as necessary to guide the manifold.

27. Install the retaining bolts and stud bolts in their original locations. Torque the retaining bolts in numerical sequence to the following specifications in 3 steps.
   a. Step 1 — 8 ft. lbs. (10 Nm)
   b. Step 2 — 15 ft. lbs. (20 Nm)
   c. Step 3 — 24 ft. lbs. (32 Nm)

28. Connect the rear PCV line to up-

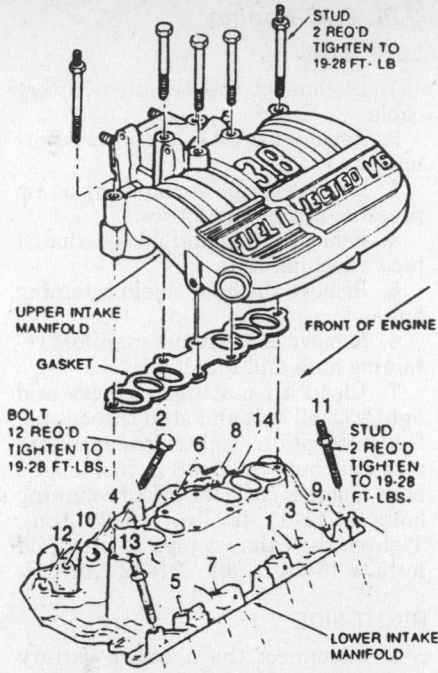

View of the upper and lower intake manifold used on 3.8L engines. Torque lower intake manifold bolts in sequence as shown

per intake tube and install the front PCV tube so the mounting bracket sits over the lower intake stud.

29. Install the injectors and fuel rail assembly.

30. Position the upper intake gasket and manifold on top of the lower intake. Use locating pins to secure position of gasket between manifolds.

31. Install bolts and studs in their original locations. Tighten the 4 center bolts, then tighten the end bolts. Repeat Step 27.

32. Install the EGR valve assembly on the manifold. Tighten the attaching bolt to 15–22 ft. lbs. (20–30 Nm).

33. Install the throttle body. Cross-tighten the retaining nuts to 15–22 ft. lbs. (20–30 Nm).

34. Connect the rear PCV line at PCV valve and upper intake manifold connections. If equipped with air conditioning, install the compressor support bracket. Tighten attaching fasteners to 15–22 ft. lbs.

35. Connect all electrical connectors and vacuum hoses.

36. Connect the heater tube hose to the heater elbow. Position the heater tube support bracket and tighten attaching nut to 15–22 ft. lbs. Connect the heater hose to the rear of the heater tube and tighten hose clamp.

37. Connect coolant bypass and upper radiator hoses and secure with hose clamps.

38. Connect the fuel line(s) at injector fuel rail assembly and connect the flexible fuel lines to steel lines.

39. Position the accelerator cable mounting bracket and install and tighten attaching bolts to 15–22 ft. lbs.

40. Connect the speed control cable, if equipped. Connect the transaxle linkage at upper intake manifold.

41. Fill the cooling system to the proper level.

42. Start the engine and check for coolant or fuel leaks.

43. Check and, if necessary, adjust engine idle speed, transaxle throttle linkage and speed control.

44. Install the air cleaner assembly and air intake duct.

Exhaust Manifold

REMOVAL & INSTALLATION

2.5L Engine

1. Open and secure the hood.
2. Disconnect the negative battery cable.
3. Drain the cooling system.
4. Remove the accelerator cable and position to the side.
5. Remove air cleaner assembly and heat stove tube at heat shield.
6. Identify, tag and disconnect all necessary vacuum lines.
7. Disconnect the exhaust pipe-to-exhaust manifold retaining nuts.
8. Remove exhaust manifold heat shield. Disconnect the oxygen sensor wire at the connector.
9. Disconnect EGR sensor wire at the connector.
10. Disconnect the thermactor check valve hose at tube assembly. Remove bracket-to-EGR valve attaching nuts.
11. Disconnect water inlet tube at intake manifold.
12. Disconnect EGR tube from the EGR valve.
13. Remove the intake manifold.
14. Remove the exhaust manifold retaining nuts. Remove the exhaust manifold from the vehicle.

To install:

15. Position exhaust manifold to the cylinder head using guide bolts in holes 2 and 3.
16. Install the remaining attaching bolts.
17. Tighten the attaching bolts until snug, then remove guide bolts and install attaching bolts in holes 2 and 3.
18. Tighten all exhaust manifold bolts to specification using the following tightening procedure: torque retaining bolts in sequence to 5–7 ft. lbs. (7–10 Nm), then retorque in sequence to 20–30 ft. lbs. (27–41 Nm).
19. Install the intake manifold gasket and bolts. Tighten the intake manifold retaining bolts to 15–23 ft. lbs. (20–30 Nm).
20. Connect the water inlet tube at intake manifold.

21. Connect thermactor check valve hose at tube assembly. Install bracket to EGR valve attaching nuts.

22. Connect the EGR sensor wire and the oxygen sensor wire at their proper connector.

23. Connect the EGR tube to EGR valve.

24. Install exhaust manifold studs.

25. Connect exhaust pipe to exhaust manifold.

26. Install vacuum lines.

27. Install air cleaner assembly and heat stove tube.

28. Install accelerator cable.

29. Connect the negative battery cable.

30. Fill the cooling system.

31. Start engine and check for leaks.

3.0L Engine

LEFT SIDE

1. Disconnect the negative battery cable. Remove the oil level indicator support bracket.

2. Remove the power steering pump pressure and return hoses. Remove the manifold exhaust pipe attaching nuts and remove the exhaust pipe from the exhaust manifold.

3. Raise the vehicle and support it safely. Remove the exhaust manifold attaching bolts and remove the manifold from the vehicle.

4. Clean all mating surfaces and lightly oil all bolt and stud threads prior to installation. Complete the installation of the left hand exhaust manifold by reversing the removal procedure. Tighten the exhaust manifold retaining bolts to 19 ft. lbs. (25 Nm) and tighten the exhaust pipe attaching nuts to 19 ft. lbs. (25 Nm).

RIGHT SIDE

1. Disconnect the negative battery cable. Remove the heater hose support bracket.

2. Disconnect and plug the heater hoses. Remove the EGR tube from the exhaust manifold. Use a back-up wrench on the lower adapter.

3. Raise the vehicle and support it safely. Remove the manifold-to-exhaust pipe attaching nuts and remove the pipe from the manifold.

4. Remove the exhaust manifold attaching bolts and remove the exhaust manifold from the vehicle.

5. Clean all mating surfaces and lightly oil all bolt and stud threads prior to installation. Complete the installation of the right hand exhaust manifold by reversing the removal procedure. Tighten the exhaust manifold retaining bolts to 19 ft. lbs. (25 Nm) and tighten the exhaust pipe attaching nuts to 19 ft. lbs. (25 Nm). Tighten the EGR tube to the exhaust manifold to 31 ft. lbs. (42 Nm).

3.0L SHO Engine

LEFT SIDE

1. Disconnect the negative battery cable.

2. Remove the oil level tube support bracket.

3. Remove the power steering pump pressure and return hoses.

4. Remove the manifold to exhaust pipe attaching nuts.

5. Remove the heat shield retaining bolts.

6. Remove the exhaust manifold retaining nuts and manifold.

7. Clean all mating surfaces and lightly oil all bolt and stud threads before installation. Tighten the manifold retaining nuts to 26–38 ft. lbs. (35–52 Nm). Tighten the heat shield retaining bolts to 11–17 ft. lbs. (15–23 Nm). Tighten the exhaust pipe to manifold nuts to 16–24 ft. lbs. (21–32 Nm).

RIGHT SIDE

1. Disconnect the negative battery cable.

2. Remove the right hand cylinder head.

3. Remove the heat shield retaining bolts.

4. Remove the exhaust manifold retaining nuts and manifold.

5. Clean all mating surfaces and lightly oil all bolt and stud threads prior to installation. Tighten the manifold retaining nuts to 26–38 ft. lbs. (35–52 Nm). Tighten the heat shield retaining bolts to 11–17 ft. lbs. (15–23 Nm).

3.8L Engine

LEFT SIDE

1. Disconnect the negative battery cable. Remove the oil level dipstick tube support bracket.

2. Tag and disconnect the spark plug wires.

3. Raise the vehicle and support safely.

4. Remove the manifold-to-exhuast pipe attaching nuts.

5. Lower the vehicle.

6. Remove the exhaust manifold retaining bolts and remove the manifold from vehicle. Discard the gasket and replace with new.

To install:

7. Lightly oil all bolt and stud threads before installation. Clean the mating surfaces on the exhaust manifold, cylinder head and exhaust pipe so they are free of the old gasket material.

8. Position the gasket and exhaust manifold on the cylinder head. Install the lower front bolt hole on No. 5 cylinder as a pilot bolt.

9. Install the remaining manifold

retaining bolts. Tighten the bolts 15–22 ft. lbs. (20–30 Nm).

NOTE: A slight warpage in the exhaust manifold may cause a misalignment between the bolt holes in the head and the manifold. Elongate the holes in the exhaust manifold as necessary to correct the misalignment, if apparent. Do not elongate the pilot hole, the lower front bolt on No. 5 cylinder.

10. Raise the vehicle and support safely.

11. Connect the exhaust pipe to the manifold. Tighten the attaching nuts to 16–24 ft. lbs. (21–32 Nm).

12. Lower the vehicle.

13. Connect the spark plug wires. Install dipstick tube support bracket attaching nut. Tighten to 15–22 ft. lbs. (20–30 Nm).

14. Start the engine and check for exhaust leaks.

RIGHT SIDE

1. Disconnect the negative battery cable. Remove the air cleaner outlet tube assembly. On Taurus and Sable, disconnect the thermactor hose from the downstream air tube check valve.

2. Tag and disconnect the coil secondary wire from coil and the wires from spark plugs. Remove the spark plugs.

3. Disconnect the EGR tube.

4. Raise the vehicle and support safely.

5. Remove the transaxle dipstick tube. On the Taurus and Sable, remove the thermactor air tube by cutting the tube clamp at the underbody catalyst fitting with a suitable cutting tool.

6. Remove the manifold-to-exhaust pipe attaching nuts.

7. Lower the vehicle.

8. Remove the exhaust manifold retaining bolts. Remove the manifold and heat shroud on Taurus and Sable. Discard the gasket and replace with new.

To install:

9. Lightly oil all bolt and stud threads before installation. Clean the mating surfaces on exhaust manifold cylinder head and exhaust pipe so they are free of the old gasket material.

10. Position the gasket, inner half of the heat shroud (if equipped) and exhaust manifold on cylinder head. Start 2 attaching bolts to align the manifold with the cylinder head. Install the remaining retaining bolts and tighten to 15–22 ft. lbs. (20–30 Nm).

11. Raise the vehicle and support safely.

12. Connect the exhaust pipe to manifold. Tighten the attaching nuts to

16–24 ft. lbs. (21–32 Nm). On the Taurus and Sable, position the thermactor hose to the downstream air tube and clamp tube to the underbody catalyst fitting.

13. Install the transaxle dipstick tube and lower vehicle.

14. Install the outer heat shroud and tighten the retaining screws to 50–70 inch lbs.

15. Install the spark plugs. Connect the wires to their respective spark plugs and connect coil secondary wire to coil.

16. Connect the EGR tube. On the Taurus and Sable, connect the thermactor hose to the downstream air tube and secure with clamp. Install the air cleaner outlet tube assembly.

17. Start the engine and check for exhaust leaks.

Timing Chain Front Cover

REMOVAL & INSTALLATION

2.5L Engine

1. Remove the engine and transaxle from the vehicle as an assembly and position in a suitable holding fixture. Remove the dipstick.

2. Remove accessory drive pulley, if equipped. Remove the crankshaft pulley attaching bolt and washer and remove pulley.

3. Remove front cover attaching bolts from front cover. Pry the top of the front cover away from the block.

4. Remove the oil pan.

5. Clean all dirt and old gasket material from all mating surfaces.

To install:

6. Clean and inspect all parts before installation. Clean the oil pan, cylinder block and front cover of gasket material and dirt.

7. Apply oil resistant sealer to a new front cover gasket and position gasket into front cover.

8. Remove the front cover oil seal and position the front cover on the engine.

9. Position the front cover alignment tool onto the end of the crankshaft, ensuring the crank key is aligned with the keyway in the tool. Bolt the front cover to the engine and tighten the bolts to 6–8 ft. lbs. (10–12 Nm). Remove the front cover alignment tool.

10. If the front cover oil seal is damaged or worn, replace with new. Lubricate the hub of the crankshaft pulley with polyethylene grease to prevent damage to the seal during installation and initial engine start. Install crankshaft pulley.

11. Install the oil pan.

12. Install the accessory drive pulley, if equipped.

13. Install crankshaft pulley attaching bolt and washer. Tighten to 140–170 ft. lbs.

14. Remove engine from work stand and install in vehicle.

3.0L Engine

1. Disconnect the negative battery cable.

2. Loosen the 4 water pump pulley bolts while the water pump drive belt is in place.

3. Loosen the alternator belt-adjuster jackscrew to provide enough slack in the alternator drive belt for removal.

4. Using a ½ in. drive breaker bar, rotate the automatic belt tensioner down and to the left to remove the water pump drive belt.

5. Drain the cooling system.

6. Remove the lower radiator hose and the heater hose from the water pump.

7. Remove the crankshaft pulley and damper.

8. Drain and remove the oil pan.

9. Remove the retaining bolts from the timing cover to the block and remove the timing cover.

NOTE: The timing cover and water pump may be removed as an assembly by not removing bolt 11–15.

To install:

10. Lightly oil all bolt and stud threads except those specifying special sealant.

11. Clean all old gasket material and sealer from the timing cover, oil pan and cylinder block.

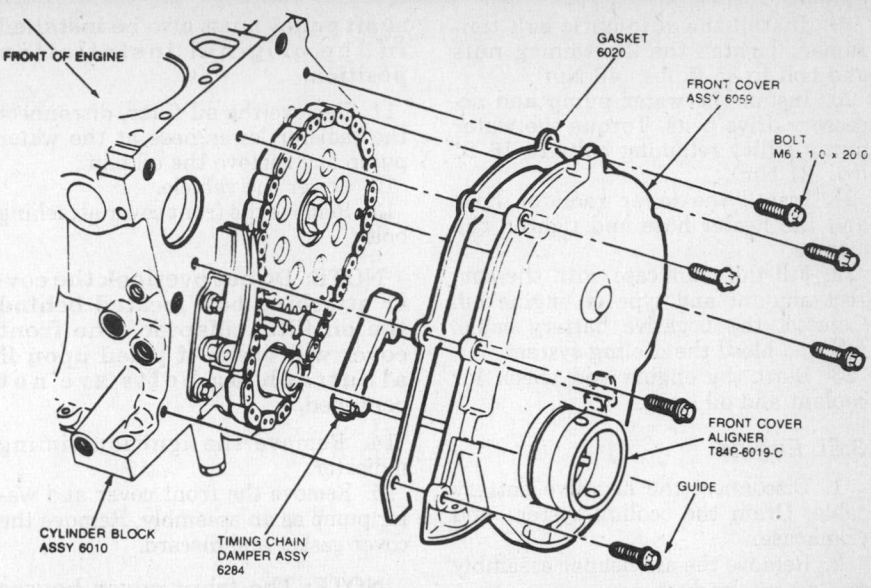

Exploded view of the front cover—2.5L engine

12. Inspect the timing cover seal for wear or damage and replace if necessary.

13. Align a new timing cover gasket over the cylinder block dowels.

14. Install the timing cover/water pump assembly onto the cylinder block with the water pump pulley loosely attached to the water pump hub.

15. Apply pipe sealant to bolt numbers 1, 2 and 3 and hand start them along with the rest of the cover retaining bolts. Tighten bolts 1–10 to 19 ft. lbs. (25 Nm) and numbers 11–15 to 7 ft. lbs. (10 Nm).

16. Install the oil pan and tighten the retaining bolts to 9 ft. lbs. (12 Nm).

17. Hand tighten the water pump pulley retaining bolts.

18. Install the crankshaft damper and pulley. Torque the damper bolt to 107 ft. lbs. (145 Nm) and the 4 pulley bolts to 26 ft. lbs. (35 Nm).

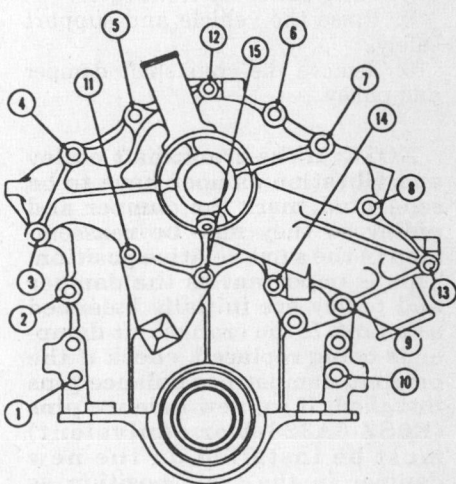

Water pump and front cover—3.0L engine

19. Install the automatic belt tensioner. Tighten the 2 retaining nuts and bolt to 35 ft. lbs. (48 Nm).

20. Install the water pump and accessory drive belts. Torque the water pump pulley retaining bolts to 16 ft. lbs. (21 Nm).

21. Install the lower radiator hose and the heater hose and tighten the clamps.

22. Fill the crankcase with the correct amount and type of engine oil. Connect the negative battery cable. Fill and bleed the cooling system.

23. Start the engine and check for coolant and oil leaks.

3.8L Engine

1. Disconnect the negative battery cable. Drain the cooling system and crankcase.

2. Remove the air cleaner assembly and air intake duct.

3. Remove the fan shroud attaching screws and unbolt the fan/clutch assembly. On Taurus and Sable, remove the fan/clutch assembly from the vehicle.

4. Loosen the accessory drive belt idler. Remove the drive belt and water pump pulley.

5. Remove the power steering pump mounting bracket attaching bolts. Leaving the hoses connected, place the pump/bracket assembly in a position that will prevent the loss of power steering fluid.

6. If equipped with air conditioning, remove the compressor front support bracket. Leave the compressor in place.

7. Disconnect coolant bypass and heater hoses at the water pump. Disconnect radiator upper hose at thermostat housing.

8. Disconnect the coil wire from distributor cap and remove cap with secondary wires attached. Remove the distributor retaining clamp and lift distributor out of the front cover.

9. Raise the vehicle and support safely.

10. Remove the crankshaft damper and pulley.

NOTE: If the crankshaft pulley and vibration damper have to be separated, mark the damper and pulley so they may be reassembled in the same relative position. This is important as the damper and pulley are initially balanced as a unit. If the crankshaft damper is being replaced, check if the original damper has balance pins installed. If so, new balance pins (E0SZ-6A328-A or equivalent) must be installed on the new damper in the same position as the original damper. The crank-

shaft pulley must also be installed in the original installation position.

11. Remove the oil filter, disconnect the radiator lower hose at the water pump and remove the oil pan.

12. Lower the vehicle.

13. Remove the front cover attaching bolts.

NOTE: Do not overlook the cover attaching bolt located behind the oil filter adapter. The front cover will break if pried upon if all attaching bolts are not removed.

14. Remove the ignition timing indicator.

15. Remove the front cover and water pump as an assembly. Remove the cover gasket and discard.

NOTE: The front cover houses the oil pump. If a new front cover is to be installed, remove the water pump and oil pump from the old front cover.

To install:

16. Lightly oil all bolt and stud threads before installation. Clean all gasket surfaces on the front cover, cylinder block and fuel pump. If reusing the front cover, replace crankshaft front oil seal.

17. If a new front cover is to be installed, complete the following:
   a. Install the oil pump gears.
   b. Clean the water pump gasket surface. Position a new water pump gasket on the front cover and install the water pump. Install the pump attaching bolts and tighten to 15–22 ft. lbs.

18. Rotate the crankshaft, as necessary, to position piston No. 1 at TDC.

19. Lubricate the crankshaft front oil seal with clean engine oil.

20. Position a new cover gasket on the cylinder block and install the front cover/water pump assembly using dowels for proper alignment. A suitable contact adhesive is recommended to hold the gasket in position while the front cover is installed.

21. Position the ignition timing indicator.

22. Install the front cover attaching bolts. Apply Loctite® or equivalent to the threads of the bolt installed below the oil filter housing prior to installation. This bolt is to be installed and tightened last. Tighten all bolts to 15–22 ft. lbs. (20–30 Nm).

23. Raise the vehicle and support safely.

24. Install the oil pan. Connect the radiator lower hose. Install a new oil filter.

25. Coat the crankshaft damper sealing surface taith clean engine oil.

26. Position the crankshaft pulley key in the crankshaft keyway.

27. Install the damper with damper washer and attaching bolt. Tighten the bolt to 104–132 ft. lbs. (140–180 Nm).

28. Install the crankshaft pulley and tighten the attaching bolts 19–28 ft. lbs. (26–28 Nm).

29. Lower the vehicle.

30. Connect the coolant bypass hose.

31. Install the distributor with rotor pointing at No. 1 distributor cap tower. Install the distributor cap and coil wire.

32. Connect the radiator upper hose at thermostat housing.

33. Connect the heater hose.

34. If equipped with air conditioning, install compressor and mounting brackets.

35. Install the power steering pump and mounting brackets.

36. Position the accessory drive belt over the pulleys. On the Taurus and Sable, install the fan/clutch assembly and fan shroud. Cross tighten the attaching bolts to 12–18 ft. lbs.

37. Install the water pump pulley. Position the accessory drive belt over water pump pulley and tighten the belt.

38. Connect battery ground cable. Fill the crankcase and cooling system to the proper level.

39. Start the engine and check for leaks.

40. Check the ignition timing and curb idle speed, adjust as required.

41. Install the air cleaner assembly and air intake duct.

Front Cover Oil Seal

REPLACEMENT

2.5L Engine

NOTE: The removal and installation of the front cover oil seal on these engines can only be accomplished with the engine removed from the vehicle.

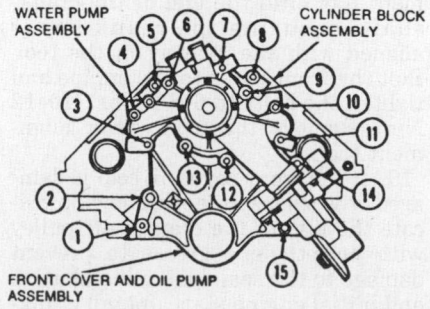

Front cover and water pump assembly—3.8L engine

1. Remove the engine from the vehicle and position in a suitable holding fixture.

2. Remove the bolt and washer at the crankshaft pulley.

3. Remove the crankshaft pulley.

4. Remove the front cover oil seal.

5. Coat a new seal with grease. Install and drive the seal until it is fully seated. Check the seal after installation to be sure the spring is properly positioned in the seal.

6. Install the crankshaft pulley, attaching bolt and washer. Tighten the crankshaft pulley bolt to 140–170 ft. lbs.

3.0L Except SHO Engine

1. Disconnect the negative battery cable and loosen the accessory drive belts.

2. Raise the front of the vehicle and support safely and remove the right front wheel.

3. Remove the pulley-to-damper attaching bolts. Disengage the accessory drive belts and remove the crankshaft pulley.

4. Remove the damper from the crankshaft using a damper removal tool.

5. Pry the seal from the timing cover with a suitable tool and be careful not to damage the front cover and crankshaft.

To install:

NOTE: Before installation, inspect the front cover and shaft seal surface of the crankshaft damper for damage, nicks, burrs or other roughness which may cause the new seal to fail. Service or replace components as necessary.

6. Lubricate the seal lip with clean engine oil and install the seal using a seal installer tool.

7. Coat the crankshaft damper sealing surface with clean engine oil. Apply RTV to the keyway of the damper prior to installation. Install the damper using a damper seal installer tool.

8. Position the crankshaft pulley and install the attaching bolts. Tighten the attaching bolts to 26 ft. lbs. (35 Nm).

9. Position the drive belt over the crankshaft pulley. Check the drive belt for proper routing and engagement in the pulleys.

10. Reconnect the negative battery cable and start the engine and check for oil leaks.

3.8L Engine

1. Disconnect the negative battery cable.

2. On Taurus and Sable, remove the fan shroud attaching screws and posi-

tion the shroud back over the fan.

3. On Tarus and Sable, unbolt the fan clutch assembly and remove.

4. Loosen the accessory drive belt idler.

5. Raise the vehicle and support safely.

6. Disengage the accessory drive belt and remove crankshaft pulley.

7. Remove the crankshaft damper.

8. Remove the seal from the front cover with a suitable prying tool. Use care to prevent damage to front cover and crankshaft.

To install:

NOTE: Inspect the front cover and crankshaft damper for damage, nicks, burrs or other roughness which may cause the seal to fail. Service or replace components as necessary.

9. Lubricate the seal lip with clean engine oil and install the seal using suitable seal installer.

10. Lubricate the seal surface on the damper with clean engine oil. Install damper and pulley assembly. Install the damper attaching bolt and tighten to 103–132 ft. lbs.

11. Position accessory drive belt over crankshaft pulley.

12. Lower the vehicle.

13. Check accessory drive belt for proper routing and engagement in the pulleys. Adjust the drive belt tension.

14. On Taurus and Sable, install the fan/clutch assembly and reposition the fan shroud with the attaching screws.

15. Connect the negative battery cable. Start the engine and check for leaks.

Timing Chain and Sprockets

REMOVAL & INSTALLATION

2.5L Engine

1. Remove the engine and transaxle from the vehicle as an assembly and position in a suitable holding fixture. Remove the dipstick.

2. Remove accessory drive pulley, if equipped, Remove the crankshaft pulley attaching bolt and washer and remove pulley.

3. Remove front cover attaching bolts from front cover. Pry the top of the front cover away from the block.

4. Clean any gasket material from the surfaces.

5. Check timing chain and sprockets for excessive wear. If the timing chain and sprockets are worn, replace with new.

6. Check timing chain tensioner blade for wear depth. If the wear depth

exceeds specification, replace tensioner.

7. Turn engine over until the timing marks are aligned. Remove camshaft sprocket attaching bolt and washer. Slide both sprockets and timing chain forward and remove as an assembly.

8. Check timing chain vibration damper for excessive wear. Replace if necessary; the damper is located inside the front cover.

9. Remove the oil pan.

To install:

10. Clean and inspect all parts before installation. Clean the oil pan, cylinder block and front cover of gasket material and dirt.

11. Slide both sprockets and timing chain onto the camshaft and crankshaft with timing marks aligned. Install camshaft bolt and washer and tighten 41–56 ft. lbs. (55–75 Nm). Oil timing chain, sprockets and tensioner after installation with clean engine oil.

12. Apply oil resistant sealer to a new front cover gasket and position gasket into front cover.

13. Remove the front cover oil seal and position the front cover on the engine.

14. Position a suitable front cover alignment tool onto the end of the crankshaft, ensuring the crank key is aligned with the keyway in the tool. Bolt the front cover to the engine and tighten the bolts to 6–8 ft. lbs. (8–12 Nm). Remove the front cover alignment tool.

15. If the front cover oil seal is damaged or worn, replace with new. Lubricate the hub of the crankshaft pulley with polyethylene grease to prevent damage to the seal during installation and initial engine start. Install crankshaft pulley.

16. Install the oil pan.

17. Install the accessory drive pulley, if equipped.

18. Install crankshaft pulley attaching bolt and washer. Tighten to 140–170 ft. lbs.

19. Remove engine from work stand and install in vehicle.

3.0L Engine

1. Disconnect the negative battery cable. Drain the cooling system. Remove the crankshaft pulley and front cover assemblies. Cover the oil pan opening to prevent dirt from entering.

2. Rotate the crankshaft until the No. 1 piston is at the TDC on its compression stroke and the timing marks are aligned.

3. Remove the camshaft sprocket attaching bolts and washer. Slide both sprockets and timing chain forward and remove as an assembly.

4. Check the timing chain and

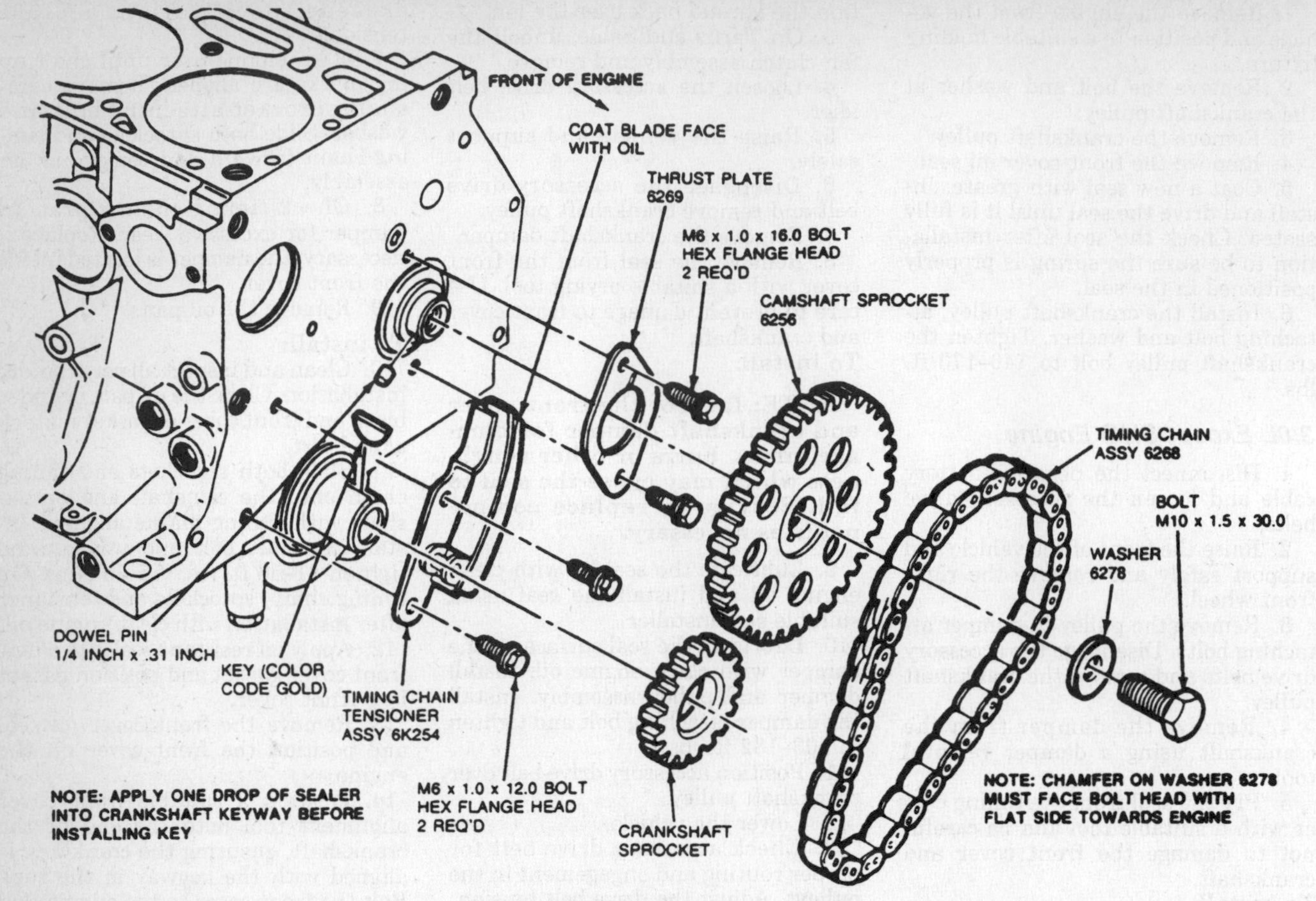

FRONT OF ENGINE

COAT BLADE FACE WITH OIL

THRUST PLATE 6269

M6 x 1.0 x 16.0 BOLT HEX FLANGE HEAD 2 REQ'D

CAMSHAFT SPROCKET 6256

TIMING CHAIN ASSY 6268

BOLT M10 x 1.5 x 30.0

WASHER 6278

TIMING CHAIN TENSIONER ASSY 6K254

DOWEL PIN 1/4 INCH x .31 INCH

KEY (COLOR CODE GOLD)

NOTE: APPLY ONE DROP OF SEALER INTO CRANKSHAFT KEYWAY BEFORE INSTALLING KEY

M6 x 1.0 x 12.0 BOLT HEX FLANGE HEAD 2 REQ'D

CRANKSHAFT SPROCKET

NOTE: CHAMFER ON WASHER 6278 MUST FACE BOLT HEAD WITH FLAT SIDE TOWARDS ENGINE

Timing chain installation—2.5L engine

sprockets for excessive wear. Replace if necessary.

To install:

NOTE: Before installation, clean and inspect all parts. Clean the gasket material and dirt from the oil pan, cylinder block and front cover.

5. Slide both sprockets and timing chain onto the camshaft and crankshaft with the timing marks aligned. Install the camshaft bolt and washer and torque to 40–51 ft. lbs. Apply clean engine oil to the timing chain and sprockets after installation.

NOTE: The camshaft bolt has a drilled oil passage in it for timing chain lubrication. If the bolt is damaged, do not replace it with a standard bolt.

6. Cut a new oil pan gasket and install it on the oil pan using a suitable contact adhesive to hold it in place. Apply a bead of RTV sealant on the gap at the cylinder block.

7. Apply an oil resistant sealer to a new front gasket and position the gasket onto the front cover.

8. Position the front cover on the engine taking care not to damage the front seal. Make sure the cover is in-

stalled over the alignment dowels.

9. Bolt the front cover to the engine and tighten it to specifications. Make sure the oil pan seal is not dislodged.

10. If the front cover seal is damaged or worn, replace the seal with a new one. Install the seal using a suitable seal installer. Install the water pump.

11. Install the crankshaft pulley and front seal. Fill the crankcase with the correct viscosity and amount of engine oil. Fill and bleed the cooling system.

12. Start the engine and check for oil and coolant leaks.

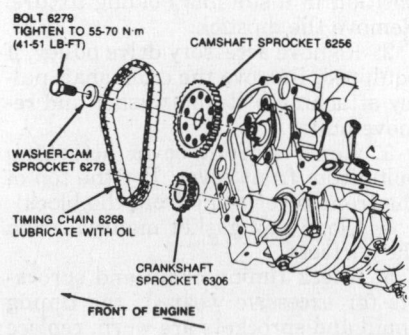

BOLT 6279 TIGHTEN TO 55-70 N·m (41-51 LB-FT)

CAMSHAFT SPROCKET 6256

WASHER-CAM SPROCKET 6278

TIMING CHAIN 6268 LUBRICATE WITH OIL

CRANKSHAFT SPROCKET 6306

FRONT OF ENGINE

Exploded view of the timing chain and sprockets—3.0L engine

3.8L Engine

1. Disconnect the negative battery cable. Drain the cooling system and crankcase.

2. Remove the air cleaner assembly and air intake duct.

3. Remove the fan shroud attaching screws and unbolt the fan/clutch assembly. On Taurus and Sable, remove the fan/clutch assembly from the vehicle.

4. Loosen the accessory drive belt idler. Remove the drive belt and water pump pulley.

5. Remove the power steering pump mounting bracket attaching bolts. Leaving the hoses connected, place the pump/bracket assembly in a position that will prevent the loss of power steering fluid.

6. If equipped with air conditioning, remove the compressor front support bracket. Leave the compressor in place.

7. Disconnect coolant bypass and heater hoses at the water pump. Disconnect radiator upper hose at thermostat housing.

8. Disconnect the coil wire from distributor cap and remove cap with secondary wires attached. Remove the distributor retaining clamp and lift distributor out of the front cover.

9. Raise the vehicle and support safely.

10. Remove the crankshaft damper and pulley.

NOTE: If the crankshaft pulley and vibration damper have to be separated, mark the damper and pulley so they may be reassembled in the same relative position. This is important as the damper and pulley are initially balanced as a unit. If the crankshaft damper is being replaced, check if the original damper has balance pins installed. If so, new balance pins (E0SZ-6A328-A or equivalent) must be installed on the new damper in the same position as the original damper. The crankshaft pulley must also be installed in original installation position.

11. Remove the oil filter, disconnect the radiator lower hose at the water pump and remove the oil pan.

12. Lower the vehicle.

13. Remove the front cover attaching bolts.

NOTE: Do not overlook the cover attaching bolt located behind the oil filter adapter. The front cover will break if pried upon if all attaching bolts are not removed.

14. Remove the ignition timing indicator.

15. Remove the front cover and water pump as an assembly. Remove the cover gasket and discard.

16. Remove the camshaft bolt and washer from end of the camshaft. Remove the distributor drive gear.

17. Remove the camshaft sprocket, crankshaft sprocket and timing chain.

18. Remove the chain tensioner assembly from the front of the cylinder block. This is accomplished by pulling back on the ratcheting mechanism and installing a pin through the hole in the bracket to relieve tension.

NOTE: The front cover houses the oil pump. If a new front cover is to be installed, remove the water pump and oil pump from the old front cover.

To install:

19. Lightly oil all bolt and stud threads before installation. Clean all gasket surfaces on the front cover, cylinder block and fuel pump. If reusing the front cover, replace crankshaft front oil seal.

20. If a new front cover is to be installed, complete the following:

　a. Install the oil pump gears.

　b. Clean the water pump gasket surface. Position a new water pump gasket on the front cover and install

water pump. Install the pump attaching bolts and tighten to 15–22 ft. lbs.

21. Rotate the crankshaft as necessary to position piston No. 1 at TDC.

22. Install the tensioner assembly. Make sure the ratcheting mechanism is in the retracted position with the pin pointing outward from the hole in the bracket assembly. Tighten the retaining bolts to 6–10 ft. lbs. (8–14 Nm).

23. Lubricate timing chain with clean engine oil. Install the camshaft sprocket, crankshaft sprocket and timing chain.

24. Remove the pin from the tensioner assembly. Make certain the timing marks are positioned across from each other.

25. Install the distributor drive gear.

26. Install the washer and bolt at end of camshaft and tighten to 54–67 ft. lbs.

27. Lubricate the crankshaft front oil seal with clean engine oil.

28. Position a new cover gasket on the cylinder block and install the front cover/water pump assembly using dowels for proper alignment. A suitable contact adhesive is recommended to hold the gasket in position while the front cover is installed.

29. Position the ignition timing indicator.

30. Install the front cover attaching bolts. Apply Loctite® or equivalent to the threads of the bolt installed below the oil filter housing prior to installation. This bolt is to be installed and tightened last. Tighten all bolts to 15–22 ft. lbs.

31. Raise the vehicle and support safely.

32. Install the oil pan. Connect the radiator lower hose. Install a new oil filter.

33. Coat the crankshaft damper sealing surface with clean engine oil.

34. Position the crankshaft pulley key in the crankshaft keyway.

35. Install the damper with damper washer and attaching bolt. Tighten the bolt to 104–132 ft. lbs.

36. Install the crankshaft pulley and tighten the attaching bolts 19–28 ft. lbs.

37. Lower the vehicle.

38. Connect the coolant bypass hose.

39. Install the distributor with rotor pointing at No. 1 distributor cap tower. Install the distributor cap and coil wire.

40. Connect the radiator upper hose at thermostat housing.

41. Connect the heater hose.

42. If equipped with air conditioning, install compressor and mounting brackets.

43. Install the power steering pump and mounting brackets.

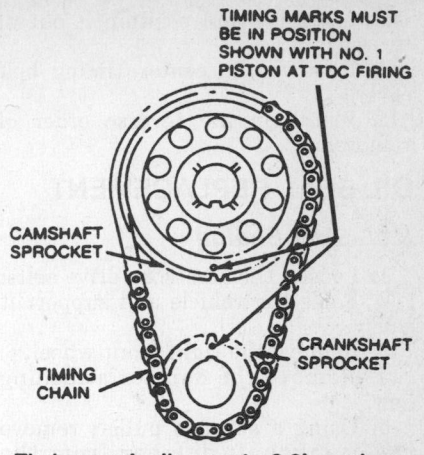

TIMING MARKS MUST BE IN POSITION SHOWN WITH NO. 1 PISTON AT TDC FIRING

CAMSHAFT SPROCKET

CRANKSHAFT SPROCKET

TIMING CHAIN

Timing mark alignment—3.0L engines

44. Position the accessory drive belt over the pulleys. On the Taurus and Sable, install the fan/clutch assembly and fan shroud. Cross tighten the attaching bolts to 12–18 ft. lbs.

45. Install the water pump pulley. Position the accessory drive belt over water pump pulley and tighten the belt.

46. Connect battery ground cable. Fill the crankcase and cooling system to the proper level.

47. Start the engine and check for leaks.

48. Check the ignition timing and curb idle speed, adjust as required.

49. Install the air cleaner assembly and air intake duct.

Timing Belt Front Cover

REMOVAL & INSTALLATION

3.0L SHO Engine

NOTE: The front cover on the 3.0L SHO engine is made up of 3 sections.

1. Disconnect the negative battery cable.

2. Remove the left idler pulley and bracket assembly.

3. Remove the drive and accessory belts.

4. Remove the right front wheel and the inner fender panel splash panel.

5. Disconnect the electrical connector from the ignition module.

6. Loosen the hose clamps and remove the bolts from the intake connector tube and remove the tube.

7. Remove the upper timing belt cover.

8. Remove the crankshaft damper using the proper puller tool.

9. Remove the lower timing belt cover.

10. Disconnect the crankshaft sensor

wire assembly and position it out of the way.

11. Remove the center timing belt cover.

12. Install in the reverse order of removal.

OIL SEAL REPLACEMENT

3.0L SHO Engine

1. Loosen the accessory drive belts.
2. Raise the vehicle and support it safely.
3. Remove the right front wheel.
4. Remove the damper attaching bolt.
5. Using a suitable puller, remove the crankshaft damper from the crankshaft.
6. Remove the timing belt.
7. Remove the crankshaft timing gear using a suitable puller.

NOTE: Be careful not to damage the crankshaft sensor or shutter.

8. Remove the crankshaft front oil seal using a suitable puller.

To install:

9. Inspect the front cover and shaft seal surface of the crankshaft damper for damage, nicks, burrs or other roughness which may cause the new seal to fail. Repair or replace as necessary.

10. Using suitable tools, install a new crankshaft front oil seal and the crankshaft timing gear.

11. Install the timing belt.

12. Install the crankshaft damper using a suitable tool. Tighten the damper attaching bolt to 113–126 ft. lbs. (152–172 Nm).

13. Install the accessory drive belts.

14. Lower the vehicle.

15. Start the engine and check for oil leaks.

Timing Belt and Tensioner

REMOVAL & INSTALLATION

3.0L SHO Engine

1. Disconnect the battery cables.
2. Remove the battery.
3. Remove the engine roll damper.
4. Disconnect the wiring to the DIS module.
5. Remove the intake manifold crossover tube bolts. Loosen the intake manifold tube hose clamps. Remove the intake manifold crossover tube.
6. Loosen the alternator/air conditioning belt tensioner pulley and relieve the tension on the belt by backing out the adjustment screw. Remove the alternator/air conditioning belt.

7. Loosen the water pump/power steering belt tensioner pulley and relieve the tension on the belt by backing out the adjustment screw. Remove the water pump/power steering belt.

8. Remove the alternator/air conditioning belt tensioner pulley and bracket assembly.

9. Remove the water pump/power steering belt tensioner pulley only.

10. Remove the upper timing belt cover.

11. Disconnect the crankshaft sensor connectors.

12. Place the gear selector in **N**.

13. Set the engine to the TDC on No. 1 cylinder position. Make sure the white mark on the crankshaft damper aligns with the 0 degree index mark on the lower timing belt cover and that the marks on the intake camshaft pulleys align with the index marks on the metal timing belt cover.

14. Raise the vehicle and support safely.

15. Remove the right front wheel.

16. Loosen the fender splash shield and place it out of the way.

17. Using a suitable tool, remove the crankshaft damper.

18. Remove the lower timing belt cover.

19. Remove the center timing belt cover and disconnect the crankshaft sensor wire and grommet from the slot in the cover and the stud on the water pump.

20. Loosen the timing belt tensioner, rotate the pulley 180 degrees clockwise and tighten the tensioner nut to hold the pulley in the unload position.

21. Lower the vehicle and remove the timing belt.

To install:

NOTE: Before installing the timing belt, inspect it for cracks, wear or other damage and replace, if necessary. Do not allow the timing belt to come into contact with gasoline, oil, water, coolant or steam. Do not twist or turn the belt inside out.

22. Make sure the engine is at TDC on the No. 1 cylinder. Check that the camshaft pulley marks line up with

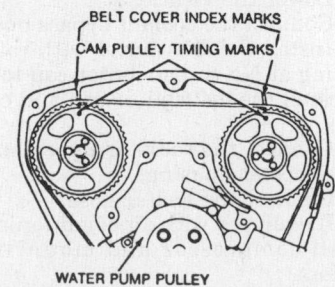

Camshaft pulley to belt cover index marks—3.0L SHO engine

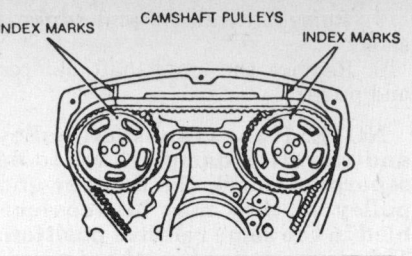

Timing belt index marks

the index marks on the upper steel belt cover and that the crankshaft pulley aligns with the idex mark on the oil pump housing.

NOTE: The timing belt has 3 yellow lines. Each line aligns with the index marks.

23. Install the timing belt over the crankshaft and camshaft pulleys. The lettering on the belt **KOA** should be readable from the rear of the engine; top of the lettering to the front of the engine. Make sure the yellow lines are aligned with the index marks on the pulleys.

24. Release the tensioner locknut and leave the nut loose.

25. Raise the vehicle and support safely.

26. Install the center timing belt cover. Make sure the crankshaft sensor wiring and grommet are installed and routed properly. Tighten the mounting bolts to 60–90 inch lbs. (7–11 Nm).

27. Install the lower timing belt cover. Tighten the bolts to 60–90 inch lbs. (7–11 Nm).

28. Using a suitable tool, install the crankshaft damper. Tighten the damper attaching bolt to 113–126 ft. lbs. (152–172 Nm).

29. Rotate the crankshaft 2 revolutions in the clockwise direction until the yellow mark on the damper aligns with the 0 degree mark on the lower timing belt cover.

30. Remove the plastic door in the lower timing belt cover. Tighten the tensioner locknut to 25–37 ft. lbs. (33–51 Nm) and install the plastic door.

31. Rotate the crankshaft 60 degrees more in the clockwise direction until the white mark on the damper aligns with the 0 degree mark on the lower timing belt cover.

32. Lower the vehicle.

33. Make sure the index marks on

the camshaft pulleys align with the marks on the rear metal timing belt cover.

34. Route the crankshaft sensor wiring and connect with the engine wiring harness.

35. Install the upper timing belt cover. Tighten the bolts to 60–90 inch lbs. (7–11 Nm).

36. Install the water pump/power steering tensioner pulley. Tighten the nut to 11–17 ft. lbs. (15–23 Nm).

37. Install the alternator/air conditioning tensioner pulley and bracket assembly. Tighten the bolts to 11–17 ft. lbs. (15–23 Nm).

38. Install the water pump/power steering and alternator/air conditioning belts and set the tension. Tighten the idler pulley nut to 25–36 ft. lbs. (34–50 Nm).

39. Install the intake manifold crossover tube. Tighten the bolts to 11–17 ft. lbs. (15–23 Nm).

40. Install the engine roll damper and the battery.

41. Connect the battery cables.

42. Raise the vehicle and support safely.

43. Install the splash shield and the right front wheel.

44. Lower the vehicle.

Timing Sprockets

REMOVAL & INSTALLATION

3.0L SHO Engine

1. Disconnect the negative battery cable.

2. Remove the timing belt.

3. Remove the camshaft and crankshaft timing belt sprockets.

4. Install in the reverse order of removal. Tighten the camshaft timing belt sprocket bolts to 15–18 ft. lbs. (21–25 Nm) and the crankshaft pulley bolt to 113–126 ft. lbs. (152–172 Nm).

Camshaft

REMOVAL & INSTALLATION

2.5L Engine

1. Drain the cooling system, fuel system and crankcase.

2. Remove the engine from the vehicle and position in a suitable holding fixture. Remove the engine oil dipstick.

3. Remove necessary drive belts and pulleys.

4. Remove cylinder head.

5. Using a magnet, remove the hydraulic lifter and label them so they can be installed in their original positions. If the tappets are stuck in the bores by excessive varnish, etc., use a

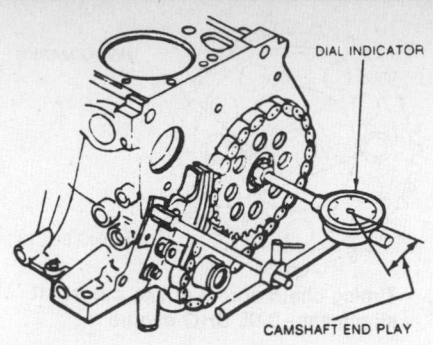

Using a dial micrometer to check the camshaft end play

suitable claw-type puller to remove the tappets.

6. Loosen and remove the drive belt, fan and pulley and crankshaft pulley.

7. Remove the oil pan.

8. Remove the cylinder front cover and gasket.

9. Check the camshaft endplay as follows:

   a. Push the camshaft toward the rear of the engine and install a dial indicator tool, so the indicator point is on the camshaft sprocket attaching screw.

   b. Zero the dial indicator. Position a small pry bar or equivalent between the camshaft sprocket or gear and block.

   c. Pull the camshaft forward and release it. Compare the dial indicator reading with the camshaft endplay specification of 0.009 in.

   d. If the camshaft endplay is over the amount specified, replace the thrust plate.

10. Remove the fuel pump, gasket and fuel pump pushrod.

11. Remove the timing chain, sprockets and timing chain tensioner.

12. Remove camshaft thrust plate. Carefully remove the camshaft by pulling it toward the front of the engine. Use caution to avoid damaging bearings, journals and lobes.

To install:

13. Clean and inspect all parts before installation.

14. Lubricate camshaft lobes and journals with heavy engine oil. Carefully slide the camshaft through the bearings in the cylinder block.

15. Install the thrust plate. Tighten attaching bolts to 6–9 ft. lbs. (8–12 Nm).

16. Install the timing chain, sprockets and timing chain tensioner.

17. Install the cylinder front cover and crankshaft pulley.

18. Clean the oil pump inlet tube screen, oil pan and cylinder block gasket surfaces. Prime oil pump by filling the inlet opening with oil and rotate the pump shaft until oil emerges from

the outlet tube. Install oil pump, oil pump inlet tube screen and oil pan.

19. Install the accessory drive belts and pulleys.

20. Lubricate the lifters and lifter bores with heavy engine oil. Install tappets into their original bores.

21. Install cylinder head.

22. Install the fuel pump pushrod and fuel pump.

23. Complete the installation of the engine by reversing the removal procedure.

24. Position No. 1 piston at TDC after the compression stroke. Position distributor in the block with the rotor at the No. 1 firing position. Install distributor retaining clamp.

25. Connect engine temperature sending unit wire. Connect coil primary wire. Install distributor cap. Connect spark plug wires and the coil high tension lead.

26. Fill the cooling system and crankcase to the proper levels.

27. Start the engine. Check and adjust ignition timing. Connect distributor vacuum line to distributor. Check for leaks. Adjust engine idle speed and idle fuel mixture.

3.0L Except SHO Engine

1. Drain the cooling system, fuel system and crankcase.

2. Remove the engine from the vehicle and position in a suitable holding fixture.

3. Remove the idler pulley and bracket assembly. Remove the drive and accessory belts. Remove the water pump.

4. Remove the crankshaft pulley and damper. Remove the lower radiator hose. Remove the oil pan to timing cover bolts. Unbolt the front timing cover and remove the cover from the engine. Remove the intake manifold.

5. Remove and tag the spark plug wires and rocker arm covers. Loosen the rocker arm fulcrum nuts and position the rocker arms to the side for easy access to the pushrods. Remove the pushrods and label so they may be installed in their original positions.

6. Using a suitable magnet or lifter removal tool, remove the hydraulic lifters and keep them in order so they can be installed in their original positions. If the lifters are stuck in the bores by excessive varnish use a hydraulic lifter puller to remove the lifters.

7. Check the camshaft endplay as follows:

   a. Push the camshaft toward the rear of the engine and install a dial indicator tool, so the indicator point is on the camshaft sprocket attaching screw.

   b. Zero the dial indicator. Position a small pry bar or equivalent between the camshaft sprocket or gear and block.

c. Pull the camshaft forward and release it. Compare the dial indicator reading with the camshaft endplay service limit specification of 0.005 in.

d. If the camshaft endplay is over the amount specified, replace the thrust plate.

8. Remove the timing chain and sprockets.

9. Remove the camshaft thrust plate. Carefully remove the camshaft by pulling it toward the front of the engine. Remove it slowly to avoid damaging the bearings, journals and lobes.

To install:

10. Clean and inspect all parts before installation.

11. Lubricate camshaft lobes and journals with heavy engine oil. Carefully insert the camshaft through the bearings in the cylinder block.

12. Install the thrust plate.

13. Install the timing chain and sprockets. Check the camshaft sprocket bolt for blockage of drilled oil passages prior to installation.

14. Install the front timing cover and crankshaft damper and pulley.

15. Lubricate the lifters and lifter bores with a heavy engine oil. Install the lifters into their original bores. Install the cylinder head throttle body, intake manifold, valve rocker arm, pushrods and rocker arm covers.

16. Install the accessory drive belts and pulleys. Complete the installation of the engine by reversing the removal procedure.

17. Install the spark plug wires. Fill and the cooling system and crankcase to the proper level.

18. Start the engine. Check and adjust the ignition timing and engine idle speed as necessary. Check for leaks of any kind.

3.0L SHO Engine

1. Disconnect the negative battery cable. Properly relieve the fuel system pressure.

2. Set the engine on TDC on No. 1 cylinder.

3. Remove the intake manifold assembly.

4. Remove the timing cover and belt.

5. Remove the cylinder head covers.

6. Remove the camshaft pulleys, noting the location of the dowel pins.

7. Remove the upper rear timing belt cover.

8. Uniformly loosen the camshaft bearing caps.

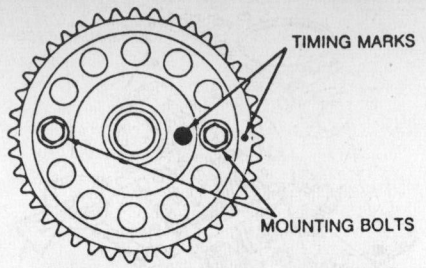

Timing chain sprocket and camshaft alignment—3.0L SHO engine

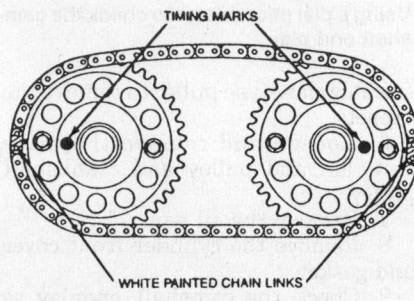

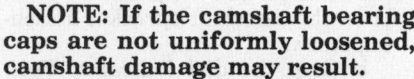

Aligning the chain with the timing marks 3.0L SHO engine.

NOTE: If the camshaft bearing caps are not uniformly loosened, camshaft damage may result.

9. Remove the bearing caps and note their positions for installation.

10. Remove the camshaft chain tensioner mounting bolts.

11. Remove the camshafts together with the chain and tensioner.

12. Remove and discard the camshaft oil seal.

13. Remove the chain sprocket from the camshaft.

To install:

14. Align the timing marks on the chain sprockets with the camshaft and install the sprockets. Tighten the bolts to 10–13 ft. lbs. (14–18 Nm).

15. Install the chain over the camshaft sprockets. Align the white painted link with the timing mark on the sprocket.

16. Rotate the camshafts 60 degrees counterclockwise. Set the chain tensioner between the sprockets and install the camshafts on the cylinder head.

NOTE: The left and right chain tensioners are not interchangeable.

17. Apply a thin coat of engine oil to the camshaft journals and install bearing caps No. 2 through No. 5 and loosely install the bolts.

NOTE: The arrows on the bearing caps point to the front of the engine when installed.

18. Apply silicone sealer to outer di-

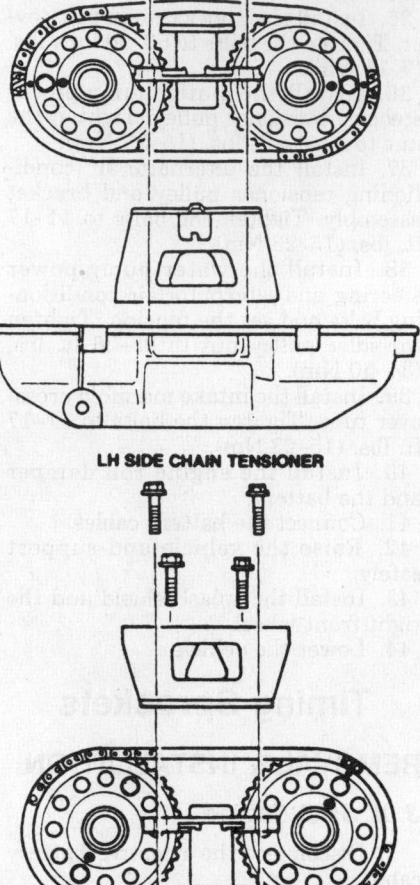

LH SIDE CHAIN TENSIONER

RH SIDE CHAIN TENSIONER

Installing the chain tensioners 3.0L SHO engine.

ameter of the new camshaft seal and the seal seating area on the cylinder head. Install the camshaft seal.

19. Apply silicone sealer the No. 1 bearing cap and install the bearing cap.

20. Tighten the bearing caps in sequence using a 2 step method. Tighten to 12–16 ft. lbs. (16–22 Nm).

NOTE: For left camshaft installation, apply pressure to the chain tensioner to avoid damage to the bearing caps.

21. Install the chain tensioner and tighten the bolts to 11–14 ft. lbs. (15–19 Nm). Rotate the camshafts 60 de-

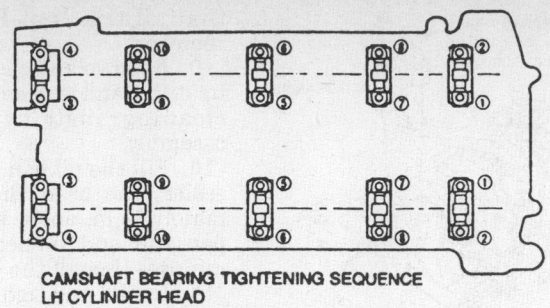

CAMSHAFT BEARING TIGHTENING SEQUENCE
LH CYLINDER HEAD

← FRONT OF ENGINE

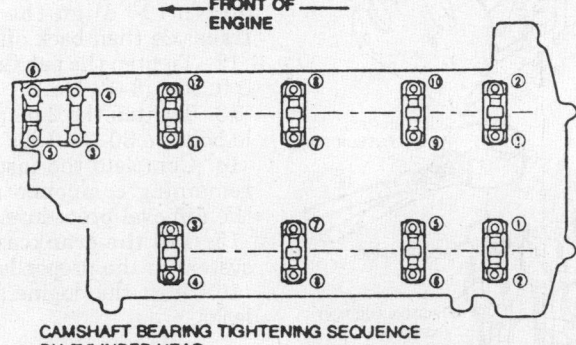

CAMSHAFT BEARING TIGHTENING SEQUENCE
RH CYLINDER HEAD

Camshaft bearing tightening sequence 3.0L SHO engine.

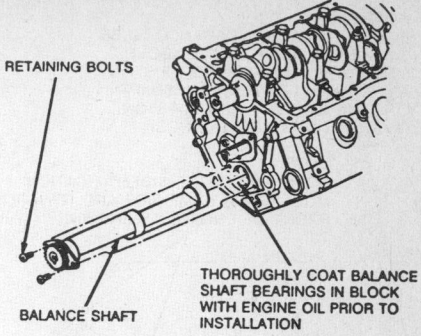

RETAINING BOLTS

THOROUGHLY COAT BALANCE
SHAFT BEARINGS IN BLOCK
WITH ENGINE OIL PRIOR TO
INSTALLATION

BALANCE SHAFT

Balancer shaft—3.8L engine

just the ignition timing and engine idle speed as necessary. Check for leaks of any kind.

Balance Shaft

REMOVAL & INSTALLATION

3.8L Engine

1. Remove the engine from the vehicle.
2. Remove the intake manifolds.
3. Remove the oil pan.
4. Remove the front cover and timing chain and camshaft sprocket.
5. Remove the balance shaft drive gear and spacer.
6. Remove the balance shaft gear, thrust plate and shaft assembly.
To install:
7. Thoroughly coat the balance shaft bearings in the block with engine oil.
8. Install the balance shaft gear.
9. Install the balance shaft, thrust plate and gear and tighten the retaining bolts to 6–10 ft. lbs. (8–14 Nm).
10. Install the timing chain and camshaft sprocket.
11. Install the oil pan.
12. Install the timing cover.
13. Install the intake manifolds.
14. Install the engine in the vehicle.

Piston and Connecting Rod

POSITIONING

grees clockwise and check for proper alignment of the timing marks.

22. Install the camshaft positioning tool T89P–6256–C or equivalent on the camshafts to check for correct positioning. The flats on the tool should align with the flats on the camshaft. If the tool does not fit and/or timing marks will not line up, repeat the procedure from Step 14.
23. Install the timing belt rear cover and tighten the bolts to 70 inch lbs. (8.8 Nm).
24. Install the camshaft pulleys and tighten the bolts to 15–18 ft. lbs. (21–25 Nm).
25. Install the timing belt and cover.
26. Install the cylinder head covers and tighten the bolts to 8–11 ft. lbs. (10–16 Nm).
27. Install the intake manifold assembly.

3.8L Engine

1. Disconnect the negative battery cable.
2. Properly relieve the fuel system pressure.
3. Drain the cooling system and crankcase.
4. Remove the engine from the vehicle and position in a suitable holding fixture.
5. Remove the intake manifold.
6. Remove the valve covers, rocker arms, pushrods and lifters.
7. Remove the oil pan.
8. Remove the front cover and timing chain.

9. Remove the camshaft through the front of the engine, being careful not to damage bearing surfaces.
To install:
10. Lightly oil all attaching bolts and stud threads before installation. Lubricate the cam lobes, thrust plate and bearing surfaces with a suitable heavy engine oil.
11. Install the camshaft being careful not to damage bearing surfaces while sliding into position.
12. Install the front cover and timing chain.
13. Install the oil pan.
14. Install the lifters.
15. Install the intake upper and lower intake manifolds.
16. Complete the installation of the engine by reversing the removal procedure.
17. Fill the cooling system and crankcase to the proper level and connect the negative battery cable.
18. Start the engine. Check and ad-

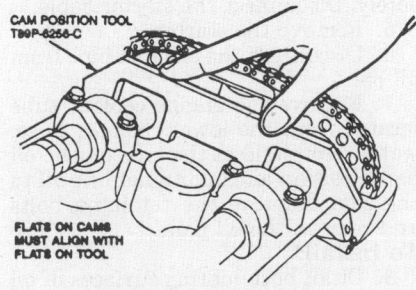

CAM POSITION TOOL
T89P-6256-C

FLATS ON CAMS
MUST ALIGN WITH
FLATS ON TOOL

Camshaft positioning tool.

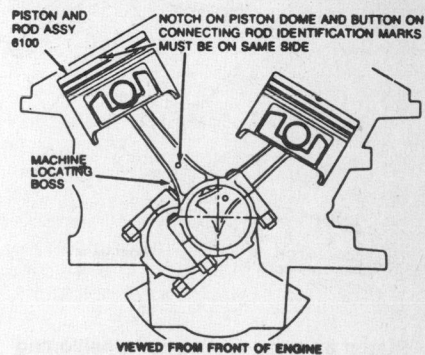

PISTON AND
ROD ASSY
6100

NOTCH ON PISTON DOME AND BUTTON ON
CONNECTING ROD IDENTIFICATION MARKS
MUST BE ON SAME SIDE

MACHINE
LOCATING
BOSS

VIEWED FROM FRONT OF ENGINE

3.0L engine piston and rod assembly

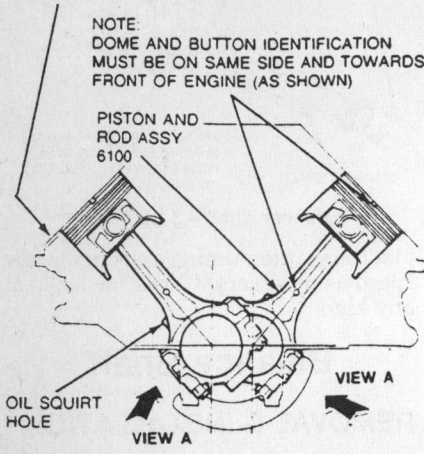

NOTE:
PISTON TO DECK CLEARANCE TO BE 0.27 BELOW DECK TO 0.25 ABOVE DECK WHEN MEASURED AT PISTON T.D.C. PARALLEL TO CRANKSHAFT ON TRUE CENTERLINE OF PISTON. (AVERAGE OF TWO READINGS)

NOTE:
DOME AND BUTTON IDENTIFICATION MUST BE ON SAME SIDE AND TOWARDS FRONT OF ENGINE (AS SHOWN)

PISTON AND ROD ASSY 6100

OIL SQUIRT HOLE

VIEW A

VIEW A

VIEW A

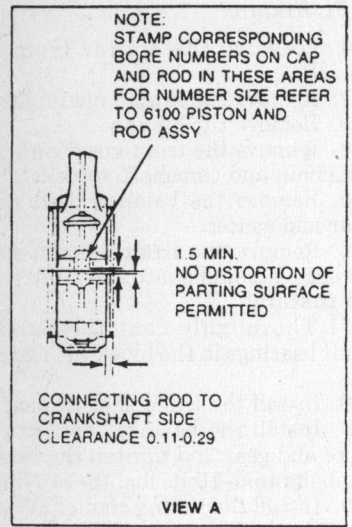

NOTE:
STAMP CORRESPONDING BORE NUMBERS ON CAP AND ROD IN THESE AREAS FOR NUMBER SIZE REFER TO 6100 PISTON AND ROD ASSY

1.5 MIN.
NO DISTORTION OF PARTING SURFACE PERMITTED

CONNECTING ROD TO CRANKSHAFT SIDE CLEARANCE 0.11-0.29

VIEW A

3.8L engine piston and rod assembly

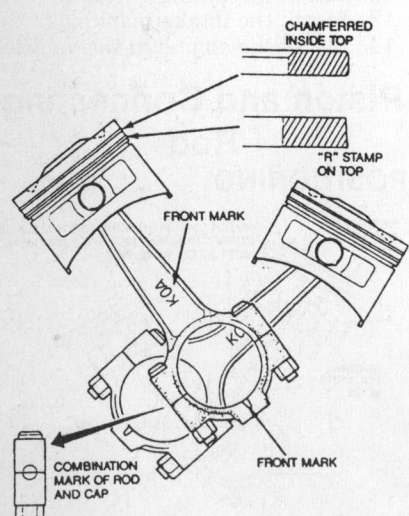

CHAMFERRED INSIDE TOP

"R" STAMP ON TOP

FRONT MARK

FRONT MARK

COMBINATION MARK OF ROD AND CAP

Piston and connecting rod positioning 3.0L SHO engine.

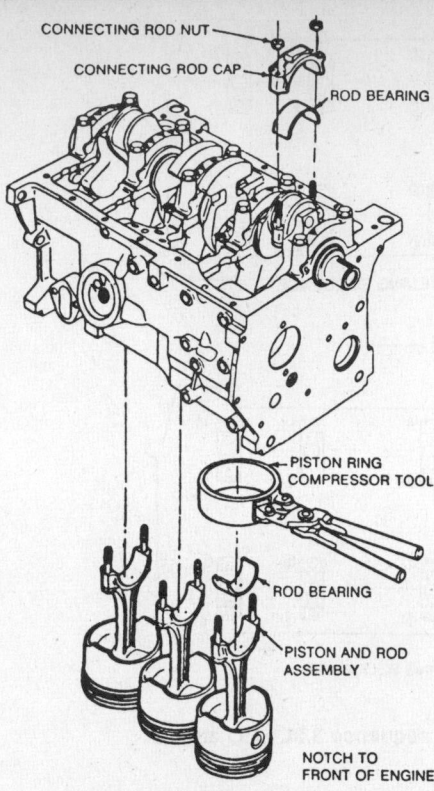

CONNECTING ROD NUT

CONNECTING ROD CAP

ROD BEARING

PISTON RING COMPRESSOR TOOL

ROD BEARING

PISTON AND ROD ASSEMBLY

NOTCH TO FRONT OF ENGINE

Piston and rod assembly—2.5L engine

ENGINE LUBRICATION

Oil Pan

REMOVAL & INSTALLATION

2.5L Engine

1. Disconnect the negative battery cable. Raise the vehicle and support safely.
2. Drain the crankcase and drain the cooling system by removing the lower radiator hose.
3. Remove the roll restrictor on manual transaxle equipped vehicles.
4. Raise the vehicle and support it safely. Disconnect the starter cable.
5. Remove the starter.
6. Disconnect the exhaust pipe from oil pan.
7. Remove the engine coolant tube located from the lower radiator hose, water pump and at the tabs on the oil pan. Position air conditioner line off to the side. Remove the retaining bolts and remove the oil pan.
To install:
8. Clean both mating surfaces of oil pan and cylinder block making certain

that all traces of RTV sealant are removed.
9. Remove and clean oil pump pick-up tube and screen assembly. After cleaning, install tube and screen assembly.
10. Fill the oil pan groove with RTV sealer; the bead should be approximately 1/8 in. above the surface of the pan rail and immediately (within 5 minutes) install the oil pan.
11. Install and tighten the 2 oil pan-to-transaxle bolts to 30–39 ft. lbs. (40–50 Nm) to align the pan with the transaxle then back off 1/2 turn.
12. Tighten the pan flange bolts to 6–8 ft. lbs. (8–12 Nm).
13. Tighten the 2 oil pan-to-transaxle bolts to 30–39 ft.lbs (40–50 Nm).
14. Complete the installation of the remaining components by reversing the removal procedure.
15. Fill the crankcase and cooling system to the proper level.
16. Start the engine and inspect for leaks.

3.0L Except SHO Engine

1. Disconnect the negative battery cable and remove the oil level dipstick.
2. Raise the vehicle and support safely. If equipped with a low level sensor, remove the retainer clip at the sensor. Remove the electrical connector from the sensor.
3. Drain the crankcase. Remove the starter motor and disconnect the electrical connector from the oxygen sensor.
4. Remove the catalyst and pipe assembly. Remove the lower engine/flywheel dust cover from the torque converter housing.
5. Remove the oil pan attaching bolts and slowly remove the oil pan from the engine block. Remove the oil pan gasket.
To install:
6. Clean the gasket surfaces on the cylinder block and oil pan. Apply a 3/16 in. bead of silicone sealer to the junction of the rear main bearing cap and cylinder block junction of the front cover assembly and cylinder block.

NOTE: When using a silicone sealer, the assembly process should occur within 15 minutes after the sealer has been applied. After this time, the sealer may start to set-up and its sealing effectiveness may be affected.

7. Position the oil pan gasket over the oil pan and secure the gasket with a suitable sealer contact adhesive.
8. Position the oil pan on the engine block and install the oil pan attaching bolts. Torque the bolts to 8 ft. lbs. (10 Nm).

9. Install the lower engine/flywheel dust cover to the torque converter housing. Install the catalyst and pipe assembly. Connect the oxygen sensor connector.

10. Install the starter motor. Install the low oil level sensor connector to the sensor and install the retainer clip. Lower the vehicle and replace the oil level dipstick.

11. Connect the negative battery cable. Fill the crankcase. Start the engine and check for oil and exhaust leaks.

3.0L SHO Engine

1. Disconnect the negative battery cable.

2. Remove the oil level dipstick.

3. Remove the accessory drive belts.

4. Remove the timing belt.

5. Raise the vehicle and support it safely.

6. If equipped with a low oil level sensor, remove the retainer clip and the electrical connector from the sensor.

7. Drain the engine oil.

8. Remove the starter motor.

9. Disconnect the HEGO sensors.

10. Remove the catalyst and pipe assembly.

11. Remove the lower flywheel dust cover from the converter housing.

12. Remove the oil pan attaching bolts and the oil pan.

To install:

13. Clean the gasket surfaces of the cylinder block and the oil pan.

14. Install the crankshaft timing belt pulley.

15. Position the oil pan gasket on the oil pan and secure with suitable silicone sealer.

16. Position the oil pan and tighten the retaining bolts to 11–17 ft. lbs. (15–23 Nm).

17. Install the lower flywheel dust cover to the converter housing.

18. Install the catalyst and pipe assembly and connect the HEGO sensors.

19. Install the starter and connect the low oil level sensor connector to the sensor. Install the retainer clip.

20. Lower the vehicle and install the accessory drive belts.

21. Replace the oil level dipstick and connect the negative battery cable.

22. Fill the crankcase with the proper type and quantity of oil. Start the vehicle and check for leaks.

3.8L Engine

1. Disconnect the negative battery cable.

2. Raise the vehicle and support safely.

3. Drain the crankcase and remove the oil filter element.

4. Remove the converter assembly, starter motor and converter housing cover.

5. Remove the retaining bolts and remove the oil pan.

To install:

6. Clean the gasket surfaces on cylinder block, oil pan and oil pickup tube.

7. Trial fit oil pan to cylinder block. Ensure enough clearance has been provided to allow oil pan to be installed without sealant being scraped off when pan is positioned under engine.

8. Apply a bead of silicone rubber sealer to the oil pan flange. Also apply a bead of sealer to the front cover/cylinder block joint and fill the grooves on both sides of the rear main seal cap.

NOTE: When using silicone rubber sealer, assembly must occur within 15 minutes after sealer application. After this time, the sealer may start to harden and its sealing effectiveness may be reduced.

9. Install the oil pan and secure to the block with the attaching screws. Tighten the screws to 7–9 ft. lbs. (9–12 Nm).

10. Install a new oil filter element. Install the converter housing cover and starter motor.

11. Install the converter assembly and lower the vehicle.

12. Fill the crankcase and connect the negative battery cable.

13. Start the engine and check for leaks.

Oil Pump

REMOVAL & INSTALLATION

2.5L Engine

1. Remove oil pan.

2. Remove oil pump attaching bolts and remove oil pump and intermediate driveshaft.

To install:

3. Prime oil pump by filling inlet port with engine oil. Rotate pump shaft until oil flows from outlet port.

4. If screen and cover assembly have been removed, replace gasket. Clean screen and reinstall screen and cover assembly and tighten attaching bolts and nut.

5. Position intermediate driveshaft into distributor socket.

6. Insert intermediate driveshaft into oil pump. Install pump and shaft as an assembly.

NOTE: Do not attempt to force the pump into position if it will not seat. The shaft hex may be mis-aligned with the distributor shaft. To align, remove the oil pump and rotate the intermediate driveshaft into a new position.

7. Tighten the oil pump attaching bolts to 15–22 ft. lbs. (20–30 Nm).

8. Complete the installation of the oil pan by reversing the removal procedure.

9. Fill the crankcase. Start engine and check for leaks.

3.0L Except SHO Engine

1. Remove the oil pan.

2. Remove the oil pump attaching bolts. Lift the oil pump off the engine and withdraw the oil pump driveshaft.

To install:

3. Prime the oil pump by filling either the inlet or the outlet port with engine oil. Rotate the pump shaft to distribute the oil within the oil pump body cavity.

4. Insert the oil pump intermediate shaft assembly into the hex drive hole in the oil pump assembly until the retainer "clicks" into place. Place the oil pump in the proper position with a new gasket and install the retaining bolt.

5. Torque the oil pump retaining bolt to 35 ft. lbs. (48 Nm).

6. Install the oil pan with new gasket.

7. Fill the crankcase. Start engine and check for leaks.

3.0L SHO Engine

1. Disconnect the negative battery cable.

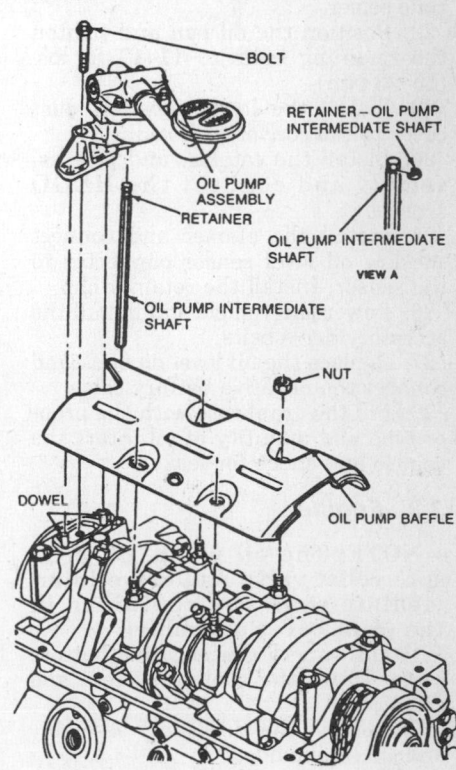

Oil pump Installation—3.0L engine

2. Remove the oil level dipstick.

3. Remove the accessory drive belts.

4. Remove the timing belt.

5. Raise the vehicle and support it safely.

6. If equipped with a low oil level sensor, remove the retainer clip and the electrical connector from the sensor.

7. Drain the engine oil.

8. Remove the starter motor.

9. Disconnect the HEGO sensors.

10. Remove the catalyst and pipe assembly.

11. Remove the lower flywheel dust cover from the converter housing.

12. Remove the oil pan attaching bolts and the pan.

13. Remove the pan gasket.

14. Remove the crankshaft timing belt pulley.

15. Remove the sump to oil pump bolts.

16. Remove the oil pump to block bolts and remove the pump.

To install:

17. Clean the gasket surfaces on the cylinder block and oil pan.

18. Align the oil pump on the crankshaft and install the oil pump retaining bolts. Tighten the bolts to 11–17 ft. lbs. (15–23 Nm).

19. Install the oil sump to oil pump retaining bolts and tighten to 6–8 ft. lbs. (7–11 Nm).

20. Install the crankshaft timing belt pulley.

21. Position the oil pan gasket on the oil pan and secure with suitable silicone sealer.

22. Position the oil pan and tighten the retaining bolts to 11–17 ft. lbs. (15–23 Nm).

23. Install the lower flywheel dust cover to the converter housing.

24. Install the catalyst and pipe assembly and connect the HEGO sensors.

25. Install the starter and connect the low oil level sensor connector to the sensor. Install the retainer clip.

26. Lower the vehicle and install the accessory drive belts.

27. Replace the oil level dipstick and connect the negative battery cable.

28. Fill the crankcase with the proper type and quantity of oil. Start the vehicle and check for leaks.

3.8L Engine

NOTE: The oil pump, oil pressure relief valve and drive intermediate shaft are contained in the front cover assembly.

1. Disconnect the negative battery cable. Drain the cooling system and crankcase.

2. Remove the air cleaner assembly and air intake duct.

3. Remove the fan shroud attaching screws and unbolt the fan/clutch assembly. Remove the fan/clutch assembly from the vehicle.

4. Loosen the accessory drive belt idler. Remove the belt and water pump pulley.

5. Remove the power steering pump mounting bracket attaching bolts. Leaving the hoses connected, place the pump/bracket assembly in a position that will prevent the loss of power steering fluid.

6. If equipped with air conditioning, remove the compressor front support bracket. Leave the compressor in place.

7. Disconnect coolant bypass and heater hoses at the water pump. Disconnect radiator upper hose at thermostat housing.

8. Disconnect the coil wire from distributor cap and remove cap with secondary wires attached. Remove the distributor hold-down clamp and lift distributor out of the front cover.

9. Raise the vehicle and support safely.

10. Remove the crankshaft damper and pulley.

NOTE: If the crankshaft pulley and vibration damper have to be separated, mark the damper and pulley so they may be reassembled in the same relative position. This is important as the damper and pulley are initially balanced as a unit. If the crankshaft damper is being replaced, check if the original damper has balance pins installed. If so, new balance pins (E0SZ-6A328-A or equivalent) must be installed on the new damper in the same position as the original damper. The crankshaft pulley must also be installed in original installation position.

11. Remove the oil filter, disconnect the radiator lower hose at the water pump and remove the oil pan.

12. Lower the vehicle.

13. Remove the front cover.

NOTE: Do not overlook the cover attaching bolt located behind the oil filter adapter. The front cover will break if pried upon if all attaching bolts are not removed.

14. Remove the oil pump cover attaching bolts and remove the cover. Lift the pump gears off the front cover pocket. Remove the cover gasket and replace with new.

To install:

15. Clean the front cover gasket contact surface. Place a straight edge across the front cover mounting surface and check for wear or warpage using a feeler gauge. If the surface is out of flat by more than 0.0016 in., replace the cover.

16. Lightly pack the gear pocket with petroleum jelly or coat all pump gear surfaces with oil conditioner.

17. Install the gears in the pocket. Make certain that the petroleum jelly fills the gap between the gears and the pocket.

18. Position the cover gasket and install the front cover. Tighten the cover retaining bolts to 18–22 ft. lbs.

19. Install the front cover attaching bolts. Apply Loctite® or equivalent to the threads of the bolt installed below the oil filter housing prior to installation. This bolt is to be installed and tightened last. Tighten all bolts to 15–22 ft. lbs.

20. Raise the vehicle and support safely.

21. Install the oil pan. Connect the radiator lower hose. Install a new oil filter.

22. Coat the crankshaft damper sealing surface with clean engine oil.

23. Position the crankshaft pulley key in the crankshaft keyway.

24. Install the damper with damper washer and attaching bolt. Tighten the bolt to 104–132 ft. lbs.

25. Install the crankshaft pulley and tighten the attaching bolts 19-28 ft. lbs.

26. Lower the vehicle.

27. Connect the coolant bypass hose.

28. Install the distributor with rotor pointing at No. 1 distributor cap tower. Install the distributor cap and coil wire.

29. Connect the radiator upper hose at thermostat housing.

30. Connect the heater hose.

31. If equipped with air conditioning, install compressor and mounting brackets.

32. Install the power steering pump and mounting brackets.

33. Position the accessory drive belt over the pulleys. Install the fan/clutch assembly and fan shroud. Cross tighten the attaching bolts to 12–18 ft. lbs.

34. Install the water pump pulley. Position the accessory drive belt over water pump pulley and tighten the belt.

35. Connect battery ground cable. Fill the crankcase and cooling system to the proper level.

36. Start the engine and check for leaks.

37. Check the ignition timing and curb idle speed, adjust as required.

38. Install the air cleaner assembly and air intake duct.

Checking

Except 3.8L Engine

1. Remove the oil pump from the vehicle.

2. Inspect the inside of the pump housing for damage or excessive wear.

3. Check the mating surface for wear. Minor scuff marks are normal but if the cover, gears or housing are excessively worn, scored or grooved, replace the pump.

4. Inspect the rotor for nicks, burrs, or score marks. Remove minor imperfections with an oil stone.

5. Measure the inner-to-outer rotor tip clearance. The clearance must not exceed 0.010 in. with a feeler gauge inserted ½ in. minimum with the rotors removed from the pump housing.

6. With the rotor assembly installed in the housing, place a straight edge across the rotor assembly and housing. Measure the clearance (rotor endplay) between the the inner and outer rotors. The clearance is 0.04 in. maximum.

7. Check the relief valve spring tension. If the spring is worn or damaged, replace the pump. Check the relief valve piston for freedom of movement in the bore.

3.8L Engine

1. Remove the oil pump from the vehicle.

2. Wash all parts in a solvent and dry them thoroughly with compressed air. Use a brush to clean the inside of the pump housing and the pressure relief valve chamber. Ensure all dirt and metal particles are removed.

3. Check the inside of the pump housing and the 2 gears for excessive wear. Check the mating surface of the pump cover for wear. Minor scuff marks are normal, but if the cover mating service is worn, scored or grooved, replace the pump. Inspect the gears for nicks, burrs or score marks. Remove all high points with an oil stone.

4. Measure the gear radial clearance. The clearance should be 0.0055–0.002 in. Idler and driver gear radial clearance must not exceed 0.005 in. with feeler gauge inserted ½ in.

5. With the gears installed in the housing, place a straightedge over the gears and the housing. Measure the clearance, rotor endplay, between the straight-edge and the rotor and outer race. Inspect the relief valve spring to see if it is collapsed or worn. Check the relief valve spring for wear or damage. If the spring is worn or damaged, replace the pump. Check the relief valve piston for free operation in the bore.

NOTE: Internal components are not serviced. If any component is out of specification, the complete pump must be replaced.

Rear Main Bearing Oil Seal

REMOVAL & INSTALLATION

Except 3.0L SHO Engine

1. Disconnect the negative battery cable.

2. Raise the vehicle and support it safely. Remove the transaxle.

3. Remove flywheel.

4. With a suitable tool, remove the oil seal.

NOTE: Use caution to avoid damaging the oil seal surface.

To install:

5. Inspect the crankshaft seal area for any damage which may cause the seal to leak. If damage is evident, service or replace the crankshaft as necessary.

6. Coat the crankshaft seal area and the seal lip with engine oil.

7. Using a seal installer tool, install the seal. Tighten the 2 bolts of the seal installer tool evenly so the seal is straight and seats without misalignment.

8. Install the flywheel. Tighten attaching bolts to 54–64 ft. lbs.

9. Install rear cover plate.

10. Complete the installation of the transaxle by reversing the removal procedure.

3.0L SHO Engine

1. Disconnect the negative battery cable.

2. Raise the vehicle and support it safely.

3. Remove the sub-frame.

4. Remove the transaxle.

5. Remove the clutch cover, disc and flywheel.

6. Remove the oil pan.

7. Remove the oil baffle plate and the oil pickup tube.

8. Remove the oil seal carrier.

9. Remove the rear crankshaft oil seal using tool T87P–3504–N or equivalent.

10. Install a new rear crankshaft seal in the carrier and reverse the removal procedure for installation.

MANUAL TRANSAXLE

For further information on transmissions/transaxles, please refer to "Chilton's Guide to Transmission Repair".

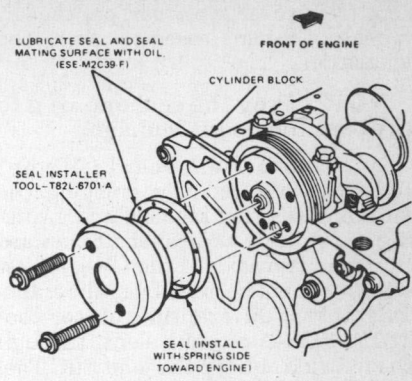

Installing the rear main oil seal—typical

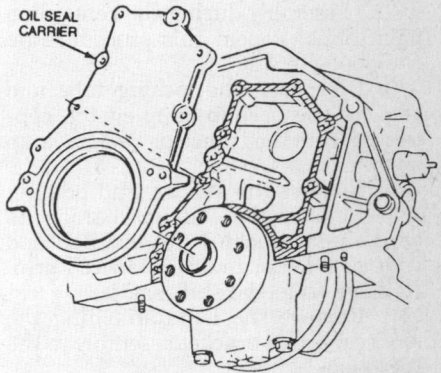

Rear crankshaft seal 3.0L SHO engine.

Transaxle Assembly

REMOVAL & INSTALLATION

1987–88

1. Disconnect the negative battery cable. Wedge a wood block approximately 7 in. long under the clutch pedal to hold the pedal up slightly beyond its normal position. Grasp the clutch cable and pull forward, disconnecting it from the clutch release shaft assembly. Remove the clutch casing from the rib on the top surface of the transaxle case.

2. Remove the 2 top transaxle-to-engine mounting bolts.

3. Raise the vehicle and support safely.

4. Remove the nut and bolt that secures the lower control arm ball joint to the steering knuckle assembly. Discard the nut and bolt. Repeat this procedure on the opposite side.

5. Using a large pry bar, pry the lower control arm away from the knuckle.

NOTE: Exercise care not to damage or cut the ball joint boot. Pry bar must not contract the lower arm.

6. Using a large pry bar, pry the left inboard CV-joint assembly from the transaxle.

NOTE: Plug the seal opening to prevent lubricant leakage.

7. Remove the inboard CV-joint from the transaxle by grasping the left-hand steering knuckle and swinging the knuckle and halfshaft outward from the transaxle.If the CV-joint assembly cannot be pried from the transaxle, insert differential rotator tool T81P-4026-A or equivalent, through the left side and tap the joint out. Tool can be used from either side of transaxle.

8. Wire the halfshaft assembly in a near level position to prevent damage to the assembly during the remaining operations. Repeat this procedure on the opposite side.

9. Disengage the locking tabs and remove the backup lamp switch connector from the transaxle backup lamp switch.

10. Remove the starter stud bolts.

11. Remove the shift mechanism to shift shaft attaching nut and bolt and control selector indicator switch arm. Remove from the shift shaft.

12. Remove the bolts attaching the shift cable and bracket assembly to the transaxle.

13. Remove the speedometer cable from the transaxle.

14. Remove the stiffener brace attaching bolts from the lower position of the clutch housing.

15. Remove the sub-frame.

16. Position a suitable jack under the transaxle.

17. Lower the transaxle support jack.

18. Remove the lower engine to transaxle attaching bolts.

19. Remove the transaxle from the rear face of the engine and lower it from the vehicle.

To install:

20. Raise the transaxle into position with the support jack. Engage the input shaft spline into the clutch disc and work the transaxle onto the dowel sleeves. Make sure the transaxle assembly is flush with the rear face of the engine prior to installation of the attaching bolts.

21. Install the lower engine to transaxle attaching bolts and tighten them to 28–31 ft. lbs. (38–42 Nm).

22. Install the speedometer cable.

23. Install the 10M and 12M bolts attaching the the shift cable and bracket to the transaxle. Tighten the 10M bolt to 16–22 ft.lbs (22–30 Nm) and the 12m bolt to 22–35 ft. lbs. (31–48 Nm).

24. Install the backup lamp switch connector to the transaxle switch.

25. Remove the seal plugs and install the inner CV-joints into the transaxle.

26. Install the center bearing to the bracket on the right hand side halfahaft.

NOTE: New circlips are required on both inner C-V joints prior to installation. Make sure both C-V joints are seated in the transaxle.

27. Attach the sub-frame and the lower ball joint to the steering knuckle. Insert a new service pinch bolt and a new nut. Tighten the nut to 37–44 ft. lbs. (50–60 Nm) but do not tighten the bolt.

28. Fill the transaxle with the proper type and quantity of transmission fluid.

29. Install the top transaxle to engine mounting bolts and tighten to 28–31 ft. lbs. (38–42 Nm).

30. Connect the clutch cable to the clutch release shaft assembly.

31. Remove the wood block from under the clutch pedal. Prior to starting the engine, set the hand brake and pump the clutch pedal a minimum of 2 times to ensure proper clutch adjustment.

1989–91

1. Disconnect the negative battery cable.

2. Wedge a 7 in. block of wood under the clutch pedal to hold the pedal up beyond it's normal position.

3. Remove the air cleaner hose.

4. Grasp the clutch cable and pull it forward, disconnecting it from the clutch release shaft assembly.

5. Disconnect the clutch cable casing from the rib on top of the transaxle case.

6. Install engine lifting eyes.

7. Tie up the wiring harness and power steering cooler hoses.

8. Disconnect the speedometer cable and speed sensor wire.

9. Support the engine using a suitable engine support fixture.

10. Raise the vehicle and support it safely. Remove the wheel and tire assemblies.

11. Remove the nut and bolt retaining the lower control arm ball joint to the steering knuckle assembly. Discard the removed nut and bolt. Repeat the procedure on the opposite side.

12. Using a suitable halfshaft remover, pry the lower control arm away from the knuckle.

NOTE: Be careful not to damage or cut the ball joint boot.

13. Remove the upper nut from the stabilizer bar and separate the stabilizer bar from the knuckle.

14. Remove the tie rod nut and separate the tie rod end from the knuckle.

15. Disconnect the heated exhaust oxygen sensor.

16. Remove the exhaust catalyst assembly.

17. Disconnect the power steering cooler from the subframe and place it out of the way.

18. Disconnect the battery cable bracket from the subframe.

19. Using a suitable pry bar, pry the left hand inboard CV-joint assembly from the transaxle. Install a plug into the seal to prevent fluid leakage. Remove the CV-joint from the transaxle by grasping the left hand steering knuckle and swinging the knuckle and halfshaft outward from the transaxle. Repeat the procedure on the right hand side.

NOTE: If the CV-joint assembly cannot be pried from the transaxle, insert a suitable tool through the left hand side and tap the joint out. The tool can be used from either side of the transaxle.

20. Support the halfshaft assembly with wire in a near level position to prevent damage to the assembly during the remaining operations. Repeat the procedure on the opposite side.

21. Remove the retaining bolts from the center support bearing and remove the right hand halfshaft from the transaxle.

22. Remove the 2 steering gear retaining nuts from the sub-frame. Support the steering gear by wiring up the tie rod ends to the coil springs.

23. Remove the transaxle to engine retaining bolts.

24. Disconnect the 2 shift cables from the transaxle.

25. Remove the engine mount bolts.

26. Position jacks under the body mount positions and remove the 4 bolts, lower the sub-frame and position it out of the way.

27. Remove the starter motor assembly.

28. Remove the left hand engine vibration dampener lower bracket.

29. Remove the backup lamp switch connector from the transaxle backup lamp switch, located on top of the transaxle and remove the backup lamp switch.

30. Position a suitable support jack under the transaxle.

31. Lower the transmission, remove it from the engine and lower it from the vehicle.

To install:

32. Raise the transaxle into position. Engage the input shaft spline into the clutch disc and work the transaxle onto the dowel sleeves. Make sure the transaxle assembly is flush with the rear face of the engine before installation of the retaining bolts.

33. Install the engine to transaxle retaining bolts. Tighten to 28–31 ft. lbs. (38–42 Nm).
34. Install the backup lamp switch and connect the electrical connector.
35. Install the starter motor. Tighten the retaining bolts to 30–40 ft. lbs. (41–54 Nm).
36. Using jacks, position the subframe and raise it into position. Install the 4 bolts and tighten to 65–85 ft. lbs. (90–115 Nm).
37. Install the left hand vibration dampener lower bracket.
38. Install the engine mount bolts and tighten to 40–55 ft. lbs. (54–75 Nm).
39. Connect the shift cables to the transaxle.
40. Install the engine to transaxle bolts and tighten to 28–31 ft. lbs. (38–42 Nm).
41. Install the steering gear retaining nuts and tighten to 85–100 ft. lbs. (115–135 Nm).
42. Install the center support bearing retaining bolts and tighten to 85–100 ft. lbs. (115–135 Nm).
43. Install the right hand halfshaft into the transaxle.
44. Install the left hand inboard C-V joint assembly into the transaxle.
45. Connect the battery cable bracket to the sub-frame.
46. Connect the power steering cooler to the subframe.
47. Install the exhaust catalyst retaining bolts and tighten to 25–34 ft. lbs. (34–47 Nm).
48. Connect the heated exhaust gas oxygen sensor.
49. Install the tie rod in the knuckle and the tie rod retaining nut. Tighten to 35–47 ft. lbs. (47–64 Nm).
50. Position the stabilizer bar to the knuckle and install the nut.
51. Install the lower control arm ball joint to steering knuckle assembly. Install and tighten a new retaining nut and bolt to 37–44 ft. lbs. (50–60 Nm).
52. Install the wheel and tire assemblies.
53. Check the transaxle fluid level.
54. Lower the vehicle.
55. Remove the engine support tool.
56. Install the speedometer cable. Connect the speedometer cable and speed sensor wire.
57. Remove the engine lifting eyes.
58. Connect the clutch cable to the transaxle.
59. Install the air cleaner hose and remove the wood block from the clutch pedal.
60. Connect the negative battery cable and check the transaxle for fluid leaks.

LINKAGE ADJUSTMENT

The manual shift mechanism and ca-bles incorporate no adjustable features, therefore adjustments are neither possible or necessary.

CLUTCH

Clutch Assembly

REMOVAL & INSTALLATION

1. Disconnect the negative battery cable. Raise the vehicle and support it safely. Remove the transaxle.
2. Mark the pressure plate assembly and the flywheel so they can be assembled in the same position.
3. Loosen the attaching bolts 1 turn at a time, in sequence, until spring tension is relieved to prevent pressure plate cover distortion.
4. Support the pressure plate and remove the bolts. Remove the pressure plate and clutch disc from the flywheel.
5. Inspect the flywheel, clutch disc, pressure plate, throwout bearing and the clutch fork for wear. Replace parts as required. If the flywheel shows any signs of overheating (blue discoloration) or if it is badly grooved or scored, it should be refaced or replaced.

To install:
6. Clean the pressure plate and flywheel surfaces thoroughly. Position the clutch disc and pressure plate into the installed position, aligning the marks made previously. Support them with a suitable dummy shaft or clutch aligning tool.
7. Install the pressure plate-to-flywheel bolts. Tighten them gradually in a cross pattern to 12–24 ft. lbs. (17–32 Nm). Remove the alignment tool.
8. Lubricate the release bearing and install it in the fork.
9. Complete the installation of the transaxle by reversing the removal procedure.

PEDAL HEIGHT/FREE-PLAY ADJUSTMENT

The free-play in the clutch is adjusted by a built in mechanism that allows the clutch controls to be self-adjusted during normal operation. The self-adjusting feature should be checked every 5000 miles. This is accomplished by insuring that the clutch pedal travels to the top of its upward position. Grasp the clutch pedal by hand or put a foot under the clutch pedal; pull up on the pedal until it stops. Very little effort is required (about 10 lbs.). During the application of upward pressure, a click may be heard which means an adjustment was necessary and has been accomplished.

Clutch Cable

REMOVAL & INSTALLATION

NOTE: Whenever the clutch cable is disconnected for any reason, such as transaxle removal or clutch, clutch pedal components or clutch cable replacement, the proper method for installing the clutch cable must be followed.

1. Disconnect the negative battery cable.
2. Prop up the clutch pedal to lift the pawl free of the quadrant which is part of the self-adjuster mechanism.
3. Remove the air cleaner assembly to gain access to the clutch cable.
4. Grasp the end of the clutch cable using a suitable tool and unhook the clutch cable from the clutch bearing release lever.

NOTE: Do not grasp the wire strand portion of the inner cable since this might cut the wires and result in cable failure.

5. Disconnect the cable from the insulator that is located on the rib of the transaxle.
6. Position the clutch shield away from the mounting plate bracket by removing the rear retaining screw. Loosen the front retaining screw located near the toe board and rotate the shield out of the way.
7. With the clutch pedal lifted up tp release the pawl, rotate the gear quadrant forward. Unhook the clutch cable from the gear quadrant. Let the quadrant swing rearward but do not let it snap back.
8. Remove the cable by withdrawing it through the engine compartment.

To install:

NOTE: The clutch pedal must be lifted to disengage the adjusting mechanism during cable installation. Failure to do so will result in damage to the self adjuster mechanism. A prying instrument must never be used to install the cable into the quadrant.

9. Insert the clutch cable assembly from the engine or passenger compartment through the dash panel and dash panel grommet. Make sure the cable is routed inboard of the brake lines and not trapped at the spring tower by the brake lines.
10. Push the clutch cable through the insulator on the stop bracket and

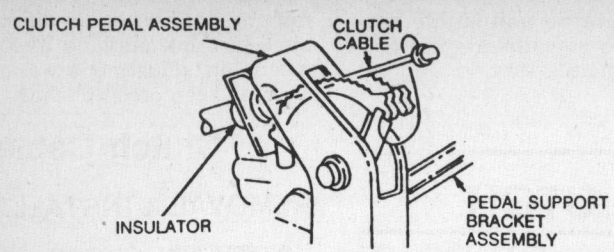

CLUTCH PEDAL ASSEMBLY

CLUTCH CABLE

INSULATOR

PEDAL SUPPORT BRACKET ASSEMBLY

Clutch cable installation

through the recess between the pedal and the gear quadrant.

11. With the clutch pedal lifted up to release the pawl, rotate the gear quadrant forward. Hook the cable into the gear quadrant.

12. Secure the clutch shield on the clutch mounting plate.

13. Using a suitable device, secure the pedal in the upper most position.

14. Install the clutch cable in the insulator on the rib of the transaxle.

15. Hook the cable into the clutch release lever in the engine compartment.

16. Remove the device that was used to temporarily secure the pedal against it's stop.

17. Adjust the clutch by depressing the clutch pedal several times.

18. Install the air cleaner and connect the negative battery cable.

AUTOMATIC TRANSAXLE

For further information on transmissions/transaxles, please refer to "Chilton's Guide to Transmission Repair".

Transaxle Assembly

REMOVAL & INSTALLATION

Except Automatic Overdrive Transaxle

1. Disconnect the negative battery cable and remove the air cleaner assembly.

2. Position the engine control wiring harness away from the transaxle converter housing.

3. Disconnect the TV linkage and manual lever cable at the respective levers. Failure to disconnect the linkage during transaxle removal and allowing the transaxle to hang will fracture the throttle valve cam shaft joint, which is located under the transaxle cover.

4. Remove the power steering hose brackets.

5. Remove the upper transaxle-to-engine attaching bolts.

6. Install suitable engine lifting brackets to the right and left areas of the cylinder head and attach with bolts. Install 2 suitable engine support bars.

NOTE: An engine support bar may be fabricated from a length of 4 × 4 wood cut to 57 in.

7. Place 1 of the engine support bars across the vehicle in front of each engine shock tower. Place another support bar across the vehicle approximately between the alternator and valve cover. Attach chains to the lifting brackets. Raise the vehicle and support safely. Remove the wheel and tire assemblies.

8. Remove the catalytic converter inlet pipe and disconnect the exhaust air hose assembly.

9. Remove each tie rod end from it's spindle. Separate the lower ball joints from the struts and remove the lower control arm from each spindle.

10. Disconnect the stabilizer bar by removing the retaining nuts.

11. Disconnect and remove the rack and pinion and auxiliary cooler from the sub-frame. Position the rack and pinion away from the sub-frame and secure with wire.

12. Remove the right front bearing support assembly retaining bolts.

13. Remove the halfshaft and link shaft assembly out of the right side of the transaxle.

14. Disengage the left halfshaft from the differential side gear. Pull the halfshaft from the transaxle.

NOTE: Support and secure the halfshaft from an underbody component with a length of wire. Do not allow the halfshafts to hang unsupported.

15. Plug the seal holes.

16. Remove the front support insulator and position the left front splash shield aside.

17. Properly support the sub-frame and lower the vehicle onto the subframe support. Remove the sub-frame and disconnect the neutral start switch wire assembly.

18. Raise the vehicle after the subframe is removed. Disconnect the speedometer cable.

19. Disconnect and remove the shift cable from the transaxle.

20. Disconnect the oil cooler lines and remove the starter.

21. Remove the dust cover from the torque converter housing and remove the torque converter-to-flywheel housing nuts.

22. Position a suitable transaxle jack under the transaxle.

23. Remove the remaining transaxle-to-engine attaching bolts.

NOTE: Before the transaxle can be lowered from the vehicle, the torque converter studs must be clear of the flywheel. Insert a suitable tool between the flywheel and converter and carefully guide the transaxle and converter away from the engine.

24. Lower the transaxle from the engine.

To install:

25. Installation is the reverse of the removal procedure. During installation be sure to observe the following:

a. Clean the transaxle oil cooler lines.

b. Install new circlips on the CV-joint seals.

c. Carefully install the halfshafts in the transaxle by aligning the splines of the CV-joint with the splines of the differential.

d. Attach the lower ball joint to the steering knuckle with a new nut and bolt. Tighten the nut to 37–44 ft. lbs. Torquing of the bolt is not required.

e. When installing the transaxle to the engine, verify that the converter-to-transaxle engagement is maintained. Prevent the converter from moving forward and disengaging during installation.

f. Adjust the TV and manual linkages. Check the transaxle fluid level.

g. Tighten the following bolts to the torque specifications listed:

Transaxle-to-engine bolts: 25–33 ft. lbs. (34–45 Nm)

Control arm-to-knuckle bolts: 36–44 ft. lbs. (50–60 Nm)

Stabilizer U-clamp-to-bracket bolts: 60–70 ft. lbs. (81–95 Nm)

Tie rod-to-knuckle nut: 23–35 ft. lbs. (31–47 Nm)

Starter-to-transaxle bolts: 30–40 ft. lbs. (41–54 Nm)

Converter-to-flywheel bolts: 23–39 ft. lbs. (31–53 Nm)

Insulator-to-bracket bolts: 55–70 ft. lbs. (75–90 Nm)

Automatic Overdrive Transaxle

1. Disconnect the negative battery

cable. Raise and support the vehicle safely. Remove the air cleaner assembly.

2. Remove the bolt retaining the shift cable and bracket assembly to the transaxle.

NOTE: Hold the bracket with a pry bar in the slot to prevent the bracket from moving.

3. Remove the shift cable bracket bolts and bracket from the transaxle. Disconnect the electrical connector from the neutral safety switch.

4. Disconnect the electrical bulkhead connector from the rear of the transaxle. Remove the dipstick. On vehicles with 3.8L engines, remove the throttle valve cable cover. Unsnap the throttle valve cable from the throttle body lever. Remove the throttle valve cable from the transaxle case.

5. Carefully pull up on the throttle valve cable and disconnect the throttle valve cable from the TV link.

NOTE: Pulling to hard on the throttle valve may bend the internal TV bracket.

6. Install engine lifting brackets.
7. Disconnect the power steering pump pressure and return line bracket.
8. Remove the converter housing bolts from the top of the transaxle.
9. Install a suitable engine support fixture.
10. Raise the vehicle and support it safely. Remove both front wheels. Remove the left hand outer tie rod end.
11. Remove the lower ball joint attaching nuts and bolts. Remove the lower ball joints and remove the lower control arms from each spindle. Remove stabilizer bar nuts.
12. Remove the rack and pinion from the sub frame. Support the steering gear with a piece of wire from the tie rod end to the coil spring. Secure the housing of the gear to a suitable support to hold it in position.
13. Remove the nuts from the engine mounts. Disconnect the oxygen sensor electrical connection. Remove the exhaust Y-pipe from the engine and rear portion of the exhaust system.
14. Remove the two 15mm bolts from the transaxle mount. Remove the four 15mm bolts from the left hand engine support and remove the bracket.
15. Position the sub-frame removal tool.
16. Remove the sub-frame to body retaining bolts and lower the sub-frame.
17. Remove the dust cover and the starter assembly.
18. Rotate the engine by the crankshaft pulley bolt to align the torque

converter bolts with the starter drive hole. Remove the torque converter-to-flywheel retaining nuts.

19. Remove the transaxle cooler line retaining clips. Disconnect the transaxle cooler lines.
20. Remove the engine to transmission retaining bolts.
21. Remove the speedometer sensor heat shield.
22. Remove the vehicle speed sensor from the transaxle.

NOTE: Vehicles with electronic instrument clusters do not use a speedometer cable.

23. Position the transmission jack. Remove the halfshafts.
24. Remove the last 2 torque converter housing bolts.
25. Seperate the transaxle from the engine and carefully lower the transaxle from the vehicle.

To install:

26. Installation is the reverse of the removal procedure. During installation be sure to observe the following:

a. Clean the transaxle oil cooler lines.

b. Install new circlips on the CV-joint seals.

c. Carefully install the halfshafts in the transaxle by aligning the splines of the CV-joint with the splines of the differential.

d. Attach the lower ball joint to the steering knuckle with a new nut and bolt. Tighten the nut to 37–44 ft. lbs. Torquing of the bolt is not required.

e. When installing the transaxle to the engine, verify that the converter-to-transaxle engagement is maintained. Prevent the converter from moving forward and disengaging during installation.

f. Adjust the TV and manual linkages. Check the transaxle fluid level.

g. Tighten the following bolts to the torque specifications listed:
Transaxle-to-engine bolts: 25–33 ft. lbs. (34–45 Nm)
Control arm-to-knuckle bolts: 36–44 ft. lbs. (50–60 Nm)
Stabilizer U-clamp-to-bracket bolts: 60–70 ft. lbs. (81–95 Nm)
Tie rod-to-knuckle nut: 23–35 ft. lbs. (31–47 Nm)
Starter-to-transaxle bolts: 30–40 ft. lbs. (41–54 Nm)
Converter-to-flywheel bolts: 23–39 ft. lbs. (31–53 Nm)
Insulator-to-bracket bolts: 55–70 ft. lbs. (75–90 Nm)

SHIFT CABLE ADJUSTMENT

Except Automatic Overdrive Transaxle

1. Position the selector lever in the

D position against the drive stop. The shift lever must be held in the **D** position while the linkage is being adjusted.

2. Loosen the transaxle manual lever-to-control cable adjustment trunnion bolt.
3. Move the transaxle manual lever to the **D** position, second detent from the most rearward position.
4. Tighten the adjustment trunnion bolt to 12–20 ft. lbs. (16–27 Nm).
5. Check the operation of the transaxle in each selector lever position. Make sure the neutral start switch functions properly in **P** and **N** and the back-up lamps are on in **R**.

Automatic Overdrive Transaxle

1. Position the selector lever in the **OD** position against the rearward stop. The shift lever must be held in the rearward position using a constant force of 8 lbs. (3.6 Kg) while the linkage is being adjusted.
2. Loosen the manual lever-to-control cable retaining nut.
3. Move the transaxle manual lever to the **OD** position, second detent from the most rearward position.
4. Tighten the retaining nut to 12–20 ft. lbs. (16–27 Nm).
5. Check the operation of the transaxle in each selector lever position. Make sure the park and neutral start switch are functioning properly.

THROTTLE CABLE ADJUSTMENT

3.0L and 3.8L Engine

The Throttle Valve (TV) cable normally does not need adjustment. The cable should be adjusted only if one of the following components is removed for service or replacement:
Main control assembly
Throttle valve cable
Throttle valve cable engine mounting bracket
Throttle control lever link or lever assembly
Engine throttle body
Transaxle assembly

1. Connect the TV cable eye to the transaxle throttle control lever link and attach the cable boot to the chain cover.
2. On vehicles equipped with the 3.0L engine, with the TV cable mounted in the engine bracket, make sure the threaded shank is fully retracted. To retract the shank, pull up on the spring rest with the index fingers and wiggle the top of the thread shank while pressing the shank through the spring with the thumbs.
3. On vehicles equipped with the 3.8L engine, the TV cable must be un-

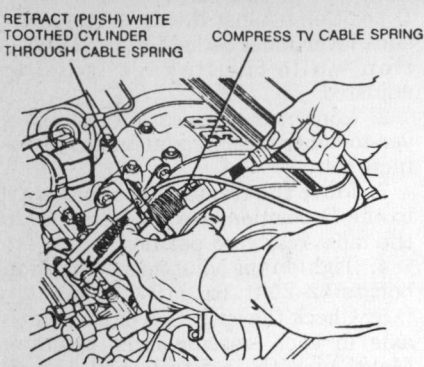

RETRACT (PUSH) WHITE TOOTHED CYLINDER THROUGH CABLE SPRING   COMPRESS TV CABLE SPRING

Throttle valve cable adjustment

clipped from the right hand intake manifold clip. To retract the shank, span the crack between the two 180 degree segments of the adjuster spring rest with a suitable tool. Comprees the spring by pushing the rod toward the throttle body with the right hand. While the spring is compressed, push the threaded shank toward the spring with the index and middle fingers of the left hand. Do not pull on the cable sheath.

4. Attach the end of the TV cable to the throttle body.

5. On vehicles equipped with the 3.8L engine, rotate the throttle body primary lever by hand, the lever to which the TV-driving nailhead is attached, to the wide-open-throttle position. The white adjuster shank must be seen to advance. If not, look for cable sheath/foam hang-up on engine/body components. Attach the TV cable into the top position of the right hand intake manifold clip.

NOTE: The threaded shank must show movement or "ratchet" out of the grip jaws. If there is no movement, inspect the TV cable system for broken or disconnected components and repeat the procedure.

DRIVE AXLE

Halfshaft

When removing both the left and right halfshafts, install suitable shipping plugs to prevent dislocation of the differential side gears. Should the gears become misaligned, the differential will have to be removed from the transaxle to re-align the side gears.

NOTE: Due to the automatic transaxle case configuration, the right halfshaft assembly must be removed first. Differential Rota-

tor T81P–4026–A or equivalent is then inserted into the transaxle to drive the left inboard CV-joint assembly from the transaxle. If only the left halfshaft assembly is to be removed for service, remove only the right halfshaft assembly from the transaxle. After removal, support it with a length of wire. Then drive the left halfshaft assembly from the transaxle.

REMOVAL & INSTALLATION

1. Remove the wheel cover/hub cover from the wheel and tire assembly and loosen the wheel nuts. Remove the hub retainer and washer. The nut must be discarded after removal.

2. Raise the vehicle and support safely. Remove the wheel assembly, remove the hub nut and washer. Discard the old hub nut. Remove the nut from the ball joint to steering knuckle attaching bolts.

3. Drive the bolt out of the steering knuckle using a suitable punch and hammer. Discard this bolt and nut after removal. Separate the ball joint from the steering knuckle using a suitable pry bar. If equipped with anti-lock brakes, remove the anti-lock brake sensor from the steering knuckle and remove the height sensor link at the lower arm ball stud attachment.

4. Position the end of the pry bar outside of the bushing pocket to avoid damage to the bushing. Use care to prevent damage to the ball joint boot. Remove the stabilizer bar link at the stabilizer bar.

5. The following removal procedure applies to the right side halfshaft/link shaft for the ATX/FLC automatic transaxle and the manual transaxle. For the AXOD automatic transaxle, proceed to Step 6:

a. Remove the bolts attaching the bearing support to the bracket. Slide the link shaft out of the transaxle. Support the end of the shaft by suspending it from a convenient underbody component with a piece of wire. Do not allow the shaft to hang unsupported, damage to the outboard CV-joint may occur.

b. Separate the outboard CV-joint from the hub.

NOTE: Never use a hammer to separate the outboard CV-joint stub shaft from the hub. Damage to the CV-joint threads and internal components may result. The right side link shaft and halfshaft assembly is removed as a complete unit.

6. The following removal procedure applies to the right and left side halfshafts for the AXOD automatic

transaxle and the left side halfshaft on the manual transaxle:

a. Install the CV-joint puller tool T86P–3514–A1 or equivalent between CV-joint and transaxle case. Turn the steering hub and or wire strut assembly out of the way.

b. Screw extension tool T86P–3514–A2 or equivalent, into the CV-joint puller and hand tighten. Screw an impact slide hammer onto the extension and remove the CV-joint.

c. Support the end of the shaft by suspending it from a convenient underbody component with a piece of wire. Do not allow the shaft to hang un-supported, damage to the outboard CV-joint may occur.

d. Separate the outboard CV-joint from the hub using front hub remover tool T81P–1104–C or equivalent and metric adapter tools T83–P–1104–BH, T86P–1104–Al and T81P–1104–A or equivalent.

e. Remove the halfshaft assembly from the vehicle.

7. The following removal procedure applies to the left side halfshaft for the automatic transaxle:

NOTE: Due to the automatic transaxle case configuration, the right halfshaft assembly must be removed first. Differential rotator tool T81P–4026–A or equivalent is then inserted into the transaxle to drive the left inboard CV-joint assembly from the transaxle. If only the left halfshaft assembly is to be removed for service, remove only the right halfshaft assembly from the transaxle. After removal, support it with a length of wire. Then drive the left halfshaft assembly from the transaxle.

a. Support the end of the shaft by suspending it from a convenient underbody component with a piece of wire. Do not allow the shaft to hang unsupported as damage to the outboard C-V joint may occur.

b. Separate the outboard CV-joint from the hub.

c. Remove the halfshaft assembly from the vehicle.

To install:

8. Install a new circlip on the inboard CV-joint stub shaft and or link shaft. The outboard CV-joint does not have a circlip. When installing the circlip, start one end in the groove and work the circlip over the stub shaft end into the groove. This will avoid over expanding the circlip.

NOTE: The circlip must not be re-used. A new circlip must be installed each time the inboard CV-joint is installed into the transaxle differential.

9. Carefully align the splines of the inboard CV-joint stub shaft with the splines in the differential. Exerting some force, push the CV-joint into the differential until the circlip is felt to seat in the differential side gear. Use care to prevent damage to the differential oil seal. Torque the link shaft bearing to 16–23 ft. lbs.

NOTE: A non-metallic mallet may be used to aid in seating the circlip into the differential side gear groove. If a mallet is necessary, tap only on the outboard CV-joint stub shaft.

10. Carefully align the splines of the outboard CV-joint stub shaft with the splines in the hub and push the shaft into the hub as far as possible.

11. Temporarily fasten the rotor to the hub with washers and 2 wheel lug nuts. Insert a steel rod into the rotor and rotate clockwise to contact the knuckle to prevent the rotor from turning during the CV-joint installation.

12. Install the hub nut washer and a new hub nut. Manually thread the retainer onto the CV-joint as far as possible.

13. Connect the control arm to the steering knuckle and install a new nut and bolt. Tighten the nut to 37–44 ft. lbs. for 1987 vehicles or 40–55 ft. lbs. on 1988–91 vehicles. A new bolt must be installed also.

14. Install the hub retainer washer and a new hub retainer. Manually thread the retainer onto the CV-joint as far as possible. A new retainer must be installed. Connect the stabilizer bar link to the stabilizer bar and tighten to 35–38 ft. lbs.

15. Install the wheel and tire assembly and lower the vehicle. Tighten the wheel nuts to 80–105 ft. lbs. Tighten the hub nut to 180–200 ft. lbs. Fill the transaxle to the proper level with the specified fluid.

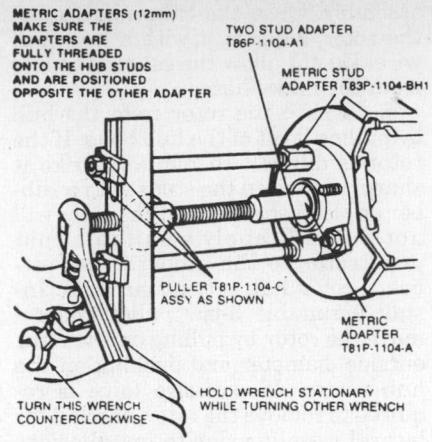

Removing the halfshaft from the hub

CV-Boot

REMOVAL & INSTALLATION

1. Clamp the halfshaft in a vise that is equipped with soft jaw covers. Do not allow the vise jaws to contact the boot or boot clamp.

2. Cut the large boot clamp with a pair of side cutters and peel the clamp away from the boot. Roll the boot back over the shaft after the clamp has been removed.

3. Clamp the interconnecting shaft in a soft jawed vise with the CV-joint pointing downward so the inner bearing race is exposed.

4. Use a brass drift and hammer, give a sharp tap to the inner bearing race to dislodge the internal snapring and separate the CV-joint from the interconnecting shaft. Take care to secure the CV-joint so it does not drop after separation. Remove the clamp and boot from the shaft.

5. Remove and discard the circlip at the end of the interconnecting shaft. The stop ring, located just below the circlip should be removed and replaced only if damaged or worn.

To install:

6. Clean the joints and repack with fresh grease. Do not reuse the old grease Install a new boot or reinstall the old boot with a new clamp.

7. The left and right interconnect-

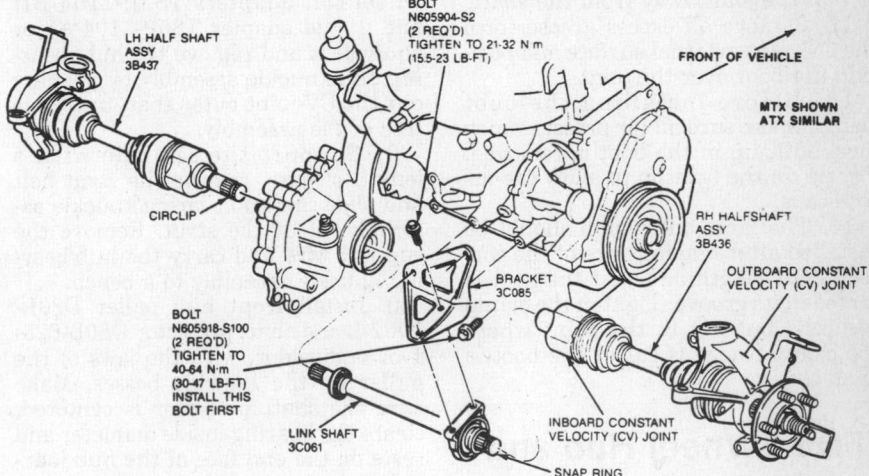

Exploded view of the halfshaft assembly—used with the MTX and ATX

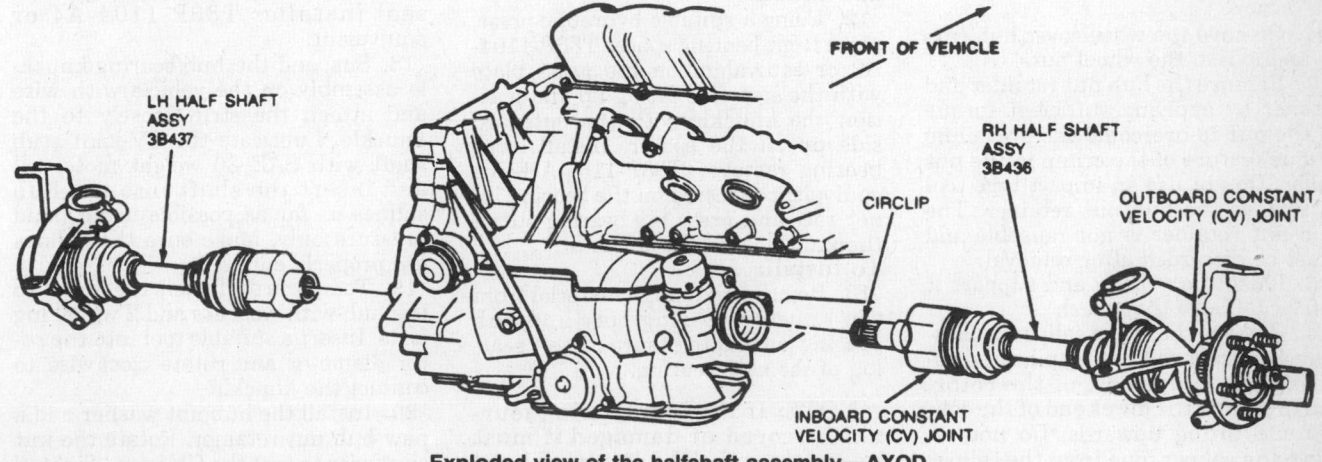

Exploded view of the halfshaft assembly—AXOD

ing shafts are different, depending on year and vehicle application. The outboard end of the shaft is shorter from the end of the shaft to the end of the boot grove than the inboard end. Take a measurement to insure correct installation.

8. Install the new boot. Make sure the boot is seated in the mounting groove and secure it in position with a new clamp. Tighten the clamp securely, but not to the point where the clamp bridge is cut or the boot is damaged.

9. Clean the interconnecting shaft splines and install a new circlip and stop ring if removed. To install the circlip correctly, start one end in the groove and work the circlip over the shaft end and into the groove.

10. Pack the CV-joint and boot with grease.

11. With the boot peeled back, position the CV-joint on the shaft and tap into position using a plastic tipped hammer. The CV-joint is fully seated when the circlip locks into the groove cut into the CV-joint inner bearing race. Check for seating by attempting to pull the joint away from the shaft.

12. Remove all excess grease form the CV-joint external surface and position the boot over the joint.

13. Before installing the boot clamp, make sure all air pressure may have built up in the boot is removed. Pry up on the boot lip to allow the air to escape.

14. The large end clamp should be installed after making sure of the correct shaft length and that the boot is seated in its groove. Tighten the clamp securely, but not to the point where the clamp bridge is cut or the boot is damaged.

Front Wheel Hub and Bearings

REMOVAL & INSTALLATION

1. Remove the wheelcover/hub cover and loosen the wheel nuts.

2. Remove the hub nut retainer and washer by applying sufficient torque to the nut to overcome the prevailing torque feature of the crimp in the nut collar. Do not use an impact-type tool to remove the hub nut retainer. The hub nut retainer is not reusable and must be discarded after removal.

3. Raise the vehicle and support it safely. Remove the wheel.

4. Remove the brake caliper by loosening the caliper locating pins and rotating the caliper off of the rotor, starting from the lower end of the caliper and lifting upwards. Do not remove the caliper pins from the caliper

assembly. Once the caliper is free of the rotor, support it with a length of wire. Do not allow the caliper to hang from the brake hose.

5. Remove the rotor from the hub by pulling it off of the hub bolts. If the rotor is difficult to remove, strike it sharply betwwen the studs with a rubber or plastic hammer. If the rotor will not pull off, apply a suitable rust penetrator to the inboard and outboard rotor hub mating surfaces. Install a suitable 3-jaw puller and remove the rotor by pulling on the rotor outside diameter and pushing on the hub center. If excessive force is required to remove the rotor, check it for lateral runout prior to installation. Lateral runout must be checked with the nuts clamping the stamped hat section of the rotor.

6. Remove the rotor splash shield.

7. Disconnect the lower control arm and tie rod from the knuckle but leave the strut attached. Loosen the 2 strut top mount-to-apron nuts.

8. Install hub remover/installer adapter T81P-1104-A with front hub remover/installer T81P-1104-C and wheel bolt adapters T83P-1104-BH and 2 stud adapter T86P-1104-A1 or equivalent and remove the hub, bearing and knuckle assembly by pushing out the CV-joint outer shaft until it is free of the assembly.

9. Support the knuckle with a length of wire, remove the strut bolt and slide the hub/bearing/knuckle assembly off of the strut. Remove the support wire and carry the hub/bearing/knuckle assembly to a bench.

10. Install front hub puller D80L-1002-L and shaft protector D80L-625-1 or equivalent, with the jaws of the puller on the knuckle bosses. Make sure the shaft protector is centered, clears the bearing inside diameter and rests on the end face of the hub journal. Remove the hub.

11. Remove the snapring that retains the bearing in the knuckle assembly and discard.

12. Using a suitable hydraulic press, place front bearing spacer T86P-1104-A2 or equivalent on the press plate with the step side facing up and position the knuckle with the outboard side up on the spacer. Install front bearing remover T83P-1104-AH2 or equivalent centered on the bearing inner race and press the bearing out of the knuckle and discard.

To install:

13. Remove all foreign material from the knuckle bearing bore and hub bearing journal to ensure correct seating of the new bearing.

NOTE: If the hub bearing journal is scored or damaged it must be replaced. The front wheel

bearings are pregreased and sealed and require no scheduled maintenance. The bearings are preset and cannot be adjusted. If a bearing is disassembled for any reason, it must be replaced as a unit, as individual service seals, rollers and races are not available.

14. Place front bearing spacer T86P-1104-A2 or equivalent with the step side down on the hydraulic press plate and position the knuckle with the outboard side down on the spacer. Position a new bearing in the inboard side of the knuckle. Install bearing installer T86P-1104-A3 or equivalent with the undercut side facing the bearing, on the bearing outer race and press the bearing into the knuckle. Make surethe bearing seats completely against the shoulder of the knuckle bore.

NOTE: Bearing installer T86P-1104-A3 or equivalent must be positioned as indicated above to prevent bearing damage during installation.

15. Install a new snapring (part of the bearing kit) in the knuckle groove.

16. Place front bearing spacer T86P-1104-A2 or equivalent on the press plate and position the hub on the tool with the lugs facing downward. Position the knuckle assembly with the outboard side down on the hub barrel. Place bearing remover T83P-1104-AH2 or equivalent flat side down, centered on the inner race of the bearing and press down on the tool until the bearing is fully seated onto the hub. Make sure the hub rotates freely in the knuckle after installation.

17. Prior to hub/bearing/knuckle installation, replace the bearing dust seal on the outboard CV-joint with a new seal from the bearing kit. Make sure the seal flange faces outboard toward the bearing. Use drive tube T83T-3132-A1 and front bearing dust seal installer T86P-1104-A4 or equivalent.

18. Suspend the hub/bearing/knuckle assembly on the vehicle with wire and attach the strut loosely to the knuckle. Lubricate the CV-joint stub shaft with SAE 30 weight motor oil and insert the shaft into the hub splines as far as possible using hand pressure only. Make sure the splines are properly engaged.

19. Temporarily fasten the rotor to the hub with washers and 2 wheel lug nuts. Insert a suitable tool into the rotor diameter and rotate clockwise to contact the knuckle.

20. Install the hub nut washer and a new hub nut retainer. Rotate the nut clockwise to seat the CV-joint. Tighten

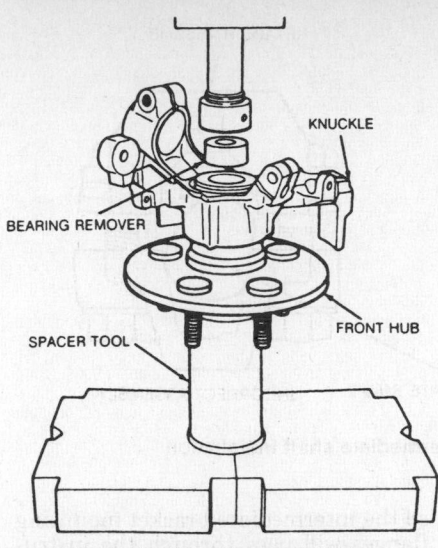

Front wheel bearing installation

the nut to 180–200 ft. lbs. (245–270 Nm). Remove the washers and lug nuts.

NOTE: Do not use power or impact-type tools to tighten the hub nut.

21. Install the remainder of the front suspension components and the rotor splash shield.
22. Install the disc brake rotor and caliper. Make sure the outer brake pad spring hook is seated under the upper arm of the knuckle.
23. Install the wheel and tighten the wheel nuts finger tight.
24. Lower the vehicle. Tighten the wheel nuts to 85–105 ft. lbs. (115–142 Nm). Install the wheelcover/hub cover.

STEERING

Steering Wheel
——— CAUTION ———

On vehicles equipped with an air bag, the negative battery cable must be disconnected, before working on the system. Failure to do so may result in deployment of the air bag and possible personal injury.

REMOVAL & INSTALLATION

Taurus, Sable and 1988 Continental

1. Center the front wheels to the straight ahead position. Disconnect the negative battery cable. Remove the steering wheel center horn pad cover by removing the retaining screws from the steering wheel assembly.

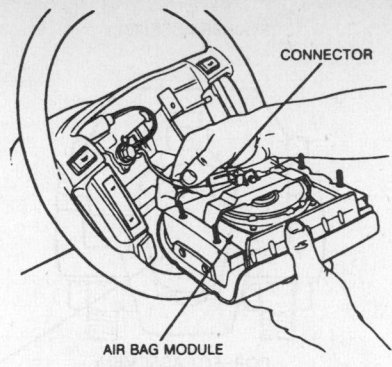

Air bag module removal—Taurus and Sable

NOTE: The emblem assembly is removed after the horn pad cover is removed, by pushing it out from the backside of the emblem.

2. Remove the energy absorbing foam from the wheel assembly, if equipped. Remember the energy absorbing foam must be installed when the steering wheel is assembled. Disconnect the horn pad wiring connector.
3. On vehicles equipped with air bag restraint system, remove the 4 nuts holding the air bag module to the steering wheel, the nuts are located on the back of the steering wheel.
4. Lift the air bag module from the wheel and disconnect the air bag module to slip-ring clock spring connector.
5. On all vehicles, loosen and remove the center mounting nut or bolt and on the vehicles equipped with speed control system, remove the electrical connectors. Discard the center nut or bolt and replace with new.
6. Grasp the rim of the steering wheel and pull the steering wheel from the upper shaft on 1987–89 vehicles. On 1990-91 a suitable puller is required to remove the steering wheel. Route the contact assembly wire through the steering wheel as the wheel is lifted off of the shaft.

To install:

NOTE: The multi-switch lever switch must be in the middle position before installing the steering wheel or damage to the switch cam may result.

7. Position the steering wheel on the end of the steering wheel shaft. Align the mark on the steering wheel with the mark on the shaft to assure the straight-ahead steering wheel position corresponds to the straight-ahead position of the front wheels. Route the contact wire harness on 1990–91 vehicles through the steering wheel opening at the 3 o'clock position. Be sure the air bag contact wire is not pinched, on vehicles so equipped.
8. Install a new service wheel locknut or bolt. Torque the nut to 35–55 ft. lbs. (47–68 Nm) and the bolt to 23–33 ft. lbs. (31–48 Nm). Connect all the electrical connectors on the vehicles equipped with speed control.
9. On vehicles equipped with air bags, connect the air bag module wire to slip ring connector and place the module on the steering wheel with the 4 attaching nuts, torque the nuts to 3–4 ft. lbs. (4–6 Nm).
10. On the other vehicles install the steering wheel hub cover and torque the nuts to 5–10 inch lbs. (0.5–1.1 Nm).
11. Reconnect the negative battery cable and check the steering wheel for proper operation.

1989–91 Continental

1. Center the front wheels to the straight ahead position. Disconnect the negative battery cable.
2. Remove the lower instrument panel cover.
3. Remove the steering column lock cylinder and the tilt release lever.
4. Remove the lower steering column shroud.
5. Disconnect the contact assembly at the body wire harness and remove

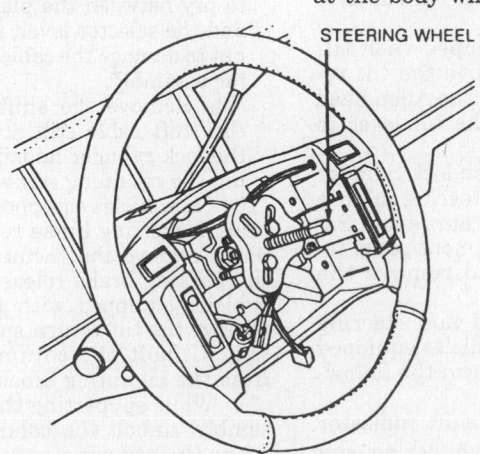

Steering wheel removal—1990–91 Taurus and Sable

the contact assembly ground wire screw located at the lock cylinder housing.

6. Remove the 4 air bag module retaining nuts and remove the air bag module from the steering wheel and disconnect the contact as an assembly at the module.

7. Remove and discard the steering wheel attaching bolt.

8. Remove the steering wheel and contact assembly. Make sure the cotact assembly is locked in the straight ahead position. Do not allow the contact assembly to rotate out of position.

To install:

9. Install the steering wheel and contact assembly onto the steering column. Make sure the drive pin on the speed control/horn brush assembly engages in the drive socket on the contact assembly housing.

10. Install a new steering wheel bolt and tighten to 23–33 ft. lbs. (31–45 Nm).

11. Install the ground wire and retaining screw.

12. Connect the contact assembly wire harness and connect the cotact assembly at the module.

13. Install the module to the steering wheel and tighten the retaining nuts.

14. Install the lower steering column shroud, lock cylinder, tilt release lever and the lower instrument panel cover.

15. Connect the negative battery cable and check the steering column for proper operation.

Steering Column

REMOVAL & INSTALLATION

1. Disconnect the negative battery cable.

2. Remove the steering column cover from lower portion of instrument panel. Remove the right hand and left hand lower instrument panel mouldings on 1990–91 Taurus and Sable.

3. On vehicles equipped with tilt steering columns, remove the tilt release lever by removing the Allen head cap screw that holds the tilt lever to the steering column.

4. Remove the ignition lock cylinder and remove the lower steering column shrouds. On 1990–91 Taurus and Sable, remove the 2 instrument panel reinforcement bolts and remove the reinforcement.

5. Remove horn pad and steering wheel assembly. On vehicles equipped with column shift perform the following steps:

a. Disconnect the shift indicator cable from the lock cylinder housing by removing the retaining screw.

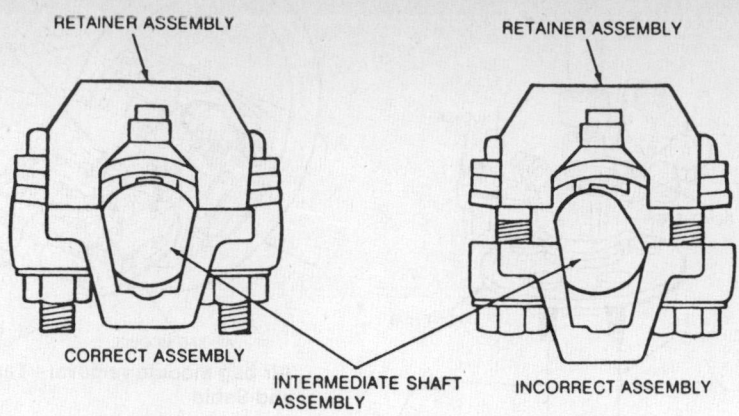

Steering column to intermediate shaft installation

Disconnect the shift indicator cable from the shift socket. Remove the hood release cable from the handle.

b. Remove the shift indicator cable from the retaining hook on the bottom of the lock cylinder housing.

6. Disconnect the speed control/horn brush wiring connector from the main wiring harness.

7. Remove the multi-function switch wiring harness retainer from the lock cylinder housing by squeezing the end of the retainer and pushing out. Disconnect the multi-function switch connector from the switch and remove the multi-function switch from the lock cylinder housing by removing the self-tapping screws.

8. Disconnect the key warning buzzer switch wiring connector from the main wiring harness. Disconnect the wiring connector from the ignition switch.

9. Disconnect the steering shaft from the intermediate shaft by removing the 2 nuts and 1 U-clamp. On vehicles equipped with column shift, perform the following steps:

a. Remove the shift cable plastic terminal from the column selector lever pilot ball using a suitable tool to pry between the plastic terminal and the selector lever. Make certain not to damage the cable during or after assembly.

b. Remove the shift cable, with the shift cable still attached, from the lock cylinder housing by removing the retaining screws.

10. On vehicles equipped with an automatic parking brake release mechanism, remove the vacuum hose from the parking brake release switch. On vehicles equipped with tilt columns, remove the tilt return spring.

11. Unbolt the column assembly from the mounting bracket.

12. While supporting the column assembly, unbolt the column assembly from the steering column support bracket. Rotate the column assembly

so the intermediate bracket mounting flanges will pass through the instrument panel opening and slowly pull the column assembly from the instrument panel.

To install:

13. Rotate the column assembly so the intermediate bracket mounting flanges will pass through the instrument panel opening and slowly slide the column assembly forward while feeding the steering shaft universal joint tongue over the forward mounting bracket.

14. Raise the steering column into position and align the 4 mounting holes over the 4 support bracket studs. Center the column in the instrument panel opening and tighten the 4 nuts to 15–25 ft. lbs. (21–33 Nm).

16. On the tilt column equipped vehicles, attach the tilt return spring. On vehicles equipped with automatic parking brake release mechanisms, install the vacuum hose on the parking brake release switch.

17. On vehicles equipped with column shift, perform the following steps.

a. Attach the shift cable bracket, with the shift cable attached, to the lock cylinder housing with the retaining screws. Torque the screws to 30–60 inch lbs.

b. Snap the transaxle shift cable terminal to the selector lever pivot ball on the steering column.

18. Connect the steering shaft to the intermediate shaft with the U-clamp and hex nuts. Make sure the "vee-angle" of the intermediate shaft fits correctly into the "vee-angle" of the mating steering column yoke. Tighten the nuts to 15–25 ft. lbs. (21–33 Nm). On the tilt column equipped vehicles, the column must be in the middle tilt position before the nuts are tightened.

19. Install the main harness wiring connector to the ignition switch. Install the key warning buzzer switch

wiring connector to the main wiring harness.

20. Install the multi-function switch to the lock cylinder housing with the self-tapping screws. Torque the screws to 18–26 inch lbs. Install the multi-function switch wiring harness retainer over the shroud mounting boss and snap it into the slot in the lock cylinder housing.

21. Connect the speed control/horn brush wiring connector to the main harness. On shift column equipped vehicles, perform the following steps:

a. Install the shift indicator cable into the retaining hook on the cylinder housing. Connect the shift indicator cable to the shift socket.

b. Loosely install the shift indicator cable onto the lock cylinder housing with one retaining screw. Adjust the shift indicator cable as follows: Place the shift lever in the **D** position with the regular transaxles and **OD** position with overdrive transaxles. Adjust the cable until the shift indicator pointer is centered on the **D** position or the **OD** position depending on the type of transaxle. Tighten the hex head screw to 18–30 inch lbs. (2.0–3.4 Nm).

22. Install the steering wheel and horn pad. Install the steering column shrouds with retaining screws. On tilt column equipped vehicles, install the tilt release lever with one socket head cap screw. On 1990–91 Taurus and Sable, install the instrument panel reinforcement brace and the right hand and left hand lower instrument panel mouldings.

23. Install the ignition lock cylinder. Install the steering column cover from the lower portion of the instrument panel with self-tapping screws.

24. Reconnect the negative battery cable and check the steering column and its components for proper operation.

the intermediate shaft. Raise the vehicle and support safely.

4. Remove the left hand side front wheel assembly. Remove the heat shield. Cut the bundling strap retaining the lines to the gear.

5. Remove the tie rod ends from the spindles. Place a drain pan under the vehicle and remove the hydraulic pressure and return lines from the steering gear.

NOTE: The pressure and return lines are on the front of the housing. Do not confuse them with the transfer lines on the side of the valve.

6. Remove the nut from the gear mounting bolts. The bolts are pressed into the gear housing and should not be removed during gear removal.

7. Push the weather boot end into the vehicle and lift the gear out of the mounting holes. Rotate the gear so the input shaft will pass between the brake booster and the floor pan. Carefully start working the steering gear out through the left hand fender apron opening.

8. Rotate the input shaft so it clears the left fender apron opening and complete the removal of the steering gear. If the steering gear seems to be stuck, check the right tie rod to ensure the stud is not caught on anything.

To install:

9. Install new plastic seals on the hydraulic line fittings.

10. Insert the steering gear through the left fender apron. Rotate the input shaft forward to completely clear the fender apron opening.

11. To allow the gear to pass between the brake booster and the floorpan, rotate the input shaft rearward. Align the steering gear bolts to the bolt holes. Install the mounting nuts and torque them to 85–100 ft. lbs. (115–135 Nm). Lower the vehicle.

12. From inside the engine compartment, install the hydraulic pressure and return lines. Tighten the pressure line to 20–25 ft. lbs. (28–33Nm) and the return line to 15–20 ft. lbs. (20–28 Nm). Swivel movement of the lines is normal when the fittings are properly tightened.

13. Raise the vehicle and support safely. Secure the pressure and return lines to the transfer tube with the bundle strap. Install the heat shield.

14. Install the tie rod ends to spindles. Torque the castle nuts to 35 ft. lbs. (48 Nm) and if necessary, torque the nuts a little bit more to align the slot in the nut for the cotter pin. Install the cotter pin.

15. Install the left front wheel assembly and lower the vehicle. Working from inside the vehicle, pull the weather boot end out of the vehicle and install it over the valve housing. Install the intermediate shaft to the steering gear input shaft. Install the the inner weather boot to the floor pan.

16. Install the intermediate shaft to the steering column shaft. Fill the power steering system.

17. Check the system for leaks and proper operation. Adjust the toe setting as necessary.

Variable Assist Power Steering System (VAPS)—Taurus LX, 3.8L Sable and Continental

The Variable Assist Power Steering System (VAPS) used on these vehicles consists of a micro-processor based module, a power rack and pinion steering gear, an actuator valve assembly, hose assemblies and a high efficiency power steering pump.

1. Disconnect the negative battery cable. Remove the primary steering column boot attachments.

2. Remove the intermediate shaft retaining bolts and remove the intermediate shaft.

Power Rack and Pinion

REMOVAL & INSTALLATION

Integral Power Rack and Pinion—Taurus and Sable

1. Disconnect the negative battery cable. Working from inside the vehicle, remove the nuts retaining the steering shaft weather boot to the dash panel.

2. Remove the bolts retaining the intermediate shaft to the steering column shaft. Set the weather boot aside.

3. Remove the pinch bolt at the steering gear input shaft and remove

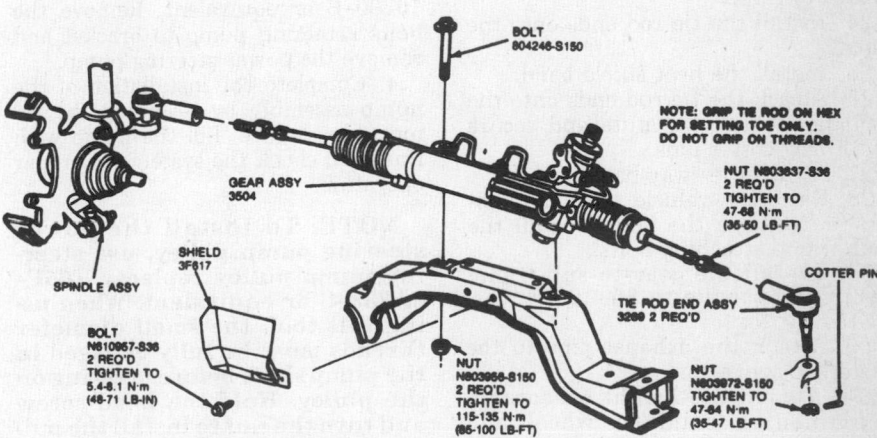

Exploded view of the power steering gear assembly

3. From inside the passenger compartment, remove the secondary steering column boot.

4. Raise the vehicle and support safely. Remove the front wheels. Support the vehicle under the rear edge of the sub-frame.

5. Remove the tie rod cotter pins and nuts. Remove the tie rod ends from the spindle.

6. Remove the tie rod ends from the shaft. Mark the position of the jam nut to maintain the alignment.

7. Remove the nuts from the gear-to-sub-frame attaching bolts.

8. Remove both height sensor attachments on Continental.

9. Remove the rear sub-frame-to-attaching bolts.

10. Remove the exhaust pipe-to-catalytic converter attachment.

11. Lower the vehicle approximately 4 in. or until the subframe separates from the body.

12. Remove the heat shield band and fold the shield down.

13. Disconnect the VAPS electrical connector from the actuator assembly.

14. Rotate the gear to clear the bolts from the sub-frame and pull to the left to facilitate line fitting removal.

15. Position a drain pan under the vehicle and remove the line fittings. Remove the O-rings from the fiting connections and replace with new.

16. Remove the left sway bar.

17. Remove the steering gear assembly through the left hand wheel well.

To install:

18. Install new O-rings into the line fittings.

19. Place the gear attachment bolts in the gear housing.

20. Install the steering gear assembly through the left hand wheel well.

21. Connect and tighten the line fittings to the steering gear assembly.

22. Connect the VAPS electrical connector.

23. Position the steering gear into the sub-frame.

24. Install the tie rod ends onto the shaft.

25. Install the heat shield band.

26. Attach the tie rod ends onto the spindle. Install the nuts and secure with new cotter pins.

27. Attach the sway bar links.

28. Raise the vehicle until the subframe contacts the body. Install the sub-frame attaching bolts.

29. Install the gear-to-sub-frame nuts and torque to 85–100 ft. lbs. (115–135 Nm).

30. Attach the exhaust pipe to the catalytic converter.

31. Attach the height sensors on Continental, install the wheels and lower the vehicle.

32. Fill the power steering system.

33. Install the secondary steering

VAPS power rack and pinion

column boot and attach the intermediate shaft to the steering column.

34. Bleed the system and align the front end.

Power Steering Pump

REMOVAL & INSTALLATION

2.5L and 3.8L Engines

1. Disconnect the negative battery cable. Loosen the tensioner pulley attaching bolts and using the ½ in. drive hole provided in the tensioner pulley, rotate the tensioner pulley clockwise and remove the belt from the alternator and power steering pulley.

2. Position a drain pan under the power steering pump from underneath the vehicle. Disconnect the hydraulic pressure and return lines.

3. Remove the pulley from the pump shaft using hub puller T69L–10300–B or equivalent. Remove the bolts retaining pump to bracket and remove the power steering pump.

4. Complete the installation of the pump assembly by reversing the removal procedure. Fill the pump with fluid and check the system for proper operation.

NOTE: To install the power steering pump pulley, use steering pump pulley replacer T65P–3A733–C or equivalent. When using this tool, the small diameter threads must be fully engaged in the pump shaft before pressing on the pulley. Hold the head screw and turn the nut to install the pulley. Install the pulley face flush with the pump shaft within ± 0.100 in.

3.0L Engine Except SHO

1. Disconnect the negative battery cable. Loosen the idler pulley and remove the power steering belt.

2. Remove the radiator overflow bottle in order to gain access to the 3 screws attaching the pulleys to the pulley hub.

3. Matchmark both pulley to hub positions.

4. Remove the pulleys from the pulley hub.

5. Remove the return line from the pump. Be prepared to catch any spilled fluid in a suitable container.

6. Back off the pressure line attaching nut completely. The line will separate from the pump connection when the pump is removed.

7. Remove the pump mounting bolts and remove the pump.

8. Installation is the reverse of the removal procedure. Fill the pump with fluid and check for proper operation.

3.0L SHO Engine

1. Disconnect the negative battery cable.

2. Remove the engine damper strut.

3. Remove the power steering belt.

4. Raise and support the vehicle safely.

5. Remove the right front wheel and tire assembly.

6. Position a jack under the engine and remove the right rear engine mount.

7. Remove the power steering pump pulley.

8. Place a drain pan under the pump and remove the pressure and return lines from the pump.

9. Remove the 4 pump retaining bolts and remove the pump.

10. Installation is the reverse of the removal procedure. Tighten the pump retaining bolts to 15–24 ft. lbs. (20–33 Nm).

BELT ADJUSTMENT

Except 3.0L SHO Engine

Belt tension is maintained by an automatic tensioner and does not require adjustment.

3.0L SHO Engine

1. Loosen the idler pulley nut and turn the adjusting screw until the belt is adjusted. Measure the belt tension using a suitable offset belt tension gauge. New belts should measure 154–198 lbs. and used belts 112–157 lbs. The allowable minimum belt tension is 80 lbs.
2. Tighten the idler pulley nut to 25–37 ft. lbs. (34–50 Nm).

SYSTEM BLEEDING

If air bubbles are present in the power steering fluid, bleed the system by performing the following:
1. Fill the reservoir to the proper level.
2. Operate the engine until the fluid reaches normal operating temperature (165–175°F).
3. Turn the steering wheel all the way to the left then all the way to the right several times. Do not hold the steering wheel in the far left or far right position stops.
4. Check the fluid level and recheck the fluid for the presence of trapped air. If apparent that air is still in the system, fabricate or obtain a vacuum tester and purge the system as follows:
   a. Remove the pump dipstick cap assembly.
   b. Check and fill the pump reservoir with fluid to the **COLD FULL** mark on the dipstick.
   c. Disconnect the ignition wire and raise the front of the vehicle and support safely.
   d. Crank the engine with the starter and check the fluid level. Do not turn the steering wheel at this time.
   e. Fill the pump reservoir to the **COLD FULL** mark on the dipstick. Crank the engine with the starter while cycling the steering wheel lock-to-lock. Check the fluid level.
   f. Tightly insert a suitable size rubber stopper and air evacuator pump into the reservoir fill neck. Connect the ignition coil wire.
   g. With the engine idling, apply a 15 in. Hg vacuum to the reservoir for 3 minutes. As air is purged from the system, the vacuum will drop off. Maintain the vacuum on the sys-

tem as required throughout the 3 minutes.
   h. Remove the vacuum source. Fill the reservoir to the **COLD FULL** mark on the dipstick.
   i. With the engine idling, re-apply 15 in. Hg vacuum source to the resrevoir. Slowly cycle the steering wheel to lock-to-lock stops for approximately 5 minutes. Do not hold the steering wheel on the stops during cycling. Maintain the vacuum as required.
   j. Release the vacuum and disconnect the vacuum source. Add fluid as required.
   k. Start the engine and cycle the wheel slowly and check for leaks at all connections.
   l. Lower the front wheels.
5. In cases of severe aeration, repeat the procedure.

Tie Rod Ends

REMOVAL & INSTALLATION

1. Remove and discard the cotter pin and nut from the worn tie rod end ball stud.
2. Disconnect the tie rod end from the steering spindle, using tie rod remover tool 3290-D or equivalent.
3. Hold the tie rod end with a wrench and loosen the tie rod jam nut.
4. Note the depth to which the tie rod is located, then grip the tie rod with a pair of suitable pliers and remove the tie rod end assembly from the tie rod.
To install:
5. Clean the tie rod threads. Thread the new tie rod end into the tie rod to the same depth as the removed tie rod end.
6. Place the tie rod end stud into the steering spindle. Make sure the front wheels are pointed straight ahead before connecting the stud to the spindle.
7. Install a new nut on the tie rod end stud. Tighten the nut to 35 ft. lbs. (48 Nm) and continue tightening until the next castellation on the nut is aligned with the cotter pin hole in the stud. Install a new cotter pin.
8. Set the toe to specification. Tighten the jam nut to 35–50 ft. lbs. (47–68 Nm).

BRAKES

For all brake system repair and service procedures not detailed below, please refer to "Brakes" in the Unit Repair section.

Master Cylinder

REMOVAL & INSTALLATION

1. Disconnect the negative battery cable. On vehicles equipped with anti-lock brakes, depress the brake pedal several times to exhaust all vacuum in the system.
2. Disconnect the brake lines from the primary and secondary outlet ports of the master cylinder and the pressure control valve.
3. Remove the nuts attaching the master cylinder to the brake booster assembly. Disconnect the brake warning lamp wire. On vehicles equipped with anti-lock brakes, disconnect the hydraulic control unit (HCU) supply hose at the master cylinder and secure in a position to prevent loss of brake fluid.
4. Slide the master cylinder forward and upward from the vehicle.
To install:
5. Mount the master cylinder on the booster. Install a new seal in the groove in the master cylinder mounting face on vehicles equipped with anti-lock brakes. Attach the brake fluid lines to the master cylinder. On vehicles equipped with anti-lock brakes, install the HCU supply hose to the master cylinder.
6. Install the brake warning lamp wire.
7. Fill the reservoirs with fresh brake fluid and bleed the system. Operate the brakes several times, then check for external hydraulic leaks.

Proportioning Valve

REMOVAL & INSTALLATION

1. Raise the vehicle and support it safely.
2. Disconnect the brake lines from the valve assembly and note their position.
3. Remove the screw retaining the valve bracket to the lower suspension arm. Remove the 2 screws retaining the valve bracket to the underbody and remove the assembly.

NOTE: The service replacement valve will have a red plastic gauge clip on the valve and must not be removed until it is installed on the vehicle.

To install:
4. Make sure the rear suspension is in the full rebound position.
5. Make sure the red plastic gauge clip is in position on the valve and that the operating rod lower adjustment screw is loose.

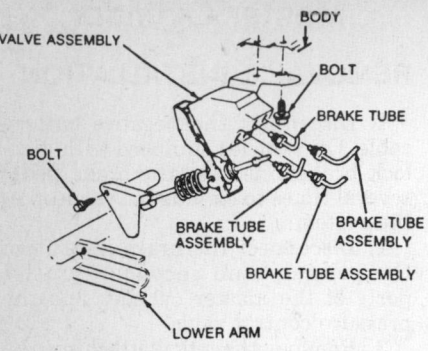

Brake pressure control valve

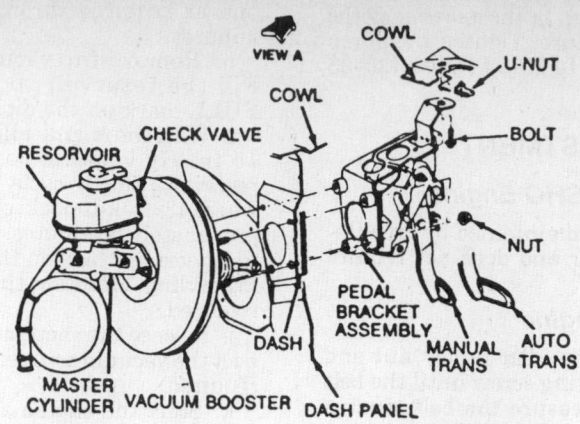

Brake booster assembly with anti-lock brakes

6. Position the valve lower mounting bracket to the lower suspension arm. Install 1 retaining screw. Make sure the valve adjuster is resting on the lower bracket and tighten the set screw.

7. Connect the brake lines in the same position as removed. Bleed the rear brakes.

8. Remove the red plastic gauge clip and lower the vehicle.

Power Brake Booster

REMOVAL & INSTALLATION

Without Anti-lock Brakes

1. Disconnect the battery ground cable and remove the brake lines from the master cylinder.

2. Remove the retaining nuts and the master cylinder.

3. From under the instrument panel, remove the stoplight switch wiring connector from the switch. Remove the pushrod retainer and outer nylon washer from the brake pin, slide the stoplight switch along the brake pedal pin, far enough for the outer hole to clear the pin.

4. Remove the switch by sliding it upward. Remove the booster to dash panel retaining nuts. Slide the booster pushrod and pushrod bushing off the brake pedal pin.

5. Remove the screws and position the vacuum tee out of the way. Position the wire harness out of the way. Remove the transaxle shift cable and bracket.

6. Disconnect the manifold vacuum hose from the booster check valve and move the booster forward until the booster studs clear the dash panel and remove the booster.

7. Installation is the reverse of the removal procedure. Bleed the brake system.

NOTE: On vehicles equipped with speed control, the vacuum dump valve must be adjusted if the brake booster has been removed.

With Anti-lock Brakes

1. Disconnect the negative battery cable. Pump the brake pedal until all vacuum is removed from the booster. This will prevent the O-ring from being sucked into the booster during disassembly.

2. Disconnect the manifold vacuum hose from the booster check valve and the electrical connector from the master cylinder reservoir cap.

3. Remove the brake lines from the primary and secondary outlet ports of the master cylinder and remove the hydraulic control unit (HCU) supply hose. Plug the ports and reservoir feed to prevent brake fluid from leaking onto paint and wiring.

4. Under the instrument panel, remove the stoplight switch wiring connector from the switch. Disengage the pedal position switch from the stud. Remove the hairpin retainer and outer nylon washer from the pedal pin. Slide the stoplight switch off of the brake pedal just far enough for the outer arm to clear the pin. Remove the switch.

5. Remove the booster to dash panel attaching nuts. Slide the bushing and booster push rod off of the brake pedal pin.

6. Move the booster forward until the booster studs clear the dash panel. Remove the booster and master cylinder assembly.

7. Place the booster and master cylinder assembly on a bench. Remove the 2 nuts attaching the master cylinder to the booster and remove the master cylinder.

To install:

8. Slide the master cylinder onto the booster studs. Make sure the O-ring is in place in the groove on the master cylinder and install the 2 attaching nuts. Tighten the nuts to 13–

25 ft. lbs. (18–34 Nm).

9. Under the instrument panel, install the booster push rod and bushing on the brake pedal pin. Fasten the booster to the dash panel with self-locking nuts. Tighten the nuts to 13–25 ft. lbs. (18–34 Nm).

10. Position the stoplamp switch so it straddles the booster push rod with the switch slot towards the pedal blade and hole just clearing the pin. Slide the switch completely onto the pin.

11. Install the outer nylon washer on the pin and secure all parts to the pin with the hairpin retainer. Make sure the retainer is fully installed and locked over the pedal pin. Install the stoplight switch wiring connector.

12. Install the pedal travel switch. To adjust the switch, push the switch plunger fully into the switch housing. This zeros out the switch adjustment so it can be automatically reset to the correct dimension during the following steps:

   a. Slowly pull the arm back out of the switch housing past the detent point. At this point it should be impossible to reattach the arm to the pin unless the brake pedal is forced down.

   b. Depress the brake pedal until the switch hook can be snapped onto the pin. Snap the hook onto the pin and pull the brake pedal back up to it's normal at rest position. This automatically sets the switch to the proper adjustment.

13. Connect the brake lines to the master cylinder and tighten to 10–18 ft. lbs. (14–24 Nm). Connect the HCU supply hose to the resorvoir.

14. Connect the manifold vacuum hose to the booster check valve and the electrical connector to the master cylinder reservoir cap.

15. Connect the negative battery cable and bleed the brake system.

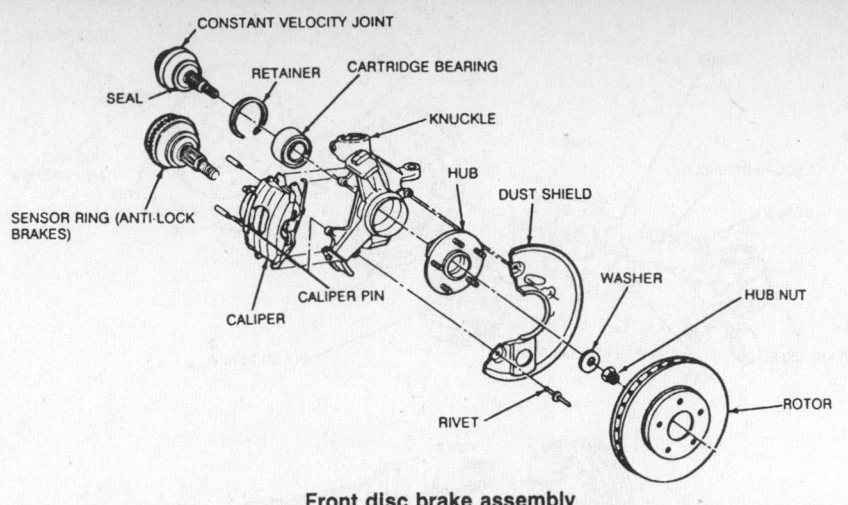

Front disc brake assembly

Brake Caliper

REMOVAL & INSTALLATION

Front

1. Raise and support the vehicle safely.

2. Remove the wheel and tire assembly. Mark the caliper to ensure that it is reinstalled on the correct knuckle.

3. Disconnect the flexible brake hose from the caliper. Remove the hollow retaining bolt that connects the hose fitting to the caliper. Remove the hose assembly from the caliper and plug the hose.

4. Remove the caliper locating pins.

5. Lift the caliper off of the rotor, integral knuckle and anchor plate using a rotating motion.

NOTE: Do not pry directly against the plastic piston or damage to the piston will result.

To install:

6. Retract the piston fully in the piston bore. Position the caliper assembly above the rotor with the anti-rattle spring under the upper arm of the knuckle. Install the caliper over the rotor with a rotating motion. Make sure the inner and outer shoes are properly positioned and the outer anti-rattle spring is properly positioned. Make sure the correct caliper assembly, as marked during removal, is installed on the correct knuckle. The caliper bleed screw should be positioned on top of the caliper when assembled on the vehicle.

7. Lubricate the locating pins and the inside of the insulators with silicone grease. Install the locating pins through the caliper insulators and hand start the threads into the knuckle attaching holes. Tighten the locating pins to 18–25 ft. lbs. (24–34 Nm).

8. Remove the plug and install the brake hose on the caliper with a new copper washer on each side of the fitting outlet. Insert the attaching bolt through the washers and fittings and tighten to 30–45 ft. lbs. (40–60 Nm).

9. Bleed the brake system, filling the master cylinder as required.

10. Install the wheel and lower the vehicle. Pump the brake pedal prior to moving the vehicle to position the brake linings.

Rear

1. Raise and support the vehicle safely.

2. Remove the wheel and tire assembly.

3. Remove the brake flex hose from the caliper assembly.

4. Remove the retaining clip from the parking brake at the caliper. Disengage the parking brake cable end from the lever arm.

5. Hold the slider pin hex-heads with an open-end wrench and remove the pinch bolts. Lift the caliper assembly away from the anchor plate. Remove the slider pins and boots from the anchor plate.

To install:

6. Apply silicone dielectric compound to the inside of the slider pin boots and to the slider pins.

7. Position the slider pins and boots in the anchor plate. Position the caliper assembly on the anchor plate. Make sure the brake shoes are installed correctly.

8. Remove the residue from the pich bolt threads and apply 1 drop of threadlock and sealer EOAZ-19554-A or equivalent. Install the pinch bolts and tighten to 23–26 ft. lbs. (31–35 Nm) while holding the slider pins with an open-end wrench.

9. Attach the cable end to the parking brake lever. Install the cable re-

taining clip on the caliper assembly.

10. Using new washers, connect the brake flex hose to the caliper. Tighten the retaining bolt to 8–11 ft. lbs. (11–16 Nm).

11. Bleed the brake system, filling the master cylinder as required.

12. Install the wheel and lower the vehicle. Pump the brake pedal prior to moving the vehicle to position the brake pads.

Disc Brake Pads
REMOVAL & INSTALLATION

Front

1. Remove the master cylinder cap and check the fluid level in the reservoir. Remove the brake fluid until the reservoir is half full. Discard the removed fluid.

2. Raise the vehicle and support it safely. Remove the wheel and tire assembly.

3. Remove the caliper locating pins. Lift the caliper assembly from the integral knuckle and anchor plate and rotor using a rotating motion. Suspend the caliper inside the fender housing with wire. Do not allow the caliper to hang from the brake hose.

NOTE: Do not pry directly against the plastic piston or damage will result.

4. Remove the inner and outer brake pads. Inspect the rotor braking surfaces for scoring and machine as necessary. Refer to the mimimum rotor thickness specification when machining. If machining is not necessary, hand sand the glaze from the braking surfaces with medium grit sand paper.

To install:

5. Use a 4 in. C-clamp and a wood block 2¾ in. × 1 in. × ¾ in. thick to seat the caliper piston in it's bore. This must be done to provide clearance for the caliper assembly with the new brake pads to fit over the rotor during installation. Care must be taken during this procedure to prevent damage to the plastic piston. Do not allow metal or sharp objects to come into direct contact with the piston surface or damage will result.

6. Remove all rust buildup from the inside of the caliper legs. Install the inner pad in the caliper piston. Do not bend the pad clips during installation in the piston or distortion and rattles can occur. Install the outer pad. Make sure the clips are properly seated.

7. Install the caliper over the rotor and install the wheel. Lower the vehicle.

8. Pump the brake pedal prior to moving the vehicle to position the brake linings. Refill the master cylinder.

Rear

1. Raise the vehicle and support it safely.
2. Remove the wheel and tire assembly.
3. Remove the screw retaining the brake hose bracket to the shock absorber bracket. Remove the retaining clip from the parking brake cable at the caliper. Remove the cable end from the parking brake lever.
4. Hold the slider pin hex-heads with an open-end wrench. Remove the upper pinch bolt. Rotate the caliper away from the rotor.
5. Remove the brake pads.

To install:

6. Using a suitable brake piston turning tool, rotate the piston clockwise until it is fully seated. Make sure 1 of the 2 slots in the piston face is positioned so it will engage the nib on the brake pad.
7. Install the brake pads in the anchor plate. Rotate the caliper assembly over the rotor into position on the anchor plate. Make sure the brake pads are installed correctly.
8. Remove the residue from the pinch bolt threads and apply 1 drop of threadlock and sealer. Install and tighten the pinch bolts to 23–26 ft. lbs. (31–35 Nm) while holding the slider pins with an open-end wrench.
9. Attach the cable end to the parking brake lever. Install the cable retaining clip on the caliper assembly. Position the brake flex hose and bracket assembly to the shock absorber bracket and install the retaining screw. Tighten the screw to 8–11 ft. lbs. (11–16 Nm).
10. Install the wheel and lower the vehicle.

Brake Rotor

REMOVAL & INSTALLATION

Front

1. Raise the vehicle and support it safely.
2. Remove the wheel and tire assembly.
3. Remove the caliper assembly from the rotor. Position the caliper out of the way and support it with a length of wire. Do not allow the caliper to hang by the brake hose.
4. Remove the rotor from the hub assembly by pulling it off of the hub studs. If additional force is required to remove the rotor, apply rust penetrator on the front and rear rotor/hub mating surfaces and then strike the rotor between the studs with a plastic hammer. If this does not work, attach a 3-jaw puller and remove the rotor.

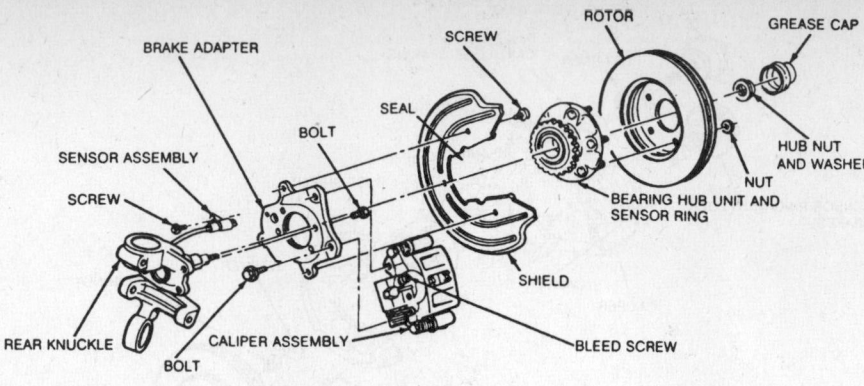

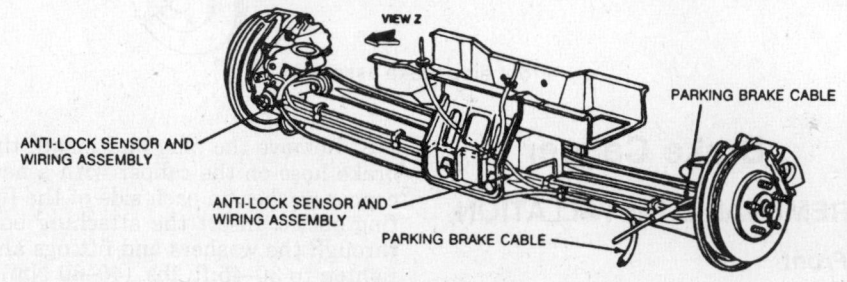

Rear disc brake assembly

NOTE: If excessive force must be used to remove the rotor, it should be checked for lateral run-out before installation.

5. Install in the reverse order of removal.

Rear

1. Raise the vehicle and support it safely.
2. Remove the wheel and tire assembly.
3. Remove the caliper assembly from the rotor and support it with a length of wire. Do not let the caliper hang from the brake line.
4. Remove the 2 rotor retaining nuts and remove the rotor from the hub.
5. Install in the reverse order of removal.

Brake Drums

REMOVAL & INSTALLATION

1. Raise the vehicle and support it safely.
2. Remove the wheel cover.
3. Remove the lugnuts and the wheel.
4. Remove the 2 drum retaining nuts and the drum.
5. Install in the reverse order of removal.

NOTE: If the drum will not come off, pry the rubber plug from the backing plate inspection

hole. Remove the brake line-to-axle retention bracket. This will allow sufficient room to insert suitable brake tools through the inspection hole to disengage the adjusting lever and back off the adjusting screw.

Brake Shoes

REMOVAL & INSTALLATION

1. Raise the vehicle and support it safely.
2. Remove the wheel and tire assembly and the brake drum.
3. Remove the 2 shoe hold-down springs and pins.
4. Lift the brake shoes, springs and adjuster assembly off of the backing plate and wheel cylinder assembly. When removing the assembly, be careful not to bend the adjusting lever.
5. Remove the parking brake cable from the parking brake lever.
6. Remove the retracting springs from the lower brake attachments and upper shoe-to-adjusting lever attachment points. This will seperate the brake shoes and disengage the adjuster mechanism.
7. Remove the horse shoe retaining clip and spring washer and slide the lever off the parking brake lever pin on the trailing shoe.

To install:

8. Apply a light coating of disc brake caliper slide grease at the points where the brake shoes contact the backing plate.

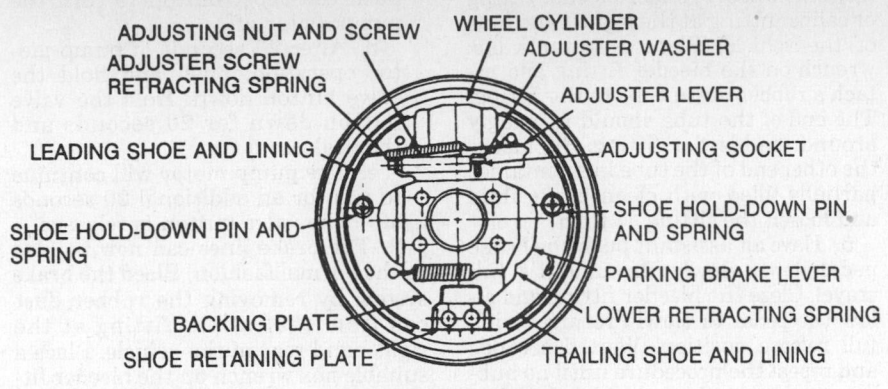

ADJUSTING NUT AND SCREW
ADJUSTER SCREW
RETRACTING SPRING
LEADING SHOE AND LINING
SHOE HOLD-DOWN PIN AND SPRING
BACKING PLATE
SHOE RETAINING PLATE

WHEEL CYLINDER
ADJUSTER WASHER
ADJUSTER LEVER
ADJUSTING SOCKET
SHOE HOLD-DOWN PIN AND SPRING
PARKING BRAKE LEVER
LOWER RETRACTING SPRING
TRAILING SHOE AND LINING

Brake shoe assembly

9. Apply a thin coat of lubricant to the adjuster screw threads and socket end of the adjusting screw. Install the stainless steel washer over the socket end of the adjusting screw and install the socket. Turn the adjusting screw into the adjusting pivot nut to the limit of the threads and then back off ½ turn.

10. Assemble the parking brake lever to the trailing shoe by installing the spring washer and a new horse shoe retaining clip. Crimp the clip until it retains the lever to the shoe securely.

11. Attach the parking brake cable to the parking brake lever.

12. Attach the lower shoe retracting spring to the leading and trailing shoe and install to the backing plate. It will be necessary to stretch the retracting spring as the shoes are installed downward over the anchor plate to the inside of the shoe retaining plate.

13. Assemble the adjuster lever in the groove located in the parking brake lever pin and into the slot of the adjuster socket that fits into the trailing shoe web.

14. Attach the upper retracting spring to the leading shoe slot. Using a suitable spring tool, stretch the other end of the spring into the notch on the adjuster lever. If the adjuster lever does not contact the star wheel after installing the spring, it is possible that the adjuster socket is installed incorrectly.

NOTE: The adjuster socket blade is marked R for the right-hand or L for the left-hand brake assemblies. The R or L adjuster blade must be installed with the letter R or L in the upright position, facing the wheel cylinder, on the correct side to ensure that the deeper of the 2 slots in the adjuster sockets fits into the parking brake lever.

15. Install the brake drum and wheel. Lower the vehicle.

Wheel Cylinder

REMOVAL & INSTALLATION

1. Raise and support the vehicle safely.

2. Remove the wheel and tire assembly.

3. Remove the hub grease cap and the cotter pin and nut retainer.

4. Remove the hub nut, thrust washer, outer bearing and the brake drum assembly.

5. Remove the brake shoes, retainers and springs from the backing plate.

6. Disconnect and plug the brake line at the rear-side of the wheel cylinder.

7. Remove the wheel cylinder-to-backing plate bolts and remove the wheel cylinder.

8. To install, reverse the order of removal. Tighten the wheel cylinder-to-backing plate bolts to 7.5–10 ft.lbs (10–14 Nm). Adjust the rear wheel bearing and bleed the rear brake system.

Parking Brake Cable

ADJUSTMENT

1. Make sure the parking brake is fully released. Place the transaxle in the **N** position.

2. Raise the vehicle and support it safely. Working in front of the left rear wheel, tighten the adjusting nut against the cable equalizer, or against the cable adjuster bracket on Taurus SHO and Continental. Then loosen the adjusting nut until the rear brakes are fully released. There should be no brake drag.

3. If the brake cables were replaced, stroke the parking brake several times, then release control and repeat Step 2.

4. Check for operation of the parking brake with the vehicle supported

and the parking brake fully released. If there is any slack in the cables or if the rear brakes drag when the wheels are turned, adjust as required.

5. Lower the vehicle.

REMOVAL & INSTALLATION

Front Cable

1. Raise the front of the vehicle and support safely.

2. Loosen the adjuster nut at the cable adjuster bracket.

3. Lower the vehicle.

4. Disconnect the cable from the control assembly at the clevis.

5. Raise the vehicle and support safely.

6. At the cable connector, disconnect the front cable from the rear cable.

7. Remove the cable and push-in prong retainer from the cable bracket, using a 13mm box end wrench to depress the retaining prongs. Allow the cable to hang.

8. Push the grommet up through the floor pan and lower the vehicle.

9. Remove the left hand cowl side panel.

10. From inside the vehicle, remove the cable end from the clevis and remove the conduit retainer from the control assembly.

11. Installation is the reverse of the removal procedure. Adjust the parking brake and check the brake for proper operation.

Rear Cable

LEFT SIDE

1. Raise the vehicle and support safely.

2. Remove the parking brake cable adjusting nut.

3. Remove the rear cable end fitting from the front cable connector.

4. Remove the wheel and drum assembly on vehicles equipped with drum brakes.

5. Disconnect the brake cable from the parking brake actuating lever. On drum brake vehicles, use a 13mm box end wrench to depress the conduit retaining prongs and remove the cable end pronged fitting from the backing plate. On disc brake vehicles, remove the E-clip from the conduit end of the fitting at the caliper.

6. Push the plastic snap-in grommet rearward to disconnect it from the side rail bracket.

7. Remove the pronged connector from the parking park adjuster bracket. Remove the cable assembly.

8. Installation is the reverse of the removal procedure. Ensure that the all pronged connectors are locked in place.

RIGHT SIDE

1. Raise the vehicle and support it safely.

2. Remove the parking brake cable adjuster nut.

3. Use a 13mm box wrench to remove the conduit retainer prongs and remove the cable from the frame side rail bracket.

4. Remove the rear wheel and drum assembly on vehicles equipped with drum brakes.

5. Disconnect the brake cable from the parking brake actuating lever. On drum brake vehicles, use a 13mm box end wrench to depress the conduit retaining prongs and remove the cable end pronged fitting from the backing plate. On disc brake vehicles, remove the E-clip from the conduit end of the fitting at the caliper.

6. On Taurus/Sable sedan vehicles, perform the following:

    a. Remove the brake pressure control valve bracket at the control arm.

    b. Remove the cable retaining screw and clip from the lower suspension arm.

    c. Remove one screw from the cable bracket at the crossmember.

    d. Remove the entire right hand cable assembly.

7. On station wagon vehicles, perform the following:

    a. Remove the cable retaining clip and screw from each lower suspension arm.

    b. Remove the cable clip retaining screw from lower suspension arm inner mounting bracket.

8. Installation is the reverse of the removal procedure. Ensure the pronged fitting is securely locked in place.

Brake System Bleeding

Without Anti-lock Brakes

1. Clean all dirt from the master cylinder filler cap.

2. If the master cylinder is known or suspected to have air in the bore, it must be bled before any of the wheel cylinders or calipers. To bleed the master cylinder, loosen the upper secondary left front outlet fitting approximately ¾ turn. Have an assistant depress the brake pedal slowly through it's full travel. Close the outlet fitting and let the pedal return slowly to the fully released position. Wait 5 seconds and then repeat the operation until all air bubbles disappear.

3. Repeat Step 2 with the right-hand front outlet fitting.

4. Continue to bleed the brake system by removing the rubber dust cap from the wheel cylinder bleeder fitting or caliper fitting at the right-hand rear of the vehicle. Place a suitable box wrench on the bleeder fitting and attach a rubber drain tube to the fitting. The end of the tube should fit snugly around the bleeder fitting. Submerge the other end of the tube in a container partially filled with clean brake fluid and loosen the fitting ¾ turn.

5. Have an assistant push the brake pedal down slowly through it's full travel. Close the bleeder fitting and allow the pedal to slowly return to it's full release position. Wait 5 seconds and repeat the procedure until no bubbles appear at the submerged end of the bleeder tube. Secure the bleeder fitting and remove the bleeder tube. Install the rubber dust cap on the bleeder fitting.

6. Repeat the procedure in Steps 4 and 5 in the following sequence: left front, left rear and right front. Refill the master cylinder reservoir after each wheel cylinder or caliper has been bled and install the master cylinder cover and gasket. When brake bleeding is completed, the fluid level should be filled to the maximum level indicated on the reservoir.

7. Always make sure the disc brake pistons are returned to their normal positions by depressing the brake pedal several times until normal pedal travel is established. If the pedal feels spongy, repeat the bleeding procedure.

With Anti-lock Brakes

The anti-lock brake system must be bled in 2 steps.

1. The master cylinder and hydraulic control unit must be bled using the Rotunda Anti-Lock Brake Breakout Box/Bleeding Adapter tool No. T90P-50-ALA or equivalent. If this procedure is not followed, air will be trapped in the hydraulic control unit which will eventually lead to a spongy brake pedal. To bleed the master cylinder and the hydraulic control unit, disconnect the 55-pin plug from the electronic control unit and install the Anti-Lock Brake Breakout Box/Bleeding Adapter to the wire harness 55-pin plug.

    a. Place the Bleed/Harness switch in the **BLEED** position.

    b. Turn the ignition to the **ON** position. At this point the red off light should come ON.

    c. Push the motor button on the adapter down to start the pump motor. The red OFF light will turn OFF and the green ON light will come ON. The pump motor will run for 60 seconds after the motor button is pushed. If the pump motor is to be turned off for any reason before the 60 seconds has elapsed, push the abort button to turn the pump motor off.

    d. After 20 seconds of pump motor operation, push and hold the valve button down. Hold the valve button down for 20 seconds and then release it.

    e. The pump motor will continue to run for an additional 20 seconds after the valve button is released.

2. The brake lines can now be bled in the normal fashion. Bleed the brake system by removing the rubber dust cap from the caliper fitting at the right-hand rear of the vehicle. Place a suitable box wrench on the bleeder fitting and attach a rubber drain tube to the fitting. The end of the tube should fit snugly around the bleeder fitting. Submerge the other end of the tube in a container partially filled with clean brake fluid and loosen the fitting ¾ turn.

3. Have an assistant push the brake pedal down slowly through it's full travel. Close the bleeder fitting and allow the pedal to slowly return to it's full release position. Wait 5 seconds and repeat the procedure until no bubbles appear at the submerged end of the bleeder tube. Secure the bleeder fitting and remove the bleeder tube. Install the rubber dust cap on the bleeder fitting.

4. Repeat the bleeding procedure at the left front, left rear and right front in that order. Refill the master cylinder reservoir after each caliper has been bled and install the master cylinder and gasket. When brake bleeding is completed, the fluid level should be filled to the maximum level indicated on the reservoir.

5. Always make sure the disc brake pistons are returned to their normal positions by depressing the brake pedal several times until normal pedal travel is established. If the pedal feels spongy, repeat the bleeding procedure.

Anti-Lock Brake System Service

PRECAUTION

Failure to observe the following precautions may result in system damage.

• Before servicing any high pressure component, be sure to discharge the hydraulic pressure from the system.

• Do not allow the brake fluid to contact any of the electrical connectors.

• Use care when opening the bleeder screws due to the high pressures available from the accumulator.

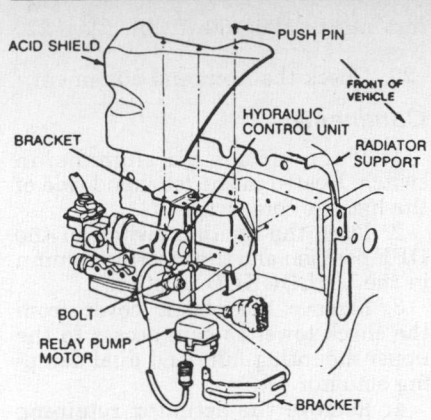

Hydraulic control unit—anti-lock brakes

Relieving Anti-Lock Brake System Pressure

Before servicing any components which contain high pressure, it is mandatory that the hydraulic pressure in the system be discharged. To discharge the system, turn the ignition **OFF** and pump the brake pedal a minimum of 20 times until an increase in pedal force is clearly felt.

Hydraulic Control Unit (HCU)

REMOVAL & INSTALLATION

1. On all vehicles except Taurus SHO, disconnect the battery cables and remove the battery from the vehicle. Remove the battery tray. Remove the 3 plastic push pins holding the acid shield to the HCU mounting bracket and remove the acid shield. On Taurus SHO it is only necessary to disconnect the negative battery cable and remove the electronic control unit and it's mounting bracket from the top of the HCU mounting bracket.

4. Disconnect the 19-pin connector from the HCU to the wiring harness and disconnect the 4-pin connector from the HCU to the pump motor relay.

5. Remove the 2 lines from the inlet ports and the 4 lines from the outlet ports of the HCU. Plug each port to prevent brake fluid from spilling onto the paint and wiring.

6. Remove the 3 nuts retaining the HCU assembly to the mounting bracket and remove the assembly from the vehicle. The nut on the front of the HCU also retains the relay mounting bracket.

7. Install in the reverse order of removal. Tighten the 3 retaining nuts to 12–18 ft. lbs. (16–24 Nm) and the brake lines to 10–18 ft. lbs. (14–24 Nm). Bleed the brake system and check for fluid leaks.

Wheel Sensors

REMOVAL & INSTALLATION

Front

1. Disconnect the sensor connector located in the engine compartment.

2. For the right front sensor, remove the 2 plastic push studs to loosen the front section of the splash shield in the wheel well. For the left front sensor, remove the 2 plastic push studs to loosen the rear section of the splash shield.

3. Thread the sensor wires through the holes in the fender apron. For the right front sensor, remove the 2 retaining clips behind the splash shield.

4. Raise and support the vehicle safely. Remove the wheel.

5. Disengage the sensor wire grommets at the height sensor bracket and from the retainer clip on the shock strut just above the spindle.

6. Loosen the sensor retaining screw and remove the sensor assembly from the front knuckle.

7. Install in the reverse order of removal. Tighten the sensor retaining screws to 40–60 inch lbs. (4.5–6.8 Nm).

Rear

TAURUS AND SABLE

1. Remove the rear seat and seat back insulation.

2. Disconnect the sensor from the harness and tie the sensor connector to the rear seat sheet metal bracket with wire or string.

3. Push the sensor wire grommet and connector through the floorpan drawing the string or wire with the sensor connector.

4. Disconnect the string or wire from the sensor from underneath the vehicle.

5. Disconnect the routing clips from the suspension arms and remove the sensor retaining bolts from the rear brake adapters.

6. Install in the reverse order of removal. Use string or wire to pull the new sensor connector through the hole in the floorpan. Tighten the sensor retaining bolt to 40–60 inch lbs. (4.6–6.8 Nm).

CONTINENTAL

1. Turn the air suspension switch in the luggage compartment to the **OFF** position. Disconnect the sensor connector in the luggage compartment.

2. Push the rubber grommet through the sheet metal floorpan.

3. Raise and safely support the vehicle. Remove the retainer clips for the sensor wire and remove the wire from it's routing position.

4. Loosen the sensor retaining screw at the caliper anchor plate and remove the sensor.

5. Install torsion spring replacement tool T88P-5310-A or equivalent on the front suspension arm. Using a suitable breaker bar, lower the arm to provide clearance for the sensor wire connector to pass through.

6. Installation is the reverse of the removal procedure. Tighten the sensor retaining screw to 40–60 inch lbs. (4.5–6.8 Nm).

Electronic Control Unit (ECU)

REMOVAL & INSTALLATION

Taurus and Sable

The ECU is located on the front right-hand side of the engine compartment next to the washer bottle except on Taurus SHO. On Taurus SHO it is mounted on the left-hand side on top of the HCU mounting bracket.

1. Disconnect the negative battery cable.

2. Disconnect the 55-pin connector from the ECU. Unlock the connector by completely pulling up the lever. Move the top of the connector away from the ECU until all terminals are clear, then pull the connector up out of the slots in the ECU.

3. Remove the screws attaching the ECU and remove the ECU.

4. Install in the reverse order of removal. Connect the 55-pin connector by installing the bottom part of the connector into the slots in the ECU and pushing the top portion of the connector into the ECU. Then pull the locking lever completely down to ensure proper installation. Tighten the retaining screws to 15–20 inch lbs. (1.7–2.3 Nm).

Continental

1. Disconnect the negative battery cable.

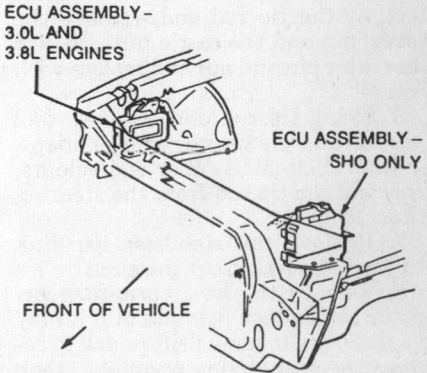

Anti-lock brake system electronic control unit location—Taurus and Sable

2. Remove the trim panel in the luggage compartment (behind the back seat) to gain access to the ECU.

3. Disconnect the 55-pin connector from the ECU. Unlock the connector by completely pulling up the lever. Move the top of the connector away from the ECU until all terminals are clear, then pull the connector up out of the slots in the ECU.

4. Remove the 3 screws attaching the ECU to the panel and remove the ECU.

5. Install in the reverse order of removal. Connect the 55-pin connector by installing the bottom part of the connector into the slots in the ECU and pushing the top portion of the connector into the ECU. Then pull the locking lever completely down to ensure proper installation. Tighten the retaining screws to 15–20 inch lbs. (1.7–2.3 Nm).

FRONT SUSPENSION

MacPherson Strut

REMOVAL & INSTALLATION

Taurus and Sable

1. Place the ignition switch in the **OFF** position and the steering column in the **UNLOCKED** position.

2. Remove the hub nut. Loosen the 3 top mount-to-shock tower nuts; do not remove the nuts at this time.

3. Raise and support the front of the vehicle safely.

NOTE: When raising the vehicle, do not lift by using the lower control arms.

4. Remove the tire and wheel assembly. Remove the brake caliper, supporting it on a wire, and the rotor.

5. At the tie rod end, remove the cotter pin and the castle nut. Discard the cotter pin and nut and replace with new.

6. Using tie rod end remover tool 3290–D and the tie rod remover adapter tool T81P-3504-W or equivalents, separate the tie rod from the steering knuckle.

7. Remove the stabilizer bar link nut and the link from the strut.

8. Remove the lower arm-to-steering knuckle pinch bolt and nut; it may be necessary to use a drift punch to remove the bolt. Using a suitable tool, spread the knuckle-to-lower arm pinch joint and remove the lower arm from

the steering knuckle. Discard the pinch nut/bolt and replace with new.

9. Remove the halfshaft from the hub and support it on a wire.

NOTE: When removing the halfshaft, do not allow it to move outward as the internal parts of the tripod CV-joint could separate, causing failure of the joint.

10. Remove the strut-to-steering knuckle pinch bolt. Using a small pry bar, spread the pinch bolt joint and separate the strut from the steering knuckle. Remove the steering knuckle/hub assembly from the strut tower.

11. Remove the 3 top mount-to-shock tower nuts and the strut assembly from the vehicle.

To install:

12. Install the strut assembly and the 3 top mount-to-shock tower nuts.

13. Install the steering knuckle and hub assembly to the strut.

14. Install a new strut-to-steering knuckle pinch bolt. Tighten the bolt to 70–95 ft. lbs. (95–129 Nm).

15. Install the halfshaft into the hub.

16. Install the lower arm to the steering knuckle and install a new pinch bolt and nut. Tighten to 40–55 ft. lbs. (54–74 Nm).

17. Install the stabilizer link to the strut and install a new stabilizer bar link nut. Tighten to 55–75 ft. lbs. (75–101 Nm).

18. Install the tie rod end onto the knuckle using a new castle nut. Tighten the castle nut to 23–35 ft. lbs. (31–47 Nm). Retain the castle nut with a new cotter pin.

19. Install the disc brake rotor, caliper and tire and wheel assembly.

20. Tighten the 3 top mount-to-shock tower nuts to 22–32 ft. lbs. (30–43 Nm).

21. Lower the vehicle and tighten the

hub nut to 180–200 ft. lbs. (244–271 Nm).

22. Check the front end alignment.

Continental

1. Turn off the air suspension switch, located in the left-hand side of the luggage compartment.

2. Place the ignition switch in the **OFF** position and the steering column in the **UNLOCKED** position.

3. Remove the plastic cover from the shock tower to gain access to the upper mounting nuts and dual damping actuator.

4. Remove the actuator retaining screws. Remove the actuator and place it aside.

5. Remove the hub nut.

6. Loosen the 3 top mount-to-shock tower nuts but do not remove them at this time.

7. Raise the front of the vehicle and support it safely.

NOTE: Do not raise the vehicle by the lower control arms.

8. Remove the tire and wheel assembly.

9. Remove the brake line bracket from the strut assembly.

10. Disconnect the height sensor link from the ball stud pin at the lower control arm.

11. Disconnect the air line from the solenoid valve.

12. Disconnect the electrical connector at the solenoid valve.

13. Remove the brake caliper and the disc brake rotor. Support the caliper with wire.

14. Remove the cotter pin and castle nut from the tie rod end. Discard the cotter pin and castle nut.

15. Using tie rod end remover TOOL-3290-D and tie rod end remover adapter T81P-3504-W or equiva-

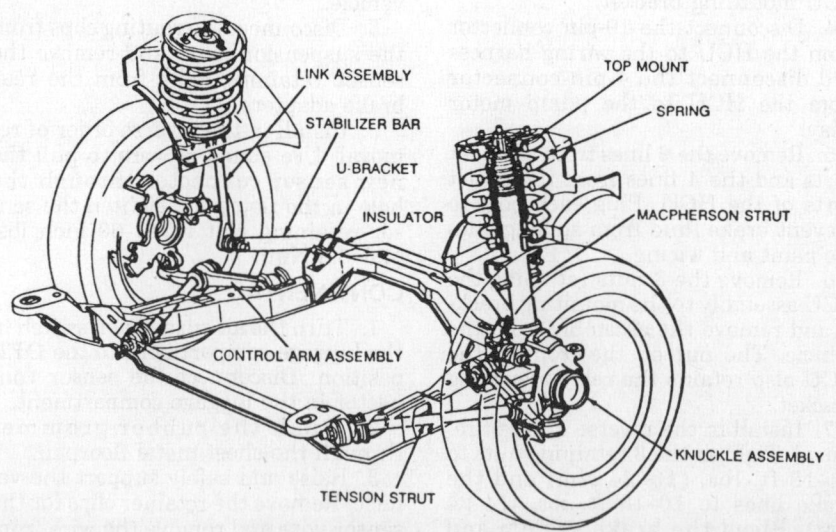

Front suspension—Taurus and Sable

LINK ASSEMBLY
STABILIZER BAR
U-BRACKET
INSULATOR
CONTROL ARM ASSEMBLY
TENSION STRUT
TOP MOUNT
SPRING
MACPHERSON STRUT
KNUCKLE ASSEMBLY

lent, remove the tie rod from the knuckle.

16. Remove the stabilizer bar link nut and the link from the strut.

17. Remove and discard the lower arm-to-steering knuckle pinch bolt and nut. A suitable drift punch may be used to remove the bolt. Using a suitable tool, slightly spread the knuckle-to-lower arm pinch joint and remove the lower arm from the steering knuckle.

18. Remove the halfshaft from the hub.

NOTE: When removing the halfshaft, do not allow the halfshaft to move outward. This could result in seperation of the internal parts of the tripod CV-joint, causing failure of the joint.

19. Remove the strut-to-steering knuckle pinch bolt. Using a suitable prying tool, slightly spread the knuckle-to-strut pinch joint to remove the strut from the steering knuckle.

20. Remove the 3 top mount-to-shock tower nuts and the strut from the vehicle.

To install:

21. Install the strut with the 3 top mount-to-shock tower nuts and leave the nuts loose.

22. Install the steering knuckle and hub assembly to the strut. Install a new strut-to-steering knuckle pinch bolt. Tighten the bolt to 70–95 ft. lbs. (95–129 Nm).

23. Install the halfshaft into the hub.

24. Install the lower arm to the steering knuckle and install a new pinch bolt and nut. Tighten to 55–75 ft. lbs. (75–101 Nm).

25. Install the tie rod end onto the knuckle using a new castle nut. Before tightening the nut, make sure the steering wheel and wheels are in the straight-ahead position. Tighten the castle nut to 23–35 ft. lbs. (31–47 Nm). Install a new cotter pin in the castle nut.

26. Install the brake caliper and rotor.

27. Connect the electrical connector and the air line to the solenoid valve and position them properly.

28. Install the height sensor link on the ball stud pin on the control arm.

29. Install the brake line bracket to the strut assembly.

30. Install the wheel and tire assembly.

31. Tighten the 3 top mount-to-shock tower nuts to 22–32 ft. lbs. (30–43 Nm).

32. Install the dual damping actuator and the plastic shock tower cover. Correctly position the actuator wiring.

33. Refill the air spring prior to fully lowering the vehicle. The refill procedure is as follows:

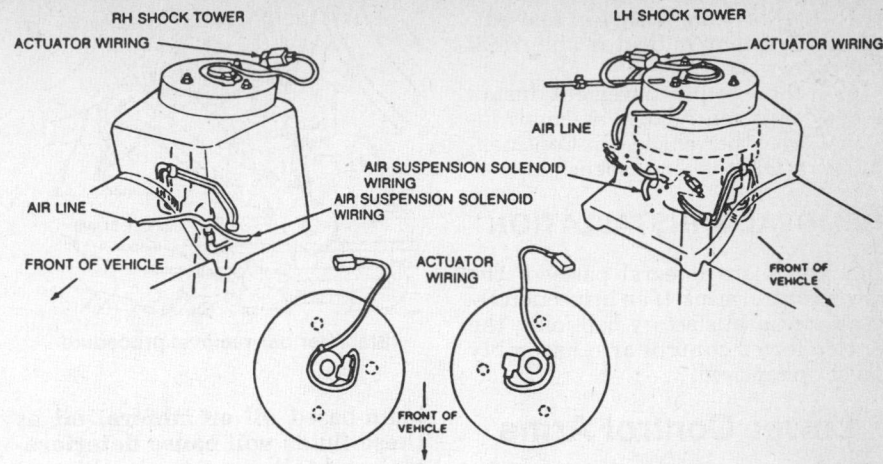

Air line and actuator wiring positioning—Continental

a. Place the air suspension service switch in the **ON** position.

b. Turn the ignition switch **OFF**.

c. Connect a battery charger to reduce battery drain.

d. Open the access door in the left-hand luggage compartment trim panel to plug the super star II tester or equivalent into the air suspension diagnostics wiring harness connector.

e. The tester button should be in the **HOLD** (up) position.

f. With the brake pedal depressed hard, turn the ignition switch to the **RUN** position.

g. Move the tester button to the **TEST** (down) position.

h. The air suspension control module will now start sending out the spring fill selection codes to be displayed on the tester. These codes will be displayed in a scrolling manner.

i. Select the desired spring fill operation by releasing the tester button when the desired code is displayed. Select either Code 24 or Code 25 to inflate either the right front or left front air spring. As long as the tester button is released the inflation will continue. To stop inflation, move the tester button back

down to the **TEST** position. The spring fill codes will again be displayed.

NOTE: Do not apply a load to the suspension until after the air spring has been inflated at least 60 seconds.

j. To exit the spring fill mode, turn the ignition switch to the **OFF** position and unplug the tester.

34. Lower the vehicle and tighten the hub nut to 180–200 lbs. (244–271 Nm).

35. Turn on the air suspension.

36. Check the front end alignment.

Lower Ball Joints

INSPECTION

1. Turn **OFF** the air suspension switch, located in the left-hand side of the luggage compartment on Continental.

2. Raise the vehicle and safely support it so the wheels fall to the full-down position.

3. Have an assistant grasp the lower edge of the tire and move the wheel and tire assembly in and out.

4. Observe the lower end of the knuckle and the lower control arm as

Code	Description
21	Vent R.F.
22	Vent L.F.
23	Vent R.R.
24	Inflate R.F.
25	Inflate L.F.
26	Inflate R.R.
27	Vent L.R.
28	Inflate L.R.

Air suspension spring fill codes.

the wheel is being moved in and out. Any movement indicates abnormal ball joint wear.

5. If there is any movement, install a new lower control arm assembly.

6. Lower the vehicle. On Continental, turn **ON** the air suspension.

REMOVAL & INSTALLATION

Ball joints are integral parts of the lower control arms. If an inspection reveals an unsatisfactory ball joint, the entire lower control arm assembly must be replaced.

Lower Control Arms

REMOVAL & INSTALLATION

1. Turn **OFF** the air suspension switch, located in the left-hand side of the luggage compartment on Continental.

2. Raise and support the front of the vehicle safely. Remove the wheel and tire assembly. Position the steering column in the unlocked position.

3. Disconnect the height sensor link from the ball stud pin on Continental.

4. Remove the tension strut-to-control arm nut and the dished washer.

5. Remove and discard the control arm-to-steering knuckle pinch bolt. Using a small pry bar, spread the pinch joint and separate the control arm from the steering knuckle.

NOTE: When separating the control arm from the steering knuckle, do not use a hammer. Be careful not to damage the bolt seal.

6. Remove the control arm-to-frame nut/bolt, then the control arm from the frame and the tension strut.

NOTE: Do not allow the halfshaft to move outward or the tripod CV-joint internal parts could separate, causing failure of the joint.

7. To install, use a new pinch nut/bolt and reverse the removal procedures. Tighten the bolts to the following torque specifications:

Control arm-to-frame 70–95 ft. lbs. (95–129 Nm)

Control arm-to-steering knuckle 40–55 ft. lbs. (54–74 Nm)

Tension strut-to-control arm 70–95 ft. lbs. (95–129 Nm)

Wheel lug nuts 80–105 ft. lbs. (109–142 Nm)

8. Check the front end alignment.

NOTE: When installing a new control arm, be sure to saturate the new bushing with vegetable oil; do not use brake fluid, petro-

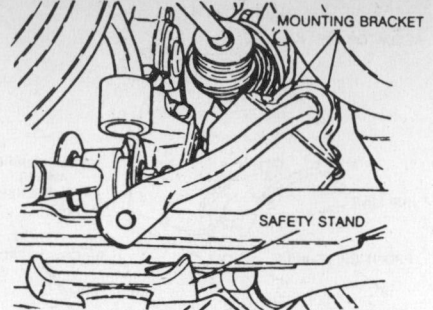

Stabilizer bar removal procedure

leum-based oil or mineral oil as these fluids will cause deterioration and failure of the bushing.

Stabilizer Bar

REMOVAL & INSTALLATION

1. Raise and support the front of the vehicle on jackstands behind the subframe.

NOTE: Do not raise or support the vehicle on the front control arms.

2. Remove and discard the stabilizer bar link-to-stabilizer bar nut, the stabilizer bar link-to-strut nut and the link from the vehicle.

3. Remove the steering gear-to-subframe nuts and the gear from the sub-frame.

4. Position another set of jackstands under the subframe and remove the rear subframe-to-frame bolts. Lower the subframe rear to gain access to the stabilizer bar brackets.

5. Remove the stabilizer bar U-bracket bolts and the stabilizer bar from the vehicle.

NOTE: When removing the stabilizer bar, replace the insulators and the U-bracket bolts with new ones.

To install:

6. To install, reverse the removal procedure. Tighten the bolts to the folowing torque specifications:

U-bracket-to-subframe 21–32 ft. lbs. (28–43 Nm)

Subframe-to-steering gear 85–100 ft. lbs. (115–135 Nm)

Stabilizer bar-to-stabilizer bar link 35–48 ft. lbs. (47–65 Nm)

Stabilizer bar-to-strut 55–75 ft. lbs. (75–101 Nm)

7. Coat the inside diameter of the new insulators with No. E25Y-19553–A or equivalent lubricant. Do not use any mineral or petroleum base lubricants as they will cause deterioration of the rubber insulators.

REAR SUSPENSION

Shock Absorbers

REMOVAL & INSTALLATION

Taurus and Sable Wagon

1. Raise and support the vehicle safely.

2. Remove the wheel and tire assembly.

3. Position a jack stand under the lower suspension arm. Remove the 2 nuts retaining the shock absorber to the lower suspension arm.

4. From inside the vehicle, remove the rear compartment access panels.

5. Remove and discard the top shock absorber attaching nut using a suitable crow's foot wrench and ratchet while holding the shock absorber shaft stationary with an open end wrench.

NOTE: If the shock absorber is to be reused, do not grip the shaft with pliers or vise grips. Gripping the shaft in this manner will damage the shaft surface finish that will result in severe oil leakage.

6. Remove the rubber insulator from the shock and the shock from the vehicle.

NOTE: The shocks are gas filled. It will require an effort to remove the shock from the lower arm.

To install

7. Install a new washer and insulator on the upper shock absorber rod.

8. Maneuver the upper part of the shock absorber into the shock tower opening in the body. Push slowly on the lower part of the shock absorber until the mounting studs are aligned with the mounting holes in the lower suspension arm.

9. Install new lower attaching nuts but do not tighten at this time.

10. Install a new insulator, washer and nut on top of the shock absorber. Torque the nut to 19–27 ft. lbs. (26–37 Nm.).

11. Install the rear compartment access panel.

12. Torque the 2 lower attaching nuts to 13–20 ft. lbs. (17–27 Nm).

13. Install the wheel and tire assembly. Remove the safety stand supporting the lower suspension arm and lower the vehicle.

MacPherson Strut

REMOVAL & INSTALLATION

Taurus and Sable Sedan

1. Raise and support the rear of the vehicle safely. Remove the wheel and tire.

NOTE: Do not raise or support the vehicle using the tension struts.

2. Raise the luggage compartment lid and loosen but do not remove, the upper strut-to-body nuts.

3. Remove the brake differential control valve-to-control arm bolt. Using a wire, secure the control arm to the body to ensure proper support leaving at least 6 in. clearance to aid in the strut removal.

4. Remove the brake hose-to-strut bracket clip and move the hose out of the way.

5. If equipped, remove the stabilizer bar U-bracket from the vehicle.

6. If equipped, remove the stabilizer bar-to-stabilizer link nut, washer and insulator, then separate the stabilizer bar from the link.

NOTE: When removing the strut, be sure the rear brake flex hose is not stretched or the steel brake tube is not bent.

7. Remove the tension strut-to-spindle nut, washer and insulator. Move the spindle rearward to separate it from the tension strut.

8. Remove the shock strut-to-spindle pinch bolt. If necessary, use a medium pry bar, spread the strut-to-spindle pinch joint to remove the strut. Discard the bolt and replace it.

9. Lower the jackstand and separate the shock strut from the spindle.

10. Support the shock strut, then loosen the top strut-to-body nuts completely and remove the strut from the vehicle.

To install:

11. Position the stabilizer bar link in the strut bracket. Install the insulator, washer and nut and tighten to 5–7 ft. lbs. (7–9.5 Nm).

12. Insert the 3 upper mount studs into the strut tower in the apron and hand start 3 new nuts. Do not tighten the nuts at this time.

13. Partially raise the vehicle.

14. Install the strut into the spindle pinch joint. Install a new pinch bolt into the spindle and through the strut bracket. Tighten the bolt to 50–70 ft. lbs. (68–95 Nm).

15. Move the spindle rearward and install the tension strut into the spindle. Install the insulator, washer and nut on the tension strut. Tighten the nut to 35–50 ft. lbs. (48–68 Nm).

16. Position the link into the stabilizer bar. Install the insulator, washer and nut on the link. Tighten to 5–7 ft. lbs. (7–9.5 Nm).

17. Position the stabilizer bar U-bracket on the body. Install the bolt and tighten to 25–37 ft. lbs. (34–50 Nm).

18. Install the brake hose to the strut bracket.

19. Install the brake control differential valve on the control arm and remove the retaining wire.

20. Install the top mount-to-body nuts and tighten to 19–26 ft. lbs. (26–35 Nm).

21. Install the wheel and tire assembly and lower the vehicle.

Continental

1. Turn off the air suspension switch located in the luggage compartment.

2. From inside the luggage compartment, disconnect the electrical connector from the dual dampening actuator.

3. Loosen but do not remove the 3 nuts retaining the strut to the upper body.

4. Raise and support the vehicle safely. Remove the wheel and tire assembly.

NOTE: Do not raise the vehicle by the tension strut.

5. Disconect the air line and electrical connector from the solenoid valve.

6. Remove the brake hose retainer at the strut bracket.

7. Disconnect the parking brake cable from the brake caliper. Remove all the wire retainers and parking brake cable retainers from the lower suspension arm.

8. Disconnect the height sensor link from the ball stud pin on the lower arm.

9. Remove the caliper assembly from the spindle and position it off to the side with a piece of wire. Do not kink or place a load on the brake hose.

10. Bleed the air spring by performing the following:
    a. Remove the solenoid clip.
    b. Rotate the solenoid counterclockwise to the first stop.
    c. Slowly pull the solenoid straight out to the second stop and bleed the air from the system.

——————— CAUTION ———————

Do not fully release the solenoid until the air is fully bled from the spring.

———————————————————————

    d. After the air is fully bled from the system, rotate the solenoid to the third stop and remove the solenoid from the housing.

11. Mark the position of the notch on the toe adjustment cam.

12. Remove the torsion spring clamp from the spindle-to-strut bolt.

13. Remove the nut from the inboard bushing on the suspension arm.

14. Install torsion spring remover tool T88P-5310-A or equivalent on the suspension arm. Pry up on the tool and arm using a ¾ in. drive ratchet to relieve the pressure on the pivot bolt. An assistant may be required to pull outboard on the spindle simultaneously to fully relieve the tension on the bolt. Remove the bolt and lower arm. Repeat this procedure for the opposite arm.

15. Remove the torsion spring from the arms.

16. Remove the stabilizer U-bracket from the body.

17. Remove the nut, washer and insulator attaching the stabilizer bar to the link. Separate the stabilizer bar from the link.

18. Remove the nut washer and insulator retaining the tension strut to the spindle. Move the spindle rearward enough to separate it from the tension strut.

19. Remove and discard the shock strut-to-spindle pinch bolt. With a suitable prying tool, spread the strut-to-spindle pinch joint as required to assist in removing the bolt.

20. Separate the spindle from the strut. Remove the spindle as an assembly with the arms attached.

21. From inside the luggage compartment area, support the shock strut by hand and remove and discard the 3 upper mount-to-body nuts. Care should be taken not to drop the shock strut when removing the upper nuts. Guide the electric actuator wire through the opening to prevent snagging and damage while removing the strut assembly.

To install:

22. Install the solenoid valve on the air spring.

23. Guide the electric actuator wire through the opening and install the strut assembly. Install 3 new upper mount nuts.

24. Install the spindle and arms to the strut. Install a new strut-to-spindle pinch bolt. Do not tighten the bolt until the control arms are attached to the body and the cams are centered.

25. Position the tension strut to the spindle. Install the insulator, washer and nut retaining the tension strut to the spindle. Tighten the nut to 35–50 ft. lbs. (48–68 Nm).

26. Install the stabilizer bar to the link. Install the insulator, washer and retaining nut. Tighten the nut to 5–7 ft. lbs. (7–9.5 Nm).

27. Install the stabilizer U-bracket to the body. Tighten the bolt to 25–37 ft. lbs. (34–50 Nm).

28. Install the torsion spring to the arms.

29. Position the inboard bushing using torsion spring remover T88P-5310-A or equivalent and install the bolt. An assistant may be required to pull outboard on the spindle to align the bushing so the bolt can be inserted. Repeat the procedure for the opposite lower arm.

30. Install the nut to the inboard bushing on the suspension arm but do not tighten at this time.

31. Tighten the spindle-to-strut bolt to 51–70 ft. lbs. (68–95 Nm).

32. Set the toe adjustment cam to the alignment mark.

33. Remove the wire from the caliper and install the caliper to the spindle.

34. Connect the height sensor link to the ball stud pin on the lower arm.

35. Install the torsion spring clamp and secure.

36. Install all wire retainers and parking brake cable retainers to the lower suspension arm.

37. Connect the parking brake cable to the brake caliper and install the brake hose retainer at the strut bracket.

38. Connect the air line and the electrical connector to the solenoid valve.

39. Install the wheel and tire assembly and partially lower the vehicle.

40. Tighten the 3 nuts retaining the strut to the upper body to 19–26 ft. lbs. (26–35 Nm).

41. From inside the luggage compartment, connect the electrical connector for the dual dampening actuator.

42. Turn on the air suspension switch and fill the air spring as follows:

    a. Place the air suspension service switch in the **ON** position.

    b. Turn the ignition switch **OFF**.

    c. Connect a battery charger to reduce battery drain.

    d. Open the access door in the left-hand luggage compartment trim panel to plug the super star II tester or equivalent into the air suspension diagnostics wiring harness connector.

    e. The tester button should be in the **HOLD** (up) position.

    f. With the brake pedal depressed hard, turn the ignition switch to the **RUN** position.

    g. Move the tester button to the **TEST** (down) position.

    h. The air suspension control module will now start sending out the spring fill selection codes to be displayed on the tester. These codes will be displayed in a scrolling manner.

    i. Select the desired spring fill operation by releasing the tester but-

Code	Description
21	Vent R.F.
22	Vent L.F.
23	Vent R.R.
24	Inflate R.F.
25	Inflate L.F.
26	Inflate R.R.
27	Vent L.R.
28	Inflate L.R.

Air suspension spring fill codes

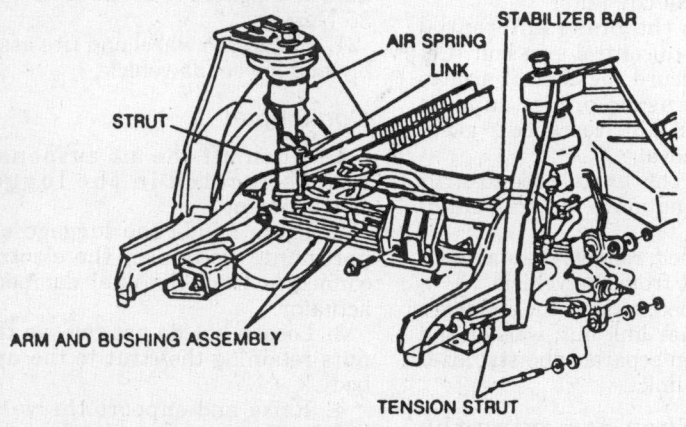

Rear suspension—Continental

ton when the desired code is displayed. Select either Code 26 or Code 28 to inflate either the right rear or left rear air spring. As long as the tester button is released the inflation will continue. To stop inflation, move the tester button back down to the **TEST** position. The spring fill codes will again be displayed.

NOTE: Do not apply a load to the suspension until after the air spring has been inflated at least 60 seconds.

    j. To exit the spring fill mode, turn the ignition switch to the **OFF** position and unplug the tester.

43. Lower the vehicle all of the way. Check the toe setting and adjust if necessary.

44. Tighten the inboard bushing nut to 45–65 ft. lbs. (61–88 Nm).

Coil Springs

REMOVAL & INSTALLATION

Taurus and Sable Wagon

1. Raise the rear of the vehicle and support safely on the pads of the underbody forward of the tension strut bracket. Position a floor jack under the lower suspension arm and raise the lower arm to normal curb height.

2. Remove the wheel and tire assembly.

3. Locate the bracket retaining the flexible hose to the body. Remove the bracket retaining bolt and bracket from the body.

4. Remove the stabilizer bar U-bracket from the lower suspension arm.

5. Remove and discard the nuts attaching the shock absorber to the lower suspension arm.

6. Disconnect and remove the parking brake cable and clip from the lower suspension arm.

7. Remove and discard the bolt and nut attaching the tension strut to the lower suspension arm.

8. Suspend the spindle and upper suspension arms from the body with a piece of wire to prevent them from dropping.

9. Remove the nut, bolt, washer and adjusting cam that retain the lower suspension arm to the spindle. Discard the nut, bolt and washer and replace with new. Set the cam aside.

10. With the floor jack, slowly lower the suspension arm until the spring, lower and upper insulators can be removed. Replace the spring and insulators as required.

To install:

11. Position the lower insulator on the lower suspension arm and press the insulator downward into place. Make certain that the insulator is properly seated.

12. Position the upper insulator on top of the spring. Install the spring on the lower suspension arm. Make certain that the spring is properly seated.

13. With the floor jack, slowly raise the suspension arm. Guide the upper spring insultor onto the upper spring underbody seat.

14. Position the spindle in the lower suspension arm with a new bolt, nut washer, and the existing cam. Install the bolt with the head of the bolt toward the front of the vehicle. Do not tighten the bolt at this time.

15. Remove the wire supporting the spindle and suspension arms.

16. Install the tension strut in the lower suspension arm using a new nut and bolt. DO NOT tighten at this time.

17. Attach the parking brake cable and clip to the lower suspension arm.

18. Position the shock absorber on the lower suspension arm and install 2 new nuts. Torque the nuts to 13–20 ft. lbs. (17–27 Nm).

19. Attach the stabilizer U-bracket to the lower suspension arm using a new bolt. Torque the bolt to 20–30 ft. lbs. (27–40 Nm).

20. Attach the flexible brake hose to the body and tighten the bolt to 8–12 ft. lbs. (11–16 Nm).

21. With the floor jack, raise the lower suspension to normal curb height. Torque the lower suspension arm to 40–55 ft. lbs. (54–74 Nm). Torque the bolt that attaches the tension strut to the body bracket to 40–55 ft. lbs. (54–74 Nm).

22. Install the wheel and tire assembly. Remove the floor jack and lower the vehicle.

23. Check the rear wheel alignment and adjust if necessary.

Rear Control Arms

REMOVAL & INSTALLATION

Taurus and Sable Sedan

1. Raise the vehicle and support it safely. Do not raise the vehicle by the tension strut.

2. Disconnect the brake proportioning valve from the left side front arm.

3. Disconnect the parking brake cable from the front arms.

4. Remove and discard the arm-to-spindle bolt, washer and nut.

5. Remove and discard the arm-to-body bolt and nut.

6. Remove the arm from the vehicle.

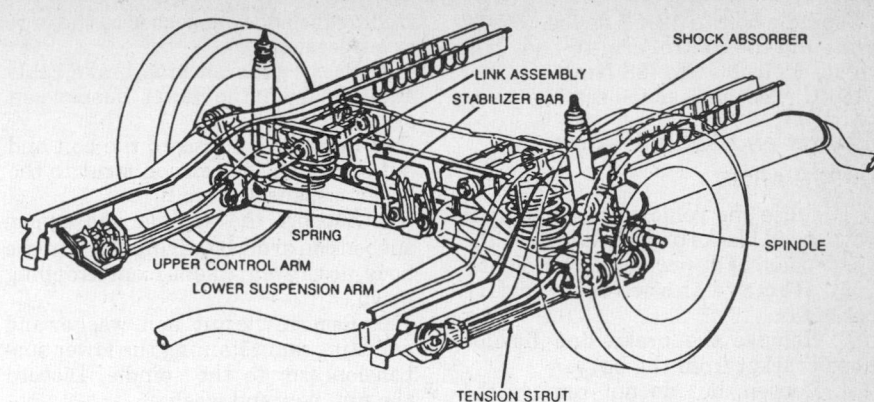

Rear suspension—Taurus and Sable wagon

To install:

NOTE: When installing new control arms, the offset on all arms must face up. The arms are stamped "bottom" on the lower edge. The flange edge of the right side rear arm stamping must face the front of the vehicle. The other 3 must face the rear of the vehicle. The rear control arms have 2 adjustment cams that fit inside the bushings at the arm-to-body attachment. The cam is installed from the rear on the left arm and from the front on the right arm.

7. Position the arm and cam where required, at the center of the vehicle. Insert a new bolt and nut but do not tighten at this time.

8. Move the arm end up to the spindle and insert a new bolt, washer and nut. Tighten the nut to 42–57 ft. lbs. (57–77 Nm).

9. Tighten the arm-to-body nut to 45–65 ft. lbs. (61–88 Nm).

10. Attach the parking brake cable to the front arms and the brake proportioning valve to the left side front arm.

11. Lower the vehicle and check the alignment.

Continental

1. Turn **OFF** the air suspension switch located in the luggage compartment.

2. Raise and support the vehicle safely.

3. Remove all wire retainers and parking brake cable retainers from the lower suspension arm.

4. Disconnect the height sensor link from the ball stud pin on the lower arm.

5. Mark the position of the notch on the toe adjustment cam.

6. Remove the torsion spring retaining clamp at the spindle.

7. Remove the nut from the inboard bushing on the suspension arm.

8. Install torsion spring remover T88P-5310-A or equivalent on the arm. Using a ¾ in. ratchet, pry up on the tool and arm to relieve the pressure on the pivot bolt. An assistant may also be required to pull outward on the spindle at the same time to fully relieve the tension on the bolt. Remove the bolt and lower the arm.

9. Remove the nut retaining the torsion spring to the arm and seperate the spring from the arm.

10. Remove the outboard attaching bolt at the spindle.

11. Repeat the removal procedure for the other arm.

To install:

NOTE: When installing new control arms, the offset must face up. The arms are stamped "bottom" on the lower edge. The rear control arms have adjustment cams that fit inside the bushings at the arm-to-body attachment. The cams are installed from the front of both arms.

12. Loosely attach the arm(s) at the spindle. Attach the torsion spring(s) to the arm(s).

13. Position the inboard bushing using torsion spring remover T88P-5310-A or equivalent and install the bolt. It may be required to have an assistant pull outward on the spindle to align the bushing so the bolt can be inserted. Repeat this step for the opposite side.

14. Set the toe adjustment cam to the alignment mark (rear arm only).

15. Connect the height sensor link to the ball stud pin on the lower arm (right-hand front only).

16. Install all wire retainers and parking brake cable retainers to the lower suspension arm.

17. Lower the vehicle and then turn **ON** the air suspension switch.

18. With the vehicle suspension at curb height, tighten the control arm-

to-spindle bolt to 42–57 ft. lbs. (57–77 Nm) and the control arm-to-body bolt to 45–65 ft. lbs. (61–88 Nm).

19. Check the rear toe setting.

Taurus and Sable Wagon

UPPER ARMS

1. Raise the vehicle and support it with wood blocks on jack stands so the suspension is at normal curb height.

2. Remove the wheel and tire assembly.

3. Remove the brake line flexible hose bracket from the body.

4. Loosen, but do not remove the nuts attaching the spindle to the upper and lower suspension arms.

5. Remove and discard the nuts and bolts attaching the front and rear upper suspension arms to the body brackets. Make sure the spindle does not fall outward.

6. Tilt the top of the spindle outward, letting it pivot on the lower suspension arm attaching bolt until the ends of the upper suspension arms are clear of the body bracket. Support the spindle with wire in this position.

7. Remove and discard the nut attaching the upper suspension arms to the spindle and remove the arms from the vehicle.

To install:

8. Install the upper suspension arms on the spindle and install a new nut, but do not tighten the nut at this time.

9. Position the upper suspension arm ends to the body bracket and install new nuts and bolts. Tighten to 70–95 ft. lbs. (95–129 Nm). Remove the wire from the spindle.

10. Tighten the nut attaching the upper suspension arms to the spindle to 150–190 ft. lbs. (204–257 Nm). Tighten the nut attaching the lower suspension arm to the spindle to 40–55 ft. lbs. (54–74 Nm).

11. Install the brake line bracket to the body.

12. Install the wheel and tire assembly, remove the jackstand and wood block and lower the vehicle.

13. Check the rear wheel alignment.

LOWER ARM

1. Raise and support the vehicle safely on the lifting pads on the underbody forward of the tension strut body bracket.

2. Remove the wheel and tire assembly.

3. Place a floor jack under the lower suspension arm.

4. Remove the bracket retaining the flexible brake hose to the body.

5. Remove the stabilizer bar U-bracket from the lower suspension arm.

6. Remove and discard the nuts at-taching the shock absorber to the lower suspension arm.

7. Remove the parking brake cable and clip from the lower suspension arm.

8. Remove and discard the bolt and nut attaching the tension strut to the lower suspension arm.

9. Support the spindle and upper suspension arms by wiring them to the body, to prevent them from dropping down.

10. Remove the nut, bolt, washer and adjusting cam retaining the lower suspension arm to the spindle. Discard the nut, bolt and washer.

11. Lower the suspension arm with the floor jack until the spring can be removed.

12. Remove and discard the bolt and nut attaching the lower suspension arm to the center body bracket and remove the arm.

To install:

13. Position the lower suspension arm-to-center body bracket and install, but do not tighten, a new bolt and nut with the bolt head toward the front of the vehicle.

14. Position the lower insulator on the lower suspension arm and press the insulator downward into place. Make sure the insulator is properly seated.

15. Position the upper insulator on top of the spring. Install the spring on the lower suspension arm, making sure the spring is properly seated.

16. Raise the suspension arm with the floor jack and guide the upper spring insulator onto the upper spring seat on the underbody.

17. Position the spindle in the lower suspension arm and install, but do not tighten, a new bolt, nut, washer and the existing cam, with the bolt head toward the front of the vehicle.

18. Remove the wire from the spindle and suspension arms.

19. Install the tension strut in the lower suspension arm using a new bolt and nut, but do not tighten at this time.

20. Install the parking brake cable and clip to the lower suspension arm.

21. Position the shock absorber on the lower suspension arm and install 2 new nuts. Tighten the nuts to 13–20 ft. lbs. (17–27 Nm).

22. Install the stabilizer bar and U-bracket to the lower suspension arm using a new bolt. Tighten the bolt to 20–30 ft. lbs. (27–40 Nm).

23. Install the flexible brake hose bracket to the body. Tighten the bolt to 8–12 ft. lbs. (11–16 Nm).

24. Using the floor jack, raise the lower suspension arm to normal curb height. Tighten the following to 40–55 ft. lbs. (54–74 Nm):

Lower suspension arm-to-body bracket nut

Lower suspension arm-to-spindle nut

Tension strut-to-body bracket bolt

25. Install the wheel and tire assembly and lower the vehicle.

26. Check the rear wheel alignment.

Rear Wheel Bearings

REMOVAL & INSTALLATION

Drum Brakes

1987–89

1. Raise the vehicle and support it safely. Remove the wheel from the hub and drum.

2. Remove the grease cap from the hub. Remove the cotter pin, nut retainer, adjusting nut and keyed flat washer from the spindle. Discard the cotter pin.

3. Pull the hub and drum assembly off of the spindle. Remove the outer bearing assembly.

4. Using seal remover tool 1175-AC or equivalent, remove and discard the grease seal. Remove the inner bearing assembly from the hub.

5. Wipe all lubricant from the spindle and inside of the hub. Cover the spindle with a clean cloth and vacuum all loose dust and dirt from the brake assembly. Carefully remove the cloth to prevent dirt from falling on the spindle.

6. Clean both bearing assemblies and cups using a suitable solvent. Inspect the bearing assemblies and cups for excessive wear, scratches, pits or other damage and replace as necessary.

7. If the cups are to be replaced, remove them with impact slide hammer T50T-100-A and bearing cup puller T77F-1102-A or equivalent.

To install:

8. If the inner and outer bearing cups were removed, install the replacement cups using driver handle T80T-4000-W and bearing cup replacers T73T-1217-A and T77F-1217-A or equivalent. Support the drum hub on a block of wood to prevent damage. Make sure the cups are properly seated in the hub.

NOTE: Do not use the cone and roller assembly to install the cups. This will result in damage to the bearing cup and the cone and roller assembly.

9. Make sure all of the spindle and bearing surfaces are clean.

10. Using a bearing packer, pack the bearing assemblies with a suitable wheel bearing grease. If a packer is not available, work in as much grease as

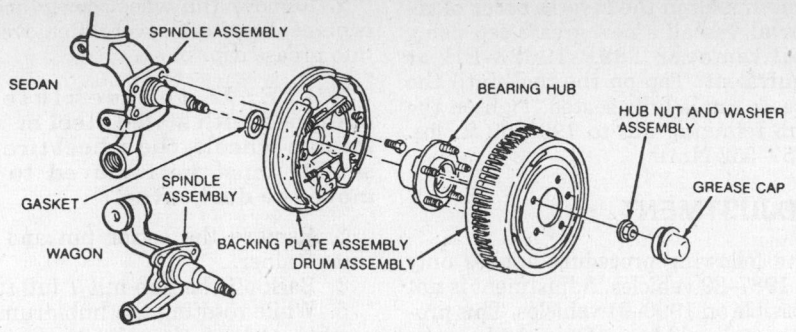

Rear wheel hub and bearing assembly—1990–91 vehicles with drum brakes

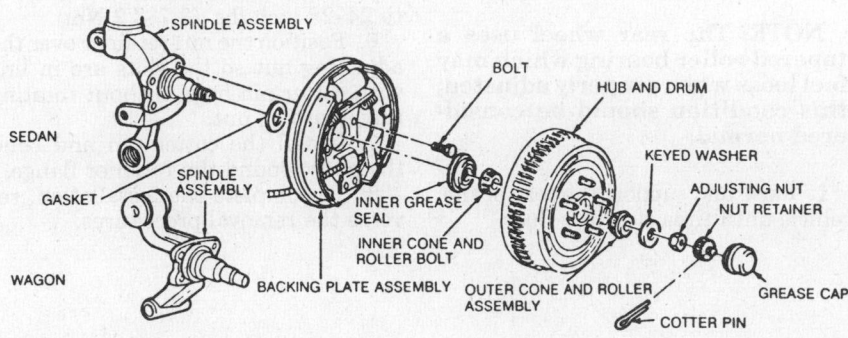

Rear wheel hub and bearing assembly—1987–89 vehicles with drum brakes

possible between the rollers and cages. Grease the cup surfaces.

NOTE: Allow all of the cleaning solvent to dry before repacking the bearings. Do not spin-dry the bearings with air pressure.

11. Install the inner bearing cone and roller assembly in the inner cup. Apply a light film of grease to the lips of a new grease seal and install the seal with rear hub seal replacer T56T-4676-B or equivalent. Make sure the retainer flange is seated all around.

12. Apply a light film of grease on the spindle shaft bearing surfaces. Install the hub and drum assembly on the spindle. Keep the hub centered on the spindle to prevent damage to the grease seal and spindle threads.

13. Install the outer bearing assembly and the keyed flatwasher on the spindle. Install the adjusting nut and adjust the wheel bearings. Install a new cotter pin. Install the grease cap.

14. Install the wheel and tire assembly and lower the vehicle.

1990–91

1. Raise the vehicle and support it safely.

2. Remove the wheel.

3. Remove the 2 pushnuts retaining the drum to the hub and remove the drum.

4. Remove the grease cap from the bearing and hub assembly and discard it.

5. Remove the hub retaining nut and remove the bearing and hub assembly from the spindle.

6. Install in the reverse order of removal. Use coil remover T89P-19623-FH or equivalent to install the new grease cap. Tap on the tool to make sure the grease cap is fully seated. Tighten the hub retaining nut to 190–260 ft. lbs. (257–352 Nm).

Disc Brakes

1987–89

1. Raise the vehicle and support it safely. Remove the tire and wheel assembly from the hub.

2. Remove the brake caliper by removing the 2 bolts that attach the caliper support to the cast iron brake adapter. Do not remove the caliper pins from the caliper assembly. Lift the caliper off of the rotor and support it with a length of wire. Do not allow the caliper assembly to hang from the brake hose.

3. Remove the rotor from the hub by pulling it off of the hub bolts. If the rotor is difficult to remove, strike the rotor sharply between the studs with a rubber or plastic hammer.

4. Remove the grease cap from the hub. Remove the cotter pin, nut retainer, adjusting nut and keyed flat washer from the spindle. Discard the cotter pin.

5. Pull the hub assembly off of the

spindle. Remove the outer bearing assembly.

6. Using seal remover tool 1175-AC or equivalent, remove and discard the grease seal. Remove the inner bearing assembly from the hub.

7. Wipe all of the lubricant from the spindle and inside of the hub. Cover the spindle with a clean cloth and vacuum all of the loose dust and dirt from the brake assembly. Carefully remove the cloth to prevent dirt from falling on the spindle.

8. Clean both bearing assemblies and cups using a suitable solvent. Inspect the bearing assemblies and cups for excessive wear, scratches, pits or other damage and replace as necessary.

9. If the cups are being replaced, remove them with impact slide hammer T50T-100-A and bearing cup puller T77F-1102-A or equivalent.

To install:

10. If the inner and outer bearing cups were removed, install the replacement cups using driver handle T80T-4000-W and bearing cup replacers T73F-1217-A and T77F-1217-B or equivalent. Support the hub on a block of wood to prevent damage. Make sure the cups are properly seated in the hub.

NOTE: Do not use the cone and roller assembly to install the cups. This will result in damage to the bearing cup and the cone and roller assembly.

11. Make sure all of the spindle and bearing surfaces are clean.

12. Pack the bearing assemblies with a suitable wheel bearing grease using a bearing packer. If a packer is not available, work in as much grease as possible between the rollers and the cages. Grease the cup surfaces.

NOTE: Allow all of the cleaning solvent to dry before repacking the bearings. Do not spin-dry the bearings with air pressure.

13. Place the inner bearing cone and roller assembly in the inner cup. Apply a light film of grease to the lips of a new grease seal and install the seal with rear hub seal replacer T56T-4676-B or equivalent. Make sure the retainer flange is seated all around.

14. Apply a light film of grease on the spindle shaft bearing surfaces. Install the hub assembly on the spindle. Keep the hub centered on the spindle to prevent damage to the grease seal and spindle threads.

15. Install the outer bearing assembly and keyed flat washer on the spindle. Install the adjusting nut and ad-

just the wheel bearings. Install a new cotter pin. Install the grease cap.

16. Install the disc brake rotor to the hub assembly. Install the disc brake caliper over the rotor.

17. Install the wheel and tire assembly and lower the vehicle.

1990–91

1. Raise the vehicle and support it safely.

2. Remove the wheel.

3. Remove the caliper assembly from the brake adapter. Support the caliper assembly with a length of wire.

4. Remove the push on nuts that retain the rotor to the hub and remove the rotor.

5. Remove the grease cap from the bearing and hub assembly and discard the grease cap.

6. Remove the bearing and hub assembly retaining nut and remove the bearing and hub assembly from the spindle.

7. Install in the reverse order of removal. Install a new grease cap using coil remover T89P-19623-FH or equivalent. Tap on the tool until the grease cap is fully seated. Tighten the hub retaining nut to 190–260 ft. lbs. (257–352 Nm).

ADJUSTMENT

The following procedure applies only to 1987–89 vehicles. Adjustment is not possible on 1990–91 vehicles. This procedure should be performed whenever the wheel is excessively loose on the spindle or it does not rotate freely.

NOTE: The rear wheel uses a tapered roller bearing which may feel loose when properly adjusted; this condition should be considered normal.

1. Raise and support the rear of the vehicle until tires clear the floor.

2. Remove the wheel cover or the ornament and nut covers. Remove the hub grease cap.

NOTE: If the vehicle is equipped with styled steel or aluminum wheels, the wheel/tire assembly must be removed to remove the dust cover.

3. Remove the cotter pin and the nut retainer.

4. Back off the hub nut 1 full turn.

5. While rotating the hub/drum assembly, tighten the adjusting nut to 17–25 ft. lbs. (23–24 Nm). Back off the adjusting nut ½ turn, then retighten it to 24–28 inch lbs. (2.7–3.2 Nm).

6. Position the nut retainer over the adjusting nut so the slots are in line with cotter pin hole, without rotating the adjusting nut.

7. Install the cotter pin and bend the ends around the retainer flange.

8. To complete the installation, reverse the removal procedures.

Ford Motor Co.
Front Wheel Drive
Mercury Tracer

SPECIFICATIONS

VEHICLE IDENTIFICATION CHART

It is important for servicing and ordering parts to be certain of the vehicle and engine identification. The VIN (vehicle identification number) is a 17 digit number visible through the windshield on the driver's side of the dash and contains the vehicle and engine identification codes. The tenth digit indicates model year, and the eighth digit indicates engine code. It can be interpreted as follows:

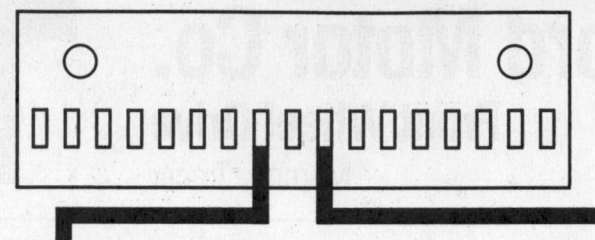

Engine Code						Model Year	
Code	Cu. In.	Liters	Cyl.	Fuel Sys.	Eng. Mfg.	Code	Year
7	98	1.6	4	2 bbl	Ford ①	J	1988
5	98	1.6	4	EFI	Ford ①	K	1989
① Mexico						L	1990
						M	1991

ENGINE IDENTIFICATION

Year	Model	Engine Displacement cu. in. (liter)	Engine Series Identification (VIN)	No. of Cylinders	Engine Type
1988	Tracer	98 (1.6)	7	4	OHC
	Tracer	98 (1.6)	5	4	OHC
1989	Tracer	98 (1.6)	7	4	OHC
	Tracer	98 (1.6)	5	4	OHC
1990	Tracer	98 (1.6)	5	4	OHC

GENERAL ENGINE SPECIFICATIONS

Year	VIN	No. Cylinder Displacement cu. in. (liter)	Fuel System Type	Net Horsepower @ rpm	Net Torque @ rpm (ft. lbs.)	Bore × Stroke (in.)	Compression Ratio	Oil Pressure @ rpm
1988	5	4-98 (1.6)	EFI	82 @ 5000	92 @ 2500	3.07 × 3.29	9:3.1	50–64 ①
	7	4-98 (1.6)	2 bbl	82 @ 5000	92 @ 2500	3.07 × 3.29	9:3.1	50–64 ①
1989	5	4-98 (1.6)	EFI	82 @ 5000	92 @ 2500	3.07 × 3.29	9:3.1	50–64 ①
1990	5	4-98 (1.6)	EFI	82 @ 5000	92 @ 2500	3.07 × 3.29	9:3.1	50–64 ①

NA Not available
① 3000 rpm—hot

GASOLINE ENGINE TUNE-UP SPECIFICATIONS

Year	VIN	No. Cylinder Displacement cu. in. (liter)	Spark Plugs Type	Gap (in.)	Ignition Timing (deg.) MT	AT	Compression Pressure (psi)	Fuel Pump (psi)	Idle Speed (rpm) MT	AT	Valve Clearance (in.) In.	Ex.
1988	5	4-98 (1.6)	AGS32C	0.044	7B ①	7B ①	③	64–85	800–900	800–900	0.012H	0.012H
	7	4-98 (1.6)	AGS32C	0.044	1–3B ②	1–3B ②	③	4–5	800–900	950–1050	0.012H	0.012H
1989	5	4-98 (1.6)	AGS32C	0.044	7B ①	7B ①	③	64–85	800–900	800–900	0.012H	0.012H
1990	5	4-98 (1.6)	AGS32C	0.044	7B ①	7B ①	③	64–85	800–900	800–900	0.012H	0.012H
1991		SEE UNDERHOOD SPECIFICATIONS STICKER										

H Hot
① Vacuum hose connected
② Vacuum hose disconnected
③ All cylinders must be within 75% of each other

FIRING ORDERS

NOTE: To avoid confusion, always replace spark plug wires one at a time.

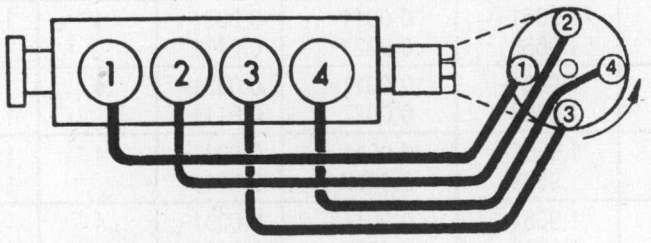

Ford 98 cu. in. (1.6L)
Firing order: 1–3–4–2
Distributor rotation: Counterclockwise

CAPACITIES

Year	Model	VIN	No. Cylinder Displacement cu. in. (liter)	Engine Crankcase (qts.) with Filter	without Filter	Transmission (pts.) 4-Spd	5-Spd	Auto.	Drive Axle (pts.)	Fuel Tank (gals.)	Cooling System (qts.)
1988	Tracer	5	4-98 (1.6)	3.5	3.2	—	3.4	6.0	NA	11.9	①
	Tracer	7	4-98 (1.6)	3.5	3.2	—	3.4	6.0	NA	11.9	①
1989	Tracer	5	4-98 (1.6)	3.5	3.2	—	3.4	6.0	NA	11.9	①
1990	Tracer	5	4-98 (1.6)	3.5	3.2	—	3.4	6.0	NA	11.9	①

① Manual transaxle—5.3 qts.
Automatic transaxle—6.3 qts.

CAMSHAFT SPECIFICATIONS

All measurements given in inches.

Year	VIN	No. Cylinder Displacement cu. in. (liter)	Journal Diameter 1	2	3	4	5	Lobe Lift In.	Ex.	Bearing Clearance	Camshaft End Play
1988	5	4-98 (1.6)	1.7103–1.7112	1.6870–1.7091	1.7103–1.7112	—	—	NA	NA	0.006	0.002–0.007
	7	4-98 (1.6)	1.7103–1.7112	1.6870–1.7091	1.7103–1.7112	—	—	NA	NA	0.006	0.002–0.007
1989	5	4-98 (1.6)	1.7103–1.7112	1.6870–1.7091	1.7103–1.7112	—	—	NA	NA	0.006	0.002–0.007
1990	5	4-98 (1.6)	1.7103–1.7112	1.6870–1.7091	1.7103–1.7112	—	—	NA	NA	0.006	0.002–0.007

NA Not available

CRANKSHAFT AND CONNECTING ROD SPECIFICATIONS

All measurements are given in inches.

Year	VIN	No. Cylinder Displacement cu. in. (liter)	Crankshaft Main Brg. Journal Dia.	Main Brg. Oil Clearance	Shaft End-play	Thrust on No.	Connecting Rod Journal Diameter	Oil Clearance	Side Clearance
1988	5	4–98 (1.6)	1.9661–1.9668	0.0011–0.0027	0.0031–0.0111	4	1.7693–1.7699	0.0009–0.0017	0.012
	7	4–98 (1.6)	1.9661–1.9668	0.0011–0.0027	0.0031–0.0111	4	1.7693–1.7699	0.0009–0.0017	0.012
1989	5	4–98 (1.6)	1.9661–1.9668	0.0011–0.0027	0.0031–0.0111	4	1.7693–1.7699	0.0009–0.0017	0.012
1990	5	4–98 (1.6)	1.9661–1.9668	0.0011–0.0027	0.0031–0.0111	4	1.7693–1.7699	0.0009–0.0017	0.012

VALVE SPECIFICATIONS

Year	VIN	No. Cylinder Displacement cu. in. (liter)	Seat Angle (deg.)	Face Angle (deg.)	Spring Test Pressure (lbs.)	Spring Installed Height (in.)	Stem-to-Guide Clearance (in.) Intake	Exhaust	Stem Diameter (in.) Intake	Exhaust
1988	5	4-98 (1.6)	45	45	NA	NA	0.008	0.008	0.2744 0.2750	0.2742 0.2748
	7	4-98 (1.6)	45	45	NA	NA	0.008	0.008	0.2744 0.2750	0.2742 0.2748
1989	5	4-98 (1.6)	45	45	NA	NA	0.008	0.008	0.2744 0.2750	0.2742 0.2748
1990	5	4-98 (1.6)	45	45	NA	NA	0.008	0.008	0.2744 0.2750	0.2742 0.2748

NA Not available

PISTON AND RING SPECIFICATIONS

All measurements are given in inches.

Year	VIN	No. Cylinder Displacement cu. in. (liter)	Piston Clearance	Ring Gap			Ring Side Clearance		
				Top Compression	Bottom Compression	Oil Control	Top Compression	Bottom Compression	Oil Control
1988	5	4-98 (1.6)	0.006	0.006–0.012	0.006–0.012	0.008–0.028	0.001–0.003	0.001–0.003	Snug
	7	4-98 (1.6)	0.006	0.006–0.012	0.006–0.012	0.008–0.028	0.001–0.003	0.001–0.003	Snug
1989	5	4-98 (1.6)	0.006	0.006–0.012	0.006–0.012	0.008–0.028	0.001–0.003	0.001–0.003	Snug
1990	5	4-98 (1.6)	0.006	0.006–0.012	0.006–0.012	0.008–0.028	0.001–0.003	0.001–0.003	Snug

TORQUE SPECIFICATIONS

All readings in ft. lbs.

Year	VIN	No. Cylinder Displacement cu. in. (liter)	Cylinder Head Bolts ①	Main Bearing Bolts ①	Rod Bearing Bolts	Crankshaft Pulley Bolts	Flywheel Bolts	Manifold		Spark Plugs
								Intake	Exhaust	
1988	5	4-98 (1.6)	56–60	40–43	37–41	71–76	71–76	14–19	12–20	11–17
	7	4-98 (1.6)	56–60	40–43	37–41	71–76	71–76	14–19	12–20	11–17
1989	5	4-98 (1.6)	56–60	40–43	37–41	71–76	71–76	14–19	12–20	11–17
1990	5	4-98 (1.6)	56–60	40–43	37–41	71–76	71–76	14–19	12–20	11–17

① Using 2 steps

BRAKE SPECIFICATIONS

All measurements in inches unless noted.

Year	Model	Lug Nut Torque (ft. lbs.)	Master Cylinder Bore	Brake Disc		Standard Brake Drum Diameter	Minimum Lining Thickness	
				Minimum Thickness	Maximum Runout		Front	Rear
1988	Tracer	65–87	0.875	0.630	0.003	7.870	0.120	0.040
1989	Tracer	65–87	0.875	0.630	0.003	7.870	0.120	0.040
1990	Tracer	65–87	0.875	0.630	0.003	7.870	0.120	0.040

WHEEL ALIGNMENT

Year	Model		Caster Range (deg.)	Caster Preferred Setting (deg.)	Camber Range (deg.)	Camber Preferred Setting (deg.)	Toe-in (in.)	Steering Axis Inclination (deg.)
1988	Tracer	Front	$5/6$P–$2^2/3$P	$1^7/12$P	$1/20$P–$1^{11}/20$P	$12/15$P	0.04N–0.20P	—
		Rear	—	—	$3/4$N–$3/4$P ①	0	0–0.16	—
1989	Tracer	Front	$5/6$P–$2^2/3$P	$1^7/12$P	$1/20$P–$1^{11}/20$P	$12/15$P	0.04N–0.20P	—
		Rear	—	—	$3/4$N–$3/4$P ①	0	0–0.16	—
1990	Tracer	Front	$5/6$P–$2^2/3$P	$1^7/12$P	$1/20$P–$1^{11}/20$P	$12/15$P	0.04N–0.20P	—
		Rear	—	—	$3/4$N–$3/4$P ①	0	0–0.16	—

① Not adjustable

ENGINE ELECTRICAL

NOTE: Disconnecting the negative battery cable on some vehicles may interfere with the functions of the on board computer systems and may require the computer to undergo a relearning process, once the negative battery cable is reconnected.

Distributor

REMOVAL

1. Disconnect the negative terminal from the battery.
2. Remove the distributor cap-to-distributor screws and move the cap (wires attached) aside. Remove the gasket.
3. Disconnect the vacuum hose (carbureted) or hoses (EFI) from the distributor vacuum advance.

NOTE: On the EFI equipped engines, label the hoses for reinstallation purposes.

4. Disconnect the electrical connector(s) from the distributor; note the wire locations for reinstallation purposes.
5. Mark the relationship of the distributor-to-engine and the rotor-to-

distributor housing for reinstallation purposes.
6. Remove the distributor-to-engine hold-down bolts and the distributor from the engine. Remove and discard the O-ring from the distributor.

INSTALLATION

Timing Not Disturbed

1. Using a new O-ring, lubricated with clean engine oil, align the matchmarks made during removal and install the distributor. Make sure the dog on the distributor aligns with the camshaft slot.
2. Install the hold-down bolts and connect the wiring to the distributor.
3. Connect the vacuum hoses.
4. Install the distributor cap.
5. Connect the negative battery cable and check the ignition timing.

Timing Disturbed

1. Remove the No. 1 spark plug.
2. Rotate the crankshaft to position the No. 1 piston on the TDC of its compression stroke.

NOTE: To locate the TDC of the compression stroke of the No. 1 piston, stuff a clean shop rag in the spark plug hole. Rotate the crankshaft until compression is noticed and adjust the crankshaft pulley notch to align the with the 1–3 degree mark on the timing plate.

3. Rotate the rotor to position it with the No. 1 spark plug wire on the distributor cap and reinstall the distributor; be sure to align the distributor drive dog with the slot in the camshaft.
4. Install the hold-down bolts and connect the wiring to the distributor.
5. Connect the vacuum hoses.
6. Install the distributor cap.
7. Connect the negative battery cable and check the ignition timing.

Ignition Timing

ADJUSTMENT

1. Operate the engine until normal operating temperatures are reached.
2. Check and/or adjust the idle speed.
3. Turn off all of the accessories.
4. On engines equipped with EFI, disconnect and plug the vacuum lines at the distributor vacuum advance.

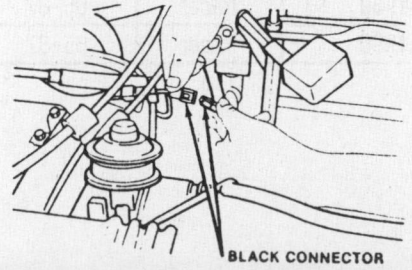

Disconnect the black electrical connector near the distributor—EFI models

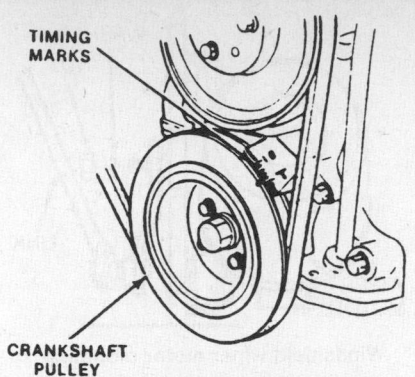

View of the ignition timing marks

5. On carbureted engines, do not disconnect the vacuum line at the distributor.

NOTE: If using 2 vacuum lines, be sure to mark them for installation purposes.

6. If equipped with EFI, disconnect the black electrical connector at the distributor.

7. Using timing light tool No. 059-00005 or equivalent, connect it to the engine.

8. Aim the timing light at the crankshaft pulley/timing plate location; the crankshaft pulley notch should align with the 1–3 degree BTDC mark on the timing plate.

9. If necessary to adjust the ignition timing, perform the following procedures:

a. Loosen the distributor hold-down bolts, just enough so the distributor can be turned.

b. Rotate the distributor clockwise (to advance) or counterclockwise (to retard) the timing.

c. With the timing corrected, tighten the distributor hold-down bolts.

d. Recheck the timing.

10. To complete the operation, reverse the removal procedures. Check and/or adjust the idle speed.

Alternator

For further information on the charging system, please refer to "Charging and Starting" in the Unit Repair section.

PRECAUTIONS

Several precautions must be observed with alternator equipped vehicles to avoid damage to the unit.

• If the battery is removed for any reason, make sure it is reconnected with the correct polarity. Reversing the battery connections may result in damage to the one-way rectifiers.

• When utilizing a booster battery as a starting aid, always connect the positive to positive terminals and the negative terminal from the booster battery to a good engine ground on the vehicle being started.

• Never use a fast charger as a booster to start vehicles.

• Disconnect the battery cables when charging the battery with a fast charger.

• Never attempt to polarize the alternator.

• Do not use test lamps of more than 12 volts when checking diode continuity.

• Do not short across or ground any of the alternator terminals.

• The polarity of the battery, alternator and regulator must be matched and considered before making any electrical connections within the system.

• Never separate the alternator on

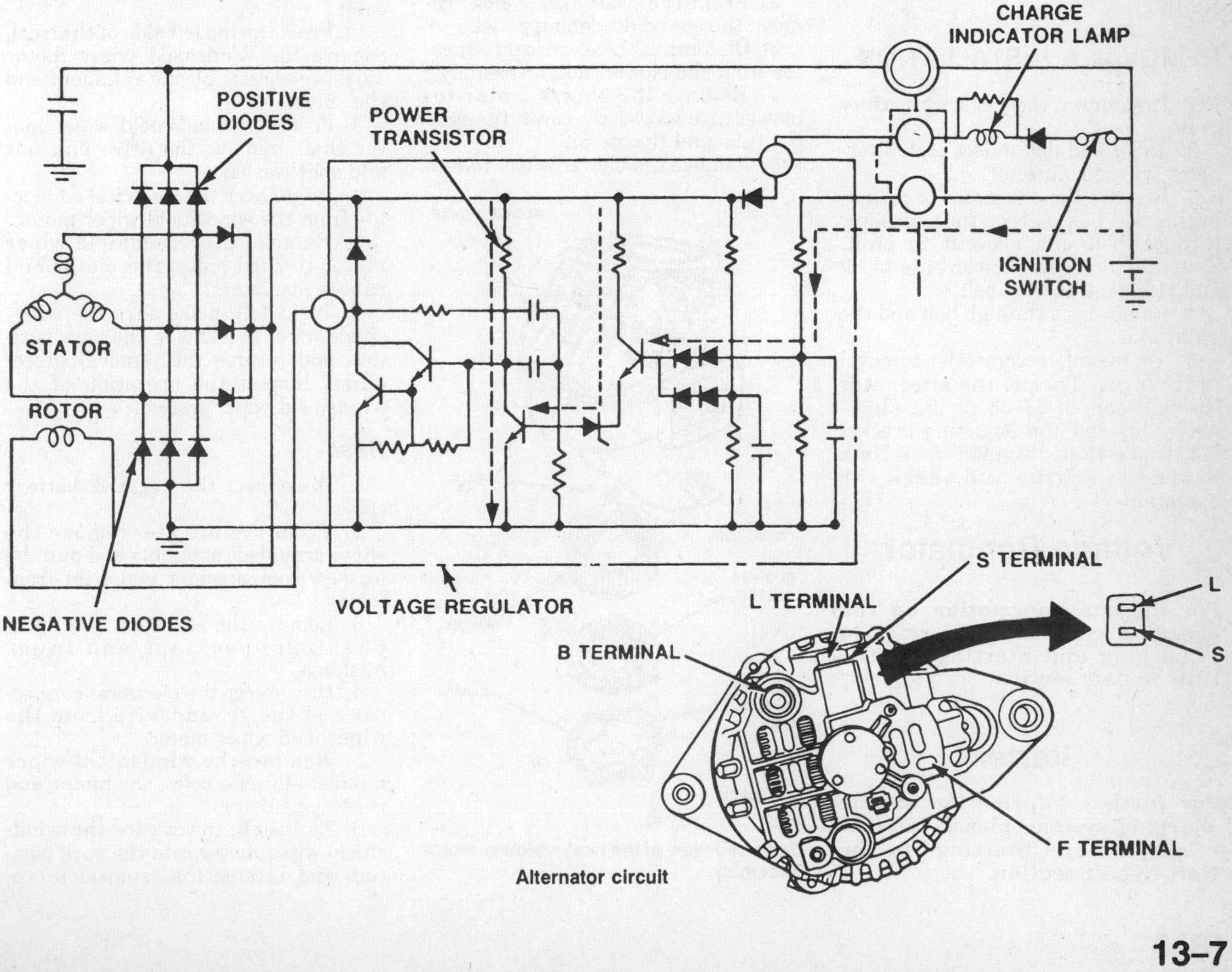

Alternator circuit

an open circuit. Make sure all connections within the circuit are clean and tight.

● Disconnect the battery ground terminal when performing any service on electrical components.

● Disconnect the battery if arc welding is to be done on the vehicle.

Belt Tension Adjustment

The belt tension on most components is adjusted by moving the component (alternator) within the range of the slotted bracket. Check the belt tension every 12 months or 10,000 miles. Push in on the drive belt about midway between the water pulley and the alternator. Belt deflection should be: New—0.31–0.35 in. (7.87–8.89mm), Used—0.35–0.39 in. (8.89–9.90mm).

1. Loosen the adjustment nut and bolt in the slotted bracket. Slightly loosen the pivot bolt.

2. Pull (don't pry) the component outward to increase tension. Push inward to reduce tension. Tighten the adjusting nut/bolt and the pivot bolt.

3. Recheck the drive belt tension and readjust, if necessary. Torque the alternator mounting bolt to 27–38 ft. lbs. (36.6–49.4 Nm) and the alternator pivot bolt to 14–19 ft. lbs. (18.9–25.8 Nm).

REMOVAL & INSTALLATION

1. Disconnect the negative battery cable.

2. Label and disconnect each alternator wiring connector.

3. Remove the alternator-to-adjusting bracket bolt. Loosen the alternator through bolt and allow it to pivot. Shift the alternator toward the block and remove the drive belt.

4. Remove the through bolt and the alternator.

5. To install, reverse the removal procedures. Torque the alternator through bolt to 27–38 ft. lbs. (36.6–49.4 Nm) and the adjusting bracket bolt to 35–45 ft. lbs. (45.5–58.5 Nm). Start the engine and check the operation.

Voltage Regulator

For further information on the charging system, please refer to "Charging and Starting" in the Unit Repair section.

Starter

For further information on the charging system, please refer to "Charging and Starting" in the Unit Repair section.

REMOVAL & INSTALLATION

1. Disconnect the negative terminal from the battery.

2. Disconnect the electrical connectors from the starter terminals.

3. Remove the starter-to-bracket bolts, the support bracket bolts and the brackets.

4. Remove the starter-to-transaxle bolts and the starter from the vehicle.

5. To install, reverse the removal procedures. Torque the starter-to-engine bolts to 23–30 ft. lbs. (40.6 Nm) and the support bracket thru bolt to 54–71 inch lbs. (5.94–7.81 Nm).

CHASSIS ELECTRICAL

Heater Blower Motor

REMOVAL & INSTALLATION

1. Disconnect the negative battery cable.

2. From the passenger's side, remove the sound deadening panel.

3. Disconnect the electrical connector from the blower motor assembly.

4. Remove the blower motor-to-blower case screws, the cover, the cooling tube and the motor.

5. Remove the blower wheel-to-mo-

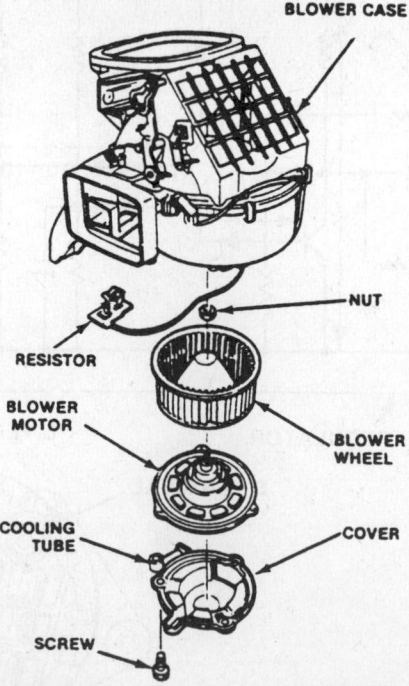

Exploded view of the heater blower motor assembly

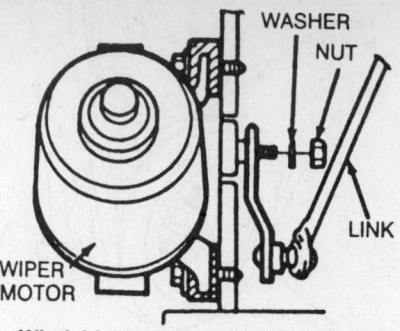

Windshield wiper motor mounting

tor nut and pull the wheel straight off the motor. Remove the gasket from the motor.

6. To install, reverse the removal procedures. Check the blower motor operation.

Windshield Wiper Motor

REMOVAL & INSTALLATION

Front

1. Disconnect the negative battery cable.

2. From the top left side of the cowl, remove the windshield wiper motor shield-to-chassis plastic retainers and the shield.

3. From the windshield wiper motor shaft, remove the drive link nut and split washer.

4. Disconnect the electrical connector from the windshield wiper motor.

5. Remove the windshield wiper motor-to-cowl bolts, the motor and rubber insulators.

6. To install, make sure the windshield wiper motor is in the park position and reverse the removal procedures. Inspect the operation of the windshield wiper system.

Rear

1. Disconnect the negative battery cable.

2. From the liftgate, remove the wiper arm/blade assembly and pull the luggage compartment end trim from inside.

3. Remove the seal cap, nut, outer bushings, packings and inner bushings.

4. Disconnect the electrical connector and the ground wire from the windshield wiper motor.

5. Remove the windshield wiper motor-to-liftgate bolts, the motor and rubber insulators.

6. To install, make sure the windshield wiper motor is in the park position and reverse the removal proce-

dures. Inspect the operation of the windshield wiper system.

Instrument Cluster

REMOVAL & INSTALLATION

1. Disconnect the negative battery cable.
2. Remove the steering wheel.
3. Remove the instrument cluster bezel-to-instrument panel screws and bezel.
4. Remove the instrument cluster-to-instrument panel screws.
5. From under the dash, depress the speedometer lock tab and pull the speedometer cable from the instrument cluster.
6. Pull the instrument cluster outward, depress the lock tab (located in the center of the connector) of the 3 electrical harness connectors and pull the connectors from the cluster.
7. To install, reverse the removal procedures. Inspect the operation of the instruments.

Speedometer

REMOVAL & INSTALLATION

1. Disconnect the negative battery cable.
2. Remove the instrument cluster.
3. Remove the lens from the instrument cluster.
4. Remove the indicator lamp overlay from the instrument cluster.
5. Remove the speedometer-to-instrument cluster screws and the speedometer.
6. To install, reverse the removal procedures. Check the operation of the speedometer.

Radio

REMOVAL & INSTALLATION

1. Disconnect the negative battery cable.
2. Remove the radio trim cover from the instrument panel.
3. Remove the radio retaining screws and pull the radio from the instrument panel.
4. Disconnect the electrical and antenna leads from the radio.
5. Installation is the reverse of the removal procedure.

Combination Switch

The combination switch assembly controls the turn signal, hedalight, dimmer and windshield wiper switch functions.

REMOVAL & INSTALLATION

1. Disconnect the negative battery cable and remove the steering wheel.
2. Remove the steering column covers-to-steering column screws and the covers.
3. Depress the small tang on the electrical harness clip and disconnect the clip; move the electrical harness aside.
4. Loosen the combination switch-to-steering column clamp, slide the switch slightly forward and disconnect the electrical connector from the rear of the combination switch.
5. Remove the combination switch from the steering column.
6. To install, reverse the removal procedures. Check the switch operations.

Ignition Lock/Switch

REMOVAL & INSTALLATION

1. Disconnect the negative battery cable.
2. Grasp the black trim ring around the ignition lock switch and pull it straight out.
3. From the driver's side, remove the sound deadening panel and the lap duct cover.
4. If equipped with air conditioning, remove the air conditioning duct assembly-to-access panel support bracket center screw, the access panel support bracket screws and the bracket.
5. From under the steering column, grasp the side window defogger duct ends, pull it outward, while twisting it slightly. From the ignition switch, located under the steering column, disengage the plastic strap connector locking tang and remove the plastic strap.
6. Remove the steering column-to-instrument panel bolts and lower the column.
7. Lift the upper steering column shroud and remove it from the steering column.
8. Remove the ignition switch-to-ignition switch housing screw, grasp the ignition switch body and pull it straight outward.
9. To disengage the electrical connectors from the ignition switch, perform the following procedures:
   a. Disengage the electrical connector locking tang.
   b. Grasp an electrical connector in each hand and pull them straight apart.

NOTE: Be aware of the electrical connector cavity position for reassembly purposes.

10. Using a straightened paper clip, disengage the 2 in-key buzzer wires from the 4-terminal connector; the wire colors are red and red wire/orange tracer.

To install:

11. To install, wires and connector, perform the following procedures:
    a. Align the wire end flat sides with the grooved portion of the connector and push the wire inward until the locking tang engages wire end.
    b. Push the 4-terminal connector into the housing connector until the locking tangs are in place.
    c. Using electrical tape, wrap it around the ignition switch wires.
12. Install the ignition switch-to-ignition switch housing screw and the plastic snap connector around the ignition switch wiring. Attach the connector peg to the steering column mounting bracket.
13. Using electrical tape, wrap it around the ignition switch wiring and steering column.
14. To complete the installation, reverse the removal procedures. Check the ignition switch operation.

Stoplight Switch

REMOVAL & INSTALLATION

1. Disconnect the negative battery cable.
2. Disconnect the electrical connector from the stoplight switch.
3. Remove the stoplight switch-to-bracket nut and unscrew the switch from the bracket.
4. To install, screw the stoplight into the bracket until the brake pedal height is 8.62–8.82 in.

NOTE: Brake pedal height is the distance from the cowl to the front center of the brake pedal.

5. Tighten the switch locknut and install the electrical connector. Test the switch operation.

Neutral Safety Switch

The neutral safety switch is mounted on the top right side of the automatic transaxle. No adjustment is possible on the neutral safety switch. If the engine will not start while the selector lever is in the **P** or **N** positions and the back-up lamps do not operate, check the shift control cable for proper adjustment. If shift cable adjustment is correct, the switch is defective and must be replaced.

REMOVAL & INSTALLATION

1. Disconnect the negative battery cable.

2. Raise and support the vehicle safely.

3. Disconnect the electrical connector from the neutral safety switch.

4. Using a wrench, remove the switch from the transaxle.

5. To install, apply sealant to the switch threads and reverse the removal procedures. Torque the neutral safety switch-to-transaxle to 14–19 ft. lbs.

Fuses, Circuit Breakers and Relays

LOCATION

Circuit Breakers

A circuit breaker is mounted on the interior fuse panel which is located above the left side kick panel. This breaker controls vehicle electrical system components.

Fuse Pane

The main fuse panel is located on the right side of the engine compartment.

An electrical equipment panel is located on under the left side of the instrument panel; it is part of the fuse panel and incorporates plug-in relays, a flasher, a buzzer and a circuit breaker.

Various Relays

Horn Relay—is located in the engine compartment on the left inner fender.

A/C Cut-utT Relay—located in the front of the left front shock tower in the engine compartment.

A/C Relay No. 1—located on the left front shock tower in the engine compartment.

A/C Relay No. 2—located on the left front shock tower in the engine compartment.

A/C Relay No. 3—located on the left front shock tower in the engine compartment.

Cooling Fan Relay—located in the left front side of the engine compartment, next to the coolant recovery bottle.

Door Buzzer Relay—located in the electrical equipment panel, above the fuse block.

Fuel Pump Relay—mounted under the center of the instrument panel.

PTC Heater Relay—located in the engine compartment on the inner fender apron, next to the coolant recovery reservoir.

Computers

LOCATION

The Electronic Control Unit (ECU) is located behind the center of the instrument panel. The RPM control module is also located near the ECU.

Flashers

LOCATION

The turn signal/hazard flasher unit, is located on the main fuse panel, at the right side of the engine compartment.

Cruise Control

ADJUSTMENT

Actuator Inner Cable Free-Play

1. With the engine off, remove the clip from the actuator cable and adjust the locknut while pressing down on the cable until free-play is 0.04–0.12 in. (1–3mm).

2. Check the system operation and adjust as needed.

Clutch Pedal Height

Pedal height is the distance from the cowl to the center of the clutch pedal pad.

1. Remove the necessary instrument panel components which block access to the clutch pedal.

2. Loosen the clutch pedal locknut.

3. Turn the stop bolt to obtain the correct pedal height of 8.4–8.6 in. Tighten the locknut.

4. If components from the instrument panel were removed, reinstall them.

Brake Pedal Height

Measure the distance from the center of the brake pedal to lower dash panel. Pedal height must be 8.62–8.82 in. (214.5–219.5mm). If the brake pedal height is not within these specifications, adjustment is necessary.

1. Disconnect the negative battery cable.

2. Adjust the pedal height by adjusting the stop light switch.

3. Disconnect the connector on the stoplight switch.

4. Loosen the stoplight switch locknut and rotate the switch until the pedal height is 8.62–8.82 in. (214.5–219.5mm).

5. Tighten the switch locknut.

6. Connect the stoplight switch connector.

7. Connect the negative battery cable and check stoplight operation.

ENGINE COOLING

Radiator

REMOVAL & INSTALLATION

1. Disconnect the negative battery cable.

2. Disconnect the coolant recovery hose from the filler neck.

3. Loosen the retaining clamp and disconnect the upper radiator hose from the radiator.

4. Disconnect the cooling fan wiring harness connector. Disengage the wiring harness from the routing clamp on the cooling fan shroud.

5. Remove the radiator cap from the filler neck. Raise the vehicle and support safely.

6. Position a fluid catch pan under the radiator. Open the drain valve and drain the cooling system.

7. Disconnect the radiator temperature switch wires.

8. Loosen the retaining clamp and disconnect the lower radiator hose.

9. Lower the vehicle.

10. Support the radiator by hand and remove the 4 bolts attaching the radiator support brackets to the vehicle body. Raise the radiator/cooling fan/shroud assembly from the crossmember mounting insulator supports and remove from vehicle. Disconnect the cooling fan and shroud from the radiator as required.

To install:

11. Lower the radiator into the normal operating position making certain the mounting insulators engage with their supports. Attach the radiator to the support brackets with the 4 bolts.

12. Connect the upper radiator hose. Raise the vehicle and connect the lower radiator hose and temperature switch wires.

13. Close the drain valve and lower the vehicle. Connect the negative battery cable. Fill the cooling system to the proper level.

14. Start the engine and allow to reach normal operating temperature. Inspect for coolant leaks and correct as required.

Electric Cooling Fan

TESTING

1. Disconnect the negative battery cable. Disconnect the fan electrical connector.

2. Using a 12 volt DC power supply,

connect it to the electrical connector (fan side); the fan should operate.

3. If the fan does not operate, inspect the temperature coolant switch and/or the fan relay.

Radiator Fan Switch

The radiator fan switch is mounted on the outflow side of the thermostat housing. The switch will open at 207°F and close at temperatures below 194°F.

NOTE: The cooling fan will turn ON if a wire is disconnected from the coolant temperature switch when the ignition switch is in the ON position.

REMOVAL & INSTALLATION

1. Disconnect the negative battery cable.
2. Disconnect the fan electrical wiring harnesses from the clamps.
3. Disconnect the electrical connector from the cooling fan.
4. Remove the fan shroud-to-radiator screws and the shroud/fan assembly from the vehicle.
5. Remove the fan from the shroud.
6. To install, reverse the removal procedures. Start the engine, allow it to reach normal operating temperature and the system operation.

Heater Core

REMOVAL & INSTALLATION

The heater core is mounted in the heater case inside the vehicle behind the instrument panel.

1. Disconnect the negative battery cable.
2. From under the instrument panel, remove both sound deadening panels and the lap duct register panel.
3. From the blower motor case and heater case, disconnect the 3 air door control cables.
4. From behind the instrument cluster, depress the speedometer lock tab and pull the speedometer cable from the cluster.
5. From behind the instrument cluster, depress the lock tab (located in the center of the connector) of the 3 electrical harness connectors and pull the connectors from the cluster.
6. From under the steering column, remove the lap duct brace-to-instrument panel screws, the brace, the lap duct and the driver's demister tube.
7. Remove the lower cover-to-steering column screws and the lower cover.
8. Remove the steering column-to-

instrument panel bolts and lower the steering column.

9. Remove the glove box-to-instrument panel screws and the glove box.
10. Remove the hood release-to-instrument panel nut and move the release cable aside.
11. Remove the center floor console-to-chassis screws and the cover.
12. From below the radio, remove the lower trim panel-to-instrument panel screws and the lower panel.
13. Using a small prybar, pry the instrument panel-to-chassis bolt covers from the perimeter of the instrument panel. Remove the instrument panel-to-chassis nuts/bolts. Lift and pull the panel out slightly.
14. Disconnect the electrical connector from the blower motor assembly.
15. From the rear of the radio, disconnect the antenna cable.
16. From the left corner of the instrument panel, disconnect the 3 instrument panel harness connectors and remove the instrument panel.
17. Using a clean drain pan, place it under the radiator, open the radiator drain cock, remove the radiator cap and drain the cooling system to a level below the heater case.
18. Disconnect and plug the heater hoses from the heater case.
19. Remove the defroster tubes-to-heater case push pins and the defroster tubes from the heater case. Remove the main air duct-to-heater case push pins and the main air duct.
20. From under the heater case, remove the lower carpet panel push pins, screw and the panel.
21. From the heater case, disconnect the electrical harness braces and remove the lower brace screws and brace.
22. Remove the heater case-to-chassis nut and bolts. Remove the lower duct-to-heater case push pins and lower duct. Remove the heater case by pulling it straight out; be careful not to damage the extension tubes.
23. Remove the heater core cover-to-heater case screws and the cover. Remove the tube braces and pull the heater core straight out.
24. Remove the outlet extension tube clip and tube. Loosen the inlet extension tube clamp and the extension tube.

To install:

25. To install, use a new O-ring (outlet extension tube) and reverse the removal procedures.
26. Refill the cooling system.
27. Start the engine, allow it to reach normal operating temperature and turn the heater control to full heat. Inspect the system for leakage and operation.
28. Connect the negative battery cable.

Water Pump

REMOVAL & INSTALLATION

1. Disconnect the negative battery cable. Remove the timing belt.
2. Place a clean drain pan under the radiator. Remove the radiator drain plug and the radiator cap; drain the cooling system to a level below the water pump.
3. Remove the coolant inlet pipe-to-water pump bolts and the inlet pipe.
4. Remove the water pump-to-engine bolts and the water pump.
5. Using a putty knife, clean the gasket mounting surfaces. Inspect the parts for wear and/or damage, if necessary, replace the parts.

To install:

6. To install, use new gaskets, sealant and reverse the removal procedures.
7. Torque the water pump-to-engine bolts to 14–19 ft. lbs., the water inlet pipe-to-water pump bolts to 14–19 ft. lbs. and the water pump pulley-to-water pump bolts to 11–13 ft. lbs.
8. Refill the cooling system. Start the engine, allow it to reach normal operating temperature and check for leaks.

Thermostat

REMOVAL & INSTALLATION

The thermostat is located on the rear of the cylinder head.

1. Disconnect the negative battery cable.
2. Disconnect the electrical leads from the cooling fan switch.
3. Drain the cooling system to a level below the thermostat housing.
4. Disconnect the upper radiator hose from the housing.
5. Remove the thermostat housing bolts and remove the thermostat.
6. Clean the cylinder and housing mating surfaces. Install the thermo-

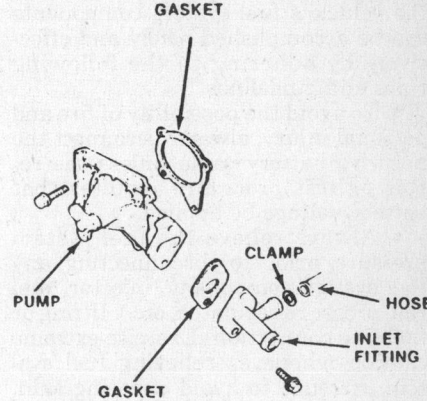

Exploded view of the water pump

stat, using a new gasket. Torque the housing bolts to 14–22 ft. lbs. (18–29 Nm).

Cooling System Bleeding

After working on the cooling system, even to replace the thermostat, the system must have the air bled from it. Air trapped in the system will prevent proper system filling and leave the coolant level low, risking possible overheating.

1. Fill the radiator to about 1 in. below the filler neck.
2. Start the engine and run it at slightly above normal idle speed. If air bubbles appear and the coolant level drops, fill the system with the correct anti-freeze/water mixture to bring the level to normal.
3. Run the engine until the thermostat opens and the water begins to move abruptly in the radiator.
4. Check the level of the coolant again, top it off if needed. Stop the engine.
5. Put the radiator cap on and check the coolant level in the overflow tank. Bring the overflow tank up to the correct level.

FUEL SYSTEM

Fuel System Service Precautions

Safety is the most important factor when performing not only fuel system maintenance but any type of maintenance. Failure to conduct maintenance and repairs in a safe manner may result in serious personal injury or death. Maintenance and testing of the vehicle's fuel system components can be accomplished safely and effectively by adhering to the following rules and guidelines.

• To avoid the possibility of fire and personal injury, always disconnect the negative battery cable unless the repair or test procedure requires that battery voltage be applied.

• Always relieve the fuel system pressure prior to disconnecting any fuel system component (injector, fuel rail, pressure regulator, etc.), fitting or fuel line connection. Exercise extreme caution whenever relieving fuel system pressure to avoid exposing skin, face and eyes to fuel spray. Please be advised that fuel under pressure may

penetrate the skin or any part of the body that it contacts.

• Always place a shop towel or cloth around the fitting or connection prior to loosening to absorb any excess fuel due to spillage. Ensure that all fuel spillage (should it occur) is quickly removed from engine surfaces. Ensure that all fuel soaked cloths or towels are deposited into a suitable waste container.

• Always keep a dry chemical (Class B) fire extinguisher near the work area.

• Do not allow fuel spray or fuel vapors to come into contact with a spark or open flame.

• Always use a backup wrench when loosening and tightening fuel line connection fittings. This will prevent unnecessary stress and torsion to fuel line piping. Always follow the proper torque specifications.

• Always replace worn fuel fitting O-rings with new. Do not substitute fuel hose or equivalent where fuel pipe is installed.

RELIEVING FUEL SYSTEM PRESSURE

Vane Air Meter Method

1. Start the engine and disconnect the vane air flow meter.
2. When the engine stalls, turn the ignition switch **OFF**.
3. Reconnect the vane air flow meter.

Fuel Pump Connector Method

1. Remove the back seat cushion.
2. Operate the engine.
3. Disconnect the fuel pump electrical connector.
4. Allow the engine to stall.
5. Turn the ignition switch **OFF** and reconnect the electrical connector.

Fuel Filter

REMOVAL & INSTALLATION

The fuel filter is located in the engine

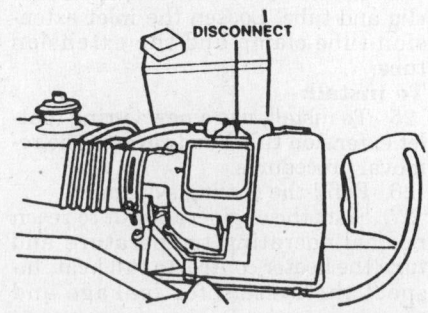

View of the vane air flow meter with electrical connector—EFI system

compartment, connected to the fuel inlet line, mounted to the inner fender well.

1. Disconnect the negative battery cable.
2. Place a shop cloth around the fuel filter fitting and disconnect the fitting.
3. Remove the fuel filter mounting brace and remove the filter.
4. Installation is the reverse of the removal procedure. Be sure to note the installation direction of the filter.

Mechanical Fuel Pump

PRESSURE TESTING

1. Connect a fuel pressure gauge between the fuel pump and the carburetor.
2. Run the engine at idle speed and check the gauge reading.
3. The fuel pump pressure should be 4–5 psi. If the pump pressure is not to specification, the pump may be bad.
4. Remove the gauge from the fuel line.

REMOVAL & INSTALLATION

1. Disconnect the negative battery cable.
2. Label and disconnect the fuel lines.
3. Remove the fuel pump retaining bolts and the pump.
4. Installation is the reverse of the removal procedure. Clean all mounting surfaces. Be sure to use a new gasket. Torque the mounting bolts to 17–22 ft. lbs. (23–30 Nm).

Electric Fuel Pump

The electric fuel pump is located in the fuel tank, on the level sending unit.

PRESSURE TESTING

1. Releive the fuel system pressure. Connect a fuel gauge in the fuel filter and the fuel rail.
2. Jumper the fuel pump check connector, so that the pump will run with the key in the **ON** position.
3. Observe the pressure reading. If the fuel pressure is below 60 psi, check the system for restrictions. Replace the pump as needed.
4. Relieve the fuel pressure. Remove the fuel pressure gauge.

REMOVAL & Installaltion

1. Relieve the fuel pressure. Disconnect the negative battery cable.
2. Disconnect the fuel lines from the fuel sending unit at the fuel tank.

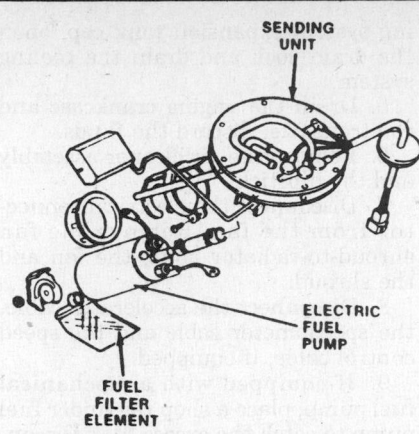

Exploded view of the electric fuel pump — EFI models

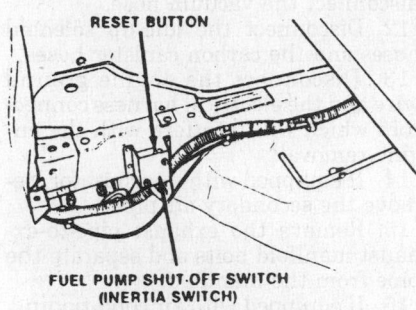

View of the fuel pump inertia switch — EFI equipped 3/5 door models

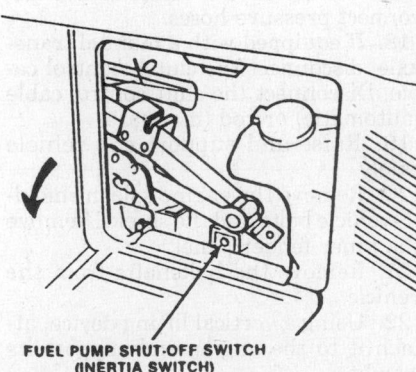

View of the fuel pump inertia switch — EFI equipped station wagon models

3. Remove the fuel sending unit-to-fuel tank bolts and the sending unit.

4. Remove the fuel filter from the fuel pump.

5. Disconnect the electrical connectors from the fuel pump.

6. Remove the retaining clamp screw, the outlet hose clamp and the fuel pump.

7. To install, use a new sending unit-to-fuel tank gasket and reverse the removal procedures.

Carburetor

REMOVAL & INSTALLATION

1. Disconnect the negative battery cable.

2. Remove the air cleaner assembly.

3. Disconnect and plug the fuel line to prevent leakage.

4. Label and disconnect the vacuum lines from the carburetor.

5. Disconnect the electrical harness connector from the carburetor.

6. Disconnect the choke heater wire from the rear of the alternator.

7. Fully open the throttle and disconnect the throttle cable.

8. Remove the carburetor-to-intake manifold nuts. Lift the carburetor and remove the idle-up diaphragm link from the carburetor linkage.

NOTE: If the PTC heater sticks to the carburetor, carefully remove it.

9. Clean the gasket mounting surfaces.

10. To install, use new gaskets and reverse the removal procedures. Start the engine. Check and/or adjust the idle mixture and idle speed. Check the fuel float level.

IDLE SPEED ADJUSTMENT

NOTE: The idle mixture and timing must be adjusted before the idle speed is adjusted; adjustment must be done with cooling fan inoperative.

1. Place the transaxle in **N** or **P**.

2. Start the engine and allow it to reach normal operating temperature.

3. Turn off all lights and accessories.

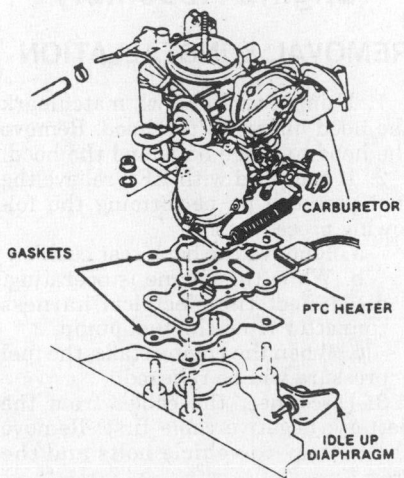

Exploded view of the carburetor assembly

4. Using a tachometer, install it to the engine.

5. Check the idle speed; if necessary, to adjust the idle speed, turn the idle speed screw at the base of the carburetor.

6. If equipped with a manual transaxle, adjust the dashpot.

IDLE MIXTURE ADJUSTMENT

The carburetor is equipped with a non-tamperable feature: A roll pin blocks the entry to the idle mixture screw and cannot be driven downward.

1. To remove the roll pin from the carburetor's idle mixture screw, perform the following procedures.

a. Remove the carburetor.

b. Invert the carburetor.

c. Using a pin punch and a hammer, drive the roll pin toward the top of the carburetor.

d. Using new gaskets, reinstall the carburetor and the air filter (secure the wing nut).

2. At the air filter housing, disconnect air injection hoses; plug the front air injection hose. Using an Exhaust Gas Analyzer tool, install and seal the probe into the rear air injection hose to prevent leakage.

3. Start the engine and allow it to reach normal operating temperature.

4. Turn the idle mixture screw to obtain a carbon monoxide (CO) reading of 1.5–2.5 percent.

5. Adjust the idle speed.

6. When the idle speed and idle mixture are balanced, perform the following procedures:

a. Remove the air cleaner housing.

b. Using a hammer and a punch, install the roll pin to block the idle mixture screw.

7. To complete the installation, reverse the removal procedures. Check for leaks.

SERVICE ADJUSTMENTS

For all carburetor service adjustment procedures and specifications, please refer to "Carburetor Service" in the Unit Repair section.

Fuel Injection

IDLE SPEED ADJUSTMENT

NOTE: The timing must be adjusted before the idle speed is adjusted; adjustment must be done with the cooling fan inoperative. The idle mixture screw is preset/sealed at the factory and must not be adjusted.

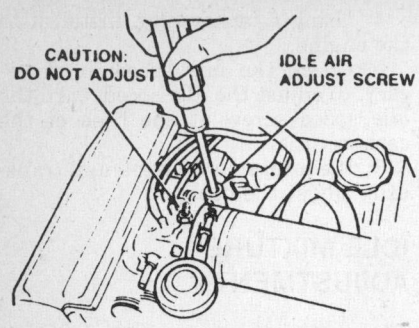

Adjusting the idle speed by turning the idle air adjusting screw—EFI engines

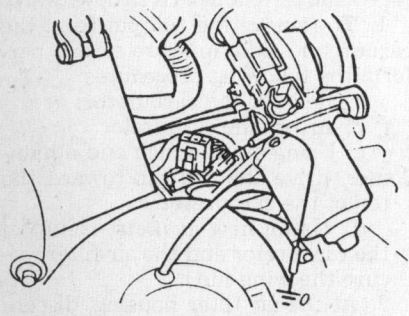

View of the jumper wire connected to the test connector—EFI engines

1. Operate the engine until normal operating temperature is reached.

2. Using a tachometer, connect it to Pin 1 (white) of the test connector and check the idle speed.

3. If necessary to adjust the idle speed, connect a jumper wire between Pin 1 (green) of the test connector and ground and turn the air adjustment screw to obtain the correct idle speed.

NOTE: Do not turn the adjustment screw located to the right of the idle adjustment screw, for it will affect the driveability and may damage the throttle body.

4. After adjustment, remove the jumper wire and the test equipment.

Fuel Injector

REMOVAL & INSTALLATION

1. Relieve the fuel pressure. Disconnect the negative battery cable.

2. Remove the intake plenum-to-intake manifold bolts and the plenum.

3. Remove the fuel lines from the fuel rail.

4. Label and disconnect the fuel injector electrical connectors.

5. Remove the fuel pressure regulator.

6. Remove the fuel rail-to-engine bolts and the fuel rail from the engine.

7. Separate the fuel injectors from the fuel rail. Remove the O-rings from the fuel injectors.

8. Clean the gasket mounting surfaces.

9. To install, use new O-rings, gasket(s) and reverse the removal procedures. Start the engine and check for leaks.

EMISSION CONTROLS

Please refer to "Emission Control" in the Unit Repair section for system maintenance procedures. Due to the complex nature of modern electronic engine control systems, comprehensive diagnosis and testing procedures fall outside the confines of this repair manual. For complete information on diagnosis, testing and repair procedures concerning all modern engine and emission control systems, please refer to "Chilton's Guide to Electronic Engine Controls".

ENGINE MECHANICAL

NOTE: Disconnecting the negative battery cable on some vehicles may interfere with the functions of the on board computer systems and may require the computer to undergo a relearning process, once the negative battery cable is reconnected.

Engine Assembly

REMOVAL & INSTALLATION

1. Using a scratch awl, matchmark the hood hinges to the hood. Remove the hood-to-hinge bolts and the hood.

2. If equipped with EFI, relieve the fuel pressure by performing the following procedures:

   a. Remove the back seat cushion.

   b. While the engine is operating, disconnect the electrical harness connector from the fuel pump.

   c. When the engine stalls, the fuel pressure will be relieved.

3. Disconnect the cables from the battery; negative cable first. Remove the battery-to-vehicle bolts and the tray.

4. Using a clean drain pan, place it under the radiator. Remove the cooling system expansion tank cap, open the drain cock and drain the cooling system.

5. Drain the engine crankcase and the transaxle; discard the fluids.

6. Remove the air cleaner assembly and the dipstick.

7. Disconnect the electrical connector from the fan. Remove the fan shroud-to-radiator bolts, the fan and the shroud.

8. Disconnect the accelerator cable, the speedometer cable and the speed control cable, if equipped.

9. If equipped with a mechanical fuel pump, place a shop rag under fuel pump to catch the excess fuel. Disconnect and plug the fuel lines.

10. Disconnect the heater hoses and the radiator hoses from the engine.

11. From the power brake booster, disconnect the vacuum hose.

12. Disconnect the idle-up solenoid hoses and the carbon canister hoses.

13. Disconnect the engine ground wire and the electrical harness connectors which will interfere with the engine removal.

14. If equipped with a carburetor, remove the secondary air pipe.

15. Remove the exhaust pipe-to-exhaust manifold bolts and separate the pipe from the manifold.

16. If equipped with air conditioning, remove the compressor from the engine bracket and move it aside.

17. If equipped with power steering, remove the pump from the engine bracket and move it aside; do not disconnect pressure hoses.

18. If equipped with a manual transaxle, disconnect the clutch control cable. Disconnect the shift control cable (automatic) or rod (manual).

19. Raise and support the vehicle safely.

20. Remove the engine splash shield-to-vehicle bolts and the shield. Remove the inner fender panel.

21. Remove the halfshafts from the vehicle.

22. Using a vertical lifting device, attach it to the engine and support its weight.

23. Remove the engine mount bolts and lift the engine/transaxle assembly from the vehicle. After removal, separate the engine from the transaxle.

To install:

24. Lower the engine/transaxle assembly into the vehicle.

25. Install the engine mount bolts.

26. Connect the halfshafts to the transaxle. Install the lower engine splash shield.

27. Connect the shift control cables. On manual transaxle equipped vehicles, connect the clutch cable.

28. Lower the vehicle. Connect the exhaust system components to the manifold.

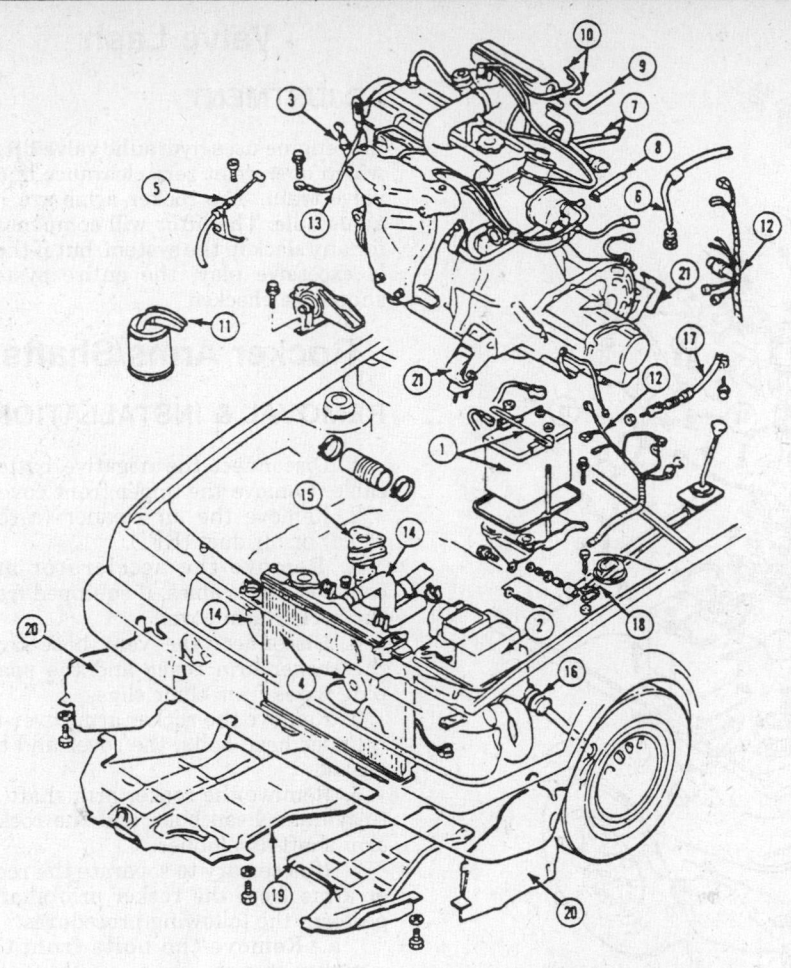

1. Battery and carrier
2. Air cleaner assembly
3. Dipstick
4. Cooling fan and radiator cowling
5. Accelerator cable and cruise control cable (if equipped)
6. Speedometer cable
7. Fuel hoses
8. Heater hoses
9. Brake vacuum hose
10. Idle-up solenoid valve hoses
11. Canister hoses
12. Engine harness connectors
13. Engine ground
14. Upper and lower radiator hose
15. Exhaust pipe
16. Halfshafts
17. Clutch control cable (manual transaxle)
18. Shift control rod
19. Engine splash shield
20. Inner fender panel
21. Engine mounts

Exploded view of the engine/transaxle assembly removal and installation—EFI

29. Install the airconditioning compressor, if equipped.

30. Reconnect all hoses and wires. Install the fan and fan shroud.

31. Install the remaining components in the reverse order of removal.

32. Refill the cooling system, the crankcase and the transaxle. Connect the battery. Install the hood.

33. Start the engine, allow it to reach normal operating temperature and check for leaks.

Engine Mounts

REMOVAL & INSTALLATION

1. Disconnect the negative battery cable.

2. Raise and support the vehicle safely. Drain the cooling system.

3. Disconnect the upper and lower radiator hoses.

4. Position a suitable jack with a block of wood, under the engine.

5. Remove the engine-to-mount bolts and the mount-to-frame bolts.

6. Relieve the pressure from the mount by jacking the engine until the mount can be removed. Remove the mount.

7. Installation is the reverse order of the removal procedure.

8. Fill the cooling system to correct level. Connect the negative battery cable.

9. Road test the vehicle and check mounts for looseness.

Cylinder Head

REMOVAL & INSTALLATION

1. Disconnect the negative battery cable.

2. Remove the timing belt and rocker arm assembly.

3. Remove the exhaust manifold.

4. Using a clean drain pan, place it under the radator. Open the drain cock and drain the cooling system.

5. Remove the spark plug wires and the spark plugs.

6. Remove the distributor-to-cylinder head bolts and the distributor from the engine.

7. From the front/rear of the engine, remove the engine lifting eyes. Disconnect the ground wire from the engine.

8. Disconnect the electrical harness connectors which may interfere with the cylinder head removal.

9. Remove the upper radiator hose, the water bypass hose and bracket.

10. Remove the cylinder head-to-engine bolts and the cylinder head.

11. Clean the gasket mounting surfaces. Check and/or replace the damaged or worn parts.

To install:

12. Prior to installation, clean the mating surfaces of the cylinder head and cylinder block throughly of any gasket material.

13. Position the cylinder head gasket on the engine block and install the cylinder head.

14. Coat the cylinder head bolts with oil and install them into the head. Tighten the cylinder head bolts in sequence to 50–60 ft. lbs. (75–81 Nm) in 2 steps.

15. Install the water bypass hose and bracket and upper radiator hose.

16. Reconnect the wire harness connectors.

17. Install the front and rear engine lifting eyes to the cylinder head and the engine ground wire.

18. Install the distributor, spark plugs and spark plug wires.

19. Install the intake and exhaust manifolds. Torque the intake manifold-to-cylinder head bolts to 14–19 ft. lbs.

Valve Lash

ADJUSTMENT

The engine uses hydraulic valve lifters which operate at zero clearance in the valve train. The rocker arms are not adjustable. The lifter will compensate for any slack in the system, but if there is excessive play, the entire system should be checked.

Rocker Arms/Shafts

REMOVAL & INSTALLATION

1. Disconnect the negative battery cable. Remove the upper front cover.
2. Remove the air cleaner (carbureted) or air duct (EFI).
3. Remove the accelerator and cruise control cables, if equipped from the rocker arm cover.
4. Disconnect the vent hose from the rocker arm cover and the spark plug wires from their clips.
5. Remove the rocker arm cover-to-cylinder head bolts, the cover and the gasket.
6. Remove the rocker arm shaft(s)-to-cylinder head bolts and the rocker arm shaft assemblies.
7. If necessary to separate the rocker arms from the rocker arm shafts, perform the following procedures:
    a. Remove the bolts from the rocker arm(s).
    b. Slide the rocker arm and springs from the shafts.

NOTE: Be sure to keep all the parts in order of disassembly for reinstallation purposes. The rocker arm shafts can only be installed in 1 position.

8. Clean the gasket mounting surfaces. Check and/or replace the parts if worn or damaged.

NOTE: To prevent damage to the O-ring on the hydraulic lash adjuster of the rocker arm, do not tamper with it unless replacement is necessary.

To install:
9. To install, use new gasket or seal-

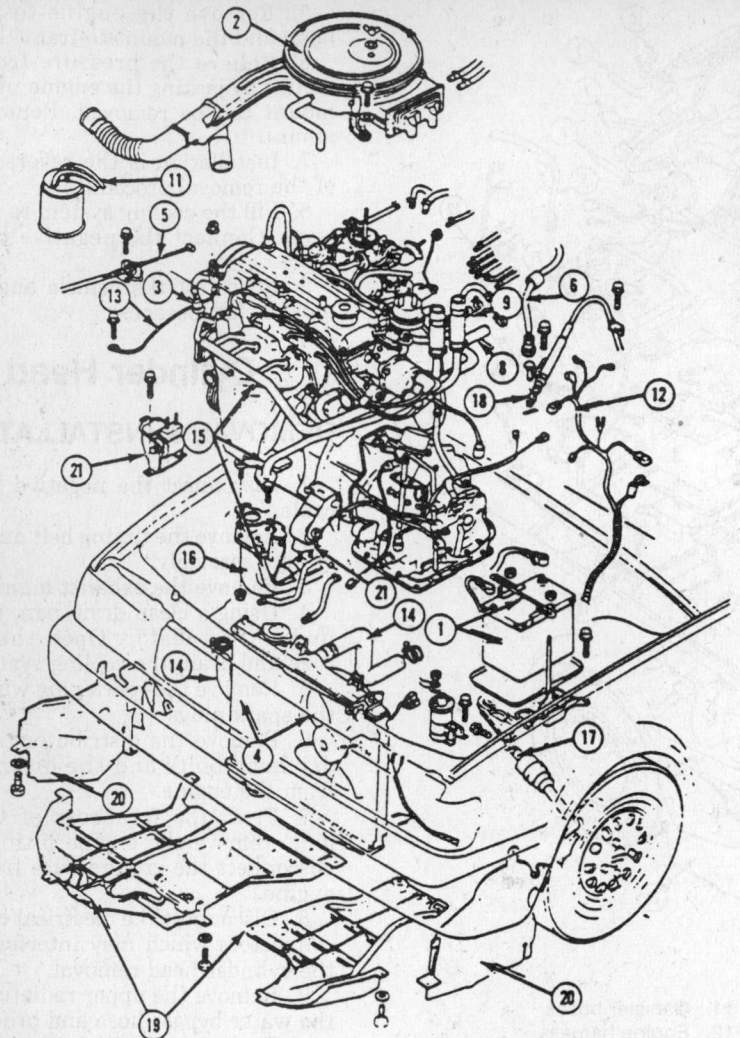

1. Battery and carrier
2. Air cleaner assembly
3. Dipstick
4. Cooling fan and radiator cowling
5. Accelerator cable and cruise control cable (if equipped)
6. Speedometer cable
7. Fuel hoses
8. Heater hoses
9. Brake vacuum hose
10. 3-way solenoid valve hoses
11. Canister hoses
12. Engine harness connectors
13. Engine ground
14. Upper and lower radiator hose
15. Secondary air pipe
16. Exhaust pipe
17. Halfshafts
18. Shift control cable or rod
19. Engine splash shield
20. Inner fender panel
21. Engine mounts

Exploded view of the engine/transaxle assembly removal and installation—carbureted

and the exhaust manifold-to-cylinder head bolts to 23–34 ft. lbs.
20. Install the rocker arm cover, timing belt and timing belt cover.
21. Install the water pump pulley and drive belts.
22. Fill the cooling system to the correct level.
23. The remainder of the installation is the reverse order of the removal procedure.
24. Torque the air injection pipes-to-exhaust manifold bolts to 12–20 ft. lbs.
25. Connect the negative battery cable.
26. Start the engine, allow it to reach normal operating temperature and check for leaks.

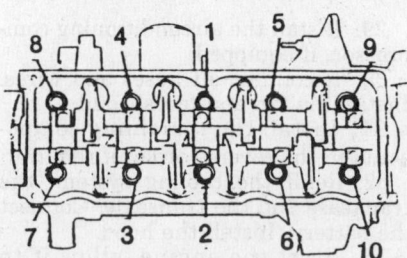

View of the cylinder head torque sequence

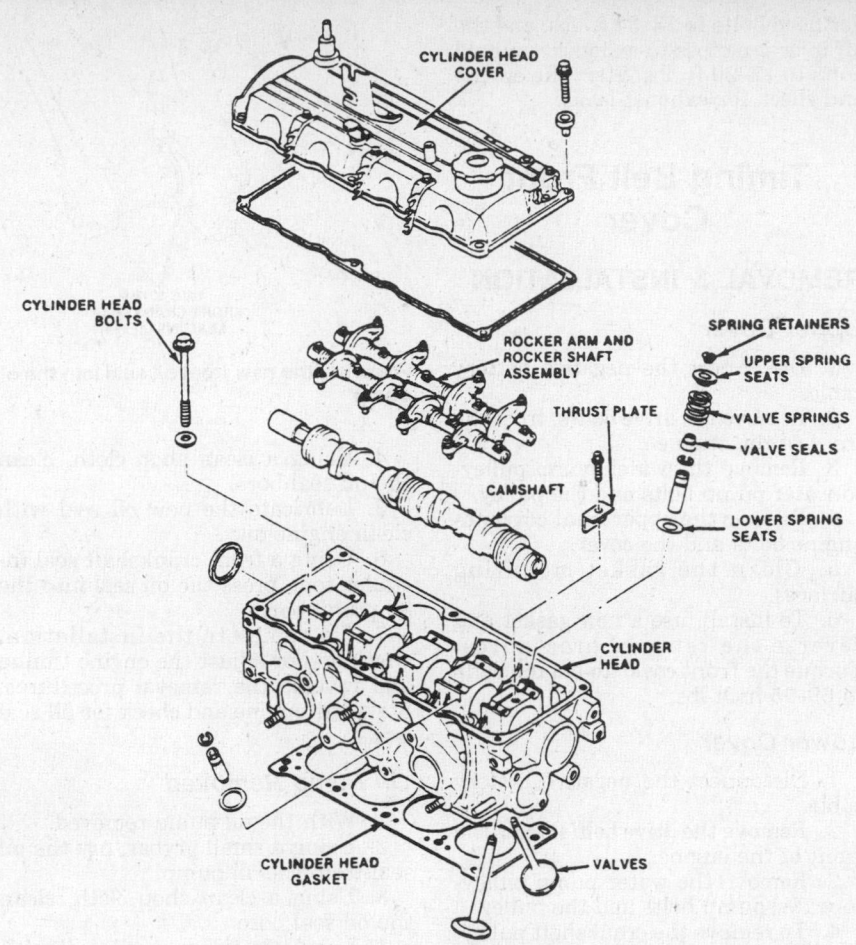

Exploded view of the cylinder head assembly

ant and reverse the removal procedures. Torque the rocker arm shaft(s)-to-cylinder head (oil holes facing downward) bolts to 16–21 ft. lbs. and the rocker arm cover-to-cylinder head bolts to 44–79 inch lbs.

NOTE: When torquing the rocker arm shaft(s)-to-cylinder head bolts, start in the center and move outwards in both directions.

10. To complete the installation, reverse the removal procedures. Start the engine and check for leaks.

Intake Manifold

REMOVAL & INSTALLATION

1. Disconnect the negative battery cable.

2. Using a clean drain pan, place it under the radiator. Remove the cooling system expansion tank cap, open the drain cock and drain the cooling system.

3. Disconnect the accelerator cable.

4. Label and disconnect all of the necessary wiring and hoses which may interfere with the intake manifold removal.

5. Remove the carburetor, if equipped. Remove the throttle body and the intake plenum, if equipped.

6. Remove the intake manifold-to-cylinder head bolts, the intake manifold and the gasket.

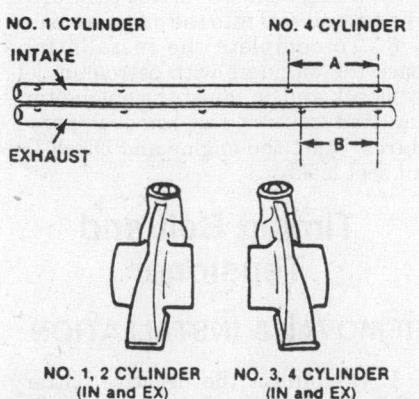

View of the rocker arm shafts and rocker arms

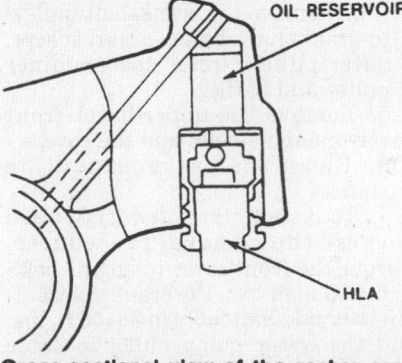

Cross-sectional view of the rocker arm, showing the Hydraulic Lash adjuster (HLA)

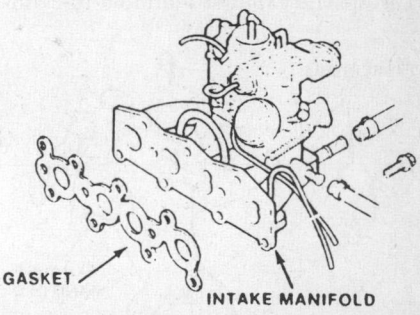

View of the intake manifold—carbureted engines

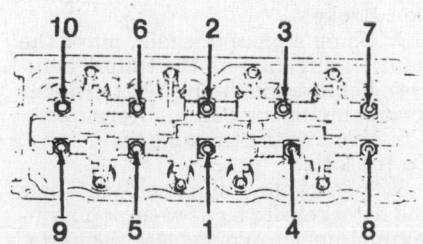

View of the rocker arm assembly torquing sequence

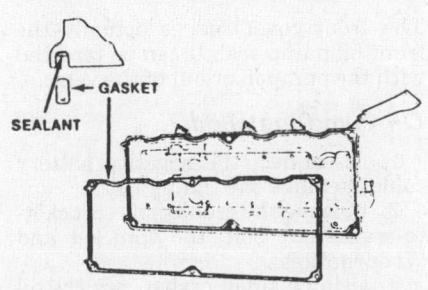

Preparing the valve cover for installation

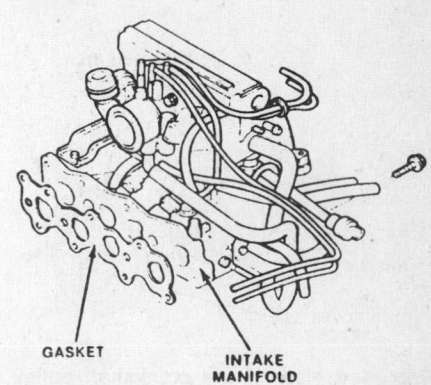

View of the intake manifold—EFI engines

13–17

7. Clean the gasket mounting surfaces. Clean and inspect the parts for damage and/or wear; replace the parts, if necessary.

8. To install, use new gaskets and reverse the removal procedures. Torque the intake manifold-to-cylinder head bolts to 14–19 ft. lbs. Refill the cooling system. Start the engine, allow it to reach normal operating temperature and check for leaks.

Exhaust Manifold

REMOVAL & INSTALLATION

1. Disconnect the negative battery cable.

2. If equipped with a carburetor, remove air cleaner and the air injection pipes from the exhaust manifold.

3. If equipped with EFI, disconnect the electrical connector from the oxygen sensor.

4. Remove the exhaust insulators-to-exhaust manifold bolts and the insulators.

5. Remove the exhaust pipe-to-exhaust manifold nuts and separate the exhaust pipe from the manifold.

6. Remove the exhaust manifold-to-cylinder head bolts, the manifold and the gasket.

7. Clean the gasket mounting surfaces. Inspect the parts for damage and replace them, if necessary.

8. To install, use new gaskets and reverse the removal procedures. Torque the exhaust manifold-to-cylin-

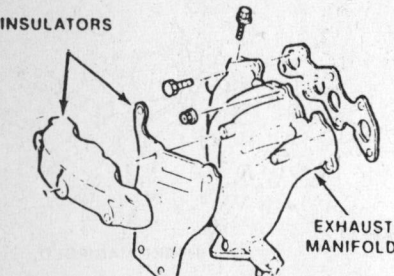

Exploded view of the exhaust manifold

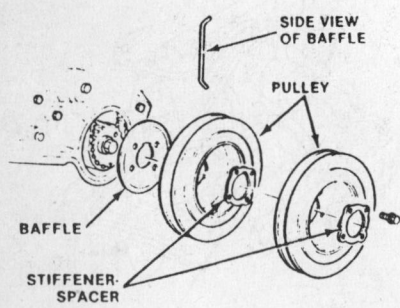

Exploded view of the crankshaft pulley assembly

der head bolts to 23–34 ft. lbs. and the air injection pipes-to-exhaust manifold bolts to 12–20 ft. lbs. Start the engine and check for exhaust leaks.

Timing Belt Front Cover

REMOVAL & INSTALLATION

Upper Cover

1. Disconnect the negative battery cable.

2. Remove the drive belt(s) from the front of the engine.

3. Remove the water pump pulley-to-water pump bolts and the pulley.

4. Remove the upper front cover-to-engine bolts and the cover.

5. Clean the gasket mounting surfaces.

6. To install, use a new gasket and reverse the removal procedures. Torque the front cover-to-engine bolts to 69–95 inch lbs.

Lower Cover

1. Disconnect the negative battery cable.

2. Remove the drive belt(s) from the front of the engine.

3. Remove the water pump pulley-to-water pump bolts and the pulley.

4. To remove the crankshaft pulley, perform the following procedures:
   a. Remove the right inner fender panel.
   b. Remove the crankshaft pulley-to-crankshaft bolts, outer spacer, outer pulley, inner spacer, inner pulley and baffle.

5. Remove the upper/lower front cover-to-engine bolts and the covers.

6. Clean the gasket mounting surfaces.

7. To install, use a new gasket and reverse the removal procedures. Torque the front cover-to-engine bolts to 69–95 inch lbs., the crankshaft pulley-to-crankshaft bolts to 36–45 ft. lbs. and the water pump pulley-to-water pump bolts to 36–45 ft. lbs.

OIL SEAL REPLACEMENT

The front cover seal is actually the front oil pump seal. It can be replaced with the pump in or out of the vehicle.

Oil Pump Installed

1. Disconnect the negative battery cable. Remove the timing belt.

2. Remove the crankshaft sprocket-to-crankshaft bolt, the sprocket and Woodruff key.

3. Using a small prybar, pry the oil seal from the oil pump housing.

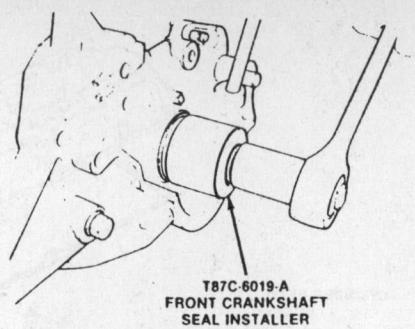

T87C-6019-A
FRONT CRANKSHAFT SEAL INSTALLER

Pressing the new front oil seal into the oil pump

4. Using a clean shop cloth, clean the oil seal bore.

5. Lubricate the new oil seal with clean engine oil.

6. Using a front crankshaft seal installer tool, press the oil seal into the oil pump bore.

7. To complete the installation, check and/or adjust the engine timing and reverse the removal procedures. Start the engine and check for oil seal leaks.

Oil Pump Removed

1. With the oil pump removed.

2. Using a small prybar, pry the oil seal from the oil pump.

3. Using a clean shop cloth, clean the oil seal bore.

4. Lubricate the new oil seal with clean engine oil.

5. Using a oil seal driver tool, drive the new oil seal into the oil pump bore.

6. To complete the installation, pack the oil pump with petroleum jelly, check and/or adjust the engine timing and reverse the removal procedures. Start the engine and check for oil seal leaks.

Timing Belt and Tensioner

REMOVAL & INSTALLATION

1. Disconnect the negative battery cable. Remove the front covers.

2. Remove the No. 1 spark plug. Rotate the crankshaft to position the No. 1 cylinder on the TDC of its compression stroke.

3. Using a piece of chalk, mark the rotation direction on the timing belt.

4. Remove the timing belt tensioner spring, mounting bolt and tensioner.

5. Remove the timing belt.

To install:

6. Inspect the timing belt tensioner and sprockets for signs wear or oil contamination, clean or replace the parts.

7. Check and/or align the camshaft and crankshaft sprockets with the cyl-

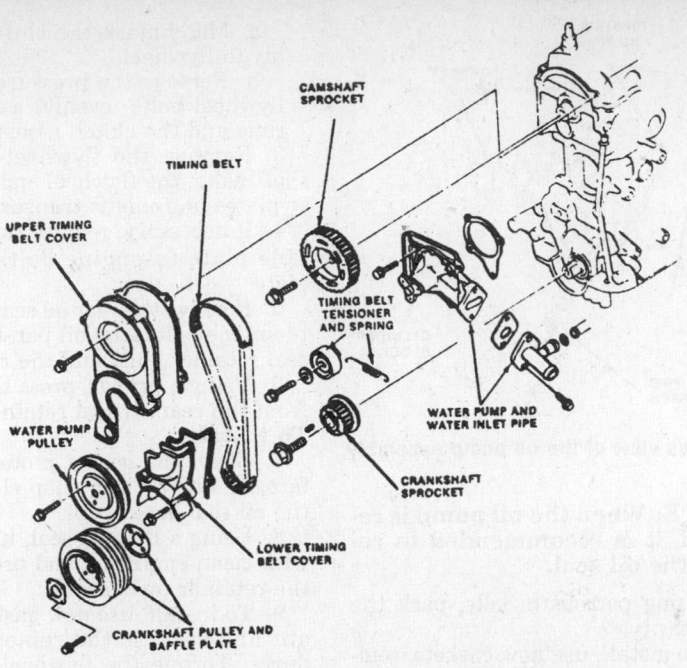

Exploded view of the timing belt assembly

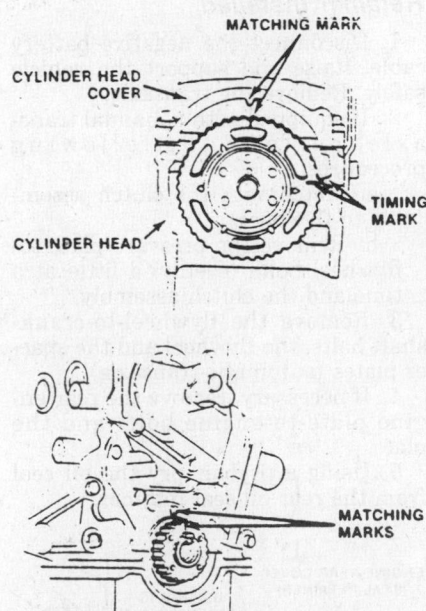

View of the camshaft and crankshaft sprocket alignment marks

inder head and oil pump alignment marks.

NOTE: If the No. 1 cylinder is not on the TDC of its compression stroke, rotate the crankshaft 1 complete revolution and realign the timing mark on the oil pump housing.

8. If reusing the timing belt, install it in the direction of the rotation mark.
9. Install the timing belt tensioner

and spring; tighten the timing belt tensioner finger-tight.
10. Rotate the crankshaft 2 complete revolutions and realign the timing marks. Reaffirm that the timing marks are aligned, if not, repeat the alignment procedures.
11. Torque the tensioner bolt to 14–19 ft. lbs. and check the timing belt deflection; the timing belt deflection should be 0.35–0.39 in. at 22 lbs.
12. To complete the installation, reverse the removal procedures. Torque the front cover-to-engine bolts to 69–95 inch lbs., the crankshaft pulley-to-crankshaft bolts to 36–45 ft. lbs. and the water pump pulley-to-water pump bolts to 36–45 ft. lbs. Start the engine and allow it to reach normal operating temperature. Check and/or adjust the ignition timing.

Camshaft

REMOVAL & INSTALLATION

1. Disconnect the negative battery cable.
2. Remove the timing belt and rocker arm assembly.
3. Matchmark the distributor housing-to-cylinder head and rotor-to-distributor housing. Remove the distributor hold-down bolts and the distributor from the rear end of the camshaft.
4. Using a medium prybar (to prevent the camshaft from turning), remove the camshaft sprocket-to-camshaft bolt and the sprocket.

5. Using a small prybar, pry the camshaft oil seal from the cylinder.
6. From the rear camshaft bearing journal, remove the thrust plate-to-cylinder head bolt and the thrust plate.
7. Slide the camshaft forward and from the cylinder head; be careful not to damage the journals and/or the lobes.
To install:
8. Clean the gasket mounting surfaces. Clean and inspect the parts for damage and/or wear; replace the parts, if necessary.
9. To install, lubricate the parts with clean engine oil, use new gaskets or sealant and reverse the removal procedures. Torque the camshaft thrust plate bolt to 6–9 ft. lbs., the camshaft sprocket-to-camshaft bolt to 36–45 ft. lbs., the distributor hold-down bolt to 14–22 ft. lbs.
10. To complete the installation, reverse the removal procedures. Refill the cooling system. Check the ignition timing. Start the engine, allow it to reach normal operating temperature and check for leaks.

Piston and Connecting Rod

POSITIONING

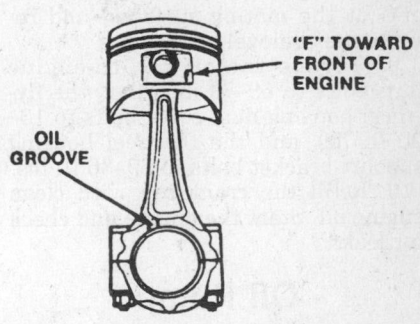

View of the piston and connecting rod positioning

ENGINE LUBRICATION

Oil Pan

REMOVAL & INSTALLATION

1. Disconnect the negative battery cable.
2. Raise and support the vehicle safely.
3. Remove the under engine splash

13 Ford Motor Co. TRACER

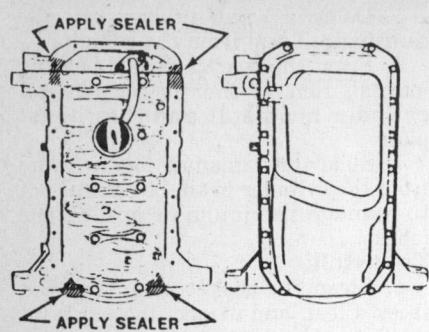

Apply sealant to oil pan-to-engine mating surfaces

shields and the right front inner fender panel.

4. Using a drain pan, place it under the engine, remove the oil pan plug and drain the crankcase.

5. Remove the flywheel-to-engine support housing bracket and the dust cover from the flywheel housing.

6. Remove the oil pan-to-engine nuts, bolts and stiffeners.

NOTE: If might be necessary to rotate the crankshaft to clear the oil pan.

To install:

7. Clean the gasket mounting surfaces. Clean and inspect the parts for damage; replace the parts, it necessary.

8. To install, use new gaskets, sealant (at the mating surfaces) and reverse the removal procedures.

9. Torque the oil pan-to-engine nuts/bolts to 69–79 inch lbs., the flywheel housing dust cover bolts to 13–20 ft. lbs. and the flywheel housing support bracket bolts to 69–86 ft. lbs.

10. Refill the crankcase with clean engine oil. Start the engine and check for leaks.

Oil Pump

REMOVAL & INSTALLATION

The oil pump is located on the front of the engine, behind the crankshaft pulley.

1. Disconnect the negative battery cable.

2. Remove the timing belt and the oil pan.

3. Remove the crankshaft sprocket-to-crankshaft bolt and the sprocket.

4. Remove the oil pickup tube-to-oil pump bolts and the tube. Remove the dipstick and the dipstick tube.

5. Remove the oil pump-to-engine bolts and the oil pump.

To install:

6. Clean the gasket mounting surfaces. Clean and inspect the parts for wear and/or damage, replace the parts, if necessary.

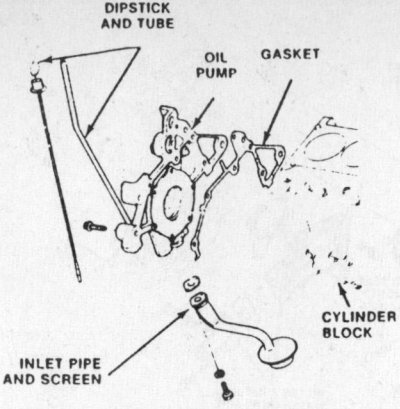

Exploded view of the oil pump assembly

NOTE: When the oil pump is removed, it is recommended to replace the oil seal.

7. Using petroleum jelly, pack the pump cavity.

8. To install, use new gaskets, sealant and reverse the removal procedures. Torque the oil pump-to-engine bolts to 14–19 ft. lbs. Refill the crankcase with clean engine oil. Start the engine and check for leaks.

CHECKING

1. With the oil pump disassembled, inspect the body for scoring damage and/or wear; if necessary, discard the worn parts.

2. Using a feeler gauge, inspect the pump body-to-outer gear clearance; it should not be greater than 0.0087 in.

3. Using a feeler gauge, inspect the inner gear tip-to-outer gear clearance; the maximum clearance should be 0.0078 in.

4. Using a feeler gauge, inspect the gears-to-pump housing endplay; the clearance should be no greater than 0.0055 in.

NOTE: If the above measurements are not within limits, replace the necessary parts.

5. Be sure to clean the relief valve, the screen and the pick-up tube.

Rear Main Bearing Oil Seal

REMOVAL & INSTALLATION

Retainer Removed

1. Disconnect the negative battery cable. Raise and support the vehicle safely. Remove the transaxle.

2. If equipped with a manual transaxle, perform the following procedures:

a. Matchmark the clutch assembly-to-flywheel.

b. Remove the pressure plate-to-flywheel bolts (evenly) a little at a time and the clutch assembly.

3. Remove the flywheel-to-crankshaft bolts, the flywheel and the spacer plates (automatic transaxle).

4. If necessary, remove the rear engine plate-to-engine bolts and the plate.

5. Remove the rear oil seal retainer-to-engine bolts, the oil pan-to-rear oil seal retainer bolts and the retainer.

6. Using a prybar, press the oil seal from the rear oil seal retainer.

To install:

7. Clean the gasket mounting surfaces. Using a clean shop cloth, clean the oil seal bore.

8. Using a new oil seal, lubricate it with clean engine oil and press it into the retainer until seats.

9. To install, use new gaskets, sealant and reverse the remove procedures. Torque the flywheel-to-crankshaft bolts to 71–76 ft. lbs. and the transaxle-to-engine bolts to 16–40 ft. lbs. (manual) or 47–66 ft. lbs.

Retainer Installed

1. Disconnect the negative battery cable. Raise and support the vehicle safely. Remove the transaxle.

2. If equipped with a manual transaxle, perform the following procedures:

a. Matchmark the clutch assembly-to-flywheel.

b. Remove the pressure plate-to-flywheel bolts (evenly) a little at a time and the clutch assembly.

3. Remove the flywheel-to-crankshaft bolts, the flywheel and the spacer plates (automatic transaxle).

4. If necessary, remove the rear engine plate-to-engine bolts and the plate.

5. Using a prybar, pry the oil seal from the rear oil seal retainer.

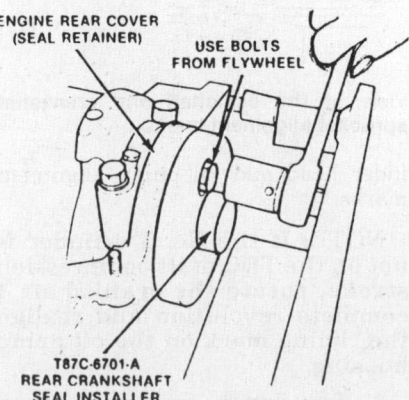

Using the oil seal installation tool to install the rear main oil seal.

To install:

6. Using a clean shop cloth, clean the oil seal bore.

7. Lubricate the new seal with clean engine.

8. Using a rear main seal installer tool, press the new oil seal into the retainer until it seats.

9. To complete the installation, reverse the removal procedures. Torque the flywheel-to-crankshaft bolts to 71–76 ft. lbs. and the transaxle-to-engine bolts to 16–40 ft. lbs. (manual) or 47–66 ft. lbs. (automatic).

MANUAL TRANSAXLE

For further information on transmissions/transaxles, please refer to "Chilton's Guide to Transmission Repair".

Transaxle Assembly

REMOVAL & INSTALLATION

1. Disconnect the negative battery cable.

2. Remove the air cleaner. Loosen the front wheel lug nuts.

3. From the transaxle, disconnect the speedometer cable.

4. From the clutch release lever, remove the adjusting nut, pin and the clutch cable. Remove the clutch cable bracket-to-transaxle bolts and the bracket. Remove the ground wire bolt and ground wire.

5. Remove the coolant pipe bracket bolt and the bracket.

6. Remove the secondary air pipe, the EGR pipe bracket and the electrical harness clip.

7. Disconnect the neutral switch/back-up light switch coupler and the body ground connector.

8. Remove the upper 2 transaxle-to-engine bolts.

9. Using a engine support bar tool, attach it to the rear engine lifting hook and support the engine's weight.

10. Raise and support the vehicle safely.

11. Place a drain pan under the transaxle, remove the drain plug and drain the transaxle.

12. Remove the front wheel lug nuts and the wheels. Remove the engine undercover and side covers.

13. Remove the front stabilizer bar. From both sides, remove the lower control arm ball joint-to-steering knuckle nut/bolt, pull the control arm

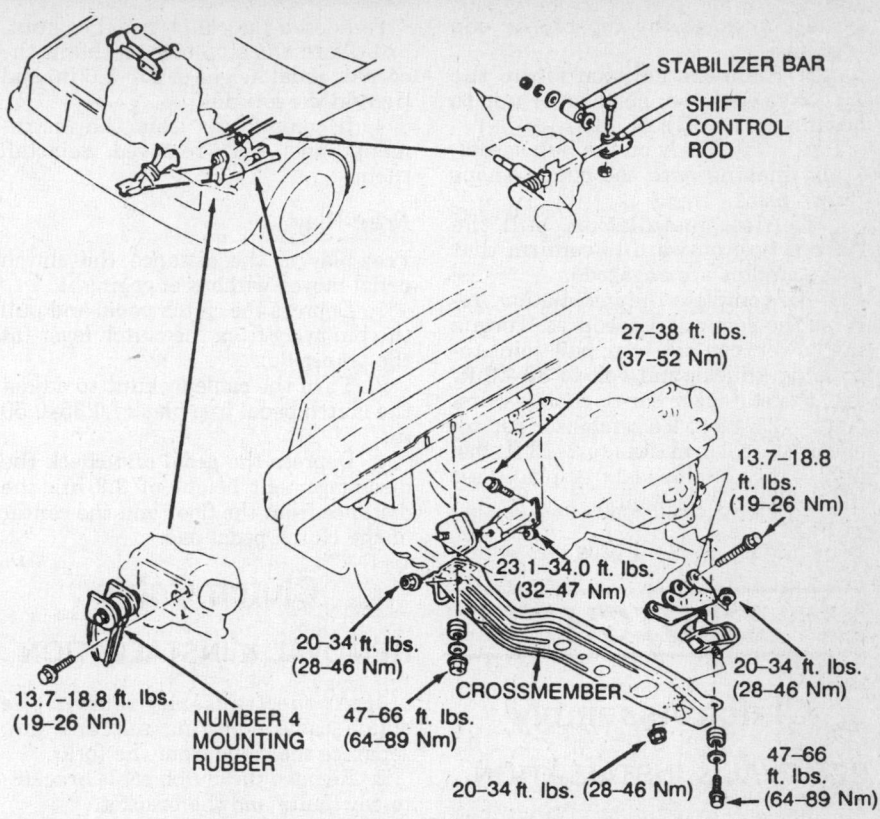

Exploded view of the crossmember and bracket assemblies

downward and separate the lower control arm from the steering knuckle.

NOTE: When separating the ball joint, be careful not to damage the ball joint dust boot.

14. Using both hands, grasp the steering knuckle/hub assembly, apply even pressure (gradually increasing), pull both halfshafts from the transaxle.

NOTE: When removing the halfshafts, withdraw them completely from the transaxle (to prevent damage to the oil seal lips), do not move the CV-joints in excess of a 20 degree angle (damage to the boots and/or joint may occur) and use a wire to support the halfshaft in the horizontal position.

15. From under the vehicle, remove the crossmember-to-chassis bolts and the crossmember.

16. Remove the shift control rod-to-transaxle nut/bolt and slide the control rod aside. Remove the shift extension bar-to-bracket bolt and slide the extension bar off the bracket.

17. Remove the starter's positive cable-to-solenoid nut and the solenoid wire by pulling the wire from the connector.

18. Remove the starter-to-engine

bolts and the starter. Remove the dust cover-to-clutch housing bolts and the cover.

19. Loosen the bracket bar on the engine support tool to lower the transaxle. Using a floor jack, support the transaxle.

20. Remove the No. 2 engine mount-to-transaxle nut/bolt, the transaxle-to-engine bolts and lower the transaxle from the vehicle.

To install:

21. Install the transaxle by performing the following procedures:

a. Apply a small amount of clutch grease to the input shaft spline and reverse the removal procedures.

b. Torque the transaxle-to-engine bolts to 47–66 ft. lbs., the No. 2 engine mount-to-transaxle nut/bolt to 27–38 ft. lbs., the starter to engine bolts to 23–34 ft. lbs., the extension bar-to-transaxle bracket bolt to 23–34 ft. lbs., the control rod-to-transaxle nut/bolt to 12–17 ft. lbs., the crossmember-to-chassis bolts to 47–66 ft. lbs., the rear engine mount-to-crossmember nut to 20–34 ft. lbs.

c. Refill the transaxle with Dexron®II or equivalent.

22. To install the halfshaft into the transaxle, perform the following procedures:

a. Install a new locking clip on the halfshaft spline; be sure the gap in the clip is at the top of the clip groove.

b. Slide the halfshafts into the transaxle bore; be careful not to damage the oil seal lip.

c. Push firmly on the hub assembly, making sure the circlip snaps into place.

d. After installation, pull the front hub outward to confirm that the circlips are engaged.

23. To complete the installation, reverse the removal procedures. Torque the lower control arm ball joint-to-steering knuckle nut/bolt to 32–40 ft. lbs., the stabilizer bar-to-chassis nuts/bolts to 23–33 ft. lbs., stabilizer bar-to-lower control arm nuts to 9–13 ft. lbs. Adjust the clutch pedal free-play. Test the vehicle performance.

CLUTCH

Clutch Assembly

REMOVAL & INSTALLATION

1. Disconnect the negative battery cable. Raise and support the vehicle safely. Remove the transaxle.

2. Using a flywheel locking tool, install it onto the engine, engage the flywheel ring gear tooth (to secure the flywheel). Using a clutch aligning tool, install it into the clutch disc and pilot shaft; this will support the clutch assembly.

3. Matchmark the pressure plate-to-flywheel for reinstallation purposes.

4. Remove the pressure plate-to-flywheel bolts, evenly, a little at a time.

5. Remove the pressure plate and clutch disc.

6. Inspect the pilot bearing, the flywheel, the pressure plate and clutch disc for wear and/or damage; replace the parts, if necessary.

7. To install, reverse the removal procedures. Torque the flywheel-to-crankshaft bolts to 71–75 ft. lbs., the pressure plate-to-flywheel bolts to 13–20 ft. lbs. Adjust the clutch pedal free-play.

PEDAL HEIGHT/FREE-PLAY ADJUSTMENT

Pedal Height

Pedal height is the distance from the cowl to the center of the clutch pedal pad.

1. Remove the necessary instrument panel components which block access to the clutch pedal.

2. Loosen the clutch pedal locknut.

3. Turn the stop bolt to obtain the correct pedal height of 8.4–8.6 in. and tighten the locknut.

4. If components from the instrument panel were removed, reinstall them.

Free-Play

Free-play is the distance the clutch pedal moves without engaging it.

1. Depress the clutch pedal and pull the pin away from the clutch lever (at the transaxle).

2. Turn the cable locknut to adjust the clutch pedal free-play of 0.35–0.59 in.

3. Depress the pedal and check the disengagement height of 3.3 in.; the distance from the floor and the center of the clutch pedal pad.

Clutch Cable

REMOVAL & INSTALLATION

1. At the transaxle, remove the clutch cable adjusting nut and pin; separate the cable from the fork.

2. Remove the clutch cable bracket-to-cowl nuts and the bracket.

3. From under the instrument panel, separate the clutch cable from the top of the clutch pedal.

4. Pull the cable through the cowl and remove the cable assembly from the engine side.

5. Inspect the clutch cable housing for frayed wire, cracked or worn housing and the cable for smooth operation; replace the cable assembly, if necessary.

6. To install, lubricate the cable with multi-purpose grease and reverse the removal procedures. Adjust the clutch pedal free-play.

AUTOMATIC TRANSAXLE

For further information on transmissions/transaxles, please refer to "Chilton's Guide to Transmission Repair".

Transaxle Assembly

REMOVAL & INSTALLATION

1. Disconnect the negative battery cable.

2. Remove the air cleaner. Loosen the front wheel lug nuts.

3. From the transaxle, disconnect the speedometer cable.

4. Disconnect the shift control cable-to-transaxle clip and 2 bracket bolts. Remove the ground wire from the cylinder head.

5. Remove the water pipe bracket bolt and the bracket.

6. Remove the secondary air pipe, the EGR pipe bracket and the electrical harness clip.

7. Disconnect the electrical connectors from the inhibitor switch, the neutral switch and the kickdown solenoid. Disconnect the body ground connector.

8. Remove the upper 2 transaxle-to-engine bolts.

9. Remove the vacuum hose from the vacuum diaphragm line. Disconnect and plug the oil cooler line at the transaxle.

10. Using a engine support bar tool, attach it to the rear engine lifting hook and support the engine's weight.

11. Raise and support the vehicle safely.

12. Place a drain pan under the transaxle, remove the drain plug and drain the transaxle.

13. Remove the front wheel lug nuts and the wheels. Remove the engine undercover and side covers.

14. Remove the front stabilizer bar. From both sides, remove the lower control arm ball joint-to-steering knuckle nut/bolt, pull the control arm downward and separate the lower control arm from the steering knuckle.

NOTE: When separating the ball joint, be careful not to damage the ball joint dust boot.

15. Using a medium prybar, insert it between the halfshaft and the transaxle (a notch is provided), pry both halfshafts from the transaxle.

NOTE: When removing the halfshafts, withdraw them completely from the transaxle (to prevent damage to the oil seal lips), do not move the CV-joints in excess of a 20 degree angle (damage to the boots and/or joint may occur) and use a wire to support the halfshaft in the horizontal position.

16. From under the vehicle, remove the crossmember-to-chassis bolts and the crossmember.

17. Remove the starter's positive cable-to-solenoid nut and the solenoid wire by pulling the wire from the connector.

18. Remove the starter-to-engine bolts and the starter. Remove the dust cover-to-clutch housing bolts and the cover.

19. Matchmark the torque converter-to-flexplate location. Remove the

torque converter-to-flexplate bolts and slide the torque converter back into the transaxle.

20. Loosen the bracket bar on the engine support tool to lower the transaxle. Using a floor jack, support the transaxle.

21. Remove the No. 2 engine mount-to-transaxle nut/bolt, the transaxle-to-engine bolts and lower the transaxle from the vehicle.

To install:

22. To install the transaxle, reverse the removal procedures. Torque the transaxle-to-engine bolts to 47–66 ft. lbs., the No. 2 engine mount-to-transaxle nut/bolt to 27–38 ft. lbs., the starter to engine bolts to 23–34 ft. lbs., the crossmember-to-chassis bolts to 47–66 ft. lbs., the rear engine mount-to-crossmember nut to 20–34 ft. lbs. Refill the transaxle with Dexron®II or equivalent.

23. To install the halfshaft into the transaxle, perform the following procedures:

   a. Install a new locking clip on the halfshaft spline; be sure the gap in the clip is at the top of the clip groove.

   b. Slide the halfshafts into the transaxle bore; be careful not to damage the oil seal lip.

   c. Push firmly on the hub assembly, making sure the circlip snaps into place.

   d. After installation, pull the front hub outward to confirm that the circlips are engaged.

24. To complete the installation, reverse the removal procedures. Torque the lower control arm ball joint-to-steering knuckle nut/bolt to 32–40 ft. lbs., the stabilizer bar-to-chassis nuts/bolts to 23–33 ft. lbs., stabilizer bar-to-lower control arm nuts to 9–13 ft. lbs. Test the vehicle performance.

MANUAL SHIFT LINKAGE ADJUSTMENT

1. Place the gear selector lever in the **N** position.

2. At the transaxle, remove the shift cable trunnion-to-transaxle shift lever spring clip and pin.

3. Rotate the transaxle shift lever fully counterclockwise to place it in the **P** position.

4. Move the transaxle shift lever clockwise 2 detents to place it in the **N** position.

NOTE: When moving the transaxle shift lever, be sure to position it between the ends of the shift cable trunnion.

5. If the trunnion holes align with the shift lever hole, the cable is adjusted, replace the pin and spring clip. If

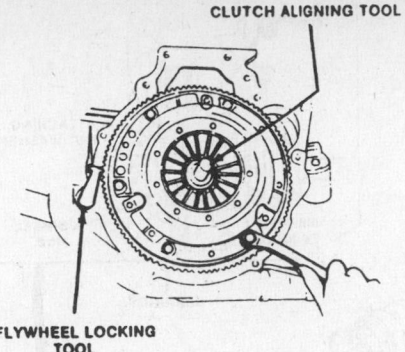

Using tools to replace the clutch assembly

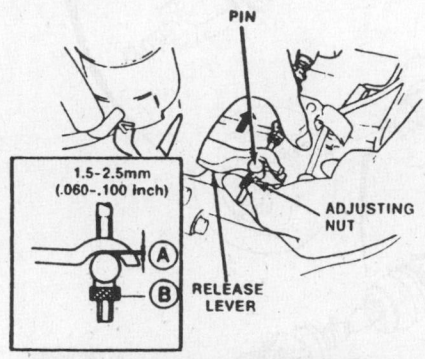

Adjusting the clutch pedal free-play

the holes are not aligned, proceed with the remaining adjustment procedures.

6. From inside the vehicle, remove the shift quadrant bezel-to-console screws. Lift the front of the bezel to disengage it from the console and rotate it to provide access to the cable adjusting nuts.

7. At the shift cable, loosen the adjusting nuts.

8. Position the gear selector lever in the **P** position and inspect the detent spring roller. If the spring is not centered, perform the following procedures:

   a. Loosen the detent spring roller screws and move the spring to center it in the **P** position.

   b. Position the shift quadrant in the **P** position and reinstall the screws.

9. Move the shift selector lever to the **N** position.

10. Move the shift cable adjuster nuts until the holes in the cable trunnion and transaxle shift lever are aligned. Torque the shift cable adjuster nuts to 69–95 inch lbs.

11. Recheck the cable trunnion and transaxle shift lever holes for alignment. If aligned, install the pin and spring clip.

12. Using an assistant to watch the transaxle shift lever movement, start with the gear selector lever in the **N** position, push the shift interlock button and carefully move the shift lever

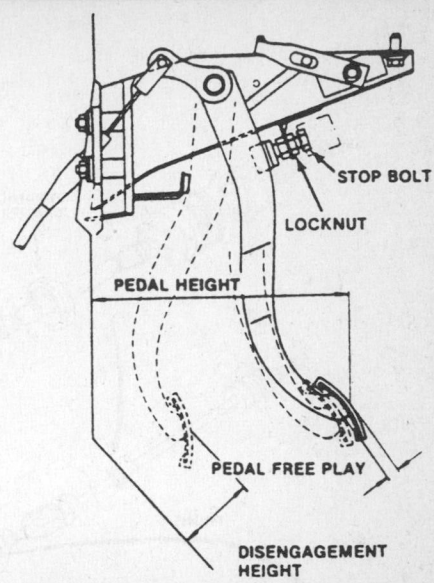

Adjusting the clutch pedal height and free-play

rearward until the transaxle shift lever begins to move; note the amount of shift selector movement.

13. If the shift selector lever forward movement **a** does not equal the rearward movement **b**, turn the adjuster nuts until the movement is equal.

NOTE: Make sure the adjustment procedure does not affect the neutral safety switch operation. Apply the parking brakes and try to start the enigne in the N and P positions. If the engine starts in any other gear selector lever positions, check and adjust the linkage adjustment and the neutral safety switch adjustment.

14. To complete the installation, reverse the removal procedures.

DRIVE AXLE

Halfshaft

REMOVAL & INSTALLATION

1. Raise and support the vehicle safely.

2. Remove the necessary splash covers from under the vehicle.

3. Remove the stabilizer bar-to-lower control arm nuts, bolt, washers and bushing.

4. Remove the wheel/tire assembly and the hub grease cap.

5. Using a stake chisel and a hammer, raise the staked portion of the hub nut.

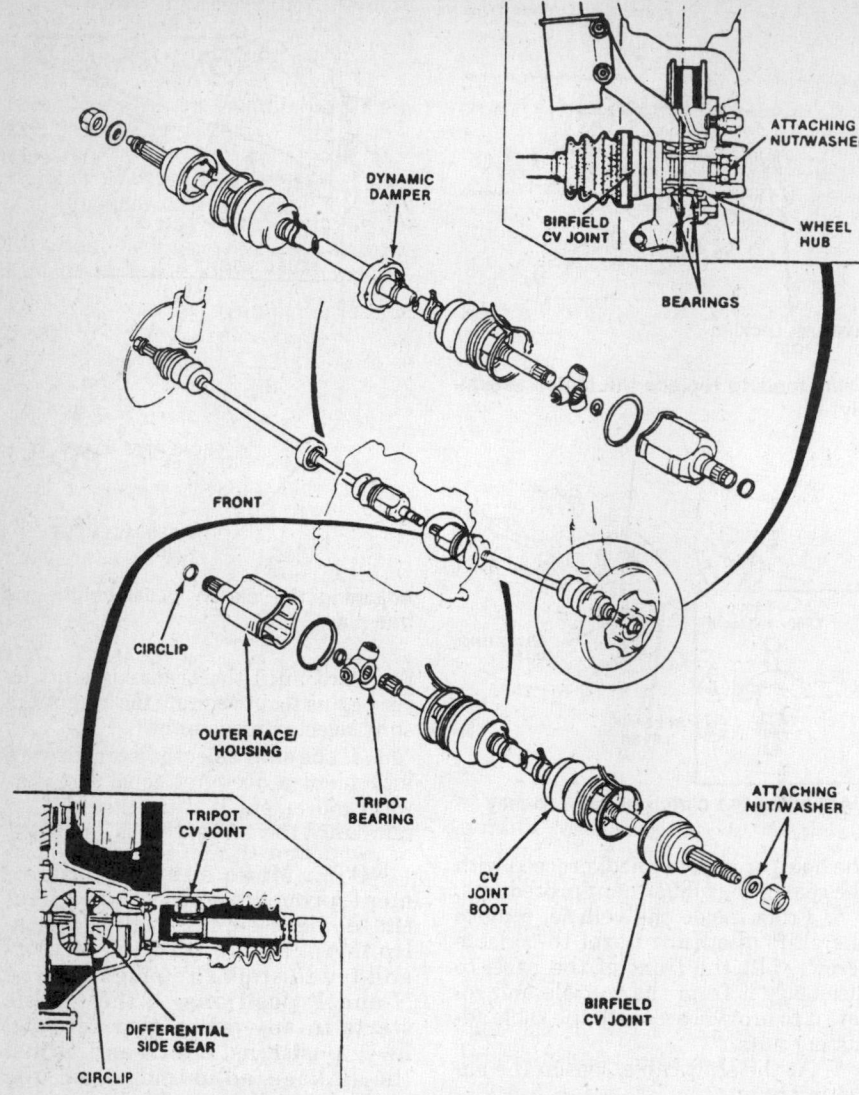

Exploded view of the halfshaft assemblies

Labels in figure: ATTACHING NUT/WASHER, DYNAMIC DAMPER, BIRFIELD CV JOINT, WHEEL HUB, BEARINGS, FRONT, CIRCLIP, OUTER RACE/HOUSING, TRIPOT CV JOINT, TRIPOT BEARING, CV JOINT BOOT, ATTACHING NUT/WASHER, BIRFIELD CV JOINT, DIFFERENTIAL SIDE GEAR, CIRCLIP

To install:

12. To install the halfshaft into the transaxle, perform the following procedures:

  a. Install a new locking clip on the halfshaft spline; be sure the gap in the clip is at the top of the clip groove.

  b. Slide the halfshafts into the transaxle bore; be careful not to damage the oil seal lip.

  c. Push firmly on the hub assembly, making sure the circlip snaps into place.

  d. After installation, pull the front hub outward to confirm that the circlips are engaged.

13. Using multi-purpose grease, lubricate the halfshaft splines, lightly.

14. To complete the installation, reverse the removal procedures. Torque the lower control arm ball joint-to-steering knuckle bolt to 32–40 ft. lbs. and a new halfshaft nut to 157–235 ft. lbs. Using a cold chisel (with the cutting edge rounded), stake the hub nut.

CV-Boot

REMOVAL & INSTALLATION

Tri-Pot (Inner)

The tri-pot joints are used only with an automatic transaxle.

1. Remove the halfshaft from the vehicle and position it in a vise.

NOTE: The vise should be equipped with jaw caps to prevent damaging the halfshaft.

2. Using diagonal cutters, remove the boot clamps and roll the boot backward.

3. Using paint, matchmark the bearing outer race, the tri-pot bearing and the halfshaft.

4. Using a pair of needle-nose pliers, remove the wire ring bearing retainer from the bearing outer race. Remove the outer race.

5. Remove the tri-pot bearing-to-halfshaft snaping. Using a brass drift and a hammer, drive the tri-pot bearing from the halfshaft.

6. If the boot is to be reused, wrap tape around the halfshaft splines and remove the boot.

To install:

7. Inspect the bearing grease for grit; if necessary, replace or repack the bearing.

8. To install outer bearing race, lubricate it with 3.5 ounces of high temperature constant velocity grease. Extend and contract the joint several times until the distance between the boot clamp land areas is 3.5 in.

9. Using a dulled prybar, lift the

6. Using an assistant to apply the brakes, loosen the hub nut.

7. Remove the lower control arm ball joint-to-steering knuckle clamp bolt, pull the lower control arm downward to separate the ball joint from the steering knuckle.

NOTE: When separating the ball joint, be careful not to damage the ball joint dust boot.

8. If equipped with a manual transaxle, use both hands, grasp the steering knuckle/hub assembly, apply even pressure (gradually increasing), pull both halfshafts from the transaxle. If equipped with an automatic transaxle, insert a medium prybar between the halfshaft and the transaxle (a notch is provided), pry both halfshafts from the transaxle.

NOTE: When removing the halfshafts, withdraw them completely from the transaxle (to pre-

vent damage to the oil seal lips), do not move the CV-joints in excess of a 20 degree angle (damage to the boots and/or joint may occur) and use a wire to support the halfshaft in the horizontal position.

9. Remove the hub nut (discard it) and washer. Pull the halfshaft from the steering knuckle assembly.

NOTE: If the wheel hub binds on the halfshaft splines, use a puller tool, to press the halfshaft from the wheel hub. Never use a hammer to separate the halfshaft from the wheel hub, for damage to the CV-joint may occur.

10. Using differential plug tool(s), plug the transaxle bore(s) to prevent oil leakage.

11. Check the halfshaft for damage, wear and/or good working order; replace the halfshaft, if necessary.

large end of the boot to remove any trapped air.

10. Install new boot clamps.

11. To complete the installation, reverse the removal procedures.

Rzeppa (Inner)

The Rzeppa or double-offset joint is used only with a manual transaxle.

1. Remove the halfshaft from the vehicle and position it in a vise.

NOTE: The vise should be equipped jaw caps to prevent damaging the halfshaft.

2. Using diagonal cutters, remove the boot clamps and roll the boot backward.

NOTE: If it boot is being replaced because it is damaged, inspect the bearing grease for grit. If grit is present, the entire bearing must be disassembled and repacked.

3. Using paint, matchmark the housing outer race to halfshaft.

4. Using a small prybar, remove the wire ring bearing retainer from the housing outer race. Remove the outer race.

5. Using paint, matchmark the inner bearing race-to-halfshaft.

6. Remove the inner bearing race-to-halfshaft snapring. Remove the inner bearing race, the cage and the ball bearings as an assembly.

7. If separating the inner bearing race assembly, perform the following procedures:

   a. Carefully pry ball bearings from the cage with a blunt prybar.

NOTE: Be careful not to damage the ball bearings.

   b. Matchmark the inner race-to-cage.

   c. Rotate the inner race to align the bearing lands with the cage windows and separate them.

8. Inspect the bearing grease for grit; if necessary, replace or repack the bearing.

To install:

9. If the boot is to be reused, wrap tape around the halfshaft splines and remove the boot.

10. To assemble bearing inner race assembly, perform the following procedures:

   a. Lubricate the parts with high temperature constant velocity grease.

   b. Align and install the inner race into the cage.

NOTE: Make sure inner race the chamfered splines are facing the large end of the cage.

   c. Using the heel portion of hand,

press the ball bearings into the cage windows.

11. Install the boot onto the halfshaft.

12. Align the matchmarks and install the inner race assembly onto the halfshaft, secure it with the snapring.

13. To install housing outer race, lubricate it with 1.4–2.1 oz. of high temperature constant velocity grease and install it.

14. Lubricate the housing outer race with another 0.7–1.0 oz. of high temperature constant velocity grease and install the wire ring bearing retainer.

15. Slide the boot over the housing outer race.

16. Extend and contract the joint several times until the distance between the boot clamp land areas is 3.5 in.

17. Using a dulled prybar, lift the large end of the boot to remove any trapped air.

18. Install new boot clamps.

19. To complete the installation, reverse the removal procedures.

Birfield (Outer)

The Birfield joint is outer joint used with either automatic or manual transaxles. The joint is not to be disassembled.

1. Remove the halfshaft from the vehicle and position it in a vise.

NOTE: The vise should be equipped with jaw caps to prevent damaging the halfshaft.

2. Using diagonal cutters, remove the boot clamps.

3. Remove the inner joint assembly from the halfshaft.

4. Slide the outer boot from the inboard side of the halfshaft.

5. To install, reverse the removal procedures.

Front Wheel Hub, Knuckle and Bearings

REMOVAL & INSTALLATION

1. Disconnect the negative battery cable. Raise and support the vehicle safely. Remove the halfshaft.

2. Disconnect the U-shaped clip from the center section of the caliper hose; do not disconnect the hose from the caliper. Remove the brake caliper-to-steering knuckle bolts and support the caliper on a length of wire; do not allow the caliper to hang by the brake hose.

3. Remove the tie rod-to-steering knuckle ball joint cotter pin and nut. Using a hammer and a tie rod separa-

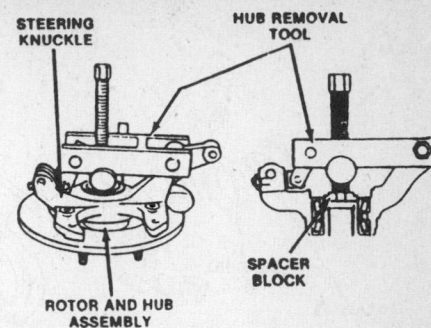

Separating the hub from the steering knuckle

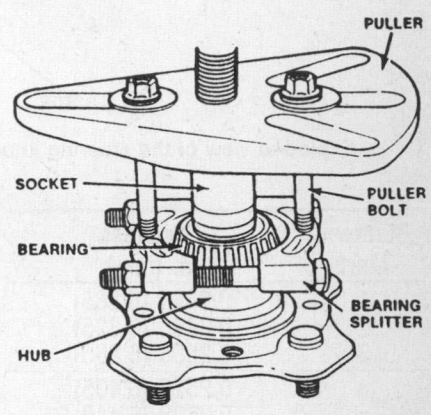

Pressing the wheel bearing from the hub

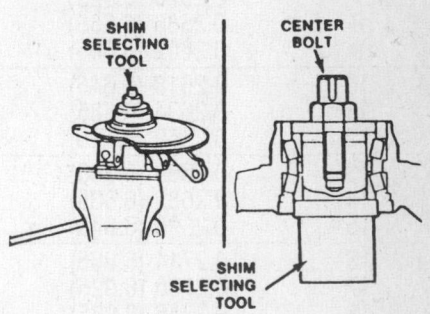

Installing wheel bearing races and adjusting the rotating torque

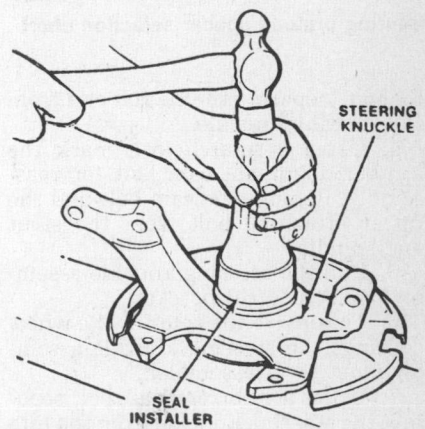

Driving the new grease seal into the steering knuckle

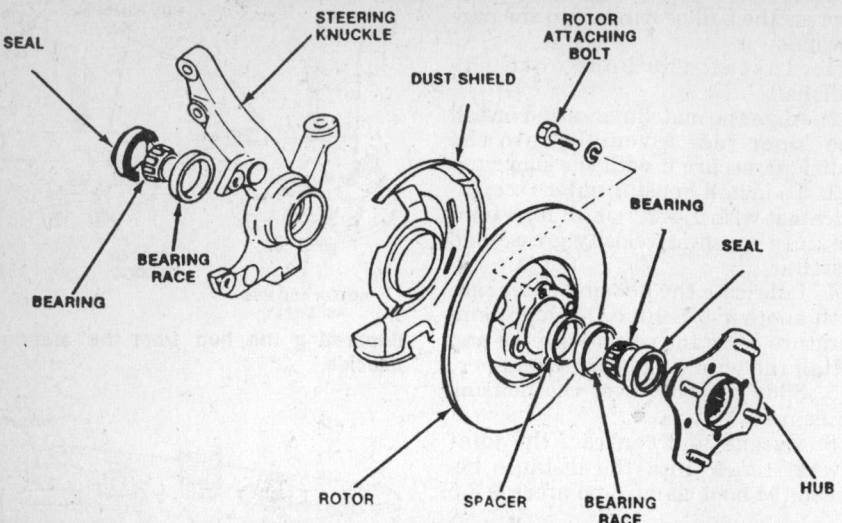

Exploded view of the steering knuckle/hub/wheel bearing assembly

Stamped Mark	Thickness in. (mm)
1	0.2474 (6.285)
2	0.2490 (6.325)
3	0.2506 (6.365)
4	0.2522 (6.405)
5	0.2538 (6.445)
6	0.2554 (6.485)
7	0.2570 (6.525)
8	0.2586 (6.565)
9	0.2602 (6.605)
10	0.2618 (6.645)
11	0.2634 (6.685)
12	0.2650 (6.725)
13	0.2666 (6.765)
14	0.2682 (6.805)
15	0.2698 (6.845)
16	0.2714 (6.885)
17	0.2730 (6.925)
18	0.2746 (6.965)
19	0.2762 (7.005)
20	0.2778 (7.045)
21	0.2794 (7.085)

Bearing preload spacer selection chart

tor tool, separate the tie rod end from the steering knuckle.

4. Using a scratch awl, mark the camber alignment cam bolt for reassembly. Remove the cam bolt and the upper attaching bolt from the strut and spindle.

5. Pull the steering knuckle assembly from the strut bracket.

6. To remove the rotor or the wheel bearings the steering knuckle assembly must be disassembled.

7. Using a hub removal tool, separate the steering knuckle from the hub assembly.

8. From the rear of the hub assembly, remove the bearing preload spacer.

NOTE: The bearing spacer, located between the bearings, determines the bearing preload; do not discard it.

9. Using paint or chalk, matchmark the rotor-to-hub alignment for reassembly purposes.

10. Unless the brake disc is damaged, it should remain attached to the hub. Remove the rotor-to-hub bolts and the rotor.

11. Using the bearing puller tool D–1123–A or equivalent and the puller tool D80L–927–A or equivalent, or a bearing splitter tool, press the wheel bearing from the hub. A socket may have to be used to complete the bearing removal. Remove the outer grease seal from the hub and discard it.

To install:

12. Using a small prybar at the inner side of the steering knuckle, pry the grease seal from the knuckle and discard it. Lift the inner wheel bearing from the steering knuckle.

13. If necessary to replace the bearing races in the steering knuckle, perform the following procedures:

   a. Using a brass drift and a hammer, drive the bearing races from the steering knuckle.

   b. Clean and inspect the steering knuckle for wear and/or damage, replace the steering knuckle, if necessary.

   c. To install, new or used bearing races, lubricate them with wheel bearing grease. Assemble the parts into the steering knuckle.

   d. Using a bearing race driver tool and a spacer selector tool, install the tools onto the steering knuckle assembly and the assembly onto a vise.

   e. Tighten the tool's center bolt

in increments, to 36, 72, 108 and 145 ft. lbs. After the final torque is reached, rotate the steering knuckle to seat the bearings. Retorque the center bolt to 145 ft. lbs.

   f. Remove the assembly from the vise and reinstall the steering knuckle into the vise; mount it by means of the shock absorber mount.

   g. Using a socket and an inch lb. torque wrench, position it on the space selector tool. Measure the torque required to just move the assembly. The torque should be 2.21–10.44 inch lbs. If the torque is less than 2.21 inch lbs., a thinner spacer should be used; if the torque is more than 10.44 inch lbs., a thicker spacer should be used.

14. Clean and inspect all of the parts for wear and/or damage; replace the parts, if necessary. Using new wheel bearing grease, pack the inside of the steering knuckle.

15. Install a greased inner bearing into the steering knuckle. Using a new inner grease seal, lubricate with wheel bearing grease and drive it into the steering knuckle using a seal installer tool.16. Lubricate and position the bearing preload spacer and the outer wheel bearing in the steering knuckle.17. If the rotor was removed from the hub, align the matchmarks and install the hub-to-rotor bolts. Torque the hub-to-rotor bolts to 33–40 ft. lbs.18. Position the hub/rotor assembly onto the steering knuckle. Using a hydraulic press, press the assembly together until the parts seat.19. To install the hub/rotor assembly, use a new cotter pin (tie rod end) and reverse the removal procedures. Torque the steering knuckle-to-strut bolts to 69–86 ft. lbs., the lower control arm-to-steering knuckle clamp bolt to 32–40 ft. lbs., the tie rod-to-steering knuckle nut to 22–33 ft. lbs. and the caliper-to-steering knuckle bolts to 29–36 ft. lbs.20. Lower the vehicle to the ground and torque the hub nut to 116–174 ft. lbs.(157–235 Nm); stake the hub nut. Check and/or adjust the front wheel alignment.

STEERING

Steering Wheel

REMOVAL & INSTALLATION

1. Disconnect the negative battery cable.

2. From the rear of the steering wheel, remove the cover pad-to-steering wheel screws and the pad.

3. Remove the steering wheel-to-steering column nut.

4. Remove the steering wheel cover pad bracket-to-steering wheel screws and the bracket.

5. Using white paint, matchmark the steering wheel-to-steering column position.

6. Using a steering wheel puller tool, press the steering wheel from the steering column.

7. To install, align the matchmarks and reverse the removal procedures.

Steering Column

REMOVAL & INSTALLATION

1. Disconnect the negative battery cable.

2. Remove the lap duct register panel screws, the lap duct brace screws, the brace and the lap duct.

3. Remove the combination switch lower cover screws and the cover.

4. Using paint, matchmark the lower universal joint-to-intermediate shaft.

5. Remove the lower steering column nuts, the lower steering column universal joint bolt and the upper steering column bolts.

6. Lower the steering column and

disconnect the electrical harness connectors from the lower steering column.

7. Remove the steering column from the vehicle.

8. To install, align the universal joint-to-intermediate shaft and reverse the removal procedures. Inspect the operation of the steering column.

Manual Steering Rack and Pinion

ADJUSTMENT

1. Remove the steering rack from the vehicle and place it in a vise.

2. Using an inch lb. Torque wrench and a pinion torque adapter tool place the assembly on the pinion and measure the pinion turning torque; the torque should be 8–11 inch lbs.

3. To adjust the pinion torque, perform the following procedures:

   a. Loosen the adjusting bolt locknut.

   b. Make sure the rack is centered in the housing.

   c. Move the adjusting bolt slightly and recheck the pinion torque.

   d. When the pinion torque of 8–11 inch lbs. is reached, retorque the

adjusting bolt locknut to 7–11 ft. lbs.

4. To install the steering gear, reverse the removal procedures. Check the steering operation.

REMOVAL & INSTALLATION

1. Disconnect the terminals from the battery (negative cable first) and remove the battery from the vehicle.

2. Raise and support the vehicle safely. Remove the front wheel assemblies.

3. Remove the tie rod end-to-steering knuckle cotter pins and nuts. Using a tie rod separator tool, separate the tie rod end from the steering knuckle.

4. From the right side lower inner fender, remove the plastic dust shield.

5. Using a pair of diagonal cutters, cut the steering column dust boot-to-steering gear plastic wire tie clamp. Pull the dust boot back. Have an assistant turn the steering wheel until the steering column shaft bolt is accessible and lock the steering column.

6. Using white paint, matchmark the steering rack pinion shaft-to-intermediate lower shaft universal joint.

7. Remove the steering gear pinion shaft-to-intermediate lower shaft universal joint clamp bolt.

8. Remove the steering rack-to-chassis bolts, lower the steering gear to disengage it from the intermediate shaft universal joint. Carefully slide the steering gear out through the right side fender well.

9. To install, align the matchmarks and reverse the removal procedures. Torque the tie rod end-to-steering knuckle nut to 25–30 ft. lbs. Install a plastic strap over the steering column dust boot. Inspect the steering operation.

Power Steering Rack and Pinion

ADJUSTMENT

1. Remove the power steering rack from the vehicle and place it in a vise.

2. Using an inch lb. torque wrench and a pinion torque adapter tool, place the assembly on the pinion and measure the pinion turning torque; the torque should be 0.52–1.3 inch lbs.

3. To adjust the pinion torque, perform the following procedures:

   a. Loosen the adjusting bolt locknut.

   b. Make sure the rack is centered in the housing.

   c. Move the adjusting bolt slightly and recheck the pinion torque.

   d. When the pinion torque of 0.52–1.3 inch lbs. is reached, re-

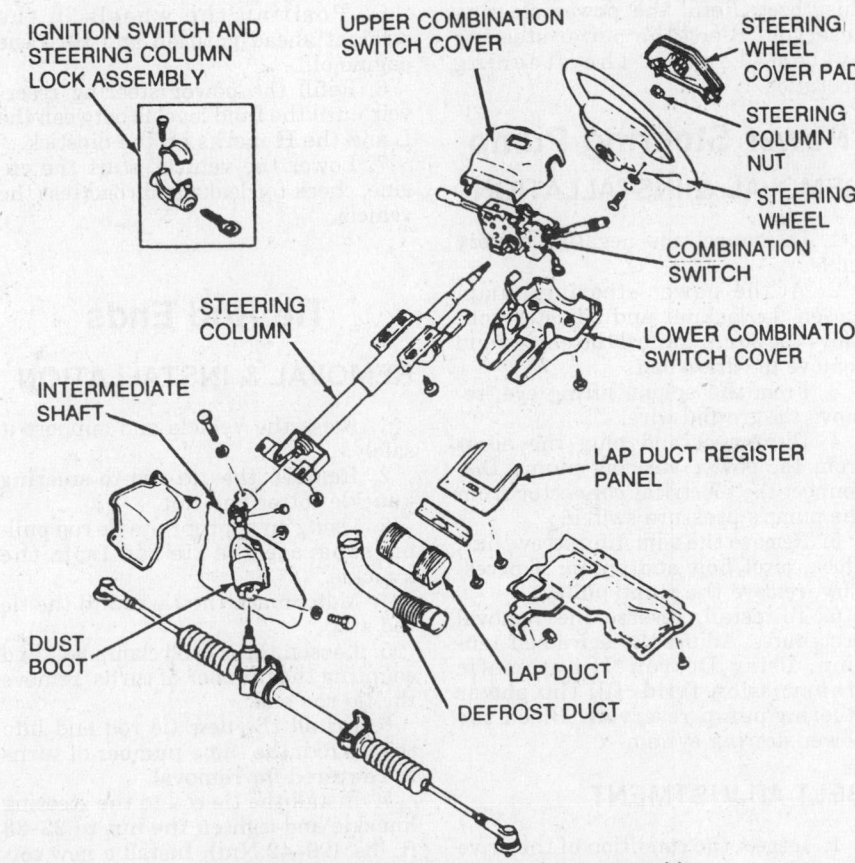

IGNITION SWITCH AND STEERING COLUMN LOCK ASSEMBLY

UPPER COMBINATION SWITCH COVER

STEERING WHEEL COVER PAD

STEERING COLUMN NUT

STEERING WHEEL

COMBINATION SWITCH

LOWER COMBINATION SWITCH COVER

STEERING COLUMN

INTERMEDIATE SHAFT

LAP DUCT REGISTER PANEL

DUST BOOT

LAP DUCT

DEFROST DUCT

Exploded view of the steering column assembly

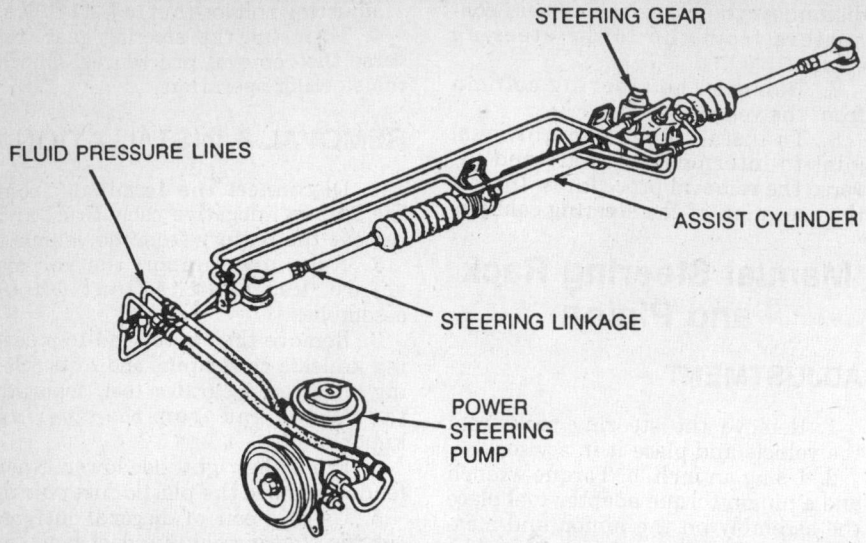

STEERING GEAR

FLUID PRESSURE LINES

ASSIST CYLINDER

STEERING LINKAGE

POWER STEERING PUMP

View of the power steering system

torque the adjusting bolt locknut to 29–36 ft. lbs.

4. To install the steering rack, reverse the removal procedures. Check the steering operation.

REMOVAL & INSTALLATION

1. Disconnect the terminals from the battery (negative cable first) and remove the battery from the vehicle.

2. Raise and support the vehicle safely. Remove the front wheel assemblies.

3. Remove the tie rod end-to-steering knuckle cotter pins and nuts. Using a tie rod separator tool, separate the tie rod end from the steering knuckle.

4. From the right side lower inner fender, remove the plastic dust shield.

5. Using a pair of diagonal cutters, cut the steering column dust boot-to-steering gear plastic wire tie clamp. Pull the dust boot back. Have an assistant turn the steering wheel until the steering column shaft bolt is accessible and lock the steering column.

6. Using white paint, matchmark the steering gear pinion shaft-to-intermediate lower shaft universal joint.

7. Remove the steering gear pinion shaft-to-intermediate lower shaft universal joint clamp bolt.

8. Using a 17mm crowsfoot tubing wrench, disconnect and plug the fluid return line from the power steering rack.

9. Using a 14mm socket, remove the banjo bolt from the pressure line at the power steering gear and discard the copper washers.

NOTE: Be sure to position the pressure lines out of the way.

10. Remove the steering rack-to-

chassis bolts, lower the steering gear to disengage it from the intermediate shaft universal joint. Carefully slide the steering rack out through the right side fender well.

11. To install, align the matchmarks, use 2 new washers at the banjo fitting and reverse the removal procedures. Torque the tie rod end-to-steering knuckle nut to 22–33 ft. lbs. Install a plastic strap over the steering column dust boot. Refill the power steering reservoir. Bleed the power steering system. Inspect the steering operation.

Power Steering Pump
REMOVAL & INSTALLATION

1. Disconnect the negative battery cable.

2. At the power steering pump, loosen the locknut and adjuster bolt. Move the pump toward the engine and remove the drive belt.

3. From the engine lifting eye, remove the ground wire.

4. Disconnect and plug the hoses from the power steering pump. Disconnect the electrical connector from the pump's pressure switch.

5. Remove the adjusting screw, nut, block, pivot bolt and pump; if necessary, remove the pump pulley.

6. To install, reverse the removal procedures. Adjust the drive belt tension. Using Dexron®II automatic transmission fluid, fill the power steering pump reservoir. Bleed the power steering system.

BELT ADJUSTMENT

1. Inspect the condition of the drive belt; replace it, if necessary.

2. At the power steering pump, loosen the locknut and adjuster bolt.

3. Using a drive belt tension gauge tool, position it between the power steering pump pulley and the crankshaft pulley. The drive belt deflection should be 0.31–0.35 in. (new belt) or 0.35–0.39 in. (used belt) at 22 lbs. pressure.

NOTE: A used belt is one that has at least 10 minutes run time.

4. If the power steering pump locknut was loosened, torque it to 32–45 ft. lbs.

BLEEDING SYSTEM

1. Raise and support the vehicle safely.

2. Using Dexron®II automatic transmission fluid, fill the power steering reservoir to the L mark on the dipstick.

3. Start the engine and allow it to reach normal operating temperature.

4. Slowly turn the steering wheel (back and forth) lock-to-lock about 10 times, until all of the air is bled from the system and the reservoir is maintaining a full level.

NOTE: When bleeding the system, be sure to refill the reservoir several times.

5. Position the wheels in the straight ahead position and turn the engine off.

6. Refill the power steering reservoir until the fluid level is between the L and the H marks on the dipstick.

7. Lower the vehicle, start the engine, check for leaks and road test the vehicle.

Tie Rod Ends
REMOVAL & INSTALLATION

1. Raise the vehicle and support it safely.

2. Remove the tie rod-to-steering knuckle cotter and nut.

3. Using an appropriate tie rod puller, separate the tie rod from the knuckle.

4. Matchmark the tie rod to the tie rod end.

5. Loosen the tie rod clamp bolt and counting the number of turns, remove the tie rod end.

6. Install the new tie rod end into the tie rod, the same number of turns as rewuired for removal.

7. Install the tie rod to the steering knuckle and tighten the nut to 22–33 ft. lbs. (29–42 Nm). Install a new cotter pin.

BRAKES

For all brake system repair and service procedures not detailed below, please refer to "Brakes" in the Unit Repair section.

Master Cylinder

REMOVAL & INSTALLATION

1. Disconnect the negative battery cable. Disconnect the low fluid level sensor wiring connector.
2. Disconnect and plug the brake tubes from the master cylinder. Cap the master cylinder tube openings.
3. Remove the master cylinder-to-cowl (manual brakes) or master cylinder-to-power booster (power brakes) nuts and the master cylinder from the vehicle.
4. To install, reverse the removal procedures. Torque the master cylinder mounting nuts to 15–25 ft. lbs. Using DOT 3 brake fluid, fill the master cylinder reservoir. Bleed the brake system.

Proportioning Valve

REMOVAL & INSTALLATION

1. Disconnect and plug the brake lines leading to the valve.
2. Remove the valve mounting bolts from the firewall.
3. Remove the valve.
4. Installation is the reverse of the removal procedure.
5. Bleed the brake system.

Power Brake Booster

REMOVAL & INSTALLATION

1. Remove the cables from the battery (negative cable first) and the battery from the vehicle.
2. Remove the master cylinder and move it aside; if possible, do not disconnect the brake tubes from the master cylinder.
3. Remove the vacuum hose from the brake booster.
4. From under the instrument panel, remove the spring clip and the clevis pin from the brake pedal.
5. Remove the brake booster-to-cowl nuts and the brake booster.

6. To install, reverse the removal procedures. If necessary, adjust the master cylinder pushrod. Check the brake operation. If the brake tubes were disconnected from the master cylinder, bleed the brake system.

Brake Caliper

REMOVAL & INSTALLATION

1. Raise and safely support the vehicle.
2. Remove the wheel and tire assembly.
3. Remove the brake pads. Remove the brake hose attaching bolt, plug the hose end. Discard the O-rings.
4. Remove the caliper attaching bolts and the anit-squeak caps.
5. Remove the caliper from the vehicle.
6. Installation is the reverse of the removal procedure.
7. Use new O-rings on the brake hose and bleed the brake system. Tighten the caliper mounting bolts to 29–36 ft. lbs.

Disc Brake Pads

REMOVAL & INSTALLATION

1. Remove some of the brake fluid from the master cylinder. Raise and support the vehicle safely.
2. Remove the tire and wheel assembly.
3. Remove the brake pad pin retainer. Disengage the anti-rattle spring from the brake pads.
4. Remove the brake pad pins and the anti-rattle spring.
5. Remove the brake pads and shims. Do not discard the shims that are located behind the inner brake pad.
6. Installation is the reverse of the removal procedure. Be sure to refill the brake fluid resivior, as required.

Brake Rotor

REMOVAL & INSTALLATION

1. Raise and safely support the vehicle.
2. Remove the wheel and tire assembly.
3. Remove the brake pads and remove the brake caliper from the rotor, do not disconnect the brake hose from the rotor. Support the caliper aside.
4. Bend back the staked edge of the halfshaft retaining nut washer.
5. Remove the halfshaft attaching nut. Discard the nut.
6. Remove the rotor and bearing

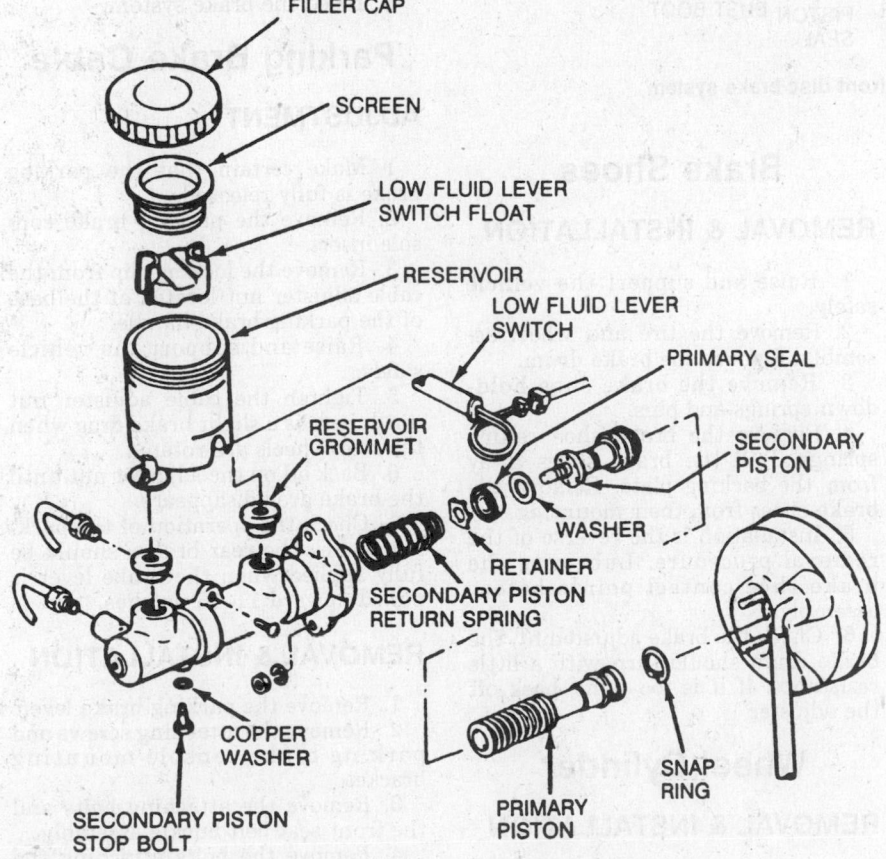

Exploded view of the master cylinder

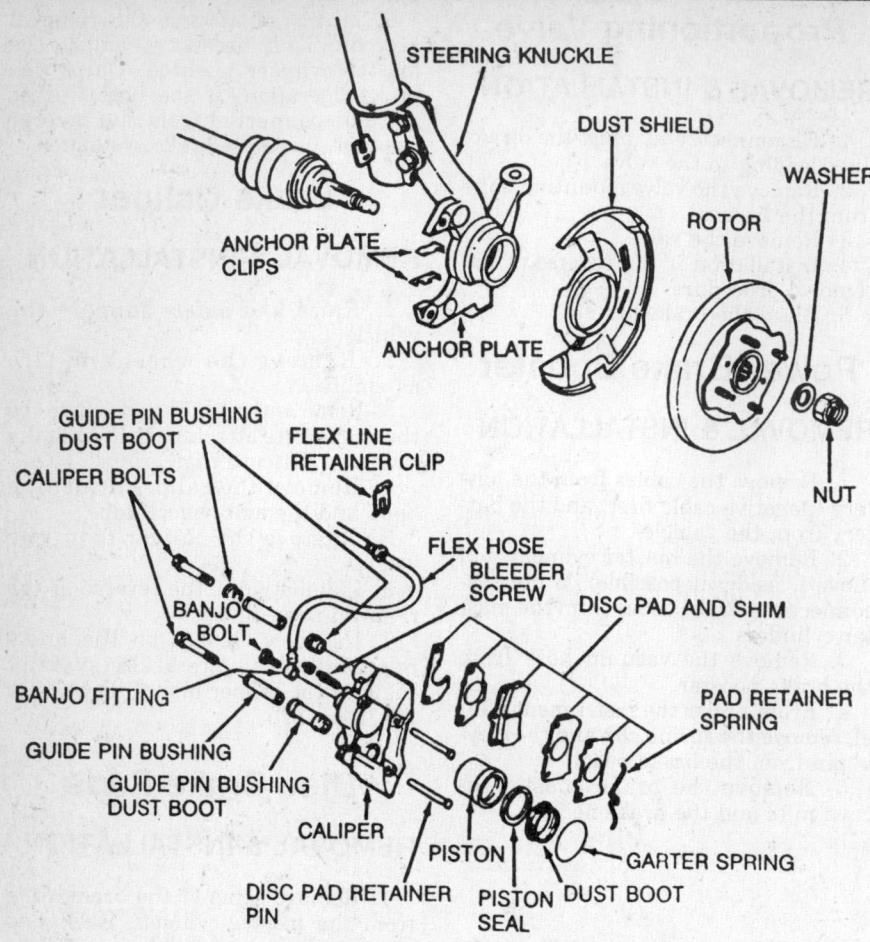

Exploded view of the front disc brake system

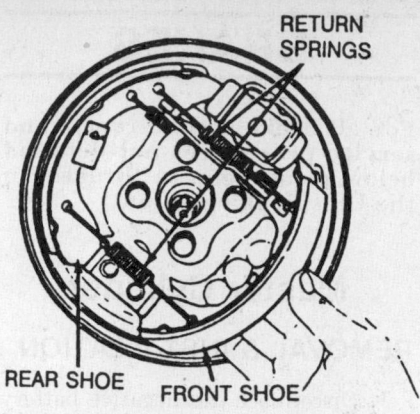

Removing the brake shoe assembly

hub from the halfshaft end, using a suitable puller.

7. Remove the rotor-to-bearing hub retaining bolts. Tighten to 33–40 ft. lbs.

8. Installation is the reverse of the removal procedure. Replace the halfshaft retaining nut.

Brake Drums

REMOVAL & INSTALLATION

1. Raise and safely support the vehicle.

2. Remove the tire and wheel assembly.

3. Remove the grease cap from the brake drum. Bend back the flat washer on the retaining nut.

4. Remove and discard the retaining nut.

5. Remove the brake drum and bearings as an assembly.

6. Installation is the reverse of the removal procedure. Use a new retaining nut for the drum and bearing assembly.

Brake Shoes

REMOVAL & INSTALLATION

1. Raise and support the vehicle safely.

2. Remove the tire and wheel assembly. Remove the brake drum.

3. Remove the brake shoe hold-down springs and pins.

4. Remove the brake shoe return springs. Pull the brake shoes away from the backing plate. Remove the brake shoes from their mounting.

5. Installation is the reverse of the removal procedure. Lubricate the brake shoe contact points before assembly.

6. Check the brake adjustemnt, the brake drum should turn with a little resistance. If it is too tight, back off the adjuster.

Wheel Cylinder

REMOVAL & INSTALLATION

1. Raise and support the vehicle safely.

2. Remove the rear brake shoes.

3. Disconnect the brake line from the wheel cylinder. Plug or cover the brake line opening to prevent the entry of dirt or grease.

4. Remove the 2 wheel cylinder attaching bolts and remove the wheel cylinder from the backing plate.

5. Position the wheel cylinder onto the backing plate and install the retaining bolts. Torque the retaining bolts to 7–9 ft. lbs.

6. Connect the brake line to the wheel cylinder.

7. Install the rear brake shoes.

8. Bleed the brake system.

Parking Brake Cable

ADJUSTMENT

1. Make certain that the parking brake is fully released.

2. Remove the parking brake console insert.

3. Remove the locking clip from the cable adjuster nut located at the base of the parking brake handle.

4. Raise and support the vehicle safely.

5. Tighten the cable adjuster nut until there is a slight brake drag when the rear wheels are rotated.

6. Back off on the adjuster nut until the brake drag disappears.

7. Check the operation of the parking brake. The rear brakes should be fully applied when the brake lever is pulled upward 11–16 notches.

REMOVAL & INSTALLATION

1. Remove the parking brake lever.

2. Remove the attaching screws and parking brake console mounting bracket.

3. Remove the attaching bolts and the front seat belt buckle assembly.

4. Remove the bolts attaching the lower half of the rear seat hinge to the floor pan.

5. Fold the rear seat forward and remove the bolts attaching the upper half of the rear seat hinge to the floor pan.

6. Remove the rear seat.

7. Remove the rear carpet push retainers and carefully pull the carpeting forward to expose the park brake cable guide.

8. Disconnect the park brake cable guide by removing the attaching screws.

9. Loosen the wheel bolts. Raise and support the vehicle safely.

10. Remove the rear wheels.

11. Remove the cotter pin and clevis pin attaching the park brake cable ends to the rear brake levers.

12. Remove the routing bracket retaining clips.

13. Disengage the park brake routing sleeves from the torsion beam routing brackets.

14. Remove the nut and bolt attaching the park brake to the fuel tank.

15. Remove the park brake cable equalizer attaching bolts.

16. Withdraw the lever end of the cable through the body opening and remove from the vehicle.

To install:

17. Position the lever end of the cable through the body opening.

18. Position the cable routing bracket on the fuel tank and install the attaching bolt.

19. Make certain that the cable seal is properly positioned in the floor pan.

20. Position the cable equalizer and install the attaching bolts. Make certain that the equalizer spacers are in position before tightening the attaching bolts.

21. Route the cable ends through the body brackets and install the retaining clips.

22. Seat the cable sleeves in the torsion beam routing brackets.

23. Attach the cable ends to the brake levers using the clevis pins and new cotter pins.

24. Install the rear wheels and lower the vehicle.

25. Route the end of the cable through the park brake lever.

26. Position the cable guide and secure with the attaching screws.

27. Position the carpet and install the push retainers. Install the rear seat and torque the retaining bolts to 28–38 ft. lbs.

28. Position the seat belt assembly and install the attaching bolts and bolt spacers. Torque the bolts to 28–58 ft. lbs. The spacers must be installed on the bolts.

29. Position the console mounting bracket and install the attaching screws.

30. Install the parking brake adjuster nut and adjust the parking brake.

Install the adjuster nut locking clip.

31. Raise the park brake handle and align with the parking brake console. Install the parking brake console.

32. Install the front push retainer and push insert. Install the park brake console insert.

33. Slide the front seats to their most forward postion. Install the park brake console attaching screws.

34. Position the front seats in their adjusted position.

Brake System Bleeding

1. Using DOT 3 brake fluid, check and/or refill the master cylinder reservoir until it is at least ½ full.

2. If the master cylinder has air trapped in the bore, perform the following procedures:

   a. Disconnect the front brake tube from the master cylinder and allow the fluid to flow from the master cylinder port.

   b. Reconnect and tighten the tube-to-master cylinder.

   c. Have an assistant depress the brake pedal (slowly) and hold it. Loosen the front tube-to-master cylinder, allow the air to purge, retighten the connection and release the pedal (slowly).

   d. After the air has been purged from the front tube, bleed the rear tube in the same manner.

3. To bleed the wheel cylinders or calipers, perform the following procedures:

   a. Connect a clear tube to the bleeder screw of the wheel cylinder or caliper.

   b. Have an assistant pump the brake pedal repeatedly and hold it. Loosen the bleeder screw, allow the air/fluid mixture to escape, retighten the screw and release the brake pedal (slowly). Perform this Step repeatedly until all air is removed from the fluid.

   c. Bleed all of the wheel cylinders or calipers using the following sequence: right rear, left front, left rear and right front.

4. After bleeding, check the pedal for sponginess. Check and/or refill the master cylinder reservoir.

FRONT SUSPENSION

MacPherson Strut

REMOVAL & INSTALLATION

1. Raise the vehicle and support it safely.

2. Remove the wheel and tire assembly.

3. Remove the brake line clip from the strut lower mounting bracket cutout and disengage the brake line.

4. Remove the 2 nuts and bolts securing the strut lower bracket to the steering knuckle.

5. In the engine compartment, remove the 2 nuts securing the strut mounting block to the strut tower mounting studs.

6. Disengage the strut lower bracket from the steering knuckle and lower the strut assembly and spacer plate clear of the wheel well.

To install:

7. Place the strut assembly with spacer plate onto the strut tower with the white alignment mark facing outward.

8. Install the upper mounting block stud nuts and torque to 32–45 ft. lbs.

9. Engage the steering knuckle in the strut tower lower bracket and install the mounting bolts. Torque the bolts to 69–86 ft. lbs.

10. Postion the brake line into the strut lower mounting bracket cutout and install the retaining clip.

11. Install the wheel and tire assembly.

12. Connect the negative battery cable.

Lower Ball Joints

INSPECTION

1. Rasie the vehicle and support it safely.

2. Grab the wheel top and bottom, shake the wheel in and out.

3. If any movement is seen in the steering knuckle relative to the control arm, the ball joint is bad and must be replaced.

4. If the ball stud is disconnected from the knuckle and any looseness is noted, the joint is defective.

REMOVAL & INSTALLATION

1. Raise the vehicle and support it safely.

2. Rmove the wheel and tire assembly.

3. Remove the brake caliper, do not disconnect the brake line and support it aside.

4. Separate the stabilizer bar from the control arm.

5. Remove the tie rod end cotter pin and nut. Separate the tie rod from the knuckle, using the proper removal tool.

6. Remove the ball joint-to-knuckle clamp bolt and pry the lower control arm from the knuckle.

7. Remove the ball joint-to-knuckle bolts and remove the ball joint.

8. Installation is the reverse of the removal procedure. Torque the ball joint clamp bolt to 32–40 ft. lbs. (42–50 Nm).

Lower Control Arms
REMOVAL & INSTALLATION

1. Raise and support the vehicle safely. Remove the lower control arm pivot bolt at the frame bracket.

2. Remove the ball joint clamp bolt and and nut from the steering knuckle assembly.

3. Remove the stabilizer bar bushing retaining nut from the rear of the control arm and remove the rear bushing washer and bushing.

4. Lower the control arm, prying the ball joint stud out of the steering knuckle, if necessary. Disengage and remove the control arm from the stabilizer end.

5. Inspect the control arm for deformation or cracks, and check the pivot bushing for deterioration. Verify that the ball joint swivels freely but is not loose. If the control arm pivot bushing is to be replaced, center the new bushing in the center of the control arm eye and install using the proper tools. Replace the lower control arm/ball joint assembly, as required.

6. If the ball joint boot is damaged or deteriorated, replace the joint.

To install:

7. Position the front bushing washer (with "dished" side forward) and bushing onto the stabilizer end. Engage the control arm with the stabilizer.

8. Raise the control arm inner end onto the pivot bracket on the frame and start the pivot bolt to hold the control arm in place. Do not completely tighten the bolt at this time.

9. Engage the control arm ball joint stud with the clamp bore in the steering knuckle and install the clamp bolt and nut.

10. Install the stabilizer rear bushing and washer (with "dished" side forward) onto the stabilizer end with the retaining nut. Torque the retaining nut to 43–52 ft. lbs.

11. Torque the pivot bolt at the control arm frame bracket to 32–40 ft. lbs.

REAR SUSPENSION

MacPherson Strut
REMOVAL & INSTALLATION

1. Raise the vehicle and support it safely.

2. Remove the rear wheel and tire assembly.

3. Install a spring compressor tool and release the strut spring tension.

4. From the cargo compartment, remove the rear quarter panel trim.

5. Remove the jam nut and flanged nut from the strut rod and remove the bushing washer and upper bushing.

6. Remove the strut lower end mounting bolt from the wheel support arm.

7. Withdraw the strut assembly downward from the wheel well and separate it from the spring and seat insulator. Remove the spring compressor.

8. Remove the lower grommet and jounce bumper seat from the strut rod. Slide the jounce bumper and shield off the strut.

9. Inspect the material condition of the jounce bumper, spring seat insulator and strut rod bushings. Inspect the strut for leakage, endplay or erratic action. Inspect the strut lower end bushing for damage or deterioration. Replace any damaged or deteriorated components, as required.

To install:

10. Slide the jounce bumper and shield onto the strut rod. Install the bumper seat and and lower grommet on the strut rod.

11. Position the coil spring on the strut, making certain that the end of the coil seats against the end of the step in the strut spring seat. When the spring is properly seated, reinstall the spring compressor.

12. Guide the strut tower into the strut mounting hole through the wheel well.

13. Align the strut lower end with the mounting hole in the wheel support arm. Start the mounting bolt in by hand to hold the strut in position.

14. From the cargo compartment, install the rod upper end bushing, bushing washer and flanged nut. Torque the flanged nut to 12–18 ft. lbs. Hold the flanged nut stationary and tighten the locknut.

15. Torque the lower strut mounting bolt to 40–50 ft. lbs.

16. Back off on the spring compressor slowly to release the spring tension. Remove the spring compressor.

17. Install the wheel and tire assembly. Lower the vehicle.

Rear Control Arms and Trailing Arms

The rear control arms and the rear trailing arms are removed using the same procedure for each.

REMOVAL & INSTALLATION

1. Raise the vehicle and support it safely.

2. Remove the wheel and tire assembly. Remove the brake drum and backing plate, if equipped with drum brakes. If equipped with disc brakes, remove the caliper and rotor.

3. Matchmark the rear toe adjusting cam, the control arm bushings and the control arm to the crossmember.

4. Remove the strut from the vehicle.

5. Remove the stabilizer bar mounting bolts and remove the stabilizer bar.

6. Remove the trailing arm mounting bolts and remove the parking brake cable from the trailing arm.

7. Remove the control arm and the trailing arm from the vehicle.

NOTE: All final tightening of bolts, should be done with the vehicle on the ground and the suspension fully loaded.

8. Installation is the reverse of the removal procedure. Torque the spindle-to-control arm bolts to 69–86 ft. lbs., the control arm-to-crossmember bolts to 69–86 ft. lbs. and the stabilizer bar mounting bolts to 32–40 ft. lbs.

Rear Wheel Bearings
REMOVAL & INSTALLATION

1. Raise and support the rear of the vehicle safely.

2. Remove the wheel and tire assembly.

3. Remove the grease cup from the rear wheel hub.

4. Using a small cape chisel and a hammer, carefully raise the staked portion of locknut; remove the discard the locknut.

NOTE: The locknuts are threaded for left and right hand applications; be sure to acquire the right one.

5. Remove the outer wheel bearing from the hub and the brake drum/bearing hub assembly.

6. Using a small prybar, pry the grease seal from the rear of the drum. Remove the inner wheel bearing from the hub.

7. To replace the bearing races, perform the following procedures:

a. Using a brass drift and a hammer, drive the races from the drum.

b. Clean and inspect the parts for wear and/or damage; replace the parts, if necessary.

c. To install the races, use a brass drift and a hammer, lubricate the races with wheel bearing grease and drive the races into the hub until they seat.

8. Using wheel bearing grease, pack the inside of the hub and the wheel bearings. Install the inner bearing into the hub.

9. To install the new grease seal, lubricate it with wheel bearing grease. Using a seal installation tool, drive the seal into the rear of the wheel hub.

10. To complete the installation, reverse the removal procedures and adjust the bearing preload.

ADJUSTMENT

1. Raise and support the vehicle safely.

2. Remove the wheel and tire assembly.

3. Remove the grease cup from the rear wheel hub.

4. Rotate the brake drum to make sure there is no brake drag; if there is drag, adjust the brake shoes.

5. Using a small cape chisel and a hammer, carefully raise the staked portion of locknut; remove the discard the locknut.

NOTE: The locknuts are threaded for left and right hand applications; be sure to acquire the right one.

6. Install the new locknut, rotate the drum and torque it to 18–21 ft. lbs.; loosen the locknut (slightly) until it can be turned by hand.

NOTE: Before the bearing preload can be set, the amount of seal drag must be measured and added to the preload torque.

7. Using an inch lb. torque wrench, position it (12 o'clock position) on 1 of the lug nuts and measure the torque necessary to start the wheel hub to turn.

8. To calculate the new torque, perform the following procedures:

   a. The required preload torque is 1.3–4.3 inch lbs.

   b. If the measure (seal drag) turning torque is 2.2 inch lbs., add it to the lowest and highest preload torque.

   c. The newly calculated preload torque is 3.5–6.5 inch lbs.

9. Torque the wheel bearing lock-nut slightly and recheck the wheel hub turning torque. When the wheel bearing torque falls within the newly calculated torque range, the torquing sequence is complete. Using a rounded cold chisel, stake the wheel locknut and reverse the removal procedures.

Rear Axle Spindle

REMOVAL & INSTALLATION

1. Raise and safely support the vehicle.

2. Remove the wheel and tire assembly. Remove the brake drum and backing plate or the rotor assembly.

3. Disconnect the spindle-to-strut bolt and the control arm bolt.

4. Remove the spindle assembly from the strut.

5. Inspect the spindle for damage and replace as necessary.

6. Installation is the reverse of the removal procedure. Torque the spindle-to-strut bolt to 69–86 ft. lbs. and the outer rear control arm bolt to 69–86 ft. lbs.

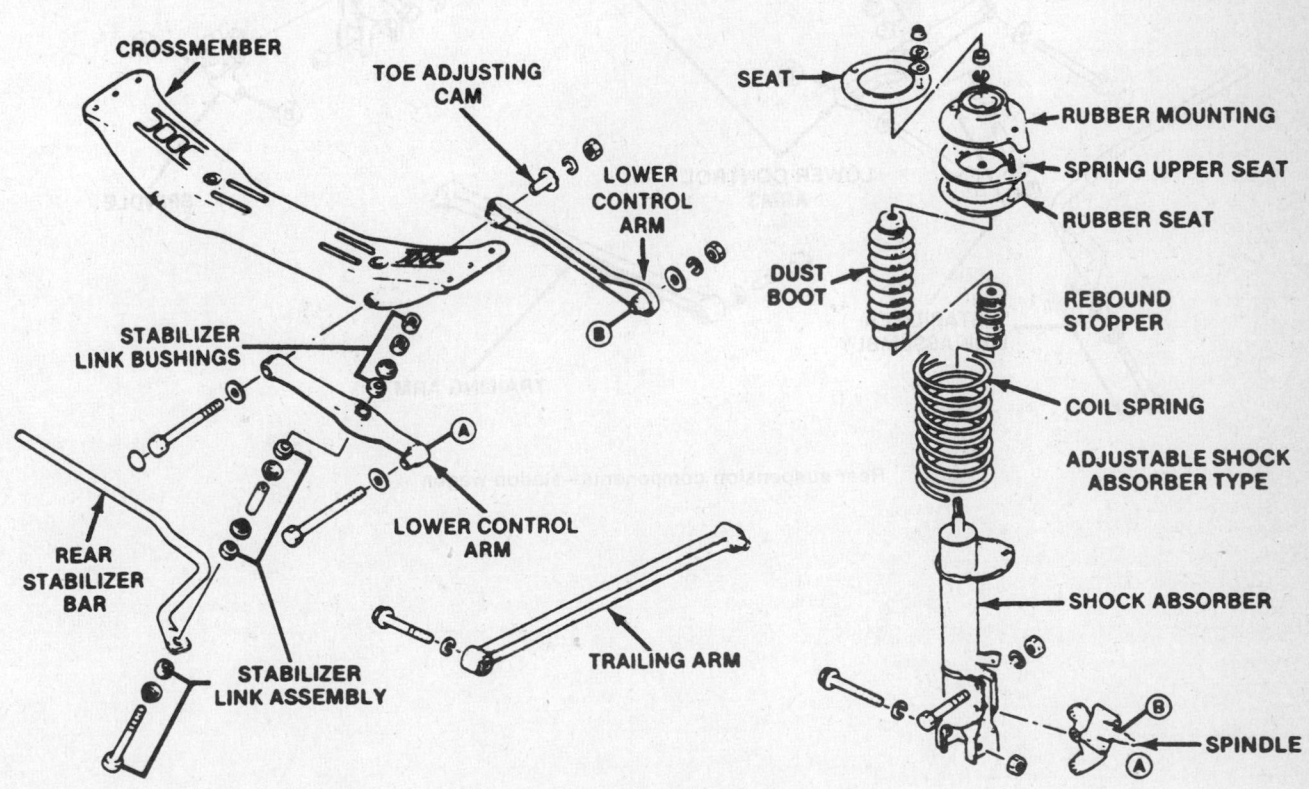

Rear suspension components—3 and 5 door

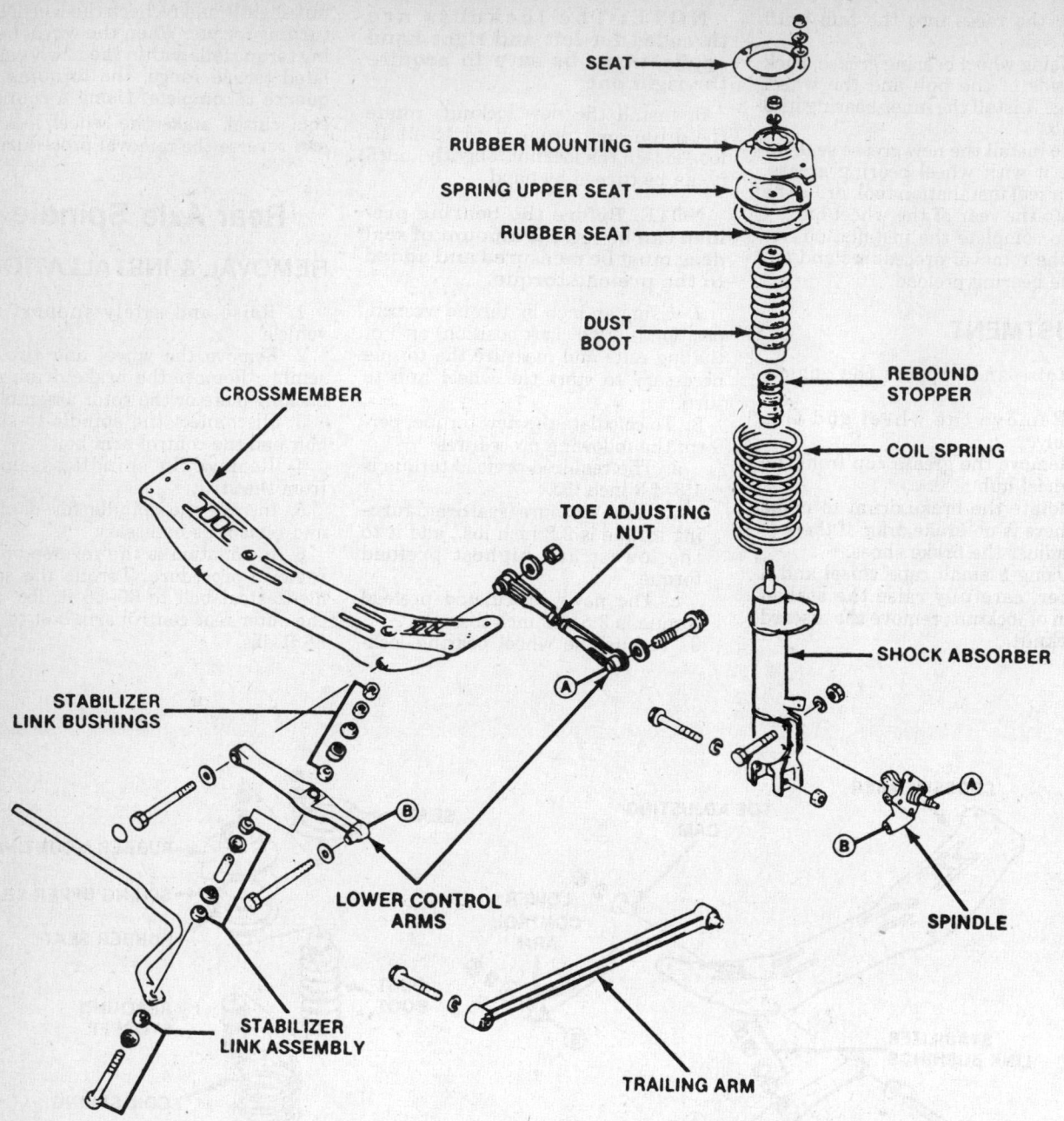

SEAT

RUBBER MOUNTING

SPRING UPPER SEAT

RUBBER SEAT

DUST BOOT

REBOUND STOPPER

COIL SPRING

SHOCK ABSORBER

CROSSMEMBER

TOE ADJUSTING NUT

STABILIZER LINK BUSHINGS

SPINDLE

LOWER CONTROL ARMS

STABILIZER LINK ASSEMBLY

TRAILING ARM

Rear suspension components—station wagon

Buick/Chevrolet Oldsmobile/Pontiac

Rear Wheel Drive

Buick—Estate Wagon, Regal
Chevrolet—Caprice, Caprice Wagon, Monte Carlo
Oldsmobile—Cutlass, Custom Cruiser
Pontiac—Grand Prix, Safari

SPECIFICATIONS

VEHICLE IDENTIFICATION CHART

It is important for servicing and ordering parts to be certain of the vehicle and engine identification. The VIN (vehicle identification number) is a 17 digit number visible through the windshield on the driver's side of the dash and contains the vehicle and engine identification codes. The tenth digit indicates model year, and the eighth digit indicates engine code. It can be interpreted as follows:

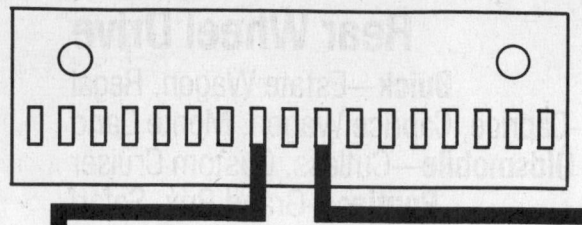

Engine Code					
Code	Cu. In.	Liters	Cyl.	Fuel Sys.	Eng. Mfg.
A	231	3.8	V6	2 bbl	Buick
7 (87)	231	3.8	V6	SFI/Turbo	Buick
Z	262	4.3	V6	EFI	Chevrolet
E	305	5.0	V8	EFI	Chevrolet
G	305	5.0	V8	4 bbl	Chevrolet
H	305	5.0	V8	4 bbl	Chevrolet
9	307	5.0	V8	4 bbl	Oldsmobile
Y	307	5.0	V8	4 bbl	Oldsmobile
6	350	5.7	V8	4 bbl	Chevrolet
7 (89–90)	350	5.7	V8	EFI	Chevrolet

Model Year	
Code	Year
G	1986
H	1987
J	1988
K	1989
L	1990
M	1991

ENGINE IDENTIFICATION

Year	Model	Engine Displacement cu. in. (liter)	Engine Series Identification (VIN)	No. of Cylinders	Engine Type
1987	Estate Wagon	307 (5.0)	Y	8	OHV
	Regal	231 (3.8)	A	6	OHV
	Regal	231 (3.8)	7	6	OHV
	Caprice Sedan	262 (4.3)	Z	6	OHV
	Caprice Sedan	305 (5.0)	H	8	OHV
	Caprice Wagon	307 (5.0)	Y	8	OHV
	Monte Carlo	262 (4.3)	Z	6	OHV
	Monte Carlo	305 (5.0)	G	8	OHV
	Monte Carlo	305 (5.0)	H	8	OHV
	Cutlass	231 (3.8)	A	6	OHV
	Cutlass	305 (5.0)	H	8	OHV
	Cutlass	307 (5.0)	Y	8	OHV
	Cutlass	307 (5.0)	9	8	OHV
	Custom Cruiser	307 (5.0)	Y	8	OHV
	Grand Prix	231 (3.8)	A	6	OHV
	Grand Prix	262 (4.3)	Z	6	OHV
	Grand Prix	305 (5.0)	H	8	OHV
	Safari	307 (5.0)	Y	8	OHV

ENGINE IDENTIFICATION

Year	Model	Engine Displacement cu. in. (liter)	Engine Series Identification (VIN)	No. of Cylinders	Engine Type
1988	Estate Wagon	307 (5.0)	Y	8	OHV
	Caprice Sedan	262 (4.3)	Z	6	OHV
	Caprice Sedan	305 (5.0)	H	8	OHV
	Caprice Wagon	307 (5.0)	Y	8	OHV
	Monte Carlo	262 (4.3)	Z	6	OHV
	Monte Carlo	305 (5.0)	H	8	OHV
	Monte Carlo	307 (5.0)	Y	8	OHV
	Cutlass	307 (5.0)	Y	8	OHV
	Custom Cruiser	307 (5.0)	Y	8	OHV
	Safari	307 (5.0)	Y	8	OHV
1989	Estate Wagon	307 (5.0)	Y	8	OHV
	Caprice Sedan ①	262 (4.3)	Z	6	OHV
	Caprice Sedan	305 (5.0)	E	8	OHV
	Caprice Wagon	307 (5.0)	Y	8	OHV
	Caprice Sedan	350 (5.7)	7	8	OHV
	Custom Cruiser	307 (5.0)	Y	8	OHV
	Safari	307 (5.0)	Y	8	OHV
1990–91	Estate Wagon	307 (5.0)	Y	8	OHV
	Caprice Sedan ①	262 (4.3)	Z	6	OHV
	Caprice Sedan	305 (5.0)	E	8	OHV
	Caprice Wagon	307 (5.0)	Y	8	OHV
	Caprice Sedan ②	350 (5.7)	7	8	OHV
	Custom Cruiser	307 (5.0)	Y	8	OHV

① Fleet only
② Police

GENERAL ENGINE SPECIFICATIONS

Year	VIN	No. Cylinder Displacement cu. in. (liter)	Fuel System Type	Net Horsepower @ rpm	Net Torque @ rpm (ft. lbs.)	Bore × Stroke (in.)	Compression Ratio	Oil Pressure @ rpm
1987	A	6-231 (3.8)	2 bbl	110 @ 3800	190 @ 1600	3.800 × 3.400	8.0:1	37 @ 2400
	7	6-231 (3.8)	SFI/Turbo	235 @ 4400	330 @ 2800	3.800 × 3.400	8.0:1	37 @ 2400
	Z	6-262 (4.3)	EFI	140 @ 3800	225 @ 2200	4.000 × 3.480	9.3:1	45 @ 2000
	H	8-305 (5.0)	4 bbl	165 @ 4200	245 @ 2400	3.736 × 3.480	9.5:1	45 @ 2000
	G	8-305 (5.0)	4 bbl	105 @ 3200	240 @ 2400	3.736 × 3.480	9.5:1	45 @ 2000
	9	8-307 (5.0)	4 bbl	148 @ 3800	250 @ 2400	3.800 × 3.385	8.0:1	30 @ 1500
	Y	8-307 (5.0)	4 bbl	148 @ 3800	250 @ 2400	3.800 × 3.385	8.0:1	40 @ 2000
	6	8-350 (5.7)	4 bbl	205 @ 4200	290 @ 4200	4.000 × 3.480	8.2:1	45 @ 2000
1988	Z	6-262 (4.3)	EFI	140 @ 4200	225 @ 2000	4.000 × 3.480	9.3:1	45 @ 2000
	H	8-305 (5.0)	4 bbl	165 @ 4200	245 @ 2400	3.736 × 3.480	8.6:1	45 @ 2000
	Y	8-307 (5.0)	4 bbl	148 @ 3800	250 @ 2400	3.800 × 3.385	8.0:1	40 @ 2000
1989	Z	6-262 (4.3)	EFI	140 @ 4000	225 @ 2000	4.000 × 3.480	9.3:1	18 @ 2000
	E	8-305 (5.0)	EFI	170 @ 4400	255 @ 2400	3.740 × 3.480	9.3:1	18 @ 2000
	Y	8-307 (5.0)	4 bbl	148 @ 3800	250 @ 2400	3.800 × 3.385	8.0:1	40 @ 2000
	7	8-350 (5.7)	EFI	NA	NA	3.740 × 3.480	9.3:1	18 @ 2000

GENERAL ENGINE SPECIFICATIONS

Year	VIN	No. Cylinder Displacement cu. in. (liter)	Fuel System Type	Net Horsepower @ rpm	Net Torque @ rpm (ft. lbs.)	Bore × Stroke (in.)	Compression Ratio	Oil Pressure @ rpm
1990–91	Z	6-262 (4.3)	EFI	140 @ 4000	225 @ 2000	4.000 × 3.480	9.3:1	18 @ 2000
	E	8-305 (5.0)	EFI	170 @ 4400	255 @ 2400	3.740 × 3.480	9.3:1	18 @ 2000
	Y	8-307 (5.0)	4 bbl	140 @ 3200	255 @ 2000	3.800 × 3.385	8.0:1	18 @ 2000
	7	8-350 (5.7)	EFI	NA	NA	3.740 × 3.480	9.3:1	18 @ 2000

GASOLINE ENGINE TUNE-UP SPECIFICATIONS

Year	VIN	No. Cylinder Displacement cu. in. (liter)	Spark Plugs Type	Gap (in.)	Ignition Timing (deg.) MT	Ignition Timing (deg.) AT	Compression Pressure (psi)	Fuel Pump (psi)	Idle Speed (rpm) MT	Idle Speed (rpm) AT	Valve Clearance In.	Valve Clearance Ex.
1987	A	6-231 (3.8)	R45TSX	0.060	—	15	②	5.5–6.5	—	700	Hyd.	Hyd.
	7	6-231 (3.8)	R44TS	0.035	—	①	②	26–51	—	700	Hyd.	Hyd.
	Z	6-262 (4.3)	R-45TS	0.035	—	0	②	—	—	400	Hyd.	Hyd.
	H	8-305 (5.0)	R-44TS	0.035	—	0	②	7.5–9.0	—	500	Hyd.	Hyd.
	G	8-305 (5.0)	R-44TS	0.035	—	6	②	7.5–9.0	—	500	Hyd.	Hyd.
	9	8-307 (5.0)	FR3LS	0.060	—	20B	②	5.5–6.5	—	600	Hyd.	Hyd.
	Y	8-307 (5.0)	FR3CLS6	0.060	—	20	②	6.0–7.5	—	450	Hyd.	Hyd.
	6	8-350 (5.7)	FR3CLS6	0.060	—	6	②	—	—	500	Hyd.	Hyd.
1988	Z	6-262 (4.3)	R-45TS	0.035	—	①	②	9.0–13.0	—	400	Hyd.	Hyd.
	H	8-305 (5.0)	R-45TS	0.035	—	①	②	7.5–9.0	—	500 ①	Hyd.	Hyd.
	Y	8-307 (5.0)	FR3L56	0.060	—	①	②	6.0–7.5	—	450	Hyd.	Hyd.
1989	Z	6-262 (4.3)	R-45TS	0.035	—	①	②	9–13	—	①	Hyd.	Hyd.
	E	8-305 (5.0)	R-45TS	0.035	—	①	②	11	—	①	Hyd.	Hyd.
	Y	8-307 (5.0)	FR3L56	0.060	—	①	②	6.0–7.5	—	①	Hyd.	Hyd.
	7	8-350 (5.7)	R-45TS	0.035	—	①	②	11	—	①	Hyd.	Hyd.
1990	Z	6-262 (4.3)	R-45TS	0.035	—	①	②	9–13	—	①	Hyd.	Hyd.
	E	8-305 (5.0)	R-45TS	0.035	—	①	②	9–13	—	①	Hyd.	Hyd.
	Y	8-307 (5.0)	FR3LS6 ③	0.060	—	①	②	6.0–7.5	—	①	Hyd.	Hyd.
	7	8-350 (5.7)	R-43TS	0.035	—	①	②	9–13	—	①	Hyd.	Hyd.
1991		See Underhood Specifications Sticker										

① See the Emission Control Label
② The lowest cylinder compression reading should not be less than 70% of the highest reading, and no cylinder should be less than 100 PSI
③ FR3CLS6 may also be used.

FIRING ORDERS

NOTE: To avoid confusion, always replace spark plug wires one at a time.

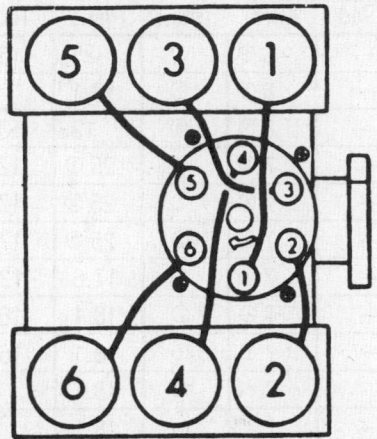

3.8L Engine
Engine Firing Order: 1–6–5–4–3–2
Distributor Rotation: Clockwise

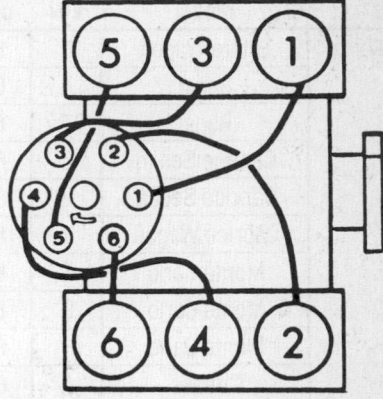

4.3L Engine
Engine Firing Order: 1–6–5–4–3–2
Distributor Rotation: Clockwise

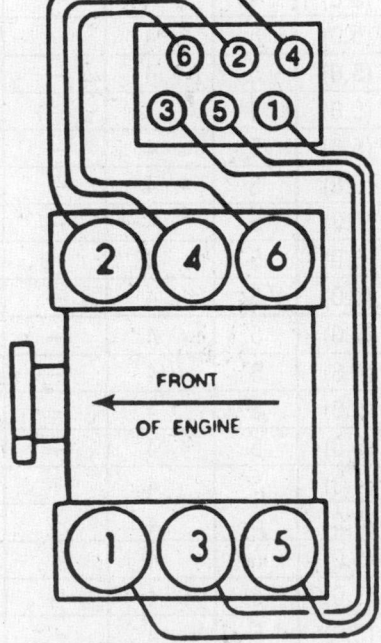

FRONT OF ENGINE

3.8L Engine (Turbo)
Engine Firing Order: 1–6–5–4–3–2
Distributorless Ignition System

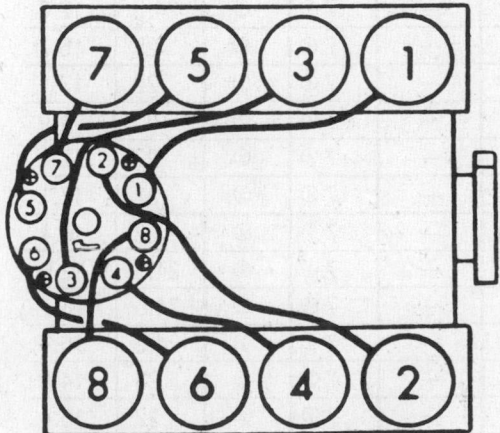

5.0L (VIN E, G, H) and 5.7L Engine
Engine Firing Order: 1–8–4–3–6–5–7–2
Distributor Rotation: Clockwise

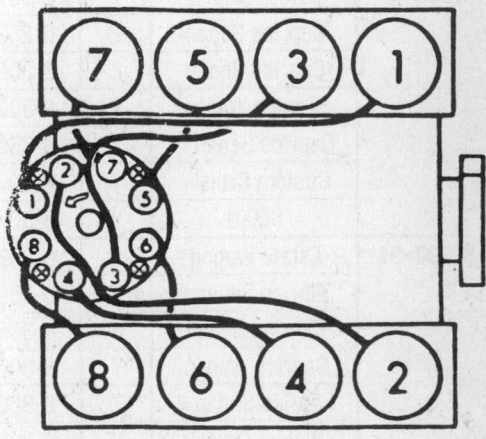

5.0L (VIN Y, 9) Engines
Engine Firing Order: 1–8–4–3–6–5–7–2
Distributor Rotation: Counterclockwise

CAPACITIES

Year	Model	VIN	No. Cylinder Displacement cu. in. (liter)	Engine Crankcase with Filter	Engine Crankcase without Filter	Transmission (pts.) 4-Spd	Transmission (pts.) 5-Spd	Transmission (pts.) Auto.	Drive Axle (pts.)	Fuel Tank (gal.)	Cooling System (qts.)
1987	Estate Wagon	Y	8-307 (5.0)	5	4	—	—	8 ①	②	25	16.2
	Regal	A	6-231 (3.8)	5	4	—	—	8 ①	②	18.1	13
	Regal	7	6-231 (3.8)	6	5	—	—	8 ①	②	19	13.1
	Caprice Sedan	Z	6-262 (4.3)	5	4	—	—	7 ④	②	25 ③	12.5
	Caprice Sedan	H	8-305 (3.0)	5	4	—	—	7 ④	②	25 ③	17.5
	Caprice Wagon	Y	8-307 (5.0)	5	4	—	—	7 ④	②	25 ③	17.5
	Monte Carlo	Z	6-262 (4.3)	5	4	—	—	7 ④	②	17.6	13.1
	Monte Carlo	G	8-305 (5.0)	5	4	—	—	7 ④	②	18.1	16.7
	Monte Carlo	H	8-305 (5.0)	5	4	—	—	7 ④	②	18.1	16.5
	Cutlass	A	6-231 (3.8)	5	4	—	—	7	②	18.1	13
	Cutlass	H	8-305 (5.0)	5	4	—	—	7	②	18.1	16
	Cutlass	Y	8-307 (5.0)	5	4	—	—	7	②	18.1	15.5
	Cutlass	9	8-307 (5.0)	5	4	—	—	7	②	18.1	15.5
	Custom Cruiser	Y	8-307 (5.0)	5	4	—	—	7	②	18.1 ③	15.5
	Grand Prix	A	6-231 (3.8)	5	4	—	—	⑤	②	17.5	13.1
	Grand Prix	Z	6-262 (4.3)	5	4	—	—	⑤	②	17.5	13.1
	Grand Prix	H	8-305 (5.0)	5	4	—	—	⑤	②	17.5	16
	Safari	Y	8-307 (5.0)	5	4	—	—	⑤	②	22	15
1988	Estate Wagon	Y	8-307 (5.0)	5	4	—	—	10.1	4.25	22	15
	Caprice Sedan	Z	6-262 (4.3)	5	4	—	—	7 ④	②	25 ③	12.5
	Caprice Sedan	H	8-305 (5.0)	5	4	—	—	7 ④	②	25 ③	16.8
	Caprice Wagon	Y	8-307 (5.0)	5	4	—	—	7 ④	②	25 ③	17.1
	Monte Carlo	Z	6-262 (4.3)	5	4	—	—	7 ④	②	17.6	13.1
	Monte Carlo	H	8-305 (5.0)	5	4	—	—	7 ④	②	18.1	16.5
	Monte Carlo	Y	8-307 (5.0)	5	4	—	—	7 ④	②	18.1	16.7
	Cutlass	Y	8-307 (5.0)	5	4	—	—	7	②	18.1	15.5
	Custom Cruiser	Y	8-307 (5.0)	5	4	—	—	7	②	22	15.5
	Safari	Y	8-307 (5.0)	5	4	—	—	10.1	4.25	22	15
1989	Estate Wagon	Y	8-307 (5.0)	5	4	—	—	7 ④	②	22	17.1
	Caprice Sedan	Z	6-262 (4.3)	4 ⑧	4	—	—	7 ④	②	24.5	12.0
	Caprice Sedan	E	8-305 (5.0)	5	4	—	—	7 ④	②	25	16.7
	Caprice Wagon	Y	8-307 (5.0)	5	4	—	—	7 ④	②	22	17.1
	Caprice Sedan ⑦	7	8-350 (5.0)	5	4	—	—	7 ④	②	25	14.9
	Custom Cruiser	Y	8-307 (5.0)	5	4	—	—	7 ④	②	22	17.1
	Safari	Y	8-307 (5.0)	5	4	—	—	7 ④	②	22	17.1
1990–91	Estate Wagon	Y	8-307 (5.0)	5	4	—	—	7 ⑨	②	22	16.4
	Caprice Sedan ⑥	Z	6-262 (4.3)	4 ⑧	4	—	—	7 ⑨	②	24.5	12.0
	Caprice Sedan	E	8-305 (5.0)	5	4	—	—	7 ⑨	②	24.5	16.7
	Caprice Wagon	Y	8-307 (5.0)	5	4	—	—	7 ⑨	②	24.5	16.7
	Caprice Sedan ⑦	7	8-350 (5.7)	5	4	—	—	7 ⑨	②	22	14.8
	Custom Cruiser	Y	8-305 (5.0)	5	4	—	—	7 ⑨	②	22	16.4

① Additional transmission fluid may be required to bring level to full mark if overhauled or torque converter drained

② 7½ in. ring gear—3.5 pts.
8½ in. ring gear—4.25 pts.
8¾ in. ring gear—5.4 pts.

③ Wagon—22 gals.

④ 700R4—10 pts.
⑤ 200R4—10.1 pts.
200C—8.5 pts.
⑥ Fleet only

⑦ Police
⑧ Add as necessary to bring to appropriate level.
⑨ Hydra-matic 4L60-10.0 pts.

CAMSHAFT SPECIFICATIONS

Year	VIN	No. Cylinder Displacement cu. in. (liter)	Journal Diameter					Lobe Lift		Bearing Clearance	Camshaft End Play
			1	2	3	4	5	In.	Ex.		
1987	A	6-231 (3.8)	1.785–1.786	1.7850–1.7860	1.7850–1.7860	1.7850–1.7860	1.7850–1.7860	NA	NA	0.0010–0.0030	NA
	7	6-231 (3.8)	1.785–1.786	1.7850–1.7860	1.7850–1.7860	1.7850–1.7860	1.7850–1.7860	NA	NA	0.0010–0.0030	NA
	Z	6-262 (4.3)	1.868–1.869	1.8682–1.8692	1.8682–1.8692	1.8682–1.8692	1.8682–1.8692	0.234	0.257	NA	0.004–0.012
	H	8-305 (5.0)	1.868–1.869	1.8682–1.8692	1.8682–1.8692	1.8682–1.8692	1.8682–1.8692	0.234	0.257	NA	0.004–0.012
	G	8-305 (5.0)	1.868 1.869	1.8682 1.8692	1.8682 1.8692	1.8682 1.8692	1.8682 1.8692	0.269	0.276	NA	0.004–0.012
	Y	8-307 (5.0)	2.036	2.0360	1.9959	1.9759	1.959	0.247	0.251	0.0038–	0.006–0.022
	9	8-307 (5.0)	2.036	2.0360	1.9959	1.9759	1.9559	0.272	0.274	0.0038–	0.006–0.022
	6	8-350 (5.7)	1.868–1.869	1.8682–1.8692	1.8682–1.8692	1.8682–1.8692	1.8682–1.8692	0.257	0.269	NA	0.004–0.012
1988	Z	6-262 (4.3)	1.868–1.869	1.8682–1.8692	1.8682–1.8692	1.8682–1.8692	1.8682–1.8692	0.234	0.257	NA	0.004–0.012
	H	8-305 (5.0)	1.868–1.869	1.8682–1.8692	1.8682–1.8692	1.8682–1.8692	1.8682–1.8692	0.234	0.257	NA	0.004–0.012
	Y	8-307 (5.0)	2.036	2.0360	1.9959	1.9759	1.9559	0.247	0.251	0.0038–	0.006–0.022
1989	Z	6-262 (4.3)	1.868–1.869	1.8682–1.8692	1.8682–1.8692	1.8682–1.8692	1.8682–1.8692	0.234	0.257	NA	0.004–0.012
	E	8-305 (5.0)	1.868–1.869	1.8682–1.8692	1.8682–1.8692	1.8682–1.8692	1.8682–1.8692	NA	NA	NA	0.004–0.012
	Y	8-307 (5.0)	2.036	2.0360	1.9959	1.9759	1.9559	0.247	0.251	0.0038	0.006–0.022
	7	8-350 (5.7)	1.868–1.869	1.8682–1.8692	1.8682–1.8692	1.8682–1.8692	1.8682–1.8692	0.257	0.269	NA	0.004–0.012
1990–91	Z	6-262 (4.3)	1.868–1.869	1.8682–1.8692	1.8682–1.8692	1.8682–1.8692	1.8682–1.8692	0.234	0.257	NA	0.004–0.012
	E	8-305 (5.0)	1.868–1.869	1.8682–1.8692	1.8682–1.8692	1.8682–1.8692	1.8682–1.8692	0.234	0.257	NA	0.004–0.012
	Y	8-307 (5.0)	2.036	2.0360	1.9959	1.9759	1.9559	0.247	0.251	0.0038	0.006–0.022
	7	8-350 (5.7)	1.868–1.869	1.8682–1.8692	1.8682–1.8692	1.8682–1.8692	1.8682–1.8692	0.257	0.269	NA	0.004–0.012

CRANKSHAFT AND CONNECTING ROD SPECIFICATIONS

All measurements are given in inches.

Year	VIN	No. Cylinder Displacement cu. in. (liter)	Crankshaft				Connecting Rod		
			Main Brg. Journal Dia.	Main Brg. Oil Clearance	Shaft End-play	Thrust on No.	Journal Diameter	Oil Clearance	Side Clearance
1987	A	6-231 (3.8)	2.4995	0.0003–0.0018	0.003–0.011	2	2.2487–2.2495	0.0005–0.0026	0.003–0.015
	7	6-231 (3.8)	2.4995	0.0003–0.0018	0.003–0.011	2	2.2487–2.2495	0.0005–0.0026	0.003–0.015

CRANKSHAFT AND CONNECTING ROD SPECIFICATIONS

All measurements are given in inches.

Year	VIN	No. Cylinder Displacement cu. in. (liter)	Crankshaft				Connecting Rod		
			Main Brg. Journal Dia.	Main Brg. Oil Clearance	Shaft End-play	Thrust on No.	Journal Diameter	Oil Clearance	Side Clearance
	Z	6-262 (4.3)	2.4484–2.4493 ①	0.0008–0.0020 ③	0.002–0.006	4	2.2487–2.2498	0.0013–0.0035	0.006–0.014
	H	8-305 (5.0)	2.4484–2.4493 ①	0.0008–0.0020 ③	0.002–0.006	5	2.0986–2.0998	0.0013–0.0035	0.006–0.014
	G	8-305 (5.0)	2.4484–2.4493 ①	0.0008–0.0020 ③	0.002–0.006	5	2.0986–2.0998	0.0013–0.0035	0.006–0.014
	9	8-307 (5.0)	2.4990–2.4995 ①	0.0005–0.0021 ③	0.003–0.013	3	2.1238–2.1248	0.0004–0.0033	0.006–0.020
	Y	8-305 (5.0)	2.4985–2.4995 ⑤	0.0005–0.0221 ③	0.003–0.013	3	2.1238–2.1248	0.0004–0.0033	0.006–0.020
	6	8-350 (5.7)	2.4484–2.4493 ①	0.0008–0.0020 ②	0.002–0.006	5	2.0986–2.0998	0.0013–0.0035	0.006–0.014
1988	Z	6-262 (4.3)	2.4484–2.4493 ①	0.0008–0.0020 ③	0.002–0.006	4	2.2487–2.2498	0.0013–0.0035	0.006–0.014
	H	8-305 (5.0)	2.4484–2.4493 ①	0.0008–0.0020 ③	0.002–0.006	5	2.0986–2.0998	0.0013–0.0035	0.006–0.014
	Y	8-307 (5.0)	2.4985–2.4995 ①	0.0005–0.0021 ③	0.003–0.013	3	2.1238–2.1248	0.0004–0.0033	0.006–0.020
1989	Z	6-262 (4.3)	2.4484–2.4493 ①	0.0008–0.0020 ③	0.002–0.006	4	2.2487–2.2498	0.0013–0.0035	0.006–0.014
	E	8-305 (5.0)	2.4481–2.4490 ④	0.0011–0.0020 ⑤	0.001–0.007	5	NA	0.0013–0.0035	0.006–0.014
	Y	8-307 (5.0)	2.4985–2.4995 ①	0.0005–0.0021 ③	0.003–0.013	3	2.1238–2.1248	0.0004–0.0033	0.006–0.020
	7	8-350 (5.7)	2.4481–2.4990 ④	0.0011–0.0020 ⑤	0.001–0.007	5	NA	0.0013–0.0035	0.006–0.014
1990-91	Z	6-262 (4.3)	2.4484–2.4493 ①	0.0008–0.0020 ③	0.002–0.006	4	2.2487–2.2498	0.0013–0.0035	0.006–0.014
	E	8-305 (5.0)	2.4481–2.4490 ④	0.0011–0.0020 ⑤	0.001–0.007	5	NA	0.0013–0.0035	0.006–0.014
	Y	8-307 (5.0)	2.4985–2.4995 ①	0.0005–0.0021 ③	0.003–0.013	3	2.1238–2.1248	0.0004–0.0033	0.006–0.020

CRANKSHAFT AND CONNECTING ROD SPECIFICATIONS

All measurements are given in inches.

Year	VIN	No. Cylinder Displacement cu. in. (liter)	Crankshaft				Connecting Rod		
			Main Brg. Journal Dia.	Main Brg. Oil Clearance	Shaft End-play	Thrust on No.	Journal Diameter	Oil Clearance	Side Clearance
	7	8-350 (5.7)	2.4481–2.4990 ④	0.0011–0.0020 ⑤	0.001–0.007	5	NA	0.0013–0.0035	0.006–0.014

① Intermediate—2.4481–2.4490
  Rear—2.4479–2.4488
② Intermediate—0.0011–0.0023
  Rear—0.0017–0.0032
③ Intermediate—0.0011–0.0034
  Rear—0.0015–0.0031
④ Front: 2.4488–2.4493
  rear: 2.4481–2.4488
⑤ Rear: 0.0020–0.0032

VALVE SPECIFICATIONS

Year	VIN	No. Cylinder Displacement cu. in. (liter)	Seat Angle (deg.)	Face Angle (deg.)	Spring Test Pressure (lbs.)	Spring Installed Height (in.)	Stem-to-Guide Clearance (in.)		Stem Diameter (in.)	
							Intake	Exhaust	Intake	Exhaust
1987	A	6-231 (3.8)	46	45	182	1.73	0.0015–0.0035	0.0015–0.0032	0.3412–0.3401	0.3412–0.3401
	7	6-231 (3.8)	45	45	185	1.73	0.0015–0.0035	0.0015–0.0032	0.3401–0.3412	0.3405–0.3412
	Z	6-262 (4.3)	46	45	200	1.70	0.0010–0.0027	0.0010–0.0027	0.3414	0.3414
	H	8-305 (5.0)	46	45	200	1.70	0.0010–0.0027	0.0010–0.0027	0.3414	0.3414
	G	8-305 (5.0)	46	45	200	1.70	0.0010–0.0027	0.0010–0.0027	0.3414	0.3414
	Y	8-307 (5.0)	③	④	194	1.72	0.0010–0.0027	0.0015–0.0032	0.3425–0.3432	0.3420–0.3427
	9	8-307 (5.0)	46	45	194	1.72	0.0010–0.0027	0.0015–0.0032	0.3425–0.3432	0.3420–0.3427
	6	8-350 (5.7)	46	45	200	1.70	0.0010–0.0027	0.0010–0.0027	0.3414	0.3414
1988	Z	6-262 (4.3)	46	45	200	1.70	0.0010–0.0027	0.0010–0.0027	0.3414	0.3414
	H	8-305 (5.0)	46	45	200	1.70	0.0010–0.0027	0.0010–0.0027	0.3414	0.3414
	Y	8-307 (5.0)	①	②	194	1.70	0.0010–0.0027	0.0015–0.0032	0.3425–0.3432	0.3420–0.3427
1989	Z	6-262 (4.3)	46	45	200	1.70	0.0010–0.0027	0.0010–0.0027	0.3414	0.3414
	E	8-305 (5.0)	46	45	200	1.72	0.0011–0.0027	0.0011–0.0027	NA	NA
	Y	8-307 (5.0)	①	②	194	1.72	0.0010–0.0027	0.0015–0.0032	0.3425–0.3432	0.3420–0.3427
	7	8-350 (5.7)	46	45	200	1.72	0.0011–0.0027	0.0011–0.0027	NA	NA

VALVE SPECIFICATIONS

Year	VIN	No. Cylinder Displacement cu. in. (liter)	Seat Angle (deg.)	Face Angle (deg.)	Spring Test Pressure (lbs.)	Spring Installed Height (in.)	Stem-to-Guide Clearance (in.)		Stem Diameter (in.)	
							Intake	Exhaust	Intake	Exhaust
1990–91	Z	6-262 (4.3)	46	45	200	1.70	0.0010–0.0027	0.0010–0.0027	0.3414	0.3414
	E	8-305 (5.0)	46	45	200	1.70	0.0011–0.0027	0.0011–0.0027	NA	NA
	Y	8-307 (5.0)	①	②	194	1.70	0.0010–0.0027	0.0015–0.0032	0.3425–0.3432	0.3420–0.3427
	7	8-350 (5.7)	46	45	200	1.70	0.0011–0.0027	0.0011–0.0027	NA	NA

① Intake—45°, Exhaust—31°
② Intake—44°, Exhaust—30°
③ Intake—45°, Exhaust—59°
④ Intake—46°, Exhaust—60°

PISTON AND RING SPECIFICATIONS

Year	VIN	No. Cylinder Displacement cu. in. (liter)	Piston Clearance	Ring Gap			Ring Side Clearance		
				Top Compression	Bottom Compression	Oil Control	Top Compression	Bottom Compression	Oil Control
1987	A	6-231 (3.8)	0.0008–0.0020	0.010–0.020	0.010–0.020	0.015–0.055	0.0030–0.0050	0.0030–0.0050	0.0035 Max
	7	6-231 (3.8)	0.0008 0.0020	0.010–0.020	0.010–0.020	0.015–0.055	0.0030–0.0050	0.0030–0.0050	0.0035 Max
	Z	6-262 (4.3)	0.0012–0.0032	0.010–0.020	0.010–0.020	0.015–0.055	0.0012–0.0032	0.0012–0.0032	0.0020–0.0070
	H	8-305 (5.0)	0.0012–0.0032	0.010–0.020	0.010–0.025	0.015–0.055	0.0012–0.0032	0.0012–0.0032	0.0020–0.0070
	G	8-305 (5.0)	0.0012–0.0032	0.010–0.020	0.010–0.025	0.015–0.055	0.0012–0.0032	0.0012–0.0032	0.0020–0.0070
	9	8-307 (5.0)	0.0007–0.0017	0.009–0.019	0.009–0.019	0.015–0.055	0.0018–0.0038	0.0018–0.0038	0.0010–0.0050
	Y	8-307 (5.0)	0.0008–0.0018	0.009–0.019	0.009–0.019	0.015–0.055	0.0018–0.0038	0.0018–0.0038	0.0010–0.0050
	6	8-350 (5.7)	0.0012–0.0032	0.010–0.020	0.010–0.020	0.015–0.055	0.0012–0.0032	0.0012–0.0032	0.0020–0.0070
1988	Z	6-262 (4.3)	0.0027	0.010–0.020	0.010–0.025	0.015–0.055	0.0012–0.0032	0.0012–0.0032	0.0020–0.0070
	H	8-305 (5.0)	0.0027	0.010–0.020	0.010–0.025	0.015–0.055	0.0012–0.0032	0.0012–0.0032	0.0020–0.0070
	Y	8-307 (5.0)	0.0008–0.0018	0.009–0.019	0.009–0.019	0.015–0.055	0.0018–0.0038	0.0018–0.0038	0.0010–0.0050
1989	Z	6-262 (4.3)	0.0027	0.010–0.020	0.010–0.025	0.015–0.055	0.0012–0.0032	0.0012–0.0032	0.0020–0.0070
	E	8-305 (5.0)	0.0070–0.0170	0.010–0.020	0.010–0.025	0.015–0.055	0.0012–0.0032	0.0012–0.0032	0.0020–0.0070
	Y	8-307 (5.0)	0.0008–0.0018	0.009–0.019	0.009–0.019	0.015–0.055	0.0018–0.0038	0.0018–0.0038	0.0010–0.0050
	7	8-350 (5.7)	0.0070–0.0170	0.010–0.020	0.010–0.025	0.015–0.055	0.0012–0.0032	0.0012–0.0032	0.0020–0.0070

PISTON AND RING SPECIFICATIONS

Year	VIN	No. Cylinder Displacement cu. in. (liter)	Piston Clearance	Ring Gap			Ring Side Clearance		
				Top Compression	Bottom Compression	Oil Control	Top Compression	Bottom Compression	Oil Control
1990–91	Z	6-262 (4.3)	0.0012 0.0021	0.010– 0.020	0.010– 0.020	0.015– 0.055	0.0012– 0.0032	0.0012– 0.0032	0.0020– 0.0070
	E	8-305 (5.0)	0.0070– 0.0021	0.010– 0.020	0.010– 0.025	0.015– 0.055	0.0012– 0.0032	0.0012– 0.0032	0.0020– 0.0070
	Y	8-307 (5.0)	0.0008– 0.0018	0.009– 0.019	0.009– 0.019	0.015– 0.055	0.0018– 0.0038	0.0018– 0.0038	0.0010– 0.0050
	7	8-350 (5.7)	0.0070– 0.0021	0.010– 0.020	0.010– 0.025	0.015– 0.055	0.0012– 0.0032	0.0012– 0.0032	0.0020– 0.0070

TORQUE SPECIFICATIONS

All readings in ft. lbs.

Year	VIN	No. Cylinder Displacement cu. in. (liter)	Cylinder Head Bolts	Main Bearing Bolts	Rod Bearing Bolts	Crankshaft Pulley Bolts	Flywheel Bolts	Manifold		Spark Plugs
								Intake	Exhaust	
1987	A	6-231 (3.8)	②	100	40	219	60	45	37	20
	7	6-231 (3.8)	②	100	40	219	60	45	37	20
	Z	6-262 (4.3)	60–75	70–85	42–47	70	70	25–45	20	22
	H	8-305 (5.0)	60–75	70–85	42–47	70	70	25–45	20	22
	G	8-305 (5.0)	60–75	70–85	42–47	70	70	25–45	20	22
	9	8-307 (5.0)	130	80 ①	48	200–310	60	40	25	25
	Y	8-307 (5.0)	125 ③	80	42	300	60	40	25	25
	6	8-350 (5.7)	60–75	70–85	42–47	70	70	25–45	20	22
1988	Z	6-262 (4.3)	60–75	70–85	42–47	—	50–70	25–45	20	22
	H	8-305 (5.0)	60–75	70–85	42–47	—	70	25–45	14–26	22
	Y	8-307 (5.0)	130 ③	①	18 ⑤	200–310	60	40 ③	25	25
1989	Z	6-262 (4.3)	60–75	70–85	42–47	—	50–70	25–45	20	22
	E	8-305 (5.0)	68	77	44	70	74	35	26	22
	Y	8-307 (5.0)	40 ④	①	18 ⑤	200–310	60	40 ③	25	25
	7	8-350 (5.7)	68	77	44	70	74	35	26	22
1990–91	Z	6-262 (4.3)	65	65	44	70 ⑦	70	35	⑥	22
	E	8-305 (5.0)	68	77	44	70 ⑦	74	35	⑥	22
	Y	8-307 (5.0)	40 ④	①	18 ⑤	200–310	60	40 ③	25	25
	7	8-350 (5.7)	68	77	44	70 ⑦	74	35	⑥	22

① 80 ft. lbs. on Nos. 1–4; 120 ft. lbs. on No. 5

② Torque cylinder head bolts to 25 ft. lbs. in tightening sequence. Continue the torquing sequence, tightening each bolt 1/4 turn (90 degrees) until 60 ft. lbs. is read on any one cylinder head bolt. Do not continue sequence at this point.

③ Dip in clean engine oil before tightening

④ Rotate position 1, 7 & 9—120°
Rotate position 8 & 10—95°

⑤ Torque in 2 steps:
1st step—18 ft.lbs.
2nd step—additional 70 degrees turn further

⑥ Bolts—26 ft. lbs.
Studs—20 ft. lbs.

⑦ Torque listed is for torsioner damper, crankshaft pulley is 43 ft. lbs.

BRAKE SPECIFICATIONS
All measurements in inches unless noted

Year	Model	Lug Nut Torque (ft. lbs.)	Master Cylinder Bore	Brake Disc Minimum Thickness	Brake Disc Maximum Runout	Standard Brake Drum Diameter	Minimum Lining Thickness Front	Minimum Lining Thickness Rear
1987	Estate Wagon	①	1.125	0.965	0.004	11.00	0.125	0.125
	Regal	100	0.931	0.965	0.004	9.50	0.125	0.125
	Monte Carlo, Caprice	80②	NA	0.965	0.980	9.50	0.030	0.030
	Cutlass	100	0.931	0.980	0.004	9.50	0.030	0.030③
	Custom Cruiser	100	1.125	0.980	0.004	11.00	0.030	0.030③
	Safari	100	1.125	0.980	0.004	9.50	0.030	—
	Grand Prix	100	0.931	0.980	0.004	9.50	0.030	—
1988	Estate Wagon	①	1.125	0.965	0.004	11.00	0.125	0.125
	Monte Carlo, Caprice	80②	1.125④	0.965	0.004	11.00	0.030	0.030
	Cutlass	100	0.931	0.980	0.004	9.50	0.030	0.030③
	Custom Cruiser	100	1.125	0.980	0.004	11.00	0.030	0.030③
	Safari	100	1.125	0.980	0.004	9.50	0.030	—
1989	Estate Wagon	①	1.125	0.980	0.004	11.00	0.030	0.030③
	Caprice	80	1.125	0.980	0.004	11.00⑤	0.030	0.030③
	Custom Cruiser	100	1.125	0.980	0.004	11.00	0.030	0.030③
	Safari	100	1.125	0.980	0.004	11.00	0.030	0.030③
1990-91	Estate Wagon	①	1.125	0.980	0.004	11.00	0.030	0.030③
	Caprice	⑥	1.125	0.980	0.004	11.00	0.030	0.030③
	Custom Cruiser	100	1.125	0.980	0.004	11.00	0.030	0.030③

① Wheel lug type: 1/2 × 20—100 ft. lbs.
7/16 × 20 Steel—80 ft. lbs.
7/16 × 20 Aluminum—90 ft. lbs.

② 88 with 7/16 in. stud; 100 with 11 in. brake drums
③ If Bonded use .062
④ Hydroboost—1 3/16 in.

⑤ Sedan—9.50
⑥ 1990 Sedan—81 ft. lbs.
1990 Wagon and Police Sedan—103 ft. lbs.
1991 Caprice—100 ft. lbs.

WHEEL ALIGNMENT

Year	Model	Caster Range (deg.)	Caster Preferred Setting (deg.)	Camber Range (deg.)	Camber Preferred Setting (deg.)	Toe-in (in.)	Steering Axis Inclination (deg.)
1987	Estate Wagon	1 13/16P–3 13/16P	2 13/16P	0–1 5/8P	13/16P	3/64	NA
	Regal	1 13/16P–3 13/16P	2 13/16P	5/16N–1 5/16P	1/2P	3/64	8
	Monte Carlo	1 13/16P–3 13/16P	2 13/16P	5/16N–1 5/16P	1/2P	3/64	7 7/8
	Caprice	1 13/16P–3 13/16P	2 13/16P	0–1 5/8P	13/16P	3/32	7 7/8
	Cutlass	1 13/16P–3 13/16P	2 13/16P	5/16N–1 5/16P	1/2P	3/64	—
	Custom Cruiser	1 13/16P–3 13/16P	2 13/16P	0–1 5/8P	13/16P	3/64	—
	Grand Prix	1 13/16P–3 13/16P	2 13/16P	5/16N–1 5/16P	1/2P	3/32	8
	Safari	1 13/16P–3 13/16P	2 13/16P	0–1 5/8P	13/16P	1/16	7 9/16

WHEEL ALIGNMENT

Year	Model	Caster Range (deg.)	Caster Preferred Setting (deg.)	Camber Range (deg.)	Camber Preferred Setting (deg.)	Toe-in (in.)	Steering Axis Inclination (deg.)
1988	Monte Carlo	$1^{13}/_{16}$P–$3^{13}/_{16}$P	$2^{13}/_{16}$P	$5/_{16}$N–$1^5/_{16}$P	$1/_2$P	$3/_{64}$	$7^7/_8$
	Caprice	$1^{13}/_{16}$P–$3^{13}/_{16}$P	$2^{13}/_{16}$P	$5/_{16}$N–$1^5/_{16}$P	$13/_{16}$P	$3/_{32}$	$7^7/_8$
	Estate Wagon	$1^{13}/_{16}$P–$3^{13}/_{16}$P	$2^{13}/_{16}$P	0–$1^5/_8$P	$13/_{16}$P	$3/_{64}$	NA
	Cutlass	$1^{13}/_{16}$P–$3^{13}/_{16}$P	$2^{13}/_{16}$P	$5/_{16}$N–$1^5/_{16}$P	$1/_2$P	$3/_{64}$	—
	Custom Cruiser	$1^{13}/_{16}$P–$3^{13}/_{16}$P	$2^{13}/_{16}$P	0–$1^5/_8$P	$13/_{16}$P	$3/_{64}$	—
	Safari	$1^{13}/_{16}$P–$3^{13}/_{16}$P	$2^{13}/_{16}$P	0–$1^5/_8$P	$13/_{16}$P	$1/_{16}$	$7^9/_{16}$
1989	Estate Wagon	2P–4P	3P	0–$1^5/_8$P	$13/_{16}$P	$1/_{32}$	NA
	Caprice	2P–4P	3P	0–$1^5/_8$P	$13/_{16}$P	$1/_{32}$	$7^7/_8$
	Custom Cruiser	2P–4P	3P	0–$1^5/_8$P	$13/_{16}$P	$1/_{32}$	—
	Safari	2P–4P	3P	0–$1^5/_8$P	$13/_{16}$P	$1/_{16}$	$7^9/_{16}$
1990–91	Estate Wagon	2P–4P	3P	0–$1^5/_8$P	$13/_{16}$P	$1/_{32}$	NA
	Custom Cruiser	2P–4P	3P	0–$1^5/_8$P	$13/_{16}$P	$1/_{32}$	—
	Caprice (1990)	2P–4P	3P	0–$1^5/_8$P	$13/_{16}$P	$1/_{32}$	$7^7/_8$
	Caprice (1991) ①	$1^{25}/_{32}$P–$3^{25}/_{32}$P	$2^{25}/_{32}$P	0–$1^7/_{32}$P	$25/_{32}$P	$1/_{16}$–$3/_8$	NA

NA—Not Available
N—Negative
P—Positive
① Sedan

ENGINE ELECTRICAL

NOTE: Disconnecting the negative battery cable on some vehicles may interfere with the functions of the on board computer systems and may require the computer to undergo a relearning process, once the negative battery cable is reconnected.

Distributor

Two types of ignition systems are used. Most engines use the High Energy Ignition (HEI) system. The Computer Controlled Coil Ignition (C^3I) is used with the 3.8L V6 turbocharged engine equipped with the SFI injection system. With the C^3I system, no distributor is used. The system utilizes a coil pack and ignition module, along with crankshaft and camshaft sensors.

NOTE: When troubleshooting a no start/no spark condition, if equipped with C^3I system, make sure the ignition module is properly grounded to it's mounting bracket.

REMOVAL

1. Disconnect the negative battery cable.
2. Disconnect and tag the ignition wire (pink), tachometer wire, if equipped, and 3 terminal connector from distributor cap.

NOTE: Use care when releasing the connector locking tabs on the distributor cap.

3. Remove distributor cap with the spark plug wires attached and position it out of the way.
4. Disconnect the 4 terminal connector from the distributor.
5. Remove the distributor hold-down bolt and clamp. Mark the position of the rotor in relation to the engine. Pull the distributor from the engine until the rotor just stops turning counterclockwise. Again mark the position of rotor.

INSTALLATION
Timing Not Disturbed

NOTE: To insure correct ignition timing if the engine has not been disturbed, the distributor must be installed with the rotor in the same position as when removed.

1. Align the rotor to the last mark made and install the distributor in the engine.
2. The rotor should turn and end up at the first mark made.
3. Check the timing when finished.

Timing Disturbed

1. Remove the No. 1 spark plug. Place a finger over the spark plug hole and rotate the engine in the normal direction of rotation slowly, until compression is felt.
2. Align the timing mark on the pulley to the **0** on the engine timing indicator by rotating the engine in the same direction slowly.
3. Position the rotor between No. 1 and No. 8 spark plug towers on V8 engine and between No. 1 and No. 6 spark plug towers on V6 engine.
4. Install the distributor, distributor cap, spark plug, wiring and connectors.
5. Check the engine timing and adjust, as required.

Distributorless Ignition

3.8L Turbocharged Engine

The C^3I ignition system consists of the ECM, ignition module, ignition coils

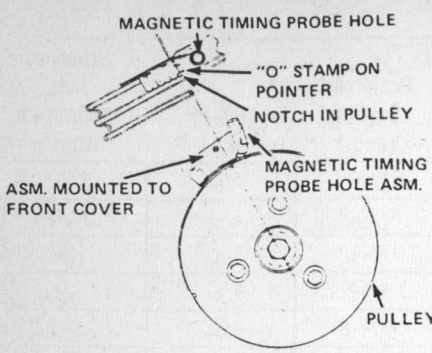

MAGNETIC TIMING PROBE HOLE

"O" STAMP ON POINTER

NOTCH IN PULLEY

ASM. MOUNTED TO FRONT COVER

MAGNETIC TIMING PROBE HOLE ASM.

PULLEY

Location of hole for magnetic timing probe

and Hall Effect camshaft and crankshaft sensors. The crankshaft sensor is mounted at the harmonic balancer and the camshaft sensor is mounted at the camshaft gear.

The spark distribution is accomplished by a signal from the crankshaft sensor which is used by the ignition module to determine the proper time to trigger the next ignition coil.

The camshaft sensor provides the C³I module with a signal pulse as pistons No. 1 and 4 are approximately 25 degrees past TDC. The signal in fact, represents the camshaft's actual location, due to the sensors location. The camshaft sensor is also used to properly time the fuel injection system.

REMOVAL & INSTALLATION

Camshaft Sensor

NOTE: If only the camshaft sensor is being replaced, it is not necessary to remove the entire drive assembly. The sensor can be replaced separately.

1. Disconnect the negative battery cable.
2. Disconnect the 14 way ignition module connector.
3. Disconnect the spark plug wire at the coil assemblies.
4. Remove the ignition module bracket assembly.
5. Disconnect the sensor wiring.
6. Remove the mounting screws and remove the sensor from the engine.
7. Install the sensor in the engine and install the mounting screws.
8. Connect the sensor wiring and install the ignition module mounting bracket.
9. Connect the spark plug wires, ignition module connector and negative battery cable.

NOTE: If the camshaft sensor drive was not removed, there is no reason to adjust the sensor's timing. If the sensor drive was removed, follow the adjustment

procedure after installing the sensor and drive. The adjustment will not affect the spark timing.

Crankshaft Sensor

1. Disconnect the negative battery cable.
2. Disconnect the crankshaft sensor connector.
3. Slowly rotate the engine until any window (slot) in the reluctor wheel on the balancer is aligned with the sensor.
4. Loosen the pinch bolt on the sensor pedestal until the sensor can freely slide in the pedestal.
5. Remove the pedestal to engine mounting bolts.
6. Carefully remove the pedestal and sensor as an assembly from the engine. The sensor will move in the pedestal and care must be used when removing.
7. Before installing the new sensor, loosen the sensor in the pedestal until it can be moved freely.
8. Verify that the reluctor is still in alignment and install the pedestal and sensor on the engine.
9. Tighten the pedestal mounting bolts to 22 ft. lbs.
10. Adjust the sensor when finished.

Ignition Coil

1. Disconnect the negative battery cable.
2. Disconnect the spark plug wires.
3. Remove the 6 Torx® screws securing the coil to the ignition module.
4. Tilt the coil assembly back, disconnect the module to coil connectors and remove the coil.
5. Installation is the reverse of removal.

Ignition Module

1. Disconnect the negative battery cable.
2. Disconnect the 14 way connector at the ignition module.
3. Disconnect the spark plug wires at the module.
4. Disconnect the ignition module from the bracket.
5. Remove the 6 Torx® screws securing the coil to the ignition module.
6. Disconnect the wires between the ignition coil and the ignition module and remove the module.
7. Installation is the reverse of removal.

ADJUSTMENT

Camshaft Sensor

1. Remove the No. 1 spark plug and rotate the engine until the No. 1 cylinder is at TDC on the compression stroke.

2. Mark the harmonic balancer and rotate the engine an additional 25 degrees past TDC.
3. Remove the spark plug wires from the ignition coil.
4. Using tool J–28742–A or equivalent, remove terminal B of the camshaft sensor plug, on the ignition module side of the plug.
5. Insert a jumper wire into terminal B of the plug and connect a voltmeter between the wire and ground.
6. Place the ignition switch in the **ON** position with the engine **OFF**.
7. Rotate the sensor counterclockwise until the sensor switch just closes. This is indicated by a voltage going from a high of 5–12 volts, to a low of 0–2 volts. The low voltage indicates the switch is closed.
8. With voltage in the low range, tighten the mounting bolts and recheck the voltage.
9. Remove the jumper wire and voltmeter. Reconnect the sensor and run the engine.

Crankshaft Sensor

1. With the sensor installed on the engine, insert adjustment tool J–36179 or equivalent, into the gap between the sensor and the reluctor wheel on the balancer.
2. Make sure the interrupter is sandwiched between the blades of the adjustment tool and both blades are properly inserted into the sensor slot.
3. Tighten the sensor pinch bolt to 30 inch lbs. while maintaining light pressure on the sensor and interrupter ring.
4. Check this clearance again at every 120 degree interval.

NOTE: If the sensor touches the interrupter ring at any point, the ring is bent and must be replaced.

Ignition Timing

ADJUSTMENT

NOTE: If equipped with the C³I ignition system, the timing is adjusted automatically by the ECM. Manual adjustment of the C³I ignition timing is not possible.

4.3L Engine

1. Run the engine until normal operating temperature is reached. Be sure the air cleaner is installed and the air conditioner is off.
2. Connect a timing light with the pickup lead on the No. 1 plug wire.
3. Disconnect the 4 wire electrical connector at the distributor. The check engine light will come on.

4. If the timing requires adjustment, loosen the distributor and set the timing to the specifications as noted on the vehicle emission information label.

5. After the timing has been set, remove the ECM fuse from the fuse block for 15 seconds to cancel any stored trouble codes.

NOTE: Some engines will incorporate a magnetic timing probe hole for the use with electronic timing equipment. Be sure to consult the equipment manufactures instructions for the use of this equipment.

5.0L and 5.7L Engines

1. Run the engine until operating temperature has been reached. Be sure the choke is fully open and the air conditioning is off.

2. With the engine running, ground the diagnostic terminal of the 12 terminal ALDL connector.

3. Connect the timing light with the pickup lead on the No. 1 plug wire.

4. If the timing requires adjustment, loosen the distributor and set the timing to the specifications noted on the vehicle emission information label.

5. Once the timing has been set and with the engine still running, unground the diagnostic terminal.

6. Clear any stored trouble codes by removing the ECM fuse for 15 seconds.

Alternator

For further information on the charging system, please refer to "Charging and Starting" in the Unit Repair section.

PRECAUTIONS

Several precautions must be observed with alternator equipped vehicles to avoid damage to the unit.

- If the battery is removed for any reason, make sure it is reconnected with the correct polarity. Reversing the battery connections may result in damage to the one-way rectifiers.
- When utilizing a booster battery as a starting aid, always connect the positive to positive terminals and the negative terminal from the booster battery to a good engine ground on the vehicle being started.
- Never use a fast charger as a booster to start vehicles.
- Disconnect the battery cables when charging the battery with a fast charger.
- Never attempt to polarize the alternator.

- Do not use test lamps of more than 12 volts when checking diode continuity.
- Do not short across or ground any of the alternator terminals.
- The polarity of the battery, alternator and regulator must be matched and considered before making any electrical connections within the system.
- Never separate the alternator on an open circuit. Make sure all connections within the circuit are clean and tight.
- Disconnect the battery ground terminal when performing any service on electrical components.
- Disconnect the battery if arc welding is to be done on the vehicle.

BELT TENSION ADJUSTMENT

V-Belts are normally adjusted by loosening the bolts of the accessory being driven and moving that accessory on its pivot points until the proper tension is applied to the belt. The accessory is held in this position while the bolts are tightened. To determine proper belt tension, a belt tension gauge will be needed or simply use the deflection method. To determine deflection, press inward on the belt at the mid-point of the longest straight run. The belt should deflect (move inward) ⅜–½ in. Some long V-belts have idler pulleys which are used for adjusting purposes. With these systems, loosen the idler pulley and move it to take up tension on the belt.

Serpentine belts are automatically adjusted by the tensioner on the engine. If the belt is loose, check the condition of the belt and tensioner. The tensioner should place enough tension on the belt so it can only be twisted 90 degrees at it's longest run.

REMOVAL & INSTALLATION

1. Disconnect the negative battery cable.

2. Disconnect and tag the electrical connections.

3. With V-Belts, remove the bolt holding the slotted adjusting bracket to the alternator and remove the belt.

4. With serpentine belts, loosen and rotate the tensioner to release the drive belt.

5. Remove the thru-bolt to release the alternator from the engine.

To install:

6. When reinstalling, reverse the removal procedure.

7. Adjust the drive belt to allow ½ in. play on the longest run between pulleys.

8. On some models, it may be necessary to loosen and rotate the fan shroud.

9. On models with air conditioning, it may be necessary to remove the compressor bracket. Do not discharge the air conditioning system.

Voltage Regulator

For further information on the charging system, please refer to "Charging and Starting" in the Unit Repair section.

Starter

For further information on the charging system, please refer to "Charging and Starting" in the Unit Repair section.

REMOVAL & INSTALLATION

1. Disconnect the negative battery cable.

2. Raise and support the vehicle safely.

3. Remove upper support attaching bolts and the brace and wire guide tube bolt, if equipped.

4. Remove the flywheel housing cover, as required.

5. If necessary, remove the exhaust crossover pipe.

6. If necessary, disconnect the transmission oil cooler lines.

7. Remove the starter mounting bolts and lower the starter.

8. Disconnect the wiring and remove starter.

9. If equipped with dual exhaust, it may be necessary to remove the left exhaust pipe.

10. Install by reversing the removal procedure.

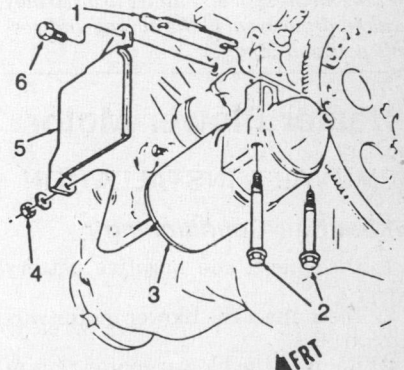

1. Shim
2. Bolts 35 ft. lbs.
3. Starter assy.
4. Nut – 13 ft. lbs.
5. Shield
6. Bolt – 20 ft. lbs.

Typical starter mounting – except 1991 Caprice

1. Nut
2. Washer
3. Bracket only on 5.7L engine
4. Bolt
5. Starter motor
6. Bolts
7. Double shim on 5.0L (VIN E, G, H) engine
8. Single shim on 5.0L (VIN E, G, H) and 5.7L engine
9. Double shim on 5.7L engine

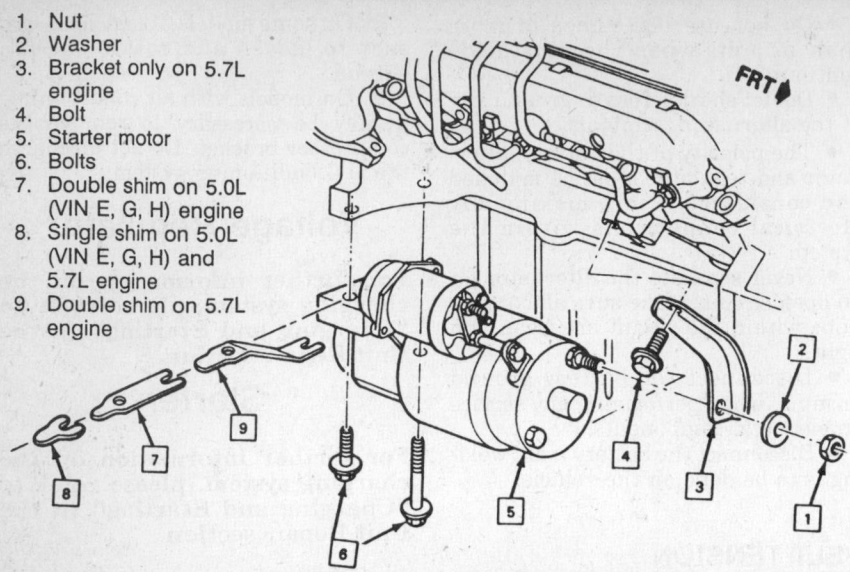

FRT

Starter mounting—1991 Caprice

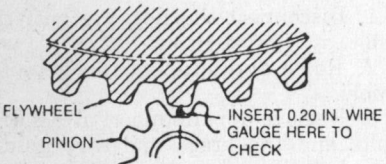

FLYWHEEL

PINION

INSERT 0.20 IN. WIRE GAUGE HERE TO CHECK

Flywheel to pinion mounting

11. If shims were removed, they must be installed in their original location to assure proper drive pinion to flywheel engagement.

CHASSIS ELECTRICAL

CAUTION

If equipped with an air bag, the negative battery cable must be disconnected, before working on the system. Failure to do so may result in deployment of the air bag and possible personal injury.

Heater Blower Motor

REMOVAL & INSTALLATION

Without Air Conditioning

1. Disconnect the negative battery cable.
2. Disconnect the blower motor wiring harness.
3. Remove the blower motor retaining screws and pull the blower motor and fan straight forward out of the heater module.
4. Installation is the reverse of removal. Clean and replace sealer as necessary.

With Air Conditioning

EXCEPT 1991 CAPRICE

1. Disconnect the negative battery cable.
2. Disconnect the blower motor wiring harness.
3. Remove the blower motor cooling tube.
4. Remove the blower motor retaining screws and lift the blower motor and fan straight up and out of the upper case of the air conditioning module.
5. Installation is the reverse of removal. Clean and replace sealer as necessary.

1991 CAPRICE

1. Disconnect the negative battery cable.
2. Remove the 4 retaining screws and remove the right hand instrument panel sound insulator.
3. Disconnect the blower motor electrical connector.
4. Remove the right hand hinge pillar trim finish panel by pulling it away from the front body hinge pillar.
5. Remove the screw from the secondary ECM bracket and swing the ECM module and bracket aside to provide access to the blower motor.
6. Remove the blower mounting mounting screws and remove the blower motor and fan assembly.
7. Installation is the reverse of removal.

Windshield Wiper Motor

REMOVAL & INSTALLATION

1. Disconnect the negative battery cable.

2. Raise the hood and remove the cowl screen.

NOTE: On the 1991 Caprice, the left hand cowl screen must be removed before the right hand cowl screen to prevent possible windshield damage.

3. Remove the linkage access hole cover, if equipped.
4. Loosen the transmission drive link to crank arm retaining bolts. Remove the drive link from the motor crank arm.
5. Disconnect the electrical wiring and the washer hoses from the motor assembly.
6. Remove the motor retaining screws. Remove the windshield wiper motor while guiding the crank arm through the hole.
7. Installation is the reverse of the removal procedure. The motor must be in the **P** position before assembling the crank arm to the drive link.

NOTE: On the 1991 Caprice, the right hand cowl screen must be installed before the left hand cowl screen to prevent possible windshield damage.

Windshield Wiper Switch

REMOVAL & INSTALLATION

1. Disconnect the negative battery cable. Remove the steering wheel.
2. It may be necessary to loosen the column mounting nuts and remove the bracket to mast jacket screws, then separate the bracket from the mast jacket to allow the connector clip on the ignition switch to be pulled out of the column assembly.
3. Disconnect the washer/wiper switch lower connector.
4. Remove the screws attaching the column housing to the mast jacket. Be sure to note the position of the dimmer switch actuator rod for reassembly in the same position. Remove the column housing and switch as an assembly.

NOTE: The tilt and travel columns have a removable plastic cover on the column housing. This provides access to the wiper switch without removing the entire column housing.

5. Turn upside down and use a drift to remove the pivot pin from the washer/wiper switch. Remove the switch.
To install:
6. Place the switch into position in the housing and install the pivot pin.
7. Position the housing onto the mast jacket and attach by installing

the screws. Install the dimmer switch actuator rod in the same position as noted earlier. Check switch operation.

8. Reconnect lower end of switch assembly.

9. Install remaining components in reverse order of removal. Be sure to attach column mounting bracket in original position.

Instrument Cluster

REMOVAL & INSTALLATION

Estate Wagon

1. Disconnect the negative battery cable. Remove the defroster grille.

2. Remove the 10 screws retaining the instrument panel top cover to the instrument panel.

3. If equipped with a twilight sentinel, pop up the photocell retainer, turn the photocell counterclockwise in the retainer and pull it down and out.

4. Slide the instrument panel top cover out far enough to disconnect the aspirator hose, electrical connector to the in-vehicle sensor and the electrical connector to the electro-luminescent inverter.

5. Remove the instrument panel top cover from the instrument panel. If equipped with quartz electronic speedometer clusters, remove the steering column trim cover, so the shift indicator can be removed.

6. Remove the 5 screws from the instrument cluster to the instrument panel carrier.

7. Disconnect the speedometer cable and pull the cluster housing assembly straight out, this will also separate the electrical connectors to the cluster.

NOTE: If equipped with tilt steering wheel, it may be helpful to tilt the wheel all the way down and pull the gear select lever to low, when removing the cluster.

8. Installation is the reverse of the removal procedure.

Regal

1. Disconnect the negative battery cable. Remove the left side trim cover.

2. Remove the retaining screws holding the cluster carrier to the instrument panel.

3. If a 2 piece speedometer cable is used, disconnect the speedometer cable at the split in the engine compartment.

4. Remove the steering column trim cover.

5. Disconnect the shift indicator clip.

6. Lower the steering column. If equipped with a tilt wheel it will be necessary to lower the wheel as far as

possible and unscrew the tilt lever.

7. Remove the cluster mounting screws and pull the instrument cluster forward enough to disconnect the speedometer cable from the rear of the cluster. Disconnect the wiring for instrument panel lighting.

8. Pull the gear selector lever down into the low position.

9. Pull the cluster out far enough to remove the screw retaining the Vehicle Speed Sensor (VSS) to the head of the speedometer.

10. Remove the cluster.

11. The installation of the cluster assembly is the reverse of the removal procedure.

12. Check that all lights, gauges and the speedometer work after installation.

Caprice

1987–90

1. Disconnect the negative battery cable.

2. Remove the steering column lower cover screws and the cover.

3. If equipped with automatic transmission, disconnect the shift indicator cable from the steering column.

4. Remove the steering column to instrument panel screws. Lower the steering column.

NOTE: Use extreme care when lowering the steering column in order to prevent damage to column assembly.

5. Remove the screws and the snap in fasteners from the perimeter of the instrument cluster lens.

6. Remove the screws from the lower corner of the cluster.

7. Remove the stud nuts from the lower corner of the cluster.

8. Disconnect the speedometer cable and pull cluster from the instrument panel.

9. Disconnect the electrical connec-

tors from the cluster and remove the assembly from the vehicle.

10. Installation is the reverse of the removal procedure.

1991

1. Disconnect the negative battery cable.

2. Remove the left hand trim plate:

   a. Remove the steering column opening filler.

   b. Open the instrument panel compartment door and unsnap the right hand moulding from the carrier.

   c. Loosen the capsule nuts attaching the steering column support bracket to the carrier, to the end of the threads but do not remove from the bolts. Gently lower the steering column.

   d. Remove the 6 screws attaching the trim plate to the carrier and carefully unsnap and pull away.

3. Remove the 5 screws attaching the cluster to the carrier.

4. Disconnect the shift indicator cable from the steering column.

5. Remove the cluster from the vehicle and disconnect the electrical connector.

6. Installation is the reverse of removal. Adjust the shift indicator as follows:

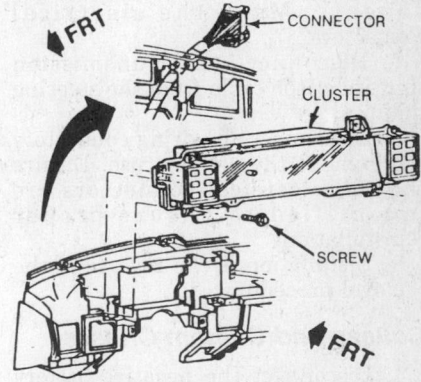

Instrument cluster—1991 Caprice

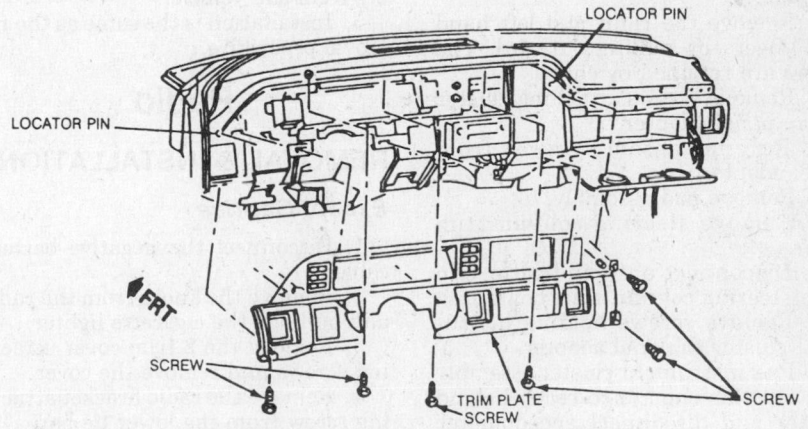

Left hand trim plate installation—1991 Caprice

a. Remove the steering column opening filler.

b. The shift lever should be in the **N** gate notch.

c. Position the guide clip on the edge of the gearshift lever bowl to centrally position the pointer on **N**. Push the guide clip onto the gearshift lever bowl.

Monte Carlo

1. Disconnect the negative battery cable. Remove the clock set stem and radio knobs.

2. Remove the instrument bezel retaining screws.

3. Slightly pull the bezel rearward. Disconnect the rear defogger switch. Remove the remote control mirror control knob, if equipped.

4. Remove the dash panel bezel. Remove the speedometer assembly retaining screws. Pull the assembly from the cluster, disconnect the speedometer cable from the assembly and remove the speedometer from the vehicle.

5. Remove the fuel gauge or the tachometer retaining screws, disconnect the electrical connectors and remove the components.

6. Remove the clock or voltmeter retaining screws, disconnect the electrical connectors and remove the components. Mark the electrical connectors.

7. Disconnect the transmission shift indicator cable from the steering column.

8. Disconnect all wiring connectors and remove the cluster case. Ensure that all electrical connectors are indentified to ensure proper reinstallation.

9. Installation is the reverse of the removal procedure.

Cutlass and Custom Cruiser

1. Disconnect the negative battery cable. Disconnect speedometer cable at transducer, if equipped with cruise control.

2. Remove the right and left hand trim covers by pulling outward. The covers are retained by clips.

3. Remove screws attaching cluster pad to panel adapter.

4. Pull pad assembly away from panel adapter.

5. Remove pad assembly.

6. Remove steering column trim cover.

7. Disconnect shift indicator clip from steering column shift bowl.

8. Remove screws holding instrument cluster to panel adapter.

9. Pull instrument cluster assembly rearward far enough to reach behind cluster and disconnect speedometer cable.

10. Disconnect speed sensor, if equipped.

11. Remove instrument cluster.

12. Installation is the reverse of removal.

Grand Prix

1. Disconnect battery ground cable.

2. Remove steering column lower cover screws and cover.

3. Disconnect shift indicator cable from steering column.

4. Remove steering column to instrument panel screws and lower steering column.

NOTE: Use extreme care when lower steering to prevent damage to column assembly.

5. Remove the screws and the snap-in fasteners from perimeter of instrument cluster lens.

6. Remove screws from upper surface of grey sheet metal trim plate.

7. Remove stud nuts from lower corner of cluster.

8. Disconnect speedometer cable and pull cluster from instrument panel.

9. Disconnect electrical connectors from cluster and remove from vehicle.

10. Installation is the reverse removal.

Speedometer

REMOVAL & INSTALLATION

Except 1991 Caprice

1. Disconnect the negative battery cable.

2. Remove the instrument cluster.

3. Remove the speedometer retaining screws. Pull the assembly forward in order to disconnect the speedometer cable. To gain slack, it may be necessary to disconnect the cable at the cruise control transducer or the transmission.

4. Remove the speedometer assembly from the vehicle.

5. Installation is the same as the removal procedure.

Radio

REMOVAL & INSTALLATION

Except Caprice

1. Disconnect the negative battery cable.

2. Remove the knobs from the radio and pull out the cigarette lighter.

3. Remove the 2 trim cover attaching screws and remove the cover.

4. Remove the radio bracket attaching screw from the lower tie bar.

5. Remove the 4 mounting plate screws and pull the radio out to obtain access to the electrical connections. Detach the wiring harness and the antenna lead.

6. Remove the mounting plate nuts and remove the radio. Installation is in the reverse order of removal.

Caprice

1987–90

1. Disconnect the negative battery cable.

2. Remove the ash tray.

3. Remove the instrument panel compartment.

4. Disconnect the air conditioning and heater cables.

5. Remove the air conditioning and radio trim plate.

6. Remove the radio and air conditioning heater control assembly.

7. Remove the screws holding the bracket to the trim plate and remove the bracket.

8. Remove the screws holding the radio to the trim plate and remove the radio.

9. Installation is the reverse of removal.

1991

1. Disconnect the negative battery cable.

2. Remove the left side trim plate:

a. Remove the steering column opening filler.

b. Open the instrument panel compartment door and unsnap the right hand moulding from the carrier.

c. Loosen the capsule nuts attaching the steering column support bracket to the carrier, to the end of the threads but do not remove from the bolts. Gently lower the steering column.

d. Remove the 6 screws attaching the trim plate to the carrier and carefully unsnap and pull away.

3. Remove the 3 screws attaching the bracket to the carrier and remove the bracket and the attached radio from the carrier.

4. Disconnect the body harness connector and the antenna lead from the radio.

5. Remove the 3 nuts attaching the bracket to the radio and remove the 3 bolts from the radio, if necessary.

6. Installation is the reverse of removal.

Headlight Switch

REMOVAL & INSTALLATION

Except 1991 Caprice
ROCKER TYPE SWITCH

1. Disconnect the negative battery cable.

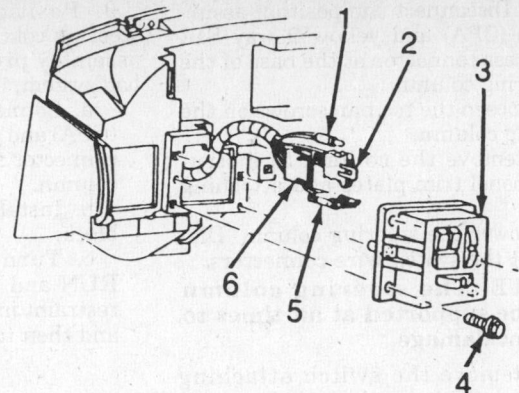

1. Headlight switch indicator light (with twilight sentinel)
2. Panel light dimmer switch connector
3. Switch
4. Screw
5. Twilight sentinel switch connector
6. Headlight switch connector

Headlight and instrument panel dimmer switch installation—1991 Caprice

2. Remove the left hand sound insulator and trim plate or cover, as necessary.

3. Remove the left side switch trim cover.

4. Remove the screws. Center screw shares the top of the switch and the bottom of the interior light rheostat.

5. Pull the switch and rheostat straight outwards, disconnect the wiring and remove the switch.

6. Installation is the reverse of the removal procedure.

KNOB TYPE SWITCH

1. Disconnect the negative battery cable.

2. Pull the headlight switch to the **ON** position.

3. Depending upon the switch mechanism, pull the trim knob from the switch by either reaching under the dash and depressing the switch shaft release button while pulling the knob and shaft from the light switch or by using a suitable tool and pushing the tang under the trim knob while pulling the knob from the shaft.

4. Remove the ferrule nut retaining the switch to the dash panel. Disconnect the electrical connector and remove the switch.

5. Installation is the reverse of the removal procedure.

1991 Caprice

1. Disconnect the negative battery cable.

2. Remove the left side trim plate:

a. Remove the steering column opening filler.

b. Open the instrument panel compartment door and unsnap the right hand moulding from the carrier.

c. Loosen the capsule nuts attaching the steering column support bracket to the carrier, to the end of the threads but do not remove from the bolts. Gently lower the steering column.

d. Remove the 6 screws attaching the trim plate to the carrier and carefully unsnap and pull away.

3. Remove the 3 screws attaching the switch to the instrument carrier and remove the switch.

4. Installation is the reverse of removal.

Dimmer Switch

REMOVAL & INSTALLATION

1. Disconnect the negative battery cable.

2. The dimmer switch is attached to the lower steering column jacket. Disconnect all electrical connections from the switch.

3. Remove the nut and screw that attach the switch to the steering column jacket and remove switch.

4. Install the dimmer switch and depress it slightly to insert a $3/32$ in. drill. Force switch up to remove lash, then tighten screw and nut to 4.0 ft. lbs.

Turn Signal Switch

REMOVAL & INSTALLATION

Except 1991 Caprice

1. Disconnect the negative battery cable.

2. Disconnect turn signal switch wire connector at lower end of steering column.

3. Remove the steering wheel and shaft lock cover.

4. Remove retaining ring and shaft lock using tool J–23653 or equivalent.

5. Remove cancelling cam and spring assembly.

6. Remove screws attaching the switch to the housing. Pull switch out. If equipped with cruise control, the wiring harness will have to be pulled up through the steering column.

7. Installation is the reverse of the removal procedure.

1991 Caprice

1. Disable the Supplemental Air Restraint (SIR) system.

a. Turn the steering wheel so the vehicles wheels are pointing straight ahead.

b. Turn the ignition switch to **LOCK**.

c. Remove the SIR fuse from the fuse block.

d. Disconnect the position assurance (CPA) and yellow 2 way SIR harness connector at the base of the steering column.

2. Remove the Torx® screws from in back of the steering wheel, disconnect the connector and remove the the inflator module.

CAUTION

To avoid personal injury when carrying a live inflator module, make sure the bag and trim cover are pointed away. When placing a live inflator module on a bench or other surface, always face the bag and trim cover up and away from the surface, also never carry the inflator module by the wires or connector on the underside of the module otherwise personal injury may result if bag is deployed.

---

3. Disconnect the negative battery cable.

4. Remove the steering wheel.

5. Remove the coil assembly retaining ring and allow it to hang.

CAUTION

Use a ½ in. wrench to hold the shaft of tool J–23653–C stationary when releasing the nut. Failure to do so may cause tool J–23653–C to fly off and cause personal injury.

---

6. Remove the wave washer.

7. Remove the shaft lock retaining ring using tool J–23653–C or equivalent.

8. Remove the shaft lock, turn signal canceling cam, upper bearing spring, inner race seat and inner race.

9. Remove the multi-function lever.

10. Remove the signal switch arm retaining screw.

11. Remove the hazard warning knob retaining screw.

12. Remove the wiring protector

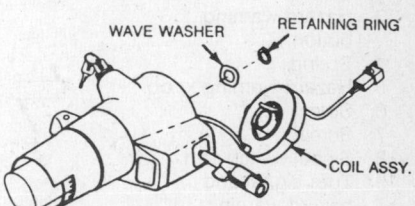

Removing the coil assembly from the steering shaft—1991 Caprice

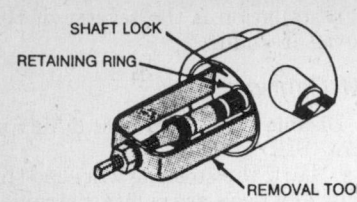

SHAFT LOCK
RETAINING RING
REMOVAL TOOL

Removing the shaft lock retaining ring using tool J–26653 or equivalent.

from the steering column then disconnect the switch connector.

13. Remove the screws retaining the turn signal and hazard warning switch to the steering column, using care not to drop the screws in the column.

14. Installation is the reverse of removal. Enable the SIR system as follows:

a. Connect the position assurance (CPA) and yellow 2 way SIR harness connector at the base of the steering column.

b. Install the SIR fuse to the fuse block.

c. Turn the ignition switch to **RUN** and verify that the inflatable restraint indicator flashes 7–9 times and then turns off.

Ignition Switch

REMOVAL & INSTALLATION

1. Disconnect the negative battery cable and disable the air bag system, if equipped, as follows:

a. Turn the steering wheel so the vehicles wheels are pointing straight ahead.

b. Turn the ignition switch to **LOCK**.

c. Remove the SIR fuse from the fuse block.

1. Shaft lock
2. Turn signal cancelling cam
3. Upper bearing spring
4. Upper bearing inner race seat
5. Inner race

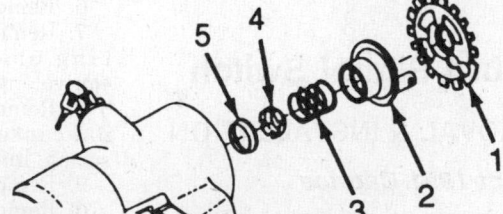

Removing the upper bearing shaft components—1991 Caprice

1. Multi-function lever
2. Screw
3. Hazard warning button
4. Spring
5. Hazard warning knob
6. Screw
7. Screw
8. Signal switch arm
9. Turn signal and hazard warning switch

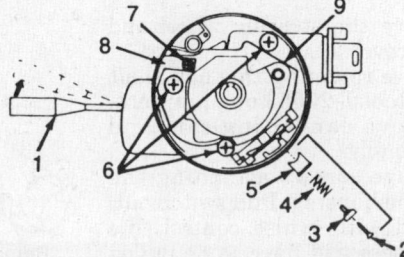

Turn signal and hazard switch removal—1991 Caprice

d. Disconnect the position assurance (CPA) and yellow 2 way SIR harness connector at the base of the steering column.

2. Loosen the toe pan screws on the steering column.

3. Remove the column to instrument panel trim plates and attaching nuts.

4. Lower the steering column. Disconnect the switch wire connectors.

NOTE: The steering column must be supported at all times to prevent damage.

5. Remove the switch attaching screws and remove the switch.

To install:

6. Move the key lock to the **LOCK** position.

7. Move the actuator rod hole in the switch to the **LOCK** position.

8. Install the switch with the rod in the hole. Adjust the ignition switch as follows:

a. 1987—Move the switch slider to the extreme right position **ACC**.

b. 1988—Move the switch slider to the extreme left **ACC** position, then move the slider 2 detents to the right to the **OFF-UNLOCK** position.

c. 1989–90—Place a $^3/_{32}$ in. drill bit in the hole on the switch to lock the switch into position. Move the switch slider to the extreme left position then move the slider one detent to the right **OFF LOCK** position. Remove the drill bit.

d. 1991—Install the ignition switch in the **OFF-UNLOCK** position. The gearshift lever bowl must not be in the **P** position. Move the switch slider to the extreme right position and move the slider 1 detent to the left **OFF LOCK** position.

9. Position and reassemble the steering column in reverse of the disassembly procedure. Enable the air bag system, if so equipped, as follows:

a. Connect the position assurance (CPA) and yellow 2 way SIR harness connector at the base of the steering column.

b. Install the SIR fuse to the fuse block.

c. Turn the ignition switch to **RUN** and verify that the inflatable restraint indicator flashes 7–9 times and then turns off.

Ignition Lock Cylinder

REMOVAL & INSTALLATION

1. Disconnect the negative battery cable and disable the air bag system, if equipped, as follows:

a. Turn the steering wheel so the vehicles wheels are pointing straight ahead.

b. Turn the ignition switch to **LOCK**.

c. Remove the SIR fuse from the fuse block.

d. Disconnect the position assurance (CPA) and yellow 2 way SIR harness connector at the base of the steering column.

2. Position the ignition lock cylinder in the **RUN** position.

3. Remove the steering wheel. Remove the lock plate, turn signal switch and the buzzer switch.

4. Remove the lock cylinder retaining screw. Remove the lock cylinder.

5. To install, rotate the lock cylinder clockwise to align the cylinder key with the keyway in the lock housing.

6. Push the lock all the way in. Install the screw.

7. Continue the installation in the reverse order of the removal procedure. Enable the air bag system, if equipped, as follows:

a. Connect the position assurance (CPA) and yellow 2 way SIR harness connector at the base of the steering column.

b. Install the SIR fuse to the fuse block.

c. Turn the ignition switch to **RUN** and verify that the inflatable restraint indicator flashes 7–9 times and then turns off.

Stoplight Switch

REMOVAL & INSTALLATION

1. Disconnect the negative battery cable.

2. Disconnect the electrical connection from the switch.

NOTE: If equipped with cruise control, there will be 2 switches mounted on the brake pedal support. The stoplight switch does not incorporate a vacuum hose.

3. Remove the switch from the tubular clip on the brake pedal mounting bracket.

4. To install and adjust, insert the switch into the clip until the switch body seats on the clip.

5. Pull the brake pedal rearwards against internal pedal stop. The switch will be moved in tubular clip, when no clicks are heard while pulling the pedal and the brake lamps do not stay on, proper adjustment has been reached.

Neutral Safety Switch

All steering columns use a mechanical neutral start system. This system has a mechanical block which prevents starting the engine in positions other than **P** or **N**. The mechanical block is achieved by a wedge shaped finger added to the ignition switch actuator rod. The finger will only pass through the bowl plate when in the **P** and **N** quadrant positions. This prevents the lock cylinder from being turned to the **START** position when in other quadrant positions. When in either **P** or **N** quadrant positions, the finger is allowed to pass through the bowl plate notches, allowing the lock cylinder to rotate to the **START** position.

Fuses, Circuit Breakers and Relays

LOCATION

Fusible Links

Fusible links are used to prevent major wire harness damage in the event of a short circuit or an overload condition in the wiring circuits which are normally not fused, due to carrying high amperage loads or because of their locations within the wiring harness. Each fusible link is of a fixed value for a specific electrical load and should a link fail, the cause of the failure must be determined and repaired prior to installing a new fusible link of the same value.

Circuit Breakers

Various circuit breakers are located under the instrument panel. In order to gain access to these components it may be necessary to first remove the under–dash padding.

Fuse Panel

The fuse panel is located on the left side of the vehicle. It is under the instrument panel assembly. In order to gain access to the fuse panel, it may be necessary to first remove the under–dash padding.

Various Relays

A/C Blower—located in the right hand front of the dash, behind the accumulator.

A/C Compressor Control—located on the right hand front of the dash, near the blower motor.

Antenna—located behind the right hand side of the instrument panel compartment.

Choke Heater—located on the left hand front of the dash, beside the brake booster.

Power Door Locks—located on the lower right hand shroud, lower access hole.

Early Fuel Evaporation (EFE)—located in the right hand side of the engine compartment, top of the wheel house.

Electronic Level Control—located on the left hand front fender behind the battery.

Rear Defogger Timer Relay—located on top of the fuse block.

Wiper Motor Relay—located inside the connector, on the wiper/washer assembly.

Horn—is attached to the left hand side of the fuse block.

A/C Programmer Unit—located behind the right side of the instrument panel.

A/C Temperature Cut-Out Relay—located behind the right front fender apron or at the center of the firewall.

Fast Idle Relay—located on the same bracket as the electronic spark control module, which is located at the top of the right front fender well.

Fast Idle Relay (4.3L Engine)—located in the center of the firewall in the engine compartment.

Fuel Pump Relay—located on a bracket in the right side of the engine compartment.

Headlight Relay—located at the front side of the engine compartment, near the headlight.

Power Master Brake Relay—located on top of the electro-hydraulic pump motor below the master cylinder.

Starter Interrupt Relay—located under the left side of the dash panel, above the steering column.

Wide Open Throttle Relay—located in the engine compartment at the center of the firewall.

Theft Deterrent Relay—located behind the instrument panel to the left of the steering column.

Power Seat Relay—located on under the right or left seat.

Rear Hatch Release Relay—located at the rear hatch release latch.

Turn Signal Flasher

The turn signal flasher is located inside the convenience center. In order to gain access to the turn signal flasher it may be necessary to first remove the under dash padding.

Hazard Flasher

The hazard flasher is located in the fuse block. It is positioned on the lower right hand corner of the fuse block assembly.

Computer (ECM)

The electronic control module is located in the passenger compartment. It is positioned in front of the right hand kick panel. In order to gain access to the assembly, first remove the trim panel.

Cruise Control

ADJUSTMENT

Servo

5.0L (VIN Y) ENGINE

Adjust the rod length to minimum slack with the carburetor lever on the slow idle screw and the engine not running. The idle load control must be fully retracted when the retainer is installed.

Electric Brake Rekease Switch and Vacuum Release Valve

The switch and valve cannot be adjusted until after the brake booster pushrod is assembled to the brake pedal assembly. To adjust use the following procedure.

1. Depress brake pedal and insert switch and valve into their proper retaining clips until fully seated.

2. Slowly pull pedal back to its fully retracted position, the switch and valve will move within the retainers to their adjusted position.

a. Cruise control switch contacts must open at $1/8$–$1/2$ in. (3.5–12.5mm) brake pedal travel, measured at the centerline of the brake pedal pad.

b. Vacuum release valve assembly must open at $1^1/16$–$1^5/16$ in. (27.0–33.0mm) brake pedal travel, measured at the centerline of the brake pedal pad.

NOTE: Nominal actuation of stoplight contacts is about $3/16$ in. (4.5mm) after cruise control contacts open.

ENGINE COOLING

Radiator

REMOVAL & INSTALLATION

1. Disconnect the negative battery cable.
2. Drain the radiator and remove the fan shrouds.
3. Disconnect the radiator inlet and outlet hoses.
4. Disconnect and plug the transmission fluid and oil cooler lines from the radiator.
5. Disconnect the low fluid sensor connector, if equipped.
6. Disconnect the coolant reservoir hose from the radiator.
7. Disconnect the heater hose and remove the radiator from the vehicle.
8. Installation is the reverse of removal. Add coolant and check for leaks.

Electric Cooling Fan

SYSTEM OPERATION

On the 3.8L turbocharged engine, 2 electric cooling fans are used. The fans are energized through a low speed, high speed and delay relay. Power to the fan motors comes from the fusible link to terminal 1 on all relays. The relays are energized when the current flows to ground, through the activation of the air conditioning coolant switches and/or ECM.

The low speed relay is energized by the ECM or air conditioner pressure switch. The ECM energizes the relay through terminal D2 when the coolant temperature reaches 208°F and the vehicle speed is less than 45 mph. The relay can also be energized by the air conditioning pressure switch when the refrigerant pressure reaches 150 psi.

The high speed relay is energized by the air conditioning high pressure switch and coolant temperature override switch. If the air conditioning pressure reaches 27 psi or the coolant temperature reaches 226°F, the relay will be energized.

The delay relay is energized by the temperature switch. When the coolant temperature reaches 226°F or above and the ignition switch is turned OFF, the delay relay is energized for 10 minutes or until the coolant temperature is below 226°F.

TESTING

1. Grounding of the diagnostic test terminal should cause the ECM to ground CKT 535 and the cooling fan should run in low speed.
2. Grounding the temperature switch harness will check CKT 335 and the high speed relay.
3. Check CKT 533 between the high speed relay terminal 4 and the fan motor. If the fan does not run, CKT 533 is open or the motor is faulty.
4. When the ignition switch is OFF, with the temperature switch grounded, the delay relay is activated. This will cause the fan to turn on for up to 10 minutes after the engine is off, depending on the coolant temperature.
5. Connect a set of air conditioning gauges to the system and start the engine. The low speed fan should operate when the high side pressure reaches 260 psi and the high speed fan should operate when the pressure reaches 300 psi.

REMOVAL & INSTALLATION

——— CAUTION ———
Always keep hands and tools away from the fan motors, even when the engine is not running. The fan motors will run at any time the coolant temperature is at 226°F and may cause injury. Always disconnect the negative battery cable before servicing the fan motors.

1. Disconnect the negative battery cable.
2. Disconnect the fan motor wiring.
3. Remove the fan and mounting bracket from the radiator supports.
4. Remove the motor from the mounting bracket and transfer the fan from the old motor to the new motor.
5. Installation is the reverse of the removal procedure.

Heater Core

REMOVAL & INSTALLATION

Without Air Conditioning

1. Disconnect the battery ground. Drain the radiator.
2. Disconnect the blower wiring.
3. Disconnect the heater hoses.
4. Remove the blower cover housing screws and remove the cover housing.
5. Remove the heater core.
6. Installation is the reverse of removal. Remove and replace sealer, as necessary.

With Air Conditioning
EXCEPT 1991 CAPRICE

1. Disconnect the negative battery cable. Drain the radiator.
2. Disconnect the blower wiring.
3. Remove the thermostatic switch and diagnostic connector, if necessary.
4. Remove the hood cowl seal and the air inlet screen screws.
5. Remove the right side windshield wiper arm.
6. Remove the air conditioning module ground strap from the dash panel.
7. Remove the flange mounting screws and lift the upper case straight up and off the lower case and remove the heater core.
8. Installation is the reverse of removal.

1991 CAPRICE

1. Disconnect the negative battery cable. Drain the radiator.
2. Remove the screw holding the hot water bypass valve to the cowl panel.
3. Squeeze both release tabs at the base of the heater core tubes and remove the heater inlet and outlet pipe quick connect fittings from the heater core tubes.
4. Remove the air conditioning module lower evaporator case.
   a. Remove the right side instrument panel sound insulator.
   b. Remove the instrument panel lower reinforcement.
   c. Remove the 2 vacuum harness connectors at the lower evaporator case.
   e. Remove the right side hinge pillar trim finish panel by pulling away from the front body hinge pillar.
   f. Roll back the carpeting to provide access to the forward lower area of the air conditioning module.
   g. Remove the lower evaporator case attaching screws and remove the lower evaporator case.
5. Remove the heater core mounting mounting straps and screws and pull the heater rearward, working the heater core tubes out of the seal.
6. Installation is the reverse of removal. Make sure the quick connect tabs are aligned correctly when connecting the inlet and outlet tubes. Pull back on the sleeve to check for proper installation of the connector. Fill with coolant and check for leaks.

Water Pump

REMOVAL & INSTALLATION

1. Disconnect the negative battery cable.
2. Drain the cooling system.
3. Unfasten the heater, bypass and lower radiator hoses from the pump.
4. Loosen the drive belts and remove the fan assembly and the spacer

bolts. If with air conditioning, remove the fan and clutch assembly.

NOTE: Keep the fan in an upright position during removal to prevent the silicone fluid from leaking out of the fan clutch.

5. Remove the alternator, air conditioning compressor and power steering brackets, if equipped.
6. Unfasten the bolts which secure the water pump and remove it.
7. Clean all gasket mating surfaces and use a new gasket.
8. Installation is the reverse of the removal procedure.

Thermostat

REMOVAL & INSTALLATION

1. Disconnect the negative battery cable.
2. Drain the coolant from the radiator to below the level of the thermostat housing.
3. Remove the radiator inlet hose from the thermostat housing.
4. Remove the thermostat housing bolts and remove the thermostat.
5. Installation is the reverse of removal. Clean the sealing surfaces, use a new gasket and tighten the housing retaining bolts to 13 ft. lbs. on the V6 engine and 19–21 ft. lbs. on the V8 engine.

FUEL SYSTEM

Fuel System Service Precautions

Safety is the most important factor when performing not only fuel system maintenance but any type of maintenance. Failure to conduct maintenance and repairs in a safe manner may result in serious personal injury or death. Maintenance and testing of the vehicle's fuel system components can be accomplished safely and effectively by adhering to the following rules and guidelines.

• To avoid the possibility of fire and personal injury, always disconnect the negative battery cable unless the repair or test procedure requires that battery voltage be applied.

• Always relieve the fuel system pressure prior to disconnecting any fuel system component (injector, fuel rail, pressure regulator, etc.), fitting or fuel line connection. Exercise extreme caution whenever relieving fuel system pressure to avoid exposing skin,

face and eyes to fuel spray. Please be advised that fuel under pressure may penetrate the skin or any part of the body it contacts.

• Always place a shop towel or cloth around the fitting or connection prior to loosening to absorb any excess fuel due to spillage. Ensure that all fuel spillage (should it occur) is quickly removed from engine surfaces. Ensure that all fuel soaked cloths or towels are deposited into a suitable waste container.

• Always keep a dry chemical (Class B) fire extinguisher near the work area.

• Do not allow fuel spray or fuel vapors to come into contact with a spark or open flame.

• Always use a backup wrench when loosening and tightening fuel line connection fittings. This will prevent unnecessary stress and torsion to fuel line piping. Always follow the proper torque specifications.

• Always replace worn fuel fitting O-rings with new. Do not substitute fuel hose or equivalent where fuel pipe is installed.

RELIEVING FUEL SYSTEM PRESSURE

3.8L Engine

1. Disconnect the fuel tank harness connector.
2. Crank the engine. The engine will start and run until the fuel supply remaining in the fuel pipes is consumed.
3. Engage the starter for 3 seconds to assure the relief of any remaining pressure.
4. With the ignition **OFF**, connect the fuel tank harness connector.
5. Disconnect the negative battery cable.

Except 3.8L Engine

1. Disconnect the negative battery cable.
2. Loosen the fuel filler cap to relieve tank vapor pressure.

NOTE: The internal constant bleed feature of the Model 220 TBI relieves fuel pump system pressure when the engine is turned OFF. Therefore, no further relief procedure is required.

3. Disconnect the negative battery cable.

Fuel Filter

REMOVAL & INSTALLATION

Carbureted Engine

1. Disconnect the negative battery cable.

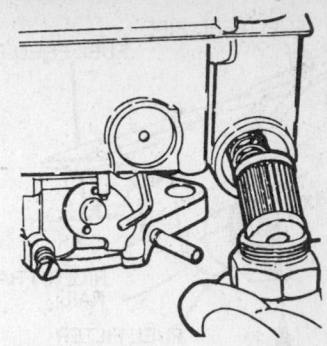

Fuel filter installation—carburetor models

2. Disconnect the fuel line connection at the fuel inlet filter nut on the carburetor.
3. Remove the fuel inlet filter nut and gasket from the carburetor.
4. Remove the filter, filter check valve and spring.
5. Remove the gasket from the fuel inlet nut. Discard the gasket, filter check valve and filter.

To install:

6. Install the fuel filter spring and the fuel filter with check valve into the carburetor opening.
7. Ensure that the filter assembly is installed with the check valve end facing the fuel inlet line. Ribs on the closed end of the filter prevent the filter from being installed incorrectly.
8. Install a new gasket onto the fuel line nut and tighten the nut into the carburetor opening.
9. Reconnect and tighten the fuel inlet line to the fuel nut.
10. Start the engine and inspect for leaks. Correct fuel leaks immediately.

Fuel Injected Engine

The fuel injection system uses an inline filter located in the fuel feed line under the hood, attached to the frame rail or on the rear crossmember of the vehicle. Always use a backup wrench on the fittings any time a fuel filter is removed or installed, and never replace a metal fuel line with a rubber insert. The high pressure fuel system used with all fuel injection systems requires metal fuel lines to contain the pressure. Replace the O-ring at the connection and torque the fuel fitting to 22 ft. lbs.

1. Relieve the fuel system pressure and disconnect the negative battery cable.
2. Disconnect the fuel lines. Use a back-up wrench to hold the fuel filter connector nut stationary while disconnecting the inlet and outlet lines.
3. Remove the O-rings from the fuel line connections. Inspect the O-rings for damage and make replacements, as required.
4. Remove the fuel filter from the retainer. Discard the filter.

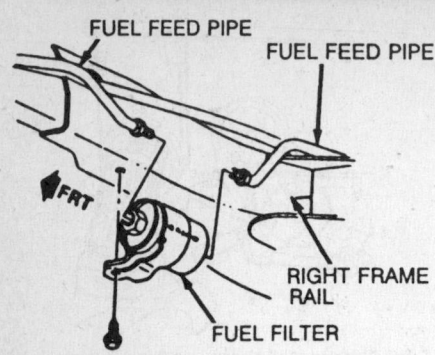

FUEL FEED PIPE
FUEL FEED PIPE
FRT
RIGHT FRAME RAIL
FUEL FILTER

Typical in-line fuel filter installation

To install:

5. Installation is the reverse of the removal procedure. The filter has an arrow (fuel flow direction) on the side of the case to ensure proper installation.

6. Install the filter in the retainer with the arrow facing away from the fuel tank, toward the front of the engine.

7. Start the engine and inspect for leaks. Correct fuel leaks immediately.

Mechanical Fuel Pump

PRESSURE TESTING

1. Disconnect the negative battery cable. Disconnect the fuel line at the carburetor and install a rubber hose approximately 8–10 in. long over the line and attach a low reading pressure gauge.

2. Hold the gauge up so it is approximatey 16 inches. above the fuel pump. Pinch the fuel return line, if equipped.

3. Start the engine and run at slow idle using the fuel in the carburetor.

4. Note the reading on the pressure gauge, if the pump is operating properly, the pressure should be 5½–6½ psi constant.

REMOVAL & INSTALLATION

1. Disconnect the fuel inlet hose from the pump.
2. Disconnect the vapor return hose, if equipped.
3. Disconnect the inlet hose.
4. Remove the 2 mounting bolts.
5. Remove the fuel pump.
To install:
6. Clean the mating surfaces and install a new gasket.
7. Install the fuel pump and tighten the bolts.
8. Reconnect the hoses, start the engine and check for leaks.

Electric Fuel Pump

PRESSURE TESTING

1987 SFI (Turbo)

NOTE: To perform all of the steps of this test, it will be necessary to supply a source of 12–14 in. Hg of vacuum to the fuel pressure regulator. A hand vacuum pump of some sort is useful in doing this; an accurate gauge and fittings needed to tee it into the vacuum line are required. Rig a vacuum line from an alternate tap on the intake manifold in place of using the vacuum pump. A length of 5/16 in. inside diameter flexible hose will also be needed.

1. Wrap a rag around the pressure tap to absorb any leakage that may occur when installing the gauge and connect pressure gauge J–34730–1 or equivalent, to the fuel pressure test point on the fuel rail. This is located between the No. 6 injector and the pressure regulator on the injector fuel rail.

2. Make sure the ignition switch has been **OFF** for at least 10 seconds and the air conditioning is **OFF**, if equipped. Then, turn the ignition switch **ON**, noting the sound of the fuel pump.

3. Verify that the pump runs for about 2 seconds. Then, check fuel pressure. It should be 25–35 psi. If there is some pressure but it is outside of specification, go to Step 6. If there is no pressure at all, see the procedure below for checking the fuel system wiring. Turn **OFF** the ignition switch. Note if the pressure holds by watching the gauge for more than 10 seconds. If it does, proceed with the next step; if the pressure is correct but does not hold, proceed with the rest of this step:

a. Pinch the fuel supply hose closed tightly at the flex hose on the down stream (pressure regulator) side of the fuel pressure gauge test fitting.

b. Turn **ON** the ignition switch just until the pressure rises to specification. Then, turn it back **OFF**. Watch the pressure to see if it holds. If it drops off, check for a leaking

flex coupling at the pump. Otherwise, check and, if necessary, replace the in-tank fuel pump. If the pressure does not hold, proceed with Step C.

c. Move the pinching device or fingers, to the flex hose on the down stream side of the fuel pressure regulator. Then, repeat the application of power to the fuel pump by turning on the ignition switch for a few

seconds and turn it back **OFF** after the pump stops.

d. If the pressure holds now, replace the pressure regulator assembly. If not, remove the spark plugs to check for a flooded cylinder. If the cylinder is flooding, the plugs will show evidence of dry, soft, black soot in most cases. If the engine has been cranked a great deal recently, there may actually be a smell of raw fuel on the plug. If the cylinder has been flooding, this will be due to a leaking injector. Replace that cylinder's injector unit.

e. If the problem is not due to a leaking injector, check for small but visible leaks in the injector pipe, connections or flexible hoses and repair, as necessary.

4. Start the engine and allow it to idle. If necessary, run it until it warms up; this test must be done with the engine at normal operating temperature. With the engine idling and at operating temperature, so warm coolant is flowing through the radiator, and read the fuel pressure. It should be 25–35 psi. If the system meets this specification, search for trouble in areas other than fuel pump and pressure regulator performance.

5. If the pressure is outside this range, continue running the test and disconnect the vacuum hose from the fuel pressure regulator. Supply a vacuum of 12–14 in. Hg to the vacuum connection on the regulator. The fuel pressure should be 24–35 psi. If it is now within the specified range, locate and correct the cause of insufficient vacuum to the regulator. This might be a broken connection, cracked or soft line that pinches closed under high vacuum or a clogged line or connection. If the fuel pressure is still incorrect, replace the pressure regulator.

6. This Step is for fuel pressure that is too low; if pressure is too high, go to Step 8. Depressurize the system, remove the fuel filter and tilt it to drain the intake (tank) side into a metal container. Check for the presence of water and dirt. If there is evidence of more than a minimal amount of either, install a new filter and recheck the pressures.

7. Pinch the fuel return line down stream of the pressure regulator to close it off tightly. Then, turn **ON** the ignition switch until the pressure stabilizes and read the pressure gauge. Pressure should be above 75 psi. If it is, check for a restricted pressure line or flexible hose in the line somewhere between the tank and the test gauge. If all the lines are okay, replace the pressure regulator. If the pressure is below 75 psi, check the hose coupling the tank to the pressure line and, if okay, replace the pump, which must be

faulty or of incorrect specification.

8. Depressurize the system and then disconnect the flexible hose from the return line. Attach the $5/16$ in. inside diameter flexible hose to the return line connection on the pressure regulator. Insert the downstream end into a metal container. Turn the ignition switch **ON** for just 2 seconds and read the fuel pressure. It should be 37–43 psi. If it is, clean or repair the return line to the tank to remove an obstruction. If it is not, replace the fuel pressure regulator.

1987–88 TBI

1. Turn the ignition **OFF** to relieve the fuel pressure.
2. Remove the air cleaner and plug the THERMAC vacuum port on the TBI unit.
3. Uncouple the fuel supply flexible hose in the engine compartment. Install fuel pressure gauge J-29658A/BT8205 and adapter 29658A-85 between the steel line and the flexible hose.
4. Tighten the gauge in the line to ensure no leaks occur during testing.
5. Start the vehicle and observe the fuel pressure reading. It should be between 9–13 psi.
6. Relieve the fuel system pressure and remove the gauge.
7. Reinstall the fuel line, start the car and check for leaks.
8. Remove the plug from the vacuum port and install the air cleaner.

1989–91 TBI

When the ignition switch is turned **ON**, the ECM will turn **ON** the in-tank fuel pump. It will remain **ON** as long as the engine is cranking or running and the ECM is receiving ignition reference pulses. If there are no reference pulses, the ECM will shut **OFF** and the fuel pump within 2 seconds after the key is **ON**. The pump will deliver fuel to the TBI unit, where the system pressure is controlled to 9–13 psi. Excess fuel is then returned to the fuel tank.

The fuel pump pressure terminal is located in the passenger side of the engine compartment.

NOTE: Fuel pressure should be noted while the fuel pump is running. Fuel pressure will drop immediately after the fuel pump stops running due to the controlled bleed in the fuel system.

1. Turn the ignition **OFF**.
2. Uncouple the fuel supply flexible hose in the engine compartment. Install fuel pressure gauge between the steel line and the flexible hose.
3. Tighten the gauge in the line to ensure no leaks occur during testing.

4. Apply battery voltage to the fuel pump test connector.
5. The fuel pressure should be 9–13 psi.

REMOVAL & INSTALLATION

1. Relieve the fuel system pressure.
2. Disconnect the negative battery cable.
3. Raise and support the vehicle safely.
4. Remove the fuel tank.
5. Remove the fuel tank sending unit and pump assembly by turning the cam lock ring counterclockwise. Lift the assembly from the fuel tank and remove the fuel pump from the sending unit.
6. Pull the fuel pump up into the attaching hose while pulling outward away from the bottom support. Take care to prevent damage to the rubber insulator and strainer during removal. After the pump assembly is clear of the bottom support, pull the pump assembly out of the rubber connector for removal.
7. Inspect the pump attaching hose for any signs of deterioration and replace, if necessary. Check the rubber sound insulator at the bottom of the pump and replace, as required.
8. Push the fuel pump into the attaching hose.
9. Install the tank sending unit and pump assembly into the fuel tank. Use a new O-ring during assembly.
10. Install the cam lock over the assembly and lock into place by turning clockwise.
11. Install the fuel tank.

Carburetor

REMOVAL & INSTALLATION

1. Disconnect the negative battery cable. Remove air cleaner.
2. Disconnect accelerator linkage.
3. Disconnect transmission detent cable.
4. Disconnect cruise control, if equipped.
5. Disconnect all necessary electrical connectors.
6. Disconnect all necessary vacuum lines.
7. Disconnect fuel line at carburetor inlet.
8. Remove the attaching bolts and remove carburetor.
9. Reverse removal procedure to install.
10. Check idle speeds.

IDLE SPEED ADJUSTMENT

Idle Speed Control (ISC)

The Idle Speed Control (ISC) is con-

trolled by the Electronic Control Module (ECM), which has the desired idle speed programmed in its memory. The ECM compares the actual idle speed to the desired idle speed and the plunger is moved in or out. This automatically adjusts the throttle to hold an idle rpm independent of the engine loads.

An integral part of the ISC is the throttle contact switch. The position of the switch determines whether or not the ISC should control idle speed. When the throttle lever is resting against the ISC plunger, the switch contacts are closed, at which time the ECM moves the ISC to the programmed idle speed. When the throttle lever is not contacting the ISC plunger, the switch contacts are open; the ECM stops sending idle speed commands and the drive controls engine speed.

NOTE: Before starting engine, place transmission selector lever in P or N position, set the parking brake and block the drive wheels.

When a new ISC assembly is installed, a base (minimum authority) and high (maximum authority) rpm speed check must be performed and adjustments made as required. These adjustments limit the low and high rpm speeds to the ECM. When making a low and high speed adjustment, the low speed adjustment is always made first. Do not use the ISC plunger to adjust curb idle speed as the idle speed is controlled by the ECM.

NOTE: Do not disconnect or connect the ISC connector with the ignition in the ON position or damage to the ECM may occur.

1. Connect a tachometer to the engine; distributor side of tach filter, if used.
2. Connect a dwell meter to the Mixture Control (M/C) solenoid dwell lead. Remember to set the dwell meter on the 6 cylinder scale, regardless of the engine being tested.
3. Turn the air conditioning off.
4. Start and run the engine until it is stabilized by entering closed loop. The dwell meter needle starts to vary.
5. Turn the ignition **OFF**.
6. Unplug the connector from ISC motor.
7. Fully retract the ISC plunger by applying 12 volts DC (battery voltage) to terminal **C** of the ISC motor connection and ground lead to terminal **D** of the ISC motor connection. It may be necessary to install jumper leads from the ISC motor in order to make proper connections.

NOTE: Do not apply battery voltage to the motor longer than necessary to retract the ISC

plunger. **Prolonged contact will damage the motor. Also, never connect a voltage source across terminals A and B or damage to the internal throttle contact switch will result.**

8. Start the engine and wait until the dwell meter needle starts to vary, indicating "closed loop" operation.

9. With the parking brake applied and the drive wheels blocked, place the transmission in **D**.

10. With the ISC plunger fully retracted, adjust carburetor base (slow) idle stop screw to the minimum idle specified rpm. The ISC plunger should not be left in the fully retracted position.

11. Place the transmission in the **P** or **N** position and fully extend the ISC plunger by applying 12 volts DC to terminal **D** of the ISC motor connection and ground lead to terminal **C** of the ISC motor connection.

NOTE: Never connect voltage source across terminals A and B as damage to the internal throttle contact switch will result.

12. With the transmission in **P**, using tool J–29607 or BT–8022 or equivalent, preset ISC plunger to obtain 1500 rpm.

13. With parking brake set and drive wheels blocked, place transmission in **D** position. Using tool J–29607 or BT–8022 or equivalent, turn ISC plunger to obtain ISC adjustment rpm (maximum authority).

14. Recheck ISC adjustment rpm with voltage applied to motor. Motor will ratchet at full extension with power applied.

15. Fully retract ISC plunger. Place transmission in **P** or **N** position and turn ignition in **OFF** position. Disconnect 12 volt power source, ground lead, tachometer and dwell meter. With ignition in **OFF** position, reconnect 4 terminal harness connector to ISC motor. To prevent internal damage to ISC, apply finger pressure to ISC plunger while retracting.

16. Remove block from drive wheels.

Idle Air Bleed Valve

1. Engage the parking brake and block the drive wheels. Disconnect and plug the hoses as directed on the vehicle emission control label.

2. Check and adjust ignition timing. Connect a dwell meter to the carburetor mixture solenoid and a tachometer to the engine's distributor electrical system.

3. Start engine and with transmission in **P**, run engine at idle until fully warm and a varying dwell is noted on the dwell meter. The engine now in closed loop operation. It is essential that the engine is operated for a sufficient length of time to ensure that the engine coolant sensor and the oxygen sensor in the exhaust, are at full operational temperature.

4. Check engine idle speed and compare to specifications on the underhood emission label. If necessary, adjust curb idle speed. On models with Idle Speed Control (ISC) or Idle Load Compensator (ILC), idle speeds are controlled by signals from the computer.

5. With engine idling in **D**, observe dwell reading on the 6 cylinder scale. If varying within the 10–50 degree range, adjustment is correct. If not, perform the following:

a. Remove the idle air bleed valve cover. If the cover is staked in place, pry it off using a suitable tool.

b. If the cover is riveted, cover the internal bowl vents to the bleed valve with masking tape.

c. Cover carburetor air intakes with masking tape to prevent metal chips from entering carburetor and engine.

d. Carefully align a No. 35 (0.110 in.) drill bit on a steel rivet head holding the idle air bleed valve cover in place. Drill only enough to remove rivet head. Drill the remaining rivet head located on the other side of the tower. Use a drift and small hammer to drive the remainder of the rivets out of the idle air bleed valve tower in the air horn casting. Use care in drilling to prevent damage to the air horn casting.

e. Lift out cover over the idle air bleed valve and remove the rivet pieces from inside the idle air bleed valve tower.

f. Using shop air, carefully blow out any remaining chips from inside the tower. Discard cover after removal. A missing cover indicates the idle air bleed valve setting has been changed from its original factory setting.

g. With cover removed, look for presence or absence, of a letter identification on top of idle air bleed valve.

h. If an identifying letter appears on top of the valve proceed to the procedure outlined under Type 2. If an identifying letter does not appear on the top of the valve proceed to the procedure outlined under Type 1.

TYPE 1

1. Presetting the idle air bleed valve to a gauge dimension if the idle air bleed valve was serviced prior to on-vehicle adjustment.

a. Install idle air bleed valve gauging tool J–33815–2, BT–8253– B or equivalent, in throttle side D–shaped vent hole in the air horn casting. The upper end of the tool should be positioned over the open cavity next to the idle air bleed valve.

b. While holding the gauging tool down lightly, so the solenoid plunger is against the solenoid stop, adjust the idle air bleed valve so the gauging tool will pivot over and just contact the top of the valve. The valve is now preset for on-vehicle adjustment.

c. Remove the gauging tool.

2. Adjusting the idle air bleed valve on the vehicle to obtain correct dwell reading.

a. Start engine and allow it to reach normal operating temperature.

b. While idling in **D**, use a suitable tool to slowly turn valve counterclockwise or clockwise, until the dwell reading varies within the 25–35 degree range, attempting to be as close to 30 degrees as possible. Perform this Step carefully. The air bleed valve is very sensitive and should be turned in ⅛ turn increments only.

c. If, after performing Steps a and b above, the dwell reading does not vary and is not within the 25–35 degree range, it will be necessary to remove the plugs and to adjust the idle mixture needles.

3. Idle mixture needle plug removal, only if necessary.

a. Remove the carburetor from the engine, following normal service procedures, to gain access to the plugs covering the idle mixture needles.

b. Invert carburetor and drain fuel into a suitable container.

c. Place carburetor on a suitable holding fixture, with manifold side up. Use care to avoid damaging linkage, tubes and parts protruding from air horn.

d. Make 2 parallel cuts in the throttle body, on each side of the locator points beneath the idle mixture needle plug on the manifold side, with a hacksaw.

e. The cuts should reach down to the steel plug but should not extend more than ⅛ in. beyond the locator points. The distance between the saw cuts depends on the size of the punch to be used.

f. Place a flat punch near the ends of the saw marks in the throttle body. Hold the punch at a 45 degrees angle and drive it into the throttle body until the casting breaks away, exposing the steel plug.

g. The hardened plug will break, rather than remaining intact. It is not necessary to remove the plug as a whole but remove the loose pieces.

h. Repeat this procedure with the other mixture needle.

4. Setting the idle mixture needles, if necessary, where correct dwell reading could not be obtained with the idle air bleed valve adjustment.

a. Using tool J–29030, BT–7610B or equivalent, turn both idle mixture needles clockwise until they are lightly seated, then turn each mixture needle counterclockwise the number of turns specified.

b. Reinstall carburetor on engine using a new flange mounting gasket but do not install air cleaner and gasket at this time.

5. Readjust the idle air bleed valve to finalize correct dwell reading. The following is necessary if idle mixture needles required setting in Step 4, above.

a. Start engine and run until fully warm, and repeat Step 2, above.

b. If unable to set dwell to 25–35 degrees and the dwell is below 25 degrees, turn both mixture needles counterclockwise an additional turn. If dwell is above 35 degrees, turn both mixture needles clockwise an additional turn. Readjust idle air bleed valve to obtain dwell limits.

c. After adjustments are complete, seal the idle mixture needle openings in the throttle body, using silicone sealant, RTV rubber or equivalent. The sealer is required to discourage unnecessary adjustment of the setting and to prevent fuel vapor loss in that area.

d. On vehicles without a carburetor-mounted idle speed control or idle load compensator, adjust curb idle speed, if necessary.

e. Check and only if necessary adjust, fast idle speed as described on emission control information label.

TYPE 2

1. Setting the idle air bleed valve to a gauge dimension;

a. Install air bleed valve, gauging tool J–33815–2, BT–8253–B or equivalent, in throttle side **D** shaped vent hole in the air horn casting. The upper end of the tool should be positioned over the open cavity next to the idle air bleed valve.

b. While holding the gauging tool down lightly, so the solenoid plunger is against the solenoid stop, adjust the idle air bleed valve so the gauging tool will pivot over and just contact the top of the valve.

c. The valve is now set properly. No further adjustment of the valve is necessary.

d. Remove gauging tool.

2. Adjusting the idle mixture needles on the vehicle to obtain correct dwell readings.

a. Remove idle mixture needle plugs, following instructions in the information given for type 1.

b. Using tool J–29030–B, BT–7610–B or equivalent, turn each idle mixture needle clockwise until lightly seated, then turn each mixture needle counterclockwise 3 turns.

c. Reinstall carburetor on engine, using a new flange mounting gasket, but do not install air cleaner or gasket.

d. Start engine and allow it to reach normal operating temperature.

e. While idling in **D**, adjust both mixture needles equally, in ⅛ turn increments, until dwell reading varies within the 25–35 degree range, attempting to be as close to 30 degrees as possible. If reading is too low, turn mixture needles counterclockwise. If reading is too high, turn mixture needles clockwise. Allow time for dwell reading to stabilize after each adjustment.

f. After adjustments are complete, seal the idle mixture needle openings in the throttle body, using silicone sealant, RTV rubber or equivalent. The sealer is required to discourage unnecessary readjustment of the setting, and to prevent fuel vapor loss in that area.

g. On vehicles without a carburetor-mounted idle speed control or idle load compensator, adjust curb idle speed, if necessary.

h. Check and, if necessary, adjust fast idle speed, as described on the emission control information label.

Idle Load Compensator (ILC)

1. Prepare vehicle for adjustments—see vehicle emission information label.

2. Connect tachometer to distributor side of tach filter, if used.

3. Remove air cleaner and plug vacuum hose to Thermal Vacuum Valve (TVV).

4. Disconnect and plug vacuum hose to EGR.

5. Disconnect and plug vacuum hose to canister purge port.

6. Disconnect and plug vacuum hose to ILC.

7. Back out idle stop screw on carburetor 3 turns.

8. Turn the air conditioning to **OFF** position.

NOTE: Before starting engine, place transmission in P, set parking brake and block drive wheels.

9. With engine running, engine warm, choke off, transmission in **D** and ILC plunger fully extended (no vacuum applied), using tool J–29607, BT–8022 or equivalent, adjust plunger

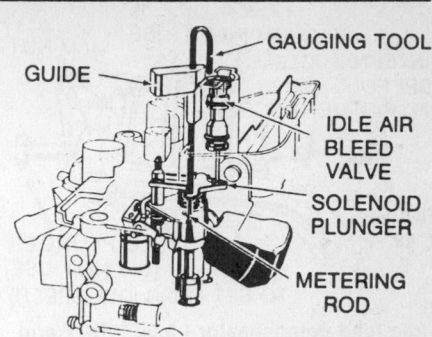

Installing idle air bleed valve gauging tool

to obtain 750 rpm on E2MC carburetor models or 725 rpm on E4MC carburetor models. Jam nut on plunger must be held with wrench to prevent damage to guide tabs when tightening.

10. Remove plug from vacuum hose, reconnect hose to ILC and observe idle speed. Idle speed should be 500 rpm in **D**.

11. If rpm in Step 10 is correct, proceed to Step 13. No further adjustment of the ILC is necessary.

12. If rpm in Step 10 is not correct:

a. Stop engine and remove the ILC. Plug vacuum hose to ILC.

b. With the ILC removed, remove the rubber cap from the center outlet tube and then remove the metal plug if used from this same tube.

c. Install ILC on carburetor and re-attach throttle return spring and any other related parts removed during disassembly. Remove plug from vacuum hose and reconnect hose to ILC.

d. Using a spare rubber cap with hole punched to accept a 0.090 in. (³/₃₂ in.) hex key wrench, install cap on center outlet tube, to seal against vacuum loss and insert wrench through cap to engage adjusting screw inside tube. Start engine and turn adjusting screw with wrench to obtain 550 rpm in **D**. Turning the adjusting screw will change the idle speed approximately 75–100 rpm for each complete turn. Turning the screw counterclockwise will increase the engine speed.

e. Remove wrench and cap, with hole, from center outlet tube and install new rubber cap.

f. Engine running, transmission in **D**, observe idle speed. If a final adjustment is required, it will be necessary to repeat Steps 12a through 12e.

13. After adjustment of the ILC plunger, measure distance from the jam nut to tip of the plunger, dimension must not exceed 1.000 in. (25mm).

14. Disconnect and plug vacuum hose to ILC. Apply vacuum source,

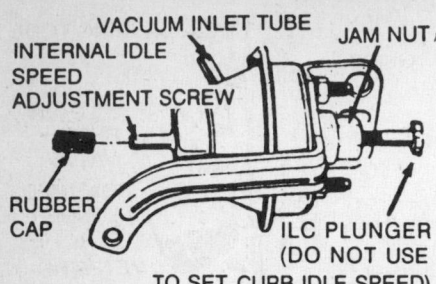

Idle load compensator—5.0L (VIN Y and 9) engines

such as hand vacuum pump J-23768, BT-7517 or equivalent, to ILC vacuum inlet tube to fully retract the plunger.

15. Adjust the idle stop on the carburetor float bowl to obtain 500 rpm in **D**.

16. Place transmission in **P** and stop engine.

17. Remove plug from vacuum hose and install hose on ILC vacuum inlet tube.

18. Remove plugs and reconnect all vacuum hoses.

19. Install air cleaner and gasket.

20. Remove block from drive wheels.

Throttle Position Sensor (TPS)

NOTE: The plug covering the TPS adjustment screw is used to provide a tamper resistant design and retain the factory setting during vehicle operation. Do not remove the plug unless diagnosis indicates the TPS sensor is not adjusted correctly or it is necessary to replace the air horn assembly, float bowl, TPS sensor to TPS adjustment screw. This is a critical adjustment that must be performed accurately and carefully to ensure proper vehicle performance and control of exhaust emissions.

1. If necessary to adjust the TPS sensor, perform the following:

   a. Using a $5/64$ in. (2mm) drill, drill hole in aluminum plug covering TPS adjustment screw, drilling only enough to start self-tapping screw.

   b. Use care in drilling to prevent damage to adjustment screw head.

   c. Start a No. 8, ½ in. long self-tapping screw in drilled hole in plug, turning screw in only enough to ensure good thread engagement in hole.

   d. Using a suitable tool placed between the screw head and air horn casting, pry against screw head to remove plug. Discard plug.

   e. Using tool J-28696, BT-7967A or equivalent, remove screw.

   f. Connect digital voltmeter, such as J-29125 or equivalent from TPS

connector center terminal (B) to bottom terminal (C). Jumpers for access can be made using terminals 12014836 and 12014837.

   g. With ignition on, engine stopped, reinstall TPS adjustment screw and with tool J-28696, BT7967A or equivalent turn screw to obtain specified voltage at specified throttle position with air conditioning off.

   h. After adjustment, install new plug (supplied in service kits) in air horn, driving plug in place until flush with raised pump lever boss on casting.

2. Remove ECM fuse from fuse block to clear any stored trouble codes.

NOTE: After TPS screw is adjusted, a new plug should be installed. If a new plug is not available, a locking type of sealer should be placed on the screw threads to prevent movement of the screw after installation.

IDLE MIXTURE ADJUSTMENT

1. Run the engine until it reaches normal operating temperature.

2. Check the ignition timing and set to specifications.

3. Remove the factory installed plugs from the mixture screws.

NOTE: Carburetor must be removed from engine to gain access to the idle mixture needle plugs.

4. Using tool J-29030-B, BT-7610-B or equivalent, turn both mixture needles clockwise until lightly seated.

5. Turn each mixture needle counterclockwise 3 turns.

6. Remove air cleaner. Disconnect vacuum hose to canister purge valve and plug it.

7. Run engine until it reaches normal operating temperature.

8. Block rear wheels and put gear selector in **D**.

9. Adjust both mixture needles equally, in ⅛ turn increments, until dwell reading varies within the 25–35 degree range, as close to 30 degrees as possible.

10. If reading is too high, turn needles clockwise. If reading is too low, turn needles counterclockwise. Install new plugs over mixture needle adjustment holes.

11. Reconnect all lines and make all necessary adjustments.

SERVICE ADJUSTMENTS

For all carburetor service adjustment procedures and specifica-

tions, please refer to "Carburetor Service" in the Unit Repair section.

Fuel Injection

Turbocharged 3.8L V6 engine is equipped with Sequential Fuel Injection (SFI). Each fuel injector is opened independently of the others, 1 time for every 2 revolutions of the crankshaft and, prior to the opening of the intake valve for the cylinder to be fired, the Electronic Control Module (ECM) is in complete control of the system during all phases of engine operation.

On the 4.3L, 5.0L and 5.7L engines, the EFI system centrally locates a single Model 220 Throttle Body Injection (TBI) unit on the intake manifold where air and fuel are distributed through a single bore in the unit. The air used for combustion is controlled by a single throttle valve which is connected to the accelerator pedal linkage through a throttle shaft and lever assembly. A special plate is located under the throttle valve to aid in uniform mixture distribution. Fuel for combustion is supplied by a single fuel injector mounted on the TBI unit. The metering tip of the fuel injector is positioned directly above the throttle valve. The injector metering tip is "pulsed" or "timed" open or closed by an electronic output signal received from the ECM. The ECM receives inputs from the the various engine sensors concerning engine operating conditions, coolant temperature, exhaust gas oxygen content, etc. The ECM uses this information to calculate the engines fuel requirements by controlling the injector pulse openings to provide an ideal fuel/air mixture ratio.

IDLE SPEED ADJUSTMENT

3.8L Engine

NOTE: This adjustment should be performed only when the injection parts have been replaced. Engine must be at normal operating temperature before making an adjustment.

1. With a suitable tool, piece the idle stop screw plug and apply leverage to remove it.

2. Ground diagnostic lead and turn ignition to **ON** position, with out starting engine, for at least 30 seconds.

3. With the ignition still **ON**, disconnect Idle Air Control (IAC) electrical connector.

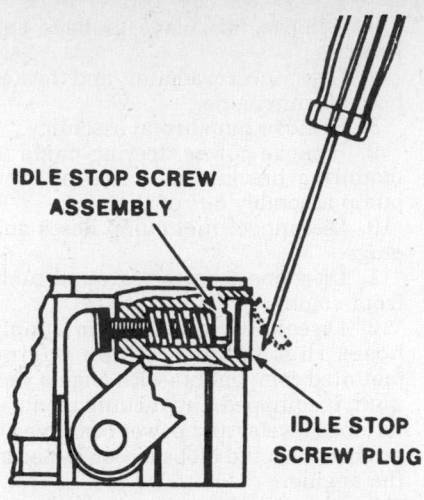

**IDLE STOP SCREW
ASSEMBLY**

**IDLE STOP
SCREW PLUG**

Removing the idle stop screw plug

4. Remove the ground from diagnostic lead and start engine.
5. Adjust the idle speed to 500 ± 50 rpm in **D** position.
6. Turn the ignition **OFF** and reconnect connector at IAC motor.
7. Adjust the Throttle Position Sensor (TPS) to 0.36–0.44 volts.
8. Recheck the setting, start the engine and check for proper idle operation.

Except 3.8L Engine

1. Plug any vacuum ports as required.
2. Remove the idle speed stop screw cover, if installed.
3. Connect a tachometer to the engine.
4. Leaving the IAC valve connected, ground the ALDL diagnostic terminal.
5. Turn the ignition switch to the **ON** position but do not start the engine. Allow the ignition switch to remain in the **ON** position (engine off) for a period of 45 seconds. This allows the IAC valve pintle to extend and seat in the valve body.
6. With the ignition switch **ON** (engine stopped) and the diagnostic terminal grounded, disconnect the IAC valve electrical connector.
7. Remove the diagnostic terminal ground and start the engine. Place the transmission in **P** and allow the engine rpm to stabilize.
8. The tachometer should read between 400–450 rpm. Adjust the idle stop screw as required until the idle speed is within the specified range.
9. Turn the ignition switch **OFF** and reconnect the IAC valve connector.
10. Apply a bead of RTV sealant to cover the idle stop screw hole. Unplug and reconnect the vacuum hoses.

Fuel Injector

REMOVAL & INSTALLATION

3.8L Engine

NOTE: **Care must be taken when removing injectors to prevent damage to the electrical connector pins on the injector and the nozzle. The injectors are serviced as a complete assembly only. Injectors are an electrical component and should not be immersed in any type of cleaner.**

1. Relieve the fuel system pressure. Connect fuel gauge J–34730–1 or equivalent, to the fuel pressure valve. Wrap a shop rag around fitting while connecting gauge to avoid fuel spill.
2. Install bleed hose into an approved container and open valve to bleed the excess system pressure.
3. With the ignition **OFF**, remove the electrical connections.
4. Remove the fuel rail.

NOTE: **Precautions must be taken to prevent dirt and other contaminants from entering the fuel passages. It is recommended that fittings be capped and holes plugged, during servicing. The fuel rail assembly should be cleaned with AC-Delco® X–30A or equivalent, engine spray cleaner before disassembly.**

5. Remove the fuel injector retaining clips, if used.
6. Remove the injectors.

To install:

7. When installing the injectors, always use new O-rings and coat them with clean engine oil.
8. The remainder of the installation is the reverse of the removal procedure.
9. When finished, start and run the engine while checking for leaks.

Except 3.8L Engine

NOTE: **Exercise care when removing the fuel injectors to prevent damage to the electrical connector terminals, the injector filter and the fuel nozzle. Also, since the injectors are electrical components, they should not be immersed in any type of liquid solvent of cleaner as damage may occur.**

1. Relieve the fuel system pressure. Disconnect the electrical connectors from the fuel injectors by squeezing the plastic tabs and pulling straight up.
2. Remove the fuel meter cover assembly in the same manner as the electrical connectors.
3. With fuel meter cover gasket in place, to prevent damage to casting, carefully lift out each injector and set aside.
4. Remove the lower (small) O-rings from the injector nozzles. Discard the O-rings and replace with new.
5. Remove the fuel meter cover gasket and discard.
6. Remove the upper (large) O-rings and steel backup washers from top of each fuel injector cavity. Discard the O-rings and replace with new.

To install:

7. Inspect the fuel injector filter for evidence of dirt and contamination. If present, check for presence of dirt in fuel lines and fuel tank.

NOTE: **If replacements are required, ensure that the injector is replaced with an identical part. The model 220 TBI is capable of accepting other types of injectors but other injectors are calibrated for different flow rates.**

8. Lubricate new lower (small) O-ring with automatic transmission fluid and push on nozzle end of injector until it seats against injector fuel filter.
9. Install the steel injector backup washer in counterbore of fuel meter body.
10. Lubricate new upper (large) O-ring with automatic transmission fluid and install directly over the backup washer. Ensure the O-ring is seated properly and is flush with top of fuel meter body surface.

NOTE: **Backup washers and O-rings must be installed before the injectors or improper seating of large O-ring could cause fuel to leak.**

11. Align the raised lug on each injector base with notch in fuel meter body cavity and install the injector. Push down with moderate pressure on injector until it is fully seated in fuel meter body. The electrical terminals of injector should be parallel with throttle shaft.
12. Install the fuel meter cover gasket.
13. Install the fuel meter cover.
14. Coat the threads of the fuel meter attaching screw with a suitable thread locking compound. Install and tighten the screws.
15. Reconnect the electrical connectors to their respective fuel injectors.
16. Turn the ignition switch to the **ON** position, engine not running and check for fuel leaks.

EMISSION CONTROLS

Please refer to "Emission Control" in the Unit Repair section for system maintenance procedures. Due to the complex nature of modern electronic engine control systems, comprehensive diagnosis and testing procedures fall outside the confines of this repair manual. For complete information on diagnosis, testing and repair procedures concerning all modern engine and emission control systems, please refer to "Chilton's Guide to Electronic Engine Controls".

Emission Warning Lamps

RESETTING

Although this light may indicate either wording depending on the vehicle, it has the same function in either case. The terms are interchangeable. This light is on the instrument panel and has 2 functions:

1. It is used to tell the driver a problem has occurred and the vehicle should be taken for service as soon as reasonably possible.

2. It is also used by technicians to read out "Trouble Codes" when diagnosing system problems.

As a bulb and system check, the "Check Engine/Service Engine Soon" light will come on with the key on and the engine not running. When the engine is started, the "Check Engine/Service Engine Soon" light will turn off.

If the "Check Engine/Service Engine Soon" light remains on, the self-diagnostic system has detected a problem. If the problem goes away, the light will go out in most cases after 10 seconds but a Trouble Code will remain in the ECM memory.

CLEARING TROUBLE CODES

When the ECM finds a problem, the "Check Engine/Service Engine Soon" light will come on and a trouble code will be recorded in the ECM memory. If the problem is intermittent, the "Check Engine/Service Engine Soon" light will go out after 10 seconds, when the fault goes away. However, the trouble code will stay in the ECM

memory until the battery voltage to the ECM is removed. Removing battery voltage for 10 seconds will clear all stored trouble codes. Do this by disconnecting the ECM harness from the positive battery pigtail for 10 seconds with the ignition OFF, or by disconnecting the ECM fuse, designated ECM or ECM/Bat., from the fuse holder.

NOTE: To prevent ECM damage, the key must be OFF when disconnecting or reconnecting power to ECM (for example battery cable, ECM pigtail, ECM fuse, jumper cables, etc.).

ECM LEARNING ABILITY

The ECM has a "learning" ability. If the battery is disconnected to clear diagnostic codes, or for repair, the "learning" process has to begin all over again. A change may be noted in the vehicle's performance to "teach" the vehicle, make sure the vehicle is at operating temperature and drive at part throttle, with moderate acceleration and idle conditions, until normal performance returns.

ENGINE MECHANICAL

NOTE: Disconnecting the negative battery cable on some vehicles may interfere with the functions of the on board computer systems and may require the computer to undergo a relearning process, once the negative battery cable is reconnected.

Engine Assembly

REMOVAL & INSTALLATION

3.8L and 4.3L Engines

1. Remove the hood.
2. Relieve the fuel system pressure and disconnect the negative battery cable.
3. Drain coolant into a suitable container.
4. Remove air cleaner.
5. If equipped with air conditioning, disconnect compressor ground wire from the mounting bracket. Remove the electrical connector from the compressor clutch, remove the compressor to mounting bracket attaching bolts and position the compressor out of the way.

6. Remove fan blade, pulleys and belts.
7. Disconnect radiator and heater hoses from engine.
8. Remove fan shroud assembly.
9. Remove power steering pump to mounting bracket bolts and position pump assembly out of the way.
10. Disconnect fuel pump hoses and plug.
11. Disconnect battery ground cable from engine.
12. Disconnect the vacuum supply hoses that supply all non-engine mounted components with engine vacuum. If equipped, the vacuum modulator, load leveler and power brake vacuum hoses should all be disconnected at the engine.
13. Disconnect accelerator cable.
14. Disconnect generator, oil and coolant sending unit switch connections at the engine. Remove the alternator.
15. Disconnect engine to body ground strap(s) at engine.
16. Raise and safely support the vehicle, disconnect the cable shield from the engine if equipped.
17. Disconnect exhaust pipes from exhaust manifolds.
18. Remove lower flywheel or converter cover.
19. Remove flywheel to converter attaching bolts. Scribe chalk mark on the flywheel and converter for reassembly alignment.
20. Remove transmission to engine attaching bolts.
21. Remove motor mount through bolts and cruise control bracket if equipped.
22. Lower the vehicle and support the automatic transmission.
23. Attach a lifting device to the engine and raise the engine enough so mounting through bolts can be removed. Make certain wiring harness, vacuum hoses and other parts are free and clear before lifting engine out of the vehicle.
24. Raise engine far enough to clear engine mounts, raise transmission support accordingly and alternately until engine can be disengaged from the transmission and removed.

To install:
25. With the engine and transmission safely supported, lower into position with the lift chain.
26. Install the motor mount through bolts and cruise control bracket if equipped.
27. Install transmission to engine attaching bolts.
28. Install the flywheel to converter attaching bolts, matching the scribe chalk marks on the flywheel and converter.

29. Install the lower flywheel or converter cover.

30. Connect the exhaust pipes to the exhaust manifolds.

31. Lower the vehicle, connect the cable shield to the engine, if equipped.

32. Connect the engine to body ground strap(s), at engine.

33. Install the alternator. Connect alternator, oil and coolant sending unit switch connections at the engine.

34. Disconnect accelerator cable.

35. Connect the vacuum supply hoses that supply all non-engine mounted components with engine vacuum.

36. Connect the battery ground cable to the engine.

37. Connect the fuel pump hoses.

38. Install the power steering pump to mounting bracket bolts.

39. Install the fan shroud assembly.

40. Connect the radiator and heater hoses to the engine.

41. Install fan blade, pulleys and belts.

42. If equipped with air conditioning, install the air conditioning compressor.

43. Install the air cleaner and fill the cooling system.

44. Connect the battery cable and install the hood.

5.0L and 5.7L Engines

1. Drain the cooling system.

2. Remove air cleaner and hot air pipe.

3. Remove hood from hinges, mark hood for reassembly.

4. Disconnect the negative battery cable. Relieve the fuel system pressure.

5. Disconnect radiator hoses, automatic transmission cooler lines, heater hoses, vacuum hoses, power steering hose bracket from engine, air conditioning compressor with brackets and hoses attached, fuel hose from fuel line, wiring and throttle cable.

6. Remove upper radiator support and radiator.

7. Raise and support the vehicle safely.

8. Disconnect exhaust pipes at manifold.

9. Remove torque converter cover and the bolts holding converter to flywheel.

10. Remove engine mount bolts or nuts.

11. Remove the transmission to engine retaining bolts and remove the starter.

12. Lower the vehicle. Secure lift chain to engine.

13. Support the transmission and remove the engine.

To install:

14. With the engine safely supported, lower into position with the lift chain.

15. Install the transmission to engine retaining bolts and install the starter.

16. Install the engine mount bolts or nuts.

17. Install the torque converter cover and the bolts holding converter to flywheel.

18. Connect the exhaust pipes at manifold.

19. Lower the vehicle.

20. Install the upper radiator support and radiator.

21. Connect radiator hoses, automatic transmission cooler lines, heater hoses, vacuum hoses, power steering hose bracket from engine, air conditioning compressor with brackets and hoses attached, fuel hose from fuel line, wiring and throttle cable.

22. Connect the negative battery cable.

23. Install the hood, aligning the marks made during removal.

24. Fill the cooling system.

25. Install the air cleaner and hot air pipe.

Engine Mounts

REMOVAL & INSTALLATION

1. Disconnect the negative battery cable.

2. Raise and support the vehicle safely.

3. Properly support the weight of the engine at the forward edge of the oil pan.

4. Remove the mount to engine block bolts.

5. Raise the engine slightly and remove the mount to mount bracket bolt and nut. Remove the engine mount.

6. Installation is the reverse of the removal procedure.

Cylinder Head

REMOVAL & INSTALLATION

3.8L and 4.3L Engines

1. Relieve the fuel system pressure and disconnect negative battery cable.

2. Remove intake manifold.

3. Loosen and remove belt(s).

4. When removing left cylinder head;

   a. Remove oil dipstick.

   b. Remove air and vacuum pumps with mounting bracket if present and move out of the way with hoses attached.

5. When removing right cylinder head:

   a. Remove alternator.

   b. Disconnect power steering gear pump and brackets attaching to cylinder head.

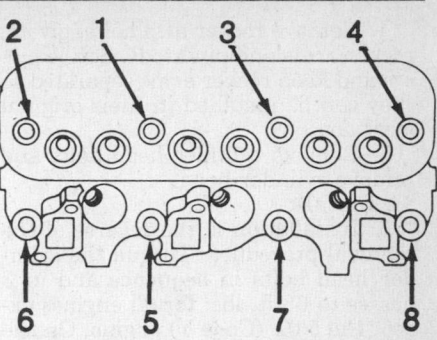

Buick V6 cylinder head bolt torque sequence

6. Disconnect wires from spark plugs, and remove the spark plug wire clips from the rocker arm cover studs.

7. Remove exhaust manifold bolts from the head being removed.

8. With air hose and cloths, clean dirt off cylinder head and adjacent area to avoid getting dirt into engine.

9. Remove rocker arm cover and rocker arm and shaft assembly from cylinder head. Lift out pushrods.

10. Loosen all cylinder head bolts, remove bolts and lift off the cylinder head.

To install:

11. Installation is the reverse of the removal procedure. On the 3.8L engine torque the cylinder head bolts in sequence to 25 ft. lbs., continue the torquing sequence, tightening each bolt ¼ turn (90 degrees) until 60 ft. lbs. is reached. Once 60 ft. lbs. is reached on any one cylinder bolt, do not tighten the bolt any more. On the 4.3L engine torque the cylinder head bolts in sequence to 65 ft. lbs.

5.0L and 5.7L Engines

1. Relieve the fuel system pressure and disconnect the negative battery cable. Drain the radiator.

2. Remove the intake manifold. Remove the exhaust manifolds.

3. Remove the valve cover. Remove the ground strap from the left cylinder head.

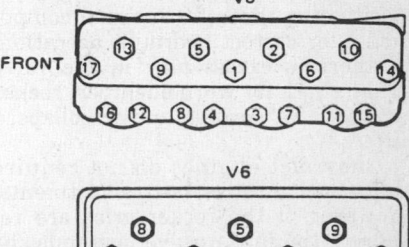

Cylinder head bolt torque sequence— 5.0L (VIN E, G, H) and 5.7L engines

4. Remove rocker arm bolts, pivots, rocker arms and pushrods. Scribe pivots and keep rocker arms separated so they can be installed in their original locations.

5. Remove cylinder head bolts and remove cylinder head.

To install:

6. Installation is the reverse of the removal procedure. Torque the cylinder head bolts in sequence and in 3 passes to 68 ft. lbs. for all engines except the 5.0L (Code Y) engine. On the 5.0L (Code Y) engine torque in sequence to 125 ft. lbs.

Valve Lifters

REMOVAL & INSTALLATION

1. Disconnect the negative battery cable.

2. Drain the coolant.

3. Remove rocker arm covers.

4. Remove the intake manifold assembly.

5. Remove the rocker arm assembly or the rocker and pivot. Remove the pushrods. Be sure to keep them in order as they must be installed in the same bores as they were removed.

6. Remove the valve lifter retainer and the restrictor, if equipped.

7. Remove the valve lifters, using the proper valve lifter removal tool.

8. Installation is the reverse of the removal procedure.

9. Soak the lifter assemblies with clean engine oil prior to installation. Coat the valve lifter rollers with Molykote® or equivalent. Use new gaskets as required.

Valve Lash

ADJUSTMENT

The Buick and Oldsmobile engines use hydraulic valve lifters, which are not adjustable. The rocker arm shaft assembly or the rockers, with pivot, are bolted to the cylinder head with a specific torque pressure, automatically positioning the lifter internal components for correct hydraulic operation. If there is excess play in the valve train, check for worn pushrods, rocker arms, valve springs and/or collapsed lifters.

Chevrolet engines do not require any routine valve lash adjustments. However, if the rocker arms are removed, the initial valve lash must be adjusted before the engine is started. Use the following procedure for Chevrolet engines.

1. Remove the valve covers.

2. By rotating the crankshaft and by positioning each valve on its base

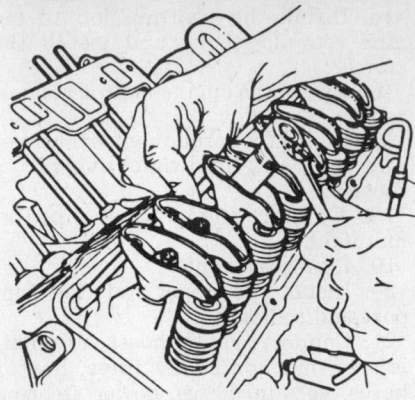

Typical valve adjustment—4.3L, 5.0L (VIN E, G, H) and 5.7L engines

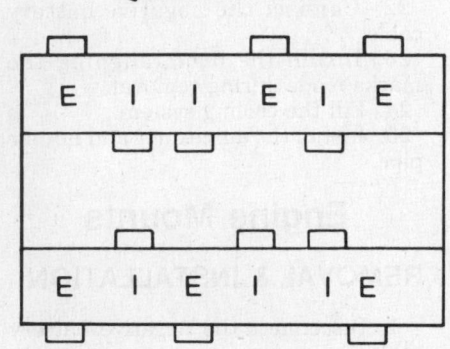

Intake and exhaust valve arrangements—4.3L engine

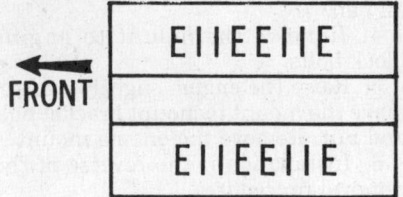

Intake and exhaust valve arrangements—5.0L (VIN E, G, H) and 5.7L engines

circle of the camshaft, remove the lash from each rocker arm and pushrod.

3. To adjust the valves, crank the engine until the mark on the vibration damper aligns with the center or **0** mark on the timing tab fastened to the crankcase front cover. The engine will be either in the No. 1 firing position or its opposite cylinder No. 6 on V8 engine and No. 4 on V6 engine, firing position.

NOTE: The firing cylinder may be determined by placing a finger on the No. 1 cylinder valve rocker arms as the mark on the damper comes near the 0 mark on the crankcase front cover. If the valve rocker arms moves as the mark comes up to the timing tab,

the engine is in the opposite cylinder, No. 6 on V8 engine and No. 4 on V6 engine, firing position and should be turned over a complete revolution to reach the No. 1 cylinder firing position.

4. With the engine in the No. 1 firing position, adjust the following valves:

  a. V8 engine—Exhaust—1, 3, 4, 8
  b. V8 engine—Intake—1, 2, 5, 7
  c. V6 engine—Exhaust—1, 5, 6
  d. V6 engine—Intake—1, 2, 3

5. Back out adjusting nut until lash is felt at the pushrod, then turn in adjusting nut until all lash is removed. This can be determined by rotating pushrod while turning adjusting nut. When play has been removed, turn adjusting nut in a full additional turn, which centers the lifter plunger.

6. Crank the engine 1 revolution until the pointer **0** mark and the vibration damper mark are again in alignment. This is the No. 1 firing position.

7. With the engine in this position, adjust the following valves:

  a. V8 engine—Exhaust—2, 5, 6, 7
  b. V8 engine—Intake—3, 4, 6, 8
  c. V6 engine—Exhaust—2, 3, 4
  d. V6 engine—Intake—4, 5, 6

8. Install the rocker arm covers.

9. Start the engine and adjust the idle speed, as required.

Rocker Arms/Shafts

REMOVAL & INSTALLATION

3.8L Engine

1. Disconnect the negative battery cable.

2. Remove the rocker arm cover.

3. Remove the rocker arm shaft assembly bolts and the assembly.

4. Wear eye protection and remove the nylon arm retainers by prying them out.

5. Remove the rocker arms from the shaft.

To install:

6. Install the rocker arms on the shaft and lubricate them with oil.

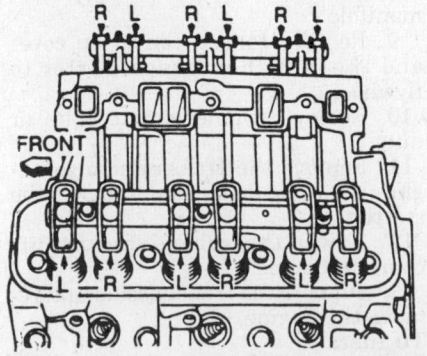

Rocker arm and shaft assembly—3.8L V6 engine

7. Center each arm on the ¼ in. hole in the shaft.

8. Install new nylon rocker arm retainers in the holes using a ½ in. drift.

9. Locate the pushrods in the rocker arms and insert the shaft-to-cylinder head bolts. Tighten each bolt a little at a time until they are tightened to 25 ft. lbs. (35 Nm).

10. Install the rocker cover using a new gasket.

4.3L, 5.0L (VIN E, G, H) and 5.7L Engines

1. Disconnect the negative battery cable.

2. Remove the air cleaner.

3. Disconnect the Computer Command Control (CCC) harness from the intake manifold and the oxygen sensor.

4. Disconnect the the power brake pipe at the carburetor and booster.

5. Disconnect the Air Injection Reaction (AIR) hose from the exhaust manifold.

6. Disconnect the alternator and choke wires.

7. Disconnect the wiring harness attached to the rocker arm cover and route away from the cover.

8. Disconnect the PCV valve.

9. Disconnect the oxygen sensor electrical lead.

10. Loosen the air conditioning compressor upper rear bracket mounting bolts with drive belt and position the unit to the side so the right hand rocker arm cover retaining bolts are accessible and there is sufficient clearance to remove the right hand rocker arm cover.

11. Loosen the retaining bolts and remove the left and right rocker arm covers. Remove the spark plug wires.

12. Remove the rocker arm nuts, rocker arm balls and rocker arm pushrods. Identify each rocker arm assembly to ensure installation in the original positions.

To install:

NOTE: If new rocker arms or rocker arm balls are being installed, coat the bearing surfaces with Molycoat® or equivalent.

13. Install the pushrods. Ensure the pushrods seat properly in the lifter socket.

14. Install the rocker arms, rocker arm balls and nuts. Tighten the rocker arm nuts until all the valve lash is eliminated.

15. Adjust the valves and air conditioning belt tension.

16. Install the rocker arm covers and all associated components in the reverse of the removal procedure.

17. Start the engine. Check the curb idle speed and adjust, if necessary.

5.0L (VIN Y, 9) Engines

1. Disconnect the negative battery cable.

2. Remove the air cleaner from the crankcase inlet pipe and filter.

3. Disconnect the heater hoses and position them to the side.

4. Disconnect the PCV valve and hose.

5. Disconnect the Idle Load Compensator (ILC) anti-dieseling solenoid vacuum hoses.

6. Disconnect the following wires from their respective connectors:

   a. Alternator

   b. ILC anti-dieseling solenoid

   c. Air Injection Reaction (AIR) and oxygen sensor

   d. Rear Vacuum Break (RVB), Idle Load Compensator (ILC), Exhaust Gas Recirculation (EGR) solenoid assembly

   e. Oil pressure, temperature and coolant sensor

7. Remove the ILC anti-dieseling solenoid.

8. Remove the alternator drive belt and rear bracket.

9. Remove the canister purge hose.

10. Loosen the right hand exhaust manifold upper shroud. Remove the EGR valve and the oil level indicator.

11. Disconnect and remove the following AIR system components:

   a. AIR hoses to the AIR switching valve and catalytic converter pipe

   b. AIR switching valve

   c. AIR/AC drive belt

   d. AIR pump pulley

12. Remove the air conditioning compressor rear bracket.

13. Loosen the retaining screws/nuts and remove the left and right valve covers.

14. Remove the rocker arm bolts, pivots and rocker arms. Indentify each rocker arm assembly to ensure installation in the original position.

To install:

15. Lubricate all wear points with 1050169 lubricant or equivalent.

16. Install the pivots, rocker arms and bolts.

17. Tighten the bolts evenly to 22 ft. lbs.

18. Install the valve covers and associated components in reverse of the removal procedure.

CHECKING VALVE TIMING

There is no recommended procedure for valve timing adjustment. It is advisable to verify camshaft lobe lift and camshaft/crankshaft relationship through crankshaft pulley location and valve operation.

PROCEDURE

NOTE: The following procedure applies to Chevrolet produced V6 and V8 engines only. For Buick and Oldsmobile engines, the camshaft lobe lift can be checked with the camshaft removed from the engine.

1. Valve keys
2. Intake valve seal
3. Spring
4. Dampener rotator
5. Valve rotator
6. Exhaust valve seal
7. Identification pad
8. 22 ft. lbs.
9. Rocker arm pivot
10. Rocker arms
11. Pushrods
12. Coil spring
13. Body
14. Collar
15. Valve spring
16. Flat washer
17. Intake valve
18. Exhaust valve

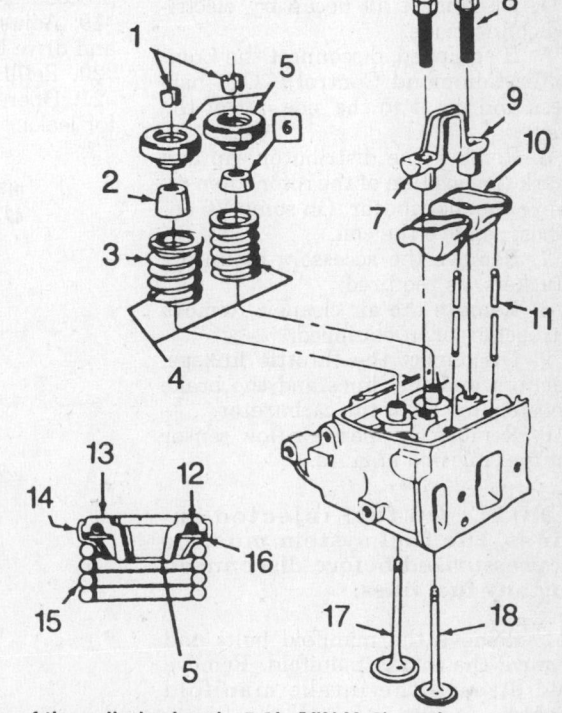

Disassembled view of the cylinder head–5.0L (VIN Y, 9) engine

1. Remove the distributor cap. Remove the right valve cover. Remove the No. 4 intake and exhaust rocker arm assembly.

2. Remove the wire from the BAT terminal of the distributor cap.

3. Turn ignition switch on. Crank engine until rotor is in line with No. 4 spark plug wire position. No. 4 piston will be approximately at the top of cylinder.

4. Measure from pivot boss on head surface to top of No. 4 intake pushrod. Record measurement.

5. Slowly turn engine 1½ revolutions until rotor approaches No. 1 spark plug wire position. Continue to turn engine until timing mark on crank puller is aligned with 0 on indicator. This is top dead center of No. 1 piston.

6. Again measure from pivot boss surface to top of No. 4 cylinder intake pushrod.

7. Measurement should increase over the first measurement.

8. If measurement increase is not within $\frac{1}{32}$ in. of first measurement, camshaft is advanced or retarded.

Intake Manifold

REMOVAL & INSTALLATION

1. Relieve the fuel system pressure and disconnect the negative battery cable.

2. Drain the radiator.

3. Disconnect the upper radiator hose, bypass hose and heater hose from the manifold.

4. Disconnect all necessary electrical connections.

5. If equipped, disconnect the Computer Command Control (CCC) harness and lay it to the side out of the way.

6. Remove the distributor cap and mark the position of the rotor, then remove the distributor. On some V6 engines, remove the coil.

7. Remove the accessory mounting brackets, as required.

8. Remove the air cleaner. Remove turbocharger, if equipped.

9. Disconnect the throttle linkage, vacuum and fuel lines and the brake booster line from the carburetor.

10. Remove the mass air flow sensor on fuel injected engines.

NOTE: On fuel injected engines, the fuel system must be depressurized before disconnecting any fuel lines.

11. Remove the manifold bolts and remove the intake manifold. Remove and discard the intake manifold gaskets.

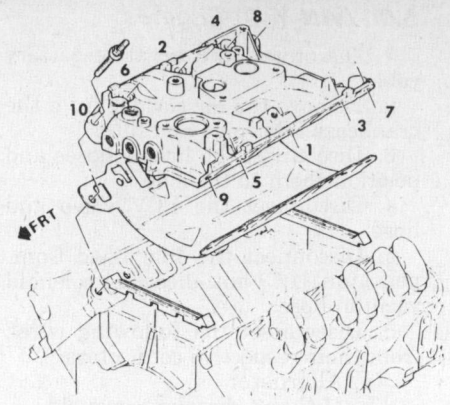

Intake manifold torque sequence— 3.8L engine

12. Thoroughly clean the intake manifold and cylinder block surfaces to remove any trace of gasket material or sealant.

To install:

13. Apply an even coat of sealer to both sides of the new intake manifold gasket. Coat the new front and rear seals with RTV sealant.

14. Position and install the intake manifold gasket onto the cylinder head surface. Install the front and rear seals.

15. Support the intake manifold and lower into position.

16. Coat the intake manifold retaining bolts with clean engine oil and tighten by hand.

17. Torque the bolts to specification following the proper sequence.

18. Install the remaining components in the reverse of the removal procedure.

19. Adjust the throttle valve cable and drive belt tension.

20. Refill the cooling system.

21. Operate the engine and inspect for leaks.

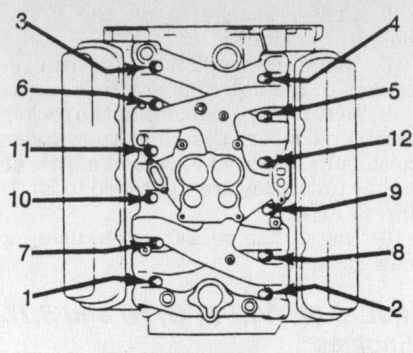

Intake manifold torque sequence— 5.0L (VIN Y and 9) engines

Exhaust Manifold

REMOVAL & INSTALLATION

3.8L and 4.3L Engines

RIGHT SIDE

1. Disconnect the negative battery cable.

2. Disconnect the oxygen sensor and flatten the exhaust manifold mounting bolt lock tabs.

3. Disconnect the exhaust pipe at the exhaust manifold flange. On turbocharged engine, disconnect exhaust pipe from and crossover from exhaust manifold.

4. Raise the vehicle and support it safely.

5. Remove the right front wheel assembly.

6. Remove the exhaust manifold mounting bolts. Remove the exhaust manifold from the engine.

7. Installation is the reverse of the removal procedure. Bend the exhaust manifold bolt's lock tabs after installing the mounting bolts.

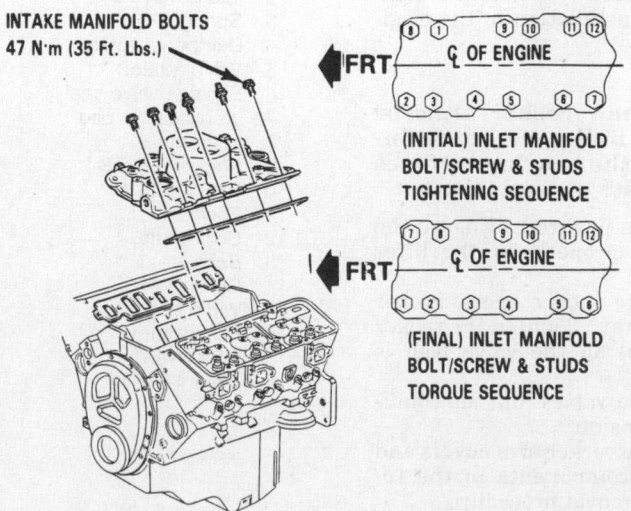

Intake manifold torque sequence—4.3L engine

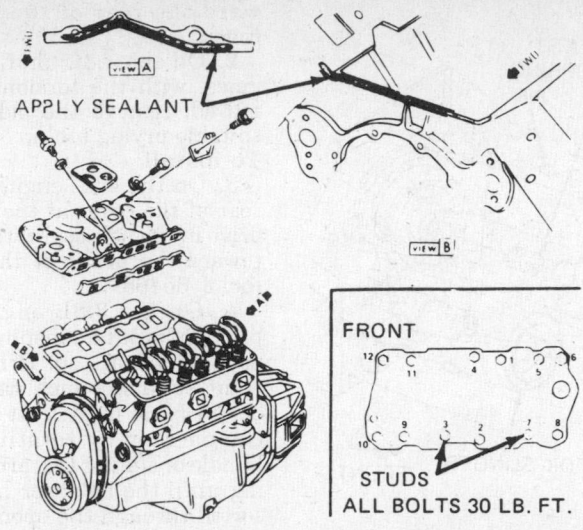

Intake manifold torque sequence—5.0L (VIN E, G, H) and 5.7L engines

FRONT

STUDS
ALL BOLTS 30 LB. FT.

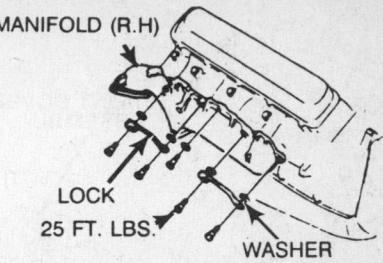

MANIFOLD (R.H)

LOCK
25 FT. LBS.

WASHER

AFTER BOLTS ARE TORQUED TO SPECIFICATION,
BEND LOCK TAB AROUND BOLT HEADS

Right exhaust manifold mounting—
5.0L (VIN Y and 9) engines

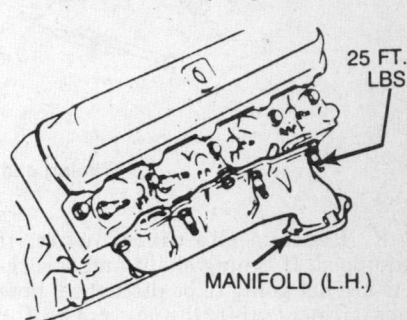

25 FT. LBS.

MANIFOLD (L.H.)

Left exhaust manifold mounting—
5.0L (VIN Y and 9) engines

LEFT SIDE

1. Disconnect the negative battery cable.
2. On carbureted engines, remove the air cleaner.
3. Disconnect the EFE pipe and flatten the exhaust manifold lock tabs.
4. Disconnect the exhaust pipe from the exhaust manifold. On turbocharged engines, disconnect the exhaust manifold from the crossover pipe.
5. Remove the air conditioning compressor and rear adjusting bracket.
6. Remove the power steering pump and the lower rear adjusting bracket.
7. Disconnect the spark plug wires at the plugs.
8. Remove the exhaust manifold mounting bolts.
9. Remove the exhaust manifold from the engine.
10. Installation is the reverse of the removal procedure.
11. Start the engine and check for leaks.

5.0L and 5.7L EngieE
RIGHT SIDE

1. Disconnect the negative battery cable.
2. Raise the vehicle and support it safely. Remove the right front wheel, the exhaust and crossover pipe(s).
3. Flatten the lock tabs on the manifold bolts and remove. If equipped, disconnect the oxygen sensor lead.
4. Remove the lower engine mounting bolt and raise the engine slightly, if necessary for clearance.
5. Remove the manifold from below.

6. To install, use new gaskets and reverse the removal procedure. Torque the manifold bolts to specification, bend bolt lock tabs back into position.

LEFT SIDE

1. Remove the air cleaner.
2. Remove the hot air shroud and the hot air tube.
3. Remove the lower alternator bracket, air conditioning drive belt and the air pump pulley.
4. Remove all air pump hoses and the AIR switching valve.
5. Raise the vehicle and remove the crossover pipe.
6. Lower the vehicle and, flatten the lock tabs on the manifold bolts and remove.
7. To install, use a new gasket and reverse the removal procedures. Torque the exhaust manifold mounting bolts to specifications, bend bolt lock tabs back into position.

Turbocharger

REMOVAL & INSTALLATION

1. Disconnect the negative battery cable.
2. Remove the air inlet hose from the compressor section of the turbocharger.
3. Disconnect the compressor outlet pipe from the compressor.
4. Disconnect the oil breather and turbocharger heat shields.
5. Remove the exhaust pipe from the turbine outlet.
6. Remove the oil breather vent from the valve cover. Disconnect and plug the oil pressure feed line at the turbocharger assembly.

7. Remove the turbocharger mounting bracket nuts. Disconnect the turbine inlet pipe from the exhaust manifold.
8. Disconnect the oil return line from turbocharger.
9. Remove the vacuum line from the turbocharger wastegate actuator.
10. Disconnect the intercooler outlet to throttle body pipe.
11. Remove the turbocharger assembly from the manifold adapter.
12. Installation is the reverse of the removal procedure. Always use new gaskets during installation. Add oil to turbocharger, as necessary.

Timing Chain Front Cover

REMOVAL & INSTALLATION

3.8L Engine

1. Disconnect the negative battery cable.
2. Drain the radiator.
3. Disconnect the radiator hoses and the heater return hose at the water pump.
4. Remove the fan assembly and pulleys.
5. Remove the crankshaft vibration damper.
6. Remove the fuel pump, if carbureted.
7. Remove the alternator.

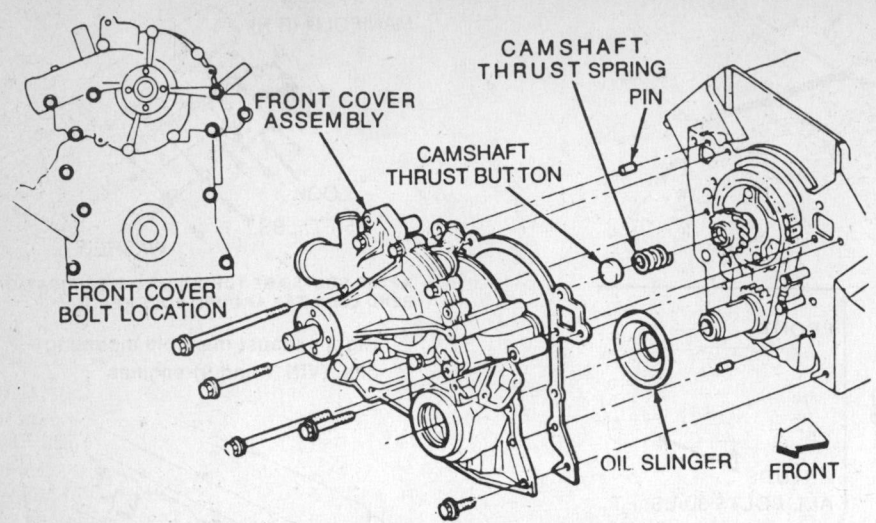

Timing chain cover—3.8L engine

8. Remove the distributor, if equipped. If timing chain and sprockets are not going to be disturbed, note position of distributor rotor for reinstallation in same position.

9. Loosen and slide front clamp on thermostat bypass hose rearward.

10. Remove bolts attaching timing chain cover to cylinder block.

11. Remove 2 oil pan to timing chain cover bolts.

12. Remove timing chain cover assembly and gasket.

13. Thoroughly clean the cover, taking care to avoid damage to the gasket surface.

To install:

14. Installation is the reverse of the removal procedure.

15. Remove oil pump cover and pack the space around the oil pump gears completely full of petroleum jelly. There must be no air space left inside the pump. Reinstall cover using new gasket.

16. To replace the front oil seal, use a punch and drive out the old seal and shedder. Drive the seal out from the front toward the rear of the timing chain cover.

17. Coil new packing around opening so ends of packing are at top. Drive in shedder using suitable punch. Stake the shedder in place in at least 3 places.

18. Size the packing by rotating a hammer handle or similar tool around the packing until the balancer hub can be inserted through the opening.

19. Torque the front cover retaining bolts to 28 ft. lbs. (39 Nm).

4.3L, 5.0L (VIN E, G, H) and 5.7L Engines

1. Disconnect the negative battery cable.

2. Remove the vibration damper assembly.

3. Remove the water pump.

4. Remove the crankcase front cover retaining bolts. Remove the front cover and discard the gasket.

5. Installation is the reverse of the removal procedure.

5.0L (VIN Y, 9) Engines

1. Disconnect the negative battery cable.

2. Drain the coolant. Disconnect the radiator hose and the bypass hose. Remove the fan, belts and pulley. Remove the air conditioner compressor, if equipped, and bracket.

3. Remove the vibration damper and crankshaft pulley.

4. Remove the front cover attaching bolts and remove the cover, timing indicator and water pump from the front of the engine.

5. Remove the dowel pins. If necessary grind a flat surface on the dowel pins to aid in removal. When installing the dowel pins, they must be inserted chamfered end first.

6. Install in the reverse order of removal using new gaskets. Apply RTV sealer around the coolant holes of the new cover gasket. Trim about ⅛ in. from each end of the new front pan seal and trim any excess material from the front edge of the oil pan gasket. Be sure all mating surfaces are clean.

Front Cover Oil Seal

REPLACEMENT

Except 5.0L (VIN Y, 9) Engines

1. On the 3.8L engine, use a punch and drive out the old seal and shedder. Drive the seal out from the front toward the rear of the timing chain cover.

2. On the 4.3L, 5.0L and 5.7L engines, with the torsional damper removed, remove the old seal using a suitable prying tool.

To install:

3. On the 4.3L engine, support the rear of the cover at the seal area and drive in the new seal with the open end toward the inside of the cover using tool J–35468.

4. On the 3.8L engine, coil new packing around opening so ends of packing are at top. Drive in shedder using suitable punch. Stake the shedder in place in at least 3 places. Size the packing by rotating a hammer handle or similar tool around the packing until the balancer hub can be inserted through the opening.

5.0L (VIN Y, 9) Engines

1. Disconnect the negative battery cable.

2. Remove the crankshaft pulley and balancer.

3. Remove the oil seal using tool BT–6406 or J–23129 and J–1859–03 or their equivalents.

To install:

4. Coat the outside diameter of the new seal with sealer.

5. Install seal with lip facing the engine, using tool BT–6405 or J–25264–A.

6. Install crankshaft pulley and balancer.

7. Install belts and adjust tension.

Timing Chain and Sprockets

REMOVAL & INSTALLATION

3.8L Engine

1. Disconnect the negative battery cable.

2. Drain the cooling system.

3. Remove the engine front cover.

4. With timing chain cover removed, temporarily install balancer bolt and washer in end of crankshaft. Turn crankshaft so the timing marks on the sprockets are as close together as possible. Remove balancer bolt and washer using a sharp blow on the wrench handle, so the bolt can be started out without changing position of sprockets.

5. Remove front crankshaft oil slinger.

6. Remove the camshaft sprocket bolts.

7. Use 2 large suitable tools to alternately pry the camshaft sprocket then the crankshaft sprocket forward until the camshaft sprocket is free, then remove the camshaft sprocket and chain

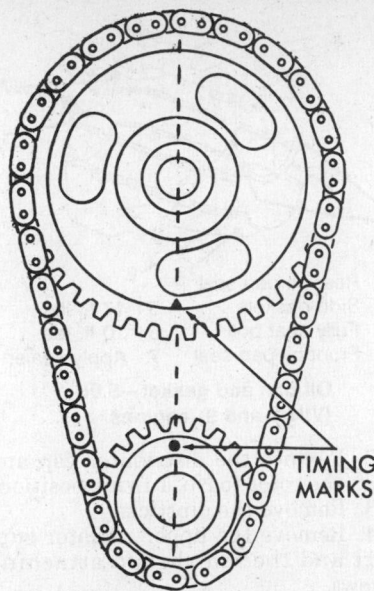

Timing gear alignment marks—
3.8L engine

and finish working crankshaft sprocket off crankshaft.

To install:

8. Thoroughly clean the timing chain, sprockets, distributor drive gear, fuel pump eccentric, if equipped and crankshaft oil slinger.

9. If the pistons have not been moved in the engine, go to Step 12. If the engine has been turned over or the pistons moved, start with Step 10.

10. Turn crankshaft so No. 1 piston is at top dead center, until timing mark on crankshaft sprocket is straight up.

11. Turn camshaft slowly, with sprocket temporarily installed, until timing mark on camshaft sprocket is straight down. Remove sprocket.

12. Assemble timing chain on sprockets and slide the sprocket and chain assembly on the shafts with the timing marks in their closest position and in line with the sprocket hubs.

13. Assemble slinger on crankshaft with large part of cone to front of engine.

14. Install camshaft sprocket bolts. Torque to specification.

15. Install camshaft thrust button and spring and timing chain dampers.

16. Install timing chain cover. Continue the installation in the reverse order of the removal procedure.

5.0L (VIN Y, 9) Engines

1. Disconnect the negative battery cable.

2. Remove the front cover and gasket.

3. Remove the crankshaft oil slinger.

4. Remove the camshaft thrust button and spring.

5. Remove the fuel pump, fuel pump gasket and fuel pump eccentric.

6. Remove the camshaft sprocket with a suitable gear puller, and remove the timing chain.

7. Remove the spark plugs.

NOTE: The crankshaft key has a blind keyway. The key must be removed before removing the crankshaft sprocket.

8. Remove the crankshaft key.

9. With sprocket removal tool BT–6812, J–25287, J–21052 or equivalents, remove the crankshaft sprocket.

To install:

10. Place the timing chain on a flat surface.

11. Insert the camshaft and crankshaft timing sprockets into the timing chain with the timing marks aligned. Ensure this alignment is maintained through out the procedure.

12. Install the sprockets with the timing chain and place them into position.

13. Rotate the camshaft sprocket as required until it engages with the camshaft. With the camshaft sprocket engaged, install the fuel pump eccentric or flat side toward the engine. Install the camshaft sprocket, fuel pump eccentric, bolt and make finger tight.

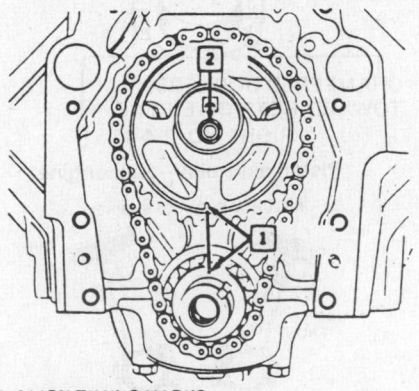

1. ALIGN TIMING MARKS
2. 88 N·m (65 LBS. FT.)

Timing gear alignment marks—
5.0L (VIN Y and 9) engines

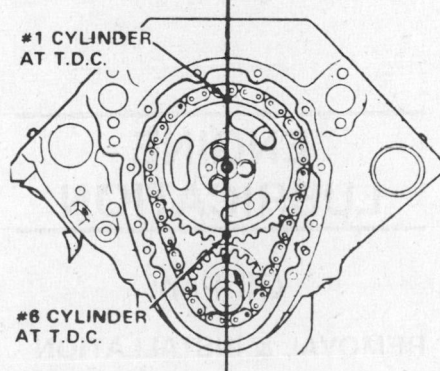

Timing gear alignment marks—
5.0L (VIN E, G, H) and 5.7L engines

14. Rotate the crankshaft until the crankshaft and crankshaft timing sprocket keyways are in alignment. When the keyways are aligned, tap the crankshaft key into place with a brass hammer until the key bottoms in the keyway.

15. Check the timing marks are still in alignment.

NOTE: When the timing marks are aligned, the No. 6 piston is at TDC. When the timing marks are on top, the No. 1 piston is in the firing position.

16. After the timing gear alignment is verified, torque the camshaft sprocket (fuel pump eccentric) bolt to 65 ft. lbs.

17. Install the remaining components in the reverse of the removal procedure using new gaskets where required.

4.3L, 5.0L (VIN E, G, H) and 5.7L Engines

1. Disconnect the negative battery cable. Remove the engine front cover.

2. Rotate the engine until the marks on both the camshaft sprocket and crankshaft sprocket align with the shaft centers.

3. Remove the camshaft sprocket retaining bolts. Remove the camshaft sprocket along with the timing chain.

4. If necessary for replacement, use a crankshaft sprocket removal tool and remove the crankshaft sprocket. Remove the crankshaft sprocket key, if required.

To install:

5. Installation is the reverse of removal.

6. Ensure that the timing marks on the crankshaft sprocket and the camshaft sprocket are aligned with the shaft centers.

7. Torque the camshaft sprocket bolts to 21 ft. lbs.

Camshaft

REMOVAL & INSTALLATION

3.8L and 4.3L Engines

NOTE: This procedure requires that the air conditioner system be discharged and recharged.

1. Disconnect the negative battery cable.

2. Drain the radiator.

3. Remove the intake manifold.

4. Remove the valve covers.

5. Remove the rocker arm assemblies, pushrods and valve lifters, noting location.

6. Remove the radiator and the air condition condenser, as required.

7. Remove timing chain cover, timing chain and sprocket.

8. Align timing marks of camshaft and crankshaft sprocket. This avoids burring of the camshaft journals by the crankshaft during removal.

9. Slide camshaft forward out of bearing bores carefully to avoid marring the bearing surfaces.

To install:

10. Installation is the reverse of the removal procedure.

11. Before installing the camshaft and the lifters, be sure to coat them with clean engine oil.

12. Be sure to use new gaskets and seals as required.

5.0L and 5.7L Engines

1. Disconnect the negative battery cable.

2. Drain the radiator.

3. Remove the upper radiator baffle.

4. Disconnect the upper radiator hose.

5. Remove the radiator.

6. Disconnect the fuel line at the fuel pump.

7. Remove the air cleaner.

8. Disconnect the throttle cable.

9. Remove the alternator belt. Remove the alternator bracket attaching bolts.

10. Remove power steering pump bracket attaching bolts and remove pump.

11. Remove air conditioning compressor mounting bracket attaching bolts and support compressor to side for access. The air conditioning lines at the compressor are flexible and should be left attached to the compressor.

— CAUTION —

Do not disconnect the air conditioning lines. Personal injury could result.

12. Disconnect thermostat bypass hose at water pump.

13. Disconnect electrical and vacuum connections.

14. Remove distributor with cap and wiring intact.

15. Remove balancer pulley. Remove balancer.

16. Remove engine front cover.

17. Remove both valve covers.

18. Remove intake manifold and gasket, front and rear seal.

19. Remove rocker arms, pushrods and valve lifters.

NOTE: All parts for each assembly must be kept together and reinstalled in the same location.

20. If equipped with air conditioning, discharge the system, remove condenser attaching bolts and remove condenser.

21. Remove bolt securing fuel pump eccentric, remove eccentric, camshaft gear, oil slinger and timing chain.

22. Remove camshaft by carefully sliding it out the front of the engine.

23. Installation is the reverse of the removal procedure. Be sure to coat the camshaft and the lifters with clean engine oil prior to installation. Be sure to use new gaskets, as required.

Piston and Connecting Rod

POSITIONING

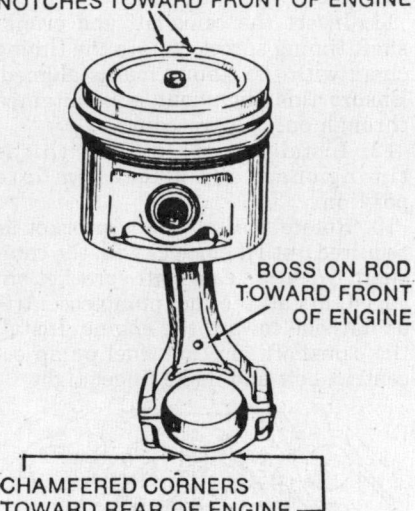

NOTCHES TOWARD FRONT OF ENGINE

BOSS ON ROD TOWARD FRONT OF ENGINE

CHAMFERED CORNERS TOWARD REAR OF ENGINE RIGHT NO. 2-4-6

Piston assembly—3.8L engine

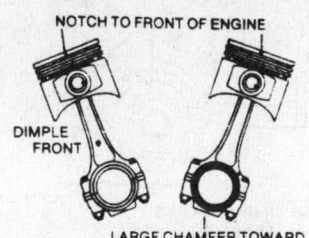

NOTCH TO FRONT OF ENGINE

DIMPLE FRONT

LARGE CHAMFER TOWARD FRONT OF ENGINE

Piston assembly—5.0L (VIN E, G, H) and 5.7L engines

ENGINE LUBRICATION

Oil Pan

REMOVAL & INSTALLATION

1. Disconnect the negative battery cable.

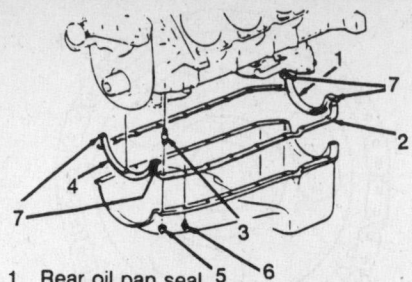

1. Rear oil pan seal
2. Side gaskets
3. Fully seat bolt
4. Front oil pan seal
5. 17 ft. lbs.
6. 10 ft. lbs.
7. Apply sealer

Oil pan and gasket—5.0L (VIN Y and 9) engines

2. Remove the distributor cap and align the rotor to No. 1 firing position.

3. Remove the dipstick.

4. Remove the upper radiator support and the fan shroud attaching screws.

5. Raise the vehicle and drain the oil.

6. Remove the flywheel cover.

7. Remove the starter motor assembly.

8. Disconnect the exhaust pipes and the crossover pipe.

9. Disconnect the engine mounts and raise the front of the engine as far as possible.

10. Remove the oil pan attaching bolts and remove the pan.

11. Installation is in the reverse order of removal. Torque the attaching bolts to 10 ft. lbs.

Oil Pump

REMOVAL & INSTALLATION

Except 3.8L Engine

1. Disconnect the negative battery cable.

2. Drain the engine oil, remove the oil pan and baffle, if equipped.

3. Remove the pump attaching bolts and remove the pump.

4. Reinstall in reverse order. Tighten the pump retaining bolts to 35 ft. lbs. (5.0L VIN Y, 9) engines, 77 ft. lbs. (5.7L and 5.0L VIN E, G, H) engines and 65 ft. lbs. (4.3L) engine. To insure immediate oil pressure on start up, the oil pump gear cavity should be packed with petroleum jelly.

3.8L Engine

NOTE: The oil pump is located on the left side of the timing chain cover. It is connected by a drilled passage in the cylinder crankcase, to an oil screen housing and stand pipe assembly.

1. Remove the oil filter.

2. Unbolt the pump cover assembly from the timing chain cover.

3. Remove the cover assembly and slide out the pump gears.

4. Remove the oil pressure relief valve cap, spring and valve. Do not remove the oil filter bypass valve and spring.

5. Check that the relief valve spring is not worn on the side, or collapsed.

6. Check that the relief valve is no more than an easy "slip-fit" in the bore in the cover.

NOTE: If there is any perceptible side play in the relief valve, replace the valve. If there is still side play, replace the cover also.

7. Check the filter bypass valve for wear. Replace if necessary.

To install:

8. Lubricate and install the pressure relief valve and spring in the cover bore.

9. Install the gasket and cap, torquing the cap to 35 ft. lbs.

10. Install the gears and check that gear-to-cover end clearance is between 0.002–0.006 in. If the clearance is less, check the timing cover gear pocket for wear.

11. Remove the gears and pack the gear pocket full of petroleum jelly. Don't use grease.

NOTE: Unless the pump is primed this way, it won't produce any oil pressure when the engine is started.

12. Install the gears. Install a new gasket and the cover. Torque the bolts evenly to 10 ft. lbs. Replace the oil filter when finshed. Tighten the oil pump screen housing to cylinder block bolts to 96 inch lbs.

Rear Main Bearing Oil Seal

REMOVAL & INSTALLATION

3.8L and 5.0L (VIN Y, 9) Engines

1. Remove the oil pan. Remove the oil pump where required. Remove the rear main bearing cap.

2. Pry the lower seal out of the bearing cap with a suitable tool, being careful not to gouge the cap surface.

3. Remove the upper seal by lightly tapping on one end with a brass pin punch until the other end can be grasped and pulled out.

4. Clean the bearing cap, cylinder block and crankshaft mating surfaces with solvent. Inspect all these surfaces for gouges, nicks and burrs.

5. Apply a light coat of engine oil on the seal lips and bead but keep the seal ends clean.

6. Insert the tip of the installation tool between the crankshaft and the seal of the cylinder block. Place the seal between the crankshaft and the seal of the cylinder block. Place the seal between the tip of the tool and the crankshaft, so the bead contacts the tip of the tool.

7. Be sure the seal lip is facing the front of the engine, and work the seal around the crankshaft using the installation tool to protect the seal from the corner of the cylinder block.

NOTE: Do not remove the tool until the opposite end of the seal is flush with the cylinder block surface.

8. Remove the installation tool, being careful not to pull the seal out at the same time.

9. Using the same procedure, install the lower seal into the bearing cap. Use a finger and thumb to lever the seal into the cap.

10. Apply sealer to the cylinder block only where the cap mates to the surface. Do not apply sealer to the seal ends.

11. Install the rear cap and torque the bolts to specifications.

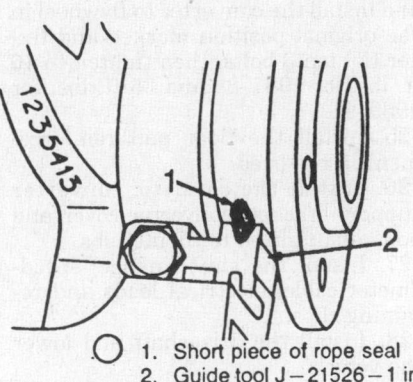

1. Short piece of rope seal
2. Guide tool J—21526—1 installed

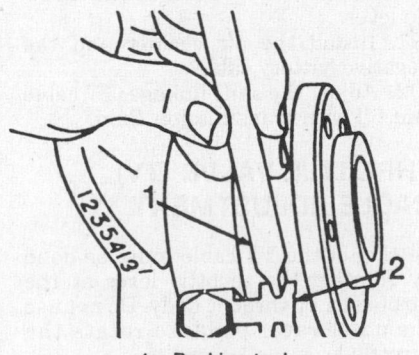

1. Packing tool
2. Guide tool

Rear main oil seal Installation— 3.8L engine

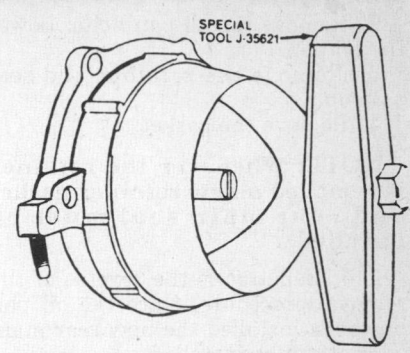

SPECIAL TOOL J-35621

One piece rear main oil seal removal tool—4.3L, 5.0L (VIN E, G, H) and 5.7L engines

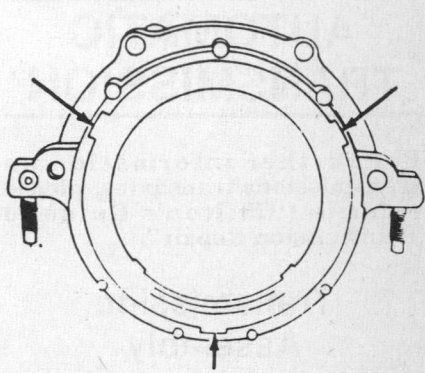

Removing the seal from the seal retainer—4.3L, 5.0L (VIN E, G, H) and 5.7L engines

4.3L, 5.0L (VIN E, G, H) and 5.7L Engines

ONE PIECE SEAL

1. Remove the transmission from the vehicle.

2. Using the notches provided in the rear seal retainer, pry out the seal using the proper tool.

NOTE: Care should be taken when removing the seal so as not to nick the crankshaft sealing surface.

3. Before installation lubricate the inside and outside diameter of the new seal with clean engine oil.

4. Install the seal on tool J–3561 or equivalent. Thread the tool into the rear of the crankshaft. Tighten the screws snugly, this is to insure the seal will be installed squarely over the crankshaft. Tighten the tool wing nut until it bottoms.

5. Remove the tool from the crankshaft.

6. Install the transmission.

4.3L, 5.0L (VIN E, G, H) and 5.7L Engines

ONE PIECE SEAL RETAINER AND GASKET

1. Remove the transmission from the vehicle.

2. Remove the oil pan bolts. Lower the oil pan.

3. Remove the retainer and seal assembly.

4. Remove the gasket.

NOTE: Whenever the retainer is removed a new retainer gasket and rear main seal must be installed.

5. Installation is the reverse of the removal procedure. Once the oil pan has been installed the new rear main oil seal can be installed.

AUTOMATIC TRANSMISSION

For further information on transmissions/transaxles, please refer to ''Chilton's Guide to Transmission Repair''.

Transmission Assembly

REMOVAL & INSTALLATION

1. Disconnect the battery.

2. Disconnect the TV cable at the throttle lever.

3. Remove the transmission dipstick. Remove the bolt retaining the filler tube to the transmission.

4. Raise the vehicle and support it safely.

5. Remove the driveshaft. The floor pan reinforcement, if used, may need to be removed if it interferes with removal of the driveshaft.

6. Disconnect the speedometer cable and the shift linkage at the transmission.

7. Disconnect all electrical leads at the transmission and any clips that retain the leads to the transmission.

8. Remove the flywheel cover.

9. Mark flywheel and converter for installation reference.

10. Remove the torque converter to flywheel bolts.

11. Remove the catalytic converter support bracket.

12. Remove the transmission mount to support bolt and the transmission support to frame bolts and insulators.

13. Support and raise the transmission slightly.

14. Slide the transmission support rearward.

15. Lower the transmission to gain access to the oil cooler lines. Disconnect the lines and cap all openings.

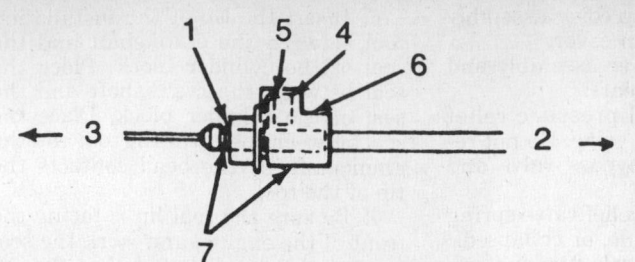

1.	Slider against fitting (zero or reset position)
2.	Direction of cable actuating lever
3.	Reset direction
4.	Reset tab
5.	Fitting
6.	Cable
7.	Slider

TV cable adjustment

16. Support the engine with a suitable jack and remove the transmission to engine bolts.

17. Slide the transmission rearward and install tool J–21366 to the converter to hold it in place.

18. Remove the transmission assembly from the vehicle.

To install:

19. Raise the transmission into place and remove tool J–21366.

20. Install the transmission to engine bolts and tighten to 35 ft. lbs.

21. Install the oil cooler pipe and TV cable.

22. Install the the transmission support to frame bolts and tighten to 41 ft. lbs.

23. Install the the transmission support to transmission mount bolts and tighten to 35 ft. lbs.

24. Remove the transmission jack and install the converter to flywheel in the original position marked and finger tighten 3 bolts, then tighten to 46 ft. lbs. for 1987–88 and 35 ft. lbs. for 1989–91.

25. Install the floor pan reinforcement, if removed.

26. Install the catalytic converter support bracket, converter cover and bolts and tighten to 89 inch lbs.

27. Install the shift linkage, speedometer cable, electrical leads and retaining clips.

28. Install the driveshaft and lower the vehicle.

29. Install the fluid filler tube and a new seal.

30. Install the TV cable at the throttle lever.

31. Install the air cleaner and the negative battery cable.

32. Adjust the shift linkage, TV cable and fill with transmission fluid.

THROTTLE VALVE (TV) CABLE ADJUSTMENT

Setting of the TV cable must be done by rotating the throttle lever at the carburetor or throttle body. Do not use the accelerator pedal to rotate the throttle lever.

1. With the engine off, depress and hold the reset tab at the engine end of the TV cable.

2. Move the slider until it stops against the fitting.

3. Release the rest tab.

4. Rotate the throttle lever to its full travel.

5. The slider must move (ratchet) toward the lever when the lever is rotated to its full travel position.

6. Recheck after the engine is hot and road test the vehicle.

DRIVE AXLE

Driveshaft

REMOVAL & INSTALLATION

1. Raise the vehicle and support it safely.

2. Matchmark the relationship of the driveshaft to the differential flange.

3. Unbolt the straps or flange. Tape the bearing caps in place to prevent losing the bearing rollers. Support the driveshaft to prevent excessive strain on the universal joint.

4. Position a suitable drain pan under the transmission end to catch any fluid that may drain out when the driveshaft is removed. Pull the shaft back and remove it. Be careful not to damage the splines at the transmission end.

5. If the transmission splined slip yoke does not have a vent hole at the center, it should be lubricated for installation with engine oil. If it does have a vent hole, it should be lubricated with grease. Slide the slip yoke into place.

6. Align the matchmarks and tighten the bolts. Tighten the U-bolts to 16 ft. lbs.

Universal Joints

REMOVAL & INSTALLATION

Snapring Type

1. Raise and support the vehicle

safely and matchmark and remove the driveshaft.

2. Support the lock rings from the yoke and remove the lubrication fitting.

3. Support the yoke in a bench vise. Never clamp the driveshaft tube.

4. Use a socket to press against one trunnion bearing to press the opposite bearing from the yoke.

5. Grasp the cap and work it out.

6. Support the other side of the yoke and press the other bearing cap from the yoke and remove as in Steps 4 and 5.

7. Remove the trunnion from the driveshaft yoke.

8. If equipped with a sliding sleeve, remove the trunnion bearings from the sleeve yoke. Remove the seal retainer from the end of the sleeve and pull the seal and washer from the retainer.

9. Disassemble the other U-joint. Clean and check the condition of all parts. Use U-joint repair kits to replace all the wearing parts.

To assemble the trunnion bearings:

10. Repack the bearings with grease and replace the trunnion dust seals after any operation that requires disassembly of the U-joint. Be sure the lubricant reservoir at the end of the trunnion is full of lubricant. Fill the reservoirs with lubricant from the bottom.

11. Install the trunnion into the driveshaft yoke and press the bearings into the yoke over the trunnion hubs as far as it will go.

12. Install the lockrings.

13. Hold the trunnion in one hand and tap the yoke slightly to seat the bearings against the lock rings.

14. Replace the driveshaft.

Molded Retainer Type

NOTE: **Don't disassemble these joints unless a repair kit is available. The factory installed joints cannot be reassembled.**

1. Raise and support the vehicle safely and remove the driveshaft.

2. Support the dirvshaft in a horizontal position. Place the U-joint so the lower ear of the shaft yoke is supported by a 1⅛ in. socket. Press the lower bearing cup of the yoke ear. This will shear the plastic retaining the lower bearing cup.

NOTE: **Never clamp the driveshaft tubing in a vise.**

3. If the bearing cup is not completely removed, lift the cross, insert a spacer and press the cup completely out.

4. Rotate the driveshaft, shear the

opposite plastic retainer, and press the other bearing cup out in the same manner.

5. Remove the cross from the yoke. Production U-joints cannot be reassembled. There are no bearing retainer grooves in the cups. Discard all parts that were removed and substitute those in the overhaul kit.

6. Remove the sheared plastic bearing retainer from the yoke. Drive a small pin or punch through the injection holes to aid in removal.

7. If the other U-joint is to be serviced, remove the bearing cups from the slip yoke.

8. Be sure the seals are installed on the service bearing cups to hold the needle bearings in place for handling. Grease the bearings, if not pregreased.

9. Install one bearing cup part way into one side of the yoke and turn this ear to the bottom.

10. Insert the cross into the yoke so the trunnion seats freely in the bearing cup.

11. Install the opposite bearing cup part way. Be sure both trunnions are started straight into the bearing cups.

12. Press against opposite bearing cups, working the cross constantly to be sure it is free in the cups. If binding occurs, check the needle rollers to be sure one needle has not become lodged under and end of the trunnion.

13. As soon as one bearing retainer groove is exposed, stop pressing and install the bearing retainer snapring.

14. Continue to press until the opposite bearing retainer can be installed. If difficulty installing the snaprings is encountered, rap the yoke with a hammer to spring the yoke ears slightly.

15. Assemble the other half of the U-joint in the same manner.

16. Check that the cross is free in the cups. If it is too tight, rap the yoke ears again to help seat the bearing retainers.

17. Replace the driveshaft.

Rear Axle Shaft, Bearing and Seal

REMOVAL & INSTALLATION

1. Raise vehicle and support it safely. Remove the tire and wheel assembly. Remove the brake drum.

2. Drain the fluid. Remove the rear carrier cover. Discard the gasket.

3. Remove the rear axle pinion shaft lock screw and the rear axle pinion shaft.

4. Push flanged end of axle shaft toward center of the vehicle and remove C-lock from button end of shaft.

5. Remove axle shaft from housing,

being careful not to damage oil seal, if not being replaced.

6. Remove seal from housing with a pry bar behind steel case of seal, being careful not to damage housing.

7. Insert tool J–23689 or equivalent, into bore and position it behind bearing so tangs on tool engage bearing outer race. Remove bearing, using slide hammer.

To install:

8. Lubricate the new bearing with gear lubricant and install bearing so tool bottoms against shoulder in housing, using tool J–23690 or equivalent.

9. Lubricate seal lips with gear lubricant. Position seal on tool J–21128 or equivalent, and position seal into housing bore. Tap seal into place so it is flush with axle tube.

10. Insert the axle into the place while engaging the splines on the end of the shaft with the splines of the rear axle side gear. Be careful not to damage the seal.

11. Install the C-lock on the bottom of the axle shaft and push the shaft outward so the lock seats in the counterbore of the rear axle side gear.

12. Install the rear axle pinion gear shift through the differential case, thrust washers and pinions, align the hole in the shaft with the lock bolt hole. Install the lock bolt and tighten to 24 ft. lbs. for 7½ in. ring gears and 20 ft. lbs. for 8½ in. ring gears.

13. Install the carrier cover and bolts using a new gasket.

14. Fill the rear assembly with the proper grade and type gear oil.

15. Install the brake drum and wheel and lower the vehicle.

Pinion Seal

REMOVAL & INSTALLATION

1. Raise and support the vehicle safely. It would help to have the front end slightly higher than the rear to avoid fluid loss.

2. Matchmark and remove the driveshaft.

3. Release the parking brake.

4. Remove the rear wheels. Rotate the rear wheels by hand to make sure there is absolutely no brake drag. If there is brake drag, remove the drums.

5. Using a torque wrench on the pinion nut, record the force needed to rotate the pinion.

6. Matchmark the pinion shaft, nut and flange. Count the number of exposed threads on the pinion shaft.

7. Install a holding tool on the pinion. A very large adjustable wrench will do or if one is not available, put the drums back on and set the parking brake as tightly as possible.

8. Remove the pinion nut.

1. Cover bolt
2. Cover gasket
3. Differential bearing cap bolt
4. Differential bearing cap
5. Drive pinion
6. Shim
7. Rear pinion bearing
8. Inner race
9. Spacer
10. Rear axle housing
11. Outer race
12. Front pinion bearing
13. Pinion yoke oil seal
14. Pinion yoke
15. Washer
16. Pinion yoke nut
17. Axle shaft
18. Bearing assy.
19. Oil seal
20. Backing plate
21. Shim
22. Side bearing
23. Bolt
24. Pinion gear shaft
25. Differential case
26. Lock bolt
27. Ring gear
28. Thrust washer
29. Pinion gear
30. Side gear
31. ABS sensor ring

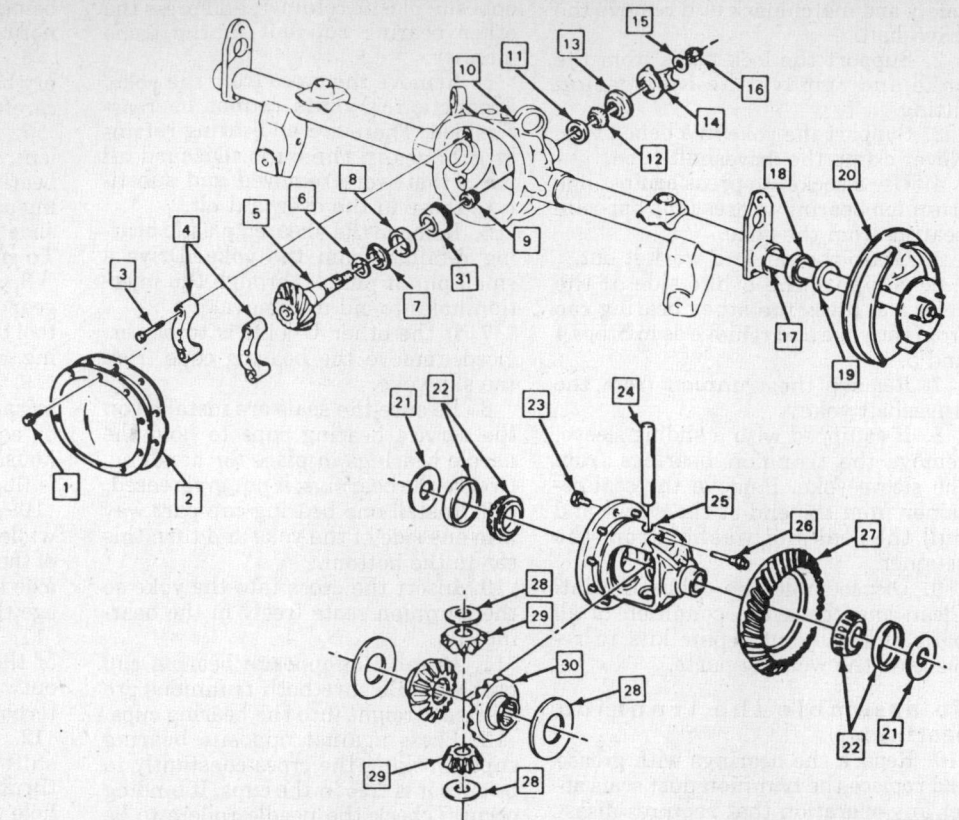

Disassembled view of the standard rear axle

9. Slide the flange off of the pinion. A puller may be necessary.

10. Center punch the oil seal to distort it and pry it out of the bore. Be careful to avoid scratching the bore.

To install:

11. Pack the cavity between the lips of the seal with lithium-based chassis lube.

12. Use a seal installer, as necessary, and position the seal in the bore and carefully drive it into place.

13. Place the flange on the pinion and push it on as far as it will go.

14. Install the pinion washer and nut on the shaft and force the pinion into place by turning the nut.

NOTE: Never hammer the flange into place.

16. Tighten the nut until the exact number of threads previously noted appear and the matchmarks align.

17. Measure the rotating torque of the pinion under the same circumstances as before. Compare both readings. As necessary, tighten the pinion nut in very small increments until the torque necessary to rotate the pinion is 3 inch lbs. higher than the originally recorded torque.

18. Install the driveshaft.

Rear Axle Housing

REMOVAL & INSTALLATION

1. Raise the vehicle and support it safely. Be sure the rear axle assembly is supported safely.

2. Disconnect shock absorbers from axle.

3. Mark driveshaft and pinion flange, disconnect driveshaft and support it out of the way.

4. Remove brake line junction block bolt at axle housing, disconnect brake

lines at junction block. On some vehicles, disconnect brake line at wheel cylinder.

5. Disconnect upper control arms from axle housing.

6. Lower rear axle assembly on hoist and remove springs.

7. Remove rear wheels and drums.

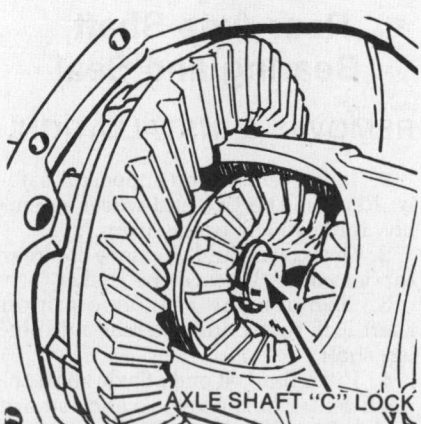

Removing the axle shaft C lock

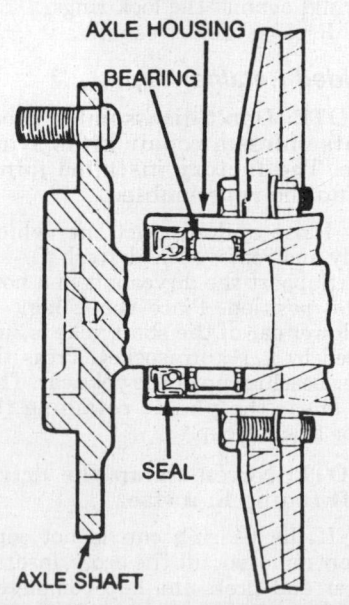

Axle shaft, bearing and seal—cutaway view

8. Disconnect brake lines from axle housing clips.

9. Disconnect lower control arms from axle housing.

10. Remove rear axle housing.

11. Installation is the reverse of the removal procedure.

12. Be sure to bleed the brake system, as required.

STEERING

CAUTION

If equipped with the Supplemental Inflatable Restraint System (SIR), the system must be disabled, before working on any part of the system. Failure to do so may result in deployment of the air bag and possible personal injury.

Supplemental Inflatable Restraint (SIR) System

DISABLING

1991 Caprice

1. Turn the steering wheel so the vehicles wheels are pointing straight ahead.

2. Turn the ignition switch to **LOCK**.

3. Remove the SIR fuse from the fuse block.

4. Disconnect the Connector Position Assurance (CPA) and yellow 2 way SIR harness connector at the base of the steering column.

ENABLING

1. Connect the Connector Position Assurance (CPA) and yellow 2 way SIR harness connector at the base of the steering column.

2. Install the SIR fuse to the fuse block.

3. Turn the ignition switch to **RUN** and verify that the inflatable restraint indicator flashes 7–9 times and then turns off.

Steering Wheel

REMOVAL & INSTALLATION

Except 1991 Caprice

NOTE: Do not pound on the steering wheel or the steering shaft. The collapsible column could be damaged enough to require replacement.

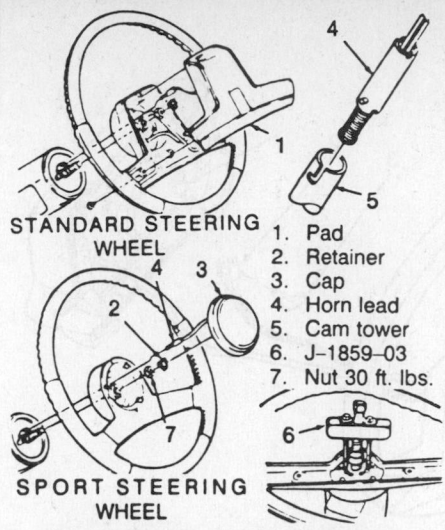

STANDARD STEERING WHEEL

1. Pad
2. Retainer
3. Cap
4. Horn lead
5. Cam tower
6. J–1859–03
7. Nut 30 ft. lbs.

SPORT STEERING WHEEL

REMOVING STEERING WHEEL

Steering wheel and horn contact assembly with standard steering column except 1991 Caprice

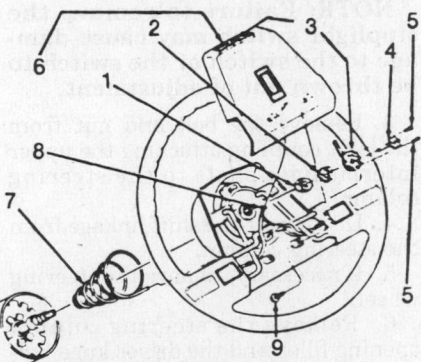

1. Steering wheel nut 30 ft. lbs.
2. Steering wheel nut retainer
3. Telescoping adjusting lever
4. Steering shaft lock knob bolt
5. Steering shaft lock knob bolt positioning screw (2)
6. Steering wheel pad
7. Horn contact spring
8. Horn lead
9. Fully driven, seated and not stripped

Steering wheel and horn contact assembly with tilt and telescoping steering column except 1991 Caprice

1. Disconnect the battery ground cable.

2. On the stock wheel, remove the screws attaching the horn pad assembly to the wheel. Disconnect the horn contact from the pad assembly.

3. On the deluxe wheel, remove the pad attaching screws, lift up the pad and disconnect the horn wire by pushing on the insulator and turning counterclockwise.

4. On the sport steering wheel, pull up on the emblem to remove it. Re-

move the contact assembly attaching screws and the contact assembly.

5. On all columns, remove the steering wheel nut retainer.

6. Remove the retaining nut and the steering wheel, using a puller.

7. Installation is the reverse of removal. Align the marks on the wheel hub and the steering shaft. Torque the attaching bolt to 30 ft. lbs.

1991 Caprice

1. Disable the SIR system.

2. Remove the Torx® screws from in back of the steering wheel, disconnect the connector and remove the the inflator module.

CAUTION

To avoid personal injury when carrying a live inflator module, make sure the bag and trim cover are pointed away. When placing a live inflator module on a bench or other surface, always face the bag and trim cover up and away from the surface, also never carry the inflator module by the wires or connector on the underside of the module otherwise personal injury may result if bag is deployed.

3. Disconnect the negative battery cable.

4. Remove the hexagon locking nut.

5. Use a suitable wheel puller and remove the steering wheel and horn contact.

NOTE: When attaching the wheel puller to the wheel, use care to prevent threading the side screws into the coil assembly and damaging the coil assembly.

To install:

6. Route the coil assembly connector to the steering wheel.

7. Install the horn contact.

8. Install the steering wheel by aligning the block tooth on the steering wheel with the block tooth on the steering shaft with one female serration and install the locking nut.

9. Connect the coil assembly, install the inflator module to the wheel and tighten the bolts to 25 inch lbs.

10. Enable the SIR system

Steering Column

REMOVAL & INSTALLATION

Except 1991 Caprice

NOTE: Handle the steering column very carefully. Rapping on the end of it or leaning on it could shear off the inserts which allow the column to collapse in a crash.

On 1990–91 vehicles the wheels must be in the straight ahead position and the key must be in the **LOCK** position when removing or installing the steering column

1. Terminal from inflatable restraint module
2. Terminal from coil assembly
3. Connector position assurance
4. Inflator module
5. Steering wheel
6. Screw

Inflator module removal—1991 Caprice

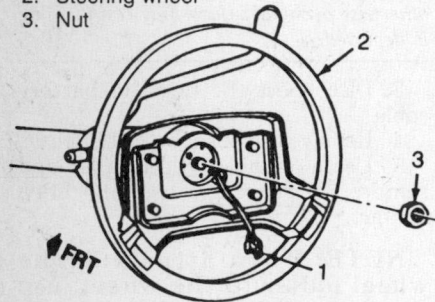

1. Terminal from coil assembly
2. Steering wheel
3. Nut

Steering wheel removal—1991 Caprice

1. Disconnect negative battery cable.
2. Disconnect flexible coupling.
3. Remove cover and toe-pan attaching screws.
4. If necessary, remove instrument panel lower trim.
5. Disconnect shift linkages, wiring, etc.
6. Remove lower column mounts, the upper column mounts and pull column up and out of the vehicle.
7. When installing, check that flexible coupling alignment is correct.

NOTE: When installing, use only the specified hardware. Over length bolts could prevent the column from properly collapsing in a crash.

1991 Caprice

NOTE: The vehicle must be in the straight ahead position and the key must be in the LOCK position when removing or installing the steering column.

1. Disable the SIR system.
2. Remove the stoplight switch.

NOTE: Failure to remove the stoplight switch may cause damage to the switch or the switch to be thrown out of adjustment.

3. Remove the bolt and nut from the joint coupling attaching the upper intermediate shaft to the steering column.
4. Disconnect the shift linkage from the steering column.
5. If necessary, remove the steering wheel.
6. Remove the steering column opening filler and the driver knee bolster and deflector.
7. Remove the bolts attaching the toe plate to the cowl and remove the shift indicator cable from the steering column.
8. Remove all electrical connections.
9. Remove the capsule nuts attaching the column support bracket to the instrument panel and remove the steering column from the vehicle.
10. Installation is the reverse of removal. Tighten the capsule nuts attaching the column support bracket to the instrument panel to 20 ft. lbs. Tighten the bolt and nut at the joint coupling attaching the upper intermediate shaft to the steering column to 46 ft. lbs. Enable the SIR system.

Power Steering Gear

REMOVAL & INSTALLATION

1. Disconnect the negative battery cable.
2. Disconnect the power steering hoses from the gear and cap the hose fittings.

3. Raise the vehicle and support it safely.
4. Disconnect intermediate shaft from the gear.
5. Remove the pitman arm from the steering gear using tool J–29107 or equivalent.
6. Remove the bolts that hold gear to frame and lower gear assembly.
7. Installation is the reverse of the removal procedure.
8. Before positioning the gear, note that the flat on the gear lower shaft must index with the flat in the intermediate shaft.
9. Make certain there is a minimum of 0.040 in. (1.02mm) clearance between intermediate shaft coupling and steering gear upper seal. Tighten mounting bolts to 80 ft. lbs. for 1987–88 or 70 ft. lbs. for 1989–91.

Power Steering Pump

REMOVAL & INSTALLATION

1. Disconnect the negative battery cable.
2. Loosen and remove power steering pump belt.
3. Remove bolts and nut from adjuster bracket.
4. Disconnect both lines at the pump and cap the lines.
5. Remove the pump assembly. Remove the pulley and bracket from the pump.
6. Installation is the reverse of the removal procedure. Connect power steering lines and tighten fittings to 20 ft. lbs. (27 Nm).
7. Fill with fluid, bleed the system and adjust belt to proper tension.

BELT ADJUSTMENT

V-Belt

EXCEPT 5.0L (Y, 9) ENGINES

Use a belt tension gauge and if the tension is below 50 lbs. (222 N), adjust to 70–80 ft. lbs. (312–356 N) on used belts and 120–130 ft. lbs. (534–578 N) on new belts

5.0L (Y, 9) ENGINES

Use a belt tension gauge and if the tension is below 67.5 ft. lbs. (300 N), adjust to 90 ft. lbs. (400 N) on used belts and 135 ft. lbs. (600 N) on new belts.

Serpentine Belt

If belt slippage occurs and the drive belt tensioner is within its operating range, check the belt tension as follows:

1. Run the engine for 10 minutes, shut off the engine, then using a tension gauge between the 2 pulleys, record the belt tension.

2. Run the engine for 30 seconds and repeat Step 1.

3. Again run the engine for 30 seconds and repeat Step 1.

4. The belt tension is the average of the 3 readings. Serpentine belt tension should be 105–125 ft. lbs. (467–556 N).

5. Replace the belt tensioner if the tension is below the minimum specified and the drive belt tensioner is within its operating range.

SYSTEM BLEEDING

When the power steering system has been serviced, air must be bled from the system by using the following procedure:

1. Turn wheels all the way to the left, add power steering fluid to the cold mark on the level indicator.

2. Start engine and run at fast idle momentarily, shut engine off and recheck the fluid level. If necessary add fluid to the cold mark.

3. Start engine and bleed system by turning wheels from side to side without hitting stops. Keep the fluid level at the cold mark. Fluid with air in it has a light tan or red appearance, this air must be eliminated before normal steering action can be achieved.

4. Return the wheels to the center position and continue running the engine for a few minutes. Road test to check the operation of the steering.

5. Recheck the fluid level it should now be stabilized at the Hot level on the indicator.

Tie Rod Ends

REMOVAL & INSTALLATION

1. Raise and support the vehicle safely.

2. Remove the cotter pins from the ball studs and remove the castellated nuts.

3. Disconnect the tie rod end from the steering arm or knuckle with a ball joint separator.

4. Remove the inner ball stud from the intermediate rod with a puller. Mark the tie rod end position before removal.

5. Loosen the clamp bolts and unscrew the ends from the adjuster tubes. If a force of more than 7 ft. lbs. is required to remove the ends after break away, the fasteners should be replaced.

6. Clean and inspect all parts. When installing, run the tie rod end to the position marked. Torque the ball stud nuts to 30 ft. lbs. for 1987–88 or 35 ft. lbs. for 1989–91.

BRAKES

For all brake system repair and service procedures not detailed below, please refer to "Brakes" in the Unit Repair section.

Master Cylinder

REMOVAL & INSTALLATION

NOTE: Be sure the area where the master cylinder is mounted is clean, before beginning removal.

1. Disconnect and cap or plug hydraulic lines. Disconnect the electrical lead, if equipped.

2. On non-power brakes, disconnect the pushrod at the brake pedal.

3. Remove the attaching bolts and master cylinder.

4. Install in the reverse order of removal. Fill with fluid and bleed.

Powermaster

REMOVAL & INSTALLATION

Regal
1987

1. Depessurize the Powermaster unit as follows:

   a. With the ignition **OFF**, apply and release the brake pedal a minimum of 10 times usuing approximately 50 lbs. force on the pedal.

2. Disconnect the negative battery cable.

3. Disconnect the electrical connector from the pressure switch.

4. Disconnect the electrical connector from the electro-hydraulic pump.

5. Disconnect the brake pipes from the powermaster unit.

6. Remove the 2 attaching nuts, disconnect the pushrod from the brake pedal and remove the powermaster unit.

To install:

7. Install the powermaster unit and pushrod and tighten the attaching nuts to 22–30 ft. lbs.

8. Tighten the brake pipe nuts to 120–180 inch lbs.

9. Reconnect the electrical connectors.

Combination Valve

REMOVAL & INSTALLATION

1. Remove the electrical wire connector from the pressure differential switch.

2. Disconnect the hydraulic lines at the combination valve.

3. Plug the lines to prevent loss of fluid and entrance of dirt.

4. Remove the combination valve.

5. Installation is the reverse of the removal procedure. Bleed the entire brake system.

Power Brake Booster

REMOVAL & INSTALLATION

1. Remove the 2 nuts holding the master cylinder to the power unit. Carefully position the master cylinder out of the way, being careful not to kink any of the hydraulic lines. It is not necessary to disconnect the brake lines.

2. Disconnect the vacuum hose from the vacuum check valve on the front housing. Plug the hose. Plug the lines immediately.

3. Loosen the 4 nuts that hold the power unit mounted on the firewall.

4. Disconnect the pushrod from the brake pedal. Do not force the pushrod to the side when disconnecting.

5. Remove the 4 mounting nuts and lift the power unit off the studs.

6. Installation is in the reverse order of removal. Torque the master cylinder-to-power brake unit mounting studs to specifications. Refill power steering pump reservoir.

Brake Caliper

REMOVAL & INSTALLATION

1. Remove ⅔ of the brake fluid from the master cylinder.

2. Raise the vehicle and support it safely.

3. Remove the tire and wheel assembly.

4. Position a C-clamp over the outboard shoe and lining and the caliper housing and bottom the piston into the caliper bore.

NOTE: If removing the caliper assembly only to access other brake parts go to Step 5. If removing the caliper from the vehicle the brake system will have to be bled.

5. Remove the bolt copper washers and inlet fitting from the caliper housing and plug to prevent fluid loss and contamination.

6. Remove the mounting bolts and the sleeves and remove the caliper from the rotor.

7. Installation is the reverse of removal. Tighten the mounting bolts to 38 ft. lbs.

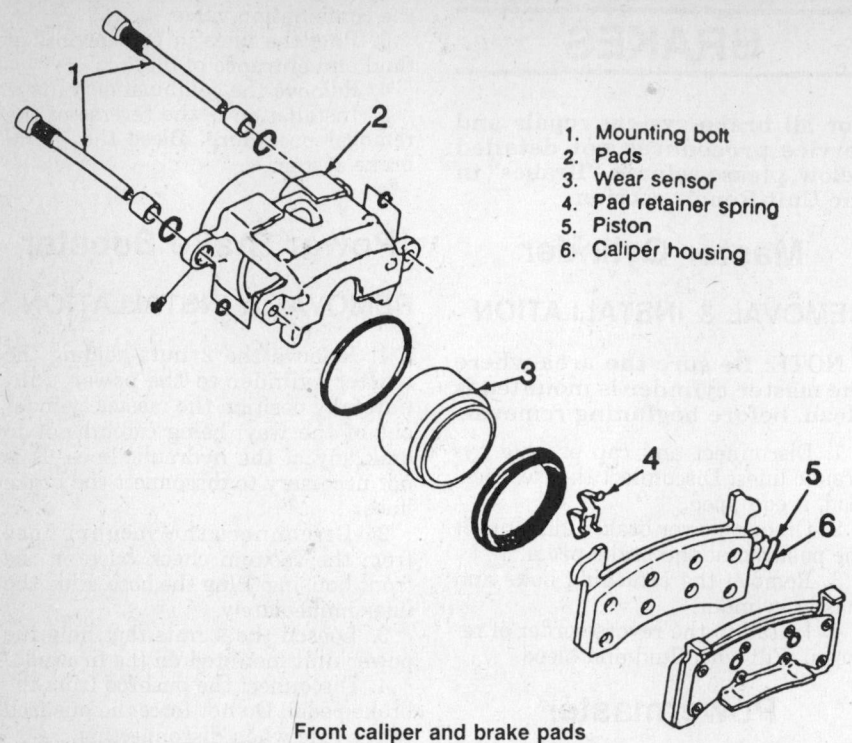

1. Mounting bolt
2. Pads
3. Wear sensor
4. Pad retainer spring
5. Piston
6. Caliper housing

Front caliper and brake pads

Disc Brake Pads

REMOVAL & INSTALLATION

1. Raise the vehicle and support it safely.
2. Remove the tire and wheel assembly.
3. Remove the caliper assembly and suspend it from the front suspension using a fabricated wire hanger.
4. Remove the inner and outer brake pads from the caliper.
5. Remove the bushings from the grooves in the caliper housing.
6. Remove the shoe retainer spring from the inboard pad.

To install

7. Lubricate new bushings and sleeves with silicone grease.
8. Install the bushings in the grooves in the caliper housing.
9. Install the shoe retainer spring on the inboard pad.
10. Install the inboard pad. Be sure to seat the shoe retainer spring in the piston.

NOTE: The wear sensor should be at the leading edge of the inboard pad during forward wheel rotation.

11. Install the outboard pad.
12. Install the caliper assembly.
13. Apply the brake pedal 3 times to seat the pads.

Brake Rotor

REMOVAL & INSTALLATION

1. Disconnect the negative battery cable.
2. Raise and support the vehicle safely.
3. Disconnect the ABS wheel speed sensor from the steering knuckle and secure, on vehicles with anti-lock brakes.
4. Remove the brake caliper.
5. Remove the dust cap from the

hub then remove the cotter pin, nut and washer from the spindle. Carefully remove the hub and rotor from the spindle.

6. Installation is the reverse of removal. Initially torque the wheel hub spindle nut to 12 ft. lbs. while turning the wheel forward by hand. Install the ABS wheel sensor, if equipped.

Brake Drums

REMOVAL & INSTALLATION

1. Raise and support the vehicle safely.
2. Mark the relationship of the wheel to the axle flange and remove the wheel.
3. Make sure the parking brake is released and remove the adjusting hole or knockout plate from the backing plate and back off the adjusting screw with a suitable tool.
4. Use a rubber mallet to tap gently on the outer rim of the drum and/or the inner drum diameter by the spindle and remove the drum.
5. Installation is the reverse of removal. Adjust the parking brake and brakes, as necessary.

Brake Shoes

REMOVAL & INSTALLATION

1. Raise the vehicle and support it safely.
2. Remove the tire and wheel assembly.
3. Remove the brake drum. If the brake drum cannot be removed, try the following:
   a. Make sure the parking brake is released.

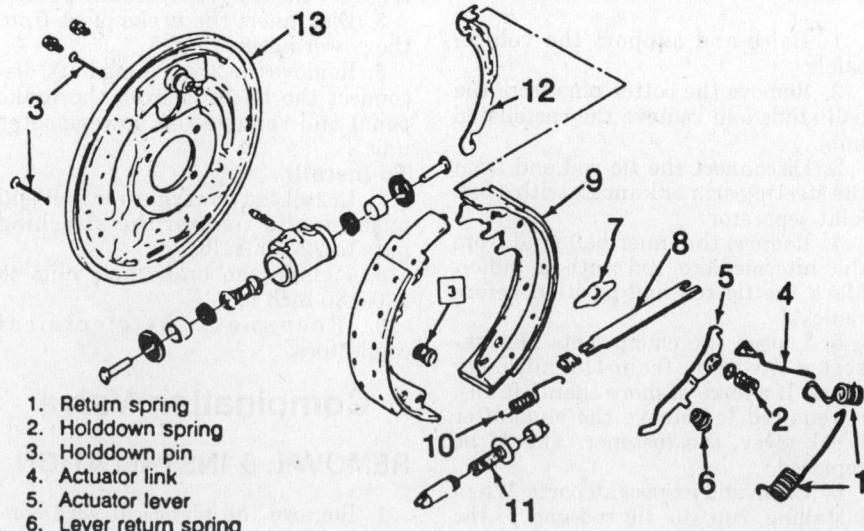

1. Return spring
2. Holddown spring
3. Holddown pin
4. Actuator link
5. Actuator lever
6. Lever return spring
7. Shoe guide
8. Parking brake strut
9. Brake shoes

Rear drum brakes

b. Back off the parking brake cable adjustment.

c. Remove the adjusting hole knockout plate from the backing plate and back off the adjusting screw.

d. Use a rubber mallet to tap on the outer rim of the drum and around the inner drum diameter by the spindle.

4. Remove the return springs.

5. Remove the hold-down springs and hold-down pins.

6. Remove the actuator lever pivot.

7. Lift up on the actuator lever to remove the actuator link. Remove the lever and the return spring.

8. Remove the shoe guide and the parking brake strut and spring.

9. Remove the brake shoes from the backing plate and the parking brake cable.

10. Remove the adjusting screw assembly and spring from the brake shoes.

11. Remove the parking brake lever by unhooking the lever tab from the slot in the brake shoe.

12. Clean the backing plate and lubricate the shoe pads.

13. Clean the adjusting screw and lubricate the screw threads for smooth rotation over the full length.

14. Install in the reverse order of removal.

15. Adjust the brake shoes. The outside diameter of both shoe and linings should be 0.050 in. (1.27mm) less than the inside diameter of the brake drum on each wheel.

Wheel Cylinder

REMOVAL & INSTALLATION

1. Raise the vehicle and support it safely.

2. Remove the wheel and brake drum.

3. Clean dirt and foreign material from around wheel cylinder assembly.

4. Disconnect the inlet tube nut and line from the cylinder.

5. Plug the opening in the line to prevent fluid loss or contamination.

6. Remove the cylinder to shoe links.

7. Remove the 2 attaching bolts and the cylinder assembly.

8. Installation is the reverse of the removal procedure. Bleed the wheel cylinder.

Parking Brake Cable

ADJUSTMENT

1. Apply the parking brake exactly 2 clicks, then raise and support the vehicle safely.

2. Loosen the locknut at the rear of the equalizer adjusting nut. Tighten the adjusting nut until the rear wheels can barely be turned backward, using 2 hands, but lock up when moved forward. Rear disc brakes will not lock up but will have a drag. Tighten the nut against the adjusting nut.

3. With the parking brake disengaged the rear wheel should turn freely in either direction with no brake drag.

REMOVAL & INSTALLATION

Front

1. Raise the vehicle and support it safely.

2. Loosen adjuster nut and disconnect the cable from the connector. Loosen the retainer at the frame.

3. Lower the vehicle.

4. Remove the lower rear bolt from the wheel house panel and pull the panel out to gain access to the front cable.

5. Disconnect the cable from the parking brake pedal assembly and remove the cable.

6. Installation is the reverse of removal procedure. Adjust the parking brake.

Rear

1. Raise the vehicle and support it safely.

2. Remove the adjuster nut, compress the retainer fingers and loosen the cable from all retainers. On the left side remove the cable from the equalizer.

3. Mark the relationship of the wheel to the axle flange and remove the tire and wheel assembly.

4. Remove the brake drum, the primary shoe return spring and the parking brake strut. On the right side also remove the secondary shoe hold-down spring.

5. Compress the retainer fingers and loosen the cable from the backing plate. Disconnect the cable from the parking brake lever and remove the cable.

6. Installation is the reverse of removal procedure. Adjust the parking brake.

Brake System Bleeding

The brake system must be bled when any brake line is disconnected or there is air in the system.

NOTE: Never bleed a wheel cylinder when a drum is removed.

1. Clean the master cylinder of excess dirt and remove the cylinder cover and the diaphragm.

2. Fill the master cylinder to the proper level. Check the fluid level periodically during the bleeding process and replenish it, as necessary. Do not allow the master cylinder fall below ½ full.

3. If the master cylinder is suspected or known to have air in the bore, bleed it before any wheel cylinder or caliper as follows:

a. Disconnect the forward brake line connection at the master cylinder.

b. Allow brake fluid to fill the master cylinder bore until it begins to flow from the forward line connector port.

c. Connect the forward brake line to the master cylinder and tighten.

d. Have a helper depress the brake pedal slowly one at a time and hold. Loosen the forward brake line connection at the master cylinder to purge the air from the bore. Tighten the connection and then have a helper release the brake pedal slowly. Wait 15 seconds and repeat the sequence. Repeat the sequence including the 15 second wait until all air is removed from the bore.

e. After all air is removed at the forward connection, repeat the above procedure for the rear connection at the master cylinder.

4. Bleed the individual wheel cylinders or calipers only after all air is removed from the master cylinder.

a. Attach the proper size box end wrench over the bleeder valve.

b. Attach a length of vinyl hose to the bleeder screw of the brake to be bled. Insert the other end of the hose into a clear jar half full of clean brake fluid, so the end of the hose is beneath the level of fluid. The correct sequence for bleeding is to work from the brake farthest from the master cylinder to the one closest; right rear, left rear, right front, left front.

5. Have an assistant depress and release the brake pedal one time and hold. Loosen the bleeder valve to purge the air from the cylinder. Tighten the bleeder screw and slowly release the pedal and wait 15 seconds. Repeat the sequence including the 15 second wait until all air is removed.

NOTE: Make sure an assistant presses the brake pedal to the floor slowly. Rapid pumping of the brake pedal pushes the master cylinder secondary piston down the bore in a way that makes it difficult to bleed the rear side of the system.

6. Repeat this procedure at each of the brakes. Remember to check the master cylinder level occasionally. Use only fresh fluid to refill the master cylinder, not the stuff bled from the system.

7. When the bleeding process is complete, refill the master cylinder, install its cover and diaphragm and discard the fluid bled from the brake system.

Anti-Lock Brake System Service

PRECAUTION

Failure to observe the following precautions may result in system damage.

• Before performing electric arc welding on the vehicle, disconnect the Electronic Brake Control Module (EBCM) and the hydraulic modulator connectors.

• When performing painting work on the vehicle, do not expose the Electronic Brake Control Module (EBCM) to temperatures in excess of 185°F (85°C) for longer than 2 hrs. The system may be exposed to temperatures up to 200°F (95°C) for less than 15 min.

• Never disconnect or connect the Electronic Brake Control Module (EBCM) or hydraulic modulator connectors with the ignition switch ON.

• Never disassemble any component of the Anti-Lock Brake System (ABS) which is designated non-servicable; the component must be replaced as an assembly.

• When filling the master cylinder, always use Delco Supreme 11 brake fluid or equivalent, which meets DOT-3 specifications; petroleum base fluid will destroy the rubber parts.

Modulator Valve

REMOVAL & INSTALLATION

— CAUTION —

The modulator is not repairable and no screws on the modulator may be loosened. If the screws are loosened, it will not be possible to to get the brake circuits leak-tight and personal injury injury may result.

1. Disconnect the negative battery cable.

2. Remove the air intake duct and resonator and move the upper coolant hose out of the way.

3. Disconnect the canister purge line at the canister and move out of the way.

4. Remove the retaining screw and remove the modulator valve cover.

5. Unlock the tab and disconnect the modulator valve electrical connector.

6. Remove the nut and disconnect the ground wire from the modulator.

7. Note the locations then disconnect the hydraulic brake pipes from the modulator.

— CAUTION —

If brake pipes are switched (inlet vs. outlet) wheel lockup will occur and personal injury may result.

8. Remove the 3 nuts retaining the modulator to the bracket.

9. Remove the insulators from the modulator valve.

To install:

10. Install the insulators to the modulator valve.

11. Install the modulator valve to the bracket and tighten the 3 nuts to 89 inch lbs.

12. Connect the hydraulic brake pipes to their original locations in the modulator and tighten to 11 ft. lbs.

— CAUTION —

If brake pipes are switched (inlet vs. outlet) wheel lockup will occur and personal injury may result.

13. Install the ground wire and nut to the modulator.

14. Install the modulator valve electrical connector.

15. Install the the modulator valve cover with the retaining screw.

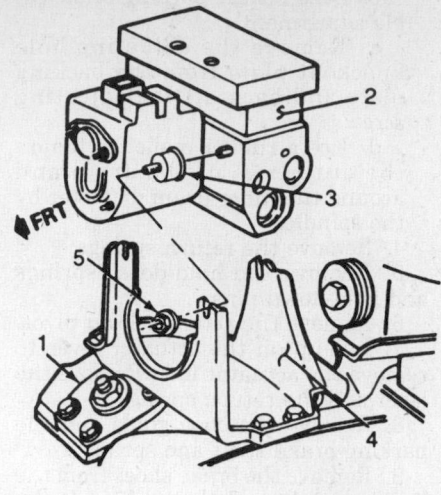

1. Steering gear
2. Hydraulic modulator valve
3. Insulator
4. Bracket
5. Nut

Hydraulic modulator valve removal

16. Connect the canister purge line to the canister.

17. Install the air intake duct and resonator and move the upper coolant hose into position.

18. Connect the negative battery cable.

19. Use only DOT 3 hydraulic brake fluid, fill and bleed the brake system.

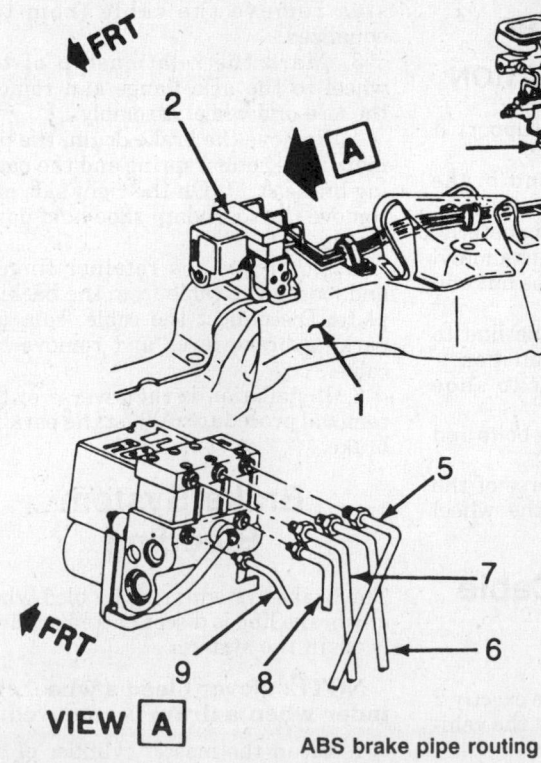

1. Left front frame rail
2. Hydraulic modulator valve
3. Master cylinder
4. Combination valve
5. Rear brake pipe
6. Right front brake pipe
7. Left front brake pipe
8. Rear modulator valve brake pipe
9. Front modulator valve brake pipe

ABS brake pipe routing

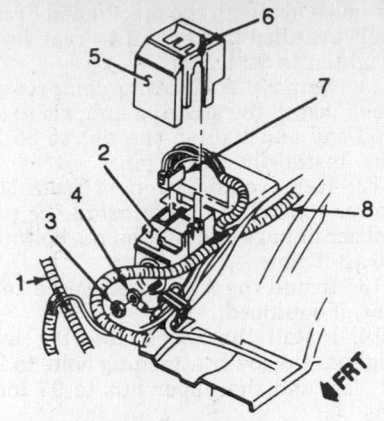

1. Forward lamp harness
2. Hydraulic modulator valve
3. Nut
4. Ground wire
5. Modulator valve cover
6. Screw
7. Modulator valve electrical connector
8. ABS wiring harness

Hydraulic modulator valve electrical connections

Electronic Brake Control Module

REMOVAL & INSTALLATION

1. Disconnect the negative battery cable.
2. Move rear carpet out of the way.
3. Remove the EBCM from its retaining bracket.
4. Installation is the reverse of the removal procedure.

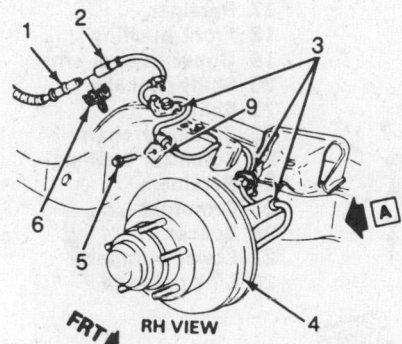

1. ABS lead (part of forward lamp harness)
2. Sensor assembly connector
3. Bracket
4. Steering knuckle assembly
5. Bolt
6. Clip
7. Wheel speed sensor
8. Bolt
9. Bracket

Front wheel speed sensor mounting

Front Wheel Speed Sensor

REMOVAL & INSTALLATION

1. Disconnect the negative battery cable.
2. For the right side speed sensor, unclip the connectors from the clip and separate.
3. For the left side speed sensor, raise and support the vehicle safely, then unclip the connectors from the clip and separate.
4. Remove the sensor wiring harness mounting bolt from the frame rail.
5. Remove the sensor retaining bolt and remove the sensor from the knuckle assembly.

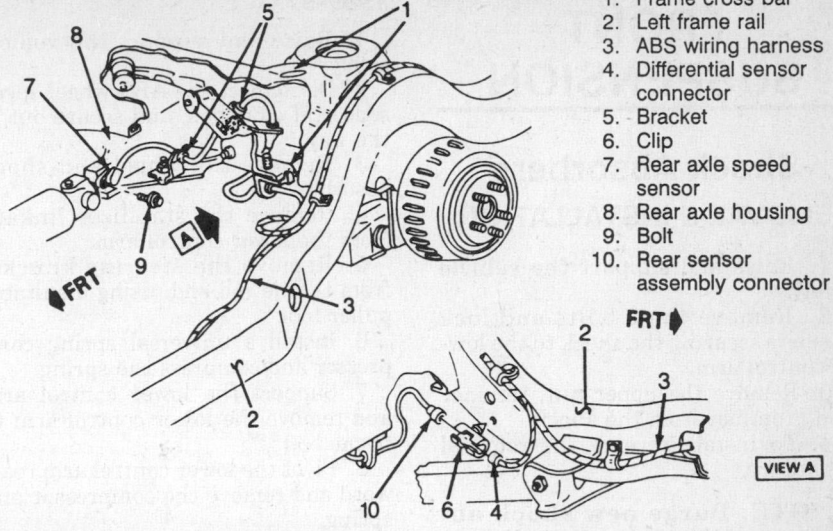

1. Frame cross bar
2. Left frame rail
3. ABS wiring harness
4. Differential sensor connector
5. Bracket
6. Clip
7. Rear axle speed sensor
8. Rear axle housing
9. Bolt
10. Rear sensor assembly connector

Rear wheel speed sensor mounting

6. Installation is the reverse of the removal procedure. Sensor retaining bolt torque is 71 inch lbs. Be sure to coat the sensor body, where it comes in contact with the knuckle with anti corrosion compound GM part number 1052856 or equivalent.

NOTE: Proper installation of the wheel speed sensor cables is critical to proper operation of the ABS system. Make sure the cables are installed in the retainers. Failure to do this may result in contact with moving parts and the over extension of the cables, resulting in an open circuit.

Rear Axle Speed Sensor

REMOVAL & INSTALLATION

1. Disconnect the negative battery cable. Raise and support the vehicle safely.
2. Disconnect the rear sensor assembly from the differential sensor connector.
3. Remove the sensor wiring harness from the retainer brackets.
4. Remove the sensor retaining bolt and remove the speed sensor from the rear axle housing.
5. Installation is the reverse of the removal procedure. Sensor retaining bolt torque is 71 inch lbs.

NOTE: Proper installation of the wheel speed sensor cables is critical to proper operation of the ABS system. Make sure the cables are installed in the retainers. Failure to do this may result in contact with moving parts and the over extension of the cables, resulting in an open circuit.

FRONT SUSPENSION

Shock Absorbers

REMOVAL & INSTALLATION

1. Raise and support the vehicle safely.
2. Remove the 2 bolts and lock washers securing the shock to the lower control arm.
3. Remove the upper nut, retainer and grommet from the shock.
4. To install, reverse the removal procedure.

NOTE: Purge new shock absorbers of air by repeatedly extending in their normal position and compressing while inverted.

Coil Spring

REMOVAL & INSTALLATION

1987–88

1. Raise and support the vehicle safely.
2. Disconnect the shock absorber from the lower control arm and push the shock up into the spring.
3. Install a safety chain around the spring and control arm.
4. While the vehicle is supported so the control arms hang free, place the spring removal/installer tool into position cradling the inner bushings. The tool should be bolted to a suitable floor jack.
5. Remove the stabilizer to the lower control arm attachment.
6. Raise the jack to remove the tension on the lower control arm pivot bolts. Remove the nuts and bolts. Remove the rear bolt first.
7. Lower the control arm by slowly lowering the jack.
8. When the tension is released from the spring, remove the chain and spring.
To install:
9. Properly position the spring onto the lower control arm, using installer tool.
10. Position the control arm into the frame and install the pivot bolts. Front bolt installed from front to rear first.
11. Torque the lower control arm nuts to 92 ft. lbs., except Monte Carlo and 65 ft. lbs. for Monte Carlo.
12. Lower the jack and install the stabilizer bar link and tighten the bolt to 15 ft. lbs.
13. Install the shock absorber and tighten the lower bolts to 20 ft. lbs.
14. Lower the vehicle.

1989–91

1. Raise and support the vehicle safely.
2. Disconnect the ABS wheel speed sensor, if equipped, and secure out of the way.
3. Remove the wheel and shock absorber.
4. Remove the stabilizer linkage from the lower control arm.
5. Remove the steering knuckle from the tie rod end, using a suitable puller tool.
6. Install a universal spring compressor and compress the spring.
7. Support the lower control arm and remove the lower control arm to frame bolts.
8. Pivot the lower control arm rearward and remove the compressor and spring.
To install:
9. Properly position the spring onto the lower control arm, using spring compressor tool.
10. Position the control arm into the frame and install the pivot bolts. Front bolt installed from front to rear first. Tighten to 92 ft. lbs.
11. Remove the spring compressor tool, install the steering knuckle to tie rod end and tighten the nut to 35 ft. lbs. Install the cotter pin.
12. Remove the support from the lower control arm and install the stabilizer linkage and tighten the bolt/nut to 13 ft. lbs.
13. Install the ABS wheel speed sensor, if equipped.
14. Install the shock absorber and tighten the lower attaching bolts to 20 ft. lbs. and the upper nut to 97 inch lbs.
15. Install the wheel and lower the vehicle. Tighten the wheel lug nuts to 100 ft. lbs.

Torsion Bars

REMOVAL & INSTALLATION

1. Raise the vehicle and support it safely.

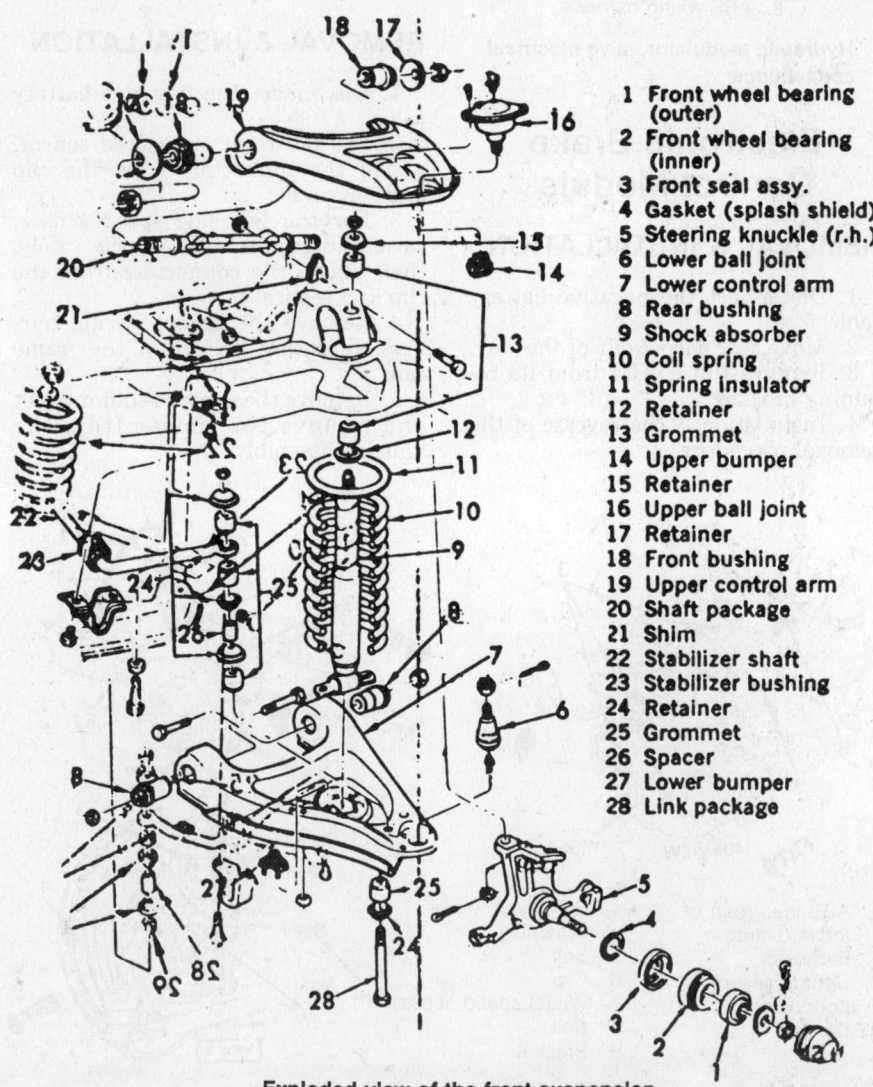

1 Front wheel bearing (outer)
2 Front wheel bearing (inner)
3 Front seal assy.
4 Gasket (splash shield)
5 Steering knuckle (r.h.)
6 Lower ball joint
7 Lower control arm
8 Rear bushing
9 Shock absorber
10 Coil spring
11 Spring insulator
12 Retainer
13 Grommet
14 Upper bumper
15 Retainer
16 Upper ball joint
17 Retainer
18 Front bushing
19 Upper control arm
20 Shaft package
21 Shim
22 Stabilizer shaft
23 Stabilizer bushing
24 Retainer
25 Grommet
26 Spacer
27 Lower bumper
28 Link package

Exploded view of the front suspension

2. Disconnect each side of the torsion bar by removing the nut from the link bolt. Pull the bolt from the linkage and remove retainers, grommets and spacer.

3. Remove bracket to frame or body bolts and remove torsion bar, rubber bushings and brackets.

4. Installation is the reverse of the removal procedure. Install the torsion bar with the identification forming on the right side of the vehicle and the slit in the rubber bushings facing the front of the vehicle.

5. Tighten torsion bar link nut to 13 ft. lbs. (18 Nm) and the bracket bolts to 24 ft. lbs. (33 Nm).

Upper Ball Joints

INSPECTION

1. Raise the vehicle and position floor stands under the left and right lower control arm as near as possible to each lower ball joint. Upper control arm bumper must not contact frame.

2. Position a dial indicator against the wheel rim.

3. Grasp the front wheel and push in on bottom of the tire while pulling out at the top. Read the gauge, then reverse the push–pull procedure. Horizontal deflection on the dial indicator should not exceed 1.25 in. (3.18mm).

4. If the indicator exceeds 1.25 in. (3.18mm) or if ball stud, when disconnected from the knuckle assembly, can be twisted in its socket by hand, replace the ball joint.

REMOVAL & INSTALLATION

1. Raise and safely support the vehicle; place floor stands under the lower control arm between the spring seats and the ball joints.

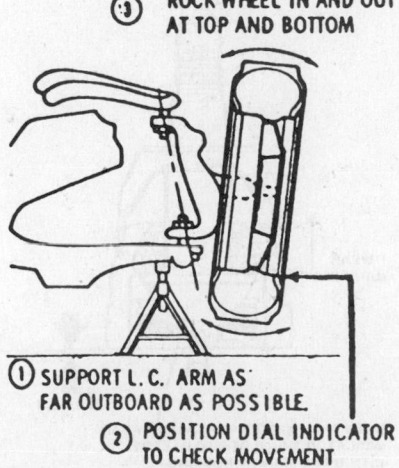

① SUPPORT L.C. ARM AS FAR OUTBOARD AS POSSIBLE.
② POSITION DIAL INDICATOR TO CHECK MOVEMENT AT THIS POINT
Checking the upper ball joint

NOTE: Leave the jack under the spring seat during removal and installation, in order to keep the spring and control arm positioned.

2. Remove the wheel.

3. Remove the cotter pin from the upper ball joint stud and loosen the upper ball joint nut.

4. Using a ball joint remover tool, break the stud loose and remove the nut and pull the stud out of the knuckle. Support the steering knuckle to prevent damage to the brake line.

5. Using a ⅛ in. diameter drill bit, drill into each of the 4 rivet heads to a depth of ½ in.

6. Drill off the rivet heads with a ½ in. diameter bit.

7. Punch out the rivets and remove the ball joint.

8. To install, place the new ball joint in the upper control arm and secure it with 4 bolts and nuts in place of rivets. Torque the nuts to specifications.

9. Connect the ball joint to steering knuckle. Torque the nut to specifications.

NOTE: When replacing ball joints, use only high-quality replacement parts and bolts and nuts specified to be strong enough to endure the stress. Always advance the ball stud nut to align the cotter pin hole.

10. Install the grease fitting and lubricate until grease appears at the seal.

11. Install the wheel.

Lower Ball Joints

INSPECTION

These lower ball joints contain a visual wear indicator. The lower ball joint grease plug screws into the wear indi-

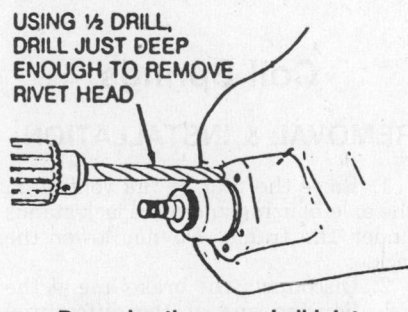

USING ½ DRILL, DRILL JUST DEEP ENOUGH TO REMOVE RIVET HEAD
Removing the upper ball joint

cator which protrudes from the bottom of the ball joint housing. As long as the wear indicator extends out of the ball joint housing, the ball joint is not worn. If the tip of the wear indicator is parallel with or recessed into the

ball joint housing, the ball joint is defective.

REMOVAL & INSTALLATION

1. Raise the vehicle and support the frame safely.

2. Remove the tire and wheel.

3. Place a floor jack under the control arm spring seat.

NOTE: Leave the jack under the spring seat during removal and installation, in order to keep the spring and control arm positioned.

4. Remove the cotter pin from the ball joint stud. Using a ball joint stud removal tool, separate the ball joint from the steering knuckle.

5. When the stud comes loose, remove the stud nut.

6. Guide the lower control arm through the opening in the splash shield using a suitable tool.

7. Block the steering knuckle out of the way by using a block of wood between the frame and the upper control arm.

8. Pry the retainer off the ball joint seal with a drift pin and remove the seal.

9. Using a ball joint remover, remove the lower ball joint from the control arm.

10. Press in a new ball joint until it bottoms on the lower control arm.

NOTE: On disc brake vehicles, make sure the grease purge on the seal faces away from the brakes.

11. Assemble the suspension and torque the nut to specifications. Install the cotter pin and bend it to the side, not over the top of the nut. The cotter pin on the Cutlass must be installed parallel to the center line of the vehicle.

12. Install the ball joint fitting and lube until grease appears at the seal.

13. Install the tire and wheel assembly.

Upper Control Arms

REMOVAL & INSTALLATION

1. Raise the vehicle and safely support it between the spring seats and the ball joints of the lower control arms.

2. Remove the tire and wheel assembly.

3. Place a floor jack under the lower control arm spring seat.

NOTE: Leave the floor jack under the spring seat during removal and installation, in order to keep the spring and control arm positioned.

4. Remove the ball joint from the steering knuckle. Support the hub assembly to prevent damage to the brake line.

5. Loosen pivot shaft to frame nuts and remove alignment shims. Remove the bolts to allow clearance and remove the control arm assembly from the vehicle.

6. Installation is the reverse of the removal procedure. Install alignment shims in the same position from which they were removed and tighten all bolts to specifications. Check the wheel alignment.

Lower Control Arm
REMOVAL & INSTALLATION

1. Loosen the wheel nuts. Raise and support the vehicle safely. Remove the wheel.

2. Remove the front coil spring and the lower ball joint.

3. Remove the lower control arm.

4. Installation is the reverse of removal. Torque the lower control arm to frame bolts to 90–92 ft. lbs. except Monte Carlo or 65 ft. lbs. for the Monte Carlo. Torque at curb height. Torque the lower ball joint to knuckle nut to 83 ft. lbs.

Front Wheel Bearings
ADJUSTMENT

1. Raise the vehicle so the wheel can spin freely. Remove the dust cap.

2. Tighten the adjusting nut to 12 ft. lbs. (16 Nm) while turning the wheel, this will seat the bearings and remove any burrs on the threads.

3. Back off the nut until it is just loose.

4. Finger tighten the nut and install the cotter pin or the retaining ring.

NOTE: If the cotter pin cannot be installed, back off the nut until the slot aligns with the serrations on the nut. Do not back off the nut more than ¼ of a turn.

5. Once adjusted, the front wheel bearings should have 0.001–0.005 in. (0.03–0.13mm) endplay.

REMOVAL & INSTALLATION

1. Remove the caliper and hub assembly.

2. Remove the outer roller bearing assembly.

3. Pry the seal from the hub, then remove the inner roller bearing assembly.

4. If necessary, remove the inner bearing outer race using tool J–29117.

5. To remove outer bearing outer race, insert a brass drift into hub, indexing end of drift with notches in hub and tap with a hammer.

6. Using clean solvent, clean all old grease from hub, spindle and bearings.

7. If outer races were removed, press the races into the hub using tool J–8092 with J–8850 or J–8457.

8. Pack the bearings with a high temperature wheel bearing grease and reassemble the hub. Install the hub on the steering knuckle and adjust the wheel bearings.

REAR SUSPENSION

Shock Absorbers
REMOVAL & INSTALLATION

NOTE: Purge new shock absorbers of air by repeatedly extending in their normal position and compressing while inverted.

1. Raise the vehicle and support the rear axle housing.

2. Remove the lower shock mounting bolt from the shock absorber eye.

3. Unfasten the upper mounting bracket bolts and remove the shock.

4. Installation is in the reverse order of removal, except that the upper attaching bolts should remain loose while the lower eye is being tightened.

Coil Springs
REMOVAL & INSTALLATION

1. Raise the rear of the vehicle on the axle housing and place jack stands under the frame. Do not lower the jack.

2. Disconnect the brake line at the axle housing and at the differential housing.

3. Disconnect the upper control arms at the differential.

4. Remove the shock absorber lower mount and lower the jack. Be careful not to stretch the brake hose.

5. Remove the spring.

6. Installation is in the reverse order of removal.

Rear Control Arms
REMOVAL & INSTALLATION
Upper Arm

NOTE: If both control arms are to be replaced, remove and replace one control arm at a time to prevent the axle from rolling or slipping sideways as this might occur with both upper control arms removed.

1. Remove the nut from the rear arm to rear axle housing bolt and while rocking axle, remove the bolt.

2. Remove front and rear arm attaching nuts and bolts.

3. Remove the suspension arm and inspect the bushing for damage.

4. Installation is the reverse of the removal procedure. Torque nuts to specifications.

Lower Arm

1. Raise the vehicle and support it under the axle housing.

2. Remove the rear arm to axle housing bracket bolt.

3. Remove the front arm to bracket bolts and remove the lower control arm.

4. Installation is the reverse of the removal procedure. Torque nuts to specifications.

Rear Wheel Bearings

For all rear wheel bearing removal and installation procedures, refer to Drive Axle section.

Rear Axle Assembly

For rear axle removal and installation procedures, refer to Drive Axle section.

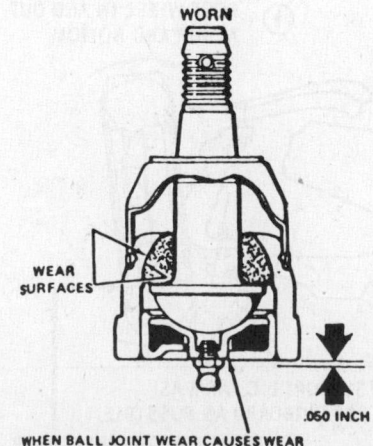

Lower ball joint wear indicator

Cadillac
Rear Wheel Drive
Brougham

15

SPECIFICATIONS

VEHICLE IDENTIFICATION CHART

It is important for servicing and ordering parts to be certain of the vehicle and engine identification. The VIN (vehicle identification number) is a 17 digit number visible through the windshield on the driver's side of the dash and contains the vehicle and engine identification codes. The tenth digit indicates model year and the eighth digit indicates engine code. It can be interpreted as follows:

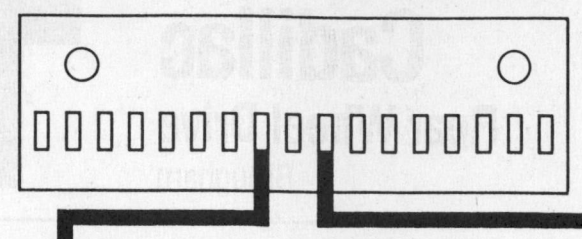

Engine Code

Code	Cu. In.	Liters	Cyl.	Fuel Sys.	Eng. Mfg.
Y	307	5.0	8	Carburetor	Oldsmobile
7	350	5.7	8	TBI	Chevrolet

Model Year

Code	Year
H	1987
J	1988
K	1989
L	1990
M	1991

ENGINE IDENTIFICATION

Year	Model	Engine Displacement cu. in. (liter)	Engine Series Identification (VIN)	No. of Cylinders	Engine Type
1987	Brougham	8-307 (5.0)	Y	8	OHV
1988	Brougham	8-307 (5.0)	Y	8	OHV
1989	Brougham	8-307 (5.0)	Y	8	OHV
1990-91	Brougham	8-307 (5.0)	Y	8	OHV
	Brougham	8-350 (5.7)	7	8	OHV

GENERAL ENGINE SPECIFICATIONS

Year	VIN	No. Cylinder Displacement cu. in. (liter)	Fuel System Type	Net Horsepower @ rpm	Net Torque @ rpm (ft. lbs.)	Bore × Stroke (in.)	Compression Ratio	Oil Pressure @ rpm
1987	Y	8-307 (5.0)	4 bbl	140 @ 3200	255 @ 2000	3.800 × 3.385	8.0:1	30 ①
1988	Y	8-307 (5.0)	4 bbl	140 @ 3200	255 @ 2000	3.800 × 3.385	8.0:1	30–45 ①
1989	Y	8-307 (5.0)	4 bbl	140 @ 3200	255 @ 2000	3.800 × 3.385	8.0:1	30–45 ①
1990-91	Y	8-307 (5.0)	4 bbl	140 @ 3200	255 @ 2000	3.800 × 3.385	8.0:1	30–45 ①
	7	8-350 (5.7)	TBI ②	180 @ 4300	240 @ 3200	4.000 × 3.480	9.3:1	18 ③

① @ 1500 rpm
② Throttle Body Injection
③ @ 2000 rpm

GASOLINE ENGINE TUNE-UP SPECIFICATIONS

Year	VIN	No. Cylinder Displacement cu. in. (liter)	Spark Plugs Type	Gap (in.)	Ignition Timing (deg.) MT	AT	Compression Pressure (psi)	Fuel Pump (psi)	Idle Speed (rpm) MT	AT	Valve Clearance In.	Ex.
1987	Y	8-307 (5.0)	FR3LS6	.060	—	20B	NA	5.5–6.5	—	475	Hyd.	Hyd.
1988	Y	8-307 (5.0)	FR3LS6	.060	—	20B	NA	6.0–7.5	—	450	Hyd.	Hyd.
1989	Y	8-307 (5.0)	FR3LS6	.060	—	20B	NA	6.0–7.5	—	450	Hyd.	Hyd.
1990	Y	8-307 (5.0)	R46TSX	.060	—	②	NA	6.0–7.5	—	②	Hyd.	Hyd.
	7	8-350 (5.7)	R45TS	.035	—	②	NA	9.0–13.0	—	②	①	①
1991		SEE UNDERHOOD SPECIFICATIONS STICKER										

① 0.0011–0.0027 inch
② Use date on vehicle emission decal

FIRING ORDERS

NOTE: To avoid confusion, always replace spark plugs and wires one at a time.

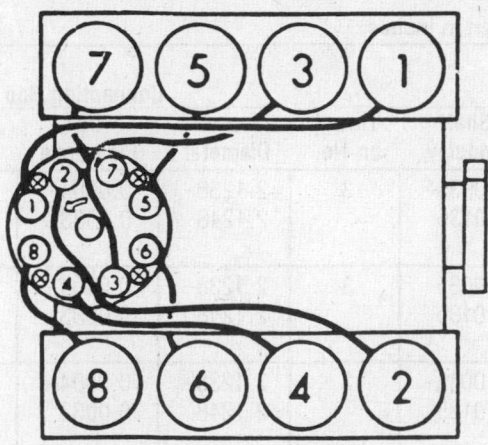

5.0L Engine
Engine Firing Order: 1-8-4-3-6-5-7-2
Distributor Rotation: Counterclockwise

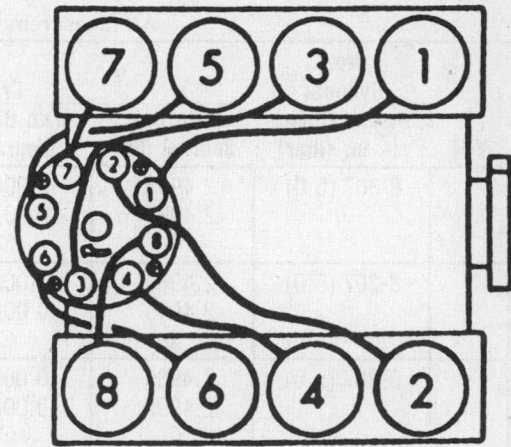

5.7L Engine
Engine Firing Order: 1-8-4-3-6-5-7-2
Distributor Rotation: Clockwise

CAPACITIES

Year	Model	VIN	No. Cylinder Displacement cu. in. (liter)	Engine Crankcase qts. with Filter	without Filter	Transmission (pts.) 4-Spd	5-Spd	Auto.	Drive Axle (pts.)	Fuel Tank (gal.)	Cooling System (qts.)
1987	Brougham	Y	8-307 (5.0)	5.0	4.0	—	—	⑤	3.50	20.7	15.3
1988	Brougham	Y	8-307 (5.0)	5.0	4.0	—	—	⑤	4.25	20.7	15.2 ①
1989	Brougham	Y	8-307 (5.0)	5.0	4.0	—	—	⑤	3.50 ②	20.7	15.2 ①
1990–91	Brougham	Y	8-307 (5.0)	5.5	5.0	—	—	③	⑥	25.0	15.2 ①
	Brougham	7	8-350 (5.7)	5.0	4.0	—	—	④	⑥	25.0	16.5

① Heavy duty—15.6
② Optional 3.23—4.25
③ Pan 6.0, overhaul 20.0
④ Pan 9.0, overhaul 21.0
⑤ Pan 10.6, overhaul 22.0

CAMSHAFT SPECIFICATIONS

All measurements given in inches.

Year	VIN	No. Cylinder Displacement cu. in. (liter)	Journal Diameter 1	2	3	4	5	Lobe Lift In.	Ex.	Bearing Clearance	Camshaft End Play
1987	Y	8-307 (5.0)	2.0352–2.0365	2.0152–2.0166	1.9952–1.9965	1.9752–1.9765	1.9552–1.9565	0.247	0.251	0.0020–0.0058	0.006–0.022
1988	Y	8-307 (5.0)	2.0352–2.0365	2.0152–2.0166	1.9952–1.9965	1.9752–1.9765	1.9552–1.9565	0.247	0.251	0.0020–0.0058	0.006–0.022
1989	Y	8-307 (5.0)	2.0352–2.0365	2.0152–2.0166	1.9952–1.9965	1.9752–1.9765	1.9552–1.9565	0.247	0.251	0.0020–0.0058	0.006–0.022
1990-91	Y	8-307 (5.0)	2.0352–2.0365	2.0152–2.0166	1.9952–1.9965	1.9752–1.9765	1.9552–1.9565	0.247	0.251	0.0020–0.0058	0.006–0.022
	7	8-350 (5.7)	1.8682–1.8692	1.8682–1.8692	1.8682–1.8692	1.8682–1.8692	1.8682–1.8692	NA	NA	NA	0.004–0.012

CRANKSHAFT AND CONNECTING ROD SPECIFICATIONS

All measurements are given in inches.

Year	VIN	No. Cylinder Displacement cu. in. (liter)	Crankshaft Main Brg. Journal Dia.	Main Brg. Oil Clearance	Shaft Endplay	Thrust on No.	Connecting Rod Journal Diameter	Oil Clearance	Side Clearance
1987	Y	8-307 (5.0)	2.4985–2.4995 ②	0.0005–0.0021 ①	0.0035–0.0135	3	2.1238–2.1248	0.0004–0.0033	0.006–0.020
1988	Y	8-307 (5.0)	2.4985–2.4995 ②	0.0005–0.0021 ①	0.0035–0.0135	3	2.1238–2.1248	0.0004–0.0033	0.006–0.020
1989	Y	8-307 (5.0)	2.4985–2.4995 ②	0.0005–0.0021 ①	0.0035–0.0135	3	2.1238–2.1248	0.0004–0.0033	0.006–0.020
1990-91	Y	8-305 (5.0)	2.4985–2.4995 ②	0.0005–0.0021 ①	0.0035–0.0135	3	2.1238–2.1248	0.0004–0.0033	0.006–0.020
	7	8-350 (5.7)	④	③	0.001–0.007	3	0.0013–0.0035	0.006–0.014	NA

① No. 5—0.0015–0.0031
② No. 1—2.4988–2.4998
③ No. 1—0.0008–0.0020
No. 2-No. 4—0.0011–0.0020
No. 5—0.0017–0.0032
④ No. 1—2.4488–2.4493
No. 2-No. 4—2.4481–2.4490
No. 5—2.4481–2.4488

VALVE SPECIFICATIONS

Year	VIN	No. Cylinder Displacement cu. in. (liter)	Seat Angle (deg.)	Face Angle (deg.)	Spring Test Pressure (lbs.)	Spring Installed Height (in.)	Stem-to-Guide Clearance (in.) Intake	Exhaust	Stem Diameter (in.) Intake	Exhaust
1987	Y	8-307 (5.0)	45 ①	44 ①	180–194 @ 1.27	$1^{43}/_{64}$	0.0010–0.0027	0.0015–0.0032	0.3425–0.3432	0.3420–0.3427
1988	Y	8-307 (5.0)	45 ①	44 ①	180–194 @ 1.27	$1^{43}/_{64}$	0.0010–0.0027	0.0015–0.0032	0.3425–0.3432	0.3420–0.3427
1989	Y	8-307 (5.0)	45 ①	44 ①	180–194 @ 1.27	$1^{43}/_{64}$	0.0010–0.0027	0.0015–0.0032	0.3425–0.3432	0.3420–0.3427

VALVE SPECIFICATIONS

Year	VIN	No. Cylinder Displacement cu. in. (liter)	Seat Angle (deg.)	Face Angle (deg.)	Spring Test Pressure (lbs.)	Spring Installed Height (in.)	Stem-to-Guide Clearance (in.)		Stem Diameter (in.)	
							Intake	Exhaust	Intake	Exhaust
1990–91	Y	8-307 (5.0)	45 ①	44 ①	180–194 @ 1.27	1⁴³/₆₄	0.0010–0.0027	0.0015–0.0032	0.3425–0.3432	0.3420–0.3427
	7	8-350 (5.7)	46	45	194–206 @ 1.25	1²³/₃₂	0.0011–0.0027	0.0011–0.0027	NA	NA

① Exhaust Valve—31° Seat, 30° Face

PISTON AND RING SPECIFICATIONS

All measurements are given in inches.

Year	VIN	No. Cylinder Displacement cu. in. (liter)	Piston Clearance	Ring Gap			Ring Side Clearance		
				Top Compression	Bottom Compression	Oil Control	Top Compression	Bottom Compression	Oil Control
1987	Y	8-307 (5.0)	0.00075–0.00175 ①	0.009–0.019	0.009–0.019	0.015–0.055	0.0018–0.0038	0.0018–0.0038	0.001–0.005
1988	Y	8-307 (5.0)	0.00075–0.00175 ①	0.009–0.019	0.009–0.019	0.015–0.055	0.0018–0.0038	0.0018–0.0038	0.001–0.005
1989	Y	8-307 (5.0)	0.00075–0.00175 ①	0.009–0.019	0.009–0.019	0.015–0.055	0.0018–0.0038	0.0018–0.0038	0.001–0.005
1990–91	Y	8-307 (5.0)	0.00075–0.00175 ①	0.009–0.019	0.009–0.019	0.015–0.055	0.0018–0.0038	0.0018–0.0038	0.001–0.005
	7	8-350 (5.7)	0.0007–0.0021	0.010–0.020	0.010–0.025	0.015–0.055	0.0012–0.0032	0.0012–0.0032	0.002–0.007

① Clearance to bore (selective)

TORQUE SPECIFICATIONS

All readings in ft. lbs.

Year	VIN	No. Cylinder Displacement cu. in. (liter)	Cylinder Head Bolts	Main Bearing Bolts	Rod Bearing Bolts	Crankshaft Pulley Bolts	Flywheel Bolts	Manifold		Spark Plugs
								Intake	Exhaust	
1987	Y	8-307 (5.0)	130 ①	80 ④	48	200–310	60	40 ①	25	25
1988	Y	8-307 (5.0)	130 ①	80 ④	48	200–310	60	40 ①	25	25
1989	Y	8-307 (5.0)	40 ①③	70 ⑥	18 ⑦	255	46	40 ①	25	25
1990–91	Y	8-307 (5.0)	40 ①③	70 ⑥	18 ⑦	255	46	40 ①	25	25
	7	8-350 (5.7)	70	75	44	45	75	35	26 ②	22

① Dip bolt in oil before installation
② Stud 20
③ Rotate bolts 1–7 and 9—120°
  Roate bolts 8 and 10—95°
④ Rear main bearing torque 120
⑥ Rear main bearing torque 105
⑦ Rotate 70°

BRAKE SPECIFICATIONS
All measurements in inches unless noted

Year	Model	Lug Nut Torque (ft. lbs.)	Master Cylinder Bore	Brake Disc Minimum Thickness	Brake Disc Maximum Runout	Standard Brake Drum Diameter	Minimum Lining Thickness Front	Minimum Lining Thickness Rear
1987	Brougham	100	NA	0.980	0.965	11.000	0.030	0.030 ①
1988	Brougham	100	NA	0.980	0.965	11.000	0.030	0.030 ①
1989	Brougham	100	NA	0.980	0.965	11.000	0.030	0.030 ①
1990–91	Brougham	100	NA	0.980	0.965	11.000	0.030	0.030 ①

① Bonded lining 0.062

WHEEL ALIGNMENT

Year	Model	Caster Range (deg.)	Caster Preferred Setting (deg.)	Camber Range (deg.)	Camber Preferred Setting (deg.)	Toe-in (in.)	Steering Axis Inclination (deg.)
1987	Brougham	2P–4P	3P	$3/16$P–$13/16$P	$5/16$P	$3/64$	$10^{19}/32$
1988	Brougham	2P–4P	3P	$3/16$P–$13/16$P	$5/16$P	$3/64$	$10^{19}/32$
1989	Brougham	2P–4P	3P	$3/16$P–$13/16$P	$5/16$P	$3/64$	$10^{19}/32$
1990–91	Brougham	2P–4P	3P	$3/16$P–$13/16$P	$5/16$P	$3/64$	$10^{19}/32$

ENGINE ELECTRICAL

NOTE: Disconnecting the negative battery cable on some vehicles may interfere with the functions of the on board computer systems and may require the computer to undergo a relearning process, once the negative battery cable is reconnected.

Distributor

REMOVAL

1. Disconnect the negative battery cable. Remove the air cleaner assembly, as required. Remove the spark plug wires from the distributor cap.
2. On 5.0L engine, disconnect the coil locking tab connectors. On the 5.7L engine, disconnect the wiring harness connectors at the side of the distributor cap.
3. Remove the distributor cap retaining screws. Remove the distributor cap and position it to the side.
4. On the 5.0L engine, disconnect the 4 terminal ECM harness from the distributor.
5. Remove the distributor assembly retaining bolt.

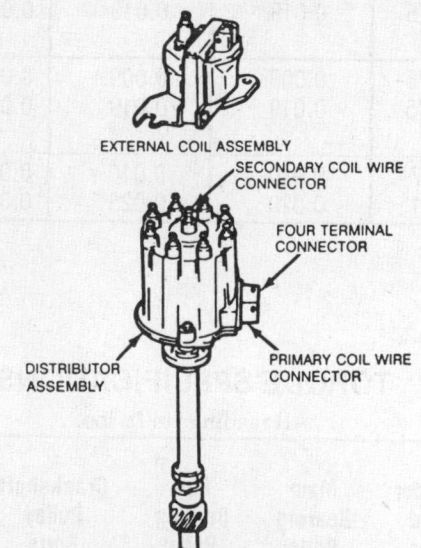

EXTERNAL COIL ASSEMBLY
SECONDARY COIL WIRE CONNECTOR
FOUR TERMINAL CONNECTOR
DISTRIBUTOR ASSEMBLY
PRIMARY COIL WIRE CONNECTOR

Distributor assembly—5.7L engine

6. Note and mark the position of the rotor. Pull the distributor upward until the rotor stops turning and again note the position of the rotor. Remove the distributor assembly from the vehicle.

INSTALLATION

Timing Not Disturbed

1. To install the distributor, position the rotor in the last position as marked and lower the assembly into the distributor bore of the engine. When the distributor rotor stops turning and the unit is seated, the rotor should be pointing to the first mark made.
2. Tighten the distributor retaining bolt.
3. Install the distributor cap. Install the spark plug wires. Connect all required electrical connections.
4. As required, install the air cleaner assembly. Connect the negative battery cable.

Timing Disturbed

1. If the engine has been accidently cranked with the distributor out, remove the No. 1 spark plug. Place a finger over the No. 1 spark plug hole and crank the engine slowly until a compression build up can be felt in that cylinder.
2. Carefully align the timing mark on the crankshaft pulley to the **O** mark on the timing indicator of the engine. Turn the distributor rotor to point between the No. 1 and No. 8 spark plug towers on the distributor cap.
3. To install the distributor, position it as previously marked and lower the assembly into the distributor bore of the engine. When the distributor rotor stops turning and the unit is seated, the rotor should be pointing to No.

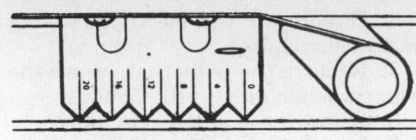

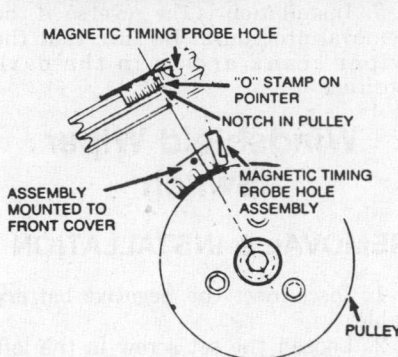

Magnetic timing probe hole location — 250 V8

1 cylinder segment on the distributor cap.

4. Tighten the distributor retaining bolt.

5. Install the distributor cap. Install the spark plug wires. Connect all required electrical connections.

6. As required, install the air cleaner assembly. Connect the negative battery cable.

Ignition Timing

ADJUSTMENT

All engines incorporate a magnetic timing probe hole for use with special electronic timing equipment.

NOTE: Always follow the timing procedures listed on the Emission Control Information Label if they disagree with the following data.

1. Connect a tachometer and a timing light to the engine.

2. Start the engine and operate until normal operating temperature is reached.

3. Turn all accessories **OFF**. Ground the diagnostic terminal of the ALDL terminal using a jumper.

4. Check the ignition timing at the specified rpm. If the ignition timing is not within specification, loosen the distributor clamp bolt and rotate the distributor until the specified timing is obtained.

5. Tighten the distributor clamp bolt making sure the distributor does not change position. Recheck the ignition timing.

6. With the engine still running, remove the jumper from the ALDL terminal.

7. Adjust the carburetor idle speed, as required.

8. Turn the engine **OFF**. Remove the tachometer and timing light.

Alternator

For further information on the charging system, please refer to "Charging and Starting" in the Unit Repair section.

PRECAUTIONS

Several precautions must be observed with alternator equipped vehicles to avoid damage to the unit.

• If the battery is removed for any reason, make sure it is reconnected with the correct polarity. Reversing the battery connections may result in damage to the one-way rectifiers.

• When utilizing a booster battery as a starting aid, always connect the positive to positive terminals and the negative terminal from the booster battery to a good engine ground on the vehicle being started.

• Never use a fast charger as a booster to start vehicles.

• Disconnect the battery cables when charging the battery with a fast charger.

• Never attempt to polarize the alternator.

• Do not use test lamps of more than 12 volts when checking diode continuity.

• Do not short across or ground any of the alternator terminals.

• The polarity of the battery, alternator and regulator must be matched and considered before making any electrical connections within the system.

• Never separate the alternator on an open circuit. Make sure all connections within the circuit are clean and tight.

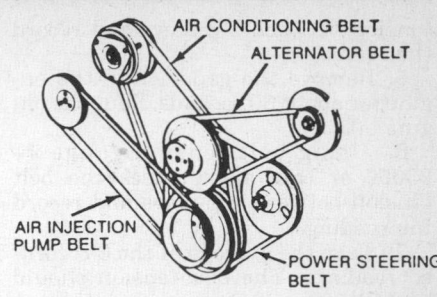

Accessory drive belts — 5.0L engine

• Disconnect the battery ground terminal when performing any service on electrical components.

• Disconnect the battery if arc welding is to be done on the vehicle.

BELT TENSION ADJUSTMENT

5.0L Engine

1. Using belt tension gauge J–23600 or equivalent, adjust the alternator belt if the tension is below 300N, as indicated on the gauge.

2. If the belt is used, the correct belt tension is 500N, as indicated on the gauge. If the belt is new, the correct tension is 700N, as indicated on the gauge.

5.7L Engine

1. Run the engine for about 10 minutes. Shut the engine off.

2. Using belt tension gauge J–23600 or equivalent, check the belt tension between 2 pulleys and record the reading.

3. Remove the gauge. Run the engine for about 30 seconds. Shut the engine off.

4. Using belt tension gauge J–23600 or equivalent, check the belt

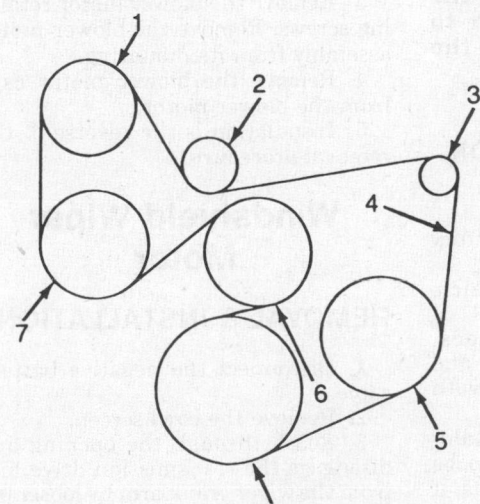

1. Air conditioning compressor belt
2. Drive belt tensioner
3. Alternator pulley
4. Serpentine drive belt
5. Power steering pump pulley
6. Water pump pulley
7. Air injection pump pulley
8. Crankshaft pulley

Accessory drive belt — 5.7L engine

tension between 2 pulleys and record the reading.

5. Remove the gauge. Run the engine for about 30 seconds. Shut the engine off.

6. Using belt tension gauge J-23600 or equivalent, check the belt tension between 2 pulleys and record the reading.

7. Take the average of the 3 recorded readings. The belt tension should be 440–538.

8. Replace the belt tensioner if the belt tension is below specification.

REMOVAL & INSTALLATION

1. Disconnect the negative battery cable.

2. Disconnect the electrical leads from the alternator.

3. Remove the bolt from the alternator adjusting bracket.

4. Remove the bolt from the rear of the alternator. If equipped with shims, save them for reinstallation.

5. Loosen the alternator pivot bolt and remove the drive belt.

6. Loosen the bolts securing the front bracket to the engine.

7. Remove the alternator along with the spacer and lower through bolt.

8. Installation is the reverse of the removal procedure.

Voltage Regulator

For further information on the charging system, please refer to "Charging and Starting" in the Unit Repair section.

Starter

For further information on the charging system, please refer to "Charging and Starting" in the Unit Repair section.

REMOVAL & INSTALLATION

5.0L Engine

1. Disconnect the negative battery cable.

2. Raise and support the vehicle safely.

3. Remove the starter braces, shields, flywheel housing cover and other items that may interfere with the starter removal.

4. Remove the starter motor retaining bolts and allow the starter to be lowered. Remove any starter shims, if equipped.

5. Remove the solenoid wires and the battery cable while supporting the starter. Be sure to note the position of the wires for reinstallation. Remove the starter from the vehicle.

6. Installation is the reverse of the removal procedure. Be sure to reuse the starter shims, if equipped.

5.7L Engine

1. Disconnect the negative battery cable.

2. Raise and support the vehicle safely.

3. Remove the front starter bracket. Disconnect the battery cable and the solenoid wire from the starter assembly.

4. Disconnect the exhaust pipe on the left side. Loosen the exhaust pipe on the right side.

5. Remove the starter retaining bolts. Remove the starter. If equipped, remove the starter shims.

6. Installation is the reverse of the removal procedure. Be sure to use shims, as required.

CHASSIS ELECTRICAL

Heater Blower Motor

REMOVAL & INSTALLATION

1. Disconnect the negative battery cable.

2. Disconnect the electrical connector from the blower motor assembly. Disconnect the ground wire, if equipped. Disconnect the blower motor cooling tube.

3. Remove the blower motor retaining screws. Remove the blower motor assembly from its mounting.

4. Remove the blower motor cage from the blower motor.

5. Installation is the reverse of the removal procedure.

Windshield Wiper Motor

REMOVAL & INSTALLATION

1. Disconnect the negative battery cable.

2. Remove the cowl screen.

3. Reach through the opening and disengage the transmission drive link from the wiper crank arm by loosening the nuts.

4. Disconnect the electrical wiring and washer hoses.

5. Remove the bolts that secure the wiper/washer unit to the firewall.

6. Remove the entire assembly.

7. Installation is the reverse of the removal procedure. Be sure that the wiper crank arm is in the park position.

Windshield Wiper Switch

REMOVAL & INSTALLATION

1. Disconnect the negative battery cable.

2. Loosen the set screw in the left climate control outlet door knob and remove the knob.

3. Remove the left climate control air outlet grille.

4. Remove the left trim plate attaching screws. One screw is located inside the left air conditioning outlet grille opening.

5. Remove the lower steering column cover.

6. Disconnect the steering column seal from lower surface and remove the trim plate.

7. Remove the wiper switch mounting screws. Remove the switch and seperate the electrical connector.

8. Installation is the reverse of the removal procedure.

Instrument Cluster

REMOVAL & INSTALLATION

1. Disconnect the negative battery cable.

2. Remove the instrument panel insert.

3. With the shift lever in the **P** position, remove the shift indicator cable and clip retaining screw from the steering column.

4. Remove the upper and lower cluster assembly retaining screws. Remove the screw directly above the steering column which retains the cluster to the speedometer mounting plate.

5. Pull the cluster outward and disengage the speedometer cable, if equipped. Disconnect all electrical connections.

6. If equipped, disconnect the speed control sensor from the cluster assembly. Disconnect other connectors as required.

7. Place the shift lever in the **L** position and if equipped with tilt wheel, place the wheel in its lowest position. Remove the cluster assembly from the dash.

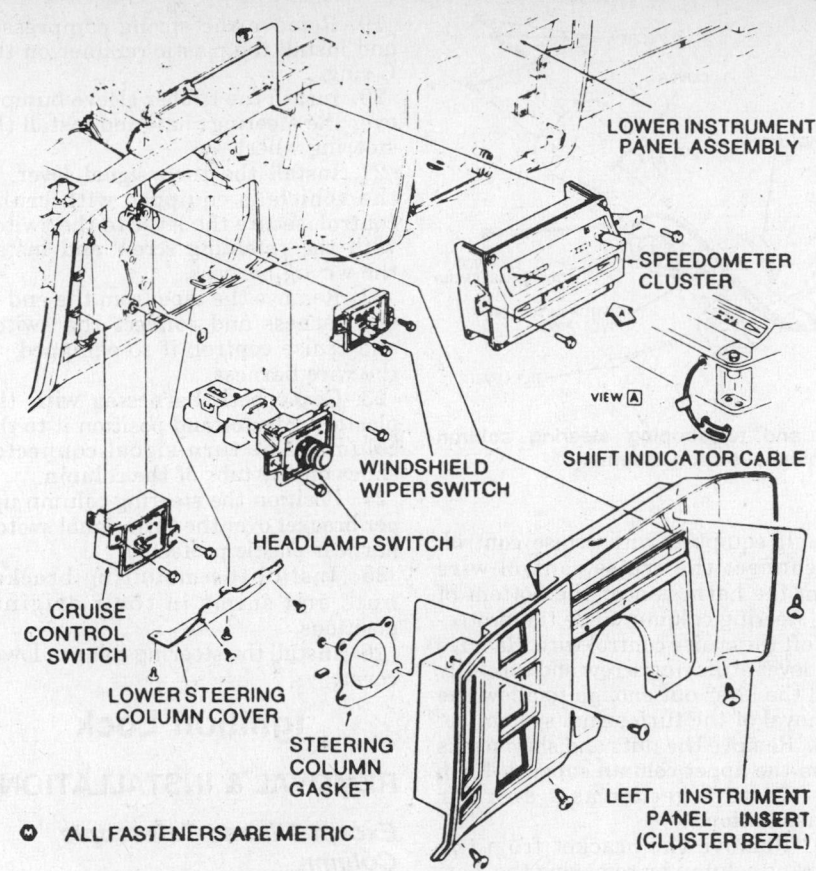

LOWER INSTRUMENT PANEL ASSEMBLY

SPEEDOMETER CLUSTER

VIEW A

SHIFT INDICATOR CABLE

WINDSHIELD WIPER SWITCH

HEADLAMP SWITCH

CRUISE CONTROL SWITCH

LOWER STEERING COLUMN COVER

STEERING COLUMN GASKET

LEFT INSTRUMENT PANEL INSERT (CLUSTER BEZEL)

Ⓜ **ALL FASTENERS ARE METRIC**

Instrument panel and related components

8. Installation is the reverse of the removal procedure. Set the shift, indicator cable in the **N** position and adjust the cable accordingly.

Radio

REMOVAL & INSTALLATION

1. Disconnect the negative battery cable.
2. To remove the center air conditioning outlets on some vehicles it will be necessary to use tool J24612 or equivalent.
3. Remove the center panel retaining screws, once the outlets are removed.
4. Remove the radio assembly retaining knobs, as required.
5. Remove the remaining trim plate screws and remove the trim plate from the vehicle.
6. Remove the radio retaining screws and pull the radio assembly forward. Disconnect the electrical connections. Disconnect the radio antenna. Remove the radio assembly from the vehicle.

7. Installation is the reverse of the removal procedure.

Headlight Switch

REMOVAL & INSTALLATION

1. Disconnect the negative battery cable.
2. Remove the instrument panel insert.
3. Remove the screws securing the switch to the instrument panel.
4. On vehicles equipped with cruise control and twilight sentinel, remove the screws securing the cruise control switch to the instrument panel.
5. Slide the cruise control switch forward to remove the light switch. If equipped, disconnect the 2 piece connector from the headlight switch. Disconnect the guidematic and twilight sentinel electrical connectors from under the instrument panel.
6. Remove the headlight switch retaining screws. Remove the switch assembly from the vehicle.

7. Installation is the reverse of the removal procedure.

Dimmer Switch

REMOVAL & INSTALLATION

1. Disconnect negative battery cable.
2. Remove left sound insulator.
3. Remove 2 nuts securing steering column to upper mounting bracket.
4. Lower steering column and remove 2 screws securing ignition switch and dimmer switch.
5. Disconnect electrical connections and remove switch.
6. Installation is the reverse of the removal procedure. Check the dimmer switch adjustment.

ADJUSTMENT

1. Insert the proper alignment tool (drill bit) through the locating hole.
2. Loosen both screws attaching the dimmer switch mounting bracket.
3. Slide the dimmer switch firmly against the actuator arm and tighten both adjusting screws.

Turn Signal Switch

REMOVAL & INSTALLATION

Except Tilt and Telescopic Column

1. Disconnect the negative battery cable.
2. Remove the steering wheel.
3. Insert a suitable tool into the lock plate and remove the lock plate cover assembly.
4. Install a spring compressor onto the steering shaft. Tighten the tool to compress the lock plate and the spring. Remove the snapring from the groove in the shaft.
5. Remove the lock plate, the turn signal cam, and the upper bearing preload spring and the thrust washer off the upper steering shaft.

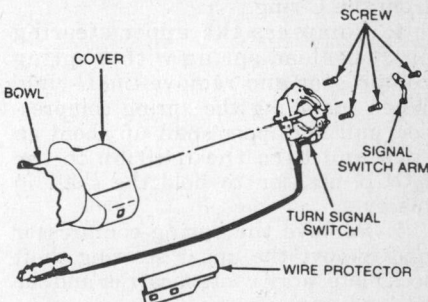

SCREW

COVER

BOWL

SIGNAL SWITCH ARM

TURN SIGNAL SWITCH

WIRE PROTECTOR

Standard steering column turnsignal switch assembly

6. Remove the steering column lower cover.

7. Remove the turn signal lever from the column.

8. On vehicles equipped with cruise control, disconnect the cruise control wire from the harness near the bottom of the column. Remove the harness protector from the cruise control wire. Do not remove the wire from the column.

9. Remove the vertical bolts at the steering column upper support. Remove the shim packs. Keep the shims in order for reinstallation.

10. Remove the screws securing the column upper mounting bracket to the column. Remove the bracket.

11. Disconnect the turn signal wiring and remove the wires from the plastic protector.

12. Remove the turn signal switch mounting screws.

13. Slide the switch connector out of the bracket on the steering column.

14. If the switch is known to be bad, cut the wires and discard the switch. Tape the connector of the new switch to the old wires, and pull the new harness down through the steering column while removing the old wires.

15. If the original switch is to be reused, wrap tape around the wire and connector and pull the harness up through the column. It may be helpful to attach a length of wire to the harness connector before pulling it up through the column to facilitate installation.

16. After freeing the switch wiring protector from its mounting, pull the turn signal switch straight up and remove the switch, switch harness and the connector from the column.

17. Installation is the reverse of the removal procedure.

Tilt and Telescopic Column

1. Disconnect the negative battery cable. Remove the steering wheel.

2. Remove the rubber sleeve bumper from the steering shaft.

3. Remove the plastic retainer and disengage the tabs on the retainer from the C-ring.

4. Compress the upper steering shaft preload spring with a spring compressor and remove the C-ring. When installing the spring compressor, pull the upper shaft up about an inch and turn the ignition to the **LOCK** position to hold the shaft in place.

5. Remove the spring compressor and remove the upper steering shaft lock plate, horn contact carrier and the preload spring.

6. Remove the steering column lower cover. Unscrew and remove the turn signal lever.

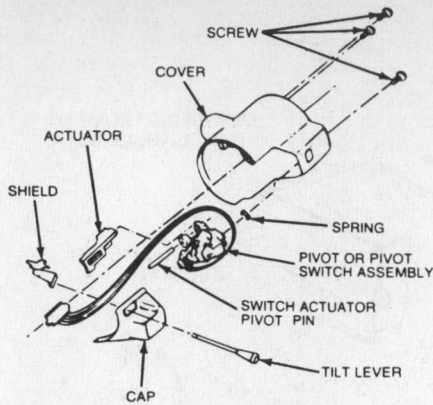

Tilt and telescoping steering column turnsignal switch assembly

7. If equipped with cruise control, disconnect the cruise control wire from the harness near the bottom of the steering column. Slide the protector off the cruise control wire. Remove the lever attaching screw and carefully pull the lever out enough to allow the removal of the turn signal switch.

8. Remove the nuts and shim packs from the upper column support. Keep the shims together as a unit for reinstallation.

9. Remove the bracket from the steering column by removing the 2 attaching screws from each side.

10. Disconnect the turn signal wiring harness and remove the wires from the plastic protector.

11. Remove the turn signal switch retaining screws and pull the switch up and out of the steering column.

12. If the switch is to be replaced, cut the wires from the switch and tape the new switch connector to the old wires. Carefully pull the new harness down through the column as the old wires are removed.

13. If the old switch is to be reused, tape the connector to the wires and carefully pull the harness up out of the column.

14. Feed the wiring harness down through the steering column to replace the old switch.

15. Secure the switch in the steering column.

16. Install the upper shaft preload spring.

17. Install the lock plate and carrier assembly. Make sure that the flat on the lower end of the steering shaft is pointing up and that the small plastic tab on the carrier is up or nearest the top of the column. The flat surface of the lock plate must be installed facing down against the turn signal switch.

18. Install the spring compressor, compress the preload spring and lock plate and install the C-ring with the wide side toward the keyway.

19. Remove the spring compressor and install the plastic retainer on the C-ring.

20. Install the rubber sleeve bumper over the steering shaft and install the steering wheel.

21. Install the turn signal lever. If the vehicle is equipped with cruise control, secure the lever to the switch with the retaining screw and install the wiring harness.

22. Remove the tape from the end of the harness and connect the switch and cruise control, if so equipped, to the wire harness.

23. Cover both harnesses with the plastic protector and position it to the column. The turn signal connector slides on the tabs of the column.

24. Position the steering column upper bracket over the turn signal switch harness plastic protector.

25. Install the mounting bracket nuts and shims in their original positions.

26. Install the steering column lower cover.

Ignition Lock

REMOVAL & INSTALLATION

Except Tilt and Telescopic Column

1. Disconnect the negative battery cable. Remove the steering wheel.

2. Remove the lock plate cover assembly.

3. After compressing the lock plate spring, remove the snapring from the groove in the shaft.

4. Remove the lock plate and slide the turn signal cam and the upper bearing preload spring off the upper steering shaft.

5. Remove the thrust washer from the shaft.

6. Remove the hazard warning switch knob from the column along with the turn signal lever.

7. If the vehicle is equipped with cruise control attach a piece of wire to the connector on the cruise control switch harness. Gently pull the harness up and out of the column.

8. Remove the turn signal switch mounting screws.

9. Slide the switch connector out of the bracket on the steering column.

10. As required, free the turn signal switch wiring protector from its mounting after disconnecting the turn signal switch electrical connectors, then pull the turn signal switch straight up and out of the steering column along with the switch harness and the connector from the steering column.

11. Turn the ignition switch to the **ON** or **RUN** position. Insert a small

drift pin into the slot next to the switch mounting screw boss. Push the lock cylinder tab and remove the lock cylinder.

12. Installation is the reverse of the removal procedure.

Tilt and Telescopic Column

1. Disconnect the negative battery cable. Remove the steering wheel.

2. Remove the rubber sleeve bumper from the steering shaft.

3. Using an appropriate tool, remove the plastic retainer.

4. Using a spring compressor, compress the upper steering shaft spring and remove the C-ring. Release the steering shaft lock plate, the horn contact carrier, and the upper steering shaft preload spring.

5. Remove the 4 screws which hold the upper mounting bracket and then remove the bracket.

6. Slide the harness connector out of the bracket on the steering column. Tape the upper part of the harness and connector.

7. Disconnect the hazard button and position the shift bowl in **P**. Remove the turn signal lever from the column.

8. If the vehicle is equipped with cruise control, remove the harness protector from the harness. Attach a piece of wire to the switch harness connector. Before removing the turn signal lever, loop a piece of wire and insert it into the turn signal lever opening. Use the wire to pull the cruise control harness out through the opening. Pull the rest of the harness up through and out of the column. Remove the guide wire from the connector and secure the wire to the column. Remove the turn signal lever.

9. Pull the turn signal switch up until the end connector is within the shift bowl. Remove the hazard flasher lever. Allow the switch to hang.

10. Place the ignition key in the **RUN** position.

11. Depress the center of the lock cylinder retaining tab with a suitable tool and then remove the lock cylinder.

12. Installation is the reverse of the removal procedure.

Ignition Switch

REMOVAL & INSTALLATION

1. Disconnect the negative battery cable.

2. Position lock cylinder in **LOCK** position.

3. Remove steering column lower cover.

4. Loosen the nuts on the upper steering column. Allow the column to drop and be supported by the seat.

5. Disconnect the ignition switch connector at switch.

6. Remove the screws securing the dimmer switch and ignition switch to the steering column. Position the dimmer switch out of the way and remove the screw securing the ignition switch to the steering column. Remove the ignition switch from the vehicle.

To install:

7. Assemble the ignition switch on the actuator rod and adjust it to the **LOCK** position.

8. If the vehicle is equipped with a standard column, hold the switch actuating rod stationary with while moving the switch toward the bottom of the column until it reaches the end of its travel, which is the **ACC** position. Back off 2 detents to the right, which is the **OFF/UNLOCK** position, then with the key also in the **OFF/UN-LOCK** position, tighten the switch mounting screws to 35 inch lbs.

9. If the vehicle is equipped with a tilt wheel, hold the switch actuating rod stationary with one hand while moving the switch toward the upper end of column until it reaches the end of its travel, which is the **ACC** position. Back off 1 detent and with the key in **LOCK** position, tighten the switch mounting screws to 35 inch lbs.

10. Continue the installation in the reverse order of the removal procedure. Test the starting system to start in **P** and **N** only.

Stoplight Switch

REMOVAL & INSTALLATION

NOTE: The cruise control release switch and the stoplight switch are adjusted or replaced in the same manner.

1. Disconnect the negative battery cable. Remove the underneath trim panel, as required. Disconnect the wire harness connector from the switch.

2. Remove the switch from the clip and then remove the clip from the bracket.

To install:

3. Place the clip in its bore on the bracket.

4. With the brake pedal depressed, insert the switch into the clip and depress the switch body. Clicks can be heard as the threaded portion of the switch is pushed through the clip towards the brake pedal.

5. Pull the brake pedal fully rearward against the pedal stop until the clicking sounds cannot be heard. The switch can be moved in the clip to correct the adjustment.

6. Release the brake pedal and repeat Step 5 to assure that no clicking sounds remain. The switch is now correctly adjusted.

7. Install the harness connector and verify the stoplights operate correctly.

Neutral Safety Switch

These vehicles incorporate a mechanical neutral start system. This system relies on a mechanical block, rather than the starter safety switch to prevent starting the engine in other than **P** or **N** positions.

The mechanical block is achieved by a cast in finger added to the switch actuator rack, which interferes with the bowl plate in all shift positions except **N** or **P**. This interference prevents rotation of the lock cylinder into the **START** position.

In either **P** or **N**, this finger passes through the bowl plate slots allowing the lock cylinder full rotational travel into the **START** position.

Fuses, Circuit Breakers and Relays

LOCATION

Fusible Links

Fusible links are used to prevent major wire harness damage in the event of a short circuit or an overload condition in the wiring circuits which are normally not fused, due to carrying high amperage loads or because of their locations within the wiring harness. Each fusible link is of a fixed value for a specific electrical load and should a link fail, the cause of the failure must be determined and repaired prior to installing a new fusible link of the same value.

Circuit Breakers

Various circuit breakers are located under the instrument panel. In order to gain access to these components, it may be necessary to first remove the under dash padding.

Fuse Panel

The fuse panel is located on the left side of the vehicle. It is under the instrument panel assembly. In order to gain access to the fuse panel, it may be necessary to first remove the under dash padding.

Relays

All vehicles use a combination of the following electrical relays in order to function properly.

Defogger Relay—is located on the relay panel under the instrument panel to the left of the fuse block.

Door Lock Relay—is attached to the lower right shroud panel behind the kick panel.

Power Antenna Relay—is located on the relay panel under the instrument panel to the left of the fuse block.

Fuel Pump Relay—is located on the relay panel under the instrument panel to the left of the fuse block.

Horn Relay—is located on the relay panel under the instrument panel to the left of the fuse block.

Starter Interrupt Relay—is located on a bracket under the left side of the dash panel, to the left of the steering column.

Power Seat Relay—is located under the seat.

Stop/turn Light Relays—is located at the left rear quarter panel.

Guidematic Power Relay—is located under the dash panel, near the fuse block.

Theft Deterrent Relay—is located behind a bracket under the left side of the instrument panel.

Air Cnditioning Compressor Control Relay—is located on the right side of the firewall in the engine compartment.

Electronic Level Control Relay—is located to the left of the level control compressor.

Memory Disable Relay—is located behind the right side of the dash near the connector.

Low Brake Vacuum Relay—is located behind the right side of the dash near the connector.

Illuminated Entry Timer—is located behind the right side of the dash near the connector.

Horn Relay—is located under the left side of the dash panel, to the left of the steering column.

Headlight Washer Relay—is located on the fluid reservoir on the front of the right front shock tower.

High Mount Stop Light Relays—are located on the left rear wheelwell inside the trunk.

Computers

LOCATION

ECM

The electronic control module is located on the right side of the vehicle. It is positioned in front of the right hand kick panel. In order to gain access to the assembly, the trim panel must first be removed.

BCM

The body computer module is located under the right side of the dash above the relay center. In order to gain ac-

cess to the assembly, the trim panel must first be removed.

Flashers

LOCATION

Turn Signal

The turn signal flasher is located behind the instrument panel bracket to the right of the steering column. In order to gain access to the turn signal flasher, it may be necessary to first remove the under dash padding.

Hazard Flasher

The hazard flasher is located in the fuse block. It is positioned on the lower right hand corner of the fuse block assembly. In order to gain access to the turn signal flasher, it may be necessary to first remove the under dash padding.

ENGINE COOLING

Radiator

REMOVAL & INSTALLATION

1. Disconnect the negative battery cable. Properly drain the cooling system.
2. Disconnect the top and bottom radiator hoses from the radiator. Remove the reservoir hose from the radiator filler neck.
3. Disconnect and plug the transmission fluid cooler lines. On the 5.7L engine, disconnect and plug the oil cooler lines.
4. Remove the bolts retaining the engine compartment rod to the radiator core support. Loosen each anchor bolt and position the support rods aside.
5. Remove the fan shroud retaining bolts. Position the fan shroud assembly aside.
6. Remove the radiator core support cover retaining bolts. Remove the radiator core support cover.
7. Carefully lift the radiator assembly upward and out of the vehicle.
8. Installation is the reverse of the removal procedure. Refill the cooling system with the proper coolant mixture.

Heater Core

REMOVAL & INSTALLATION

1. Disconnect the negative battery cable. Disconnect and tag all electrical wiring from the heater core housing, as required.
2. Remove the right windshield washer nozzle.
3. Remove the right air inlet screen from the plenum. Partially remove the rubber molding above the plenum (1 screw on the right hand side). Drain the radiator.
4. Remove the remaining screws and remove the primary inlet screen. Remove the blower motor.
5. Remove the 2 screws holding the compressor cycling switch to the module and carefully reposition the switch off of the module cover.
6. Remove the screws retaining the case module cover. Remove the cover. Remove and plug the heater hoses from the heater core nipples.
7. Remove the screw and the retainer holding the heater core to the frame at the top of the assembly.
8. With the temperature door in the max/hot position, reach through the temperature housing and push the lower forward corner of the heater core away from the housing.
9. Rotate the core parallel to the housing. This will cause the core to snap out of the lower clamp. The core can now be removed in a vertical direction due to the configuration of the component.
10. Installation is the reverse order of the removal procedure. Be sure to install a new module cover seal as required.

Water Pump

REMOVAL & INSTALLATION

1. Disconnect the negative battery cable.
2. Drain the radiator. Disconnect the lower radiator hose at the water pump. On the 5.0L engine, remove the bypass hose and the heater hose from the water pump.
3. Remove the drive belts on the 5.0L engine. Remove the serpentine drive belt on the 5.7L engine.
4. Remove the radiator fan and water pump pulley.
5. Remove the front air conditioning compressor bracket. Remove the front alternator bracket. Remove the power steering pump adjusting bracket. Remove the air pump mounting bracket.
6. Remove the water pump retaining bolts. Remove the water pump from the engine.

7. Installation is the reverse of the removal procedure. Use a new gasket or RTV sealant, as required.

8. Install the drive belts and tighten them to the proper tension.

9. Refill the cooling system with the correct mixture of antifreeze and water. Start the engine and check for leaks.

Thermostat

REMOVAL & INSTALLATION

1. Disconnect the negative battery cable. Drain the cooling system.

2. Remove the radiator hose from the thermostat housing. On the 5.0L engine, remove the coolant bypass hose.

3. Remove the thermostat housing retaining bolts. Remove the thermostat housing assembly from the engine.

4. Remove the thermostat and discard the gasket.

5. Installation is the reverse of the removal procedure. Be sure to use a new gasket or RTV sealant, as required. Refill the cooling system using the proper coolant mixture.

FUEL SYSTEM

Fuel System Service Precautions

Safety is the most important factor when performing not only fuel system maintenance but any type of maintenance. Failure to conduct maintenance and repairs in a safe manner may result in serious personal injury or death. Maintenance and testing of the vehicle's fuel system components can be accomplished safely and effectively by adhering to the following rules and guidelines.

● To avoid the possibility of fire and personal injury, always disconnect the negative battery cable unless the repair or test procedure requires that battery voltage be applied.

● Always relieve the fuel system pressure prior to disconnecting any fuel system component (injector, fuel rail, pressure regulator, etc.), fitting or fuel line connection. Exercise extreme caution whenever relieving fuel system pressure to avoid exposing skin, face and eyes to fuel spray. Please be advised that fuel under pressure may penetrate the skin or any part of the body that it contacts.

● Always place a shop towel or cloth around the fitting or connection prior to loosening to absorb any excess fuel due to spillage. Ensure that all fuel spillage, should it occur, is quickly removed from engine surfaces. Ensure that all fuel soaked cloths or towels are deposited into a suitable waste container.

● Always keep a dry chemical (Class B) fire extinguisher near the work area.

● Do not allow fuel spray or fuel vapors to come into contact with a spark or open flame.

● Always use a backup wrench when loosening and tightening fuel line connection fittings. This will prevent unnecessary stress and torsion to fuel line piping. Always follow the proper torque specifications.

● Always replace worn fuel fitting O-rings with new. Do not substitute fuel hose or equivalent where fuel pipe is installed.

RELIEVING FUEL SYSTEM PRESSURE

5.0L Engine

1. Release the fuel vapor pressure in the fuel tank by removing the fuel tank cap.

2. Be sure that the engine is cold. Disconnect the negative battery cable.

3. Cover the fuel line with an absorbent shop cloth and loosen the connection slowly, using the proper tool, to release the fuel pressure gradually.

5.7L Engine

1. Release the fuel vapor pressure in the fuel tank by removing the fuel tank cap.

2. Be sure that the engine is cold. Disconnect the negative battery cable.

3. The internal constant bleed feature to throttle body injection relieves the fuel pump system pressure when the engine is not running. Therefore, no further action is required.

Fuel Filter

REMOVAL & INSTALLATION

5.0L Engine

1. Be sure that the engine is cold. Disconnect the negative battery cable.

2. Properly relieve the fuel pump pressure. Remove the air cleaner assembly.

3. Using the proper tools disconnect the fuel line from the fuel filter at the base of the carburetor.

4. Using the proper tools remove the fuel filter housing from the carburetor. Remove the fuel filter, gasket and spring.

5. Installation is the reverse of the removal procedure.

5.7L Engine

1. Be sure that the engine is cold. Disconnect the negative battery cable.

2. Properly relieve the fuel pump pressure. Raise and support the vehicle safely.

3. Grasp the fuel filter and one of the fuel line fittings. Twist the quick connect assembly about a ¼ turn in each direction to loosen any dirt within the fitting.

4. Grasp the fuel filter and the other fuel line fitting. Twist the quick connect assembly about a ¼ turn in each direction to loosen any dirt within the fitting.

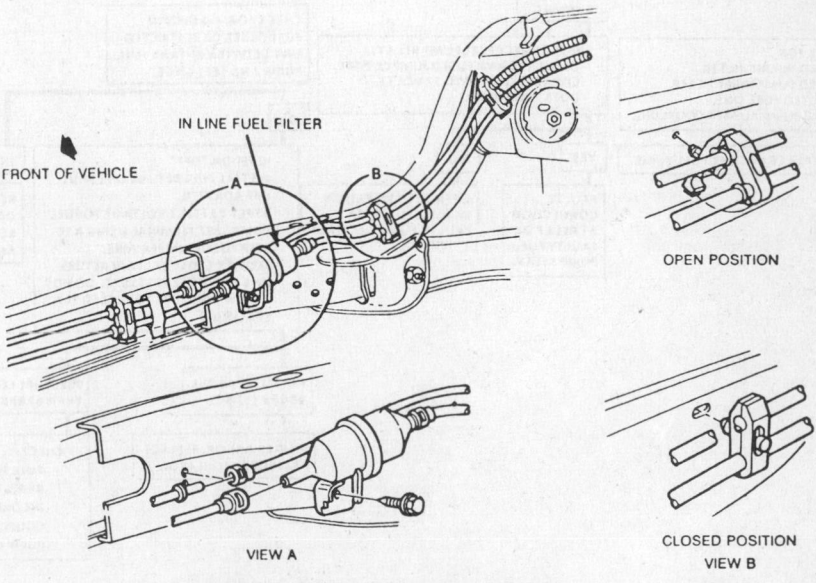

Fuel filter location and related fuel lines — 5.7L engine

5. Squeeze the plastic tabs of the connector and pull the connection apart.

6. Remove the fuel filter retaining bolts. Remove the fuel filter from its mounting.

7. Installation is the reverse of the removal procedure. Prior to installation, apply a few drops of clean engine oil to both tube ends of the filter.

NOTE: The application of clean engine oil will ensure proper reconnection and prevent a possible fuel leak. During normal operation the O-ring that is located in the connector will swell and may prevent proper reconnection if not lubricated. If the new filter is nicked, scratched or damaged during installation it must be replaced.

Mechanical Fuel Pump

PRESSURE TESTING

1. Be sure that the engine is cold. Disconnect the negative battery cable.

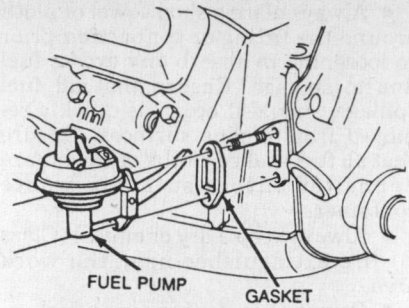

Fuel pump location—5.0L engine

2. Properly relieve the fuel pump pressure. Remove the air cleaner assembly.

3. Using the proper tools disconnect the fuel line from the fuel filter at the base of the carburetor.

4. Install a rubber hose about 8–10 in. long over the fuel line and connect a low reading pressure gauge.

5. Position the pressure gauge upward about 16 inches above the fuel pump. If the vehicle is equipped with a fuel return line, pich it.

6. Start the engine and run at slow idle using the fuel in the carburetor.

7. If the fuel pump is performing properly the pressure should be 5.5–6.5 psi. If not within specification, replace the fuel pump.

REMOVAL & INSTALLATION

1. Be sure that the engine is cold. Disconnect the negative battery cable. Properly relieve the fuel pump pressure.

2. Remove the air conditioning compressor drive belt.

3. If equipped with an air pump, loosen the air pump pulley bolts and remove the air pump hoses and electrical leads to the air pump. Remove the air pump pulley and the air pump from the engine.

4. Remove the compressor front bracket. Remove the fuel inlet hose from the fuel pump. Disconnect the vapor return hose, if equipped.

5. Remove the fuel outlet pipe. Remove the nuts securing the fuel pump to the engine. Remove the fuel pump from the engine. Discard the gasket.

6. Installation is the reverse order of the removal procedure. Be sure to

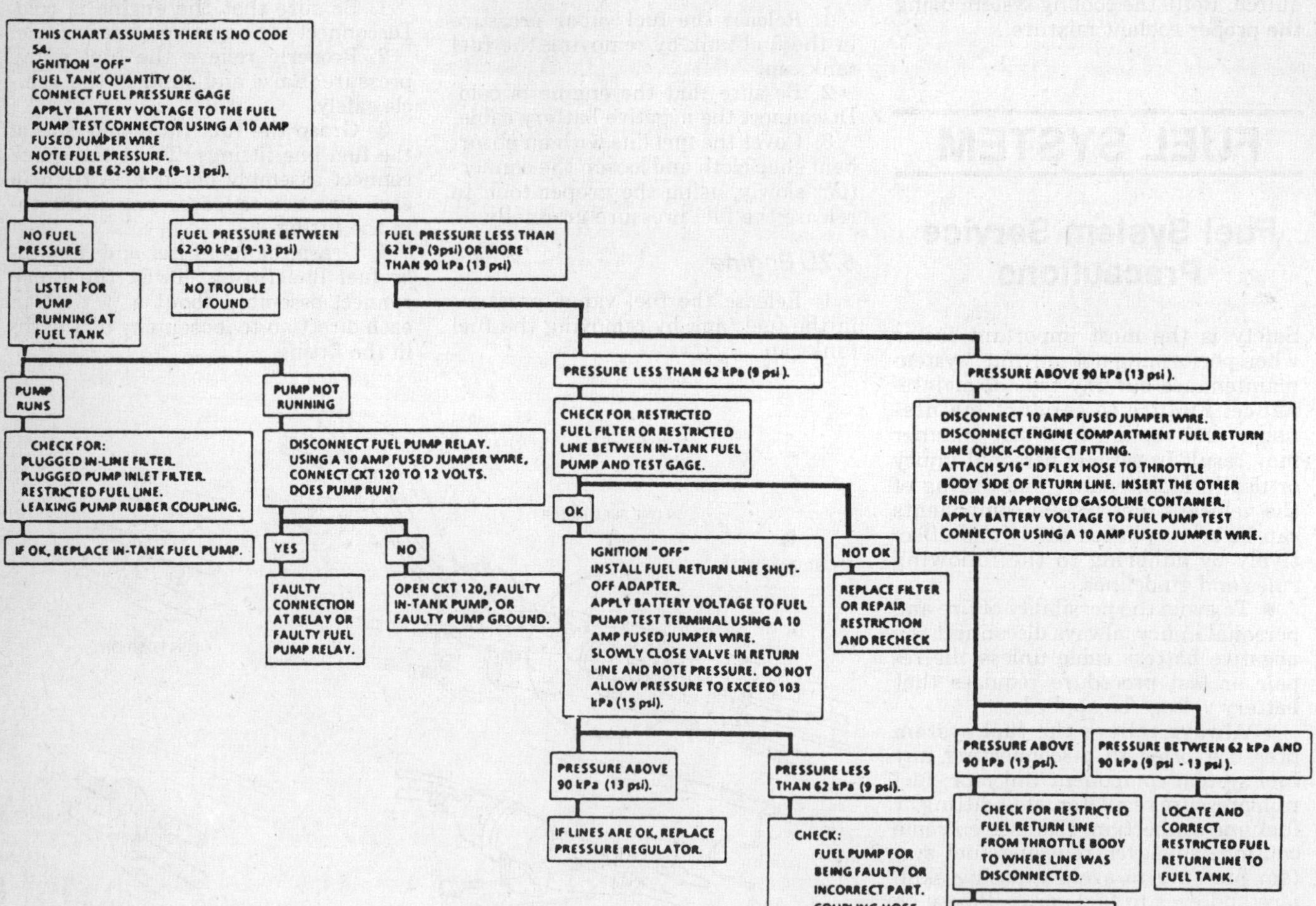

THIS CHART ASSUMES THERE IS NO CODE 54.
IGNITION "OFF"
FUEL TANK QUANTITY OK.
CONNECT FUEL PRESSURE GAGE
APPLY BATTERY VOLTAGE TO THE FUEL PUMP TEST CONNECTOR USING A 10 AMP FUSED JUMPER WIRE
NOTE FUEL PRESSURE.
SHOULD BE 62-90 kPa (9-13 psi).

NO FUEL PRESSURE

FUEL PRESSURE BETWEEN 62-90 kPa (9-13 psi)

FUEL PRESSURE LESS THAN 62 kPa (9psi) OR MORE THAN 90 kPa (13 psi)

LISTEN FOR PUMP RUNNING AT FUEL TANK

NO TROUBLE FOUND

PUMP RUNS

PUMP NOT RUNNING

CHECK FOR:
PLUGGED IN-LINE FILTER.
PLUGGED PUMP INLET FILTER.
RESTRICTED FUEL LINE.
LEAKING PUMP RUBBER COUPLING.

DISCONNECT FUEL PUMP RELAY. USING A 10 AMP FUSED JUMPER WIRE, CONNECT CKT 120 TO 12 VOLTS. DOES PUMP RUN?

IF OK, REPLACE IN-TANK FUEL PUMP.

YES

NO

FAULTY CONNECTION AT RELAY OR FAULTY FUEL PUMP RELAY.

OPEN CKT 120, FAULTY IN-TANK PUMP, OR FAULTY PUMP GROUND.

PRESSURE LESS THAN 62 kPa (9 psi).

CHECK FOR RESTRICTED FUEL FILTER OR RESTRICTED LINE BETWEEN IN-TANK FUEL PUMP AND TEST GAGE.

OK

IGNITION "OFF"
INSTALL FUEL RETURN LINE SHUT-OFF ADAPTER.
APPLY BATTERY VOLTAGE TO FUEL PUMP TEST TERMINAL USING A 10 AMP FUSED JUMPER WIRE.
SLOWLY CLOSE VALVE IN RETURN LINE AND NOTE PRESSURE. DO NOT ALLOW PRESSURE TO EXCEED 103 kPa (15 psi).

PRESSURE ABOVE 90 kPa (13 psi).

DISCONNECT 10 AMP FUSED JUMPER WIRE.
DISCONNECT ENGINE COMPARTMENT FUEL RETURN LINE QUICK-CONNECT FITTING.
ATTACH 5/16" ID FLEX HOSE TO THROTTLE BODY SIDE OF RETURN LINE. INSERT THE OTHER END IN AN APPROVED GASOLINE CONTAINER.
APPLY BATTERY VOLTAGE TO FUEL PUMP TEST CONNECTOR USING A 10 AMP FUSED JUMPER WIRE.

NOT OK

REPLACE FILTER OR REPAIR RESTRICTION AND RECHECK

PRESSURE ABOVE 90 kPa (13 psi).

IF LINES ARE OK, REPLACE PRESSURE REGULATOR.

PRESSURE LESS THAN 62 kPa (9 psi).

CHECK:
FUEL PUMP FOR BEING FAULTY OR INCORRECT PART.
COUPLING HOSE.
PUMP INLET FILTER.

PRESSURE ABOVE 90 kPa (13 psi).

PRESSURE BETWEEN 62 kPa AND 90 kPa (9 psi - 13 psi).

CHECK FOR RESTRICTED FUEL RETURN LINE FROM THROTTLE BODY TO WHERE LINE WAS DISCONNECTED.

LOCATE AND CORRECT RESTRICTED FUEL RETURN LINE TO FUEL TANK.

IF LINE IS OK, REPLACE PRESSURE REGULATOR.

Fuel system diagnosis—5.7L engine

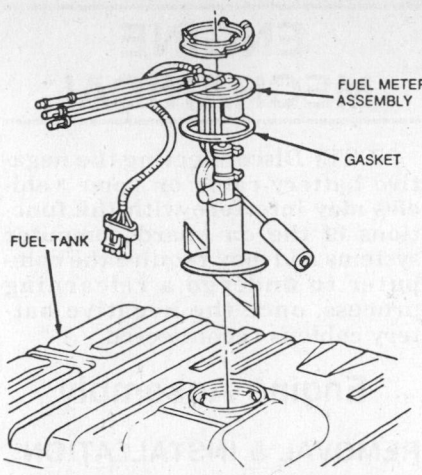

Fuel pump location—5.7L engine

use a new fuel pump gasket. Start the engine and check for leaks.

Electric Fuel Pump

PRESSURE TESTING

NOTE: The fuel pressure should be recorded while the fuel pump is operating. Fuel pump pressure will drop immediately after the fuel pump stops running due to a controlled bleed within the fuel system. The fuel pump test terminal is located on the right side of the engine compartment.

REMOVAL & INSTALLATION

1. Be sure that the engine is cold. Disconnect the negative battery cable.
2. Properly relieve the fuel pump pressure. Drain the fuel tank. Raise and support the vehicle safely.

NOTE: If the nylon fuel feed or return lines become kinked and cannot be straightened, they must be replaced. Do not attempt to repair sections of nylon fuel lines, they must be replaced.

3. Disconnect and plug the fuel line fittings at the fuel meter assembly. Disconnect all electrical connections.
4. Properly support the fuel tank. Remove the fuel tank retaining strap bolts. Remove the retaining straps. Carefully remove the empty fuel tank from the vehicle.
5. Using tool J–24187 or equivalent, remove the fuel level meter assembly retaining cam. Remove the fuel level meter assembly from the tank and discard the O-ring.
6. Installation is the reverse of the removal procedure. Be sure to use a new O-ring.

Carburetor

REMOVAL & INSTALLATION

1. Disconnect the negative battery cable. Remove the air cleaner assembly. Disconnect the accelerator linkage.
2. Disconnect the transmission detent cable. Disconnect the cruise control linkage, if equipped.
3. Remove and tag all vacuum and electrical lines to the carburetor. Disconnect the choke heat pipe.
4. Disconnect and plug the fuel line at the carburetor inlet. Remove the carburetor mounting bolts. Remove the carburetor from the manifold.
5. Installation is the reverse of the removal procedure. Be sure to install a new carburetor base gasket.
6. Torque the carburetor retaining bolts to 12 ft. lbs. in the following sequence, left rear, right front, right rear, left front.

IDLE SPEED ADJUSTMENT

1. Place the transmission selector lever in the **P** position, set the parking brake and block the drive wheels. Connect a suitable tachometer to the engine. Remove the air cleaner assembly and plug the vacuum hose to the Thermal Vacuum Valve (TVV).
2. Disconnect and plug the vacuum hose to the EGR valve and the vacuum hose to the canister purge port.
3. Disconnect and plug the vacuum hose to the idle load compensator (ILC). Back out the idle stop screw on the carburetor 3 turns.
4. Turn the air conditioning control switch to the **OFF** position. With the engine running and at normal operating temperature, place the transmission selector lever in the **D** position. Fully extend the idle load compensator plunger (no vacuum applied).
5. Using tool J–29607, BT–8022 or equivalent, adjust the ILC plunger to obtain a 725 ± 50 rpm. The jam nut on the plunger must be held with a suitable wrench to prevent damage to the guide tabs.
6. Measure the distance from the jam nut to the tip of the plunger. The dimension must not exceed 1 inch. If the dimension is not as specified check for a low idle condition. Remove the plug from the ILC vacuum hose and plug the hose back into the manifold. Adjust the idle speed to specification with the transmission selector lever in the **D** position.
7. If the idle speed is correct, then the adjustment is over. If the idle speed does not meet specification, perform the following:

8. Stop the engine and remove the idle load compensator.

NOTE: It will not be necessary to remove the idle load compensator if a hex wrench is modified to clear the obstructions.

9. Remove the rubber cap from the center outlet tube. Using a $^3/_{32}$ in. hex key wrench, insert it through the open center tube to engage the idle speed adjusting screw inside the tube.
10. If the idle speed was low, turn the adjusting screw counterclockwise a complete turn for every 75–100 rpm. If the idle was high, turn the adjusting screw clockwise a complete turn for every 75–100 rpm. Reinstall the plug on the center of the outlet tube.
11. Reinstall the idle load compensator on the carburetor and attach the throttle return spring and any other related parts that were removed. Recheck the idle speed with the transmission selector lever in the **D** position. Be sure that the system is in the closed loop mode. If the idle speed is still not within specification, repeat the procedure.
12. Disconnect the power feed (fuse) to the ECM with the ignition **OFF**, for 10 seconds. This will allow the ECM to reset the throttle position sensor value.
13. Disconnect and plug the vacuum source to the ILC. Apply a vacuum source using a hand held vacuum pump or equivalent to the ILC vacuum inlet tube to fully retract the plunger.
14. Adjust the idle stop screw on the carburetor float bowl to obtain 450 rpm, with the transmission selector lever in the **D** position. Place the transmission selector lever in the **P** and shut off the engine.
15. Remove the plug from the vacuum hose and install the hose on the ILC vacuum inlet tube. Remove all the plugs from the disconnected vacuum lines and reconnect the vacuum lines to their proper ports.
16. Install the air cleaner and gasket, remove the blocks from the drive wheels and road test the vehicle.

IDLE MIXTURE ADJUSTMENT

All carburetors have mixture needles concealed under staked in plugs. Mixture adjustments should be performed only during carburetor overhaul.

SERVICE ADJUSTMENTS

For all carburetor service adjustment procedures and specifications, please refer to "Carburetor Service" in the Unit Repair section.

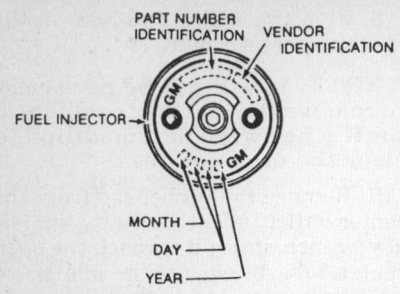

Fuel Injector identification data

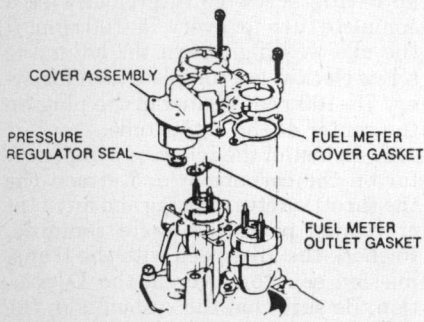

Fuel meter cover assembly and related components—5.7L engine

Fuel Injection

IDLE SPEED ADJUSTMENT

The idle speed is controlled by the ECM and is not adjustable.

IDLE MIXTURE ADJUSTMENT

The idle mixture is set at the factory and is not adjustable.

Fuel Injector

REMOVAL & INSTALLATION

1. Disconnect the negative battery cable. Properly relieve the fuel system pressure.
2. Remove the air cleaner assembly and extension. Disconnect the electrical connectors to the fuel injectors.
3. Remove the fuel meter cover retaining screws. Remove the fuel meter cover assembly.
4. Remove the fuel meter outlet passage gasket. Remove the pressure regulator dust seal.

NOTE: If the fuel meter cover gasket is stuck to the fuel meter body, leave it in place. If it is stuck to the fuel meter cover, remove it and place it on the fuel meter body.

5. Once the fuel meter cover gasket is on the fuel meter body, use the proper tool and fulcrum to carefully pry out the fuel injector.
6. Remove and discard the small O-ring from the nozzle end of the fuel injector.
7. Remove and discard the fuel meter cover gasket. Remove and discard the large O-ring and fuel injector washer from the top of the injector cavity.
8. Installation is the reverse of the removal procedure.

NOTE: When installing the injectors, install the fuel injector washer and large O-ring before the injector, to be sure that the O-ring is properly seated. Reversing these procedures could result in a fuel leak and possible engine fire.

EMISSION CONTROLS

Please refer to "Emission Control" in the Unit Repair section for system maintenance procedures. Due to the complex nature of modern electronic engine control systems, comprehensive diagnosis and testing procedures fall outside the confines of this repair manual. For complete information on diagnosis, testing and repair procedures concerning all modern engine and emission control systems, please refer to "Chilton's Guide to Electronic Engine Controls".

Emission Warning Lamps

RESETTING

A service engine soon telltale light located on the instrument panel alerts the driver that the vehicle should be taken for service as soon as possible. If the light remains on, the self-diagnostic system has detected a problem. After the system has been repaired, all trouble codes must be cleared from the ECM memory. To clear the trouble codes, remove the 3 amp ECM fuse for 10 seconds with the ignition switch turned **OFF**.

ENGINE MECHANICAL

NOTE: Disconnecting the negative battery cable on some vehicles may interfere with the functions of the on board computer systems and may require the computer to undergo a relearning process, once the negative battery cable is reconnected.

Engine Assembly

REMOVAL & INSTALLATION

5.0L Engine

1. Disconnect the negative battery cable. Properly relieve the fuel system pressure. Remove the air cleaner assembly.
2. Remove the hood, after scribing hood hinge outline for proper alignment.
3. Remove the air cleaner and heat shroud. Disconnect and plug the transmission oil cooler lines.
4. Drain the cooling system. Disconnect the heater hoses from the engine. Unfasten the fender struts from the radiator shroud. Remove the radiator hose bracket, radiator shroud and fan. Remove the radiator hoses. Remove the radiator.
5. If equipped, disconnect the throttle and cruise control linkage at the carburetor.
6. Disconnect the brake vacuum hose from the vacuum pipe. Remove the cruise control power unit, if equipped.
7. Disconnect the power steering pump bracket and position the pump out of the way with the hoses still connected.
8. Remove the air conditioning compressor bracket bolts and position the compressor out of the way with the hoses still connected. Do not discharge the system.
9. Disconnect all electrical wires and vacuum lines that will interfere with the removal of the engine.
10. Disconnect the automatic level control line, if equipped. Remove the alternator. Remove the air pump, if equipped.
11. Raise and support the vehicle safely. Remove the engine to transmission bolts. Remove each engine mount through bolt.
12. Remove the starter. Disconnect the exhaust pipes from the exhaust manifolds. Drain the engine oil.
13. Remove the bolts attaching the flywheel inspection cover to the transmission. Remove the cover. Remove

the bolts attaching the flywheel to the converter.

16. Disconnect and plug the fuel line and the vapor return line at the fuel pump, as required.

17. Lower the vehicle. Install the lifting equipment to the engine. Support the transmission properly. Raise the engine slightly and pull it forward to disengage it from the transmission. Remove the engine from the vehicle.

18. Installation is the reverse of the removal procedure.

5.7L Engine

1. Disconnect the negative battery cable. Properly relieve the fuel system pressure. Remove the air cleaner assembly.

2. Remove the hood, after scribing hood hinge outline for proper alignment.

3. Drain the cooling system. Disconnect the radiator hoses. Disconnect the heater hose from the radiator. Disconnect and plug the transmission cooler lines.

4. Remove the radiator cover and tie struts. Disconnect the fan shroud from the radiator assembly and position it aside. Remove the radiator from the vehicle.

5. Remove the cooling fan assembly. Remove the fan shroud assembly from the vehicle. Disconnect the heater hose at the rear of the intake manifold.

6. As required, disconnect and plug the power steering hoses at the power steering gear.

7. Remove the serpentine drive belt. Remove the air conditioning compressor and position it aside. Remove the alternator assembly.

8. Disconnect the accelerator, cruise control and throttle valve cables from their mountings. Remove the retaining brackets from the intake manifold and position them aside.

9. Disconnect the fuel line clips at the thermostat housing and air pump. Position the fuel lines aside. As required, remove the air pump assembly.

10. Disconnect and plug all required electrical connectors and vacuum hoses. Remove the distributor cap. Remove the negative battery cable at the cylinder head.

11. Raise and support the vehicle safely. Drain the engine oil. Disconnect the exhaust pipes at the crossover pipe.

12. Disconnect the starter electrical connectors. Remove the starter retaining bolts. Remove the starter from the vehicle. As required, disconnect and plug the fuel line.

13. Remove the flywheel cover. Remove the transmission to flywheel re-

taining bolts. Remove the motor mount bolts.

14. Disconnect the transmission oil cooler lines at the clip on the oil pan. Disconnect all necessary electrical connectors. Remove the oil cooler hose shield.

15. Remove the transmission to engine retaining bolts. Lower the vehicle.

16. Install the lifting equipment to the engine. Support the transmission properly. Raise the engine slightly and pull it forward to disengage it from the transmission. Remove the engine from the vehicle.

17. Installation is the reverse of the removal procedure.

Engine Mounts

REMOVAL & INSTALLATION

1. Disconnect the negative battery cable. Raise and support the vehicle safely.

2. Remove the engine through bolt. Properly raise the engine enough to remove the engine mount. Once the engine is raised be sure to properly support it.

3. Remove the engine mount retaining bolts. Remove the engine mount.

4. Installation is the reverse of removal procedure.

Cylinder Head

REMOVAL & INSTALLATION

5.0L Engine

1. Disconnect the negative battery cable. Properly relieve the fuel system pressure. Remove the air cleaner assembly.

2. Drain the radiator. Remove the intake manifold. Remove the exhaust manifolds. Remove the alternator, power steering pump, air pump and air conditioning compressor, as required.

3. Remove the valve covers, rocker assemblies and pushrods. Note the location of each part so they can be reassembled in the proper location.

6. Remove the cylinder head retaining bolts. Remove the cylinder head and discard the old gasket.

7. Installation is the reverse of the removal procedure. Before installing

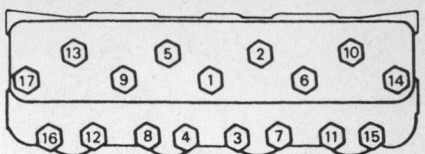

Cylinder head bolt torque sequence—5.7L engine

the cylinder head bolts, dip them in clean engine oil. Torque the cylinder head bolts in sequence to the proper torque specification.

5.7L Engine

1. Disconnect the negative battery cable. Properly relieve the fuel system pressure. Remove the air cleaner assembly.

2. Drain the radiator. Remove the intake manifold. Remove the exhaust manifolds. Remove the alternator, power steering pump, air pump and air conditioning compressor, as required. Remove the diverter valve.

3. Remove the valve covers, rocker assemblies and pushrods. Note the location of each part so they can be reassembled in the proper location.

6. Remove the cylinder head retaining bolts. Remove the cylinder head and discard the old gasket.

7. Installation is the reverse of the removal procedure. Before installing the cylinder head bolts, coat the threads with sealing compound, GM part number 1052080, or equivalent. Torque the cylinder head bolts in sequence to the proper torque specification.

Valve Lifters

REMOVAL & INSTALLATION

1. Disconnect the negative battery cable. Properly relieve the fuel system pressure. Remove the air cleaner assembly.

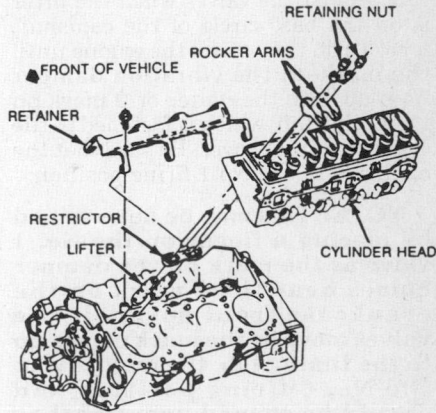

Rocker arm assembly and related components—5.7L engine

Cylinder head bolt torque sequence—5.0L engine

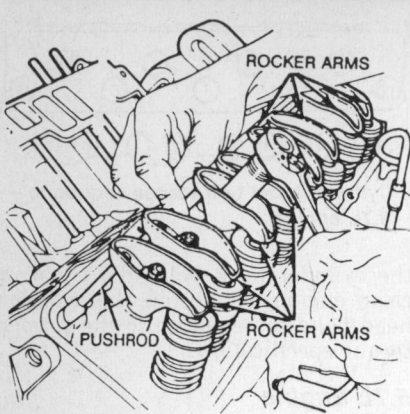

Valve adjustment procedure

2. Remove the valve covers. Remove the rocker arms and pivot assemblies. Remove the pushrods.

3. Remove the intake manifold.

4. Remove the lifter guide retainer bolts and remove the lifter guide. Using the proper valve lifter removal tool, remove the valve lifters.

5. Installation is the reverse of the removal procedure. Be sure to coat the lifters in clean engine oil before installing them.

6. As required, adjust the valves.

Valve Lash

ADJUSTMENT

5.0L Engine

The rocker arm assembly on this engine is equipped with rocker arm pivots. The hydraulic lifters are properly position in the lifter bores once the rocker arm pivots are torque to specification, thereby eliminating the need for valve adjustment.

5.7L Engine

1. Disconnect the negative battey cable. Remove the valve covers.

2. Tighten the rocker arm nuts until all lash is eliminated, if necessary.

3. Adjust the valves when the lifter is on the base circle of the camshaft lobe. To do this, crank the engine until the mark on the vibration damper lines up with the center or **0** mark on the timing tab, which is fastened to the crankcase front cover. Be sure that the engine is in the No.1 firing position.

NOTE: This may be determined by placing a finger on the No. 1 valve as the mark on the damper comes near the 0 mark on the crankcase front cover. If the valves move as the mark comes up to the timing tab, the engine is in the No. 6 firing position and should be turned over another time to reach to No. 1 firing position.

Valve cover removal tool positioning— 5.0L engine

4. With the engine in the No. 1 firing position, adjust the following valves. Exhaust—1, 3, 4, 8 Intake—1, 2, 5, 7.

5. Back out adjusting nut until lash is felt at the pushrod, then turn in adjusting nut until all lash is removed. This can be determined by rotating pushrod while turning the adjusting nut. When play has been removed, turn the adjusting nut in an additional turn.

6. Crank the engine one revolution until the pointer, **0** mark and the vibration damper mark are again in alignment. This is the No. 6 firing position.

7. With the engine in this position, adjust the following valves. Exhaust—2, 5, 6, 7 Intake—3, 4, 6, 8.

8. Install the valve covers.

9. Start the engine and adjust the idle speed, as required.

Rocker Arms

REMOVAL & INSTALLATION

5.0L Engine

1. Disconnect the negative battery cable. Properly relieve the fuel system pressure. Remove the air cleaner assembly.

2. Disconnect and tag any electrical leads or hoses preventing access to the valve cover retaining bolts. Remove the spark plug wires.

3. Remove the accessory drive belts and brackets, as required. On the left side remove the EGR valve and the exhaust manifold upper shroud.

4. Remove the air pump and drive belts, as required.

5. Remove the valve cover retaining bolts. Install tool BT-8315 or J-34144 midway between the ends of the valve cover on the upper side. Tighten the tool screw and apply pressure on the valve cover.

6. Using a rubber mallet, hit the side of the valve cover above where the tool is installed. Be sure to use a shop towel to absorb the blow from the mallet, otherwise damage to the valve cover may result.

7. Remove the valve cover from the engine. Clean the valve cover and mating surfaces.

8. Installation is the reverse of the removal procedure. Apply a ¼ in. (6mm) bead of RTV sealant or equivalent to the valve cover.

5.7L Engine

1. Disconnect the negative battery cable. Properly relieve the fuel system pressure. Remove the air cleaner assembly.

2. Disconnect the computer command control harness from the intake manifold and oxygen sensor. Remove the required electrical and vacuum connections. Remove the spark plug wires.

3. Disconnect the harness from the right valve cover. Remove the crankcase air inlet hose and connector.

4. Remove the EGR valve solenoid bracket. Disconnect the power brake vacuum pipe. Remove the AIR hose at the manifold check valve. Remove the PCV valve and hose from the valve cover.

5. Disconnect the fuel lines, as required. Remove the alternator rear support bracket and wire harness.

6. Remove the valve cover retaining bolts. Remove the valve covers from the engine. Discard the gaskets.

7. Installation is the reverse of the removal procedure. Be sure to use new gaskets or RTV sealant, as required.

Intake Manifold

REMOVAL & INSTALLATION

5.0L Engine

1. Disconnect the negative battery cable. Properly relieve the fuel system pressure. Remove the air cleaner assembly.

2. Drain the radiator. Remove the upper radiator hose, thermostat, bypass hose, and heater hose at the rear of the manifold. Remove and tag all vacuum lines from the intake manifold.

3. Disconnect and plug the fuel line. Remove the throttle cable, detent cable and cruise control rod.

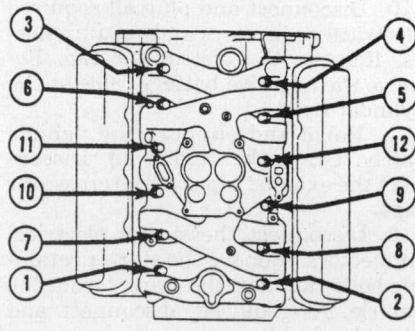

Intake manifold torque sequence—5.0L engine

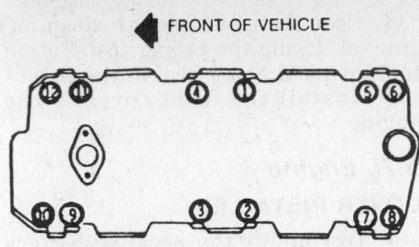

◄ FRONT OF VEHICLE

Intake manifold torque sequence — 5.7L engine

4. Remove the drive belts, alternator rear brace, air conditioning compressor rear brace and all necessary electrical leads.

5. Remove the computer command control solenoid assembly and the idle load compensator and bracket assembly. Remove the EGR valve, as necessary.

6. As required, remove the carburetor assembly from the intake manifold.

7. Remove the intake manifold retaining bolts. Remove the intake manifold from the vehicle and discard the gasket.

8. Installation is the reverse order of the removal procedure. Be sure to apply a suitable RTV sealant to the head side of the manifold gasket and to the corners of the front and rear manifold seals. Tighten the intake manifold attaching bolts in sequence to the proper specification.

5.7L Engine

1. Disconnect the negative battery cable. Properly relieve the fuel system pressure. Remove the air cleaner assembly.

2. Drain the radiator. Remove the radiator hose at the thermostat housing. Remove the heater hose from the intake manifold.

3. Remove the thermostat housing and gasket, as required. Remove the throttle body assembly.

4. Disconnect the computer command control harness and position it aside. Disconnect the power brake vacuum pipe. Disconnect the accelerator cable and throttle valve cable retaining bracket.

5. Disconnect the fuel line clips, as required. Remove the spark plug wires at the distributor cap.

6. Remove the distributor cap. Matchmark and remove the distributor assembly from the engine. Remove the coil.

7. Remove the coolant temperature sensor. Disconnect the air conditioning compressor brace and the alternator brace.

8. Remove the intake manifold retaining bolts. Remove the intake manifold from the engine. Discard the gaskets.

To install:

9. Position new gaskets on the cylinder heads. Apply a 5mm bead of RTV sealant, part number 1052289 or equivalent on the front and rear of the cylinder block.

10. Extend the bead of RTV sealant 13mm up each cylinder head to seal and retain the gaskets in position.

11. Install the intake manifold to the engine. Install the retaining bolts. Torque the bolts to specification and in the proper sequence.

12. Install the coolant temperature sensor. Connect the air conditioning compressor brace and the alternator brace.

13. Install the distributor assembly. Install the distributor cap. Install the coil.

14. Connect the fuel line clips, as required. Install the spark plug wires at the distributor cap.

15. Connect the computer command control harness. Connect the power brake vacuum pipe. Connect the accelerator cable and throttle valve cable retaining bracket.

16. Install the thermostat housing and gasket, as required. Install the throttle body assembly.

17. Fill the radiator, using the proper grade and type coolant. Install the radiator hose at the thermostat housing. Install the heater hose at the intake manifold.

18. Connect the negative battery cable. Install the air cleaner assembly.

Exhaust Manifold

REMOVAL & INSTALLATION

5.0L Engine

LEFT SIDE

1. Disconnect the negative battery cable. Remove the air cleaner assembly.

2. Flatten the exhaust manifold bolt lock tabs. Remove the heat shroud shield retaining bolts. Remove the heat shroud shield.

3. Raise and support the vehicle safely. Remove the exhaust pipe from the exhaust manifold. Lower the vehicle.

4. Remove the spark plug wires. Loosen the alternator bracket bolts and move the bracket aside.

5. Remove the exhaust manifold retaining bolts and remove the exhaust manifold from the engine.

6. Installation is the reverse order of the removal procedure. Be sure to install new gaskets, as required.

RIGHT SIDE

1. Disconnect the negative battery cable. Remove the air cleaner assembly. Remove the spark plug wires.

2. Remove the oxygen sensor lead wire. Raise and support the vehicle safely.

3. Remove the crossover pipe. Disconnect the exhaust pipe from the exhaust manifold.

4. Remove the front wheel to gain access to the exhaust manifold bolts, if necessary. Flatten the exhaust manifold bolt lock tabs.

5. Remove the exhaust manifold retaining bolts and remove the exhaust manifold from the engine.

6. Installation is the reverse order of the removal procedure. Be sure to install new gaskets, as required.

5.7L Engine

LEFT SIDE

1. Disconnect the negative battery cable. Remove the air cleaner assembly.

2. Raise and support the vehicle safely. Remove the crossover pipe. Lower the vehicle.

3. Remove the spark plug wires and wire clips. Disconnect the oxygen sensor connector. Disconnect the AIR hose at the check valve.

4. Flatten the exhaust manifold bolt lock tabs. Remove the exhaust manifold retaining bolts. Remove the exhaust manifold and heat shield from the engine.

5. Installation is the reverse of the removal procedure. Be sure to use new gaskets, as required.

RIGHT SIDE

1. Disconnect the negative battery cable. Remove the air cleaner assembly. Flatten the exhaust manifold bolt lock tabs.

2. Raise and support the vehicle safely. Disconnect the crossover pipe at both exhaust manifolds.

3. Remove the exhaust mount at the rear of the catalytic converter. Remove the back two exhaust manifold retaining bolts. Lower the vehicle.

4. Disconnect the spark plug wires at the distributor cap. Remove the diverter valve.

5. Remove the remaining exhaust manifold bolts. Remove the exhaust manifold and heat shield from the engine.

6. Installation is the reverse of the removal procedure. Be sure to use new gaskets, as required.

Timing Chain Front Cover

REMOVAL & INSTALLATION

5.0L Engine

1. Disconnect the negative battery

cable. Properly relieve the fuel system pressure.

2. Drain the cooling system. Remove the drive belts. Remove the fan shroud. Remove the fan assembly and fan pulley. Use hub balancer puller J–8614 or equivalent and remove the hub balancer.

3. Remove the power steering pump and position it to the side with the hoses attached.

4. Remove the AIR pump pulley. Remove the air conditioning compressor front bracket and position the compressor to the side.

5. For convenience, remove the water pump assembly from the front cover shield.

6. Remove the front cover retaining bolts, timing indicator and front cover. Discard the gasket.

NOTE: It may be necessary to grind a flat surface on the dowel pins to aid in the removal of the front cover.

7. Clean the front cover and engine mating surfaces. Remove the front cover oil seal using an appropriate oil seal removal tool.

To install:

8. Coat the outside diameter of the new seal with an approved sealer and install the seal using an approciate seal installer tool.

9. After installing the oil pan seal to the front cover, trim ⅛ in. (3.2mm) from each end of the seal.

10. Apply an approved sealer around coolant holes of the new front cover gasket and install the front cover. Install the timing indicator.

11. Apply a suitable sealer to crankshaft key and inside the crankshaft balancer hub. Apply a suitable seal lubricant to the seal contact area of the balancer hub.

12. Install the crankshaft balancer on the crankshaft. Check the clearance between the front of the engine and balancer hub while installing the hub. The proper balancer to engine clearance is 0.001 in. tight to 0.0007 in. loose.

13. Torque the crankshaft hub bolt to specification and torque the crankshaft pulley bolts to 28 ft. lbs.

14. Complete installation by reversing the removal procedure.

5.7L Engine

1. Disconnect the negative battery cable. Properly relieve the fuel system pressure.

2. Remove the serpentine drive belt. Raise and support the vehicle safely. Remove the vibration damper retaining bolt.

3. Remove the crankshaft pulley bolts and the crankshaft pulley. Using

tool J–23523 or equivalent remove the vibration damper.

4. Drain the engine oil. Remove the oil pan retaining bolts. Remove the oil pan.

5. Lower the vehicle. Remove the water pump assembly.

6. Remove the front cover retaining bolts. Remove the front cover. Discard the gasket.

7. Clean the front cover and engine mating surfaces. Remove the front cover oil seal using an appropriate oil seal removal tool.

To install:

8. Coat the outside diameter of the new seal with an approved sealer and install the seal using an approciate seal installer tool.

9. Position the cover and the gasket over the crankshaft end.

10. Loosely install the cover to block upper retaining bolts.

NOTE: Do not force the cover over the dowels to the point where the cover flange or the dowels become distorted.

11. Tighten the bolts in a alternate pattern and evenly while pressing downward on the cover so that the dowels in the block are aligned with the corresponding holes in the cover. Position the engine front cover so that the dowels enter the holes in the cover without binding.

12. Continue the installation in the reverse order of the removal procedure.

Front Cover Oil Seal

REPLACEMENT

5.0L Engine

COVER INSTALLED

1. Disconnect the negative battery cable. Properly relieve the fuel system pressure.

2. Remove the crankshaft pulley retaining bolts. Remove the crankshaft pulley.

3. Remove the harmonic balancer, using the proper tools.

4. Using seal removal tool J–23129 and J–185903 remove the oil seal from the front cover.

5. Installation is the reverse of the removal procedure. Coat the outside diameter of the new seal with sealing compound, or equivalent.

COVER REMOVED

1. Disconnect the negative battery cable. Properly relieve the fuel system pressure.

2. Remove the front cover from the engine.

3. Using the proper tool remove the old seal and discard it.

4. Coat the new seal with clean engine oil. Using the proper installation tool install the new seal in the cover.

5. Install the front cover to the engine.

5.7L Engine

COVER INSTALLED

1. Disconnect the negative battery cable. Properly relieve the fuel system pressure.

2. Remove the serpentine drive belt. Raise and support the vehicle safely. Remove the vibration damper retaining bolt.

3. Remove the crankshaft pulley bolts and the crankshaft pulley. Using tool J–23523 or equivalent remove the vibration damper.

4. Pry the seal from the cover, using the proper tool. Care should be used as not to damage the cover.

5. Installation is the reverse of the removal procedure. Be sure to use tool J–35468 or equivalent to properly align the new oil seal.

COVER REMOVED

1. Disconnect the negative battery cable. Properly relieve the fuel system pressure.

2. Remove the front cover from the engine.

3. Using the proper tool remove the old seal and discard it.

4. Coat the new seal with clean engine oil. Using the proper installation tool install the new seal in the cover.

5. Install the front cover to the engine.

Timing Chain and Sprockets

REMOVAL & INSTALLATION

5.0L Engine

1. Disconnect the negative battery cable. Properly relieve the fuel system pressure. Remove the engine front cover.

2. Remove the fuel pump.

3. Remove the crankshaft oil slinger, camshaft thrust button and spring.

4. Remove the camshaft sprocket retaining bolt and the fuel pump eccentric. Remove the camshaft sprocket and timing chain assembly.

5. Remove the crankshaft key before attempting to remove the crankshaft sprocket. Using an appropriate puller tool, remove the crankshaft sprocket.

To install:

6. Insert the camshaft sprocket and crankshaft sprocket into the timing chain, with the timing marks aligned. Lube the thrust surface with Molykote or equivalent.

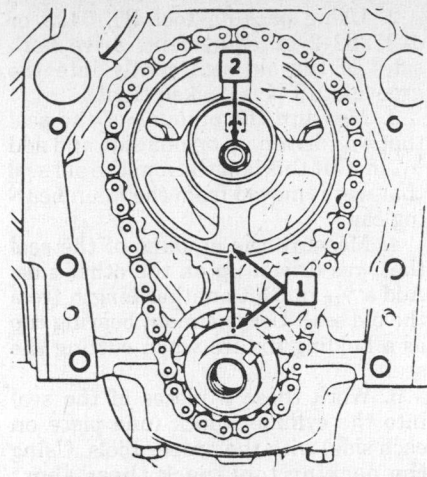

Timing mark alignment—5.0L engine

7. Grasp both sprockets and the timing chain together and put them into their prospective places. Rotate the camshaft sprocket and engage it on the camshaft.

8. Install the fuel pump eccentric, flat side toward the engine. Install the camshaft sprocket bolt finger tight. Rotate the crankshaft until the keyways are aligned. Install the crankshaft sprocket key, tap it in with a brass hammer until the key bottoms.

9. When the timing marks are in alignment, the No. 6 cylinder should be at TDC. When both timing marks are on the top, the No. 1 cylinder is at TDC of the compression stroke.

10. Slowly and evenly draw the camshaft sprocket onto the camshaft, using the mounting bolt and torque the bolt to 65 ft. lbs.

11. Lubricate the timing chain and finish the installation by reversing the order of the removal procedure.

12. When installing the front cover, apply a suitable RTV sealant around the coolant holes of the new front cover. Be sure to trim the ends of the oil pan seal and install the seal onto the timing chain cover.

5.7L Engine

1. Disconnect the negative battery cable. Properly relieve the fuel system pressure. Remove the engine front cover.

2. Rotate the engine until the marks on both the camshaft sprocket and crankshaft sprocket align with the shaft centers.

3. Remove the camshaft sprocket retaining bolts. Remove the camshaft sprocket along with the timing chain.

4. Using a crankshaft sprocket removal tool, remove the crankshaft sprocket. Remove the crankshaft sprocket key, if required.

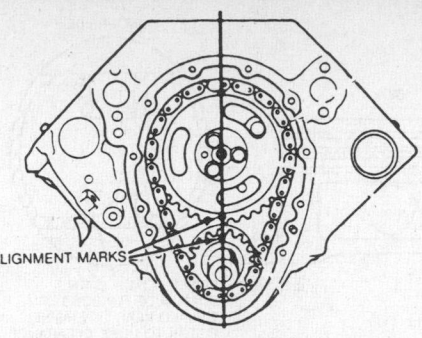

Timing mark alignment—5.7L engine

5. Installation is the reverse of the removal procedure.

Camshaft

REMOVAL & INSTALLATION

5.0L Engine

1. Disconnect the negative battery cable. Properly relieve the fuel system pressure. Drain the cooling system.

2. Remove the intake manifold. Remove the valve covers, rocker arm assemblies, pushrods and lifters. Be sure to note the location of each component for proper installation.

3. Remove the radiator shroud assembly. Remove the radiator. Remove the front grille, if necessary. Remove the cooling fan and water pump pulley.

4. Remove the power steering pump and position it to the side. Remove the alternator. Remove the air pump. Remove the crankshaft pulley and vibration damper.

5. Properly discharge the air conditioning system. Remove the compressor mount bolts, brackets and compressor assembly. Remove the condenser assembly and seal all openings.

6. Remove the water pump. Remove the fuel pump. Remove the front engine cover. Remove the camshaft thrust button and spring. Rotate the crankshaft and align the timing marks.

7. Remove the camshaft retaining bolt, gear and chain. Remove the camshaft retaining plate and camshaft flange adapter and carefully remove the camshaft. The camshaft sprocket is a tight fit. If the sprocket does not come off easily, a light blow on the lower edge of the sprocket with a soft face mallet should dislodge the sprocket.

8. Installation is the reverse of the removal procedure. Lubricate the camshaft journals with a suitable engine oil supplement, before installing the camshaft.

5.7L Engine

1. Disconnect the negative battery cable. Properly relieve the fuel system pressure. Drain the cooling system.

2. Remove the intake manifold. Remove the valve covers, rocker arm assemblies, pushrods and lifters Be sure to note the location of each component for proper installation.

3. Remove the radiator tie struts at the radiator cradle. Remove the radiator. Remove the serpentine drive belt. Remove the clutch fan assembly.

4. Remove the engine front cover. Remove the timing chain. Remove the camshaft sprocket.

5. As required, properly discharge the air conditioning system and remove the condenser assembly. As required, remove the grille assembly.

6. Install three $5/16$–18×4 in. bolts in the camshaft timing gear bolt holes. Carefully pull the camshaft partially out of the engine using the bolts as a handle. Remove the bolts from the camshaft. Remove the camshaft from the engine.

7. Installation is the reverse of the removal procedure. Lubricate the camshaft journals with a suitable engine oil supplement, before installing the camshaft.

Piston and Connecting Rod

POSITIONING

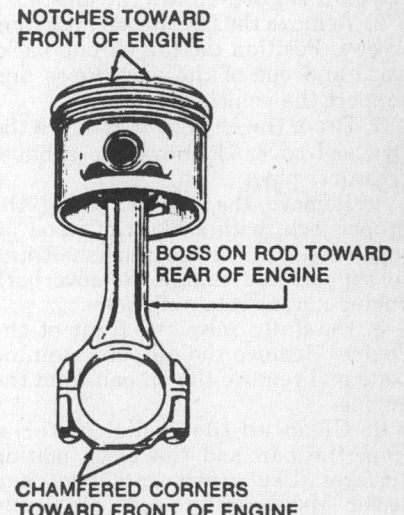

NOTCHES TOWARD FRONT OF ENGINE

BOSS ON ROD TOWARD REAR OF ENGINE

CHAMFERED CORNERS TOWARD FRONT OF ENGINE

Piston positioning and identification—5.0L engine

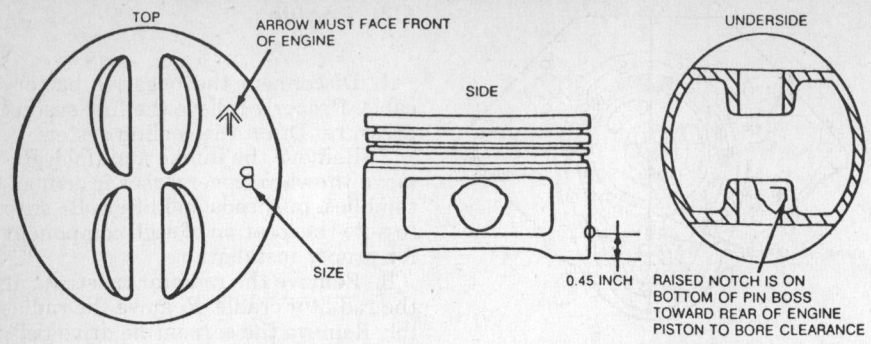

Piston positioning and identification—5.7L engine

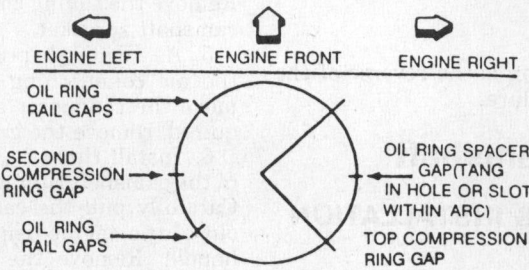

Piston ring gap locations—5.7L engine

ENGINE LUBRICATION

Oil Pan

REMOVAL & INSTALLATION

1. Disconnect the negative battery cable. Remove the air cleaner assembly. On the 5.7L engine, remove the AIR pipe diverter valve outlet hose. On the 5.0L engine remove the dipstick.

2. Remove the fan shroud attaching screws. Position the fan shroud backward and out of the way. Raise and support the vehicle safely.

3. Drain the engine oil. Remove the flywheel cover. Remove the exhaust crossover pipe.

4. Remove the starter. Using the proper jack, with a block of wood on top, place it under the crankshaft hub to support the engine. Remove both engine mount retaining bolts.

5. Carefully raise the front of the engine. Remove the oil pan retaining bolts and remove the oil pan from the engine.

6. Clean all the gasket material from the pan and the block mating surfaces. Use a new gasket kit and sealer. Make sure the seals are firmly positioned on the flange surfaces with each seal properly located in the cut out notches of the gm-pan gasket.

7. Installation is the reverse of the removal procedure.

Oil Pump

REMOVAL & INSTALLATION

1. Disconnect the negative battery cable. Raise and support the vehicle safely. Drain the engine oil. Remove the oil pan.

2. Remove the oil pump retaining bolts. Remove the oil pump with the pump driveshaft from the engine.

3. Before installing the oil pump to the engine, remove the pump cover and fill the cavities with petroleum jelly.

4. Installation is the reverse of the removal procedure. Be sure that the oil pump driveshaft extension is fully engaged.

5. After completing installation, remove the oil pressure sending unit and install an oil pressure guage. Start the engine and check the oil pressure.

Rear Main Bearing Oil Seal
REMOVAL & INSTALLATION

5.0L Engine

1. Disconnect the negative battery cable. Raise and support the vehicle safely. Drain the engine oil. Remove the oil pan. Remove the rear main bearing cap.

2. Using packing tool BT-6433 or J-25282-2 or equivalent, drive both sides of the old seal gently into the groove until it is packed tight.

3. Measure the amount of the seal that was driven up on one side and add $\frac{1}{16}$ in. Cut this length from the old seal that was removed from the main bearing cap.

4. Measure the amount of the seal that was driven up on the other side. Add a $\frac{1}{16}$ in. Cut another length from the old seal. Use the main bearing cap as a holding fixture when cutting the seal.

5. Work these 2 pieces of the seal into the cylinder block (one piece on each side) with the proper tools. Using the packing tool, pack these short pieces up into the block using tool BT-6436 or equivalent.

6. Place a piece of shim stock between the seal and the crankshaft to protect the bearing surface before trimming the seal.

7. Form a new rope seal in the rear main bearing cap. Place a drop of a suitable sealer on each end of the seal and cap. Install the main bearing cap. Do not use the attaching bolts to pull down the bearing cap. Tap gently into place with a suitable tool.

8. Continue the installation in the reverse order of the removal procedure.

5.7L Engine

1. Disconnect the negative battery cable. Raise and support the vehicle safely. Remove the transmission. As

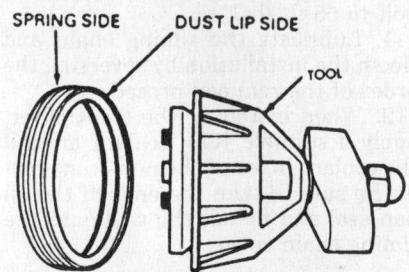

Rear main seal installation tool— 5.7L engine

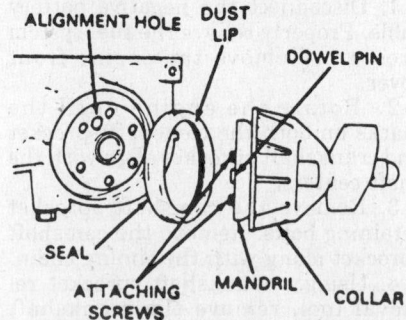

Installing one piece rear main seal— 5.7L engine

required, remove the flywheel.

2. Drain the engine oil. Lower the oil pan.

3. Remove the rear crankshaft seal retaining nuts and bolts.

4. Remove the crankshaft seal retainer along with the assembled seal and gasket.

5. Remove the rear crankshaft seal from the rear crankshaft seal retainer.

6. Using the proper installation tool, install the seal to the rear of the crankshaft then install the retainer with the tool attached. Tighten the wing nut of the tool until it bottoms. Remove the tool from the retainer.

7. Continue the installation in the reverse of the removal procedure.

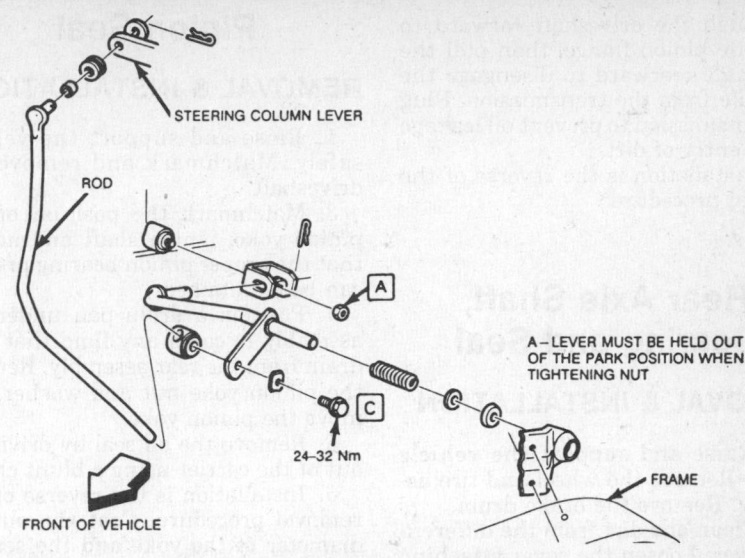

Shift linkage adjustment

AUTOMATIC TRANSMISSION

For further information on transmissions/transaxles, please refer to "Chilton's Guide to Transmission Repair".

Transmission Assembly

REMOVAL & INSTALLATION

1. Disconnect the negative battery cable. Position the selector lever in the **N** detent.

2. Remove the air cleaner assembly. Disconnect the accelerator cable and detent cable, as required.

3. Remove the transmission dipstick and the dipstick tube retaining bolt.

4. Raise and support the vehicle safely.

5. Matchmark the driveshaft so it can be reinstalled in its original position. Remove the driveshaft.

6. Disconnect the shift linkage, speedometer cable and all electrical connections at the transmission. Remove the starter.

7. Remove the flexplate cover and mark the flexplate and converter so they can be reinstalled in their original location. Remove the flexplate to converter bolts.

8. Position a transmission jack under the transmission and remove the transmission mount.

9. Remove the crossmember attaching bolts and remove the crossmember. If necessary, remove the floor pan reinforcement.

10. Remove the transmission to en-

gine bolts. Support the engine with a suitable support tool.

11. Lower the transmission slightly. Disconnect the transmission lines and required cables. Plug all openings.

12. Install a torque converter holding tool and remove the transmission assembly from the vehicle.

13. Installation is the reverse of the transmission removal procedure.

SHIFT LINKAGE ADJUSTMENT

1. With the transmission selector lever in the **N** detent, tighten the linkage rod retaining bolt to the proper torque.

2. The linkage is correctly adjusted if at final vehicle inspection with the selector lever raised and centered in the **N** detent, the column lever can be lowered and will engage in the column neutral notch.

3. Adjustment is unacceptable if any rotation of the selector lever is required to engage the column neutral notch.

DETENT CABLE ADJUSTMENT

1. Remove the air cleaner assembly.

2. Depress and hold down the metal reset tab at the engine side of the throttle valve cable.

3. Move the slider until it stops against the fitting. Release the reset tab.

4. Rotate the throttle lever to its full travel position.

5. The slider must ratchet toward the lever when the lever is rotated to its full travel position.

DRIVE AXLE

Driveshaft and U-Joints

REMOVAL & INSTALLATION

1. Raise and support the vehicle safely. Position a drain pan under the transmission.

2. Matchmark the driveshaft so it can be reinstalled in its original position. Remove the rear driveshaft flange capscrews.

NOTE: Never let the full weight of the driveshaft be supported only by the front universal joint.

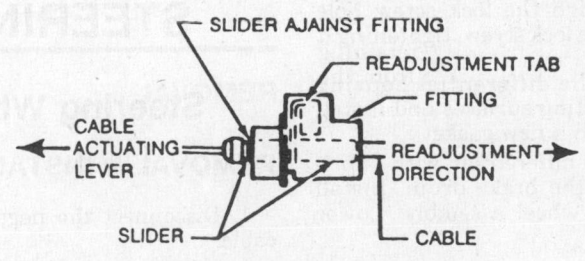

Throttle valve cable adjustment

3. Push the driveshaft forward to clear the pinion flange, then pull the driveshaft rearward to disengage the slip yoke from the transmission. Plug the transmission to prevent oil leakage or the entry of dirt.

4. Installation is the reverse of the removal procedure.

Rear Axle Shaft, Bearing and Seal

REMOVAL & INSTALLATION

1. Raise and support the vehicle safely. Remove the wheel and tire assembly. Remove the brake drum.

2. Clean any dirt from the differential cover. Loosen the cover attaching bolts. Drain the lubricant.

3. Remove the pinion cross shaft lockscrew and remove the cross shaft.

4. Push in on the flanged end of the axle shaft and remove the C-lock from the splined end of the axle shaft.

5. Remove the axle shaft from the housing, being cautious not to damage the oil seal.

6. Use a suitable tool to pry the oil seal out of the bore. Use an axle shaft bearing puller or a slide hammer to remove the axle bearing from the bearing bore.

7. Lubricate the new bearing with gear lubricant. Use bearing installer tool J–23690 or equivalent and install the bearing so that the tool bottoms out against the shoulder in the housing. Lubricate the lips of the seal with gear lubricant. Position the new seal on seal installer tool J–23771 or equivalent, and position the seal into the housing bore. Tap the seal into place so that it is flush with the axle tube.

8. Slide the axle shaft into the housing until the splines on the end of the shaft engage the splines of the differential side gear. Handle the shaft gently when trying to engage to splines.

9. Install the axle shaft C-lock on the splined end of the axle shaft in the differential. Push the shaft outward so that the shaft lock seats in the counterbore of the differential side gear.

10. Install the pinion cross shaft through the differential case and pinion gears. Align the lock screw hole and install the lock screw, tightening it to 25 ft. lbs.

11. Clean the differential housing and cover mating surfaces and install the cover with a new gasket.

12. Fill the differential with lubricant. Install the brake drum. Install the tire and wheel assembly. Lower the vehicle.

Pinion Seal

REMOVAL & INSTALLATION

1. Raise and support the vehicle safely. Matchmark and remove the driveshaft.

3. Matchmark the position of the pinion yoke, pinion shaft and nut so that the proper pinion bearing preload can be maintained.

4. Position a drain pan under the assembly to catch any fluid that may drain from the rear assembly. Remove the pinion yoke nut and washer. Remove the pinion yoke.

5. Remove the oil seal by driving it out of the carrier using a blunt chisel.

6. Installation is the reverse of the removal procedure. Coat the outside diameter of the yoke and the sealing lip of the new seal with seal lubricant, part number 1050169 or equivalent.

7. Tighten the yoke nut to the position marked from Step 3. While holding the pinion yoke tighten the nut an additional $1/16$ in. beyond the alignment marks.

Axle Housing

REMOVAL & INSTALLATION

1. Raise and support the vehicle safely. Remove the tire and wheel assemblies. Remove the brake drums. Properly support the rear axle.

2. Disconnect the shock absorbers from axle. Matchmark the driveshaft and disconnect it from the rear axle pinion flange.

3. Remove the brake line junction block bolt at axle housing. Disconnect the brake lines at the junction block. If equipped with ABS disconnect all required electrical connectors.

4. Disconnect the upper control arms from axle housing. Lower the rear axle assembly slightly and remove the springs.

5. Continue lowering the rear axle assembly and remove it from the vehicle.

6. Installation is the reverse of the removal procedure.

STEERING

Steering Wheel

REMOVAL & INSTALLATION

1. Disconnect the negative battery cable.

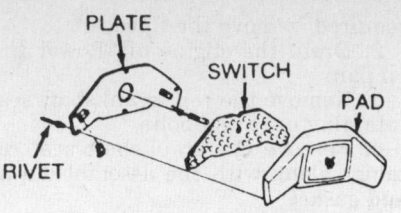

PAD AND HORN SWITCH

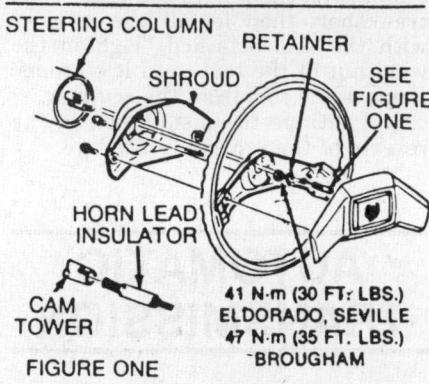

FIGURE ONE

41 N·m (30 FT. LBS.)
ELDORADO, SEVILLE
47 N·m (35 FT. LBS.)
BROUGHAM

STANDARD COLUMN

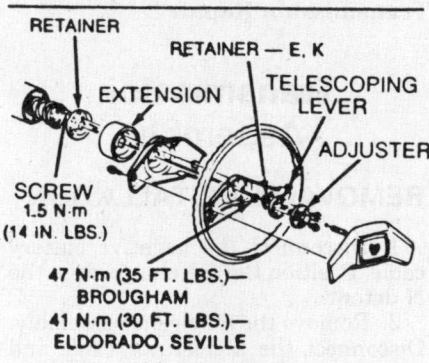

47 N·m (35 FT. LBS.)—
BROUGHAM
41 N·m (30 FT. LBS.)—
ELDORADO, SEVILLE

TILT AND TELESCOPING COLUMN

Steering wheel and related components

2. Remove the horn pad retaining screws. Remove the horn pad assembly.

3. Remove the horn contact wire from the plastic tower by pushing in on the wire and turning counterclockwise. The wire will spring out of the tower. It may be necessary to turn the ignition to the **ON** position in order to facilitate removal.

4. If the vehicle is equipped with a tilt and telescoping steering wheel, remove the screws that secure the telescope locking lever assembly to the adjuster. Unscrew and remove the adjuster from the steering shaft.

5. Remove the locking lever assembly. Scribe an alignment mark on the steering wheel hub in line with the

slash mark on the steering shaft.

6. Loosen the locknut on the steering shaft and position it flush with the end of the shaft. Using the proper steering wheel removal tool, remove the wheel from its mounting on the steering shaft.

7. Remove the steering wheel removal tool from the steering wheel. Remove the locknut from the steering shaft. Remove the steering wheel from the vehicle.

8. Installation is the reverse of the removal procedure. When installing the steering wheel, it should not be driven on the steering shaft as damage to the steering column and its components could occur.

Steering Column

REMOVAL & INSTALLATION

1. Disconnect the negative battery cable.

2. Center the steering wheel and remove the upper coupling pinch bolt and nut.

3. Disconnect the transmission shift linkage at the lower shift lever.

4. Remove the steering column lower cover from the instrument panel, exposing the upper support bolts.

5. Disconnect the turn signal wiring connector. If equipped with cruise control, disconnect the harness.

6. As required, remove the lower instrument panel trim cover. Remove the screw securing the shift cable to the shift bowl.

7. Loosen bolts at the steering column upper support. Do not completely remove the upper support nuts or bolts as the steering column could bend under its own weight.

8. Move the rubber carpet seal up the steering column as far as possible and position the carpet to gain access to the toe plate.

9. Remove the screws retaining the toe plate to the floor pan.

10. Remove the bolts at the upper column bracket, disconnect the remaining electrical connectors and vacuum connectors while supporting the column.

11. Carefully pull the steering column up and out of the vehicle. If the shaft hangs up in the upper coupling, secure the upper mounting bracket and free the coupling from the steering shaft. Remove the column assembly.

12. Installation is the reverse of the removal procedure. A clearance of $^5/_{16}$ in. should exist between the shaft and the upper coupling when the installation is complete or lower steering column bearing damage could result.

Power Steering Gear

REMOVAL & INSTALLATION

1. Disconnect the negative battery cable. Position a drain pan under the steering gear. Disconnect the pressure and return lines from the steering gear assembly. Plug the opening to prevent the entrance of dirt.

2. If equipped, disconnect the stone shield from the return pipe.

3. Remove the pinch bolt from the flex coupling and disconnect the coupling from the gear.

NOTE: Failure to disconnect the flexible coupling from the steering gear stub shaft can result in damage to the steering gear and or the intermediate shaft. This damage can cause the loss of steering control which could result in a vehicle crash and bodily injuries.

4. Raise the vehicle and support it safely.

5. Remove the pitman arm nut and washer. Remove the pitman arm from the sector shaft using a pitman arm puller tool.

6. Remove the retaining bolts and washers holding the steering gear to the side rail. Lower the gear assembly from the vehicle.

7. The installation is the reverse of the removal procedure. Tighten the pitman arm nut to 185 ft. lbs., the mounting bolts to 70 ft. lbs. and the flex coupling pinch bolt to 30 ft. lbs.

Power Steering Pump

REMOVAL & INSTALLATION

5.0L Engine

1. Disconnect the negative battery cable. Disconnect and relocate the air cleaner inlet tube and the upper radiator hose to gain access to the pump.

2. Remove the alternator belt. Loosen the alternator mounting bolts, except for the long bolt. Rotate the unit upward to gain access by pivoting the long bolt.

3. Remove and plug the pressure and return hoses from the pump. Remove the front pump bracket mounting bolts and spacer. Remove the rear pump mounting nut.

4. Remove the power steering pump drive belt. Remove the pump and bracket from the engine as an assembly.

5. Installation is the reverse order of the removal procedure. Be sure to bleed the air from the system.

5.7L Engine

1. Disconnect the negative battery cable. Remove the serpentine drive belt.

2. Remove the power steering pump pulley. Raise and support the vehicle safely.

3. Remove and plug the pressure and return hoses from the pump. Remove the 3 Torx head screws an separate the pump from the bracket.

4. Remove the power steering pump from the vehicle.

5. Installation is the reverse of the removal procedure. Bleed the system, as required.

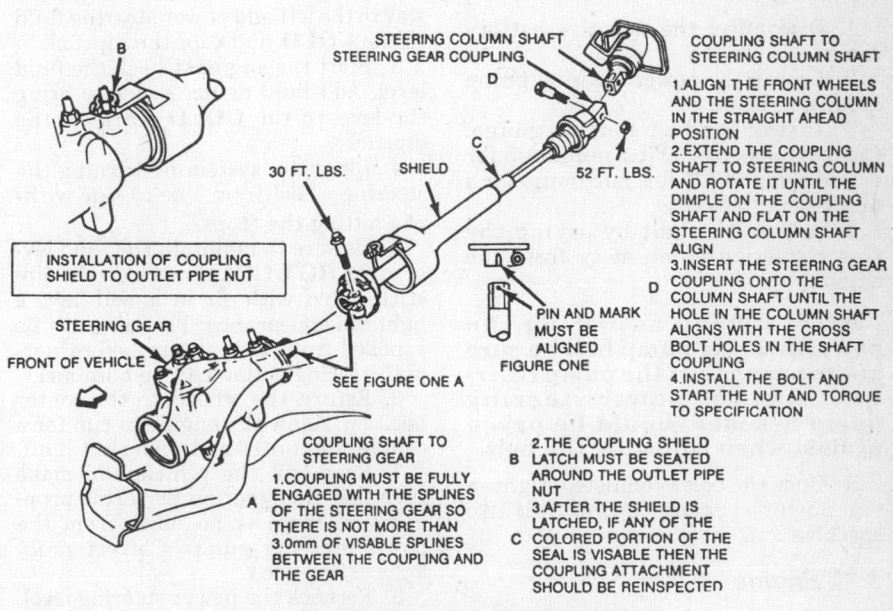

Steering gear and alignment data

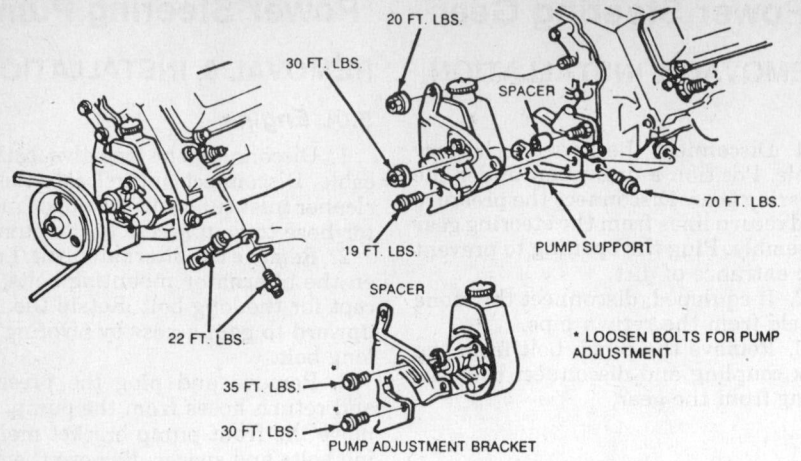

Power steering pump mounting—5.0L engine

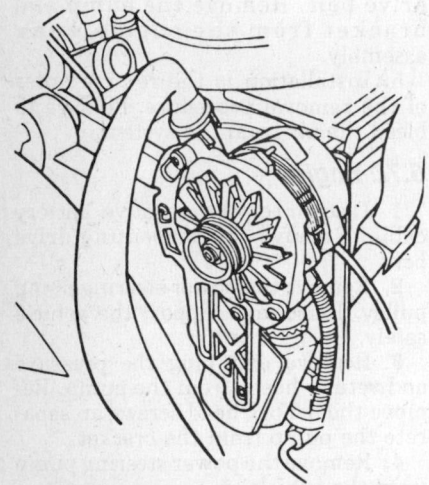

Power steering pump mounting—5.7L engine

BELT ADJUSTMENT

5.0L Engine

1. Disconnect the negative battery cable.

2. Loosen the power steering pump mounting bolts.

3. Install the belt tension gauge. Correct tension is 90 lbs. minimum for a used belt and 170 lbs. maximum for a new belt.

4. Adjust the belt by prying the power steering pump away from the engine.

NOTE: When adjusting the power steering pump belt be sure not to pry against the pump reservoir. Only the power steering pump bracket should be pryed against when adjusting the belt.

5. Once the belt is adjusted, tighten the power steering pump bolts to specification.

5.7L Engine

The serpentine drive belt is self adjust-

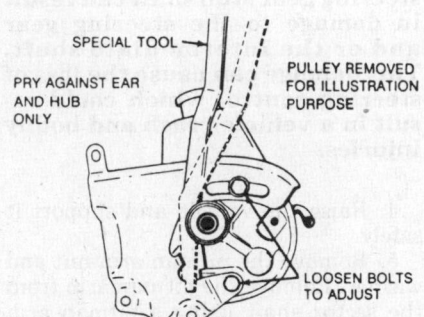

Power steering pump adjustment—5.0L engine

ing within the tensioner operating limits.

SYSTEM BLEEDING

1. Raise and support the vehicle safely.

2. With the wheels turned all the way to the left add power steering fluid to the **COLD** mark on the dipstick.

3. Start the engine. Check the fluid level. Add fluid as necessary to bring the level to the **COLD** mark on the dipstick.

4. Bleed the system by turning the steering wheel from side to side without hitting the stops.

5. Be sure to maintain the fluid level at the **HOT/COLD** mark on the dipstick. Fluid with air in it will have a light tan appearance. This air must be expelled from the system before normal steering action can be obtained.

6. Return the wheels to the center position. Allow the engine to run for a couple of minutes and then shut it off.

7. Road test the vehicle and make sure that the steering performs properly and there is no noise from the power steering pump. Correct problems as required.

8. Recheck the power steering level. Be sure that the fluid level is at the

HOT mark on the dipstick after the system has stabilized at its normal operating temperature.

Tie Rod Ends

REMOVAL & INSTALLATION

1. Raise and support the vehicle safely.

2. Remove the cotter pin and castellated nut from the outer tie rod end. Discard the nut, do not reuse.

3. Using the proper tool disconnect the tie rod end from the steering knuckle.

4. Using the proper tool remove the inner ball stud from the intermediate rod.

NOTE: When disconnecting a linkage joint no attempt should be made to disengage the joint by driving a wedge between the joint and the retained part as seal damage may result.

5. Remove the tie rod from the adjuster tube by loosening the clamp bolts and unscrewing the end assemblies.

6. Installation is the reverse of the removal procedure. Check and adjust front end alignment, as required.

BRAKES

For all brake system repair and service procedures not detailed below, please refer to "Brakes" in the Unit Repair section.

Master Cylinder

REMOVAL & INSTALLATION

1. Disconnect the negative battery cable. Disconnect and plug the brake lines at the master cylinder.

2. Remove the nuts securing the master cylinder to the power booster.

3. Remove the master cylinder from the vehicle. Be sure not to lose the master cylinder pushrod.

4. Bench bleed the master cylinder before installing on the vehicle.

5. Installation is the reverse of the removal procedure. As required, bleed the system.

Combination Valve

REMOVAL & INSTALLATION

1. Disconnect the negative battery cable. Disconnect the electrical con-

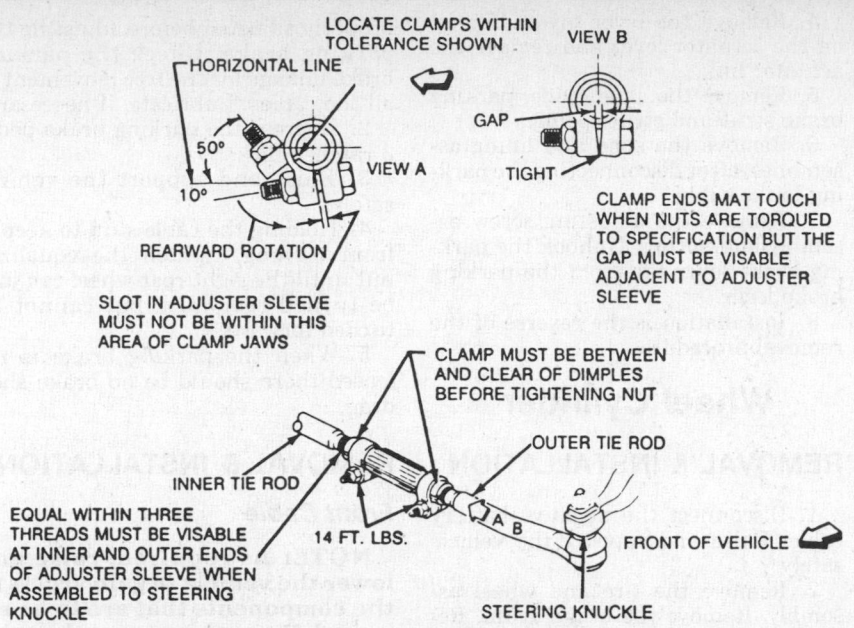

LOCATE CLAMPS WITHIN TOLERANCE SHOWN

VIEW B

HORIZONTAL LINE

50°

10°

VIEW A

GAP

TIGHT

REARWARD ROTATION

CLAMP ENDS MAT TOUCH WHEN NUTS ARE TORQUED TO SPECIFICATION BUT THE GAP MUST BE VISABLE ADJACENT TO ADJUSTER SLEEVE

SLOT IN ADJUSTER SLEEVE MUST NOT BE WITHIN THIS AREA OF CLAMP JAWS

CLAMP MUST BE BETWEEN AND CLEAR OF DIMPLES BEFORE TIGHTENING NUT

OUTER TIE ROD

INNER TIE ROD

EQUAL WITHIN THREE THREADS MUST BE VISABLE AT INNER AND OUTER ENDS OF ADJUSTER SLEEVE WHEN ASSEMBLED TO STEERING KNUCKLE

14 FT. LBS.

A B

FRONT OF VEHICLE

STEERING KNUCKLE

Positioning the tie rod adjuster tube clamp

nector from the valve assembly.

2. Disconnect and plug the brake lines at the valve.

3. Remove the valve retaining bolt. Remove the valve from its mounting.

4. Installation is the reverse of the removal procedure. As required, bleed the system.

Power Brake Booster

REMOVAL & INSTALLATION

1. Disconnect the negative battery cable. Remove the master cylinder retaining nuts and position the assembly out of the way.

2. Be sure not to lose the mater cylinder pushrod. Disconnect vacuum line from vacuum check valve on unit.

3. Remove steering column lower cover.

4. Remove cotter pin, washer and spring spacer that secures power unit pushrod to brake pedal arm.

5. Remove the nuts that secure the power unit to the firewall. Remove the power unit.

6. Installation is the reverse of the removal procedure. As required, bleed the system.

Brake Caliper

REMOVAL & INSTALLATION

1. Disconnect the negative battery cable. Partially drain the master cylinder assembly.

2. Raise and support the vehicle

safely. Remove the tire and wheel assembly.

3. Disconnect and plug the brake line hose at the caliper. If equipped, disconnect any required electrical connectors.

4. Remove the caliper retaining bolts. Remove the caliper assembly from its mounting.

5. Installation is the reverse of the removal procedure. As required, bleed the brake system.

Disc Brake Pads

REMOVAL & INSTALLATION

1. Disconnect the negative battery cable. Partially drain the master cylinder assembly.

2. Raise and support the vehicle safely. Remove the tire and wheel assembly.

3. Remove the caliper retaining bolts. Remove the caliper assembly from its mounting. Do not allow the caliper to hang by the brake line hose.

4. Remove the outboard shoe and lining. Remove the inboard shoe and lining.

5. Installation is the reverse of the removal procedure. As required, bleed the brake system. Be sure to use a new inboard shoe retainer spring.

6. Apply about 175 lbs. of force to the brake pedal 3 times to seat the linings.

7. Position a pair of channel lock pliers over the brake shoe ears and bottom edge of the caliper. While applying about 50 lbs. of force on the brake pedal, clinch the outboard shoe ears to the caliper.

Brake Rotor

REMOVAL & INSTALLATION

1. Disconnect the negative battery cable. Partially drain the master cylinder assembly.

2. Raise and support the vehicle safely. Remove the tire and wheel assembly.

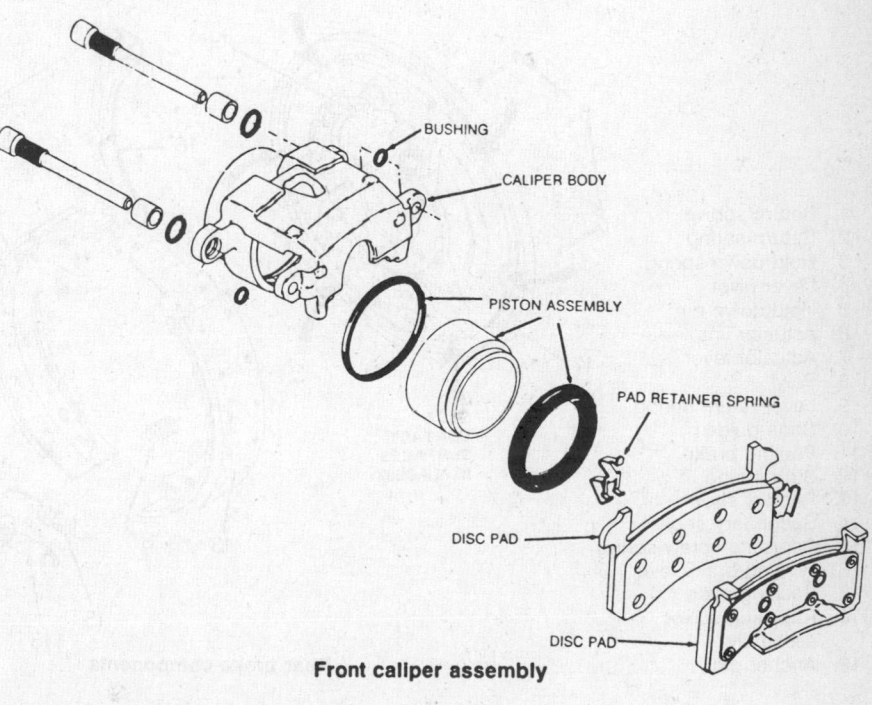

BUSHING

CALIPER BODY

PISTON ASSEMBLY

PAD RETAINER SPRING

DISC PAD

DISC PAD

Front caliper assembly

3. Remove the caliper retaining bolts. Remove the caliper assembly from its mounting and properly position it aside.

4. Remove the dust cap. Remove the cotter pin, locknut, washer and outer bearing assembly.

5. Remove the rotor assembly from the spindle.

6. Installation is the reverse of the removal procedure. Adjust the wheel bearings, as required.

Brake Drums

REMOVAL & INSTALLATION

1. Disconnect the negative battery cable.

2. Raise and support the vehicle safely. Remove the tire and wheel assembly.

3. Remove the drum locking tabs, if equipped. Remove the rear brake drum from the vehicle.

4. Installation is the reverse of the removal procedure.

Brake Shoes

REMOVAL & INSTALLATION

1. Disconnect the negative battery cable. Raise and support the vehicle safely.

2. Remove the tire and wheel assembly. Remove the brake drum.

3. Using the proper tool, remove the return springs. Remove the hold down springs and pins.

4. Remove the lever pivot. Lift up on the actuator lever and remove the actuator link.

5. Remove the shoe guide, parking brake strut and strut spring.

6. Remove the shoe and lining assemblies, after disconnecting the parking brake cable.

7. Remove the adjusting screw assembly and spring. Unhook the parking brake lever tab from the parking brake lever.

8. Installation is the reverse of the removal procedure.

Wheel Cylinder

REMOVAL & INSTALLATION

1. Disconnect the negative battery cable. Raise and support the vehicle safely.

2. Remove the tire and wheel assembly. Remove the brake drum. Remove the brake shoes.

3. Disconnect and plug the brake line at the wheel cylinder. Remove the wheel cylinder links from the wheel cylinder.

4. Remove the wheel cylinder retaining bolts or clips. Remove the wheel cylinder from its mounting.

5. Installation is the reverse of the removal procedure. As required, bleed the brake system.

Parking Brake Cable

ADJUSTMENT

1. Be sure that the rear brakes are properly adjusted before adjusting the parking brake. Check the parking brake linkage for the free movement of all the cables. Lubricate, if necessary.

2. Depress the parking brake pedal 3 ratchet clicks.

3. Raise and support the vehicle safely.

4. Holding the cable stud to keep it from turning, tighten the equalizer nut until the right rear wheel can just be turned rearward, but cannot be turned forward.

5. When the parking brake is released there should be no brake shoe drag.

REMOVAL & INSTALLATION

Front Cable

NOTE: As required, raise and lower the vehicle to gain access to the components that are to be removed. Properly support the vehicle at all times.

1. Release the parking brake.

2. Remove the equalizer nut and separate the cable stud from the equalizer.

3. Remove the front cable from the cable connector. Loosen the adjuster nut and disconnect the front cable from the connector.

4. Compress the cable retainer fingers and loosen the assembly at the frame.

5. Remove the cable at the pedal assembly. Remove the cable end from the parking brake assembly clevis.

6. Pull the cable through the hole in

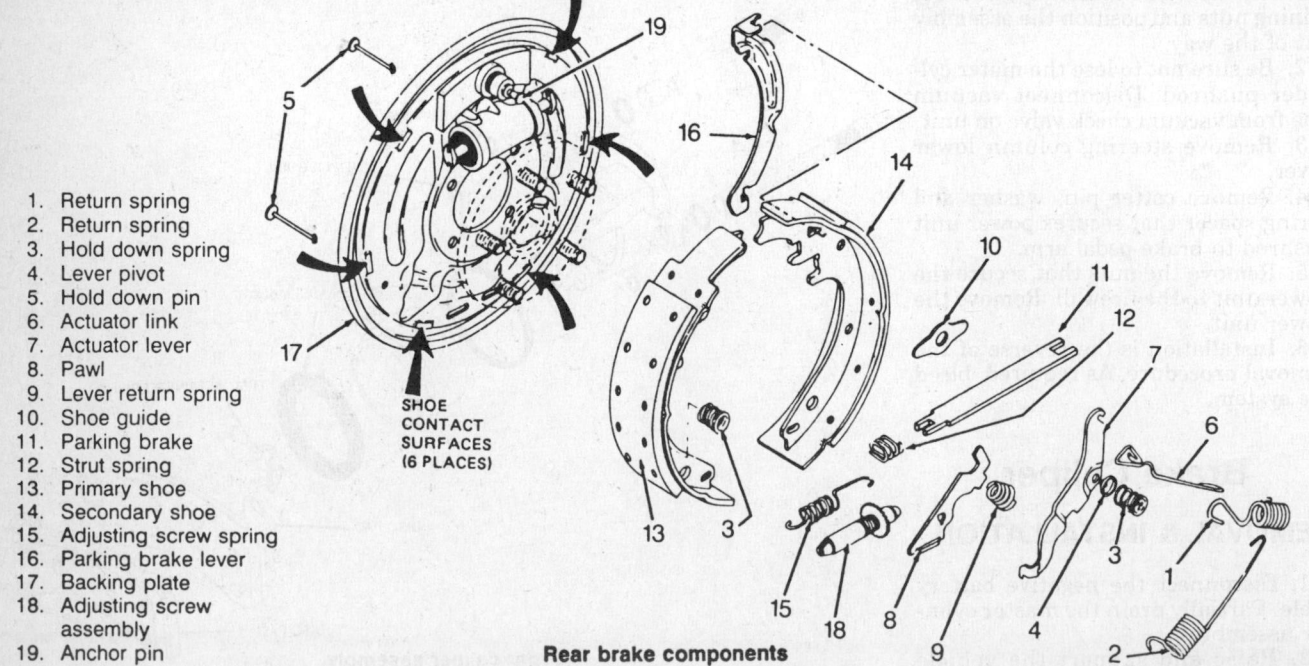

1. Return spring
2. Return spring
3. Hold down spring
4. Lever pivot
5. Hold down pin
6. Actuator link
7. Actuator lever
8. Pawl
9. Lever return spring
10. Shoe guide
11. Parking brake
12. Strut spring
13. Primary shoe
14. Secondary shoe
15. Adjusting screw spring
16. Parking brake lever
17. Backing plate
18. Adjusting screw assembly
19. Anchor pin

SHOE CONTACT SURFACES (6 PLACES)

Rear brake components

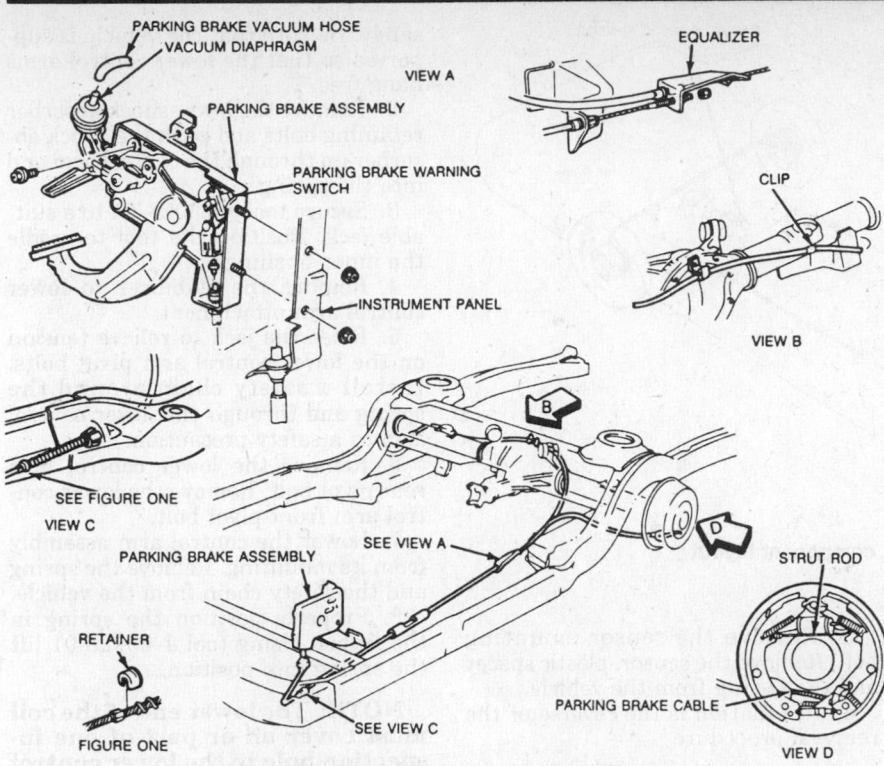

Parking brake vacuum hose
VACUUM DIAPHRAGM
VIEW A
PARKING BRAKE ASSEMBLY
PARKING BRAKE WARNING SWITCH
INSTRUMENT PANEL
EQUALIZER
CLIP
VIEW B
SEE FIGURE ONE
VIEW C
PARKING BRAKE ASSEMBLY
SEE VIEW A
SEE VIEW C
RETAINER
FIGURE ONE
STRUT ROD
PARKING BRAKE CABLE
VIEW D

Parking brake assembly and related components

the frame and remove it from the vehicle.

7. Installation is the reverse of the removal procedure. Adjust the parking brakes.

Rear Cable

1. Release the parking brake. Raise and support the vehicle safely.
2. Remove the tire and wheel assembly. Remove the brake drum.
3. Remove the equalizer nut and the retainer. Separate the equalizere from the right rear cable stud.
4. Remove the end of the left rear cable from the cable connector and equalizer.
5. Remove the clip retaining the right rear cable to the control arm bracket. Pull the cable rearward and remove it from the bracket.
6. Remove the cable from the brake backing plate. Remove the pawl spring and pawl lever from the actuating lever.
7. Remove the cable end from the operating lever. Remove the cable from the backing plate.
8. Installation is the reverse of the removal procedure. Adjust the parking brakes.

Brake System Bleeding

1. Fill the master cylinder to within ¼ in. of the reservoir rim.

2. Raise and support the vehicle safely.
3. Bleed the system in the following sequence: — right rear, left rear, right front and left front.
4. Bleed one wheel at a time.
5. Install a transparent tube on the bleeder screw of the caliper or wheel cylinder to be bled and place the opposite end of the hose in a container partially filled with brake fluid.
6. Open the bleeder screw ¾ turn. Depress the brake pedal to the floor, then tighten the bleeder screw. Slowly release the brake pedal.
7. Repeat the bleeding operation until clear brake fluid flows without air bubbles.

NOTE: Check the master cylinder fluid level frequently during the bleeding procedure and refill, if necessary.

8. After bleeding operation is completed, discard the fluid in the container. Fill the master cylinder to ¼ in. from the reservoir rim and check the brake system operation.

Anti-Lock Brake System Service

PRECAUTIONS

Failure to observe the following pre-

cautions may result in system damage.

- Before performing electric arc welding on the vehicle, disconnect the Electronic Brake Control Module (EBCM) and the hydraulic modulator connectors.
- When performing painting work on the vehicle, do not expose the Electronic Brake Control Module (EBCM) to temperatures in excess of 185°F (85°C) for longer than 2 hrs. The system may be exposed to temperatures up to 200°F (95°C) for less than 15 min.
- Never disconnect or connect the Electronic Brake Control Module (EBCM) or hydraulic modulator connectors with the ignition switch ON.
- Never disassemble any component of the Anti-Lock Brake System (ABS) which is designated non-servicable; the component must be replaced as an assembly.
- When filling the master cylinder, always use Delco Supreme 11 brake fluid or equivalent, which meets DOT-3 specifications; petroleum base fluid will destroy the rubber parts.

Hydraulic Modulator

REMOVAL & INSTALLATION

1. Disconnect the negative battery cable. Remove the left front radiator brace.
2. Remove the air cleaner intake hose. Remove the ABS modulator intake cover.
3. Disconnect the modulator 12 pin connector and ground strap.
4. Disconnect and plug the brake line connections at the modulator assembly.
5. Remove the modulator retaining bolts. Remove the modulator assembly from its mounting.
6. Installation is the reverse of the removal procedure. Bleed the brake system.

Electronic Brake Control Module

REMOVAL & INSTALLATION

1. Disconnect the negative battery cable.
2. Remove the left side close out panel. Remove the glove box liner.
3. Remove the EBCM from its retaining bracket.
4. Installation is the reverse of the removal procedure.

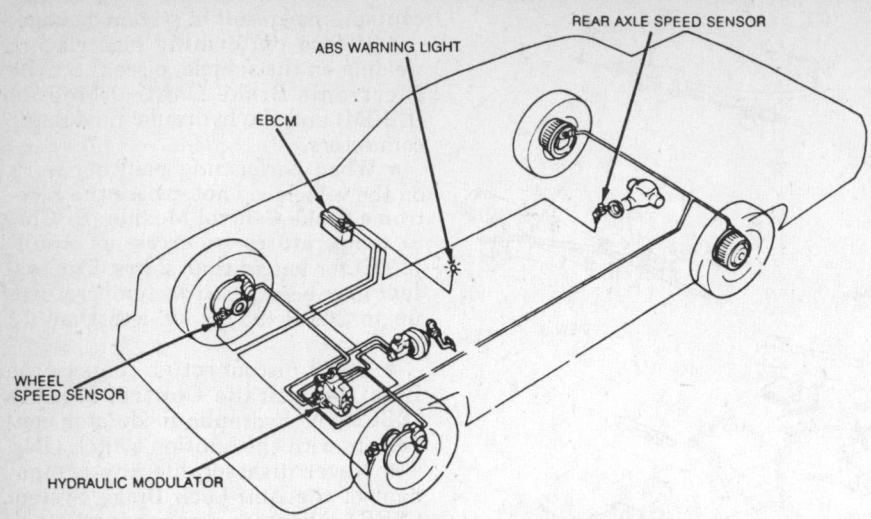

ABS WARNING LIGHT

REAR AXLE SPEED SENSOR

EBCM

WHEEL
SPEED SENSOR

HYDRAULIC MODULATOR

ABS braking system component layout

Front Wheel Speed Sensor

REMOVAL & INSTALLATION

1. Disconnect the negative battery cable.
2. Disconnect the sensor connector from the harness and the fenderwell clip from under the hood.
3. Raise and support the vehicle safely.
4. Remove the sensor cable from the retainers. Remove the sensor mounting bolt. Remove the sensor from the vehicle.
5. Installation is the reverse of the removal procedure. Be sure to coat the sensor body, where it comes in contact with the knuckle with anti corrosion compound GM part number 1052856 or equivalent.

NOTE: Proper installation of the wheel speed sensor cables is critical to proper operation of the ABS system. Make sure that the cables are installed in the retainers. Failure to do this may result in contact with moving parts and the over extension of the cables, resulting in an open circuit.

Rear Axle Speed Sensor

REMOVAL & INSTALLATION

1. Disconnect the negative battery cable. Raise and support the vehicle safely.
2. Disconnect the sensor connector. Remove the sensor cable from the retainer brackets.

3. Remove the sensor mounting bolt. Remove the sensor, plastic spacer and the O-ring from the vehicle.
4. Installation is the reverse of the removal procedure.

NOTE: Proper installation of the wheel speed sensor cables is critical to proper operation of the ABS system. Make sure that the cables are installed in the retainers. Failure to do this may result in contact with moving parts and the over extension of the cables, resulting in an open circuit.

FRONT SUSPENSION

Shock Absorbers

REMOVAL & INSTALLATION

1. Disconnect the negative battery cable.
2. Remove the top shock absorber retaining nut.
3. Raise and support the vehicle safely.
4. Remove the bottom shock absorber retaining bolts. Remove the shock absorber from the vehicle.
5. Installation is the reverse of the removal procedure.

Coil Springs

REMOVAL & INSTALLATION

1. Raise and support the vehicle

safely. Be sure that the vehicle is supported so that the lower control arms hang free.
2. Remove the lower shock absorber retaining bolts and push the shock absorber up through the control arm and into the spring.
3. Secure tool J–23028–01 to a suitable jack. Position the tool to cradle the inner bushings.
4. Remove the stabilizer to lower control arm attachment.
5. Raise the jack to relieve tension on the lower control arm pivot bolts. Install a safety chain around the spring and through the lower control arm as a safety precaution.
6. Remove the lower control arm rear pivot bolt. Remove the lower control arm front pivot bolt.
7. Lower the control arm assembly from its mounting. Remove the spring and the safety chain from the vehicle.
8. Properly position the spring in the frame. Using tool J–23028–01 lift the spring into position.

NOTE: The lower end of the coil must cover all or part of one inspection hole in the lower control arm. The second hole must be partly or completely uncovered.

9. Continue the installation in the reverse order of the removal procedure.

Upper Ball Joints

INSPECTION

1. Raise and support the vehicle safely.
2. Position jack stands under the lower control arms as near as possible to each lower ball joint.
3. The upper control arm bumpers must not contact the frame. Position a dial indicator gauge against the wheel rim.
4. Grasp the front wheel and push in on the bottom of the tire while pulling at the top.
5. Read and record the gauge reading. Reverse the push pull procedure. Read and record the gauge reading.

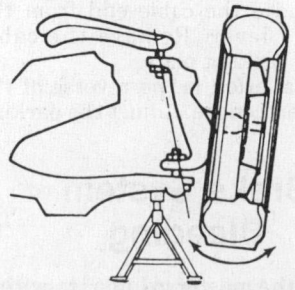

Checking upper ball joints

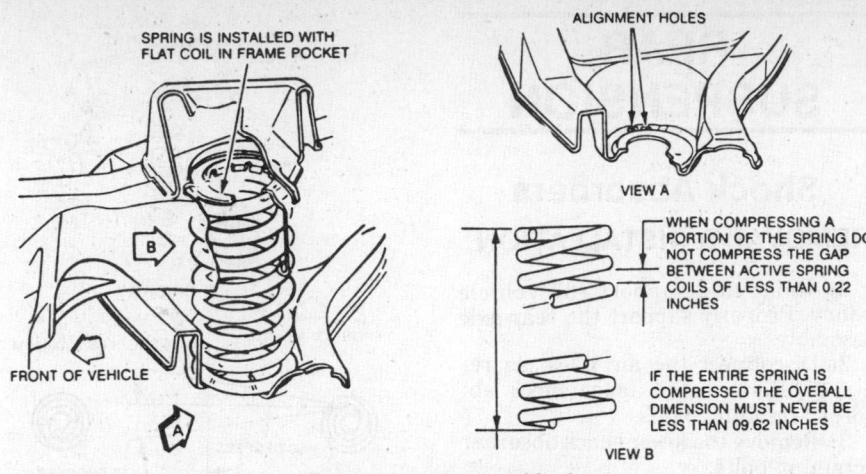

Front coil spring positioning

Horizontal deflection should not exceed 0.125 inch.

6. If the horizontal deflection exceeds 0.125 inch, if the ball joint has been disconnected from the knuckle assembly and looseness is detected, or the joint can be twisted in the socket ball joint replacement is necessary.

REMOVAL & INSTALLATION

1. Raise and support the vehicle safely. Remove the tire and wheel assembly.

2. Remove the caliper and properly support it so that the brake hose is not damaged.

3. Remove the cotter pin from the ball joint. Loosen, but do not remove the locknut. Properly support the lower control arm.

4. Using the proper ball joint removal tool, separate the ball joint from its mounting. Remove the locknut.

5. Lift the upper control arm upward and position a block of wood between the frame and the upper arm to act as a support.

6. Grind off the heads of the rivets retaining the ball joint in place. Remove the ball joint from its mounting.

7. Installation is the reverse of the removal procedure. Be sure to use new bolts to hold the ball joint in place. Check and adjust the front end alignment, as required.

Lower Ball Joints

INSPECTION

The vehicle must be supported by the wheel so that the weight of the vehicle will properly load the ball joints. The lower ball joint is checked for wear by visual inspection. Wear is indicated by protrusion of the ½ inch diameter nipple into which the grease fitting is

threaded. The round nipple projects 0.050 inch beyond the surface of the ball joint cover on a new ball joint. Normal wear will result in the surface of this nipple retreating slowly inward.

REMOVAL & INSTALLATION

1. Raise and support the vehicle safely. Remove the tire and wheel assembly.

2. Remove the cotter pin from the ball joint. Loosen, but do not remove the locknut. Properly support the lower control arm.

3. Using the proper ball joint removal tool, separate the ball joint from its mounting. Remove the locknut.

5. Lift the upper control arm with the knuckle and hub assembly attached and position a block of wood between the frame and the upper arm to act as a support.

NOTE: Do not pull on the brake hose when lifting the knuckle and hub assembly as damage may occur.

6. As required, remove the tie rod end from the steering knuckle. Using the proper ball joint removal tool press the ball joint from its mounting.

7. Installation is the reverse of the removal procedure. Be sure to adjust the front end alignment, as required.

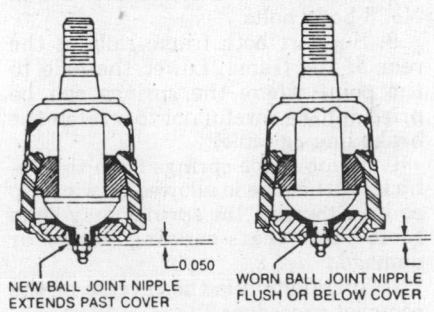

Checking lower ball joints

Upper Control Arms

REMOVAL & INSTALLATION

1. Raise and support the vehicle safely. Remove the tire and wheel assembly.

2. Properly support the lower control arm assembly.

3. Separate the upper ball joint from the steering knuckle, using the proper tools.

4. Remove the upper control arm shaft to frame bracket nuts. Be sure to replace the shims exactly in the same position that they were removed.

5. Remove the upper control arm assembly from the vehicle.

6. Installation is the reverse of the removal procedure. Be sure to adjust the front end alignment, as required.

Lower Control Arms

REMOVAL & INSTALLATION

1. Raise and support the vehicle safely. Remove the tire and wheel assembly.

2. Remove the spring. Disconnect the lower ball joint from the steering knuckle, using the proper tools.

3. Remove the lower control arm retaining bolts. Remove the lower control arm from the vehicle.

4. Installation is the reverse of the removal procedure. Be sure to adjust the front end alignment, as required.

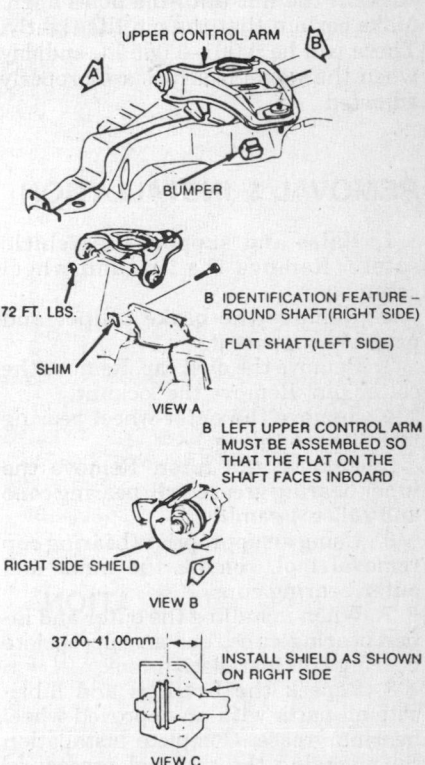

Upper control arm adjustment data

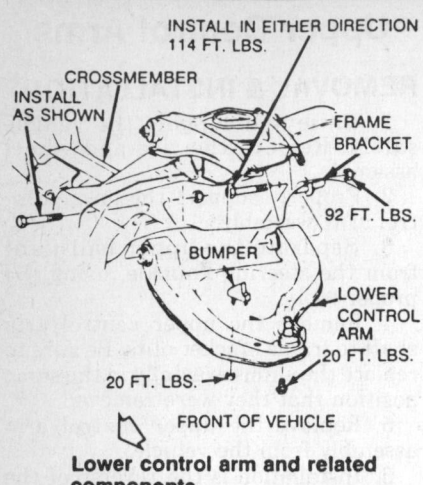

INSTALL IN EITHER DIRECTION
114 FT. LBS.

CROSSMEMBER

INSTALL
AS SHOWN

FRAME
BRACKET

92 FT. LBS.

BUMPER

LOWER
CONTROL
ARM

20 FT. LBS.   20 FT. LBS.

FRONT OF VEHICLE

**Lower control arm and related
components**

Front Wheel Bearings

ADJUSTMENT

1. Raise and support the vehicle safely.
2. Remove the dust cap and cotter pin from the spindle nut. Be sure that the hub is fully seated on the spindle.
3. To adjust, spin the wheel and tighten the locknut nut to 12 ft. lbs. Stop the wheel.
4. Back off the nut until it is free and then tighten it finger tight.
5. Insert the cotter pin. If the pin cannot be installed in this position, back off the nut until the holes align. Make certain that the pin fits tightly. There will be 0.001–0.005 in. endplay when the wheel bearings are properly adjusted.

REMOVAL & INSTALLATION

1. Raise and support the vehicle safely. Remove the tire and wheel assembly.
2. Remove the brake caliper and properly support it.
3. Remove the dust cap. Remove the cotter pin. Remove the locknut.
4. Remove the outer wheel bearing from its mounting.
5. Remove the rotor. Remove the inner bearing grease seal, bearing cone and roller assembly.
6. Using an appropriate bearing cup removal tool, remove the inner and outer bearing cups.
7. When installing the outer and inner bearing cups, use an appropriate bearing cup installation tool.
8. Repack the bearings and lubricate all parts with an approved wheel bearing grease. Complete installation by reversing the removal procedure. Adjust the wheel bearings.

REAR SUSPENSION

Shock Absorbers
REMOVAL & INSTALLATION

1. Raise and support the vehicle safely. Properly support the rear axle assembly.
2. Disconnect the air lines, as required. Remove the upper shock absorber retaining bolts.
3. Remove the lower shock absorber retaining bolts.
4. Remove the shock absorber from the vehicle.
5. Installation is the reverse of the removal procedure.

Coil Springs
REMOVAL & INSTALLATION

1. Raise and support the vehicle safely. Properly support the rear axle assembly. Remove the shock absorbers.
2. Remove the stabilizer shaft.

NOTE: Do not lower the axle assembly to the point at which the brake hoses become taut, as damage may result.

3. Remove the bolt that secures the brake hose junction block to the rear axle assembly. Remove the link on the height sensor arm, if equipped.
4. Remove the driveshaft retaining bolts. Remove the driveshaft and position it to the side.
5. Remove the upper control arm pivot bolts at the rear axle housing.
6. Disconnect the left side parking brake cable at the equalizer and disconnect the cable at the frame near the No. 4 body bolt by removing the clip. Slide the cable through the hole.
7. Disconnect the cable from the clip at the center of the rear crossmember and disconnect the cable at the C connector which is located at the left of the frame between No. 2 and No. 3 body bolts.
8. Support both frame rails at the rear of the frame. Lower the axle to the point where the springs can be pried out. Be careful not to stretch the brake line or cable.
9. Remove the springs from the vehicle. If the axle is allowed to wind up as it is lowered, the springs may snap from their seats causing injury or damage.
10. Installation is the reverse of the removal procedure.
11. Tape the upper rubber insulator

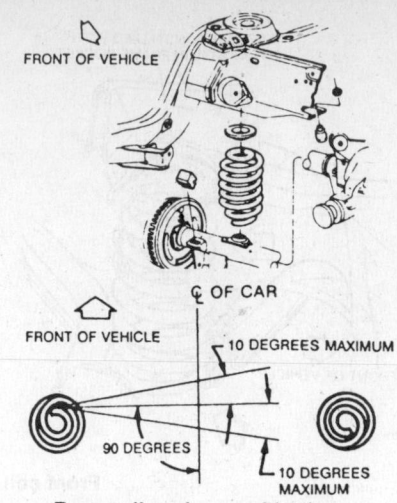

FRONT OF VEHICLE

¢ OF CAR

FRONT OF VEHICLE

10 DEGREES MAXIMUM

90 DEGREES

10 DEGREES MAXIMUM

Rear coil spring positioning

to the top of the spring and position the upper end of the left rear spring coil toward the left frame side rail. Position the upper right end of the right spring coil toward the right frame side rail.
12. Adjust the parking brakes, as required

Upper Control Arms
REMOVAL & INSTALLATION

NOTE: If both control arms are being replaced, only replace them one at a time to prevent the rear axle from slipping sideways

1. Raise and support the vehicle safely.
2. If equipped with electronic level control, remove the height sensor link retaining nut.
3. Properly support the rear axle assembly.
4. Remove the upper control arm retaining bolts. Remove the upper control arm from the vehicle.
5. Installation is the reverse of the removal procedure.

Lower Control Arms
REMOVAL & INSTALLATION

NOTE: If both control arms are being replaced, only replace them one at a time to prevent the rear axle from slipping sideways

1. Raise and support the vehicle safely. Properly support the rear axle assembly.
2. Disconnect the stabilizer arm bracket at the lower control arm. Remove the front and rear lower control arm retaining bolts.
3. Remove the lower control arm assembly from the vehicle.
4. Installation is the reverse of the removal procedure.

SPECIFICATIONS

VEHICLE IDENTIFICATION CHART

It is important for servicing and ordering parts to be certain of the vehicle and engine identification. The VIN (vehicle identification number) is a 17 digit number visible through the windshield on the driver's side of the dash and contains the vehicle and engine identification codes. The tenth digit indicates model year and the eighth digit indicates engine code. It can be interpreted as follows:

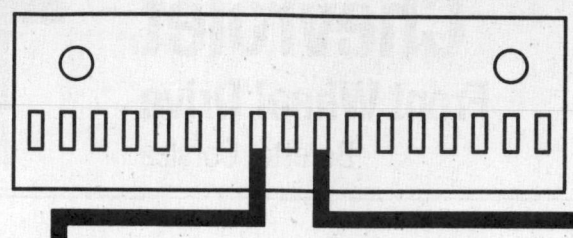

Engine Code						Model Year	
Code	Cu. In.	Liters	Cyl.	Fuel Sys.	Eng. Mfg.	Code	Year
1	121	2.0	4	TBI	Chevrolet	H	1987
G	133	2.2	4	TBI	Chevrolet	J	1988
A	138	2.3	4	MPI	Chevrolet	K	1989
W	173	2.8	V6	MPI	Chevrolet	L	1990
T	191	3.1	V6	MPI	Chevrolet	M	1991

ENGINE IDENTIFICATION

Year	Model	Engine Displacement cu. in. (liter)	Engine Series Identification (VIN)	No. of Cylinders	Engine Type
1987	Beretta	121 (2.0)	1	4	OHV
	Beretta	173 (2.8)	W	6	OHV
	Corsica	121 (2.0)	1	4	OHV
	Corsica	173 (2.8)	W	6	OHV
1988	Beretta	121 (2.0)	1	4	OHV
	Beretta	173 (2.8)	W	6	OHV
	Corsica	121 (2.0)	1	4	OHV
	Corsica	173 (2.8)	W	6	OHV
1989	Beretta	121 (2.0)	1	4	OHV
	Beretta	173 (2.8)	W	6	OHV
	Corsica	121 (2.0)	1	4	OHV
	Corsica	173 (2.8)	W	6	OHV
1990–91	Beretta	133 (2.2)	G	4	OHV
	Beretta	138 (2.3)	A	4	OHV
	Beretta	191 (3.1)	T	6	OHV
	Corsica	133 (2.2)	G	4	OHV
	Corsica	138 (2.3)	A	4	OHV
	Corsica	191 (3.1)	T	6	OHV

OHV Overhead Valves

GENERAL ENGINE SPECIFICATIONS

Year	VIN	No. Cylinder Displacement cu. in. (liter)	Fuel System Type	Net Horsepower @ rpm	Net Torque @ rpm (ft. lbs.)	Bore × Stroke (in.)	Compression Ratio	Oil Pressure @ rpm
1987	1	4-121 (2.0)	TBI	90 @ 5600	108 @ 3200	3.500 × 3.150	9.0:1	63-77 @ 1200
	W	6-173 (2.8)	MPI	125 @ 4500	160 @ 3600	3.500 × 2.990	8.9:1	50-65 @ 1200
1988	1	4-121 (2.0)	TBI	90 @ 5600	108 @ 3200	3.500 × 3.150	9.0:1	63-77 @ 1200
	W	6-173 (2.8)	MPI	125 @ 4500	160 @ 3600	3.500 × 2.990	8.9:1	50-65 @ 1200
1989	1	4-121 (2.0)	TBI	90 @ 5600	108 @ 3200	3.500 × 3.150	9.0:1	63-77 @ 1200
	W	6-173 (2.8)	MPI	125 @ 4500	160 @ 3600	3.500 × 2.990	8.9:1	50-65 @ 1200
1990-91	G	4-133 (2.2)	TBI	95 @ 5200	120 @ 3200	3.500 × 3.460	9.0:1	63-77 @ 1200
	A	4-138 (2.3)	MPI	180 @ 6200	160 @ 5200	3.630 × 3.350	10.0:1	30 @ 2000
	T	6-191 (3.1)	MBI	135 @ 4200	180 @ 3600	3.600 × 3.400	8.8:1	50-65 @ 2400

MPI Multi-Port Fuel Injection
TBI Throttle Body Injection

GASOLINE ENGINE TUNE-UP SPECIFICATIONS

Year	VIN	No. Cylinder Displacement cu. in. (liter)	Spark Plugs Type	Gap (in.)	Ignition Timing (deg.) MT	AT	Compression Pressure (psi)	Fuel Pump (psi)	Idle Speed (rpm) MT	AT	Valve Clearance In.	Ex.
1987	1	4-121 (2.0)	FR3LM	0.035	①	①	②	10–12	①	①	Hyd.	Hyd.
	W	6-173 (2.8)	R43CTLSE	0.045	①	①	②	10–12	①	①	Hyd.	Hyd.
1988	1	4-121 (2.0)	FR3LM	0.035	①	①	②	10–12	①	①	Hyd.	Hyd.
	W	6-173 (2.8)	R43CTLSE	0.045	①	①	②	10–12	①	①	Hyd.	Hyd.
1989	1	4-121 (2.0)	FR3LM	0.035	①	①	②	10–12	①	①	Hyd.	Hyd.
	W	6-173 (2.8)	R43CTLSE	0.045	①	①	②	10–12	①	①	Hyd.	Hyd.
1990	G	4-133 (2.2)	R44LTSM	0.035	①	①	②	9–13	①	①	Hyd.	Hyd.
	A	4-138 (2.3)	FR3LS	0.035	①	①	②	30–47	①	①	Hyd.	Hyd.
	T	6-191 (3.1)	R43CTLSF	0.045	①	①	②	30–47	①	①	Hyd.	Hyd.
1991			SEE UNDERHOOD SPECIFICATIONS STICKER									

① Ignition timing and idle speed is controlled by the electronic control module. No adjustments are possible
② When analyzing compression test results, look for uniformity among cylinders rather than specific pressures

FIRING ORDERS

NOTE: To avoid confusion, always replace spark plug wires 1 at a time.

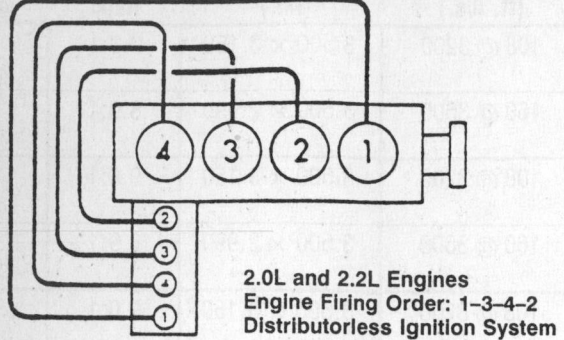

2.0L and 2.2L Engines
Engine Firing Order: 1–3–4–2
Distributorless Ignition System

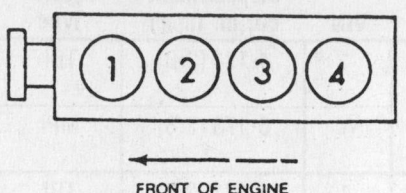

2.3L Engine
Engine Firing Order: 1–3–4–2
Distributorless Ignition System

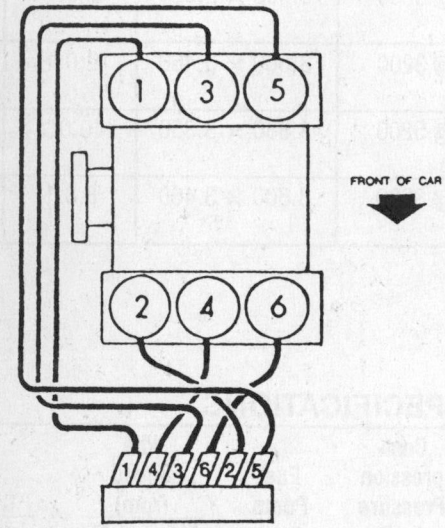

2.8L Engine (1988)
Engine Firing Order: 1–2–3–4–5–6
Distributorless Ignition System

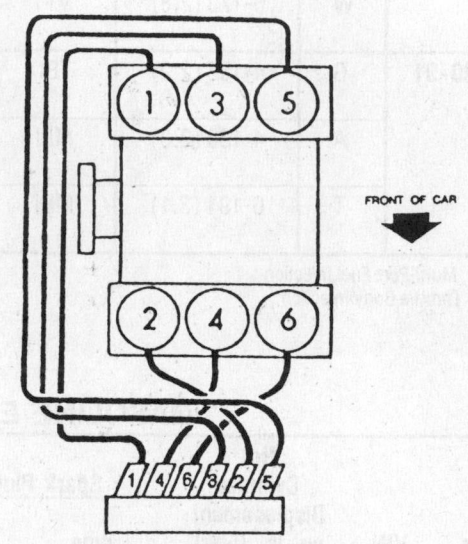

2.8L (1989–91) and 3.1L Engine
Engine Firing Order: 1–2–3–4–5–6
Distributorless Ignition System

CAPACITIES

Year	Model	VIN	No. Cylinder Displacement cu. in. (liter)	Engine Crankcase (qts.) with Filter	without Filter	Transmission (pts.) 4-Spd	5-Spd	Auto.	Drive Axle (pts.)	Fuel Tank (gal.)	Cooling System (qts.)
1987	Beretta	1	4-121 (2.0)	4.5	4.0	NA	5.4 ①	8.0 ②	NA	13.6	8.8
		W	6-173 (2.8)	4.5	4.0	NA	5.4 ①	8.0 ②	NA	13.6	11.4
	Corsica	1	4-121 (2.0)	4.5	4.0	NA	5.4 ①	8.0 ②	NA	13.6	8.8
		W	6-173 (2.8)	4.5	4.0	NA	5.4 ①	8.0 ②	NA	13.6	11.4
1988	Beretta	1	4-121 (2.0)	4.0	4.0	NA	5.4 ①	8.0 ②	NA	14	9.6 ③
		W	6-173 (2.8)	4.0	4.0	NA	5.4 ①	8.0 ②	NA	14	11 ④
	Corsica	1	4-121 (2.0)	4.0	4.0	NA	5.4 ①	8.0 ②	NA	14	9.6 ③
		W	6-173 (2.8)	4.0	4.0	NA	5.4 ①	8.0 ②	NA	14	11 ④
1989	Beretta	1	4-121 (2.0)	4.0	4.0	NA	4.0	8.0 ②	NA	14	14.1 ⑤
		W	6-173 (2.8)	4.0	4.0	NA	4.0	8.0 ②	NA	14	⑥
	Corsica	1	4-121 (2.0)	4.0	4.0	NA	4.0	8.0 ②	NA	14	14.1 ⑤
		W	6-173 (2.8)	4.0	4.0	NA	4.0	8.0 ②	NA	14	⑥

CAPACITIES

Year	Model	VIN	No. Cylinder Displacement cu. in. (liter)	Engine Crankcase (qts.) with Filter	without Filter	Transmission (pts.) 4-Spd	5-Spd	Auto.	Drive Axle (pts.)	Fuel Tank (gal.)	Cooling System (qts.)
1990-91	Beretta	G	4-133 (2.2)	4.0	4.0	NA	4.0	14.0 ⑦	NA	15.6	⑧⑨
		A	4-138 (2.3)	4.0	4.0	NA	4.0	14.0 ⑦	NA	15.6	⑨
		T	6-191 (3.1)	4.0	4.0	NA	4.0	14.0 ⑦	NA	15.6	⑩
	Corsica	G	4-133 (2.2)	4.0	4.0	NA	4.0	14.0 ⑦	NA	15.6	⑧⑨
		A	4-138 (2.3)	4.0	4.0	NA	4.0	14.0 ⑦	NA	15.6	⑨
		T	6-191 (3.1)	4.0	4.0	NA	4.0	14.0 ⑦	NA	15.6	⑩

NA Not applicable
① 5 speed (Getrag)—4 pts.
② This figure is for drain and refill. After a complete overhaul, use 16.0 pts. If the torque converter is replaced, use 18.0 pts.
③ With air conditioning—9.8 qts.
④ With air conditioning—11.1 qts.
⑤ Without air conditioning—13.1 qts.
⑥ Automatic transaxle
   With air conditioning—16.6 qts.
   Without air conditioning—16.7 qts.
 Manual transaxle
   With air conditioning—16.1 qts.
   Without air conditioning—16.2 qts.
⑦ This figure is for drain and refill. After a complete overhaul, use 18.0 pts.
⑧ Automatic transaxle
   With air conditioning—9.5 qts.
   Without air conditioning—9.6 qts.
⑨ Manual transaxle
   With or without air conditioning—9.5 qts.
⑩ Automatic transaxle—12.4 qts.
   Manual transaxle—11.8 qts.

CAMSHAFT SPECIFICATIONS

All measurements given in inches.

Year	VIN	No. Cylinder Displacement cu. in. (liter)	Journal Diameter 1	2	3	4	5	Lobe Lift In.	Ex.	Bearing Clearance	Camshaft End Play
1987	1	4-121 (2.0)	1.867–1.869	1.867–1.869	1.867–1.869	1.867–1.869	1.867–1.869	0.260	0.260	0.001–0.004	NA
	W	6-173 (2.8)	1.867–1.881	1.867–1.881	1.867–1.881	1.867–1.881	—	0.262	0.273	0.001–0.004	NA
1988	1	4-121 (2.0)	1.867–1.869	1.867–1.869	1.867–1.869	1.867–1.869	1.867–1.869	0.260	0.260	0.001–0.004	NA
	W	6-173 (2.8)	1.867–1.881	1.867–1.881	1.867–1.881	1.867–1.881	—	0.262	0.273	0.001–0.004	NA
1989	1	4-121 (2.0)	1.867–1.869	1.867–1.869	1.867–1.869	1.867–1.869	1.867–1.869	0.260	0.260	0.001–0.004	NA
	W	6-173 (2.8)	1.867–1.881	1.867–1.881	1.867–1.881	1.867–1.881	—	0.262	0.273	0.001–0.004	NA
1990-91	G	4-133 (2.2)	1.867–1.869	1.867–1.869	1.867–1.869	1.867–1.869	1.867–1.869	0.259	0.259	0.001–0.004	NA
	A	4-138 (2.3)	1.572–1.573	1.375–1.376	1.375–1.376	1.375–1.376	1.375–1.376	0.410	0.410	0.002–0.004	0.001–0.009
	T	6-191 (3.1)	1.868–1.881	1.868–1.881	1.868–1.881	1.868–1.881	—	0.263	0.273	0.001–0.004	NA

NA Not available

CRANKSHAFT AND CONNECTING ROD SPECIFICATIONS

All measurements are given in inches.

Year	VIN	No. Cylinder Displacement cu. in. (liter)	Crankshaft Main Brg. Journal Dia.	Crankshaft Main Brg. Oil Clearance	Crankshaft Shaft End-play	Thrust on. No.	Connecting Rod Journal Diameter	Connecting Rod Oil Clearance	Connecting Rod Side Clearance
1987	1	4-121 (2.0)	2.4945–2.4954	0.0006–0.0019	0.002–0.008	1	1.9983–1.9994	0.001–0.003	0.004–0.015
	W	6-173 (2.8)	2.6473–2.6483	0.0016–0.0033	0.0024–0.0083	4	1.9983–1.9993	0.001–0.003	0.006–0.017
1988	1	4-121 (2.0)	2.4945–2.4954	0.0006–0.0019	0.002–0.008	1	1.9983–1.9994	0.001–0.003	0.004–0.015
	W	6-173 (2.8)	2.6473–2.6483	0.0016–0.0033	0.0024–0.0083	4	1.9983–1.9993	0.001–0.003	0.006–0.017
1989	1	4-121 (2.0)	2.4945–2.4954	0.0006–0.0019	0.002–0.008	1	1.9983–1.9994	0.001–0.003	0.004–0.015
	W	6-173 (2.8)	2.6473–2.6483	0.0016–0.0033	0.0024–0.0083	4	1.9983–1.9993	0.001–0.003	0.006–0.017
1990–91	G	4-133 (2.2)	2.4945–2.4954	0.0006–0.0019	0.002–0.007	4	1.9983–1.9994	0.001–0.003	0.004–0.015
	A	4-138 (2.3)	2.0470–2.0480	0.0005–0.0023	0.003–0.009	3	1.8887–1.8897	0.001–0.002	0.006–0.018
	T	6-191 (3.1)	2.6473–2.6483	0.0012–0.0030	0.0024–0.0083	3	1.9983–1.9994	0.001–0.004	0.014–0.027

PISTON AND RING SPECIFICATIONS

All measurements are given in inches.

Year	VIN	No. Cylinder Displacement cu. in. (liter)	Piston Clearance	Ring Gap Top Compression	Ring Gap Bottom Compression	Ring Gap Oil Control	Ring Side Clearance Top Compression	Ring Side Clearance Bottom Compression	Ring Side Clearance Oil Control
1987	1	4-121 (2.0)	0.0010–0.0022	0.010–0.020	0.010–0.020	0.010–0.050	0.001–0.003	0.001–0.003	0.0080
	W	6-173 (2.8)	0.0020–0.0030	0.010–0.020	0.010–0.020	0.020–0.055	0.001–0.003	0.001–0.003	0.0080
1988	1	4-121 (2.0)	0.0010–0.0022	0.010–0.020	0.010–0.020	0.010–0.050	0.001–0.003	0.001–0.003	0.0080
	W	6-173 (2.8)	0.0020–0.0030	0.010–0.020	0.010–0.020	0.020–0.055	0.001–0.003	0.001–0.003	0.0080
1989	1	4-121 (2.0)	0.0010–0.0022	0.010–0.020	0.010–0.020	0.010–0.050	0.001–0.003	0.001–0.003	0.0080
	W	6-173 (2.8)	0.0020–0.0030	0.010–0.020	0.010–0.020	0.020–0.055	0.001–0.003	0.001–0.003	0.0080
1990–91	G	4-133 (2.2)	0.0007–0.0017	0.010–0.020	0.010–0.020	0.010–0.050	0.002–0.003	0.002–0.003	0.0020–0.0082
	A	4-138 (2.3)	0.0007–0.0020	0.014–0.024	0.016–0.026	0.016–0.055	0.003–0.005	0.002–0.003	—
	T	6-191 (3.1)	0.0010–0.0022	0.010–0.020	0.020–0.028	0.010–0.030	0.002–0.003	0.002–0.003	0.0080

VALVE SPECIFICATIONS

Year	VIN	No. Cylinder Displacement cu. in. (liter)	Seat Angle (deg.)	Face Angle (deg.)	Spring Test Pressure (lbs.)	Spring Installed Height (in.)	Stem-to-Guide Clearance (in.)		Stem Diameter (in.)	
							Intake	Exhaust	Intake	Exhaust
1987	1	4-121 (2.0)	46	45	73-81	1.60 ①	0.0011–0.0023	0.0014–0.0028	NA	NA
	W	6-173 (2.8)	46	45	90	1.70 ①	0.0010–0.0027	0.0010–0.0027	NA	NA
1988	1	4-121 (2.0)	46	45	73-81	1.60 ①	0.0011–0.0023	0.0014–0.0028	NA	NA
	W	6-173 (2.8)	46	45	90	1.70 ①	0.0010–0.0027	0.0010–0.0027	NA	NA
1989	1	4-121 (2.0)	46	45	73-81	1.60 ①	0.0011–0.0023	0.0014–0.0028	NA	NA
	W	6-173 (2.8)	46	45	90	1.70 ①	0.0010–0.0027	0.0010–0.0027	NA	NA
1990–91	G	4-133 (2.2)	46	45	100-110	1.60 ①	0.0011–0.0026	0.0014–0.0030	NA	NA
	A	4-138 (2.3)	45	44	71-79	1.44 ①	0.0010–0.0027	0.0010–0.0027	0.274–0.275	0.274–0.275
	T	6-191 (3.1)	46	45	90	1.60 ①	0.0010–0.0027	0.0010–0.0027	NA	NA

NA Not available
① With valve closed

TORQUE SPECIFICATIONS

All readings in ft. lbs.

Year	VIN	No. Cylinder Displacement cu. in. (liter)	Cylinder Head Bolts	Main Bearing Bolts	Rod Bearing Bolts	Crankshaft Pulley Bolts	Flywheel Bolts	Manifold		Spark Plugs
								Intake	Exhaust	
1987	1	4-121 (2.0)	62-70 ①	63-77	34-43	66-89	45-59 ②	15-22	6-13	20
	W	6-173 (2.8)	③	63-83	34-44	67-85	45-59 ②	18	15-23	20
1988	1	4-121 (2.0)	62-70 ①	63-77	34-43	66-89	45-59 ②	15-22	6-13	20
	W	6-173 (2.8)	③	63-83	34-44	67-85	45-59 ②	18	15-23	20
1989	1	4-121 (2.0)	62-70 ①	63-77	34-43	66-89	45-59 ②	15-22	6-13	20
	W	6-173 (2.8)	③	63-83	34-44	67-85	45-59 ②	18	15-23	20
1990–91	G	4-133 (2.2)	62-70 ①	70	38	85 ④	52 ⑤	18	7 ⑥	11
	A	4-138 (2.3)	26 ⑦	15 ⑧	18 ⑨	75 ⑩	22 ⑪	18	27	6
	T	6-191 (3.1)	③	73	39	66-85	45-59 ②	15-24	18	20

① Specification is for the shorter bolts. Torque the longer bolts to 73–83 ft. lbs.
② Specification is for automatic transaxle. Torque the manual transaxle bolts to 47–63 ft. lbs.
③ Cylinder head bolts should first be torqued to 33 ft. lbs. Then tighten the bolts by rotating the torque wrench an additional 90 degrees.
④ Specification is for the crankshaft center bolt. Torque the pulley to hub bolts to 37 ft. lbs.
⑤ Specification is for automatic transaxle. Torque the manual transaxle bolts to 55 ft. lbs.
⑥ Specification is for exhaust manifold nuts. Torque exhaust manifold studs to 9 ft. lbs.
⑦ Cylinder head bolts should first be torqued in sequence to 26 ft. lbs. Then tighten the bolts by rotating the torque wrench an additional:
100 degrees for short bolts
110 degrees for long bolts
⑧ Main bearing bolts should first be torqued to 15 ft. lbs. Then tighten the bolts by rotating the torque wrench an additional 90 degrees.
⑨ Connecting rod bolts should first be torqued to 18 ft. lbs. Then tighten the bolts by rotating the torque wrench an additional 80 degrees.
⑩ Crankshaft balancer to crankshaft bolt should first be torqued to 74 ft. lbs. Then tighten an additional 90 degrees.
⑪ Flywheel bolts should first be torqued to 22 ft. lbs. Then tighten an additional 45 degrees.

BRAKE SPECIFICATIONS

All measurements in inches unless noted.

Year	Model	Lug Nut Torque (ft. lbs.)	Master Cylinder Bore	Brake Disc Minimum Thickness	Brake Disc Maximum Runout	Standard Brake Drum Diameter	Minimum Lining Thickness Front	Minimum Lining Thickness Rear
1987	Beretta	100	0.945	0.830	0.004	7.879	3/32	3/32
	Corsica	100	0.945	0.830	0.004	7.879	3/32	3/32
1988	Beretta	100	0.945	0.830	0.004	7.879	3/32	3/32
	Corsica	100	0.945	0.830	0.004	7.879	3/32	3/32
1989	Beretta	100	0.945	0.830	0.004	7.879	3/32	3/32
	Corsica	100	0.945	0.830	0.004	7.879	3/32	3/32
1990–91	Beretta	100	0.875	0.830	0.004	7.879	3/32	3/32
	Corsica	100	0.875	0.830	0.004	7.879	3/32	3/32

WHEEL ALIGNMENT

Year	Model		Caster Range (deg.)	Caster Preferred Setting (deg.)	Camber Range (deg.)	Camber Preferred Setting (deg.)	Toe-in (in.)	Steering Axis Inclination (deg.)
1987	Beretta	Front	7/10P–27/10P	17/10P ①	3/10P–13/10P	8/10P	1/16N–1/16P	—
		Rear	—	—	0–13/10P	1/10P	1/8P	—
	Corsica	Front	7/10P–27/10P	17/10P ①	3/10P–13/10P	4/5P	1/16N–1/16P	—
		Rear	—	—	3/10P–12/10P	1/4P	1/8P	—
1988	Beretta	Front	7/10P–27/10P	17/10P ①	3/10P–13/10P	8/10P	1/16N–1/16P	—
		Rear	—	—	0–13/10P	1/10P	1/8P	—
	Corsica	Front	7/10P–27/10P	17/10P ①	3/10P–13/10P	4/5P	1/16N–1/16P	—
		Rear	—	—	3/10P–12/10P	1/4P	1/8P	—
1989	Beretta	Front	2/5P–19/10P	12/10P	0–12/10P	6/10P	0	—
		Rear	—	—	9/10N–4/10P	1/4P	5/16P	—
	Corsica	Front	2/5P–19/10P	12/10P	0–12/10P	6/10P	0	—
		Rear	—	—	8/10N–3/10P	1/4P	1/4P	—
1990–91	Beretta	Front	2/5P–19/10P	12/10P	0–12/10P	6/10P	0	—
		Rear	—	—	9/10N–4/10P	1/4P	5/16P	—
	Corsica	Front	2/5P–19/10P	12/10P	0–12/10P	6/10P	0	—
		Rear	—	—	8/10N–3/10P	1/4P	1/4P	—

① Not adjustable

ENGINE ELECTRICAL

NOTE: Disconnecting the negative battery cable on some vehicles may interfere with the functions of the on board computer systems and may require the computer to undergo a relearning process, once the negative battery cable is reconnected.

Distributorless Ignition

Two types of distributorless ignition systems will be covered in this section. The first type is the Direct Ignition System (DIS); the second type is the Integrated Direct Ignition System (IDIS).

The distributorless ignition systems use of a waste spark method of spark distribution. Each cylinder is paired with its comparison cylinder in the firing order. This places 1 cylinder on the compression stroke with the compari-

son cylinder on the exhaust stroke. The cylinder that is on the exhaust stroke uses very little spark allowing most of the spark to go to the cylinder on the compression stroke. This process reverses when the cylinder roles reverse. There are 2 coils for the 4 cylinder engines and 3 coils for the 6 cylinder engines. The Direct Ignition System (DIS) is used on the 2.0L, 2.2L, 2.8L and 3.1L engines. The Integrated Direct Ignition System (IDIS) is use on the 2.3L engine only.

Since no distributor is used, the tim-

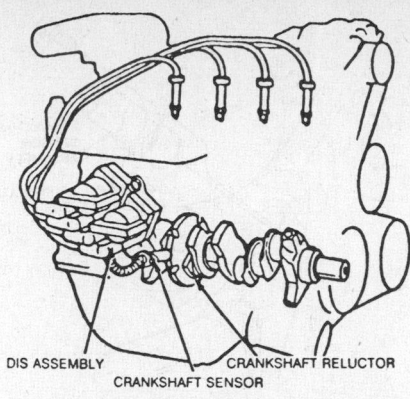

View of the Direct Ignition System (DIS) 2.0L, 2.2L and 3.1L engines

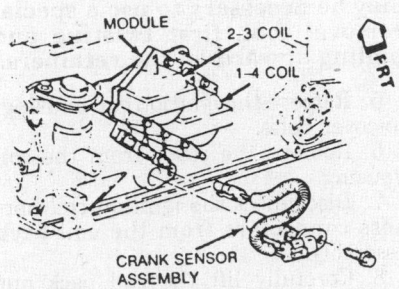

Removing the coil pack from the engine

ing references are gathered from the engine sensors.

REMOVAL & INSTALLATION

Coil Pack

1. Disconnect the negative battery cable.
2. Disconnect the electrical connectors from the coil pack.
3. Mark the spark plug wires for correct installation and remove them from each coil.
4. Remove the coil pack-to-engine bolts and remove the coil pack from the engine.
To install:
5. Position the coil pack to the engine block and install the retaining bolts. Torque the retaining bolts to 15–21 ft. lbs. (20–30 Nm).
6. Connect the spark plug wires to their respective positions, marked during removal, on the ignition coils.
7. Connect the electrical connectors to the coil pack.
8. Connect the negative battery cable.
9. Start the engine and test the engine performance.

Crankshaft Sensor

1. Disconnect the negative battery cable.
2. Disconnect the sensor harness

connector at the ignition module.
3. Remove the crankshaft sensor retaining bolt and remove the sensor from the engine.

NOTE: Prior to installing the crankshaft sensor, inspect the O-ring for wear, cracks or signs of leakage. Replace it, if necessary. If it is necessary to replace the seal, lubricate it with engine oil prior to installation.

To install:
4. Position the crankshaft sensor to the engine block.
5. Install the crankshaft sensor retaining bolt. Torque the retainer bolt to 53–107 inch lbs. (6–12 Nm).
6. Connect the negative battery cable.

Ignition Coils

1. Disconnect the negative battery cable.
2. Remove the retaining bolts attaching the ignition coil to the ignition module.
3. Remove the coil from the module.
To install:
4. Position the ignition coil to the module and install the retaining bolts.
5. Torque the ignition coil retaining bolts to 40 inch lbs. (4.5 Nm). Connect the negative battery cable.
6. Start the engine and check performance.

Ignition Module

1. Disconnect the negative battery cable.
2. Disconnect the electrical connectors from the coil pack.
3. Mark the spark plug wires for correct installation and remove them from each ignition coil.
4. Remove the bolts retaining the coil pack to the engine block.
5. Remove the coil pack from the engine.
6. Remove the ignition coils from the ignition module.
7. Remove the ignition module from the assembly plate.
To install:
8. Place the module onto the assembly plate and assemble the ignition coils to the module with the retaining bolts.
9. Torque the retaining bolts to 40 inch lbs. (4.5 Nm).
10. Position the coil pack to the engine block and install the retaining bolts. Torque the retaining bolts to 15–21 ft. lbs. (20–30 Nm).
11. Connect the spark plug wires to on the ignition coils (marked during removal).
12. Connect the electrical connectors to the coil pack.
13. Connect the spark plug wires and

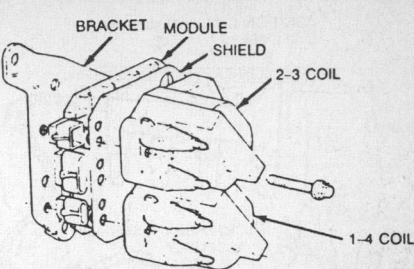

Removing the ignition coils and module from the assembly plate

electrical connectors to their respective places.
14. Connect the negative battery cable.
15. Start the engine and check performance.

INTEGRATED DIRECT IGNITION SYSTEM

The Integrated Direct Ignition System (IDIS) consist of 2 separate ignition coils an ignition module and a secondary conductor housing mounted to an aluminum cover plate. A crankshaft sensor, related connecting wires and an Electronic Spark Timing (EST) portion of the Electronic Control Module (ECM) make up the remainder of the system.

This system, being a distributorless ignition system, uses a waste spark method of spark distribution. Each cylinder is paired with its comparison cylinder in the firing order. This places 1 cylinder on the compression stroke with the comparison cylinder on the exhaust stroke. The cylinder that is on the exhaust stroke uses very little spark allowing most of the spark to go to the cylinder on the compression stroke. This process reverses when the cylinder roles reverse.

Because of the direction of current flow in the primary winding and thus, into the secondary winding, 1 plug will fire from the center electrode to the side electrode while the other fires from the side electrode.

The magnetic pick-up sensor is mounted on the side of engine block, in proximity to the crankshaft reluctor ring. Notches in the crankshaft reluctor ring trigger the magnetic pick-up sensor to provide timing information to the Electronic Control Module. The magnetic pick-up sensor provides a cam signal to identify correct firing sequence and crank signals to trigger each coil at the proper time.

The Electronic Control Module (ECM) sends a signal from the Electronic Spark Control (EST) to control spark timing. Under 700 rpm, the ignition module controls spark timing when the system is in the module or

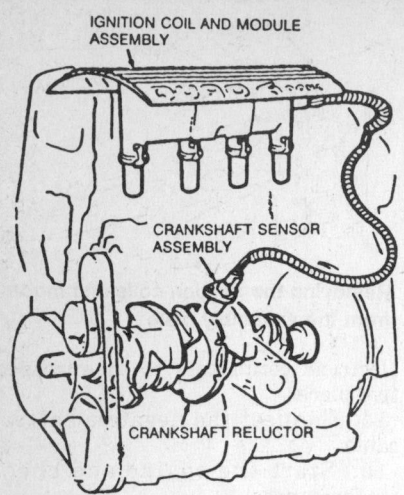

View of the Integrated Direct Ignition System (IDIS) 2.3L engine

Removing the IDS ignition assembly from the engine

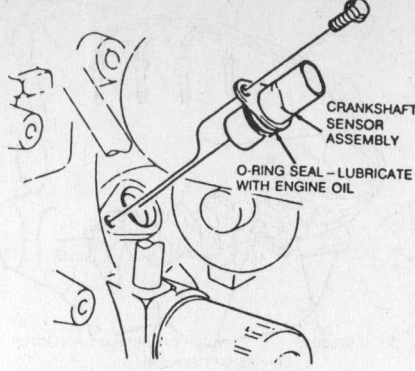

Removing crankshaft sensor from the engine

bypass timing mode. When over 700 rpm, the Electronic Control Module controls spark timing, when the system is in the EST mode.

Since no distributor is used, the timing references are gathered from the engine sensors.

REMOVAL & INSTALLATION

Ignition Assembly

1. Disconnect the negative battery cable.
2. Disconnect the harness connector from the coil and module assembly.
3. Remove the ignition assembly-to-camshaft housing retaining bolts.
4. Carefully remove the ignition assembly from the the engine.

NOTE: If the spark plug boots present a problem coming off, it may be necessary to use a special removal tool, first twisting and pulling upward on the retainers.

To install:

5. Install the spark plug boots and retainers on the ignition assembly housing secondary terminals.

NOTE: If the boots and retainers are not in place on the housing secondary terminals prior to installing the ignition assembly, damage to the ignition system may result.

6. Position the ignition assembly to the engine while carefully aligning the boots to the spark plug terminals.
7. Coat the ignition assembly-to-camshaft housing retaining bolts with an approved lubricant and install them into the housing.
8. Torque the retaining bolts to 19 ft. lbs. (26 Nm).

9. Connect the harness connector to the ignition coil module assembly.
10. Connect the negative battery cable.
11. Start the engine and test the engine performance.

Crankshaft Sensor

1. Disconnect the negative battery cable.
2. Disconnect the harness connector at the crankshaft sensor.
3. Remove the sensor retaining bolt.
4. Remove the crankshaft sensor from the engine.
5. Inspect the sensor O-ring for wear, cracks or signs of leakage. Replace it if necessary.

To install:

6. Lubricate the O-ring with engine oil and install it on the sensor.
7. Position the sensor to the engine block and install the retaining bolt. Torque the retaining bolt to 88 inch lbs. (10 Nm).
8. Connect the sensor harness connector.
9. Connect the negative battery cable.
10. Start the engine and test engine performance.

Ignition Coil

1. Disconnect the negative battery cable.
2. Disconnect the harness connector from the coil and module assembly.
3. Remove the ignition assembly-to-camshaft housing retaining bolts.
4. Carefully remove the ignition assembly from the engine.

NOTE: If the spark plug boots present a problem coming off, it

may be necessary to use a special removal tool, first twisting and pulling upward on the retainers.

5. Remove the ignition coil housing-to-cover bolts.
6. Remove the cover from the coil housing.
7. Disconnect the ignition coil harness connectors from the coil pack assembly.
8. Carefully lift the coil pack out and remove the contacts and seals from the housing.

To install:

9. Install new coil seals into the coil housing.
10. Install the coil contacts to the coil housing and retain with petroleum jelly.
11. Place the coil pack into the housing and connect the harness connectors.
12. Assemble the cover to the coil housing and install the retaining bolts. Torque the retaining bolts to 35 inch lbs. (4 Nm).
13. Install the spark plug boots and retainers on the ignition assembly housing secondary terminals.

NOTE: If the boots and retainers are not in place on the housing secondary terminals prior to installing the ignition assembly, damage to the ignition system may result.

14. Position the ignition assembly to the engine while carefully aligning the boots to the spark plug terminals.
15. Coat the ignition assembly-to-camshaft housing retaining bolts with an approved lubricant and install them into the housing.
16. Torque the retaining bolts to 19 ft. lbs. (26 Nm).
17. Connect the harness connector to the ignition coil module assembly.
18. Connect the negative battery cable.
19. Start the engine and test the engine performance.

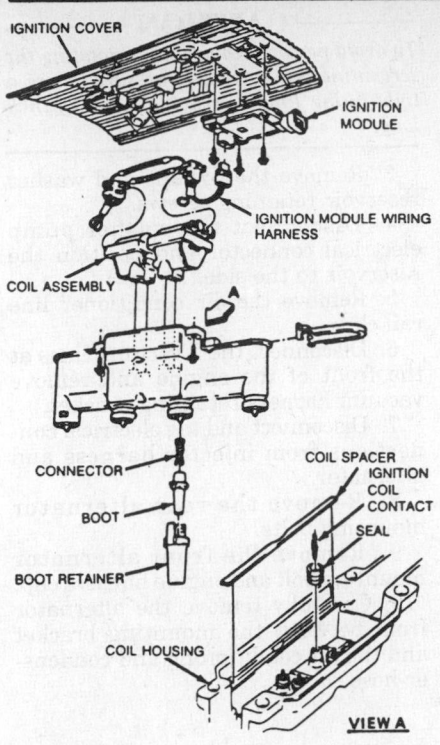

Exploded view of the IDIS Ignition assembly

Ignition Module

1. Disconnect the negative battery cable.

2. Disconnect the harness connector from the coil and module assembly.

3. Remove the ignition assembly-to-camshaft housing retaining bolts.

4. Carefully remove the ignition assembly from the engine.

NOTE: If the spark plug boots present a problem coming off, it may be necessary to use a special removal tool, first twisting and pulling upward on the retainers.

5. Remove the ignition coil housing-to-cover bolts.

6. Remove the cover from the coil housing.

7. Disconnect the coil harness connector from the module.

8. Remove the screws retaining the module to the ignition assembly cover.

NOTE: If the same module is going to be replaced, take care not to remove the grease from the module or coil. If a new module is to be installed, a package of silicone grease will be included with it. This grease aids in preventing the module from overheating.

To install:

9. Place the module on the ignition cover and install the retaining bolts. Torque the retaining bolts to 35 inch lbs. (4 Nm).

10. Connect the coil harness connector to the module.

11. Assemble the module cover to the coil housing and install the retaining bolts. Torque the retaining bolts to 35 inch lbs. (4 Nm).

12. Install the spark plug boots and retainers on the ignition assembly housing secondary terminals.

NOTE: If the boots and retainers are not in place on the housing secondary terminals prior to installing the ignition assembly, damage to the ignition system may result.

13. Position the ignition assembly to the engine while carefully aligning the boots to the spark plug terminals.

14. Coat the ignition assembly-to-camshaft housing retaining bolts with an approved lubricant and install them into the housing.

15. Torque the retaining bolts to 19 ft. lbs. (26 Nm).

16. Connect the harness connector to the ignition coil module assembly.

17. Connect the negative battery cable.

18. Start the engine and test the engine performance.

Ignition Timing

ADJUSTMENT

Ignition timing is controlled by the Electronic Control Module (ECM). No adjustments are possible.

Alternator

For further information on the charging system, please refer to "Charging and Starting" in the Unit Repair section.

PRECAUTIONS

Several precautions must be observed with alternator equipped vehicles to avoid damage to the unit.

• If the battery is removed for any reason, make sure it is reconnected with the correct polarity. Reversing the battery connections may result in damage to the one-way rectifiers.

• When utilizing a booster battery as a starting aid, always connect the positive to positive terminals and the negative terminal from the booster battery to a good engine ground on the vehicle being started.

• Never use a fast charger as a booster to start vehicles.

• Disconnect the battery cables when charging the battery with a fast charger.

• Never attempt to polarize the alternator.

• Do not use test lamps of more than 12 volts when checking diode continuity.

• Do not short across or ground any of the alternator terminals.

• The polarity of the battery, alternator and regulator must be matched and considered before making any electrical connections within the system.

• Never separate the alternator on an open circuit. Make sure all connections within the circuit are clean and tight.

• Disconnect the battery ground terminal when performing any service on electrical components.

• Disconnect the battery if arc welding is to be done on the vehicle.

BELT TENSION ADJUSTMENT

A single (serpentine) belt is used to drive all engine mounted components.

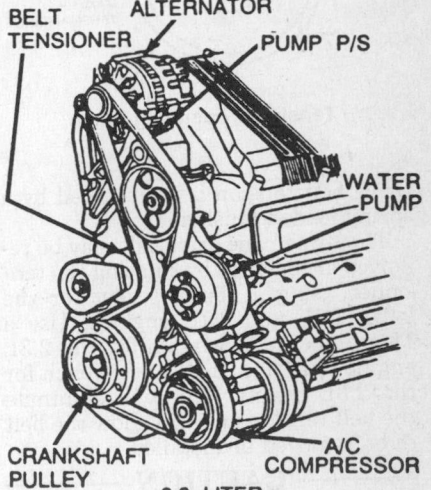

Drive belt routing—2.8L engine with air conditioning

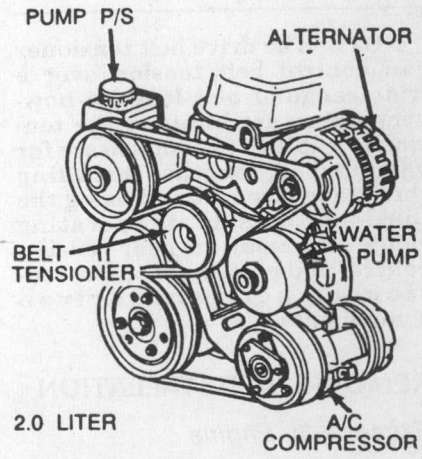

View of the drive belt routing—2.0L engine with air conditioning

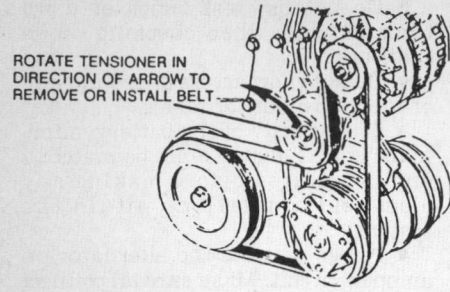

ROTATE TENSIONER IN DIRECTION OF ARROW TO REMOVE OR INSTALL BELT

View of the drive belt routing— 2.3L engine

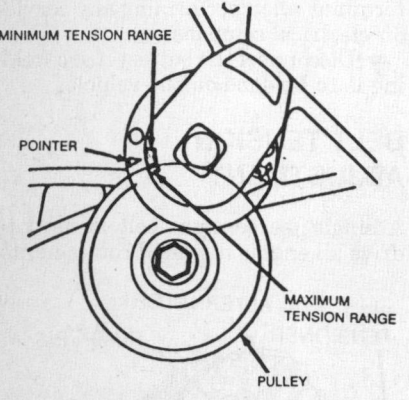

MINIMUM TENSION RANGE

POINTER

MAXIMUM TENSION RANGE

PULLEY

Tensioner operating range

Drive belt tension is maintained by a spring loaded tensioner.

The serpentine drive belt may be removed or installed by rotating the tensioner using a 15mm socket for the 2.0L, 2.2L and 3.1L engines. Use a 13mm open end wrench for the 2.3L engine or a ¾ in. open end wrench for the 2.8L engine. This will eliminate the belt tension and will allow the belt to be removed or installed.

CAUTION

To avoid personal injury when rotating the serpentine belt tensioner on the 2.3L engine, be sure to use a tight fitting 13mm wrench at least 24 inch long.

NOTE: The drive belt tensioner can control belt tension over a wide range of belt lengths; however, there are limits to the tensioner's ability to compensate for various belt lengths. Installing the wrong size belt and using the tensioner outside its operating range can result in poor tension control and/or damage to the tensioner, belt and driven components.

REMOVAL & INSTALLATION

Except 2.3L Engine

1. Disconnect the negative battery cable.

2. Label and disconnect the electrical connectors from the back of the alternator.
3. Remove the alternator mounting bolts.
4. Remove the serpentine drive belt.
5. Remove the alternator-to-bracket bolts and the alternator.

To install:

6. Position the alternator to the the mounting bracket and install the retaining bolts.
7. Connect the alternator electrical connectors to the rear of the alternator.
8. Install the serpentine drive belt adjust the belt tension.
9. Connect the negative battery cable.
10. Start the engine and perform a charging system test.

2.3L Engine

1. Disconnect the negative battery cable.
2. Remove the serpentine drive belt.

CAUTION

To avoid personal injury when rotating the serpentine belt tensioner, be sure to use a tight fitting 13mm wrench at least 24 inch long.

3. Remove the coolant and washer reservoir retaining screws.
4. Disconnect the washer pump electrical connector and position the reservoir to the side.
5. Remove the air conditioner line rail clip.
6. Disconnect the 2 vacuum lines at the front of the engine and remove vacuum harness retaining bracket.
7. Disconnect and tag electrical connections from injector harness and alternator.
8. Remove the rear alternator mounting bolts.
9. Remove the front alternator mounting bolt and engine harness clip.
10. Carefully remove the alternator from between the mounting bracket and the air conditioning and condenser hose.

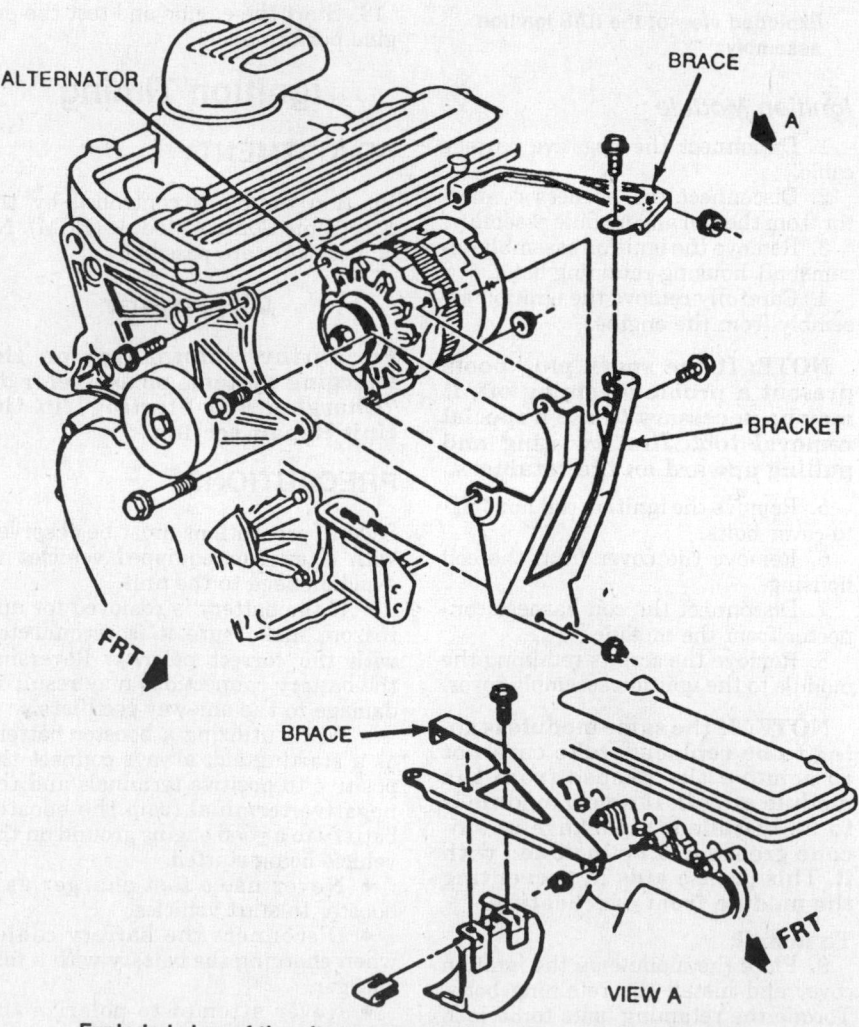

ALTERNATOR

BRACE

A

BRACKET

BRACE

FRT

FRT

VIEW A

Exploded view of the alternator mounting—2.0L and 2.2L engines

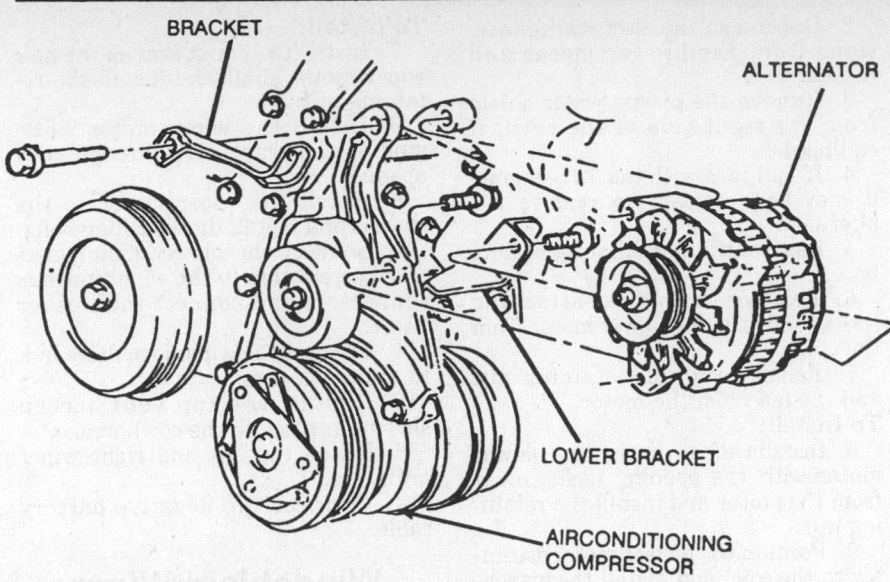

BRACKET

ALTERNATOR

LOWER BRACKET

AIRCONDITIONING COMPRESSOR

Exploded view of the alternator mounting—2.3L engine

NOTE: Extreme care must be taken when removing or installing the alternator as not to damage the air conditioner compressor and condenser hoses.

To install:

11. Place the alternator between the air conditioner compressor and condenser hoses and install it on the bracket.

12. Install the rear mounting bolts. Torque the mounting bolts to 20 ft. lbs. (26 Nm).

13. Install the front mounting bolts. Torque to 37 lbs. (50 Nm).

14. Install the serpentine drive belt and adjust the belt tension.

—————— CAUTION ——————

To avoid personal injury when rotating the serpentine belt tensioner, be sure to use a tight fitting 13mm wrench at least 24 in. long.

15. Install the air conditioner rail clip.

16. Connect the washer pump electrical connector.

17. Install the coolant and washer pump reservoir.

18. Connect the electrical connections for the alternator and injector harness.

19. Install the vacuum harness retaining bracket and connect the vacuum lines at the front of the engine.

20. Connect the negative battery cable.

21. Start the engine and perform a charging system test.

Starter

For further information on the charging system, please refer to "Charging and Starting" in the Unit Repair section.

REMOVAL & INSTALLATION

Except 2.3L Engine

1. Disconnect the negative battery cable.

2. Remove the air cleaner assembly.

3. Raise and support the vehicle safely.

NOTE: Engines equipped with an oil cooler, remove the oil filter and position the hose next to the starter to the side.

4. Remove the air conditioning compressor brace retaining nuts and remove the brace from the engine.

5. Remove flywheel inspection cover bolts and remove the inspection cover.

6. Remove the starter retaining bolts.

7. Carefully lower the starter and the shims.

8. Disconnect the electrical wiring connections at the starter.

To install:

9. Connect the electrical connections to the starter.

10. Position the shims in place and install the starter and mounting bolts. Torque the bolts to 32 ft. lbs. (43 Nm).

NOTE: Engines equipped with an oil cooler, position the cooler hose next to the starter motor and install the oil filter.

11. Install the flywheel inspection cover and retaining bolts.

12. Install the air conditioning compressor brace and retaining nuts.

13. Lower vehicle and connect the negative battery cable.

14. Crank the engine and check the starter operation.

2.3L Engine

1. Disconnect the negative battery cable.

2. Disconnect the electrical connector from the cooling fan.

3. Remove the cooling fan mounting bolts and remove the fan assembly.

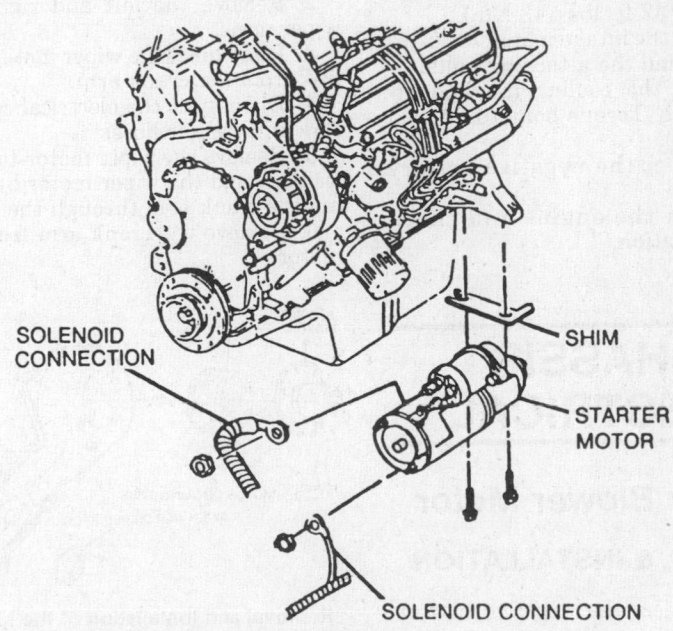

SOLENOID CONNECTION

SHIM

STARTER MOTOR

SOLENOID CONNECTION

Starter removal and installation—2.0L and 2.2L engines

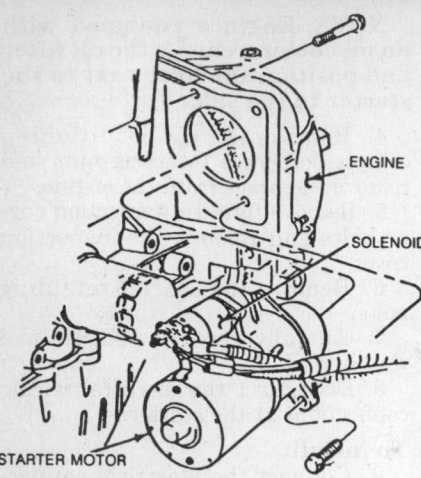

**Starter removal and installation—
2.8L and 3.1L engines**

4. Remove the intake manifold-to-engine brace bolts and remove the the brace from the engine.

5. Remove the starter mounting bolts.

6. Carefully lift the starter away from the engine with the solenoid harness attached to it.

7. When the starter is clear, disconnect the solenoid harness connections and lift the starter up and out toward the front of the vehicle.

To install:

8. Connect the solenoid harness connections to the starter, while supporting the starter toward the mounting position.

9. Rotate the starter so the solenoid faces the engine at a slight angle to clear the bottom of the intake manifold.

10. Install the starter to the engine and install the mounting bolts. Torque the bolts to 32 ft. lbs. (43 Nm).

11. Install the intake manifold-to-engine brace and the attaching bolts.

12. Install the cooling fan and attaching bolts. Torque bolts to 89 inch lbs. (10 Nm).

13. Connect the negative battery cable.

14. Crank the engine and check starter operation.

CHASSIS ELECTRICAL

Heater Blower Motor

REMOVAL & INSTALLATION

1. Disconnect the negative battery cable.

2. Disconnect the electrical connections from the blower motor and resistor.

3. Remove the plastic water shield from the right side of the cowl, if equipped.

4. If equipped with the 3.1L engine, it may be necessary to remove the alternator.

5. Remove the blower motor cooling hose.

6. Remove the blower attaching screws and pull the blower motor from the cowl.

7. Remove the fan retaining nut and the fan from the motor.

To install:

8. Install the fan on the new blower motor with the opening facing away from the motor and install the retaining nut.

9. Position the blower motor assembly to the cowl and install the attaching screws.

10. Install the blower motor cooling hose.

11. If equipped with the 3.1L engine, install the alternator if previously removed.

12. Install the plastic water shield on the right side of the cowl, if equipped.

13. Connect the electrical connections to the blower motor and resistor.

14. Connect the negative battery cable.

Windshield Wiper Motor

REMOVAL & INSTALLATION

1. Disconnect the negative battery cable.

2. Remove the left and right side wiper arms.

3. Disconnect the wiper motor drive link from the crank arm.

4. Disconnect the electrical connectors and washer hoses.

5. Remove the wiper motor-to-chassis bolts and the wiper motor by guiding the crank arm through the hole.

6. Remove the crank arm from the motor.

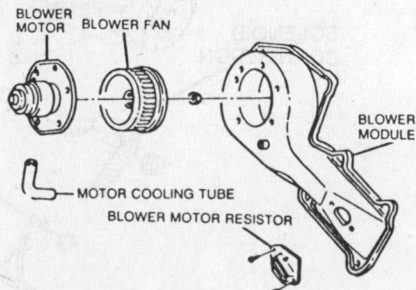

Removal and installation of the blower motor assembly

To install:

7. Install the crank arm on the new wiper motor shaft and install the retaining nut.

8. Install the wiper motor while guiding the crank arm through cowl opening.

9. Install the wiper motor to the chassis and install the attaching bolts.

10. Connect the blower motor electrical connectors to the wiper harness connectors and connect the washer hoses.

11. Connect the wiper arm drive link to the crank arm.

12. Install the top vent screen shroud in place to the cowl area.

13. Install the left and right wiper arms.

14. Connect the negative battery cable.

Windshield Wiper Switch

REMOVAL & INSTALLATION

1. Disconnect the negative battery cable.

2. Remove the switch by gently prying behind the switch.

3. Disconnect and label the wiring.

4. To install, connect the wires to the new switch and press it into the instrument panel to the same depth as the old switch.

5. Reconnect the negative battery cable and check the wiper operation.

Instrument Cluster

REMOVAL & INSTALLATION

The speedometer and gauge cluster are replaced as an assembly only.

NOTE: Whenever working on any electronic equipment, make sure to have a clean, static free environment in which to work. Always cover the work surface with a mat that is grounded and static free. Static electricity from walking across the floor or sliding across a car seat is enough to damage any equipment.

1. Disconnect the negative battery cable.

2. Remove the left sound insulator retaining screws and remove the insulator from the lower dash and cowl.

3. Remove the screws from the upper, center instrument cluster trim plate.

4. Slide the steering column seal out and remove the trim plate by pulling it straight outward.

5. Remove both upper instrument cluster-to-dash screws and pull the in-

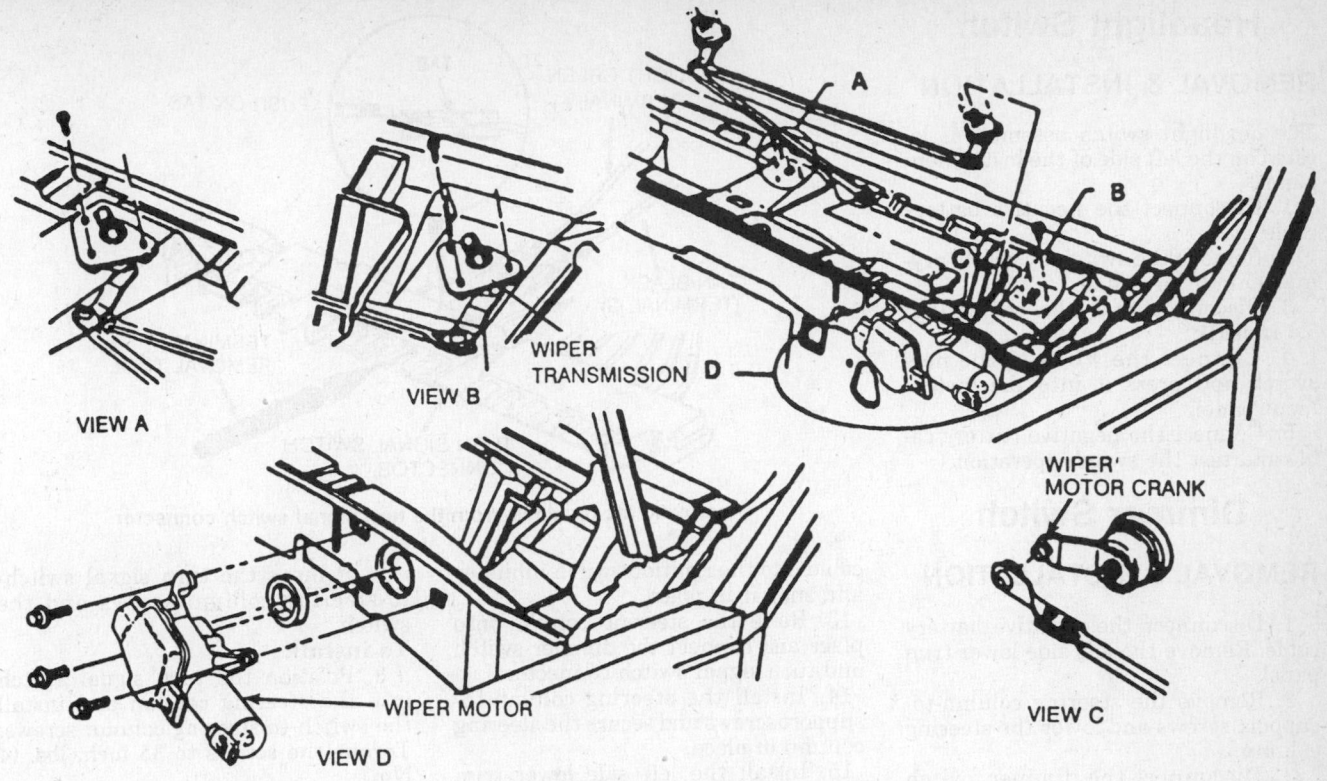

VIEW A

VIEW B

WIPER TRANSMISSION **D**

WIPER MOTOR CRANK

VIEW C

WIPER MOTOR

VIEW D

Removal and installation of the wiper motor assembly

strument cluster straight outward. Disconnect and label the electrical connectors.

To install:

6. Position the instrument cluster close to the wiring harness and connect the harness.

7. Slide the instrument cluster into the mounting clips and install the mounting screws.

8. Install the cluster trim plate, slide the steering column seal in place and connect the negative battery cable.

9. Install the left sound insulator to the lower dash panel and cowl.

10. Disconnect the negative battery cable.

Radio

REMOVAL & INSTALLATION

The radio is in housed as a part of the accessory center, which incorporates the heater and air conditioning controls. This is removed as a unit.

1. Disconnect the negative battery cable.

2. Remove left sound insulator retaining screws and remove the insulator from the lower dash.

3. On the Beretta, remove the lower trim panel screws and pull the trim panel out to release the taps at the top and remove the trim panel.

4. On Corsica, the trim panel has no screws retaining it. Carefully pull the trim panel out and release it from the retaining taps and remove the trim panel.

5. Remove the accessory center attaching screws from the top and from the bottom.

6. Pull the accessory center away from the carrier.

7. On vehicles with air conditioning, remove the electrical and vacuum harness from the back of the heater and air conditioning control assembly.

8. On vehicles without air conditioning, remove the cables from the control module.

9. Disconnect the antenna connection and unplug a label the attaching electrical connections.

10. Pull the accessory center assembly from the dash.

11. Place the assembly on a clean working area.

12. Remove all controls knobs by pulling off.

13. Remove the screws attaching the trim plate to the radio. Separate the radio from the trim plate.

To install:

14. Assemble the radio to the trim plate and accessory center. Install the retaining screws.

15. Install the knobs by pushing in place.

16. Position the accessory center as-

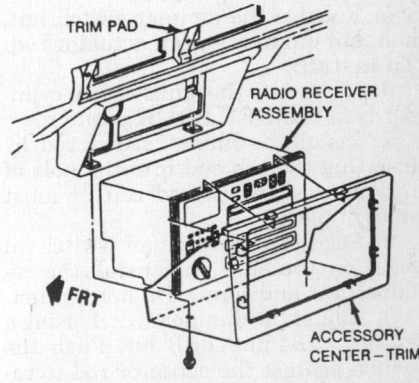

TRIM PAD

RADIO RECEIVER ASSEMBLY

FRT

ACCESSORY CENTER—TRIM

Removing and installing the accessory center assembly from the dash

sembly to the dash and connect the electrical harness connections.

17. On vehicles with air conditioning, connect the electrical and vacuum harnesses at the rear of the heater and air conditioning control assembly.

18. On vehicles without air conditioning, connect the control cables to the control module.

19. Connect the antenna lead to the radio.

20. Slide the accessory center in place in the dash. Install the attaching screws at top and bottom.

21. Install the trim panel in place.

22. Install the sound insulator at lower dash and cowl and install the retaining screws.

Headlight Switch

REMOVAL & INSTALLATION

The headlight switch assembly is located on the left side of the instrument panel.

1. Disconnect the negative battery cable.
2. Remove the switch by gently prying behind the switch.
3. Disconnect and label the wiring.

To install:

4. Connect the wires to the new switch and press it into the instrument panel.
5. Connect the negative battery cable and test the switch operation.

Dimmer Switch

REMOVAL & INSTALLATION

1. Disconnect the negative battery cable. Remove the left side lower trim panel.
2. Remove the steering column-to-support screws and lower the steering column.
3. Disconnect the dimmer switch and turn signal switch connectors.
4. Place the ignition lock cylinder in the **OFF LOCK** position.
5. Remove the dimmer switch nut, bolt and dimmer switch actuator rod.

To install:

6. Make sure the ignition lock cylinder is in the **OFF LOCK** position.
7. Install the dimmer switch rod, by inserting the tab end into the hole of the dimmer switch rod cap. It must snap in place.
8. Position the dimmer switch in place on the stud and install the retainer nut and screw. Do not tighten.
9. Adjust the dimmer switch using a 3/32 in. (2.34mm) drill bit. Push the switch against the actuator rod to remove all lash.
10. Remove the adjustment tool from the dimmer switch.
11. Torque the dimmer switch stud nut and screw to 35 inch lbs.
12. If equipped, install the park lock

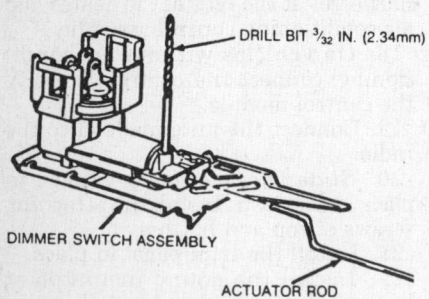

DRILL BIT 3/32 IN. (2.34mm)

DIMMER SWITCH ASSEMBLY

ACTUATOR ROD

Adjusting the dimmer switch

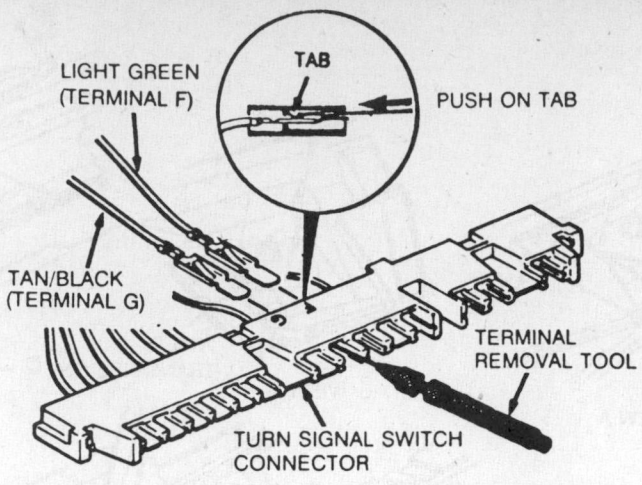

LIGHT GREEN (TERMINAL F)

TAB

PUSH ON TAB

TAN/BLACK (TERMINAL G)

TERMINAL REMOVAL TOOL

TURN SIGNAL SWITCH CONNECTOR

Removing the terminals from the turn signal switch connector

cable into the ignition switch inhibiter and snap it in place.

13. Raise the steering column into place and connect the dimmer switch and turn signal switch connectors.
14. Install the steering column-to-support screws and secure the steering column in place.
15. Install the left side lower trim panel.
16. Connect the negative battery cable.

Combination Switch

REMOVAL & INSTALLATION

NOTE: A special terminal remover tool is required to remove the terminals from the connector on the turn signal switch.

1. Disconnect the negative battery cable. Remove the steering wheel.
2. Pull the turn signal canceling cam assembly from the steering shaft.
3. Remove the hazard warning knob-to-steering column screw and the knob.

NOTE: Before removing the turn signal assembly, position the turn signal lever so the turn signal assembly-to-steering column screws can all be removed.

4. Remove the column housing cover-to-column housing bowl screw and the cover.

NOTE: If equipped with cruise control, disconnect the cruise control electrical connector.

5. Remove the turn signal lever retaining screw and the lever.
6. Using a terminal remover tool, disconnect and label the wires F and G on the connector at the buzzer switch assembly from the turn signal switch electrical harness connector.

7. Remove the turn signal switch-to-steering column screws and the switch.

To install:

8. Position the turn signal switch into the steering column and install the switch-to-steering column screws. Torque the screws to 35 inch. lbs. (4 Nm).
9. Connect wires F and G of the buzzer switch assembly, to the turn signal switch harness connector.
10. Install the turn signal lever and screw retaining screw. Torque the retaining screw to 20 inch lbs. (2.3 Nm).

NOTE: If equipped with cruise control, connect the cruise control electrical connector.

11. Install the column housing cover and retaining screw. Torque the retaining screw to 35 inch lbs. (4 Nm).
12. Install the hazard warning knob and retaining screw.
1. Install the turn signal canceling cam assembly over the steering shaft, install the steering wheel and retaining nut. Torque the nut to 30 ft. lbs. (41 Nm).
14. Connect the negative battery cable. Check the switch operation.

Ignition Lock/Switch

REMOVAL & INSTALLATION

The manufacturer recommends the steering column be removed from the vehicle prior to ignition lock removal and installation.

Standard Steering Column

1. Disconnect the negative battery cable. Remove the left side lower trim panel.
2. Remove the steering column-to-support screws and lower the steering column.

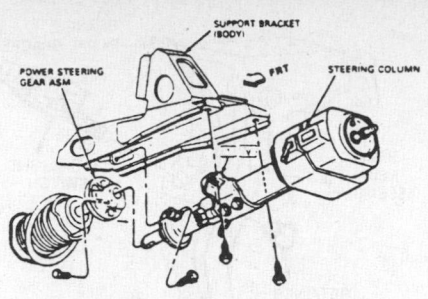

Steering column mounting

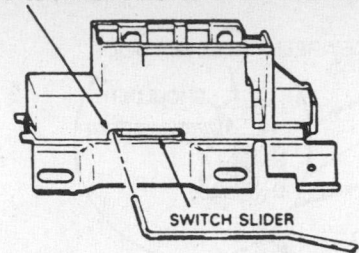

PLACE SWITCH SLIDER IN FAR LEFT POSITION

SWITCH SLIDER

Ignition switch installation position

2. Remove the steering column-to-support screws and lower the steering column.

3. Disconnect the dimmer switch and turn signal switch connectors.

4. Remove the wiring harness-to-firewall nuts and steering column.

5. If equipped with a park lock cable, insert a small prybar into the ignition switch inhibiter switch access hole, depress the locking tab and disconnect the park lock cable from the inhibiter switch.

6. Remove the steering column-to-steering gear bolt and the steering column from the vehicle.

7. Remove the combination switch.

8. Using a flat type pry blade, position it in the square opening of the spring retainer, push downward to the left, to release the spring retainer. Remove the wheel tilt spring.

9. Remove the spring retainer, the tilt spring and the tilt spring guide.

10. Remove the shoe pin retaining cap. Using a pivot pin removal tool, remove both pivot pins.

11. Place the lock cylinder in the **RUN** position.

12. Pull the shoe release lever and release the steering column housing.

13. Remove the column housing, the steering shaft assembly and turn signal switch housing as an assembly.

14. Using a terminal remover tool, disconnect and label the wires F and G on the connector at the buzzer switch assembly from the turn signal switch electrical harness connector.

15. Place the lock cylinder in the **RUN** position and remove the buzzer switch.

16. Place the lock cylinder in the **ACC** position. Remove the lock cylinder retaining screw and the lock cylinder.

17. Remove the dimmer switch nut/bolt, the dimmer switch and actuator rod.

18. Remove the dimmer switch mounting stud, the mounting nut was mounted to it.

19. Remove the ignition switch-to-steering column screws and the ignition switch.

20. Remove the lock bolt screws and the lock bolt.

21. Remove the switch actuator rack and ignition switch.

22. Remove the steering shaft lock and spring.

To install:

23. To install the lock bolt, lubricate it with lithium grease and install the lock bolt, spring and retaining plate.

24. Lubricate the teeth on the switch actuator rack. Install the rack and the ignition switch through the opening in the steering bolt until it rests on the retaining plate.

---

3. Disconnect the dimmer switch and turn signal switch connectors.

4. Remove the wiring harness-to-firewall nuts and steering column.

5. If equipped with a park lock cable, insert a small prybar into the ignition switch inhibiter switch access hole, depress the locking tab and disconnect the park lock cable from the inhibiter switch.

6. Remove the steering column-to-steering gear bolt and the steering column from the vehicle.

7. Remove the combination switch.

8. Place the lock cylinder in the **RUN** position.

9. Remove the steering shaft assembly and turn signal switch housing as an assembly.

10. Using a terminal remover tool, disconnect and label the wires F and G on the connector at the buzzer switch assembly from the turn signal switch electrical harness connector.

11. Place the lock cylinder in the **RUN** position and remove the buzzer switch.

12. Place the lock cylinder in the **ACC** position. Remove the lock cylinder retaining screw and the lock cylinder.

13. Remove the dimmer switch nut/bolt, the dimmer switch and actuator rod.

14. Remove the dimmer switch mounting stud, the mounting nut was mounted to it.

15. Remove the ignition switch-to-steering column screws and the ignition switch.

Ignition lock cylinder removal

16. Remove the lock bolt screws and the lock bolt.

17. Remove the switch actuator rack and ignition switch.

18. Remove the steering shaft lock and spring.

To install:

19. To install the lock bolt, lubricate it with lithium grease and install the lock bolt, spring and retaining plate.

20. Lubricate the teeth on the switch actuator rack. Install the rack and the ignition switch through the opening in the steering bolt until it rests on the retaining plate.

21. Install the steering column lock cylinder set by holding the barrel of the lock cylinder, insert the key and turn it to the **ACC** position.

22. Install the lock set in the steering column while holding the rack against the lock plate.

23. Install the lock retaining screw and torque the screw to 27 inch lbs. Insert the key in the lock cylinder and turn the lock cylinder to the **START** position and the rack will extend.

24. Center the slotted holes on the ignition switch mounting plate and install the ignition switch mounting screw and nut.

25. Install the dimmer switch and actuator rod into the center slot on the switch mounting plate. Torque the dimmer switch stud to 35 inch lbs.

26. Install the buzzer switch and turn the lock cylinder to the **RUN** position. Push the switch in until it is bottomed out with the plastic tab that covers the lock retaining screw.

27. Install the steering shaft and turn signal housing as an assembly.

28. Install the turn signal switch. Torque the turn signal switch housing screws to 88 inch lbs., the turn signal switch screws to 35 inch lbs. and the steering wheel locknut to 30 ft.lbs.

29. To complete the installation, reverse the removal procedures.

Tilt Steering Column

1. Disconnect the negative battery cable. Tilt the column up as far as it will go and remove the left side lower trim panel.

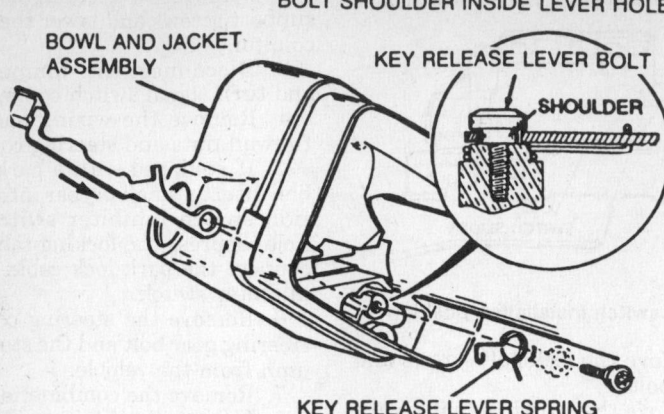

Removing the key release lever

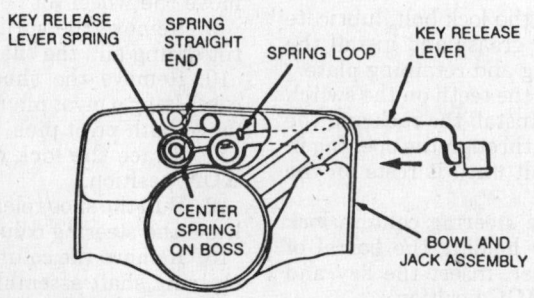

Key release lever spring installation position

25. Install the steering column lock cylinder set by holding the barrel of the lock cylinder, insert the key and turn the key to the **ACC** position.

26. Install the lock set in the steering column while holding the rack against the lock plate.

27. Install the lock retaining screw and torque the screw to 27 inch lbs. Insert the key in the lock cylinder. Turn the lock cylinder to the **START** position and the rack will extend.

28. Center the slotted holes on the ignition switch mounting plate. Install the ignition switch mounting screw and nut.

29. Install the dimmer switch and actuator rod into the center slot on the switch mounting plate. Torque the dimmer switch stud to 35 inch lbs.

30. Install the buzzer switch and turn the lock cylinder to the **RUN** position. Push the switch in until it is bottomed out with the plastic tab that covers the lock retaining screw.

31. Install the steering shaft and turn signal housing as an assembly.

32. Install the turn signal switch. Torque the turn signal switch housing screws to 88 inch lbs., the turn signal switch screws to 35 inch lbs. and the steering wheel locknut to 30 ft. lbs.

33. Connect the negative battery cable.

Stoplight Switch

ADJUSTMENT

1. Disconnect the negative battery cable.

2. Remove the lower, left trim panel and locate the stoplight switch on the brake pedal support.

3. Disconnect the electrical connector from the switch and remove the switch by twisting it out of the tubular retaining clip.

4. Pull back on the brake pedal and push the switch through the retaining clip noting the clicks; repeat this procedure until no more clicks can be heard.

5. Connect the electrical connector to the switch.

6. Connect the negative battery cable and check the switch operation.

REMOVAL & INSTALLATION

1. Disconnect the negative battery cable.

2. Remove the lower, left trim panel. Locate the stoplight switch on the brake pedal support.

3. Disconnect the electrical connector from the switch and remove the

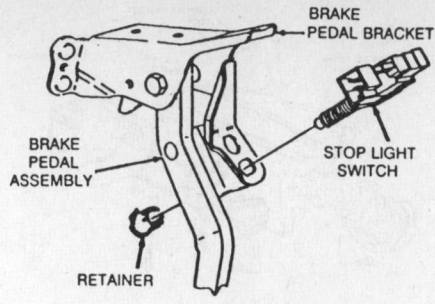

Removing the stoplight switch

switch by twisting it out of the tubular retaining clip.

To install:

4. Using a new retaining clip, install the switch and connect the electrical connector.

5. To adjust the switch, pull back on the brake pedal, push the switch through the retaining clip noting the clicks; repeat this procedure until no more clicks can be heard.

6. Connect the negative battery cable and check the switch operation.

Clutch Switch

ADJUSTMENT

1. Disconnect the negative battery cable.

2. Remove the lower, left trim panel and locate the switch on the clutch pedal support.

3. Disconnect the electrical connector from the switch and remove the switch by twisting it out of the tubular retaining clip.

4. Pull back on the clutch pedal and push the switch through the retaining clip noting the clicks; repeat this procedure until no more clicks can be heard.

5. Connect the electrical connector to the switch.

6. Connect the negative battery cable and check the switch operation.

REMOVAL & INSTALLATION

1. Disconnect the negative battery cable.

2. Remove the lower, left trim panel. Locate the switch on the clutch pedal support.

3. Disconnect the electrical connector from the switch and remove the switch by twisting it out of the tubular retaining clip.

To install:

4. Using a new retaining clip, install the switch and connect the electrical connector.

5. To adjust the switch, pull back on the clutch pedal, push the switch

through the retaining clip noting the clicks; repeat this procedure until no more clicks can be heard.

6. Connect the negative battery cable and check the switch operation.

Neutral Safety Switch

The automatic transaxle utilizes the neutral safety switch and back-up light switch as a combined unit. This switch is located on top of the of the transaxle.

ADJUSTMENT

1. Disconnect the negative battery cable.
2. Loosen the switch retaining screws.
3. Rotate the switch on the shifter assembly to align the service adjustment hole with the carrier tang hole.
4. Using a $3/32$ in. drill bit or gauge pin, insert it into the service adjustment hole to a depth of $3/8$ in. (9mm).
5. Tighten the switch-to-transaxle screws and remove the drill bit or gauge pin.
6. Connect the negative battery cable and test the switch operation.

REMOVAL & INSTALLATION

1. Disconnect the negative battery cable and the electrical connector from the switch.

2. Remove the switch-to-transaxle screws and the switch.
To install:
3. Place the transaxle's shift control lever in the **N** notch in the detent plate.
4. Position the switch onto the transaxle and install the screws loosely.
5. Perform a switch adjustment.
6. Connect the negative battery cable.
7. Start the engine and check the switch operation.

Back-up Light Switch

The back-up light switch applies to the manual transaxle only and is located on top of the transaxle.

REMOVAL & INSTALLATION

1. Disconnect the negative battery cable.
2. Disconnect the electrical connector at the switch.
3. Screw the back-up light switch out of the transaxle.
To install:
4. Prior to installing the switch, apply an approved thread sealant to the threads of the new switch.
5. Thread the back-up light switch into the transaxle.
6. Torque the switch to 84 inch lbs. (9 Nm) and connect the electrical connector.

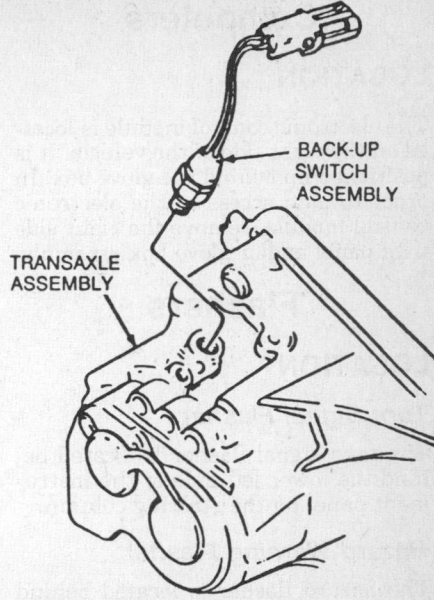

Removing the back-up light switch — manual transaxle

7. Connect the negative battery cable.

Fuses, Circuit Breakers and Relays

LOCATION

Fuse Panel
The fuse panel is located on the left side of the instrument panel assembly. In order to gain access to the fuse panel, it is necessary to first remove the lower trim panel.

Fusible Links
Fusible links—A and E are located rear of the engine compartment, at the battery junction box.
Fusible links—B, C and D are located at the front section of the engine at the starter solenoid.
Fusible link—F is located on the left side of the engine compartment, near the battery.

Circuit Breakers
Circuit breakers No. 12 and No. 15 are located in fuse block.

Various Relays
The coolant fan, air conditioning compressor, air conditioning high blower speed and fuel pump relays are all located in the engine compartment mounted to the center of the firewall on the relay bracket.

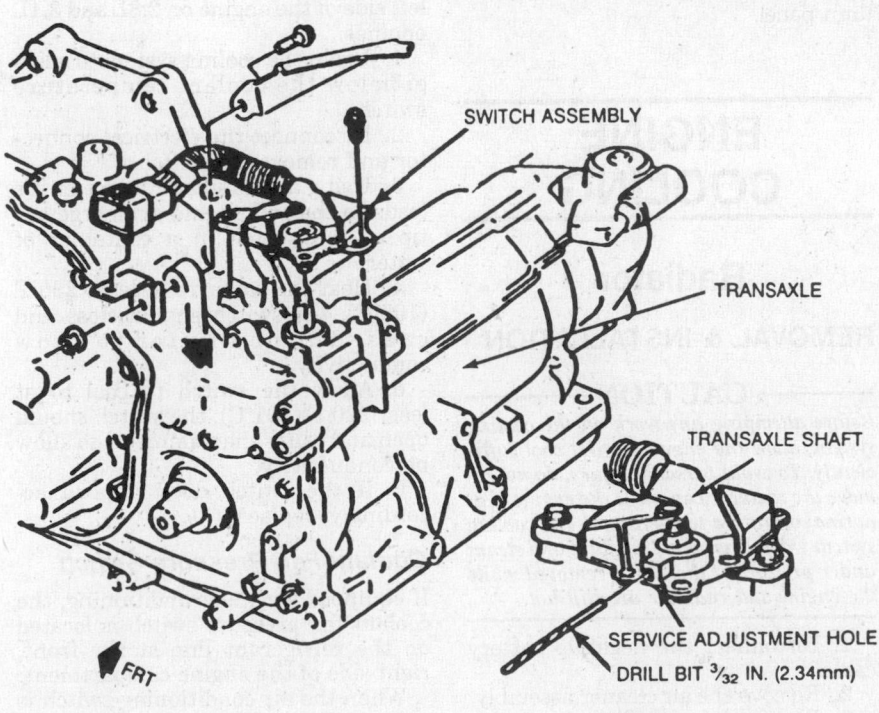

Removing the neutral safety switch — automatic transaxle

Computers

LOCATION

The electronic control module is located on the right side of the vehicle. It is positioned up behind the glove box. In order to gain access to the electronic control module, remove the right side trim panel and/or glove box assembly.

Flashers

LOCATION

Turn Signal Flasher

The turn signal flasher is located behind the lower left side of the instrument panel on the steering column.

Hazard Warning Flasher

The hazard flasher is located behind the lower left side of the instrument panel on the steering column.

Cruise Control

ADJUSTMENT

Control Cable

1. With the servo cable installed on the brackets, place the cable over the stud on the servo lever so the stud engages the slot in the cable end.
2. Connect the cable to the throttle lever and release the lever.
3. Pull the servo end of the cable towards the servo as far as possible without moving the throttle.
4. Attach the cable to the servo in the closest alignment holes without moving the throttle.

NOTE: Do not stretch the cable to attach it to the servo. This will not allow the engine to return to idle.

5. The cable is now adjusted properly.
6. Start the engine and turn ON the speed control main switch.
7. Drive the vehicle above 25 mph.
8. Engage the speed control and check the following functions: set, disengage, coast and resume.

Brake Pedal Release Switch

The brake pedal release switch is located at the top of the brake pedal, directly above the brake pedal switch.
1. Remove the lower steering column cover.
2. Pull the brake pedal release switch from the mounting bracket.
3. Depress the brake pedal and insert the brake pedal release switch into the tubular retainer bracket until it seats on the retainer.

NOTE: Note that clicks can be heard as the threaded portion of the valve passes through the retainer toward the brake pedal.

4. Pull the brake pedal rearward against the pedal stop until audible clicks can no longer be heard.
5. Release the brake pedal and again, pull the pedal rearward to make sure no more clicks can be heard.
6. Install the lower steering column panel.

Clutch Pedal Release Switch

The clutch pedal release switch is located at the top of the clutch pedal.
1. Remove the lower steering column cover.
2. Pull the clutch pedal release switch from the mounting bracket.
3. Depress the clutch pedal and insert the clutch pedal release switch into the tubular retainer bracket until it seats on the retainer.

NOTE: Note that clicks can be heard as the threaded portion of the valve passes through the retainer toward the clutch pedal.

4. Pull the clutch pedal rearward against the pedal stop until audible clicks can no longer be heard.
5. Release the clutch pedal and again, pull the pedal rearward to make sure no more clicks can be heard.
6. Reinstall the lower steering column panel.

ENGINE COOLING

Radiator

REMOVAL & INSTALLATION

— CAUTION —

Before attemping any work on the cooling system, allow the engine to first cool sufficiently. To avoid personal injury, do not remove the radiator cap while the engine is at normal operation temperature. The cooling system will release scalding fluid and steam under pressure if the cap is removed while the engine and radiator are still hot.

1. Disconnect the negative battery cable.
2. Remove the air cleaner assembly.
3. Place and drain pan under the radiator, release the drain plug and drain the engine coolant.
4. Disconnect the electrical connection from the electric fan.
5. Remove the fan-to-chassis mounting bolts and remove the fan assembly.
6. Disconnect the radiator upper and lower hoses at the radiator end.
7. If equipped with an automatic transaxle, disconnect the transaxle cooler lines and plug.
8. Remove the upper radiator mounting bolts.
9. Remove the condenser-to-radiator mounting bolts.
10. Carefully lift the radiator out.
To install:
11. Reverse the installation procedure.
12. Torque the radiator mounting bolts to 89 inch lbs. (10 Nm).
13. Refill the cooling system with an approved coolant mixture.
14. Connect the negative battery cable.
15. Start the engine, allow it to reach operating temperature and check for leaks.

Electric Cooling Fan

TESTING

Coolant Temperature Switch

The coolant temperature switch is located at the left side of the engine on the coolant outlet on 2.0L and 2.2L engines. On the left rear of side of the engine on the 2.3L engine and on the top left side of the engine on 2.8L and 3.1L engines.
1. Drain the cooling system to a level below the coolant temperature switch.
2. Disconnect the electrical connector and remove the switch.
3. Using an ohmmeter, connect it's leads to the switch and submerge the tip of the switch in a container of water.
4. Heat the water to at least 230°F (108°C); the switch should close and cause the ohmmeter to show conductivity.
5. Allow the switch to cool to at least 220°F (101°C); the switch should open and cause the ohmmeter to show no conductivity.
6. If the switch does respond accordingly, replace it.

Coolant Fan Pressure Switch

If equipped with air conditioning, the coolant fan pressure switch is located on the refrigerant line at the front, right side of the engine compartment.

When the air conditioning switch is turned ON and the low pressure switch is CLOSED, the cooling fan will turn ON.

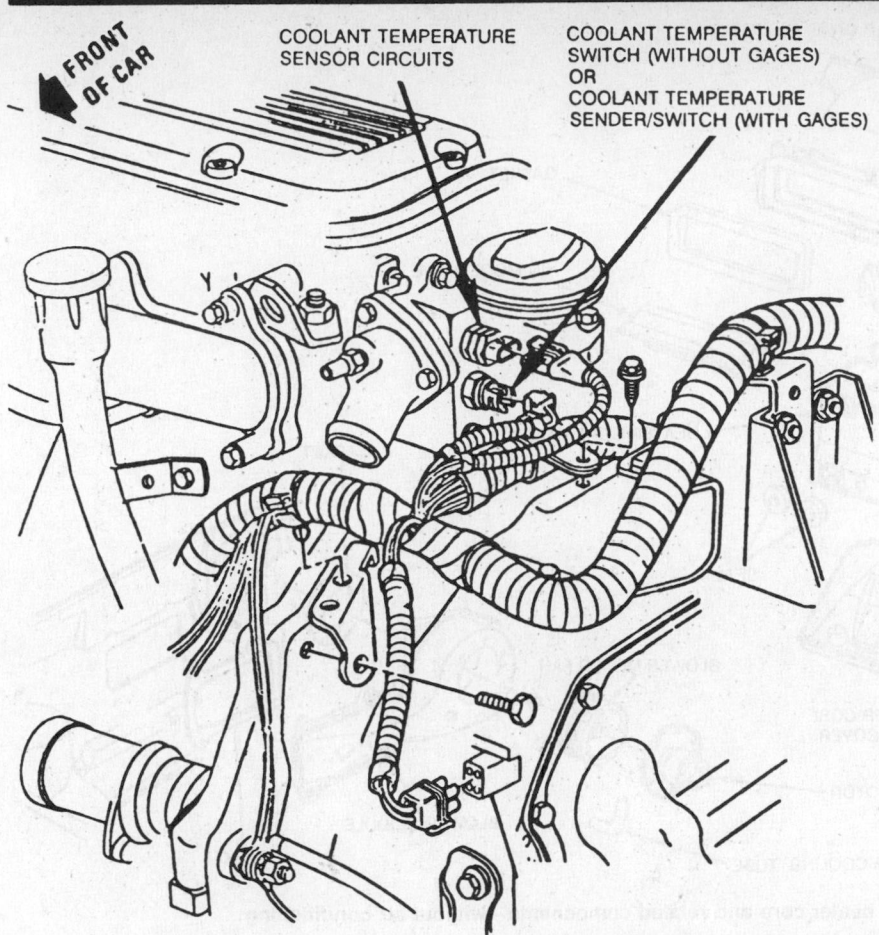

COOLANT TEMPERATURE SENSOR CIRCUITS

COOLANT TEMPERATURE SWITCH (WITHOUT GAGES) OR COOLANT TEMPERATURE SENDER/SWITCH (WITH GAGES)

FRONT OF CAR

Coolant temperature switch location – typical

Electric Fan Relay

The electric fan relay is located at the center, front of the dash on the relay block.

The ECM reads the sensor information and sends an electrical impulse to the relay's primary circuit causing the cooling fan to turn ON.

REMOVAL & INSTALLATION

1. Disconnect the negative battery cable.
2. Disconnect the electrical wiring harness from the cooling fan frame.
3. Remove the fan assembly from the radiator support.
4. To install, reverse the removal procedures. Torque the fan assembly-to-radiator support bolts to 7 ft. lbs.

Heater Core

REMOVAL & INSTALLATION

Without Air Conditioning

1. Disconnect the negative battery cable. Drain the cooling system.

2. Remove heater hoses from the heater core.
3. Remove the right and left hush panels and the steering column trim cover.
4. Remove the heater air outlet deflector.
5. Remove the heater core cover, the heater core and retaining straps.
6. Reverse the removal procedures. Refill and bleed the cooling system. Start the engine, allow it to reach normal operating temperatures and check for leaks.

With Air Conditioning

1. Disconnect the negative battery cable. Drain the cooling system.
2. Raise and safely support the vehicle.
3. Remove the drain tube from the heater case and the heater hoses from the heater core. Lower the vehicle.
4. Remove the right and left hush panels and the steering column trim cover.
5. Remove the heater air outlet deflector and the glove box.
6. Remove the heater core cover, the heater core and retaining straps.

7. Reverse the removal procedures. Refill and bleed the cooling system. Start the engine, allow it to reach normal operating temperatures and check for leaks.

Water Pump

REMOVAL & INSTALLATION

Except 2.3L Engine

1. Disconnect the negative battery cable.
2. Drain engine coolant from the radiator and engine.
3. Remove the serpentine drive belt.
4. On the 2.0L engine, remove the alternator and bracket with wires attached and position it out of the way.
5. On the 3.1L engine remove the radiator and heater hoses.
6. Remove the water pump pulley bolts and remove the pulley.
7. Remove the water pump-to-engine bolts and the pump.
To install:
8. Clean the gasket mounting surfaces.

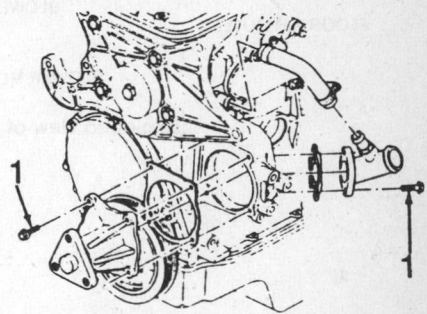

1. 14–22 ft. lbs.

Water pump installation – 2.0L and 2.2L engines

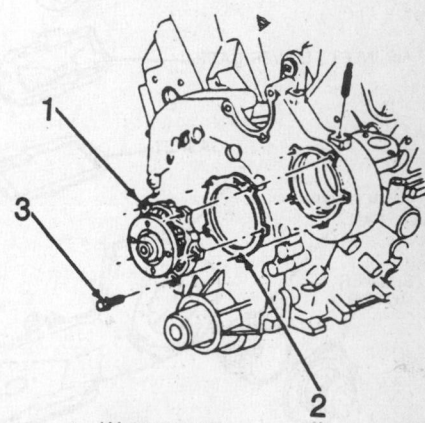

1. Water pump
2. Gasket
3. 6–9 ft. lbs.

Water pump installation – 2.8 and 3.1L engines

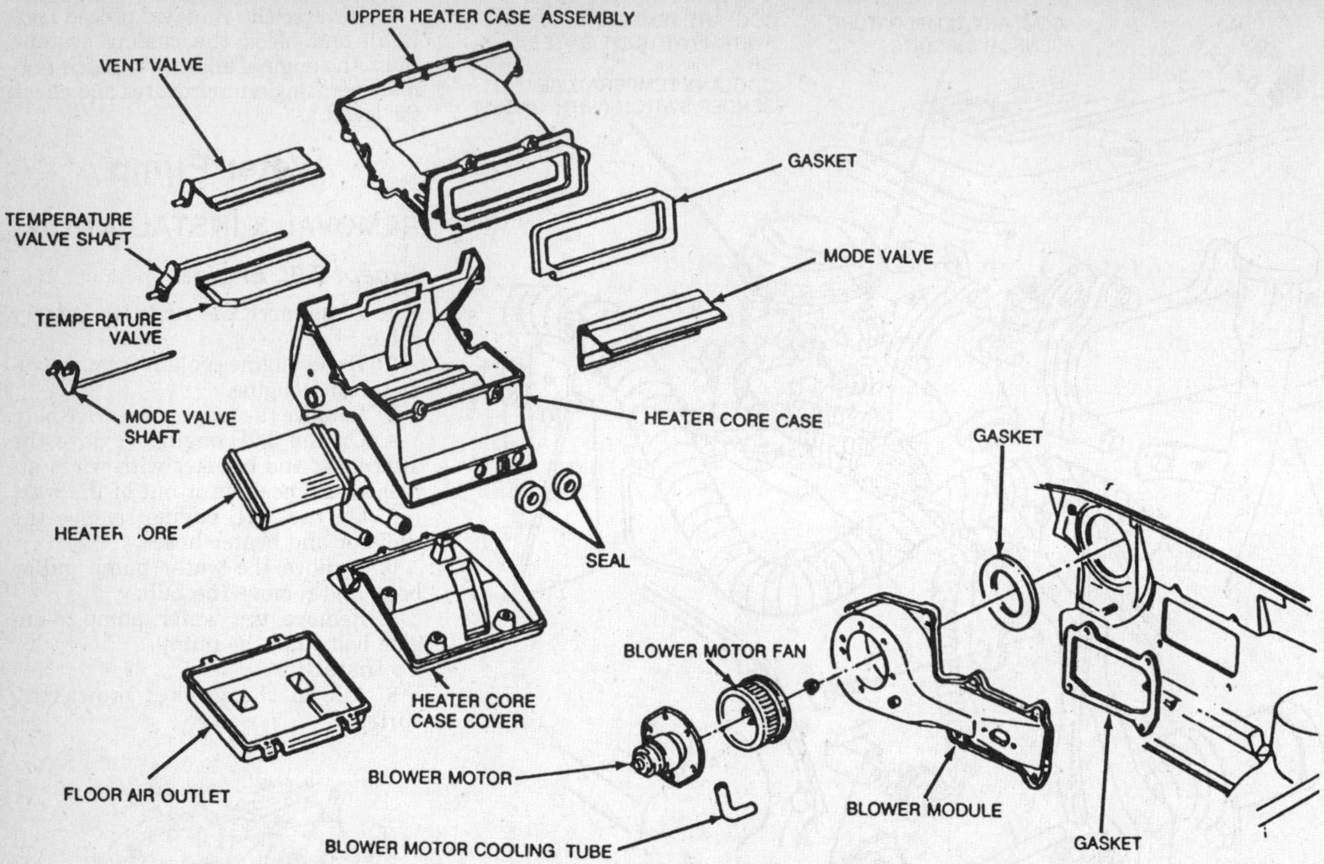

UPPER HEATER CASE ASSEMBLY

VENT VALVE

GASKET

TEMPERATURE VALVE SHAFT

MODE VALVE

TEMPERATURE VALVE

MODE VALVE SHAFT

HEATER CORE CASE

GASKET

HEATER CORE

SEAL

FLOOR AIR OUTLET

BLOWER MOTOR FAN

HEATER CORE CASE COVER

GASKET

BLOWER MOTOR

BLOWER MODULE

BLOWER MOTOR COOLING TUBE

GASKET

Exploded view of the heater core and related components – without air conditioning

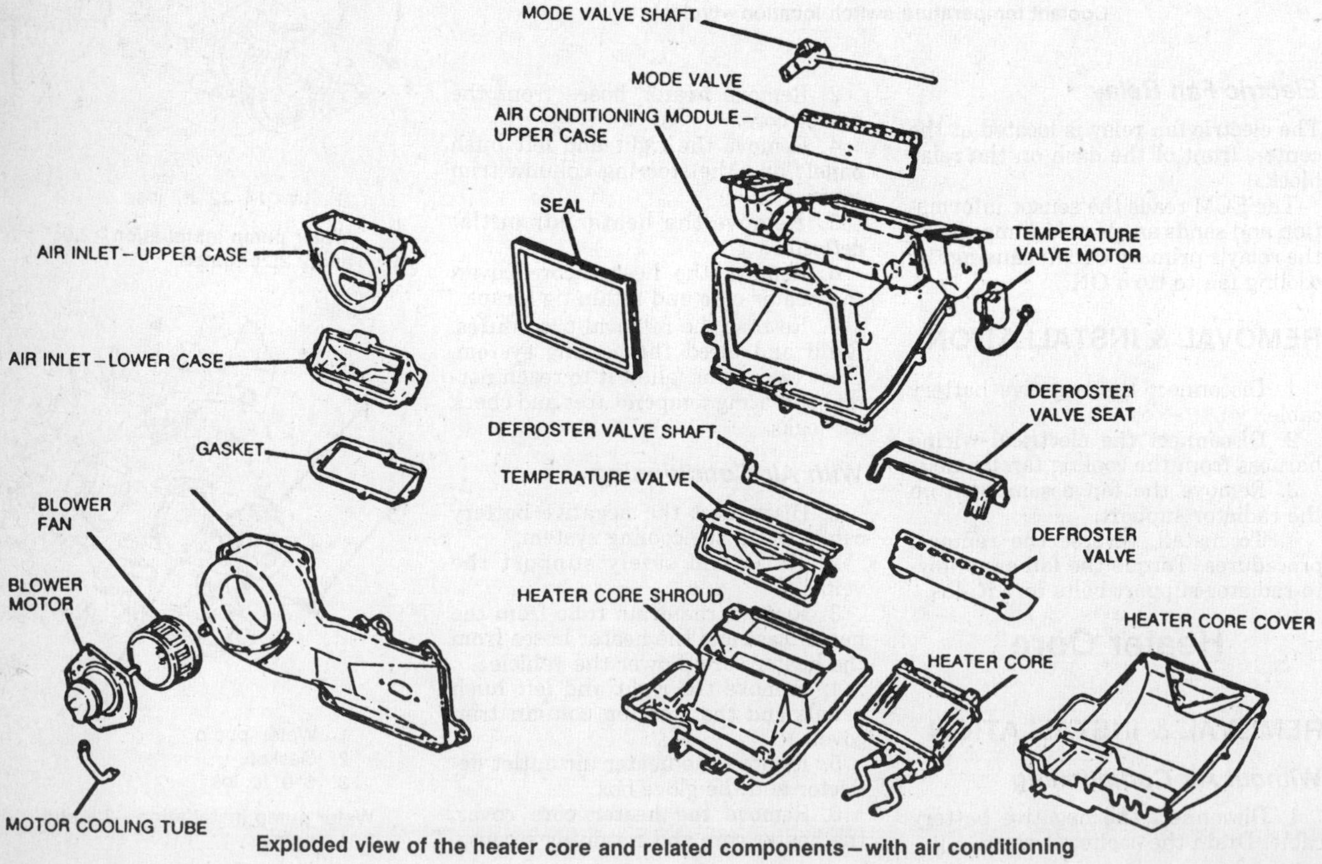

MODE VALVE SHAFT

MODE VALVE

AIR CONDITIONING MODULE – UPPER CASE

SEAL

TEMPERATURE VALVE MOTOR

AIR INLET – UPPER CASE

AIR INLET – LOWER CASE

DEFROSTER VALVE SEAT

GASKET

DEFROSTER VALVE SHAFT

TEMPERATURE VALVE

DEFROSTER VALVE

BLOWER FAN

BLOWER MOTOR

HEATER CORE COVER

HEATER CORE SHROUD

HEATER CORE

MOTOR COOLING TUBE

Exploded view of the heater core and related components – with air conditioning

9. Using new gaskets and sealant, if necessary, reverse the removal procedures. Torque the water pump-to-engine bolts to 14–22 ft. lbs. on the 2.0L and 2.2L engines or to 6–9 ft. lbs. on the 2.8L and 3.1L engines.

10. To complete the installation, reverse the removal procedures.

11. Refill and bleed the cooling system. Start the engine, allow it to reach normal operating temperature and check for leaks.

2.3L Engine

1. Disconnect the negative battery cable.

2. Drain the engine coolant at the radiator.

NOTE: Remove the heater hose from the thermostat housing for additional draining.

3. Remove the oxygen sensor connector.

4. Remove the upper and lower exhaust manifold heat shield retaining bolts and remove the shields.

5. Remove the exhaust manifold brace-to-mainfold retaining bolt.

6. Using a 13mm box wrench, loosen the exhaust pipe-to-manifold spring bolts from the engine compartment.

7. Raise the vehicle and support it safely.

8. From below, remove the bolts from the exhaust flange using a 7/32 in. (5.5mm) socket an 1 bolt rotate clockwise first.

NOTE: Rotating the bolt clockwise is necessary to relieve the spring pressure from the 1st bolt prior to removing the 2nd bolt, otherwise the exhaust pipe will twist and bind the bolt as it is removed.

9. Thread the bolt with least pressure on it out 4 turns.

10. Move the other bolt and turn it all the way out of the exhaust pipe flange.

11. Return to the 1st bolt and rotate it the rest of the way out.

12. Pull the exhaust pipe back from the exhaust manifold.

13. Remove the radiator outlet pipe from the oil pan and transaxle.

14. Remove the exhaust manifold brace.

15. Pull down on the radiator outlet pipe to disengage it from the water pump.

16. Lower the vehicle.

17. Remove the exhaust manifold-to-cylinder head retaining nuts.

18. Remove the exhaust manifold, seals and gaskets.

19. Remove the water pump cover-to-engine retaining bolts.

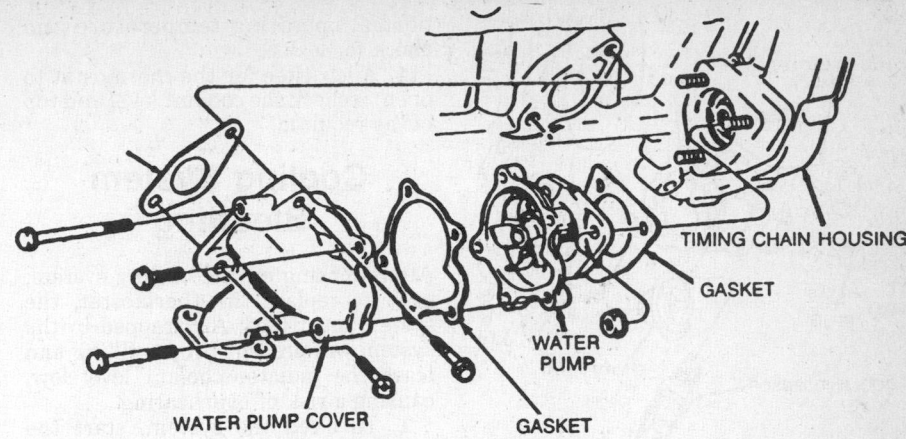

Water pump removal and installation – 2.3L engine

20. Remove the water pump-to-timing chain housing retaining nuts.

21. Remove the water pump and cover assembly from the engine.

22. Remove the water pump cover-to-radiator pump assembly.

To install:

NOTE: Before installing the water pump it is important to first read over the entire procedure. Pay special attention to the tightening sequence, to avoid part damage and to insure proper sealing.

23. Clean all mating surfaces throughly and use new gaskets.

24. Position the water pump cover to the radiator pump assembly and install the retaining bolts. Do not tighten.

25. Lubricate the splines of the radiator pump drive with the an approved chassis grease and install the pump and cover assembly.

26. Install the pump cover-to-engine retaining bolts. Do not tighten.

27. Install the timing chain housing nuts. Do not tighten.

28. Lubricate the O-ring on the radiator outlet pipe with a solution of antifreeze and slide the pipe into the radiator pump cover. Install the retaining bolts. Do not tighten.

29. Tighten the bolts and nuts in following order:

   a. Pump assembly-to-timing chain housing nuts – 19 ft. lbs (26 Nm).

   b. Water pump-to-pump cover assembly – 106 inch lbs. (12 Nm).

   c. Water Pump cover-to-engine (tighten the bottom bolt first) – 19 ft. lbs (26 Nm).

   d. Radiator outlet pipe assembly-to-pump cover – 125 ft. lbs. (14 Nm).

30. Install the exhaust manifold with new gaskets.

31. In the the exhaust manifold-to-cylinder head retaining nuts. Torque

the retaining nuts in sequence to 22 ft. lbs. (30 Nm).

32. Raise and support the vehicle safely.

33. Seat the exhaust manifold bolts into the exhaust pipe flange.

34. Using a 7/32 in. (5.5mm) socket start both bolts. Rotate the bolts counterclockwise.

35. Turn both bolts in evenly to avoid cocking the exhaust pipe and binding the bolts. Turn the bolts in until fully seated.

36. Install the radiator outlet pipe to the transaxle and to the oil pan and install the exhaust manifold brace.

37. Lower the vehicle.

38. Install the exhaust manifold brace-to-manifold retaining bolt.

39. Using a 13mm wrench, tighten the exhaust pipe-to-manifold nuts to 22 ft. lbs. (30 Nm).

40. Install the lower heat shields.

41. Connect the oxygen connector to the oxygen sensor.

42. Connect the negative battery cable.

43. Refill and bleed the cooling system. Start the engine, allow it to reach normal operating temperature and check for leaks.

Thermostat

REMOVAL & INSTALLATION

1. Disconnect the negative battery cable.

2. Remove the air cleaner assembly.

3. Drain the engine coolant level below the thermostat housing.

4. Remove the upper radiator hose from the thermostat water outlet and position it to the side.

5. On the 2.3L engine, remove the heater and throttle body coolant hoses from the thermostat housing and disconnect the electrical connector from the coolant temperature sensor.

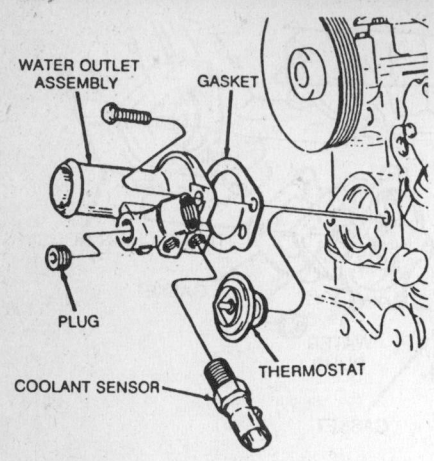

Thermostat removal and installation—2.3L engine

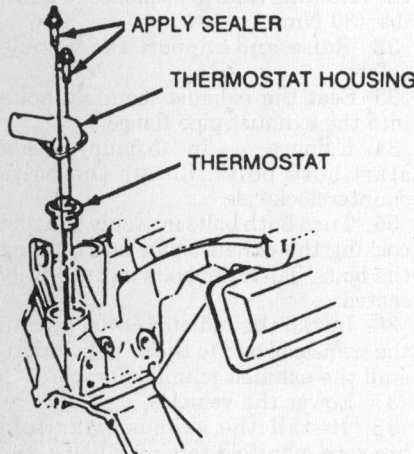

Thermostat removal and installation—2.8L and 3.1L engines

6. Remove the thermostat retaining bolts.

7. Remove the thermostat housing gasket and thermostat.

To install:

8. Throughly clean the mating surfaces of the engine and thermostat.

9. Install the new thermostat, gasket and housing, being careful not to allow the thermostat to slip out of position.

10. Install the retaining bolts and torque to 6–9 ft. lbs. (8–12 Nm) for 2.0L and 2.2L engines, 15–22 ft. lbs (20–30 Nm) for the 2.8L and 3.1L engines and 19 ft. lbs. (26 Nm) for the 2.3L engine.

11. On 2.3L engine, connect the heater and throttle body coolant hoses the thermostat housing and connect the coolant temperature sensor connector.

12. Connect the upper radiator hose to the thermostat housing water outlet.

13. Refill and bleed the cooling system. Start the engine, allow it to reach normal operating temperature and check for leaks.

14. Allow time for the thermostat to open, recheck the coolant level and top off as required.

Cooling System Bleeding

After working on the cooling system, even to replace the thermostat, the system must bled. Air trapped in the system will prevent proper filling and leave the radiator coolant level low, causing a risk of overheating.

1. To bleed the system, start the system cool, the radiator cap off and the radiator filled to about an inch below the filler neck.

2. Start the engine and run it at slightly above normal idle speed. This will insure adequate circulation. If air bubbles appear and the coolant level drops, fill the system with a mixture of anti-freeze and water to bring the level back to the proper level.

3. Run the engine this way until the thermostat opens. When this happens, the coolant will move abruptly across the top of the radiator and the temperature of the radiator will suddenly rise.

4. At this point, air is often expelled and the level may drop quite a bit. Keep refilling the system until the level is near the top of the radiator and remains constant.

5. If the vehicle has an overflow tank, fill the radiator up to the top of the filler neck.

FUEL SYSTEM

Fuel System Service Precautions

Safety is the most important factor when performing not only fuel system maintenance but any type of maintenance. Failure to conduct maintenance and repairs in a safe manner may result in serious personal injury or death. Maintenance and testing of the vehicle's fuel system components can be accomplished safely and effectively by adhering to the following rules and guidelines.

• To avoid the possibility of fire and personal injury, always disconnect the negative battery cable unless the repair or test procedure requires that battery voltage be applied.

• Always relieve the fuel system pressure prior to disconnecting any fuel system component (injector, fuel rail, pressure regulator, etc.), fitting or fuel line connection. Exercise extreme caution whenever relieving fuel system pressure to avoid exposing skin, face and eyes to fuel spray. Please be advised that fuel under pressure may penetrate the skin or any part of the body that it contacts.

• Always place a shop towel or cloth around the fitting or connection prior to loosening to absorb any excess fuel due to spillage. Ensure that all fuel spillage (should it occur) is quickly removed from engine surfaces. Ensure that all fuel soaked cloths or towels are deposited into a suitable waste container.

• Always keep a dry chemical (Class B) fire extinguisher near the work area.

• Do not allow fuel spray or fuel vapors to come into contact with a spark or open flame.

• Always use a backup wrench when loosening and tightening fuel line connection fittings. This will prevent unnecessary stress and torsion to fuel line piping. Always follow the proper torque specifications.

• Always replace worn fuel fitting O-rings with new. Do not substitute fuel hose or equivalent where fuel pipe is installed.

RELIEVING FUEL SYSTEM PRESSURE

NOTE: Make sure the engine is cold before disconnecting any portion of the fuel system.

Throttle Body Injection

1. Disconnect the negative battery cable.

2. Remove the fuel filler cap the relieve tank vapor pressure.

3. Using a shop rag, wrap it around the fuel line fitting.

4. Open the fuel line and absorb any excess fuel remaining in the line.

5. When the line fitting is reconnected, use a new O-ring.

Multi Port Fuel Injection

1. Disconnect the negative battery cable.

2. Remove the fuel filler cap the relieve tank vapor pressure.

3. Using a fuel gauge tool, connect it to the fuel pressure connector.

NOTE: Be sure to wrap a shop cloth around the fuel line fitting when connecting the fuel gauge tool to the fuel pressure connector.

4. Place the bleeder hose and shop cloth in an approved fuel container.

Open the pressure valve to bleed the fuel pressure from the system.

5. After the fuel pressure is bled, re-tighten the fuel pressure valve.

Fuel Filter

REMOVAL & INSTALLATION

An inline fuel filter is used on all engines. It is located on a frame cross-member near the rear of the vehicle.

1. Relieve the fuel system pressure.
2. Raise and support the the vehicle safely.
3. Using a backup wrench, remove the fuel line fittings from the fuel filter.
4. Remove the fuel filter-to-cross-member screws and the filter from the vehicle.
5. Installation is the reverse of the removal procedure. Use a new fuel filter and O-rings. Torque the fuel line-to-filter connectors to 22 ft. lbs.

Electric Fuel Pump

PRESSURE TESTING

TBI System

1. Disconnect the negative battery cable. Relieve the fuel system pressure.
2. Remove the air cleaner and plug the thermac vacuum port on the throttle body.
3. Disconnect the quick-connect fuel supply fitting and install a fuel line adapter and fuel pressure gauge tool between the fittings.

NOTE: Before connecting the quick-connnect fitting, use air pressure to blow any dirt from the fitting that would otherwise enter and contaminate the fuel system.

4. Connect the negative battery cable. Start the engine and read the fuel pressure on the gauge, it should be 9–13 psi.
5. Turn the ignition **OFF**, relieve the fuel system pressure and remove the fuel pressure gauge.
6. When connecting the quick-connect fittings, apply a few drops of clean engine oil to the male tube ends. Make sure the connections are tight.
7. Remove the plug from the thermac vacuum port at the throttle body and install the air cleaner.
8. Connect the negative battery cable. Start the engine and check for fuel leaks.

MFI System

1. Relieve the fuel system pressure.

2. Using a fuel pressure gauge tool, connect it to the fuel pressure connection fitting on the fuel rail.
3. Using a clean shop cloth, wrap it around the fitting to catch any fuel leakage when connecting the gauge.
4. Turn the ignition **ON** and read the fuel pressure on the gauge, it should be 37–43 psi.
5. Start the engine and again note the fuel pressure on the gauge.
6. With the engine idling, the fuel pressure should be 33–40 psi. This idle pressure will vary somewhat depending on barometric pressure, but in any case it should be lower.
7. Relieve the fuel system pressure and disconnect the gauge.

REMOVAL & INSTALLATION

The fuel pump is located in the fuel tank. Removal and installation procedures require the fuel tank to be removed from the vehicle.

── **CAUTION** ──

The fuel system pressure must be relieved before attempting any service procedures. Use caution to avoid the risk of fire by disposing of any fuel and fuel soaked rags properly.

1. Relieve the fuel pressure.
2. Disconnect the negative battery cable.
3. Using a siphon hose and pump, drain the fuel from the fuel tank.
4. Raise and safely support the vehicle.
5. Support the fuel tank and disconnect the retaining straps.
6. Lower the tank enouph to disconnect the sending unit wire, the hoses and the ground strap. Remove the fuel tank from the vehicle.
7. Using a locking cam tool, remove the sending unit retaining cam from the fuel tank.
8. Remove the fuel pump and sending unit assembly from the tank. Remove and discard the O-ring gasket.
To install:
9. Install a new O-ring and gasket. Carefully install the fuel pump and sending unit assembly into the fuel tank.
10. Install the retaining cam and lock and secure the sending unit in place to the fuel tank.
11. Raise the tank in position to connect the sending unit wire, the hoses and the ground strap. Install the tank retaining straps and secure the tank in place.
12. Lower the vehicle and refill the tank with fuel.
13. Connect the negative battery cable. Turn the ignition switch to the **ON** position, to restore system pressure.

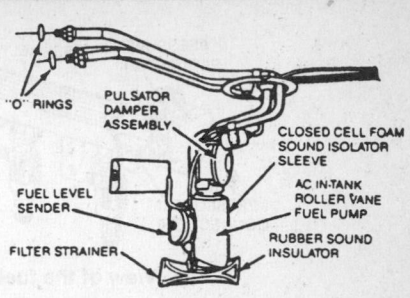

Fuel pump and sending unit assemblies

14. Start the engine and check for fuel leaks.

Fuel Injection

Throttle Body Injection (TBI)

The 2.0L and 2.2L engines are equipped with Throttle Body Injection (TBI).

This injection system uses a single throttle body injection unit (model 700 TBI). It is located on the intake manifold where the carburetor is normally mounted. The TBI unit is computer controlled and supplies the correct amount of fuel during all engine operating conditions. In the TBI system, a single fuel injector mounted at the top of the throttle body, sprays fuel through the throttle valve and into the intake manifold. The activating signal for the injector originates with the electronic control module ECM, which monitors engine temperature, throttle position, vehicle speed and several other engine related conditions. A fuel pressure regulator inside the throttle body maintains fuel pressure at 9–13 psi and routes unused fuel back to the fuel tank through a fuel return line.

Multi-Port Fuel Injection (MFI)

The 2.3L, 2.8L and 3.1L engines or equipped with Multi-port Fuel Injection (MFI).

This system uses Bosch fuel injectors, 1 at each intake port. The injectors are mounted on a fuel rail and are activated by a signal from the Electronic Control Module (ECM). The injector is a solenoid operated valve which remains open depending on the width of the electronic pulses, length of the signal from the ECM; the longer the open time, the more fuel is injected. In this manner, the air/fuel mixture can be precisely controlled for maximum performance with minimum emissions. A pressure regulator maintains 28–36 psi in the fuel line to the injectors and the excess fuel is fed back to the tank.

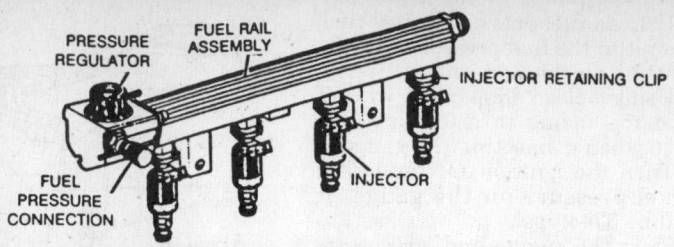

View of the fuel rail assembly—2.3L engine

IDLE SPEED AND IDLE MIXTURE ADJUSTMENT

Idle speed and mixture are controlled by the Electronic Control Module (ECM). No adjustments are possible.

Fuel Injector

REMOVAL & INSTALLATION

2.0 and 2.2L Engines

1. Relieve the fuel system pressure.
2. Remove the air cleaner. Disconnect the negative battery cable from the battery.
3. Disconnect the electrical connector from the fuel injector.
4. Remove the injector retainer-to-throttle body screw and the retainer.
5. Using a small pry bar and a fulcrum, carefully lift the injector until it is free from the fuel meter body.
6. Remove the O-rings form the nozzle end of the injector.
7. Inspect the fuel injector filter for dirt and/or contamination.

To install:
8. Lubricate the O-rings with automatic transmission fluid and place them on the fuel injector.
9. Push the fuel injector straight into the fuel meter body, apply thread locking compound on the fuel injector retainer screw and install.
10. Connect the electrical connector to the fuel injector.
11. Install the air cleaner. Connect the negative battery cable.
12. Turn the ignition switch to the **ON** position, to restore system pressure. Start the engine and check for fuel leaks.

2.3L, 2.8L and 3.1L Engines

1. Relieve the fuel system pressure.
2. Disconnect the negative battery cable from the battery.
3. Disconnect the fuel line from the fuel rail.
4. Remove the fuel rail-to-intake manifold bolts and the fuel rail assembly from the intake manifold.

NOTE: When removing the fuel rail, the fuel injectors will pull straight out of the intake manifold.

5. Remove the fuel injector-to-fuel rail retaining clips and the injectors from the fuel rail.
6. Installation is the reverse order of the removal procedure. Use new O-rings on the fuel injectors. Connect the negative battery cable.

EMISSION CONTROLS

Please refer to "Emission Control" in the Unit Repair section for system maintenance procedures. Due to the complex nature of modern electronic engine control systems, comprehensive diagnosis and testing procedures fall outside the confines of this repair manual. For complete information on diagnosis, testing and repair procedures concerning all modern engine and emission control systems, please refer to "Chilton's Guide to Electronic Engine Controls".

Emission Warning Lamps

RESETTING

When the ECM finds a problem, the Service Engine Soon light will turn ON and a trouble code will be recorded in the ECM memory. If the problem is intermittent, the Service Engine Soon light will light go out after 10 seconds, when the fault goes away. However, the trouble code will stay in the ECM memory until the battery voltage to the ECM is removed. Removing the battery voltage for 10 seconds will clear all stored trouble codes. This is done by disconnecting the ECM harness from the positive battery pigtail for 30 seconds with the ignition **OFF** or by disconnecting the ECM fuse, designated ECM or ECM/BAT, from the fuse holder.

NOTE: To prevent ECM damage, the ignition switch must be OFF when disconnecting or reconnecting power to ECM (for example battery cable, ECM pigtail, ECM fuse, jumper cables, etc.). Disconnecting the negative battery cable on some vehicles may interfere with the functions of the on board computer systems and may require the computer to undergo a relearning process, once the negative battery cable is reconnected.

ENGINE MECHANICAL

NOTE: Disconnecting the negative battery cable on some vehicles may interfere with the functions of the on board computer systems and may require the computer to undergo a relearning process, once the negative battery cable is reconnected.

Engine Assembly

REMOVAL & INSTALLATION

2.0L, 2.2L and 2.3L Engines

1. Relieve the fuel pressure. Disconnect the battery cables (negative cable first). Remove the battery from the vehicle.
2. Position a clean drain pan under the radiator, open the drain cock and drain the cooling system. Remove the air intake hose.
3. From the throttle body, disconnect the TV and accelerator cables. Disconnect the ECM electrical harness connector from the engine.
4. Remove all vacuum hoses, not a part of the engine assembly, the upper/lower radiator hoses and the heater hoses from the engine.
5. Remove the heat shield from the exhaust manifold. Disconnect and label the engine wiring harness from the firewall.
6. Disconnect the windshield washer hoses and the bottle. Rotate the tensioner pulley, to reduce the belt tension and remove the serpentine drive belt.
7. Disconnect and plug the fuel hoses. Raise and safely support the vehicle.

8. Remove the right side inner fender splash shield.

9. Remove the air conditioning compressor-to-bracket bolts and move it aside, so it will not interfere with the engine removal; do not disconnect the refrigerant lines.

10. Remove the flywheel splash shield. Label and disconnect electrical wires from the starter.

11. Remove the front starter brace, the starter-to-engine bolts and the starter.

12. If equipped with an automatic transaxle, remove the torque converter-to-flywheel bolts and push the converter back into the transaxle.

13. Remove the crankshaft pulley-to-crankshaft bolt. Using a crankshaft pulley hub remover tool, press the pulley from the crankshaft.

14. Remove the oil filter. Remove the engine-to-transaxle support bracket.

15. Disconnect the right rear engine mount.

16. Remove the exhaust pipe-to-exhaust manifold bolts, the exhaust pipe from the center hanger and loosen the muffler hanger.

17. Remove the TV and shift cable bracket. Remove both lower engine-to-transaxle bolts.

18. Lower the vehicle. From the intake manifold, remove the TV and accelerator cable bracket.

19. Remove the right front engine mount nuts. Disconnect the electrical connectors. Remove the alternator-to-bracket bolts and the alternator.

20. Remove the master cylinder-to-booster nuts, move the master cylinder and support it out of the way; do not disconnect the brake lines.

21. Using a vertical lifting device, install to the engine and lift it slightly.

22. Remove the right front engine mount bracket. Remove the remaining engine-to-transaxle bolts.

23. Remove the power steering pump-to-engine bolts and move it aside; do not disconnect the high pressure hoses.

24. Carefully lift and remove the engine from the vehicle.

To install:

25. Secure the engine on a engine suitable lifting device.

26. Support the transaxle with floor jack.

27. Carefully lower the engine into the vehicle, aligning it to the transaxle.

28. Install the engine-to-transaxle bolts. Install the right front engine mount bracket and retaining nuts.

29. Install the right rear engine mount and retaining bolts.

30. Install the engine-to-transaxle support bracket and retaining bolts.

31. Lower the transaxle jack and remove it from the vehicle.

32. Install the power steering pump and pump-to-engine retaining bolts.

33. Install the master cylinder and the master cylinder-to-booster retaining nuts.

34. Install the alternator, bracket and retaining bolts. Connect the electrical connectors to the alternator.

35. Install the TV and accelerator cable bracket.

36. Install the TV and shift cable bracket.

37. Raise the vehicle and support it safely.

38. Install the exhaust pipe to the exhaust manifold and install the center hanger. Install the exhaust pipe-to-exhaust manifold retaining bolts.

39. Install the oil filter.

40. Install the crankshaft pulley on the crankshaft and install the pulley-to-crankshaft retaining bolt.

41. If equipped with an automatic transaxle, install the torque converter-to-flywheel retaining bolts.

42. Install the starter, front starter brace and the starter-to-engine retaining bolts.

43. Connect the electrical wires to the starter.

44. Install the flywheel splash shield.

45. Lower the vehicle.

46. Install the air conditioning compressor, with the refrigerant lines attached. Install the air conditioning compressor-to-bracket bolts.

47. Install the right side inner fender splash shield.

48. Connect the fuel hoses.

49. Install the windshield washer bottle and connect the washer hoses.

50. Rotate the tensioner pulley and install the serpentine drive belt.

51. Install the heat shield to the exhaust manifold. Connect the engine wiring harness to the firewall.

52. Install all vacuum hoses, the upper and lower radiator hoses and heater hoses to the engine.

53. Connect the TV and accelerator cables to the throttle body.

54. Connect the ECM electrical harness connector to the engine.

55. Install the air intake hose.

56. Close the radiator pet cock and refill the cooling system.

57. Install the battery and secure it in place. Connect the battery cables (the negative cable first).

58. Start the engine, allow it to reach normal operating temperatures and check for leaks.

2.8L and 3.1L Engines

1. Relieve the fuel pressure. Disconnect the battery cables (negative cable first). Remove the battery from the vehicle.

2. Remove the air cleaner, the air inlet hose and the mass air flow sensor.

3. Position a clean drain pan under the radiator, open the drain cock and drain the cooling system. Remove the exhaust manifold crossover assembly bolts and separate the assembly from the exhaust manifolds.

4. Remove the serpentine belt tensioner and the drive belt. Remove the power steering pump-to-bracket bolts and support the pump out of the way.

5. Disconnect the radiator hose from the engine.

6. Disconnect the TV and accelerator cables from the throttle valve bracket on the plenum.

7. Disconnect the electrical connectors. Remove the alternator-to-bracket bolts and the alternator. Label and disconnect the electrical wiring harness from the engine.

8. Disconnect and plug the fuel hoses. Remove the coolant overflow and bypass hoses from the engine.

9. From the charcoal canister, disconnect the purge hose. Label and disconnect all the necessary vacuum hoses.

10. Using a engine holding fixture tool, support the engine.

11. Raise and safely support the vehicle.

12. Remove the right inner fender splash shield. Remove the crankshaft pulley-to-crankshaft bolt. Using a wheel puller, press the crankshaft pulley from the crankshaft.

13. Remove the flywheel cover. Label and disconnect the starter wires. Remove the starter-to-engine bolts and the starter.

14. Disconnect the wires from the oil pressure sending unit.

15. Remove the air conditioning compressor-to-bracket bolts and the bracket-to-engine bolts. Support the compressor so it will not interfere with the engine; do not disconnect the refrigerant lines.

16. Disconnect the exhaust pipe from the rear of the exhaust manifold.

17. If equipped with an automatic transaxle, remove the torque converter-to-flywheel bolts and push the converter into the transaxle.

18. Remove the front and rear engine mount bolts along with the mount brackets.

19. Remove the intermediate shaft bracket from the engine.

20. Disconnect the shifter cable from the transaxle.

21. Remove the lower engine-to-transaxle bolts and lower the vehicle.

22. Disconnect the heater hoses from the engine.

23. Using an vertical engine lift, install it to the engine and lift it slightly. Remove the engine holding fixture. Using a floor jack, support the transaxle.

24. Remove the upper engine-to-

transaxle bolts. Remove the front engine mount bolts and transaxle mounting bracket.

25. Remove the engine from the vehicle.

To install:

26. Secure the engine on a engine suitable lifting device.

27. Carefully lower the engine into the vehicle, aligning it to the transaxle.

28. Install the upper engine-to-transaxle bolts. Torque bolts to 55 ft. lbs. (75 Nm).

29. Install the transaxle mount bracket and front engine mount retaining bolts. Torque the bolts to 65 ft. lbs. (88 Nm).

30. Using a floor jack, support the transaxle and remove the engine lifting device from the engine.

31. Install the lower engine-to-transaxle.

32. Connect the heater hoses to the engine.

33. Connect the shifter cable to the transaxle.

34. Install the intermediate shaft bracket to the engine.

35. Install the front and rear engine mount bolts along with the mount brackets.

36. Lower the jack and remove it from the transaxle.

37. Raise the vehicle and support it safely.

38. If equipped with an automatic transaxle, install the torque converter-to-flywheel bolts.

39. Install the flywheel cover and retaining bolts.

40. Connect the exhaust pipe to the the exhaust manifold and install the retaining bolts.

41. Lower the vehicle.

42. Position the air conditioning compressor, with the lines attached, in place and install the compressor-to-bracket bolts.

43. Install the compressor bracket-to-engine bolts.

44. Connect the wires to the oil pressure sending unit.

45. Connect the starter wires. Position the starter in place and install the starter-to-engine bolts.

46. Install the crankshaft pulley and install the pulley-to-crankshaft bolt. Install the right inner fender splash shield.

47. Connect the purge hose to the charcoal canister. Connect all the necessary vacuum hoses.

48. Connect the coolant overflow and bypass hoses to the engine.

49. Connect the fuel delivery hoses to the engine.

50. Position the alternator in place and install the alternator-to-bracket bolts. Connect the GM electrical connec-

tors to the alternator.

51. Connect all electrical wiring harnesses to the engine.

52. Connect the TV and accelerator cables to the throttle valve bracket on the plenum.

53. Connect the radiator hoses to the engine.

54. Install the serpentine belt tensioner and the drive belt.

55. Position the power steering pump in place and install the power steering pump-to-bracket bolts.

56. Connect the crossover pipe to the exhaust manifold and install the retaining bolts.

57. Install the air cleaner, air inlet hose and the mass air flow sensor.

58. Close the radiator cock and refill the cooling system.

59. Install the battery and secure it in place. Connect the battery cables (the negative cable first).

60. Start the engine, allow it to reach normal operating temperatures and check for leaks.

Engine Mounts

REMOVAL & INSTALLATION

Front

1. Disconnect the negative battery cable.

2. Remove the upper mount-to-body bracket bolts.

3. Raise and safely support the vehicle.

4. Using an engine holding fixture tool, support the engine.

5. Remove the left side inner fender shield.

6. Remove the lower engine mount-to-body bracket bolt.

7. Raise the engine (slightly) and remove the engine mount through bolt.

8. Remove the lower engine mount-to-engine bracket bolt and the mount.

To install:

9. Reverse the removal procedures. Torque the engine mount through bolt to 66–81 ft. lbs. and the engine mount-to-bracket bolts to 55–66 ft. lbs.

10. Lower the vehicle and connnect the negative battery cable.

Rear

1. Disconnect the negative battery cable.

2. Raise and safely support the vehicle.

3. Using an engine holding fixture tool, support the engine.

4. Remove the engine mount nuts/bolts and the engine mount.

To install:

5. Reverse the removal procedures. Torque the mounting bolts to 44–56 ft. lbs. and nuts to 14–20 ft. lbs.

6. Lower the vehicle and connnect the negative battery cable.

Cylinder Head

REMOVAL & INSTALLATION

2.0L and 2.2L Engines

1. Relieve the fuel pressure. Disconnect the negative battery cable.

2. Drain the cooling system. Remove the TBI cover.

3. Raise and safely support the vehicle.

4. Disconnect the exhaust pipe-to-exhaust manifold bolts and separate the exhaust pipe from the manifold.

5. Lower the vehicle. Disconnect the heater hose from the intake manifold.

6. Disconnect the TV and accelerator cable bracket.

7. Label and disconnect the vacuum hoses from the intake manifold and thermostat.

8. Disconnect the accelerator linkage from the TBI unit.

9. Label and disconnect the electrical wiring from the engine.

10. Disconnect the upper radiator hose from the thermostat. Remove the serpentine belt.

11. Remove the power steering pump-to-bracket bolts and support the pump out of the way; do not disconnect the high pressure hoses from the pump.

12. Disconnect and plug the fuel lines. Remove the alternator-to-bracket bolts and the alternator. Position it out of the way, with electrical connectors attached.

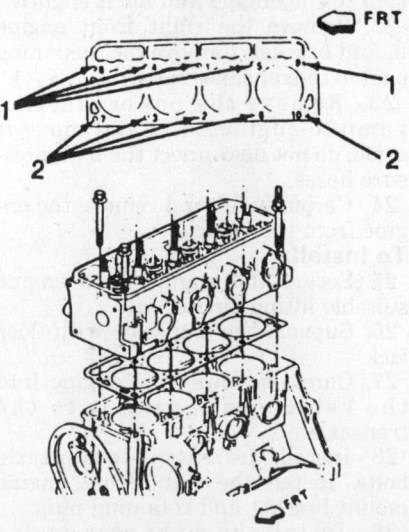

1. 73–83 ft. lbs.
2. 62–70 ft. lbs.

Cylinder head bolt torque sequence—2.0L and 2.2L engines

13. Remove the alternator rear brace.

14. Remove the rocker arm cover-to-cylinder head bolts and the cover. Remove the rocker arm bolts, the rocker arms and pushrods; be sure to keep valve train components in the order that they were removed.

15. Starting with the outer bolts, remove the cylinder head-to-engine bolts.

To install:

16. Clean and inspect the gasket mounting surfaces. Make sure the threads on the cylinder head bolts and in the block are clean.

17. Position the cylinder head gasket in place on the engine block dowel pins.

18. Install the cylinder head and tighten the head bolts hand tight.

19. Following the torquing sequence, torque the head bolts, in 3 steps, to 73–83 ft. lbs. (intake side) and 62–70 ft. lbs. (exhaust side).

20. Install the pushrods and rocker arms in the same order they were removed. Torque the rocker arm nuts to 7–11 ft. lbs.

21. To complete the installation, reverse the removal procedures. Refill the cooling system. Start the engine, allow it to reach normal operating temperatures and check for leaks.

2.3L Engine

1. Relieve the fuel system pressure. Remove negative battery cable and drain cooling system.

2. Disconnect heater inlet and throttle body heater hoses from water outlet. Disconnect upper radiator hose from water outlet.

3. Remove exhaust manifold.

4. Remove intake and exhaust camshaft housings.

5. Remove oil cap and dipstick. Pull oil fill tube upward to unseat from block.

6. Disconnect and tag injector harness electrical connector.

7. Disconnect throttle body to air cleaner duct. Remove throttle cable and bracket and position aside.

8. Remove throttle body from intake manifold with electrical harness, hoses, cable attached and position aside.

9. Disconnect and tag MAP sensor vacuum hose from intake manifold.

10. Remove intake manifold bracket to block bolt.

11. Disconnect and tag 2 coolant sensor connections.

12. Remove cylinder head to block bolts.

NOTE: When removing cylinder head to block bolts follow reverse of tighten sequence.

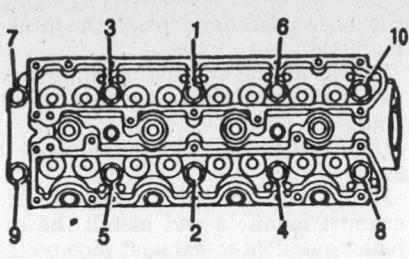

▼ FRONT OF ENGINE

Cylinder head bolt torque sequence–2.3L engine

13. Remove cylinder head and gasket.

NOTE: Clean all gasket surfaces with plastic or wood scraper. Do not use any sealing material.

To install;

14. Install the cylinder head gasket to the cylinder block and carefully position the cylinder head in place.

15. Coat the head bolt threads with clean engine oil and allow the oil to drain off before installing.

16. Torque the cylinder head bolts in sequence in 2 steps as follows:

Step 1: in sequence, torque the long and short cylinder head to block bolts–26 ft. lbs. (35 Nm).

Step 2: in sequence, tighten the short bolts–80 degree turn and the long bolts–90 degree turn.

17. Install the intake manifold-to-block bracket bolt and bracket.

18. Connect the MAP sensor vacuum hose to the intake manifold.

19. Install the throttle body on the intake manifold with electrical harness, hoses and cable attached.

20. Connect the throttle body-to-air cleaner duct. Install the throttle cable and bracket.

21. Connect the injector harness electrical connector.

22. Connect the 2 coolant sensor connections.

23. Install the oil cap and dipstick. Install the oil fill tube into the block.

24. Install the exhaust and intake camshaft housings.

25. Install the exhaust manifold.

26. Connect the heater inlet and throttle body heater hoses to the water outlet. Connect the upper radiator hose to the water outlet.

27. Fill the cooling system and connect the negative battery cable.

28. Start the engine, allow it to reach operating temperature and check for leaks.

2.8L and 3.1L Engines

LEFT SIDE

1. Relieve the fuel pressure.

2. Disconnect the negative battery cable.

3. Place a drain pan under the radiator and drain the cooling system.

4. Remove the rocker cover retaining bolts and remove rocker cover.

5. Remove the intake manifold-to-cylinder head bolts and the remove the intake manifold.

6. Remove the fuel plenum and fuel rail assembles.

7. Disconnect the exhaust crossover from the right exhaust manifold.

8. Disconnect the oil level indicator tube bracket.

9. Loosen the rocker arms nuts, turn the rocker arms and remove the pushrods.

NOTE: Be sure to keep the parts in order for installation purposes.

10. Remove the cylinder head-to-engine bolts; start with the outer bolts and work toward the center. Remove the cylinder head with the exhaust manifold.

To install:

11. Clean the gasket mounting surfaces. Inspect the surfaces of the cylinder head, block and intake manifold damage and/or warpage. Clean the threaded holes in the block and the cylinder head bolt threads.

12. Using new gaskets, align the new cylinder head gasket over the dowels on the block with the note **This Side Up** facing the cylinder head.

13. Install the cylinder head and exhaust manifold crossover assembly on the engine.

14. Coat the cylinder head bolt threads with engine oil and install the hand tight.

15. Using the torquing sequence, torque the bolts to 33 ft.lbs. After all bolts are torqued to 33 ft. lbs., rotate the torque wrench another 90 degrees or ¼ turn. This will apply the correct torque to the bolts.

HEAD TORQUE SEQUENCE

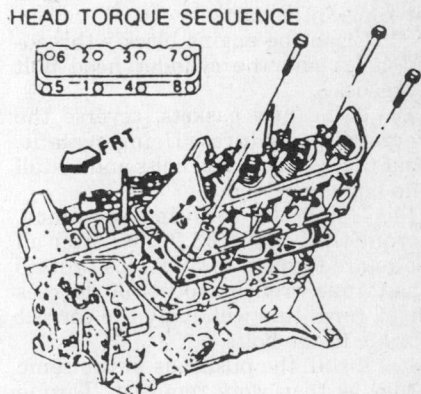

Cylinder head bolt torque sequence–2.8L and 3.1L engines

16. Install the pushrods in the same order that they were removed. Torque the rocker arm nuts to 14–20 ft. lbs.

17. Install the intake manifold using a new gasket and following the correct sequence, torque the bolts to 24 ft. lbs. and nuts to 18 ft. lbs.

18. Install the fuel plenum and fuel rail. Torque the plenum bolts to 16 ft. lbs. (21 Nm).

19. Connect the exhaust crossover to the right exhaust manifold.

20. Connect the oil level indicator tube bracket.

21. Refill the cooling system. Connect the negative battery cable.

22. Operate the engine until normal operating temperatures are reached and check for leaks.

RIGHT SIDE

1. Relieve the fuel pressure. Disconnect the negative battery cable. Drain the cooling system.

2. Raise and safely support the vehicle. Remove the exhaust manifold-to-exhaust pipe bolts and separate the pipe from the manifold.

3. Lower the vehicle. Remove the exhaust manifold-to-cylinder head bolts and exhaust manifold.

4. Remove the rocker arm cover. Remove the intake manifold-to-cylinder head bolts and the intake manifold.

5. Loosen the rocker arms nuts, turn the rocker arms and remove the pushrods.

NOTE: Be sure to keep the components in order for reassembly purposes.

6. Remove the cylinder head-to-engine bolts, starting with the outer bolts, working towards the center of the head.

7. Lift the cylinder head from the engine.

To install:

8. Clean the gasket mounting surfaces. Inspect the parts for damage and/or warpage; if necessary, machine or replace the parts.

9. Clean the engine block's threaded holes and the cylinder head bolt threads.

10. Using new gaskets, reverse the removal procedures. Using sealant, coat the cylinder head bolts and install the bolts hand tight.

11. Using the torquing sequence, torque the bolts to 33 ft. lbs. After all bolts are torqued to 33 ft. lbs., rotate the torque wrench another 90 degrees or ¼ turn; this will apply the correct torque to the bolts.

12. Install the pushrods in the same order as they were removed. Torque the rocker arm nuts to 14–20 ft. lbs.

13. Follow the torquing sequence,

use a new gasket and install the intake manifold.

14. Install the exhaust manifold and exhaust manifold-to-cylinder head bolts.

15. Raise the vehicle and support it safely.

16. Connect the exhaust pipe to the exhaust manifold and install the exhaust manifold-to-exhaust pipe bolts.

17. Lower the vehicle. Refill the cooling system.

18. Connect the negative battery cable. Start the engine, allow it to reach normal operating temperatures and check for leaks.

Valve Lifters

REMOVAL & INSTALLATION

2.0L and 2.2L Engines

1. Disconnect the negative battery cable. Remove the rocker arm cover.

2. Loosen the rocker arms nuts enough to move the rocker arms aside and remove the pushrods.

3. Using a valve lifter remover tool, remove the lifters from the engine.

To install:

4. Using Molykote® or equivalent, coat the base of the new lifters. Using a valve lifter remover tool, install the lifters into the engine.

5. To complete the installation, reverse the removal procedures. Torque the rocker arm nuts to 7–11 ft. lbs. and the rocker arm cover bolts to 8 ft. lbs.

6. Connect the negative battery cable.

2.3L Engine

The valve train consists of 2 chain driven overhead camshafts with direct acting lifters, therefore, camshaft removal is necessary in order to gain access to the lifers. Once the camshafts are removed from their mountings the valve lifters can be removed from their bores.

2.8L and 3.1L Engines

1. Disconnect the negative battery cable.

2. Drain the cooling system.

3. Remove the rocker arm covers and intake manifold.

4. Loosen the rocker arms nuts enough to move the rocker arms aside and remove the pushrods.

5. Remove the lifters from the engine.

To install:

6. Using Molykote® or equivalent, coat the base of the new lifters and install them into the engine.

7. To complete the installation, position the pushrods and the rocker arms correctly into their original posi-

tions. Torque the rocker arm nuts to 18 ft. lbs. and the intake manifold-to-cylinder head bolts to 20 ft. lbs.

8. Connect the negative battery cable.

Valve Lash

ADJUSTMENT

Hydraulic valve lifters are used in the 2.0L, 2.2L, 2.8L and 3.1L engines and are not adjustable. If valve system noise is present, check the torque on the rocker arm nuts. The correct torque should be 7–11 ft. lbs. (2.0L and 2.2L) or 14–20 ft. lbs. (2.8L and 3.1L). If noise is still present, check the condition of the camshaft, lifters, rocker arms, pushrods and valves.

On the 2.3L engine, direct acting hydraulic valve lifters are used. The valve lifter body includes a harden iron contact foot bonded to a steel shell. These lifters are not serviceable or adjustable.

Rocker Arms

REMOVAL & INSTALLATION

2.0L and 2.2L Engines

1. Disconnect the negative battery cable. Remove the air hose from the TBI unit and the air cleaner.

2. Remove the intake manifold-to-rocker cover hose.

3. Remove the rocker arm cover bolts and the cover.

4. Remove the rocker arm nuts and the rocker arms.

NOTE: Be sure to keep the components in order for installation purposes.

To install:

5. Using new gaskets and sealant, if necessary, reverse the removal procedures. Torque the rocker arm nuts to 7–11 ft. lbs.

6. Complete the installation in the reverse order of the removal procedures. Connect the negative battery cable.

2.3L Engine

The valve train consists of 2 chain driven overhead camshafts with direct acting lifters.

2.8L and 3.1L Engines

LEFT SIDE

1. Disconnect the negative battery cable. Disconnect the bracket tube from the rocker cover.

2. Remove the spark plug wire cover. Drain the cooling system and re-

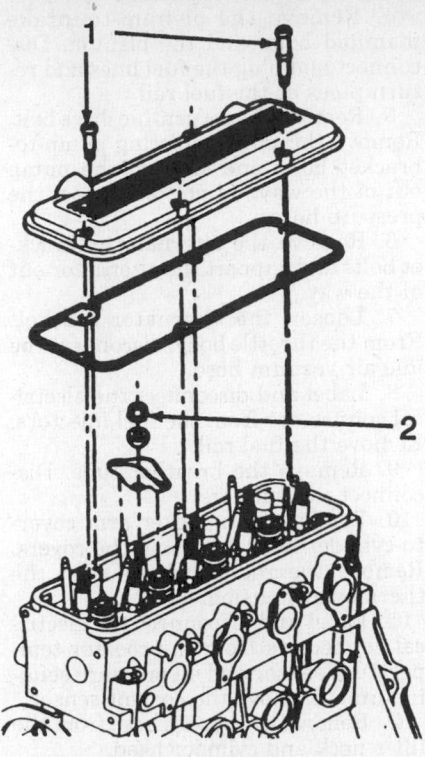

1. 6–9 ft. lbs.
2. 11–18 ft. lbs.

**Rocker arm and cover Installation—
2.0L and 2.2L engines**

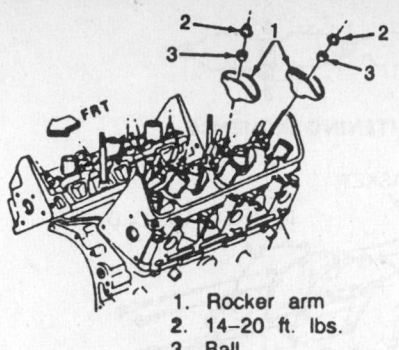

1. Rocker arm
2. 14–20 ft. lbs.
3. Ball

**Rocker arm Installation—2.8L and
3.1L engines**

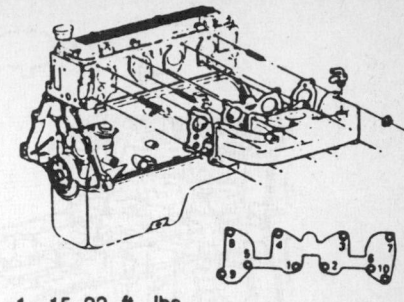

1. 15–22 ft. lbs.

**Intake manifold bolt torque sequence—
2.0L and 2.2L engines**

move the heater hose from the filler neck.

3. Remove the rocker arm cover-to-cylinder head bolts and the rocker cover.

NOTE: If the rocker arm cover will not lift off the cylinder head easily, strike the end with the palm of the hand or a rubber mallet.

4. Remove the rocker arm nuts and the rocker arms; be sure to keep the components in order for installation purposes.
To install:
5. Clean the gasket mounting surfaces.
6. Using new gaskets and sealant, reverse the removal procedures.
7. Torque the rocker arm nuts to 14–20 ft. lbs.
8. Start the engine and check for leaks. Connect the negative battery cable.

RIGHT SIDE

1. Disconnect the negative battery cable. Disconnect the brake booster vacuum line from the bracket.
2. Disconnect the cable bracket from the plenum.
3. Disconnect the vacuum line bracket from the cable bracket.

4. Disconnect the lines from the alternator brace stud.
5. Remove the rear alternator brace and the serpentine drive belt.
6. Remove the alternator and support it out of the way.
7. Remove the PCV valve.
8. Loosen the alternator bracket.
9. Disconnect the spark plug wires from the spark plugs. Remove the rocker cover-to-cylinder head bolts and the rocker cover.

NOTE: If the rocker arm cover will not lift off the cylinder head easily, strike the end with the palm of the hand or a rubber mallet.

10. Remove the rocker arm nuts and the rocker arms; be sure to keep the components in order for installation purposes.
To install:
11. Clean the gasket mounting surfaces.
12. Using new gaskets and sealant, reverse the removal procedures.
13. Torque the rocker arm nuts to 14–20 ft. lbs. Connect the negative battery cable.

Intake Manifold

REMOVAL & INSTALLATION

2.0L and 2.2L Engines

1. Disconnect the negative battery cable. Relieve the fuel pressure. Remove the TBI cover.
2. Drain the cooling system. Label and disconnect the vacuum lines and electrical connectors from the intake manifold.
3. Disconnect and plug the fuel line.
4. Disconnect the TBI linkage. Remove the throttle body-to-intake manifold bolts and the throttle body.
5. Remove the serpentine drive belt. Remove the power steering pump-to-bracket bolts and support the pump out of the way; do not disconnect the pressure hoses.

6. Raise and safely support the vehicle.
7. Disconnect the TV cable, accelerator cable and brackets.
8. Remove the heater hose from the bottom of the intake manifold. Lower the vehicle.
9. Remove the intake manifold-to-cylinder head nuts/bolts and the manifold.
To install:
10. Clean the gasket mounting surfaces.
11. Using new gaskets, reverse the removal procedures. Torque the intake manifold-to-cylinder heads bolts, in the proper sequence to 15–22 ft. lbs.
12. Refill the cooling system. Connect the negative battery cable.
13. Start the engine, allow it to reach normal operating temperatures and check for leaks.

2.3L Engine

1. Disconnect the negative battery cable.
2. Remove the coolant fan shroud, vacuum hose and electrical connector from the MAP sensor.
3. Disconnect the throttle body to air cleaner duct.
4. Remove the throttle cable bracket.
5. Remove the power brake vacuum hose, including the retaining bracket to power steering bracket and position it to the side.
6. Remove the throttle body from the intake manifold with electrical harness, coolant hoses, vacuum hoses and throttle cable attached. Position these components aside.
7. Remove the oil/air separator bolts and hoses. Leave the hoses attached to the separator, disconnect from the oil fill, chain housing and the intake manifold. Remove as an assembly.
8. Remove the oil fill cap and oil level indicator stick.
9. Pull the oil tube fill upward to unseat from block and remove.

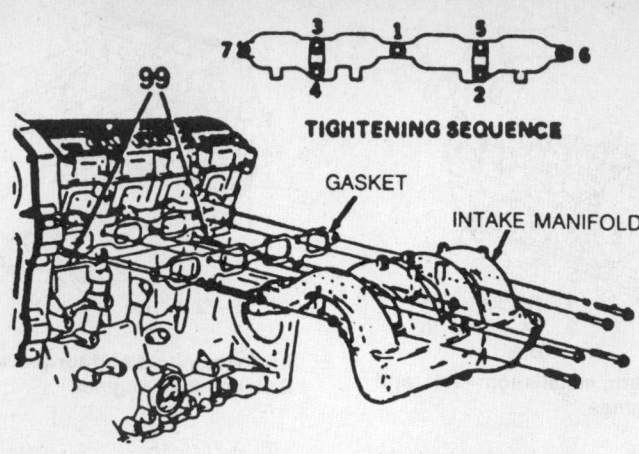

Intake manifold installation—2.3L engine

10. Disconnect the injector harness connector.

11. Remove the fill tube out top, rotating as necessary to gain clearance for the oil/air separator nipple between the intake tubes and fuel rail electrical harness.

12. Remove the intake manifold support bracket bolts and nut. Remove the intake manifold retaining nuts and bolts.

13. Remove the intake manifold.

NOTE: Intake manifold mounting hole closest to chain housing is slotted for additional clearance.

To install:

14. Install the intake manifold and gasket. Tightening the intake manifold bolts/nuts in sequence and to 18 ft. lbs. (25 Nm). Tighten intake manifold brace and retainers hand tight. Tighten to specifications in the following sequence:

    a. Nut to stud bolt—18 ft. lbs. (25 Nm).

    b. Bolt to intake manifold—40 ft. lbs. (55 Nm).

    c. Bolt to cylinder block—40 ft. lbs. (55 Nm).

15. Lubricate a new oil fill tube ring seal with engine oil. Install the tube between No. 1 and 2 intake tubes. Rotate as necessary to gain clearance for oil/air separator nipple on fill tube.

16. Locate the oil fill tube in its cylinder block opening. Align the fill tube so it is approximately in its installed position. Place the palm of your hand over the oil fill opening and press straight down to seat fill tube and seal into cylinder block.

17. Install oil/air separator assembly, it may be necessary to lubricate the hoses for ease of assembly.

18. Install throttle body to intake manifold using a new gasket.

19. Reverse the remaining removal procedures. Torque intake manifold to the following:

    Brace-to-block—40 ft. lbs. (55 Nm).

    Brace-to-manifold—40 ft. lbs. (55 Nm).

    Brace-to- manifold stud 18 ft. lbs. (25 Nm).

    Intake manifold-to-cylinder head bolts in sequence—18 ft. lbs. (25 Nm).

20. Connect the negative battery cable.

2.8L and 3.1L Engines

1. Disconnect the negative battery cable. Relieve the fuel pressure. Drain the cooling system.

2. Disconnect the TV and accelerator cables from the plenum.

3. Remove the throttle body-to-plenum bolts and the throttle body. Remove the EGR valve.

4. Remove the plenum-to-intake manifold bolts and the plenum. Disconnect and plug the fuel lines and return pipes at the fuel rail.

5. Remove the serpentine drive belt. Remove the power steering pump-to-bracket bolts and support the pump out of the way; do not disconnect the pressure hoses.

6. Remove the alternator-to-bracket bolts and support the alternator out of the way.

7. Loosen the alternator bracket. From the throttle body, disconnect the idle air vacuum hose.

8. Label and disconnect the electrical connectors from the fuel injectors. Remove the fuel rail.

9. Remove the breather tube. Disconnect the runners.

10. Remove both rocker arm cover-to-cylinder head bolts and the covers. Remove the radiator hose from the thermostat housing.

11. Label and disconnect the electrical connectors from the coolant temperature sensor and oil pressure sending unit. Remove the coolant sensor.

12. Remove the bypass hose from the filler neck and cylinder head.

13. Remove the intake manifold-to-cylinder head bolts and the manifold.

14. Loosen the rocker arm nuts, turn them 90 degrees and remove the pushrods; be sure to keep the components in order for installation purposes.

To install:

15. Clean all gasket mounting surfaces.

16. Using new gaskets, place a $\frac{3}{16}$ in. bead of RTV sealant on the ridges of the manifold and reverse the removal procedures.

INTAKE MANIFOLD BOLT
TORQUE SEQUENCE
7 4 3 6
8 1 2 5

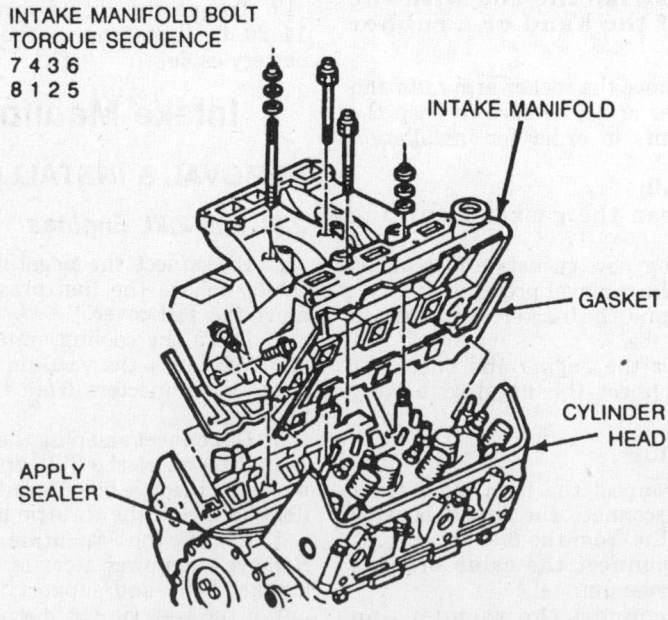

Intake manifold installation—2.8L and 3.1L engines

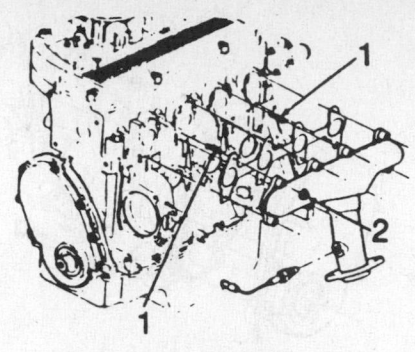

1. 3–11 ft. lbs.
2. 6–13 ft. lbs.

Exhaust manifold installation—
2.0L and 2.2L engines

17. Torque the intake manifold-to-cylinder head bolts, following the torquing sequence, to 24 ft. lbs. and the nuts to 18 ft. lbs.
18. Refill the cooling system. Connect the negative battery cable.
19. Start the engine, allow it to reach normal operating temperatures and check for leaks.

Exhaust Manifold

REMOVAL & INSTALLATION

2.0L and 2.2L Engines

1. Disconnect the negative battery cable.
2. Disconnect the oxygen sensor wire.
3. Remove the serpentine belt.
4. Remove the alternator-to-bracket bolts and position the alternator, with the wires attached, out of the way.
5. Raise and safely support the vehicle.
6. Disconnect the exhaust pipe-to-exhaust manifold bolts and lower the vehicle.
7. Remove the exhaust manifold-to-cylinder head bolts.
8. Remove the exhaust manifold from the exhaust pipe flange and the manifold from the vehicle.
To install:
9. Clean the gasket mounting surfaces.
10. Using new gaskets, reverse the removal procedures. Torque the exhaust manifold-to-cylinder head nuts to 3–11 ft. lbs. and bolts to 6–13 ft. lbs.
11. Connect the negative battery cable. Start the engine and check for leaks.

2.3L Engine

1. Disconnect the negative battery cable and oxygen sensor connector.
2. Remove upper and lower exhaust manifold heat shields.

3. Remove exhaust manifold brace to manifold bolt.
4. Break loose the manifold to exhaust pipe spring loaded bolts using a 13mm box wrench.
5. Raise and support vehicle safely.
6. Remove the manifold to exhaust pipe bolts out of the exhaust pipe flange by using a $\frac{7}{32}$ in. (5.5mm) socket and rotate clockwise as if tightening a bolt with right hand threads or removing a bolt with left hand threads. It is necessary to relieve the spring pressure from 1 bolt prior to removing the second bolt. If the spring pressure is not relieved, it will cause the exhaust pipe to twist and bind the bolt as it is removed. Relieve the spring pressure by:
    a. Thread 1 bolt out 4 turns.
    b. Move to the other bolt and turn it all the way out of the exhaust pipe flange.
    c. Return to the first bolt and rotate it the rest of the way out of the exhaust pipe flange.
7. Pull down and back on the exhaust pipe to disengage it from the exhaust manifold bolts.
8. Lower vehicle.
9. Remove exhaust manifold to cylinder head retaining nuts and remove exhaust manifold.
To install:
10. Installation is the reverse of the removal procedures. In sequence torque exhaust manifold bolts to head 27 ft. lbs., manifold to exhaust pipe 22 ft. lbs. and manifold to brace 19 ft. lbs.
11. Connect the negative battery cable.

NOTE: Turn bolts in evenly to avoid cocking the exhaust pipe and binding the bolts. Turn bolts in until fully seated.

2.8L and 3.1L Engines
LEFT SIDE

1. Disconnect the negative battery cable. Drain the cooling system.
2. Remove the air cleaner, air inlet hose and the mass air flow sensor.
3. Remove the coolant bypass pipe. Remove the manifold heat shield.
4. Disconnect the exhaust manifold crossover assembly at the right manifold.
5. Remove the exhaust manifold-to-cylinder head attaching bolts.
6. From the right manifold, remove the exhaust manifold with the crossover assembly.
To install:
7. Clean the gasket mounting surfaces.
8. Using new gaskets, reverse the removal procedures. Torque the exhaust manifold-to-cylinder head bolts to 19 ft. lbs. and the crossover bolts to 25 ft. lbs.
9. Connect the negative battery cable. Start the engine and check for exhaust leaks.

RIGHT SIDE

1. Disconnect the negative battery cable.
2. Raise and safely support the vehicle.
3. Remove the heat shield.

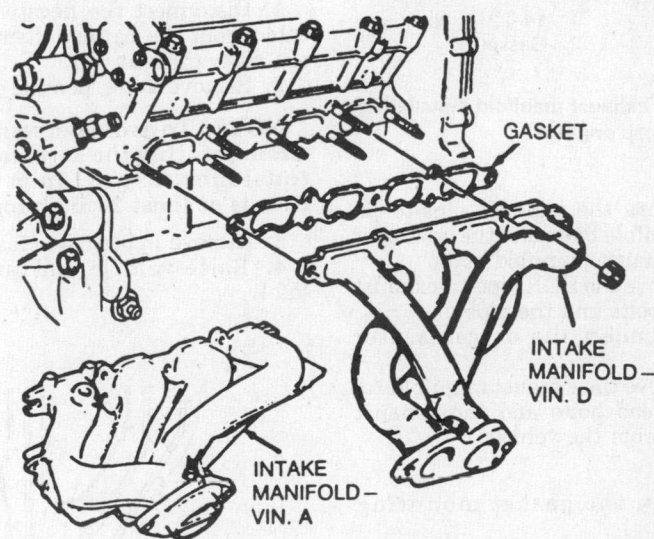

GASKET

INTAKE MANIFOLD – VIN. D

INTAKE MANIFOLD – VIN. A

TIGHTENING SEQUENCE

Exhaust manifold installation—2.3L engine

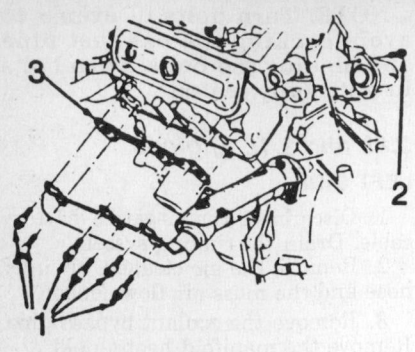

1. 14–22 ft. lbs.
2. 22–30 ft. lbs.
3. Gasket

Left side exhaust manifold installation– 2.8L and 3.1L engines

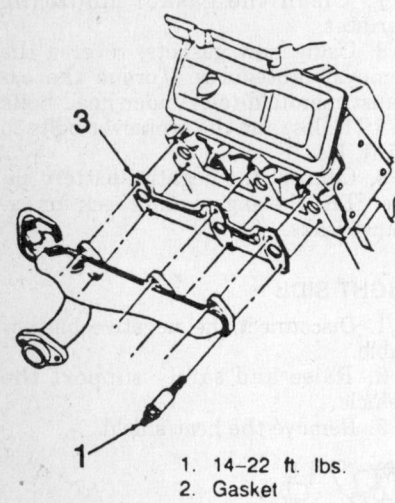

1. 14–22 ft. lbs.
2. Gasket

Right side exhaust manifold installation– 2.8L and 3.1L engines

4. Remove the exhaust pipe-to-exhaust manifold bolts and the crossover pipe-to-exhaust manifold bolts.
5. Remove the EGR pipe-to-exhaust manifold bolts and the pipe.
6. Disconnect the oxygen sensor wire.
7. Remove the exhaust manifold-to-cylinder head bolts and the exhaust manifold from the vehicle.

To install:
8. Clean the gasket mounting surfaces.
9. Using new gaskets, reverse the removal procedures. Torque the exhaust manifold-to-cylinder head bolts to 19 ft. lbs. and the crossover pipe bolts to 25 ft. lbs.
10. Connect the negative battery cable. Start the engine and check for leaks.

Timing Chain Front Cover

REMOVAL & INSTALLATION

2.0L and 2.2L Engines

1. Disconnect the negative battery cable.
2. Raise and safely support the vehicle.
3. Drain the engine oil and remove the oil pan.
4. Lower the vehicle.
5. Remove the serpentine belt and the belt tensioner.
6. Remove the crankshaft pulley retaining bolt. Using a crankshaft pulley puller tool, remove the crankshaft pulley.
7. Remove the timing case cover bolts. Tap the cover with a rubber mallet and remove the cover.

To install:
8. Clean gasket mounting surfaces.
9. Using new gaskets, install the timing case cover over the dowels on the block and reverse the removal procedures. Torque the timing case cover-to-engine bolts to 6–9 ft. lbs.
10. Using a crankshaft pulley installer tool, press the pulley onto the crankshaft. Torque the crankshaft pulley bolt to 66–88 ft. lbs.
11. To complete the installation, reverse the removal procedures. Connect the negative battery cable. Start the engine and check for leaks.

2.3L Engine

1. Disconnect the negative battery cable from the battery. Remove coolant recovery reservoir.
2. Remove the serpentine drive belt.

NOTE: To avoid personal injury when rotating the serpentine belt tensioner, use a 13mm wrench that is at least 24 inch long.

3. Remove upper cover fasteners.
4. Raise vehicle and support it safely.

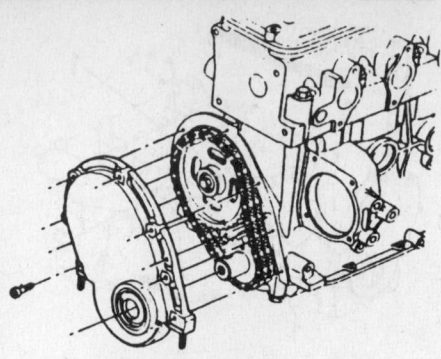

Front cover installation–2.0L and 2.2L engines

5. Remove right front wheel assembly.
6. Remove right lower splash shield.
7. Remove crankshaft balancer assembly.
8. Remove lower cover fasteners and lower vehicle.
9. Remove the front cover.

To install:
10. Installation is the reverse of the removal procedure. Torque retaining bolt and washer for balancer assembly to 74 ft. lbs.

NOTE: The automatic transaxle crankshaft balancer must not be installed on a manual transaxle engine.

2.8L and 3.1L Engines

1. Disconnect the negative battery cable. Drain the cooling system.
2. Remove the serpentine belt and the belt tensioner.
3. Remove the alternator-to-bracket bolts and with the wires attached to the alternator, position it out of the way.
4. Remove the power steering pump-to-bracket bolts and support it out of the way; do not disconnect the pressure hoses.

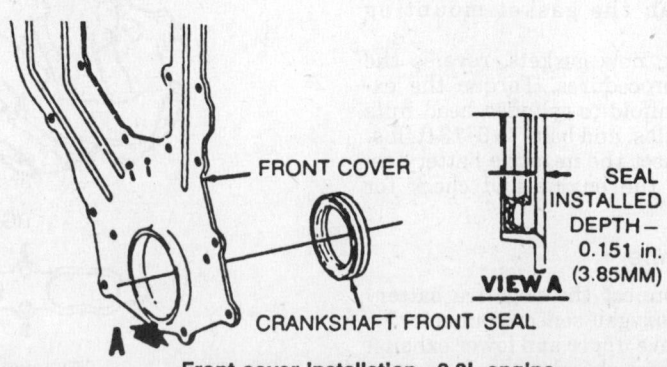

Front cover installation–2.3L engine

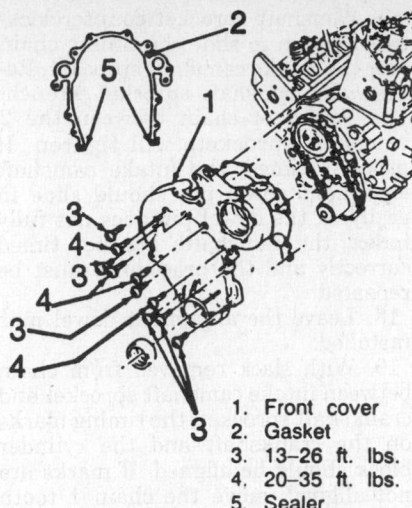

1. Front cover
2. Gasket
3. 13–26 ft. lbs.
4. 20–35 ft. lbs.
5. Sealer

Front cover installation—2.8L and 3.1L engines

5. Raise and safely support the vehicle.
6. Remove the right side inner fender splash shield and the flywheel dust cover.
7. Using a crankshaft pulley puller tool, remove the crankshaft damper.
8. Label and disconnect the starter wires and remove the starter.
9. Loosen the front 5 oil pan bolts, on both sides, enough to lower the oil pan ½ in.
10. Lower the vehicle. Disconnect the radiator hose from the water pump.
11. Disconnect the heater coolant hose from the cooling system filler pipe.
12. Remove the bypass and overflow hoses.
13. Remove the water pump pulley. Disconnect the canister purge hose.
14. Remove the spark plug wire shield from the water pump.
15. Remove the upper timing case cover-to-engine bolts and the timing case cover.

To install:
16. Clean gasket mounting surfaces.
17. Using silicone sealant and a new gasket, apply a thin bead to the front cover mating surface, install the timing case cover on the engine. Apply silicone sealant to the sections of the oil pan rails that were lowered and install the mounting bolts.
18. Using a crankshaft pulley installer tool, press the damper pulley onto the crankshaft.
19. Installation is the reverse of removal procedures. Lower the vehicle and connect the negative battery cable.
20. Start the engine and check for oil leaks.

Front Cover Oil Seal

REPLACEMENT

2.0L and 2.2L Engines

1. Disconnect the negative battery cable. Remove the serpentine belt.
2. Raise and safely support the vehicle. Remove the right front wheel and tire assembly.
3. Remove the inner fender splash shield.
4. Remove the crankshaft pulley bolt.
5. Using a crankshaft pulley puller tool, remove the crankshaft pulley.
6. Using a small pry bar, pry the oil seal from the front cover.

NOTE: Use care not to damage the seal seat or the crankshaft while removing or installing the seal. Inspect the sealing surface of the crankshaft for grooves or other wear.

To install:
7. Using an oil seal centering tool, drive the new seal into the cover with the lip facing towards the engine.
8. Install a crankshaft pulley installer tool, onto the crankshaft pulley and press the pulley onto the crankshaft.
9. To complete the installation, reverse the removal procedures. Torque the pulley bolt to 66–88 ft. lbs.

2.3L Engine

1. Disconnect the negative battery cable from the battery. Remove coolant recovery reservoir.
2. Remove the serpentine drive belt.

NOTE: To avoid personal injury when rotating the serpentine belt tensioner, use a 13mm wrench that is at least 24 in. long.

3. Remove upper cover retaining bolts.
4. Raise vehicle and support it safely.
5. Remove right front wheel assembly.
6. Remove right lower splash shield.
7. Remove crankshaft balancer assembly.
8. Remove lower cover retaining bolts and lower the vehicle.
9. Remove the front cover.
10. Installation is the reverse of the removal procedure. Torque the front cover retaining bolts to 106 inch lbs. (12 Nm). Torque retaining bolt and washer for balancer assembly to 74 ft. lbs.

NOTE: The automatic transaxle crankshaft balancer must not

be installed on a manual transaxle engine.

11. Connect the negative battery cable.

2.8L and 3.1L Engines

1. Disconnect the negative battery cable. Remove the serpentine belt.
2. Raise and safely support the vehicle. Remove the right side inner fender splash shield.
3. Remove the damper retaining bolt.
4. Using a crankshaft pulley puller tool, press the damper pulley from the crankshaft.
5. Using a small pry bar, pry out the seal in the front cover.

NOTE: Use care not to damage the seal seat or the crankshaft while removing or installing the seal. Inspect the crankshaft seal surface for signs of grooves or wear.

To install:
6. Using a seal installer tool, drive the new seal in the cover with the lip facing towards the engine.
7. Using a crankshaft pulley installer tool, press the crankshaft pulley onto the crankshaft. Torque the damper bolt to 67–85 ft. lbs.
8. To complete the installation, reverse the removal procedures.

Timing Chain and Sprockets

REMOVAL & INSTALLATION

2.0L and 2.2L Engines

1. Disconnect the negative battery cable. Remove the timing case cover.
2. Rotate the crankshaft to until the marks on the crankshaft and camshaft sprockets are aligned.
3. Remove the timing chain tensioner upper bolt.
4. Loosen the timing chain tensioner nut as far as possible but do not remove the nut.
5. Remove the timing chain and camshaft sprocket.
6. Using a gear puller, remove the crankshaft sprocket.

To install:
7. Before installing the camshaft sprocket, lubricate the thrust side with Molykote® or equivalent. Using a sprocket installer tool, install the crankshaft sprocket.
8. Align the camshaft sprocket mark with the crankshaft sprocket marks. Install the timing chain and camshaft sprocket.
9. Press the camshaft sprocket onto the camshaft using the camshaft

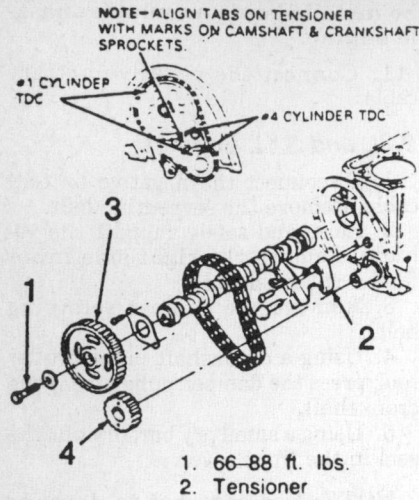

NOTE—ALIGN TABS ON TENSIONER WITH MARKS ON CAMSHAFT & CRANKSHAFT SPROCKETS.

#1 CYLINDER TDC

#4 CYLINDER TDC

1. 66–88 ft. lbs.
2. Tensioner
3. Camshaft sprocket
4. Crankshaft sprocket

Timing chain and sprockets installation— 2.0L and 2.2L engines

sprocket bolt. Torque the camshaft sprocket bolt to 66–88 ft. lbs.

10. Align the tabs on the tensioner with the marks on the camshaft and crankshaft sprockets and tighten the tensioner.

11. Installation is the reverse of the removal procedures. Connect the negative battery cable.

2.3L Engine

NOTE: Prior to removing the timing chain, review the entire procedure.

1. Disconnect the negative battery cable.

2. Remove front engine cover and crankshaft oil slinger.

3. Rotate the crankshaft clockwise, as viewed from front of engine/normal rotation until the camshaft sprockets' timing dowel pin holes line up with the holes in the timing chain housing. The mark on the crankshaft sprocket should line up with the mark on the cylinder block. The crankshaft sprocket keyway should point upwards and line up with the centerline of the cylinder bores. This is the timed position.

4. Remove 3 timing chain guides.

5. Raise vehicle and support in safely.

6. Gently pry off timing chain tensioner spring retainer and remove spring.

NOTE: Two styles of tensioner are used. One with a spring post, early production and 1 without a spring post, late production. Both styles are identical in operation and are interchangeable.

7. Remove timing chain tensioner shoe retainer.

8. Make sure all the slack in the timing chain is above the tensioner assembly; remove the chain tensioner shoe. The timing chain must be disengaged from the wear grooves in the tensioner shoe in order to remove the shoe. Slide a prybar under the timing chain while pulling shoe outward.

9. If difficulty is encountered removing chain tensioner shoe, proceed as follows:

a. Lower the vehicle.

b. Hold the intake camshaft sprocket with a holding tool and remove the sprocket bolt and washer.

c. Remove the washer from the bolt and re-thread the bolt back into the camshaft by hand, the bolt provides a surface to push against.

d. Remove intake camshaft sprocket using a 3-jaw puller in the 3 relief holes in the sprocket. Do not attempt to pry the sprocket off the camshaft or damage to the sprocket or chain housing could occur.

10. Remove tensioner assembly retaining bolts and tensioner.

─────── CAUTION ───────
Tensioner piston is spring loaded and could fly out causing personal injury.
────────────────────────

11. Remove chain housing to block stud, timing chain tensioner shoe pivot.

12. Remove timing chain.

NOTE: Failure to follow this procedure could result in severe engine damage.

To install:

13. Tighten intake camshaft sprocket retaining bolt and washer, to specification while holding sprocket in place.

14. Install a special tool through holes in camshaft sprockets into holes in timing chain housing, this positions the camshafts for correct timing.

15. If the camshafts are out of position and must be rotated more than ⅛ turn in order to install the alignment dowel pins, perform the following:

a. The crankshaft must be rotated 90 degrees clockwise off of TDC in order to give the valves adequate clearance to open.

b. Once the camshafts are in position and the dowels installed, rotate the crankshaft counterclockwise back to top dead center. Do not rotate the crankshaft clockwise to TDC, valve or piston damage could occur.

16. Install timing chain over exhaust camshaft sprocket, around idler sprocket and around crankshaft sprocket.

17. Remove the alignment dowel pin from the intake camshaft. Using a dowel pin remover tool rotate the intake camshaft sprocket counterclockwise enough to slide the timing chain over the intake camshaft sprocket. Release the camshaft sprocket wrench. The length of chain between the 2 camshaft sprockets will tighten. If properly timed, the intake camshaft alignment dowel pin should slide in easily. If the dowel pin does not fully index, the camshafts are not timed correctly and the procedure must be repeated.

18. Leave the alignment dowel pins installed.

19. With slack removed from chain between intake camshaft sprocket and crankshaft sprocket, the timing marks on the crankshaft and the cylinder block should be aligned. If marks are not aligned, move the chain 1 tooth forward or rearward, remove slack and recheck marks.

20. Tighten chain housing to block stud, timing chain tensioner shoe pivot. Stud is installed under the timing chain. Tighten to 19 ft. lbs.

21. Reload timing chain tensioner assembly to its zero position as follows:

a. Assemble restraint cylinder, spring and nylon plug into plunger. Index slot in restraint cylinder with peg in plunger. While rotating the restraint cylinder clockwise, push the restraint cylinder into the plunger until it bottoms. Keep rotating the restraint cylinder clockwise but allow the spring to push it out of the plunger. The pin in the plunger will lock the restraint in the loaded position.

b. Install a special plunger installer tool into plunger assembly.

c. Install plunger assembly into tensioner body with the long end toward the crankshaft when installed.

22. Install tensioner assembly to chain housing. Recheck plunger assembly installation. It is correctly installed when the long end is toward the crankshaft.

23. Install and tighten timing chain tensioner bolts and tighten to 10 ft. lbs.

24. Install tensioner shoe and tensioner shoe retainer.

25. Remove the special tool from the plunger and squeeze plunger assembly into tensioner body to unload the plunger assembly.

26. Lower vehicle enough to reach and remove the alignment dowel pins. Rotate crankshaft clockwise 2 full rotations. Align crankshaft timing mark with mark on cylinder block and reinstall alignment dowel pins. Alignment dowel pins will slide in easily if engine is timed correctly.

NOTE: If the engine is not correctly timed, severe engine damage could occur.

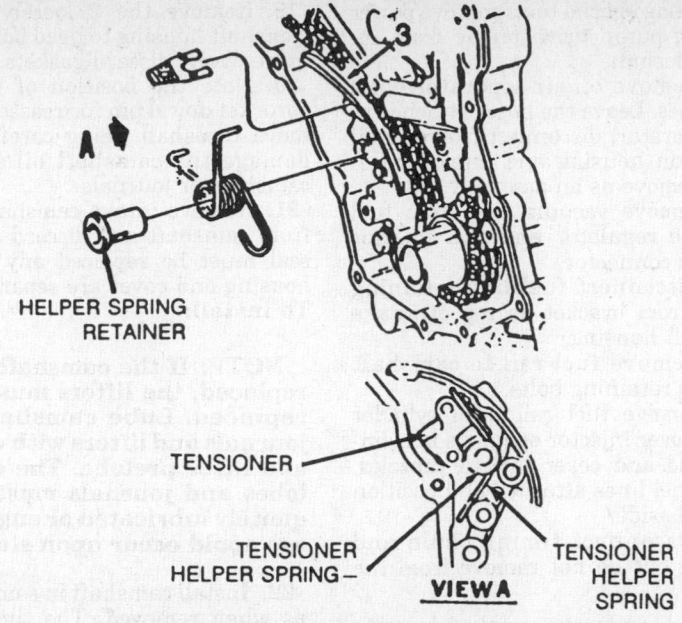

HELPER SPRING RETAINER

TENSIONER

TENSIONER HELPER SPRING—

VIEW A

TENSIONER HELPER SPRING

Installing the timing chain tensioner—2.3L engine

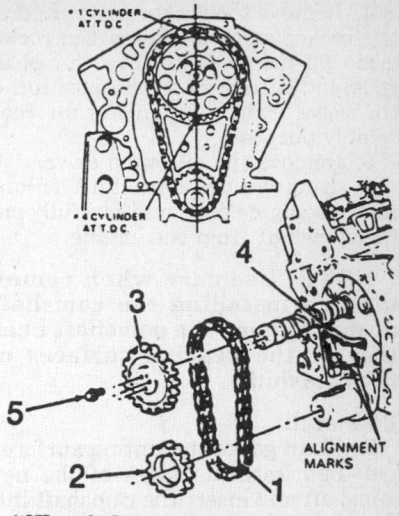

• 1 CYLINDER AT T D C

• 4 CYLINDER AT T D C

ALIGNMENT MARKS

NOTE—ALIGN TIMING MARKS ON CAM & CRANK SPROCKETS USING ALIGNMENT MARKS ON DAMPER STAMPING OR CAST ALIGNMENT MARKS ON CYL & CASE.

1. Timing chain
2. Crankshaft sprocket
3. Camshaft sprocket
4. Damper
5. 15–20 ft. lbs.

Timing chain and sprockets installation— 2.8L and 3.1L engines

To install:

5. Before installing the sprockets, apply Molykote® or equivalent, to the thrust face of the sprocket(s).
6. Install the sprocket on the crankshaft.
7. Hold the camshaft sprocket with the chain hanging down. Align the marks on the camshaft and crankshaft sprockets.
8. Align the dowel in the camshaft with the sprocket. Install the sprocket and timing chain using a camshaft bolt to pull the sprocket into position.
9. Torque the camshaft bolts to 15– 20 ft. lbs.
10. Lubricate the new timing chain with clean engine oil.
11. Installation is the reverse of the removal procedures.
12. Connect the negative battery cable. Start the engine and check for leaks.

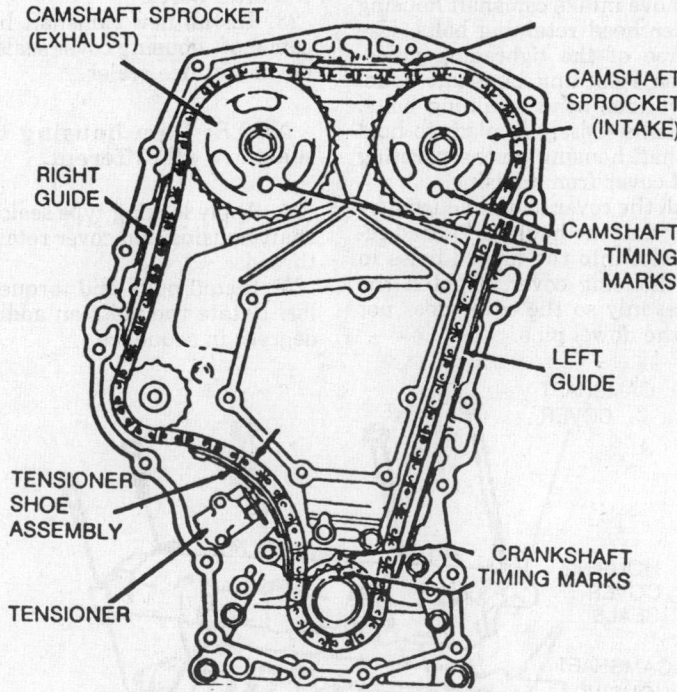

CAMSHAFT SPROCKET (EXHAUST)

CAMSHAFT SPROCKET (INTAKE)

RIGHT GUIDE

CAMSHAFT TIMING MARKS

LEFT GUIDE

TENSIONER SHOE ASSEMBLY

TENSIONER

CRANKSHAFT TIMING MARKS

Timing chain installation—2.3L engine

27. Install 3 timing chain guides and crankshaft oil slinger.
28. Install engine front cover.
29. Connect the negative battery cable. Start engine and check for oil leaks.

2.8L and 3.1L Engines

1. Disconnect the negative battery cable. Remove the front cover.
2. Rotate the crankshaft to position the No. 1 piston at TDC with the crankshaft and camshaft sprockets aligned.

NOTE: When the camshaft and crankshaft marks are aligned, the No. 4 piston is on the TDC of its compression stroke.

3. Remove the camshaft sprocket bolts, the sprocket and the timing chain.
4. Remove the crankshaft sprocket.

Camshaft

REMOVAL & INSTALLATION

2.0L and 2.2L Engines

1. Relieve the fuel pressure. Disconnect the negative battery cable. Remove the engine and attach it to an engine stand.
2. Remove the timing chain and sprocket from the engine.
3. Drain the engine oil and remove the oil filter.

4. Remove the rocker cover. Loosen the rocker arms and turn the rocker arms 90 degrees. Remove the pushrods and lifters; note the position of the valve train components for reassembly purposes.

5. Remove the oil pump drive.

6. Remove the camshaft thrust plate-to-engine bolts and carefully pull the camshaft from the engine.

NOTE: Use care when removing and installing the camshaft; do not damage the camshaft bearings or the bearing surfaces on the camshaft.

To install:

7. Clean gasket mounting surfaces.

8. Lubricate the lobes of the new camshaft and insert the camshaft into the engine.

NOTE: If a new camshaft is being used replace all of the lifters. Used lifters can only be used on the camshaft that they were originally installed with; provided they are installed in the exact same position they were removed.

9. Align the marks on the camshaft and crankshaft sprockets Install the timing chain and sprocket.

10. To complete the installation, use new gaskets and reverse the removal procedures. Torque the rocker arm nuts to 11–18 ft. lbs.

11. Connect the negative battery cable and adjust the ignition timing.

2.3L Engine

INTAKE CAMSHAFT

NOTE: Any time the camshaft housing to cylinder head bolts are loosened or removed, the camshaft housing to cylinder head gasket must be replaced.

1. Relieve the fuel system pressure. Disconnect the negative battery cable.

2. Remove ignition coil and module assembly electrical connections mark or tag, if necessary.

3. Remove 4 ignition coil and module assembly to camshaft housing bolts and remove assembly by pulling straight up. Use a special spark plug boot wire remover tool to remove connector assemblies if stuck to the spark plugs.

4. Remove the idle speed power steering pressure switch connector.

5. Loosen 3 power steering pump pivot bolts and remove drive belt.

6. Disconnect the 2 rear power steering pump bracket to transaxle bolts.

7. Remove the front power steering pump bracket to cylinder block bolt.

8. Disconnect the power steering pump assembly and position aside.

9. Using special tools remove power steering pump drive pulley from intake camshaft.

10. Remove oil/air separator bolts and hoses. Leave the hoses attached to the separator, disconnect from the oil fill, chain housing and intake manifold. Remove as an assembly.

11. Remove vacuum line from fuel pressure regulator and fuel injector harness connector.

12. Disconnect fuel line retaining clamp from bracket on top of intake camshaft housing.

13. Remove fuel rail to camshaft housing retaining bolts.

14. Remove fuel rail from cylinder head. Cover injector openings in cylinder head and cover injector nozzles. Leave fuel lines attached and position fuel rail aside.

15. Disconnect timing chain and housing but do not remove from the engine.

16. Remove intake camshaft housing cover to camshaft housing retaining bolts.

17. Remove intake camshaft housing to cylinder head retaining bolts. Use the reverse of the tightening procedure when loosening camshaft housing to cylinder head retaining bolts. Leave 2 bolts loosely in place to hold the camshaft housing while separating camshaft cover from housing.

18. Push the cover off the housing by threading 4 of the housing to head retaining bolts into the tapped holes in the cam housing cover. Tighten the bolts in evenly so the cover does not bind on the dowel pins.

19. Remove the 2 loosely installed camshaft housing to head bolts and remove cover, discard gaskets.

20. Note the position of the chain sprocket dowel pin for reassembly. Remove camshaft being careful not to damage the camshaft oil seal from camshaft or journals.

21. Remove intake camshaft oil seal from camshaft and discard seal. This seal must be replaced any time the housing and cover are separated.

To install:

NOTE: If the camshaft is being replaced, the lifters must also be replaced. Lube camshaft lobes, journals and lifters with camshaft and lifter prelube. The camshaft lobes and journals must be adequately lubricated or engine damage could occur upon start up.

22. Install camshaft in same position as when removed. The timing chain sprocket dowel pin should be straight up and line up with the centerline of the lifter bores.

23. Install new camshaft housing to camshaft housing cover seals into cover, do not use sealer.

NOTE: Cam housing to cover seals are all different.

24. Apply locking type sealer to camshaft housing and cover retaining bolt threads.

25. Install bolts and torque to 11 ft. lbs. Rotate the bolts an additional 75 degrees in sequence.

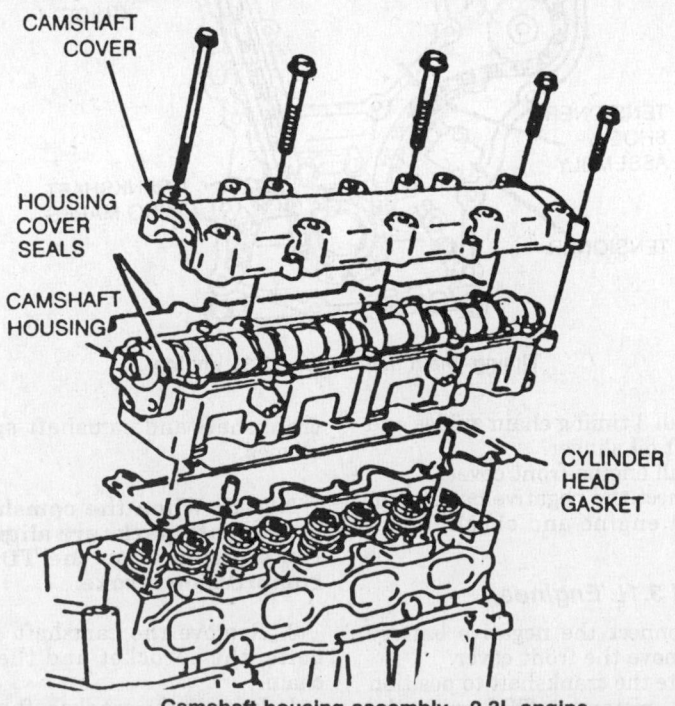

Camshaft housing assembly—2.3L engine

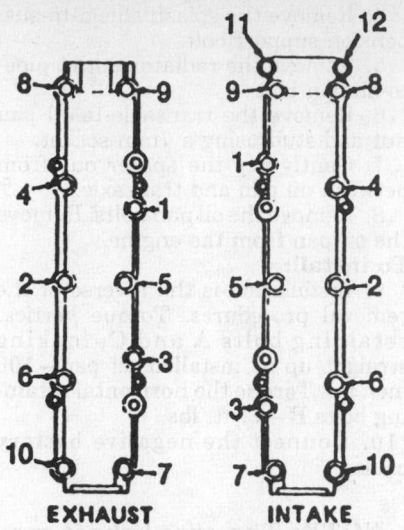

Camshaft housing bolt torque sequence – 2.3L engine

NOTE: The 2 rear bolts that hold fuel pipe to camshaft housing are torque to 11 ft. lbs. Rotate the bolts additional 25 degrees.

26. Install timing chain housing and timing chain.
27. Uncover fuel injectors and install new fuel injector ring seals lubed with engine oil.
28. Reverse the remaining removal procedures. Connect the negative battery cable. Check and adjust the ignition timing.

NOTE: Clean any loose lubricant that is present on the ignition coil and module assembly to camshaft housing bolts. Apply Loctite® 592 or equivalent onto the ignition coil and module assembly to camshaft housing bolts. Install the bolts and torque to 13 ft. lbs.

EXHAUST CAMSHAFT

NOTE: Any time the camshaft housing to cylinder head bolts are loosened or removed the camshaft housing to cylinder head gasket must be replaced.

1. Relieve the fuel system pressure. Disconnect the negative battery cable.
2. Remove electrical connection from ignition coil and module assembly.
3. Remove 4 ignition coil and module assembly to camshaft housing bolts and remove assembly by pulling straight up. Use a special tool to remove connector assembly if stuck to the spark plugs.
4. Remove electrical connection from oil pressure switch.
5. Remove transaxle fluid level indicator tube assembly from exhaust camshaft cover and position aside.
6. Remove exhaust camshaft cover and gasket.
7. Disconnect timing chain and housing, but do not remove from the engine.
8. Remove exhaust camshaft housing to cylinder head bolts. Use the reverse of the tightening procedure when loosening camshaft housing while separating camshaft cover from housing.
9. Push the cover off the housing by threading 4 of the housing to head retaining bolts into the tapped holes in the camshaft cover. Tighten the bolts in evenly so the cover does not bind on the dowel pins.
10. Remove the 2 loosely installed camshaft housing to cylinder head bolts and remove cover, discard gaskets.
11. Loosely reinstall 1 camshaft housing to cylinder head bolt to hold the camshaft housing in place during camshaft and lifter removal.

12. Note the position of the chain sprocket dowel pin for reassembly. Remove camshaft being careful not to damage the camshaft or journals.
To install:
NOTE: If the camshaft is being replaced, the lifters must also be replaced. Lube camshaft lobe, journals and lifters with camshaft and lifter prelube. The camshaft lobes and journals must be adequately lubricated or engine damage could occur upon start up.

13. Install camshaft in same position as when removed. The timing chain sprocket dowel pin should be straight up and line up with the centerline of the lifter bores.
14. Install new camshaft housing to camshaft housing cover seals into cover, no sealer is needed.

NOTE. Cam housing to cover seals are all different.

15. Apply locking type sealer to camshaft housing and cover retaining bolt threads.
16. Install camshaft housing cover to camshaft housing.
17. Install bolts and torque in sequence to 11 ft. lbs. Then rotate the bolts 75 degrees in sequence.
18. Install timing chain housing and timing chain.
19. Install exhaust camshaft housing cover and new gasket and torque to 10 ft. lbs.
20. Reverse the remaining removal procedures.

NOTE: Clean any loose lubricant that is present on the ignition coil and module assembly to camshaft housing bolts. Apply Loctite® 592 or equivalent onto the ignition coil and module assembly to camshaft housing bolts. Install the bolts and torque to 13 ft. lbs.

2.8L and 3.1L Engines

1. Relieve the fuel pressure. Disconnect the negative battery cable. Remove the engine and attach it to an engine stand.
2. Remove the intake manifold, the timing chain and sprockets.

NOTE: Be sure to keep the valve train components in order for reassembly purposes.

3. Remove the valve lifters.
4. Carefully pull the camshaft from the front of the engine.

NOTE: The camshaft journals are all the same size. Use extreme care when removing or installing the camshaft not to damage the camshaft bearings or the bearing journals of the camshaft.

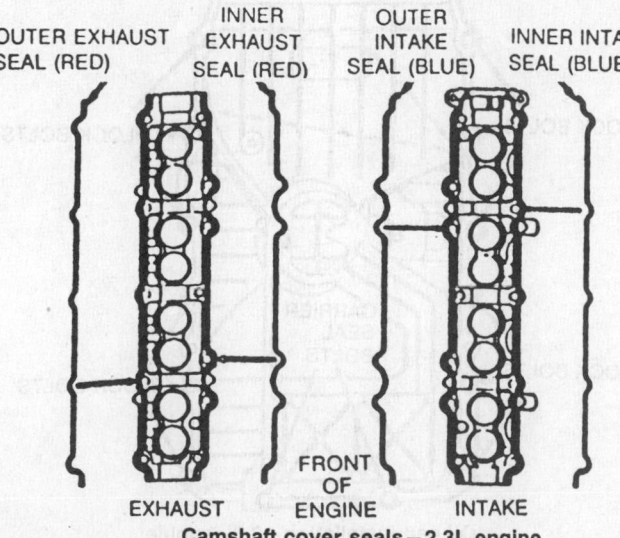

Camshaft cover seals – 2.3L engine

To install:

5. Clean gasket mounting surfaces.

6. If installing a new camshaft, lubricate the camshaft lobes and insert the camshaft in the engine.

NOTE: If a new camshaft is being used, replace all of the lifters. Used lifters can only be used on the camshaft that they were originally installed with; provided they are installed in the exact same position they were removed.

7. Align the camshaft and crankshaft sprocket marks. Install the timing chain and sprocket.

8. Install the front cover and valve train components. Torque the rocker arm nuts to 14–20 ft. lbs.

9. Installation is the reverse of the removal procedures. Connect the negative battery cable.

10. Start the engine, allow it to reach normal operating temperatures and check for leaks.

Piston and Connecting Rod

POSITIONING

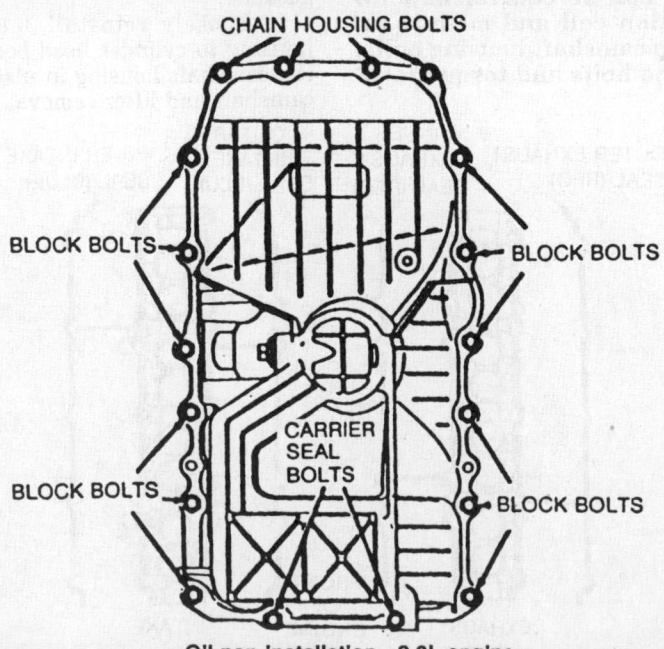

NOTCH TOWARD FRONT OF ENGINE

Piston and connecting rod installation position—typical

ENGINE LUBRICATION

Oil Pan

REMOVAL & INSTALLATION

2.0L and 2.2L Engines

1. Disconnect the negative battery cable. Remove the exhaust pipe shield.

2. Raise and safely support the vehicle. Drain the engine oil.

3. Disconnect the air conditioning brace from the starter and the air conditioning bracket.

4. Disconnect the starter brace from the block. Label and disconnect the starter wires. Remove the starter.

5. Remove the flywheel dust cover.

6. Remove the right support bolts and lower the support for clearance to remove the oil pan. If equipped with an automatic transaxle, remove the oil filter and extension.

7. Remove the oil pan-to-engine bolts and the oil pan.

To install:

8. Clean gasket mounting surfaces.

9. Using new gaskets and sealant, reverse the removal procedures. Torque the oil pan-to-engine bolts to 6 ft. lbs.

NOTE: Place a small bead of RTV sealant on the oil pan-to-engine block sealing surface. Apply a thin layer of RTV sealant on the ends of the oil pan rear seal.

10. Installation is the reverse of the removal procedures. Install a new oil filter. Connect the negative battery cable.

11. Refill the engine with the clean engine oil. Start the engine and check for leaks.

2.3L Engine

1. Disconnect the negative battery cable.

2. Raise and support the vehicle safely.

3. Remove the flywheel inspection cover.

4. Remove the splash shield-to-suspension support bolt.

5. Remove the radiator outlet pipe-to-oil pan bolt.

6. Remove the transaxle-to-oil pan nut and stud using a 7mm socket.

7. Gently pry the spacer out from between oil pan and transaxle.

8. Remove the oil pan bolts. Remove the oil pan from the engine.

To install:

9. Installation is the reverse of the removal procedures. Torque vertical retaining bolts **A** and **C**, looking straight up at installed oil pan—106 inch lbs. Torque the horizontal retaining bolts **B**—17 ft. lbs.

10. Connect the negative battery cable.

NOTE: The crankshaft may have to be rotated to gain clearance.

2.8L and 3.1L Engines

1. Disconnect the negative battery cable.

2. Raise and safely support the vehicle. Drain the engine oil.

3. Remove the flywheel dust cover.

4. Label and disconnect the starter wires. Remove the starter.

5. Remove the oil pan-to-engine nuts/bolts and the oil pan.

To install:

6. Clean gasket mounting surfaces.

7. Using new gaskets and sealant, reverse the removal procedures. Torque the oil pan nuts to 6–9 ft. lbs. or bolts to 15–22 ft. lbs. Install a new oil filter. Refill the engine with the correct engine oil.

CHAIN HOUSING BOLTS

BLOCK BOLTS

BLOCK BOLTS

BLOCK BOLTS

CARRIER SEAL BOLTS

BLOCK BOLTS

Oil pan installation—2.3L engine

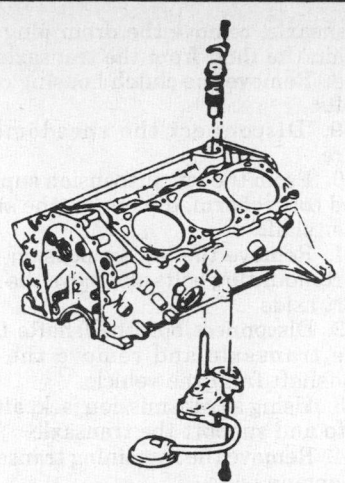

Oil pump installation—2.8L and 3.1L engines

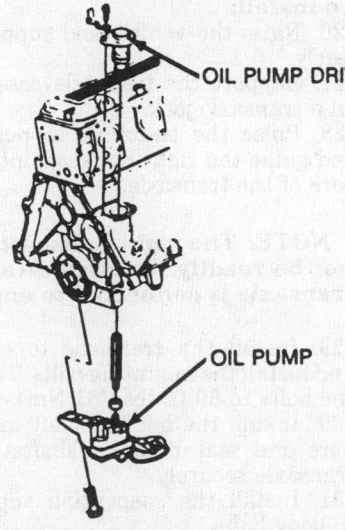

OIL PUMP DRIVE

OIL PUMP

Oil pump installation—2.0L and 2.2L engines

8. Connect the negative battery cable. Start the engine and check for leaks.

Oil Pump

REMOVAL & INSTALLATION

Except 2.3L Engine

1. Disconnect the negative battery cable. Raise and safely support the vehicle. Drain the engine oil.
2. Remove the oil pan-to-engine bolts and the oil pan.
3. Remove the oil pump-to-rear main bearing cap bolt, the oil pump and extension shaft.
To install:
4. Using new gaskets and sealant, reverse the removal procedures. Torque the oil pump-to-bearing cap bolt to 25–38 ft. lbs. and the upper oil pump drive bolt to 14–22 ft. lbs., on

the 2.0L and 2.2L engines or to 25–38 ft. lbs. on the 2.8L and 3.1L engine.
5. Refill the engine with clean engine oil. Connect the negative battery cable. Start the engine and check for oil pressure and leaks.

2.3L Engine

1. Disconnect the negative battery cable.
2. Raise and support the vehicle safely.
3. Remove the retaining bolts and the oil pan.
4. Remove the oil pump assembly retainers, bolts and nut.
5. Remove the oil pump assembly and shims if equipped.

NOTE: Oil pump drive gear backlash must be checked when any of the following components are replaced: oil pump assembly, oil pump drive gear, crankshaft and cylinder block.

To install:
6. Installation is the reverse of the removal procedure. Adjust the pump gear backlash. Torque oil pump to block bolts to 33 ft. lbs.
7. Adjust oil pump drive gear backlash as follows:
   a. With oil pump assembly off engine, remove 3 retaining bolts and separate the driven gear cover and screen assembly from the oil pump.
   b. Install the oil pump on the block using the original shims. Tighten the bolts to 33 ft. lbs.
   c. Install the dial indicator assembly to measure backlash between oil pump to drive gear.
   d. Record oil pump drive to driven gear backlash correct backlash clearance is 0.010–0.014 in. When taking measurement crankshaft cannot move.
   e. Remove shims to decrease clearance and add shims to increase clearance.

f. When proper clearance is reached rotate crankshaft ½ turn and recheck clearance.
g. Remove oil pump from block reinstall driven gear cover and screen assembly to pump and tighten to 106 inch lbs.
h. Reinstall the pump assembly on block. Torque oil pump-to-block bolts 33 ft. lbs.

CHECKING

1. If foreign matter is present, determine it's source.
2. Check the pump cover and housing for cracks, scoring and/or damage; if necessary, replace the housings.
3. Inspect the idler gear shaft for looseness in the housing; if necessary, replace the pump or timing chain, depending on the model.
4. Inspect the pressure regulator valve for scoring or sticking; if burrs are present, remove them with an oil stone.
5. Inspect the pressure regulator valve spring for loss of tension or distortion; if necessary, replace it.
6. Inspect the suction pipe for looseness, if pressed into the housing and the screen for broken wire mesh; if necessary, replace them.
7. Inspect the gears for chipping, galling and/or wear; if necessary, replace them.
8. Inspect the driveshaft and driveshaft extension for looseness and/or wear; if necessary, replace them.

Rear Main Bearing Oil Seal

REMOVAL & INSTALLATION

NOTE: This procedure should only be performed if tool No. J-34686 or equivalent, is available. This is a special tool designed for this application.

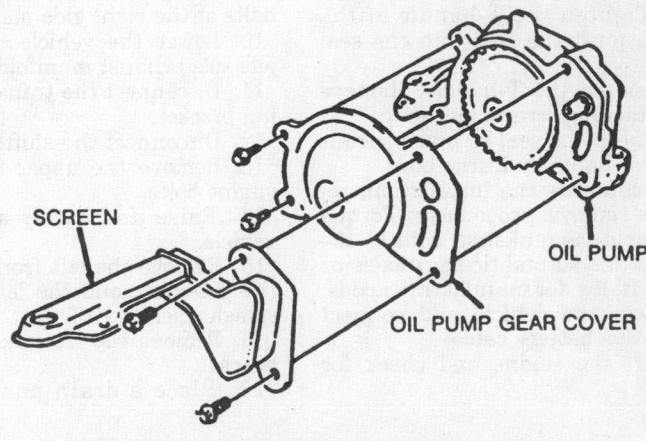

SCREEN

OIL PUMP

OIL PUMP GEAR COVER

Exploded view of the oil pump—2.3L engine

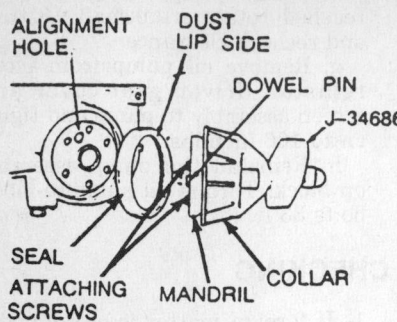

Rear main bearing oil seal Installation— Typical

1. Disconnect the negative battery cable. Remove the transaxle.

2. If equipped with a manual transaxle, matchmark and remove the clutch/flywheel assembly. If equipped with an automatic transaxle, remove the flywheel.

3. Using a small pry bar, pry the rear main seal from the engine.

NOTE: Use care when removing or installing the seal to avoid damage to the crankshaft sealing surface. If equipped with a manual transaxle, inspect the condition of the clutch to insure that the clutch was not damaged by oil loss from the rear main seal.

To install:

4. To install the rear main oil seal, perform the following procedures:

   a. Lubricate the seal bore and seal surface with engine oil.

   b. Using a seal installation tool, press the new rear oil seal into the engine. The seal must fit squarely against the back of the tool.

   c. Align the dowel pin of the tool with the dowel pin in the crankshaft and tighten the attaching screws on the tool to 2–5 ft. lbs.

   d. Tighten the T-handle of the tool to push the seal into the seal bore.

   e. Loosen the T-handle. Remove the attaching screws and tool.

   f. Check the seal to make sure it is seated squarely in the bore.

5. To complete the installation, reverse the removal procedures. Torque the flywheel-to-crankshaft bolts to 45–59 ft. lbs. for automatic transaxles or to 47–63 ft. lbs. for manual transaxles.

6. Lower the vehicle and connect the negative battery cable.

7. Start the engine and check for leaks.

MANUAL TRANSAXLE

For further information on transmissions/transaxles, please refer to "Chilton's Guide to Transmission Repair".

Transaxle Assembly

REMOVAL & INSTALLATION

NOTE: Before performing any maintenance that requires the removal of the slave cylinder, transaxle or clutch housing, the clutch master cylinder pushrod must first be disconnected from the clutch pedal. Failure to disconnect the pushrod will result in permanent damage to the slave cylinder if the clutch pedal is depressed with the slave cylinder disconnected.

Muncie

1. Disconnect the negative battery cable.

2. Using an engine support fixture tool and an adapter, install them on the engine and raise the engine enough to take the engine weight off of the engine mounts.

3. Remove the left side sound insulator.

4. Disconnect the clutch master cylinder pushrod from the clutch pedal.

5. Remove the air cleaner and duct assembly.

6. Disconnect the clutch slave cylinder-to-transaxle support bolts and position the cylinder aside.

7. Remove the transaxle-to-mount through bolt.

8. Raise and safely support the vehicle.

9. Remove both exhaust crossover bolts at the right side manifold.

10. Lower the vehicle. Remove the left side exhaust manifold.

11. Disconnect the transaxle mounting bracket.

12. Disconnect the shifter cables.

13. Remove the upper transaxle-to-engine bolts.

14. Raise and safely support the vehicle.

15. Remove the left front wheel and tire assembly and the left side inner splash shield.

16. Remove the transaxle strut and bracket.

17. Place a drain pan under the transaxle, remove the drain plug and drain the fluid from the transaxle.

18. Remove the clutch housing cover bolts.

19. Disconnect the speedometer wire.

20. From the left suspension support and control arm, disconnect the stabilizer shaft.

21. Remove the left suspension support mounting bolts and move the support aside.

22. Disconnect both halfshafts from the transaxle and remove the left halfshaft from the vehicle.

23. Using a transmission jack, attach it to and support the transaxle.

24. Remove the remaining transaxle-to-engine bolts.

25. Slide the transaxle away from the engine, lower it and remove the right side halfshaft.

To install:

26. Raise the vehicle and support it safely.

27. Support the transaxle assembly on a transaxle jack.

28. Raise the transaxle in position and guide the right halfshaft into the bore of the transaxle.

NOTE: The right halfshaft cannot be readily installed after the transaxle is connected to engine.

29. Install the transaxle to engine and install the mounting bolts. Torque the bolts to 60 ft. lbs. (81 Nm).

30. Install the left halfshaft into its bore and seat both halfshafts to the transaxle securely.

31. Install the suspension support-to-body bolts.

32. Install the stabilizer shaft-to-suspension support and install the control arm.

33. Install the speedometer wire connector.

34. Install the clutch housing cover bolts.

35. Install the strut bracket to transaxle and install the strut.

36. Install the inner splash shield.

37. Tire and wheel assembly and lower the vehicle.

38. Install the upper transaxle-to-engine bolts.

39. Connect the shift cables.

40. Install left side exhaust manifold.

41. Raise vehicle and support it safely.

42. Install both exhaust crossover bolts at the right side manifold.

43. Lower the vehicle.

44. Install the transaxle-to-mount thru bolt.

45. Install the clutch slave cylinder to the support bracket.

46. Install the air cleaner and air intake duct assembly.

47. Remove engine support fixture.

48. Install the clutch master cylinder pushrod to clutch pedal.

49. Install the left sound insulator.

50. Refill the transaxle and check for leaks.

51. Connect the negative battery cable.

Isuzu

1. Disconnect the negative battery cable.

2. Using an engine support fixture tool and an adapter, install them on the engine and raise the engine enough to take the engine weight off the engine mounts.

3. Remove the left side sound insulator.

4. Disconnect the clutch master cylinder pushrod from the clutch pedal.

5. Disconnect the clutch slave cylinder-to-transaxle support bolts and position the cylinder aside.

6. Remove the wiring harness from the transaxle mount bracket and the shift wire electrical connector.

7. Remove the transaxle-to-mount bolts and the transaxle mount bracket-to-chassis nuts/bolts.

8. Disconnect the shift cables and remove the retaining clamp from the transaxle. Remove the ground cables from the transaxle mounting studs.

9. Raise and safely support the vehicle.

10. Remove the left front wheel and tire assembly and the left side inner splash shield.

11. Remove the transaxle front strut and bracket.

12. Remove the clutch housing cover bolts. Disconnect the speedometer wire connector.

13. From the left suspension support and control arm, disconnect the stabilizer shaft.

14. Remove the left suspension support mounting bolts and move the support aside.

15. Disconnect both halfshafts from the transaxle and remove the left halfshaft from the vehicle.

16. Place a drain pan under the transaxle, remove the drain plug and drain the fluid from the transaxle.

17. Using a transmission jack, attach it to and support the transaxle.

18. Remove the transaxle-to-engine bolts.

19. Slide the transaxle away from the engine, lower it and remove the right side halfshaft.

To install:

20. Raise the vehicle and support it safely.

21. Support the transaxle assembly on a transaxle jack.

22. Raise the transaxle in position and guide the right halfshaft into the bore of the transaxle.

NOTE: The right halfshaft cannot be readily installed after the transaxle is connected to engine.

23. Install the transaxle to engine and install the mounting bolts. Torque the bolts to 60 ft. lbs. (81 Nm).

24. Install the left halfshaft into its bore and seat both halfshafts to the transaxle securely.

25. Install the suspension support-to-body bolts.

26. Install the stabilizer shaft-to-suspension support and install the control arm.

27. Install the speedometer wire connector.

28. Install the clutch housing cover bolts.

29. Install the front strut bracket to transaxle and install the front strut.

30. Install the inner splash shield.

31. Install the tire and wheel assembly and lower the vehicle.

32. Install the ground cables at the mounting studs.

33. Install the electrical connections for the shift light.

34. Install the slave cylinder to the transaxle bracket aligning the pushrod into the pocket of the clutch release lever. Install the retaining nuts and tighten evenly to prevent damage to the cylinder.

35. Install the transaxle mount bracket.

36. Install the transaxle mount to the side frame and install the retaining bolts.

37. Connect the wire harness at the mount bracket.

38. Remove the engine support.

39. Install the shift cables.

40. Refill the transaxle and check for leaks.

41. Connect the negative battery cable.

LINKAGE ADJUSTMENT

No adjustments are possible on the manual transaxle shifting cables or linkage. If the transaxle is not engaging completely, check for stretched cables or broken shifter components or a faulty transaxle.

Clutch Assembly
REMOVAL & INSTALLATION

1. Raise and safely support the vehicle. Disconnect the negative battery cable.

2. From inside the vehicle, remove the hush panel.

3. Disconnect the clutch master cylinder pushrod from the clutch pedal.

4. Remove the transaxle.

5. Using paint or chalk, matchmark the pressure plate and flywheel assembly to insure proper balance during reassembly.

6. Loosen the pressure plate-to-flywheel bolts, 1 turn at a time, until the spring pressure is removed.

7. Support the pressure plate and remove the bolts.

8. Remove the pressure plate and disc assembly; be sure to note the flywheel side of the clutch disc.

9. Clean and inspect the clutch assembly, flywheel, release bearing, clutch fork and pivot shaft for signs of wear. Replace any necessary parts.

To install:

10. Position the clutch disc and pressure plate in the appropriate position, support the assembly with an alignment tool.

NOTE: Make sure the clutch disc is facing the same direction it was when removed. If the same pressure plate is being reused, align the marks made during the removal, install the pressure plate retaining bolts. Tighten them gradually and evenly.

11. Remove the alignment tool and torque the pressure plate-to-flywheel bolts to 15 ft. lbs. Lightly lubricate the clutch fork ends. Fill the recess ends of the release bearing with grease. Lubricate the input shaft with a light coat of grease.

12. To complete the installation, reverse the removal procedures.

NOTE: The clutch lever must not be moved towards the flywheel until the transaxle is bolted to the engine. Damage to the transaxle, release bearing and clutch fork could occur if this is not followed.

13. Bleed the clutch system and check the clutch operation when finished. Connect the negative battery cable.

PEDAL HEIGHT/FREE-PLAY ADJUSTMENT

Push the clutch pedal all the way to the floor; the distance of travel should be 6–7 in. (163mm). If the measurement is not correct check the following areas:

Clutch pedal assembly distorted

Clutch master cylinder pushrod lenght—incorrect

Dash mat under the nuetral start switch
Mislocated neutral start switch

Clutch Master and Slave Cylinder

A hydraulic clutch mechanism is used on all clutch equipped vehicles. This mechanism uses a clutch master cylinder with a remote reservoir and a slave cylinder connected to the master cylinder. Whenever the system is disconnected for repair or replacement, the clutch system must be bled to insure proper operation.

REMOVAL & INSTALLATION

The clutch master and slave cylinders are removed from the vehicle as an assembly. After installation the clutch hydraulic system must be bled.
1. Disconnect the negative battery cable.
2. From inside the vehicle, remove the hush panel.

NOTE: If equipped with a 2.8L engine, remove the air cleaner, the mass air flow sensor and the air intake duct as an assembly.

3. Disconnect the clutch master cylinder pushrod from the clutch master cylinder.
4. From the front of the dash, remove the trim cover.
5. Remove the clutch master cylinder-to-clutch pedal bracket nuts and the remote reservoir-to-chassis screws.
6. Remove the slave cylinder-to-transaxle nuts and the slave cylinder.

7. Remove the hydraulic system (as a unit) from the vehicle.

To install:
8. Install the slave cylinder-to-transaxle support, align the pushrod to the clutch fork outer lever pocket. Torque the slave cylinder-to-transaxle support nuts to 14–20 ft. lbs.

NOTE: If installing a new clutch hydraulic system, do not break the pushrod plastic retainer; the straps will break on the first pedal application.

9. Install the master cylinder-to-clutch pedal bracket. Torque the nuts evenly, to prevent damaging the master cylinder, to 15–20 ft. lbs. and reverse the removal procedures. Remove the pedal restrictor from the pushrod. Lubricate the pushrod bushing on the clutch pedal; if the bushing is cracked or worn, replace it.
10. If equipped with cruise control, check the switch adjustment at the clutch pedal bracket.

NOTE: When adjusting the cruise control switch, do not exert more than 20 lbs. of upward force on the clutch pedal pad for damage to the master cylinder pushrod retaining rod can result.

11. Depress the clutch pedal several times to break the plastic retaining straps; do not remove the plastic button from the end of the pushrod.
12. Installation is the reverse the removal procedures. If necessary, bleed the clutch hydraulic system.
13. Connect the negative battery cable.

Hydraulic Clutch System Bleeding

PROCEDURE

1. Remove any dirt or grease around the reservoir cap so dirt cannot enter the system.
2. Fill the reservoir with an approved DOT 3 brake fluid.
3. Loosen but do not remove, the bleeder screw on the slave cylinder.
4. Fluid will now flow from the master cylinder to the slave cylinder.

NOTE: It is important that the reservoir remain filled throughout the procedure.

5. Air bubbles should now appear at the bleeder screw.
6. Continue this procedure until a steady stream of fluid without any air bubbles is present.
7. Tighten the bleeder screw. Check the fluid level in the reservoir and refill to the proper mark.
8. The system is now fully bled. Check the clutch operation by starting the engine, pushing the clutch pedal to the floor and placing the transmission in reverse.
9. If any grinding of the gears is noted, repeat the procedure.

NOTE: Never under any circumstances reuse fluid that has been in the system. The fluid may be contaminated with dirt and moisture.

AUTOMATIC TRANSAXLE

For further information on transmissions/transaxles, please refer to "Chilton's Guide to Transmission Repair".

Transaxle Assembly

REMOVAL & INSTALLATION

2.0L, 2.2L and 2.3L Engines

1. Disconnect the negative battery cable. Remove the air cleaner and air intake assembly.
2. Disconnect the TV cable from the throttle lever and the transaxle.
3. Remove the fluid level indicator and the filler tube.
4. Using an engine support fixture tool and an adapter, install them onto the engine.

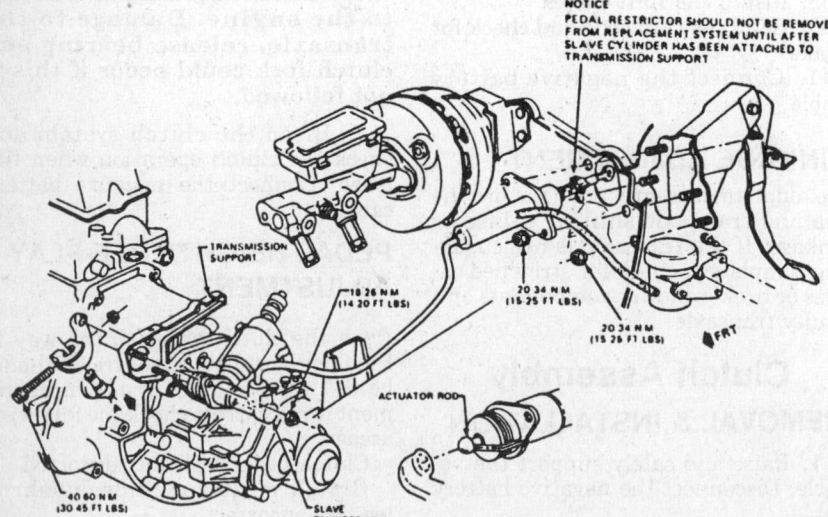

NOTICE
PEDAL RESTRICTOR SHOULD NOT BE REMOVE FROM REPLACEMENT SYSTEM UNTIL AFTER SLAVE CYLINDER HAS BEEN ATTACHED TO TRANSMISSION SUPPORT

TRANSMISSION SUPPORT

18 26 N M (14 20 FT LBS)

20 34 N M (15 25 FT LBS)

20 34 N M (15 25 FT LBS)

FRT

ACTUATOR ROD

40 60 N M (30 45 FT LBS)

SLAVE CYLINDER ASM

Clutch master and slave cylinder installation

5. Remove the wiring harness-to-transaxle nut.

6. Label and disconnect the electrical connectors for the speed sensor, TCC connector and the neutral safety/backup light switch.

7. Disconnect the shift linkage from the transaxle.

8. Remove the upper transaxle-to-engine bolts, the transaxle mount and bracket assembly.

9. Disconnect the rubber hose that runs from the transaxle to the vent pipe.

10. Raise and safely support the vehicle.

11. Remove the front wheels and tire assemblies.

12. Disconnect the shift linkage and bracket from the transaxle.

13. Remove the left side splash shield.

14. Using a modified halfshaft seal protector tool, install 1 on each halfshaft to protect the seal from damage and the joint from possible failure.

15. Using care not to damage the halfshaft boots, disconnect the halfshafts from the transaxle.

16. Remove the transaxle strut. Remove the left side stabilizer link pin bolt and bushing clamp nuts from the support.

17. Remove the left frame support bolts and move it out of the way.

18. Disconnect the speedometer wire from the transaxle.

19. Remove the transaxle converter cover and matchmark the torque converter-to-flywheel for reassembly.

20. Disconnect and plug the transaxle cooler pipes.

21. Remove the transaxle-to-engine support.

22. Using a transmission jack, position and secure the jack to the transaxle. Remove the remaining transaxle-to-engine bolts.

23. Making sure the torque converter does not fall out, remove the transaxle from the vehicle.

NOTE: The transaxle cooler and lines should be flushed any time the transaxle is removed for overhaul or replacing the pump, case or converter.

To install:

24. Put a small amount of grease on the pilot hub of the converter and make sure the converter is properly engaged with the pump.

25. Raise the transaxle to the engine while guiding the right side halfshaft into the transaxle.

26. Install the lower transaxle mounting bolts and remove the jack.

27. Align the converter with the matchmarks on the flywheel and install the bolts hand tight.

28. Torque the converter bolts to 46 ft. lbs.; retorque the first bolt after the others.

29. To complete the installation, reverse the removal procedures.

30. Connect the negative battery cable. Check the fluid level when finished.

2.8L and 3.1L Engines

1. Disconnect the negative battery cable. Remove the air cleaner, bracket, Mass Air Flow (MAF) sensor and air tube as an assembly.

2. Disconnect the exhaust crossover from the right side manifold and remove the left side exhaust manifold. Raise and support the manifold/crossover assembly.

3. Disconnect the TV cable from the throttle lever and the transaxle.

4. Remove the vent hose and the shift cable from the transaxle.

5. Remove the fluid level indicator and the filler tube.

6. Using an engine support fixture tool and an adapter, install them on the engine.

7. Remove the wiring harness-to-transaxle nut.

8. Label and disconnect the wires for the speed sensor, TCC connector and the neutral safety/backup light switch.

9. Remove the upper transaxle-to-engine bolts.

10. Remove the transaxle-to-mount through bolt, the transaxle mount bracket and the mount.

11. Raise and safely support the vehicle.

12. Remove the front wheel and tire assemblies.

13. Disconnect the shift cable bracket from the transaxle.

14. Remove the left side splash shield.

15. Using a modified halfshaft seal protector tool, install 1 on each halfshaft to protect the seal from damage and the joint from possible failure.

16. Using care not to damage the halfshaft boots, disconnect the halfshafts from the transaxle.

17. Remove the torsional and lateral strut from the transaxle. Remove the left side stabilizer link pin bolt.

18. Remove the left frame support bolts and move it out of the way.

19. Disconnect the speedometer wire from the transaxle.

20. Remove the transaxle converter cover and matchmark the converter-to-flywheel for assembly.

21. Disconnect and plug the transaxle cooler pipes.

22. Remove the transaxle-to-engine support.

23. Using a transmission jack, position and secure it to the transaxle. Remove the remaining transaxle-to-engine bolts.

24. Make sure the torque converter does not fall out and remove the transaxle from the vehicle.

NOTE: The transaxle cooler and lines should be flushed any time the transaxle is removed for overhaul, to replace the pump, case or converter.

To install:

25. Put a small amount of grease on the pilot hub of the converter and make sure the converter is properly engaged with the pump.

26. Raise the transaxle to the engine while guiding the right side halfshaft into the transaxle.

27. Install the lower transaxle mounting bolts and remove the jack.

28. Align the converter with the matchmarks on the flywheel and install the bolts hand tight.

29. Torque the converter bolts to 46 ft. lbs.; retorque the first bolt after the others.

30. To complete the installation, reverse the removal procedures.

31. Connect the negative battery cable. Check the fluid level when finished.

SHIFT CONTROL LINKAGE ADJUSTMENT

1. Loosen the cable-to-transaxle shift lever nut so the cable is free.

2. Position the gear shift selector and the transaxle shift lever into the **N** position.

3. While holding transaxle's shift lever out of the **P** position, torque the shift cable-to-shift lever nut to 11 ft. lbs. (15 Nm) for floor shift or 15 ft. lbs. (20 Nm) for column shift.

THROTTLE VALVE ADJUSTMENT

1. Turn the engine **OFF**.

2. At the end of the TV cable (engine side), depress and hold down the cable's metal readjustment tab.

3. Move the slider until it stops against the fitting and release the readjustment tab.

4. Rotate the throttle lever (by hand) to it's full travel position; the TV slider should move (ratchet) toward the lever when the lever. Release the TV.

5. After adjustment, make sure the cable moves freely and road test the vehicle.

NOTE: Even if the cable appears to function properly when the engine is cold or stopped, recheck it after the engine is hot.

Park/Neutral and Back-up Light Switch

The switch assembly is located on top of the transaxle.

1. Place the transaxle's shift control lever in the **N** notch in the detent plate.

2. Loosen the switch-to-transaxle screws.

3. Rotate the switch on the shifter assembly to align the service adjustment hole with the carrier tang hole.

4. Using a $\frac{3}{32}$ in. drill bit or gauge pin, insert it into the service adjustment hole to a depth of $\frac{3}{8}$ in. (9mm).

5. Tighten the switch-to-transaxle screws and remove the drill bit or gauge pin.

DRIVE AXLE

Halfshaft

REMOVAL & INSTALLATION

If equipped with an automatic transaxle, the inner joint on the right side halfshaft uses a male spline that locks into the transaxle gears. The left side halfshaft uses a female spline that is installed over the stub shaft on the transaxle.

An intermediate shaft is installed between the transaxle and the right halfshaft.

Except Intermediate Shaft

1. With the weight of the vehicle on the tires, loosen the hub nut.

2. Raise and safely support the vehicle.

3. Remove the hub nut.

4. Install boot protectors on the boots.

5. Remove the brake caliper with the line attached and support it (on a wire) out of the way; do not allow the caliper to hang from the line.

6. Remove the brake rotor and caliper mounting bracket.

7. Remove the strut to steering knuckle bolts. Pull the steering knuckle out of the strut bracket.

8. Using a halfshaft removal tool and an extension, remove the halfshafts from the transaxle and support them safely.

9. Using a spindle remover tool, remove the halfshaft from the hub and bearing.

To install:

10. Loosely place the halfshaft on the transaxle and in the hub and bearing.

11. Properly position the steering knuckle to the strut bracket and in-

stall the bolt. Torque the bolts to 133 ft. lbs.

12. Install the brake rotor, caliper bracket and caliper. Place a holding device in the rotor to prevent it from turning.

13. Install the hub nut and washer. Torque the nut to 71 ft. lbs.

14. Seat the halfshafts into the transaxle using a prybar on the groove on the inner retainer.

15. Verify that the shafts are seated by grasping the CV-joint and pulling outwards; do not grasp the shaft. If the snapring is seated, the halfshaft will remain in place.

16. To complete the installation, reverse the removal procedures. When the vehicle is lowered with the weight on the wheels, final torque the hub nut to 191 ft. lbs.

Intermediate Shaft

1. Raise and safely support the vehicle. Remove the front right wheel and tire assembly.

2. Drain the transaxle.

3. Using a modified seal protector, place it over the outer seal.

4. Remove the stabilizer bar from the right control arm.

5. Remove the right ball joint-to-steering knuckle cotter pin and nut. Using a ball joint remover tool, separate the ball joint from the steering knuckle.

6. Pull the steering knuckle outward and separate the halfshaft from the intermediate shaft.

7. Remove the intermediate shaft housing-to-bracket bolts and the lower bracket-to-engine bolt. Loosen the upper bracket-to-engine bolt and swing the bracket out of the way.

8. Remove the intermediate shaft housing-to-transaxle bolts, disengage

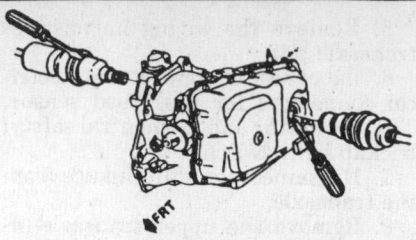

Removing halfshafts from transaxle — automatic shown — manual similar

the housing from the transaxle and remove the intermediate shaft assembly.

To install:

9. Lubricate the intermediate shaft splines with grease and reverse the removal procedures. Torque the intermediate shaft housing-to-transaxle bolts to 18 ft. lbs. (25 Nm), the intermediate shaft housing-to-bracket bolts to 37 ft. lbs. (50 Nm) and the bracket-to-engine bolts to 37 ft. lbs. (50 Nm).

10. To complete the installation reverse the removal procedures. Refill the transaxle.

CV-Boot

REMOVAL & INSTALLATION

Inner

1. Remove the halfshaft.

2. Remove the CV-joint housing-to-transaxle bolts.

3. Cut the seal retaining clamps and remove the old boot from the shaft.

4. Using a pair of snapring pliers, remove the retaining ring from the shaft and remove the spider assembly.

To install:

5. Using solvent, clean the splines of the shaft and repack the joint.

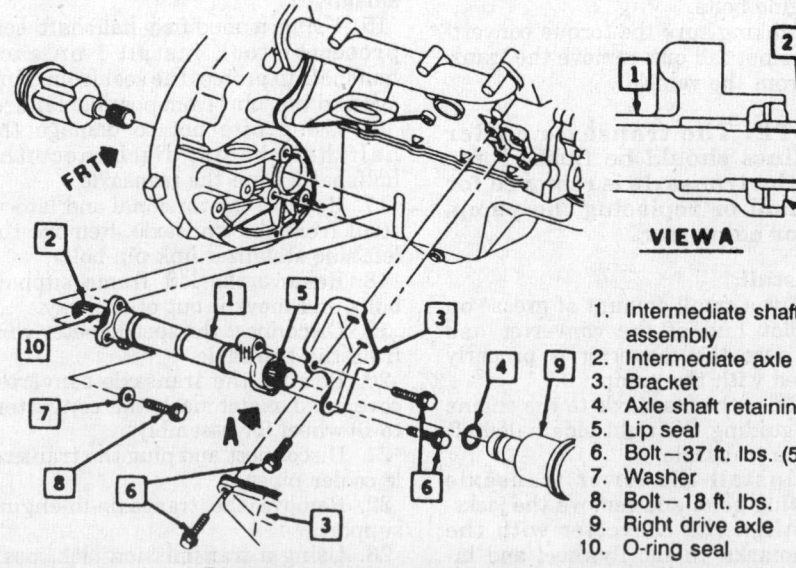

1. Intermediate shaft assembly
2. Intermediate axle shaft
3. Bracket
4. Axle shaft retaining ring
5. Lip seal
6. Bolt — 37 ft. lbs. (50 Nm)
7. Washer
8. Bolt — 18 ft. lbs.
9. Right drive axle
10. O-ring seal

Exploded view of the intermediate shaft assembly

6. Install the inner boot clamp first and the new boot second.

7. Push the CV-joint assembly onto the shaft until the retaining ring is seated on the shaft.

8. Slide the boot onto the joint. Install both the inner and outer clamps.

9. To complete the installation, reverse the removal procedures.

Outer

1. Remove the halfshaft from the vehicle.

2. Cut off the boot retaining clamps and discard them. Remove the old boot.

3. If equipped with a deflector ring, use a brass drift and carefully tap it off.

4. Using a pair of snapring pliers, spread the retaining ring inside the outer CV-joint and tap the joint off the halfshaft.

To install:

5. Using solvent, clean the splines of the halfshaft and the CV-joint and repack the joint. Install a new retaining ring inside the joint.

6. Install the inner boot clamp first, the new boot second.

7. Push the joint assembly onto the halfshaft until the ring is seated on the shaft.

8. Slide the boot onto the joint and install the clamps on both the inner and outer part of the boot.

9. To complete the installation, reverse the removal procedures.

Front Wheel Hub, Knuckle and Bearings

REMOVAL & INSTALLATION

The hub and bearing are replaced as an assembly only.

1. With the vehicle weight on the tires, loosen the hub nut.

2. Raise and safely support the vehicle. Remove the wheel and tire assembly.

3. Install a boot cover over the outer CV-joint boot.

4. Remove the hub nut. Remove the brake caliper and support it out of the way (on a wire); do not allow the caliper to hang on the brake line.

5. Remove the hub and bearing mounting bolts.

6. Remove the brake rotor splash shield.

7. Using a hub puller tool, press the hub and bearing from the halfshaft.

8. Disconnect the stabilizer link from the lower control arm.

9. Remove the cotter pin and the ball joint-to-knuckle retaining nut.

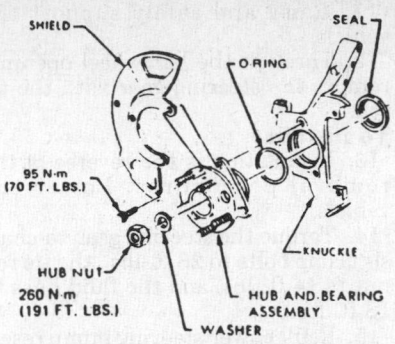

Hub, knuckle and bearing—exploded view

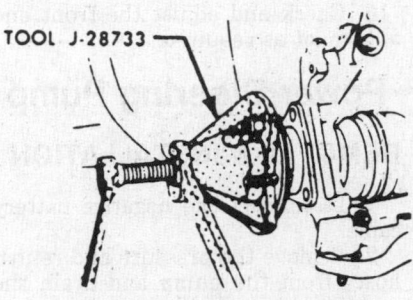

Removing halfshaft from steering knuckle bearing

10. Disconnect the ball joint from the steering knuckle, using a ball joint separator tool.

11. Remove the halfshaft from the knuckle and support it out of the way.

12. Matchmark the strut in relationship to the knuckle, for alignment purposes and remove the strut-to-knuckle retaining nuts.

13. Remove the knuckle from the strut.

14. Using a brass drift, remove the inner knuckle seal.

To install:

15. Clean and inspect the steering knuckle bore and the bearing mating surfaces.

16. Using a seal driver tool, install it into the steering knuckle; be sure to lubricate the new seal and the bearing with a high temperature wheel bearing grease.

17. Connect the ball joint to the knuckle and install the ball joint-to-knuckle retaining nut, hand tight.

18. Position the knuckle to the strut and install the retaining bolts. Align the matchmarks and torque the retaining bolts to 129 ft. lbs. (175 Nm). Torque the ball joint-to-knuckle retaining nut to 55 ft. lbs (75 Nm).

19. Install a new O-ring between the bearing and knuckle assembly.

20. Install the splash shield, hub/bearing assembly, to the knuckle and install the retaining bolts. Torque the retaining bolts to 67 ft. lbs. (90 Nm).

21. Remove the boot cover from the outer CV-joint boot and slide the halfshaft into the knuckle assembly.

22. Install the hub washer and retaining nut, (use and new nut) on the halfshaft. Torque the retaining nut to 71 ft. lbs (100 Nm).

23. Connect the stabilizer link to the lower control arm.

24. Install the brake rotor, caliper and the wheel/tire assembly.

25. Lower the vehicle and torque the hub nut to 191 ft. lbs.

STEERING

Steering Wheel

REMOVAL & INSTALLATION

1. Disconnect the negative battery cable. Turn the steering wheel so the wheels are in the straight ahead position.

2. From the rear of the steering wheel, remove the horn cover-to-steering wheel screws. Disconnect the horn electrical connector from the steering wheel.

3. Remove the steering wheel-to-column retainer, nut, washer, if equipped and damper assembly.

4. Using a marking tool, mark the steering wheel alignment with the steering shaft for realignment purposes.

5. Using a steering wheel puller, press the steering wheel from the steering column.

6. Installation is the reverse of the removal procedures. Torque the steering wheel nut to 30 ft. lbs. Connect the negative battery cable.

Steering Column

REMOVAL & INSTALLATION

1. Disconnect the negative battery cable. Remove the left side lower trim panel.

2. Remove the upper steering column mounting bolts. Lower the steering column onto the seat.

3. Disconnect the dimmer switch and turn signal switch electrical connectors.

4. Remove the wiring harness-to-firewall/steering column nuts.

NOTE: If the vehicle is equipped with a park lock, the park lock cable must be disconnected by pressing the locking tab at the ignition switch inhibiter before removing the column from the vehicle.

5. Remove both lower steering column-to-steering rack bolts and the steering column from the vehicle.

To install:

6. Push the convoluted seal over the rag joint.

7. Connect the electrical connectors. Insert the steering column into the rag coupling. Raise the column and loosely assembly the capsule bolts.

8. Install and torque the lower shackle bolt to 29 ft. lbs. (40 Nm).

9. Torque the capsule bolts to 20 ft. lbs. (27 Nm).

10. To complete the installation, reverse the removal procedures. Connect the negative battery cable.

Power Steering Rack

ADJUSTMENT

1. Disconnect the negative battery cable. Raise and safely support the vehicle.

2. With the front tires off the ground, loosen the locknut on the bottom of the steering rack.

3. Turn the adjuster plug clockwise until it bottoms out in the housing.

4. Turn the adjuster plug in the opposite direction 50–70 degrees.

5. While holding the adjuster plug, torque the locknut to 50 ft. lbs.

NOTE: If the adjuster plug is not held, damage to the pinion teeth on the steering rack may occur.

6. Check to make sure the steering wheel returns to center.

REMOVAL & INSTALLATION

1. Disconnect the negative battery cable. From inside the vehicle, remove the left side lower sound insulator.

2. Remove the upper steering shaft-to-steering rack coupling pinch bolt.

3. Place a drain pan under the steering gear and disconnect the pressure lines from the steering gear.

4. Raise and safely support the vehicle.

5. Remove both front wheel and tire assemblies.

6. Using a ball joint remover, disconnect the tie rod ends from the steering knuckles.

7. Lower the vehicle.

8. Remove both steering gear-to-chassis clamps.

9. Slide the steering gear forward and remove the lower steering shaft-to-steering rack coupling pinch bolt.

10. From the firewall, disconnect the coupling and seal from the steering gear.

11. Raise and safely support the vehicle.

12. Through the left wheel opening, remove the steering gear with the tie rods.

To install:

13. Installation is the reverse of the removal procedures. Lower the vehicle.

14. Torque the steering gear-to-chassis clamp bolts to 28 ft. lbs., the tie rod nut to 44 ft. lbs. and the fluid lines to 18 ft. lbs.

15. Refill power steering pump reservoir and bleed the power steering system. Connect the negative battery cable.

16. Check and adjust the front end alignment as required.

Power Steering Pump

REMOVAL & INSTALLATION

1. Disconnect the negative battery cable.

2. Remove the pressure and return hoses from the pump and drain the system into a suitable container.

3. Cap the fittings at the pump.

4. Remove the serpentine belt.

5. Locate the pump attaching bolts through the pulley and remove the bolts.

6. Remove the pump assembly.

7. Installation is the reverse of the removal procedures. Torque the power steering pump bolts to 20 ft. lbs. Refill power steering pump reservoir and bleed the system. Connect the negative battery cable.

BELT ADJUSTMENT

1. Install a belt tension gauge on the power steering belt.

2. Loosen pump adjustment bolts.

3. Tighten the front bracket-to-engine bolt **A**, to 9 inch lbs. (1 Nm).

4. Set the belt tension by turning adjustment stud.

NOTE: The adjustment bolts are all tighten to different torque specifications. Tighten each bolt as follows:

5. Tighten adjustment bolts A to 67 ft. lbs. (91 Nm), bolts B to 19 ft. lbs. (26 Nm) and bolts C to 40 ft. lbs. (54 Nm).

6. Start engine and run it for a minimum of 2 minutes. Re-adjust the belt tension.

SYSTEM BLEEDING

NOTE: Automatic transmission fluid is not compatible with the seals and hoses of the power steering system. Under no cir-

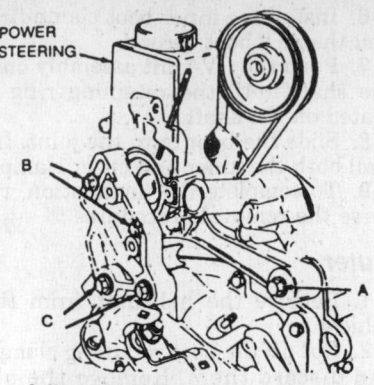

Adjusting the power steering belt tension—2.3L engine

cumstances should automatic transmission be used in place of power steering fluid in this system.

1. With the engine turned **OFF**, turn the wheels all the way to the left.

2. Fill the reservoir with power steering fluid until the level is at the **COLD** mark on the reservoir.

3. Start and operate the engine at fast idle for 15 seconds. Turn the engine **OFF**.

4. Recheck the fluid level and fill it to the **COLD** mark.

5. Start the engine and bleed the system by turning the wheels in both directions slowly to the stops.

6. Stop the engine and check the fluid. Fluid that still has air in it will be a light tan color.

7. Repeat this procedure until all air is removed from the system.

BRAKES

For all brake system repair and service procedures not detailed below, please refer to "Brakes" in the Unit Repair section.

Master Cylinder

REMOVAL & INSTALLATION

1. Disconnect the negative battery cable and the electrical connector from the fluid level sensor.

2. Disconnect and plug the 4 brake lines on the master cylinder.

3. Remove the master cylinder-to-power booster nuts and the master cylinder with the reservoir attached.

To install:

4. Bench bleed the new master cylinder and reverse the removal procedures. Torque the master cylinder-to-power booster nuts to 20 ft. lbs. and

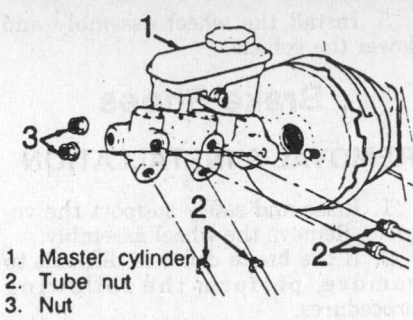

1. Master cylinder
2. Tube nut
3. Nut

Master cylinder mounting

1 Master cylinder
2 Proportioning valve cap
3 O-ring
4 Spring
5 Proportioning valve piston
6 Proportioning valve seal

MAKE SURE SEAL LIPS POINT
UPWARD TOWARD CAP

Proportioning valve installation

the brake lines-to-master cylinder to 13 ft. lbs.

5. Connect the fluid level electrical sensor wires. Refill the reservoir with an approved DOT 3 brake fluid and bleed the brake system. Connect the negative battery cable.

BENCH BLEEDING

This procedure is used to bench bleed the master cylinder.
1. Refill the master cylinder reservoir.
2. Push the plunger several times to force fluid into the piston.
3. Continue pumping the plunger until the fluid is free of the air bubbles.
4. Plug the outlet ports and install the master cylinder.

Proportioning Valve

REMOVAL & INSTALLATION

NOTE: It may be necessary to remove the resevoir in order to remove the proportioning valve. If the resevoir is removed, bleed the brake system when finished.

1. Disconnect the negative battery cable.
2. Remove the proportioning valve cap on the master cylinder.
3. Remove and discard the O-rings.
4. Remove the springs, the proportioning valve pistons and the seals from the valves.
5. Inspect the valves for corrosion or abnormal wear, replace as required.
6. Clean all parts in denatured alcohol or an equivalent. Dry all parts with air before reassembling.
To install:
7. Assemble the springs, proportioning valve pistons and the seals on the valves.
8. Install new O-ring seals.
9. Install the proportioning valve cap on the master cylinder.
10. Torque the caps to 20 ft. lbs. (27 Nm). Refill the resevoir and bleed the brake system.
11. Connect the negative battery cable.

Power Brake Booster

REMOVAL & INSTALLATION

1. Disconnect the negative battery cable. Remove the master cylinder.

NOTE: Place the master cylinder in an upright position to prevent fluid loss.

2. Remove the lower-left trim panel inside the vehicle and disconnect the brake pedal-to-booster pushrod from the brake pedal.
3. Disconnect the vacuum line from the booster.
4. Remove the brake booster mounting nuts and the booster.
To install:
5. Installation is the reverse of the removal procedures. Torque the master cylinder-to-power booster to 20 ft. lbs. and the power booster mounting nuts to 20 ft. lbs.
6. Bleed the brake system. Connect the negative battery cable.

Brake Caliper

REMOVAL & INSTALLATION

1. Disconnect the negative battery cable.
2. Remove half of the brake fluid from the master cylinder.
3. Raise and support the vehicle safely and remove the wheel assembly.

NOTE: Remove the brake hose retaining bolt, only if the caliper is going to be overhauled or replaced.

4. Position a large C-clamp over the caliper with the screw end against the outboard brake pad. Tighten the clamp until the caliper piston is pushed out enough to bottom the piston.
5. Remove the C-clamp. Remove the caliper guide pins and lift the caliper off of the rotor.
6. Support the caliper so there is no strain on the brake hose.
7. Press the inboard pad outward and remove it from the caliper.

8. Remove and discard the O-ring bushings and steel sleeves, new parts are to be installed.
9. Check the condition of the rotor. If rotor measurements exceed manufacture's specifications or has mild scoring, machine the rotor.
To install:
10. Lubricate and install the O-ring bushings. Install the sleeves by pressing them through the O-rings until the sleeve end on the pad side is flush with caliper ear.
11. Position the inboard pads so the pad contacts the piston and the support spring ends. The inboard and outboard pads are similar but not interchangeable.
12. Press down on the ears at the top of the inboard pad until the pad lies flat and the spring ends are just inside the lower edge of the pad.
13. Position the outboard pad with the ears toward the positioning pin holes and the tab on the inner edge of the pad resting in the notch in the edge of the caliper. Bend the ears to provide a slight interference fit in the caliper.
14. Press the outboard pad tightly into position and clinch the ears of the outboard pad over the outboard caliper half.
15. Position the caliper over the rotor.
16. Install the caliper over the rotor.
17. Install the caliper mounting bolts and tighten to 38 ft. lbs. (51 Nm).
18. If the brake hose retaining nut was disconnected, reconnect it and torque to 33 ft. lbs. (45 Nm).
19. Install the wheel assembly and lower the vehicle.
20. Fill the master cylinder with brake fluid and bleed the system.
21. Connect the negative battery cable.

Disc Brake Pads

REMOVAL & INSTALLATION

1. Raise and safely support the front of the vehicle. Remove the wheel assembly; reinstall 2 lug nuts to retain the rotor to the axle hub.

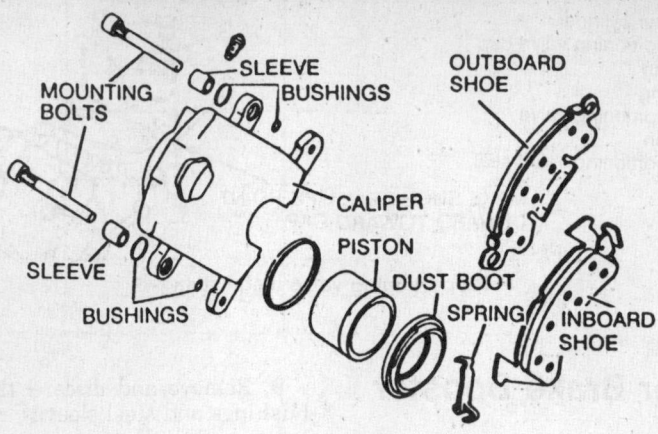

Exploded view of the brake caliper assembly

2. Using a siphon, remove ⅔ of the brake fluid from the master cylinder.

3. Using a pair of large adjustable pliers, position the jaws over the inboard pad tab and the inboard caliper housing. Squeeze the pliers to bottom the piston in the caliper housing.

4. Remove the caliper-to-caliper bracket boots, bolt coverings, the bolts and sleeve assemblies.

5. Remove the caliper from the rotor. Using a wire, suspend the caliper from the strut.

6. Remove the outboard pad, the inboard pad and the bushing from the mounting bolt hole groves.

To install:

7. Using silicone grease, lubricate the new mounting bolt bushings and install them in the holes.

8. Install the retainer spring onto the inboard pad and the pad into the caliper by snapring the retaining spring into the piston; the inboard pad must lay flat against the piston.

NOTE: On some models, the retaining spring is already staked to the inboard pad.

9. Install the outboad pad with the wear sensor at the leading edge of the forward wheel rotating; the pad must lay flat against the caliper.

10. Position the caliper assembly over the rotor in the mounting bracket. Torque the caliper-to bracket bolts to 38 ft. lbs. (51 Nm).

11. Using a small prybar, position it between the outboard pad and the rotor hub to hold the pad in position. Have an assistant, apply approximately 50 lbs pressure on the brake pedal.

12. While the assistant is applying pressure, position a ball peen hammer on the outboard pad tab and tap it with another hammer to drive the tab downward to a 45 degree angle to lock the pad into position.

13. Remove the 2 rotor-to-wheel hub nuts and install the wheel.

14. Lower the vehicle. Refill the master cylinder reservoir and road test the vehicle.

Brake Rotor

REMOVAL & INSTALLATION

1. Raise and safely support the vehicle. Remove wheel assembly.

2. Remove caliper retaining bolts and remove the caliper. Using a wire suspend the caliper from the strut.

3. Remove the rotor by sliding it off of the hub assembly.

To install:

4. Slide the caliper on the hub assembly and install 2 lug nuts to hold it in place.

5. Install the brake pads into the caliper and place the caliper assembly over the rotor.

6. Install the caliper mounting bolts and torque to 38 ft. lbs. (51 Nm).

7. Remove the lug nuts from the caliper and install the wheel assembly.

8. Lower the vehicle.

9. Fill the master cylinder with brake fluid.

10. Depress the brake pedal 3–4 times to seat the brake linings and to restore pressure in the system.

Brake Drums

REMOVAL & INSTALLATION

1. Raise and safely support the vehicle.

2. Remove the wheel assembly.

3. Remove the brake drum from the spindle.

To install:

4. Using a brake adjusting tool, adjust the brake shoe to 0.50 in. (1.27mm) less than the brake drum diameter. Install the brake drum to the axle.

5. Install the wheel assembly and lower the vehicle.

Brake Shoes

REMOVAL & INSTALLATION

1. Raise and safely support the vehicle. Remove the wheel assembly.

2. If the brake drum is difficult to remove, perform the following procedures:

a. Make sure the parking brake is released.

b. Back off the parking brake cable adjustment.

c. Remove the adjusting hole knockout plate and back off the adjusting screw.

NOTE: On some drum designs, the knockout plate must be drilled out using a ⁷⁄₁₆ in. (11mm) drill bit. A rubber adjusting hole cover is available for installation purposes.

d. Using a rubber mallet, tap the drum from the spindle.

3. Remove the return springs, the hold-down springs and the lever pivot. While lifting up on the actuator lever, remove the actuator link.

4. Remove the actuator lever, the lever return spring, the parking brake strut and the strut spring.

5. Disconnect the parking brake cable and remove the primary brake shoe.

6. Remove the adjusting screw, the spring, the retaining ring, the pin, the parking brake lever and the secondary shoe.

7. If any parts are of doubtful strength or quality, due to discoloration from heat, stress or wear, replace them.

To install:

8. Clean all of the parts in denatured alcohol. Lubricate the necessary parts.

9. To install, reverse the removal procedures and install all of the parts, except the brake drum.

10. Using a brake adjusting tool, adjust the brake shoe to 0.50 in. (1.27mm) less than the brake drum diameter. Install the brake drum.

11. To complete the installation, reverse the removal procedures. Road test the vehicle.

Wheel Cylinder

REMOVAL & INSTALLATION

1. Raise and safely support the vehicle. Remove the wheel assembly and brake drum Remove the brake shoes and attaching hardware.

2. Clean any dirt from around the wheel cylinder.

3. Disconnect and plug the brake line from the wheel cylinder.

4. Remove the wheel cylinder-to-backing plate bolt and lockwasher.

5. Remove the wheel cylinder.

To install:

6. Apply a liquid gasket to the shoulder of the wheel cylinder that faces the backing plate and reverse the removal procedures. Torque the wheel cylinder-to-backing plate bolt to 106 inch lbs. and the brake line-to-wheel cylinder to 13 ft. lbs.

7. Bleed the brake system. Lower the vehicle and check the brake operation.

Parking Brake Cable

ADJUSTMENT

1. Apply and release the parking brake lever (10 clicks) at least 6 times. Apply the parking brake lever 4 clicks.

2. Raise and safely support the vehicle.

3. Locate the access hole in the backing plate and adjust the parking brake cable until a ⅛ in. drill bit can be inserted between the the brake shoe webbing and the parking brake lever.

4. Check to make sure a ¼ in. drill bit will not fit in the same position.

5. Release the parking brake and check to see if both wheels turn freely by hand.

6. Lower the vehicle.

REMOVAL & INSTALLATION

Front Cable

1. Raise and safely support the vehicle.

2. Loosen but do not remove, the equalizer nut to remove the cable.

3. Disconnect the cable from the equalizer and right side cable.

4. Remove the hand grip from the parking brake lever inside the vehicle.

5. Remove the console.

6. Disconnect the cable from the parking brake lever.

7. Remove the nut holding the cable to the floor.

8. Remove the exhaust hanger bracket mounting nuts.

9. Remove the catalytic converter shield.

10. Remove the cable.

11. To install, Lubricate the cable and reverse the removal procedures. Adjust the parking brake.

Rear Cable

1. Raise and safely support the vehicle.

2. Loosen the equalizer nut until

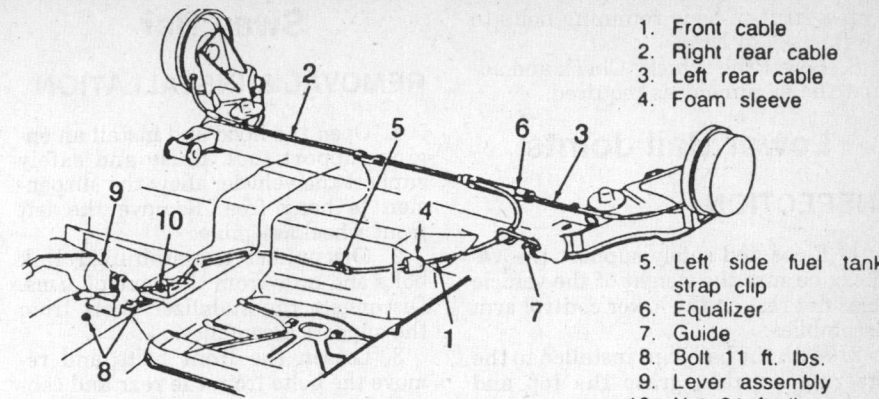

1. Front cable
2. Right rear cable
3. Left rear cable
4. Foam sleeve
5. Left side fuel tank strap clip
6. Equalizer
7. Guide
8. Bolt 11 ft. lbs.
9. Lever assembly
10. Nut 24 ft. lbs.

View of the parking brake cables—Beretta shown—Corsica similar

the cable tension is released.

3. Disconnect the right side cable button from the connector.

4. Disconnect the conduit end of the cable from the bracket on the axle.

5. Remove the wheel/tire assembly and the brake drum.

6. Disconnect the cable from the parking brake lever attached to the brake shoes.

7. Remove the conduit end from the brake shoe backing plate.

8. To install, lubricate the cable and reverse the removal procedures. Adjust the parking brake.

Brake System Bleeding

1. Clean the bleeder screw at each wheel.

2. Attach a small rubber hose to the bleed screw and place the end in a clear container of fresh brake fluid.

3. Fill the master cylinder reservoir with fresh brake fluid. The master cylinder reservoir level should be checked and filled often during the bleeding procedure.

4. Have an assistant slowly pump the brake pedal and hold the pressure.

5. Open the bleeder screw about ¼ turn. The pedal should fall to the floor as air and fluid are pushed out. Close the bleeder screw while the assistant holds the pedal to the floor. Slowly release the pedal and wait 15 seconds. Repeat the process until no more air bubbles are forced from the system when the brake pedal is applied. It may be necessary to repeat this 10 or more times to get all of the air from the system.

6. Repeat this procedure on the remaining wheel cylinders and calipers. Make sure the master cylinder does not run out of brake fluid.

NOTE: Remember to wait 15 seconds between each bleeding and do not pump the pedal rapid-

ly. Rapid pumping of the brake pedal pushes the master cylinder secondary piston down the bore in a manner that makes it difficult to bleed the system.

7. Check the brake pedal for sponginess and the brake warning light for an indication of unbalanced pressure. Repeat the entire bleeding procedure to correct either of these conditions. Check the fluid level when finished.

FRONT SUSPENSION

MacPherson Strut

REMOVAL & INSTALLATION

1. Disconnect the upper strut-to-body retaining bolts.

2. Raise and safely support the vehicle. Allow the suspension to hang free. Remove the wheel assembly. Install a halfshaft boot protector.

3. Remove the cotter pin and tierod retaining nut. Using a tierod separator tool, separate the tie rod from the strut.

4. Support the steering knuckle to prevent tension from being applied to the brake line.

5. Matchmark the strut in relationship to the knuckle and remove both strut-to-knuckle retaining bolts. Remove the strut assembly from the vehicle.

6. Installation is the reverse of the removal procedures. When installing the mounting bolts be sure to place the flats of the bolts in the horizontal position.

7. Torque the strut-to-knuckle bolts to 129 ft. lbs. (175 Nm) and the

upper strut-to-body retaining bolts to 18 ft. lbs. (25 Nm).

8. Lower the vehicle. Check and adjust the alignment as required.

Lower Ball Joints

INSPECTION

1. Raise and safely support the vehicle; be sure the weight of the vehicle does not rest on the lower control arm assemblies.

2. With the ball joint installed to the steering knuckle, grasp the top and bottom of the wheel, then move the wheel using an in and out shaking motion. Observe any movement between the steering knuckle and the control arm. If movement exists, replace the ball joint.

REMOVAL & INSTALLATION

1. Raise and safely support the vehicle and remove the wheel assembly.

2. If no countersink is found on the lower side of the rivets, carefully locate the center of the rivet body and mark it using a punch.

3. Properly drill out the rivets of the ball joint assembly. Using a ball joint separator tool, separate the ball joint from the steering knuckle.

4. Disconnect the stabilizer bar from the lower control arm. Remove the ball joint from the vehicle.

5. Installation is the reverse of the removal procedures.

6. Attach the ball joint the lower control arm with the retaining bolts and nuts. Torque the retaining bolts and nuts to 50 ft. lbs. (68 Nm).

7. Lower the vehicle. Check and align the front end as required.

Lower Control Arms

REMOVAL & INSTALLATION

1. Raise and safely support the vehicle and remove the wheel assembly.

2. Disconnect the stabilizer bar from the lower control arm assembly. Using a ball joint separator tool, separate the ball joint from the steering knuckle.

3. Remove the lower control arm retaining bolts and remove the lower control arm from the vehicle.

4. Installation is the reverse of the removal procedures. Torque the lower control arm bolts to 63 ft. lbs. (85 Nm). Torque the ball joint-to-knuckle retaining nut to 55 ft. lbs. (75 Nm). Check and align the front end as required.

Sway Bar

REMOVAL & INSTALLATION

1. Open the hood and install an engine support tool. Raise and safely support the vehicle; allow the suspension to hang free. Remove the left front wheel assembly.

2. Disconnect the stabilizer link bolts and nuts from the control arms. Disconnect the stabilizer shaft from the support assemblies.

3. Loosen the front bolts and remove the bolts from the rear and center of the support assemblies, allowing the supports to be lowered enough to remove the stabilizer bar assembly. Remove the assembly from the vehicle.

4. Installation is the reverse of the removal procedures. Loosely assemble all components while insuring that the stabilizer bar is centered, side-to-side. Torque the stabilizer bar support assemblies to 14 ft. lbs. Torque the stabilizer link bolts and nuts 14 ft. lbs. (18 Nm).

5. Lower the vehicle.

REAR SUSPENSION

Shock Absorbers

REMOVAL & INSTALLATION

1. Open the trunk and remove the shock absorber trim cover, if equipped. Remove the upper shock absorber retaining bolt. Remove each shock absorber separately when both assemblies are being replaced.

2. Raise and safely support the vehicle and the rear axle assembly.

3. Remove the lower shock retaining bolts. Remove the shock absorber from the vehicle.

4. Installation is the reverse of the removal procedures. Torque the lower shock retaining bolt to 35 ft. lbs. (48 Nm) and the upper shock retaining bolt to 22 ft. lbs. (30 Nm).

Coil Springs

REMOVAL & INSTALLATION

1. Raise and safely support the vehicle under the rear control arms. Sup-

port the rear axle assembly with and jack.

2. Remove the wheel assembly. Remove the right and left brake line bracket retaining screws from the body and allow the brake line to hang free.

3. Remove the shock absorber lower retaining bolts. Lower the rear axle assembly to remove the coil springs. Do not allow the axle assembly to hang in this position.

4. Installation is the reverse of the removal procedures. Before installing the coil springs it is necessary to install the insulators to the body using adhesive.

5. Position the spring and insulator in the spring seat and raise the axle. The upper ends of the coil must be positioned properly in the seat of the body.

6. Torque the shock aborber lower retaining bolts to 21 ft lbs. (28 Nm).

7. Install the wheel assemblies and lower the vehicle.

Stabilizer Bar

REMOVAL & INSTALLATION

1. Raise and safely support the vehicle.

2. Remove the nuts and bolts at both axle and control arm attachments.

3. Remove the bracket. Remove the insulator and the stabilizer bar assembly assembly.

4. Installation is the reverse of the removal procedures. Torque the bracket-to-axle bolts to 13 ft. lbs. (18 Nm) and the bracket-to-control arm bolts to 16 ft. lbs. (22 Nm).

Rear Wheel Bearings

REMOVAL & INSTALLATION

The rear wheel hub and bearing are replaced as an assembly only.

1. Raise and safely support the vehicle.

2. Remove the wheel and tire assembly and the brake drum.

3. Remove the hub/bearing assembly-to-rear axle nuts/bolts.

NOTE: The top mounting bolt will not clear the brake shoe when removing the hub and bearing. The hub and bearing must be partially removed while the top bolt is being turned out.

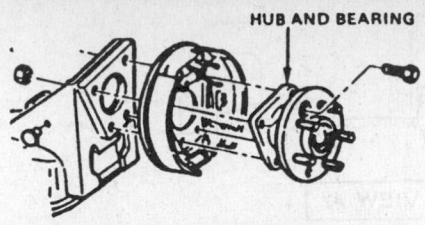

Rear wheel hub and bearing mounting

To install:

4. To install, insert and turn the top bolt in while installing the hub and bearing. Install the retaining bolts.

5. Torque the hub/bearing assembly-to-rear axle nuts/bolts to 38 ft. lbs.

6. Install the brake drum and wheel and tire assembly.

Rear Axle Assembly

REMOVAL & INSTALLATION

1. Raise and safely support the vehicle under the rear control arms. Support the rear axle assembly with and jack.

2. Remove the wheel assembly. Remove the right and left brake line bracket retaining screws from the body and allow the brake line to hang free.

3. Remove the stabilizer bar brackets. Remove the insulator and the stabilizer bar assembly assembly.

4. Remove the shock absorber lower retaining bolts. Lower the rear axle assembly to remove the coil springs. Do not allow the axle assembly to hang in this position.

5. Remove the control arm retaining bolts from the underbody bracket and lower the axle.

6. Remove the hub retaining bolts an remove the hub, bearing and backing plate assembly.

NOTE: Be careful not to drop the hub/bearing assembly, damage to the bearing could result.

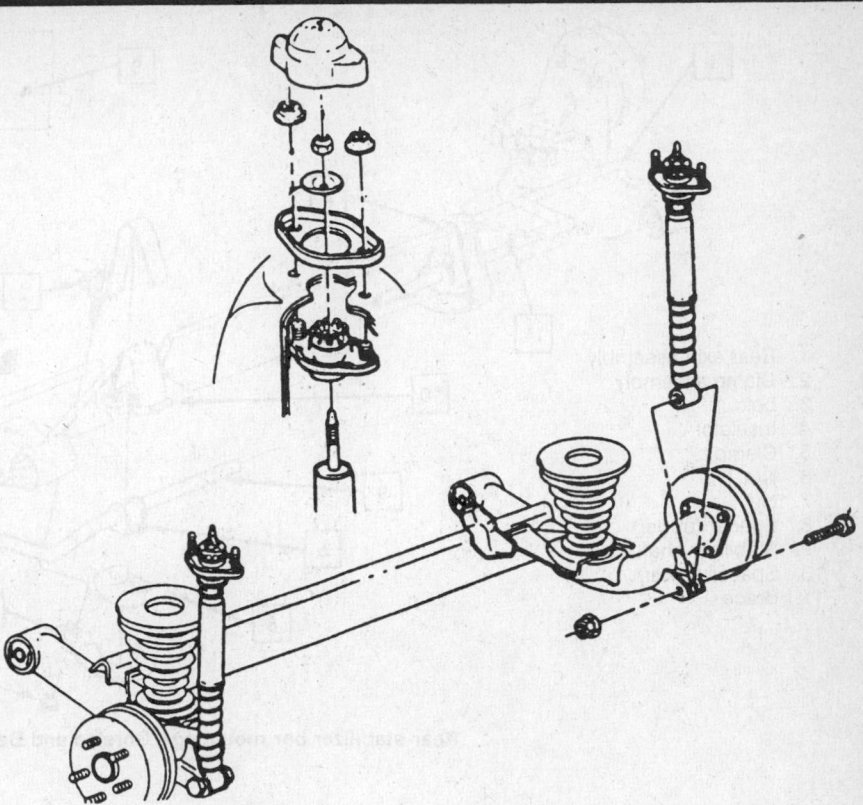

Rear shock absorber mounting – Corsica shown. Beretta similar

To install:

7. Install the backing plate and hub/bearing assembly to the rear axle assembly. Install the retaining bolts and nuts and torque to 38 ft. lbs. (52 Nm).

8. Install the stabilizer bar to the rear axle assembly and install the attaching nuts and bolts. Torque the bracket-to-axle bolts to 13 ft. lbs. (18 Nm) and the bracket-to-control arm bolts to 16 ft. lbs. (22 Nm).

9. Secure the axle assembly on a transmission jack and raise it into position.

10. Install the control arms to the underbody bracket and install the mounting nuts and bolts. Do not torque the bolts at this time. The bolts must be torque and curb height.

NOTE: The control arm mounting bolts must be install from the inboard side.

11. Connect the brake line connections and install the brake cable to the rear axle assembly.

12. Position the springs and insulators in the spring seat and raise the axle. The upper ends of the coil must be positioned properly in the seat of the body.

13. Connect the shock absorber at the lower end and install retaining bolt. Torque the retaining bolt to 35 ft. lbs. (48 Nm).

14. Connect the parking brake to the guide hook. Adjust the cable as required.

15. Bleed the brake system and refill the reservoir. Adjust the brakes as required.

16. Lower the axle to curb height and torque the axle-to-body mounting bolts. Torque the bolts to 66 ft. lbs. (90 Nm).

17. Install the wheel assemblies and lower the vehicle. Torque the lug nuts to 100 ft. lbs. (140 Nm).

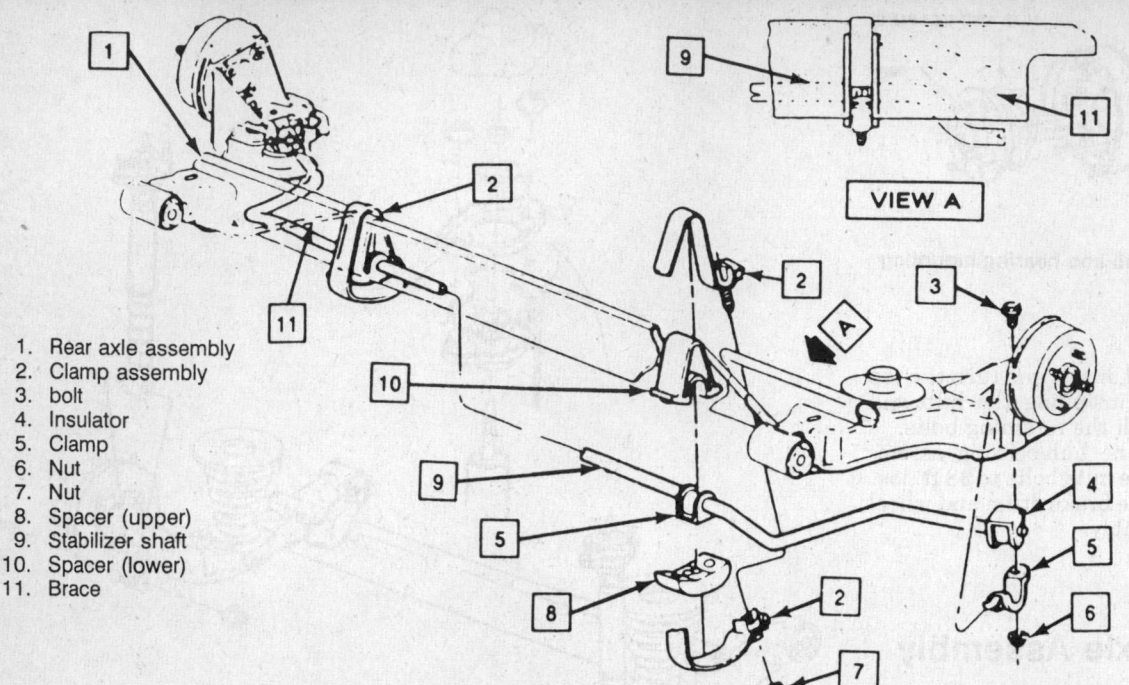

1. Rear axle assembly
2. Clamp assembly
3. bolt
4. Insulator
5. Clamp
6. Nut
7. Nut
8. Spacer (upper)
9. Stabilizer shaft
10. Spacer (lower)
11. Brace

VIEW A

Rear stabilizer bar mounting—Corsica and Beretta

Chevrolet
Rear Wheel Drive
Corvette

17

SPECIFICATIONS

VEHICLE IDENTIFICATION CHART

It is important for servicing and ordering parts to be certain of the vehicle and engine identification. The VIN (vehicle identification number) is a 17 digit number visible through the windshield on the driver's side of the dash and contains the vehicle and engine identification codes. The tenth digit indicates model year, and the eighth digit indicates engine code. It can be interpreted as follows:

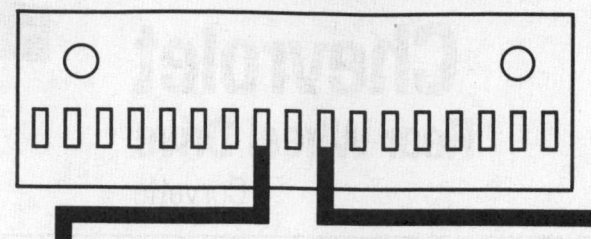

Engine Code						Model Year	
Code	Cu. In.	Liters	Cyl.	Fuel Sys.	Eng. Mfg.	Code	Year
8	350	5.7	8	PFI	Chevrolet	H	1987
J	350	5.7	8	PFI	Chevrolet	J	1988
						K	1989
						L	1990
						M	1991

ENGINE IDENTIFICATION

Year	Model	Engine Displacement cu. in. (liter)	Engine Series Identification (VIN)	No. of Cylinders	Engine Type
1987	Corvette	350 (5.7)	8	8	OHV
1988	Corvette	350 (5.7)	8	8	OHV
1989	Corvette	350 (5.7)	8	8	OHV
1990–91	Corvette	350 (5.7)	8	8	OHV
	Corvette ZR-1	350 (5.7)	J	8	DOHV

GENERAL ENGINE SPECIFICATIONS

Year	VIN	No. Cylinder Displacement cu. in. (liter)	Fuel System Type	Net Horsepower @ rpm	Net Torque @ rpm (ft. lbs.)	Bore × Stroke (in.)	Compression Ratio	Oil Pressure @ rpm
1987	8	8-350 (5.7)	PFI	230 @ 4000	330 @ 3200	4.000 × 3.480	9.5:1	50–65 @ 2000
1988	8	8-350 (5.7)	PFI	245 @ 4300	340 @ 3200	4.000 × 3.480	9.5:1	50–65 @ 2000
1989	8	8-350 (5.7)	PFI	240 @ 4300	335 @ 3200	4.000 × 3.480	9.5:1	50–65 @ 2000
1990–91	8	8-350 (5.7)	PFI	245 @ 4000	345 @ 3200	4.000 × 3.480	10.25:1	50–65 @ 2000
	J	8-350 (5.7)	PFI	375 @ 5800	370 @ 5600	3.897 × 3.661	11:1	50–60 @ 2000

PFI   Port Fuel Injection

GASOLINE ENGINE TUNE-UP SPECIFICATIONS

Year	VIN	No. Cylinder Displacement cu. in. (liter)	Spark Plugs Type	Spark Plugs Gap (in.)	Ignition Timing (deg.) MT	Ignition Timing (deg.) AT	Compression Pressure (psi)	Fuel Pump (psi)	Idle Speed (rpm) MT	Idle Speed (rpm) AT	Valve Clearance In.	Valve Clearance Ex.
1987	8	8-350 (5.7)	R43CTS	0.035	6B	6B	②	9–13	450	400 ①	Hyd.	Hyd.
1988	8	8-350 (5.7)	FR3CLS	0.035	④	④	②	3–10	450 ③	450 ③	Hyd.	Hyd.
1989	8	8-350 (5.7)	FR3CLS	0.035	④	④	②	3–10	450 ③	450 ③	Hyd.	Hyd.
1990	8	8-350 (5.7)	FR5LS	0.035	④	④	②	3–10	450 ③	450 ③	Hyd.	Hyd.
	J	8-350 (5.7)	FR2LS	0.035	④	④	②	3–10	450 ③	450 ③	Hyd.	Hyd.
1991			SEE UNDERHOOD SPECIFICATIONS STICKER									

① In Drive
② When checking cylinder compression pressures, the throttle should be open, all spark plugs should be removed and the battery should be near or at full charge. The lowest reading cylinder should not be less than 70% of the highest cylinder. No individual cylinder reading should be less than 100 lbs.

③ Minimum idle speed specification shown. Idle speed is usually a non-adjustable specification controlled by the ECM
④ Refer to Vehicle Emission Control Information label for ignition timing specifications. If no specifications are shown, no adjustment is required

FIRING ORDERS

NOTE: To avoid confusion, always replace spark plug wires one at a time.

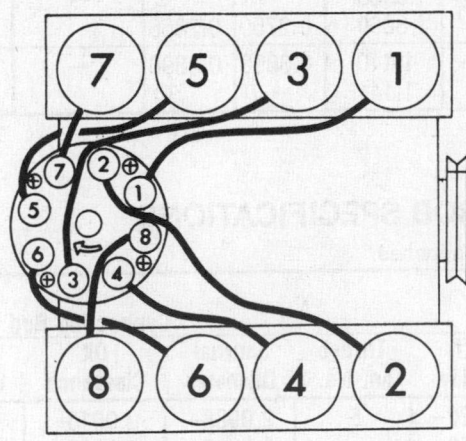

5.7L Engine
Engine Firing Order: 1–8–4–3–6–5–7–2
Distributor Rotation: Clockwise

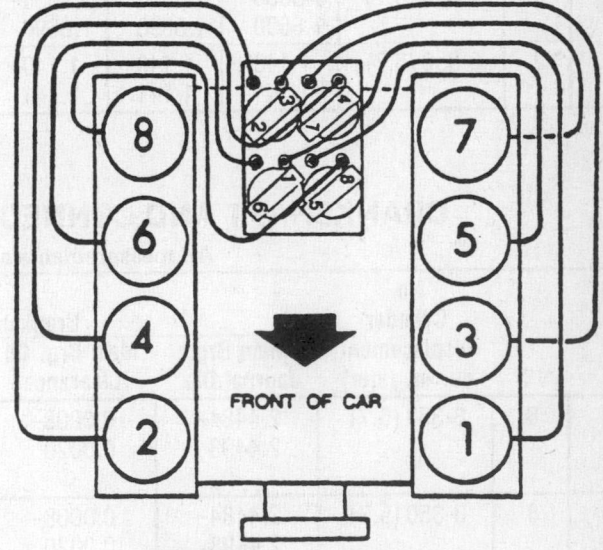

5.7L Engine
Engine Firing Order: 1–8–4–3–6–7–2
Distributorless Ignition System

CAPACITIES

Year	Model	VIN	No. Cylinder Displacement cu. in. (liter)	Engine Crankcase (qts.) with Filter	Engine Crankcase (qts.) without Filter	Transmission (pts.) 4-Spd	Transmission (pts.) 5-Spd	Transmission (pts.) Auto.	Drive Axle (pts.)	Fuel Tank (gal.)	Cooling System (qts.)
1987	Corvette	8	8-350 (5.7)	5.0	4.0	3.5 ①	—	10	3.75	20	14.0
1988	Corvette	8	8-350 (5.7)	5.0	4.0	3.5 ①	—	10	3.75	20	14.0

CAPACITIES

Year	Model	VIN	No. Cylinder Displacement cu. in. (liter)	Engine Crankcase (qts.) with Filter	Engine Crankcase (qts.) without Filter	Transmission (pts.) 4-Spd	Transmission (pts.) 5-Spd	Transmission (pts.) Auto.	Drive Axle (pts.)	Fuel Tank (gal.)	Cooling System (qts.)
1989	Corvette	8	8-350 (5.7)	5.0	4.0	—	②	10	3.75	20	14.0
1990–91	Corvette	8	8-350 (5.7)	5.0	4.0	—	②	10	3.75	20	14.5
	Corvette ZR-1	J	8-350 (5.7)	8.6	7.6	—	②	10	3.75	20	15.8

① 4 speed overdrive uses Dexron®II in the overdrive section and 80WGL5 in the transmission section

② ZF 6 speed transmission—4.4 pts.

CAMSHAFT SPECIFICATIONS

All measurements given in inches.

Year	VIN	No. Cylinder Displacement cu. in. (liter)	Journal Diameter 1	Journal Diameter 2	Journal Diameter 3	Journal Diameter 4	Journal Diameter 5	Lobe Lift In.	Lobe Lift Ex.	Bearing Clearance	Camshaft End Play
1987	8	8-350 (5.7)	1.8680–1.8690	1.8680–1.8690	1.8680–1.8690	1.8680–1.8690	1.8680–1.8690	0.2733 ①	0.2820 ①	—	0.004–0.012
1988	8	8-350 (5.7)	1.8680–1.8690	1.8680–1.8690	1.8680–1.8690	1.8680–1.8690	1.8680–1.8690	0.2733 ①	0.2820 ①	—	0.004–0.012
1989	8	8-350 (5.7)	1.8680–1.8690	1.8680–1.8690	1.8680–1.8690	1.8680–1.8690	1.8680–1.8690	0.2733 ①	0.2820 ①	—	0.004–0.012
1990	8	8-350 (5.7)	1.8680–1.8690	1.8680–1.8690	1.8680–1.8690	1.8680–1.8690	1.8680–1.8690	① 0.2750	① 0.2856	—	0.004–0.012
	J	8-350 (5.7)	1.140–1.141	1.140–1.141	1.140–1.141	1.140–1.141	1.140–1.141	0.3898 ①	0.3898 ①	—	0.005–0.014

① ± 0.002

CRANKSHAFT AND CONNECTING ROD SPECIFICATIONS

All measurements are given in inches.

Year	VIN	No. Cylinder Displacement cu. in. (liter)	Crankshaft Main Brg. Journal Dia.	Crankshaft Main Brg. Oil Clearance	Crankshaft Shaft End-play	Crankshaft Thrust on. No.	Connecting Rod Journal Diameter	Connecting Rod Oil Clearance	Connecting Rod Side Clearance
1987	8	8-350 (5.7)	2.4484–2.4493 ①	0.0008–0.0020 ②	0.0020–0.0060	5	2.0988–2.0998	0.0013–0.0035	0.006–0.014
1988	8	8-350 (5.7)	2.4484–2.4493 ①	0.0008–0.0020 ②	0.0020–0.0060	5	2.0988–2.0998	0.0013–0.0035	0.006–0.014
1989	8	8-350 (5.7)	2.4484–2.4493 ①	0.0008–0.0020 ②	0.0020–0.0060	5	2.0988–2.0998	0.0013–0.0035	0.006–0.014
1990–91	8	8-350 (5.7)	2.4484–2.4493 ①	0.0008–0.0030 ②	0.0020–0.0060	5	2.0988–2.0998	0.0013–0.0035	0.006–0.014
	J	8-350 (5.7)	2.7550–2.7560	0.0007–0.0023	0.0006–0.0010	3	2.0993–2.1000	0.0007–0.0027	NA NA

① Specification applies to the No. 1 bearing.
Nos. 2, 3, 4—2.4481–2.4490
No. 5—2.4479–2.4488

② Specification applies to the No. 1 bearing.
Nos 2, 3, 4—0.0011–0.0023
No. 5—0.0017–0.0032
Specifications shown apply to new components

③ Specification applies to the No. 1 bearing
Nos 2, 3, 4—0.0011–0.0023
No. 5—0.0017–0.0042

VALVE SPECIFICATIONS

Year	VIN	No. Cylinder Displacement cu. in. (liter)	Seat Angle (deg.)	Face Angle (deg.)	Spring Test Pressure (lbs.)	Spring Installed Height (in.)	Stem-to-Guide Clearance (in.)		Stem Diameter (in.)	
							Intake	Exhaust	Intake	Exhaust
1987	8	8-350 (5.7)	46	45	194–206 @ 1.25 ①	1^{23}/$_{32}$ ②	0.0010– 0.0027	0.0010– 0.0027	0.3410– 0.3417	0.3410– 0.3417
1988	8	8-350 (5.7)	46	45	194–206 @ 1.25 ①	1^{23}/$_{32}$ ②	0.0010– 0.0027	0.0010– 0.0027	0.3410– 0.3417	0.3410– 0.3417
1989	8	8-350 (5.7)	46	45	194–206 @ 1.25 ①	1^{23}/$_{32}$ ②	0.0010– 0.0027	0.0010– 0.0027	0.3410– 0.3417	0.3410– 0.3417
1990–91	8	8-350 (5.7)	46	45	194–206 @ 1.25 ③	1^{23}/$_{32}$ ③	0.0010– 0.0037	0.0010– 0.0047	—	—
	J	8-350 (5.7)	46	45	146.8–166.4 @ 0.95 ③	1.34	0.0012– 0.0026	0.0014– 0.0030	—	—

① Exhaust valve—1.16
② Exhaust—1^{19}/$_{32}$
③ Intake and Exhaust.

PISTON AND RING SPECIFICATIONS
All measurements are given in inches.

Year	VIN	No. Cylinder Displacement cu. in. (liter)	Piston Clearance	Ring Gap			Ring Side Clearance		
				Top Compression	Bottom Compression	Oil Control	Top Compression	Bottom Compression	Oil Control
1987	8	8-350 (5.7)	0.0007– 0.0017 ①	0.0100– 0.0200	0.0130– 0.0250	0.0150– 0.0550	0.0012– 0.0029	0.0012– 0.0029	0.002– 0.008
1988	8	8-350 (5.7)	0.0007– 0.0017 ①	0.0100– 0.0200	0.0130– 0.0250	0.0150– 0.0550	0.0012– 0.0029	0.0012– 0.0029	0.002– 0.008
1989	8	8-350 (5.7)	0.0007– 0.0017 ①	0.0100– 0.0200	0.0130– 0.0170	0.0100– 0.0300	0.0012– 0.0029	0.0012– 0.0029	0.0012– 0.0029
1990–91	8	8-350 (5.7)	—	0.0100– 0.0300	0.0130– 0.0270	0.0100– 0.0400	0.0012– 0.0039	0.0012– 0.0039	0.0014– 0.0034
	J	8-350 (5.7)	—	0.0160– 0.0260	0.0310– 0.0390	0.0120– 0.0240	0.0020– 0.0390	0.0120– 0.0030	0.001– 0.002

① 0.0025 maximum
② 0.0027 maximum

TORQUE SPECIFICATIONS
All readings in ft. lbs.

Year	VIN	No. Cylinder Displacement cu. in. (liter)	Cylinder Head Bolts	Main Bearing Bolts	Rod Bearing Bolts	Crankshaft Pulley Bolts	Flywheel Bolts	Manifold		Spark Plugs
								Intake	Exhaust	
1987	8	8-350 (5.7)	65 ①	80	45	60	60	30	20	22
1988	8	8-350 (5.7)	65	80	45	59–81	60	35	20	22

17 GM–CHEVROLET CORVETTE

TORQUE SPECIFICATIONS

All readings in ft. lbs.

Year	VIN	No. Cylinder Displacement cu. in. (liter)	Cylinder Head Bolts	Main Bearing Bolts	Rod Bearing Bolts	Crankshaft Pulley Bolts	Flywheel Bolts	Manifold Intake	Manifold Exhaust	Spark Plugs
1989	8	8-350 (5.7)	67	80	45	70	60	35	19	22
1990–91	8	8-350 (5.7)	67	80	45	70	60	35 ②	19	22
	J	8-350 (5.7)	③	⑤	22 ⑥	148	74	20 ④	22	15

① Long and medium; short—60 ft. lbs.
② All except Nos. 1 and 4; 1 and 4, 45 ft. lbs.
③ Torque bolts in 3 steps: 1st at 45 ft. lbs.; 2nd at 75 ft. lbs.; and final at 118 ft. lbs.
④ Injector Housing Bolts
⑤ Torque bolts on No. 1, 3 and 5 to 30 ft. lbs. (40Nm) plus 45–50° turn
   Torque bolts on No. 2 and 4 to 15 ft. lbs. (20Nm), plus 77½–82½° turn
⑥ Plus 80–85° turn

BRAKE SPECIFICATIONS

All measurements in inches unless noted

Year	Model	Lug Nut Torque (ft. lbs.)	Master Cylinder Bore	Brake Disc Minimum Thickness	Brake Disc Maximum Runout	Standard Brake Drum Diameter	Minimum Lining Thickness Front	Minimum Lining Thickness Rear
1987	Corvette	100 ①	—	0.724	0.006	—	0.062	0.062
1988	Corvette	100	—	0.724	0.006	—	0.062	0.062
1989	Corvette	100	—	0.724 ②	0.006	—	0.062	0.062
1990–91	Corvette	100	—	0.724 ②	0.006	—	0.062	0.062

① Aluminum wheels—80
② Heavy duty—1.039

WHEEL ALIGNMENT

Year	Model		Caster Range (deg.)	Caster Preferred Setting (deg.)	Camber Range (deg.)	Camber Preferred Setting (deg.)	Toe-in (in.)	Axis Inclination (deg.)
1987	Corvette	Front	4¹¹/₁₆–6⁵/₁₆	5½	⁵/₁₆–1⁵/₁₆	¹³/₁₆	³/₃₂	8³/₄
		Rear	—	—	¹/₁₆N–²⁹/₃₂P	¹³/₃₂	³/₃₂	
1988	Corvette	Front	4¹¹/₁₆–6⁵/₁₆	5½	⁵/₁₆–1⁵/₁₆	¹³/₁₆	³/₃₂	8³/₄
		Rear	—	—	¹/₁₆N–²⁹/₃₂P	¹³/₃₂	³/₃₂	—
1989	Corvette	Front	5⁵/₁₆–6⁵/₁₆	5¹³/₁₆	0–1			
		Rear	—	—	⁵/₁₆N–¹¹/₁₆P	³/₁₆	³/₆₄	—
1990–91	Corvette	Front	5½–6½	6	0–1P	½P	0±0.10° ①	—
		Rear	—	0	½N–¹/₂P	0	0±0.10° ①	—

N Negative
P Positive
① In degrees

ENGINE ELECTRICAL

NOTE: Disconnecting the negative battery cable on some vehicles may interfere with the functions of the on board computer systems and may require the computer to undergo a relearning process, once the negative battery cable is reconnected.

Distributor

REMOVAL

1. Disconnect the negative battery cable.
2. Remove the air cleaner cover and distributor shield.
3. Disconnect the ignition switch battery feed wire and tachometer wire from the distributor cap, if equipped.
4. Disconnect all electrical connections from the unit. Release the coil connectors from the distributor cap.
5. Remove the distributor cap retaining screws and remove the cap. Disconnect the 4 terminal harness from the distributor.
6. Remove the distributor hold-down bolt. Note the position of the rotor and then pull the distributor assembly from the engine.

INSTALLATION

Timing Not Disturbed

NOTE: To insure correct ignition timing the distributor must be installed with the rotor in the same position as it was removed.

1. Install distributor into distributor housing.
2. Install distributor hold-down clamp and bolt.
3. Install the distributor cap, then connect the coil connector to distributor.
4. Connect the ignition switch battery feed wire and tachometer wire.
5. Install harness retainer and secondary wires, if removed.
6. Install air cleaner cover and distributor shield. Connect battery negative cable.
7. Check ignition timing.

Timing Disturbed

1. If the engine has been cranked with the distributor out, remove the No. 1 spark plug. Place a finger over the hole and crank the engine slowly until compression is felt.
2. Align the timing mark on the pul-

ley to **0** on the engine timing indicator. Position the rotor between the No. 1 and No. 8 spark plug towers.
3. The distributor can now be correctly installed in the engine.
4. Once the distributor has been installed, check the engine timing and adjust as required.

Distributorless Ignition

REMOVAL & INSTALLATION

Crankshaft Sensor

1. Disconnect battery negative cable.
2. Raise and support vehicle.
3. Disconnect crankshaft sensor electrical connector.
4. Remove the crankshaft sensor mounting bolt, crankshaft sensor and sensor shim, if applicable.
5. Reverse procedure to install.
6. Coat crankshaft sensor O-ring with engine oil. Torque crankshaft sensor bolt to 71 inch lbs. (10 Nm).
7. Lower vehicle and connect battery negative cable.

Ignition Module

NOTE: Before removing the ignition module, refer to manufacture's instructions provided with the replacement ignition module.

1. Disconnect battery negative cable.
2. Remove intake plenum.
3. Disconnect all electrical connectors from the ignition module.
4. Remove 4 mounting bolts, then the ignition module.
5. Reverse procedure to install.
6. Apply a suitable dielectric grease

to the back of the ignition module as shown. Torque the 4 mounting bolts to 89 inch lbs. (10 Nm), then connect the battery negative cable.

Ignition Coil

1. Disconnect battery negative cable.
2. Remove the intake plenum.
3. Disconnect and tag spark plug wires from the ignition coil pack.
4. Remove the 2 mounting bolts, the remove the ignition coil pack.
5. Reverse procedure to install.
6. Torque mounting bolts to 40 inch lbs. (4.5 Nm), then connect battery negative cable.

Ignition Housing

1. Disconnect battery negative cable.
2. Remove intake plenum.
3. Disconnect and tag all electrical connectors and spark plug wires.
4. Remove 4 ignition housing brack-

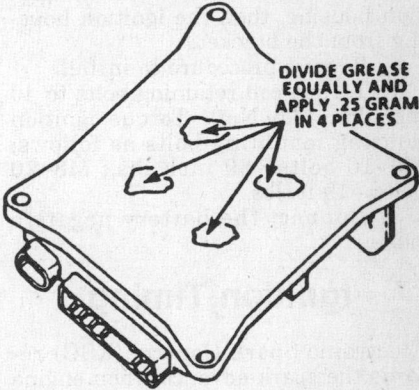

DIVIDE GREASE EQUALLY AND APPLY .25 GRAM IN 4 PLACES

Ignition module grease application

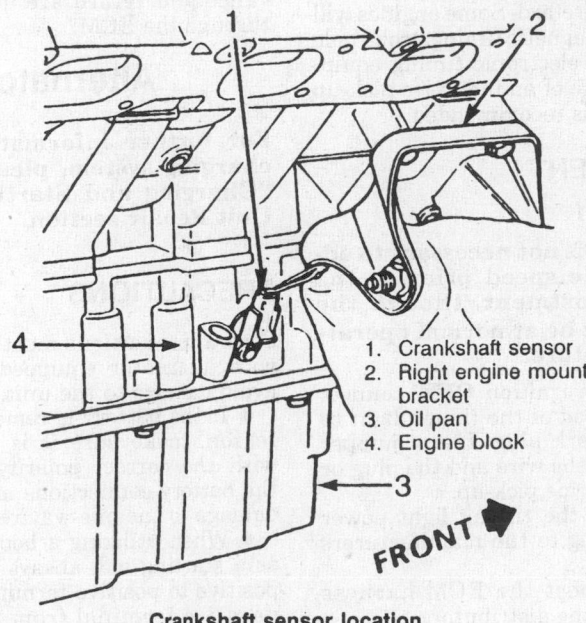

1. Crankshaft sensor
2. Right engine mount bracket
3. Oil pan
4. Engine block

FRONT

Crankshaft sensor location

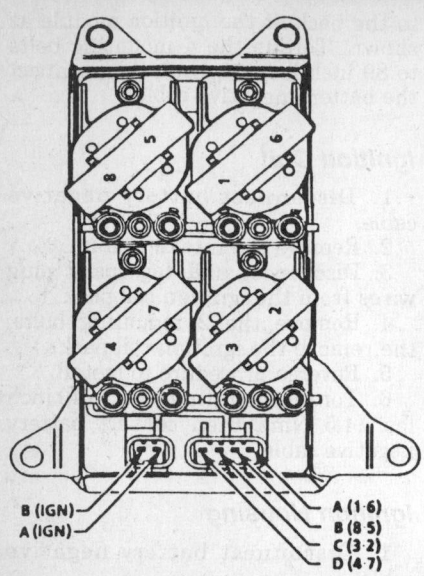

B (IGN)
A (IGN)

A (1-6)
B (8-5)
C (3-2)
D (4-7)

Ingition coil pack

et mounting bolts, then 2 ignition coil mounting bolts. Note position of coils.

5. Remove the coils from the ignition housing, then the ignition housing from the bracket.

6. Reverse procedure to install.

7. Torque coil retaining bolts to 40 inch lbs. (4.5 Nm). Torque ignition housing mounting bolts as follows: M6–16 bolts—89 inch lbs.; M8–20 bolts—19 ft. lbs.

8. Connect the battery negative cable.

Ignition Timing

Electronic Spark Control (ESC) retards the spark advance when engine detonation occurs. If the controller fails, the result could be no ignition, no retard or full retard. Some engines will also have a magnetic timing probe hole for use with electronic timing equipment. The use of an inductive pick-up timing light is recommended.

ADJUSTMENT

Except ZR-1

NOTE: It is not necessary to adjust the idle speed prior to the timing adjustment, though the engine must be at normal operating temperature.

1. With the ignition **OFF**, connect the pick-up lead of the timing light to the No. 1 spark plug. Use a jumper lead between the wire and the plug or an inductive type pick-up.

2. Connect the timing light power leads according to the manufacturers instructions.

3. Disconnect the ECM harness connector at the distributor.

4. Start the engine and run it at idle speed. Aim the timing light at the timing mark. The line on the balancer or pulley will align with the timing mark.

5. If required, adjust the timing by loosening the securing clamp hold-down bolt and rotating the distributor until the desired ignition advance is achieved, then tighten the bolt.

6. To advance the timing, rotate the distributor opposite to the normal direction of rotor rotation. Retard the timing by rotating the distributor in the normal direction of rotor rotation.

7. Tighten the hold-down bolt to 25 ft. lbs. (34 Nm).

8. Turn the ignition **OFF** and remove the timing light. Reconnect the No. 1 spark plug wire and connect the ECM harness connector.

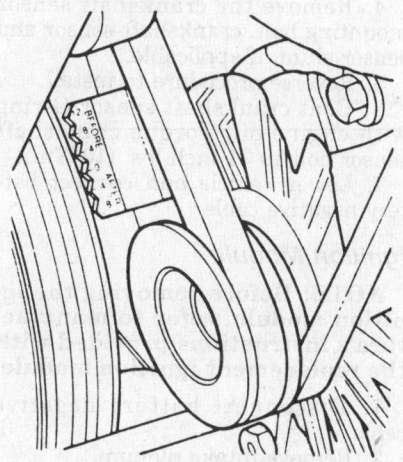

Timing mark—typical

ZR-1

Base timing is preset at the factory, no adjustment is possible. Timing advance and retard are accomplished through the ECM.

Alternator

For further information on the charging system, please refer to "Charging and Starting" in the Unit Repair section.

PRECAUTIONS

Several precautions must be observed with alternator equipped vehicles to avoid damage to the unit.

• If the battery is removed for any reason, make sure it is reconnected with the correct polarity. Reversing the battery connections may result in damage to the one-way rectifiers.

• When utilizing a booster battery as a starting aid, always connect the positive to positive terminals and the negative terminal from the booster

battery to a good engine ground on the vehicle being started.

• Never use a fast charger as a booster to start vehicles.

• Disconnect the battery cables when charging the battery with a fast charger.

• Never attempt to polarize the alternator.

• Do not use test lamps of more than 12 volts when checking diode continuity.

• Do not short across or ground any of the alternator terminals.

• The polarity of the battery, alternator and regulator must be matched and considered before making any electrical connections within the system.

• Never separate the alternator on an open circuit. Make sure all connections within the circuit are clean and tight.

• Disconnect the battery ground terminal when performing any service on electrical components.

• Disconnect the battery if arc welding is to be done on the vehicle.

BELT TENSION ADJUSTMENT

A single serpentine belt is used to drive all accessories. Belt tension is maintained by a spring loaded tensioner which has the ability to maintain belt tension over a broad range of belt lengths. There is an indicator to make sure the tensioner is adjusted to within its operating range.

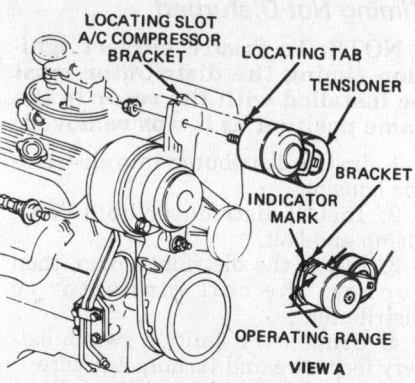

LOCATING SLOT
A/C COMPRESSOR BRACKET
LOCATING TAB
TENSIONER
BRACKET
INDICATOR MARK
OPERATING RANGE
VIEW A

Drive belt tension location and adjustments

To check the belt tension, install belt tension gauge J-23600 between the alternator and the air pump. The correct belt tension should be 120–140 lbs. (534–623 N) on 1987–89 vehicles and 60–90 lbs. on 1990–91 vehicles.

REMOVAL & INSTALLATION

1. Disconnect the battery negative cable.

2. Remove the air intake duct hose.
3. Rotate the tensioner using a ½ inch breaker bar, then remove the belt.
4. Reverse procedure to install.

Starter

For further information on the charging system, please refer to "Charging and Starting" in the Unit Repair section.

REMOVAL & INSTALLATION

Except ZR-1

1. Disconnect the negative battery cable.
2. Raise and support the vehicle safely.
3. Remove the flywheel cover.
4. Disconnect the wiring from the starter solenoid. Replace each connector nut as the terminals are removed as the thread sizes differ between connectors. Tag the wiring positions to avoid improper connections during installation.
5. Loosen the 2 starter mounting bolts, support the starter and remove the bolts. Lower the starter from the vehicle.
6. Installation is the reverse of the removal procedure.
7. Check the flywheel to pinion clearance. The clearance should be 0.020 in. (0.5mm).
8. Torque the 2 starter mounting bolts to 35 ft. lbs. (47 Nm).
9. Lower vehicle and connect the battery negative cable.

ZR-1

1. Disconnect battery negative cable.
2. Remove intake plenum.
3. Remove coil pack.
4. Disconnect the wiring from the starter solenoid. Replace each connector nut as the terminals are removed as the thread sizes differ between connectors. Tag the wiring positions to avoid improper connections during installation.
5. Remove the 2 starter mounting bolts, then remove the starter from the vehicle.
6. Installation is the reverse of the removal procedure.
7. Torque starter mounting bolts to 38 ft. lbs. (52 Nm). Coat bolt threads with Loctite.

CHASSIS ELECTRICAL

CAUTION

If equipped with an air bag, the negative battery cable must be disconnected, before working on the system. Failure to do so may result in deployment of the air bag and possible personal injury.

Heater Blower Motor

REMOVAL & INSTALLATION

1. Disconnect the negative battery cable.
2. Remove the front wheel house rear panel. Move the wheel hose seal aside.
3. Remove the heat motor cooling tube.
4. Remove the heater motor relay.
5. Remove the motor retaining screws and remove the motor assembly from the vehicle.
6. Installation is the reverse of the removal procedure. Connect the battery negative cable.

Windshield Wiper Motor

REMOVAL & INSTALLATION

1. Disconnect the negative battery cable.
2. Remove wiper arms.
3. Remove air inlet leaf screen.
4. Turn ignition **ON** and activate motor with wiper switch. Allow motor crank arm to rotate to point to a position of 4–5 o'clock as viewed from passenger compartment. Stop crank arm in this position by turning **OFF** ignition switch.
5. Disconnect battery ground cable.
6. Disconnect upper motor electrical connectors.
7. Remove motor mounting bolts.

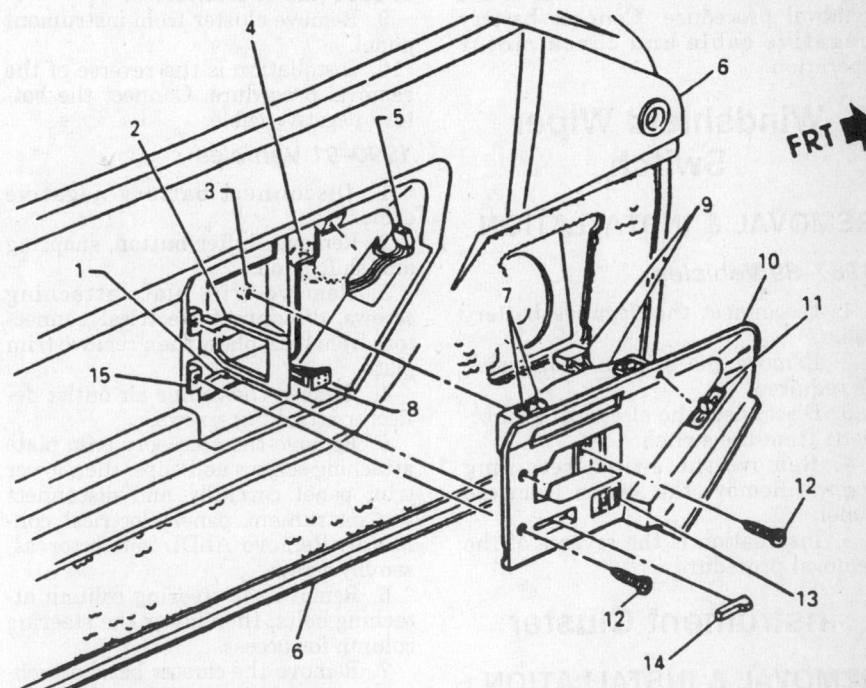

1. Door lock remote rod
2. Door inside handle
3. Accessory trim plate nut
4. Courtesy light electrical harness
5. Windshield wiper/ washer electrical harness
6. Door trim panel
7. Accessory trim plate retainer tabs
8. Door lock electrical harness
9. Courtesy light
10. Accessory trim plate
11. Windshield/wiper washer switch
12. Accessory trim plate screw
13. Door lock switch
14. Door lock rod knob
15. Accessory trim plate U-nut

Windshield wiper/washer switch removal–1987-89 vehicles

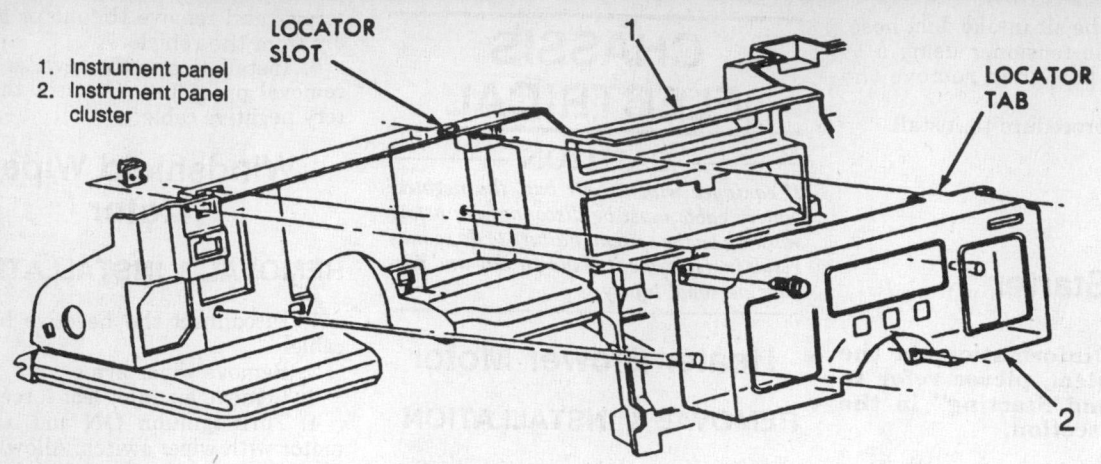

1. Instrument panel
2. Instrument panel cluster

LOCATOR SLOT

LOCATOR TAB

Instrument panel cluster—1987–89 vehicles

8. With crank arm in position described in Step 4 above, motor may now be removed from vehicle. Lower electrical connector may be disconnected as motor is partially removed.

9. Installation is the reverse of the removal procedure. Connect battery negative cable and check motor operation.

Windshield Wiper Switch

REMOVAL & INSTALLATION

1987–89 Vehicles

1. Disconnect the negative battery cable.

2. Remove the drivers door panel, as required.

3. Disconnect the electrical connections from the switch.

4. Remove the switch retaining screws. Remove the switch from the panel.

5. Installation is the reverse of the removal procedure.

Instrument Cluster

REMOVAL & INSTALLATION

1987–89 Vehicles

1. Disconnect battery ground cable.

2. Remove light switch knob (spring loaded) and light switch nut.

3. Remove steering column trim cover.

4. Remove the steering column attaching bolts and lower steering column for access.

5. Remove cluster bezel front and left side attaching screws.

6. Remove cluster bezel from instrument panel.

7. Remove the cluster to instrument panel attaching screws.

8. Pull cluster rearward for access to disconnect cluster electrical connectors. Metal retaining clips are located at back side of connectors.

9. Remove cluster from instrument panel.

10. Installation is the reverse of the removal procedure. Connect the battery negative cable.

1990–91 Vehicles

1. Disconnect battery negative cable.

2. Remove shifter button, snapring and shift knob.

3. Remove trim plate attaching screws, disconnect electrical connectors from trim plate, then remove trim plate.

4. Remove the center air outlet deflector attaching screws.

5. Remove the accessory trim plate attaching screws and clips, then lower trim panel carefully and disconnect the instrument panel electrical connector. Remove ALDL connector assembly screw.

6. Remove the steering column attaching bolts, then lower the steering column for access.

7. Remove the cluster bezel attaching screws, cluster screws and disconnect the instrument panel cluster electrical connector. Remove the instrument panel cluster.

8. Reverse procedure to install. Torque cluster bezel screws to 29 inch lbs. (3.3 Nm). Connect the battery negative cable.

Radio

REMOVAL & INSTALLATION

1. Disconnect battery negative cable.

2. Remove the instrument panel trim plates as necessary.

3. Remove radio attaching screws and pull radio carefully outwards.

4. Disconnect electrical connectors from radio and remove radio from vehicle.

5. Reverse procedure to install. Connect the battery negative cable.

Concealed Headlights

MANUAL OPERATION

1. Open the hood.

2. Rotate the manual control knob in the direction of the arrow on the assembly. Turn the knob until it will not go any further.

3. Position the retainer wire over the control knob to hold the headlight door open.

4. Be sure to use the retainer or the headlight door may be jarred out of position.

Headlight Switch

REMOVAL & INSTALLATION

1987–89 Vehicles

1. Disconnect the negative battery terminal.

2. Remove the left air distribution duct.

3. Remove the instrument cluster attaching screws and pull the cluster rearward.

4. Disconnect the speedometer cable, electrical connectors and remove the cluster.

5. Remove the instrument panel to left door pillar attaching screws and pull the left side of the instrument panel slightly forward for access.

6. Depress the shaft retainer, pull

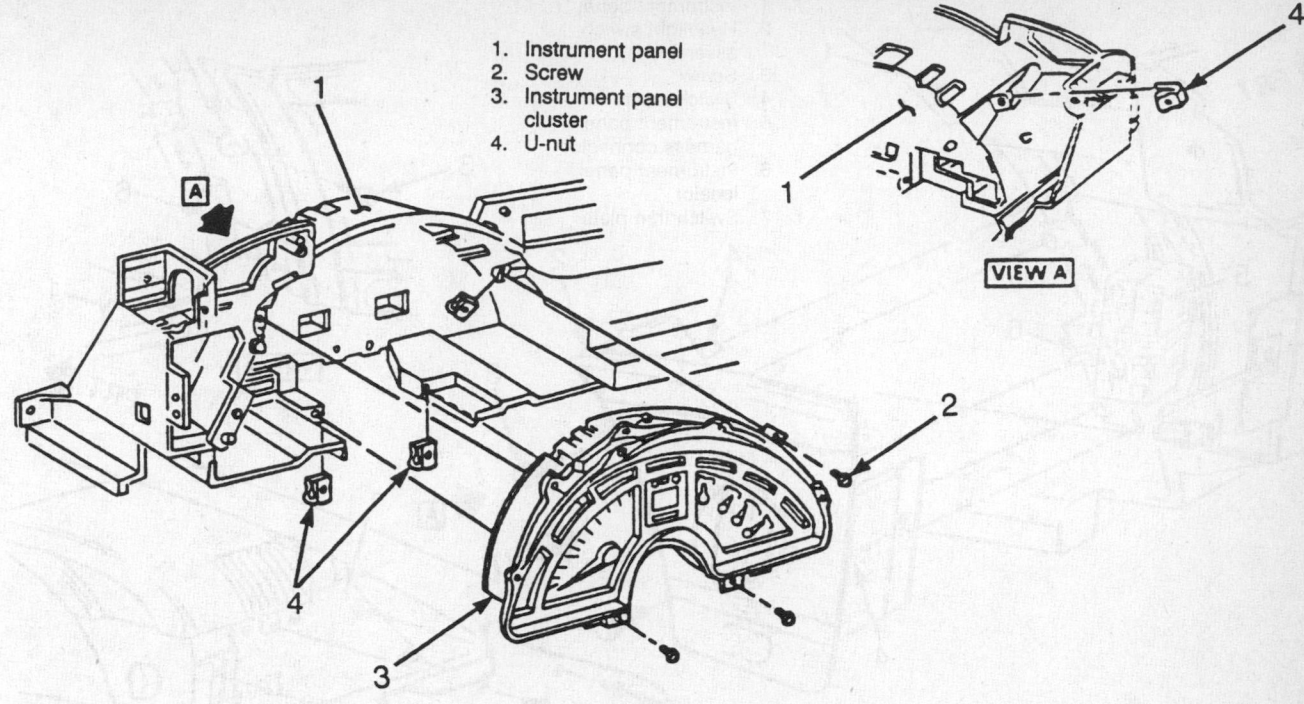

1. Instrument panel
2. Screw
3. Instrument panel cluster
4. U-nut

VIEW A

Instrument panel cluster–1990–91 vehicles

the knob and shaft assembly out and remove the switch bezel.

7. Disconnect all connections from the switch. Mark the connections for reinstallation.

8. Pry the connector from the switch and remove the switch from the panel.

9. Installation is the reverse of the removal procedure. Connect the battery negative cable and check operation of switch.

1990–91 Vehicles

1. Disconnect battery negative cable.

2. Remove the instrument panel cluster.

3. Remove headlight switch attaching screws and disconnect electrical connectors.

4. Remove headlight switch.

5. Reverse procedure to install. Connect the battery negative cable.

Combination Switch

REMOVAL & INSTALLATION

1. Disconnect the negative battery cable.

2. Remove the steering wheel.

3. Remove the steering column/ dash trim cover.

4. Remove the C-ring plastic retainer.

5. Install the lock plate compressing tool over the steering shaft. Position a

1. Instrument panel
2. Headlight switch

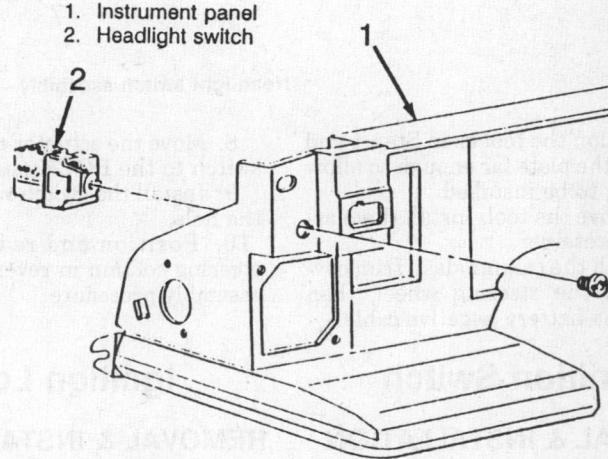

Headlight switch–1987–89 vehicles

$5/16$ in. nut under each tool leg and reinstall the star screw to prevent the shaft from moving.

6. Compress the lock plate by turning the shaft nut clockwise until the C-ring can be removed.

7. Remove the tool and lift out the lock plate, horn contact carrier and the upper bearing preload spring.

8. Pull the switch connector out of the mast jacket and tape the upper part to facilitate switch removal.

9. Remove the turn signal lever. Push the flasher in and unscrew it.

10. Position the turn signal and shifter housing in Low position. Remove the switch by pulling it straight

up while guiding the wiring harness out of the housing.

To install:

11. Install the replacement switch by working the harness connector down through the housing and under the mounting bracket.

12. Install the harness cover and clip the connector to the mast jacket.

13. Install the switch mounting screws, signal lever and the flasher knob.

14. With the turn signal lever in neutral and the flasher knob out, install the upper bearing preload spring, horn contact carrier and lock plate onto the shaft.

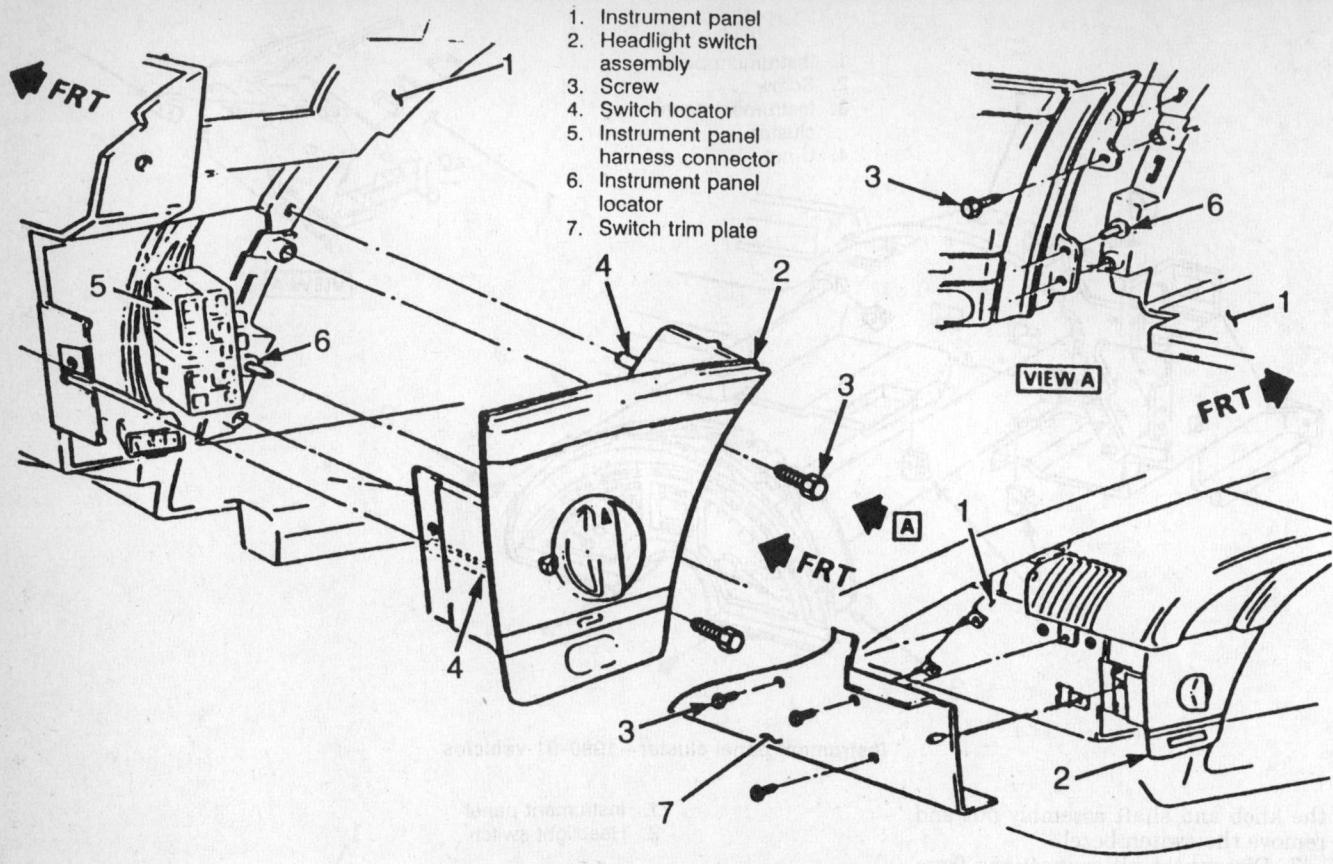

1. Instrument panel
2. Headlight switch assembly
3. Screw
4. Switch locator
5. Instrument panel harness connector
6. Instrument panel locator
7. Switch trim plate

VIEW A

Headlight switch assembly—1990–91 vehicles

15. Position the tool as in Step 4 and compress the plate far enough to allow the C-ring to be installed.

16. Remove the tool. Install the plastic C-ring retainer.

17. Install the column/dash trim cover. Install the steering wheel, then connect the battery negative cable.

Ignition Switch

REMOVAL & INSTALLATION

1. Disconnect the negative battery terminal.

2. Loosen the retaining screws on the steering column.

3. Remove the column to instrument panel trim plates and attaching nuts.

4. Lower the steering column.

NOTE: Be sure the steering column is supported at all times in order to prevent damage to the column.

5. Disconnect the switch wire connectors.

6. Remove the switch attaching screws and remove the switch.
To install:

7. Move the key lock to the LOCK position.

8. Move the actuator rod hole in the switch to the LOCK position.

9. Install the switch with the rod in the hole.

10. Position and reassemble the steering column in reverse of the disassembly procedure.

Ignition Lock

REMOVAL & INSTALLATION

1. Disconnect the negative battery cable.

2. Remove the steering wheel.

3. Remove the rubber sleeve bumper from the steering shaft.

4. Using an appropriate tool, remove the plastic retainer.

5. Using a spring compressor, compress the upper steering shaft spring and remove the C-ring. Release the steering shaft lock plate, the horn contact carrier and the upper steering shaft preload spring.

6. Remove the 4 screws which hold the upper mounting bracket and then remove the bracket.

7. Slide the harness connector out of the bracket on the steering column. Tape the upper part of the harness and connector.

8. Disconnect the hazard button and position the shift bowl in park.

9. Remove the turn signal lever from the column.

10. If equipped with cruise control, remove the harness protector from the harness. Attach a piece of wire to the switch harness connector. Before removing the turn signal lever, loop a piece of wire and insert it into the turn signal lever opening. Use the wire to pull the cruise control harness out through the opening. Pull the rest of the harness up through and out of the column.

11. Remove the guide wire from the connector and secure the wire to the column.

12. Remove the turn signal lever.

13. Pull the turn signal switch up until the end connector is within the shift bowl.

14. Remove the hazard flasher lever. Allow the switch to hang.

15. Place the ignition key in the RUN position.

16. Depress the center of the lock cylinder retaining tab with a suitable tool and then remove the lock cylinder.

17. On some vehicles, it will be necessary to cut and splice an electrical wire which is a part of the lock cylinder.
To install:

18. Install the cylinder assembly wir-

ing harness through the lock housing cover, column housing and the column housing shroud.

19. Install lock cylinder, then the retaining screw.

20. Position the key in the **RUN** position.

21. Install the buzzer switch and clip, then connect the wiring harness.

22. Install wiring protector, then the turn signal switch.

23. Install the upper bearing race seat, spring, shaft lock and carrier assembly.

24. Using a suitable tool, depress shaft and install lock retainer.

25. Install the snapring retainer, spacer, bumper and bumper spacer.

26. Install the turn signal lever to the switch actuator pivot assembly.

27. Install the steering wheel.

28. Install the instrument panel sound insulator, if removed.

29. Connect the battery negative cable.

Stoplight Switch

ADJUSTMENT

NOTE: Do not use excessive **force while adjusting the stoplight switch as damage to the power booster may occur.**

Due to the mounting of the switch, it provides for automatic adjustment when the brake pedal is manually returned to its mechanical stop.

Pull the brake pedal fully rearward against the pedal stop until the clicking sounds cannot be heard. The switch will move into the retainer providing proper adjustment. Release the brake pedal and repeat, to ensure no clicking sounds remain.

REMOVAL & INSTALLATION

1. Disconnect the battery negative cable.

2. Disconnect electrical connector from switch.

3. Remove the retainer from the switch, then the switch from the vehicle.

4. Reverse procedure to install. Connect the battery negative cable.

Clutch Switch

REMOVAL & INSTALLATION

1. Disconnect the negative battery cable.

2. Remove the hush pad from under the dash panel.

3. Remove the bolt and switch from the clutch bracket and rotate the switch slightly so the actuating rod retainer can be pulled from the hole of the clutch pedal.

To install:

4. Place a new switch in position so the actuating rod retainer is in line with the hole in the clutch pedal and reinstall the bolt.

5. Connect the electrical connector to the switch and depress the clutch pedal fully to the floor to adjust the switch.

6. Connect the battery negative cable.

Neutral Safety Switch

ADJUSTMENT

1. Disconnect battery negative cable.

2. Remove shifter knob assembly.

3. Remove console.

4. Remove neutral switch mounting bolts, then the switch.

5. Position the shift control lever in **N.**

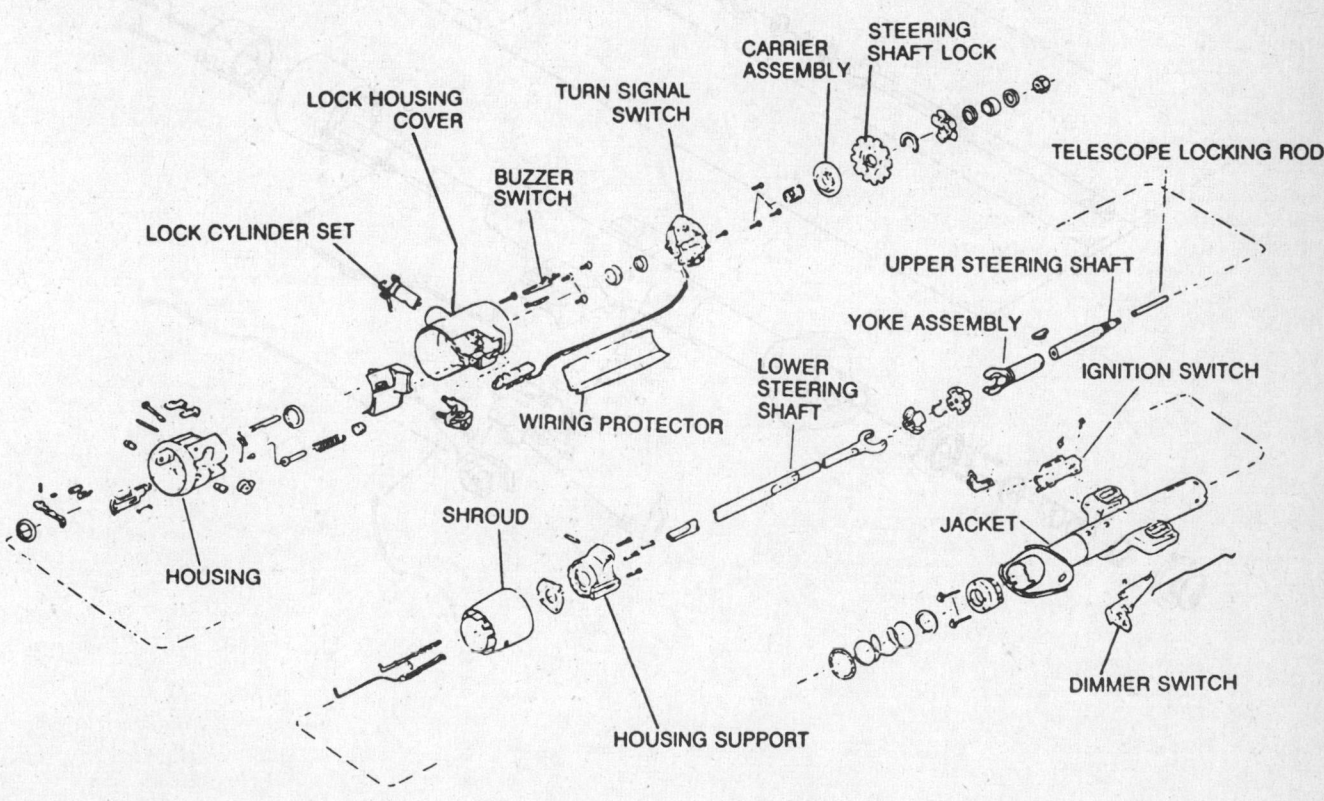

Exploded view of steering column—1987–89 vehicles

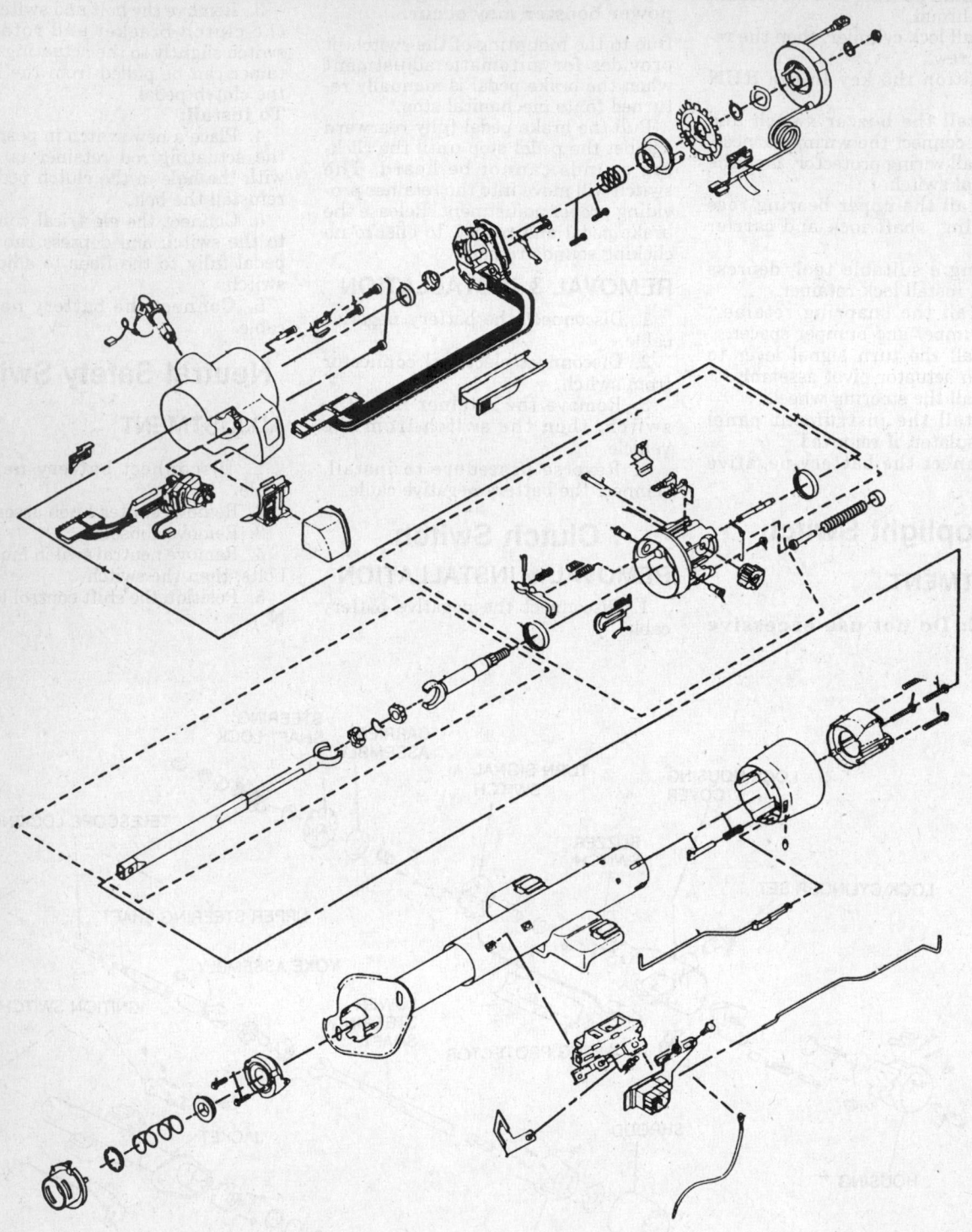

Exloded view of steering column—1990–91 vehicles

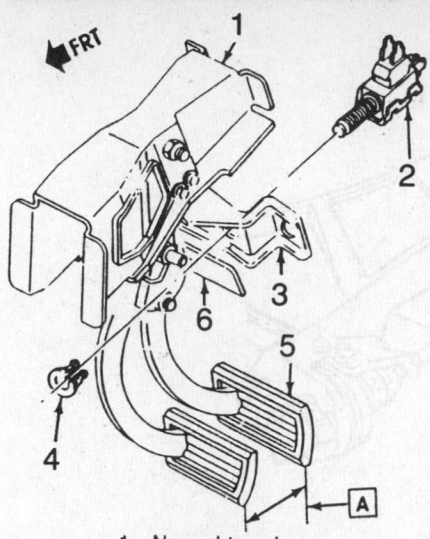

1. Normal travel
2. Brake pedal bracket
3. Stoplight switch
4. Retainer
5. Brake pedal
6. Actuator

Stoplight switch adjustemnt

6. Align tang on switch with the tang slot on the shift control.

7. Insert gauge pin $^3/_{32}$ in. (2.34mm) in service adjustment hole and rotate switch until pin drops to a depth of $^{19}/_{32}$ inch (15mm).

8. Install switch mounting bolts and torque to 26 inch lbs. (3 Nm).

9. Install console and shifter knob assembly. Connect battery negative cable.

REMOVAL & INSTALLATION

NOTE: This procedure applies only to a new switch being installed.

1. Disconnect battery ground cable.
2. Remove shifter knob assembly.
3. Remove console.
4. Remove neutral switch mounting bolts, then the switch.

To install:

5. Position shifter lever in the **N** position.

6. Insert carrier tang on the new switch in slot on shifter. Torque switch mounting bolts to 26 inch lbs. (3 Nm).

NOTE: If holes do not align with shifter control, check that the shifter control lever is in N, do not rotate switch. The switch is pinned in the N position. If switch was rotated and the pin broken, switch adjustment must be performed.

7. Move shift control lever out of the **N** position to shear the pin. Check that engine starts only in the **P** or **N** positions. If engine starts in any other position, readjust neutral switch.

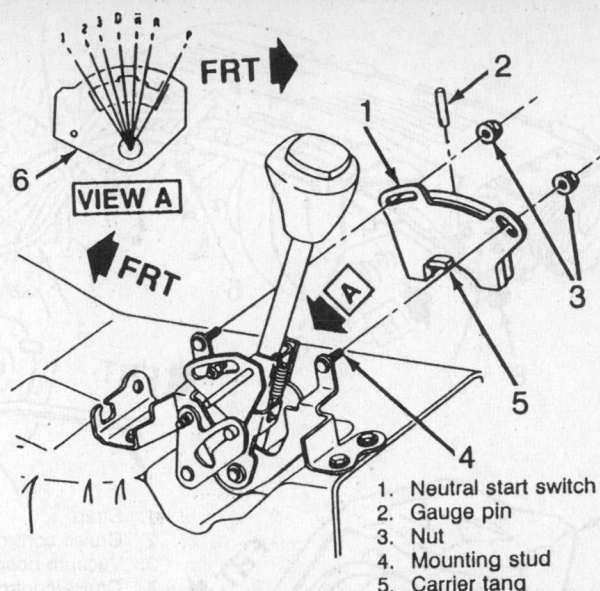

1. Neutral start switch
2. Gauge pin
3. Nut
4. Mounting stud
5. Carrier tang
6. Detent plate

Neutral switch

8. Install console and shifter knob assembly.

9. Connect battery negative cable.

Fuses, Circuit Breakers and Relays

LOCATION

Fusible Links

Fusible links, located at the jump start junction block, are used to prevent major wire harness damage in the event of a short circuit or an overload condition in the wiring circuits which are normally not fused, due to carrying high amperage loads or because of their location within the wiring harness. Each fusible link is of a fixed value for a specific electrical load and should a link fail, the cause of the failure must be determined and repaired prior to installing a new fusible link of the same value.

Circuit Breakers

Various circuit breakers are located in the fuse block.

Fuse Block

The fuse block assembly is located behind the right side of the instrument panel.

Relays

Listed below are the following relays that are mounted on the instrument panel harness.

Power Antenna Relay (1987–89 Coupe)—located in the left hand rear of cargo compartment, on the end panel.

Power Antenna Relay (Convertible and 1990–91 Coupe)—located on the left hand of the cargo compartment above the rear of the wheel house.

Anti-Lock Brake Module Relay—located under the left hand side of the cargo compartment, behind the driver's seat.

Amplifier Relay—located behind the center of the instrument panel, to the right of the radio.

Auxiliary Engine Cooling Fan Relay—located in the left rear corner of the engine compartment.

Fuel Pump Relay (1987–89)—located to the right of the master cylinder.

Fuel Pump Relay (1990–91)—located below right hand side of the instrument panel.

ABS Control Module Relay—located under the corner of the rear floor, in storage compartment.

Computers

LOCATION

Electronic Control Module (1987–89)—located behind the right side of the dash.

Electronic Control Module (1990–91)—located in the engine compartment, near battery.

ABS Control Module—located under the left corner of rear floor, in storage compartment.

Central Control Module (CCM, 1990–91)—located behind the middle of the instrument panel.

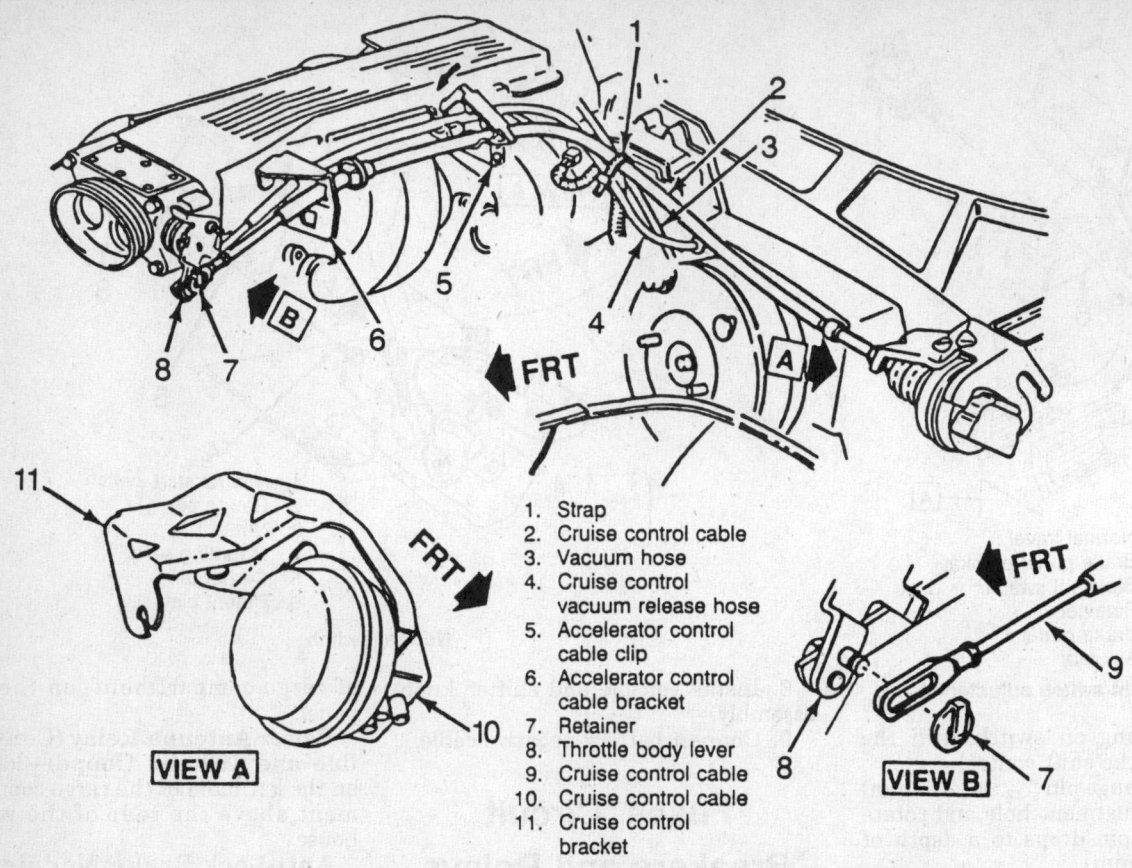

1. Strap
2. Cruise control cable
3. Vacuum hose
4. Cruise control vacuum release hose
5. Accelerator control cable clip
6. Accelerator control cable bracket
7. Retainer
8. Throttle body lever
9. Cruise control cable
10. Cruise control cable
11. Cruise control bracket

Cruise control cable routing and adjustment—1990–91 Except ZR-1

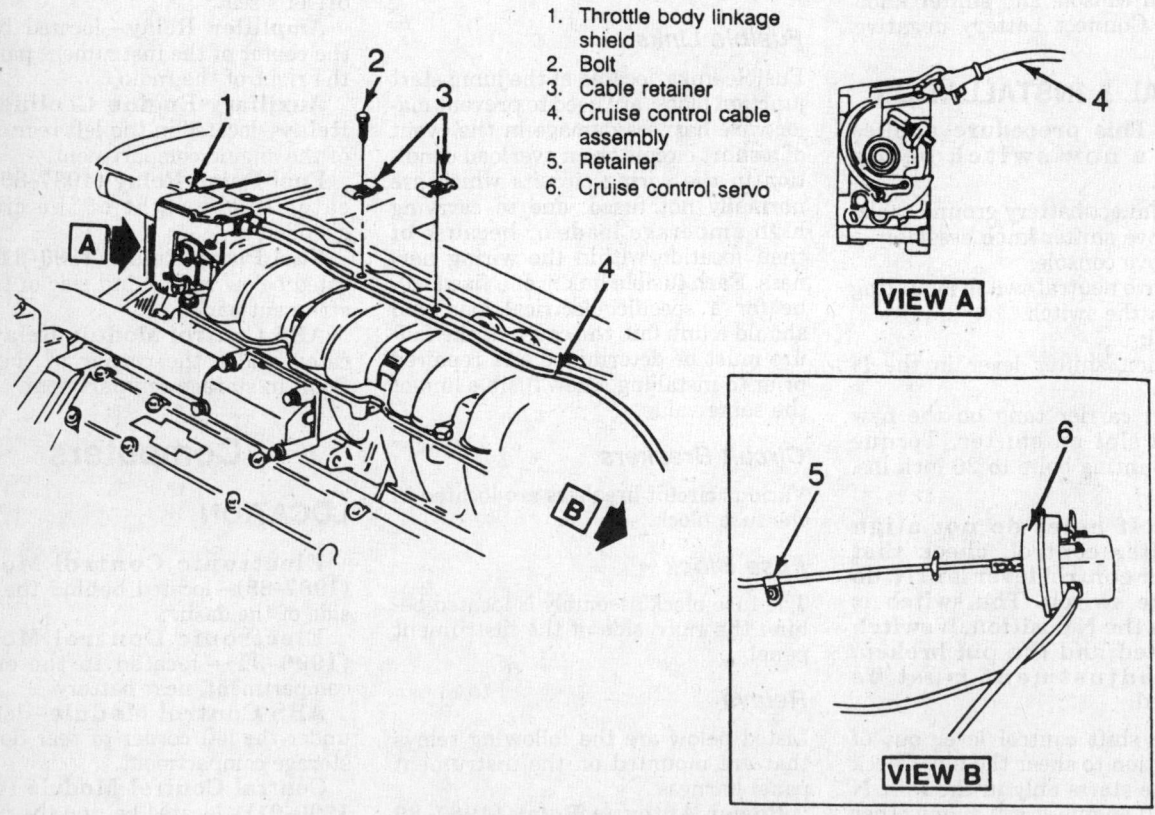

1. Throttle body linkage shield
2. Bolt
3. Cable retainer
4. Cruise control cable assembly
5. Retainer
6. Cruise control servo

Cruise control cable routing and adjustment—1990–91 ZR-1

Select Ride Control Module—located under left corner of rear floor, in storage compartment.

Electronic Spark Control Module—located on the right side of air conditioning heater blower housing.

Flashers

LOCATION

Turn Signal—located behind the right side of the dash panel, near the fuse panel.

Hazard Flasher—located in the convenience center.

Cruise Control

ADJUSTMENT

Servo Linkage

1987–89 VEHICLES

1. With the cable installed to the cable bracket and throttle lever, install the cable to the clip and servo bracket using the first ball on the servo chain.
2. Connect the servo chain to the cable assembly connector leaving a space of 4 ball links.
3. With the ignition **OFF**, close the throttle completely.
4. Adjust the cable jam nuts until the cable sleeve at the throttle lever is tight but not holding the throttle open.
5. Tighten the jam nuts.
6. Pull the servo boot over the washer on the cable.

1990–91 VEHICLES

1. With the cruise control cable installed in the cable clips and throttle lever, insert cable into servo bracket.
2. Pull servo assembly end of cable toward servo without moving the throttle lever.
3. If 1 out of the 5 holes in the servo assembly tab aligns with the cable pin, push pin through hole and connect pin to tab with retainer.
4. If the tab holes does not align with the pin, move the cable away from the servo assembly until the next closest tab hole aligns and connect the pin to the tab with the retainer.

ENGINE COOLING

Radiator

REMOVAL & INSTALLATION

1987–89 Vehicles

1. Disconnect battery negative cable.

---

2. Drain cooling system.
3. On 1989 vehicles, remove air cleaner and intake duct assembly, then disconnect MAF electrical connector.
4. Remove the upper radiator hose.
5. Remove the lower radiator hose.
6. Remove the radiator overflow hose.
7. Remove the air conditioning accumulator and position aside.
8. Disconnect transmission oil cooler line.
9. Disconnect cooling fan wires from the fan and fan shroud.
10. Remove the fan to gain access to the lower transmission cooler line. Remove the lower transmission cooler line.
11. On 1989, remove the power steering reservoir bracket bolts from the fan shroud and from the frame.
12. Remove the upper fan shroud attaching bolts.
13. Remove the radiator.

To install:
14. Install the radiator, shroud and retaining screws.
15. On 1989 vehicles, install the power steering reservoir bracket bolts at the shroud and frame.
16. Install the wiring harness and relay onto the shroud.
17. Connect the automatic transmission oil cooler line.
18. Install the air conditioning accumulator bracket.
19. Install cooling fan, if removed.
20. Install the radiator overflow hose, then the upper and lower radiator hoses.
21. Install the air cleaner and intake duct assembly.
22. Connect the MAF electrical connector.
23. Fill cooling system. Start engine and check for leaks, then connect the battery negative cable.

1990–91 Vehicles

1. Disconnect battery negative cable.
2. Remove radiator pressure cap.
3. Drain coolant into a suitable container.
4. Remove the air cleaner assembly.
5. On ZR-1, remove the radiator upper air deflector.
6. Disconnect the electrical connectors from the cooling fan relays.
7. Remove the bolts attaching the accumulator bracket to the radiator upper support.
8. Remove the fan shroud to upper support attaching bolts.
9. Remove the rubber access plug from the top of the radiator.
10. Remove the radiator air bleed hose clamp, then the hose.
11. Remove the upper bolts attach-

---

ing the upper support to the front side member.
12. On ZR-1, proceed as follows:
   a. Remove seal retainers and seal from oil cooler and air conditioning line.
   b. Remove AIR pump assembly and position aside.
   c. Remove the bolt attaching the AIR pump bracket at the rear and loosen the front bolt.
   d. Remove the AIR pump intake duct.
13. Remove screws attaching the upper support to the lower support. Remove upper support.
14. Remove the radiator upper and lower hose clamps, then the hoses.
15. On all Except ZR-1, disconnect oil cooler lines from the radiator.
16. Remove the radiator from the vehicle.

To install:
17. Install radiator.
18. Connect transmission cooler lines to the radiator, if equipped.
19. Install the upper and lower radiator hoses.
20. Install upper support. Torque the upper support to front side member nuts and bolts to 18 ft. lbs. (25 Nm).
21. On ZR-1 vehicles, install the AIR pump duct, bolt retaining the bracket and the AIR pump.
22. Connect cooling fan electrical connectors.
23. Install fan shroud to upper support attaching bolts. Torque bolts to 80 inch lbs.
24. Install accumulator bracket to upper support attaching bolts. Torque bolts to 80 inch. lbs. (9 Nm).
25. On ZR-1 vehicles, install retainers to oil cooler/air conditioning line seal an connect cooler line. Torque cooler line bolt to 89 inch lbs. (10 Nm).
26. Connect the air bleed hoses.
27. Install access plug, then the air cleaner.
28. Fill cooling system. Connect battery negative cable, then start engine and check for leaks.

Electric Cooling Fans

REMOVAL & INSTALLATION

1987–89 Vehicles

1. Disconnect battery negative cable.
2. Remove the air cleaner and the intake air duct assembly.
3. Disconnect the MAF sensor and cooling fan electrical connector.
4. Remove fan assembly upper screws. Raise and support vehicle.
5. Remove cooling fan lower mounting screws, then remove engine cooling fan.

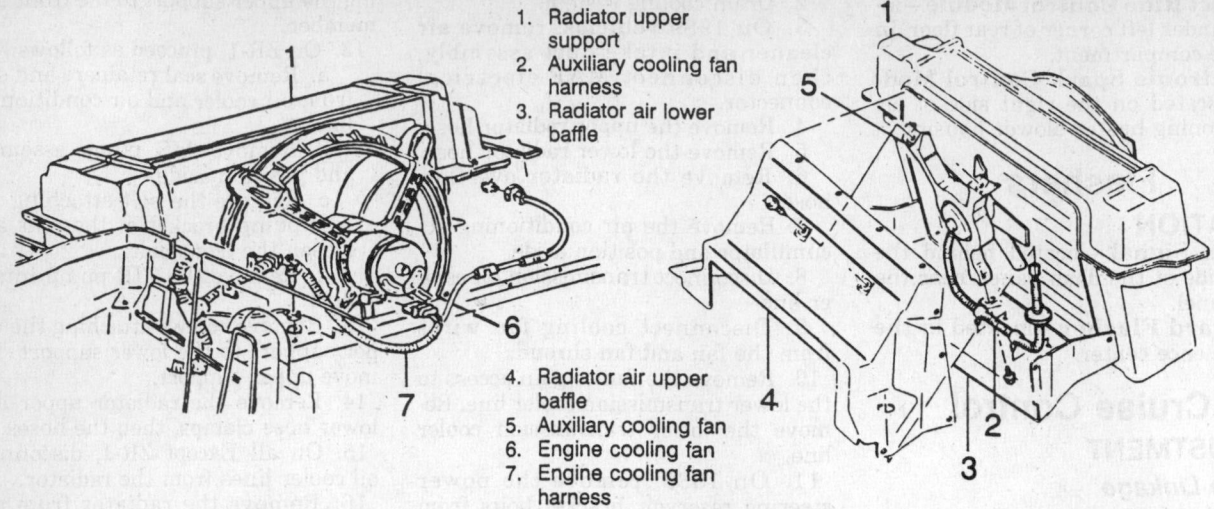

1. Radiator upper support
2. Auxiliary cooling fan harness
3. Radiator air lower baffle
4. Radiator air upper baffle
5. Auxiliary cooling fan
6. Engine cooling fan
7. Engine cooling fan harness

Cooling fan—1987–89 vehicles

6. Remove auxiliary cooling fan upper and lower mounting bolts.

7. Disconnect electrical connector and remove auxiliary fan from vehicle.

8. Reverse procedure to install. Connect the battery negative cable.

1990–91 Vehicles

1. Disconnect battery negative cable.

2. Remove air intake duct assembly.

3. Remove the power steering pump reservoir bracket to front crossmember bolts and position aside.

4. Disconnect the electrical connector from the primary cooling fan.

5. Remove the screws attaching the fan motor to the motor support.

6. Remove the bolts attaching the primary fan assembly to the fan shroud.

7. Remove the end cap from the power steering pump pulley.

8. Remove the primary fan assembly from the vehicle.

9. Remove the auxiliary fan upper right mounting bolt.

10. Raise and support the vehicle.

11. Disconnect auxiliary cooling fan electrical connector.

12. Remove remaining auxiliary cooling fan mounting bolts, then remove auxiliary cooling fan from the vehicle.

To install:

13. Install primary and secondary cooling fans. Torque all bolts to 89 inch lbs. (10 Nm).

14. Connect cooling fan electrical connectors.

15. Install air conditioning discharge line bolt, then the end cap on the power steering pump pulley.

16. Connect all radiator hoses, if disconnected.

17. Connect battery negative cable.

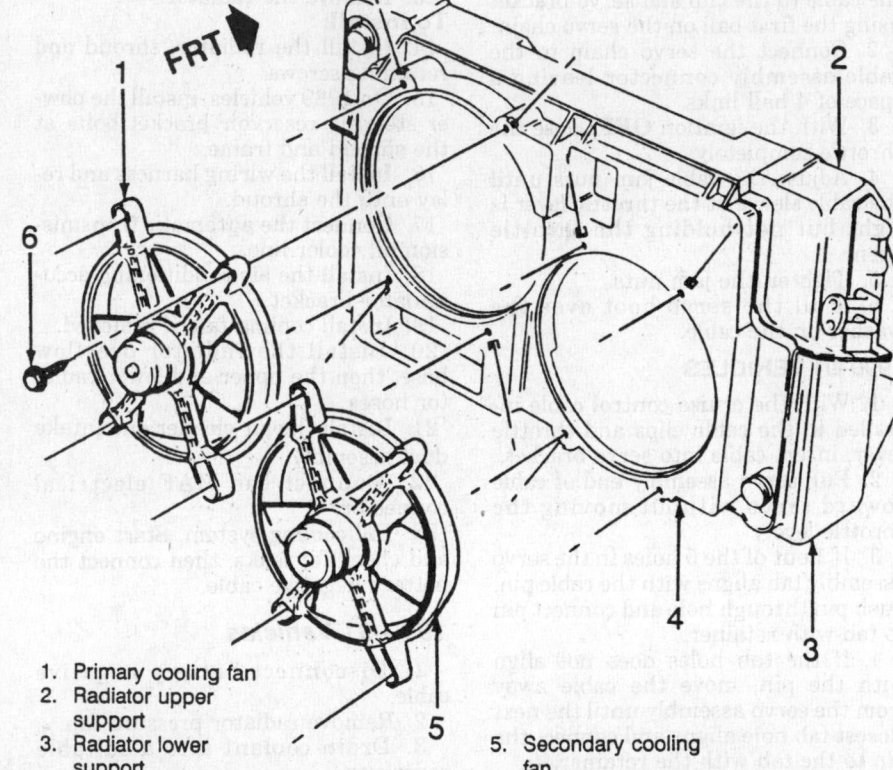

1. Primary cooling fan
2. Radiator upper support
3. Radiator lower support
4. Fan shroud
5. Secondary cooling fan
6. Screw

Cooling fan—1990–91 vehicles

Fill cooling system. Start engine and check for leaks.

Heater Core

REMOVAL & INSTALLATION

1987–89 Vehicles

1. Disconnect the negative battery cable.

2. Drain the cooling system.

3. Remove the instrument cluster bezel including the tilt wheel lever and instrument panel pad.

4. Remove the air conditioning distributor duct and disconnect the flex hose.

5. Remove the right side hush panel.

6. Remove the side window defroster flex hose.

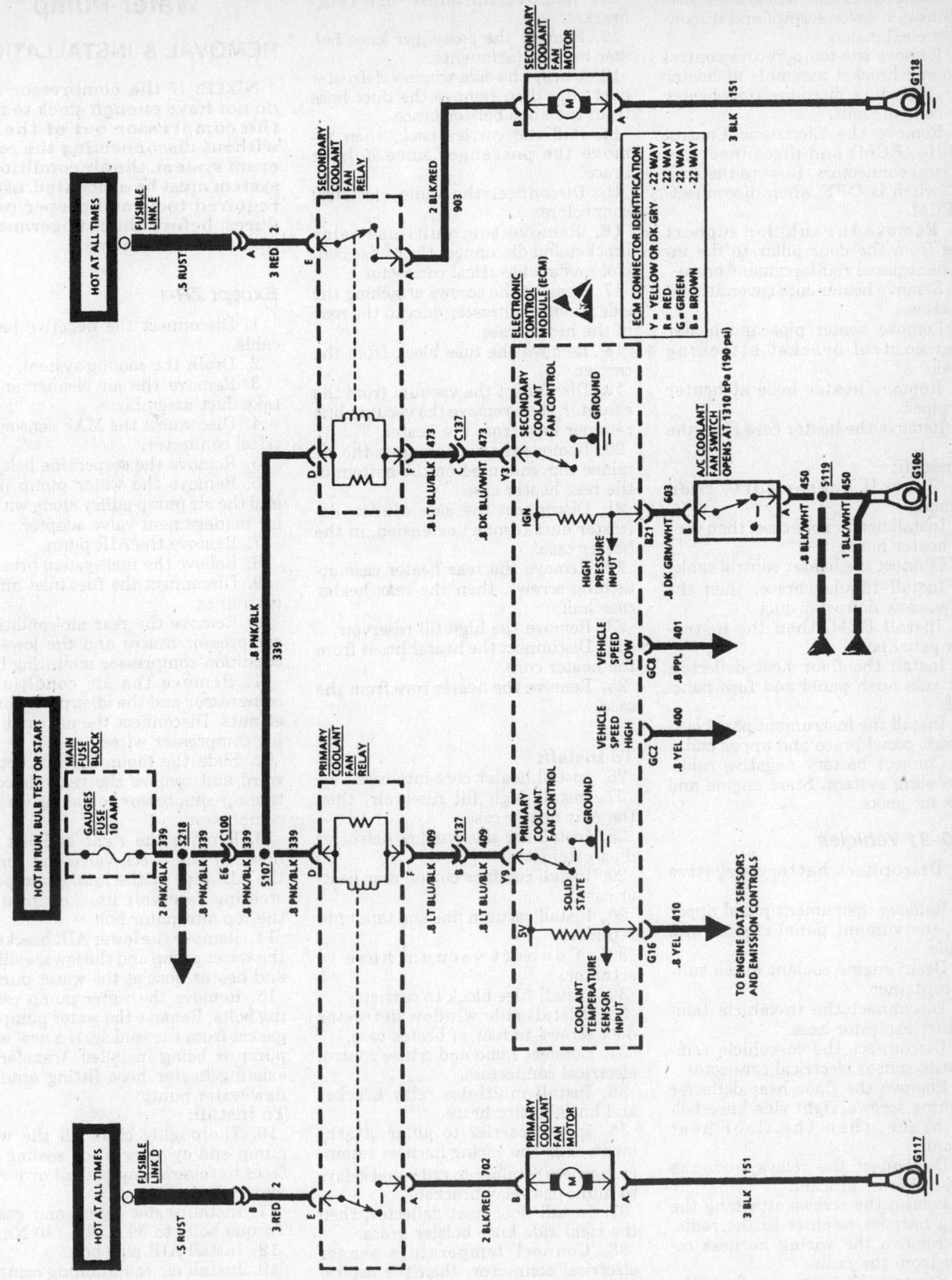

Cooling fan schematic—1990–91

7. Remove the side window defroster to heater cover screws and disconnect the extension.

8. Remove the temperature control cable and bracket assembly at heater cover including disconnecting heater door control shaft.

9. Remove the Electronic Control Module (ECM) and disconnect the electrical connectors. Be sure the ignition switch is **OFF** when disconnecting ECM.

10. Remove the tubular support brace from the door pillar to the instrument panel reinforcement brace.

11. Remove heater core cover attaching screws.

12. Remove heater pipe and heater water control bracket attaching screws.

13. Remove heater hose at heater core pipes.

14. Remove the heater core from the case.

To install:

15. Install heater core, then retainers.

16. Install heater core case, then connect heater hoses.

17. Connect the heater control cable.

18. Install tubular brace, then the side window defroster duct.

19. Install ECM, then the instrument panel pad.

20. Install the floor heat deflector, right side hush panel and fuse panel bezel.

21. Install the instrument panel outlet duct, panel brace and upper pad.

22. Connect battery negative cable. Fill cooling system. Start engine and check for leaks.

1990–91 Vehicles

1. Disconnect battery negative cable.

2. Remove instrument panel upper trim, instrument panel cluster and console.

3. Drain engine coolant into a suitable container.

4. Disconnect the in-vehicle temperature aspirator hose.

5. Disconnect the in-vehicle temperature sensor electrical connector.

6. Remove the floor heat deflector attaching screws, right side knee bolster brace, then the floor heat deflector.

7. Disconnect the relays from the multi-use relay bracket.

8. Loosen the screws attaching the wiring harness retainer to the radio, then remove the wiring harness retainer from the radio.

9. Remove the harnesses from the wiring harness retainer, then remove the wiring harness retainer.

10. Remove the carrier nuts from the right side pillar.

11. Remove the multi-use relay bracket.

12. Remove the passenger knee bolster brace attachments.

13. Unclip the side window defroster duct clip, then remove the duct hose from the knee bolster brace.

14. Pull the carrier back, then remove the passenger knee bolster brace.

15. Disconnect the radio electrical connectors.

16. Remove the multi-use relay bracket and disconnect the cruise control module electrical connector.

17. Remove the screws attaching the side window defroster duct to the rear of the heater case.

18. Remove the fuse block from the carrier.

19. Disconnect the vacuum from the actuator, then remove the vacuum line retainer tape from the heater.

20. Remove the harness from the retainer clip, mounted on the bottom of the rear heater case.

21. Disconnect the side window defroster duct (center) extension, in the heater case.

22. Remove the rear heater case attaching screws, then the rear heater case half.

23. Remove the high fill reservoir.

24. Disconnect the heater hoses from the heater core.

25. Remove the heater core from the case.

To install:

26. Install heater core into case.

27. Install high fill reservoir, then the rear heater case.

28. Install the side window defroster duct extension.

29. Install retainer clip on rear heater case.

30. Install vacuum line and tape onto retainer.

31. Connect vacuum hose to actuator.

32. Install fuse block to carrier.

33. Install side window defroster duct screws to rear of heater case.

34. Connect radio and cruise control electrical connectors.

35. Install multi-use relay bracket and knee bolster brace.

36. Install carrier to pillar attachment, then the wiring harness retainer, harness retainer to radio and relays to multi-use relay bracket.

37. Install floor heat deflector, then the right side knee bolster brace.

38. Connect temperature sensor electrical connector, then the aspirator hose.

39. Install instrument panel pad. Fill cooling system and connect battery negative cable. Start engine and check for leaks.

Water Pump

REMOVAL & INSTALLATION

NOTE: If the compressor lines do not have enough slack to move the compressor out of the way without disconnecting the refrigerant system, the air conditioning system must be evacuated, use the required tools and proper procedures, before the refrigerant system are disconnected.

Except ZR-1

1. Disconnect the negative battery cable.

2. Drain the cooling system.

3. Remove the air cleaner and intake duct assembly.

4. Disconnect the MAF sensor electrical connector.

5. Remove the serpentine belt.

6. Remove the water pump pulley and the air pump pulley along with the air management valve adapter.

7. Remove the AIR pump.

8. Relieve the fuel system pressure.

9. Disconnect the fuel inlet and return lines.

10. Remove the rear air conditioner compressor braces and the lower air condition compressor mounting bolt.

11. Remove the air conditioning compressor and the idler pulley bracket nuts. Disconnect the air conditioning compressor wires.

12. Slide the mounting bracket forward and remove the rear air conditioning compressor bolt along with the compressor.

13. Remove the right and left AIR hoses at the check valve and remove the AIR pipe at the intake and power steering reservoir bracket including the top alternator bolt.

14. Remove the lower AIR bracket on the water pump and the lower radiator and heater hose at the water pump.

15. Remove the water pump retaining bolts. Remove the water pump and gasket from the vehicle. If a new water pump is being installed, transfer the existing heater hose fitting onto the new water pump.

To install:

16. Thoroughly clean all the water pump and cylinder block sealing surfaces to remove any sealant or foreign material.

17. Install water pump and gasket. Torque bolts to 30 ft. lbs. (40 Nm).

18. Install AIR pipe bolt.

19. Install air conditioning compressor bracket mounting bolt.

20. Install radiator lower hose, then the AIR bracket bolts.

21. Connect fuel lines, then install belt tensioner bolt.

22. Install the AIR pipe and control valve attaching bolt.

23. Connect electrical connector at control valve, then upper hose onto AIR control valve.

24. Install cover onto AIR control valve, then the AIR pump attaching bolts.

25. Install the AIR pump brace bolt. Torque bolt to 25 ft. lbs. (33 Nm).

26. Install air conditioning compressor mounting bolts.

27. Install the pulley and damper. Torque bolts to 22 ft. lbs. (29 Nm).

28. Install serpentine belt, then the air cleaner and intake duct assembly.

29. Connect battery negative cable and fill cooling system. Start engine and check for leaks.

ZR-1

1. Disconnect the battery negative cable.

2. Drain engine coolant into a suitable container.

3. Disconnect the air intake duct.

4. Remove the screws attaching the throttle body extension to the throttle body, then remove the throttle body extension and gasket.

5. Remove clamps and hoses from the coolant outlets, radiator inlet and inlet pipe.

6. Remove the inlet pipe assembly and hose from the vehicle.

7. Loosen the coolant pump pulley attaching bolts, then rotate the belt tensioner.

8. Remove the bolts from the pulley, then the pulley from the vehicle.

9. Release the belt tensioner, then remove the belt from the vehicle.

10. Remove the water pump hose clamp, then the hose from the water pump.

11. Remove the alternator lower bracket mounting bolts, then remove the bracket from the vehicle.

12. Remove the water pump attaching bolts, bolt attaching the air conditioning compressor to the water pump, then remove the water pump from the vehicle.

To install:

13. Clean pump and front cover sealing surfaces.

14. Install water pump, gasket and bolts, finger tight only.

15. Install bolt attaching air conditioning compressor to pump.

16. Torque air conditioning compressor bolt and water pump attaching bolts to 20 ft. lbs. (26 Nm).

17. Install engine hose.

18. Install alternator bolts. Apply Loctite to bolt threads. Torque alternator mounting bolts to 39 ft. lbs. (52 Nm) and bracket bolts to 20 ft. lbs. (26 Nm).

19. Install belt tensioner. Torque belt tensioner bolt to 45 ft. lbs. (60 Nm).

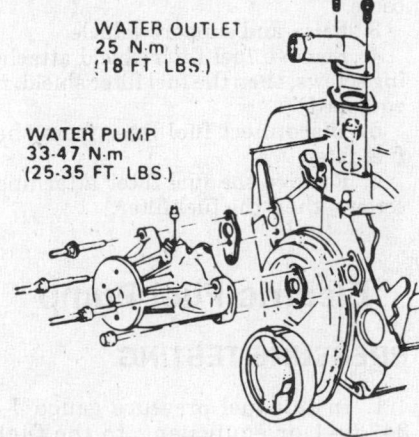

WATER OUTLET
25 N·m
(18 FT. LBS.)

WATER PUMP
33-47 N·m
(25-35 FT. LBS.)

Water pump assembly—Except ZR-1

20. Install serpentine belt. Torque water pump pulley bolts to 89 inch lbs. (10 Nm).

21. Install water pump hose and inlet pipe assembly.

22. Install throttle body extension and gasket. Torque bolts to 53 inch lbs. (6 Nm).

23. Install air intake duct, then fill cooling system.

24. Connect battery negative cable. Start engine and check for leaks.

Thermostat

REMOVAL & INSTALLATION

Except ZR-1

1. Disconnect the battery negative cable.

2. Drain engine coolant into a suitable container.

3. Remove the air cleaner and intake duct assembly, then disconnect the radiator upper hose from the outlet.

4. Remove the coolant hose from the throttle body.

5. Disconnect EGR electrical connector and vacuum harness from the EGR solenoid.

6. Remove the thermostat housing attaching bolts, then the thermostat.

7. Reverse procedure to install. Connect battery negative cable and torque thermostat housing mounting bolts to 25 ft. lbs. (34 Nm).

ZR-1

1. Disconnect battery negative cable.

2. Drain engine coolant into a suitable container.

3. Raise and support vehicle.

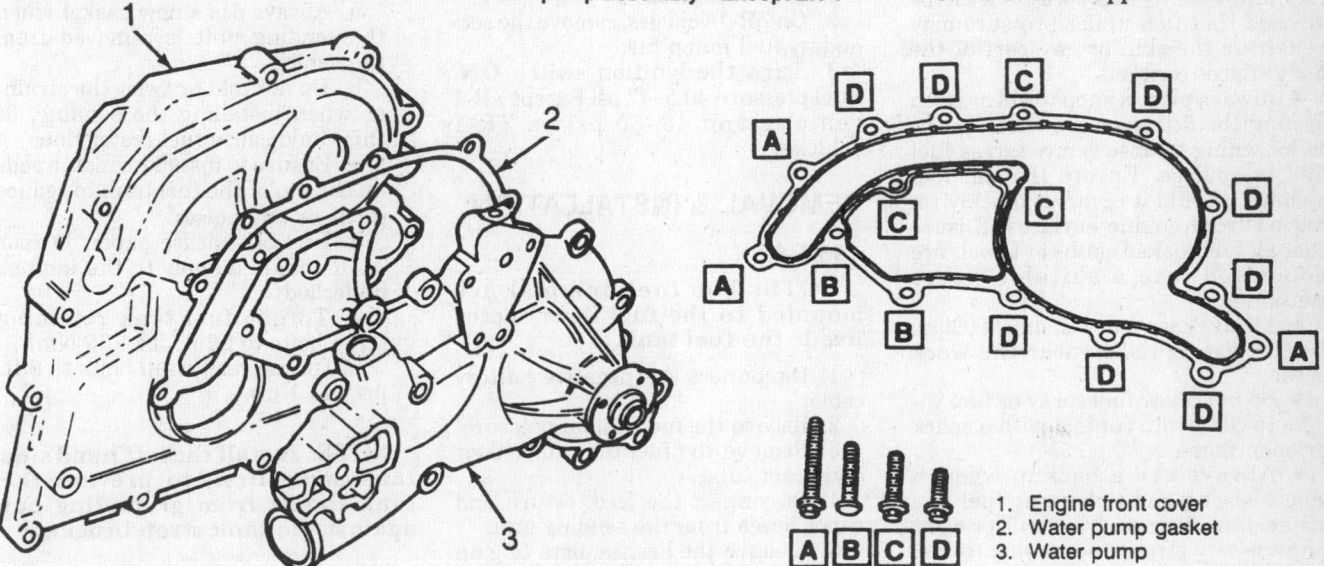

1. Engine front cover
2. Water pump gasket
3. Water pump

Water pump assembly—ZR-1

4. Remove thermostat housing attaching bolts.

5. Loosen the bolts attaching the housing assembly bracket to the front side member.

6. Remove the thermostat and gasket from housing.

7. Reverse procedure to install. Connect battery negative cable and torque thermostat housing bolts and bracket to front side member bolts to 18 ft. lbs. (25 Nm).

FUEL SYSTEM

Fuel System Service Precautions

Safety is the most important factor when performing not only fuel system maintenance but any type of maintenance. Failure to conduct maintenance and repairs in a safe manner may result in serious personal injury or death. Maintenance and testing of the vehicle's fuel system components can be accomplished safely and effectively by adhering to the following rules and guidelines.

• To avoid the possibility of fire and personal injury, always disconnect the negative battery cable unless the repair or test procedure requires that battery voltage be applied.

• Always relieve the fuel system pressure prior to disconnecting any fuel system component (injector, fuel rail, pressure regulator, etc.), fitting or fuel line connection. Exercise extreme caution whenever relieving fuel system pressure to avoid exposing skin, face and eyes to fuel spray. Please be advised that fuel under pressure may penetrate the skin or any part of the body that it contacts.

• Always place a shop towel or cloth around the fitting or connection prior to loosening to absorb any excess fuel due to spillage. Ensure that all fuel spillage (should it occur) is quickly removed from engine surfaces. Ensure that all fuel soaked cloths or towels are deposited into a suitable waste container.

• Always keep a dry chemical (Class B) fire extinguisher near the work area.

• Do not allow fuel spray or fuel vapors to come into contact with a spark or open flame.

• Always use a backup wrench when loosing and tightening fuel line connection fittings. This will prevent unnecessary stress and torsion to fuel line piping. Always follow the proper torque specifications.

• Always replace worn fuel fitting O-rings with new. Do not substitute fuel hose or equivalent where fuel pipe is installed.

RELIEVING FUEL SYSTEM PRESSURE

1. Disconnect the negative battery cable.

2. Loosen the fuel filler cap to relieve the tank pressure.

3. Connect fuel gauge J–34730–1 or equivalent, to the fuel pressure tap.

4. Wrap a shop towel around the fitting while connecting the gauge to catch any fuel spray.

5. Install a bleed hose into a suitable container, then open the valve to bleed the fuel system pressure.

Fuel Filter

REMOVAL & INSTALLATION

1. Relieve fuel system pressure.

2. Disconnect battery negative cable.

3. Raise and support vehicle.

4. Remove fuel filter shield attaching screws, then the fuel filter shield, if equipped.

5. Disconnect fuel lines from the fuel filter.

6. Remove the fuel filter attaching screws, then the fuel filter.

Electric Fuel Pump

PRESSURE TESTING

1. Install fuel pressure gauge J–34730–1 or equivalent, to the fuel pressure connection.

2. On ZR-1 vehicles, remove the secondary fuel pump fuse.

3. Turn the ignition switch **ON**. Fuel pressure 40.5–47 psi Except ZR-1 vehicles and 48–55 psi on ZR-1 vehicles.

REMOVAL & INSTALLATION

1987–89

NOTE: The fuel pump(s) are mounted to the fuel lever meter inside the fuel tank.

1. Disconnect the negative battery cable.

2. Relieve the fuel system pressure.

3. Remove the fuel tank filler door and drain tube.

4. Disconnect the feed, return and vapor hoses from the sending unit.

5. Remove the license plate to gain access for removal of the 2 bolts securing the fascia to impact bar.

6. Raise the vehicle and support it safely.

7. Remove the spare tire and carrier from the frame.

8. Disconnect the intermediate exhaust pipe at the converter. Remove the intermediate pipe and mufflers as an assembly from the vehicle.

9. Remove both rear inner fender braces at the frame.

10. Remove both rear inner fender panels.

11. Remove the antenna ground strap and clip.

12. Disconnect the fuel vapor pipe from the left hand fuel tank strap.

13. Disconnect the fuel tank cables from the rear stabilizer shaft brackets.

14. Remove the screws securing the bottom edge of the fascia to the energy absorber pad.

15. Remove all rear lamps.

16. Disconnect each side of the fascia from the horizontal body retainer.

17. Disconnect the right and left vertical retainers securing the fascia to the body.

18. Remove the 6 frame bolts and loosen the 2 front frame bolts.

19. Remove the front frame bolts. Pull the tank and frame assembly to the rear pushing the cover outward and letting the rear of the frame assembly down to clear the cover.

20. Remove the vapor hose from the vapor connector and remove the tank and frame assembly.

21. Remove the fuel sending unit and pump assembly by turning the cam lock ring counterclockwise. Lift the assembly from the fuel tank.

22. Disconnect the fuel pump from the fuel level sending unit.

To install:

23. Reverse the removal procedure, noting the following:

a. Always use a new gasket when the sending unit is removed from the vehicle.

b. Do not fold or twist the strainer when installing the sending, as this could cause fuel restriction.

c. Ensure to install insulator pads on the top of the fuel tank to reduce rattle or any noises.

d. Peel off release paper on rear insulators and apply to the tank or underbody.

e. Torque fuel tank retaining strap bolts to 26 ft. lbs. (35 Nm).

f. Torque rear strap bolts to 8 ft. lbs. (11 Nm).

NOTE: Install the left hand side tank strap first, to prevent the tank flange from grounding out against the tank strap bracket.

g. Connect the battery negative cable and check for leaks.

1990–91

NOTE: The fuel pump(s) are mounted on the sending unit, therefore, removal of the gas tank is unnecessary.

1. Disconnect the negative battery cable.
2. Relieve the fuel system pressure.
3. Remove the filler door bezel attaching screws, then the filler door bezel.
4. Remove gas cap, then lift the fuel tank filler neck housing and disconnect the drain hose.
5. Remove filler neck housing, then disconnect the fuel pipes and fuel vapor pipe.
6. Disconnect the sending unit electrical connector, remove the attaching bolts, then the sending unit assembly from the vehicle.
7. Reverse procedure to install. Connect the battery negative cable.

Fuel Injection

IDLE SPEED ADJUSTMENT

NOTE: The idle stop screw used to adjust the minimum engine idle speed is adjusted at the factory. The idle speed should only be adjusted if it is absolutely necessary. Prior to adjusting the idle speed, ensure the ignition timing is correct and the throttle body is clean around the throttle plates.

1. Using the proper tool, pierce the idle stop plug and remove it.
2. Leave the idle air control motor connected and ground the diagnostic lead. Turn the ignition to the **ON** position, but do not start the engine.
3. Wait 30 seconds, then disconnect the idle air control connector.
4. Remove the ground from the diagnostic lead and start the engine.
5. Allow the engine to go into the closed loop mode and adjust the idle screw to 450 rpm in **N**.
6. Turn the ignition **OFF** and reconnect the idle speed control connector.
7. Adjust the throttle position sensor as follows:
   a. With the ignition switch in the **ON** position, connect a scan tool or 3 jumper wires to the TPS.
   b. Adjust the TPS to obtain a reading from 0.46–0.62 volts.
8. Start the engine and check for proper idle operation.

Fuel Injector

REMOVAL & INSTALLATION

1. Relieve the fuel system pressure,

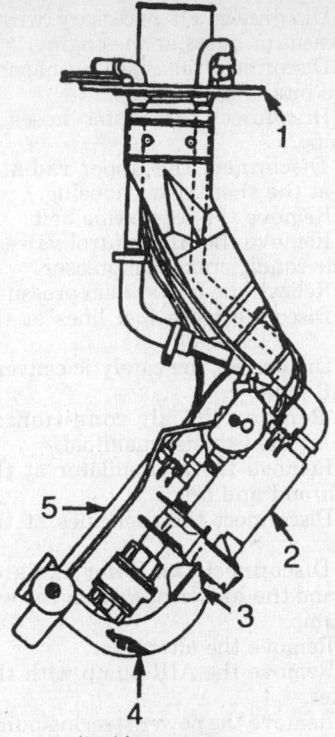

1. Fuel lever meter
2. Primary fuel pump
3. Primary fuel pump filter
4. Secondary fuel pump filter
5. Secondary fuel pump

Fuel pump assembly—1990–91 ZR-1

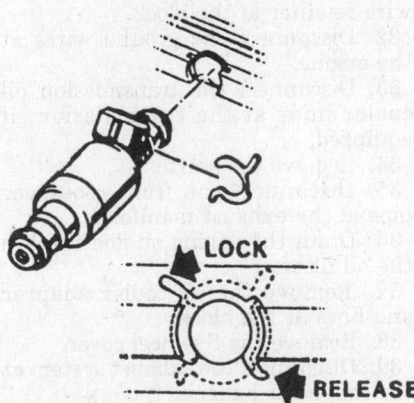

Injector removal—Except ZR-1

then disconnect the battery negative cable.
2. Remove the plenum, cold start valve line, if necessary, runners and cold start valve.
3. Disconnect the fuel lines and the fuel line connectors.
4. Loosen the fuel injector rail retaining bolts and raise the rail, with fuel injectors, upward and away from the manifold.
5. Except ZR-1 vehicles, rotate the injector retaining clips to the unlocked

Injector removal—ZR-1

position to release the injector. On ZR-1 vehicles, remove retaining clip. Withdraw the injector from the fuel rail opening.
6. Remove the O-ring seals from both ends of the injector. Discard and replace the seals.
7. Installation is the reverse of the removal procedure. Connect the battery negative cable.

EMISSION CONTROLS

Please refer to "Emission Control" in the Unit Repair section for system maintenance procedures. Due to the complex nature of modern electronic engine control systems, comprehensive diagnosis and testing procedures fall outside the confines of this repair manual. For complete information on diagnosis, testing and repair procedures concerning all modern engine and emission control systems, please refer to "Chilton's Guide to Electronic Engine Controls".

Emission Warning Lamps

RESETTING

The light is on the instrument panel and has the following functions:
It informs the driver that a problem has occurred and the vehicle should be serviced as soon as possible.
It displays trouble codes stored by the ECM.
It indicates Open Loop or Closed Loop operation.
The light will come ON with the key

ON and the engine not running. When the engine is started, the light will turn OFF. If the light remains ON, the self-diagnostic system has detected a problem. If the problem goes away, the light will go out in most cases after 10 seconds but a trouble code will remain stored in the ECM.

To clear the codes from the memory of the ECM, either to determine if the malfunction will occur again or because repair has been completed, the ECM power feed must be disconnected for at least 30 seconds.

Depending on how the vehicle is equipped, the ECM power feed can be disconnected at the positive battery terminal pigtail. The inline fuse holder that originates at the positive or the ECM fuse in the fuse block.

If the negative battery terminal is disconnected, other on-board memory data, such as pre-set radio tuning will also be lost.

ENGINE MECHANICAL

NOTE: Disconnecting the negative battery cable on some vehicles may interfere with the functions of the on board computer systems and may require the computer to undergo a relearning process, once the negative battery cable is reconnected.

Engine Assembly

REMOVAL & INSTALLATION

Except ZR-1

1. Mark the relationship between each hood hinge and the hood. Remove the hood.
2. Disconnect the negative battery cable and relieve fuel system pressure.
3. Drain the coolant.
4. Disconnect the throttle, TV and cruise control cables at the engine.
5. Disconnect the spark plug wires from the plugs. Remove the wires and distributor cap as an assembly.
6. Remove the distributor.
7. Remove the cowl screen. Remove the nut from the wiper motor arm.
8. Disconnect the wiper motor wires, remove the wiper motor cover and remove the wiper motor.
9. Remove the air intake duct with the MAF sensor.
10. Disconnect the brake booster vacuum hose.
11. Disconnect the canister hose at the PCV pipe.

12. Disconnect all necessary wiring and vacuum hoses at the engine.
13. Disconnect the injection harness at the intake manifold.
14. Disconnect the heater hoses at the pipe.
15. Disconnect the upper radiator hose at the thermostat housing.
16. Remove the serpentine belt.
17. Remove the AIR control valve at the air conditioning compressor.
18. Relieve the fuel system pressure.
19. Disconnect the fuel lines at the rail.
20. Disconnect the catalytic converter AIR pipe.
21. Remove the air conditioning brace at the exhaust manifold.
22. Remove the accumulator at the fan shroud and brace.
23. Disconnect the fuel lines at the block.
24. Disconnect the lower radiator hose and the heater hose from the water pump.
25. Remove the alternator.
26. Remove the AIR pump with the bracket.
27. Remove the power steering pump from the engine and wire it aside.
28. Remove the water pump pulley and the crankshaft pulley.
29. Raise the vehicle and support it safely.
30. Disconnect the wires at the oxygen, Electronic Spark Control (ESC) system harness and temperature sensors.
31. Remove the temperature sensor wire retainer at the block.
32. Disconnect the ground wires at the engine.
33. Disconnect the transmission oil cooler lines at the transmission, if equipped.
34. Remove the starter.
35. Disconnect the front crossover pipe at the exhaust manifolds.
36. Drain the engine oil and remove the oil filter.
37. Remove the oil cooler adapter and lines at the block.
38. Remove the flywheel cover.
39. Disconnect the exhaust system at the converter hanger.
40. Disconnect the clutch system, if equipped with a manual transmission.
41. Remove the engine mount through bolts and nuts.
42. Remove the transmission to engine bolts.
43. Lower the vehicle.
44. Support the transmission with a transmission jack.
45. Install a suitable lifting device and remove the engine from the vehicle.

To install:

46. Using a suitable lifting device, install the engine.

47. Remove the lifting device, then raise and support vehicle.
48. Support the transmission with a suitable jack.
49. Install the engine mount through bolts.
50. If equipped with automatic transmission, install the engine to transmission attaching bolts.
51. If equipped with manual transmission, install the clutch assembly.
52. Install the exhaust system, if removed.
53. Connect the oil cooler line at the oil pan.
54. Install the starter, then the transmission cooler lines at the flywheel cover.
55. Connect the catalytic converter AIR pipe at the manifold.
56. Connect the ground wire to the engine block.
57. Connect the temperature sensor, oxygen sensor and ESC electrical connectors.
58. Lower vehicle, then install the crankshaft pulley and water pump pulley.
59. Install the power steering pump, then the power steering pump reservoir at the fan shroud.
60. Install the alternator, then connect the heater hoses to the water pump.
61. Connect fuel lines to engine, then install the accumulator.
62. Install the air conditioning compressor bracket, then the brace.
63. Install the catalytic converter AIR pipe, then the AIR control valve.
64. Connect fuel lines at the fuel rail.
65. Install the serpentine belt, then the radiator upper hose.
66. Connect heater hoses, then the injector harness.
67. Connect all vacuum hoses and wires that were disconnect during removal.
68. Connect the canister hose to the PCV, then the brake booster hose.
69. Install the wiper motor and cowl screen.
70. Install the distributor, cap and wires.
71. Connect the throttle, TV and cruise control cables.
72. Fill crankcase with oil, then the cooling system.
73. Connect the battery negative cable. Start engine and check for leaks.

ZR-1

1. Mark the relationship between each hood hinge and the hood. Remove the hood.
2. Disconnect the battery negative cable, then relieve fuel system pressure.
3. Raise and support vehicle safely.

4. Drain engine coolant into a suitable container.

5. Drain engine oil.

6. Remove exhaust system, then the driveshaft.

7. Position a suitable transmission support stand under transmission and remove the transmission support beam.

8. Remove transmission from vehicle.

9. Remove the clutch actuator cylinder, left side converter shield, clutch housing cover, then the clutch cover and disc.

10. Install engine lift hook J–37307–2 to rear of engine.

11. Remove the AIR tube center section from the AIR hose and oil pan.

12. Disconnect oxygen sensor electrical connectors.

13. Remove the power steering lower hose from the oil cooler.

14. Remove the battery negative cable from the cylinder case.

15. Remove the nuts attaching the engine mounts to the driveline and the frame.

16. Lower the vehicle.

17. Remove the air cleaner assembly and air duct.

18. Disconnect the engine oil cooler lines from the oil filter housing.

19. Raise rear of engine.

20. Loosen fuel tank filler cap, then release fuel system pressure.

22. Disconnect the fuel lines from the fuel rail.

23. Remove the evaporator housing panel and the resistor.

24. Remove the attaching the right bulkhead connector, then the engine right side wiring harness.

25. Remove the instrument panel right lower sound insulator panel.

26. Disconnect the bulkhead wiring harness connectors from under the dash.

27. Remove the air bleed hose from the plenum.

28. Remove the radiator upper and lower hoses, then disconnect the power steering pump vacuum lines.

29. Discharge the air conditioning system.

30. Remove the air conditioning suction discharge line flange from the compressor.

31. Remove the air conditioning compressor to accumulator line from the accumulator.

32. Remove the air conditioning accumulator and position aside.

33. Remove the air conditioning accumulator bracket from the vehicle.

34. Remove the power steering pressure line at the power steering gear.

35. Disconnect the throttle body linkage shield, then remove the throttle body cable to plenum retainers.

36. Disconnect the accelerator and cruise control cables from the throttle body.

37. Install engine lift hook J–37307–1 to front of engine.

38. Remove the ECM from the ECM bracket, then disconnect ECM harness connectors.

39. Remove the left front fender.

40. Remove the positive cable from the battery, battery hold-down clamp, then the battery from the vehicle.

41. Disconnect the engine left side bulkhead block electrical connector.

42. Disconnect the engine wiring harness fusible links at the junction block.

43. Disconnect the engine harness connectors from the following:
   Secondary injector modules
   Battery positive cable at junction block
   Differential pressure switch vacuum and electrical connectors
   Air conditioning cutout relay
   Air conditioning high blower relay
   Transmission shift solenoid relay
   Fuel pump fuse
   Forward lamp link connector
   Battery positive lead
   Air conditioning blower resistor
   Air conditioning pressure sensor
   Air conditioning cooling fan switch
   Windshield washer pump
   Low coolant sensor
   Blower motor
   ESC knock sensor
   ESC knock sensor relay

44. Disconnect hoses from the vacuum pump.

45. Disconnect the front and rear vacuum connections. Reposition engine harness aside.

46. Remove the braided ground strap from the left hand frame rail. Reposition positive battery cable aside.

47. Remove the left hand side plenum panel screen.

48. Disconnect the brake booster vacuum hose.

49. Remove the windshield wiper motor from the vehicle.

50. Disconnect the MAP electrical connector, then remove the MAP sensor bracket from the plenum.

51. Disconnect the AIR hose from the left exhaust manifold.

52. Install a suitable lifting device and remove the engine from the vehicle.

To install:

53. Install the engine mounts.

54. Using a suitable lifting device, install the engine into vehicle.

55. Install the engine/bracket bolts, then remove the the lifting device from the brackets.

56. Connect the AIR hose to the left exhaust manifold.

57. Install the MAP sensor and MAP sensor bracket.

58. Install the wiper motor.

59. Install the left side plenum panel screen.

60. Route left side wiring harness into position, then install the ground strap to the frame rail.

61. Connect the left hand side bulkhead block connector.

62. Connect the engine harness fusible links and relays.

63. Install the battery, then hold-down clamps.

64. Connect the battery negative cable, then install the left front fender.

65. Install the ECM to the ECM bracket, then connect the electrical connector.

66. Remove the engine front lift hook.

67. Connect power brake booster vacuum hose to the plenum.

68. Connect the cruise control and throttle cables to the throttle body, then install cable shield.

69. Install cable retainers to the plenum.

70. Install the power steering pressure line to the power steering gear.

71. Connect the engine oil cooler lines to the engine.

72. Install the accumulator to the accumulator bracket.

73. Connect air conditioning lines.

74. Connect the vacuum lines to the power steering pump.

75. Connect the radiator upper and lower hoses.

76. Connect the air bleed hose to the plenum.

77. Connect the bulkhead connector to the bulkhead.

78. Connect the evaporator housing panel resistor electrical connector.

79. Install hose onto vacuum pump, then the front and rear vacuum connections.

80. Connect the engine harness connectors to the following:
   Air conditioning blower resistor
   Air conditioning pressure sensor
   Air conditioning cooling fan
   Windshield washer pump
   Low coolant sensor
   Blower motor
   ESC knock sensor
   ESC knock sensor relay
   Differential pressure switch

81. Connect the fuel lines to the fuel rail.

82. Install the engine right side wiring harness under the dash.

83. Install the instrument panel right sound insulator panel.

84. Raise and support vehicle, then install the engine/bracket bolts and nuts. Torque to 40 ft. lbs. (54 Nm). Lower vehicle.

85. Install the power steering hose to power steering oil cooler.

86. Install the oxygen sensors, if removed.

87. Connect the AIR tube center section to the AIR hose and oil pan.

88. Connect the negative battery cable, then remove the engine rear lift hook.

89. Raise and support vehicle, then install the clutch assembly and housing.

90. Install transmission and support beam, then the driveshaft.

91. Install the exhaust system.

92. Lower the vehicle and fill cooling system.

93. Fill engine crankcase with oil.

94. Charge the air conditioning system, then reset the change oil monitor if the oil was drained during removal.

Engine Mounts

REMOVAL & INSTALLATION

1987–88 Vehicles

1. Disconnect the negative battery cable, then raise and support vehicle.

2. Remove engine mount through bolt.

3. Raise the engine enough to allow for sufficient clearance.

4. Remove engine mount to block bolts.

5. When removing the right engine mount, remove 1 exhaust manifold shroud screw.

6. Remove engine mount.

To install:

7. Replace mount to engine and lower engine into place.

8. Install and tighten the retaining bolts.

9. When installing the right engine mount, install the exhaust manifold shroud screw. Connect the battery negative cable.

1989–91 Vehicles

EXCEPT ZR-1

1. Disconnect battery negative cable.

2. Remove the air intake duct from the air cleaner assembly.

3. Raise and support vehicle.

4. When removing the right engine mount, remove the Electronic Spark Control (ESC) sensor shield.

5. Remove the engine mount through bolts and nuts.

6. Raise engine slightly for sufficient clearance, then remove engine mount bolts and engine mount from vehicle.

7. Reverse procedure to install. Torque engine mount bolts and through bolts to 41 ft. lbs. (56 Nm) Connect the battery negative cable.

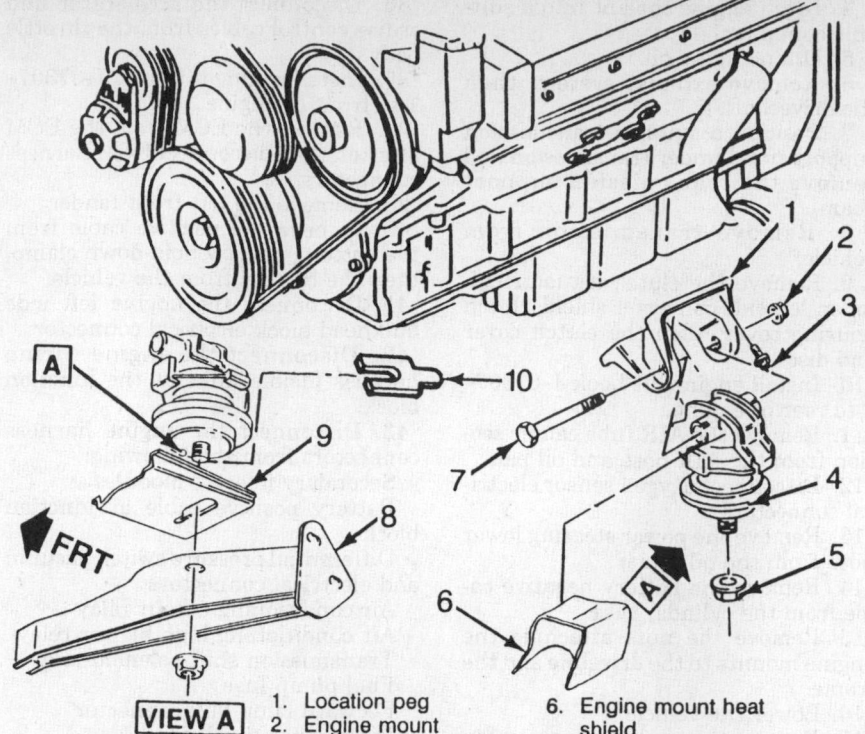

1. Location peg	6. Engine mount heat
2. Engine mount	shield
bracket	7. Engine mount
3. Engine mount	through bolt
bracket bolt	8. Front side member
4. Engine hydraulic	9. Frame
mount	10. Engine mount spacer
5. Engine mount nut	

Engine mounts – 1990–91 ZR-1

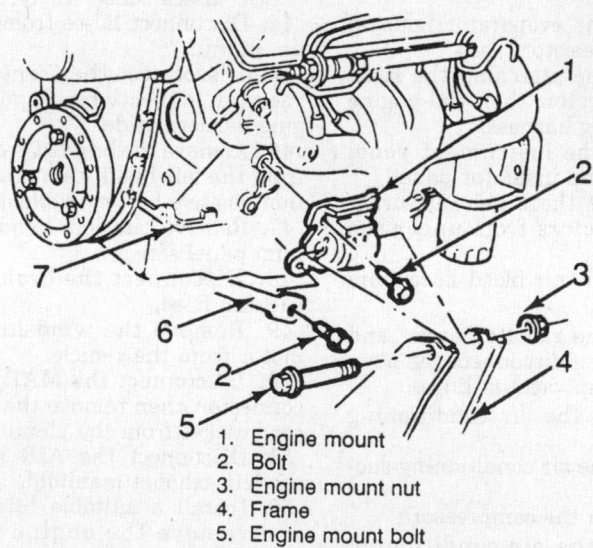

1. Engine mount	
2. Bolt	
3. Engine mount nut	
4. Frame	
5. Engine mount bolt	
6. Support brace	
7. Engine block	

Engine mounts – 1989–91 Except ZR-1

ZR-1

1. Disconnect battery negative cable, then remove the right or left exhaust manifold.

2. Remove the nut attaching the engine mount to drivetrain and frame.

3. Raise engine slightly to allow for sufficient clearance.

4. Remove the engine mount bracket nut and bolt from bracket.

5. Remove the engine mount and mount shield from the vehicle.

6. Remove the bolts attaching the bracket to the cylinder case, then the bracket from the vehicle.

7. Reverse procedure to install. Torque engine mount bracket bolts to 38 ft. lbs. (52 Nm). Torque engine mount nuts and bolts to 40 ft. lbs. (54 Nm). Connect the battery negative cable.

Cylinder Head

REMOVAL & INSTALLATION

1987–88 Vehicles
RIGHT

1. Disconnect the negative battery cable, then relieve the fuel system pressure.
2. Drain the cooling system.
3. Remove the intake manifold.
4. Disconnect the rear air conditioning brace at the exhaust manifold.
5. Disconnect and remove the dipstick tube assembly.
6. Remove the check valve from the AIR manifold.
7. Disconnect the AIR hose at the catalytic converter AIR pipe.
8. Disconnect the temperature sending unit wire.
9. Disconnect the plug wires from the spark plugs and cylinder head/rocker arm attachment points.
10. Remove the spark plugs.
11. Raise and properly support the vehicle.
12. Disconnect the converter AIR pipe clamp at the manifold.
13. Disconnect the exhaust pipe at both manifolds.
14. Remove the front converter hanger bolts.
15. Remove the converter AIR pipe.
16. Lower the vehicle.
17. Remove the exhaust manifold bolts.
18. Remove the exhaust manifold with the EGR pipe.
19. Remove the spark plug wire retainers.
20. Remove the rocker arm cover.
21. Disconnect the serpentine belt at the air conditioning compressor.
22. Disconnect the air conditioning wire connectors.
23. Loosen the rear air conditioning mounting bolts.
24. Loosen and remove the air conditioning bracket nuts from the water pump studs.
25. Loosen the front air conditioning mounting bolt and slide the air conditioning unit with bracket forward.
26. Remove the pushrods.
27. Loosen and remove the head bolts.
28. Remove the right cylinder head

from the cylinder head from the engine block surface.
29. Remove and discard the cylinder head gasket. Thoroughly clean all gasket mating surfaces.
To install:

NOTE: The cylinder head and engine block surfaces must be completely free of existing gasket material and free of nicks and grooves. Throughly clean and inspect the cylinder head bolt threads for damage and wear. The use of dirty or damaged bolts may produce false and inaccurate torque readings. Replace all damaged bolts as required.

30. Use a new cylinder head gasket installed with the bead facing up. Installation of the cylinder head is the reverse of the removal procedure.

NOTE: If the steel type gaskets were removed, coat both sides of the new steel gasket, lightly but thoroughly, with a suitable sealing compound. If composite type gaskets were removed, the new gaskets must be installed dry.

31. Coat the threads of the cylinder head bolts with a suitable sealing compound. Install the bolts finger tight.
32. Torque the bolts to the proper specification and in the proper sequence. Connect the battery negative cable.

LEFT

1. Disconnect the negative battery cable, then relieve the fuel system pressure.
2. Drain the cooling system.
3. Remove the intake manifold.
4. Disconnect the AIR hose at the check valve.
5. Remove the alternator brace.
6. Disconnect the fan temperature sensor wire.
7. Raise and safely support the vehicle.
8. Disconnect the exhaust pipe at the manifold.
9. Lower the vehicle.
10. Remove the exhaust manifold bolts.
11. Support and remove the left hand exhaust manifold.
12. Disconnect the serpentine belt at the AIR pump.
13. Remove the rocker arm cover.
14. Remove the spark plugs.
15. Disconnect the power steering, alternator mounting bracket at the cylinder head.
16. Remove the pushrods.
17. Loosen and remove the head bolts. Remove the left cylinder head from the engine block surface.
18. Remove the cylinder head gasket

and discard. Thoroughly clean all gasket mating surfaces.
To install:

NOTE: The cylinder head and engine block surfaces must be completely free of existing gasket material and free of nicks and grooves. Throughly clean and inspect the cylinder head bolt threads for damage and wear. The use of dirty or damaged bolts may produce false and inaccurate torque readings. Replace all damaged bolts as required.

19. Use a new cylinder head gasket installed with the bead facing up. Installation of the cylinder head is the reverse of the removal procedure.

NOTE: If steel type gaskets were removed, coat both sides of the new steel gasket (thinly and evenly) with a suitable sealing compound. It is important to apply the proper amount of sealant because too much can cause the gasket to move away from the cylinder head and block surfaces. If composite type gaskets were removed, the new gaskets must be installed dry.

20. Coat the threads of the cylinder head bolts with a suitable sealing compound. Install the bolts finger tight.
21. Torque bolts in the specified pattern to 67 ft. lbs. (91 Nm).

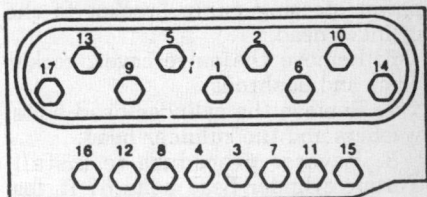

Cylinder head bolt torque sequence—1987–88 vehicles

1989–91 Vehicles Except ZR-1
RIGHT

1. Disconnect battery negative cable, then relieve the fuel system pressure.
2. Remove the intake manifold.
3. Remove the right exhaust manifold.
4. Remove the air conditioning compressor mounting bracket attaching bolts, then the mounting bracket.
5. Remove the valve cover, rocker arms and pushrods.
6. Remove the cylinder head bolts, washers and the cylinder head.
7. Reverse procedure to install. Torque cylinder head bolts 67 ft. lbs. (97 Nm). Connect battery negative cable and check for leaks.

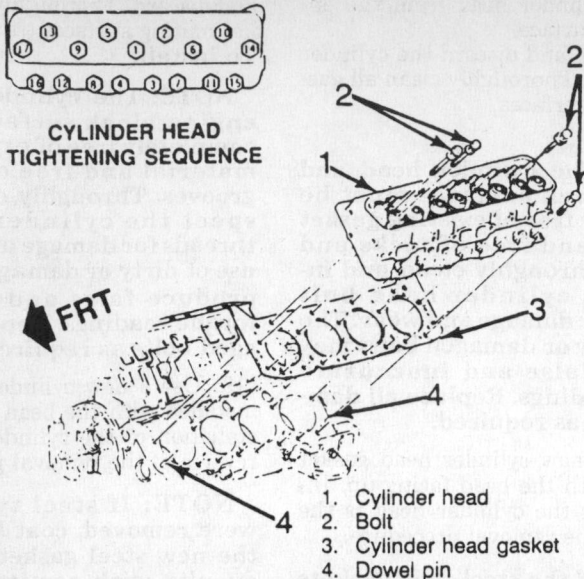

CYLINDER HEAD TIGHTENING SEQUENCE

1. Cylinder head
2. Bolt
3. Cylinder head gasket
4. Dowel pin

Cylinder head bolt torque sequence—1989–91 Except ZR-1

LEFT

1. Disconnect battery negative cable and relieve fuel system pressure.
2. Remove the left exhaust manifold.
3. Remove the alternator.
4. Remove the 2 bolts and 1 nut attaching the AIR pump bracket to the head. Position pump and bracket assembly aside.
5. Remove the bolt attaching the power steering pump bracket to the cylinder head.
6. Remove the valve cover, rocker arms and pushrods.
7. Remove the cylinder head bolts, washers and the culinder head.
8. Reverse procedure to install. Torque cylinder head bolts 67 ft. lbs. (97 Nm). Connect the battery negative cable and check for leaks.

1990–91 ZR-1

RIGHT

1. Disconnect the battery negative cable.
2. Drain engine coolant into a suitable container.
3. Relieve fuel system pressure.
4. Remove plenum assembly.
5. Disconnect the fuel lines from the right fuel rail.
6. Disconnect electrical connectors from the fuel injectors.
7. Remove the bolts attaching the fuel rail assembly to the injector housing.
8. Remove the injectors from the housing, then the fuel rail assembly from the vehicle.
9. Remove and clamp the hose from the right coolant outlet pipe.

10. Remove the oil pressure sensor from the oil filter housing.
11. Remove the bolt attaching the outlet pipe bracket to the alternator bracket.
12. Remove the screws attaching the outlet pipe to the injector housing, then remove the outlet pipe and gasket.
13. Remove PCV grommet from the injector housing. Plug the ventilation hose from the injector housing.
14. Removing the bolt attaching the alternator rear support bracket to the alternator.
15. Remove the bolt attaching the alternator rear support bracket and right side ventilation pipe to the injector housing.
16. Remove the ventilation pipe and bracket from the vehicle.
17. Remove the bolts attaching the injector housing to the cylinder head.
18. Remove the injector housing and gasket from the vehicle.
20. Remove the right bank valve lifters.
21. Remove alternator.
22. Remove the right exhaust manifold, if necessary.
23. Remove the fuel filter heat shield.
24. Remove the vacuum hose from secondary port throttle valve actuator.
25. Remove the access plug from the right cylinder head.
26. Remove the bolt attaching the right secondary timing chain guide.
27. Remove cylinder head and gasket from vehicle.
To install:
28. Install the cylinder head locating dowels into block, if removed during removal.

29. Install the cylinder head gasket, head washers and bolts. Coat bolt threads with engine oil.
30. Torque cylinder head bolts as follows:
   1st–45 ft. lbs. (60 Nm)
   2nd–74 ft. lbs. (100 Nm)
   3rd–118 ft. lbs. (160 Nm)
31. Install the fixed guide bolt. Apply Loctite to bolt threads and torque to 20 ft. lbs. (26 Nm).
32. Install the access plug into the cylinder head and torque to 15 ft. lbs. (20 Nm).
33. Connect the vacuum hose to the actuator.
34. Raise and support vehicle, then drain engine oil.
35. Install the fuel filter heat shield, then the exhaust manifold.
36. Install the alternator.
37. Install valve lifters, then the injector housing.
38. Fill crankcase with engine oil and connect the battery negative cable.

LEFT

1. Disconnect battery negative cable.
2. Drain engine coolant into a suitable container.
3. Relieve fuel system pressure.
4. Remove plenum assembly.
5. Disconnect fuel lines from the left fuel rail.
6. Disconnect electrical connectors from the injectors.
7. Remove the bolts attaching the fuel rail assembly to the injector housing.
8. Remove the injectors from the housing, then the fuel rail assembly from the vehicle.
9. Remove and plug hose from left coolant outlet pipe.
10. Remove bolt attaching the outlet pipe bracket to the power steering pump bracket.
11. Remove bolts attaching the outlet pipe to the injector housing, then remove the outlet pipe and gasket from vehicle.
12. Remove PCV grommet from injector housing.
13. Disconnect and plug ventilation hose from injector housing.
14. Disconnect the coolant temperature sensor and cooling fan switch electrical connectors.
15. Remove bolts attaching the injector housing to the cylinder head, then remove the injector housing and gasket from vehicle.
16. Remove the vacuum hose from the secondary port throttle valve actuator.
17. Remove the power brake booster assembly.
18. Remove the left bank valve lifters.

19. Remove the AIR control valve hoses, then disconnect the electrical connectors.

20. Disconnect the camshaft sensor electrical connector.

21. Remove the left exhaust manifold, if necessary.

22. Remove the access plug from the left cylinder head.

23. Remove the bolt attaching the left secondary timing chain guide.

24. Remove the cylinder head bolts, then the cylinder head and gasket from the vehicle.

To install:

25. Install cylinder head locating dowels into cylinder head, if removed during removal.

26. Install cylinder head gasket, head, washers and bolts. Coat bolt threads with engine oil.

27. Torque cylinder head bolts as follows:

    1st—45 ft. lbs. (60 Nm)
    2nd—74 ft. lbs. (100 Nm)
    3rd—118 ft. lbs. (160 Nm)

28. Install fixed guide bolt. Coat bolt threads with Loctite. Torque bolt to 20 ft. lbs. (26 Nm).

29. Install access plug into cylinder head. Torque plug to 15 ft. lbs. (20 Nm).

30. Connect vacuum hose to actuator.

31. Raise and support vehicle, then drain engine oil. Lower vehicle.

32. Install exhaust manifold, then connect the camshaft position sensor electrical connector.

33. Connect the AIR control valve hoses and electrical connectors.

34. Install the valve lifters, then the injector housing.

35. Fill engine crankcase with oil. Reset the change oil monitor if oil was drained during removal. Connect battery and check for leaks.

Valve Lifters

REMOVAL & INSTALLATION

Except ZR-1

1. Disconnect the negative battery cable.

2. Drain the cooling system.

3. Remove the intake manifold assembly.

4. Remove the rocker arm covers.

5. Remove the rocker arms and pushrods. Be sure to keep them in order as they must be installed in the same bores as they were removed.

6. As required, remove the valve lifter guide retaining bolts. Remove the valve lifter guide, if equipped with roller lifters.

7. Remove the valve lifters using the proper valve lifter removal tool.

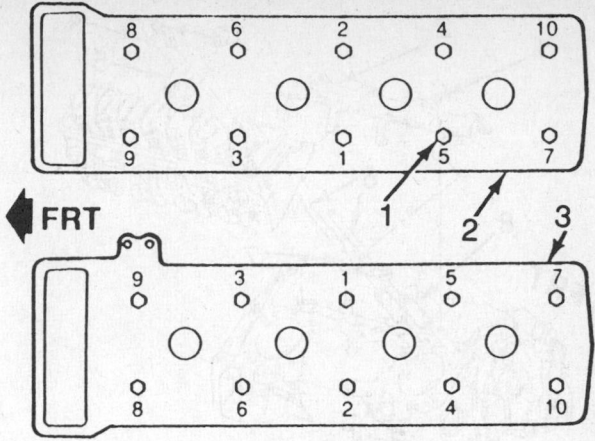

1. Cylinder head bolt
2. Right cylinder haed
3. Left cylinder haed

Cylinder head bolt torque sequence—1990–91 ZR-1

8. Place the lifters in a rack so they may be installed in their original locations.

9. Coat the base of the lifters with Molycoat® or equivalent prior to installation. Installation is the reverse of the removal procedure.

ZR-1

1. Disconnect battery negative cable.

2. Remove camshafts.

3. Remove lifters from bores.

4. Reverse procedure to install. Lubricate lifter bores with engine oil. Connect the battery negative cable

NOTE: Ensure that the lifters, that are to be reused, are retained in proper order so each lifter can be returned to its original bore. Pre-oil any new lifter being installed.

Valve Lash

ADJUSTMENT

Except ZR-1

NOTE: This engine utilizes hydraulic lifters that normally require very little maintenance or adjustment. These components are simple in design and are best maintained through regular, scheduled engine oil changes. If the engine is running well and no audible clicking sounds are heard from the valve train, do not attempt to remove or disassemble the valve lifters.

1. Disconnect the negative battery cable.

2. Remove the valve covers.

3. Tighten the rocker arm nuts until all lash is eliminated.

4. Adjust the valves when the lifter is on the base circle of the camshaft lobe by cranking the engine until the mark on the vibration damper aligns with the center or **0** mark on the timing tab fastened to the crankcase front cover and the engine is in the No. 1 firing position.

NOTE: This may be determined by placing fingers on the No. 1 valve as the mark on the damper comes near the 0 mark on the crankcase front cover. If the valves move as the mark comes up to the timing tab, the engine is in the No. 6 firing position and should be turned over one more time to reach to No. 1 firing position.

5. With the engine in the No. 1 firing position, adjust the following valves:

    a. Exhaust—1, 3, 4, 8
    b. Intake—1, 2, 5, 7

6. Back out adjusting nut until lash is felt at the pushrod then turn in adjusting nut until all lash is removed. This can be determined by rotating pushrod while turning adjusting nut. When play has been removed, turn adjusting nut in one full additional turn.

7. Crank the engine one revolution until the pointer **0** mark and the vibration damper mark are again in alignment. This is the No. 6 firing position.

8. With the engine in this position, adjust the following valves:

    a. Exhaust—2, 5, 6, 7
    b. Intake—3, 4, 6, 8

9. Install the rocker arm covers.

10. Connect the battery negative cable, then start the engine and adjust the idle speed as required.

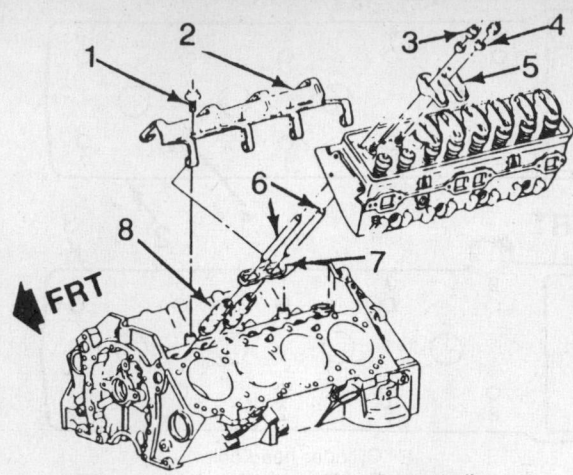

1. Retainer bolt
2. Valve lifter restrictor retainer
3. Valve rocker arm adjustment nut
4. Rocker arm ball
5. Valve rocker arm
6. Pushrod
7. Valve lifter guide
8. Lifter

Rocker arms and pushrods—Except ZR-1

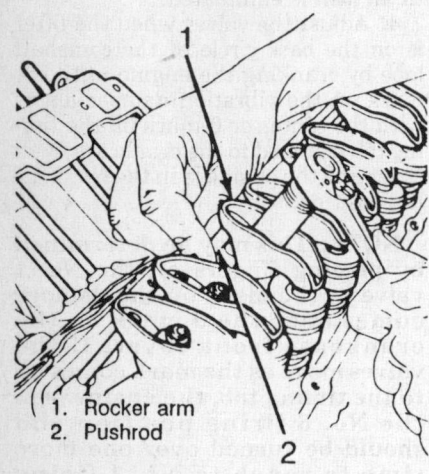

1. Rocker arm
2. Pushrod

Valve adjustment—Except ZR-1

Rocker Arms

REMOVAL & INSTALLATION

Except ZR-1

1. Disconnect the negative battery cable. Remove the air cleaner.
2. Remove the right rocker arm cover as follows:

a. Remove the EGR pipe assembly.

b. Remove the crankcase vent pipe.

c. Loosen the spark plug wire retainer on the right cylinder head and remove the remaining wire retainers.

d. Remove the injector harness retaining nuts and position the harness off to the side.

e. On 1987–88 vehicles, discon-

nect the heater control valve harness vacuum hose.

f. On 1989–91 vehicles, remove the engine cooling air pipe assembly. Disconnect the heater core to plenum coolant hose and AIR hoses from the control valve.

g. On 1989–91 vehicles, remove the bolts attaching the air conditioning compressor and position aside.

h. Remove the rocker arm retaining bolts. Remove the rocker arm cover and gasket. Replace the gasket as required.

3. Remove the left rocker arm cover as follows:

a. Disconnect the PCV valve and hose.

b. Disconnect the injector harness and position to the side.

c. On 1989–91 vehicles, remove spark plug wire retainers, then the spark plug wires. Remove the serpentine belt from the AIR pump.

d. On 1987–88 vehicles, disconnect the canister hose at the purge pipe.

e. On 1987–88 vehicles, disconnect the power brake booster vacuum line. Disconnect the brake booster pipe at the plenum.

f. Loosen the AIR pump pulley bolts and disconnect the serpentine belt from the AIR pump.

f. Remove the AIR pump pulley and loosen the AIR pump lower mounting bolt.

g. Remove the rocker cover retaining bolts and remove the cover and cover gasket.

4. Remove the rocker arm nuts, rocker arm balls and the rocker arms. Identify the rocker arm nuts, rocker arm balls, rocker arms and pushrods

so they may be installed in their original locations. If new rocker arms and/or rocker arm balls are being installed, place a coat of Molycoat® or equivalent, onto the bearing surfaces prior to installation.

To install:

5. Install the pushrods making certain they seat in the lifter sockets.

6. Install the rocker arms, rocker arm balls and rocker arm nuts in their original positions.

7. Tighten the rocker arm nuts until all lash is eliminated.

8. Adjust the valves and the air conditioning belt tension.

9. Reinstall the rocker arm covers and connect the battery negative cable.

10. Start the engine and inspect for leaks. Check and adjust the curb idle speed.

Intake Manifold

REMOVAL & INSTALLATION

1987–88 Vehicles

1. Disconnect the negative battery cable.

2. Relieve the fuel system pressure.

3. Drain the cooling system.

4. Remove the fuel injection subassembly: mass air flow sensor, plenum, runners and the fuel rail assembly.

5. Disconnect and mark all necessary vacuum and electrical connections.

6. Remove the distributor cap, mark the position of the rotor and the distributor. Remove the distributor.

7. Disconnect the upper radiator hose at the thermostat outlet opening.

8. Remove the air pump brace.

9. Disconnect the EGR pipe at the inlet opening.

10. Disconnect the heater control vacuum line at the intake.

11. Remove the thermostat outlet.

12. Remove the intake manifold retaining bolts.

13. Lift the intake manifold upward and away from the intake surface.

14. Remove the gaskets from the cylinder head surfaces.

To install:

15. Thoroughly clean the cylinder block, intake manifold and cylinder head surfaces with the proper cleaning

compound to remove any traces of gasket material and RTV sealant. Any material left on these surfaces will cause installation interference and improper sealing.

16. Install the cylinder head gaskets so the blocked openings are positioned toward the rear of the engine. Locate the gasket tabs and bend the tabs so they are flush with the rear surface of

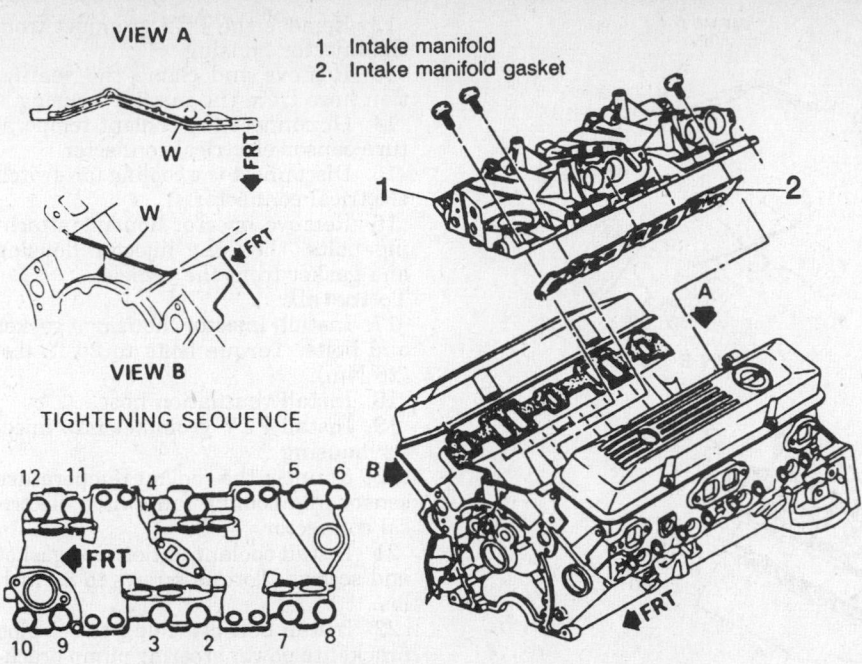

VIEW A

1. Intake manifold
2. Intake manifold gasket

VIEW B

TIGHTENING SEQUENCE

Intake manifold bolt torque sequence—1987–88 vehicles

the cylinder head. After the tabs are bent into place, apply a $^3/_{16}$ bead of RTV onto the front and rear cylinder case ridges.

17. Apply Loctite to the threads of the intake manifold retaining bolts.

18. Install the intake manifold in the reverse order of the removal procedure. Torque the intake manifold retaining bolts in sequence to 35 ft. lbs. (47 Nm). Connect battery negative cable.

1989–91 Vehicles Except ZR-1

1. Disconnect battery negative cable.
2. Relieve system fuel pressure.
3. Drain engine coolant into a suitable container.
4. Disconnect the throttle and cruise control cables from the throttle body and cable bracket.
5. Disconnect the TV cable from the throttle body and bracket.
6. Remove the bracket from the plenum and position aside.
7. Disconnect the following electrical connectors:
Throttle position sensor
Idle air control valve
Mass air flow sensor (1989 only)
Coolant temperature sensor (1990–91)
Manifold absolute pressure sensor (1990–91)
Manifold air temperature sensor (1990–91)
8. Remove the air intake duct from the throttle body.
9. Disconnect vacuum hoses from the throttle body and the plenum.

10. Disconnect the heater hoses from the throttle body.
11. Remove the power brake vacuum booster fitting from the plenum.
12. Remove the runner to plenum bolts, then remove the plenum from the vehicle.
13. On 1990–91 vehicles, remove the vacuum harness from the EGR solenoid.
14. On 1990–91 vehicles, remove the EGR solenoid assembly from the coolant outlet, then the EGR valve from the intake manifold.
15. Remove the injector harness attaching bolts, then disconnect the injector harness connectors.
16. Remove the runner to manifold attaching bolts, then the runner.
17. Disconnect the fuel lines.
18. Remove the fuel rail and injector assembly.
19. Remove the distributor.
20. Remove the radiator upper hose, then the AIR pump brace.
21. Remove the EGR valve pipe and position aside.
22. Remove the PCV valve from the manifold.
23. Remove the crankshaft vent pipe.
24. Remove the intake manifold attaching bolts, then the intake manifold and gaskets.

To install:

25. Thoroughly clean the cylinder block, intake manifold and cylinder head surfaces with the proper cleaning compound to remove any traces of gasket material and RTV sealant. Any material left on these surfaces will

cause installation interference and improper sealing.

26. Install the cylinder head gaskets so the blocked openings are positioned at the front of the engine. Locate the gasket tabs and bend the tabs so they are flush with the rear surface of the cylinder head. After the tabs are bent into place, apply a $^3/_{16}$ bead of RTV onto the front and rear cylinder case ridges.

27. Apply Loctite to the threads of the intake manifold retaining bolts.

28. Install the intake manifold in the reverse order of the removal procedure. Torque the intake manifold retaining bolts in sequence to 35 ft. lbs. (47 Nm). Connect the battery negative cable.

Injector Housing

REMOVAL & INSTALLATION

1990–91 ZR-1
RIGHT

1. Disconnect battery negative cable.
2. Drain engine coolant into a suitable container.
3. Relieve the fuel system pressure.
4. Remove the plenum assembly.
5. Disconnect the fuel lines from the right fuel rail.
6. Disconnect the electrical connectors from the fuel injectors.
7. Remove the bolts attaching the fuel rail assembly to the injector housing.
8. Remove the injectors from the housing, then the fuel rail assembly from the vehicle.
9. Remove and clamp the right coolant outlet pipe hose.
10. Remove the oil pressure sensor from the oil filter housing.
11. Remove the bolt attaching the outlet pipe bracket to the alternator bracket.
12. Remove the bolt attaching the outlet pipe to the injector housing, then the outlet pipe and gasket from the vehicle.
13. Remove the PCV grommet from the injector housing.
14. Remove and clamp the ventilation hose from the injector housing.
15. Remove the bolt attaching the alternator rear support bracket to the alternator.
16. Remove the bolt attaching the alternator rear support bracket and right side ventilation pipe to the injector housing.
17. Remove the ventilation pipe and bracket from the vehicle.
18. Remove the injector housing attaching bolts, then the injector housing and gasket from the vehicle.

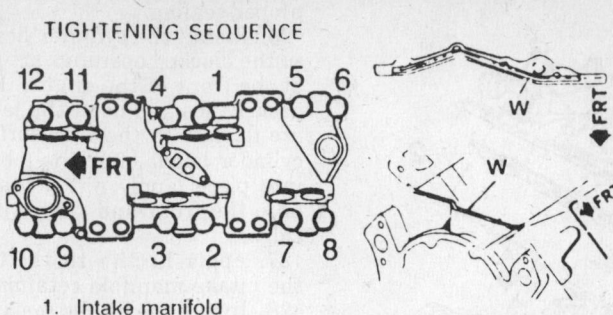

VIEW A

TIGHTENING SEQUENCE

VIEW B

1. Intake manifold
2. Intake manifold bolt
3. Intake manifold gasket

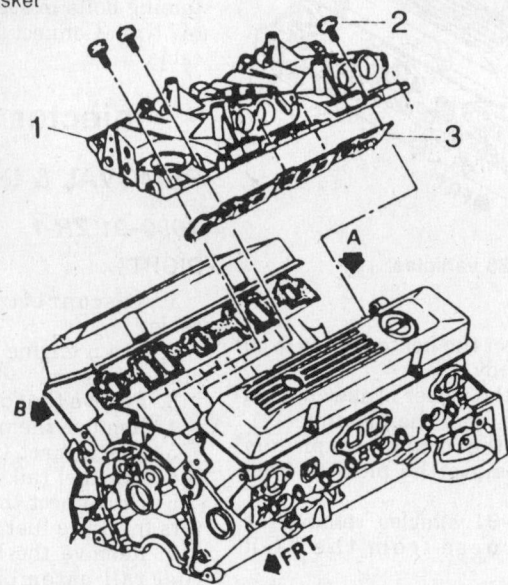

Intake manifold bolt torque sequence—1989–91 Except ZR-1

To install:

19. Install injector housing, gasket, alternator bracket, right ventilation pipe and bolts. Torque bolts to 20 ft. lbs. (26 Nm).
20. Install ventilation hose.
21. Install PCV grommet into injector housing.
22. Install coolant outlet gasket, outlet and screws. Torque screws to 89 inch lbs. (10 Nm).
23. Install bolt attaching the outlet pipe bracket to alternator bracket. Torque bolt to 38 ft. lbs. (52 Nm).
24. Install the oil pressure sensor. Apply Loctite to sensor threads.
25. Install the hose and clamp onto the right coolant outlet pipe.
26. Install the fuel rail assembly to the injector housing. Torque bolts to 20 ft. lbs. (26 Nm).
27. Connect injector electrical connectors.
28. Install fuel lines to right fuel rail, then the plenum assembly.
29. Fill cooling system and connect the battery negative cable.

LEFT

1. Disconnect the battery negative cable.
2. Drain engine coolant into a suitable container.
3. Relieve the fuel system pressure.
4. Remove the plenum assembly.
5. Disconnect the fuel lines from the right fuel rail.
6. Disconnect the electrical connectors from the injectors.
7. Remove the bolts attaching the fuel rail assembly to the injector housing.
8. Remove the injectors from the housing, then the fuel rail assembly from the vehicle.
9. Remove and clamp the hose from the left coolant outlet pipe.
10. Remove the bolt attaching the outlet pipe bracket to the power steering pump bracket.
11. Remove the bolts attaching the outlet pipe to the injector housing, then the outlet pipe and gasket from the vehicle.

12. Remove the PCV grommet from the injector housing.
13. Remove and clamp the ventilation hose from the injector housing.
14. Disconnect the coolant temperature sensor electrical connector.
15. Disconnect the cooling fan switch electrical connector.
16. Remove injector housing attaching bolts, then the injector housing and gasket from the vehicle.

To install:

17. Install injector housing, gasket and bolts. Torque bolts to 20 ft. lbs. (26 Nm).
18. Install ventilation hose.
19. Install PCV grommet into injector housing.
20. Connect the coolant temperature sensor and cooling fan switch electrical connector.
21. Install coolant outlet pipe gasket and screws. Torque screws to 89 inch lbs.
22. Install bolt attaching outlet pipe bracket to power steering pump bracket. Torque bolts to 20 ft. lbs. (26 Nm).
23. Install the hose to the left coolant outlet pipe.
24. Install the fuel rail assembly to the injector housing. Torque bolts to 20 ft. lbs. (26 Nm).
25. Connect injector electrical connectors.
26. Install fuel lines to right fuel rail, then the plenum assembly.
27. Fill cooling system and connect battery negative cable.

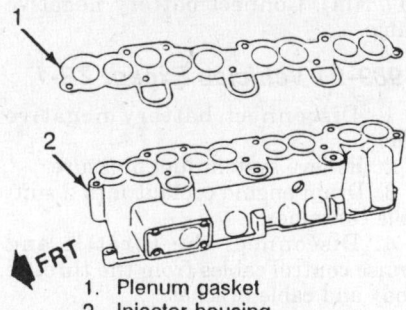

1. Plenum gasket
2. Injector housing

Injector housing—1990–91 ZR-1

Exhaust Manifold

REMOVAL & INSTALLATION

Except ZR-1

RIGHT

1. Disconnect the negative battery cable.
2. Remove the plenum extension.
3. Disconnect the EGR sensor wire.
4. Remove the EGR pipe bolts at the intake manifold.

5. Remove the rear air conditioning compressor brace and allow it to hang from the compressor.

6. Disconnect the dipstick tube at the manifold and remove the dipstick/tube as an assembly.

7. Remove the AIR check valve at the manifold.

8. Disconnect the AIR hose at the catalytic air pipe opening.

9. Disconnect the temperature sending unit wire.

10. Disconnect the spark plug wires from the plugs, cylinder head and the valve covers.

11. Remove the spark plugs.

12. Raise and properly support the vehicle.

13. Remove the catalytic converter AIR pipe at the manifold.

14. Disconnect the exhaust crossover pipe at the manifold.

15. Remove the bolts from the catalytic front support hanger.

16. Remove the catalytic converter AIR pipe.

17. Lower the vehicle.

18. Support the exhaust manifold and remove the retaining bolts.

19. Remove the exhaust manifold and EGR assembly from the vehicle. If the manifold is being replaced, remove the EGR pipe clamp and EGR pipe.

To install:

20. Install exhaust manifold, gasket and bolts. Torque bolts to 19 ft. lbs. (26 Nm).

21. Raise and support vehicle.

22. Install front crossover pipe to manifold flange nuts. Torque nuts to 15 ft. lbs. (21 Nm).

23. Install to AIR to the manifold.

24. Lower vehicle.

25. Install spark plugs, wires and retainers, if removed.

26. Connect the temperature sensor electrical connector.

27. Install the AIR check valve to manifold.

28. Install the oil dipstick and tube.

29. Install the oil dipstick tube, then the dipstick.

30. Install the air conditioning compressor brace.

31. Install the EGR assembly, if removed.

32. Connect battery negative cable. Start engine and check for leaks.

LEFT

1. Disconnect the negative battery cable.

2. On 1987–88 vehicles, remove the air cleaner.

3. On 1987–88 vehicles, disconnect the PCV hose from the intake and rocker arm cover.

4. Disconnect the AIR hose at the exhaust check valve.

5. Disconnect the rear alternator brace and allow to hang from the alternator.

6. On 1989–91 vehicles, remove the spark plug wires from the plugs, then from the wire retainers and position aside.

7. On 1989–91 vehicles, remove the spark plugs.

8. Raise and properly support the vehicle.

7. Disconnect the exhaust pipe at the manifold.

8. Lower the vehicle.

9. Support the manifold and remove the retaining bolts.

10. Remove the exhaust manifold from the vehicle.

To install:

11. Install gasket, manifold and bolts. torque bolts to 19 ft. lbs.

12. Raise and support vehicle.

13. Install front crossover pipe to manifold flange nuts. Torque bolts to 15 ft. lbs. (21 Nm).

14. On 1989–91 vehicles, install spark plugs, spark plug wires and retainers.

15. On 1987–88 vehicles, install the PCV hose to intake and rocker arm cover.

16. Install alternator brace, if removed.

17. Install the AIR hose to check valve.

18. Connect battery negative cable. Start engine and check for leaks.

ZR-1

RIGHT

1. Disconnect battery negative cable.

2. Remove the wheel house lower rear and center panels.

3. Remove bolt attaching the oil dipstick and guide tube to thew exhaust manifold, then remove oil dipstick and tube from the vehicle.

4. Remove the front exhaust manifold to cylinder head attaching bolts.

5. Remove the stud nut from the center of the manifold.

6. Raise and support vehicle.

7. Disconnect the catalytic converter oxygen sensor electrical connector. To gain access to the connector, it may be necessary to perform the following steps:

   a. Remove the bolts located at the right front of the oil pan, attaching the ignition timing sensor/oxygen sensor connector bracket.

   b. Slide the connector bracket assembly to the rear.

8. Disconnect the AIR hose from the manifold.

9. Remove the screws attaching the manifold/converter flanges to the exhaust pipe flanges.

10. Remove the rear manifold to head attaching bolts, then the manifold and gasket from the vehicle.

To install:

11. Install manifold/converter assembly to engine.

12. Install bolts attaching manifold/converter flanges to the exhaust pipe flanges. Finger tighten bolts.

13. Lower vehicle.

14. Install manifold gasket to head, then install the front manifold to head attaching bolts.

15. Install stud nut at center manifold, if removed. Coat threads with Loctite and torque to 11 ft. lbs. (15 Nm).

16. Raise and support vehicle.

17. Install the rear manifold to head attaching bolts. Torque rear bolts to 11 ft. lbs. (15 Nm) and exhaust flange bolts to 15 ft. lbs. (20 Nm).

18. Install the converter heat shields and screws.

19. Connect the oxygen sensors electrical connectors.

20. Connect the AIR hose to the manifold and lower vehicle.

21. Torque manifold front bolts and stud to 11 ft. lbs. (15 Nm).

22. Install the wheel house panels and connect the battery negative cable. Start engine and check for leaks.

LEFT

1. Disconnect the battery negative cable.

2. Remove the wheelhouse lower rear and center panels.

3. Disconnect the AIR hose from the manifold.

4. Remove the bolts attaching the manifold to the head.

5. Remove the stud nut from the center of the manifold.

6. Remove the gasket from the manifold.

7. Raise and support vehicle.

8. Disconnect the converter oxygen sensor electrical connector.

9. Remove the screws attaching the converter heat shields, then remove the heat shield from the vehicle.

10. Remove the bolts attaching the manifold/converter flange to the front exhaust pipe flange, then remove manifold/converter from the vehicle.

To install:

11. Install manifold/converter to the engine.

12. Install bolts attaching manifold/converter flange to the exhaust pipe flange. Finger tight only.

13. Lower vehicle.

14. Install the manifold gasket to head.

15. Install bolts attaching manifold to head. Finger tight.

16. Install stud nut, if removed. Torque manifold bolts and stud nut to 11 ft. lbs. (15 Nm).

17. Raise and support vehicle.

18. Torque exhaust pipe flange bolts to 15 ft. lbs. (20 Nm).

19. Install the converter heat shields and screws.

20. Connect the oxygen sensors electrical connectors.

21. Lower vehicle, then connect the AIR hose to the exhaust manifold.

22. Install wheel house panels and connect the battery negative cable. Start engine and check for leaks.

Timing Chain Front Cover

REMOVAL & INSTALLATION

Except ZR-1

1. Disconnect the negative battery cable.

2. Disconnect the drive belt and remove the crankshaft pulley.

3. Install tool J–23523 onto the vibration dampener assembly. Remove the vibration damper from the face of the crankcase front cover.

NOTE: The use of pullers, such as the universal claw type, that pull on the outside of the hub may damage the torsional dampener. The outside ring of the dampener is bonded to the hub with rubber. The use of the wrong type puller may disturb this bond.

4. Raise the vehicle and support it safely.

5. Drain the engine oil and remove the oil pan.

6. Lower the vehicle. Remove the AIR management valve adapter.

7. Remove the AIR pump pulley and air pump retaining bolts. Remove the air pump.

8. Relieve the fuel system pressure and disconnect the fuel inlet and return pipes.

9. Disconnect the air conditioner compressor mounting bracket nuts at the water pump. Slide the mounting bracket forward and remove the compressor mounting bolt. Disconnect the electrical wires and position the unit to the side.

10. Disconnect the AIR hose from the right exhaust manifold.

11. Remove the air conditioning compressor mounting bracket.

12. Remove the upper AIR pump bracket with the power steering reservoir.

13. Remove the lower AIR pump bracket.

14. Drain the radiator and disconnect the radiator and heater hoses at the water pump. Remove the water pump.

15. Remove the front cover retaining

screws. Remove the front cover and discard the gasket.

16. Thoroughly clean the gasket mating surfaces on the cylinder block and front cover. Inspect the front cover for damage and distortion. Replace the front cover, if necessary. Replace the oil seal.

17. With a suitable cutting tool, remove any excess gasket material that may be protruding at the oil pan to engine block surface.

To install:

18. Coat the new cover gasket with a suitable sealing compound and apply the gasket onto the front cover sealing surface.

19. Position the front cover and gasket onto the cylinder block surface and hold in place. Install the cover retaining screws and make them finger tight.

20. Tighten the retaining screws evenly in an alternate pattern. While tightening the retaining screws, readjust the position of the front cover, as required, to ensure the cylinder block locating dowels are evenly aligned with the holes in the cover. Do not force the cover over the locating dowels.

21. When the front cover is properly in place, torque the retaining screws to 90 inch lbs. (9 Nm) on 1987–89 vehicles and 98 inch lbs. (11 Nm) on 1990–91 vehicles.

22. Prior to installing the oil pan, apply an even coating of sealant 1052080 or equivalent, onto the front corners where the front cover and the rear main seal mate with the crankcase. Reinstall the oil pan and pan gasket.

23. Install the remaining compo-

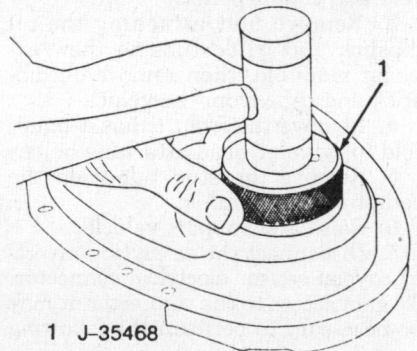

1 J–35468

Installing front cover oil seal – Except ZR-1

nents in reverse of the removal procedure. Connect the battery negative cable.

ZR-1

1. Disconnect battery negative cable, then drain engine coolant into a suitable container.

2. Remove water pump, discharge the air conditioning system, then the air conditioning compressor.

3. Remove the power steering pump assembly, then the serpentine belt.

4. Remove the bolt and washer attaching the torsional damper to the crankshaft.

5. Using tool J–24420–C or equivalent, remove the torsional damper and drift key from the crankshaft.

6. Remove front cover attaching nuts and bolts, then remove the front cover and gasket from the vehicle.

7. Reverse procedure to install. Apply Loctite to bolt threads.

8. Torque crankshaft damper bolt to 148 ft. lbs. (200 Nm).

9. Torque front cover attaching nuts and bolts to 89 inch lbs. (10 Nm). Connect the battery negative cable.

Front Cover Oil Seal

REPLACEMENT

Except ZR-1

FRONT COVER REMOVED

1. Pry the oil seal from the front cover with the appropriate tool.

2. Discard the oil seal. Exercise caution when removing the seal to prevent damaging the front cover.

3. With a clean rag, ensure the front cover sealing surfaces are free from dirt and grease.

4. Support the rear of the front cover and position the new seal so the open end of the seal is toward the the inside of the front cover.

5. With tool J–35468 or equivalent, drive the new seal into the front cover. Visually inspect the seal to ensure it is seated evenly in the front cover.

FRONT COVER INSTALLED

1. Disconnect the negative battery cable.

2. Loosen and remove the drive belt from the crankshaft pulley.

3. Remove the crankshaft pulley.

4. Install tool J–23523 onto the vibration dampener assembly. Remove the vibration damper from the face of the crankcase front cover.

NOTE: The use of pullers, such as the universal claw type, that pull on the outside of the hub may damage the torsional dampener. The outside ring of the dampener is bonded to the hub with rubber. The use of the wrong type puller may disturb this bond.

5. Pry the oil seal from the front cover with the appropriate tool. Discard the oil seal. Exercise caution when removing the seal to prevent

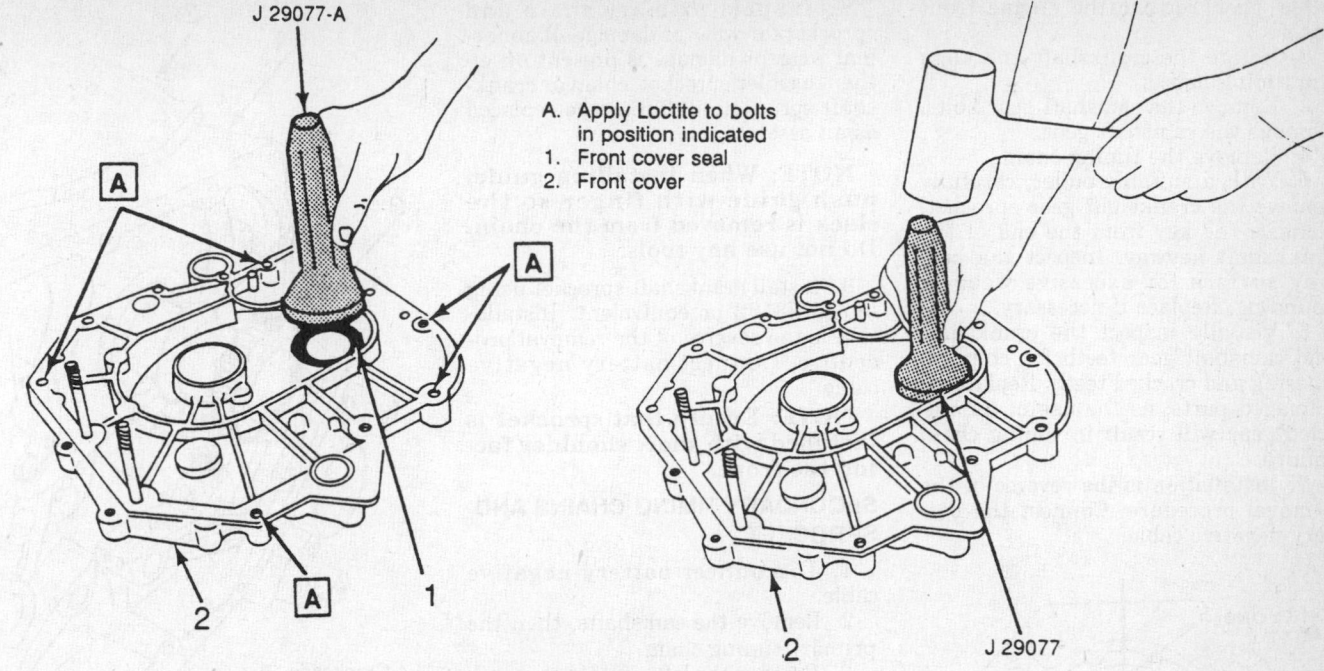

A. Apply Loctite to bolts in position indicated
1. Front cover seal
2. Front cover

Removing front oil seal—ZR-1

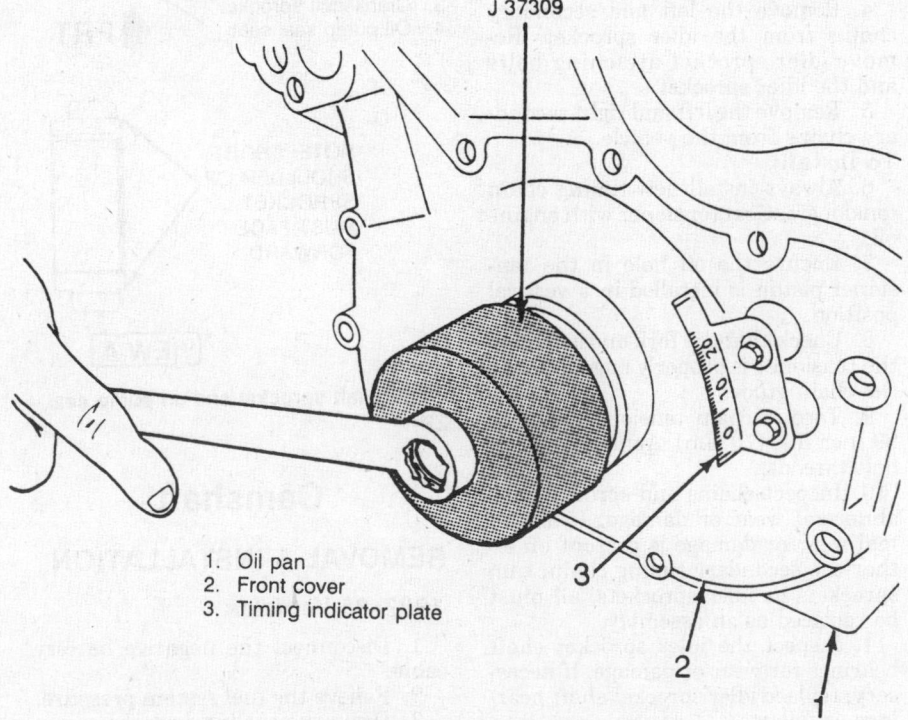

1. Oil pan
2. Front cover
3. Timing indicator plate

Installing front cover oil seal—ZR-1

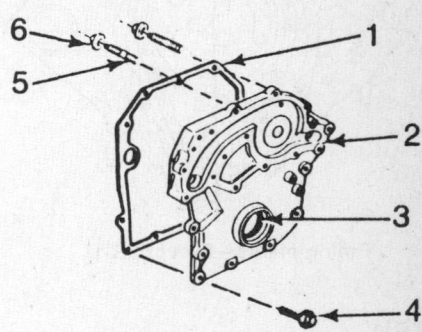

1. Front cover gasket
2. Front cover
3. Front cover seal
4. Front cover bolt
5. Front cover stud
6. Front cover stud nut

Removing front cover—ZR-1

damaging the front cover and crank-shaft surfaces.

6. With a clean rag, ensure the front cover sealing surfaces are free from dirt and grease.

7. With tool J–35468 or equivalent, drive the new seal into the front cover. Visually inspect the seal to ensure it is seated evenly in the front cover.

8. With the removal tool, reinstall the vibration dampener.

9. Reinstall the crankshaft pulley and reconnect the drive belt. Adjust the drive belt tension. Connect the battery negative cable.

ZR-1

1. Disconnect the battery negative cable, then remove the front cover.

2. Using tool J–29077-A or equivalent, remove the seal from the front cover.

3. Install new seal coated with engine oil using tool J–37309 or equivalent.

4. Reverse procedure to install. Connect the battery negative cable.

NOTE: Do not remove seal installing tool J–37309, until the front cover has been installed and the bolts torqued.

Timing Chain and Sprockets

REMOVAL & INSTALLATION

Except ZR-1

1. Disconnect the negative battery

17–35

cable, then remove the engine front cover.

2. Rotate the crankshaft and align the timing marks.

3. Remove the camshaft gear bolts. Remove the camshaft gear.

4. Remove the timing chain.

5. With a suitable puller, carefully remove the crankshaft gear sprocket. Remove the key from the end of the crankshaft keyway. Inspect the keyway surface for excessive wear or rounding. Replace if necessary.

6. Visually inspect the crankshaft and camshaft gear teeth for chipped, missing and cracked teeth. Replace all damaged parts, as the use of a damaged gear will result in timing chain failure.

7. Installation is the reverse of the removal procedure. Connect the battery negative cable.

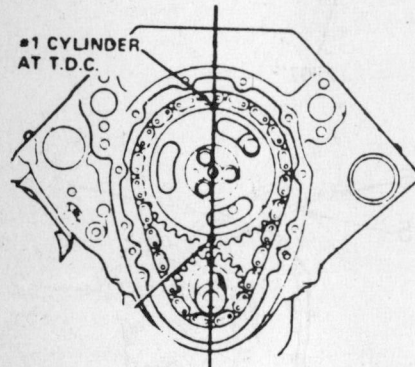

Timing marks—Except ZR-1

ZR-1

PRIMARY TIMING CHAIN AND SPROCKET

1. Disconnect battery negative cable, then remove the front cover.

2. Remove the left and right intake camshafts. Remove the bolts attaching the primary chain guide to the oil pump, then the guide from the vehicle.

3. Remove the idler sprocket assembly attaching bolts, then the primary chain from the idler sprocket and crankshaft sprocket.

4. Remove the bolts attaching the primary chain guide to the oil pump and the chain guide.

5. Using tool J-38211 or equivalent, remove the crankshaft sprocket.

6. Remove the drift key and oil pump seal from crankshaft.

To install:

7. Inspect the primary chain guide for excessive wear. Wear groove should not exceed a depth of 0.040 in. (1.0mm). If necessary, replace wear strip. Apply Loctite to chain guide bolt threads. Torque bolts to 89 inch lbs. (10 Nm).

8. Inspect primary chain and sprocket for wear or damage. If abnormal wear or damage is present on either the idler sprocket, chain or crankshaft sprocket, all 3 must be replaced as an assembly.

NOTE: When installing guide, push guide with finger so the slack is removed from the chain. Do not use any tools.

9. Install crankshaft sprocket using tool J-38132 or equivalent. Installation is the reverse of the removal procedure. Connect battery negative cable.

NOTE: Ensure that sprocket is installed with short shoulder facing the front.

SECONDARY TIMING CHAINS AND SPROCKET

1. Disconnect battery negative cable.

2. Remove the camshafts, then the primary timing chain.

3. Remove the left and right secondary timing chain tensioners.

4. Remove the left and secondary chains from the idler sprocket. Remove idler sprocket attaching bolts and the idler sprocket.

5. Remove the left and right secondary chains from the vehicle.

To install:

6. Always install new timing chain tensioners. Coat tensioner with engine oil.

7. Ensure the oil hole in the tensioner piston is installed in a vertical position.

8. Check that the fork on the end of the tensioner is properly engaged onto the chain guide.

9. Torque chain tensioner bolts to 89 inch lbs. (10 Nm). Apply Loctite to bolt threads.

10. Inspect chains and sprockets for abnormal wear or damage. If abnormal wear or damage is present on either the secondary timing chain, cam sprockets or idler sprockets, all must be replaced as an assembly.

11. Inspect the idler sprocket shaft bearings for wear or damage. If necessary, replace idler sprocket shaft bearings as follows:

a. Using tool J-37328 or equivalent, remove bearings from idler sprocket.

b. When installing bearings, ensure the manufacture's name and part No. are visible from either end of the sprocket assembly.

c. Using a suitable press, press in bearings until bearings are flush with idler sprocket. Apply minimum pressure to obtain a 0.0–1.3mm below the surface.

12. Reverse procedure to install.

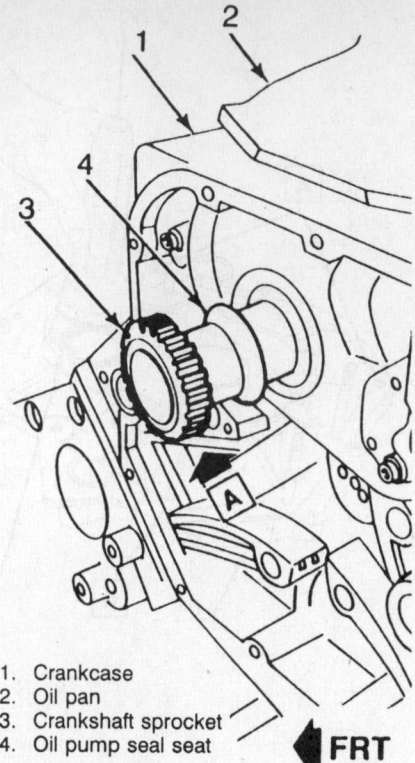

1. Crankcase
2. Oil pan
3. Crankshaft sprocket
4. Oil pump seal seat

◄ FRT

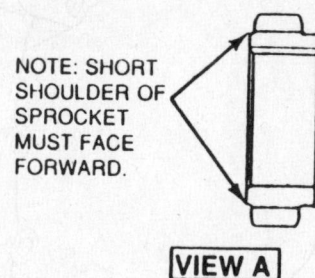

NOTE: SHORT SHOULDER OF SPROCKET MUST FACE FORWARD.

VIEW A

Crankshaft sprocket and oil pump seal— ZR-1

Camshaft

REMOVAL & INSTALLATION

1987–88 Vehicles

1. Disconnect the negative battery cable.

2. Relieve the fuel system pressure.

3. Drain the cooling system.

4. Disconnect air conditioning accumulator from shroud and lay aside.

5. Disconnect upper transmission cooler line at radiator.

6. Disconnect fan wire at fan and fan shroud. Remove cooling fan.

7. Disconnect lower transmission cooler line and remove fitting at radiator.

8. Remove upper fan shroud bolts and remove shroud.

9. Remove the radiator and air conditioning condenser.

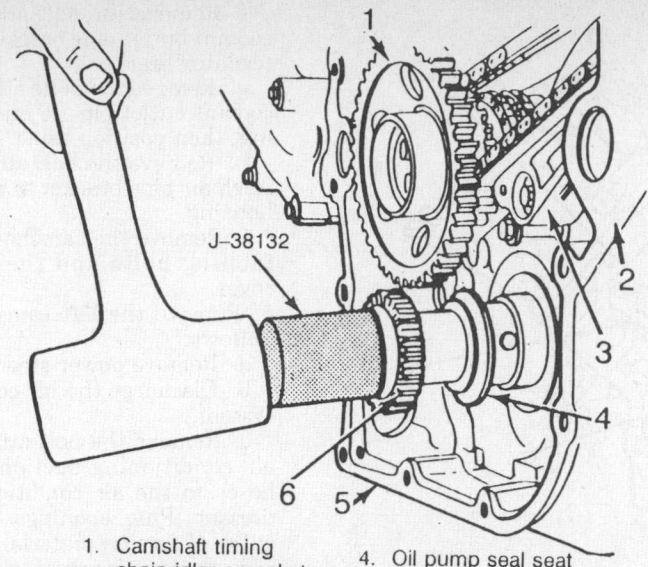

1. Camshaft timing chain idler sprocket
2. Cylinder case
3. Camshaft secondary timing chain fixed left side guide
4. Oil pump seal seat
5. Crankcase
6. Crankshaft sprocket

Installing crankshaft sprocket—ZR-1

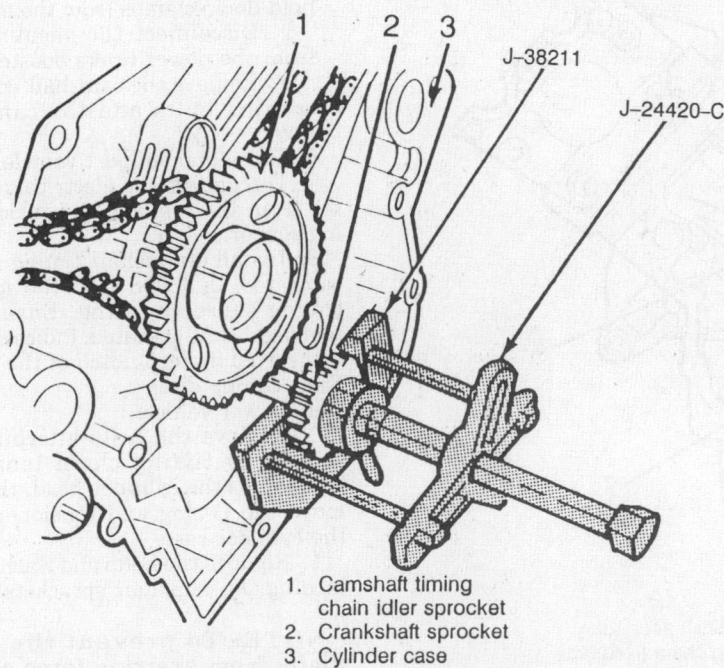

1. Camshaft timing chain idler sprocket
2. Crankshaft sprocket
3. Cylinder case

Removing crankshaft sprocket—ZR-1

10. Remove the intake manifold.
11. Remove the serpentine drive belt.
12. Remove the water pump damper and the crankshaft pulley.
13. Disconnect the power steering line.
14. Remove the vibration damper.
15. Raise the vehicle and support it safely.
16. Drain the engine oil and remove the oil pan.
17. Lower the vehicle.

18. Remove the AIR pump.
19. Disconnect the fuel inlet and return lines.
20. Remove the air conditioning compressor brackets and position the compressor to the side.
21. Remove the water pump.
22. Remove front cover bolts. Remove front cover.
23. Rotate crankshaft and align timing marks.

24. Remove cam gear bolts remove chain and gear.
25. Remove camshaft, using care not to damage the camshaft bearings.
To install:
26. When installing a new camshaft, coat camshaft lobes with Molykote® or equivalent.
27. Lubricate camshaft journals with engine oil, then install camshaft.
28. Install the timing chain on the camshaft sprocket. Position the sprocket vertically with the chain hanging down and align the marks on the camshaft with the marks on the camshaft sprockets.
29. Align the dowel in the camshaft with the dowel hole in the camshaft sprocket, then install the sprocket on the camshaft. Torque bolts to 20 ft. lbs. (27 Nm).
30. Install crankcase front cover.
31. Install valve lifters, then reverse remaining removal procedures for installation.

1989–91 Except ZR-1

1. Disconnect battery negative cable, then remove the radiator and air conditioning condenser assembly.
2. Relieve fuel system pressure, then remove the intake manifold, rocker arms, pushrods and valve lifters.
3. Remove timing chain, the camshaft retainer bolts and the retainer.
4. Remove the camshaft from the vehicle.

NOTE: When removing the camshaft, rotate and support the camshaft as it is drawn out from the cylinder block.

To install:
5. Using a micrometer, check the camshaft bearing journals for an out-of-round condition. If journals exceed 0.001 in. out-of-round, the camshaft should be replaced.
6. Inspect the camshaft bearings for wear or damage. Replace as necessary.
7. When installing the camshaft, coat the camshaft lobes and distributor drive gear with a suitable camshaft prelube.
8. Reverse procedure to install.

1990–91 ZR-1

1. Disconnect battery negative cable.
2. When removing right bank camshafts, remove the oil filter housing.
3. When removing the left bank camshafts, remove the air conditioning compressor.
4. Remove the right camshaft cover as follows:
   a. Drain engine coolant into a suitable container.

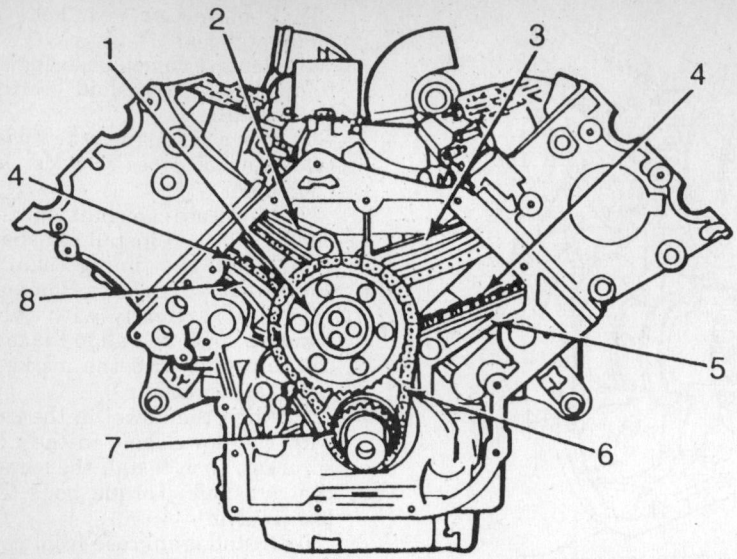

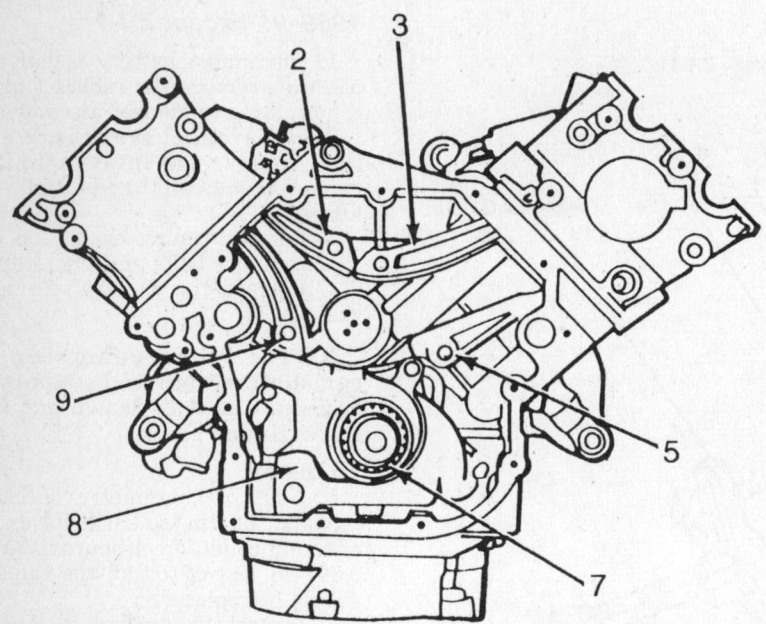

1. Camshaft timing chain idler sprocket assembly
2. Camshaft secondary timing chain fixed right side guide
3. Camshaft secondary timing chain fixed right side guide
4. Camshaft secondary timing chain
5. Camshaft secondary timing chain fixed left side guide
6. Camshaft primary timing chain
7. Crankshaft sprocket
8. Oil pump
9. Camshaft timing chain pivot right side guide

Timing chain and guide location – ZR-1

b. Remove spark plug wires from plugs.

c. Disconnect the electrical connector from the blower motor resistor block.

d. Remove the screws attaching the evaporator housing quarter panel, then remove the panel.

e. Remove the oil pressure sensor from the oil filter housing.

f. Remove the bolt attaching the coolant outlet pipe bracket to the alternator bracket.

g. Remove the bolts attaching the coolant outlet pipe to injector housing, then position aside.

h. Remove the bolt attaching the fresh air pipe bracket to the injector housing.

i. Remove the camshaft cover attaching bolts and the camshaft cover.

5. Remove the left camshaft cover as follows:

a. Remove power steering pump.

b. Discharge the air conditioning system.

c. Remove the bolt attaching the air conditioning suction/discharge hoses to the air conditioning compressor. Plug openings to prevent entry of foreign material.

d. Remove spark plug wires from spark plugs.

e. Disconnect the ventilation breather hose from the camshaft cover.

f. Remove the bolts attaching the throttle and cruise control cable hold-down clamps from the plenum.

g. Disconnect the vacuum hose from the power brake booster.

h. Remove the camshaft cover attaching bolts and the camshaft cover.

6. Raise and support vehicle.

7. Disconnect the electrical connector from the crankshaft ignition timing sensor.

8. Install crankshaft timing slot locator tool J–38098 into the ignition timing sensor opening. Ensure the tool head is fully seated, indicating pin is inserted in deep notch of the crankshaft timing disc.

9. Lower vehicle.

10. Remove the bolts attaching the secondary timing chain tensioner housing to the cylinder head, then remove the O-ring and tensioner from the cylinder case.

11. Remove the bolts and washers attaching the camshaft sprockets.

NOTE: To prevent the camshafts from exerting force on the crankshaft timing slot locator tool J–38098, install a wrench on the rear camshaft hex when removing the sprocket bolts.

12. Remove the camshaft timing plates and pins.

13. Remove the camshaft retainers and thrust washers.

14. Remove the camshafts and sprockets from the vehicle. Install timing chain retainers J–38099 to retain secondary chain loops.

15. Remove lifters from bores. Make sure any lifters, to be reused, are re-

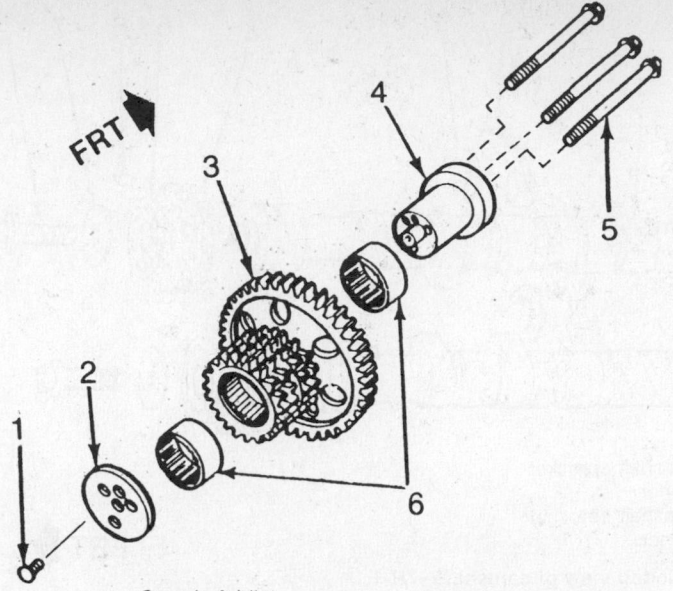

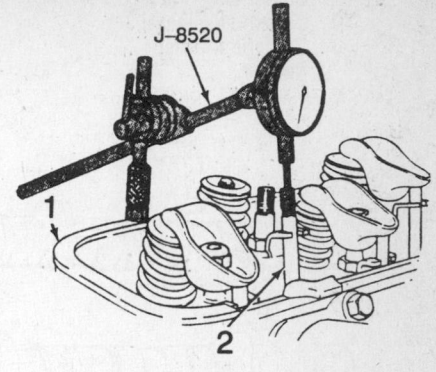

1. Cylinder head
2. Pushrod

Checking camshaft lobe lift—1989–91 Except ZR-1

1. Camshaft idler sprocket assembly screw
2. Camshaft timing chain idler sprocket washer
3. Camshaft timing chain idler sprocket
4. Camshaft timing chain idler sprocket shaft
5. Camshaft idler sprocket bolt
6. Camshaft idler sprocket bolt
7. Camshaft timing chain idler sprocket bearing

Camshaft timing chain idler sprocket assembly—ZR-1

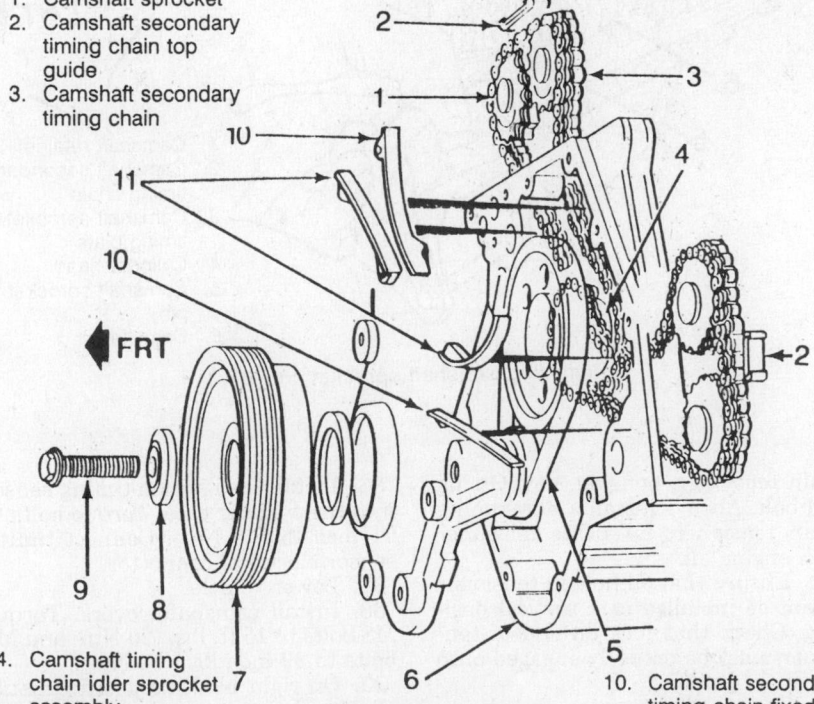

1. Camshaft sprocket
2. Camshaft secondary timing chain top guide
3. Camshaft secondary timing chain
4. Camshaft timing chain idler sprocket assembly
5. Camshaft primary timing chain
6. Cylinder case
7. Torsional damper
8. Crankshaft damper washer
9. Crankshaft damper bolt
10. Camshaft secondary timing chain fixed guide
11. Camshaft secondary timing chain pivot guide

Installing torsional damper—ZR-1

tained in proper order so each one can be returned to its original bore.

To install:
16. Inspect the camshaft bearing journals for wear or damage.
17. Inspect the camshaft bearing surfaces in the cylinder head and camshaft cover for wear or damage.

NOTE: The camshaft cover and cylinder head must be replaced as a set if excessive wear or damage to the bearing surfaces is found.

18. Lubricate lifters and bores with engine oil, then install lifters into bores.
19. Install the camshaft sprocket onto the secondary timing chain, while removing the timing chain retainers J–38099.
20. Slide camshaft into the sprocket, noting the position of the alignment hole for timing pin tool installation. Position the camshaft in the neutral position, no valves opened.
21. Lubricate camshaft journals, lobes, thrust washers and retainers with clean engine oil.
22. Install the camshaft thrust washers, retainers and the bolts. Torque bolts to 89 inch lbs. (10 Nm).
23. Repeat steps 18 through 22 for the remaining camshafts.
24. Install timing pins J–37326 into camshaft retainers and indexing holes in camshafts. The camshafts can not be rotated to align holes.
25. Install camshaft secondary chain pre-tensioner J–37305. Tighten until all the slack has been removed from the timing chain.
26. Install timing plate pin. If no holes line up on the timing plate, reverse plate.
27. Install bolts finger tight. New

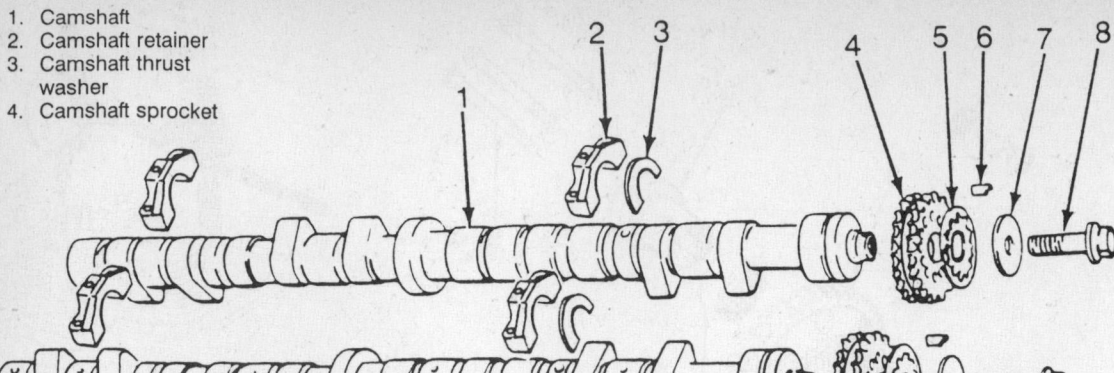

1. Camshaft
2. Camshaft retainer
3. Camshaft thrust washer
4. Camshaft sprocket

5. Camshaft sprocket timing plate
6. Camshaft sprocket pin

7. Camshaft sprocket washer
8. Camshaft sprocket washer

FRT ▶

Exploded view of camshaft—ZR-1

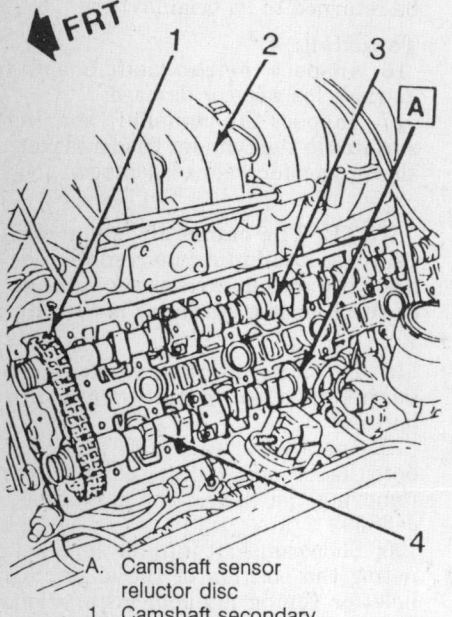

◀ FRT

A. Camshaft sensor reluctor disc
1. Camshaft secondary timing chain
2. Plenum
3. Intake left side camshaft
4. Exhaust left side camshaft

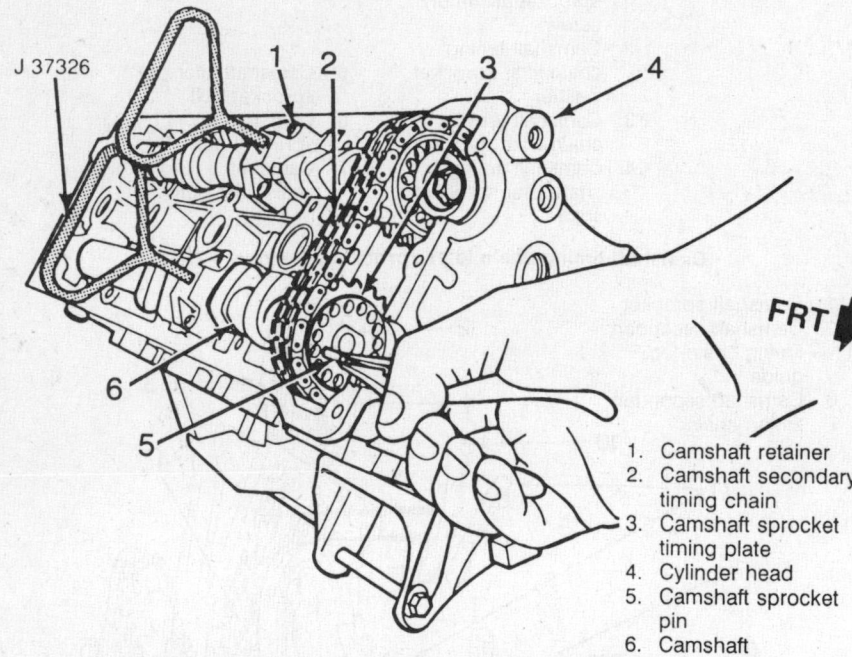

FRT ▶

1. Camshaft retainer
2. Camshaft secondary timing chain
3. Camshaft sprocket timing plate
4. Cylinder head
5. Camshaft sprocket pin
6. Camshaft

Installing camshaft sprocket pin—ZR-1

Camshaft replacement—ZR-1

camshaft bolts should be used each time a bolt is removed.

28. Apply Loctite on the camshaft sprocket bolts and torque bolts to 19 ft. lbs. (25 Nm) and turn 80–85 degrees using torque angle meter J–36660. Install a backup wrench on the camshaft hex on the rear of the camshaft.

29. Remove timing pins J–37326.

30. Remove the secondary timing chain pre-tensioner tool J–37305.

31. Install the GM secondary timing

chain tensioner, housing, new O-ring and bolt. Always install a new timing chain tensioner. Lubricate tensioner with engine oil.

32. Ensure that oil hole in tensioner piston be installed in a vertical position. Check that fork on end of tensioner must be properly engaged onto the chain guide.

33. Torque chain tensioner bolts to 89 inch lbs. (10 Nm).

34. Raise and support vehicle.

35. Remove crankshaft timing slot locator J–38098 from the cylinder case.

36. Install the ignition timing sensor into the cylinder case. Torque bolts to 71 inch lbs. (8 Nm). Connect timing sensor electrical connector.

37. Lower vehicle.

38. Install camshaft covers. Torque M8 bolts to 15 ft. lbs. (20 Nm) and M6 bolts to 89 inch lbs. (10 Nm).

39. On right bank camshafts, install oil filter housing.

40. On left bank camshafts, install air conditioning compressor.

41. Reconnect battery negative cable.

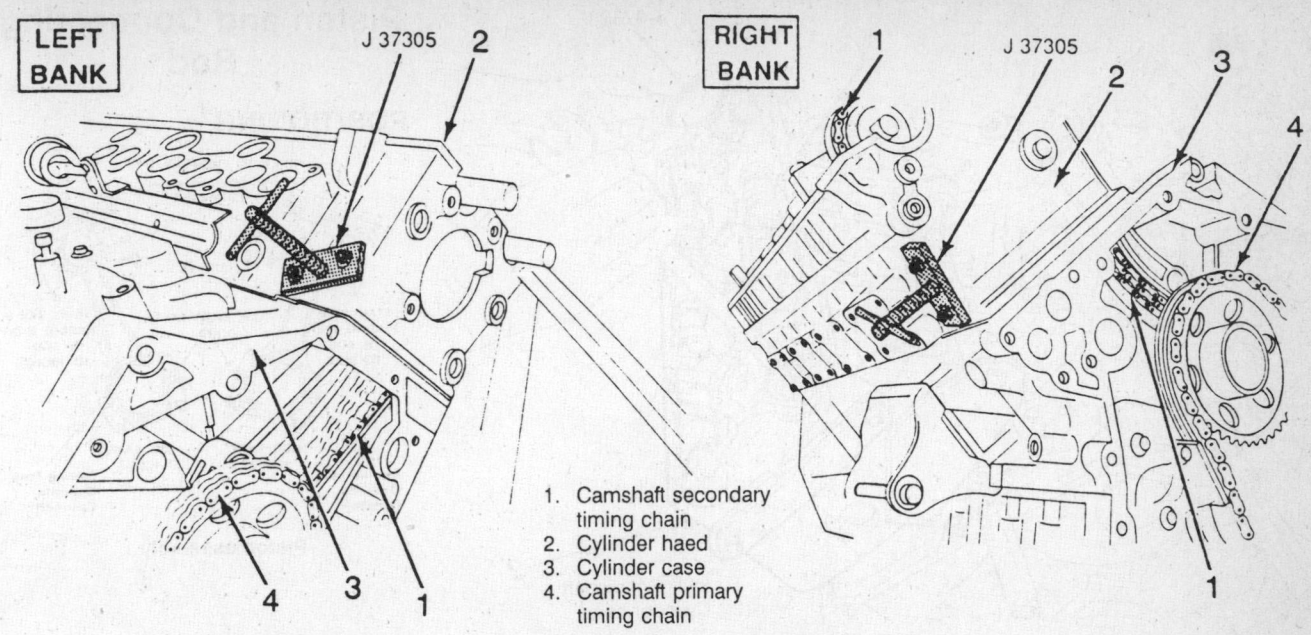

1. Camshaft secondary timing chain
2. Cylinder haed
3. Cylinder case
4. Camshaft primary timing chain

Secondary timing chain pre-tensioners

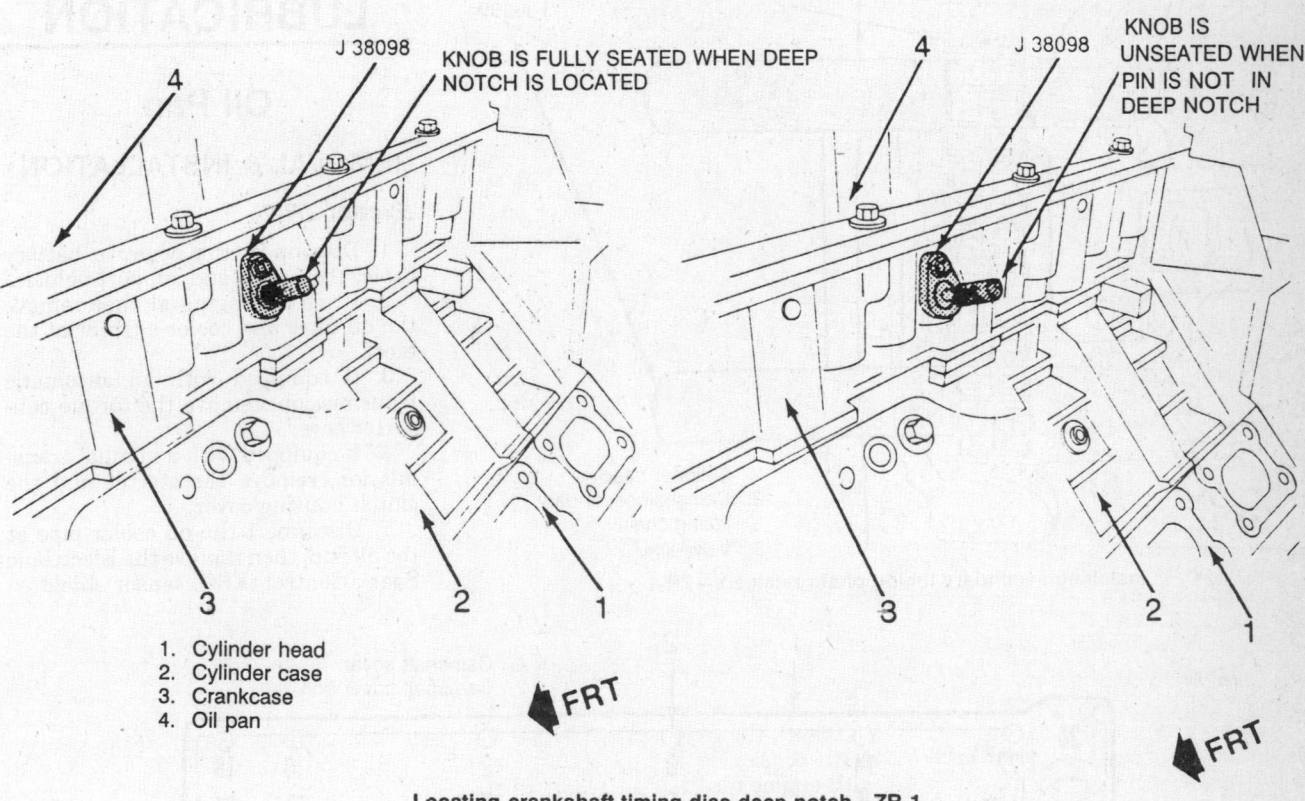

1. Cylinder head
2. Cylinder case
3. Crankcase
4. Oil pan

Locating crankshaft timing disc deep notch—ZR-1

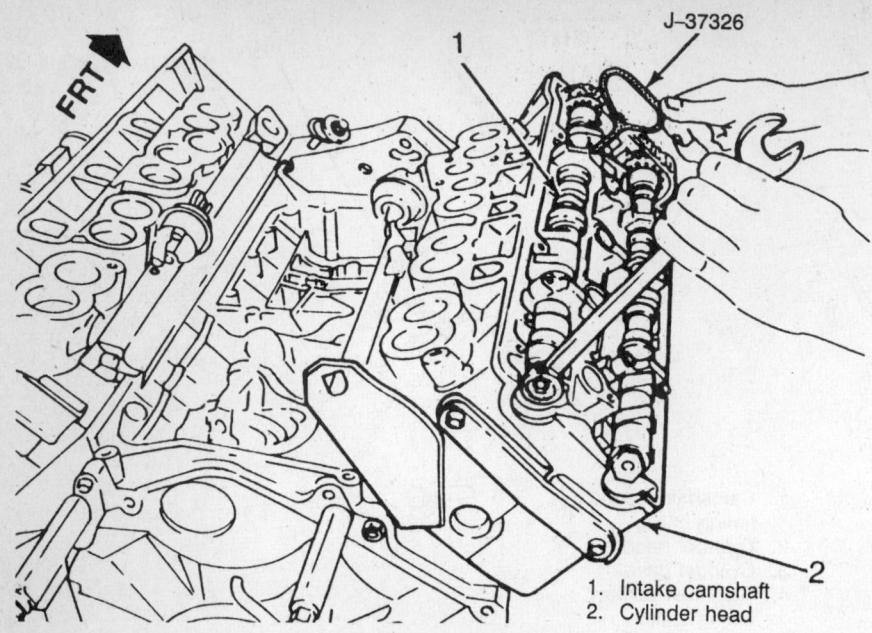

1. Intake camshaft
2. Cylinder head

Installing camshaft timing pin tool

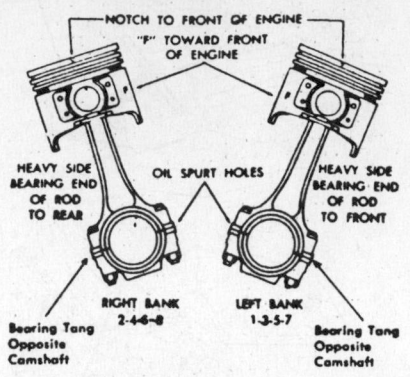

Piston and Connecting Rod

POSITIONING

Piston assembly

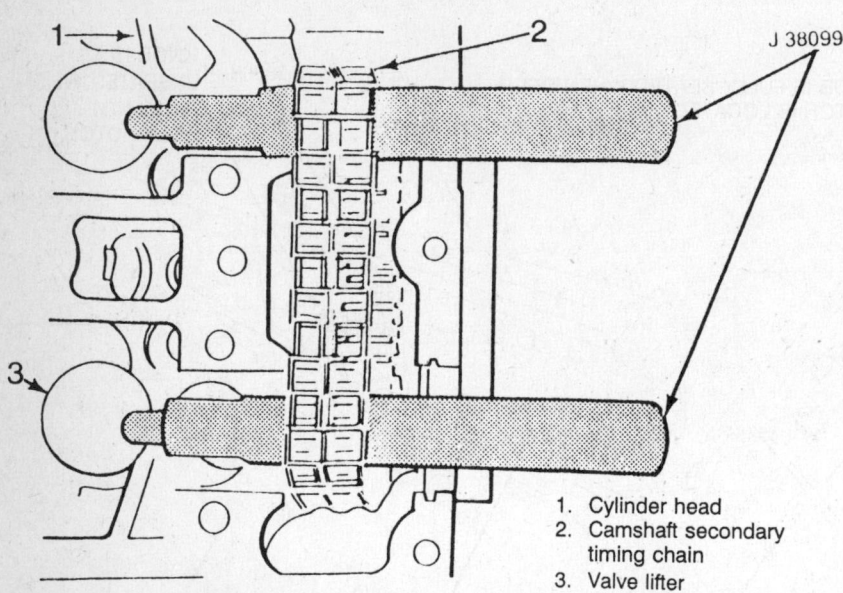

1. Cylinder head
2. Camshaft secondary timing chain
3. Valve lifter

Installing secondary timing chain retainers — ZR-1

ENGINE LUBRICATION

Oil Pan

REMOVAL & INSTALLATION

Except ZR-1

1. Disconnect the negative battery cable, then raise and support vehicle.

2. Drain the engine oil, then remove the oil filter and cooler adapter at the block.

3. If equipped with an automatic transmission, remove the torque converter cover.

4. If equipped with a manual transmission, remove the starter and the clutch housing cover.

5. Disconnect the oil cooler pipe at the oil pan, then remove the Electronic Spark Control (ESC) sensor shield.

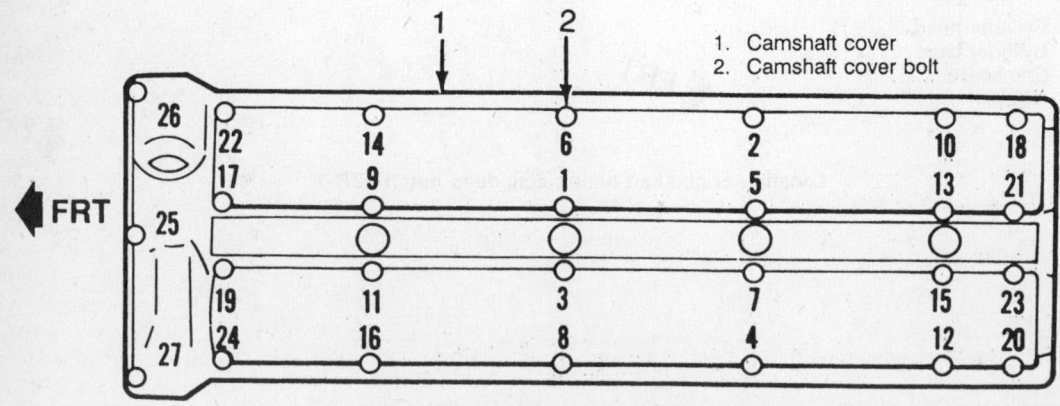

1. Camshaft cover
2. Camshaft cover bolt

Camshaft cover torque sequence — ZR-1

6. Remove the front crossmember braces, then the oil pan bolts and the pan.

7. Installation is the reverse of the removal procedure. Tighten the bolts to 16 ft. lbs. (22 Nm). Connect the battery negative cable.

ZR-1

1. Disconnect battery negative cable, then remove the oil lever indicator from the guide tube.

2. Raise and support vehicle, then drain the engine oil.

3. Remove the clutch housing cover attaching bolts, then the clutch housing from the vehicle.

4. Remove the bolts attaching the AIR pipe to the oil pan, then remove the right and left converter heat shields.

5. Remove the right and left nuts attaching the engine mounts at the front crossmember rear brace, then the bolts attaching the front crossmember rear braces to the front crossmember.

6. Remove the bolts attaching the left front crossmember rear brace to the left front side member and brace from the vehicle.

7. Remove the bolts attaching the right front crossmember rear brace to the right front side member, then remove brace from vehicle.

8. Remove the oil pan attaching bolts, the oil pan and gasket from vehicle.

To install:

9. Apply Loctite to bolt threads. Torque oil pan front screws to 89 inch lbs. (10 Nm). Torque oil pan bolts to 20 ft. lbs. (26 Nm).

10. Torque left and right front crossmember rear brace to front crossmember bolts to 59 ft. lbs. (80 Nm).

11. Torque the left and right front crossmember rear brace to front side member bolts to 46 ft. lbs. (62 Nm).

12. Torque engine mounts to front crossmember bolts to 40 ft. lbs. (54 Nm).

13. Installation is the reverse of the removal procedure. Connect the battery negative cable.

Oil Pump

REMOVAL & INSTALLATION

Except ZR-1

1. Disconnect the negative battery cable.

2. Raise the vehicle and support it safely.

3. Drain the engine oil and remove the oil pan.

4. Support the oil pump by hand and remove the main bearing cap bolt.

5. Carefully remove the pump with the extension shaft.

To install:

6. Support the oil pump with extension shaft and assemble to the rear main bearing cap.

7. Ensure the slot on the top of the extension shaft is aligned with the drive tang on the lower end of the distributor driveshaft.

8. Torque the main bearing cap bolt to 80 ft. lbs. (108 Nm). Connect the battery negative cable and refill crankcase.

ZR-1

1. Disconnect battery negative cable.

2. Remove crankshaft sprocket.

3. Remove bolts attaching the oil pump to cylinder case, then remove the oil pump from the vehicle.

4. Remove O-ring from crankshaft.

To install:

5. Install new O-ring onto crankshaft.

6. Install oil pump and bolts. Finger tight only.

NOTE: Apply Loctite to bolt threads. Ensure the 2 flats of the pump drive gear align with the 2 flats on the crankshaft. Do not force pump onto crankshaft.

7. Using oil pump aligning tool J–38383, align oil pump on the crank-

shaft. Torque oil pump bolts to 20 ft. lbs. (26 Nm).

8. Install a new oil pump shaft seal using tools J–38135 and J–38463.

NOTE: Ensure to install a new oil pump shaft seal whenever the pump is removed from the vehicle.

Rear Main Bearing Oil Seal

REMOVAL & INSTALLATION

Except ZR-1

1. Disconnect the negative battery cable.

2. Raise the vehicle and support it safely.

3. Remove the transmission.

4. Drain the engine oil and remove the oil pan.

5. Remove the studs from the retainer.

6. Remove the retainer and seal assembly.

7. Using the notches provided in the retainer, pry out the seal.

8. Remove the gasket.

NOTE: Whenever the retainer is removed, a new retainer gasket and rear main seal must be installed.

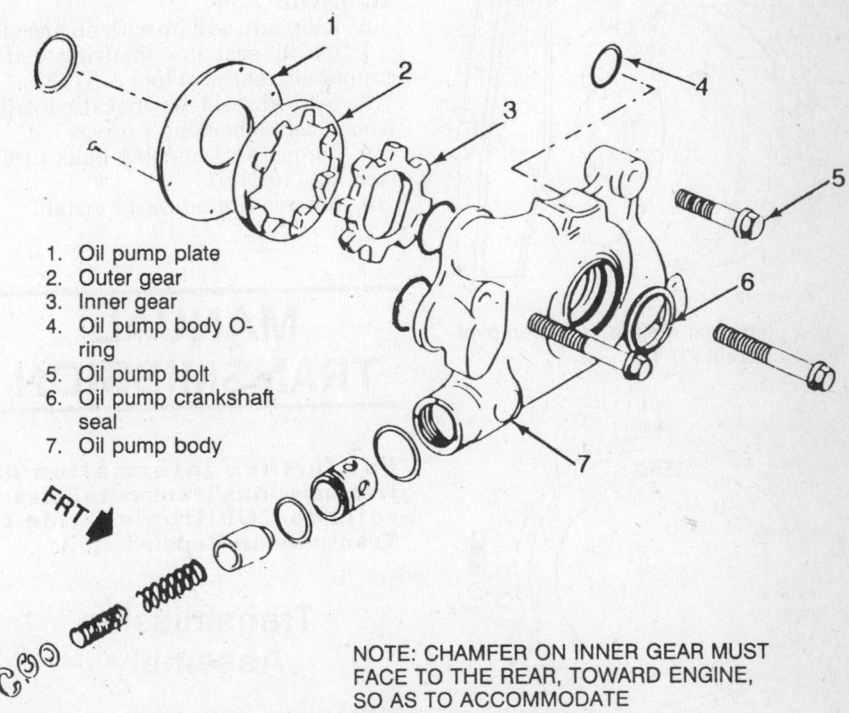

1. Oil pump plate
2. Outer gear
3. Inner gear
4. Oil pump body O-ring
5. Oil pump bolt
6. Oil pump crankshaft seal
7. Oil pump body

NOTE: CHAMFER ON INNER GEAR MUST FACE TO THE REAR, TOWARD ENGINE, SO AS TO ACCOMMODATE CRANKSHAFT O-RING.

Oil pump assembly–ZR-1

To install:

9. Clean the mating surfaces of the case and the retainer assembly.

10. Install a new gasket on the studs in the engine case.

NOTE: It is not necessary to use any type of sealant to retain the gasket in place.

11. Install the retainer-to-case bolts. Torque the bolts to 90–120 inch lbs. (10–13 Nm) on 1987–88 vehicles and 11 ft. lbs. (15 Nm) on 1989–91 vehicles.

12. Install a new gasket on the oil pan. Apply sealant onto the 2 front corners where the cover meets the case and where the rear seal retainer meets the case.

13. Install the oil pan and gasket.

14. Lubricate the inside and outside diameters of the oil seal with engine oil.

15. Install the seal on tool J–35621.

16. Thread the screws into the rear of the crankshaft. Tighten the screws snugly to insure the seal will be installed squarely over the crankshaft.

17. Tighten the wing nut on the tool until it bottoms.

18. Remove the tool from the crankshaft.

ZR-1

1. Disconnect battery negative cable.

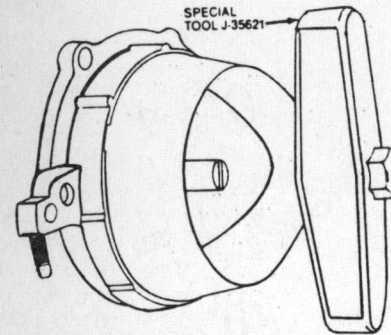

One piece rear main oil seal removal tool—Except ZR-1

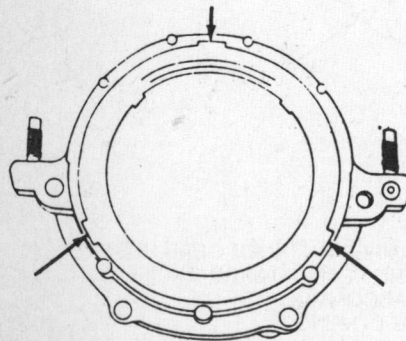

Removing the seal from seal retainer— Except ZR-1

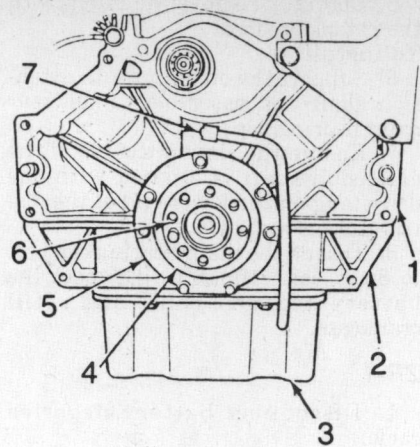

1. Cylinder case
2. Crankcase
3. Oil pan
4. Crankcase rear seal
5. Rear oil seal housing
6. Crankshaft
7. Cylinder case drain pipe

Crankshaft rear seal—ZR-1

2. Remove transmission and flywheel.

3. Remove the screws attaching the crankshaft rear main oil seal/housing assembly to the cylinder case.

4. Remove the seal/housing assembly from the vehicle.

5. Remove the seal from the housing.

To install:

6. Lubricate seal lip with engine oil.

7. Install seal into housing using crankshaft rear seal tool J–37312.

8. Seal should be installed 1.0–1.5mm below housing surface.

9. Torque seal housing bolts to 89 inch lbs. (10 Nm).

10. Reverse procedure to install.

MANUAL TRANSMISSION

For further information on transmissions/transaxles, please refer to "Chilton's Guide to Transmission Repair".

Transmission Assembly

REMOVAL & INSTALLATION

1. Disconnect the negative battery cable.

2. On 1987–88 vehicles, remove the distributor cap.

3. On 1989–91 vehicles, remove the console trim plate, then the shift knob assembly and reverse lockout collar.

4. Raise the vehicle and support it safely.

5. On 1987–88 vehicles, if equipped with a convertible top, remove the upper and lower underbody braces.

6. Remove the complete exhaust system as an assembly.

7. Remove the exhaust hanger at the transmission.

8. Support the transmission using the proper equipment.

9. Remove the bolts attaching the driveline support beam at the axle and the transmission. Remove the driveline support beam from the vehicle.

10. Mark the relationship of the driveshaft to the axle companion flange. Remove the trunnion bearing straps and disengage the rear universal joint from the axle. Slide the driveshaft slip yoke out of the overdrive unit and remove the shaft from the vehicle.

11. Disconnect the transmission cooler lines at the overdrive unit, if equipped.

12. Disconnect the shift linkage at the side cover.

13. Disconnect the electrical connectors at the side cover. Disconnect the backup light switch, 1st gear switch, overdrive unit and speedometer sensor switch.

14. Lower the transmission and support the engine.

15. Remove the bolts attaching the transmission to the bell housing. Slide the transmission to the rear to disengage the input shaft from the clutch. Remove the transmission from the vehicle.

To install:

16. Clean and repack the clutch release bearing.

17. Install the transmission and attaching bolts.

18. Connect the oil cooler line pipes to the overdrive unit, if equipped. Torque the connector fittings to 8–12 ft. lbs. (11–16 Nm).

19. Install and align the driveline support beam.

20. Install the driveshaft.

21. Connect and adjust the throttle shift linkage.

22. Connect the backup light switch, overdrive unit, if equipped, speedometer sensor and 1st gear electrical connectors.

23. Refill transmission to proper level. The 4 or 6 speed section uses SAE-80 W or SAE-80 W-90 GL-5 gear lube. The overdrive unit, if equipped uses Dexron®II automatic transmission fluid.

24. Install the exhaust system components. Reinstall upper and lower underbody braces, if removed. Connect the battery negative cable.

CLUTCH

Clutch Assembly

REMOVAL & INSTALLATION

1. Remove the transmission from the vehicle.
2. Disconnect the clutch fork pushrod and spring.
3. Remove the slave cylinder attaching bolts.
4. Remove the flywheel housing.
5. Slide the clutch fork from the ball stud and remove the fork from the dust boot. The ball stud is threaded into the clutch housing and is easily replaced, if necessary.
6. Install a clutch pilot tool.

NOTE: Look for the assembly markings X on the flywheel and the clutch cover, pressure plate

assembly. If there are none, scribe marks to identify the position of the clutch cover relative to the flywheel.

7. Loosen the clutch cover bolts evenly, until the spring pressure is relieved, then remove the bolts and clutch assembly.
8. Clean the pressure plate and the flywheel face.
To install:
9. Position the disc and pressure plate assembly on the flywheel and install a pilot tool.
10. Install the pressure plate assembly bolts. Make sure the mark on the cover is aligned with the mark on the flywheel. Tighten the bolts alternately and evenly to 30 ft. lbs. (41 Nm).
11. Remove the pilot tool.
12. Remove the release fork and lubricate the ball socket and the fork fingers at the throw-out bearing with graphite or Molycoat® grease. Reinstall the release fork.
13. Lubricate the inside recess and the fork groove of the throw-out bearing with a light coat of graphite or Molycoat® grease.
14. Install the clutch release fork and dust boot in the clutch housing and the throw-out bearing on the fork, then install the flywheel housing. Tighten flywheel housing bolts to 30 ft. lbs. (41 Nm). Reinstall the slave cylinder.

15. Connect the fork pushrod and spring.
16. Adjust the shift linkage.
17. Adjust the clutch pedal free-play. Bleed the hydraulic clutch system.

Clutch Master Cylinder

REMOVAL & INSTALLATION

1. Disconnect the negative battery cable.
2. Remove the hush panel from underneath of the dash.
3. Disconnect the pushrod from the clutch pedal.
4. Disconnect the hydraulic line at the master cylinder.
5. Remove the clutch master cylinder retaining bolts. Remove the clutch master cylinder from the vehicle.
6. Installation is the reverse of the removal procedure. Bleed the system, as required. Connect battery negative cable.

1. Master cylinder
2. Clutch pedal
3. Gasket
4. Clutch master cylinder bolt

Clutch master cylinder

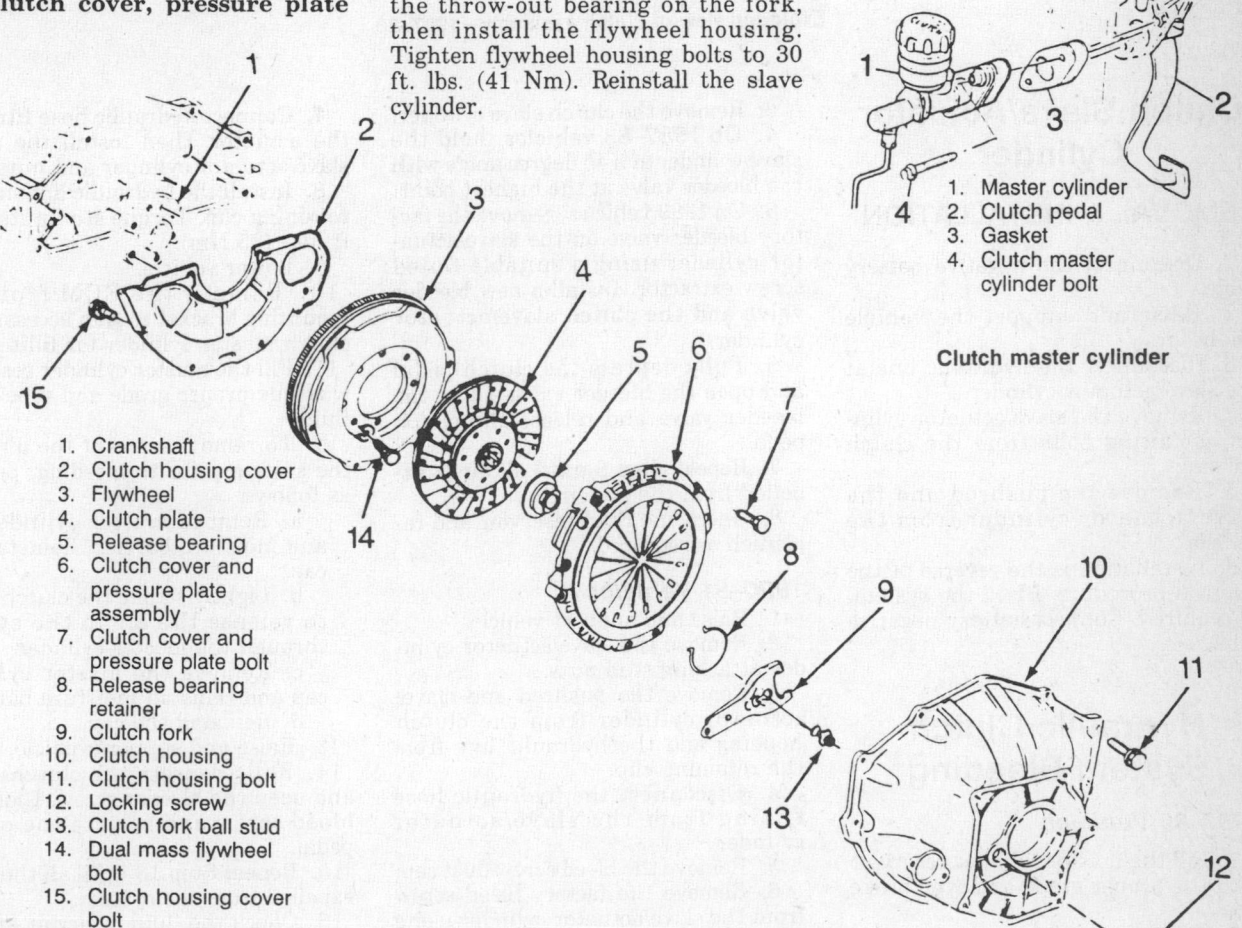

1. Crankshaft
2. Clutch housing cover
3. Flywheel
4. Clutch plate
5. Release bearing
6. Clutch cover and pressure plate assembly
7. Clutch cover and pressure plate bolt
8. Release bearing retainer
9. Clutch fork
10. Clutch housing
11. Clutch housing bolt
12. Locking screw
13. Clutch fork ball stud
14. Dual mass flywheel bolt
15. Clutch housing cover bolt

Exploded view of clutch assembly—1989–91

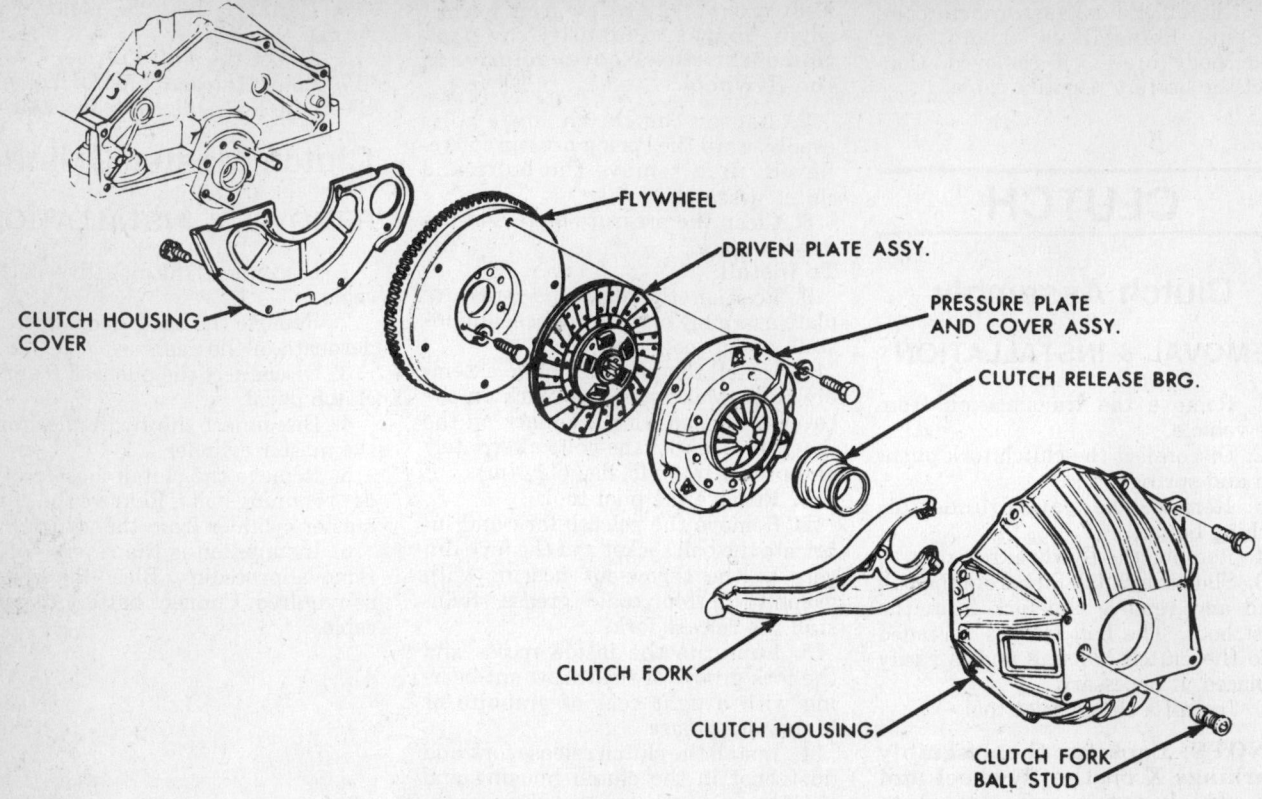

Exploded view of clutch assembly—1987–88

CLUTCH HOUSING COVER

FLYWHEEL

DRIVEN PLATE ASSY.

PRESSURE PLATE AND COVER ASSY.

CLUTCH RELEASE BRG.

CLUTCH FORK

CLUTCH HOUSING

CLUTCH FORK BALL STUD

Clutch Slave/Actuator Cylinder

REMOVAL & INSTALLATION

1. Disconnect the negative battery cable.
2. Raise and support the vehicle safely.
3. Disconnect the hydraulic line at the slave/actuator cylinder.
4. Remove the slave/actuator cylinder mounting bolts from the clutch housing.
5. Remove the pushrod and the slave/actuator cylinder from the vehicle.
6. Installation is the reverse of the removal procedure. Bleed the system, as required. Connect battery negative cable.

Hydraulic Clutch System Bleeding

1987–89 Vehicles

1. Fill the master cylinder reservoir with the proper grade and type brake fluid.
2. Raise the vehicle and support it safely.

3. Remove the clutch slave cylinder.
4. On 1987–88 vehicles, hold the slave cylinder at a 45 degree angle with the bleeder valve at the highest point.
5. On 1989 vehicles, remove the factory bleeder valve on the slave/actuator cylinder using a suitable fluted screw extractor. Install a new bleeder valve and the clutch slave/actuator cylinder.
6. Fully depress the clutch pedal and open the bleeder valve. Close the bleeder valve and release the clutch pedal.
7. Repeat Step 6 until all air is expelled from the system.
8. Check the fluid reservoir and replenish as required.

1990–91 Vehicles

1. Raise and support vehicle.
2. Remove the slave/actuator cylinder attaching stud nuts.
3. Remove the pushrod and slave/actuator cylinder from the clutch housing and the hydraulic line from the retaining clip.
4. Disconnect the hydraulic hose fitting from the slave/actuator cylinder.
5. Remove the bleed screw dust cap.
6. Remove the factory bleed screw from the slave/actuator cylinder using a fluted screw extractor. Install a new bleed screw.

7. Connect hydraulic hose fitting to the actuator, then install the clutch slave/actuator cylinder and nuts.
8. Install the hydraulic line into the retaining clip. Torque stud nuts to 19 ft. lbs. (25 Nm).
9. Lower vehicle.
10. Remove the ECM from the mounting bracket to gain access to the clutch master cylinder for filling.
11. Fill the master cylinder reservoir with the proper grade and type brake fluid.
12. To remove some of the air from the system prior to bleeding, proceed as follows:
    a. Remove master cylinder cap and moisture barrier. Reinstall the cap.
    b. Lightly stroke the clutch pedal to release the air in the system through the master cylinder.
    c. Remove the master cylinder cap and reinstall moisture barrier.
    d. Reinstall the cap.
13. Raise and support vehicle.
14. Fully depress the clutch pedal and open the bleeder screw. Close the bleed screw and release the clutch pedal.
15. Repeat Step 13 until all the air is expelled from the system.
16. Check the fluid reservoir and replenish, as required.
17. Torque bleeder screw until screw

breaks, requires for body clearance. Screw should break at approximately 10–14 ft. lbs. (14–19 Nm).

18. Install dust cap on the bleeder screw.

19. Lower the vehicle and install the ECM.

AUTOMATIC TRANSMISSION

For further information on transmissions/transaxles, please refer to "Chilton's Guide to Transmission Repair".

Transmission Assembly

REMOVAL & INSTALLATION

1. Disconnect the negative battery cable.

2. Raise and support the vehicle safely.

3. Disconnect the TV cable at the transmission.

4. Disconnect the oil cooler lines at the transmission.

5. Remove the complete exhaust system.

6. Remove the transmission inspection cover.

7. Remove the torque convertor to flywheel bolts. The relationship between the flywheel and convertor must be marked so proper balance is maintained after installation.

8. Matchmark the driveshaft and the rear yoke, for reinstallation purposes. With a drain pan positioned under the front yoke, unbolt and remove the driveshaft.

9. Mark and disconnect vacuum lines, wiring and the speedometer cable from the transmission, as required.

10. Place a transmission jack up against the transmission oil pan, then secure the transmission to the jack.

11. Remove the transmission mounting pad bolt(s), then carefully raise the transmission just enough to take the weight, of the transmission, off the supporting crossmember. Remove the transmission mounting pad.

NOTE: Exercise extreme care to avoid damage to underhood components while raising or lowering the transmission.

12. Remove the transmission dipstick, then unbolt and remove the filler tube.

1. Bolt 35 ft. lbs. (47 Nm)

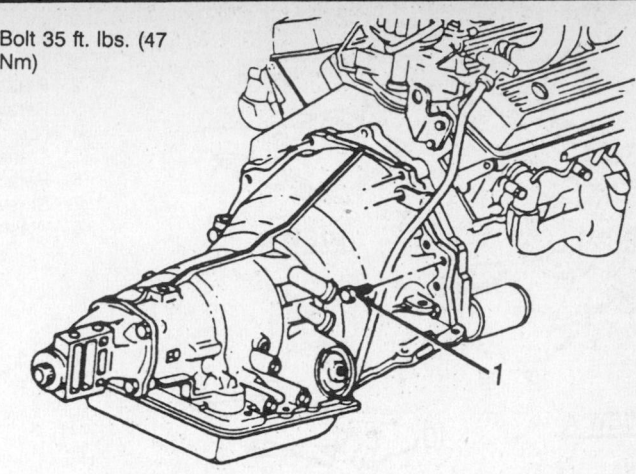

Installing the automatic transmission to the engine

13. Disconnect the floor shift cable. Disconnect the oil cooler lines from the transmission.

14. Support the engine using a jack placed beneath the engine oil pan. Be sure to put a block of wood between the jack and the oil pan, to prevent damage to the pan.

15. With the proper gauge wire, fasten the torque convertor to the transmission case.

16. Remove the transmission to engine mounting bolts, then carefully move the transmission rearward, downward and out from under the vehicle.

NOTE: If interference is encountered with the cable(s), cooler lines, etc., remove the component(s) before finally lowering the transmission.

To install:

17. Support transmission with jack, then install transmission.

18. Torque transmission to engine bolts to 35 ft. lbs.

19. Torque converter to flywheel bolts to 46 ft. lbs. (62 Nm). Ensure align marks made during removal.

20. Install converter cover and torque screws to 89 inch lbs.

21. Connect the oil cooler lines, then the TV cable.

22. Connect the electrical connectors to transmission.

23. Connect the speedometer electrical connector.

24. Connect the shift control cable.

25. Install the driveshaft, then the driveline support beam.

26. Install the exhaust system, if removed.

27. Connect the TV cable to the throttle lever.

28. Connect the battery negative cable and install the air cleaner.

29. Adjust the shift control cable and

TV cable. Refill the transmission to the proper level with Dexron®II automatic transmission fluid.

SHIFT LINKAGE ADJUST

1. Disconnect and remove the battery negative cable.

2. Place the control lever in the **N** position.

3. Raise and support vehicle.

4. Loosen the cable attachment at the shift lever.

5. Rotate the shift lever clockwise to **P** detent and then back to **N**.

6. Tighten the cable attachment to 15 ft. lbs. (20 Nm).

NOTE: The lever must be be held out of the P position when tightening the nut.

7. Lower the vehicle.

8. Check the cable adjustment by rotating the control lever through the detents.

9. Connect the battery negative cable.

THROTTLE LINKAGE CABLE

1. Check that the cable slider is in the 0 or fully re-adjusted position.

2. Rotate the throttle idler lever to the full travel stop position.

3. Slider must move toward the lever, when the lever is rotated to the full travel stop position.

4. Release lever.

5. Check TV cable operation. If readjustment is necessary, proceed as follows:

    a. Depress and hold the metal readjustment tab.

    b. Move the slider back through fitting in the direction opposite of the throttle idler lever, until slider stops against fitting.

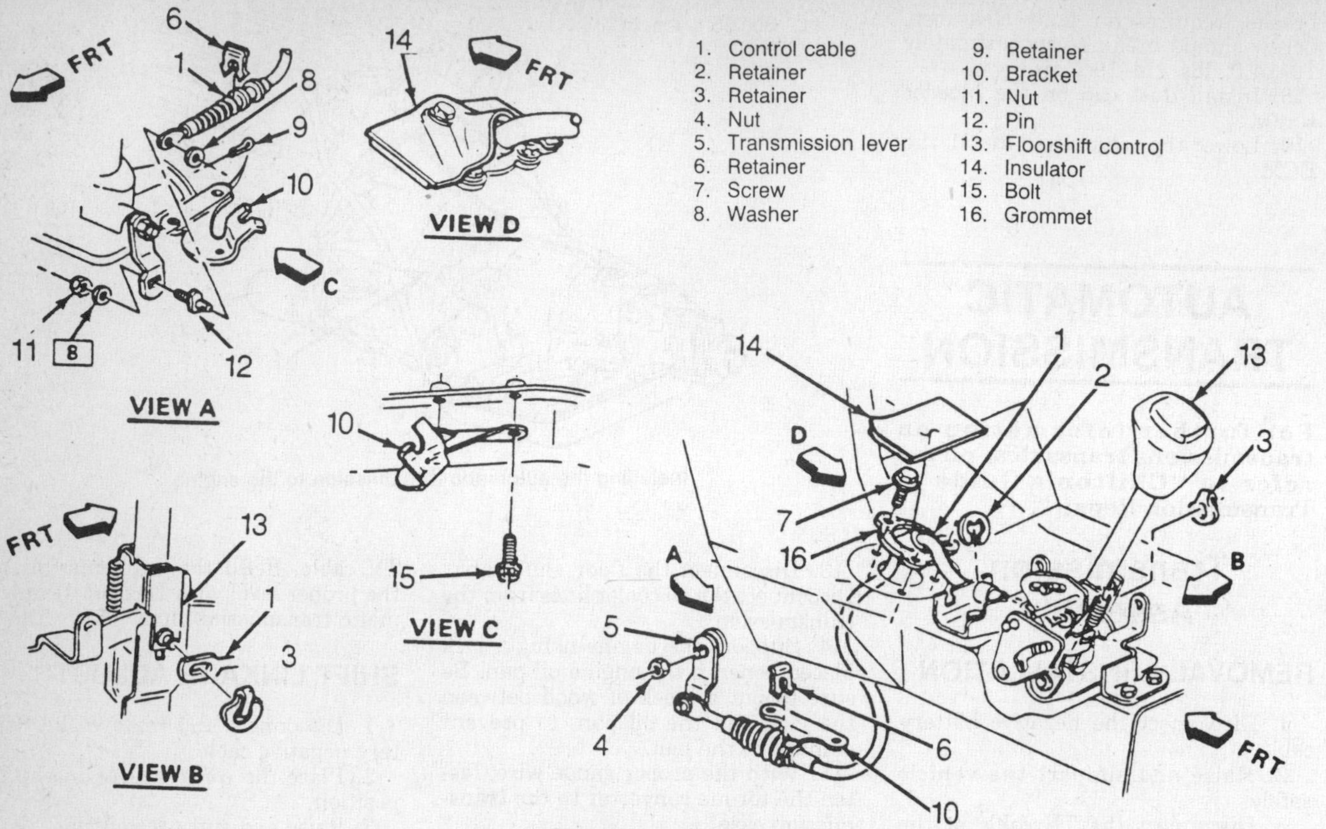

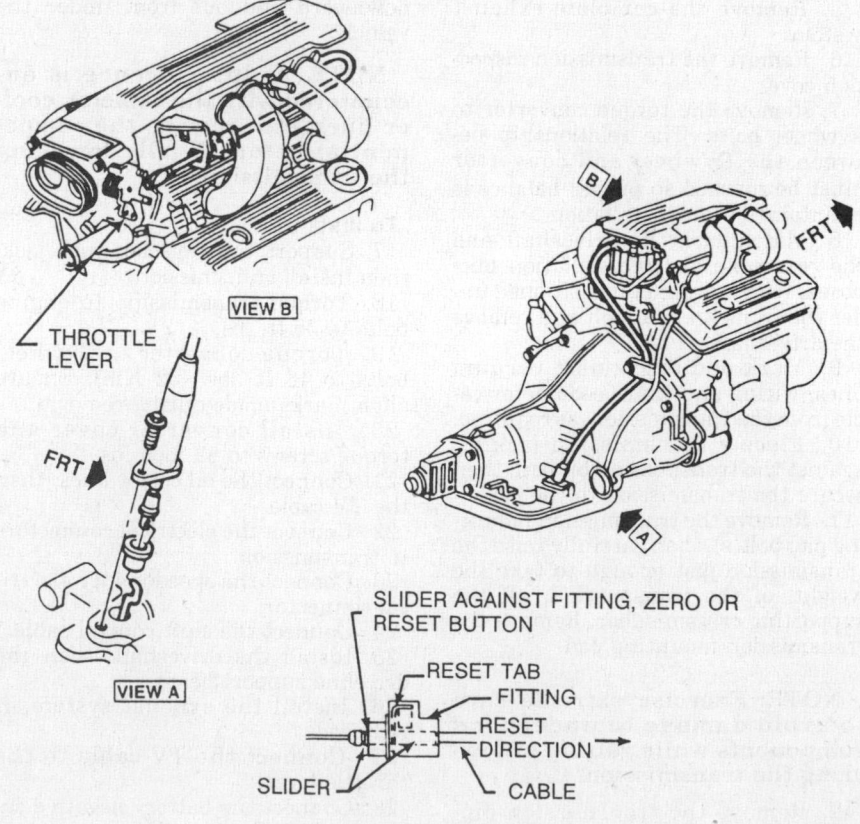

1. Control cable
2. Retainer
3. Retainer
4. Nut
5. Transmission lever
6. Retainer
7. Screw
8. Washer
9. Retainer
10. Bracket
11. Nut
12. Pin
13. Floorshift control
14. Insulator
15. Bolt
16. Grommet

VIEW A

VIEW D

VIEW B

VIEW C

Shift control cable

c. Release re-adjustment tab.
d. Repeat Steps 5b. and 5c. until proper adjustment is obtained.

DRIVE AXLE

Driveshaft and U-Joints

REMOVAL & INSTALLATION

1. Raise the vehicle and support it safely, then remove the complete exhaust system, if necessary.

2. Remove the bolts attaching the support beam at the axle and transmission. Remove support beam from the vehicle.

3. Mark relationship of shaft to companion flange and disconnect the rear universal joint by removing trunnion bearing straps. Tape bearing cups to trunnion to prevent dropping and loss of bearing rollers.

4. Slide slip yoke from the transmission and remove shaft. Watch for oil leakage from transmission output shaft housing.

5. Remove the universal joint

THROTTLE LEVER

VIEW B

VIEW A

SLIDER AGAINST FITTING, ZERO OR RESET BUTTON

RESET TAB
FITTING
RESET DIRECTION
SLIDER
CABLE

Throttle valve cable

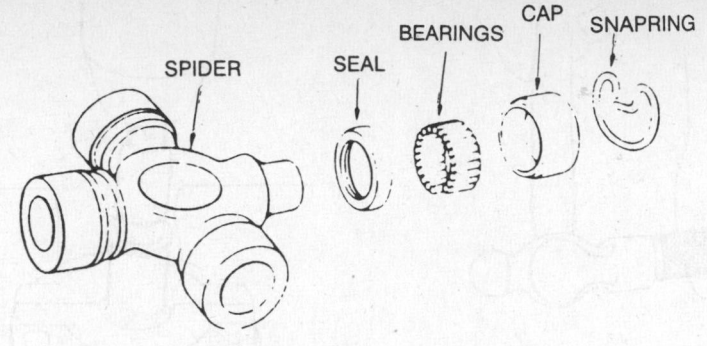

Universal joint assembly

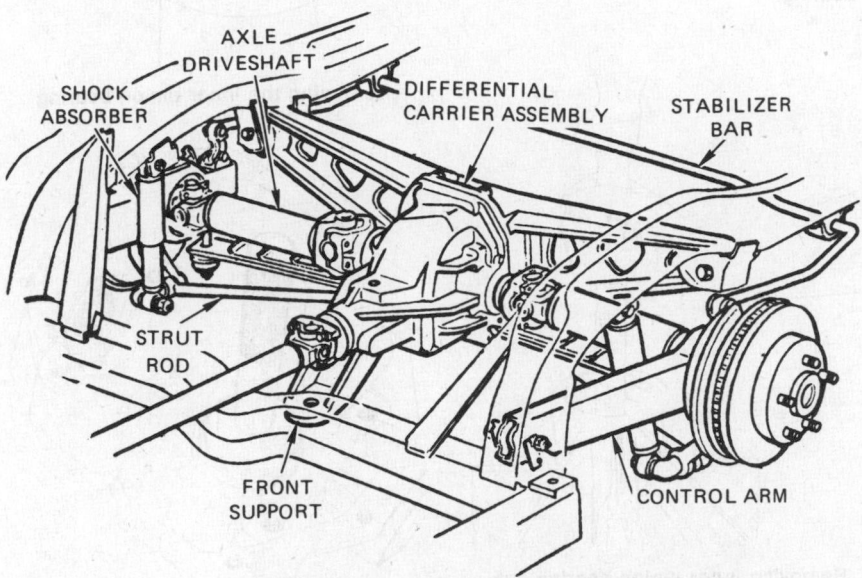

Rear suspension and related components

snapring, then place the drive shaft into suitable holding fixture.

6. Press the lower bearing cap out from the yoke. Rotate the driveshaft, then remove the the other bearing cap.

7. Remove the universal joint from the yoke.

8. Installation is the reverse of the removal procedure.

Rear Axle Shaft, Bearing and Seal

REMOVAL & INSTALLATION

1. Raise the vehicle and support it safely, then disconnect the leaf spring and tie rod from the knuckle.

2. Scribe a mark on the cam bolt and the knuckle for realignment, then remove the cam bolt.

3. Separate the spindle support rod from the mounting bracket at the carrier.

4. Remove the axle shaft trunnion straps at the spindle and side gear yoke.

5. Push out on the wheel and tire assembly and remove the axle shaft, then remove the differential carrier from the differential case.

6. Using tools J–34171 (7.875 in. axle) or J–35510 (8.5 in. axle), and driver handle J–8592, drive out oil seal and bearing assembly. Discard seal and bearing.

To install:

7. Installation is the reverse of the removal procedure.

8. Install new bearing using tools J–34172 (7.875 in. rear) or J–35510 (8.5 in. axle) and driver J–8592. Lubricate bearings with a suitable hypoid lubricate.

9. Apply a light coat of hypoid lubricant on the lip of the axle shaft seal.

10. Install axle shaft seal using tools J–26938 (7.875 in. axle) or J–35511 (8.5 in. axle) and driver J–8592.

11. Tighten the trunnion strap retaining bolts to 26 ft. lbs. (35 Nm). Tighten the cam bolt to 187 ft. lbs. (253 Nm).

Front Wheel Hub, Knuckle and Seal

REMOVAL & INSTALLATION

1. Raise and support vehicle, then remove tire and wheel assembly.

2. Remove brake caliper and rotor, wheel hub attaching bolts, then the wheel hub. Remove hub O-ring from knuckle.

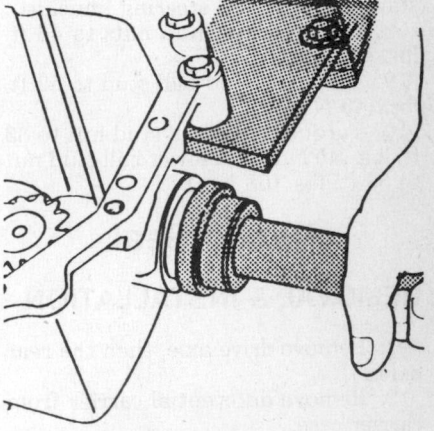

Installing axle seal

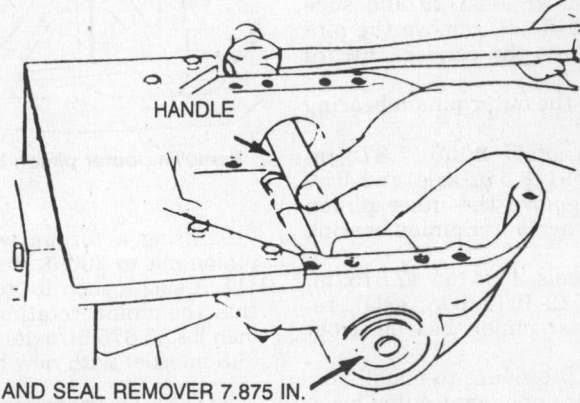

BEARING AND SEAL REMOVER 7.875 IN. AXLE OR 8.5 IN. AXLE

Removing axle shaft seal

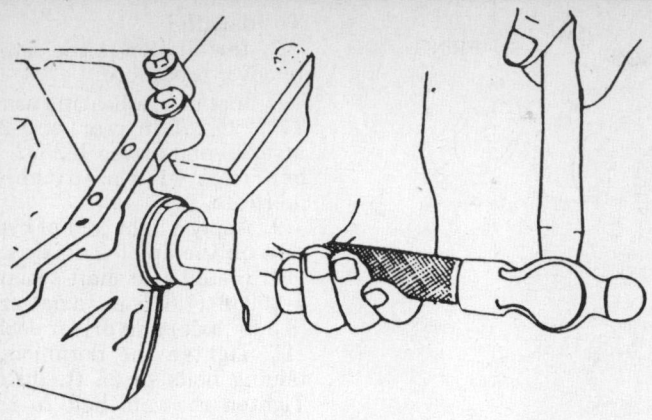

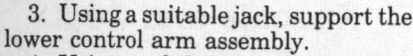
Installing axle bearing

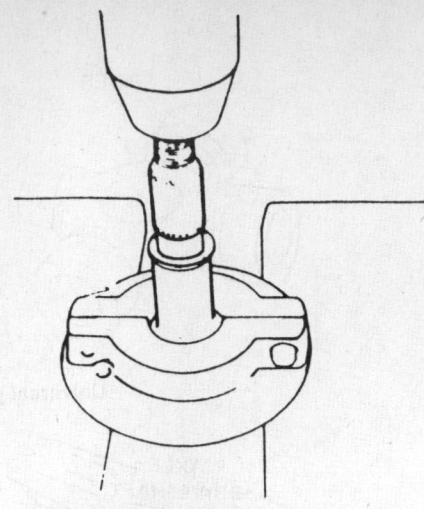
Removing the inner pinion bearing

3. Using a suitable jack, support the lower control arm assembly.

4. Using tool J–33436, remove the upper and lower ball studs.

5. Using tool J–6627–A, disconnect tie rod ball stud from the steering knuckle.

6. Remove the knuckle from the vehicle.

To install:

7. Reverse procedure to install. Install new 0-ring in steering knuckle.

8. Torque wheel hub nuts to 46 ft. lbs. (62 Nm).

9. Torque tie rod ball stud to 32 ft. lbs. (43 Nm).

10. Torque upper ball stud nut to 33 ft. lbs. (45 Nm) and lower ball stud nut to 50 ft. lbs. (68 Nm).

Pinion Seal

REMOVAL & INSTALLATION

1. Remove drive axle, then the rear axle.

2. Remove differential carrier from carrier case.

3. Place differential carrier case into a suitable holding fixture.

4. Using puller J–23129 and slide hammer J–6215–1B, remove the pinion oil seal from the carrier. Discard seal.

5. Remove the outer pinion bearing and spacer.

6. Using tools J–2935 (7.875 in. axle) or J–35591 (8.5 in. axle) and driver J–8592, remove the inner pinion bearing cup, then outer pinion bearing cup.

7. Using tools J–34165 (7.875 in. axle) or J–8612–B (8.5 in. axle), remove the inner pinion bearing from the pinion.

8. Reverse procedure to install.

9. Lubricate inner and outer bearings using a suitable lube. Apply a light coat of engine oil to the lip of the new pinion seal.

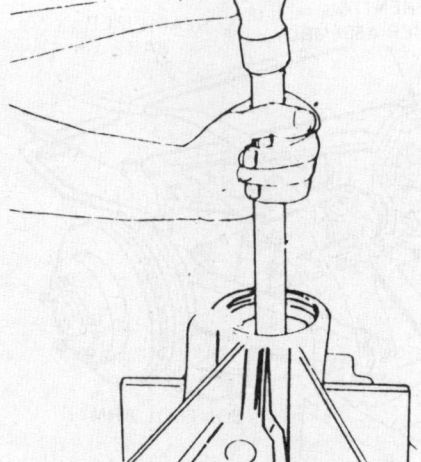
Removing inner pinion bearing cup

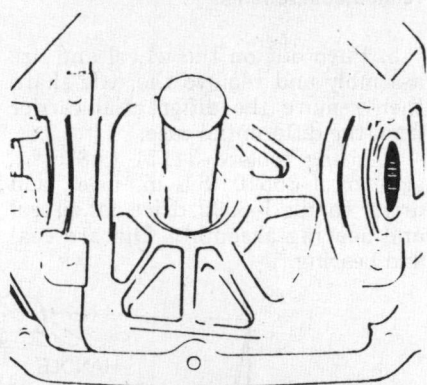
Removing outer pinion bearing cup

10. Using a torque wrench, torque pinion nut to 200 ft. lbs. (270 Nm).

11. Using a inch lb. torque wrench, that the pinion rotating torque is 25 inch lbs. (7.875 in. axle) or 30 inch lbs. (8.5 in. axle) with new bearings.

NOTE: To increase preload, remove shims as necessary. To decrease preload, add shims as necessary.

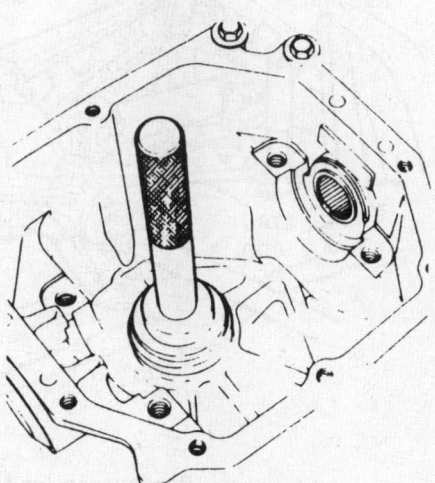
Installing inner pinion bearing cup

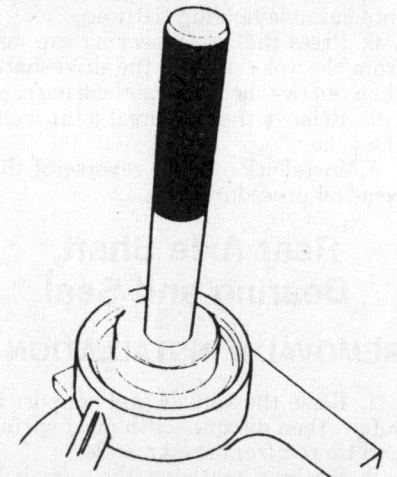
Installing the outer pinion bearing cup

Differential Carrier

REMOVAL & INSTALLATION

1. Raise and support vehicle.

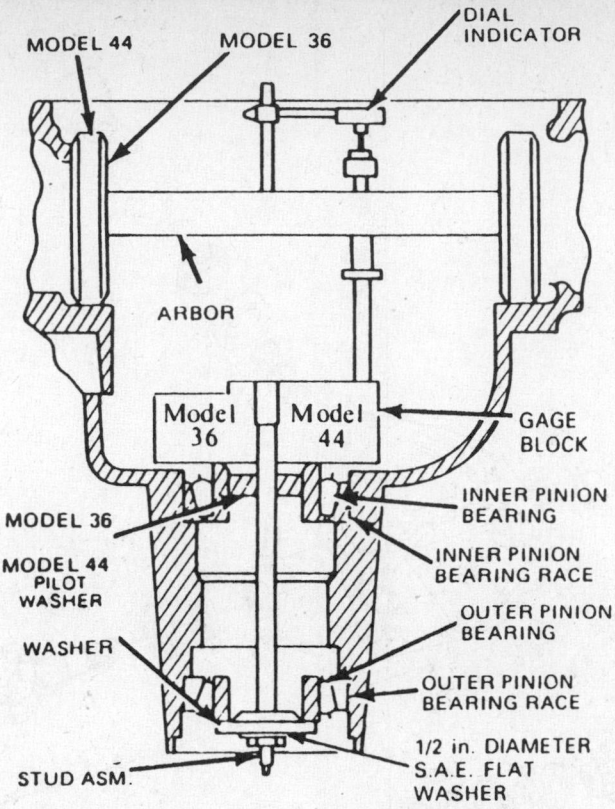

Pinion depth gauge assembly

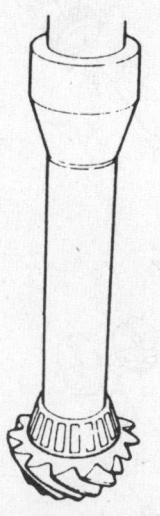

Installing the inner pinion bearing

2. Remove the spare tire. Remove tire cover by removing support hooks.

3. Remove the upper and lower underbody braces, if necessary.

4. Remove the complete exhaust system, if necessary.

5. Remove leaf spring from the knuckles and attaching bolts from the cover. Remove leaf spring from vehicle.

6. On ZR-1 vehicles, remove exhaust hangers.

7. Scribe alignment marks on cam bolts and brackets for ease of installation.

8. Remove cam bolts and mounting bracket from carrier.

9. Remove both tie rod ends from knuckles.

10. Remove the axle shaft trunnion straps from side gear yokes. Push wheel and tire assembly outward to disengage trunnions from side gear yokes.

11. Scribe alignment marks on driveshafts and companion flanges for ease of installation.

12. Remove the driveshafts trunnion straps from the pinion flange. Push driveshaft forward into transmission and tie shaft to driveline support beam.

13. Support transmission.

14. Remove the differential cover beam attaching bolts at the frame brackets.

15. Remove the drive line support beam attaching bolts at the frame brackets.

16. Remove the differential carrier assembly from the vehicle.

To install:

17. Install differential carrier cover assembly onto vehicle.

18. Apply suitable sealant to driveline support and differential carrier.

19. Install the driveline support attaching bolts at the front of the differential carrier cover. Torque cover attaching bolts to 23 ft. lbs. (31 Nm) on models 36 and 35 ft. lbs. (48 Nm). on model 44.

20. Align marks on driveshaft and yoke, and install driveshaft. Torque shaft trunnion retainers to 18 ft. lbs. (24 Nm).

21. Install wheel shaft trunnions into yoke.

22. Install rear wheel driveshaft universal joint retainers onto yoke shaft. Torque retainers to 26 ft. lbs. (35 Nm).

23. Install tie rod ends into knuckle. Torque tie rod nut to 33 ft. lbs. (45 Nm) to align slot in nut with hole in stud.

24. Install mounting bracket onto carrier. Torque bolts to 60 ft. lbs. (80 Nm).

25. Install spring, then the exhaust system hangers and nuts. Torque nuts to 13 ft. lbs. (17 Nm).

26. Install exhaust system.

27. If equipped with convertible top, install upper and lower underbody braces.

28. Install spare tire cover and spare tire.

29. Fill rear axle with suitable lubricant, then lower vehicle.

STEERING

Steering Wheel
──── CAUTION ────

If equipped with an air bag, the negative battery cable must be disconnected, before working on the system. Failure to do so may result in deployment of the air bag and possible personal injury.

REMOVAL & INSTALLATION
1978–89 Vehicles

1. Disconnect battery negative cable, then remove the horn from the steering wheel.

2. Remove the horn button wire.

3. Remove the telescope lever attaching screws and the shaft lock knob screw.

4. Remove the steering wheel nut retainer, then the steering wheel nut.

5. Using tool J–1859–03, remove the steering wheel from the vehicle.

NOTE: Before removing steering wheel, scribe marks on steering wheel hub and steering wheel shaft for ease of installation.

6. Reverse procedure to install.

7. Torque steering wheel nut to 30 ft. lbs. (40 Nm). Connect battery negative cable.

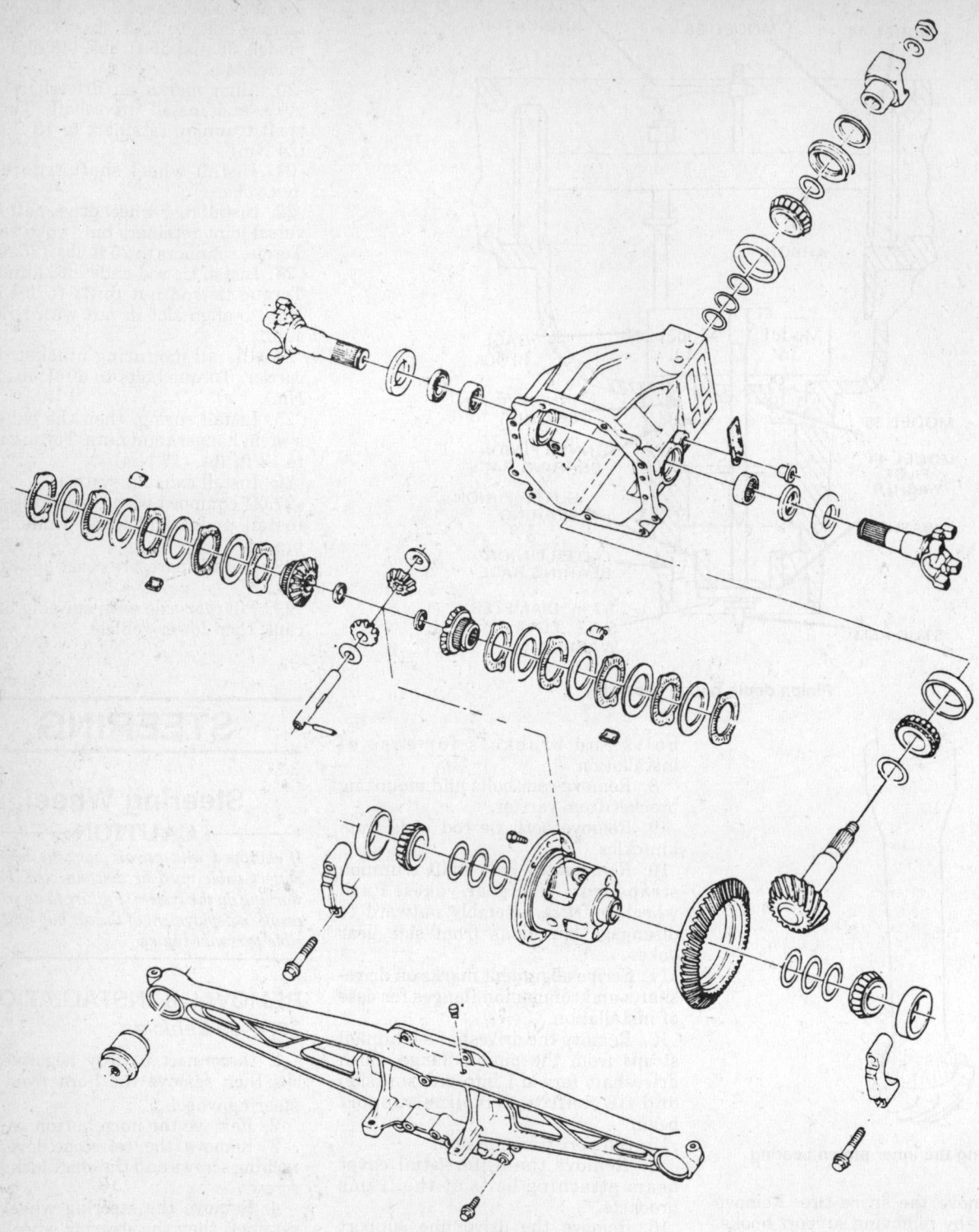

Exploded view of rear axle

1990–91 Vehicles

1. Ensure the ignition switch is in the **OFF** position, disconnect battery negative cable and remove the left sound insulator.

2. Disconnect the Connector Position Assurance (CPA) and Supplemental Inflatable Restraint (SIR) harness connectors at base of the steering column.

3. Install SIR Load tool J–37808 according to manufacturer instructions.

4. Remove screws attaching the back of the steering wheel to the inflator module, then remove the inflator module from the steering wheel.

5. Disconnect the SIR electrical connector at inflator module, then remove the steering wheel attaching nut.

6. Using tool J–1859–03, remove the steering wheel. Disconnect the horn electrical connector.

7. Reverse procedure to install.

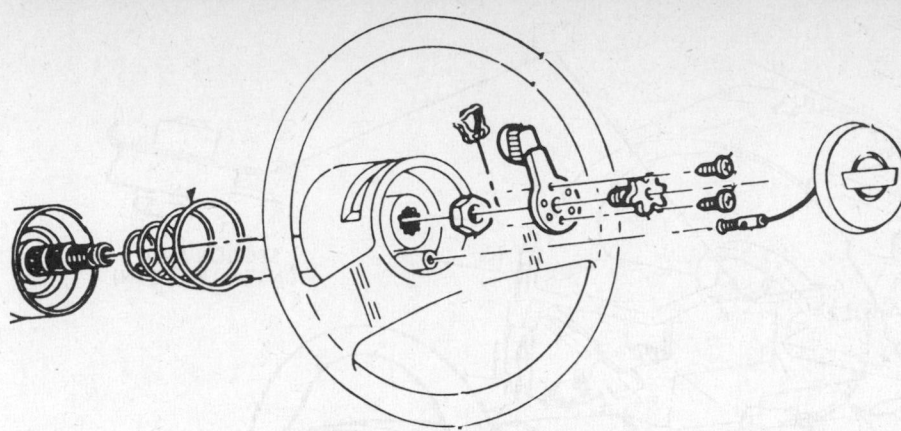

Steering wheel assembly—1987–89

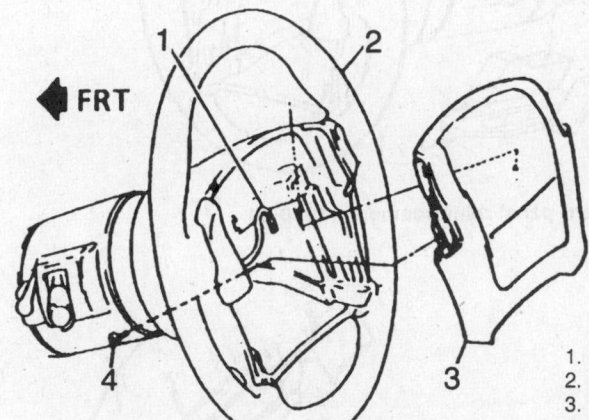

1. Connector
2. Steering wheel
3. Inflator module
4. Screw

Steering wheel assembly—1990–91

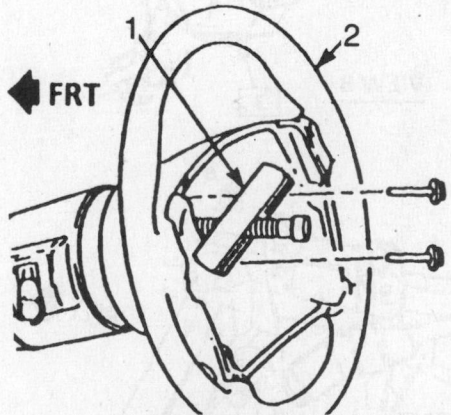

1. Steering wheel puller J-1859-03
2. Steering wheel

Removing steering wheel—1990–91

8. Torque steering wheel nut to 30 ft. lbs. (41 Nm).

Steering Column

REMOVAL & INSTALLATION
1987–89 Vehicles

NOTE: Handle the steering col-

umn very carefully. Hammering the end of it or leaning on it could shear off the plastic type inserts which allow the column to collapse in a collision.

1. Disconnect the negative battery cable, then remove the steering wheel.
2. Remove the nut and bolt from the upper intermediate shaft coupling.
3. Separate the coupling from the lower end of steering column.
4. Remove the left hand instrument panel sound insulator and lower trim pad, then disconnect all electrical connectors from the column assembly.
5. Remove the screws securing the toe pan cover to the floor.
6. Remove the nuts securing the bracket to the instrument panel.
7. Withdraw the steering column.
8. Installation is the reverse of the removal procedure. Use only the specified hardware. Over length bolts could prevent the column from properly collapsing in a crash.

1990–91 Vehicles

1. Disconnect battery negative cable, then remove steering wheel.
2. Remove the intermediate shaft

upper bolt, then the ALDL connector and the lamp from the sound insulator.
3. Remove the left sound insulator, then the column housing cover end cap by pulling toward front of vehicle.
4. Disconnect the multi-function lever electrical connector.
5. Remove the multi-function lever by pulling toward driver side door, then the drivers side knee bolster.
6. Remove the tilt lever, nuts from the lower support plate and capsule bolts from the reinforcement assembly, then disconnect all electrical connectors from the steering column.
7. Remove the sound insulator to steering column lower support bracket, accelerator pedal bracket nuts, then remove the steering column assembly from the vehicle.
8. Reverse procedure to install.

Power Steering Rack

REMOVAL & INSTALLATION
1987–89 Vehicles

1. Disconnect the battery negative cable, the inlet and outlet hoses, then the pipe from gear valve.
2. Loosen the front lug nuts, raise and support vehicle, then remove both wheel and tire assemblies.
3. Using tool J-24319-01, disconnect both tie rod ends.
4. Remove the stabilizer bar assembly, including both holding brackets, then the return pipe, mounted on the gear.
5. Disconnect the left cylinder feed pipe from the cylinder, then remove the rack mounting through bolts.
6. Remove the front saddle mounting nut and bolt, then lower the vehicle.
7. Remove the steering gear pinch bolt from the gear, then the rack and pinion assembly.
8. Reverse procedure to install. Connect battery negative cable.

1990–91 Vehicles

1. Disconnect battery negative cable.
2. Remove the power steering gear inlet hose assembly from the steering gear.
3. Remove the power steering gear outlet hose assembly from the steering gear.

NOTE: If equipped with a power steering fluid cooling pipe, disconnect fluid cooling pipe outlet hose from the fluid cooling pipe.

4. Remove the steering gear coupling shield.
5. Remove the intermediate shaft

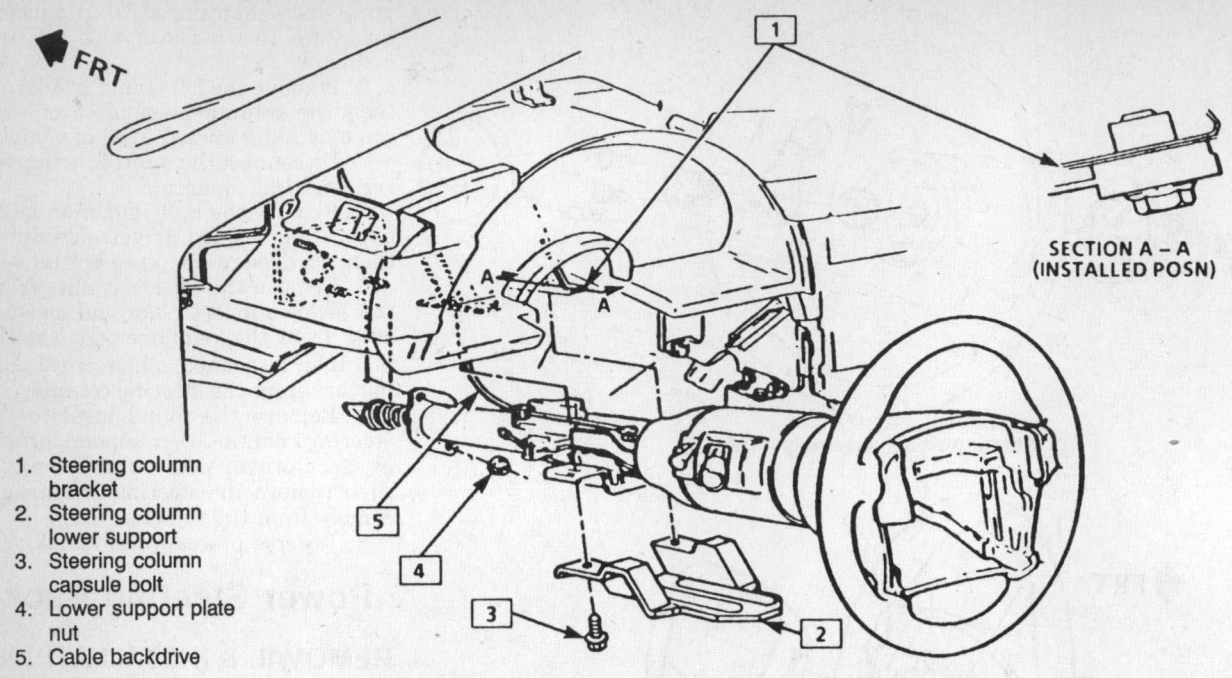

FRT

SECTION A – A
(INSTALLED POSN)

1. Steering column bracket
2. Steering column lower support
3. Steering column capsule bolt
4. Lower support plate nut
5. Cable backdrive

Steering column-to-instrument panel reinforcement—1990–91

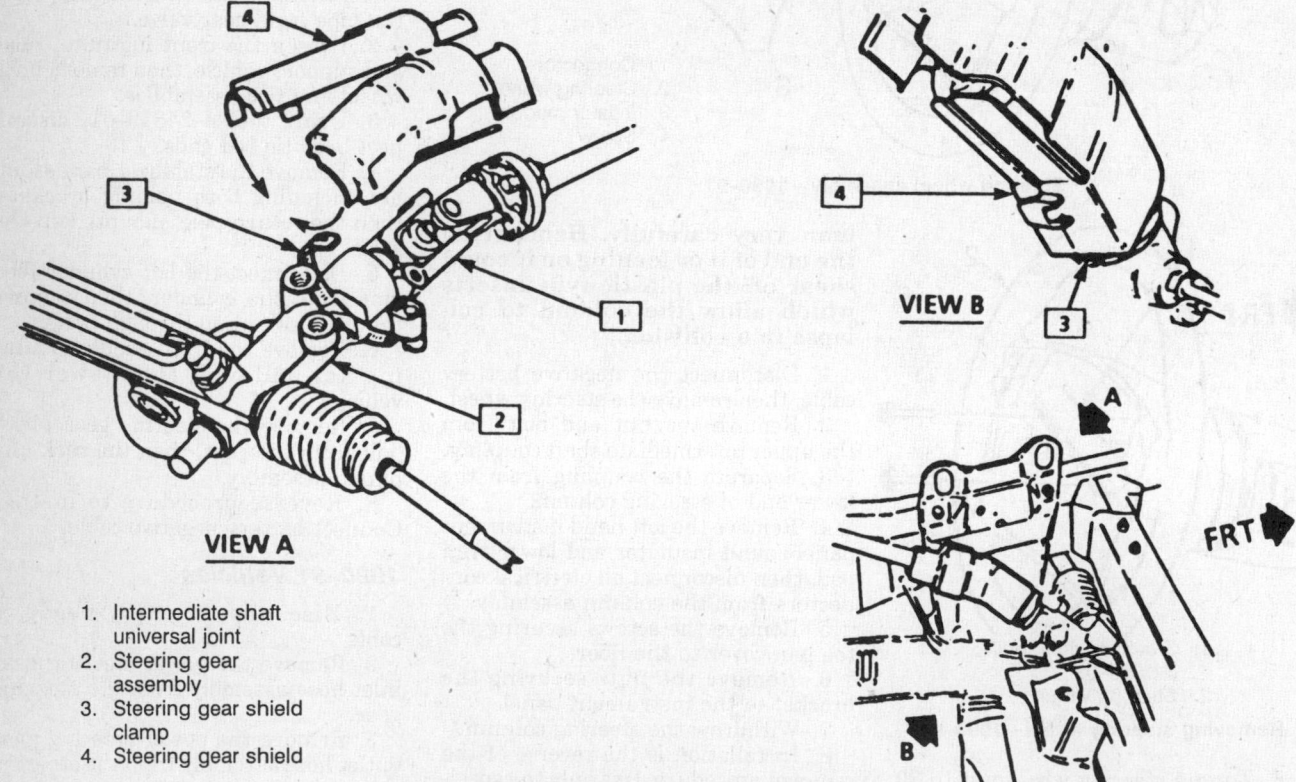

VIEW A

VIEW B

FRT

1. Intermediate shaft universal joint
2. Steering gear assembly
3. Steering gear shield clamp
4. Steering gear shield

Steering gear-to-steering column coupling shield

from the power steering gear and lower steering shaft, and position aside.

6. Raise and support vehicle.

7. Remove the tire and wheel assemblies.

8. Remove both outer tie rods from the knuckles.

9. Remove the power steering cooler assembly, if equipped.

10. Remove the stabilizer shaft.

11. Remove the steering gear to frame attaching clamp nuts, then the bolts and clamp from the vehicle.

12. Remove the power steering gear attaching attaching nuts and bolts.

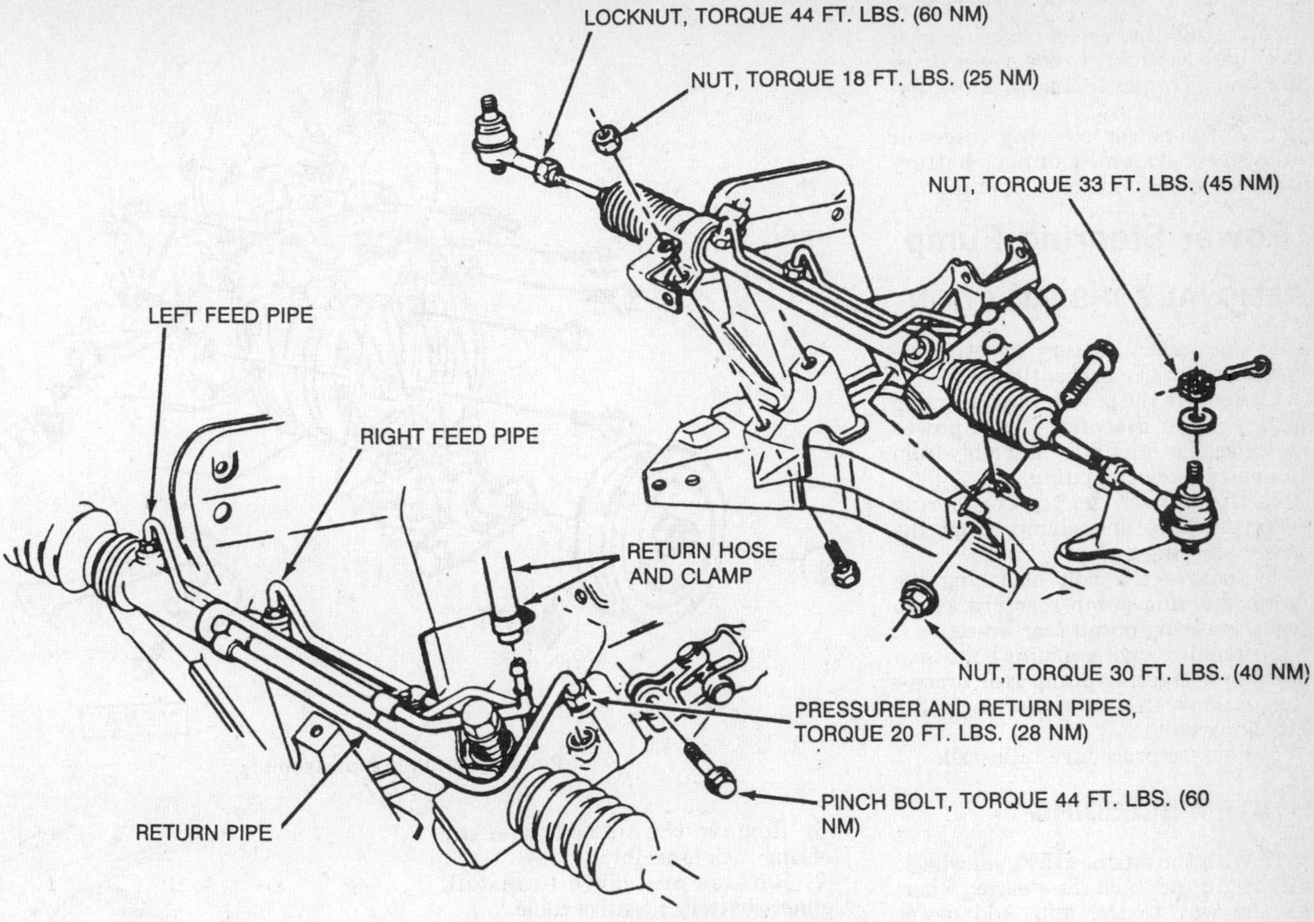

LOCKNUT, TORQUE 44 FT. LBS. (60 NM)

NUT, TORQUE 18 FT. LBS. (25 NM)

NUT, TORQUE 33 FT. LBS. (45 NM)

LEFT FEED PIPE

RIGHT FEED PIPE

RETURN HOSE
AND CLAMP

NUT, TORQUE 30 FT. LBS. (40 NM)

PRESSURER AND RETURN PIPES,
TORQUE 20 FT. LBS. (28 NM)

RETURN PIPE

PINCH BOLT, TORQUE 44 FT. LBS. (60
NM)

Power rack and pinion assembly—1987–89

13. Remove the power steering gear from the vehicle.
14. Remove the outer tie rods from the power steering gear, if necessary.
15. Remove rack and pinion boots, if necessary.
16. Remove the inner tie rods if necessary.

To install:
17. Install tie rods, if removed.
18. Install the rack and pinion boots, if removed.
19. Connect the power steering cooling pipe, if removed.
20. Install the power steering gear, nuts and bolts. Torque nuts to 30 ft. lbs. (40 Nm). Torque the steering gear clamp nuts to 18 ft. lbs. (25 Nm).
21. Install the stabilizer shaft and the power steering cooler assembly, if removed.
22. Install both outer tie rods to the steering knuckle.
23. Install tire and wheel assemblies and lower the vehicle.
24. Install the intermediate shaft and the steering gear coupling shield.
25. Install the power steering gear outlet hose assembly to the power

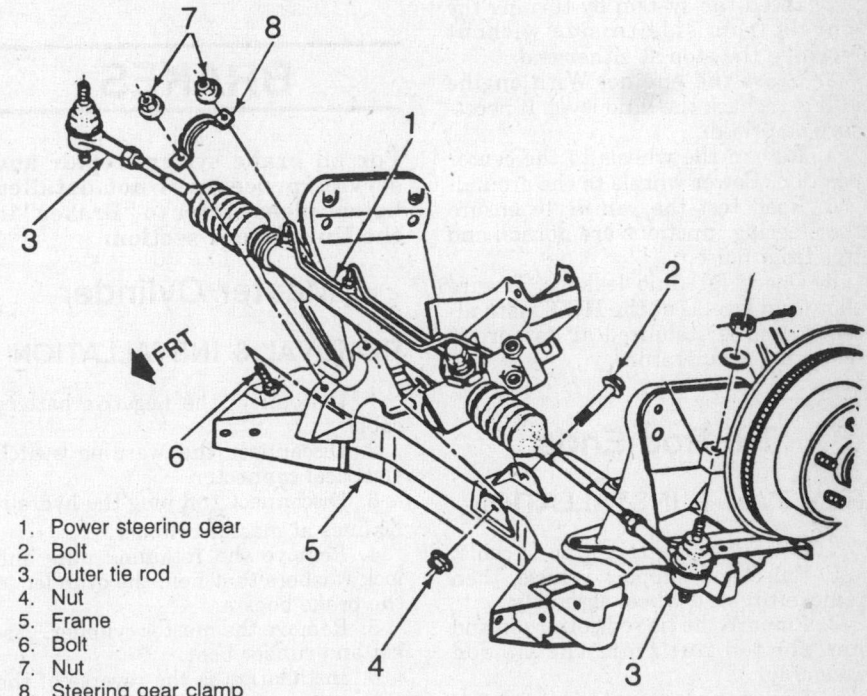

1. Power steering gear
2. Bolt
3. Outer tie rod
4. Nut
5. Frame
6. Bolt
7. Nut
8. Steering gear clamp

Power rack and pinion assembly—1990–91

steering gear. Torque fitting to 21 ft. lbs. (28 Nm).

26. Install the power steering gear inlet hose assembly to the power steering gear. Torque fitting to 21 ft. lbs. (28 Nm).

27. Refill power steering reservoir and bleed system. Connect battery negative cable and check operation.

Power Steering Pump

REMOVAL & INSTALLATION

1. Disconnect battery negative cable, then remove serpentine belt.

2. Remove the power steering pump pulley, then disconnect the power steering gear inlet hose assembly from the power steering pump.

3. Disconnect the power steering reservoir hose and clamp, from the power steering pump.

4. Remove the bolt attaching the power steering pump rear bracket to power steering pump rear brace.

5. Remove engine mount bolt, then the power steering pump rear brace.

6. Remove the power steering pump attaching bolts.

7. Reverse procedure to install.

SYSTEM BLEEDING

1. With the engine **OFF** and wheels off the ground, turn the steering wheel all the way to the left. Add power steering fluid to the **COLD** mark on the fluid level indicator.

2. Bleed the system by turning the wheels from side to side without reaching the stop at either end.

3. Start the engine. With engine idling, recheck the fluid level. If necessary add fluid.

4. Return the wheels to the center position. Lower wheels to the ground.

5. Road test the vehicle to ensure the steering functions are normal and free from noise.

6. Check for fluid leakage. Ensure that fluid level is at the **HOT** mark after system is stabilized at its normal operating temperature.

Tie Rod Ends

REMOVAL & INSTALLATION

1. Disconnect battery ground cable.

2. Raise and support vehicle, then remove tire and wheel assembly.

3. Remove the tie rod cotter pin and hex slotted nut from the tie rod assembly.

4. Loosen tie rod jam nut.

5. Using tool J–24319–01, remove tie rod from steering knuckle.

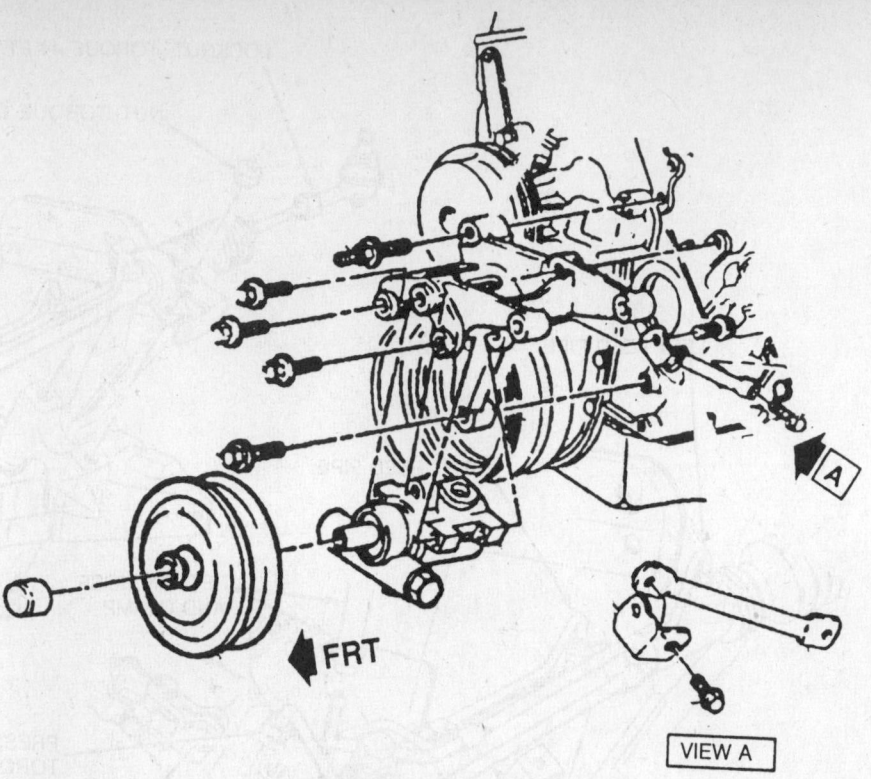

Power steering pump assembly

6. Remove the tie rod from the steering rack assembly.

7. Reverse procedure to install. Connect battery negative cable.

8. Torque tie rod jam nuts to 50 ft. lbs.

BRAKES

For all brake system repair and service procedures not detailed below, please refer to "Brakes" in the Unit Repair section.

Master Cylinder

REMOVAL & INSTALLATION

1. Disconnect the negative battery cable.

2. Disconnect the warning switch electrical connector.

3. Disconnect and plug the hydraulic lines at master cylinder.

4. Remove the retaining nuts and lock washers that hold the cylinder to the brake booster.

5. Remove the master cylinder, gasket and rubber boot.

6. Installation is the reverse of the removal procedure. Bleed the system, as required.

7. Torque master cylinder to brake

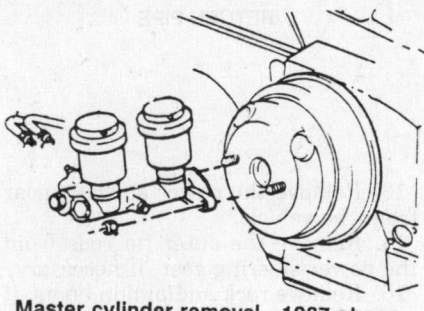

Master cylinder removal—1987 shown, 1988–91 similar

booster nuts to 15–25 ft. lbs. (20–34 Nm) on 1987 vehicles and 13 ft. lbs. (18 Nm) on 1988–91 vehicles.

Proportioning Valve

REMOVAL & INSTALLATION

1. Disconnect battery negative cable and warning switch assembly electrical connector.

2. Remove the end plug and O-ring.

3. Remove the proportioning valve with the ground spring attached.

NOTE: Gently tap the cylinder body against a piece of wood to dislodge the proportioning valve assembly.

4. Reverse procedure to install. Connect the battery negative cable and bleed system.

Power Brake Booster

REMOVAL & INSTALLATION

1987–89 Vehicles

1. Disconnect battery negative cable.
2. Remove the master cylinder from the vehicle.
3. Disconnect the vacuum hose from the vacuum check valve.
4. Remove the pushrod end of the valve assembly from the brake pedal by removing the retaining clip.
5. Remove the brake booster attaching nuts, then the power booster assembly from the cowl.
6. Reverse procedure to install.
7. Torque power booster attaching bolts to 15 ft. lbs. (21 Nm). Connect battery negative cable and bleed system.

1990–91 Vehicles

1. Disconnect battery negative cable.
2. Remove the ECM, then the ECM housing bracket attaching bolt.
3. Remove the cruise control cable from the cruise control servo, then the servo mounting bracket.
4. Disconnect the pressure differential sensor electrical connector, then the vacuum hose.
5. Disconnect the master cylinder warning switch electrical connector, then remove the nuts attaching the master cylinder to the power booster assembly. Position master cylinder, cruise control cable and battery cable aside.
6. Remove the power booster vacuum check valve from the power booster assembly.
7. Remove the instrument panel left sound insulator, then the input

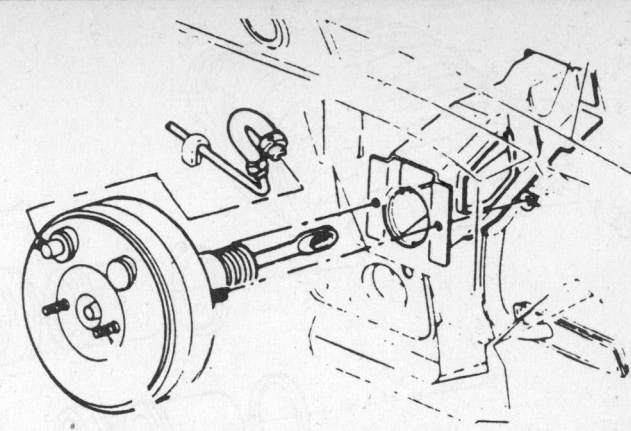

Power booster removal—1987–89

pushrod assembly retaining ring and washer from the brake pedal.
8. Remove the power booster assembly attaching nuts and washers, then power booster assembly with seals and the ECM bracket.
9. Reverse procedure to install.
10. Torque power booster attaching nuts to 15 ft. lbs. (21 Nm). Connect battery negative cable and bleed system.

Brake Caliper

REMOVAL & INSTALLATION

Front

1. Remove ⅔ of the brake fluid from the master cylinder reservoir.
2. Raise and support the vehicle.
3. Mark the relationship between the wheel and axle flange.
4. Remove the tire and wheel assembly. Install 2 wheel nuts to retain the brake rotor.
5. Depress the caliper pistons into

the caliper bores to provide clearance between the pads and the rotor.
6. Remove the inlet fitting bolt, 2 gaskets and brake hose inlet fitting. Plug all opening to prevent brake fluid loss or contamination.
7. Remove the circlip and the retainer pin, then the caliper housing from the rotor and the caliper mounting bracket.
8. Reverse procedure to install.

Rear

1. Disengage the parking brake automatic adjuster.
2. Remove ⅔ of the brake fluid from the master cylinder reservoir.
3. Raise and support the vehicle.
4. Mark the relationship between the wheel and axle flange, then remove the tire and wheel assembly. Install 2 wheel nuts to retain the brake rotor.
5. Remove the inlet fitting bolt, inlet fitting and 2 gaskets. discard gaskets. Plug all openings.
6. Remove the lever return spring,

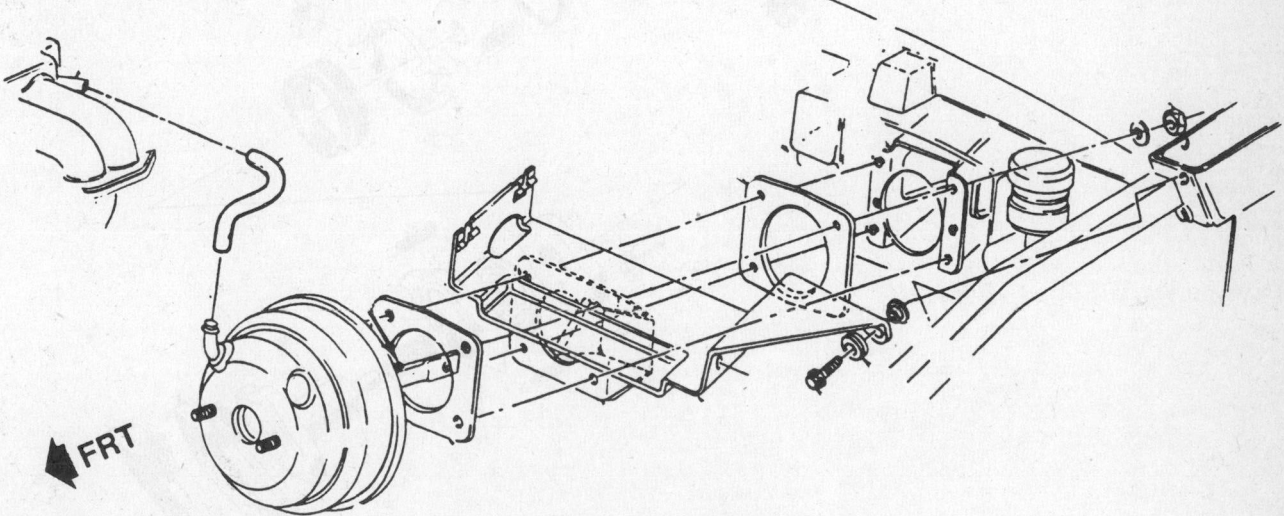

Power booster removal—1990–91

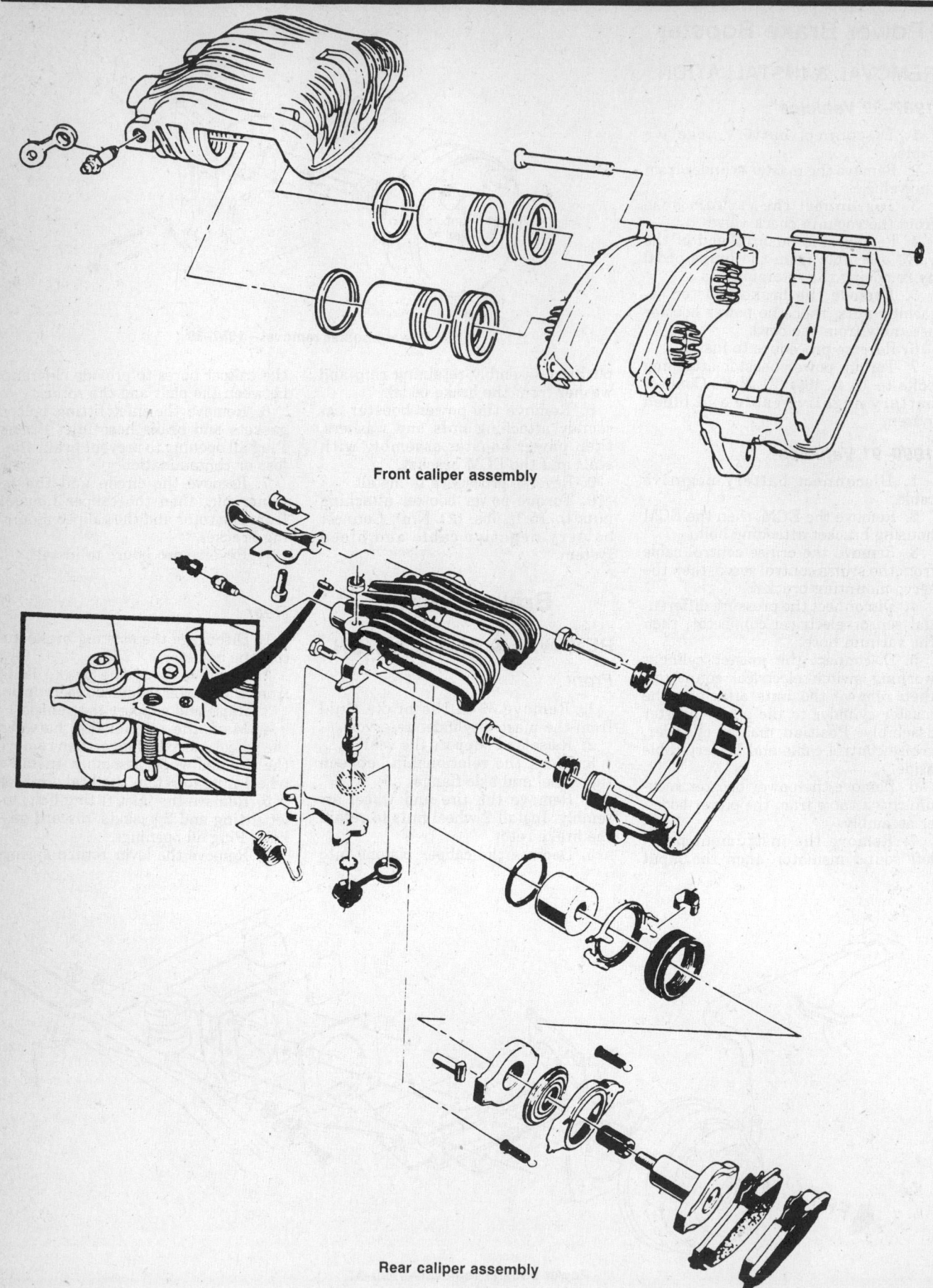

Front caliper assembly

Rear caliper assembly

then the brake cable from the lever and bracket.

7. Remove the 2 guide pins bolts, then the caliper housing from the brake rotor and caliper mounting bracket.

8. Reverse procedure to install.

Disc Brake Pads

REMOVAL & INSTALLATION

Front

1. Remove ⅔ of the brake fluid from the master cylinder reservoir.

2. Raise and support the vehicle, then mark the relationship between the wheel to the axle flange.

3. Remove the tire and wheel assembly. Install 2 wheel nuts to retain the brake rotor.

4. Depress the caliper pistons into the caliper bores to provide clearance between the pads and the rotor, then remove the circlip and the retainer clip.

5. Lift the caliper from the rotor and the mounting bracket.

6. Remove the pads from the caliper.

7. Suspend the caliper from the upper control arm with wire to avoid damage to the brake hose.

8. Reverse procedure to install.

Rear

1. Remove ⅔ of the brake fluid from the master cylinder reservoirs.

2. Raise and support the vehicle.

3. Mark the relationship between the wheel to the axle flange.

4. Remove the tire and wheel assembly. Install 2 wheel nuts to retain the brake rotor.

5. Depress the caliper pistons into the caliper bores to provide clearance between the pads and the rotor.

6. Remove the caliper upper guide pin bolt, then rotate the caliper at the lower guide pin bolt and guide pin within the caliper mounting bracket.

7. Remove the pads from the caliper.

8. Reverse procedure to install.

Brake Rotor

REMOVAL & INSTALLATION

1. Disconnect battery negative cable.

2. Raise and support vehicle.

3. Remove the tire and wheel assembly.

4. Remove brake caliper.

5. Remove the rotor from the vehicle.

6. Reverse procedure to install.

Parking Brake Cable

ADJUSTMENT

1987 Vehicles

1. Raise the vehicle and support it safely.

2. Remove the rear wheels. Install 2 wheel nuts to insure correct rotor positioning.

3. Back the caliper piston into its bore.

4. Loosen the parking brake cable so there is no tension on the park brake shoes.

5. Rotate the rotor until the hole in the rotor face will align with the star adjuster.

6. To make the adjustment, insert the proper brake adjusting tool through the hole in the rotor. For the driver's side, move the handle of the tool upward to adjust the shoes out and downward to adjust the shoes in. For the passenger's side, move the handle of the tool downward to adjust the shoes out and upward to adjust the shoes in.

7. Adjust 1 side at a time until there is no rotation of the rotor. Then back the star adjuster off 5–7 notches. Then go to the opposite side and do the same procedure.

8. Apply the park brake lever 2 notches.

9. Adjust the cable at the equalizer so the wheel has a drag.

10. Release the park brake lever and check the wheel for free rotation.

11. Correct adjustment will result in no drag on the wheel.

1988–91 Vehicles

The parking brake lever/cable adjustment is automatic. The only adjustment required is a free-travel adjustment and should only be made if the caliper housing has been disassembled.

The adjustment process requires a second person to apply a light brake pedal load. Lever free-travel is set by the position of the adjusting screw. Turning the adjustment screw clockwise increases the free-travel; turning the adjustment screw counterclockwise decreases the free-travel. Measure the free-travel between the lever and the caliper housing. Free-travel must be 0.024–0.028 in. (0.6–0.7mm).

NOTE: Cycling the lever 3 times should result in parking brake lever movement of 7–9 notches when a 50 lb. (220 N) force is applied.

REMOVAL & INSTALLATION

Front Cable

1. Raise the vehicle and support it safely.

2. Disconnect the left rear cable at the equalizer.

3. Disconnect the right rear cable at the retainer.

4. Lower the vehicle in order to remove the lower door sill moulding.

5. Remove the cable nut, cable guide and cable, in the sequence given.

6. Installation is the reverse of the removal procedure. Adjust the parking brake, as required.

Rear Cable

LEFT

1. Raise the vehicle and support it safely.

2. Disconnect the left rear cable at the equalizer.

3. Remove the cable at the frame. Remove the caliper mounting bracket and parking brake lever at the wheel.

4. Installation is the reverse of the removal procedure. Adjust the parking brake, as required.

RIGHT

1. Raise the vehicle and support it safely.

2. Remove enough tension at the equalizer to disconnect the right rear parking brake at the retainer.

3. Remove the cable at the frame. Remove the caliper mounting bracket and the parking brake lever at the wheel.

4. Installation is the reverse of the removal procedure. Adjust the parking brake as required.

Brake System Bleeding

1. Clean the bleed screw at wheel.

2. Start the wheel furthest from the master cylinder, right-rear.

3. Attach a small rubber hose to the bleed screw and place the end in a clear container of brake fluid.

4. Fill the master cylinder with brake fluid, check often during bleeding. Have an assistant slowly pump up the brake pedal and hold the pressure.

5. Open the bleed screw approximately ¼ turn, press the brake pedal to the floor, close the bleed screw and slowly release the pedal. Continue until no more air bubbles are forced from the cylinder on application of the brake pedal.

6. Repeat procedure on remaining wheel cylinders and calipers, still working from cylinder/caliper furthest from the master cylinder.

NOTE: The bleeder valve at the wheel cylinder must be closed at the end of each stroke and before the brake pedal is released, to insure that no air can enter the system. It is also important that the brake pedal be returned to the full up position so the piston in the master cylinder moves back enough to clear the bypass outlets.

Anti-Lock Brake System Service

PRECAUTION

Failure to observe the following precautions may result in system damage.

• Before performing electric arc welding on the vehicle, disconnect the Electronic Brake Control Module (EBCM) and the hydraulic modulator connectors.

• When performing painting work on the vehicle, do not expose the Electronic Brake Control Module (EBCM) to temperatures in excess of 185°F (85°C) for longer than 2 hrs. The system may be exposed to temperatures up to 200°F (95°C) for less than 15 min.

• Never disconnect or connect the Electronic Brake Control Module (EBCM) or hydraulic modulator connectors with the ignition switch ON.

• Never disassemble any component of the Anti-Lock Brake System (ABS) which is designated non-servicable; the component must be replaced as an assembly.

1. Wheel speed sensor (1 at each wheel)
2. Tooth ring (1 at each wheel)
3. Caliper (1 at each wheel)
4. Master cylinder
5. Power booster
6. Lateral accelerometer
7. Anti-lock warning lamp
8. Module relay
9. Control module
10. Modulator valve

• When filling the master cylinder, always use Delco Supreme 11 brake fluid or equivalent, which meets DOT-3 specifications; petroleum base fluid will destroy the rubber parts.

Modulator Valve

REMOVAL & INSTALLATION

1. Disconnect the battery negative cable.
2. Remove the storage tray and insulator.
3. Disconnect the modulator valve ground wire from the body wiring harness.
4. Disconnect the brake pipes from the modulator valve.
5. Remove the modulator valve attaching nuts, the the modulator valve.

Disconnect modulator valve brake pipes

Remove the ground wire and insulators when replacing the valve.

6. Reverse procedure to install. Connect battery negative cable.

Lateral Accelerometer

REMOVAL & INSTALLATION

1. Disconnect battery negative cable.
2. Remove the console trim plate.
3. Remove the radio.
4. Remove the lateral accelerometer to instrument panel carrier assembly attaching screws. Disconnect electrical connector.
5. Remove the lateral accelerometer from the vehicle.
6. Reverse procedure to install. Connect battery negative cable.

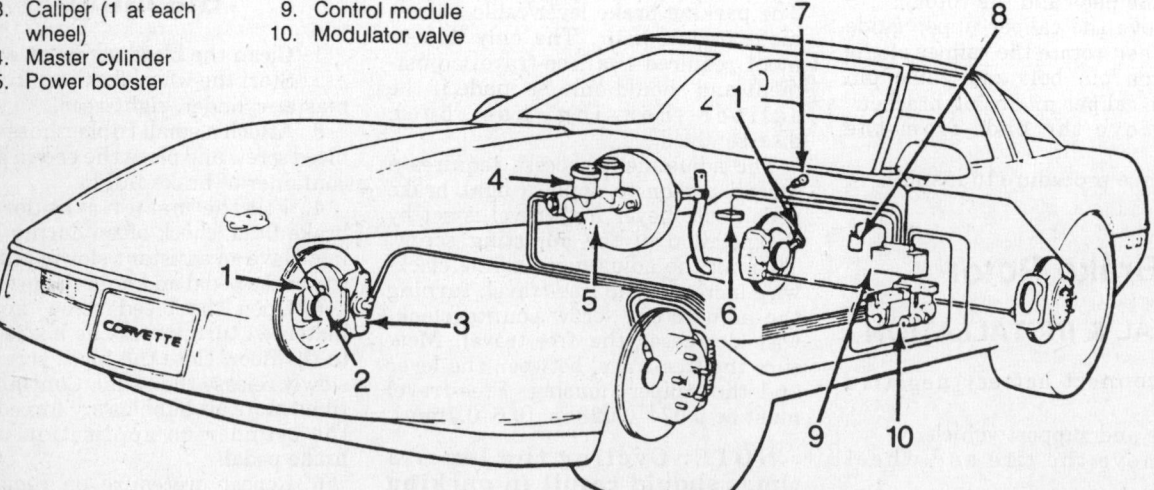

Anti-lock brake system layout and component location

Wheel Speed Sensor

REMOVAL & INSTALLATION

1. Disconnect battery negative cable.
2. Raise and support vehicle.
3. Remove the tire and wheel assembly.
4. Disconnect the sensor harness connector from the ABS harness connector.
5. When working on the rear sensors, remove the bracket and bolt from the knuckle.
6. Remove sensor wiring harness with the grommets from the bracket.
7. Remove the wheel speed sensor attaching bolt, then the wheel speed sensors from the knuckle.
8. Reverse procedure to install. Connect battery negative cable.

Control Module

REMOVAL & INSTALLATION

1. Disconnect battery ground cable.
2. Remove the storage tray and insulator.
3. Disconnect the electrical connector from the control module.
4. Remove the module relay from the brackets.
5. Remove the control module attaching bolts, then the control module from the vehicle.
6. Reverse procedure to install.

1. Control module
2. Bolt
3. Bracket
4. Rivet
5. Nut
6. Storage compartment
7. Module relay

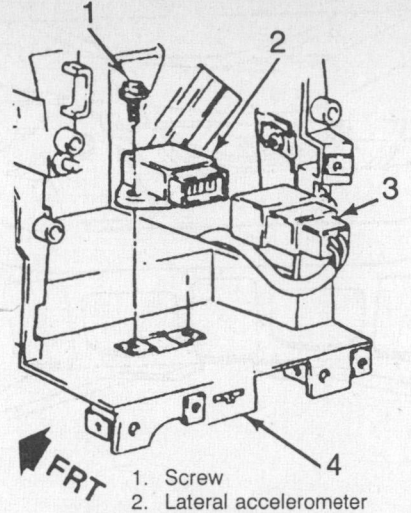

1. Screw
2. Lateral accelerometer
3. Electrical connector
4. Instrument panel

Lateral accelerometer location

Pump Motor Relay and Solenoid Relay

REMOVAL & INSTALLATION

1. Disconnect battery negative cable.
2. Remove the storage tray and insulator.
3. Remove the retainer screw and retainer, then the appropriate relay.
4. Reverse procedure to install. Connect battery negative cable.

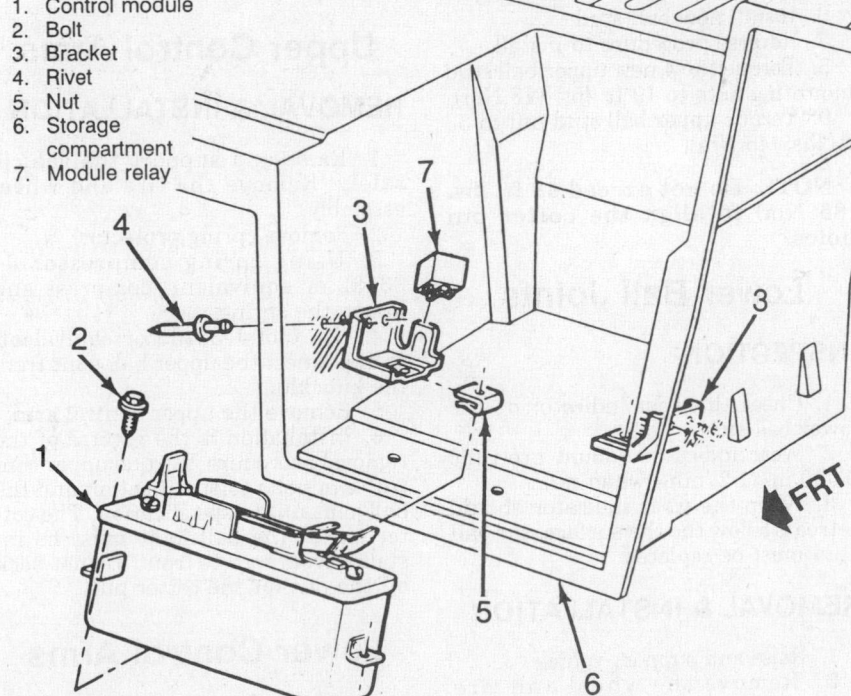

Anti-lock system control module

Module Relay

REMOVAL & INSTALLATION

1. Disconnect battery negative cable.
2. Remove the storage tray and insulator.
3. Disconnect the control module electrical connector.
4. Remove the screws from the wiring harness retention clip.
5. Remove the retention clip from the wiring harness.
6. Disconnect the module valve electrical connector.
7. Disconnect the battery feed (red) wire connector from the harness connector.
8. Disconnect the wheel speed sensor electrical connectors from the wiring harness connector.
9. Remove the module relay from the bracket.
10. Reverse procedure to install. Connect battery negative cable.

FRONT SUSPENSION

Shock Absorbers

REMOVAL & INSTALLATION

1. If equipped with selective ride control shock absorbers, disconnect the negative battery cable.
2. Raise and support vehicle, then remove the tire and wheel assembly.
3. Support the front knuckle with a suitable jack.
4. If equipped with selective ride control shock absorbers, remove the actuator retaining clip. Remove the actuator from the cup retainer. Note the position of the actuator electrical leads for installation purposes.
5. Remove the shock absorber upper mounting nut.
6. If equipped with selective ride control shock absorbers, remove the cup retainer.
7. Remove the shock absorber lower mounting bolts and nuts, then compress the shock absorber and remove it from the vehicle.
8. Installation is the reverse of the removal procedure.

Transverse Springs

REMOVAL & INSTALLATION

1. Raise the vehicle and support it

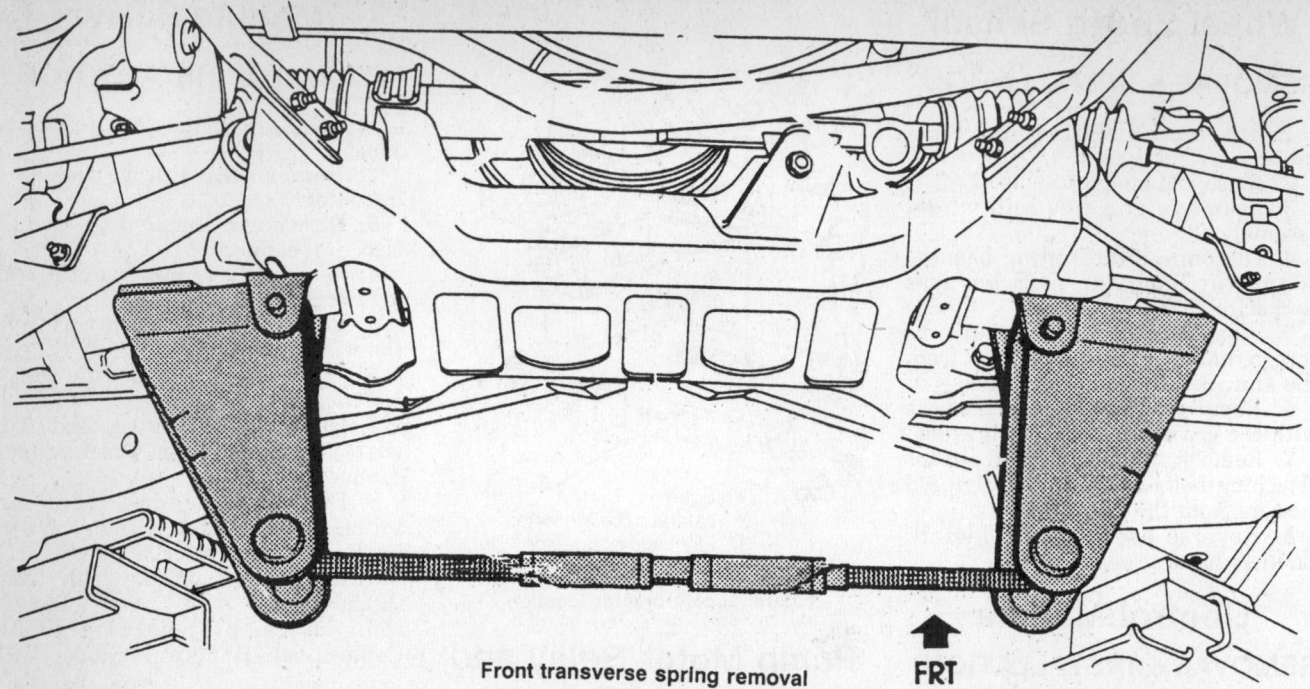

Front transverse spring removal

FRT

safely, then remove both front tire and wheel assemblies.

2. Remove the shock absorbers, then disconnect the stabilizer shaft links from both lower control arms.

3. Remove the anti-lock brake sensor brackets from the knuckles, then remove the spring protectors.

4. Compress the front leaf springs using the proper tools, then disconnect the lower control arms from the steering knuckles.

5. Remove the spring retainer nuts and retainers, then pull both lower control arms downward to release the spring ends from the lower control arms.

6. Remove the springs and retainer shims from the vehicle.

7. Installation is the reverse of the removal procedure.

Upper Ball Joints

INSPECTION

1. Raise and support the vehicle.

2. Position jackstands under the left and right lower control arms.

3. Position a dial indicator against the wheel rim.

4. Grasp the front tire and push in on the bottom while pulling out at the top. Check dial indicator. Reverse the push-pull procedure.

5. Horizontal deflection on the dial indicator must not exceed 0.125 in. (3.18mm).

6. If specifications are not as indicated, replace ball stud.

REMOVAL & INSTALLATION

1. Raise and support vehicle.

2. Support the lower control arm with jack stands.

3. Remove the tire and wheel assembly.

4. Using tool J–33436, remove the ball stud from the knuckle.

5. Grind or chisel off the ball stud rivets.

6. Install new ball stud.

7. Reverse procedure to install.

8. Torque the 4 new upper ball stud mounting nuts to 19 ft. lbs. (25 Nm).

9. Torque upper ball stud nut to 33 ft. lbs. (45 Nm).

NOTE: Do not exceed 63 ft. lbs. (85 Nm) to align the cotter pin holes.

Lower Ball Joints

INSPECTION

1. Check the wear indicator on the lower ball stud.

2. Wear indicator should protrude 0.050 in. (1.27mm) when new.

3. When the wear indicator should retreats below the the surface, the ball stud must be replaced.

REMOVAL & INSTALLATION

1. Raise and support vehicle.

2. Remove the wheel and tire assembly.

3. Support the lower control arm using jack stands.

4. Using tool J–33436, remove the ball stud from the knuckle.

5. Using tool J–9519–E, remove the ball stud from the control arm.

6. Reverse procedure to install.

7. Torque lower control arm ball stud nut to 50 ft. lbs. (68 Nm).

NOTE: Do not exceed 88 ft. lbs. (120 Nm) to align the cotter pin holes.

Upper Control Arms

REMOVAL & INSTALLATION

1. Raise and support the vehicle safely. Remove the tire and wheel assembly.

2. Remove spring protector.

3. Using spring compressor J–33432 or equivalent, compress and loosen the spring.

4. Use tool J–33436 or equivalent, to disconnect the upper ball joint from the knuckle.

5. Remove the upper control arm.

6. Installation is the reverse of the removal procedure. Torque upper control arm bolts to specification and the ball joint nut to specification. The cotter pin at the ball joint must be installed from rear to front. Do not back off the nut for the cotter pin.

Lower Control Arms

REMOVAL & INSTALLATION

1. Raise and support the vehicle

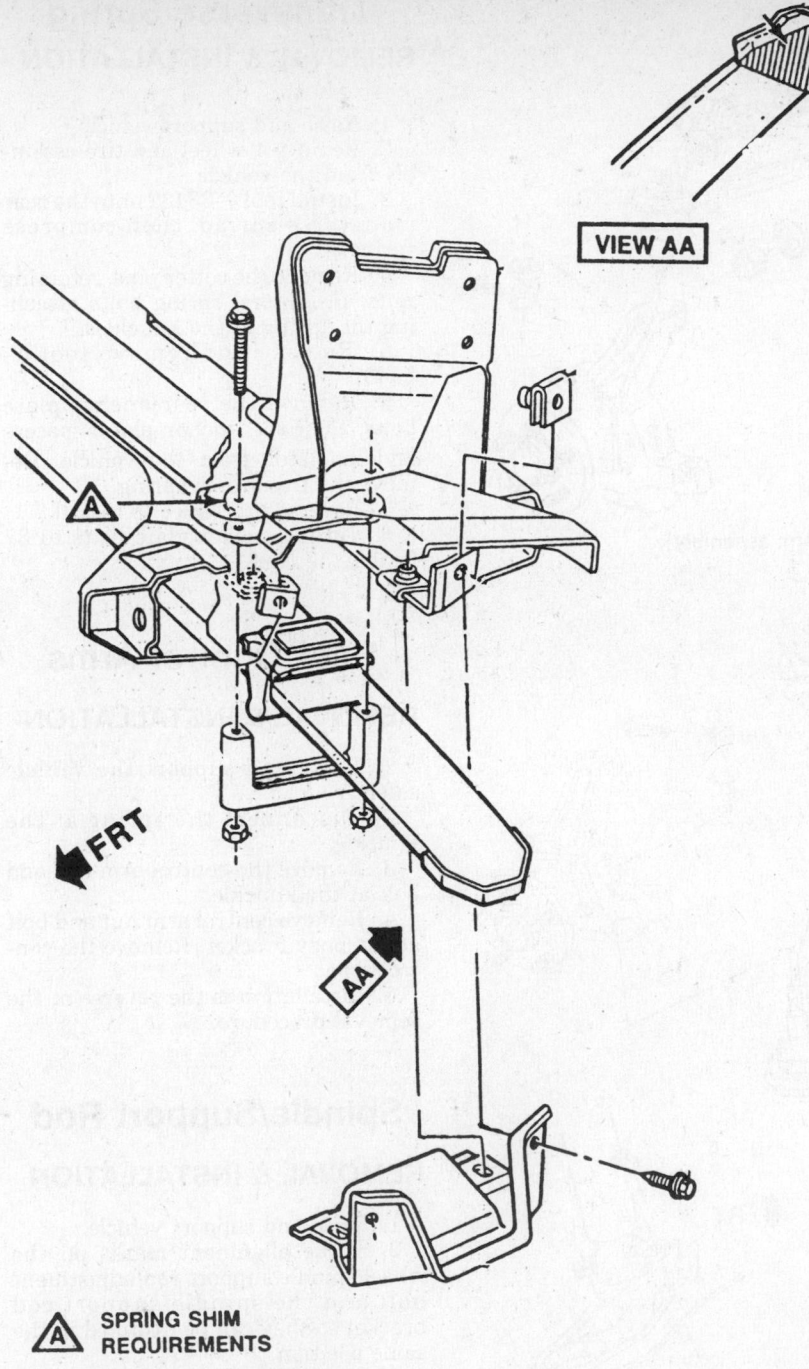

VIEW AA

◄ **FRT**

AA

⚠️ A **SPRING SHIM REQUIREMENTS**

SPRING COLOR CODE	NUMBER OF SHIMS REQUIRED PER SIDE
BLUE	0
YELLOW	1
GREEN	2

Front transverse spring installation

removal procedure. Torque the ball joint nut to 50 ft. lbs. (68 Nm).

Stabilizer Shaft

REMOVAL & INSTALLATION

1. Raise and support vehicle.
2. Remove the tire and wheel assembly.
3. Support the lower control arm using jackstands.
4. Remove the stabilizer shaft insulator clamp bolts and brackets from the frame.
5. Remove the stabilizer shaft to links attaching bolts.
6. Remove the stabilizer shaft from the vehicle.
7. Reverse procedure to install.

Front Wheel Bearings

REMOVAL & INSTALLATION

1. Raise and support the vehicle safely.
2. Remove the tire and wheel assembly.
3. Remove the caliper assembly and position it out of the way.
4. Remove the hub and bearing assembly.
5. Installation is the reverse of the removal procedure. The bearings do not require adjustment.

REAR SUSPENSION

Shock Absorbers

REMOVAL & INSTALLATION

NOTE: Purge new shocks of air by repeatedly extending them in their normal position and compressing them while inverted.

1. If equipped with selective ride control, disconnect the battery negative cable.
2. Raise and support the vehicle safely.
3. Remove the rear wheels.
4. Remove the upper bolt and nut.
5. Remove the lower mounting nut and washers.
6. Pivot the top of the shock absorber out of the frame bracket and pull the bottom off the strut shaft.

safely. Remove the tire and wheel assembly.
2. Remove spring protector.
3. Using tool J–3432 or equivalent, compress spring.

4. Remove lower shock bracket.
5. Using tool J–3436 or equivalent, disconnect lower ball joint.
6. Remove lower control arm.
7. Installation is the reverse of the

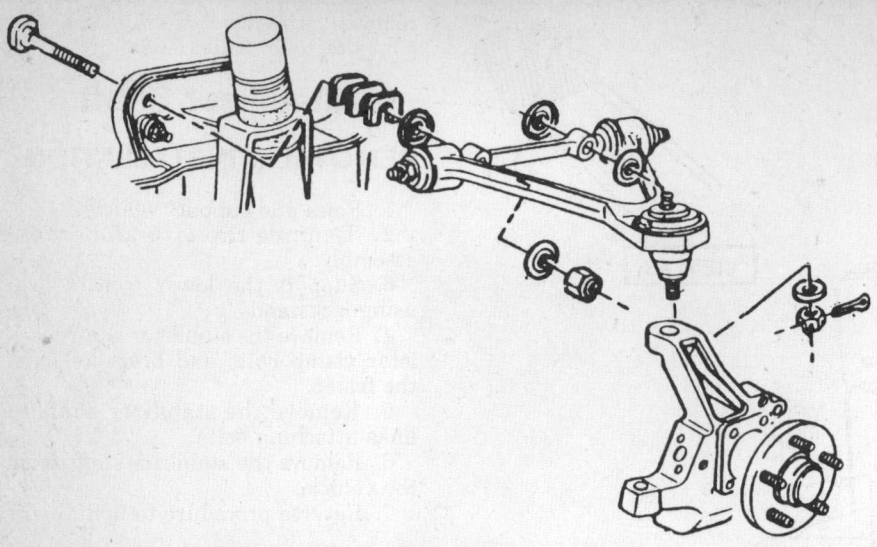

Exploded view of upper control arm assembly

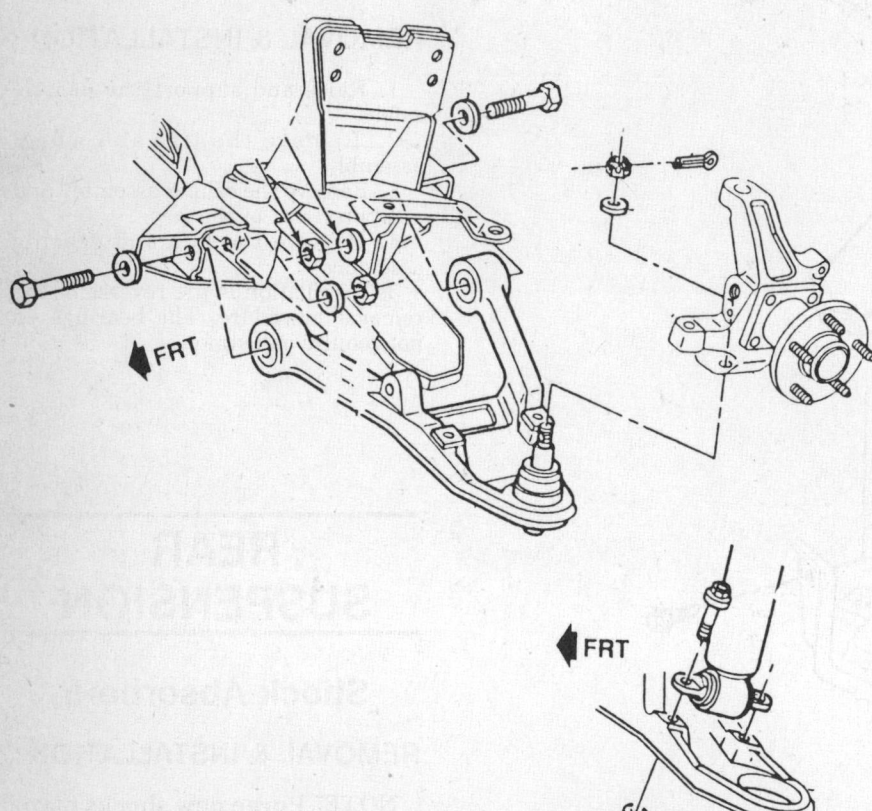

Exploded view of lower control arm assembly

To install:

7. Slide the upper shock absorber eye into the frame bracket and install the bolt, lockwasher and nut.

8. Install the rubber grommets on the lower shock eye and place the shock over the strut shaft. Install the washers and nut.

9. Lower the vehicle.

10. If equipped with selective ride control, connect the battery negative cable.

Transverse Spring
REMOVAL & INSTALLATION

1. Raise and support vehicle.
2. Remove 1 wheel and tire assembly from the vehicle.
3. Install tool J–33432 onto the rear transverse spring, then compress spring.
4. Remove the cotter pins, retaining nuts, insulators, spring bolts attaching the spring to the knuckles.
5. Release and remove tool J–33432.
6. Remove the rear anchor plate bolts, then the anchor plate, spacers and insulator from the vehicle. Remove the transverse spring.
7. Reverse procedure to install.
8. Torque anchor plate bolts to 37 ft. lbs. (50 Nm).

Rear Control Arms
REMOVAL & INSTALLATION

1. Raise and support the vehicle safely.
2. Disconnect the spring at the knuckle.
3. Remove the control arm nut and bolt at the knuckle.
4. Remove control arm nut and bolt at the body bracket. Remove the control arm.
5. Installation is the reverse of the removal procedure.

Spindle/Support Rod
REMOVAL & INSTALLATION

1. Raise and support vehicle.
2. Scribe alignment marks on the wheel spindle/support rod adjustment bolt and the spindle/support rod bracket so they can be installed in the same position.
3. Remove the adjustment bolt, cam and nut, then separate the spindle/support rod from the bracket.
4. Remove the spindle/support bolt, washer and nut at the spindle, then remove the spindle/support rod from the vehicle.
5. Reverse procedure to install.
6. Torque spindle/support rod to knuckle nut to 107 ft. lbs. (145 Nm). Torque spindle/support rod adjustment nut to 186 ft. lbs. (253 Nm).

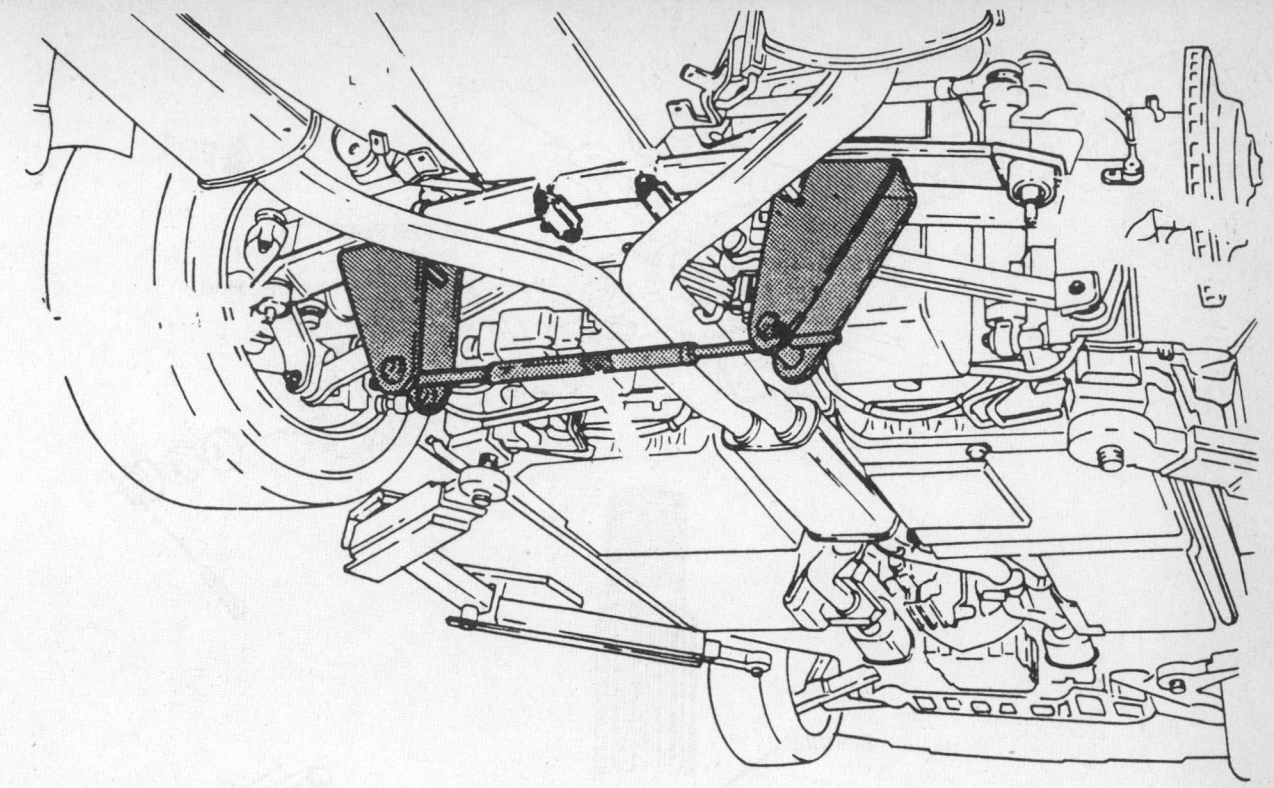

Removing rear transverse spring

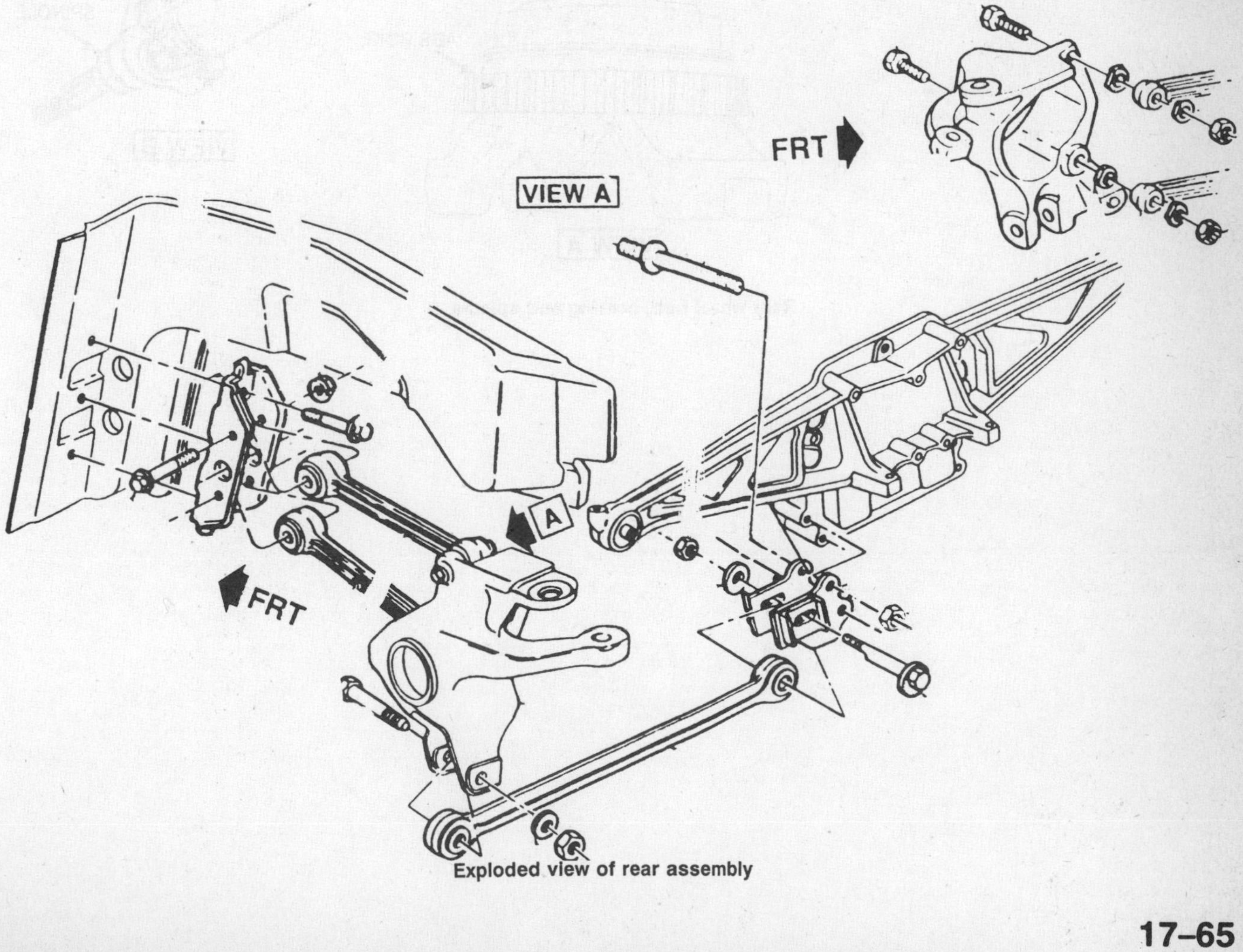

VIEW A

FRT ▶

Exploded view of rear assembly

FRT ◀

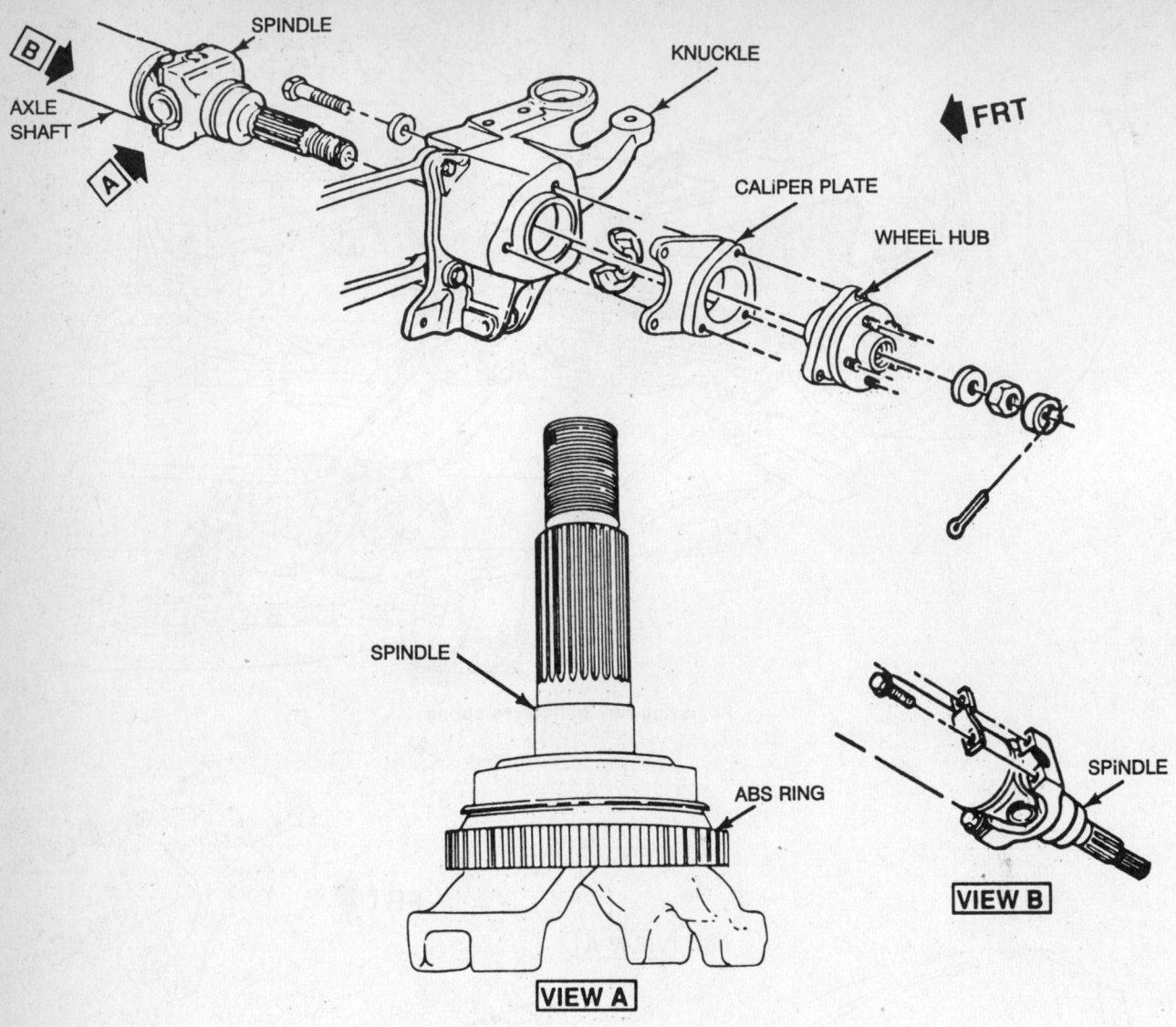

SPINDLE

AXLE SHAFT

B

A

KNUCKLE

CALIPER PLATE

WHEEL HUB

FRT

SPINDLE

ABS RING

VIEW A

SPINDLE

VIEW B

Rear wheel hub, bearing and spindle

Chevrolet/Pontiac
Rear Wheel Drive
Chevrolet—Chevette   Pontiac—1000

SPECIFICATIONS

VEHICLE IDENTIFICATION CHART

It is important for servicing and ordering parts to be certain of the vehicle and engine identification. The VIN (vehicle identification number) is a 17 digit number visible through the windshield on the driver's side of the dash and contains the vehicle and engine identification codes. The tenth digit indicates model year and the eigth digit indicates engine code. It can be interpreted as follows:

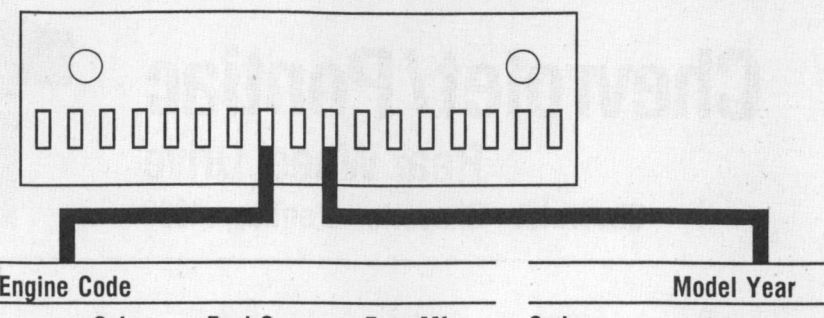

Engine Code					Model Year	
Code	Cu. In.	Liters	Cyl.	Fuel Sys.	Eng. Mfg.	Code	Year
C	97.6	1.6	4	2 bbl	Chevy	H	1987

ENGINE IDENTIFICATION

Year	Model	Engine Displacement cu. in. (liter)	Engine Series Identification (VIN)	No. of Cylinders	Engine Type
1987	Chevette	4-98 (1.6)	C	4	OHC
	1000	4-98 (1.6)	C	4	OHC

GENERAL ENGINE SPECIFICATIONS

Year	VIN	No. Cylinder Displacement cu. in. (liter)	Fuel System Type	Net Horsepower @ rpm	Net Torque @ rpm (ft.lbs.)	Bore × Stroke (in.)	Compression Ratio	Oil Pressure @ rpm
1987	C	4-98 (1.6)	2 bbl	65 @ 5200	80 @ 2400	3.228 × 2.980	9.0:1	55 @ 2000

GASOLINE ENGINE TUNE-UP SPECIFICATIONS
Refer to Section 41 for all spark plug recommendations

Year	VIN	No. Cylinder Displacement cu. in. (liter)	Spark Plugs Gap (in.)	Ignition Timing (deg.)		Compression Pressure (psi)	Fuel Pump (psi)	Idle Speed (rpm)		Valve Clearance	
				MT	AT			MT	AT	In.	Ex.
1987	C	4-98 (1.6)	.035	8B	8B	—	5.5-6.5	800	700	Hyd.	Hyd.

FIRING ORDERS

NOTE: To avoid confusion, always replace spark plug wires one at a time.

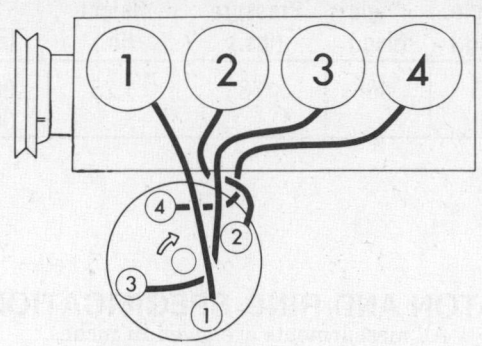

Chevrolet 98 cu. in. (1.6 liter) 4 cyl.
Engine firing order: 1-3-4-2
Distributor rotation: clockwise

CAPACITIES

Year	Model	VIN	No. Cylinder Displacement cu. in. (liter)	Engine Crankcase with Filter	Engine Crankcase without Filter	Transmission (pts.) 4-Spd	Transmission (pts.) 5-Spd	Transmission (pts.) Auto.	Drive Axle (pts.)	Fuel Tank (gal.)	Cooling System (qts.)
1987	Chevette	C	4-98 (1.6)	4	4	5.9	5.3	6①	1.75	12.2	9②
	1000	C	4-98 (1.6)	4	4	5.9	5.3	6①	1.75	12.2	9②

① Overhaul—9.7 pts.
② With air conditioning—9.2

CRANKSHAFT AND CONNECTING ROD SPECIFICATIONS
All measurements are given in inches.

Year	VIN	No. Cylinder Displacement cu. in. (liter)	Crankshaft Main Brg. Journal Dia.	Crankshaft Main Brg. Oil Clearance	Crankshaft Shaft End-play	Crankshaft Thrust on No.	Connecting Rod Journal Diameter	Connecting Rod Oil Clearance	Connecting Rod Side Clearance
1987	C	4-98 (1.6)	2.0078–2.0088	①	.004–.008	4	1.809–1.810	.0014–.0031	.004–.012

① No.5—.0009-.0026
All others—.0005-.0018

VALVE SPECIFICATIONS

Year	VIN	No. Cylinder Displacement cu. in. (liter)	Seat Angle (deg.)	Face Angle (deg.)	Spring Test Pressure (lbs.)	Spring Installed Height (in.)	Stem-to-Guide Clearance (in.)		Stem Diameter (in.)	
							Intake	Exhaust	Intake	Exhaust
1987	C	4-98 (1.6)	45	46	173	1.25	.0006–.0017	.0014–.0025	.3141	.3133

PISTON AND RING SPECIFICATIONS
All measurments are given in inches.

Year	VIN	No. Cylinder Displacement cu. in. (liter)	Piston Clearance	Ring Gap			Ring Side Clearance		
				Top Compression	Bottom Compression	Oil Control	Top Compression	Bottom Compression	Oil Control
1987	C	4-98 (1.6)	.0008–.0016	.009–.019	.008–.018	.015–.055	.0012–.0027	.0012–.0032	.0003–.0050

TORQUE SPECIFICATIONS
All readings in ft. lbs.

Year	VIN	No. Cylinder Displacement cu. in. (liter)	Cylinder Head Bolts	Main Bearing Bolts	Rod Bearing Bolts	Crankshaft Pulley Bolts	Flywheel Bolts	Manifold		Spark Plugs
								Intake	Exhaust	
1987	C	4-98 (1.6)	75	50	40	100	50	18	25	22

BRAKE SPECIFICATIONS
All measurements in inches unless noted

Year	Model	Lug Nut Torque (ft. lbs.)	Master Cylinder Bore	Brake Disc		Standard Brake Drum Diameter	Minimum Lining Thickness	
				Minimum Thickness	Maximum Runout		Front	Rear
1987	Chevette	80	.847	.374	.0005	7.874	.030	①
	1000	80②	.874	.374	.0005	7.874	.030	①

① Bonded Shoes — .062 in.
　Riveted Shoes — .030 in. over rivet head.
② Aluminum alloy wheels — 100 ft. lbs.

WHEEL ALIGNMENT

Year	Model	Caster		Camber		Toe-in (in.)	Steering Axis Inclination (deg.)
		Range (deg.)	Preferred Setting (deg.)	Range (deg.)	Preferred Setting (deg.)		
1987	All	4P-6P	5P	¼P-½P	¼P	¹⁄₁₆P	NA

ENGINE ELECTRICAL

NOTE: Disconnecting the negative battery cable on some vehicles may interfere with the functions of the on board computer systems and may require the computer to undergo a relearning process, once the negative battery cable is reconnected.

Distributor

REMOVAL & INSTALLATION

Timing Not Disturbed

1. Disconnect the negative battery cable.
2. If the vehicle is equipped with air conditioning, disconnect the electrical lead at the air conditioning compressor. Remove the compressor mounting thru bolt and 2 adjusting bolts. Remove the compressor upper mounting bracket.
3. Raise and safely support the vehicle. Remove the 2 bolts securing the compressor lower mounting bracket and pull the bracket outward for clearance. Do not disconnect any refrigerant lines.
4. Lower the vehicle.
5. Remove the air cleaner.
6. Remove the distributor cap.
7. Remove the ignition coil cover by prying on the flat on the front edge of the cover.

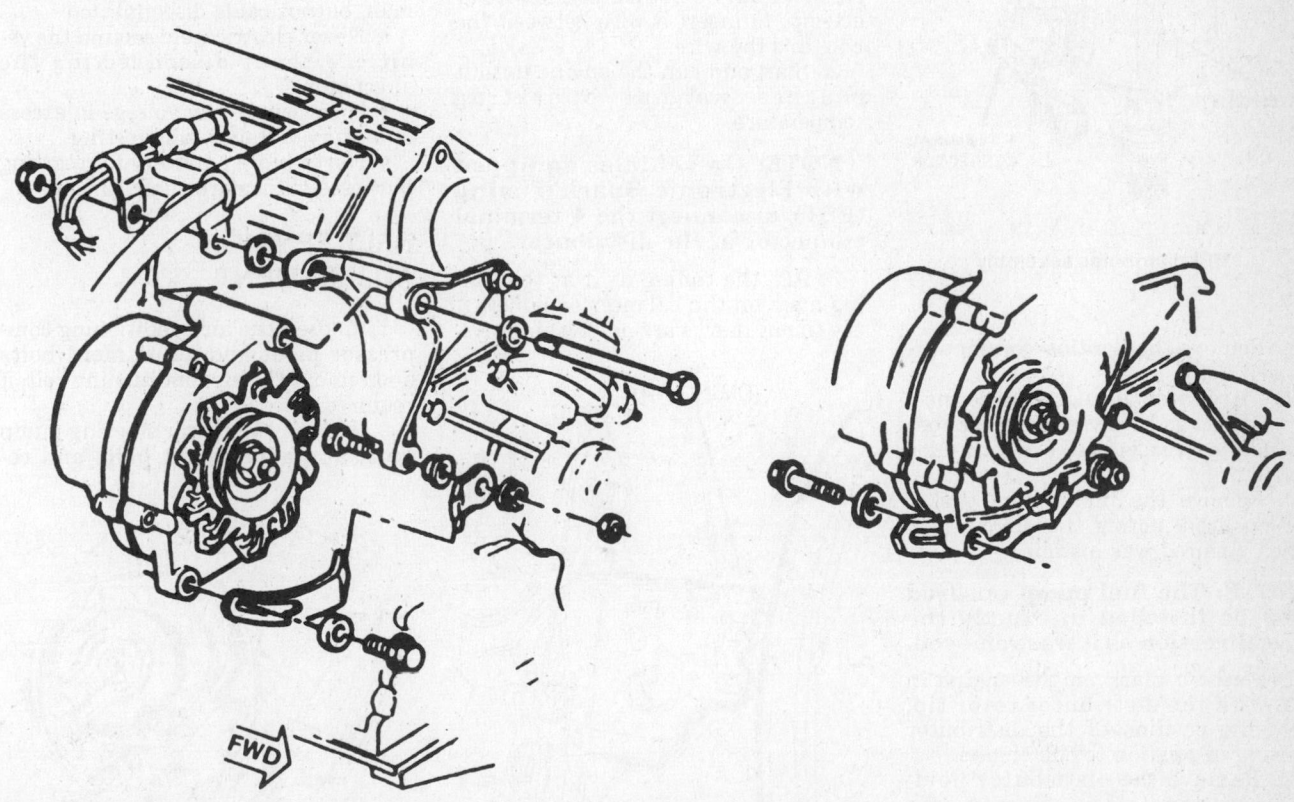

Alternator mounting and adjustment

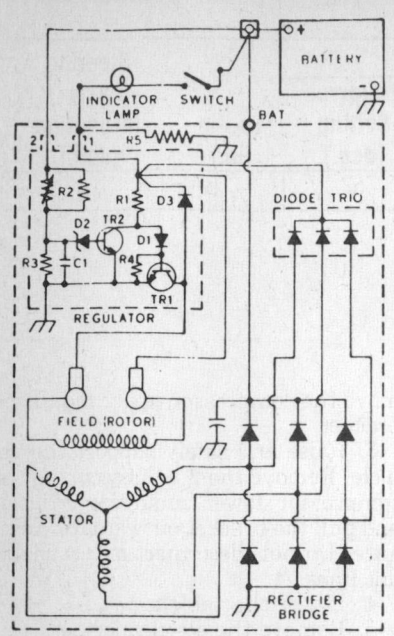

Charging system schematic

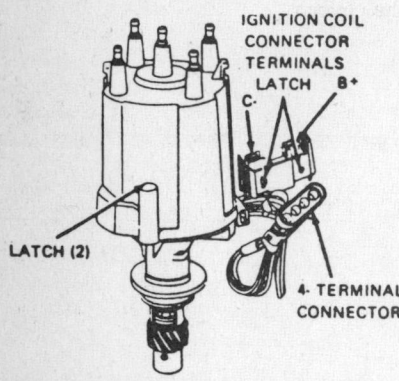

HEI distributor assembly

8. Remove the ignition coil mounting bracket bolts.

9. Disconnect the electrical connector with red and brown wires that goes from the ignition coil to the distributor.

10. Remove the fuel pump, gasket and pushrod, noting the direction in which pushrod was installed.

NOTE: The fuel pump pushrod must be installed in exactly the same direction as it was removed.

11. Scribe a mark on the engine in line with the distributor rotor tip. Note the position of the distributor housing in relation to the engine.

12. Remove the distributor hold-down bolt and clamp. Remove the distributor.

13. Complete installation by reversing the removal procedure. Aligning the marks made during removal.

Timing Disturbed

1. Remove the No. 1 spark plug and place a finger over the spark plug hole.

2. Manually turn the engine in the normal direction of rotation until compression is felt.

3. Align the timing marks to TDC. Align the marks made during removal and install the distributor.

Ignition Timing

Vehicles equipped with Electronic Spark Timing (EST) can be identified by the absence of a vacuum and a mechanical spark advance on the distributor. EST allows continuous spark timing adjustments to be made by the ECM (Electronic Control Module).

ADJUSTMENT

NOTE: Refer to and follow all instructions on the Vehicle Emissions Control information label located on the radiator support panel for the latest service procedures or specification changes.

1. Connect a timing light to the No. 1 spark plug. Use a jumper lead or adapter between the wire and plug, or use a timing light with an inductive type pick-up. Do not pierce the wire or attempt to insert a wire between the boot and the wire.

2. Start and run the engine until it reaches normal operating temperature.

NOTE: On vehicles equipped with Electronic Spark Timing (EST), disconnect the 4 terminal connector at the distributor.

3. Aim the timing light at the timing mark on the balancer or pulley, if the timing marks are not within speci-

TIMING TAB

CRANKSHAFT PULLEY

Ignition timing marks

fications, loosen the distributor hold-down clamp bolt. Rotate the distributor until the timing marks indicates the correct timing.

4. Tighten the distributor hold-down bolt and recheck the timing.

5. Vehicles equipped with EST, reconnect the 4 terminal connector at the distributor.

6. Turn the engine off and disconnect the timing light and reconnect the No. 1 spark wire, if removed.

Alternator

For further information on the charging system, please refer to "Charging and Starting" in the Unit Repair section.

PRECAUTIONS

The following precautions should be observed when working on any charging system:

• Never switch battery polarity
• When installing a battery, always connect the positive terminal first
• Never disconnect the battery while the engine is running
• If the molded connector is is disconnected from the alternator, never ground the hot wire
• Never run the alternator with the main output cable disconnected
• Never electric weld around the vehicle without disconnecting the alternator
• Never apply any voltage in excess of battery voltage while testing
• Never jump a battery for starting purposes with more than 12 volts

BELT TENSION ADJUSTMENT

1. Loosen the air conditioning compressor pivot and adjustment bolts and remove the air conditioning belt, if required.

2. Loosen the power steering pump pivot and adjustment bolts and re-

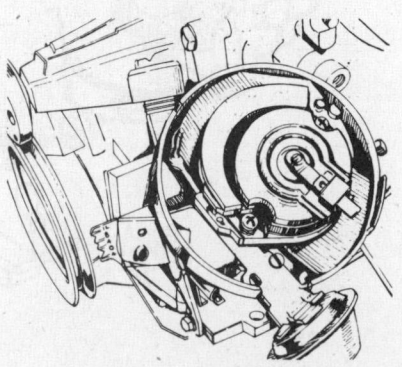

Correct distributor rotor alignment

move the power steering belt, if required.

3. Loosen the alternator pivot and adjustment bolt and remove the alternator belt.

4. Install the new alternator belt making sure the belt is on the correct pulleys.

5. Adjust the alternator belt to a maximum tension of 146 lbs. for a new belt and 70 lbs. for a used belt.

NOTE: Never apply pressure to the frame end of the aternator when adjusting the belt tension. Apply the pressure to the center of the alternator housing.

6. Install the power steering belt, if required, and adjust the belt to a maximum tension of 146 lbs. for a new belt and 70 lbs. for a used belt.

7. Install the air conditioning belt, if required and adjust the belt to a maximum tension of 168 lbs. for a new belt and 90 lbs. for a used belt.

8. Start the engine and make sure the belts are running properly.

BELT TENSION CHART

	New Belt (lbs.)	Used Belt (lbs.)
Alternator	146	70
Power Steering	146	70
Air Conditioning	168	90

REMOVAL & INSTALLATION

1. Disconnect the negative battery cable.

2. Disconnect the alternator wiring.

3. Remove the brace bolt and the drive belt.

4. Support the alternator. Remove the mounting bolt and remove the alternator.

5. Installation is the reverse of removal. Adjust the alternator belt to the correct specification.

Voltage Regulator

For further information on the charging system, please refer to "Charging and Starting" in the Unit Repair section.

ADJUSTMENT

The voltage regulator is a solid state unit mounted inside the alternator. The voltage regulator voltage setting cannot be adjusted. Replacement of the voltage regulator requires disassembling of the alternator.

Starter

For further information on the charging system, please refer to "Charging and Starting" in the Unit Repair section.

REMOVAL & INSTALLATION

Without Power Brakes

1. Disconnect the battery negative cable.

2. Remove the air cleaner.

3. Disconnect and plug the fuel line at the carburetor and move it aside.

4. Disconnect and tag the vacuum hoses at the carburetor.

5. Remove the splash shield from the distributor coil and move it aside.

6. Using a 6 in. and 12 in. extension with a universal socket, remove the upper starter bolt.

7. Remove the lower starter bolt.

8. Disconnect and tag the starter wiring.

NOTE: The master cylinder mounting nuts can be removed for access to remove the starter. Take care not to bend any of the brakes lines.

9. Installation is the reverse of removal.

With Power Brakes

1. Disconnect the battery ground cable.

2. Remove the air cleaner.

3. Disconnect and plug the fuel line at the carburetor.

4. Remove the splash shield from the distributor coil.

5. Using a 6 in. and 12 in. extension with a universal socket, remove the upper starter bolt.

6. Remove the steering column cover screws and remove the cover.

7. Remove the steering column upper nuts and toe pan screw.

8. Raise and safely support the vehicle. Remove the steering shaft from the steering coupling.

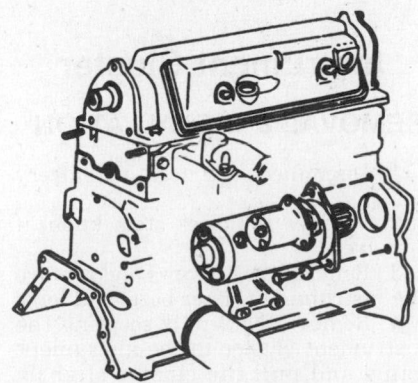

Starter motor mounting

9. Lower the vehicle and move the steering column from inside the vehicle to gain access to the starter.

10. Disconnect and tag the starter wiring.

11. Remove the starter lower bolt and remove the starter.

12. Installation is the reverse of removal.

CHASSIS ELECTRICAL

Heater Blower Motor

REMOVAL & INSTALLATION

1. Disconnect the negative battery cable.

2. Disconnect the electrical lead from the blower motor.

3. Scribe a mark to reference the blower motor flange-to-case position.

4. Remove the blower motor-to-case attaching screws and remove the blower motor and wheel as an assembly. Pry the flange gently if the sealer acts as an adhesive.

5. Remove the blower wheel retaining nut and separate the motor and wheel.

6. Reverse the removal procedure to complete installation. Be sure to align the scribe marks made during removal.

NOTE: Assemble the blower wheel to the motor with the open end of the wheel away from the motor. If necessary, replace the sealer at the motor flange.

Windshield Wiper Motor

REMOVAL & INSTALLATION

1. Disconnect the negative battery cable. Working inside the vehicle, reach up under the instrument panel above the steering column and loosen, but do not remove, the transmission drive link-to-motor crank arm attaching nuts.

2. Disconnect the transmission drive link from the wiper rotor crank arm.

3. Raise the hood and disconnect the wiper motor wiring.

4. Remove the 3 motor attaching bolts.

5. Remove the motor while guiding the crank arm through the hole.

6. Align the sealing gasket to the base of the motor and reverse the removal procedure to complete installation.

NOTE: If the wiper motor-to-firewall sealing gasket is damaged during removal, it should be replaced with a new gasket to prevent possible water leaks.

Windshield Wiper Linkage

REMOVAL & INSTALLATION

1. Disconnect the negative battery cable. Remove or loosen the instrument panel cover and the instrument panel cluster housing.
2. On vehicles equipped with air conditioning, remove screws and push the left air conditioning duct aside for better access to linkage attaching bolts (left side). Remove the left side air outlet duct, the speedometer cable shield and the instrument panel brace (left side).
3. Working from inside the vehicle, loosen transmission drive link to motor crank arm attaching nuts and disengage drive link.
4. Remove wiper arm and blade assemblies. Remove wiper linkage to dash panel attaching bolts.
5. Move the linkage assembly to the left while rotating the assembly, work it out through instrument panel access hole at right upper center of instrument panel.
To install:
6. Install the assembly through instrument panel access hole and insert serrated shafts through holes in upper dash panel, then install the attaching bolts.
7. Cycle the wiper motor to insure that motor crank arm is in the park position.
8. Attach wiper linkage drive link to wiper motor crank arm.
9. Complete installation by reversing the removal procedure.

Windshield Wiper Switch

The windshield wiper switch is part of the combination switch assembly. The combination switch consists of the windshield wiper/washer, headlight beam selector and turn signal.

REMOVAL & INSTALLATION

1. Disconnect the negative battery cable. Remove the steering wheel and turn signal switch. It may be necessary

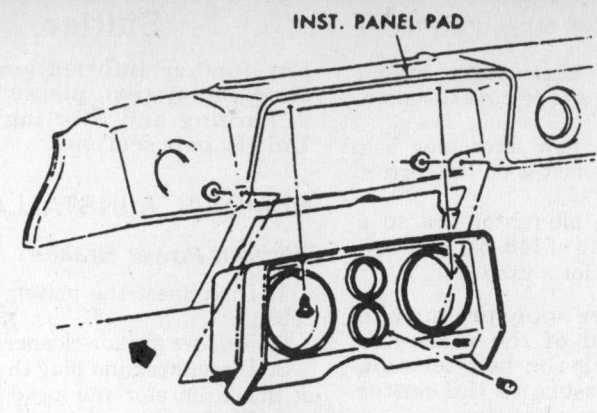

INST. PANEL PAD

Instrument cluster removal

to loosen the 2 steering column mounting nuts and remove the 4 bracket to mast jacket screws, then separate the bracket from the mast jacket to allow the connector clip on the ignition switch to be pulled out of the column assembly.
2. Disconnect the washer/wiper switch lower connector.
3. Remove the screws attaching the column housing to the mast jacket. Be sure to note the position of the dimmer switch actuator rod for reassembly in the same position. Remove the column housing and switch as an assembly.
4. Turn the switch upside down and use a drift to remove the pivot pin from the washer/wiper switch. Remove the switch.
To install:
5. Place a new switch into position in the housing and install the pivot pin.
6. Position the housing onto the mast jacket and attach it by installing the screws. Install the dimmer switch actuator rod in the same position as noted earlier. Check the switch operation.
7. Reconnect lower end of switch assembly.
8. Install remaining components in reverse order of removal. Be sure to attach column mounting bracket in its original position.

Instrument Cluster

REMOVAL & INSTALLATION

1. Disconnect the negative battery cable.
2. Remove the clock stem knob, if equipped.
3. Remove the 4 screws and remove the instrument cluster bezel and lens.
4. Remove the 2 nuts securing the instrument cluster to the instrument panel and pull the cluster slightly forward.

5. Disconnect the electrical connector and speedometer cable from the cluster and remove it.
6. Installation is the reverse of removal procedures. Be sure to connect the speedometer cable to the cluster before installation.

Speedometer

REMOVAL & INSTALLATION

1. Disconnect the negative battery cable. Remove the instrument cluster assembly.
2. Remove the speedometer retaining screws from the instrument cluster.
3. Separate the speedometer head from the instrument cluster.
4. Installation is the reverse of the removal procedure.

Speedometer Cable

REMOVAL & INSTALLATION

1. Disconnect the negative battery cable. Remove the instrument cluster assembly.
2. Pull the core from the speedometer cable housing. If the core is broken in the middle, it will be necessary to disconnect the speedometer cable at the transmission and insert the new core through the top of the housing.
3. Attach the cable housing to the transmission and insert the new core through the top of the housing.
4. Attach the speedometer cable to the rear of the speedometer.
5. Install the instrument cluster assembly and check the speedometer operation.

Radio

REMOVAL & INSTALLATION

1. Disconnect the negative battery cable.

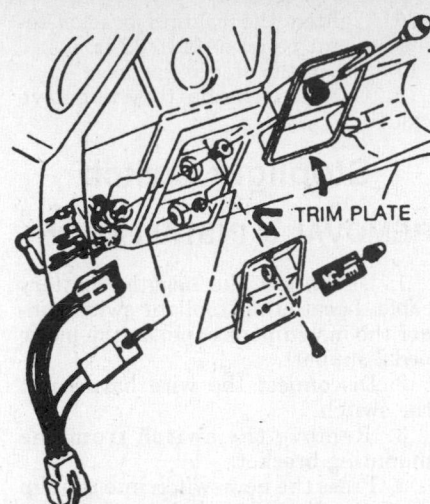

Headlight switch mounting

2. Remove the nut from the mounting stud on the bottom of the radio.

3. Remove all control knobs and/or spacers from the right and left radio control shafts.

4. Remove the 4 screws from the center trim plate and pull the trim plate and the radio forward slightly.

5. Disconnect the antenna lead from the rear of the radio.

6. Disconnect the speaker and electrical connectors from the radio harness.

7. Disconnect the electrical connectors from the rear window defogger and cigarette lighter.

8. Use a deep well socket to remove the retaining nuts from both control shafts and remove the radio.

9. Installation is the reverse of the removal procedure.

Headlight Switch

REMOVAL & INSTALLATION

1. Disconnect the negative battery cable.

2. Pull the headlight switch control knob to the On position.

3. Reach up under the instrument panel and depress the switch shaft retainer button while pulling on the switch control shaft knob.

4. Remove the 3 screws and remove the headlight switch trim plate.

5. Remove the light switch ferrule nut from the front of the instrument panel.

6. Disconnect the multi-contact connector from the bottom of the headlight switch.

7. Installation is the reverse of removal.

Combination Switch

NOTE: The turn signal switch is incorporated into the combination switch.

REMOVAL & INSTALLATION

1. Disconnect the negative battery cable. Remove the steering wheel.

2. Position a suitable tool into 1 of the 3 cover slots. Pry up and out on at least 2 slots to free the cover.

3. Press down on the lock plate, but do not relieve the full load of the spring because the ring will rotate and make the removal difficult. Pry the round wire snapring out of the shaft groove and discard it. Lift the lock plate off the end of the shaft.

4. Slide the turn signal canceling cam, upper bearing preload spring and thrust washer off the end of the shaft.

5. Remove the lever by rotating it clockwise to its stop (OFF position), then pull the lever straight out to disengage it.

6. Push the hazard warning knob in and unscrew the knob.

7. Remove the 2 screws, pivot arm and spacer.

8. Wrap the upper part of the connector with tape to prevent snagging the wires during switch removal.

9. Remove the 3 switch mounting screws and pull the switch straight up, guiding the wiring harness through the column housing.

To install:

NOTE: During installation, it is extremely important that only the specified screws, bolts and nuts be used. The use of overlength screws could prevent the steering column from compressing under impact.

10. Position the new switch into the housing.

11. Install the 3 switch mounting screws. Replace the spacer and pivot arm. Be sure the spacer protrudes through the hole in the arm and that the arm finger encloses the turn signal switch frame.

12. Install the hazard warning knob.

13. Make sure the turn signal switch is in the neutral position and that the hazard warning knob is out. Slide the thrust washer, upper bearing preload spring and the canceling cam into the upper end of the shaft.

14. Place the lock plate and a new snapring onto the end of the shaft. Compress the lock plate as far as possible. Slide the new snapring into the shaft groove and remove the lockplate compressor tool.

15. Install the lever, guiding the wire harness through the column housing. Align the lever pin with the switch slot. Push on the end of the lever until it is seated securely.

16. Install the steering wheel.

Ignition Lock

REMOVAL & INSTALLATION

The ignition lock is located on the right side of the steering column and should be removed only in the **RUN** position. Removal in any other position will damage the key buzzer switch. The ignition lock cannot be disassembled; if replacement is required, a new cylinder coded to the old key must be installed.

1. Disconnect the negative battery cable. Remove the steering wheel and turn signal switch.

2. Do not remove the buzzer switch or damage to the lock cylinder will result.

3. Place the lock cylinder in the **RUN** position. Remove the securing screw and remove the cylinder.

To install:

4. Hold the cylinder sleeve and rotate knob (key in) clockwise to stop. (This retracts the actuator). Insert the cylinder into the housing bore with the key on the cylinder sleeve aligned with the keyway in the housing. Push the

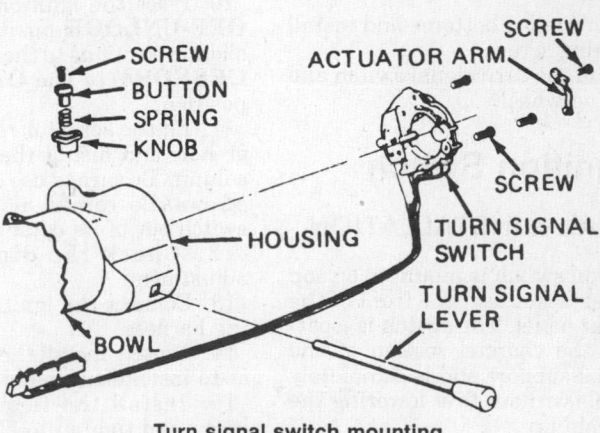

Turn signal switch mounting

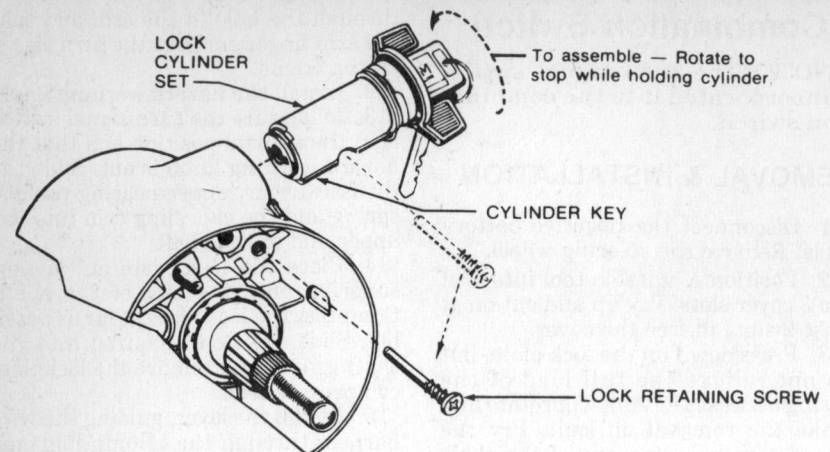

Lock cylinder installation details

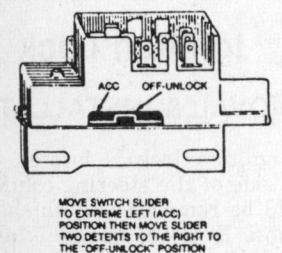

Ignition switch — positioning for installation

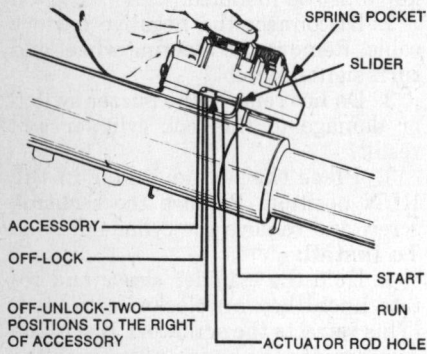

Postioning the ignition switch for installation

cylinder in until it bottoms and install the retaining screw.

5. Install the turn signal switch and the steering wheel.

Ignition Switch

REMOVAL & INSTALLATION

The ignition switch is mounted on top of the mast jacket near the front of the instrument panel. The switch is located inside the channel section of the brake pedal support and is completely inaccessible without first lowering the steering column.

1. Disconnect the negative battery cable.
2. Remove the steering wheel.
3. Move the driver's seat as far back as possible.
4. Remove the floor pan bracket screw.
5. Remove the 2 column bracket-to-instrument panel nuts and lower the column far enough to disconnect the ignition switch wiring harness.

NOTE: **Be sure the steering column is properly supported before proceeding.**

6. The switch should be in the **LOCK** position before removal. If the lock cylinder has already been removed, the actuating rod to the switch should be pulled up until there is a definite stop, then moved down 1 detent to the **LOCK** position.
7. Remove the 2 mounting screws and remove the ignition and dimmer switch.
To install:
8. Install the lock cylinder.
9. Turn the cylinder clockwise to **STOP** and then counterclockwise to stop, then counterclockwise again to stop (**OFF-UNLOCK**) position.
10. Place the ignition switch in the **OFF-UNLOCK** position. Move the slider 2 positions to the right from **ACCESSORY** to the **OFF-UNLOCK** position.
11. Fit the actuator rod into the slider hole and install the switch on the column. Be sure to use only the correct screws. Be careful not to move the switch out of its detent.
12. Check the dimmer switch adjustment.
13. Connect the ignition switch wiring harness.
14. Loosely install the column bracket-to-instrument panel nuts.
15. Install the floor pan bracket screw and tighten to 20 ft. lbs.

16. Tighten the column bracket-to-instrument panel nuts to 22 ft. lbs.
17. Install the steering wheel.
18. Connect the battery negative cable.

Stoplight Switch

REMOVAL & INSTALLATION

1. Disconnect the negative battery cable. Locate the stoplight switch under the instrument panel on the brake pedal support.
2. Disconnect the wire harness at the switch.
3. Remove the switch from the mounting bracket.
4. Press the new switch into the clip until the shoulder of the switch bottoms out against the clip.
5. Adjust the switch by pulling the brake pedal back to its normal position.
6. Check the operation of the switch. Contact should be made when the brake pedal is depressed 0.53 in. (13.5mm).

Clutch Start Switch

The clutch start switch is located on the top of the clutch pedal.

ADJUSTMENT

The clutch start switch is self-adjusting and does not require any adjustment.

REMOVAL & INSTALLATION

1. Disconnect the negative battery cable. Remove the electrical connection from the switch.
2. Compress the switch retainer and remove the safety switch from the bracket. Rotate the switch slightly so the actuating shaft retainer can be pulled from the hole of the clutch pedal.
3. Place the new switch in position so the actuating shaft retainer is in line with the hole of the clutch pedal and then push the switch into the hole of the clutch bracket.
4. Reconnect the electrical connection on the switch and the negative battery cable.

NOTE: **The engine should only start with the clutch pedal fully depressed and the ignition switch in the START position.**

Neutral Safety Switch

REMOVAL & INSTALLATION

1. Remove the floor console cover.

2. Disconnect the electrical connectors on the back-up, seat belt warning and neutral starter contacts on the switch.

3. Position the shift lever in **N**.

4. Remove the 2 switch attaching screws and remove the switch.

To install:

5. Make sure the shift lever is in the **N** position before installing the switch assembly.

6. Place the neutral start switch assembly in position on the shift lever making sure the pin on the lever is in the slot of the switch.

NOTE: When installing the same switch, align the contact support slot with the service adjustment hole in the switch and insert a 3/32 in. drill bit to hold the switch in Neutral. Remove the drill bit after the switch is fastened to the shift lever mounting bracket.

7. Install the 2 switch attaching screws.

8. Move the shift lever out of **N** in order to shear the plastic pin.

9. Connect the electrical connectors to the switch contacts. Apply the parking brake and start the engine. Check to make sure the engine starts only in **P** or **N**. Make sure the back-up lights work only in **Re**. Check that the seatbelt warning system operates properly.

10. Stop the engine and install the floor console cover.

Fuses, Circuit Breakers and Relays

LOCATION

Fusible Links

Fusible links are provided in all battery feed circuits and other selected circuits. This is a short piece of copper wire approximately 4 in. long in series with the circuit and acts as a fuse. Fusible links are generally located at the starter motor electrical junction.

Circuit Breakers

A circuit breaker is an electrical switch which breaks the circuit during an electrical overload. The circuit breaker will remain open until the short or overload condition in the circuit is corrected. Circuit breakers are located in the fuse panel.

Fuse Panel

The fuse block on some vehicles is a swing-down unit located in the underside of the instrument panel adjacent to the steering column. On other vehi-

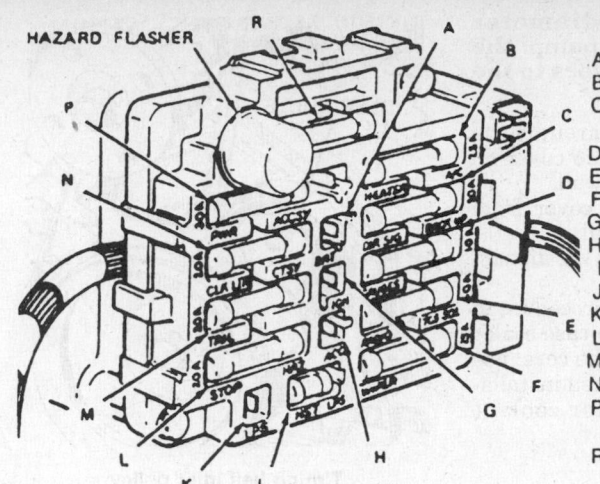

A. Battery receptacle
B. Heater/air conditioner
C. Directional signal/backup lamp
D. Gauges
E. Radio/tcs solenoid
F. Windshield wipers
G. Ignition receptacle
H. Accessory receptacle
I. Hazard flasher
J. Instrument lights
K. Lamp receptacle
L. Stop/hazard warning lamps
M. Tail lamp
N. Clock/lighter/courtesy lamps
P. Power accessory fuse/receptacle
R. Electric choke

Fuse box—fuse locations

cles, the fuse block is located behind the glove box and access is gained through the glove box opening.

Various Relays

Horn Relay—located below the left side of the instrument panel near the fuse box.

A/C Blower Relay—located under the right side of the dash on the A/C module.

Rear Window Defogger Relay—located behind the left side of the instrument panel.

Computer

LOCATION

Electronic Control Module

The electronic control module is located below the right hand side of the instrument panel.

Flashers

LOCATION

Turn Signal Flasher

The turn signal flasher is located above the brake pedal bracket and to the left of the steering column.

Hazard Flasher

The hazard flasher is located behind the left side of the instrument panel on the fuse box.

ENGINE COOLING

Radiator

REMOVAL & INSTALLATION

1. Disconnect the negative battery cable.

2. Drain the cooling system.

3. Remove the upper radiator support or the upper fan shroud.

4. Disconnect the coolant hoses. On vehicles equipped with automatic transmission, disconnect and plug the cooler lines from the radiator.

5. Remove the radiator.

6. Installation is the reverse of the removal.

Heater Core

REMOVAL & INSTALLATION

Without Air Conditioning

1. Disconnect the negative battery cable.

2. Drain the radiator.

3. Disconnect the heater hoses at the heater core tube connections. Use care when removing the hoses as the core tube attachment seams can be easily damaged if too much force is used on them. When the hoses are removed, install plugs in the core tubes to avoid spilling coolant when removing the core.

NOTE: The larger diameter hose goes to the water pump: the smaller diameter hose goes to the thermostat housing.

4. Remove the screws around the perimeter of the heater core cover on the engine side of the firewall.

5. Pull the heater core cover from its mounting in the firewall.

6. Remove the core from the distributor assembly.

7. Reverse the removal procedure to install. Be sure the core-to-case sealer is intact before replacing the core; use new sealer if necessary. When installation is complete, check for coolant leaks.

With Air Conditioning

1. Disconnect the negative battery cable.

2. Disconnect the heater hoses at the core with a drain pan under the vehicle. Plug the hoses to prevent spillage.

3. Remove the A/C hose bracket.

4. Removes the heater core case cover and remove the core from the case.

5. Installation is the reverse of removal.

Water Pump

REMOVAL & INSTALLATION

1. Disconnect the battery negative cable. Remove the alternator and air conditioning compressor drive belts.

2. Remove the engine fan, spacer (air conditioned vehicles) and the pulley.

3. Remove the timing belt front cover by removing the 2 upper bolts, center bolt and 2 lower nuts. Remove the timing belt lower cover retaining nut and remove the cover.

4. Drain the coolant from the engine.

5. Remove the lower radiator hose and the heater hose at the water pump.

6. Turn the crankshaft pulley so the mark on the pulley is aligned with the 0 mark on the timing scale and that a ⅛ in. drill bit can be inserted through the timing belt upper rear cover and camshaft sprocket.

7. Remove the idler pulley and pull the timing belt off the sprocket. Do not disturb the crankshaft position.

8. Remove the water pump retaining bolts and remove the pump and gasket from the engine.

9. Clean off all the old gasket material from the engine.

To install:

10. With a new gasket in place on the water pump, position the water pump

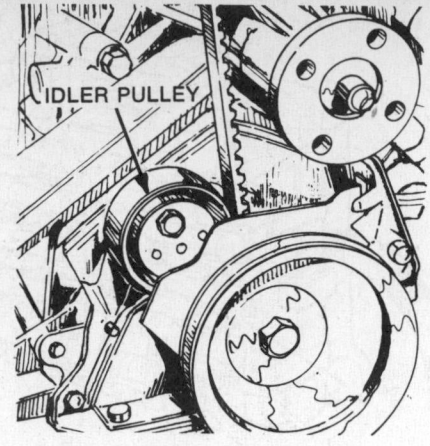

Timing belt idler pulley

in place on the engine and install the retaining bolts.

11. Install the timing belt onto the cam sprocket.

12. Apply sealer to the idler pulley attaching bolt and install the bolt and the idler pulley. Turn the idler pulley counterclockwise on its mounting bolt to remove the slack in the timing belt.

13. Use a tension gauge to adjust timing belt tension. Check belt tension midway between the tensioner and the cam sprocket on the idler pulley side. Correct belt tension is 70 lbs. Torque the idler pulley mounting bolt to 13–18 ft. lbs.

14. Remove the ⅛ in. drill bit from the upper rear timing belt cover and cam sprocket.

15. Install the lower radiator hose and the heater hose to the water pump.

16. Install the timing belt front covers.

17. Install the water pump pulley, spacer (if equipped) and engine fan.

18. Install the engine drive belt(s).

19. Refill the cooling system.

20. Connect the battery negative cable.

21. Start the engine and check for leaks. Run the engine with the heater on until the thermostat opens, then recheck the coolant level.

Thermostat

REMOVAL & INSTALLATION

1. Drain the radiator and remove the radiator hose at the water outlet.

2. Remove the thermostat housing bolts and remove the housing, gasket and thermostat.

3. Remove any old gasket material. Install the thermostat. Use a new gasket on the thermostat housing and install the thermostat housing bolts.

4. Install the radiator hose at the water outlet.

5. Fill the cooling system. Run the engine with the heater on until the thermostat opens, then recheck the coolant level.

Cooling System Bleeding

After working on the cooling system, even to replace the thermostat, it must be bled. Air trapped in the system will, otherwise, prevent proper filling, leaving the radiator coolant level low and causing risk of overheating.

To bleed the system, start with the system cool, the radiator cap off and the radiator filled to about 1 in. below the filler neck. Start the engine and run it at slightly above normal idle speed, to ensure adequate circulation. If air bubbles appear and the coolant level drops, fill the system with an antifreeze/water mixture to bring the level back to the proper level. Run the engine this way until the thermostat opens. When this happens, coolant will move abruptly across the top of the radiator and the temperature of the radiator will suddenly rise. At this point, air is often expelled and the level may drop quite a bit. Keep refilling the system until the level is near the top of the radiator and remains constant. If the vehicle has an overflow tank, fill the radiator right up to the filler neck. Replace the radiator filler cap.

FUEL SYSTEM

Fuel System Service Precautions

Safety is the most important factor when performing not only fuel system maintenance but any type of maintenance. Failure to conduct maintenance and repairs in a safe manner may result in serious personal injury or death. Maintenance and testing of the vehicle's fuel system components can be accomplished safely and effectively by adhering to the following rules and guidelines.

• To avoid the possibility of fire and personal injury, always disconnect the negative battery cable unless the repair or test procedure requires that battery voltage be applied.

• Always relieve the fuel system pressure prior to disconnecting any fuel system component (injector, fuel rail, pressure regulator, etc.), fitting or fuel line connection. Exercise extreme caution whenever relieving fuel system pressure to avoid exposing skin, face and eyes to fuel spray. Please be advised that fuel under pressure may penetrate the skin or any part of the body that it contacts.

• Always place a shop towel or cloth around the fitting or connection prior to loosening to absorb any excess fuel due to spillage. Ensure that all fuel spillage (should it occur) is quickly removed from engine surfaces. Ensure that all fuel soaked cloths or towels are deposited into a suitable waste container.

• Always keep a dry chemical (Class B) fire extinguisher near the work area.

• Do not allow fuel spray or fuel vapors to come into contact with a spark or open flame.

• Always use a backup wrench when loosening and tightening fuel line connection fittings. This will prevent unnecessary stress and torsion to fuel line piping. Always follow the proper torque specifications.

• Always replace worn fuel fitting O-rings with new. Do not substitute fuel hose or equivalent where fuel pipe is installed.

Fuel Filter

REMOVAL & INSTALLATION

—— CAUTION ——

Do not perform this operation on a hot engine. Place rags under the fuel fitting to catch any spilled fuel.

1. Disconnect the small fuel line connection nut, using a flare nut wrench, while holding the large fitting nut with a standard open end wrench. A flared nut wrench is preferred over a standard open end wrench since it will not slip off and round off the corners of the tubing nut.
2. Remove the large filter retaining nut from the carburetor. There is a spring behind the filter. Remove the filter and spring.
3. Install the spring and new filter element in the same order as removal.
4. Install the new gasket on the retaining nut and tighten it into place. Do not overtighten the nut.
5. Run the engine and check for leaks.

Mechanical Fuel Pump

PRESSURE TESTING

1. Disconnect the fuel line at the carburetor.
2. Attach a hose with a low pressure gauge at one end to the fuel line.
3. Start and run the engine using the gas still in the carburetor.

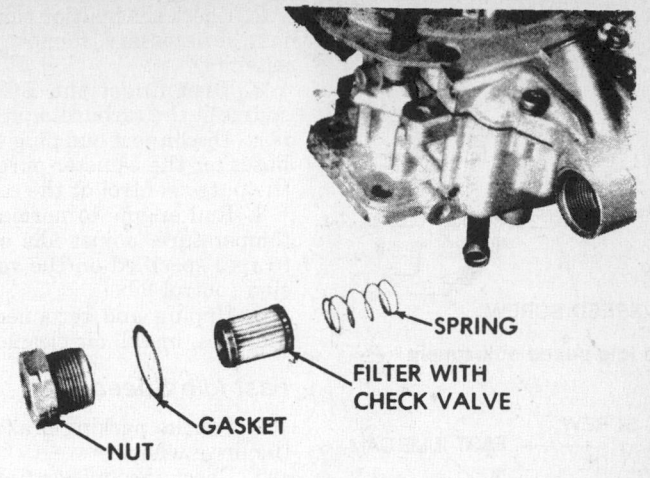

Fuel filter

4. Hold the gauge about 16 in. above the fuel pump and note the reading on the gauge. The correct pressure should be 5–6 psi constant.
5. If the pressure is too high or too low, replace the pump.

REMOVAL & INSTALLATION

NOTE: Vehicles equipped with air conditioning requires the removal of the rear compressor bracket for access to the pump.

1. Disconnect the negative battery cable.
2. Remove the distributor cap and the spark plug wire retaining clips.
3. Remove the coil wire and the coil assembly.
4. It may be necessary to remove the air cleaner on some models.
5. Disconnect the fuel pump hoses and remove the pump.
6. Remove the fuel pump pushrod.
7. Installation is the reverse of the removal. Check for any leaks when finished.

Carburetor

REMOVAL & INSTALLATION

1. Remove air cleaner and gasket.
2. Disconnect the fuel and vacuum lines from the carburetor.
3. Disconnect the accelerator linkage and the electrical connectors.
4. Remove the carburetor attaching nuts and remove the carburetor.
5. Remove the electric Early Fuel Evaporation (EFE) heater (if equipped) and the insulator gasket.
6. Be sure the throttle body and intake manifold sealing surfaces are clean.

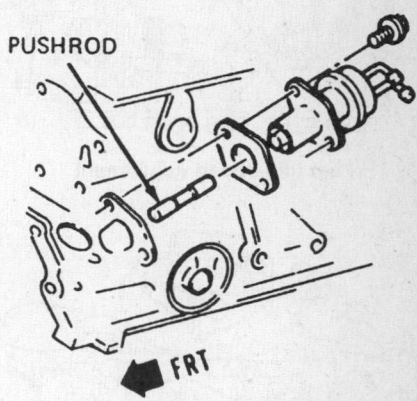

Fuel pump mounting

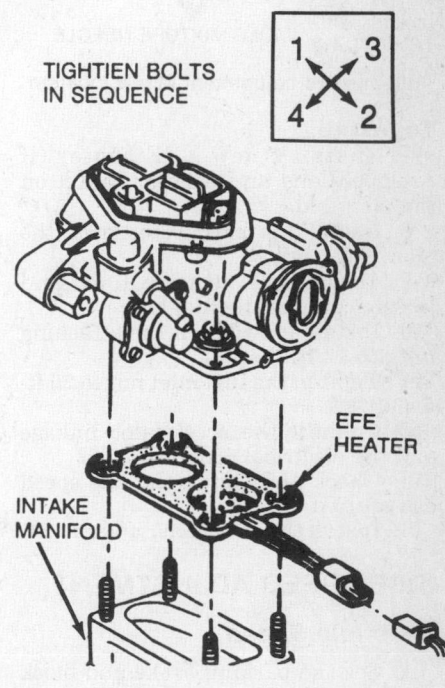

Carburetor mounting

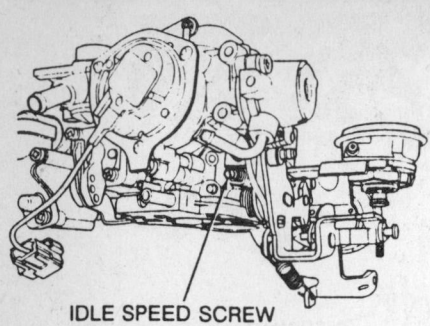

IDLE SPEED SCREW

Curb idle speed adjustment

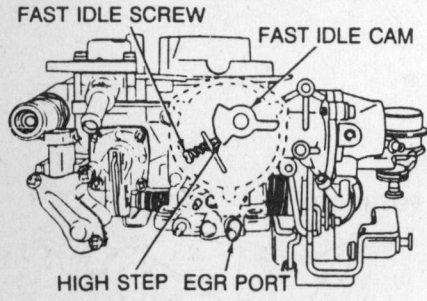

FAST IDLE SCREW   FAST IDLE CAM

HIGH STEP   EGR PORT

Fast idle speed adjustment

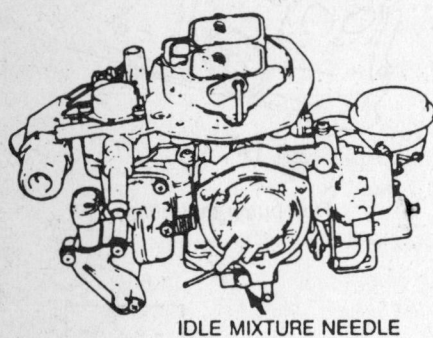

IDLE MIXTURE NEEDLE

Idle misture adjustment screw location

To install:

7. Install a new EFE heater (if equipped) and an insulator gasket on the manifold.

8. Install the carburetor over the manifold studs.

9. Install the vacuum lines and loosely connect the fuel line.

10. Install and tighten the attaching nuts to 12 ft. lbs.

11. Tighten the fuel inlet nut to 25 ft. lbs.

12. Connect the accelerator linkage and the electrical connectors.

13. Check and adjust the idle speed as required.

14. Install the air cleaner and gasket.

IDLE SPEED ADJUSTMENT

Curb Idle Speed

1. Set the parking brake and block the drive wheels.

---

2. Check the ignition timing and adjust, if necessary. Remove air cleaner assembly.

3. Disconnect the EGR vacuum source at the carburetor and block the port. Disconnect and plug the vacuum hoses for the canister purge tank and the purge control at the canister.

4. Run engine to normal operating temperature, adjust idle speed screw to rpm specified on the vehicle emission control label.

5. Unplug and reconnect all vacuum lines, install air cleaner.

Fast Idle Speed

1. Set the parking brake and block the drive wheels.

2. Check the ignition timing and adjust, if necessary. Remove air cleaner assembly.

3. Disconnect the EGR vacuum source at the carburetor and block the port. Disconnect and plug the vacuum hoses for the canister purge tank and the purge control at the canister.

4. Place fast idle screw on highest step of fast idle cam, adjust to rpm specified on vehicle emission control label.

5. Unplug and reconnect all vacuum lines, install air cleaner assembly.

IDLE MIXTURE ADJUSTMENT

NOTE: The idle mixture needle has been preset at the factory and sealed. Do not remove the plug during normal engine maintenance. Idle mixture should be adjusted only in the case of major carburetor overhaul, throttle body replacement or high emissions.

1. Remove the carburetor.

2. Place inverted carburetor on a suitable holding fixture, manifold side up. Use care to avoid damaging linkage tubes and parts protruding from air horn.

3. Remove the idle mixture needle plug as follows:

  a. Position a punch in the locator point of throttle body, beneath idle mixture needle plug (manifold side).

  b. Drive out the hardened steel plug covering the mixture needle.

  c. Using tool J–29030 or equivalent, lightly seat the needle and then it back out 2 turns as a preliminary idle mixture adjustment.

4. Install the carburetor.

5. Perform the idle mixture needle adjustment.

6. After the adjustment is complete, seal the idle mixture needle setting using RTV or equivalent.

7. If necessary, reset the idle speed.

SERVICE ADJUSTMENTS

For all carburetor service adjustment procedures and specifications, please refer to "Carburetor Service" in the Unit Repair section.

EMISSION CONTROLS

Please refer to "Emission Control" in the Unit Repair section for system maintenance procedures. Due to the complex nature of modern electronic engine control systems, comprehensive diagnosis and testing procedures fall outside the confines of this repair manual. For complete information on diagnosis, testing and repair procedures concerning all modern engine and emission control systems, please refer to "Chilton's Guide to Electronic Engine Controls".

Emission Warning Lamps

When the ECM finds a problem, the "Check Engine/Service Engine Soon" light will come ON and a trouble code will be recorded in the ECM memory. If the problem is intermittent, the "Check Engine/Service Engine Soon" light will go out after 10 seconds, when the fault goes away. However, the trouble code will stay in the ECM memory until the battery voltage to the ECM is removed.

RESETTING

Removing battery voltage for 10 seconds will clear all stored trouble codes. Disconnecting the ECM harness from the positive battery pigtail for 10 seconds with the ignition OFF, or by disconnecting the ECM fuse, designated ECM or ECM/Bat., from the fuse holder.

NOTE: To prevent ECM damage, the key must be OFF when disconnecting or reconnecting power to ECM; for example battery cable, ECM pigtail, ECM fuse, jumper cables, etc.

ENGINE MECHANICAL

NOTE: Disconnecting the negative battery cable on some vehicles may interfere with the functions of the on board computer systems and may require the computer to undergo a relearning process, once the negative battery cable is reconnected.

Engine Assembly

REMOVAL & INSTALLATION

1. Disconnect the battery cables.
2. Matchmark the hood to the hinges and remove the hood.
3. Remove the battery cable clips from the frame rail.
4. Drain the cooling system. Disconnect the radiator hoses from the engine and the heater hoses at the heater.
5. Tag and disconnect any wires leading from the engine.
6. Remove the radiator upper support and remove the radiator and engine fan.
7. Remove the air cleaner assembly.
8. Disconnect the following items:
   a. Fuel line at the rubber hose along the left frame rail.
   b. Automatic transmission throttle valve linkage.
   c. Accelerator cable.
9. On air conditioned vehicles, remove the compressor from its mount and lay it aside. If equipped with power steering, remove the power steering pump and bracket and lay it aside.
10. Raise and safely support the vehicle.
11. Disconnect the exhaust pipe at the exhaust manifold.
12. Remove the flywheel dust cover on manual transmission vehicles or the torque converter underpan on automatic transmission vehicles.
13. If equipped with automatic transmission, remove the torque converter-to-flywheel bolts.
14. Remove the converter housing or flywheel housing-to-engine retaining bolts and lower the vehicle.
15. Position a floor jack or other suitable support under the transmission.
16. Remove the safety straps from the front engine mounts and remove the mount nuts.
17. Install the engine lifting apparatus.
18. Remove the engine by pulling it forward to clear the transmission while lifting slowly. Check to make sure all necessary disconnections have

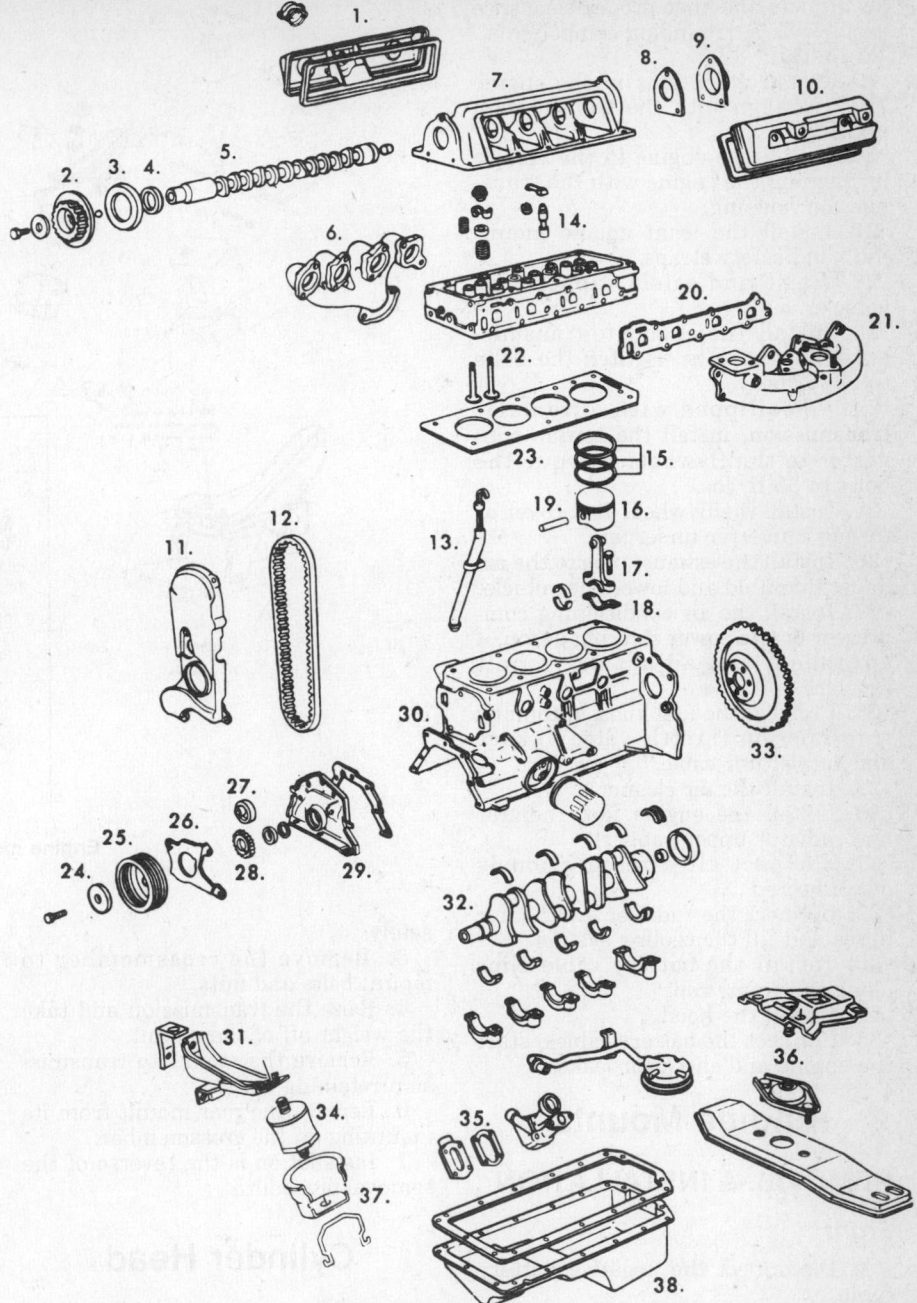

1. Camshaft Cover and Gasket	14. Rocker Arm, Adjuster, Valve Springs, Valve Spring Cap, and Keys	26. Lower Cover
2. Camshaft Sprocket		27. Idler
3. Camshaft Sprocket Guide	15. Piston Rings	28. Crankshaft Sprocket
4. Camshaft Oil Seal	16. Piston	29. Crankcase Front Cover
5. Camshaft	17. Connecting Rod	30. Cylinder Block
6. Exhaust Manifold	18. Connecting Rod Bearing and Cap	31. Engine Mounting Bracket
7. Camshaft Housing		32. Crankshaft and Bearings
8. Camshaft Rear Cover Gasket	19. Piston Pin	33. Flywheel
9. Camshaft Rear Cover	20. Intake Manifold Gasket	34. Engine Mount
10. Camshaft Housing Cover and Gasket	21. Intake Manifold	35. Oil Pump Assembly
	22. Valves	36. Transmission Mounting and Support
11. Timing Belt Cover	23. Cylinder Head Gasket	37. Engine Mounting Plate and Spring
12. Timing Belt	24. Washer	38. Oil Pan and Gasket
13. Oil Dipstick and Tube	25. Crankshaft Pulley	

Exploded view of the engine

been made and that proper clearance exists with surrounding components.

To install:

19. Install guide pins in the engine block to align with the transmission housing.

20. Install the engine in the vehicle by aligning the engine with the transmission housing.

21. Install the front engine mount nuts and safety straps.

22. Raise and safely support the vehicle.

23. Install the engine-to-transmission housing bolts. Tighten the bolts to 25 ft. lbs.

24. If equipped with automatic transmission, install the torque converter to the flywheel. Torque the bolts to 35 ft. lbs.

25. Install the flywheel dust cover or torque converter underpan.

26. Install the exhaust pipe to the exhaust manifold and lower the vehicle.

27. Install the air conditioning compressor or the power steering pump, if equipped, and adjust drive belt tension.

28. Connect the fuel lines, automatic transmission throttle valve linkage and accelerator cable.

29. Install the air cleaner.

30. Install the engine fan, radiator and radiator upper support.

31. Connect all wires previously disconnected.

32. Connect the radiator and heater hoses and fill the cooling system.

33. Install the battery cable clips along the frame rail.

34. Install the hood.

35. Connect the battery cables, start the engine and check for leaks.

Engine Mounts

REMOVAL & INSTALLATION

Front

1. Disconnect the negative battery cable.

2. Remove the heater assembly and position it on top of the engine.

3. Remove the upper radiator support.

4. Remove the engine mount nuts and retaining wire.

5. Raise the vehicle and support it safely. Using a lifting device, raise the engine.

6. Remove the mount to engine bracket. Remove the engine mount from the vehicle.

7. Installation is the reverse of the removal procedure.

Rear

1. Disconnect the negative battery cable.

2. Raise the vehicle and support it

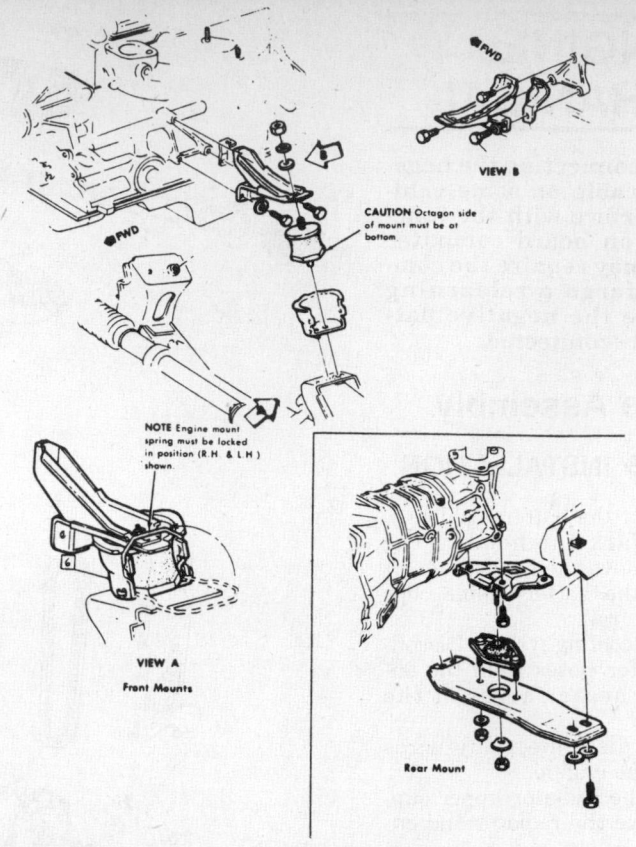

Engine mounts

safely.

3. Remove the crossmember to mount bolts and nuts.

4. Raise the transmission and take the weight off of the mount.

5. Remove the mount to transmission retaining bolts.

6. Remove the rear mount from its mounting on the crossmember.

7. Installation is the reverse of the removal procedure.

Cylinder Head

REMOVAL & INSTALLATION

1. Disconnect the negative battery cable.

2. Remove all accessory drive belts.

3. Remove the engine fan, timing belt cover and timing belt.

4. Remove the air cleaner and snorkel assembly.

5. Drain the cooling system and disconnect the upper radiator hose and heater hose at the intake manifold.

6. Remove the accelerator cable support bracket.

7. Disconnect and label the spark plug wires.

8. Disconnect and label the wires from the idle solenoid, choke, temperature sender and alternator.

9. Raise the vehicle and disconnect the exhaust pipe from the exhaust manifold.

10. Remove the dipstick tube bracket-to-manifold attaching bolt.

11. Disconnect the fuel line at the carburetor.

12. Take off the coil cover. Remove the coil bracket bolts and remove the coil.

13. Remove the camshaft cover.

14. Remove the camshaft cover-to-camshaft housing attaching stubs.

15. Remove the rocker arms, rocker arm guides and valve lash adjusters. Keep the parts in order so they can be installed in their original locations.

16. Remove the camshaft carrier to cylinder head attaching bolts and remove the camshaft carrier. A sharp wedge may be necessary to separate the camshaft carrier from the cylinder head. Be very cautious not to damage the mating surfaces.

17. Remove the manifold and cylinder head as an assembly.

To install:

18. Install a new cylinder head gasket with the words **THIS SIDE UP** facing up over dowel pins in the block. Make sure the gasket is absolutely clean.

19. Install the manifold and cylinder head assembly.

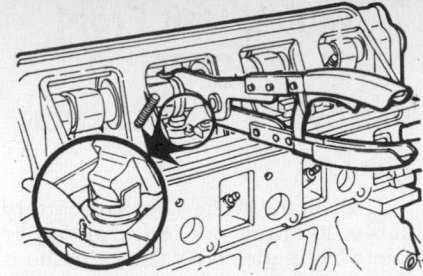

Cylinder head torque sequence—gasoline engine

20. Apply a light, thin continuous bead of sealant to the jointing surfaces of the cylinder head and the camshaft carrier and install the camshaft carrier. Clean any excess sealer from the cylinder head. Apply sealing compound to the camshaft carrier/cylinder head bolts and install the bolts finger-tight. Tighten the bolts a little at a time and in the correct sequence until the final specified torque figure is reached.
21. Install the camshaft cover-to-camshaft housing attaching studs.
22. Install the valve lash adjusters and rocker arm guides. Prelube the rocker arms with engine assembly lubricant and install the rocker arms.
23. Using new gaskets, install the camshaft covers.
24. Install the coil bracket mounting bolt.
25. Connect the fuel line to the carburetor.
26. Install the dipstick tube bracket-to-manifold attaching bolt.
27. Attach the exhaust pipe to the exhaust manifold.
28. Connect the wires to the idle solenoid, choke, temperature sender and alternator.
29. Connect the spark plug wires.
30. Apply Teflon® tape or its equivalent to the threads of the accelerator cable support bracket attaching bolts and install the bracket.
31. Install the air cleaner assembly.
32. Connect the upper radiator hose and heater hose to the intake manifold.
33. Fill the cooling system.
34. Install the timing belt, timing belt cover, engine fan, drive belts and connect the negative battery cable.

Valve Lash

ADJUSTMENT

Adjustment of the hydraulic valve lash adjusters is automatic. No servicing of the lash adjusters is required, except cleanliness should be exercised when handling the valve lash adjusters. Before installation of the valve lash adjusters, fill them with oil and check the lash adjuster oil hole in the cylinder head to make sure it is unclogged and free of foreign matter.

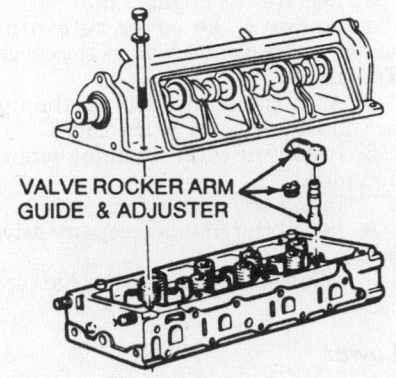

Depressing the valve spring using the special tool—gasoline engine

Rocker arm guide and adjuster—gasoline engine

Rocker Arms/Shafts

REMOVAL & INSTALLATION

1. Disconnect the negative battery cable. Remove the camshaft cover and carburetor from the engine.
2. Using tool J-25477 or equivalent, depress the valve spring and remove the rocker arms. Note the location of all parts so they can be reinstalled in their original location.
3. Remove the spark plugs and install an air line adapter tool J-23590 or equivalent into a spark plug port. Pressurize the cylinder to hold the valves in place.
4. Using tool J-25477 or equivalent, depress the valve spring and remove the rocker guides, valve locks, caps and valve spring. Remove the valve stem oil seal, as required.
To install:
5. Position the valve stem seal over the valve stem and seat against hand. Place the valve spring and cap over the valve stem, compress and install the valve lock.

NOTE: Grease may be used to hold the lock in place while working with the valve spring compressor tool.

6. Install the rocker guides and rocker arms, then remove the compressor tool.

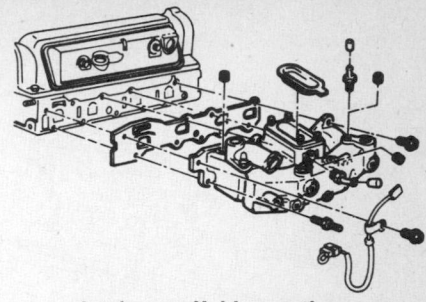

Intake manifold mounting

7. Remove the air line adapter tool and install the spark plugs. Install the cam cover.

Intake Manifold

REMOVAL & INSTALLATION

1. Disconnect the negative battery cable.
2. Drain the cooling system.
3. Remove the air cleaner.
4. Disconnect the upper radiator and heater hoses.
5. Remove the EGR valve.
6. Disconnect all electrical wiring, vacuum hoses and the accelerator linkage from the carburetor.
7. Disconnect the fuel line from the carburetor.
8. Remove the coil.
9. Remove the intake manifold retaining bolts. Remove the intake manifold from the engine.
10. Installation is the reverse of removal. Torque all intake manifold bolts to 15 ft. lbs. (20 Nm).

Exhaust Manifold

REMOVAL & INSTALLATION

1. Disconnect the negative battery cable.
2. Raise and safely support the vehicle.
3. Disconnect the exhaust pipe from the flange.
4. Lower the vehicle.
5. Remove the carburetor heat tube.

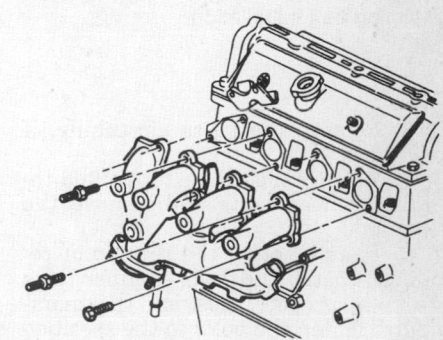

Exhaust manifold

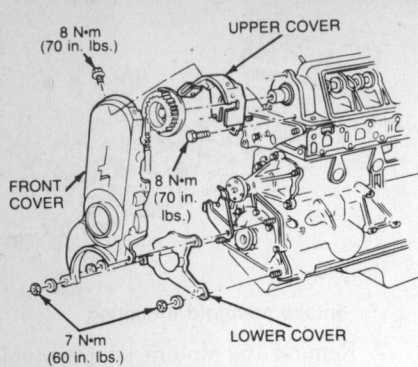

Timing belt cover mounting

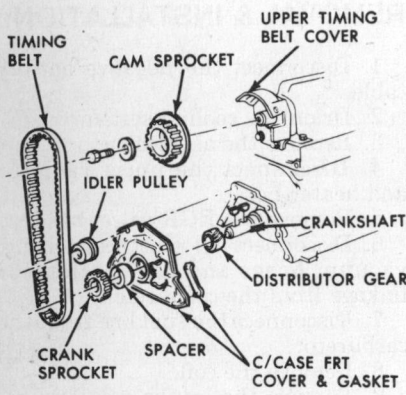

Timing belt and gears

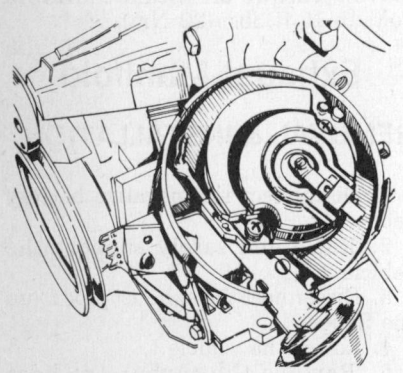

Correct distributor rotor alignment for timing belt installation

6. Remove the pulse air tubing, if equipped.

7. Remove the exhaust manifold-to-cylinder head bolts and remove the manifold.

8. Installation is the reverse of removal. Install the 2 upper inner bolts first, to properly position the manifold. Tighten the bolts to the specified torque.

Timing Belt Front Cover

REMOVAL & INSTALLATION

Front

1. Disconnect the negative battery cable. Remove the radiator upper mounting panel on vehicles without air conditioning or fan shroud on models with A/C.

2. Remove engine accessory drive belts.

3. Remove the engine fan.

4. Remove the cover retaining screws and nuts and remove the cover.

To install:

5. Align the screw slots on the upper and lower parts of the cover.

6. Install the cover retaining screws and nuts.

7. Install the engine fan.

8. Install the engine accessory drive belts.

9. Connect the negative battery cable.

Lower

1. Disconnect the negative battery cable.

2. Loosen the alternator and the air conditioning compressor bolts, if equipped. Remove the drive belts.

3. Remove the damper pulley-to-crankshaft bolt and washer and remove the pulley.

4. Remove the upper front timing belt cover.

5. Remove the lower cover retaining nut. Remove the lower cover.

To install:

6. Align the lower timing belt cover with the studs on the engine block.

7. Install the lower front cover retaining nut.

8. Install the upper front timing belt cover.

9. Install the crankshaft damper pulley. Torque the retaining bolt to the specified torque.

10. Install the drive belts and tighten the alternator and compressor mounting bolts.

11. Connect the negative battery cable.

Upper

1. Crank the engine so No. 1 cylinder is at TDC of the compression stroke.

2. Disconnect the negative battery cable.

3. Remove the upper and lower front cover, the timing belt and the camshaft timing sprocket.

4. Remove the 3 bolts retaining the camshaft sprocket cover to the camshaft carrier.

5. Inspect the condition of the cam seal. Replace the seal if necessary.

6. Position and align a new gasket over the end of the camshaft and against the camshaft carrier.

7. Install the 3 camshaft sprocket cover retaining screws.

8. Install the camshaft sprocket, timing belt and the upper and lower front covers.

9. Connect the negative battery cable.

Front Cover Oil Seal

REPLACEMENT

1. Remove the front timing cover.

2. Using puller tools J–24420 and J–34984–6 or their equivalent, remove the crankshaft sprocket spacer assembly.

3. Carefully pry the seal from the crankcase front cover.

4. Apply clean engine oil to the seal lip. Position the new seal on seal installer tool J–26434 or equivalent, with the open end of the seal toward the rear of the crankcase front cover and install the seal. Install the crankshaft sprocket spacer assembly.

5. Install the front cover.

Timing Belt and Sprockets

ADJUSTMENT

1. Remove the fan, fan belt, water

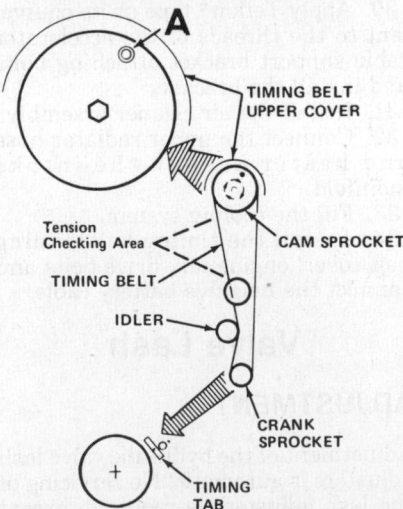

Quick Check Hole (In Sprocket) should align with hole in Timing Belt Upper Cover (A) when #1 Cyl. is at T.D.C.

Pulley timing mark should align with 0° mark on timing tab.

Timing belt installation—1.6 L Chevette. When camshaft is aligned at No. 1 cylinder TDC compression stroke, a 1/8 in. drill bit should fit through rear timing belt cover and into quick check hole in sprocket.

pump pulley and upper cam belt cover.

2. Rotate the crankshaft clockwise a minimum of one revolution. Stop with No. 1 piston at TDC.

3. Install a belt tension gauge on the same side as the idler pulley midway between the cam sprocket and the idler pulley. Be sure the center finger of the gauge extension fits in a notch between the teeth on the belt. Correct belt tension is 70 lbs.

4. If the tension is incorrect, loosen the idler pulley attaching bolt and using a ¼ in. Allen wrench, rotate the pulley counterclockwise on its attaching bolt until the correct tension is obtained. Torque the bolt to 15 ft. lbs.

5. The remainder of the installation is the reverse of the removal procedure.

REMOVAL & INSTALLATION

1. Rotate the engine to bring No. 1 cylinder to TDC. The timing mark should be at the **0** degree mark on the timing scale. With No. 1 cylinder at TDC, a ⅛ in. drill bit may be inserted through a hole in the timing belt upper rear cover into a hole in the camshaft drive sprocket. These holes are provided to facilitate and verify camshaft timing. Aligning these holes now will make installation of the new belt much easier.

2. Disconnect the negative battery cable.

3. Remove the alternator and air conditioning compressor drive belts.

4. Remove the engine fan and pulley.

5. Remove the engine upper and lower front timing belt covers.

6. Remove the timing belt idler pulley.

7. Remove the timing belt from the camshaft and crankshaft timing sprockets.

8. With the distributor cap off, mark the location of the rotor in the No. 1 spark plug firing position on the distributor housing. If equipped with air conditioning, remove the compressor and lower its mounting bracket. Do not discharge the air conditioning system.

9. Remove the camshaft timing sprocket bolt and washer and remove the camshaft sprocket.

10. Remove the crankshaft sprocket using tool J–28509 or equivalent.

To install:

11. Position the crankshaft sprocket on the crankshaft making sure the locating tabs face outward.

12. Install the crankshaft sprocket.

13. Align the camshaft sprocket dowel with the hole in the end of the camshaft and install the sprocket on the camshaft.

14. Apply thread locking compound to the camshaft sprocket retaining bolt and washer and torque to 65–85 ft. lbs.

15. Position the timing belt over the crankshaft sprocket.

16. Install the crankshaft pulley.

17. Align the crankshaft pulley timing mark with the **0** mark on the timing scale and the distributor rotor with the scribed mark on the distributor housing.

18. Align the hole in the camshaft sprocket with the hole in the upper rear timing belt cover. Insert a ⅛ in. drill bit to hold the sprocket in alignment.

19. Install the timing belt on the camshaft and crankshaft sprockets.

20. Using the correct procedure, adjust the timing belt tension.

21. Install the distributor cap. On air conditioned vehicles, install the lower compressor bracket and the compressor.

22. Install the upper and lower front timing belt covers.

23. Install the engine fan and pulley.

24. Install the alternator and, if necessary, the air conditioning compressor drive belts.

25. Connect the negative battery cable.

Camshaft
REMOVAL & INSTALLATION

NOTE: A special valve spring compressor is necessary for this procedure. If replacing the camshaft or rocker arms, prelubricate new parts with engine assembly lubricant.

1. Disconnect the negative battery cable.

2. Remove engine accessory drive belts.

3. Remove the engine fan and pulley.

4. Remove the upper and lower front timing belt covers.

5. Loosen the idler pulley and remove the timing belt from the camshaft sprocket.

6. Remove the camshaft sprocket attaching bolt and washer and remove the camshaft sprocket.

7. Remove the camshaft cover. Using the valve spring compressor, remove the rocker arms and guides. Keep the rocker arms and guides in order so they can be installed in their original locations.

8. Remove the heater assembly.

9. Remove the camshaft carrier rear cover.

10. Remove the camshaft thrust plate bolts. Slide the camshaft slightly to the rear and remove the thrust plate.

11. Remove the engine mount nuts and wire retainers.

12. Using a floor jack, raise the front of the engine.

13. Remove the camshaft from the camshaft carrier. Heavy pressure will be needed to pull the camshaft and seal forward.

To install:

14. Position the camshaft into the camshaft carrier.

15. Lower the engine on the motor mounts.

16. Install the engine mount nuts and attach the retaining wires.

17. Slide the camshaft slightly to the rear and install the thrust plate. Slide the camshaft forward and install the carrier rear cover.

18. Position and align a new gasket over the end of the camshaft, against the camshaft carrier.

19. Install the heater assembly.

20. Install the valve rocker arms and guides in their original locations using the special valve spring compressor. Install the camshaft covers.

21. Align the dowel in the camshaft sprocket with the hole in the end of the camshaft and install the sprocket.

22. Apply thread locking compound to the sprocket retaining bolt threads and install the bolt and washer. Torque the sprocket retaining bolt to 65–85 ft. lbs.

23. Turn the crankshaft clockwise to bring the No. 1 cylinder to TDC. Make sure the distributor rotor is in position to fire the No. 1 spark plug. Align the hole in the camshaft sprocket with the hole in the upper rear timing belt cover and install the timing belt on the camshaft sprocket.

24. Adjust timing belt tension.

25. Install the upper and lower front timing belt covers.

26. Install the engine fan and pulley.

27. Install the engine accessory drive belts.

28. Connect the negative battery cable.

Piston and Connecting Rod
POSITIONING

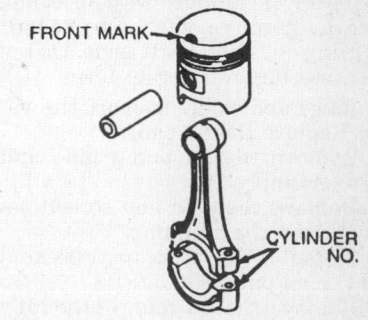

Piston and connecting rod positioning

ENGINE LUBRICATION

Oil Pan

REMOVAL & INSTALLATION

1. Disconnect the negative battery cable.
2. Drain the cooling system.
3. Remove the upper radiator support and fan shroud.
4. Disconnect the heater hoses at the heater core.
5. Remove the heater core housing.
6. Remove the engine mount retaining nuts and clips.
7. Raise and safely support the vehicle.
8. Drain the engine oil.
9. Disconnect the power steering line, if equipped.
10. Disconnect the rack and pinion unit from the crossmember and steering shaft and pull it aside.
11. Remove the flywheel shield.
12. Remove the heater pipe at the oil pan.
13. Remove the oil pan retaining bolts.
14. Raise the engine.
15. Remove the oil pan, oil pipe and suction screen.
16. Installation is the reverse of the removal procedure. Fill the engine with oil and check for leaks. Start the engine and check for leaks.

Oil Pump

REMOVAL & INSTALLATION

1. Disconnect the negative battery cable. Remove the ignition coil attaching bolts and lay the coil aside.
2. Raise and safely support the vehicle. Remove the fuel pump, pushrod and gasket. Note the direction the pushrod comes out for reference during installation.
3. Lower the vehicle and remove the distributor. If equipped with air conditioning, remove the compressor mounting bolts and lay it aside. Do not disconnect any refrigerant lines.
4. Raise and safely support the vehicle. Remove the oil pan.
5. Remove the oil pump pipe and screen assembly.
6. Remove the pipe and screen assembly from the oil pump.
7. Remove the pick-up tube seal from the oil pump.
8. Remove the oil pump attaching bolts and remove the oil pump.

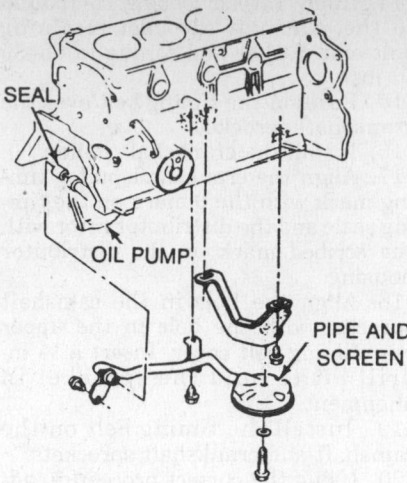

Oil pump and screen mounting

To install:

9. Position the oil pump in place and torque the oil pump mounting bolts to 15 ft. lbs.

NOTE: Make certain that the pilot on the oil pump engages the case.

10. Install the pick-up tube seal in the oil pump.
11. Install the pick-up pipe and screen assembly in the oil pump. Install the pick-up pipe and screen clamp. Torque the clamp bolt 6–8 ft. lbs. Torque the pick-up tube and screen mounting bolt 19–25 ft. lbs.
12. Install the oil pan.
13. Install the fuel pump and pushrod in the same direction as removal.
14. Lower the vehicle and install the distributor and the ignition coil.

Rear Main Bearing Oil Seal

REMOVAL & INSTALLATION

1. Disconnect the negative battery cable.
2. Remove the transmission.
3. Remove the flywheel or flexplate.
4. Remove the rack and pinion unit mounting bolts.
5. Remove the left side strut.
6. Remove the flexible coupling and pull the gear down.
7. Drain the engine oil.
8. Remove the oil pan, suction pipe and screen.
9. Remove the rear main cap.
10. Remove the seal.
To install:
11. Before replacing the seal, clean all bearing cap and case surfaces.
12. Inspect the crankshaft seal surface for any wear or nicks.

13. Install the new seal against the rear main bearing bulkhead. Apply RTV sealer or equivalent to the verticle grooves of the bearing cap. Wipe off any excess sealer.
14. Torque the bearing bolts to 10–12 ft. lbs. Tap the end of the crankshaft rearward then forward. Retorque the bearing cap bolts to 40–52 ft. lbs.
15. Reverse the removal procedure for the remainder of the installation.

MANUAL TRANSMISSION

For further information on transmissions/transaxles, please refer to "Chilton's Guide to Transmission Repair".

Transmission Assembly

REMOVAL & INSTALLATION

1. Disconnect the negative battery cable. Remove the floor console and shifter boot retainer.
2. Lift up the shifter boot to gain access to the locknut on the shift lever. Loosen the locknut and remove the upper portion of the shift lever with the knob attached.
3. Remove the foam insulator.
4. Remove the 3 bolts on the extension and remove the control assembly.
5. Carefully remove the retaining clip.
6. Remove the locknut, boot retainer and seat from the threaded end of the control lever.
7. Remove the spring and the guide from the forked end of the control lever.
8. Raise and safely support the vehicle. Drain the lubricant from the transmission.
9. Remove the driveshaft.
10. Disconnect the speedometer cable and back-up light switch.
11. Disconnect the return spring and clutch cable at the clutch release fork.
12. Remove the crossmember-to-transmission mount bolts.
13. Remove the exhaust manifold nuts and converter-to-tailpipe bolts and nuts. Remove the converter-to-transmission bracket bolts and remove the converter.
14. Remove the crossmember-to-frame bolts and remove the crossmember.
15. Remove the dust cover.

16. Remove the clutch housing-to-engine retaining bolts, slide the transmission and clutch housing to the rear and remove the transmission.

To install:

17. Place the transmission in gear, position the transmission and clutch housing and slide forward. Turn the output shaft to align the input shaft splines with the clutch hub.

18. Install the clutch housing retaining bolts and lock washers. Torque the bolts to 25 ft. lbs.

19. Install the dust cover.

20. Position the crossmember to the frame and loosely install the retaining bolts. Install the crossmember-to-transmission mounting bolts. Torque the center nuts to 33 ft. lbs.; the end nuts to 21 ft. lbs. Torque the crossmember-to-frame bolts to 40 ft. lbs.

21. Install the exhaust pipe to the manifold and the converter bracket on the transmission.

22. Connect the clutch cable. Adjust clutch pedal free-play.

23. Connect the speedometer cable and back-up light switch.

24. Install the driveshaft.

25. Fill the transmission to the correct level with SAE 80W or SAE 80W–90 GL-5 gear lubricant. Lower the vehicle.

26. Install the shift lever and check operation of the transmission.

CLUTCH

Clutch Assembly

REMOVAL & INSTALLATION

1. Disconnect the negative battery cable. Raise the vehicle and support it safely.

2. Remove the transmission.

3. Remove the throwout bearing from the clutch fork by sliding the fork off the ball stud against spring tension. If the ball stud is to be replaced, remove the locknut and stud from the bell housing.

4. If the balance marks on the pressure plate and the flywheel are not easily seen, remark them with paint or a center punch.

5. Alternately loosen the pressure plate to flywheel attaching bolts 1 turn at a time until spring tension is released.

6. Support the pressure plate and cover assembly, then remove the bolts and the clutch assembly.

7. Check the pressure plate, clutch plate and flywheel for wear. If the flywheel is scored, worn or discolored from overheating, it should be either refaced or replaced. Replace the clutch disc as necessary.

To install:

8. Align the balance marks on the clutch assembly and the flywheel. Place the clutch disc on the pressure plate with the long end of the splined hub facing forward and the damper springs inside the pressure plate. Insert a dummy shaft through the cover and clutch disc.

9. Position the assembly against the flywheel and insert the dummy shaft into the pilot bearing in the crankshaft.

10. Align the balance marks and install the pressure plate to flywheel bolts finger tight. Tighten all bolts evenly and gradually until tight, to avoid possible clutch distortion. Torque the bolts to 18 ft. lbs. and remove the dummy shaft.

11. Pack the groove on the inside of the throwout bearing with graphite grease. Also coat the fork groove and ball stud depression with the lubricant.

12. Install the throwout bearing and release fork assembly in the bell housing with the fork spring hooked under the ball stud and the fork spring fingers inside the bearing groove.

13. Position the transmission and clutch housing and install the clutch housing attaching bolts and lock washers. Torque the bolts to 25 ft. lbs.

14. Complete the transmission installation. Check the position of the engine in the front mounts and realign as necessary. A special gauge J–23644, or equivalent, is necessary to adjust ball stud position, if removed.

15. Adjust clutch pedal free-play as required.

16. Lower the vehicle and check operation of the clutch and transmission.

CLUTCH BALL STUD INITIAL ADJUSTMENT

1. Install throw-out bearing assembly, clutch fork and ball stud to transmission.

2. Mount and secure transmission to engine.

3. Cycle clutch 1 time.

4. Place gauge J–28449, or equivalent, so the flat end is against the front face of clutch housing and the hooked end is aligned with the bottom depression in the clutch fork.

5. Turn ball stud clockwise by hand until clutch release bearing makes contact with the clutch spring and the fork is snug on the gauge.

6. Install locknut and tighten to 25 ft. lbs., being careful not to change the ball stud adjustment.

7. Remove the gauge by pulling outward at the housing end.

PEDAL HEIGHT/FREE-PLAY ADJUSTMENT

Adjustment is made at the firewall end of the outer clutch cable. Pedal free-play should be ½–1 in. at the pedal.

1. Pull the adjusting ring clip from the cable at the firewall.

2. To increase free-play, move the cable into the firewall, one notch at a time and replace the clip.

3. To decrease free-play, pull the cable out, one notch at a time and replace the clip.

4. If, after the adjustment, the pedal won't return tight against the bumper, the ball stud will have to be adjusted. Use the special gauge mentioned in the clutch replacement procedure.

Clutch Cable

ADJUSTMENT

Adjustment is made at the firewall end of the outer clutch cable. Pedal free-play should be ½ in. at the pedal.

1. Pull the adjusting ring clip from the cable at the firewall.

2. To increase free-play, move the cable into the firewall, 1 notch at a time and replace the clip.

3. To decrease free-play, pull the cable out, 1 notch at a time and replace the clip.

4. If, after the adjustment, the pedal won't return tight against the bumper, the ball stud will have to be adjusted.

REMOVAL & INSTALLATION

1. Disconnect the negative battery cable. Raise and safely support the vehicle.

2. Disconnect the clutch return spring and cable from the clutch fork.

3. Disconnect the clutch cable from the upper end of the clutch pedal.

4. Pull the clutch cable assembly through the firewall and disconnect it at the cable retainer on the fender.

5. Insert the new cable through the firewall and attach it to the clutch pedal.

6. Secure the new cable to the clutch fork.

7. Check the clutch operation and adjust the clutch as necessary.

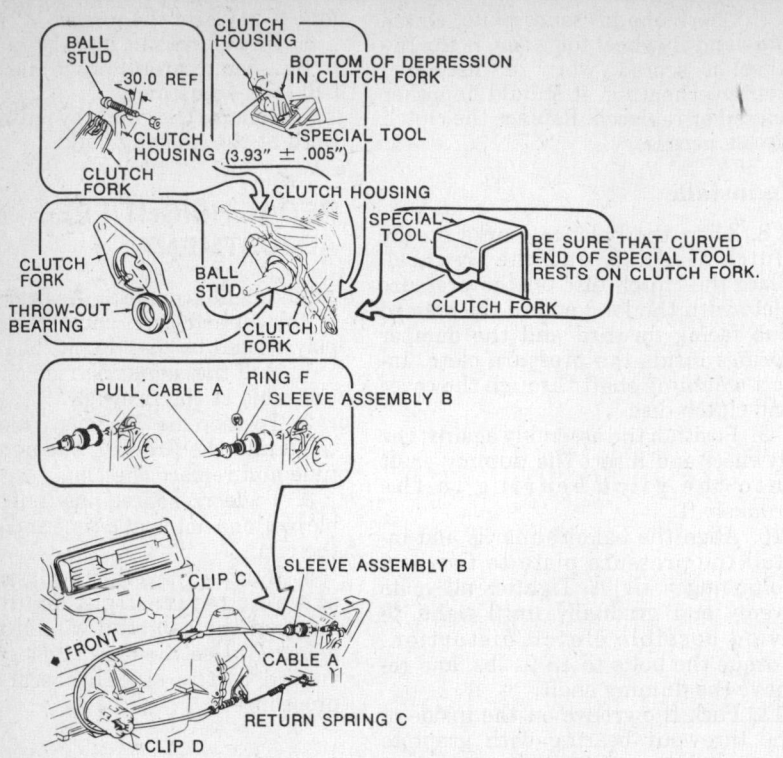

Clutch cable and ball stud adjustment details

AUTOMATIC TRANSMISSION

For further information on transmissions/transaxles, please refer to "Chilton's Guide to Transmission Repair".

Transmission Assembly

REMOVAL & INSTALLATION

1. Disconnect the negative battery cable. Remove the TV/detent cable at the bracket and carburetor or injection pump.
2. Remove the air cleaner and dipstick.
3. On vehicles with air conditioning, remove the heater core cover screws from the heater assembly. Disconnect the wire connector and with hoses attached, place the heater core cover aside.
4. Raise and safely support the vehicle. Remove the driveshaft.
5. Disconnect the speedometer cable, electrical lead to case connector and oil cooler pipes.
6. Disconnect the shift control linkage.

7. Support the transmission with suitable transmission jack and remove the rear transmission support bolts.
8. Remove the nuts holding the converter bracket to the support.
9. Disconnect the exhaust pipe at the rear of the catalytic converter.
10. Disconnect the exhaust pipe at manifold and remove the exhaust pipe, catalytic converter and converter bracket as an assembly.
11. Remove the torque converter dust cover, if equipped.
12. Remove converter to flexplate bolts.
13. Lower transmission until jack is just supporting it and remove the transmission to engine mounting bolts.
14. Raise the transmission to its normal position, then place a 2 in. block of wood between the rack-and-pinion housing and the engine oil pan.
15. Support the engine properly and slide the transmission rearward from the engine and lower it away from the vehicle.
NOTE: **The use of a converter holding tool is necessary when lowering the transmission. If a converter holding tool is not available, keep the rear of the transmission lower than the front so the converter will not fall out.**
16. Installation is the reverse of removal procedure.

17. When installing the flexplate-to-converter bolts, make certain that the weld nuts on the converter are flush with the flexplate and the converter rotates freely by hand in this position.
18. Hand start the 3 flexplate-to-converter bolts and tighten them finger tight, then torque to specifications. This will insure proper converter alignment. Install a new oil seal on the oil filler tube before installing the tube. Make all necessary linkage adjustments.

DRIVE AXLE

Driveshaft and U-Joints

REMOVAL & INSTALLATION

1. Disconnect the negative battery cable. Raise and safely support the vehicle. Scribe matchmarks on the driveshaft and the companion flange and disconnect the rear universal joint by removing the trunnion bearing straps.
2. Move the driveshaft to the rear under the axle to remove the slip yoke from the transmission. Watch for leakage from the transmission output shaft housing.
3. Install the driveshaft in the reverse order of removal. Tighten the trunnion strap bolts to 16 ft. lbs.

Rear Axle Shaft, Bearing and Seal

REMOVAL & INSTALLATION

1. Raise the vehicle and support it safely. Remove the wheel and the brake drum.
2. Clean the area around the differential carrier cover.
3. Remove the differential carrier cover to drain the rear axle lubricant.
4. Use a metric Allen wrench to remove the differential pinion shaft lock screw and remove the differential pinion shaft. It may be necessary to shorten the Allen wrench to do this.
5. Push the flanged end of the axle shaft toward the center of the vehicle and remove the C-lock from the inner end of the shaft.
6. Remove the axle shaft from the housing making sure not to damage the oil seal.
7. If replacing the seal only, remove the oil seal by using the inner end of the axle shaft. Insert the end of the shaft behind the steel case of the oil

seal and carefully pry the seal out of the bore.

8. To remove the bearings, insert a bearing and seal remover into the bore so the tool head grasps behind the bearing. Slide the washer against the seal or bearing and turn the nut against the washer. Attach a slide hammer and remove the bearing.

9. Lubricate a new bearing with hypoid lubricant and install it into the housing with a bearing installer tool. Make sure the tool contacts the end of the axle tube to ensure that the bearing is at the correct depth.

10. Lubricate the cavity between the seal lips with a high temperature wheel bearing grease. Place a new oil seal on the seal installation tool and position the seal in the axle housing bore. Tap the seal into the bore flush with the end of the housing.

11. Slide the axle shaft into place making sure the splines on the end of the shaft do not damage the oil seal and that they engage the splines of the differential side gear. Install the C-lock on the inner end of the axle shaft and push the shaft outward so the shaft lock seats in the counterbore of the differential side gear.

12. Position the differential pinion shaft through the case and pinions, aligning the hole in the shaft with the lockscrew hole. Install the lockscrew.

13. Clean the gasket mounting surfaces on the differential carrier and the carrier cover. Install the carrier cover using a new gasket and tighten the cover bolts in a crosswise pattern to 22 ft. lbs.

14. Fill the rear axle with the correct lubricant to the bottom of the filler hole.

15. Install the brake drum and the wheel and tire assembly.

16. Lower the vehicle.

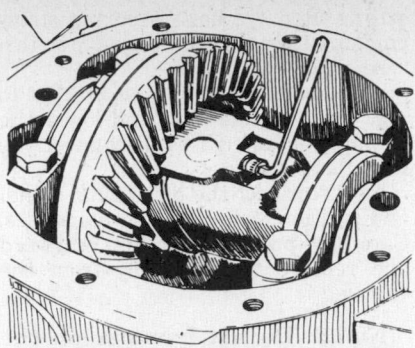

Removing the differential pinion shaft lockscrew

Rear Axle Housing

REMOVAL & INSTALLATION

1. Disconnect the negative battery cable. Raise vehicle and support it safely.

2. Remove the rear wheels and tires.

3. Disconnect the parking brake equalizer spring.

4. Remove the equalizer bracket attaching nut and separate the parking brake cable(s).

5. Clean dirt from the brake line and separate the brake hose running from the frame to the axle. Plug both ends of the brake line to prevent contamination.

6. Disconnect the stabilizer bar, if equipped.

7. Safely support the rear axle with an adjustable lifting device.

8. Disconnect both rear shock absorbers from the lower brackets.

9. Disconnect the rear axle extension bracket.

10. Lower the axle and remove the springs.

11. Remove the control arm front attaching bolts.

12. Lower the rear axle housing and remove from the vehicle.

13. Installation is the reverse of the removal procedure.

14. After the rear axle has been completely installed. Bleed the brake system and adjust the parking brake.

STEERING

NOTE: The steering column is designed to collapse in the event of a collision. When working on the steering column or any related components, it is important that the column not be hammered on or banged in any way which may cause damage to the column.

Steering Wheel

REMOVAL & INSTALLATION

1. Disconnect the negative battery cable.

2. Pull up on the horn cap to remove it. Remove the horn ring-to-steering wheel attaching screws and remove the ring.

3. Remove the wheel nut retainer and the wheel nut.

NOTE: Do not overexpand the retainer.

4. Using a suitable steering wheel puller, thread the puller anchor screws into the threaded holes in the steering wheel. With the center bolt of the puller butting against the steering shaft, turn the center bolt to remove the steering wheel.

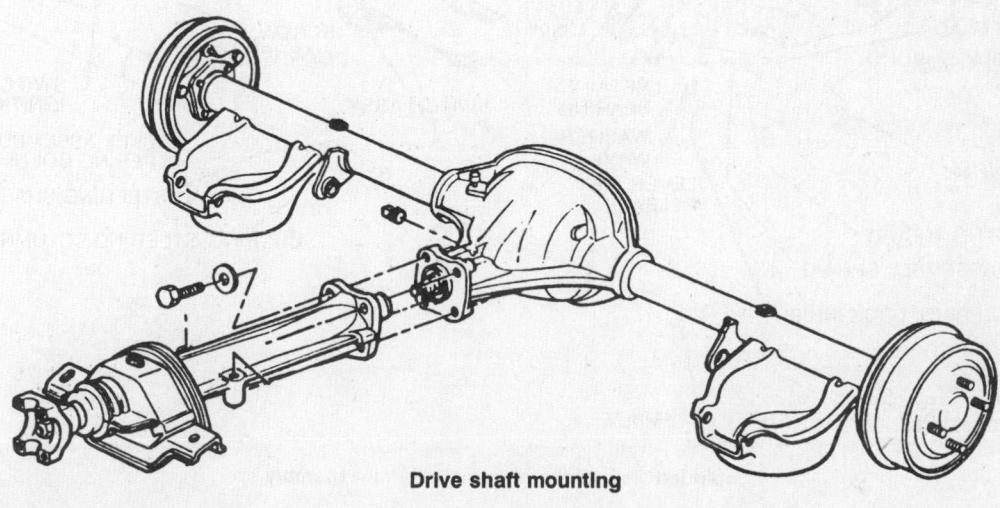

Drive shaft mounting

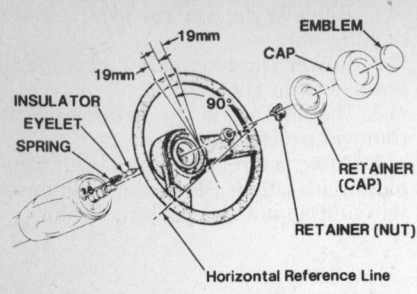

Chevette steering wheel assembly

To install:

5. Place the turn signal lever in the **N** position and install the steering wheel. Torque the steering wheel nut to 30 ft. lbs. and install the nut retainer. Use caution not to over-expand the nut retainer.

6. Connect the negative battery cable.

Steering Column

REMOVAL & INSTALLATION

1. Disconnect the negative battery cable.

2. Remove the steering wheel. Move the front seat rearward as far as possible.

3. Remove the floor pan bracket

screws. Remove bolts securing steering column to rack and pinion assembly.

4. Remove the 2 column bracket to instrument panel nuts and lower the column far enough to disconnect the wiring harnesses.

5. Disconnect the directional signal and ignition switch wiring harnesses. Carefully pull the column rearward and remove the assembly from the vehicle.

NOTE: Do not hammer on the end of the steering shaft. The plastic injection break-away pins will shear, causing the shaft to collapse.

6. Installation is the reverse order of the removal. Special attention must be given to the installation of the bolts and brackets during the assembly.

Manual Steering Rack

REMOVAL & INSTALLATION

1. Disconnect the negative battery cable. Raise and safely support the vehicle.

2. Remove the wheels and tires. Remove the bolts and shield.

3. Remove the outer tie rod cotter pins and nuts on both sides.

4. Remove the tie rods from the steering knuckle using tool BT–7101 or equivalent. Remove the tie rods.

5. Remove the flexible coupling pinch bolt to the shaft.

6. Remove the four bolts at the clamps and remove the assembly from the vehicle.

To install:

7. Position the assembly to the vehicle with the stub shaft in position with the flexible coupling and install the clamps and 4 new bolts.

8. Install the flexible coupling pinch bolt to the shaft.

9. Install the tie rods into the steering knuckles and torque the nuts to 30 ft. lbs. Install a new cotter pin.

10. Install the bolts and shield.

11. Install the wheels and tires. Lower the vehicle.

12 Check for proper steering operation before moving the vehicle.

Power Steering Rack

REMOVAL & INSTALLATION

1. Disconnect the negative battery cable. Raise and safely support the vehicle.

2. Remove the wheels and tires. Remove the bolts and shield.

3. Remove the outer tie rod cotter pins and nuts on both sides.

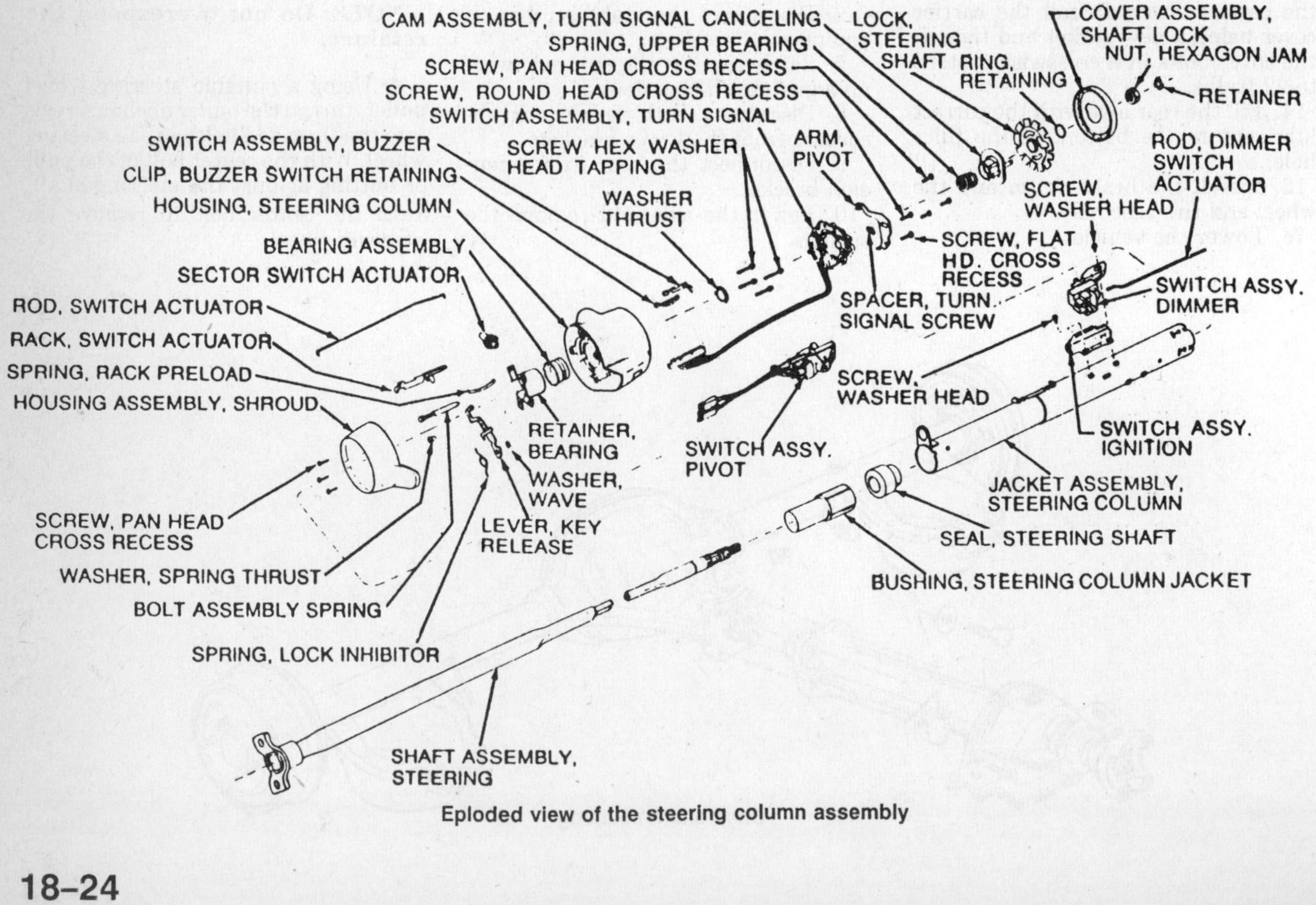

Eploded view of the steering column assembly

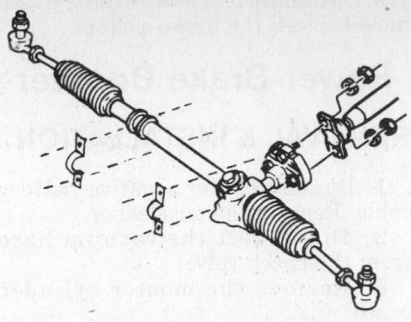

Manual rack and pinion assembly

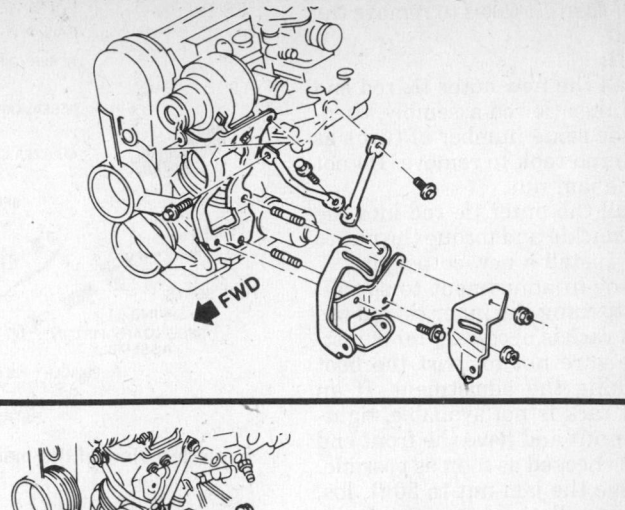

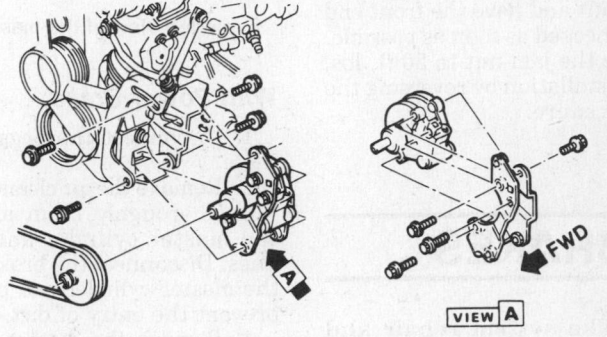

Power steering pump mounting

4. Using a tie rod separating tool, disconnect the tie rods from the steering knuckles.

5. Remove the 2 hydraulic lines from the steering gear. Remove the flexible coupling pinch bolt to the shaft.

6. Remove the 4 bolts at the clamps and remove the assembly from the vehicle.

To install:

7. Position the assembly to the vehicle with the stub shaft in position with the flexible coupling and install the clamps and four new bolts.

8. Install the flexible coupling pinch bolt to the shaft.

9. Install the tie rods into the steering knuckles and torque the nuts to 30 ft. lbs. Install a new cotter pin.

10. Install the 2 hydraulic hoses and bleed the system.

11. Install the bolts and shield.

12. Install the wheels and tires. Lower the vehicle.

13. Check for proper steering operation before moving the vehicle.

Power Steering Pump

REMOVAL & INSTALLATION

1. Disconnect the negative battery cable. Remove the upper adjusting bolt.

2. Remove the lower brace bolt-to-pump bracket.

3. Remove the left hand crossmember brace to body.

4. Remove the pressure line and the reservoir line at the pump.

5. Remove the rear pump adjusting bracket.

6. Remove the front pivot bolt at the pump and remove the bolt.

7. Remove the front pump bracket at the bolt-to-engine. Remove the bracket and pump.

8. Installation is the reverse of the removal procedure. In addition, adjust the belt tension, fill the reservoir and bleed the system.

BELT ADJUSTMENT

1. Loosen the pump attaching bolts and nut.

2. Adjust the belt tension to the proper specification by moving the pump with a suitable tool.

3. Tighten the pump attaching bolts and nut once the proper tension is reached.

4. Run the engine to assure proper operation.

SYSTEM BLEEDING

When the power steering system has been serviced, air must be bled from the system by using the following procedure:

1. Turn wheels all the way to the left, add power steering fluid to the COLD mark on the level indicator.

2. Start engine and run at fast idle momentarily, shut engine off and recheck the fluid level. If necessary add fluid to the COLD mark.

3. Start engine and bleed system by turning wheels from side to side without hitting stops. Keep the fluid level at the Cold mark. Fluid with air in it has a light tan or red appearance, this air must be eliminated before normal steering action can be achieved.

4. Return the wheels to the center position and continue running the engine for 2–3 minutes. Road test to check the operation of the steering.

5. Recheck the fluid level it should now be stabilized at the HOT level on the indicator.

Tie Rod Ends

REMOVAL & INSTALLATION

1. Disconnect the negative battery cable. Raise and support the vehicle safely. Remove the wheels and tires.

2. Loosen the jam nut located on the inner tie rod.

3. Remove the outer tie rod cotter pin and nut.

4. Using a tie rod end separating tool, remove the tie rod from the steering knuckle.

5. Remove the outer tie rod from the inner tie rod assembly. Count the

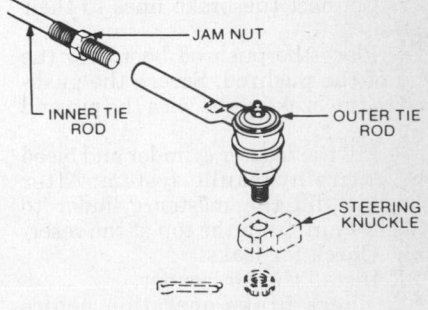

Tie rod end assembly

number of turns it takes to remove the tie rod end.

To install:

6. Install the new outer tie rod end onto the inner tie rod assembly, turning it in the same number of turns as the old tie rod took to remove. Do not tighten the jam nut.

7. Install the outer tie rod into the steering knuckle and torque the nut to 32 ft. lbs. Install a new cotter pin.

8. Set toe-in adjustment to specification by turning the inner tie rod (an alignment rack is necessary for adjustment). Be sure not to twist the boot when making the adjustment. If an alignment rack is not available, tighten the jam nut and have the front end alignment checked as soon as possible.

9. Torque the jam nut to 50 ft. lbs. Complete installation by reversing the removal procedure.

BRAKES

For all brake system repair and service procedures not detailed below, please refer to "Brakes" in the Unit Repair section.

Master Cylinder

REMOVAL & INSTALLATION

Without Power Brake

1. Disconnect the negative battery cable. Disconnect the master cylinder pushrod from the brake pedal.

2. Remove the pushrod boot.

3. Remove the air cleaner.

4. Thoroughly clean all dirt from the master cylinder and the brake lines. Disconnect the brake lines from the master cylinder and plug them to prevent the entry of dirt.

5. Remove the master cylinder attaching nuts and remove the master cylinder.

To install:

6. Install the master cylinder with its spacer. Tighten the securing nuts.

7. Connect the brake lines to their ports.

8. Place the pushrod boot over the end of the pushrod. Secure the pushrod to the brake pedal with the pin and clip.

9. Fill the master cylinder and bleed the entire hydraulic system. After bleeding, fill the master cylinder to within ¼ in. from the top of the reservoir. Check for leaks.

10. Install the air cleaner.

11. Check brake operation before moving the car.

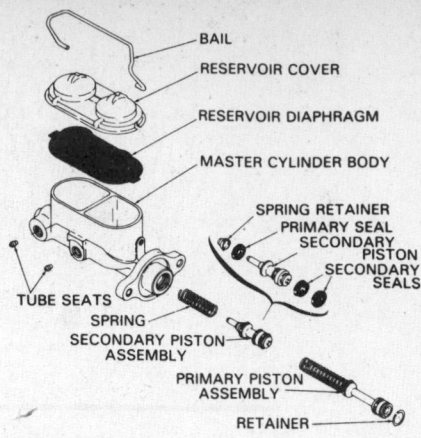

Exploded view of the master cylinder

With Power Brake

1. Disconnect the negative battery cable.

2. Remove the air cleaner assembly.

3. Thoroughly clean all dirt from the master cylinder and the brake lines. Disconnect the brake lines from the master cylinder and plug them to prevent the entry of dirt.

4. Remove the master cylinder attaching nuts and brace rod. Remove the master cylinder.

To install:

5. Place the master cylinder into position on the power brake booster. Install the brace rod and attaching nuts. Tighten the attaching nuts to 150 inch lbs. (17 Nm).

6. Connect the brake lines to their ports.

7. Fill the master cylinder and bleed the entire hydraulic system. After bleeding, fill the master cylinder to within ¼ in. from the top of the reservoir. Check for leaks.

8. Install the air cleaner assembly.

Combination Valve

REMOVAL & INSTALLATION

NOTE: If the combination valve is found defective it must be replaced.

1. Disconnect the negitive battery cable.

2. Clean all the dirt from the switch and connections.

3. Disconnect he electrical lead from the switch connection.

4. Disconnect the hydraulic lines from the connections at the switch. It may be necessary to loosen the line conncections at the master cylinder to loosen lines. Cover the open ends with a clean, lint-free rag.

5. Remove the mounting screw and remove the combination valve.

6. Installation is the reverse of removal. Bleed the brake system.

Power Brake Booster

REMOVAL & INSTALLATION

1. Disconnect the negative battery cable. Remove the air cleaner.

2. Disconnect the vacuum hose from the check valve.

3. Remove the master cylinder brace.

4. Remove the master cylinder-to-power cylinder nut and pull forward on the master cylinder until it clears the power cylinder mounting studs. Move the master cylinder aside and support it, being careful of the brake lines.

5. Remove the nuts securing the power cylinder to the firewall.

6. Remove the pushrod-to-pedal retainer and slip the pushrod off the pedal pin. Remove the power cylinder.

7. Installation is the reverse of removal.

Brake Caliper

REMOVAL & INSTALLATION

1. Remove ⅔ of the brake fluid from the master cylinder assembly.

2. Raise the vehicle and support with jackstands.

3. Mark the relationship of the wheel to the axle, then remove the wheel.

4. Position a C-clamp as shown in the illustration and tighten until the piston bottoms in the bore, then remove the C-clamp.

5. Remove the bolt holding the inlet fitting.

NOTE: If only the shoe and lining are being replaced, do not remove the inlet fitting.

6. Remove the 2 bolt covers and Allen head mounting bolts.

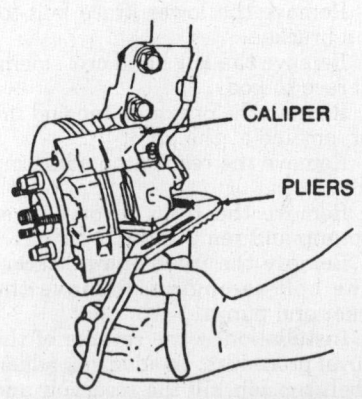

Compressing the caliper piston

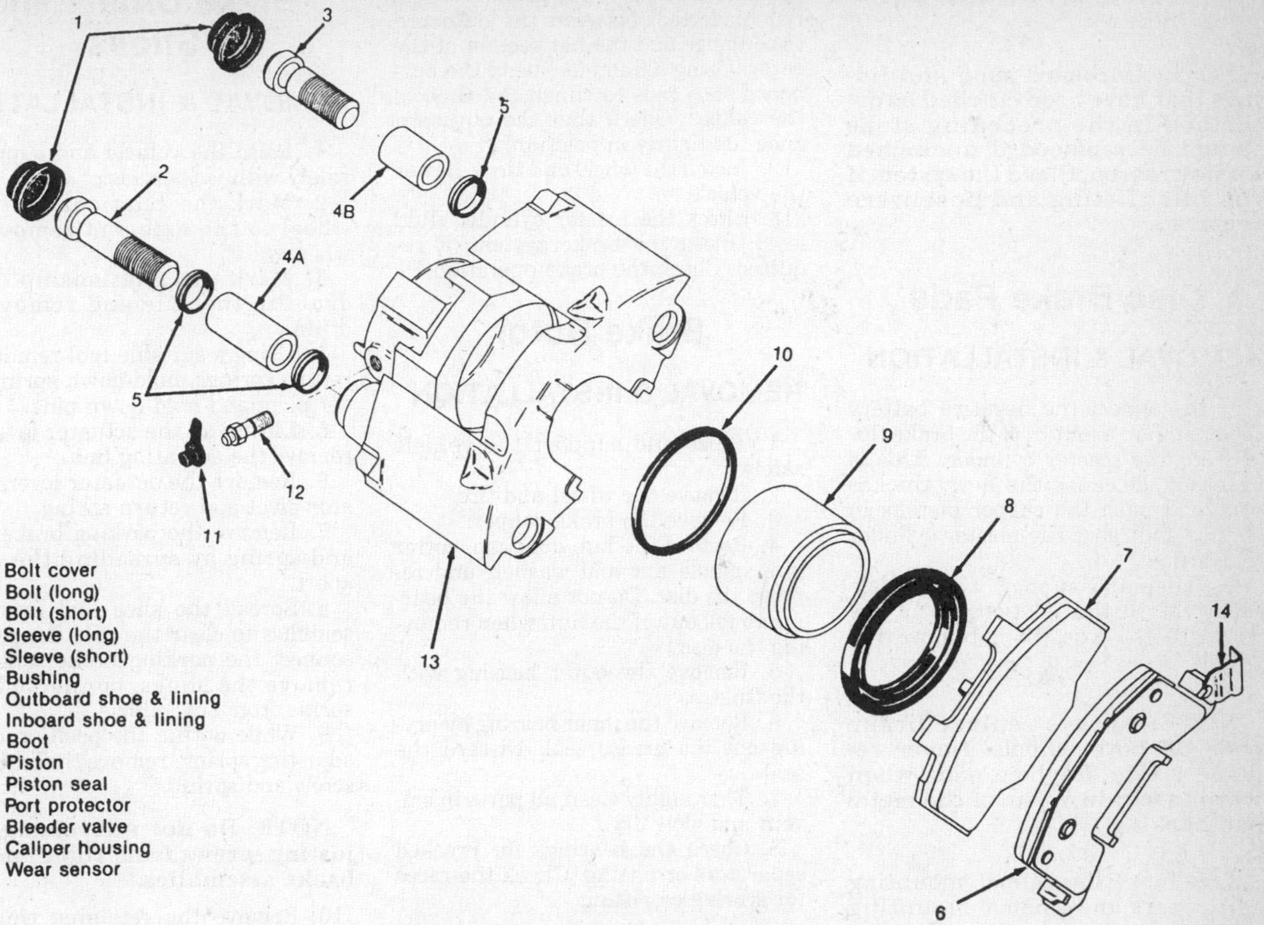

Exploded view of the disc brake caliper

1. Bolt cover
2. Bolt (long)
3. Bolt (short)
4A. Sleeve (long)
4B. Sleeve (short)
5. Bushing
6. Outboard shoe & lining
7. Inboard shoe & lining
8. Boot
9. Piston
10. Piston seal
11. Port protector
12. Bleeder valve
13. Caliper housing
14. Wear sensor

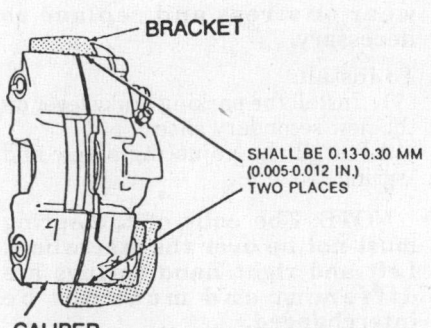

SHALL BE 0.13-0.30 MM
(0.005-0.012 IN.)
TWO PLACES

Proper clearance between the caliper and bracket stops

NOTE: If the mounting bolts show signs of corrosion replace them with new ones.

7. If only the shoe and linings are being replaced, remove the caliper from the rotor and suspend it from the suspension so there isn't any tension on the brake hose.

8. Remove the shoe and lining assemblies from the caliper. To remove the outboard shoe and lining, use 12

inch channel lock pliers to straighten bent over shoe tabs.

9. Remove the sleeves from the mounting bolt holes.

10. Remove the bushings from the grooves in the mounting bolt holes.

To install:

11. Prior to installation, lubricate and install new bushing and sleeves.

12. Install the inboard shoe and lining positioning the shoe retainer spring into the piston.

13. Install the outboard shoe and lining with the wear sensor at the leading edge of the shoe during forward wheel rotation.

14. Position the caliper over the rotor in the mounting bracket.

15. Coat the threads and shoulder of the mounting bolts with silicone grease. Install the mounting bolts and torque to 21–25 ft. lbs.

16. Check the clearance between the caliper and bracket stops as shown in the illustration and, if necessary, file the ends of the bracket to provide the proper clearance.

17. Install the inlet fitting if removed and torque to 18–30 ft. lbs.

18. Cinch the outboard shoe by performing the following steps:

a. Wedge a prying tool between the outboard shoe flange and the hat section of the rotor to seat the shoe flange in the caliper.

b. Have an assistant lightly press on the brake pedal to clamp the outboard shoe tightly to the caliper. Maintain pressure on the hydraulic system to keep the tool wedged in place during the remaining steps.

NOTE: Make sure the master cylinder is filled to the proper level and the cover is in place before performing the previous step.

c. Bend the outboard shoe tabs and cinch the shoe to the caliper by positioning an 8 ounce machinists hammer as shown in the illustration, then striking it with a 16 ounce brass hammer.

d. Check that the shoe tabs are bent to an angle of approximately 45 degrees. After both tabs are bent and hydraulic pressure released, check that the outboard shoe is locked tightly in position. If not, repeat Steps a–c.

NOTE: Outboard shoe and linings that have been cinched as described in the preceding steps should be replaced if uncinched for any reason. Bleed the system if the inlet fitting and hose were removed.

Disc Brake Pads

REMOVAL & INSTALLATION

1. Disconnect the negative battery cable. Siphon about ½ of the brake fluid from the master cylinder. This is necessary because the new, thicker pads will push the caliper pistons in farther and cause the master cylinder to overflow.
2. Raise and support the vehicle safely. Mark the relationship of the wheel to the axle, then remove the wheel.

NOTE: Always replace brake pads on both wheels. Never replace 1 side. Replace pads when worn to within $\frac{1}{32}$ in. of the metal pad backing.

3. Remove the caliper mounting bolt covers and remove mounting bolts.
4. Position a 4 in. adjustable pliers over the inboard pad tab and the inboard caliper housing. Compress the piston back into the caliper bore.
5. Remove the caliper from its mounting bracket.
6. Remove the inboard and outboard pads. Remove the sleeves and bushings from the caliper mounting bolt holes. Suspend the caliper assembly with a wire hook.

NOTE: Do not allow the caliper to hang by the brake hose.

To install:
7. Lubricate the new bushings and sleeves with silicone grease and install into the caliper mounting bolt holes.
8. Install the inboard pad. Install the outboard pad with the wear sensor at the leading edge of the shoe during forward wheel rotation.
9. Position the caliper assembly over the rotor on its mounting bracket and install the mounting bolts. Torque to 21–25 ft. lbs. (28–47 Nm).
10. Check the clearance between the caliper and the bracket stop. If necessary, file the ends of the bracket stops to provide proper clearance.
11. Apply the brake pedal several times to seat the brake pads. Wedge a flat blade tool between the outboard shoe flange and the hat section of the rotor. Using a hammer, bend the outboard shoe tabs to clinch the shoe to the caliper. Check that the outboard shoe fits tightly in position.
12. Install the wheel and tires. Lower the vehicle.
13. Check the master cylinder fluid level. Bleed the brake system, if required. Check the brake operation.

Brake Rotor

REMOVAL & INSTALLATION

1. Raise and support the vehicle safely.
2. Remove the wheel and tire.
3. Remove the brake caliper.
4. Remove the hub dust cap, cotter pin, spindle nut and washer, and remove the disc. Do not allow the bearing to fall out of the hub when removing the disc.
5. Remove the outer bearing with the fingers.
6. Remove the inner bearing by prying out the grease seal. Discard the seal.
7. Thoroughly clean all parts in solvent and blow dry.
8. Check the bearings for cracked separators or pitting. Check the races for scoring or pitting.

NOTE: If it is necessary to replace either the inner or outer bearing it will also be necessary to replace the race for that bearing.

9. Drive out the old race from the hub with a brass drift inserted behind the race in the notches in the hub.
10. Lubricate the new race with a light film of grease.
11. Use the proper tool to start the race squarely into the hub and carefully seat it.
12. Pack the inner and outer bearings with high melting point wheel bearing grease.
13. Place the inner bearing in the hub and install a new grease seal. The seal should be installed flush with the hub surface. Use a block of wood to seat the seal.
14. Install the disc over the spindle.
15. Press the outer bearing firmly into the hub by hand.
16. Install the spindle washer and nut. Adjust the wheel bearings.
17. Install the brake caliper. Tighten the brake caliper mounting bolts to 70 ft. lbs.
18. Install the wheel and tire.
19. Lower the car.

Brake Drums and Shoes

REMOVAL & INSTALLATION

1. Raise the vehicle and support it safely with jackstands.
2. Mark the relationship of the wheel to the axle and remove the wheel.
3. Mark the relationship of the drum to the axle and remove the drum.
4. Using a suitable tool remove the return springs, hold-down springs, lever pivot and hold-down pins.
5. Lift up on the actuator lever and remove the actuating link.
6. Remove the actuator lever, actuator pivot and return spring.
7. Remove the parking brake strut and spring by spreading the shoes apart.
8. Spread the shoe and lining assemblies to clear the axle flange. Disconnect the parking brake cable and remove the shoes, connected by a spring from the vehicle.
9. While noting the position of the adjusting spring, remove the adjusting screw and spring.

NOTE: Do not interchange adjusting screws from right and left brake assemblies.

10. Remove the retaining ring and pin then remove the parking brake lever from the secondary shoe.

NOTE: Examine all parts for wear or stress and replace as necessary.

To install:
11. Install the parking brake lever on the new secondary shoe.
12. Install the adjusting screw and spring.

NOTE: The coils of the spring must not be over the star wheel. Left and right hand springs are different and must not be interchanged.

13. Spread the shoe and lining assemblies to clear the axle flange and connect the parking brake cable.
14. Install the parking brake strut and spring by spreading the shoes apart.

NOTE: The end of the strut without the spring engages the parking brake lever. The end with the spring engages the primary shoe.

15. Install the actuator pivot, lever and return spring.
16. Install the actuating link in the shoe retainer.

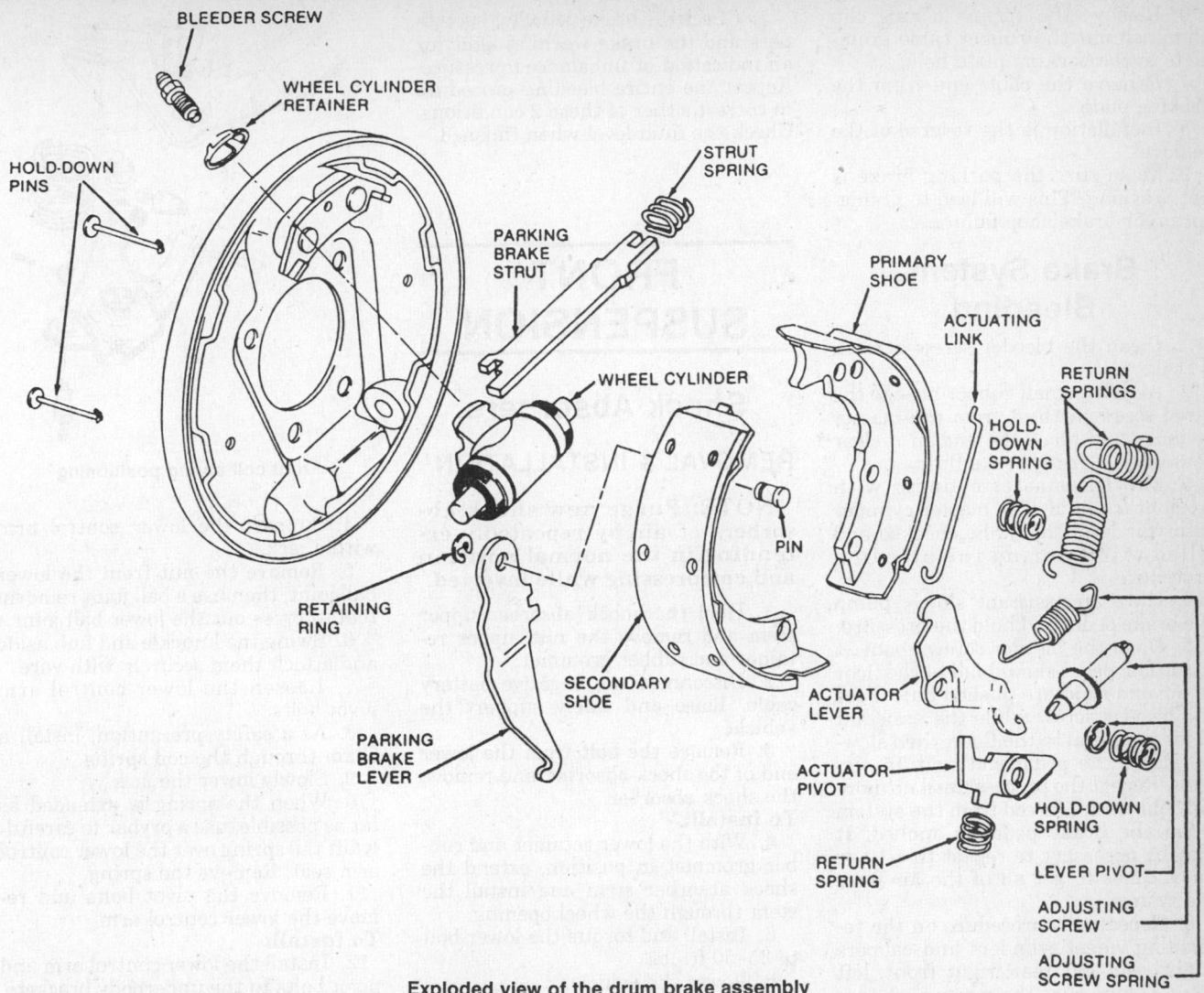

Exploded view of the drum brake assembly

17. Lift up on the actuator lever and hook the link into the lever.

18. Install the hold-down pins, lever pivot and hold-down springs.

19. Install the shoe return springs.

20. Install the drum and wheel. Adjust the brakes by applying the brake several times until the pedal is firm. Check the fluid level and adjust the parking brake.

Wheel Cylinder
REMOVAL & INSTALLATION

1. Disconnect the negative battery cable. Raise and support the vehicle safely.

2. Remove the wheel and tire. Remove the brake drum and brake shoe assembly.

3. Clean the area around the inlet tube line and disconnect the tube line.

4. Remove the wheel cylinder retainer by inserting 2 awls into the access slots between the wheel cylinder pilot and the retainer locking tabs.

Bend both tabs away simutaneously and remove.

To install:

5. Place the wheel cylinder into position and hold in place using a wooden block between the cylinder and axle flange.

6. Use a 1⅛ in., 12 point socket and socket extension to aid in installing a new retainer over the wheel cylinder abutment.

7. Connect the inlet tube and torque the nut to 120–180 inch lbs.

8. Install the brake shoe assembly and brake drum. Install the wheel and tire and lower the vehicle.

9. Fill the master cylinder and bleed the brake system.

Parking Brake Cable
ADJUSTMENT

1. Raise and safely support the vehicle.

2. Apply the parking brake 3 notches from the fully released position.

3. Tighten the parking brake cable equalizer adjusting nut under the vehicle until a light drag is felt when the rear wheels are rotated forward.

4. Fully release the parking brake and rotate the rear wheels. There should be no drag.

5. Lower the vehicle.

REMOVAL & INSTALLATION

1. Disconnect the negative battery cable. Raise and safely support the vehicle.

2. Disconnect the parking brake equalizer spring and equalizer.

3. Remove the parking brake cable from all underbody mounting brackets.

4. Remove the rear wheels and brake drums.

5. Remove the parking brake cable from the parking brake lever.

6. Remove the spring locking clip and push out the rubber cable grommets in the backing plate hole.

7. Remove the cable end from the backing plate.

8. Installation is the reverse of the removal.

9. Make sure the parking brake is not dragging. This will lead to premature rear brake shoe failure.

Brake System Bleeding

1. Clean the bleeder screw at each wheel.

2. Attach a small rubber hose to the bleed screw farthest from the master cylinder and place the end in a clear container of fresh brake fluid.

3. Fill the master cylinder with fresh brake fluid. The master cylinder reservoir level should be checked and filled often during the bleeding procedure.

4. Have an assistant slowly pump the brake pedal and hold the pressure.

5. Open the bleeder screw about ¼ turn. The pedal should fall to the floor as air and fluid are pushed out. Close the bleeder screw while the assistant holds the pedal to the floor, then slowly release the pedal and wait 15 seconds. Repeat the process until no more air bubbles are forced from the system when the brake pedal is applied. It may be necessary to repeat this 10 or more times to get all of the air from the system.

6. Repeat this procedure on the remaining wheel cylinders and calipers (right rear, left rear, right front, left front). Make sure the master cylinder does not run out of brake fluid.

NOTE: Remember to wait 15 seconds between each bleeding and do not pump the pedal rapidly. Rapid pumping of the brake pedal pushes the master cylinder secondary piston down the bore in a manner that makes it difficult to bleed the system.

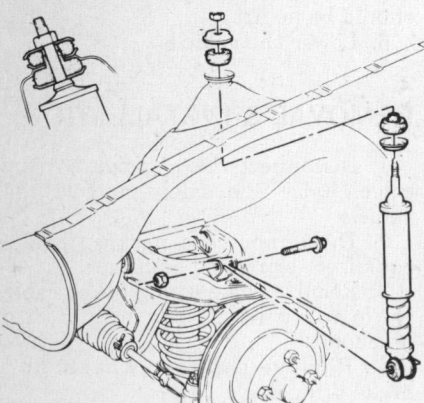

Front shock absorber

7. Check the brake pedal for sponginess and the brake warning light for an indication of unbalanced pressure. Repeat the entire bleeding procedure to correct either of these 2 conditions. Check the fluid level when finished.

FRONT SUSPENSION

Shock Absorbers

REMOVAL & INSTALLATION

NOTE: Purge new shock absorbers of air by repeatedly extending in the normal position and compressing while inverted.

1. Hold the shock absorber upper stem and remove the nut, upper retainer and rubber grommet.

2. Disconnect the negative battery cable. Raise and safely support the vehicle.

3. Remove the bolt from the lower end of the shock absorber and remove the shock absorber.

To install:

4. With the lower retainer and rubber grommet in position, extend the shock absorber stem and install the stem through the wheel opening.

5. Install and torque the lower bolt to 35–50 ft. lbs.

6. Lower the vehicle.

7. Install the upper rubber grommet, retainer and nut to the shock absorber stem.

8. Hold the shock absorber upper stem and torque the nut to 7 ft. lbs.

Coil Springs

REMOVAL & INSTALLATION

NOTE: The ball joint studs use a special nut which must be discarded whenever loosened and removed. During reassembly, use a standard nut to draw the ball joint into position on the knuckle, then remove the standard nut and install a new special nut for final installation.

1. Disconnect the negative battery cable. Raise and safely support the vehicle at the frame.

2. Remove the wheel and tire.

3. Disconnect the stabilizer bar from the lower control arm and disconnect the tie rod from the steering knuckle.

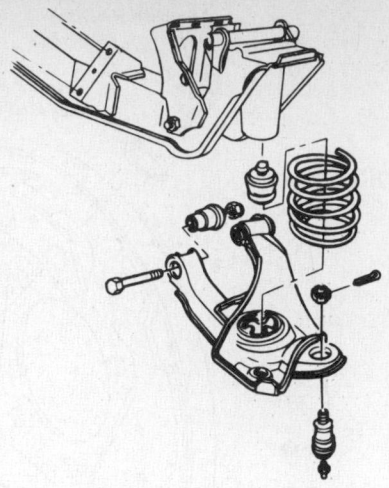

Front coil spring positioning

4. Support the lower control arm with a jack.

5. Remove the nut from the lower ball joint, then use a ball joint removal tool to press out the lower ball joint.

6. Swing the knuckle and hub aside and attach them securely with wire.

7. Loosen the lower control arm pivot bolts.

8. As a safety precaution, install a chain through the coil spring.

9. Slowly lower the jack.

10. When the spring is extended as far as possible, use a prybar to carefully lift the spring over the lower control arm seat. Remove the spring.

11. Remove the pivot bolts and remove the lower control arm.

To install:

12. Install the lower control arm and pivot bolts to the underbody brackets. Torque the lower control arm pivot bolts to 49 ft. lbs.

13. Position inspring correctly and install it in the upper pocket. Use tape to hold the insulator onto the spring.

14. Install the lower end of the spring onto the lower control arm. An assistant may be necessary to compress the spring far enough to slide it over the raised area of the lower control arm seat.

15. Use a jack to raise the lower control arm and compress the coil spring.

16. Install the ball joint through the lower control arm and into the steering knuckle. Install the nut on the ball stud and torque to 41–54 ft. lbs.

17. Connect the stabilizer bar to the lower control arm. Connect the tie rod to the steering knuckle. Install the wheel and tire.

18. Lower the vehicle.

Upper Ball Joints

INSPECTION

1. Disconnect the negative battery

cable. Raise the vehicle and position floor stands under the left and right lower control arm as near as possible to each lower ball joint. Upper control arm bumper must not contact frame.

2. Position a dial indicator against the wheel rim.

3. Grasp the front wheel and push in on bottom of the tire while pulling out at the top. Read the guage, then reverse the push — pull procedure. Horizontal deflection on the dial indicator should not exceed 1.25 in. (3.18mm).

4. If the indicator exceeds 1.25 in. (3.18mm), or if ball stud (when disconnected from the knuckle assembly) can be twisted in its socket with your fingers, replace the ball joint.

REMOVAL & INSTALLATION

NOTE: The ball joint studs use a special nut which must be discarded whenever loosened and removed. During reassembly, use a standard nut to draw the ball joint into position on the knuckle, then remove the standard nut and install a new special nut for the final installation.

1. Disconnect the negative battery cable. Raise and safely support the vehicle.

2. Remove the tire and wheel.

3. Support the lower control arm with a floor jack.

4. Loosen, but do not remove the upper ball stud nut.

5. Install a ball joint removal tool with the cup end over the lower ball stud nut.

6. Turn the threaded end of the ball joint removal tool until the upper ball stud is free of the steering knuckle.

7. Remove the ball joint removal tool and remove the nut from the ball stud.

8. Remove the 2 nuts and bolts attaching the ball joint to the upper control arm and remove the ball joint.

NOTE: Inspect the tapered hole in the steering knuckle. Clean the area. If any deformation or damage is found, the steering knuckle must be replaced.

To install:

9. Install the nuts and bolts attaching the ball joint to the upper control arm. Torque the nuts to 29 ft. lbs. Then mate the upper control arm ball stud to the steering knuckle.

10. Install and torque the ball stud nut to 29–36 ft. lbs.

11. Install the tire and wheel.

12. Lower the vehicle.

Lower Ball Joints

INSPECTION

These lower ball joints contain a visual wear indicator. The lower ball joint grease plug screws into the wear indicator which protrudes from the bottom of the ball joint housing. As long as the wear indicator extends out of the ball joint housing, the ball joint is not worn. If the tip of the wear indicator is parallel with, or recessed into the ball joint housing, the ball joint is defective.

REMOVAL & INSTALLATION

NOTE: The ball joint studs use a special nut which must be discarded whenever loosened and removed. During assembly, use a standard nut to draw the ball joint into position on the knuckle, then remove the standard nut and install a new special nut for final installation.

1. Disconnect the negative battery cable. Raise and safely support the vehicle.

2. Remove the tire and wheel.

3. Support the lower control arm with a hydraulic floor jack.

4. Loosen, but do not remove the lower ball stud nut.

5. Install a ball joint removal tool with the cup end over the upper ball stud nut.

6. Turn the threaded end of the ball joint removal tool until the ball stud is free of the steering knuckle.

7. Remove the ball joint removal tool and remove the nut from the ball stud.

8. Remove the ball joint.

NOTE: Inspect the tapered hole in the steering knuckle. Clean the area. If any deformation or damage is found, the steering knuckle must be replaced.

To install:

9. Mate the ball stud through the lower control arm and into the steering knuckle.

10. Install and torque the ball stud nut to 41–54 ft. lbs.

11. Install the tire and wheel.

12. Lower the vehicle.

Upper Control Arms

REMOVAL & INSTALLATION

NOTE: The ball joint studs use a special nut which must be discarded whenever loosened and removed. During reassembly, use a

standard nut to draw the ball joint into position on the knuckle, then remove the standard nut and install a new special nut for final installation.

1. Disconnect the negative battery cable. Raise the vehicle and support it safely.

2. Remove the tire and wheel.

3. Support the lower control arm with a floor jack.

4. Remove the upper ball joint from the steering knuckle.

5. Remove the upper control arm pivot bolts and remove the upper control arm.

To install:

6. Install the upper control arm with its pivot bolts.

NOTE: The inner pivot bolt must be installed with the bolt head toward the front.

7. Install the pivot bolt nut.

8. Position the upper control arm in a horizontal plane and torque the nut to 43–50 ft. lbs.

9. Install the ball joint to the upper control arm and to the steering knuckle. Torque the ball joint-to-upper control arm attaching bolts to 29 ft. lbs. Torque the ball stud nut to 29–36 ft. lbs.

10. Install the tire and wheel.

11. Lower the vehicle.

Lower Control Arms
REMOVAL & INSTALLATION

NOTE: The ball joint studs use a special nut which must be discarded whenever loosened and removed. During reassembly, use a standard nut to draw the ball joint into position on the knuckle, then remove the standard nut and install a new special nut for final installation.

1. Disconnect the negative battery cable. Raise and safely support the vehicle on a frame contact hoist.

2. Remove the wheel and tire.

3. Disconnect the stabilizer bar from the lower control arm and disconnect the tie rod from the steering knuckle.

4. Support the lower control arm with a jack.

5. Remove the nut from the lower ball joint, then use a ball joint removal tool to press out the lower ball joint.

6. Swing the knuckle and hub aside and attach them securely with wire.

7. Loosen the lower control arm pivot bolts.

8. As a safety precaution, install a chain through the coil spring.

9. Slowly lower the jack.

10. When the spring is extended as

far as possible, use a prybar to carefully lift the spring over the lower control arm seat. Remove the spring.

11. Remove the pivot bolts and remove the lower control arm.

To install:

12. Install the lower control arm and pivot bolts to the underbody brackets. Torque the lower control arm pivot bolts to 49 ft. lbs.

13. Position spring correctly and install it in the upper pocket. Use tape to hold the insulator onto the spring.

14. Install the lower end of the spring onto the lower control arm. An assistant may be necessary to compress the spring far enough to slide it over the raised area of the lower control arm seat.

15. Use a jack to raise the lower control arm and compress the coil spring.

16. Install the ball joint through the lower control arm and into the steering knuckle. Install the nut on the ball stud and torque to 41–54 ft. lbs.

17. Connect the stabilizer bar to the lower control arm. Connect the tierod to the steering knuckle. Install the wheel and tire.

18. Lower the vehicle.

Front Wheel Bearings

ADJUSTMENT

1. Disconnect the negative battery cable. Raise and safely support the vehicle.

2. Remove the hub cap or wheel cover from the wheel. Remove the dust cap from the hub.

3. Remove the cotter pin from the spindle and spindle nut.

4. Spin the wheel forward by hand and tighten the spindle nut to 12 ft. lbs. This will fully seat the bearings.

5. Back off the nut to a just loose position.

6. Hand-tighten the spindle nut. Loosen the spindle nut until either hole in the spindle aligns with a slot in the nut, but not more than ½ flat.

7. Install a new cotter pin, bend the ends of the pin against the nut and cut off any extra length to avoid interference with the dust cap.

8. Proper bearing adjustment should give 0.001–0.005 in. of endplay.

9. Install the dust cap on the hub and the hub cap or wheel cover on the wheel.

10. Lower the vehicle.

REMOVAL & INSTALLATION

1. Disconnect the negative battery cable. Raise and safely support the vehicle.

2. Remove the wheel and tire.

3. Remove the brake caliper leaving the brake line attached and support it so it is not hanging on the brake line.

4. Remove the dust cap, cotter pin spindle nut and washer making sure the rotor does not fall off.

5. Place one hand over the outer bearing and remove the rotor.

6. Using a suitable tool, drive out the inner seal and bearing race.

7. Using a suitable tool, drive out the outer bearing race.

To install:

8. Clean out the bearing seats in the rotor thoroughly.

9. Use a bearing driver and drive the inner and outer races in their proper positions.

10. Make sure the new bearings are packed with grease properly. Place the inner bearing in the rotor and install the inner grease seal with the lip facing inward.

11. Place the outer bearing in its position and install the rotor onto the spindle. The remainder of the installation is the reverse of the removal. Adjust the bearings properly.

REAR SUSPENSION

Shock Absorbers

REMOVAL & INSTALLATION

NOTE: Purge new shock absorbers of air by repeatedly extending them in the normal position and compressing them while inverted.

1. Disconnect the negative battery cable. Raise and safely support the vehicle.

2. Support the rear axle.

3. Remove the shock absorber upper attaching nut and lower attaching bolt and nut and remove the shock absorber.

To install:

4. Install the retainer and the rubber grommet onto the shock absorber.

5. Place the shock absorber into its installed position and install and tighten the upper retaining nut to 7 ft. lbs.

6. Install the lower shock absorber nut and bolt and torque to 21 ft. lbs.

7. Remove the rear axle supports and lower the vehicle.

Coil Springs

REMOVAL & INSTALLATION

1. Disconnect the negative battery

cable. Raise and safely support the vehicle.

2. Support the rear axle with a floor jack.

3. Disconnect both shock absorbers from their lower brackets.

4. Disconnect the rear axle extension center support bracket from the underbody. Use caution when disconnect the extension and safely support it when disconnected.

5. Lower the rear axle and remove the springs and spring insulators.

NOTE: Do not stretch the rear brake hoses when lowering the rear axle.

To install:

6. Position the insulators on top and on the bottom of the springs and position the springs between their upper and lower seats.

7. Raise the rear axle. Connect the rear axle extension center support bracket to the underbody. Torque the bolts to 37 ft. lbs.

8. Connect the shock absorbers to their lower brackets. Torque the nuts to 21 ft. lbs.

9. Remove the jack from the axle.

10. Lower the vehicle.

Rear Control Arms

REMOVAL & INSTALLATION

NOTE: If both control arms are going to be replaced, only replace one control arm at a time. This will prevent the axle from rolling or sliding sideways.

1. Disconnect the negative battery cable. Raise and safely support the vehicle.

2. Disconnect the stabalizer bar, if equipped.

3. Remove the front and rear control arm mounting bolts.

4. Remove the control arm.

5. Installation is the reverse of the removal.

Rear Wheel Bearings

For rear wheel bearing removal and installation procedures, please refer to Rear Axle Shaft, Bearing and Seal in the Drive Axle section.

Rear Axle Assembly

For rear axle removal and installation procedures, please refer to Rear Axle Assembly in the Drive Axle section.

GM—Pontiac

Rear Wheel Drive
Fiero

SPECIFICATIONS

VEHICLE IDENTIFICATION CHART

It is important for servicing and ordering parts to be certain of the vehicle and engine identification. The VIN (vehicle identification number) is a 17 digit number visible through the windshield on the driver's side of the dash and contains the vehicle and engine identification codes. The tenth digit indicates model year, and the eighth digit indicates engine code. It can be interpreted as follows:

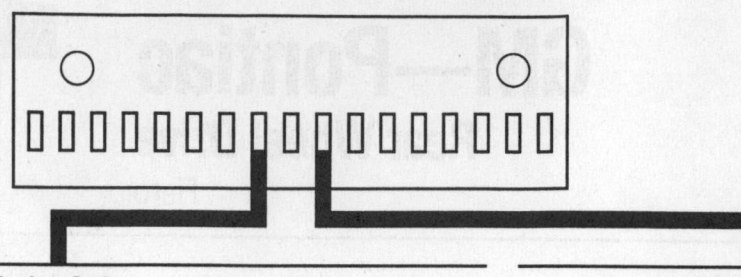

Engine Code						Model Year	
Code	Cu. In.	Liters	Cyl.	Fuel Sys.	Eng. Mfg.	Code	Year
R	151	2.5	4	TBI	Pontiac	H	1987
9	173	2.8	6	MFI	Chevrolet	J	1988

ENGINE IDENTIFICATION

Year	Model	Engine Displacement cu. in. (liter)	Engine Series Identification (VIN)	No. of Cylinders	Engine Type
1987	Fiero	151 (2.5)	R	4	OHV
	Fiero	173 (2.8)	9	4	OHV
1988	Fiero	151 (2.5)	R	4	OHV
	Fiero	173 (2.8)	9	4	OHV

GENERAL ENGINE SPECIFICATIONS

Year	VIN	No. Cylinder Displacement cu. in. (liter)	Fuel System Type	Net Horsepower @ rpm	Net Torque @ rpm (ft.lbs.)	Bore × Stroke (in.)	Compression Ratio	Oil Pressure @ rpm
1987	R	4-151 (2.5)	TBI	92 @ 4400	134 @ 2800	4.000 × 3.000	8.3:1	36–41 @ 2000
	9	6-173 (2.8)	MFI	140 @ 5200	170 @ 3600	3.500 × 3.000	8.5:1	30–45 @ 2000
1988	R	4-151 (2.5)	TBI	98 @ 4500	134 @ 2800	4.000 × 3.000	8.3:1	36–41 @ 2000
	9	6-173 (2.8)	MFI	135 @ 4500	170 @ 3600	3.500 × 3.000	8.5:1	30–45 @ 2000

TBI—Throttle Body Fuel Injection
MFI—Multiport Fuel Injection

GASOLINE ENGINE TUNE-UP SPECIFICATIONS

Year	VIN	No. Cylinder Displacement cu. in. (liter)	Spark Plugs Type	Gap (in.)	Ignition Timing (deg.) MT	AT	Com-pression Pressure (psi)	Fuel Pump (psi)	Idle Speed (rpm) MT	AT	Valve Clearance In.	Ex.
1987	R	4-151 (2.5)	R43CTS	.060	①	①	NA	9-13	①	①	Hyd.	Hyd.
	9	6-173 (2.8)	R42CTS	.045	①	①	NA	41-47	①	①	Hyd.	Hyd.
1988	R	4-151 (2.5)	R42CTS	.060	①	①	NA	9-13	①	①	Hyd.	Hyd.
	9	6-173 (2.8)	R42CTS	.060	①	①	NA	41-47	①	①	Hyd.	Hyd.

NOTE: The underhood specifications sticker often reflects tune-up specification changes made in production. Sticker figures must be used if they disagree with those in this chart
NA—Not available
① See underhood sticker

FIRING ORDERS

NOTE: To avoid confusion, always replace spark plug wires one at a time.

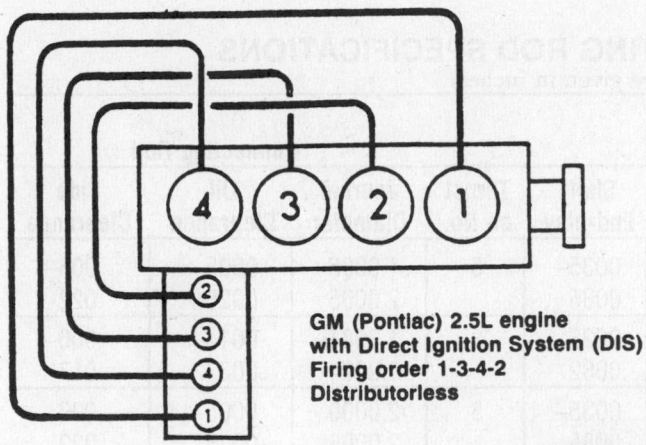

GM (Pontiac) 2.5L engine
with Direct Ignition System (DIS)
Firing order 1-3-4-2
Distributorless

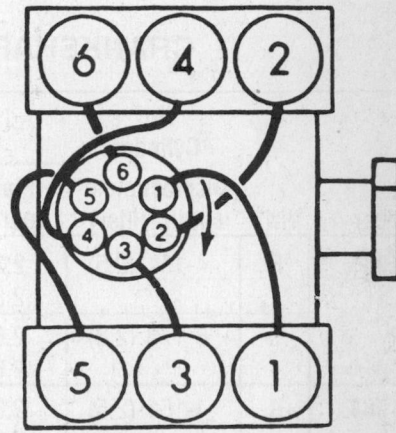

GM (Chevrolet) 173 V6 (2.8 L)
Engine firing order: 1-2-3-4-5-6
Distributor rotation: clockwise

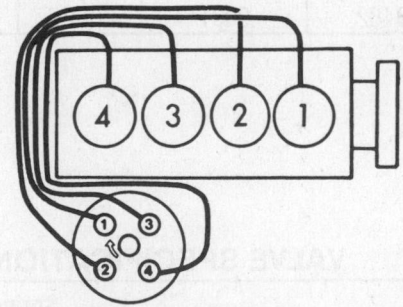

GM (Pontiac) 2.5L engine
Firing order: 1–3–4–2
Distributor rotation: clockwise

CAPACITIES

Year	Model	VIN	No. Cylinder Displacement cu. in. (liter)	Engine Crankcase with Filter	without Filter	Transmission (pts.) 4-Spd	5-Spd	Auto.	Drive Axle (pts.)	Fuel Tank (gal.)	Cooling System (qts.)
1987	Fiero	R	4-151 (2.5)	3	3	—	4.1	8.0	—	11.9	13.8
	Fiero	9	6-173 (2.8)	4	4	—	5.3	8.0	—	11.9	13.8
1988	Fiero	R	4-151 (2.5)	4	4	—	4.1②	8.0①	—	11.9	13.8
	Fiero	9	6-173 (2.8)	4	4	—	5.3②	8.0①	—	11.9	13.8

① Overhaul—10.0
② Isuzu—5.3

CAMSHAFT SPECIFICATIONS
All measurements given in inches.

Year	VIN	No. Cylinder Displacement cu. in. (liter)	Journal Diameter 1	2	3	4	5	Lobe Lift In.	Ex.	Bearing Clearance	Camshaft End Play
1987	R	4-151 (2.5)	1.869	1.869	1.869	1.869	—	0.232	0.232	.0007–.0027	.0015–.0050
	9	6-173 (2.8)	1.869	1.869	1.869	1.869	—	0.231	0.231	.0010–.0040	—
1988	R	4-151 (2.5)	1.869	1.869	1.869	1.869	—	0.232	0.232	.0007–.0027	.0015–.0050
	9	6-173 (2.8)	1.869	1.869	1.869	1.869	—	0.231	0.263	.0010–.0040	—

CRANKSHAFT AND CONNECTING ROD SPECIFICATIONS
All measurements are given in inches.

Year	VIN	No. Cylinder Displacement cu. in. (liter)	Crankshaft Main Brg. Journal Dia.	Main Brg. Oil Clearance	Shaft End-play	Thrust on No.	Connecting Rod Journal Diameter	Oil Clearance	Side Clearance
1987	R	4-151 (2.5)	2.2995–2.3005	.0005–.0022	.0035–.0085	5	1.9995–2.0005	.0005–.0026	.006–.022
	9	6-173 (2.8)	2.6473–2.6482	.0016–.0031	.0023–.0082	3	1.9984–1.9994	.0014–.0037	.006–.017
1988	R	4-151 (2.5)	2.3000–2.3005	.0005–.0022	.0035–.0085	5	2.0000–2.0005	.0005–.0026	.006–.022
	9	6-173 (2.8)	2.6473–2.6482	.0016–.0031	.0023–.0082	3	1.9984–1.9994	.0014–.0037	.006–.017

VALVE SPECIFICATIONS

Year	VIN	No. Cylinder Displacement cu. in. (liter)	Seat Angle (deg.)	Face Angle (deg.)	Spring Test Pressure (lbs.)	Spring Installed Height (in.)	Stem-to-Guide Clearance (in.) Intake	Exhaust	Stem Diameter (in.) Intake	Exhaust
1987	R	4-151 (2.5)	45	45	176	1.69	.0010–.0027	.0010–.0027	.3418–.3425	.3418–.3425
	9	6-173 (2.8)	46	45	195	1.57	.0010–.0027	.0010–.0027	.3410–.3425	.3410–.3426
1988	R	4-151 (2.5)	46	45	178	1.44	.0010–.0027	.0010–.0027	.3130–.3140	.3120–.3130
	9	6-173 (2.8)	46	45	195	1.57	.0010–.0027	.0010–.0027	.3410–.3425	.3410–.3426

PISTON AND RING SPECIFICATIONS
All measurments are given in inches.

Year	VIN	No. Cylinder Displacement cu. in. (liter)	Piston Clearance	Ring Gap			Ring Side Clearance		
				Top Compression	Bottom Compression	Oil Control	Top Compression	Bottom Compression	Oil Control
1987	R	4-151 (2.5)	.0014–.0022 ①	.010–.020	.010–.020	.020–.060	.002–.003	.001–.003	.015–.055
	9	6-173 (2.8)	.0007–.0017	.0098–.0197	.0098–.0197	.020–.055	.0012–.0028	.0016–.0037	.008 Max
1988	R	4-151 (2.5)	.0014–.0022 ①	.010–.020	.010–.020	.020–.060	.002–.003	.002–.003	.015–.055
	9	6-173 (2.8)	.0007–.0017	.0098–.0197	.0098–.0197	.020–.055	.0012–.0028	.0016–.0037	.008 Max

① Measured 1.8 in. down from piston top

TORQUE SPECIFICATIONS
All readings in ft. lbs.

Year	VIN	No. Cylinder Displacement cu. in. (liter)	Cylinder Head Bolts	Main Bearing Bolts	Rod Bearing Bolts	Crankshaft Pulley Bolts	Flywheel Bolts	Manifold		Spark Plugs
								Intake	Exhaust	
1987	R	4-151 (2.5)	①	70	32	162	44	25	44	7-15
	9	6-173 (2.8)	65-90	63-74	34-40	66-84	45-55	20-25	22-28	7-15
1988	R	4-151 (2.5)	①	70	32	162	44	25	44	7-15
	9	6-173 (2.8)	65-90	63-74	34-40	66-84	45-55	22-28	44	7-15

① Stage 1 – 18
Stage 2 – 35 except bolts 9–18
Stage 3 – Torque all bolts 90 degrees

BRAKE SPECIFICATIONS
All measurements in inches unless noted

Year	Model	Lug Nut Torque (ft. lbs.)	Master Cylinder Bore	Brake Rotor		Standard Brake Drum Diameter	Minimum Lining Thickness	
				Minimum Thickness	Maximum Runout		Front	Rear
1987	Fiero	①	1.00	③	0.005	②	0.062	0.062
1988	Fiero	①	1.00	③	0.003	②	0.062	0.062

① Steel 80; aluminum 100
② Cars equipped with 4 wheel disc brakes

③ Minimum refinish thickness (front) – 0.445
Discard thickness (front) – 0.390
Minimum refinish thickness (rear) – 0.0500
Discard thickness (rear) – 0.450

WHEEL ALIGNMENT

Year	Model	Caster		Camber		Toe-in (in.)	Steering Axis Inclination (deg.)
		Range (deg.)	Preferred Setting (deg.)	Range (deg.)	Preferred Setting (deg.)		
1987	Fiero	3N-7P	5P	$^5/_{16}$N-1$^5/_{16}$P	½P	$^1/_{16}$ ± $^1/_{32}$	NA
1988	Fiero	3N-7P	5P	$^5/_{16}$N-1$^5/_{16}$P	½P	$^1/_{16}$ ± $^1/_{32}$	NA

N Negative
P Positive

ENGINE ELECTRICAL

NOTE: Disconnecting the negative battery cable on some vehicles may interfere with the functions of the on board computer systems and may require the computer to undergo a relearning process, once the negative battery cable is reconnected.

Distributor

REMOVAL & INSTALLATION

Timing Not Disturbed

1. Position the engine at TDC on the compression stroke. Disconnect the negative battery cable.
2. If required, remove the air cleaner assembly. Tag and disconnect all electrical wires.
3. Remove the spark plug wires. Remove the distributor cap.
4. Matchmark the distributor assembly in relation to where the rotor is pointing, to aid in reassembly.
5. Remove the distributor retaining bolt. Carefully remove the distributor from the engine.
6. Installation is the reverse of the removal procedure. Check and adjust the engine timing as required.

Timing Disturbed

If the engine was cranked while the distributor was removed, place the engine on TDC of the compression stroke to obtain proper ignition timing.

1. Remove the No. 1 spark plug.
2. Place a thumb or finger over the spark plug hole. Crank the engine slowly until compression is felt.
3. Align the timing mark on the crankshaft pulley with the 0 degree

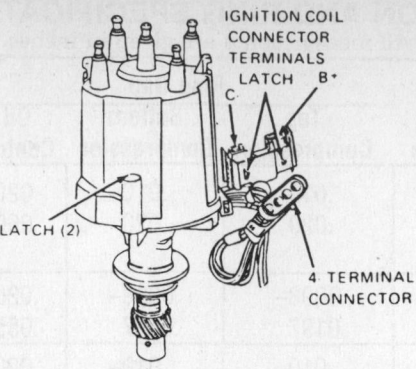

Typical distributor used with a separately mounted coil

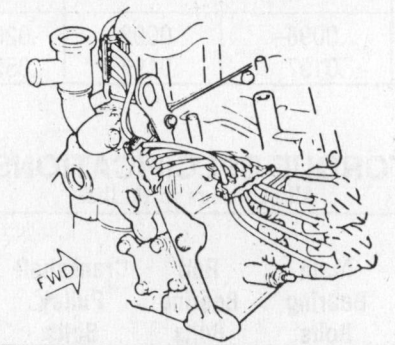

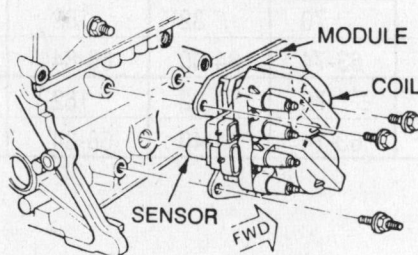

Distributorless ignition assembly—2.5L engine

mark on the timing scale attached to the front of the engine. This places the engine at TDC of the compression stroke.

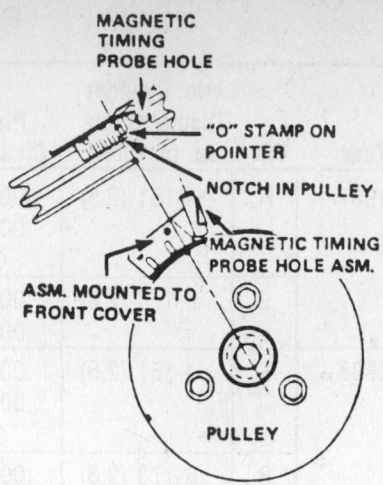

Location of the magnetic timing probe hole

4. Turn the distributor shaft until the rotor points between the No. 1 and No. 3 spark plug towers on the cap for the 2.5L engine. If equipped with the 2.8L engine, turn the distributer shaft until the rotor points between the No. 1 and No. 6 spark plug towers on the cap.
5. Continue the installation in the reverse order of the removal.

Distributorless Ignition

Distributorless ignition systems use a Waste Spark method of spark distribution making the timing non adjustable. Each cylinder is paired with its opposing cylinder in the firing order, so that 1 cylinder on compression fires at the same time with its opposing cylinder on exhaust. The process reverses when the cylinders reverse roles. 1 coil per cylinder is needed, since 1 coil fires 2 cylinders. An ignition module is located under the coil pack and is connected to the Electronic Control Module (ECM), by a 6 pin connector. The ignition module controls the primary circuit to the coils, by turning them on and off. It also controls spark timing below 400 rpm and if the ECM bypass circuit becomes open or grounded.

The magnetic pickup sensor inserts through the engine block, just above the pan rail, in proximity to the crankshaft reluctor ring. Notches in the crankshaft reluctor ring trigger the magnetic pickup sensor to provide timing information to the ECM. The magnetic pickup sensor provides a cam signal to identify correct firing sequence and crank signal to trigger each coil at the proper time.

This system uses EST and control wires from the ECM, as with distributor systems. The ECM controls timing using crankshaft position, engine rpm, engine temperature and manifold absolute pressure, (MAP), sensing.

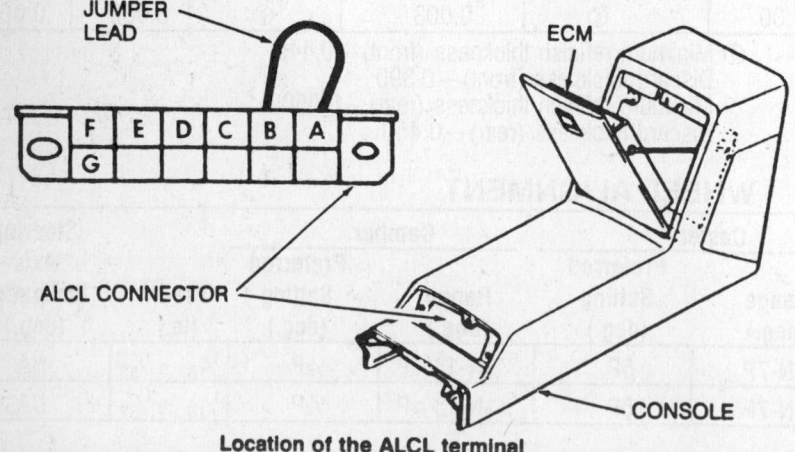

Location of the ALCL terminal

Ignition Timing

ADJUSTMENT

Except Distributorless Ignition

NOTE: If these timing procedures differ from the information found on the vehicle identification label, use the data on the vehicle information label.

1. Connect a timing light according to the manufacturer's instructions.
2. Follow the instructions on the underhood engine decal.
3. The **ALCL** terminal must be grounded before the ignition timing can be properly checked. The **ALCL** terminal is located in the front lower section of the console. Connect terminals **A** and **B** with a jumper wire. The engine is now in the bypass mode, thus enabling the engine timing to be checked. Do not disconnect the 4 wire connector at the distributor.
4. Start the engine and run it at idle speed.
5. Aim the timing light at the degree scale just over the harmonic balancer.
6. Adjust the timing by loosening the securing clamp and rotating the distributor until the desired ignition advance is achieved, then tighten the clamp.
7. Loosen the distributor clamp outer bolt, then slide the clamp back slightly. Do not remove the retaining bolt.
8. Adjust the timing, then replace and tighten the clamp. To advance the timing, rotate the distributor opposite the normal direction of rotor rotation. Retard the timing by rotating the distributor in the normal direction of rotor rotation.

Alternator

For further information on the charging system, please refer to "Charging and Starting" in the Unit Repair section.

PRECAUTIONS

Several precautions must be observed with alternator equipped vehicles to avoid damage to the unit.

● If the battery is removed for any reason, make sure it is reconnected with the correct polarity. Reversing the battery connections may result in damage to the one-way rectifiers.
● When utilizing a booster battery as a starting aid, always connect the positive to positive terminals and the negative terminal from the booster battery to a good engine ground on the vehicle being started.
● Never use a fast charger as a booster to start vehicles.
● Disconnect the battery cables when charging the battery with a fast charger.
● Never attempt to polarize the alternator.
● Do not use test lamps of more than 12 volts when checking diode continuity.
● Do not short across or ground any of the alternator terminals.
● The polarity of the battery, alternator and regulator must be matched and considered before making any electrical connections within the system.
● Never separate the alternator on an open circuit. Make sure all connections within the circuit are clean and tight.
● Disconnect the battery ground terminal when performing any service on electrical components.
● Disconnect the battery if arc welding is to be done on the vehicle.

BELT TENSION ADJUSTMENT

2.5L Engine

A single (serpentine) belt is used to drive all engine mounted components on 1987–88 vehicles. Drive belt tension is maintained by a spring loaded tensioner. The drive belt tensioner can control belt tension over a wide range of belt lengths; however, there are limits to the tensioner's ability to compensate. Using the tensioner outside its operating range can result in poor tension control and/or damage to the tensioner.

2.8L Engine

The drive belt tension is 145 lbs. for a new belt and 70 lbs. for a used belt.

REMOVAL & INSTALLATION

2.5L Engine

1. Disconnect the negative battery cable.
2. Remove the air cleaner, as required.
3. Disconnect the upper strut mount, as required.
4. Disconnect the alternator adjusting bolts and upper adjusting bracket. remove the drive belt.
5. Disconnect the wiring from the back of the alternator.
6. Lower the alternator mounting bracket and remove the alternator from the vehicle.
7. Installation is the reverse of the removal procedure. Adjust the drive belt, as required.

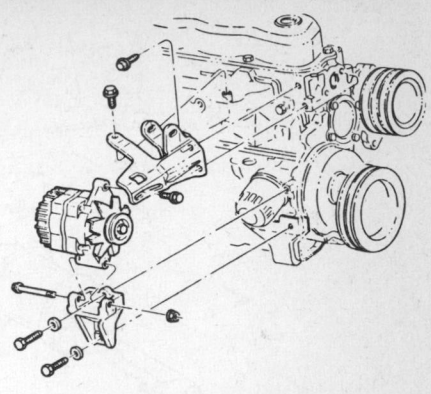

Alternator mounting

2.8L Engine

1. Disconnect the negative battery cable.
2. Loosen the top alternator bracket retaining bolts.
3. Raise and support the vehicle safely. Remove the right rear tire and wheel assembly.
4. Remove the splash guards. Remove the toe link rod outer end and swing it up and to the left.
5. Remove the lower alternator bracket. Remove the alternator adjusting bolt.
6. Remove the drive belt. Disconnect the upper alternator bracket bolt.
7. Disconnect the electrical connections from the alternator.
8. Rotate the alternator bracket lower end toward the engine. Remove the alternator from the vehicle. Remove the alternator shield.
9. Installation is the reverse of the removal procedure. Adjust the drive belt, as required.

Voltage Regulator

For further information on the charging system, please refer to "Charging and Starting" in the Unit Repair section.

ADJUSTMENT

An alternator with an integral voltage regulator is standard equipment. There are no adjustments possible with this unit. The alternator must be disassembled in order to service the regulator.

Starter

For further information on the charging system, please refer to "Charging and Starting" in the Unit Repair section.

REMOVAL & INSTALLATION

1. Disconnect the negative battery cable.

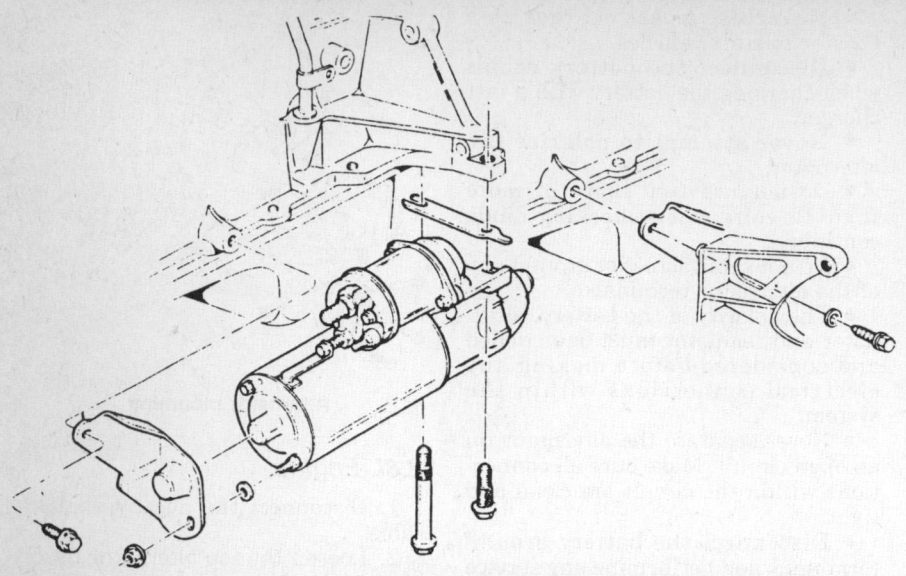

Starter motor mounting

2. Raise and support the vehicle safely.

3. Disconnect all wires at solenoid terminals. Note color coding of wires for reinstallation.

4. Remove the starter support bracket mount bolts, as required. Loosen the front bracket bolt or nut and rotate the bracket clear.

5. Remove the starter retaining bolts. Remove the starter. Note the location of any shims so that they may be replaced in the same positions upon installation.

6. Installation is the reverse of the removal procedure.

CHASSIS ELECTRICAL

Heater Blower Motor

REMOVAL & INSTALLATION

1. Disconnect the negative battery cable.

2. Remove the cooling tube.

3. Disconnect all electrical connections.

4. Remove the heater motor retaining screws. Remove the heater motor from its mounting.

5. Installation is the reverse order of the removal procedure.

Windshield Wiper Motor

REMOVAL & INSTALLATION

1. Disconnect the negative battery cable. Remove the wiper arms and the shroud top vent grille, as necessary.

2. Loosen, but do not remove the transmission drive link to motor crank arm retaining nuts.

3. Detach the drive link from the motor crank arm.

4. Disconnect the electrical leads.

5. Remove the attaching screws and remove the wiper motor.

6. Installation is the reverse of removal. Be sure the wiper motor is in the park position before installing the wiper arms and the shroud top screen.

Delay Wiper Controls

OPERATION

Pulse Position

With the wiper/washer switch in

PULSE voltage is applied to the solid state pulse/speed/wash control through the gray (No. 91) wire. This voltage signals the solid state pulse/speed/wash control to momentarily ground the coil of the park/run relay. With the park/run relay energized, voltage is applied through the contacts of the relay to the wiper motor.

After the wipers have started, the park/run switch supplies battery voltage until the wipers return to park position. The wipers remain parked until the solid state pulse/speed/wash control again grounds the park/run relay coil.

The length of the delay time between strokes is controlled by the variable pulse delay resistor. From the low position, the delay cycles are 18, 10, 6, 3 and 1.25 seconds.

Mist Position

When the control is moved to the mist position and released, the wipers make 1 sweep at low speed and return to the park position. The circuit operation is the same as that of the low speed.

Windshield Wiper Linkage

REMOVAL & INSTALLATION

1. Disconnect the negative battery cable. Remove the wiper arms.

2. Remove the shroud top vent screen.

3. Remove the drive link from the crank arm.

4. Remove the transmission to cowl panel attaching bolts.

5. Remove wiper transmission.

6. Installation is the reverse of the removal procedure.

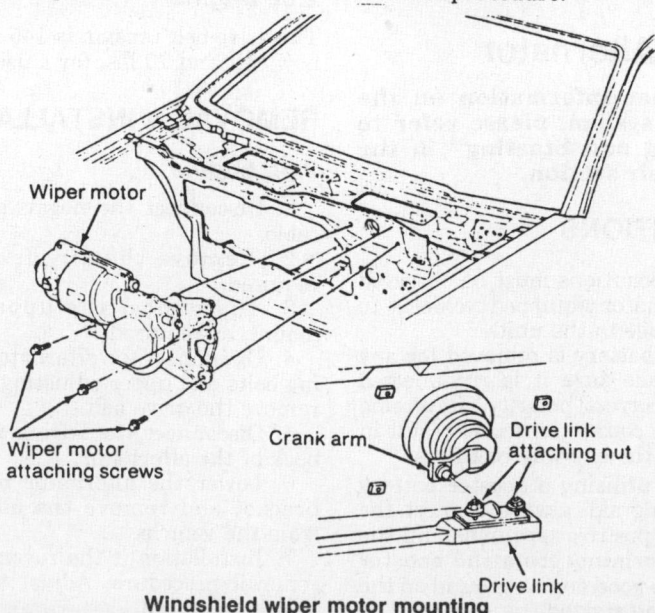

Windshield wiper motor mounting

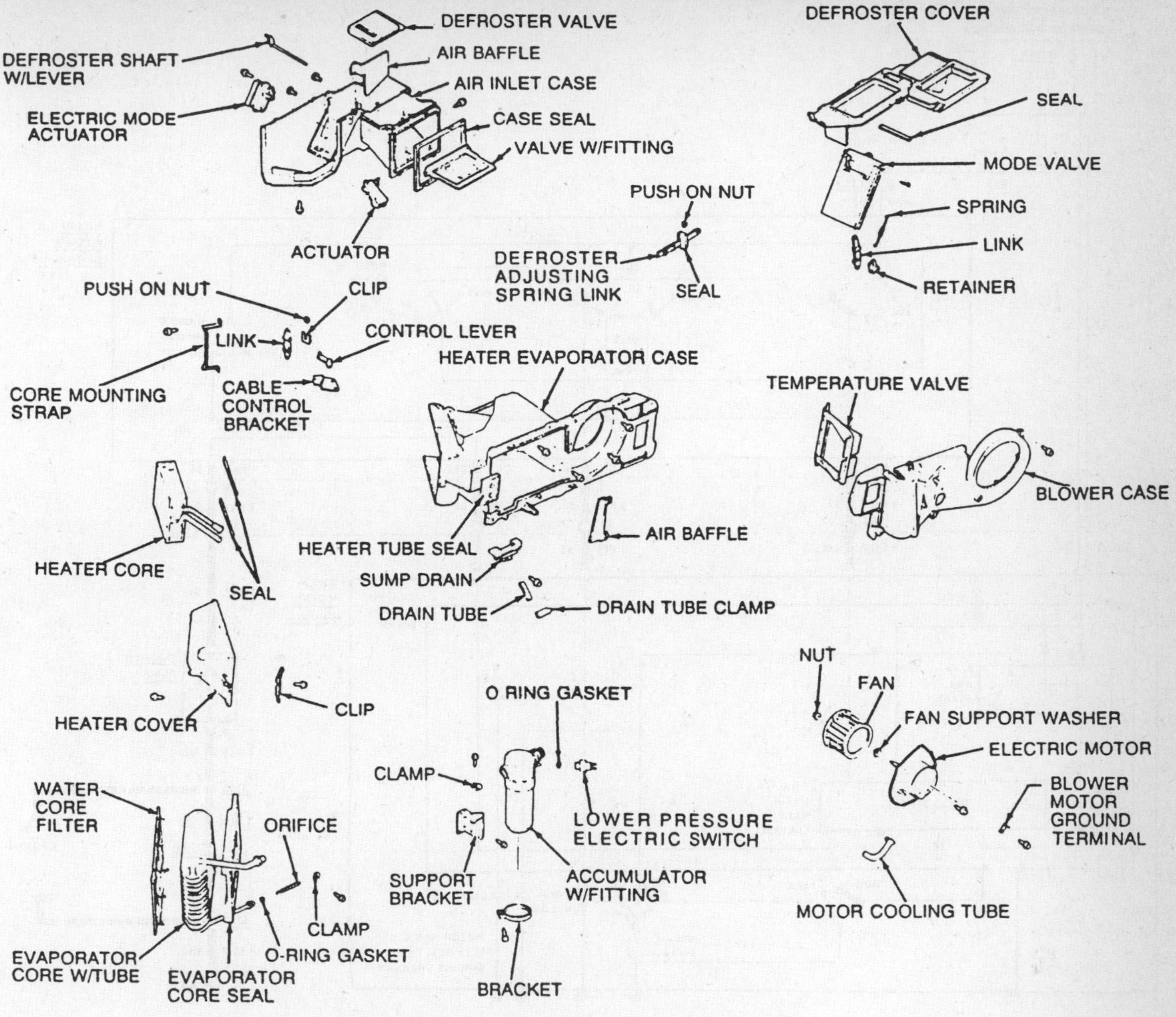

DEFROSTER VALVE

DEFROSTER COVER

DEFROSTER SHAFT W/LEVER

AIR BAFFLE

AIR INLET CASE

SEAL

ELECTRIC MODE ACTUATOR

CASE SEAL

VALVE W/FITTING

MODE VALVE

SPRING

PUSH ON NUT

LINK

ACTUATOR

DEFROSTER ADJUSTING SPRING LINK

SEAL

RETAINER

PUSH ON NUT

CLIP

CONTROL LEVER

LINK

HEATER EVAPORATOR CASE

CORE MOUNTING STRAP

CABLE CONTROL BRACKET

TEMPERATURE VALVE

HEATER CORE

SEAL

AIR BAFFLE

HEATER TUBE SEAL

SUMP DRAIN

BLOWER CASE

DRAIN TUBE

DRAIN TUBE CLAMP

HEATER COVER

CLIP

O RING GASKET

NUT

FAN

FAN SUPPORT WASHER

WATER CORE FILTER

CLAMP

ELECTRIC MOTOR

ORIFICE

LOWER PRESSURE ELECTRIC SWITCH

BLOWER MOTOR GROUND TERMINAL

SUPPORT BRACKET

ACCUMULATOR W/FITTING

CLAMP

EVAPORATOR CORE W/TUBE

EVAPORATOR CORE SEAL

O-RING GASKET

BRACKET

MOTOR COOLING TUBE

Exploded view of the heater/air conditioning case

Windshield Wiper Switch

REMOVAL & INSTALLATION

Instrument Cluster

REMOVAL & INSTALLATION

1. Disconnect the negative battery cable.
2. Remove the rear cluster cover.
3. Remove the front trim plate.
4. Remove the steering column cover.
5. Remove the cluster attaching screws. Disconnect the wiring harness and remove the cluster assembly.

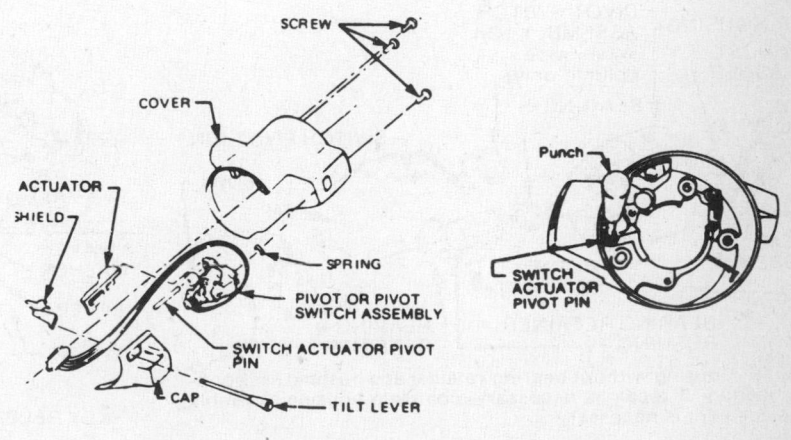

SCREW

COVER

ACTUATOR

SHIELD

SPRING

Punch

PIVOT OR PIVOT SWITCH ASSEMBLY

SWITCH ACTUATOR PIVOT PIN

SWITCH ACTUATOR PIVOT PIN

CAP

TILT LEVER

Wiper switch removal—adjustable columns

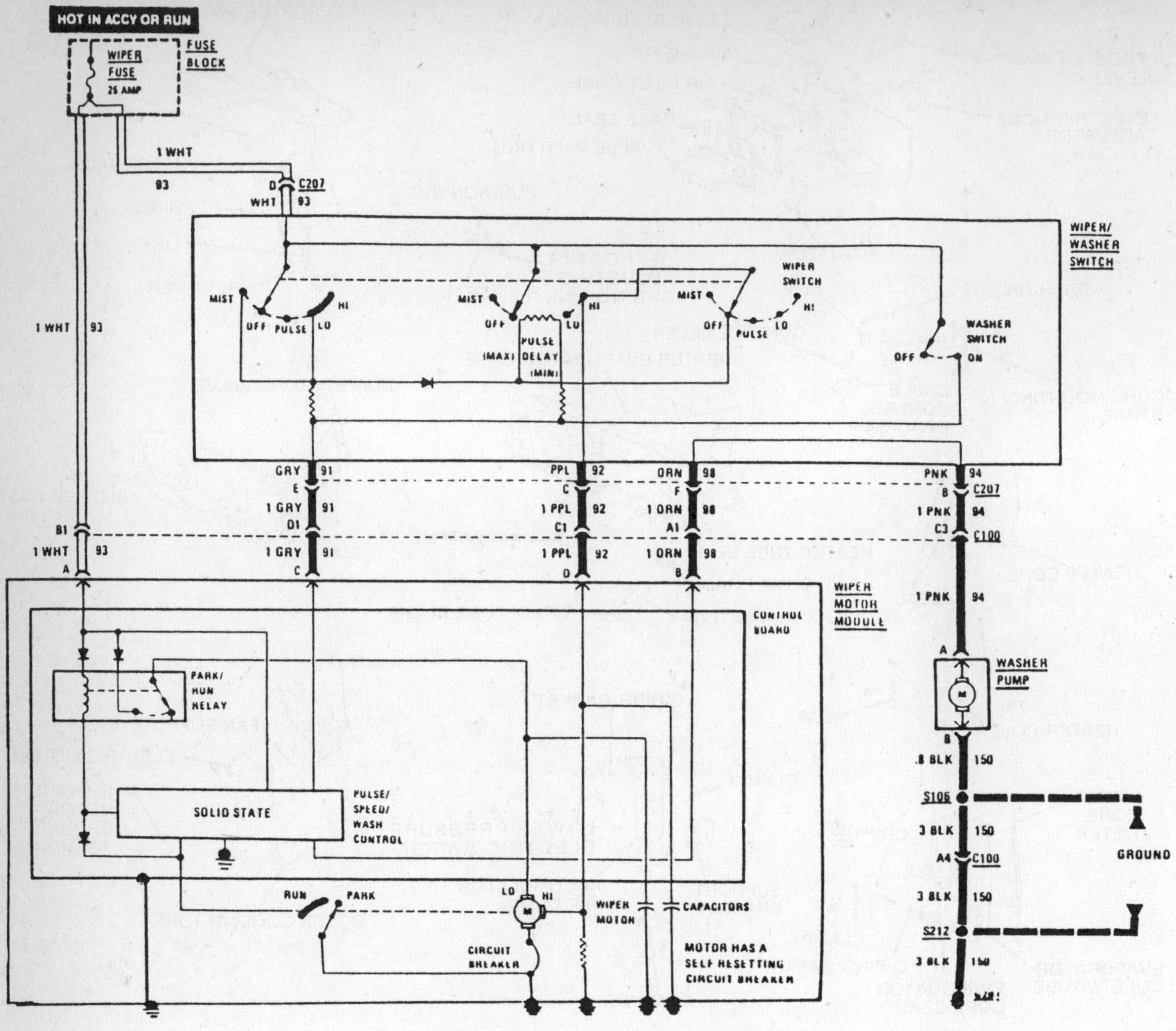

FUSE BLOCK

WIPER FUSE 25 AMP

1 WHT
93

D | C207
WHT | 93

1 WHT | 93

WIPER/WASHER SWITCH

MIST | OFF PULSE | LO | HI

MIST | OFF | PULSE DELAY (MIN) | LO | HI

WIPER SWITCH

MIST | OFF | PULSE | LO | HI!

WASHER SWITCH

OFF | ON

(MAX)

GRY | 91
E
1 GRY | 91
D1
1 WHT | 93
A

PPL | 92
C
1 PPL | 92
C1
1 GRY | 91
C

ORN | 98
F
1 ORN | 98
A1
1 PPL | 92
D

PNK | 94
C207
1 PNK | 94
C100
1 ORN | 98
B

WIPER MOTOR MODULE

CONTROL BOARD

PARK/RUN RELAY

SOLID STATE

PULSE/SPEED/WASH CONTROL

RUN | PARK

LO | M | HI
WIPER MOTOR

CAPACITORS

CIRCUIT BREAKER

MOTOR HAS A SELF RESETTING CIRCUIT BREAKER

1 PNK | 94

A
WASHER PUMP
M
B

.8 BLK | 150

S106

3 BLK | 150

A4 | C100

3 BLK | 150

S212

3 BLK | 150

GROUND

Windshield wiper system schematic

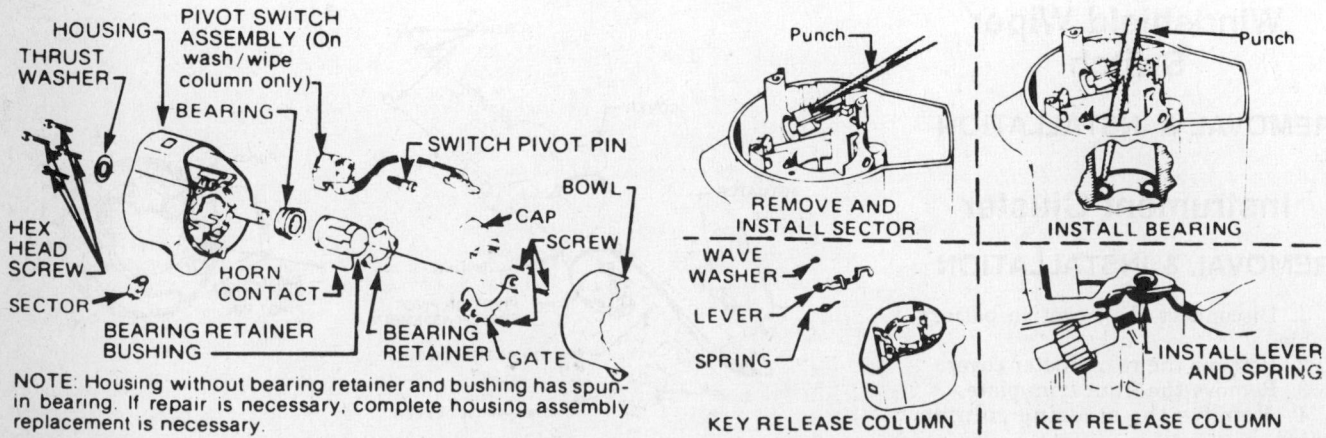

HOUSING THRUST WASHER

HOUSING

PIVOT SWITCH ASSEMBLY (On wash/wipe column only)

BEARING

SWITCH PIVOT PIN

BOWL

CAP

SCREW

GATE

HEX HEAD SCREW

SECTOR

HORN CONTACT

BEARING RETAINER BUSHING

BEARING RETAINER

NOTE: Housing without bearing retainer and bushing has spun-in bearing. If repair is necessary, complete housing assembly replacement is necessary.

Punch

REMOVE AND INSTALL SECTOR

WAVE WASHER

LEVER

SPRING

KEY RELEASE COLUMN

Punch

INSTALL BEARING

INSTALL LEVER AND SPRING

KEY RELEASE COLUMN

Wiper switch removal—standard columns

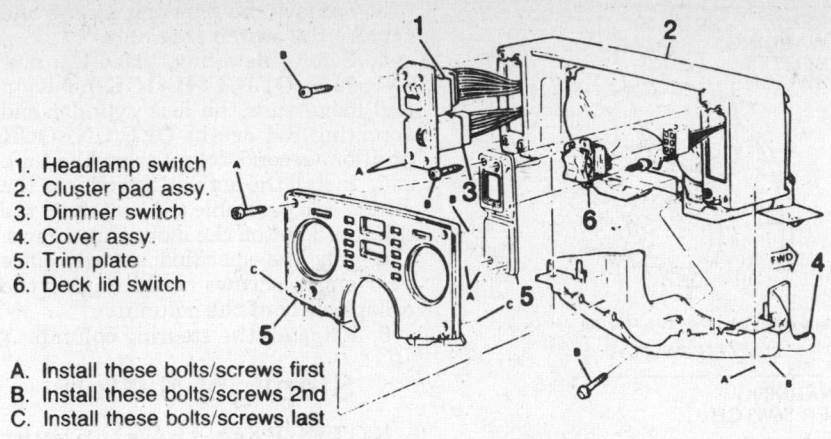

1. Headlamp switch
2. Cluster pad assy.
3. Dimmer switch
4. Cover assy.
5. Trim plate
6. Deck lid switch

A. Install these bolts/screws first
B. Install these bolts/screws 2nd
C. Install these bolts/screws last

Instrument cluster trim plates

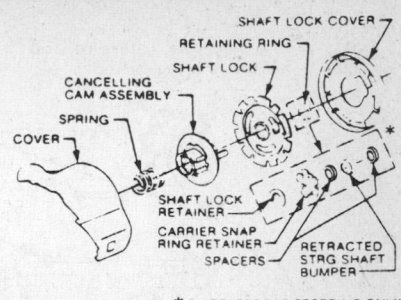

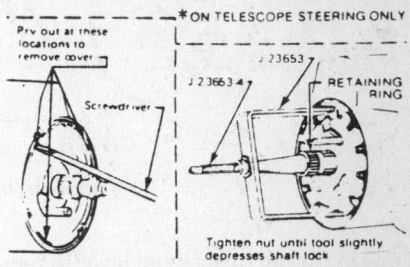

These parts must be removed to remove the turn signal switch

6. The speedometer, tachometer and gauges may be serviced by removing the front cluster lens.

7. Installation is the reverse of the removal procedure.

Speedometer Cable

REMOVAL & INSTALLATION

1. Disconnect the negative battery cable.
2. Remove the instrument cluster retaining screws.
3. Pull the cluster outwards and disengage the cable.
4. Pull the core from the cable. If the core is frayed or broken on the transaxle end, raise and support the vehicle safely. Disconnect the cable from the transaxle. Make sure that the entire cable has been removed.
5. Installation is the reverse order of the removal procedure.

Radio

REMOVAL & INSTALLATION

1. Disconnect the negative battery cable. Remove the console trim plate assembly.
2. Disconnect the side retaining nuts and the rear retaining bolt.
3. Disconnect the electrical and the antenna connections.
4. Remove the radio from its mounting.
5. Installation is the reverse of removal.

Concealed Headlights

MANUAL OPERATION

In the event of system failure, the

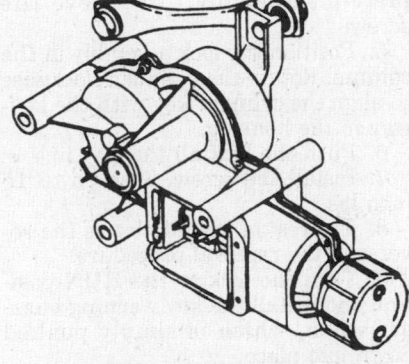

Headlight motor assembly

headlights may be raised or lowered manually.

1. Locate the headlight door motors in each headlight assembly under the front compartment.
2. Rotate the knob on each headlight door motor in the direction of the arrow until each headlight door fully open.

Headlight Switch

REMOVAL & INSTALLATION

1. Disconnect the negative battery cable.
2. Remove the headlight/dimmer switch trim plate screws.
3. Disconnect the electrical connector and remove the switch assembly.
4. Installation is the reverse order of the removal procedure.

Combination Switch

REMOVAL & INSTALLATION

1. Disconnect the negative battery cable. Remove the steering wheel.
2. Remove the trim cover from the steering column.

3. Position a U-shaped lockplate compressing tool on the end of the steering shaft and compress the lock plate by turning the shaft nut clockwise. Pry the wire snapring out of the shaft groove.
4. Remove the tool and lift the lockplate off the shaft.
5. Slip the canceling cam, upper bearing preload spring and thrust washer off the shaft.
6. Remove the turn signal lever. Remove the hazard flasher button retaining screw and remove the button, spring and knob.
7. Pull the switch connector out of the mast jacket and tape the upper part to facilitate switch removal. Attach a long piece of wire to the turn signal switch, feed this wire through the column first and then use this wire to pull the switch connector into position. On vehicles equipped with tilt wheel, place the turn signal and shifter housing in low position and remove the harness cover.
8. Remove the 3 switch mounting screws. Remove the switch by pulling it straight up while guiding the wiring harness cover through the column.
9. Install the replacement switch by working the connector and cover down through the housing and under the bracket. On vehicles equipped with tilt wheel, the connector is worked down through the housing, under the bracket and then the cover in installed on the harness.
10. Install the switch mounting screws and the connector on the mast jacket bracket. Install the column to dash trim plate.
11. Install the flasher knob and the turn signal lever.

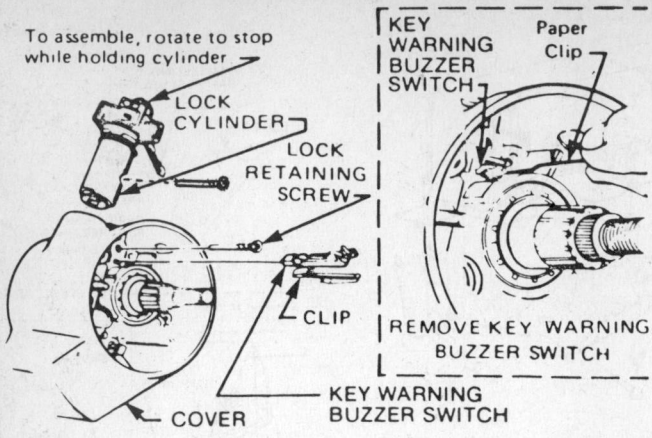

Ignition lock cylinder removal

12. With the turn signal lever in neutral and the flasher knob out, slide the thrust washer, upper bearing preload spring and canceling cam onto the shaft.

13. Position the lock plate on the shaft and press it down until a new snapring can be inserted in the shaft groove. Always use a new snapring when assembling.

14. Install the cover and the steering wheel.

Ignition Lock

REMOVAL & INSTALLATION

1. Disconnect the negative battery cable. Remove the steering wheel.

2. Turn the lock to the **RUN** position.

3. Remove the lock plate, turn signal switch or combination switch and the key warning buzzer switch. The warning buzzer switch can be fished out using a suitable tool.

4. Remove the lock cylinder retaining screw and lock cylinder. If the screw is dropped on removal, it could fall into the column, requiring complete disassembly to retrieve the screw.

5. Position the lock assembly in the column. Rotate the cylinder clockwise to align the cylinder key with the keyway in the housing.

6. Push the lock all the way in.

7. Install the screw. Tighten to 15 inch lbs.

8. The rest of installation is the reverse of the removal procedure.

9. Turn the lock to the **RUN** position and install the key warning buzzer switch, which is simply pushed down into place.

Ignition Switch

REMOVAL & INSTALLATION

1. Disconnect the negative battery cable. Lower the steering column and support it properly.

2. Put the switch in the **OFF/UN-LOCK** position. With the cylinder removed, the rod is in an **OFF/UN-LOCK** position when it is in the next to the uppermost detent.

3. Remove the 2 switch screws and remove the switch assembly.

4. Before installing, place the new switch in **OFF/UNLOCK** position and make sure the lock cylinder and actuating rod are in **OFF/UNLOCK** position (second detent from the top).

5. Install the activating rod into the switch and assemble the switch on the column. Tighten the mounting screws. Use only the specified screws, since overlength screws could impair the collapsibility of the column.

6. Reinstall the steering column.

Stoplight Switch

NOTE: Both the stoplight switch and the speed control switch are mounted on the brake pedal support bracket, the stoplight switch is located directly above the speed control switch.

ADJUSTMENT

1. With the brake pedal depressed, insert the switch into the retainer until the switch body seats on the retainer.

2. Note that audible clicks can be heard as the threaded portion of the switch is pushed through the retainer toward the brake pedal.

3. Pull the brake pedal fully rearward against the pedal stop until the audible click sound can no longer be heard. The switch will be moved in the retainer providing the correct adjustment.

4. Release the the brake pedal and repeat Step 3 to assure that no audible click sounds remain.

REMOVAL & INSTALLATION

1. Disconnect the negative battery cable. Disconnect the wiring harness from the switch which is located under the instrument panel at the brake pedal support.

2. Remove the retaining nut from the switch and remove the switch from the bracket.

3. Installation is the reverse order of the removal procedure.

Clutch Switch

REMOVAL & INSTALLATION

1. Disconnect the negative battery cable. Disconnect the electrical connector at the clutch switch, which is located at the top of the clutch pedal.

2. Remove the bolt attaching the switch to the clutch bracket.

3. Rotate the clutch switch slightly to disconnect the shaft from the clutch pedal hole.

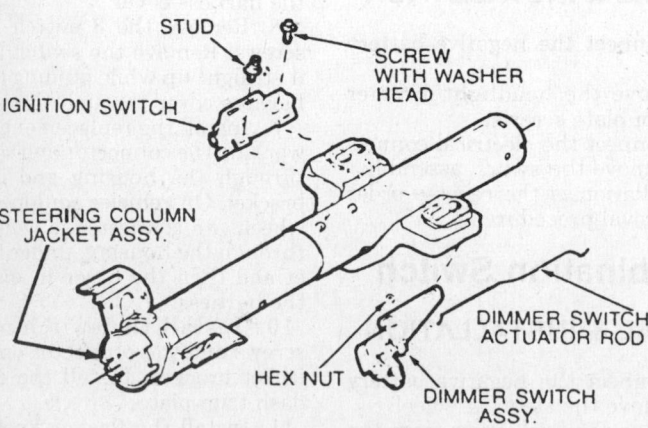

Ignition and dimmer switch removal

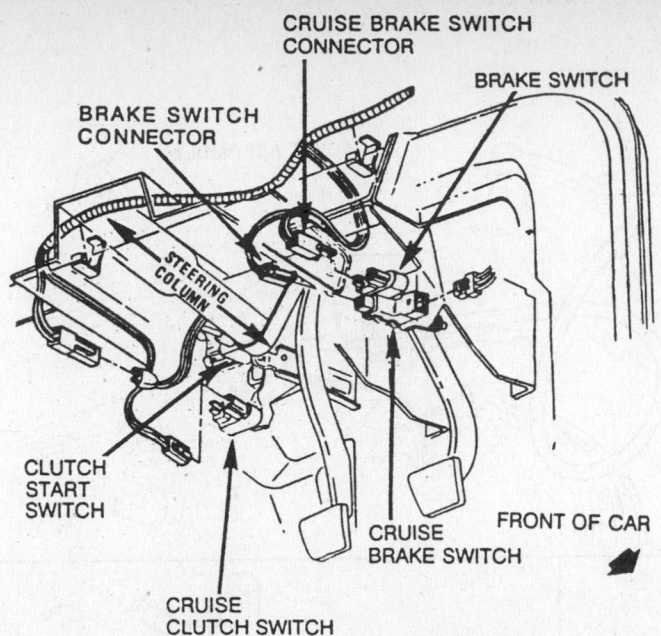

Stoplight and clutch switch location

4. Installation is the reverse order of the removal procedure.

Neutral Safety Switch

This vehicle is equipped with a mechanical neutral start system. This system relies on a mechanical block, rather than the starter safety switch to prevent starting the engine in any gear except **P** or **N.** This unit is mounted on top of the steering column and has a manual actuated cable leading from the shifter to the column. When the shifter is in the **P** or **N** position the cable positions a locking pin against a cam in relationship to the ignition switch, thus preventing the ignition from moving to the start position.

Fuses, Circuit Breakers and Relays

LOCATIONS

Fusible Link

Added protection is provided in all bat-tery feed circuits and other selected circuits by a fusible link. This link is a short piece of copper wire approximately 4 in. long inserted in series with the circuit and acts as a fuse. The link is 2 or more gauges smaller in size than the circuit wire it is protecting and will burn out without damage to the circuit in case of current overload.

1. Fuse block – Behind the left side of instrument panel.
2. Fusible link B – right front of engine compartment at battery junction block.
3. Fusible link C – In front lights harness, right of master cylinder.
4. Fusible link D – In front lights harness, right of master cylinder.

Fuse Panel

The fuse panel is a swing down unit located in the underside of the instrument panel, left of the steering column. The fuse panel uses miniaturized fuses, designed for increased circuit protection and greater reliability. Various convenience connectors, which snap into the fuse panel, add to the serviceability of this unit.

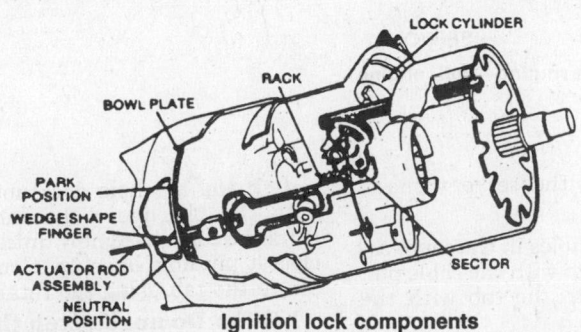

Ignition lock components

Computer

LOCATION

The electronic control module (ECM) is located between the seats and is mounted to the rear bulkhead. Access to the computer can be gained by removing the console. The computer is not a serviceable part and can only be replaced if diagnosed to be faulty.

Turn Signal/Hazard Flasher

LOCATION

The turn signal and hazard flasher is located on the left side of the steering column bracket

Convenience Center

LOCATION

The convenience center is a stationary unit. It is located on the right side of the heater or air conditioning module in the vehicle under the instrument panel. This location provides easy access to the audio alarm, hazard warnings, the horn relay and the seatbelt key and headlamp warning alarm. All units are serviced by plug-in replacements.

Speed Control

SERVO CABLE

Adjustment

2.5L ENGINE

1. Be sure that the cruise control cable is attached to the engine bracket. Insert the cable snug in the cruise pulley slot.
2. Insert the cable in the servo bracket. Pull the servo assembly end of the cable toward the servo without moving the idler pulley.
3. If 1 of the 6 holes in the servo assembly lines up with the cable pin, push the pin through the hole and connect the pin to the tab with the retainer.
4. If the tab hole does not line up with the pin, move the cable away from the servo assembly until the next closest tab hole lines up. Connect the pin to the tab using the retainer.

NOTE: Do not stretch the cable so as to make a particular tab hole connect to the pin. This could prevent the engine from returning to idle.

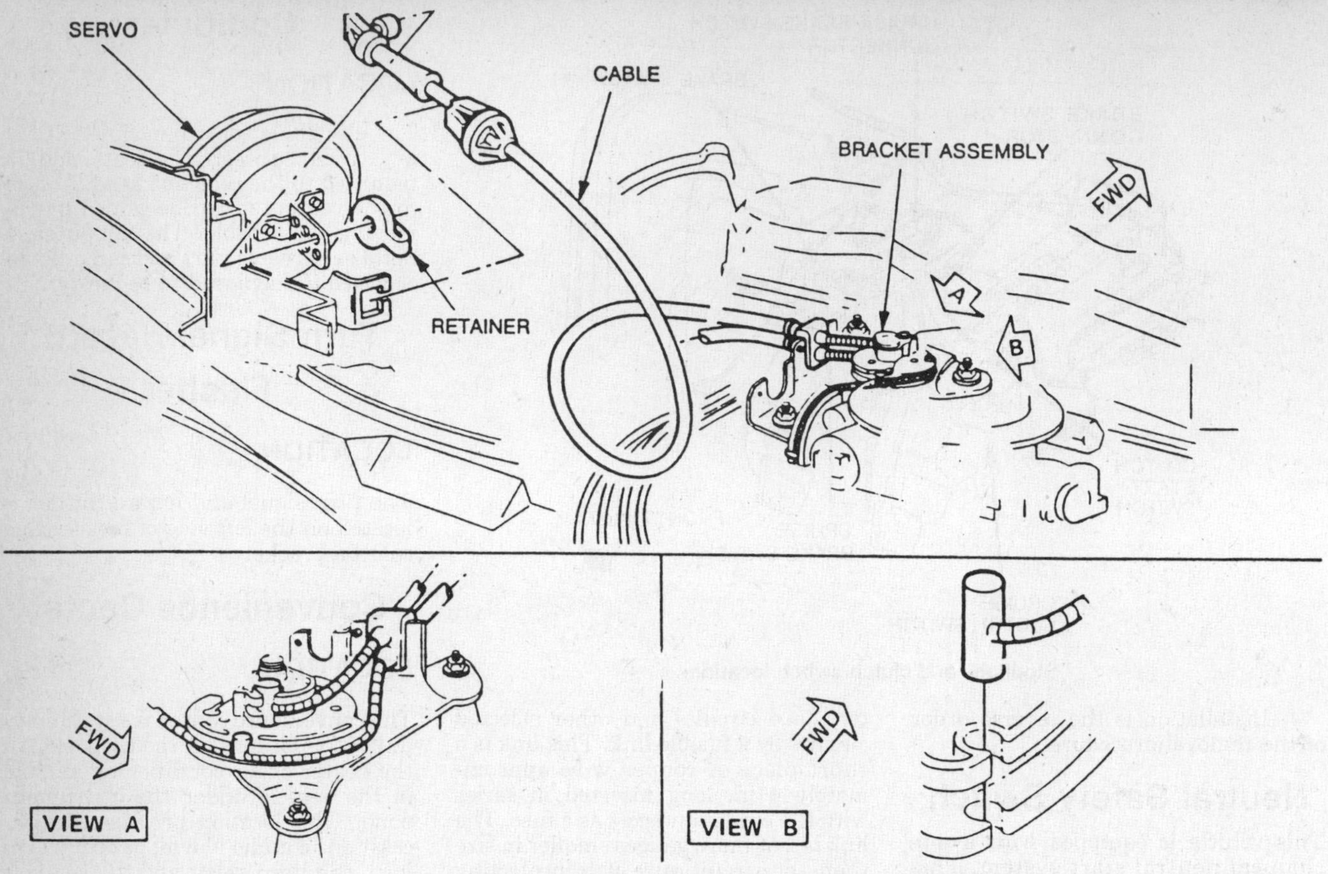

19 GM—PONTIAC FIERO

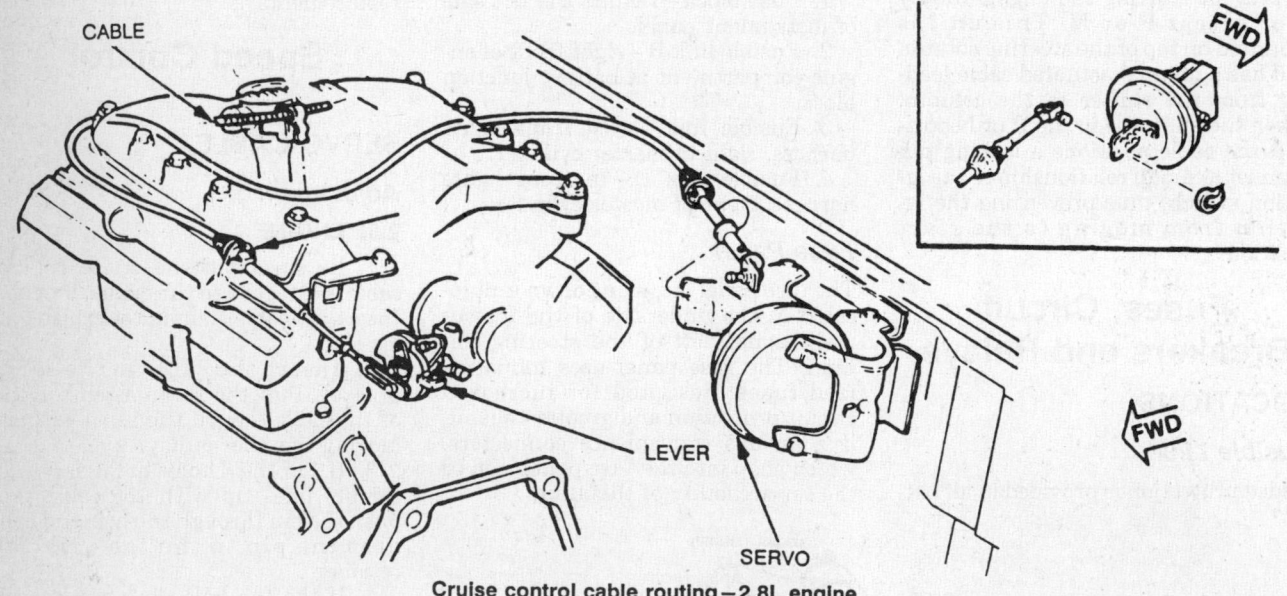

SERVO

CABLE

BRACKET ASSEMBLY

FWD

RETAINER

A

B

FWD

VIEW A

VIEW B

FWD

Cruise control cable routing—2.5L engine

CABLE

FWD

LEVER

SERVO

FWD

Cruise control cable routing—2.8L engine

2.8L ENGINE

1. With the cable assembly installed in the bracket, install the cable assembly end on to the stud of the accelerator control lever.

2. Pull the servo assembly end of the cable toward the servo without moving the lever.

3. If 1 of the 6 holes in the servo assembly tab lines up with the cable pin, connect the pin to the tab with the retainer.

4. If the tab hole does not line up with the pin, move the cable away from the servo assembly until the next closest tab hole lines up. Connect the pin to the tab using the retainer.

NOTE: Do not stretch the cable

19-14

SYSTEM CHECK TABLE

	Action	Correct Result
1	Drive car faster than 25 mph. Turn Cruise switch ON. Depress Set button at the end of the Multi-function lever	Car should maintain speed
2	Hold Set button in and take foot off accelerator	Car should coast to slower speed
3	Release Set Button	Cruise Control should engage and hold a slower speed, if the new speed remains above 25 mph
4	Slide Cruise switch to R/A and hold it there	Car should accelerate
5	Release Cruise switch back to ON	Car should hold new faster speed
6	Tap brake pedal	Car should coast slower (Cruise disengages)
7	Slide Cruise switch momentarily to R/A	Car should accelerate to former Set speed
8	While cruising, accelerate, then remove foot from accelerator	Car should coast back to set speed
9	While cruising, tap Cruise switch to R/A	Car should increase 1 mph for each tap, up to ten taps, then system may have to be reset to a new speed
10	While cruising, tap Set button	Car should decrease by 1 mph for each tap, until 25 mph is reached when Cruise Control will not operate
11	Slide Cruise switch to OFF	Cruise Control turns off

so as to make a particular tab hole connect to the pin. This could prevent the engine from returning to idle.

ENGINE COOLING

Radiator

REMOVAL & INSTALLATION

1. Disconnect the negative battery cable. Drain the engine coolant.
2. Disconnect the wiring harness from the fan and fan frame.
3. Remove the fan and frame assembly.
4. Disconnect the upper radiator support bracket.
5. Disconnect the coolant hoses at the radiator.
6. Disconnect the transaxle/engine oil cooler lines at the radiator.
7. Remove the radiator retaining bolts. Remove the radiator from the vehicle.
8. Installation is the reverse of removal. After installation run the engine and check for leaks.

Electric Cooling Fan

SYSTEM OPERATION

The fan motor is activated by a coolant temperature fan switch. If the vehicle is equipped with air conditioning, a second switch can activate the circuit, depending upon air conditioning compressor head pressure to the condenser. The coolant temperature fan switch regulates voltage to the coolant fan relay, which operates the fan whenever the coolant temperature exceeds 230°F (110°C).

REMOVAL & INSTALLATION

1. Disconnect the negative battery cable.
2. Disconnect the harness from the fan motor and the fan frame.
3. Remove the fan frame to radiator support attaching bolts.
4. Remove the fan and frame assembly.
5. Installation is the reverse order of the removal procedure.

TESTING

1. With the engine cold and idling, move the A/C Function selector to the **NORM** position. The coolant fan and engine blower will turn on.
2. With the engine coolant below operating temperature, move the A/C function selector to the **OFF** position. The coolant fan and engine blower will turn off.
3. With the engine warm, run the engine at a fast idle for several minutes. The coolant fan and the engine blower will turn on before the coolant temperature indicator on the instrument panel comes on.

Heater Core

REMOVAL & INSTALLATION

With Air Conditioning

1. Disconnect the negative battery cable. Drain the cooling system. Disconnect and plug the heater hoses at the heater.
2. Remove the speaker grille and the speaker.
3. Remove the heater core cover retainers and the heater core.
4. Installation is the reverse order of the removal procedure.
5. Refill the cooling system as required.

Without Air Conditioning

1. Disconnect the negative battery cable.
2. Disconnect the following wire connections, heater relay, heater blower resistor, heater blower switch, heater ground connection and forward courtesy lamp socket.

3. Remove the windshield washer fluid container.

4. Drain the radiator. Disconnect the heater core inlet and outlet hoses.

5. Remove the heater core grommets.

6. Remove the heater case cover.

7. Remove the heater core retainer and remove the heater core.

8. Installation is the reverse order of the removal procedure.

9. Refill the cooling system as required.

Water Pump

REMOVAL & INSTALLATION

2.5L Engine

1. Disconnect battery negative cable. Drain the engine coolant.

2. Remove accessory drive belts. Remove all components in order to gain access to the water pump retaining bolts.

3. Remove the water pump attaching bolts and remove the pump.

4. If installing a new water pump, transfer the pulley from the old unit. With sealing surfaces cleaned, place a ⅛ in. bead of RTV gasket sealant or an equivalent, on the water pump sealing surface. While sealer is still wet, install pump and torque bolts to 6 ft. lbs. Be

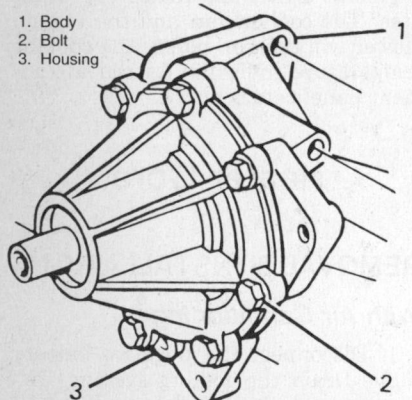

1. Body
2. Bolt
3. Housing

Water pump mounting-four cylinder engine

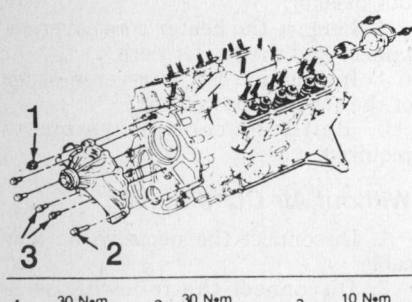

1— 30 N•m (22 FT-LBS)	2— 30 N•m (22 FT-LBS)	3— 10 N•m (7 FT-LBS)

Water pump bolt torques for the V6 engine

sure to coat the bolts with RTV sealant in order to prevent coolant leakage.

5. Install accessory drive belts.

6. Connect battery negative cable.

2.8L Engine

1. Disconnect the negative battery cable. Drain the engine coolant.

2. Remove the fan shroud and the drive belts. Remove all the necessary components in order to gain access to the water pump retaining bolts.

3. Remove the radiator hoses and the heater hose running to the water pump.

4. Remove the bolts attaching the water pump to the engine block and remove the water pump and gasket.

5. Installation is the reverse order of the removal procedure, be sure to apply a thin bead of RTV sealant or an equivalent, to the water pump mounting surface and the water pump bolts. Torque the bolts to 6–9 ft. lbs. Do not over torque the water pump bolts, because the pump is aluminum and will crack very easily.

Thermostat

REMOVAL & INSTALLATION

1. Disconnect the negative battery cable. As required, drain the coolant. Remove the thermostat cap.

2. Grasp the thermostat handle and gently pull up.

3. Before installing, clean the thermostat housing and O-ring. Apply a suitable lubricant to the O-ring for easier installation.

4. Push the thermostat down into the housing until it is properly seated and install the cap.

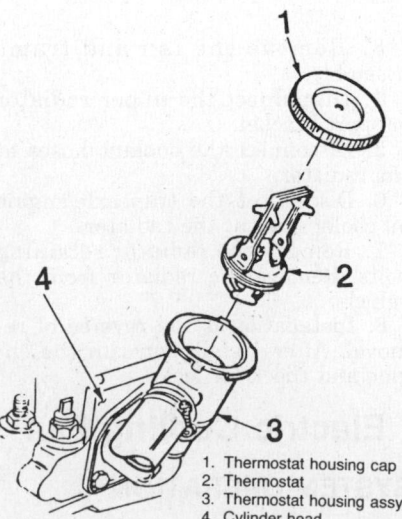

1. Thermostat housing cap
2. Thermostat
3. Thermostat housing assy
4. Cylinder head

Thermostat and housing

FUEL SYSTEM

Fuel System Service Precautions

Safety is the most important factor when performing not only fuel system maintenance but any type of maintenance. Failure to conduct maintenance and repairs in a safe manner may result in serious personal injury or death. Maintenance and testing of the vehicle's fuel system components can be accomplished safely and effectively by adhering to the following rules and guidelines.

• To avoid the possibility of fire and personal injury, always disconnect the negative battery cable unless the repair or test procedure requires that battery voltage be applied.

• Always relieve the fuel system pressure prior to disconnecting any fuel system component (injector, fuel rail, pressure regulator, etc.), fitting or fuel line connection. Exercise extreme caution whenever relieving fuel system pressure to avoid exposing skin, face and eyes to fuel spray. Please be advised that fuel under pressure may penetrate the skin or any part of the body that it contacts.

• Always place a shop towel or cloth around the fitting or connection prior to loosening to absorb any excess fuel due to spillage. Ensure that all fuel spillage (should it occur) is quickly removed from engine surfaces. Ensure that all fuel soaked cloths or towels are deposited into a suitable waste container.

• Always keep a dry chemical (Class B) fire extinguisher near the work area.

• Do not allow fuel spray or fuel vapors to come into contact with a spark or open flame.

• Always use a backup wrench when loosening and tightening fuel line connection fittings. This will prevent unnecessary stress and torsion to fuel line piping. Always follow the proper torque specifications.

• Always replace worn fuel fitting O-rings with new. Do not substitute fuel hose or equivalent where fuel pipe is installed.

RELIEVING FUEL SYSTEM PRESSURE

2.5L Engine

1. Be sure that the engine is cold. Remove the fuel pump fuse from the fuse panel.

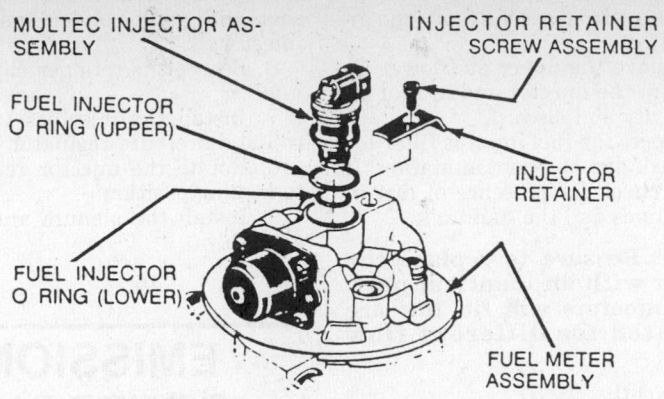

Throttle body injection system—2.5L engine

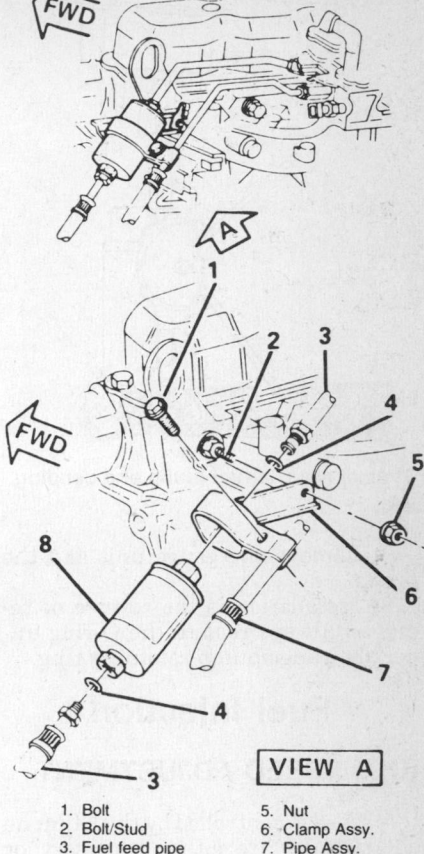

1. Bolt
2. Bolt/Stud
3. Fuel feed pipe
4. "O-ring
5. Nut
6. Clamp Assy.
7. Pipe Assy.
8. Filter Assy.

Fuel filter

2. Start the engine and let it run until all fuel in the line is used.

3. Crank the starter an additional 3 seconds to relieve any residual pressure.

4. With the ignition **OFF**, replace the fuse.

5. Disconnect the negative battery cable. Disable the fuel pump by disconnecting the electrical connectors at the pump.

2.8L Engine

1. Be sure that the engine is cold. Connect the fuel gauge J-34730-1 or equivalent to the fuel pressure valve, located on the fuel rail.

2. Wrap a shop towel around the fitting while connecting the gauge to avoid any spillage.

3. Install the bleed hose into a suitable container and open the valve to bleed off the fuel pressure.

4. Disconnect the negative battery cable. Disable the fuel pump by disconnecting the electrical connectors at the pump.

Fuel Filter

REMOVAL & INSTALLATION

1. Properly relieve the fuel system pressure. Disconnect the negative battery cable.

2. Disconnect the inlet and outlet hoses from the fuel filter.

3. Remove the filter retaining clamps, as required.

4. Remove the filter from the engine.

5. Installation is the reverse of the removal procedure.

Electric Fuel Pump

PRESSURE TESTING

1. Properly relieve the fuel system pressure.

2. Remove the air cleaner and plug the thermal vacuum port on the throttle body assembly.

3. Remove the steel pipe between

the throttle body and the fuel filter. Install a fuel pressure gauge between the throttle body and the fuel filter.

4. Start the vehicle. Record the fuel pressure, it should be within specification.

5. If not within specification, repair or replace defective components, as required.

6. Before removing the test equipment, relieve the fuel system pressure.

REMOVAL & INSTALLATION

1. Relieve the fuel system pressure. Disconnect the negative battery cable.

2. Drain the fuel tank. Raise and support the vehicle safely.

3. Disconnect the wiring from the tank.

4. Remove the ground wire retaining screw from under the body.

5. Disconnect all hoses from the tank.

6. Properly support the tank and remove the retaining strap nuts.

7. Remove the fuel tank from the vehicle.

8. Remove the fuel gauge/pump retaining ring using spanner wrench tool J-24187 or equivalent.

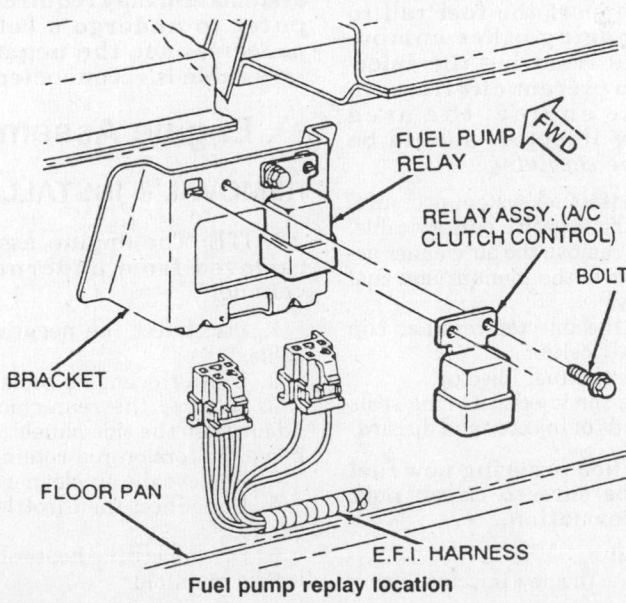

Fuel pump replay location

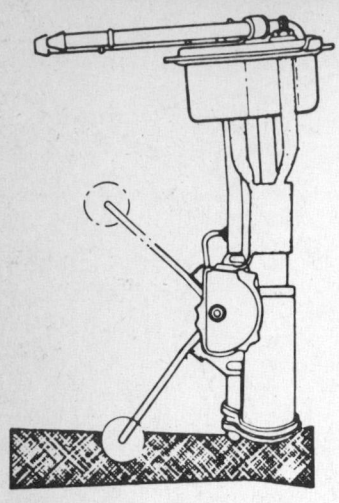

Typical electric fuel pump and sending unit

9. Remove the gauge unit and the pump.

10. Installation is the reverse of removal. Always replace the O-ring under the gauge/pump retaining ring.

Fuel Injection

IDLE SPEED ADJUSTMENT

Idle speed is controlled by the ECM; no adjustments are either necessary or possible.

IDLE MIXTURE ADJUSTMENT

Idle mixture is controlled by the ECM; no adjustments are either necessary or possible.

Fuel Injector

REMOVAL & INSTALLATION

2.5L Engine

NOTE: Use care in removing the injector in order to prevent damage to the electrical connector on top of the injector and nozzle. Also, because the fuel injector is an electrical component, it should not be immersed in any type of liquid solvent or cleaner, as damage may occur. The fuel injector is serviced only as a complete assembly.

1. Relieve the fuel system pressure. Disconnect the negative battery cable. Remove the air cleaner assembly.

2. Disconnect the electrical connector to the fuel injector. Remove the injector retainer screw and the retainer.

3. Using a fulcrum, place a flat blade tool under the ridge opposite the connector end and carefully pry the injector out.

4. Remove the upper and lower O-rings from the injector and in fuel injector cavity and discard.

5. Inspect the fuel injector filter for evidence of dirt and contamination. If present, check for presence of dirt in the fuel lines and the fuel tank.

NOTE: Be sure to replace the injector with an identical part. Other injectors will fit, but are calibrated for different flow rates.

To Install:

6. Lubricate the new upper and lower O-rings with automatic transmission fluid and place them on injector. (Make sure the upper O-ring is in the groove and the lower 1 is flush up against filter.)

7. Install the injector assembly, pushing it straight into fuel injector cavity.

8. Install the injector retainer and attaching screw, using an appropriate thread locking compound.

9. Reconnect the electrical connector to the fuel injector. Torque the injector retainer attaching screw to 27 inch lbs.

10. Be sure the electrical connector end on the injector is facing in the general direction of the cut-out in the fuel meter body to accommodate the wire grommet.

2.8L Engine

NOTE: Use care in removing the injectors to prevent damage to the electrical connector pins on the injector and the nozzle. The fuel injector is serviced as a complete assembly. Since it is an electrical component, it should not be immersed in any type of cleaner. Support the fuel rail to avoid damaging other components while removing the injector. Also, to prevent dirt from entering the engine, the area around the injectors should be clean before servicing.

1. Relieve the fuel system pressure. Disconnect the negative battery cable. As required, remove the air cleaner assembly. Remove the plenum and fuel rail assembly.

2. Rotate the injector retainer clip to the release position.

3. Remove the fuel injector.

4. Remove the injector O-ring seals from both ends of injector and discard.

NOTE: When ordering new fuel injectors, be sure to check part number information.

To Install:

5. Lubricate the new injector O-ring seals with engine oil and install on the injector.

6. Secure the retainer clip onto the injector.

7. Install the injectors to the fuel rail and pressure regulator assembly.

8. Rotate the injector retainer clip to locking position.

9. Install the plenum and fuel rail assembly.

EMISSION CONTROLS

Please refer to "Emission Control" in the Unit Repair section for system maintenance procedures. Due to the complex nature of modern electronic engine control systems, comprehensive diagnosis and testing procedures fall outside the confines of this repair manual. For complete information on diagnosis, testing and repair procedures concerning all modern engine and emission control systems, please refer to "Chilton's Guide to Electronic Engine Controls".

ENGINE MECHANICAL

NOTE: Disconnecting the negative battery cable on some vehicles may interfere with the functions of the on board computer systems and may require the computer to undergo a relearning process, once the negative battery cable is reconnected.

Engine Assembly

REMOVAL & INSTALLATION

NOTE: The engine assembly is removed from underneath the vehicle.

1. Disconnect the negative battery cable.

2. Drain the engine coolant.

3. Remove the rear compartment lid and also the side panels. Do not remove the torsion rod retaining bolts.

4. Remove the air cleaner assembly.

5. Disconnect the throttle and shift cables.

6. Disconnect the heater hose at the intake manifold.

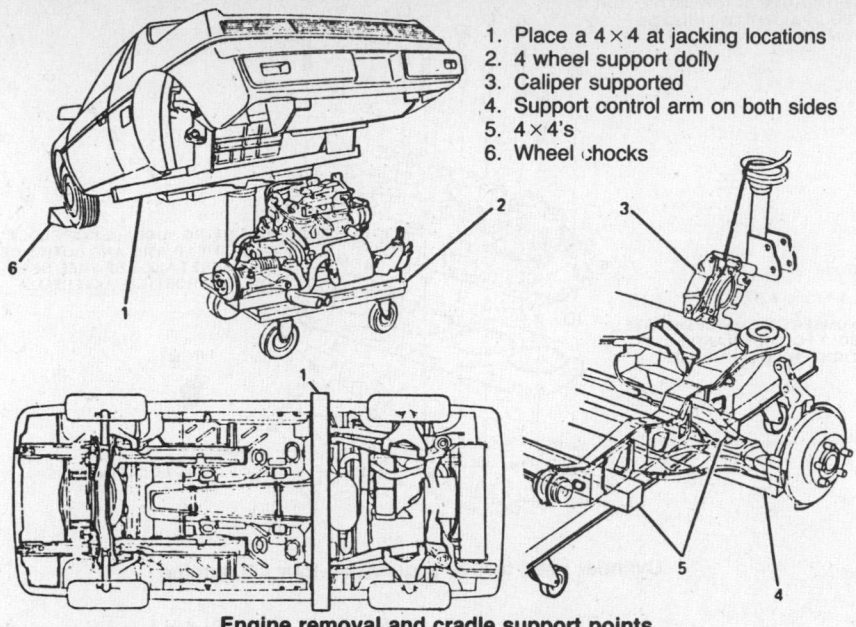

1. Place a 4×4 at jacking locations
2. 4 wheel support dolly
3. Caliper supported
4. Support control arm on both sides
5. 4×4's
6. Wheel chocks

Engine removal and cradle support points

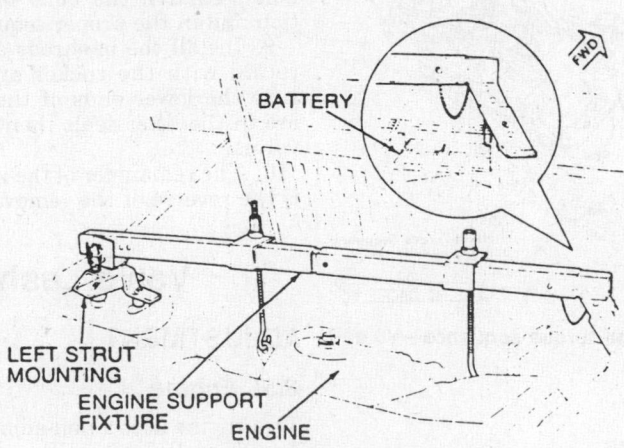

BATTERY
FWD
LEFT STRUT
MOUNTING
ENGINE SUPPORT
FIXTURE
ENGINE

Engine holding fixture mounting

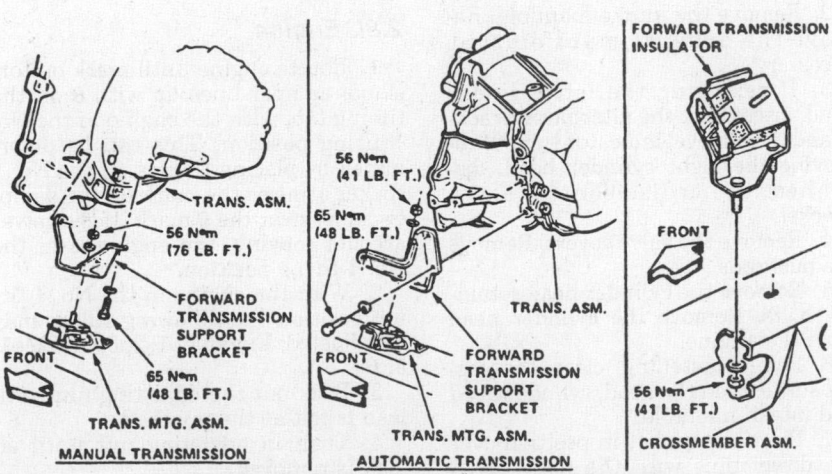

MANUAL TRANSMISSION

TRANS. ASM.
56 N•m (76 LB. FT.)
FORWARD TRANSMISSION SUPPORT BRACKET
65 N•m (48 LB. FT.)
TRANS. MTG. ASM.
FRONT

AUTOMATIC TRANSMISSION

56 N•m (41 LB. FT.)
65 N•m (48 LB. FT.)
TRANS. ASM.
FRONT
FORWARD TRANSMISSION SUPPORT BRACKET
TRANS. MTG. ASM.

FORWARD TRANSMISSION INSULATOR
FRONT
56 N•m (41 LB. FT.)
CROSSMEMBER ASM.

Forward transaxle mount and mounting brackets

7. Disconnect the vacuum hoses from all non-engine components.
8. Properly relieve the fuel system pressure. Disconnect the fuel lines and filter.
9. Disconnect the fuel pump relay and the oxygen sensor.
10. On vehicles equipped with automatic transaxle, disconnect the transaxle cooler lines.
11. Disconnect the slave cylinder from the manual transaxle equipped vehicles.
12. Disconnect the engine to chassis ground strap.
13. If equipped with airconditioning, properly discharge the system. Disconnect and plug the refrigerant lines at the compressor and seal the end.
14. Remove the rear console.
15. Remove the ECM harness through the bulkhead panel.
16. Install an engine support fixture.
17. Remove the engine strut bracket and mark the bolt and bracket for reassembly.
18. Raise and support the vehicle safely.
19. Remove the rear wheels.
20. On vehicles equipped with an automatic transaxle, remove the torque converter bolts.
21. Remove the parking brake cable and calipers. Do not disconnect the brake hoses. Support the caliper out of the way.
22. Remove the strut bolts and mark the struts for realignment.
23. Disconnect the air conditioning wiring, if equipped.
24. Loosen the 4 engine cradle bolts.
25. On the 2.5L engine, release the parking brake cables at the cradle using tool J-34065 or equivalent.

NOTE: Support the engine/transaxle and cradle assembly on the proper equipment. Be sure to support the outboard ends of the lower control arms. Disconnect the engine support fixture.

26. Lower the vehicle and attach the engine/transaxle assembly to a dolly. Remove the cradle bolts. Raise the vehicle and roll the dolly from under the vehicle.
27. Separate the engine and transaxle.
28. Installation is the reverse of removal.

Engine Mounts

REMOVAL & INSTALLATION

1. Disconnect the negative battery cable. Support engine using and engine support tool.
2. Remove the bolt for the forward torque reaction rod.

3. Raise the vehicle and support it safely..

4. Remove the engine mount to chassis nuts.

5. Remove the upper engine mount to support bracket nuts.

6. Remove the mount.

7. Installation is the reverse order of the removal procedure.

8. Torque engine mount to specification.

9. Torque engine mount to support bracket to specification.

Cylinder Head

REMOVAL & INSTALLATION

2.5L Engine

1. Relieve the fuel system pressure. Disconnect the negative battery cable. Drain the cooling system.

2. Raise the vehicle and support it safely.

3. Remove the exhaust pipe.

4. Lower the vehicle.

5. Remove the oil level indicator tube.

6. Remove the air cleaner assembly.

7. Disconnect the EFI electrical connections and vacuum hoses.

8. Remove the EGR base plate.

9. Remove the heater hose from the intake manifold.

10. Remove the ignition coil lower mounting bolt and wiring connections.

11. Remove all wiring connections from the intake manifold and cylinder head.

12. Remove the engine strut bolt from the upper support. Remove the power steering pump and position it to the side, as required.

13. Remove the alternator belt. Remove the air conditioning compressor and position to the side, as required.

14. Remove the throttle cables from the intake manifold. Remove the intake manifold.

15. Remove the valve cover, rocker arms and pushrods.

16. Remove the cylinder head bolts and remove the cylinder head.

17. Before installing, clean the gasket surfaces of the head and block.

18. Make sure the retaining bolt threads and the cylinder block threads are clean since dirt could affect bolt torque.

19. Install a new gasket over the dowel pins in the cylinder block. Install the cylinder head into place over the dowel pins.

20. Tighten the cylinder head bolts to specification gradually and in the proper sequence.

21. The remainder of the installation is the reverse order of the removal procedure.

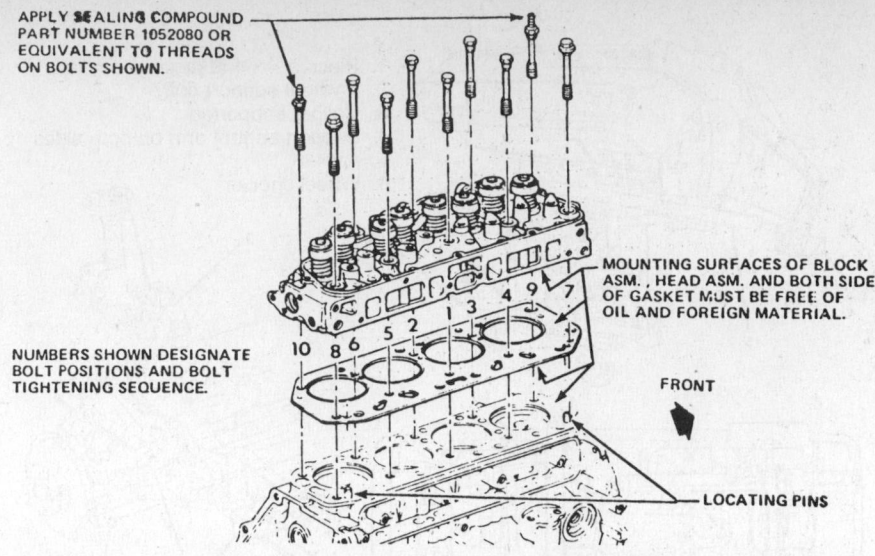

APPLY SEALING COMPOUND PART NUMBER 1052080 OR EQUIVALENT TO THREADS ON BOLTS SHOWN.

MOUNTING SURFACES OF BLOCK ASM., HEAD ASM. AND BOTH SIDES OF GASKET MUST BE FREE OF OIL AND FOREIGN MATERIAL.

NUMBERS SHOWN DESIGNATE BOLT POSITIONS AND BOLT TIGHTENING SEQUENCE.

FRONT

LOCATING PINS

Cylinder head torque sequence—four cyl. engine

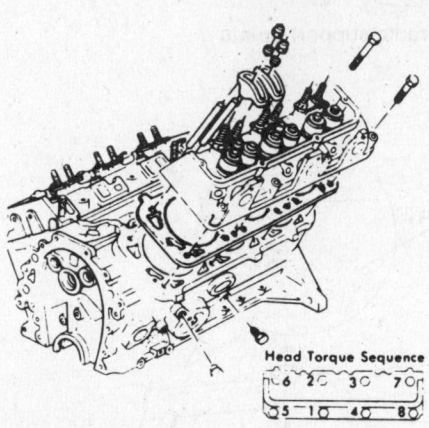

Head Torque Sequence

Cylinder head torque sequence—V6 engine

2.8L Engine

1. Relieve the fuel system pressure. Disconnect the negative battery cable. Drain the radiator.

2. Remove the intake manifold. Remove the exhaust manifolds, as necessary.

3. If removing the left cylinder head, disconnect the alternator bracket and the oil level indicator tube. If removing the right cylinder head, disconnect the cruise control servo bracket.

4. Remove the valve covers. Remove the pushrods.

5. Remove the cylinder head retaining bolts. Remove the cylinder head from the engine.

6. Before installing, clean the gasket surfaces on the head, cylinder head and intake manifold.

7. Place the gasket in position over the dowel pins with the note **THIS SIDE UP** showing.

8. Place the cylinder head into position. Coat the cylinder head bolts threads with a sealer and install the bolts. Tighten the bolts to specification and in the proper sequence.

9. Install the pushrods and loosely retain with the rocker arms. Make sure the lower ends of the pushrods are in the lifter seals then adjust the valves.

10. The remainder of the installation is the reverse of the removal.

Valve Lash

ADJUSTMENT

2.5L Engine

This engine uses a non-adjustable, hydraulic, roller lifter. Excessive valve lash indicates either a worn pushrod, a worn rocker arm, a worn camshaft, or a worn valve lifter.

2.8L Engine

1. Rotate engine until mark on torsional damper lines up with **0** on the timing tab, with the engine in the No. 1 firing position. This can be determined by placing fingers on the No. 1 rocker arms as the mark on the damper comes near the **0** mark. If the valves are not moving, the engine is in the No. 1 firing position.

2. With the engine in the No. 1 firing position the following valves may be adjusted: Exhaust–1, 2, 3; Intake–1, 5, 6.

3. Back out the adjusting nut until lash is felt at the pushrod.

4. Turn in adjusting nut until all lash is removed.

5. When all lash has been removed,

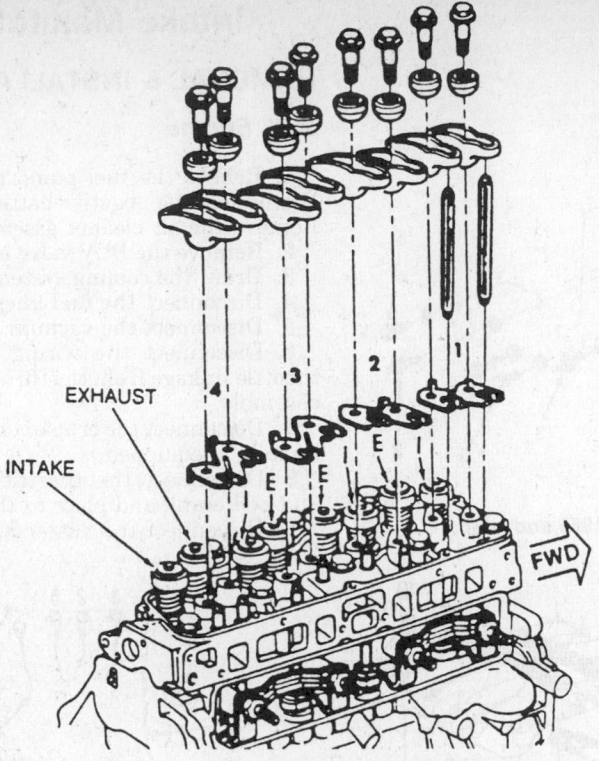

Valve arrangement—2.5L engine

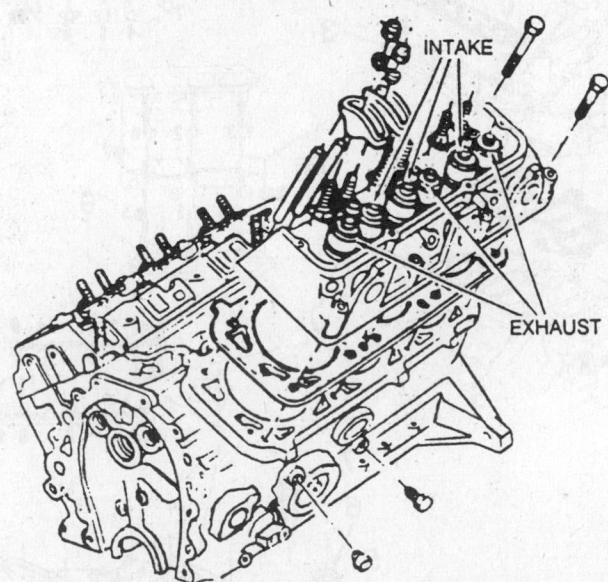

Valve arrangement—2.8L engine

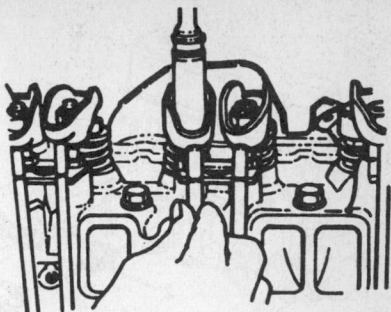

Adjusting valve lash-V6 engine

turn in adjusting nut 1½ additional turns.

6. Crank the engine 1 turn until the timing tab **0** mark and torsional damper mark are again in alignment. This is the No. 4 firing position.

7. With the engine in the No. 4 firing position the following valves may be adjusted: exhaust—4, 5, 6; intake—2, 3, 4.

8. Install rocker arm covers.

9. Start engine, check timing and idle speed, check for oil leaks.

Rocker Arms/ Pushrods

REMOVAL & INSTALLATION

2.5L Engine

1. Disconnect the negative battery cable. Remove the air cleaner.

2. Remove the PCV valve and hose.

3. Disconnect the wires from the spark plugs and clips.

4. Remove the valve cover retaining bolts.

5. Remove the valve cover by tapping lightly with a rubber hammer. Prying on the cover could cause damage to the sealing surfaces.

6. Remove the rocker arm bolt.

7. If replacing the pushrod only, loosen the rocker arm bolt and swing the arm clear of the pushrod.

8. Remove the pushrod retainers, if equipped. Remove the rocker arm and pushrod.

9. Installation is the reverse order of the removal procedure.

10. Torque the rocker arm bolt to specification. Apply a continuous $3/16$ in. diameter bead of RTV sealant or equivalent around the cylinder head sealant surfaces inboard at the bolt holes.

2.8L Engine

1. Disconnect the negative battery cable.

2. Remove the engine compartment lid and both side covers. Do not remove the torsion rod retaining bolts.

3. Disconnect the vacuum boost line and tube.

4. Disconnect the throttle and downshift cables and bracket.

5. Disconnect the cruise control cable, if applicable.

6. Disconnect the ground cable.

7. Remove the PCV from the cover.

8. Remove the oil dip stick tube.

9. Disconnect the plug wires and bracket.

10. Remove the engine lift hook.

11. Remove the rocker arm cover bolts and carefully remove the cover by taping with a rubber mallet. If prying is necessary do not distort the sealing flange.

12. Remove the rocker arm nuts. Keep all components in order so that they may be reinstalled in the same location.

13. Remove the rocker arm pivot balls, arms and pushrods.

14. Before installation, coat the bearing surfaces of the rocker arms and pivot balls with Molykote® or equivalent.

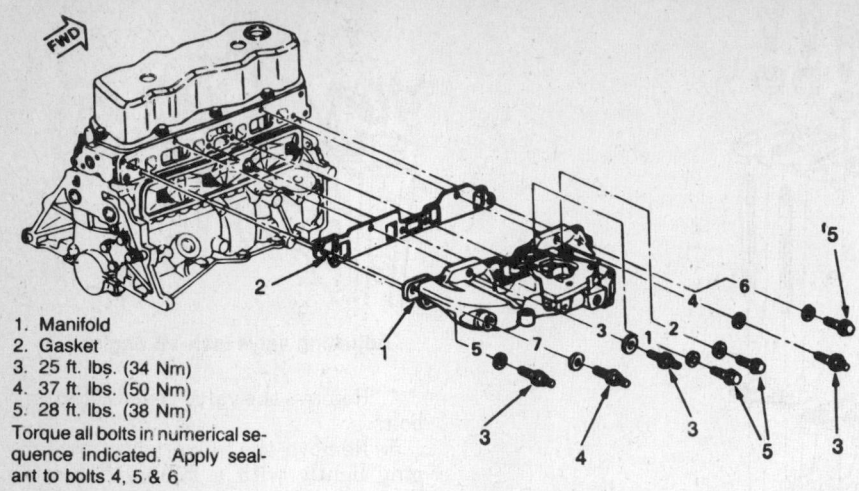

1. Manifold
2. Gasket
3. 25 ft. lbs. (34 Nm)
4. 37 ft. lbs. (50 Nm)
5. 28 ft. lbs. (38 Nm)
Torque all bolts in numerical sequence indicated. Apply sealant to bolts 4, 5 & 6.

Intake manifold torque sequence—four cyl. engine, 1986 and later

Intake Manifold

REMOVAL & INSTALLATION

2.5L Engine

1. Relieve the fuel pump pressure. Disconnect the negative battery cable. Remove the air cleaner assembly.
2. Remove the PCV valve and hose.
3. Drain the cooling system.
4. Disconnect the fuel lines.
5. Disconnect the vacuum hoses.
6. Disconnect the wiring and the throttle linkage from the throttle body assembly.
7. Disconnect the cruise control and linkage, if equipped.
8. Disconnect the throttle linkage and bell crank and place to the side.
9. Disconnect the heater hose.

15. Insert the pushrods, rocker arms and pivot balls. Make sure the pushrods are seated in the valve lifters.

16. Adjust the rocker arm nuts until lash is eliminated. Rotate the engine until the mark on the torsional damper lines up with the **0** mark on the timing tab, with the engine in the No. 1 firing position. This may be determined by placing fingers on the No. 1 rocker arms as the mark on the damper comes near the 0 mark. If the valves are not moving, the engine is in the No. 1 firing position. With the engine in the No. 1 firing position the following valves may be adjusted, Exhaust–4, 5, 6; Intake–2, 3, 4.

17. Install the rocker arm covers. Clean the surfaces on the cylinder head and rocker arm cover. Place a ⅛ in. dot of RTV sealant or an equivalent, at the intake manifold and cylinder head split line. Install the rocker arm cover gasket, using care to line up the holes in the gasket with the bolt holes in the cylinder head.

18. Install the rocker arm cover bolts and torque to specification.

19. The remainder of the installation is the reverse order of the removal procedure

Pushrod Cover

REMOVAL & INSTALLATION

2.5L Engine

1. Disconnect the negative battery cable.
2. Remove the intake manifold assembly.
3. Remove the pushrod cover retaining bolts. Remove the pushrod cover.
4. Installation is the reverse of the removal procedure. Be sure to use new gaskets or RTV sealant, as required.

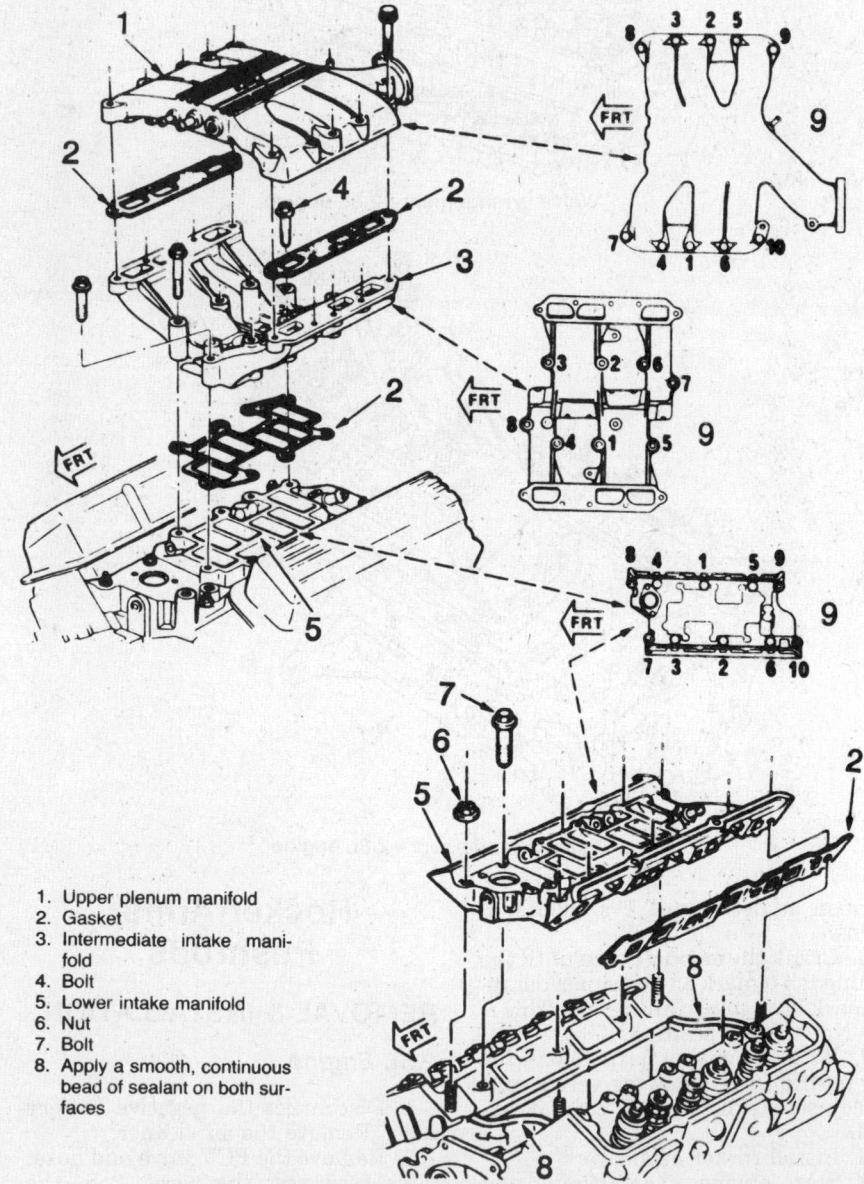

1. Upper plenum manifold
2. Gasket
3. Intermediate intake manifold
4. Bolt
5. Lower intake manifold
6. Nut
7. Bolt
8. Apply a smooth, continuous bead of sealant on both surfaces

Intake manifold installation and torque sequence—V6 engine

10. Remove the generator upper bracket.

11. Remove the ignition coil.

12. Remove the retaining bolts and remove the manifold.

13. Installation is the reverse of removal. Be sure to use new gaskets, as required. Torque all bolts in the proper sequence.

2.8L Engine

1. Position the engine at TDC on the compression stroke. Properly relieve the fuel system pressure.

2. Disconnect the negative battery cable. Remove the valve covers.

3. Drain the engine coolant.

4. Disconnect the throttle body to elbow intake hose.

5. Remove the distributor. Disconnect the vacuum booster pipe and bracket.

6. Disconnect the shift and throttle linkage.

7. Remove the throttle body to upper plenum.

8. Disconnect the heater and radiator hoses.

9. Disconnect all wiring harness and vacuum hoses while noting their locations for reassembly.

10. Disconnect the EGR pipe.

11. Remove the upper manifold plenum and gaskets.

12. Remove the intermediate intake manifold and gasket.

13. Remove the lower intake manifold and gaskets.

14. Clean all gasket surfaces on the intake manifolds and cylinder head.

15. Install the lower intake manifold and gasket and torque to specification in the proper sequence.

16. Install the intermediate intake manifold and gaskets and torque in sequence to specification.

17. Install the upper manifold ple-

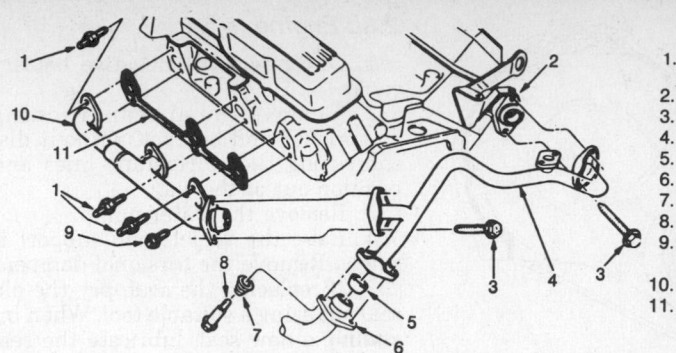

Exhaust manifold installation—V6 engine

1. Bolt/stud lockwasher assembly
2. Exhaust manifold
3. Bolt
4. Crossover pipe
5. Seal
6. Muffler
7. Spring
8. Bolt
9. Bolt and lockwasher assembly
10. Exhaust manifold
11. Gasket

num and gaskets and torque in sequence.

18. The remainder of the installation is the reverse of the removal. Check engine timing, coolant level and for leaks.

Exhaust Manifold

REMOVAL & INSTALLATION

2.5L Engine

1. Disconnect the negative battery cable. Remove the air cleaner and the EFI bracket tube.

2. Raise and support the vehicle safely.

3. Remove the exhaust pipe and lower the vehicle. As required, remove the battery side cover.

4. Remove the exhaust manifold retaining bolts. Remove the exhaust manifold and gasket from the engine.

5. Installation is the reverse of removal. Clean the sealing surfaces and use a new gasket. Torque the retaining bolts in sequence.

2.8L Engine

FRONT

1. Disconnect the negative battery cable.

2. Remove the rear compartment lid. Do not remove the torsion rod retaining bolts.

3. Remove the brake vacuum hose.

4. Remove the manifold heat shield.

5. Remove the front crossover bolts.

6. Raise and support the vehicle safely. Remove the front converter heat shield and the lower manifold bolts.

7. Lower the vehicle and remove the upper manifold bolts then remove the manifold.

8. Installation is the reverse of the removal procedure. Be sure to use a new gasket. Torque the manifold to specification.

2.8L Engine

REAR

1. Disconnect the negative battery cable. Disconnect the manifold to crossover bolts.

2. Remove the manifold retaining bolts. remove the manifold.

3. Installation is the reverse order of the removal procedure.

4. Torque the manifold bolts to specification.

Timing Chain Front Cover and Oil Seal

REMOVAL & INSTALLATION

2.5L Engine

1. Disconnect the negative battery cable. Remove the engine compartment lid and side panels. Remove the trim at the sail panel below the battery side panel.

2. Remove the drive belt. Raise and support the vehicle safely.

3. Remove the right rear tire and

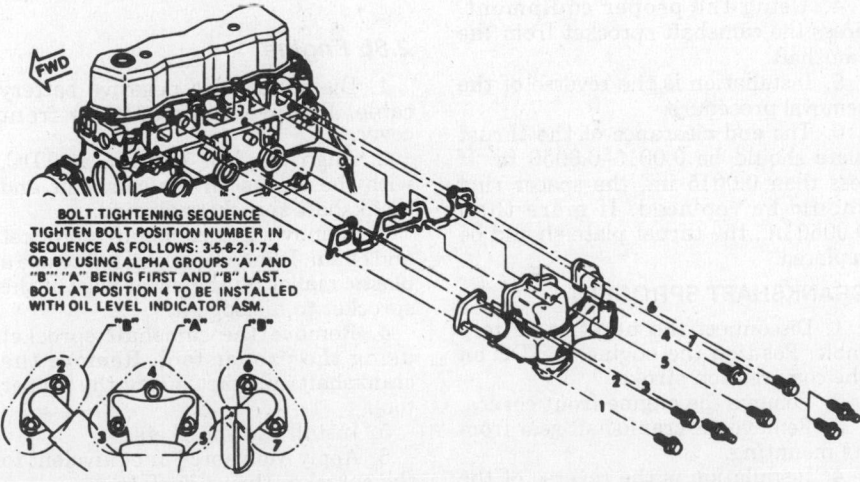

BOLT TIGHTENING SEQUENCE
TIGHTEN BOLT POSITION NUMBER IN SEQUENCE AS FOLLOWS: 3-5-6-2-1-7-4 OR BY USING ALPHA GROUPS "A" AND "B": "A" BEING FIRST AND "B" LAST. BOLT AT POSITION 4 TO BE INSTALLED WITH OIL LEVEL INDICATOR ASM.

Exhaust manifold torque sequence—four cyl. engine, 1985 and later

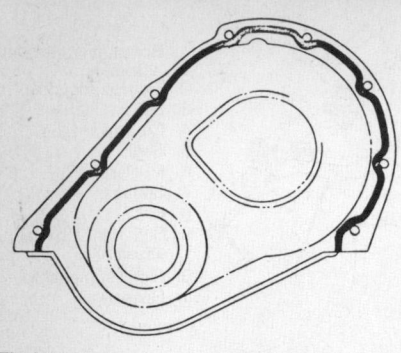

Timing cover sealer application—four cyl. engine

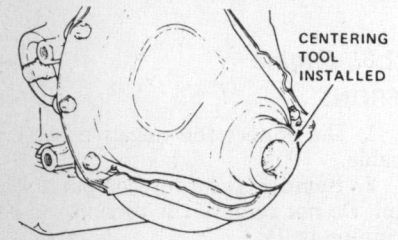

Front cover centering tool installed—four cyl. engine

CENTERING TOOL INSTALLED

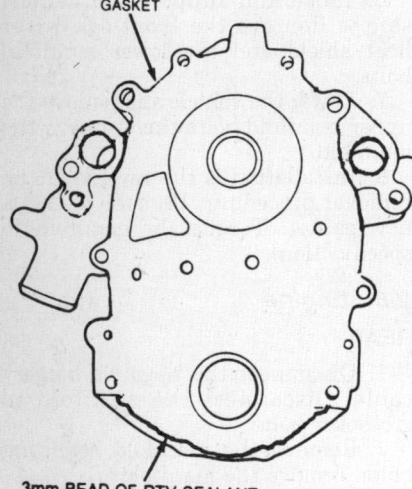

GASKET

3mm BEAD OF RTV SEALANT #1052366 OR EQUIVALENT

Applying sealer to the front cover on the V6 engine

wheel assembly. Remove the inner splash shield.

4. Remove the starter assembly. Remove the flywheel cover.

5. Remove the pulley and hub. Lower the vehicle.

6. Properly support the engine using the required equipment. Remove the engine torque strut.

7. Raise and support the vehicle safely. Remove the engine mounts.

8. Remove the timing gear cover bolts. Remove the timing gear cover.

9. Installation is the reverse of the removal procedure. Be sure to use new gaskets or RTV sealant, as required.

2.8L Engine

1. Disconnect the negative battery cable.

2. Remove the air conditioning compressor and bracket, without disconnecting the refrigerant lines and position out of the way.

3. Remove the water pump.

4. Raise the vehicle and support it safely. Remove the torsional damper.

5. If replacing the seal, pry the old seal out using a suitable tool. When installing a new seal, lubricate the seal with clean engine oil. Insert the seal in the front cover with the lip facing the engine. Using the proper tool, drive the seal into place.

6. Remove the oil pan to cover bolts.

7. Lower the vehicle and remove the front cover.

8. Before installing, clean the sealing surfaces on the front cover and cylinder block. Install a new gasket and apply a ⅛ in. bead of RTV sealer to the oil pan sealing surface of the front cover.

9. Place the front cover on the engine and install the stud bolt and bolts.

10. The remainder of the installation is the reverse order of the removal procedure.

Timing Chain and Sprockets

REMOVAL & INSTALLATION

2.5L Engine
CAMSHAFT SPROCKET

1. Disconnect the negative battery cable. Remove the engine from the vehicle.

2. Position the engine assembly in a suitable holding fixture.

3. Position the engine at TDC on the compression stroke. Remove the front cover. Remove the camshaft.

4. Using the proper equipment, press the camshaft sprocket from the camshaft.

5. Installation is the reverse of the removal procedure.

6. The end clearance of the thrust plate should be 0.0015–0.0050 in. If less than 0.0015 in., the spacer ring should be replaced. If more than 0.0050 in., the thrust plate should be replaced.

CRANKSHAFT SPROCKET

1. Disconnect the negative battery cable. Position the engine at TDC on the compression stroke.

2. Remove the engine front cover.

3. Remove the crankshaft gear from its mounting.

4. Installation is the reverse of the removal procedure.

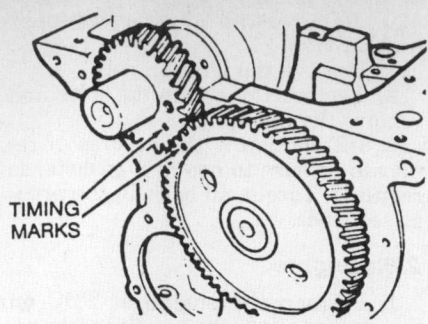

TIMING MARKS

Aligning timing marks—2.5L engine

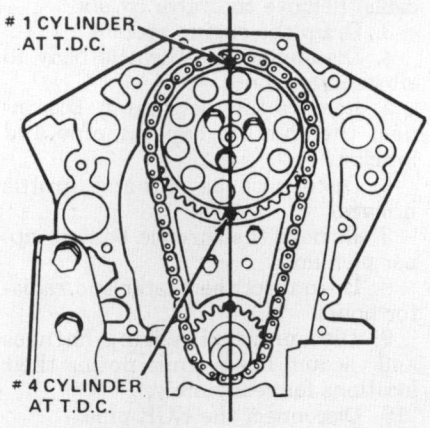

#1 CYLINDER AT T.D.C.

#4 CYLINDER AT T.D.C.

Align the timing marks for the camshaft and crankshaft sprockets as shown

V-6 timing chain and sprockets—exploded view

2.8L Engine

1. Disconnect the negative battery cable. Remove the crankcase front cover.

2. Align the No. 1 piston at TDC, with the marks on the camshaft and crankshaft sprockets aligned.

3. Remove the camshaft sprocket and chain. It may be necessary to use a plastic mallet on the lower edge of the sprocket to dislodge it.

4. Remove the camshaft sprocket using the proper tool. Remove the crankshaft sprocket, using the proper tool.

5. Install the sprockets.

6. Apply Molykote® or equivalent to the sprocket thrust surface.

7. Hold the sprocket with the chain

hanging down and align the marks on the camshaft and crankshaft sprockets.

8. Align the dowel in the camshaft with the dowel hole in the camshaft sprocket.

9. Draw the camshaft sprocket onto the camshaft, using the mounting bolts and torque 15–25 ft. lbs.

10. Lubricate the timing chain with engine oil.

11. Install the crankcase front cover.

Camshaft

REMOVAL & INSTALLATION

2.5L Engine

1. Disconnect the negative battery cable. Remove the engine from the vehicle and position it in a suitable holding fixture.

2. Remove the valve cover. Remove the pushrods.

3. Remove the distributor and fuel pump.

4. Remove the pushrod cover, and valve lifters.

5. Remove the alternator, lower alternator bracket and front engine mount bracket assembly.

6. Remove the oil pump driveshaft and gear assembly. Remove the front pulley hub and timing gear cover.

7. Remove the 2 camshaft thrust plate screws by working through holes in the camshaft gear.

8. Remove the camshaft and gear assembly by pulling it out through the front of the block. Support the camshaft carefully when removing so as not to damage camshaft bearings.

Removing the camshaft thrust screws— four cyl. engine

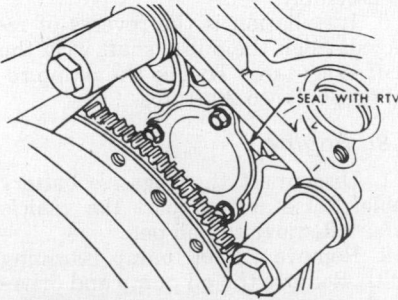

The camshaft rear cover on the V6

9. As required, remove the gear from the camshaft.

10. Installation is the reverse of the removal procedure. The end clearance of the thrust plate should be 0.0015–0.0050 in. If less than 0.0015 in., the spacer ring should be replaced. If more than 0.0050 in., the thrust plate should be replaced.

11. Thoroughly coat the camshaft journals with a high quality engine oil supplement.

12. Install the camshaft assembly in the engine block, be careful not to damage the cam bearings or the camshaft.

13. Turn crankshaft and camshaft so that the valve timing marks on the gear teeth will line up. The engine is now in the No. 4 cylinder firing position. Install camshaft thrust plate to block screws and tighten to 75 inch lbs.

14. Install timing gear cover and gasket. Line up keyway in hub with key on crankshaft and slide hub onto shaft. Install center bolt and torque to 160 ft. lbs. (212 Nm).

15. Install the lifters, pushrods, pushrod cover, oil pump shaft and gear assembly and fuel pump. Install the distributor.

16. Install front mount assembly lower alternator bracket and alternator.

17. Install the engine in the vehicle.

2.8L Engine

1. Disconnect the negative battery cable. Remove the engine from the vehicle and position it in a suitable holding fixture.

2. Remove the intake manifold. Remove the valve covers. Remove rocker arm assemblies, pushrods and lifters.

3. Remove the crankcase front cover.

4. Remove the timing chain and sprocket.

5. Remove the engine rear cover.

6. Carefully remove the camshaft to avoid damage to the cam bearings.

7. Before installation, lubricate the camshaft journals with engine oil. If a new camshaft is to be installed, coat the lobes with clean engine oil.

8. The remainder of the installation is the reverse of removal.

Piston and Connecting Rod

POSITIONING

To properly install the piston and connecting rod assembly. Align the piston and connecting rod assembly with the piston mark (notch) toward the front of the engine.

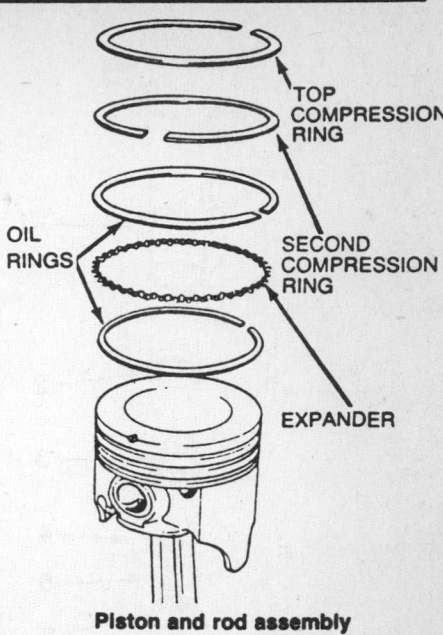

OIL RINGS

TOP COMPRESSION RING

SECOND COMPRESSION RING

EXPANDER

Piston and rod assembly

ENGINE LUBRICATION

Force Balancer Assembly

REMOVAL & INSTALLATION

2.5L Engine

1. Disconnect the negative battery cable. Raise and support the vehicle safely.

2. Drain the engine oil. Remove the oil pan.

3. Remove the balancer assembly.

4. Installation is the reverse of the removal procedure. Torque the short bolts to 9 ft. lbs. plus a 75 degree turn. Torque the long bolts 9 ft. lbs. plus a 90 degree turn.

1-11/16" (42.9mm)

Crankshaft position movement

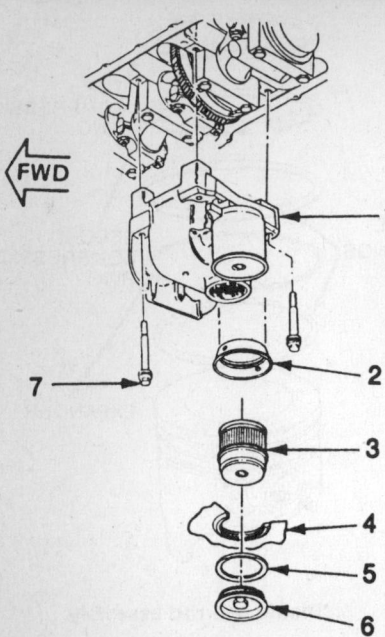

FWD

Correct counterweight installation

COUNTER WEIGHTS

Balancer assembly—2.5L engine

5. Rotate the engine to TDC on the No. 1 and No. 4 cylinders. Measure from the block to the first cut of the double notch on the reluctor ring.

6. The measurement should be $1^{11}/_{16}$ in. Mount the balancer with the counterweights parallel and pointing away from the crankshaft. Be sure not to move the crankshaft.

7. Be sure to use new gaskets or RTV sealant, as required.

Oil Pan

REMOVAL & INSTALLATION

2.5L Engine

1. Disconnect the negative battery cable. Remove the engine compartment lid and side panels.

2. On 1988 vehicles, remove the sail panel below the battery side panel trim. Remove the battery side shield.

3. Raise and support the vehicle

safely. Drain the engine oil. On 1988 vehicles, remove the oil filter. On 1988 vehicles, remove the serpentine drive belt.

4. Remove the engine mount to cradle nuts. Remove the flywheel cover. Remove the starter.

5. As required, remove the right rear tire and wheel assembly. Remove the splash shield. Loosen the alternator bracket. As required, remove the alternator.

6. On 1988 vehicles, remove the heat shield at the air conditioning compressor. Remove the air conditioning compressor mounting bolts. Position the compressor to the side.

7. Lower the vehicle. Remove the engine strut. Properly support the engine using tool J28467, or equivalent.

8. Raise and support the vehicle safely. Remove the engine front support bracket and mount.

9. Remove the oil pan retaining bolts. Remove the oil pan from the vehicle.

10. Installation is the reverse of the removal procedure. Be sure to use new gaskets or RTV sealant, as required.

2.8L Engine

1. Disconnect the negative battery cable.

2. Raise the vehicle and support it safely.

3. Drain the oil.

4. Remove the flywheel shield or clutch housing cover.

5. Remove the starter.

6. Remove the oil pan retaining bolts. Remove the oil pan from the engine.

7. Before installation, clean all mating surfaces.

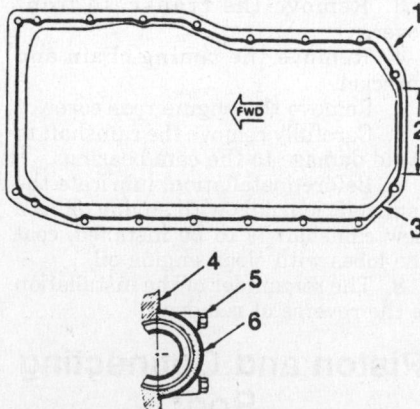

FWD

1. Oil pan
2. Apply a ⅜" thick bead of RTV sealer in area indicated
3. Apply a ³⁄₁₆" wide by ⅛" thick bead of RTV sealer in area indicated
4. Engine block assy.
5. Rear bearing
6. Groove in main bearing cap must be filled flush to ⅛" above surface with RTV

Oil pan sealer application-four cylinder engine

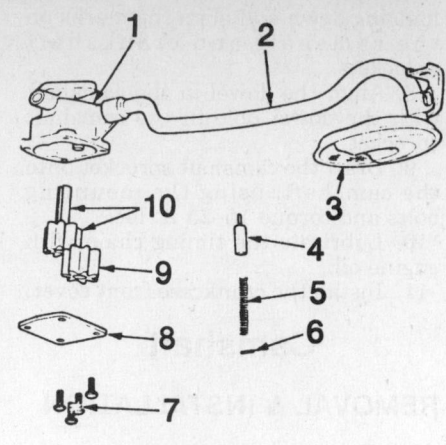

1. Pump body
2. Pickup tube
3. Pickup screen assy.
4. Pressure regulator valve
5. Pressure regulator spring
6. Spring retainer
7. Cover Screws
8. Cover
9. Idler gear
10. Drive gear and shaft

Oil pump - exploded view

8. Place a ⅛ in. bead of RTV sealant or an equivalent, on the oil pan sealing flange.

9. Install the oil pan and torque the 1 in. bolts to 6–9 ft. lbs. and the 1.5 in. bolts to 14–22 ft. lbs.

10. The remainder of the installation is the reverse of removal.

Oil Pump

REMOVAL & INSTALLATION

2.5L Engine

1. Disconnect the negative battery cable. Raise and support the vehicle safely.

2. Remove the oil pan. On 1988 vehicles, it is not necessary to remove the balancer assembly in order to service the oil pump.

3. Remove the 2 flange mounting bolts and the nut from the main bearing cap bolt.

4. Remove the pump and screen as an assembly.

5. Installation is the reverse of removal. Align the pump shaft with the drift shaft tang. Torque the pump retaining bolts to 20 ft. lbs.

2.8L Engine

1. Disconnect the negative battery cable. Raise and support the vehicle safely. Remove the oil pan.

2. Remove the oil pump retaining bolts. Remove the oil pump and driveshaft extension.

3. To install, engage the driveshaft extension in the cover end of the distributor drive gear.
4. Install the pump to rear bearing cap bolt and torque 26 to 35 ft. lbs.
5. Install the oil pan and refill with oil.

Rear Main Bearing Oil Seal

REMOVAL & INSTALLATION

One Piece Seal

1. Disconnect the negative battery cable. Raise and support the vehicle safely.
2. Remove the transaxle assembly. Remove the flywheel.
3. If equipped with a manual transaxle, remove the pressure plate and clutch.
4. Pry out of the rear main seal.
5. Before installing, clean the block and crankshaft to seal mating surfaces.
6. Lubricate the outside of the seal for ease of installation and press into the block with fingers.
7. Install the flywheel and torque the bolts to 44 ft. lbs.
8. Install the transaxle assembly.

Thin Seal

1. Remove the engine and mount on a suitable stand.
2. Remove the oil pan and oil pump assembly.
3. Remove the front cover, then the lock chain tensioner with a pin.
4. Rotate the crankshaft until the timing marks on the cam and crank sprockets align.
5. Remove the camshaft bolt, cam sprocket and timing chain.
6. Rotate the crankshaft to the horizontal position.
7. Remove the rod bearing nuts, caps and bolts.
8. Remove the crankshaft and the old oil seal.
9. Apply a light coat of GM 1052726 or equivalent to the outside of the seal.
10. Install the new seal and tool in the rear area of the crankshaft.
11. Install the crankshaft and tool in the engine.
12. Position the seal tool so that the arrow points towards the cylinder block and remove the tool.
13. Put a light coat of oil on the crankshaft journals.
14. Seal the rear main bearing split line surface with GM 1052726 or equivalent.
15. The remainder of the installation is the reverse of removal. Torque to specifications.

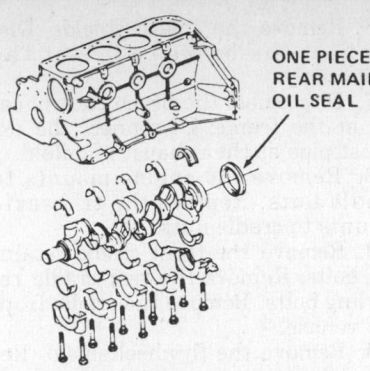

Crankshaft bearings and rear seal

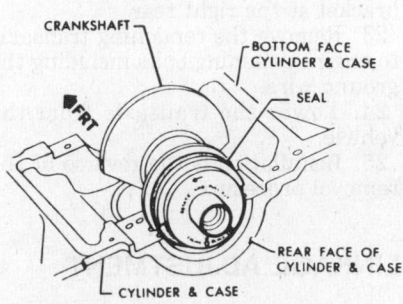

CAUTION RETAINER SPRING SIDE OF SEAL MUST FACE TOWARD FRONT OF CYLINDER & CASE.

Installing the thin type oil seal— V6 engine

Connecting Rod and Main Bearing

Replacement

1. Remove the engine from the vehicle. Position the assembly in a suitable holding fixture.
2. Remove the cylinder head assembly, as required. Remove the flywheel.
3. Remove the timing belt covers. Remove the timing belt. Remove the oil pan. Remove the oil screen assembly.
4. Matchmark and remove the main bearing caps. Remove the upper half of the main bearing shells.
5. Matchmark and remove the connecting rod caps. Remove the upper half of the connecting rod bearing shells.
6. Carefully push the pistons up into the cylinder head or remove them.
7. Remove the lower half of the connecting rod bearing shells.
8. Carefully lift the crankshaft from its mounting. Remove the lower half of the main bearing shells.
9. Installation is the reverse of the removal procedure.

MANUAL TRANSAXLE

For further information on transmissions/transaxles, please refer to "Chilton's Guide to Transmission Repair".

Transaxle Assembly

REMOVAL & INSTALLATION

1987 Vehicles

1. Remove the air cleaner assembly.
2. Disconnect the negative battery cable.
3. Disconnect the ground cable at the transaxle.
4. Disconnect the shift and select cable at the transaxle.
5. Remove the upper transaxle to engine bolts.
6. Install an engine support fixture J-28467 or equivalent.
7. Raise and support the vehicle safely.
8. Remove the rear wheels and tires.
9. Remove the axle shafts.
10. Remove the heat shield from the catalytic converter.
11. Disconnect the exhaust pipe at the exhaust manifold.
12. Remove the engine mount to cradle nuts.
13. Support the cradle with an adjustable stand.
14. Remove the rear cradle to body bolts.
15. Remove the forward cradle to body through bolts.
16. Lower the cradle and move out of the way.
17. Remove the starter and inspection cover shields and remove the starter.
18. Position a transaxle jack under the transaxle.
19. Remove the transaxle to engine bolts. Carefully remove the transaxle from the vehicle.
20. Installation is the reverse of the removal procedure.

1988 Vehicles

1. Disconnect the negative battery cable.
2. Remove the air cleaner assembly.
3. Remove the right engine vent cover.
4. Remove the left engine vent cover.
5. Remove the throttle valve cable.
6. Remove the shift cable at the transaxle bracket.

7. Disconnect the neutral start switch electrical connection.

8. Disconnect the transaxle converter clutch electrical connection.

9. Disconnect the speedometer pick-up electrical connection.

10. Remove the wire harness at the transaxle to engine retaining bolts.

11. Remove the transaxle to engine retaining bolts. Remove the shift cable bracket to remove the neutral start switch harness.

12. Install the engine fixture tool J–28467–A or equivalent. Raise the vehicle and support it safely. Remove the rear wheels.

13. Install rear axle boot protectors. Remove the fixed adjusting link/lateral control arm through bolts.

14. Disconnect the trailing arms at knuckles.

NOTE: On vehicles equipped with Tri-Pot joints, care must be exercised not to allow the Tri-Pot joints to become overextended. When either end or both ends of the shaft are disconnected, overextending the joint could result in separation of internal components. This could cause failure of the joint. Therefore, it is important to handle the drive axle in a manner that prevents overextending.

15. Remove rear axle shafts from transaxle. Support the rear axle shafts.

16. Remove the splash shields. Disconnect the brake cables at the calipers.

17. Disconnect the brake control cable at the frame. Disconnect the exhaust pipe at the exhaust manifold.

18. Remove the engine mounts to cradle nuts. Remove the transaxle mounts to cradle nuts.

19. Remove the front cradle retaining bolts. Remove the rear cradle retaining bolts. Remove the cradle from the vehicle.

20. Remove the flywheel shield. Remove the starter.

21. Install the transaxle support jack.

22. Remove the transaxle support bracket at the right rear.

23. Remove the remaining transaxle to engine retaining bolts including the ground wire.

24. Lower the transaxle from the vehicle.

25. Installation is the reverse of the removal procedure.

LINKAGE ADJUSTMENT

1. Disconnect the negative battery cable.

2. Place the transaxle in 1st gear.

3. Loosen the shift cable attaching nuts at the transaxle levers.

4. Remove the console and trim plates as required for access to shifter.

5. With the shifter lever in the 1st gear position, insert the proper alignment pins.

6. Remove the lash from transaxle by first compressing the selector cable and then tightening the nut. The levers should be kept from moving during this process. Similarly, the shift cable is first compressed and then the nut is tightened. Again the levers are to remain stationary. The nut on these levers is tightened to 20 ft. lbs. (27 Nm).

7. Ensure that the reverse inhibit cam is against roller and align if necessary.

8. Remove the alignment pins at shifter assembly.

NOTE: While cycling from 1st to 2nd and 2nd to 1st, the select cable should not move. Difficulty in shifting the transaxle to reverse may be corrected by moving select lever inboard toward the 1st-3rd-Reverse position during the shift cable adjustment.

CLUTCH

Clutch Assembly

REMOVAL & INSTALLATION

1. Disconnect the negative battery cable. Raise and support the vehicle safely. Remove the transaxle.

2. Mark the pressure plate assembly and the flywheel so that they can be assembled in the same position..

3. Loosen the attaching bolts 1 turn at a time until spring tension is relieved.

4. Support the pressure plate and remove the bolts. Remove the pressure plate and clutch disc. Do not disassemble the pressure plate assembly, replace it if defective.

5. Inspect the flywheel, clutch disc, pressure plate, throwout bearing and the clutch fork and pivot shaft assembly for wear. Replace the parts as required. If the flywheel shows any signs of overheating, or if it is badly grooved or scored, it should be replaced.

6. Clean the pressure plate and flywheel mating surfaces thoroughly. Position the clutch disc and pressure plate into the installed position and support with a dummy shaft or clutch aligning tool. The clutch plate is assembled with the damper springs offset toward the transaxle. One side of the factory supplied clutch disc is stamped **FLYWHEEL SIDE**.

7. Install the pressure plate to flywheel bolts. Tighten them gradually in a crisscross pattern.

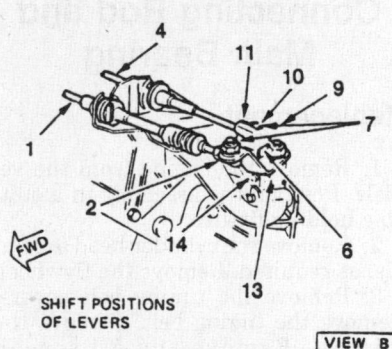

TYPICAL CABLE ATTACHMENT   VIEW A

SHIFT POSITIONS OF LEVERS   VIEW B

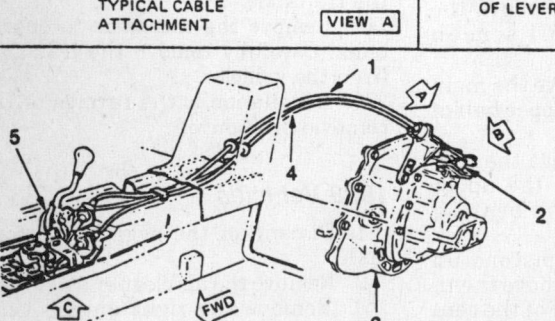

VIEW C

1. Cable A	5. Trans. control assy.	9. R	13. R/3rd/1st
2. Lever F	6. Lever D	10. 1st/2nd	14. 2nd/4th
3. Tansaxle assy.	7. Nut E	11. 4th/3rd	15. Alignment pin F
4. Cable B	8. Washer P	12. Retainer clip J	16. Alignment pin G

Manual transaxle cable adjustment

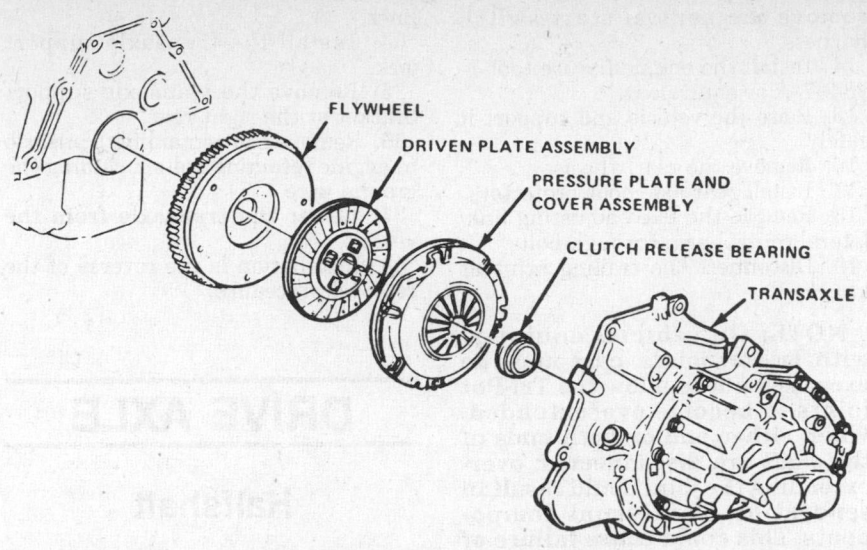

Exploded view of clutch assembly

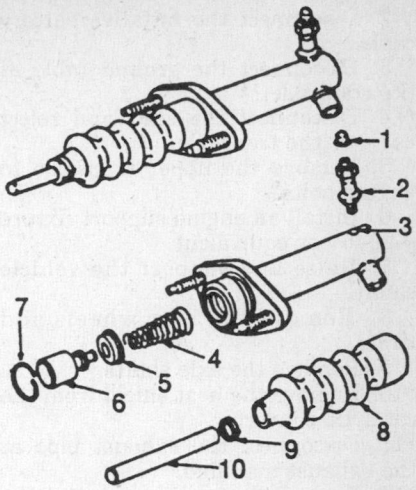

1. Bleedscrew Dust Cover
2. Bleedscrew
3. Cylinder Bolt
4. Spring
5. Seal
6. Plunger
7. Retaining Ring
8. Dust Cover
9. Retaining Band
10. Push Rod

Clutch slave cylinder components

8. Lubricate the outside groove and the inside recess of the release bearing with high temperature grease. Wipe off any excess. Install the release bearing.

9. Install the transaxle.

Clutch Master Cylinder

REMOVAL & INSTALLATION

1. Disconnect the negative battery cable. Disconnect clutch pushrod at clutch pedal assembly.

2. Remove the hydraulic line at the clutch master cylinder.

3. Remove the 2 nuts attaching the cylinder to cowl wall.

4. Remove the clutch cylinder.

5. To install, postion clutch rod through the the cowl opening and install the cylinder to cowl nuts loosely.

6. Place the clutch master cylinder rod on the clutch pedal assembly. Install washer and clip.

7. Torque the cylinder to cowl nuts to 13 ft. lbs.

8. Reconnect the hydraulic line to the master cylinder and torque to 13 ft. lbs.

9. Fill the master cylinder with recommended fluid and bleed the system.

Clutch Slave Cylinder

REMOVAL & INSTALLATION

1. Disconnect the negative battery cable. Remove the hydraulic line at the slave cylinder.

2. Remove the slave cylinder to bracket bolts and remove the cylinder.

3. To install, position slave cylinder at the bracket mounting and pilot the cylinder into the clutch release lever.

4. Install slave cylinder to bracket nuts and torque to 16 ft. lbs.

5. Install hydraulic line to slave cylinder, torque to 13 ft. lbs.

6. Fill master cylinder with recommended fluid and bleed system.

Hydraulic Clutch System Bleeding

1. Fill the master cylinder reservoir with brake fluid.

2. Have an assistant pump the clutch pedal 2–3 times and hold to the floor.

3. Open the bleeder screw at the slave cylinder ½ turn and allow all air in the system to escape, close the bleeder screw as soon as brake fluid begins to flow.

4. Repeat this procedure until all air is completely out of the system.

AUTOMATIC TRANSAXLE

For further information on transmissions/transaxles, please refer to "Chilton's Guide to Transmission Repair".

Transaxle Assembly

REMOVAL & INSTALLATION

1987 Vehicles

1. Remove the air cleaner assembly.

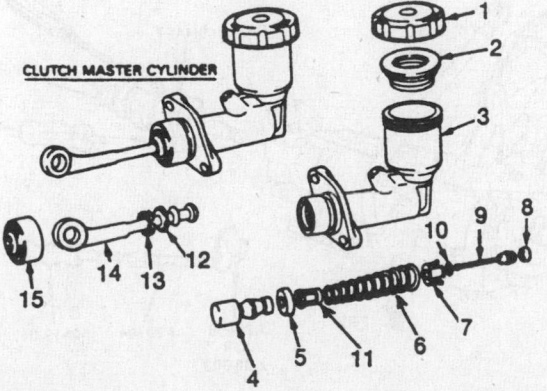

1. Reserve Cap
2. Baffle
3. Cylinder Body and Reservoir Assembly
4. Plunger
5. Seal
6. Spring
7. Valve Spacer
8. Center Valve Seal
9. Valve Stem
10. Spring
11. Spring Retainer
12. Retaining Washer
13. Circlip
14. Push Rod
15. Dust Cover

Clutch master cylinder components

2. Disconnect the negative battery cable.

3. Disconnect the ground cable at the transaxle.

4. Disconnect the shift and select cable at the transaxle.

5. Remove the upper transaxle to engine bolts.

6. Install an engine support fixture J-28467 or equivalent.

7. Raise and support the vehicle safely.

8. Remove the rear wheels and tires.

9. Remove the axle shafts.

10. Remove the heat shield from the catalytic converter.

11. Disconnect the exhaust pipe at the exhaust manifold.

12. Remove the engine mount to cradle nuts.

13. Support the cradle with an adjustable stand.

14. Remove the rear cradle to body bolts.

15. Remove the forward cradle to body through bolts.

16. Lower the cradle and move out of the way.

17. Remove the starter and inspection cover shields and remove the starter.

18. Remove the flywheel to converter bolts.

19. Disconnect and plug the cooler lines.

20. Position a transaxle jack under the transaxle.

21. Remove the transaxle to support mounting bolts on the right side.

22. Remove the transaxle to engine bolts. Carefully remove the transaxle from the vehicle.

23. Installation is the reverse of the removal procedure.

1988 Vehicles

1. Disconnect the negative battery cable.

2. Remove the air cleaner assembly.

3. Remove the right engine vent cover.

4. Remove the left engine vent cover.

5. Remove the throttle valve cable.

6. Remove the shift cable at the transaxle bracket.

7. Disconnect the neutral start switch electrical connection.

8. Disconnect the transaxle converter clutch electrical connection.

9. Disconnect the speedometer pick-up electrical connection.

10. Remove the wire harness at the transaxle to engine retaining bolts.

11. Remove the transaxle cooler line support bracket.

12. Remove the transaxle to engine retaining bolts.

13. Remove the shift cable bracket to remove the neutral start switch harness.

14. Install the engine fixture tool J-28467-A or equivalent.

15. Raise the vehicle and support it safely.

16. Remove the rear wheels.

17. Install rear axle boot protectors.

18. Remove the fixed adjusting link/lateral control arm through bolts.

19. Disconnect the trailing arms at knuckles.

NOTE: On vehicles equipped with Tri-Pot joints, care must be exercised not to allow the Tri-Pot joints to become overextended. When either end or both ends of the shaft are disconnected, overextending the joint could result in separation of internal components. This could cause failure of the joint. Therefore, it is important to handle the drive axle in a manner that prevents overextending.

20. Remove rear axle shafts from transaxle.

21. Support the rear axle shafts.

22. Remove the splash shields.

23. Disconnect the brake cables at the calipers.

24. Disconnect the brake control cable at the frame.

25. Disconnect the exhaust pipe at the exhaust manifold.

26. Remove the engine mounts to cradle nuts.

27. Remove the transaxle mounts to cradle nuts.

28. Remove the front cradle retaining bolts.

29. Remove the rear cradle retaining bolts.

30. Remove the cradle from the vehicle.

31. Remove the flywheel shield. Remove the starter.

32. Remove the flexplate bolts.

33. Disconnect and plug the cooler lines.

34. Install the transaxle support jack.

35. Remove the transaxle support bracket at the right rear.

36. Remove the remaining transaxle to engine retaining bolts including the ground wire.

37. Lower the transaxle from the vehicle.

38. Installation is the reverse of the removal procedure.

DRIVE AXLE

Halfshaft

REMOVAL & INSTALLATION

1987 Vehicles

1. Remove the hub nut and discard.

2. Raise the vehicle and remove the wheel and tire.

3. Install a drive boot seal protector on the outer seal.

4. Disconnect the toe link rod at the knuckle assembly.

5. Disconnect the parking brake cables at the cradle.

6. Disconnect the brake line bracket at the underbody in the inner wheel housing opening.

7. Using tool J-28733 or equivalent, remove the axle shaft from the hub and bearing assembly.

8. Support the axle shaft.

9. Remove the clamp bolt from the lower control arm ball stud.

10. Separate the knuckle from the lower control arm.

11. Pull the strut, knuckle and caliper assembly away from the body and secure in this position.

12. Using tool J-33008 and J-2619-01 or equivalents, disengage the

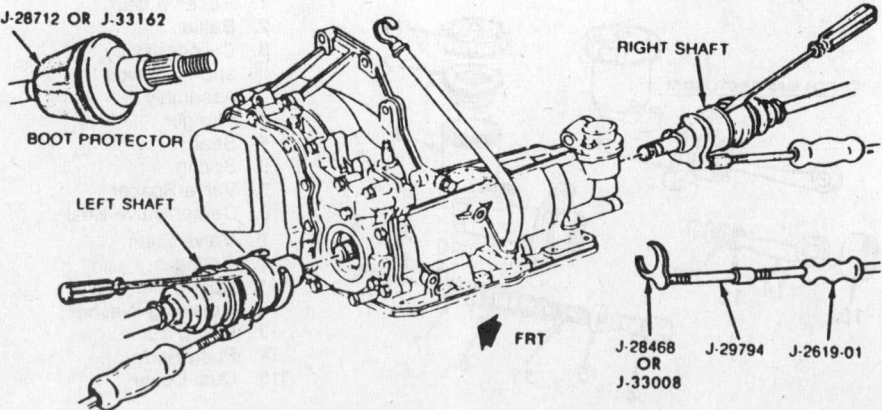

Removing the drive axle from the transaxle

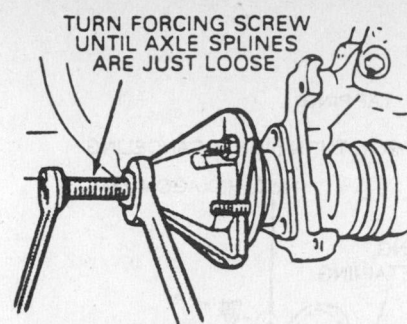

TURN FORCING SCREW
UNTIL AXLE SPLINES
ARE JUST LOOSE

Pressing half shaft the from hub

snaprings which are retaining the drive axle at the transaxle and remove the drive axle. If the drive axle is being replaced, replace the knuckle seal.

13. When installing the drive to the transaxle, seat the axle positioning a suitable tool inside the groove provided on the inner retainer. The remainder of the installation is the reverse of removal. Torque the hub nut to 225 ft. lbs.

1988 Vehicles

NOTE: **Vehicles equipped with a silicone (gray) boot on the drive axle joints, use boot protector J-33162 on these boots. All other boots are made of thermoplastic material (black) and do not require use of the boot protector.**

1. Position the selector lever in the **N** detent.
2. Raise and support the vehicle safely.
3. Remove the tire and wheel assembly.
4. Install a drift punch through rotor and remove hub nut and washer (discard nut).
5. Remove the caliper and rotor.
6. Disconnect the trailing arm at the knuckle.
7. Remove the fixed adjusting link, lateral control arm through bolt.
8. Scribe a matchmark on the strut and knuckle assembly.
9. Remove the strut mounting bolts.
10. Press the hub from the halfshaft.

NOTE: **On vehicles equipped with Tri-Pot joints, care must be exercised not to allow Tri-Pot joints to become overextended. When either end or both ends of the shaft are disconnected, overextending the joint could result in separation of internal compounds. This could cause failure of the joint. Therefore, it is important to handle the drive axle in a manner that prevents overextending.**

11. Install special tools J-28468 or J-33008 with J-29794 and J-2619-01 or equivalent slide and remove haftshaft from the transaxle.
12. Installation is the reverse of removal. Install the hub and washer and replace with a new nut. Torque the nut to 183–208 ft. lbs.

Rear Axle Shaft, Bearing and Seal

REMOVAL & INSTALLATION

1. Remove the hub cap and loosen the hub nut.
2. Raise and support the vehicle safely and remove the tire and wheel assembly.
3. Install the drive axle boot protectors. Remove and discard the hub nut.
4. Remove the caliper and rotor and remove the hub and bearing attaching bolts. If the bearing assembly is being reused, mark the attaching bolts and corresponding holes for installation.
5. Install tool J-28733 or equivalent and remove the hub and bearing assembly.
6. If installing a new bearing, be sure to replace the knuckle seal. Clean and inspect the bearing mating surfaces and knuckle bore for dirt, nicks and burrs.
7. If installing a knuckle seal, use tool J-28671 or equivalent and apply grease to the seal and knuckle bore.
8. Place the hub and bearing on the axle shaft and install all other components at this time.
9. Apply a torque of 74 ft. lbs. to the new hub nut, until the hub and bearing assembly is seated properly.

10. Install the rotor and caliper and apply a final torque of 200 ft. lbs. to the hub nut.
11. Install the tire and wheel assembly and lower the vehicle.

STEERING

Steering Wheel

REMOVAL & INSTALLATION

1. Disconnect the negative battery cable. Remove the center cap, retainer clip and nut.
2. Remove the steering wheel retaining nut. Remove the wheel using a steering wheel puller.
3. When installing, align the index mark on the steering wheel with the index mark on the steering shaft. Torque the retaining nut to 35 ft. lbs.
4. The canceling cam tower must be centered in the slot of the lock plate cover before assembling the wheel.

Steering Column

REMOVAL & INSTALLATION

1. Disconnect the battery negative cable.
2. Remove the left instrument panel sound absorber. Remove the left instrument panel trim pad and steering column trim collar.
3. Remove the bolt at the flex joint. Remove 2 nuts from the lower support and 2 bolts from the upper support.

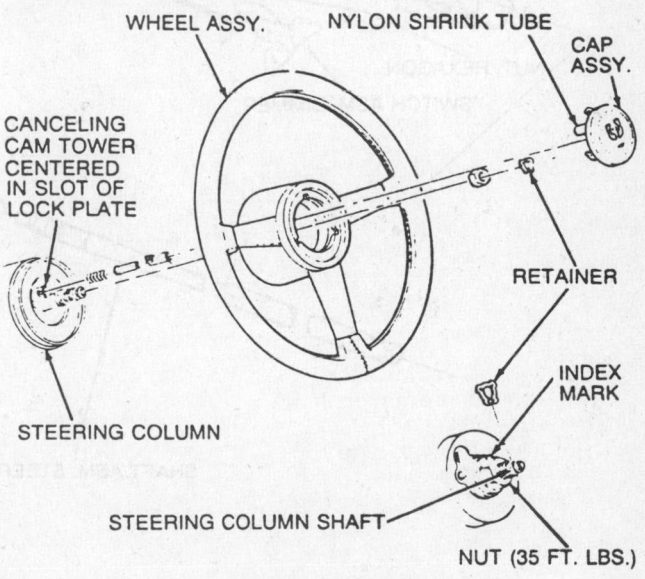

WHEEL ASSY.   NYLON SHRINK TUBE   CAP ASSY.

CANCELING CAM TOWER CENTERED IN SLOT OF LOCK PLATE

RETAINER

INDEX MARK

STEERING COLUMN

STEERING COLUMN SHAFT

NUT (35 FT. LBS.)

Steering wheel removal

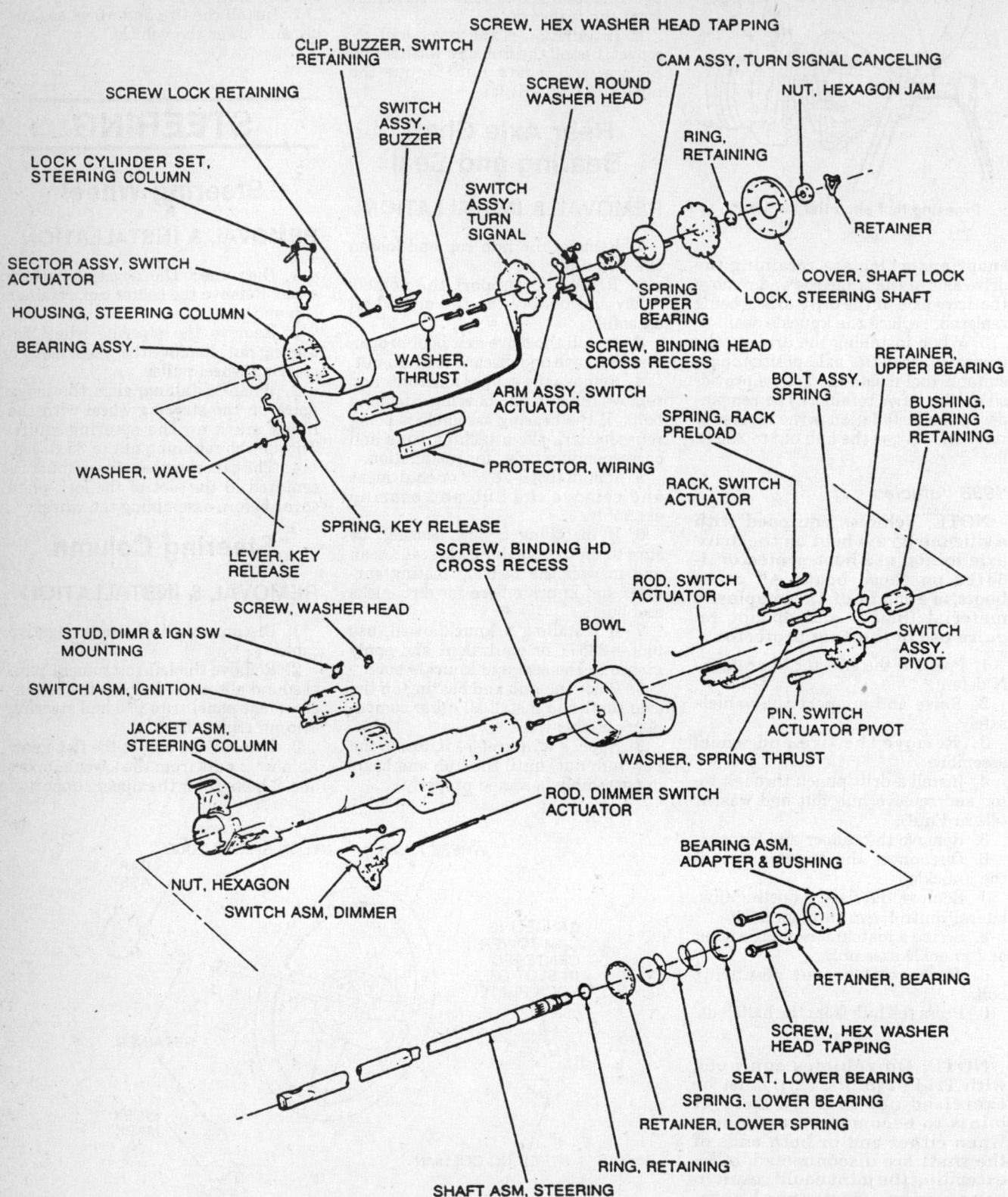

SCREW, HEX WASHER HEAD TAPPING

CLIP, BUZZER, SWITCH RETAINING

CAM ASSY, TURN SIGNAL CANCELING

SCREW LOCK RETAINING

SWITCH ASSY, BUZZER

SCREW, ROUND WASHER HEAD

NUT, HEXAGON JAM

RING, RETAINING

LOCK CYLINDER SET, STEERING COLUMN

SWITCH ASSY, TURN SIGNAL

RETAINER

SECTOR ASSY, SWITCH ACTUATOR

COVER, SHAFT LOCK

LOCK, STEERING SHAFT

SPRING UPPER BEARING

HOUSING, STEERING COLUMN

BEARING ASSY.

SCREW, BINDING HEAD CROSS RECESS

RETAINER, UPPER BEARING

WASHER, THRUST

BOLT ASSY, SPRING

BUSHING, BEARING RETAINING

ARM ASSY, SWITCH ACTUATOR

SPRING, RACK PRELOAD

PROTECTOR, WIRING

RACK, SWITCH ACTUATOR

WASHER, WAVE

SPRING, KEY RELEASE

SCREW, BINDING HD CROSS RECESS

ROD, SWITCH ACTUATOR

LEVER, KEY RELEASE

SWITCH ASSY, PIVOT

SCREW, WASHER HEAD

BOWL

STUD, DIMR & IGN SW MOUNTING

PIN, SWITCH ACTUATOR PIVOT

SWITCH ASM, IGNITION

WASHER, SPRING THRUST

JACKET ASM, STEERING COLUMN

BEARING ASM, ADAPTER & BUSHING

ROD, DIMMER SWITCH ACTUATOR

NUT, HEXAGON

RETAINER, BEARING

SWITCH ASM, DIMMER

SCREW, HEX WASHER HEAD TAPPING

SEAT, LOWER BEARING

SPRING, LOWER BEARING

RETAINER, LOWER SPRING

RING, RETAINING

SHAFT ASM, STEERING

Exploded view of the standard steering column

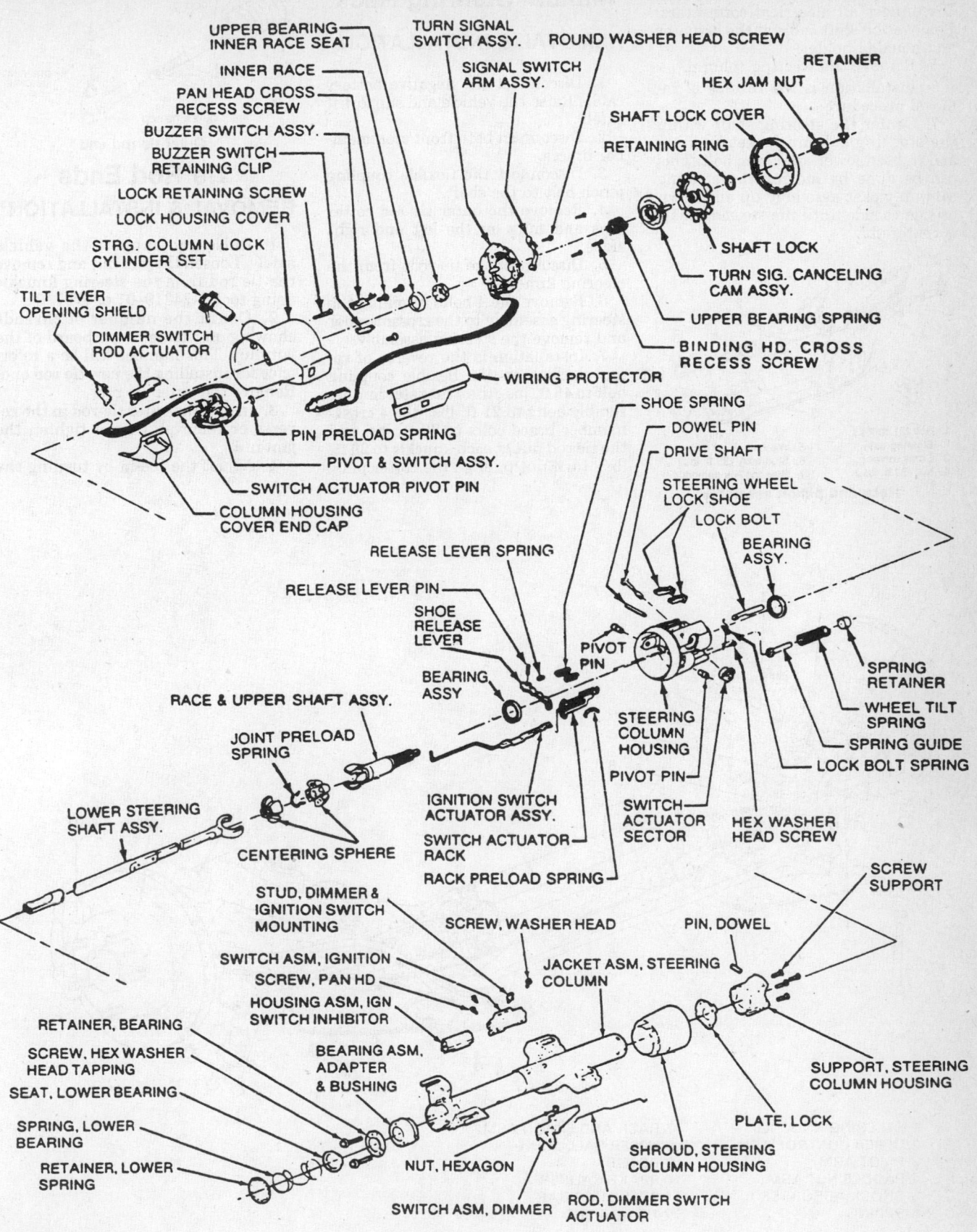

UPPER BEARING INNER RACE SEAT

INNER RACE

PAN HEAD CROSS RECESS SCREW

BUZZER SWITCH ASSY.

BUZZER SWITCH RETAINING CLIP

LOCK RETAINING SCREW

LOCK HOUSING COVER

STRG. COLUMN LOCK CYLINDER SET

TILT LEVER OPENING SHIELD

DIMMER SWITCH ROD ACTUATOR

COLUMN HOUSING COVER END CAP

SWITCH ACTUATOR PIVOT PIN

PIVOT & SWITCH ASSY.

PIN PRELOAD SPRING

TURN SIGNAL SWITCH ASSY.

SIGNAL SWITCH ARM ASSY.

ROUND WASHER HEAD SCREW

HEX JAM NUT

RETAINER

SHAFT LOCK COVER

RETAINING RING

SHAFT LOCK

TURN SIG. CANCELING CAM ASSY.

UPPER BEARING SPRING

BINDING HD. CROSS RECESS SCREW

WIRING PROTECTOR

SHOE SPRING

DOWEL PIN

DRIVE SHAFT

STEERING WHEEL LOCK SHOE

LOCK BOLT

BEARING ASSY.

RELEASE LEVER SPRING

RELEASE LEVER PIN

SHOE RELEASE LEVER

BEARING ASSY

PIVOT PIN

STEERING COLUMN HOUSING

PIVOT PIN

SWITCH ACTUATOR SECTOR

HEX WASHER HEAD SCREW

SPRING RETAINER

WHEEL TILT SPRING

SPRING GUIDE

LOCK BOLT SPRING

RACE & UPPER SHAFT ASSY.

JOINT PRELOAD SPRING

LOWER STEERING SHAFT ASSY.

CENTERING SPHERE

IGNITION SWITCH ACTUATOR ASSY.

SWITCH ACTUATOR RACK

RACK PRELOAD SPRING

STUD, DIMMER & IGNITION SWITCH MOUNTING

SCREW, WASHER HEAD

SCREW SUPPORT

PIN, DOWEL

SWITCH ASM, IGNITION

SCREW, PAN HD

HOUSING ASM, IGN SWITCH INHIBITOR

JACKET ASM, STEERING COLUMN

RETAINER, BEARING

SCREW, HEX WASHER HEAD TAPPING

SEAT, LOWER BEARING

SPRING, LOWER BEARING

RETAINER, LOWER SPRING

BEARING ASM, ADAPTER & BUSHING

NUT, HEXAGON

SWITCH ASM, DIMMER

ROD, DIMMER SWITCH ACTUATOR

SHROUD, STEERING COLUMN HOUSING

PLATE, LOCK

SUPPORT, STEERING COLUMN HOUSING

Exploded view of the tilt steering column

4. Remove the shift indicator cable. Disconnect all electrical connectors. Remove the shift cable at the actuator and housing holder.

5. Remove the steering column.

6. Installation is the reverse of removal procedure.

7. Center the steering shaft within the steering column jacket bushing and tighten lower attaching bolt. This can be done by moving the steering column jacket assembly up and down or side to side until the steering shaft is centered.

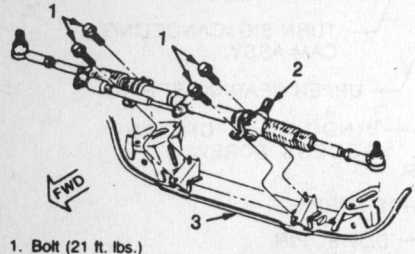

1. Bolt (21 ft. lbs.)
2. Steering assy.
3. Cross member
4. Nut (32 ft. lbs.)
5. Washer
6. Stud assy (36 ft. lbs.)
7. Steering link damper

Rack and pinion assembly

Manual Steering Rack
REMOVAL & INSTALLATION

1. Disconnect the negative battery cable. Raise the vehicle and support it safely.

2. Disconnect both front crossmember braces.

3. Disconnect the flexible coupling pinch bolt to the shaft.

4. Remove the outer tie rod cotter pins and nuts on the left and right sides.

5. Disconnect the tie rods from the steering knuckle.

6. Remove the 4 bolts retaining the steering assembly to the crossmember and remove the steering assembly.

7. Installation is the reverse of removal. Tighten the flexible coupling bolt to 46 ft. lbs., the 4 new steering assembly bolts to 21 ft. lbs., the 4 crossmember brace bolts to 20 ft. lbs. and the tie rod nut at each knuckle to 29 ft. lbs., turn nut to align the cotter pin.

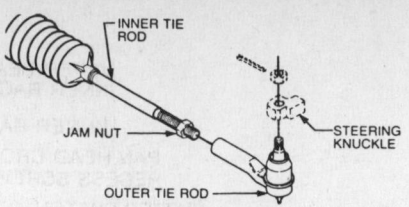

Outer tie rod end

Tie Rod Ends
REMOVAL & INSTALLATION

1. Raise and support the vehicle safely. Loosen the jam nut and remove the tie rod from the steering knuckle using tool J–24319–01 or BT7101.

2. Count the number of threads showing on the tie rod, inboard of the jam nut. This number will be a reference for installing the new tie rod end. Remove the outer tie rod.

3. Install the outer tie-rod in the reverse or removal. Do not tighten the jam nut.

4. Adjust the toe-in by turning the

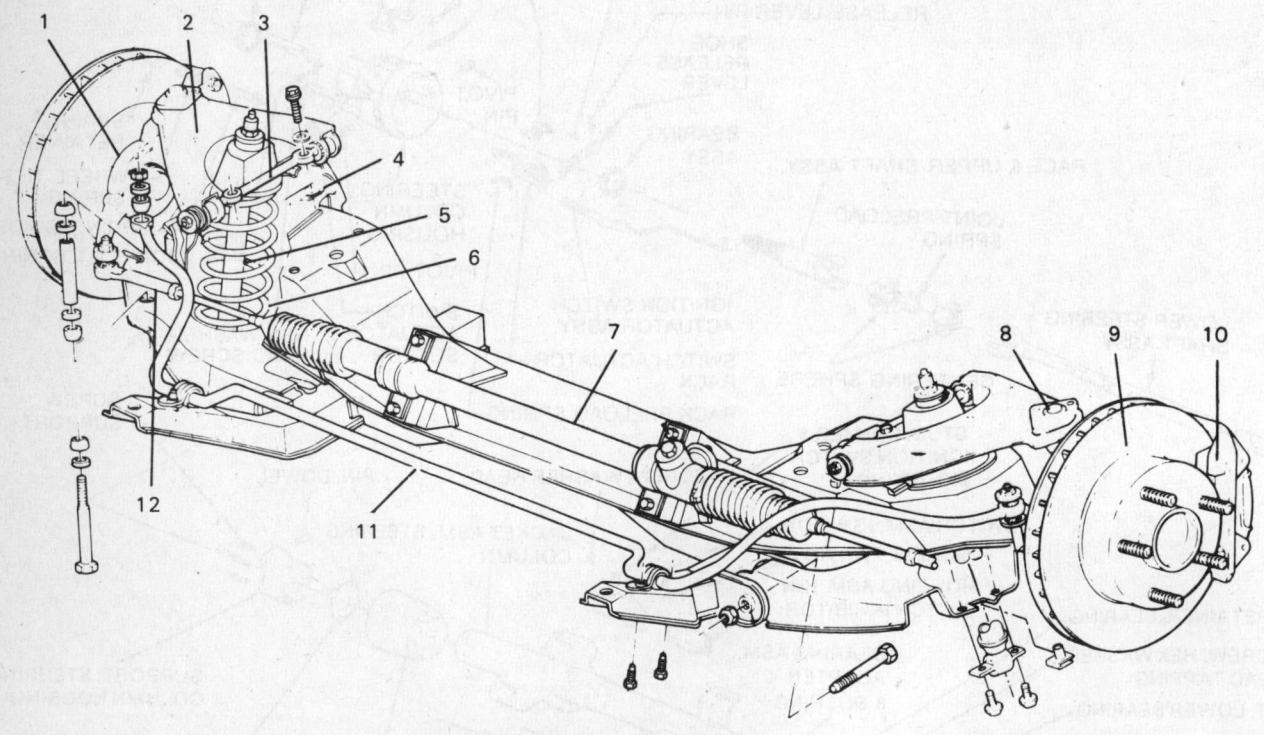

1. STEERING KNUCKLE
2. UPPER CONTROL ARM
3. PIVOT ARM
4. PADDLE NUT ASM.
5. SHOCK ABSORBER
6. SPRING
7. RACK AND PINION ASM.
8. UPPER BALL JOINT
9. ROTOR
10. BRAKE CALIPER
11. STABILIZER BAR
12. TIE ROD END

Steering gear and related components

inner tie-rod the required number of turns.

5. Make sure the boot is not twisted then torque the jam nut to 50 ft. lbs.

BRAKES

For all brake system repair and service procedures not detailed below, please refer to "Brakes" in the Unit Repair section.

Master Cylinder

REMOVAL & INSTALLATION

1. Disconnect the negative battery cable. Disconnect and plug the hydraulic lines at the master cylinder.
2. Remove the 2 nuts attaching the master cylinder to its mounting. Remove the master cylinder from the vehicle.
3. Installation is the reverse of the removal procedure. Be sure to bleed the master cylinder. prior to installation.

Combination Valve

REMOVAL & INSTALLATION

NOTE: The combination valve is not repairable and must be replaced if found defective.

1. Disconnect the negative battery cable. Disconnect and plug the hydraulic lines at the combination valve.
2. Disconnect the warning switch wiring harness from the valve switch terminal.
3. Remove the bolt attaching the valve to the bracket.
4. Remove the combination valve.
5. Installation is the reverse of removal.
6. Bleed the system.

Power Brake Booster

REMOVAL & INSTALLATION

1. Disconnect the negative battery cable. Disconnect the master cylinder from the booster and position it to the side.
2. Remove the booster attaching nuts.
3. Remove the booster pushrod from the brake pedal assembly.
4. Remove the booster from the vehicle.
5. Installation is the reverse of removal.

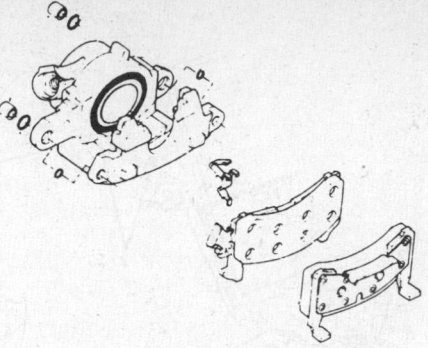

Front brake pads—1987 vehicles

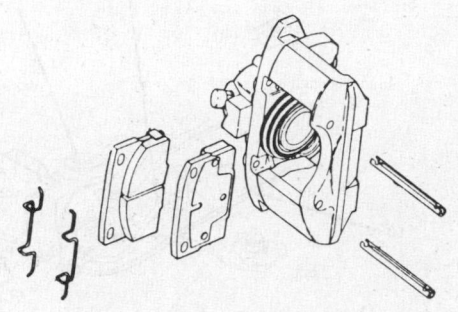

Front brake pads—1988 vehicles

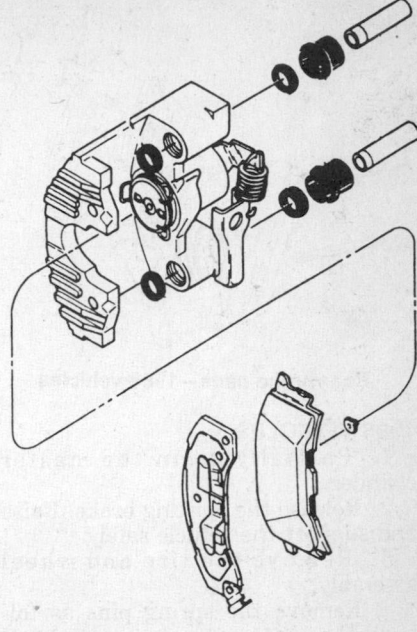

Rear brake pads—1987 vehicles

NOTE: If any hydraulic component is removed or brake line disconnected, bleed the brake system after installation, as necessary.

Disc Brake Pads

REMOVAL & INSTALLATION

Front Pads

1987 VEHICLES
1. Partially drain the master cylinder.
2. Raise and support the vehicle safely.
3. Remove the tire and wheel assembly.
4. Remove the caliper retaining bolts. Remove the caliper.
5. Remove the pads from the caliper.
6. Installation is the reverse of the removal procedure. Be sure to add brake fluid, as required.

1988 VEHICLES
1. Partially drain the master cylinder.
2. Raise and support the vehicle safely.
3. Remove the tire and wheel assembly.
4. Bottom the piston in the caliper bore to provide clearance between the linings and rotor.

5. Remove the spring pins as follows. Connect spring pin removal tool J-36620 to a slide hammer tool.
6. Remove the threaded tip from the rod on the spring pin tool. Insert the rod completely through the pin and install the threaded tip as far as it will go.
7. Use the slide hammer to drive out the pin.

NOTE: Be prepared to catch the springs when removing the spring pins, as the springs may fly out.

8. Remove the springs from the shoe flanges. Remove the disc brake linings from the caliper.
9. Installation is the reverse of the removal procedure.

Rear Pads

1987 VEHICLES
1. Partially drain the master cylinder.
2. Raise and support the vehicle safely.
3. Remove the tire and wheel assembly.
4. Loosen the tension on the parking brake cable at the equalizer.
5. Remove the caliper retaining bolts. Remove the caliper.
6. Remove the pads from the caliper.
7. Installation is the reverse of the removal procedure. Be sure to add brake fluid, as required.

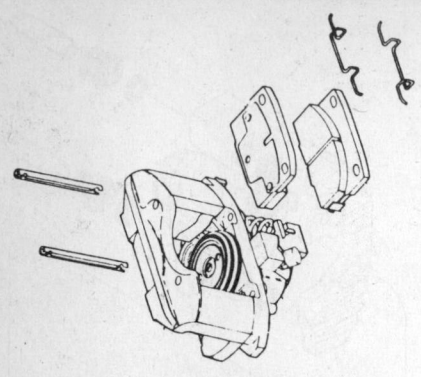

Rear brake pads—1988 vehicles

1988 VEHICLES

1. Partially drain the master cylinder.

2. Release the parking brake. Raise and support the vehicle safely.

3. Remove the tire and wheel assembly.

4. Remove the spring pins as follows. Connect spring pin removal tool J-36620 to a slide hammer tool.

5. Remove the threaded tip from the rod on the spring pin tool. Insert the rod completely through the pin and install the threaded tip as far as it will go.

6. Use the slide hammer to drive out the pin.

NOTE: Be prepared to catch the springs when removing the spring pins, as the springs may fly out.

7. Remove the springs from the shoe flanges. Remove the disc brake linings from the caliper.

8. Installation is the reverse of the removal procedure.

Parking Brake Cable

ADJUSTMENT

Adjustment of parking brake cable is necessary whenever the rear brake cables have been disconnected. Need for parking brake adjustment is indicated if the hydraulic brake system operates with good reserve, but the parking

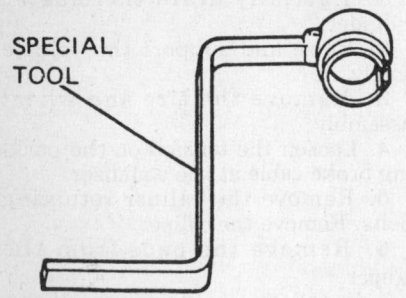

SPECIAL TOOL

Special tool used to disconnect parking brake cables

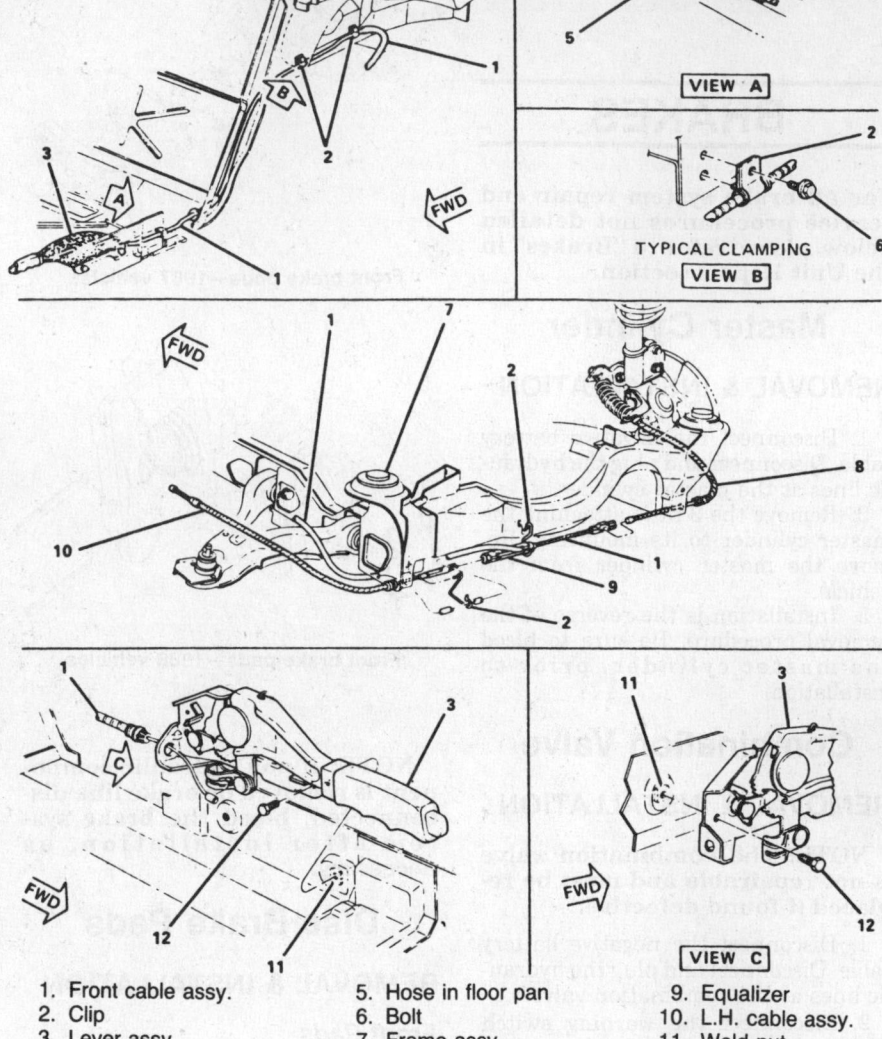

1. Front cable assy.	5. Hose in floor pan	9. Equalizer
2. Clip	6. Bolt	10. L.H. cable assy.
3. Lever assy.	7. Frame assy.	11. Weld nut
4. Grommet	8. R.H. cable assy.	12. Bolt/Screw

Parking brake assembly

brake hand level travel is more than 9 ratchet clicks.

1. Place parking brake hand lever in the released position.

2. Raise and support the vehicle safely.

3. Apply lubricant to groove in the equalizer nut.

4. Hold the brake cable stud from turning and tightening equalizer nut until cable slack is removed.

5. Make sure the caliper levers are against stops on the caliper housing after tightening the equalizer nut.

6. If levers are off the stops, loosen the cable until the levers do return to the stops.

7. Operate the parking brake lever several times to check adjustment. Properly adjusted parking brake shoes

and properly adjusted parking brake cable will result in a parking brake handle movement of 5–8 notches when a force is applied perpendicularly at the handle grip midpoint.

8. Lower the rear wheels. The levers must be on the caliper stops after completion of adjustment. Back off the parking brake adjuster if necessary to keep the levers on the stops.

REMOVAL & INSTALLATION

1. Raise and safely support the vehicle.

2. Loosen the adjusting nut at the equalizer and separate the cables.

3. Remove the cables at the calipers.

4. Disconnect the cables at the cra-

dle with tool J–34065 and remove the cables.

5. Install the new cables by reversing the removal procedure. Adjust the cables after installation.

FRONT SUSPENSION

Shock Absorbers

REMOVAL & INSTALLATION

1. Raise the vehicle and support safely.
2. Remove the wheel and tire assembly.
3. Remove the lower retaining bolts.
4. Remove the nut and bolt from the top of the shock absorber.
5. Remove the shock from the vehicle through the lower control arm.
6. Installation is the reverse of the removal procedure.

Coil Springs

REMOVAL & INSTALLATION

1. Raise the vehicle and support it safely. Properly support the lower control arm, using a suitable jack.
2. Remove wheel and tire assembly.
3. Remove the shock absorber. Disconnect the stabilizer bar from the lower control arm. Disconnect the lower ball joint from the steering knuckle.
4. Install a safety chain through the spring, as a safety precaution. Remove the lower control arm bolts.
5. Slowly lower the jack under the lower control arm and remove the spring from the vehicle.
6. Installation is the reverse of the removal procedure.

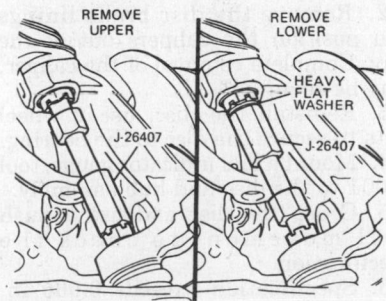

Ball joint removal

Upper Ball Joints

INSPECTION

1. Raise the front of the vehicle with a lift placed under the engine cradle. The front wheels should be clear of the ground.
2. Grasp the wheel at the top and bottom and shake the wheel in and out.
3. If any movement is seen of the steering knuckle relative to the control arm, the ball joints are defective and must be replaced. Note, movement elsewhere may be due to loose wheel bearings or other troubles. Watch the knuckle-to-control arm connection.
4. If the ball stud is disconnected from the steering knuckle and any looseness is noted, often the ball joint stud can be twisted in its socket with your fingers, replace the ball joints.

REMOVAL & INSTALLATION

1. Raise the vehicle and support it safely. Properly support the lower control arm, using a suitable jack.
2. Remove wheel and tire assembly.
3. Remove the bolt that retains the brake line clip to the upper control arm.
4. Disconnect the tie rod end from the steering knuckle, swing the knuckle outboard.
5. Using a ball joint removal tool, remove the ball joint from the steering knuckle.
6. Remove the upper control arm retaining bolts. Remove the upper control arm from the vehicle.
7. Position the control arm in a suitable holding fixture. Drill out the ball joint retaining rivets. Remove the ball joint from the control arm.
8. Install a new ball joint, using the retaining bolts provided with the ball joint.
9. Installation is the reverse of the removal procedure. Be sure to check the front end alignment.

Lower Ball Joints

INSPECTION

1. Raise the front of the vehicle with a lift placed under the engine cradle. The front wheels should be clear of the ground.
2. Grasp the wheel at the top and bottom and shake the wheel in and out.
3. If any movement is seen of the steering knuckle relative to the control arm, the ball joints are defective and must be replaced. Note, movement elsewhere may be due to loose wheel

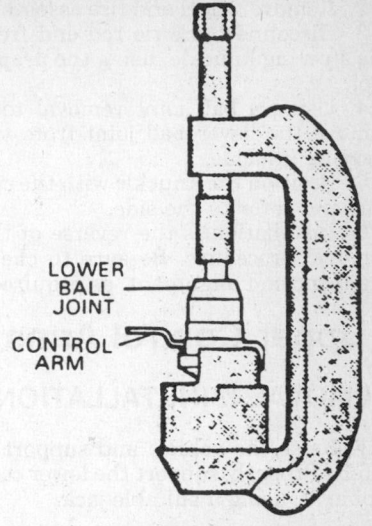

REMOVING LOWER BALL JOINT

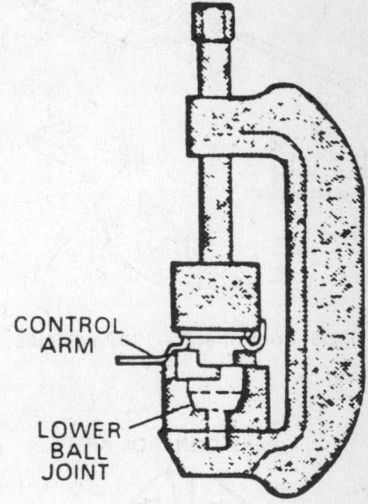

INSTALLING LOWER BALL JOINT

Lower ball joint removal and installation

bearings or other troubles. Watch the knuckle-to-control arm connection.

4. If the ball stud is disconnected from the steering knuckle and any looseness is noted, often the ball joint stud can be twisted in its socket with your fingers, replace the ball joints.

REMOVAL & INSTALLATION

1987 Vehicles

The lower ball joint is welded to the lower control arm, if the lower ball joint requires replacement the lower control arm must also be replaced.

1988 Vehicles

1. Raise the vehicle and support it safely. Properly support the lower control arm, using a suitable jack.

2. Remove wheel and tire assembly.

3. Disconnect the tie rod end from the steering knuckle, using the proper tool.

4. Using a ball joint removal tool, remove the lower ball joint from the steering knuckle.

5. Position the knuckle with the caliper and rotor to the side.

6. Installation is the reverse of the removal procedure. Be sure to check the front end alignment, as required.

Upper Control Arms

REMOVAL & INSTALLATION

1. Raise the vehicle and support it safely. Properly support the lower control arm, using a suitable jack.

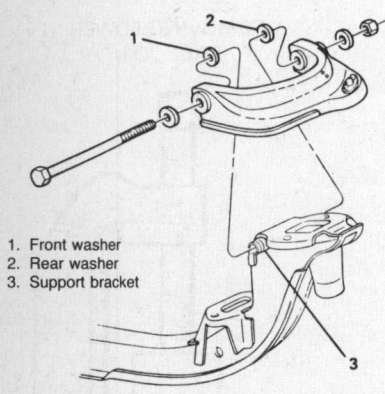

1. Front washer
2. Rear washer
3. Support bracket

Upper control arm—1987 vehicles

2. Remove wheel and tire assembly.

3. Remove the bolt that retains the brake line clip to the upper control arm.

4. Disconnect the tie rod end from the steering knuckle, swing the knuckle outboard.

5. Using a ball joint removal tool, remove the ball joint from the steering knuckle.

6. Remove the upper control arm retaining bolts. Remove the upper control arm from the vehicle.

7. Installation is the reverse of the removal procedure. Be sure to check the front end alignment.

Lower Control Arms

REMOVAL & INSTALLATION

1. Raise the vehicle and support it

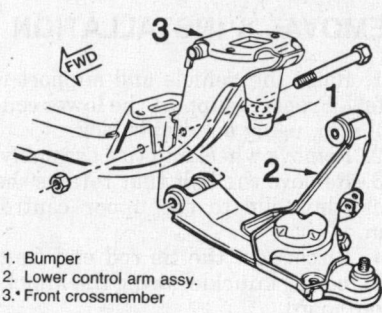

1. Bumper
2. Lower control arm assy.
3. Front crossmember

Lower control arm

safely. Properly support the lower control arm, using a suitable jack.

2. Remove wheel and tire assembly. Remove the spring assembly.

3. Remove the lower control arm retaining bolts. Remove the lower control arm from the vehicle.

4. Installation is the reverse of the removal procedure. Be sure to check the front end alignment, as required.

Front Wheel Bearings

ADJUSTMENT

Tapered Wheel Bearings

1. Raise the vehicle and support it safely.

2. Remove the wheel and tire assembly.

3. Remove the dust cap from the hub.

4. Remove cotter pin from spindle and spindle nut.

5. Tighten the spindle nut to 12 ft. lbs. while turning the wheel assembly forward by hand to fully seat the bearings. This will remove any grease or burrs which could cause excessive wheel bearing play later.

6. Back off the nut to the just loose position.

7. Hand tighten the spindle nut. Loosen the spindle nut until either hole in the spindle lines up with a slot in the nut. (Not more than ½ flat).

8. Install a new cotter pin. Bend the ends of the cotter pin against nut, cut off extra length to ensure ends will not interfere with the dust cap.

9. Measure the looseness in the hub assembly. There will be from 0.001–0.005 in. endplay when properly adjusted.

10. Install the dust cap on the hub.

11. Replace the wheel cover or hub cap.

12. Lower the vehicle to the floor.

SEALED WHEEL BEARINGS

1. Raise and support the vehicle safely. Remove the tire and wheel assemblies.

2. Remove the disc brake linings and position the calipers out of the way. Complete removal of the caliper, may be required.

3. Reinstall the disc, use 2 wheel nuts to secure the disc to the bearing.

4. Mount a dial indicator gauge, tool J8001 to the disc and hub assembly.

5. Grasp the disc and use a push pull movement to check the specification.

6. Specification exceeds 0.005 in. (0.1270mm), replace the hub and bearing assembly.

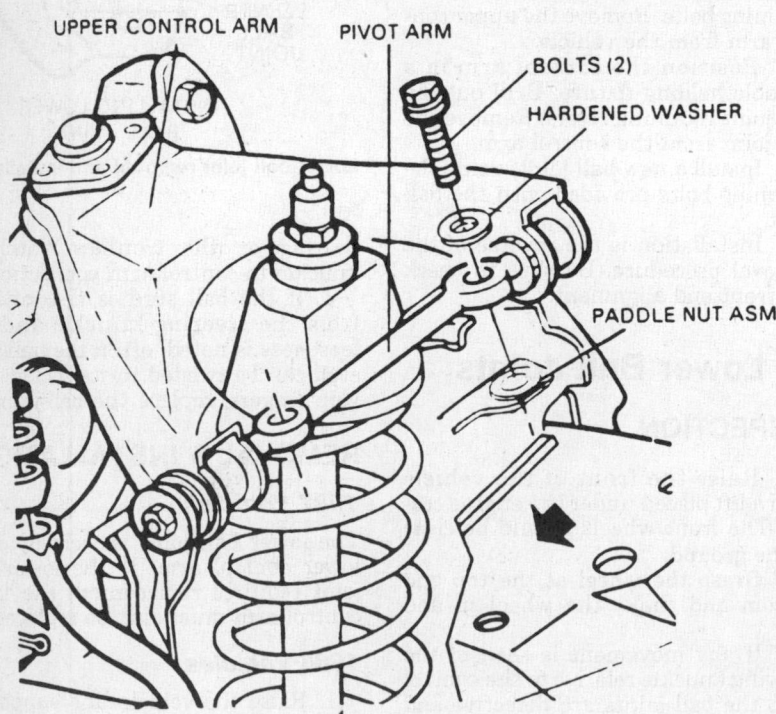

UPPER CONTROL ARM   PIVOT ARM   BOLTS (2)   HARDENED WASHER   PADDLE NUT ASM

Upper control arm—1988 vehicles

REMOVAL & INSTALLATION

1987 Vehicles

1. Raise and safely support the vehicle.

2. Remove the wheel and tire assembly.

3. Remove the brake caliper from the knuckle.

4. Remove the dust cup, cotter pin, spindle nut and washer.

5. Remove the hub and bearings. Do not allow the bearings to fall on the ground.

6. Remove the outer bearing. Remove the inner bearing by prying out the grease seal. Discard the seal.

7. Drive out the old races from the hub with a brass drift inserted behind the races in the notches in the hub.

8. Lubricate the new race with a light film of oil.

9. Start the new race squarely in the hub and using an appropriate tool, seat the race in the hub.

10. Istallation is the reverse of the removal. After assembly adjust the bearings correctly.

1988 Vehicles

1. Raise the vehicle and support it safely.

2. Remove the wheel and tire assembly.

3. Remove the bolt attaching the brake line clip to the upper control arm.

4. Remove the caliper and suspend with a wire.

5. Remove the rotor.

6. Remove the 3 bolts attaching the hub and bearing assembly to the steering knuckle.

7. Remove the bearing and hub assembly.

8. Install the hub and bearing assembly. Torque the hub and bearing to steering knuckle bolt to 220 ft. lbs.

NOTE: When ever the brake rotor has been separated from the wheel bearing, remove any rust or other foreign material from the mating surfaces of the wheel bearing flange and rotor. Failure to do so may result in lateral run-out of the rotor, causing brake pedal pulsation.

9. Install the rotor and caliper.

10. Install the bolt attaching the brake line clip to the upper control arm.

11. Install the wheel and tire assembly.

12. Lower the vehicle to the ground.

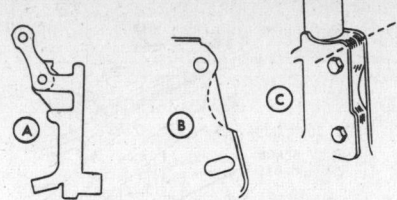

Scribing the strut and knuckle

REAR SUSPENSION

MacPherson Strut

REMOVAL & INSTALLATION

1. Remove the engine compartment cover.

2. Remove the 3 upper strut nuts and washers.

3. Loosen the wheel lug nuts.

4. Raise the vehicle and support it safely. Support the rear control arm with a floor jack.

5. Remove the wheel and tire. Remove the brake line clip.

6. Scribe the strut and knuckle. Remove the 2 strut mounting nuts and bolts. Remove the strut assembly and spacer plate from the vehicle.

7. Installation is the reverse of removal. Align the scribe marks on the strut and knuckle and replace the bolts in the same order in which they were removed. Tighten the strut mounting nuts to 140 ft. lbs. and the upper strut nuts to l8 ft. lbs.

Lower Control Arm

REMOVAL & INSTALLATION

1987 Vehicles Only

1. Raise the vehicle and support it safely.

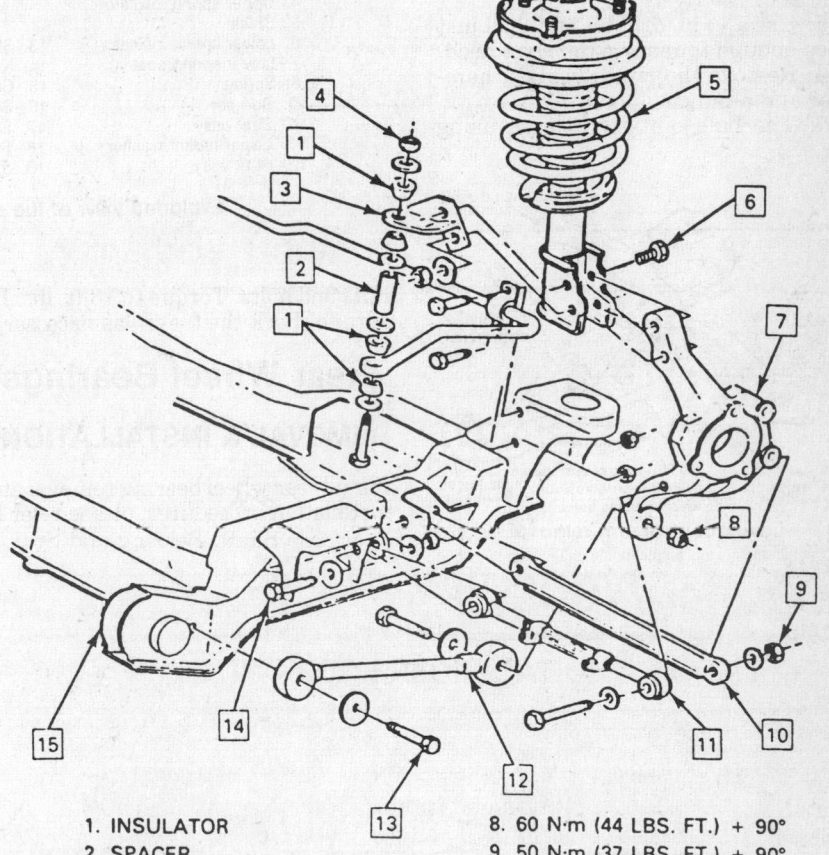

1. INSULATOR
2. SPACER
3. BRACKET
4. 17 N·m (13 LBS. FT.)
5. STRUT ASSEMBLY
6. INSTALL IN DIRECTION SHOWN
7. KNUCKLE
8. 60 N·m (44 LBS. FT.) + 90°
9. 50 N·m (37 LBS. FT.) + 90°
10. LATERAL CONTROL ARM
11. FIXED ADJUSTING LINK
12. TRAILING ARM
13. 51 N·m (37 LBS. FT.)
14. 55 N·m (41 LBS. FT.)
15. FRAME

Exploded view of the rear suspension—1988

2. Remove the ball joint clamping bolt.

3. Separate the knuckle from the ball joint.

4. Remove the lower control arm pivot bolts at the frame and the control arm.

5. Installation is the reverse of removal. Be sure to check the toe-in and camber settings, as required.

Lower Ball Joint

REMOVAL & INSTALLATION

1987 Vehicles Only

1. Raise the vehicle and support it safely, then remove the wheel.

2. Remove the clamp bolt from the lower control arm ball stud.

3. Disconnect the ball joint from the knuckle.

NOTE: It may be necessary to tap the ball stud with a mallet.

4. Using an ⅛ in. drill, drill the rivets approximately ¼ in. deep in the center of the rivet.

5. Use a ½ in. drill bit and drill just deep enough to remove the rivet head.

6. Remove the rivets using a hammer and a punch.

7. The ball joint is replaced using

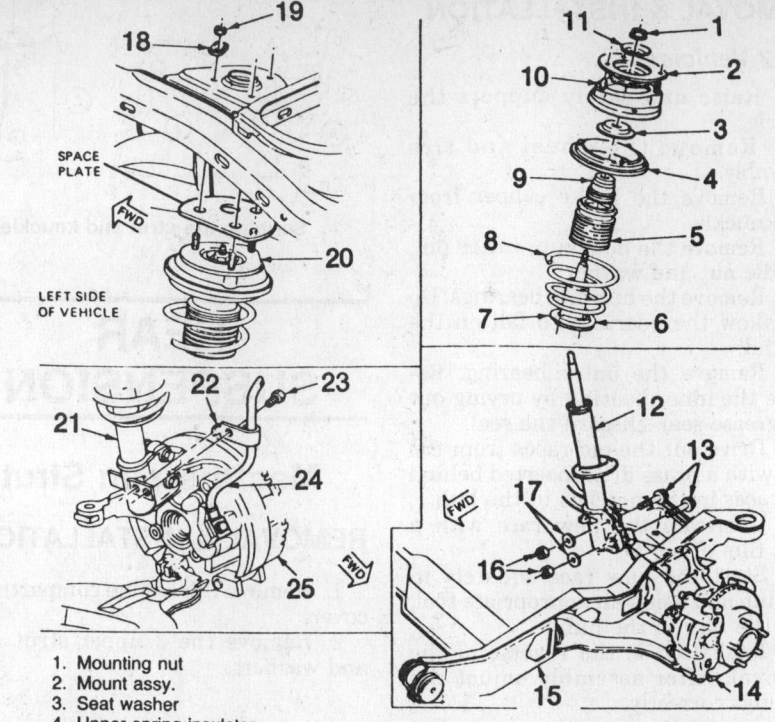

1. Mounting nut
2. Mount assy.
3. Seat washer
4. Upper spring insulator
5. Shield
6. Lower spring insulator
7. Lower spring seat
8. Spring
9. Bumper
10. Seat assy.
11. Upper mount washer
12. Strut assy.
13. Strut mounting bolts
14. Knuckle and hub assy.
15. Cradle assy.
16. Strut mounting nuts
17. Strut lower washers
18. Strut upper washers
19. Strut upper nuts
20. Rear strut mount assy.
21. Strut assy.
22. Brake line clip
23. Brake line clip bolt
24. Rear brake hose
25. Caliper assy.

Exploded view of the rear suspension—1987 vehicles

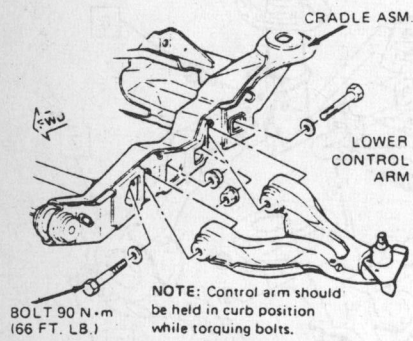

BOLT 90 N·m
(66 FT. LB.)

NOTE: Control arm should be held in curb position while torquing bolts.

Lower control arm removal

nuts and bolts. Torque to 13 ft. lbs. Be sure to check the toe-in, as necessary.

Rear Wheel Bearings

REMOVAL & INSTALLATION

For all rear wheel bearing removal and installation procedures, please refer to Rear Axle Shaft, Bearing and Seal in

the Drive Axle section.

Rear Axle Assembly

REMOVAL & INSTALLATION

For all rear axle (halfshaft) removal and installation procedures, please refer to Halfshaft in the Drive Axle section.

Pontiac
Front Wheel Drive
LeMans

SPECIFICATIONS

VEHICLE IDENTIFICATION CHART

It is important for servicing and ordering parts to be certain of the vehicle and engine identification. The VIN (vehicle identification number) is a 17 digit number visible through the windshield on the driver's side of the dash and contains the vehicle and engine identification codes. The tenth digit indicates model year and the eighth digit indicates engine code. It can be interpreted as follows:

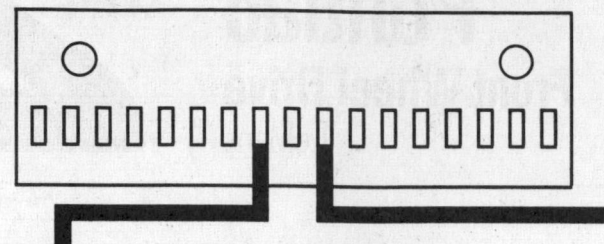

Engine Code

Code	Cu. In.	Liters	Cyl.	Fuel Sys.	Eng. Mfg.
6	98	1.6	4	TBI	GM
K	121	2.0	4	TBI	GM

Model Year

Code	Year
J	1988
K	1989
L	1990
M	1991

ENGINE IDENTIFICATION

Year	Model	Engine Displacement cu. in. (liter)	Engine Series Identification (VIN)	No. of Cylinders	Engine Type
1988	Lemans	98 (1.6)	6	4	OHC
1989	Lemans	98 (1.6)	6	4	OHC
	Lemans	121 (2.0)	K	4	OHC
1990-91	Lemans	98 (1.6)	6	4	OHC
	Lemans	121 (2.0)	K	4	OHC

GENERAL ENGINE SPECIFICATIONS

Year	VIN	No. Cylinder Displacement cu. in. (liter)	Fuel System Type	Net Horsepower @ rpm	Net Torque @ rpm (ft. lbs.)	Bore × Stroke (in.)	Compression Ratio	Oil Pressure @ rpm
1988	6	4-98 (1.6)	TBI	74 @ 5200	88 @ 3400	3.11 × 3.20	8.5:1	55 @ 2000
1989	6	4-98 (1.6)	TBI	74 @ 5600	88 @ 3400	3.11 × 3.20	8.5:1	55 @ 2000
	K	4-121 (2.0)	TBI	96 @ 4800	118 @ 3600	3.39 × 3.39	8.8:1	55 @ 2000
1990-91	6	4-98 (1.6)	TBI	74 @ 5600	88 @ 3400	3.11 × 3.20	8.5:1	55 @ 2000
	K	4-121 (2.0)	TBI	96 @ 4800	118 @ 3600	3.39 × 3.39	8.8:1	55 @ 2000

ENGINE TUNE-UP SPECIFICATIONS

Year	VIN	No. Cylinder Displacement cu. in. (liter)	Spark Plugs Type	Gap (in.)	Ignition Timing (deg.) MT	AT	Compression Pressure (psi)	Fuel Pump (psi)	Idle Speed (rpm) MT	AT	Valve Clearance In.	Ex.
1988	6	4-98 (1.6)	ACR44XLS6	0.060	①	①	②	9-13	①	①	HYD.	HYD.
1989	6	4-98 (1.6)	ACR44XLS6	0.060	①	①	②	9-13	①	①	HYD.	HYD.
	K	4-121 (2.0)	ACR44XLS6	0.060	①	①	②	9-13	①	①	HYD.	HYD.
1990	6	4-98 (1.6)	ACR45XLS	0.045	①	①	②	9-13	①	①	HYD.	HYD.
	K	4-121 (2.0)	ACR45XLS	0.045	①	①	②	9-13	①	①	HYD.	HYD.
1991		SEE UNDERHOOD SPECIFICATIONS STICKER										

① See underhood specifications sticker
② Lowest reading not less than 70% of highest. No reading less than 100 psi.

FIRING ORDERS

NOTE: To avoid confusion, always replace spark plug wires one at a time.

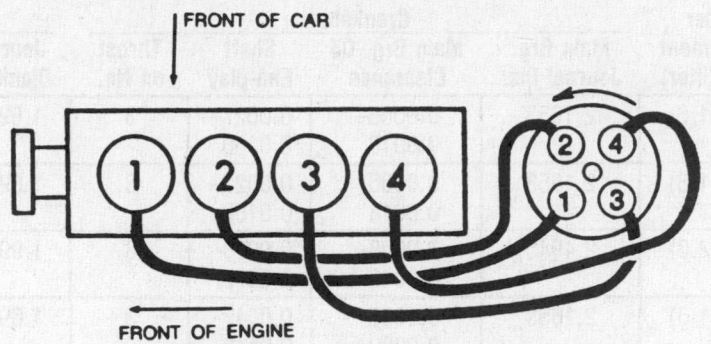

1.6L and 2.0L Engines
Engine Firing Order: 1–3–4–2
Distributor Rotation: Counterclockwise

CAPACITIES

Year	Model	VIN	No. Cylinder Displacement cu. in. (liter)	Engine Crankcase with Filter	without Filter	Transmission (pts.) 4-Spd.	5-Spd.	Auto.	Drive Axle (pts.)	Fuel Tank (gal.)	Cooling System (qts.)
1988	Lemans	6	4-98 (1.6)	5	4	3.5	3.5	8 ①	—	13.2	8.1
1989	Lemans	6	4-98 (1.6)	5	4	4.5	4.5	8 ①	—	13.0	8.1
	Lemans	K	4-121 (2.0)	5	4	4.5	4.5	8 ①	—	13.0	8.1
1990-91	Lemans	6	4-98 (1.6)	5	4	4.5	4.5	8 ①	—	13.0	8.1
	Lemans	K	4-121 (2.0)	5	4	4.5	4.5	8 ①	—	13.0	8.1

① Overhaul—12 pts.

CAMSHAFT SPECIFICATIONS
All measurements given in inches.

Year	VIN	No. Cylinder Displacement cu. in. (liter)	Journal Diameter 1	2	3	4	5	Lobe Lift In.	Ex.	Bearing Clearance	Camshaft End Play
1988	6	4-98 (1.6)	1.578–1.577	1.588–1.590	1.598–1.597	1.608–1.607	1.618–1.617	0.224	0.245	0.0018–0.0020	0.002 0.006

CAMSHAFT SPECIFICATIONS

All measurements given in inches.

Year	VIN	No. Cylinder Displacement cu. in. (liter)	Journal Diameter 1	2	3	4	5	Lobe Lift In.	Ex.	Bearing Clearance	Camshaft End Play
1989	6	4-98 (1.6)	1.578–1.577	1.588–1.590	1.598–1.597	1.608–1.607	1.618–1.617	0.224	0.245	0.0018–0.0020	0.002 0.006
	K	4-121 (2.0)	1.867–1.869	1.867–1.869	1.867–1.869	1.867–1.869	1.867–1.869	0.259	0.259	0.0010–0.0039	0.002 0.006
1990–91	6	4-98 (1.6)	1.578–1.577	1.588–1.587	1.600–1.597	1.608–1.607	1.618–1.617	0.224	0.245	0.0020–0.0035	0.002 0.004
	K	4-121 (2.0)	1.670–1.671	1.671–1.672	1.691–1.692	1.701–1.702	1.710–1.711	0.237	0.251	0.0011–0.0035	0.002 0.006

CRANKSHAFT AND CONNECTING ROD SPECIFICATIONS

All measurements are given in inches.

Year	VIN	No. Cylinder Displacement cu. in. (liter)	Crankshaft Main Brg. Journal Dia.	Main Brg. Oil Clearance	Shaft End-play	Thrust on No.	Connecting Rod Journal Diameter	Oil Clearance	Side Clearance
1988	6	4-98 (1.6)	2.1653	0.0005–0.0018	0.0027–0.0100	3	1.6929	0.0014–0.0031	0.0027–0.0095
1989	6	4-98 (1.6)	2.1653	0.0006–0.0018	0.0027–0.0100	3	1.6929	0.0014–0.0031	0.0027–0.0095
	K	4-121 (2.0)	2.4945	0.0006–0.0019	0.0020–0.0070	3	1.9983	0.0010–0.0031	0.0039–0.0149
1990–91	6	4-89 (1.6)	2.1653	0.0006–0.0020	0.0047–0.0140	3	1.6929	0.0007–0.0025	0.0028–0.0095
	K	4-121 (2.0)	2.2828	0.0006–0.0016	0.0028–0.0118	3	1.9279	0.0007–0.0025	0.0028–0.0095

VALVE SPECIFICATIONS

Year	VIN	No. Cylinder Displacement cu. in. (liter)	Seat Angle (deg.)	Face Angle (deg.)	Spring Test Pressure (lbs.)	Spring Installed Height (in.)	Stem-to-Guide Clearance (in.) Intake	Exhaust	Stem Diameter (in.) Intake	Exhaust
1988	6	4-98 (1.6)	45	46	62	1.26	0.0006–0.0017	0.0014–0.0025	0.275	0.275
1989	6	4-98 (1.6)	45	46	62	1.26	0.0006–0.0017	0.0014–0.0025	0.275	0.275
	K	4-121 (2.0)	45	46	63	1.48	0.0011–0.0026	0.0014–0.0030	0.275	0.276
1990–91	6	4-98 (1.6)	46	46	62	1.24	0.0008–0.0020	0.0016–0.0030	0.276	0.276
	K	4-121 (2.0)	45	46	63	1.48	0.0006–0.0017	0.0012–0.0024	0.275	0.275

PISTON AND RING SPECIFICATIONS

All measurements are given in inches.

Year	VIN	No. Cylinder Displacement cu. in. (liter)	Piston Clearance	Ring Gap Top Compression	Bottom Compression	Oil Control	Ring Side Clearance Top Compression	Bottom Compression	Oil Control
1988	6	4-98 (1.6)	0.0008–0.0016	0.012–0.020	0.012–0.020	0.016–0.055	0.0012–0.0027	0.0012–0.0032	0.0000–0.0050

PISTON AND RING SPECIFICATIONS
All measurements are given in inches.

Year	VIN	No. Cylinder Displacement cu. in. (liter)	Piston Clearance	Ring Gap			Ring Side Clearance		
				Top Compression	Bottom Compression	Oil Control	Top Compression	Bottom Compression	Oil Control
1989	6	4-98 (1.6)	0.0008	0.012-0.020	0.012-0.020	0.016-0.055	0.0012-0.0027	0.0012-0.0032	0.0000-0.0050
	K	4-121 (2.0)	0.0098 0.0022	0.010-0.020	0.010-0.020	0.010-0.050	0.0019-0.0027	0.0019-0.0027	0.0019-0.0032
1990-91	6	4-98 (1.6)	0.0008	0.012-0.020	0.012-0.020	0.016-0.055	0.0019-0.0027	0.0012-0.0032	0.0000-0.0050
	K	4-121 (2.0)	0.0004-0.0012	0.010-0.018	0.012-0.020	0.010-0.050	0.0019-0.0027	0.0019-0.0027	0.0019-0.0032

TORQUE SPECIFICATIONS
All readings in ft. lbs.

Year	VIN	No. Cylinder Displacement cu. in. (liter)	Cylinder Head Bolts	Main Bearing Bolts	Rod Bearing Bolts	Crankshaft Pulley Bolts	Flywheel Bolts	Manifold		Spark Plugs
								Intake	Exhaust	
1988	6	4-98 (1.6)	18 ①	36 ②	18 ③	40	25 ④	16	16	18
1989	6	4-98 (1.6)	18 ①	36 ②	18 ③	40	25 ④	16	16	18
	K	4-121 (2.0)	18 ①	70	38	20	⑤	16	16	18
1990-91	6	4-98 (1.6)	18 ①	36 ②	18 ③	41	25 ④	16	16	15
	K	4-121 (2.0)	18 ①	70	38	20	⑤	16	16	15

① Cold—plus 2 turns of 60 degrees each and 1 turn of 30 degrees
  Warm—plus 30-50 degree turn after warm up (thermostat open)
② Plus a 45-60 degree turn
③ Plus a 30 degree turn
④ Plus a 30-45 degree turn
⑤ Automatic—52 ft. lbs.
  Manual —55 ft. lbs.

BRAKE SPECIFICATIONS
All measurements in inches unless noted.

Year	Model	Lug Nut Torque (ft. lbs.)	Master Cylinder Bore	Brake Disc		Standard Brake Drum Diameter	Minimum Lining Thickness	
				Minimum Thickness	Maximum Runout		Front	Rear
1988	Lemans	65	0.813	0.460	0.004	7.900	0.28 ②	0.02 ①
1989	Lemans	66	0.813	0.460	0.004	7.900	0.28 ②	0.02 ①
1990-91	Lemans	66	0.874	0.420	0.004	7.900	0.28 ②	0.02 ①

① Above rivet head
② Shoe and lining

WHEEL ALIGNMENT

Year	Model		Caster		Camber		Toe-in (in.)	Steering Axis Inclination (deg.)
			Range (deg.)	Preferred Setting (deg.)	Range (deg.)	Preferred Setting (deg.)		
1988	Lemans	Front	3/4P-2 3/4P	NA	1 1/4N-1/4P	NA	0	—
		Rear	—	—	1N-0	NA	1/3	—
1989	Lemans	Front	3/4P-2 3/4P	NA	1 1/4N-1/4P	NA	0	—
		Rear	—	—	1N-0	NA	1/3	—
1990-91	Lemans	Front	3/4P-2 3/4P	NA	1 1/4N-1/4P	NA	0	—
		Rear	—	—	1N-0	NA	1/3	—

NA Not adjustable   P Positive   N Negative

ENGINE ELECTRICAL

NOTE: Disconnecting the negative battery cable on some vehicles may interfere with the functions of the on board computer systems and may require the computer to undergo a relearning process, once the negative battery cable is reconnected.

Distributor

REMOVAL

1. Disconnect the negative battery cable.
2. Remove the distributor cap.
3. Mark and remove all electrical leads connected to the distributor assembly.
4. Mark the relationship of the rotor to the distributor housing and the distributor housing to the engine.
5. Remove the hold-down bolt, clamp and distributor.

INSTALLATION

Timing Not Disturbed

1. Turn the distributor shaft until the rotor points to the No. 1 spark plug tower on the cap.
2. Align the marks on the distributor housing and the engine.
3. Install the distributor into the engine.
4. Tighten the distributor hold-down bolt and reconnect the electrical connections.
5. Check and/or adjust the ignition timing.

Timing Disturbed

If the engine was cranked with the distributor removed, it will be necessary to position the No. 1 cylinder at TDC on the compression stroke. Follow the procedure listed here. This will enable the proper setting of the ignition timing.

1. Remove the No. 1 spark plug.
2. Place a finger over the spark plug hole. Crank the engine slowly until compression is felt.
3. Align the timing mark on the crankshaft pulley with the **0** degree mark on the timing scale attached to the front of the engine. This places the No. 1 cylinder at the TDC of the compression stroke.
4. Turn the distributor shaft until the rotor points to the No. 1 spark plug tower on the cap.

5. Install the distributor into the engine.
6. Tighten the distributor hold-down bolt and reconnect the electrical connections. Check the timing and adjust, as necessary.

Ignition Timing

ADJUSTMENT

1.6L Engine

1. Make sure the ignition switch is turned **OFF** when connecting electrical equipment to the engine.
2. Using an induction type timing light, connect the pickup lead of the light to the No. 1 spark plug wire.
3. Connect the timing light positive and negative leads to the battery positive and negative terminals.

NOTE: When connecting a timing light to the No. 1 spark plug wire, be sure to use a jumper wire between the spark plug and boot; do not pierce or cut the high tension wire.

4. Refer to the vehicle emission information label for the correct specification. Start the engine and aim the timing light at the timing mark.
5. The line on the harmonic balancer or crankshaft pulley should align with the mark on the timing plate. If adjustment is necessary, loosen the distributor hold-down bolt and rotate the distributor until the timing mark indicates that the correct timing has been reached.
6. Tighten the distributor hold-down bolt and recheck the timing, adjust as necessary.

NOTE: If using a magnetic timing probe, install the probe at the lower-left side of the engine. Using the meter and the same procedure as with the timing light, set the timing to 10 degrees BTDC.

2.0L Engine

Timing procedure and specifications are provided on the vehicle emission information label located in the engine compartment.

Alternator

For further information on the charging system, please refer to "Charging and Starting" in the Unit Repair section.

PRECAUTIONS

Several precautions must be observed with alternator equipped vehicles to avoid damage to the unit.

- If the battery is removed for any reason, make sure it is reconnected with the correct polarity. Reversing the battery connections may result in damage to the one-way rectifiers.
- When utilizing a booster battery as a starting aid, always connect the positive to positive terminals and the negative terminal from the booster battery to a good engine ground on the vehicle being started.
- Never use a fast charger as a booster to start vehicles.
- Disconnect the battery cables when charging the battery with a fast charger.
- Never attempt to polarize the alternator.
- Do not use test lamps of more than 12 volts when checking diode continuity.
- Do not short across or ground any of the alternator terminals.
- The polarity of the battery, alternator and regulator must be matched and considered before making any electrical connections within the system.
- Never separate the alternator on an open circuit. Make sure all connections within the circuit are clean and tight.
- Disconnect the battery ground terminal when performing any service on electrical components.
- Disconnect the battery if arc welding is to be done on the vehicle.

BELT TENSION ADJUSTMENT

NOTE: The following procedure requires the use of a belt tension gauge.

1. If the belt is cold, operate the engine at idle speed, until it reaches normal operating temperature; the belt will seat itself in the pulleys allowing the belt fibers to relax or stretch. If the belt is hot, allow it to cool, until it is warm to the touch.

NOTE: A used belt is one that has been rotated at least 1 complete revolution on the pulleys. This begins the belt seating process and it must never be tensioned to the new belt specifications.

2. Loosen the alternator mounting bolts.
3. Using a belt tension gauge tool, place the tension gauge at the center of the belt between the pulleys on its longest section.
4. While applying pressure on the component, adjust the drive belt tension to the following:

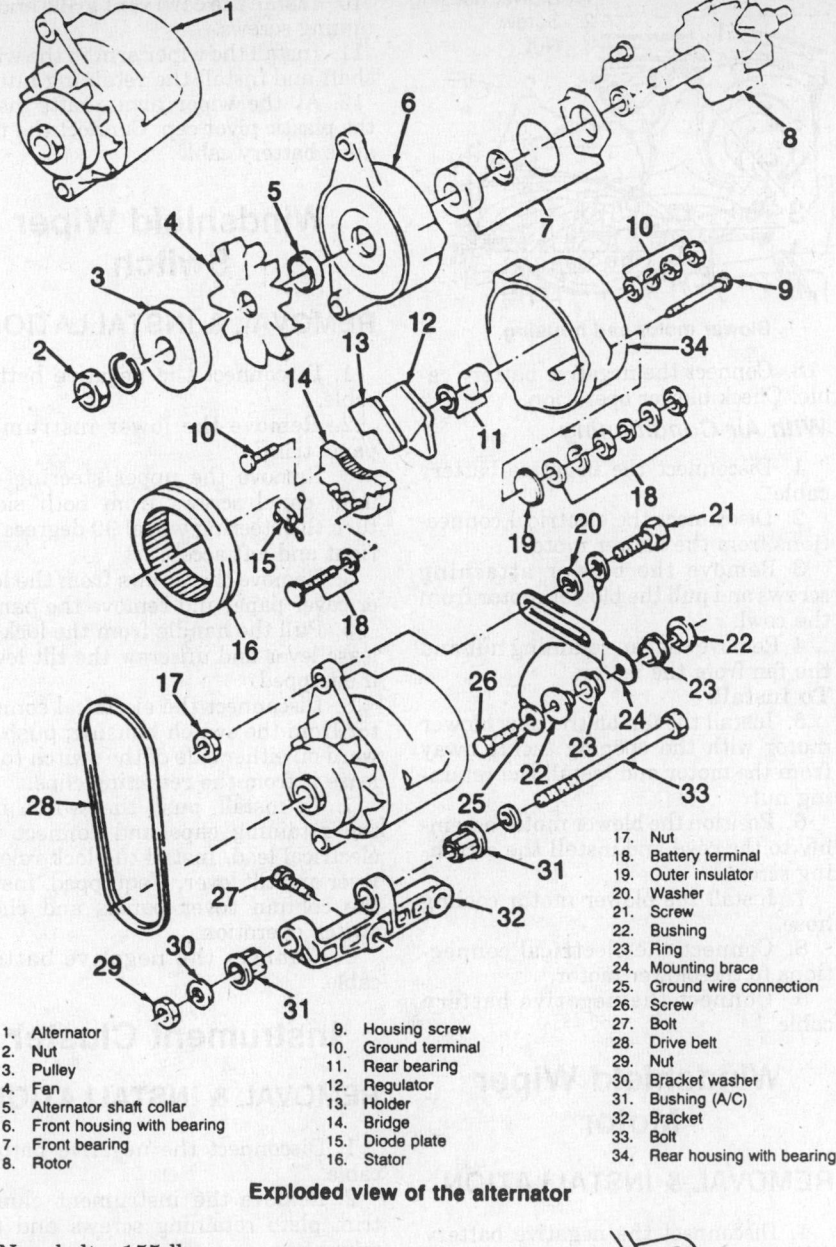

1. Alternator
2. Nut
3. Pulley
4. Fan
5. Alternator shaft collar
6. Front housing with bearing
7. Front bearing
8. Rotor
9. Housing screw
10. Ground terminal
11. Rear bearing
12. Regulator
13. Holder
14. Bridge
15. Diode plate
16. Stator
17. Nut
18. Battery terminal
19. Outer insulator
20. Washer
21. Screw
22. Bushing
23. Ring
24. Mounting brace
25. Ground wire connection
26. Screw
27. Bolt
28. Drive belt
29. Nut
30. Bracket washer
31. Bushing (A/C)
32. Bracket
33. Bolt
34. Rear housing with bearing

Exploded view of the alternator

New belt—155 lbs.
Used belt—80 lbs.
5. While holding tension on the component, tighten the component mounting bolts and remove the tension gauge.

REMOVAL & INSTALLATION

1. Disconnect the negative battery cable.

NOTE: Failure to disconnect the negative cable may result in injury from the positive battery lead at the alternator and may short the alternator and regulator during the removal process.

2. Disconnect and label the electrical terminal plug and the battery lead from the rear of the alternator.

3. Loosen the mounting bolts. Push the alternator inwards and slip the drive belt off the pulley.
4. Remove the mounting bolts and the alternator.
5. Install in the reverse order of removal. Install the electrical leads and the negative battery cable. Adjust the belt tension.

Starter

For further information on the charging system, please refer to "Charging and Starting" in the Unit Repair section.

REMOVAL & INSTALLATION

1. Disconnect the negative battery cable.
2. Disconnect the ignition switch lead wire and the battery cable from the starter motor terminal.
3. Remove the starter mounting bolts and the starter.
4. To install, hold the starter in place and install the mounting bolts. Torque the starter mounting bolts to 33 ft. lbs. (45 Nm).
5. Connect the electrical wiring to the starter.
6. Connect the negative battery cable. Start the engine and test starter performance.

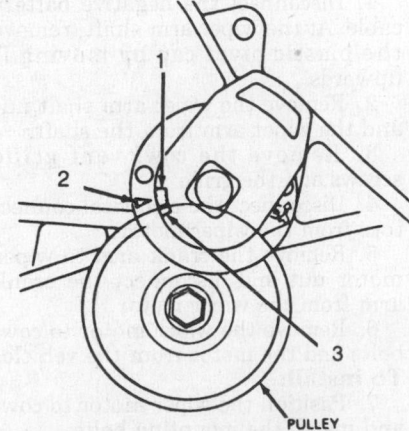

1. Minimum tension range   2. Pointer
3. Maximum tension range

Adjusting the serpentine belt tension

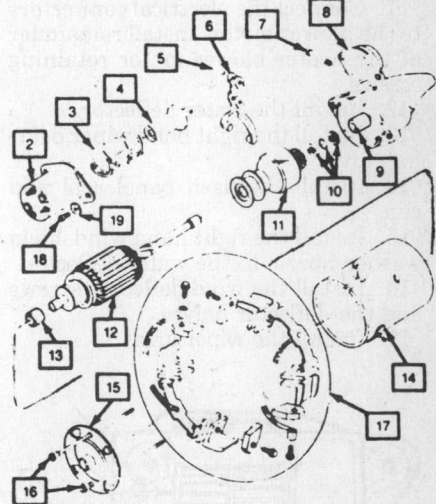

1. Starter motor assembly
2. Starter solenoid switch
3. Spring
4. Plunger
5. Pin
6. Lever
7. Shaft
8. Housing
9. Starter drive end bushing
10. Starter drive pinion bushing
11. Starter drive pinion
12. Armature
13. Starter cummulator end bushing
14. Frame and field
15. Frame end
16. Bolt
17. Starter holder with brush
18. Bolt
19. Washer

Exploded view of the starter

CHASSIS ELECTRICAL

Heater Blower Motor

The heater blower motor is located in the engine compartment, attached to the cowl.

REMOVAL & INSTALLATION

Without Air Conditioning

1. Disconnect the negative battery cable.
2. Remove the wiper arms.
3. Remove the wind deflector screws and the deflector halves.
4. Remove the right hand windshield washer nozzle from the water deflector.
5. Remove the dash panel seal and clip.
6. Remove the right hand wiper bearing nut.
7. Remove the water deflector.
8. Disconnect the electrical connectors from the blower motor. Remove the heater blower motor retaining screws.
9. Remove the housing, the motor and the housing cover.
To install:
10. Align the motor by first inserting the lower screw, then the upper.
11. Connect the electrical connectors to the blower motor. Install remainder of the heater blower motor retaining screws.
12. Install the water deflector.
13. Install the right hand wiper bearing nut.
14. Install the dash panel seal and clip.
15. Install the right hand windshield washer nozzle to the water deflector.
16. Install the wind deflector screws and the deflector halves.
17. Install the wiper arms.

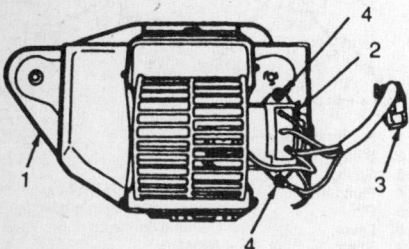

1. Blower motor housing
2. Blower motor
3. Harness connector
4. Screw

View of the blower motor—without air conditioning

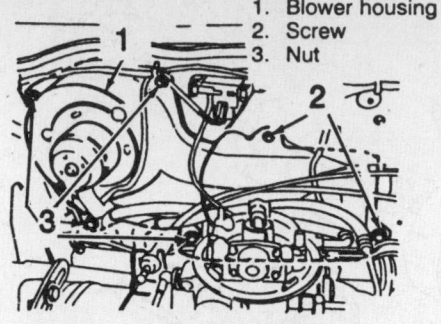

1. Blower housing
2. Screw
3. Nut

Blower motor and housing

18. Connect the negative battery cable. Check blower operation.

With Air Conditioning

1. Disconnect the negative battery cable.
2. Disconnect the electrical connections from the blower motor.
3 Remove the blower attaching screws and pull the blower motor from the cowl.
4 Remove the fan retaining nut and the fan from the motor.
To install:
5. Install the fan on the new blower motor with the opening facing away from the motor and install the retaining nut.
6. Position the blower motor assembly to the cowl and install the attaching screws.
7. Install the blower motor cooling hose.
8. Connect the electrical connections to the blower motor.
9. Connect the negative battery cable.

Windshield Wiper Motor

REMOVAL & INSTALLATION

1. Disconnect the negative battery cable. At the wiper arm shaft, remove the plastic pivot cap by moving it upwards.
2. Remove the wiper arm shaft nut and the wiper arm from the shaft.
3. Remove the cowl vent grille screws and the grille.
4. Disconnect the electrical connectors from the wiper motor.
5. Remove the crank arm to wiper motor nut and disconnect the crank arm from the wiper motor.
6. Remove the wiper motor to cowl bolts and the motor from the vehicle.
To install:
7. Position the wiper motor to cowl and install the mounting bolts.
8. Connect the crank arm to wiper motor and install the retaining nut.
9. Connect the electrical connectors to the wiper motor.

10. Install the cowl vent grille and retaining screws.
11. Install the wiper arm to the wiper shaft and install the retaining nut.
12. At the wiper arm shaft, install the plastic pivot cap. Connect the negative battery cable.

Windshield Wiper Switch

REMOVAL & INSTALLATION

1. Disconnect the negative battery cable.
2. Remove the lower instrument panel trim.
3. Remove the upper steering column panel screws from both sides; turn the steering wheel 90 degrees for right and left access.
4. Remove the screws from the lower cover panel and remove the panel.
5. Pull the handle from the lock release lever and unscrew the tilt lever, if equipped.
6. Disconnect the electrical connector from the switch housing; push inward on either side of the switch to release it from the retaining clips.
7. To install, push the switch into the retaining clips and connect the electrical lead. Install the lock release lever and tilt lever, if equipped. Install the column cover panels and check switch operation.
8. Connect the negative battery cable.

Instrument Cluster

REMOVAL & INSTALLATION

1. Disconnect the negative battery cable.
2. Remove the instrument cluster trim plate retaining screws and the trim plate.
3. Pull the instrument cluster forward, disconnect the speedometer cable and the electrical connectors from the rear of the instrument cluster.
4. To install, connect the speedometer and the electrical connectors to the instrument cluster. Install the cluster in the dash and install the retaining screws. Check for the proper operation of the speedometer and the gauges.
5. Connect the negative battery cable.

Speedometer

REMOVAL & INSTALLATION

1. Disconnect the negative battery cable.

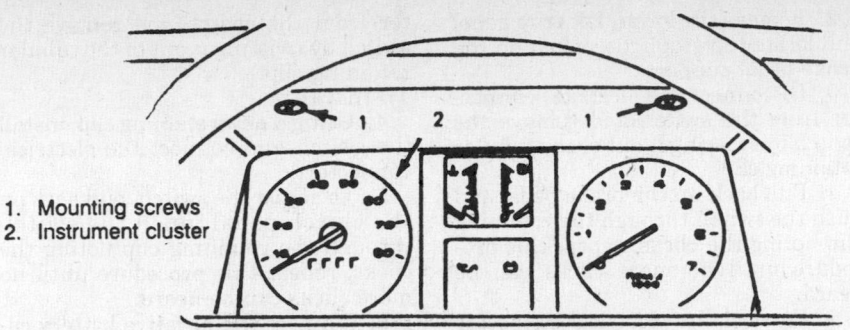

1. Mounting screws
2. Instrument cluster

Instrument cluster retaining screw locations

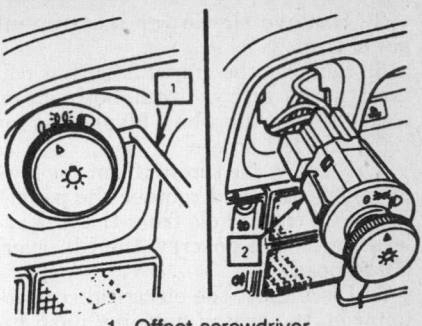

1. Offset screwdriver
2. Retainer

Replacing the headlight switch in the instrument panel

2. Remove the instrument panel cluster lens, the face plate and the instrument cluster from the instrument panel.

3. Press the speedometer cable retainer and separate the speedometer cable from the speedometer.

4. Remove the speedometer retaining screws. Remove the speedometer from the cluster.

To install:

5. Install the speedometer into the cluster and install the retaining screws.

6. Position the cluster assembly to the dash, while inserting the speedometer cable into the speedometer, push in securely.

7. Install the instrument cluster face plate and lens to the panel.

8. Connect the negative battery cable.

Radio

REMOVAL & INSTALLATION

1. Disconnect the negative battery cable.

2. Turn the key to the **ON** position. Move the shift lever in to **1ST** gear.

3. Remove the storage pocket panel and the front center console.

4. Remove the retaining screws at the top of the console and slide the center console back.

5. Using a center punch on each side of the radio bracket, release the radio by inserting the center punch into the each hole in the control panel and push to the right.

6. Reach behind the radio and push rearward toward the shift lever until the radio is free. Disconnect the antenna and harness connections from the radio.

To install:

7. Connect the antenna and harness connections. Position the radio to the dash and slide it in until it seats into the bracket.

8. Slide the console forward to the dash and install the retaining screws.

9. Move the shift lever in to **P** or **N** position.

10. Install the front center console and storage pocket panel.

11. Connect the negative battery cable. Check radio operation.

Headlight Switch

REMOVAL & INSTALLATION

1. Disconnect the negative battery cable.

2. Using an offset tool, depress the headlight switch retaining clips and pull the switch from the dash.

3. Disconnect the electrical connector from the rear of the switch. Remove the switch from the vehicle.

4. To install, connect the electrical lead and push switch into position in the dash. Connect the negative battery cable.

Combination Switch

The combination switch consists of the turn signal switch and the dimmer switch which is connected to the steering column.

REMOVAL & INSTALLATION

1. Disconnect the negative battery cable.

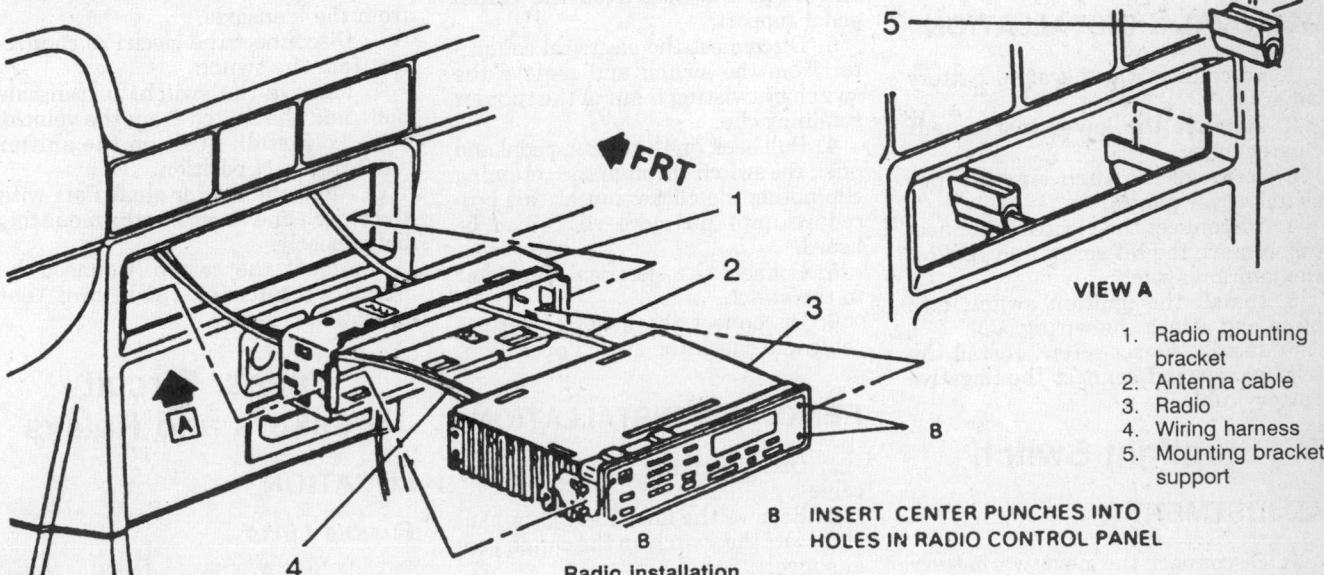

FRT

VIEW A

1. Radio mounting bracket
2. Antenna cable
3. Radio
4. Wiring harness
5. Mounting bracket support

B INSERT CENTER PUNCHES INTO HOLES IN RADIO CONTROL PANEL

Radio installation

2. Remove the lower instrument panel trim.

3. Remove the upper steering column panel screws from both sides; turn the steering wheel 90 degrees for right and left access.

4. Remove the screws from the lower cover panel and remove the panel.

5. Pull the handle from the lock release lever and unscrew the tilt lever, if equipped.

6. Disconnect the electrical connector from the switch housing; push inward on either side of the switch to release it from the retaining clips.

7. To install, push the switch into the retaining clips and connect the electrical lead. Install the lock release lever and tilt lever, if equipped. Install the column cover panels and check switch operation.

8. Connect the negative battery cable.

Ignition Lock

REMOVAL & INSTALLATION

1. Disconnect the negative battery cable.

2. Remove the lower instrument cluster trim.

3. Remove the turn signal/wiper switch cover panels.

4. With the key in the ignition switch, turn the key to the **2ND** position.

5. Using a small Allen wrench, press downward on the detent spring and remove the ignition lock cylinder.

6. To install, place the key in the cylinder and install it into the ignition switch. Install the trim panels. Connect the negative battery cable.

Ignition Switch

REMOVAL & INSTALLATION

1. Disconnect the negative battery cable.

2. Remove the lower instrument cluster trim.

3. Remove the turn signal/wiper switch cover panels.

4. Disconnect the electrical connector, remove the set screw and remove the ignition switch.

5. Install the ignition switch into place and attach the wiring.

6. Install the set screw. Install the trim panels and connect the negative battery cable.

Stoplight Switch

ADJUSTMENT

1. Disconnect the negative battery cable.

2. Remove the lower, left trim panel and locate the stoplight switch on the brake pedal support.

3. Disconnect the electrical connector from the switch and remove the switch by twisting it out of the tubular retaining clip.

4. Pull back on the brake pedal and push the switch through the retaining clip noting the clicks; repeat this procedure until no more clicks can be heard.

5. Connect the electrical connector to the switch.

6. Connect the negative battery cable and check the switch operation.

REMOVAL & INSTALLATION

1. Disconnect the negative battery cable.

2. Disconnect the electrical connector from the brake light switch, located above the brake pedal.

3. Remove the switch from the tubular clip on the brake pedal mounting bracket.

To install:

4. Insert the switch into the clip until the switch body seats on the clip.

5. Pull the brake pedal rearward against the internal pedal stop. The switch will be moved in the tubular clip providing the proper adjustment.

6. Connect the electrical connector to the switch.

7. Connect the negative battery cable and check the switch operation.

Clutch Switch

ADJUSTMENT

1. Disconnect the negative battery cable.

2. Remove the lower, left trim panel and locate the switch on the clutch pedal support.

3. Disconnect the electrical connector from the switch and remove the switch by twisting it out of the tubular retaining clip.

4. Pull back on the clutch pedal and push the switch through the retaining clip noting the clicks; repeat this procedure until no more clicks can be heard.

5. Connect the electrical connector to the switch.

6. Disconnect the negative battery cable and check the switch operation.

REMOVAL & INSTALLATION

1. Disconnect the negative battery cable.

2. Remove the lower, left trim panel. Locate the switch on the clutch pedal support.

3. Disconnect the electrical connec-
tor from the switch and remove the switch by twisting it out of the tubular retaining clip.

To install:

4. Using a new retaining clip, install the switch and connect the electrical connector.

5. To adjust the switch, pull back on the clutch pedal, push the switch through the retaining clip noting the clicks; repeat this procedure until no more clicks can be heard.

6. Connect the negative battery cable and check the switch operation.

Neutral Safety Switch

ADJUSTMENT

1. Disconnect the negative battery cable.

2. Raise the vehicle and support it safely.

3. Loosen the switch to transaxle bolts. Insert $3/32$ in. (2.34mm) drill in the service adjustment hole and rotate the switch until the drill drops into the a depth of $9/64$ in. (9mm).

4. Torque the mounting bolts to 22 ft. lbs. (30 Nm). Remove the drill gauge.

5. Lower the vehicle and connect the negative battery cable.

6. Start the engine and vary that the engine will start in **P** and **N** positions.

NOTE: If the engine will start in any other position other than P or N, readjust the switch.

REMOVAL & INSTALLATION

1. Disconnect the negative battery cable.

2. Raise the vehicle and support it safely. Disconnect the shift linkage from the transaxle.

3. Disconnect the electrical connector from the switch.

4. Remove the switch to transaxle bolts and the switch from the vehicle.

5. To install, position the shifter shaft in the **N** position.

6. Align the shifter shaft flats with the switch and assemble the mounting bolts loosely.

7. Adjust the switch. Connect the negative battery cable and test operation.

Fuses, Circuit Breakers and Relays

LOCATION

Fusible Links

Fusible link **A** is located at the lower rear of the engine, near the starter so-

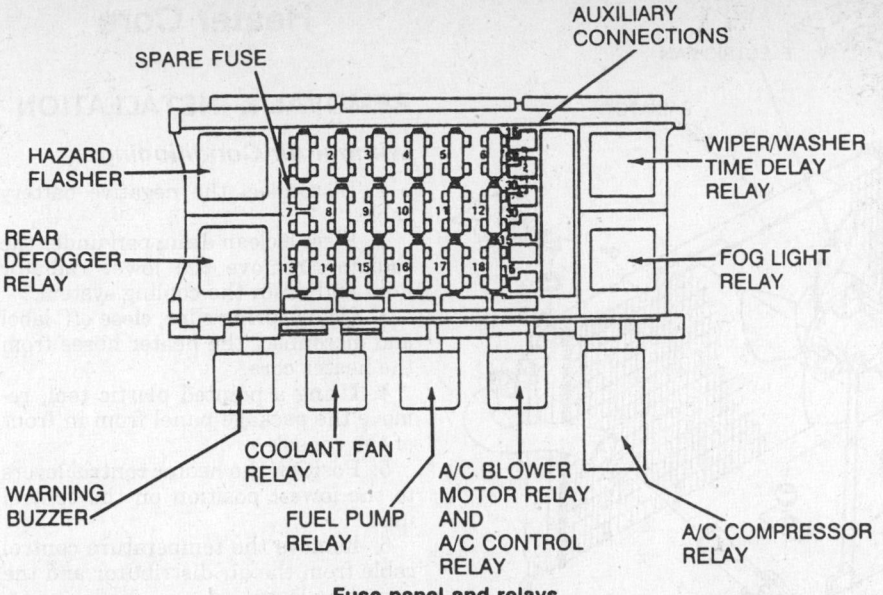

Fuse panel and relays

lenoid. Fusible link **B** is located at the positive battery terminal.

Circuit Breakers

Circuit breakers **12** and **15** are located in the fuse panel.

Fuse Panel

The fuse panel is located at the left side of the instrument panel and is reached by pulling the release handle and swinging the panel downward. Always return the fuse panel to its full upward, latched position before driving the vehicle.

Various Relays

All relays for this vehicle are located on the fuse block, under the left side of the instrument panel.

Computers

LOCATION

The Electronic Control Module (ECM) is located behind the kick panel at the passenger-side door jam (under the dash).

Memory Calibration Unit

The memory calibration unit is located inside the ECM. It contains programmed information tailored to the vehicle's weight, engine, transmission, axle ratio and etc. Even though a single ECM unit can be used for many vehicles, a specific memory calibration unit must be used for each vehicle.

Flashers

LOCATION

Turn Signal Flasher

The turn signal flasher is located on the fuse block, under the left side of the instrument panel.

Hazard Warning Flasher

The hazard warning flasher is located on the fuse block, under the left side of the instrument panel.

Cruise Control

ADJUSTMENT

Control Cable

1. Disconnect the negative battery cable.
2. Pull the cable end of the servo assembly toward the servo without moving the idler pulley cam.
3. If 1 of the 6 holes in the servo assembly tab lines up with the cable pin, connect the pin to the tab with retainer 7.
4. If a tab hole does not line up with the pin, move the cable away from the servo assembly until the next closest tab hole lines up. Connect the pin-to-tab with retainer 7.

NOTE: Do not stretch the cable so as to make a particular tab hole connect to the pin. This could prevent the engine from returning to idle.

5. Connect the battery cable and test operation.

Vacuum Release Valve

1. Disconnect the negative battery cable.
2. With the brake pedal depressed, insert the valve into the tubular retainer until the valve seats on the retainer.

NOTE: Audible clicks can be heard as the threaded portion of the valve is pushed through the retainer toward the brake pedal.

3. Pull the brake pedal fully rearward against the pedal stop until the audible click sounds can no longer be heard. The valve will be moved in the tubular retainer providing the adjustment.
4. Release the brake pedal and repeat Step 3 to insure that no audible click sounds remain.
5. Connect the battery cable and test operation.

ENGINE COOLING

Radiator

REMOVAL & INSTALLATION

— CAUTION —

Before attempting any work on the cooling system, allow the engine to first cool sufficiently. To avoid personal injury, do not remove the radiator cap while the engine is at normal operation temperature. The cooling system will release scalding fluid and steam under pressure if the cap is removed while the engine and radiator are still hot.

1. Disconnect the negative battery cable.
2. Place and drain pan under the radiator. Remove the lower radiator hose and drain the cooling system.
3. Remove the coolant recovery bottle hose and the upper radiator hose.
4. Disconnect the electrical connections from the electric fan motor, the oxygen sensor and the temperature sensor.
5. Remove the upper fan mounting bolts and remove the fan and shroud as an assembly.
6. If equipped with automatic transaxle, disconnect the transaxle cooler lines and plug.
7. Remove the radiator support mounting bolts. Carefully lift the radiator out.
To install:
8. Carefully lower the radiator into

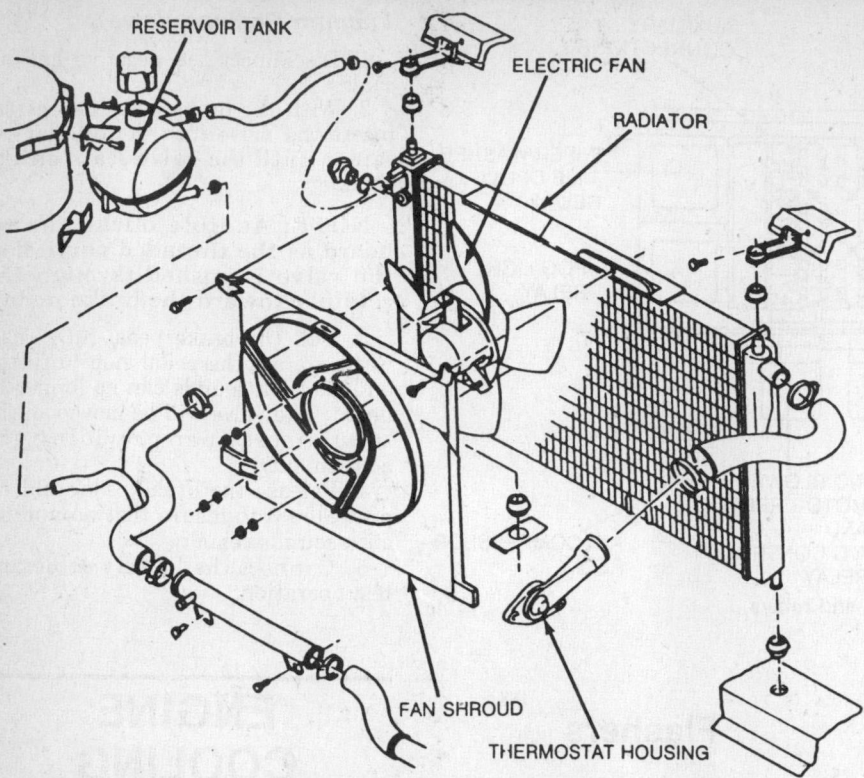

RESERVOIR TANK

ELECTRIC FAN

RADIATOR

FAN SHROUD

THERMOSTAT HOUSING

Exploded view of the radiator and electric cooling fan assembly

Heater Core

REMOVAL & INSTALLATION

Without Air Conditioning

1. Disconnect the negative battery cable.
2. Place a clean drain pan under the radiator, remove the lower radiator hose and drain the cooling system.
3. Using spring clips, close off, label and disconnect the heater hoses from the heater core.
4. Using a pointed plastic tool, remove the package panel from in front of the console.
5. Position the heater control levers to the lowest position on the control unit.
6. Remove the temperature control cable from the air distributor and the actuating lever.
7. From under the glove box, remove the kick panel.
8. Remove the temperature valve linkage from the right side of the air distributor.
9. At the lower right side of the air distributor cover, pull back the carpet to access the screw.
10. Remove the air distributor housing cover screws and the cover.
11. Position the temperature valve to access the upper heater core screws.
12. Remove the heater core housing screws and the heater core.

To install:

13. Install the heater core into the heater core housing and install the retaining screws.
14. Install the air distributor housing cover and retaining screws.
15. Install the temperature valve linkage to the right side of the air distributor.
16. Install the lower left kick panel under the glove box.
17. Install the temperature control cable to the air distributor and the actuating lever.
18. Install the package panel in front of the console.
19. Remove the spring clips from the heater hoses. Connect the heater hoses to the heater core.
20. Install the lower radiator hose. Connect the negative battery cable.
21. Refill the cooling system, start the engine and check for leaks.

With Air Conditioning

1. Disconnect the negative battery cable.
2. Place a clean drain pan under the radiator, remove the lower radiator hose and drain the cooling system.
3. Using spring clips, close off, label

the engine compartment. Install the support mounting bolts.

9. If equipped with automatic transaxle, connect the transaxle cooler lines.
10. Install the fan and shroud as an assembly and install the upper fan mounting bolts.
11. Connect the electrical connections to the electric fan motor, the oxygen sensor and the temperature sensor.
12. Install the coolant recovery bottle hose and the upper radiator hose.
13. Connect the upper and lower radiator hoses. Refill the cooling system with an approved coolant mixture.
14. Connect the negative battery cable.
15. Start the engine, allow it to reach operating temperature and check for leaks.

Electric Cooling Fan

TESTING

1. Start the engine and allow it to reach normal operating temperature.
2. When the radiator temperature reaches 230°F, the electric cooling fan should turn **ON**.

3. If the fan fails to operate, perform the following procedures:
   a. Disconnect the electrical connector from the electric cooling fan.
   b. Using a fused jumper wire, connect it from the battery to the cooling fan.
   c. The electric cooling fan should turn **ON**; if not, replace the fan motor.
   d. If the fan still will not operate, inspect the fuse, the fan switch and/or the fan switch relay.
4. If the electrical connector has been disconnected, reconnect it.

REMOVAL & INSTALLATION

1. Disconnect the negative battery cable.
2. Remove the upper cooling fan shroud to radiator support bolts.
3. Disconnect the electrical leads from the fan motor. Remove the fan and shroud as an assembly.
4. To install, position the fan and shroud as an assembly to the radiator support and install the mounting bolts.
5. Connect the electrical leads to the fan motor. Connect the negative battery cable.
6. Connect the negative battery cable. Start the engine and check the fan operation.

and disconnect the heater hoses from the heater core.

4. Remove the evaporator drain hose at the heater case.

5. If equipped with manual transaxle, remove the gear shift boot.

6. Using a pointed plastic tool, remove the package panel from in front of the console.

7. Remove the console shift plate and remove the front center console.

8. Remove the glove box retaining straps and screws. Remove the glove box.

9. Remove the hush panel retainers and remove the outer heater case cover.

10. Remove move the heater cover case retaining clips and remove the case cover.

11. Remove the heater core retaining clamps and remove the heater core from the case.

To install:

12. Position the heater core into the case housing and secure in place with retaining clamps.

13. Install the heater case cover and secure in place with the retaining clips. Install the hush panel and retainers.

14. Install the glove box, retaining straps and screws.

15. Install the front center console and install the console shift plate.

16. Install the package panel in front of the console.

17. If equipped with manual transaxle, install the gear shift boot.

18. Install the evaporator drain hose to the heater case.

19. Remove the spring clips and connect the heater hoses to the heater core.

20. Install the lower radiator hose. Connect the negative battery cable.

21. Refill the cooling system, start the engine, allow it to reach normal operating temperature and check for leaks.

Water Pump

REMOVAL & INSTALLATION

1. Disconnect the negative battery cable. Drain the cooling system.

2. Remove the front cover, the timing belt and the rear cover.

3. Remove the water pump mounting bolts and the water pump from the engine.

4. Clean the seal mounting surfaces.

To install:

5. Use a new water pump seal. Coat the sealing surface and the seal ring with grease.

6. Torque the water pump bolts to 71 inch lbs. Refill the cooling system.

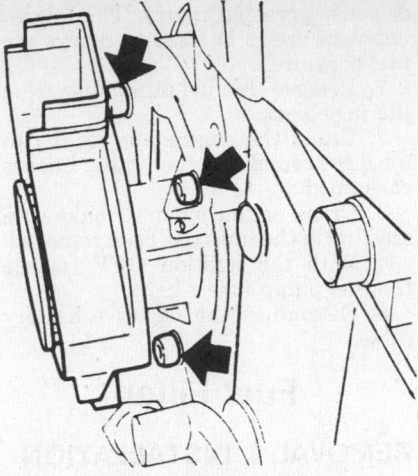

View of the water pump

7. Start the engine, allow it to reach normal operating temperature and check for leaks, bleed cooling system.

8. Check and adjust the ignition timing if needed.

Thermostat

REMOVAL & INSTALLATION

1.6L Engine

1. Disconnect the negative battery cable.

2. Using a clean drain pan, place it under the radiator, remove the lower radiator hose and drain the cooling system.

3. Remove the front cover, the timing belt and the rear cover; slip it over the water pump rear cover piece.

4. Remove the water inlet bolts, the water inlet housing and the thermostat.

5. Clean the gasket mounting surfaces.

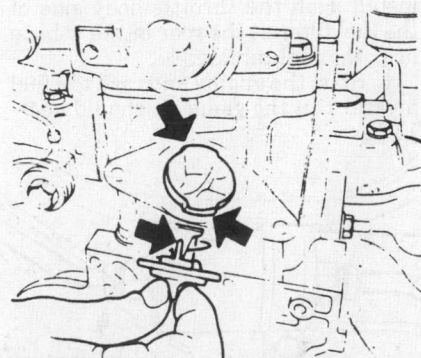

Exploded view of the thermostat and engine location.

6. To install, use a new seal. Torque the thermostat housing bolts to 78 inch lbs. Refill the cooling system and bleed the air from the system. Connect the negative battery cable.

2.0L Engine

1. Disconnect the negative battery cable.

2. Using a clean drain pan, place it under the radiator, remove the lower radiator hose and drain the cooling system.

3. Remove the upper radiator hose.

4. Remove the thermostat housing bolts and remove the thermostat.

To install:

5. Clean the sealing surfaces of the cylinder head and thermostat housing.

6. Install the thermostat to the cylinder head.

7. Install the thermostat housing using a new O-ring seal. Torque the housing bolts to 7.5 ft. lbs. (10 Nm).

8. Install the upper and lower radiator hoses.

9. Refill the cooling system and connect the battery cable. Start the engine and check thermostat operation and for leaks.

Cooling System Bleeding

After working on the cooling system, even to replace the thermostat, the system must bled. Air trapped in the system will prevent proper filling and leave the radiator coolant level low, causing a risk of overheating.

1. To bleed the system, start the system cool, the radiator cap OFF and the radiator filled to about an inch below the filler neck.

2. Start the engine and run it at slightly above normal idle speed. This will insure adequate circulation. If air bubbles appear and the coolant level drops, fill the system with a mixture of anti-freeze and water to bring the level back to the proper level.

3. Run the engine this way until the thermostat opens. When this happens, the coolant will move abruptly across the top of the radiator and the temperature of the radiator will suddenly rise.

4. At this point, air is often expelled and the level may drop quite a bit. Keep refilling the system until the level is near the top of the radiator and remains constant.

5. If the vehicle has an overflow tank, fill the radiator to the top of the filler neck.

FUEL SYSTEM

Fuel System Service Precautions

Safety is the most important factor when performing not only fuel system maintenance but any type of maintenance. Failure to conduct maintenance and repairs in a safe manner may result in serious personal injury or death. Maintenance and testing of the vehicle's fuel system components can be accomplished safely and effectively by adhering to the following rules and guidelines.

• To avoid the possibility of fire and personal injury, always disconnect the negative battery cable unless the repair or test procedure requires that battery voltage be applied.

• Always relieve the fuel system pressure prior to disconnecting any fuel system component (injector, fuel rail, pressure regulator, etc.), fitting or fuel line connection. Exercise extreme caution whenever relieving fuel system pressure to avoid exposing skin, face and eyes to fuel spray. Please be advised that fuel under pressure may penetrate the skin or any part of the body that it contacts.

• Always place a shop towel or cloth around the fitting or connection prior to loosening to absorb any excess fuel due to spillage. Ensure that all fuel spillage (should it occur) is quickly removed from engine surfaces. Ensure that all fuel soaked cloths or towels are deposited into a suitable waste container.

• Always keep a dry chemical (Class B) fire extinguisher near the work area.

• Do not allow fuel spray or fuel vapors to come into contact with a spark or open flame.

• Always use a backup wrench when loosening and tightening fuel line connection fittings. This will prevent unnecessary stress and torsion to fuel line piping. Always follow the proper torque specifications.

• Always replace worn fuel fitting O-rings with new. Do not substitute fuel hose or equivalent where fuel pipe is installed.

RELIEVING FUEL SYSTEM PRESSURE

Modern fuel injection systems operate under high pressure, this makes it necessary to first relieve the system of pressure before servicing. The pressurized fuel when released may ignite or cause personal injury. The following steps are to be used to relieve the fuel pressure.

1. Remove the fuel pump fuse from the fuse block.
2. Crank the engine and let it run until the remaining fuel in the lines is consumed.
3. Crank engine again to make sure any fuel in the lines has been removed.
4. With the ignition **OFF** replace the fuel pump fuse.
5. Disconnect the negative battery cable.

Fuel Filter

REMOVAL & INSTALLATION

The inline fuel filter is located on the rear crossmember of the vehicle. Always use a back-up wrench for removing or installing the fuel line fittings.

1. Relieve the fuel system pressure.
2. Disconnect the negative battery cable. Raise safely and support the vehicle.
3. Disconnect the fuel lines from the fuel filter.
4. Remove the fuel filter bracket mounting bolt and remove the filter from the frame.
To install:
5. Use a new fuel filter and O-rings. Install the filter and bracket to the frame and install the mounting bolt.
6. Connect the fuel lines to the filter. Torque the fuel line-to-filter connectors to 22 ft. lbs.
6. Lower the vehicle. Connect the negative battery cable.
7. Start the engine and check for leaks.

Electric Fuel Pump

PRESSURE TESTING

1. Relieve the fuel system pressure.
2. Remove the air cleaner and plug the thermac vacuum port on the throttle body.
3. Connect a pressure gauge tool, install it on the throttle body side of the fuel filter at the rear of the vehicle near the fuel tank.
4. Start the engine and read the fuel pressure on the gauge, it should be 9–13 psi.

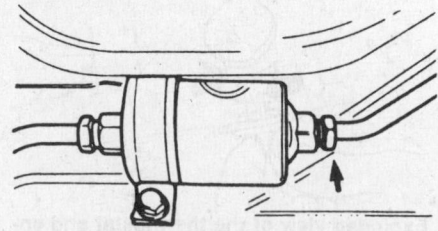
View of the inline fuel filter

5. Turn the ignition **OFF**, relieve the fuel system pressure and remove the fuel pressure gauge. Reconnect all fuel and vacuum lines. Install the air cleaner.

REMOVAL & INSTALLATION

The electric fuel pump is attached to the sending unit and is located in the fuel tank.
1. Relieve the fuel system pressure.
2. Disconnect the negative battery cable.
3. Raise the rear seat and remove the floor pan cover.
4. Disconnect the electrical connectors and fuel line from the pump.
5. Remove the fuel pump retaining bolts and lift the fuel pump and sending unit assembly from the fuel tank.
To install:
6. Use new O-rings. Place the fuel pump in position to the fuel tank and install the retaining screws.
7. Connect the fuel line and electrical connectors to the pump. Connect the negative battery cable.
8. Turn the ignition switch to the **ON** position to pressurize the fuel system. Start the engine and check for leaks.
9. Install the floor pan cover and seat.

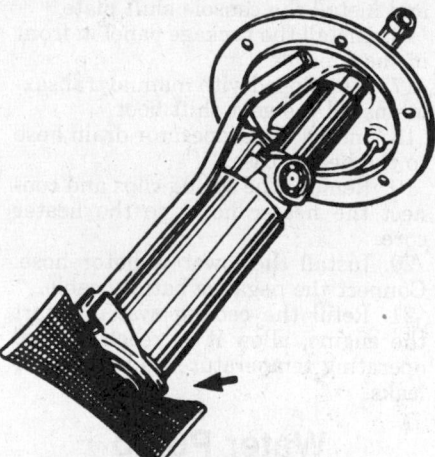
View of the electric fuel pump

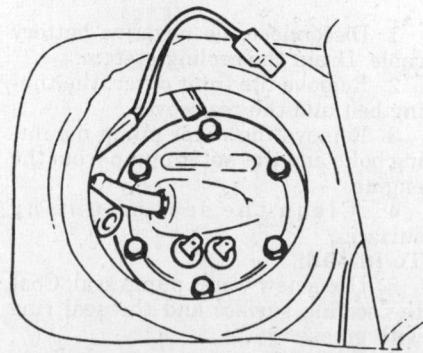
Fuel pump and sending unit mounting— under rear seat

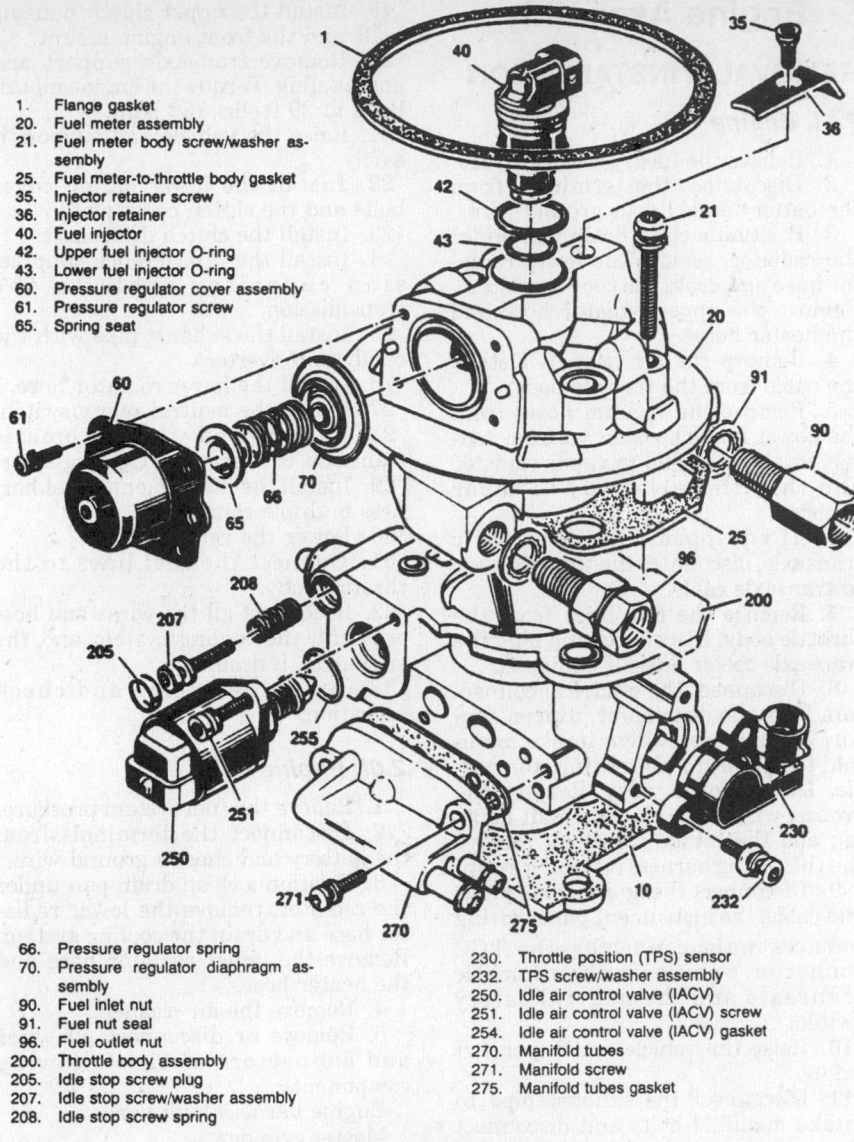

1. Flange gasket
20. Fuel meter assembly
21. Fuel meter body screw/washer assembly
25. Fuel meter-to-throttle body gasket
35. Injector retainer screw
36. Injector retainer
40. Fuel injector
42. Upper fuel injector O-ring
43. Lower fuel injector O-ring
60. Pressure regulator cover assembly
61. Pressure regulator screw
65. Spring seat

66. Pressure regulator spring
70. Pressure regulator diaphragm assembly
90. Fuel inlet nut
91. Fuel nut seal
96. Fuel outlet nut
200. Throttle body assembly
205. Idle stop screw plug
207. Idle stop screw/washer assembly
208. Idle stop screw spring

230. Throttle position (TPS) sensor
232. TPS screw/washer assembly
250. Idle air control valve (IACV)
251. Idle air control valve (IACV) screw
254. Idle air control valve (IACV) gasket
270. Manifold tubes
271. Manifold screw
275. Manifold tubes gasket

Exploded view of the throttle body

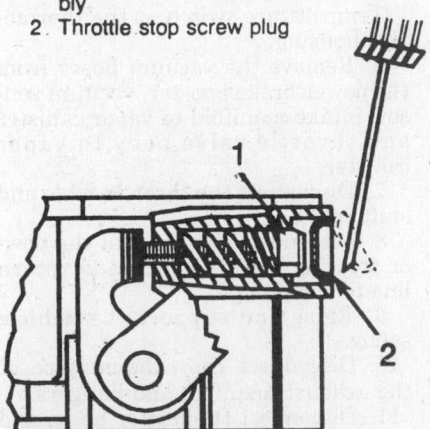

1. Throttle stop screw assembly
2. Throttle stop screw plug

Removing the idle stop screw plug

Fuel Injection

IDLE SPEED ADJUSTMENT

The throttle body is adjusted and sealed at the factory, no adjustment should be performed. All fuel control functions are controlled by the Electronic Control Module (ECM). However, if it is necessary to adjust the minimum idle speed, perform the following procedures.

1. Remove the air cleaner.
2. Using a scratch awl, pierce the idle stop screw plug, apply leverage and remove the plug.
3. Using a tachometer, follow the manufacturer's recommendations and connect it to the engine.
4. Position the transaxle in **P**, for automatic transaxle or **N**, for manual

transaxle. Start the engine and allow the rpm to stabilize.

5. Using the special tool BT–8528A or equivalent, position it fully into the idle air passage so that no air leak exists.

6. Using a No. 20 Torx® Bit tool, turn the idle stop screw until the engine speed is 525–575 rpm, for automatic transaxle or 575–625 rpm, for manual transaxle.

7. After adjustment, stop the engine, remove the tool BT–8528A or equivalent. Using silicone sealant, cover the idle stop screw.

IDLE MIXTURE ADJUSTMENT

The idle mixture is electronically controlled by the Electronic Control Module (ECM), no adjustment is necessary.

Fuel Injector

REMOVAL & INSTALLATION

NOTE: When removing the injector, be careful not to damage the electrical connector pins, on top of the injector, the injector fuel filter and the nozzle. The fuel injector is serviced as a complete assembly only. It is an electrical component and should not be immersed in any kind of cleaner.

1. Relieve the fuel system pressure.
2. Remove the air cleaner. Disconnect the negative battery cable.
3. Disconnect the electrical connector from the fuel injector.
4. Remove the injector retainer to throttle body screw and the retainer.
5. Using a small pry bar and a fulcrum, carefully lift the injector until it is free from the fuel meter body.
6. Remove the O-rings from the nozzle end of the injector.
7. Inspect the fuel injector filter for dirt and/or contamination.
To install:
8. Lubricate the O-rings with automatic transmission fluid and place them on the fuel injector.
9. Push the fuel injector straight into the fuel meter cavity, place thread locking compound on the fuel injector retainer bolt and install. Torque the retainer bolt to 27 inch lbs. (3 Nm).
10. Connect the electrical connector to the fuel injector.

NOTE: It is important that the replacement injector is identical. Although different injectors may fit in the 700 TBI throttle body, the calibrated flow rates may be different.

11. Connect the negative battery cable.

12. Turn the ignition switch to the **ON** position to pressurize the fuel system.

13. Start the engine and check for leaks. Install the air cleaner.

EMISSION CONTROLS

Please refer to "Emission Control" in the Unit Repair section for system maintenance procedures. Due to the complex nature of modern electronic engine control systems, comprehensive diagnosis and testing procedures fall outside the confines of this repair manual. For complete information on diagnosis, testing and repair procedures concerning all modern engine and emission control systems, please refer to "Chilton's Guide to Electronic Engine Controls".

Emission Warning Lamps

RESETTING

When the "Service Engine Soon" light turns **ON**, a trouble code is stored in the ECM memory. If the problem is periodic, the light will turn **OFF** when the problem goes away. However, the trouble code will stay in the ECM memory until the battery voltage is removed from the ECM.

To erase the ECM memory, turn **OFF** the ignition switch, then disconnect the battery negative cable, the ECM pigtail or the ECM fuse for 10 seconds.

ENGINE MECHANICAL

NOTE: Disconnecting the negative battery cable on some vehicles may interfere with the functions of the on board computer systems and may require the computer to undergo a relearning process, once the negative battery cable is reconnected.

Engine Assembly

REMOVAL & INSTALLATION

1.6L Engine

1. Relieve the fuel system pressure.
2. Disconnect the terminals from the battery and chassis ground wire.
3. Position a clean drain pan under the radiator, remove the lower radiator hose and drain the cooling system. Remove the upper radiator hose and the heater hoses.
4. Remove the air cleaner. Detach the cable from the throttle body.
5. Remove the vacuum hoses from the power brake booster, vacuum sensor, intake manifold to vapor canister and throttle valve body to vapor canister.
6. If equipped with automatic transaxle, disconnect the throttle body to transaxle cable.
7. Remove the fuel lines from the throttle body. Disconnect and plug the transaxle cooler lines, if equipped.
8. Disconnect the electrical connectors from the distributor, oxygen sensor, oil pressure switch, intake manifold temperature sensor, injector nozzle, IAC, throttle valve. Remove the ground wires from the camshaft housing and the intake manifold, remove the the wiring harness retaining strap.
9. Disconnect the ignition coil plugs and cable, the instrument panel wiring harness multi-connector, the TCC connector, vehicles with automatic transaxle and the neutral safety switch.
10. Raise the vehicle and support it safely.
11. Disconnect the exhaust pipe to intake manifold bolts and disconnect the rear exhaust pipe from the catalytic converter. Remove the exhaust pipe/catalytic converter assembly from the vehicle.
12. Remove the closure plug and the halfshaft from the transaxle.
13. Remove the clutch cover plate and the clutch housing to lower engine block bolts.
14. Lower the vehicle.
15. Using an engine sling, attach it to the engine hooks and support the engine weight.
16. Using the proper equipment, support the transaxle.
17. Remove the front engine mount and the clutch housing to upper engine bolts. Separate the engine from the clutch housing and lift the engine from the vehicle.

To install:

18. Lower the engine into the engine compartment and align it with the clutch housing.

19. Install the upper clutch housing bolts and the front engine mount.
20. Remove transaxle support and engine sling. Torque the engine mount bolts to 29 ft. lbs. (39 Nm).
21. Raise the vehicle and support it safely.
22. Install the lower clutch cover bolts and the clutch cover plate.
23. Install the clutch driveshaft.
24. Install the interference suppression capacitor cable to the transmission.
25. Install the exhaust pipe with the catalytic converter.
26. Install the lower radiator hose.
27. Install the neutral safety switch.
28. If equipped with automatic transaxle, connect the TCC connector.
29. Install the instrument panel harness multiple connector.
30. Lower the vehicle.
31. Connect the fuel lines to the throttle body.
32. Reconnect all the wires and hoses. Refill the cooling system and the engine oil, if drained.
33. Start the engine and check operation.

2.0L Engine

1. Relieve the fuel system pressure.
2. Disconnect the terminals from the battery and chassis ground wire.
3. Position a clean drain pan under the radiator, remove the lower radiator hose and drain the cooling system. Remove the upper radiator hose and the heater hoses.
4. Remove the air cleaner.
5. Remove or disconnect all wires and connectors at the following components:
   Engine harness bulk head
   Master cylinder
   Air conditioning relay cluster switches
   Wiper motor
   Cooling fan, relay and ground connection
   ECM
   Temperature switch at the thermostat housing.
6. Remove the vacuum hoses from the power brake booster, vacuum sensor, intake manifold to vapor canister and throttle valve body to vapor canister.
7. Disconnect the throttle cable and shift cable.
8. Disconnect the hoses at the power steering cut off switch and return line to the pump.
9. Raise and support the vehicle safely.
10. Disconnect the exhaust pipe at the exhaust manifold and hangers.
11. Disconnect the heater hoses and fuel lines. If equipped with automatic transaxle, disconnect the cooler lines.

12. Remove the front wheel assemblies.

13. Remove the brake calipers and suspend by a wire or hanger.

14. Disconnect wire connections at the air conditioning compressor and discharge the system.

15. Remove the suspension supports by removing the 2 center bolts on each side, removing 1 bolt at each end and loosen the remaining bolt.

NOTE: Insure that the vehicle, engine and transaxle weight are supported properly during the the following procedure.

16. If equipped with automatic transaxle, remove the rear transaxle lateral strut.

17. Remove the front transaxle strut.

18. Support the vehicle under the radiator support frame section.

19. Reposition the jack to the rear of the cowl with a 4×4 × 6 ft. board spanning the width of the vehicle.

20. Raise the vehicle enough to position and dolly under the transaxle with the 4 × 4 × 12 blocks as support.

21. Lower the vehicle weight onto the dolly.

22. Remove the remaining bolt at each end of the right and left front suspension supports.

23. Remove the transaxle mount and the rear engine mount.

24. Remove the strut bolts.

NOTE: Carefully scribe the position of the strut on the hub to maintain camber adjustments for reassembly purposes.

25. Raise the vehicle leaving the engine, transaxle and suspension on the dolly.

26. Separate the engine from the transaxle.

To install:

27. Raise and support the vehicle safely.

28. Assemble the engine to the transaxle.

29. Place the engine and transaxle assembly on a dolly and position it in the chassis.

30. Install the transaxle mount, rear engine mount and front engine mounts and related bolts.

31. Loosely install each end of the right and left suspension supports.

32. Install the steering knuckle-to-strut bolts and position the strut in the previously scribed location.

33. Raise the vehicle and remove the dolly.

34. Install the remaining bolts in the right and left suspension supports. Install the front and rear transaxle struts.

35. Install the rear transaxle lateral strut.

36. Install the suspension supports and install the 2 center bolts on each side, install the 1 bolt at each end and tighten the remaining bolt.

37. Connect the wire connections at the air conditioning compressor.

38. Install the brake calipers and bleed the brake system as required.

39. Install the front wheel assemblies.

40. Connect the heater hoses and fuel lines. If equipped with automatic transaxle, connect the cooler lines to the transaxle.

41. Connect the exhaust pipe to the exhaust manifold with the bracket hangers.

42. Lower the vehicle.

43. Connect the power steering hoses to the pump.

44. Connect the throttle cable and shift cable. Adjust as required.

45. Install the vacuum hoses to the power brake booster, vacuum sensor, intake manifold to vapor canister and throttle valve body to vapor canister.

46. Install or connect all wires and connectors at the following components:
Engine harness bulk head
Master cylinder
Air conditioning relay cluster switches
Wiper motor
Cooling fan, relay and ground connection
ECM
Temperature switch at the thermostat housing.

47. Install the air cleaner.

48. Install the radiator and heater hoses. Fill the cooling system with coolant.

49. Connect the fuel lines to the throttle body.

50. Connect the chassis ground wire. Reconnect all remaining wires.

51. Refill the engine with oil. Connect the negative battery cable.

52. Start the engine and check proper operation.

Engine Mounts

REMOVAL & INSTALLATION

1. Disconnect the negative battery cable.

2. Using an engine support fixture tool, center it on the cowl and attach it to the engine. Raise the engine slightly to take the weight off of the engine mounts.

3. From the front of the engine, remove the engine mount bolts and the mount.

4. Inspect the engine mount for deterioration and replace it, if necessary.

5. To install, support the engine using a engine support fixture tool.

6. Install the engine mounts and the retaining bolts to the engine.

7. Torque the engine mount to bracket bolts to 29 ft. lbs. (39 Nm) and the engine mount to engine bolts to 29 ft. lbs. (39 Nm).

8. Connect the negative battery cable.

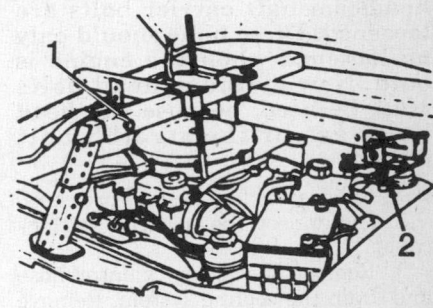

1. J-28467-A Engine support fixture
2. J-28467-20 Adapters
Supporting the engine

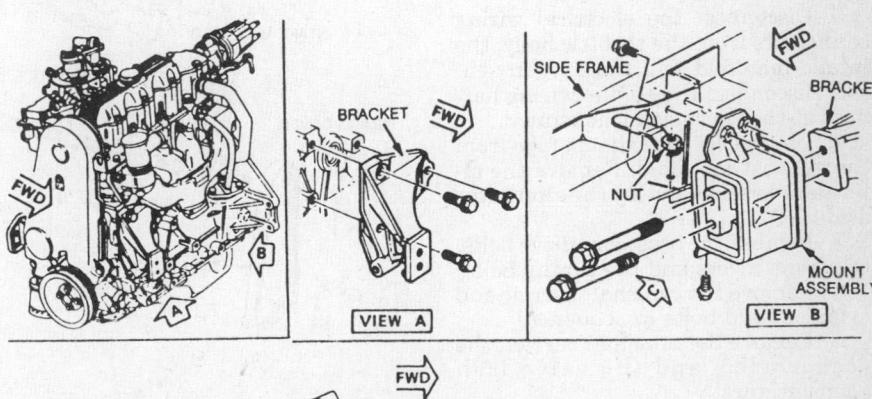

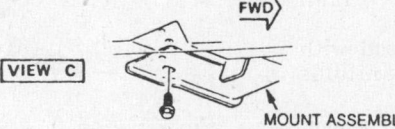

View of the front engine mount—2.0L engine

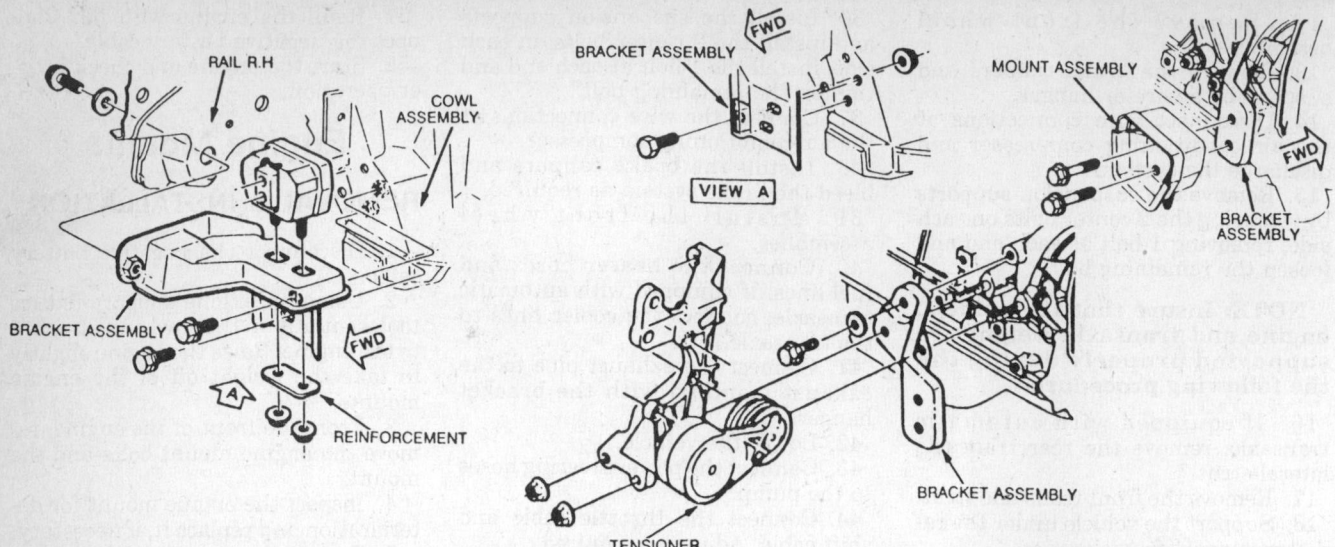

View of the rear engine mount—2.0L engine

Cylinder Head

REMOVAL & INSTALLATION

NOTE: Cylinder head gasket replacement is necessary if cylinder head/camshaft carrier bolts are loosened. These bolts should only be loosened when the engine is cold. New cylinder head bolts must be used, because the head bolts are of the stretch bolt design.

1. Relieve the fuel system pressure.
2. Disconnect the negative battery cable.
3. Remove the lower radiator hose and drain the cooling system. Remove the upper radiator hose and the heater hoses.
4. Remove the air cleaner. Detach the throttle cable and remove it from the intake manifold. Remove the downshift cable.
5. Disconnect the electrical wiring connectors from the throttle body, the intake manifold and the oxygen sensor. Disconnect the engine wiring harness at the thermostat housing.
6. Disconnect the exhaust pipe from the exhaust manifold. Remove the alternator bracket and lay the alternator aside.
7. Remove the accessory drive belts, the front covers and the timing belt.
8. Remove the camshaft carrier and cylinder head bolts in sequence.
9. Remove the camshaft carrier, the rocker arms and the valve lash compensators.
10. Remove the cylinder head with the intake and exhaust manifolds attached.
11. Clean the cylinder head gasket mounting surfaces.

To install:

13. Apply a 3mm bead of anerobic sealant to the camshaft carrier sealing surface.
14. Assemble the intake and exhaust manifolds to the cylinder head. Use a new head gasket and install the assembly in place on the engine.
15. Install the valve lash compensators and the rocker arms.
16. Install the camshaft carrier on the cylinder head. Use new camshaft carrier and cylinder head bolts.

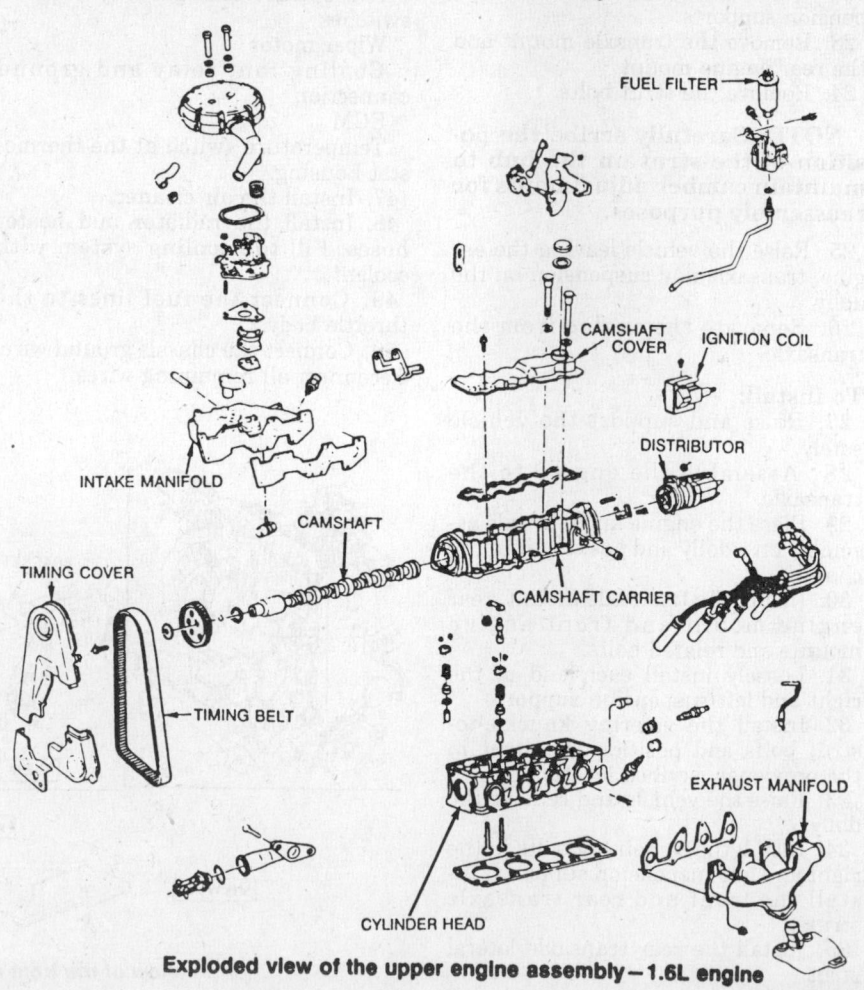

Exploded view of the upper engine assembly—1.6L engine

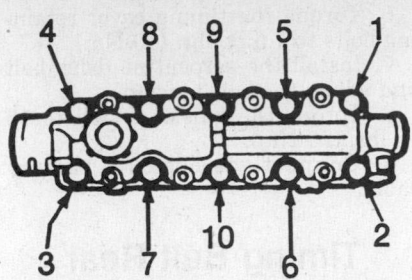

The camshaft carrier/cylinder head bolt removal sequence

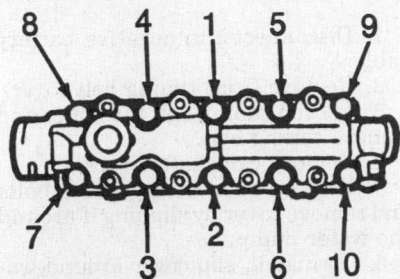

The camshaft carrier/cylinder head bolt torquing sequence

NOTE: New cylinder head bolts must be used, because the head bolts are of the stretch bolt design.

17. Torque the camshaft carrier and cylinder head bolts to 18 ft. lbs. (24 Nm) in sequence, turn an additional 60 degrees, turn another 60 degrees (to 120 degrees) and finally to 150 degrees for the 1.6L engine and 180 degrees for the 2.0L engine.

18. Install the rear cover, timing belt, the front cover and the accessory drive belts.

19. Connect the exhaust pipe to the exhaust manifold. Install the alternator bracket and the thermostat housing.

20. Connect the electrical wiring connectors to the throttle body, the intake manifold and the oxygen sensor. Connect the engine wiring harness to the thermostat housing.

21. Install the air cleaner. Connect the throttle cable to the throttle body. Connect the downshift cable.

22. Install the lower radiator hose, the upper radiator hose and the heater hoses.

23. Refill the cooling system. Connect the negative battery cable.

24. Start the engine and allow it to reach normal operating temperature. After operating temperature is reached, torque the camshaft carrier and cylinder head bolts an additional 30–50 degrees. Check for coolant and oil leaks.

25. Check the ignition timing and adjust, if necessary.

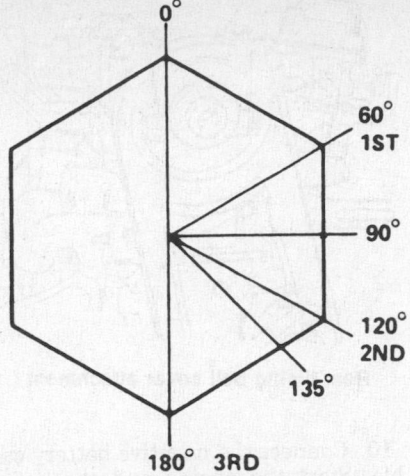

View of the camshaft carrier/cylinder head bolt torque degree chart

Valve Lifters/Rocker Arms

REMOVAL & INSTALLATION

1. Disconnect the negative battery cable.
2. Remove the camshaft carrier cover bolts and the cover.
3. Remove the spark plugs.

NOTE: When working on a particular cylinder, be sure to rotate the crankshaft until the piston of that cylinder is located on the TDC of its compression stroke.

4. Using a air line adapter tool, install it into the spark plug hole of the cylinder being serviced and apply compressed air.

NOTE: Engine components could move due to compressed air, causing belts and pulleys to rotate with considerable force.

5. Using a valve spring compressor tool, compress the valve springs.
6. Remove the rocker arms and the valve lifters; it is important that all of the valve train parts are kept in the order that they were removed.
7. Inspect and/or replace the worn parts.
8. Clean the gasket mounting surfaces of the camshaft carrier and cover.
To install:
9. Using a air line adapter tool, install it into the spark plug hole of the cylinder being serviced and apply compressed air.
10. Using a special valve spring compressing tool, compress the valve springs.
11. Coat the lifters with an engine oil prior to installation.

12. If using the same lifters, install each lifter in the same bore of which it came.
13. If using the same rocker arms, install each rocker arm in its original position.
14. Release the valve spring compressor tool and remove it from the carrier.
15. Install a new camshaft carrier cover gasket, install the carrier cover and retaining bolts. Torque the camshaft carrier cover bolts to 6 ft. lbs. (8 Nm).
16. Install the spark plugs and wires. Connect the negative battery cable.

Valve Lash

ADJUSTMENT

The valve train uses hydraulic valve compensators, located in the cylinder head, which eliminate the need for valve lash adjustment.

Intake Manifold

REMOVAL & INSTALLATION

1. Relieve the fuel system pressure.
2. Disconnect the negative battery cable.
3. Position a clean drain pan under the radiator, remove the lower radiator hose and drain the cooling system.
4. Remove the air cleaner. Detach the cable from the throttle body, the intake manifold bracket and the downshift cable.
5. Loosen the alternator and swing it aside.
6. Disconnect the electrical wiring connectors from the throttle body, the intake manifold, the engine wiring harness and the thermostat housing.
7. Remove the intake manifold mounting nuts and washers, remove the manifold from the engine.
8. Clean the gasket mounting surfaces.
To install:
9. Install a new manifold gasket. Install the intake manifold on the engine and install the mounting nuts and

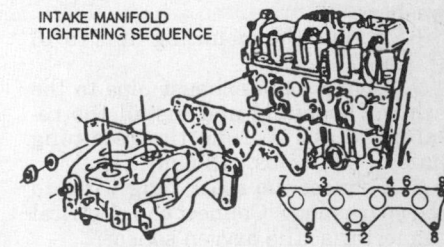

Installation of the intake manifold— 2.0L engine

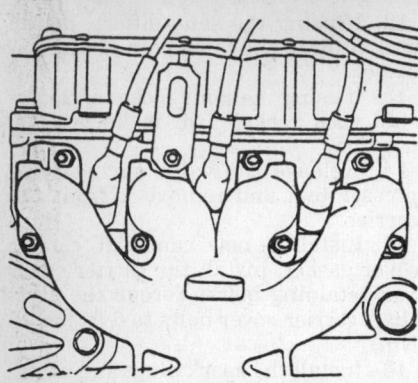

Exhaust manifold mounting

Rear timing belt cover attachment

washers. Torque the manifold mounting nuts to 16 ft. lbs. (22 Nm).

10. Connect the electrical wiring connectors to the throttle body, the intake manifold, the engine wiring harness and the thermostat housing.

11. Position the alternator in place and install the retaining bolts.

12. Install the intake manifold bracket and connect the downshift cable to the throttle body. Install the air cleaner.

13. Install the the lower radiator hose. Refill the cooling system.

14. Connect the negative battery cable. Start the engine and check for coolant leaks.

Exhaust Manifold

REMOVAL & INSTALLATION

1. Disconnect the negative battery cable.

2. Remove the air cleaner. Disconnect the spark plug wires from the spark plugs and the electrical connector at the oxygen sensor. Remove the manifold pre-heater.

3. Remove the exhaust pipe nuts and the exhaust manifold mounting nuts/washers. Remove the exhaust manifold from the engine.

4. Clean the gasket mounting surfaces.

To install:

5. To install, use a new gasket, position the exhaust manifold to the engine and install the mounting nuts/washers.

6. Torque the mounting nuts to 16 ft. lbs. (22 Nm).

7. Connect the exhaust pipe to the exhaust manifold and install the retaining nuts. Torque the retaining nuts to 9.5 ft. lbs. (13 Nm).

8. Connect the spark plug wires to the spark plugs. Connect the electrical connector at the oxygen sensor.

9. Install the manifold pre-heater and air cleaner.

10. Connect the negative battery cable. Start the engine and check for coolant leaks.

Timing Belt Front Cover

REMOVAL & INSTALLATION

1.6L Engine

1. Disconnect the negative battery cable.

2. Loosen the alternator mounting bolts and remove the drive belt from the alternator pulley.

3. Loosen the air conditioning compressor mounting bolts and remove the drive belt from the compressor pulley.

4. Remove the power steering pump lines and mounting bolts, remove the pump.

5. Unsnap the front cover, upper half first and remove it from the engine.

To install:

6. Snap the front cover into place, bottom first. Install the power steering pump and lines.

7. Adjust the drive belt tensions. Check power steering fluid level, fill as required. It is recommended that the power steering system be bled to insure proper operation.

8. Connect the negative battery cable.

2.0L Engine

1. Disconnect the negative battery cable.

2. Loosen the serpentine belt tensioner bolt and allow the tensioner to swing downward.

3. Remove the serpentine belt.

4. Remove the timing cover retaining bolts and remove the timing cover.

To install:

5. Position the timing cover in place and install the retaining bolts.

6. Torque the timing cover retaining bolts to 7.5 ft. lbs. (10 Nm).

7. Install the serpentine drive belt and adjust the belt tension.

8. Torque the tensioner bolt to 18 ft. lbs. (25 Nm).

9. Connect the negative battery cable.

Timing Belt Rear Cover

REMOVAL & INSTALLATION

1. Disconnect the negative battery cable.

2. Remove front timing belt cover.

3. Loosen timing belt tensioner and remove timing belt.

4. Remove camshaft sprocket.

5. Remove rear timing cover bolts and remove cover by slipping it around the water pump.

6. To install, slip cover around water pump and install the retaining bolts. Install the camshaft sprocket, tighten to 34 ft. lbs. (46 Nm). Slide the timing belt over sprocket and adjust tension to specification. Install front cover.

7. Connect the negative battery cable.

OIL SEAL REPLACEMENT

1. Disconnect the negative battery cable.

2. Remove the timing belt front cover.

3. Mark the relationship of the timing belt to the crankshaft and camshaft sprockets. Loosen the timing belt tensioner and remove the timing belt.

4. Remove the crankshaft pulley retaining bolt. Remove the crankshaft sprocket and the rear thrust washer. Remove the rear timing cover mounting screws and remove the cover.

5. Using a small pry bar, pry the front oil seal from the oil pump housing.

6. Using the protective sleeve of the seal installation tool, install it onto the crankshaft.

To install:

7. Using a new front oil seal, lubricate the seal lips with engine oil and install it onto the protective sleeve.

8. Using the seal installation tool, install the new oil seal into the oil pump until it seats.

9. Install the rear timing cover and mounting screws. Install the crankshaft sprocket, thrust washer retaining bolt. Torque the crankshaft sprocket bolt to 114 ft. lbs. (155 Nm).

10. Install the crankshaft pulley and

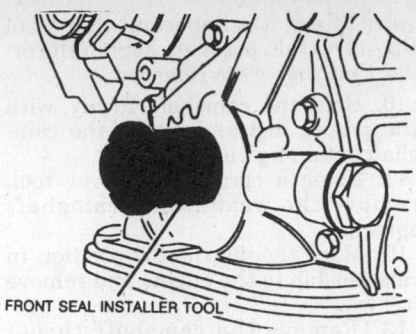

FRONT SEAL INSTALLER TOOL

Installation of the front cover seal

retaining bolt. Torque the retaining bolt to 40 ft. lbs. (55 Nm).

11. Align the timing marks made prior to disassembly and install the timing belt. Adjust the belt tension.

10. Install the front timing cover and adjust all accessory drive belts to specification.

11. Connect the negative battery cable. Check ignition timing.

Timing Belt and Tensioner

ADJUSTMENT

1.6L Engine

1. Disconnect the negative battery cable.

2. Remove the drive belts from the alternator and air conditioning compressor pulleys.

4. Remove the power steering pump lines and mounting bolts, remove the pump.

5. Remove the front cover from the engine.

6. Loosen the water pump retaining bolts and release the timing belt tension.

7. Using a special timing belt tension adjustment tool, turn the water pump eccentric clockwise until the tensioner contacts the high torque stop. Tighten the water pump retaining bolts slightly.

8. Rotate the crankshaft 2 rotations counterclockwise to insure the belt is fully seated into the gear.

9. Rotate the water pump eccentric counterclockwise until the hole in the tensioner arm is aligned with the hole in the base.

10. Tighten the water pump retaining bolts to 18 ft. lbs. (25 Nm). Make sure the tensioner holes remain in alignment. If not readjust.

11. Snap the front cover into place, bottom first. Install the power steering pump and lines.

12. Install the alternator and air conditioning compressor drive belts.

13. Install the power steering pump. Connect the power steering lines and fill the fluid level as required. It is recommended that the power steering system be bled to insure proper operation.

14. Connect the negative battery cable.

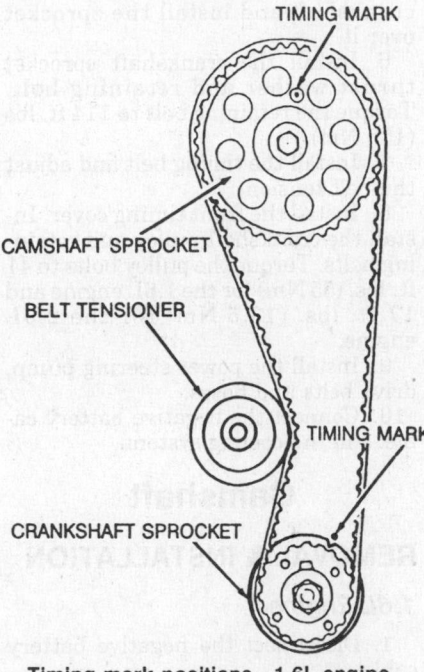

TIMING MARK

CAMSHAFT SPROCKET

BELT TENSIONER

TIMING MARK

CRANKSHAFT SPROCKET

Timing mark positions—1.6L engine

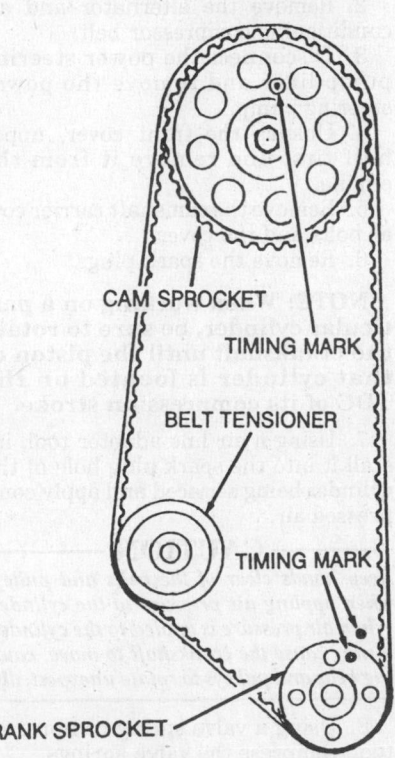

CAM SPROCKET

TIMING MARK

BELT TENSIONER

TIMING MARK

CRANK SPROCKET

Timing mark positions—2.0L engine

2.0L Engine

1. Disconnect the negative battery cable. Drain the cooling system.

2. Remove the power steering pump, bracket and serpentine belt tensioner.

3. Remove the serpentine belt.

4. Remove the timing cover retaining bolts and remove the timing cover.

5. Loosen the water pump retaining bolts and release the timing belt tension.

6. Using a special timing belt tension adjustment tool, turn the water pump eccentric clockwise until the tensioner contacts the high torque stop. Tighten the water pump retaining bolts slightly.

7. Rotate the crankshaft 2 rotations counterclockwise to insure the belt is fully seated into the gear.

8. Rotate the water pump eccentric counterclockwise until the hole in the tensioner arm is aligned with the hole in the base.

9. Tighten the water pump retaining bolts to 18 ft. lbs. (25 Nm). Make sure the tensioner holes remain in alignment. If not readjust.

10. Install the timing belt front cover and retaining bolts. Torque the retaining bolts to 7.5 ft. lbs. (10 Nm).

11. Install the serpentine drive belt and adjust the belt tension.

12. Connect the negative battery cable.

REMOVAL & INSTALLATION

1. Disconnect the negative battery cable. Drain the cooling system.

2. Remove the timing belt front cover.

3. Mark the relationship of the timing belt to the crankshaft and camshaft sprockets. Loosen the timing belt tensioner and remove the timing belt.

4. On the 2.0L engine, the crankshaft gear must be removed in order to remove the timing belt.

To install:

5. Set the crankshaft and camshaft sprockets at top center TDC compression stroke. Align the sprockets with the timing marks on the rear cover.

6. Install the timing belt over the camshaft sprocket and allow the belt to hang free.

7. Install the crankshaft gear and position the timing belt over it. Adjust the timing belt tension.

8. Install the front timing cover. Install the power steering pump, drive belts and hoses.

9. Connect the negative battery cable. Fill the cooling system.

10. Check and adjust the ignition timing as required.

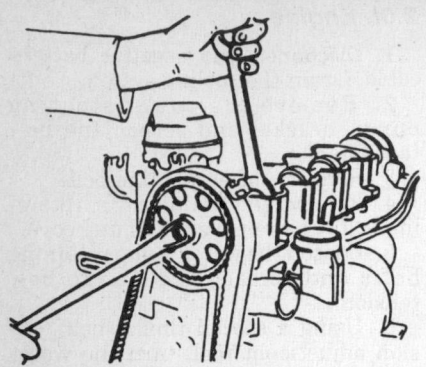

Removing the camshaft sprocket from the camshaft

Timing Sprockets

REMOVAL & INSTALLATION

Camshaft Sprocket

1. Disconnect the negative battery cable.
2. Remove the timing belt front cover.
3. Mark the relationship of the timing belt to the crankshaft and camshaft sprockets. Loosen the timing belt tensioner and remove the timing belt.
4. Remove the camshaft carrier cover to camshaft carrier bolts and remove the cover from the engine.
5. Hold the camshaft in place with an open end wrench and remove the sprocket bolt, washer and sprocket.

To install:

6. Install the camshaft sprocket, washer and retaining bolt. Hold the camshaft in place with an open end wrench and tighten the sprocket retaining bolt. Torque the camshaft sprocket bolt to 34 ft. lbs (45 Nm).
7. Install the timing belt, aligning the marks made prior to removal.
8. Install the front timing cover.
9. Install the power steering pump, drive belts and hoses.
10. Connect the negative battery cable. Fill the cooling system.
11. Install the camshaft carrier cover and retaining bolts. Torque the bolts to 6 ft. lbs. (8 Nm). Check and adjust the ignition timing as needed.
12. Connect the negative battery cable.

Crankshaft Sprocket

1. Disconnect the negative battery cable.
2. Remove the timing belt front cover.
3. Mark the relationship of the timing belt to the crankshaft and camshaft sprockets. Loosen the timing belt tensioner and remove the timing belt.
4. Remove the crankshaft pulley bolt, pulley and thrust washer. Remove the crankshaft sprocket and the Woodruff® key.

NOTE: **It is recommended to replace the front oil seal when the crankshaft pulley is removed.**

To install:

5. Insert the Woodruff® key in the crankshaft and install the sprocket over it.
6. Install the crankshaft sprocket thrust washer and retaining bolt. Torque the retaining bolt to 114 ft. lbs (155 Nm).
7. Install the timing belt and adjust the belt tension.
8. Install the front timing cover. Install the crankshaft pulley and retaining bolts. Torque the pulley bolts to 41 ft. lbs. (55 Nm) for the 1.6L engine and 17 ft. lbs. (13.5 Nm) for the 2.0L engine.
9. Install the power steering pump, drive belts and hoses.
10. Connect the negative battery cable. Fill the cooling system.

Camshaft

REMOVAL & INSTALLATION

1.6L Engine

1. Disconnect the negative battery cable.
2. Remove the alternator and air conditioning compressor belt.
3. Disconnect the power steering pump lines and remove the power steering pump.
4. Unsnap the front cover, upper half first and remove it from the engine.
5. Remove the camshaft carrier cover bolts and the cover.
6. Remove the spark plugs.

NOTE: **When working on a particular cylinder, be sure to rotate the crankshaft until the piston of that cylinder is located on the TDC of its compression stroke.**

7. Using a air line adapter tool, install it into the spark plug hole of the cylinder being serviced and apply compressed air.

――――― CAUTION ―――――
Keep hands clear of the belts and pulleys when appling air pressure to the cylinder. When air pressure is appied to the cylinder, it may cause the crankshaft to move, causing belts and pulleys to rotate unexpectedly.

8. Using a valve spring compressor tool, compress the valve springs.
9. Remove the rocker arms and the valve lifters; it is important that all of the valve train parts are kept in the order that they were removed.
10. Hold the camshaft firmly with the proper tool and loosen the camshaft retaining bolt.
11. Using a sprocket remover tool, remove the washer and camshaft sprocket.
12. Mark the distributor position in relationship to the engine and remove it.
13. Remove the camshaft thrust plate from the rear carrier.
14. Slide the camshaft out from the rear.
15. Clean the gasket mounting surfaces of the carrier and the cover. Inspect and replace any worn or damaged parts.

To install:

16. Using a seal installer tool, install a new camshaft carrier front seal.
17. Coat camshaft bearings and camshaft with an approved camshaft lubricant. Carefully slide the camshaft into the carrier from the rear. Be careful not to damage the front carrier seal.
18. Install the camshaft thrust plate at the rear of the carrier. Torque the trust plate retaining bolts to 70 inch lbs. (8 Nm).
19. Using a feeler gauge, check the camshaft endplay; it should be 0.016–0.064 in. (0.04–0.16mm), if not, replace the rear thrust washer.
20. Install the camshaft sprocket and retaining bolt. Hold the camshaft firmly with the proper tool and tighten the camshaft retaining bolt. Torque the bolt to 34 ft. lbs. (46 Nm).
21. Align the marks on the crankshaft gear and camshaft sprocket with the timing marks on the rear timing cover.
22. Install the timing belt and cover.
23. Install the distributor in the engine, aligning the marks previously made during disassembly.
24. Using a air line adapter tool, install it into the spark plug hole of the cylinder being serviced and apply compressed air.

NOTE: **When working on a particular cylinder, be sure to rotate the crankshaft until the piston of that cylinder is located on the TDC of its compression stroke.**

25. Using a valve spring compressor tool, compress the valve springs.
26. Install the rocker arms and the valve lifters; it is important that all of the valve train parts installed in the same order that they were removed.
27. Disconnect the air line and adapter from the engine. Remove the valve spring compressor tool.
28. Install the spark plugs.

29. Using a new gasket install the camshaft carrier cover and retaining bolts. Torque the bolts to 6 ft. lbs. (9 Nm).

30. Snap the front cover in place on the engine, lower half first and snap the upper cover in place.

31. Install the power steering pump and connect the power steering pump lines.

32. Install the alternator and air conditioning compressor belts. Check and adjust the ignition timing as needed.

33. Connect the negative battery cable.

2.0L Engine

1. Disconnect the negative battery cable.

2. Remove the air cleaner and breather hoses.

3. Remove the camshaft carrier cover bolts and the cover.

4. Remove the serpentine belt.

5. Remove the alternator and bracket from the carrier.

6. Using a valve spring compressor tool, compress the valve springs.

7. Remove the rocker arms and the valve lifters; it is important that all of the valve train parts are kept in the order that they were removed.

8. Hold the camshaft firmly with the proper tool and loosen the camshaft retaining bolt.

9. Using a sprocket remover tool, remove the washer and camshaft sprocket.

10. Mark the distributor position in relationship to the engine and remove it.

11. Remove the camshaft thrust plate from the rear carrier.

12. Slide the camshaft out from the rear.

13. Clean the gasket mounting surfaces of the carrier and the cover. Inspect and replace any worn or damaged parts.

To install:

14. Oil the camshaft carrier seal with oil prior to installing the camshaft.

15. Coat camshaft bearings and camshaft with an approved camshaft lubricant. Carefully slide the camshaft into the carrier from the rear. Be careful not to damage the front carrier seal.

16. Install the camshaft thrust plate at the rear of the carrier. Torque the trust plate retaining bolts to 70 inch lbs. (8 Nm).

17. Using a feeler gauge, check the camshaft endplay; it should be 0.016–0.064 in. (0.04–0.16mm), if not, replace the rear thrust washer.

18. Install the camshaft sprocket and retaining bolt. Hold the camshaft firmly with the proper tool and tighten the camshaft retaining bolt. Torque

the bolt to 34 ft. lbs. (46 Nm).

19. Align the marks on the crankshaft gear and camshaft sprocket with the timing marks on the rear timing cover.

20. Install the timing belt, front cover and retaining bolts. Torque the front cover bolts to 7.5 ft. lbs. (10 Nm).

21. Install the distributor in the engine, aligning the marks previously made during disassembly.

22. Using a valve spring compressor tool, compress the valve springs.

23. Install the rocker arms and the valve lifters; it is important that all of the valve train parts installed in the same order that they were removed.

24. Using a new gasket install the camshaft carrier cover and retaining bolts. Torque the bolts to 6 ft. lbs. (9 Nm).

25. Install the alternator and bracket to the carrier.

26. Install the power steering pump and serpentine belt tensioner as an assembly. Install the serpentine belt.

27. Install the alternator and air conditioning compressor belts.

28. Install the air cleaner and breather hoses.

29. Connect the negative battery cable. Check and adjust the ignition timing as needed.

Piston and Connecting Rod

POSITIONING

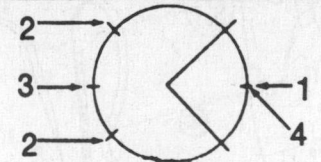

ENGINE LEFT ENGINE FRONT ENGINE RIGHT

1. Oil ring spacer gap
   (Tang in hole or slot with arc)
2. Oil ring rail gaps
3. 2nd compression ring gap
4. Top compression ring gap

Location of the piston ring gaps

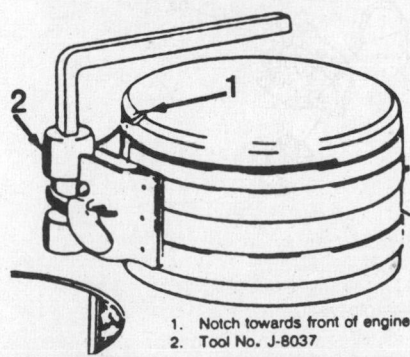

1. Notch towards front of engine
2. Tool No. J-8037

Installing the piston assembly into the engine block

ENGINE LUBRICATION

Oil Pan

REMOVAL & INSTALLATION

1. Disconnect the negative battery cable.

2. Raise and safely support the vehicle.

3. Place a drain pan under the engine, remove the drain plug from the oil pan and drain the oil from the crankcase.

4. Remove the exhaust pipe from the exhaust manifold.

5. Remove the oil pan to engine bolts and the oil pan from the engine.

6. Clean the gasket mounting surfaces.

7. To install, use a new gasket, RTV sealant and reverse the removal procedures. Be sure to coat the oil pan rail seams with sealant.

8. Torque the oil pan bolts to 4 ft. lbs. (5 Nm) and the oil pan plug to 34 ft. lbs. (46 Nm).

9. Install the exhaust pipe to manifold and tighten the nuts to 19 ft. lbs. (26 Nm).

10. Refill the crankcase with new oil.

Oil Pump

REMOVAL & INSTALLATION

1. Disconnect the negative battery cable.

2. Remove the accessory drive belts on the 1.6L engine and the serpentine belt on the 2.0L engine. Remove the crankshaft pulley assembly.

3. Remove the front timing belt cover and the timing belt.

4. Remove the rear timing belt cover bolts and the cover from the engine.

5. Disconnect the electrical connector from the oil pressure switch.

6. Raise and support the vehicle safely.

7. Drain the engine oil.

8. Remove the oil pan bolts and the oil pan from the engine.

9. Remove the oil filter and the pick up tube. Remove the oil pump bolts and the oil pump from the engine.

To install:

NOTE: When the oil pump has been removed from the engine, it is recommended to replace the front oil seal.

10. Clean the gasket mounting surfaces and the oil pump, if it is going to be re-used.

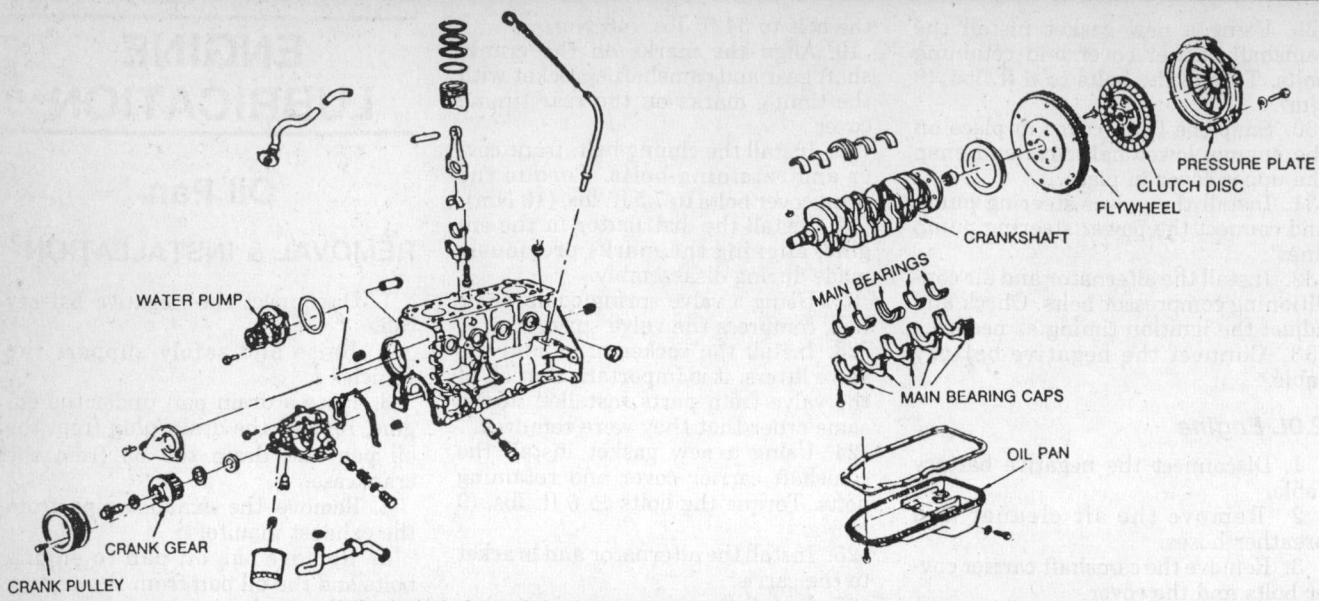

Exploded view of the lower engine assembly—1.6L engine

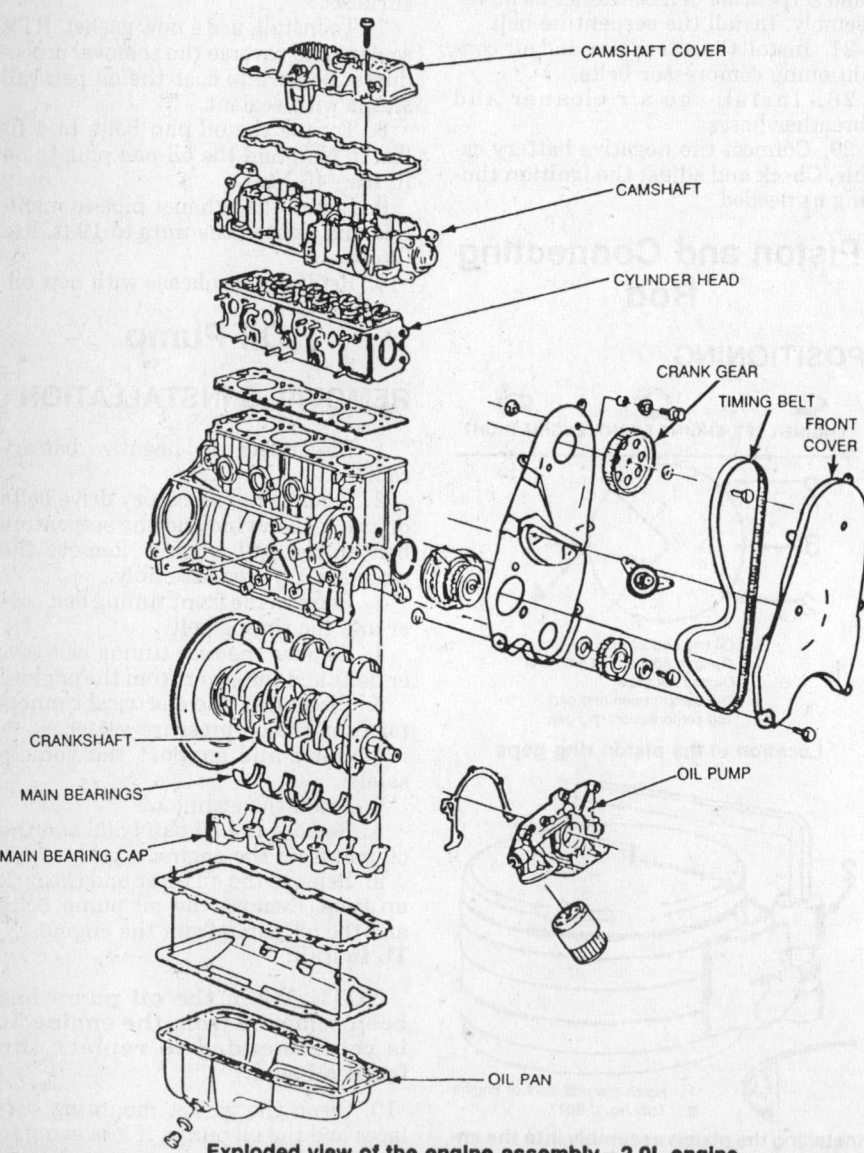

Exploded view of the engine assembly—2.0L engine

11. To install, use new oil pan and pump gaskets. Use an approved sealant on the gasket surfaces. Torque the oil pump to engine bolts to 5 ft. lbs. (7 Nm) and the oil pan bolts to 6 ft. lbs. (8 Nm).

12. Install the timing belt cover, the crankshaft sprocket and the timing belt. Install and adjust the accessory drive belts. Use a new oil filter and fill the crankcase with clean engine oil.

13. Run the engine and check for leaks, also check ignition timing. Connect the negative battery cable.

CHECKING

1. If foreign matter is present, determine it's source.

2. Check the pump cover and housing for cracks, scoring and/or damage; if necessary, replace the housings.

3. Inspect the idler gear shaft for looseness in the housing; if necessary, replace the pump or timing chain, depending on the model.

4. Inspect the pressure regulator valve for scoring or sticking; if burrs

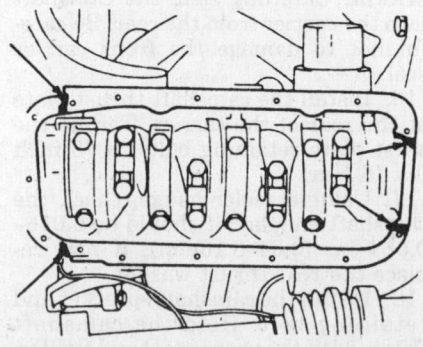

Installing sealant to the oil pan rail seams

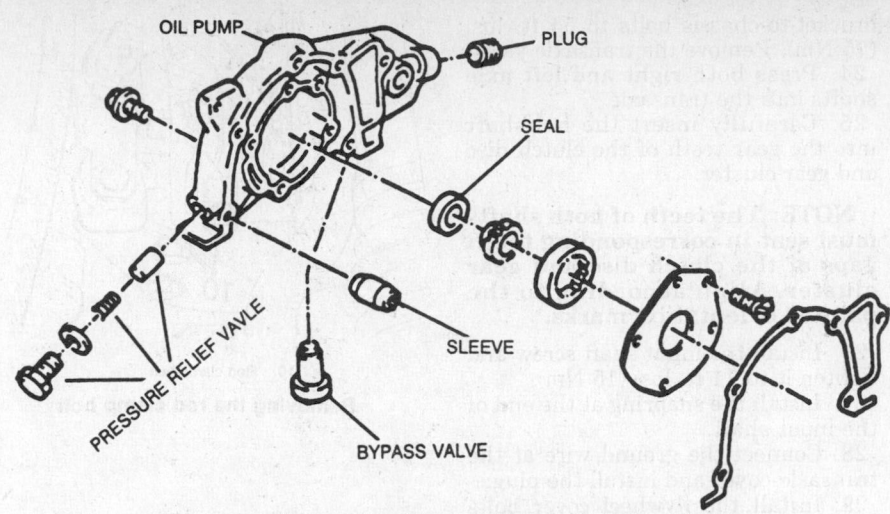

OIL PUMP   PLUG
SEAL
SLEEVE
PRESSURE RELIEF VAVLE
BYPASS VALVE

Exploded view of the oil pump—1.6L and 2.0L engines

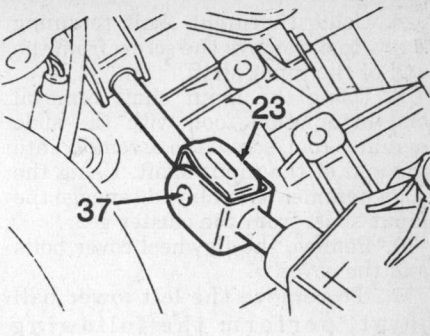

23. Clip
37. Bolt (Pin)
Removing the universal joint clip and bolt

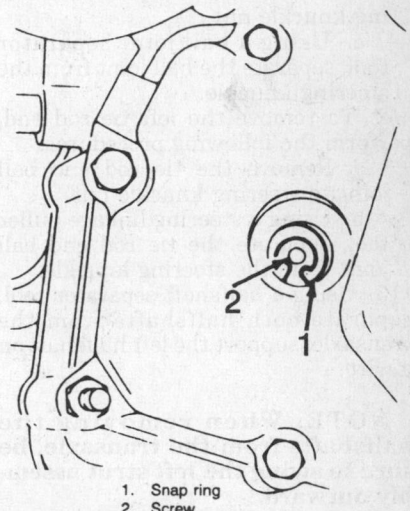

1. Snap ring
2. Screw
View of the input shaft snap ring

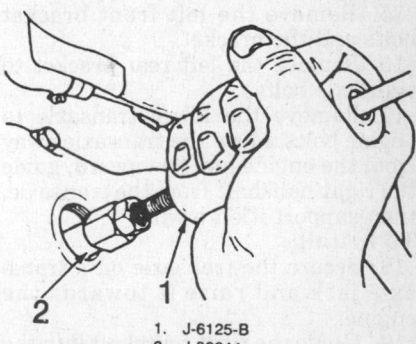

1. J-6125-B
2. J-36644
Disengaging the input shaft from the cluster gear

are present, remove them with an oil stone.

5. Inspect the pressure regulator valve spring for loss of tension or distortion; if necessary, replace it.

6. Inspect the suction pipe for looseness, if pressed into the housing and the screen for broken wire mesh; if necessary, replace them.

7. Inspect the gears for chipping, galling and/or wear; if necessary, replace them.

8. Inspect the driveshaft and driveshaft extension for looseness and/or wear; if necessary, replace them.

Rear Main Bearing Oil Seal

REMOVAL & INSTALLATION

The rear seal use in both the 1.6L and 2.0L engines is of the 1 piece lip design.

1. Disconnect the negative battery cable.

2. Raise and support the vehicle safely. Remove the transaxle.

3. If equipped with an automatic transaxle, remove flexplate retaining bolts and remove the flexplate from the engine.

4. If equipped with a manual transaxle, remove the pressure plate and clutch disc assembly. Remove the flywheel bolts and remove the flywheel from the engine.

5. Using a small pry bar, pry the rear main oil seal from its retainer. Clean all gasket mating surfaces thoroughly.

To install:

6. Lubricate the new oil seal lips with engine oil. Using the seal installation tool, drive the new rear oil seal into the block until it seats.

NOTE: When installing the flywheel, new retaining bolts must be used.

7. If equipped with a manual transaxle, install the flywheel and retaining bolts. Torque the flywheel bolts to 25 ft. lbs. (35 Nm) for 1.6L engine and 55 ft. lbs. (75 Nm) for 2.0L engine. Install the clutch disc/pressure plate assembly.

8. If equipped with automatic transaxle torque the flexplate bolts to 25 ft. lbs. (35 Nm) for 1.6L engine and 52 ft. lbs. (70 Nm) for 2.0L engine.

9. Install the transaxle.

10. Connect the negative battery cable. Fill the engine with oil and check for leaks.

MANUAL TRANSAXLE

For further information on transmissions/transaxles, please refer to "Chilton's Guide to Transmission Repair".

Transaxle Assembly

REMOVAL & INSTALLATION

1. Disconnect the negative battery cable.

2. Remove the clutch cable from the release lever.

3. From the shifter universal joint, remove the retaining clip and bolt.

4. From the transaxle, remove the speedometer cable, the speed sensor and the back-up light connector.

5. Remove the upper transaxle to engine bolts. Install the engine support fixture tool and support the engine.

6. Raise the vehicle and support it safely. Remove the left front wheel assembly.

7. From the transaxle cover, remove the plug and the ground wire. Using a pair of internal snapring pliers, remove the snapring from the end of the input shaft; mark the position of the input shaft in relation to the cluster gear.

8. Using the input shaft retaining screw tool, remove the screw from the end of the input shaft.

9. Using the input shaft removal and installation tool, with the slide hammer tool, screw the assembly into the end of the input shaft. Using the slide hammer assembly, disengage the input shaft from the cluster gear.

10. Remove the flywheel cover bolts and the cover.

11. To remove the left lower ball joint, perform the following procedures:

    a. Remove the retainer clip from the ball joint.

    b. Remove the ball joint to steering knuckle nut.

    c. Using a ball joint separator tool, separate the ball joint from the steering knuckle.

12. To remove the left tie rod end, perform the following procedures:

    a. Remove the tie rod end ball joint to steering knuckle nut.

    b. Using a steering linkage puller tool, separate the tie rod end ball joint from the steering knuckle.

13. Using a halfshaft separator tool, separate both halfshafts from the transaxle; support the left halfshaft on a wire.

NOTE: When removing the halfshafts from the transaxle, be sure to swing the left strut assembly outward.

14. Using a transxle jack, position it under the transaxle and support it.

15. Remove the left front bracket bolts and the bracket.

16. Remove the left rear bracket to transaxle bolts.

17. Remove the lower transaxle to engine bolts. Move the transaxle away from the engine and downward; guide the right halfshaft from the transaxle, then support it on a wire.

To install:

18. Secure the transaxle on a transaxle jack and raise it towards the engine.

19. Guide the right haftshaft into the transaxle, while installing the transaxle to the engine.

NOTE: The right haftshaft cannot be readily installed after the tranaxle is connected to the engine.

20. Install the lower transaxle-to-engine bolts and tighten to 55 ft. lbs. (75 Nm).

21. Install the the left rear mount bracket-to-transaxle bolts and tighten to 55 ft. lbs. (75 Nm).

22. Install the left front mount bracket-to-transaxle bolts and tighten to 47 ft. lbs. (65 Nm).

23. Install the left front mount bracket-to-chassis bolts to 55 ft. lbs. (75 Nm). Remove the transaxle jack.

24. Press both right and left axle shafts into the transaxle.

25. Carefully insert the halfshaft into the gear teeth of the clutch disc and gear cluster.

NOTE: The teeth of both shafts must seat in corresponding tooth gaps of the clutch disc and gear cluster. Align according to the painted orientation marks.

26. Install the input shaft screw and tighten it to 11 ft. lbs. (15 Nm).

27. Install the snapring at the end of the input shaft.

28. Connect the ground wire at the transaxle cover and install the plug.

29. Install the flywheel cover bolts and tighten to 55 ft. lbs. (75 Nm).

30. Install the speed sensor and the back-up light connector.

31. Install the clutch cable to the release lever.

32. Install the shifter universal and install the retaining clip and bolt.

33. Connect and tighten the ball joint-to-steering knuckle nut to 50 ft. lbs. (68 Nm).

34. Connect and tighten the tie rod end-to-steering knuckle nut to 45 ft. lbs. (61 Nm).

35. Lower the vehicle.

36. Remove the engine support fixture tool and the adaptor tool from the engine.

37. Check and replenish the transaxle fluid level. Connect the negative battery cable.

LINKAGE ADJUSTMENT

1. Disconnect the negative battery cable.

2. Position the gear shift lever in the **N** position.

3. Loosen the shift rod clamp bolt.

4. From the shift lever cover, remove the adjustment hole plug. Turn the shift rod left until a $\frac{3}{16}$ in. gauge pin can be inserted into the adjustment hole into the intermediate shift lever.

5. Remove the boot from the console, then, pull it upward to expose the shift control lever mechanism.

6. With the transaxle in **N**, place the gear shift lever into the **1ST/2ND** gear position. With the lever against the stop and the arrow aligned with the notch, torque the rod clamp bolt to 10 ft. lbs. (13.6 Nm), turn the bolt another 90–180 degrees.

7. Using a 0.120 in. dia. gauge pin, check the clearance between the **A** catch and the **B** stop.

8. Remove the gauge pin and install the plug.

9. To further adjust the shift lever,

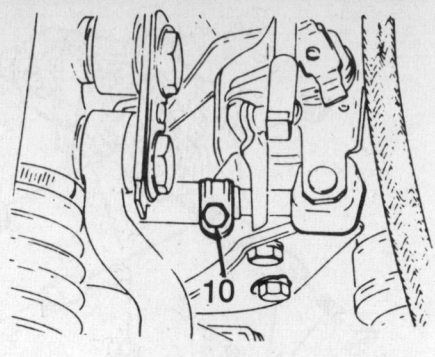

10.   Rod clamp bolt

Removing the rod clamp bolt

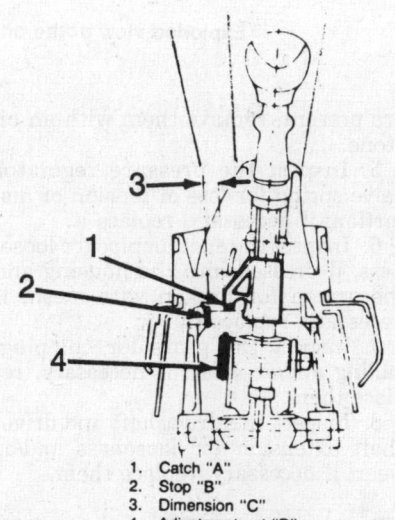

1. Catch "A"
2. Stop "B"
3. Dimension "C"
4. Adjustment nut "D"

Adjusting the shift lever measurements

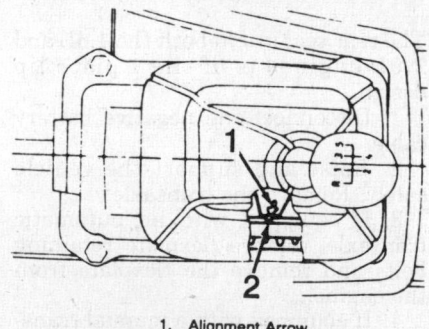

1. Alignment Arrow
2. Notch

Aligning the shift lever

bend back the adjusting nut locking tabs and turn the adjusting nut **D** until the **C** dimension is 0.449–0.465 in. Bend up the locking tabs to secure the adjusting nut.

10. Install the boot the console and center the console.

11. Connect the negative battery cable.

CLUTCH

Clutch Assembly

REMOVAL & INSTALLATION

It is not necessary to remove the transaxle from this vehicle to replace the clutch assembly.

1. Disconnect the negative battery cable. Remove the clutch cable from the release lever. Raise and safely support the vehicle.

2. From the transaxle cover, remove the plug and the ground wire. Using a pair of internal snapring pliers, remove the snapring from the end of the input shaft; mark the position of the input shaft in relation to the cluster gear.

3. Using a input shaft retaining screw tool, remove the screw from the end of the input shaft.

4. Using the input shaft removal and installation tool, with the slide hammer tool, screw the assembly into the end of the input shaft. Using the slide hammer assembly, disengage the input shaft from the cluster gear.

5. Remove the clutch cover from the bottom of the transaxle and push back the clutch release bearing. Using a set of pressure plate spring clamps tool, rotate the flywheel and install a clamp every 120 degrees.

NOTE: The pressure plate and clutch disc cannot be removed without installing the 3 spring clamps.

6. Remove the pressure plate to flywheel bolts, the pressure plate/clutch disc assembly. Be sure to support the assembly when removing the last bolt.
To install:

7. To replace the clutch disc in the assembly, perform the following procedures:

a. Using a hydraulic press, apply pressure to the pressure plate spring fingers, remove the spring clamps.

b. Reduce the pressure of the press and separate the clutch disc from the pressure plate.

c. Inspect the clutch disc and the pressure plate for wear and/or damage; if necessary, replace the disc. Be sure to install the spring clamps to the pressure plate/clutch disc assembly.

d. Using grease, lightly lubricate the clutch disc spline.

e. When installing the pressure plate/clutch disc assembly, align the pressure plate **V** mark with the dot on the flywheel. Install 2 pressure plate to flywheel bolts for support and torque the bolts to 11 ft. lbs (15 Nm).

f. Install the input shaft by aligning the input shaft with the mark on the cluster gear. Using an input shaft removal/installation tool and a slide hammer tool, seat the input shaft with the cluster gear.

g. Install the screw into the end of the input shaft; torque it to 11 ft. lbs (15 Nm).

h. Install the snapring on the end of the input shaft; the sharp edges must face the cover.

i. Install the remainder of the pressure plate retaining bolts and torque to 11 ft. lbs (15 Nm).

NOTE: When installing a new clutch disc, make sure that the long part of the clutch disc hub faces the transaxle.

8. Using Teflon® pipe thread sealer, coat the threads of the input shaft cover plug and tighten to 36 ft. lbs (50 Nm).

9. Remove the spring clamps from the pressure plate/clutch disc assembly.

10. Install the clutch cover and retaining bolts. Torque the retaining bolts to 62 inch lbs. (7 Nm). Install the left tire and wheel assembly, lower the vehicle. Install the clutch cable to the release lever. Check clutch engagement and operation.

11. Connect the negative battery cable.

Clutch Cable

ADJUSTMENT

1. Measure the distance from the center of the clutch pedal to the bottom edge of the steering wheel.

2. Depress the clutch pedal (fully) and measure the distance again. Subtract the 1st measurement from the 2nd to determine the pedal travel.

3. If the pedal travel is not 5.43–5.70 in. (138–146mm), remove the clutch cable clip and adjust the nut to bring the measurement within specifications.

NOTE: With the correct adjustment, the clutch pedal will be higher than the brake pedal and there will be no free-play operation. As the clutch disc wears, the clutch pedal will move further away from the brake pedal.

REMOVAL & INSTALLATION

1. Disconnect the negative battery cable.

2. Measure the threaded end of the clutch cable at the release lever and record the measurement for pre-adjustment procedures.

3. Remove the clutch cable clip and loosen the clutch cable adjusting nut. Disconnect the cable from the release arm and cable bracket.

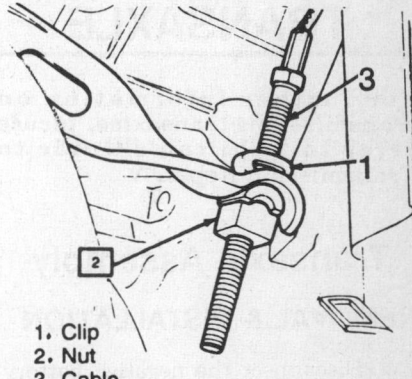

1. Clip
2. Nut
3. Cable
View of the clutch cable adjuster

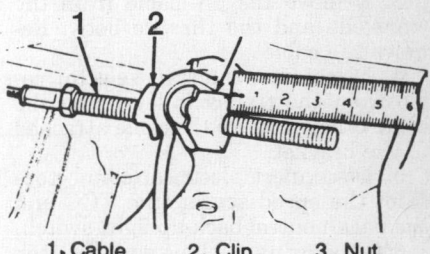

1. Cable   2. Clip   3. Nut
Measuring the end of the clutch cable

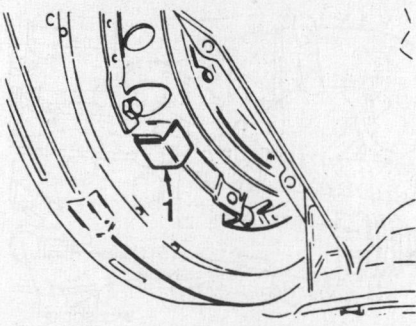

1. J-36554
View of the pressure plate spring clamps

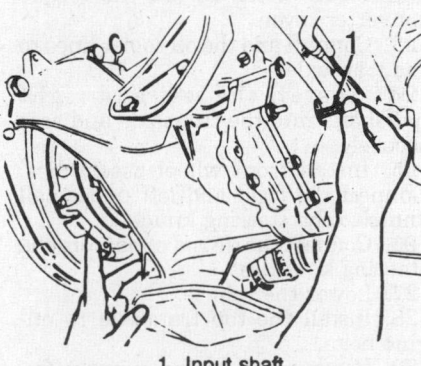

1. Input shaft
Installing the input shaft into the pressure plate/clutch disc assembly

4. Disconnect the clutch start safety switch.

5. At the clutch pedal, remove the cable return spring and brace. Remove the clutch pedal retaining nut, spring and shaft. Remove the pedal and pull the cable through the firewall.

6. Disconnect the spring and the cable from the pedal.

7. Remove the clutch cable by pulling it from the engine compartment.

To install:

8. From the engine compartment, install the clutch cable through the front dash. Place the grommet and washer the clutch cable.

9. From under the dash, connect the cable and return spring to the clutch pedal.

10. Position the clutch pedal assembly to the support brace and install the pedal support shaft through the brace and pedal. Coat the shaft prior to installing it.

11. Install the washer, shaft retaining nut, shaft spring and return spring to the brace.

12. Install the clutch start switch.

13. Install the clutch cable to the release lever and install the adjustment nut.

14. Adjust the clutch cable to the measurement taken earlier. Adjust the clutch pedal travel.

15. Connect the negative battery cable. Check the clutch operation.

AUTOMATIC TRANSAXLE

For further information on transmissions/transaxles, please refer to "Chilton's Guide to Transmission Repair".

Transaxle Assembly

REMOVAL & INSTALLATION

1. Disconnect the negative battery cable.

2. Remove the air cleaner.

3. Remove the TV cable from the transaxle and the throttle body. Remove the cable.

4. Disconnect the shift selector cable from the transaxle lever and the cable bracket; leave the cable attached to the bracket.

5. Disconnect electrical connectors from the speed sensor, the TCC and the park/neutral/back-up light switch.

6. Disconnect the speedometer drive cable from the transaxle.

7. Remove the top transaxle to engine bolts.

8. Using the engine support fixture tool and the adaptor tool, attach it to the engine and support the weight.

9. Raise and safely support the vehicle.

10. Remove both front wheels. Using the ball joint separator tool, separate the ball joints (both sides) from the steering knuckles. Remove the tie rod ends from the steering knuckles.

11. Remove the right transaxle to engine mount bolts and the remaining transaxle to engine bolts.

12. Lower the transaxle from the vehicle.

To install:

13. Apply a light coating of grease to the torque converter piolet hub. Place the torque converter on to the hub and seat it securely into the pump.

14. Secure the transaxle on a transaxle jack and position it towards the engine.

15. Install lower transaxle to engine bolts and torque to engine bolts to 54 ft. lbs. (73 Nm).

16. Install the right transaxle to engine mount bolts and torque to 30 ft. lbs. (41 Nm).

17. Install the left and rear transaxle to engine mount bolts and torque to 16 ft. lbs. (22 Nm).

18. Install the torque converter to flywheel bolts and torque to 44 ft. lbs. (60 Nm). Torque the remaining transaxle to engine bolts to 55 ft. lbs. (75 Nm).

19. Check and/or adjust the selector cable adjustment. Check and/or adjust the TV cable adjustment. Check and refill the transaxle with fluid.

20. Install the right transaxle to engine mount bolts and the remaining transaxle to engine bolts.

21. Align the marks on the torque converter and flywheel, made during disassembly and install the torque converter to flywheel bolts. Torque the bolts to 44 ft. lbs. (60 Nm).

22. Install the left transaxle to engine mount bolts. Install the torque converter cover.

23. Connect and the oil cooler lines to the transaxle.

24. Install the left and right halfshafts into the transaxle and seat securely.

25. Install front wheel assemblies. Connect the right and left upper ball joints to the steering knuckles.

26. Connect the tie rod ends from the steering knuckles.

27. Lower the vehicle.

28. Install the top transaxle to engine bolts.

29. Remove the engine support fixture tool and the adaptor tool from the engine.

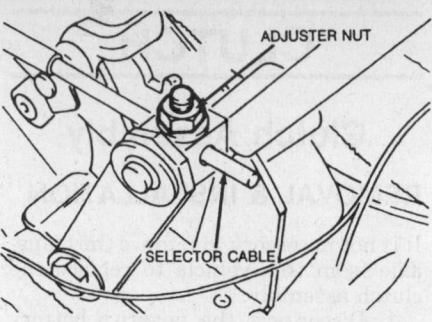

Adjusting the shift linkage—automatic transaxle

30. Connect the speedometer drive cable to the transaxle.

31. Connect the electrical connectors to the speed sensor, the TCC and the park/neutral/back-up light switch.

32. Connect the shift selector cable to the transaxle lever and the cable bracket assembly.

33. Install the TV cable to the transaxle and the throttle body. Connect the cable.

34. Check and replenish the transaxle fluid level.

35. Install the air cleaner. Connect the negative battery cable.

SHIFT LINKAGE ADJUSTMENT

1. Disconnect the negative battery cable.

2. Remove the center console.

3. Loosen the clamp at the selector lever and cable.

4. Adjust the cable so that the selector lever will catch in each position; P, R, N, D, 2 and 1.

5. Adjust the cable at the selector lever. Check the shift in all positions.

6. Install the console and connect the negative battery cable.

THROTTLE LINKAGE ADJUSTMENT

1. Disconnect the negative battery cable.

2. Remove the air cleaner.

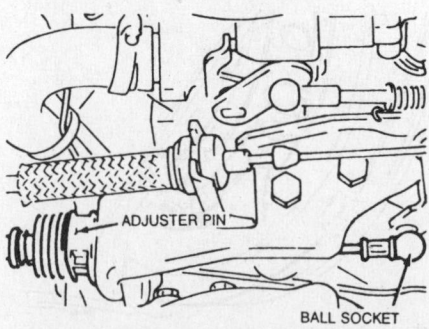

Adjusting the throttle linkage—automatic transaxle

3. Remove the locking spring clip adjuster.

4. Pull the adjuster pin out, to relieve tension on the cable.

5. Dissengage the ball socket from the lever at the transaxle end.

6. Remove the cable from the mounting bracket by pressing the retaining lugs down.

7. If equipped with 1.6L engine, disconnect the cable at the transaxle end.

8. If equipped with 2.0L engine, remove the TV cable sleeve, at the transxale. Remove the cable by pulling the sleeve up.

9. If equipped with 1.6L engine connect the cable at the transaxle.

10. If equipped with 2.0L engine, connect the cable at the transaxle and install the TV cable sleeve at the transaxle.

11. Install the cable to mounting bracket. Install the ball socket at the throttle body and secure it with locking spring clip.

12. Install the air cleaner.

13. Connect the negative battery cable.

DRIVE AXLE

Halfshaft

REMOVAL & INSTALLATION

1. Raise the hood. Loosen the upper strut to body nuts.

2. Remove the hub cap, then loosen the wheel lug nuts. Remove the grease cap, remove the cotter pin, the wheel hub nut and thrust washer.

3. Raise and safely support the vehicle. Remove the wheel/tire assembly.

4. From the lower ball joint, remove retaining clip and the nut.

5. Using the ball joint separator tool, separate the lower ball joint from the steering knuckle.

6. Remove the tie rod end-to-ball joint nut.

7. Using a special tie rod end separator tool, separate the tie rod end from the steering knuckle.

8. Using a halfshaft to hub separator tool, drive the halfshaft from the hub assembly.

9. Position a drain pan under the transaxle. Using a axle shaft to transaxle separator tool and the slide hammer tool, separate and remove the halfshaft from the transaxle.
To install:

10. Use new retaining clips, cotter pins. Torque the lower ball joint-to-steering knuckle nut to 50 ft. lbs. (70

Nm), the tie rod end-to-steering knuckle nut to 45 ft. lbs (60 Nm).

11. Lower the vehicle to the floor. Torque the hub-to-halfshaft nut to 74 ft. lbs. (100 Nm), the wheel lug nuts to 65 ft. lbs. (90 Nm) and the upper strut-to-body nuts to 22 ft. lbs. (30 Nm). Check and/or refill the transaxle.

CV-Boot

REMOVAL & INSTALLATION

Inner

1. Remove the halfshaft.

2. Remove the CV-joint housing-to-transaxle bolts.

3. Cut the seal retaining clamps and remove the old boot from the shaft.

4. Using a pair of snapring pliers, remove the retaining ring from the shaft and remove the spider assembly.
To install:

5. Using solvent, clean the splines of the shaft and repack the joint.

6. Install the inner boot clamp first and the new boot second.

7. Push the CV-joint assembly onto the shaft until the retaining ring is seated on the shaft.

8. Slide the boot onto the joint. Install both the inner and outer clamps.

9. Install the wheel assembly and lower the vehicle.

Outer

1. Remove the halfshaft from the vehicle.

2. Cut off the boot retaining clamps and discard them. Remove the old boot.

3. If equipped with a deflector ring, use a brass drift and carefully tap it off.

4. Using a pair of snapring pliers, spread the retaining ring inside the outer CV-joint and tap the joint off the halfshaft.
To install:

5. Using solvent, clean the splines of the halfshaft and the CV-joint and repack the joint. Install a new retaining ring inside the joint.

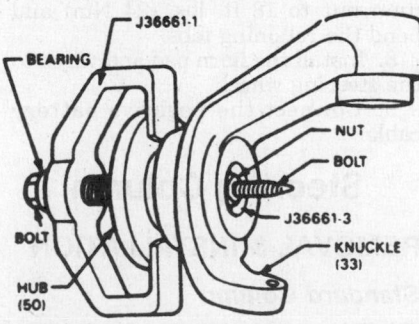

Removing the wheel hub from the steering knuckle

6. Install the inner boot clamp first, the new boot second.

7. Push the joint assembly onto the halfshaft until the ring is seated on the shaft.

8. Slide the boot onto the joint and install the clamps on both the inner and outer part of the boot.

9. Install the wheel assemblies and lower the vehicle.

Front Wheel Hub, Knuckle and Bearings

REMOVAL & INSTALLATION

1. With the vehicle weight on the tires, loosen the hub nut.

2. Raise and safely support the vehicle. Remove the wheel and tire assembly.

3. Install a boot cover over the outer CV-joint boot.

4. Remove the hub nut. Remove the brake caliper and support it out of the way (on a wire); do not allow the caliper to hang on the brake line.

5. Using a special tool, separate the halfshaft from the hub assembly.

6. Disconnect the ball joint from the knuckle and the tie rod end from the strut assembly.

7. Remove the upper strut-to-body nuts and lower the strut/knuckle assembly from the vehicle.

8. Place the knuckle/strut assembly on a work bench.

9. Using a halfshaft separator tool and the front wheel hub remover tool, press the hub from the steering knuckle.

10. Using the halfshaft separator tool, the front wheel hub remover tool and the inner bearing race remover tool, remove the inner bearing race from the hub.

11. From inside the steering knuckle, remove the internal snaprings.

12. Using the halfshaft separator tool and the bearing remover/installer tool, press the bearing from the steering knuckle.
To install:

NOTE: Whenever the wheel bearing is removed from the steering knuckle, it must be discarded and replaced with a new one.

13. Using solvent, clean all of the parts and blow dry with compressed air.

14. Before assembling the parts, be sure to coat them with a layer of wheel bearing grease.

15. Using snapring pliers, install the outer internal snapring into the steering knuckle.

16. Using the halfshaft separator

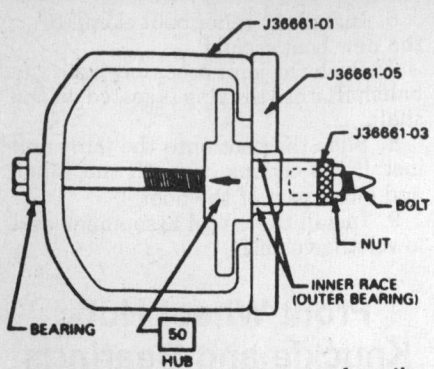

Removing the inner bearing race from the hub

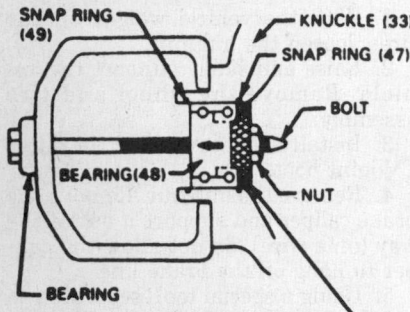

Removing the wheel bearing from the steering knuckle

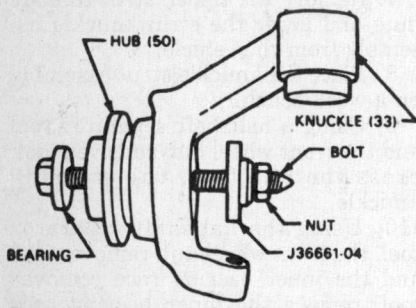

Pressing the new wheel bearing into the steering knuckle

tool and the bearing remover/installer tool, press the new wheel bearing into the steering knuckle until it butts against the snapring.

17. Using snapring pliers, install the inner internal snapring into the steering knuckle.

18. Install the strut onto the body. Remove the seal protector from the halfshaft. Install the halfshaft into the steering knuckle/strut assembly. Install the new washer and new halfshaft nut onto the halfshaft.

19. Use new cotter pins and reverse the removal procedures. Torque the steering knuckle/strut assembly to body nuts to 22 ft. lbs. (30 Nm).

20. Tighten the lower ball joint-to-steering knuckle nut 50 ft. lbs. (68 Nm), the tie rod end-to-steering

knuckle nut to 45 ft. lbs. (61 Nm), the disc rotor-to-hub screw to 3 ft. lbs. (4 Nm), the caliper-to-steering knuckle bolts to 70 ft. lbs. (95 Nm) and the wheel lug nuts to 65 ft. lbs. (88 Nm).

21. Torque the halfshaft-to-hub nut to 74 ft. lbs. (100 Nm), back it off, retighten to 15 ft. lbs. (20 Nm), then, tighten another 90 degrees. Check and/or adjust the front end alignment.

NOTE: When tightening the halfshaft nut, be sure to have the vehicle resting on its wheels. If the castellated nut does not align with a shaft hole, back off the nut until it does; do not tighten the nut to locate another shaft hole.

STEERING

Steering Wheel

REMOVAL & INSTALLATION

1. Disconnect the negative battery cable.
2. Remove the horn pad and wires from the steering wheel.
3. Using a scratch awl, mark the alignment of the steering wheel with the steering column.
4. Remove the steering wheel retaining nut and washer.
5. Using a steering wheel puller tool, remove the steering wheel from the steering column.

NOTE: It may be necessary to disconnect the horn contact ring from the steering wheel. When installing the steering wheel, be sure that the turn signal return segment is positioned on the upper left side, facing the steering column.

To install:

6. Align the steering wheel on the column with marks made during removal and install the steering wheel.
7. Torque the steering wheel column nut to 18 ft. lbs. (24 Nm) and bend the retaining tabs.
8. Install the horn pad and wires to the steering wheel.
9. Connect the negative battery cable.

Steering Column

REMOVAL & INSTALLATION

Standard Column

1. Disconnect the negative battery cable.

2. Remove the upper/lower steering column switch cover panel screws and the panels.

NOTE: When removing the steering column cover panels, it will be necessary to turn the steering 90 degrees in both directions so the screws become visible.

3. From the instrument panel, remove the lower steering column trim.
4. Disconnect the electrical harness connectors from the steering column and ignition lock switches.
5. If equipped with an automatic transmission, disconnect the park lock actuation cable.
6. Unclip the turn signal switch (left side) and the wiper switch (right side).
7. Position the steering wheel in the straight-ahead position.
8. Remove the steering column shaft to steering shaft flange pinch bolt and the steering column to dash bolts.
9. To remove the steering column to instrument panel shear bolts, perform the following procedures:
    a. Using a center punch, center punch the left side shear bolt.
    b. Using an ⅛ in. drill bit, drill a hole through the shear bolt.
    c. Using a bolt extractor tool, drive the extractor tool into the shear bolt and unscrew it.
10. Guide the steering column out of the vehicle.

NOTE: The plastic washer seated loosely on the steering shaft serves to center the steering shaft. It is placed in the steering shaft prior to mounting the assembly and must be removed after the assembly has been completed.

To install:

11. Center the steering wheel, use a new shear bolt. Torque the steering column-to-instrument panel bolt to 16 ft. lbs. (22 Nm), the steering column shaft-to-coupling pinch bolt to 16 ft. lbs. (22 Nm), the steering pinion-to-steering coupling pinch bolt to 16 ft. lbs. (22 Nm) and the steering wheel-to-steering column nut to 18 ft. lbs. (24 Nm).

Tilt Column

1. Disconnect the negative battery terminal from the battery.
2. From the steering wheel, remove the cover cap with the horn button.
3. Position the steering wheel on the straight-ahead position. Remove the steering wheel nut and washer.

4. Using a steering wheel puller tool, pull the steering wheel from the steering column. Do not pound on the steering wheel for damage may occur to the steering column.

NOTE: When removing the steering wheel, make sure the puller hook claws face outwards. If necessary, unclip the contact ring from the steering wheel and replace it with a new one. When installing, make sure the turn signal return segment points to the left. Lubricate the contact finger to contact plate surface.

5. Remove the steering wheel height adjustment lever, the turn signal switch cover screws and both covers.

6. Place the ignition switch (with key) in **2ND** position, press detent spring downward and remove the ignition lock cylinder.

7. Disconnect the electrical harness connector from the ignition contact switch, then, remove the headless set screw and the ignition switch. Remove the switch housing screws and push the switch towards the steering wheel.

8. Compress the locking tabs, remove the turn signal switch (left side) and the wiper switch (right side) from the switch housing.

9. Remove the steering column shaft-to-steering shaft flange pinch bolt and the steering column-to-dash bolts.

10. To remove the steering column-to-instrument panel shear bolts, perform the following procedures:

    a. Using a center punch, center punch the left side shear bolt.

    b. Using an 1/8 in. drill bit, drill a hole through the shear bolt.

    c. Using the bolt extractor tool, drive the extractor tool into the shear bolt and unscrew it.

11. Guide the steering column out of the vehicle.

NOTE: The plastic washer seated loosely on the steering shaft serves to center the steering shaft. It is placed in the steering shaft prior to mounting the assembly and must be removed after the assembly has been completed.

To install:

12. Center the steering wheel, use a new shear bolt. Torque the steering column-to-instrument panel bolt to 16 ft. lbs. (22 Nm), the steering column shaft-to-coupling pinch bolt to 16 ft. lbs. (22 Nm), the steering pinion-to-steering coupling pinch bolt to 16 ft. lbs. (Nm) and the steering wheel-to-steering column nut to 18 ft. lbs. (24 Nm).

Manual Steering Rack

ADJUSTMENT

1. Raise and support the vehicle safely.

2. Center the steering wheel.

3. Loosen the adjuster plug locknut. Turn the adjuster plug clockwise until it bottoms, then, back it out 50–70 degrees.

4. Inspect the steering pinion torque, it should be 8–20 inch lbs.

5. After adjusting the pinion torque, hold the adjuster stationary and torque the adjuster plug locknut to 50 ft. lbs. (68 Nm).

REMOVAL & INSTALLATION

1. Disconnect the negative battery cable.

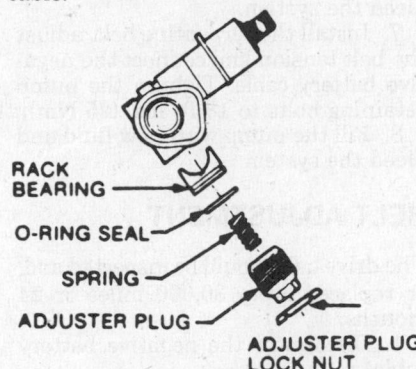

Exploded view of the manual steering gear adjustment assembly

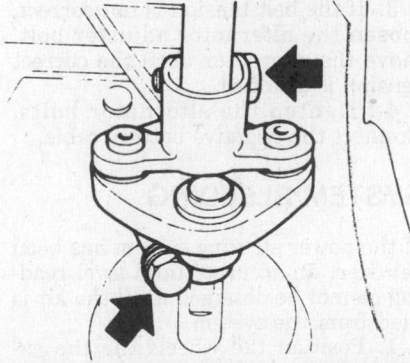

View of the steering column pinch bolts

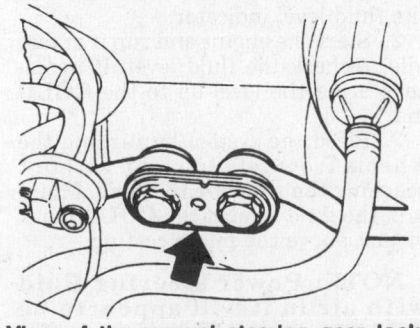

View of the manual steering gear lock plate

2. Position the steering wheel in the straight-ahead position. Remove the steering column-to-coupling pinch bolt and the pinion shaft-to-coupling pinch bolt.

3. Remove the air cleaner.

4. Raise and support the vehicle safely.

5. At the center of the manual steering assembly, cut the plate lock in half before attempting to remove the lock plate bolts; do not attempt to re-use the lock plate. Remove both ttie rod end-to-steering rack/pinion center bolts.

6. If equipped, remove both steering damper brackets.

7. Remove the steering assembly-to-chassis bolts and the dash seal from the rack/pinion. Remove the steering assembly through the right-wheel opening.

To install:

NOTE: If the studs were removed with the mounting studs, reinstall the studs and retorque. If removed for the 2nd time, reuse the stud with thread locking compound.

8. Use new self locking nuts, a new lock plate. Pay attention to the direction of the notches in the lock plate. Torque the steering rack/pinion-to-chassis nuts to 28 ft. lbs. (38 Nm) and the tie rod end-to-steering rack/pinion bolts to 65 ft. lbs. (88 Nm). Adjust the manual steering rack/pinion play.

NOTE: When installing the coupling onto the steering pinion, push it downward and torque the pinion-to-coupling pinch bolt to 29 ft. lbs. (39 Nm). When installing the steering spindle, pull it upward until it stops on the spindle ball bearing and torque the upper pinch bolt to 34 ft. lbs. (46 Nm).

Power Steering Rack

ADJUSTMENT

1. Raise and support the vehicle safely.

2. Center the steering wheel.

3. Loosen the adjuster plug locknut. Turn the adjuster plug clockwise until it bottoms, then, back it out 50–70 degrees.

4. Inspect the steering pinion torque, it should be 16 inch lbs.

5. After adjusting the pinion torque, hold the adjuster stationary and torque the adjuster plug locknut to 50 ft. lbs. (68 Nm).

REMOVAL & INSTALLATION

1. Disconnect the negative battery cable.

2. Position the steering wheel in the straight-ahead position. Remove the steering column-to-coupling pinch bolt and the pinion shaft-to-coupling pinch bolt.

3. Remove the air cleaner.

4. At the center of the steering rack, cut the plate lock in half before attempting to remove the lock plate bolts; do not attempt to reuse the lock plate. Remove both tie rod end-to-steering rack center bolts.

5. Remove the high pressure hoses from the steering rack.

6. Remove the rack-to-chassis bolts and remove the dash seal from the steering rack. Remove the steering rack through the right-wheel opening. **To install:**

NOTE: If the studs were removed with the mounting studs, reinstall the studs and retorque. If removed for the 2nd time, reuse the stud with thread locking compound.

7. Use new self locking nuts, a new lock plate. Pay attention to the direction of the notches in the lock plate. Torque the steering rack-to-chassis nuts to 28 ft. lbs. (38 Nm) and the tie rod end-to-steering rack bolts to 65 ft. lbs. (88 Nm). Adjust the steering rack play.

NOTE: When installing the coupling onto the steering pinion, push it downward and torque the pinion-to-coupling pinch bolt to 37 ft. lbs. (51 Nm). When installing the steering spindle, pull it upwards until it stops on the spindle ball bearing and torque the upper pinch bolt to 34 ft. lbs. (46 Nm).

8. Refill the power steering system reservoir and bleed the system.

Power Steering Pump

REMOVAL & INSTALLATION

1.6L Engine

1. Disconnect the negative battery cable.

2. Remove the power steering belt.

3. Remove the pressure and return lines from the power steering pump and plug.

4. Remove the upper timing belt cover.

5. Remove the pump retaining bolts and remove the pump.

6. To install, install the power steering pump and retaining bolts. Torque the pump retaining bolts to 20 ft. lbs. (27 Nm).

7. Connect the pressure and return lines. Fill the pump with new fluid and bleed the system.

8. Install the drive belt, adjust the belt tension and connect the negative battery cable.

2.0L Engine

1. Disconnect the negative battery cable.

2. Remove the serpentine belt.

3. Remove the pressure and return lines from the power steering pump and plug.

4. Remove the pump retaining bolts which are accessible through the holes of the pulley and remove the pump from the bracket.

5. To install, install the power steering pump and retaining bolts. Torque the pump retaining bolts to 18 ft. lbs. (25 Nm).

6. Connect the pressure and return lines. Fill the pump with new fluid and bleed the system.

7. Install the serpentine belt, adjust the belt tension and connect the negative battery cable. Tighten the pump retaining bolts to 18 ft. lbs. (25 Nm).

8. Fill the pump with new fluid and bleed the system.

BELT ADJUSTMENT

The drive belt should be inspected and/or replaced every 30,000 miles or 24 mouths.

1. Disconnect the negative battery cable.

2. Using a belt tension gauge tool, position it on the center of the longest belt span.

3. If the belt tension is not correct, loosen the alternator adjuster bolt, move the alternator until the correct tension is attained.

4. Tighten the alternator bolts. Connect the negative battery cable.

SYSTEM BLEEDING

If the power steering system has been serviced, an accurate fluid level reading cannot be obtained until the air is bled from the system.

1. Position the wheels the the extreme left and add an approved power steering fluid to the **COLD** mark on the fluid level indicator.

2. Start the engine and run it at fast idle, recheck the fluid level. If necessary bring the level up to the **COLD** mark.

3. Bleed the system by turning the wheels from left to right without reaching the stop at either end. Maintain the fluid level at the **COLD** mark or just above the pump casting.

NOTE: Power steering fluid with air in it will appear to be light tan or red. This air must be eliminated from the fluid before

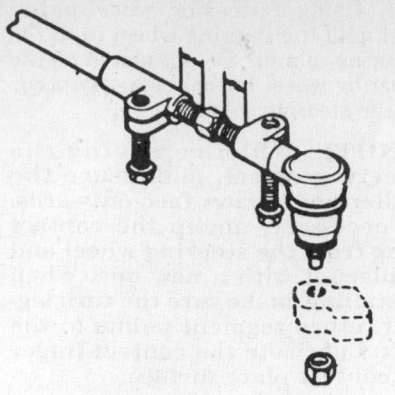

Installation of the outer tie rod end assembly

normal steering action can be obtained.

4. Return the the wheels to the center position. Continue to run the engine for 2 or 3 minutes.

5. Road test the vehicle to be sure the steering functions normal and is free of noise.

6. Recheck the fluid level. When the engine has reached normal operating temperature, the level should be at the **HOT** mark. Add fluid if necessary.

7. Check the system for leaks.

Tie Rod Ends

REMOVAL & INSTALLATION

Outer

1. Raise and safely support the vehicle.

2. Remove the tie rod end-to-steering knuckle nut.

3. Loosen the tie rod end pinch bolt.

4. Using a steering linkage puller tool, separate the tie rod end from the steering knuckle.

5. Remove the tie rod end from the tie adjuster. When unscrewing the tie rod end, record the number of revolutions to remove it, this will aid in installation.

To install:

6. Turn the new tie rod end in the number of turns of turns require to remove it. Torque the tie rod end-to-steering knuckle nut to 43–50 ft. lbs. (58–68 Nm).

7. Check and adjust the front end alignment.

Inner

1. Raise and safely support the vehicle.

2. Remove the outer tie rod end-to-steering knuckle nut.

3. Loosen the tie rod end pinch bolt.

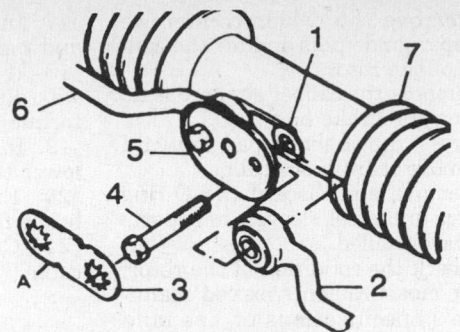

1. Washer
2. Inner tie rod end
3. Locking plate
4. Bolt
5. Inner tie rod end plate
6. Inner tie rod end
7. Rack and pinion boot

Installation of the inner tie rod end assembly

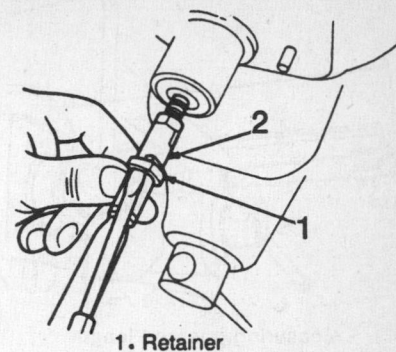

1. Retainer
2. Adjustment sleeve

Removing the retaining ring from the push rod

4. Using a steering linkage puller tool, separate the outer tie rod end from the steering knuckle.

5. Remove the outer tie rod end from the tie adjuster. When unscrewing the tie rod end, record the number of revolutions to remove it, this will aid in installation.

6. Pry of the center bolt lock plate and discard.

7. Remove the inner tie rod end retaining bolt and slide the tie rod end from behind the bolt support. Loosen the pinch bolt at the outer tie rod end and remove the inner tie rod end.

NOTE: **If both tie rod ends are to be removed the rack and pinion must be kept in position. This can be accomplished by installing a retaining bolt in the tie rod end bolt hole of the rack after removing the first the tie rod end.**

To install:

8. Install the inner tie rod end to the outer tie rod end.

9. Torque the pinch bolt to 41 ft. lbs. (56 Nm). Slip the inside end of the tie rod end behind the bolt support and install the lock plate and bolt.

10. Torque the mounting bolt to 65 ft. lbs. (88 Nm). Lower the vehicle.

BRAKES

For all brake system repair and service procedures not detailed below, please refer to "Brakes" in the Unit Repair section.

Master Cylinder

REMOVAL & INSTALLATION

1. Disconnect the negative battery cable.

2. Disconnect the electrical connector from the reservoir cap.

3. Disconnect and plug the brake lines from the master cylinder.

4. Remove the master cylinder to power brake booster nuts.

5. Remove the master cylinder from the vehicle.

6. To install, use new self locking nuts. Torque the master cylinder brake booster nuts to 13 ft. lbs. (18 Nm). Refill the master cylinder reservoir with clean brake fluid. Bleed the brake system.

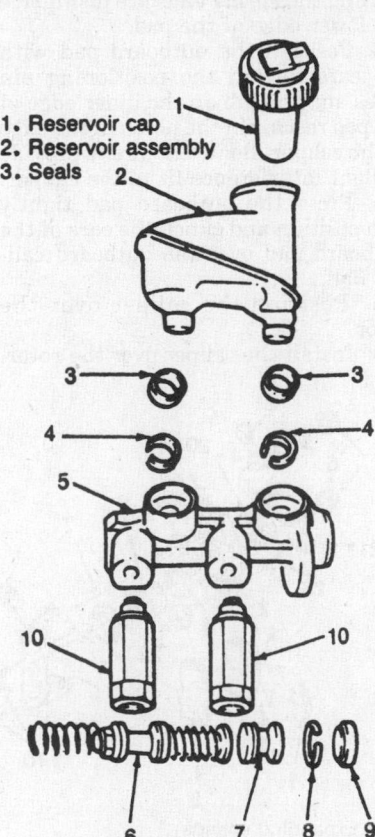

1. Reservoir cap
2. Reservoir assembly
3. Seals
4. Retaining clamps
5. Cylinder body
6. Secondary piston assembly
7. Primary piston
8. Retainer
9. Seal ring
10. Proportioning valves

Exploded view of the master cylinder

voir with clean brake fluid. Bleed the brake system.

7. Connect the negative battery cable and test the brake operation.

Proportioning Valve

Since the valves are adjusted in pairs, they must be replaced in pairs.

REMOVAL & INSTALLATION

1. Disconnect the negative battery cable.

2. Disconnect and plug the brake lines from the proportioning valves.

3. Remove the proportioning valves from the master cylinder.

NOTE: **Be sure the valves are stamped with identical part numbers.**

4. To install, Torque the proportioning valve-to-master cylinder bolts to 30 ft. lbs. (41 Nm). Refill the master cylinder reservoir with clean brake fluid. Bleed the brake system.

Power Brake Booster

REMOVAL & INSTALLATION

1. Disconnect the negative battery cable.

2. Remove the master cylinder from the booster; do not disconnect the brake lines.

3. Remove the vacuum hose from the intake manifold.

4. Remove the windshield washer reservoir.

5. From under the dash, remove the brake light switch and the brake spring.

6. Remove the pushrod to pedal pin retainer and the pin.

7. If not equipped with power steering, remove the brake pedal bracket-to-dash nuts. If equipped with power steering, remove the lower mounting

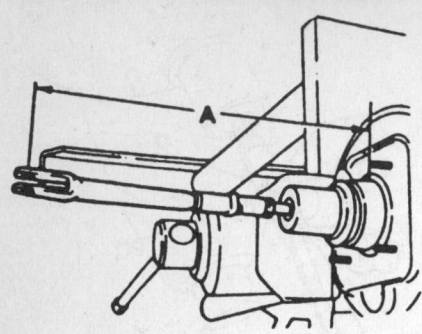

Measuring pushrod length

screw from behind the fluid lines using a flat head socket wrench.

8. To remove the power brake booster and bracket, tilt the brake servo slightly and remove it upwards.

9. From the power brake booster, remove the two-part support bracket and the rubber boot.

10. Remove the pushrod retainer and pushrod, then, unscrew and remove the adjuster sleeve from the piston rod.

11. Unscrew the hex nut.

To install:

12. Install the adjuster sleeve to the pushrod and measure the distance from the booster flange to the end of the adjustment sleeve. It should be10.96 in. (278.5 Nm). Adjust as required.

13. Position the booster and mounting bracket to the firewall and install mounting bolts. Tighten the mounting bolts to 16 ft. lbs. (22 Nm).

14. Install the master cylinder to the booster and the mounting nuts. Torque the master cylinder-to-power booster nuts to 13 ft. lbs. (18 Nm).

13. Connect the negative battery cable. Start the engine and check the brake operation.

Brake Caliper

REMOVAL & INSTALLATION

1. Disconnect the negative battery cable.

2. Remove half of the brake fluid from the master cylinder.

3. Raise and support the vehicle safely and remove the wheel assembly.

NOTE: Remove the brake hose retaining bolt, only if the caliper is going to be overhauled or replaced.

4. Position a large C-clamp over the caliper with the screw end against the outboard brake pad. Tighten the clamp until the caliper piston is pushed out enough to bottom the piston.

5. Remove the C-clamp. Remove the caliper guide pins and lift the caliper off of the rotor.

6. Support the caliper so there is no strain on the brake hose.

7. Press the inboard pad outward and remove it from the caliper.

8. Remove and discard the O-ring bushings and steel sleeves, new parts are to be installed.

9. Check the condition of the rotor. If rotor measurements exceed manufacture's specifications or has mild scoring, machine the rotor.

To install:

10. Lubricate and install the O-ring bushings. Install the sleeves by pressing them through the O-rings until the sleeve end on the pad side is flush with caliper ear.

11. Position the inboard pads so the pad contacts the piston and the support spring ends. The inboard and outboard pads are similar but not interchangeable.

12. Press down on the ears at the top of the inboard pad until the pad lies flat and the spring ends are just inside the lower edge of the pad.

13. Position the outboard pad with the ears toward the positioning pin holes and the tab on the inner edge of the pad resting in the notch in the edge of the caliper. Bend the ears to provide a slight interference fit in the caliper.

14. Press the outboard pad tightly into position and clinch the ears of the outboard pad over the outboard caliper half.

15. Position the caliper over the rotor.

16. Install the caliper over the rotor.

17. Install the caliper mounting bolts and tighten to 38 ft. lbs. (51 Nm).

18. If the brake hose retaining nut was disconnected, reconnect it and torque to 33 ft. lbs. (45 Nm).

19. Install the wheel assembly and lower the vehicle.

20. Fill the master cylinder with brake fluid and bleed the system.

21. Connect the negative battery cable.

Disc Brake Pads

REMOVAL & INSTALLATION

1. Raise and safely support the vehicle. Remove the wheel assembly; reinstall 2 lug nuts to retain the rotor to the axle hub.

2. Using a siphon, remove ⅔ of the brake fluid from the master cylinder.

3. Using a pair of large adjustable pliers, position the jaws over the inboard pad tab and the inboard caliper housing. Squeeze the pliers to bottom the piston in the caliper housing.

4. Remove the caliper-to-caliper bracket boots (bolt coverings), the bolts and sleeve assemblies.

5. Remove the caliper from the rotor. Using a wire, suspend the caliper from the strut.

6. Remove the outboard pad, the inboard pad and the bushing from the mounting bolt hole groves.

To install:

7. Using silicone grease, lubricate the new mounting bolt bushings and install them in the holes.

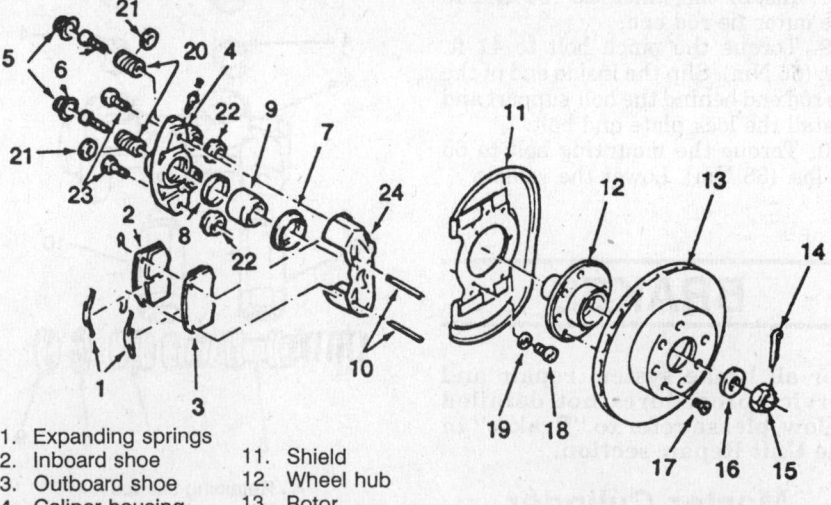

1. Expanding springs	11. Shield
2. Inboard shoe	12. Wheel hub
3. Outboard shoe	13. Rotor
4. Caliper housing	14. Cotter pin
5. Bleeder valve cap	15. Wheel hub nut
6. Bleeder valve	16. Wheel hub washer
7. Piston boot	17. Detent screw
8. Piston seal	18. Shield screw
9. Piston caliper	19. Shield washer
10. Retaining pins	

20. Bleeder valve plug	
21. Bleeder valve washer	
22. Caliper housing spacer	
23. Caliper housing bolt	
24. Retaining frame	

Exploded view of the front disc brake and related components

8. Install the retainer spring onto the inboard pad and the pad into the caliper by snapring the retaining spring into the piston; the inboard pad must lay flat against the piston.

NOTE: On some models, the retaining spring is already staked to the inboard pad.

9. Install the outboard pad with the wear sensor at the leading edge of the forward wheel rotating; the pad must lay flat against the caliper.

10. Position the caliper assembly over the rotor in the mounting bracket. Torque the caliper-to bracket bolts to 38 ft. lbs. (51 Nm).

11. Using a small prybar, position it between the outboard pad and the rotor hub to hold the pad in position. Have an assistant, apply approximately 50 lbs pressure on the brake pedal.

12. While the assistant is applying pressure, position a ball peen hammer on the outboard pad tab and tap it with another hammer to drive the tab downward to a 45 degree angle to lock the pad into position.

13. Remove the 2 rotor-to-wheel hub nuts and install the wheel.

14. Lower the vehicle. Refill the master cylinder reservoir and road test the vehicle.

Brake Rotor

REMOVAL & INSTALLATION

1. Raise and safely support the vehicle. Remove wheel assembly.

2. Remove caliper retaining bolts and remove the caliper. Using a wire suspend the caliper from the strut.

3. Remove the rotor by sliding it off of the hub assembly.

To install:

4. Slide the caliper on the hub assembly and install 2 lug nuts to hold it in place.

5. Install the brake pads into the caliper and place the caliper assembly over the rotor.

6. Install the caliper mounting bolts and torque to 38 ft. lbs. (51 Nm).

7. Remove the lug nuts from the caliper and install the wheel assembly.

8. Lower the vehicle.

9. Fill the master cylinder with brake fluid.

8. Depress the brake pedal 3–4 times to seat the brake linings and to restore pressure in the system.

Brake Drums

REMOVAL & INSTALLATION

1. Raise and safely support the rear of the vehicle.

2. Remove the wheel assembly.

3. Remove the brake drum from the axle.

To install:

4. Using a brake adjusting tool, adjust the brake shoe to 0.50 in. (1.27mm) less than the brake drum diameter. Install the brake drum to the axle.

5. Install the wheel assembly and lower the vehicle.

Brake Shoes

REMOVAL & INSTALLATION

1. Raise and safely support the rear of the vehicle. Remove the wheel assembly.

2. If the brake drum is difficult to remove, perform the following procedures:

   a. Make sure the parking brake is released.

   b. Back off the parking brake cable adjustment.

   c. Remove the adjusting hole knockout plate and back off the adjusting screw.

NOTE: On some drum designs, the knockout plate must be drilled out using a $7/16$ in. (11mm) drill bit. A rubber adjusting hole cover is available for installation purposes.

   d. Using a rubber mallet, tap the drum from the spindle.

3. Remove the return springs, the hold-down springs and the lever pivot. While lifting up on the actuator lever, remove the actuator link.

4. Remove the actuator lever, the lever return spring, the parking brake strut and the strut spring.

5. Disconnect the parking brake cable and remove the primary brake shoe.

6. Remove the adjusting screw, the spring, the retaining ring, the pin, the parking brake lever and the secondary shoe.

7. If any parts are of doubtful strength or quality, due to discoloration from heat, stress or wear, replace them.

8. Clean all of the parts in denatured alcohol. Lubricate the necessary parts.

To install:

9. Install the primary brake shoe and connect the parking brake cable.

10. Install the adjusting screw, the spring, the retaining ring, the pin, the parking brake lever and the secondary shoe.

11. Install the actuator lever, the lever return spring, the parking brake strut and the strut spring.

12. Install the return springs, the hold-down springs and the lever pivot. While lifting up on the actuator lever, install the actuator link.

13. Using a brake adjusting tool, adjust the brake shoe to 0.50 in. (1.27mm) less than the brake drum diameter. Install the brake drum.

14. Lower the vehicle. Road Test the vehicle.

Wheel Cylinder

REMOVAL & INSTALLATION

1. Raise and safely support the vehicle.

2. Using a piece of chalk, mark the relative position of the wheels to the wheel hub. Remove the wheel/tire assemblies.

3. Remove the brake drum-to-wheel hub detent screw and the brake drum.

4. Remove the upper return spring and push the brake shoes slightly outward.

NOTE: Note the position of the adjuster assembly and the adjuster actuator-to-actuator spring.

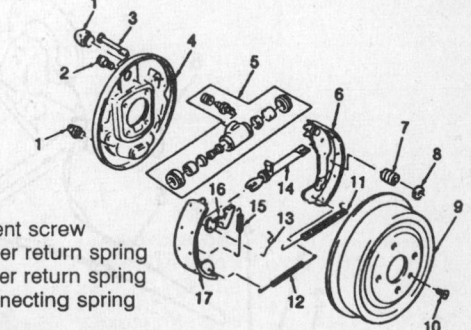

1. Access hole cover
2. Wheel cylinder retainer
3. Hold-down pin
4. Backing plate
5. Wheel cylinder assembly
6. Shoe and lining
7. Hold-down spring
8. Hold-down washer
9. Brake drum
10. Detent screw
11. Upper return spring
12. Lower return spring
13. Connecting spring link
14. Adjuster assembly
15. Adjuster spring
16. Actuator adjuster
17. Shoe adjuster

Exploded view of the rear drum and related components

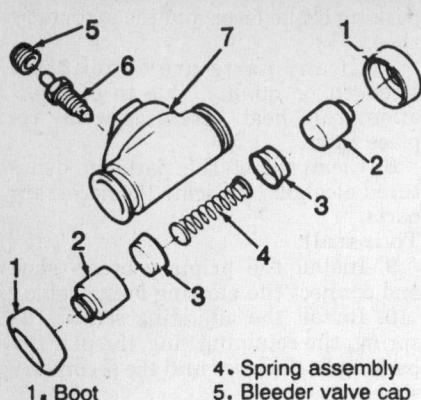

1. Boot
2. Piston
3. Seal
4. Spring assembly
5. Bleeder valve cap
6. Bleeder valve
7. Wheel cylinder

Exploded view of the rear wheel cylinder

5. Remove and plug the brake line from the wheel cylinder.

6. Remove the wheel cylinder-to-backing plate bolt and the wheel cylinder.

7. To install, position the wheel cylinder-to-the backing plate and install the retaining bolts.

8. Torque the wheel cylinder-to-backing plate bolt to 7 ft. lbs. (9.5 Nm).

9. Adjust the rear wheel brakes and the parking brake.

10. Bleed the brake system. Road test the vehicle.

Parking Brake Cable

ADJUSTMENT

1. Raise and safely support the vehicle.

2. Release the parking brake.

3. Inspect the parking brake cable for free movement.

4. At the equalizer, adjust the self-locking nut until the wheels are difficult to turn.

5. Back-off the self-locking nut until the rear wheels are just free to turn.

REMOVAL & INSTALLATION

1. Release parking brake lever.

2. Raise and safely support the vehicle. Remove the rear wheel assembly.

3. Remove the brake drum mounting screw and the brake drum.

4. At the transaxle tunnel, remove the parking brake cable from the guides.

5. Remove the plastic guides from the fuel tank bracket.

6. Remove the parking brake cable from the rear axle assembly guides.

7. Using a pointed tool, remove the retaining ring from the plastic sleeve in the backing plate.

8. Remove the parking brake cable from the parking brake shoe lever and the brake anchor plate.

To install:

9. Install the parking brake cable to the parking brake shoe lever and the brake anchor plate.

10. Install the retaining ring into the plastic sleeve and into the backing plate.

11. Install the parking brake cable from the rear axle assembly guides.

12. Install the plastic guides in the fuel tank bracket.

13. At the transaxle tunnel, secure the parking brake cable to the guides.

14. Install the brake drum mounting screw and the brake drum.

15. Install the wheel assembly and lower the vehicle.

16. Check the operation of the parking brake.

Brake System Bleeding

On diagonally split brake systems, start the manual bleeding procedure with the right rear, then the left front, the left rear and the right front.

1. Clean the bleeder screw at each wheel.

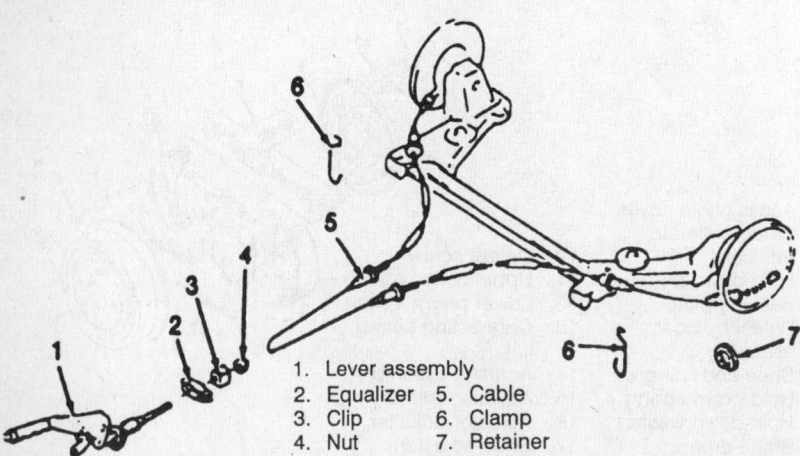

1. Lever assembly
2. Equalizer
3. Clip
4. Nut
5. Cable
6. Clamp
7. Retainer

Exploded view of the parking brake cable system

2. Attach a small rubber hose to the bleeder screw and place the other end in a clear container of fresh brake fluid.

3. Refill the master cylinder with fresh brake fluid. The master cylinder reservoir should be checked and topped off often during the bleeding procedure.

4. Have an assistant slowly pump the brake pedal and hold the pressure.

5. Open the bleeder screw about ¼ turn. The pedal should fall to the floor as air and fluid are pushed out. Close the bleeder screw while the assistant holds the pedal to the floor, then, slowly release the pedal and wait 15 seconds. Repeat the process until no more air bubbles are forced from the system when the brake pedal is applied. It may be necessary to repeat this numerous times to get all of the air from the system.

6. Repeat this procedure on the remaining wheel cylinders and calipers.

NOTE: Remember to wait 15 seconds between each bleeding and do not pump the pedal rapidly. Rapid pumping of the brake pedal pushes the master cylinder secondary piston down the bore in a manner that makes it difficult to bleed the system.

7. Check the brake pedal for sponginess and the brake warning light for an indication of unbalanced pressure. Repeat the entire bleeding procedure to correct either of these conditions.

FRONT SUSPENSION

MacPherson Strut

REMOVAL & INSTALLATION

1. Loosen the upper strut-to-body nuts and the wheel lug nuts. Remove the halfshaft-to-hub cotter pin, nut and washer.

2. Raise and safely support the vehicle; allow the wheels to hang free. Remove the wheel assembly. Using drive axle boot seal protector tools, place them on the outer CV-joints.

3. Remove the caliper-to-steering knuckle bolts. Remove the caliper and position it aside. Remove the rotor-to-wheel hub screw and the rotor.

4. Remove the outer tie rod end-to-steering knuckle nut. Using tie rod end remover tool, separate the outer tie rod end-to-steering knuckle arm.

5. Remove the lower ball joint-to-steering knuckle retaining clip and nut. To remove the clip, lift up on the rear of the clip, while pulling outward on the loops.

6. Using ball joint separator tool, separate the lower ball joint from the steering knuckle arm.

7. Using front wheel hub remover tool, separate the halfshaft from the steering knuckle hub. Properly support the halfshaft.

8. Remove the upper strut-to-body nuts and washers. Remove the strut assembly from the vehicle.

To install:

9. Install the strut assembly to the strut tower and install the upper strut-to-body nuts and washers.

10. Install the halfshaft to the steering knuckle hub.

11. Connect the lower ball joint to the steering knuckle arm and install the retaining nut.

12. Connect the outer tie rod end to the steering knuckle and install the retaining nut.

13. Install the rotor and hub nut. Install brake caliper and the caliper-to-steering knuckle bolts.

14. Remove the drive axle boot seal protector tools from the outer CV-joints.

15. Torque the following:
Steering knuckle/strut assembly nuts – 22 ft lbs. (27 Nm)
Lower ball nut – 50 ft. lbs. (68 Nm)
tie rod end nut – 45 ft. lbs. (61 Nm)
Disc rotor retaining bolts – 3 ft. lbs. (4 Nm)
Caliper retaining bolts – 7 ft. lbs. (9.5 Nm)
Halfshaft-to-hub nut – 74 ft. lbs. (100 Nm), back off the nut, retighten to 15 ft. lbs. (20 Nm), tighten another 90 degrees. Install the cotter pin.

16. Install the wheel assembly and lower the vehicle. Torque the wheel lug nuts 65 ft. lbs. (88 Nm). Check the front end alignment and adjust, as required.

Lower Ball Joints

INSPECTION

1. Raise and safely support the vehicle.

2. With the ball joint installed to the steering knuckle, Grasp the top and bottom of the wheel, then, move the wheel using an in and out shaking motion.

3. Observe any movement between the steering knuckle and the control arm. If movement exists, replace the ball joint.

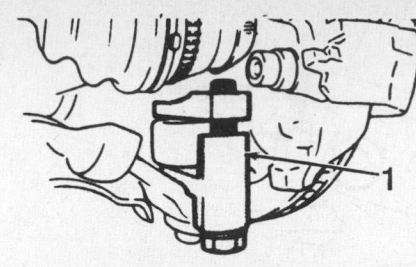

1. Ball joint separator tool No. J-36226
Separating the ball joint from the steering knuckle

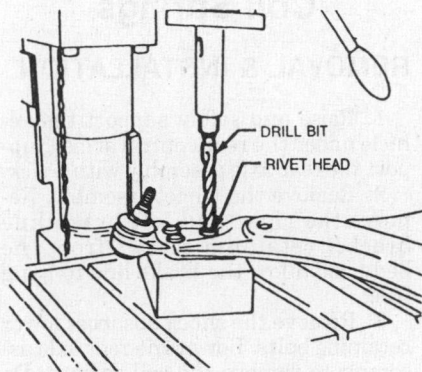

DRILL BIT
RIVET HEAD

Removing the lower ball joint

REMOVAL & INSTALLATION

1. Raise and safely support the vehicle. Lower the vehicle slightly so the weight does not rest on the control arm. Remove the wheel assembly.

2. If a silicone (gray) boot is used on the inboard axle joint, install a boot seal protector tool. If a thermoplastic (black) boot is used, no protector is necessary.

3. Remove the retaining clip from the ball joint castle nut.

4. Remove the castle nut. Using ball joint separator tool, disconnect the ball joint from the steering knuckle arm.

5. Using a drill, drill out the ball joint-to-control arm rivets. Be careful not to damage the halfshaft boot when drilling out the ball joint rivets.

6. Loosen the stabilizer shaft bushing assembly nut. Remove the ball joint from the control arm.

To install:

7. Position the new ball joint to the lower control arm. Install new retaining bolts and nuts.

8. Torque the lower ball joint retaining nuts to 51 ft lbs. (68 Nm). Install and torque the stabilizer bolts to 13 ft. lbs. (18 Nm).

9. Install and torque the ball joint-to-steering knuckle nut to 50 ft. lbs. (68 Nm).

Lower Control Arms

REMOVAL & INSTALLATION

1. Raise and safely support the vehicle. Lower the vehicle slightly so the weight does not rest on the control arm. Remove the wheel assembly.

2. Disconnect the stabilizer shaft from the control arm and the support assembly.

3. Remove the ball joint-to-steering knuckle cotter pin and nut. Using ball joint separator tool, separate the ball joint from the steering knuckle.

4. Remove the control arm-to-support arm bolts. Remove the control arm from the vehicle.

To install:

5. Install the control arm and mounting bolts, torque the front control arm-to-support arm bolt to 100 ft. lbs. (140 Nm) and the rear control arm-to-support arm bolt to 50 ft. lbs. (70 Nm).

6. Connect the ball joint to the steering knuckle and install the retaining nut. Torque the nut to 51 ft. lbs. (70 Nm).

7. Connect the stabilizer shaft to the control arm and the support assembly. Install the retaining nuts and torque to 13 ft. lbs. (17 Nm).

8. Install the wheel assembly and lower the vehicle.

Sway Bar

REMOVAL & INSTALLATION

1. Loosen the left front wheel lug nuts. Raise and safely support the vehicle; allow the suspension to hang free. Remove the wheel assembly.

2. Remove the stabilizer shaft link assemblies from the control arms.

3. Remove the stabilizer shaft bushings and brackets from the body.

4. Remove the stabilizer shaft and bushings.

To install:

5. Install the stabilizer bar bush-

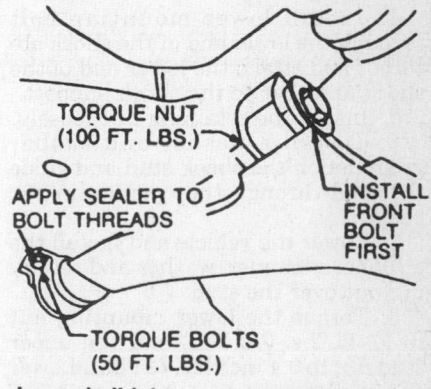

TORQUE NUT (100 FT. LBS.)
APPLY SEALER TO BOLT THREADS
INSTALL FRONT BOLT FIRST
TORQUE BOLTS (50 FT. LBS.)
Lower ball joint mounting bolt location

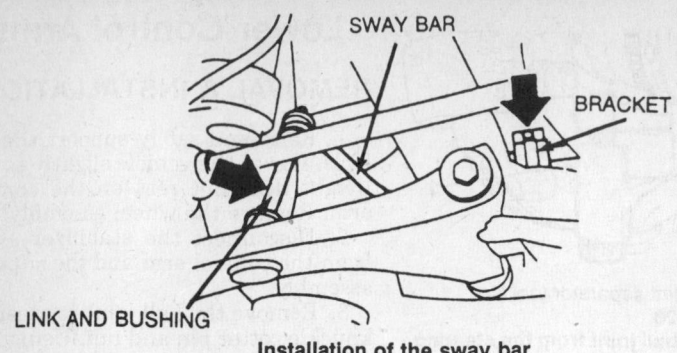

Installation of the sway bar

ings in place on the bar, position the stabilizer to the frame and install the mounting brackets a bolts. Do not tighten.

6. Install the stabilizer end links, bushings and retaining bolts. Center the stabizer bar in the proper installation position and tighten the link retaining nuts.

7. Torque the stabilizer bar bracket retaining bolts to 29 ft. lbs. (40 Nm).

8. Install the wheel assemblies and lower the vehicle.

REAR SUSPENSION

Shock Absorbers

REMOVAL & INSTALLATION

1. Open the trunk. If equipped, remove the trim cover. Remove the upper shock absorber-to-body nut.

2. Raise and safely support the vehicle and the rear axle assembly before unbolting the shock absorbers.

3. Remove the shock absorber-to-rear axle assembly bolt. Remove the shock absorber from the vehicle.

To install:

4. Install lower mounting bolt through the lower end of the shock absorber and attach the lower end of the shock absorber to the shock support.

5. Install the retaining nut loosely.

6. Install a washer and rubber grommet on the shock stud and guide the stud through the opening in the body.

7. Lower the vehicle and install the a rubber grommet, washer and retaining nut over the stud.

8. Torque the lower mounting nut to 51 ft. lbs. (70 Nm) and the upper stud nut to 0.4 inch lbs. (9 Nm). Lower the vehicle.

Coil Springs

REMOVAL & INSTALLATION

1. Raise and safely support the vehicle under the rear control arms. Support the rear axle assembly with a jack.

2. Remove the wheel assembly. Remove the right and left brake line bracket retaining screws from the body and allow the brake line to hang free.

3. Remove the shock absorber lower retaining bolts. Lower the rear axle assembly to remove the coil springs. Do not allow the axle assembly to hang in this position.

To install:

4. Installation is the reverse of the removal procedures. Before installing the coil springs, it is necessary to install the insulators to the body using adhesive.

5. Position the spring and insulator in the spring seat and raise the axle. The upper ends of the coil must be positioned properly in the seat of the body.

6. Torque the shock aborber lower retaining bolts to 51 ft. lbs. (70 Nm).

7. Install the wheel assemblies and lower the vehicle.

Rear Wheel Bearings

REMOVAL & INSTALLATION

1. Raise and safely support the vehicle.

2. Remove the wheel assembly.

3. Remove the brake drum detent screw and the drum.

NOTE: To remove the brake drum, it may be necessary to loosen the parking brake cable and press the parking brake lever inwards, with a pry bar. Do not hammer on the brake drum for damage to the bearing may result.

4. Remove the hub/bearing assembly to axle spindle grease cap, cotter pin, hub nut, thrust washer and the

outer bearing from the axle spindle.

5. Using a small pry bar, remove the grease seal from the inside of the hub. Remove the inner and outer bearing from the hub.

6. If replacing the wheel bearings, perform the following procedures:

a. Using a hammer and a drift punch, drive both outer bearing races (in opposite directions) from the wheel hub.

b. Using cleaning solvent (not gasoline), clean the bearings, races and hub. Using compressed air, blow dry the parts.

c. Inspect the parts for damage and/or wear. If necessary, replace any defective parts.

d. Using an arbor press, the rear hub inner and outer bearing race installer tool and the driver handle tool, press the outer bearing, outer race into the wheel hub until it seats.

NOTE: Before installing the wheel bearings, be sure to force wheel bearing grease into the bearing.

e. Using an arbor press, the rear hub inner and outer bearing race installer tool and the driver handle tool, press the inner bearing, outer race into the wheel hub until it seats and install the inner bearing.

f. Lubricate the lips of the new grease seal. Using the rear hub seal installation, press the new seal into the hub.

g. Install the wheel bearing hub onto the axle spindle, followed by the outer, inner bearing, thrust washer and hub nut.

h. Adjust the wheel bearing play. Adjust the parking brake.

7. Install the wheel assemblies. Torque the wheel lug nuts to 66 ft. lbs. (89 Nm).

ADJUSTMENT

1. Raise and support the vehicle.

2. Remove the grease cap from the rear wheel hub.

3. Remove the cotter pin from the spindle and the spindle nut.

4. While turning the wheel, by hand, in the forward direction, tighten the spindle nut to 12 ft. lbs. (16 Nm).

NOTE: The tightening procedure will remove any grease or burrs which could cause excessive wheel bearing play.

5. Back off the nut to the just loose position.

6. Hand tighten the spindle nut and loosen it until a spindle hole aligns with a slot in the nut.

1 COVER·TRIM
2 NUT·SHOCK UPPER
3 WASHER·SHOCK UPPER
4 BUMPER·SHOCK UPPER
5 GROMMET·SHOCK UPPER
6 WASHER·SHOCK UPPER
7 ABSORBER·SHOCK
8 BOLT·HEX
9 NUT·HEX
10 RING·SEAL
11 BEARING·WHEEL HUB INNER
12 HUB·WHEEL

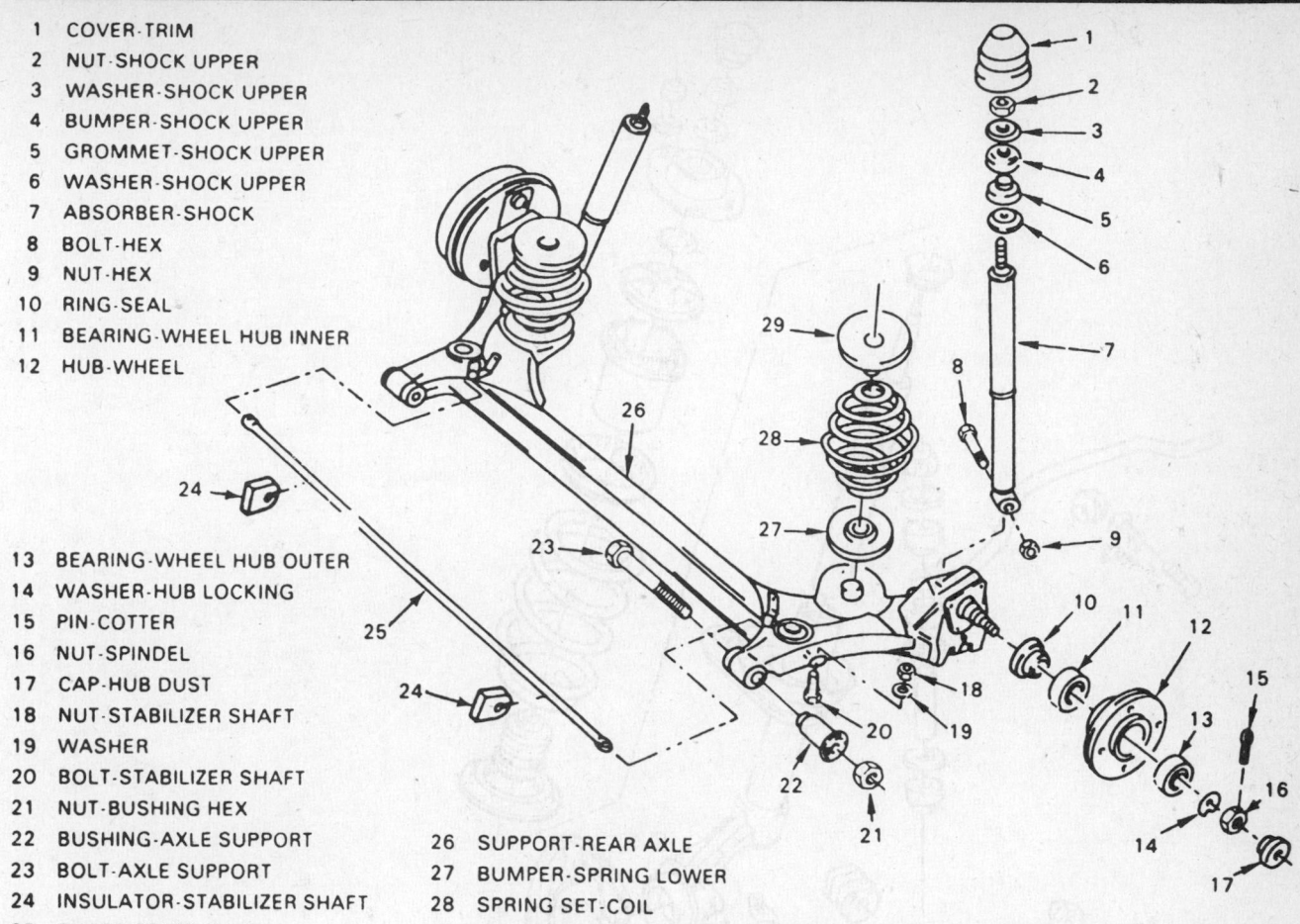

13 BEARING·WHEEL HUB OUTER
14 WASHER·HUB LOCKING
15 PIN·COTTER
16 NUT·SPINDEL
17 CAP·HUB DUST
18 NUT·STABILIZER SHAFT
19 WASHER
20 BOLT·STABILIZER SHAFT
21 NUT·BUSHING HEX
22 BUSHING·AXLE SUPPORT
23 BOLT·AXLE SUPPORT
24 INSULATOR·STABILIZER SHAFT
25 SHAFT·STABILIZER

26 SUPPORT·REAR AXLE
27 BUMPER·SPRING LOWER
28 SPRING SET·COIL
29 RING·SPRING UPPER INSULATOR

Exploded view of the rear axle assembly

7. Install a new cotter pin and bend the ends around the nut.

8. Using a feeler gauge, measure the endplay. If it is within 0.001–0.005 in., it is properly adjusted. Install the dust cap.

9. Install the wheel assembly and lower the vehicle. Torque the wheel lug nuts to 66 ft. lbs. (89 Nm).

Rear Axle Assembly

REMOVAL & INSTALLATION

1. Raise and safely support the vehicle under the rear control arms. Support the rear axle assembly with and jack.

2. Remove the wheel assembly. Remove the right and left brake line bracket retaining screws from the body and allow the brake line to hang free.

3. Remove the stabilizer bar brackets. Remove the insulator and the stabilizer bar assembly.

4. Remove the shock absorber lower retaining bolts. Lower the rear axle assembly to remove the coil springs. Do

not allow the axle assembly to hang in this position.

5. Remove the control arm retaining bolts from the underbody bracket and lower the axle.

6. Remove the hub retaining bolts an remove the hub, bearing and backing plate assembly.

NOTE: Be careful not to drop the hub/bearing assembly, damage to the bearing could result.

To install:

7. Install the backing plate and hub/bearing assembly to the rear axle assembly. Install the retaining bolts and nuts and torque to 21 ft. lbs. (28 Nm).

8. Install the stabilizer bar to the rear axle assembly and install the attaching nuts and bolts. Torque the nuts to 59 ft. lbs. (80 Nm).

9. Secure the axle assembly on a transmission jack and raise it into position.

10. Install the control arms to the underbody bracket and install the mounting nuts and bolts. Do not torque the bolts at this time. The bolts must be torque and curb height.

NOTE: The control arm mounting bolts must be install from the inboard side.

11. Connect the brake line connections and install the brake cable to the rear axle assembly.

12. Position the springs and insulators in the spring seat and raise the axle. The upper ends of the coil must be positioned properly in the seat of the body.

13. Connect the shock absorber at the lower end and install retaining bolt. Torque the retaining bolt to 51 ft. lbs. (69 Nm).

14. Connect the parking brake to the guide hook. Adjust the cable, as required.

15. Bleed the brake system and refill the reservoir. Adjust the brakes, as required.

16. Lower the axle to curb height and torque the axle-to-body mounting bolts. Torque the bolts to 70 ft. lbs. (95 Nm).

17. Install the wheel assemblies and lower the vehicle. Torque the lug nuts to 100 ft. lbs. (140 Nm).

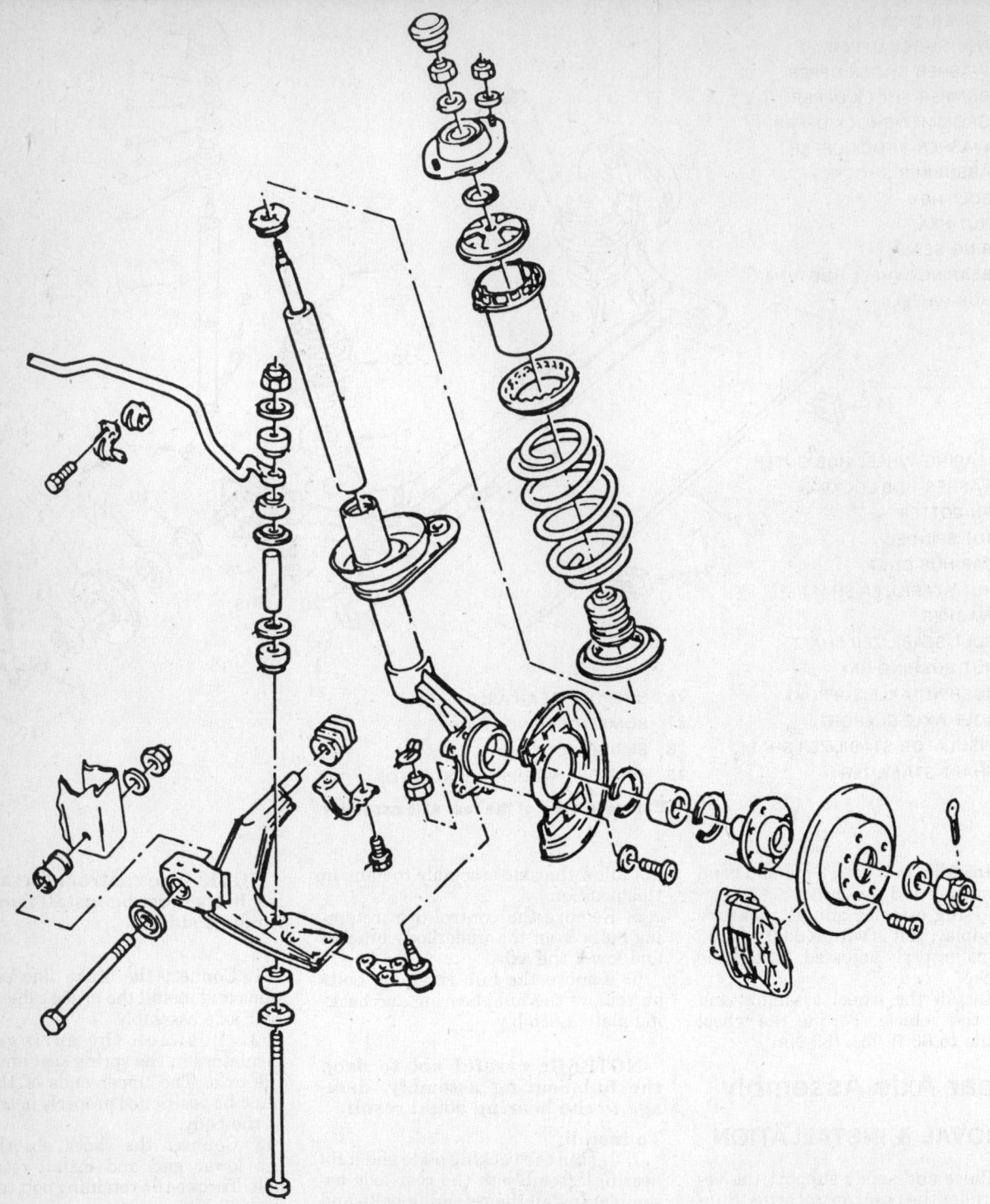

Front suspension components

GM "A" Body
Front Wheel Drive
Buick—Century **Chevrolet**—Celebrity
Oldsmobile—Cutlass Ciera, Cutlass Cruiser
Pontiac—6000

SPECIFICATIONS
VEHICLE IDENTIFICATION CHART

It is important for servicing and ordering parts to be certain of the vehicle and engine identification. The VIN (vehicle identification number) is a 17 digit number visible through the windshield on the driver's side of the dash and contains the vehicle and engine identification codes. The tenth digit indicates model year, and the eighth digit indicates engine code. It can be interpreted as follows:

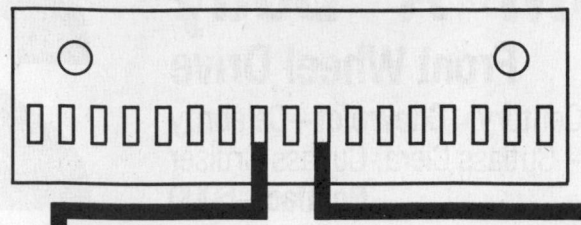

Engine Code						Model Year	
Mode	Cu. In.	Liters	Cyl.	Fuel Sys.	Eng. Mfg.	Code	Year
R	151	2.5	4	TBI	Pontiac	H	1987
W	173	2.8	6	MFI	Chevrolet	J	1988
T	192	3.1	6	MFI	Chevrolet	K	1989
N	204	3.3	6	SFI	Buick	L	1990
3	231	3.8	6	SFI	Buick	M	1991

ENGINE IDENTIFICATION

Year	Model	Engine Displacement Cu. In. (liter)	Engine Series Identification (VIN)	No. of Cylinders	Engine Type
1987	Celebrity	151 (2.5)	R	4	TBI
	Celebrity	173 (2.8)	W	6	MFI
	Century	151 (2.5)	R	4	TBI
	Century	173 (2.8)	W	6	MFI
	Century	231 (3.8)	3	6	SFI
	Cutlass Ciera	151 (2.5)	R	4	TBI
	Cutlass Ciera	173 (2.8)	W	6	MFI
	Cutlass Ciera	231 (3.8) HO	3	6	SFI
	6000	151 (2.5)	R	4	TBI
	6000	173 (2.8)	W	6	MFI
1988	Celebrity	151 (2.5)	R	4	TBI
	Celebrity	173 (2.8)	W	6	MFI
	Century	151 (2.5)	R	4	TBI
	Century	173 (2.8)	W	6	MFI
	Century	231 (3.8)	3	6	SFI
	Cutlass Ciera	151 (2.5)	R	4	TBI
	Cutlass Ciera	173 (2.8)	W	6	MFI
	Cutlass Ciera	231 (3.8)	3	6	SFI
	6000	151 (2.5)	R	4	TBI
	6000	173 (2.8)	W	6	MFI

ENGINE IDENTIFICATION

Year	Model	Engine Displacement Cu. In. (liter)	Engine Series Identification (VIN)	No. of Cylinders	Engine Type
1989	Celebrity	151 (2.5)	R	4	TBI
	Celebrity	173 (2.8)	W	6	MFI
	Century	151 (2.5)	R	4	TBI
	Century	173 (2.8)	W	6	MFI
	Century	204 (3.3)	N	6	MFI
	Cutlass Ciera	151 (2.5)	R	4	TBI
	Cutlass Ciera	173 (2.8)	W	6	MFI
	Cutlass Ciera	204 (3.3)	N	6	MFI
	6000	151 (2.5)	R	4	TBI
	6000	173 (2.8)	W	6	MFI
	6000	192 (3.1)	T	6	MFI
1990-91	Celebrity	151 (2.5)	R	4	TBI
	Celebrity	192 (3.1)	T	6	MFI
	Century	151 (2.5)	R	4	TBI
	Century	204 (3.3)	N	6	SFI
	Cutlass ①	151 (2.5)	R	4	TBI
	Cutlass ①	204 (3.3)	N	6	SFI
	6000	151 (2.5)	R	4	TBI
	6000	192 (3.1)	T	6	MFI

① Ciera & Cruiser
TBI Throttle Body Injection
MFI Multiport Fuel Injection
SFI Sequential Fuel Injection
HO High output

GENERAL ENGINE SPECIFICATIONS

Year	VIN	No. Cylinder Displacement cu. in. (liter)	Fuel System Type	Net Horsepower @ rpm	Net Torque @ rpm (ft. lbs.)	Bore × Stroke (in.)	Compression Ratio	Oil Pressure @ rpm
1987	R	4-151 (2.5)	TBI	92 @ 4000	134 @ 2800	4.000 × 3.000	8.3:1	37.5 @ 2000
	W	6-173 (2.8)	MFI	130 @ 4800	155 @ 3600	3.503 × 2.992	8.9:1	50-65 @ 1200
	3	6-231 (3.8)	SFI	150 @ 4400	200 @ 2000	3.800 × 3.400	8.0:1	37 @ 2400
1988	R	4-151 (2.5)	TBI	92 @ 4000	134 @ 2800	4.000 × 3.000	8.3:1	37.5 @ 2000
	W	6-173 (2.8)	MFI	130 @ 4800	155 @ 3600	3.503 × 2.992	8.9:1	50-65 @ 1200
	3	6-231 (3.8)	SFI	150 @ 4400	200 @ 2000	3.800 × 3.400	8.0:1	37 @ 2400
1989	R	4-151 (2.5)	TBI	92 @ 4000	134 @ 2800	4.000 × 3.000	8.3:1	37.5 @ 2000
	W	6-173 (2.8)	MFI	130 @ 4800	155 @ 3600	3.503 × 2.992	8.9:1	50-65 @ 1200
	T	6-192 (3.1)	MPFI	120 @ 4200	175 @ 2200	3.503 × 3.312	8.8:1	50-65 @ 2400
	N	6-204 (3.3)	SFI	160 @ 5200	185 @ 2000	3.700 × 3.160	9.0:1	45 @ 2000
1990-91	R	4-151 (2.5)	TBI	92 @ 4400	134 @ 2800	4.000 × 3.000	8.3:1	37.5 @ 2000
	T	6-192 (3.1)	MFI	120 @ 4200	175 @ 2200	3.503 × 3.312	8.8:1	50-65 @ 2400
	N	6-204 (3.3)	SFI	160 @ 5200	185 @ 2000	3.700 × 3.160	9.0:1	45 @ 2000

TBI Throttle Body Injection
MFI Multi-port Fuel Injection
SFI Sequential Multi-port Fuel Injection

GASOLINE ENGINE TUNE-UP SPECIFICATIONS

Year	VIN	No. Cylinder Displacement cu. in. (liter)	Spark Plugs Type	Gap (in.)	Ignition Timing (deg.) MT	AT	Compression Pressure (psi)	Fuel Pump (psi)	Idle Speed (rpm) MT	AT	Valve Clearance In.	Ex.
1987	R	4-151 (2.5)	R-43TSX	0.060	①	①	NA	6.0–7.0	①	①	Hyd.	Hyd.
	W	6-173 (2.8)	R-42CTS	0.045	①	①	NA	40.0–46.0	①	①	Hyd.	Hyd.
	3	6-231 (3.8)	R-44TS8	0.080	①	①	NA	34.0–40.0	①	①	Hyd.	Hyd.
1988	R	4-151 (2.5)	R-43TS6	0.060	①	①	NA	6.0–7.0	①	①	Hyd.	Hyd.
	W	6-173 (2.8)	R-43LTSE	0.045	①	①	NA	40.0–46.0	①	①	Hyd.	Hyd.
	3	6-231 (3.8)	R-44LTS	0.080	①	①	NA	34.0–40.0	①	①	Hyd.	Hyd.
1989	R	4-151 (2.5)	R-43TS6	0.060	①	①	NA	6.0–7.0	①	①	Hyd.	Hyd.
	W	6-173 (2.8)	R-43LTSE	0.045	①	①	NA	40.0–46.0	①	①	Hyd.	Hyd.
	T	6-192 (3.1)	R-43LTSE	0.045	①	①	NA	34.0–47.0	①	①	Hyd.	Hyd.
	N	6-204 (3.3)	R-44LTS6	0.060	①	①	NA	37.0–43.0	①	①	Hyd.	Hyd.
1990	R	4-151 (2.5)	R-43TS6	0.060	①	①	NA	6.0–7.0	①	①	Hyd.	Hyd.
	T	6-192 (3.1)	R-43LTSE	0.045	①	①	NA	34.0–47.0	①	①	Hyd.	Hyd.
	N	6-204 (3.3)	R-44LTS6	0.060	①	①	NA	37.0–43.0	①	①	Hyd.	Hyd.
1991				SEE UNDERHOOD SPECIFICATIONS STICKER								

① Refer to underhood specifications sticker

FIRING ORDERS

NOTE: To avoid confusion, always replace spark plug wires one at a time.

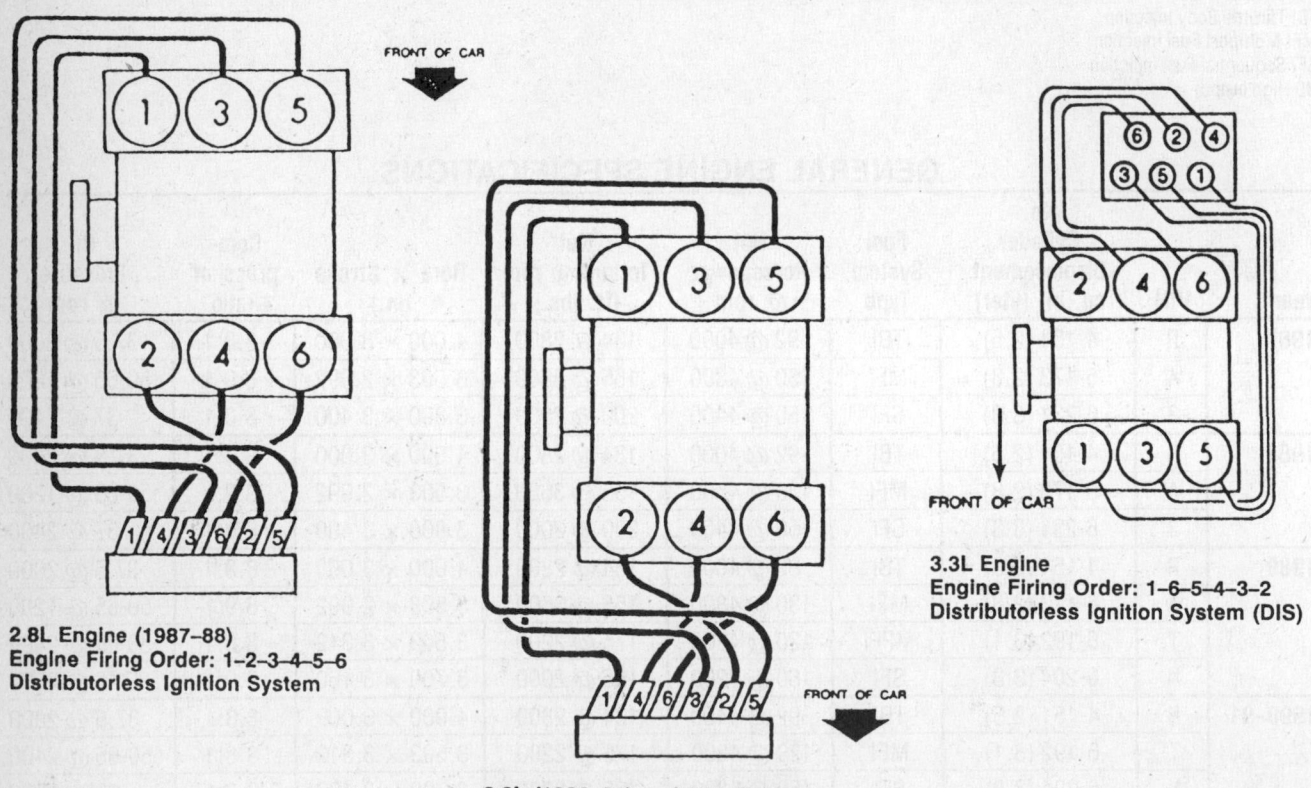

2.8L Engine (1987–88)
Engine Firing Order: 1–2–3–4–5–6
Distributorless Ignition System

2.8L (1989–91) and 3.1L Engines
Engine Firing Order: 1–2–3–4–5–6
Distributorless Ignition System

3.3L Engine
Engine Firing Order: 1–6–5–4–3–2
Distributorless Ignition System (DIS)

FRONT OF CAR

CAPACITIES

Year	Model	VIN	No. Engine Cylinder cu. in. (liter)	Engine Crankcase without filter	with filter	Transmission (pts.) 4	5	Auto.	Drive Axle (pts.)	Fuel Tank (gals.)	Cool Sys. (qts.)
1987	Celebrity	R	151 (2.5)	3.0	3.5	6	—	①	—	15.7	9.6
	Celebrity	W	173 (2.8)	4.0	4.5	6	—	①	—	15.7	12.6
	Century	R	151 (2.5)	3.0	3.5	—	—	①	—	15.5	9.7 ②
	Century	W	173 (2.8)	4.0	4.0	—	—	①	—	15.5	12.5
	Century	3	231 (3.8)	4.0	4.5	—	—	①	—	15.5	12.6
	Cutlass Ciera	R	151 (2.5)	3.0	3.5	6	6	①	—	15.7	12.0
	Cutlass Ciera	W	173 (2.8)	4.0	4.5	6	6	①	—	15.7	13.5
	Cutlass Ciera	3	231 (3.8)	4.0	4.5	6	6	①	—	15.7	12.7
	6000	R	151 (2.5)	3.0	3.5	—	4	①	—	15.7	9.7 ②
	6000	W	173 (2.8)	4.0	4.5	—	4	①	—	16.4	12.9
1988	Celebrity	R	151 (2.5)	3.0	3.5	—	4	①	—	15.7	9.7 ②
	Celebrity	W	173 (2.8)	4.0	4.0	—	4	①	—	15.7	13.5
	Century	R	151 (2.5)	3.0	3.5	—	—	①	—	15.7	9.7 ②
	Century	W	173 (2.8)	4.0	4.5	—	—	①	—	15.7	13.5
	Century	3	231 (3.8)	4.0	4.5	—	—	①	—	15.7	12.7
	Cutlass Ciera	R	151 (2.5)	3.0	3.5	6	6	①	—	15.7	12.0
	Cutlass Ciera	W	173 (2.8)	4.0	4.5	6	6	①	—	15.7	13.5
	Cutlass Ciera	3	231 (3.8)	4.0	4.5	6	6	①	—	15.7	12.7
	6000	R	151 (2.5)	4.0	4.5	—	—	①	—	15.7	9.7 ②
	6000	W	173 (2.8)	4.0	4.5	—	—	①	—	15.7	13.5
1989	Celebrity	R	151 (2.5)	4.0	4.5	—	—	①	—	15.7	9.7
	Celebrity	W	173 (2.8)	4.0	4.5	—	—	①	—	15.7	13.2
	Century	R	151 (2.5)	4.0	4.5	—	—	①	—	15.7	9.7
	Century	W	173 (2.8)	4.0	4.5	—	—	①	—	15.7	13.2
	Century	N	204 (3.3)	4.0	4.5	—	—	①	—	15.7	15.7
	Cutlass Ciera	R	151 (2.5)	4.0	4.5	—	—	①	—	15.7	9.7
	Cutlass Ciera	W	173 (2.8)	4.0	4.5	—	—	①	—	15.7	13.2
	Cutlass Ciera	N	204 (3.3)	4.0	4.5	—	—	①	—	15.7	12.7
	6000	R	151 (2.5)	4.0	4.5	—	—	①	—	15.7	9.7
	6000	W	173 (2.8)	4.0	4.5	—	—	①	—	15.7	13.2
	6000	T	192 (3.1)	4.0	4.5	—	—	①	—	15.7	12.6
1990-91	Celebrity	R	151 (2.5)	4.0	4.5	—	—	①	—	15.7	9.7
	Celebrity	T	192 (3.1)	4.0	4.5	—	—	①	—	15.7	12.8
	Century	R	151 (2.5)	4.0	4.5	—	—	①	—	15.7	9.7
	Century	N	204 (3.3)	4.0	4.5	—	—	①	—	15.7	15.7
	Cutlass	R	151 (2.5)	4.0	4.5	—	—	①	—	15.7	9.7
	Cutlass	N	204 (3.3)	4.0	4.5	—	—	①	—	15.7	13.2
	6000	R	151 (2.5)	4.0	4.5	—	—	①	—	15.7	9.7
	6000	T	192 (3.1)	4.0	4.5	—	—	①	—	15.7	12.6

① 125C—8 pts.
  Overhaul—12 pts.
  440—T4—13 pts.
  Overhaul—20 pts.
② Heavy Duty—12 qts.

CAMSHAFT SPECIFICATIONS

All measurements given in inches.

Year	VIN	No. Cylinder Displacement cu. in. (liter)	Journal Diameter 1	2	3	4	5	Lobe Lift In.	Ex.	Bearing Clearance	Camshaft End Play
1987	R	4-151 (2.5)	1.869	1.869	1.869	—	—	0.232	0.232	0.0007–0.0027	0.0015–0.0050
	W	6-173 (2.8)	1.869	1.869	1.869	1.869	—	0.263	0.273	0.0010–0.0040	—
	3	6-231 (3.8)	1.786	1.786	1.786	1.786	1.786	0.397	0.397	①	—
1988	R	4-151 (2.5)	1.869	1.869	1.869	—	—	0.232	0.232	0.0007–0.0027	0.0015–0.0050
	W	6-173 (2.8)	1.8678–1.8815	1.8678–1.8815	1.8678–1.8815	1.8678–1.8815	—	0.262	0.273	0.0010–0.0040	—
	3	6-231 (3.8)	1.785–1.786	1.785–1.786	1.785–1.786	1.785–1.786	1.785–1.786	0.245	0.245	0.0005–0.0035	—
1989	R	4-151 (2.5)	1.869	1.869	1.869	—	—	0.232	0.232	0.0007–0.0027	0.0015–0.0050
	W	6-173 (2.8)	1.8678–1.8815	1.8678–1.8815	1.8678–1.8815	1.8678–1.8815	—	0.262	0.273	0.0010–0.0040	—
	T	6-192 (3.1)	1.8678–1.8815	1.8678–1.8815	1.8678–1.8815	1.8678–1.8815	—	0.263	0.273	0.0010–0.0040	—
	N	6-204 (3.3)	1.7850–1.7860	1.7850–1.7860	1.7850–1.7860	1.7850–1.7860	—	0.250	0.255	0.0005–0.0035	—
1990–91	R	4-151 (2.5)	1.869	1.869	1.869	—	—	0.232	0.232	0.0007–0.0027	0.0015–0.0050
	T	6-192 (3.1)	1.8678–1.8815	1.8678–1.8815	1.8678–1.8815	1.8678–1.8815	—	0.263	0.273	0.0010–0.0040	—
	N	6-204 (3.3)	1.7850–1.7860	1.7850–1.7860	1.7850–1.7860	1.7850–1.7860	—	0.250	0.255	0.0005–0.0035	—

① No. 1—0.0005–0.0025
No. 2-5—0.0005–0.0035

CRANKSHAFT AND CONNECTING ROD SPECIFICATIONS

All measurements are given in inches.

Year	VIN	No. Cylinder Displacement cu. in. (liter)	Crankshaft Main Brg. Journal Dia.	Main Brg. Oil Clearance	Shaft End-play	Thrust on No.	Connecting Rod Journal Diameter	Oil Clearance	Side Clearance
1987	R	4-151 (2.5)	2.2995–2.3005	0.0005–0.0022	0.003–0.008	5	1.9995–2.0005	0.0005–0.0026	0.006–0.022
	W	6-173 (2.8)	2.6473–2.6483	0.0016–0.0033	0.002–0.008	3	1.9983–1.9993	0.0013–0.0026	0.006–0.017
	3	6-231 (3.8)	2.4995	0.0003–0.0018	0.003–0.011	2	2.2487–2.2495	0.0005–0.0026	0.004–0.015
1988	R	4-151 (2.5)	2.3000	0.0005–0.0022	0.003–0.008	5	1.9995–2.0005	0.0005–0.0026	0.006–0.022
	W	6-173 (2.8)	2.6473–2.6483	0.0016–0.0033	0.002–0.008	3	1.9983–1.9993	0.0013–0.0026	0.006–0.017
	3	6-231 (3.8)	2.4988–2.4998	0.0003–0.0018	0.003–0.011	2	2.2487–2.2495	0.0005–0.0026	0.006–0.023

CRANKSHAFT AND CONNECTING ROD SPECIFICATIONS

All measurements are given in inches.

Year	VIN	No. Cylinder Displacement cu. in. (liter)	Crankshaft				Connecting Rod		
			Main Brg. Journal Dia.	Main Brg. Oil Clearance	Shaft End-play	Thrust on No.	Journal Diameter	Oil Clearance	Side Clearance
1989	R	4-151 (2.5)	2.3000	0.0005–0.0022	0.003–0.008	5	1.9995–2.0005	0.0005–0.0026	0.006–0.022
	W	6-173 (2.8)	2.6473–2.6483	0.0016–0.0033	0.002–0.008	3	1.9983–1.9993	0.0013–0.0026	0.006–0.017
	T	6-192 (3.1)	2.6473–2.6483	0.0012–0.0027	0.002–0.008	3	1.9983–1.9994	0.0013–0.0031	0.014–0.027
	N	6-204 (3.3)	2.4988–2.4998	0.0003–0.0018	0.003–0.011	3	2.2487–2.2499	0.0003–0.0026	0.003–0.015
1990–91	R	4-151 (2.5)	2.3000	0.0005–0.0022	0.003–0.008	5	1.9995–2.0005	0.0005–0.0026	0.006–0.022
	T	6-192 (3.1)	2.6473–2.6483	0.0012–0.0027	0.002–0.008	3	1.9983–1.9994	0.0013–0.0031	0.014–0.027
	N	6-204 (3.3)	2.4988–2.4998	0.0003–0.0018	0.003–0.011	3	2.2487–2.2499	0.0003–0.0026	0.003–0.015

VALVE SPECIFICATIONS

Year	VIN	No. Cylinder Displacement cu. in. (liter)	Seat Angle (deg.)	Face Angle (deg.)	Spring Test Pressure (lbs.)	Spring Installed Height (in.)	Stem-to-Guide Clearance (in.)		Stem Diameter (in.)	
							Intake	Exhaust	Intake	Exhaust
1987	R	4-151 (2.5)	46	45	176 @ 1.254	1.690	0.0010–0.0027	0.0010–0.0032	0.3410–0.3140	0.3410–0.313
	W	6-173 (2.8)	46	45	215 @ 1.291	1.727	0.0015–0.0027	0.0015–0.0027	0.3412–0.3416	0.3412–0.3416
	3	6-231 (3.8)	45	45	195 @ 1.340	1.727	0.0015–0.0032	0.0015–0.0032	0.3405–0.3412	0.3405–0.3412
1988	R	4-151 (2.5)	46	46	176 @ 1.254	1.440	—	—	0.3130–0.3140	0.3120–0.3130
	W	6-173 (2.8)	46	45	215 @ 1.291	1.727	0.0010–0.0027	0.0010–0.0027	0.3412–0.3416	0.3412–0.3416
	3	6-231 (3.8)	45	45	195 @ 1.340	1.727	0.0015–0.0035	0.0015–0.0032	0.3405–0.3412	0.3405–0.3412
1989	R	4-151 (2.5)	46	46	176 @ 1.254	1.440	—	—	0.3130–0.3140	0.3120–0.3130
	W	6-173 (2.8)	46	45	215 @ 1.291	1.727	0.0010–0.0027	0.0010–0.0027	0.3412–0.3416	0.3412–0.3416
	T	6-192 (3.1)	46	45	215 @ 1.291	1.575	0.0010–0.0027	0.0010–0.0027	—	—
	N	6-204 (3.3)	46	45	215 @ 1.291	1.701	0.0010–0.0027	0.0010–0.0027	—	—
1990–91	R	4-151 (2.5)	46	46	176 @ 1.254	1.440	—	—	0.3130–0.3140	0.3120–0.3416
	T	6-192 (3.1)	46	45	215 @ 1.291	1.575	0.0010–0.0027	0.0010–0.0027	—	—
	N	6-204 (3.3)	46	45	215 @ 1.291	1.701	0.0010–0.0027	0.0010–0.0027	—	—

PISTON AND RING SPECIFICATIONS

All measurements are given in inches.

Year	VIN	No. Cylinder Displacement cu. in. (liter)	Piston Clearance	Ring Gap Top Compression	Ring Gap Bottom Compression	Ring Gap Oil Control	Ring Side Clearance Top Compression	Ring Side Clearance Bottom Compression	Ring Side Clearance Oil Control
1987	R	4-151 (2.5)	0.0014–0.0022 ①	0.010–0.020	0.010–0.020	0.020–0.060	0.002–0.003	0.001–0.003	0.015–0.055
	W	6-173 (2.8)	0.0020–0.0028	0.010–0.020	0.010–0.020	0.020–0.055	0.001–0.003	0.001–0.003	0.005–0.008
	3	6-231 (3.8)	0.0010–0.0020	0.013–0.023	0.013–0.023	0.015–0.035	0.003–0.005	0.003–0.005	0.003
1988	R	4-151 (2.5)	0.0014–0.0022 ①	0.010–0.020	0.010–0.020	0.020–0.060	0.002–0.003	0.001–0.003	0.015–0.055
	W	6-173 (2.8)	0.0020–0.0028	0.010–0.020	0.010–0.020	0.020–0.055	0.001–0.003	0.001–0.003	0.005–0.008
	3	6-231 (3.8)	0.0010–0.0020	0.013–0.023	0.013–0.023	0.015–0.035	0.003–0.005	0.003–0.005	0.003
1989	R	4-151 (2.5)	0.0014–0.0022 ①	0.010–0.020	0.010–0.020	0.020–0.060	0.002–0.003	0.001–0.003	0.015–0.055
	W	6-173 (2.8)	0.0020–0.0028	0.010–0.020	0.010–0.020	0.020–0.055	0.001–0.003	0.001–0.003	0.005–0.008
	T	6-192 (3.1)	0.0022–0.0028	0.010–0.020	0.010–0.020	0.010–0.050	0.002–0.004	0.002–0.004	0.008 ②
	N	6-204 (3.3)	0.0004–0.0022	0.010–0.025	0.010–0.025	0.010–0.040	0.001–0.003	0.001–0.003	0.001 0.008
1990–91	R	4-151 (2.5)	0.0014–0.0022 ①	0.010–0.020	0.010–0.020	0.020–0.060	0.002–0.003	0.001–0.003	0.015–0.055
	T	6-192 (3.1)	0.0022–0.0028	0.010–0.020	0.010–0.020	0.010–0.050	0.002–0.004	0.002–0.004	0.008 ②
	N	6-204 (3.3)	0.0004–0.0022	0.010–0.025	0.010–0.025	0.010–0.040	0.001–0.003	0.001–0.003	0.001 0.008

① Measured 1/8 in. down from piston top
② Maximum clearance

TORQUE SPECIFICATIONS

All readings in ft. lbs.

Year	VIN	No. Cylinder Displacement cu. in. (liter)	Cylinder Head Bolts	Main Bearing Bolts	Rod Bearing Bolts	Crankshaft Pulley Bolts	Flywheel Bolts	Manifold Intake	Manifold Exhaust	Spark Plugs
1987	R	4-151 (2.5)	①	70	32	162	②	25	③	15
	W	6-173 (2.8)	⑥④	68	37	75	⑤	25	15–23	10–25
	3	6-231 (3.8)	60 ⑥	100	45	219	60	32	37	20
1988	R	4-151 (2.5)	①	70	32	162	②	25	③	15
	W	6-173 (2.8)	⑥④	68	37	75	⑤	25	15–23	10–25
	3	6-231 (3.8)	60 ⑥	100	45	219	60	32	37	20

TORQUE SPECIFICATIONS
All readings in ft. lbs.

Year	VIN	No. Cylinder Displacement cu. in. (liter)	Cylinder Head Bolts	Main Bearing Bolts	Rod Bearing Bolts	Crankshaft Pulley Bolts	Flywheel Bolts	Manifold Intake	Manifold Exhaust	Spark Plugs
1989	R	4-151 (2.5)	①	70	32	162	②	25	③	15
	W	6-173 (2.8)	⑥④	68	37	75	③	25	15–23	10–25
	T	6-192 (3.1)	33 ⑥	63–83	34–40	66–85	③	25	15–23	10–25
	N	6-204 (3.3)	35	90	20	219	61 ⑤	88 ⑥	30	20
1990–91	R	4-151 (2.5)	①	70	32	162	②	25	③	15
	T	6-192 (3.1)	33 ⑥	63–83	34–40	66–85	⑤	25	15–23	10–25
	N	6-204 (3.3)	35	90	20	219	61 ⑦	88 ⑧	30	20

① Torque bolts in sequence: 1st, 18 ft. lbs.; 2nd, 22 ft. lbs. except number 9 bolt; torque number 9 bolt to 29 ft. lbs.; 3rd, turn all bolts 120 degrees except number 9 bolt; number 9 bolt turn 90 degrees
② Manual Transaxle—69 ft. lbs.
Automatic Transaxle—55 ft. lbs.
③ Torque bolts in sequence, 3-5-6-2-1-7-4; torque bolts 1, 2, 6 and 7 to 32 ft. lbs. and bolts 3, 4 and 5 to 37 ft. lbs.
④ Torque bolts to 33 ft. lbs.
⑤ Manual Transaxle—52 ft. lbs.
Automatic Transaxle—46 ft. lbs.
⑥ Rotate wrench an additional 1/4 turn
⑦ Apply P/N 1052624
⑧ Inch lbs.

BRAKE SPECIFICATIONS
All measurements in inches unless noted.

Year	Model	Lug Nut Torque (ft. lbs.)	Master Cylinder Bore	Brake Disc Minimum Thickness	Brake Disc Maximum Runout	Standard Brake Drum Diameter	Minimum Lining Thickness Front	Minimum Lining Thickness Rear
1987	Celebrity	100	0.874	0.830	0.002	8.858	0.030	①
	Century	100	0.874	0.830	0.002	8.858	0.030	①
	Cutlass Ciera	100	0.874	0.830	0.002	8.858	0.030	①
	6000	100	0.874	0.830	0.002	8.858	0.030	①
1988	Celebrity	100	0.874	0.830	0.002	8.858	0.030	①
	Century	100	0.874	0.830	0.002	8.858	0.030	①
	Cutlass Ciera	100	0.874	0.830	0.002	8.858	0.030	①
	6000	100	0.874	0.830	0.002	8.858	0.030	①
1989	Celebrity	100	0.874 ②	0.830	0.004	8.863	0.030	①
	Century	100	0.874 ②	0.830	0.004	8.863	0.030	①
	Cutlass Ciera	100	0.874 ②	0.830	0.004	8.863	0.030	①
	6000	100	0.874 ②	0.830	0.004	8.863	0.030	①
1990–91	Celebrity	100	0.874 ②	0.830 ③④	0.004 ⑤	8.863	0.030	0.030
	Century	100	0.874 ②	0.830 ③	0.004	8.863	0.030	0.030
	Cutlass	100	0.874 ②	0.830 ③	0.004	8.863	0.030	0.030
	6000	100	0.874 ②	0.830 ③④	0.004 ⑤	8.863	0.030	0.030

① 0.030 in. over rivet head; if bonded, 0.062 in. over shoe
② Medium and heavy duty—0.944
③ Medium & heavy duty—0.972
④ Rear disc—0.756
⑤ Rear disc—0.003

WHEEL ALIGNMENT

Year	Model	Caster Range (deg.)	Caster Preferred Setting (deg.)	Camber Range (deg.)	Camber Preferred Setting (deg.)	Toe-in (in.)	Steering Axis Inclination (deg.)
1987	Celebrity, Century, Cutlass Ciera, 6000	1P–3P	2P	½N–½P	0	³/₃₂N–³/₃₂P	NA
1988	Celebrity, Century, Cutlass Ciera, 6000	1P–3P	2P	½N–½P	0	³/₃₂N–³/₃₂P	NA
1989	Celebrity, Century, Cutlass Ciera, 6000	1P–3P	2P	½N–½P	0	³/₃₂N–³/₃₂P	NA
1990–91	Celebrity, Century, Cutlass, 6000	1P–3P	2P	½N–½P	0	³/₃₂N–³/₃₂P	NA

NA Not available
N Negative
P Positive

ENGINE ELECTRICAL

NOTE: Disconnecting the negative battery cable on some vehicles may interfere with the functions of the on board computer systems and may require the computer to undergo a relearning process, once the negative battery cable is reconnected.

Distributorless Ignition

REMOVAL & INSTALLATION

Ignition Coil

1. Disconnect battery negative cable.
2. Disconnect and tag spark plug wires.
3. Remove ignition coil(s) attaching bolts, then the ignition coil.
4. Reverse procedure to install.

Ignition Module

1. Disconnect battery negative cable.
2. Disconnect electrical connector from ignition module.
3. Disconnect and tag spark plug wires.
4. Remove ignition module attaching nuts and bolts, then the ignition module from the vehicle.
5. Reverse procedure to install.

Crankshaft Sensor

3.1L ENGINE

1. Disconnect battery negative cable.
2. Disconnect crankshaft sensor electrical connector.
3. Remove the crankshaft sensor attaching bolt, then remove the crankshaft sensor from thew vehicle.
3. Reverse procedure to install.

EXCEPT 3.1L ENGINE

1. Disconnect battery negative cable.
2. Disconnect serpentine belt from crankshaft pulley.
3. Raise and support vehicle.
4. Remove right front tire and wheel assembly, then the inner access cover.
5. Remove crankshaft harmonic balancer retaining bolt, then the crankshaft harmonic balancer.
6. Disconnect electrical connector from sensor, then remove the crankshaft sensor from the vehicle.
7. Reverse procedure to install.

Ignition Timing

All 1987–91 vehicles are equipped with a Distributorless Ignition System; also referred to as Direct Ignition System (DIS). The system consists of a coil pack, ignition module, crankshaft reluctor ring, magnetic sensor and an Electronic Control Module (ECM). Timing advance and retard are accomplished through the ECM with Electronic Spark Timing (EST) and Electronic Spark Control (ESC). No adjustment is possible.

Alternator

For further information on the charging system, please refer to "Charging and Starting" in the Unit Repair section.

PRECAUTIONS

Several precautions must be observed with alternator equipped vehicles to avoid damage to the unit.

• If the battery is removed for any reason, make sure it is reconnected with the correct polarity. Reversing the battery connections may result in damage to the one-way rectifiers.
• When utilizing a booster battery as a starting aid, always connect the positive to positive terminals and the negative terminal from the booster battery to a good engine ground on the vehicle being started.
• Never use a fast charger as a booster to start vehicles.
• Disconnect the battery cables when charging the battery with a fast charger.
• Never attempt to polarize the alternator.
• Do not use test lamps of more than 12 volts when checking diode continuity.
• Do not short across or ground any of the alternator terminals.

• The polarity of the battery, alternator and regulator must be matched and considered before making any electrical connections within the system.

• Never separate the alternator on an open circuit. Make sure all connections within the circuit are clean and tight.

• Disconnect the battery ground terminal when performing any service on electrical components.

• Disconnect the battery if arc welding is to be done on the vehicle.

BELT TENSION ADJUSTMENT

V-Belt

1. Place the tension gauge midway between the accessory pulleys. Install the gauge on the longest belt span possible. If the belt is notched on the inner surface, place the middle finger of the tensioner gauge into 1 of the notches.

2. To adjust, loosen the accessory adjusting and pivot bolts. Move the accessory inward or outward to obtain the correct tension listed in the specification chart, then tighten the adjusting bolt and pivot bolt.

Serpentine Belt

A single serpentine belt is used to drive all engine accessories. The belt tension is maintained by a spring loaded tensioner. The belt tensioner has the ability to control the belt tension over a broad range of belt lengths. However, there are limits to which the tensioner can compensate for varying lengths. If the belt tension is below the minimum specifications, replace the belt tensioner.

Check the serpentine belt tension with tool J-23600B or equivalent in the following manner:

1. Start the engine and run until operating temperature is reached.

2. Shut the engine OFF and place the tension gauge midway between the pulleys. Install the gauge on the longest belt span possible. If the belt is notched on the inner surface, place the middle finger of the tensioner gauge into 1 of the notches. Correct belt tension readings should be approximately 40 lbs. for 2.5L engine or 70 lbs. except 2.5L engine.

REMOVAL & INSTALLATION

1. Disconnect the negative battery cable.

2. Remove the 2 terminal plug and battery lead on the back of the alternator.

3. Loosen the alternator mounting bolts and pivot bolt.

4. Remove the alternator belt and and through bolt.

5. Remove the alternator from the engine.

6. Installation is the reverse of the removal procedure. Adjust the alternator belt to specification.

Starter

For further information on the charging system, please refer to "Charging and Starting" in the Unit Repair section.

REMOVAL & INSTALLATION

1. Disconnect the negative battery cable at the battery.

2. If necessary, remove the engine side strut bolt and upper radiator panel bracket.

3. On 3.3L and 3.8L engines, discharge the air conditioning system.

4. Raise and support the vehicle safely.

5. Remove the cooling fan lower retaining bolts and disconnect the electrical connection at the fan, as required.

6. Lower the vehicle.

7. Remove the cooling fan upper.

8. Remove the spark plug wires and oil indicator tube, as required.

9. Raise and support the vehicle safely.

10. Remove the exhaust manifold flange bolts, manifold bolts and manifold, as required.

11. Remove the air conditioning manifold retaining bolt from the air conditioning compressor and remove the air conditioning line retaining bolt, as required.

12. Remove the electrical wiring from the starter motor.

13. Remove the flywheel inspection cover.

14. Remove the starter mounting bolts and starter motor. Remove the shims, if used.

To install:

15. Raise and safely support vehicle.

16. Connect starter wiring, install shims, if used, then the starter. Torque bolts 30 ft. lbs. (40 Nm).

17. Connect the air conditioning line and manifold bolt.

18. Install the inspection cover.

19. Install the exhaust manifold.

20. Lower vehicle, then install the spark plug wires and oil tube indicator.

21. Install cooling fan.

22. On 3.3L and 3.8L charge air conditioning system.

23. Install the engine strut bolt and upper radiator panel bracket, if removed.

24. Connect battery negative cable.

CHASSIS ELECTRICAL

Heater Blower Motor

REMOVAL & INSTALLATION

1. Disconnect the negative battery cable.

2. Tag and disconnect the blower motor electrical leads.

3. Remove the motor retaining bolts and remove the blower motor.

4. Installation is the reverse of the removal procedure. Connect battery negative cable.

Windshield Wiper Motor

REMOVAL & INSTALLATION

1. Disconnect the negative battery cable.

2. Remove the air intake grille.

3. Loosen the wiper linkage to drive arm attaching nuts.

4. Remove the transmission link from the drive arm.

5. Disconnect the wiring and hoses from the motor.

6. Unbolt and remove the motor.

7. Installation is the reverse of the removal procedure. Connect battery negative cable.

Windshield Wiper Switch

REMOVAL & INSTALLATION

1. Disconnect the negative battery cable.

2. Remove the steering wheel and turn signal switch. It may be necessary to first remove the column mounting nuts and remove the 4 bracket-to-mast jacket screws, then separate the bracket from the mast jacket to allow the connector clip on the ignition switch to be pulled out of the column assembly.

3. Tag and disconnect the washer/wiper switch lower connector.

4. Remove the screws attaching the column housing to the mast jacket. Be sure to note the position of the dimmer switch actuator rod for reassembly in

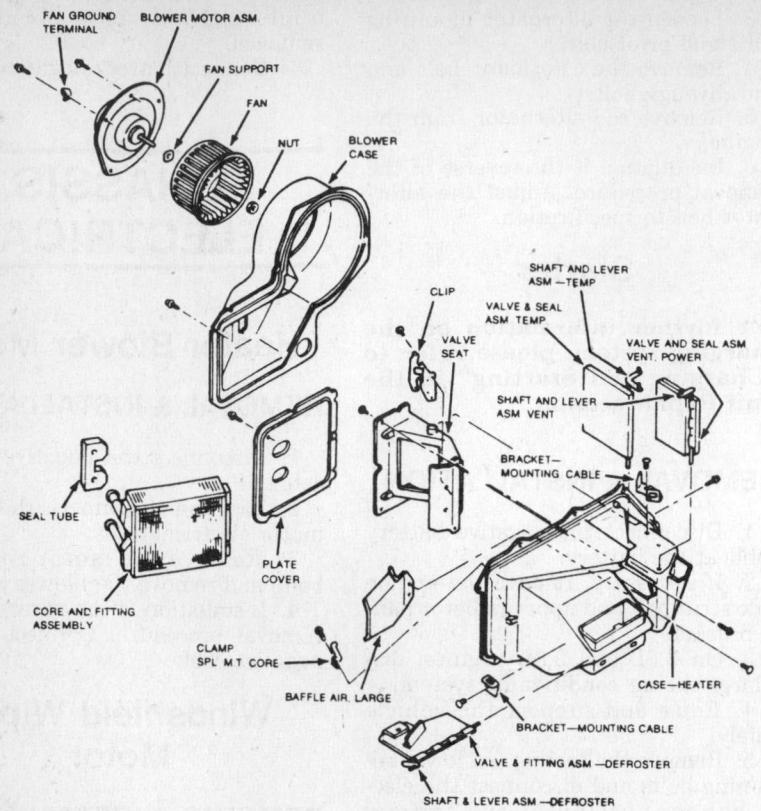

Heater core, blower motor and related components—Typical

the same position. Remove the column housing and switch as an assembly.

NOTE: Certain tilt and travel columns are equipped with a removable plastic cover on the column housing. This provides access to the wiper switch without removing the entire column housing.

5. Turn upside down and use a drift to remove the pivot pin from the washer/wiper switch. Remove the switch.
To install:
6. Place the switch into position in the housing. Install the pivot pin.
7. Position the housing onto the mast jacket and attach by installing the screws. Install the dimmer switch actuator rod in the same position as noted when removed. Check switch operation.
8. Reconnect lower end of the switch assembly.
9. Install remaining components in reverse order of the removal procedure.

Instrument Cluster

REMOVAL & INSTALLATION

Celebrity

1. Disconnect the negative battery cable.

2. Remove instrument panel hush panel.
3. Remove vent control housing, as required.
4. On non-air conditioning vehicles, remove steering column trim cover screws and lower cover with vent cables attached. On air conditioning vehicles, remove trim cover attaching screws and remove cover.
5. Remove instrument cluster trim pad.
6. Remove ash tray, retainer and fuse block, disconnect wires as necessary.
7. Remove headlight switch knob and instrument panel trim plate. Disconnect electrical connectors of any accessory switches in trim plate.
8. Remove cluster assembly and disconnect speedometer cable, **PRNDL** and cluster electrical connectors.
9. Installation is the reverse of the removal procedure.

6000

1. Disconnect the negative battery cable, and remove the center and left hand lower instrument panel trim plate.
2. Remove the screws holding the instrument cluster to the instrument panel carrier.
3. Remove the instrument cluster lens to gain access to the speedometer

head and gauges.
4. Remove right-hand and left-hand hush panels, steering column trim cover and disconnect parking brake cable and vent cables, if equipped.
5. Remove steering column retaining bolts and drop steering column.
6. Disconnect temperature control cable, inner to outer air conditioning wire harness and inner to outer air conditioning vacuum harness, if equipped.
7. Disconnect chassis harness behind left lower instrument panel and ECM connectors behind glove box. Disconnect instrument panel harness at cowl.
8. Remove center instrument panel trim plate, radio, if equipped, and disconnect neutral switch and brake light switch.
9. Remove upper and lower instrument panel retaining screws, nuts and bolts.
10. Pull instrument panel assembly out far enough to disconnect ignition switch, headlight dimmer switch and turn signal switch. Disconnect all other accessory wiring and vacuum lines necessary to remove instrument panel assembly.
11. Remove instrument panel assembly with wiring harness.
12. Installation is the reverse of the removal procedure. Connect battery negative cable.

Ciera

1. Disconnect the negative battery cable. Remove left instrument panel trim pad.
2. Remove instrument panel cluster trim cover.
3. Disconnect speedometer cable at transaxle or cruise control transducer, if equipped.
4. Remove steering column trim cover.
5. Disconnect shift indicator clip from steering column shift bowl.
6. Remove 4 screws attaching cluster assembly to instrument panel.
7. Pull assembly out far enough to reach behind cluster and disconnect speedometer cable.
8. Remove cluster assembly.
9. Installation is the reverse of the removal procedure. Connect battery negative cable.

Century

1. Disconnect the negative battery cable.
2. Disconnect the speedometer cable and pull it through the firewall.
3. Remove the left side hush panel retaining screws and nut.
4. Remove the right side hush panel retaining screws and nut.

5. Remove the shift indicator cable clip.

6. Remove the steering column trim plate.

7. Put the gear selector in **L**. Remove the retaining screws and gently pull out the instrument panel trim plate.

8. Disconnect the parking brake cable at the lever by pushing it forward and sliding it out of its slot.

9. Unbolt and lower the steering column.

10. Remove the gauge cluster retaining screws and pulling the cluster out far enough to disconnect any wires, then pull the cluster out.

11. Installation is the reverse of the removal procedure. Connect battery negative cable.

SPEEDOMETER

REMOVAL & INSTALLATION

Celebrity

1. Disconnect the negative battery cable.

2. Remove the cluster trim panel.

3. Remove the cluster lens screws. Remove the cluster lens.

4. Remove the speedometer to cluster attaching screws. Remove the speedometer from the instrument cluster.

5. Disconnect the speedometer cable and remove the speedometer assembly.

6. Installation is the reverse of the removal procedure. Connect battery negative cable.

6000

1. Disconnect the negative battery cable.

2. Remove the center and left lower trim plates.

3. Remove the screws holding the instrument cluster assembly to the dash assembly. Remove the instrument cluster.

4. Remove the instrument cluster lens screws. Remove the instrument cluster lens.

5. Remove the screws holding the speedometer to the instrument cluster. Remove the speedometer.

6. Disconnect the speedometer cable from the rear of the speedometer.

7. Installation is the reverse of the removal procedure. Connecdt battery negative cable.

Ciera

1. Disconnect the negative battery cable.

2. Remove the instrument cluster assembly.

3. Remove the vehicle speed sensor screw from the rear of the speedometer. Remove the vehicle speed sensor, if equipped.

4. Remove the speedometer lens screws and remove the speedometer lens. Remove the bezel.

5. Remove the screw that holds the speedometer to the instrument cluster.

6. Remove the speedometer head by pulling forward. Disconnect the speedometer cable by prying gently on the retainer and pulling the speedometer cable out of the speedometer head.

7. Installation is the reverse of the removal procedure. Connect battery negative cable.

Century

1. Disconnect the negative battery cable.

2. Remove the left hand trim plate.

3. Remove the instrument cluster housing screws. Remove the instrument cluster. If the vehicle is equipped with tilt-wheel steering, working room can be gained by removing the tilt-wheel cover.

4. Remove the speedometer lens screws and remove the speedometer lens.

5. Disconnect the speedometer cable by pushing in on the retaining clip and pulling back on the cable.

6. Remove the screws holding the speedometer to the instrument and remove the speedometer assembly.

7. Installation is the reverse of the removal procedure. Connect battery negative cable.

Radio

REMOVAL & INSTALLATION

1. Disconnect battery negative cable.

2. Remove the accessory trim plate.

3. Remove the instrument cluster trim plate.

4. Remove the radio attaching bolts, then disconnect electrical connectors.

5. Remove radio from vehicle.

6. Reverse procedure to install. Connect battery negative cable.

Headlight Switch

REMOVAL & INSTALLATION

CELEBRITY

1. Disconnect the negative battery cable.

2. Remove the headlight switch knob.

3. Remove the instrument panel trim pad.

4. Unbolt the switch mounting plate from the instrumnet panel carrier.

5. Disconnect trhe wiring from the switch.

6. Remove the switch.

7. Installation is the reverse of removal procedure. Connect the battery negative cable.

6000

1. Disconnect the negative battery cable.

2. Remove the steering column trim cover and headlight rod and knob by reaching behind the instrument panel and depressing the lock tab.

3. Remove the left instrument panel trim plate.

4. Unbolt and remove the switch and bracket assembly from the instrument panel.

5. Loosen the bezel and remove the switch from the bracket.

6. Installation is the reverse of removal procedure. Connect the battery negative cable.

Ciera

1. Disconnect the negative battery cable.

2. Remove the left side instrument panel trim pad.

3. Unbolt the switch from the instrument panel.

4. Pull the switch rearward and remove it.

5. Installation is the reverse of the removal procedure.

Century

1. Disconnect the negative battery cable.

2. Remove the instrument panel trim plate.

3. Remove the left side instrument panel switch trim panel by removing the 3 screws and gently rocking the panel out.

4. Remove the three screws and pull the switch straight out.

5. Installation is the reverse of the removal procedure. Connect the battery negative cable.

Dimmer Switch

REMOVAL & INSTALLATION

1. Disconnect the negative battery cable.

2. Remove the steering wheel. Remove the trim cover.

3. Remove the turn signal switch assembly.

4. Remove the ignition switch stud and screw. Remove the ignition switch.

5. Remove the dimmer switch actuator rod by sliding it from the switch assembly.

6. Remove the dimmer switch bolts and remove the dimmer switch.

7. Installation is the reverse of the removal procedure.

8. Adjust the dimmer switch by depressing the switch slightly and inserting a $3/32$ in. drill bit into the adjusting hole. Push the switch up to remove any play and tighten the dimmer switch adjusting screw. Connect the battery negative cable.

Combination Switch

REMOVAL & INSTALLATION

1. Disconnect the negative battery cable. Remove the steering wheel and trim cover.

2. Loosen the cover screws. Pry the cover upward and remove it from the shaft.

3. Position the U-shaped lock plate compressing tool on the end of the steering shaft and compress the lockplate by turning the shaft nut clockwise. Pry the wire snapring out of the shaft groove.

4. Remove the tool and lift the lock plate off the shaft.

5. Slip the cancelling cam, upper bearing preload spring and thrust washer off the shaft.

6. Remove the turn signal lever. Push the flasher knob in and unscrew it. Remove the button retaining screw and remove the button, spring and knob.

7. Pull the switch connector out the mast jacket and tape the upper part to facilitate switch removal. Attach a long piece of wire to the turn signal switch connector. When installing the turn signal switch, feed this wire through the column first, and then use this wire to pull the switch connector into position. On vehicle equipped with tilt wheel, place the turn signal and shifter housing in Low position and remove the harness cover.

8. Remove the 3 switch mounting screws. Remove the switch by pulling it straight up while guiding the wiring harness cover through the column.

To install:

9. Install the replacement switch by working the connector and cover down through the housing and under the bracket. If equipped with tilt wheel, the connector is worked down through the housing, under the bracket and then the cover is installed on the harness.

10. Install the switch mounting screws and the connector on the mast jacket bracket. Install the column-to-dash trim plate.

11. Install the flasher knob and the turn signal lever.

12. With the turn signal lever in neutral and the flasher knob out, slide the thrust washer, upper bearing preload spring and cancelling cam onto the shaft.

13. Position the lock plate on the shaft and press it down until a new snapring can be inserted in the shaft groove. Always use a new snapring when assembling.

14. Install the cover and the steering wheel. Connect the battery negative cable.

Ignition Lock

REMOVAL & INSTALLATION

1. Disconnect the negative battery cable. Place the lock in the **RUN** position. Remove the steering wheel.

2. Remove the lock plate, turn signal switch and buzzer switch.

3. Remove the screw and lock cylinder.

NOTE: If the screw is dropped on removal, it could fall into the column, requiring complete disassembly to retrieve the screw.

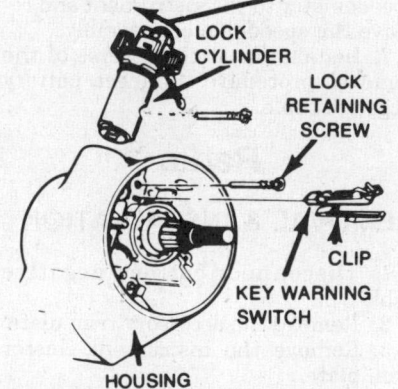

Mounting of the ignition lock cylinder assembly, removal of the key warning switch, is shown in the inset

4. Rotate the cylinder clockwise to align cylinder key with the keyway in the housing.

5. Push the lock all the way in.

6. Install the screw. Tighten the screw to 14 inch lbs. for adjustable columns and 25 inch lbs. for standard columns. Connect battery negative cable.

Ignition Switch

REMOVAL & INSTALLATION

The switch is located inside the channel section of the brake pedal support and is completely inaccessible without first lowering the steering column. The switch is actuated by a rod and rack assembly. A gear on the end of the lock cylinder engages the toothed upper end of the rod.

1. Disconnect the negative battery cable. Lower the steering column; be sure to properly support it.

2. Put the ignition switch in the **OFF–UNLOCKED** position. With the cylinder removed, the rod is in the **LOCK** position when it is in the next to the uppermost detent. **OFF–UNLOCKED** position is 2 detents from the top.

3. Remove the 2 switch screws and remove the switch assembly.

4. Before installing, place the new switch in **OFF–UNLOCKED** position and make sure the lock cylinder and actuating rod are in **OFF–UNLOCKED**, third detent from the top.

5. Install the activating rod into the switch and assemble the switch on the column. Tighten the mounting screws. Use only the specified screws since overlength screws could impair the collapsibility of the column.

6. Reinstall the steering column. Connect battery negative cable.

Stoplight Switch

ADJUSTMENT

1. The switch is mounted on the brake pedal bracket.

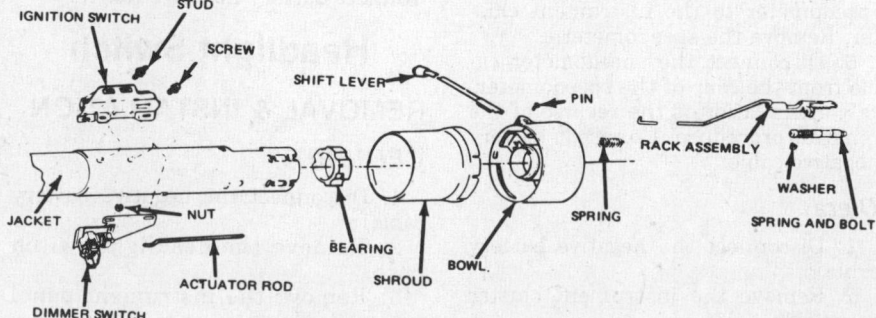

Installtion of the ignition switch

2. To adjust, depress the pedal and push the switch through the circular retaining clip until it contacts the brake pedal, then pull the pedal up against the internal pedal stop. This places the switch in the correct position within the clip.

REMOVAL & INSTALLATION

1. Disconnect the negative battery cable. Disconnect the electrical connector to the switch.
2. Remove the switch from the brake pedal bracket.
3. Install the new switch into the bracket.
4. Connect the electrical connector.
5. Adjust the switch. Connect battery negative cable.

Clutch Switch

ADJUSTMENT

1. Lift the clutch pedal to its uppermost position. Check the operation of the pawl and the quadrant. Make sure the pawl disengages from the quadrant when the pedal is pulled to this position.
2. Check the quadrant for free rotation in both directions.
3. Depress the clutch pedal slowly several times to set the pawl into mesh with the quadrant teeth.

REMOVAL & INSTALLATION

1. Disconnect the negative battery cable. Support the clutch pedal against the bumper stop in order to release the pawl from the quadrant. Disconnect the clutch cable from the release lever at the transaxle assembly.

—— CAUTION ——
Be careful to prevent the cable from snapping towards the rear of the vehicle possibly causing bodily injury. The quadrant in the adjusting mechanism can also be damaged by allowing the cable to snap rearward.

2. From inside the vehicle, disconnect the clutch cable from the quadrant. Lift the locking pawl away from the quadrant. Slide the cable away from the pedal along the right side of the quadrant.
3. Remove the neutral start switch from the pedal. Remove the pedal pivot nut, bolt and clutch pedal from the mounting bracket.
4. Note the position of the adjusting mechanism, the pawl and quadrant springs. Remove the E-ring.
5. Inspect the components for tooth damage and replace any components found to be defective.
6. Installation is the reverse of the

removal procedure. Check the clutch operation and adjust by lifting the clutch pedal up to allow the mechanism to adjust the cable length. Depress the pedal slowly several times to set the pawl into mesh with the quadrant teeth.

Neutral Safety Switch

ADJUSTMENT

1. After the switch is installed, move the housing towards the **L** gear position.
2. Shift the gear selector into the **P** position.
3. The main housing and the housing back should ratchet. This will provide proper switch adjustment.
4. Repeat if necessary.

REMOVAL & INSTALLATION

Vehicles With Console Shift

1. New switches come with a small plastic alignment pin installed. Leave this pin in place. Position the shifter assembly in **N**.
2. Disconnect the negative battery cable. Remove the old switch and install the replacement, align the pin on the shifter with the slot in the switch and fasten with the 2 screws.
3. Move the shifter from the **N** position. This shears the plastic alignment pin and frees the switch.
4. If the switch is to be adjusted, insert a 3/32 in. drill bit or similar size pin and align the hole switch. Position switch, adjust as necessary. Remove the pin before shifting from **N**. Connect battery negative cable.

Vehicles With Column Shift

1. Disconnect the negative battery cable. Remove wire connectors from the combination back-up and neutral safety switch.
2. Remove 2 screws attaching the switch to the steering column.
3. Installation is the reverse of the removal procedure. To adjust a new switch:
   a. Position the shift lever in **N**.
   b. Loosen the attaching screws. Install a 0.090 in. gauge pin into the outer hole in the switch cover.
   c. Rotate the switch until the pin goes into the alignment hole in the inner plastic slide.
   d. Tighten the switch to column attaching screws and remove the gauge pin. Torque the screws to 20 inch lbs. maximum.
   e. Make sure the engine starts only in the **P** and **N** positions. Connect battery negative cable.

Fuses, Circuit Breakers and Relays

LOCATION

Fusible Links

There are several locations where fusible links can be found. They are located ahead of the left hand front shock tower, near the positive battery connection or at the starter solenoid near the front of the engine.

Circuit Breakers

Circuit breakers are used along with the fusible links to protect the various components of the electrical system, such as headlights, the windshield wipers and electric windows. The circuit breakers are located either in the switch or mounted on or near the lower lip of the instrument panel, to the right or left of the steering column.

Fuse Panel

The fuse panel is located on the left side of the vehicle. It is under the instrument panel assembly. In order to gain access to the fuse panel, it may be necessary to first remove the under dash padding.

Relays

CELEBRITY, CIERA, 6000

A/C Compressor Relay—located on the upper right corner of the engine cowl.
A/C Delay Relay—located in the upper right corner of the engine cowl.
A/C Heater Blower Relay—located on the plenum, on the right side of the firewall.
Altitude Advance Relay—located on the left inner fender, in front of the shock tower.
Charging System Relay—located behind the instrument panel, near the fuse block.
Constant Run Relay—located on the left inner fender wheel well.
Coolant Fan Low-Speed Relay—located on the left inner fender wheel well, on a bracket on the 2.5L engines and on the fender panel in front of the left front shock tower on all except 2.5L engines.
Coolant Fan Relay—located on the left front wheel well on the bracket on the 2.5L engine and on the fender panel ahead of the left front shock tower on all except 2.5L engines.
Defogger Timer Relay—located behind the instrument panel, under the instrument cluster.
Early Fuel Evaporation Heater Relay—located on the upper right side of the engine cowl.

Electronic Level Control Relay—located on the frame behind the left rear wheel well.

Fuel Pump Relay—located on the upper right side of the engine cowl.

High Mount Stop Light Relays—located on the left rear wheel well, in the trunk.

Horn Relay—located on the convenience center.

Low Brake Vacuum Relay—taped to the instrument panel above the fuse block.

Rear Wiper Relay—located in the top center of the tailgate.

Starter Interrupt Relay—located above the ashtray, taped to the instrument panel harness.

CENTURY

F54A/C Coolant Fan Relay (2.5L Engine)—located on the right side of the firewall.

Blower Relay—located on the right side of the firewall.

Coolant Fan Delay Relay (SFI)—located in front of the left front shock tower, on a bracket.

Coolant Fan Relay—located in front of the left front shock tower.

Fuel Pump Relay (2.5L Engine)—located in the relay bracket on the right side of the firewall.

High Speed Coolant Fan Relay—located on the left front side of the engine.

Horn Relay—located under the instrument panel, in the convenience center.

Low Speed Coolant Fan Relay—located near the battery, on the left side of the radiator shroud.

Rear Wiper Relay—located in the top center of the tailgate.

Starter Interrupt Relay—taped to the instrument panel harness, above the right side ashtray.

Computers

LOCATION

Electronic Control Module (ECM)

The electronic module is located on the right side of the vehicle. It is positioned under the instrument panel. In order to gain access to the electronic control module, it will be necessary to first remove the trim panel.

Cruise Control Module

The cruise control module is located behind the instrument panel, above the accelerator pedal.

Flashers

LOCATION

Hazard

The harzard flasher is located in the convenience center. The convenience center is a swing down type, located under the instrument panel near the fuse block.

Turn Signal

The turn signal flasher is located behind the instrument panel, to the right of the steering column.

Cruise Control

ADJUSTMENT

NOTE: To keep the vehicle under control and to prevent possible vehicle damage, it is not advisable to use the cruise control on slippery roads. Disengage the cruise control in conditions such as varying or heavy traffic or when traveling down a steep graded hill.

1. Adjust the throttle lever to the idle position with the engine **OFF**. If equipped with the idle control solenoid, the solenoid must be de-energized.
2. Pull the servo assembly end of the cable towards the servo blade.
3. Line up the holes in the servo blade with the cable pin. Install the cable pin.
4. If equipped with the 2.8L engine, it will be necessary to position the ball of the chain assembly into the chain retainer. This will allow a slight slack to occur not to exceed one ball diameter. Remove the excess chain outside of the chain retainer.

ENGINE COOLING

Radiator

REMOVAL & INSTALLATION

1. Disconnect the battery ground cable, then drain the cooling system.
2. Remove the engine forward strut bracket to the radiator. Loosen the bolt to prevent damage to the bushing, then swing the strut rearward.
3. Disconnect the headlight harness connectors from the fan frame. Disconnect the electrical connector from the fan.
4. Remove the cooling fan attaching bolts, then the cooling fan.
5. Scribe the hood latch location on the radiator support, then remove the latch.
6. Disoconnect the coolant hoses from the radiator. If equipped with automatic transaxle, disconnect the oil cooler lines.
7. Remove the radiator attaching bolts, then the radiator. If equipped with air conditioning, it may be necessary to raise the left side of the radiator so the radiator neck will clear the compressor.
8. Reverse procedure to install. Refill system and connect the battery negative cable.

Electric Cooling Fan

TESTING

Coolant Fan Does Not Run

1. Turn the ignition switch to the **RUN** position. Ground the diagnostic terminal **B** of the assembly line communication link.
2. If the coolant fan runs, replace the ECM. If the coolant fan does not run, go to the next Step.
3. Remove the connector from the coolant fan relay which is located on the left front fender. Connect a test lamp to terminal **C** of the connector and ground. Turn the ignition switch to the **RUN** position.
4. If the test lamp does not light, inspect the brown and white wire for an open. Repair as necessary.
5. If the test lamp lights, move the test light from terminal **C** to terminal **E** of the coolant fan relay connector.
6. If the test lamp does not light, inspect the red wire and fusible link C, located on the engine harness near the starter solenoid. Repair as necessary.
7. If the test lamp lights, connect a fused jumper between terminals **E** and **A** of the coolant fan relay connector.
8. If the coolant fan runs, replace the coolant fan relay. If the coolant fan does not run. Go to the next Step.
9. With the fused jumper still in place, remove the coolant fan connector and connect a test lamp to terminal **B** of the connector and ground.
10. If the lamp does not light, inspect the wiring for an open and repair as necessary. If the lamp lights, go to the next Step.
11. Move the test lamp ground lead to terminal **A** of the coolant fan connector. If the test lamp does not light, check wire for an open and repair as necessary.

Coolant Fan Runs Continuously with the Ignition Switch In Run

1. Check for diagnostic Code 14 or 15. If either of these codes are present, replace the coolant sensor. If no code is present, go to the next Step.
2. Inspect the dark green and white wire for an open and repair, as necessary. If the wire shows continuity on the 2.5L, replace the coolant fan relay. On all other engines, go to the next Step.
3. Remove the connector from the fan temperature back up switch and turn the ignition switch to **RUN**.
4. If the coolant fan runs, replace the coolant fan relay. If the coolant fan does not run, replace the fan temperature back up switch located between the coolant fan relay and the ECM.

Coolant Fan Runs Continuously with the Ignition Switch In Off

1. Remove the connector from the coolant fan relay.
2. If the coolant fan runs, check for a short to battery voltage. Repair as necessary.
3. If the coolant fan stops running, replace the coolant fan relay.

REMOVAL & INSTALLATION

1. Disconnect the negative battery cable.
2. Tag and disconnect the electrical connector from the fan motor and fan frame.
3. Remove the fan frame to radiator support bolts.
4. Remove the fan and frame assembly from the vehicle.
5. Installation is the reverse of the removal procedure. Connect battery negative cable.

Heater Core

REMOVAL & INSTALLATION

Without Air Conditioning

1. Disconnect the negative battery cable. Drain the cooling system.
2. Remove the heater inlet and outlet hoses.
3. Remove the radio noise suppression strap.
4. Remove the core cover retaining screws. Remove the cover.
5. Remove the core.
6. Installation is the reverse of the removal procedure. Refill system and connect battery negative cable.

With Air Conditioning

1. Disconnect the negative battery

cable. Drain the cooling system.
2. Disconnect the heater hoses at the heater core.
3. Remove the heater duct and the lower side covers.
4. Remove the lower heater outlet.
5. Remove the housing cover-to-air valve housing clips.
6. Remove the housing cover bolts. Remove the housing cover.
7. Remove the core retaining straps. Remove the core tubing retainers. Lift out the heater core.
8. Installation is the reverse of the removal procedure. Refill system and connect battery negative cable.

Water Pump

REMOVAL & INSTALLATION

2.5L Engine

1. Disconnect the negative battery cable.
2. Drain the cooling system.
3. Remove accessory drive belts.
4. Remove water pump attaching bolts and remove pump.
To install:
5. If installing a new water pump, transfer pulley from old unit. With sealing surfaces cleaned, place a ⅛ in. (3mm) bead of RTV sealant or equivalent, on the water pump sealing surface. While sealer is still wet, install pump and torque bolts to 6 ft. lbs.
6. Install accessory drive belts.
7. Fill the cooling system. Connect battery negative cable.
8. Start the engine and check for leaks.

2.8L Engine

1. Disconnect the negative battery cable.
2. Drain cooling system and remove heater hose.
3. Remove serpentine belt.
4. Remove water pump attaching bolts and nut and remove pump.
To install:
5. Clean the sealing surfaces and place a ³⁄₃₂ in. (2mm) bead of RTV sealant or equivalent on the water pump sealing surface.
6. Coat bolt threads with pipe sealant No. 1052080 or equivalent.
7. Install pump and torque bolts to 10 ft. lbs.
8. Connect negative battery cable and refill system.

3.1L Engine

1. Disconnect the negative battery cable.
2. Drain cooling system.
3. Remove the serpentine belt.

4. Remove the heater hose and radiator hose.
5. Remove the water pump cover attaching bolts and remove the cover.
6. Remove the water pump attaching bolts and remove the water pump.
To install:
7. Position the water pump on the engine and install the attaching bolts. Torque bolts to 89 inch lbs. (10 Nm).
8. Install the water pump cover and attaching bolts.
9. Complete installation by reversing the removal procedure. Connect battery negative cable and refill system.

3.3L Engine

1. Disconnect the negative battery cable.
2. Drain cooling system.
3. Remove the accessory drive belt.
4. Remove the coolant hose at the water pump.
5. Remove the water pump pulley bolts. The long bolt should be removed through the access hole provided in the body side rail. Then, remove the pulley.
6. Remove the water pump attaching bolts and remove the water pump.
7. Installation is the reverse of the removal procedure. Connect battery negative cable and refill system.

3.8L Engine

1. Disconnect the negative battery cable.
2. Drain cooling system.
3. Remove the accessory drive belts.
4. Disconnect the radiator and heater hoses at the water pump.
5. Remove the water pump pulley bolts, long bolt removed through ac-

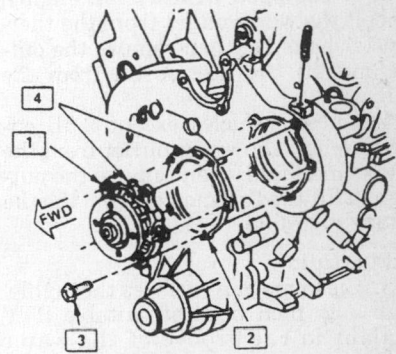

1. Water pump
2. Gasket
3. Bolt - 89 inch lbs. (10 Nm)
4. Locator - Must be vertical

Water pump mounting—2.8L and 3.1L engines

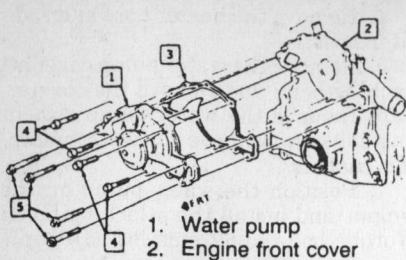

1. Water pump
2. Engine front cover
   Assembly
3. Gasket
4. Bolts - 97 inch lbs. (11 Nm)
5. Bolts - 29 ft. lbs. (39 Nm)

Water pump mounting—3.3L engine

cess hole provided in the body side rail, then remove the pulley.

6. Remove the water pump attaching bolts, then remove the water pump.

7. Clean all gasket mating surfaces.

8. Using a new gasket, install the water pump on the engine. Torque the bolts to specifications.

9. Install the water pump pulley, then torque the bolts to specifications.

10. The remainder of the installation is the reverse of removal. Connect battery negative cable and refill system.

Thermostat

REMOVAL & INSTALLATION

1. Disconnect the battery negative cable, then drain the cooling system.

2. If equipped with cruise control, remove the vacuum modulator from the thermostat housing.

3. If equipped with a 2.5L engine, unbolt the water outlet from the thermostat housing, then remove the outlet and lift the thermostat from the vehicle.

4. On all vehicles except 2.5L engine, unbolt the water outlet from the intake manifold, then remove the outlet and lift the thermostat from the the intake manifold.

To install:

5. Clean mating surfaces throughly. Run a ⅛ inch bead of suitable RTV sealant in the groove of the water outlet.

6. Install the thermostat with the spring toward the engine, then the water outlet. Torque bolts to 21 ft. lbs.

7. Complete installation by reversing the removal procedure. Fill cooling system and check for leaks. Connect battery negative cable.

FUEL SYSTEM

Fuel System Service Precautions

Safety is the most important factor when performing not only fuel system maintenance but any type of maintenance. Failure to conduct maintenance and repairs in a safe manner may result in serious personal injury or death. Maintenance and testing of the vehicle's fuel system components can be accomplished safely and effectively by adhering to the following rules and guidelines.

• To avoid the possibility of fire and personal injury, always disconnect the negative battery cable unless the repair or test procedure requires that battery voltage be applied.

• Always relieve the fuel system pressure prior to disconnecting any fuel system component (injector, fuel rail, pressure regulator, etc.), fitting or fuel line connection. Exercise extreme caution whenever relieving fuel system pressure to avoid exposing skin, face and eyes to fuel spray. Please be advised that fuel under pressure may penetrate the skin or any part of the body that it contacts.

• Always place a shop towel or cloth around the fitting or connection prior to loosening to absorb any excess fuel due to spillage. Ensure that all fuel spillage (should it occur) is quickly removed from engine surfaces. Ensure that all fuel soaked cloths or towels are deposited into a suitable waste container.

• Always keep a dry chemical (Class B) fire extinguisher near the work area.

• Do not allow fuel spray or fuel vapors to come into contact with a spark or open flame.

• Always use a backup wrench when loosening and tightening fuel line connection fittings. This will prevent unnecessary stress and torsion to fuel line piping. Always follow the proper torque specifications.

• Always replace worn fuel fitting O-rings with new. Do not substitute fuel hose or equivalent where fuel pipe is installed.

RELIEVING FUEL SYSTEM PRESSURE

Throttle Body Injection (TBI)

1. On a cold engine, remove the fuse marked "Fuel Pump" from the fuse block in the passenger compartment.

2. Crank the engine, engine will start and run until the fuel supply remaining in the fuel lines is exhausted. When the engine stops, engage the starter again for 3.0 seconds to assure dissipation of any remaining pressure.

3. With the ignition **OFF**, replace the fuel pump fuse.

4. Disconnect the negative battery cable.

Multi-Port Fuel Injection (MPFI)

1. Disconnect the negative battery cable to avoid possible fuel discharge if an accidental attempt is made to start the engine.

2. Loosen the fuel filler cap to relieve the tank pressure.

3. Connect fuel gauge J34730–1 or equivalent to fuel valve. Wrap a shop towel around the fitting while connecting gauge to avoid spillage.

4. Install bleed hose into an approved container and open valve to relieve system pressure.

Fuel Filter

REMOVAL & INSTALLATION

The filter is an inline unit located just ahead of the TBI unit or to the left of the fuel tank on later models.

1. Ensure the engine is cold, then unclamp and remove the fuel hose.

2. Unscrew the filter from the fuel line.

3. Installation is the reverse of removal.

Electric Fuel Pump

PRESSURE TESTING

1. Disconnect the fuel line from the EFI unit.

2. Install a suitable pressure gage to the fuel line.

3. Connect a jumper wire from the positive terminal on the battery to the **G** terminal of the AWLCL unit.

4. Fuel pressure gauge should be 9–13 psi if equipped with TBI or 34–46 psi if equipped with MFI.

NOTE: If fuel pressure does not meet specifications, check the fuel line for restrictions or the fuel pump for malfunctions.

REMOVAL & INSTALLATION

The fuel pump is attached to the fuel sending unit located inside the fuel tank.

1. Relieve the fuel system pressure,

then disconnect the negative battery cable.

2. Raise and support the vehicle safely. Drain the fuel tank.

3. Disconnect wiring from the tank, then remove the ground wire retaining screw from under the body.

4. Disconnect all hoses from the tank.

5. Support the tank on a jack and remove the retaining strap nuts.

6. Lower the tank and remove it from the vehicle.

7. Remove the fuel gauge/pump retaining ring using a spanner wrench such as tool J-24187 or equivalent.

8. Remove the gauge unit and the pump.

9. Installation is the reverse of the removal procedure. Always replace the O-ring under the gauge/pump retaining ring. Connect battery negative cable.

Fuel Injection

IDLE SPEED ADJUSTMENT

Throttle Body Injection (TBI)

NOTE: This procedure should be performed only when the throttle body parts have been replaced.

1. Remove the air cleaner and gasket.

2. Plug the vacuum port on the TBI marked THERMAC.

3. If the vehicle is equipped with a tamper resistant plug covering the throttle stop screw, the TBI unit must be removed from the engine.

4. Reinstall the throttle body on the engine. Remove the throtle valve cable from the throttle control bracket to allow access to the throttle stop screw.

5. Connect a tachometer to the engine.

6. Start the engine and run it to normal operating temperatures.

7. Install tool J-33047 or equivalent, into the idle air passage of the throttle body. Be sure the tool is fully seated and no air leaks exist.

8. Place the transaxle P for automatic transaxle or N for manual transaxle. Using a No. 20 Torx bit, turn the minimum air screw until the engine rpm is within specification.

9. Stop the engine and remove the special tool.

10. Install the cable on the throttle body.

11. Use RTV sealant to cover the throttle stop screw.

Multi-Port Fuel Injection (MPFI)

1. Using an suitable tool, pierce the idle stop screw plug, located on the

side of the throttle body, and remove it by prying it from the housing.

2. Using a jumper wire, ground the diagnostic lead of the IAC motor.

3. Turn the ignition ON. Do not start the engine. After 30 seconds, disconnect the IAC electrical connector. Remove the diagnostic lead ground lead and start the engine. Allow the system to go to closed loop.

4. Adjust the idle set screw to 550 rpm on automatic transaxle (in D) or 650 rpm on manual transaxle (N).

5. Turn the ignition OFF and reconnect the IAC motor lead.

6. Using a voltmeter, adjust the TPS to 0.55 ± 0.1 volt and secure the TPS.

7. Recheck the setting, then start the engine and check for proper idle operation.

8. Seal the idle stop screw with silicone sealer.

Fuel Injector

All fuel injectors are serviced as a complete assembly only. Since it is an electrical component, it should not be immersed in any type of cleaner.

REMOVAL & INSTALLATION

Throttle Body Injection

1. Relieve fuel system pressure. Disconnect the negative battery cable.

2. Remove the air cleaner assembly.

3. Squeeze the 2 tabs on the injector electrical connector together and pull straight upward.

4. Remove the fuel meter cover retaining screws. The 2 front retaining screws are shorter than the 3 rear retaining screws. Remove the fuel meter cover.

5. With the fuel meter cover gasket in place, use a prying tool and carefully lift the injector until it is free from the fuel meter body.

6. Remove the small O-ring from the injector nozzle end. Carefully rotate the injector fuel filter back and forth and remove the filter from the base of the injector.

7. Remove and discard the fuel meter cover gasket. Remove the large O-ring and steel back-up washer from the top counterbore of the fuel meter body injector cavity.

To install:

8. Install the fuel injector nozzle filter on the nozzle end of the fuel injector, with the larger end of the filter facing the injector, so the filter covers raised rib at the base of the injector.

9. Lubricate the new small O-ring with automatic transmission fluid and push the O-ring on the nozzle end of the injector until it presses against the

injector fuel filter.

10. Install the steel backup washer in the top counterbore of the fuel meter body injector cavity.

11. Lubricate the new large O-ring with automatic transmission fluid and install it directly over the backup washer. Be sure the O-ring is seated properly in the cavity and is flush with the top of the fuel meter body casting surface.

12. Install the injector into the cavity, aligning the raised lug on the injector base with cast-in notch in the fuel meter body cavity. Push down on the injector until it is fully seated in the cavity. The electrical terminals of the injector will be approximately parallel to the throttle shaft.

13. Install a new dust seal into the recess on the fuel meter body.

14. Install a new fuel outlet passage gasket on the fuel meter cover and a new cover gasket on the fuel meter body.

15. Install the fuel meter cover, making sure the pressure regulator dust seal and cover gaskets are in place; then, apply a thread locking compound to the threads on the fuel meter cover attaching screws. Install the fuel meter cover attaching screws and lock washers and torque to 28 inch lbs. (3 Nm). The 2 short screws go to the front of the injector. Connect battery negative cable.

Multi-Port Fuel Injection

NOTE: Always support the fuel rail to avoid damaging other components while removing the injectors.

1. Relieve fuel system pressure. Disconnect the negative battery cable.

2. Remove the intake manifold plenum.

3. Remove the fuel rail.

4. Remove the injector retaining clips and remove the injectors.

5. Remove the injector O-ring seals from both ends of the injector and discard.

To install:

6. Lubricate the new injector seals with clean engine oil and install on the injectors.

7. Install new injector retaining clips on the injectors. Position the open end of the clip facing the injector electrical connector.

8. Install the injectors into the fuel rail assembly. Push in far enough to engage the retainer clip with the machined slots on the injector socket.

9. Install the fuel rail assembly and intake manifold plenum.

10. Complete installation by reversing the removal procedure. Connect battery negative cable.

EMISSION CONTROLS

Please refer to "Emission Control" in the Unit Repair section for system maintenance procedures. Due to the complex nature of modern electronic engine control systems, comprehensive diagnosis and testing procedures fall outside the confines of this repair manual. For complete information on diagnosis, testing and repair procedures concerning all modern engine and emission control systems, please refer to "Chilton's Guide to Electronic Engine Controls".

Emission Warning Lamps

RESETTING

1989–91 Ciera

Vehicles equipped with an engine oil life index display as a part of the Driver Information System (DIS), have a display that will show when to change the engine oil.

The oil change interval is determined by the driver information system and will usually fall at or between the 2 recommended alternative intervals of 3000 miles and 7500 miles but it could be shorter than 3000 miles under some severe driving conditions. The driver information system will also signal the need for an oil change at 7500 miles or one year passed since the last oil change. If the drive information system does not indicate the need for an oil change after 7500 miles or one year if the engine oil life index display fails to appear, the oil should be changed and the driver information system serviced.

When the engine oil life index reaches 10 percent or less, the change oil light display will function as a reserve trip odometer, indicating the distance to an oil change. Until the engine oil lift index reset is performed, the driver information system will display the distance to the oil change and sound a beep when the ignition switch is turned to the ACCESSORY or RUN position the first time each day.

When the distance to the next oil change reaches 0, the driver information system will display the change oil now light. Until an engine oil life index reset is performed the the driver information system will display the change oil now light and sound a beep when

the ignition switch is turned to the ACCESSORY or RUN position the first time each day.

The driver information system will not detect dusty conditions or engine malfunctions which may affect the engine oil. So if driving in severe conditions exists, be sure to change the engine oil every 3000 miles or 3 months which ever comes first, unless instructed otherwise by the drive information system. The driver information center does not measure the engine oil level, it will remain the owner's responsibility to check the engine oil level. After the oil has been changed, the engine oil life index light must be reset. Reset the can be accomplished as follows:

a. The engine oil life index can be reset by pressing the RESET and OIL buttons simultaneously for at least 5 seconds while on the engine oil life index display. The driver information system will reset the engine oil life index to 100 percent and display a engine oil life index of 100 percent.

b. Oil life index 100 message appears.

NOTE: The Engine Oil Life Index is stored on a non-volatile memory chip and will not reset by disconnecting the battery and or fuse.

1987–91 6000

The Servive Reminder section of the Driver Information Center (DIC) display shows how many miles remain until service is needed. When the reset button is pressed twice, a type of service is needed, and the No. of miles remaining until the service is needed will be displayed. Each time the Reset button is pressed, another type of service and the mile remaining for it will be displayed.

With the ignition switch in the Run, Bulb, Test or Start positions, voltage is applied from the ECM fuse through the Pink/Black wire to the ECM. As the moves, the speed sensor sends electrical pulses (signals) to the ECM. The ECM then sends a signal to the speed signal input of the DIC module. The DIC module converts these pulses (signals) into miles. The module subtracts the miles travelled from the distance remaining for each item of the service reminder.

When the miles remaining for a service approaches 0, that service will be displayed on the DIC display. All 4 types of service can be shown at the same tume.

SERVICE REMINDER RESET

To reset the service light, it will be nec-

essary to subtract the mileage from the service interval light that is illuminated. The miles remaining for a certain type of service can be decreased by holding the Reset button. The miles remaining will be decreased in steps of 500 miles every 5 seconds. In the first step, the miles will decrease to a multiple of 500. For example, 2880 miles will decrease to 2500 miles. If the Reset button is held in and the miles remaining reach 0, the DIS display will show the service interval for the service selected. The service intervals are as follows:

1. Change oil – 7500 miles
2. Oil filter change – 7500 miles
3. Next filter change – 15,000 miles
4. Rotate tires – 7500 miles
5. Next tire rotation – 15,000 miles
6. Tune Up – 30,000 miles

If the Reset button is still held down, the miles will decrease in steps of 500 miles from the service interval. When the Reset button is released, the mile display shown will be the new distance until the service should be performed.

When a service distance reaches 0, the service reminder item will be displayed. If the service interval is reset within 10 miles, the display will go out immediately. If more than 10 miles passes before the service interval is reset, the item will remain displayed for another 10 miles after being reset before going out.

NOTE: On some models it may be necessary to depress the system Recall button, in order to display the service interval light on the driver information center in order to decrease the mileage from it, so as to reset the interval light.

ENGINE MECHANICAL

NOTE: Disconnecting the negative battery cable on some vehicles may interfere with the functions of the on board computer systems and may require the computer to undergo a relearning process, once the negative battery cable is reconnected.

Engine Assembly

REMOVAL & INSTALLATION

2.5L Engine

WITH MANUAL TRANSAXLE

1. Relieve the fuel system pressure.

Disconnect the negative battery cable.

2. Scribe reference marks at the hood supports and remove the hood. Install covers on both fenders.

3. Raise and support the vehicle safely. Remove front mount-to-cradle nuts.

4. Remove forward exhaust pipe.

5. Remove starter assembly.

6. Remove flywheel inspection cover.

7. Lower the vehicle.

8. Remove the air cleaner assembly.

9. Remove all bellhousing retaining bolts.

10. Remove forward torque reaction rod from engine and core support.

11. If equipped with air conditioning, remove the air conditioning belt and compressor and position to the side.

12. Remove emission hoses at canister.

13. Remove power steering hose, if equipped.

14. Remove vacuum hoses and electrical connectors at solenoid.

15. Remove heater blower motor.

16. Disconnect throttle cable.

17. Drain cooling system.

18. Disconnect heater hose.

19. Disconnect engine harness at bulkhead connector.

20. Install an engine lift support tool and partially hoist the engine. Remove heater hose at intake manifold and disconnect fuel line.

21. Completely remove the engine from the vehicle.

To install:

22. Partially lower the engine into the vehicle. Connect the heater hose and fuel line.

23. Lower the engine completely and install the 4 upper bell housing retaining bolts.

24. Raise and support the vehicle safely.

25. Install the 2 lower bell housing retaining bolts.

26. Install the front mount-to-cradle nuts.

27. Install the starter assembly and flywheel inspection cover.

28. Install the exhaust pipe and lower the vehicle.

29. Complete installation by reversing the removal procedure.

30. After the engine has been completely installed. Fill the cooling system, connect the negative battery cable, start the engine and check for leaks.

WITH AUTOMATIC TRANSAXLE

1. Relieve the fuel system pressure. Disconnect the negative battery cable.

2. Scribe reference marks at the hood supports and remove the hood. Install covers on both fenders.

3. Drain the cooling system. Re-

move the air cleaner assembly and pre-heat tube.

4. Disconnect engine harness connector.

5. Disconnect all external vacuum hose connections.

6. Remove throttle and transaxle linkage at TBI assembly and intake manifold.

7. Remove upper radiator hose.

8. If equipped with air conditioning, remove the air conditioning compressor from mounting brackets and set aside. Do not discharge the air conditioning system.

9. Remove front engine strut assembly.

10. Disconnect heater hoses.

11. Raise the vehicle and support it safely. Remove transaxle to engine bolts leaving the upper 2 bolts in place.

12. Remove front mount-to-cradle nuts.

13. Remove forward exhaust pipe.

14. Remove flywheel inspection cover and remove starter motor.

15. Remove torque converter to flywheel bolts.

16. Remove power steering pump and bracket with hoses attached and set aside.

17. Remove lower radiator hose.

18. Remove the 2 rear transaxle support bracket bolts.

19. Remove fuel supply line at fuel filter.

20. Using a floor jack and a block of wood placed under the transaxle, raise engine and transaxle until engine front mount studs clear cradle.

21. Connect engine lift equipment and put tension on engine.

22. Remove the 2 remaining transaxle bolts.

23. Slide engine forward and remove from the vehicle.

To install:

24. Position the engine inside the vehicle aligning with the transaxle bell housing.

25. With the engine supported by the lifting tool, install the 2 upper bell housing bolts. Do not lower the engine while the jack is supporting the transaxle.

26. Remove the transaxle support jack and lower the engine onto the engine mounts. Remove the engine lift tool.

27. Raise the vehicle and install the front mount-to-chassis nuts.

28. Complete installation by reversing the removal procedure. After the engine has been completely installed. Fill the cooling system, connect the negative battery cable, start the engine and check for leaks.

2.8L and 3.1L Engines

1. Relieve the fuel system pressure.

2. Disconnect the negative battery cable. Scribe reference marks at the hood supports and remove the hood. Install covers on both fenders.

3. Remove the airflow tube at the air cleaner and throttle valve.

4. Drain the cooling system.

5. Disconnect vacuum hoses from all non-engine mounted components.

6. Disconnect the accelerator linkage and TV cable. Disconnect the cruise control cable, if equipped.

7. Disconnect the engine harness connector from the ECM and pull the connector through the front of dash. Disconnect the engine harness from the junction block at the dash panel.

8. Remove the engine strut bracket from the radiator support and position aside, as required.

9. Disconnect the radiator hoses from radiator and heater hoses from engine. Disconnect and plug the transaxle cooler lines.

10. Remove the serpentine belt cover and belt.

11. On vehicles with the air conditioning compressor mounted on the upper portion of the engine, remove the AIR pump and bracket. Then, remove the air conditioning compressor from the mounting bracket and position aside.

12. If equipped, remove power steering pump from engine and set it aside.

13. Disconnect and plug the fuel lines.

14. Disconnect the EGR at the exhaust, as required.

15. Raise and support the vehicle safely.

16. On vehicles with the air conditioning compressor mounted on the lower portion of the engine, remove the air conditioning compressor from the engine. Do not discharge the air conditioning system.

17. Remove the engine front mount-to-cradle and mount-to-engine bracket retaining nuts, as required.

18. Disconnect and tag all electrical wiring at the starter. Remove the starter retaining bolts and remove the starter.

19. If equipped with automatic transaxle, remove the transaxle inspection cover and disconnect the torque converter from the flexplate.

20. Disconnect the exhaust pipe.

21. Remove the 1 transaxle-to-engine bolt from the back side of the engine.

22. Disconnect the power steering cut-off switch, if equipped.

23. Lower the vehicle.

24. Remove the exhaust crossover pipe.

25. Remove the remaining transaxle-to-engine bolts.

26. Support the transaxle by positioning a floor jack and a block of wood

under the transaxle. Install an engine lift tool and remove the engine from the vehicle.

To install:

27. Position the engine in the vehicle while aligning the transaxle. Install the transaxle-to-engine bolts. Torque the attaching bolts to 55 ft. lbs. (75 Nm).

28. Position the front engine mount studs in the cradle and engine bracket.

29. Remove the engine lift tool. Raise and support the vehicle safely.

30. Install the engine mount retaining nuts.

31. Complete installation by reversing the removal procedure. After the engine has been completely installed. Fill the cooling system, connect the negative battery cable, start the engine and check for leaks.

3.3L Engine

1. Disconnect the negative battery cable. Scribe reference marks at the hood supports and remove the hood. Install covers on both fenders.

2. Relieve the fuel system pressure.

3. Disconnect the negative battery cable.

4. Drain the cooling system. Disconnect the radiator and heater hoses. Disconnect and plug the transaxle cooler lines.

5. Remove the upper engine strut and engine cooling fan.

6. Remove the intake duct from the throttle body. Disconnect vacuum hoses from all non-engine mounted components. Disconnect all electrical connections.

7. Remove the cable bracket and cables from the throttle body.

8. Remove the serpentine belt. Remove the power steering pump and locate to the side.

9. Remove the upper transaxle to engine retaining bolts.

10. Raise and support the vehicle safely.

11. Remove the air conditioning compressor and locate to the side.

12. Remove the engine mount to frame nuts, flywheel dust cover and flywheel to converter bolts.

13. Remove the lower engine to transaxle bolts; 1 bolt is located behind the transaxle case and engine block.

14. Lower the vehicle. Install an engine lift tool and remove the engine from the vehicle.

To install:

15. Installation is the reverse of the removal procedure. After the engine has been completely installed. Fill the cooling system, connect the negative battery cable, start the engine and check for leaks.

3.8L Engine

1. Disconnect the negative battery cable. Scribe reference marks at the hood supports and remove the hood. Install covers on both fenders.

2. Remove the air cleaner assembly and drain the cooling system.

3. Disconnect vacuum hoses to all non-engine mounted components.

4. Disconnect the detent cable and accelerator linkage.

5. Disconnect the engine electrical harness and ground strap.

6. Disconnect the heater hoses from the engine and radiator hoses from the radiator. Disconnect the transaxle cooler lines, if equipped.

7. Remove the power steering pump and bracket assembly.

8. Raise and support the vehicle safely.

9. Disconnect the exhaust pipe from the manifold.

10. Disconnect the fuel lines.

11. Remove the engine front mount to cradle retaining nuts.

12. Disconnect and tag all electrical wiring at the starter. Remove the starter retaining bolts and remove the starter.

13. If equipped with automatic transaxle, remove the flexplate cover and disconnect the flexplate from the torque converter.

14. Remove the retaining bolts from the transaxle rear support bracket.

15. Lower the vehicle and place a support under the transaxle rear extension.

16. Remove the engine strut bracket from the radiator support and position aside.

17. Remove the transaxle-to-engine retaining bolts.

18. If equipped with air conditioning, remove the air conditioning compressor from the mounting bracket and lay aside.

19. Install an engine lift tool and remove the engine from the vehicle.

To install:

20. Position the engine in the vehicle and align the engine front mount studs. Align the transaxle and install the transaxle-to-engine retaining bolts.

21. Remove the engine lift tool.

22. Install the air conditioning compressor on the mounting bracket, as required.

23. Raise the vehicle. Install the retaining bolts to the transaxle rear support bracket.

24. Complete installation by reversing the removal procedure. After the engine has been completely installed. Fill the cooling system, connect the negative battery cable, start the engine and check for leaks.

Engine Mounts

REMOVAL & INSTALLATION

1. Disconnect the negative battery cable.

2. Raise and support the vehicle safely.

3. Using a suitable tool, support the engine and remove the engine mounting bracket nuts.

4. Raise the engine slightly until the engine mount is free from the vehicle chassis.

5. Remove the nuts holding the engine mount to the frame.

6. Remove the engine mounts and discard.

7. Installation is the reverse of the removal procedure. Connect the battery negative cable.

Cylinder Head

REMOVAL & INSTALLATION

2.5L Engine

1. Relieve the pressure in the fuel system before disconnecting any fuel line connections.

2. Disconnect the negative battery cable.

3. Drain the cooling system. Remove the air cleaner and the oil level indicator tube.

4. Disconnect the throttle linkage and fuel lines.

5. Disconnect the oxygen sensor connector. Remove the intake and exhaust manifolds.

6. Remove the alternator bracket to cylinder head bolts, as required.

7. If equipped with air conditioning, remove the compressor bracket bolts and position the compressor aside. Do not disconnect any of the refrigerant lines.

8. Disconnect and tag all vacuum and electrical connections from the cylinder head.

9. Disconnect the radiator hoses and engine strut rod bolt from the upper support.

10. Remove the power steering pump bracket, if top mounted.

11. Remove the rocker arm cover, rocker arms, and pushrods.

12. Remove the cylinder head bolts and remove the cylinder head from the engine.

To install:

13. Clean the cylinder head and block from any foreign matter, nicks or heavy scratches. Clean the cylinder head bolt threads and threads in the cylinder block.

14. Position the new cylinder head gasket over the dowel pins.

15. Carefully guide the cylinder head

into place. Coat the cylinder head bolts with sealing compound and install finger tight.

16. Torque the cylinder head bolts as follows:

 a. Torque the cylinder head bolts gradually to 25 ft. lbs. in the proper sequence.

 b. Torque all bolts except No. 9 in sequence again to 22 ft. lbs. Torque No. 9 to 29 ft. lbs.

 c. Repeat sequence. Turn all bolts, except No. 9, 120 degrees (2 flats). Turn No. 9 a ¼ turn (90 degrees).

17. Complete installation by reversing the removal procedure. Refill system and connect battery negative cable.

2.8L and 3.1L Engines

LEFT SIDE

1. Relieve the pressure in the fuel system before disconnecting any fuel line connections.

2. Disconnect the negative battery cable. Raise the vehicle and support it safely.

3. Drain the cylinder block and lower the vehicle.

4. Remove the oil level indicator tube, rocker arm cover, intake manifold and plenum, as required.

5. Remove the exhaust crossover, generator bracket, AIR pump and brackets.

6. Disconnect and tag all electrical wiring and vacuum hoses that may interfere with the removal of the left cylinder head.

7. Loosen the rocker arm until the pushrods can be removed. Remove the pushrods. Keep the pushrods in the same order as removed.

8. Remove the cylinder head bolts. Remove the cylinder head. Do not pry on the head to loosen it.

To install:

9. Clean the cylinder head and block from any foreign matter, nicks or heavy scratches. Clean the cylinder head bolt threads and threads in the cylinder block.

10. Position the new cylinder head gasket over the dowel pins with the words "This Side Up" facing upwards. Carefully guide the cylinder head into place.

11. Install the pushrods. Make sure the lower ends of the pushrods are in the lifter seats. Install the rocker arm nuts and torque the nuts to 14–20 ft. lbs. (20–27 Nm).

12. Install the intake manifold.

13. Complete installation by reversing the removal procedure. Refill system and connect battery negative cable.

14. Adjust the valve lash, as required.

RIGHT SIDE

1. Relieve the pressure in the fuel system before disconnecting any fuel line connections.

2. Disconnect the negative battery cable. Raise the vehicle and support it safely.

3. Drain the cylinder block and lower the vehicle.

4. If equipped, remove the cruise control servo bracket, the air management valve and hose and the intake manifold.

5. Remove the exhaust pipe at crossover, crossover and heat shield, as required.

6. Disconnect and tag all electrical wiring and vacuum hoses that may interfere with the removal of the right cylinder head.

7. Remove the rocker cover. Loosen the rocker arm nuts and remove the pushrods. Keep the pushrods in the order in which they were removed.

8. Remove the cylinder head bolts. Remove the cylinder head. Do not pry on the head to loosen it.

To install:

9. Clean the cylinder head and block from any foreign matter, nicks or heavy scratches. Clean the cylinder head bolt threads and threads in the cylinder block.

10. Position the new cylinder head gasket over the dowel pins with the words "This Side Up" facing upwards. Carefully guide the cylinder head into place. Install the pushrods and loosely retain with the rocker arms.

11. Install the pushrods. Make sure the lower ends of the pushrods are in the lifter seats. Install the rocker arm nuts and torque the nuts to 14–20 ft. lbs. (20–27 Nm).

12. Install the intake manifold.

13. Complete installation by reversing the removal procedure. Connect battery negative cable and refill system.

14. Adjust the valve lash, as required.

3.3L Engine

1. Relieve the pressure in the fuel system before disconnecting any fuel line connections.

2. Disconnect the negative battery cable. Raise the vehicle and support it safely.

3. Drain the cylinder block and lower the vehicle.

4. Remove the intake manifold and exhaust manifold.

5. Remove the valve cover.

6. Remove the ignition module and coils as a unit.

7. Disconnect and tag all electrical wiring and vacuum hoses, as necessary.

8. If equipped with air conditioning, remove the air conditioning compressor and position to the side.

9. Remove the alternator and power steering pump and position to the side. Remove the belt tensioner assembly.

10. Remove the rocker arm assembly, guide plate and pushrods.

11. Remove the cylinder head bolts and remove the cylinder head.

To install:

12. Clean the cylinder head and block from any foreign matter, nicks or heavy scratches. Clean the cylinder head bolt threads and threads in the cylinder block.

13. Position the new cylinder head gasket on the block.

14. Carefully guide the cylinder head into place. Coat the cylinder head bolts with sealing compound. Gradually tighten the cylinder head bolts 3 times around in the proper sequence to specifications.

15. Install the pushrods, guide plate

1. Apply sealing compound No. 102080 or equivalent to bolts shown

2. Mounting surfaces of block assy., head assy. and both sides of gasket must be free of oil.

3. Locating pins

NUMBERS SHOWN DESIGNATE BOLT POSITIONS AND BOLT TIGHTENING SEQUENCE.

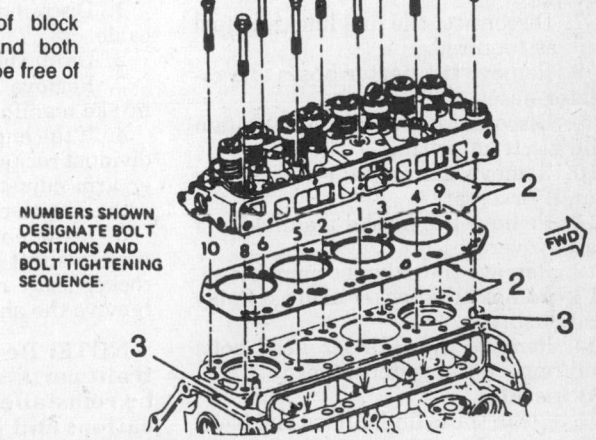

Cylinder head torque sequence—2.5L engine

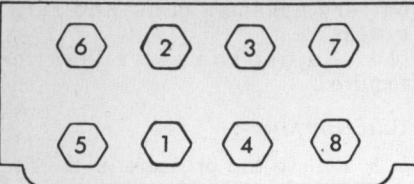

Cylinder head torque sequence— 2.8L and 3.1L engines

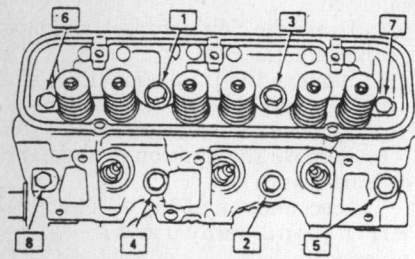

Cylinder head torque sequence— 3.3L and 3.8L engines

and rocker arm assembly. Tighten the rocker arm pivot bolts to 28 ft. lbs. (38 Nm).

16. Complete installation by reversing the removal procedure. Connecxt battery negative cable and refill system.

3.8L Engine

1. Relieve the pressure in the fuel system before disconnecting any fuel line connections.

2. Disconnect the negative battery cable. Raise the vehicle and support it safely.

3. Drain the cylinder block and lower the vehicle.

4. Remove the accessory drive belt(s).

5. Remove the alternator, AIR pump, oil indicator and power steering pump, as required. Position to the side.

6. Remove the throttle cable. Remove the cruise control cable, if equipped.

7. Disconnect the fuel lines and fuel rail, as required.

8. Remove the heater hoses and radiator hoses.

9. Disconnect and tag all vacuum and electrical wiring.

10. Remove the radiator and cooling fan, if necessary.

11. Remove the intake manifold and valve cover.

12. Remove the exhaust manifold(s).

13. Remove the rocker arm assembly and pushrods.

14. Remove the cylinder head bolts and remove the cylinder head.

To install:

15. Clean the cylinder head and block from any foreign matter, nicks or

heavy scratches. Clean the cylinder head bolt threads and threads in the cylinder block.

16. Position the new cylinder head gasket on the block.

NOTE: When using steel gaskets, use sealer part number 1050026 or equivalent on the gaskets.

17. Carefully guide the cylinder head into place. Coat the cylinder head bolts with sealing compound and install. Gradually tighten the cylinder head bolts 3 times around in the proper sequence to specifications.

18. Install the exhaust manifold.

19. Install the pushrods, rocker arm assembly and intake manifold.

20. Complete installation by reversing the removal procedure.

Valve Lifters

REMOVAL & INSTALLATION

2.5L Engine

1. Disconnect the negative battery cable.

2. Remove the intake manifold and valve cover.

3. Loosen the rocker arms and rotate to clear the pushrods.

4. Remove the pushrods, retainer and guide.

5. Remove the lifters. Keep all components separated so they may be reinstalled in the same location.

To install:

6. Lubricate the lifters with engine oil and install the lifters in their bore.

7. Install the guides, retainers and pushrods.

8. With the lifter on the base circle of the camshaft, tighten the rocker arm bolts to 24 ft. lbs. (32 Nm).

9. Complete installation by reversing the removal procedure. Connect battery negative cable.

Except 2.5L Engine

1. Disconnect the negative battery cable.

2. Drain the cooling system.

3. Remove the valve cover and the intake manifold.

4. If the engine is equipped with individual rocker arms, loosen the rocker arm adjusting nut and rotate the arm so as to clear the pushrod.

5. If the engine is equipped with a rocker shaft assembly, remove the rocker shaft retaining bolts/nuts and remove the shaft assembly.

NOTE: Be sure to keep all valve train parts in order so they may be reinstalled in their original locations and with the same mating surfaces as when removed.

6. Remove the pushrods and valve lifters using tool J3049 or equivalent.

7. Installation is the reverse of the removal procedure. Lubricate the bearing surfaces with Molykote® or its equivalent. Adjust the valves, as required. Connect battery negative cable.

Valve Lash

ADJUSTMENT

Except 2.8L Engine

Hydraulic valve lifter keep all parts of the valve train in constant contact and adjust automatically to maintain zero lash under all conditions.

2.8L Engine

Anytime the valve train has been disturbed, the valve lash must be readjusted.

1. Crank the engine until the timing mark on the damper aligns with the **0** mark on the timing scale. Both valves in the No. 1 cylinder should be closed. If the valves are moving as the timing marks align, the engine is in the No. 4 firing position. Turn the crankshaft one more revolution. With the engine in the No. 1 firing position, adjust the following valves: exhaust— 1, 2, 3 and intake—1, 5, 6.

2. Back out the adjusting nut until lash is felt at the pushrod. Then, turn in the adjusting nut until all lash is removed. This can be determine by rotating the pushrod while turning the adjusting nut. When all lash has been removed, turn the adjusting nut in 1½ additional turns to center the lifter plunger.

3. Rotate the crankshaft one full revolution, until the timing mark on the damper aligns with the **0** mark on the timing scale once again. This is the No. 4 firing position. Adjust the following valves: exhaust—4, 5, 6 and intake—2, 3, 4.

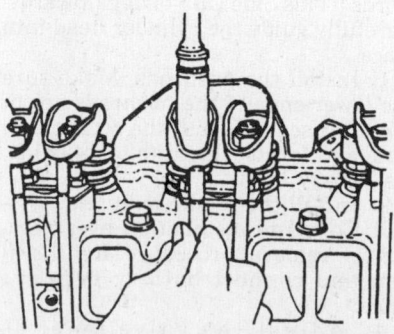

Adjusting valve lash—2.8L engine

Rocker Arms/Shafts

REMOVAL & INSTALLATION

2.5L Engine

1. Relieve pressure in the fuel system before disconnecting any fuel lines.
2. Disconnect the negative battery cable.
3. Remove the valve cover.
4. If only the pushrod is being removed, loosen the rocker arm bolt and swing the rocker arm aside.
5. Remove the rocker arm nut and ball.
6. Lift the rocker arm off the stud, keeping rocker arms in order for installation.
7. Installation is the reverse of the removal procedure. Connect battery negative cable.

2.8L and 3.1L Engines

1. Relieve pressure in the fuel system before disconnecting any fuel lines.
2. Disconnect the negative battery cable. Remove the valve covers.
3. Remove the rocker arm nuts, pivot balls, rocker arms and pushrods. Keep all components separated so they may be reinstalled in the same location.

NOTE: The intake and exhaust pushrods are of different lengths.

To install:

4. Install the pushrods in their original location. Be sure they are seated in the lifter.
5. Coat the bearing surfaces of the rocker arms and pivots balls with Molykote or equivalent.
6. If equipped with adjustable lifters, install the rocker arms and pivot balls. Loosely retain with the rocker arms nuts until the valve lash is eliminated.
7. If equipped with non-adjustable lifters, install the pushrods. Make sure the lower ends of the pushrods are in the lifter seats. Install the rocker arm nuts and torque the nuts to 14–20 ft. lbs. (20–27 Nm).
8. Complete installation by reversing the removal procedure. Connect battery negative cable.
9. Adjust valve lash, as required.

3.3L Engine

1. Relieve pressure in the fuel system before disconnecting any fuel lines. Disconnect the negative battery cable.
2. Remove the valve covers.
3. Remove the rocker arm bolts, pivots, and rocker arms assembly.

Keep all components separated so they may be reinstalled in the same location.

4. Installation is the reverse of the removal procedure. Connect battery negative cable.

3.8L Engine

1. Relieve pressure in the fuel system before disconnecting any fuel lines.
2. Disconnect the negative battery cable. Remove the valve covers.
3. Remove the rocker arm shaft(s). Place the shaft on a clean surface.
4. Remove the nylon rocker arm retainers. A pair of slip joint pliers is good for this.
5. Slide the rocker arms off the shaft and inspect them for wear or damage. Keep them in order.

NOTE: If it become necessary to replace 1 or more rocker arms, it must be noted that all service rocker arms are stamped R for right and L for left. Be sure the rocker arms are installed on the rocker arm shaft in the correct sequence.

6. Installation is the reverse of the removal procedure. Connect battery negative cable.

Intake Manifold

REMOVAL & INSTALLATION

2.5L Engine

1. Relieve the pressure in the fuel system before disconnecting any fuel line connections.
2. Disconnect the negative battery cable.
3. Remove the air cleaner and the PCV valve.
4. Drain the cooling system into a clean container.
5. Disconnect the fuel and vacuum lines and the electrical connections.
6. Disconnect the throttle linkage at the EFI unit. Disconnect the transaxle downshift linkage and cruise control linkage.
7. Remove the bell crank and the throttle linkage. Position to the side for clearance.
8. Remove the heater hose at the intake manifold.
9. Remove the pulse air check valve bracket from the manifold, as required.
10. Remove the manifold attaching bolts and remove the manifold.
To install:
11. Clean the cylinder head and intake manifold surfaces from any foreign matter, nicks or heavy scratches.
12. Install the intake manifold with a

new gasket and tighten the retaining bolts in sequence to the specified torque value.
13. Complete installation by reversing the removal procedure. Connect battery negative cable.

2.8L and 3.1L Engines

1. Relieve the pressure in the fuel system before disconnecting any fuel line connections.
2. Disconnect the negative battery cable.
3. Disconnect the accelerator and TV cable bracket at the plenum.
4. Disconnect the throttle body at the plenum.
5. Disconnect the EGR valve at the plenum.
6. Remove the plenum.
7. Disconnect the fuel inlet and return pipes at the fuel rail.
8. Remove the serpentine belt.
9. Disconnect the power steering pump and lay it aside.
10. Disconnect the generator and lay it aside.
11. Loosen the generator bracket.
12. Disconnect the idle air vacuum hose at the throttle body.
13. Disconnect the wires at the injectors.
14. Disconnect the fuel rail.
15. Remove the breather tube.
16. Remove both rocker covers.
17. Drain the cooling system.
18. Disconnect the radiator hose at the thermostat housing.
19. Disconnect the wires at the coolant sensor and the oil sending switch.
20. Remove the coolant sensor.
21. Disconnect the bypass hose at the fill neck and head.
22. Loosen the rocker arms and remove the pushrods.
23. Remove the intake manifold bolts and remove the intake manifold.
To install:
24. Place a $\frac{3}{16}$ in. (5mm) diameter bead GM sealer part 1052917 or equvalent, on each ridge.
25. Position a new intake manifold gasket.
26. Install the pushrods and tighten the rocker arm nuts to 14–20 ft. lbs.
27. Install the intake manifold and torque the bolts to specifications.
28. Complete installation by reversing the removal procedure. Adjust the valve, as required. Connect battery negative cable.

3.3L Engine

1. Relieve the pressure in the fuel system before disconnecting any fuel line connections.
2. Disconnect the negative battery cable.
3. Drain the cooling system.
4. Remove the serpentine belt, al-

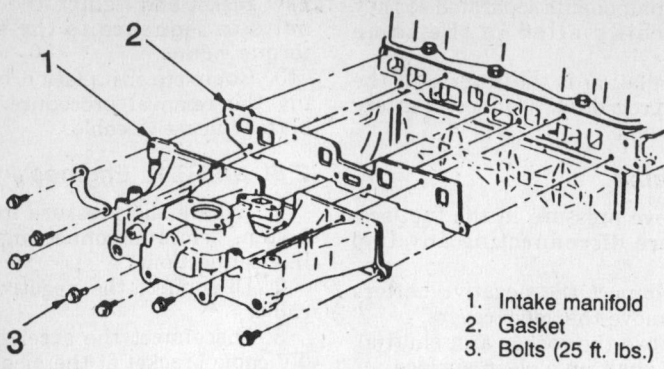

1. Intake manifold
2. Gasket
3. Bolts (25 ft. lbs.)

Intake manifold assembly—2.5L engine

ternator and braces and power steering pump braces.

5. Remove the coolant bypass hose, heater pipe and upper radiator hose.

6. Remove the air inlet duct, throttle cable bracket and cables.

7. Disconnect and tag all vacuum hoses and electrical connectors, as necessary.

8. Remove the fuel rail, vapor canister purge line and heater hose from the throttle body.

9. Remove the intake manifold retaining bolts and intake manifold.

To install:

10. Clean the cylinder head and intake manifold surfaces from any foreign matter, nicks or heavy scratches.

11. Apply sealer part number 12345336 or equivalent, to the ends of the manifold seals. Clean the intake manifold bolts and bolt holes. Apply thread lock compound part number

1052624 or equivalent, to the intake manifold bolt threads before assembly.

12. Install the new gasket and intake manifold. Tighten the intake manifold bolts twice to 88 inch lbs. (10 Nm) in the proper sequence.

13. Complete installation by reversing the removal procedure. Connect battery negative cable.

3.8L Engine

1. Relieve the pressure in the fuel system before disconnecting any fuel line connections.

2. Disconnect the negative battery cable.

3. Remove the mass air flow sensor and air intake duct.

4. Remove the serpentine accessory drive belt, alternator and bracket.

5. Remove the ignition coil module, TV cable, throttle cable and cruise control cable.

6. Disconnect and tag all vacuum hoses and electrical wiring, as necessary.

7. Drain the cooling system. Remove the heater hoses from the throttle body and upper radiator hose.

8. Disconnect the fuel lines from the fuel rail and injectors.

9. Remove the intake manifold retaining bolts and remove the intake manifold and gasket.

To install:

10. Clean the cylinder head and intake manifold surfaces from any foreign matter, nicks or heavy scratches.

11. Install the intake manifold gasket and rubber seals. Apply sealer part number 1050026 or equivalent, on the gasket. Apply sealer/lubricant part number 1052080 or equivalent, to all pipe thread fitting.

12. Carefully install the intake manifold to cylinder block. Install the intake manifold bolts and torque in sequence to the specified value.

13. Complete installation by reversing the removal procedure.

Exhaust Manifold

REMOVAL & INSTALLATION

2.5L Engine

1. Disconnect the negative battery cable. Remove the air cleaner and the TBI preheat tube.

2. Remove the manifold strut bolts from the radiator support panel and the cylinder head.

3. Remove the air conditioning compressor bracket to one side. Do not disconnect any of the refrigerant lines.

4. If necessary, remove the dipstick tube attaching bolt and the engine mount bracket from the cylinder head.

5. Raise the vehicle and support safely. Disconnect the exhaust pipe from the manifold.

6. Remove the manifold attaching bolts and remove the manifold.

7. Install the exhaust manifold and gasket to the cylinder head. Torque all bolts in sequence to the specified torque value.

8. Complete installation by reversing the removal procedure. Connect battery negative cable.

2.8L and 3.1L ENngines

LEFT SIDE

1. Disconnect the negative battery cable.

2. Remove the air supply plumbing from the exhaust manifold, as required.

3. Remove the coolant recovery bottle, if necessary.

4. Remove the serpentine belt cover and belt, as required.

5. Remove the air conditioning compressor and lay aside, if necessary.

6. Remove the right side torque strut, air conditioning and torque strut mounting bracket, as required.

8. Remove the heat shield, if equipped.

9. Remove the exhaust crossover pipe at the manifold.

10. Remove the exhaust manifold retaining bolts and manifold.

1. 16 ft. lbs. (22 Nm)
   Then 23 ft. lbs. (32 Nm)
   Retorque 23 ft. lbs. (32 Nm) in sequence
2. Intake manifold
3. Gasket
4. 24 ft. lbs. (33 Nm)
5. Sealer

Intake manifold assembly—2.8L and 3.1L engines

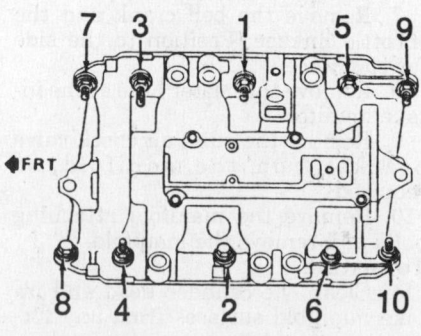

Intake manifold assembly—3.3L engine

11. Installation is the reverse of the removal procedure. Connect battery negative cable.

RIGHT SIDE

1. Disconnect the negative battery cable.
2. Raise and support the vehicle safely.
3. Disconnect the exhaust pipe and lower the vehicle.
4. Remove the air cleaner assembly, breather, mass air flow sensor and heat shield.
5. Remove the crossover at the manifold.
6. Remove the accelerator and TV cables and brackets, as required.
7. Remove the exhaust manifold retaining bolts and remove the manifold.
8. Installation is the reverse of the removal procedure. Connect battery negative cable.

3.3L Engine

LEFT SIDE

1. Disconnect the negative battery cable.
2. Remove the air cleaner inlet ducting. Remove the spark plug wires.
3. Remove the 2 bolts attaching the exhaust crossover pipe to the manifold.
4. Remove the engine lift hook, manifold heat shield and oil level indicator.
5. Remove the exhaust manifold retaining bolts and remove the manifold.
6. Installation is the reverse of the removal procedure.

RIGHT SIDE

1. Disconnect the negative battery cable.
2. Remove the spark plug wires, oxygen sensor connector, throttle cable bracket and cables.
3. Remove the brake booster hose from the manifold.

4. Remove the 2 bolts attaching the exhaust crossover pipe to the manifold.
5. Remove the exhaust pipe to manifold bolts, engine lift hook and transaxle oil level indicator tube.
6. Remove the manifold heat shield. Remove the exhaust manifold retaining bolts and remove the manifold.
7. Installation is the reverse of the removal procedure.

3.8L Engine

LEFT SIDE

1. Disconnect the battery ground.
2. Unbolt and remove the crossover pipe.
3. Remove the upper engine support strut.
4. Unbolt and remove the manifold.
5. Installation is the reverse of the removal procedure.

RIGHT SIDE

1. Disconnect the negative battery cable and remove the pinch bolt at the steering gear intermediate shaft and separate the intermediate shaft from the stub shaft.

NOTE: Failure to disconnect the intermediate shaft from the rack and pinion stub shaft can result in damage to the steering gear and/or intermediate shaft. This damage can cause loss of steering control which could result in a vehicle crash with possible bodily injury.

2. Raise and support the vehicle safely and remove the exhaust pipe from the manifold.
3. Lower the vehicle and remove the upper engine support strut.
4. Place a floor jack under the front crossmember and take up the weight of the vehicle and remove the 2 front body mount bolts along with their cushions and retainers.

5. Remove the cushions from the bolts and thread the bolts and their retainers a minimum of 3 turns into the cradle cage nuts so the bolts serve to hold the cradle and prevent movement.
6. Lower the floor jack so the crossmember contacts the body mount bolt retainers. Check for any hose or wire interference problems.
7. Remove the alternator, disconnect the power steering pump and remove its bracket.
8. Disconnect the manifold from the crossover pipe and remove the exhaust manifold retaining bolts and remove the manifold.
9. Installation is the reverse of the removal procedure. Connect battery negative cable.

Timing Chain Front Cover and Seal

REMOVAL & INSTALLATION

2.5L Engine

1. Relieve the pressure in the fuel system before disconnecting any fuel line connections.
2. Disconnect the negative battery cable.
3. Remove the inner fender splash shield. Remove the crankshaft pulley.
4. Remove the alternator lower bracket and the front engine mounts.
5. Using a floor jack, raise the engine.
6. Remove the engine mount mounting bracket-to-cylinder block bolts. Remove the bracket and mount as an assembly.
7. Remove the oil pan-to-front cover screws and front cover-to-block screws.
8. Pull the cover slightly forward, just enough to allow cutting of the oil pan front seal flush with the block on both sides.
9. Remove the front cover and attached portion of the pan seal.
10. Clean the gasket surfaces thoroughly.
To install:
11. Cut the tabs from the new oil pan front seal.
12. Install the seal on the front cover pressing the tips into the holes provided.
13. Coat the new gasket with sealer and position it on the front cover.
14. Apply a 1/8 in. bead of silicone sealer to the joint formed at the oil pan and stock.
15. Align the front cover seal with a centering tool and install the front cover. Tighten the screws. Install the pulley and connect the battery negative cable.

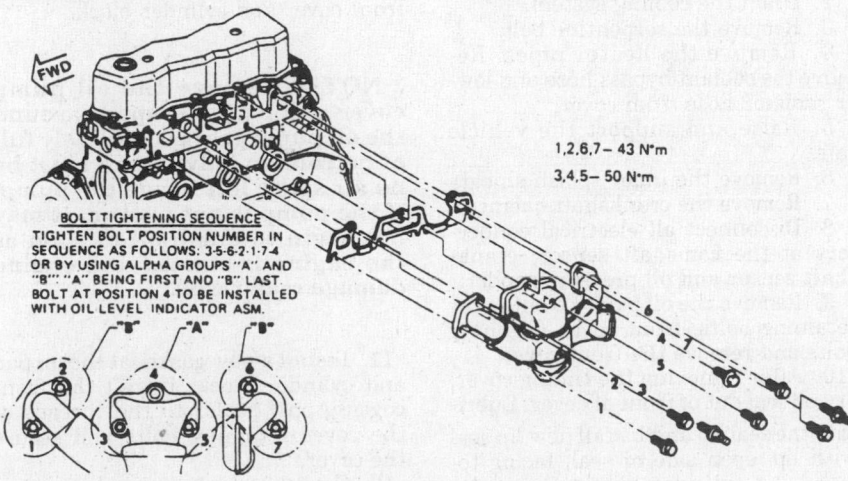

1,2,6,7 – 43 N·m
3,4,5 – 50 N·m

BOLT TIGHTENING SEQUENCE
TIGHTEN BOLT POSITION NUMBER IN SEQUENCE AS FOLLOWS: 3-5-6-2-1-7-4 OR BY USING ALPHA GROUPS "A" AND "B". "A" BEING FIRST AND "B" LAST BOLT AT POSITION 4 TO BE INSTALLED WITH OIL LEVEL INDICATOR ASM.

Exhaust manifold assembly—2.5L engine

2.8L Engine

1987

1. Relieve the pressure in the fuel system before disconnecting any fuel line connections.
2. Disconnect the negative battery cable.
3. Remove the water pump.
4. Remove the compressor without disconnecting any air conditioning lines and lay it aside.
5. Remove harmonic balancer, using a suitable puller.

NOTE: **The outer ring (weight) of the harmonic balancer is bonded to the hub with rubber. The balancer must be removed with a puller which acts on the inner hub only. Pulling on the outer portion of the balancer will break the rubber bond or destroy the tuning of the torsional damper.**

6. Disconnect the lower radiator hose and heater hose.
7. Remove timing gear cover attaching screws, cover and gasket.
8. After removing the timing cover, pry oil seal out of front of cover. Lubricate the seal lip and install new lip seal with lip, open side of seal, facing toward the cylinder block. Carefully drive or press seal into place.

To install:
9. Clean all the gasket mounting surfaces on the front cover and block. Apply a continuous $3/22$ in. bead of sealer No. 1052357 or equivalent, to front cover sealing surface and around coolant passage ports and central bolt holes.
10. Apply a bead of silicone sealer to the oil pan-to-cylinder block joint.
11. Install a centering tool in the crankshaft snout hole in the front cover and install the cover.
12. Install the front cover bolts finger tight, remove the centering tool and tighten the cover bolts.
13. Complete installation by reversing the removal procedure. Connect battery negative cable.

2.8L and 3.1L Engines

1988-91

1. Relieve the pressure in the fuel system before disconnecting any fuel line connections. Disconnect the negative battery cable.
2. Drain the cooling system.
3. Remove the tensioner and serpentine belt.
4. Remove the alternator and power steering pump. Locate and support these accessories to the side.
5. Raise and support the vehicle safely.

6. Remove the inner splash shield. Remove the torsion damper using tool J-24420-B or equivalent.
7. Remove the flywheel cover at the transaxle and starter.
8. Remove the serpentine belt idler pulley.
9. Drain the engine oil. Remove the oil pan and lower front cover bolts.
10. Lower the vehicle.
11. Remove the radiator hose at the water pump. Remove the heater hose at fill pipe.
12. Remove the bypass hose and overflow hoses. Remove the canister purge hose.
13. Remove the upper front cover retaining bolts and remove the front cover.
14. After removing the timing cover, pry oil seal out of front of cover. Lubricate the seal lip and install new lip seal with lip, open side of seal, facing toward the cylinder block. Carefully drive or press seal into place.

To install:
15. Clean the mating surfaces of the front cover and cylinder block.
16. Install a new gasket. Make sure not to damage the sealing surfaces. Apply sealer part number 1052080 or equivalent, to the sealing surface of the front cover.
17. Position the front cover on the engine block and install the upper cover bolt.
18. Raise and support the vehicle safely. Install the oil pan and lower cover bolts.
19. Complete installation by reversing the removal procedure. Connect battery negative cable.

3.3L Engine

1. Relieve the pressure in the fuel system before disconnecting any fuel line connections. Disconnect the negative battery cable.
2. Drain the cooling system.
3. Remove the serpentine belt.
4. Remove the heater pipes. Remove the coolant bypass hose and lower radiator hose from cover.
5. Raise and support the vehicle safely.
6. Remove the inner splash shield.
7. Remove the crankshaft balancer.
8. Disconnect all electrical connectors at the camshaft sensor, crankshaft sensor and oil pressure sender.
9. Remove the oil pan to front cover retaining bolts, front cover retaining bolts and remove the front cover.
10. After removing the timing cover, pry oil seal out of front of cover. Lubricate the seal lip and install new lip seal with lip, open side of seal, facing toward the cylinder block. Carefully drive or press seal into place.

To install:
11. Clean the mating surfaces of the front cover and cylinder block.
12. Install a new gasket on the cylinder block. Install the front cover. Apply sealer to the threads of the cover retaining bolts and secure the cover. Tighten the bolts to 22 ft. lbs. (30 Nm).
13. Install the oil pan to front cover bolts. Tighten the bolts to 88 inch lbs. (10 Nm).
14. Reconnect all electrical connectors. Adjust the crankshaft sensor using tool J-37087 or equivalent.
15. Complete installation by reversing the removal procedure. Connect battery negative cable.

3.8L Engine

1. Relieve the pressure in the fuel system before disconnecting any fuel line connections. Disconnect the negative battery cable.
2. Disconnect the lower radiator hose and the heater hose at the water pump.
3. Remove the 2 nuts from the front engine mount at the cradle and raise the engine using a suitable lifting device.
4. Remove the water pump pulley and all drive belts.
5. Remove the alternator and brackets.
6. Remove the balancer bolt and washer. Using a puller, remove the balancer.
7. Remove the cover-to-block bolts. Remove the 2 oil pan-to-cover bolts.
8. Remove the cover and gasket.
9. After removing the timing cover, pry oil seal out of front of cover. Lubricate the seal lip and install new lip seal with lip, open side of seal, facing toward the cylinder block. Carefully drive or press seal into place.

To install:
10. Clean the mating surfaces of the front cover and cylinder block.

NOTE: **Remove the oil pump cover and pack the space around the oil pump gears completely full of petroleum jelly. There must be no air space left inside the pump. If the pump is not packed, it may not begin to pump oil as soon as the engine is started and engine damage may result.**

11. Install a new gasket at the oil pan and cylinder block. Install the front cover. Apply sealer to the threads of the cover retaining bolts and secure the cover.
12. Complete installation by reversing the removal procedure.

Timing Chain and Sprockets

REMOVAL & INSTALLATION

2.5L Engine

NOTE: The camshaft gear is press fitted on the camshaft. If replacement of the camshaft gear is necessary, the engine must be removed from the vehicle and the camshaft and gear removed from the engine.

1. Relieve the pressure in the fuel system before disconnecting any fuel line connections.
2. Disconnect the negative battery cable.
3. Remove the engine from the vehicle.
4. Remove the camshaft and gear assembly from the engine block.
5. Using an arbor press and adapter, remove the gear from the camshaft. Position the thrust plate to avoid damage by interference with the Woodruff® key as the gear is removed.

To install:
6. Support the camshaft at the back of the front journal in the arbor press using press plate adapters.
7. Position the spacer ring thrust plate over the end of the shaft and Woodruff® key in keyway.
8. Press the gear on the shaft with the bottom against the spacer ring. Measure the end clearance at the thrust plate. Clearance should be within 0.0015–0.0050 in. (0.0381–1.270mm).
9. If the clearance is less than 0.0015 in. (0.0381mm), replace the spacer ring.
10. If more than 0.0050 in. (1.270mm), make certain the gear is seated properly against the spacer. If the clearance is still excessive, replace the thrust plate.
11. Measure the backlash at position outside the 2 retainer plate access holes and at 2 other areas 90 degrees from these holes. If the backlash is not within specifications, replace the camshaft and crankshaft gears.
12. Lubricate the camshaft journals with a high quality engine oil supplement. Install the camshaft and gear into the engine block.
13. Rotate the camshaft and crankshaft so the timing marks on the gear teeth line up. The engine is now in No. 4 cylinder firing position.
14. Install the camshaft thrust plate to block screws and tighten to 90 inch lbs. (10 Nm).
15. Complete installation by reversing the removal procedure. Connect battery negative cable.

2.8L and 3.1L Engines

1. Relieve the pressure in the fuel system before disconnecting any fuel line connections. Disconnect the negative battery cable.
2. Remove the crankcase front cover.
3. Place the No. 1 piston at TDC with the marks on the camshaft and crankshaft sprockets aligned.
4. Remove the camshaft sprocket and chain.

NOTE: If the sprocket does not come off easily, a light blow with a plastic mallet on the lower edge of the sprocket should dislodge the sprocket.

5. Remove the crankshaft sprocket.

To install:
6. Install the crankshaft sprocket. Apply Molykote or equivalent, to the sprocket thrust surface.
7. Hold the sprocket with the chain hanging down and align the marks on the camshaft and crankshaft sprockets.
8. Align the dowel in the camshaft with the dowel hole in the camshaft sprocket.
9. Draw the camshaft sprocket onto the camshaft using the mounting bolts. Tighten the camshaft sprocket mounting bolts to 18 ft. lbs. (25 Nm).
10. Lubricate the timing chain with engine oil. Install the crankcase front cover. Connect battery negative cable.

3.3L Engine

1. Relieve the pressure in the fuel system before disconnecting any fuel line connections. Disconnect the negative battery cable.
2. Remove the crankcase front cover and camshaft thrust bearing.
3. Turn the crankshaft so the timing marks are aligned.
4. Remove the timing chain dampner and camshaft sprocket bolts.
5. Remove the camshaft sprocket and chain. Remove the crankshaft sprocket.

To install:
6. Make sure the crankshaft is positioned so No. 1 piston is at TDC on compression stroke.
7. Rotate the camshaft with the sprocket temporarily installed, so the timing mark is straight down.
8. Assembly the timing chain on the sprockets with the timing marks aligned. Install the timing chain and sprocket.
9. Install the camshaft sprocket bolts. Torque the bolts to 27 ft. lbs. (37 Nm).
10. Install the timing chain dampner and engine front cover. Connect battery negative cable.

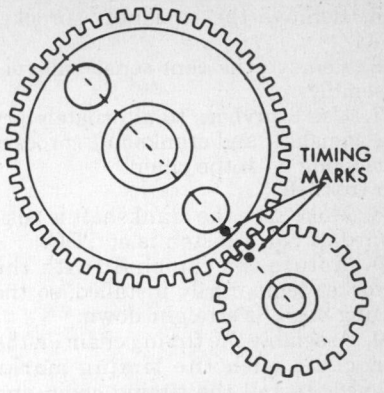

Timing gear alignment—2.5L engine

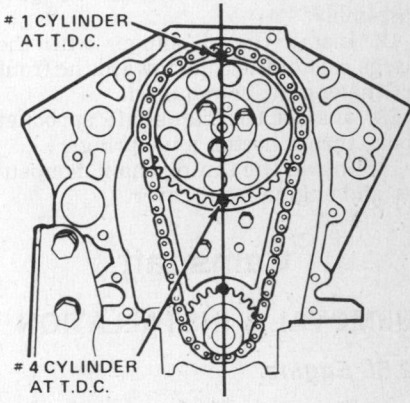

Timing gear alignment—2.8L and 3.1L engines

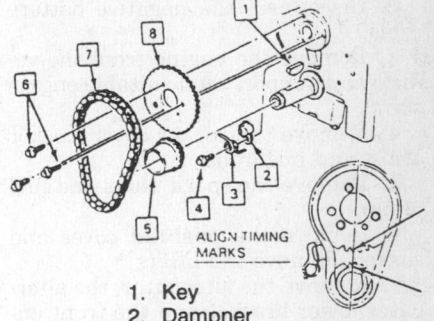

1. Key
2. Dampner
3. Spring
4. Bolt 16 ft. lbs. (22 Nm)
5. Crankshaft sprocket
6. Bolt 26 ft. lbs. (35 Nm)
7. Timing chain
8. Camshaft sprocket

Timing chain and sprockets alignment—3.3L engine

3.8L Engine

1. Relieve the pressure in the fuel system before disconnecting any fuel line connections. Disconnect the negative battery cable.
2. Remove the crankcase front cover.
3. Turn the crankshaft so the timing marks are aligned.
4. Remove the crankshaft oil slinger, as required.

5. Remove the camshaft sprocket bolts.

6. Remove the cam sensor magnet assembly.

7. Use 2 prybars to alternately pry the camshaft and crankshaft sprocket free along with the chain.

To install:

8. Make sure the crankshaft is positioned so No. 1 piston is at TDC.

9. Rotate the camshaft with the sprocket temporarily installed, so the timing mark is straight down.

10. Assembly the timing chain on the sprockets with the timing marks aligned. Install the timing chain and sprocket.

11. Install the cam sensor magnet assembly.

12. Install the oil slinger with the large part of the cone toward the front of the engine, as required.

13. Install the camshaft sprocket bolt, thrust botton and spring.

14. Install the timing chain dampener and engine front cover.

Camshaft

REMOVAL & INSTALLATION

2.5L Engine

1. Relieve the pressure in the fuel system before disconnecting any fuel line connections.

2. Disconnect the negative battery cable.

3. Remove the engine from the vehicle and support on a suitable engine stand.

4. Remove the rocker cover, rocker arms, and pushrods.

5. Remove the spark plugs and fuel pump.

6. Remove the pushrod cover and gasket. Remove the lifters.

7. Remove the alternator, the alternator lower bracket and the front engine mount bracket assembly.

8. Remove the oil pump driveshaft and gear assembly.

9. Remove the crankshaft hub and timing gear cover.

10. Remove the 2 camshaft thrust plate screws by working through the holes in the gear.

11. Remove the camshaft and gear assembly by pulling it through the front of the block. Take care not to damage the bearings.

12. If replacement of the camshaft gear is necessary, use the following procedure:

a. Remove the camshaft gear using an arbor press and adapter.

b. Position the thrust plate to avoid damage by interference with the Woodruff® key as the gear is removed.

c. When assembling the gear onto the camshaft, support the camshaft at the back of the front journal in the arbor press using press plate adapters.

d. Press the gear on the shaft until it bottoms against the spacer ring.

e. Measure the end clearance of the thrust plate. End clearance should be 0.0015–0.0050 in.

f. If clearance is less than 0.0015, replace the spacer ring.

g. If clearance is more than 0.0050, replace the thrust plate.

To install:

13. Lubricate the camshaft journals with a high quality engine oil supplement and carefully install the camshaft and gear into the cylinder block.

14. Rotate the camshaft and crankshaft so the timing marks on the gear theeth line up. The engine is now in No. 4 cylinder firing position.

15. Install the camshaft thrust plate to block screw. Torque the screw to 90 inch lbs. (10 Nm).

16. Complete installation by reversing the removal procedure. Connect battery negative cable.

2.8L, 3.1L and 3.3L Engines

1. Relieve the pressure in the fuel system before disconnecting any fuel line connections.

2. Disconnect the negative battery cable.

3. Remove the engine from the vehicle and support on a suitable engine stand.

4. Remove the intake manifold, valve cover, rocker arms, pushrods and valve lifters.

5. Remove the crankshaft balancer and front cover.

6. Remove the timing chain and sprockets.

7. Carefully remove the camshaft. Avoid marring the camshaft bearing surfaces.

To install:

8. Coat the camshaft with lubricant part number 1052365 or equivalent and install the camshaft.

9. Install the timing chain and sprocket.

10. Install the camshaft thrust button and front cover.

11. Complete installation by reversing the removal procedure. Connect battery negative cable.

12. Adjust the valves, as required.

3.8L Engine

1. Relieve the pressure in the fuel system before disconnecting any fuel line connections.

2. Disconnect the negative battery cable.

3. Remove the engine from the ve-

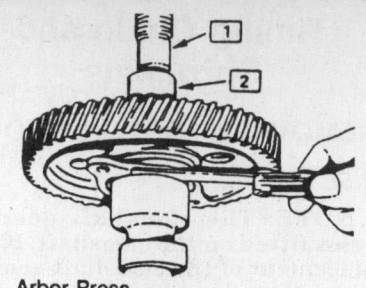

1. Arbor Press
2. Tool J–21474–13 or J– 21795–1

Camshaft timing gear/thrust plate end clearance—2.5L engine

hicle and support on a suitable engine stand.

4. Remove the intake manifold.

5. Remove the rocker arm covers.

6. Remove the rocker arm assemblies, pushrods and lifters.

7. Remove the timing chain cover.

NOTE: Align the timing marks of the camshaft and crankshaft sprockets to avoid burring the camshaft journals by the crankshaft.

8. Remove the timing chain, camshaft sensor magnet assembly and sprockets.

To install:

9. Coat the camshaft with lubricant part number 1052365 or equivalent and install the camshaft.

10. Install the timing chain, camshaft sensor magnet assembly and sprockets.

11. Install the camshaft thrust button and front cover.

12. Complete installation by reversing the removal procedure. Connect battery negative cable.

Piston and Connecting Rod
POSITIONING

Piston Identification—2.8L engine

ENGINE LUBRICATION

Oil Pan

REMOVAL & INSTALLATION

2.5L Engine

1. Disconnect the negative battery cable. Raise and support the vehicle safely. Drain the oil.
2. Remove cradle to front engine mount nuts.
3. Disconnect exhaust pipe at manifold and at rear transaxle mount.
4. Disconnect starter and remove flywheel housing inspection cover.
5. Remove upper generator bracket. Remove the splash shield, if equipped, in order to gain working clearance.
6. Install suitable engine support equipment and raise engine.
7. Remove lower generator bracket and engine support bracket.
8. Remove oil pan retaining bolts and remove oil pan.

To install:

9. Thoroughly clean all gasket sealing surfaces.
10. Install rear oil pan gasket in rear main bearing cap and apply a small quantity of sealer in depressions where pan gasket engages into block.
11. Install front oil pan gasket on timing gear cover pressing tips into holes provided in cover.
12. Install side gaskets on oil pan using grease as a retainer.
13. Apply a ⅛ inch by ¼ inch long bead of sealer at split lines of front and side gaskets.
14. Install oil pan. Bolts into timing gear cover should be installed last. They are installed at an angle and holes line up after rest of pan bolts are snugged up.
15. Complete installation by reversing the removal procedure. Connect battery negative cable. Fill crankcase with oil, run engine and check for leaks.

2.8L and 3.1L Engines

1. Disconnect the battery ground.
2. If equipped with serpentine belt, remove the serpentine belt cover, belt and tensioner.
3. If necessary, support the engine with tool J–28467–A or equivalent, using an extra support leg.
4. Raise and safely support the vehicle.
5. Drain the oil.
6. Remove the right tire and wheel assembly. Remove the splash shield.

7. Remove the steering gear pinch bolt, as required.
8. Remove the transaxle mount retaining nuts and engine to frame mount retaining nuts, as required.
9. Remove the front engine horse collar bracket from the block, as required.
10. Remove the bellhousing cover and remove the starter.
11. Possition a jackstand under the frame front center crossmember.
12. Loosen but do not remove the rear frame bolts.
13. Remove the front frame bolts and lower the front frame.
14. Remove the oil pan retaining bolts and remove the oil pan.
15. Installation is the reverse of the removal procedure. Refill crankcase and connect bvattery negative cable.

NOTE: The oil pan on some vehicles may not require a gasket. If a gasket is not required, the oil pan is installed using RTV gasket material. Make sure the sealing surfaces are free of old RTV material. Use a ⅛ inch bead of RTV material on the pan sealing flange. Torque the pan bolts to 8–10 ft. lbs.

3.3L Engine

1. Disconnect the negative battery cable.
2. Raise and support the vehicle safely.
3. Drain the engine oil.
4. Remove the transaxle converter cover and starter motor.
5. Remove the oil filter, oil pan retaining bolts and oil pan assembly.

To install:

6. Clean the oil pan and cylinder block mating surfaces.
7. Install a new oil pan gasket to the oil pan flange.
8. Install the oil pan and torque the retaining bolts 8–10 ft. lbs.
9. Complete installation by reversing the removal procedure. Refill crankcase and connect battery negative cable.

3.8L Engine

1. Disconnect the battery ground cable.
2. Raise and safely support the vehicle.
3. Drain the oil.
4. Remove the bellhousing cover.
5. Unbolt and remove the oil pan.
6. Installation is the reverse of removal. RTV gasket material is used in place of a gasket. Make sure the sealing surfaces are free of all old RTV material. Use a ⅛ inch bead of RTV material on the oil pan sealing flange. Torque the pan bolts to 10–14 ft. lbs.

7. Refill crankcase and connect battery negative cable.

Oil Pump

REMOVAL & INSTALLATION

2.5L Engine

1. Disconnect the negative battery cable.
2. Raise and support the vehicle safely.
3. Drain the engine oil and remove the oil pan.
4. Remove the 2 flange mounting bolts and nut from the main bearing cap bolt.
5. Remove the pump and screen as an assembly.

To install:

6. Remove the 4 cover attaching screws and cover from the oil pump assembly.
7. Pack the space around the oil pump gears completely full of petroleum jelly. There must be no air space left inside the pump. If the pump is not packed, it may not begin to pump oil as soon as the engine is started and engine damage may result.
8. Align the oil pump shaft to match with the oil pump drive shaft tang, then install the oil pump to the block positioning the flange over the oil pump driveshaft lower bushing. Do not use any gasket. Torque the bolts to 20 ft. lbs. (30 Nm).
9. Install the oil pan using a new gasket and seals.
10. Complete installation by reversing the removal procedure. Connect battery negative cable.

2.8L and 3.1L Engines

1. Disconnect the negative battery cable.
2. Raise and support the vehicle safely.
3. Drain the engine oil and remove the oil pan.
4. Remove the pump to rear main bearing cap bolt and remove the pump and extension shaft.

To install:

5. Remove the 4 cover attaching screws and cover from the oil pump assembly.
6. Pack the space around the oil pump gears completely full of petroleum jelly. There must be no air space left inside the pump. If the pump is not packed, it may not begin to pump oil as soon as the engine is started and engine damage may result.
7. Assemble the pump and extension shaft with retainer to rear main bearing cap, aligning the top end of the extension shaft with the lower end of the drive gear.

8. Install the pump to the rear bearing cap bolt and torque to specifications. Install the oil pan.

9. Complete installation by reversing the removal procedure. Connect battery negative cable.

3.3L and 3.8L Engines

1. Disconnect the negative battery cable.

2. Raise and support the vehicle safely.

3. Drain the engine oil.

4. Remove the oil filter.

5. Unbolt the oil pump cover from the timing chain cover.

6. Slide out the oil pump gears. Remove the oil pressure relief valve cap, spring and valve. Do not attempt to remove the oil filter bypass valve and spring. Clean all parts thoroughly in solvent and check for wear.

To install:

7. Lubricate and install the pressure relief valve and spring in the bore of the oil pump cover.

8. Install the relief valve spring retaining cap and gasket.

9. Install the oil pump drive and driven gears. Pack the gear pockets full of petroleum jelly.

10. Install the oil pump cover. Alternately tighten the cover screws.

11. Complete installation by reversing the removal procedure. Refill crankcase and connect battery negative cable.

Rear Main Bearing Oil Seal

REMOVAL & INSTALLATION

2.5L Engine

1. Disconnect the negative battery cable.

2. Support the engine. Remove the transaxle and flywheel.

3. Being careful not to scratch the crankshaft, pry out the old seal with an suitable pry tool.

4. Coat the new seal with clean engine oil and install it by hand or use seal installer tool J–34924 onto the crankshaft. The seal backing must be flush with the block opening.

5. Install all other parts in reverse of removal.

2.8L and 3.1L Engines

1. Disconnect the negative battery cable.

2. Support the engine with tool J–28467–A or equivalent.

3. Remove the transaxle and flywheel.

4. Carefully remove the old seal by inserting a prying tool through the

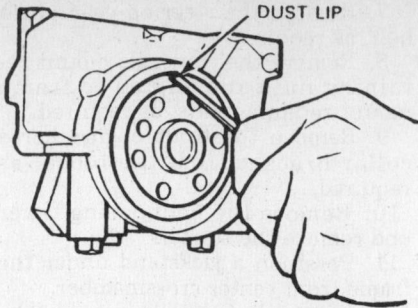

Remove rear seal—2.8L and 3.1L engines

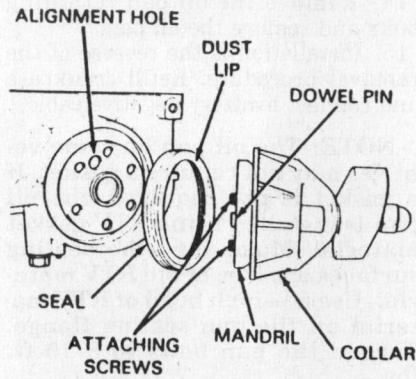

Installing main rear seal—2.8L and 3.1L engines

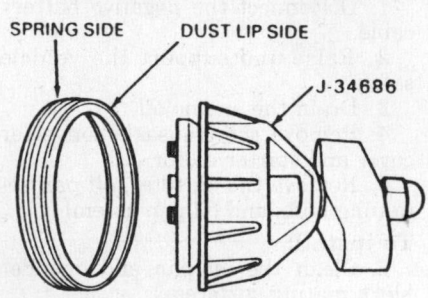

SEAL BORE TO SEAL SURFACE TO BE LUBRICATED WITH ENGINE OIL BEFORE ASSEMBLY

Rear main seal and tool—2.8L and 3.1L engines

dust lip at an angle. Pry out the old seal with an suitable pry tool.

5. Coat the new seal with clean engine oil, and install it using seal installer tool J–34686 or equivalent.

6. Complete installation by reversing the removal procedure.

3.3L and 3.8L Engines

1. Disconnect the negative battery cable.

2. Raise and support the vehicle safely.

3. Drain the engine oil and remove the oil pan.

4. Remove the rear main bearing cap. Remove the oil seal from the bearing cap.

To install:

5. Insert a packing tool J–21526–2 or equivalent against one end of the seal in the cylinder block. Pack the old seal in until it is tight. Pack the other end of seal in the same manner.

6. Measure the amount the seal was driven up into the block on one side and add approximately $\frac{1}{16}$ in. (2mm). With a single edge razor blade, cut this amount off of the old lower seal. The bearing cap can be used as a holding fixture.

7. Install the packing guide tool J–21526–1 or equivalent, onto the cylinder block.

8. Using the packing tool, work the short pieces of the seal into the guide tool and pack into the cylinder block until the tool hits the built in stop. Repeat this step on the other side. A small amount of oil on the pieces of seal may be helpful when packing into the cylinder block.

9. Remove the guide tool.

10. Install a new rope seal in the bearing cap and install the cap. Torque the retaining bolts to specifications.

11. Complete installation by reversing the removal procedure.

MANUAL TRANSAXLE

For further information on transmissions/transaxles, please refer to "Chilton's Guide to Transmission Repair".

Transaxle Assembly

REMOVAL & INSTALLATION

4 Speed

1. Disconnect the negative battery cable.

2. Remove the 2 transaxle strut bracket bolts on the left side of the engine compartment, if equipped.

3. As required, if equipped with a V6 engine, disconnect the fuel lines and fuel line clamps at the clutch cable bracket.

4. Remove the top 4 engine-to-transaxle bolts and the one at the rear near the firewall. The one at the rear is installed from the engine side.

5. Loosen the engine-to-transaxle bolt near the starter, but do not remove.

6. Disconnect the speedometer cable at the transaxle, or at the speed control transducer, if equipped.

7. Remove the retaining clip and washer from the shift linkage at the transaxle. Remove the clips holding the cables to the mounting bosses on the case.

8. Support the engine with a lifting chain.

9. Unlock the steering column. Raise and safely support the vehicle. Drain the transaxle. Remove the 2 nuts attaching the stabilizer bar to the left lower control arm. Remove the 4 bolts which attach the left retaining plate to the engine cradle. The retaining plate covers holds the stabilizer bar.

10. Loosen the 4 bolts holding the right stabilizer bracket.

11. Disconnect and remove the exhaust pipe and crossover, if necessary.

12. Pull the stabilizer bar down on the left side.

13. Remove the 4 nuts and disconnect the front and rear transaxle mounts from the engine cradle. Remove the 2 rear center crossmember bolts.

14. Remove the 3 right side front cradle attaching bolts. They are accessible under the splash shield.

15. Remove the top bolt from the lower front transaxle shock absorber, if equipped.

16. Remove the left front wheel. Remove the front cradle-to-body bolts on the left side, and the rear cradle-to-body bolts.

17. Pull the left side driveshaft from the transaxle using special tool J–28468 or equivalent. The right side halfshaft will simply disconnect from the case. When the transaxle is removed, the right shaft can be swung out of the way. A boot protector should be used when disconnecting the driveshafts.

18. Swing the cradle to the left side. Secure out of the way, outboard of the fender well.

19. Remove the flywheel and starter shield bolts and remove the shields.

20. Remove the 2 transaxle extension bolts from the engine-to-transaxle bracket, if equipped.

21. Place a jack under the transaxle case. Remove the last engine-to-transaxle bolt. Pull the transaxle to the left, away from the engine, then down and out from under the vehicle.

To install:

22. Installation is the reverse of removal. Position the right halfshaft into its bore as the transaxle is being installed. When the transaxle is bolted to the engine, swing the cradle into position and install the cradle-to-body bolts immediately. Be sure to guide the left halfshaft into place as the cradle is moved back into position. Connect battery negative cable.

5 Speed

1. Disconnect the negative battery cable.

2. Remove the air cleaner and air intake duct assembly.

3. Remove the sound insulator from inside the vehicle.

4. Remove the clutch master cylinder pushrod from the clutch pedal.

5. Remove the clutch slave cylinder from the transaxle.

6. Disconnect the exhaust crossover pipe.

7. Disconnect the shift cables at the transaxle.

8. Install the engine support fixture J–28467.

9. Remove the top engine to transaxle bolts.

10. Raise and safely support the vehicle.

11. Install the halfshaft boot seal protectors with special tool J–34754.

12. Remove the left front wheel and tire.

13. Remove the left side frame and disconnect the rear transaxle mount from the bracket.

14. Drain the transaxle.

15. Disengage the halfshafts from the transaxle.

16. Remove the clutch housing cover bolts.

17. Disconnect the speedometer cable.

18. Attach a jack to the transaxle case.

19. Remove the remaining transaxle to engine bolts.

20. Slide the transaxle away from the engine. Carefully lower the jack while guiding the right halfshaft out of the transaxle.

To install:

21. When installing the transaxle, position the right halfshaft shaft into its bore as the transaxle is being installed. The right shaft cannot be readily installed after the transaxle is connected to the engine.

22. After the transaxle is fastened to the engine and the left halfshaft is installed at the transaxle, position the left side frame and install the frame to body bolts.

23. Connect the transaxle to the front and rear mounts.

24. The remainder of the installation is the reverse of removal. Connect battery negative cable.

LINKAGE ADJUSTMENT

4 Speed

1. Remove the shifter boot and retainer from inside the vehicle. Ensure that shifter is in 1st gear.

2. Install two No. 22 drill bits, or two $5/32$ inch rods into the 2 alignment

holes in the shifter assembly to hold it in 1st gear.

3. Place the transaxle into 1st gear by pushing the rail selector down, just to the point of feeling the resistance of the inhibitor spring. Rotate the shifter lever all the way counterclockwise.

4. Install the stud, with the cable attached, into the slotted area of the select lever, while gently pulling on the lever to remove all the lash.

5. Remove the 2 drill bits or pins from the shifter.

6. Check the shifter for proper operation. It may be necessary to readjust after road test.

CLUTCH

Clutch Assembly

REMOVAL & INSTALLATION

1. Disconnect the negative battery cable.

2. Disconnect the clutch cable from the transaxle.

3. On 1987–89 vehicles, remove the hush panel from inside the vehicle and disconnect the clutch master cylinder pushrod from the clutch pedal.

4. Remove the transaxle assembly.

5. Mark the relationship between the pressure plate and flywheel.

6. Evenly and carefully loosen the pressure plate bolts until the spring pressure is relieved.

7. Support the pressure plate and remove the pressure plate retaining bolts. Remove the pressure plate and disc.

NOTE: Do not disassemble the pressure plate and disc assembly. If the unit is defective, replace as an assembly.

8. Clean and lubricate all parts as required.

9. Installation is the reverse of the removal procedure. Note that the disc is installed with the damper springs offset towards the transaxle. Most discs are marked FLYWHEEL SIDE. If the old pressure plate is to be reused, align the marks made previously.

PEDAL HEIGHT/FREE-PLAY ADJUSTMENT

All vehicles use a self-adjusting clutch mechanism which may be checked as follows. As the clutch friction material wears, the cable must be lengthened. This is accomplished by simply pulling

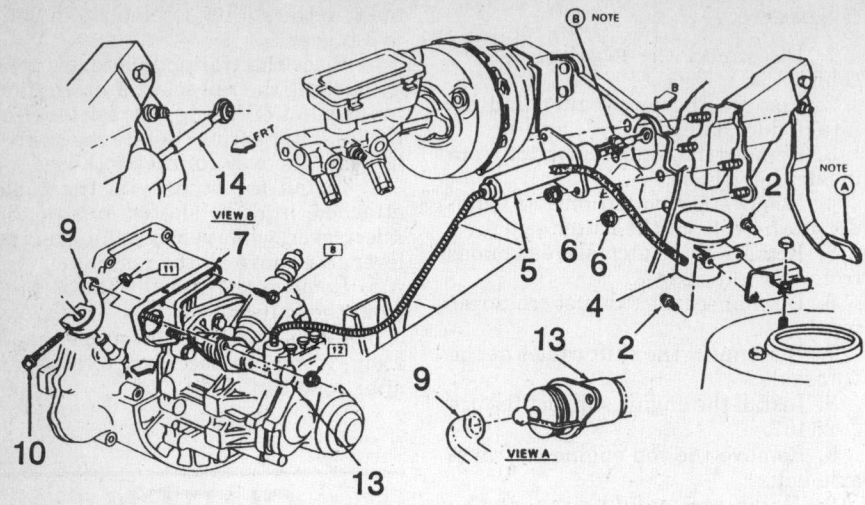

1. Clutch pedal assembly
2. Bolt
3. Bracket
4. Reservoir
5. Master cylinder
6. 20 ft. lbs.
7. Slave cylinder bracket
8. Bolt 40 ft. lbs.
9. Lever
10. Bolt 37 ft. lbs.
11. Nut
12. Nut 40 ft. lbs.
13. Slave cylinder
14 Master cylinder push rod

Clutch hydraulic system

the clutch pedal up to its rubber bumper. This action forces the pawl against its stop and rotates it out of mesh with the quadrant teeth, allowing the cable to play out until the quadrant spring load is balanced against the load applied by the release bearing. This adjustment procedure is required every 5000 miles or less.

1. With engine running and brake on, hold the clutch pedal approximately ½ inch from floor mat and move shift lever between first and reverse several times. If this can be done smoothly without clashing into reverse, the clutch is fully releasing. If shift is not smooth, clutch is not fully releasing and linkage should be inspected and corrected as necessary.

2. Check clutch pedal bushings for sticking or excessive wear.

3. Have an assistant fully apply the clutch pedal to the floor. Observe the clutch fork level travel at the transaxle. The end of the clutch fork lever should have a total travel of approximately 1.5–1.7 in.

4. If fork lever is not correct, check the adjusting mechanism by depressing the clutch pedal and looking for pawl to firmly engage with the teeth in the quadrant.

5. To check the self-adjusting mechanism for proper operation, proceed as follows:

   a. Depress the clutch pedal and look for the pawl to firmly engage with the teeth in the quadrant.

   b. Release the clutch pedal and look for the pawl to be lifted off the quadrant teeth by the bracket stop.

Clutch Cable

REMOVAL & INSTALLATION

1. Support the clutch pedal upward against the bumper stop to release the pawl from the quadrant. Disconnect the end of the cable from the clutch release lever at the transaxle. Be careful to prevent the cable from snapping rapidly toward the rear of the vehicle. The quadrant in the adjusting mechanism can be damaged by allowing the cable to snap back.

2. Disconnect the clutch cable from the quadrant. Lift the locking pawl away from the quadrant, then slide the cable out on the right side of the quadrant.

3. From the engine side of the cowl disconnect the 2 upper nuts holding the cable retainer to the upper studs. Disconnect the cable from the bracket mounted to the transaxle and remove the cable.

4. Inspect the clutch cable for frayed wires, kinks, worn ends and excessive friction. If any of these conditions exist, replace the cable.

To install:

5. With the gasket in position on the 2 upper studs, position a new cable with the retaining flange against the bracket.

6. Attach the end of the cable to the quadrant, being sure to route the cable under the pawl.

7. Attach the 2 upper nuts to the retainer mounting studs, and torque to specifications.

8. Attach the cable to the bracket mounted to the transaxle.

9. Support the clutch pedal upward against the bumper stop to release the pawl from the quadrant. Attach the outer end of the cable to the clutch release lever. Be sure not to yank on the cable, since overloading the cable could damage the quadrant.

10. Check clutch operation and adjust by lifting the clutch pedal up to allow the mechanism to adjust the cable length. Depress the pedal slowly several times to set the pawl into mesh with the quadrant teeth.

Clutch Master and Slave Cylinder

NOTE: The clutch hydraulic system is serviced as a complete unit, it has been bled of air and filled with fluid.

REMOVAL & INSTALLATION

1. Disconnect the negative battery cable.

2. Remove the hush panel from inside the vehicle.

3. Remove the clutch master cylinder retaining nuts at the front of the dash.

4. Remove the slave cylinder retaining nuts at the transaxle.

5. Remove the hydraulic system as a unit from the vehicle.

6. Install the slave cylinder to the transaxle support bracket aligning the pushrod into the pocket on the clutch fork outer lever. Tighten the retaining nuts evenly to prevent damage to the slave cylinder. Torque the nuts to 40 ft. lbs.

NOTE: Do not remove the plastic pushrod retainer from the slave cylinder. The straps will break on the first clutch pedal application.

7. Position the clutch master cylinder to the front of the dash. Torque the nuts evenly to 20 ft. lbs.

8. Remove the pedal restrictor from the pushrod. Lube the pushrod bushing on the clutch pedal. Connect the pushrod to the clutch pedal and install the retaining clip.

9. If equipped with cruise control, check the switch adjustment at the clutch pedal bracket.

NOTE: When adjusting the cruise control switch, do not exert an upward force on the clutch pedal pad of more than 20 lbs. or damage to the master cylinder pushrod retaining ring may result.

10. Install the hush panel.

11. Press the clutch pedal down several times. This will break the plastic retaining straps on the slave cylinder pushrod. Do not remove the plastic button on the end of the pushrod.

12. Connect the negative battery cable.

AUTOMATIC TRANSAXLE

For further information on transmissions/transaxles, please refer to "Chilton's Guide to Transmission Repair".

Transaxle Assembly

REMOVAL & INSTALLATION

THM 125C

NOTE: By September 1, 1991, Hydra-matic will have changed the name designation of the THM 125C automatic transaxle. The new name designation for this transaxle will be Hydra-matic 3T40. Transaxles built between 1989 and 1990 will serve as transitional years in which a dual system, made up of the old designation and the new designation will be in effect.

1. Disconnect the negative battery cable.

2. Remove the air cleaner.

3. Unbolt the detent cable attaching bracket at the transaxles.

4. Pull up on the detent cable cover at the transaxle until the cable is exposed. Disconnect the cable from the rod.

5. Remove the 2 transaxle strut bracket bolts at the transaxle, if equipped.

6. Remove all the engine-to-transaxle bolts except the one near the starter. The one nearest the firewall is installed from the engine side of the vehicle.

7. Loosen but do not remove the engine-to-transaxle bolt near the starter.

8. Disconnect the speedometer cable at the upper and lower coupling. If equipped with cruise control, remove the speedometer cable at the transducer.

9. Remove the retaining clip and washer from the shift linkage at the transaxle. Remove the 2 shift linkage at the transaxle. Remove the 2 shift linkage bracket bolts.

10. Disconnect and plug the cooler lines at the transaxle.

11. Install an engine holding fixture. Raise the engine enough to take its weight off the mounts.

12. Unlock the steering column. Raise and safely support the vehicle.

13. Remove the 2 nuts holding the anti-sway bar to the left lower control arm (driver's side).

14. Remove the 4 bolts attaching the covering plate over the stabilizer bar to the engine cradle on the left side of vehicle.

15. Loosen but do not remove the 4 bolts holding the stabilizer bar bracket to the right side of the engine cradle. Pull the bar downward.

16. Disconnect the front and rear transaxle mounts at the engine cradle.

17. Remove the 2 rear center crossmember bolts.

18. Remove the 3 right (passenger) side front engine cradle attaching bolts. The nuts are accessible under the splash shield next to the frame rail.

19. If equipped with V6 engine, remove the top bolt from the lower front transaxle shock absorber, as required.

20. Remove the left side front and rear cradle-to-body bolts.

21. Remove the left front wheel. Attach an halfshaft removing tool J-28468 or equivalent to a slide hammer. Place the tool behind the halfshaft cones and pull the cones out away from the transaxle. Remove the right shaft in the same manner. Set the shafts out of the way. Plug the openings in the transaxle to prevent fluid leakage and the entry of dirt.

22. Swing the partial engine cradle to the left (driver) side and wire it out of the way outboard of the fender well.

23. Remove the 4 torque converter and starter shield bolts. Remove the 2 transaxle extension bolts from the engine-to-transaxle bracket.

24. Attach a transaxle jack to the case.

25. Use a felt pen to matchmark the torque converter and flywheel. Remove the 3 torque converter-to-flywheel bolts.

26. Remove the transaxle-to-engine bolt near the starter. Remove the transaxle by sliding it to the left, away from the engine.

27. Installation is the reverse of the removal procedure. As the transaxle is installed, slide the right halfshaft into the case. Install the cradle-to-body bolts before the stabilizer bar is installed. To aid in stabilizer bar installation, a pry hole has been provided in the engine cradle. Connect battery negative cable.

THM 440-T4

NOTE: By September 1, 1991, Hydra-matic will have changed the name designation of the THM 440-T4 automatic transaxle. The new name designation for this transaxle will be Hydra-matic 4T60. Transaxles built between 1989 and 1990 will serve as transitional years in which a dual system, made up of the old designation and the new designation will be in effect.

1. Disconnect the negative battery cable.

2. Remove the air cleaner and disconnect the TV cable at the throttle body.

3. Disconnect the shift linkage at the transaxle.

4. Install the engine support fixture tool J-28467 or equivalent.

5. Disconnect all electrical connectors.

6. Remove the 3 bolts from the transaxle to the engine.

7. Disconnect the vacuum line at the modulator.

8. Raise and safely support the vehicle.

9. Remove the left front wheel and tire assembly.

10. Remove the left side ball joint from the steering knuckle.

11. Disconnect the brake line bracket at the strut.

NOTE: A halfshaft seal protector tool J-34754 should be modified and installed on any halfshaft prior to service procedures on or near the halfshaft. Failure to do so could result in seal damage or joint failure.

12. Remove the halfshafts from the transaxle.

13. Disconnect the pinch bolt at the intermediate steering shaft. Failure to do so could cause damage to the steering gear.

14. Remove the frame to stabilizer bolts.

15. Remove the stabilizer bolts at the control arm.

16. Remove the left front frame assembly.

17. Disconnect the speedometer cable or wire connector from the transaxle.

18. Remove the extension housing to engine block support bracket.

19. Disconnect the cooler pipes.

20. Remove the converter cover, and converter to flywheel bolts.

21. Remove all of the remaining transaxle to engine bolts except one.

22. Position a jack under the transaxle.

23. Remove the remaining transaxle to engine bolt and remove the transaxle.

24. Installation is the reverse of the

removal procedure. Torque the transaxle to engine bolts to 55 ft. lbs. Flush the oil cooler lines with using tool J-35944 or equivalent and adjust the TV cable and shift linkage as necessary.

SHIFT CONTROL CABLE ADJUSTMENT

1. Place the shift lever in **N**. To determine the **N** position, rotate the selector shaft clockwise from **P** through **R** to **N**.
2. Place the shift control assembly in **N**.
3. Push the tab on the cable adjuster to adjust the cable in cable mounting bracket.

PARK/LOCK CONTROL CABLE ADJUSTMENT

The shifter lever must not be able to move to any other positions with the shift lever in **P** and the key in the **LOCK** position. Also, with the key in the **RUN** position and the shift lever in **N**, make sure you cannot turn the key to the **LOCK** position. If these conditions cannot be met, adjustment is necessary.

1. If the key cannot be removed in the **P** position, snap the connector lock button to the **UP** position.
2. Move the cable connector nose rearward until the key can be removed from the ignition.
3. Push the snap lock button down.

TV DETENT CABLE ADJUSTMENT

1. With the engine **OFF**, depress and hold-down the readjust tab at the TV cable adjuster.
2. Move the cable conduit until it stops against the fitting. Release the readjustment tab.
3. Rotate the throttle lever by hand to its full travel position. The slider must ratchet toward the lever when the lever is rotated to its full travel.

NOTE: Check that the cable moves freely. The cable may appear to function properly with the engine OFF and COLD. Recheck after the engine is HOT.

DRIVE AXLE

Halfshaft

REMOVAL & INSTALLATION

1. Remove the hub nut and discard.

A new hub nut must be used for reassembly.

2. Raise and safely support the vehicle. Remove the wheel and tire assembly.
3. Install an halfshaft boot seal protector onto the seal.
4. Disconnect the brake hose clip from the MacPherson strut, but do not disconnect the hose from the caliper. Remove the brake caliper from the spindle and support the caliper out of the way by a length of wire. Do not allow the caliper to hang by the brake hose.
5. Mark the camber alignment cam bolt for reassembly. Remove the cam bolt and the upper attaching bolt from the strut and spindle.
6. Pull the steering knuckle assembly from the strut bracket.
7. Remove the halfshaft from the transaxle.
8. Using spindle remover tool J-28733 or the equivalent, remove the halfshaft from the hub and bearing assembly. Do not allow the halfshaft to hang free, if necessary, support using wire in order to prevent any component damage.

To install:

9. If a new halfshaft is to be installed, a new knuckle seal should be installed first along with a boot seal protector when necessary.
10. Loosely install the halfshaft into the transaxle and steering knuckle.
11. Loosely attach the steering knuckle to the suspension strut.
12. The halfshaft is an interference fit in the steering knuckle. Press the axle into place, then install the hub nut. When the shaft begins to turn with the hub, insert a drift through the caliper into one of the cooling slots in the rotor to keep it from turning.

NOTE: On some later vehicles, the hub flange has a notch in it which, when one of the hub bearing retainer bolts is removed and

a longer bolt put in its place through the notch, can be used to prevent the hub and the shaft from turning.

13. Tighten the hub nut to 70 ft. lbs. to completely seat the shaft.
14. Install the brake caliper. Tighten the caliper mounting bolts to 30 ft. lbs.
15. Load the hub assembly by lowering it onto a jackstand. Align the camber cam bolt marks made during removal, install the bolt and tighten to 140 ft. lbs. Tighten the upper nut to the same torque valve.
16. Install the halfshaft all the way into the transaxle using a suitable tool inserted into the groove provided on the inner retainer. Tap the tool until the shaft seats in the transaxle. Remove the boot seal protector.
17. Connect the brake hose clip the the strut. Install the tire and wheel, lower the vehicle and tighten the hub nut to 192 ft. lbs.

CV-Boot

REMOVAL & INSTALLATION
Outer

1. Disconnect the negative battery cable. Raise and support the vehicle safely.
2. Remove the front tire and wheel assembly.
3. Remove the caliper bolts and wire the caliper off to the side.
4. Remove the hub nut, washer and wheel bearing.
5. Using a brass drift, lightly tap around the seal retainer to loosen it. Remove the seal retainer.
6. Remove the seal retaining clamp or ring and discard.
7. Using snapring pliers, remove the race retaining ring from the halfshaft.
8. Pull the outer joint assembly and the outboard seal away from the halfshaft.

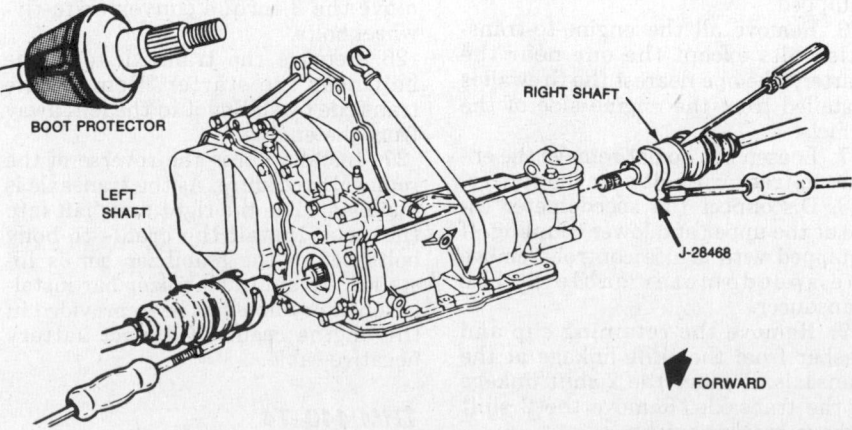

Halfshaft removal using special tools attached to slide hammers

9. Flush the grease from the joint and repack with half of the grease provided. Put the remainder of the grease in the seal.

To install:

10. Assemble the inner seal retainer, outboard seal and outer seal retainer to the halfshaft. Push the joint assembly onto toshaft until the retaining ring is seated in the groove.

11. Slide the outboard seal onto the joint assembly and secure using the outer seal retainer. Using seal clamp tool J-35910 or equivalent, torque the outer clamp to 130 ft. lbs. (176 Nm), and the inner clamp to 100 ft. lbs. (136 Nm).

Inner

1. Raise and support the vehicle safely.

2. Remove the front tire and wheel assembly.

3. Remove the caliper bolts and wire the caliper off to the side of the vehicle.

4. Remove the hub nut, washer and wheel bearing.

5. Remove the front halfshaft. Place in a suitable holding fixture being careful not place undue pressure on the halfshaft.

6. Remove the joint assembly retaining ring. Remove the joint assembly.

7. Remove the race retaining ring and remove the seal retainer.

8. Remove the inner seal retaining clamp. Remove the inner joint seal.

9. Flush the grease from the joint and repack with half of the grease provided. Put the remainder of the grease in the seal.

To install:

10. Assemble the inner seal retainer, outboard seal and outer seal retainer to the halfshaft. Push the joint assembly onto te shaft until the retaining ring is seated in the groove.

11. Slide the outboard seal onto the joint assembly and secure using the outer seal retainer. Using seal clamp tool J-35910 or equivalent, torque the outer clamp to 130 ft. lbs. (176 Nm) and the inner clamp to 100 ft. lbs. (136 Nm).

Front Wheel Hub, Knuckle and Bearings

REMOVAL & INSTALLATION

1. Disconnect battery negative cable.

2. Remove the wheel cover, loosen the hub nut, then raise and support vehicle.

3. Remove the tire and wheel assembly.

4. Install boot cover, tool J-28712, double off-set joint or J-33162 tri-pot joint.

5. Remove and discard the hub nut. Ensure to use new hub nut during assembly.

6. Remove the brake caliper and rotor.

7. Remove the 3 hub and bearing attaching bolts, then remove the hub.

NOTE: If the old bearing is to be reused, make matchmarks on the bolts and holes for installation purposes.

8. Attach bearing puller J-28733 or equivalent, then remove the bearing.

To install:

9. Clean the mating surfaces of all dirt and corrossion. Check the knuckle bore and seal for damage. If a new bearing is to be installed, remove the old knuckle seal and install a new one. Grease the lips of new seal.

10. Push the bearing onto the halfshaft. Install a new washer and hub nut.

11. Tighten the hub nut on the halftshaft until the new bearing is seated. If the rotor and hub start to rotate as the hub nut ids tightened, insert a drift through the caliper and into the rotor cooling fins to prevent rotation.

NOTE: Do not apply full torque to the hub nut at this time.

12. Install the brake shield, if removed, and the bearing retaining bolts. Torque bolts to 63 ft. lbs. (85Nm).

13. Install the caliper and rotor. Ensure the caliper hose is not twisted. Install caliper bolts.

14. Install the wheel assembly. Torque the hub nut to 192 ft. lbs. (260 Nm). Connect battery negative cable.

STEERING

Steering Wheel

REMOVAL & INSTALLATION

NOTE: When installing the steering wheel, always make sure the turn signal lever is in the neutral position.

1. Disconnect the negative battery cable. Remove the trim retaining screws from behind the wheel. On steering wheels with a center cap, pull off the cap.

2. Lift the trim off and pull the horn wires from the turn signal cancelling cam.

3. Remove the retainer and the steering wheel nut.

4. Mark the wheel-to-shaft relationship and then remove the wheel with a puller.

5. Install the wheel on the shaft, aligning the previously made marks. Tighten the nut to 30 ft. lbs.

6. Insert the horn wires into the cancelling cam.

7. Install the center trim and reconnect the battery cable.

Steering Column

NOTE: Once the steering column is removed from the vehicle, the column is extremely susceptible to damage. Dropping the column assembly on its end could collapse the steering shaft or loosen the plastic injections which maintain column rigidity. Leaning on the column assembly could cause the jacket to bend or deform. Any of the above damage could impair the column's collapsible design. If it is necessary to remove the steering wheel, use a standard wheel puller. Under no condition should the end of the shaft be hammered upon, as hammering could loosen the plastic injection which maintains column rigidity.

REMOVAL & INSTALLATION

1. Disconnect the negative battery cable.

2. If column repairs are to be made, remove the steering wheel.

3. Remove the nuts and bolts attaching the flexible coupling to the bottom of the steering column. Remove the safety strap and bolt if equipped.

4. Remove the steering column trim shrouds and column covers.

5. Disconnect all wiring harness connectors. Remove the dust boot mounting screws and column mounting bracket bolts.

6. Lower the column to clear the mounting bracket and carefully remove from the vehicle.

7. Installation is the reverse of the removal procedure.

Power Steering Rack

BEARING PRELOAD ADJUSTMENT

1. Raise and support vehicle.

2. When adjusting, ensure front

wheels are raised and the steering wheel centered.

3. Loosen the adjuster plug locknut, turn adjuster plug clockwise until it bottoms in the housing, then back adjuster plug approximately 50–70 degrees (approximately 1 flat).

4. After adjustment, check the returnabilty of the steering wheel.

REMOVAL & INSTALLATION

1. Disconnect the negative battery cable. Raise and safely support vehicle. Allow the front suspension to hang freely. Disconnect the power steering hoses from the gear, where equipped.

2. Move the intermediate shaft seal upward and remove the intermediate shaft-to-stub shaft pinch bolt.

3. Remove both front wheels.

4. Remove the cotter pins and nut from both tie rod ends. Disconnect the tie rod ends from the steering knuckles.

5. Remove the air management system pipe bracket bolt from the crossmember.

6. Support the engine cradle with a floor jack. Remove the 2 rear cradle mount bolts and, using a jack, lower the rear of the engine cradle about 4–5 in.

NOTE: Do not lower the engine cradle too far or damage to surrounding components will result.

7. Remove the rack and pinion heat shield, then the 2 rack and pinion mount bolts.

8. Remove the rack and pinion assembly through the left wheel opening.

To install:

9. Installation is the reverse of removal. Torque the mount bolts to 70 ft. lbs.; the tie rod end nuts to 30 ft. lbs. and the pinch bolt to 45 ft. lbs. Connect battery negative cable and refill system.

Power Steering Pump

REMOVAL & INSTALLATION

2.5L Engine

1. Disconnect the negative battery cable. Raise and support the vehicle safely.

2. Remove the pump drive belt and siphon the fluid from the pump reservoir.

3. Disconnect the hydraulic lines from the pump.

4. Remove the radiator hose clamp bolt.

5. Remove the upper and lower

bolts and nuts from the front pump bracket.

6. Remove the pump and bracket from the engine.

7. Installation is the reverse of the removal procedure. Be sure to adjust the drive belt tension and bleed the hydraulic system. Connect battery negative cable and refill system.

Except 2.5L Engine

1. Disconnect the negative battery cable at the battery. Remove air cleaner, if necessary.

2. Disconnect the blower motor wiring and remove the blower motor.

3. Remove the coolant hose from the water pump.

4. Siphon the fluid out of the pump reservoir, then disconnect the lines from the pump.

5. Remove the pump drive belt.

6. Remove the 1 nut which attaches the rear pump bracket to the engine bracket.

7. Remove the 2 front pump bracket-to-engine bolts, then remove the pump and bracket assembly.

8. Installation is the reverse of the removal procedure. Be sure to adjust the drive belt tension and bleed the hydraulic system. Connect battery negative cable and refill system.

BELT ADJUSTMENT

NOTE: When adjusting the power steering pump belt, do not pry against the pump reservoir. Only the bracket should be pried against when adjusting belt tension.

1. Position the belt tension gauge on the belt.

2. Loosen the pump mounting bolts.

3. Adjust the belt by prying the pump away from the engine until the correct tension is reached. Tighten pump bolts.

SYSTEM BLEEDING

1. Fill the fluid reservoir.

2. Let fluid stand undisturbed for 2 minutes, then crank engine for about 2 seconds. Refill reservoir if necessary.

3. Repeat Steps 1 and 2 until fluid level remains constant after cranking the engine.

4. Raise the front of the vehicle until both wheels are off the ground, then start the engine. Increase engine speed to 1500 rpm.

5. Turn the wheels lightly against the stop to the left and right, checking the fluid level and refilling, if necessary.

Tie Rod Ends

REMOVAL & INSTALLATION

1. Loosen the jam nut on the steering rack inner tie rod.

2. Remove the tie rod end nut. Separate the tie rod end from the steering knuckle using a suitable puller.

3. Unscrew the tie rod end, counting the number of turns.

To install:

4. Screw the tie rod end onto the steering rack inner tie rod the same number of turns as counted for removal. This will give approximately correct toe.

5. Install the tie rod end into the knuckle. Install nut and torque to 40 ft. lbs.

6. If the toe must be adjusted, use pliers to expand the boot clamp. Turn the inner tie rod to adjust. Replace clamp.

7. Torque jam nut to 59 ft. lbs.

BRAKES

For all brake system repair and service procedures not detailed below, please refer to "Brakes" in the Unit Repair section.

Master Cylinder

REMOVAL & INSTALLATION

1. Disconnect the negative battery cable. Disconnect and plug the hydraulic lines at master cylinder.

2. Remove the master cylinder retaining nuts and lock washers.

3. Remove the master cylinder from the vehicle.

4. Install the cylinder on the booster. Install nuts and lock washers. Torque the attaching nuts to 25 ft. lbs.

5. Install hydraulic lines.

6. Bleed the brakes system.

Power Brake Booster

REMOVAL & INSTALLATION

1. Disconnect the negative battery cable. Disconnect vacuum hose from vacuum check valve.

2. Unbolt the master cylinder and carefully move it aside without disconnecting the hydraulic lines.

3. Disconnect pushrod at brake pedal assembly.

4. Remove nuts and lock washers that secure booster to firewall and re-

move booster from engine compartment.

5. Install by reversing removal procedure. Torque the mounting nuts to 25 ft. lbs. Make sure to check operation of stop lights. Allow engine vacuum to build before applying brakes.

Brake Caliper

REMOVAL & INSTALLATION

1. Dsiconnect the barttery negative cable.

2. Raise and support vehicle, then remove the tire and wheel assembly.

3. Remove ⅔ of the brake fluid from the master cylinder.

4. Position a 12 inch adjustable pliers over the inboard brake shoe tab and the inboard caliper housing. Squeeze the pliers to compress the piston back into the caliper bore and to provide clearance between the lining and rotor.

5. If equipped with rear disc brakes, disconnect the parking brake cable and return spring from the parking brake lever, then the parking brake cable from the bracket.

6. On all models, remove the caliper mounting bolts, then lift caliper from bracket and remove the inner and outer pads with the anti-rattle springs.

7. Disconnect the hydraulic hose, then remove the caliper from the vehicle.

8. Reverse procedure to install. Bleed brake system.

Disc Brake Pads

REMOVAL & INSTALLATION

1. Dsiconnect the barttery negative cable.

2. Raise and support vehicle, then remove the tire and wheel assembly.

3. Remove ⅔ of the brake fluid from the master cylinder.

4. Position a 12 inch adjustable pliers over the inboard brake shoe tab and the inboard caliper housing. Squeeze the pliers to compress the piston back into the caliper bore and to provide clearance between the lining and rotor.

5. If equipped with rear disc brakes, disconnect the parking brake cable and return spring from the parking brake lever, then the parking brake cable from the bracket.

6. On all models, remove the caliper mounting bolts, then lift caliper from braket and remove the inner and outer pads with the anti-rattle springs.

7. Reverse procedure to install. Bleed brake system.

Brake Rotor

REMOVAL & INSTALLATION

1. Disconnect battery negative cable.

2. Remove the caliper.

3. Remove the hub nut and washer, the the rotor.

4. Reverse procedure to install. Torque hub nut to 63 ft. lbs. (85 Nm).

Brake Drums

REMOVAL & INSTALLATION

1. Disconnect battery negative cable.

2. Raise and safely support the vehicle, then remove the tire and wheel assembly.

3. Remove the brake drum. If the drum is difficult to remove, remove the access plug from the backing plate and back off the adjusting screw.

4. Reverse procedure to install. Connect battery negative cable.

Brake Shoes

REMOVAL & INSTALLATION

1. Disconnect battery negative cable.

2. Raise and support vehicle, then remove the tire and wheel assembly.

3. Remove the brake drum. If the drum is difficult to remove, remove the access plug from the backing plate and back off the adjusting screw.

4. Remove the return springs from the anchor using appropriate brake spring pliers.

5. Remove the hold-down springs and retaining pins. Remove the lever pivot, actuator link, actuator lever, actuator pivot and lever return spring, parking brake strut and strut spring.

6. Remove the brake shoes, then disconnect the parking brake cable.

7. Remove the adjusting screw assembly and spring. Note position of adjusting spring.

NOTE: Do not interchange the adjusting screws or adjusting screw springs from right to left brake assembly.

8. Remove the retaining ring, pin and parking brake lever from the secondary shoe.

To install:

9. Lubricate the shoe contact surfaces on the backing plate and adjusting screw assembly.

10. Install the parking brake lever on the secondary shoe with the pin and retaining ring.

11. Install the adjusting screw as-

sembly and spring. The coil of the spring must not be over the star wheel.

12. Install the shoe and lining assemblies after attaching the parking brake cable.

13. Install the parking brake strut and spring by spreading the shoes apart. Ensure the strut is properly positioned. The end with the spring engages the primary shoe and the end without the spring engages the parking brake lever.

14. Install the actuator pivot, actuator lever and return spring.

15. Install the actuator link in the shoe retainer.

16. Install the link into the lever while holding up on the lever.

17. Install the hold-down pins, lever pivot and hold-down springs.

18. Install the shoe return springs.

19. Install the brake drum, wheel and tire assembly, then lower vehicle. Apply the brake pedal several times to seat the brake shoes. Check and adjust the parking brake, as required.

20. Check the master cylinder reservoir. Reconnect the negative battery cable.

Wheel Cylinder

REMOVAL & INSTALLATION

1. Disconnet battery negative cable.

2. Loosen the wheel lug nuts, raise and support vehicle, then remove the tire and wheel assembly. Remove the drum and brake shoes. Leave the hub and wheel bearing assembly in place.

3. Remove any dirt from around the brake line fitting, then disconnect the brake line.

4. Remove the wheel cylinder retainer by using 2 awls or punches into the slots between the wheel cylinder pilot and retainer locking tabs. Bend both tabs away simultaneously. Remove the wheel cylinder from the backing plate.

To install:

5. Position the wheel cylinder against the backing plate and hold it in place with a wooden block between the wheel cylinder and the hub and bearing assembly.

6. Install a new retainer over the wheel cylinder abutment on the rear of the backing plate by pressing it into place with an 1⅛ inch 12 point socket and an extension.

7. Install a new bleeder screw into the wheel cylinder. Install brake line and torque to 10–15 ft. lbs.

8. The rest of the installation is the reverse of the removal procedure. After installing the brake drum, bleed the system.

Parking Brake Cable

ADJUSTMENT

1. Raise the rear of the vehicle and support it safely using jackstands, with both rear wheels off the ground.

2. Apply the parking brake 3 ratchet clicks from the fully released position.

3. Loosen the equalizer locknut, the tighten the adjusting nut until a light to moderate drag is felt when the rear wheels are rotate. Tighten the locknut.

4. Fully release parking brake and rotate rear wheels; no drag should be felt.

REMOVAL & INSTALLATION

Front Cable

1. Place the gear selector in **N** and apply the parking brake.

2. Disconnect the parking brake cable from the pedal.

3. Remove the cable retaining nut and the bracket securing the front cable to the floor panel.

4. Raise and support vehicle, then loosen the equalizer nut.

5. Loosen the catalytic converter shield, if necessary, and remove the parking brake cable from the body.

6. Disconnect the cable from the equalizer, then remove the cable from the guide and the underbody clips.

7. Reverse procedure to install. Adjust cable.

Rear Cables

1. Raise and support rear of vehicle, then back off the equalizer nut until the cable tension is eleminated.

2. Remove tires, wheels and brake drums.

3. Insert a suitable pry bar between the brake shoe and the top part of the brake adjuster bracket. Push the bracket to the front, then release the top brake adjuster rod.

4. Remove the rear hold-down spring. Remove the actuator lever and the lever return spring.

5. Remove the adjuster screw spring, then the top rear brake shoe return spring.

6. Unhook the parking brake cable from the parking brake pedal.

7. Depress the conduit fitting retaining tangs and then remove the conduit fitting from the backing plate.

8. Remove the cable end button from the connector.

9. Depress the conduit fitting retaining tangs and remove the conduit fitting from the axle bracket. Reverse procedure to install.

Anti-Lock Brake System Service

PRECAUTIONS

Failure to observe the following precautions may result in system damage.

• Before performing electric arc welding on the vehicle, disconnect the Electronic Brake Control Module (EBCM) and the hydraulic modulator connectors.

• When performing painting work on the vehicle, do not expose the Electronic Brake Control Module (EBCM) to temperatures in excess of 185°F (85°C) for longer than 2 hrs. The system may be exposed to temperatures up to 200°F (95°C) for less than 15 min.

• Never disconnect or connect the Electronic Brake Control Module (EBCM) or hydraulic modulator connectors with the ignition switch ON.

• Never disassemble any component of the Anti-Lock Brake System (ABS) which is designated non-servicable; the component must be replaced as an assembly.

• When filling the master cylinder, always use Delco Supreme 11 brake fluid or equivalent, which meets DOT-3 specifications; petroleum base fluid will destroy the rubber parts.

RELIEVING ANTI-LOCK BRAKE SYSTEM PRESSURE

— CAUTION —

Failure to fully depressurize the accumulator before performing any repairs could result in injury, and/or damage to the system.

With the ignition switch in the **OFF** position, apply and relase the brake pedal a minimum of 20 times using approximately 50 lbs. (222 N) of force on the pedal. A change in the pedal feel will occur when the accumulator is completely discharged.

Hydraulic Unit

REMOVAL & INSTALLATION

1. Depressureize the system, then disconnect the battery negative cable.

2. Disconnect the electrical connectors from the unit, then remove the fluid from the reservoir.

3. Remove the wire clip from the return hose fitting, then the return hose from the pump.

4. Remove the pressure hose attaching bolt, then the pressure hose and O-ring from the pump.

5. Remove the pump mounting bolt, then the energy unit from the hydraulic unit.

6. Disconnect the 4 brake lines from the valve block and hydraulic unit.

7. Disconnect the pushrod from the brake pedal, then push the dust boot forward off the rear half of the pushrod and unthread the 2 halves of the pushrod.

8. Remove the hydraulic unit attaching bolts from the pushrod bracket, then the hydraulic unit from the vehicle.

To install:

9. Install the hydraulic unit to the pushrod bracket. Torque bolts to 37 ft. lbs. (50 Nm).

10. Thread the 2 halves of pushrod together, reposition the dust boot, then

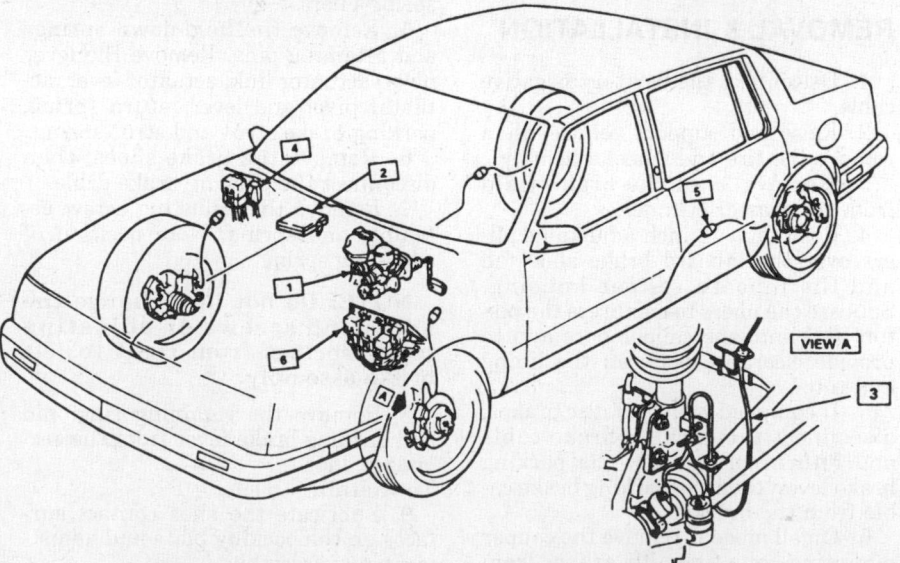

1.	HYDRAULIC UNIT	4.	RELAYS AND GROUND
2.	ELECTRONIC CONTROLLER	5.	SENSOR CONNECTION TO HARNESS
3.	FRONT WHEEL SPEED SENSOR	6.	RELAYS AND FUSE

Anti-Lock brake system components—1990 Celebritly and 1990–91 6000

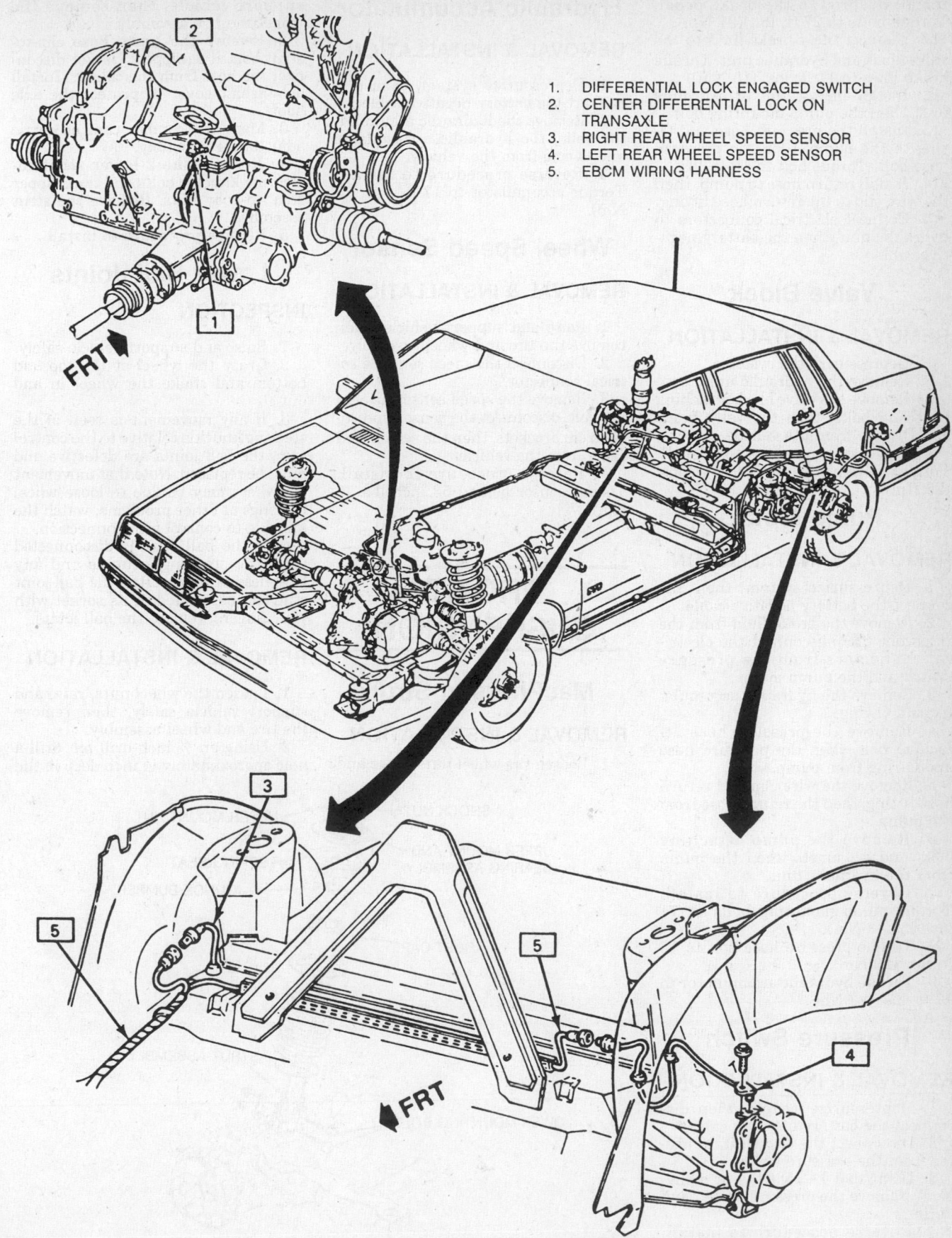

1. DIFFERENTIAL LOCK ENGAGED SWITCH
2. CENTER DIFFERENTIAL LOCK ON TRANSAXLE
3. RIGHT REAR WHEEL SPEED SENSOR
4. LEFT REAR WHEEL SPEED SENSOR
5. EBCM WIRING HARNESS

FRT

FRT

Anti-Lock brake system components (cont.) – 1990 Celebrity and 1990–91 6000

install pushrod to the brake pedal. Torque bolts to 27 ft. lbs. (37 Nm).

11. Connect the 4 brake lines to the valve block and hydraulic unit. Torque brake lines to 11 ft. lbs. (15 Nm).

12. Install energy unit to hydraulic unit, then the pump mounting bolt.

13. Install the pressure hose and O-ring to the pump, then the pressure hose bolt. Torque bolt to 15 ft. lbs.

14. Install return hose to pump, then the wire clip to the return hose fitting.

15. Connect electrical connectors to hydraulic unit, then the battery negative cable.

Valve Block

REMOVAL & INSTALLATION

1. Depressurize the system.
2. Remove the hydraulic unit.
3. Remove the valve block attaching nuts and bolts, then the valve block and O-rings from the vehicle.
4. Reverse procedure to install. Torque valve block bolts to 18 ft. lbs. (25 Nm).

Pump Motor

REMOVAL & INSTALLATION

1. Depressurize system, then disconnect the battery negative cable.
2. Remove the brake fluid from the reservoir, then disconnect the electrical connectors from the pressure switch and the pump motor.
3. Remove the hydraulic accumulator and O-ring.
4. Remove the pressure hose attaching bolt, then the pressure hose and O-ring from pump.
5. Remove the wire clip and return hose fitting, then the return hose from the pump.
6. Remove the pump attaching bolts and grommets, then the pump from the hydraulic unit.
7. Reverse procedure to install. Torque pump mounting bolts to 71 inch lbs. (8 Nm).
8. Torque pressure hose bolt to 15 ft. lbs. (20 Nm).
9. Torque hydraulic accumulator to 17 ft. lbs. (23 Nm).

Pressure Switch

REMOVAL & INSTALLATION

1. Depressurize system, then disconnect the battery negative cable.
2. Disconnect the electrical connector from the pressure switch.
3. Using tool J–35804–A or equivalent, remove the pressure switch and O-ring.
4. Reverse procedure to install. Torque pressure switch to 17 ft. lbs. (23 Nm).

Hydraulic Accumulator

REMOVAL & INSTALLATION

1. Depressurize system, then disconnect the battery negative cable.
2. Remove the hydraulic accumulator bolts, the hydraulic accumulator and O-ring from the vehicle.
3. Reverse procedure to install. Torque accumulator to 17 ft. lbs. (23 Nm).

Wheel Speed Sensor

REMOVAL & INSTALLATION

1. Raise and support vehicle, then remove the tire and wheel assembly.
2. Disconnect the speed sensor electrical connector.
3. Remove the speed sensor attaching bolt, disconnect the sensor and cable from brackets, then the sensor and cable from the vehicle.
4. Reverse procedure to install. Torque sensor bolt to 53 inch lbs. (6 Nm).

FRONT SUSPENSION

MacPherson Strut

REMOVAL & INSTALLATION

1. Loosen the wheel nuts, raise and support vehicle, then remove the wheel and tire assembly.

2. Remove the brake hose clip-to-strut bolt, if equipped. Do not disconnect the hose from the caliper. Install a halfshaft cover to protect the axle boot.

3. Mark the camber cam eccentric adjuster for assembly.

4. Remove the 2 lower strut-to-steering knuckle bolts and the 3 upper strut-to-body nuts. Remove the strut assembly.

5. Reverse procedure to install.

Lower Ball Joints

INSPECTION

1. Raise and support vehicle safely.
2. Grasp the wheel at the top and bottom and shake the wheel in and out.
3. If any movement is seen of the steering knuckle relative to the control arm, the ball joints are defective and must be replaced. Note that movement elsewhere may be due to loose wheel bearings or other problems; watch the knuckle-to-control arm connection.
4. If the ball stud is disconnected from the steering knuckle and any looseness is noted, often the ball joint stud can be twisted in its socket with your fingers, replace the ball joints.

REMOVAL & INSTALLATION

1. Loosen the wheel nuts, raise and support vehicle safely, then remove the tire and wheel assembly.

2. Using an ⅛ inch drill bit, drill a hole approximately ¼ inch deep in the

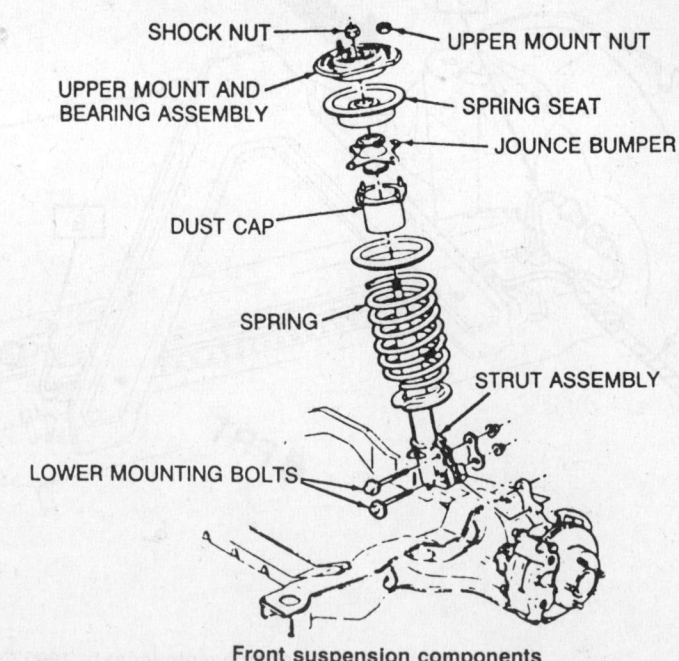

SHOCK NUT — UPPER MOUNT NUT
UPPER MOUNT AND BEARING ASSEMBLY — SPRING SEAT
— JOUNCE BUMPER
DUST CAP
SPRING
STRUT ASSEMBLY
LOWER MOUNTING BOLTS

Front suspension components

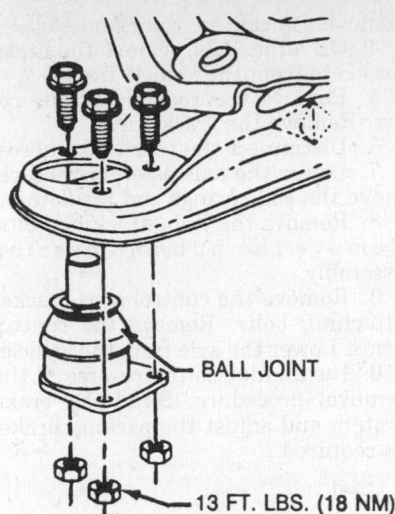

Ball joint installation

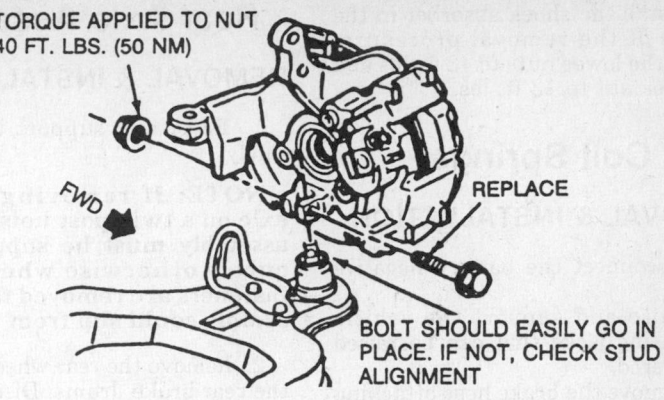

Ball joint stud should go in easily

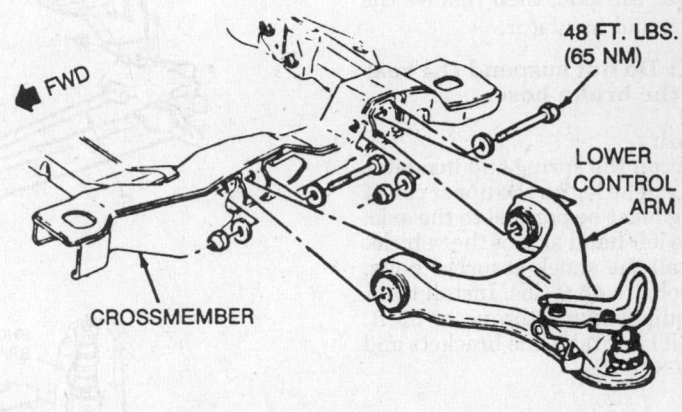

Control arm

center of each of the 3 ball joint rivets.

3. Using a ½ inch drill bit, drill off the rivet heads. Drill only enough to remove the rivet head.

4. Using a hammer and punch, remove the rivets, driving them out from the bottom.

5. Loosen the ball joint pinch bolt in the steering knuckle, then remove the ball joint.

To install:

6. Install a new ball joint in the control arm. Torque new bolts to 13 ft. lbs.

7. Install the ball stud into the steering knuckle pinch bolt fitting. It should go in easily; if not, check the stud alignment. Install the pinch bolt from the rear to the front. Torque to 45 ft. lbs.

8. Install the wheel and lower the vehicle.

Lower Control Arms

REMOVAL & INSTALLATION

1. Loosen the wheel nuts, raise and support vehicle safely, then remove the tire and wheel assembly.

2. Remove the stabilizer bar from the control arm.

3. Remove the ball joint from the steering knuckle.

4. Remove the control arm pivot bolts, then the control arm from the vehicle.

To install:

5. Install the control into the fittings. Install the pivot bolts from the rear to the front. Torque bolts to 50 ft. lbs.

6. Install the ball stud into the pinch bolt fitting. It should go in easily; if not, check the ball joint stud alignment.

7. Install the pinch bolt from the rear to the front. Torque bolts 40 ft. lbs.

8. Install the stabilizer bar attachment. Torque bolts to 35 ft. lbs.

9. Install the tire and wheel assembly and lower the vehicle.

Stabilizer Shaft

REMOVAL & INSTALLATION

1. Disconnect battery negative cable.

2. Raise and support vehicle safely.

3. Remove the stabilizer shaft insulator clamp and insulator at the control arms. Do not remove the studs from the control arm.

4. Remove the plate from the frame at each side, then the stabilizer shaft and insulator busings from the vehicle.

5. Reverse procedure to install. Torque plate to frame bolts to 40 ft. lbs. (55 Nm). Torque Insulator clamp nuts to 33 ft. lbs. (45 Nm).

REAR SUSPENSION

Shock Absorbers

REMOVAL & INSTALLATION

1. Disconnect the nagative battery cable.

2. Open the deck or trunk lid, then remove the trim cover and the upper shock nut. Remove and replace 1 shock at a time when replacing both shocks.

3. Raise and support the vehicle safely.

4. Remove the shock lower attaching bolt, then remove the shock. If equipped with air shocks, disconnect the air lines.

NOTE: Purge new shocks of air by repeatedly compressing them while inverted and extending them in their normal installed position.

5. Install the shock absorber in the reverse of the removal procedure. Torque the lower nuts to 43 ft. lbs and the upper nut to 13 ft. lbs.

Coil Springs

REMOVAL & INSTALLATION

1. Disconnect the battery negative cable.
2. Raise and support the vehicle safely using jacks that can be raised and lowered.
3. Remove the brake hose attaching brackets (right and left), allowing the hoses to hang freely. Do not disconnect the hoses.
4. Remove the track bar attaching bolts from the rear axle.
5. Lower the axle, then remove the coil spring and insulator.

NOTE: Do not suspend the rear axle by the brake hose.

To install:
6. Position the spring and insulator on the axle. The leg on the upper coil of the spring must be parallel to the axle, facing the left hand side of the vehicle.
7. Install the shock absorber bolts. Torque bolts to 43 ft. lbs. Install track bar, if equipped, and torque to 33 ft. lbs. Install the brake line brackets and torque to 8 ft. lbs.

Rear Wheel Bearings

REMOVAL & INSTALLATION

1. Disconnect battery negative cable, then raise and support vehicle.
2. Remove the wheel and brake drum. Do not hammer on the brake drum as damage to the bearing may result.
3. If equipped with anti-lock brakes, remove caliper, rotor and pads.
3. On all models, remove the hub and bearing assembly to the rear axle attaching bolts and remove the rear axle.

NOTE: The bolts which attach the hub and bearing assembly also support the brake assembly. When removing these bolts, support the brake assembly with a wire or other means. Do not let the brake line support the brake assembly.

4. Reverse procedure to install.

ADJUSTMENT

There is no adjustment to the rear wheel bearings and hub assembly.

Rear Axle Assembly

REMOVAL & INSTALLATION

1. Raise and support the vehicle safely.

NOTE: If removing the rear axle on a twin post hoist, the axle assembly must be supported securely otherwise when certain fasteners are removed the axle assembly could slip from the hoist.

2. Remove the rear wheels. Remove the rear brake drums. Disconnect the parking brake from the rear axle.
3. If equipped with anti-lock brakes, remove the caliper, rotor and pads.
4. On all models, remove the brake brackets from the vehicle frame.
5. Remove the rear shock absorbers. Remove the track bar.
6. Disconnect the rear brake hoses.
7. Lower the axle assembly and remove the coil springs and insulators.
8. Remove the hub attaching bolts. Remove the hub and bearing assembly.
9. Remove the control arm bracket attaching bolts. Remove the control arms. Lower the axle from the vehicle.
10. Installation is the reverse of the removal procedure. Bleed the brake system and adjust the parking brake, as required.

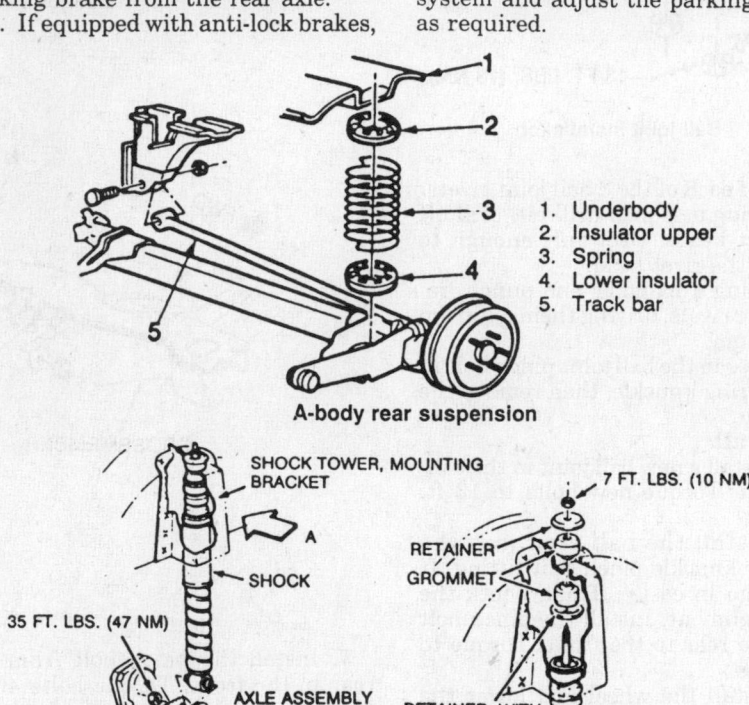

1. Underbody
2. Insulator upper
3. Spring
4. Lower insulator
5. Track bar

A-body rear suspension

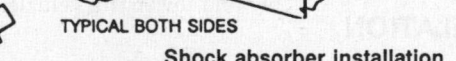

SHOCK TOWER, MOUNTING BRACKET

A

SHOCK

35 FT. LBS. (47 NM)

AXLE ASSEMBLY

FRONT

TYPICAL BOTH SIDES

7 FT. LBS. (10 NM)

RETAINER
GROMMET

RETAINER, WITH SUPER LIFT SHOCKS ONLY

SHOCK

VIEW A

Shock absorber installation

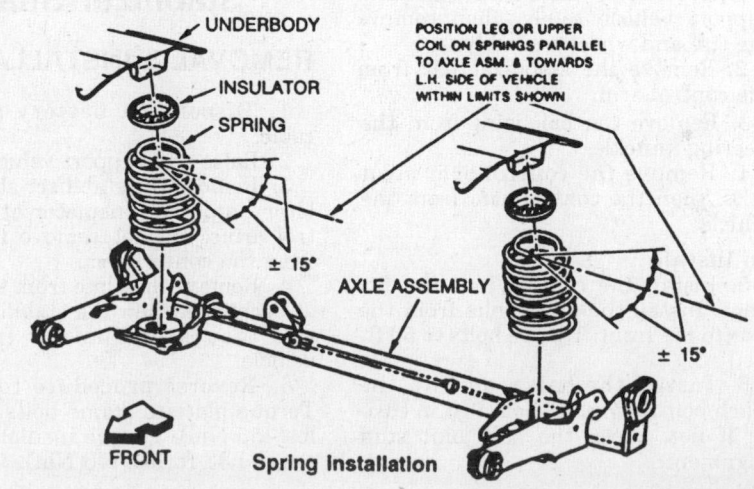

UNDERBODY

INSULATOR

SPRING

± 15°

POSITION LEG OR UPPER COIL ON SPRINGS PARALLEL TO AXLE ASM. & TOWARDS L.H. SIDE OF VEHICLE WITHIN LIMITS SHOWN

AXLE ASSEMBLY

± 15°

FRONT

Spring Installation

GM "C" & "H" Body
Front Wheel Drive
Buick—Electra, LeSabre, Park Avenue
Cadillac—DeVille, Fleetwood
Oldsmobile—Delta 88, Ninety-Eight
Pontiac—Bonneville

SPECIFICATIONS

VEHICLE IDENTIFICATION CHART

It is important for servicing and ordering parts to be certain of the vehicle and engine identification. The VIN (vehicle identification number) is a 17 digit number visible through the windshield on the driver's side of the dash and contains the vehicle and engine identification codes. The tenth digit indicates model year and the eighth digit indicates engine code. It can be interpreted as follows:

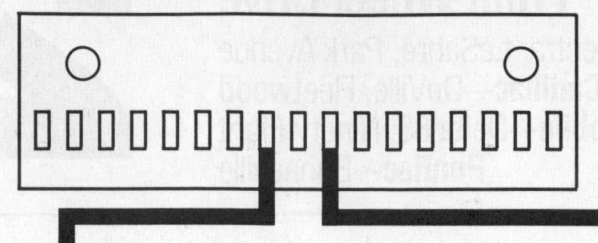

Engine Code

Code	Cu. In.	Liters	Cyl.	Fuel Sys.	Eng. Mfg.
3 ('87–'88)	231	3.8	6	SFI	Buick
C	231	3.8	6	SFI	Buick
8	250	4.1	8	DFI	Cadillac
5	273	4.5	8	DFI	Cadillac
3 ('90–'91)	273	4.5	8	DFI	Cadillac

Model Year

Code	Year
H	1987
J	1988
K	1989
L	1990
M	1991

GENERAL ENGINE SPECIFICATIONS

Year	VIN	No. Cylinder Displacement cu. in. (liter)	Fuel System Type	Net Horsepower @ rpm	Net Torque @ rpm (ft. lbs.)	Bore × Stroke (in.)	Compression Ratio	Oil Pressure @ rpm
1987	3	6-231 (3.8)	SFI	150 @ 4400	200 @ 2000	3.800 × 3.400	8.5:1	37 @ 2000
	8	8-250 (4.1)	DFI	130 @ 4200	200 @ 2000	3.465 × 3.307	9.0:1	30 @ 2000
1988	3	6-231 (3.8)	SFI	150 @ 4400	200 @ 2000	3.800 × 3.400	8.5:1	37 @ 2000
	C	6-231 (3.8)	SFI	165 @ 5200	210 @ 2000	3.800 × 3.400	8.5:1	37 @ 2400
	5	8-273 (4.5)	DFI	155 @ 4000	240 @ 2800	3.622 × 3.307	9.0:1	37 @ 1500
1989	C	6-231 (3.8)	SFI	165 @ 5200	210 @ 2000	3.800 × 3.400	8.5:1	37 @ 2400
	5	8-273 (4.5)	DFI	155 @ 4000	240 @ 2800	3.622 × 3.307	9.0:1	37 @ 1500
1990–91	C	6-231 (3.8)	SFI	165 @ 5200	210 @ 2000	3.800 × 3.400	8.5:1	40 @ 1850
	3	8-273 (4.5)	SFI	180 @ 4300	245 @ 3000	3.622 × 3.307	9.5:1	37 @ 1500

SFI Sequential Fuel Injection
DFI Digital Fuel Injection

ENGINE IDENTIFICATION

Year	Model	Engine Displacement cu. in. (liter)	Engine Series Identification (VIN)	No. of Cylinders	Engine Type
1987	DeVille	250 (4.1)	8	8	OHV
	Fleetwood	250 (4.1)	8	8	OHV
	Electra	231 (3.8)	3	6	OHV
	Park Avenue	231 (3.8)	3	6	OHV
	LeSabre	231 (3.8)	3	6	OHV
	Ninety Eight	231 (3.8)	3	6	OHV
	Delta 88	231 (3.8)	3	6	OHV
	Bonneville	231 (3.8)	3	6	OHV
1988	DeVille	273 (4.5)	5	8	OHV
	Fleetwood	273 (4.5)	5	8	OHV
	Electra	231 (3.8)	C	6	OHV
	Park Avenue	231 (3.8)	C	6	OHV
	LeSabre	231 (3.8)	3	6	OHV
	Ninety Eight	231 (3.8)	C	6	OHV
	Delta 88	231 (3.8)	3	6	OHV
	Bonneville	231 (3.8)	3	6	OHV
	Bonneville	231 (3.8)	C, 3	6	OHV
1989	DeVille	273 (4.5)	5	8	OHV
	Fleetwood	273 (4.5)	5	8	OHV
	Electra	231 (3.8)	C	6	OHV
	Park Avenue	231 (3.8)	C	6	OHV
	LeSabre	231 (3.8)	C	6	OHV
	Ninety Eight	231 (3.8)	C	6	OHV
	Delta 88	231 (3.8)	C	6	OHV
	Bonneville	231 (3.8)	C	6	OHV
1990–91	DeVille	273 (4.5)	3	8	OHV
	Fleetwood	273 (4.5)	3	8	OHV
	Electra	231 (3.8)	3	6	OHV
	Park Avenue	231 (3.8)	3	6	OHV
	LeSabre	231 (3.8)	3	6	OHV
	Ninety Eight	231 (3.8)	3	6	OHV
	Delta 88	231 (3.8)	3	6	OHV
	Bonneville	231 (3.8)	3	6	OHV

OHV—Overhead Valves

GASOLINE ENGINE TUNE-UP SPECIFICATIONS

Year	VIN	No. Cylinder Displacement cu. in. (liter)	Spark Plugs Type	Gap (in.)	Ignition Timing (deg.) MT	AT	Com- pression Pressure (psi)	Fuel Pump (psi)	Speed (rpm) MT	AT	Valve Clearance In.	Ex.
1987	3	6-231 (3.8)	R44TSX	0.045	①	①	②	37–43	①	①	Hyd.	Hyd.
	8	8-250 (4.1)	R42LTS6	0.060	①	①	140–165	9–12	①	①	Hyd.	Hyd.
1988	3	6-231 (3.8)	R44LTS	0.045	①	①	②	34–40	①	①	Hyd.	Hyd.
	C	6-231 (3.8)	R44LTS6	0.060	①	①	②	40–47	①	①	Hyd.	Hyd.
	5	8-273 (4.5)	R44LTS6	0.060	①	①	140–165	9–12	①	①	Hyd.	Hyd.
1989	C	6-231 (3.8)	R44LTS6	0.060	①	①	②	40–47	①	①	Hyd.	Hyd.
	5	8-273 (4.5)	R44LTS6	0.060	①	①	140–165	9–12	①	①	Hyd.	Hyd.
1990	C	6-231 (3.8)	R44LTS6	0.060	①	①	②	40–47	①	①	Hyd.	Hyd.
	3	8-273 (4.5)	R44LTS6	0.060	①	①	140–165	40–47	①	①	Hyd.	Hyd.
1991		SEE UNDERHOOD SPECIFICATIONS STICKER										

① These vehicles are equipped with computerized emissions systems which have no distributor vacuum advance unit. The idle speed and ignition timing are controlled by the emissions computer.

② The lowest cylinder reading should be no less than 70% of the highest and no cylinder should be less than 100 P.S.I.

FIRING ORDERS

NOTE: To avoid confusion, always replace spark plug wires one at a time.

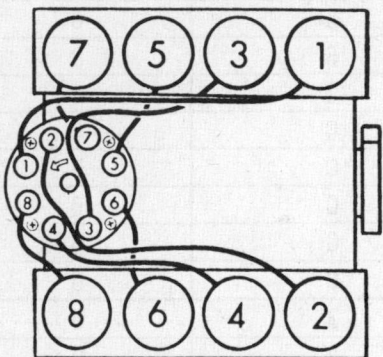

4.1L and 4.5L Engines
Engine Firing Order: 1–8–4–3–6–5–7–2
Distributor Rotation: Counterclockwise

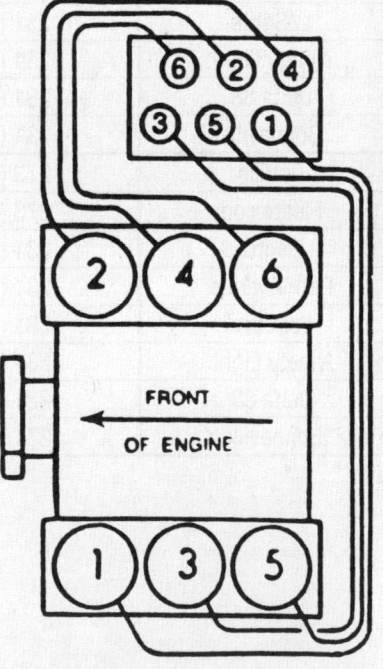

3.8L Engine VIN 3
Engine Firing Order: 1–6–5–4–3–2
Distributorless Ignition System

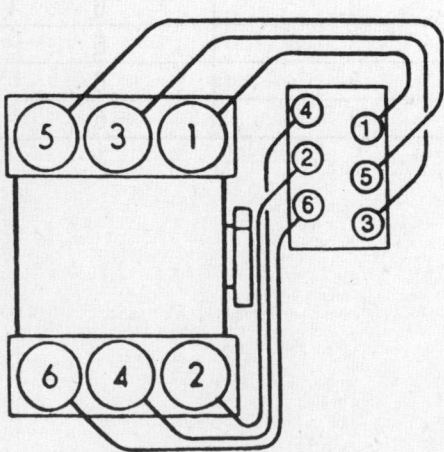

3.8L Engine VIN C
Engine Firing Order: 1–6–5–4–3–2
Distributorless Ignition System

CAPACITIES

Year	Model	VIN	No. Cylinder Displacement cu. in. (liter)	Engine Crankcase (qts.) with Filter	Engine Crankcase (qts.) without Filter	Transmission (pts.) 4-Spd	Transmission (pts.) 5-Spd	Transmission (pts.) Auto.	Drive Axle (pts.)	Fuel Tank (gal.)	Cooling System (qts.)
1987	DeVille	8	8-250 (4.1)	4.0 ①	4.0	—	—	22	—	18	13.2 ③
	Fleetwood	8	8-250 (4.1)	4.0 ①	4.0	—	—	22	—	18	13.2 ③
	Electra	3	8-231 (3.8)	4.0 ①	4.0	—	—	22	—	18	13.3
	Park Avenue	3	8-231 (3.8)	4.0 ①	4.0	—	—	22	—	18	13.3
	LeSabre	3	8-231 (3.8)	4.0 ①	4.0	—	—	22	—	18	13.0
	Ninety Eight	3	8-231 (3.8)	4.0 ①	4.0	—	—	22	—	18	13.3
	Delta 88	3	8-231 (3.8)	4.0 ①	4.0	—	—	22	—	18	13.3
	Bonneville	3	8-231 (3.8)	4.0 ①	4.0	—	—	22	—	18	13.3
1988	DeVille	5	8-273 (4.5)	5.5	5.0	—	—	22	—	18	13.0 ③
	Fleetwood	5	8-273 (4.5)	5.5	5.0	—	—	22	—	18	13.0 ③
	Electra	C	6-231 (3.8)	4.0 ①	4.0	—	—	22	—	18	13.0
	Park Avenue	C	6-231 (3.8)	4.0 ①	4.0	—	—	22	—	18	13.0
	LeSabre	3	6-231 (3.8)	4.0 ①	4.0	—	—	22	—	18	13.0
	Ninety Eight	C	6-231 (3.8)	4.0 ①	4.0	—	—	22	—	18	12.50
	Delta 88 Royale	3	6-231 (3.8)	4.0 ①	4.0	—	—	22	—	18	13.25
	Bonneville	C, 3	6-231 (3.8)	4.0	4.0	—	—	22	—	18	13.0
	Bonneville	C	6-231 (3.8)	4.0	4.0	—	—	22	—	18	13.0
1989	DeVille	5	8-273 (4.5)	5.5	5.0	—	—	22	—	18	13.0 ③
	Fleetwood	5	8-273 (4.5)	5.5	5.0	—	—	22	—	18	13.0 ③
	Electra	C	6-231 (3.8)	4.0 ①	4.0	—	—	22	—	18	13.0
	Park Avenue	C	6-231 (3.8)	4.0 ①	4.0	—	—	22	—	18	13.0
	LeSabre	C	6-231 (3.8)	4.0 ①	4.0	—	—	22	—	18	13.0
	Ninety Eight	C	6-231 (3.8)	4.0 ①	4.0	—	—	22	—	18	12.50
	Delta 88 Royale	C	6-231 (3.8)	4.0 ①	4.0	—	—	22	—	18	13.25
	Bonneville	C	6-231 (3.8)	4.0 ①	4.0	—	—	22	—	18	13.0
1990–91	DeVille	3	8-273 (4.5)	5.5 ①	5.0	—	—	22	—	18	13.2
	Fleetwood	3	8-273 (4.5)	5.5	5.0	—	—	22	—	18	13.2
	Electra	C	6-231 (3.8)	4.0 ①	4.0	—	—	22	—	18	13.0
	Park Avenuea	C	6-231 (3.8)	4.0 ①	4.0	—	—	22	—	18	13.0
	LeSabre	C	6-231 (3.8)	4.0 ①	4.0	—	—	22	—	18	13.0
	Ninety Eight	C	6-231 (3.8)	4.0 ①	4.0	—	—	22	—	18	13.0
	Delta 88 Royale	C	6-231 (3.8)	4.0 ①	4.0	—	—	22	—	18	13.0
	Bonneville	C	6-231 (3.8)	4.0 ②①	4.0	—	—	22	—	18	13.0

① Additional oil may be necessary to bring the level to full
② SSE—5.5 qts.
③ Use coolant solution specifically designed for use in aluminum engines.

CAMSHAFT SPECIFICATIONS

All measurements given in inches.

Year	VIN	No. Cylinder Displacement cu. in. (liter)	Journal Diameter					Lobe Lift		Bearing Clearance	Camshaft End Play
			1	2	3	4	5	In.	Ex.		
1987	3	6-231 (3.8)	1.7850–1.7860	1.7850–1.7860	1.7850–1.7860	1.7850–1.7860	—	0.368	0.384	①	NA
	8	8-250 (4.1)	2.035–2.036	2.015–2.016	1.995–1.996	1.975–1.976	1.955–1.956	0.384	0.396	0.0018–0.0037	NA
1988	3	6-231 (3.8)	②	②	②	②	—	0.245	0.245	①	NA
	C	6-231 (3.8)	②	②	②	②	—	0.272	0.272	①	NA
	5	8-273 (4.5)	2.0350–2.0360	2.0150–2.0160	1.9950–1.9960	1.9750–1.9760	1.9550–1.9560	0.384	0.396	0.0018–0.0037	NA
1989	C	6-231 (3.8)	1.7850–1.7860	1.7850–1.7860	1.7850–1.7860	1.7850–1.7860		0.250	0.255	①	NA
	5	8-273 (4.5)	2.0350–2.0360	2.0150–2.0160	1.9950–1.9960	1.9750–1.9760	1.9550–1.9560	0.384	0.396	0.0018–0.0037	NA
1990-91	C	6-231 (3.8)	1.7850–1.7860	1.7850–1.7860	1.7850–1.7860	1.7850–1.7860	—	0.250	0.255	①	NA
	3	8-273 (4.5)	NA	NA	NA	NA	NA	0.384	0.396	0.0018 0.0037	NA NA

① No. 1: 0.0005–0.0025
   No. 2–5: 0.0005–0.0035

CRANKSHAFT AND CONNECTING ROD SPECIFICATIONS

All measurements are given in inches.

Year	VIN	No. Cylinder Displacement cu. in. (liter)	Crankshaft				Connecting Rod		
			Main Brg. Journal Dia.	Main Brg. Oil Clearance	Shaft End-play	Thrust on. No.	Journal Diameter	Oil Clearance	Side Clearance
1987	3	6-231 (3.8)	2.4995–	0.0003–0.0018	0.0003–0.0010	2	2.2487–2.2499	0.0005–0.0026	0.003–0.015
	8	8-250 (4.1)	2.6354–2.6364	0.0004–0.0027	0.0010–0.0070	3	1.9291	0.0005–0.0028	0.008–0.020
1988	3	6-231 (3.8)	2.4988–2.4988	0.0003–0.0018	0.0030–0.0110	2	2.2487–2.2499	0.0005–0.0026	0.003–0.015
	C	6-231 (3.8)	2.4998–2.4998	0.0003–0.0018	0.0030–0.0110	2	2.2487–2.2499	0.0005–0.0026	0.003–0.015
	5	8-273 (4.5)	2.6354–2.6364	0.0004–0.0027	0.0010–0.0070	3	1.9291	0.0005–0.0028	0.008–0.020
1989	C	6-231 (3.8)	2.4988–2.4998	0.0003–0.0018	0.0030–0.0110	2	2.2487–2.2499	0.0003–0.0026	0.003–0.015
	5	8-273 (4.5)	2.6354–2.6364	0.0004–0.0027	0.0010–0.0070	3	1.9291	0.0005–0.0028	0.008–0.020
1990-91	C	6-231 (3.8)	2.4988–2.4998	0.0003–0.0018	0.0030–0.0110	2	2.2487–2.2499	0.0003–0.0026	0.003–0.015
	3	8-273 (4.5)	2.6354–2.6364	0.0004–0.0027	0.0010–0.0070	3	1.9291	0.0005–0.0028	0.008–0.020

VALVE SPECIFICATIONS

Year	VIN	No. Cylinder Displacement cu. in. (liter)	Seat Angle (deg.)	Face Angle (deg.)	Spring Test Pressure (lbs.)	Spring Installed Height (in.)	Stem-to-Guide Clearance (in.)		Stem Diameter (in.)	
							Intake	Exhaust	Intake	Exhaust
1987	3	6-231 (3.8)	46	45	90	1.690–1.750	0.0015–0.0035	0.0015–0.0032	0.3401–0.3412	0.3405–0.3412
	8	8-250 (4.1)	45	44	93–103	1.730	0.0010–0.0030	0.0010–0.0030	0.3420–0.3413	0.3401–0.3408
1988	3	6-231 (3.8)	46	45	90	1.690–1.750	0.0015–0.0035	0.0015–0.0032	0.3401–0.3412	0.3405–0.3412
	C	6-231 (3.8)	45	45	105	—	0.0015–0.0035	0.0015–0.0032	0.3401–0.3412	0.3405–0.3412
	5	8-273 (4.5)	45	44	93–103	1.730	0.0010–0.0030	0.0010–0.0030	0.3420–0.3413	0.3401–0.3408
1989	C	6-231 (3.8)	45	45	76–84	1.690–1.750	0.0015–0.0035	0.0015–0.0032	0.3401–0.3412	0.3405–0.3412
	5	8-273 (4.5)	45	44	93–103	1.730	0.0010–0.0030	0.0010–0.0030	0.3420–0.3413	0.3401–0.3408
1990–91	C	6-231 (3.8)	45	45	76–84	1.690–1.750	0.0015–0.0035	0.0015–0.0032	0.3401–0.3412	0.3405–0.3412
	3	8-273 (4.5)	45	44	93–103	—	0.0010–0.0030	0.0020–0.0040	0.3420–0.3413	0.3401–0.3408

PISTON AND RING SPECIFICATIONS

All measurements are given in inches.

Year	VIN	No. Cylinder Displacement cu. in. (liter)	Piston Clearance	Ring Gap			Ring Side Clearance		
				Top Compression	Bottom Compression	Oil Control	Top Compression	Bottom Compression	Oil Control
1987	3	6-231 (3.8)	0.0008–0.0020	0.0100–0.0200	0.0100–0.0200	0.0150–0.0550	0.0300–0.0050	0.0030–0.0050	0.0035 Max.
	8	8-250 (4.1)	0.0010–0.0018	0.0150–0.0240	0.0150–0.0240	0.0100–0.0500	0.0016–0.0037	0.0016–0.0037	None (side sealing)
1988	3	6-231 (3.8)	0.0004–0.0022	0.0100–0.0200	0.0100–0.0220	0.0150–0.0550	0.0010–0.0030	0.0010–0.0030	0.0005–0.0065
	C	6-231 (3.8)	①	0.0100–0.0250	0.0100–0.0550	0.0150–0.0055	0.0013–0.0031	0.0013–0.0031	0.0011 0.0081
	5	8-273 (4.5)	0.0010–0.0018	0.0150–0.0240	0.0150–0.0240	0.0100–0.0500	0.0016–0.0037	0.0016–0.0037	None (side sealing)
1989	C	6-231 (3.8)	①	0.0100–0.0250	0.0100–0.0250	0.0150–0.0055	0.0013–0.0031	0.0013–0.0031	0.0011 0.0081
	5	8-273 (4.5)	0.0010–0.0018	0.0150–0.0240	0.0150–0.0240	0.0100–0.0500	0.0016–0.0037	0.0016–0.0037	None (side sealing)
1990–91	C	6-231 (3.8)	0.0004–0.0022	0.0100–0.0250	0.0100–0.0250	0.0150–0.0550	0.0013–0.0031	0.0013–0.0031	0.0011–0.0081
	3	8-273 (4.5)	0.0010–0.0018	0.0150–0.0240	0.0150–0.0240	0.0100–0.0500	0.0016–0.0037	0.0016–0.0037	None (side sealing)

① Skirt top: 0.0007–0.0027
  Skirt bottom: 0.0010–0.0045

TORQUE SPECIFICATIONS
All readings in ft. lbs.

Year	VIN	No. Cylinder Displacement cu. in. (liter)	Cylinder Head Bolts	Main Bearing Bolts	Rod Bearing Bolts	Crankshaft Pulley Bolts	Flywheel Bolts	Manifold Intake	Manifold Exhaust	Spark Plugs
1987	3	6-231 (3.8)	60 ⑤	100	40	219	60	45	37	20
	8	8-250 (4.1)	①	85	22	18		③	18	11
1988	3	6-231 (3.8)	60 ⑤	100	40	219	60	80 ④	37	20
	C	6-231 (3.8)	60 ⑤	100	40	219	60	80 ④	37	20
	5	8-273 (4.5)	①	85	22	18		③	18	11
1989	C	6-231 (3.8)	60 ⑤	90	43	219	61	88	41	20
	5	8-273 (4.5)	①	85	22	18		②	18	11
1990-91	C	6-231 (3.8)	35	90	43	219	61	88 ④	41	20
	3	8-273 (4.5)	①	85	24	18	70	②	18	11

① Tighten in 3 Steps
  1. Tighten bolts in sequence to 38 ft. lbs.
  2. Tighten bolts in sequence to 68 ft. lbs.
  3. Tighten bolts, 1, 3 and 4 to 90 ft. lbs.
② Tighten in 3 Steps
  1. Tighten bolts 1, 2, 3, 4 in sequence to 8 ft. lbs.
  2. Tighten bolts 5 through 16 in sequence to 8 ft. lbs.
  3. Retighten all bolts in sequence to 12 ft. lbs.
③ Tighten in 3 Steps
  1. Tighten bolts 1, 2, 3, 4 in sequence to 15 ft. lbs.
  2. Tighten bolts 5 through 16 in sequence to 22 ft. lbs.
  3. Retighten all bolts in sequence to 22 ft. lbs.
④ Inch lbs.
⑤ 3 Step procedure: Should you reach 60 ft. lbs. at any time in step 2 or 3, stop tightening
  Do not complete the balance of the 90 degree turn of this bolt
  Step 1: 25 ft. lbs.
  Step 2: 90 degrees
  Step 3: 90 degrees

BRAKE SPECIFICATIONS
All measurements in inches unless noted

Year	Model	Lug Nut Torque (ft. lbs.)	Master Cylinder Bore	Brake Disc Minimum Thickness	Brake Disc Maximum Runout	Standard Brake Drum Diameter	Minimum Lining Thickness Front	Minimum Lining Thickness Rear
1987	DeVille	100	0.945	0.972	0.004	8.900	0.030	0.030
	Fleetwood	100	0.945	0.972	0.004	8.900	0.030	0.030
	Electra	100	0.937	0.972	0.004	8.860	0.030	0.030
	Park Ave	100	0.937	0.972	0.004	8.860	0.030	0.030
	LeSabre	100 ①	0.937	0.972	0.004	8.860	0.030	0.030
	Ninety Eight	100	0.937	0.972	0.004	8.860	0.030	0.030
	Delta 88	100 ①	0.937	0.972	0.004	8.860	0.030	0.030
	Bonneville	100 ①	0.937	0.972	0.004	8.860	0.030	0.030

BRAKE SPECIFICATIONS

All measurements in inches unless noted

Year	Model	Lug Nut Torque (ft. lbs.)	Master Cylinder Bore	Brake Disc		Standard Brake Drum Diameter	Minimum Lining Thickness	
				Minimum Thickness	Maximum Runout		Front	Rear
1988	DeVille	100	0.937 ②	0.972	0.004	8.900	0.030	0.030
	Fleetwood	100	0.937 ②	0.972	0.004	8.900	0.030	0.030
	Electra	100	0.937 ②	0.972	0.004	8.860	0.030	0.030
	Park Ave	100	0.937 ②	0.972	0.004	8.860	0.030	0.030
	LeSabre	100 ①	0.937 ②	0.972	0.004	8.860	0.030	0.030
	Ninety Eight	100	0.937 ②	0.972	0.004	8.860	0.030	0.030
	Delta 88	100 ①	0.937 ②	0.972	0.004	8.860	0.030	0.030
	Bonneville	100 ①	0.937 ②	0.972	0.004	8.860	0.030	0.030
1989	DeVille	100	0.937	0.972	0.004	8.860	0.030	0.030
	Fleetwood	100	0.937	0.972	0.004	8.860	0.030	0.030
	Electra	100	0.937	0.972	0.004	8.860	0.030	0.030
	Park Ave	100	0.937	0.972	0.004	8.860	0.030	0.030
	LeSabre	100	0.937	0.972	0.004	8.860	0.030	0.030
	Ninety Eight	100	0.937	0.972	0.004	8.860	0.030	0.030
	Delta 88	100	0.937	0.972	0.004	8.860	0.030	0.030
	Bonneville	100	0.937	0.972	0.004	8.860	0.030	0.030
1990–91	DeVille	100	0.937	0.972	0.004	8.860	0.030	0.030
	Fleetwood	100	0.937	0.972	0.004	8.860	0.030	0.030
	Electra	100	0.937	0.972	0.004	8.860	0.030	0.030
	Park Ave	100	0.937	0.972	0.004	8.860	0.030	0.030
	LeSabre	100	0.937	0.972	0.004	8.860	0.030	0.030
	Ninety Eight	100	0.937	0.972	0.004	8.860	0.030	0.030
	Delta 88	100	0.937	0.972	0.004	8.860	0.030	0.030
	Bonneville	100	0.937	0.972	0.004	8.860	0.030	0.030

① 7/16 in. stud—80 ft. lbs.
② Anti-lock brakes: standard brakes—0.945

WHEEL ALIGNMENT

Year	Model	Caster		Camber		Toe-in (in.)	Steering Axis Inclination (deg.)
		Range (deg.)	Preferred Setting (deg.)	Range (deg.)	Preferred Setting (deg.)		
1987	DeVille	1 1/2 P–3 1/2 P	2 1/2 P	5/16 N–1 1/4 P	1/2	3/32 P ①	—
	Fleetwood	1 1/2 P–3 1/2 P	2 1/2 P	5/16 N–1 1/4 P	1/2	3/32 P ①	—
	Electra	2P–3P	2 1/2 P	②	1/2 P	3/32 P ①	—
	Park Ave	2P–3P	2 1/2 P	②	1/2 P	3/32 P ①	—
	LeSabre	2P–3P	2 1/2 P	5/16 N–11/16 P	3/16 P	0	—
	Ninety Eight	2P–3P	2 1/2 P	②	②	3/32 P ①	—
	Delta 88	2P–3P	2 1/2 P	5/16 N–11/16 P	3/16 P	0	12 13/16 P
	Bonneville	2P–3P	2 1/2 P	5/16 N–11/16 P	3/16 P	0	—

WHEEL ALIGNMENT

Year	Model	Caster Range (deg.)	Caster Preferred Setting (deg.)	Camber Range (deg.)	Camber Preferred Setting (deg.)	Toe-in (in.)	Steering Axis Inclination (deg.)
1988	DeVille	$2^1/_2$P–$3^1/_2$P	3P	1N–0	$^1/_2$N	0	—
	Fleetwood	$2^1/_2$P–$3^1/_2$P	3P	1N–0	$^1/_2$N	0	—
	Electra	$2^1/_2$P–$3^1/_2$P	3P	$^1/_3$N–$^2/_3$P	$^1/_5$P	0	—
	Park Ave	$2^1/_2$P–$3^1/_2$P	3P	$^1/_3$N–$^2/_3$P	$^1/_5$P	0	—
	LeSabre	$2^1/_2$P–$3^1/_2$P	3P	$^5/_{16}$N–$^{11}/_{16}$P	$^3/_{16}$P	0	—
	Ninety Eight	2P–3P	$2^1/_2$P	$^1/_3$N–$^2/_3$P	$^1/_5$P	0	—
	Delta 88	2P–3P	$2^1/_2$P	$^5/_{16}$N–$^{11}/_{16}$P	$^3/_{16}$P	0	$12^{13}/_{16}$P
	Bonneville	2P–3P	$2^1/_2$P	$^5/_{16}$N–$^{11}/_{16}$P	$^3/_{16}$P	0	—
1989	DeVille	$2^1/_2$P–$3^1/_2$P	3P	②	②	0	—
	Fleetwood	$2^1/_2$P–$3^1/_2$P	3P	②	②	0	—
	Electra	$2^1/_2$P–$3^1/_2$P	3P	$^5/_{16}$N–$^{11}/_{16}$P	$^3/_{16}$P	0	—
	Park Ave	$2^1/_2$P–$3^1/_2$P	3P	$^5/_{16}$N–$^{11}/_{16}$P	$^3/_{16}$P	0	—
	LeSabre	$2^1/_2$P–$3^1/_2$P	3P	$^5/_{16}$N–$^{11}/_{16}$P	$^3/_{16}$P	0	—
	Ninety Eight	$2^1/_2$P–$3^1/_2$P	3P	$^5/_{16}$N–$^{11}/_{16}$P	$^3/_{16}$P	0	—
	Delta 88	$2^1/_2$P–$3^1/_2$P	3P	$^5/_{16}$N–$^{11}/_{16}$P	$^3/_{16}$P	0	—
	Bonneville	$2^1/_2$P–$3^1/_2$P	3P	$^5/_{16}$N–$^{11}/_{16}$P	$^3/_{16}$P	0	—
1990–91	DeVille	$2^1/_2$P–$3^1/_2$P	3P	②	②	0	—
	Fleetwood	$2^1/_2$P–$3^1/_2$P	3P	②	②	0	—
	Electra	$2^1/_2$P–$3^1/_2$P	3P	$^5/_{16}$N–$^{11}/_{16}$P	$^3/_{16}$P	0	—
	Park Ave	$2^1/_2$P–$3^1/_2$P	3P	$^5/_{16}$N–$^{11}/_{16}$P	$^3/_{16}$P	0	—
	LeSabre	$2^1/_2$P–$3^1/_2$P	3P	$^5/_{16}$N–$^{11}/_{16}$P	$^3/_{16}$P	0	—
	Ninety Eight	$2^1/_2$P–$3^1/_2$P	3P	$^5/_{16}$N–$^{11}/_{16}$P	$^3/_{16}$P	0	—
	Delta 88	$2^1/_2$P–$3^1/_2$P	3P	$^5/_{16}$N–$^{11}/_{16}$P	$^3/_{16}$P	0	—
	Bonneville	$2^1/_2$P–$3^1/_2$P	3P	$^5/_{16}$N–$^{11}/_{16}$P	$^3/_{16}$P	0	—

N Negative
P Positive
① In or out pref: 0
② Left wheel
    Min.—1N
    Pref.—$^1/_2$N
    Max.—0
   Right wheel
    Min.—0
    Pref.—$^1/_2$P
    Max.—1P

ENGINE ELECTRICAL

NOTE: Disconnecting the negative battery cable on some vehicles may interfere with the functions of the on board computer systems and may require the computer to undergo a relearning process, once the negative battery cable is reconnected.

Distributor

The 4.1L and 4.5L engines are equipped with High Energy Ignition (HEI) system, utilizing Electronic Spark Timing (EST). The EST distributor uses no mechanical or vacuum advance and is easily identified by the absence of a vacuum advance.

All other engines are equipped with Computer Controlled Coil Ignition (C^3I), which eliminates the distributor. The ECM provides multiport injection from processing the crankshaft signal only.

The C^3I system consists of the coil pack, ignition module, various hall effect sensors, interrupter rings and electronic control module (ECM). Since the ECM controls the ignition timing, no timing adjustments are neccessary. These systems utilize the EST signal from the ECM to control spark timing

REMOVAL

1. Disconnect the negative terminal from the battery.

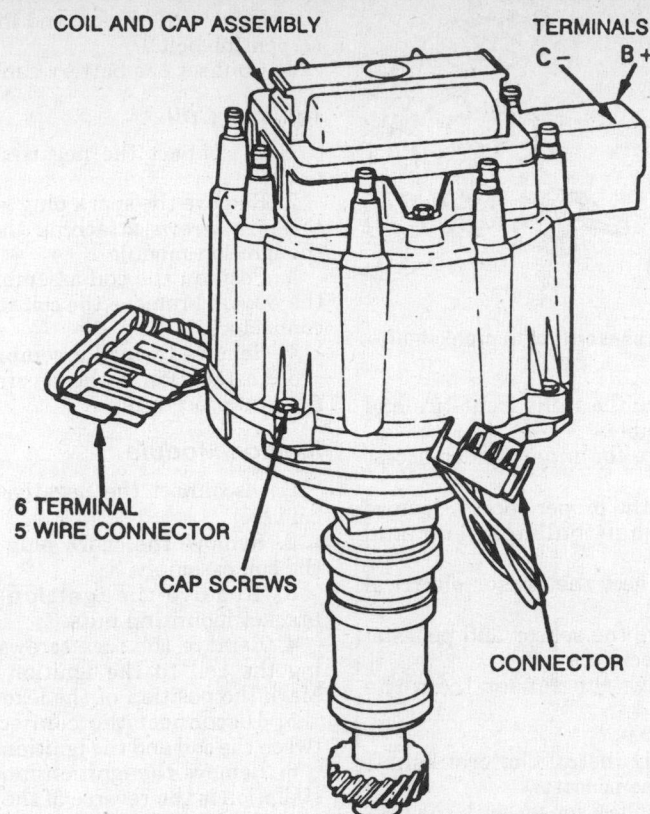

COIL AND CAP ASSEMBLY

TERMINALS
C –   B +

6 TERMINAL
5 WIRE CONNECTOR

CAP SCREWS

CONNECTOR

Distributor Assembly—1990–91 4.5L engine

2. Label and disconnect all wires leading from the distributor cap.

3. Remove the distributor cap by turning the 4 latches counterclockwise. Lift off the distributor cap and carefully move it aside.

4. Disconnect the electrical connector harness from the distributor, if not already done.

5. Remove the distributor holddown nut and clamp, using the proper tool.

6. Using a piece of chalk or paint, mark the rotor-to-distributor body and the distributor body-to-engine positions. Pull the distributor upward until the rotor just stops turning (counterclockwise); note the position of the rotor once again. Remove the distributor.

NOTE: Do not crank the engine with the distributor removed. On certain engines, a thrust washer is used between the distributor drive gear and the crankcase. This washer may stick to the bottom of the distributor when it is removed. Always make sure that this washer is at the bottom of the distributor bore before installation. On Digital Fuel Injection (DFI) systems, the malfunction trouble codes must be cleared after removal or adjustment of the

distributor. This is accomplished by removing battery voltage to terminal R of the distributor for 10 seconds.

INSTALLATION

Timing Not Disturbed

1. To install the distributor, rotate the distributor shaft until the rotor aligns with the second mark, when the shaft stopped moving. Lubricate the drive gear with clean engine oil and install the distributor into the engine. As the distributor is installed, the rotor should rotate to the first alignment mark; this will ensure proper timing. If the marks do not align properly, remove the distributor and reset; be sure to install the thrust washer, if equipped.

2. Install the clamp and hold-down nut. Tighten the nut until the distributor can just be moved with a little effort.

3. Connect all wires and hoses. Install the distributor cap. Check and/or adjust the ignition timing.

Timing Disturbed

1. Remove the No. 1 spark plug.
2. Rotate the crankshaft until No. 1 piston is at the TDC of its compression stroke.

NOTE: The compression stroke can be determined by placing a thumb over the hole while slowly cranking the engine. Crank until compression is felt at the hole and continue cranking slowly until the timing mark on the crankshaft pulley aligns with the 0 degrees timing mark located on the timing chain cover.

3. Position the distributor in the block but do not, at this time, allow it to engage with the drive gear.

4. Rotate the distributor shaft until the rotor points between No. 1 and No. 8 spark plug towers and lower the distributor to engage the camshaft.

NOTE: It may be necessary to turn the rotor a small amount in either direction in order to achieve this engagement. The rotor will rotate slightly as the distributor gear engages. If installed correctly, the rotor should point toward the No. 1 spark plug terminal in the distributor cap.

5. Press down firmly on the distributor housing. This will ensure that the distributor shaft engages the oil pump shaft, thereby allowing the distributor to fully contact the engine block.

6. Install the hold-down clamp and tighten the nut until it is snug, do not tighten.

7. Install the distributor cap, making sure that the rotor points to No. 1 terminal in the cap.

8. Attach all wires and hoses.

9. Start the engine. Check and/or adjust the ignition timing. Torque the distributor hold-down nut to 20 ft. lbs.

NOTE: Malfunction trouble codes must be cleared after removal or adjustment of the distributor. The ECM power feed must be disconnected for at least 30 seconds to clear the coded.

Distributorless Ignition

REMOVAL & INSTALLATION

Crankshaft Sensor

3.8L ENGINE (VIN 3)

1. Disconnect the negative battery cable.

2. Disconnect the crankshaft harness connector.

3. Rotate the harmonic balancer using the proper tool, until any window in the interrupter is aligned with the crank sensor.

4. Loosen the pinch bolt on the sensor pedestal until the sensor is free to slide in the pedestal.

5. Carefully remove the sensor and the pedestal as a unit.

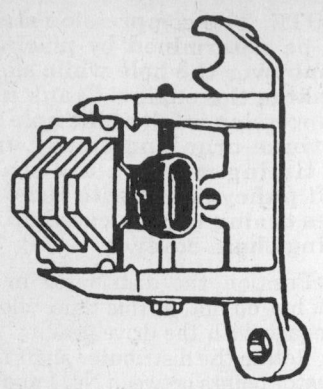

Crankshaft sensor—3.8L engine VIN C

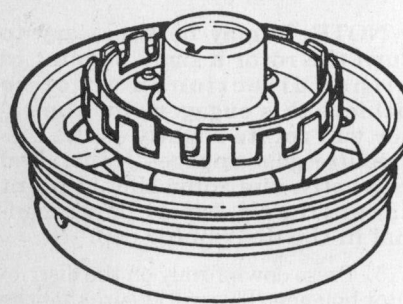

Crankshaft balancer with interrupter rings—3.8L engine

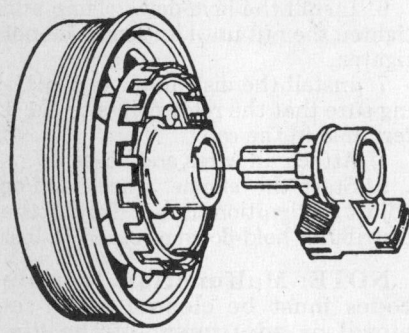

Crankshaft sensor tool to harmonic balancer—3.8L engine

6. Loosen the pinch bolt on the new sensor pedestal until the sensor is free to slide in the pedestal.

7. Verify that the window in the interrupter is still properly positioned and install the sensor and pedestal as a unit while making sure that the interrupter ring is aligned with the proper slot.

8. Install the pedestal and torque the bolts to 22 ft. lbs.

9. Reverse the removal procedure and connect the negative battery cable.

3.8L ENGINE (VIN C)

1. Disconnect the negative battery cable.

2. Remove the serpentine drive belt.

3. Raise the vehicle and support it safely.

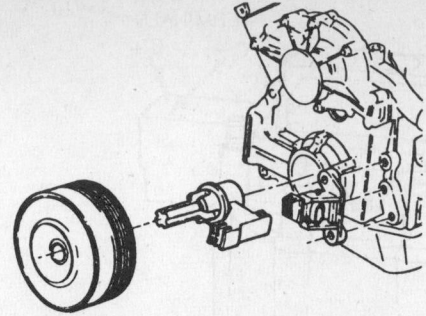

Crankshaft sensor tool to crankshaft

4. Remove the right front tire and wheel assembly.

5. Remove the inner fender access panel.

6. Using the proper socket, remove the crankshaft balancer bolt and balancer.

7. Disconnect the sensor electrical connector.

8. Remove the sensor and pedestal from the block face.

9. Remove the sensor from the pedestal.

To install:

10. Loosely install the crankshaft sensor on the pedestal.

11. Position the sensor with the pedestal attached on the proper tool.

12. Position the special tool on the crankshaft.

13. Install the bolts to hold the pedestal to the block face and torque to 14–28 ft. lbs.

14. Torque the pedestal pinch bolt to 30–35 ft. lbs.

15. Remove the tool.

16. Place special tool on the harmonic balancer and turn. If any vane of the harmonic balancer touches the tool, replace the balancer assembly.

17. Install the balancer on the crankshaft.

18. Torque the crankshaft bolt to 200–239 ft. lbs.

19. Install the inner fender access panel.

20. Install the wheel and torque the lug nuts to 100 ft. lbs.

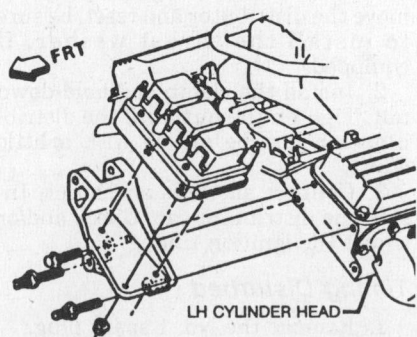

Ignition module and coil assembly—3.8L engine

21. Lower the vehicle and install the serpentine belt.

22. Connect the battery cable.

Ignition Coil

1. Disconnect the negative battery cable.

2. Remove the spark plug wires and the torx screws attaching the coil to the ignition module.

3. Position the coil assembly out of the way and remove the coil to module connectors.

4. Remove the coil assembly.

5. Installation is the reverse of the removal procedure.

Ignition Module

1. Disconnect the negative battery cable.

2. Remove the spark plug wires at the coil assembly.

3. Remove the ignition module bracket mounting nuts.

4. Remove the torx screws mounting the coil to the ignition module. Mark the position of the lead wires.

5. Disconnect the connecters between the coil and the ignition module.

6. Remove the ignition module. Installation is the reverse of the removal procedure.

Ignition Timing

ADJUSTMENT

NOTE: The 4.1L and 4.5L engines incorporate a magnetic timing probe hole for use with special electronic timing equipment. Consult the manufacturer's instructions before using this system. The following procedure is for use with the HEI-EST distributor. For placement of sensors on the C³I systems, see the underhood sticker and follow the procedure given.

The 3.8L engine uses a Computer Controlled Coil Ignition (C³I) system. The system does not use a distributor; instead, it uses a coil pack, an ignition module, a crankshaft sensor and a camshaft sensor; no adjustment is necessary.

1. Connect a timing light to the No. 1 spark plug wire according to the light manufacturer's instructions; do not pierce the spark plug wire to connect the timing light.

2. Follow the instructions on the emission control label located in the engine compartment.

3. If equipped with an Electronic Spark Timing (EST) distributor, disconnect the 4-wire terminal plug from the distributor. Some models may re-

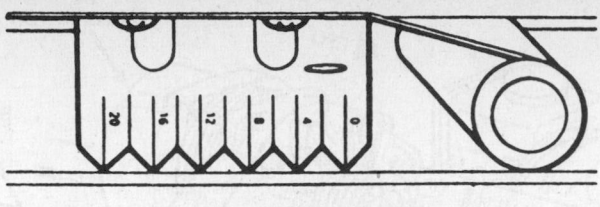

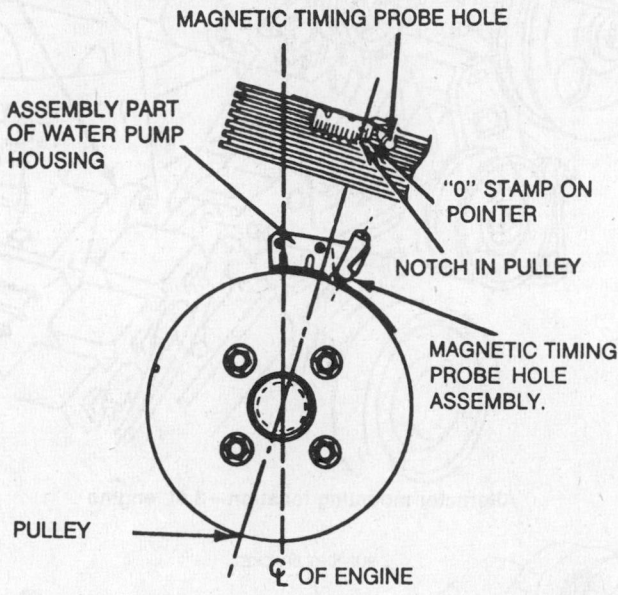

MAGNETIC TIMING PROBE HOLE

ASSEMBLY PART OF WATER PUMP HOUSING

"0" STAMP ON POINTER

NOTCH IN PULLEY

MAGNETIC TIMING PROBE HOLE ASSEMBLY.

PULLEY

℄ OF ENGINE

View of the magnetic timing probe hole—4.1L and 4.5L engines

quire grounding the diagnostic connector located under the left side of the dash.

4. Start the engine and allow it to run at idle speed.

5. Aim the timing light at the degree scale just over the harmonic balancer.

6. Adjust the timing by loosening the hold-down clamp and rotate the distributor until the desired ignition advance is achieved. When the correct timing marks are aligned, tighten the clamp.

7. Adjust the timing, replace and tighten the hold-down clamp. To advance the timing, rotate the distributor opposite the normal direction of rotor rotation. Retard the timing by rotating the distributor in the normal direction of rotor rotation.

NOTE: On Digital Fuel Injection (DFI) system, the malfunction trouble codes must be cleared after removal or adjustment of the distributor. This is accomplished by removing battery voltage to terminal R of the distributor for 10 seconds.

The 3.8L engine uses a Computer Controlled Coil Ignition (C^3I) system. The system does not use a distributor; instead, it uses a coil pack, an ignition module, a crankshaft sensor and a camshaft sensor; no adjustment is necessary.

Alternator

For further information on the charging system, please refer to "Charging and Starting" in the Unit Repair section.

PRECAUTIONS

Several precautions must be observed with alternator equipped vehicles to avoid damage to the unit.

• If the battery is removed for any reason, make sure it is reconnected with the correct polarity. Reversing the battery connections may result in damage to the one-way rectifiers.

• When utilizing a booster battery as a starting aid, always connect the positive to positive terminals and the negative terminal from the booster battery to a good engine ground on the vehicle being started.

• Never use a fast charger as a booster to start vehicles.

• Disconnect the battery cables when charging the battery with a fast charger.

• Never attempt to polarize the alternator.

• Do not use test lamps of more than 12 volts when checking diode continuity.

• Do not short across or ground any of the alternator terminals.

• The polarity of the battery, alternator and regulator must be matched and considered before making any electrical connections within the system.

• Never separate the alternator on an open circuit. Make sure all connections within the circuit are clean and tight.

• Disconnect the battery ground terminal when performing any service on electrical components.

• Disconnect the battery if arc welding is to be done on the vehicle.

BELT TENSION ADJUSTMENT

A single serpentine belt is used to drive all engine mounted accessories. Drive belt tension is maintained by a spring loaded tensioner. A belt squeak when the engine is started or stopped is normal and has no effect on belt durability. The drive belt tensioner can control belt tension over a broad range belt lengths; however, there are limits to the tensioner's ability to compensate.

1. Inspect tensioner markings to see if the belt is within operating lengths. Replace belt if the belt is excessively worn or is outside of the tensioner's operating range.

2. Run engine with the accessories **OFF** until the engine is warmed up. Turn the engine **OFF** read belt tension with a proper belt tension gauge or equivalent placed halfway between the alternator and the air conditioning compressor. For non-air conditioning applications read tension between the power steering pump and crankshaft pulley. Remove tool.

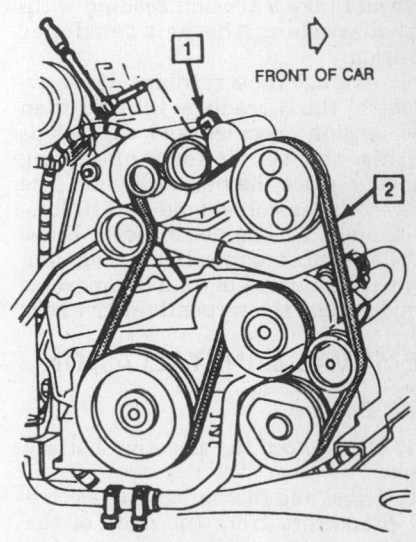

FRONT OF CAR

1. Drive belt tensioner
2. Serpentine drive belt

Drive belt—4.1L and 4.5L engines

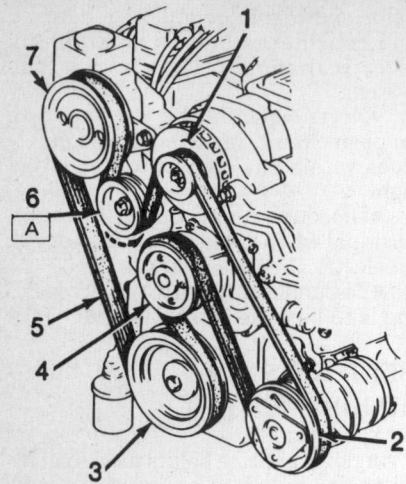

1. Generator pulley
2. A/C compressor
3. Crankshaft balancer
4. Water pump pulley
5. Serpentine belt
6. Belt tensioner
7. P/S pump pulley
A. Rotate the drive belt tensioner in direction of arrow in order to install or remove the drive belt

View of the serpentine drive belt routing—3.8L engine

Alternator mounting location—3.8L engine

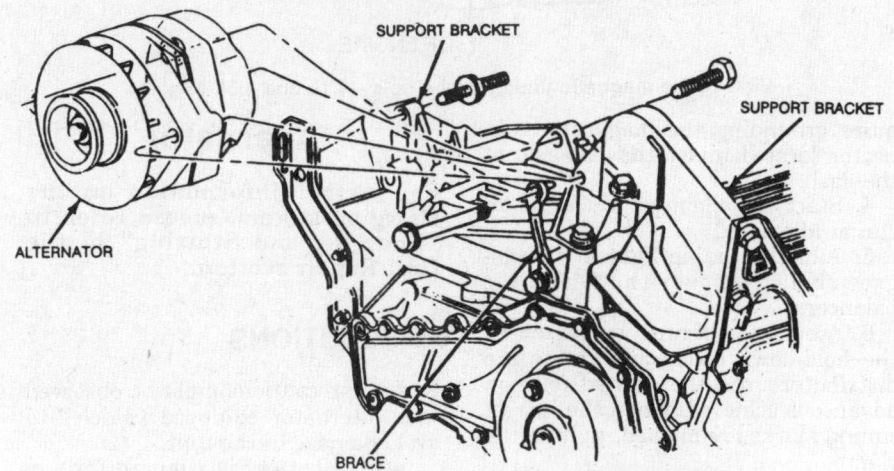

Alternator mounting location—4.1L and 4.5L engines

3. Start the engine, with accessories **OFF**, and allow the system to stabilize for 15 seconds. Turn the engine **OFF**. Using the proper tool, apply clockwise force (tighten) to the tensioner pulley bolt. Release the force and immediately take a tension reading without disturbing belt tensioner position.

4. Apply a counterclockwise force to the tensioner pulley bolt and raise the pulley to the fully raised position. Slowly lower the pulley to engage the belt and take a tension reading without disturbing the belt tensioner position.

5. Average the 3 readings. If the average of the 3 readings is lower than the tension specified and the belt is within the tensioner's operating range, replace the belt tensioner. The drive belt tension should be 110 lbs.– 4.1L and 4.5L engines or never below 67 lbs.–3.8L engine. If the belt tensioner is adjusted beyond it's movable limit, replace the serpentine drive belt.

REMOVAL & INSTALLATION

3.8L Engine

1. Disconnect the negative battery cable.

2. Label and disconnect the electrical connectors from the back of the alternator.

3. Remove the brace at the back of the alternator and the fuel rail cover, if equipped.

4. Loosen the belt tensioner and rotate it counterclockwise to remove the serpentine drive belt.

5. While supporting the alternator, remove the mounting bolts and the alternator.

6. To install, reverse the removal procedure.

4.1L and 4.5L Engines

1. Disconnect the negative battery cable.

2. Remove the air intake assembly at the throttle body.

3. Remove the serpentine belt from the tensioner pulley.

4. Remove the cover from the rear of the alternator and disconnect the electrical connections.

5. Disconnect the alternator mounting stud and the brace from the power steering pump.

6. Remove the rear alternator bolt and move the alternator upward and remove the connector.

7. Disconnect the heated windshield power module connection, if equipped.

8. Disconnect the front alternator bolt and remove the alternator.

To install:

9. Install the alternator and replace the front alternator bolt, tighten to 32 ft. lbs.

10. Connect the heated windshield power leads, if equipped.

11. Install the alternator connector and the rear mounting bolt. Tighten the bolt to 20 ft. lbs.

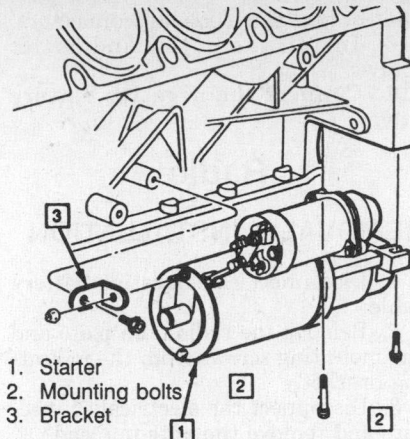

1. Starter
2. Mounting bolts
3. Bracket

Starter mounting location—4.1L and 4.5L engines

12. Install the power steering brace and replace the alternator mounting stud.
13. Connect the electrical connections and replace the cover.
14. Install the serpentine belt.
15. Replace the air intake assembly to the throttle body. Connect the negative battery cable.

Starter

For further information on the charging system, please refer to "Charging and Starting" in the Unit Repair section.

REMOVAL & INSTALLATION

1. Disconnect the negative battery cable.
2. Raise and support the vehicle safely.
3. Remove the flywheel shield, if equipped.
4. Label and disconnect the electrical connectors from the starter.
5. Remove the starter-to-engine bolts and the starter.

NOTE: Note the location of any shims so that they may be replaced in the same positions upon installation.

6. To install, reverse the removal procedures; be sure to install the shims. Check the starter operation.

CHASSIS ELECTRICAL

—— **CAUTION** ——

On vehicles equipped with an air bag, the negative battery cable must be disconnected, before working on the system. Failure to

do so may result in deployment of the air bag and possible personal injury.

Heater Blower Motor

REMOVAL & INSTALLATION

1. Disconnect the negative terminal from the battery.
2. Disconnect the electrical connections from the blower motor.
3. Disconnect the cooling hose from the blower motor.
4. Remove the mounting screws and the motor.
5. If neccessary, remove the coil and spark plug wires.
6. To install, reverse the removal procedures. Use a silicone sealer on the blower motor sealing surfaces.

Windshield Wiper Motor

REMOVAL & INSTALLATION

1. Disconnect the negative battery cable. Remove the wiper arms and the cowl cover.
2. Disconnect the wiper arm drive link from the crank arm.
3. Disconnect the electrical connectors and remove the wiper motor mounting bolts.
4. Guide the crank arm through the hole in the dash and remove the motor.
5. To install, reverse the removal procedures.

Windshield Wiper Switch

REMOVAL & INSTALLATION

1. Disconnect the negative terminal from the battery.

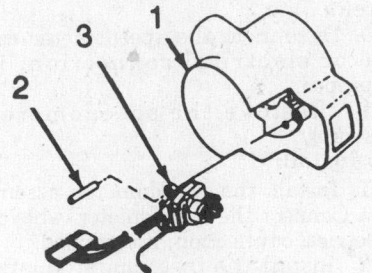

1. Cover assembly, lock housing
2. Pin, switch actuator pivot
3. Switch assembly, pivot and pulse

Windshield washer switch assembly—Cadillac

2. Remove the steering wheel, the cover and the lock plate assembly.
3. Remove the turn signal actuator arm, the lever and the hazard flasher button.
4. Remove the turn signal switch screws, the lower steering column trim panel and the steering column bracket bolts.
5. Disconnect the the turn signal switch and the wiper switch connectors.
6. Pull the turn signal switch rearward 6–8 inches, remove the key buzzer switch and cylinder lock assembly.
7. Remove and pull the steering column housing rearward. Remove the housing cover screw.
8. Remove the wiper switch pivot and the switch assembly.
To install:
9. Install the pivot and switch assembly.
10. Reposition and reinstall the steering column. Replace the housing cover screw.
11. Install the cylinder lock and key buzzer assembly. Reposition the turn signal switch.
12. Connect the turn signal switch and wiper switch connectors.
13. Install the steering column bracket bolts and the column trim panel.
14. Replace the turn signal switch screws.
15. Install the hazzard flasher button, turn signal actuator arm and lever.
16. Install the lock plate assembly, cover and the steering wheel.
17. Connect the negative battery cable.

Instrument Cluster

REMOVAL & INSTALLATION

Except Cadillac

1. Disconnect the negative terminal from the battery. Remove the defroster grille.
2. Remove the instrument panel top cover-to-instrument panel screws.
3. If equipped with a twilight sentinel, pop up the photocell retainer and turn the photocell counterclockwise in the retainer and pull it down-and-out.
4. Slide the instrument panel top cover out far enough to disconnect the aspirator hose and the electrical connector, if equipped.
5. Remove the instrument panel top cover from the instrument panel. If equipped with quartz electronic speedometer clusters, remove the steering column trim cover, so the shift indicator can be removed.
6. Remove the instrument cluster-

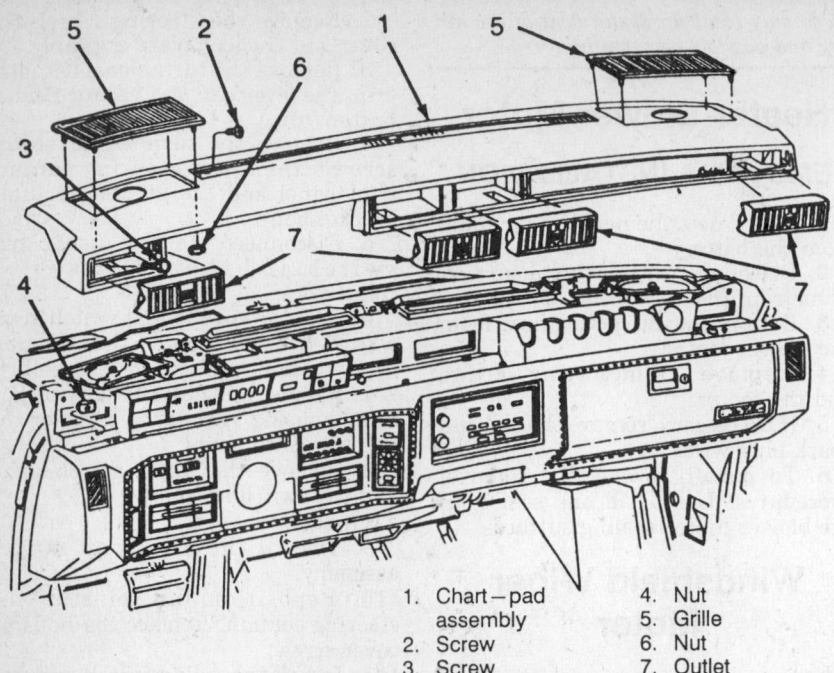

1. Chart—pad assembly
2. Screw
3. Screw
4. Nut
5. Grille
6. Nut
7. Outlet

Upper trim panel—Cadillac

to-instrument panel carrier screws. Pull the cluster housing assembly straight out; this will separate the electrical connectors from the cluster.

NOTE: It may be helpful to tilt the wheel all the way down and pull the gear select lever to low, when removing the cluster.

7. Disconnect the non-volatile memory chip, if equipped.
8. Remove the speedometer retaining screws and disconnect the speedometer cable or the electrical connection, if equipped.
9. Remove the speedometer assembly.

To install:

10. Install the speedometer assembly. Connect the speedometer cable or the electrical connection, if equipped.
11. Reconnect the non-volatile memory chip, if equipped.
12. Install the intsrument cluster and connect the electrical connections.
13. Install the instrument panel top cover and the shift indicator, if equipped.
14. Connect the aspirator hose and the electrical connections.
15. Replace the photo cell and retainer, if equipped with a twilight sentinal.
16. Replace the defroster grille and connect the negative battery cable

Cadillac

1. Disconnect the negative battery cable.
2. Remove the outlet screws and pry out each outlet, carefully.
3. Remove the glove box mounting

screws and disconnect the electrical connections. Remove the glove box assembly.
4. Disconnect the in-vehicle temperature sensor electrical connector and aspirator tube. Remove the upper trim pad.
5. Disconnect the cluster mounting screws and the electrical connectors.
6. Remove the shift indicator cable clip.
7. Remove the instrument cluster.

NOTE: On a digital cluster, remove the memory chip for the season odometer before sending the unit to an authorized repair center. The printed circuit must be lifted to gain access to the memory chip.

8. Remove the lens mounting screws and the speedometer retaining screws.
9. Disconnect the speedometer cable or electrical connection, if equipped.
10. Remove the speedometer assembly.

To install:

11. Install the speedometer assembly. Connect the speedometer cable or electrical connection, if equipped.
12. Install the instrument cluster and connect the electrical connectors.
13. Install and adjust the shift indicator clip. Replace the cluster mounting screws.
14. Install the trim pad and connect the in-vehicle temperature sensor coonnector and the aspirator tube.
15. Install the glove box assembly

and connect the electrical connectors.
16. Install the outlet and outlet screws.
17. Connect the negative battery cable.

Radio

REMOVAL & INSTALLATION

1. Disconnect the negative battery cable.
2. Remove the radio trim plate and the mounting screws from the mounting bracket.
3. Disconnect the electrical connectors and remove the antenna lead.
4. Remove the bracket mounting nuts and the bracket.
5. Remove the radio.
6. Installation is the reverse of the removal procedure.

Headlight Switch

REMOVAL & INSTALLATION

1. Disconnect negative terminal from the battery. Remove the steering column lower cover or the instrument panel trim plate covering the headlamp switch, if equipped with a rocker-type headlamp switch.
2. Disconnect the electrical harness retainer below headlight switch assembly. The switch connector is integral with the instrument panel; simply pull the switch outward to disconnect it, except on Cadillac.
3. On Cadillac, depress spring loaded release button on top of headlight switch and remove switch, knob and rod assembly with the switch in the ON position.
4. Remove screw with ground wire at bottom of switch housing and any other mounting screws.
5. Pull assembly down and rearward, disconnect wiring harness connectors, bulb(s) and remove assembly.
6. To install, reverse the removal procedures.

NOTE:. Some models are equipped with a optic fiber connector which will have to be disconnected.

Dimmer Switch

The dimmer switch is attached to the lower portion of the steering column and is controlled by an actuator rod connected to the turn signal lever.

REMOVAL & INSTALLATION

1. Disconnect the negative terminal from the battery.

2. Remove the left side sound insulator.

3. Lower the steering column trim plate.

4. Remove the steering column-to-dash screws and lower the steering column.

5. Position the ignition switch in the **OFF-UNLOCKED** position. With the cylinder removed, the rod is in **LOCK** when it is in the next to the uppermost detent; **OFF-UNLOCKED** is 2 detents from the top.

6. Remove the mounting screws and disconnect the electrical connectors. Remove the ignition switch assembly along with the dimmer switch.

7. To adjust the dimmer switch, perform the following procedures:

a. Install the dimmer switch-to-steering column screws loosely.

b. Position the switch to firmly contact the actuator rod.

c. Tighten the screws and test the actuator smoothness in all the tilt positions, if equipped with tilt wheel.

To install:

8. Install the dimmer switch and attach the mounting screws. Put the ignition switch in **OFF-UNLOCKED** position; make sure the lock cylinder and actuating rod are in **OFF-UN-LOCKED** (third detent from the top) position.

9. Install the activating rod into the switch and assemble the switch on the column. Tighten the mounting screws.

10. Connect the electrical connections to the dimmer switch.

11. Position the steering column in place and install the column mounting screws.

12. Install the column trim plate and replace the sound insulator.

13. Connect the negative battery cable.

Turn Signal Switch

REMOVAL & INSTALLATION

1. Disconnect the negative battery cable and remove the steering wheel and the shroud.

2. Remove the inflation restraint (air bag module) coil assembly-to-steering shaft lock screw (home boss) and retaining ring. Remove the coil assembly from the shaft and allow it to hang freely.

3. Using the lock plate compression tool or equivalent, position it on the end of the steering shaft and compress the lock plate by turning the shaft nut clockwise. Pry the wire snapring out of the shaft groove.

4. Remove the tool and lift the lock plate from the shaft.

5. Remove the cancelling cam, up-

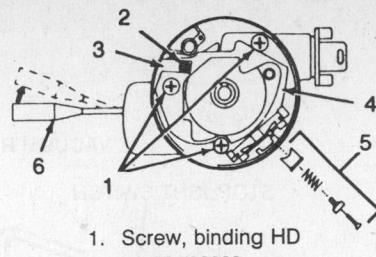

1. Screw, binding HD cross recess
2. Screw
3. Arm, signal switch
4. Switch assembly, turn signal
5. Multi-function lever
6. Hazard knob assembly

Turn signal switch

per bearing preload spring, bearing seat and inner race from the shaft.

6. Position the turn signal switch in the right turn position. Remove the turn signal lever screw and the lever.

7. To remove the turn signal switch, perform the following procedures:

a. Remove the switch-to-steering column screws, pull the switch out and allow it to hang freely.

b. From under the dash, remove the retainer spring and wiring protector.

c. Remove the hazard knob.

d. Disconnect the electrical connector from the lower steering column and gently pull the wiring connector through the gear shift lever bowl, the column housing and the lock housing cover. Remove the switch.

To install:

8. Install the turn signal switch harness through the steering column housing and connect the switch and screw.

9. Install the switch actuator arm and screw.

10. Install the inner race, bearing seat and the bearing preload spring. Replace the turn signal cancelling cam.

11. Install the lock plate, using a lock plate compression tool, compress the lock plate and install the shaft lock retaining ring.

12. Install the steering wheel and the shroud.

13. To install the inflation restraint coil, perform the following procedures:

a. Install the home boss-to-steering column lock screw, allowing the hub to rotate.

b. While holding the coil assembly (in one hand) with the steering wheel connector facing upwards, rotate the coil hub counterclockwise until it stops; the coil ribbon is now wound snug.

c. Rotate the coil hub 2½ turns clockwise until the center lock hole is even with the notch in the coil housing.

d. While holding the hub in position, install the lock screw into the center lock hole.

e. Install the coil assembly using the horn tower on the inner ring cancelling cam and outer ring projections for alignment purposes.

14. Connect the negative battery cable.

Combination Switch

The combination switch is attached to the upper portion of the steering column and is part of the turn signal lever.

REMOVAL & INSTALLATION

1. Disconnect the negative terminal from the battery.

2. Remove the left side sound insulator.

3. Lower the steering column trim plate.

4. Remove the steering column-to-dash screws and lower the steering column.

5. Remove the inflation restraint (air bag module) and the combination switch assembly.

6. Position the ignition switch in the **OFF-UNLOCKED** position. With the cylinder removed, the rod is in **LOCK** when it is in the next to the uppermost detent; **OFF-UNLOCKED** is 2 detents from the top.

7. Remove the mounting screws and disconnect the electrical connectors. Remove the ignition switch assembly along with the dimmer switch.

To install:

8. Adjust the dimmer switch.

9. Install the dimmer switch and attach the mounting screws. Put the ignition switch in **OFF-UNLOCKED** position; make sure the lock cylinder and actuating rod are in **OFF-UN-LOCKED** (third detent from the top) position.

10. Install the activating rod into the switch and assemble the switch on the column. Tighten the mounting screws.

11. Connect the electrical connections at the dimmer switch.

12. Install the combination switch and replace the air bag module.

13. Position the steering column in place and install the column mounting screws.

14. Install the column trim plate and replace the sound insulator.

15. Connect the negative battery cable.

Ignition Switch

REMOVAL & INSTALLATION

1. Disconnect the negative battery cable and lower the steering column; be sure to properly support it.
2. Position the switch in the **OFF-UNLOCKED** position. With the lock cylinder removed, the rod is in **LOCK** when it is in the next to the uppermost detent; **OFF-UNLOCKED** is 2 detents from the top.
3. Remove both switch screws and the switch assembly.
4. To install, position the new switch in **OFF-UNLOCKED** position; make sure the lock cylinder and actuating rod are in **OFF-UN-LOCKED**, 3rd detent from the top, position.
5. Install the actuating rod into the switch and assemble the switch on the column. Tighten the mounting screws.

NOTE: Use only the specified screws since over length screws could impair the collapsibility of the column.

6. To complete the installation, reverse the removal procedures.

Ignition Lock

REMOVAL & INSTALLATION

1. Disconnect the negative battery cable and remove the turn signal switch assembly.
2. Remove the key from the lock cylinder. Remove the buzzer switch and clip.
3. Reinsert the key into the lock cylinder and turn it to the **LOCK** position.
4. Remove the cylinder lock-to-steering column screw and the lock set.
5. To install the cylinder lock and torque the lock-to-steering column screw to 22 inch lbs.
6. Position the key in the **RUN** position and reverse the removal procedures. Torque the turn signal switch-to-steering column screws to 30 inch lbs. and the turn signal lever screw to 20 inch lbs.

Stoplight Switch

ADJUSTMENT

1. Install the switch into the tubular clip until the switch assembly seats itself on the tubular clip.
2. Pull the brake pedal rearward against the pedal stop.
3. The switch will be moved in the

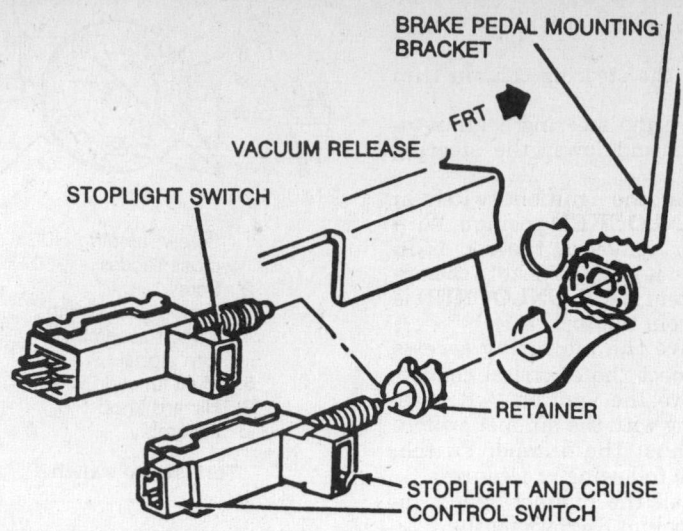

Stoplight switch location—1990–91 vehicles

tubular clip which will adjust itself properly.
4. The proper switch adjustment is achieved when no clicks are heard when the pedal is pulled upward and the brake lights stay off when the brake pedal is released.

REMOVAL & INSTALLATION

1. Disconnect the negative terminal from the battery. Remove the underdash trim panel, if equipped.
2. Loosen the tubular clip from the stoplight switch assembly.
3. Disconnect the electrical connector from the rear of the switch assembly.
4. Remove the stoplight switch from the vehicle.
5. To install, reverse the removal procedures.

Neutral Safety Switch

ADJUSTMENT

1. Disconnect the negative battery cable.
2. Place the transaxle shifter lever in the **N** position.
3. Loosen the switch mounting screws.
4. Rotate the switch on the shifter assembly to align the service adjustment holes.
5. Insert a gauge pin or equivalent, into the service slots. Tighten the mounting bolts.
6. Remove the gauge pin. Connect the negative battery cable.

REMOVAL & INSTALLATION

1. Disconnect the negative battery cable.

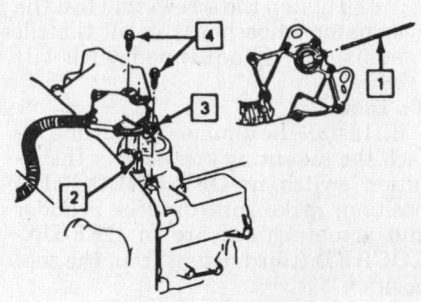

1. ³/₃₂ in. drill bit
2. Selector shaft
3. Neutral start and back up lamp switch
4. Bolts

Neutral safety switch adjustment

2. Disconnect the shift linkage and the electrical connnectors at the switch.
3. Remove the mounting bolts and the switch assembly.
4. Place the transaxle shifter lever in the **N** position.
5. Rotate the switch on the shifter assembly to align the service adjustment holes.
6. Insert a gauge pin or the equivalent into the service slots. Tighten the mounting bolts.
7. Remove the gauge pin. Connect the negative battery cable.

Fuses, Circuit Breakers and Relays

LOCATION

Fuses

The fuse panel is located on the left side of the vehicle. It is under the instrument panel assembly. In order to gain access to the fuse panel, it may be necessary to first remove the under dash padding.

Circuit Breakers

The convenience center is located on the underside of the instrument panel near the fuse panel. It provides a central location for various relays, hazard flasher units and warning buzzers/chimes. All units are replaced with plug-in modules.

Relays

The relay center is located on the right side of the instrument panel. The relay center is mounted behind the glove box assembly.

Computers

LOCATION

ECM

The electronic control module is located on the right side of the vehicle. It is positioned under the instrument panel. In order to gain access to electronic control module, it will be necessary to first remove the trim panel.

BCM

The body control module is located on the right side of the vehicle and positioned under the instrument panel. In order to gain access to body control module, it will be necessary to first remove the trim panel.

EBCM

The electronic brake control module is located on the right side of the vehicle and positioned under the right sound insulator panel. In order to gain access to electronic brake control module, it will be necessary to first remove the trim panel.

Flashers

LOCATION

The turn signal flasher unit is located behind the instrument panel near the steering column, along with the hazard flasher. It is secured in place with a plastic retainer. In order to gain access to components, it may first be necessary to remove certain under dash padding.

The hazard flasher is located on the fuse block. It is positioned on the lower right side corner of the fuse block assembly. In order to gain access to the turn signal flasher it may be necessary to first remove the under dash padding.

Cruise Control

ADJUSTMENT

1. Turn the ignition switch **OFF**.
2. Fully retract the idle speed control motor plunger.

NOTE: The throttle lever must not touch the idle speed control plunger.

3. Connect the cruise control cable to the hole in the servo blade that leaves the minimum slack.
4. Install the retainer at the servo.

ENGINE COOLING

Radiator

REMOVAL & INSTALLATION

1. Disconnect the negative battery cable.
2. Drain the radiator coolant. Remove the upper radiator panel.
3. Disconnect and remove the cooling fans, if neccessary.
4. Disconnect the coolant reservoir hoses and the radiator hoses.
5. Disconnect the engine coolant lines at the radiator, if equipped.
6. Disconnect the transaxle cooler lines. Remove the radiator.
7. The installation is the reverse of the removal procedures.

Electric Cooling Fan(s)

TESTING

1. Disconnect the electrical connector from the cooling fan.
2. Using an ammeter and jumper wires, connect the fan motor in series with the battery and ammeter. With the fan running, check the ammeter reading, it should be 3.4–5.0 amps; if not, replace the motor.
3. Reconnect the fan's electrical connector. Start the engine, allow it to reach temperatures above 194°F and confirm that the fan runs. If the fan doesn't run, replace the temperature switch.

REMOVAL & INSTALLATION

Cadillac

1. Disconnect the negative terminals from the battery.

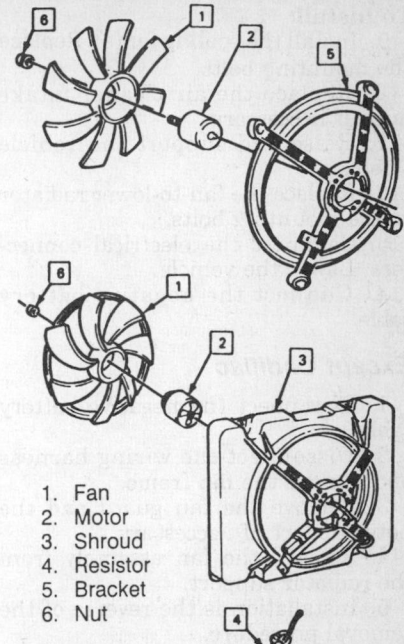

1. Fan
2. Motor
3. Shroud
4. Resistor
5. Bracket
6. Nut

Exploded view of the cooling fan

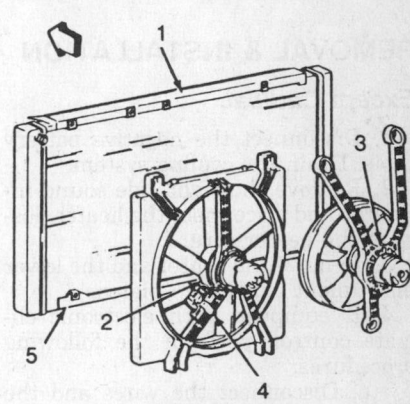

1. Radiator upper mounting panel
2. Left cooling fan
3. Right cooling fan
4. Electrical connector
5. Lower radiator cradle

Mounting location of vehicles with 2 cooling fans

2. Raise and support the vehicle safely.
3. Disconnect the electrical connectors from the rear of the fan assemblies.
4. Remove the fan-to-lower radiator cradle bolts.
5. Lower the vehicle.
6. For right fan removal, remove the air conditioning accumulator to gain working clearance. Remove the air cleaner intake duct.
7. Remove the upper fan-to-radiator panel bolts and the upper radiator panel.
8. Remove the cooling fan assemblies.

To install:

9. Install the cooling fan(s). Replace the mounting bolts.

10. Replace the air cleaner intake duct, if neccessary.

11. Raise and support the vehicle safely.

12. Replace the fan-to-lower radiator cradle mounting bolts.

13. Connnect the electrical connectors. Lower the vehicle.

14. Connect the negative battery cable.

Except Cadillac

1. Disconnect the negative battery cable.

2. Disconnect the wiring harness and remove the fan frame.

3. Remove the fan guard and the hose support, if neccessary.

4. Remove the fan assembly from the radiator support.

5. Installation is the reverse of the removal procedure.

Heater Core

REMOVAL & INSTALLATION

Except Cadillac

1. Disconnect the negative battery cable. Drain the cooling system.

2. Remove the right side sound insulator and disconnect the heater hoses at the heater core.

3. Remove the center and the lower instrument panel trim plates.

4. If equipped with electronic climate control, perform the following procedures:

   a. Disconnect the wires and the hose from the programmer.

   b. Remove the programmer linkage cover and linkage.

   c. Remove the programmer mounting bolts and the programmer.

5. Remove the heater core cover and heater core assembly.

6. Installation is the reverse of the removal procedure. Refill the cooling system and check for the proper coolant level.

Cadillac

1. Disconnect the negative battery cable. Drain the cooling system.

2. Remove the right side sound insulator and disconnect the heater hoses at the heater core.

3. Remove the intsrument panel and gauges.

4. Remove the glove box assembly and disconnect the programmer shield.

5. Disconnect the air mix valve link,

the program vacuum and electrical connectors.

6. Remove the heater core cover with the programmer attached.

7. Remove the heater core retaining screws and the heater core assembly.

8. Clean the mounting surfaces.

To install:

9. Install the heater core assembly. Replace the heater core cover with the programmer attached.

10. Connect the vacuum and electrical connections.

11. Connect the air mix valve link and adjust the air mix.

12. Install the glove box assembly and connect programmer shield.

13. Install the instrument panel and the gauges.

14. Install the right side sound insulator and connect the heater hoses at the heater core.

15. Refill the cooling system. Connect the negative battery cable.

Water Pump

REMOVAL & INSTALLATION

3.8L Engine

1. Disconnect the negative terminal from the battery. Drain the cooling system.

2. Remove the serpentine drive belt and the coolant hoses from the water pump.

3. Remove the water pump pulley bolts and the pulley; the long bolt can be removed through the access hole in the body side rail.

4. Remove the water pump-to-engine bolts and the pump.

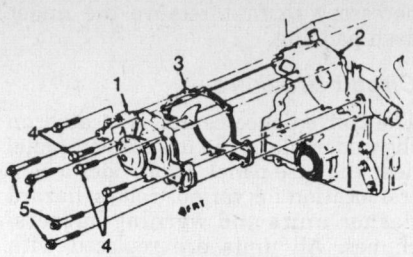

1. Water pump
2. Engine front cover assembly
3. Gasket
4. 97 inch lbs.
5. 29 ft. lbs.

Exploded view of the water pump—3.8L engine

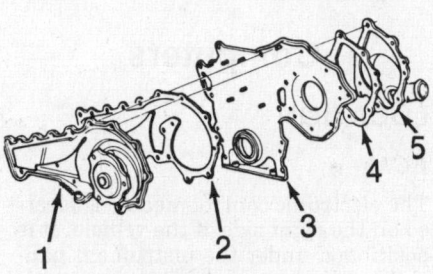

1. WATER PUMP ASSEMBLY
2. WATER PUMP GASKET
3. FRONT COVER
4. WATER PUMP INLET GASKET
5. WATER PUMP INLET

Exploded view of the water pump—4.1L and 4.5L engines

5. Clean the gasket mounting surfaces. Install a new gasket and pump assembly.

6. To install, use a new gasket with sealant, if necessary, and reverse the

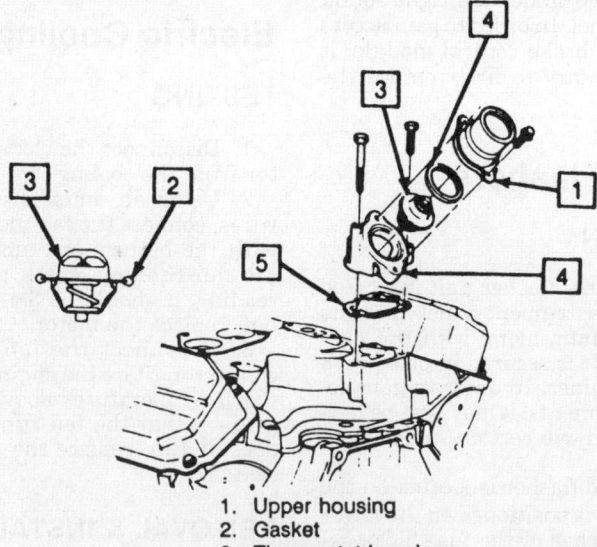

1. Upper housing
2. Gasket
3. Thermostat housing
4. Lower housing
5. Gasket

Location of thermostat—Cadillac

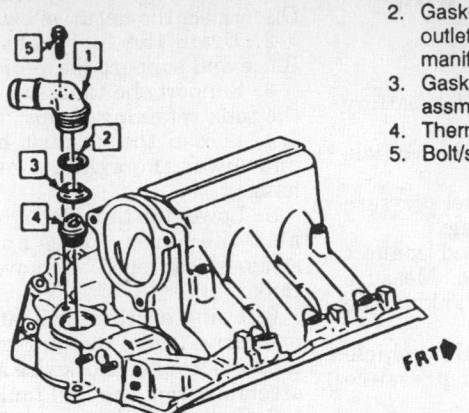

1. Water outlet assembly
2. Gasket (O-ring) water outlet assm to intake manifold
3. Gasket—thermostat assm to water outlet
4. Thermostat assembly
5. Bolt/screw

Location of thermostat—3.8L engine

removal procedures. Torque the water pump-to-engine bolts to 29 ft. lbs. for the long bolt and 97 inch lbs. for the short bolt. Refill the cooling system.

4.1L and 4.5L Engines

1. Disconnect the negative terminal from the battery. Drain the cooling system.
3. If equipped with air conditioning, remove the accumulator from its bracket, move the bracket and accumulator aside without discharging the air conditioning system.
4. Remove the right cross brace and the accessory drive belt.
5. Remove the water pump pulley-to-water pump bolts and the pulley.
6. Remove the water pump-to-engine bolts and the water pump.
7. Clean the gasket mounting surfaces.
To install:
8. Install a new gasket and pump the water pump pulley, do not fully tighten the screws.
9. Install the right cross brace.
10. Install the air conditioning accumulator bracket and accumulator.
11. Install the air conditioning accumulator bracket and accumulator.
12. Replace the accessory drive belt.
13. Tighten the water pump pulley bolts fully. Refill the engine coolant.
14. Connect the negative battery cable. Start the engine and check for leaks.

Thermostat

REMOVAL & INSTALLATION

1. Disconnect the negative battery cable. Drain the coolant to below the thermostat housing.
2. Remove the thermostat housing mounting screws/bolts.
3. Remove the thermostat housing and lift out the thermostat.

4. Clean the mounting surfaces and install new gasket(s)/O-ring.
5. Install the thermostat. The remainder of the installation is the reverse of the removal procedure.

FUEL SYSTEM

Fuel System Service Precautions

Safety is the most important factor when performing not only fuel system maintenance but any type of maintenance. Failure to conduct maintenance and repairs in a safe manner may result in serious personal injury or death. Maintenance and testing of the vehicle's fuel system components can be accomplished safely and effectively by adhering to the following rules and guidelines.

●To avoid the possibility of fire and personal injury, always disconnect the negative battery cable unless the repair or test procedure requires that battery voltage be applied.

●Always relieve the fuel system pressure prior to disconnecting any fuel system component (injector, fuel rail, pressure regulator, etc.), fitting or fuel line connection. Exercise extreme caution whenever relieving fuel system pressure to avoid exposing skin, face and eyes to fuel spray. Please be advised that fuel under pressure may penetrate the skin or any part of the body that it contacts.

●Always place a shop towel or cloth around the fitting or connection prior to loosening to absorb any excess fuel due to spillage. Ensure that all fuel spillage (should it occur) is quickly re-

moved from engine surfaces. Ensure that all fuel soaked cloths or towels are deposited into a suitable waste container.

●Always keep a dry chemical (Class B) fire extinguisher near the work area.

●Do not allow fuel spray or fuel vapors to come into contact with a spark or open flame.

●Always use a backup wrench when loosening and tightening fuel line connection fittings. This will prevent unnecessary stress and torsion to fuel line piping. Always follow the proper torque specifications.

●Always replace worn fuel fitting O-rings with new. Do not substitute fuel hose or equivalent where fuel pipe is installed.

RELIEVING FUEL SYSTEM PRESSURE

3.8L Engine

1987

1. From the fuse panel, remove the fuel pump fuse.
2. Start the engine and allow it run until it uses all the fuel.
3. Replace the fuse.
4. Disconnect the negative battery cable.

1988–91

1. Disconnect the negative battery cable.
2. Loosen the fuel filler cap to relieve the tank vapor pressure.
3. Connect a suitable fuel pressure gauge to the fuel pressure connection. Wrap a shop towel around the fitting while connecting the gauge to avoid spillage.
4. Install a bleed hose into a container and open the valve to bleed the system pressure. The system is now safe for servicing.

4.1L Engine

If the engine has been operated, allow a few minutes for it to bleed-down.

4.5L Engine

1. Disconnect the negative battery cable.
2. Loosen the fuel filler cap to relieve the tank vapor pressure.
3. Connect a suitable fuel pressure gauge to the fuel pressure connection. Wrap a shop towel around the fitting while connecting the gauge to avoid spillage.
4. Install a bleed hose into a container and open the valve to bleed the system pressure. The system is now safe for servicing.

Fuel Filter

REMOVAL & INSTALLATION

1. Disconnect the negative battery cable.
2. Raise and support the vehicle safely. The filter is located at the rear of the vehicle.
3. Disconnect the fuel lines from the filter.
4. Remove the filter from the vehicle.

To install:

5. Install the filter and connect the fuel lines to the filter.
6. Secure the filter and lower the vehicle.
7. Start the engine and check for leaks.
8. There is also a fuel filter located in the fuel tank on the lower end of the pick-up pipe.

Electric Fuel Pump

PRESSURE TESTING

1. Disconnect the negative battery cable.
2. Raise and support the vehicle safely.
3. Connect a suitable fuel pressure gauge to the fuel line fitting.
4. Lower the vehicle and connect the negative battery cable. Measure the fuel pressure while cranking the engine.
5. Raise and support the vehicle safely. Remove the fuel pressure gauge.
6. Lower the vehicle.

REMOVAL & INSTALLATION

The electric fuel pump is located in the fuel tank.

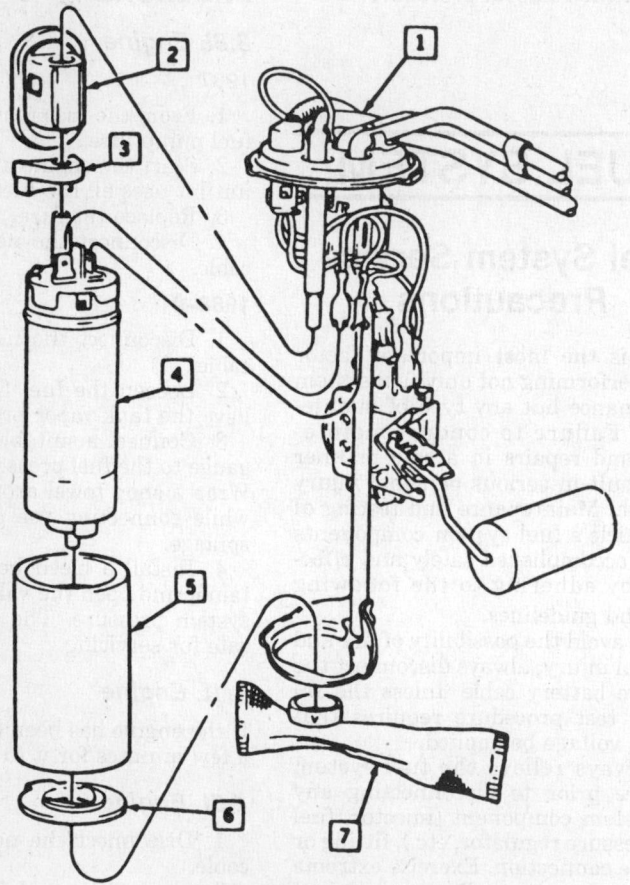

1. Fuel tank meter assembly
2. Pulsator (port injection only)
3. Bumper
4. Fuel pump
5. Sound insulator sleeve
6. Sound insulator
7. Filter

Exploded view of the fuel pump assembly

1. Relieve the fuel system pressure. Disconnect the negative battery cable.
2. Drain the fuel from the tank. Raise and support the vehicle safely.
3. Support the tank and disconnect the tank retaining straps.
4. Loosen the exhaust heat shield and lower the exhaust at the rear hanger.
5. Lower the tank enough to disconnect the wires, hoses and ground strap, if equipped. Remove the fuel tank.
6. Using a brass drift and a hammer, drive (turn) the cam lock ring-to-fuel tank counterclockwise and lift the assembly from the fuel tank.
7. Pull the fuel pump up into the attaching hose while pulling outward away from the bottom support. Take care to prevent damage to the rubber sound insulator and strainer during removal. Once the pump assembly is clear of the bottom support, pull it out of the rubber connector.
cf35To install:
uf32
8. Install the pump into the fuel tank. Connect the fuel lines, wires and the ground strap, if equipped.
9. When installing the fuel tank, make sure all rubber sound isolators or anti-squeak spacers are replaced in their original locations.
10. Support the tank and install the tank retaining straps.
11. Lower the vehicle. Refill the fuel tank.
12. Connect the negative battery cable. Start the engine and check for any leaks.

Fuel Injection

IDLE SPEED ADJUSTMENT

The idle speed is controlled by the Engine Control Module (ECM) and not adjustable.

IDLE MIXTURE ADJUSTMENT

The idle mixture is not adjustable.

Fuel Injector

REMOVAL & INSTALLATION

3.8L Engine

1. Properly relieve the fuel system pressure. Remove the air cleaner assembly. Disconnect the negative battery cable.
2. Label and disconnect the fuel injector electrical connectors.
3. Remove the fuel rail retaining

bolts. Disconnect the electrical connections and the fuel supply line.

4. Remove the fuel rail.

5. Separate the injector from the fuel rail.

6. To install, use new O-rings and reverse the removal procedures. Start the engine and check for leaks.

4.1L and 1987–89 4.5L Engines

NOTE: Care must be taken when removing injectors to prevent damage to the electrical connector pins on the injector and the nozzle. The injectors are serviced as a complete assembly only. Injectors are an electrical component and should not be immersed in any type of cleaner.

1. On the 4.1L engine, if the engine was recently operated, allow the fuel pressure to bleed down. On the 4.5L engine properly release the fuel system pressure.

2. Disconnect the negative battery cable. Remove the air cleaner assembly.

3. Disconnect the electrical connector from the fuel injector(s) by squeezing the 2 tabs together and pulling it straight up.

4. Remove the fuel meter cover-to-throttle body screws and the cover; be sure to note the position of the 4 short screws. Allow the gasket to remain in place to prevent damage to the casting housing.

5. Using a small pry bar and a ¼ in. rod, pry the fuel injector(s) from the throttle body; discard the O-rings.

To install:

6. Use new O-rings, lubricate with Dexron®II automatic transmission fluid, and install the injectors. Simply push them into the sockets.

7. Install the fuel cover-to-throttle body screws, making sure they go in the position that they were removed.

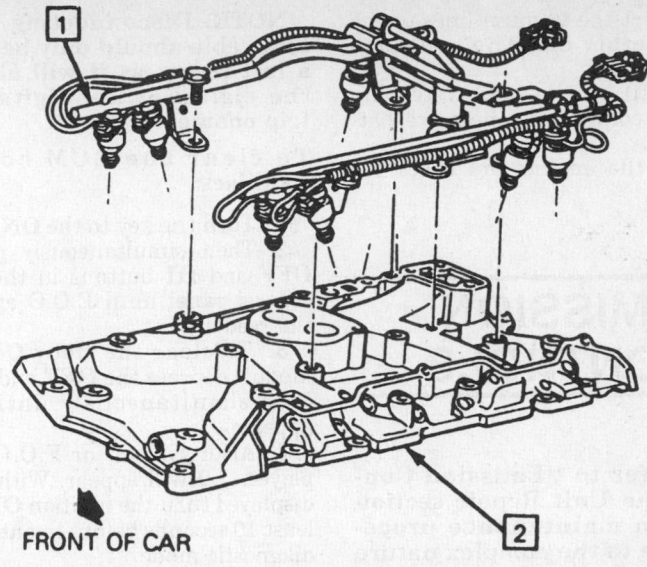

1. Fuel rail assembly
2. Intake manifold

Fuel rail assembly—1990–91 4.5L engine

8. Connect the electrical connectors at the injectors.

9. Replace the air filter assembly and connect the negative battery cable.

10. Start the engine and check for leaks.

1990–91 4.5L Engine

1. Disconnect the negative battery cable.

2. Position the power steering pump out of the way.

3. Relieve the fuel system pressure.

4. Disconnect the vacuum lines from the pressure regulator and the base assembly.

5. Disconnect the fuel feed line from the rear of the rail assembly. Discard the O-ring.

6. Remove the fuel return line. Discard the O-ring.

7. Disconnect the electrical connectors at the front and the rear of the rail assembly.

8. Remove the rail support bracket mounting bolts and remove the rail assembly from the intake manifold.

9. Disconnect the electrical connector from the fuel injector by pushing in the clip while pulling the connector body away from the injector.

10. Disconnect the injector retaining clip. Discard the clip.

11. Remove the fuel injector assembly, by twisting back and forth while removing. Remove and discard the O-rings from the injectors.

To install:

12. Lubricate new O-rings and install on the injector assembly.

13. Install a new injector clip on the injector.

14. Install the fuel injector into the fuel rail socket. Push in to engage the retainer clip with the fuel rail cup.

NOTE: The electrical connectors should be facing the engine front for injectors 1–4. The connectors should be facing the rear of the engine for injectors 5–8.

15. Install the electrical connector to the injector assembly.

16. Install the fuel rail assembly and connect the support bracket mounting bolts.

17. Connect the electrical connectors at the front and rear of the rail assembly.

18. Install the fuel return line, using a new O-ring.

19. Connect the fuel feed line at the rear of the rail assembly, using a new O-ring.

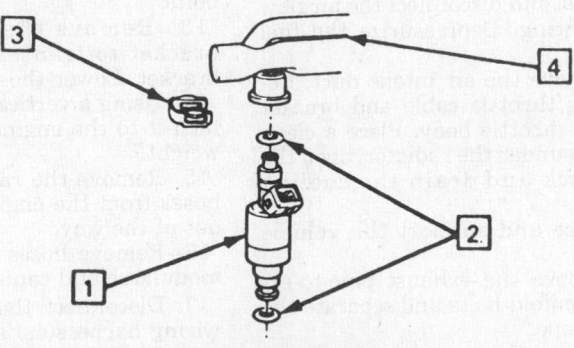

1. Injector assembly
2. Seal-O-ring injector
3. Clip-injector retainer
4. Fuel rail

Fuel injector—1990–91 4.5L engine

20. Connect the vacuum lines to the base assembly and the pressure regulator.

21. Reposition the power steering pump and connect the negative battery cable.

22. Start the engine and check for leaks.

EMISSION CONTROLS

Please refer to "Emission Control" in the Unit Repair section for system maintenance procedures. Due to the complex nature of modern electronic engine control systems, comprehensive diagnosis and testing procedures fall outside the confines of this repair manual. For complete information on diagnosis, testing and repair procedures concerning all modern engine and emission control systems, please refer to "Chilton's Guide to Electronic Engine Controls".

Emission Warning Lamps

The dash mounted "Service Soon" and "Service Now" lights are used to indicated to the mechanic or owner of a malfunction that the computer has detected in the vehicle's operation. The malfunctions can be related to the operating sensors or the electronic control module (ECM). The service light will go out automatically if the trouble is cleared or intermittent.

The ECM, however will automatically store the trouble code until the diagnostic system is "Cleared".

RESETTING

On all models, except Cadillac, this is accomplished by removing battery voltage to the ECM for 30 seconds.

To prevent ECM damage, the key must be **OFF** when disconnecting or reconnecting power to the ECM.

To disconnect battery voltage to the ECM, on all models except Cadillac, perform one of the following:

1. Remove the ECM fuse from the fuse panel.
2. Remove the ECM pigtail.
3. Disconnect the battery cable.

NOTE: Disconnecting the battery cable should only be done as a last resort as it will also clear the digital radio, digital clock, trip odometer etc.

To clear the ECM codes on Cadillacs:

1. Turn the key to the **ON** position.
2. Then simultaneously press the **OFF** and **HI** buttons in the climate control panel until E.O.O appears in the readout.
3. To clear the Body Computer Module depress the **OFF** and **LO** buttons simultaneously until F.O.O appears.
4. After E.O.O. or F.O.O. is displayed .7.0 will appear. With the .7.0 displayed turn the ignition **OFF** for at least 10 seconds before re-entering the diagnostic mode.

ENGINE MECHANICAL

NOTE: Disconnecting the negative battery cable on some vehicles may interfere with the functions of the on board computer systems and may require the computer to undergo a relearning process, once the negative battery cable is reconnected.

Engine Assembly

REMOVAL & INSTALLATION

3.8L Engine

1. Disconnect the negative terminal from the battery. Using a scribing tool, matchmark the hood hinges and remove the hood.
2. Label and disconnect the air flow sensor wiring. Depressurize the fuel system.
3. Remove the air intake duct. Remove the throttle cable and bracket from the throttle body. Place a clean drain pan under the radiator, open the drain cock and drain the cooling system.
4. Raise and support the vehicle safely.
5. Remove the exhaust pipe-to-exhaust manifold bolts and separate the exhaust pipe.
6. Remove the engine mount bolts.
7. If equipped with a driveline vibration absorber, remove the bolts and disconnect the absorber.
8. Label and disconnect the electrical connectors from the starter. Re-

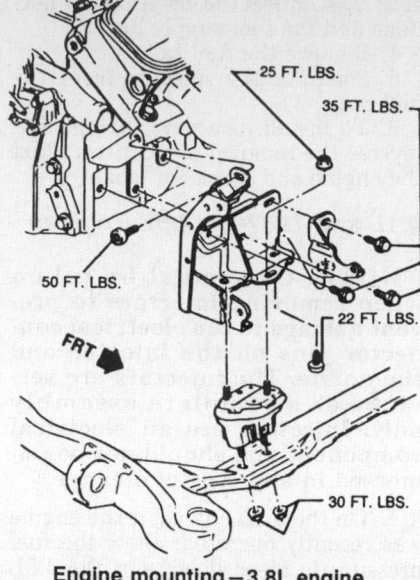

Engine mounting—3.8L engine

move the starter-to-engine bolts and the starter.

9. If equipped with air conditioning, disconnect the compressor and position it out of the way; Do not disconnect the refrigerant lines.
10. Place a catch pan under the power steering gear, disconnect the hydraulic lines, drain the fluid and wire the hoses out of the way.
11. Remove the lower transaxle-to-engine bolts.

NOTE: One bolt is situated between the transaxle case and the engine block; it is installed in the opposite direction of the other bolts.

12. Remove the flywheel cover. Matchmark the flexplate-to-torque converter relationship to insure proper alignment upon installation. Remove the flexplate-to-torque converter bolts.
13. Remove the engine support bracket-to-transaxle bolts and the bracket. Lower the vehicle.
14. Using a vertical engine hoist, attach it to the engine and support the weight.
15. Remove the radiator and heater hoses from the engine; position them out of the way.
16. Remove hoses from the vacuum modulator and canister purge lines.
17. Disconnect the engine electrical wiring harness(es) and position them out of way.
18. Remove the upper transaxle-to-engine bolts.
19. Using the proper engine removal equipment, carefully remove the engine from the vehicle.

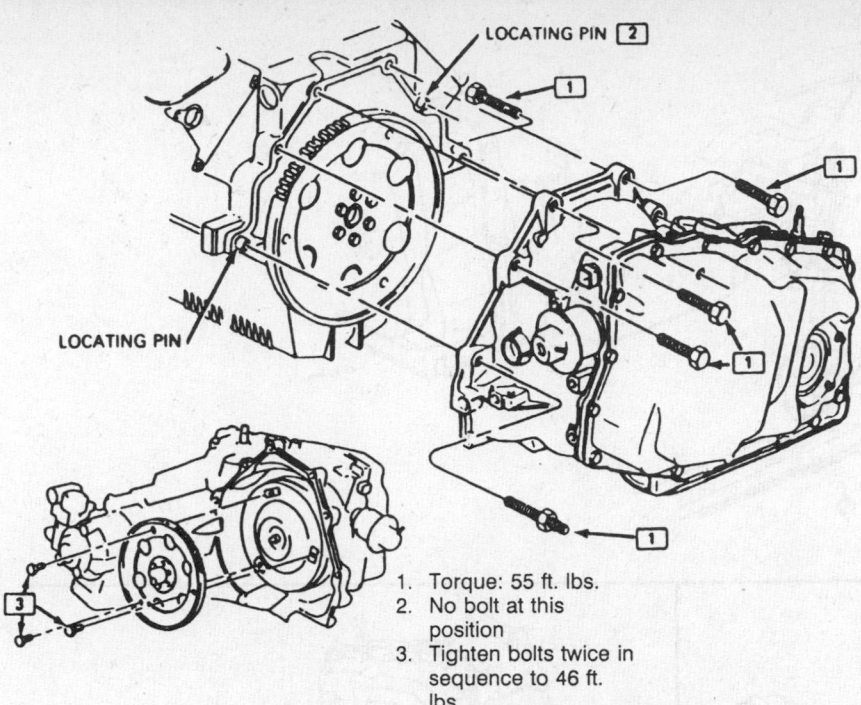

LOCATING PIN [2]

LOCATING PIN

1. Torque: 55 ft. lbs.
2. No bolt at this position
3. Tighten bolts twice in sequence to 46 ft. lbs.

Engine-to-transaxle mounting location — 3.8L engine

To install:

20. Install the engine, using a proper engine hoist.

21. Connect and reposition the engine electrical wiring harness, secure the bracket.

22. Connect the hoses to the vacuum modulator and the cannister purge lines.

23. Install the radiator and the heater hoses.

24. Remove the engine hoist. Raise and support the vehicle safely.

25. Replace the engine support bracket-to-transaxle and the install the bracket.

26. Replace the upper transaxle-to-engine bolts. Install the engine mount bolts and tighten to 70 ft. lbs.

27. Install the torque coverter and tighten the bolts to 46 ft. lbs. Replace the flywheel cover.

28. Install the lower transaxle-to-engine bolts, tighten to 55 ft. lbs.

29. Connect the power steering hydraulic lines to the power steering gear.

30. Install the air conditioning compressor, if equipped.

31. Install the starter and tighten the mounting bolts to 35 ft. lbs.

32. Connect the electrical connections at the starter motor.

33. Connect the driveline vibration absorber, if equipped.

34. Install the exhaust pipe and replace the exhaust pipe-to-manifold bolts.

35. Lower the vehicle.

36. Connect the air flow sensor wiring. Install the hood assembly.

37. Connect the negative battery cable. Refill the cooling system.

38. Start the engine, allow it to reach normal operating temperatures and check for leaks.

4.1L and 4.5L Engines

1. Disconnect the negative terminal from the battery. Place a clean drain pan under the radiator, open the drain cock and drain the cooling system.

2. Remove the air cleaner. Using a scribing tool, matchmark the hood to the support brackets and remove the hood.

3. If equipped with air conditioning, perform the following procedures:
   a. Remove the hose strap from the right-strut tower.
   b. Remove the accumulator from its bracket and position it out of the way.
   c. Remove the canister hoses from the accumulator bracket.
   d. Remove the accumulator bracket from the wheel house.

4. Remove the cooling fans, the accessory drive belt, the radiator and heater hoses.

5. Label and disconnect the electrical connectors from the following items:
   a. Oil pressure switch
   b. Coolant temperature sensor
   c. Distributor
   d. EGR solenoid
   e. Engine temperature switch

6. Label and disconnect the cables from the following items:
   a. Accelerator
   b. Cruise control linkage
   c. Transaxle throttle valve (TV) cable

7. If equipped with cruise control, remove the diaphragm with the bracket attached and move it aside.

8. Remove the vacuum supply hose and the exhaust crossover pipe.

9. Disconnect the oil cooler lines from the oil filter adapter, the oil line cooler bracket from the transaxle and position them aside.

10. Remove the air cleaner mounting bracket.

11. Using a catch pan or a shop rag, carefully bleed the fuel pressure from the schraeder valve. Disconnect the fuel lines from the throttle body. Remove the fuel line bracket from the transaxle and secure the fuel lines out of the way.

NOTE: When bleeding the fuel system, be sure to have a container or rags on hand to catch excess fuel. Take precautions to avoid the risk of fire.

12. Remove the small vacuum line from the brake booster.

13. Label and disconnect the AIR solenoid electrical and hose connections. Remove the AIR valves with the bracket.

14. Label and disconnect the electrical connectors from the following:
   a. Idle Speed Control (ISC) motor
   b. Throttle Position Switch (TPS)
   c. Fuel injectors
   d. Manifold Air Temperature (MAT) sensor
   e. Oxygen sensor
   f. Electric Fuel Evaporator (EFE) grid
   g. Alternator bracket

15. Remove the power steering pump hose strap from the stud-headed bolt in front of the right cylinder head and the stud-headed bolt.

16. Remove the AIR pipe clip located near the No. 2 spark plug, if equipped.

17. Remove the power steering pump and belt tensioner with bracket attached; wire them out of the way.

18. Raise and support the vehicle safely.

19. Label and disconnect the electrical connectors from the starter and the ground wire from the cylinder block.

20. Remove the 2 flywheel covers. Remove the starter-to-engine bolts and the starter. Matchmark the flywheel-to-torque converter location. Remove the 3 flywheel-to-torque converter bolts and slide the converter back into the bell housing.

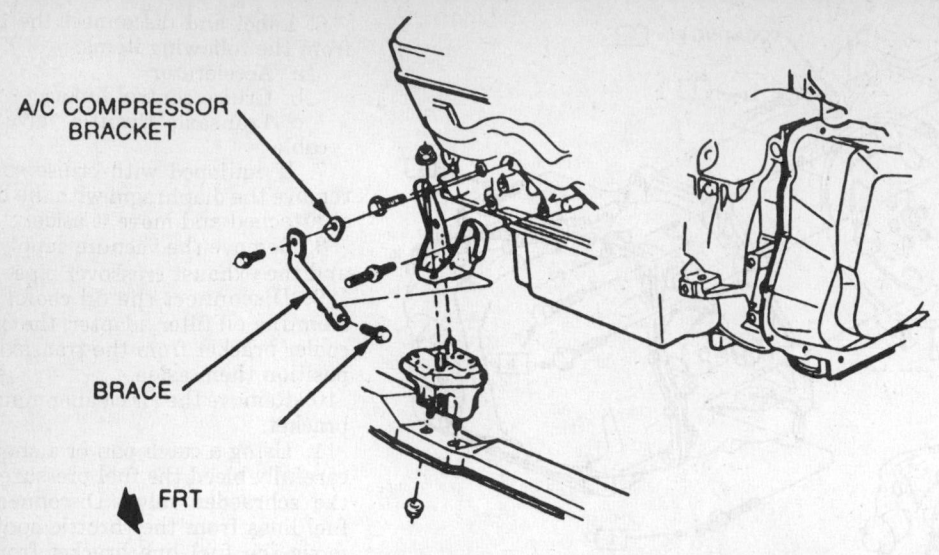

A/C COMPRESSOR
BRACKET

BRACE

FRT

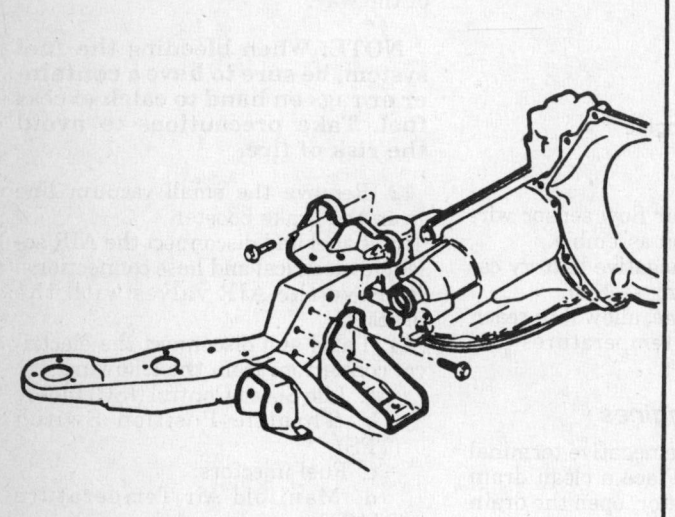

FRT

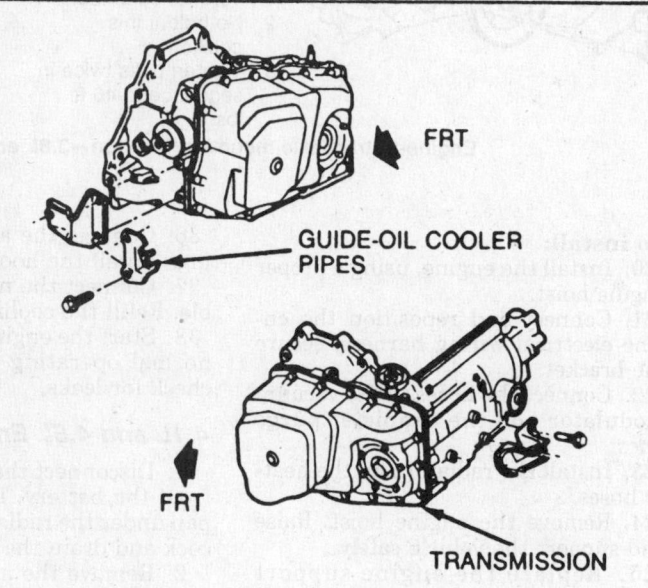

FRT

GUIDE-OIL COOLER
PIPES

FRT

TRANSMISSION

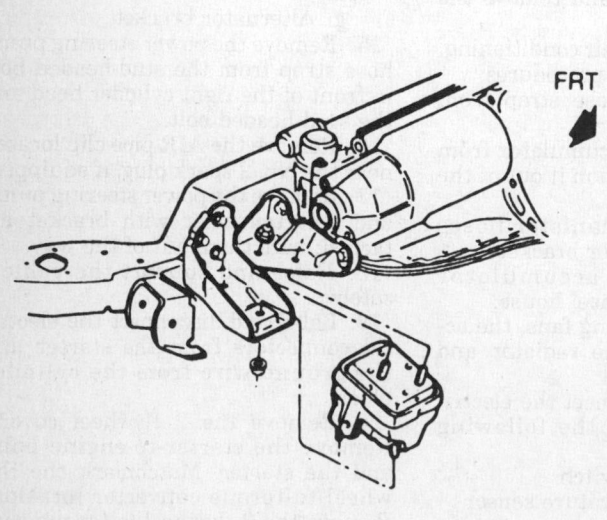

FRT

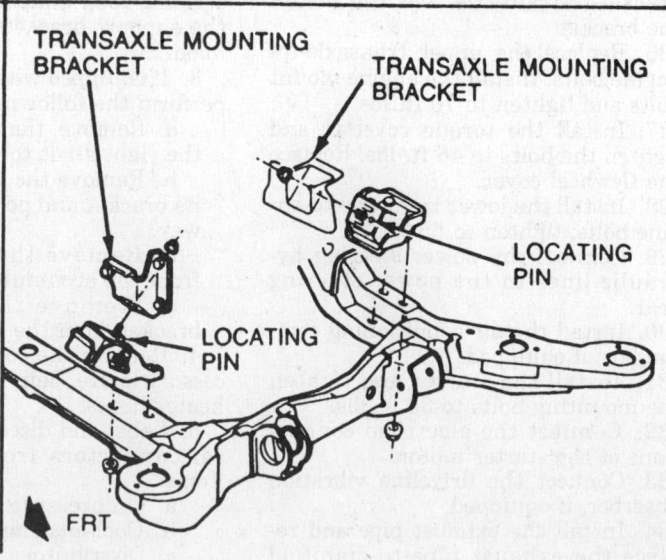

TRANSAXLE MOUNTING
BRACKET

TRANSAXLE MOUNTING
BRACKET

LOCATING
PIN

LOCATING
PIN

FRT

Engine and transmission mounts—4.5L engine

21. If equipped with air conditioning, perform the following procedures:

a. Remove the compressor lower dust shield.

b. Remove the right front wheel/tire assembly and outer wheelhouse plastic shield.

c. Remove the compressor-to-bracket bolts and lower the compressor from the engine; do not disconnect the refrigerant lines.

22. Remove the lower radiator hose.

23. From the lower right front of the engine and cradle, remove the driveline vibration dampener with the brackets, if equipped, and the engine-to-transaxle bracket bolts. Pull the alternator wire with the plastic cover down and out of the way.

24. Remove the exhaust pipe-to-manifold bolts with the springs attached and the AIR pipe-to-converter bracket from the exhaust manifold stud.

NOTE: Be careful not to lose the springs when detaching the exhaust pipe.

25. Remove the lower right side bell housing-to-engine bolt. Lower the vehicle.

26. Using a vertical engine hoist, attach it to the engine and support it.

27. Remove the upper bell housing-to-engine bolts and left front engine mount bracket-to-engine bolts. Remove the engine from the vehicle.

To install:

28. Raise the transaxle with a separate jack to engage the engine.

29. Install the engine into the vehicle, using a suitable engine hoist. Engage the dowels on the block with the transaxle case.

30. Install the transaxle bell housing-to-engine mounting bolts.

31. Lower and remove the floor jack assembly from the transaxle.

32. Lower the engine, making sure that it is seated on the mount properly.

33. Remove the engine hoist. Raise and support the vehicle safely.

34. Lower the right hand transaxle bell housing-to-engine bolt. Support the engine.

35. Install the left front engine mount bracket to engine bolts and the flexplate to converter bolts.

36. Replace the flexplate covers.

37. Install the starter motor and connect the electrical wires to the starter.

38. Connect the air pipe-to-converter bracket to the exhaust manifold stud.

39. Install the exhaust pipe to manifold bolts and springs.

40. Connect the alternator and install the plastic cover. Install the right front engine-to-transaxle bracket and tighten the bolts to 30 ft. lbs.

41. Install the lower radiator hose and replace the air conditioning compressor mounting bolts.

42. Install the air conditioning compressor lower dust shield and the outer wheel house plastic shield.

43. Install the right front tire and wheel assembly. Lower the vehicle.

44. Install the power steering pump and the belt tensioner. Replace the stud headed bolt.

45. Install the power steering hose strap to the stud headed bolt in front of the cylinder head.

46. Connect the electrical connections at these components:

a. Idle Speed Control (ISC) motor

b. Throttle Position Switch (TPS)

c. Fuel injectors

d. Manifold Air Temperature (MAT) sensor

e. Oxygen sensor

f. Electric Fuel Evaporator (EFE) grid

g. Alternator bracket

47. Replace the air valve and bracket. Connect the air solenoid electrical and hose connections.

48. Connect the vacuum line to the brake booster.

49. Connect the fuel lines at the throttle body and replace the fuel line bracket at the transaxle.

50. Replace the air cleaner mounting bracket and connect the oil cooler lines to the oil filter adapter.

51. Connect the oil cooler line bracket at the transaxle. Replace the exhaust crossover pipe.

52. Replace the cruise control diaphragm and connect the vacuum line.

53. Connect the accelerator, cruise control and the transaxle throttle valve cables to the throttle lever.

54. Connect the wire connectors to the following:

a. Oil pressure switch

b. Coolant temperature sensor

c. Distributor

d. EGR solenoid

e. Engine temperature switch

55. Replace the accessory drive belt, heater hoses and upper radiator hose.

56. Install the cooling fans and connect the air conditioning accumulator bracket.

57. Install the air conditioning accumulator and connect the wires and hoses.

58. Install the hood aasembly and replace the air cleaner.

59. Refill the engine coolant. Connect the negative battery cable.

60. Start the engine, allow it to reach normal operating temperatures and check for leaks.

Engine Mounts

REMOVAL & INSTALLATION

3.8L Engine

1. Disconnect the negative battery cable.

2. Raise and support the vehicle safely.

3. Remove the engine through mount bolt. Using a vertical lifting device, attach it to the engine and raise the engine.

4. Remove the engine mount bolts and the mount.

5. To install, reverse the removal procedures.

4.1L and 4.5L Engines

RIGHT

1. Disconnect the negative battery cable and brace from the engine bracket to the engine.

2. Remove the nuts securing the engine bracket to the mount.

3. Raise the vehicle and support it safely.

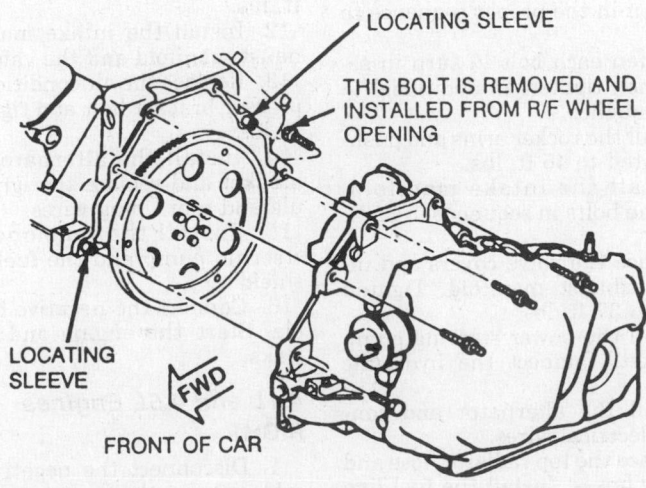

Engine-to-transaxle mounting location—4.1L and 4.5L engines

LOCATING SLEEVE

THIS BOLT IS REMOVED AND INSTALLED FROM R/F WHEEL OPENING

LOCATING SLEEVE

FWD

FRONT OF CAR

4. Support the vehicle with stands at each front frame horn.

5. Remove the nuts on the engine mount securing to the frame.

6. Remove the nuts securing the transaxle mount to the mount.

7. Remove the nuts securing the transaxle mount to the frame bracket.

8. Raise the engine using an engine support tool.

9. Raise the engine until the bracket is free from the engine mount. Remove the stud and the bolts that secure the bracket to the block. Remove the mount and bracket by pulling forward.

10. Remove the transaxle mounting bracket from the transaxle.

11. Remove the mount assembly.

To install:

12. Position the engine mount and bracket, in place between the transaxle and frame and secure the bracket to the transaxle with the 2 bolts and tighten to 34 ft. lbs.

13. While lowering the engine, guide the motor mount into location and install the engine mount to frame and transaxle mount to frame bracket with the 2 nuts each and tighten to 22 ft. lbs.

14. Install the nuts to the engine mount studs and the nuts to transaxle mount studs and tighten to 22 ft. lbs.

15. Remove the brace from the engine bracket to engine.

16. Remove the stands and lower the hoist. Connect the negative battery cable.

LEFT

1. Raise the vehicle and support it safely. Disconnect the negative battery cable.

2. Support the vehicle with stands at each front frame horn.

3. Remove the nut securing the mount to the transaxle bracket and nuts securing the mount to the frame.

4. Lift the engine using engine support tool.

5. Remove the bolts securing the bracket to the transaxle.

6. Raise the engine assembly until the brackets are free.

7. Remove the mount and bracket by pulling it upward.

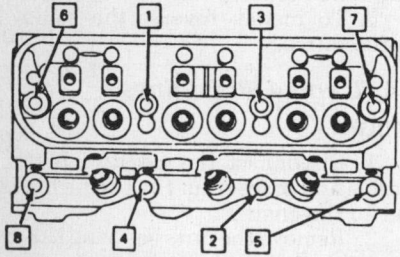

Cylinder head bolt tightening sequence— 3.8L engine

To install:

8. Position the engine mount and bracket, in place between the transaxle and frame and tighten the bracket to 41 ft. lbs. and nuts to 22 ft lbs.

9. Lower the transaxle onto the mount until it is seated.

10. Install the nut securing the mount to the bracket and tighten to 22 ft. lbs.

11. Connect the negative battery cable.

Cylinder Head
REMOVAL & INSTALLATION
3.8L Engine (VIN 3)

1. Drain the cooling system and disconnect the negative battery cable.

2. Depressurize the fuel system.

3. Disconnect Mass Air Flow (MAF) sensor wiring and air intake duct.

4. Remove TV and accelerator cables, cruise control cable, if equipped.

5. Remove crankcase ventilation pipe.

6. Remove all hoses, vacuum lines and wiring to gain access.

7. Remove the fuel rail.

8. Remove the intake manifold.

9. Disconnect the exhaust crossover pipe.

10. Remove the exhaust manifolds.

11. Remove the valve covers, rocker arms, guide plates and pushrods. Keep all parts in order so they may be reassembled in their original locations.

12. Loosen the cylinder head bolts in reverse of the torque sequence, then remove the bolts and lift off the cylinder head.

13. Clean all gasket mating surfaces and the cylinder head bolt holes in the block.

To install:

14. Install the cylinder head gasket and cylinder head.

15. Install the cylinder head bolts and tighten in the proper sequence to 25 ft. lbs.

16. Tighten each bolt ¼ turn in sequence, then tighten an additional ¼ turn in sequence.

17. Install the rocker arms and pushrods. Tighten to 45 ft. lbs.

18. Install the intake manifold. Tighten the bolts in sequence to 32 ft. lbs.

19. Replace the valve covers and install the exhaust manifold. Tighten the bolts to 37 ft. lbs.

20. Install the power steering pump and bracket. Connect the hydraulic lines.

21. Install the alternator and connect the electrical wires.

22. Replace the top radiator hose and the heater hoses. Install the fuel line and the wiring connector.

23. Install the exhaust crossover pipe and connect the vacuum lines and electrical connections.

24. Replace the crankcase ventilation pipe. Connect the TV and accelerator cables.

25. Connect the cruise control cable, if equipped.

26. Replace the mass air flow sensor and air intake duct.

27. Connect the negative battery cable. Refill the engine coolant.

28. Start the engine and check for leaks.

3.8L Engine (VIN C)

1. Disconnect the negative battery cable.

2. Remove the intake and exhaust manifolds.

3. Remove the valve covers.

4. Disconnect the ignition module wires, spark plug wires and alternator bracket. Remove air conditioning compressor bracket bolt.

5. Remove the power steering pump, tensioner assembly and the fuel line heat shield.

6. Remove the rocker arm assemblies, guide plate and the pushrods.

7. Remove the cylinder head bolts and remove the cylinder head.

8. Clean all gasket mating surfaces and the cylinder head bolt holes in the block.

To install:

9. Install the cylinder head gasket and head onto the block.

10. Install the cylinder head bolts and tighten as follows:

   a. Tighten the cylinder head bolts, in sequence, to 35 ft. lbs.

   b. Rotate each bolt 130 degrees, in sequence.

   c. Rotate each bolt an additional 30 degrees, in sequence.

11. Install the pushrods, guide plate and the rocker arm assemblies. Tighten the rocker arm pedestal bolts to 28 ft. lbs.

12. Install the intake manifold, exhaust manifold and the valve covers.

13. Replace the air conditioning compressor bracket bolt and tighten to 52 ft. lbs.

14. Install the alternator support bracket and replace the igniton module and spark plug wires.

15. Install the tensioner, power steering pump and the fuel line heat shield.

16. Connect the negative battery cable. Start the engine and check for leaks.

4.1L and 4.5L Engines
RIGHT

1. Disconnect the negative battery cable. Drain the engine coolant. Relieve the fuel pressure.

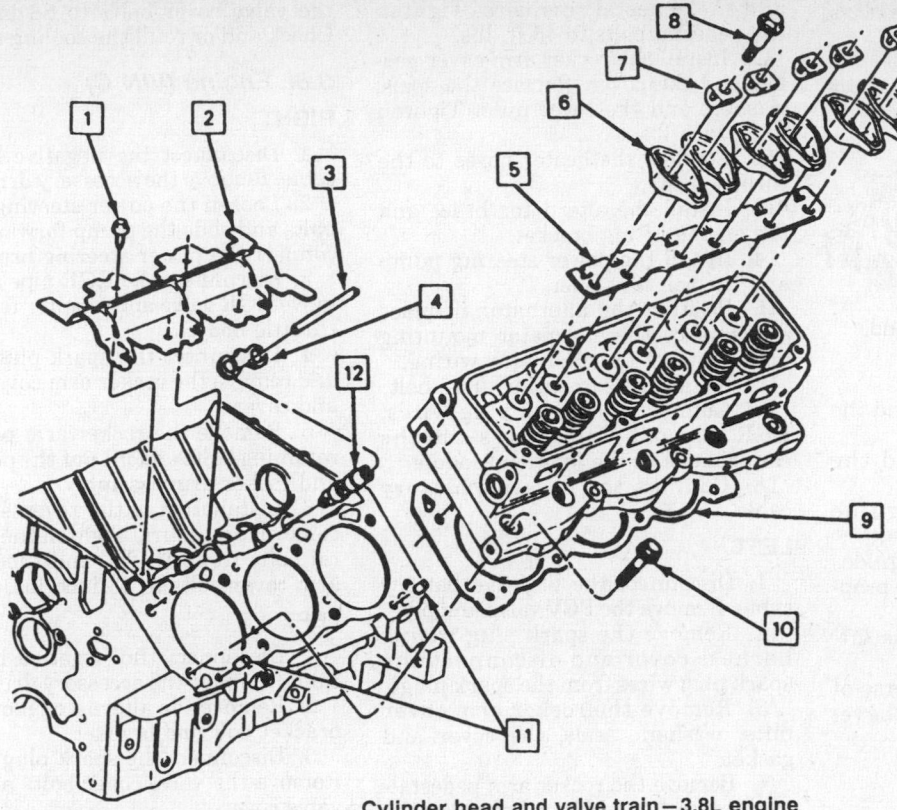

1. Bolt
2. Lifter guide retainer
3. Pushrod
4. Lifter guide
5. Pushrod guide
6. Rocker arm
7. Rocker arm pivot
8. Bolt
9. Head gasket
10. Head bolt
11. Dowel pin
12. Valve lifter

Cylinder head and valve train—3.8L engine

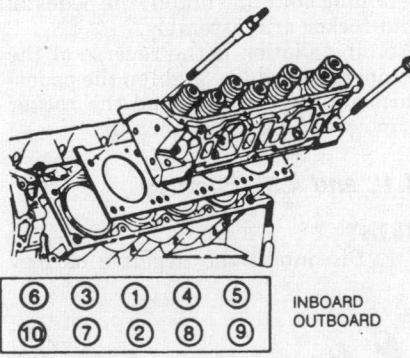

INBOARD
OUTBOARD

Cylinder head bolt tightening—4.1L and 4.5L engines

2. Remove the rocker arm covers and the intake manifold assembly.

3. Remove the right side exhaust manifold and disconnect the engine lift bracket and air pump bracket.

4. Remove the cylinder head bolts and remove the cylinder head.

5. Clean all gasket mating surfaces and the cylinder head bolt holes in the block.

To install:

6. Install the cylinder head gasket and the cylinder head.

7. Tighten the cylinder head bolts as follows:

   a. Tighten the cylinder head bolts, in sequence, to 38 ft. lbs.

   b. Tighten the cylinder head bolts, in sequence, to 68 ft. lbs.

Tighten cylinder head bolts 1, 3 and 4 to 90 ft. lbs.

8. Install the engine lift bracket and the air pump bracket.

9. Install the exhaust manifold, intake manifold and the rocker arm covers.

10. Refill the engine coolant. Connect the negative battery cable.

11. Start the engine and check for leaks.

LEFT

1. Disconnect the negative battery cable. Drain the engine coolant.

2. Remove the rocker arm covers and the intake manifold assembly.

3. Remove the left side exhaust manifold.

4. Remove the cooling fans and the dipstick tube.

5. Remove the cylinder head mounting bolts and remove the cylinder head.

6. Clean all gasket mating surfaces and the cylinder head bolt holes in the block.

To install:

7. Install a new head gasket over the dowels on the cylinder block.

8. Install the cylinder head and tighten the bolts as follows:

   a. Tighten the cylinder head bolts, in sequence, to 38 ft. lbs.

   b. Tighten the cylinder head bolts, in sequence, to 68 ft. lbs.

Tighten cylinder head bolts 1, 3 and 4 to 90 ft. lbs.

9. Install the dipstick tube and replace the cooling fans.

10. Install the exhaust manifold, intake manifold and the rocker arm covers.

11. Refill the engine coolant. Connect the negative battery cable.

12. Start the engine and check for leaks.

Valve Lifters

REMOVAL & INSTALLATION

3.8L Engine

1. Disconnect the negative battery cable.

2. Remove the valve covers and the intake manifold.

3. Remove the rocker arm bolts, rocker arms and the pedestals.

4. Remove the pushrods, guide retainer bolts and the retainer.

5. Remove the lifter guides and lift out the lifters, using the proper tool.

6. Prior to installation dip the lifters in the proper prelube. The installation is the reverse of the removal procedure.

4.1L and 4.5L Engines

1. Disconnect the negative battery cable.

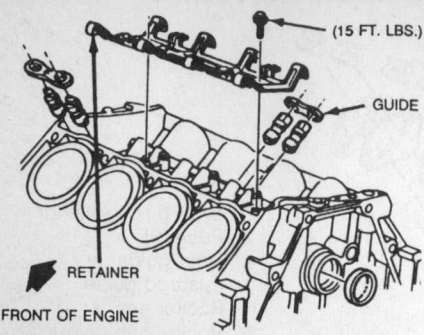

Lifter guides and retainer—4.1L and 4.5L engines

2. Remove the valve covers and the intake manifold.

3. Remove the rockers and the pushrods.

4. Disconnect the valve guide retainer.

5. Remove the valve lifter guides and pull out the lifters, using the proper tool.

6. Prior to installation dip the lifters in the proper prelube.

7. The installation is the reverse of the removal procedure. Tighten the retainer bolts to 15 ft. lbs.

Rocker Arms

REMOVAL & INSTALLATION

3.8L Engine (VIN 3)
RIGHT

1. Disconnect the negative battery cable.

2. Remove the spark plug cables, the wiring connector, the EGR solenoid wiring/hoses, the C³I module nuts and module.

3. Remove the serpentine drive belt. Disconnect the alternator wiring. Remove the alternator mounting bolt and rotate the alternator toward the front of the vehicle.

4. Remove the power steering pump and the belt tensioner.

5. Remove the engine lifting bracket and the rear alternator brace.

6. Remove the heater hoses from the throttle body.

7. Remove the rocker arm cover nuts, washers, seals, the cover and gasket. Discard the gasket.

8. Remove the rocker arm pedestal-to-cylinder head bolts, the pedestals, the rocker arms and the pedestal retainers.

NOTE: Be sure to keep the parts in order for reassembly purposes.

9. Clean the gasket mounting surfaces.

To install:

10. Install the rocker arms, pedestals

and the pedestal retainers. Tighten the pedestal bolts to 45 ft. lbs.

11. Install the rocker arm cover gasket and the cover. Replace the seals, washers and the cover nuts. Tighten to 88 inch lbs.

12. Connect the heater hoses to the throttle body.

13. Install the alternator brace and the engine lifting bracket.

14. Install the power steering pump and the belt tensioner.

15. Position the alternator in place and replace the alternator mounting bolt. Connect the alternator wiring.

16. Install the serpentine drive belt.

17. Connect the spark plug wires, EGR solenoid wiring/hoses and the connections at the ignition module.

18. Connect the negative battery cable.

LEFT

1. Disconnect the negative battery cable. Remove the PCV valve and pipe.

2. Remove the spark plug wiring harness cover and disconnect the spark plug wires from the spark plugs.

3. Remove the rocker arm cover nuts, washers, seals, the cover and gasket.

4. Remove the rocker arm pedestal-to-cylinder head bolts, the pedestals, the rocker arms and the pedestal retainers.

NOTE: Be sure to keep the parts in order for reassembly purposes.

5. Clean the gasket mounting surfaces.

6. To install, use a new gasket with sealant, if necessary, and reverse the removal procedures. Torque the rocker arm pedestal bolts to 45 ft. lbs. and

the valve cover bolts to 88 inch lbs. Check and/or refill the cooling system.

3.8L Engine (VIN C)
RIGHT

1. Disconnect the negative battery cable. Remove the accessary drive belt.

2. Loosen the power steering pump bolts and slide the pump forward. Disconnect the power steering bracket.

3. Disconnect the EGR pipe and remove EGR valve and adapter from the throttle body.

4. Disconnect the spark plug wires and remove the rocker arm cover bolts and cover.

5. Remove the rocker arm pedestal retaining bolts and lift out the pedestal and rocker arm assembly.

6. Installation is the reverse of the removal procedure. Tighten the pedestal bolts to 28 ft. lbs. and the rocker arm cover bolts to 88 inch lbs.

LEFT

1. Disconnect the negative battery cable. Remove the accessory drive belt.

2. Remove the alternator mounting bracket bolt and bracket.

3. Disconnect the spark plug wires. Remove the valve cover bolts and the valve cover.

4. Remove the rocker arm pedestal retaining bolts and lift out the pedestal and rocker arm assembly.

5. Installation is the reverse of the removal procedure. Tighten the pedestal bolts to 28 ft. lbs. and the rocker arm cover bolts to 88 inch lbs.

4.1L and 4.5L Engines
RIGHT

1. Disconnect the negative battery

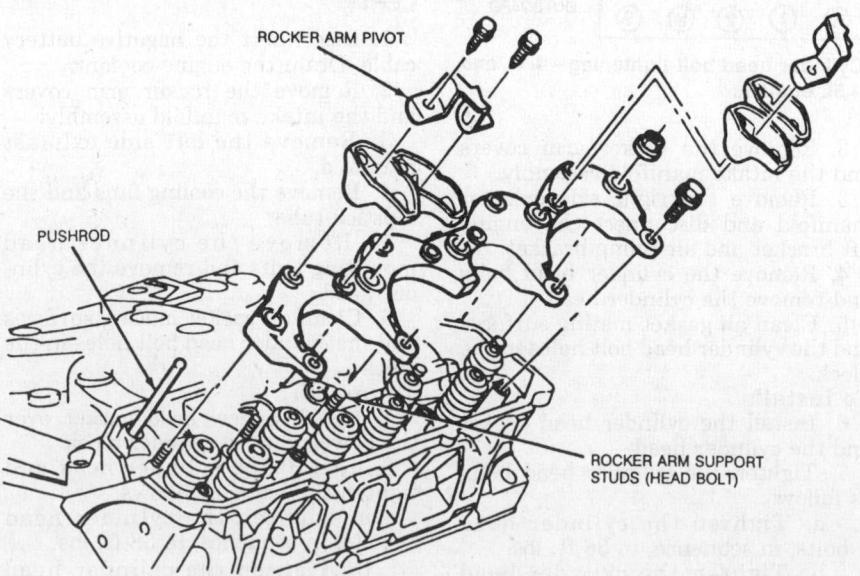

Rocker arm assembly—4.1L and 4.5L engines

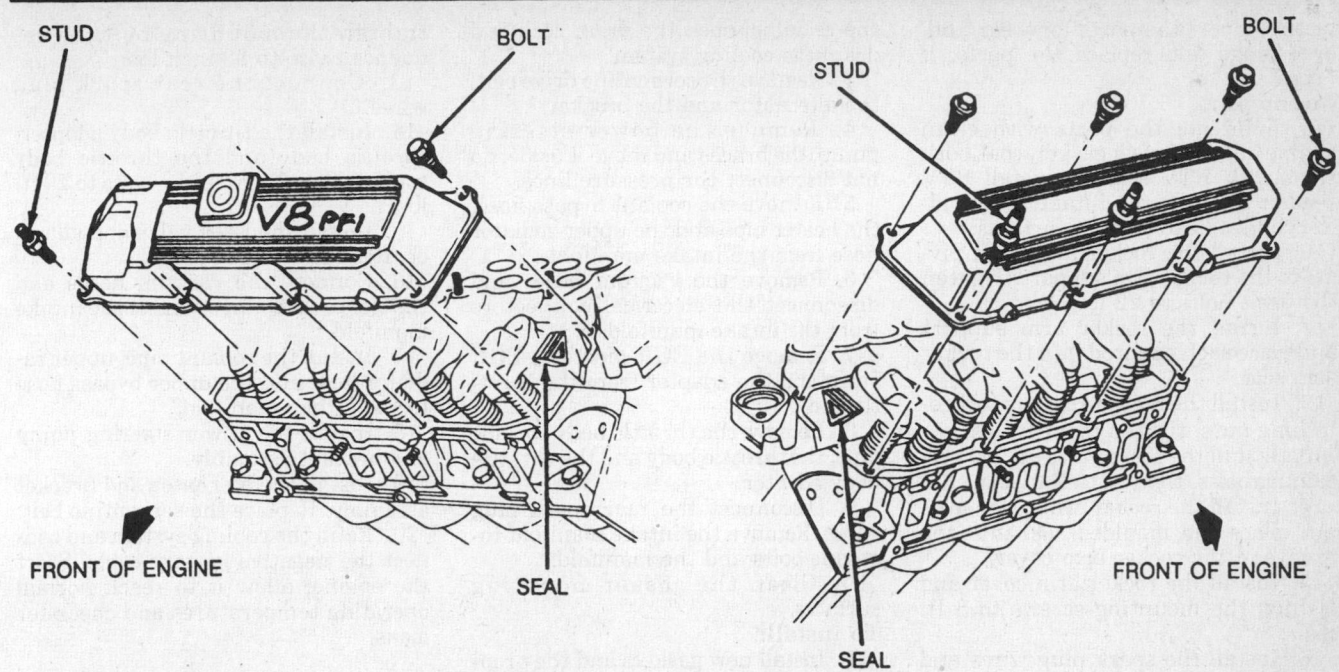

Rocker arm covers—4.1L and 4.5L engines

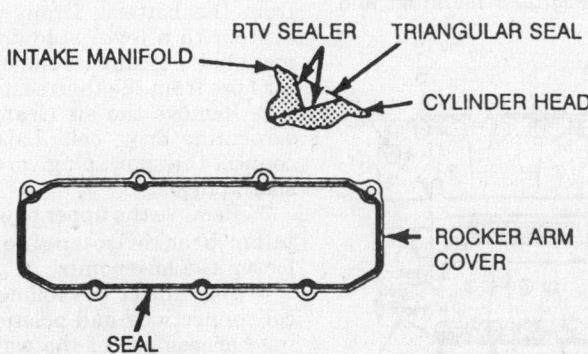

Rocker arm cover sealing—4.1L and 4.5L engines

cable. Remove the air cleaner and the AIR management valve with bracket, move the assembly aside.

2. From the throttle body, remove the Manifold Absolute Pressure (MAP) hose.

3. Remove the right side spark plug wires and conduit.

4. Remove the fuel vapor canister pipe bracket from the valve cover stud.

5. Drain the cooling system to a level below the thermostat housing. Remove the heater hose from the thermostat housing and move it aside.

6. Remove the brake booster vacuum hose from the intake manifold.

7. Remove the rocker arm cover-to-cylinder screws, the cover and the gasket/seals. Discard them.

8. Remove the rocker arm pivot-to-rocker arm support bolts, the pivots and the rocker arms.

9. If necessary, remove the rocker arm support-to cylinder head nuts/bolts and the support.

10. Clean the gasket mounting surfaces. Inspect the parts for wear and/or damage and replace the parts, if necessary.

To install:

11. Lubricate the parts with clean engine oil, use a new gasket and coat both sides with RTV sealant, install RTV sealant between the intake manifold-to-cylinder head mating surfaces.

12. Install the rocker arms and pivots to the rocker arm support. Tighten the pivot bolts to 22 ft. lbs.

13. Install the rocker arm support and place each pushrod into the rocker arm seat.

14. Install the rocker arm support retaining nuts, tighten to 37 ft. lbs.

15. Install the rocker arm support retaining bolts, tighten to 7 ft. lbs.

16. Install the rocker arm cover seals and place the moulded seal into the groove in the rocker arm cover.

17. Install the rocker arm cover and

tighten the mounting screws to 8 ft. lbs.

18. Connect the brake booster vaccum hose and the EECS pipe bracket.

19. Install the spark plug wires and conduit. Connect the MAP hose to the throttle body.

20. Install the air management and bracket assembly.

21. Replace the heater hose and air cleaner assembly.

22. Connect the negative battery cable. Start the engine and check for leaks.

LEFT

1. Disconnect the negative battery cable. Remove the air cleaner, the PCV valve, the throttle return spring and the serpentine drive belt.

2. Loosen the lower power steering pump bracket nuts.

3. Remove the power steering pump, the belt tensioner, the bracket-to-engine bolts and the bracket. Move the power steering pump assembly toward the front of the vehicle; do not disconnect the pressure hoses.

4. Remove the left side spark plug wires and conduit.

5. Remove the rocker arm cover-to-cylinder screws, the cover and the gasket/seals. Discard them.

6. Remove the rocker arm pivot-to-rocker arm support bolts, the pivots and the rocker arms.

7. If necessary, remove the rocker arm support-to cylinder head nuts/bolts and the support.

8. Clean the gasket mounting sur-

faces. Inspect the parts for wear and/or damage and replace the parts, if necessary.

To install:

9. Lubricate the parts with clean engine oil, use a new gasket, coat both sides with RTV sealant, install RTV sealant between the intake manifold-to-cylinder head mating surfaces.

10. Install the rocker arms and pivots to the rocker arm support. Tighten the pivot bolts to 22 ft. lbs.

11. Install the rocker arm support and place each pushrod into the rocker arm seat.

12. Install the rocker arm support retaining nuts, tighten to 37 ft. lbs.

13. Install the rocker arm support retaining bolts, tighten to 7 ft. lbs.

14. Install the rocker arm cover seals and place the moulded seal into the groove in the rocker arm cover.

15. Install the rocker arm cover and tighten the mounting screws to 8 ft. lbs.

16. Install the spark plug wires and conduit.

17. Install the power steering pump, belt tensioner and bracket assembly. Replace the accessory drive belt.

18. Install the throttle return spring and the PCV valve.

19. Install the air cleaner and connect the negative battery cable.

20. Start the engine and check for leaks.

Intake Manifold

REMOVAL & INSTALLATION

3.8L Engine

1. Relieve the fuel system pressure.
2. Disconnect the negative battery cable. Place a clean drain pan under the radiator, open the drain cock and drain the cooling system.

3. Remove the serpentine drive belt, the alternator and the bracket.

4. Remove the power steering pump, the braces and move it aside; do not disconnect the pressure lines.

5. Remove the coolant bypass hose, the heater pipe and the upper radiator hose from the intake manifold.

6. Remove the vacuum hoses and disconnect the electrical connectors from the intake manifold.

7. Remove the EGR pipe, the EGR valve and the adapter from the throttle body.

8. Remove the throttle body coolant pipe, the throttle body and the throttle body adapter.

9. Disconnect the rear spark plug wires. Remove the intake manifold-to-engine bolts and the manifold.

10. Clean the gasket mounting surfaces.

To install:

11. Install new gaskets and the proper sealant on the ends of the manifold seals.

12. Install the intake manifold and

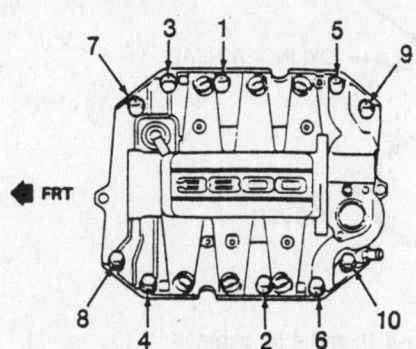

View of the intake manifold bolt torquing sequence—3.8L engine

tighten the mounting bolts in sequence twice to 88 inch lbs.

13. Connect the rear spark plug wires.

14. Install the throttle body adapter, throttle body and the throttle body coolant pipe. Tighten the bolts to 20 ft. lbs.

15. Install the EGR valve and adapter. Replace the EGR pipe.

16. Connect the vacuum hoses and the electrical connections to the intake manifold.

17. Install the coolant pipe, upper radiator hose and the upper bypass hose to the intake manifold.

18. Install the power steering pump and bracket assembly.

19. Install the aternator and bracket assembly. Replace the serpentine belt.

20. Refill the cooling system and connect the negative battery cable. Start the engine, allow it to reach normal operating temperatures and check for leaks.

4.1L and 4.5L Engines

1. Disconnect the negative terminal from the battery. Drain the cooling system to a level below the intake manifold. Disconnect the upper radiator hose from the thermostat housing.

2. Remove the air cleaner and the serpentine drive belt. Label and disconnect the spark plug wires from the spark plugs.

3. Remove the upper power steering pump bracket-to-engine bolts and loosen the lower nuts.

4. Disconnect the following electrical connections and position the wiring harness out of the way: distributor, oil pressure switch, EGR solenoid, coolant sensor, mass airflow temperature sensor, throttle position sensor, 4-way connector at the distributor,

1. Throttle body
2. Gasket
3. 20 ft. lbs.
4. Throttle body adapter
5. Gasket
6. Stud
7. Intake manifold

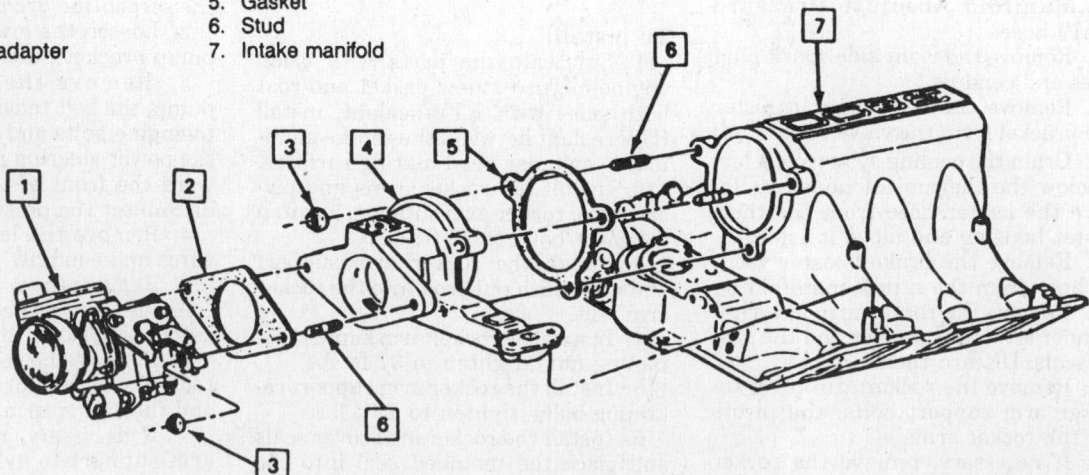

Throttle body and adapter to the Intake manifold—3.8L engine

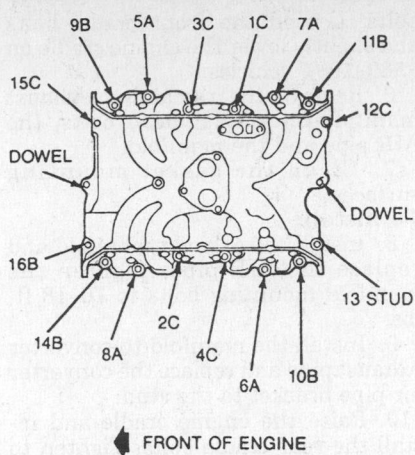

FRONT OF ENGINE

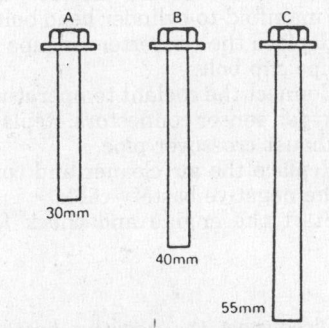

30mm

40mm

55mm

Intake manifold bolt size and torque sequence—4.1L and 4.5L engines

electric fuel evaporator grid, idle speed control motor and fuel injectors.

5. From the throttle lever, disconnect the accelerator, cruise control, if equipped, and transaxle TV cables.

6. Using a shop rag at the fuel line Schraeder valve (test port), bleed off the fuel pressure. Disconnect the fuel inlet and return lines from the throttle body. From the transaxle, remove the fuel line brackets and move the lines aside; disconnect the modulator vacuum line.

7. Disconnect the heater hose from the nipple at the rear of the intake manifold.

8. From the intake manifold, remove the cruise control bracket, if equipped. Remove the vacuum line from the left rear engine lift bracket and the throttle body.

9. Disconnect the electrical connectors from the alternator and AIR management solenoid. Remove the alternator, the idler pulley, the AIR management valve/bracket and EGR solenoid/bracket. Disconnect the hose from the MAP hose.

10. From the right cylinder head, remove the power steering pipe and the AIR pipe. Raise and support the vehicle safely.

11. Drain the engine oil and remove the oil filter. Lower the vehicle.

12. Remove the distributor. Remove

both rocker arm covers. Remove the rocker arm support with the rocker arms intact by first alternately and evenly removing the 4 bolts followed by the 5 nuts. Keep the pushrods in sequence so they may be reassembled in their original positions.

13. If equipped with air conditioning, partially remove the compressor; do not discharge the system. Remove the vacuum harness connections from the TVS at the rear of the intake manifold.

14. Remove the intake manifold bolts and remove the 2 bolts securing the lower thermostat housing to the front cover. Remove the engine lift brackets or bend them out of the way.

15. Remove the intake manifold and lower the thermostat housing as an assembly by lifting it straight up off of the dowels.

16. Clean the gasket mounting surfaces.

To install:

17. Install new gaskets and apply the proper RTV sealant to the 4 corners where the end seals meet.

18. Install the intake manifold, using new gaskets. Tighten the mounting bolts as follows:

    a. Torque the No. 1–4 bolts, in sequence, to 8 ft. lbs.

    b. Torque the No. 5–16 bolts, in sequence, to 8 ft. lbs.

    c. Retorque all bolts, in sequence, to 12 ft. lbs.

    d. Recheck all bolts, in sequence, to 12 ft. lbs.

19. Install the right side engine lift brackets.

20. Install the alternator and idler pulley mounting bracket and replace the brackets at the right cylinder head.

21. Install the pushrods and the rocker arm support assemblies.

22. Install the rocker arm covers, using new seals.

23. Replace the EGR valve and bracket assembly. Connect the MAP hose.

24. Connect the wire connectors at the ISC motor, TPS, the fuel injectors and the MAT sensor.

25. Connect the air management wires, valves and the bracket assembly.

26. Install the alternator and connect the electrical wires.

27. Install the belt tensioner, power steering pump and bracket assembly.

28. Connect the transaxle modulator vaccum line and the vacuum supply line at the throttle body.

29. Install the vacuum line bracket at the left rear engine lift bracket.

30. Install the cruise control servo bracket and connect the fuel lines at the throttle body. Connect the fuel line brackets at the transaxle.

31. Replace the upper radiator hose.

32. Connect the transmission TV, cruise control and accelerator cables at the throttle body.

33. Install the distributor cap, wires and conduit.

34. Connect the wire connectors at the distributor, oil pressure switch, coolant sensor and the EGR solenoid.

35. Replace the heater hose at the thermostat housing.

36. Raise and support the vehicle safely. Replace the oil filter and tighten the oil drain plug.

37. Install the upper left side power steering pump bracket bolts. Replace the accessory drive belt.

38. Install the air cleaner assembly and refill the cooling system.

39. Connect the negative battery cable. Start the engine and allow it to reach normal operating temperatures and check for leaks.

Exhaust Manifold

REMOVAL & INSTALLATION

3.8L Engine
RIGHT

1. Disconnect the negative battery cable.

2. If necessary, disconnect the mass air flow sensor, air intake duct, the crankcase ventilation pipe and the IAC connector from the throttle body.

3. Label and disconnect the wires from the spark plugs. Disconnect the oxygen sensor lead.

4. If equipped, disconnect the heater inlet pipe from the manifold stud. Remove the transaxle oil indicator tube for 1990–91 vehicles.

5. Remove the exhaust crossover pipe-to-exhaust manifold bolts and the pipe. Disconnect the alternator bracket, if neccessary.

6. Raise and support the vehicle safely. Remove the exhaust pipe-to-manifold bolts, the exhaust manifold-to-cylinder head bolts and the manifold.

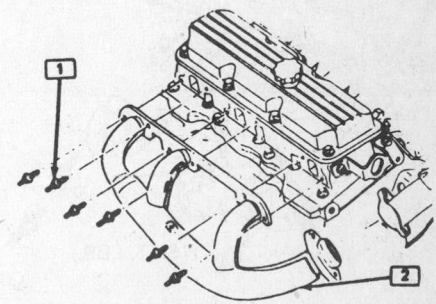

1. Stud—41 ft. lbs.
2. Left (front) exhaust manifold

Left side exhaust manifold—3.8L engine

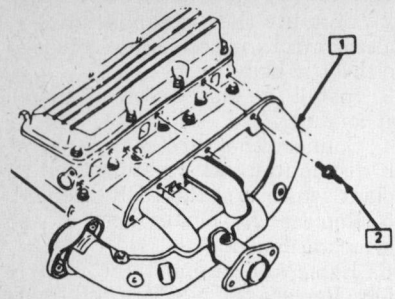

1. Right (rear) exhaust manifold
2. Stud — 41 ft. lbs.

Right side exhaust manifold — 3.8L engine

7. Remove the EGR pipe from the exhaust manifold.

8. Clean the gasket mounting surfaces.

To install:

9. Replace the EGR pipe to the exhaust manifold.

10. Install the exhaust manifold, using a new gasket. Tighten the mounting studs to 37–41 ft. lbs.

11. Lower the vehicle. Connect the alternator bracket, if neccessary.

12. Install the crossover pipe and replace the exhaust manifold-to-cylinder bolts.

13. Replace the transaxle oil indicator tube–1990 vehicles. Connect the heater inlet pipe to the manifold, if equipped.

14. Connect the oxygen sensor lead and the spark plug wires.

15. If necessary, connect the mass air flow sensor, air intake duct, the crankcase ventilation pipe and the IAC connector from the throttle body.

16. Connect the negative battery cable. Start the engine and check for leaks.

LEFT

1. Disconnect the negative battery cable. If necessary, remove the mass air flow sensor, air intake duct and crankcase ventilation pipe.

2. Remove the exhaust crossover pipe-to-exhaust manifold bolts. Label and disconnect the spark plug wires.

3. Remove the exhaust manifold-to-cylinder head bolts and the manifold.

NOTE: It may be necessary to remove the oil dipstick tube to provide additional clearance.

4. Clean the gasket mounting surfaces and install a new gasket.

5. Install the exhaust manifold and tighten the mainfold mounting studs to 37–41 ft. lbs.

6. The installation is the reverse of the removal procedure. Start the engine and check for exhaust leaks.

4.1L and 4.5L Engines

RIGHT

1. Disconnect the negative battery cable. Remove the air cleaner.

2. Remove the exhaust crossover pipe. Disconnect the oxygen and coolant temperature sensors.

3. Remove the catalytic converter-to-AIR pipe clip bolt. Remove the upper manifold-to-cylinder head bolts. Raise and support the vehicle safely.

4. Disconnect the converter air pipe bracket from the stud and remove the converter-to-manifold exhaust pipe.

5. Support the engine cradle with screw jacks and remove the rear cradle bolts. Loosen the front cradle bolts and slightly lower the engine cradle on 1989–1991 vehicles.

6. Remove the remaining exhaust manifold-to-cylinder head bolts, the AIR pipe and the manifold.

7. Clean the gasket mounting surfaces.

To install:

8. Install the exhaust manifold and replace the AIR pipe. Tighten the manifold mounting bolts to 16–18 ft. lbs.

9. Install the manifold-to-converter exhaust pipe and replace the converter air pipe bracket to the stud.

10. Raise the engine cradle and install the rear cradle bolts. Tighten to 75 ft. lbs on 1989–91 vehicle.

11. Lower the vehicle. Replace the upper manifold-to-cylinder head bolts.

12. Replace the converter air pipe to AIR pipe clip bolt.

13. Connect the coolant temperature and oxygen sensor connectors. Replace the exhaust crossover pipe.

14. Replace the air cleaner and connect the negative battery cable.

15. Start the engine and check for leaks.

LEFT

1. Disconnect the negative battery cable. Remove both cooling fans and the exhaust crossover pipe.

2. Remove the serpentine drive belt and the AIR pump pivot bolt.

3. Remove the belt tensioner and the power steering pump brace.

4. Remove the exhaust manifold-to-cylinder head bolts, the AIR pipe and the manifold.

5. Clean the gasket mounting surfaces.

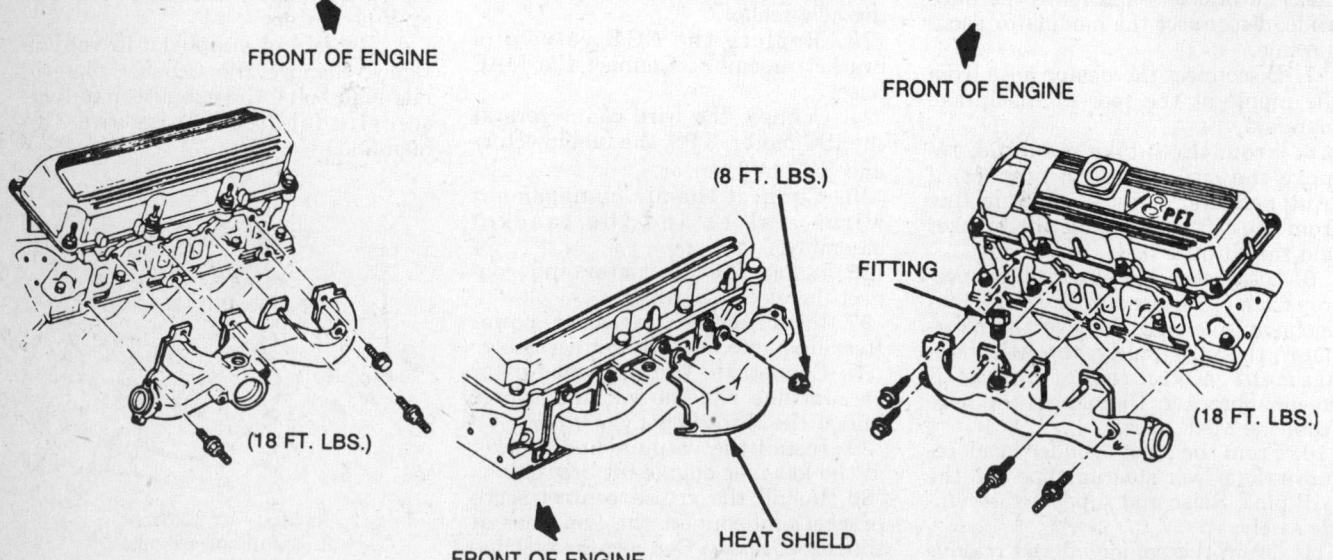

FRONT OF ENGINE

(8 FT. LBS.)

FITTING

(18 FT. LBS.)

(18 FT. LBS.)

FRONT OF ENGINE

HEAT SHIELD

FRONT OF ENGINE

Exhaust manifolds — 1990–91 Cadillac

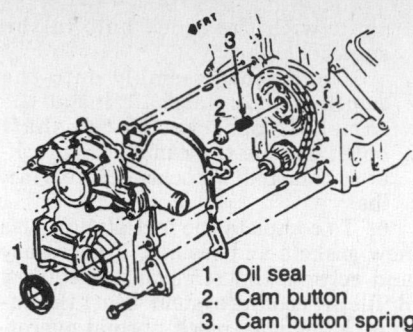

1. Oil seal
2. Cam button
3. Cam button spring

Exploded view of the front cover assembly—3.8L engine

6. To install, use new gaskets and reverse the removal procedures. Torque the exhaust manifold-to-engine bolts to 16–18 ft. lbs. Start the engine and check for exhaust leaks.

Timing Chain Front Cover

REMOVAL & INSTALLATION

3.8L Engine (VIN 3)

1. Disconnect the negative battery cable. Drain the cooling system.
2. Remove the lower radiator hose and the coolant bypass hose from the front cover. Remove the heater pipes.
3. Remove the front engine cradle mount bolts. Using a vertical lifting device, secure it to the engine and raise it slightly. Remove the alternator and mounting bracket.
4. Remove the serpentine drive belt and the water pump pulley.
5. Label and disconnect the alternator wiring. Remove the alternator and the alternator bracket.
7. Remove the crankshaft balancer bolt/washer and the balancer.
8. Remove the front cover-to-engine bolts and the front cover.
9. Remove the front cover-to-oil pan bolts and the front chain cover.
10. Install the gasket to the cylinder block and replace the front cover. Tighten the front cover bolts to 22 ft. lbs.
11. Install the balancer, bolt and the washer, Tighten the bolt to 219 ft. lbs.
12. Install the alternator and connect the alternator bracket.
13. Lower the engine and replace the front engine cradle bolts.
14. Install the serpentine belt and the water pump pulley.
15. Install the heater pipes, heater hoses and the radiator hoses.
16. Refill the cooling system and connect the negative battery cable.
17. Start the engine and check for leaks.

3.8L Engine (VIN C)

1. Disconnect the negative battery cable. Drain the cooling sytem.
2. Remove the drive belt and the heater pipes.
3. Disconnect the lower radiator and bypass hoses from the cover.
4. Raise and support the vehicle safely. Remove the right front tire and wheel assembly and replace the inner splash shield.
5. Remove the crankshaft bolt and balancer.
6. Disconnect the electrical connections at the camshaft sensor, crankshaft sensor and the oil pressure switch.
7. Remove the oil pan-to-front cover bolts.
8. Remove the front cover mounting bolts and the cover assembly.
9. Clean the gasket surfaces at the cover and the cylinder block.

To install:

10. Install the gasket to the cylinder block.
11. Install the front cover and tighten the mounting bolts to 22 ft. lbs.
12. Replace the oil pan-to-cover mounting bolts and tighten to 88 inch lbs.
13. Connect the electrical connections and replace the crankshaft balancer and tighten the bolt to 219 ft. lbs.
14. Install the inner fender splash shield and the right front tire and wheel assembly.
15. Lower the vehicle. Replace the coolant bypass hose and radiator hoses.
16. Connect the heater pipes and install the drive belt.
17. Refill the cooling system and connect the negative battery cable.
18. Start the engine and check for leaks.

4.1L and 4.5L Engines

1. Disconnect the negative terminal from the battery.
2. Place a clean drain pan under the radiator, open the drain cock and drain the engine coolant. Remove the air cleaner and move it aside.
3. Remove the serpentine belt.
4. Label and disconnect the alternator wiring. Remove the alternator and the alternator bracket.
5. Remove the air conditioner accumulator from the bracket and move it aside; do not disconnect the fittings on the accumulator.
6. Remove the water pump pulley and pump. If necessary, remove the idler pulley.
7. Raise and support the vehicle safely.
8. Remove the crankshaft pulley-to-crankshaft pulley bolt. Attach a puller tool to the crankshaft pulley; using the center bolt, press the crankshaft pulley from the crankshaft.
9. Remove the front cover-to-engine bolts, the oil pan-to-front cover bolts and the front cover.
10. Clean the gasket mounting surfaces.

To install:

11. Install the timing cover and tighten the mounting bolts to 15 ft. lbs.
12. Install the crankshaft damper and tighten the bolt to 18 ft. lbs.
13. Lower the vehicle. Replace the water pump and pulley.
14. Install the idler pulley, if needed. Install the serpentine belt.
15. Connect the alternator wiring and install the alternator and bracket.
16. Replace the air conditioner accumulator and connect the bracket.
17. Replace the air cleaner and refill the cooling system.
18. Connect the negative battery cable. Start the engine and check for leaks.

Front Cover Oil Seal

REPLACEMENT

3.8L Engine

1. Disconnect the negative battery cable.
2. Remove the serpentine drive belt. Remove the crankshaft balancer-to-crankshaft bolts.
3. Using a small pry bar, pry the oil seal from the front cover; be careful not to damage the sealing surfaces.
4. Clean the oil seal mounting surface. Using the proper lubricant coat the outside of the seal and the crankshaft balancer.
5. Using the oil seal installation tool, drive the new seal into the front cover until it seats.
6. To install, reverse the removal procedures. Torque the crankshaft balancer-to-crankshaft bolt to 219 ft. lbs.

4.1L and 4.5L Engines

1. Disconnect the negative battery cable. Remove the serpentine belt.
2. Remove the crankshaft pulley-to-crankshaft pulley bolt.
3. Attach a puller tool to the crankshaft pulley; using the center bolt, press the crankshaft pulley from the crankshaft.
4. Using the oil seal removal tools, press the oil seal from the front cover. Clean the oil seal mounting surface.
5. Lubricate the new seal with engine oil. Using a hammer and an oil seal installation tool, drive the new oil

seal in to the front cover until it seats.

6. To complete the installation, reverse the removal procedures. Torque the crankshaft pulley-to-crankshaft bolt to 18 ft. lbs.

Timing Chain and Sprockets

REMOVAL & INSTALLATION

3.8L Engine

1. Disconnect the negative battery cable. Remove the front cover.

2. Remove the button and spring from the center of the camshaft. Align the marks of the timing sprockets as they must be close together.

4. Remove the camshaft sprocket bolts, the sprocket and the timing chain.

5. Remove the crankshaft sprocket. Clean the gasket mounting surfaces.

6. To install the timing chain and sprockets, perform the following procedures:

    a. Assemble the timing chain on the camshaft sprocket and crankshaft sprockets.

    b. Align the O-marks on the sprockets; they must face each other.

    c. Slide the assembly onto the camshaft and crankshaft. Install the camshaft sprocket-to-camshaft bolts. Torque the camshaft sprocket-to-camshaft sprocket bolts to 27–28 ft. lbs.

NOTE: On the 1988–91 (VIN C) engine, align the camshaft sprocket mark with the balancer shaft sprocket mark.

7. Install the camshaft button and spring.

8. Replace the front cover assembly. Connect the negative battery cable. Refill the cooling system. Start the engine, allow it to reach normal operating temperatures and check for leaks.

4.1L and 4.5L Engines

1. Disconnect the negative battery cable. Remove the front cover.

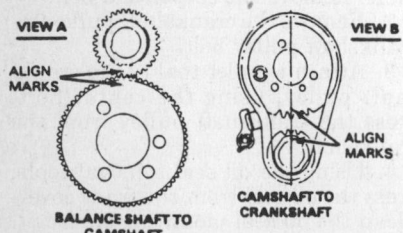

View of the timing chain, sprockets and balancer shaft alignment—3.8L engine

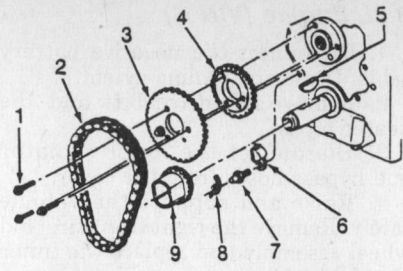

1. 27 ft. lbs.
2. Timing chain
3. Camshaft sprocket
4. Camshaft gear
5. Key
6. Damper
7. Special bolt (14 ft. lbs.)
8. Spring
9. Crankshaft sprocket

Exploded view of the timing chain, sprockets and balancer shaft sprocket—3.8L engine

2. Remove the oil slinger from the crankshaft. Rotate the engine to align the sprocket timing marks; the No.1 cylinder will be on the TDC of its compression stroke.

3. From the camshaft, remove the camshaft thrust button, replace it and the camshaft sprocket-to-camshaft screw. Slide the camshaft sprocket, the crankshaft sprocket and timing chain from the engine as an assembly.

4. Clean the gasket mounting surfaces. Inspect the parts for wear and/or damage; if necessary, replace the parts.

5. To install the timing chain and sprockets, perform the following procedures:

    a. Assemble the timing chain on the camshaft sprocket and crankshaft sprockets.

    b. Align the timing marks on the sprockets; they must face each other.

    c. Align the dowel pin in the cam-

shaft with the index hole in the sprocket.

    d. Slide the assembly onto the camshaft and crankshaft. Install the camshaft sprocket-to-camshaft bolts. Torque the camshaft sprocket-to-camshaft sprocket bolt to 37 ft. lbs.

6. To complete the installation, use new gaskets and sealant, if necessary and reverse the removal procedures. Refill the cooling system. Start the engine, allow it to reach normal operating temperatures and check for leaks.

Camshaft

REMOVAL & INSTALLATION

3.8L Engine

1. Disconnect the negative battery cable. Remove the engine assembly and position in a suitable holding fixture.

2. Remove the intake manifold, the front timing cover, timing chain and sprockets.

3. Remove the rocker arm covers, the rocker arm shaft or rocker arm assemblies, the pushrods and the hydraulic lifters.

NOTE: When removing the valve components, be sure to keep them in order for reinstallation purposes.

4. Carefully, slide the camshaft forward, out of the bearing bores; do not damage the bearing surfaces.

5. Clean the gasket mounting surfaces. Inspect the parts for wear and/or damage, replace if neccessary.

6. To install, use new gaskets and sealant, if necessary, lubricate the valve

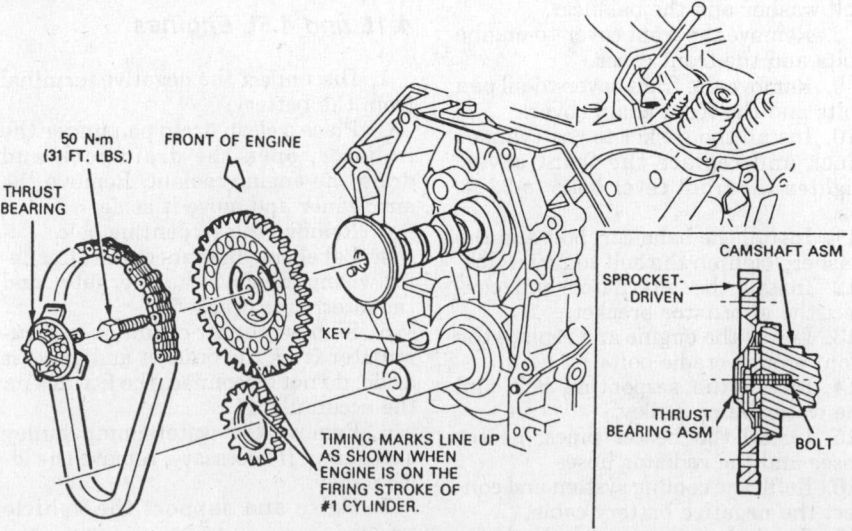

Camshaft and timing chain alignment—4.5L engine

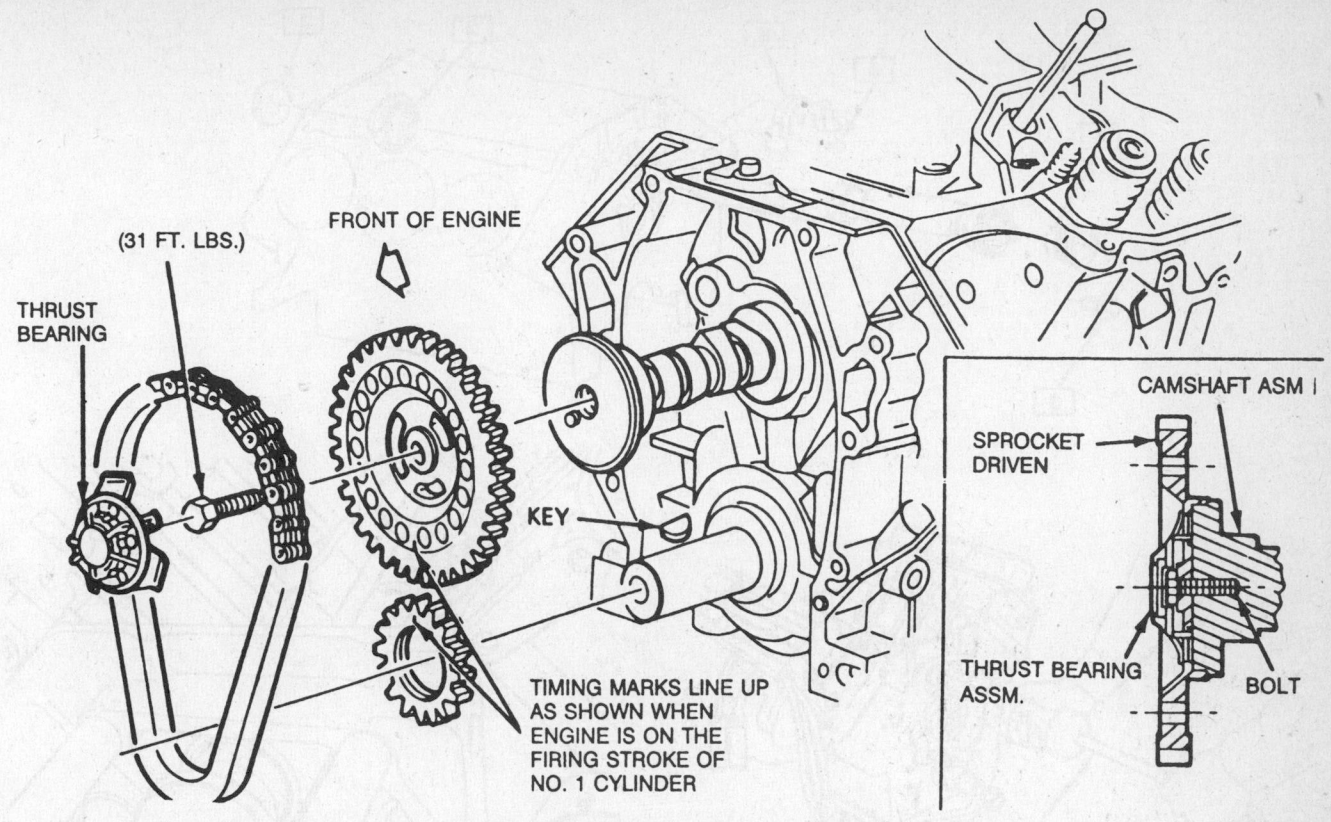

(31 FT. LBS.)

FRONT OF ENGINE

THRUST
BEARING

KEY

TIMING MARKS LINE UP
AS SHOWN WHEN
ENGINE IS ON THE
FIRING STROKE OF
NO. 1 CYLINDER

CAMSHAFT ASM

SPROCKET
DRIVEN

THRUST BEARING
ASSM.

BOLT

Timing chain and camshaft—4.5L engine

lifters and camshaft with multi-lube No. 1052365 or equivalent, and reverse the removal procedures. Refill the cooling system. Start the engine, allow it to reach normal operating temperatures and check for leaks.

NOTE: On the 1988–91 (VIN C) engine, align the camshaft gear with the balancer shaft gear timing marks.

4.1L and 4.5L Engines

1. Disconnect the negative battery cable. Remove the engine assembly and position in a suiatble holding fixture.

2. Remove the intake manifold and the timing chain and remove the valve lifters.

NOTE: When removing the valve components, be sure to keep the parts in order for reinstallation purposes.

3. Carefully slide the camshaft out from the front of the engine; be sure not to damage the camshaft bearings.

4. Clean the gasket mounting surfaces. Inspect the parts for wear and/or damage; if necessary, replace the parts.

5. To install, lubricate the camshaft with engine oil, use new gaskets and sealant, if necessary, and reverse the

removal procedures. Torque the camshaft sprocket-to-camshaft screws to 31–37 ft. lbs.

NOTE: If a new camshaft is to be installed, new lifters and a distributor drive gear must also be installed.

6. To complete the installation, reverse the removal procedures. Refill the cooling system. Start the engine, allow it to reach normal operating temperatures and check for leaks.

Balance Shaft

REMOVAL & INSTALLATION

3.8L Engine

1. Disconnect the negative battery cable. Remove the engine and secure it to a workstand.

2. Remove the flywheel-to-crankshaft bolts and the flywheel.

3. Remove the timing chain cover-to-engine bolts and the cover.

4. Remove the camshaft sprocket-to-camshaft gear bolts, the sprocket, the timing chain and the gear.

5. To remove the balance shaft, perform the following procedures:

   a. Remove the balance shaft gear-to-shaft bolt and the gear.

   b. Remove the balance shaft retainer-to-engine bolts and the retainer.

   c. Using the slide hammer tool, pull the balance shaft from the front of the engine.

To install:

6. If replacing the rear balance shaft bearing, perform the following procedures:

   a. Drive the rear plug from the engine.

   b. Using the camshaft remover/installer tool, press the rear bearing from the rear of the engine.

   c. Dip the new bearing in clean engine oil.

   d. Using the balance shaft rear bearing installer tool, press the new rear bearing into the rear of the engine.

   e. Install the rear cup plug.

7. Using the balance shaft installer tool, screw it into the balance shaft and install the shaft into the engine; remove the installer tool.

8. Clean the gasket mounting surfaces. Inspect the parts for wear and/or damage; replace the parts, if necessary.

9. Install the balance shaft retainer. Torque the balance shaft retainer-to-engine bolts to 27 ft. lbs.

10. Align the balance shaft gear with the camshaft gear timing marks. In-

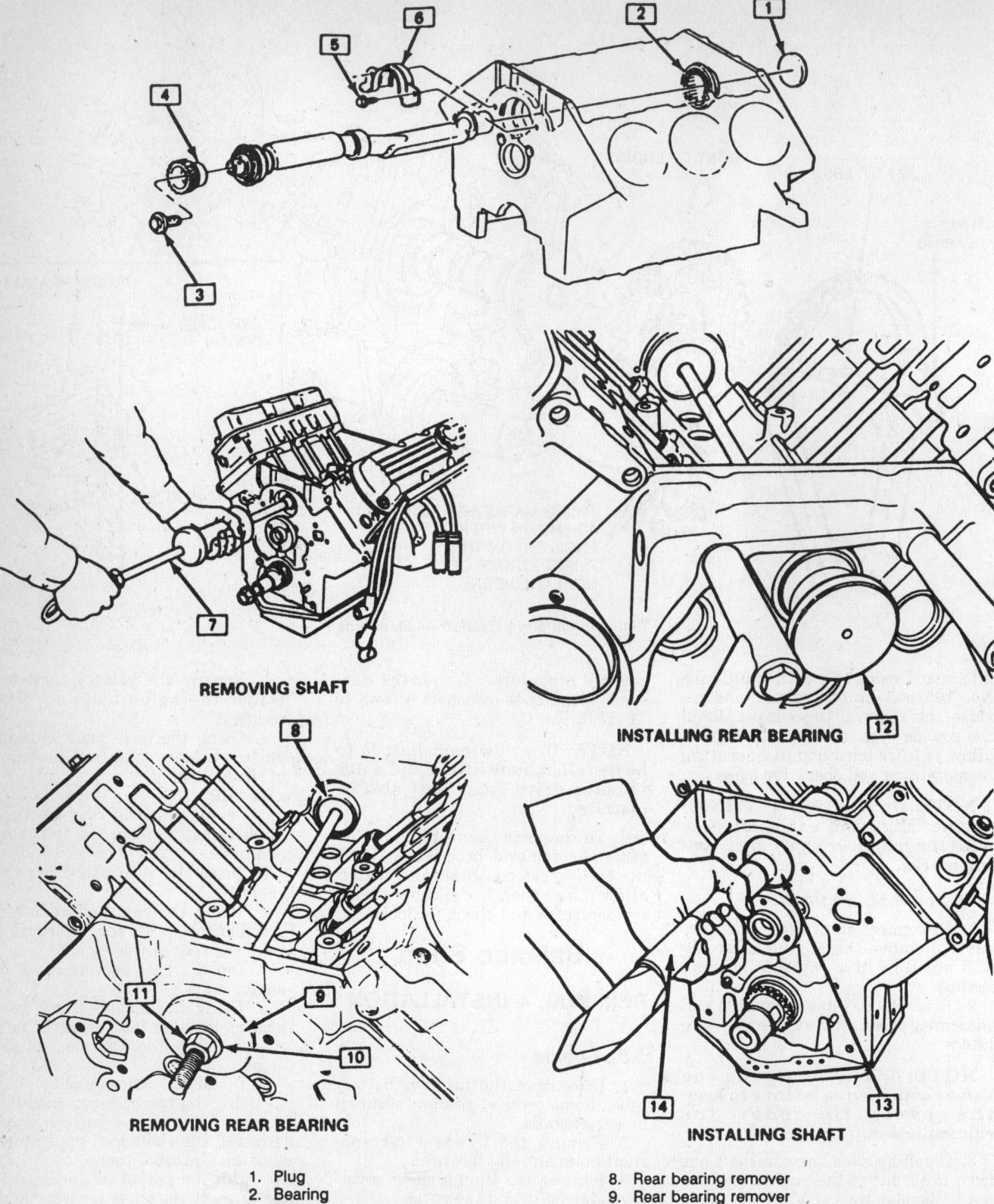

REMOVING SHAFT

INSTALLING REAR BEARING

REMOVING REAR BEARING

INSTALLING SHAFT

1. Plug
2. Bearing
3. Bolt
4. Balance shaft gear
5. Bolt
6. Retainer
7. Slide hammer

8. Rear bearing remover
9. Rear bearing remover
10. Washer
11. Nut
12. Rear bearing installer
13. Shaft installer
14. Driver handle

Balance shaft service—3.8L engine

stall the balance shaft gear onto the balance shaft. Torque the balance gear-to-balance shaft bolt to 14 ft. lbs, then using a torque angle meter tool, rotate another 35 degrees.

11. Align the marks on the balance shaft gear and the camshaft gear by turning the balance shaft.

12. Turn the crankshaft so that the No. 1 piston is at TDC.

13. Install the timing chain and sprocket.

14. Replace the balance shaft front bearing retainer and bolts. Tighten the bolts to 61 ft. lbs.

15. Install the front timing cover and the lifter guide retainer.

16. Install the intake manifold and flywheel assembly. Tighten the flywheel bolts to 61 ft. lbs.

17. Install the engine assembly and connect the negative battery cable. Start the engine and check for leaks.

Piston and Connecting Rod

POSITIONING

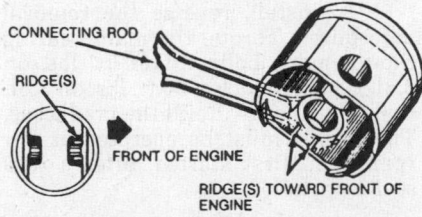

Piston installation direction—4.5L engine

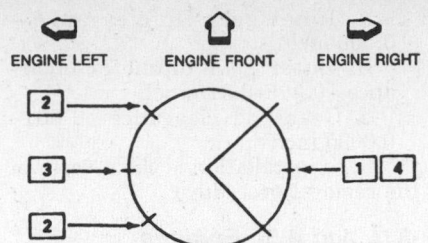

1. Oil ring spacer gap (tang in hole or slot with arc)
2. Oil ring rail gaps
3. 2nd compression ring gap
4. Top compression ring gap

Piston ring gap locations—3.8L engine

ENGINE LUBRICATION

Oil Pan

REMOVAL & INSTALLATION

3.8L Engine

1. Disconnect the negative battery cable. Raise and support the vehicle safely.

2. Drain the crankcase and remove the transaxle converter cover.

3. Remove the oil filter and the starter motor.

4. Remove the oil pan-to-engine bolts and the oil pan.

5. Clean the gasket mounting surfaces.

6. To install, use new gaskets, sealant and reverse the removal procedures. Torque the oil pan-to-engine bolts to 88 inch lbs. on Code 3 engines and 124 inch lbs. on Code C engines. Refill the crankcase. Start the engine and check for leaks.

4.1L and 4.5L Engines

1. Disconnect the negative battery cable. Raise and support the vehicle safely.

2. Drain the crankcase and remove the oil filter. Remove the flywheel inspection cover.

3. Remove the oil pan-to-engine bolts and the oil pan.

NOTE: If the pan is difficult to remove, lightly tap the edges with a plastic hammer.

4. Clean the gasket mounting surfaces.

5. To install, use a new gasket, sealant and reverse the removal procedures. Torque the oil pan-to-engine bolts to 12 ft. lbs. Refill the crankcase. Start the engine and check for leaks.

Oil Pump

REMOVAL & INSTALLATION

3.8L Engine

1. Disconnect the negative battery cable. Remove the front cover from the engine.

2. Remove the oil filter adapter, pressure regulator valve and spring.

3. Remove the oil pump cover-to-front cover screws and the cover. Remove the inner and outer pump gears.

4. Using petroleum jelly, pack the pump and reinstall the parts. Torque the oil pump cover-to-front cover screws to 88 inch lbs.

5. To complete the installation, reverse the removal prcedure.

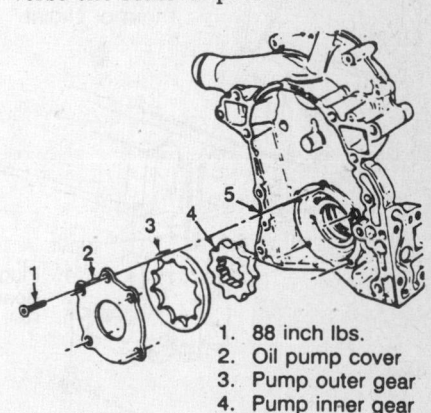

1. 88 inch lbs.
2. Oil pump cover
3. Pump outer gear
4. Pump inner gear
5. Front cover

Exploded view of the oil pump assembly—3.8L engine

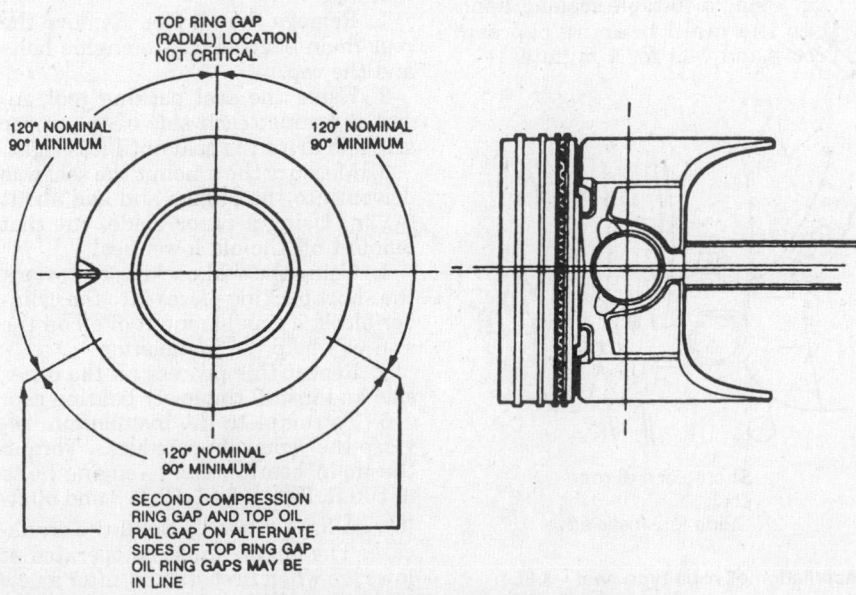

Piston ring orientation—4.5L engine

NOTE: Unless the pump is primed, it won't produce oil pressure when the engine is started.

4.1L and 4.5L Engines

1. Disconnect the negative battery cable. Raise and support the vehicle safely.
2. Remove the oil pan mounting bolts and remove the oil pan.
3. Remove the oil pump-to-engine screws/nut and the oil pump from the engine.
4. Clean the mounting surfaces. Install the pump assembly and tighten the mouning screws to 15 ft. lbs. and the nut to 22 ft. lbs.
5. The installation is the reverse of the removal procedure. Refill the crankcase start the engine and check for leaks.

CHECKING

3.8L Engine

1. Remove the front cover from the engine.
2. Remove the oil filter adapter, pressure regulator valve and spring.
3. Remove the oil pump cover-to-front cover screws and the cover. Remove the inner and outer pump gears.
4. Check the oil pump gears for:

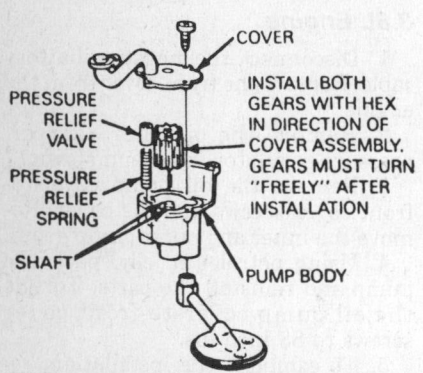

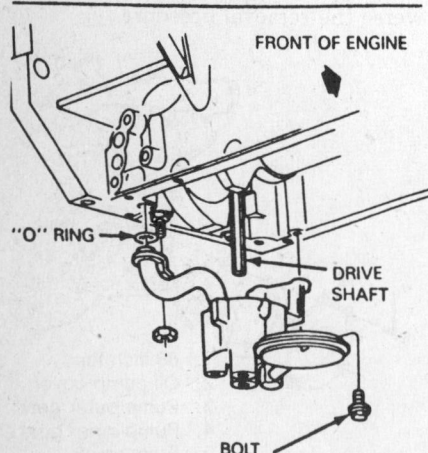

Oil pump assembly—4.1L and 4.5L engines

a. Inner gear tip clearance— 0.006 inch
b. Outer gear diameter clearance—0.008–0.015 inch
c. Gear end clearance—0.001– 0.0035 inch
5. The installation is the reverse of the removal procedure.

4.1L and 4.5L Engines

1. Raise and support the vehicle safely.
2. Remove the oil pump assembly and the screws mounting the pump cover to the housing.
3. Remove the oil pressure regulator spring from the bore in the housing. Check the free length of the regulator spring, should be 2.57–2.69 inches. A force of 9.3–10.5 lbs. should be required to comprss the spring to 1.46 inch.
4. The installation is reverse of the removal procedure.

Rear Main Bearing Oil Seal

REMOVAL & INSTALLATION

3.8L Engine

Braided fabric rope seals are used. The upper seal half cannot be replaced without removing the crankshaft.

Lower Half-Seal
1. Remove the oil pan. Remove the rear main bearing cap-to-engine bolts and the cap.
2. Remove the old seal from the bearing cap.
3. To replace the oil seal, perform the following procedures:
   a. Using a suitable sealant, apply it to the main bearing cap seal groove and wait for 1 minute.

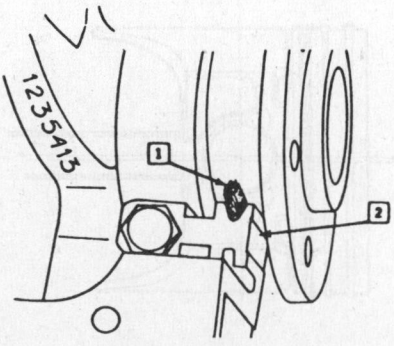

1. Short piece of rope seal
2. Guide tool installed

Installation of rope type seal—3.8L engine

b. Using a new rope seal and a wooden dowel or hammer handle, roll the new seal into the cap so both ends projecting above the parting surface of the cap; force the seal into the groove by rubbing it down, until the seal projects above the groove not more than $\frac{1}{16}$ in.
c. Using a sharp razor blade, cut the ends off flush with the surface of the cap.
d. Using chassis grease, apply a thin coat to the seals surface.
4. To install the neoprene sealing strips (side seals), perform the following procedures:
   a. Using light oil or kerosene, soak the strips for 5 minutes.

NOTE: The neoprene composition seals will swell up once exposed to the oil and heat. It is normal for the seals to leak for a short time, until they become properly seated. The seals must not be cut to fit.

b. Place the sealing strips in the grooves on the sides of the bearing cap.
5. Using sealer the proper sealer, apply it to the main bearing cap mating surface; do not apply sealer to the bolt holes.
6. To install, reverse the removal procedures. Torque the main bearing cap-to-engine bolts to 100 ft. lbs. on 3.8L Code 3 vehicles, 90 ft. lbs. on 3.8L Code C vehicles . Refill the crankcase. The engine must be operated at low rpm when first started, after a new seal is installed.

Upper Half-Seal
Engine removal is not necessary if the following time saver procedure is followed.
1. Remove the oil pan. Remove the rear main bearing cap-to-engine bolts and the cap.
2. Using the seal packing tool, insert it against each side of the upper seal and drive the seal until it is tight.
3. Measure the amount the seal was driven into the engine and add about $\frac{1}{16}$ in. Using a razor blade, cut that amount off the old lower seal.
4. Using the seal packing tool, work the short packing pieces into the cylinder block; a small amount of oil on the seal will help the installation.
5. Repeat this process on the other side and install the lower bearing cap.
6. To complete the installation, reverse the removal procedures. Torque the main bearing cap-to-engine bolts to 100 ft. lbs. on 3.8L Code 3 and 90 ft. lbs. on 3.8 L Code C. Refill the crankcase. The engine must be operated at low rpm when first started, after a new seal is installed.

4.1L and 4.5L Engines

1. Raise and support the vehicle safely.

2. Remove the tranasaxle assembly. Remove the flexplate from the crankshaft.

3. Using the proper tool, pry out the old seal from the rear of the engine.

4. Lubricate the new seal with wheel bearing grease and install on the crankshaft with the spring facing inside the engine.

5. Press the seal into position, using the proper tool.

NOTE: The seal should be flush with the block. It is neccessary to use the proper tool because the seal must be installed square or an oil leak could result.

6. The installation is the reverse of the removal procedure.

AUTOMATIC TRANSAXLE

For further information on transmissions/transaxles, please refer to "Chilton's Guide to Transmission Repair".

Transaxle Assembly

REMOVAL & INSTALLATION

3.8L Engine

1. Disconnect the negative terminal from the battery. Disconnect the wire connector at the mass air flow sensor, if equipped.

2. Remove the air intake duct and the mass air flow sensor as an assembly.

3. Disconnect the cruise control assembly and the the shift control linkage.

4. Label and disconnect the following:
  a. Park/Neutral switch
  b. Torque converter clutch
  c. Vehicle speed sensor and fuel pipe retainers
  d. Vacuum modulator hose at the modulator

5. Remove the top transaxle-to-engine block bolts and install an engine support fixture.

6. Raise the vehicle and support it safely. Remove both front tire and wheel assemblies and turn the steering wheel to the full left position.

7. Remove the right front ball joint nut and separate the control arm from the steering knuckle.

8. Remove the right halfshaft.

NOTE: Be careful not to allow the halfshaft splines to contact any portion of the lip seal.

9. Using a medium pry bar, remove the left halfshaft; be careful not to damage the pan. Install halfshaft boot seal protectors.

10. Remove the bolts at the transaxle and the nuts at the cradle member. Remove the left front transaxle mount.

11. Remove the right front mount-to-cradle nuts. Remove the left rear transaxle mount-to-transaxle bolts.

12. Remove the right rear transaxle mount. Remove the engine support bracket-to-transaxle case bolts.

13. Remove the flywheel cover, matchmark the flywheel-to-torque converter and remove the flywheel-to-converter bolts.

NOTE: Be sure to matchmark the flywheel-to-converter relationship for proper alignment upon reassembly.

14. Remove the rear cradle member-to-front cradle dog leg.

15. Remove the front left cradle-to-body bolt and the front cradle dog leg-to-right cradle member bolts.

16. Install a transaxle support fixture into position.

17. Remove the cradle assembly by swinging it aside and supporting it with jackstand.

18. Disconnect and plug the oil cooler lines at the transaxle.

NOTE: One bolt is located between the transaxle and the engine block; it is installed in the opposite direction.

19. Remove the remaining lower transaxle-to-engine bolts and lower the transaxle from the vehicle.
To install:

20. Install the transaxle into the vehicle using the dowel pin as guide. Tighten the bolts to 55 ft. lbs.

21. Connect the oil cooler lines and remove the support fixture.

22. Install the front left cradle-to-body bolts and replace the rear cradle-to-front cradle dog leg.

23. Install the flywheel and tighten the bolts to 46 ft. lbs. Replace the flywheel cove and tighten the bolts to 136 inch lbs.

24. Install the right rear transaxle mount. Replace the engine support bracket-to-transaxle case bolts and tighten to 40 ft. lbs.

25. Install the right front mount-to-cradle nuts. Replace the left rear transaxle mount-to-transaxle bolts and tighten to 30 ft. lbs.

26. Replace the bolts at the transaxle and the nuts at the cradle member. Replace the left front transaxle mount and tighten the bolts to 40 ft. lbs.

27. Install both halfshafts.

28. Connect the control arm to the steering knuckle and tighten the right front ball joint nut.

29. Install the tire and wheel assemblies. Lower the vehicle.

30. Install the top transaxle-to-engine block bolts and remove the engine support fixture.

31. Connect the following:
  a. Park/Neutral switch
  b. Torque converter clutch
  c. Vehicle speed sensor and fuel pipe retainers

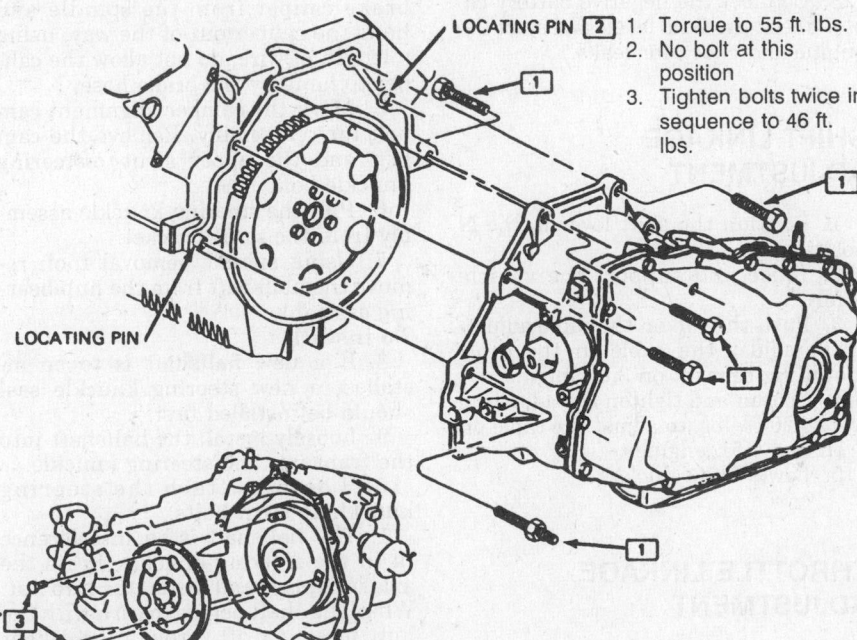

LOCATING PIN [2] 1. Torque to 55 ft. lbs.
2. No bolt at this position
3. Tighten bolts twice in sequence to 46 ft. lbs.

LOCATING PIN

Transaxle-to-engine mounting location—3.8L engine

d. Vacuum modulator hose at the modulator

32. Connect the cruise control assembly and the the shift control linkage.

33. Replce the air intake duct and the mass air flow sensor as an assembly.

34. Connect the wire connector at the mass air flow sensor, if equipped.

35. Connect the negative battery cable.

4.1L and 4.5L Engines

1. Disconnect the negative terminal from the battery. Remove the air cleaner and the TV cable.

2. Disconnect the shift linkage from the transaxle. Using an engine support fixture tool, connect it to and support the engine.

3. Label and disconnect the electrical connectors from the following items:
   a. Converter clutch
   b. Vehicle speed sensor
   c. Vacuum line at the modulator

4. Remove the upper bell housing-to-engine bolts and studs.

5. Raise and support the vehicle safely. Remove both front wheels.

6. From the left side of the vehicle, disconnect the lower ball joint from steering knuckle. Remove both drive axles from the transaxle.

7. Remove the stabilizer bar-to-left control arm bolt.

8. Remove the left front cradle assembly.

9. Remove the extension housing-to-engine support bracket.

10. Disconnect and plug the oil cooler lines at the transaxle case.

11. Remove the right and left transaxle mount attachments.

12. Remove the flywheel splash shield. Matchmark the torque converter-to-flyheel and remove the converter-to-flywheel bolts.

13. Remove the lower bell housing bolts.

14. Using a floor jack, position it under the transaxle and remove the last bell housing bolt.

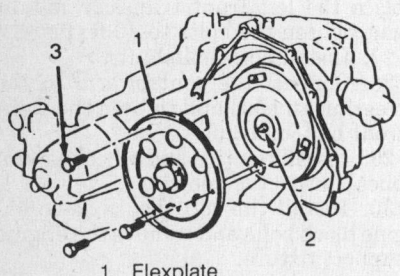

1. Flexplate
2. Torque converter
3. Bolt

Coverter-to-flexplate attachments—4.1L and 4.5L engines

NOTE: **To reach the last bell housing bolt, use a 3 in. socket wrench extension through the right wheel arch opening.**

15. Remove the transaxle assembly.

To install:

16. Install the transaxle assembly and replace the lower bell hosing bolts. Tighten the bolts to 55 ft. lbs.

17. Repace the converter-to-flexplate bolts and tighten to 46 ft. lbs. Install the flexplate splash shield.

18. Connect the oil cooler lines at the transaxle case.

19. Install the extension housing-to-engine support bracket. Replace the left front cradle assembly.

20. Replace the stabilizer bar-to-left control arm bolt.

21. Install both halfshafts. Fully seat the halfshafts by inserting the proper tool in the groove on the joint housing and tap until the joints are seated.

22. Connect the lower ball joint to the steering knuckle and replace the left and right front transaxle mount-to-cradle attachments. Tighten the nuts to 23 ft. lbs.

23. Replace both front tire and wheel assemblies. Lower the vehicle.

24. Replace the upper bell housing-to-engine bolts/studs and tighten to 55 ft. lbs.

25. Connect the electrical connectors to the converter clutch, vehicle speed sensor and the vacuum line to the modulator.

26. Connect the shift linkage to the transaxle. Remove the engine support fixture tool.

27. Replace the air cleaner and the TV cable.

28. Connect the negative battery cable. Check the fluid levels and start the engine and check for leaks.

SHIFT LINKAGE ADJUSTMENT

1. Position the shift lever in the **N** position.

2. Raise and support the vehicle safely.

3. Push the tab on the cable adjuster to adjust the cable in the cable mounting bracket on 3.8L engine.

4. Loosen and tighten the adjusting nut to 20 ft. lbs. to adjust the cable on 4.1L and 4.5L engines.

5. Lower the vehicle.

THROTTLE LINKAGE ADJUSTMENT

1. Stop the engine. Raise and support the vehicle safely.

NOTE: **Check the throttle body for full travel prior to any adjustments.**

2. Depress and hold-down the metal readjust tab at the engine end of the TV cable.

3. Move the slider until it stops against the fitting.

4. Release the readjustment tab.

5. Rotate the throttle lever to the full travel position.

6. The slider must move toward the lever when the lever is rotated to it's full travel position.

DRIVE AXLE

Halfshaft

REMOVAL & INSTALLATION

1987–88

NOTE: **Use care when removing the halfshaft. Tri-pots can be damaged if the halfshaft is overextended.**

1. Remove the hub nut.

2. Raise and support the vehicle safely. Remove the front tire and wheel assembly.

3. Using the halfshaft boot seal protector tool, install it onto the seal.

4. Disconnect the brake hose clip from the strut, do not disconnect the hose from the caliper. Remove the brake caliper from the spindle and hang the caliper out of the way, using a length of wire; do not allow the caliper to hang by the brake hose.

5. Mark the camber alignment cam bolt for reassembly. Remove the cam bolt and the upper strut-to-steering knuckle bolt.

6. Pull the steering knuckle assembly from the strut bracket.

7. Using spindle removal tool, remove the halfshaft from the hub/bearing assembly.

To install:

8. If a new halfshaft is to be installed, a new steering knuckle seal should be installed first.

9. Loosely install the halfshaft into the transaxle and steering knuckle.

10. Loosely attach the steering knuckle-to-strut bolts.

11. The halfshaft is an interference fit in the steering knuckle. Press the axle into place and install the hub nut. When the shaft begins to turn with the hub, insert a drift through the caliper into one of the cooling slots in the rotor to keep it from turning. Insert a

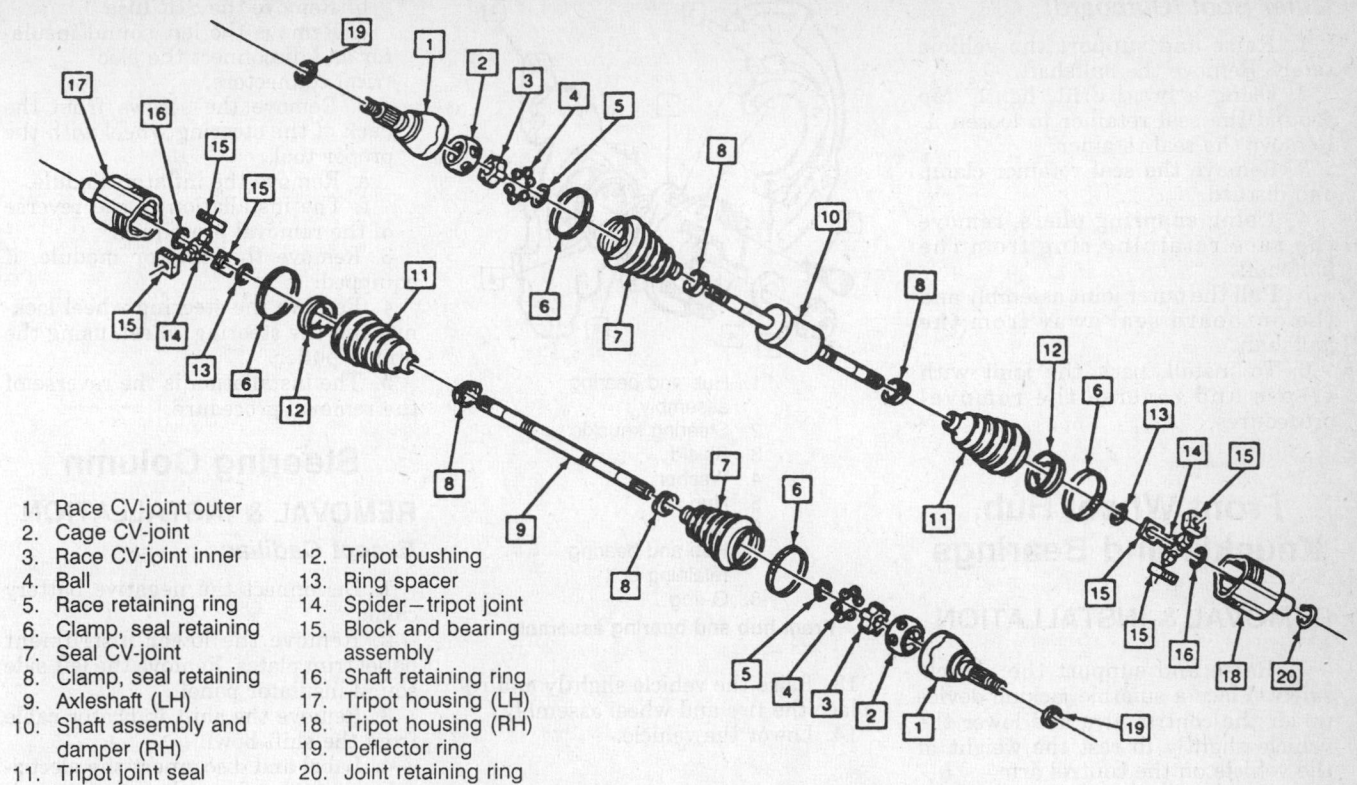

1. Race CV-joint outer
2. Cage CV-joint
3. Race CV-joint inner
4. Ball
5. Race retaining ring
6. Clamp, seal retaining
7. Seal CV-joint
8. Clamp, seal retaining
9. Axleshaft (LH)
10. Shaft assembly and
    damper (RH)
11. Tripot joint seal

12. Tripot bushing
13. Ring spacer
14. Spider—tripot joint
15. Block and bearing
    assembly
16. Shaft retaining ring
17. Tripot housing (LH)
18. Tripot housing (RH)
19. Deflector ring
20. Joint retaining ring

Exploded view of driveshaft assembly—1990–91 Cadillac

long bolt in the hub flange to prevent the shaft from turning. Torque the hub nut to 191 ft. lbs. and tighten the brake caliper-to-steering knuckle bolts.

12. Load the hub assembly by lowering it onto a jackstand. Align the camber cam bolt marks made during removal, install the bolt and tighten to 140 ft. lbs. Tighten the upper nut to the same value.

13. Install the halfshaft all the way into the transaxle, using a small prybar inserted into the groove provided on the inner retainer. Tap the pry bar until the shaft seats in the transaxle. Remove the boot seal protector.

14. Connect the brake hose clip to the strut. Install the wheel assembly and lower the vehicle.

1989–91

NOTE: Use care when removing the halfshaft. Tri-pots can be damaged if the halfshft is overextended.

1. Raise and support the vehicle safely. Remove the tire and wheel assembly.
2. Use an halfshaft boot seal protector tool and install it onto the seal.
3. Insert drift into rotor and caliper to prevent rotor from turning.
4. Remove hub nut and washer using a hub nut socket tool.

5. Remove the lower ball joint cotter pin and nut and loosen the joint using a ball joint separator tool. If removing the right halfshaft, turn the wheel to the left, if removing the left halfshaft turn the wheel to the right.
6. With a prybar between the suspension support and the lower control arm, separate the joint.
7. Pull out on the lower knuckle area and with a plastic or rubber mallet strike the end of the axle shaft to disengage the axle from the hub and bearing. The shaft nut can be partially installed to protect the threads.
8. Separate the hub and bearing assembly from the halfshaft and move the strut and knuckle assembly rearward. Remove the inner joint from the transaxle using the proper tool from the intermediate shaft, if equipped.

NOTE: On vehicles equipped with the anti-lock brake system, care must be used to prevent damage to the toothed sensor ring on the halfshaft and the wheel speed sensor on the steering knuckle.

To install:
9. Seat the halfshaft into the transaxle by placing the proper tool into the groove on the joint housing and tapping until seated.
10. Verify the halfshaft is seated into the transaxle by grasping on the hous-

ing and pulling outboard. Do not pull on the halfshaft.

11. Install the halfshaft into the hub and bearing assembly.
12. Install the lower ball joint to the knuckle. Tighten the nut to 41 ft. lbs. minimum and to 50 ft. lbs. maximum to install the cotter pin.
13. Install the cotter pin.
14. Install the washer and new shaft nut.
15. Insert drift into rotor and caliper to prevent rotor from turning.
16. Torque the shaft nut to 185 ft. lbs.
17. Remove the boot protector.
18. Install the tire and wheel assembly. Lower the vehicle.

CV-Boot

REMOVAL & INSTALLATION

Inner Boot (Inboard)

1. Raise and support the vehicle safely. Remove the halfshaft.
2. Remove the joint assembly retaining ring and the joint assembly.
3. Remove the bearing race retaining ring and the seal retainer.
4. Remove the inner seal retainer clamp and the inner joint seal.
5. To install, pack the joint with grease and reverse the removal procedures.

Outer Boot (Outboard)

1. Raise and support the vehicle safely. Remove the halfshaft.
2. Using a brass drift, lightly tap around the seal retainer to loosen it. Remove the seal retainer.
3. Remove the seal retainer clamp and discard.
4. Using snapring pliers, remove the race retaining ring from the halfshaft.
5. Pull the outer joint assembly and the outboard seal away from the halfshaft.
6. To install, pack the joint with grease and reverse the removal procedures.

Front Wheel Hub, Knuckle and Bearings

REMOVAL & INSTALLATION

1. Raise and support the vehicle safely. Place a suiatble jacking device under the control arm and lower the vehicle slightly to rest the weight of the vehicle on the control arm.
2. Remove the tire and wheel asembly. Remove the caliper bolts, remove and support the caliper out of the way.
3. Remove the rotor and using the proper tool, separate the hub from the halfshaft.
4. Remove the hub and bearing retaining bolts, shield, hub and bearing assembly and the O-ring.
5. Disconnect the ball joint from the steering knuckle, using the proper tool.
6. Remove the halfshaft assembly and tap the seal from the steering knuckle. Remove the steering knuckle from the hub.

NOTE: The hub and bearing are replaced only as an assembly.

To install:

7. Install a new hub and bearing seal in the steering knuckle with the proper seal installer tool. Install the steering knuckle to the strut.
8. Lubricate the hub and bearing with grease and install the halfshaft.
9. Connect the ball joint to the steering knuckle and insert a new O-ring around the hub and bearing assembly.
10. Install the hub and bearing assembly into the steering knuckle. Tighten the bolts to 75 ft. lbs.
11. Install the rotor and caliper assembly. Tighten the caliper bolts to 38 ft. lbs.
12. Install the shaft washer and nut. Tighten the nut to 180 ft. lbs.

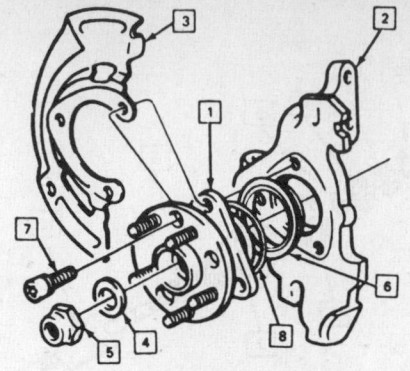

1. Hub and bearing assembly
2. Steering knuckle
3. Shield
4. Washer
5. Hub nut
6. Seal
7. Hub and bearing retaining bolt
8. O-ring

Front hub and bearing assembly

13. Raise the vehicle slightly and replace the tire and wheel assembly.
14. Lower the vehicle.

STEERING

Steering Wheel

─── CAUTION ───

On vehicles equipped with an air bag, the negative battery cable must be disconnected, before working on the system. Failure to do so may result in deployment of the air bag and possible personal injury.

REMOVAL & INSTALLATION

Except Cadillac

1. Disconnect the negative battery cable.
2. Remove the screws holding the steering pad.
3. Remove the steering pad and disconnect the horn lead.
4. Remove the retainer and nut.
5. Remove the steering wheel, using the proper tool.
6. The installation is the reverse of the removal procedure. Tighten the steering shaft nut to 30 ft. lbs.

Cadillac

1. Disconnect the negative battery cable.
2. If equipped with an inflator module, remove as follows:
   a. Turn the ignition switch to the **OFF** position.

b. Remove the SIR fuse 3.
   c. Remove the left sound insulator and disconnect the elec trical connectors.
   d. Remove the screws from the back of the steering wheel with the proper tool.
   e. Remove the inflator module.
   f. The installation is the reverse of the removal procedure.
3. Remove the inflator module, if equipped.
4. Remove the steering wheel locknut and the steering wheel, using the proper puller.
5. The installation is the reverse of the removal procedure.

Steering Column

REMOVAL & INSTALLATION

Except Cadillac

1. Disconnect the negative battery cable.
2. Remove the lower instrument panel trim plates. Remove the left side sound insulator panel.
3. Remove the shift indicator cable from the shift bowl.
4. Label and disconnect the electrical connectors from the steering column. Remove the steering column-to-dash bolts.
5. Remove the steering shaft-to-intermediate shaft bolt and the steering column from the vehicle.
6. To install, reverse of the removal procedures. Inspect the steering column operations.

Cadillac

1. Disconnect the negative battery cable. Remove the inflator module, if equipped. Remove the steering column trim plate.
2. Remove the retaining filler, the column reinforcement plate and disconnect the electrical connections and remove the shift control cable at the actuator.
3. Remove the bolts securing the seal assembly and the bolt from the upper knuckle of the intermediate steering shaft.
4. Disconnect the lower brace assembly and the lower support bracket.
5. Remove the bolts securing the column to the upper support and remove the column assembly.
6. Install the column assembly. The installation is the reverse of the removal procedure.

Power Steering Rack
ADJUSTMENT

Rack Bearing Preload

1. Loosen the adjuster plug locknut

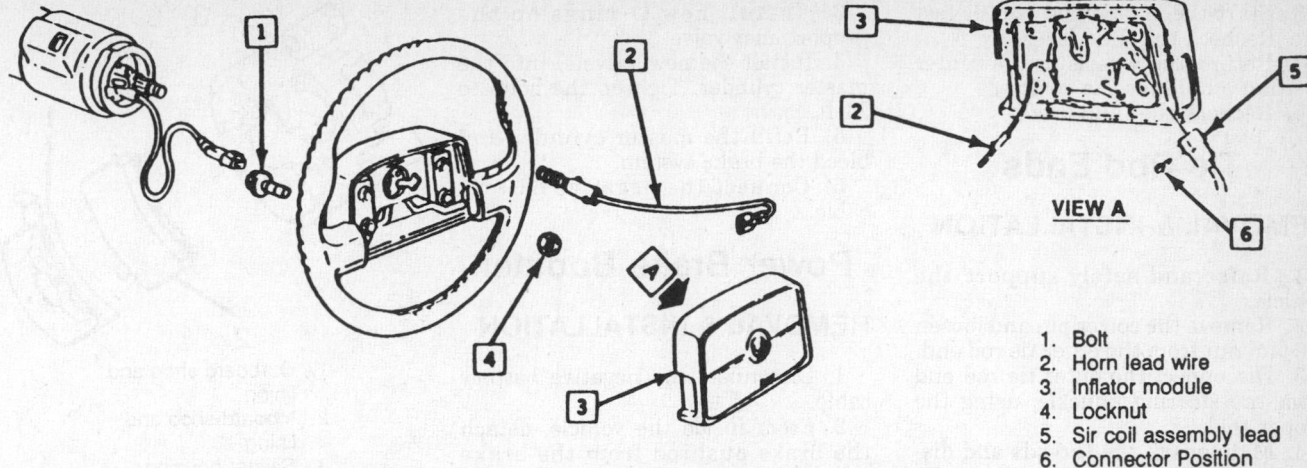

1. Bolt
2. Horn lead wire
3. Inflator module
4. Locknut
5. Sir coil assembly lead
6. Connector Position Assurance (CPA)

Steering wheel and inflator module—1990–91 Cadillac

and turn the adjuster plug clockwise until it bottoms in the housing. Then back off 50–70 degrees which is approximately one flat.

2. Raise and support the vehicle safely to make the proper adjustments. Be sure to check the returnability of the steering wheel to the center position after the adjustment.

3. Tighten the locknut to the adjuster plug to 50 ft. lbs.

REMOVAL & INSTALLATION

1. Raise and support the vehicle safely. Allow the front suspension to hang freely. Disconnect the pressure lines from the steering gear and drain the excess fluid into a container; be sure to plug the openings.

2. Move the intermediate shaft cover upward and remove the intermediate shaft-to-stub shaft pinch bolt. Remove both front tire and wheel assemblies.

3. Disconnect the tie rod ends from the steering knuckles. Remove the line retainer, outlet and pressure hoses.

4. Remove the rack/pinion assembly-to-chassis bolts.

5. Loosen the front engine cradle mounting bolts and the lower the rear of the cradle about 3 inches, if neccessary. Remove the rack and pinion assembly.

6. To install, reverse the removal procedures. Tighten the rack mounting bolts to 50 ft. lbs. Tighten the tie rod end nut to 35–52 ft. lbs. Refill the power steering pump reservoir. Bleed the power steering system and check for leaks. Check and/or adjust the front wheel alignment.

Power Steering Pump

REMOVAL & INSTALLATION

3.8L Engine

1. Disconnect the negative battery cable.

2. Remove the drive belt and disconnect the pressure and return hoses.

3. Remove the power steering pump mounting bolts.

4. Remove the pump assembly. Transfer the pulley as neccessary.

5. Installation is in the reverse order of removal. Adjust the drive belts and bleed the power steering system.

4.1L and 4.5L Engines

1. Disconnect the negative battery cable.

2. Remove the serpentine drive belt and the power steering pump pulley, using the proper tool.

3. Disconnect and plug the high

pressure and feed lines from the pump. Remove the belt tensioner, if neccessary.

4. Remove the power steering pump-to-bracket bolts and the pump.

5. To install, reverse the removal procedures. Torque the power steering pump mounting bolts to 18 ft. lbs. Refill the power steering pump reservoir. Bleed the power steering system.

BELT ADJUSTMENT

The serpentine is self adjusting within the tensioner operating limits.

SYSTEM BLEEDING

1. Raise and support the vehicle safely. Fill the fluid reservoir.

2. Bleed the system by turning the wheels from side to side, without reaching the stop ay either end. Keep the fluid level at the FULL COLD mark. Continue this until the air is eliminated from the fluid.

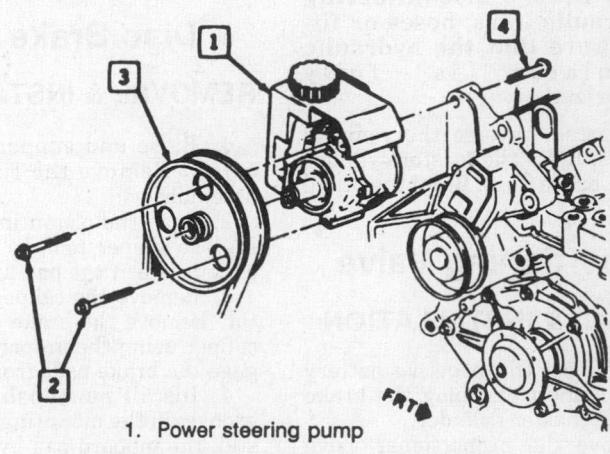

1. Power steering pump

Power steering pump assembly—3.8L engine

3. Start the engine and run at fast idle. Recheck the fluid level.

4. Return the wheels to the center position and lower the vehicle.

5. Recheck the fluid level.

Tie Rod Ends

REMOVAL & INSTALLATION

1. Raise and safely support the vehicle.

2. Remove the cotter pin and loosen the jam nut from the outer tie rod end.

3. Disconnect the outer tie rod end from the steering knuckle, using the proper tool.

4. Matchmark the threads and disconnect the outer tie rod end from the inner tie rod. Remove the tie rod end.

5. Install the tie rod end to the matchmarks on the inner tie rod.

6. The remainder of the installation is the reverse of the removal procedure. Tighten the hex nut to 35–45 ft. lbs.

BRAKES

For all brake system repair and service procedures not detailed below, please refer to "Brakes" in the Unit Repair section.

Master Cylinder

REMOVAL & INSTALLATION

1. Disconnect the negative battery cable and the electrical connector from the level sensor unit.

2. Disconnect and plug hydraulic lines from the master cylinder.

3. Remove the mounting bolts and the master cylinder assembly.

NOTE: Before disconnecting any hydraulic lines, hoses or fittings be sure that the hydraulic accumulator is fully depressurized.

4. To install, reverse the removal procedures. Refill the master cylinder with clean brake fluid. Bleed the brake system.

Proportioning Valve

REMOVAL & INSTALLATION

1. Disconnect the negative battery cable. Disconnect and plug the brake lines at the master cylinder.

2. Remove the proportioner valve and O-ring assembly.

3. Install new O-rings on the proportioner valve.

4. Install the new valve(s) into the master cylinder. Tighten the bolts to 24 ft. lbs.

5. Refill the master cylinder and bleed the brake system.

6. Connect the negative battery cable.

Power Brake Booster

REMOVAL & INSTALLATION

1. Disconnect the negative battery cable.

2. From inside the vehicle, detach the brake pushrod from the brake pedal.

3. Remove the master cylinder-to-power brake booster and move the master cylinder aside.

4. Disconnect the vacuum hose from the power brake booster.

5. Remove the power brake booster-to-cowl nuts and the booster.

6. To install, reverse the removal procedures. Perform the system bleeding procedure.

Brake Caliper

REMOVAL & INSTALLATION

1. Raise and support the vehicle safely. Remove the tire and wheel assembly.

2. Push the piston into caliper, using the proper tool, to provide clearance between the pad and the rotor.

3. Diconnect and plug the brake line and remove the mounting bolts and sleeves.

4. Remove the caliper from the rotor and the mounting bracket.

5. The installation is the reverse of the removal procedure. Tighten the caliper mounting bolts to 38 ft. lbs. Bleed the brake system.

Disc Brake Pads

REMOVAL & INSTALLATION

1. Raise and support the vehicle safely. Remove the tire and wheel assembly.

2. Push the piston into caliper, using the proper tool, to provide clearance between the pad and the rotor.

3. Remove the caliper from the rotor. Remove the brake pads from the caliper using the proper tool to disengage the brake pads from the caliper.

4. Install new bushings into the grooves in the mounting bolt holes. Install the inboard pad by snapping the retainer spring into the piston.

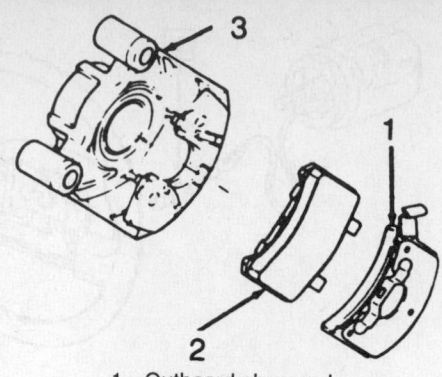

1. Outboard shoe and lining
2. Inboard shoe and lining
3. Caliper housing

Brake pad mounting

5. Install the outboard pad with the back of the pad flat against the caliper.

6. The remainder of the installation is the reverse of the removal procedure.

Brake Rotor

REMOVAL & INSTALLATION

1. Raise and support the vehicle safely. Remove the tire and wheel assembly.

2. Push the piston into caliper, using the proper tool, to provide clearance between the pad and the rotor.

3. Remove the caliper from the rotor. Suspend the caliper do not let the caliper hang free.

4. Remove the shaft nut and washer and remove the rotor assembly.

5. Install the rotor to the hub assembly. Tighten the shaft nut to 70 ft. lbs.

6. The remainder of the installation is the reverse of the removal procedure.

Brake Drums

REMOVAL & INSTALLATION

1. Raise and support the vehicle safely.

2. Matchmark the wheel to the hub flange.

3. Remove the tire and wheel assembly. Matchmark the drum to the hub flange.

4. Remove the brake drum assembly. Make sure that the parking brake is released.

5. The installation is the reverse of the removal procedure.

1. Actuator spring
2. Upper shoe return spring
3. Spring connecting link
4. Adjuster actuator
5. Spring washer
6. Lower return spring
7. Hold-down spring assembly
8. Hold-down pin
9. Adjuster shoe and lining
10. Shoe and lining
11. Adjuster socket
12. Spring clip
13. Adjuster nut
14. Adjuster screw
15. Retaining ring

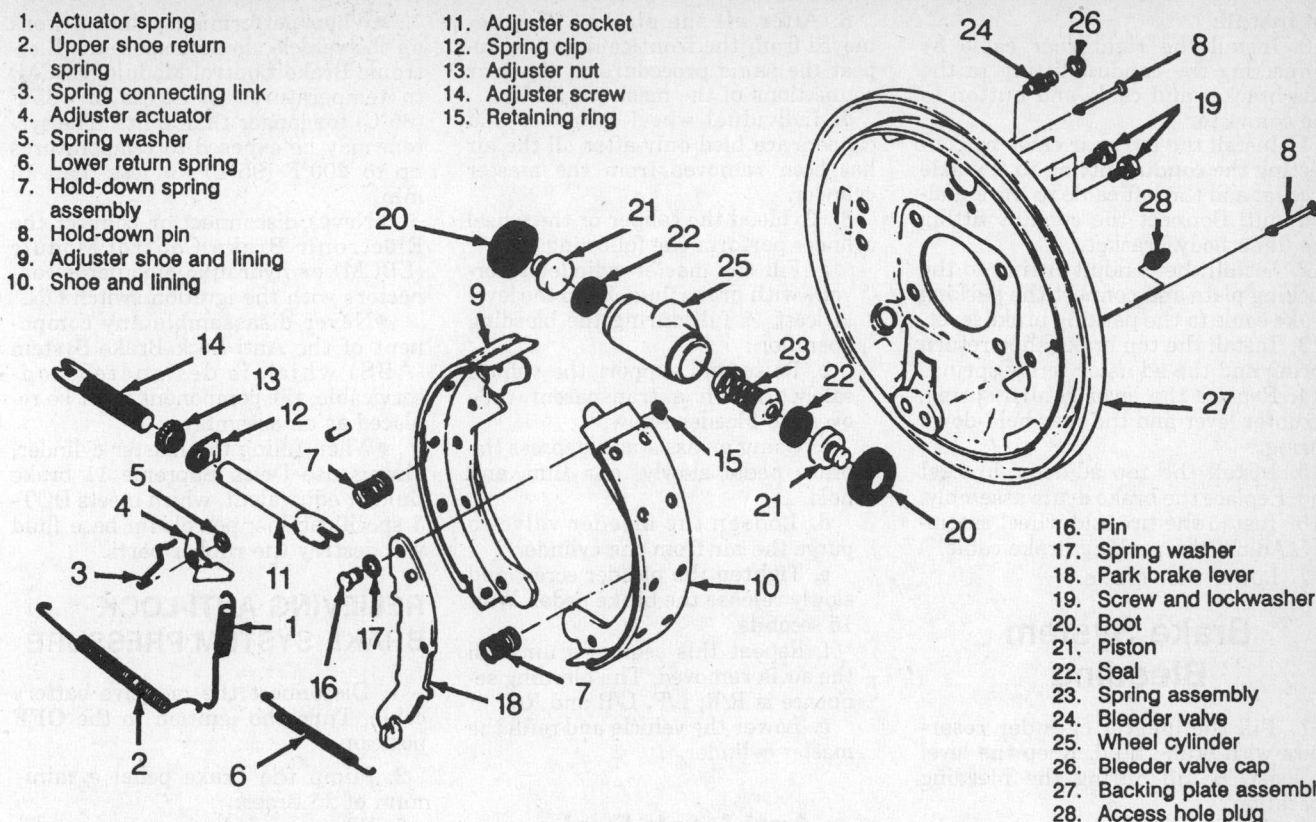

16. Pin
17. Spring washer
18. Park brake lever
19. Screw and lockwasher
20. Boot
21. Piston
22. Seal
23. Spring assembly
24. Bleeder valve
25. Wheel cylinder
26. Bleeder valve cap
27. Backing plate assembly
28. Access hole plug

Exploded view of the rear brake assembly

Brake Shoes

REMOVAL & INSTALLATION

1. Raise and support the vehicle safely. Remove the brake drum assembly.
2. Remove the actuator and the upper return spring with the proper tools.
3. Disconnect the spring connecting link, adjuster actuator and the hold-down washer.
4. Remove the hold-down springs and the pins. Disconnect the brake shoes from the parking brake cable.
5. Remove the brake shoe and lining assemblies.
6. The installation is the reverse of the removal procedure.

Wheel Cylinder

REMOVAL & INSTALLATION

1. Raise and support the vehicle safely. Remove the rear drum assembly.
2. Remove the brake shoe and lining assembly.
3. Disconnect and plug the inlet line. Remove the mounting screws and lockwashers.
4. Remove the wheel cylinder assembly.

5. The installation is the reverse of the removal procedure. Bleed the brake system.

Parking Brake Cable

ADJUSTMENT

1. Adjust the rear brakes.
2. Apply and release the parking brake 6 times to 10 clicks. Release the park brake pedal.
3. Raise and support the vehicle safely. Remove the access plug.
4. Adjust the park brake cable until a ⅛ drill can be inserted through the access hole into the space between the shoe web and the park brake lever.
5. Check for free wheel rotation. Replace the access plug.
6. Lower the vehicle.

REMOVAL & INSTALLATION

Front

1. Raise and safely support the vehicle.
2. Loosen the equalizer assembly at the front parking brake cable. Remove the front parking brake cable from the equalizer assembly.
3. Disconnect the cable casing retaining nut at the underbody. Remove the cable casing and cable from the control assembly.

4. Reverse the removal procedure for installation. Tighten the casing retaining nut to 22 ft. lbs. Adjust the cable.

Rear

1. Raise and support the vehicle safely. Remove the tire and wheel assembly.
2. Remove the brake drum and insert the proper tool between the brake shoe and the top part of the actuator bracket.
3. Push the bracket to the front and release the top adjuster bracket rod.
4. Remove the rear hold-down spring, actuator lever and the lever return spring.
5. Disconnect the adjuster screw spring and remove the top rear brake shoe return spring.
6. Disconnect the parking brake cable from the parking brake lever.
7. Depress the conduit fitting retaining tangs and remove the conduit fitting from the backing plate.
8. Remove the left rear cable by backing off the equalizer nut and disconnecting the conduit from the under body bracket.
9. Remove the right rear cable by disconnecting the cable end button from the connector and remove the conduit fitting from the axle bracket.

To install:

10. Install the right rear cable by connecting the conduit fitting to the axle bracket and cable end button to the connector.

11. Install the left rear cable by connecting the conduit fitting to the axle bracket and the left cable to the equalizer nut. Connect the conduit fitting the underbody bracket.

12. Install the conduit fitting to the backing plate and connect the parking brake cable to the parking brake lever.

13. Install the top brake shoe return spring and the adjuster screw spring.

14. Replace the lever return spring, actuator lever and the rear hold-down spring.

15. Install the top adjuster bracket rod. Replace the brake drum assembly.

16. Install the tire and wheel assembly. Adjust the parking brake cable.

17. Lower the vehicle.

Brake System Bleeding

1. Fill the master cylinder reservoirs with brake fluid. Keep the level at least ½ full during the bleeding operation.

2. Disconnect and plug the brake lines. Fill the master cylinder until fluid begins to flow from the front pipe connector port.

3. Connect the brake lines to the master cylinder and tighten.

4. Depress the brake pedal slowly one time and hold, tighten the connection and then release the brake pedal slowly. Wait 15 seconds.

5. Repeat the sequence until all the air has been removed from the master cylinder bore.

6. After all the air has been removed from the front connections repeat the same procedure at the rear connections of the master cylinder.

7. Individual wheel cylinders and calipers are bled only after all the air has been removed from the master cylinder.

8. To bleed the caliper or the wheel cylinder perform the following:

a. Fill the master cylinder reservoirs with brake fluid. Keep the level at least ½ full during the bleeding operation.

b. Raise and support the vehicle safely. Attach a transparent tube over the bleeder screw.

c. Using an assistant, depress the brake pedal slowly, one time and hold.

d. Loosen the bleeder valve to purge the air from the cylinder.

e. Tighten the bleeder screw and slowly release the brake pedal. Wait 15 seconds.

f. Repeat this sequence until all the air is removed. The bleeding sequence is R/R, L/F, L/R and R/F.

g. Lower the vehicle and refill the master cylinder.

Anti-Lock Brake System Service

PRECAUTIONS

Failure to observe the following precautions may result in system damage.

• Before performing electric arc welding on the vehicle, disconnect the Electronic Brake Control Module (EBCM) and the hydraulic modulator connectors.

• When performing painting work on the vehicle, do not expose the Electronic Brake Control Module (EBCM) to temperatures in excess of 185°F (85°C) for longer than 2 hrs. The system may be exposed to temperatures up to 200°F (95°C) for less than 15 min.

• Never disconnect or connect the Electronic Brake Control Module (EBCM) or hydraulic modulator connectors with the ignition switch ON.

• Never disassemble any component of the Anti-Lock Brake System (ABS) which is designated non-servicable; the component must be replaced as an assembly.

• When filling the master cylinder, always use Delco Supreme 11 brake fluid or equivalent, which meets DOT-3 specifications; petroleum base fluid will destroy the rubber parts.

RELIEVING ANTI-LOCK BRAKE SYSTEM PRESSURE

1. Disconnect the negative battery cable. Turn the ignition to the **OFF** position.

2. Pump the brake pedal a minimum of 25 times.

3. When a definite increase in pedal effort, stroke the pedal a few more times.

4. This should relieve all the hydraulic pressure from the system.

Hydraulic Unit

REMOVAL & INSTALLATION

1. Disconnect the negative battery cable.

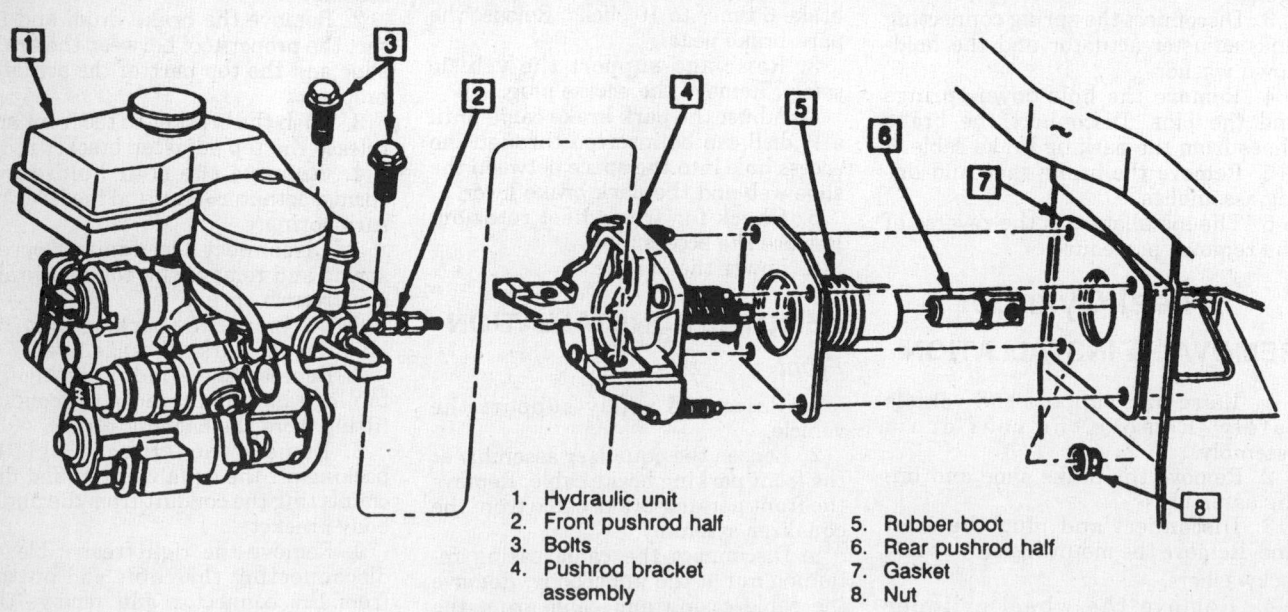

1. Hydraulic unit
2. Front pushrod half
3. Bolts
4. Pushrod bracket assembly
5. Rubber boot
6. Rear pushrod half
7. Gasket
8. Nut

Mounting of the hydraulic unit

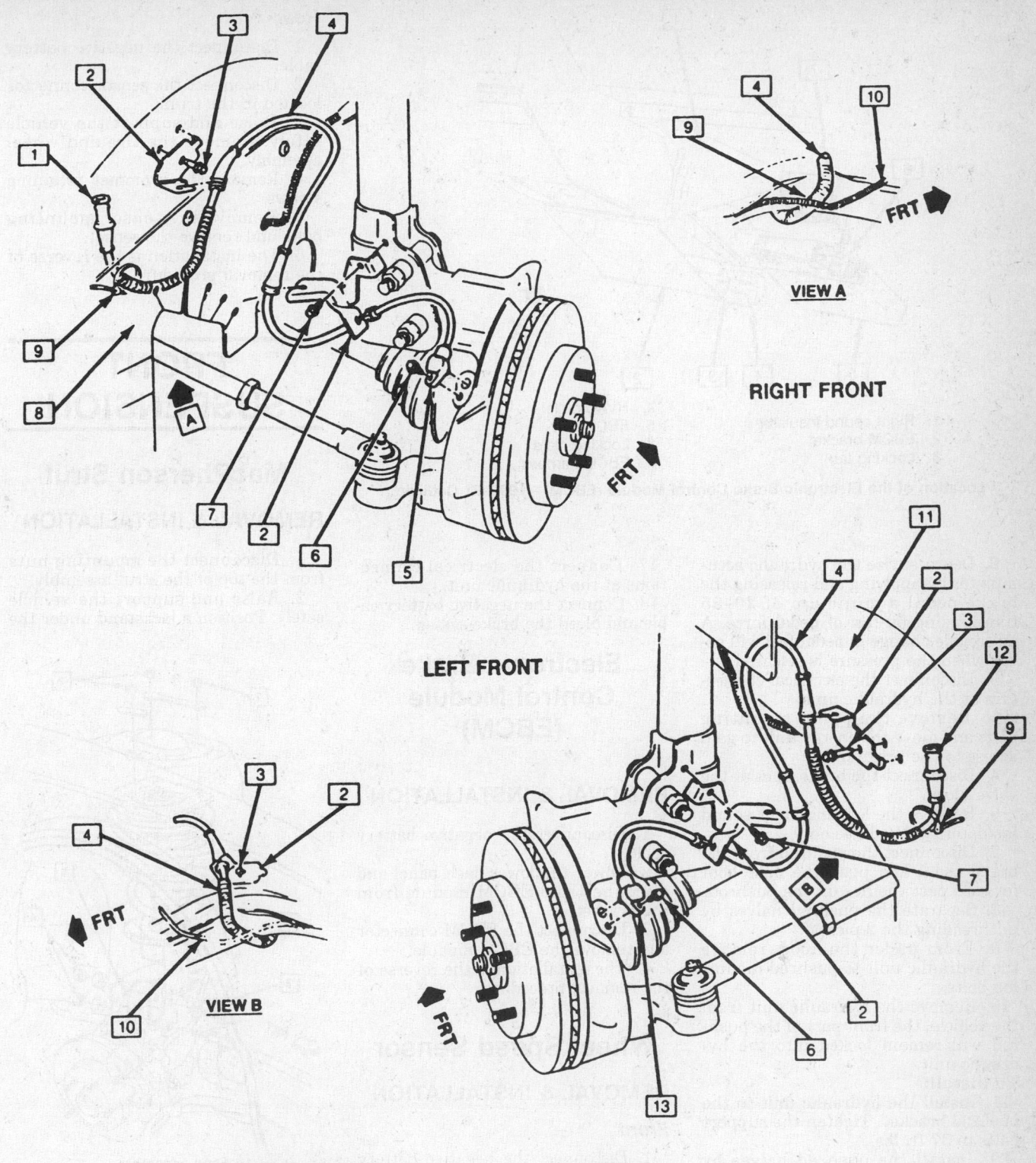

VIEW A

RIGHT FRONT

LEFT FRONT

VIEW B

1. Right wheel speed sensor connector
2. Bracket
3. Rivet
4. Wheel speed sensor lead
5. Right wheel speed sensor
6. Bolt
7. Screw
8. Shield
9. Strap
10. Brake pipe
11. Frame rail
12. Left wheel speed sensor connector
13. Left wheel speed sensor

Front wheel speed sensors

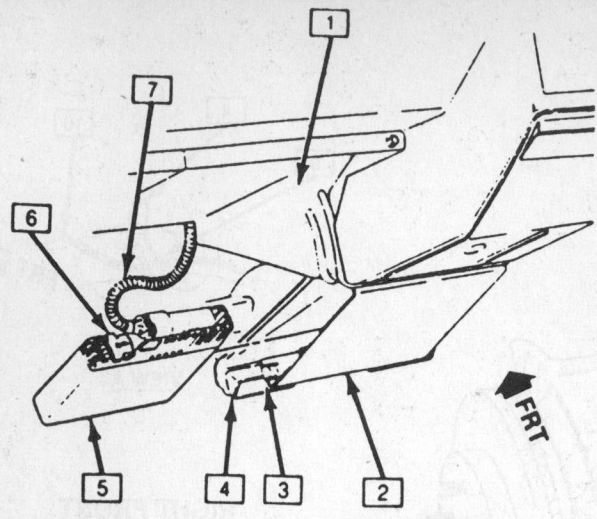

1. Right sound insulator
2. EBCM bracket
3. Locking tab
4. HVAC outlet
5. EBCM
6. Locking plate
7. EBCM harness

Location of the Electronic Brake Control Module (EBCM)—1990-91 Cadillac

2. Depressurize the hydraulic accumulator by applying and releasing the brake pedal a minimum of 20-25 times, using 50 lbs. of pedal force. A noticeable change in pedal feel will occur when the pressure is released.

3. Disconnect the electrical connectors at the hydraulic unit.

4. Remove the pump mounting bolts and move the energy unit to gain access to the brake lines.

5. Disconnect the brake lines at the valve block.

6. Remove the left and right sound insulators on Cadillac only.

7. Disconnect the pushrod from the brake pedal and push the dust boot forward past the hex on the pushrod.

8. Separate the pushrod halves by unthreading the 2 pieces.

9. From under the hood, remove the hydraulic unit-to-pushrod mounting bolts.

10. Remove the hydraulic unit from the vehicle, the front part of the pushrod will remain locked into the hydraulic unit.

To install:

11. Install the hydraulic unit to the pushrod bracket. Tighten the support bolts to 37 ft. lbs.

12. Install the pushrod halves by threading the 2 pieces together.

13. Install the pushrod to the brake pedal and reposition the dust boot.

14. Install the left and the right sound insulators on Cadillac only.

15. Connect the brake lines to the valve block and tighten to 11 ft. lbs.

16. Reposition the energy unit and replace the pump mounting bolts. Tighten to 71 inch lbs.

17. Connect the electrical connections at the hydraulic unit.

18. Connect the negative battery cable and bleed the brake system.

Electronic Brake Control Module (EBCM)

REMOVAL & INSTALLATION

1. Disconnect the negative battery cable.

2. Lower the lower dash panel and disconnect the EBCM module from the bracket.

3. Disconnect the EBCM connector and remove the EBCM module.

4. The installation is the reverse of the removal procedure.

Wheel Speed Sensor

REMOVAL & INSTALLATION

Front

1. Disconnect the negative battery cable.

2. Disconnect the sensor connector from the wiring harness.

3. Raise and support the vehicle safely. Remove the tire and wheel assembly.

4. Remove the sensor mounting screw and remove the sensor.

5. The installation is the reverse of the removal procedure.

Rear

1. Disconnect the negative battery cable.

2. Disconnect the sensor connector located in the trunk.

3. Raise and support the vehicle safely. Remove the tire and wheel assembly.

4. Remove the grommet retaining screws.

5. Remove the sensor mounting bolts and remove the sensor.

6. The installation is the reverse of the removal procedure.

FRONT SUSPENSION

MacPherson Strut

REMOVAL & INSTALLATION

1. Disconnect the mounting nuts from the top of the strut assembly.

2. Raise and support the vehicle safely. Position a jackstand under the

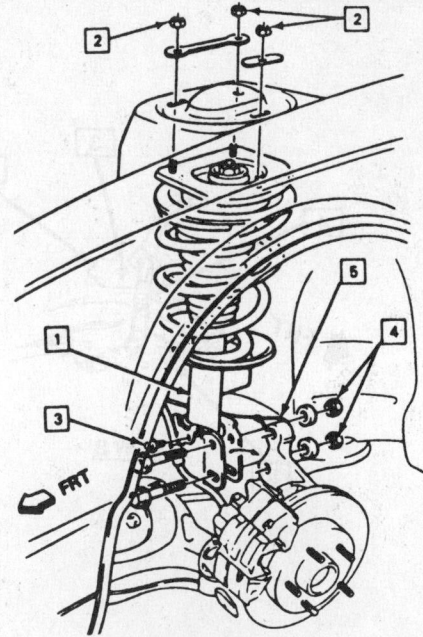

1. Strut assembly
2. Strut-to-body nuts
3. Brake line bracket bolt
4. Strut-to-steering knuckle nuts
5. Retain steering knuckle with wire once strut assembly is removed

Strut mount location

engine cradle and lower the vehicle so that the weight of the vehicle rests on the a jackstand and not the control arms.

3. Remove the tire and wheel assemblies. Disconnect the front sensor, if equipped with anti-lock brake.

4. Disconnect the brake line bracket from the strut assembly. Remove the strut-to-steering knuckle bolts.

5. Remove the strut assembly from the vehicle.

6. The installation is the reverse of the removal procedure.

Lower Ball Joints

INSPECTION

1. Raise and support the vehicle safely. Position a jackstand under the engine cradle and lower the vehicle so that the weight of the vehicle rests on the a jackstand and not the control arms.

2. Grasp the wheel at the top and the bottom and shake the wheel in and out.

3. If the is any movement of the steering knuckle in relation the control arm, the ball joints are defective and must be replaced.

REMOVAL & INSTALLATION

1. Raise and support the vehicle safely. Position a jackstand under the engine cradle and lower the vehicle so that the weight of the vehicle rests on the jackstand and not the control arms.

2. Remove the tire and wheel assembly.

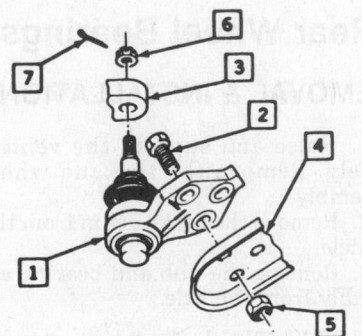

1. Ball joint
2. Ball joint mounting bolts must face down
3. Steering knuckle
4. Control arm
5. Ball joint mounting nuts
6. Ball joint-to-steering knuckle nut

Explode view of ball joint assembly

3. Disconnect the ball joint from the steering knuckle, using the proper tool.

4. Drill out the rivets retaining the ball joint and loosen the stabilizer shaft bushing assembly nut.

5. Remove the ball joint from the steering knuckle and the control arm.

6. The installation is the reverse of the removal procedure. Tighten the ball joint-to-control arm mounting bolts to 50 ft. lbs.

Lower Control Arms

REMOVAL & INSTALLATION

1. Raise and support the vehicle safely. Position a jackstand under the engine cradle and lower the vehicle so that the weight of the vehicle rests on the jackstand and not the control arms.

2. Remove the tire and wheel assembly. Disconnect the stabilizer shaft-to-control arm bolt.

3. Remove the ball joint from the steering knuckle and the control arm.

4. Remove the control arm mounting bolts and remove the control arm from the engine cradle.

To install:

5. Install the control arm to the engine cradle. Do not tighten the control arm bolts at this time.

6. Install the stabilizer shaft bushings and connect the ball joint to the steering knuckle.

7. Raise the vehicle so that the weight of the vehicle is supported by the control arm.

NOTE: The weight of the vehicle must be supported by the control arms when tightening the control arm mounting nuts.

8. Tighten the rear control arm mounting nut to 90 ft. lbs. and the front mounting nut to 140 ft. lbs.

9. Install the ball joint to the control arm and tighten the nut to 37 ft. lbs.

10. Replace the tire and wheel assembly.

11. Raise the vehicle and remove the jackstand.

12. Lower the vehicle.

Sway Bar

REMOVAL & INSTALLATION

1. Raise and support the vehicle safely. Position a jackstand under the engine cradle and lower the vehicle so that the weight of the vehicle rests on the jackstand and not the control arms.

2. Remove the tire and wheel assemblies.

3. Remove the bolts connecting the stabilizer bar bushings to the control arms.

4. Remove the stabilizer bar mounting bolts. Matchmark and disconnect the tie rod ends from the steering knuckles.

5. Disconnect the exhaust pipe from the exhaust manifold and turn the passenger side strut assembly completely to the right.

6. Slide the stabilizer bar over the steering knuckle and pull down until the stabilizer bar clears the frame.

7. Remove the stabilizer bar from the vehicle.

To install:

8. Install the stabilizer bar over the steering knuckle.

9. Raise the stabilizer bar over the frame and slide into position.

10. Loosely, install the stabilizer bar mount bushings, brackets and bolts.

11. Install the tie rod ends to the steering knuckles, tighten the nuts to 52 ft. lbs. Tighten the stabilizer bar mounting bolts to 37 ft. lbs.

12. Connect the exhaust pipe to the exhaust manifold and tighten the bolts to 15 ft. lbs.

13. Replace the tire and wheel assemblies.

14. Raise the vehicle and remove the jackstands.

15. Lower the vehicle.

REAR SUSPENSION

MacPherson Strut

REMOVAL & INSTALLATION

1. Raise and support the vehicle safely.

2. Remove the trunk side cover. Remove the tire and wheel assemblies.

3. Support the control arm with a suitable jack.

4. Disconnect the Electronic Level Control (ELC) air tube and separate from the strut air tube.

5. Disconnect the strut tower mounting nuts. The nuts are located inside the trunk.

6. Remove the strut anchor bolts, washers and nuts from the steering knuckle and bracket.

7. Remove the strut assembly from the vehicle.

To install:

8. Install the strut assembly and connect the upper strut mounting nuts.

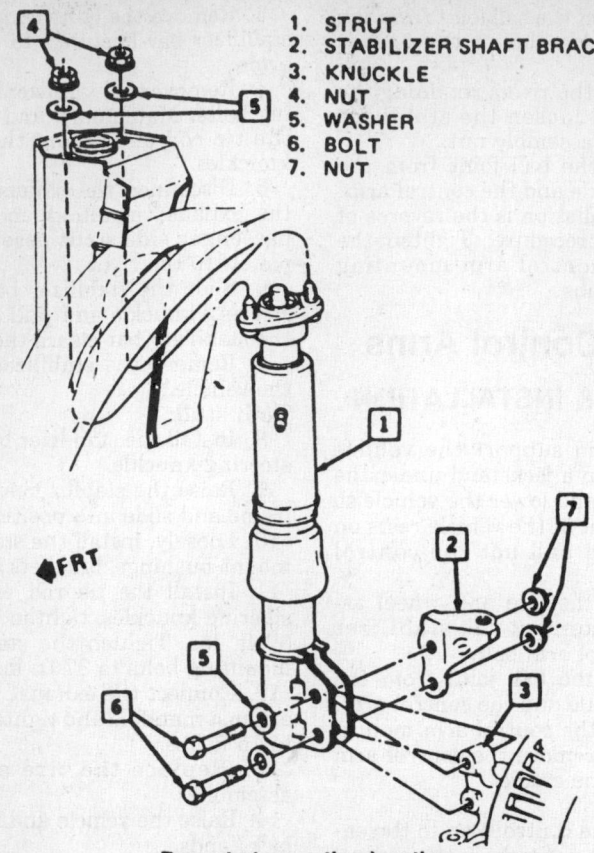

1. STRUT
2. STABILIZER SHAFT BRACKET
3. KNUCKLE
4. NUT
5. WASHER
6. BOLT
7. NUT

◀FRT

Rear strut mounting location

9. Replace the strut anchor bolts, washer, knuckle bracket and nuts.
10. Connect the ELC tube.
11. Tighten the upper mount nuts to 220 inch lbs. and the strut-to-knuckle nuts to 125 ft. lbs.
12. Replace the tire and wheel assemblies. Remove the jack from under the vehicle.
13. Replace the trunk side cover and lower the vehicle.

Coil Springs

REMOVAL & INSTALLATION

1. Raise and support the vehicle safely. Support the vehicle so that the control arms hang free.
2. Remove both tire and wheel assemblies.
3. Disconnect the ELC height sensor on the right control arm and/or the parking brake cable retaining clip on the left control arm.
4. Place a proper tool and jack into position and remove the tension from the control arm pivot bolts.

NOTE: Place a chain around the spring and through the control arm as a safety measure.

5. Remove the pivot bolt and nut from the rear of the control arm.
6. Slowly, maneuver the jack to relieve in the front control arm pivot bolt.
7. Lower the jack to allow the control arm to pivot downward.
8. When all the compression is removed from the spring remove the safety chain, spring and the insulators.

NOTE: Do not apply force to the control arm and/or ball joint to remove the spring. Proper maneuvering of the spring will allow for easy removal.

To install:

9. Snap the upper insulator on the spring prior to installation.
10. Position the lower insulator and spring in the vehicle. Install the coil springs so that the upper end of the springs are positioned properly.
11. Raise the control arm into position, using the proper tool and jack.
12. Slowly, maneuver the jack to permit the installation of the pivot bolt and nut at the front of the control arm.
13. Install the pivot bolt and nut at the rear of the control arm.
14. Attach the rear stabilizer bar to the knuckle bracket. Connect the ELC height sensor link on the right control arm and/or the parking brake cable retaining clip on the left control arm.
15. Replace both tire and wheel assemblies.
16. Remove the jack from under the vehicle. Lower the vehicle.
17. Tighten the control arm pivot nuts to 85 ft. lbs., the control arm pivot bolts to 125 ft. lbs. and the stabilizer support bolt to 160 inch lbs.

Rear Control Arms

REMOVAL & INSTALLATION

1. Raise and support the vehicle safely. Remove the tire and wheel assembly.
2. Disconnect the ELC height sensor on the right control arm and/or the parking brake cable retaining clip on the left control arm.
3. Disconnect the suspension adjustment link retaining nut and separate the link assembly from the control arm.
4. Remove the ball stud and the castellated nut. Turn over and install with the flat portion facing up. Do not tighten.
5. Separate the knuckle from the ball stud, using the proper tool. Remove the control arm.
6. The installation is the reverse of the removal procedure. Tighten the control arm pivot nuts to 85 ft. lbs. and the pivot bolts to 125 ft. lbs. Tighten the pivot nuts and bolts with the vehicle unsupported and the wheels at normal height.

Rear Wheel Bearings

REMOVAL & INSTALLATION

1. Raise and support the vehicle safely. Remove the tire and wheel assembly.
2. Remove the brake drum from the vehicle.
3. Remove the hub and bearing assembly from the axle.

NOTE: The bolts that attach the hub and bearing assembly also support the brake assembly. Do not let the brake line support the brake assembly.

4. The installation is the reverse of the removal procedure. Tighten the hub and bearing bolts to 52 ft. lbs.

GM "E", "K" & "V" Body
Front Wheel Drive
Buick—Reatta, Riviera
Cadillac—Allante, Eldorado, Seville
Oldsmobile—Toronado, Trofeo

SPECIFICATIONS

VEHICLE IDENTIFICATION CHART

It is important for servicing and ordering parts to be certain of the vehicle and engine identification. The VIN (vehicle identification number) is a 17 digit number visible through the windshield on the driver's side of the dash and contains the vehicle and engine identification codes. The tenth digit indicates model year, and the eighth digit indicates engine code. It can be interpreted as follows:

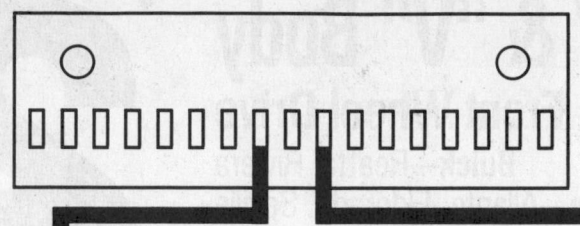

Engine Code						Model Year	
Code	**Cu. In.**	**Liters**	**Cyl.**	**Fuel Sys.**	**Eng. Mfg.**	**Code**	**Year**
3 ('87)	231	3.8	6	SFI	Buick	H	1987
C ('88–91)	231	3.8	6	SFI	Buick	J	1988
8 ('87)	250	4.1	8	DFI	Cadillac	K	1989
7 ('87–88)	250	4.1	8	MFI	Cadillac	L	1990
3 ('90–91)	273	4.5	8	MFI	Cadillac	M	1991
5 ('88–89)	273	4.5	8	DFI	Cadillac		
8 ('89–91)	273	4.5	8	MFI	Cadillac		

ENGINE IDENTIFICATION

Year	Model	Engine Displacement cu. in. (liter)	Engine Series Identification (VIN)	No. of Cylinders	Engine Type
1987	Allante	250 (4.1)	7	8	OHV
	Eldorado	250 (4.1)	8	8	OHV
	Riviera	231 (3.8)	3	6	OHV
	Seville	250 (4.1)	8	8	OHV
	Toronado	231 (3.8)	3	6	OHV
1988	Allante	250 (4.1)	7	8	OHV
	Eldorado	273 (4.5)	5	8	OHV
	Reatta	231 (3.8)	C	6	OHV
	Riviera	231 (3.8)	C	6	OHV
	Seville	273 (4.5)	5	8	OHV
	Toronado	231 (3.8)	C	6	OHV
1989	Allante	273 (4.5)	8	8	OHV
	Eldorado	273 (4.5)	5	8	OHV
	Reatta	231 (3.8)	C	6	OHV
	Riviera	231 (3.8)	C	6	OHV
	Seville	273 (4.5)	5	8	OHV
	Toronado	231 (3.8)	C	6	OHV

ENGINE IDENTIFICATION

Year	Model	Engine Displacement cu. in. (liter)	Engine Series Identification (VIN)	No. of Cylinders	Engine Type
1990–91	Allante	273 (4.5)	8	8	OHV
	Eldorado	273 (4.5)	3	8	OHV
	Reatta	231 (3.8)	C	6	OHV
	Riviera	231 (3.8)	C	6	OHV
	Seville	273 (4.5)	3	8	OHV
	Toronado	231 (3.8)	C	6	OHV
	Trofeo	231 (3.8)	C	6	OHV

OHV Overhead Valves

GENERAL ENGINE SPECIFICATIONS

Year	VIN	Cylinder Displacement cu. in. (liter)	Fuel System Type	Net Horsepower @ rpm	Net Torque @ rpm (ft. lbs.)	Bore × Stroke (in.)	Compression Ratio	Oil Pressure @ rpm
1987	3	6-231 (3.8)	SFI	140 @ 4400	200 @ 2000	3.800 × 3.400	8.0:1	37 @ 2600
	7	8-250 (4.1)	MFI	170 @ 4300	235 @ 3200	3.460 × 3.310	9.0:1	37 @ 1500
	8	8-250 (4.1)	DFI	130 @ 4200	200 @ 2200	3.465 × 3.310	9.0:1	37 @ 1500
1988	3	6-231 (3.8)	SFI	165 @ 5200	210 @ 2000	3.800 × 3.400	8.5:1	37 @ 2400
	5	8-273 (4.5)	DFI	155 @ 4200	240 @ 2800	3.620 × 3.310	9.0:1	37 @ 1500
	7	8-250 (4.1)	MFI	170 @ 4300	235 @ 3200	3.460 × 3.310	8.5:1	37 @ 1500
	C	6-231 (3.8)	SFI	165 @ 5200	210 @ 2000	3.800 × 4.060	8.5:1	37 @ 2400
1989	5	8-273 (4.5)	DFI	155 @ 4200	240 @ 2800	3.620 × 3.310	9.0:1	37 @ 1500
	8	8-273 (4.5)	MFI	200 @ 4400	270 @ 3200	3.620 × 3.310	9.0:1	37 @ 1500
	C	6-231 (3.8)	SFI	165 @ 5200	210 @ 2000	3.800 × 3.400	8.5:1	37 @ 2400
1990–91	3	8-273 (4.5)	MFI	180 @ 4000	245 @ 3000	3.620 × 3.310	9.5:1	37 @ 1500
	8	8-273 (4.5)	MFI	200 @ 4400	230 @ 3200	3.620 × 3.310	9.0:1	37 @ 1500
	C	6-231 (3.8)	SFI	165 @ 5200	210 @ 2000	3.800 × 3.400	8.5:1	37 @ 2400

PFI Port Fuel Injection   DFI Digital Fuel Injection   NA Not available
SFI Sequential Fuel Injection   MFI Multiport Fuel Injection

GASOLINE ENGINE TUNE-UP SPECIFICATIONS

Year	VIN	No. Cylinder Displacement cu. in. (liter)	Spark Plugs Type	Spark Plugs Gap (in.)	Ignition Timing (deg.) MT	Ignition Timing (deg.) AT	Compression Pressure (psi)	Fuel Pump (psi)	Idle Speed (rpm) MT	Idle Speed (rpm) AT	Valve Clearance In.	Valve Clearance Ex.
1987	3	6-231 (3.8)	R44LTS	0.045	—	①	100	38	—	500	Hyd.	Hyd.
	8	8-250 (4.1)	R44LTS6	0.060	—	10B ②	140	9–12	—	①	Hyd.	Hyd.
1988	C	6-231 (3.8)	R44LTS6	0.060	—	①	—	27–36	—	①	Hyd.	Hyd.
	5	8-273 (4.5)	R44LTS6	0.060	—	①	140–165	46.5	—	①	Hyd.	Hyd.
	7	8-250 (4.1)	R44LTS6	0.060	—	①	140–165	65–95	—	①	Hyd.	Hyd.
1989	5	8-273 (4.5)	R44LTS6	0.060	—	①	140–165	46.5	—	①	Hyd.	Hyd.
	8	8-273 (4.5)	R44LTS6	0.060	—	①	140–165	46.5	—	①	Hyd.	Hyd.
	C	6-231 (3.8)	R44LTS6	0.060	—	①	—	27–36	—	①	Hyd.	Hyd.
1990	3	8-273 (4.5)	R44LTS6	0.060	—	①	140–165	43.5	—	①	Hyd.	Hyd.
	8	8-273 (4.5)	R44LTS6	0.060	—	①	140–165	43.5	—	①	Hyd.	Hyd.
	C	6-231 (3.8)	R44LTS6	0.060	—	①	—	27–36	—	①	Hyd.	Hyd.
1991		SEE UNDERHOOD SPECIFICATIONS STICKER										

① Controlled by ECM
② 800 in Park

FIRING ORDERS

NOTE: To avoid confusion, always replace spark plug wires one at a time.

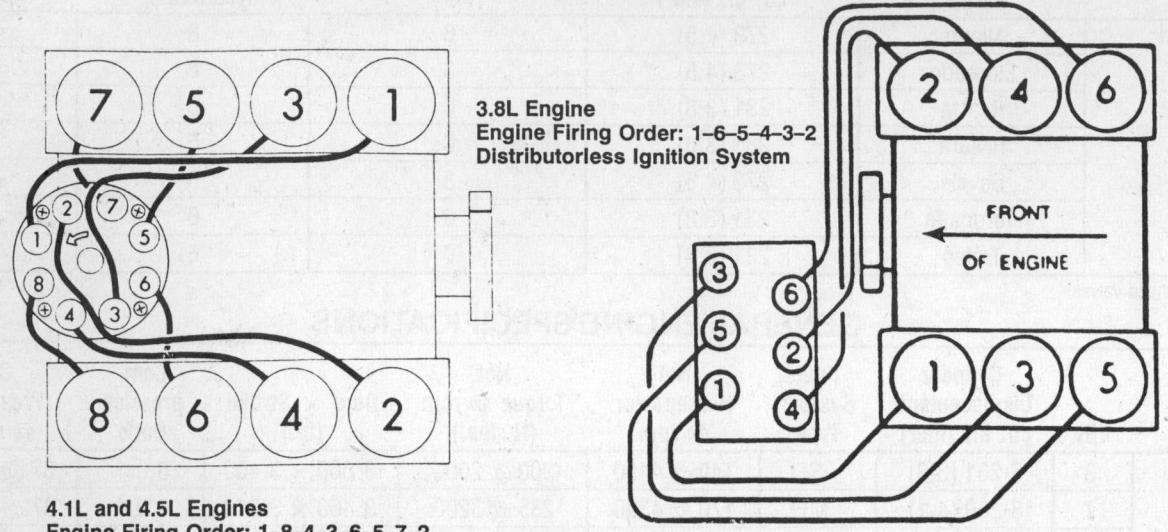

3.8L Engine
Engine Firing Order: 1–6–5–4–3–2
Distributorless Ignition System

4.1L and 4.5L Engines
Engine Firing Order: 1–8–4–3–6–5–7–2
Distributor Rotation: Counterclockwise

CAPACITIES

Year	Model	VIN	No. Cylinder Displacement cu. in. (liter)	Engine Crankcase with Filter	Engine Crankcase without Filter	Transmission (pts.) 4-Spd	Transmission (pts.) 5-Spd	Transmission (pts.) Auto.	Drive Axle (pts.)	Fuel Tank (gals.)	Cooling System (qts.)
1987	Allante	7	8-250 (4.1)	6.0	5.0	—	—	13	—	22	12.1
	Eldorado	8	8-250 (4.1)	6.0	5.0	—	—	13	—	18	12.6
	Riviera	3	6-231 (3.8)	5.0	4.0	—	—	13	—	18	13
	Seville	8	8-250 (4.1)	6.0	5.0	—	—	13	—	18	12.6
	Toronado	3	6-231 (3.8)	5.0	4.0	—	—	13	—	18	13
1988	Allante	7	8-250 (4.1)	6.0	5.0	—	—	13	—	22	12.1
	Eldorado	5	8-273 (4.5)	6.0	5.0	—	—	13	—	18.8	12.1
	Reatta	C	6-231 (3.8)	5.0	4.0	—	—	13	—	18	13
	Riviera	3	6-231 (3.8)	5.0	4.0	—	—	13	—	18	13
	Seville	5	8-273 (4.5)	6.0	5.0	—	—	13	—	18.8	12.1
	Toronado	C	6-231 (3.8)	5.0	4.0	—	—	13	—	18	13
1989	Allante	5	8-273 (4.5)	6.0	5.0	—	—	13	—	22	12.1
	Eldorado	5	8-273 (4.5)	6.0	5.0	—	—	13	—	18.8	12
	Reatta	C	6-231 (3.8)	5.0	4.0	—	—	12	—	18	13
	Riviera	C	6-231 (3.8)	5.0	4.0	—	—	12	—	18	13
	Seville	5	8-273 (4.5)	6.0	5.0	—	—	13	—	18.8	12.1
	Toronado	C	6-231 (3.8)	5.0	4.0	—	—	12	—	18	13
1990–91	Allante	8	8-273 (4.5)	6.0	5.0	—	—	13	—	22	12.1
	Eldorado	3	8-273 (4.5)	6.0	5.0	—	—	13	—	18.8	12.1
	Reatta	C	6-231 (3.8)	5.0	4.0	—	—	12	—	18	13
	Riviera	C	6-231 (3.8)	5.0	4.0	—	—	12	—	18	13
	Seville	3	8-273 (4.5)	6.0	5.0	—	—	13	—	18.8	12.1
	Toronado	C	6-231 (3.8)	5.0	4.0	—	—	12	—	18	13
	Trofeo	C	6-231 (3.8)	5.0	4.0	—	—	12	—	18	13

CAMSHAFT SPECIFICATIONS

All measurements given in inches.

Year	VIN	No. Cylinder Displacement cu. in. (liter)	Journal Diameter					Lobe Lift		Bearing Clearance	Camshaft End Play
			1	2	3	4	5	In.	Ex.		
1987	3	6-231 (3.8)	1.785–1.786	1.785–1.786	1.785–1.786	1.785–1.786	—	0.245	0.245	0.0005–0.0035 ①	NA
	8	8-250 (4.1)	NA	NA	NA	NA	NA	0.384	0.396	0.0018–0.0037	NA
	7	8-250 (4.1)	NA	NA	NA	NA	NA	0.384	0.396	0.0018–0.0037	NA
1988	C	6-231 (3.8)	1.785–1.786	1.785–1.786	1.785–1.786	1.785–1.786	—	0.245	0.245	0.0005–0.0035	NA
	7	8-250 (4.1)	NA	NA	NA	NA	NA	0.384	0.396	0.0018–0.0037	NA
	5	8-273 (4.5)	NA	NA	NA	NA	NA	0.384	0.396	0.0018–0.0037	NA
1989	5	8-273 (4.5)	NA	NA	NA	NA	NA	0.384	0.396	0.0018–0.0037	NA
	8	8-273 (4.5)	NA	NA	NA	NA	NA	0.384	0.396	0.0018–0.0037	NA
	C	6-231 (3.8)	1.785–1.786	1.785–1.786	1.785–1.786	1.785–1.786	—	0.253	0.253	0.0005–0.0035	NA
1990–91	3	8-273 (4.5)	NA	NA	NA	NA	NA	0.384	0.396	0.0018–0.0037	NA
	8	8-273 (4.5)	NA	NA	NA	NA	NA	0.384	0.396	0.0018–0.0037	NA
	C	6-231 (3.8)	1.785–1.786	1.785–1.786	1.785–1.786	1.785–1.786	—	0.253	0.253	0.0005–0.0035	NA

NA Not available
① Journal No. 1—0.0005–0.0025 in.

CRANKSHAFT AND CONNECTING ROD SPECIFICATIONS

All measurements are given in inches.

Year	VIN	No. Cylinder Displacement cu. in. (liter)	Crankshaft				Connecting Rod		
			Main Brg. Journal Dia.	Main Brg. Oil Clearance	Shaft End-play	Thrust on No.	Journal Diameter	Oil Clearance	Side Clearance
1987	3	6-231 (3.8)	2.4995	0.0003–0.0018	0.003–0.011	2	2.2487–2.2495	0.0003–0.0028	0.003–0.015
	7	8-250 (4.1)	2.6374–2.6384	0.0016–0.0039 ①	0.001–0.007	3	1.929	0.0005–0.0028	0.008–0.020
	8	8-250 (4.1)	2.6374–2.6384	0.0016–0.0039 ①	0.001–0.007	3	1.929	0.0005–0.0028	0.008–0.020
1988	C	6-231 (3.8)	2.4988 2.4998	0.0003–0.0018	0.003–0.011	2	2.2487–2.2499	0.0003–0.0028	0.003–0.015
	7	8-250 (4.1)	2.6374–2.6384	0.0016–0.0039 ①	0.001–0.007	3	1.929	0.0005–0.0028	0.008–0.020
	5	8-273 (4.5)	2.6374–2.6384	0.0016–0.0039 ①	0.001–0.007	3	1.929	0.0005–0.0028	0.008–0.020

CRANKSHAFT AND CONNECTING ROD SPECIFICATIONS

All measurements are given in inches.

Year	VIN	No. Cylinder Displacement cu. in. (liter)	Crankshaft				Connecting Rod		
			Main Brg. Journal Dia.	Main Brg. Oil Clearance	Shaft End-play	Thrust on No.	Journal Diameter	Oil Clearance	Side Clearance
1989	5	8-273 (4.5)	2.635–2.636	0.0016–0.0039 ①	0.001–0.007	3	1.927	0.0005–0.0028	0.008–0.020
	8	8-273 (4.5)	2.635–2.636	0.0016–0.0039 ①	0.001–0.007	3	1.927	0.0005–0.0028	0.008–0.020
	C	6-231 (3.8)	2.4988 2.4998	0.0003–0.0018	0.003–0.011	2	2.2487–2.2499	0.0003–0.0026	0.003–0.015
1990–91	3	8-273 (4.5)	2.635–2.636	0.0016–0.0039 ①	0.001–0.007	3	1.927	0.0005–0.0028	0.008–0.020
	8	8-273 (4.5)	2.635–2.636	0.0016–0.0039 ①	0.001–0.007	3	1.927	0.0005–0.0028	0.008–0.020
	C	6-231 (3.8)	2.4988 2.4998	0.0003–0.0018	0.003–0.011	2	2.2487–2.2499	0.0003–0.0026	0.003–0.015

① No. 1—0.0008–0.0031

VALVE SPECIFICATIONS

Year	VIN	No. Cylinder Displacement cu. in. (liter)	Seat Angle (deg.)	Face Angle (deg.)	Spring Test Pressure (lbs.)	Spring Installed Height (in.)	Stem-to-Guide Clearance (in.)		Stem Diameter (in.)	
							Intake	Exhaust	Intake	Exhaust
1987	3	6-231 (3.8)	46	45	90 @ 1.727	1²³/₃₂	0.0015–0.0035	0.0015–0.0032	0.3401–0.3412	0.3405–0.3412
	7	8-250 (4.1)	45	44	99 @ 1.730	1²³/₃₂	0.0010–0.0030	0.0010–0.0030	0.3413–0.3420	0.3411–0.3418
	8	8-250 (4.1)	45	44	99 @ 1.730	1²³/₃₂	0.0010–0.0030	0.0010–0.0030	0.3413–0.3420	0.3411–0.3418
1988	C	6-231 (3.8)	45	45	105 @ 1.730	1²³/₃₂	0.0015–0.0035	0.0015–0.0032	0.3401–0.3412	0.3405–0.3412
	7	8-250 (4.1)	45	44	99 @ 1.730	1²³/₃₂	0.0010–0.0030	0.0010–0.0030	0.3413–0.3420	0.3411–0.3418
	5	8-273 (4.5)	45	44	99 @ 1.730	1²³/₃₂	0.0010–0.0030	0.0010–0.0030	0.3413–0.3420	0.3411–0.3418
1989	5	8-273 (4.5)	45	44	93–103 @ 1.730	1²³/₃₂	0.0010–0.0030	0.0010–0.0030	0.3413–0.3420	0.3411–0.3418
	8	8-273 (4.5)	45	44	93–103 @ 1.730	1²³/₃₂	0.0010–0.0030	0.0010–0.0030	0.3413–0.3420	0.3411–0.3408
	C	6-231 (3.8)	45	45	76–84 @ 1.750	1.690–1.750	0.0015–0.0035	0.0015–0.0032	0.3401–0.3412	0.3405–0.3412
1990–91	3	8-273 (4.5)	45	44	68–76 @ 1.730	1²³/₃₂	0.0010–0.0030	0.0010–0.0030	0.3413–0.3420	0.3411–0.3418
	8	8-273 (4.5)	45	44	93–103 @ 1.730	1²³/₃₂	0.0010–0.0030	0.0010–0.0030	0.3413–0.3420	0.3411–0.3418
	C	6-231 (3.8)	45	45	76–84 @ 1.750	1²³/₃₂	0.0015–0.0035	0.0015–0.0032	0.3401–0.3412	0.3405–0.3412

PISTON AND RING SPECIFICATIONS
All measurements are given in inches.

Year	VIN	No. Cylinder Displacement cu. in. (liter)	Piston Clearance	Ring Gap			Ring Side Clearance		
				Top Compression	Bottom Compression	Oil Control	Top Compression	Bottom Compression	Oil Control
1987	3	6-231 (3.8)	0.0004–0.0022	0.0100–0.0200	0.0100–0.0220	0.0150–0.0550	0.0010–0.0030	0.0010–0.0030	0.0005–0.0065
	7	8-250 (4.1)	0.0010–0.0018	0.0150–0.0240	0.0150–0.0240	0.0100–0.0500	0.0016–0.0037	0.0016–0.0037	None ①
	8	8-250 (4.1)	0.0010–0.0018	0.0150–0.0240	0.0150–0.0240	0.0100–0.0500	0.0016–0.0037	0.0016–0.0037	None ①
1988	C	6-231 (3.8)	②	0.0100–0.0250	0.0100–0.0250	0.0150–0.0550	0.0013–0.0031	0.0013–0.0031	0.0011–0.0081
	7	8-250 (4.1)	0.0010–0.0018	0.0150–0.0240	0.0150–0.0240	0.0100–0.0500	0.0016–0.0037	0.0016–0.0037	None ①
	5	8-273 (4.5)	0.0010–0.0018	0.0150–0.0240	0.0150–0.0240	0.0100–0.0500	0.0016–0.0037	0.0016–0.0037	None ①
1989	5	8-273 (4.5)	0.0010–0.0018	0.0150–0.0240	0.0150–0.0240	0.0100–0.0500	0.0016–0.0037	0.0016–0.0037	①
	8	8-273 (4.5)	0.0010–0.0018	0.0150–0.0240	0.0150–0.0240	0.0100–0.0500	0.0016–0.0037	0.0016–0.0037	①
	C	6-231 (3.8)	②	0.0100–0.0250	0.0100–0.0250	0.0150–0.0550	0.0013–0.0031	0.0013–0.0031	0.0011–0.0081
1990–91	3	8-273 (4.5)	0.0010–0.0018	0.0150–0.0240	0.0150–0.0240	0.0100–0.0500	0.0016–0.0037	0.0016–0.0037	①
	8	8-273 (4.5)	0.0010–0.0018	0.0150–0.0240	0.0150–0.0240	0.0100–0.0500	0.0016–0.0037	0.0016–0.0037	①
	C	6-231 (3.8)	0.0004–0.0022 ③	0.0100–0.0250	0.0100–0.0250	0.0150–0.0550	0.0013–0.0031	0.0013–0.0031	0.0011–0.0081

① None—Side Sealing
② Skirt top—0.0007–0.0027
   Skirt bottom—0.0010–0.0045
③ Measure at centerline of piston pin hole

TORQUE SPECIFICATIONS
All readings in ft. lbs.

Year	VIN	No. Cylinder Displacement cu. in. (liter)	Cylinder Head Bolts	Main Bearing Bolts	Rod Bearing Bolts	Crankshaft Pulley Bolts	Flywheel Bolts	Manifold		Spark Plugs
								Intake	Exhaust	
1987	3	6-231 (3.8)	①	100	4-0	210 ⑤	60	32	37	20
	7	8-250 (4.1)	②	85	22	18	37	22 ⑦	18	11
	8	8-250 (4.1)	②	85	22	18	37	22 ⑦	18	11
1988	C	6-231 (3.8)	①	100	4-0	210 ⑤	60	88 ⑥	37	20
	7	8-250 (4.1)	②	85	22	18	37	22 ⑦	18	11
	5	8-273 (4.5)	②	85	22	18	70	22 ⑦	18	11
1989	5	8-273 (4.5)	②	85	24 ④	18	70	12 ⑧	18	11
	8	8-273 (4.5)	②	85	24 ④	18	70	12 ⑧	18	11
	C	6-231 (3.8)	③	90	43	219 ⑤	61	88 ⑥	41	20

TORQUE SPECIFICATIONS

All readings in ft. lbs.

Year	VIN	No. Cylinder Displacement cu. in. (liter)	Cylinder Head Bolts	Main Bearing Bolts	Rod Bearing Bolts	Crankshaft Pulley Bolts	Flywheel Bolts	Manifold Intake	Manifold Exhaust	Spark Plugs
1990-91	3	8-273 (4.5)	②	85	24 ④	18	70	12 ⑧	18	11
	8	8-273 (4.5)	②	85	24 ④	18	70	12 ⑧	18	11
	C	6-231 (3.8)	③	90	43	219 ⑤	61	88 ⑥	41	20

① Torque in sequence to 25 ft. lbs.; then turn each bolt an add'l ¼ turn (90 degrees) in sequence; then turn each bolt an add'l ¼ turn (90 degrees) in sequence (if torque exceeds 60 ft. lbs. at any point during last 2 steps, do not complete 90 degrees turn).
② Torque in sequence to 38 ft. lbs.; then torque to 68 ft. lbs.; then torque No. 1, 3 and 4 bolts to 90 ft. lbs.
③ Torque in seuqence to 35 ft. lbs.; then turn each bolt 130 degreese; then rotate each bolt an add'l 30 degrees.
④ Lubricate with engine oil
⑤ Crankshaft balancer assembly
⑥ Inch lbs.
⑦ Torque bolts 1, 2, 3 and 4 in sequence to 15 ft. lbs.; then tighten bolts 5 through 16 in sequence to 22 ft. lbs.; then retighten all bolts in sequence to 22 ft. lbs.; then retorque all bolts to sequence to 22 ft.lbs.
⑧ Torque bolts 1, 2, 3 and 4 in sequence to 8 ft. lbs.; then tighten bolts 5 through 16 in sequence to 8 ft. lbs; then retighten all bolts in seuqence to 12 ft. lbs.; then retorque above step until torque level is maintained.

BRAKE SPECIFICATIONS

All measurements in inches unless noted.

Year	Model	Lug Nut Torque (ft. lbs.)	Master Cylinder Bore	Brake Disc Minimum Thickness	Brake Disc Maximum Runout	Standard Brake Drum Diameter	Minimum Lining Thickness Front	Minimum Lining Thickness Rear
1987	Eldorado	100	①	0.971 ②	0.004 ③	NA	0.030	0.030
	Riviera	100	①	0.971 ②	0.004 ③	NA	0.030	0.030
	Seville	100	①	0.971 ②	0.004 ③	NA	0.030	0.030
	Toronado	100	①	0.971 ②	0.004 ③	NA	0.030	0.030
1988	Allante	100	①	0.971 ②	0.004 ③	NA	0.030	0.030
	Eldorado	100	①	0.971 ②	0.004 ③	NA	0.030	0.030
	Reatta	100	①	0.971 ②	0.004 ③	NA	0.030	0.030
	Riviera	100	①	0.971 ②	0.004 ③	NA	0.030	0.030
	Seville	100	①	0.971 ②	0.004 ③	NA	0.030	0.030
	Toronado	100	①	0.971 ②	0.004 ③	NA	0.030	0.030
1989	Allante	100	①	0.971 ②	0.004 ③	NA	0.030	0.030
	Eldorado	100	①	0.971 ②	0.004 ③	NA	0.030	0.030
	Reatta	100	①	0.971 ②	0.004 ③	NA	0.030	0.030
	Riviera	100	①	0.971 ②	0.004 ③	NA	0.030	0.030
	Seville	100	①	0.971 ②	0.004 ③	NA	0.030	0.030
	Toronado	100	①	0.971 ②	0.004 ③	NA	0.030	0.030
1990-91	Allante	100	①	0.971 ②	0.004 ③	NA	0.030	0.030
	Eldorado	100	①	0.971 ②	0.004 ③	NA	0.030	0.030
	Reatta	100	①	0.971 ②	0.004 ③	NA	0.030	0.030
	Riviera	100	①	0.971 ②	0.004 ③	NA	0.030	0.030
	Seville	100	①	0.971 ②	0.004 ③	NA	0.030	0.030
	Toronado	100	①	0.971 ②	0.004 ③	NA	0.030	0.030
	Trofeo	100	①	0.971 ②	0.004 ③	NA	0.030	0.030

NA Not available
① Standard—1.126 in.
Quick Tape-up—1.574 in.
Anti-Lock—1.000 in.
② Rear—0.444 in.
③ Rear—0.003 in.

WHEEL ALIGNMENT

Year	Model		Caster Range (deg.)	Caster Preferred Setting (deg.)	Camber Range (deg.)	Camber Preferred Setting (deg.)	Toe-in (in.)	Steering Axis Inclination (deg.)
1987	Allante	Front	2 5/16P–3 1/2P	2 13/16P	13/16N–13/16P	0	0	NA
		Rear			1/8N–1/2	7/32P	3/32	
	Eldorado	Front	1 5/16P–3 5/16P	2 5/16P	13/16N–13/16P	0	0	NA
		Rear			13/32N–3/16	3/32N	3/32	
	Riviera	Front	1 5/16P–3 5/16P	2 5/16P	13/16N–13/16P	0	0	NA
		Rear			1N–3/8N	11/16N	3/32	
	Seville	Front	1 5/16P–3 5/16P	2 5/16P	13/16N–13/16P	0	0	NA
		Rear			13/32N–3/16	3/32N	3/32	
	Toronado	Front	1 5/16P–3 5/16P	2 5/16P	13/16N–13/16P	0	0	NA
		Rear			23/32N–3/32N	13/32N	7/64	
1988	Allante	Front	2 5/16P–3 1/2P	2 13/16P	13/16N–13/16P	0	0	NA
		Rear			1/8N–1/2	7/32P	3/32	
	Eldorado	Front	1 5/16P–3 5/16P	2 5/16P	13/16N–13/16P	0	0	NA
		Rear			13/32N–3/16	3/32N	3/32	
	Reatta	Front	1 13/16P–3 13/16P	2 13/16P	13/16N–13/16P	0	0	NA
		Rear			0–1 5/16P	5/8P	3/32	
	Riviera	Front	1 5/16P–3 3/16P	2 5/16P	13/16N–13/16P	0	0	NA
		Rear			0–1 5/16P	5/8P	3/32	
	Seville	Front	1 5/16P–3 5/16P	2 5/16P	13/16N–13/16P	0	0	NA
		Rear			13/32N–3/16	3/32N	3/32	
	Toronado	Front	1 5/16P–3 5/16P	2 5/16P	13/16N–13/16P	0	0	NA
		Rear			13/32N–7/32	3/32N	7/64	
	Trofeo	Front	1 5/16P–3 5/16P	2 5/16P	13/16N–13/16P	0	0	NA
		Rear			13/32N–7/32	3/32N	7/64	
1989	Allante	Front	2P–3P	2 1/2P	13/16N–13/16P	0	3/32	NA
		Rear			1/2N–1/8	3/16N	3/32	
	Eldorado	Front	1 5/16P–3 5/16P	2 5/16P	13/16N–13/16P	0	0	NA
		Rear			13/32N–3/16	3/32N	3/32	
	Reatta	Front	1 13/16P–3 13/16P	2 13/16P	13/16N–13/16P	0	0	NA
		Rear			0–1 5/16P	5/8P	3/32	
	Riviera	Front	1 5/16P–3 3/16P	2 5/16P	13/16N–13/16P	0	0	NA
		Rear			0–1 5/16P	5/8P	3/32	
	Seville	Front	1 5/16P–3 5/16P	2 5/16P	13/16N–13/16P	0	0	NA
		Rear			13/32N–3/16	3/32N	3/32	
	Toronado	Front	1 5/16P–3 5/16P	2 5/16P	13/16N–13/16P	0	0	NA
		Rear			13/32N–7/32	3/32N	7/64	
	Trofeo	Front	1 5/16P–3 5/16P	2 5/16P	13/16N–13/16P	0	0	NA
		Rear			13/32N–7/32	3/32N	7/64	

WHEEL ALIGNMENT

Year	Model		Caster Range (deg.)	Caster Preferred Setting (deg.)	Camber Range (deg.)	Camber Preferred Setting (deg.)	Toe-in (in.)	Steering Axis Inclination (deg.)
1990-91	Allante	Front	2P–3P	$2^{1}/_{2}$P	$^{13}/_{16}$N–$^{13}/_{16}$P	0	$^{3}/_{32}$	NA
		Rear			$^{1}/_{2}$N–$^{1}/_{8}$	$^{3}/_{16}$N	$^{3}/_{32}$	
	Eldorado	Front	$1^{5}/_{16}$P–$3^{5}/_{16}$P	$2^{5}/_{16}$P	$^{13}/_{16}$N–$^{13}/_{16}$P	0	0	NA
		Rear			$^{13}/_{32}$N–$^{3}/_{16}$	$^{3}/_{32}$N	$^{3}/_{32}$	
	Reatta	Front	$1^{13}/_{16}$P–$3^{13}/_{16}$P	$2^{13}/_{16}$P	$^{13}/_{16}$N–$^{13}/_{16}$P	0	0	NA
		Rear			0–$1^{5}/_{16}$P	$^{5}/_{8}$P	$^{3}/_{32}$	
	Riviera	Front	$1^{5}/_{16}$P–$3^{3}/_{16}$P	$2^{5}/_{16}$P	$^{13}/_{16}$N–$^{13}/_{16}$P	0	0	NA
		Rear			0–$1^{5}/_{16}$P	$^{5}/_{8}$P	$^{3}/_{32}$	
	Seville	Front	$1^{5}/_{16}$P–$3^{5}/_{16}$P	$2^{5}/_{16}$P	$^{13}/_{16}$N–$^{13}/_{16}$P	0	0	NA
		Rear			$^{13}/_{32}$N–$^{3}/_{16}$	$^{3}/_{32}$N	$^{3}/_{32}$	
	Toronado	Front	$1^{5}/_{16}$P–$3^{5}/_{16}$P	$2^{5}/_{16}$P	$^{13}/_{16}$N–$^{13}/_{16}$P	0	0	NA
		Rear			$^{13}/_{32}$N–$^{7}/_{32}$	$^{3}/_{32}$N	$^{7}/_{64}$	
	Trofeo	Front	$1^{5}/_{16}$P–$3^{5}/_{16}$P	$2^{5}/_{16}$P	$^{13}/_{16}$N–$^{13}/_{16}$P	0	0	NA
		Rear			$^{13}/_{32}$N–$^{7}/_{32}$	$^{3}/_{32}$N	$^{7}/_{64}$	

P Positive
N Negative
① Degrees

ENGINE ELECTRICAL

NOTE: Disconnecting the negative battery cable on some vehicles may interfere with the functions of the on board computer systems and may require the computer to undergo a relearning process, once the negative battery cable is reconnected.

Distributor

The High Energy Ignition (HEI) distributor with Electronic Spark Timing (EST) distributor uses no mechanical or vacuum advance and is easily identified by the absence of a vacuum advance and the presence of a 6 terminal ECM connector.

REMOVAL

1. Disconnect the negative battery cable.
2. Set No. 1 cylinder to TDC of its compression stroke.
3. Remove distributor appearance cover and retainer, if equipped.
4. Remove ignition switch battery feed wire from distributor cap. Remove coil connectors from cap.

NOTE: Do not use a screwdriver to release locking tabs.

5. Remove 4 bolts from distributor cap and move cap off to the side. Note the location of the cap "doghouse" upon removal and reinstall in same position.
6. Remove 6 terminal ECM harness from distributor. Matchmark the rotor-to-housing and the housing-to-engine.
7. Remove distributor clamp nut and hold-down nut. Use special tool J-29791 or equivalent, to remove hold-down nut.
8. Note the position of rotor, then pull distributor up until rotor just stops turning counterclockwise and again note position of rotor. Remove distributor.

INSTALLATION

Timing Not Disturbed

1. Insert the distributor into the engine, making sure the tip of the rotor is aligned with the alignment marks on the distributor housing and the engine.
2. Make sure the oil pump intermediate driveshaft is properly seated in the oil pump.
3. Install the distributor lock but do not tighten.

4. Reconnect the electrical harness connector(s) to the distributor, then, install distributor cap.
5. Start the engine and allow it to reach normal operating temperatures. Check and/or adjust the timing.

Timing Disturbed

1. Remove the No. 1 spark plug and place a finger over the hole. Using a

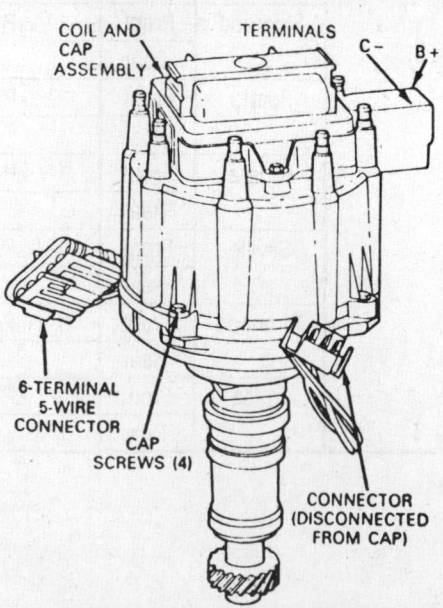

EST distributor with coil-in-cap

wrench on the crankshaft pulley bolt, slowly turn the engine until compression is felt.

2. Align the timing marks so the No. 1 cylinder is on TDC of the compression stroke.

3. Position the distributor in the engine with the rotor at No. 1 firing position. Make sure the oil pump intermediate driveshaft is properly seated in the oil pump.

4. Install the distributor retainer and lock bolt, tighten the lock bolt.

5. Reconnect the electrical harness connector(s) to the distributor and install distributor cap.

6. Start the engine and allow it to reach normal operating temperatures. Check and/or adjust the timing.

Distributorless Ignition

REMOVAL & INSTALLATION

The Computer Controlled Coil Ignition (C³I) system. It uses an ignition coil pack, an ignition module and a dual crankshaft sensor.

Ignition Coil

1. Label and remove spark plug wires.
2. Remove 6 torx screws securing coil to ignition module.
3. Tilt coil assembly back.
4. Remove coil to module connectors.
5. Remove coil assembly.

NOTE: Ensure that the replacement coil pack is identical to the one being removed. The Type I, 3.8L coil pack will physically fit, however, the position of No. 1 coil, as noted on the coil pack, is in a different location No. 1 and 4 on the 3.8L are closest to the module connector.

To install:
6. Install coil assembly and connectors.
7. Install 6 torx screws and torque to 27 inch lbs. (3 Nm).
8. Install spark plug wires.

Ignition Module

1. Remove 14-way connector at ignition module.
2. Remove spark plug wires at coil assembly.
3. Remove nuts and washers (3) securing ignition module assembly to bracket.
4. Remove 6 torx screws securing coil assembly to ignition module.
5. Note lead colors and mark for reassembly.
6. Disconnect connectors between coil and ignition module.

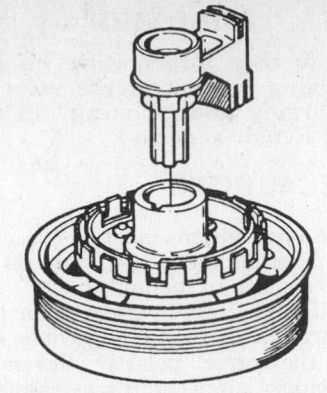
Checking vanes on harmonic balancer

7. Remove ignition module.
To install:
8. Install coil and connectors to ignition module.
9. Install 6 torx screws and torque to 27 inch lbs. (3 Nm).
10. Install nuts and washers securing assembly to bracket.
11. Install plug wires.
12. Connect 14-way connector to module.

Crankshaft Sensor

1. Remove nuts holding vibration dampner support to ignition module bracket and vibration dampner to engine bracket.
2. Remove support.
3. Remove bolts holding bracket to front of engine (2).
4. Remove nut from vibration dampner to engine cradle.
5. Remove vibration dampner and support assembly.
6. Disconnect serpentine belt from crankshaft pulley.
7. Raise and safely support the vehicle.
8. Remove right front tire and wheel assembly.
9. Remove right inner fender access cover.
10. Remove crankshaft harmonic balancer retaining bolt using 28mm socket.
11. Remove crankshaft harmonic balancer.
12. Disconnect sensor electrical connector.
13. Remove sensor and pedestal from block face.
14. Remove sensor from pedestal.
To install:
15. Loosely install crankshaft sensor on pedestal.
16. Position sensor with pedestal attached on special tool J-37089.
17. Position special tool on crankshaft.
18. Install bolts to hold pedestal to

block face. Torque to 14–28 ft. lbs. (20–40 Nm).
19. Torque pedestal pinch bolt to 36–40 ft. lbs. (3.9–4.5 Nm).
20. Remove special tool J-37089.
21. Place special tool J-37089 on harmonic balancer and turn. If any vane of the harmonic balancer touches the tool, replace the balancer assembly.
22. Install balancer on crankshaft.
23. Torque crankshaft bolt to 200–239 ft. lbs. (270–315 Nm).
24. Install inner fender shield.
25. Install tire and wheel assembly and torque to 100 ft. lbs. (140 Nm).

Ignition Timing

ADJUSTMENT

NOTE: Always consult the underhood sticker before adjusting timing. If the underhood sticker differs from the following procedures, follow the sticker.

3.8L Engine

The 3.8L (Code 3 and C) engines are equipped with a C³I ignition system which does not incorporate a distributor. There is no initial timing except replacement of sensors.

4.1L and 4.5L Engines

NOTE: The engine incorporates a magnetic timing probe hole for use with special electronic timing equipment. The following procedure is for use with the HEI−EST distributor.

1. Connect a timing light to the No. 1 spark plug wire according to the light manufacturer's instructions. Do not pierce the spark plug wire to connect the timing light.

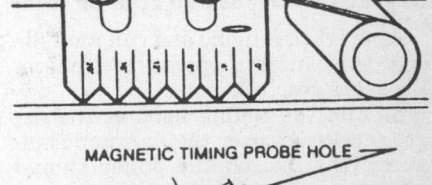

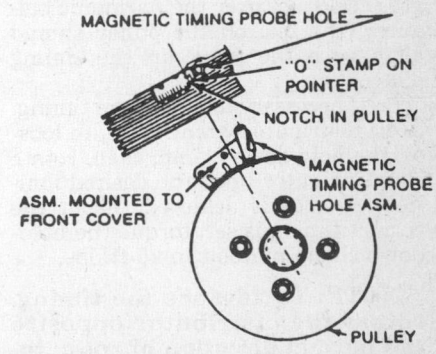
View of the magnetic timing probe holder—4.1L (250 cu. in.) and 4.5L (273 cu. in.) V8 engines

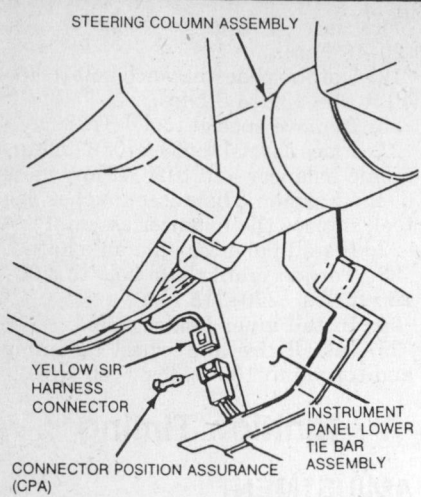

STEERING COLUMN ASSEMBLY

YELLOW SIR HARNESS CONNECTOR

INSTRUMENT PANEL LOWER TIE BAR ASSEMBLY

CONNECTOR POSITION ASSURANCE (CPA)

Yellow 2 way SIR harness connector

2. Set the parking brake and position the transaxle in the **P** position.

NOTE: Do not attempt to time the engine if it is operating on less than the designed number of cylinders, as damage to the catalytic converter may occur.

3. Follow the instructions on the emission control label located in the engine compartment.

NOTE: On the 4.5L engine, connect a jumper wire between pins A (ground) and B of the Assembly Line Data Link (ALDL) connector, located near the parking brake pedal under the dash. By jumping the Assembly Line Data Link (ALDL) connector, the ECM will command the BCM to display a SET TIMING message on the Climate Control Driver Information Panel (CCDIC). The engine will now operate at base timing. The timing can now be checked with a standard timing light at 10 degrees BTDC at 900 rpm or less.

4. Start the engine and run it at idle speed until normal operating temperatures are reached.

5. Aim the timing light at the degree scale just over the harmonic balancer; the line on the pulley should align with the mark on the timing plate.

6. If necessary to adjust the timing, use a distributor wrench tool, to loosen the hold-down clamp, then, rotate the distributor until the desired ignition advance is achieved. When the correct timing is set, torque the hold-down clamp nut/bolt to 20 ft. lbs.

NOTE: To advance the timing, rotate the distributor opposite the normal direction of rotor rotation. Retard the timing by rotating the distributor in the normal direction of rotor rotation.

Alternator

For further information on the charging system, please refer to "Charging and Starting" in the Unit Repair section.

PRECAUTIONS

Several precautions must be observed with alternator equipped vehicles to avoid damage to the unit.

• If the battery is removed for any reason, make sure it is reconnected with the correct polarity. Reversing the battery connections may result in damage to the one-way rectifiers.

• When utilizing a booster battery as a starting aid, always connect the positive to positive terminals and the negative terminal from the booster battery to a good engine ground on the vehicle being started.

• Never use a fast charger as a booster to start vehicles.

• Disconnect the battery cables when charging the battery with a fast charger.

• Never attempt to polarize the alternator.

• Do not use test lamps of more than 12V when checking diode continuity.

• Do not short across or ground any of the alternator terminals.

• The polarity of the battery, alternator and regulator must be matched and considered before making any electrical connections within the system.

• Never separate the alternator on an open circuit. Make sure all connections within the circuit are clean and tight.

• Disconnect the battery ground terminal when performing any service on electrical components.

• Disconnect the battery if arc welding is to be done on the vehicle.

BELT TENSION ADJUSTMENT

All accessories are driven by a single serpentine belt. The tension is maintained automatically by a spring-loaded tensioner. Periodic adjustment is not required.

Belt tension can be checked using a suitable belt tension gauge. The tensioner should maintain approximately 110 lbs. (490 N) of tension throughout its functional travel. If the tension is below specification and the tensioner is resting on the maximum travel stop, replace the serpentine belt.

REMOVAL & INSTALLATION

1. Disconnect the negative battery cable.

2. Label and disconnect the electrical connectors from the back of the alternator.

3. Release the tension from the drive belt and remove the belt from the alternator pulley. Do not remove the belt from any other pulleys.

4. Remove the alternator-to-bracket bolts and the alternator from the vehicle.

To install:

5. Install alternator on vehicle.

6. Reposition drive belt on alternator pulley.

7. Install electrical connectors.

8. Connect negative battery cable.

Voltage Regulator

For further information on the charging system, please refer to "Charging and Starting" in the Unit Repair section.

Starter

For further information on the charging system, please refer to "Charging and Starting" in the Unit Repair section.

REMOVAL & INSTALLATION

1. Disconnect the negative battery cable.

2. Raise and safely support the vehicle.

3. Remove starter motor shield.

4. Remove solenoid wires and battery cables.

5. Remove starter motor mounting bolts and stud.

NOTE: If the starter is mounted using shims, ensure that they are repositioned in their proper location upon installation.

To install:

6. Install starter motor mounting bolts and stud.

7. Connect solenoid wires and battery cable.

8. Install starter motor shield.

9. Lower vehicle.

10. Connect negative battery cable.

CHASSIS ELECTRICAL

— CAUTION —
On vehicles equipped with an air bag, the negative battery cable must be disconnected, before working on the system. Failure to do so may result in deployment of the air bag and possible personal injury.

Heater Blower Motor

REMOVAL & INSTALLATION

1988–89 Reatta and 1987–89 Riviera

1. Disconnect the negative battery cable.
2. Remove the front of cowl shield(s).
3. Disconnect the electrical harness from the blower motor. Remove the harness from the retaining clips and move it aside.
4. Remove the cooling tube from the blower motor.
5. Remove the blower motor screws and the motor from the vehicle.
6. To install, reverse the removal procedures.

1990–91 Reatta and Riviera

1. Disconnect the negative battery cable.
2. Remove cowl cross-tower brace; 2 nuts each side.
3. Remove both cowl relay center bracket nuts and position out of the way.
4. Remove blower motor electrical connector, cooling hose and mounting screws. Tilt blower motor in case and detach fan from motor.
5. Remove blower motor from case.
6. Remove fan from case.
7. To install, reverse the removal procedure.

Allante

1. Disconnect the negative battery cable.
2. Remove the cross tower brace.
3. Partially remove the upper intake manifold by performing the following procedures:
   a. Remove both right rear EGR pipe bolts.
   b. Remove the right rear transaxle dipstick bolt.
   c. Remove the right rear bracket bolt.
   d. Remove the right rear lower intake manifold nuts.
   e. Position the upper intake manifold aside.
4. Remove the electrical harness bracket and disconnect the electrical connector.
5. Remove the cooling hose, the mounting screws and the blower motor.
6. To install, reverse the removal procedures.

Eldorado and Seville

1987

1. Disconnect the negative battery cable.

2. Remove the air cleaner assembly and the cross tower brace.
3. Disconnect the electrical harness support bracket.
4. Label and disconnect the electrical wiring connectors. Remove the cooling hose and mounting screws.
5. Tilt the blower motor in the case and remove the fan from the blower motor.

NOTE: Be careful not to bend the fan upon removal as a fan imbalance could result after reassembly.

6. Remove the blower motor and fan assembly from the vehicle.
7. To install, reverse the removal procedures.

1988–91

1. Disconnect the negative battery cable.
2. Remove the cowl relay center bracket nuts and move the bracket aside.
3. Remove the air cleaner assembly and the cross tower brace.
4. Disconnect the electrical harness support bracket.
5. On 1990–91 vehicles, remove the MAP sensor bracket.
6. Label and disconnect the electrical wiring connectors. Remove the cooling hose and mounting screws.
7. Tilt the blower motor in the case and remove the fan from the blower motor.

NOTE: Be careful not to bend the fan upon removal as a fan imbalance could result after reassembly.

8. Remove the blower motor and fan assembly from the vehicle.
9. To install, reverse the removal procedures.

Toronado and Trofeo

1. Disconnect the negative battery cable.
2. Remove the front of the cowl shield.
3. Remove the bulkhead retaining screw and the bulkhead electrical connector.
4. Remove the Electronic Spark Control (ESC) module electrical connector.
5. Remove the ESC module and bracket assembly.
6. Remove the power steering pump bracket support.
7. Remove the coil bracket nuts. Label and disconnect the electrical connector from the coil.
8. Remove the plug wire guides. Remove the coil/bracket assembly and move it aside. Remove the wiring harness conduit.

9. Remove the blower motor cooling tube.
10. Label and disconnect the electrical connectors from the blower motor. Remove the blower motor mounting screws.
11. Remove the blower motor mounting screws and the blower motor.
To install:
12. Install blower motor fan to blower motor.
13. Install blower motor using strip caulk type sealing material between the motor and heater and air conditioning module.
14. Install blower motor mounting screws (5).
15. Install blower motor cooling tube.
16. Install blower motor electrical connector and wiring harness conduits.
17. Install plug wire guides (2).
18. Install coil electrical connector.
19. Install plug wires to coil (3).
20. Install coil bracket nuts (3).
21. Install power steering pump bracket support and bracket support bolts.
22. Install ESC module and bracket assembly.
23. Install ESC module electrical connector.
24. Install bulkhead connector.
25. Install front of cowl shield.
26. Connect negative battery cable.

Windshield Wiper Motor

REMOVAL & INSTALLATION

1. Disconnect the negative battery cable. Remove both wiper arms.
2. Remove the cowl cover.
3. Remove the wiper arm drive link from the crank arm.
4. Disconnect the electrical connectors.
5. If necessary, remove the air conditioning pipe shroud bracket.
6. Remove the wiper motor-to-chassis bolts and the motor; guide the crank arm through the hole.
7. To install, reverse the removal procedures. Check the wiper motor operation.

Windshield Wiper Switch

REMOVAL & INSTALLATION

1987 Riviera
1987–91 Toronado and Trofeo

1. Disconnect the negative battery cable. Remove the steering wheel.

2. It may be necessary to loosen both column mounting nuts and remove the bracket-to-mast jacket screws. Separate the bracket from the mast jacket to allow the connector clip on the ignition switch to be pulled out of the column assembly.

3. Disconnect the washer/wiper switch lower connector.

4. Remove the screws attaching the column housing to the mast jacket. Be sure to note the position of the dimmer switch actuator rod for reassembly in the same position. Remove the column housing and switch as an assembly.

NOTE: The tilt and travel columns have a removable plastic cover on the column housing. This provides access to the wiper switch without removing the entire column housing.

5. Turn upside down and use a drift to remove the pivot pin from the washer/wiper switch. Remove the switch.

6. Place the switch into position in the housing and install the pivot pin.

7. Position the housing onto the mast jacket and attach by installing the screws. Install the dimmer switch actuator rod in the same position as noted earlier. Check switch operation.

8. Reconnect lower end of switch assembly.

9. Install remaining components in reverse order of removal. Be sure to attach column mounting bracket in original position.

1988–91 Reatta and Riviera
1987–91 Eldorado and Seville

The windshield wiper switch is attached to switch pod, located on the instrument panel to the right side of the steering wheel.

1. Disconnect the negative battery cable.

2. Remove the switch trim panel from the instrument panel.

3. Remove the switch-to-instrument panel screws.

4. Pull the switch outward and disconnect the electrical connectors from the rear of the switch.

5. To install, reverse the removal procedures.

Allante

The windshield wiper switch is attached to switch pod, located on the instrument panel to the right side of the steering wheel.

1. Disconnect the negative battery cable.

2. Remove the bottom instrument panel trim plate.

3. Remove the switch pod-to-instrument panel screws, pull the pod outward and disconnect the electrical con-

nectors. Remove the switch pod from the vehicle.

4. To install, reverse the removal procedures. Check the switch pod operation.

Instrument Cluster

REMOVAL & INSTALLATION

Reatta and Riviera

1. Disconnect the negative battery cable.

2. Remove the center, left and right trim covers.

3. Remove the instrument cluster-to-dash screws, then, pull the cluster straight out of the housing.

4. To install, reverse removal procedures.

Allante

1. Disconnect the negative battery cable.

2. Remove the left and right switch pod trim plates.

3. Remove the cluster trim plate.

4. Remove the cluster assembly-to-dash screws, pull the cluster forward and disconnect the electrical connectors.

5. Remove the cluster assembly from the vehicle.

6. To install, reverse the removal procedures.

Eldorado and Seville

1. Disconnect the negative battery cable. Remove the screws located along the top and remove the instrument panel trim plate.

2. Remove the mounting screws and the filter lens.

3. Remove the warning light lens screws and the lens. Remove the trip odometer reset button.

4. Remove the instrument panel cluster screws. Pull the cluster off the electrical connections and remove it. Using a pair of pliers, hold the retaining tabs at either end of the cluster board and remove the board.

5. To install the cluster, align it with the electrical connectors, push it into the instrument panel and reverse the removal procedures.

Toronado and Trofeo
1987–88

1. Disconnect the negative battery cable.

2. Remove the steering column trim cover. Lower the steering column.

3. Remove the instrument panel trim plate.

4. Remove the cluster-to-instrument panel screws.

5. Pull the cluster rearward and remove it.

6. To install, reverse the removal procedures.

1989–91

1. Disconnect the negative battery cable.

2. Remove instrument panel cluster trim plate.

3. Remove screws retaining cluster to instrument panel.

4. Pull cluster out and disengage electrical connector.

5. To install, reverse the removal procedure.

Radio

REMOVAL & INSTALLATION

1987 Riviera

1. Disconnect the negative battery cable.

2. Remove transaxle selector.

3. Remove transaxle indicator assembly.

4. Remove screws securing console top trim plate (4).

5. Remove console left front floor panel.

6. Remove screws from top of bracket securing radio assembly.

7. Remove bracket, antenna and all electrical connectors to radio assembly.

To install:

8. Connect antenna and all electrical connectors to radio assembly.

9. Install radio assembly in place with bracket secured by screws (2).

10. Install console left hand floor panel.

11. Install screws securing console top trim plate.

12. Install transaxle indicator assembly.

13. Install transaxle selector handle.

14. Connect negative battery cable.

1988–91 Reatta and Riviera

The entertainment system on Reatta and Riviera vehicles consists of a remote radio receiver, an optional tape deck and an Electronic Control Center (ECC) monitor. The entertainment system is controlled by the Electronic Control Center (also known as CRT) through the use of "hard" and "soft" keys.

RADIO RECEIVER

1. Disconnect the negative battery cable.

2. Remove the gear selector handle, transaxle indicator assembly and storage compartment (lift lid) to reveal bolts retaining console assembly.

3. Remove 4 bolts retaining console assembly and remove assembly.

4. Disconnect antenna lead-in and radio harness connector from radio receiver.

5. Remove 2 bolts to radio support assembly top cover and remove radio receiver.

To install:

6. Install radio receiver and 2 bolts to radio support assembly top cover.

7. Connect radio harness connector and antenna lead-in to radio receiver.

8. Install console assembly and 4 retaining bolts.

9. Install storage compartment, transaxle indicator assembly and gear selector handle.

10. Connect negative battery cable.

Allante

The entertainment system on Allante vehicles consists of a remote radio receiver, a remote tape deck and a radio control head, below the Driver Information Center (DIC).

RADIO CONTROL HEAD AND COMBINATION PANEL

1. Disconnect the negative battery cable.

2. Remove pop-out air conditioner vent.

3. Remove 2 screws retaining the combination panel.

4. Remove left side sound insulation panel screws.

5. Remove left side sound insulation panel.

6. Remove 2 nuts and washers, at the back of tape player.

7. Remove combo panel.

8. Remove 3 electrical connectors, depress tabs, push in, then pull to release.

To install:

9. Connect electrical connectors.

10. Align combo panel.

11. Install 2 nuts and washers, at the back of the tape player.

12. Install left side sound insulation panel.

13. Install left side sound insulation panel screws.

14. Install 2 screws retaining combo panel.

15. Insert air conditioning vent.

TAPE PLAYER

1. Disconnect the negative battery cable.

2. Remove radio head/combo panel.

3. Remove 3 tape player retaining bolts, 1 on the side, 2 underneath.

4. Remove 3 bolts, open combo panel door.

5. Depress latch to open cassette door.

6. Release screw cover retaining tabs, access from inside cassette door.

7. Remove screw cover.

8. Remove 3 screws and washers.

9. Remove tape player door.

10. Remove 2 face plate retainer bolts.

11. Pull tape player out as far as it will go.

12. Disconnect 3 electrical connectors.

To install:

13. Install 3 electrical connectors.

14. Depress latch to open cassette door.

15. Slide tape player into place with door open.

16. Install 3 bolts retaining tape player in combo panel.

17. Close combo panel door and install 3 bolts.

18. Align face plate and install 2 bolts.

19. Align cassette door and install 3 screws.

20. Snap on screw cover.

21. Install radio head/combo panel.

22. Connect negative battery cable.

RADIO RECEIVER

1. Disconnect the negative battery cable.

2. Remove glove box assembly.

3. 2 screws and 1 nut and washer retaining the radio receiver.

4. Remove coaxial cable and 3 electrical connectors.

To install:

5. Install 3 electrical connectors and coaxial cable.

6. Install nut, washer and 3 screws retaining radio receiver.

7. Install glove box assembly.

8. Connect negative battery cable.

Eldorado and Seville

1. Disconnect the negative battery cable.

2. Remove radio trim plate.

3. Remove left hand air conditioning vent.

4. Remove 7 screws attaching instrument panel trim plate.

5. Loosen lower 2 mounting nuts under radio; top 2 nuts do not have to be loosened.

6. Slide radio forward and disconnect electrical connectors.

7. Remove antenna lead-in.

To install:

8. Install antenna lead-in to radio.

9. Connect electrical connectors to radio.

10. Slide radio into instrument panel bracket and tighten lower mounting nuts.

11. Install instrument panel trim plate.

12. Install radio trim plate.

13. Install air conditioning vent.

14. Connect negative battery cable.

Toronado and Trofeo

RADIO HEAD

1. Disconnect the negative battery cable.

2. Remove driver's side lower hush panel.

3. Remove knee bolster.

4. Remove instrument panel trim panel.

5. Remove screws retaining radio/ECC bracket.

6. Remove nuts to remove radio bracket from radio.

7. Remove electrical connectors.

To install:

8. Install nuts attaching radio to mounting bracket.

9. Install electrical connections to radio and ECC.

10. Carefully reposition radio and mounting bracket to instrument panel.

NOTE: If the radio buttons operate unusually or intermittently, the condition may be due to poor alignment or uneven tightening of the radio or instrument panel trim panel screws. If this occurs, remove the trim panel, loosen the radio mounting bolts and realign the radio unit.

11. Install trim plate and knee bolster.

12. Install lower hush panel.

13. Connect negative battery cable.

REMOTE RADIO RECEIVER

1. Disconnect the negative battery cable.

2. Open console storage tray and remove CD, cassette holder or phone handset, if equipped.

3. Remove T-15 torx screws and remove storage tray liner.

4. Remove electrical connectors to console seat controls and handset connector, if equipped.

5. Open ashtray and tke out cigar lighter and ashtray bucket.

6. Set emergency brake, place shift lever in **N**.

7. Pull console trim plate up, console trim plate has clip tabs in area to right and left of top edge of shifter plate.

8. Disconnect bulb and cigar lighter electrical connectors and remove console trim plate.

9. The remote chassis will be visible towards the front end of the console.

10. Remove 10mm nuts retaining chassis to CRTC bracket.

11. Remove electrical connectors to remote chassis and coaxial lead-in connector.

12. Remove radio chassis.

To install:

13. Place radio chassis in top of CRTC bracket and install 10mm nuts.

Make certain radio wiring is not trapped under radio receiver chassis.

14. Connect electrical connectors on left side of chassis.

15. Connect electrical connectors on right side of receiver. Best order is: lower white 4-pin, upper white 6-pin, lower black 6-pin and upper blue 4-pin.

16. Connect antenna coaxial lead-in.

17. Connect lower console trim plate over shift lever and reconnect electrical connectors to ashtray.

18. Carefully snap trim plate into place.

19. Return shift lever to park and release emergency brake.

20. Connect electrical connectors to remote chassis and coaxial lead-in connector.

21. Connect electrical connections to console mounted seat controls and connect phone handset connector, if equipped.

22. Connect lower console storage tray liner and fasten T-15 torx screws.

23. Reinsert CD/cassette bucket, handset, cigar lighter and ashtray.

24. Connect negative battery cable.

Concealed Headlights

MANUAL OPERATION
Reatta

1. Open the hood.

2. Turn the manual control knob in the direction of the arrow on the "Headlight Up" label. Turn the knob by hand until it stops.

3. Close the hood and check headlight operation.

Toronado and Trofeo

1. On 1987–88 vehicles, remove fuse No. 2 from engine compartment relay center. On 1989–91 vehicles, disconnect 3-way headlight door actuator connector.

2. Remove protective cover from the knob.

3. Rotate the knob clockwise until the headlight doors open.

4. To close the doors, rotate the knob counterclockwise until the headlight doors close.

5. Install protective cover over knob.

6. On 1987–88 vehicles, install fuse No. 2 in engine compartment relay center. On 1989–91 vehicles, connect 3-way headlamp door actuator connectors.

Headlight Switch

REMOVAL & INSTALLATION
1987–88

The headlight switch is located on a switch pod, located on the left side of the instrument panel.

1. Disconnect the negative battery cable. Remove the instrument panel trim plate.

2. Remove the switch pod screws and pull the switch outward. Disconnect the electrical connectors and remove the switch from the vehicle.

3. To install, reverse the removal procedures. Check the operation of the switch.

1989–91

The headlight switch is located on the left side of the instrument panel.

1. Remove the left trim plate screws and the trim plate, if equipped.

2. Remove the left air vent, if equipped.

3. Remove the headlight switch screws, pull the switch forward and disconnect the electrical connectors or the fiber optic lead, if equipped.

4. Remove the headlight switch.

5. To install, reverse the removal procedures.

Dimmer Switch

The dimmer switch is attached to the lower steering column jacket. It is activated by a rod attached to the turn signal lever.

REMOVAL & INSTALLATION

Toronado and Trofeo

1. Disconnect the negative battery cable.

2. If necessary, remove the lower steering column trim cover.

3. Disconnect the electrical connector from the dimmer switch.

4. Remove the dimmer switch-to-steering column screws and the dimmer switch.

5. To install, position the actuator rod into the dimmer switch hole and reverse the removal procedures. Adjust the dimmer switch by depressing the switch slightly and inserting a $\frac{3}{32}$ in. drill bit into the adjusting hole. Push the switch up to remove any play and tighten the dimmer switch adjusting screw.

Combination Switch

The combination switch is a multi-function switch which consists of the turn signal, headlight beam, cruise control, windshield washer and wiper switches; washer and wiper switches dash-mounted on some models.

CAUTION

Replacing the combination switch necessitates removal of the steering wheel. If equipped with the Supplemental Inflatable Restraint (SIR) system, removing the steering wheel requires temporarily disabling the SIR system and removal of the inflator module. Failure to do so could result in accidental deployment of the air bag and possible personal injury.

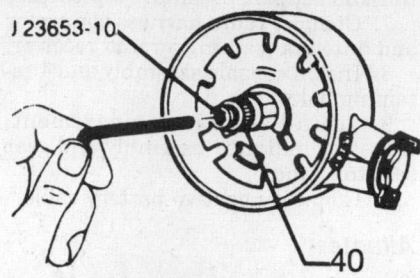

40. Upper steering shaft

Installing the lock plate compressor screw

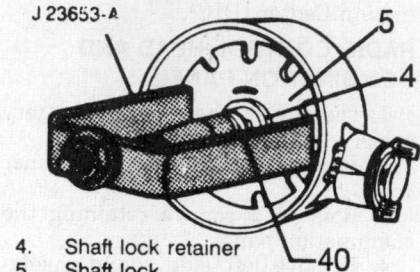

4. Shaft lock retainer
5. Shaft lock
40. Upper steering shaft

Compressing the shaft lock

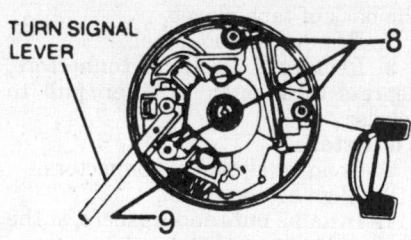

8. Screw
9. Turn signal switch assembly

Positioning the turn signal lever to remove the turn signal switch screws

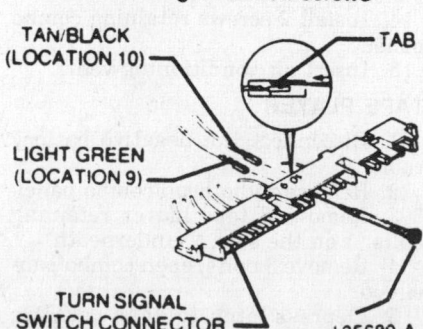

Releasing the buzzer wires from the turn signal switch connector

REMOVAL & INSTALLATION

1987–89

1. Disconnect the negative battery cable. Remove the steering wheel.
2. Remove the bumper and the carrier snapring retainer from the steering shaft.
3. Using the lock plate compressor screw tool, install it in the upper steering shaft, torque it to 40 inch lbs., to keep the shaft from telescoping.
4. Using the lock plate compressor tool, install it on the upper steering shaft, tighten it to depress the shaft lock. Remove the shaft lock retainer, the compressor tool and the steering shaft lock.
5. Remove the turn signal cancelling cam assembly. Place the turn signal switch in the **N** position and remove the upper bearing spring.
6. Position the turn signal switch so the mounting screws can be removed through the holes in the switch and remove the turn signal lever.
7. Remove the turn signal switch-to-steering column screws and lift the turn signal switch. Remove the wire protector and disconnect the turn signal switch connector.
8. Using the terminal remover tool, disconnect the buzzer switch wires from the turn signal switch connector. Using needle-nose pliers, remove the buzzer switch assembly.
9. Place the lock cylinder in the **ACCESSORY** position, remove the lock retaining screw and the lock cylinder set.
10. Lifting the turn signal switch assembly, gently pull the wires through the steering column shroud.

To install:

11. Install turn signal connector through lock housing cover and steering column housing shroud.
12. Install steering column lock cylinder set while in **ACCESSORY** position.
13. Install lock retaining screw and torque to 22 inch lbs. (2.5 Nm).
14. Install buzzer switch by pushing switch down into its retaining bore until bottomed with plastic tab covering lock retaining screw.
15. Install buzzer switch wires to turn signal switch connector: light green wire to location 9, tan/black wire to location 10.

NOTE: Wire terminal retainer must be removed and discarded from service buzzer switch wire.

16. Install wire connector retainer.
17. Install turn signal switch connector.
18. Install wire protector and turn signal switch. Install screws and torque to 59 inch lbs. (6.8 Nm).

NOTE: Position turn signal switch so screws can be installed through openings in switch.

19. Install turn signal lever. Tighten screw to 53 inch lbs. (6 Nm).
20. Place turn signal switch in **OFF** position. Install upper bearing spring.
21. Install turn signal cancel cam assembly.
22. Install steering shaft lock.
23. Install shaft lock retainer to upper steering shaft using special tool J–23653–A to slightly depress shaft lock.
24. Install carrier snapring retainer. Install steering shaft bumper.
25. Extend shaft and lock in place. Install steering wheel and jam nut. Torque to 30 ft. lbs. (41 Nm).
26. Remove lock plate compression screw J–23653–10.

1990–91

1. Disconnect the negative battery cable.
2. Place the ignition switch in the **LOCK** position to prevent uncentering of the coil assembly ring.
3. Disable the SIR system and remove the inflator module (air bag), if equipped.
4. Remove the steering wheel.
5. Remove coil assembly retaining ring.
6. Remove coil assembly from shaft end, allowing coil to hang freely.

NOTE: Coil assembly will become uncentered if the steering column is separated from steering gear and is allowed to rotate or if the centering spring is depressed, allowing hub to rotate while coil is removed from column.

7. Remove wave washer.
8. Remove shaft lock retaining ring using special tool J-23653–C to depress shaft lock.
9. Remove shaft lock.
10. Remove turn signal cancelling cam assembly.
11. Remove upper bearing spring, inner race seat and inner race.
12. Remove multi-function lever by performing the following:
   a. Ensure that the switch is in the **OFF** position before access cover from steering wheel.
   b. Remove cruise control connector from lever. Note position of connector when installed in column.
   c. Pull lever straight out of switch.
13. Remove screws and signal switch arm.
14. Remove turn signal switch screws.
15. Remove screw from end of hazard knob assembly. Remove button spring and knob from switch cavity.
16. Remove turn signal switch assembly and allow to hang freely.
17. Remove wiring protector at base of steering column.
18. Disconnect wiring harness at the base of the steering column.
19. Gently pull wire harness through instrument panel bracket and column housing.

To install:

20. Route wiring assembly for new switch through column housing and instrument panel bracket.
21. Connect wiring assembly to connector at base of the steering column.
22. Connect coil assembly wire harness through column housing and in-

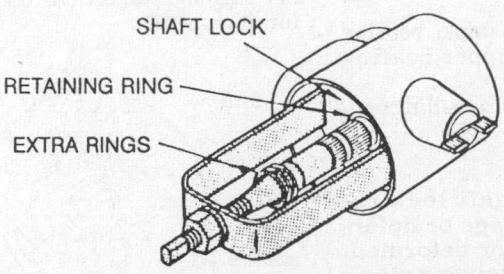

Removing shaft lock retaining ring

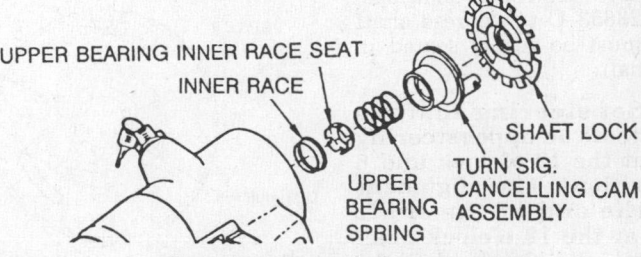

Removing upper shaft components

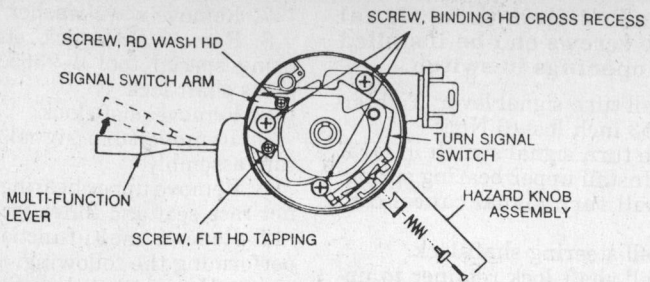

SCREW, RD WASH HD

SIGNAL SWITCH ARM

SCREW, BINDING HD CROSS RECESS

TURN SIGNAL SWITCH

MULTI-FUNCTION LEVER

HAZARD KNOB ASSEMBLY

SCREW, FLT HD TAPPING

Turn signal switch installed

strument panel bracket. Allow coil to hang freely.

23. Install turn signal switch assembly and screws. Tighten to 30 inch lbs. (3.4 Nm).

24. Install wiring protector.

25. Install signal switch arm and screws. Tighten to 20.4 inch lbs. (2.3 Nm).

26. Install hazard knob, spring and button to hazard warning switch cavity. Install switch screw; drive in fully. Do not strip.

27. Install multi-function lever by performing the following:

NOTE: Ensure that the switch is in the OFF position before installation.

a. Install lever electrical connectors.

b. With "WASH" paddle loose on the metal shaft, align shaft with the switch notch and insert shaft only.

c. Rotate "WASH" paddle into position and push into switch.

d. Push on the knob to seat lever into switch.

e. Install cruise control connector.

f. Install access cover onto steering column.

28. Install inner race, upper bearing inner race seat and upper bearing spring.

29. Install turn signal cancelling cam assembly.

30. Install shaft lock.

NOTE: Inspect shaft lock retaining ring for damage or deformation. If damaged or deformed, replace with new retaining ring.

31. Install shaft lock retaining ring. Align to block tooth on shaft using special tool J-23653-C to depress shaft lock. Ring must be firmly seated in groove on shaft.

NOTE: Set steering shaft so that block teeth on upper steering shaft are at the 12 o'clock and 6 o'clock positions. The alignment mark at the end of the shaft should be at the 12 o'clock position and vehicle wheels straight

ahead. Set the ignition switch to the LOCK position to ensure no damage occurs to the coil assembly.

32. Ensure coil assembly hub is centered by performing the following:

a. Hold coil assembly with clear bottom up to see coil ribbon.

b. There are 2 styles of coils. One rotates clockwise and the other rotates counterclockwise. While holding coil assembly, depress spring lock to rotate hub in direction of arrow until it stops.

c. The coil ribbon should be wound up snug against the center hub.

d. Rotate coil hub in opposite direction approximately 2½ turns. Release spring lock between locking tabs in front of arrow.

NOTE: If a new coil assembly is being installed, assemble the pre-centered coil assembly to column. Remove centering tab and dispose.

33. Install wave washer.

34. Install coil assembly using horn tower on cancelling cam assembly inner ring and projections on outer ring for alignment.

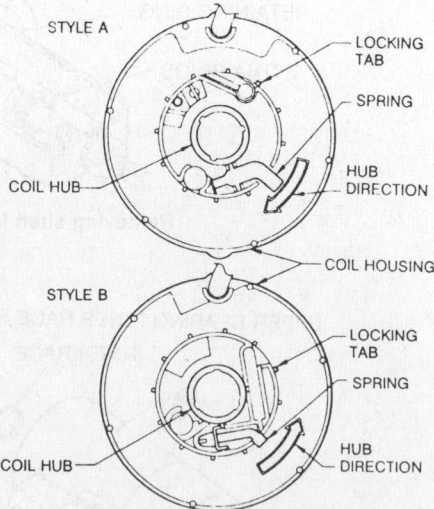

STYLE A

LOCKING TAB

SPRING

COIL HUB

HUB DIRECTION

COIL HOUSING

STYLE B

LOCKING TAB

SPRING

COIL HUB

HUB DIRECTION

Removing pass key lock cylinder set

35. Install coil assembly retaining ring. Ring must be firmly seated in groove on shaft.

NOTE: Gently pull lower coil assembly wire to remove any wire kinks that may be inside column assembly.

36. Install steering wheel.

37. Install inflator module and enable SIR system.

Ignition Lock
CAUTION

Replacing the ignition lock assembly necessitates removal of the steering wheel. If equipped with the Supplemental Inflatable Restraint (SIR) system, removing the steering wheel requires temporarily disabling the SIR system and removal of the inflator module. Failure to do so could result in accidental deployment of the air bag and possible personal injury.

REMOVAL & INSTALLATION

1987–89

1. Disconnect the negative battery cable. Remove the steering wheel.

2. Remove the bumper and the carrier snapring retainer from the steering shaft.

3. Using the lock plate compressor screw tool, install it in the upper steering shaft, torque it to 40 inch lbs., to keep the shaft from telescoping.

4. Using the lock plate compressor tool, install it on the upper steering shaft, tighten it to depress the shaft lock. Remove the shaft lock retainer, the compressor tool and the steering shaft lock.

5. Remove the turn signal cancelling cam assembly. Place the turn signal switch in the **N** position and remove the upper bearing spring.

6. Position the turn signal switch so the mounting screws can be removed through the holes in the switch and remove the turn signal lever.

7. Remove the turn signal switch-to-steering column screws and lift the

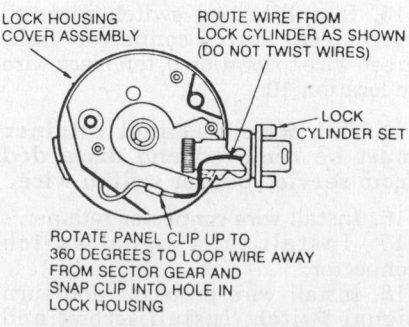

LOCK HOUSING COVER ASSEMBLY

ROUTE WIRE FROM LOCK CYLINDER AS SHOWN (DO NOT TWIST WIRES)

LOCK CYLINDER SET

ROTATE PANEL CLIP UP TO 360 DEGREES TO LOOP WIRE AWAY FROM SECTOR GEAR AND SNAP CLIP INTO HOLE IN LOCK HOUSING

Routing pass key wire harness

turn signal switch. Remove the wire protector and disconnect the turn signal switch connector.

8. Using the terminal remover tool, disconnect the buzzer switch wires from the turn signal switch connector. Using needle-nose pliers, remove the buzzer switch assembly.

9. Place the lock cylinder in the **ACC** position, remove the lock retaining screw and the lock cylinder set.

To install:

10. Reverse the removal procedures. Torque the lock retaining screw to 22 inch lbs., the turn signal switch screws to 59 inch lbs. and the turn signal lever screw to 53 inch lbs.

11. Check the operation of the switches and the steering column.

1990–91

1. Disconnect the negative battery cable.

2. Place the ignition switch in the **LOCK** position to prevent uncentering of the coil assembly ring.

3. Disable the SIR system and remove the inflator module (air bag), if equipped.

4. Remove the steering wheel.

5. Remove the combination switch assembly and allow to hang freely. Do not remove wiring harness and connector from steering column.

6. Remove key from pass key lock cylinder set.

7. Disconnect buzzer switch assembly.

8. Reinsert key in pass key lock cylinder. Turn key to **LOCK** position.

9. Remove lock retaining screw.

10. Disconnect pass key lock cylinder terminal connector.

11. Remove wiring protector.

12. Attach a length of mechanics wire to terminal connector to aid in reassembly.

13. Gently pull wire through instrument panel bracket and column housing.

14. Remove pass key lock cylinder.

To install:

NOTE: Route wire from lock cylinder through steering column using mechanics wire. Rotate panel clip 360 degrees and snap clip into hole in housing. Failure to do so may result in component damage or malfunction of pass key lock cylinder.

15. Install pass key lock cylinder.

16. Gently pull lower lock cylinder wire to remove any wire kinks that may be inside column assembly.

17. Install lock retaining screw. Tighten to 22 inch lbs. (2.5 Nm).

18. Turn key to **RUN** position.

19. Install buzzer switch assembly.

20. Install combination switch.

21. Install inflator module. Enable SIR system.

22. Install steering wheel.

23. Connect negative battery cable.

Ignition Switch

REMOVAL & INSTALLATION

1987–88

1. Disconnect the negative battery cable.

2. Place the ignition switch on the **OFF/UNLOCKED** or **ACC** (tilt wheel).

3. Remove top pan cover, if equipped, and loosen the toe clamp bolts.

4. Remove lower instrument panel trim retaining screws. Remove the panel in order to gain working clearance.

5. Remove the automatic transaxle shift indicator needle.

6. Remove the steering column instrument panel bracket and allow the steering wheel to rest on the driver's seat.

7. Remove the dimmer switch retaining screws and the switch.

8. Remove the ignition switch attaching screws and lift the switch from the actuator rod.

9. Label and disconnect the electrical connector(s) from the ignition switch.

10. Before installation, place the slider on the new switch in one of the following positions, depending on the steering column and accessories:

    a. Standard column with key release—extreme left detent.

    b. Standard column with park lock—1 detent from extreme left **OFF/LOCK** position.

    c. All other standard columns—2 detents from extreme left **OFF/UNLOCK** position.

    d. Adjustable column with key release—extreme right detent.

    e. Adjustable column with park lock—1 detent from extreme right **OFF/LOCK** position.

    f. All other adjustable columns—2 detents from extreme right **OFF/UNLOCK** position.

11. Connect the electrical connector(s) to the switch.

12. Position the switch on actuator rod, then, install the ignition switch-to-steering column screws.

13. To complete the installation, reverse the removal procedures.

1989–91

The ignition switch is hard-wired. The wiring harness with the column harness connector must be replaced with the ignition switch. Do not splice the new switch to the existing column wiring harness.

1. Disconnect the negative battery cable.

2. Remove the lower left sound insulator and the instrument panel steering column cover.

3. Remove the ignition switch wire protector and the switch-to-column screws.

4. Remove the ignition and turn signal switch column harness connectors from the dash connector.

5. Disconnect the turn signal harness connector from the column harness connector.

6. Remove the steering column bolts and nuts and gently lower steering column to the seat.

7. Remove the ignition switch assembly with the switch, harness and connector.

8. To install, reverse the removal procedures.

Stoplight Switch

ADJUSTMENT

NOTE: When the brake pedal is in the fully released position, the stoplight switch plunger should be fully depressed against the pedal arm. The switch is adjusted by moving it in or out.

1. Remove the stoplight switch from the brake pedal bracket.

2. Insert the switch into the retainer until the switch body seats on the tube clip.

3. Pull the brake pedal rearward against the internal pedal stop.

NOTE: The switch will be moved in the retainer resulting in proper adjustment.

4. When no further adjustment clicks are heard and the stoplights remain **OFF**, the stoplight switch will be properly seated.

REMOVAL & INSTALLATION

1. Disconnect the negative battery cable. Remove the underdash hush panel, if equipped.

2. Locate the stoplight switch on the brake pedal bracket.

3. Remove the tubular retaining clip.

4. Remove the stoplight switch electrical connectors.

5. Remove the switch assembly from the vehicle.

6. To install, reverse the removal procedures and perform the adjustment procedures.

Neutral Safety Switch

ADJUSTMENT

1. Place transaxle shift lever in **N**.
2. Loosen switch attaching screws.
3. Rotate switch on shifter assembly to align hole with carrier tang hole.
4. Insert $^3/_{32}$ in. (2.34mm) max. diameter gauge pin or drill bit to a depth of $^{15}/_{32}$ in. (12mm).
5. Tighten 2 attaching screws to 20 ft. lbs. (27 Nm).
6. Remove gauge pin.
7. Ensure that engine will start only in **P** and **N** positions. If engine will start in any other position, readjust switch.

REMOVAL & INSTALLATION

All neutral safety/back-up light switches come with a small plastic alignment pin installed. Leave this pin in place.

1. Place the shifter assembly in the **N** position.
2. Remove the shifter lever-to-switch nut and the lever.
3. Disconnect the electrical connector from the neutral safety/back-up light switch.
4. Remove the neutral safety/back-up light switch-to-transaxle bolts and the switch from the vehicle.

To install:

5. Position the shifter shaft in the **N** position.

NOTE: If using an old switch or the plastic pin (new switch) is broken, install a $^3/_{32}$ in. pin gauge (drill bit) into the neutral safety/back-up light switch; the switch is locked into its neutral position.

6. Align the flats of the shifter shaft and the neutral safety/back-up light, then, align the switch-to-tang on the transaxle. Torque the switch-to-transaxle bolts to 22 ft. lbs. Remove the pin gauge.
7. To complete installation, reverse the removal procedures. Make sure the engine starts only in the **P** and **N** positions.

Fuses, Circuit Breakers and Relays

LOCATION

Fuse Panels

1987

Riviera—behind center of instrument panel, front of console

Allante—center console, under ash tray

Eldorado and Seville—glove box

Toronado and Trofeo—right side of instrument panel

1988

Riviera and Reatta—behind center of instrument panel, front of console

Allante—center console, under ash tray

Eldorado and Seville—glove box

Toronado and Trofeo—right side of instrument panel

1989

Riviera and Reatta—Front right side of console

Allante—center console, under ash tray

Eldorado and Seville—glove box

Toronado and Trofeo—right side of instrument panel

1990

Riviera and Reatta—front left side of console

Allante—center console, under ash tray

Eldorado and Seville—glove box

Toronado and Trofeo—right side of instrument panel

1991

Riviera and Reatta—front left side of console

Allante—center console, under ash tray

Eldorado and Seville—glove box

Toronado and Trofeo—right side of instrument panel

Circuit Breakers

A circuit breaker is an electrical switch which breaks the circuit during an electrical overload. Some circuit breakers are designed to automatically reset after a specified period of time. Others must be manually reset after the electrical malfunction causing the overload has been corrected.

The majority of circuit breakers can be found in the fuse panel. Some, however, are installed in-line near the device they are intended to protect.

Relays

Relays are generally mounted in the vicinity of the device(s) they are intended to control. On the vehicles listed below, there is an Interior Relay Center (IRC).

Riviera and Reatta—below center of instrument panel, right front of console

Eldorado and Seville—behind right side of instrument panel, below glove box

Toronado and Trofeo—behind right side of instrument panel, behind instrument panel compartment

Computers

LOCATION

Electronic Control Module

Riviera and Reatta (1987–88)—behind instrument panel on right shroud

Riviera and Reatta (1989–91)—behind right side of instrument panel, left of heater and air conditioning programmer

Allante (1987–91)—behind right side of instrument panel, near shroud

Eldorado and Seville (1987–91)—behind right side of instrument panel

Toronado and Trofeo (1987–88)—behind instrument panel on right shroud

Toronado and Trofeo (1989–91)—behind right side of instrument panel, left of heater and air conditioner programmer

Body Computer Module

Riviera and Reatta (1987–88)—behind right side of instrument panel

Riviera and Reatta (1989–91)—behind upper right side of instrument panel, behind glove box

Allante (1987–91)—behind center of instrument panel

Eldorado and Seville (1987–91)—behind instrument panel, behind glove box

Toronado and Trofeo (1987–88)—behind right side of instrument panel, behind instrument panel compartment

Toronado and Trofeo (1989–91)—behind instrument panel, above and right of fuse panel

Turn Signal/Hazard Flashers

LOCATION

Reatta and Riviera (1987)—behind instrument panel, left of steering column

Riviera and Reatta (1988)—behind instrument panel, right of steering column

Riviera and Reatta (1989)—front center of console, beside fuse panel

Riviera and Reatta (1990–91)—right side of steering column

Allante—the turn signals and hazard warning lights are controlled by the Body Computer Module (BCM). Therefore, individual turn signal and hazard flasher units are not used

Eldorado and Seville (1987)—behind left side of instrument panel, near steering column

Eldorado and Seville (1988)—center of console

Eldorado and Seville (1989–91)—behind center of instrument panel, below radio

Toronado and Trofeo (1987–91)—behind instrument panel, right side of steering column support

Cruise Control

ADJUSTMENT

Except Allante, Eldorado and Seville

With the engine off, adjust the cable or rod length to obtain the minimum slack.

Allante, Eldorado and Seville

1. With the engine off, ensure that

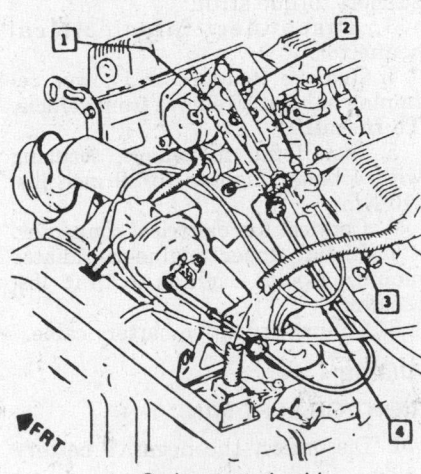

1. Cruise control cable
2. Throttle cable
3. Engine harness
4. Throttle valve cable

Adjusting cruise control cable—Reatta, Riviera, Toronado and Trofeo

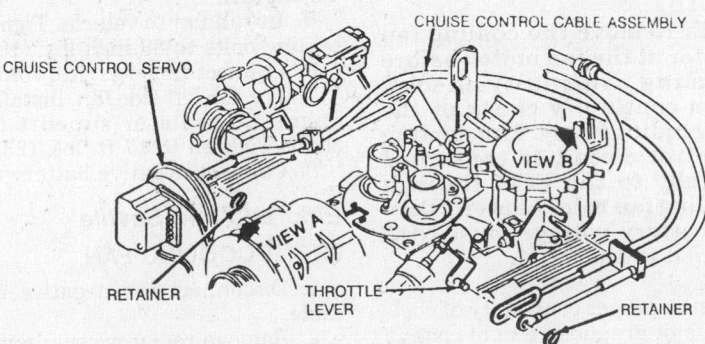

Adjusting cruise control cable—Allante, Eldorado and Seville

the idle speed motor has retracted until the throttle body lever contacts the minimum throttle angle adjusting screw.

2. Select the servo blade hole that will result in minimum cable slack.

ENGINE COOLING

Radiator

REMOVAL & INSTALLATION

1987 Riviera

1. Disconnect the negative battery cable.

2. Drain engine coolant.

3. Remove engine forward strut brace at radiator and swing strut rearward.

NOTE: To prevent shearing of rubber bushing, loosen bolt before swinging strut.

4. Remove forward lamp harness from fan frame and unplug fan connector.

5. Remove fan attaching bolts. Remove fan and frame assembly.

6. Remove hood latch from radiator support.

NOTE: Scribe latch location before removal.

7. Remove coolant hoses from radiator and coolant recovery tank hose from radiator neck.

8. Remove transaxle oil cooler lines from radiator, if applicable.

9. Remove radiator-to-radiator support attaching bolts and clamps.

10. Remove radiator from vehicle.
To install:
11. If new radiator, transfer fittings from old radiator to new radiator.

12. Install radiator in vehicle, locating bottom of radiator in lower mounting pads.

13. Install radiator-to-radiator support attaching clamp and bolts. Torque to 7 inch lbs. (10 Nm).

14. Connect transaxle oil cooler lines. Torque nuts to 6 ft. lbs. (27 Nm), if applicable.

15. Connect coolant hoses to radiator. Torque clamps to 15 inch lbs. (2 Nm).

16. Connect coolant recovery hose to radiator neck.

17. Install hood latch to radiator support. Torque bolts to 6 ft. lbs. (25 Nm).

18. Install fan assembly making sure bottom leg of frame fits into rubber grommet at lower radiator support.

19. Install fan attaching bolts; torque to 85 inch lbs. (10 Nm).

20. Install fan connector and forward lamp harness to fan frame.

21. Swing engine forward strut and brace forward until brace contacts radiator support. Install brace to radiator support attaching bolts and torque to 11 ft. lbs. (50 Nm).

NOTE: Ensure engine ground strap is reconnected to strut brace.

22. Fill engine with coolant.
23. Connect negative battery cable.
24. Start engine and check for leaks. Check transaxle fluid level and add, as necessary. Allow engine to come to normal operating temperature and check again for leaks.

1988–91 Reatta and Riviera

1. Disconnect the negative battery cable.

2. Drain coolant from radiator.

3. Remove plastic radiator support cover.

4. Remove engine-to-radiator torque strut.

5. Remove rear cooling fan.

6. Remove coolant reservoir hose at filler neck.

7. Remove upper and lower radiator hoses from radiator.

8. Remove transaxle oil cooler lines at radiator.

9. Remove radiator top support, 3 remaining bolts with torque strut removed.

10. Remove radiator from vehicle; lift radiator straight up and out.
To install:
11. Install radiator in vehicle.
12. Install radiator top support, securing with 3 retaining bolts. Tighten to 18 ft. lbs. (25 Nm).
13. Connect oil cooler lines at radiator. Tighten to 20 ft. lbs. (27 Nm).
14. Install upper and lower radiator hoses to radiator, securing hose clamps.

15. Connect reservoir hose at filler neck, securing hose clamp.

16. Install rear cooling fan.

17. Install engine-to-radiator torque strut and 2 remaining strut/radiator support retaining bolts. Tighten radiator support retaining bolts to 18 ft. lbs. (25 Nm).

18. Install plastic radiator support cover.

19. Fill radiator with coolant.

20. Connect negative battery cable.

21. Start engine and check for leaks. Check transaxle fluid level and add, as necessary. Allow engine to come to normal operating temperature and check again for leaks.

Allante, Eldorado and Seville

1. Disconnect the negative battery cable.

2. Drain cooling system.

3. Remove right and left cooling fans. On Eldorado and Seville remove rear cooling fan.

4. Disconnect coolant reservoir hose at filler neck.

5. Remove upper and lower radiator hoses from radiator.

6. Remove engine oil cooler lines from left radiator end tank.

7. Remove transaxle oil cooler lines from right radiator end tank.

8. Remove radiator top support.

9. Remove radiator from car, lifting radiator straight up and out.

To install:

10. Install radiator in vehicle.

11. Install radiator top support. Tighten radiator support retaining bolts to 18 ft. lbs. (25 Nm).

12. Connect transaxle oil cooler lines at radiator. Tighten to 20 ft. lbs. (27 Nm).

13. Connect oil cooler lines at radiator. Tighten to 13 ft. lbs. (18 Nm).

14. Install upper and lower radiator hoses to radiator securing hose clamps.

15. Connect coolant reservoir hose at filler neck.

16. Install cooling fan(s).

17. Fill cooling system.

18. Connect negative battery cable.

19. Start engine and check for leaks. Check transaxle fluid level and add, as necessary. Allow engine to come to normal operating temperature and check again for leaks.

Toronado and Trofeo

1. Disconnect the negative battery cable.

2. Drain cooling system.

3. Remove plastic radiator support cover.

4. Remove engine-to-radiator torque strut.

5. Remove rear cooling fan.

6. Remove upper air cleaner duct and/or silencer, as necessary.

7. Remove coolant reservoir hose at filler neck.

8. Remove upper and lower radiator hoses from radiator.

9. Remove transaxle oil cooler lines.

10. Remove radiator top support, 3 remaining bolts with torque strut removed.

11. Remove radiator from vehicle, lifting straight up and out.

To install:

12. Install radiator in vehicle.

13. Install radiator top support, securing with 3 retaining bolts.

14. Connect transaxle oil cooler lines at radiator. Tighten to 20 ft. lbs. (27 Nm).

15. Connect upper and lower radiator hoses to radiator, securing with clamps.

16. Connect coolant reservoir hose at filler neck, securing with hose clamp.

17. Install rear cooling fan.

18. Install upper air cleaner duct and/or silencer, if removed.

19. Install engine-to-radiator torque strut and 2 remaining strut/radiator support retaining bolts. Tighten to 18 ft. lbs. (25 Nm).

20. Install plastic radiator support cover.

21. Fill cooling system.

22. Connect negative battery cable.

23. Start engine and check for leaks. Check transaxle fluid level and add, as necessary. Allow engine to come to normal operating temperature and check again for leaks.

Electric Cooling Fan

TESTING

1. Check fuse or circuit breaker for power to cooling fan motor.

2. Remove connector(s) at cooling fan motor(s). Connect jumper wire and apply battery voltage to the positive terminal of the cooling fan motor.

3. Using and ohmmeter, check for continuity in cooling fan motor.

NOTE: Remove the cooling fan connector at the fan motor before performing continuity checks. Perform continuity check of the motor windings only. The cooling fan control circuit is connected electrically to the ECM through the cooling fan relay center. Ohmmeter battery voltage must NOT be applied to the ECM.

4. Ensure proper continuity of cooling fan motor ground circuit at chassis ground connector.

REMOVAL & INSTALLATION

Reatta and Riviera

FRONT COOLING FAN

1. Disconnect the negative battery cable.

2. Remove plastic radiator cover.

3. Remove front fan guard cover; 4 clips for Riviera. Remove front grill on Reatta.

4. Disconnect fan electrical connector.

5. Remove front cooling fan from vehicle (3 bolts).

To install:

6. Install front fan, securing with 3 bolts. Tighten to 89 inch lbs. (10 Nm).

7. Connect electrical fan connector.

8. Install front fan guard cover; 4 clips for Riviera. Install front grille on Reatta.

9. Install plastic radiator cover.

10. Connect negative battery cable.

REAR COOLING FAN

1. Disconnect the negative battery cable.

2. Remove upper engine-to-radiator support torque strut.

3. Disconnect fan electrical connector.

4. Remove 2 upper and lower retaining bolts and remove from vehicle.

To install:

5. Install fan to vehicle, securing with 4 bolts. Tighten to 89 inch lbs. (10 Nm).

6. Connect fan electrical connector.

7. Install upper engine-to-radiator mounting bolts. Tighten to 18 ft. lbs. (25 Nm).

8. Connect negative battery cable.

Allante

RIGHT OR LEFT FAN

1. Disconnect the negative battery cable.

2. Disconnect fan electrical connector.

3. For the left side fan, remove upper engine-to-radiator support torque strut; 4 bolts from radiator support.

4. Remove fan retaining bolts and remove fan from vehicle.

To install:

5. Install fan to vehicle. Tighten retaining bolts to 88 inch lbs. (10 Nm).

6. Connect fan electrical connector.

7. For the left side fan, install upper engine-to-radiator support torque strut. Tighten to 17 ft. lbs. (23 Nm).

8. Connect negative battery cable.

Eldorado and Seville

FRONT COOLING FAN

1. Disconnect the negative battery cable.

2. Remove radiator cover panel.

3. Remove electrical connector.

4. Remove fan control module and bracket (1987–89). Remove right headlight bracket (1990–91).

5. Remove front grill (1987–89).

6. Remove fan retaining bolts and remove fan from vehicle.

To install:

7. Install fan to vehicle. Tighten to 97 inch lbs. (11 Nm).

8. Connect electrical connector.

9. Install fan control module and bracket (1987–89). Install right headlight (1990–91).

10. Install front grill (1987–89).

11. Install radiator cover panel.

12. Connect negative battery cable.

REAR COOLING FAN

1. Disconnect the negative battery cable.

2. Disconnect fan electrical connector.

3. On 1987–89 vehicles, remove air cleaner duct and air conditioning hose bracket.

4. On 1990–91 vehicles, remove upper engine-to-radiator support torque strut and oil cooler line bracket from fan.

5. Remove fan retaining bolts and remove fan from vehicle.

To install:

6. Install fan in vehicle. Tighten bolts to 97 inch lbs. (11 Nm).

7. Connect electrical connector.

8. On 1987–89 vehicles, connect air cleaner duct and air conditioning hose bracket.

9. On 1990–91 vehicles, connect upper engine-to-radiator support torque strut and oil cooler line bracket to fan. Tighten torque strut-to-radiator mounting bolts to 17 ft. lbs. (23 Nm).

10. Connect negative battery cable.

Toronado and Trofeo

FRONT COOLING FAN

1. Disconnect the negative battery cable.

2. Remove plastic radiator cover.

3. Remove front grill.

4. Remove electrical connector.

5. Remove fan retaining bolts and remove fan from vehicle.

To install:

6. Install fan in vehicle. Tighten bolts to 89 inch lbs. (10 Nm).

7. Connect electrical connector.

8. Install front grill.

9. Install plastic radiator cover.

10. Connect negative battery cable.

Heater Core

REMOVAL & INSTALLATION

Reatta and Riviera

1987–89

1. Disconnect the negative battery cable.

2. Drain the cooling system.

3. Remove console and instrument panel, as required.

4. Disconnect the hoses from the heater core.

5. Remove the right side sound insulator and courtesy lamp.

6. Remove the glove box.

7. Disconnect the air conditioning programmer the electrical and vacuum connectors. Remove the air conditioning programmer screws and the programmer.

8. Disconnect the ECM electrical connectors. Remove the ECM and bracket.

9. Disconnect the BCM electrical connectors. Remove the BCM and bracket.

10. Remove the heater core cover screws, the cover, the retaining clip, the heater core screws and the heater core.

To install:

11. Install heater core cover screws, the cover, the retaining clip, heater core screws and heater core.

12. Install BCM bracket and connect BCM electrical connectors.

13. Install ECM bracket and connect ECM electrical connectors.

14. Install air conditioner programmer and connect air conditioning programmer electrical and vacuum connectors.

15. Install glove box.

16. Install right side sound insulator and courtesy lamp.

17. Connect the heater core hoses.

18. Connect negative battery cable.

19. Fill cooling system.

20. Start engine and check for coolant leaks. Allow engine to come to normal operating temperature. Recheck for coolant leaks.

1990–91

1. Disconnect the negative battery cable.

2. Drain the cooling system.

3. Remove console and instrument panel.

4. Remove programmer and electrical connectors.

5. Remove electrical connections from BCM. Remove BCM and mounting bracket.

6. Remove electrical connections from ECM. Remove ECM and mounting bracket.

7. Remove heater core from housing.

8. Disconnect inlet and outlet heater hoses from heater core.

9. Remove 2 heater retaining screws.

10. Remove heater core from vehicle.

To install:

11. Install heater core to heater case, securing with 2 screws.

12. Connect inlet and outlet heater hoses to heater core.

13. Install heater core cover.

14. Install ECM mounting bracket, ECM and electrical connectors.

15. Install BCM mounting bracket, BCM and electrical connectors.

16. Install programmer and electrical connections.

17. Install instrument panel and console.

18. Connect negative battery cable.

19. Fill cooling system.

20. Start engine and check for coolant leaks. Allow engine to come to normal operating temperature. Recheck for coolant leaks.

Allante

1. Disconnect the negative battery cable.

2. Drain the cooling system to a level below the heater core.

3. Remove the glove box screws. Label and disconnect the electrical connectors from the glove box.

4. Remove the glove box assembly from the vehicle.

5. Remove the lower sound insulator to gain working clearance.

6. Remove the radio.

7. Remove the air conditioning programmer, the Electronic Control Module (ECM) screws and the ECM.

8. Remove the module assembly heater core cover. Disconnect the hoses from the heater core.

9. Remove the heater core screws and the heater core.

To install:

10. Install heater core in vehicle.

11. Install module assembly heater core cover. Connect hoses to the heater core.

12. Install ECM bracket, ECM and electrical connectors.

13. Install air conditioning programmer.

14. Install radio and lower sound insulator.

15. Install glove box assembly and glove box electrical connectors.

16. Fill cooling system.

17. Start engine and check for coolant leaks. Allow engine to come to normal operating temperature. Recheck for coolant leaks.

Eldorado and Seville

1. Disconnect the negative battery cable.

2. Drain the cooling system to a level below the heater core.

3. Remove the glove box screws. Label and disconnect the electrical connectors from the glove box.

4. Remove the glove box assembly from the vehicle.

5. Remove the lower sound insulator to gain working clearance.

6. Remove the air conditioner programmer, the Electronic Control Module (ECM) screws and the ECM.

7. Remove the module assembly heater core cover. Disconnect the hoses from the heater core.

8. Remove the heater core screws and the heater core.

To install:

9. Install the heater core in vehicle.

10. Connect hoses to heater core. Install module assembly heater core cover.

11. Install the air conditioner programmer and the ECM.

12. Install the lower sound insulator.

13. Install the glove box assembly to vehicle. Connect the electrical connectors to the glove box.

14. Fill cooling system.

15. Start engine and check for coolant leaks. Allow engine to come to normal operating temperature. Recheck for coolant leaks.

Air Mixture Valve

ADJUSTMENT

Allante, Eldorado and Seville

1. Remove the glove box.

2. On the temperature control panel, set the temperature for 90°F, allow 1–2 minutes for the programmer arm to travel to it's **MAX HEAT** position.

3. From the programmer output arm, disconnect the threaded rod from the plastic retainer.

4. To check the air mixture valve for free travel, push the valve to the **MAX A/C** position and check for possible binding.

NOTE: Place the pre-load air mixture valve in the MAX HEAT position; pull on the threaded rod to ensure the valve is seating.

5. To avoid influencing the programmer arm or air mixture valve position, carefully snap the threaded rod into the plastic retainer.

6. Adjust the temperature setting to 60°F, then, check to verify the programmer arm and air mixture valve travel to the **MAX A/C** position.

7. After adjustment, reverse the removal procedures.

Water Pump

REMOVAL & INSTALLATION

3.8L Engine

1. Disconnect the negative battery cable.

2. Position a drain pan under the radiator, open the drain cock and drain the cooling system.

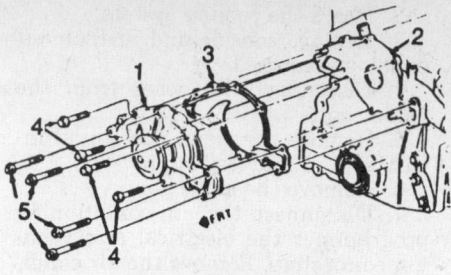

1. Water pump
2. Engine front cover assembly
3. Gasket
4. 97 inch lbs.
5. 29 ft. lbs.

Exploded view of the water pump – 3.8L engine

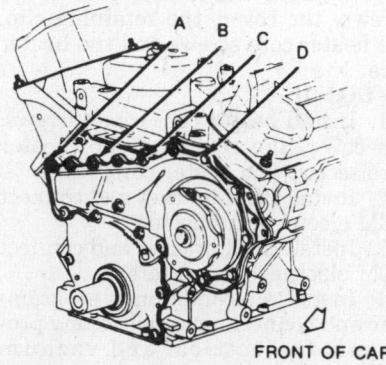

FRONT OF CAR

Locations for fasteners on the 250 V8 water pump.   A fasteners are Torx screws; B fasteners are nuts; C fasteners are studs; and D fasteners are hex screws. Torque A and C to 30 ft. lbs. and B and D to 5 ft. lbs.

3. Disconnect the hoses from the water pump.

4. Remove the drive belt(s).

5. Remove the water pump pulley bolts and the pulley.

NOTE: The long bolt is removed through the access hole provided in the body side rail.

6. Remove the water pump-to-engine bolts and the pump.

To install:

7. Clean the gasket mounting surfaces.

8. Using a new gasket and sealant, if necessary, reverse the removal procedures. Torque the water pump-to-engine long bolts to 22 ft. lbs. (1986–87) or 29 ft. lbs. (1988–90) and the short bolts to 97 inch lbs.

9. Refill the cooling system. Start the engine, allow it to reach normal operating temperatures and check for leaks. Adjust the drive belt(s) to correct tension.

NOTE: Because the radiator is made of aluminum and plastic, make sure the antifreeze solution

is approved for use in cooling systems with a high aluminum content. GM recommends the use of a supplement/sealant part number 3634621 or equivalent, specifically designed for use in aluminum engines to protect the engine from damage.

4.1L and 4.5L Engines

1. Disconnect the negative battery cable.

2. Position a drain pan under the radiator, open the drain cock and drain the cooling system.

3. Remove the air filter assembly. Disconnect and remove the coolant recovery tank.

4. Disconnect and remove the cross brace.

5. While applying tension to the drive belt, to hold the water pump pulley from moving, remove the water pulley bolts.

6. Remove the drive belt and the water pump pulley.

7. Remove the water pump-to-engine bolts and the pump.

To install:

8. Clean the gasket mounting surfaces.

9. Using a new gasket and sealant, if necessary, reverse the removal procedures. Torque the:

Pulley-to-water pump bolts to 25 ft. lbs.

Water pump-to-engine Torx® bolts to 5 ft. lbs.

Water pump-to-engine stud nuts to 30 ft. lbs.

Remaining fasteners to 5 ft. lbs.

NOTE: Because the engines use an aluminum block and the radiator is made of aluminum, make sure the antifreeze solution is approved for use in cooling systems with a high aluminum content. GM recommends the use of a supplement/sealant part number 3634621 or equivalent, specifically designed for use in aluminum engines to protect the engine from damage.

Thermostat

REMOVAL & INSTALLATION

3.8L Engine

1. Drain the coolant until it is below the level of thermostat. Remove the thermostat housing. Observe the direction of the thermostat upon removal.

2. Replace the thermostat and O-ring ensuring the proper direction of new thermostat.

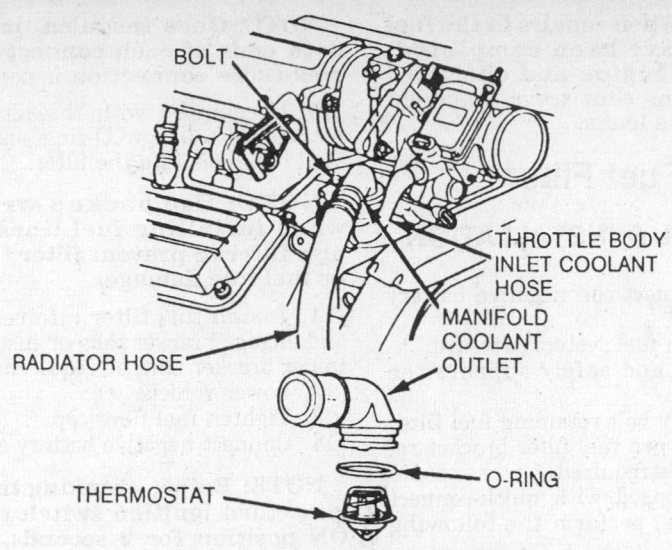

Replacing thermostat — 3.8L Engine

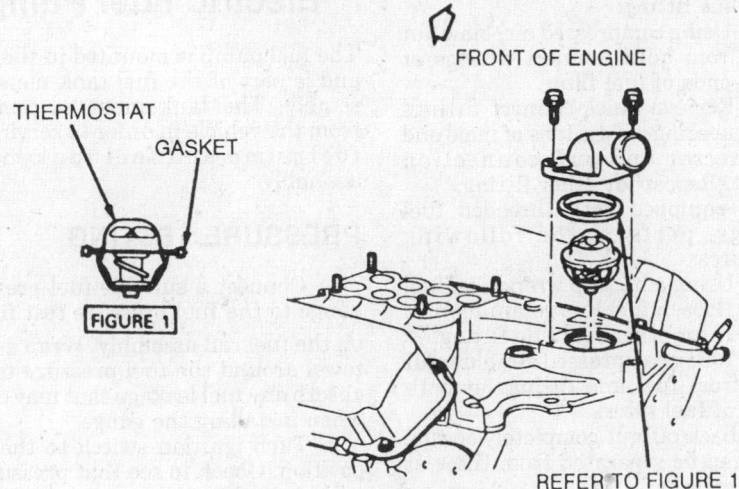

Replacing thermostat — Allante

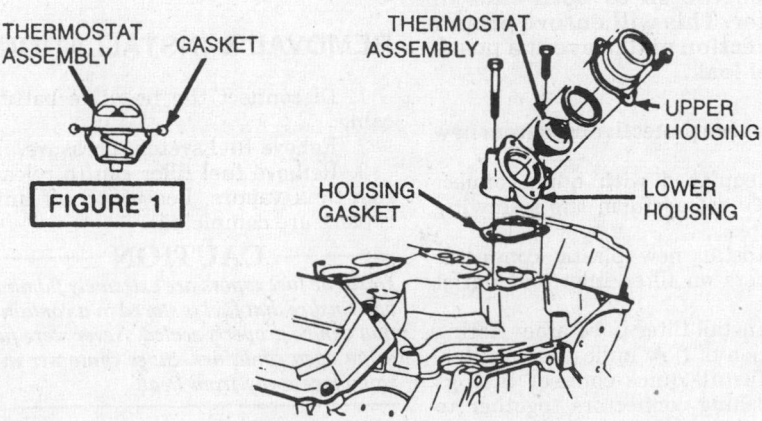

Replacing thermostat — Eldorado and Seville

3. Fill cooling system using a 50/50 mixture of water and ethylene glycol antifreeze.

4. Start engine and check for coolant leaks. Allow engine to come to normal operating temperature. Recheck for coolant leaks.

4.1L and 4.5L Engines

1. Drain coolant to a level below the thermostat housing.

2. Remove 2 bolts securing thermostat housing to intake manifold.

3. Remove thermostat housing.

4. Remove thermostat and O-ring from intake manifold.

To install:

5. Install thermostat and a new O-ring to intake manifold.

6. Install thermostat housing to intake manifold. Tighten thermostat housing bolts to 18 ft. lbs. (25 Nm).

7. Refill cooling system using a 50/50 mixture of water and ethylene glycol antifreeze.

8. Start engine and check for coolant leaks. Allow engine to come to normal operating temperature. Recheck for coolant leaks.

Cooling System Bleeding

1. With the cooling system completely drained, fill the system with at least a 50/50 mixture of ethylene glycol antifreeze and water but no more than a 70/30 mixture of water to antifreeze.

2. Fill the radiator to just below the filler neck. Fill the coolant recovery reservoir to the COLD FILL mark.

3. Run the engine with the radiator cap removed until normal operating temperature is reached, with the radiator inlet hose hot.

4. With the engine idling, add coolant to the radiator until it reaches the bottom of the filler neck.

5. Position the heating system controls on maximum; allowing coolant to circulate through the heater core.

6. Check the coolant level again and add, as necessary.

7. Install the radiator cap.

FUEL SYSTEM

Fuel System Service Precautions

Safety is the most important factor when performing not only fuel system maintenance but any type of maintenance. Failure to conduct maintenance and repairs in a safe manner may result in serious personal injury or death. Maintenance and testing of the vehicle's fuel system components can be accomplished safely and effectively by adhering to the following rules and guidelines.

- To avoid the possibility of fire and personal injury, always disconnect the negative battery cable unless the repair or test procedure requires that battery voltage be applied.
- Always relieve the fuel system pressure prior to disconnecting any fuel system component (injector, fuel rail, pressure regulator, etc.), fitting or fuel line connection. Exercise extreme caution whenever relieving fuel system pressure to avoid exposing skin, face and eyes to fuel spray. Please be advised that fuel under pressure may penetrate the skin or any part of the body that it contacts.
- Always place a shop towel or cloth around the fitting or connection prior to loosening to absorb any excess fuel due to spillage. Ensure that all fuel spillage (should it occur) is quickly removed from engine surfaces. Ensure that all fuel soaked cloths or towels are deposited into a suitable waste container.
- Always keep a dry chemical (Class B) fire extinguisher near the work area.
- Do not allow fuel spray or fuel vapors to come into contact with a spark or open flame.
- Always use a backup wrench when loosing and tightening fuel line connection fittings. This will prevent unnecessary stress and torsion to fuel line piping. Always follow the proper torque specifications.
- Always replace worn fuel fitting O-rings with new. Do not substitute fuel hose or equivalent where fuel pipe is installed.

RELIEVING FUEL SYSTEM PRESSURE

1. Disconnect the negative battery cable.
2. Loosen fuel filler cap to relieve tank vapor pressure. Do not tighten until service has been completed.
3. Connect a suitable fuel pressure gauge to fuel pressure connection on fuel rail assembly. Wrap a shop towel around fitting while connecting gauge to avoid spillage.
4. Install bleed hose into an approved container and open valve to bleed system pressure. Fuel connections are now safe for servicing.
5. Drain any fuel into an approved container.

NOTE: When repairs to the fuel system have been completed, start the engine and check all connections that were loosened for possible leaks.

Fuel Filter

REMOVAL & INSTALLATION

1. Disconnect the negative battery cable.
2. Relieve fuel system pressure.
3. Raise and safely support the vehicle.
4. Remove bolt retaining fuel filter bracket or open fuel filter bracket release tabs, as required.
5. If equipped with quick-connect fuel fittings, perform the following procedures:
   a. Grasp filter and 1 fuel line fitting. Twist quick-connect fitting ¼ turn in each direction to loosen any dirt within fitting. Repeat for other fuel line fitting.
   b. Using compressed air, blow out dirt from quick-connect fittings at both ends of fuel filter.
   c. Remove quick-connect fittings by squeezing plastic tabs of male end connector and pull connection apart. Repeat for other fitting.
6. If equipped with threaded fuel fittings, perform the following procedures:
   a. Using a backup wrench on fuel filter, loosen fuel line retaining nut. Repeat for other fuel line fitting.
   b. Using compressed air, blow out dirt from fuel line fittings at both ends of fuel filter.
   c. Back off nut completely so fuel line can be separated from filter at both ends.
7. Remove fuel filter.

To install:

NOTE: Before installing a new filter, always apply a few drops of clean engine oil to both ends of the filter. This will ensure proper reconnection and prevent a possible fuel leak.

8. Remove protective caps from new filter.
9. If equipped with quick-connect fuel fittings, perform the following procedures:
   a. Install new plastic connector retainers on filter inlet and outlet tubes.
   b. Install filter in retainer noting direction of flow indicated on filter.
   c. Install quick-connect fittings by pushing connectors together to cause the retaining tabs/fingers to snap into place.

NOTE: Once installed, pull on both ends of each connection to make sure connection is secure.

10. If equipped with threaded fuel fittings, install new O-ring seals, install fuel lines into the filter.

NOTE: Use backup wrench when installing fuel lines into new filter to prevent filter O-ring or fuel line damage.

11. Install fuel filter into retainer and engage bracket tabs or install retainer bracket bolt, as required.
12. Lower vehicle.
13. Tighten fuel filler cap.
14. Connect negative battery cable.

NOTE: Before cranking the engine, turn ignition switch to the ON position for 2 seconds, then turn switch OFF for 5 seconds. Again turn ignition switch to ON position and check for fuel leaks.

Electric Fuel Pump

The fuel pump is mounted in the tank and is part of the fuel tank meter assembly. The tank must be removed from the vehicle in order to service the fuel pump and fuel tank meter assembly.

PRESSURE TESTING

1. Connect a suitable fuel pressure gauge to the fuel pressure test fitting on the fuel rail assembly. Wrap a shop towel around the fuel pressure tap to absorb any fuel leakage that may occur when installing the gauge.
2. Turn ignition switch to the **ON** position. Check to see that pressure is within specification.
3. Turn ignition switch **OFF**. Pressure should not leak down with fuel pump **OFF**.
4. Pressure at idle should be 3–10 psi (21–69 kPa) lower than static pressure.

REMOVAL & INSTALLATION

1. Disconnect the negative battery cable.
2. Relieve fuel system pressure.
3. Remove fuel filler cap to release fuel tank vapors. Leave cap off until repairs are completed.

--- **CAUTION** ---

Gasoline fuel vapors are extremely flammable. Ensure that fuel is stored in a container that can be properly sealed. Never store fuel in an open container. Store container in a safe place away from heat.

4. Remove fuel tank by performing the following:

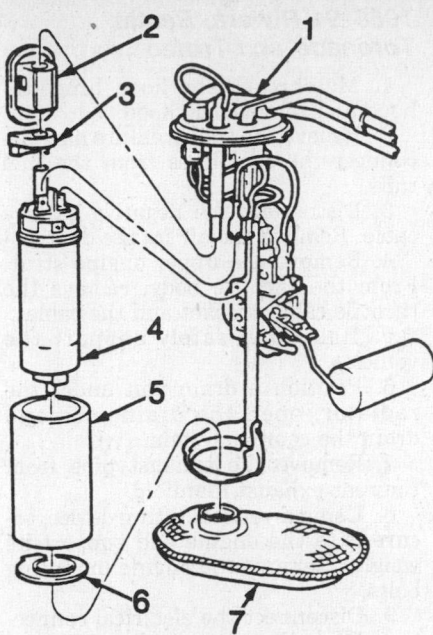

1. Fuel tank meter assembly
2. Pulsator
3. Bumper
4. Fuel pump
5. Sound isolator sleeve
6. Sound insulator
7. Filter strainer

Exploded view of the electric fuel pump/sending unit assembly

a. Drain fuel from the tank into an approved container for storage.
b. Raise and safely support the vehicle.
c. Remove rear stabilizer bar at links, pivot bar downward.
d. Remove hoses and pipes from tank unit.
e. Remove hoses at tank from filler and vent pipe.
f. Disconnect tank unit harness from rear body harness.
g. Support fuel tank and disconnect 2 fuel tank retaining straps.
h. Remove tank from vehicle.
5. Remove sending unit, gasket and pump assembly by turning cam lock ring counterclockwise. Lift assembly from fuel tank and remove fuel pump from fuel tank sending unit.
6. Pull fuel pump up into attaching hose while pulling outward away from bottom support. Take care to prevent damage to rubber insulator and strainer during removal. After pump assembly is clear of bottom support, pull pump assembly out of rubber connector for removal.
To install:
7. Push fuel pump assembly into attaching hose.
8. Install fuel tank sending unit and pump assembly into tank assembly. Use new O-ring seal during reassembly.

9. Install cam lock over assembly and lock by turning clockwise.
10. Support tank and position in vehicle. Install tank straps and secure with retaining bolts. Tighten to 25 ft. lbs. (33 Nm).
11. Connect tank unit harness to body harness.
12. Connect hoses to filler and vent pipes. Tighten clamps.
13. Connect hoses and pipes to tank unit.
14. Connect rear stabilizer bar to links. Tighten bolts to 42 ft. lbs. (58 Nm).
15. Lower vehicle.
16. Refill tank and install filler cap.
17. Connect negative battery cable.
18. Start engine and check for leaks.

Fuel Injection

IDLE SPEED ADJUSTMENT

Idle speed is controlled by the ECM. No adjustments should be attempted.

IDLE MIXTURE ADJUSTMENT

Idle mixture is maintained by the ECM. No adjustment should be attempted.

Fuel Injector

REMOVAL & INSTALLATION

Multi-Port Fuel Injection (MFI) and Sequential Fuel Injection (SFI)

1. Relieve the fuel pressure. Disconnect the negative battery cable.
2. Label and disconnect the fuel injector electrical connectors.
3. Remove the fuel rail retaining bolts. Remove the fuel rail.
4. Separate the injector from the fuel rail.
5. To install, use new O-rings and reverse the removal procedures. Start the engine and check for leaks.

Digital Fuel Injection (DFI)

NOTE: Care must be taken when removing injectors to prevent damage to the electrical connector pins on the injector and the nozzle. The injectors are serviced as a complete assembly only. Injectors are an electrical component and should not be immersed in any type of cleaner.

1. If the engine was recently operated, allow the fuel pressure to bleed down.

2. Disconnect the negative battery cable. Remove the air cleaner.
3. Disconnect the electrical connector from the fuel injector(s) by squeezing both tabs together and pulling it straight up.
4. Remove the fuel meter cover-to-throttle body screws and the cover; be sure to note the position of the short screws. Allow the gasket to remain in place to prevent damage to the casting housing.
5. Using a small prybar and a ¼ in. rod, pry the fuel injector(s) from the throttle body; discard the O-rings.
6. To install, use new O-rings, lubricate with Dexron®II automatic transmission fluid and reverse the removal procedures. When installing the injectors, push them into the sockets. Start the engine and check for leaks.

EMISSION CONTROLS

Please refer to "Emission Control" in the Unit Repair section for system maintenance procedures. Due to the complex nature of modern electronic engine control systems, comprehensive diagnosis and testing procedures fall outside the confines of this repair manual. For complete information on diagnosis, testing and repair procedures concerning all modern engine and emission control systems, please refer to "Chilton's Guide to Electronic Engine Controls".

ENGINE MECHANICAL

NOTE: Disconnecting the negative battery cable on some vehicles may interfere with the functions of the on board computer systems and may require the computer to undergo a relearning process, once the negative battery cable is reconnected.

Engine Assembly

REMOVAL & INSTALLATION

1987 Riviera and Toronado

1. Disconnect the negative battery cable. Matchmark the hood hinges and remove the hood.

2. Position a drain pan under the radiator, open the drain cock and drain the cooling system.

3. Remove the air inlet and radiator hoses.

4. Disconnect the following electrical connectors:

   a. Fuel rail and other injection system connectors

   b. Engine ground wires

   c. Oil pressure sending unit

   d. EGR solenoid

   e. Coolant temperature sending units

   f. Throttle body electrical connections

   g. Crankshaft and camshaft sensors

   h. Alternator

5. Remove the serpentine drive belt. Remove the power steering pump and move it aside; do not disconnect the pressure hoses, if possible.

6. Remove the alternator. Disconnect and remove the heater hoses.

7. Remove the throttle cable bracket and the cruise control cables from the throttle lever.

8. Disconnect both fuel lines.

9. Remove the cooling fan and radiator.

10. Disconnect the exhaust Y-pipe, remove the exhaust manifold on the forward side of the engine. Label and disconnect the vacuum lines between the engine and components mounted on the firewall.

11. Remove the engine-to-transaxle bolts, the vibration damper and bracket from the engine.

12. Remove the ground strap and wiring harness bolts. Remove the engine-to-transaxle bracket. Raise and safely support the vehicle.

13. Remove the air conditioning compressor-to-bracket bolts, move it aside and support it without disturbing the refrigerant hoses. Remove the exhaust pipe.

14. Remove the engine-to-mount nuts. Matchmark the torque converter-to-flywheel and remove the torque converter-to-flywheel bolts.

15. Remove the left front wheel and the remaining engine-to-transaxle bolts. Make sure to remove the bolt that faces in the opposite direction.

16. Remove the engine-to-transaxle bracket and lower the vehicle. Using an engine vertical lifting device, connect it to the engine and lift the engine from the vehicle.

To install:

17. Install engine assembly in vehicle.

18. Install upper engine-to-transaxle bolts and tighten until snug. Do not torque at this time.

19. Install engine mount nuts. Tighten to 70 ft. lbs. (90 Nm).

20. Raise and safely support the vehicle.

21. Install remaining engine-to-transaxle bolts. Tighten to 55 ft. lbs. (75 Nm).

NOTE: One bolt is located between the transaxle case and engine block and is installed in the opposite direction.

22. Install engine-to-transaxle bracket.

23. Install converter-to-flywheel bolts.

NOTE: Line up matchmark made during disassembly. Ensure weld nuts in the torque converter are flush with the flywheel. Rotate torque converter to ensure freedom of movement. Tighten 3 bolts finger-tight, then retighten to 46 ft. lbs. (62 Nm).

24. Install torque converter cover.

25. Install air conditioning compressor to bracket.

26. Connect starter.

27. Lower vehicle.

28. Complete final torque of upper engine-to-transaxle bolts. Tighten to 55 ft. lbs. (75 Nm).

29. Install wiring harness hold down bolts.

30. Connect ground bolts.

31. Install vibration dampener and bracket to engine. Tighten vibration dampener to 219 ft. lbs. (297 Nm).

32. Install front exhaust manifold. Tighten 37 ft. lbs. (50 Nm).

33. Install radiator and cooling fan.

34. Connect fuel supply and return lines.

35. Install throttle cable and bracket and cables to cruise control, accelerator and throttle valve.

36. Connect heater hoses.

37. Install alternator and power steering pump.

38. Install serpentine belt.

39. Connect the following electrical connections:

   a. Fuel rail and other fuel injection system connectors

   b. Engine ground connections

   c. Oil pressure sender

   d. EGR solenoid

   e. Coolant temperature

   f. Throttle body

   g. Crankshaft and camshaft sensors

   h. Alternator

40. Connect air inlet and radiator hoses.

41. Install hood and hood bolts observing marks made during removal.

42. Connect negative battery cable.

43. Start engine and check for fuel, coolant and transaxle leaks.

1988–91 Riviera, Reatta, Toronado and Trofeo

1. Matchmark the hood hinge-to-hood and remove the hood.

2. Relieve the fuel pressure and disconnect the fuel lines from the fuel rail.

3. Disconnect the negative battery cable. Remove the air intake duct.

4. Remove the upper engine strut. From the throttle body, remove the throttle cable bracket and the cables.

5. Raise and safely support the vehicle.

6. Position a drain pan under the radiator, open the drain cock and drain the cooling system.

7. Remove the exhaust pipe from the rear exhaust manifold.

8. Using a vertical lifting device, secure it to the engine and support its weight. Remove the engine mounting bolts.

9. Disconnect the electrical connectors from the starter. Remove the starter-to-engine bolts and the starter.

10. Remove the serpentine drive belt. Remove the air conditioning compressor-to-bracket bolts and move the compressor aside; do not disconnect the pressure hoses.

11. Disconnect and plug the power steering hoses at the steering gear.

12. Remove the lower transaxle-to-engine bolts.

NOTE: One of the lower transaxle bolts is located between the transaxle case and the engine block; it is installed in the opposite direction.

13. Remove the flywheel cover. Matchmark the torque converter-to-flywheel for alignment purposes. Remove the torque converter-to-flywheel bolts and slide the torque converter rearward.

14. Remove the engine support bracket-to-transaxle bolts and the bracket.

15. Lower the vehicle.

16. Disconnect the vacuum hoses from the vacuum modulator and the emission control canister. Disconnect and move aside any electrical harness connectors which may be in the way.

17. Remove the radiator and heater hoses from the engine.

18. Remove the remaining transaxle-to-engine bolts. Lift the engine assembly from the vehicle and attach it to a work stand.

To install:

19. Install engine assembly in vehicle. Install upper engine-to-transaxle bolts and tighten until snug. Do not torque at this time.

20. Install radiator and connect heater hoses to engine.

21. Connect vacuum hoses to vacuum modulator and the emission control canister. Connect electrical harness connectors previously removed.

22. Raise and safely support the vehicle.

23. Install the engine support bracket-to-transaxle bolts and bracket.

24. Install the torque convertor-to-flywheel bolts. Tighten to 46 ft. lbs. (62 Nm). Install flywheel cover aligning marks made during removal.

25. Install lower transaxle bolts. Tighten to 55 ft. lbs. (75 Nm).

NOTE: One of the lower transaxle bolts is located between the transaxle case and the engine block; it is installed in the opposite direction.

26. Connect the power steering hoses at the steering gear.

27. Install the air conditioning compressor in the bracket and install the compressor-to-bracket bolts. Install the serpentine belt.

28. Install the starter on the engine and connect starter electrical connector.

29. Install engine mounting bolts. Tighten to 70 ft. lbs. (90 Nm). Remove lifting device.

30. Connect the exhaust pipe to the rear exhaust manifold.

31. Lower the vehicle.

32. Fill the cooling system.

33. Connect the throttle cable bracket and cables to the throttle body. Install the upper engine strut.

34. Install the air intake duct. Connect negative battery cable.

35. Connect the fuel lines to the fuel rail.

36. Install the hood at matchmarks made during removal.

37. Start the engine and check for fuel, coolant and transaxle leaks.

Allante

1. Disconnect the negative battery cable. Position a drain pan under the radiator, open the drain cock and drain the cooling system.

2. Remove the air cleaner. Matchmark the hood hinge-to-hood and remove the hood.

3. Remove the cooling fans and the accessory drive belt.

4. Remove the upper intake manifold. Remove the upper radiator hose and disconnect the heater hose from the thermostat housing.

5. Disconnect the following electrical connectors, positioning the wires out of the way:
   a. Oil pressure sending unit
   b. Coolant temperature sensor
   c. Distributor
   d. EGR solenoid
   e. Engine temperature switch

   f. Idle speed control
   g. Throttle position sensor
   h. Injector electrical connections
   i. MAT sensor
   j. Oxygen sensor
   k. Throttle body base warmer
   l. Alternator
   m. Ground wires at the alternator mounting bracket

6. Disconnect the accelerator, the cruise control and the transaxle throttle valve cables from the throttle lever.

7. Disconnect the cruise control diaphragm/bracket and move them aside.

8. Disconnect the transaxle oil cooler lines from the radiator. Remove the radiator.

9. Disconnect and remove the oil cooler lines from the oil filter adapter.

10. Remove the oil cooler lines-to-transaxle bracket.

11. Remove the air cleaner bracket and the oil filter adapter.

12. Disconnect the air injection tubes from the diverter valve.

13. Remove the cross brace.

14. Remove the right front heater hose and the coolant reservoir.

15. Remove the Air Injection Reactor (AIR) filter and bracket.

16. Remove the power steering line brace from the right cylinder head. Remove the pump and belt tensioner as an assembly and position them forward of the engine.

NOTE: Make sure to follow carefully the instructions in the next 2 steps. Air conditioning refrigerant has a boiling point of −26°F.

17. Discharge the air conditioning system and remove the air conditioning lines from the accumulator and condenser.

18. Position a metal container and a rag so as to catch the fuel and carefully depress the center pin at the Schraeder valve on the fuel line until all fuel pressure is exhausted. Disconnect supply and return fuel lines from the fuel rail. Remove the fuel line bracket from the transaxle and move the fuel lines aside.

19. Raise and safely support the vehicle.

20. Label and disconnect the electrical connectors from the starter. Disconnect any ground wires still connected at the block.

21. Disconnect the oxygen level sensor wire and the remove the oxygen sensors.

22. Disconnect and remove the exhaust Y-pipe. Remove the starter-to-engine bolts and the starter.

23. Remove the torque converter covers. Matchmark the torque converter-to-flywheel and remove the flywheel-to-torque converter bolts.

24. Remove the air conditioning compressor lower dust shield, the right front tire and the outer wheel house plastic shield.

25. Remove the right rear transaxle-to-engine mount bolt, the front engine mount nuts and the right rear transaxle mount bolts.

26. Remove the alternator. Remove the oxygen sensor wires. Remove the heater bypass bracket from the right side of the vehicle.

27. Remove the right side engine brace and lower the vehicle to the ground.

28. Remove the engine-to-transaxle bolts; the bolts are accessible from the top.

29. Run a chain from a lifting crane down to both lift points on top of the engine and ensure it is secure. Lift the engine out of the vehicle.

To install:

30. Situate a floor jack under the transaxle and raise it slightly so it will align with the engine. Lower the engine into the engine compartment; be careful not to damage accessories that are still in position. Change the engine and transaxle angles as necessary to get good alignment; engage the dowels that are on the engine block with the corresponding holes in the transaxle.

31. Install the upper transaxle-to-engine bolts. Lower the engine, directing it squarely onto its mounts. Remove the lifting equipment.

NOTE: Ensure that converter is properly positioned to the flexplate and engaged in front pump of transaxle.

32. Install 5 upper transaxle bell housing-to-engine bolts.

33. Lower floor jack and remove from transaxle.

34. Lower engine making sure it is properly seated on mounts.

35. Remove lifting equipment. Raise and safely support the vehicle.

36. Install right side engine brace.

37. Remove engine support.

38. Install alternator and oxygen sensor wires and heater bypass bracket to right side of vehicle.

39. Install front engine mount nuts and right rear transaxle mounting bolts.

40. Connect oil level sensor at oil pan and both oxygen sensors.

41. Install right rear transaxle-to-engine mounting bolt.

42. Install outer wheel house plastic shield.

43. Install right front tire and wheel assembly.

44. Install air conditioning compressor lower dust shield.

45. Install 3 flexplate-to-converter bolts. Install flexplate cover.

46. Install starter. Install exhaust "Y" pipe.

47. Install electrical connectors at starter and ground wires to block.

48. Lower vehicle.

49. Install fuel line bracket. Install fuel lines at fuel rail.

50. Install air conditioning lines to accumulator and condenser.

51. Install power steering pump and tensioner. Install power steering line brace on right cylinder head.

52. Install AIR system air filter and bracket.

53. Install coolant reservoir. Install right front heater hose.

54. Install front right and rear cross braces.

55. Install AIR tubes on diverter valve.

56. Install oil filter adapter.

57. Install air cleaner mounting bracket.

58. Install oil cooler line bracket at transaxle. Install oil cooler lines to oil filter adapter.

59. Install radiator. Install engine oil and transaxle oil cooler lines to radiator.

60. Connect cruise control diaphragm with bracket.

61. Install the following wiring connectors:
   a. Injectors
   b. Ground wires at alternator bracket
   c. Oil pressure switch
   d. Coolant temperature sensor
   e. Distributor
   f. Engine temperature switch

62. Connect cables from throttle lever including: accelerator, cruise control and transaxle throttle valve.

63. Install accessory drive belt.

64. Install upper radiator hose and heater hose to thermostat housing.

65. Install cooling fan.

66. Install air conditioning accumulator hose brace.

67. Install vehicle hood.

68. Install air cleaner. Install engine coolant. Connect negative battery cable.

69. Charge air conditioning system.

70. Start engine and check for oil, coolant and transaxle leaks.

Eldorado and Seville

1. Disconnect the negative battery cable. Position a drain pan under the radiator, open the drain cock and drain the cooling system.

2. Remove the air cleaner. Matchmark the hood hinge-to-hood and remove the hood.

3. Remove the cooling fan and the accessory drive belt.

4. Remove the upper radiator hose and disconnect the heater hose from the thermostat housing.

5. Disconnect the following electrical connectors, positioning the wires out of the way:
   a. Oil pressure sending unit
   b. Coolant temperature sensor
   c. Distributor
   d. EGR solenoid
   e. Engine temperature switch
   f. Idle speed control
   g. Throttle position sensor
   h. Injector electrical connections
   i. MAT sensor
   j. Oxygen sensor
   k. Throttle body base warmer
   l. Alternator
   m. Ground wires at the alternator mounting bracket

6. Disconnect the accelerator, the cruise control and the transaxle throttle valve cables from the throttle lever.

7. Disconnect the cruise control diaphragm/bracket and move them out of the way.

8. Disconnect the transaxle oil cooler lines from the radiator. Remove the radiator.

9. Disconnect and remove the oil cooler lines from the oil filter adapter.

10. Remove the oil cooler lines-to-transaxle bracket.

11. Remove the air cleaner bracket and the oil filter housing adapter.

12. Disconnect the air injection tubes from the diverter valve.

13. Remove the right front and right rear body braces.

14. Remove the right front heater hose and the coolant reservoir.

15. Remove the Air Injection Reactor (AIR) filter box and bracket. Remove the idler pulley for the accessory drive belt.

16. Remove the power steering line brace from the right cylinder head. Remove the pump and belt tensioner as an assembly and position them forward of the engine.

NOTE: Make sure to follow carefully the instructions in the next 2 steps. Air conditioning refrigerant has a boiling point of −26°F.

17. Discharge the air conditioning system and remove the air conditioning lines from the accumulator and condenser.

18. Position a metal container and a rag so as to catch the fuel and carefully depress the center pin at the Schraeder valve on the fuel line until all fuel pressure is exhausted. Disconnect supply and return fuel lines from the throttle body. Remove the fuel line bracket from the transaxle and move the fuel lines aside.

19. Remove the EGR lines and brackets. Remove the vacuum modulator line and the fuel filter; reposition them aside.

20. Raise and safely support the vehicle.

21. Remove the starter heat shield. Label and disconnect the electrical connectors from the starter. Disconnect any ground wires still connected at the block.

22. Disconnect and remove the exhaust crossover pipe. Remove the starter-to-engine bolts and the starter.

23. Remove the torque converter covers. Matchmark the torque converter-to-flywheel and remove the flywheel-to-torque converter bolts.

24. Remove the air conditioning compressor lower dust shield, the right front tire and the outer wheel house plastic shield.

25. Remove the right rear transaxle-to-engine mount bolt and the lower engine mounting damper nut.

26. Remove the front engine mount nuts and the right rear transaxle mount nuts.

27. Remove the alternator. Remove the oxygen sensor wires. Remove the heater bypass bracket from the right side of the vehicle.

28. Remove the right side engine brace and lower the vehicle to the ground.

29. Remove the engine-to-transaxle bolts; the bolts are accessible from the top.

30. Run a chain from a lifting crane down to both lift points on top of the engine and ensure it is secure. Lift engine out of the vehicle.

To install:

31. Situate a floor jack under the transaxle and raise it slightly so it will align with the engine. Lower the engine into the engine compartment, being careful not to damage accessories that are still in position. Change the engine and transaxle angles as necessary to get good alignment and then engage the dowels that are on the engine block with the corresponding holes in the transaxle.

NOTE: Ensure that converter is properly positioned to the flexplate and engaged in the front pump of transaxle.

32. Install upper 5 transaxle bell housing-to-engine bolts.

33. Lower floor jack and remove from transaxle.

34. Lower engine making sure it is seated on the mount properly.

35. Remove lifting equipment.

36. Raise and safely support the vehicle.

37. Support the engine. Install right side engine brace. Remove engine support.

38. Install alternator and oxygen sensor wires and heater bypass bracket to right side of vehicle.

39. Install front engine mount nuts and right rear transaxle mount bolts.
40. Install lower engine damper nut.
41. Install right rear transaxle-to-engine mounting bolt.
42. Install outer wheel house plastic shield.
43. Install right front tire and wheel assembly.
44. Install air conditioner compressor lower dust shield.
45. Install 3 flexplate-to-converter bolts. Install 2 flexplate covers.
46. Install starter to engine and connect electrical connectors. Install engine ground connectors.
47. Install exhaust crossover pipe.
48. Install starter heat shield.
49. Lower vehicle.
50. Install vacuum modulator line and vacuum hose to power brake booster.
51. Install EGR lines and bracket.
52. Install fuel line bracket at transaxle. Install fuel lines at throttle body.
53. Install air conditioning lines to accumulator and condenser.
54. Install power steering pump and tensioner. Install power steering line brace on right cylinder head.
55. Install A.I.R. system air filter and bracket.
56. Install coolant reservoir. Install right front heater hose.
57. Install front right and rear cross braces.
58. Install A.I.R. tubes on diverter valve.
59. Install oil filter adapter.
60. Install air cleaner mounting bracket.
61. Install oil cooler line bracket at transaxle. Install oil cooler lines to oil filter adapter.
62. Install radiator. Install engine oil and transaxle oil cooler lines to radiator.
63. Connect cruise control diaphragm with bracket.
64. Install the following wiring connectors:
  a. ISC
  b. TPS
  c. Injectors
  d. MAT sensor
  e. Oxygen sensor
  f. Electric EFE grid
  g. Ground wires at alternator bracket
  h. Oil pressure switch
  i. Coolant temperature sensor
  j. Distributor
  k. EGR solenoid
  l. Engine temperature switch
65. Connect cables from throttle lever including: accelerator, cruise control and transaxle throttle valve.
66. Install accessory drive belt.
67. Install upper radiator hose and heater hose to thermostat housing.
68. Install cooling fan.

69. Install air conditioning accumulator hose brace.
70. Install vehicle hood.
71. Install air cleaner. Install engine coolant. Connect negative battery cable.
72. Charge air conditioning system.
73. Start engine and check for oil, coolant and transaxle leaks.

Engine Mounts

REMOVAL & INSTALLATION

Reatta, Riviera, Toronado and Trofeo

1. Disconnect the negative battery cable.
2. Safely support the engine using a suitable engine holding fixture.
3. Raise and safely support the vehicle.
4. Remove the engine mount bracket nuts.
5. Raise the engine slightly.
6. Remove the engine mount retaining bolts. Remove the engine mount.
7. To install, reverse the removal procedures.

Allante

RIGHT SIDE ENGINE AND TRANSAXLE MOUNT

1. Disconnect the negative battery cable.
2. Raise and safely support the vehicle.
3. Remove 2 heat shield screws.
4. Remove screw from engine mount brace at engine mount bracket.
5. Loosen nut at top of brace to exhaust manifold and position brace out of the way.
6. Support the engine with a transaxle jack.
7. Remove 2 screws securing mount bracket to transaxle.
8. Remove 4 nuts at top and bottom of mount.
9. Raise engine with transaxle jack.
10. Remove engine mount.
To install:
11. Position transaxle mount and bracket in place between transaxle and frame. Secure bracket to transaxle with 2 bolts. Tighten to 50 ft. lbs. (70 Nm).

NOTE: Guide engine mount into location while lowering engine.

12. Lower engine.
13. Install mount to frame and transaxle bracket with 2 nuts each. Tighten to 30 ft. lbs. (40 Nm).
14. Install brace from bracket to engine. Tighten to 25 ft. lbs. (35 Nm).
15. Install heat shield.

16. Remove transaxle jack and lower hoist.

LEFT SIDE ENGINE MOUNT

1. Disconnect the negative battery cable.
2. Remove air cleaner assembly.
3. Remove serpentine belt.
4. Discharge air conditioning system.
5. Lower center exhaust manifold nuts.
6. Raise and safely support the vehicle.
7. Remove right hand engine compartment splash shield. Remove air conditioning splash shield.
8. Remove 2 air conditioning compressor brackets. Remove air conditioning compressor.
9. Remove engine mount bracket bolts from engine block and cradle.
10. Raise engine with transaxle jack and remove mount and bracket.
To install:
11. Place mount in vise and position mount bracket onto mount. Tighten 2 nuts to 30 ft. lbs. (40 Nm).
12. Install engine mount and bracket through right hand wheel well.
13. Install engine mount bracket bolts to engine block. Tighten to 50 ft. lbs. (70 Nm).
14. Install engine mount to cradle nuts. Tighten to 30 ft. lbs. (40 Nm).
15. Install air conditioning compressor. Install 2 air conditioning compressor brackets.
16. Install air conditioning splash shield. Install right hand engine compartment splash shield.
17. Lower vehicle.
18. Install lower center exhaust manifold nut.
19. Install serpentine belt.
20. Connect negative battery cable.
21. Install air cleaner assembly.
22. Charge air conditioning system.

Eldorado and Seville

RIGHT SIDE ENGINE AND TRANSAXLE MOUNT

1. Disconnect the negative battery cable.
2. Remove the brace from the engine bracket to engine.
3. Remove 2 engine bracket-to-mount nuts.
4. Raise and safely support the vehicle.
5. Remove 2 nuts securing the engine mount to the frame. Remove 2 nuts securing transaxle bracket to mount. Remove 2 nuts securing the transaxle mount to the frame bracket.
6. Using the engine support tool, raise the engine.
7. Raise the engine slowly until the bracket is free from the engine and transaxle mount. Remove the bracket-

to-block stud and bolts. Remove the mount and bracket by pulling forward.

8. Remove the transaxle mounting bracket from the transaxle. Remove the mount assembly.

To install:

9. Position engine mount and bracket in place between cylinder block and frame. Secure bracket to block with 1 stud and 2 bolts. Tighten to 34 ft. lbs. (46 Nm).

10. Position transaxle mount and bracket in place between transaxle and frame. Secure bracket to transaxle with 2 bolts. Tighten to 34 ft. lbs. (46 Nm).

NOTE: Guide engine mount into location while lowering engine.

11. Lower engine.

12. Install engne mount to frame and transaxle mount to frame bracket with 2 nuts. Tighten to 22 ft. lbs. (31 Nm).

13. Install 2 nuts to engine mount studs and 2 nuts to transaxle mount studs. Tighten to 22 ft. lbs. (31 Nm).

14. Remove brace from engine bracket to engine.

15. Remove stands and lower vehicle.

16. Connect negative battery cable.

LEFT SIDE ENGINE MOUNT

1. Disconnect the negative battery cable. Remove the air cleaner assembly.

2. Remove the serpentine belt and discharge the air conditioning system.

3. Install the engine support tool.

4. Remove the lower center exhaust manifold nut and top nut of the engine damper.

5. Raise and safely support the vehicle.

6. Remove the right side engine compartment splash shield and air conditioning splash shield.

7. Remove the engine damper. Remove both air conditioning compressor brackets. Remove the air conditioning compressor.

8. Remove the water pipe bracket bolt.

9. Remove the engine mount bracket bolts from the engine block and cradle. Remove the engine mount and bracket through the right hand wheel well.

To install:

10. Place mount in vice and position mount bracket onto mount. Tighten 2 nuts to 31 ft. lbs. (41 Nm).

11. Install engine mount and bracket through right wheel well.

12. Install engine mount bracket bolts to engine block. Tighten to 50 ft. lbs. (68 Nm).

13. Install engine mount to cradle nuts. Tighten bolts to 31 ft. lbs. (41 Nm).

14. Install water pipe bracket bolt.

15. Install air conditioning compressor bracket.

16. Install 2 air conditioning compressor brackets.

17. Install engine damper.

18. Install air conditioning compressor splash shield.

19. Install right hand engine compartment splash shield.

20. Lower vehicle.

21. Install lower center exhaust manifold nut and top nut on engine damper.

22. Remove engine support tool.

23. Install serpentine bolt.

24. Connect negative battery cable.

25. Install air cleaner assembly.

26. Charge air conditioning system.

Cylinder Head

REMOVAL & INSTALLATION

3.8L Engine

1987

1. Disconnect the negative battery cable. Remove the air cleaner.

2. Place a drain pan under the radiator, open the drain cock and drain the cooling system.

3. Remove the serpentine belt.

4. Relieve fuel pressure in fuel rail.

5. Remove alternator electrical connections and alternator.

6. Remove bypass hose from intake manifold.

7. Remove electrical connections from intake manifold and cylinder head.

8. Remove upper radiator hose. Remove air intake duct from throttle body.

9. Remove vacuum connector block. Remove PCV and vapor canister vacuum line.

10. Remove rear engine left bracket.

11. Remove front spark plug wire harness.

12. Remove throttle cables at throttle body.

13. Remove heater hose from water outlet.

14. Remove fuel rail supply and return lines.

15. Remove intake manifold bolts, intake manifold and gaskets.

16. If removing the front (left) cylinder head, perform the following:

    a. Remove the cooling fan.

    b. Remove oil level indicator tube and indicator.

    c. Remove front exhaust manifold bolts and manifold.

17. If removing the rear (right) cylinder head, perform the following:

    a. Remove multi-pin connector from C³I unit.

    b. Remove 2 upper heat shield-to-cowl screws.

    c. Remove throttle cable bracket from cylinder head.

    d. Remove belt tensioner/power steering pump bracket and pump from cylinder head.

    e. Raise and safely support the vehicle.

    f. Remove 2 lower heat shield screws and heat shield.

    g. Remove C³I bracket from manifold studs.

    h. Remove heater tube fro manifold studs.

    i. Remove exhaust manifold-to-crossover bolts.

    j. Disconnect oxygen sensor connection.

    k. Remove exhaust manifold bolts, studs and manifold.

    l. Lower vehicle.

18. Remove valve cover nuts and valve cover.

19. Remove rocker arm bolts and studs. Remove rocker arms, pedestal and guides.

NOTE: Keep parts in order so they can be returned to their original location upon reassembly.

20. Remove cylinder head bolts. Remove cylinder head.

To install:

NOTE: Clean all gasket mating surfaces and cylinder head bolt holes in block with and appropriate tap.

21. Install cylinder head gasket on block. Install cylinder head.

22. Apply an appropriate sealant to cylinder head bolt threads. Install cylinder head bolts.

23. Tighten cylinder head bolts using the following steps:

    a. Tighten each cylinder head bolt to 25 ft. lbs. (34 Nm) following the proper sequence.

NOTE: If 60 ft. lbs. (81 Nm) is reached at any time during steps b and c, STOP. Do not complete the balance of the 90 degree turn on this bolt.

    b. Tighten each bolt ¼ turn (90 degree) in sequence.

    c. Tighten each bolt an additional ¼ turn (90 degree) in sequence.

24. Install pushrods, guide plate and rocker arm assemblies. Apply an appropriate high temperature, high strength thread sealant compound to the rocker arm pedestal bolts. Tighten to 45 ft. lbs. (60 Nm).

25. Install intake manifold.

26. Install valve cover.

27. Install exhaust manifold.

28. If the front (left) side cylinder

head was removed, perform the following:

  a. Install exhaust manifold and bolts. Tighten to 50 ft. lbs. (37 Nm).

  b. Install oil level indicator tube and indicator.

  c. Install cooling fan.

29. If the rear (right) side cylinder head was removed, perform the following:

  a. Raise and safely support the vehicle.

  b. Install exhaust manifold and bolts. Tighten to 37 ft. lbs. (50 Nm).

  c. Connect oxygen sensor connection.

  d. Install exhaust manifold-to-crossover bolts.

  e. Install heater tube.

  f. Install C³I bracket and spark plug wires.

  g. Install heat shield-to-cowl screws.

  h. Lower vehicle.

  i. Install 2 upper heat shield attaching screws.

  j. Install multi-pin connector to C³I unit.

  k. Install belt tensioner/power steering pump bracket to cylinder head.

  l. Install throttle cable bracket to cylinder head.

30. Install intake manifold gaskets and manifold. Tighten intake manifold bolts in sequence to 32 ft. lbs. (44 Nm).

31. Install fuel rail supply and return lines. Connect throttle cables to throttle body.

32. Connect front spark plug wire harness.

33. Connect rear engine lift bracket.

34. Connect PCV and vapor canister vacuum lines. Connect vacuum connector block. Install air intake duct to throttle body.

35. Install upper radiator hose.

36. Connect electrical connections to manifold and cylinder head items.

37. Install alternator and alternator electrical connections.

38. Install serpentine belt.

39. Fill cooling system.

40. Connect negative battery cable.

41. Start engine and check for coolant, oil and fuel leaks. Allow engine to come to normal operating temperature and recheck for leaks.

1988–91 3.8L Engine

1. Disconnect the negative battery cable.

2. Remove the intake and exhaust manifolds.

3. Remove the valve cover.

4. If removing the front (left) side cylinder head, perform the following:

  a. Remove the C³I and spark plug wires.

  b. Remove the alternator bracket.

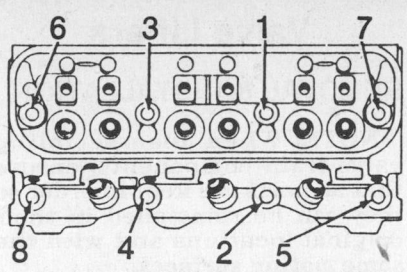

Cylinder head torque sequence— 3.8L engine

  c. Remove 1 air conditioning compressor bracket bolt.

5. If removing the rear (right) side cylinder head, perform the following:

  a. Remove the power steering pump.

  b. Remove the belt tensioner assembly.

  c. Remove fuel line heat shield.

6. Remove rocker arm assemblies, guide plate and pushrods.

7. Remove cylinder head bolts and cylinder head.

NOTE: Clean all gasket mating surfaces and cylinder head bolt holes in block.

To install:

8. Clean threads in block using an appropriate tap.

9. Install cylinder head gasket on block.

10. Apply an appropriate sealant to cylinder head bolt threads. Install cylinder head bolts.

11. On 1988 vehicles, tighten cylinder head bolts using the following steps:

  a. Tighten each cylinder head bolt to 25 ft. lbs. (34 Nm) following the proper sequence.

NOTE: If 60 ft. lbs. (81 Nm) is reached at any time during steps b and c, STOP. Do not complete the balance of the 90 degree turn on this bolt.

  b. Tighten each bolt ¼ turn (90 degree) in sequence.

  c. Tighten each bolt an additional ¼ turn (90 degree) in sequence.

12. On 1989–91 vehicles, tighten cylinder head bolts using the following steps:

  a. Tighten each cylinder head bolt to 35 ft. lbs. (47 Nm) following the proper sequence.

  b. Rotate each bolt 130 degrees, in sequence, using an appropriate torque angle meter.

  c. Rotate each bolt an additional 30 degrees, in sequence, using torque angle meter.

13. Install pushrods, guide plate and rocker arm assemblies. Apply an appropriate high temperature, high

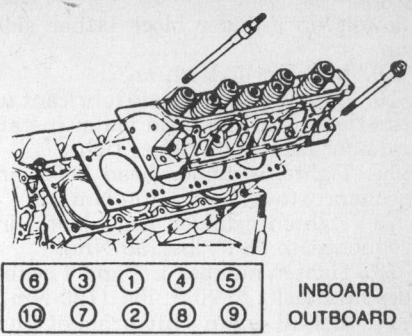

INBOARD
OUTBOARD

Cylinder head torque sequence— 4.1L and 4.5L engines

strength thread sealant compound to the rocker arm pedestal bolts. Tighten to 28 ft. lbs. (38 Nm).

14. Install intake manifold.

15. Install valve cover.

16. Install exhaust manifold.

17. If the front (left) side cylinder head was removed, perform the following:

  a. Install air conditioning compressor bracket bolt. Tighten to 52 ft. lbs. (80 Nm).

  b. Install alternator support bracket to cylinder head.

  c. Install alternator.

  d. Install C³I and spark plug wires.

18. If the rear (right) side cylinder head was removed, perform the following:

  a. Install belt tensioner assembly.

  b. Install power steering pump.

  c. Install fuel line heat shield.

19. Connect negative battery cable.

20. Start engine and check for coolant, oil and fuel leaks. Allow engine to come to normal operating temperature and recheck for leaks.

4.1L and 4.5L Engines

RIGHT SIDE

1. Disconnect the negative battery cable. Drain the engine coolant.

2. Remove rocker arm covers.

3. Remove the lower intake and right hand exhaust manifolds.

4. Remove engine lift bracket and oil dipstick tube.

5. Reposition AIR bracket.

6. Remove 10 cylinder head bolts.

7. Remove cylinder head.

To install:

NOTE: Clean sealing surfaces of cylinder head, block and liners. Clean cylinder head bolt holes with an appropriate tap. Ensure that bolt holes are free of shavings, oil and coolant.

8. Install new head gasket over

dowels on cylinder block either side up.

9. Install cylinder head.

10. Apply an appropriate lubricant to the threads of the head bolts. Install cylinder head bolts finger tight.

11. Tighten cylinder head bolts, in sequence, to 38 ft. lbs. (50 Nm).

12. Tighten cylinder head bolts, in sequence, to 68 ft. lbs. (90 Nm).

13. Tighten number 1, 3 and 4 cylinder head bolts to 90 ft. lbs. (120 Nm).

14. Install engine lift bracket and AIR bracket.

15. Install lower intake and right hand exhaust manifolds.

16. Install rocker arm covers.

17. Fill cooling system.

18. Connect negative battery cable.

19. Start engine and check for coolant, oil and fuel leaks. Allow engine to come to normal operating temperature and recheck for leaks.

LEFT SIDE

1. Disconnect the negative battery cable.

2. Drain the cooling system.

3. Remove the rocker arm covers.

4. Remove the intake manifold-to-engine bolts and intake manifold.

5. Disconnect the exhaust manifold crossover pipe, the exhaust pipe-to-exhaust manifold bolts, the exhaust manifold-to-cylinder head bolts and the exhaust manifold.

6. Remove the engine lifting bracket and the dipstick tube.

7. Remove the AIR bracket-to-engine bolts and move the bracket aside.

8. Remove the cylinder head-to-engine bolts and the cylinder head.

To install:

9. Clean the gasket mounting surfaces.

10. Install new head gasket over dowels on cylinder block either side up.

11. Install cylinder head.

12. Apply a suitable lubricant to the cylinder head bolt threads.

13. Install cylinder head bolts finger tight.

14. Tighten bolts, in sequence, to 38 ft. lbs. (50 Nm).

15. Tighten cylinder head bolts, in sequence, to 68 ft. lbs. (90 Nm).

16. Tighten number 1, 3 and 4 cylinder head bolts to 90 ft. lbs. (120 Nm).

17. Install AIR bracket. Install dipstick tube and engine lift bracket.

18. Install exhaust manifold. Install lower intake manifold.

19. Install rocker arm covers.

20. Fill cooling system.

21. Connect negative battery cable.

22. Start engine and check for coolant, oil and fuel leaks. Allow engine to come to normal operating temperature and recheck for leaks.

Valve Lifters

REMOVAL & INSTALLATION

NOTE: When disassembling valve train components, ensure that all parts are kept in order so they can be reinstalled in their original locations and with the same mating surfaces.

1. Disconnect the negative battery cable. Remove the intake manifold.

2. Remove the rocker arm cover and discard the old gasket.

3. Remove the rocker arm assemblies. Remove the pushrods.

4. Remove the lifter guide retainer bolts and retainer.

5. Remove the lifter retainers.

6. Using the valve lifter removal tool, remove the valve lifters.

To install:

7. Clean the gasket mounting surfaces.

8. Lubricate the lifters with clean engine oil, use new gaskets and/or sealant and reverse the removal procedures.

Valve Lash

All engines use hydraulic lifters which are non-adjustable. Hydraulic valve lifters keep all parts of the valve train in constant contact and adjust automatically to maintain **0** lash under all operating conditions.

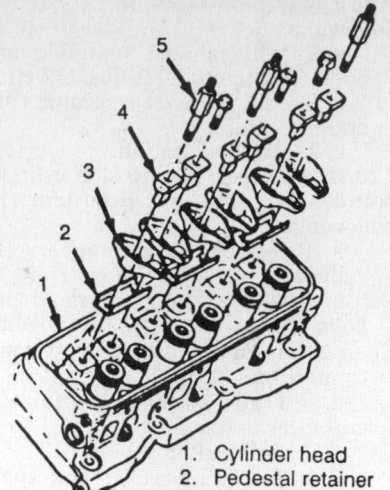

1. Cylinder head
2. Pedestal retainer
3. Rocker arm
4. Pedestal
5. Double ended bolt

Exploded view of the rocker arm assembly—1987 3.8L engine

Rocker Arms

REMOVAL & INSTALLATION

3.8L Engine

1987

1. Disconnect the negative battery cable. Remove the rocker arm cover nuts, washers, seals, the cover and gasket, discard the gasket.

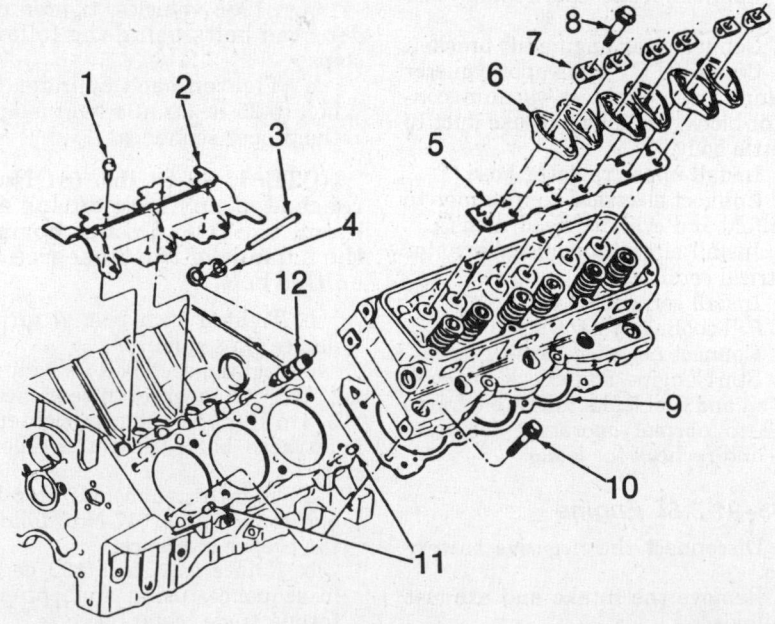

1.	Bolt (27 ft. lbs.)	5.	Pushrod guide	9.	Head gasket
2.	Lifter guide retainer	6.	Rocker arm	10.	Head bolt
3.	Pushrod	7.	Rocker arm pivot	11.	Dowel pin
4.	Lifter guide	8.	Bolt (28 ft. lbs.)	12.	Valve lifter

Exploded view of the rocker arm assembly—1988–91 3.8L engine

2. Remove the rocker arm pedestal-to-cylinder head bolts, the pedestals, the rocker arms and the pedestal retainers. Note the position of the double-ended bolts on disassembly.

NOTE: Be sure to keep the parts in order for reassembly purposes.

3. Clean the gasket mounting surfaces.

4. Using a new gasket and sealant, if necessary, reverse the removal procedures. Torque the rocker arm bolts to 43 ft. lbs. (58 Nm). Check and/or refill the cooling system. Start the engine, allow it to reach normal operating temperatures and check for fluid leaks.

1988–91

1. Disconnect the negative battery cable. Remove the rocker arm cover nuts, washers, seals, the cover and gasket, discard the gasket.

2. Remove the rocker arm pivot-to-cylinder head bolts, the pivots, the rocker arms and the pushrod guide.

NOTE: Be sure to keep the parts in order for reassembly purposes.

3. Clean the gasket mounting surfaces.

4. Using a new gasket and sealant, if necessary, reverse the removal procedures. Torque the rocker arm bolts to 28 ft. lbs. Check and/or refill the cooling system. Check and/or refill the

cooling and lubrication systems. Start the engine, allow it to reach normal operating temperatures and check for leaks.

4.1L and 4.5L Engines

1. Disconnect the negative battery cable. Remove the rocker arm cover.

2. Remove the rocker arm support-to-cylinder head bolts.

3. Remove the rocker arm support-to-cylinder head stud nuts.

NOTE: This method of removal is preferred as the pivot assemblies may be damaged if the pivot bolt torque is not removed evenly against the valve spring tension.

4. Place the rocker arm support in a vise and remove the rocker arm pivot-to-rocker arm support bolts.

To install:

5. Lubricate all parts with axle lube 1052271 or equivalent, and reverse the removal procedures. Torque the rocker arm pivot-to-rocker arm support bolts to 22 ft. lbs. (30 Nm).

NOTE: The pivot bolts are self-tapping.

6. Position the pushrod into the seat of each rocker arm and loosely install the retaining nuts.

7. Recheck the pushrods for being seated correctly. Tighten the nuts alternately and evenly, checking the position of the pushrods while tightening.

8. When the nuts have been seated and the pushrods are correct. Torque the rocker arm support-to-cylinder head nuts to 37 ft. lbs. (50 Nm) and the bolts to 7 ft. lbs. (10 Nm).

9. To complete the installation, reverse the removal procedures. Start the engine and check for leaks.

Intake Manifold

REMOVAL & INSTALLATION

3.8L Engine
1987

1. Relieve the fuel pressure.

2. Disconnect the negative battery cable. Drain the cooling system. Remove the air intake duct and mass air flow sensor.

3. Remove the serpentine drive belt, alternator and alternator bracket.

4. Remove the ignition module and associated wiring. Disconnect wiring and vacuum lines that will interfere with removal of the manifold.

5. Disconnect and remove the throttle, cruise control and transaxle throttle valve cables from the throttle body.

6. Remove the upper radiator hose. Disconnect the heater hoses at the throttle body.

7. Disconnect the electrical connections for the injectors.

8. Remove the fuel rail bolts and the fuel rail. Replace all O-rings on injectors that are to be reused.

9. Label and remove the spark plug wires.

10. Remove the intake manifold bolts, the manifold and gasket.

To install:

11. Clean all mating surfaces.

12. Using new gaskets and sealant 1050026, for a steel gasket, reverse the removal procedures. Pipe thread fittings must be sealed with a sealer and lubricant such as 1052080 or equivalent. Torque the intake manifold-to-engine bolts, in sequence, to 32 ft. lbs. (44 Nm).

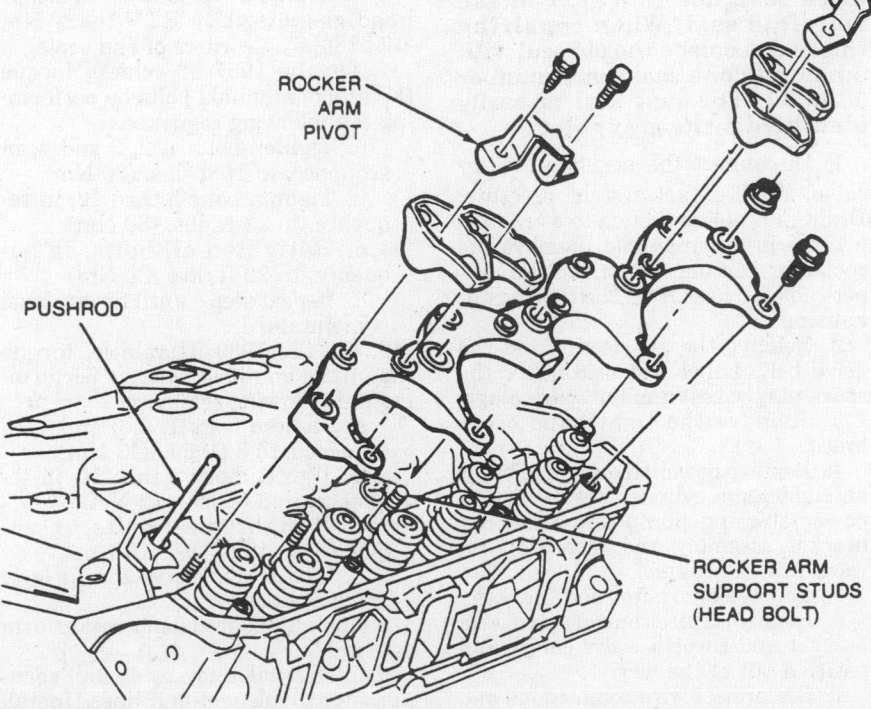

Exploded view of the rocker arm assembly—1987-88 4.1L and 1988-91 4.5L engines

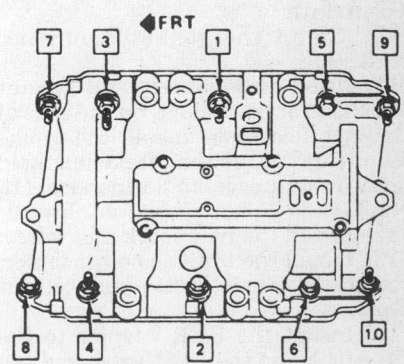

Intake manifold bolt tightening sequence—1987 3.8L engine

13. Install fuel rail assembly and fuel rail bolts. Replace all O-rings on injectors. Torque fuel rail bolts to 120 inch lbs. (15 Nm). Connect electrical connections to fuel injectors.

14. Connect upper radiator hose. Connect heater hoses at the throttle body.

15. Connect the throttle, cruise control and transaxle throttle valve cables to the throttle body.

16. Install the ignition module and associated wiring. Connect wiring and vacuum lines that were removed for ease of disassembly. Install spark plug wires.

17. Install alternator bracket and alternator. Install serpentine belt.

18. Install air intake duct and mass air flow sensor.

19. Fill the cooling system.

20. Connect negative battery cable.

21. Start engine and check for coolant, oil and fuel leaks. Allow engine to come to normal operating temperature and recheck for leaks.

1988–91

1. Relieve the fuel pressure.

2. Disconnect the negative battery cable. Place a clean drain pan under the radiator, open the drain cock and drain the cooling system.

3. Remove the serpentine drive belt, the alternator and the bracket.

4. Remove the power steering pump, the braces and move it aside; do not disconnect the pressure lines.

5. Remove the coolant bypass hose, the heater pipe and the upper radiator hose from the intake manifold.

6. Remove the vacuum hoses and disconnect the electrical connectors from the intake manifold.

7. Remove the EGR pipe, the EGR valve and the adapter from the throttle body.

8. Remove the throttle body coolant pipe, the throttle body and the throttle body adapter.

9. Disconnect the rear spark plug wires. Remove the intake manifold-to-engine bolts and the manifold.

To install:

10. Clean the gasket mounting surfaces.

11. Using new gaskets and sealant 12345336 or equivalent, on the ends of the manifold seals, install the intake manifold. Torque the intake manifold bolts, in sequence, to 88 inch lbs. (10 Nm).

12. Install the rear spark plug wires.

13. Install the throttle body adapter, throttle body and throttle body coolant pipe.

14. Install the EGR adapter to the throttle body, the EGR valve and the EGR pipe.

15. Install the vacuum hoses and

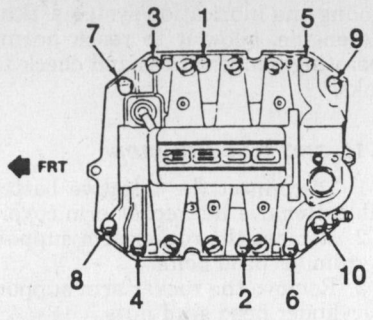

Intake manifold bolt torque sequence— 1988–91 3.9L engine

connect electrical connectors to the intake manifold.

16. Connect the upper radiator hose, heater pipe and coolant bypass hose to the intake manifold.

17. Install the power steering pump braces and power steering pump.

18. Install the alternator bracket and alternator. Install the serpentine drive belt.

19. Fill the cooling system.

20. Connect negative battery cable.

21. Start the engine and check for coolant, oil and fuel leaks. Allow the engine to come to normal operating temperature and recheck for leaks.

4.1L and 4.5L Engines

EXCEPT ALLANTE

NOTE: Some vehicles equipped with the 4.1L and 4.5L engines have been experiencing oil leakage at the intake manifold to block seal, due to a split intake manifold seal. When repairing this leak, replace the old seal with a new silicone seal (part number 3634619). The new seal is easily identified by its gray color.

1. Disconnect the negative battery cable. Relieve fuel system pressure. Drain the cooling system to a level below the intake manifold. Remove the coolant reservoir. Disconnect the upper radiator hose from the thermostat housing.

2. Remove the air cleaner and the drive belt. Label and disconnect the spark plug wires from the spark plugs.

3. Remove the tight hand cross brace.

4. Remove power steering line brace on right hand cylinder head. Remove power steering pump and tensioner bracket assembly and reposition toward front of engine.

5. Remove alternator and bracket.

6. Remove cruise control servo with bracket and throttle valve cables and position out of the way.

7. Disconnect wire connections and reposition:

a. Distributor
b. Oil pressure switch
c. Coolant temperature sensor
d. EGR solenoid
e. ISC motor
f. Throttle position switch
g. Electric EFE grid
h. Injectors
i. MAT sensor

8. Remove upper radiator hose and heater hose. remove air conditioning hose bracket.

9. Disconnect spark plug wire protectors and reposition cap.

10. Mark the distributor rotor position and remove distributor.

NOTE: Do not crank or in any other way rotate crankshaft with the distributor removed.

11. Disconnect fuel and vacuum lines from throttle body. Disconnect vacuum supply solenoid and lines.

12. Remove valve covers. Remove rocker arms and pushrods.

NOTE: Pushrods should be marked or retained in sequence so that they may be reinstalled in their original positions.

13. Remove intake manifold bolts and remove intake manifold, gaskets and seals. Discard gaskets and seals.

14. Clean sealing surfaces fo intake manifold, cylinder head and cylinder block.

To install:

15. Install new end seals. Use RTV (part No. 1052366) at 4 corners where end seals will meet side gaskets.

16. Install new intake to cylinder head gaskets. Use RTV (part No. 1052366) at 4 corners of end seals.

17. On the 1987–88 vehicle, torque the intake manifold bolts by performing the following sequence:

a. Tighten bolts 1, 2, 3 and 4, in sequence, to 15 ft. lbs. (20 Nm).

b. Tighten bolts 5 thru 16, in sequence, to 22 ft. lbs. (30 Nm).

c. Retighten all bolts, in sequence, to 22 ft. lbs. (30 Nm).

d. Repeat step c until torque level is maintained.

18. On the 1989–91 vehicle, torque the intake manifold bolts by performing the following sequence:

a. Tighten bolts 1, 2, 3 and 4, in sequence, to 8 ft. lbs. (12 Nm).

b. Tighten bolts 5 thru 16, in sequence, to 8 ft. lbs. (12 Nm).

c. Retighten all bolts, in sequence, to 12 ft. lbs. (16 Nm).

d. Repeat step c until torque level is maintained.

19. Install pushrods and rocker arm assembly.

20. Install valve covers. Install vacuum supply solenoid and lines. Install fuel and vacuum lines to throttle body.

21. Install distributor in original position. Install distributor cap and wire protectors.

22. Install air conditioning hose bracket.

23. Install upper radiator hose and heater hose.

24. Connnect following wire connectors:
   a. Distributor
   b. Oil pressure switch
   c. Coolant temperature sensor
   d. EGR solenoid
   e. ISC motor
   f. Throttle position switch
   g. Electric EFE grid
   h. Injectors
   i. MAT sensor

25. Install cruise control servo and throttle valve cables.

26. Install alternator bracket and alternator.

27. Install power steering pump and tensioner assembly. Install power steering line brace to right hand cylinder head.

28. Install accessory drive belt. Install coolant reservoir.

29. Install right hand cross brace.

30. Fill cooling system.

31. Install air cleaner assembly.

32. Connect negative battery cable.

33. Start engine and check for coolant, oil and fuel leaks. Allow engine to come to normal operating temperature and recheck for leaks.

ALLANTE

NOTE: Some vehicles equipped with the 4.1L and 4.5L engines have been experiencing oil leakage at the intake manifold to block seal, due to a split intake manifold seal. When repairing this leak, replace the old seal with a new silicone seal (part number 3634619). The new seal is easily identified by its gray color.

1. Disconnect the negative battery cable. Relieve fuel system pressure. Drain the cooling system to a level below the lower intake manifold. Remove the coolant reservoir. Remove accessory drive belt.

2. Remove shock tower support bracket.

3. Disconnect accelerator, cruise control and throttle valve cables.

4. Remove appropriate vacuum lines.

5. Remove 2 EGR pipe-to-upper intake bolts. Remove EGR tube gasket.

6. Remove MAP and MAT sensor and electrical connections. Remove PCV hose.

7. Remove transaxle dipstick tube bolt. Remove fuel line support bracket.

8. Remove upper intake support bracket. Remove heater assembly and discard gasket.

9. Remove upper intake from lower intake manifold and discard gaskets.

10. Remove power steering pump accessory drive bracket bolts on right hand cylinder head. Loosen power steering pump and tensioner and position toward the front of the engine.

11. Remove vacuum line from pressure regulator and base assembly.

12. Remove inlet fitting screw assemblies and bracket from rear fuel rail and pressure regulator assemblies.

13. Remove fuel feed line and O-ring from rear fuel rail assembly. Discard O-ring. Remove fuel return line from return fitting.

14. Remove 4 rail support bracket attaching bolts. Disconnect electrical connectors at front and rear wiring assemblies.

15. Remove fuel rail assembly from manifold.

16. Remove alternator with bracket and idler pulley.

17. Remove cruise control servo with bracket and cables. Reposition out of the way.

18. Remove wire connections as follows:
   a. Distributor
   b. Oil pressure switches
   c. Coolant temperature sensor
   d. Ground wires

19. Disconnect the upper radiator hose and 2 heater hose connections.

20. Disconnect spark plug wire protectors and reposition cap.

21. Mark distributor rotor position and remove distributor.

NOTE: Do not crank or in any other way rotate crankshaft with the distributor removed.

22. Remove valve covers. Remove rocker arms and pushrods.

NOTE: Pushrods should be marked or retained in sequence so they may be reinstalled in their original positions.

23. Remove intake manifold bolts and remove intake manifold, gaskets and seals. Discard gaskets and seals.

24. Clean sealing surfaces of intake manifold, cylinder head and cylinder block.

To install:

25. Install new end seals. Use RTV at 4 corners where end seals will meet side gaskets.

26. Install new intake to cylinder head gaskets. Use RTV at 4 corners of end seals.

27. On the 1987–88 vehicle, torque the intake manifold bolts by performing the following sequence:
   a. Tighten bolts 1, 2, 3 and 4, in sequence, to 15 ft. lbs. (20 Nm).
   b. Tighten bolts 5 thru 16, in sequence, to 22 ft. lbs. (30 Nm).
   c. Retighten all bolts, in sequence, to 22 ft. lbs. (30 Nm).
   d. Repeat step c until torque level is maintained.

28. On the 1989–91 vehicle, torque the intake manifold bolts by performing the following sequence:
   a. Tighten bolts 1, 2, 3 and 4, in sequence, to 8 ft. lbs. (12 Nm).

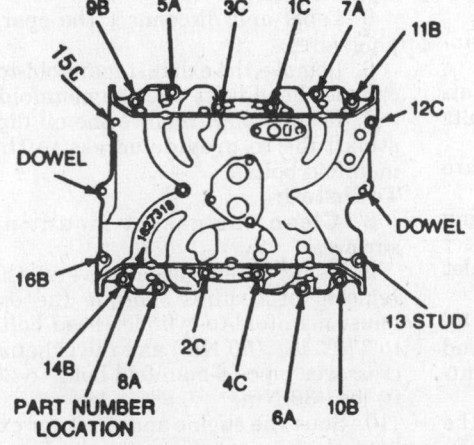

FRONT OF ENGINE

BOLT TIGHTENING SEQUENCE

1. TIGHTEN BOLTS 1, 2, 3, & 4 IN SEQUENCE TO 20.0 N·m (15 FT-LBS).

2. TIGHTEN BOLTS 5 THRU 16 IN SEQUENCE TO 30.0 N·m (22 FT-LBS).

3. RETIGHTEN ALL BOLTS IN SEQUENCE TO 30.0 N·m (22 FT-LBS).

4. REPEAT STEP 3.

Intake manifold bolt torque sequence—1987–88 4.1L and 1988–91 4.5L engines

b. Tighten bolts 5 thru 16, in sequence, to 8 ft. lbs. (12 Nm).

c. Retighten all bolts, in sequence, to 12 ft. lbs. (16 Nm).

d. Repeat step c until torque level is maintained.

29. Install pushrods and rocker arm assembly.

30. Install valve covers. Install vacuum supply solenoid and lines. Install fuel and vacuum lines to throttle body.

31. Install distributor in original position. Install distributor cap and wire protectors.

32. Install air conditioning hose bracket.

33. Install upper radiator hose and heater hose.

34. Connnect following wire connectors:

a. Distributor

b. Oil pressure switch

c. Coolant temperature sensor

d. Ground wires

35. Install cruise control servo and throttle valve cables.

36. Install alternator bracket and alternator.

37. Install power steering line brace to right hand cylinder head. Install power steering pump and tensioner assembly.

38. Install accessory drive belt. Install coolant reservoir.

39. Lubricate new injector O-ring seals and install on spray tip end of each fuel injector.

NOTE: If new rail support brackets have to be installed, tighten the attaching screw assemblies to 44 inch lbs. (5 Nm).

40. Install fuel rail assembly in intake manifold.

41. Install rail support bracket attaching bolts. Tighten attaching bolts to 18 ft. lbs. (24 Nm).

42. Install vacuum line to pressure regulator.

43. Lubricate new inlet fitting O-ring and install on fuel feed line. Connect fuel feed line into rear fuel rail inlet port.

44. Connect inlet fitting bracket and screw assemblies to rear fuel rail and pressure regulator assemblies. Tighten to 44 inch lbs. (5 Nm).

45. Connect fuel return line to the return line fitting. Tighten to 22 ft. lbs. (30 Nm). Use backup wrench on fitting to prevent it from turning.

46. Connect electrical connectors at front and rear wiring assemblies.

47. Install new upper intake-to-lower intake gaskets.

48. Install upper intake attaching nuts to lower intake manifold. Tighten to 15 ft. lbs. (20 Nm).

49. Install heater assembly and gasket.

50. Install throttle body and gasket. Tighten throttle body bolts to 15 ft. lbs. (20 Nm).

51. Install EGR pipe. Tighten EGR pipe bolts to 18 ft. lbs. (24 Nm).

52. Install upper intake support bracket. Install rear fuel line support bracket. Install transaxle dipstick tube bolt.

53. Connect PCV hose. Connect MAT and MAP sensors and electrical connectors.

54. Install vacuum lines. Install shock tower support bracket.

55. Install accelerator, cruise control and throttle valve cables.

56. Fill cooling system.

57. Install air cleaner assembly.

58. Connect negative battery cable.

59. Start engine and check for coolant, oil and fuel leaks. Allow engine to come to normal operating temperature and recheck for leaks.

Exhaust Manifold

REMOVAL & INSTALLATION

3.8L Engine

LEFT SIDE

1. Disconnect the negative battery cable.

2. If necessary, remove the mass air flow sensor, air intake duct and crankcase ventilation pipe.

3. Remove the exhaust crossover pipe-to-exhaust manifold bolts.

4. Remove the cooling fan assembly, as required.

5. Label and disconnect the spark plug wires.

6. Remove the exhaust manifold-to-cylinder head bolts and the manifold.

7. If necessary, remove the oil dipstick tube to provide access to the manifold bolts.

To install:

8. Clean the gasket mounting surfaces.

9. Using a new gasket, reverse the removal procedures. Torque the exhaust manifold-to-cylinder head bolts to 37 ft. lbs. (50 Nm) and the exhaust crossover pipe-to-manifold bolts to 22 ft. lbs. (30 Nm).

10. Start the engine and check for exhaust leaks.

RIGHT SIDE

1. Disconnect the negative battery cable.

2. Remove heater hose from heater pipe.

3. Remove power steering support bracket from intake manifold and C^3I bracket from stud.

4. Remove throttle bracket from cylinder head.

5. Remove exhaust crossover bolts from rear exhaust manifold.

6. Remove 2 upper heat shield screws.

7. Raise and safely support the vehicle.

8. Disconnect exhaust pipe from exhaust manifold.

9. Remove 2 lower heat shield screws and heat shield.

10. Remove spark plug wires from spark plugs.

11. Disconnect oxygen sensor connection. Remove EGR pipe, as required.

12. Remove heater pipe-to-manifold nuts. Remove C^3I bracket-to-manifold nuts.

13. Remover manifold bolts and studs. Remove manifold.

To install:

14. Install exhaust manifold. Install manifold bolts and studs. Tighten to 37 ft. lbs. (50 Nm).

15. Install C^3I bracket bracket and nuts.

16. Install heater pipe on studs and tighten nuts.

17. Connect oxygen sensor connection. Install EGR pipe, if removed.

18. Connect spark plug wires to spark plugs.

19. Install heat shield with 2 lower attaching screws.

20. Install exhaust pipe to manifold.

21. Lower vehicle.

22. Install heater hose to heater pipe.

23. Install power steering support bracket and C^3I bracket to intake manifold stud.

24. Install exhaust crossover to rear manifold.

25. Install throttle bracket to cylinder head.

26. Install 2 upper heat shield screws to cowl.

27. Connect negative battery cable.

4.1L and 4.5L Engines

LEFT SIDE

1. Disconnect the negative battery cable, the oxygen sensor wire and the spark plug wires.

2. Remove both cooling fan; both fans, if equipped.

3. Remove the serpentine drive belt and the AIR pipe from the air pump. Remove the starter shield, as required.

4. Remove the belt tensioner and the power steering pump brace.

5. Raise and safely support the vehicle.

6. Remove the exhaust Y-pipe and the air conditioning-to-manifold brace.

7. Remove the exhaust manifold-to-cylinder head bolts, the AIR pipe and the manifold.

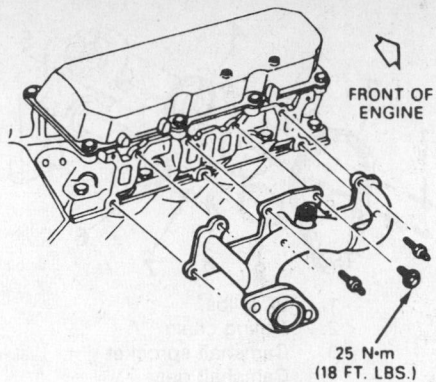

Exploded view of the exhaust manifolds —
4.1L and 4.5L engines

25 N·m
(18 FT. LBS.)

FRONT OF
ENGINE

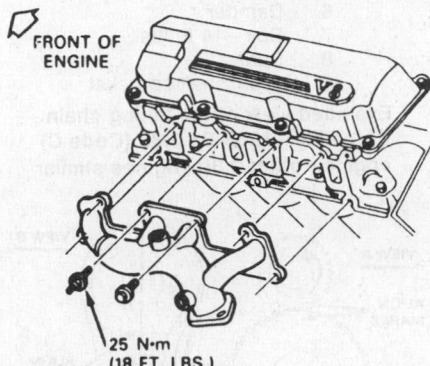

To install:

8. Clean the gasket mounting surfaces.

9. Using new gaskets, reverse the removal procedures. Torque the exhaust manifold-to-engine bolts to 16 ft. lbs. (21 Nm). Start the engine and check for exhaust leaks.

RIGHT SIDE

1. Disconnect the negative battery cable. Remove the air cleaner.

2. Remove the EGR pipe from the manifold. Remove 2 heat shield screws.

3. Raise and safely support the vehicle.

4. Disconnect the Y-pipe from the manifold.

5. From the front of the manifold, remove the engine mount brace.

6. Disconnect the oxygen sensor wire. Remove heat shield.

7. If required, support engine cradle with screw jacks and remove rear cradle bolts on both sides. Loosen front cradle bolts. Slightly lower engine cradle.

8. Remove the exhaust manifold-to-cylinder head bolts and the manifold.

To install:

9. Clean the gasket mounting surfaces.

10. Using new gaskets, reverse the removal procedures. Torque the exhaust manifold-to-engine bolts to 16

ft. lbs. (20 Nm). Start the engine and check for exhaust leaks.

Timing Chain Front Cover

REMOVAL & INSTALLATION

3.8L Engine

1. Disconnect the negative battery cable.

2. Drain the cooling system. Remove the lower radiator hose and the coolant bypass hose from the timing case cover. Remove the heater pipes.

3. Install a vertical lifting device and raise the engine slightly. Remove the front engine cradle mount bolts.

4. Remove the serpentine drive belt and the water pump pulley.

5. Label and disconnect the alternator wiring. Remove the alternator and the alternator bracket.

6. Raise and safely support the vehicle.

7. Remove right front tire and wheel assembly.

8. On 1988–91 vehicles, remove the inner splash shield.

9. Remove the crankshaft balancer bolt/washer and the balancer.

10. Disconnect the electrical connectors from the crankshaft sensor, the camshaft sensor and the oil pressure switch.

11. Remove the oil pan-to-timing case cover bolts, the timing case cover-to-engine bolts and the cover.

To install:

12. Clean the gasket mounting surfaces.

13. Using a new gasket and sealant 1052080 or equivalent, reverse the removal procedures. Torque the:

Timing case cover-to-engine bolts to 22 ft. lbs. (30 Nm).

Oil pan-to-timing case cover bolts to 88 inch lbs. (10 Nm).

Crankshaft balancer-to-crankshaft bolt to 219 ft. lbs. (298 Nm).

14. Refill the cooling system. Start the engine, allow it to reach normal operating temperatures and check for leaks.

4.1L and 4.5L Engines

1. Disconnect the negative battery cable.

2. Drain the cooling system. Remove the air cleaner.

3. Remove the serpentine belt.

4. Remove the right cross brace.

5. Remove the AIR air filter and bracket.

6. Remove the water pump pulley bolts and the pulley. If necessary, remove the idler pulley.

7. Raise and safely support the vehicle.

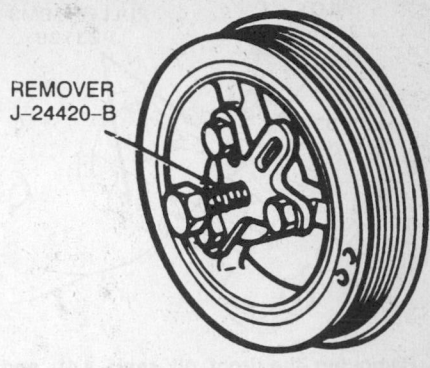

REMOVER
J–24420–B

Using the Wheel Puller tool to remove the damper pulley — 4.1L and 4.5L engines

8. Remove the crankshaft pulley-to-crankshaft pulley bolt. Attach a wheel puller to the crankshaft pulley. Using a pilot between the crankshaft and the center bolt, press the crankshaft pulley from the crankshaft. Remove the Woodruff® key from the crankshaft.

9. Remove the timing case cover-to-engine bolts, the oil pan-to-timing case cover bolts and the cover.

10. Clean the gasket mounting surfaces.

11. To complete the installation, use a new gasket, RTV sealant (on the oil pan lip) and reverse the removal procedures. Torque the timing case cover-to-engine bolts to 15 ft. lbs. (20 Nm) and the crankshaft pulley-to-crankshaft bolt to 18 ft. lbs. (25 Nm).

Front Cover Oil Seal

REPLACEMENT

3.8L Engine

1. Disconnect the negative battery cable.

2. Remove the drive belt.

3. Remove the crankshaft balancer-to-crankshaft bolts.

4. Using a small prybar, pry the oil seal from the timing case cover; be careful not to damage the sealing surfaces.

To install:

5. Clean the oil seal mounting surface.

6. Using GM lubricant 1050169 or equivalent, coat the outside of the seal and the crankshaft balancer.

7. Using the oil seal installation tool, drive the new seal into the timing case cover until it seats.

8. To complete the installation, reverse the removal procedures. Torque the crankshaft balancer-to-crankshaft bolt to 219 ft. lbs. (297 Nm).

4.1L and 4.5L Engines

1. Disconnect the negative battery cable.

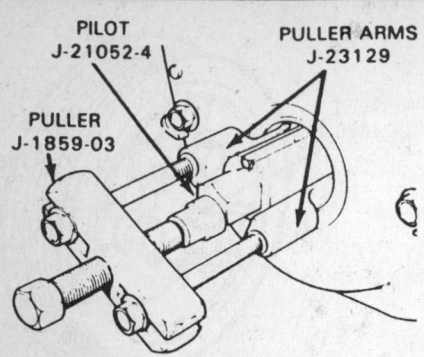

Removing the front oil seal—4.1L and 4.5L engines

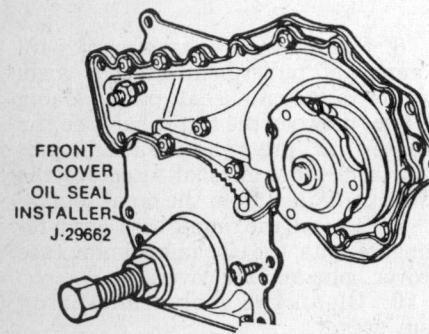

Installing the front oil seal—4.1L and 4.5L engines

2. Remove the serpentine belt.

3. Raise and safely support the vehicle.

4. Remove right front tire. Remove right front air deflector.

5. Loosen and reposition the heater bypass line.

6. Remove the crankshaft pulley-to-crankshaft pulley bolt. Attach a wheel puller to the crankshaft pulley. Using a pilot between the crankshaft and the center bolt, press the crankshaft pulley from the crankshaft. Remove the Woodruff® key from the crankshaft.

7. Using a small prybar, pry the oil seal from the timing case cover, discard it.

To install:

8. Clean the oil seal mounting surface. Lubricate the new seal with engine oil.

9. Using a hammer and the oil seal installation tool, drive the new oil seal in to the timing case cover until it seats.

10. Lubricate bore of hub and inside diameter of seal with EP lubricant to prevent seizure to crankshaft and provide lubrication of oil seal lip.

11. Position damper on crankshaft, lining up key slot in hub with key on crankshaft.

12. Position installer on end of crankshaft. Position thrust bearing with inner race forward, then washer

and installer nut last. Install damper on crankshaft by tightening installer nut.

13. Hub will bottom out on crankshaft. Torque installer nut to 65 ft. lbs. (90 Nm) to ensure balancer and timing gear are fully seated. Remove installer and reinstall bolt/washer in crankshaft. Torque to 65 ft. lbs. (90 Nm).

14. Install heater bypass line.

15. Install right front air deflector. Install right front tire.

16. Install serpentine belt.

17. Connect negative battery cable.

Timing Chain and Sprockets

REMOVAL & INSTALLATION

3.8L Engine

1. Disconnect the negative battery cable. Remove the front cover.

2. Remove the button and spring from the center of the camshaft.

3. Rotate the crankshaft to align the marks of the timing sprockets; they must be close together.

4. Remove the camshaft sprocket bolts, the sprocket and the timing chain.

5. Remove the crankshaft sprocket and the Woodruff® key; be sure not to lose the key.

To install:

6. Clean the gasket mounting surfaces. Inspect the parts for wear and/or damage; if necessary, replace the parts.

7. To install the timing chain and sprockets, perform the following procedures:

   a. Assemble the timing chain on the camshaft sprocket and crankshaft sprockets.

   b. Align the **0** marks on the sprockets; they must face each other.

   c. Slide the assembly onto the camshaft and crankshaft. Install the camshaft sprocket-to-camshaft bolts. Torque the camshaft sprocket-to-camshaft sprocket bolts to 27 ft. lbs. (37 Nm).

NOTE: On the 1988–91 (VIN C) engine, align the camshaft sprocket mark with the balancer shaft sprocket mark.

8. Using petroleum jelly, pack the oil pump.

9. To complete the installation, use new gaskets, sealant, if necessary, and reverse the removal procedures. Refill the cooling system. Start the engine, allow it to reach normal operating temperatures and check for leaks.

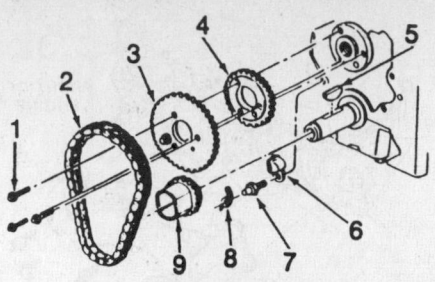

1. 27 ft. lbs.
2. Timing chain
3. Camshaft sprocket
4. Camshaft gear
5. Key
6. Damper
7. Bolt – 14 ft. lbs.
8. Spring
9. Crankshaft sprocket

Exploded view of the timing chain assembly—1988–91 3.8L (Code C) engine—other 3.8L engines similar

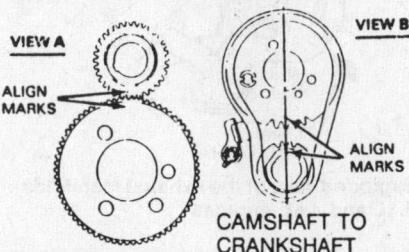

View of the timing sprocket alignment—3.8L engine–balance shaft gear alignment is used on the 1988–91 3.8L (Code C) engine only

4.1L and 4.5L Engines

1. Disconnect the negative battery cable. Drain the cooling system.

2. Remove engine front cover.

3. Remove oil slinger from crankshaft.

4. Rotate the engine until the crankshaft and camshaft timing marks are aligned.

5. Remove thrust button and screw securing camshaft sprocket to camshaft. Discard thrust button.

6. Remove camshaft and crankshaft sprockets with chain attached.

To install:

7. If timing was disturbed, rotate crankshaft until timing mark on crank sprocket is positioned straight up.

8. Install timing chain over camshaft sprocket.

9. Install cam sprocket, crank sprocket and timing chain over crankshaft, ensuring that timing marks are aligned.

10. Move camshaft until the dowel pin mates with the index hole in the sprocket.

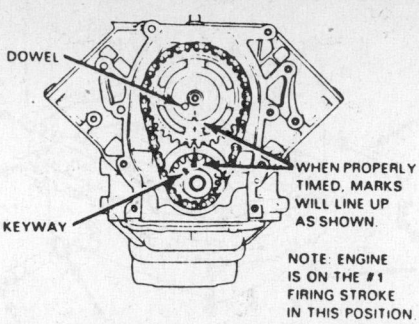

DOWEL

KEYWAY

WHEN PROPERLY TIMED, MARKS WILL LINE UP AS SHOWN.

NOTE: ENGINE IS ON THE #1 FIRING STROKE IN THIS POSITION.

Aligning the timing marks — 4.1L and 4.5L V8 engines

11. Hold camshaft sprocket in position against end of camshaft and press sprocket on camshaft by hand, being sure index pin in camshaft is aligned with index hole in sprocket.

12. Install screw securing camshaft sprocket to camshaft. Tighten to 37 ft. lbs. (50 Nm).

NOTE: It may be necessary to keep the engine from rotating while setting the torque.

13. Install new thrust button.

14. Install oil slinger on crankshaft with smaller end of slinger against crankshaft sprocket.

15. Install engine front cover.

16. Connect negative battery cable.

Camshaft

REMOVAL & INSTALLATION

3.8L Engine

1. Disconnect the negative battery cable. Remove the intake manifold, the timing chain and camshaft sprockets.

2. Remove the rocker arm covers, the rocker arm shaft or rocker arm assemblies, the pushrods and the hydraulic lifters.

NOTE: When removing the valve components, be sure to keep them in order for reinstallation purposes.

3. On the 1988–91 (VIN C) engine, remove the camshaft gear from the camshaft.

4. On 1987 engines, remove the camshaft thrust bearing-to-engine bolts.

5. Carefully, slide the camshaft forward, out of the bearing bores; do not damage the bearing surfaces.

To install:

6. Clean the gasket mounting surfaces. Inspect the parts for wear and/or damage; if necessary, replace the parts.

7. Using new gaskets, sealant, if necessary, lubricate the valve lifters

and camshaft with multi-lube 1052365 or equivalent, and reverse the removal procedures. Refill the cooling system. Start the engine, allow it to reach normal operating temperatures and check for leaks.

NOTE: On the 1988–91 (VIN C) engine, align the camshaft gear with the balancer shaft gear timing marks.

4.1L and 4.5L Engines

To perform this procedure, the engine must be removed from the vehicle and attached to an engine stand.

1. Disconnect the negative battery cable. Remove the intake manifold and the timing chain.

2. Remove the valve lifters.

NOTE: When removing the valve components, be sure to keep the parts in order for reinstallation purposes.

3. Carefully slide the camshaft out from the front of the engine; be sure not to damage the camshaft bearings.

To install:

4. Clean the gasket mounting surfaces. Inspect the parts for wear and/or damage; if necessary, replace the parts.

5. Lubricate the camshaft with engine oil, use new gaskets, sealant, if necessary, and reverse the removal procedures. Torque the camshaft sprocket-to-camshaft screws to 37 ft. lbs. (50 Nm).

NOTE: If a new camshaft is to be installed, new lifters and a distributor drive gear must also be installed.

6. To complete the installation, reverse the removal procedures. Refill the cooling system. Start the engine, allow it to reach normal operating temperatures and check for leaks.

Auxiliary/Silent Shaft

REMOVAL & INSTALLATION

1988–91 3.8L Engine

1. Disconnect the negative battery cable. Remove the engine and secure it to a workstand.

2. Remove the flywheel-to-crankshaft bolts and the flywheel.

3. Remove the timing chain cover-to-engine bolts and the cover.

4. Remove the camshaft sprocket-to-camshaft gear bolts, the sprocket, the timing chain and the gear.

5. To remove the balance shaft, perform the following procedures:

   a. Remove the balance shaft gear-to-shaft bolt and the gear.

   b. Remove the balance shaft retainer-to-engine bolts and the retainer.

   c. Using the slide hammer tool, pull the balance shaft from the front of the engine.

6. If replacing the rear balance shaft bearing, perform the following procedures:

   a. Drive the rear plug from the engine.

   b. Using the camshaft remover/installer tool, press the rear bearing from the rear of the engine.

   c. Dip the new bearing in clean engine oil.

   d. Using the balance shaft rear bearing installer tool, press the new rear bearing into the rear of the engine.

   e. Install the rear cup plug.

To install:

7. Using the balance shaft installer tool, screw it into the balance shaft and install the shaft into the engine; remove the installer tool.

8. Clean the gasket mounting surfaces. Inspect the parts for wear and/or damage; replace the parts, if necessary.

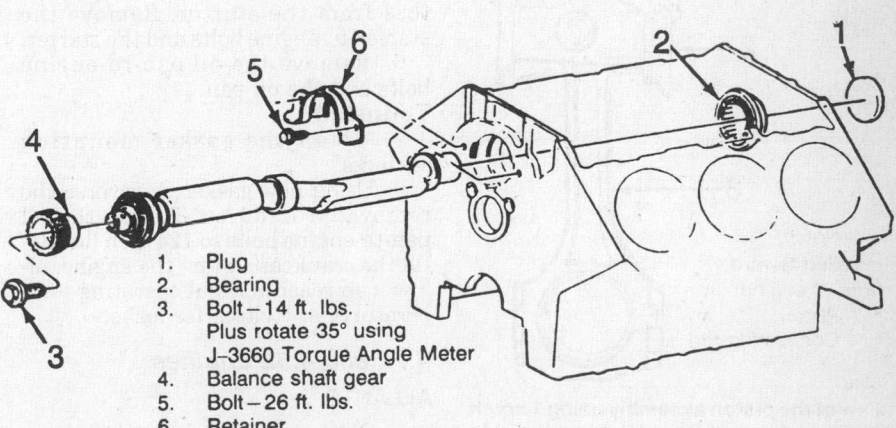

1. Plug
2. Bearing
3. Bolt — 14 ft. lbs.
   Plus rotate 35° using
   J–3660 Torque Angle Meter
4. Balance shaft gear
5. Bolt — 26 ft. lbs.
6. Retainer

Exploded view of the balance shaft assembly — 1988–91 3.8L (Code C) engine

9. Install the balance shaft retainer. Torque the balance shaft retainer-to-engine bolts to 27 ft. lbs.

10. Align the balance shaft gear with the camshaft gear timing marks. Install the balance shaft gear onto the balance shaft. Torque the balance gear-to-balance shaft bolt to 45 ft. lbs. (61 Nm).

11. To complete the installation, use new gaskets, sealant, if necessary, and reverse the removal procedures. Torque the flywheel-to-crankshaft bolts to 60 ft. lbs. (81 Nm). Refill the cooling system. Start the engine, allow it reach normal operating temperatures and check for leaks.

Piston and Connecting Rod

POSITIONING

NOTCHES TOWARD FRONT OF ENGINE

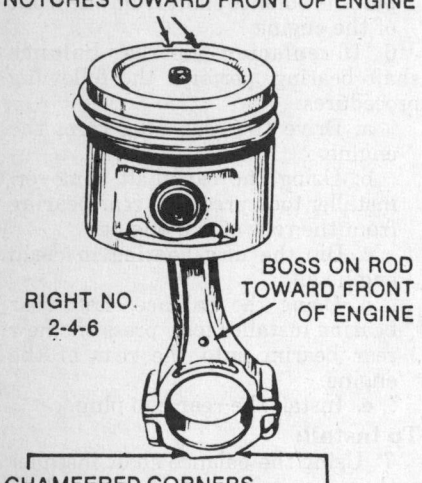

RIGHT NO. 2-4-6

BOSS ON ROD TOWARD FRONT OF ENGINE

CHAMFERED CORNERS TOWARD REAR OF ENGINE

View of the right-bank piston and rod positioning — 3.8L and 4.1L V6 engines

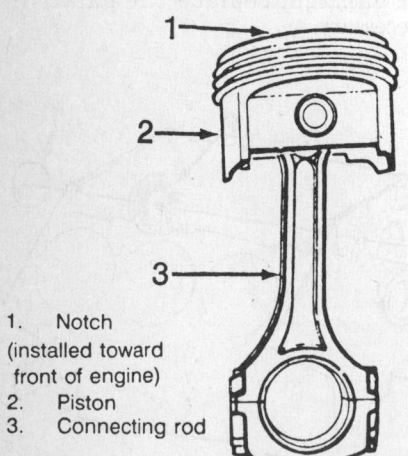

1. Notch (installed toward front of engine)
2. Piston
3. Connecting rod

View of the piston assembly using 1 notch on the piston and the oil hole on the side of the connecting rod

---

NOTCHES TOWARD FRONT OF ENGINE

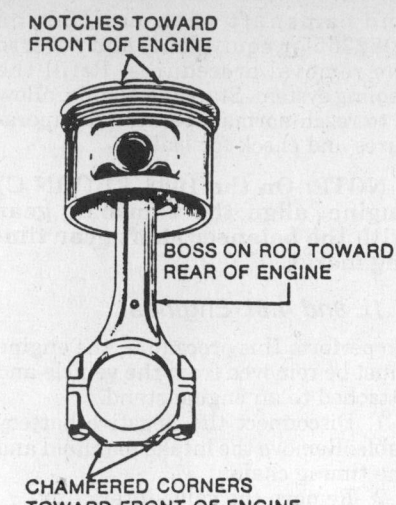

BOSS ON ROD TOWARD REAR OF ENGINE

CHAMFERED CORNERS TOWARD FRONT OF ENGINE

LEFT NO. 1-3-5

View of the left-bank piston and rod positioning — 3.8L and 4.1L V6 engines

ENGINE LUBRICATION

Oil Pan

REMOVAL & INSTALLATION

3.8L Engine

1. Disconnect the negative battery cable.

2. Raise and safely support the vehicle.

3. Drain the crankcase.

4. Remove the torque converter cover and the oil filter.

5. Disconnect the electrical connectors from the starter. Remove the starter-to-engine bolts and the starter.

6. Remove the oil pan-to-engine bolts and the oil pan.

To install:

7. Clean the gasket mounting surfaces.

8. Using new gasket(s), reverse the removal procedures. Torque the oil pan-to-engine bolts to 124 inch lbs. Refill the crankcase. Start the engine, allow it to reach normal operating temperatures and check for leaks.

4.1L and 4.5L Engines

ALLANTE

1. Disconnect the negative battery cable.

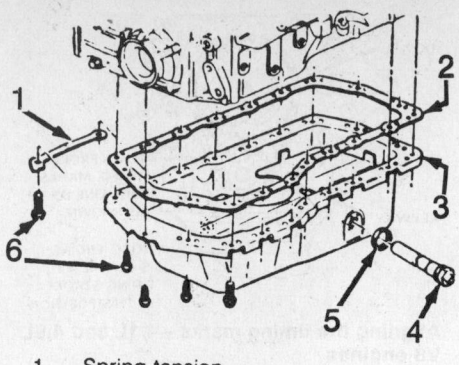

1. Spring tension
2. Oil pan gasket
3. Oil pan
4. Oil level indicator switch — 40 ft. lbs.
5. Seal
6. Bolt — 124 inch lbs.

Exploded view of the oil pan assembly — 1988–91 3.8L (Code C) engine

2. Raise and safely support the vehicle.

3. Drain the crankcase and disconnect the oil level sensor.

4. Remove the torque converter cover.

5. Remove the exhaust Y-pipe.

6. Remove the oil pan-to-engine bolts/nuts and the oil pan.

To install:

7. Clean the gasket mounting surfaces.

8. Using a new gasket, place RTV sealant at the rear main bearing cap and the front cover-to-block joints and reverse the removal procedures. Torque the oil pan-to-engine bolts to 15 ft. lbs. (20 Nm). Fill the crankcase. Start the engine and check for leaks.

ELDORADO AND SEVILLE

1. Disconnect the negative battery cable. Raise and safely support the vehicle. Drain the crankcase.

2. Remove the 2 torque converter covers from the lower side of the transaxle.

3. Remove the exhaust crossunder pipe and reposition.

4. Remove the oil pan-to-engine bolts and the pan.

To install:

4. Clean the gasket mounting surfaces.

5. Using new gaskets and sealant, reverse the removal procedures. Torque the oil pan-to-engine bolts to 12 ft. lbs. (16 Nm). Refill the crankcase. Start the engine and check for leaks.

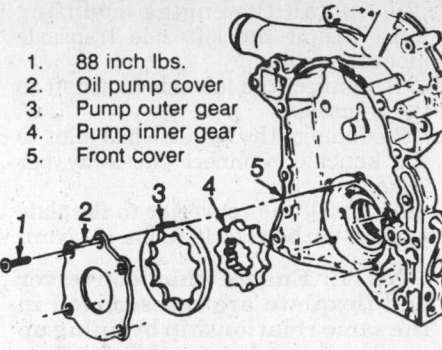

1. 88 inch lbs.
2. Oil pump cover
3. Pump outer gear
4. Pump inner gear
5. Front cover

Exploded view of the oil pump assembly—3.8L engine—4.1L V6 similar

Oil Pump

REMOVAL & INSTALLATION

3.8L Engine

The oil pump, located in the bottom of the front cover, is an integral part of the front cover; the crankshaft passes through it.

1. Disconnect the negative battery cable. Remove the front cover.
2. Clean the gasket mounting surfaces.
3. To inspect the pump gears, perform the following procedures:

   a. Remove the oil pump cover-to-front cover screws and the cover.

   b. Remove the inner and outer pump gears.

   c. Using solvent, clean the gears.

   d. Inspect the gears for wear and/or damage; if necessary, replace the parts.

To install:

4. Using petroleum jelly, pack the pump and reinstall the parts. Torque the oil pump cover-to-front cover screws to 88 inch lbs. (11 Nm).

NOTE: Unless the pump is properly primed this way, it won't produce any oil pressure when the engine is started.

5. To complete the installation, use new gaskets, sealant, if necessary, and reverse the removal procedures. Check and/or refill the crankcase. Replace the oil filter. Start the engine and check for leaks.

4.1L and 4.5L Engines

1. Disconnect the negative battery cable. Remove the oil pan.
2. Remove the oil pump-to-engine screws/nut and the oil pump from the engine.
3. To disassemble, remove the oil pump cover-to-housing screws, slide the driveshaft, drive gear and driven gear from the pump housing.

4. Remove the oil pressure regulator valve and spring from the bore in the housing assembly.
5. Inspect the oil pressure regulator valve for nicks and burrs.
6. Measure the free length of the regulator valve spring. It should be 2.57–2.69 in. (65.28–68.32mm).
7. Inspect the drive gear and driven gear for nicks and burrs.
8. Assemble the pump drive gear over the driveshaft so the retaining ring is inside the gear. Position the drive gear over the pump housing shaft closest to the pressure regulator bore.
9. Slide the driven gear over the remaining shaft in the pump housing, meshing the driven gear with the drive gear.
10. Install the oil pressure regulator spring and valve in the bore of the pump housing assembly.
11. Install the pump cover-to-pump housing screws to 5 ft. lbs. (7 Nm), the oil pump-to-engine screws to 15 ft. lbs. (20 Nm) and nut to 22 ft. lbs. (30 Nm).
12. To complete the installation, use new gaskets and reverse the removal procedures. Refill the crankcase. Start the engine and check for leaks.

CHECKING

1. If foreign matter is present, determine it's source.
2. Check the pump cover and housing for cracks, scoring and/or damage; if necessary, replace the housing(s).
3. Inspect the idler gear shaft for looseness in the housing; if necessary, replace the pump or timing chain, depending on the model.
4. Inspect the pressure regulator valve for scoring or sticking; if burrs are present, remove them with an oil stone.
5. Inspect the pressure regulator valve spring for loss of tension or distortion; if necessary, replace it.
6. Inspect the suction pipe for looseness, if pressed into the housing, and the screen for broken wire mesh; if necessary, replace them.
7. Inspect the gears for chipping, galling and/or wear; if necessary, replace them.
8. Inspect the driveshaft and driveshaft extension for looseness and/or wear; if necessary, replace them.

Rear Main Bearing Oil Seal

REMOVAL & INSTALLATION

3.8L Engine

Braided fabric rope seals are used. The

upper seal half cannot be replaced without removing the crankshaft.

LOWER HALF-SEAL

1. Disconnect the negative battery cable. Remove the oil pan.
2. Remove the rear main bearing cap-to-engine bolts and the cap.
3. Remove the old seal from the bearing cap.

To install:

4. To replace the oil seal, perform the following procedures:

   a. Using sealant GM 1052621, Loctite® 414 or equivalent, apply it to the main bearing cap seal groove and wait for 1 minute.

   b. Using a new rope seal and a wooden dowel or hammer handle, roll the new seal into the cap so both ends projecting above the parting surface of the cap; force the seal into the groove by rubbing it down, until the seal projects above the groove not more than $\frac{1}{16}$ in.

   c. Using a sharp razor blade, cut the ends off flush with the surface of the cap.

   d. Using chassis grease, apply a thin coat to the seals surface.

5. To install the neoprene sealing strips (side seals), perform the following procedures:

   a. Using light oil or kerosene, soak the strips for 5 minutes.

NOTE: The neoprene composition seals will swell up once exposed to the oil and heat. It is normal for the seals to leak for a short time, until they become properly seated. The seals must not be cut to fit.

   b. Place the sealing strips in the grooves on the sides of the bearing cap.

6. Using sealer GM 1052621 or equivalent, apply it to the main bearing cap mating surface; do not apply sealer to the bolt holes.

7. To complete the installation, reverse the removal procedures. Torque the main bearing cap-to-engine bolts to 90 ft. lbs. (122 Nm). Refill the crankcase. The engine must be operated at low rpm when first started, after a new seal is installed.

UPPER HALF-SEAL

Engine removal is not necessary if the following time saver procedure is followed.

1. Disconnect the negative battery cable. Remove the oil pan.
2. Remove the rear main bearing cap-to-engine bolts and the cap.

To install:

3. Using the seal packing tool, insert it against each side of the upper seal and drive the seal until it is tight.

4. Measure the amount the seal was

driven into the engine and add about $\frac{1}{16}$ in. Using a razor blade, cut that amount off the old lower seal.

5. Using the seal packing tool, work the short packing pieces into the cylinder block; a small amount of oil on the seal will help the installation.

6. Repeat this process on the other side.

7. Install the lower bearing cap.

8. To complete the installation, reverse the removal procedures. Torque the main bearing cap-to-engine bolts to 90 ft. lbs. (122 Nm). Refill the crankcase. The engine must be operated at low rpm when first started, after a new seal is installed.

4.1L and 4.5L Engines

NOTE: To perform this procedure, use a seal removal tool and a seal installer tool.

1. Disconnect the negative battery cable. Remove the transaxle.

2. Unbolt and remove the flexplate from the rear end of the crankshaft.

3. Using a seal removal tool, remove the old seal. Throughly clean the seal bore of any left over seal material with a clean rag.

To install:

4. Lubricate the lip of the new seal with wheel bearing grease. Position it over the crankshaft and into the seal bore with the spring facing inside the engine.

5. Using a seal installer tool, press the seal into place. The seal must be square, this is the purpose of the installer, and flush with the block to 1mm indented.

6. To complete the installation, reverse the removal procedures. On Allante (1987-88) and Eldorado/Seville (1987), torque the flexplate-to-crankshaft bolts to 37 ft. lbs. (50 Nm). On Allante (1989-91) and Eldorado/Seville (1988-91), torque the flexplate-to-crankshaft bolts to 70 ft. lbs. (95 Nm). Refill the crankcase. Operate the engine and check for leaks.

AUTOMATIC TRANSAXLE

For further information on transmissions/transaxles, please refer to "Chilton's Guide to Transmission Repair".

Transaxle Assembly

REMOVAL & INSTALLATION

1987 Riviera and Toronado

NOTE: To perform this procedure, an engine support tool and a halfshaft remover tool are necessary.

1. Disconnect the negative battery cable. Install the engine support fixture.

2. Disconnect the vacuum line from the modulator; electrical connections involved with the transaxle; transaxle valve cable at the throttle body and at the transaxle; the cruise control servo.

3. Disconnect the shift selector bracket and cable from the transaxle. Disconnect the neutral start switch.

4. Remove the top transaxle mounting bolts.

5. Remove the bolts that fasten the wiring harness to the transaxle. Remove the driveline dampener bracket.

6. Raise and safely support the vehicle.

7. Disconnect and drain the transaxle oil cooler lines at the transaxle.

8. Remove the torque converter cover. Scribe the relationship between the flexplate and the converter so the same relationship may be established on reinstallation for balance. Remove the converter-to-flexplate bolts, turning the crankshaft, as necessary.

9. Remove the left side transaxle mounting bolts. Remove the engine mounting nuts.

10. Disconnect the sway bar links. Disconnect the left side ball joint from the knuckle.

11. Disconnect the left side halfshaft from the transaxle using a special tool J-33008 or equivalent.

12. Disconnect the left side of the frame by removing the bolts.

13. Position a floor jack under the transaxle and support it securely.

14. Remove both remaining engine-to-transaxle bolts.

NOTE: One of the bolts is located between the transaxle case and the block, it is installed in the direction opposite to the others.

15. Remove the engine-to-transaxle bracket.

16. Remove the right halfshaft from the transaxle and hang it securely.

17. Remove the transaxle.

To install:

18. Slide the transaxle into position, install the lower engine-to-transaxle bolts and torque to 55 ft. lbs. (75 Nm).

19. Install the engine-to-transaxle bracket. Install the left side frame assembly bolts.

20. Install the engine mounting nuts. Install the left side transaxle mounting bolts.

21. Connect the left side halfshaft to the transaxle.

22. Connect the left side ball joint to the knuckle. Connect the sway bar links.

23. Install the converter to flexplate and tighten bolts to 46 ft. lbs. (62 Nm).

NOTE: Ensure that converter and flexplate are reassembled in the same relationship by lining up scribe marks made during disassembly.

24. Install the torque converter cover.

25. Connect transaxle oil cooler lines.

26. Lower vehicle.

27. Install driveline dampener bracket. Install wiring harness bolts to transaxle.

28. Install top transaxle mounting bolts.

29. Connect neutral start switch. Connect shift selector bracket and cable to transaxle.

30. Connect vacuum line to the modulator; electrical connections to transaxle; transaxle throttle valve cable and cruise control servo.

31. Remove engine support fixture.

32. Connect negative battery cable.

33. Start engine and check transaxle fluid level. Add as necessary.

1988-91 Reatta, Riviera, Toronado and Trofeo

1. Disconnect the negative battery cable. Remove the air intake duct.

2. Disconnect the Throttle Valve (TV) cable from the transaxle and the throttle body. Disconnect the cruise control servo and cable.

3. Remove the exhaust pipe crossover.

4. Disconnect the shift control linkage lever from from the manual shaft and the mounting bracket from the transaxle.

5. Disconnect the electrical harness connectors from the neutral start/backup light switch, the torque converter clutch (TCC) and the vehicle speed sensor (VSS).

6. From the vacuum modulator, disconnect the hose.

7. Remove the upper transaxle-to-engine bolts.

8. Using the engine support fixture tool, attach it to the engine, turn the wing nuts to relieve the tension on the engine cradle and mounts.

9. Turn the steering wheel to the full left position.

10. Raise and safely support the vehicle. Remove both from wheel assemblies.

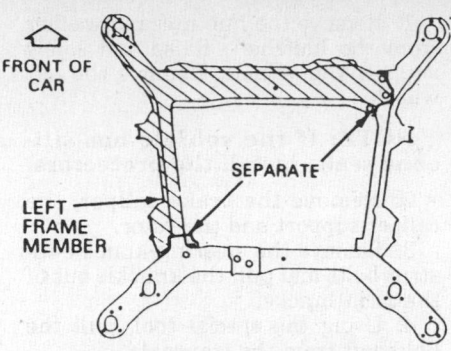

View of the frame separation points

11. Using the halfshaft seal protector tool, install one on each halfshaft. Remove both front ball joint-to-steering knuckle nuts and separate the control arms from the steering knuckles.

12. Using a medium prybar, pry the halfshaft from the transaxle and support it on a wire; do not remove the halfshaft from the steering knuckle.

NOTE: When removing the halfshaft, be careful not to damage the seal lips.

13. Remove the right rear transaxle-to-frame nuts, the left rear transaxle mount-to-transaxle bolts and the right rear transaxle mount.

14. From the left control arm, remove the stabilizer shaft.

15. Remove the flywheel cover bolts and the cover.

16. Matchmark the torque converter-to-flywheel bolts for reinstallation purposes. Remove the torque converter-to-flywheel bolts and push the torque converter back into the transaxle.

17. Remove the partial frame-to-main frame bolts, the partial frame-to-body bolts and the partial frame.

18. Disconnect and plug the oil cooler tubes from the transaxle.

19. Remove the lower transaxle-to-engine bolts.

NOTE: One bolt is located between the engine and the transaxle case and is positioned in the opposite direction.

20. Lower the transaxle from the vehicle; be careful not to damage the hoses, lines and wiring.
To install:
21. Raise transaxle into position. Install the lower transaxle bolts.

NOTE: Ensure that the opposite-facing bolt is reinstalled in the proper direction.

22. Unplug and connect the oil cooler tubes to the transaxle.

23. Install the partial frame. Secure with the partial frame-to-body and the partial frame-to-main frame bolts.

24. Install the torque converter observing matchmarks made on disassembly and secure with torque converter-to-flywheel bolts. Tighten to 46 ft. lbs. (62 Nm). Install flywheel cover and secure with flywheel cover bolts.

25. Install left control arm and stabilizer shaft.

26. Install right rear transaxle mount, right rear transaxle-to-frame nuts and the left rear transaxle mount-to-frame nuts.

27. Install halfshaft into transaxle.

NOTE: When installing halfshafts, be sure not to damage seals.

28. Connect the control arms to the transaxle and secure with both front ball joint-to-steering knuckle nuts.

29. Install both wheel and tire assemblies.

30. Lower the vehicle.

31. Remove engine support fixture tool.

32. Install the upper transaxle-to-engine bolts.

33. Connect vacuum modulator hose.

34. Connect electrical harness connectors to neutral start/backup light switch, Torque Converter Clutch (TCC) and the Vehicle Speed Sensor (VSS).

35. Connect shift control linkage lever to manual shaft and mounting bracket to transaxle.

36. Install exhaust crossover pipe.

37. Connect Throttle Valve (TV) cable to the transaxle and throttle body. Connect cruise control servo.

38. Install air intake duct. Connect negative battery cable.

39. Start engine and check for transaxle leaks. Refill as necessary.

Eldorado, Seville and Allante

1. Disconnect the negative battery cable. Remove the air cleaner assembly. Disconnect the transaxle throttle valve cable.

2. Remove the cruise control servo and bracket assembly. Disconnect the electrical connectors going to the distributor, oil pressure sending unit and transaxle.

3. Remove the bracket for the engine oil cooler lines.

4. Remove the shift linkage bracket from the transaxle and the manual shift lever from the manual shift shaft; leave the cable attached to the lever and bracket.

5. Remove the fuel line bracket and disconnect the neutral safety switch connector.

6. Remove the vacuum modulator.

7. Remove the throttle valve cable support bracket and engine oil cooler

line bracket. Remove the bell housing bolts except the left and right side bolts; note the bolt lengths and positions.

8. Remove the air injection reactor crossover pipe fitting and reposition the pipe. Remove the radiator hose bracket and transaxle mount-to-bracket nuts.

9. Install an engine support fixture, noting the positions of the hooks.

10. Raise and safely support the vehicle.

11. Remove both front wheels, the right and left stabilizer link bolts. Remove the ball joint cotter pins and nuts and press the ball joints from the steering knuckles.

12. Remove the air conditioner splash shield and the mount cover for the forward most cradle insulator.

13. Remove the hose connections from the ends of the air injection reactor pipes. Remove the vacuum hoses and the wire loom from the clips at the front of the cradle.

14. Remove the engine mount and dampener-to-cradle attachments. Remove the transaxle mount-to-cradle attachments. Remove the wire loom clip from the transaxle mount bracket and lower the vehicle.

15. Using both left side support hooks on the engine support fixture to raise the transaxle 2 in. from its normal position. Raise and safely support the vehicle.

16. Remove the right front and left rear transaxle-to-cradle bolts and the left stabilizer mount bolts. Remove the foremost cradle mount insulator bolt and the left cradle member, separate the right front corner first.

17. Remove the air injection reactor management valve/bracket assembly from the transaxle mount bracket and reposition the bracket to the transaxle stud bolts.

18. Lower the vehicle. Lower the transaxle to its normal position to gain access to the transaxle mounting bracket. Remove the mounting bracket.

19. Raise and safely support the vehicle. Remove the right rear transaxle mount-to-transaxle bracket. Remove the engine-to-transaxle brace bolts that pass into the transaxle VSS connector.

20. Mark the relationship between torque converter and flexplate for reassembly in the same position. Remove the flywheel covers, then, remove the torque converter bolts, rotating the crankshaft with a socket wrench as necessary to gain access. Position a jack under the transaxle to support it.

21. Remove the left and right bell housing bolts; note the bolt lengths and positions.

NOTE: Access may be gained through the right wheelhouse opening to remove the bolt on the right side; use a 3 foot long socket extension to reach it.

22. Disconnect the oil cooler lines at the transaxle, drain them and plug the openings. Then, install halfshaft boot seal protectors and disconnect the halfshafts at the transaxle. Suspend the halfshafts out of the way and remove the transaxle.

To install:
23. Reverse the removal procedures placing the bolts in their original positions. Torque the bell housing bolts to 55 ft. lbs. (75 Nm).
24. Turn the converter until it is aligned with the flexplate as originally installed. Install the converter-to-flexplate bolts and torque to 46 ft. lbs. (63 Nm). Install the splash shield under the converter. Unplug and reconnect the oil cooler lines to the transaxle case. Torque the fittings to 15 ft. lbs. (21 Nm).
25. To complete the installation, reverse the removal procedures, observing the following torque figures:
   Forward most insulator mount bolt – 74 ft. lbs. (100 Nm).
   Cradle-to-cradle mounting bolts – 74 ft. lbs. (100 Nm)
   Upper transaxle mount bracket stud bolts – 74 ft. lbs. (100 Nm).
   Side transaxle mount bracket stud bolts – 50 ft. lbs. (70 Nm).
   Left or rear transaxle mount nuts – 35 ft. lbs. (45 Nm).
   Engine mount-to-cradle attachments – 35 ft. lbs. (45 Nm).
   Right rear mount bracket-to-transaxle bolts – 50 ft. lbs. (70 Nm).
   Right rear mount bracket nuts – 35 ft. lbs. (45 Nm).
   Stabilizer mount bolts – 38 ft. lbs. (50 Nm).
   Ball joint nuts – 81 ft. lbs. (110 Nm).
   Shift cable bracket-to-transaxle bolts – 18 ft. lbs. (24 Nm).
   Lug nuts – 100 ft. lbs. (140 Nm).
26. Adjust the transaxle valve cable and the shift linkage. Refill the transaxle to the proper level. Start engine and allow to come to normal operating temperature. Check transaxle fluid level and adjust as necessary.

SHIFT LINKAGE ADJUSTMENT

Except 440-T4 Transaxle

1. Disconnect the shift cable. Move the shift lever to the N position.
2. Place the transaxle lever in the N detent.
3. Attach the shift cable to the pin and tighten the retaining nut.
4. Assemble the bushing and the re-

tainer at the shift cable; tighten the attaching nut.

440-T4 Transaxle

1. Disconnect the shift cable. Move the shift lever to the N position.
2. Place the transaxle lever in the N detent.

NOTE: The N detent can be found by rotating the selector shaft clockwise from P through R to N.

3. Push the cable adjuster tab to adjust the cable in the cable mounting bracket.

THROTTLE LINKAGE ADJUSTMENT

1. With the engine stopped, depress the accelerator pedal fully and have an assistant check the throttle body for wide open throttle.

NOTE: If the throttle body cannot achieve full throttle, repair the accelerator system.

2. At the engine end of the TV cable, depress and hold down the metal readjust tab, move the slider until it stops against the fitting and release the readjustment tab.
3. Rotate the throttle lever, by hand, to it's full travel position.
4. The slider must move, ratchet, toward the lever when the lever is rotated to it's full travel position.

DRIVE AXLE

Halfshaft
REMOVAL & INSTALLATION

Left Side

1987 RIVIERA AND TORONADO
NOTE: Secure a halfshaft spindle remover set tool. Also, if the vehicle uses silicone boot seals, halfshaft boot seal protectors must be installed before the halfshaft is disconnected. If the vehicle uses thermoplastic seals, these are not required. They are needed with the silicone seals because, without them, the joint may turn to too sharp an angle, causing the seal to be damaged in a way that is not readily detectible. These are identified by GM tool J–28712 or equivalent (for the outer seal), and tool J–33162 or equivalent (for the inner seal).

1. Remove the hub nut and washer from the halfshaft. Raise and safely support the vehicle. Remove the left wheel.

NOTE: If the vehicle has silicone seals, install the protectors.

2. Remove the brake caliper, the caliper support and the rotor.
3. Remove the steering knuckle-to-strut bolts and pull the knuckle out of the strut bracket.
4. Using the special tool, pull the halfshaft from the transaxle.

NOTE: Support the shaft at the center so there will be no downward force on the outer joint.

5. Using a spindle removal tool, remove the halfshaft from the hub/bearing assembly and the vehicle. Do not remove the boot seal protector unless complete disassembly is necessary.
To install:
6. Loosely position the halfshaft into the steering knuckle and transaxle.
7. Place the the steering knuckle into position in the strut bracket and install the bolts. Torque to 144 ft. lbs. (196 Nm).
8. To complete the installion, reverse the removal procedures.

NOTE: If the vehicle uses a prevailing torque hub nut, use a new nut, torque it to specifications, making sure the threads are undamaged, free of oil and grease. Otherwise, the halfshaft may not be retained safely.

9. Install a new prevailing torque hub nut and washer and torque it to 74 ft. lbs. (100 Nm). Remove the object used to hold the rotor stationary.
10. Seat the halfshaft into the transaxle with a prybar resting against the groove provided on the inner retainer. Tap the prybar lightly to seat the snapring and lock the halfshaft into the transaxle. Verify that the snapring has been seated by grasping the housing (not the shaft) and pulling it outboard. If the shaft is locked, it will not pull free.
11. Torque the lug nuts to 100 ft. lbs. (136 Nm).

1987 ELDORADO AND SEVILLE
NOTE: To perform this procedure, use a special puller tool and a new prevailing torque nut from the halfshaft.

1. Remove the hub nut and washer. Raise and safely support the vehicle.
2. Remove the wheel/tire assembly.
3. Remove the brake caliper and rotor.
4. Disconnect the stabilizer bar from the control arm, the tie rod end

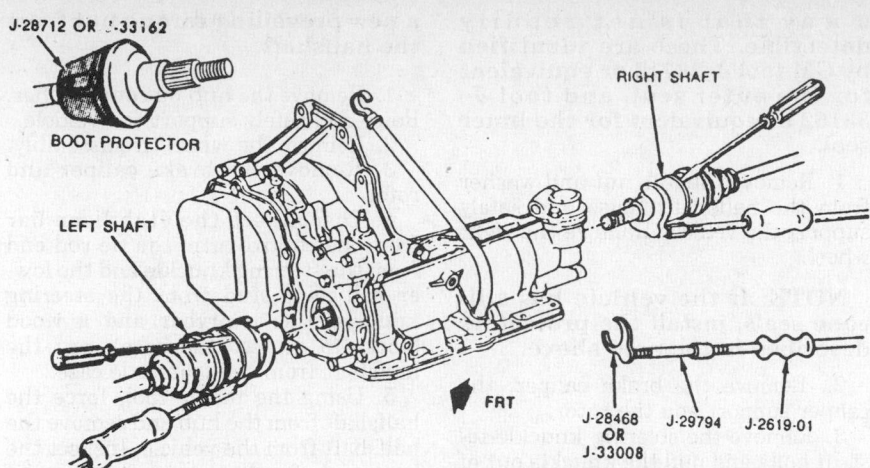

Use a screwdriver and the special tool shown to pull the drive axles out of the transaxle. Make sure to support the axles at the center to avoid putting downward force on the outer joint

from the steering knuckle and the lower ball joint stud from the steering knuckle. Use a prybar and a wood block (to protect the case), pry the halfshaft from the transaxle case.

5. Using the puller tool, force the halfshaft from the hub and remove the halfshaft from the vehicle. Inspect the boot seals for damage and replace, if necessary.

To install:

6. Position the halfshaft ends into the steering knuckle and transaxle without fully seating them.

7. Reconnect the lower ball joint-to-steering knuckle and torque the nut 37 ft. lbs. (50 Nm). Reconnect the stabilizer bar-to-lower control arm and the tie rod end-to-steering knuckle.

8. Using new bolts, reinstall the brake caliper.

9. Install a washer and new prevailing torque nut; torque the nut to 74 ft. lbs. (100 Nm). Insert a prybar into a slot in the brake caliper to prevent the halfshaft from turning when torquing the nut.

10. Position a prybar into the CV-

joint housing groove, tap it with a hammer until the halfshaft is seated in the transaxle. Grab the halfshaft housing, not the halfshaft, and pull it outward to make sure the halfshaft is properly seated.

11. To complete the installation, reverse the removal procedures. Torque the hub nut to 183 ft. lbs. (249 Nm).

1988-91 ALL VEHICLES

1. Remove the hub nut and washer.
2. Raise and safely support the vehicle. Remove the front wheel.
3. Remove the brake caliper and rotor.
4. Remove the stabilizer link from the control arm.
5. Remove the tie rod end-to-steering knuckle cotter pin and nut. Using a ball joint removal tool, separate the tie rod end from the steering knuckle.
6. Remove the lower ball joint-to-steering knuckle cotter pin and nut. Using a ball joint removal tool, separate the lower ball joint from the steering knuckle.
7. Using a prybar and a wooden block, pry the halfshaft from the steering knuckle and suspend it on a wire.

NOTE: When removing the halfshaft, be careful not to allow the shaft to drop causing damage to the CV-joints. Do not allow the halfshaft to overextend for the Tri-Pot (S-plan) joint can disengage from the bearing blocks.

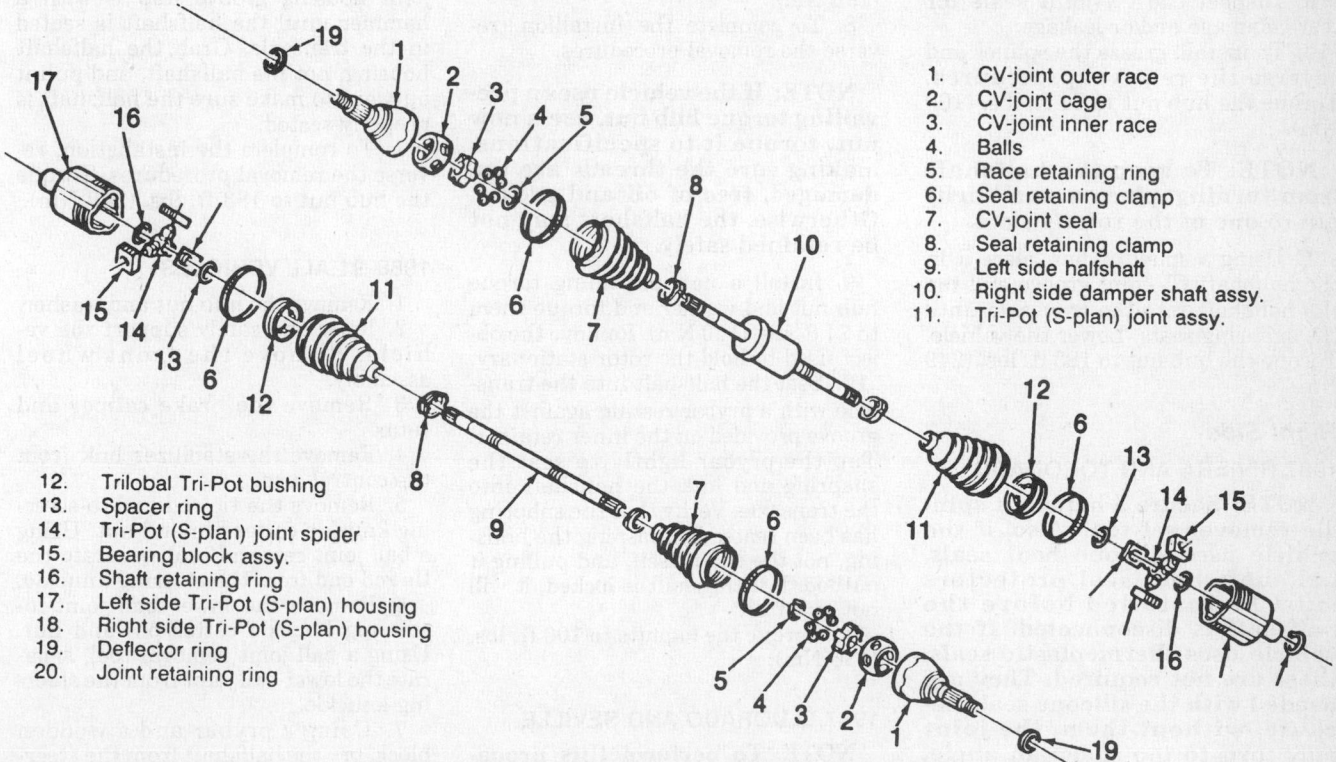

1. CV-joint outer race
2. CV-joint cage
3. CV-joint inner race
4. Balls
5. Race retaining ring
6. Seal retaining clamp
7. CV-joint seal
8. Seal retaining clamp
9. Left side halfshaft
10. Right side damper shaft assy.
11. Tri-Pot (S-plan) joint assy.

12. Trilobal Tri-Pot bushing
13. Spacer ring
14. Tri-Pot (S-plan) joint spider
15. Bearing block assy.
16. Shaft retaining ring
17. Left side Tri-Pot (S-plan) housing
18. Right side Tri-Pot (S-plan) housing
19. Deflector ring
20. Joint retaining ring

Exploded view of the halfshaft assemblies—Tri-Pot (S-plan)—1988-91

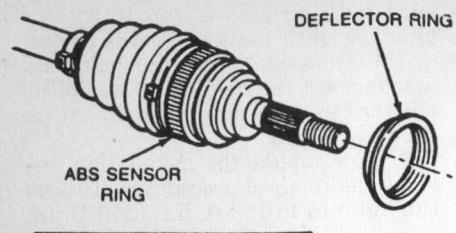

ANTI-LOCK BRAKE EQUIPPED

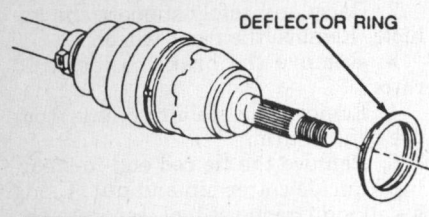

STANDARD BRAKE EQUIPPED

View of the 2 types of outer CV-joint assemblies and deflector rings— 1988–91

8. Using the halfshaft removal tool, press the halfshaft from the steering knuckle hub and remove it from the vehicle.

NOTE: If equipped with an anti-lock brake system, be careful not to damage the toothed sensor ring (on halfshaft) and the wheel speed sensor (on steering knuckle).

To install:

9. Inspect the CV-joint seals for tears, damage and/or leakage.

10. To install, grease the splines and reverse the removal procedures. Torque the hub nut to 74 ft. lbs. (100 Nm).

NOTE: To keep the halfshaft from turning, place a small drift pin in one of the rotor's slots.

11. Using a small prybar, place it in the halfshaft CV-joint groove and tap the halfshaft into the transaxle until the snapring seats. Lower the vehicle. Torque the hub nut to 183 ft. lbs. (249 Nm).

Right Side

1987 RIVIERA AND TORONADO

NOTE: Secure a halfshaft spindle remover set tool. Also, if the vehicle uses silicone boot seals, halfshaft boot seal protectors must be installed before the halfshaft is disconnected. If the vehicle uses thermoplastic seals, these are not required. They are needed with the silicone seals because, without them, the joint may turn to too sharp an angle, causing the seal to be damaged in

a way that is not readily detectible. These are identified by GM tool J–28712 or equivalent for the outer seal, and tool J–33162 or equivalent for the inner seal.

1. Remove the hub nut and washer from the halfshaft. Raise and safely support the vehicle. Remove the right wheel.

NOTE: If the vehicle has silicone seals, install the protectors described in the note above.

2.. Remove the brake caliper, the caliper support and the rotor.

3. Remove the steering knuckle-to-strut bolts and pull the knuckle out of the strut bracket.

4. Using the special tool, pull the halfshaft from the transaxle.

NOTE: Support the shaft at the center so there will be no downward force on the outer joint.

5. Using the spindle removal tool, remove the halfshaft from the hub/bearing assembly and the vehicle. Do not remove the boot seal protector unless complete disassembly is necessary.

To install:

6. Loosely position the halfshaft into the steering knuckle and transaxle.

7. Place the the steering knuckle into position in the strut bracket and install the bolts. Torque to 144 ft. lbs. (196 Nm).

8. To complete the installion, reverse the removal procedures.

NOTE: If the vehicle uses a prevailing torque hub nut, use a new nut, torque it to specifications, making sure the threads are undamaged, free of oil and grease. Otherwise, the halfshaft may not be retained safely.

9. Install a new prevailing torque hub nut and washer and torque them to 74 ft. lbs. (100 Nm). Remove the object used to hold the rotor stationary.

10. Seat the halfshaft into the transaxle with a prybar resting against the groove provided on the inner retainer. Tap the prybar lightly to seat the snapring and lock the halfshaft into the transaxle. Verify that the snapring has been seated by grasping the housing, not the shaft itself, and pulling it outboard. If the shaft is locked, it will not pull free.

11. Torque the lugnuts to 100 ft. lbs. (136 Nm).

1987 ELDORADO AND SEVILLE

NOTE: To perform this procedure, use a special puller tool and

a new prevailing torque nut from the halfshaft.

1. Remove the hub nut and washer. Raise and safely support the vehicle.

2. Remove the wheel/tire assembly.

3. Remove the brake caliper and rotor.

4. Disconnect the stabilizer bar from the control arm, the tie rod end from the steering knuckle and the lower ball joint stud from the steering knuckle. Use a prybar and a wood block (to protect the case), pry the halfshaft from the transaxle case.

5. Using the puller tool, force the halfshaft from the hub and remove the halfshaft from the vehicle. Inspect the boot seals for damage and replace, if necessary.

To install:

6. Position the halfshaft ends into the steering knuckle and transaxle without fully seating them.

7. Reconnect the lower ball joint-to-steering knuckle and torque the nut 37 ft. lbs. (50 Nm). Reconnect the stabilizer bar-to-lower control arm and the tie rod end-to-steering knuckle.

8. Using new bolts, reinstall the brake caliper.

9. Install a washer and new prevailing torque nut; torque the nut to 74 ft. lbs. (100 Nm). Insert a prybar into a slot in the brake caliper to prevent the halfshaft from turning when torquing the nut.

10. Position a prybar into the CV-joint housing groove, tap it with a hammer until the halfshaft is seated in the transaxle. Grab the halfshaft housing, not the halfshaft, and pull it outward to make sure the halfshaft is properly seated.

11. To complete the installation, reverse the removal procedures. Torque the hub nut to 183 ft. lbs. (249 Nm).

1988–91 ALL VEHICLES

1. Remove the hub nut and washer.

2. Raise and safely support the vehicle. Remove the front wheel assembly.

3. Remove the brake caliper and rotor.

4. Remove the stabilizer link from the control arm.

5. Remove the tie rod end-to-steering knuckle cotter pin and nut. Using a ball joint removal tool, separate the tie rod end from the steering knuckle.

6. Remove the lower ball joint-to-steering knuckle cotter pin and nut. Using a ball joint removal tool, separate the lower ball joint from the steering knuckle.

7. Using a prybar and a wooden block, pry the halfshaft from the steering knuckle and suspend it on a wire.

NOTE: When removing the halfshaft, be careful not to allow the shaft to drop causing damage to the CV-joints. Do not allow the halfshaft to overextend for the Tri-Pot (S-plan) joint can disengage from the bearing blocks.

8. Using a halfshaft removal tool, press the halfshaft from the steering knuckle hub and remove it from the vehicle.

NOTE: If equipped with an anti-lock brake system, be careful not to damage the toothed sensor ring (on halfshaft) and the wheel speed sensor (on steering knuckle).

To install:

9. Inspect the CV-joint seals for tears, damage and/or leakage.

10. To install, grease the splines and reverse the removal procedures. Torque the hub nut to 74 ft. lbs. (100 Nm).

NOTE: To keep the halfshaft from turning, place a small drift pin in one of the rotor's slots.

11. Using a small prybar, place it in the halfshaft CV-joint groove and tap the halfshaft into the transaxle until the snapring seats. Lower the vehicle. Torque the hub nut to 183 ft. lbs. (249 Nm).

CV-Boot

REPLACEMENT

Inner (Inboard)

1. Disconnect the negative battery cable.
2. Raise and safely support the vehicle. Remove the front wheels.
3. Remove the outer boot assembly.
4. Remove the boot retaining clamps and the spacer ring.
5. Slide the halfshaft and the spider bearing assembly out of the tri-pot housing. Install the spider retainer onto the spider bearing assembly.
6. Remove the spider assembly and the boot from the halfshaft.
7. To install, pack the new boot with grease and reverse the removal procedures.

Outer (Outboard)

1. Disconnect the negative battery cable.
2. Raise and safely support the vehicle. Remove the front wheels.
3. Remove the brake caliper and support on a wire. Remove the rotor.
4. Slide the outer CV-joint assembly off the halfshaft.
5. Remove the bearing retaining

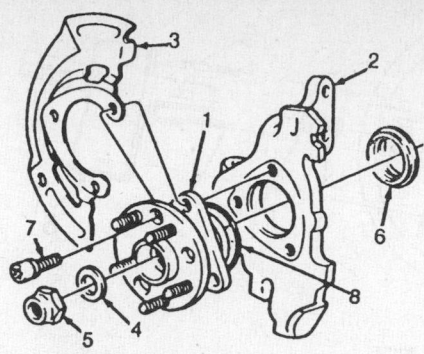

1. Hub and bearing assembly
2. Steering knuckle
3. Shield
4. Washer
5. Hub nut — 180 ft. lbs.
6. Seal
7. Hub and bearing retaining bolt — 70 ft. lbs.
8. O-ring

Exploded view of the hub/bearing assembly

ring, the boot retainer, the clamp and the outer boot.
6. To install, pack the new boot with grease and reverse the removal procedures.

Front Wheel Hub, Spindle and Bearing

NOTE: The bearings are preadjusted and require no lubrication, maintenance or adjustment. There are darkened areas on the bearing assembly which are the result of a heat treating process.

REMOVAL & INSTALLATION

1. Raise and safely support the vehicle.
2. Place jackstands under the cradle and lower the vehicle slightly so the weight of the vehicle rests on the jackstands and not on the control arms.
3. Remove the wheel assembly.
4. Insert a drift punch into the rotor and remove the hub nut/washer.
5. Remove the brake caliper, support and the rotor.
6. Using the front hub spindle remover tool, separate the halfshaft from the hub.
7. Remove the hub/bearing assembly-to-steering knuckle bolts and the hub/bearing assembly.
To install:
8. If replacing the seal, drive the seal towards the engine. Cut the seal off the halfshaft; be careful not to damage the halfshaft boot.

NOTE: If the speed sensor bracket is removed or loosened from the steering knuckle, the speed sensor gap must be adjusted. If the speed sensor is removed from the bracket, speed sensor wax must be applied to the sensor before it is reinstalled in the bracket. Failure to apply the wax will permit corrosion and may result in sensor failure.

9. To install the new grease seal, lubricate the with wheel bearing grease and using the hub seal installer tool, install the seal.
10. To complete the installation, reverse the removal procedures. Torque the:
   Hub/bearing assembly-to-steering knuckle bolts to 70 ft. lbs. (95 Nm).
   Hub nut to 180 ft. lbs. (244 Nm).
   Wheel nuts to 100 ft. lbs. (136 Nm).

STEERING

Steering Wheel

——— CAUTION ———

On vehicles equipped with an air bag, the Supplemental Inflatable Restraint (SIR) system must be disabled before working on the steering system or its components. Failure to do so may result in accidental deployment of the air bag and possible personal injury.

When carrying a live Inflator Module, ensure that the bag and trim are facing away. Never carry the Inflator Module by the wires or conductor on the underside of the module.

Always place a live Inflator Module on the bench so the bag and trim face up.

REMOVAL & INSTALLATION

Reatta, Riviera, Toronado and Trofeo

1987–89

1. Disconnect the negative battery cable.
2. Remove the steering wheel-to-horn pad screws, located behind the steering wheel, and lift the pad from the steering wheel.
3. If the steering wheel is equipped with control buttons, disconnect the electrical connector(s).
4. Remove the steering wheel-to-shaft retainer, if equipped and nut.
5. Scribe an alignment mark on the steering wheel hub in line with the slash mark on the steering shaft.
6. Using the steering wheel puller, press the steering wheel from the steering shaft.

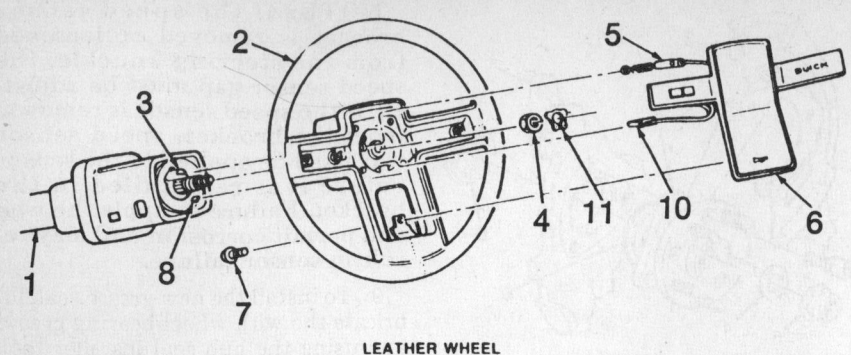

LEATHER WHEEL

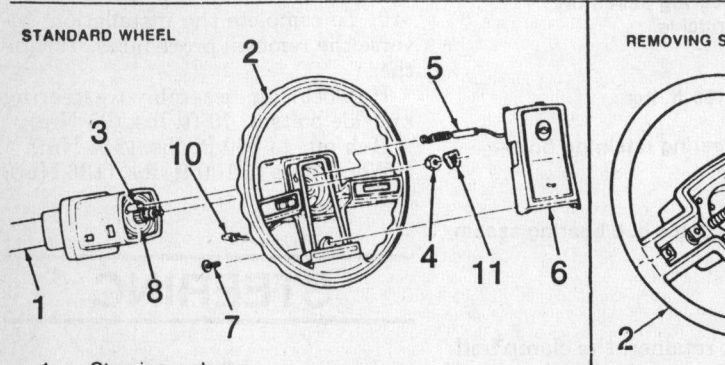

STANDARD WHEEL

REMOVING STEERING WHEEL

1. Steering column
2. Steering wheel
3. Cam tower
4. Nut – 35 ft. lbs.
5. Horn lead
6. Horn pad
7. Horn pad mounting screws – 13 inch lbs.
8. Cruise control connector (column)
9. Steering Wheel Puller tool No. J–23072
10. Cruise control connector
11. Retainer

Exploded view of the steering wheel assembly – Reatta, Riviera and Toronado

NOTE: If equipped with steering wheel controls, do not install steering wheel puller bolts beyond 5 turns as damage to electronic components behind the wheel may result.

7. To install, reverse the removal procedures. Torque the steering wheel-to-steering shaft nut to 35 ft. lbs. (47 Nm).

1990–91

1. Disconnect the negative battery cable. Ensure that ignition switch is in the **OFF** position.
2. Remove SIR fuse from fuse panel as follows:
Reatta and Riviera – Fuse No. 14
Toronado and Trofeo – Fuse No. 9
3. Remove left-side sound insulator.
4. Remove left-side courtesy lamp as required to ease removal of sound insulator.
5. Remove Connector Position Assurance (CPA) pin and yellow 2 way connector at the base of the steering column.
6. Loosen inflator module screws from back of steering wheel.
7. Remove horn contact by pushing

slightly and twisting counterclockwise.
8. Remove Connector Position Assurance (CPA) pin and coil assembly connector from inflator module.
9. Remove steering column shaft nut.
10. Remove steering wheel using a suitable steering wheel puller.
To install:
11. Feed SIR coil assembly lead

through slot in steering wheel.
12. Install steering wheel onto column shaft.
13. Install column shaft nut. Tighten to 30 ft. lbs. (41 Nm).
14. Install horn contact, coil assembly connector and CPA to inflator module.
15. Install inflator module onto steering wheel, securing with 4 screws behind steering wheel. Tighten to 27 inch lbs. (3 Nm).
16. Connect negative battery cable.
17. Connect yellow 2 way connector and CPA pin at the base of the steering column.
18. Install fuse in fuse panel.
19. Install left-side sound insulator and connect courtesy lamp, if removed

Allante, Eldorado and Seville

1987–89

1. Disconnect the negative battery cable.
2. For the Allante, pry the horn trim pad from the steering wheel. For the Eldorado and Seville, remove the steering wheel-to-horn pad screws, located behind the steering wheel, and the horn trim pad. Remove the horn contact wire, ground connector and cruise control wiring connector.
3. Remove the telescope locking lever assembly-to-adjuster screws. Unscrew and remove the telescoping adjuster from the steering shaft.
4. Remove the telescoping lever assembly. Scribe an alignment mark on the steering wheel hub-in-line with the slash mark on the steering shaft.
5. Remove the steering wheel-to-steering shaft locknut. Using the steering wheel puller, press the steering wheel from the steering shaft.

NOTE: When removing the steering wheel, be sure to remove the cruise control wire from it.

To install:
6. Feed the cruise control wire

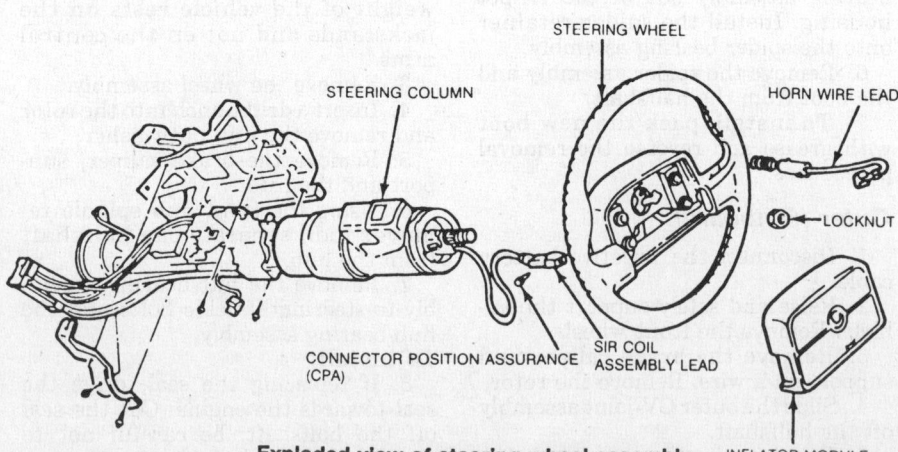

Exploded view of steering wheel assembly

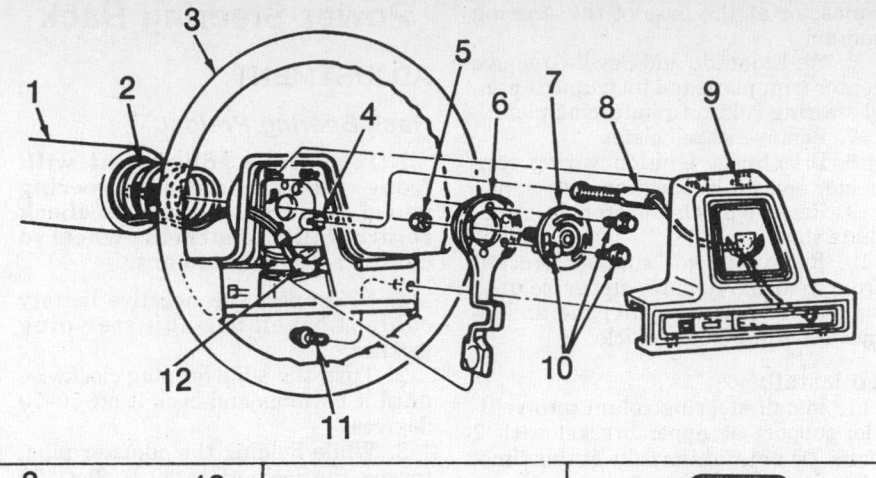

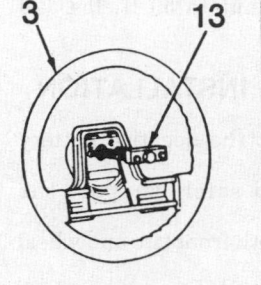
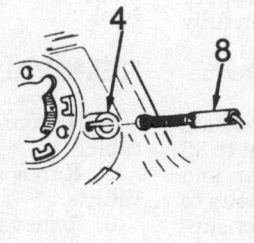
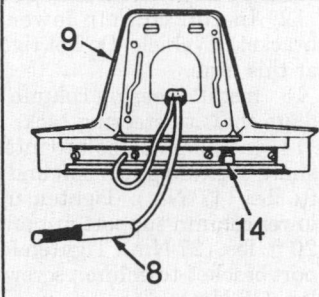

1. Steering column	8. Horn lead
2. Telescoping spring	9. Horn pad
3. Steering wheel	10. Telescope adjuster screws – 13 inch lbs.
4. Cam tower	11. Horn pad mounting screws – 13 inch lbs.
5. Nut – 35 ft. lbs.	12. Cruise control connector (column)
6. Telescope lever	13. Steering Wheel Puller tool No. J–23072
7. Telescope adjuster	14. Cruise control connector

Exploded view of the steering wheel assembly – Eldorado and Seville

through the steering wheel, align the matchmark and reverse the removal procedures. Torque the steering wheel-to-steering shaft to 35 ft. lbs. (47 Nm).

NOTE: For ease of installation, fully extend the steering shaft and install the lock plate compressor screw tool, hand tight; this will keep the shaft extended when installing the steering wheel. Feed the cruise control wire through the wheel.

7. Remove the tool and place the telescoping lever in the 5 o'clock position.

8. Thread the telescope adjuster assembly finger tight onto the shaft. Install the screws into the telescoping adjuster lever.

9. Move the adjuster lever all the way to the right. The steering wheel should move freely in and out. Move the adjuster lever to the left. The steering wheel should be locked in place with the telescope lever approximately ¼ in. from the left side of the

shroud opening. The lever must not contact the shroud in the full locked position. Loosen and adjust the lever as required.

1990–91

1. Disconnect the negative battery cable. Ensure that ignition switch is in the **OFF** position.

2. Remove SIR fuse from fuse panel as follows:
   Allante – Fuse No. 12
   Eldorado and Seville – Fuse No. 19

3. Remove left-side sound insulator.

4. Remove left-side courtesy lamp, as required, to ease removal of sound insulator.

5. Remove Connector Position Assurance (CPA) pin and yellow 2 way connector at the base of the steering column.

6. Loosen inflator module screws from back of steering wheel.

7. Remove horn contact by pushing slightly and twisting counterclockwise.

8. Remove Connector Position Assurance (CPA) pin and coil assembly

connector from inflator module.

9. Remove steering column shaft nut.

10. Remove steering wheel using a suitable steering wheel puller.

To install:

11. Feed SIR coil assembly lead through slot in steering wheel.

12. Install steering wheel onto column shaft.

13. Install column shaft nut. Tighten to 30 ft. lbs. (41 Nm).

14. Install horn contact, coil assembly connector and CPA to inflator module.

15. Install inflator module onto steering wheel, securing with 4 screws behind steering wheel. Tighten to 27 inch lbs. (3 Nm).

16. Connect negative battery cable.

17. Connect yellow 2 way connector and CPA pin at the base of the steering column.

18. Install fuse in fuse panel.

19. Install left-side sound insulator and connect courtesy lamp, if removed.

Steering Column

REMOVAL & INSTALLATION

1987–89 Reatta, Riviera, Toronado and Trofeo

1. Disconnect the negative battery cable.

2. Remove the left side sound absorber from the dash area.

3. Remove the steering column trim cover.

4. Label and disconnect the electrical connectors from the steering column. Remove the wiring harness protector.

5. Remove the park lock cable from the ignition switch, if equipped.

6. Remove the lower column mounting bolts.

NOTE: On the Toronado, remove the pinch bolt.

7. If equipped with a column shifter, disconnect the shift linkage at the column.

8. Remove the upper steering column-to-instrument panel bolts and the column assembly from the vehicle.

To install:

9. Reverse the removal procedures. Loosely install the upper steering column bolts and torque the lower column bolts to 20 ft. lbs. (27 Nm).

NOTE: Failure to install the upper bolts first may result in a cracked lower bearing casting.

10. To complete the installation, reverse the removal procedures and check the operation of the steering column.

1987–89 Allante, Eldorado and Seville

1. Disconnect the negative battery cable.
2. Remove left dash close-out panel.
3. Remove column wiring connector from left hand hard shell grommet.
4. Remove park lock cable from ignition switch.
5. Remove bolt connecting steering shaft to intermediate shaft.
6. Remove bolts and nut connecting steering column to instrument panel bracket.

NOTE: When removing the steering column, the lower column bracket nut and bolts must be removed first. After removing lower bolts, remove upper column bracket bolts. Failure to remove lower nut and bolt first may result in a cracked lower bearing casting.

7. Remove column from the car.
To install:
8. Install steering column mounting bolts and nut.

NOTE: When installing column, loosely install the upper column bracket bolts first. Before tightening upper bracket bolts, install lower column nuts and bolt. Failure to install upper bolts first may result in a cracked lower bearing casting.

9. Install intermediate shaft coupling to steering column shaft. Tighten intermediate shaft bolt to 35 ft. lbs. (47 Nm) and steering column bolts to 20 ft. lbs. (27 Nm).
10. Connect park lock cable to ignition switch.
11. Connect steering column wiring connector to left hand hard shell grommet.
12. Install dash close-out panel.
13. Connect negative battery cable.

1990–91 Reatta, Riviera, Allante, Eldorado, Seville, Toronado and Trofeo

1. Disconnect the negative battery cable. Ensure that ignition switch is in the **OFF** position.
2. Remove SIR fuse from fuse panel as follows:
   Reatta and Riviera—Fuse No. 14
   Allante—Fuse No. 12
   Eldorado and Seville—Fuse No. 19
   Toronado and Trofeo—Fuse No. 9
3. Remove left-side sound insulator.
4. Remove left-side courtesy lamp, as required, to ease removal of sound insulator.
5. Remove Connector Position Assurance (CPA) pin and yellow 2 way

connector at the base of the steering column.
6. On Eldorado and Seville, remove center trim plate and instrument panel steering column reinforcing plate.
7. Remove knee bolster.
8. Disconnect ignition wiring connector and multi-function connector.
9. Remove pinch bolt from intermediate shaft.
10. Remove lower support bracket from vehicle. Remove upper column support from instrument panel and remove column from vehicle.

To install:
11. Install steering colum into vehicle; support at upper bracket with 2 bolts. Do not tighten fully at this time.
12. Install column lower support bracket to vehicle. Do not tighten fully at this time.
13. Install steering column intermediate shaft to steering rack.
14. Install pinch bolt to intermediate shaft. Tighten pinch bolt and nut to 35 ft. lbs. (47 Nm). Tighten upper and lower column support nut and bolts to 20 ft. lbs. (27 Nm). Tighten lower support bracket-to-column screws to 12 ft. lbs. (16 Nm).
15. Connect multi-function switch connector and ignition wiring connector.
16. On Eldorado and Seville, install instrument panel steering column reinforcement plate and center trim plate.
17. Install knee bolster.
18. Connect negative battery cable.
19. Connect yellow 2 way connector and CPA pin at the base of the steering column.
20. Install fuse in fuse panel.
21. Install left-side sound insulator and connect courtesy lamp, if removed.

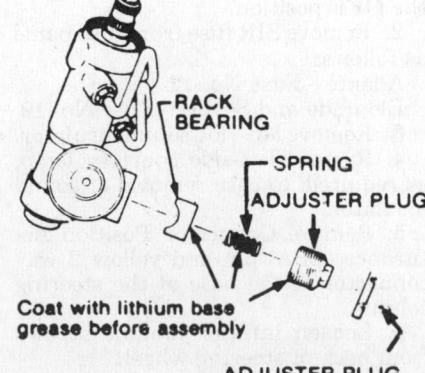

RACK BEARING

SPRING

ADJUSTER PLUG

Coat with lithium base grease before assembly

ADJUSTER PLUG LOCK NUT

Exploded view of the power steering rack adjustment assembly

Power Steering Rack

ADJUSTMENT

Rack Bearing Preload

NOTE: Make adjustment with front wheels raised and steering wheel centered. Be sure to check returnability of steering wheel to center after adjustment.

1. Disconnect the negative battery cable. Loosen the adjuster plug locknut.
2. Turn the adjuster plug clockwise until it bottoms and back it off 50–70 degrees.
3. While holding the adjuster plug, torque the locknut to 50 ft. lbs. (70 Nm).

REMOVAL & INSTALLATION

1. Disconnect the negative battery cable.
2. Raise and safely support the vehicle.
3. Remove both front tire and wheel assemblies.
4. Remove the intermediate shaft lower pinch bolt.
5. Remove the tie rod ends from the steering knuckles.
6. Remove the line retainer. Disconnect and plug the return and pressure hose from the steering rack and pinion.
7. Label and disconnect the electrical connection at the idle speed power steering switch.
8. Remove the rack and pinion assembly retaining bolts. Remove the rack and pinion assembly.
To install:
9. Reverse the removal procedures. Torque the:
   Rack and pinion attaching bolts to 50 ft. lbs.
   Tie rod end nuts to 7.5 ft. lbs., plus an additional ⅓ turn
   Tie rod-to-steering knuckle the nut to 33 ft. lbs.
   Intermediate shaft coupling bolt to 30 ft. lbs.

NOTE: After tightening the castellated nut, align the nut slot to cotter pin hole by tightening only; do not loosen.

10. Bleed the power steering system and check for leaks.

Power Steering Pump

REMOVAL & INSTALLATION

3.8L Engine

1. Disconnect the negative battery cable.

2. Remove the serpentine drive belt, the alternator bolts and the alternator.

3. Raise and safely support the vehicle.

4. Disconnect and plug the pressure and return lines from the pump.

5. Remove the rear pump adjustment bracket-to-pump nut.

6. Remove the alternator adjustment bracket and support brace.

7. Remove the rear pump adjustment bracket and the pump assembly.

8. Remove the front pump adjustment bracket and the pulley.

9. To install, reverse the removal procedures. Refill the power steering pump reservoir. Bleed the power steering system.

4.1L and 4.5L Engines

1. Disconnect the negative battery cable.

2. Remove the serpentine drive belt, the power steering pump pulley.

3. Disconnect and plug the high pressure and feed lines from the pump.

4. Remove the power steering pump-to-bracket bolts and the pump.

5. To install, reverse the removal procedures. Torque the power steering pump-to-bracket bolts to 30 ft. lbs. Refill the power steering pump reservoir. Bleed the power steering system.

BELT ADJUSTMENT

All accessories are driven by a single serpentine belt. The serpentine belt tension is maintained automatically by a spring tensioner. No adjustment is necessary or possible. If the belt tension is not within specification, replace the belt tensioner.

SYSTEM BLEEDING

1. Fill the fluid reservoir.

2. Let the fluid stand undisturbed for 2 minutes, crank the engine for about 2 seconds. Refill the reservoir, if necessary.

3. Repeat above steps until the fluid level remains constant after cranking the engine.

4. Raise and safely support the vehicle, until the wheels are off the ground. Start the engine and increase the engine speed to about 1500 rpm.

5. Turn the wheels lightly against the stops to the left and right, checking the fluid level and refilling, if necessary.

Outer Tie Rod Ends

REMOVAL & INSTALLATION

1. Disconnect the negative battery cable.

2. Raise and safely support the vehicle.

3. Remove cotter pin and hex slotted nut from outer tie rod assembly. Loosen jam nut.

4. Disconnect outer tie rod from steering knuckle using a suitable steering linkage separator tool.

5. Remove outer tie rod from inner tie rod.

To install:

6. Install outer tie rod assembly to inner tie rod. Do not tighten jam nut.

7. Connect outer tie rod to steering knuckle, hex slotted nut to outer tie rod stud. Tighten hex slotted nut to 35 ft. lbs. (50 Nm). Check for cotter pin slot alignment. Maximum torque is 45 ft. lbs. (60 Nm) to align slot. Do not back off for cotter pin insertion.

8. Install cotter pin into hole in tie rod stud.

9. Check toe and adjust by turning inner tie rod.

NOTE: Be sure rack and pinion boot is not twisted or puckered during toe adjustment.

10. Tighten jam nut against outer tie rod to 50 ft. lbs. (70 Nm).

BRAKES

For all brake system repair and service procedures not detailed below, please refer to "Brakes" in the Unit Repair section.

Master Cylinder

REMOVAL & INSTALLATION

Diagonal Split System

1. Disconnect the negative battery cable. If equipped with a fluid level sensor switch, disconnect the electrical connector.

2. Disconnect and plug hydraulic lines. Drain the master cylinder.

3. Remove the master cylinder-to-power brake booster nuts and the master cylinder.

4. To install, reverse the removal procedures. Torque the mounting nuts to 26 ft. lbs. (35 Nm). Refill the master cylinder and bleed the system.

Proportioning Valve

REMOVAL & INSTALLATION

Diagonal Split System

NOTE: Individual proportioning valves are installed on the master cylinder outlets.

1. Disconnect the negative battery cable. Disconnect and plug the fluid lines from the proportioning valves.

2. Remove the proportioning valves and O-rings from the master cylinder.

3. To install, use new O-rings and reverse the removal procedures. Torque the proportioning valve-to-master cylinder to 18–30 ft. lbs. (24–41 Nm). Refill the master cylinder reservoir with clean brake fluid. Bleed the brake system.

Teves Anti-Lock System

The Teves system uses a single proportioner valve located near the left rear wheel. The valve is not to be disassembled.

1. Disconnect the negative battery cable. Turn the ignition switch **OFF** throughout this procedure.

2. Using at least 50 lbs. (68 Nm) pressure on the brake pedal, depress the pedal at least 25 times; a noticable change in pedal pressure will be noticed when the accumulator is discharged.

3. Disconnect the fluid lines from the proportioner valve and the valve from the vehicle.

4. To install, reverse the removal procedures. Bleed the rear brake system.

Bosch III System

The Bosch III system uses individual proportioning valves installed to the master cylinder. The valves are not to be disassembled.

1. Disconnect the negative battery cable. Turn the ignition switch **OFF** throughout this procedure.

2. Using at least 50 lbs. pressure on the brake pedal, depress the pedal at least 25 times; a noticable change in pedal pressure will be noticed when the accumulator is discharged.

3. Disconnect and plug the fluid line(s) from the proportioning valve(s).

4. Remove the proportioning valve(s) from the hydraulic unit.

5. To install, reverse the removal procedures. Torque the proportioning valve(s)-to-hydraulic unit to 11 ft. lbs. (15 Nm). Bleed the brake circuit(s).

Power Brake Booster

NOTE: This procedure is used only with the diagonal split system.

REMOVAL & INSTALLATION

1. Disconnect the negative battery cable. Remove the master cylinder-to-power brake booster nuts and move the master cylinder aside.

2. From inside the vehicle, detach

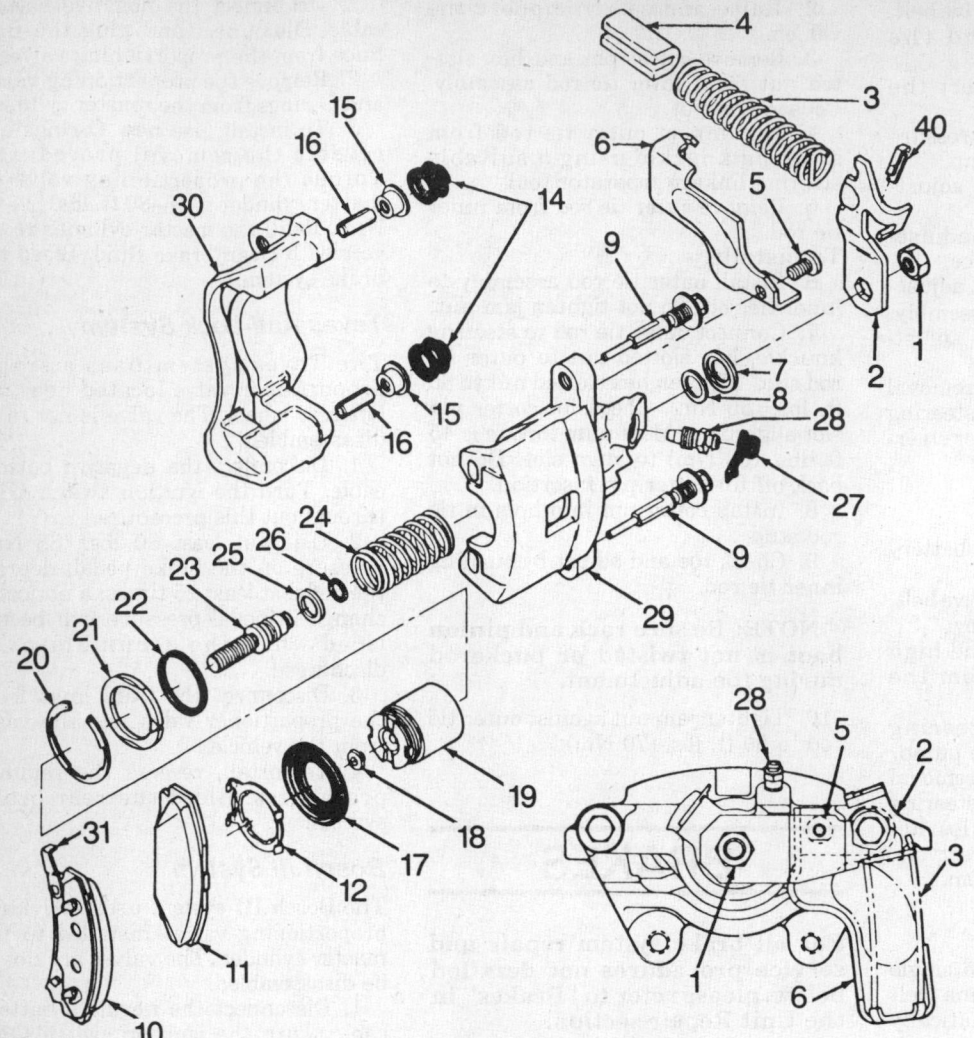

1. Nut
2. Park brake lever
3. Return spring
4. Damper
5. Bolt
6. Bracket
7. Lever seal
8. Anti-friction washer
9. Mounting bolt
10. Outboard shoe and lining
11. Inboard shoe and lining
12. Shoe retainer
14. Bolt boot
15. Support bushing
16. Bushing
17. Caliper piston boot
18. Two-way check valve
19. Piston assembly
20. Retainer
21. Piston locator
22. Piston seal
23. Actuator screw
24. Balance spring and retainer
25. Thrust washer
26. Shaft seal
27. Cap
28. Bleeder valve
29. Caliper housing
30. Bracket
31. Wear sensor
40. Retaining clip

Rear brake caliper assembly

the brake pushrod from the brake pedal.

3. Detach the vacuum hose at the vacuum cylinder.

4. Remove the nuts from the mounting studs which hold the unit to the dash panel. Remove the unit and clean it prior to installation.

5. To install, reverse the removal procedures. Torque the power booster-to-cowl nuts to 28 ft. lbs. (38 Nm) and the master cylinder-to-power booster nuts to 28 ft. lbs. (38 Nm).

6. Bleed the brake system.

Brake Caliper

REMOVAL & INSTALLATION

Front

1. Remove ⅔ of brake fluid from master cylinder assembly.

2. Raise and safely support the vehicle. Mark the relationship of the wheel to axle flange.

3. Remove wheel and tire assembly. Reinstall 2 wheel nuts to retain rotor.

4. Remove bolt attaching inlet fitting. Plug openings in caliper and pipe to prevent fluid loss and contamination.

5. Remove mounting bolts.

6. Remove caliper from rotor and mounting bracket.

To install:

7. Install caliper over rotor in mounting bracket. Ensure that bolt boots are in place.

8. Lubricate entire shaft of mounting bolts with silicone grease. Tighten mounting bolts to 63 ft. lbs. (85 Nm).

9. Connect inlet fitting to 24 ft. lbs. (32 Nm).

10. Remove wheel nuts securing rotor to hub. Install wheels and tires, aligning previous marks.

11. Lower vehicle.

12. Torque wheel nuts to 100 ft. lbs. (140 Nm).

13. Fill master cylinder to proper level with clean brake fluid.

14. Bleed caliper.

Rear

1. Remove ⅔ of brake fluid from master cylinder assembly.

2. Raise and safely support the vehicle.

3. Mark the relationship of wheel to axle flange. Remove wheel and tire assembly. Reinstall 2 wheel nuts to retain rotor.

4. Loosen tension on parking brake cable at equalizer.

5. Remove retaining clip from lever.

6. Remove cable, return spring and damper from return spring.

7. Remove locknut while holding lever.

8. Remove lever, lever seal and anti-friction washer.

9. Compress bottom piston into caliper bore to provide clearance between linings and rotor.

10. Reinstall anti-friction washer, lever seal (sealing bead against housing), lever and nut.

11. Remove bolt attaching inlet fitting. Plug openings in caliper and pipe to prevent fluid loss and contamination.

12. Remove mounting bolts.

13. Remove caliper from rotor and mounting bracket.

To install:

14. Install caliper over rotor in mounting bracket, making sure that boots are in place.

15. Lubricate entire shaft of mounting bolts with silicone grease.

16. Install mounting bolts and tighten to 63 ft. lbs. (85 Nm).

17. Connect inlet fittings and tighten to 15 ft. lbs. (20 Nm).

NOTE: Ensure that parking brake components are clean and free of corrosion. Parts found to be corroded should be replaced. Do not try to polish corrosion away.

18. Install anti-friction washer.

19. Install lever seal with sealing bead against caliper housing. Lubricate seal prior to installation.

20. Install lever on actuator screw hex, with lever pointing down.

21. Install nut while holding rotated lever toward front of vehicle and tighten to 35 ft. lbs. (48 Nm). Rotate lever back against stop on caliper.

22. Install damper and return spring.

23. Connect parking brake cable and adjust.

24. Install retaining clip on lever so it retains parking brake cable from sliding out of the slot in lever.

25. Remove 2 wheel nuts securing rotor to hub. Install wheel and tire assembly aligning previous marks.

26. Lower vehicle.

27. Torque wheel nuts to 100 ft. lbs. (140 Nm).

28. Fill master cylinder to proper level with clean brake fluid.

29. Bleed caliper.

Disc Brake Pads

REMOVAL & INSTALLATION

1. Remove disc brake caliper from mounting bracket and support with a length of mechanics wire. Do not allow caliper to hang by the brake line unsupported.

2. Remove outboard shoe and lining. Use a suitable tool to disengage shoe springs from holes in caliper housing.

3. Remove inboard shoe and lining, unsnapping shoe spring from piston.

4. If installing new shoe and linings, bottom piston in caliper bore using large pliers. Take care not to damage piston or piston boot.

5. Remove bushings from mounting bolt holes in bracket.

To install:

6. Install new bushings in mounting bolt holes in bracket. Lubricate bushings with silicone grease before installation.

7. Install inboard shoe and lining by snapping shoe retainer spring into piston. Shoe retainer spring is already staked to the inboard shoe. Shoe must lay flat against piston.

8. Install outboard shoe and lining by snapping shoe springs into holes in caliper housing. Wear sensor should be at the trailing edge of shoe during forward wheel rotation. Back of shoe must lay flat against caliper.

9. Install caliper.

10. Apply approximately 175 lbs. (778 N) of force 3 times to brake pedal to seat linings.

Brake Rotor

REMOVAL & INSTALLATION

1. Remove disc brake caliper from mounting bracket and support with a length of mechanics wire. Do not allow caliper to hang by the brake line unsupported.

2. Remove 2 bolts retaining caliper mounting bracket, remove bracket and set aside.

3. Remove brake rotor taking care not to damage wheel nut threads.

4. Complete the installation of the brake rotor by reversing the removal procedure.

Parking Brake Cable

ADJUSTMENT

1. Lube the cables at the underbody rub points and at the equalizer hooks. Set and release the parking brake several times and check for free movement of all cables.

NOTE: With the ignition switch turned ON, the parking brake warning light should be OFF.

2. Set the parking brake pedal in the fully released position, raise and safely support the vehicle.

3. Hold the brake cable stud and tighten the equalizer nut until all cable slack is removed. Make sure the caliper levers are against the stops on the caliper housing; if not, loosen the cable until they are.

4. Operate the parking brake pedal several times to check the adjustment; the pedal should become firm after 3½ strokes.

5. Lower the vehicle and check that the caliper levers are still on their stops. If not, back off the parking brake adjuster until they are.

REMOVAL & INSTALLATION

The parking brake cable system consists of 4 separate cables: front, intermediate, left and right. The front and intermediate cables are joined at the adjuster screw. The left and right cables are joined to the intermediate cable through an equalizer.

1. Ensure that the parking brake is fully released.

2. Release the cable adjustment enough to allow removal of the desired cable(s).

NOTE: To prevent damage to threaded parking brake adjusting rod clean the exposed threads on each side of the nut and lubricate threads on the adjusting rod before turning the nut.

3. Remove old cable(s) and connect replacement cable(s).

4. Adjust new cable and check operation of parking brake.

Brake System Bleeding

Diagonal Split System

MASTER CYLINDER

1. Refill the master cylinder reservoir.

2. Push the plunger several times to force fluid into the piston.

3. Continue pumping the plunger until the fluid is free of the air bubbles.

4. Plug the outlet ports and install the master cylinder.

SYSTEM BLEEDING

1. Fill the master cylinder with fresh brake fluid. Check the level often during the procedure.

2. Starting with the right rear wheel, remove the protective cap from the bleeder, if equipped, and place where it will not be lost. Clean the bleed screw.

——— **CAUTION** ———

When bleeding the brakes, keep face away from the brake area. Spewing fluid may cause facial and/or visual damage. Do not allow brake fluid to spill on the car's finish; it will remove the paint.

3. If the system is empty, the most effecient way to get fluid down to the wheel is to loosen the bleeder about ½–¾ turn, place a finger firmly over the bleeder and have a helper pump the brakes slowly until fluid comes out the bleeder. Once fluid is at the bleeder, close it before the pedal is released inside the vehicle.

NOTE: If the pedal is pumped rapidly, the fluid will churn and create small air bubbles, which are difficult to remove from the system. These air bubbles will eventually congregate resulting in a spongy pedal.

4. Once fluid has been pumped to the caliper or wheel cylinder, open the bleed screw again, have the helper press the brake pedal to the floor, lock the bleeder and have the helper slowly release the pedal. Wait 15 seconds and repeat the procedure (including the 15 second wait) until no more air comes out of the bleeder upon application of the brake pedal. Remember to close the bleeder before the pedal is released inside the vehicle each time the bleeder is opened. If not, air will be induced into the system.

5. If a helper is not available, connect a small hose to the bleeder, place the end in a container of brake fluid and proceed to pump the pedal from inside the vehicle until no more air comes out the bleeder. The hose will prevent air from entering the system.

6. Repeat the procedure on remaining wheel cylinders in order:
   a. left front
   b. left rear
   c. right front

7. Hydraulic brake systems must be totally flushed if the fluid becomes contaminated with water, dirt or other corrosive chemicals. To flush, bleed the entire system until all fluid has been replaced with the correct type of new fluid.

8. Install the bleeder cap(s) on the bleeder to keep dirt out. Always road test the vehicle after brake work of any kind is done.

Teves Anti-Lock Brake System

FRONT BRAKES

1. Turn the ignition switch OFF throughout this procedure.

2. Using at least 50 lbs. pressure on the brake pedal, depress the pedal at least 25 times; a noticable change in pedal pressure will be noticed when the accumulator is discharged.

3. Remove the reservoir cap. Check and/or refill the master cylinder reservoir.

4. Using the bleeder adapter tool, install it onto the fluid reservoir.

5. Attach a diaphragm type pressure bleeder to the adapter and charge the bleeder to 20 psi.

6. Using a transparent vinyl tube, connect it to either front wheel caliper and insert the other end in a beaker ½ full of clean brake fluid.

7. Open the bleeder valve ½–¾ turn and purge the caliper until bubble free fluid flows from the hose.

8. Tighten the bleeder screw and remove the bleeder equipment.

9. Turn the ignition switch ON and allow the pump to charge the accumulator.

10. After bleeding, inspect the pedal for sponginess and the brake warning light for unbalanced pressure; if either of the conditions exist, repeat the bleeding procedure.

REAR BRAKES

1. Turn the ignition switch OFF.

2. Using at least 50 lbs. pressure on the brake pedal, depress the pedal at least 25 times; a noticable change in pedal pressure will be noticed when the accumulator is discharged.

3. Check and/or refill the master cylinder reservoir.

4. Turn the ignition switch ON and allow the system to charge.

NOTE: The pump will turn OFF when the system is charged.

5. Using a transparent vinyl tube, connect it to a rear wheel bleeder valve and insert the other end in a beaker ½ full of clean brake fluid.

6. Open the bleeder valve ½–¾ turn and slightly depress the brake pedal for at least 10 seconds or until air is removed from the brake system. Close the bleeder valve.

NOTE: It is a good idea to check the fluid level several times during the bleeding operation. Remember, depressurize the system before checking the reservoir fluid.

7. Repeat the bleeding procedure for the other rear wheel.

8. After bleeding, inspect the pedal for sponginess and the brake warning light for unbalanced pressure; if either of the conditions exist, repeat the bleeding procedure.

Bosch III Anti-Lock Brake System

PUMP AND BOOSTER

1. Turn the ignition switch OFF.

2. Using at least 50 lbs. pressure on the brake pedal, depress the pedal at least 25 times; a noticable change in pedal pressure will be noticed when the accumulator is discharged.

3. Check and/or refill the reservoir to the full mark.

4. Using a transparent vinyl hose, connect it to a pump bleeder screw and insert the other end in a beaker ½ full of clean brake fluid.

5. Loosen the bleeder screw ½–¾ turn. Turn the ignition switch ON; the pump should run forcing fluid from the hose. When the fluid becomes bub-ble-free, turn the ignition switch OFF, tighten the bleeder screw.

6. Move the transparent vinyl hose to the hydraulic unit bleeder screw. Loosen the bleeder screw ½–¾ turn. Turn the ignition switch ON; the pump should run forcing fluid from the hose. When the fluid becomes bubble-free, turn the ignition switch OFF, tighten the bleeder screw.

7. Disconnect the bleeder hose.

8. Turn the ignition switch ON and allow the hydraulic unit to charge; the pump should turn OFF after 30 seconds.

Anti-Lock Brake System Service

PRECAUTIONS

Failure to observe the following precautions may result in system damage.

• Before performing electric arc welding on the vehicle, disconnect the Electronic Brake Control Module (EBCM) and the hydraulic modulator connectors.

• When performing painting work on the vehicle, do not expose the Electronic Brake Control Module (EBCM) to temperatures in excess of 185°F (85°C) for longer than 2 hrs. The system may be exposed to temperatures up to 200°F (95°C) for less than 15 min.

• Never disconnect or connect the Electronic Brake Control Module (EBCM) or hydraulic modulator connectors with the ignition switch ON.

• Never disassemble any component of the Anti-Lock Brake System (ABS) which is designated non-serviceable; the component must be replaced as an assembly.

• When filling the master cylinder, always use Delco Supreme 11 brake fluid or equivalent, which meets DOT-3 specifications; petroleum base fluid will destroy the rubber parts.

RELIEVING ANTI-LOCK BRAKE SYSTEM PRESSURE

NOTE: Unless otherwise specified, the hydraulic accumulator should be depressurized before disassembling any portion of the hydraulic system.

1. With the ignition switch in the OFF position, sensor block connector disconnected from the hydraulic unit or the negative battery cable disconnected, pump the brake pedal a minimum of 25 times using approximately 50 lbs. (222 N) of pedal force. When a noticeable change in pedal feel occurs, the accumulator is discharged.

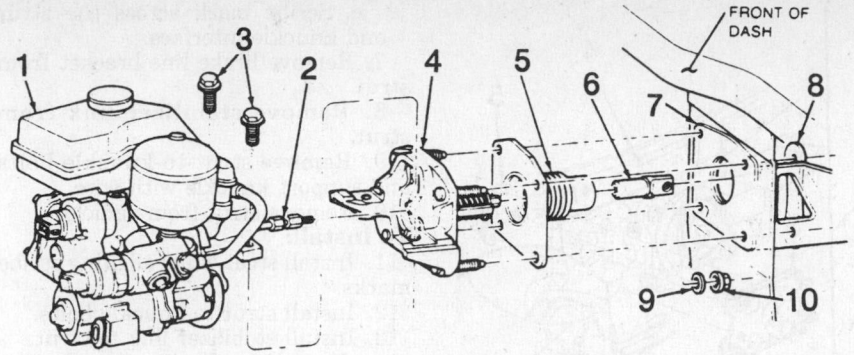

1. Hydraulic unit
2. Front pushrod half
3. Bolts — 37 ft. lbs.
4. Pushrod bracket assembly
5. Rubber boot
6. Rear pushrod half
7. Gasket
8. Reinforcement washer
9. Washer — used on lower right stud only
10. Nuts — 15 ft. lbs.

Exploded view of the anti-lock brake system hydraulic unit — Teves — all except Allante

2. When a definite increase in pedal effort is felt, stroke the pedal a few additional times.

Hydraulic Modulator

REMOVAL & INSTALLATION

Teves System

NOTE: The hydraulic accumulator is under pressure and must be depressurized before attempting to dismantle the system.

1. Disconnect the negative battery cable.
2. Firmly apply the parking brake.
3. Using at least 50 lbs. pressure on the brake pedal, depress the pedal at least 20 times; a noticeable change in pedal pressure will be noticed when the accumulator is discharged.
4. Disconnect the electrical connectors from the hydraulic brake unit.
5. Remove the pump-to-hydraulic unit bolt and move the unit aside to gain access to the hydraulic lines.
6. Using a back-up wrench, disconnect the hydraulic lines from the hydraulic unit.
7. From under the dash, disconnect the pushrod from the brake pedal.
8. Move the dust boot forward, past the pushrod hex and unscrew both pushrod halves.
9. Remove the hydraulic unit-to-pushrod bracket bolts and separate the hydraulic unit from the pushrod bracket; half of the pushrod will remain locked in the hydraulic unit.
10. Disassemble the master cylinder from the hydraulic unit.
11. To install, assemble the master cylinder to the hydraulic unit and reverse the removal procedures. Torque the hydraulic unit-to-pushrod bracket

bolts to 37 ft. lbs. Bleed the brake system.

Bosch III System

NOTE: The hydraulic accumulator is under pressure and must be depressurized before attempting to dismantle the system.

1. Disconnect the negative battery cable.
2. Firmly apply the parking brake.
3. Using at least 50 lbs. pressure on the brake pedal, depress the pedal at least 25 times; a noticable change in pedal pressure will be noticed when the accumulator is discharged.
4. If working on an Allante, remove the air intake duct from the air cleaner and the throttle body.
5. Remove the cross brace.
6. Disconnect the electrical connectors from the hydraulic brake unit and the pump motor. Using a siphon, remove as much fluid from the reservoir as possible.
7. Remove the pressure hose fitting (banjo bolt) from the hydraulic unit; be careful not to drop the fitting washers. Disconnect the return hose from the reservoir fitting.
8. Using a back-up wrench, disconnect the hydraulic lines from the hydraulic unit.
9. From under the dash, remove the driver's side sound insulator panel. From the pedal hub pin, remove the pushrod retainer and the foam washer.
10. From the engine compartment, remove the hydraulic unit-to-mounting adapter nuts.
11. Move the hydraulic unit to disengage the pushrod-to-pedal hub pin.
12. Remove the hydraulic unit from the vehicle.

13. To install, reverse the removal procedures. Torque the hydraulic unit-to-mounting bracket nuts to 20 ft. lbs. Refill the reservoir to the **FULL** mark. Turn the ignition **ON** and allow the pump to charge the hydraulic accumulator. Bleed the brake system.

Wheel Speed Sensor

REMOVAL & INSTALLATION

Front Sensor

1. Disconnect sensor connector from underhood area near strut tower.
2. Raise and safely support the vehicle.
3. Disengage sensor cable grommet from wheel house pass-through hole and remove sensor cable from retainers.
4. Remove sensor mounting bolt and remove sensor from vehicle.

To install:

5. Route sensor cable and install retainers. Install wheelhouse pass-through grommet.

NOTE: Proper installation of wheel speed sensor cables is critical to continued system operation. Be sure that cables are installed in retainers. Failure to install cables in retainers properly may result in contact with moving parts and/or over-extension of cables, resulting in circuit damage.

6. Position sensor in knuckle and install mounting bolt. Tighten mounting bolt to 9 ft. lbs. (12 Nm).

NOTE: If the wheel speed sensor is removed or replaced, the sensor body must be coated with a suitable anti-corrosion compound where the sensor comes in contact with the knuckle.

7. Lower vehicle.
8. Connect wheel speed sensor connector underhood.

Rear Sensor

1. Raise and safely support the vehicle.
2. Disconnect sensor connector and remove sensor cable from retainer brackets.
3. Remove sensor mounting bolt and remove sensor from vehicle.

To install:

4. Position sensor in knuckle and install mounting bolt. Tighten to 9 ft. lbs. (12 Nm).

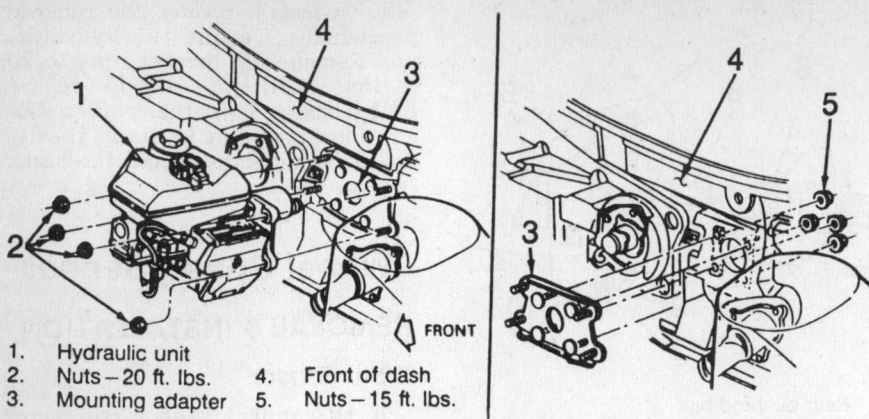

1. Hydraulic unit
2. Nuts – 20 ft. lbs.
3. Mounting adapter
4. Front of dash
5. Nuts – 15 ft. lbs.

View of the anti-lock brake system hydraulic unit and mounting bracket – Bosch III – Allante

NOTE: If the wheel speed sensor is removed or replaced, the sensor body must be coated with a suitable anti-corrosion compound where the sensor comes in contact with the knuckle.

5. Install wheel speed sensor cable in retainers.
6. Connect wheel speed sensor connector.
7. Lower vehicle.

Electronic Brake Control Module (EBCM)

REMOVAL & INSTALLATION

Except Allante

1. Disconnect the negative battery cable.
2. Open trunk lid. Remove left trunk carpet trim.
3. Remove velcro-attached cover concealing the EBCM.
4. Disconnect EBCM 35-pin connector.
5. Remove EBCM.
6. Complete installation of EBCM by reversing the removal procedure.

Allante

1. Disconnect the negative battery cable.
2. Remove driver's side insulator panel.
3. Remove EBCM connector by disengaging retainer and rotating connector toward the driver's seat.
4. Remove EBCM retaining bolts.
5. Disengage EBCM from mounting bracket and remove from vehicle.
To install:
6. Position EBCM in mounting bracket and install retaining bolts.
7. Install EBCM connector.

8. Install driver's side sound insulator panel.
9. Connect negative battery cable.

FRONT SUSPENSION

MacPherson Strut

REMOVAL & INSTALLATION

1. Disconnect the negative battery cable.
2. Remove nut attaching top of strut assembly to body.
3. If equipped, remove electrical connector from top of strut.
4. Raise and safely support the vehicle.
5. Remove tire and wheel assembly.

NOTE: Whenever working near the halfshafts, care must be taken to prevent inner tri-pot joints from being overextended. Overextension of the joint could result in separation of internal components which could go undetected and result in failure of the joint. Care should be taken to avoid scratching or cracking the spring coating when handling the front suspension coil spring. Damage to the spring coating could result in premature failure.

6. In order to reassemble the knuckle and strut in the same relationship, make the following scribe marks:
   a. Using a sharp tool, scribe the inboard surface of the strut along the upper knuckle radius.
   b. Scribe the knuckle along the lower curve. of the strut.

   c. Scribe mark across the strut and knuckle interface.
7. Remove brake line bracket from strut.
8. Remove stabilizer link from strut.
9. Remove strut-to-knuckle bolts and support knuckle with wire.
10. Remove strut from vehicle.
To install:
11. Install strut while aligning scribe marks.
12. Install strut-to-knuckle bolts.
13. Install stabilizer link to strut.
14. Install brake line bracket to strut.
15. Install nuts attaching top of strut to body. Tighten stabilizer link nuts to 48 ft. lbs. (65 Nm). Tighten strut assembly-to-body nuts to 18 ft. lbs. (24 Nm). Tighten steering knuckle-to-strut nuts to 136 ft. lbs. (184 Nm).
16. Install tire and wheel assembly.
17. Lower vehicle.
18. Tighten wheel mounting nuts to 100 ft. lbs. (140 Nm).
19. If equipped, connect electrical connector to top of strut.
20. Connect negative battery cable.

Lower Ball Joints

INSPECTION

1. Raise and safely support the vehicle. Install jackstands under both lower control arms as far outboard as possible.
2. Lower the vehicle onto the jackstands so the downward tension exerted by the stabilizer bar is relieved.
3. Install a dial indicator and clamp the assembly to the lower control arm.
4. Position the dial indicator plunger tip against the knuckle arm. Zero the dial indicator gauge.
5. Measure the axial travel fo the knuckle arm with respect to the control arm, by raising and lowering the wheel using a prybar under the center of the tire.
6. During the measurement, if the axial travel of the control arm is 0.030 in. or more, relative to the knuckle arm, the ball joint should be replaced.

REMOVAL & INSTALLATION

1. Raise and safely support the vehicle.
2. Place jackstands under cradle and lower vehicle slightly so weight of the vehicle rests on the jack stands and not on the control arms.
3. Remove tire and wheel assembly.
4. Install a suitable outer CV-joint boot protector.
5. Remove stabilizer bar insulators, retainers, spacer and bolt.

6. Remove ball joint from knuckle.

NOTE: If equipped with anti-lock brakes, ensure that there is enough clearance between the ball joint stud and speed sensor ring. If not remove the halfshaft hub nut. Install special tool J-28733 or equivalent halfshaft remover. Tighten tool until halfshaft moves inboard enough to provide clearance for ball joint removal.

7. Drill out 3 rivets retaining ball joint starting with ¼ in. drill bit and finishing with ½ in. drill bit.
8. Remove ball joint.
To install:
9. Install new ball joint into control arm.
10. Install ball joint bolts.
11. Connect ball joint to knuckle. Tighten ball joint bolts to 50 ft. lbs. (68 Nm). Tighten ball joint nut to 7 ft. lbs. (10 Nm). Tighten nut an additional ½ turn (3 flats.)

NOTE: When tightening nut, a minimum torque of 48 ft. lbs. (65 Nm) must be obtained. If 48 ft. lbs. (65 Nm) is not obtained, inspect for stripped threads. If threads are satisfactory, replace ball joint and knuckle. If required, turn the nut up to an additional ⅛ of a turn to allow for installation of the cotter pin. Bend both ends of the cotter pin.

12. If removed, tighten the hub nut to 183 lbs. (245 N), to assure proper bearing clamp load.
13. Remove CV-joint boot protector.
14. Install tire and wheel assembly.
15. Raise vehicle enough to allow removal or jackstands.
16. Lower vehicle. Tighten wheel nuts to 100 ft. lbs. (140 Nm).

Lower Control Arms

REMOVAL & INSTALLATION

1. Raise and safely support the vehicle.
2. Place jackstands under cradle and lower vehicle slightly so weight of the vehicle rests on the jackstands and not the control arms.
3. Remove the tire and wheel assembly.

NOTE: Care must be taken not to overextend Tri-Pot joints. Overextension of the joint could result in separation if internal components which could go undetected and result in failure of the joint.

4. Install a suitable CV-joint boot protector.

5. Remove stabilizer shaft insulator, retainers, spacer and bolt to control arm.
6. Lower ball joint from knuckle.
7. Remove control arm bushing bolt and front nut, retainer and insulator.
8. Remove control arm from frame.
To install:
9. Connect control arm to frame.
10. Install control arm bushing bolt and front nut, retainer and insulator. Do not tighten at this time.
11. Connect lower ball joint to knuckle.
12. Install stabilizer shaft insulator, retainers, spacer and bolt. Tighten stabilizer shaft nut and bolt to 13 ft. lbs. (17 Nm).

NOTE: Tighten ball joint nut to 7 ft. lbs. (10 Nm). Tighten nut an additional ½ turn (3 flats). When tightening nut a minimum torque of 48 ft. lbs. (65 Nm) must be obtained. If 48 ft. lbs. (65 Nm) is not obtained, inspect for stripped threads. If threads are satisfactory, replace ball joint and knuckle. If required, turn the nut up to an additional ⅛ of a turn to allow for installation of the cotter pin. Bend both ends of the cotter pin.

13. Remove outer CV-joint boot protector.
14. Install tire and wheel assembly.
15. Raise vehicle slightly so weight of vehicle is supported by the control arms. Tighten control arm bushing bolt to 100 ft. lbs. (140 Nm) or nut to 91 ft. lbs. (123 Nm). Tighten retainer to 52 ft. lbs. (70 Nm).
16. Remove jackstands and lower vehicle.
17. Tighten wheel nuts to 100 ft. lbs. (140 Nm).

Sway Bar

REMOVAL & INSTALLATION

1. Disconnect the negative battery cable.
2. Raise and safely support the vehicle.
3. Place jackstands under cradle and lower vehicle slightly so the weight of the vehicle rests on the jackstands and not on the control arms.
4. Remove right side wheel assembly.
5. Remove left and right insulators, retainers, spacers and bolts.
6. Remove left and right bracket bolts, brackets and insulators.
7. Remove exhaust pipe from rear manifold and move pipe up.
8. Remove stabilizer shaft.
To install:
9. Install stabilizer shaft.

10. Install exhaust pipe to rear manifold.
11. Install left and right insulators, brackets and loosely install bolts.
12. Install left and right insulators, retainers, spacers and bolts.
13. Center stabilizer on frame and check clearance. Tighten bracket to frame bolts to 33 ft. lbs. (45 Nm). Tighten nuts to 13 ft. lbs. (17 Nm).
14. Raise vehicle enough to allow for removal of jackstands.
15. Lower vehicle. Tighten wheel nuts to 100 ft. lbs. (140 Nm).

REAR SUSPENSION

MacPherson Strut

REMOVAL & INSTALLATION

1. Disconnect the negative battery cable.
2. Raise and safely support the vehicle.
3. Reinstall 2 wheel nuts to hold rotor on hub and bearing assembly.
4. Remove brake caliper and support with a length of mechanics wire.

NOTE: Do not allow caliper to hang by the brake hose unsupported.

5. Loosen knuckle pivot bolt on outboard end of control arm. Do not remove.
6. Remove upper strut rod cap, mounting nut, retainer and insulator.
7. Compress strut by hand and remove lower insulator.
8. Rotate strut and knuckle assembly outward by pivoting on knuckle pivot bolt.
9. Remove knuckle pinch bolt.
10. Remove strut from knuckle.
To install:
11. Position strut in knuckle. Strut must by fully seated in knuckle with tang on strut bottomed in knuckle slot.
12. Install knuckle pinch bolt. Tighten to 44 ft. lbs. (60 Nm).
13. Install lower insulator on strut and position strut rod in suspension support.
14. Install upper strut insulator, retainer and nut. Tighten upper strut nut to 65 ft. lbs. (88 Nm) Tighten knuckle pivot bolt to 59 ft. lbs. (80 Nm).
15. Install strut rod cap.
16. Install caliper and new caliper bracket mounting bolts.

17. Remove 2 wheel nuts previously installed to retain rotor.
18. Install wheel and tire assembly.
19. Lower vehicle. Tighten wheel nuts to 100 ft. lbs. (140 Nm).

Transverse-Mounted Leaf Spring

REMOVAL & INSTALLATION

NOTE: Removal and installation of the transverse-mounted rear spring requires disassembly of either the left or right suspension while leaving the other side intact. The spring may be removed from either side of the vehicle.

1. Disconnect the negative battery cable.
2. Raise and safely support the vehicle.
3. Remove tire and wheel assembly.
4. Disconnect height sensor link, if disassembling left control arm.
5. Remove stabilizer shaft mounting bolt at strut, if equipped with stabilizer.
6. Reinstall 2 wheel nuts to hold rotor on hub and bearing assembly.
7. Remove brake caliper and support with a length of wire.

NOTE: Do not allow caliper to hang by the brake hose unsupported.

8. Loosen knuckle pivot bolt on outboard end of control arm. Do not remove pivot bolt.
9. Support outboard end of control arm with a suitable lifting device to slightly compress spring.
10. Remove strut rod cap, mounting nut, retainer and upper insulator.
11. Slowly remove lifting device to relieve spring pressure.
12. Compress strut by hand and remove lower insulator.
13. Remove wheel speed sensor, if equipped with anti-lock brakes.
14. Remove inner control arm nuts.
15. While supporting the knuckle and control arm, remove inner control arm bolts and remove the control arm, knuckle, strut, hub and bearing and rotor from vehicle as an assembly.
16. Place a jackstand under the outboard end of spring.
17. Lower the vehicle so the weight loads the spring downward on jackstand.
18. Remove the 3 spring retainer bolts, retainer and lower insulator from retainer nearest the supported end of spring.
19. Slowly raise vehicle, allowing spring to deflect downward until

spring no longer exerts force on the lifting device. Remove lifting device.
20. Remove spring retainer bolts, retainer and lower insulator from retainer on opposite side of vehicle.
21. Withdraw spring from rear suspension support through disassembled side of vehicle suspension.
22. Remove upper spring insulators, as required.

NOTE: Inspect all spring insulators, insulator locating pads, retainers and control arm contact pads for cuts, cracks, tears or other damage. Replace worn or damaged parts.

To install:
23. Install spring insulators which were previously removed. Ensure that molded arrow on the insulator points toward the centerline of the vehicle when installing upper outboard insulators. Tighten center and upper outboard insulator nuts to 21 ft. lbs. (28 Nm).

NOTE: When positioning spring in suspension support, outboard and center insulator locating bands must be centered on spring insulators. Failure to position spring correctly may result in reduced vehicle handling characteristics.

24. With spring properly located, install lower insulator and spring retainer on side of vehicle opposite the disassembled portion of suspension.
25. Place suitable lifing device under free end of spring.
26. Lower vehicle, allowing weight to load spring and deflect free end of spring into position in suspension support.
27. Install lower insulator and spring retainer on disassembled side of suspension support. Tighten spring retainer bolts to 21 ft. lbs. (28 Nm).
28. Raise the vehicle and remove spring lifting device.
29. Position the assembled control arm, knuckle, strut, hub and bearing and rotor assembly in suspension support and install inner control arm bolts and nuts. Do not tighten at this time.
30. Connect wheel sensor, if equipped with anti-lock brakes.
31. Install lower strut insulator and position strut rod in suspension support assembly.
32. Position suitable lifting under outboard end of lower control arm to slightly compress spring.
33. Install strut insulator, retainer and nut. Tighten upper strut nut to 65 ft. lbs. (88 Nm). Tighten knuckle pivot bolt to 59 ft. lbs. (80 Nm). Tighten in-

ner control arm bolts to 66 ft. lbs. (90 Nm).
34. Remove lifing device.
35. Install strut rod cap.
36. Install stabilizer shaft mounting bolt, if equipped with stabilizer. Tighten stabilizer shaft mounting bolt to 43 ft. lbs. (58 Nm).
37. Remove 2 wheel nuts previously installed to retain motor.
38. Install caliper and new caliper mounting bracket bolts. Tighten caliper mounting bracket bolts to 83 ft. lbs. (113 Nm).
39. Connect height sensor link, if left side of suspension was disassembled.
40. Install wheel and tire assembly.
41. Lower vehicle. Tighten wheel nuts to 100 ft. lbs. (140 Nm).

NOTE: Vehicle must have rear wheel alignment performed after removal and installation of rear spring.

Rear Control Arms

REMOVAL & INSTALLATION

1. Disconnect the negative battery cable.
2. Raise and safely support the vehicle.
3. Remove wheel and tire assembly.
4. If equipped with anti-lock brakes, remove speed sensor from knuckle.
5. Reinstall 2 wheel nuts to hold rotor on hub and bearing assembly.
6. Remove brake caliper and support with a length of mechanics wire.

NOTE: Do not allow caliper to hang by the brake hose unsupported.

7. Loosen knuckle pivot bolt on outboard end of control arm. Do not remove.
8. Remove upper strut rod cap, mounting nut, retainer and insulator.
9. Compress strut by hand and remove lower insulator.
10. While supporting the knuckle, remove knuckle pivot bolt and remove the knuckle, strut, hub and bearing and rotor from car as an assembly.
11. Remove both inner control arm bolts and remove control arm from vehicle.

To install:
12. Position control arm in vehicle and install both inner control arm bolts. Do not tighten bolts at this time.
13. Position the assembled knuckle, strut, hub and bearing and rotor assembly in control arm and install knuckle pivot bolt. Do not tighten bolt at this time.
14. Install lower strut insulator and position strut rod in suspension support.

15. Install upper strut insulator, retainer and nut. Tighten upper strut nut to 65 ft. lbs. (88 Nm). Tighten knuckle pivot bolt to 59 ft. lbs. (80 Nm). Tighten inner control arm bolts to 66 ft. lbs. (90 Nm).

16. Install strut rod cap.

17. Remove 2 wheel nuts previously installed to retain rotor.

18. Install caliper and new caliper bracket mounting bolts.

19. If equipped, install speed sensor to knuckle.

20. Install wheel and tire assembly.

21. Lower vehicle. Tighten wheel nuts to 100 ft. lbs. (140 Nm).

Rear Wheel Bearings
REMOVAL & INSTALLATION

1. Disconnect the negative battery cable.

2. Raise and safely support the vehicle.

3. Remove wheel and tire assembly.

4. If equipped with anti-lock brakes, remove speed sensor from knuckle.

5. Reinstall 2 wheel nuts to hold rotor on hub and bearing assembly.

6. Remove brake caliper and support with a length of mechanics wire.

NOTE: Do not allow caliper to hang by the brake hose unsupported.

7. Remove rotor.

8. Remove 4 hub mounting bolts.

9. Remove hub and bearing assembly.

To install:

10. Position hub and bearing assembly on knuckle.

11. Install 4 hub mounting bolts. Tighten to 52 ft. lbs. (70 Nm).

12. Install rotor.

13. Install caliper and new caliper bracket mounting bolts. Tighten to 83 ft. lbs. (113 Nm).

14. Install wheel and tire assemby.

15. Lower vehicle. Tighten wheel nuts to 100 ft. lbs. (140 Nm).

ADJUSTMENT

The hub and bearing are installed as an assembly. No periodic adjustment is required. If the bearing is found to have excessive play, the assembly must be replaced.

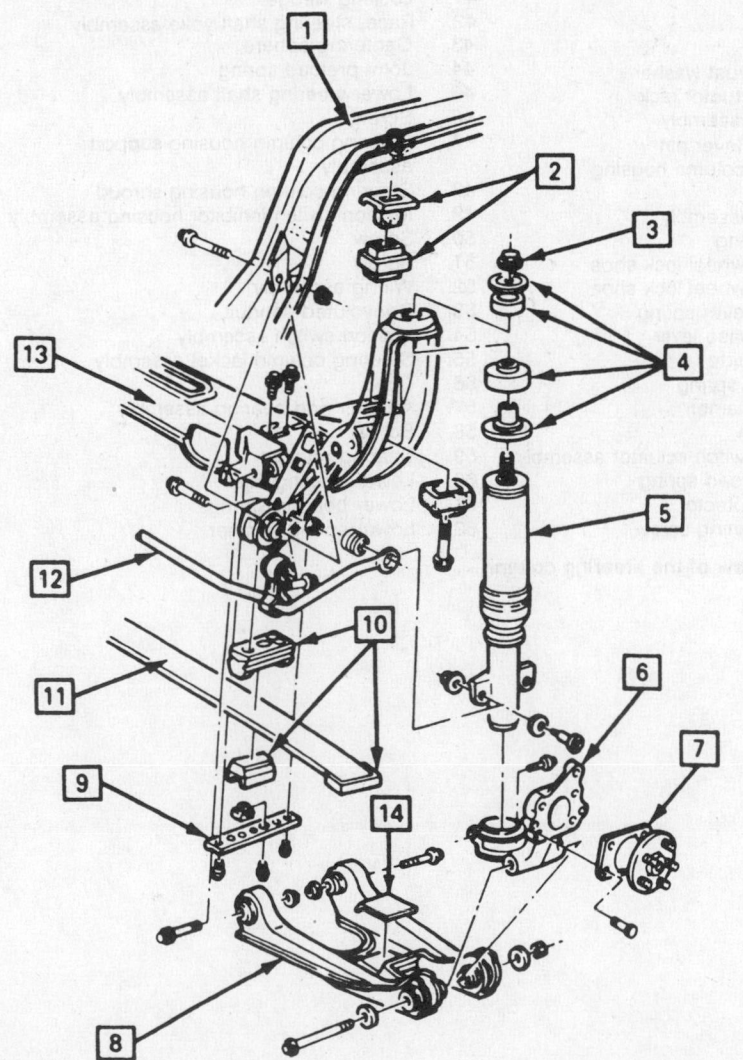
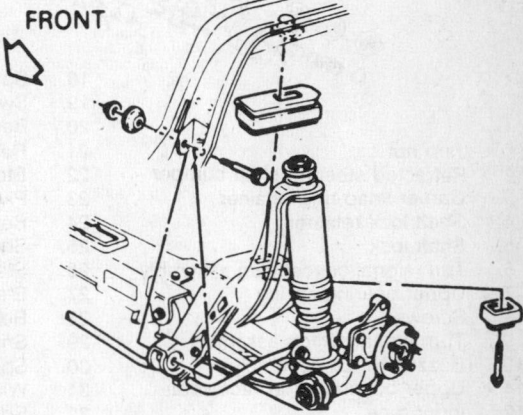

FRONT

1. Underbody assembly
2. Suspension support insulators
3. Upper strut mounting nut
4. Strut mount insulators
5. Strut
6. Knuckle
7. Hub/bearing assembly
8. Control arm
9. Spring retainer
10. Spring insulators
11. Single leaf spring
12. Stabilizer shaft
13. Suspension support
14. Trim height adjustment spacer

Rear suspension assembly

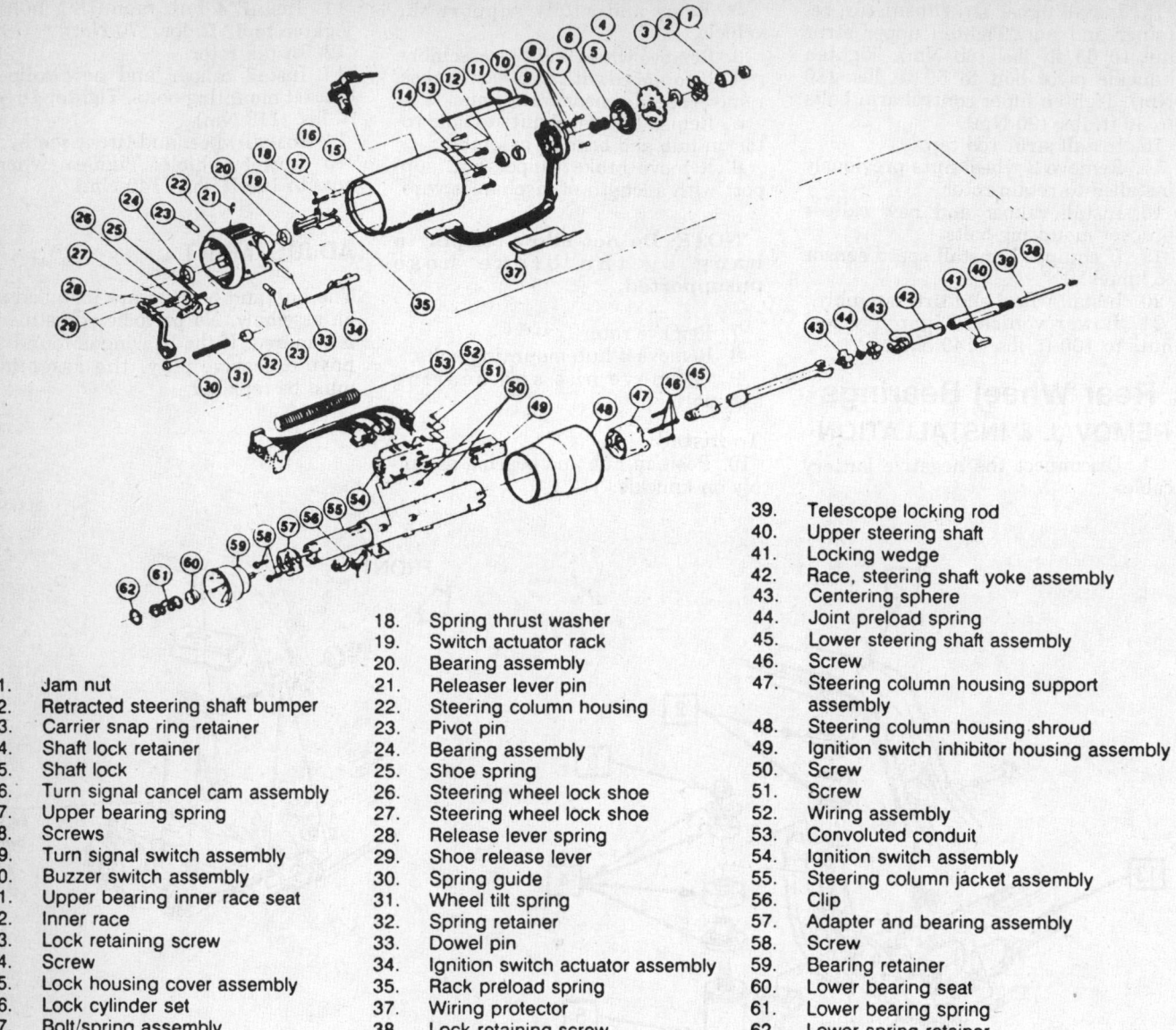

39. Telescope locking rod
40. Upper steering shaft
41. Locking wedge
42. Race, steering shaft yoke assembly
43. Centering sphere
44. Joint preload spring
45. Lower steering shaft assembly
46. Screw
47. Steering column housing support assembly
48. Steering column housing shroud
49. Ignition switch inhibitor housing assembly
50. Screw
51. Screw
52. Wiring assembly
53. Convoluted conduit
54. Ignition switch assembly
55. Steering column jacket assembly
56. Clip
57. Adapter and bearing assembly
58. Screw
59. Bearing retainer
60. Lower bearing seat
61. Lower bearing spring
62. Lower spring retainer

18. Spring thrust washer
19. Switch actuator rack
20. Bearing assembly
21. Releaser lever pin
22. Steering column housing
23. Pivot pin
24. Bearing assembly
25. Shoe spring
26. Steering wheel lock shoe
27. Steering wheel lock shoe
28. Release lever spring
29. Shoe release lever
30. Spring guide
31. Wheel tilt spring
32. Spring retainer
33. Dowel pin
34. Ignition switch actuator assembly
35. Rack preload spring
37. Wiring protector
38. Lock retaining screw

1. Jam nut
2. Retracted steering shaft bumper
3. Carrier snap ring retainer
4. Shaft lock retainer
5. Shaft lock
6. Turn signal cancel cam assembly
7. Upper bearing spring
8. Screws
9. Turn signal switch assembly
10. Buzzer switch assembly
11. Upper bearing inner race seat
12. Inner race
13. Lock retaining screw
14. Screw
15. Lock housing cover assembly
16. Lock cylinder set
17. Bolt/spring assembly

Exploded view of the steering column

GM "F" Body
Rear Wheel Drive
Chevrolet—Camaro
Pontiac—Firebird

24

SPECIFICATIONS

VEHICLE IDENTIFICATION CHART

It is important for servicing and ordering parts to be certain of the vehicle and engine identification. The VIN (vehicle identification number) is a 17 digit number visible through the windshield on the driver's side of the dash and contains the vehicle and engine identification codes. The tenth digit indicates model year and the eighth digit indicates engine code. It can be interpreted as follows:

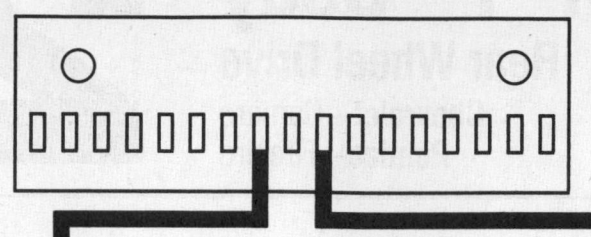

Engine Code						Model Year	
Code	Cu. In.	Liters	Cyl.	Fuel Sys.	Eng. Mfg.	Code	Year
S	173	2.8	6	MFI	Chevrolet	H	1987
H	305	5.0	8	Carb.	Chevrolet	J	1988
F	305	5.0	8	TPI	Chevrolet	K	1989
E	305	5.0	8	TBI	Chevrolet	L	1990
8	350	5.7	8	TPI	Chevrolet	M	1991
T	191	3.1	6	MFI	CPC		
7	231	3.8	6	SFI-Turbo	Buick		

ENGINE IDENTIFICATION

Year	Model	Engine Displacement cu. in. (liter)	Engine Series Identification (VIN)	No. of Cylinders	Engine Type
1987	Camaro	173 (2.8)	S	6	OHV
	Firebird	173 (2.8)	S	6	OHV
	Camara	305 (5.0)	H	8	OHV
	Firebird	305 (5.0)	H	8	OHV
	Camara	305 (5.0)	F	8	OHV
	Firebird	305 (5.0)	F	8	OHV
	Camaro	350 (5.7)	8	8	OHV
	Firebird	350 (5.7)	8	8	OHV
1988	Camaro	173 (2.8)	S	6	OHV
	Firebird	173 (2.8)	S	6	OHV
	Camaro	305 (5.0)	F	8	OHV
	Firebird	305 (5.0)	F	8	OHV
	Camaro	305 (5.0)	E	8	OHV
	Firebird	305 (5.0)	E	8	OHV
	Camaro	350 (5.7)	8	8	OHV
	Firebird	350 (5.7)	8	8	OHV

ENGINE IDENTIFICATION

Year	Model	Engine Displacement cu. in. (liter)	Engine Series Identification (VIN)	No. of Cylinders	Engine Type
1989	Camaro	173 (2.8)	S	6	OHV
	Firebird	173 (2.8)	S	6	OHV
	Camaro	305 (5.0)	F	8	OHV
	Firebird	305 (5.0)	F	8	OHV
	Camaro	305 (5.0)	E	8	OHV
	Firebird	305 (5.0)	E	8	OHV
	Camaro	350 (5.7)	8	8	OHV
	Firebird	350 (5.7)	8	8	OHV
	Firebird	231 (3.8)	7	6	OHV
1990–91	Camaro	191 (3.1)	T	6	OHV
	Firebird	191 (3.1)	T	6	OHV
	Camaro	305 (5.0)	F	8	OHV
	Firebird	305 (5.0)	F	8	OHV
	Camaro	305 (5.0)	E	8	OHV
	Firebird	305 (5.0)	E	8	OHV
	Camaro	350 (5.7)	8	8	OHV
	Firebird	350 (5.7)	8	8	OHV

OHV Over Head Valve

GENERAL ENGINE SPECIFICATIONS

Year	VIN	No. Cylinder Displacement cu. in. (liter)	Fuel System Type	Net Horsepower @ rpm	Net Torque @ rpm (ft. lbs.)	Bore × Stroke (in.)	Compression Ratio	Oil Pressure @ 2000 rpm
1987	S	6-173 (2.8)	MFI	135 @ 5100	165 @ 3600	3.500 × 3.000	8.9:1	55
	H	8-305 (5.0)	Carb.	150 @ 4000	240 @ 2400	3.736 × 3.480	8.6:1	55
	F	8-305 (5.0)	TPI	190 @ 4800	240 @ 3200	3.740 × 3.480	9.3:1	55
	8	8-350 (5.7)	TPI	230 @ 4000	300 @ 3200	4.000 × 3.480	9.5:1	55
1988	S	6-173 (2.8)	MFI	135 @ 5100	165 @ 3600	3.500 × 3.000	8.9:1	55
	F	8-305 (5.0)	TPI	190 @ 4800	240 @ 3200	3.736 × 3.480	9.3:1	55
	E	8-305 (5.0)	TBI	150 @ 4000	240 @ 3200	3.736 × 3.480	9.3:1	55
	8	8-350 (5.7)	TPI	230 @ 4000	300 @ 3200	4.000 × 3.480	9.5:1	55
1989	S	6-173 (2.8)	MFI	135 @ 5100	165 @ 3600	3.500 × 3.000	8.9:1	55
	F	8-305 (5.0)	TPI	190 @ 4800	240 @ 3200	3.736 × 3.480	9.3:1	55
	E	8-305 (5.0)	TBI	150 @ 4000	240 @ 3200	3.736 × 3.480	9.3:1	55
	8	8-350 (5.7)	TPI	230 @ 4000	300 @ 3200	4.000 × 3.480	9.5:1	55
	7	6-231 (3.8)	SFI-Turbo	235 @ 4400	330 @ 2800	3.800 × 3.400	8.0:1	37
1990–91	T	6-191 (3.1)	MFI	140 @ 4400	180 @ 3600	3.500 × 3.310	8.9:1	55
	F	8-305 (5.0)	TPI	230 @ 4400	300 @ 3200	3.736 × 3.480	9.3:1	55
	E	8-305 (5.0)	TBI	170 @ 4000	255 @ 2400	3.736 × 3.480	9.3:1	55
	8	8-350 (5.7)	TPI	240 @ 4400	345 @ 3200	4.000 × 3.480	9.3:1	55

GASOLINE ENGINE TUNE-UP SPECIFICATIONS

Year	VIN	No. Cylinder Displacement cu. in. (liter)	Spark Plugs Type	Spark Plugs Gap (in.)	Ignition Timing (deg.) MT	Ignition Timing (deg.) AT	Compression Pressure (psi)	Fuel Pump (psi)	Speed (rpm) MT	Speed (rpm) AT	Valve Clearance In.	Valve Clearance Ex.
1987	S	6-173 (2.8)	R-43LTSE	0.045	10	10	NA	40–47	600	500	Hyd.	Hyd.
	H	8-305 (5.0)	R-44TS	0.035	6	6	NA	4.0–6.5	500	500	Hyd.	Hyd.
	F	8-305 (5.0)	R-44TS	0.035	6	6	NA	40–47	500	500	Hyd.	Hyd.
	8	8-350 (5.7)	R-44TS	0.035	6	6	NA	40–47	450	400	Hyd.	Hyd.
1988	S	6-173 (2.8)	R-42CTS	0.045	10	10	NA	40–47	450	400	Hyd.	Hyd.
	F	8-305 (5.0)	R-43TS	0.035	6	6	NA	40–47	500	500	Hyd.	Hyd.
	E	8-305 (5.0)	R-45TS	0.035	6	6	NA	9.0–13.0	450	400	Hyd.	Hyd.
	8	8-350 (5.7)	R-43TS	0.035	6	6	NA	40–47	450	400	Hyd.	Hyd.
1989	S	6-173 (2.8)	R-42CTS	0.045	10	10	NA	40–47	450	400	Hyd.	Hyd.
	F	8-305 (5.0)	R-43TS	0.035	6	6	NA	40–47	500	500	Hyd.	Hyd.
	E	8-305 (5.0)	R-45TS	0.035	6	6	NA	9.0–13.0	450	400	Hyd.	Hyd.
	8	8-350 (5.7)	R-43TS	0.035	6	6	NA	40–47	450	400	Hyd.	Hyd.
	7	6-231 (3.8)	R-43TS	0.035	①	①	NA	34–40	①	①	Hyd.	Hyd.
1990	T	6-191 (3.0)	R-43TS	0.045	10	10	NA	40–47	①	①	Hyd.	Hyd.
	F	8-305 (5.0)	R-45TS	0.035	6	6	NA	40–47	①	①	Hyd.	Hyd.
	E	8-305 (5.0)	R-45TS	0.035	0	0	NA	9.0–13.0	①	①	Hyd.	Hyd.
	8	8-350 (5.7)	R-45TS	0.035	6	6	NA	40–47	①	①	Hyd.	Hyd.
1991		SEE UNDERHOOD SPECIFICATIONS STICKER										

① See Emission Decal

FIRING ORDERS

NOTE: To avoid confusion, always replace spark plug wires one at a time.

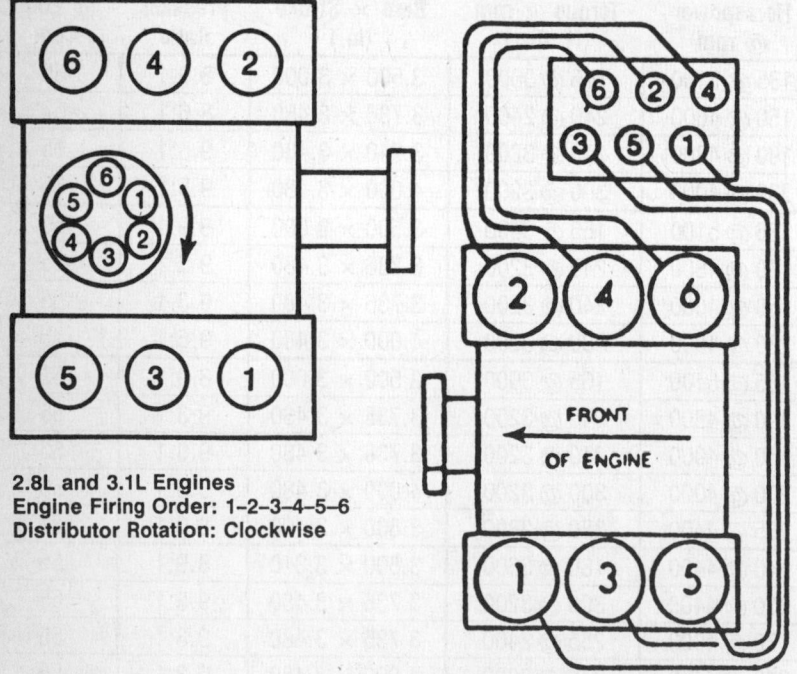

2.8L and 3.1L Engines
Engine Firing Order: 1–2–3–4–5–6
Distributor Rotation: Clockwise

FRONT OF ENGINE

3.8L Engine
Engine Firing Order: 1–6–5–4–3–2
Distributorless Ignition System

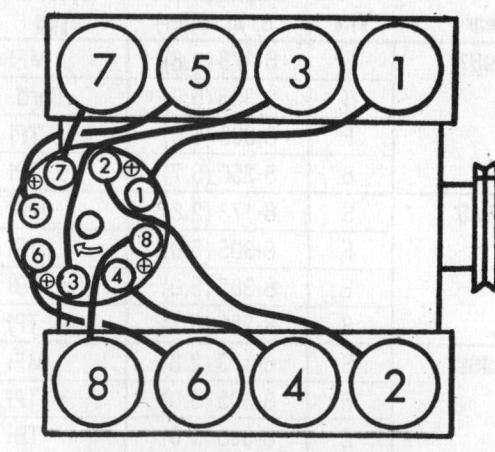

5.0L and 5.7L Engines
Engine Firing Order: 1–8–4–3–6–5–7–2
Distributor Rotation: Clockwise

CAPACITIES

Year	Model	VIN	No. Cylinder Displacement cu. in. (liter)	Engine Crankcase (qts.) with Filter	Engine Crankcase (qts.) without Filter	Transmission (pts.) 4-Spd	Transmission (pts.) 5-Spd	Transmission (pts.) Auto.	Drive Axle (pts.)	Fuel Tank (gal.)	Cooling System (qts.)
1987	Camaro	S	6-173 (2.8)	4.0	4.0	—	6.6	8.5 ①	3.5	16	13
	Camaro	H	8-305 (5.0)	5.0	4.0	—	6.6	8.5 ①	3.5	16	17
	Camaro	F	8-305 (5.0)	5.0	4.0	—	6.6	8.5 ①	3.5	16	17
	Camaro	8	8-350 (5.7)	5.0	4.0	—	6.6	8.5 ①	3.5	16	17
	Firebird	S	6-173 (2.8)	4.0	4.0	—	6.6	8.5 ①	3.5	16	13
	Firebird	H	8-305 (5.0)	5.0	4.0	—	6.6	8.5 ①	3.5	16	17
	Firebird	F	8-305 (5.0)	5.0	4.0	—	6.6	8.5 ①	3.5	16	17
	Firebird	8	8-350 (5.7)	5.0	4.0	—	6.6	8.5 ①	3.5	16	17
1988	Camaro	S	6-173 (2.8)	4.0	4.0	—	6.6	8.5 ①	3.5	16	13
	Camaro	F	8-305 (5.0)	5.0	4.0	—	6.6	8.5 ①	3.5	16	17
	Camaro	E	8-305 (5.0)	5.0	4.0	—	6.6	8.5 ①	3.5	16	15.5
	Camaro	8	8-305 (5.7)	5.0	4.0	—	6.6	8.5 ①	3.5	16	17
	Firebird	S	6-173 (2.8)	4.0	4.0	—	6.6	8.5 ①	3.5	16	13
	Firebird	F	8-305 (5.0)	5.0	4.0	—	6.6	8.5 ①	3.5	16	17
	Firebird	E	8-305 (5.0)	5.0	4.0	—	6.6	8.5 ①	3.5	16	15.5
	Firebird	8	8-350 (5.7)	5.0	4.0	—	6.6	8.5 ①	3.5	16	17
1989	Camaro	S	6-173 (2.8)	4.0	4.0	—	6.6	8.5 ①	3.5	16	13
	Camaro	F	8-305 (5.0)	5.0	4.0	—	6.6	8.5 ①	3.5	16	17
	Camaro	E	8-305 (5.0)	5.0	4.0	—	6.6	8.5 ①	3.5	16	15.5
	Camaro	8	8-305 (5.7)	5.0	4.0	—	6.6	8.5 ①	3.5	16	17
	Firebird	S	6-173 (2.8)	4.0	4.0	—	6.6	8.5 ①	3.5	16	13
	Firebird	F	8-305 (5.0)	5.0	4.0	—	6.6	8.5 ①	3.5	16	17
	Firebird	E	8-305 (5.0)	5.0	4.0	—	6.6	8.5 ①	3.5	16	15.5
	Firebird	8	8-350 (5.7)	5.0	4.0	—	6.6	8.5 ①	3.5	16	17
	Firebird	7	6-231 (3.8)	—	4.0	—	—	10	3.5	15.5	16.5
1990–91	Camaro	T	6-191 (3.1)	4.0	4.0	—	5.9	10	3.5	15.5	14.5
	Camaro	F	8-305 (5.0)	5.0	4.0	—	5.9	10	3.5	15.5	17.5
	Camaro	E	8-305 (5.0)	5.0	4.0	—	5.9	10	3.5	15.5	17.5
	Camaro	8	8-350 (5.7)	5.0	4.0	—	5.9	10	3.5	15.5	16.5
	Firebird	T	6-191 (3.1)	4.0	4.0	—	5.9	10	3.5	15.5	14.5
	Firebird	F	8-305 (5.0)	5.0	4.0	—	5.9	10	3.5	15.5	17.5
	Firebird	E	8-305 (5.0)	5.0	4.0	—	5.9	10	3.5	15.5	17.5
	Firebird	8	8-350 (5.7)	5.0	4.0	—	5.9	10	3.5	15.5	16.5

① 10.0 if equipped with overdrive

CAMSHAFT SPECIFICATIONS

All measurements given in inches.

Year	VIN	No. Cylinder Displacement cu. in. (liter)	Journal Diameter					Lobe Lift		Bearing Clearance	Camshaft End Play
			1	2	3	4	5	In.	Ex.		
1987	S	6-173 (2.8)	1.8976–1.8996	1.8976–1.8996	1.8976–1.8996	1.8976–1.8996		0.2350	0.2660	NA	NA
	H	8-305 (5.0)	1.8682–1.8692	1.8682–1.8692	1.8682–1.8692	1.8682–1.8692	1.8682–1.8692	0.2340 ①②	0.2570 ①②	NA	0.004–0.012
	F	8-305 (5.0)	1.8682–1.8692	1.8682–1.8692	1.8682–1.8692	1.8682–1.8692	1.8682–1.8692	0.2340 ①②	0.2570 ①②	NA	0.004–0.012
	8	8-350 (5.7)	1.8682–1.8692	1.8682–1.8692	1.8682–1.8692	1.8682–1.8692	1.8682–1.8692	0.2730	0.2828	NA	0.004–0.012
1988	S	6-173 (2.8)	1.8976–1.8996	1.8976–1.8996	1.8976–1.8996	1.8976–1.8996		0.2350	0.2660	NA	NA
	F	8-305 (5.0)	1.8682–1.8692	1.8682–1.8692	1.8682–1.8692	1.8682–1.8692	1.8682–1.8692	0.2690	0.2760	NA	0.004–0.012
	E	8-305 (5.0)	1.8682–1.8692	1.8682–1.8692	1.8682–1.8692	1.8682–1.8692	1.8682–1.8692	0.2340	0.2570	NA	0.004–0.012
	8	8-350 (5.7)	1.8682–1.8692	1.8682–1.8692	1.8682–1.8692	1.8682–1.8692	1.8682–1.8692	0.2730	0.2820	NA	0.004–0.012
1989	S	6-173 (2.8)	1.8976–1.8996	1.8976–1.8996	1.8976–1.8996	1.8976–1.8996		0.2350	0.2660	NA	NA
	F	8-305 (5.0)	1.8682–1.8692	1.8682–1.8692	1.8682–1.8692	1.8682–1.8692	1.8682–1.8692	0.2690	0.2760	NA	0.004–0.012
	E	8-305 (5.0)	1.8682–1.8692	1.8682–1.8692	1.8682–1.8692	1.8682–1.8692	1.8682–1.8692	0.2340	0.2570	NA	0.004–0.012
	8	8-350 (5.7)	1.8682–1.8692	1.8682–1.8692	1.8682–1.8692	1.8682–1.8692	1.8682–1.8692	0.2730	0.2820	NA	0.004–0.012
	7	6-231 (3.8)	1.7850 1.7860	1.7850 1.7860	1.7850 1.7860	1.7850 1.7860	—	NA	NA	③	NA
1990–91	T	6-191 (3.1)	1.8678–1.8697	1.8678–1.8697	1.8678–1.8697	1.8678–1.8697	—	0.2626	0.2732	0.0010–0.0040	NA
	F	8-305 (5.0)	1.8682–1.8692	1.8682–1.8692	1.8682–1.8692	1.8682–1.8692	1.8682–1.8692	④	④	NA	0.004–0.012
	E	8-305 (5.0)	1.8682–1.8692	1.8682–1.8692	1.8682–1.8692	1.8682–1.8692	1.8682–1.8692	0.234	0.257	NA	0.004–0.012
	8	8-350 (5.7)	1.8682–1.8692	1.8682–1.8692	1.8682–1.8692	1.8682–1.8692	1.8682–1.8692	⑤	⑤	NA	0.004–0.012

① TBI—0.2750-Intake; 0.2690 = Exhaust
② 4 bbl HO—0.2690-Intake; 0.2760 = Exhaust
③ No. 1—0.0005-0.0025
   No. 2,3,4—0.0005-0.0035
④ 1990-INT.—0.269 Ex. 0.276
   1991-INT.—0.275 Ex. 0.285
⑤ 1990-INT.—0.273 Ex. 0.282
   1991-INT.—0.275 Ex. 0.285

CRANKSHAFT AND CONNECTING ROD SPECIFICATIONS

All measurements are given in inches.

Year	VIN	No. Cylinder Displacement cu. in. (liter)	Crankshaft				Connecting Rod		
			Main Brg. Journal Dia.	Main Brg. Oil Clearance	Shaft End-play	Thrust on No.	Journal Diameter	Oil Clearance	Side Clearance
1987	S	6-173 (2.8)	2.6473–2.6483	0.0017–0.0029	0.0019–0.0066	3	1.998–1.999	0.0014–0.0035	0.0060–0.0170
	H	8-305 (5.0)	①	②	0.0020–0.0060	5	2.098–2.099	0.0018–0.0039	0.0080–0.0140
	F	8-305 (5.0)	①	②	0.0020–0.0060	5	2.098–2.099	0.0018–0.0039	0.0080–0.0140
	8	8-350 (5.7)	①	②	0.0020–0.0060	5	2.098–2.099	0.0013–0.0035	0.0060–0.0140
1988	S	6-173 (2.8)	2.6473–2.6483	0.0017–0.0029	0.0019–0.0066	3	1.998–1.999	0.0014–0.0035	0.0060–0.0170
	F	8-305 (5.0)	①	②	0.0020–0.0060	5	2.098–2.099	0.0018–0.0039	0.0080–0.0140
	E	8-305 (5.0)	①	②	0.0020–0.0060	5	2.098–2.099	0.0018–0.0039	0.0080–0.0140
	8	8-350 (5.7)	①	②	0.0020–0.0060	5	2.098–2.099	0.0013–0.0035	0.0060–0.0140
1989	S	6-173 (2.8)	2.6473 2.6483	0.0017–0.0029	0.0019–0.0066	3	1.998–1.999	0.0014–0.0035	0.0060–0.0170
	F	8-305 (5.0)	①	②	0.0020–0.0060	5	2.098–2.099	0.0018–0.0039	0.0080–0.0140
	E	8-305 (5.0)	①	②	0.0020–0.0060	5	2.098–2.099	0.0018–0.0039	0.0080–0.0140
	8	8-350 (5.7)	①	②	0.0020–0.0060	5	2.098–2.099	0.0013–0.0035	0.0060–0.0140
	7	6-231 (3.8)	2.4995	0.0003–0.0018	0.003–0.011	2	2.2487–2.2495	0.0005–0.0026	0.0030–0.0150
1990–91	T	6-191 (3.1)	2.6473–2.6483	③	0.0024–0.0083	3	1.9983–1.9994	④	0.0140–0.0290
	F	8-305 (5.0)	①	②	0.001–0.007	5	2.098–2.099	0.0013–0.0035	0.0060–0.0140
	E	8-305 (5.0)	①	②	0.001–0.007	5	2.098–2.099	0.0013–0.0035	0.0060–0.0140
	8	8-350 (5.7)	①	②	0.001–0.007	5	2.098–2.099	0.0013–0.0035	0.0060–0.0140

① No. 1—2.4484-2.4493
 Nos. 2, 3, 4—2.4481-2.4490
 No. 5—2.4479-2.4488

① No. 1—0.0008-0020
 Nos. 2, 3, 4—0.0011-0.0023
 No. 5—.0-017-0.0032

③ 1990—Main Bearing Clearance—0.0012-0.0027
 Main Thrust Bearing Clearance—0.0016-0.0027

 1990—Main Bearing Clearance—0.0012-0.0030
 Main Thrust Bearing Clearance—0.0016-0.0030

④ 1990—0.0014-0.0036
 1991—0.0011-0.0033

VALVE SPECIFICATIONS

Year	VIN	No. Cylinder Displacement cu. in. (liter)	Seat Angle (deg.)	Face Angle (deg.)	Spring Test Pressure (lbs.)	Spring Installed Height (in.)	Stem-to-Guide Clearance (in.)		Stem Diameter (in.)	
							Intake	Exhaust	Intake	Exhaust
1987	S	6-173 (2.8)	46	45	194 @ 1.18	1.57	0.0010–0.0027	0.3410–0.0027	0.3410–0.3420	0.3410–0.3420
	H	8-305 (5.0)	46	45	194-206 @ 1.25	1.72	0.0010–0.0027	0.0010–0.0027	0.3410–0.3420	0.3410–0.3420
	F	8-305 (5.0)	46	45	194-206 @ 1.25	1.72	0.0010–0.0027	0.0010–0.0027	0.3410–0.3420	0.3410–0.3420
	8	8-350 (5.7)	46	45	194-206 @ 1.25	1.72	0.0010–0.0027	0.0010–0.0027	0.3410–0.3420	0.3410–0.3420
1988	S	6-173 (2.8)	46	45	194 @ 1.18	1.57	0.0010–0.0027	0.3410–0.0027	0.3410–0.3420	0.3410–0.3420
	E	8-305 (5.0)	46	45	194-206 @ 1.25	①	0.0010–0.0027	0.0010–0.0027	0.3410–0.3420	0.3410–0.3420
	F	8-305 (5.0)	46	45	194-206 @ 1.25	①	0.0010–0.0027	0.0010–0.0027	0.3410–0.3420	0.3410–0.3420
	8	8-350 (5.7)	46	45	194-206 @ 1.25	①	0.0010–0.0027	0.0010–0.0027	0.3410–0.3420	0.3410–0.3420
1989	S	6-173 (2.8)	46	45	194 @ 1.18	1.57	0.0010–0.0027	0.3410–0.0027	0.3410–0.3420	0.3410–0.3420
	E	8-305 (5.0)	46	45	194-206 @ 1.25	①	0.0010–0.0027	0.0010–0.0027	0.3410–0.3420	0.3410–0.3420
	F	8-305 (5.0)	46	45	194-206 @ 1.25	①	0.0010–0.0027	0.0010–0.0027	0.3410–0.3420	0.3410–0.3420
	8	8-350 (5.7)	46	45	194-206 @ 1.25	①	0.0010–0.0027	0.0010–0.0027	0.3410–0.3420	0.3410–0.3420
	7	6-231 (3.8)	45	NA	185 @ 1.340	1.73	0.0015–0.0035	0.0015–0.0032	0.3420–0.3401	0.3412–0.3405
1990-91	T	6-191 (3.1)	46	45	190 @ 1.20	1.60	0.0014–0.0025	0.0016–0.0029	0.3410–0.3420	0.3410–0.3420
	F	8-305 (5.0)	46	45	194-206 @ 1.25	①	0.0010–0.0027	0.0010–0.0027	0.3410–0.3420	0.3410–0.3420
	E	8-305 (5.0)	46	45	194-206 @ 1.25	①	0.0010–0.0027	0.0010–0.0027	0.3410–0.3420	0.3410–0.3420
	8	8-350 (5.7)	46	45	194-206 @1.25	①	0.0010–0.0027	0.0010–0.0027	0.3410–0.3420	0.3410–0.3420

① Intake—1.72
Exhaust—1.59

PISTON AND RING SPECIFICATIONS
All measurements are given in inches.

Year	VIN	No. Cylinder Displacement cu. in. (liter)	Piston Clearance	Ring Gap			Ring Side Clearance		
				Top Compression	Bottom Compression	Oil Control	Top Compression	Bottom Compression	Oil Control
1987	S	6-173 (2.8)	0.017–0.043	0.0098–0.0196	0.0098–0.0196	0.0200–0.0550	0.0011–0.0027	0.0015–0.0037	0.0078 Max.
	H	8-305 (5.0)	0.0027	0.0100–0.0200	0.0100–0.0250	0.0150–0.0550	0.0012–0.0032	0.0012–0.0032	0.0020–0.0070
	F	8-305 (5.0)	0.0027	0.0100–0.0200	0.0100–0.0250	0.0150–0.0550	0.0012–0.0032	0.0012–0.0032	0.0020–0.0070
	8	8-350 (5.7)	0.0045	0.0100–0.0200	0.0100–0.0250	0.0150–0.0550	0.0012–0.0032	0.0012–0.0032	0.0020–0.0070

PISTON AND RING SPECIFICATIONS
All measurements are given in inches.

Year	VIN	No. Cylinder Displacement cu. in. (liter)	Piston Clearance	Ring Gap			Ring Side Clearance		
				Top Compression	Bottom Compression	Oil Control	Top Compression	Bottom Compression	Oil Control
1988	S	6-173 (2.8)	0.017–0.043	0.0098–0.0196	0.0098–0.0196	0.0200–0.0550	0.0011–0.0027	0.0015–0.0037	0.0078 Max.
	F	8-305 (5.0)	NA	0.0100–0.0200	0.0100–0.0250	0.0150–0.0550	0.0012–0.0032	0.0012–0.0032	0.0020–0.0070
	E	8-305 (5.0)	0.0027	0.0100–0.0200	0.0100–0.0250	0.0150–0.0550	0.0012–0.0032	0.0012–0.0032	0.0020–0.0070
	8	8-350 (5.7)	0.0027	0.0100–0.0200	0.0100–0.0250	0.0150–0.0550	0.0012–0.0032	0.0012–0.0032	0.0020–0.0070
1989	S	6-173 (2.8)	0.017–0.043	0.0098–0.0196	0.0098–0.0196	0.0200–0.0550	0.0300–0.0070	0.0040–0.0950	0.0078 Max.
	F	8-305 (5.0)	NA	0.0100–0.0200	0.0100–0.0250	0.0150–0.0550	0.0012–0.0032	0.0012–0.0032	0.0020–0.0070
	E	8-305 (5.0)	0.0027	0.0100–0.0200	0.0100–0.0250	0.0150–0.0550	0.0012–0.0032	0.0012–0.0032	0.0020–0.0070
	8	8-350 (5.7)	0.0027	0.0100–0.0200	0.0100–0.0250	0.0150–0.0550	0.0012–0.0032	0.0012–0.0032	0.0020–0.0070
	7	6-231(3.8)	0.0013 0.0035	0.0100–0.0200	0.0100–0.0200	0.0150–0.0550	NA	NA	NA
1990–91	T	6-191 (3.1)	0.0012–0.0028	0.0100–0.0200	①	0.0100–0.0300	0.0020–0.0035	0.0020–0.0035	0.0075 Max.
	F	8-305 (5.0)	0.0007–0.0027	0.0100–0.0200	0.0100–0.0250	0.0650 Max.	0.0012–0.0032	0.0012–0.0032	0.008 Max.
	E	8-305 (5.0)	0.0007–0.0027	0.0100–0.0200	0.0100–0.0250	0.0650 Max.	0.0012–0.0032	0.0012–0.0032	0.008 Max.
	8	8-350 (5.7)	0.0007–0.0027	0.0100 0.0200	0.0180–0.0260	0.0650 Max.	0.0012–0.0032	0.0012–0.0032	0.008 Max.

① 1990—0.010–0.020
1991—0.020–0.028

TORQUE SPECIFICATIONS
All readings in ft. lbs.

Year	VIN	No. Cylinder Displacement cu. in. (liter)	Cylinder Head Bolts	Main Bearing Bolts	Rod Bearing Bolts	Crankshaft Pulley Bolts	Flywheel Bolts	Manifold		Spark Plugs
								Intake	Exhaust	
1987	S	6-173 (2.8)	③	63–83	34–45	75	50	13–25	25	7–15
	H	8-305 (5.0)	60–70	63–85	42–47	60	75	25–45	②	15–20
	F	8-305 (5.0)	60–75	63–85	42–47	60	75	25–45	②	15–20
	8	8-350 (5.7)	60–75	63–85	42–47	60	75	25–45	②	15–20
1988	S	6-173 (2.8)	③	63–83	34–45	75	50	13–25	19–31	7–15
	F	8-305 (5.0)	60–75	63–85	42–47	60	75	25–45	②	15–20
	E	8-305 (5.0)	60–75	63–85	42–47	60	75	25–45	②	15–20
	8	8-350 (5.7)	60–75	63–85	42–47	60	75	25–45	②	15–20
1989	S	6-173 (2.8)	③	63–83	34–45	75	50	13–25	19–31	7–15
	F	8-305 (5.0)	60–75	63–85	42–47	60	75	25–45	②	15–20
	E	8-305 (5.0)	60–75	63–85	42–47	60	75	25–45	②	15–20
	8	8-350 (5.7)	60–75	63–85	42–47	60	75	25–45	②	15–20
	7	6-231 (3.8)	①	100	40	219	60	45	37	20

TORQUE SPECIFICATIONS
All readings in ft. lbs.

Year	VIN	No. Cylinder Displacement cu. in. (liter)	Cylinder Head Bolts	Main Bearing Bolts	Rod Bearing Bolts	Crankshaft Pulley Bolts	Flywheel Bolts	Manifold		Spark Plugs
								Intake	Exhaust	
1990–91	T	6-191 (3.1)	③	73	39	70	52	19	25	25
	F	8-305 (5.0)	68	77	44	70	74	35	②	15–20
	E	8-305 (5.0)	68	77	44	70	74	35	②	15–20
	8	8-350 (5.7)	68	77	44	70	74	35	②	15–20

① Torque in 3 steps:
1st step: Tighten to 2.5 ft. lbs.
2nd step: Rotate wrench an additional 90 degrees.
3rd step: Rotate wrench an additional 90 degrees.
(Should 60 ft. lbs. be reached at any time in steps 2 & 3—STOP—do not turn any further)
② Outer bolts—14–26
Inner bolts—20–32
③ Torque in 2 steps:
1st step: Tighten to 40 ft. lbs.
2nd step: Rotate wrench an additional 90 degrees.

BRAKE SPECIFICATIONS
All measurements in inches unless noted.

Year	Model	Lug Nut Torque (ft. lbs.)	Master Cylinder Bore	Brake Disc		Standard Brake Drum Diameter	Minimum Lining Thickness	
				Minimum Thickness	Maximum Runout		Front	Rear
1987	Camaro, Firebird	80	NA	0.965	0.005	9.500	0.030	0.030 ①③
1988	Camaro, Firebird	80	NA	0.965	0.005	9.500	0.030	0.030 ①③
1989	Camaro, Firebird	80	NA	0.965	0.005	9.500	0.030	0.030 ①③
1990–91	Camaro, Firebird	80	④	②	0.005	9.500	0.030	0.030 ③

① 0.062—bonded
② Front rotor—0.965
Rear rotor—0.724
③ Rear disc—0.030
④ Disc/Drum—0.945
Disc/Disc—1.00

WHEEL ALIGNMENT

Year	Model	Caster		Camber		Toe-in (in.)	Steering Axis Inclination (deg.)
		Range (deg.)	Preferred Setting (deg.)	Range (deg.)	Preferred Setting (deg.)		
1987	Camaro, Firebird	4$\frac{1}{2}$P–5$\frac{1}{2}$P	5P	$\frac{1}{2}$P–1$\frac{1}{2}$P	1P	$\frac{3}{64}$P	NA
1988	Camaro, Firebird	4$\frac{1}{2}$P–5$\frac{1}{2}$P	5P	$\frac{1}{2}$N–1$\frac{1}{2}$P	0	$\frac{3}{64}$P	NA
1989	Camaro, Firebird	4$\frac{3}{16}$P–5$\frac{3}{16}$P	4$\frac{11}{16}$P	$\frac{3}{16}$N–$\frac{13}{16}$P	$\frac{5}{16}$P	0	NA
1990–91	Camaro, Firebird	4$\frac{1}{2}$P–5$\frac{1}{2}$P	5P	$\frac{1}{2}$P–1$\frac{1}{2}$P	1P	$\frac{3}{64}$P	NA

NA Not available
P Positive
N Negative

ENGINE ELECTRICAL

NOTE: Disconnecting the negative battery cable on some vehicles may interfere with the functions of the on board computer systems and may require the computer to undergo a relearning process, once the negative battery cable is reconnected.

Distributor

REMOVAL

1. Disconnect the negative battery cable. Remove all the necessary components in order to gain access to the distributor assembly.
2. Disconnect all electrical connections from the distributor. Release the coil connectors from the distributor cap.
3. Remove the distributor cap retaining screws and remove the cap. Mark the position of the distributor housing in relation to the block and the distributor rotor in relation to the distributor housing.
4. Remove the distributor hold-down clamp and bolt and pull the distributor assembly from the engine.

INSTALLATION

Timing Not Disturbed

1. Install the distributor, aligning the marks that were made during the removal procedure.
2. Install the distributor hold-down clamp and bolt and temporarily tighten.
3. Install the distributor cap and connect the electrical connectors.
4. Install the remainder of the com-

ponents that were removed to gain access to the distributor.
5. Connect the negative b007815 cable.
6. Start the engine and set the ignition timing. Tighten the hold-down clamp bolt to 27 ft. lbs. (36 Nm) and recheck the timing.

Timing Disturbed

1. Remove the No. 1 cylinder spark plug.
2. Place a finger over the spark plug hole and crank the engine slowly until compression is felt.
3. Align the timing mark on the crankshaft pulley with the **0** mark on the timing scale attached to the front of the engine. This places the engine at TDC of the compression stroke for No. 1 cylinder.
4. Rotate the distributor shaft until the rotor points to the No. 1 spark plug tower on the distributor cap.
5. Install the distributor in the engine.
6. Install the hold-down clamp and bolt and tighten temporarily.
7. Install the distributor cap and connect the electrical connectors.
8. Install the remainder of the components that were removed to gain access to the distributor.
9. Connect the negative battery cable.
10. Start the engine and set the ignition timing. Tighten the hold-down clamp bolt to 27 ft. lbs. (36 Nm) and recheck the timing.

Distributorless Ignition

The 20th anniversary Trans AM, offered during the 1989 model year, is equipped with a 3.8L SFI turbocharged engine that features distributorless ignition. This system uses a "waste spark" method of spark distribution. Each cylinder is paired

with it's opposite in the firing order, so 1 cylinder on the compression stroke fires simultaneously with it's opposing cylinder on the exhaust stroke. The cylinder on the exhaust stroke requires very little voltage to fire it's plug, so most of the available voltage is used to fire the plug of the cylinder that is on the compression stroke. The process reverses when the cylinders reverse roles.

The distributorless ignition system consists of a coil pack, the ignition module, a dual hall effect sensor, interrupter rings and the electronic control module (ECM). The coil pack contains 3 separate ignition coils (1 for each pair of 2 cylinders) enclosed in 1 housing and serviced as a unit. The ignition module is located under the coil pack and is connected to the ECM. The ignition module controls the primary circuit to the coils, turning them on and off and controls the spark timing below 400 rpm and if the ECM bypass circuit becomes open or grounded. The dual hall effect sensor is a combination camshaft and crankshaft sensor, mounted on the front cover behind the crankshaft balancer. Interrupter rings, mounted on the crankshaft balancer, pass through slots in the dual hall effect sensor and provide timing information to the ECM.

The distributorless ignition system uses electronic spark control (EST). The ECM controls timing with inputs concerning crankshaft position, engine rpm, engine temperature and volume of intake air.

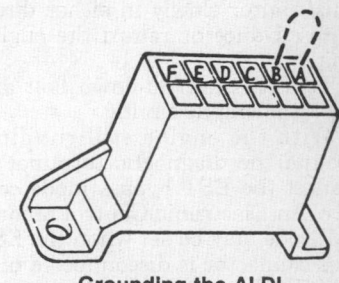

Grounding the ALDL

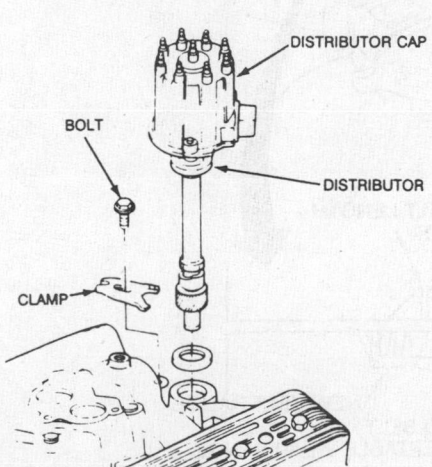

Typical HEI distributor

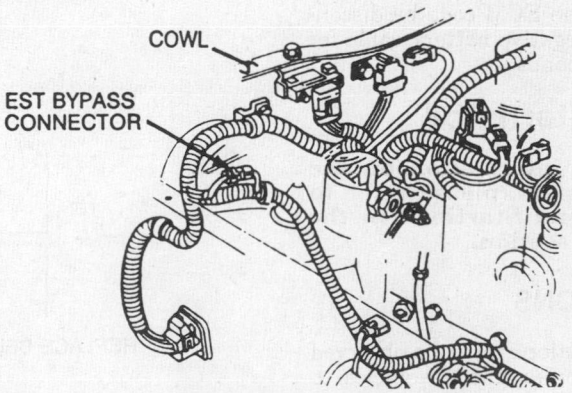

EST bypass connector location

Ignition Timing

ADJUSTMENT

NOTE: On all 1987–88 and 1991 vehicles, it will be necessary to put the Electronic Spark Timing (EST) in the bypass mode by disconnecting the single wire timing connector. This wire is tan with a black tracer and breaks out of the wiring harness near the rear of the right hand valve cover. Do not disconnect the 4 prong EST connector from the distributor assembly. On 1989–90 vehicles, with the engine running, ground the diagnostic terminal (A and B) of the Assembly Line Diagnostic Link (ALDL) connector.

1. Refer to the Vehicle Emission Information label which is located on the radiator support panel, for the proper timing information.
2. With the ignition **OFF**, connect the pick-up lead of an inductive timing light to the No. 1 spark plug wire. Connect the timing light power leads according to the manufacturers instructions.
3. Run engine to normal operating temperature. Disconnect the EST bypass mode connector or ground the diagnostic terminal of the ALDL connector.
4. Check the timing by aiming the timing light at the timing mark and harmonic balancer. If the engine timing requires adjustment, loosen the distributor hold-down bolt and rotate the distributor slowly in either direction, to advance or retard the engine timing.
5. Tighten the hold-down bolt and recheck the engine timing.
6. With the engine still running, unground the diagnostic terminal or reconnect the EST bypass mode connector. An Electronic Control Module (ECM) code may be set when the EST bypass connector is disconnected or if the ALDL diagnostic terminal is ungrounded after the engine is shut **OFF**. Clear the ECM code by disconnecting the negative battery cable for at least 30 seconds.

Alternator

For further information on the charging system, please refer to "Charging and Starting" in the Unit Repair section.

PRECAUTIONS

Several precautions must be observed with alternator equipped vehicles to avoid damage to the unit.

- If the battery is removed for any reason, make sure it is reconnected with the correct polarity. Reversing the battery connections may result in damage to the one-way rectifiers.
- When utilizing a booster battery as a starting aid, always connect the positive to positive terminals and the negative terminal from the booster battery to a good engine ground on the vehicle being started.
- Never use a fast charger as a booster to start vehicles.
- Disconnect the battery cables when charging the battery with a fast charger.
- Never attempt to polarize the alternator.
- Do not use test lamps of more than 12 volts when checking diode continuity.
- Do not short across or ground any of the alternator terminals.
- The polarity of the battery, alternator and regulator must be matched and considered before making any electrical connections within the system.
- Never separate the alternator on an open circuit. Make sure all connections within the circuit are clean and tight.
- Disconnect the battery ground terminal when performing any service on electrical components.
- Disconnect the battery if arc welding is to be done on the vehicle.

BELT TENSION ADJUSTMENT

A drive belt tensioner is used on all vehicles to keep the drive belt in proper

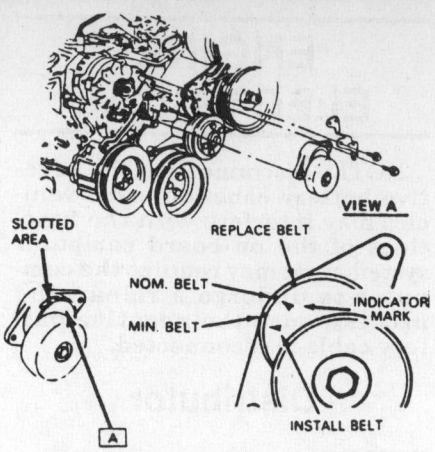

THE INDICATOR MARK ON THE MOVEABLE PORTION OF THE TENSIONER MUST BE WITHIN THE LIMITS OF THE SLOTTED AREA ON THE STATIONARY PORTION OF THE TENSIONER. ANY READING OUTSIDE THESE LIMITS INDICATES EITHER A DEFECTIVE BELT OR TENSIONER.

Drive belt tensioner—2.8L and 3.1L engines

adjustment. Check the belt length scale on the drive belt tensioner for the proper installed length and replace as necessary. If belt slippage occurs and the drive belt tensioner is within it's operating range, check the belt tension.

1. Run the engine for 5–10 minutes.
2. Shut **OFF** the engine and check the belt tension at the following locations using J–23600–B V-belt tension gauge or equivalent:

a. V6 engine (except 3.8L engine): On vehicles without air conditioning, check the belt tension between the tensioner and the power steering pump pulley. On vehicles with air conditioning, check the belt ten-

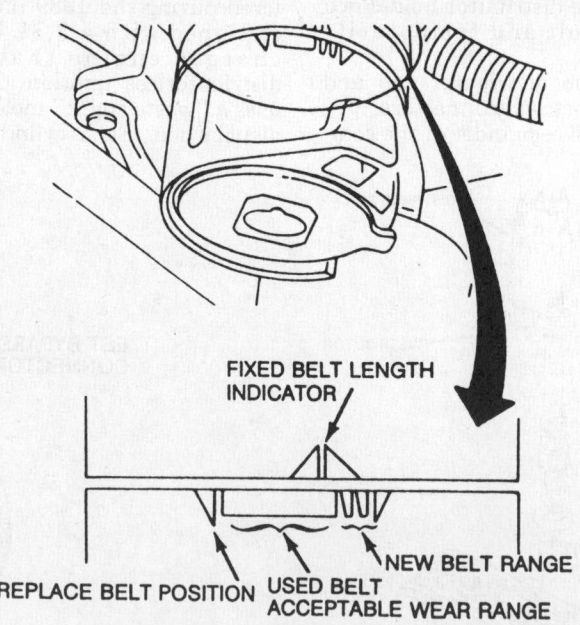

Drive belt tensioner—5.0L and 5.7L engines

sion between the tensioner and the air conditioner compressor pulley.

b. V8 engine: Check the belt tension between any 2 pulleys.

3. Run the engine for 30 seconds and recheck the belt tension.

4. Repeat Step No. 3. The belt tension is the average of the 3 readings.

a. V6 engine (except 3.8L engine): Belt tension should be 116–142 lbs. (516–631 N) on vehicles without air conditioning. On vehicles with air conditioning the belt tension should be 103–127 lbs. (460–563 N).

b. V8 engine: Belt tension should be 99–121 lbs. (440–538 N).

5. Replace the drive belt tensioner if the belt tension is below the minimum specified and if the drive belt tensioner is within it's operating range.

REMOVAL & INSTALLATION

1. Disconnect the negative battery cable.

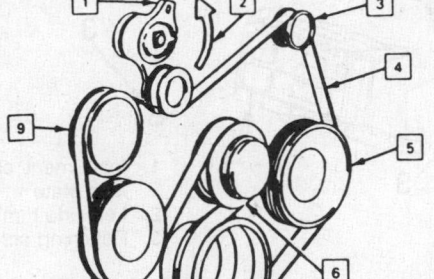

2. Tag and disconnect the alternator wiring.

3. Remove the alternator brace bolt. As required, loosen the power steering pump brace and mount nuts. Remove the drive belt.

4. Support the alternator and remove the mount bolts. Remove the unit from the vehicle.

5. Installation is the reverse of the removal procedure.

Voltage Regulator

For further information on the charging system, please refer to "Charging and Starting" in the Unit Repair section.

Starter

For further information on the charging system, please refer to "Charging and Starting" in the Unit Repair section.

1. Tensioner assembly
2. Rotate tensioner in direction shown to install or remove belt
3. Alternator assembly
4. Accessory drive belt
5. Power steering belt
6. Water pump
7. Crankshaft
8. Air pump
9. Air conditioning compressor or belt idler

Drive belt and pulleys—5.0L and 5.7L engines

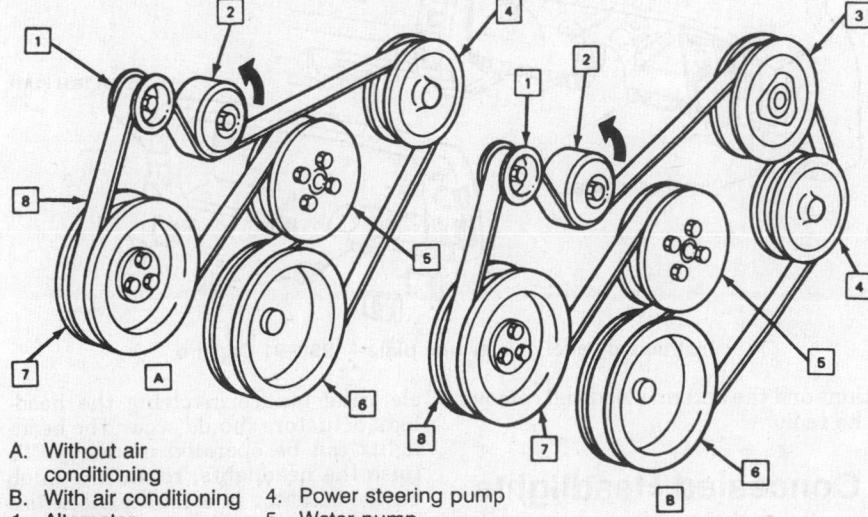

A. Without air conditioning
B. With air conditioning
1. Alternator
2. Tensioner
3. Air conditioning compressor
4. Power steering pump
5. Water pump
6. Crankshaft
7. AIR pump
8. Belt

Drive belt and pulleys—2.8L and 3.1L engines

REMOVAL & INSTALLATION

1. Disconnect the negative battery cable.

2. Raise the vehicle and support it safely.

3. Disconnect all wiring from the starter.

4. Remove the flywheel housing cover. Remove the starter brace as required.

5. Remove the starter motor retaining bolts and any shims.

6. Remove the starter from the vehicle.

7. Installation is the reverse of the removal procedure.

8. If shims were used, they must be replaced in their original locations.

CHASSIS ELECTRICAL

— CAUTION —
On vehicles equipped with an air bag, the negative battery cable must be disconnected, before working on the system. Failure to do so may result in deployment of the air bag and possible personal injury.

Heater Blower Motor

REMOVAL & INSTALLATION

1. Disconnect the negative battery cable. If necessary, remove the diagonal fender brace at the right rear corner of the engine compartment to gain access to the blower motor.

2. Disconnect the electrical wiring from the blower motor. If equipped with air conditioning, remove the blower relay and bracket as an assembly and swing them up and out of the way.

3. Remove the blower motor cooling tube.

4. Remove the blower motor retaining screws.

5. Remove the blower motor and fan as an assembly from the case.

6. Installation is the reverse of the removal procedure.

Windshield Wiper Motor

REMOVAL & INSTALLATION

1. Disconnect the negative battery cable.

2. Remove the left and right wiper arms.

3. Remove the cowl screen on 1987–

90 vehicles. On 1991 vehicles remove the shroud vent grille.

4. Loosen the transmission drive link to crank arm retaining bolts. Remove the drive link from the motor crank arm.

5. Disconnect the electrical wiring and the washer hoses from the motor assembly.

6. Remove the motor retaining screws. Remove the windshield wiper motor while guiding the crank arm through the hole.

7. Installation is the reverse of the removal procedure. The motor must be in the park position before assembling the crank arm to the drive link.

Windshield Wiper Switch

The windshield wiper switch is incorporated in the combination switch.

Instrument Cluster

REMOVAL & INSTALLATION

1. Disconnect the negative battery cable.

2. On 1987–89 Firebird with digital cluster, remove the right and left lower trim plates. Removal of lower instrument panel covers is not required.

3. On 1990–91 Firebird, remove the instrument panel knee bolster and the instrument panel cluster trim plate. On 1990–91 Camaro, remove the instrument panel knee bolster and the headlight switch knob. Remove the cluster trim plate screws and pull the cluster trim plate forward. Disconnect the electrical connectors and remove the cluster trim plate.

4. Remove the retaining screws from the instrument cluster, pull the cluster back and disconnect the electrical connectors. Remove the instrument cluster.

5. Installation is the reverse of removal procedure.

Radio

REMOVAL & INSTALLATION

1. Disconnect the negative battery cable.

2. On 1990–91 Camaro, remove the knee bolster.

3. Remove the front/accessory trim plate.

4. Remove the radio mounting screws and pull the radio towards the rear of the vehicle to gain access to the electrical connections and antenna lead.

5. Disconnect the electrical connec-

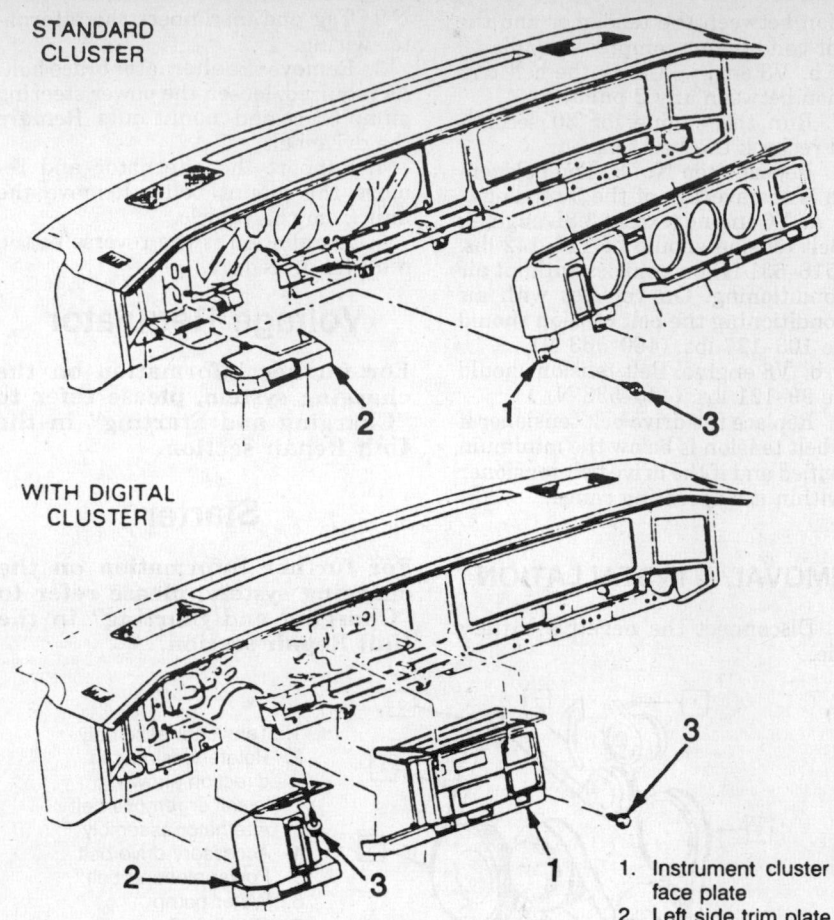

1. Instrument cluster face plate
2. Left side trim plate
3. Retaining screws

Digital and standard instrument cluster trim plates—1987–89 Firebird

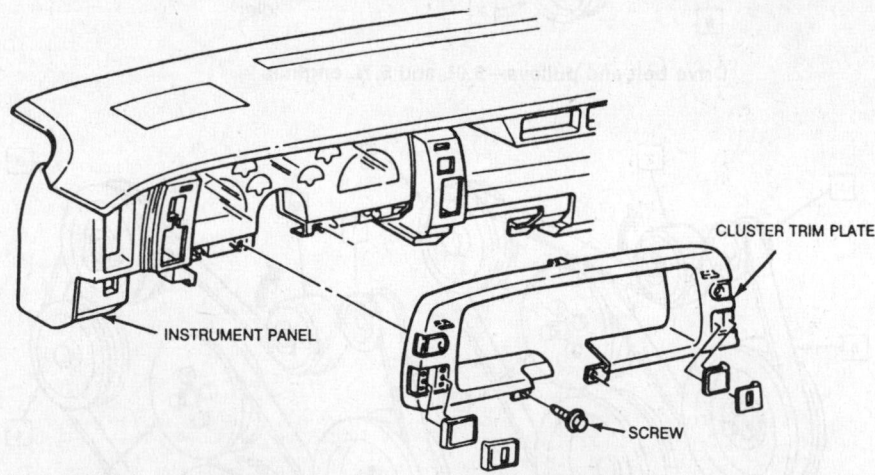

Instrument panel cluster trim plate—1990–91 Camaro

tions and the antenna lead and remove the radio.

Concealed Headlights

MANUAL OPERATION

The concealed headlights used on the Firebird are electrically operated. If an electrical failure involving the headlight actuators should occur, the headlights can be operated manually. To raise the headlights, rotate the knob on the actuator in a counterclockwise direction until the headlights are fully open. Lower the headlights by turning the actuator knob in a clockwise direction until the headlights are fully closed.

Headlight Switch

REMOVAL & INSTALLATION

1987–88 Camaro and 1987–89 Firebird

1. Disconnect the negative battery cable.
2. Remove the right and left lower trim plates. Removal of the lower instrument panel covers is not required.
3. Remove the instrument panel cluster trim plate.
4. Remove the 2 switch assembly retaining screws.
5. Depress the side tangs and pull the switch assembly from the instrument panel. Disconnect the electrical connectors and remove the switch assembly.
6. Installation is the reverse of the removal procedure.

1989 Camaro

1. Disconnect the negative battery cable.
2. Remove the insulator screws and nut from under the instrument panel and remove the insulator.
3. Remove the headlight switch knob assembly by depressing the release button on the headlight switch from under the instrument panel.
4. Remove the headlight switch knob trim plate screws and remove the trim plate.
5. Unscrew the retainer attaching the headlight switch to the instrument panel, disconnect the electrical connectors and remove the headlight switch from under the instrument panel.
6. Installation is the reverse of the removal procedure.

1990–91 Camaro

1. Disconnect the negative battery cable.
2. Remove the instrument panel knee bolster.
3. Remove the switch knob by depressing the release button on the switch from under the instrument panel.
4. Remove the retaining screws from the instrument panel cluster trim plate and pull it forward away from the instrument panel. Disconnect the electrical connectors and remove the cluster trim plate.
5. Remove the retaining nut from the headlight switch and lower the switch out through the bottom of the instrument panel.
6. Disconnect the electrical connec-

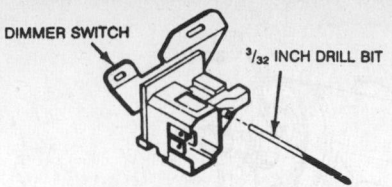

DIMMER SWITCH   3/32 INCH DRILL BIT

Dimmer switch adjustment

tors and remove the switch assembly.
7. Installation is the reverse of the removal procedure.

1990–91 Firebird

1. Disconnect the negative battery cable.
2. Remove the instrument panel knee bolster.
3. Remove the instrument panel cluster trim plate.
4. Remove the headlight switch retaining screws.
5. Disconnect the electrical connectors and remove the switch assembly.
6. Installation is the reverse of the removal procedure.

Dimmer Switch

REMOVAL & INSTALLATION

1. Disconnect the negative battery cable.
2. Remove the steering column to instrument panel trim plates. Loosen the toe plate retaining screws and remove the capsule nuts to lower the steering column. Support the column to prevent it from being damaged.
3. Remove the electrical connector and the retaining nut and remove the dimmer switch.
4. Installation is the reverse of the removal procedure. Adjust the dimmer switch by depressing the mechanism slightly to insert a $^3/_{32}$ inch drill bit. Move the switch to remove the lash and tighten the retaining nut to 35 inch lbs. (4 Nm).

Turn Signal Switch

REMOVAL & INSTALLATION

1. Disconnect the negative battery cable.
2. Remove the inflator module on air bag equipped vehicles.
3. Remove the steering wheel.
4. Remove the coil assembly retaining ring on air bag equipped vehicles. Pull the coil assembly out and allow it to hang.
5. Using a suitable tool, depress the lock plate to gain access to the snapring. Remove the snapring and remove the lockplate.
6. Remove the turn signal cancelling cam, upper bearing spring and signal switch arm.
7. Remove the hazard warning knob, turn signal lever and steering column wiring protector.
8. Disconnect the turn signal switch connector from the harness connector. Remove the switch retaining screws and remove the turn signal switch.
9. Installation is the reverse of the removal procedure.

Combination Switch

REMOVAL & INSTALLATION

1. Disconnect the negative battery cable.
2. Remove the tilt lever on vehicles equipped with tilt wheel and cruise control, by grasping the lever firmly and turning counterclockwise.
3. Make sure the combination switch lever is in the center or **OFF** position.
4. Remove the housing cover end cap and disconnect the cruise control connector, if equipped with cruise control.
5. Remove the combination switch lever by pulling straight out of the turn signal switch.
6. Installation is the reverse of the removal procedure.

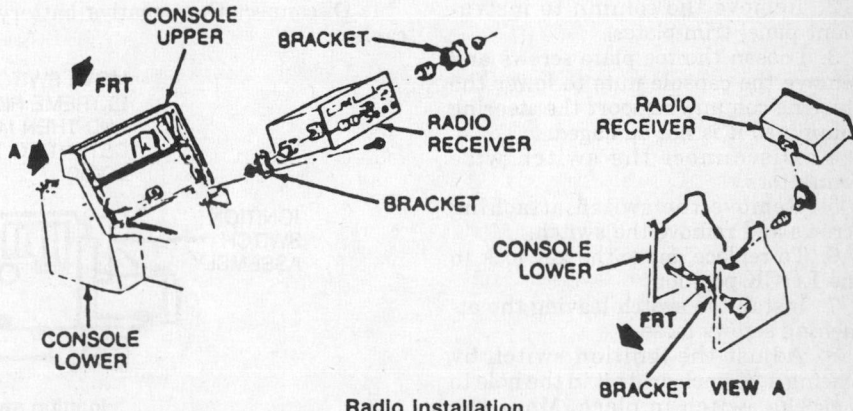

CONSOLE UPPER   BRACKET

FRT   RADIO RECEIVER

BRACKET

RADIO RECEIVER

CONSOLE LOWER

CONSOLE LOWER   FRT

BRACKET   VIEW A

Radio Installation

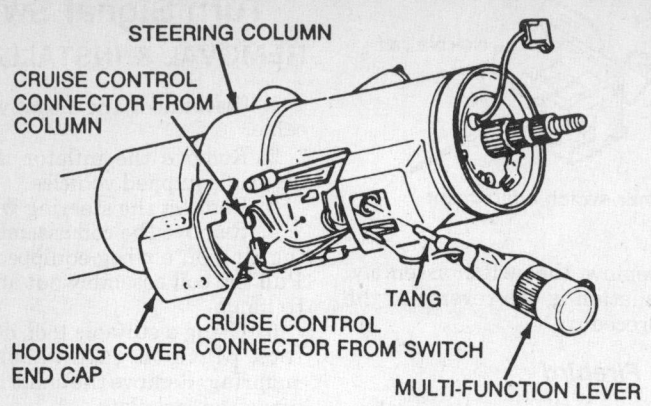

CRUISE CONTROL CONNECTOR FROM COLUMN

STEERING COLUMN

HOUSING COVER END CAP

CRUISE CONTROL CONNECTOR FROM SWITCH

TANG

MULTI-FUNCTION LEVER

Combination switch—turn signal lever

Ignition Lock

REMOVAL & INSTALLATION

1. Disconnect the negative battery cable.
2. Remove the turn signal switch.
3. On 1987 vehicles, turn the lock cylinder to the **RUN** position and remove the key warning buzzer switch. On 1988–91 vehicles, remove the key from the lock cylinder, remove the buzzer switch and reinsert the key in the **LOCK** position.
4. Remove the lock retaining screw and remove the lock cylinder. If equipped with Vehicle Anti-Theft System (VATS), disconnect the terminal connector and gently pull the wire through the steering column housing shroud, steering column housing and lock housing cover.
5. Installation is the reverse of the removal procedure. Place the lock cylinder in the **RUN** position before installing the buzzer switch.

Ignition Switch

REMOVAL & INSTALLATION

1. Disconnect the negative battery terminal.
2. Remove the column to instrument panel trim plates.
3. Loosen the toe plate screws and remove the capsule nuts to lower the steering column. Support the steering column so it is not damaged.
4. Disconnect the switch wire connectors.
5. Remove the switch attaching screws and remove the switch.
6. To replace, move the key lock to the **LOCK** position.
7. Install the switch leaving the attaching screws loose.
8. Adjust the ignition switch by placing a 3/32 inch drill bit in the hole to lock the switch in place. Move the

switch slider to the extreme right position and then move the slider 1 detent to the left (OFF LOCK). Tighten the attaching screws to 35 inch lbs. (4 Nm).
9. Reassemble the remaining components of the steering column in reverse of the disassembly procedure.

Stoplight Switch

ADJUSTMENT

With the brake pedal in the fully released position, the stoplight switch plunger should be fully depressed against the brake pedal shank. Adjust the switch by moving it in or out, as necessary.

1. Insert the switch into the retainer until the switch body seats on the retainer.
2. Pull the brake pedal to the rear against the internal pedal stop. The stoplight switch will be moved in the retainer giving the proper adjustment. The proper adjustment is obtained when no clicks are heard when the brake pedal is pulled up and the brake lights do not stay ON without the brakes being applied.

REMOVAL & INSTALLATION

1. Disconnect the negative battery cable.

2. Remove the electrical connectors and remove the stoplight switch by pulling it out of the retainer.
3. Install the replacement stoplight switch by inserting it into the retainer. Connect the electrical connectors.
4. Adjust the stoplight switch.

Clutch Switch

ADJUSTMENT

The clutch switch should be adjusted so that the vehicle cannot be started unless the clutch pedal is fully depressed.

REMOVAL & INSTALLATION

1. Disconnect the negative battery cable.
2. Remove the sound insulator on 1987–89 vehicles and the console trim plate on 1990–91 vehicles.
3. Disconnect the clutch switch connector.
4. Remove the switch attaching bolt and remove the clutch switch.
5. Installation is the reverse of the removal procedure.

Neutral Safety Switch

ADJUSTMENT

1. Position the transmission control shifter assembly in the **N** notch in the detent plate.
2. Loosen the switch attaching screws.
3. Rotate the switch on the shifter assembly to align the service adjustment hole with the carrier tang hole. Insert a 2.34mm diameter gauge pin to a depth of 15mm.
4. Tighten the attaching screws.
5. Remove the gauge pin.

REMOVAL & INSTALLATION

1. Disconnect the negative battery cable.
2. Remove the console assembly to

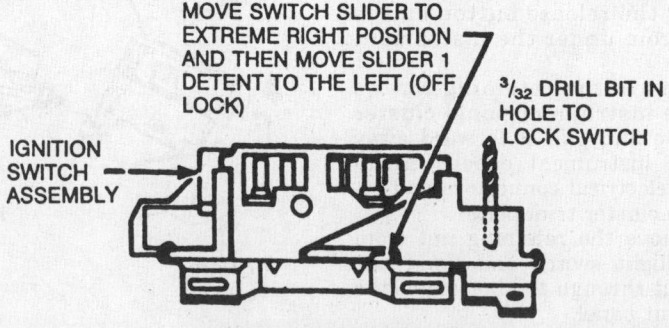

MOVE SWITCH SLIDER TO EXTREME RIGHT POSITION AND THEN MOVE SLIDER 1 DETENT TO THE LEFT (OFF LOCK)

IGNITION SWITCH ASSEMBLY

3/32 DRILL BIT IN HOLE TO LOCK SWITCH

Ignition switch adjustment

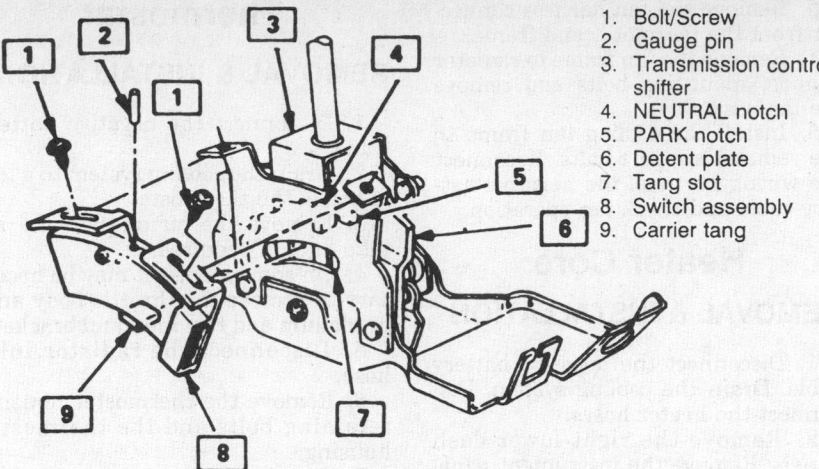

1. Bolt/Screw
2. Gauge pin
3. Transmission control shifter
4. NEUTRAL notch
5. PARK notch
6. Detent plate
7. Tang slot
8. Switch assembly
9. Carrier tang

Neutral safety switch

gain access to the neutral safety switch.

3. Disconnect the electrical connectors.

4. Remove the switch attaching screws and remove the neutral safety switch.

5. Position the transmission control shifter assembly in the **N** notch in the detent plate.

6. Install the switch assembly to the transmission control shifter assembly by inserting the carrier tang into the hole in the shifter lever assembly. Tighten the attaching screws.

7. Move the transmission control shifter assembly out of the **N** position. This will shear the switch internal plastic pin.

8. Assemble the remaining components in the reverse order of their removal.

Fuses, Circuit Breakers and Relays

LOCATION

Fuse Panel

The fuse panel is located on the left side of the vehicle, under the instrument panel assembly. In order to gain access to the fuse panel it may be necessary to first remove the under dash padding.

Circuit Breakers

Circuit breakers are located on the fuse panel.

Relays

All vehicles use a combination of the following electrical relays in order to function properly.

Throttle Kicker Relay (VIN–H)—located on the left side of the engine cowl or the right front inner fender panel.

Air Conditioner Blower Speed High Speed Relay—located near the blower module on the air conditioner module.

Burn Off Relay (1987–89)—located behind the ECM.

Choke Heater Relay—located in the right-hand front corner of the engine compartment.

Power Door Lock Relay—located in the left-hand shroud in the lower access hole.

Air Conditioner Compressor Relay—located on the left side engine cowl near the brake booster.

Radio Amplifier Relay—located behind the right-hand side of the instrument panel.

Power Antenna Relay (1987–89)—located behind the right side of the instrument panel lower cover.

Horn Relay—located in the convenience center, behind the instrument panel to the right of the steering column.

Fuel Pump Relay—located on the left side of the engine cowl.

Hatch Release Relay—located under the front part of the console.

Cooling Fan Relay (V6 engine)—located on the left side of the firewall.

Cooling Fan Relay (V8 engine)—located on the right side of the radiator or the left side of the firewall.

Fog Light Relay (1987–89)—located in the left-hand front corner of the engine compartment. **1990**—located in the left-hand rear corner of the engine compartment. **1991**—located behind the left side instrument panel, near the fuse panel.

Mass Air Flow Relay (1987–89)—located in the left-hand rear of the engine compartment.

Computers

LOCATION

The engine electronic control module, cruise control module, PASS key decoder theft deterrent module and the diagnostic/energy reserve module for air bag equipped vehicles are all located under the right-hand side of the instrument panel. The resistor module for air bag equipped vehicles and the daytime running lights module are located under the left-hand side of the instrument panel.

Flashers

LOCATION

The hazard flasher is located in the convenience center, behind the instrument panel to the right of the steering column. The turn signal flasher is also located in the convenience center on 1987–90 vehicles. On 1991 vehicles, the turn signal flasher is attached to the fuse panel.

Cruise Control

ADJUSTMENT

1. With the cable assembly installed in the servo bracket, install the cable assembly end onto the stud of the lever assembly. Secure the component with the retainer.

2. Pull the servo assembly end of the cable toward the servo assembly without moving the lever assembly.

3. If one of the 6 holes in the servo assembly tab lines up with the cable assembly pin, connect the pin to the tab with the retainer.

4. If the tab hole does not line up with the pin, move the cable assembly away from the servo assembly until the next closest hole lines up. Secure the component with the retainer.

5. Do not stretch the cable assembly so as to make a particular tab hole connect to the pin, as this will prevent the engine from returning to idle.

ENGINE COOLING

Radiator

REMOVAL & INSTALLATION

1. Disconnect the negative battery cable.

24 GM "F" BODY

2. Drain the cooling system.
3. Remove the intake duct, air duct bracket and air cleaner top, if equipped.
4. Remove the Mass Air Flow (MAF) sensor, if equipped.
5. Remove the engine cooling fan. If equipped with a fan clutch, the clutch should be set aside in an upright position to prevent seal leakage.
6. Disconnect the radiator hoses from the radiator.
7. If equipped with an automatic transmission, disconnect and plug the transmission cooler lines at the radiator.
8. If equipped, remove the fan shield assembly.
9. Remove the radiator and shroud assembly, then lift the radiator straight up and out of the vehicle.
10. Install radiator and shroud assembly by reversing removal procedures. Make sure the radiator is positioned in the lower cradle properly.
11. Reconnect all hoses, install the cooling fan and refill the cooling system with the proper type and quantity of coolant. Connect the negative battery cable.

Electric Cooling Fan

NOTE: Keep hands, tools and clothing away from cooling fan. Electric cooling fans can come on whether or not the engine is running. The fan may start automatically in response to a heat sensor with the ignition in the ON position.

TESTING

1. Disconnect the cooling fan electrical connector from the wire harness.
2. Connect a jumper wire from the positive terminal of the battery to one of the terminals of the cooling fan electrical connector.
3. Ground the other terminal of the cooling fan electrical connector using a jumper wire.
4. If the cooling fan does not run, the cooling fan motor must be replaced.
5. If the cooling fan runs during the test procedure but does not run during normal vehicle operation, check the coolant temperature sensor, the cooling fan relay and the electronic control module.

REMOVAL & INSTALLATION

1. Disconnect the negative battery cable.
2. Remove the air cleaner top, if equipped.

3. Remove the fan harness connector from the fan motor and frame.
4. Remove the fan frame to radiator support mounting bolts and remove the fan assembly.
5. Install the cooling fan frame to the radiator support bolts. Reconnect the wiring harness, the negative battery cable and check fan operation.

Heater Core

REMOVAL & INSTALLATION

1. Disconnect the negative battery cable. Drain the cooling system. Disconnect the heater hoses.
2. Remove the right lower dash panels. Remove the instrument panel lower trim pad and the console.
3. Disconnect the electronic control module retaining screws and position it to the side.
4. Remove the heater case retaining screws and remove the heater case.
5. Remove the core shroud screws and remove the core shroud, heater core and mounting strap as an assembly.
6. Remove the core mounting strap and remove the heater core from the core shroud.
7. Installation is the reverse of the removal procedure.

Water Pump

REMOVAL & INSTALLATION

1. Disconnect the negative battery cable.
2. Drain the cooling system.
3. Remove the air intake duct, if equipped.
4. Remove the water pump drive belt.
5. Disconnect the radiator and heater hoses from the thermostat housing and water pump.
6. Remove the accessory mounting brackets.
7. Remove the water pump pulley bolts and water pump pulley.
8. Remove the water pump retaining bolts and remove the water pump.
9. Installation is the reverse of the removal procedure. Make sure all gasket mating surfaces are clean before installation. Tighten the water pump retaining bolts as follows:
5.0L and 5.7L engines—30 ft. lbs. (41 Nm).
3.8L engine—115 inch lbs. (13 Nm).
1987–88 2.8L engine: Small bolt—7 ft. lbs. (10 Nm), large bolt and nut—15 ft. lbs. (20 Nm).
1989 2.8L engine and 1990–91 3.1L engine—to specification.
10. Refill the cooling system with the proper type and quantity of coolant.

Thermostat

REMOVAL & INSTALLATION

1. Disconnect the negative battery cable.
2. Drain the cooling system to a level below the thermostat.
3. Remove the air cleaner and intake duct, if required.
4. On some models it may be necessary to remove the throttle body and/or plenum and fuel lines and brackets.
5. Disconnect the radiator inlet hose.
6. Remove the thermostat housing retaining bolts and the thermostat housing.
7. Remove the thermostat.
8. Installation is the reverse of the removal procedure. Make sure all gasket mating surfaces are clean before installation. Tighten the thermostat housing retaining bolts as follows:
5.0L and 5.7L TPI engines—25 ft. lbs. (34 Nm).
5.0L TBI engine—21 ft. lbs. (28 Nm).
3.8L engine—13 ft. lbs. (18 Nm).
2.8L and 3.1L engines—15 ft. lbs. (21 Nm).
9. Refill the cooling system with the proper type and quantity of coolant.

Cooling System Bleeding

1. Drain the cooling system.
2. Fill the cooling system with a 50/50 mix of ethylene glycol antifreeze and water to a level just below the filler neck.
3. Fill the coolant recovery reservoir to the COLD FILL mark and install the reservoir cap.
4. Run the engine with the radiator cap removed until the normal operating temperature is reached.
5. With the engine idling, add coolant to the radiator until the level reaches the bottom of the filler neck.

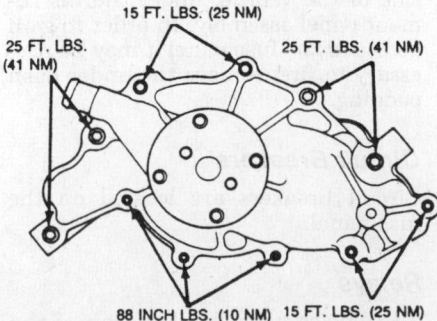

Water pump bolt torque specifications—1989 2.8L and 1990–91 3.1L engines

6. Install the radiator cap. The arrows on the cap must line up with the coolant recovery reservoir hose.

FUEL SYSTEM

Fuel System Service Precautions

Safety is the most important factor when performing not only fuel system maintenance but any type of maintenance. Failure to conduct maintenance and repairs in a safe manner may result in serious personal injury or death. Maintenance and testing of the vehicle's fuel system components can be accomplished safely and effectively by adhering to the following rules and guidelines.

• To avoid the possibility of fire and personal injury, always disconnect the negative battery cable unless the repair or test procedure requires that battery voltage be applied.

• Always relieve the fuel system pressure prior to disconnecting any fuel system component (injector, fuel rail, pressure regulator, etc.), fitting or fuel line connection. Exercise extreme caution whenever relieving fuel system pressure to avoid exposing skin, face and eyes to fuel spray. Please be advised that fuel under pressure may penetrate the skin or any part of the body that it contacts.

• Always place a shop towel or cloth around the fitting or connection prior to loosening to absorb any excess fuel due to spillage. Ensure that all fuel spillage (should it occur) is quickly removed from engine surfaces. Ensure that all fuel soaked cloths or towels are deposited into a suitable waste container.

• Always keep a dry chemical (Class B) fire extinguisher near the work area.

• Do not allow fuel spray or fuel vapors to come into contact with a spark or open flame.

• Always use a backup wrench when loosening and tightening fuel line connection fittings. This will prevent unnecessary stress and torsion to fuel line piping. Always follow the proper torque specifications.

• Always replace worn fuel fitting O-rings with new. Do not substitute fuel hose or equivalent where fuel pipe is installed.

RELIEVING FUEL SYSTEM PRESSURE

Carbureted Engine

1. Disconnect the negative battery cable.
2. Loosen the fuel filler cap to relieve the tank pressure.
3. Cover the fuel fitting to be disconnected with an absorbent shop cloth and slowly loosen the fitting to release the fuel pressure gradually.

TBI Engine

1. Disconnect the negative battery cable.
2. Loosen the fuel filler cap to relieve the tank pressure.
3. Fuel system pressure is automatically relieved when the engine is turned **OFF**. No further relieving is necessary.

TPI Engine

1. Disconnect the negative battery cable.
2. Loosen the fuel filler cap to relieve the tank pressure.
3. Connect J–34730–1 fuel pressure gauge or equivalent, to the fuel pressure valve. Wrap a shop cloth around the fitting while connecting the gauge to avoid spillage.
4. Place the end of the bleed hose into a container and open the valve to relieve the fuel system pressure.

Fuel Filter

REMOVAL & INSTALLATION

Carbureted Engine

1. Disconnect the negative battery cable.
2. Disconnect the fuel line at the fuel inlet filter nut.
3. Remove the fuel inlet filter nut from the carburetor and remove the filter and spring.
To install:
4. If removed, install the check valve in the fuel inlet filter. The fuel inlet check valve must be installed in the filter to meet motor vehicle safety standards for roll-over. A new service replacement filter must include the check valve.
5. Install the fuel inlet filter spring, filter and check valve assembly in the carburetor. Make sure the valve end of the filter faces toward the fuel line. The ribs on the closed end of the filter element prevent the filter from being

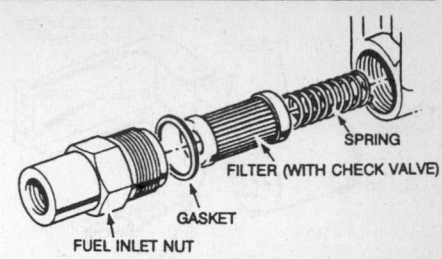

Carburetor fuel filter

installed incorrectly unless force is used.

6. Install the fuel inlet nut and tighten to 46 ft. lbs. (62 Nm).
7. Connect the fuel line and tighten the fitting.
8. Connect the negative battery cable, start the engine and check for leaks.

Fuel Injected Engines

1. Disconnect the negative battery cable.
2. Relieve the fuel system pressure.
3. Raise and safely support the vehicle.
4. Clean the fuel filter connections before disconnecting to prevent contamination of the fuel system. Disconnect the fuel lines from the fuel filter.
5. Remove the filter bracket screw and remove the fuel filter from the fuel filter bracket.
To install:
6. Check the fuel line O-rings for cuts, nicks, swelling or distortion and replace as necessary.
7. Position the replacement filter in the fuel filter bracket with the flow arrow pointing toward the engine.
8. Install the fuel filter bracket screw and the fuel lines. Tighten the in-line fuel filter fittings to 20 ft. lbs. (27 Nm), using a back-up wrench to prevent the filter from turning.
9. Lower the vehicle, connect the negative battery cable and tighten the fuel filler cap.
10. Turn the ignition switch to the **ON** position for 2 seconds and then **OFF** for 5 seconds. Again turn to the **ON** position and check for fuel leaks.

Mechanical Fuel Pump

A mechanical fuel pump is used with carbureted engines.

PRESSURE TESTING

1. Disconnect the fuel line at the carburetor.
2. Install a low pressure gauge onto the fuel line.
3. Start the engine.
4. The fuel pump pressure should be 4–6.5 psi.

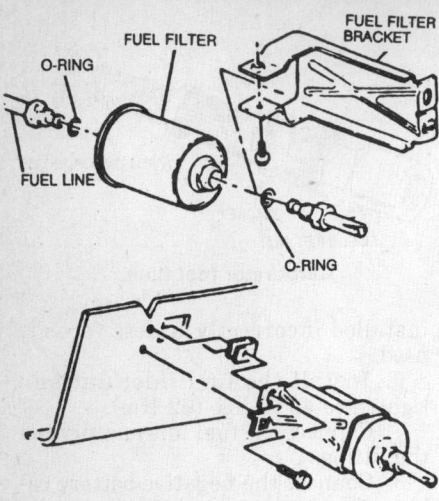

Fuel Injection fuel filter

5. If the fuel pressure is less, check for restrictions in the fuel tank sender filter, fuel lines or hoses.

6. Remove the pressure gauge and reconnect the fuel line.

VACUUM TESTING

1. Disconnect the inlet hose at the fuel pump and connect a vacuum gauge.

2. Crank run the engine until maximum vacuum is reached. If the vacuum reading is less than 15 in. Hg., replace the fuel pump.

REMOVAL & INSTALLATION

1. Disconnect the negative battery cable.

2. Disconnect the fuel inlet hose and outlet line and the vapor return hose, if equipped.

3. Remove the 2 fuel pump retaining bolts and remove the fuel pump. If the fuel pump pushrod is to be removed, remove the 2 mounting plate retaining bolts and remove the pushrod, gasket and mounting plate.

4. Installation is the reverse of the removal procedure. Make sure all gasket mating surfaces are clean before installation. Tighten the fuel pump retaining bolts to 27 ft. lbs. (37 Nm). The mounting plate retaining bolts are tightened to 36 inch lbs. (4 Nm).

Electric Fuel Pump

PRESSURE TESTING

5.0L TBI Engine

1. Make sure there is an adequate quantity of fuel in the tank.

2. Make sure the ignition switch is in the **OFF** position.

3. Connect a fuel pressure gauge to the fuel pump outlet line.

4. Apply battery voltage to the fuel pump test connector using a 10 amp fused jumper wire.

5. The fuel pressure should be 9–13 psi.

6. Disconnect the fuel pressure gauge.

Except 5.0L TBI Engine

1. Make sure there is an adequate quantity of fuel in the tank.

2. Connect a fuel pressure gauge to the fuel pump outlet line.

3. Make sure the ignition switch has been in the **OFF** position for at least 10 seconds and the air conditioning is turned **OFF**.

4. Turn the ignition switch **ON**. The pump will run for about 2 seconds. The fuel pump pressure should be 40.5–47 psi. except for 3.8L engine or 34–40 psi. for 3.8L engine, while the pump is running and hold steady when the pump stops.

NOTE: The ignition switch may have to be cycled to ON more than once to obtain maximum pressure. It is also normal for the pressure to drop slightly when the pump stops.

5. Disconnect the fuel pressure gauge.

REMOVAL & INSTALLATION

The electric fuel pump is located inside the fuel tank.

1. Release the fuel pressure and disconnect the negative battery cable. Drain the fuel from the fuel tank.

2. Raise and support the vehicle safely. Disconnect the exhaust pipe at the catalytic convertor and the rear hanger. Allow the exhaust system to hang over the rear axle assembly.

3. Remove the tail pipe and muffler heat shields. Remove the fuel filler neck shield from behind the left rear tire.

4. Remove the rear suspension track bar and the track bar brace.

5. Disconnect the fuel pump/sending unit electrical connector, at the body harness connector. Do not pry up on the cover connector, as the pump/sending unit wiring harness is an integral part of the sending unit.

6. Disconnect the fuel pipes. Remove the fuel pipe retaining bracket on the left side and the brake line clip from the retaining bracket.

7. Position a jack under the rear axle assembly in order to support the rear axle.

8. Disconnect the lower ends of the shock absorbers, lower the axle assembly enough to release the tension on the coil springs. Remove the coil springs.

9. Lower the rear axle assembly as far as possible without causing damage to the brake lines and cables.

10. Remove the fuel tank strap bolts. Remove the tank by rotating the front of the tank downward and sliding it to the right side.

11. Remove the fuel pump/sending unit from the tank, by loosening the cam nut. When removing the cam nut, use brass tool or equivalent to tap the nut loose.

12. Remove the O-ring from beneath the unit. Replace the O-ring if defective.

13. Separate the fuel pump from the sending unit.

To install:

14. Install the fuel pump to the sending unit.

15. Install the O-ring in the groove around the tank opening and install the fuel pump/sending unit. Install the cam nut and tighten until it is against the stop.

16. Raise the fuel tank into position and install the tank strap bolts.

17. Install the coil springs and raise the rear axle into position. Connect the shock absorbers.

18. Connect the fuel lines and the electrical connector.

19. Install the rear suspension track bar and the track bar brace.

20. Install the fuel filler neck shield and the tail pipe and muffler heat shields.

21. Connect the exhaust system and lower the vehicle.

22. Fill the fuel tank.

23. Connect the negative battery cable, start the engine and check for fuel leaks.

Carburetor

REMOVAL & INSTALLATION

1. Disconnect the negative battery cable. Remove the air cleaner assembly.

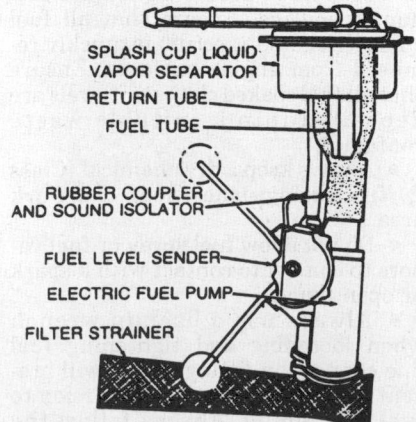

Electric fuel pump and fuel gauge meter assembly of a TBI-equipped engine

2. Disconnect the accelerator linkage and the detent cable.

3. Separate the necessary electrical connectors and remove vacuum lines.

4. Remove the fuel line at the carburetor inlet.

5. Remove the 4 attaching bolts. Remove the carburetor from the vehicle.

6. Installation is the reverse of removal. Be sure to use a new gasket. Tighten hold-down bolts to 144 inch lbs. (16 Nm) in an "X" pattern.

IDLE SPEED ADJUSTMENTS

The engine must be running in Closed Loop for all idle speed adjustments.

Carburetor Idle Speed Screw

1. Run the engine until it reaches normal operating temperature. Make sure the choke is open and the air conditioning is **OFF**.

2. Connect a tachometer and a timing light.

3. Set the parking brake and block the wheels.

4. Set the ignition timing according to the underhood emission decal.

5. Disconnect the electrical connection from the idle solenoid.

6. Adjust the carburetor idle speed screw. Refer to the underhood emission decal for vehicle specification.

Idle Stop Solenoid

1. If the vehicle is equipped with air conditioning, disconnect the electrical lead from the compressor and turn the air conditioning switch **ON**. If the vehicle is not equipped with air conditioning, disconnect the electrical lead from the solenoid and connect a jumper wire from a 12 volt supply to the solenoid.

2. Partially open the throttle to assure that the solenoid plunger is fully extended and allow the throttle to close on the plunger.

3. Adjust the solenoid plunger. Refer to the underhood emission decal for vehicle specification.

4. Reconnect the electrical leads and turn the air conditioning **OFF** or disconnect the jumper wire.

Fast Idle Speed

1. Disconnect and plug the vacuum hose to the EGR valve.

2. Place the fast idle cam follower on the highest step of the fast idle cam.

3. Adjust the fast idle cam screw. Refer to the underhood emission decal for vehicle specification.

4. Release the fast idle cam and stop the engine. Unplug the EGR valve vacuum hose and reconnect it to the valve.

IDLE MIXTURE ADJUSTMENTS

Fuel mixture is controlled by the Electronic Control Module (ECM). The ECM controls the mixture through the Mixture Control solenoid mounted in the float bowl. The Mixture Control solenoid can be monitored with a dwell meter set on the 6 cylinder scale. Connect the dwell meter to the Mixture Control solenoid dwell connector (green) located in the harness near the solenoid.

On a normal operating engine the dwell meter needle, at both idle and part throttle, will be between 10–50 degrees dwell and varying. This is called "closed loop" operation. This means that the oxygen sensor affects control of the fuel delivery. The oxygen sensor does not affect fuel control in the "open loop" operation and the dwell reading will not vary. Open loop operation occurs when the engine is cold, the oxygen sensor is below 600°F (315°C) or at wide-open throttle.

External Gauge

With the engine **OFF**, air cleaner and gasket removed, measure the Mixture Control solenoid travel as follows:

1. Insert float gauge J–34935–1, BT–8420–A or equivalent, down the **D** shaped vent hole in the air horn casting. Press down on gauge and release, observing that gauge moves freely and does not bind. With the gauge released (solenoid UP position), record mark on gauge (in inches) that lines up with top of air horn casting.

2. Lightly press down on gauge un-

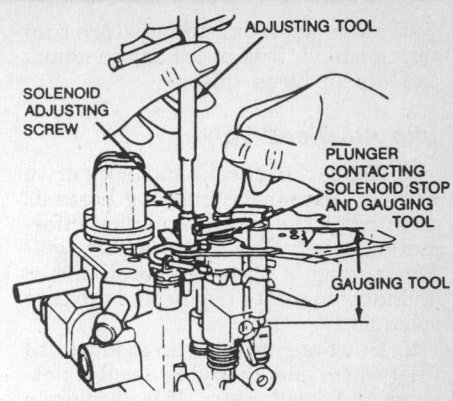

Mixture control solenoid adjustment

til bottom (solenoid DOWN position). Record in inches the mark on the gauge that lines up with top of air horn casting.

3. Subtract the gauge UP dimension (Step 1) from the gauge DOWN dimension (Step 2) and record the difference in inches. The difference in dimensions is the total solenoid travel.

4. If the Mixture Control (M/C) plunger travel is between $1/16$–$3/16$ inch (2.4–4.8mm) and the mixture control dwell at 3000 rpm was varying between 10–50 degrees, the mixture control solenoid and solenoid adjustments are correct. If not, the mixture control solenoid must be adjusted.

Mixture Control Solenoid

1. Remove the air horn.

2. Install mixture control solenoid gauging tool J–33815–1, BT–8253–A, or equivalent, over the throttle side metering jet rod guide. Temporarily reinstall the solenoid plunger (removed during air horn removal) into the solenoid body.

3. Holding the solenoid plunger in the DOWN position against the solenoid stop, use tool J–28696–10, BT–7928 or equivalent, to turn the adjusting screw (lean stop screw) until the solenoid plunger just contacts the gauging tool. The adjustment is correct when the solenoid plunger is contacting both the solenoid stop and the gauging tool.

4. Remove the solenoid plunger and gauging tool and reinstall the metering rod and float bowl insert.

5. Invert the air horn and remove the solenoid stop screw from the bottom side of the air horn, using tool J–28696–4, BT–7967–A or equivalent.

6. Remove the solenoid adjusting screw plug and the rich mixture stop screw plug from the air horn.

7. Reinstall the solenoid stop screw in the air horn and bottom lightly, then back out the screw ¼ turn.

8. Install the air horn.

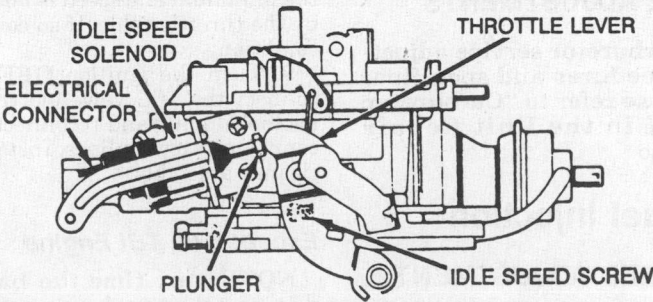

4 barrel carburetor

9. After adjusting the mixture control solenoid, it is necessary to adjust the idle air bleed valve.

Idle Air Bleed Valve

1. Set parking brake and block drive wheels. Disconnect and plug hoses as directed on the vehicle emission information label. Check and adjust ignition timing. Connect a dwell meter and tachometer to engine and mixture solenoid.

2. Start engine and run at idle until fully warm and a varying dwell is noted on the dwell meter. It is absolutely essential that the engine is operated for a sufficient length of time to ensure the engine coolant sensor and the oxygen sensor in the exhaust, are at full operational temperature.

3. Adjust curb idle speed, if necessary. With engine idling, observe dwell reading on the 6 cylinder scale. If within or varying between 25–35 degree range, no further adjustment is necessary. If dwell does not vary and/or falls outside of the 10–50 degree range, perform the following.

   a. With engine OFF, cover primary and secondary carburetor air intake with a shop cloth to prevent metal chips from entering carburetor and engine, also place masking tape over side air top vents on bleed valve tower.

   b. Carefully align a No. 35 drill (0.110 in.) on the steel rivet head holding the idle air bleed valve cover in place and drill only enough to remove rivet head. Use a drift and small hammer to drive the remainder of the rivets out of the idle air bleed value tower in the air horn casting. Use care in drilling to prevent damage to the air horn casting.

   c. Remove idle air bleed valve cover and remove remainder of rivets from inside tower in air horn casting. Discard cover after removal. Carefully blow out any chips or dirt which may be in air bleed valve cavity. A missing cover indicates the idle air bleed valve setting has been changed from its original factory setting.

   d. While idling in D or N, slowly turn valve up or down until dwell reading varies within the 25–35 degree range, attempting to be as close to 30 degree as possible. Perform this step carefully. The idle air bleed valve is very sensitive and should be turned only in ⅛ turn increments.

   e. If after performing Step d, the dwell reading does not vary and is not within the 25–35 degree range, it will be necessary to remove the carburetor to gain access to the plugs covering the idle mixture needles and readjust the idle mixture.

Idle Mixture

1. Remove the carburetor from the engine.
2. Invert the carburetor and drain the fuel into a container.
3. Place the inverted carburetor on a suitable holding fixture.
4. Remove the idle mixture needle plugs as follows:

   a. With a hacksaw, make 2 parallel cuts in the throttle body, 1 on each side of the locator points beneath the idle mixture needle plug (manifold side). The cuts should reach down to the steel plug, but should not extend more than ⅛ inch beyond the locator points. The distance between the saw cuts depends upon the size of the punch to be used.

   b. Hold a suitable punch at a 45 degree angle and drive it into the throttle body until the casting breaks away, exposing the steel plugs.

   c. Drive out the hardened steel plugs covering the mixture needles. Hardened plugs will shatter rather than remaining intact. It is not necessary to remove the plug completely; instead, remove loose pieces to allow the use of the idle mixture adjusting tool J–29030–B, BT–7610–B or equivalent.

5. Using the mixture adjusting tool, turn each idle mixture needle inward until lightly seated. Back out each mixture needle 3 turns.

6. Reinstall the carburetor. Do not install the air cleaner and gasket. Start engine, run until fully warm and repeat idle air bleed valve adjustment until dwell reading is varying and within specified limits. If unable to achieve varying dwell and specified limits, turn each mixture needle out 1 additional turn. Reset idle air bleed valve to obtain dwell limit specifications.

7. If necessary, reset curb idle speed to specification.

8. Check and, if necessary, adjust fast idle speed. Disconnect dwell meter and tachometer. Unplug and reconnect vacuum hoses.

SERVICE ADJUSTMENTS

For all carburetor service adjustment procedures and specifications, please refer to "Carburetor Service" in the Unit Repair section.

Fuel Injection

IDLE SPEED ADJUSTMENT

The idle speed and mixture are electronically controlled by the Electronic Control Module (ECM). All adjustments are preset at the factory. The only time the idle speed should need adjustment is when the throttle body assembly has been replaced. The throttle stop screw, used in regulating the minimum idle speed, is adjusted at the factory and should not require further adjustment. This adjustment should be performed only when the throttle body has been replaced

5.0L TBI Engine

1. Block the drive wheels and apply the parking brake. Remove the air cleaner assembly and or air duct. Remove and plug any vacuum hoses on the tube manifold assembly, if so equipped. Disconnect the throttle cable.

NOTE: If present, pierce the idle stop screw plug with an awl and apply leverage to remove it.

2. Ground the diagnostic test terminal in the ALDL connector. Turn the ignition ON and leave the engine OFF. Wait at least 45 seconds, this will allow the Idle Air Control (IAC) pintle to seat in the throttle body.

3. With the ignition still in the ON position and the engine OFF, with the ALDL test terminal still grounded, disconnect the IAC valve electrical connector.

4. Connect a tachometer to the engine to monitor the engine speed.

5. Remove the ground from the ALDL connector test terminal.

6. Place the transmission in the P or N position. Start and run the engine until it reaches normal operating temperature. It may be necessary to depress the accelerator pedal in order to start the engine. Allow the engine idle speed to stabilize.

NOTE: The engine should be at normal operating temperature with the accessories and cooling fan OFF.

7. The idle speed should be at 400–450 rpm, if not within specification adjust as necessary.

8. Install the throttle cable, be sure the minimum idle speed is not affected by the throttle cable. If so correct this condition.

9. Turn the ignition OFF and reconnect the IAC valve electrical connector. Unplug and reconnect the disconnected vacuum lines. Install the air cleaner assembly.

Except 5.0L TBI Engine

NOTE: Any time the battery is disconnected on vehicles equipped with the 3.1L engine, the programmed position of the IAC valve pintle is lost and replaced with a "default" value. To return the IAC valve pintle to the correct position, restore the battery power and connect a scan tool. Select "IAC System," then select "Idle Learn" in the "Miscellaneous Test" mode. Proceed with idle learn as directed. This procedure allows the ECM memory to be updated with the correct IAC valve pintle position for the vehicle and provide a stable idle speed.

1. Apply the parking brake and block the drive wheels. Remove the plug from the idle stop screw (except 3.8L) by piercing it first with a suitable tool, then applying leverage to the tool to lift the plug out.

2. Leave the Idle Air Control (IAC) valve connected and ground the diagnostic terminal (ALDL).

3. Turn the ignition switch to the ON position but do not start the engine. Wait for at least 30 seconds. This allows the IAC valve pintle to extend and seat in the throttle body.

4. With the ignition switch still in the ON position, disconnect IAC electrical connector.

5. Remove the ground from the diagnostic terminal. Disconnect the distributor set-timing connector on 5.0L and 5.7L engines. Start the engine and allow the engine to reach normal operating temperature.

6. With the engine in the D position, adjust the idle stop screw to obtain the correct specifications:

2.8L engine with automatic transmission: 550 rpm in D.

2.8L engine with manual transmission: 650 rpm in N.

3.8L engine with automatic transmission: 500 ± 50 rpm in D.

5.0L engine, all transmissions: 400 rpm in N.

5.7L engine, all transmissions: 450 rpm in N.

7. Turn the ignition OFF and reconnect the connector at the IAC motor.

8. Adjust the TPS if necessary. Start the engine and inspect for proper idle operation.

Fuel Injector

REMOVAL & INSTALLATION

2.8L and 3.1L Engines

1. Disconnect the negative battery cable.

2. Relieve the fuel system pressure.

3. Disconnect the air inlet duct at the throttle body and the crankcase vent pipe at the valve cover grommet.

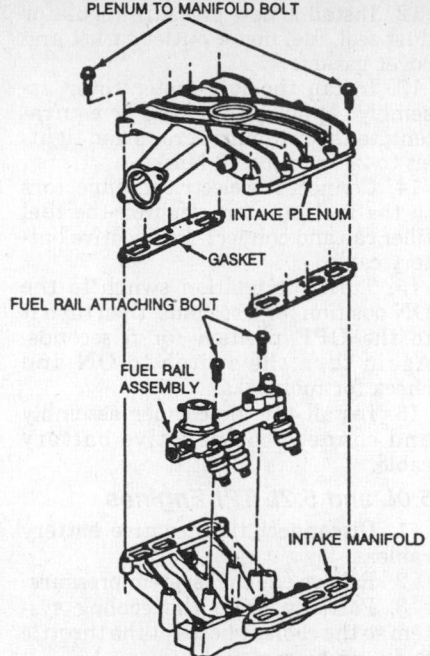

Removing plenum and fuel rail— 2.8L and 3.1L engines

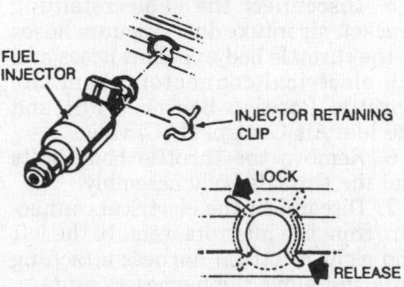

Fuel injector and retaining clip assembly

4. Disconnect the vacuum harness connector from the throttle body.

5. Remove the throttle cable bracket bolt, the throttle body attaching bolts and the throttle body and gasket. Discard the gasket.

6. Remove the EGR transfer tube to plenum bolts, the EGR transfer tube and gasket. Discard the gasket.

7. Remove the air conditioning compressor to plenum bracket attaching hardware and the bracket.

8. Remove the plenum bolts and studs and the plenum and gaskets. Discard the gaskets.

9. Disconnect the fuel feed and return lines at the fuel rail. Remove the fuel line O-rings and discard.

10. Disconnect the vacuum line at the pressure regulator, the injector electrical connectors and remove the fuel rail attaching bolts and the fuel rail assembly.

11. Rotate the injector retaining clip to the release position and remove the injector. Discard the O-ring seals and the injector retaining clip.

To install:

12. Lubricate new O-ring seals with engine oil and install on the injector. Install a new retaining clip on the injector.

13. Install the injector into the fuel rail injector socket with the electrical connectors facing outward. Rotate the injector retaining clip to the lock position.

14. Install the fuel rail assembly onto the intake manifold. Tilt the rail assembly to install the injectors.

15. Install the fuel rail attaching bolts and tighten to 18 ft. lbs. (25 Nm).

16. Connect the electrical connectors to the fuel injectors. Rotate the injectors as required to avoid stretching the wire harness.

17. Connect the vacuum line to the pressure regulator.

18. Install new O-rings on the fuel feed and return lines and connect the lines to the fuel rail. Tighten the fuel line nuts to 20 ft. lbs. (27 Nm).

19. Temporarily connect the negative battery cable. With the engine OFF and the ignition ON, check for fuel leaks. Disconnect the negative battery cable.

20. Clean the gasket sealing surfaces of the intake manifold plenum.

21. Install new plenum gaskets, the plenum and the plenum bolts and studs. Tighten the plenum bolts and studs to 18 ft. lbs. (25 Nm).

22. Install the air conditioning compressor to plenum bracket and attaching hardware, the EGR tube with a new gasket and the EGR transfer tube bolts. Tighten the bolts to 19 ft. lbs. (26 Nm).

23. Install the throttle body with a new gasket and the throttle body bolts. Tighten the bolts to 20 ft. lbs. (27 Nm).

24. Install the throttle cable bracket bolt and connect the vacuum harness connector to the throttle body.

25. Connect the air inlet duct to the throttle body and the crankcase vent pipe to the valve cover grommet.

26. Tighten the fuel filler cap and connect the negative battery cable.

3.8L Engine

1. Disconnect the negative battery cable.

2. Relieve the fuel system pressure.

3. Disconnect the electrical connectors from the fuel injectors.

4. Disconnect the vacuum hose from the pressure regulator.

5. Disconnect the fuel feed and return lines from the fuel rail.

6. Remove the fuel rail attaching bolts and remove the fuel rail and the fuel injectors.

7. Installation is the reverse of the removal procedure. Use new O-rings on the injectors and coat the O-rings with engine oil.

5.0L TBI Engine

1. Disconnect the negative battery cable.
2. Relieve the fuel system pressure.
3. Remove the air cleaner assembly.
4. Remove the electrical connectors from the fuel injectors by squeezing the plastic tabs and pulling straight up.
5. Remove the fuel meter cover attaching screws and remove the fuel meter cover assembly.
6. Remove the fuel meter outlet passage gasket and pressure regulator dust seal. If the fuel meter cover gasket is stuck to the fuel meter body, leave it in place. If it is stuck to the fuel meter cover, remove it and place it on the fuel meter body.
7. With the fuel meter cover gasket in place to protect the fuel meter body, use a suitable pry bar and fulcrum to carefully pry out the injector.
8. Discard both injector O-rings and the fuel meter cover gasket.

To install:

NOTE: Be sure to replace the injector with an identical part. Injectors from other models can fit, but are calibrated for different flow rates. Service fuel injector packages may contain a fuel injector washer (spacer). The washer is not required for this application.

9. Lubricate a new upper (large) O-ring with engine oil and install in the fuel meter body cavity. Make sure the O-ring is seated properly and is flush with the top of the fuel meter body surface.
10. Lubricate a new lower (small) O-ring with engine oil and install on the nozzle end of the injector. Push the O-ring on far enough to contact the filter.
11. Install the injector by aligning the raised lug on the injector base with the notch in the fuel meter body cavity. Push down on the injector until it is fully seated in the fuel meter body. The electrical terminals of the injector should be parallel with the throttle shaft.

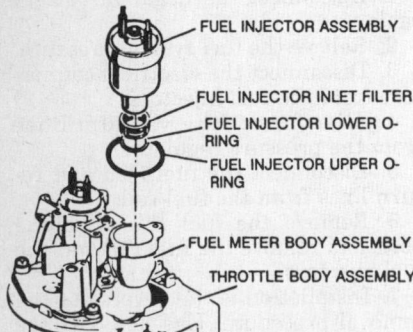

FUEL INJECTOR ASSEMBLY

FUEL INJECTOR INLET FILTER
FUEL INJECTOR LOWER O-RING
FUEL INJECTOR UPPER O-RING

FUEL METER BODY ASSEMBLY
THROTTLE BODY ASSEMBLY

Fuel injector and O-rings—TPI

12. Install a new pressure regulator dust seal, fuel meter outlet gasket and cover gasket.
13. Install the fuel meter cover assembly. Apply Loctite 262 or equivalent, to the retaining screws and tighten to 27 inch lbs. (3 Nm).
14. Connect the electrical connectors to the fuel injectors, tighten the fuel filler cap and connect the negative battery cable.
15. Turn the ignition switch to the **ON** position for 2 seconds, then turn it to the **OFF** position for 5 seconds. Again turn the switch to **ON** and check for fuel leaks.
16. Install the air cleaner assembly and connect the negative battery cable.

5.0L and 5.7L TPI Engines

1. Disconnect the negative battery cable.
2. Relieve the fuel system pressure.
3. Partially drain the cooling system so the coolant hoses at the throttle body can be removed.
4. Disconnect the throttle, TV and cruise control cables.
5. Disconnect the cable retaining bracket, air intake duct, vacuum hoses at the throttle body, coolant hoses and the electrical connectors from the Throttle Position Sensor (TPS) and the Idle Air Control (IAC) valve.
6. Remove the throttle body bolts and the throttle body assembly.
7. Disconnect the electrical connectors from the injectors, remove the left and right electrical harness attaching nuts and move the harnesses aside.
8. Disconnect the power brake vacuum hose at the plenum and remove the runner to plenum bolt attaching the Manifold Absolute Pressure (MAP) sensor. Disconnect the MAP sensor and vacuum hoses at the plenum.
9. Remove the remaining runner to plenum bolts. Lift the plenum and disconnect the Manifold Air Temperature sensor electrical connector. Remove the plenum and discard the plenum gaskets.
10. Remove the runner to manifold bolts, PCV valve and hose, EGR solenoid and the left and right side runners and gaskets. Discard the gaskets.
11. Disconnect the fuel feed and return lines. Discard the fuel line O-rings.
12. Remove the fuel tube bracket bolt.
13. Disconnect the vacuum line at the pressure regulator.
14. Remove the fuel rail attaching bolts and the fuel rail assembly.
15. Rotate the injector retainer clip to the release position and remove the injector. Discard the O-rings and retainer clips.

To install:

NOTE: There are 2 injector part numbers used in production for the 5.0L engine and 2 different part numbers for the 5.7L engine. Do not intermix injectors with different part numbers, as this will result in engine roughness and excessive emissions.

16. Lubricate new injector O-ring seals with engine oil and install on the injector.
17. Install a new retainer clip onto the injector and install the injector into the fuel rail injector socket, with the electrical connector facing outward. Rotate the injector retainer clip to the locking position.
18. Install the fuel rail assembly in the intake manifold. Install the attaching bolts to 15 ft. lbs. (20 Nm). Install the fuel tube bracket bolt and tighten to 25 ft. lbs. (34 Nm).
19. Connect the vacuum line to the pressure regulator.
20. Install new O-rings on the fuel feed and return lines and connect the fuel lines to the fuel rail. Tighten the fuel line nuts to 20 ft. lbs. (27 Nm).
21. Temporarily connect the negative battery cable. Turn the ignition switch to **ON** for 2 seconds and then to **OFF**. Again turn to the **ON** position and check for fuel leaks. Disconnect the negative battery cable.
22. Clean all plenum and runner gasket mating surfaces.
23. Install new gaskets, the runners and manifold to runner bolts to the intake manifold. Tighten the bolts to 25 ft. lbs. (34 Nm).
24. Install the EGR solenoid.
25. Install the right and left hand runner to manifold bolts finger tight only.
26. Support the plenum above the runners, connect the MAT sensor electrical connector and lower the plenum into position. Start a few bolts to hold the plenum in position.
27. Connect the vacuum hoses and MAP sensor.
28. Tighten all bolts to 25 ft. lbs. (34 Nm), starting in the center of the plenum/manifold and working outward.
29. Install the PCV valve and hose.
30. Connect the power brake vacuum hose to the fitting on the plenum, the left and right injector electrical harnesses, the attaching nuts and the electrical connectors to the injectors.
31. Install the throttle body with a new gasket and tighten the attaching bolts to 18 ft. lbs. (24 Nm).
32. Connect the electrical connectors to the TPS and IAC valve, coolant hoses, vacuum hoses, throttle cable bracket and the throttle, TV and cruise control cables.

33. Refill the cooling system, tighten the fuel filler cap and connect the negative battery cable.

EMISSION CONTROLS

Please refer to "Emission Control" in the Unit Repair section for system maintenance procedures. Due to the complex nature of modern electronic engine control systems, comprehensive diagnosis and testing procedures fall outside the confines of this repair manual. For complete information on diagnosis, testing and repair procedures concerning all modern engine and emission control systems, please refer to "Chilton's Guide to Electronic Engine Controls".

Emission Warning Lamps

RESETTING

All vehicles feature a "Service Engine Soon" light on the instrument panel. This light has the following functions:

It informs the driver that a problem has occured and the vehicle should be taken in for service.

It displays diagnostic codes stored by the ECM.

It indicates "Open Loop" or "Closed Loop" operation.

When the ECM sets a trouble code, the "Service Engine Soon" light will come ON and a trouble code will be stored in the memory. The light will not go out until the problem is rectified. If the problem is intermittent, the light will go out after 10 seconds, when the fault goes away. Even after the light goes out, there is still a trouble code stored in the memory of the ECM.

To clear the code from memory, the ECM power feed must be disconnected for at least 30 seconds. The ECM power feed can be disconnected at the positive battery terminal pigtail, the inline fuse holder that originates at the positive connection at the battery or the ECM fuse in the fuse block. The negative battery cable may be disconnected but other on-board memory data, such as preset radio tuning, will also be lost.

ENGINE MECHANICAL

NOTE: Disconnecting the negative battery cable on some vehicles may interfere with the functions of the on board computer systems and may require the computer to undergo a relearning process, once the negative battery cable is reconnected.

Engine Assembly

REMOVAL & INSTALLATION

2.8L and 3.1L Engines

1. Disconnect the negative battery cable.
2. Remove the air cleaner duct.
3. Mark the hood location on the hood supports and remove the hood.
4. Remove the water pump drive belt.
5. Drain the radiator and remove the radiator hoses. Disconnect the heater hoses and the transmission cooler lines.
6. Remove the fan shroud, fan and radiator.
7. Disconnect the throttle linkage, including the cruise control detent cable.
8. Disconnect the air conditioning compressor and lay aside. Remove the power steering pump and lay aside.
9. Remove the vacuum brake booster line.
10. Remove the distributor cap and lay the wiring aside.
11. Disconnect the necessary wires and hoses.
12. Raise and safely support the vehicle.
13. Disconnect the exhaust pipes at the exhaust manifolds.
14. Remove the dust cover and remove the converter bolts.
15. Disconnect the starter wires.
16. Remove the bell housing bolts and the motor mount through bolts.
17. Lower the vehicle.
18. Relieve the fuel system pressure. Disconnect the fuel lines.
19. Support the transmission with a suitable jack. Attach an engine lifting device.
20. Remove the engine, including removing the wire from the bracket at the rear left of the engine.
To install:
21. Position the engine assembly in the vehicle.
22. Attach the motor mount to engine brackets and lower the engine in

place. Remove the engine lifting device and the transmission jack.
23. Raise and support the vehicle safely.
24. Install the motor mount through bolts and tighten the nuts to 50 ft. lbs. (68 Nm). Install the bell housing bolts and tighten to 35 ft. lbs. (47 Nm).
25. On vehicles with automatic transmissions, install the converter to flywheel attaching bolts to 46 ft. lbs. (63 Nm).
26. Install the flywheel splash shield and tighten to 89 inch lbs. (10 Nm).
27. Connect the starter wires and the fuel lines.
28. Install the exhaust pipe on the exhaust manifold.
29. Lower the vehicle.
30. Install the power steering pump and the air conditioning compressor.
31. Connect the necessary wires and hoses.
32. Install the radiator, fan and fan shroud. Connect the radiator and heater hoses and the transmission cooler lines.
33. Connect the vacuum brake booster line, the throttle linkage and cruise control cable. Install the distributor cap.
34. Fill the cooling system with the proper type and amount of coolant and the crankcase with the proper type of oil to the correct level.
35. Install the water pump drive belt, the air cleaner duct and the hood.
36. Connect the negative battery cable, start the engine and check for leaks.

3.8L Engine

1. Disconnect the negative battery cable.
2. Mark the location of the hood on the hood hinges and remove the hood.
3. Drain the engine coolant.
4. Remove the fan, pulleys and belts. Remove the radiator hoses and the radiator and fan shroud.
5. Disconnect the power steering pump and air conditioning compressor from their mounting brackets and position them out of the way.
6. Relieve the fuel system pressure. Disconnect the fuel line and the battery ground cable from the engine.
7. Disconnect the necessary hoses and wiring.
8. Disconnect the throttle cable.
9. Remove the alternator.
10. Disconnect the engine to body ground straps at the engine.
11. Raise and safely support the vehicle.
12. Disconnect the crossover pipe from the exhaust manifolds.
13. Remove the flywheel cover and use a scribe to mark the relationship of the torque converter to the flywheel.

Remove the converter to flywheel bolts.

14. Disconnect the starter wiring.

15. Remove the transmission to engine attaching bolts and the motor mount to frame bracket attaching bolts.

16. Lower the vehicle.

17. Support the transmission with a suitable jack and install an engine lifting device.

18. Remove the engine assembly.

To install:

19. Position the engine in the vehicle.

20. Install the transmission to engine attaching bolts and tighten to 35 ft. lbs. (48 Nm).

21. Raise and safely support the vehicle.

22. Install the motor mount to frame bracket attaching bolts and tighten to 48 ft. lbs. (65 Nm).

23. Install the converter to flywheel bolts making sure the scribed marks are aligned. Tighten the bolts to 46 ft. lbs. (63 Nm). Install the flywheel cover.

24. Connect the crossover pipe to the exhaust manifold.

25. Lower the vehicle.

26. Connect the engine to body ground straps and install the alternator.

27. Connect all necessary hoses and wiring.

28. Connect the throttle cable and the negative battery cable at the engine.

29. Connect the fuel lines.

30. Install the power steering pump and air conditioning compressor in their respective brackets.

31. Install the radiator, fan shroud, radiator and heater hoses and the fan, pulleys and belts.

32. Fill the cooling system with the proper type and quantity of coolant and the engine with the proper type of oil to the correct level.

33. Connect the negative battery cable, start the engine and check for leaks.

5.0L and 5.7L Engines

1. Disconnect the negative battery cable.

2. Mark the location of the hood on the hood hinges and remove the hood.

3. Remove the air cleaner.

4. Drain the cooling system.

5. Remove the radiator hoses.

6. Disconnect the transmission cooler lines, the electrical connectors and retaining clips at the fan and remove the fan and shroud.

7. Remove the radiator.

8. Remove the accessory drive belt.

9. Disconnect the throttle cable.

10. Remove the plenum extension

screws and the plenum extension, if equipped.

11. Disconnect the spark plug wires at the distributor and remove the distributor.

12. Disconnect the necessary hoses and wiring.

13. Disconnect the power steering and air conditioning compressors from their respective brackets and lay them aside.

14. Relieve the fuel system pressure. Disconnect the fuel lines.

15. Disconnect the negative battery cable at the engine block.

16. Raise and safely support the vehicle.

17. Remove the exhaust pipes at the exhaust manifolds.

18. Remove the flywheel cover and remove the converter to flywheel bolts.

19. Disconnect the starter wires.

20. Remove the bell housing bolts and the motor mount through bolts.

21. Lower the vehicle.

22. Support the transmission with a suitable jack.

23. Remove the AIR/converter bracket and ground wires from the rear of the cylinder head.

24. Attach a suitable lifting device and remove the engine assembly.

To install:

25. Position the engine assembly in the vehicle.

26. Attach the motor mount to engine brackets and lower the engine into place.

27. Remove the engine lifting device and the transmission jack.

28. Raise and safely support the vehicle.

29. Install the motor mount through bolts and tighten to 50 ft. lbs. (68 Nm).

30. Install the bell housing bolts and tighten to 35 ft. lbs. (47 Nm).

31. On vehicles with automatic transmissions, install the converter to flywheel bolts. Tighten the bolts to 46 ft. lbs. (63 Nm). Install the flywheel cover.

32. Connect the starter wires and the fuel lines.

33. Connect the exhaust pipe at the exhaust manifold.

34. Lower the vehicle.

35. Connect the necessary wires and hoses.

36. Install the power steering pump and air conditioning compressor in their respective brackets.

37. Install the radiator, fan and fan shroud, radiator hoses and heater hoses.

38. Connect the transmission cooler lines and cooling fan electrical connectors.

39. Install the distributor.

40. Install the plenum extension, if equipped.

41. Fill the cooling system with the proper type and quantity of coolant and the crankcase with the proper type of oil to the correct level.

42. Install the air cleaner and the hood.

43. Connect the negative battery cable, start the engine, check for leaks and check the timing.

Engine Mounts

REMOVAL & INSTALLATION

2.8L and 3.1L Engines

1. Disconnect the negative battery cable. Remove the top half of the radiator shroud. Raise and support the vehicle safely.

2. Remove the engine mount through bolt. Using a suitable engine lift, raise the front of the engine and remove the mount to engine bolts and remove the mount.

NOTE: Raise the engine only enough for sufficient clearance. Check for interference between the rear of the engine and the cowl panel which could cause distributor damage.

3. Installation is the reverse order of the removal procedure. Tighten the engine mount through bolt nut to 50 ft. lbs. (68 Nm).

3.8L Engine

1. Disconnect the negative battery cable.

2. Raise and safely support the vehicle.

3. Support the weight of the engine at the forward edge of the oil pan.

4. Remove the mount to cylinder block bolts.

5. Raise the engine slightly and remove the mount to mount bracket bolt and nut. Remove the engine mount.

6. Installation is the reverse of the removal procedure. Tighten the mount to cylinder block bolts to 59 ft. lbs. (80 Nm) and the bolt and nut to 48 ft. lbs. (65 Nm).

5.0L and 5.7L Engines

1. Disconnect the negative battery cable.

2. Raise the vehicle and support safely.

3. Support the engine with a suitable jack to unload the engine mount. Remove the engine mount retaining bolt from below the the frame mounting bracket.

NOTE: Do not use a jack under the oil pan, crankshaft pulley or

any sheet metal when supporting the engine. Due to the small clearance between the oil pan and the oil pump screen, jacking against the oil pan may cause it to be bent against the pump screen, resulting in a damaged oil pickup.

4. Using a suitable engine lift, raise the front of the engine and remove the mount and bracket to engine bolts and nuts and remove the mount.

NOTE: Raise the engine only enough for sufficient clearance. Check for interference between the rear of the engine and the cowl panel which could cause distributor damage.

5. Installation is the reverse of the removal procedure. Tighten the mount and bracket bolts to 38 ft. lbs. (52 Nm) and the mount and bracket nuts to 30 ft. lbs. (41 Nm). Tighten the through bolt nut to 50 ft. lbs. (68 Nm).

Cylinder Head

REMOVAL & INSTALLATION

2.8L and 3.1L Engines

1. Disconnect the negative battery cable.
2. Relieve the fuel system pressure and drain the engine coolant from the radiator.
3. Remove the intake manifold and the spark plugs.
4. Remove the dipstick tube and bracket.
5. Remove the exhaust manifolds.
6. Remove the drive belt and remove the air conditioning compressor and lay aside.
7. Remove the power steering pump and bracket and lay aside.
8. Remove the ground cable from the rear of the cylinder head and remove the engine lift bracket.
9. Loosen the rocker arms until the pushrods can be removed.
10. Remove the belt tensioner and remove the alternator and brackets.
11. Remove the AIR bracket.
12. Remove the cylinder head bolts and remove the cylinder heads.
To install:
13. Clean the gasket mating surfaces of all components. Be careful not to nick or scratch any surfaces as this will allow leak paths. Clean the bolt threads in the cylinder block and on the head bolts. Dirt will affect bolt torque.
14. Place the head gaskets in position over the dowel pins, with the note "This Side Up" showing.
15. Install the cylinder heads.
16. Coat the cylinder head bolts threads with sealer No. 1052080 or

equivalent, and install the bolts. Tighten the bolts in the proper sequence. Tighten the head bolts on 1987 vehicles to 70 ft. lbs. (95 Nm). On 1988–91 vehicles, the head bolts should be tightened in 2 steps. First tighten in sequence to 40 ft. lbs. (55 Nm), then turn each bolt in sequence an additional ¼ turn (90 degrees).
17. Install the pushrods and loosely retain them with the rocker arms. Make sure the lower ends of the pushrods are in the lifter seats.
18. Install the power steering pump bracket and pump and the air conditioning compressor bracket and compressor.
19. Install the ground cable to the rear of the cylinder head.
20. Install the exhaust manifolds.
21. Install the dipstick tube and bracket.
22. Adjust the valve lash.
23. Install the intake manifold.
24. Install the AIR bracket and the belt tensioner.
25. Install the alternator bracket and alternator.
26. Install the accessory drive belt.
27. Install the spark plugs.
28. Fill the cooling system with the proper type and quantity of coolant.
29. Connect the negative battery cable, start the vehicle and check for leaks.

3.8L Engine

1. Disconnect the negative battery cable.
2. Drain the cooling system and relieve the fuel system pressure.
3. Remove the accessory drive belt.
4. If removing the right cylinder head, remove the air conditioning compressor with the hoses attached, the alternator and the alternator bracket.
5. If removing the left cylinder head, remove the oil level indicator, power steering pump with the hoses connected and the power steering pump mounting bracket.
6. Remove the spark plug wires and the exhaust manifolds.

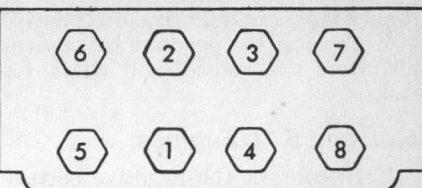
Cylinder head bolt torque sequence— 2.8L engine

7. Remove the intake manifold, valve covers, rocker arm shafts, pushrods, cylinder head bolts and the cylinder heads.

To install:
8. Clean the gasket mating surfaces of all components. Be careful not to nick or scratch any surfaces as this will allow leak paths. Clean the bolt threads in the cylinder block and on the head bolts. Dirt will affect bolt torque.
9. Install the cylinder head gasket on the block and install the cylinder head.
10. Coat the head bolt threads with a suitable thread sealer and install. Tighten the head bolts in 3 steps as follows:
   a. Tighten in sequence to 25 ft. lbs. (34 Nm).
   b. Tighten in sequence an additional ¼ turn (90 degrees).
   c. Tighten in sequence an additional ¼ turn (90 degrees).

NOTE: If 60 ft. lbs. (81 Nm) is reached at any time in Steps b and c, stop at this point. Do not complete the balance of the 90 degree turn.

11. Install the exhaust manifolds, pushrods, rocker arm shaft, intake manifold, valve cover and spark plug wires.
12. For the right side cylinder head, install the alternator and it's mounting bracket and the air conditioning.
13. For the left side cylinder head, install the power steering pump and it's mounting bracket and the oil level indicator.
14. Install the accessory drive belt and fill the cooling system with the

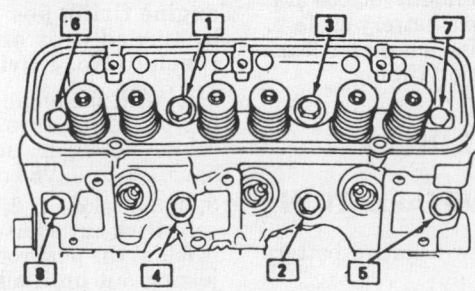
Cylinder head bolt torque sequence—3.8L engine

proper type and quantity of coolant.

15. Connect the negative battery cable, start the vehicle and check for leaks.

5.0L and 5.7L Engines

1. Disconnect the negative battery cable.

2. Drain the cooling system and relieve the fuel system pressure.

3. Remove the accessory drive belt and remove the intake manifold.

4. Remove the power steering pump and alternator bracket or the air conditioning compressor mounting bracket, as necessary.

5. Remove the exhaust manifolds and the valve covers.

6. Remove the rocker arms and pushrods.

7. Disconnect the ground wires and the catalytic converter AIR pipe bracket at the rear of the cylinder heads.

8. Remove the cylinder head bolts and the cylinder head.

To install:

9. Clean the gasket mating surfaces of all components. Be careful not to nick or scratch any surfaces as this will allow leak paths. Clean the bolt threads in the cylinder block and on the head bolts. Dirt will affect bolt torque.

10. Position the head gasket over the dowel pins with the bead up. Install the cylinder head over the dowel pins and gasket.

11. Coat the threads of the head bolts with No. 1052080 thread sealer or equivalent. Install the head bolts and tighten in sequence to 68 ft. lbs. (92 Nm).

12. Install the exhaust manifolds.

13. Install the pushrods and rocker arms and adjust the valve lash. Install the valve covers.

14. Install the power steering pump and alternator bracket, or air conditioning compressor mounting bracket, as necessary.

15. Connect the ground wires and the catalytic converter AIR bracket to the rear of the cylinder head.

16. Install the intake manifold.

17. Install the accessory drive belt.

18. Fill the cooling system with the proper type and amount of coolant. Connect the negative battery cable.

19. Start the engine, check for leaks and check the ignition timing.

Valve Lifters

REMOVAL & INSTALLATION

1. Disconnect the negative battery cable.

2. Drain the cooling system and relieve the fuel system pressure.

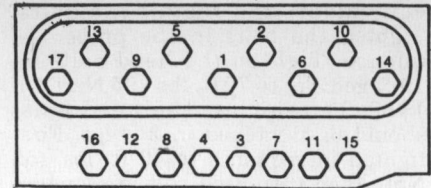

Cylinder head bolt torque sequence – V8 Chevy produced engine

3. Remove the intake manifold assembly. Remove the valve covers.

4. Remove the pushrods and rocker arms or rocker shafts. Remove the valve lifter retainer assembly, if equipped with roller lifters. Using the proper valve lifter removal tool, remove the valve lifters.

5. Installation is the reverse of the removal procedure. Install the lifters in the same position they were before removal. Coat the lifters in clean engine oil before installing them.

Valve Lash

ADJUSTMENT

3.8L Engine

Valve adjustments are not possible on this engine

Except 3.8L Engine

1. Disconnect the negative battery cable. Remove the valve covers.

2. Tighten the rocker arm nuts until all lash is eliminated if necessary.

3. Adjust the valves when the lifter is on the base circle of the camshaft lobe by cranking the engine until the mark on the vibration damper lines up with the center or 0 mark on the timing tab fastened to the crankcase front cover and the engine is in the No. 1 firing position.

NOTE: This may be determined by placing a finger on the No. 1 valve as the mark on the damper comes near the 0 mark on the crankcase front cover. If the valves move as the mark comes up to the timing tab, the engine is in the No. 6 – V8 engine or No. 4 – V6 engine firing position and should be turned over one more time to reach to No. 1 firing position.

4. With the engine in the No. 1 firing position, adjust the following valves. V6 engine: intake – 1, 5, 6 exhaust – 1, 2, 3; V8 engine: exhaust – 1, 3, 4, 8 intake – 1, 2, 5, 7.

5. Back out adjusting nut until lash is felt at the pushrod, then turn in adjusting nut until all lash is removed. This can be determined by rotating pushrod while turning adjusting nut.

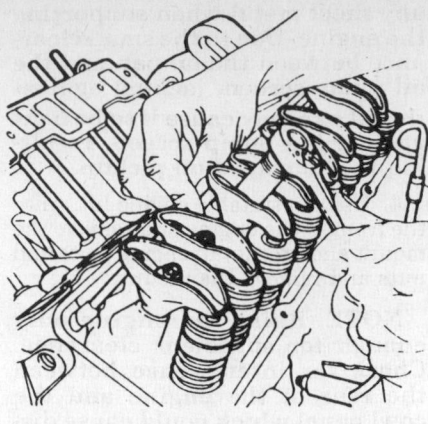

Typical valve adjustment procedure

When play has been removed, turn adjusting nut in one full additional turn.

6. Crank the engine one revolution until the pointer, **0** mark and the vibration damper mark are again in alignment. This is the No. 6 – V8 engine or No. 4 – V6 engine firing position.

7. With the engine in this position, adjust the following valves. V6 engine: intake – 2, 3, 4 exhaust – 4, 5, 6; V8 engine: exhaust – 2, 5, 6, 7 intake – 3, 4, 6, 8.

8. Install the valve covers and connect the negative battery cable.

9. Start the engine and adjust the idle speed as required.

Rocker Arms/Shafts

REMOVAL & INSTALLATION

2.8L and 3.1L Engines

1. Disconnect the negative battery cable.

2. For left side valve cover removal, remove the accessory drive belt and the transmission dipstick. Remove the air management hose and air conditioning bracket, if equipped.

3. For right side valve cover removal, remove the EGR valve adapter with the EGR valve and shield from the exhaust manifold. Remove the coil and coil mounting bracket from the cylinder head. Disconnect the crankcase vent pipe.

4. Relieve the fuel system pressure and remove the plenum and fuel rail and disconnect the throttle body.

5. Remove the center intake manifold on 1990–91 vehicles.

6. Remove the valve cover reinforcements and nuts and remove the valve cover.

7. Remove the rocker arm nuts, rocker arm balls and rocker arms. Place the components in a rack so they can be reinstalled in the same location.

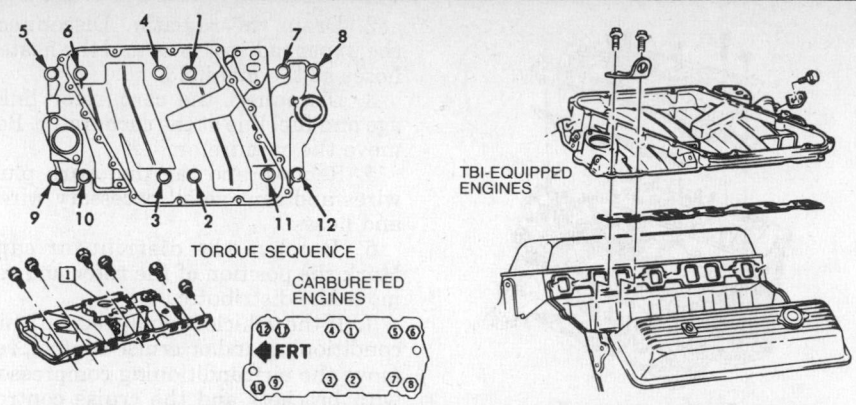

Intake manifold bolt tightening sequence of all Chevrolet-built V8 engines. Note that the lower sequence is used for all carbureted engines, whereas the upper sequence is used for all TBI-equipped engines

8. Install in the reverse order of removal. Make sure all gasket mating surfaces are clean before installing. Adjust the valve lash before installing the valve covers.

3.8L Engine

1. Disconnect the negative battery cable.

2. If removing the right side valve cover, remove the PCV pipe to the air cleaner, the necessary computer command control hoses and leads and the hot air tube.

3. Remove the spark plug wires and the accessory mounting brackets, as required.

4. Remove the valve cover attaching bolts and remove the valve cover.

5. Remove the rocker arm shaft retaining bolts and the rocker arm shaft.

6. If the rocker arms are being replaced, remove the nylon rocker arm retainers and discard. Install the replacement rocker arm using a new nylon retainer. Install the nylon retainers with a suitable drift of at least ½ inch diameter.

NOTE: Service rocker arms are stamped (R) for right and (L) for left. Make sure the rocker arms are installed on the rocker shaft in the correct sequence.

7. Install in the reverse order of removal. Make sure all gasket mating surfaces are clean before installation. Tighten the rocker arm shaft retaining bolts to 25 ft. lbs. (35 Nm).

5.0L and 5.7L Engines

1. Disconnect the negative battery cable.

2. Remove the air cleaner, if necessary.

3. To remove the right side valve cover, perform the following:
  a. 1987–88 vehicles: Remove the air management hoses and disconnect the wires and hoses from the EGR solenoid and the alternator.

Remove the EGR solenoid. Remove the air management valve bracket and move aside. Remove the air management tubes.
  b. 1989–91 vehicles: Remove the EGR pipe assembly, if necessary. Disconnect the electrical connections and wiring harnesses as necessary. Disconnect the spark plug wires from the distributor. Remove the crankcase vent hoses and valves. Remove the coil and disconnect the heater hose from the throttle body on 1991 vehicles. Remove the AIR control valve, check valve, pipes and hoses.

4. To remove the left side valve cover, perform the following:
  a. 1987–88 vehicles: Remove the power brake booster line. Disconnect the AIR hoses and the PCV hose and move the wiring harness.
  b. Disconnect the electrical connections and move the wiring harnesses, as necessary. Remove the alternator and disconnect the crankcase hoses and the PCV valve.

5. Remove the valve cover retaining bolts and washers and remove the valve cover.

6. Remove the rocker arm assemblies and place them in a rack so they may be reinstalled in the same location.

7. Install in the reverse order of removal. Make sure all gasket mating surfaces are clean before installation. Adjust the valve lash before installing the valve cover.

Intake Manifold
REMOVAL & INSTALLATION

2.8L and 3.1L Engines

1. Disconnect the negative battery cable.

2. Drain the cooling system and relieve the fuel system pressure.

3. Disconnect the air inlet duct at the throttle body and the crankcase

vent pipe at the valve cover grommet.

4. Disconnect the vacuum harness connector from the throttle body.

5. Remove the throttle cable bracket bolt, the throttle body attaching bolts and remove the throttle body. Discard the throttle body gasket.

6. Remove the EGR transfer tube to plenum bolts and remove the EGR transfer tube. Discard the EGR transfer tube gasket.

7. Remove the air conditioning compressor to plenum bracket attaching hardware and the bracket.

8. Remove the plenum bolts/studs and the plenum. Discard the plenum gaskets.

9. Disconnect the fuel feed and return lines at the fuel rail. Discard the fuel line O-rings.

10. Disconnect the vacuum line at the pressure regulator and the injector electrical connectors.

11. Remove the fuel rail attaching bolts and the fuel rail assembly.

12. Remove the spark plug wires and the distributor cap. Mark the distributor position and remove the hold-down bracket and the distributor.

13. Remove the air management hose and bracket, if equipped.

14. Disconnect the emission canister hoses.

15. Remove the valve covers.

16. Remove the upper radiator hose at the manifold and disconnect the heater hose.

17. Disconnect the coolant switch sensors.

18. Remove the transmission dipstick.

19. Remove the center intake manifold bolts and the center intake manifold on 1990–91 vehicles.

20. Remove the intake manifold bolts and remove the intake manifold.
To install:

21. Make sure all gasket mating surfaces are clean and free of oil or water prior to installation.

22. Place a $^3/_{16}$ inch diameter bead of RTV sealer on each ridge. Install new gaskets on the cylinder heads and hold in place by extending the ridge RTV bead up ¼ inch onto the gasket ends. The new gaskets will have to be cut, where indicated, to install behind the pushrods. Cut only those areas that are necessary.

23. Install the intake manifold on the engine. Make sure the areas between the case ridges and intake are completely sealed.

24. Install the intake manifold retaining bolts and nuts and tighten to 19 ft. lbs. (26 Nm) in the proper sequence.

25. Install the center intake manifold on 1990–91 vehicles. Tighten the retaining bolts to 15 ft. lbs. (21 Nm).

26. Install the upper radiator hose

and the valve covers and connect the heater hose and the coolant switch sensors.

27. Install the air management hose and bracket, if equipped.

28. Install the distributor, distributor cap and spark plug wires.

29. Install the fuel rail assembly in the intake manifold. Tighten the attaching bolts to 18 ft. lbs. (25 Nm).

30. Connect the injector electrical connectors and the vacuum line to the pressure regulator.

31. Install new O-rings on the fuel feed and return lines and connect the lines to the fuel rail. Tighten the fuel line nuts to 20 ft. lbs. (27 Nm).

32. Temporarily connect the negative battery cable. With the engine **OFF** and the ignition **ON**, check for fuel leaks. Disconnect the negative battery cable.

33. Install the plenum with a new gasket and install the bolts/studs. Tighten to 18 ft. lbs. (25 Nm).

34. Install the air conditioning compressor to plenum bracket and attaching hardware. Install the EGR transfer tube with a new gasket. Tighten the attaching bolts to 19 ft. lbs. (26 Nm).

35. Install the throttle body with a new gasket and tighten the retaining bolts to 20 ft. lbs. (27 Nm).

36. Install the throttle cable bracket bolt and connect the vacuum harness connector to the throttle body.

37. Connect the air inlet duct to the throttle body and the crankcase vent pipe to the valve cover grommet.

38. Install the transmission dipstick and connect the necessary wires and hoses.

39. Connect the negative battery cable.

40. Fill the cooling system with the proper type and amount of coolant. Do not install the radiator cap.

41. Start the engine and set the initial timing. Tighten the distributor hold-down clamp bolt to 25 ft. lbs. (34 Nm) after setting.

42. Let the engine run until the upper radiator hose becomes hot (thermostat open). With the engine idling, add coolant to the radiator, if necessary, until the level reaches the bottom of the filler neck. Install the radiator cap, making sure the arrows on the cap line up with the overflow tube.

3.8L Engine

1. Disconnect the negative battery cable.

2. Drain the cooling system and relieve the fuel system pressure.

3. Remove the air inlet tube.

4. Disconnect the fuel line at the fuel rail and at the pressure regulator.

5. Disconnect the injector wiring

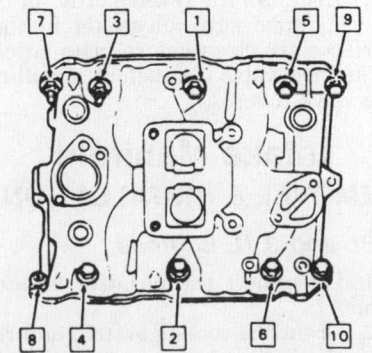

Intake manifold bolt tightening sequence—2.8L engine

harness connectors located just behind the coil.

6. Disconnect the coolant temperature sensor wire connectors located at the front of the manifold.

7. Disconnect the heater, bypass and upper radiator hoses, the vacuum lines and hoses from the EGR, fuel pressure regulator and PCV valve and the throttle, cruise control and TV cables from the throttle body.

8. Remove the EGR vacuum control valve and the ignition wires from the spark plugs.

9. Remove the lower right side turbo mounting bracket to intake and bracket support to plenum. Remove the intake manifold bolts and remove the intake manifold.

10. Installation is the reverse of the removal procedure. Make sure all gasket mating surfaces are clean prior to installation. Tighten the intake manifold bolts to 44 ft. lbs. (60 Nm) in the proper sequence.

5.0L Carbureted Engine

1. Disconnect the negative battery cable. Remove the air cleaner assembly.

Intake manifold bolt torque sequence—3.8L engine

2. Drain the radiator. Disconnect the upper radiator hose and the heater hoses at the manifold.

3. Disconnect the carburetor linkage and fuel line at the carburetor. Remove the carburetor.

5. Remove and tag the spark plug wires and remove all necessary wires and hoses.

6. Remove the distributor cap. Mark the position of the rotor and remove the distributor.

7. If the vehicle is equipped with air conditioning and/or cruise control, remove the air conditioning compressor with brackets and the cruise control servo assembly with bracket.

8. Loosen the alternator belt and remove the upper mounting bracket. Remove the EGR solenoids and brackets. Remove the vacuum brake line.

9. Remove the intake manifold attaching bolts. Remove the intake manifold.

10. Installation is the reverse of the removal procedure. Make sure all gasket mating surfaces are clean before installation. Apply a $3/16$ inch bead of RTV sealant on the front and rear ridge of the cylinder case. Extend the bead about 1/2 inch up each cylinder head in order to seal and retain the manifold side gaskets. Also use RTV sealant at the water passages. Tighten the intake manifold bolts to 35 ft. lbs. (47 Nm) in the proper sequence.

5.0L TBI Engine

1. Disconnect the negative battery cable.

2. Drain the radiator, relieve the fuel system pressure and remove the air cleaner.

3. Disconnect the electrical connectors to the IAC valve, TPS and fuel injectors. Remove the injector wiring harness. Tag and disconnect the vacuum hoses. Disconnect all wires and hoses as necessary.

4. Disconnect the throttle, transmission control and cruise control cables. Disconnect the fuel feed and return lines and discard the O-rings.

5. Remove the TBI unit attaching bolts and remove the TBI unit.

6. Disconnect the ECM engine control harness and lay aside. Disconnect the upper radiator hose and heater hose at the manifold. Remove the EGR valve and solenoid and remove the coolant temperature sensor.

7. Disconnect the fuel line clips and lines at the cylinder head and intake manifold. Disconnect the power brake vacuum pipe at the manifold.

8. Disconnect the spark plug wires at the distributor cap and remove the distributor cap. Mark the position of the rotor and the distributor housing and remove the distributor.

9. Remove the intake manifold bolts and studs and remove the intake manifold.

10. Install in the reverse order of removal. Make sure all gasket mating surfaces are clean before installation. Apply a $^3/_{16}$ bead of RTV sealant on the front and rear of the cylinder block. Extend the bead ½ inch up each cylinder head to seal and retain the intake manifold gaskets. Tighten the intake manifold bolts to 35 ft. lbs. (47 Nm) in the proper sequence.

5.0L and 5.7L TPI Engines

1. Disconnect the negative battery cable.

2. Drain the cooling system and relieve the fuel system pressure.

3. Disconnect the accelerator, TV and cruise control cables.

4. Remove the air intake duct. Disconnect the

5. Disconnect the heater hoses and the electrical connections at the throttle body and the intake manifold.

6. Disconnect the vacuum and breather hoses at the throttle body.

7. Remove the throttle body from the plenum.

8. Disconnect the electrical connectors from the injectors, remove the left and right electrical harness attaching nuts and move the harnesses aside.

9. Disconnect the power brake vacuum hose at the plenum and remove the runner to plenum bolt attaching the Manifold Absolute Pressure (MAP) sensor. Disconnect the MAP sensor and vacuum hoses at the plenum.

10. Remove the remaining runner to plenum bolts. Lift the plenum and disconnect the manifold air temperature sensor electrical connector. Remove the plenum and discard the plenum gaskets.

11. Remove the runner to manifold bolts, PCV valve and hose, EGR solenoid and the left and right side runners and gaskets. Discard the gaskets.

12. Disconnect the fuel feed and return lines. Discard the fuel line O-rings.

13. Remove the fuel tube bracket bolt.

14. Disconnect the vacuum line at the pressure regulator.

15. Remove the fuel rail attaching bolts and the fuel rail assembly.

16. Rotate the injector retainer clip to the release position and remove the injector. Discard the O-rings and retainer clips.

17. Remove the ignition coil and the EGR solenoid.

18. Disconnect the upper radiator hose at the thermostat housing.

19. Disconnect the spark plug wires at the distributor cap. Remove the distributor cap. Mark the position of the rotor and the distributor housing and remove the distributor.

20. Remove the EGR valve and pipe. Disconnect wires as necessary.

21. Remove the intake manifold bolts and studs and remove the intake manifold.

To install:

22. Make sure all gasket mating surfaces are clean and free of oil or water. Install the intake manifold gaskets. Apply a $^3/_{16}$ bead of RTV sealant to the front and rear ridges of the cylinder case. Extend the RTV bead ½ inch up each cylinder head to seal and retain the intake manifold gaskets.

23. Install the intake manifold and tighten the bolts and studs to 35 ft. lbs. (47 Nm) in the proper sequence.

24. Connect the electrical wires and the upper radiator hose.

25. Install the EGR valve and pipe and the ignition coil and EGR solenoid.

26. Lubricate new injector O-ring seals with engine oil and install on the injector.

NOTE: There are 2 injector part numbers used in production for the 5.0L engine and 2 different part numbers for the 5.7L engine. Do not intermix injectors with different part numbers, as this will result in engine roughness and excessive emissions.

27. Install a new retainer clip onto the injector and install the injector into the fuel rail injector socket, with the electrical connector facing outward. Rotate the injector retainer clip to the locking position.

28. Install the fuel rail assembly in the intake manifold. Install the attaching bolts to 15 ft. lbs. (20 Nm). Install the fuel tube bracket bolt and tighten to 25 ft. lbs. (34 Nm).

29. Connect the vacuum line to the pressure regulator.

30. Install new O-rings on the fuel feed and return lines and connect the fuel lines to the fuel rail. Tighten the fuel line nuts to 20 ft. lbs. (27 Nm).

31. Temporarily connect the negative battery cable. Turn the ignition switch to **ON** for 2 seconds and then to **OFF**. Again turn to the **ON** position and check for fuel leaks. Disconnect the negative battery cable.

32. Install new gaskets, the runners and manifold to runner bolts to the intake manifold. Tighten the bolts to 25 ft. lbs. (34 Nm).

33. Install the EGR solenoid.

34. Install the right and left hand runner to manifold bolts finger tight only.

35. Support the plenum above the runners, connect the MAT sensor electrical connector and lower the plenum into position. Start a few bolts to hold the plenum in position.

36. Connect the vacuum hoses and MAP sensor.

37. Tighten all bolts to 25 ft. lbs. (34 Nm), starting in the center of the plenum/manifold and working outward.

38. Install the PCV valve and hose.

39. Connect the power brake vacuum hose to the fitting on the plenum, the left and right injector electrical harnesses, the attaching nuts and the electrical connectors to the injectors.

40. Install the throttle body with a new gasket and tighten the attaching bolts to 18 ft. lbs. (24 Nm).

41. Connect the electrical connectors to the TPS and IAC valve, coolant hoses, vacuum hoses, throttle cable bracket and the throttle, TV and cruise control cables.

42. Connect the upper radiator hose to the thermostat housing.

43. Install the distributor and the distributor cap. Connect the spark plug wires. Install the plenum extension.

44. Install the air intake duct and fill the cooling system with the proper type and quantity of coolant.

45. Connect the negative battery cable and start the engine and check for leaks. Check the ignition timing.

Exhaust Manifold

REMOVAL & INSTALLATION

2.8L and 3.1L Engines

1. Disconnect the negative battery cable.

2. Raise and safely support the vehicle.

3. Disconnect the exhaust croossover pipe and lower the vehicle.

4. To remove the right side manifold, perform the following procedure:

   a. 1987–88 vehicles: Remove the air management valve from the AIR pump, remove the alternator bracket and disconnect the air management hose.

   b. 1989–91 vehicles: Remove the throttle body air duct and the accessory drive belt. Disconnect the EGR transfer tube at the plenum and remove the EGR valve adapter with the EGR valve and shield from the exhaust manifold. Disconnect the vacuum line and the electrical connector from the diverter valve. Remove the AIR pump pulley and bracket and disconnect the AIR hose from the check valve. Remove the AIR pump bolt and AIR pump with diverter valve from the lower bracket. Remove the AIR pipe from the exhaust manifold and remove the alternator brace.

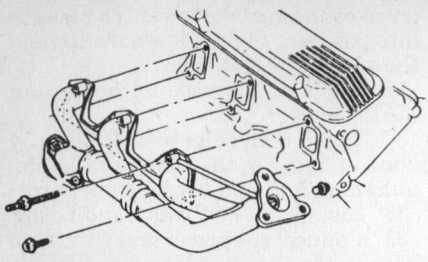

Right exhaust manifold installation—3.8L engine

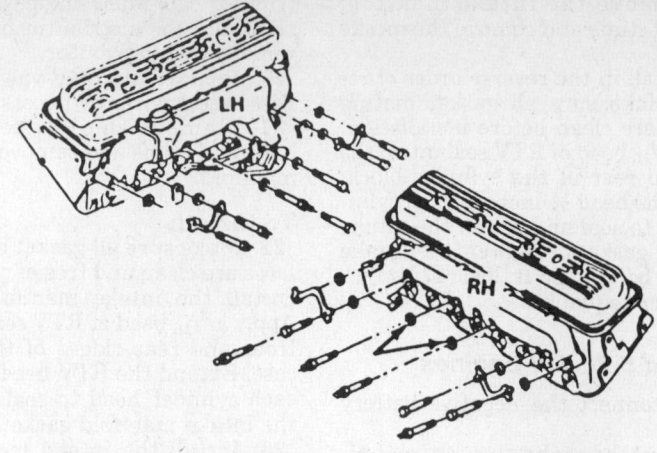

Exhaust manifold installation—5.0L and 5.7L engines

5. To remove the left side manifold, perform the following procedure:

a. 1987–88 vehicles: Disconnect the air management hoses and wires and remove the power steering and fuel line bracket.

b. 1989–91 vehicles: Remove the rear power steering pump bracket.

6. Remove the exhaust manifold bolts and nut and remove the exhaust manifold.

7. Install in the reverse order of removal. Make sure all mating surfaces are clean before installation. Tighten the exhaust manifold bolts and nut to 25 ft. lbs. (34 Nm).

3.8L Engine

1. Disconnect the negative battery cable.

2. Remove the exhaust pipe from the turbocharger and disconnect the oxygen sensor wire on the right side exhaust manifold.

3. Raise and safely support the vehicle.

4. Remove the exhaust manifold to croossover pipe and lower the vehicle.

5. Remove the exhaust manifold to cylinder head bolts and remove the exhaust manifold.

6. Install in the reverse order of removal. Make sure all mating surfaces are clean before installation. Tighten the exhaust manifold to cylinder head bolts to 37 ft. lbs. (50 Nm).

5.0L and 5.7L Engines

1. Disconnect the negative battery cable.

2. Disconnect the spark plug wires, if necessary.

3. Disconnect the AIR hoses and remove the AIR valve.

4. Remove the air management valve, if equipped.

5. Remove the air conditioning compressor and power steering pump and lay them aside. Remove the brackets.

6. Raise and safely support the vehicle.

7. Remove the exhaust pipes from the exhaust manifolds and lower the vehicle.

8. Remove the exhaust manifold bolts and studs and remove the exhaust manifold.

9. Install in the reverse order of removal. Make sure all mating surfaces are clean before installation. Tighten the 4 outside exhaust manifold bolts and studs to 20 ft. lbs. (27 Nm) and the inside bolts to 26 ft. lbs. (35 Nm).

Turbocharger

REMOVAL & INSTALLATION

3.8L Engine

1. Disconnect the negative battery cable.

2. Remove the air inlet hose from the compressor section of the turbocharger.

3. Disconnect the compressor outlet pipe from the compressor.

4. Disconnect the oil breather and turbocharger heat shields.

5. Remove the exhaust pipe from the turbine outlet.

6. Remove the oil breather vent from the valve cover. Disconnect and plug the oil pressure feed line at the turbocharger assembly.

7. Remove the turbocharger mounting bracket nuts. Disconnect the turbine inlet pipe from the exhaust manifold.

8. Disconnect the oil return line from turbocharger.

9. Remove the vacuum line from the turbocharger wastegate actuator.

10. Disconnect the intercooler outlet to throttle body pipe.

11. Remove the turbocharger assembly from the manifold adapter.

12. Install in the reverse order of removal. Always use new gaskets. Make sure all gasket mating surfaces are clean before installation. Tighten the turbocharger bracket to cylinder head bolts to 37 ft. lbs. (50 Nm). Tighten the

turbocharger to bracket nuts to 20 ft. lbs. (27 Nm). Tighten the heat shield retaining bolts to 20 ft. lbs. (27 Nm).

Timing Chain Front Cover

REMOVAL & INSTALLATION

2.8L and 3.1L Engines

1. Disconnect the negative battery cable.

2. Drain the cooling system and remove the accessory drive belt. Disconnect the lower radiator hose at the front cover and heater hose at the water pump.

3. Raise and safely support the vehicle.

4. Remove the oil pan.

5. Lower the vehicle.

6. On 1987–88 vehicles, remove the air conditioning compressor from it's mounting bracket and lay aside. Remove the compressor mounting bracket. On 1989–91 vehicles, remove the power steering pump and lay aside. Remove the power steering pump bracket.

7. Remove the water pump.

8. Using a suitable puller, remove the vibration damper.

9. Remove the front cover bolts and remove the front cover.

10. Install in the reverse order of removal. Make sure all gasket mating surfaces are clean before installation. Tighten the front cover bolts to 15 ft. lbs. (21 Nm) and the vibration damper bolt to 76 ft. lbs. (103 Nm).

3.8L Engine

1. Disconnect the negative battery cable.

2. Drain the radiator.

3. Disconnect the radiator hoses and the heater return hose at the water pump.

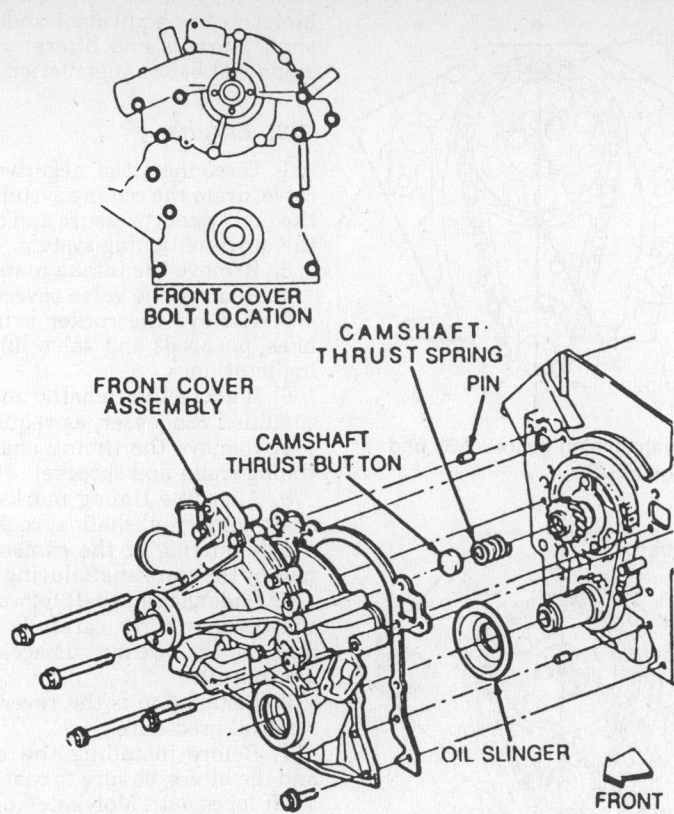

FRONT COVER BOLT LOCATION

FRONT COVER ASSEMBLY

CAMSHAFT THRUST SPRING

PIN

CAMSHAFT THRUST BUTTON

OIL SLINGER

FRONT

Timing chain cover installation—3.8L engine

4. Remove the fan assembly and pulleys.

5. Remove the crankshaft vibration damper.

6. Remove the alternator.

7. Remove the distributor, if equipped. If timing chain and sprockets are not going to be disturbed, note position of distributor rotor for reinstallation in same position.

8. Loosen and slide front clamp on thermostat bypass hose rearward.

9. Remove bolts attaching timing chain cover to cylinder block.

10. Remove 2 oil pan to timing chain cover bolts.

11. Remove timing chain cover assembly and gasket.

To install:

12. Thoroughly clean the cover, taking care to avoid damage to the gasket surface.

13. Installation is the reverse of the removal procedure.

14. Remove oil pump cover and pack the space around the oil pump gears completely full of petroleum jelly. There must be no air space left inside the pump. Reinstall cover using new gasket.

15. Tighten the front cover retaining bolts to 22 ft. lbs. (30 Nm) and the vibration damper bolt to 200 ft. lbs. (270 Nm).

5.0L and 5.7L Engines

1. Disconnect the negative battery cable.

2. Drain the cooling system and remove the accessory drive belt and pulleys.

3. Remove the water pump.

4. Using a suitable puller, remove the vibration damper.

5. Raise and safely support the vehicle.

6. Working from the front of the oil pan, remove 3 oil pan bolts on each side of the oil pan and loosen the next 3. Lower the vehicle.

7. Remove the front cover bolts. Using suitable prying tools, pry down on each side of the oil pan just enough to remove the front cover. Be careful not to damage the oil pan gasket or the oil pan.

To install:

8. Install in the reverse order of removal. Make sure all gasket mating surfaces are clean prior to installation.

9. Apply RTV sealant to the exposed portion of the oil pan rails and the oil pan seal on the bottom of the front cover. Pry down on the pan rails just enough to install the front cover. Put pressure down on the front cover as it is installed to align the front cover dowel pins. Be careful not to damage the front cover.

10. Tighten the front cover and oil pan bolts to 100 inch lbs. (11 Nm). Tighten the vibration damper bolt to 70 ft. lbs. (95 Nm).

Front Cover Oil Seal

REPLACEMENT

Except 3.8L Engine
FRONT COVER REMOVED

1. Using a suitable tool, pry the seal out from the front of the cover.

2. Using a suitable tool, install the new seal with the open end of the seal toward the inside of the front cover. Support the rear of the cover at the seal area while installing.

3. Inspect the sealing area of the vibration damper for damage or grooving and replace, as necessary. Coat the area which contacts the seal prior to installing. Tighten the vibration damper bolt to 70 ft. lbs. (95 Nm).

FRONT COVER INSTALLED

1. Disconnect the negative battery cable.

2. Remove the accessory drive belt and pulleys.

3. Remove the vibration damper using a suitable puller.

4. Pry the seal out of the front cover with a suitable prying tool.

5. Using a suitable installation tool, install the new seal with the open end of the seal toward the inside of the front cover.

6. Inspect the sealing area of the vibration damper for damage or grooving and replace as necessary. Coat the area which contacts the seal prior to installing. Tighten the vibration damper bolt to 70 ft. lbs. (95 Nm).

7. Install the accessory drive belt and pulleys and connect the negative battery cable.

3.8L Engine

1. Disconnect the negative battery cable.

2. Remove the front cover.

3. Use a suitable drift to drive out the old seal and shedder from the front toward the rear of the cover.

4. Coil new packing around the front cover opening so the ends of the packing are at the top.

5. Drive in the shedder using a suitable punch and stake the shedder in place at 3 locations.

6. Size the packing by rotating a suitable tool around the packing until the vibration damper hub can be inserted through the opening.

7. Installation is the reverse of the removal procedure. Inspect the sealing area of the vibration damper for damage or grooving and replace, as neces-

sary. Coat the area which contacts the seal prior to installing. Tighten the vibration damper bolt to 200 ft. lbs. (270 Nm).

Timing Chain and Sprockets

REMOVAL & INSTALLATION

1. Remove the timing chain cover. Remove the crankshaft oil slinger, if so equipped.

2. Crank the engine until the No. 1 piston is at TDC and the timing marks on the camshaft and crankshaft sprockets are aligned.

3. Remove the camshaft sprocket bolts and remove the camshaft sprocket and chain. Using a suitable puller, remove the crankshaft sprocket.

NOTE: The sprocket is a tight fit on the camshaft. If the sprocket does not come off easily, use a plastic mallet and strike the lower edge of the sprocket. This should dislodge the sprocket, allowing it to be removed from the shaft.

To install:

4. Install the crankshaft sprocket using a suitable installation tool. Install the timing chain on the camshaft sprocket and lube the thrust surface with Molykote® or equivalent.

5. Hold the sprocket vertically with the chain hanging down and align the marks on the camshaft and crankshaft sprockets.

6. Align the dowel in the camshaft with the dowel hole in the camshaft sprocket and install the sprocket on the camshaft.

7. Slowly and evenly draw the camshaft sprocket onto the camshaft using the mounting bolts and torque the bolts to 21 ft. lbs. (28 Nm) except 3.8L engines which are tightened to 31 ft. lbs. (42 Nm).

NOTE: Do not drive the sprocket onto the camshaft, this could cause the rear camshaft core plug to be dislodged.

8. Lubricate the timing chain and install the timing chain cover.

Camshaft

REMOVAL & INSTALLATION

2.8L and 3.1L Engines

1. Disconnect the negative battery cable. Relieve fuel pressure, discharge the air conditioning system and drain the cooling system.

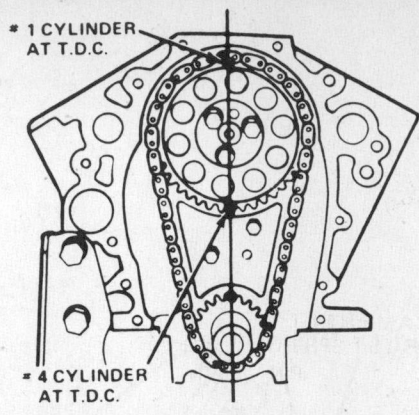

Aligning the timing gears—2.8L and 3.1L engines

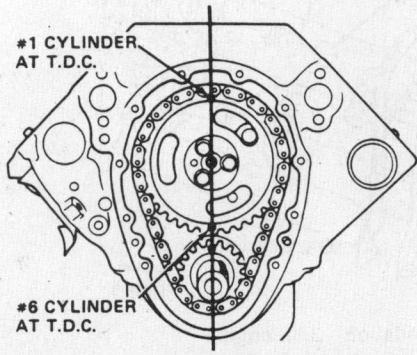

Timing chain alignment—Chevy produced V8 engine

2. Remove the valve covers. Remove the rocker arm assemblies and pushrods. Remove the intake manifold.

3. Remove the valve lifters.

4. As required, remove the radiator, grille and air conditioning condenser.

5. Remove the front engine cover.

6. Remove the timing chain and sprockets. Carefully remove the camshaft.

7. Installation is the reverse order of the removal procedure. Be sure to coat the camshaft lobes with

Molykote® or equivalent and the camshaft journals and lifters with clean engine oil before installation.

3.8L Engine

1. Disconnect the negative battery cable, drain the cooling system, relieve the fuel system pressure and discharge the air conditioning system.

3. Remove the intake manifold.

4. Remove the valve covers.

5. Remove the rocker arm assemblies, pushrods and valve lifters, noting location.

6. Remove the radiator and the air condition condenser, as required.

7. Remove the timing chain cover, timing chain and sprocket.

8. Align the timing marks of camshaft and crankshaft sprocket. This avoids burring of the camshaft journals by the crankshaft during removal.

9. Slide the camshaft forward out of the bearing bores carefully to avoid marring the bearing surfaces.

To install:

10. Installation is the reverse of the removal procedure.

11. Before installing the camshaft and the lifters, be sure to coat the camshaft lobes with Molykote® or equivalent, and the camshaft journals and lifters with clean engine oil.

12. Be sure to use new gaskets and seals, as required.

5.0L and 5.7L Engines

1. Disconnect the negative battery cable. Relieve fuel pressure as necessary and drain the cooling system.

2. Remove the intake manifold. Remove the valve covers, rocker arm assemblies, pushrods and lifters, keep all parts in order.

3. Remove all necessary wires and hoses. Disconnect the upper and lower transmission cooler lines.

4. Remove the radiator shroud assembly and radiator. Remove the front

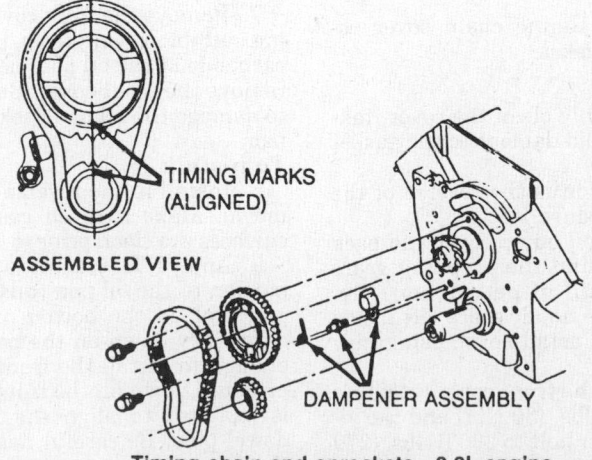

TIMING MARKS (ALIGNED)

ASSEMBLED VIEW

DAMPENER ASSEMBLY

Timing chain and sprockets—3.8L engine

grille, if necessary. Remove the cooling fan.

5. Remove the power steering pump and lay aside. Remove the drive belts, crankshaft pulley and vibration damper.

6. Remove the air conditioning compressor mount bolts, brackets, accumulator and compressor and position it out of the way. Remove the air injection pump with brackets and set it aside.

7. Remove the water pump assembly, remove the front engine cover. Remove the fuel pump pushrod, if equipped, with mechanical pump. Rotate the crankshaft and align the timing marks.

8. Remove the camshaft bolts, gear and chain. Install two $5/16$ in. × 4 in. bolts or equivalent, in the camshaft bolt holes and carefully remove the camshaft.

9. Installation is the reverse order of the removal procedure. Lubricate the camshaft lobes with Molykote® and the journals and lifters with a suitable engine oil supplement, before installing the camshaft.

Piston and Connecting Rod

POSITIONING

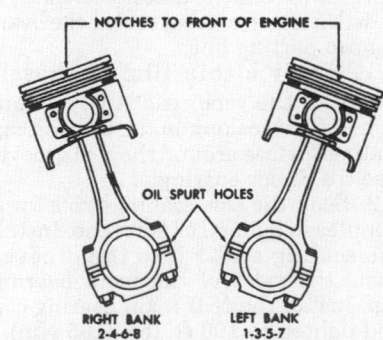

Piston identification—Chevy produced engines

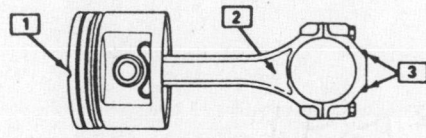

1. Notch on piston towards front of engine
2. Left bank: No. 1, 3 and 5—2 bosses on rod towards rear of engine
   Right bank: No. 2, 4 and 6—2 bosses on rod towards front of engine
3. Left bank: Chamfered corners on rod cap towards front of engine
   Right bank: Chamfered corners on rod cap towards rear of engine

Piston and rod positioning—3.8L engine

ENGINE LUBRICATION

Oil Pan

REMOVAL & INSTALLATION

1. Disconnect the negative battery cable. Remove the air cleaner assembly. Remove the plenum extension, if equipped. Remove the distributor cap and lay it aside.

2. Remove the upper half of the fan shroud assembly. Remove the air conditioning compressor, if necessary, and lay aside.

3. Raise the vehicle and support it safely. Drain the engine oil.

4. Remove the air injection pipe at the catalytic convertor. Remove the catalytic converter hanger bolts.

5. Remove the torque converter dust shield. If equipped with manual transmission, it may be necessary to remove the oil filter in order to remove the dust shield.

6. Remove the exhaust pipe at the manifolds.

7. Remove the starter bolts, loosen the starter brace, then lay the starter aside. On V8 engines, remove the front starter brace.

8. Disconnect the transmission oil cooler lines at the clips on the oil pan. Remove the front engine mount through bolts.

9. Raise the engine enough to provide sufficient clearance for oil pan removal.

10. Remove the oil pan bolts. If the front of the crankshaft prohibits removal of the pan, turn the crankshaft to position it horizontally.

11. Remove the oil pan from the vehicle.

12. Remove all old RTV from the oil pan and engine block.

To install:

13. Run a ⅛ in. bead of RTV around the oil pan sealing surface. Remember to keep the RTV on the inside of the bolt holes.

14. Install the oil pan. Tighten the 2 rear oil pan retaining bolts on the 2.8L and 3.1L engines to 18 ft. lbs. (25 Nm) and the rest of the retaining bolts and nuts to 89 inch lbs. (10 Nm). Tighten the oil pan retaining bolts on the 3.8L engine to 88 inch lbs. (10 Nm). Tighten the oil pan retaining bolts on 5.0L and 5.7L engines to 101 inch lbs. (11 Nm) and the retaining nuts to 17 ft. lbs. (23 Nm).

15. Lower the engine and install the remainder of the components.

16. Lower the vehicle and fill the engine with the proper type of motor oil to the required level.

17. Connect the negative battery cable, start the engine and check for leaks.

Oil Pump

REMOVAL & INSTALLATION

Except 3.8L Engine

1. Raise the vehicle and support safely.
2. Drain the oil.
3. Remove the oil pan.
4. Remove the oil pump bolt. Remove the oil pump with the extension shaft.
5. Installation is the reverse of the removal procedure. Using a suitable tool, install a new pickup screen and pipe to the replacement pump.
6. Prime the pump by turning it upside down and pouring clean oil into the pickup screen while turning the pump extension clockwise.
7. Align the slot on the end of the shaft extension with the drive tang on the distributor shaft.
8. Tighten the oil pump bolt on 2.8L and 3.1L engines to 30 ft. lbs. (41 Nm) and to 65 ft. lbs. (88 Nm) on 5.0L and 5.7L engines

3.8L Engine

NOTE: The oil pump is located on the left side of the timing chain cover. It is connected by a drilled passage in the cylinder crankcase, to an oil screen housing and stand pipe assembly.

1. Disconnect the negative battery cable.
2. Remove the oil filter.
3. Unbolt the pump cover assembly from the timing chain cover.
4. Remove the cover assembly and slide out the pump gears.
5. Remove the oil pressure relief valve cap, spring and valve. Do not remove the oil filter bypass valve and spring.
6. Check that the relief valve spring is not worn on the side, or collapsed.
7. Check that the relief valve is no more than an easy "slip-fit" in the bore in the cover.

NOTE: If there is any perceptible side play in the relief valve, replace the valve. If there is still side play, replace the cover also.

8. Check the filter bypass valve for wear. Replace if necessary.
To install:
9. Lubricate and install the pressure relief valve and spring in the cover bore.
10. Install the gasket and cap, torquing the cap to 35 ft. lbs.

11. Install the gears and check that gear-to-cover end clearance is between 0.002–0.006 in. If the clearance is not as specified, check the timing cover gear pocket for wear. If the gear pocket is worn, the timing cover must be replaced.

12. Remove the gears and pack the gear pocket full of petroleum jelly. Don't use grease.

NOTE: Unless the pump is primed this way, it won't produce any oil pressure when the engine is started.

13. Install the gears. Install a new gasket and the cover. Torque the bolts evenly to 10 ft. lbs. Replace the oil filter and check the oil level. Connect the negative battery cable.

CHECKING

NOTE: The oil pump housing on the 3.8L engine is part of the timing cover. If the housing is worn, the timing cover must be replaced.

1. Inspect pump housing and cover for cracks, scoring, casting imperfections and damaged threads.

2. Check idler gear shaft for play in pump body. If loose replace the oil pump except on 3.8L engine, where the timing cover should be replaced.

3. Check pressure regulator valve for sticking and pressure regulator spring for loss of tension.

4. Inspect the gears for chipping, galling or wear.

5. Inspect pick-up screen and pipe assembly for broken wire mesh or looseness. The pick-up screen and pipe are serviced as an assembly. The oil pan must be removed to check the pick-up screen and pipe on 3.8L engines.

Rear Main Bearing Oil Seal

REMOVAL & INSTALLATION

Except 3.8L Engine

1. Remove the transmission.
2. Remove the flywheel or flexplate.
3. Using a suitable prying tool, pry the old seal from the engine.
4. Coat the new seal with clean oil. Using tool J-34686 or equivalent, install the new seal.
5. Install the remainder of the components in the reverse order of their removal.

3.8L Engine

NOTE: The following procedure is only to be used as an oil

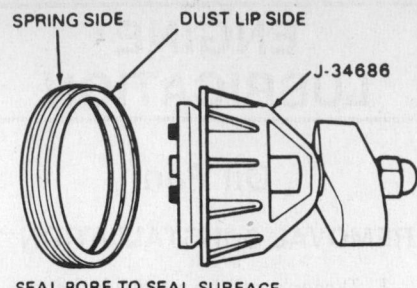

SPRING SIDE   DUST LIP SIDE   J-34686

SEAL BORE TO SEAL SURFACE
TO BE LUBRICATED
WITH ENGINE OIL BEFORE
ASSEMBLY

One piece seal installation tool positioning

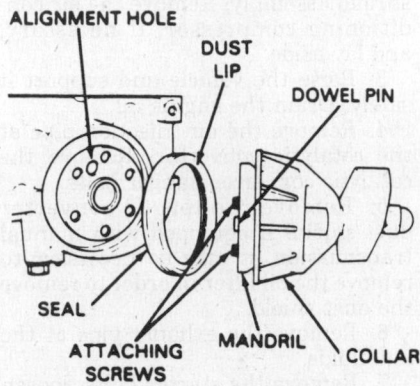

ALIGNMENT HOLE
DUST LIP
DOWEL PIN
SEAL
ATTACHING SCREWS
MANDRIL
COLLAR

One piece seal installation procedure

seal repair while the engine is in the vehicle. Whenever possible the crankshaft should be removed to install this type of rear main seal.

1. Disconnect the negative battery cable.

2. Drain the engine oil and remove the oil pan.

3. Remove the rear main bearing cap.

4. Insert packing tool J–21526–2 or equivalent, against 1 end of the seal in

the cylinder block. Drive the old seal gently into the groove until it is packed tight. This will vary from ¼ inch to ¾ inch depending on the amount of pack required.

5. Repeat Step 4 on the other end of the seal.

To install:

6. Measure the amount the seal was driven up on 1 side and add $\frac{1}{16}$ inch. Using a suitable cutting tool, cut that length from the old seal removed from the rear main bearing cap. Repeat the procedure for the other side. Use the rear main bearing cap as a holding fixture when cutting the seal.

7. Install guide tool J–21526–1 or equivalent, onto the cylinder block.

8. Using the packing tool, work the short pieces cut in Step 6 into the guide tool and then pack into the cylinder block. The guide tool and packing tool are machined to provide a built in stop. Use this procedure for both sides. It may help to use oil on the short pieces of the rope seal when packing into the cylinder block.

9. Remove the guide tool.

10. Apply Loctite 414 or equivalent, to the seal groove in the rear main bearing cap. Within 1 minute, insert a new seal into the groove and roll into place with a suitable tool until no more than $\frac{1}{16}$ inch of the seal projects above the groove. Cut the excess seal material with a sharp cutting tool at the bearing cap parting line.

11. Apply a thin film of chassis grease to the rope seal. Apply a thin film of RTV sealant on the bearing cap mating surface around the seal groove. Use the sealer sparingly.

12. Soak the side sealing strips for 5 minutes in light oil or kerosene. Install the sealing strips into the grooves along the sides of the main bearing cap. Install the rear main bearing cap and tighten to 100 ft. lbs. (135 Nm).

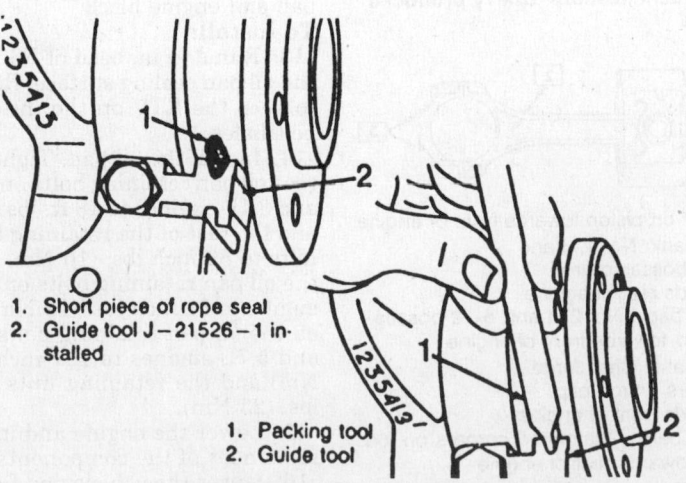

1. Short piece of rope seal
2. Guide tool J–21526–1 installed

1. Packing tool
2. Guide tool

Rear main seal installation—3.8L engine

13. Installation of the remainder of the components is the reverse of the removal procedure.

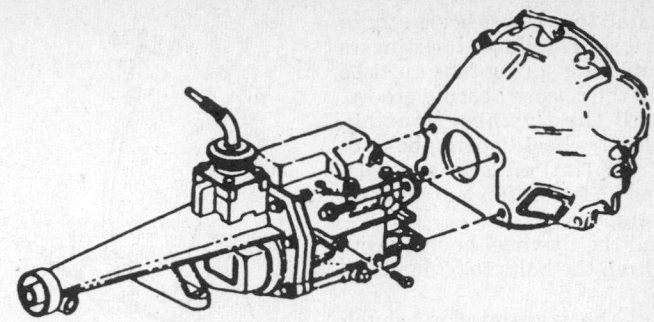

Transmission to engine attachment

MANUAL TRANSMISSION

For further information on transmissions/transaxles, please refer to "Chilton's Guide to Transmission Repair".

Transmission Assembly

REMOVAL & INSTALLATION

1. Disconnect the negative battery cable.
2. Remove the shift lever knob.
3. Raise and safely support the vehicle.
4. Drain the transmission fluid.
5. Remove the driveshaft.
6. Support the left side of the rear axle with an adjustable lifting device.

NOTE: The rear axle must be supported on the left side only or damage to the brake lines could result.

7. Remove the torque arm rear attaching bolts, the front torque arm outer bracket and the torque arm.
8. Disconnect the speed sensor connector or speedometer cable. Disconnect the backup light wiring harness connector.
9. Remove the catalytic converter hanger nuts and bolts and remove the catalytic converter hanger.
10. Support the engine with a suitable jackstand.
11. Remove the transmission mount nuts at the support, the support bolts and the support.
12. Lower the transmission enough to reach the shift lever control assembly. This may require the assistance of a helper.

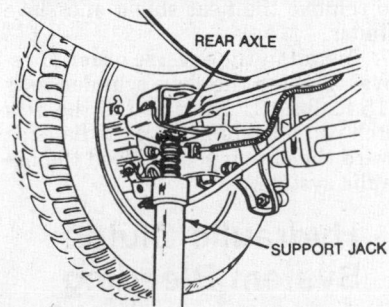

REAR AXLE

SUPPORT JACK

Rear axle support—left side

13. Remove the shift control assembly bolts and remove the shift control assembly from the extension housing.
14. Remove the transmission to flywheel housing bolts and with the aid of a helper, remove the transmission.
15. Installation is the reverse of the removal procedure.

LINKAGE ADJUSTMENT

The M39, MK6 and MB1 5-speed transmissions are designed with an internal shift mechanism. External linkage adjustment is not possible.

CLUTCH

Clutch Assembly

REMOVAL & INSTALLATION

1. Disconnect the negative battery cable.
2. Raise and safely support the vehicle.
3. Remove the transmission.
4. Remove the clutch slave cylinder heat shield and the slave cylinder from the flywheel housing. Remove the flywheel housing.
5. Slide the clutch fork from the ball stud and remove the fork from the dust boot.
6. Install tool J–33169 or equivalent to support the clutch assembly during removal. Look for a mark or white painted letters on the pressure plate and an **X** mark on the flywheel. If the **X** or letter is not evident, mark the flywheel and clutch cover for indexing purposes during installation.
7. Loosen the clutch-to-flywheel attaching bolts evenly 1 turn at a time until the spring pressure is released.
8. Remove the clutch and pressure plate assembly.
9. Inspect the flywheel for cracks, heat checks or other damage. Replace or machine as necessary. Check the clutch disc, pressure plate and release bearing for wear and oil, grease or metal contamination and replace as necessary. Check the pilot bearing for excessive wear or damage and replace, if necessary.

To install:

10. Clean the pilot bearing and lubricate with machine oil. Install the flywheel if it was removed and install the flywheel bolts. Tighten the bolts to 52 ft. lbs. (70 Nm) on 2.8L and 3.1L engines and 74 ft. lbs. (100 Nm) on 5.0L and 5.7L engines.
11. Position the clutch disc and pressure plate in the installed position and support them with a suitable alignment tool or a drive gear. The clutch disc is installed with the damper springs toward the transmission. The flywheel side is marked. Align the index marks on the pressure plate with the index marks on the flywheel. Install the clutch-to-flywheel bolts. Tighten alternate bolts, 1 turn at a time to avoid distorting the clutch assembly. Tighten the bolts to 15 ft. lbs. (21 Nm) on 2.8L and 3.1L engines and 30 ft. lbs. (40 Nm) on 5.0L and 5.7L engines.
12. Remove the alignment tool. Lubricate the clutch fork ball socket and the fingers at the release bearing using wheel bearing grease.

NOTE: If replacing the clutch fork, be sure to install the correct part number. The forks for the V6 and V8 engines appear very similar. Installing the wrong fork may destroy the clutch slave cylinder.

13. Inspect the clutch fork ball stud and replace if worn or damaged.
14. Install the clutch fork with the retaining spring onto the ball stud. The retaining spring tangs must be installed to the rear of the shoulder on the ball stud. Install the dust boot onto the clutch fork.
15. Lubricate the recess inside the release bearing collar and the clutch fork groove using wheel bearing

grease. Install the release bearing onto the clutch fork. The clutch fork fingers and the retaining spring tabs must be installed in the release bearing groove.

16. Install the flywheel housing. Tighten the flywheel housing bolts to 35 ft. lbs. (47 Nm) on 2.8L and 3.1L engines and 70 ft. lbs. (95 Nm) on 5.0L and 5.7L engines.

17. Install the flywheel housing cover and tighten the bolts to 53 inch lbs. (6 Nm).

18. Install the transmission, clutch slave cylinder and heat shield. Tighten the slave cylinder and heat shield bolts to 15 ft. lbs. (21 Nm).

19. Connect the negative battery cable.

PEDAL HEIGHT/FREE-PLAY ADJUSTMENT

The hydraulic clutch system locates the clutch pedal height and provides automatic clutch adjustment. No adjustment of clutch linkage or pedal position is required.

Clutch Master Cylinder

REMOVAL & INSTALLATION

1. Disconnect the negative battery cable.

2. Remove the steering column trim cover and lower panel or sound insulator, as necessary, to gain access to the clutch pedal.

3. Disconnect the brake vacuum booster pushrod from the brake pedal. Remove the retainer and washer.

4. Disconnect the clutch master cylinder input rod from the pedal. Use a sharp cutting tool to cut the bushing retaining tabs.

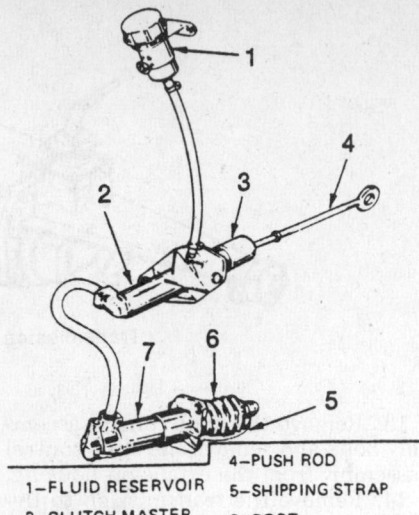

1—FLUID RESERVOIR
2—CLUTCH MASTER CYLINDER
3—BOOT
4—PUSH ROD
5—SHIPPING STRAP
6—BOOT
7—CLUTCH SLAVE CYLINDER

Hydraulic clutch assembly

5. Remove the clutch master cylinder-to-cowl nuts and the brake vacuum booster-to-cowl nuts.

6. Remove the hose clamp and the clutch fluid reservoir hose. Catch the fluid from the reservoir in a container.

7. Pull the brake vacuum booster forward to gain access to the clutch master cylinder. Remove the clutch master cylinder with U-bolt from the cowl. Lower the master cylinder down to the clutch housing area.

8. Raise and safely support the vehicle.

9. Disconnect the high pressure hose and remove the clutch master cylinder.

To install:

10. Connect the high pressure hose and place the master cylinder up near

the brake vacuum booster. Lower the vehicle.

11. Install the clutch master cylinder to the cowl with the U-bolt.

12. Install a new bushing to the pedal. Install the flat end of the bushing toward the pedal.

13. Install the clutch master cylinder input rod to the pedal. Install the retainer and washer.

14. Attach the brake vacuum booster to the cowl, connect the clutch fluid reservoir hose with the hose clamp and install the clutch master cylinder-to-cowl nuts. Tighten the nuts to 115 inch lbs. (13 Nm). Tighten the brake vacuum booster-to-cowl nuts to 15 ft. lbs. (21 Nm).

15. Replace the sound insulator or steering column trim panel and lower panel.

16. Connect the brake vacuum pushrod to the brake pedal.

17. Fill and bleed the hydraulic system. Connect the negative battery cable.

Clutch Slave Cylinder

REMOVAL & INSTALLATION

1. Disconnect the negative battery cable.

2. Remove the steering column trim cover and lower panel or sound insulator as necessary to gain access to the clutch pedal.

3. Disconnect the clutch master cylinder input rod from the clutch pedal. Using a sharp cutting tool, cut the bushing retaining tabs.

NOTE: Disconnect the clutch master cylinder input rod before removing the slave cylinder. If it is not disconnected, permanent damage to the slave cylinder will occur if the clutch pedal is depressed while the slave cylinder is disconnected.

4. Raise and safely support the vehicle.

5. Disconnect the pressure hose, catching the hydraulic fluid in a container.

6. Remove the slave cylinder bolts and remove the heat shield and slave cylinder.

7. Install in the reverse order of removal. Tighten the slave cylinder bolts to 15 ft. lbs. (21 Nm). Install the new clutch pedal bushing with the flat side toward the clutch pedal. Bleed the hydraulic system.

Hydraulic Clutch System Bleeding

1. Clean all dirt and grease from the

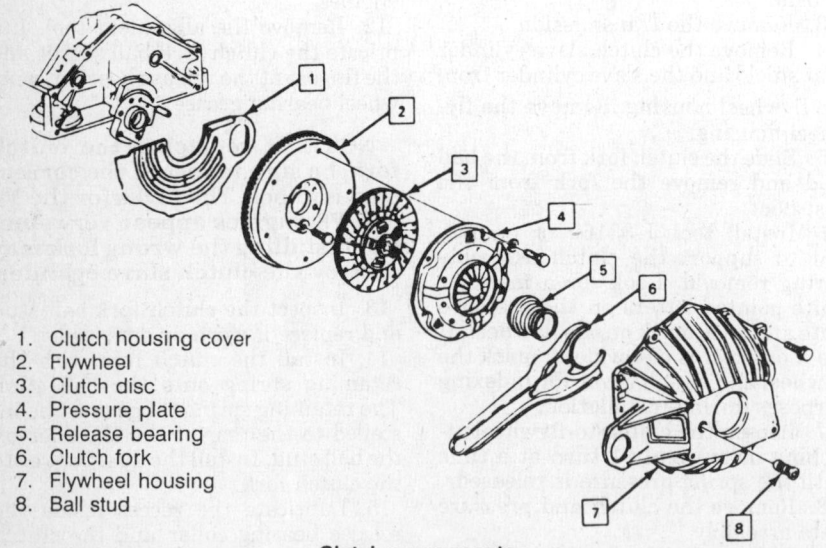

1. Clutch housing cover
2. Flywheel
3. Clutch disc
4. Pressure plate
5. Release bearing
6. Clutch fork
7. Flywheel housing
8. Ball stud

Clutch components

cap to make sure no foreign substances enter the system.

2. Remove the cap and diaphragm and fill the reservoir to the top with the approved DOT 3 brake fluid. Fully loosen the bleed screw which is in the slave cylinder body next to the inlet connection.

3. At this point, bubbles of air will appear at the bleed screw outlet. When the slave cylinder is full and a steady stream of fluid comes out of the slave cylinder bleeder, tighten the bleed screw to 18 inch lbs. (2 Nm).

4. Assemble the diaphragm and cap to the reservoir. Fluid in the reservoir should be level with the step. Exert a light load of about 20 lbs. to the slave cylinder piston by pushing the clutch fork towards the cylinder and loosening the bleed screw. Maintain a constant light load. Fluid and any air that is left will be expelled through the bleed port. Tighten the bleed screw when a steady flow of fluid and no air is being expelled.

5. Fill the reservoir fluid level back to normal capacity.

6. Exert a light load to the release lever but do not open the bleeder screw as the piston in the slave cylinder will move slowly down the bore. Repeat this operation 2–3 times. The fluid movement will force any air left in the system into the reservoir. The hydraulic system should now be fully bled.

7. Check the operation of the clutch hydraulic system and repeat this procedure if necessary. Check the push-rod travel at the slave cylinder to insure the minimum travel is 0.43 in. for 2.8L and 3.1L engines and 0.57 inch for 5.0L and 5.7L engines.

AUTOMATIC TRANSMISSION

For further information on transmissions/transaxles, please refer to "Chilton's Guide to Transmission Repair".

Transmission Assembly

REMOVAL & INSTALLATION

1. Disconnect the negative battery cable.
2. Remove the air cleaner assembly, if necessary.
3. Disconnect the Throttle Valve (TV) control cable at the throttle lever.
4. Remove the transmission oil dip-

stick. Unbolt and remove the dipstick tube.
5. Raise the vehicle and support it safely.
6. Mark the relationship between the driveshaft and the rear pinion flange so the driveshaft may be reinstalled in its original position.
7. Remove the driveshaft from the vehicle.
8. Disconnect the catalytic converter support bracket at the transmission.
9. Disconnect the speedometer cable, electrical connectors and the shift control cable from the transmission.
10. Remove the torque arm to transmission bolts.

NOTE: The rear spring force will cause the torque arm to move toward the floor pan. When disconnecting the arm from the transmission, carefully place a piece of wood between the floor pan and the torque arm. This will prevent possible personal injury and/or floor pan damage.

11. Remove the flywheel cover, then mark the relationship between the torque converter and the flywheel.
12. Remove the torque converter to flywheel attaching bolts.
13. Support the transmission with a jack, then remove the transmission mount bolt.
14. Unbolt and remove the transmission crossmember.
15. Lower the transmission slightly. Disconnect the TV cable and oil cooler lines from the transmission.
16. Support the engine. Remove the transmission to engine mounting bolts.
17. Remove the transmission from the vehicle. Keep the rear of the transmission lower than the front to avoid the possibility of the torque converter disengaging from the transmission.
To install:
18. Install the transmission in the vehicle.

19. Install and tighten the transmission to engine bolts to 35 ft. lbs. (47 Nm).
20. Connect the TV cable and oil cooler lines.
21. Install the crossmember.
22. Install and tighten the transmission crossmember to frame bolts to 40 ft. lbs. (54 Nm) and the crossmember to transmission mount nut to 35 ft. lbs. (47 Nm).
23. Install the torque converter to the flywheel, aligning the marks that were made prior to removal. Tighten the converter to flywheel bolts to 46 ft. lbs. (63 Nm).
24. Install the flywheel cover.
25. Connect the torque arm to the transmission.
26. Connect the speedometer cable, electrical connectors and the shift control cable.
27. Connect the catalytic converter support bracket.
28. Install the driveshaft, aligning the marks that were made on the driveshaft and pinion flange prior to removal.
29. Lower the vehicle.
30. Install the transmission dipstick and dipstick tube.
31. Connect the TV control cable at the throttle lever.
32. Install the air cleaner assembly, if necessary, and connect the negative battery cable.
33. Start the engine and check the transmission fluid.

SHIFT CONTROL CABLE ADJUSTMENT

1. Raise and safely support the vehicle.
2. Loosen the shift control cable attachment at the shift lever.
3. Rotate the shift lever clockwise to the **P** detent and then back to the **N** detent.
4. Tighten the cable attaching nut to 11 ft. lbs. (15 Nm). The lever must be held out of **P** when tightening the nut.

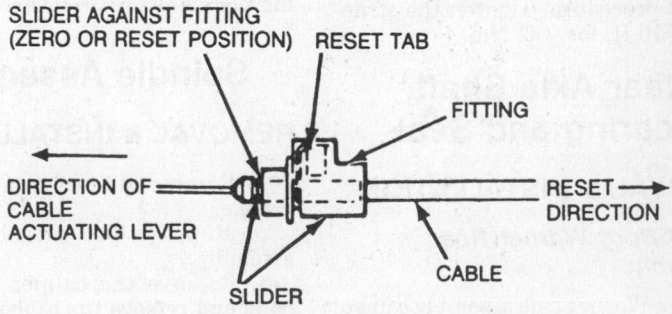

TV cable adjustment (part rotated 90 degrees)

5. Check cable adjustment by rotating the control lever through the detents.

THROTTLE VALVE CABLE ADJUSTMENT

Setting of the TV cable must be done by rotating the throttle lever at the carburetor or throttle body. Do not use the accelerator pedal to rotate the throttle body lever.

1. Stop the engine.
2. Depress and hold-down the metal reset tab at the engine end of the TV cable.
3. Move the slider until it stops against the fitting.
4. Release the reset tab.
5. Rotate the throttle lever to it's full travel position.
6. The slider must move (ratchet) toward the lever when the lever is rotated to it's full travel position.
7. Check that the cable moves freely. The cable may appear to function properly with the engine stopped and cold. Recheck after the engine is hot.

DRIVE AXLE

Driveshaft and U-Joints

REMOVAL & INSTALLATION

1. Raise and support the vehicle safely. Matchmark the pinion flange and driveshaft for assembly.
2. Remove the drive shaft strap bolts and remove the retaining straps.
3. Drop the driveshaft down at the rear, then pull it backwards out from the transmission extension housing. The transmission housing should be plugged to prevent leakage. If the bearing caps are loose, tape them together to prevent dropping and losing the bearing rollers.
4. Installation is the reverse of the removal procedure. Tighten the strap bolts to 16 ft. lbs. (22 Nm).

Rear Axle Shaft, Bearing and Seal

REMOVAL & INSTALLATION

Except Borg Warner Rear Assembly

The Borg Warner axle assembly can be quickly identified by checking the axle

code. The Borg Warner axle numbers are 4EW, 4EU and 4ET on 1987–88 vehicles, BET, BEU and BEW on 1989 vehicles and 9EQ and 9ER on 1990 vehicles.

1. Raise the vehicle and support it safely. Remove the rear wheels and drums or rotors.
2. Remove the carrier cover and drain.
3. Remove the rear axle pinion shaft lock screw. Remove the rear axle pinion shaft.
4. Remove the C-clip from the bottom end of the shaft by pushing the flanged end of the axle shaft into the axle housing.
5. Remove the axle shaft from the axle housing.
6. Using a suitable tool, remove the oil seal from the axle housing. Be careful not to damage the housing.
7. Install tool J–22813–01 or equivalent, into the bore of the axle housing, making sure it engages the bearing outer race. Remove the bearing, using slide hammer.
8. Installation is the reverse of the removal procedure. Lubricate the new bearing and sealing lips with gear lube before installing. Tighten the pinion gear shaft lock screw to 27 ft. lbs. (36 Nm). Tighten the carrier cover bolts to 22 ft. lbs. (30 Nm).

Borg Warner Rear Assembly

1. Raise the vehicle and support it safely.
2. Remove the rear wheels and drums or rotors. Remove the brake components as required.
3. Remove the 4 nuts holding the brake anchor plate and outer bearing retainer.
4. Remove the axle shaft and wheel bearing assembly using axle shaft removal tool J–21597 and slide hammer J–2619-01 or equivalent.
5. To remove the inner bearing retainer and the bearing from the axle shaft, split the retainer with a chisel and remove it from the shaft. Using tool J–22912–01, press the bearing off the shaft.
6. Installation is the reverse of the removal procedure. Tighten the backing plate bolts to 36 ft. lbs. (49 Nm).

Spindle Assembly

REMOVAL & INSTALLATION

1. Raise and safely support the vehicle.
2. Remove the wheel and tire assembly.
3. Remove the caliper mounting bolts and remove the caliper. Support the caliper with mechanics wire. Do

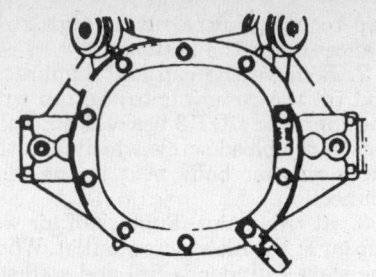

Rear axle cover—except Borg Warner

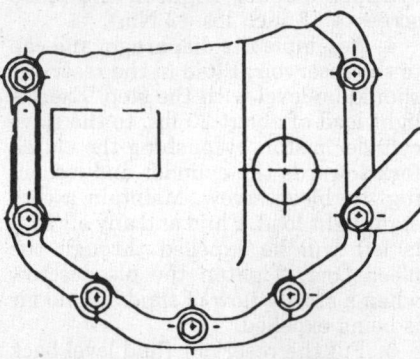

Rear axle cover—Borg Warner

not let the caliper hang by the brake hose.
4. Remove the dust cap from the hub and remove the cotter pin, nut and washer from the spindle. Remove the hub and rotor assembly from the spindle. Remove the splash shield.
5. Remove the outer wheel bearing assembly from the hub. Using a suitable tool, pry out the inner bearing lip seal and remove the inner wheel bearing assembly.
6. Using a suitable tool, disconnect the tie rod from the spindle.
7. Support the lower control arm. Using a suitable tool, disconnect the ball joint from the spindle.
8. Remove and discard 2 bolts, washers and nuts attaching the strut to the spindle and remove the spindle.
To install:
9. Position the spindle to the strut. Install new strut-to-spindle bolts, washers and nuts to the strut. Tighten the 2 nuts to 125 ft. lbs. (170 Nm) followed by an additional 120 degree turn. The final torque must exceed 148 ft. lbs. (200 Nm).
10. Connect the ball joint stud and nut to the spindle. Tighten the castle nut to 83 ft. lbs. (113 Nm) and install a new cotter pin. If the hole in the stud does not line up with a slot in the castle nut, continue to tighten the nut just enough to allow insertion of the cotter pin. Do not back off the nut to insert the cotter pin.
11. Connect the tie rod. Tighten the castle nut to 35 ft. lbs. (48 Nm). If the hole in the stud does not line up with a slot in the castle nut, continue to tight-

en the nut just enough to allow insertion of the cotter pin. Do not back off the nut to insert the cotter pin.

12. Install the splash shield.

13. Clean the hub, spindle and bearings of old grease and air dry. Inspect the bearings for cracked cages and worn or pitted rollers. Inspect the races for cracks or scores. Replace the bearings and races as assemblies, if necessary. If the bearings are to be replaced, remove the old bearing races with a suitable drift inserted behind the races.

14. If the races were removed, drive or press new races into the hub.

15. Apply a thin film of high temperature wheel bearing grease to the bearing and seal seat areas of the spindle. Put a small quantity of grease inboard of each bearing cup in the hub. Pack the wheel bearings with grease using a bearing packer. If a bearing packer is not available, the bearings may be greased by hand. If hand packing is used, it is extremely important to work the grease thoroughly into the bearings between the rollers, cone and cage.

16. Place the inner bearing into the hub. Put an additional quantity of grease outboard of the bearing. Install a new grease seal using a suitable tool. Lubricate the seal lip with a thin layer of grease.

17. Install the hub and rotor assembly. Place the outer bearing in the outer bearing cup and install the washer and nut.

18. Tighten the nut to 12 ft. lbs. (16 Nm) while turning the hub and rotor assembly forward by hand. This will seat the bearing. Put an additional quantity of grease outboard of the bearing. Back off the nut to the just loose position. Hand tighten the spindle nut. Loosen the spindle nut just enough that either hole in the spindle lines up with a slot in the nut (not more than ½ flat). Install a new cotter pin and the dust cap.

19. Using a dial indicator, check the hub assembly. There should be from 0.001–0.005 inch (0.03–0.13mm) endplay when properly adjusted.

20. Install the caliper to the steering knuckle. Tighten the caliper mounting bolts to 38 ft. lbs. (51 Nm).

21. Install the wheel and tire assembly and lower the vehicle. Check the brake fluid level.

Pinion Seal

REMOVAL & INSTALLATION

1. Raise and safely support the vehicle.

2. Remove both rear wheel and tire assemblies.

3. Remove the brake drums or rotors.

4. Matchmark the driveshaft and pinion yoke so they may be reassembled in the same position. Remove the driveshaft.

5. Using a suitable inch pound torque wrench, check the pinion preload and record. This will give the combined pinion bearing, carrier bearing, axle bearing and seal preload.

6. Using a suitable tool to hold the pinion flange in place, remove the pinion flange nut and washer.

7. Place a suitable container beneath the differential to catch any fluid that may drain from the rear axle. Using a suitable tool, remove the pinion flange.

8. Use a suitable tool to remove the pinion seal.

To install:

9. Inspect the seal surface of the pinion flange for tool marks, nicks or damage and replace, as necessary. Examine the carrier bore and remove any burrs that might cause leaks around the outside of the seal.

10. Install the seal using a suitable seal installer.

11. Apply suitable seal lubricant to the outer diameter of the pinion flange and the sealing lip of the new seal.

12. Install the pinion flange on the drive pinion by tapping with a suitable soft hammer until a few pinion threads project through the pinion flange.

13. Install the washer and pinion flange nut. While holding the pinion flange, tighten the nut a little at a time and turn the drive pinion several revolutions after each tightening, to set the bearing rollers. Check the preload each time with a suitable inch pound torque wrench until the preload is 3–5 inch lbs. (0.3–0.6 Nm) more than the reading obtained in Step 5.

14. Install the drive shaft and the drums or rotors.

15. Install the rear wheels and tires. Check and add the correct lubricant, as necessary.

Differential Carrier

REMOVAL & INSTALLATION

1. Raise and safely support the vehicle.

2. Place a suitable container beneath the differential to hold the differential fluid and remove the carrier cover.

3. Remove the axles.

4. Mark the differential bearing caps **L** and **R** to make sure they will be reassembled in their original location.

5. Using a suitable prying tool, remove the differential carrier. Be careful not to damage the gasket sealing surface when prying. Place the right and left bearing outer races of the side bearing assemblies and shims in sets with the marked differential bearing caps so they can be reinstalled in their original positions.

To install:

6. Inspect the differential carrier housing for foreign material. Check the ring and pinion for chipped teeth, excessive wear and scoring. Check the carrier bearings visually and by feel. Clean the differential housing and replace components, as necessary.

7. Install the differential carrier. Check the carrier bearing preload and ring and pinion backlash and adjust, as necessary. Tighten the differential bearing cap bolts to 55 ft. lbs. (75 Nm) except on Borg-Warner rear axles which are tightened to 40 ft. lbs. (54 Nm).

8. Install the axles.

9. Install the carrier cover using a new gasket. Tighten the carrier cover bolts to 20 ft. lbs. (27 Nm).

10. Lower the vehicle.

Axle Housing

REMOVAL & INSTALLATION

1. Raise the vehicle and support it safely.

2. Disconnect the shock absorbers from the axle. Remove the tire and wheel assemblies.

3. Mark the driveshaft and pinion flange, then disconnect the driveshaft and support out of the way.

4. Remove the brake line junction block bolt at the axle housing and disconnect the brake lines at the junction block.

5. Disconnect the control arms and the track bar from the axle housing.

6. Lower the rear axle assembly. Remove the springs.

7. Continue lowering the rear axle assembly and remove it from the vehicle.

8. Installation is the reverse of the removal procedure.

STEERING

Steering Wheel

CAUTION

On vehicles equipped with an air bag, the negative battery cable must be disconnected, before working on the system. Failure to do so may result in deployment of the air bag and possible personal injury.

REMOVAL & INSTALLATION

1987–89

1. Disconnect the negative battery cable.

2. Remove the horn pad.

3. Disconnect the horn contact lead.

4. Remove the retainer and steering wheel nut.

5. Using a suitable steering wheel puller, remove the steering wheel.

6. Installation is the reverse of the removal procedure. Make sure the turn signal lever is in the neutral position before installation. Tighten the steering wheel nut to 31 ft. lbs. (42 Nm).

1990–91

1. Disconnect the negative battery cable.

2. Disable the Supplemental Inflatable Restraint (SIR) system as follows:

  a. Turn the steering wheel so the vehicle's wheels are pointing straight ahead.

  b. Remove the SIR fuse from the fuse block.

  c. Remove the left sound insulator by removing the nut from the stud and gently prying the insulator from the knee bolster.

  d. Disconnect the Connector Position Assurance (CPA) and yellow 2-way SIR harness connector at the base of the steering column.

3. Loosen the screws and locknuts from the back of the steering wheel using a suitable Torx® driver or equivalent until the inflator module can be released from the steering wheel. Remove the inflator module from the steering wheel.

───────── CAUTION ─────────

When carrying a live inflator module, make sure the bag and trim cover are pointed away from the body. In case of an accidental deployment, the bag will then deploy with minimal chance of injury. When placing a live inflator module on a bench or other surface, always face the bag and trim cover up, away from the surface. This is necessary so a free space is provided to allow the air bag to expand in the unlikely event of accidental deployment. Otherwise, personal injury may result. Also, never carry the inflator module by the wires or connector on the underside of the module.

4. Disconnect the coil assembly connector and CPA from the inflator module terminal.

5. Remove the steering wheel locking nut.

6. Using a suitable puller, remove the steering wheel and horn contact. When attaching the steering wheel puller, use care to prevent threading the side screws into the coil assembly and damaging the coil assembly.

To install:

7. Route the coil assembly connector through the steering wheel.

8. Connect the horn contact and install the steering wheel. When installing the steering wheel, align the block tooth on the steering wheel with the block tooth on the steering shaft within 1 female serration.

9. Install the steering wheel locking nut. Tighten the nut to 31 ft. lbs. (42 Nm).

10. Connect the coil assembly connector and CPA to the inflator module terminal.

11. Install the inflator module. Make sure the wiring is not exposed or trapped between the inflator module and the steering wheel. Tighten the inflator module screws to 25 inch lbs. (2.8 Nm).

12. Connect the negative battery cable.

13. Enable the SIR system as follows:

  a. Connect the yellow 2-way SIR harness connector to the base of the steering column and CPA.

  b. Install the left sound insulator.

  c. Install the SIR fuse in the fuse block.

  d. Turn the ignition switch to **RUN** and verify that the inflatable restraint indicator flashes 7–9 times and then turns OFF. If the indicator does not respond as stated, a problem within the SIR system is indicated.

Steering Column

REMOVAL & INSTALLATION

1. Disconnect the negative battery cable.

2. On 1990–91 vehicles, disable the Supplemental Inflatable Restraint (SIR) system as follows:

  a. Turn the steering wheel so the vehicle's wheels are pointing straight ahead.

  b. Remove the SIR fuse from the fuse block.

  c. Remove the left sound insulator by removing the nut from the stud and gently prying the insulator from the knee bolster.

  d. Disconnect the Connector Position Assurance (CPA) and yellow 2-way SIR harness connector at the base of the steering column.

3. Remove the nut and bolt from the upper intermediate shaft coupling. Separate the coupling from the lower end of the steering column.

4. Remove the steering wheel, if the column is to be replaced or repaired on the bench.

5. Remove the knee bolster and bracket, if equipped.

6. Remove the bolts attaching the toe plate to the cowl.

7. Disconnect the electrical connectors.

8. Remove the capsule nuts attaching the steering column support bracket to the instrument panel.

9. Disconnect the park lock cable from the ignition switch inhibitor, on vehicles with automatic transmission.

10. Remove the steering column from the vehicle.

To install:

NOTE: **If a service replacement steering column is being installed, do not remove the anti-rotation pin until after the steering column has been connected to the steering gear. Removing the anti-rotation pin before the steering column is connected to the steering gear may damage the SIR coil assembly.**

11. Position the steering column in the vehicle.

12. Connect the park lock cable to the ignition switch inhibitor on vehicles with automatic transmission.

13. Install the capsule nuts attaching the steering column support bracket to the instrument panel and tighten to 20 ft. lbs. (27 Nm).

14. Install the nut and bolt to the upper intermediate shaft coupling attaching the upper intermediate shaft to the steering column. Tighten the nut to 44 ft. lbs. (60 Nm).

15. Install the bolts attaching the toe plate to the cowl and tighten to 58 inch lbs. (6.5 Nm).

16. Connect the electrical connectors.

17. Remove the anti-rotation pin if a service replacement steering column is being installed.

18. Install the knee bolster and bracket, if equipped.

19. Install the sound insulator panel.

20. If a service replacement steering column is being installed, remove the locking nut, remove the coil assembly shipping cover and disengage the connector from the cover.

21. Install the steering wheel.

22. Connect the negative battery cable.

23. Enable the SIR system as follows:

  a. Connect the yellow 2-way SIR harness connector to the base of the steering column and CPA.

  b. Install the left sound insulator.

  c. Install the SIR fuse in the fuse block.

  d. Turn the ignition switch to **RUN** and verify that the inflatable restraint indicator flashes 7–9 times

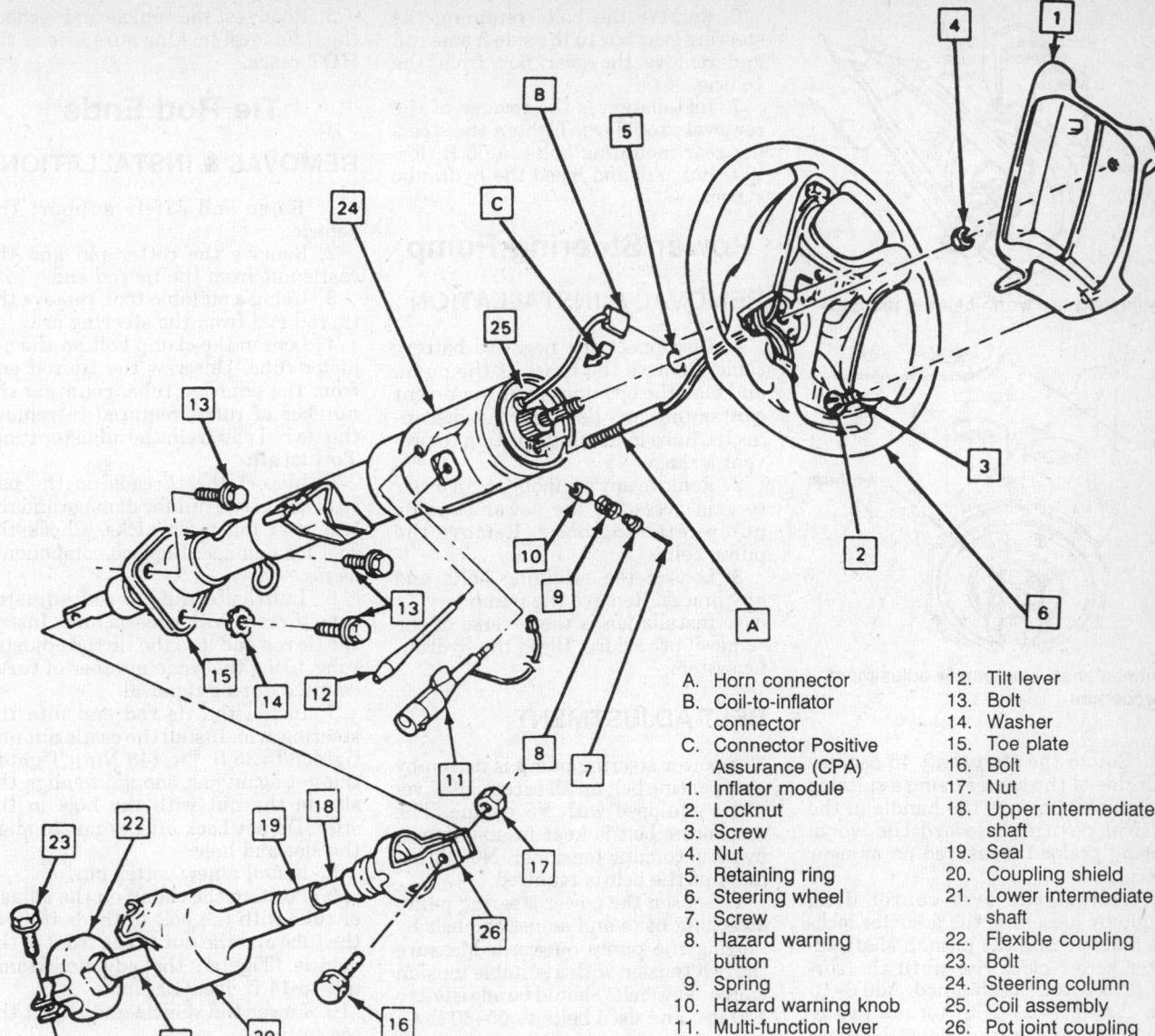

A. Horn connector
B. Coil-to-inflator connector
C. Connector Positive Assurance (CPA)
1. Inflator module
2. Locknut
3. Screw
4. Nut
5. Retaining ring
6. Steering wheel
7. Screw
8. Hazard warning button
9. Spring
10. Hazard warning knob
11. Multi-function lever
12. Tilt lever
13. Bolt
14. Washer
15. Toe plate
16. Bolt
17. Nut
18. Upper intermediate shaft
19. Seal
20. Coupling shield
21. Lower intermediate shaft
22. Flexible coupling
23. Bolt
24. Steering column
25. Coil assembly
26. Pot joint coupling

Steering column assembly with air bag

and then turns OFF. If the indicator does not respond as stated, a problem within the SIR system is indicated.

Power Steering Gear

ADJUSTMENT

Worm Bearing Preload

1. Disconnect the negative battery cable.
2. Remove the steering gear.
3. Rotate the stub shaft back and forth to drain the power steering fluid.
4. Remove the adjuster plug nut.
5. Turn the adjuster plug in (clockwise) using a suitable spanner wrench until the adjuster plug and thrust bearing are firmly bottomed in the housing. Tighten the adjuster plug to 20 ft. lbs. (27 Nm).
6. Place an index mark on the housing even with 1 of the holes in the adjuster plug.
7. Measure back counterclockwise ½ inch (13mm) and place a second mark on the housing.
8. Turn the adjuster plug counterclockwise until the hole in the adjuster plug is aligned with the second mark on the housing.
9. Install the adjuster plug nut and using a suitable punch in a notch, tighten securely. Hold the adjuster plug to maintain alignment of the marks.
10. Install the steering gear and connect the negative battery cable.

Pitman Shaft Over-Center

1. Disconnect the negative battery cable.
2. Remove the steering gear.
3. Rotate the stub shaft back and forth to drain the power steering fluid.
4. Turn the pitman shaft adjuster screw counterclockwise until fully extended, then turn back 1 full turn.
5. Rotate the stub shaft from stop to stop and count the number of turns.
6. Starting at either stop, turn the stub shaft back ½ the total number of turns. This is the "center" of the gear. When the gear is centered, the flat on the stub shaft should face upward and be parallel with the side cover and the master spline on the pitman shaft should be in line with the adjuster screw.

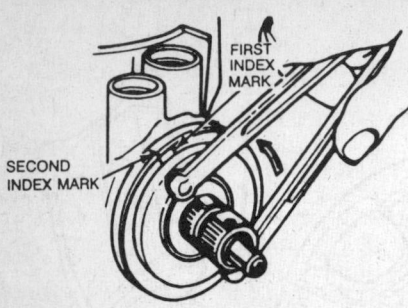

Adjusting the worm bearing preload

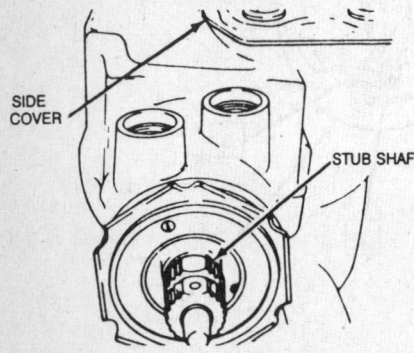

Pitman shaft over-center adjustment procedure

7. Rotate the stub shaft 45 degrees each side of the center using a suitable torque wrench with the handle in the vertical position. Record the worm bearing preload measured on or near the center.

8. Adjust the over-center drag torque by loosening the adjuster locknut and turning the pitman shaft adjuster screw clockwise until the correct drag torque is obtained: Add 6–10 inch lbs. (0.7–1.1 Nm) torque to the previously measured worm bearing preload torque. Tighten the adjuster locknut to 20 ft. lbs. (27 Nm). Prevent the adjuster screw from turning while tightening the adjuster screw locknut.

9. Install the steering gear and connect the negative battery cable.

REMOVAL & INSTALLATION

1. Disconnect the negative battery cable. Remove coupling shield, if equipped.

2. Remove the retaining nuts, lock washers and bolts at the steering coupling to steering shaft flange.

3. Disconnect and plug the pressure and return lines from the steering gear box. Plug the hoses and gearbox openings. Raise and safely support the vehicle.

4. Remove the pitman arm nut and washer. Matchmark the arm to the shaft.

5. With a puller, remove the pitman arm from the shaft.

6. Remove the bolts retaining the steering gear box to the side frame rail and remove the gear box from the vehicle.

7. Installation is the reverse of the removal procedure. Tighten the steering gear mounting bolts to 66 ft. lbs. (90 Nm). Fill and bleed the hydraulic system.

Power Steering Pump

REMOVAL & INSTALLATION

1. Disconnect the negative battery cable. Remove the hoses at the pump and tape the openings shut to prevent contamination. Position the disconnected lines in a raised position to prevent leakage.

2. Remove any components in order to gain access to the power steering pump retaining bolts. Remove the pump belt.

3. Loosen the retaining bolts and any braces. Remove the pump.

4. Installation is the reverse of the removal procedure. Bleed the hydraulic system.

BELT ADJUSTMENT

The power steering pump is driven by a serpentine belt on all except 1987 vehicles equipped with V8 engine. The serpentine belt is kept in adjustment by an automatic tensioner. No adjustment of the belt is required.

1. Loosen the power steering pump attaching bolts and adjust the belt by moving the pump outward. Measure the belt tension with a suitable tension gauge. New belts should be adjusted to 130 lbs. and used belts to 65–80 lbs.

NOTE: Do not move the pump by prying against the reservoir or by pulling on the filler neck, or damage may occur.

2. Tighten all pump mounting bolts and recheck the belt tension.

SYSTEM BLEEDING

1. With the wheels turned all the way to the left, add power steering fluid to the **COLD** mark on the fluid level indicator.

2. Start the engine and run at fast idle momentarily, shut the engine **OFF** and recheck the fluid level. If necessary, add fluid to to bring level to the **COLD** mark.

3. Start the engine and bleed the system by turning the wheels from side to side without hitting the stops.

4. Return the wheels to the center position and keep the engine running for a few minutes.

5. Road test the vehicle and recheck the fluid level making sure it is at the **HOT** mark.

Tie Rod Ends

REMOVAL & INSTALLATION

1. Raise and safely support the vehicle.

2. Remove the cotter pin and the castle nut from the tie rod end.

3. Using a suitable tool, remove the tie rod end from the steering arm.

4. Loosen the clamp bolt on the adjuster tube. Unscrew the tie rod end from the adjuster tube, counting the number of turns required to remove the tie rod end from the adjuster tube.

To install:

5. Inspect the threads on the ball stud and castle nut for damage and the ball stud taper for nicks. Check the seal for damage. Replace components as necessary.

6. Lubricate the tie rod adjuster tube threads with chassis lube. Install the tie rod end into the tie rod adjuster tube, using the same number of turns counted during removal.

7. Install the tie rod end into the steering arm. Install the castle nut and tighten to 35 ft. lbs. (48 Nm). Tighten the nut again just enough to align the slot in the nut with the hole in the stud. Do not back off the nut to align the slot and hole.

8. Install a new cotter pin.

9. Position the clamp on the adjuster tube with the bolt to the bottom of the tube and the nut to the front of the vehicle. Tighten the adjuster clamp nut to 14 ft. lbs. (19 Nm).

10. Lower the vehicle and adjust the toe setting.

BRAKES

For all brake system repair and service procedures not detailed below, please refer to "Brakes" in the Unit Repair section.

Master Cylinder

REMOVAL & INSTALLATION

1. Disconnect the negative battery cable.

2. Disconnect and plug the brake lines at the master cylinder.

3. Remove the 2 master cylinder attaching nuts.

4. On vehicles with manual transmission, move the clutch master cylinder and bracket out of the way.

5. Move the combination valve out of the way.

6. Remove the master cylinder.

7. Installation is the reverse of the removal procedure. Bench bleed the master cylinder prior to installation. Tighten the 2 attaching nuts to 18 ft. lbs. (25 Nm). Fill the master cylinder to the proper level and bleed the brake system.

Combination Valve

REMOVAL & INSTALLATION

1. Disconnect the negative battery cable.

2. Disconnect and plug the brake lines at the combination valve.

3. Disconnect the electrical connector from the combination valve switch terminal.

4. Remove the 2 nuts attaching the combination valve to the booster.

5. On vehicles with manual transmission, move the clutch master cylinder and bracket out of the way.

6. Remove the combination valve.

7. Installation is the reverse of the removal procedure. Tighten the 2 combination valve attaching nuts to 18 ft. lbs. (25 Nm). Bleed the brake system.

Power Brake Booster

REMOVAL & INSTALLATION

1. Disconnect the negative battery cable.

2. Disconnect the vacuum hose from the vacuum check valve.

3. On vehicles with manual transmission, remove the clutch master cylinder bracket with the clutch master cylinder and move out of the way.

4. Remove the combination valve with the attached combination valve bracket and move out of the way.

5. Remove the master cylinder from the booster.

6. Working inside the vehicle, remove the retainer and disconnect the booster pushrod from the brake pedal. Remove the booster attaching nuts.

7. Remove the power brake booster.

8. Install in the reverse order of removal. Tighten the booster attaching nuts to 15 ft. lbs. (21 Nm). Tighten the master cylinder attaching nuts to 18 ft. lbs. (25 Nm).

Brake Caliper

REMOVAL & INSTALLATION
Front

SINGLE PISTON

1. Remove ⅔ of the brake fluid from the master cylinder.

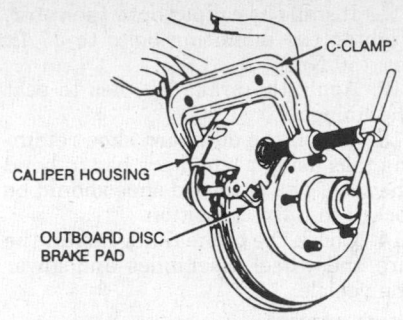

Compressing the caliper piston

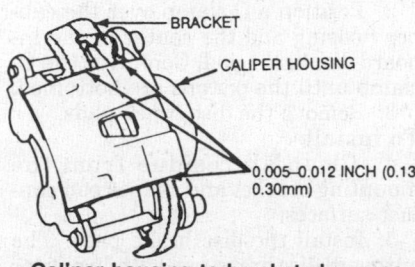

Caliper housing to bracket clearance

2. Raise and safely support the vehicle.

3. Remove the wheel and tire assembly.

4. Bottom the piston into the caliper bore using a suitable C-clamp. Position the C-clamp over the outboard disc brake pad and the caliper housing.

5. Remove the bolt, copper washers and inlet fitting from the caliper housing. Plug the openings in the inlet fitting and caliper housing to prevent fluid loss and contamination.

6. Remove the mounting bolts and sleeves.

7. Remove the caliper assembly from the rotor and bracket.

To install:

8. Inspect the mounting bolts and sleeves for damage or corrosion and replace as necessary. Check the inlet fitting bolt for blockage.

9. Lubricate the sleeves and bushings with silicone grease and install the sleeves into the caliper housing.

10. Install the caliper assembly onto the rotor and bracket. Install the mounting bolts and tighten to 37 ft. lbs. (50 Nm).

11. Measure the clearance between the caliper housing and the stops on the bracket. The clearance should be 0.005–0.012 inch (0.13–0.30mm). If necessary, remove the caliper assembly and file the ends of the stops on the bracket to provide proper clearance.

12. Install the bolt, new copper washers and the inlet fitting to the caliper housing. Tighten the bolt to 32 ft. lbs. (44 Nm).

13. Install the wheel and tire assembly and lower the vehicle.

14. Fill the master cylinder and bleed the caliper.

DUAL PISTON

1. Remove ⅔ of the brake fluid from the master cylinder.

2. Raise and support the vehicle safely.

3. Remove the wheel and tire assembly.

4. Remove the bolt, inlet fitting and 2 washers from the caliper housing. Plug the openings in the caliper housing and inlet fittings.

5. Remove the circlip and retainer pin.

6. Remove the caliper housing from the rotor and mounting bracket.

To install:

7. Check the inlet fitting bolt for blockage and clear or replace as necessary.

8. Install the caliper housing over the rotor and onto the mounting bracket. Make sure the guiding surfaces on the inboard and outboard disc brake pads and mounting bracket are seated correctly.

9. Press the caliper housing down to compress the bias springs and slide a new retainer pin into position and install a new circlip.

10. Install the inlet fitting, bolt and 2 new washers. Tighten the bolt to 30 ft. lbs. (40 Nm).

11. Bleed the brakes.

12. Install the wheel and tire assembly and lower the vehicle.

13. With the engine running, pump the brake pedal slowly and firmly 3 times to seat the brake pads.

Rear

1. Raise and safely support the vehicle.

2. Loosen the parking brake cable at the equalizer.

3. Remove the wheel and tire assembly. Install 2 wheel nuts to retain the rotor.

4. Remove the bolt, inlet fitting and washers from the caliper housing. Plug the holes in the caliper housing and inlet fitting.

5. Remove the caliper lever return spring only if it is defective. Discard the spring if the coils are opened.

6. Disconnect the parking brake cable from the caliper lever and caliper bracket.

7. Remove the 2 caliper guide pin bolts.

8. Remove the caliper housing from the rotor and mounting bracket.

To install:

9. Inspect the guide pins and boots and replace if corroded, worn or damaged. Check the inlet fitting bolt for blockage.

10. Install the caliper housing over the rotor and into the mounting bracket. Install the 2 caliper guide pin bolts. Tighten the upper caliper guide pin

bolt to 26 ft. lbs. (35 Nm) and the lower guide pin bolt to 16 ft. lbs. (22 Nm).

11. Connect the parking brake cable to the caliper bracket and caliper lever. Install the caliper lever return spring, if removed.

12. Install the inlet fitting, bolt and 2 new washers to the caliper housing. Tighten the bolt to 22 ft. lbs. (30 Nm).

13. Bleed the brake system.

14. Adjust the parking brake free travel if the caliper was overhauled.

15. Lower the vehicle and cycle the parking brake.

16. Raise and safely support the vehicle.

17. Inspect the caliper parking brake levers to make sure they are against the stops on the caliper housing. If the levers are not on their stops, check the parking brake adjustment.

18. Remove the 2 nuts securing the rotor and install the wheel and tire assembly. Lower the vehicle.

19. With the engine running, pump the brake pedal slowly and firmly 3 times to seat the disc brake pads. Check the hydraulic system for leaks.

Disc Brake Pads

REMOVAL & INSTALLATION

Front

SINGLE PISTON

1. Raise and safely support the vehicle.

2. Remove the wheel and tire assemblies.

3. Remove the caliper mounting bolts.

4. Position a C-clamp over the outboard disc brake pad and the caliper housing. Tighten it until the caliper piston bottoms in its bore. Remove the C-clamp.

5. Pivot the caliper off of the rotor. Do not allow the caliper to hang by the brake hose, suspend it with a length of wire.

6. Remove the disc brake pads.

7. Remove the bushings from the mounting bolt holes.

To install:

8. Lubricate the bushings with silicone grease and install the bushings into the mounting bolt holes.

9. Install the retaining spring on the inboard pad in the correct position. Install the inboard pad into the caliper with the wear sensor at the leading edge of the pad. Snap the retaining spring into position. The pad must lay flat against the piston. If it does not, use a large pair of pliers to compress the piston.

10. Install the outboard pad. The pad must lay flat against the caliper housing.

11. Install the caliper onto the rotor. Tighten the mounting bolts to 37 ft. lbs. (50 Nm).

12. Apply the brake 3 times to seat the linings.

13. Clinch the outboard shoe retaining tabs using a small pry bar to bend the tabs. The outboard shoe should be locked in a fixed position.

14. Check the brake fluid. Install the tire and wheel assemblies and lower the vehicle.

DUAL PISTON

1. Remove the caliper assembly.

2. Position a C-clamp over the caliper housing and the center of the inboard disc brake pad. Compress the C-clamp until the pistons are bottomed.

3. Remove the disc brake pads.

To install:

4. Clean all residue from the mounting bracket and caliper pad contact surfaces.

5. Install the disc brake pads. The outboard disc brake pad with insulator is installed in the caliper housing. The inboard brake pad with wear sensor is pressed into the caliper pistons. Push the pads in firmly until they are flush and fully seated in the caliper housing.

6. Install the caliper and bleed the brake system.

Rear

1. Remove ⅔ of the brake fluid from the master cylinder reservoir.

2. Raise and safely support the vehicle.

3. Remove the wheel and tire assembly. Install 2 wheel nuts to retain the rotor.

4. Position a C-clamp and tighten until the piston bottoms in the base of the caliper housing. Make sure 1 end of the C-clamp rests on the inlet fitting bolt and the other against the outboard disc brake pad.

NOTE: It is not necessary to remove the parking brake caliper lever return spring to replace the disc brake pads.

5. Remove the upper caliper guide pin bolt and discard.

6. Rotate the caliper housing about the lower caliper mounting bolt and guide pin. Be careful not to strain the hose or cable conduit.

7. Lift out the disc brake pads.

To install:

8. Clean all residue from the pad guide surfaces on the mounting bracket and caliper housing. Inspect the guide pins for free movement in the mounting bracket. Replace the guide pins or boots, if they are corroded or damaged.

9. Install the disc brake pads. The outboard pad with insulator is installed toward the caliper housing. The inboard pad with the wear sensor is installed nearest the caliper piston. The wear sensor must be in the trailing position with forward wheel rotation.

10. Rotate the caliper housing into it's operating position. The springs on the outboard brake pad must not stick through the inspection hole in the caliper housing. If the springs are sticking through the inspection hole in the caliper housing, lift the caliper housing and make the necessary corrections to the outboard brake pad positions.

11. Install a new upper caliper guide pin bolt and tighten to 26 ft. lbs. (35 Nm). Tighten the lower caliper guide pin bolt to 16 ft. lbs. (22 Nm).

12. With the engine running, pump the brake pedal slowly and firmly to seat the brake pads.

13. Check the caliper parking brake levers to make sure they are against the stops on the caliper housing. If the levers are not on their stops, check the parking brake adjustment.

14. Remove the 2 wheel nuts from the rotor and install the wheel and tire assembly.

15. Lower the vehicle and fill the master cylinder reservoir.

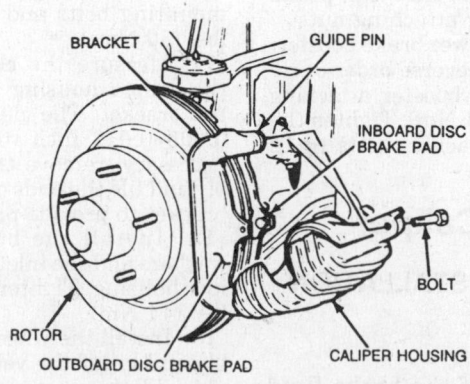

Rear disc brake pad installation

Brake Rotor

REMOVAL & INSTALLATION

Front

1. Raise and support the vehicle safely.
2. Remove the wheel and tire assembly.
3. Remove the caliper assembly.
4. Remove the dust cap from the hub. Remove the cotter pin, nut and washer from the spindle.
5. Remove the hub and rotor assembly.
6. Install in the reverse order of removal. Check the rotor for scoring or damage and machine or replace, as necessary. If machining, check the minimum thickness specification. Adjust the wheel bearings as follows:

   a. Tighten the spindle nut to 12 ft. lbs. (16 Nm) while turning the rotor forward by hand to fully seat the bearings.

   b. Back off the nut to the just loose position.

   c. Hand tighten the spindle nut. Loosen the spindle nut just enough that either hole in the spindle lines up with a slot in the nut, not more than ½ flat.

   d. Install a new cotter pin.

   e. Using a dial indicator, check the hub and rotor assembly. There should be 0.001–0.005 inch (0.03–0.13mm) endplay when properly adjusted.

Rear

1. Raise and support the vehicle safely.
2. Remove the wheel and tire assembly.
3. Remove the caliper assembly.
4. Remove the caliper mounting bracket.
5. Remove the brake rotor.
6. Install in the reverse order of removal.
7. Apply bolt adhesive to 2 new caliper mounting bracket bolts and tighten them to 70 ft. lbs. Recheck the torque on both bolts immediately. Allow the bolt adhesive to dry for 2 hours before operating the vehicle.
8. Tighten the upper caliper guide pin bolt to 26 ft. lbs. (35 Nm) and the lower caliper guide pin bolt to 16 ft. lbs. (22 Nm).

Brake Drums

REMOVAL & INSTALLATION

1. Raise and support the vehicle safely.
2. Remove the wheel and tire assembly.

3. Remove the brake drum. If the brake drum is difficult to remove, try the following:

   a. Make sure the parking brake is released.

   b. Back off the parking brake cable adjustment.

   c. Remove the adjusting hole cover or knockout plate from the backing plate and back off the adjusting screw, using suitable brake adjusting tools.

   d. Use a suitable rubber mallet to tap gently on the outer rim of the drum and/or around the inner drum diameter by the spindle. Be careful not to deform the drum by excessive use of force.
4. Install in the reverse order of removal. Adjust the brake shoes.

Brake Shoes

REMOVAL & INSTALLATION

1. Raise and safely support the vehicle.
2. Remove the wheel and tire assemblies.
3. Remove the brake drum.
4. Remove the return springs.
5. Remove the hold-down springs and pins. Remove the lever pivot.
6. Remove the actuator link while lifting up on the actuator lever.
7. Remove the actuator lever and lever return spring.
8. Remove the shoe guide, parking brake strut and strut spring.
9. Remove the brake shoes, after removing the parking brake cable from the shoe.
10. Remove the adjusting screw assembly and spring. Remove the retaining ring, pin and parking brake lever from the secondary shoe.

To install:

NOTE: Any part or spring which may appear worn should be replaced. The short shoe (primary) should be installed to the front of the vehicle and the long shoe (secondary) should be installed to the rear. After complete installation of the brake shoes a clicking sound should be heard when turning the adjusting screw or self-adjuster.

11. Install the parking brake lever on the secondary shoe with the pin and new retaining ring.
12. Install the adjusting screw and spring. Lubricate the adjusting screw with brake (white) grease.
13. Install the brake shoe assemblies after installing the parking brake cable on the shoe.

14. Install the parking brake strut and strut spring by spreading the shoes apart.
15. Install the shoe guide, actuator lever and lever return spring.
16. Install the hold-down pins, lever pivot and springs. Install the actuator link on the anchor pin.
17. Install the actuator link into the actuator lever while holding up on the lever.
18. Install the shoe return springs. Install the brake drum. Install the wheel and tire assemblies.
19. Adjust the brake shoes and lower the vehicle.

Wheel Cylinder

REMOVAL & INSTALLATION

1. Raise and support the vehicle safely.
2. Remove the tire and wheel assembly.
3. Remove the brake components.
4. Insert awls or pins, ⅛ in. diameter or less, into the access slots between the wheel cylinder pilot and retainer locking tabs.
5. Bend both tabs away simultaneously until they spring over the abutment shoulder releasing the wheel cylinder. Discard the old retaining clip.

To install:

6. For ease of installation hold the wheel cylinder against the backing plate by inserting a block betwen the wheel cylinder and the axle shaft flange.
7. Position the wheel cylinder retainer clip so the tabs will be away from and in a horizontal position with the backing plate when installing.
8. Press the new retaining clip over the wheel cylinder abutment and into position using a 1⅛ in. 12 point socket. Make sure the retainer tabs are properly snapped under the abutment shoulder.
9. Install the brake components, drum and wheel and tire assembly. Bleed the hydraulic system.

Parking Brake Cable

ADJUSTMENT

The parking brake cable is adjustable only on 1987–89 vehicles. 1990–91 vehicles feature a self-adjusting parking brake.

Except Rear Disc Brakes

1987–89

1. Pull the parking brake hand lever exactly 2 ratchet clicks.

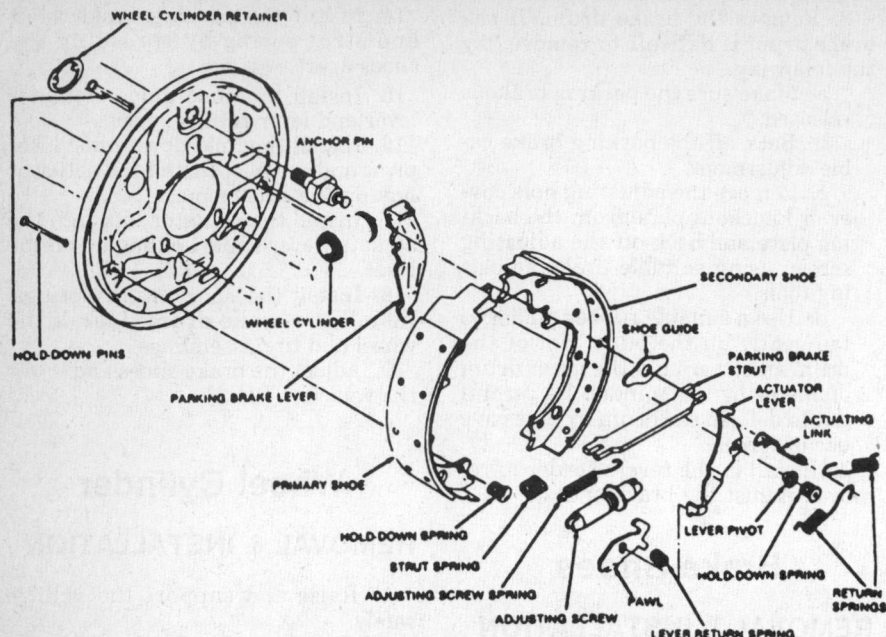

Rear brake shoe assembly

2. Raise the rear of the vehicle and support it safely.

3. Tighten the brake cable adjusting nut until the left rear wheel can be turned rearward with both hands but locks when forward rotation is attempted.

4. Release the parking brake pedal; both rear wheels must turn freely in either direction without brake drag. Be sure the parking brake cables are not adjusted too tightly causing the brakes to drag.

5. Lower the vehicle.

Rear Disc Brakes

1987–89

1. Apply the brake pedal 3 times with a pedal force of approximately 175 lbs. Apply and release the parking brake 3 times.

2. Raise and safely support the vehicle.

3. Check the parking brake hand lever for full release:

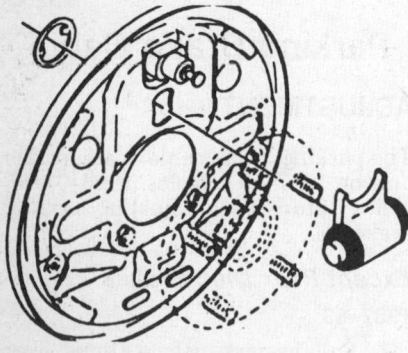

Wheel cylinder mounting

a. Turn the ignition switch **ON**.

b. The brake warning lamp should be OFF. If the brake warning lamp is still ON and the parking brake hand lever is completely released, pull downward on the front parking brake cable to remove slack from the lever assembly.

c. Turn the ignition switch **OFF**.

4. Remove the rear wheels and tires. Reinstall 2 wheel nuts on each side to retain the brake rotors.

5. The parking brake levers on both calipers should be against the lever stops on the caliper housings. If the levers are not against the stops, check for binding in the rear cables and/or loosen the cables at the equalizer adjusting nut until both left and right levers are against their stops.

6. Adjust the equalizer adjusting nut until the parking brake levers on both calipers just begin to move off of their stops.

7. Back off the adjuster nut until the levers move back, barely touching their stops.

8. Operate the parking brake hand lever several times to check adjustment. After cable adjustment, the parking brake hand lever should travel no more than 16 ratchet clicks. The rear wheels should not turn forward when the parking brake hand lever is applied 12–16 ratchet clicks.

9. Release the parking brake hand lever. Both rear wheels must turn freely in both directions. The parking brake levers on both calipers should be resting on their stops.

10. Remove the wheel nuts retaining the rotors. Install the wheels and tires.

11. Lower the vehicle.

REMOVAL & INSTALLATION

Front Cable

1987–89

1. Raise and safely support the vehicle.

2. Remove the adjusting nut at the equalizer and remove the front cable from the equalizer and bracket.

3. Lower the vehicle.

4. Remove the upper console and lower console rear screws. Lift the rear of the lower console to gain access to the parking brake control.

5. Remove the pin and retainer from the control assembly and front cable.

6. Remove the cable and casing from the control assembly and bracket and remove the cable and grommet from the vehicle.

7. Installation is the reverse of the removal procedure. Adjust the parking brake.

1990–91

1. Remove the carpet finish moulding.

2. Remove the console.

3. With the parking brake lever in the down position, rotate the arm toward the front of the vehicle until a 3mm metal pin can be inserted into the hole. Insert the metal pin into the hole, locking out the self adjuster.

4. Raise and safely support the vehicle.

5. Disconnect the rear cables from the equalizer.

6. Remove the front cable from the bracket using a fabricated parking brake cable retainer compressor tool.

7. Remove the grommet from the hole.

8. Lower the vehicle.

9. Remove the barrel-shaped button from the adjuster track.

10. Remove the front cable and casing from the control assembly using a fabricated parking brake cable retainer compressor tool.

11. Remove the front cable from the floor pan.

12. Install in the reverse order of removal.

Rear Cable

EXCEPT REAR DISC BRAKES

1. Raise and safely support the vehicle.

2. Pull the equalizer rearward to gain the necessary cable slack. Insert a spacer to hold the equalizer in place. Remove the left and/or right rear cable from the equalizer.

3. Compress the retainer fingers on the casing and pull the left and/or

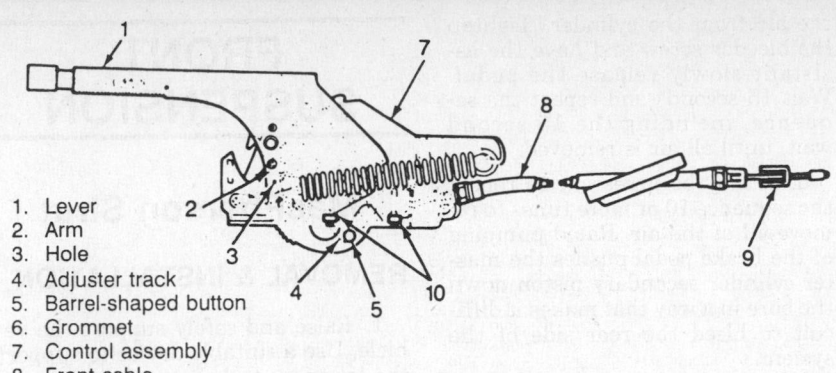

1. Lever
2. Arm
3. Hole
4. Adjuster track
5. Barrel-shaped button
6. Grommet
7. Control assembly
8. Front cable
9. Equalizer
10. Bolt

Parking brake control and front cable—1989–91

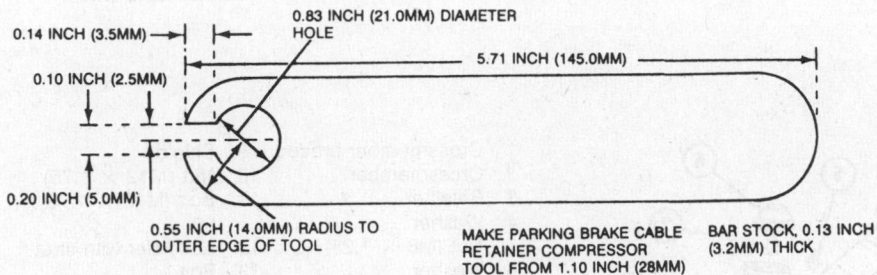

0.14 INCH (3.5MM)
0.10 INCH (2.5MM)
0.20 INCH (5.0MM)
0.55 INCH (14.0MM) RADIUS TO OUTER EDGE OF TOOL
0.83 INCH (21.0MM) DIAMETER HOLE
5.71 INCH (145.0MM)
MAKE PARKING BRAKE CABLE RETAINER COMPRESSOR TOOL FROM 1.10 INCH (28MM)
BAR STOCK, 0.13 INCH (3.2MM) THICK

Fabricated parking brake cable retainer compressor tool

right rear cable out of the seat belt plate.

4. On the left side, pull the left rear cable through the clip on the axle housing.

5. On the right side, remove the screw and clamp from the right rear cable.

6. Remove the wheel(s) and tire(s).

7. Remove the brake drum(s).

8. Disconnect the left and/or right rear cable from the brake shoe operating lever.

9. Compress the retainer fingers and pull the left and/or right cable from the backing plate.

10. Install in the reverse order of removal. Adjust the parking brake on 1987–89 vehicles.

REAR DISC BRAKES

1. Raise and safely support the vehicle.

2. Pull the equalizer rearward to gain the necessary cable slack. Insert a spacer to hold the equalizer in place. Remove the left and/or right rear cable from the equalizer.

3. Compress the retainer fingers on the casing and pull the left and/or right rear cable out of the seat belt plate.

4. On the left side, pull the left rear cable through the clip on the axle housing.

5. On the right side, remove the

screw and clamp from the right rear cable.

6. Remove the wheel(s) and tire(s).

7. Push forward on the caliper lever(s). Remove the left and/or right rear cable from the tang on the caliper lever(s). Release the caliper lever(s).

8. Compress the retainer fingers on the cable casing and pull out of the bracket(s).

9. Install in the reverse order of removal. Adjust the parking brake on 1987–89 vehicles.

Parking Brake Free-Travel

ADJUSTMENT

Parking brake free-travel adjustment is possible only on 1989–91 rear disc brake equipped vehicles.

Rear Disc Brakes

1989–91

NOTE: Disc brake pads must be new or parallel to within 0.006 inch (0.15mm). Parking brake adjustment is not valid with heavily tapered pads and may cause caliper/parking brake binding. Replace tapered brake pads. Parking brake free-travel should only be made if the caliper has been

taken apart. This adjustment will not correct a condition where the caliper levers will not return to their stops.

1. Have an assistant apply a light brake pedal load, enough to stop the rotor from turning by hand. This takes up all clearances and ensures that components are correctly aligned.

2. Apply light pressure to the caliper lever.

3. Measure the free-travel between the caliper lever and the caliper housing. The free-travel must be 0.024–0.028 inch (0.6–0.7mm).

4. If the free-travel is incorrect, do the following:

a. Remove the adjuster screw.

b. Clean the thread adhesive residue from the threads.

c. Coat the threads with adhesive.

d. Screw in the adjuster screw far enough to obtain 0.024–0.028 inch (0.6–0.7mm) free-travel between the caliper lever and the caliper housing.

5. Have an assistant release the brake pedal, then apply the brake pedal firmly 3 times. Recheck the free-travel and adjust as necessary.

Brake System Bleeding

1. Remove the vacuum reserve by applying the brakes several times, with the engine **OFF**.

2. Fill the master cylinder reservoir with brake fluid and keep it at least half full of fluid during the bleeding operation.

3. If the master cylinder is known or suspected to have air in the bore, bleed it before any wheel cylinder or caliper in the following manner:

a. Disconnect the forward brake line connection at the master cylinder.

b. Allow brake fluid to fill the master cylinder bore until it begins to flow from the forward brake line connector port.

c. Connect the forward brake line to the master cylinder and tighten.

d. Have an assistant depress the brake pedal slowly 1 time and hold. Loosen the forward brake line connection at the master cylinder to purge air from the bore. Tighten the connection and have the assistant release the pedal slowly. Wait 15 seconds and repeat the sequence, including the 15 second wait, until all air is removed from the bore. Make sure brake fluid does not contact any painted surface.

e. Repeat the procedure at the rear master cylinder brake line connection.

f. If it is known that the calipers and wheel cylinders do not contain any air, it will not be necessary to bleed them.

4. If it necessary to bleed all of the wheel cylinders and calipers, follow this sequence: Right rear, left rear, right front, left front.

5. Bleed individual wheel cylinders or calipers only after all air is removed from the master cylinder.

a. Place a suitable bleeder wrench over the bleeder valve.

b. Attach a clear tube over the bleeder valve and allow the tube to hang submerged in a clear container partially filled with brake fluid.

c. Have an assistant depress the brake pedal slowly 1 time and hold. Loosen the bleeder valve to purge

the air from the cylinder. Tighten the bleeder screw and have the assistant slowly release the pedal. Wait 15 seconds and repeat the sequence, including the 15 second wait, until all air is removed.

d. It may be necessary to repeat the sequence 10 or more times to remove all of the air. Rapid pumping of the brake pedal pushes the master cylinder secondary piston down the bore in a way that makes it difficult to bleed the rear side of the system.

6. Check the brake pedal for sponginess and the red brake warning lamp for an indication of unbalanced pressure. Repeat the bleeding procedure to correct either of these conditions.

FRONT SUSPENSION

MacPherson Strut

REMOVAL & INSTALLATION

1. Raise and safely support the vehicle. Use a suitable device to support the lower control arm.

2. Remove the wheel and tire assembly.

3. Remove the brake hose bracket.

4. Remove and discard the strut-to-knuckle bolts, washers and nuts.

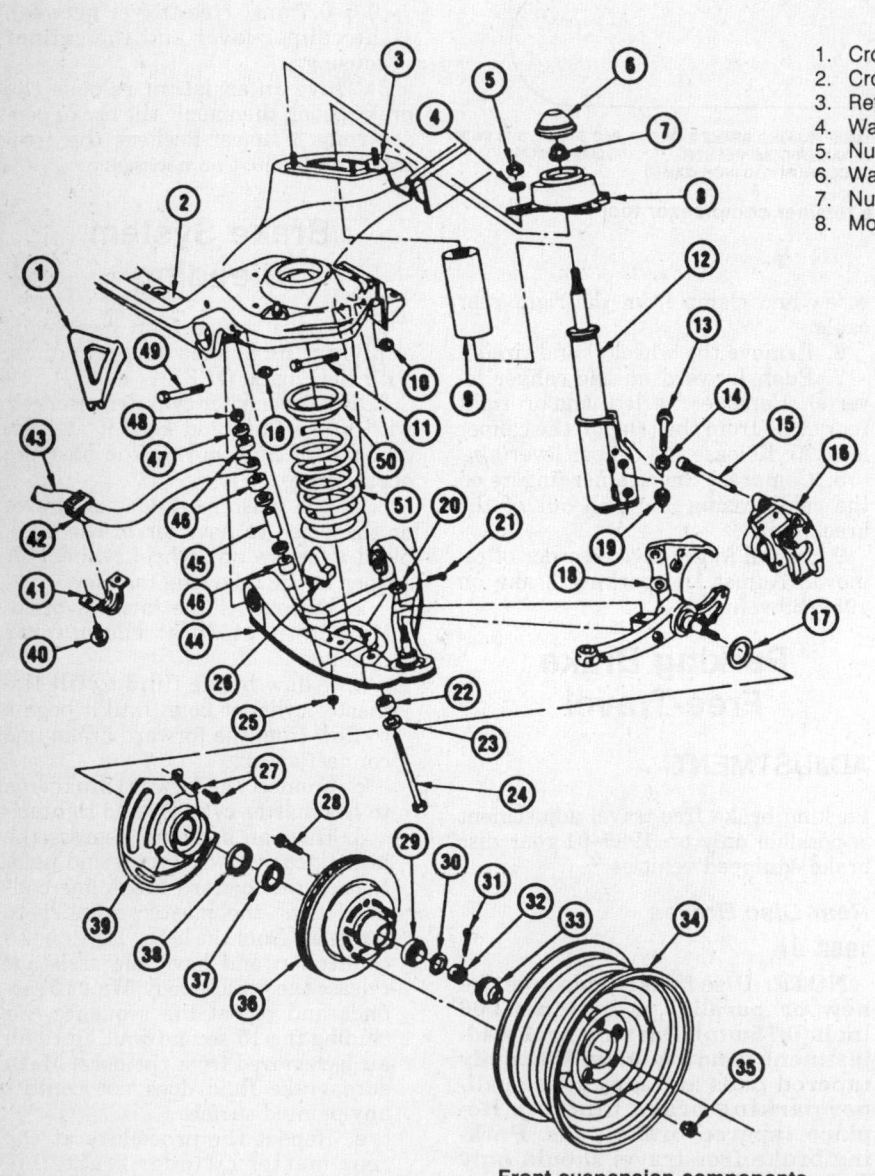

Front suspension components

1. Crossmember brace
2. Crossmember
3. Retainer
4. Washer
5. Nut (M8 × 1.25)
6. Washer
7. Nut (M14 × 2)
8. Mount
9. Shield
10. Nut (M12 × 1.75)
11. Bolt (M12 × 1.75 × 95)
12. Absorber with strut
13. Bolt
14. Washer
15. Bolt
16. Caliper
17. Gasket
18. Spindle
19. Nut (M16 × 2)
20. Nut ($^9/_{16}$–18)
21. Cotter pin ($^1/_8$ × 1)
22. Grommet
23. Retainer
24. Bolt ($^5/_{16}$–18 × 7)
25. Nut ($^7/_{16}$–14)
26. Bumper
27. Bolt
28. Bolt
29. Outer front wheel bearing
30. Washer
31. Cotter pin (M3.2 × 25)
32. Nut
33. Cap
34. Wheel
35. Nut
36. Hub
37. Inner front wheel bearing
38. Seal
39. Shield
40. Bolt (M10 × 1.5 × 30)
41. Bracket
42. Insulator
43. Front stabilizer shaft
44. Lower control arm
45. Spacer
46. Grommet
47. Retainer
48. Nut
49. Bolt (M12 × 1.75 × 115)
50. Insulator

5. Remove the cover from the upper mount assembly.

6. Remove the nut from the upper end of the strut.

7. Remove the strut and shield.

8. Install in the reverse order of removal. Tighten the upper strut nut to 46 ft. lbs. (63 Nm). Use new strut-to-knuckle bolts, washers and nuts. Tighten the strut-to-knuckle nuts to 125 ft. lbs. (170 Nm) followed by a 120 degree turn. Final torque must exceed 148 ft. lbs. (200 Nm). Check the front end alignment.

Coil Springs

REMOVAL & INSTALLATION

1. Raise and safely support the vehicle.

2. Remove the wheel and tire assembly.

3. Remove the stabilizer link and bushings at the lower control arm.

4. Remove the cotter pin and nut from the tie rod end. Using a suitable tool, remove the steering knuckle from the tie rod ball joint stud.

5. Install a suitable spring compressor and compress the spring.

6. Remove the lower control arm pivot bolt and pivot the lower control arm rearward.

7. Remove the spring compressor and remove the spring.

To install:

8. Properly position the spring on the control arm, making sure the spring insulator is in place. The bottom of the spring is coiled helical and the top is coiled flat, with a gripper notch near the end of the wire. After assembly, the end of the spring coil must cover all or part of 1 inspection drain hole. The other hole must be completely uncovered.

9. Install the spring compressor and compress the spring.

10. Pivot the lower control arm forward into position in the frame.

11. Install the bolts. The front bolt installs from front to rear first. Tighten the lower control arm pivot bolt/nuts to 66 ft. lbs. (90 Nm).

12. Remove the spring compressor.

13. Install the stabilizer linkage. Tighten the stabilizer link nut to 16 ft. lbs. (22 Nm).

14. Install the steering knuckle to the tie rod ball joint stud. Tighten the nut to 83 ft. lbs. (113 Nm).

15. Install a new cotter pin. If the hole in the stud does not line up with a slot in the nut, tighten the nut until it does. Do not back off the nut to install the cotter pin.

16. Install the wheel and tire assembly and lower the vehicle.

Lower Ball Joints

INSPECTION

1. Raise and safely support the vehicle. Use a suitable device to support the lower control arm in it's normal ride height position.

2. Grasp the wheel at the top and bottom. Alternately push and pull on the top and the bottom of the wheel in an attempt to move it toward and away from the vehicle. Check for any horizontal movement of the steering knuckle relative to the lower control arm. If there is any movement the ball joint must be replaced.

3. Check the ball joint when it is disconnected from the steering knuckle. If there is any looseness in the ball stud, if the ball stud can be twisted in it's socket using finger pressure or if there are any cuts or tears in the ball joint seal, replace the ball joint.

REMOVAL & INSTALLATION

1. Disconnect the negative battery cable. Raise and safely support the vehicle. Remove the wheel and tire assembly.

2. Support the lower control arm under the spring seat with a suitable jack.

3. Remove the cotter pin and loosen the lower ball stud nut. Remove the grease fitting.

4. Using a suitable tool, break the ball stud loose from the steering knuckle. Separate the lower control arm from the steering knuckle.

5. Using ball joint tools J–9519–23, J–9519–18 and adapter tool J–9519–9 or equivalents, press the ball joint from the lower control arm.

To install:

6. Install the new ball joint to the lower control arm. Using ball joint tools J–9519–23, J–9519–18 and adapter tool J–9519–9 or equivalents, press the ball joint into the lower control arm until it bottoms on the arm.

NOTE: When installing the new ball joint, position the purge vent in the rubber boot facing inward.

7. Connect the ball joint to the steering knuckle. Install the ball stud nut and tighten to 83 ft. lbs. (113 Nm). Then tighten enough to align the nut slot with the stud hole and install the cotter pin. Do not back off the nut to align the slot and hole.

8. Install and lubricate the ball joint fitting until grease appears at the seal.

9. Install the wheel and tire assembly.

10. Lower the vehicle and check the front alignment.

Lower Control Arms

REMOVAL & INSTALLATION

1. Raise and safely support the vehicle.

2. Remove the wheel and tire assembly.

3. Remove the stabilizer link and bushings at the lower control arm.

4. Remove the cotter pin and nut from the tie rod end. Using a suitable tool, remove the steering knuckle from the tie rod ball joint stud.

5. Install a suitable spring compressor and compress the coil spring.

6. Remove the lower control arm pivot bolt and pivot the lower control arm rearward.

7. Remove the spring compressor and remove the spring.

To install:

8. Properly position the spring on the control arm, making sure the spring insulator is in place. The bottom of the spring is coiled helical and the top is coiled flat, with a gripper notch near the end of the wire. After assembly, the end of the spring coil must cover all or part of 1 inspection drain hole. The other hole must be completely uncovered.

9. Install the spring compressor and compress the spring.

10. Pivot the lower control arm forward into position in the frame.

11. Install the bolts. The front bolt installs from front to rear first. Tighten the lower control arm pivot bolt/nuts to 66 ft. lbs. (90 Nm).

12. Remove the spring compressor.

13. Install the stabilizer linkage. Tighten the stabilizer link nut to 16 ft. lbs. (22 Nm).

14. Install the steering knuckle to the tie rod ball joint stud. Tighten the nut to 83 ft. lbs. (113 Nm).

15. Install a new cotter pin. If the hole in the stud does not line up with a slot in the nut, tighten the nut until it does. Do not back off the nut to install the cotter pin.

16. Install the wheel and tire assembly and lower the vehicle.

Sway Bar

REMOVAL & INSTALLATION

1. Raise and safely support the vehicle.

2. Remove each side of the sway bar linkage by removing the nut from the link bolt, pulling the bolt from the linkage and removing the retainers, grommets and spacer.

3. Remove the bracket-to-frame or body bolts and remove the sway bar, rubber bushings and brackets. Remove the lower structure brace, if equipped.

4. Installation is the reverse of the removal procedure. Install the sway bar with the identification tag on the right side of the vehicle. The rubber bushings should be positioned squarely in the bracket with the slit in the bushings facing the front of the vehicle. Tighten the sway bar link nut/bolt to 16 ft. lbs. (22 Nm) and the bracket bolts to 39 ft. lbs. (53 Nm).

Front Wheel Bearings

ADJUSTMENT

1. Raise and safely support the vehicle.
2. Remove the wheel cover or center cap.
3. Remove the dust cap from the hub.
4. Remove the cotter pin from the spindle nut.
5. Tighten the spindle nut to 12 ft. lbs. (16 Nm) while turning the wheel forward by hand to fully seat the bearings. This will remove any grease or burrs which could cause excessive wheel bearing play later.
6. Back off the nut to the just loose position.
7. Hand tighten the spindle nut. Loosen the spindle nut just enough that either hole in the spindle lines up with a slot in the nut, not more than ½ flat.
8. Install a new cotter pin. Bend the ends of the cotter pin against the nut and cut off the extra length to ensure the ends will not interfere with the dust cap.
9. Using a dial indicator, check the hub assembly. There should be 0.001–0.005 inch (0.03–0.13mm) endplay when properly adjusted.
10. Install the dust cap on the hub. Install the wheel cover or center cap.
11. Lower the vehicle.

REMOVAL & INSTALLATION

1. Raise and support the vehicle safely.
2. Remove the wheel and tire assembly.
3. Remove the caliper assembly.
4. Remove the dust cap from the hub. Remove the cotter pin, nut and washer from the spindle.
5. Remove the hub and rotor assembly.
6. Remove the outer bearing assembly from the hub. The inner bearing assembly will remain in the hub and may be removed after prying out the inner seal. Discard the seal after removal.

7. Remove the old bearing races from the hub with a suitable drift inserted behind the races.
8. Clean all parts in clean solvent and air dry. Do not spin the bearing with compressed air while drying or the bearing may be damaged.

To install:

9. Inspect the bearings for cracked cages and worn or pitted rollers. Check the bearing races for cracks, scores or brinelled condition. Replace as necessary.
10. If the races were removed, drive or press the races into the hub.
11. Apply a thin film of high temperature wheel bearing grease to the spindle at the outer bearing seat and at the inner bearing seat, shoulder and seal seat.
12. Put a small quantity of grease inboard of each bearing cup in the hub.
13. Pack the wheel bearings using a suitable bearing packer. If a bearing packer is not available, the bearings can be packed by hand. If hand packing is used, it is extremely important to work the grease thoroughly into the bearings between the rollers, cone and cage.
14. Place the inner bearing cone and roller assembly in the hub. Put an additional quantity of grease outboard of the bearing.
15. Install a new grease seal using a suitable tool until the seal is flush with the hub. Lubricate the seal lip with a thin layer of grease.
16. Carefully install the hub and rotor assembly. Place the outer bearing assembly in the outer bearing race. Install the washer and nut and tighten to 12 ft. lbs. (16 Nm).
17. Install the remainder of the components in the reverse of the removal procedure. Adjust the wheel bearings.

REAR SUSPENSION

Shock Absorbers

REMOVAL & INSTALLATION

1. Raise and support the vehicle safely.
2. Pull back the carpet in the rear hatch area and disconnect the upper shock attaching nut.
3. Remove the lower shock mounting nut. Remove the shock absorber from the vehicle.

4. Installation is the reverse of the removal procedure. Tighten the upper shock attaching nut to 13 ft. lbs. (17 Nm) and the lower attaching nut to 70 ft. lbs. (95 Nm).

Coil Springs

REMOVAL & INSTALLATION

1. Raise and safely support the vehicle so the rear axle can be independently raised and lowered.
2. Support the rear axle with a suitable jack.
3. If equipped with brake hose attachment brackets, disconnect the brackets allowing the hoses to hang free. Do not disconnect the hoses. Perform this step only if the hoses will be unduly stretched when the axle is lowered.
4. Disconnect the track bar from the axle.
5. Remove the lower shock absorber nuts and lower the axle. Make sure the axle is supported securely on the floor jack and that there is no chance of the axle slipping after the shock absorbers are disconnected.
6. Lower the axle and remove the coil spring. Do not lower the axle past the limits of the brake lines or the lines will be damaged.
7. To install, reverse the removal procedure. Make sure the spring is seated in the same position as before removal. Tighten the track bar mounting nut to 80 ft. lbs. (108 Nm) and bracket nut to 61 ft. lbs. (83 Nm). Tighten the shock mounting nuts to 70 ft. lbs. (95 Nm).

Rear Control Arms

REMOVAL & INSTALLATION

NOTE: If both control arms are being replaced, remove and replace 1 control arm at a time to prevent the axle from rolling or slipping sideways, making replacement difficult.

1. Raise and safely support the vehicle. Using a suitable jack, support the rear axle at the curb height position.
2. Remove the control arm-to-axle housing bolt and control arm-to-underbody bolt.
3. Remove the control arm.
4. Install in the reverse order of removal. Tighten the front and rear bolts to 85 ft. lbs. (115 Nm).

GM "J" Body
Front Wheel Drive
Buick—Skyhawk **Cadillac**—Cimarron
Chevrolet—Cavalier **Oldsmobile**—Firenza
Pontiac—Sunbird

SPECIFICATIONS

VEHICLE IDENTIFICATION CHART

It is important for servicing and ordering parts to be certain of the vehicle and engine identification. The VIN (vehicle identification number) is a 17 digit number visible through the windshield on the driver's side of the dash and contains the vehicle and engine identification codes. The tenth digit indicates model year and the eighth digit indicates engine code. It can be interpreted as follows:

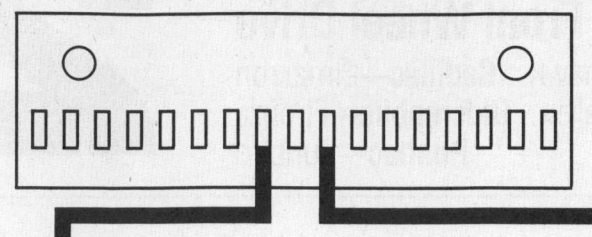

Engine Code							Model Year	
Code	Cu. In.	Liters	Cyl.	Fuel Sys.	Eng. Mfg.		Code	Year
M	121 (OHC)	2.0	4	MFI Turbo	①		H	1987
1	121 (OHV)	2.0	4	TBI HO	Chevrolet		J	1988
K	121 (OHC)	2.0	4	TBI	①		K	1989
G	134 (OHV)	2.2	4	TBI	Chevrolet		L	1990
W	173 (OHV)	2.8	6	MFI	Chevrolet		M	1991
T	192 (OHV)	3.1	6	MFI	Chevrolet			

HO High Output   OHC Overhead Cam engine   MFI Multi-Port Fuel Injection
OHV Overhead Valve engine   TBI Throttle Body Injection   ① Chevrolet-Pontiac-GM of Canada

ENGINE IDENTIFICATION

Year	Model	Engine Displacement cu. in. (liter)	Engine Series Identification (VIN)	No. of Cylinders	Engine Type
1987	Cavalier	121 (2.0)	1	4	OHV
	Cavalier	173 (2.8)	W	6	OHV
	Cimarron	121 (2.0)	1	4	OHV
	Cimarron	173 (2.8)	W	6	OHV
	Firenza	121 (2.0)	1	4	OHV
	Firenza	121 (2.0)	K	4	OHC
	Firenza	173 (2.8)	W	6	OHV
	Sunbird	121 (2.0)	K	4	OHC
	Sunbird	121 (2.0)	M	4	OHC—Turbo
	Skyhawk	121 (2.0)	1	4	OHV
	Skyhawk	121 (2.0)	K	4	OHC
	Skyhawk	121 (2.0)	M	4	OHC—Turbo
1988	Cavalier	121 (2.0)	1	4	OHV
	Cavalier	173 (2.8)	W	6	OHV
	Cimarron	173 (2.8)	W	6	OHV
	Firenza	121 (2.0)	1	4	OHV
	Firenza	121 (2.0)	K	4	OHC
	Sunbird	121 (2.0)	K	4	OHC
	Sunbird	121 (2.0)	M	4	OHC—Turbo
	Skyhawk	121 (2.0)	K	4	OHC

ENGINE IDENTIFICATION

Year	Model	Engine Displacement cu. in. (liter)	Engine Series Identification (VIN)	No. of Cylinders	Engine Type
1989	Cavalier	121 (2.0)	1	4	OHV
	Cavalier	173 (2.8)	W	6	OHV
	Sunbird	121 (2.0)	K	4	OHC
	Sunbird	121 (2.0)	M	4	OHC—Turbo
	Skyhawk	121 (2.0)	1	4	OHV
1990	Cavalier	134 (2.2)	G	4	OHV
	Cavalier	192 (3.1)	T	6	OHV
	Sunbird	121 (2.0)	K	4	OHC
	Sunbird	121 (2.0)	M	4	OHC
1991	Cavalier	134 (2.2)	G	4	OHV
	Cavalier	192 (3.1)	T	6	OHV
	Sunbird	121 (2.0)	K	4	OHC
	Sunbird	192 (3.1)	T	6	OHV

OHV—Overhead valve
OHC—Overhead cam
OHC—Turbo overhead cam with turbocharger

GENERAL ENGINE SPECIFICATIONS

Year	VIN	No. Cylinder Displacement cu. in. (liter)	Fuel System Type	Net Horsepower @ rpm	Net Torque @ rpm (ft. lbs.)	Bore × Stroke (in.)	Compression Ratio	Oil Pressure @ rpm
1987	M	4-121 (2.0)	MFI Turbo	160 @ 5600	160 @ 2800	3.38 × 3.38	8.0:1	65 @ 2500
	1	4-121 (2.0)	TBI (HO)	90 @ 5600	108 @ 3200	3.50 × 3.15	9.0:1	63–77 @ 1200
	K	4-121 (2.0)	TBI	102 @ 5200	130 @ 2800	3.38 × 3.38	8.8:1	45 @ 2000
	W	6-173 (2.8)	MFI	120 @ 4800	155 @ 3600	3.50 × 2.99	8.9:1	50 @ 2400
1988	M	4-121 (2.0)	MFI Turbo	160 @ 5600	160 @ 2800	3.38 × 3.38	8.0:1	65 @ 2500
	1	4-121 (2.0)	TBI (HO)	90 @ 5600	108 @ 3200	3.50 × 3.15	9.0:1	63–77 @ 1200
	K	4-121 (2.0)	TBI	102 @ 5200	130 @ 2800	3.38 × 3.38	8.8:1	45 @ 2000
	W	6-173 (2.8)	MFI	120 @ 4800	155 @ 3600	3.50 × 2.99	8.9:1	50 @ 2400
1989	M	4-121 (2.0)	MFI Turbo	160 @ 5600	160 @ 2800	3.38 × 3.38	8.0:1	65 @ 2500
	1	4-121 (2.0)	TBI (HO)	90 @ 5600	108 @ 3200	3.50 × 3.15	9.0:1	63–77 @ 1200
	K	4-121 (2.0)	TBI	102 @ 5200	130 @ 2800	3.38 × 3.38	8.8:1	45 @ 2000
	W	6-173 (2.8)	MFI	120 @ 4800	155 @ 3600	3.50 × 2.99	8.9:1	50 @ 2400
1990	K	4-121 (2.0)	TBI	102 @ 5200	108 @ 3200	3.39 × 3.39	8.8:1	—
	M	4-121 (2.0)	MFI Turbo	160 @ 5600	160 @ 2800	3.39 × 3.39	8.0:1	—
	G	4-134 (2.2)	TBI	95 @ 5200	120 @ 3200	3.50 × 3.46	9.0:1	63–77 @ 1200
	T	6-192 (3.1)	MFI	140 @ 4500	180 @ 3600	3.50 × 3.31	8.8:1	—
1991	K	4-121 (2.0)	TBI	96 @ 4800	118 @ 3600	3.39 × 3.39	8.8:1	—
	G	4-134 (2.2)	TBI	95 @ 5200	120 @ 3200	3.50 × 3.46	9.0:1	63–77 @ 1200
	T	6-192 (3.1)	MFI	140 @ 4500	180 @ 3600	3.50 × 3.31	8.8:1	—

GASOLINE ENGINE TUNE-UP SPECIFICATIONS

Year	VIN	No. Cylinder Displacement cu. in. (liter)	Spark Plugs Type	Spark Plugs Gap (in.)	Ignition Timing (deg.) MT	Ignition Timing (deg.) AT	Compression Pressure (psi)	Fuel Pump (psi)	Idle Speed (rpm) MT	Idle Speed (rpm) AT	Valve Clearance In.	Valve Clearance Ex.
1987	M	4-121 (2.0)	RN9YC4	0.060	①	①	NA	25–30	①	①	Hyd.	Hyd.
	1	4-121 (2.0)	RC12LYC	0.035	①	①	NA	10–12	①	①	Hyd.	Hyd.
	K	4-121 (2.0)	RN12YC6	0.060	①	①	NA	10	①	①	Hyd.	Hyd.
	W	6-173 (2.8)	R-42CTS	0.045	①	①	NA	30–37	①	①	Hyd.	Hyd.
1988	M	4-121 (2.0)	RN9YC4	0.060	①	①	NA	25–30	①	①	Hyd.	Hyd.
	1	4-121 (2.0)	RC12LYC	0.035	①	①	NA	10–12	①	①	Hyd.	Hyd.
	K	4-121 (2.0)	RN12YC6	0.060	①	①	NA	10	①	①	Hyd.	Hyd.
	W	6-173 (2.8)	RS13LYC	0.045	①	①	NA	30–37	①	①	Hyd.	Hyd.
1989	M	4-121 (2.0)	RN9YC4	0.060	①	①	NA	25–30	①	①	Hyd.	Hyd.
	1	4-121 (2.0)	RC12LYC	0.035	①	①	NA	10–12	①	①	Hyd.	Hyd.
	K	4-121 (2.0)	RN12YC6	0.060	①	①	NA	10	①	①	Hyd.	Hyd.
	W	6-173 (2.8)	RS13LYC	0.045	①	①	NA	30–37	①	①	Hyd.	Hyd.
1990	K	4-121 (2.0)	R44XLS	0.045	①	①	NA	9–13	①	①	Hyd.	Hyd.
	M	4-121 (2.0)	R42XLS	0.035	①	①	NA	35–38	①	①	Hyd.	Hyd.
	G	4-134 (2.2)	R44LTSM	0.035	①	①	NA	9–13	①	①	Hyd.	Hyd.
	T	6-192 (3.1)	R44LTSM	0.045	①	①	NA	40.5–47	①	①	Hyd.	Hyd.
1991					SEE UNDERHOOD SPECIFICATIONS STICKER							

NOTE: The underhood specifications sticker often reflects tune-up specifications changes made in production. Sticker figures must be used if they disagree with those in this chart.

Part numbers in this chart are not recommendations by Chilton for any product by brand name

NA Not available at time of publication

① See underhood specifications sticker

FIRING ORDERS

NOTE: To avoid confusion, always replace spark plug wires one at a time.

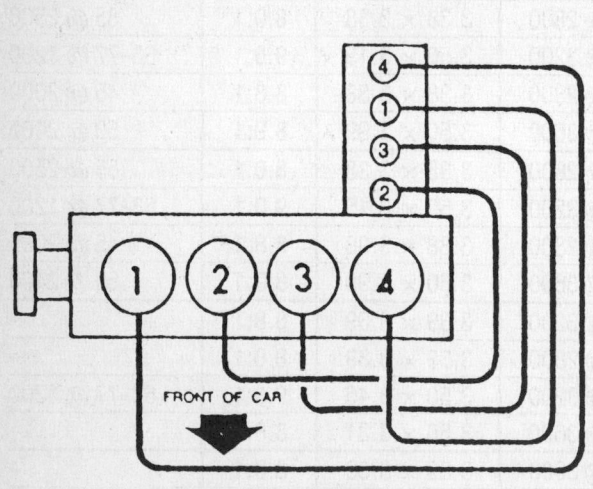

2.0L (VIN 1) and 2.2L Engines
Engine Firing Order: 1–3–4–2
Distributorless Ignition System

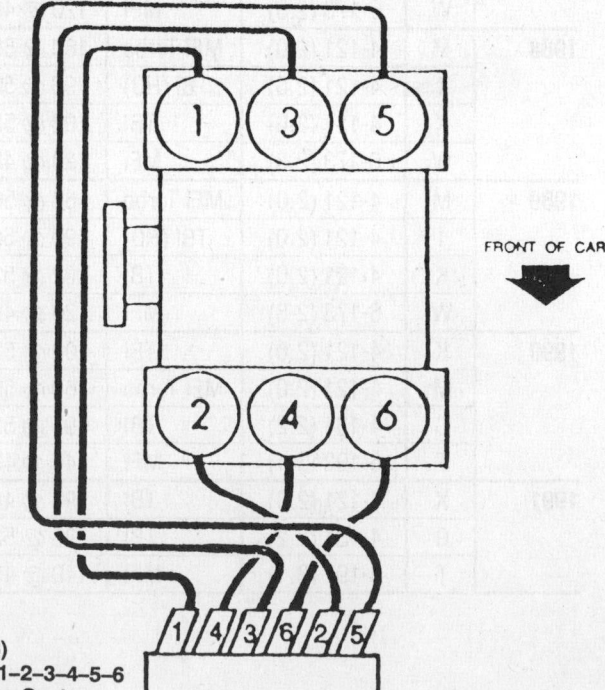

2.8L Engine (1987–88)
Engine Firing Order: 1–2–3–4–5–6
Distributorless Ignition System

FIRING ORDERS

NOTE: To avoid confusion, always replace spark plug wires one at a time.

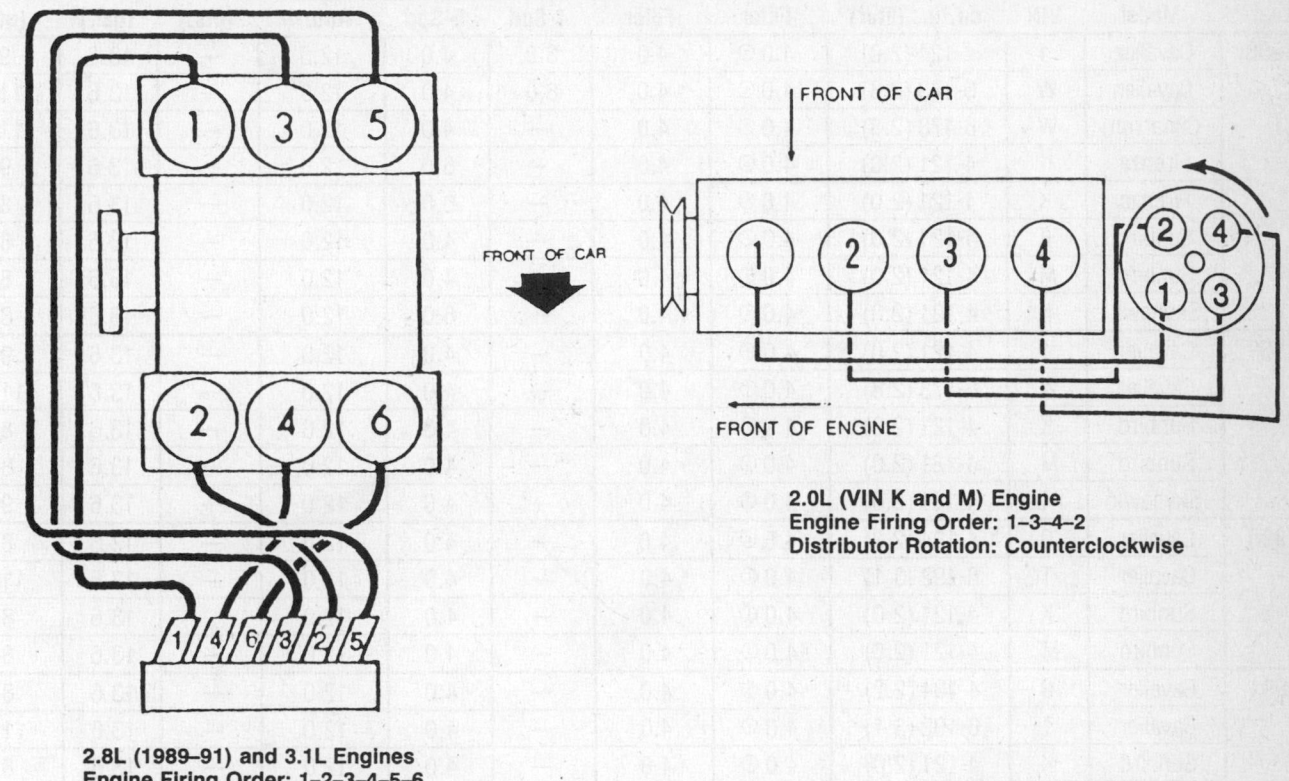

2.8L (1989–91) and 3.1L Engines
Engine Firing Order: 1–2–3–4–5–6
Distributorless Ignition System

2.0L (VIN K and M) Engine
Engine Firing Order: 1–3–4–2
Distributor Rotation: Counterclockwise

CAPACITIES

Year	Model	VIN	No. Cylinder Displacement cu. in. (liter)	Engine Crankcase with Filter	Engine Crankcase without Filter	Transmission (pts.) 4-Spd	Transmission (pts.) 5-Spd	Transmission (pts.) Auto ②	Drive Axle (pts.)	Fuel Tank (gal.)	Cooling System (qts.)
1987	Cavalier	1	4-121 (2.0)	4.0 ①	4.0	6.0	4.0	12.0	—	13.6	9.7
	Cavalier	W	6-173 (2.8)	4.0 ①	4.0	6.0	4.0	12.0	—	13.6	11.0
	Cimarron	1	4-121 (2.0)	4.0 ①	4.0	—	4.0	12.0	—	13.6	9.7
	Cimarron	W	6-173 (2.8)	4.0 ①	4.0	—	4.0	12.0	—	13.6	11.0
	Firenza	1	4-121 (2.0)	4.0 ①	4.0	—	6.0	12.0	—	13.6	9.7
	Firenza	K	4-121 (2.0)	4.0 ①	4.0	—	6.0	12.0	—	13.6	8.5
	Firenza	W	6-173 (2.8)	4.0 ①	4.0	—	6.0	12.0	—	13.6	11.0
	Sunbird	K	4-121 (2.0)	4.0 ①	4.0	—	4.0	12.0	—	13.6	8.5
	Sunbird	M	4-121 (2.0)	4.0 ①	4.0	—	4.0	12.0	—	13.6	8.5
	Skyhawk	1	4-121 (2.0)	4.0 ①	4.0	—	6.0	12.0	—	13.6	9.7
	Skyhawk	K	4-121 (2.0)	4.0 ①	4.0	—	6.0	12.0	—	13.6	8.5
	Skyhawk	M	4-121 (2.0)	4.0 ①	4.0	—	6.0	12.0	—	13.6	8.5

CAPACITIES

Year	Model	VIN	No. Cylinder Displacement cu. in. (liter)	Engine Crankcase with Filter	Engine Crankcase without Filter	Transmission (pts.) 4-Spd	Transmission (pts.) 5-Spd	Transmission (pts.) Auto ②	Drive Axle (pts.)	Fuel Tank (gal.)	Cooling System (qts.)
1988	Cavalier	1	4-121 (2.0)	4.0 ①	4.0	6.0	4.0	12.0	—	13.6	9.7
	Cavalier	W	6-173 (2.8)	4.0 ①	4.0	6.0	4.0	12.0	—	13.6	11.0
	Cimarron	W	6-173 (2.8)	4.0 ①	4.0	—	4.0	12.0	—	13.6	11.0
	Firenza	1	4-121 (2.0)	4.0 ①	4.0	—	6.0	12.0	—	13.6	9.7
	Firenza	K	4-121 (2.0)	4.0 ①	4.0	—	6.0	12.0	—	13.6	8.5
	Sunbird	K	4-121 (2.0)	4.0 ①	4.0	—	4.0	12.0	—	13.6	8.5
	Sunbird	M	4-121 (2.0)	4.0 ①	4.0	—	4.0	12.0	—	13.6	8.5
	Skyhawk	K	4-121 (2.0)	4.0 ①	4.0	—	6.0	12.0	—	13.6	8.5
1989	Cavalier	1	4-121 (2.0)	4.0 ①	4.0	—	4.0	12.0	—	13.6	9.7
	Cavalier	W	6-173 (2.8)	4.0 ①	4.0	—	4.0	12.0	—	13.6	11.0
	Sunbird	K	4-121 (2.0)	4.0 ①	4.0	—	4.0	12.0	—	13.6	8.5
	Sunbird	M	4-121 (2.0)	4.0 ①	4.0	—	4.0	12.0	—	13.6	8.5
	Skyhawk	1	4-121 (2.0)	4.0 ①	4.0	—	4.0	12.0	—	13.6	9.7
1990	Cavalier	G	4-134 (2.2)	4.0 ①	4.0	—	4.0	12.0	—	13.6	8.5
	Cavalier	T	6-192 (3.1)	4.0 ①	4.0	—	4.0	12.0	—	13.6	11.0
	Sunbird	K	4-121 (2.0)	4.0 ①	4.0	—	4.0	12.0	—	13.6	8.5
	Sunbird	M	4-121 (2.0)	4.0 ①	4.0	—	4.0	12.0	—	13.6	8.5
1991	Cavalier	G	4-134 (2.2)	4.0 ①	4.0	—	4.0	12.0	—	13.6	8.5
	Cavalier	T	6-192 (3.1)	4.0 ①	4.0	—	4.0	12.0	—	13.6	11.0
	Sunbird	K	4-121 (2.0)	4.0 ①	4.0	—	4.0	12.0	—	13.6	8.5
	Sunbird	T	6-192 (3.1)	4.0 ①	4.0	—	4.0	12.0	—	13.6	11.0

① When changing the oil filter, additional oil will be needed
② Overhaul capacity, refill capacity is approximately 8 pts.

CAMSHAFT SPECIFICATIONS

All measurements given in inches.

Year	VIN	No. Cylinder Displacement cu. in. (liter)	Journal Diameter 1	Journal Diameter 2	Journal Diameter 3	Journal Diameter 4	Journal Diameter 5	Lobe Lift In.	Lobe Lift Ex.	Bearing Clearance	Camshaft End Play
1987	M	4.121 (2.0)	1.6714–1.6720	1.6812–1.6816	1.6911–1.6917	1.7009–1.7015	1.7108–1.7114	0.2409	0.2409	0.0008	0.0160–0.0640
	1	4.121 (2.0)	1.8670–1.8690	1.8670–1.8690	1.8670–1.8690	1.8670–1.8690	1.8670 1.8690	0.2600	0.2600	0.0010–0.0040	NA
	K	4-121 (2.0)	1.6714–1.6720	1.6812–1.6816	1.6911–1.6917	1.7009–1.7015	1.7108–1.7114	0.2409	0.2409	0.0008	0.0160–0.0640
	W	6.173 (2.8)	1.8678–1.8815	1.8678–1.8815	1.8678–1.8815	1.8678–1.8815	1.8678–1.8815	0.2626	0.2732	NA	NA
1988	M	4-121 (2.0)	1.6714–1.6720	1.6812–1.6816	1.6911–1.6917	1.7009–1.7015	1.7108–1.7114	0.2409	0.2409	0.0008	0.0160–0.0640
	1	4-121 (2.0)	1.8670–1.8690	1.8670–1.8690	1.8670–1.8690	1.8670–1.8690	1.8670–1.8690	0.2600	0.2600	0.0010–0.0040	NA
	K	4-121 (2.0)	1.6714–1.6720	1.6812–1.6816	1.6911–1.6917	1.7009–1.7015	1.7108–1.7114	0.2409	0.2409	0.0008	0.0160–0.0640
	W	6-173 (2.8)	1.8678–1.8815	1.8678–1.8815	1.8678–1.8815	1.8678–1.8815	1.8678–1.8815	0.2626	0.2732	NA	NA

CAMSHAFT SPECIFICATIONS
All measurements given in inches.

Year	VIN	No. Cylinder Displacement cu. in. (liter)	Journal Diameter					Lobe Lift		Bearing Clearance	Camshaft End Play
			1	2	3	4	5	In.	Ex.		
1989	M	4-121 (2.0)	1.6714–1.6720	1.6812–1.6816	1.6911–1.6917	1.7009–1.7015	1.7108–1.7114	0.2409	0.2409	0.0008	0.0160–0.0640
	1	4-121 (2.0)	1.8670–1.8690	1.8670–1.8690	1.8670–1.8690	1.8670–1.8690	1.8670–1.8690	0.2600	0.2600	0.0018–0.0040	NA
	K	4-121 (2.0)	1.6714–1.6720	1.6812–1.6816	1.6911–1.6917	1.7009–1.7015	1.7108–1.7114	0.2409	0.2409	0.0008	0.0160–0.0640
	W	6-173 (2.8)	1.8678–1.8815	1.8678–1.8815	1.8678–1.8815	1.8678–1.8815	1.8678–1.8815	0.2626	0.2732	NA	NA
1990–91	K	4-121 (2.0)	1.6714–1.6720	1.6812–1.6816	1.6911–1.6917	1.7009–1.7015	1.7108–1.7114	0.2366	0.2515	0.0011–0.0035	0.0016–0.0063
	M	4-121 (2.0)	1.6714–1.6720	1.6812–1.6816	1.6911–1.6917	1.7009–1.7015	1.7108–1.7114	0.2625	0.2625	0.0011–0.0035	0.0016–0.0063
	G	4-134 (2.2)	1.8670–1.8690	1.8670–1.8690	1.8670–1.8690	1.8670–1.8690	1.8670–1.8690	0.2590	0.2590	0.0001–0.0039	NA
	T	6192 (3.1)	1.8678–1.8815	1.8678–1.8815	1.8678–1.8815	1.8678–1.8815	1.8678–1.8815	0.2626	0.2732	NA	NA

NA Not available

CRANKSHAFT AND CONNECTING ROD SPECIFICATIONS
All measurements are given in inches.

Year	VIN	No. Cylinder Displacement cu. in. (liter)	Crankshaft				Connecting Rod		
			Main Brg. Journal Dia.	Main Brg. Oil Clearance	Shaft End-play	Thrust on No.	Journal Diameter	Oil Clearance	Side Clearance
1987	M	4-121 (2.0)	①	0.0006–0.0016	0.0030–0.0120	3	1.9278–1.9286	0.0007–0.0024	0.0027–0.0095
	1	4-121 (2.0)	2.4945–2.4954	0.0006–0.0019	0.0020–0.0080	4	1.9983–1.9994	0.0010–0.0031	0.0040–0.0150
	K	4-121 (2.0)	①	0.0006–0.0016	0.0030–0.0120	3	1.9278–0.9286	0.0007–0.0024	0.0027–0.0095
	W	6-173 (2.8)	2.6473–2.6482	0.0016–0.0033	0.0024–0.0083	3	1.9983–1.9994	0.0014–0.0037	0.0063–0.0173
1988	M	4-121 (2.0)	①	0.0006–0.0016	0.0030–0.0120	3	1.9278–1.9286	0.0007–0.0024	0.0027–0.0095
	1	4-121 (2.0)	2.4945–2.4954	0.0006–0.0019	0.0020–0.0080	4	1.9983–1.9994	0.0010–0.0031	0.0040–0.0150
	K	4-121 (2.0)	①	0.0006–0.0016	0.0030–0.0120	3	1.9278–1.9286	0.0007–0.0024	0.0027–0.0095
	W	6-173 (2.8)	2.6473–2.6482	0.0016–0.0033	0.0024–0.0083	3	1.9983–1.9994	0.0014–0.0037	0.0063–0.0173
1989	M	4-121 (2.0)	①	0.0006–0.0016	0.0030–0.0120	3	1.9278–1.9286	0.0007–0.0024	0.0027–0.0095
	1	4-121 (2.0)	2.4945–2.4954	0.0006–0.0019	0.0020–0.0080	4	1.9983–1.9994	0.0010–0.0031	0.0040–0.0150
	K	4-121 (2.0)	①	0.0016–0.0016	0.0030–0.0120	3	1.9278–1.9286	0.0007–0.0024	0.0027–0.0095
	W	6-173 (2.8)	2.6473–2.6482	0.0016–0.0033	0.0024–0.0083	3	1.9983–1.9994	0.0014–0.0037	0.0063–0.0173

CRANKSHAFT AND CONNECTING ROD SPECIFICATIONS

All measurements are given in inches.

Year	VIN	No. Cylinder Displacement cu. in. (liter)	Crankshaft				Connecting Rod		
			Main Brg. Journal Dia.	Main Brg. Oil Clearance	Shaft End-play	Thrust on No.	Journal Diameter	Oil Clearance	Side Clearance
1990–91	K	4-121 (2.0)	2.2828–2.2833	0.0006–0.0016	0.0028–0.0118	3	1.9279–1.9287	0.0007–0.0025	0.0028–0.0095
	M	4-121 (2.0)	2.2828–2.2833	0.0006–0.0016	0.0028–0.0118	3	1.9279–1.9287	0.0007–0.0025	0.0028–0.0095
	G	4-134 (2.2)	2.4945–2.4954	0.0006–0.0019	0.002–0.007	4	1.9983–1.9994	0.0098–0.0031	0.0039–0.0149
	T	6-192 (3.1)	2.6473–2.6483	0.0012–0.0030	0.0024–0.0083	3	1.9983–1.9994	0.0011–0.0034	0.014–0.027

① Bearings are identified by color:
Brown 2.2830–2.2832;
Green 2.2827–2.2830

VALVE SPECIFICATIONS

Year	VIN	No. Cylinder Displacement cu. in. (liter)	Seat Angle (deg.)	Face Angle (deg.)	Spring Test Pressure (lbs.)	Spring Installed Height (in.)	Stem-to-Guide Clearance (in.)		Stem Diameter (in.)	
							Intake	Exhaust	Intake	Exhaust
1987	M	4-121 (2.0)	45	46	NA	NA	0.0006–0.0020	0.0010–0.0024	NA	NA
	1	4-121 (2.0)	46	45	183 @ 1.33	1.60	0.0011–0.0026	0.0014–0.0030	0.0490–0.0560	0.0630–0.0750
	K	4-121 (2.0)	45	46	NA	NA	0.0006–0.0020	0.0010–0.0024	NA	NA
	W	6-173 (2.8)	46	45	195 @ 1.18	1.57	0.0010–0.0027	0.0010–0.0027	0.0610–0.0730	0.0670–0.0790
1988	M	4-121 (2.0)	45	46	NA	NA	0.0006–0.0020	0.0010–0.0024	NA	NA
	1	4-121 (2.0)	46	45	183 @ 1.33	1.60	0.0011–0.0026	0.0014–0.0030	0.0490–0.0560	0.0630–0.0750
	K	4-121 (2.0)	45	46	NA	NA	0.0006–0.0020	0.0010–0.0024	NA	NA
	W	6-173 (2.8)	46	45	195 @ 1.18	1.57	0.0010–0.0027	0.0010–0.0027	0.0610–0.0730	0.0670–0.0790
1989	M	4-121 (2.0)	45	46	NA	NA	0.0006–0.0020	0.0010–0.0024	NA	NA
	1	4-121 (2.0)	46	45	183 @ 1.33	1.60	0.0011–0.0026	0.0014–0.0030	0.0490–0.0560	0.0630–0.0750
	K	4-121 (2.0)	45	46	NA	NA	0.0006–0.0020	0.0010–0.0024	NA	NA
	W	6-173 (2.8)	46	45	195 @ 1.18	1.57	0.0010–0.0027	0.0010–0.0027	0.0610–0.0730	0.0670–0.0790
1990–91	K	4-121 (2.0)	45	46	180 @ 1.043	NA	0.0006–0.0017	0.0012–0.0024	0.2760–0.2755	0.2753–0.2747
	M	4-121 (2.0)	45	46	172 @ 1.043	NA	0.0006–0.0017	0.0012–0.0024	0.2760–0.2755	0.2753–0.2747
	G	4-134 (2.2)	46	45	212 @ 1.22	NA	0.0011–0.0026	0.0014–0.0030	0.0490–0.0590	0.063–0.075
	T	6-192 (3.1)	46	45	215 @ 1.291	1.57	0.0010–0.0027	0.0010–0.0027	0.0610–0.0730	0.0670–0.0027

NA—Not available

PISTON AND RING SPECIFICATIONS
All measurements are given in inches.

Year	VIN	No. Cylinder Displacement cu. in. (liter)	Piston Clearance	Ring Gap			Ring Side Clearance		
				Top Compression	Bottom Compression	Oil Control	Top Compression	Bottom Compression	Oil Control
1987	M	4-121 (2.0)	0.0012–0.0020	0.0120–0.0200	0.0120–0.0200	0.0160–0.0550	0.0020–0.0030	0.0010–0.0024	—
	1	4-121 (2.0)	0.0098–0.0220	0.0100–0.0200	0.0100–0.0200	0.0100–0.0500	0.0010–0.0030	0.0010–0.0030	0.0006–0.0090
	K	4-121 (2.0)	0.0004–0.0012	0.0120–0.0200	0.0120–0.0200	0.0160–0.0550	0.0020–0.0030	0.0010–0.0024	—
	W	6-173 (2.8)	0.0007–0.0017	0.0098–0.0197	0.0098–0.0197	0.0200–0.0550	0.0012–0.0027	0.0016–0.0037	0.0078 Max
1988	M	4-121 (2.0)	0.0012–0.0020	0.0120–0.0200	0.0120–0.0200	0.0160–0.0550	0.0020–0.0030	0.0010–0.0024	—
	1	4-121 (2.0)	0.0098–0.0220	0.0100–0.0200	0.0100–0.0200	0.0100–0.0500	0.0010–0.0030	0.0010–0.0030	0.0006–0.0090
	K	4-121 (2.0)	0.0004–0.0012	0.0120–0.0200	0.0120–0.0200	0.0160–0.0550	0.0020–0.0030	0.0010–0.0024	—
	W	6-173 (2.8)	0.0022–0.0035	0.0100–0.0200	0.0100–0.0200	0.0100–0.0500	0.0020–0.0035	0.0020–0.0035	0.0080 Max
1989	M	4-121 (2.0)	0.0012–0.0020	0.0120–0.0200	0.0120–0.0200	0.0160–0.0550	0.0020–0.0030	0.0010–0.0024	—
	1	4-121 (2.0)	0.0098–0.0220	0.0100–0.0200	0.0100–0.0200	0.0010–0.0500	0.0010–0.0030	0.0010–0.0030	0.0006–0.0090
	K	4-121 (2.0)	0.0004–0.0012	0.0120–0.0200	0.0120–0.0200	0.0160–0.0550	0.0020–0.0030	0.0010–0.0024	—
	W	6-173 (2.8)	0.0022–0.0035	0.0100–0.0200	0.0100–0.0200	0.0100–0.0500	0.0020–0.0035	0.0020–0.0035	0.0080 Max
1990–91	K	4-121 (2.0)	0.0004–0.0012	0.0098–0.0177	0.0118–0.0197	NA	0.0024–0.0036	0.0019–0.0032	NA
	M	4-121 (2.0)	0.0012–0.0020	0.0098–0.0177	0.0118–0.0197	NA	0.0024–0.0036	0.0019–0.0032	NA
	G	4-134 (2.2)	0.0007–0.0017	0.0100–0.0200	0.0100–0.0200	0.0100–0.0500	0.0019 0.0027	0.0019 0.0027	0.0019–0.0082
	T	6-191 (3.1)	0.00093–0.00222	0.0100–0.0200	0.0200–0.0280	0.0100–0.0300	0.0020–0.0035	0.0020–0.0035	0.008 Max

NA—Not available

TORQUE SPECIFICATIONS
All readings in ft. lbs.

Year	VIN	No. Cylinder Displacement cu. in. (liter)	Cylinder Head Bolts	Main Bearing Bolts	Rod Bearing Bolts	Crankshaft Pulley Bolts	Flywheel Bolts	Manifold		Spark Plugs
								Intake	Exhaust	
1987	M	4-121 (2.0)	②	44 ③	26 ④	20 ⑤	48 ⑥	16	16	15
	1	4-121 (2.0)	⑦	63–77	34–43	68–89	63 ①	15–22	6–13	15
	K	4-121 (2.0)	②	44 ③	26 ④	20 ⑤	48 ⑥	16	16	15
	W	6-173 (2.8)	33 ⑧	63–83	34–45	66–84	45	18	14–22	15

TORQUE SPECIFICATIONS
All readings in ft. lbs.

Year	VIN	No. Cylinder Displacement cu. in. (liter)	Cylinder Head Bolts	Main Bearing Bolts	Rod Bearing Bolts	Crankshaft Pulley Bolts	Flywheel Bolts	Manifold		Spark Plugs
								Intake	Exhaust	
1988	M	4-121 (2.0)	②	44 ③	26 ④	20 ⑤	48 ⑥	16	16	15
	1	4-121 (2.0)	①	63–77	34–43	68–89	63 ①	15–22	6–13	15
	K	4-121 (2.0)	②	44 ③	26 ④	20 ⑤	48 ⑥	16	16	15
	W	6-173 (2.8)	33 ⑧	63–83	34–45	66–84	45	18	14–22	15
1989	M	4-121 (2.0)	②	44 ③	26 ④	20 ⑤	48 ⑥	16	16	15
	1	4-121 (2.0)	⑦	63–77	34–43	68–89	63 ①	15–22	6–13	15
	K	4-121 (2.0)	②	44 ③	26 ④	20 ⑤	48 ⑥	16	16	15
	W	6-173 (2.8)	33 ⑧	63–83	34–45	66–84	45	18	14–22	15
1990–91	K	4-121 (2.0)	②	44 ③	26 ④	114	46	16	⑫	15
	M	4-121 (2.0)	②	44 ③	26 ④	114	46	18	⑫	15
	G	4-134 (2.2)	⑩	70	38	85	46	18	⑪	7–15
	T	6-191 (3.1)	33 ⑧	73	39	76	46	⑨	18	7–15

CAUTION: Verify the correct original equipment engine is in the vehicle by referring to the VIN engine code before torquing any bolts.

① Auto. Trans.—45–59
② Step 1—18 ft. lbs.
  Step 2—Tighten additional 180 degrees in 3 steps of 60 degrees each
  Step 3—Warm engine—tighten bolts additional 30–50 degree turn
③ Plus additional 45–50 degree turn
④ Plus additional 45 degree turn
⑤ Crankshaft pulley to sprocket bolts
⑥ Plus additional 30 degree turn
⑦ Long bolts—73–83 ft. lbs.
  Short bolts—62–70 ft. lbs.
⑧ Coat thread with sealer an additional 90 degree turn

⑨ Tighten in sequence to 15 ft. lbs., then retighten to 24 ft. lbs.
⑩ Step 1—Tighten all bolts initially to 41 ft. lbs.
  Step 2—Tighten all bolts an additional 45 degrees in sequence
  Step 3—Tighten all bolts an additional 45 degrees in sequence
  Step 4—Tighten the long bolts—8, 4, 1, 5 and 9 an additional 20 degrees and tighten the short bolts—7, 3, 2, 6 and 10 an additional 10 degrees
⑪ Nuts—115 inch lbs.
  Studs—89 inch lbs.
⑫ 115 inch lbs.

BRAKE SPECIFICATIONS
All measurements in inches unless noted

Year	Model	Lug Nut Torque (ft. lbs.)	Master Cylinder Bore	Brake Disc		Maximum Brake Drum Diameter	Minimum Lining Thickness	
				Minimum Thickness	Maximum Runout		Front	Rear
1987	Cavalier	100	0.940	0.815	0.004	7.929	1/8	1/8
	Sunbird	100	0.940	0.815	0.004	7.929	1/8	1/8
	Firenza	100	0.940	0.815	0.004	7.929	1/8	1/8
	Skyhawk	100	0.940	0.815	0.004	7.929	1/8	1/8
	Cimarron	100	0.940	0.815	0.004	7.929	1/8	1/8
1988	Cavalier	100	0.940	0.815	0.004	7.929	1/8	1/8
	Sunbird	100	0.940	0.815	0.004	7.929	1/8	1/8
	Firenza	100	0.940	0.815	0.004	7.929	1/8	1/8
	Skyhawk	100	0.940	0.815	0.004	7.929	1/8	1/8
	Cimarron	100	0.940	0.815	0.004	7.929	1/8	1/8
1989	Cavalier	100	0.940	0.815	0.004	7.929	1/8	1/8
	Sunbird	100	0.940	0.815	0.004	7.929	1/8	1/8
	Skyhawk	100	0.940	0.815	0.004	7.929	1/8	1/8
1990–91	Cavalier	100	0.874	0.815	0.004	7.929	1/8	1/8
	Sunbird	100	0.874	0.815	0.004	7.929	1/8	1/8

WHEEL ALIGNMENT

Year	Model	Caster Range (deg.)	Caster Preferred Setting (deg.)	Camber Range (deg.)	Camber Preferred Setting (deg.)	Toe-in (in.)	Steering Axis Inclination (deg.)
1987	Cavalier	23/32P–2 23/32P	1 23/32P	3/16P–1 3/16P	13/16P	0 ②	13 1/2
	Sunbird	11/16P–2 11/16P	1 11/16P	3/16P–1 3/16P	13/16P	0 ②	13 1/2
	Firenza	11/16P–2 11/16P	1 11/16P	3/16P–1 3/16P	13/16P	0 ②	13 1/2
	Skyhawk	23/32P–2 23/32P	1 23/32P	3/16P–1 3/16P	13/16P	0 ②	13 1/2
	Cimarron	23/32P–2 23/32P	1 23/32P	3/16P–1 3/16P	13/16P	0 ②	13 1/2
1988	Cavalier	13/16N–4 3/16P	1 11/16P	3/16P–1 3/16P ②	13/16P ①	0	13 1/2
	Sunbird	13/16N–4 3/16P	1 11/16P	3/16P–1 3/16P	13/16P	0	13 1/2
	Firenza	13/16N–4 3/16P	1 11/16P	3/16P–1 3/16P	13/16P	0	13 1/2
	Skyhawk	13/16N–4 3/16P	1 11/16P	3/16P–1 3/16P	13/16P	0	13 1/2
	Cimarron	13/16N–4 3/16P	1 11/16P	3/16P–1 3/16P	13/16P	0	13 1/2
1989	Cavalier	11/16P–2 11/16P	1 11/16P	3/16P–1 3/16P ②	13/16P ①	0	13 1/2
	Sunbird	11/16P–2 11/16P	1 11/16P	3/16P–1 3/16P	13/16P	0	13 1/2
	Skyhawk	11/16P–2 11/16P	1 11/16P	3/16P–1 3/16P	13/16P	0	13 1/2
1990–91	Cavalier	11/16P–2 11/16P	1 11/16P	3/16P–1 3/16P ②	13/16P ①	0	13 1/2
	Sunbird	11/16P–2 11/16P	1 11/16P	3/16P–1 3/16P	13/16P	0	13 1/2

① Z-24; 1N–P. Preferred setting is 0 camber
② If vehicle is equipped with P215-60R14 tires setting is 1/8 degree out

ENGINE ELECTRICAL

NOTE: Disconnecting the negative battery cable on some vehicles may interfere with the functions of the on board computer systems and may require the computer to undergo a relearning process, once the negative battery cable is reconnected.

Distributor

REMOVAL

2.0L (VIN M and K) Engine

1. Disconnect the negative battery cable.
2. Tag the spark plug wires and remove the wires and ignition coil from the distributor.
3. Disconnect the wiring from the distributor.
4. Remove the 2 distributor hold-down nuts.
5. Mark the tang drive and camshaft for correct reassembly.
6. Remove the distributor.

INSTALLATION

Timing Not Disturbed

1. Align the tang drive according to the previous marking and install the distributor.
2. Torque the hold-down nuts to 13 ft. lbs.
3. Connect the wiring to the distributor.
4. Reconnect the cap and spark plug wires and connect the negative battery cable.
5. Check and/or adjust the ignition timing.

Timing Disturbed

1. Remove the No. 1 cylinder spark plug.
2. Place a finger over the spark plug hole while rotating the engine slowly by hand, until compression is felt.
3. Align the timing mark on the crankshaft pulley with the **0** degree mark on the timing scale on the front of the engine. This places the engine at TDC of the compression stroke for No. 1 cylinder.
4. Rotate the distributor shaft until the rotor points to the No. 1 spark plug tower on the distributor cap.
5. Install the distributor in the engine. Be sure to align the distributor-to-engine matchmarks.
6. Install and torque the hold-down nuts to 13 ft. lbs.
7. Connect all wiring to the distributor.
8. Start and run the engine.
9. Check and adjust the ignition timing.

Distributorless Ignition

The Distributor Ignition System (DIS) is used on the 2.0L (VIN 1), 2.2L (VIN G) and all V6 engines.

REMOVAL & INSTALLATION

DIS Assembly

1. Disconnect the negative battery cable.
2. Disconnect the electrical wires from the DIS assembly.
3. Mark the location of the spark plug wires on the DIS assembly and remove the wires.
4. Remove the DIS assembly mounting bolts and remove the assembly from the block.

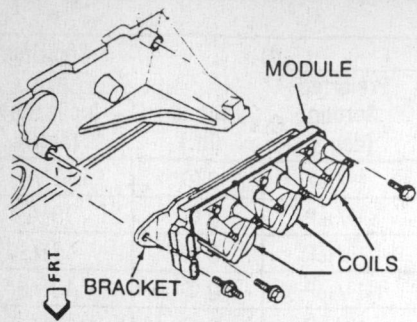

Ignition coil pack (DIS)—2.8L and 3.1L engines

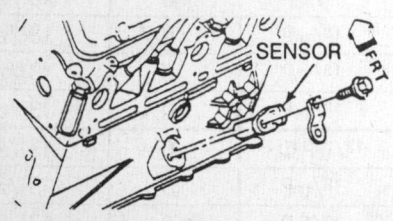

Crankshaft sensor removal— 2.8L and 3.1L engines

NOTE: With the coil pack removed, the coils can each be removed and the ignition module can be removed as well.

To install:

5. Install the DIS assembly on the block.

6. Reconnect the plug wires to their original location.

7. Connect the DIS assembly wiring.

8. Connect the negative battery cable.

9. If equipped with the 3.1L engine, perform the idle learn procedure to allow the ECM memory to be updated with the correct IAC valve pintle position and provide for a stable idle speed.

   a. Install a Tech 1 scan tool.

   b. Turn the ignition to the **ON** position, engine not running.

   c. Select **IAC SYSTEM**, then **IDLE LEARN** in the **MISC TEST** mode.

   d. Proceed with idle learn as directed by the scan tool.

Crankshaft Sensor

1. Disconnect the negative battery cable.

2. Disconnect the sensor harness plug.

3. Remove the sensor-to-block bolt and remove the sensor from the engine.

4. To install the sensor, position the sensor in the block and install the sensor bolt. Torque the sensor bolt to 71 inch lbs.

5. Reconnect the sensor harness plug.

Ignition Timing

ADJUSTMENT

2.0L (VIN 1 and G), 2.8L and 3.1L Engines

The ignition timing on engines with distributorless ignitions, is controlled by the Electronic Control Module (ECM). No adjustments are possible.

2.0L (VIN K and M) Engine

AVERAGING METHOD

1. Refer to the underhood emission control label and follow all of the timing instructions if they differ from below.

2. Warm the engine to normal operating temperature.

3. Place the transmission in **N** or **P**. Apply the parking brake and block wheels.

4. Air conditioning, cooling fan and choke must be **OFF**. Do not remove the air cleaner, except as noted.

5. Ground the ALCL connector under the dash by installing a jumper wire between the **A** and **B** terminals. The Check Engine light should begin flashing.

6. Connect an inductive timing light to the No. 1 spark plug wire lead and record timing.

7. Connect an inductive timing light to the No. 4 spark plug wire lead and record timing.

8. Add the 2 timing numbers and divide by 2 to obtain "average timing".

NOTE: For example: No. 1 timing = 4 degrees and No. 4 timing = 8 degrees; 4 + 8 = 12 ÷ 2 = 6 degrees average timing. If a change is necessary, subtract the average timing from the timing specification to determine the amount of timing change to No. 1 cylinder. For example: if the timing specification is 8 degrees and the average timing is 6 degrees, advance the No. 1 cylinder 2 degrees to set the timing.

9. To correct the timing, loosen the distributor hold-down clamp, adjust the distributor and retighten the hold-down bolt.

10. Once the timing is properly set, remove the jumper wire from the ALCL connector.

11. If necessary to clear the ECM memory, disconnect the ECM harness from the positive battery pigtail for 10 seconds with the key in the **OFF** position.

Alternator

For further information on the charging system, please refer to "Charging and Starting" in the Unit Repair section.

PRECAUTIONS

Several precautions must be observed with alternator equipped vehicles to avoid damage to the unit.

• If the battery is removed for any reason, make sure it is reconnected with the correct polarity. Reversing the battery connections may result in damage to the one-way rectifiers.

• When utilizing a booster battery as a starting aid, always connect the positive to positive terminals and the negative terminal from the booster battery to a good engine ground on the vehicle being started.

• Never use a fast charger as a booster to start vehicles.

• Disconnect the battery cables when charging the battery with a fast charger.

• Never attempt to polarize the alternator.

• Do not use test lamps of more than 12 volts when checking diode continuity.

• Do not short across or ground any of the alternator terminals.

• The polarity of the battery, alternator and regulator must be matched and considered before making any electrical connections within the system.

1. 2-3 coil
2. 1-4 coil
3. Module
4. Crank sensor assembly
5. Bolt—tighten to 71 inch lbs.

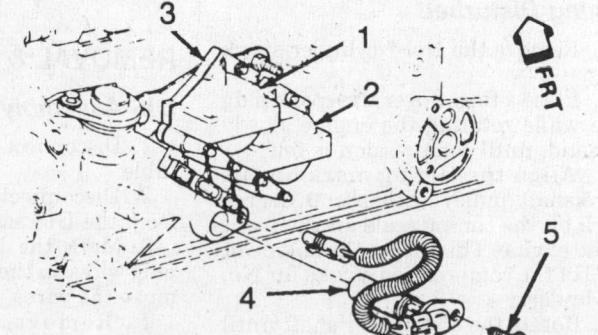

Ignition coils, module and sensor—2.0L and 2.2L engines

- Never separate the alternator on an open circuit. Make sure all connections within the circuit are clean and tight.
- Disconnect the battery ground terminal when performing any service on electrical components.
- Disconnect the battery if arc welding is to be done on the vehicle.

BELT TENSION ADJUSTMENT

V-Belts

Using belt tension gauge J–23600 or equivalent, adjust the alternator belt, if the tension is below 300N, as indicated on the gauge. If the old belt is used, the correct belt tension is 350N, as indicated on the gauge. If the belt is new, the correct tension is 600N, as indicated on the gauge.

Serpentine Belts

Serpentine belts are tensioned by loosening and rotating the belt tensioner. The correct belt tension is indicated on the indicator mark of the belt tensioner. If the indicator mark is not within specification, replace the belt or the tensioner.

NOTE: To remove or install the belt, push and rotate the tensioner. Care should be taken to avoid twisting or bending the tensioner when applying torque.

REMOVAL & INSTALLATION

V-Belt

1. Disconnect the negative battery cable.

——————— CAUTION ———————

Failure to disconnect the negative cable may result in injury from the positive battery lead at the alternator and may short the alternator and regulator during the removal process.

2. Disconnect and tag the 2 terminal plug and the battery lead from the rear of the alternator.
3. Loosen the mounting bolts. Push the alternator inwards and slip the drive belt off the pulley.
4. Remove the mounting bolts and remove the alternator.
To install:
5. Position the alternator in its brackets and install the mounting bolts. Do not tighten the bolts.
6. Slip the drive belt over the pulley. Pull outward on the alternator and adjust the belt tension. Tighten the mounting and adjusting bolts.
7. Connect the electrical leads.

8. Connect the negative battery cable.

Serpentine Belts

Serpentine belts are tensioned by loosening and rotating the belt tensioner. The correct belt tension is indicated on the indicator mark of the belt tensioner. If the indicator mark is not within specification, replace the belt or the tensioner.
1. Disconnect the negative battery cable.
2. Disconnect and tag the alternator wiring at the rear of the alternator.
3. Loosen the belt tensioner pivot bolt and rotate the tensioner to remove the belt.
4. Support the alternator and remove the mounting bolts.
5. Remove the alternator from the engine.
6. To install, place the alternator in the mounts and install the bolts.
7. Install the serpentine belt and tighten the belt tensioner.
8. Connect the alternator wiring and negative battery cable.

Voltage Regulator

For further information on the charging system, please refer to "Charging and Starting" in the Unit Repair section.

Starter

For further information on the charging system, please refer to "Charging and Starting" in the Unit Repair section.

REMOVAL & INSTALLATION

2.0L (VIN 1), 2.2L, 2.8L and 3.1L Engines

1. Disconnect the negative battery cable. Raise and support the vehicle safely.
2. Disconnect and tag the solenoid wires and battery cable at the starter.
3. Remove the rear starter support bracket. Remove the air conditioning compressor support rod, if equipped.
4. Support the starter and remove the 2 starter-to-engine bolts.
5. Remove the starter. Note the location and number of any shims.
To install:
6. Install the starter, placing any amount of shims removed in the original location.
7. Tighten the mounting bolts to 25–35 ft. lbs.
8. Install the support bracket and air conditioning compressor rod, if removed.
9. Connect the starter wiring.

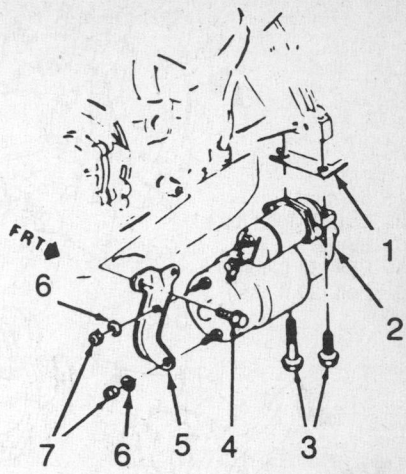

1. Shim
2. Starter
3. Bolt (32 ft. lbs.)
4. Bolt (9 ft. lbs.)
5. Bracket
6. Washer
7. Nut (24 ft. lbs.)

Starter mounting—2.0L (VIN 1) and 2.2L engines

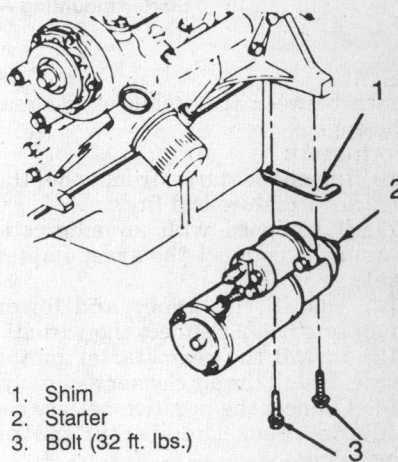

1. Shim
2. Starter
3. Bolt (32 ft. lbs.)

Starter mounting—2.8L and 3.1L engines

10. Connect the negative battery cable and check the starter operation.

2.0L (VIN K and M) Engine

1. Disconnect the negative battery cable.
2. Remove the air cleaner assembly.
3. Remove the lower starter mounting bolt.
4. Remove the rear starter brace.
5. Disconnect and tag the wiring at the starter.
6. Remove the upper starter mounting bolt.
7. Raise and support the vehicle safely.
8. If equipped with an automatic transaxle, disconnect the speedometer cable.
9. Push the shifter cable up and guide the starter, armature end first,

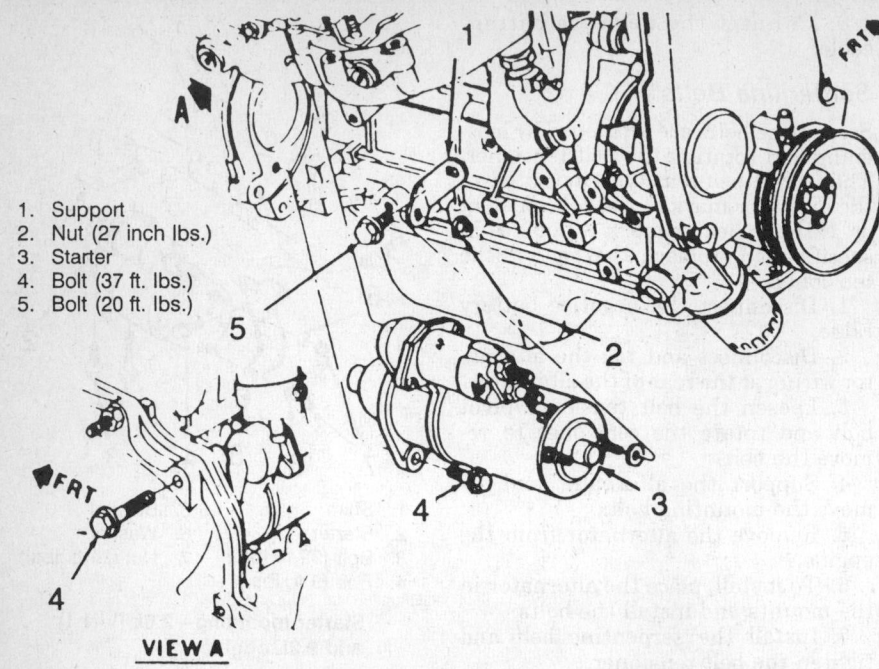

1. Support
2. Nut (27 inch lbs.)
3. Starter
4. Bolt (37 ft. lbs.)
5. Bolt (20 ft. lbs.)

VIEW A

Starter mounting—2.0L (VIN K and M) engine

down between the stabilizer bar and the engine.

To install:

10. Install the starter from under the vehicle, armature end first.

11. If equipped with an automatic transaxle, connect the speedometer cable.

12. Install the upper and lower mounting bolts. Connect the wiring.

13. Install the rear starter motor brace. Install the air cleaner assembly.

14. Connect the negative battery cable and check the starter motor operation.

CHASSIS ELECTRICAL

Heater Blower Motor

REMOVAL & INSTALLATION

1. Disconnect the negative battery cable.

2. Disconnect the electrical connections at the blower motor and blower resistor.

3. Remove the plastic water shield from the right side of the cowl.

4. Remove the blower motor retaining screws and remove the blower motor and cage.

5. Hold the blower motor cage and remove retaining nut from the blower motor shaft.

6. Remove the blower motor and cage.

To install:

7. Install the cage on the new motor.

8. Check that the retaining nut is on tight, the motor rotates and the fan cage is not interferring with the motor.

9. Install the motor in the heater assembly, connect the wiring and check the motor operation in all speeds.

Windshield Wiper Motor

REMOVAL & INSTALLATION

1. Disconnect the negative battery cable. Loosen, but do not remove the drive link-to-crank arm attaching nuts to detach the drive link from the motor crank arm.

2. Tag and disconnect all electrical leads from the wiper motor.

3. Unscrew the mounting bolts, rotate the motor up, outward and remove it.

4. Guide the crank arm through the opening in the body and then tighten the mounting bolts to 4–6 ft. lbs.

5. Install the drive link to the crank arm with the motor in the park position.

6. Installation is the reverse of the removal procedure.

Windshield Wiper Switch

REMOVAL & INSTALLATION

1. Disconnect the negative battery cable. Remove the steering wheel and turn signal switch.

NOTE: **It may be necessary to loosen the 2 column mounting nuts and remove the 4 bracket-to-mast jacket to allow the connector clip on the ignition switch to be pulled out of the column assembly.**

2. Disconnect the wiper switch lower connector.

3. Remove the screws attaching the column housing to the mast jacket. Note the position of the dimmer switch actuator rod for reassembly. Remove the column housing and switch as an assembly.

NOTE: **Tilt and travel columns have a removable plastic cover on the column housing. This provides access to the wiper switch without removing the entire column housing.**

4. Turn the switch upside down and use a drift to remove the pivot pin from the switch. Remove the switch.

To install:

5. Place the switch into the housing and install the pivot pin.

6. Position and attach the housing onto the mast jacket by installing the screws.

7. Install the dimmer switch actuator rod in the same position as noted earlier. Check the switch operation.

8. Reconnect lower switch wiring.

9. Install the remaining components in reverse order of removal. Be sure to attach column mounting bracket in the original position.

Instrument Cluster

REMOVAL & INSTALLATION

Cavalier, Cimarron and Sunbird

1. Disconnect the negative battery cable.

2. Remove the speedometer cluster trim plate.

3. Remove the speedometer cluster attaching screws.

4. Lower the steering column. Pull the cluster away from the instrument panel and disconnect the speedometer cable.

5. Disconnect the vehicle speed sensor connector from the cluster. Disconnect all other electrical connectors as required.

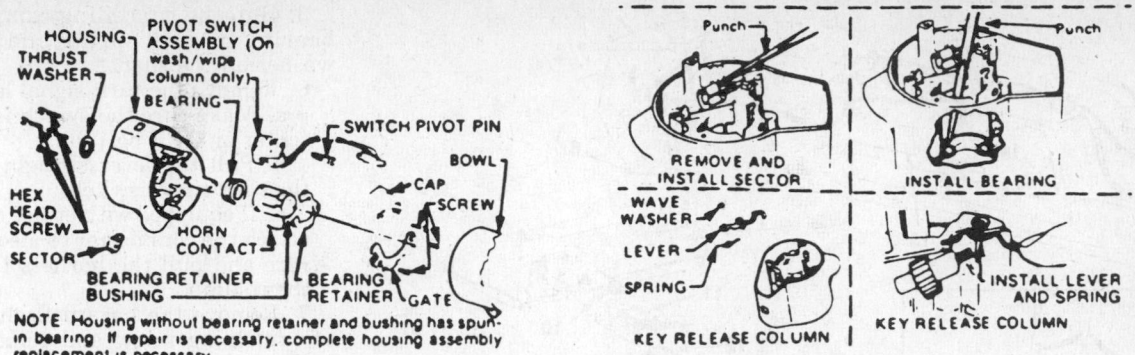

NOTE: Housing without bearing retainer and bushing has spun-in bearing. If repair is necessary, complete housing assembly replacement is necessary

Wiper switch and related parts—standard steering column

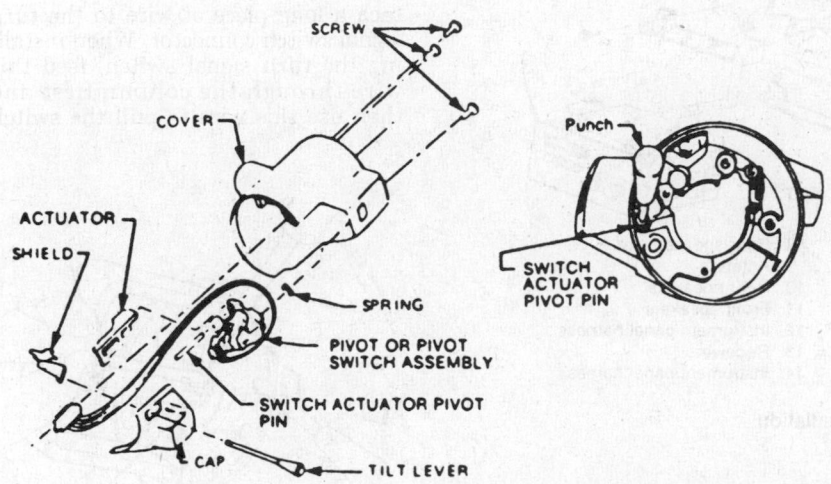

Wiper switch and related parts—adjustable steering column

6. Remove the cluster housing from the vehicle.

7. Installation is the reverse of the removal procedure.

Skyhawk and Firenza

1. Disconnect the negative battery cable.

2. Remove the steering column trim cover. Remove the left and right hand trim cover.

3. Remove the cluster trim cover.

4. Remove the screws attaching the lens and bezel to the cluster carrier.

5. Lower the steering wheel column by removing the 2 upper steering column attaching bolts.

6. Remove the screws attaching the cluster housing to the cluster carrier. Pull the cluster out slightly from the instrument panel and disconnect the speedometer cable. Disconnect all others connectors.

7. Remove the cluster housing from the vehicle.

8. Installation is the reverse of the removal procedure.

NOTE: Some 1987–88 Firenza vehicles, equipped with manual control air conditioning, may exhibit metallic rattle or buzzing noise coming from the center of the instrument panel. Under certain road or engine load conditions, with the air conditioning ON, the metal defroster valve in the air conditioning module assembly may vibrate against the case causing the noise. The noise may be heard in all modes except defrost.

Speedometer

REMOVAL & INSTALLATION

1. Disconnect the negative battery cable.

2. Remove speedometer cluster from instrument panel.

3. Remove cluster lens and face plate.

4. Remove screws securing speedometer to cluster assembly and re-move speedometer and disconnect the cable.

5. Installation is the reverse of the removal procedure.

Radio

REMOVAL & INSTALLATION

NOTE: Do not operate the radio with the speaker leads disconnected. Operating the radio without an electrical load will damage the output transistors.

1. Disconnect the negative battery cable.

2. Remove the center instrument panel trim plate.

3. Check the right side of the radio to determine whether a nut or a stud is used for side retention.

4. If a nut is used, remove the hush panel and loosen the nut from below, on vehicles without air conditioning. On vehicles with air conditioning, remove the hush panel, air conditioning duct and air conditioning control head for access to the nut. Do not remove the nut; loosen it just enough to pull the radio out. If a rubber stud is used, go to Step 5.

5. Remove the 2 radio bracket-to-instrument panel attaching screws. Pull the radio forward far enough to disconnect and tag the wiring and antenna. Remove the radio.

6. Installation is the reverse of the removal procedure.

Headlight Switch

REMOVAL & INSTALLATION

Cavalier, Cimarron and Sunbird

1. Disconnect the negative battery cable.

2. Pull the knob out fully. Remove the knob from rod by depressing the retaining clip from the underside of the knob.

3. Remove the trim plate.

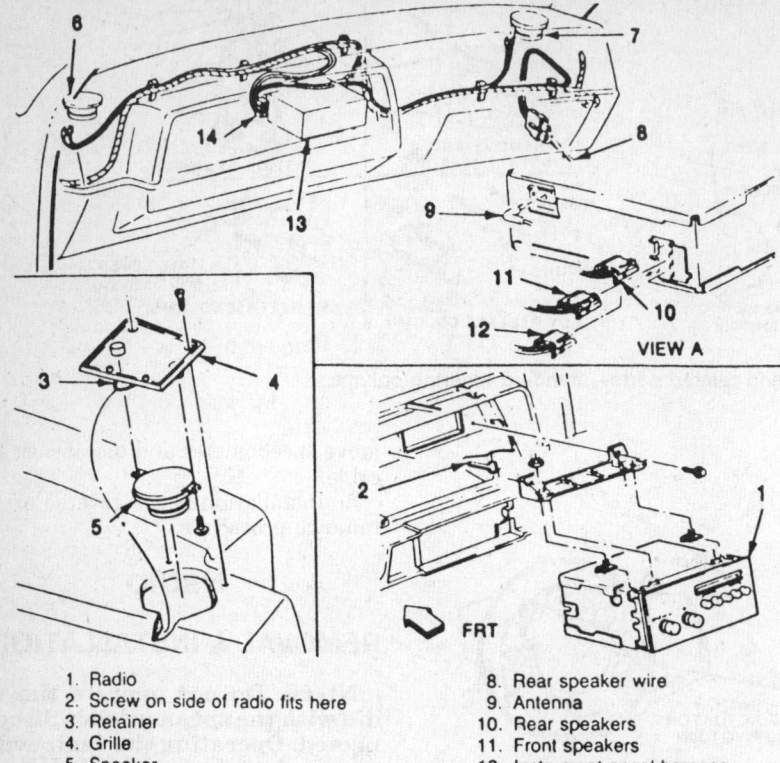

1. Radio
2. Screw on side of radio fits here
3. Retainer
4. Grille
5. Speaker
6. Front speaker
7. Front speaker
8. Rear speaker wire
9. Antenna
10. Rear speakers
11. Front speakers
12. Instrument panel harness
13. Receiver
14. Instrument panel harness

Typical radio installation

4. Remove the switch by removing nut, rotating the switch 180 degrees, then tilting forward and pulling it out. Disconnect the wire harness.

5. Installation is the reverse of the removal procedure.

Skyhawk and Firenza

1. Disconnect the negative battery cable.
2. Remove the left side trim cover.
3. Remove the screws attaching the headlight switch to the instrument panel.
4. Pull the switch rearward in order to remove it from the vehicle.
5. Installation is the reverse of the removal procedure.

Dimmer Switch

REMOVAL & INSTALLATION

1. Disconnect the negative battery cable. Remove the steering wheel. Remove the trim cover.
2. Remove the turn signal switch assembly.
3. Remove the ignition switch stud and screw. Remove the ignition switch.
4. Remove the dimmer switch actu-

ator rod by sliding it from the switch assembly.

5. Remove the dimmer switch bolts and remove the dimmer switch.

6. Installation is the reverse of the removal procedure.

7. Adjust the dimmer switch by depressing the switch slightly and inserting a $\frac{3}{32}$ in. drill bit into the adjusting hole. Push the switch up to remove any play and tighten the dimmer switch adjusting screw.

Turn Signal Switch

REMOVAL & INSTALLATION

NOTE: Before removing the turn signal switch, be sure the lever is in the OFF or CENTER position.

1. Disconnect the negative battery cable. Remove the steering wheel. Remove the trim cover.
2. Pry the cover from the steering column.
3. Position a U-shaped lockplate compressing tool on the end of the steering shaft nut clockwise. Pry the wire snapring on the shaft groove off.
4. Remove the tool and lift the lockplate off the shaft.

5. Slip the cancelling cam, upper bearing preload spring and thrust washer off the shaft.

6. Remove the turn signal lever.

   a. Make sure the switch is in the center or **OFF** position.

   b. Pull the lever straight out of the turn signal switch.

   c. If equipped with cruise control, attach the connnector to mechanic's wire and pull the harness through the column.

7. Remove the hazard flasher button retaining screw and remove the button, spring and knob.

8. Pull the switch connector out of the mast jacket and tape the upper part to facilitate switch removal. Attach a long piece of wire to the turn signal switch connnector. When installing the turn signal switch, feed this wire through the column first and then use this wire to pull the switch

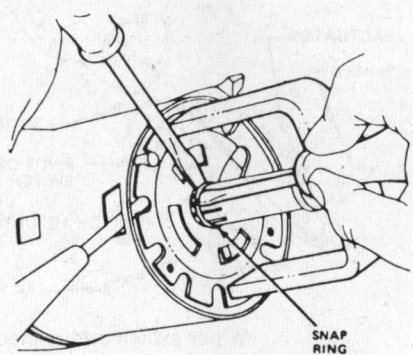

Using the lock plate depressing tool to remove the snapring

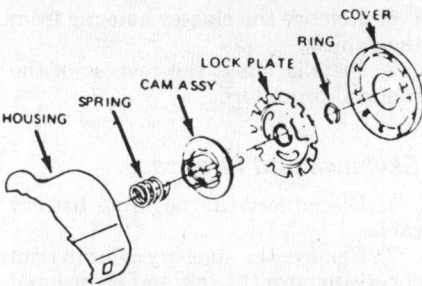

Remove these parts for removal of the turn signal switch

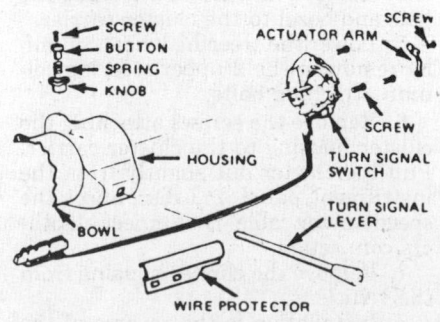

Turn signal switch removal details

connector into position. On tilt columns, place the turn signal and shifter housing in **LOW** position and remove the harness cover.

9. Remove the 3 switch mounting screws. Remove the switch by pulling it straight up while guiding the wire harness cover through the column.

To install:

10. Install the replacement switch by working the connector and cover down through the housing and under the bracket. If equipped with tilt steering, the connector is worked down through the housing, under the bracket and then the cover is installed on the harness.

11. Install the switch mounting screws and the connector on the mast jacket bracket. Install the column-to-dash trim plate.

12. Install the flasher knob and turn the signal lever.

13. With the turn signal lever in middle position and the flasher knob out, slide the thrust washer, upper bearing preload spring and cancelling cam onto the shaft.

14. Position the lock plate on the shaft and press it down until a new snapring can be inserted in the shaft groove. Always use a new snapring when assembling.

15. Install the cover and steering wheel. Connect the negative battery cable.

Ignition Switch

REMOVAL & INSTALLATION

The switch is located inside the channel section of the brake pedal support and is completely inaccessible without first lowering the steering column. The switch is actuated by a rod and rack assembly. A gear on the end of the lock cylinder engages the toothed upper end of the rod.

1. Lower the steering column; be sure to properly support it.

2. Put the switch in the **OFF-LOCKED** position. With the cylinder removed, the rod is in **OFF-UN-LOCKED** position when it is in the next to the upper most detent.

3. Remove the 2 switch screws and remove the switch assembly.

4. Before installing, move the slider on the switch to the following positions:

 a. Key release columns—Leave the slider to the extreme left.

 b. Park lock columns—Move the slider 1 detent to the right in the **OFF-LOCK** position.

 c. All other columns—Move the slider 2 detents to the left in the **OFF-UNLOCKED** position on 1987 vehicles. Move the slider 2 detents to the right in the **OFF-UN-LOCKED** position on 1988–91 vehicles.

5. Install the activating rod into the switch and assemble the switch on the column. Tighten the mounting screws. Use only the specified screws, since over length screws could impair the effectiveness of the column to collapse.

6. Install the steering column.

Ignition Lock Cylinder

REMOVAL & INSTALLATION

Standard Steering Column

1. Remove the steering wheel.

2. Turn the ignition key to the **RUN** position.

3. Remove the lock plate, turn signal or combination switch and the key warning buzzer switch. The warning buzzer switch is pulled out with small tool.

4. Remove the lock cylinder retaining screw and lock cylinder.

NOTE: If the retaining screw is dropped during removal, it could fall into the column, requiring complete column disassembly to retrieve the screw.

5. Rotate the cylinder clockwise to align the cylinder key with the keyway in the housing.

6. Push the lock all the way in.

7. Install the screw. Tighten to 15 inch lbs.

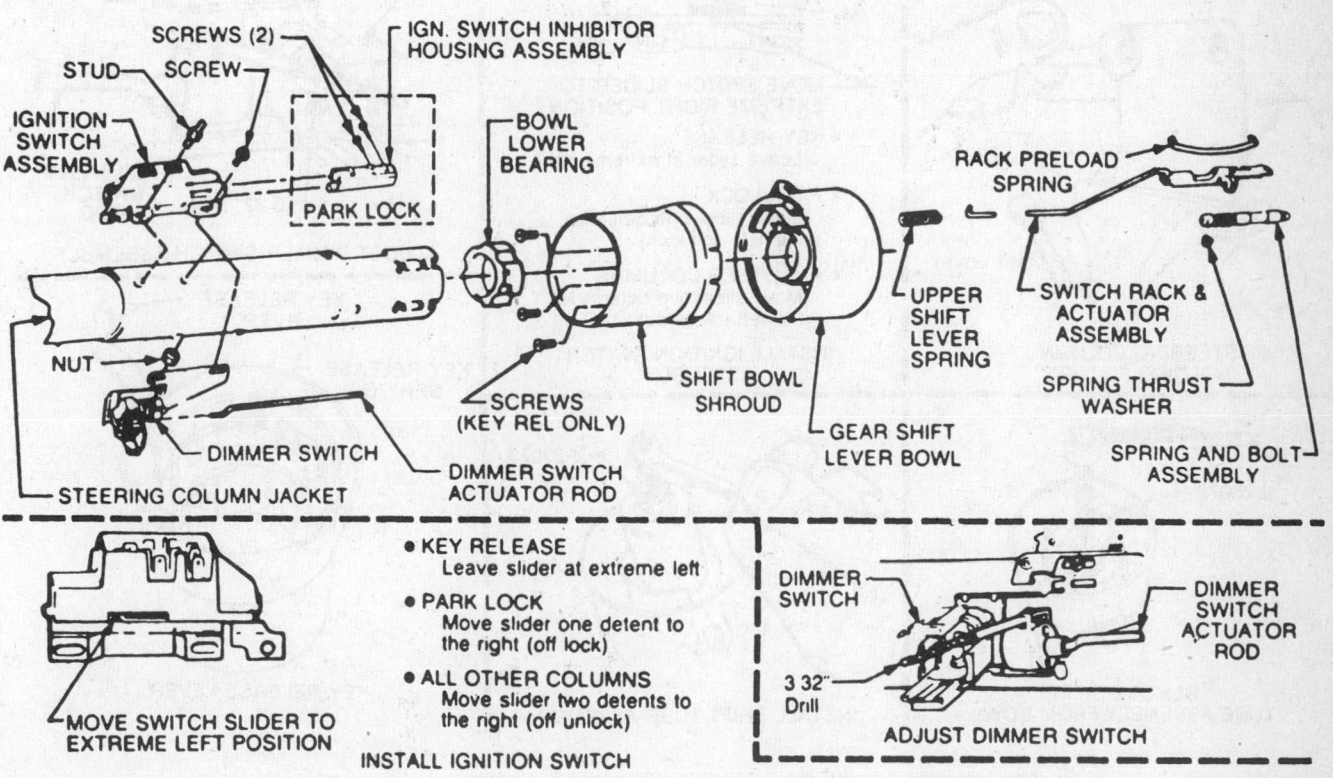

Ignition switch and dimmer switch removal and installation—standard column

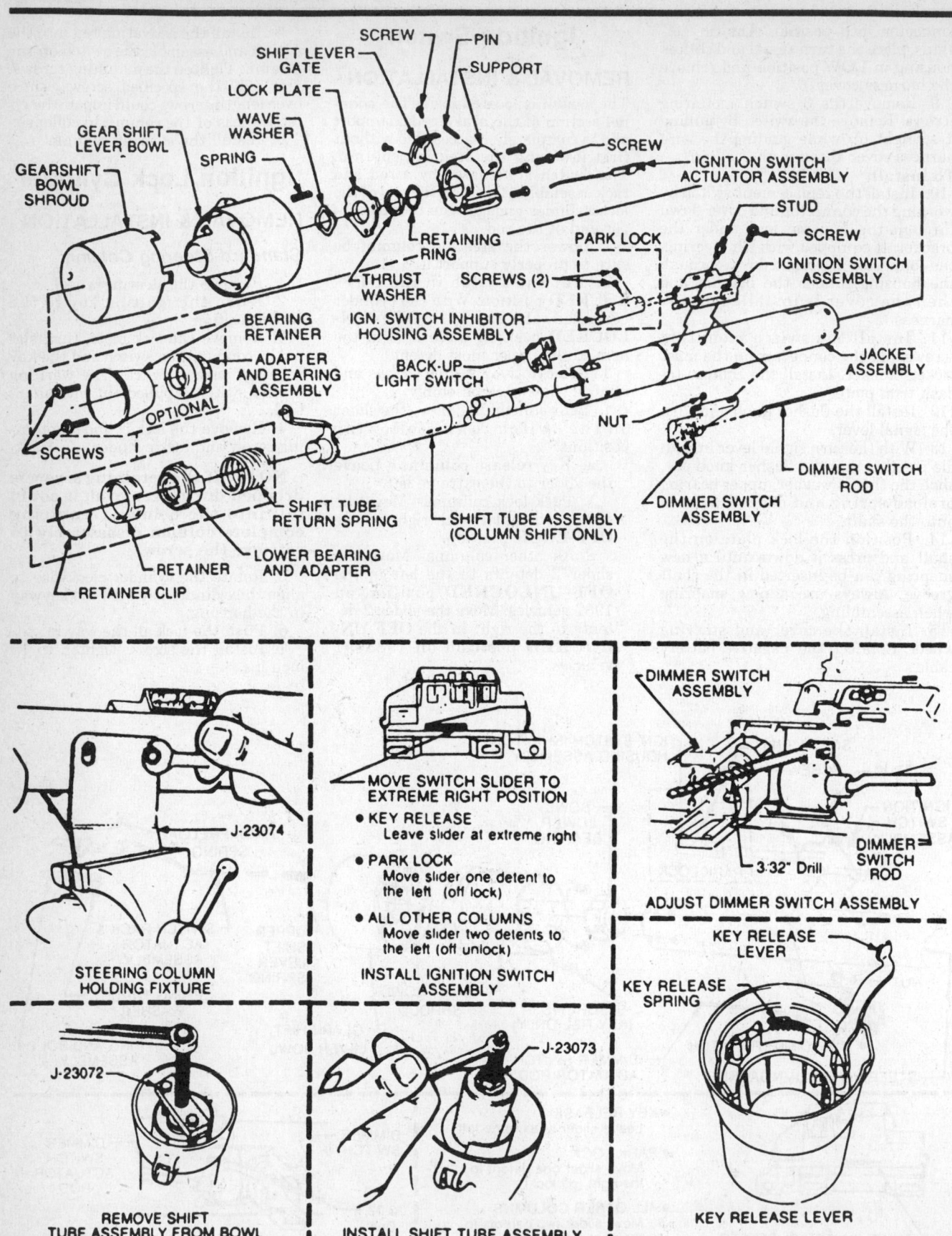

SCREW — PIN
SHIFT LEVER GATE — SUPPORT
LOCK PLATE
GEAR SHIFT LEVER BOWL — WAVE WASHER
GEARSHIFT BOWL SHROUD — SPRING
SCREW
IGNITION SWITCH ACTUATOR ASSEMBLY
STUD
SCREW
IGNITION SWITCH ASSEMBLY
PARK LOCK
RETAINING RING
THRUST WASHER
SCREWS (2)
IGN. SWITCH INHIBITOR HOUSING ASSEMBLY
BEARING RETAINER
ADAPTER AND BEARING ASSEMBLY
OPTIONAL
BACK-UP LIGHT SWITCH
JACKET ASSEMBLY
NUT
SCREWS
SHIFT TUBE RETURN SPRING
SHIFT TUBE ASSEMBLY (COLUMN SHIFT ONLY)
DIMMER SWITCH ASSEMBLY
DIMMER SWITCH ROD
LOWER BEARING AND ADAPTER
RETAINER
RETAINER CLIP

J-23074

STEERING COLUMN HOLDING FIXTURE

MOVE SWITCH SLIDER TO EXTREME RIGHT POSITION
• KEY RELEASE Leave slider at extreme right
• PARK LOCK Move slider one detent to the left (off lock)
• ALL OTHER COLUMNS Move slider two detents to the left (off unlock)

INSTALL IGNITION SWITCH ASSEMBLY

DIMMER SWITCH ASSEMBLY
3/32" Drill
DIMMER SWITCH ROD

ADJUST DIMMER SWITCH ASSEMBLY

KEY RELEASE LEVER
KEY RELEASE SPRING

J-23072

REMOVE SHIFT TUBE ASSEMBLY FROM BOWL

J-23073

INSTALL SHIFT TUBE ASSEMBLY

KEY RELEASE LEVER

Ignition switch and dimmer switch removal and installation—adjustable column

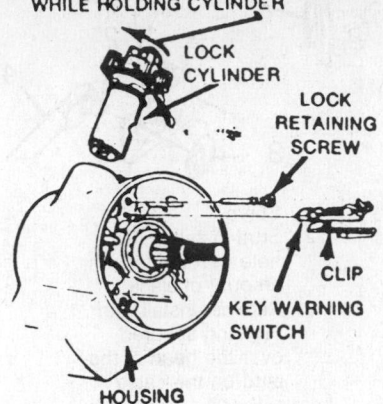

Lock cylinder installation

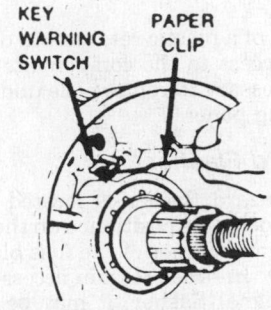

Removing the key warning buzzer

8. The remainder of the installation is the reverse of the removal. Turn the lock to **RUN** position and push the key warning buzzer switch into place.

Tilt Steering Column

1. Disconnect the negative battery cable. Remove the steering wheel.
2. Remove the rubber sleeve bumper from the steering shaft.
3. Using an appropriate tool, remove the plastic retainer.
4. Using a spring compressor, compress the upper steering shaft spring and remove the C-ring. Release the steering shaft lock plate, the horn contact carrier and the upper steering shaft preload spring.
5. Remove the 4 screws which hold the upper mounting bracket and then remove the bracket.
6. Slide the harness connector out of the bracket on the steering column. Tape the upper part of the harness and connector.
7. Disconnect the hazard button and position the shift bowl, on automatic transmission equipped vehicles in the **P** position. Remove the turn signal lever from the column.
8. If equipped with cruise control, remove the harness protector from the harness. Attach a piece of wire to the

switch harness connector. Before removing the turn signal lever, loop a piece of wire and insert it into the turn signal lever opening. Use the wire to pull the cruise control harness out through the opening. Pull the rest of the harness up through and out of the column. Remove the guide wire from the connector and secure the wire to the column. Remove the turn signal lever.
9. Pull the turn signal switch up until the end connector is within the shift bowl. Remove the hazard flasher lever. Allow the switch to hang.
10. Place the ignition key in the **RUN** position.
11. Depress the center of the lock cylinder retaining tab with a suitable tool and then remove the lock cylinder.
12. Installation is the reverse of the removal procedure.

Stoplight Switch

REMOVAL & INSTALLATION

The stoplight, cruise control and cruise control vacuum switch are all located on the brake pedal mounting bracket and are adjusted in an identical manner.
1. Remove the wiring from switch and remove the switch.
2. To install, insert the retaining tubular clip in bracket on the pedal assembly.
3. With the pedal depressed, insert the switch into the tubular clip until the switch body seats on clip.

NOTE: Audible clicks can be heard as threaded portion of switch is pushed through the clip toward the brake pedal. Vacuum release valve and stoplight switch are self-adjusting.

4. Connect the wiring for the switch.

Clutch Switch

ADJUSTMENT

The clutch start switch is used on vehicles equipped with a manual transaxle. The switch prevents the engine from starting unless the clutch pedal is depressed.

REMOVAL & INSTALLATION

1. Disconnect the negative battery cable.
2. Unbolt the switch from the clutch pedal assembly and disconnect the wiring.
3. Install the new switch in reverse order of removal.

Neutral Safety System

All column shift automatic transaxle models use a mechanical neutral start system. This system has a mechanical block which prevents cranking the engine when the shift lever is in any position except **P** or **N**.

All floor shift automatic transaxle models use a park lock system. This system uses a flexible cable actuator which is attached at one end to the shift lever and the other end is attached to the column mounted ignition switch where it actuates a locking pin. The locking pin engages an ignition switch sliding contact when the shift lever is in **R**, **N** or **D** and does not allow the ignition switch slider to move to the **LOCK** position. When the shift lever is in **P**, the pin disengages from the slider and allows it to move to the **LOCK** position.

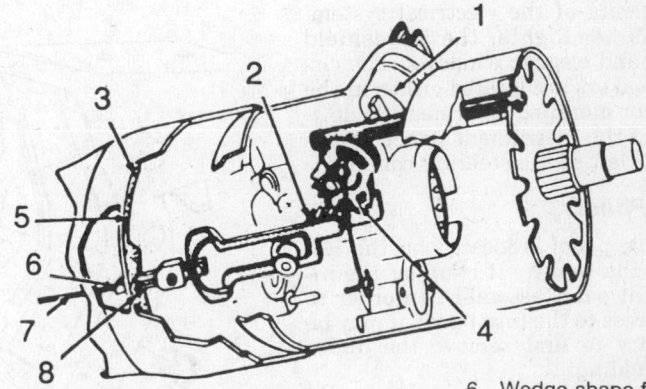

1. Lock cylinder
2. Rack
3. Bowl plate
4. Sector
5. Park position
6. Wedge shape finger
7. Actuator rod assembly
8. Neutral position

Mechanical neutral start system

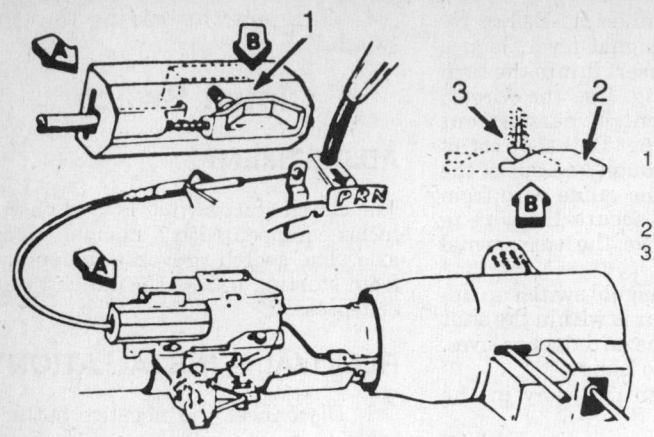

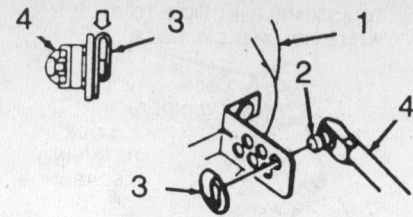

1. Position of locking pin and cam with shift lever in park
2. Cam
3. Locking pin

1. Servo
2. Stud-install in the hole with the least amount of slack
3. Retainer-install with the tang secured over the head of the stud on the cable

Park lock system

Servo cable adjustment

Fuses, Circuit Breakers and Relays

LOCATION

Fusible Links

Fusible links are used to prevent major wire harness damage in the event of short circuit or an overload condition in the wiring circuits which are normally not fused, due to carrying high amperage loads or because of their locations within the wiring harness. Each fusible link is of a fixed value for a specific electrical load and should a link fail, the cause of failure must be determined and repaired prior to installing a new fusible link of the same value. Fusible links are located in the engine harness at the starter solenoid and the left hand front of the dash at the battery junction block.

Circuit Breakers

Circuit breakers are used along with the fusible links to protect the various components of the electrical system, such as headlights, the windshield wipers and electric windows. The circuit breakers are located either in the switch or mounted on or near the lower lip of the instrument panel, to the right or left of the steering column.

Fuse Panels

The fuse panel is located on the left side of the vehicle. It is under the instrument panel assembly. In order to gain access to the fuse panel, it may be necessary to first remove the under dash padding.

Convenience Center and Various Relays

The convenience center is located on the underside of the instrument panel

near the fuse panel. It provides a central location for various relays, hazard flasher units and buzzers. All units are easily replaced with plug-in modules.

Computer

LOCATION

The Electronic Control Module (ECM) is located on the right side of the vehicle. It is positioned in front of the right hand kick panel. In order to gain access to the assembly, remove the trim panel.

Flashers

LOCATION

Turn Signal Flasher

The turn signal flasher is located directly under the steering column of the vehicle. It is secured in place by

means of a plastic retainer. In order to gain access to the component, it may be necessary to remove the underdash padding panel.

Hazard Flasher

The hazard flasher is located in the fuse block. It is positioned on the lower right hand corner of the fuse block assembly. In order to gain access to the turn signal flasher, it may be necessary to first remove the under dash padding.

Cruise Control

ADJUSTMENT

Release Switch and Valve

1. Depress the brake pedal and insert the vacuum release valve into the retainer until a click is heard indicating that the valve switch is seated.

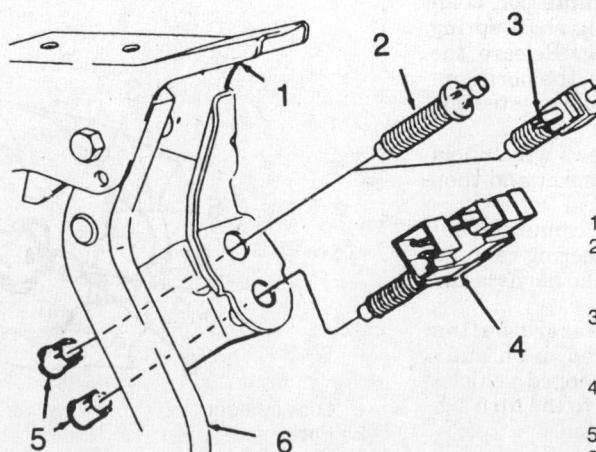

1. Brake pedal bracket
2. Vacuum release valve-manual transaxle
3. Vacuum release valve/switch-automatic transaxle
4. Stoplight and cruise control switch
5. Retainer
6. Brake pedal

Cruise control vacuum valve/switch installation

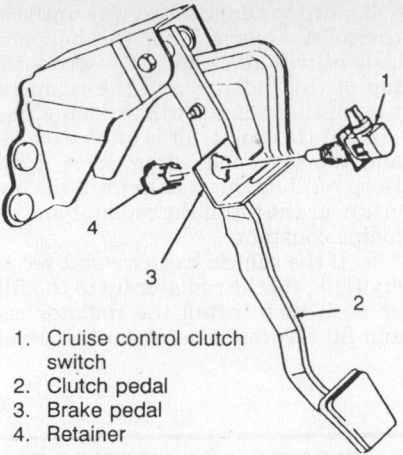

1. Cruise control clutch switch
2. Clutch pedal
3. Brake pedal
4. Retainer

Cruise control clutch switch installation

2. Allow the brake pedal to travel rearward to the positive stop.

3. The valve switch will be moved through the retainer into the proper position.

NOTE: Audible clicks can be heard as threaded portion of switch is pushed through the clip toward the brake pedal. Vacuum release valve and stoplight switch are self-adjusting.

Servo Cable

1. Install the cable into the engine bracket. Route the cable assembly to the servo bracket.

2. Pull the servo end of the cable towards the servo assembly without moving the throttle lever.

3. Line up the pin in the end of the cable with 1 of the holes in the servo assembly tab.

4. Insert the cable pin into 1 of the 6 holes in the servo bracket. Install the retainer.

NOTE: Do not stretch the cable to make a certain connection as this will prevent the engine from returning to idle. Use the next closest hole.

ENGINE COOLING

Radiator

REMOVAL & INSTALLATION

1. Disconnect the negative battery cable.
2. Drain the cooling system.

3. Disconnect the electrical lead at the fan motor.

4. Remove the fan frame-to-radiator support bolts and remove the fan assembly.

5. Disconnect the upper and lower radiator hoses and the coolant recovery hose from the radiator.

6. Disconnect the transaxle oil cooler lines, on automatic transaxle equipped models, from the radiator and wire them out of the way.

7. Remove the radiator-to-radiator support attaching bolts and clamps. Remove the radiator.

To install:

8. Place the radiator in the vehicle so the bottom is located in the lower mounting pads. Tighten the attaching bolts and clamps.

9. Connect the transaxle oil cooler lines and tighten the bolts to 20 ft. lbs.

10. Installation of the remaining components is in the reverse order of the removal procedure. Fill and bleed the cooling system.

Electric Cooling Fan

The coolant fan relay is activated by the Electronic Control Module (ECM) when the coolant temperature sensor recognizes temperature readings above 230°F (108°C) on 2.0L engine and 223°F (106°C) on all other engines. The coolant fan is also activated if a coolant temperature sensor failure is detected Code 14 or 15 or if the ECM is in the back up mode. The ECM will also activate the cooling fan relay on 2.8L and 3.1L engines when the air conditioning pressure exceeds 200 psi. and on engines, when air conditioning is turned on and low pressure switch is closed.

NOTE: The ECM controls the cooling fan by grounding CKT 335 green/yellow wire. Once the ECM turns the fan relay on, it will keep fan on for a minimum of 30 seconds, or until vehicle speed exceeds 70 mph on the 2.8L and 3.1L engine.

TESTING

NOTE: If the fan does not run while connected to the electrical wiring connector, inspect for a defective coolant temperature switch or air conditioning relay, if equipped. Always check body wiring for frayed or loose connections.

1. Disconnect the electrical wiring connector from the electric cooling fan.

2. Using a 14 gauge jumper wire, connect it between the fan and the

positive battery terminal; the fan should run.

3. If the fan does not run when connected to the jumper wire, replace the fan assembly.

REMOVAL & INSTALLATION

1. Disconnect the negative battery cable.

2. Tag and disconnect the wiring harness from the fan frame and motor assembly.

3. Remove the fan assembly retaining bolts. Remove the fan and motor assembly from the vehicle.

4. Installation is the reverse of the removal procedure.

Heater Core

REMOVAL & INSTALLATION

Without Air Conditioning

1. Disconnect the negative battery cable and drain the cooling system.

2. Remove the heater hoses at the heater core.

3. Remove the heater outlet deflector.

4. Remove the heater core cover retaining screws. Remove the heater core cover.

5. Remove the heater core retaining straps and remove the heater core.

To install:

6. Install the new heater core and retaining straps.

7. Install the heater outlet deflector and heater core cover.

8. Connect the heater hoses to the core.

9. Fill and bleed the cooling system when finished. Check for leaks and the heater operation.

With Air Conditioning

1. Disconnect the negative battery cable and drain the cooling system.

2. Raise and safely support the vehicle.

3. Disconnect the drain tube from the heater case.

4. Remove the rear lateral transaxle support.

5. Remove the heater hoses and evaporator lines from the heater core and evaporator.

6. Lower the vehicle. Remove the right and left hush panels, steering column trim cover, heater outlet duct and glove box.

7. Remove the heater core cover. Pull the cover straight to the rear so it does not damage the drain tube.

8. Remove the heater core clamps and remove the heater core.

To install:

9. Install the heater core and clamps.

10. Install the heater core cover using care not to damage the drain tube.

11. Install the glove box, heater outlet duct, steering column trim cover and hush panels.

12. Raise and support the vehicle safely.

13. Connect the heater hoses and evaporator lines to the heater core and evaporator, connect the drain tube to the case. Install the rear transaxle lateral support.

14. Lower the vehicle, fill the cooling system and connect the negative battery cable.

15. Check the heater operation and bleed the cooling system. Check for leaks.

Water Pump

REMOVAL & INSTALLATION

2.0L (VIN 1), 2.2L, 2.8L and 3.1L Engines

1. Disconnect the negative battery cable.

2. Drain the cooling system.

3. Remove all drive belts.

4. Remove the alternator.

5. Unscrew the water pump pulley mounting bolts and remove the pulley.

6. Remove the mounting bolts and remove the water pump.

7. To install the pump, place a 1/8 in. bead of RTV sealant on the water pump sealing surface. While the sealer is still wet, install the pump and tighten the bolts to 15–22 ft. lbs. on 4 cylinder engines and 6–9 ft. lbs. on 6 cylinder engines.

8. Installation of the remaining components is in the reverse order of removal.

2.0L (VIN M and K) Engine

1. Disconnect negative battery cable.

2. Drain cooling system.

3. Remove timing belt.

4. Remove water pump retaining bolts, water pump and seal ring.

5. To install reverse removal procedures. Torque water pump bolts to 18 ft. lbs. Be sure to properly install the accessory drive belt.

Thermostat

REMOVAL & INSTALLATION

2.0L (VIN 1), 2.2L, 2.8L and 3.1L Engines

The thermostat is located inside a housing either on the cylinder head (4 cylinder) or in the thermostat housing on the intake manifold (V6 engine). It is not necessary to remove the radiator hose from the thermostat housing when removing the thermostat.

1. Disconnect the negative battery cable.

2. Drain the cooling system and remove the air cleaner.

3. Disconnect the AIR pipe at the upper check valve and the bracket at the water outlet.

4. Disconnect the electrical lead.

5. Remove the 2 retaining bolts from the thermostat housing and lift up the housing with the hose attached. Lift out the thermostat.

6. Insert the new thermostat, spring end down. Apply a thin bead of silicone sealer to the housing mating surface and install the housing while the sealer is still wet. Tighten the housing retaining bolts to 15–22 ft. lbs. on 6 cylinder engines or 6–9 ft. lbs. on 4 cylinder engines.

7. Installation of the remaining components is in the reverse order of removal.

2.0L (VIN M and K) Engine

NOTE: The engine must be COLD for this procedure.

1. Disconnect the negative battery cable.

2. Remove the thermostat housing cap.

3. Grasp the handle of the thermostat assembly and gently pull upward.

4. Clean the thermostat housing and O-ring.

5. Apply a suitable lubricant to the O-ring, then install the thermostat into the housing, pushing down to ensure that the thermostat is firmly seated.

6. Replace the thermostat housing cap.

Cooling System Bleeding

After working on the cooling system, even to replace the thermostat, it must be bled. Air trapped in the system will prevent proper filling and leave the radiator coolant level low, causing a risk of overheating.

1. To bleed the system, start with the system cool, the radiator cap off and the radiator filled to about an inch below the filler neck.

2. Start the engine and run it at slightly above normal idle speed. This will insure adequate circulation. If air bubbles appear and the coolant level drops, fill the system with an antifreeze/water mixture to bring the level back to the proper level.

3. Run the engine this way until the thermostat opens. When this happens, coolant will move abruptly across the top of the radiator and the temperature of the radiator will suddenly rise.

4. At this point, air is often expelled and the level may drop quite a bit. Keep refilling the system until the level is near the top of the radiator and remains constant.

5. If the vehicle has a coolant recovery tank, fill the radiator up to the filler neck then install the radiator cap and fill recovery tank to correct level.

FUEL SYSTEM

Fuel System Service Precautions

Safety is the most important factor when performing not only fuel system maintenance but any type of maintenance. Failure to conduct maintenance and repairs in a safe manner may result in serious personal injury or death. Maintenance and testing of the vehicle's fuel system components can be accomplished safely and effectively by adhering to the following rules and guidelines.

• To avoid the possibility of fire and personal injury, always disconnect the negative battery cable unless the repair or test procedure requires that battery voltage be applied.

• Always relieve the fuel system pressure prior to disconnecting any fuel system component (injector, fuel rail, pressure regulator, etc.), fitting or fuel line connection. Exercise extreme caution whenever relieving fuel system pressure to avoid exposing skin, face and eyes to fuel spray. Please be advised that fuel under pressure may penetrate the skin or any part of the body that it contacts.

• Always place a shop towel or cloth around the fitting or connection prior to loosening to absorb any excess fuel due to spillage. Ensure that all fuel spillage (should it occur) is quickly removed from engine surfaces. Ensure that all fuel soaked cloths or towels are deposited into a suitable waste container.

• Always keep a dry chemical (Class B) fire extinguisher near the work area.

• Do not allow fuel spray or fuel vapors to come into contact with a spark or open flame.

• Always use a backup wrench when loosening and tightening fuel line connection fittings. This will prevent unnecessary stress and torsion to fuel line piping. Always follow the proper torque specifications.

• Always replace worn fuel fitting O-rings with new. Do not substitute fuel hose or equivalent where fuel pipe is installed.

RELIEVING FUEL SYSTEM PRESSURE

The fuel delivery pipe is under high pressure even after the engine is stopped. Direct removal of the fuel line, may result in dangerous fuel spray. Make sure to release the fuel pressure according to the following procedures:

2.0L (VIN 1) and 2.2L Engines

1987

1. Release the fuel vapor pressure in the fuel tank by removing the fuel tank cap and reinstalling it.
2. Disconnect the fuel pump at the rear body connector and wait until the engine stops.
3. Start the engine and allow it to run a few seconds until it runs out of fuel.
4. Once the engine is stopped, crank it a few times with the starter for about 3 seconds to dissipate the fuel in the lines.

1988

1. Release the fuel vapor pressure in the fuel tank by removing the fuel tank cap and reinstalling it.
2. Remove the fuel pump fuse from the fuse block or from the underhood fuse holder.
3. Start the engine and allow it to run a few seconds until it runs out of fuel.
4. Once the engine is stopped, crank it a few times with the starter for about 3 seconds to dissipate the fuel in the lines.
5. If the fuel pressure can't be released in the above manner because the engine failed to run, disconnect the negative battery cable, cover the union bolt of the fuel line with an absorbant rag and loosen the union bolt slowly to release the fuel pressure gradually.

1989–91

1. Disconnect the negative battery cable.
2. Release the fuel vapor pressure in the fuel tank by removing the fuel tank cap and reinstalling it.
3. The internal constant bleed feature of the TBI Models 700/220, relieves the fuel pump system pressure when the engine is turned **OFF** and no further pressure relive procedure is required.

2.0L (VIN K) Engine

1987–91

1. Release the fuel vapor pressure in the fuel tank by removing the fuel tank cap and reinstalling it.
2. Remove the fuel pump fuse from the fuse block.
3. Start the engine and allow it to run a few seconds until it runs out of fuel.
4. Once the engine is stopped, crank it a few times with the starter for about 3 seconds to dissipate the fuel in the lines.
5. If the fuel pressure can't be released in the above manner because the engine failed to run, disconnect the negative battery cable, cover the union bolt of the fuel line with an absorbant rag and loosen the union bolt slowly to release the fuel pressure gradually.

2.0L (VIN M) Engine

1987–88

1. Release the fuel vapor pressure in the fuel tank by removing the fuel tank cap and reinstalling it.
2. Disconnect the fuel tank harness connector.
3. Start the engine and allow it to run a few seconds until it runs out of fuel.
4. Once the engine is stopped, crank it a few times with the starter for about 3 seconds to dissipate the fuel in the lines.
5. If the fuel pressure can't be released in the above manner because the engine failed to run, disconnect the negative battery cable, cover the union bolt of the fuel line with an absorbant rag and loosen the union bolt slowly to release the fuel pressure gradually.

1989–91

1. Disconnect the negative battery cable.
2. Disconnect the fuel filler cap.
3. Connect gauge J–34730–1 or equivalent, to the fuel pressure connection. Wrap a cloth around the fitting to absorb any fuel leakage.
4. Install the bleed hose into an approved container and open the valve to bleed system pressure.

2.8L and 3.1L Engines

1987

1. Disconnect the negative battery cable.
2. Disconnect the fuel filler cap.
3. Connect gauge J–34730–1 or equivalent, to the fuel pressure connection. Wrap a cloth around the fitting to absorb any fuel leakage.
4. Install the bleed hose into an approved container and open the valve to bleed system pressure.

1988

1. Release the fuel vapor pressure in the fuel tank by removing the fuel tank cap and reinstalling it.
2. Disconnect the fuel tank harness connector.
3. Start the engine and allow it to run a few seconds until it runs out of fuel.
4. Once the engine is stopped, crank it a few times with the starter for about 3 seconds to dissipate the fuel in the lines.
5. If the fuel pressure can't be released in the above manner because the engine failed to run, disconnect the negative battery cable, cover the union bolt of the fuel line with an absorbant rag and loosen the union bolt slowly to release the fuel pressure gradually.

1989–91

1. Disconnect the negative battery cable.
2. Disconnect the fuel filler cap.
3. Connect gauge J–34730–1 or equivalent, to the fuel pressure connection. Wrap a cloth around the fitting to absorb any fuel leakage.
4. Install the bleed hose into an approved container and open the valve to bleed system pressure.

Fuel Filter

REMOVAL & INSTALLATION

The fuel filter is located under the rear of the vehicle near the fuel tank.

1. Relieve the fuel system pressure.
2. Disconnect the negative battery cable.
3. Raise and safely support the vehicle.
4. Disconnect the fuel lines from the filter.
5. Remove the filter retaining bolt and remove the filter from the vehicle.
6. Install the new filter in position, using new O-ring seals, and connect the fuel lines. Tighten the fuel lines to 20 ft. lbs.
7. Lower the vehicle.
8. Connect the negative battery cable and run the engine. Check for leaks.

Electric Fuel Pump

PRESSURE TESTING

Throttle Body Injection

1. Relieve the fuel system pressure.
2. Remove the air cleaner and plug the thermal vacuum port on the throttle body unit.
3. Remove the steel fuel line from between the throttle body unit and the fuel filter.

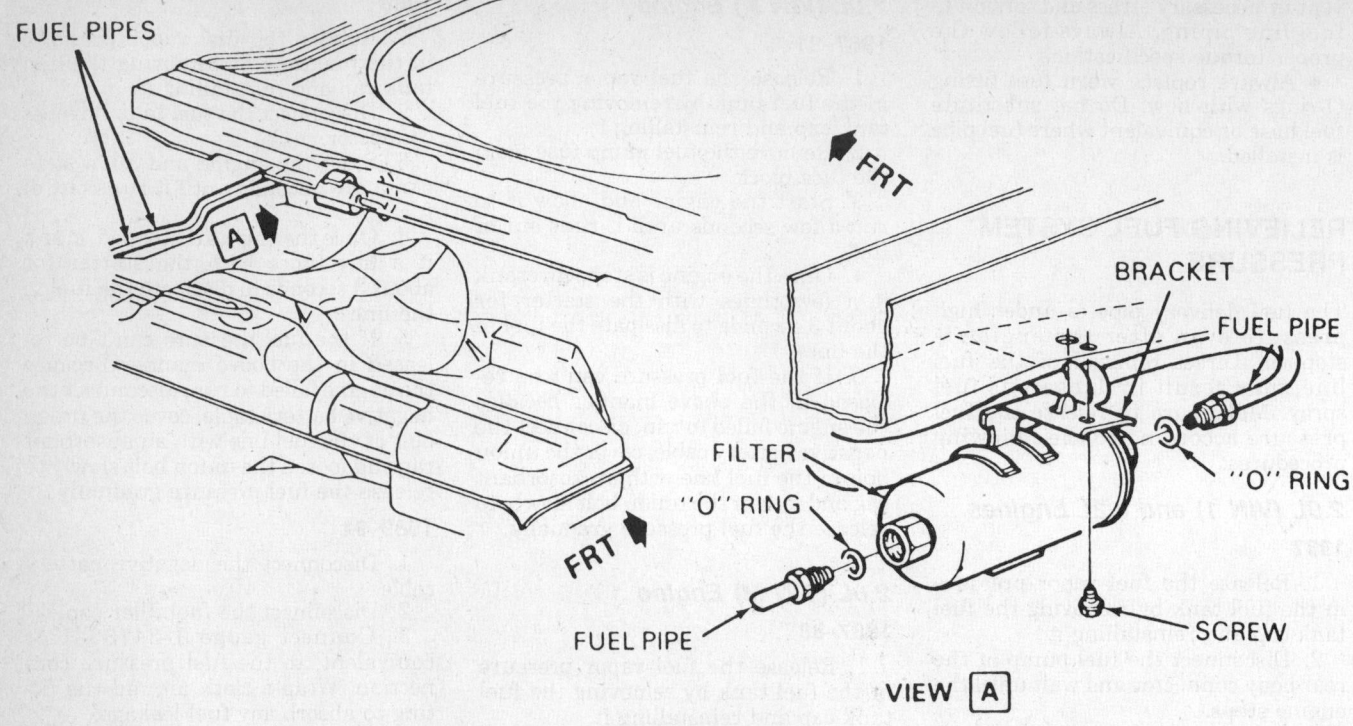

FUEL PIPES

A

FRT

FRT

BRACKET

FUEL PIPE

FILTER

"O" RING

"O" RING

FUEL PIPE

SCREW

VIEW A

Fuel filter installation

4. Install a fuel pressure gauge with at least a 15 psi capacity between the throttle body and the filter.

5. Start the engine and observe the pressure reading. Pressure should be 9–13 psi. If the pressure is not within these limits, one or more of the following could be at fault:

    a. A short in the system

    b. A clogged fuel filter

    c. A shorted or defective oil pressure switch

    d. Defective fuel pump relay

    e. Defective fuel pump

NOTE: Check each of these components in turn to diagnose the problem before replacing the pump.

6. Follow the cautions at the start of this procedure to depressurize the system. Remove the pressure gauge and install the fuel line. Torque the nuts to 19–25 ft. lbs.

7. Start the engine and check for leaks.

8. Unplug the thermal vacuum port on the throttle body.

Multi-Port Injection

1. Release the fuel system pressure. Wrap a shop towel around fuel pressure connector on the fuel rail to absorb any leakage that may occur when installing gauge.

2. Install a fuel pressure gauge J–34730–1 or equivalent, to pressure connector.

3. With ignition **ON** pump pressure should be as follows:

    a. 40.5–47 psi on 2.8L and 3.1L engines

    b. 35–38 psi on 2.0L (Code M) engine

4. When engine is idling, pressure should drop 3–10 psi on 2.8L and 3.1L engines or 25–30 psi on 2.0L (Code M) engine.

NOTE: The application of vacuum to the pressure regulator should result in a fuel pressure drop.

5. Remove fuel pressure gauge J–34730–1 or equivalent, from pressure connector.

REMOVAL & INSTALLATION

The electric fuel pump is located in the fuel tank.

1. Relieve the fuel system pressure.

2. Disconnect the battery ground.

3. Raise and support the vehicle safely.

4. Remove the fuel filler cap.

5. Drain the fuel tank.

6. Disconnect the filler neck hose and the vent hose.

7. Disconnect the filler neck hose and the vent hose.

8. Remove the fuel tank strap rear support bolts and lower the tank on a jack, just enough, to disconnect the fuel feed line, return and vapor lines from the fuel meter.

9. Remove the tank.

10. Remove the fuel meter/pump as-

sembly by turning the cam lock ring counterclockwise. Lift the assembly from the tank and remove the pump from the meter.

11. Pull the pump up onto the attaching hose while pulling outward from the bottom support. Take care not to damage the rubber insulator and strainer. After the pump is clear of the bottom support pull it out of the rubber connector.

12. Installation is the reverse of removal. Use a new O-ring on the tank cam lockring.

Fuel Injection

IDLE SPEED AND MIXTURE ADJUSTMENT

All fuel control functions are controlled by the Electronic Control Module (ECM). No adjustments are necessary.

Fuel Injector

REMOVAL & INSTALLATION

NOTE: Use care in removing injector to prevent damage to the electrical pins on top of the injector. The fuel injectors are an electrical component. Do not immerse in any type of cleaner.

Throttle Body Injection

1. Relieve the fuel pump pressure.
2. Disconnect the negative battery cable.
3. Remove the TBI cover and gasket.
4. Disconnect the electrical connector to fuel injector.
5. Remove the injector retainer.
6. Using a fulcrum, place a suitable tool under the ridge opposite the connector end and carefully pry injector out.
7. To install, reverse the removal procedures. Be sure the electrical connector end, on the injector is facing in the direction to the cut-out in the fuel meter body for the wire grommet to fit properly.

NOTE: Remove the upper and lower O-rings from injector body and in fuel injector cavity and replace with new O-rings before installing injector.

Multi Port Injection

NOTE: The fuel rail is removed as an assembly, then the injectors can be removed.

1. Disconnect the negative battery cable. Relieve the fuel system pressure.
2. Tag and disconnect the fuel injection electrical connections.
3. Remove the upper intake manifold plenum asssmbly. Remove the necessary components in order to gain access to the fuel rail retaining bolts.
4. Remove the fuel rail retaining bolts. Remove the fuel rail assembly.
5. Separate the fuel injector from the fuel rail.
6. Installation is the reverse of the removal procedure. Replace the O-rings when installing the injectors.

EMISSION CONTROLS

Please refer to "Emission Control" in the Unit Repair section for system maintenance procedures. Due to the complex nature of modern electronic engine control systems, comprehensive diagnosis and testing procedures fall outside the confines of this repair manual. For complete information on diagnosis, testing and repair procedures concerning all modern engine and emission control systems, please refer to "Chilton's Guide to Electronic Engine Controls".

Emission Warning Lamps

RESETTING

When the Electronic Control Module (ECM) finds a problem, the CHECK ENGINE light will come on and a trouble code will be stored in the ECM. In order to clear the stored trouble code, it is necessary to remove the battery voltage for 10 seconds. This will clear all stored codes in ECM memory. Do this by disconnecting the ECM harness from the positive battery cable with the ignition in the **OFF** position or by removing the ECM fuse.

NOTE: In order to prevent damage to the ECM, the key must be OFF when connecting or disconnecting power to the ECM.

ENGINE MECHANICAL

NOTE: Disconnecting the negative battery cable on some vehicles may interfere with the functions of the on board computer systems and may require the computer to undergo a relearning process, once the negative battery cable is reconnected.

Engine Assembly

REMOVAL & INSTALLATION

2.0L (VIN 1) and 2.2L Engines

NOTE: Special tool J-24420 crankshaft pulley hub remover is required. The engine is removed from the top of vehicle.

1. Disconnect the negative battery cable and relieve the fuel system pressure.
2. Drain the cooling system.
3. Remove the air cleaner.
4. Disconnect the accelerator and TV cables.
5. Disconnect the ECM harness at engine.
6. Disconnect the necessary vacuum hoses.
7. Disconnect all of the cooling hoses at engine.
8. Remove the exhaust heat shield.
9. If equipped with air conditioning, remove the adjustment bolt at motor mount.
10. Disconnect engine wiring harness at bulkhead.
11. Remove the windshield washer bottle.
12. Remove the alternator and power steering belt.
13. Disconnect the fuel hoses.
14. Raise and safely support the vehicle. If equipped with air conditioning, remove the air conditioning brace.
15. Remove inner fender splash shield.
16. If equipped with air conditioning, remove the air conditioning compressor.
17. Remove flywheel splash shield.
18. Disconnect and the tag starter wires.
19. Disconnect the front starter brace.
20. Remove the starter.
21. Remove the torque converter bolts.
22. Remove the crankshaft pulley and hub using tool J-24420 or equivalent.
23. Remove the oil filter.
24. Disconnect the engine-to-transaxle bracket.
25. Disconnect the right rear mount.
26. Disconnect exhaust at manifold and at center hanger.
27. Disconnect the TV and shift cable.
28. Remove the lower bell housing bolts.
29. Lower the vehicle.
30. Remove the right front motor mount nuts.
31. Remove alternator and adjusting brace.
32. Disconnect the master cylinder and push it aside.
33. Install a suitable lifting device.
34. Remove the right front motor mount bracket.
35. Remove upper bell housing bolts.
36. Remove the power steering pump while lifting engine.
37. Carefully remove the engine from the vehicle.

To install:
38. Install the engine mount alignment bolt M6X1X65 to ensure proper power train alignment.
39. Slowly lower the engine into the vehicle, leaving the lifting device attached.
40. Install the transaxle bracket. Install the mount to the side frame and secure with new bolts.
41. With the engine weight not on the mounts, tighten the transaxle bolts to 48–63 ft. lbs.
42. Tighten the right front mount nuts.
43. Lower the engine weight onto the mounts. Remove the lifting device. Raise and support the vehicle safely.
44. Installation of the remaining components is in the reverse order of removal. Check the powertrain align-

ment bolt; if excessive force is required to remove the bolt, loosen the transaxle bolts and realign the powertrain.

2.0L (VIN K and M) Engine

NOTE: This procedure requires the use of a special powertrain alignment bolt M6X1X65. The engine is removed from the bottom of the vehicle.

1. Disconnect the negative battery cable and relieve fuel pressure.
2. Drain the cooling system.
3. Remove the air cleaner assembly.
4. Disconnect the engine electrical harness at bulkhead.
5. Disconnect the electrical connector at brake cylinder.
6. Remove the throttle cable from bracket and EFI assembly.
7. Remove and tag the vacuum hoses from EFI assembly.
8. Remove the power steering high pressure hose at cut-off switch.
9. Remove and tag the vacuum hoses at map sensor and canister.
10. Disconnect the air conditioning relay cluster switches.
11. Remove the power steering return hose at pump.
12. Disconnect the ECM wire connections, feed the harness through bulkhead and lay harness over engine.
13. Remove the upper and lower radiator hoses from engine.
14. Remove the electrical connections from the temperature switch at thermostat housing.
15. Raise and support the vehicle safely.
16. Disconnect the transaxle shift cable at transaxle.
17. Remove the speedometer cable at transaxle and bracket.
18. Disconnect the exhaust pipe at the exhaust manifold.
19. Remove the exhaust pipe from converter.
20. Remove the heater hoses from heater core.
21. Remove fuel lines at the flex hoses.
22. Remove the transaxle cooler lines at flex hoses.
23. Remove the left and right front wheels.
24. Remove the right hand spoiler section and splash shield.
25. Remove the right and left brake calipers and support with wire.
26. Remove right and left tie rod ends.
27. Disconnect the electrical connections at air conditioning compressor.
28. Remove the air conditioning compressor and mounting brackets, support the air conditioning compressor by wiring it in a wheel opening.
29. Remove the front suspension

support attachment bolts; 6 bolts each side.
30. Lower the vehicle.
31. Support the front of vehicle by placing 2 short stands under core support.
32. Position a front post hoist to the rear of cowl.
33. Position a 4 × 4 × 6 timber on the front post hoist.
34. Raise the vehicle enough to remove stands.
35. Position a 4-wheel dolly under engine and transaxle assembly.
36. Position three 4 × 4 × 12 blocks under the engine and transaxle assembly only, letting support rails hang free.
37. Lower the vehicle onto 4-wheel dolly slightly.
38. Remove the rear transaxle mount attachment bolts.
39. Remove the left front engine mount attachment bolts.
40. Remove the 2 engine support to body attachment bolts behind right hand inner axle U-joint.
41. Remove 1 attaching bolt and nut from right hand chassis side rail to engine mount bracket.
42. Remove 6 strut attachment nuts.
43. Raise the vehicle, letting the engine, transaxle and suspension rest on the 4-wheel dolly.

To install:
44. Position the engine and transaxle assembly in chassis.
45. Install transaxle and left front mounts to side rail bolts loosely.
46. Install M6X1X65 alignment bolt in left front mount to prevent powertrain misalignment.
47. Torque transaxle mount bolts to 42 ft. lbs. and left front mount bolts to 18 ft. lbs.
48. Install right rear mount to body bolts and torque to 38 ft. lbs.
49. Install right rear mount to chassis side rail bolt and nut torque to 38 ft. lbs.
50. Place a lifting device under the control arms. Raise them into position and install retaining nuts.
51. Raise and support the vehicle safely.
52. Using suitable lifting equipment, raise the control arms and attach tie rod ends.
53. Complete the installation by installing the remaining components in reverse order.

2.8L and 3.1L Engines

NOTE: Always release the fuel pressure before starting repair. The engine is removed from the top of the vehicle.

1. Disconnect the negative battery cable. Drain the cooling system and remove the air cleaner assembly. Mark

the bolt location and remove the hood.
2. Remove the air flow sensor. Remove the exhaust crossover heat shield and remove the crossover pipe.
3. Remove the serpentine belt tensioner and belt.
4. Remove the power steering pump mounting bracket. Disconnect the heater pipe at the power steering pump mounting bracket.
5. Disconnect the radiator hoses from the engine.
6. Disconnect the accelerator and throttle valve cable at the throttle valve.
7. Remove the alternator. Tag and disconnect the wiring harness at the engine.
8. Relieve the fuel pressure and disconnect the fuel hose. Disconnect the coolant bypass and the over flow hoses at the engine.
9. Tag and remove the vacuum hoses to the engine.
10. Raise the vehicle and support it safely.
11. Remove the inner fender splash shield. Remove the harmonic balancer.
12. Remove the flywheel cover. Remove the starter bolts. Tag and disconnect the electrical connections to the starter. Remove the starter.
13. Disconnect the wires at the oil sending unit.
14. Remove the air conditioning compressor and related brackets.
15. Disconnect the exhaust pipe at the rear of the exhaust manifold.
16. Remove the flexplate-to-torque converter bolts.
17. Remove the transaxle-to-engine bolts. Remove the engine-to-rear mount frame nuts.
18. Disconnect the shift cable bracket at the transaxle. Remove the lower bell housing bolts.
19. Lower the vehicle and disconnect the heater hoses at the engine.

NOTE: It may be necessary to remove the engine hood. Using an awl, scribe marks around the hood hinges to help aid correct hood alignment upon installation.

20. Install a suitable engine lifting device. While supporting the engine and transaxle, remove the upper bell housing bolts.
21. Remove the front mounting bolts.
22. Remove the master cylinder from the booster.
23. Remove the engine assembly from the vehicle.

To install:
24. Install the engine in position in the vehicle.

25. Install the upper transaxle-to-engine bolts.

26. Raise and safely support the vehicle.

27. Install the lower transaxle-to-engine bolts.

28. Reconnect the shift cable bracket to the transaxle.

29. Install the engine mounts, tightening the front mount-to-frame bolts to 61 ft. lbs. and the engine mount to bracket bolts to 50 ft. lbs.

30. Install the flywheel to converter bolts.

31. Reconnect the exhaust pipe and install the air conditioning compressor. Install the flywheel cover.

32. Reconnect the coolant hoses and the fuel lines.

33. Install the wiring harness at the engine and install the alternator.

34. Lower the vehicle and install the accessory drive belt.

35. Refill all of the fluids and connect the negative battery cable.

36. Install the hood. Install the air cleaner assembly.

37. Road test the vehicle.

Engine Mounts

REMOVAL & INSTALLATION

Front

1. Disconnect the negative battery cable.

2. Raise the vehicle and support safely.

3. Using a suitable fixture, support the engine and remove the engine mount nuts.

4. Remove the inner fender shield.

5. Remove the engine mount bolts. The manufacturer recommends discarding the engine mount bolts and replacing with new bolts. Note the location and length of each bolt for reassembly.

6. Remove the engine mount.

7. Installation is the reverse of the removal procedure.

Rear

1. Disconnect the negative battery cable.

2. Raise the vehicle and support safely.

3. If equipped with manual transaxle, remove the oil filter in order to gain working clearance.

4. Using a suitable fixture, support the engine and remove the engine mounting nuts.

5. Remove the engine mounting bolts. Remove the engine mount.

6. Installation is the reverse of the removal procedure.

NOTE: On some 1987 Sunbirds, engine Codes K and M, fatigue fracture of the rear engine mount may occur. The ignition coil and bracket are mounted to the rear engine mount. If the mount fractures, the coil may become unsupported.

Cylinder Head

REMOVAL & INSTALLATION

2.0L (VIN 1) and 2.2L Engines

NOTE: The engine must be cold before removing the cylinder head. Always release the fuel pressure before starting repair.

1. Disconnect the negative battery cable.

2. Drain the cooling system.

3. Remove the TBI cover. Raise and safely support the vehicle.

4. Remove the exhaust shield. Disconnect the exhaust pipe.

5. Remove the heater hose from the intake manifold. Lower the vehicle.

6. Disconnect the accelerator and TV cable bracket.

7. Lower the vehicle.

8. Tag and disconnect the vacuum lines at the intake manifold and thermostat.

9. Disconnect the accelerator linkage at the TBI unit and remove the linkage bracket.

10. Tag and disconnect all necessary wires. Remove the upper radiator hose at the thermostat.

11. Remove the serpentine belt.

12. Remove the power steering pump and lay aside.

13. Make sure the fuel system pressure is released and disconnect and plug the fuel lines.

14. Remove the alternator. Remove the alternator brace from the head and remove the upper mounting bracket.

15. Remove the cylinder head cover. Remove the rocker arms and pushrods keeping all parts in order for correct installation.

19. Remove the cylinder head bolts. Remove the cylinder head with the TBI unit, intake and exhaust manifolds still attached.

To install:

20. The gasket surfaces on both the head and the block must be clean of any foreign matter and free of any nicks or heavy scratches. Bolt threads in the block and the bolts must be clean.

21. Place a new cylinder head gasket in position over the dowel pins on the block. Carefully guide the cylinder head into position.

22. Coat the cylinder bolts with sealing compound and install them finger tight.

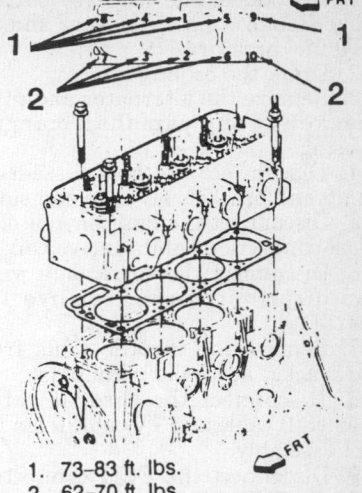

1. 73–83 ft. lbs.
2. 62–70 ft. lbs.

Cylinder head bolt torque sequence— 2.0L (VIN 1) and 2.2L engines

23. If equipped with the 2.0L engine, torque the short bolts in sequence to 62–70 ft. lbs. and torque the long bolts in sequence to 73–83 ft. lbs.

24. If equipped with the 2.2L engine, tighten the bolts in the following sequence:

   a. Tighten all bolts initially to 41 ft. lbs.

   b. Tighten all bolts 45 degrees in sequence.

   c. Tighten all bolts an additional 45 degrees in sequence.

   d. Tighten the long bolts 8, 4, 1, 5 and 9 an additional 20 degrees.

   e. Tighten the short bolts 7, 3, 2, 6 and 10 an additional 10 degrees.

NOTE: The short bolts, exhaust side, should end up with a total rotation of 100 degrees and the long bolts, intake side, should end up with a total rotation of 110 degrees.

25. Reinstall the alternator. Install the power steering pump and brackets.

26. Reconnect the fuel lines and the hoses. Connect the exhaust pipe to the manifold.

27. Install the valve cover and connect the linkage at the TBI unit. Install the air cleaner and fill all the fluids.

28. Run the engine and check for leaks.

2.0L (VIN K and M) Engine

NOTE: Cylinder head gasket replacement is necessary if camshaft carrier/cylinder head bolts are loosened. The head bolts should always be loosened when cold. New head bolts should be used every time camshaft carrier/ cylinder head or gasket are replaced.

1. Disconnect the negative battery cable. Remove the air cleaner and relieve fuel pressure.

2. Drain the cooling system.

3. Remove the alternator and pivot bracket at the camshaft carrier housing.

4. Disconnect the power steering pump and bracket, lay it to one side.

5. Disconnect the ignition coil electrical connections and remove coil.

6. Disconnect the spark plug wires and distributor cap, remove the distributor.

7. Remove the throttle cable from the bracket at intake manifold.

8. Disconnect the throttle cable, downshift cable and TV cable from the EFI assembly.

9. Disconnect the ECM connectors from the EFI assembly.

10. Remove the vacuum brake hose at filter.

11. Disconnect the inlet and return fuel lines at flex joints.

12. Remove the water pump bypass hose at the intake manifold and water pump.

13. Disconnect the ECM harness connectors at intake manifold.

14. Disconnect the heater hose from intake manifold.

15. Disconnect the exhaust pipe at exhaust manifold.

NOTE: On engine Code M, remove the exhaust manifold to turbo connection and O_2 sensor connection.

16. Disconnect the breather hose at camshaft carrier.

17. Remove the upper radiator hose.

18. Disconnect the engine electrical harness and wires from thermostat housing.

19. Remove the timing cover.

20. Remove the timing probe holder.

21. Loosen the water pump retaining bolts and remove timing belt.

22. Loosen the camshaft carrier and cylinder head attaching bolts, a little at a time, in sequence.

23. Remove the camshaft carrier assembly.

24. Remove the cylinder head, intake manifold and exhaust manifold as an assembly.

To install:

25. Install a new cylinder head gasket in position on the block.

26. Apply a continuous bead of sealer to the cam carrier.

27. Install the cylinder head, reassembled with the intake and exhaust manifolds, if removed.

28. Install the camshaft carrier on the cylinder head and tighten the bolts, in following sequence, to the correct torque.

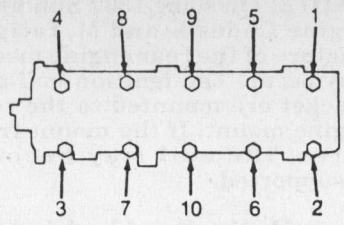

Camshaft carrier/cylinder head bolt loosening sequence—2.0L (VIN K and M) engine

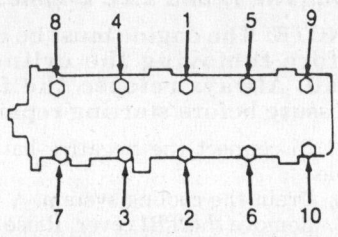

Camshaft carrier/cylinder head bolt torque sequence—2.0L (VIN K and M) engine

a. Tighten all bolts in sequence to 18 ft. lbs.

b. Tighten all bolts an additional 180 degrees in 3 steps of 60 degrees each.

29. Install the timing belt.

30. Reconnect the electrical harness and the breather hose at the camshaft carrier.

31. Connect the exhaust pipe at the manifold and attach the heater hose to the intake manifold.

32. Connect the brake hose at the filter. Connect the throttle and TV cable.

33. Refill the cooling system and connect the negative battery cable.

34. Run the engine, until warm, thermostat open, and tighten all of the the cylinder head/cam carrier bolts an additional 30–50 degrees, in sequence. Check for leaks.

2.8L and 3.1L Engines

LEFT SIDE

1. Relieve the fuel system pressure and disconnect the negative battery cable. Drain the cooling system. Remove the rocker cover.

2. Remove the intake manifold. Disconnect the exhaust crossover at the right exhaust manifold.

3. Disconnect the oil level indicator tube bracket.

4. Loosen the rocker arms nuts enough to remove the pushrods.

5. Starting with the outer bolts, remove the cylinder head bolts. Remove the cylinder head with the exhaust manifold.

6. Clean and inspect the surfaces of the cylinder head, block and intake manifold. Clean the threads in the block and the threads on the bolts.

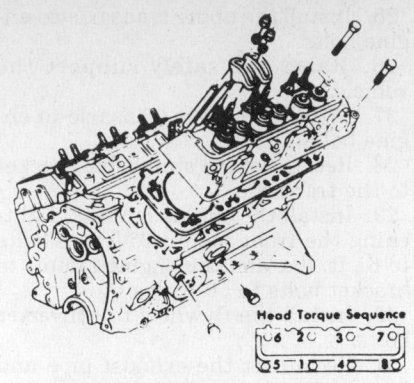

Cylinder head torque sequence—2.8L and 3.1L engines

To install:

7. Align the new gasket over the dowels on the block with the note **THIS SIDE UP** facing the cylinder head.

8. Install the cylinder head and exhaust manifold crossover assembly on the engine.

9. Coat the cylinder head bolts with a proper sealer and install the bolts hand tight.

10. Torque the bolts, in the correct sequence, to 33 ft. lbs., then rotate an additional 90 degree (¼ turn).

11. Install the pushrods in the same order they were removed.

12. Install the rocker arms. The correct rocker arm torque is 18 ft. lbs.

13. Install the intake manifold using a new gasket and following the correct sequence, torque the bolts to the correct specification.

14. The remainder of the installation is the reverse of the removal.

RIGHT SIDE

1. Disconnect the negative battery cable. Drain the cooling system.

2. Raise and safely support the vehicle. Disconnect the exhaust manifold from the exhaust pipe.

3. Lower the vehicle. Disconnect the exhaust manifold from the cylinder head and remove the manifold.

4. Remove the rocker cover. Remove the intake manifold.

5. Loosen the rocker arms enough so the pushrods can be removed. Note the position of the pushrods for assembly.

6. Starting with the outer bolts, remove the cylinder head bolts and remove the cylinder head.

7. Inspect and clean the surfaces of the cylinder head, engine block and intake manifold.

8. Clean the threads in the engine block and the threads on the cylinder head bolts.

To install:

9. Align the new gasket on the dowels on the engine block with the note

THIS SIDE UP facing the cylinder head.

10. Install the cylinder head on the engine. Coat the head bolts with a proper sealer. Install and tighten the bolts hand tight.

11. Torque the bolts, in sequence, to 33 ft. lbs., then rotate an additional 90 degree (¼ turn).

12. Install the pushrods in the same order as they were removed.

13. Install the rocker arms. The correct rocker arm torque is 18 ft. lbs.

14. Install the intake manifold using a new gasket. Following the correct sequence, torque the bolts to the proper specification.

15. The remainder of the installation is the reverse of the removal.

Valve Lifters

REMOVAL & INSTALLATION

1. Disconnect the negative battery cable.

2. On the 2.8L and 3.1L engines, remove the intake manifold.

3. Remove the rocker arm cover.

4. Loosen the rocker arm holding nut and move the rocker arm to the side.

5. Remove the pushrods.

6. Using a suitable tool, remove the valve lifter.

7. Installation is the reverse of removal procedure. Tighten the rocker arm nut to 10 ft. lbs on the 2.0L engine, 14 ft. lbs. on the 2.2L engine, 18 ft. lbs. on the 2.8L and 3.1L engines. Fill lifter assembly with engine oil and lubricate the bottom of the valve lifter with Molykote® or equivalent, prior to installation.

Rocker Arms

REMOVAL & INSTALLATION

2.0L (VIN K and M) Engine

1. Disconnect the negative battery cable. Remove camshaft carrier cover.

2. Hold the valves in place with compressed air, using air adapter J–22794 or equivalent, in spark plug hole.

3. Compress the valve springs with special tool J–33302–25 or equivalent.

4. Remove the rocker arms. Keep the rocker arms in order for reassembly.

5. To install, reverse the removal procedures using new gasket.

2.0L (VIN 1) and 2.2L Engines

1. Disconnect the negative battery cable. Remove the air cleaner. Remove the rocker cover.

2. Remove the rocker arm nut and ball. Lift the rocker arm off the stud and the pushrods from the engine. Always keep the valve system parts in order.

To install:

3. Coat the rocker arm balls with Molykote® or equivalent.

4. Install the pushrods in the order removed, making sure they seat properly in the lifter.

5. Install the rocker arms, balls and nuts in the order removed and adjust the valve lash.

NOTE: The valve system on these engines is not adjustable. The correct rocker arm torque is 11–18 ft. lbs.

6. Installation of the remaining components is in the reverse order of removal.

2.8L and 3.1L Engines

LEFT SIDE

1. Disconnect the negative battery cable. Disconnect the bracket tube at the rocker cover.

2. Remove the spark plug wire cover. Drain the cooling system and remove the heater hose at the filler neck.

3. Remove the rocker arm cover bolts and remove the rocker cover.

4. Remove the rocker arm nuts and remove the rocker arms. Note the order of removal for installation.

5. Install the rocker arms in the correct order. The correct rocker arm torque is 14–20 ft. lbs.

6. The remainder of the installation is the reverse of the removal.

RIGHT SIDE

1. Disconnect the negative battery cable. Disconnect the brake booster vacuum line at the bracket.

2. Disconnect the cable bracket at the plenum.

3. Disconnect the vacuum line bracket at the cable bracket.

4. Disconnect the lines at the alternator brace stud.

5. Remove the rear alternator brace.

6. Remove the serpentine belt.

7. Remove the alternator and support it out of the way.

8. Remove the PCV valve.

9. Loosen the alternator bracket.

10. Remove the spark plug wires. Remove the rocker cover bolts and remove the rocker cover.

11. Remove the rocker arm nuts and remove the rocker arms. Note the order of removal for installation.

12. Install the rocker arms in the correct order. The correct rocker arm torque is 14–20 ft. lbs.

13. The remainder of the installation is the reverse of the removal.

Intake Manifold

REMOVAL & INSTALLATION

2.0L (VIN K and M) Engines

1. Release the fuel pressure. Disconnect the negative battery terminal from the battery.

2. Remove induction tube and hoses.

3. Disconnect and tag wiring to throttle body, fuel injectors, MAP sensor and wastegate, if equipped.

4. Disconnect and tag PCV hose and vacuum hoses on the throttle body.

5. Remove the throttle cable and the cruise control cable, if equipped.

6. Remove wiring to the ignition coil and remove the manifold support bracket.

7. Remove the rear bolt from alternator bracket, power steering adjusting bracket and front alternator adjusting bracket.

8. Remove the fuel lines to the fuel rail and regulator outlet.

9. Remove the retaining nuts and washers and intake manifold.

To install:

10. Use a new gasket on the manifold surface and mount the manifold in position.

11. Tighten the bolts to 16 ft. lbs. (VIN K) and 18 ft. lbs. (VIN M), in the correct sequence.

12. Reconnect the fuel lines. Install the bolt for the power steering adjusting bracekt and the alternator.

13. Connect the ignition coil wiring and connect the vacuum hoses.

14. Connect the induction tube and hoses.

15. Reconnect all of the electrical wiring and the battery cable.

2.0L (VIN 1) and 2.2L Engines

1. Disconnect the negative battery cable and relieve fuel pressure.

2. Remove the air cleaner assembly.

3. Drain the coolant.

4. Remove and tag the vacuum lines and wires as necessary.

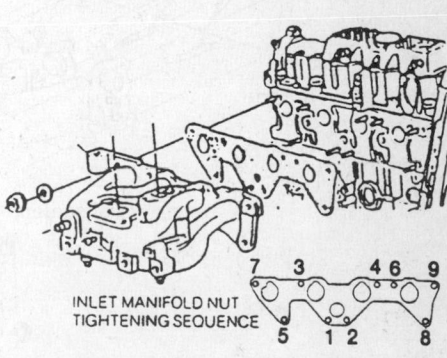

INLET MANIFOLD NUT
TIGHTENING SEQUENCE

7 3   4 6 9

5   1 2   8

Intake manifold torque sequence— 2.0L (VIN K) engine

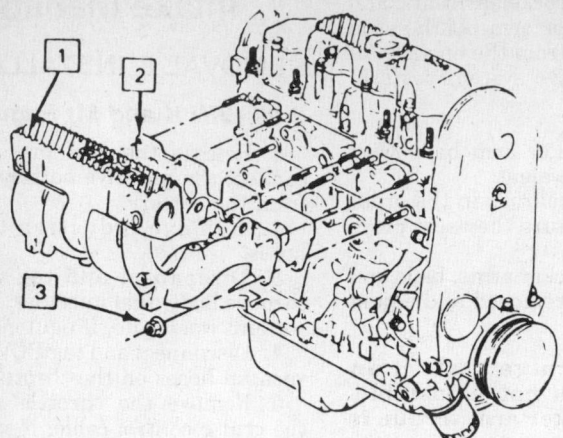

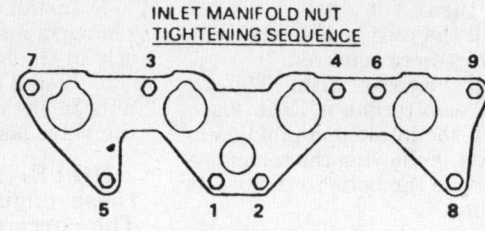

1. Intake manifold
2. Gasket
3. Nut (18 ft. lbs.)

INLET MANIFOLD NUT
TIGHTENING SEQUENCE

Intake manifold torque sequence–2.0L (VIN M) engine

5. Disconnect the fuel line, TBI linkakage and remove the TBI unit.

6. Remove the power steering pump and lay aside.

7. Disconnect the coolant hose at the manifold.

8. Raise and support the vehicle safely.

9. Disconnect the coolant pipe retaining nut, located at the top of the DIS, and move the pipe rearward.

10. Disconnect the accelerator and TV cables and bracket.

11. Remove the lower intake manifold nuts.

12. Lower the vehicle, remove the remaining intake manifold bolts and nuts and remove the manifold.

To install:

13. Use a new gasket on the manifold surface and mount the manifold in position.

14. Tighten the nuts to 15–22 ft. lbs., in the correct sequence.

15. The remainder of ther installation is the reverse of removal.

2.8L and 3.1L Engines

1. Disconnect the negative battery cable and relieve fuel pressure. Remove the air cleaner inlet tube.

2. Disconnect the accelerator cable bracket at the plenum.

3. Disconnect the throttle body and the EGR pipe from the EGR valve. Remove the plenum assembly.

4. Disconnect the fuel line along the fuel rail.

5. Disconnect the serpentine drive belt. Remove the power steering pump mounting bracket.

6. Remove the heater pipe at the power steering pump bracket.

7. Tag and disconnect the wiring at the alternator, remove the alternator.

8. Disconnect the wires from the cold start injector assembly. Remove the injector assembly from the intake manifold.

9. Disconnect the idle air vacuum hose at the throttle body. Disconnect the wires at the injectors.

10. Remove the fuel rail, breather tube and the fuel runners from the engine.

11. Tag and disconnect the coil wires.

12. Remove the rocker arm covers. Drain the cooling system, disconnect the radiator hose at the thermostat housing. Disconnect the heater hose from the thermostat housing and the thermostat wiring.

13. Remove the thermostat assembly housing.

14. Remove the intake manifold bolts and remove the intake manifold from the engine.

To install:

15. Apply a bead of sealant to the points where the manifold meets the block and install new gaskets. The gaskets are marked left and right.

16. Install the intake manifold assembly and tighten the bolts, in sequence, to 15 ft. lbs., then retighten, in sequence, to 24 ft. lbs.

17. Install the thermostat housing assembly. Install the rocker arm covers.

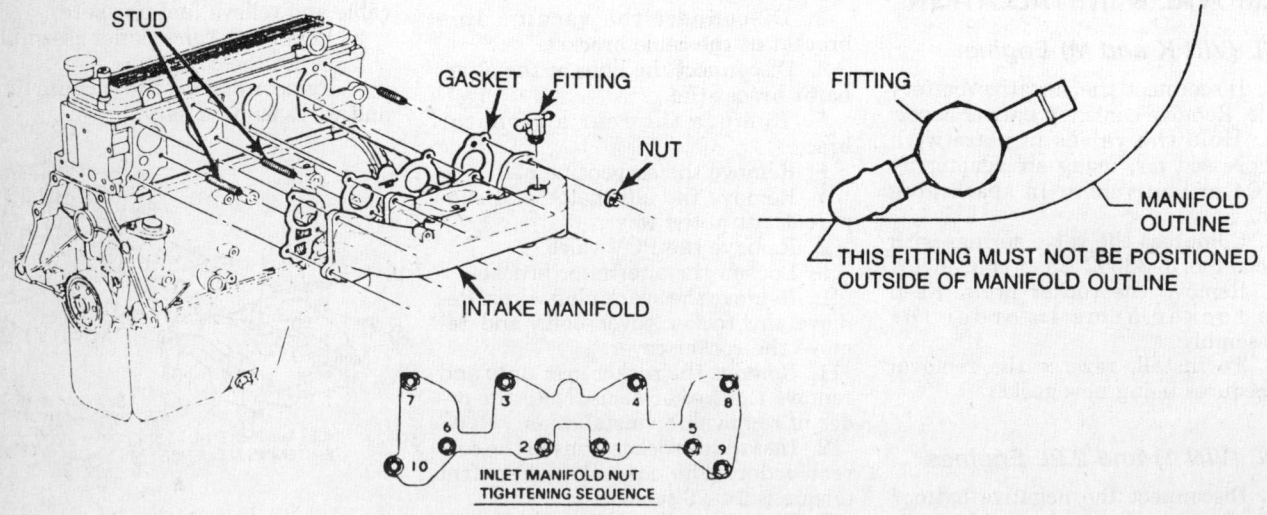

STUD

GASKET FITTING

NUT

FITTING

MANIFOLD OUTLINE

THIS FITTING MUST NOT BE POSITIONED OUTSIDE OF MANIFOLD OUTLINE

INTAKE MANIFOLD

INLET MANIFOLD NUT
TIGHTENING SEQUENCE

Intake manifold torque sequence –2.0L (VIN 1) and 2.2L engines

"J" BODY GM 25

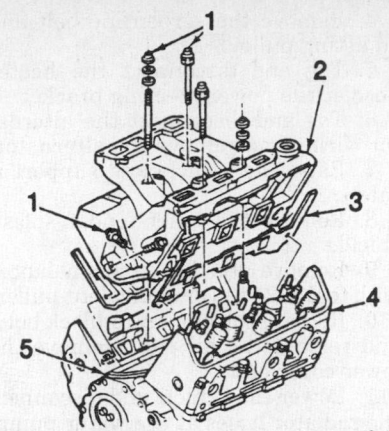

1.
Tighten in proper
sequence to 15 ft. lbs.
(20Nm), then retighten
to 24 ft. lbs. (33Nm)

2. Intake manifold
3. Gasket
4. Cylinder head
5. Sealer

⑦ ④ ③ ⑥
⑧ ① ② ⑤

**Intake manifold torque sequence—
2.8L and 3.1L engines**

18. Reconnect the coil wires. Install the fuel rail, runners and the breather tube.

19. Install the alternator and connect the wiring. Connect the EGR tube to the EGR valve.

20. Install the power steering pump bracket and pump. Install the serpentine belt.

21. Connect the accelerator cable at the plenum and connect the negative battery cable.

22. Install the air cleaner inlet tube.

Exhaust Manifold

REMOVAL & INSTALLATION

2.0L (VIN K and M) Engine

1. Disconnect the negative battery cable.

2. Remove turbocharger induction tube, if equipped.

3. Remove and tag spark plug wires.

4. Remove turbocharger assembly from exhaust manifold, if equipped.

5. Remove exhaust manifold retaining nuts and manifold.

6. Installation is in the reverse order of removal. Torque exhaust manifold bolts to 16 ft. lbs. and turbocharger-to-exhaust manifold to 18 ft. lbs., if equipped.

NOTE: Torque No. 2 and 3 exhaust manifold retaining nuts prior to No. 1 and 4.

2.0L (VIN 1) and 2.2L Engines

1. Disconnect the negative battery cable.

2. Remove the air cleaner. Remove

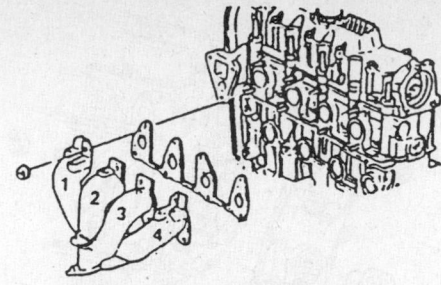

Exhaust manifold installation torque sequence—2.0L (VIN K) engine

the exhaust manifold shield. Raise and safely support the vehicle.

3. Disconnect the exhaust pipe at the manifold and lower the vehicle.

4. Disconnect the air management-to-check valve hose and remove the bracket. Disconnect the oxygen sensor lead wire.

5. Remove the alternator belt. Remove the alternator adjusting bolts, loosen the pivot bolt and pivot the alternator upward.

6. Remove the alternator brace and the AIR pipes bracket bolt.

7. Unscrew the mounting bolts and remove the exhaust manifold. The manifold should be removed with the AIR plumbing as an assembly. If the manifold is to be replaced, transfer the plumbing to the new one.

8. Clean the mating surfaces on the manifold and the head, position the manifold and tighten the nuts to 6–13 ft. lbs. in the proper sequence.

9. Installation of the remaining components is in the reverse order of removal.

2.8L and 3.1L Engines

LEFT SIDE

1. Disconnect the negative battery cable.

2. Remove the air cleaner assembly.

3. Remove the air flow sensor. Remove the engine heat shield.

4. Remove the crossover pipe at the manifold.

5. Remove the exhaust manifold bolts.

6. Remove the exhaust manifold.

7. Installation is the reverse of the removal procedure.

RIGHT SIDE

1. Disconnect the negative battery cable.

2. Remove the air cleaner assembly.

3. Remove the air flow sensor. Remove the engine heat shield.

4. Disconnect the crossover pipe at the manifold.

5. Disconnect the accelerator and throttle valve cable at the throttle lever and the plenum. Move aside to gain working clearance.

6. Disconnect the power steering line at the power steering pump.

7. Remove the EGR valve assembly.

8. Raise the vehicle and support safely.

9. Disconnect the exhaust pipe at the exhaust manifold.

10. Lower the vehicle.

11. Remove the manifold bolts. Remove the exhaust manifold.

12. Installation is the reverse of the removal procedure.

Turbocharger

REMOVAL & INSTALLATION

1. Disconnect the negative battery cable.

2. Raise and safely support the vehicle.

3. Remove the Lower fan retaining screws.

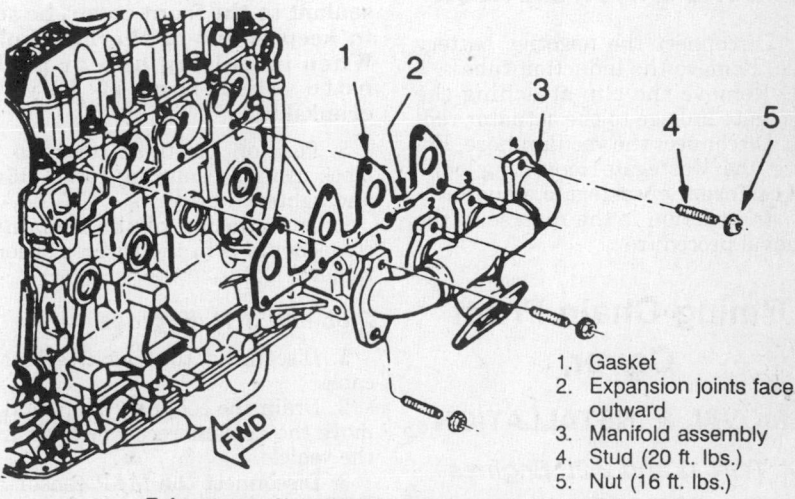

1. Gasket
2. Expansion joints face outward
3. Manifold assembly
4. Stud (20 ft. lbs.)
5. Nut (16 ft. lbs.)

Exhaust manifold torque sequence–2.0L (VIN M) engine

25–31

4. Disconnect the exhaust pipe at the turbocharger.

5. Remove air conditioning rear support bracket.

6. Remove the turbocharger support bracket from the engine.

7. Disconnect the oil drain and water return pipes at turbo.

8. Lower the vehicle and remove coolant recovery pipe.

9. Remove induction tube, coolant fan and oxygen sensor.

10. Disconnect the oil and water feed pipes.

11. Remove the air intake duct and vacuum hose at the actuator.

12. Remove the exhaust manifold retaining nuts, remove the turbocharger and manifold as an assembly.

13. Remove the turbocharger from exhaust manifold.

To install:

14. Install the turbocharger to the exhaust manifold and torque the bolts to 18 ft. lbs.

15. Install a new manifold gasket and install the manifold in position on the block. Tighten the bolts to 16 ft. lbs.

16. Install the air intake duct and the vacuum hose actuator.

17. Install the induction tube and O₂ sensor. Install the coolant recovery tube.

18. Raise and safely support the vehicle. Connect the oil drain and water return pipe to the turbocharger.

19. Install the turbocharger support bracket. Connect the exhaust pipe to the turbocharger and install the rear air conditioning support bracket.

20. Install the lower fan retaining screws. Lower the vehicle and connect the negative battery cable. Check all fluid levels.

Turbocharger Wastegate Unit

REMOVAL & INSTALLATION

1. Disconnect the negative battery cable. Remove the induction tube.

2. Remove the clip attaching the wastegate linkage to the actuator rod.

3. Disconnect the vacuum hose. Remove the wastegate mounting bolts and remove the wastegate actuator.

4. Installation is the reverse of the removal procedure.

Timing Chain Front Cover

REMOVAL & INSTALLATION

2.0L (VIN 1) and 2.2L Engines

NOTE: The following proce-

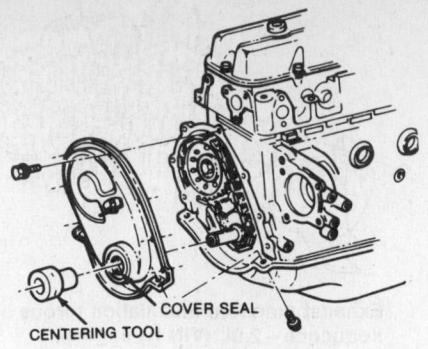

Front cover removal—2.0L (VIN 1) and 2.2L engines

dure requires the use of a front cover centering tool J–35468 and crankshaft puller J–24420.

1. Disconnect the negative battery cable. Remove the engine accessory drive belts.

2. Although not absolutely necessary, removal of the right front inner fender splash shield will facilitate access to the front cover.

3. Remove the center bolt from the crankshaft pulley and retaining bolts, remove the pulley. Using a puller J–24420 or equivalent, remove hub from the crankshaft.

4. Remove the alternator lower bracket.

5. Remove the oil pan-to-front cover bolts.

6. Remove the front cover-to-block bolts and remove the front cover. If the front cover is difficult to remove, use a rubber mallet to loosen it.

To install:

7. The surfaces of the block and front cover must be clean and free of oil. Apply a ⅛ in. bead of RTV sealant to the cover. The sealant must be wet to the touch when the bolts are torqued down.

NOTE: When applying RTV sealant to the front cover, be sure to keep it out of the bolt holes. When installing hub or pulley note position of key on crankshaft.

8. Position the front cover on the block using a centering tool J–35468 and tighten the screws.

9. Installation of the remaining components is in the reverse order of removal.

2.8L and 3.1L Engines

1. Disconnect the negative battery cable.

2. Drain the cooling system and remove the coolant recovery tank from the vehicle.

3. Disconnect the MAP sensor and EGR sensor solenoids.

4. Remove the serpentine belt and adjusting pulley.

5. Tag and disconnect the heater hose at the power steering bracket.

6. Tag and disconnect the alternator wiring and remove the alternator.

7. Raise the vehicle and support it safely.

8. Remove the inner fender splash shield.

9. Remove the harmonic balancer with tool J–24420 or equivalent puller.

10. Remove the oil pan-to-block bolts and remove the oil pan. Remove the lower cover bolts.

11. Lower the vehicle and disconnect the radiator hoses at the water pump.

12. Remove the heater hose from the thermostat housing.

13. Disconnect the overflow hoses and the canister purge hose.

14. Remove the front cover.

To install:

15. Apply a bead of sealer to the front cover surface.

16. Install a new front cover gasket and front oil seal.

17. Install the front cover and tighten to 20–28 ft. lbs.

18. Raise and safely support the vehicle. Install the oil pan and the lower front cover bolts.

19. Install the crankshaft balancer.

20. Install the inner splash shield and lower the vehicle.

21. Install the radiator hoses and the power steering pump.

22. Install the alternator and the accessory drive belt.

23. Refill the fluids and connect the negative battery cable.

Front Cover Oil Seal

REPLACEMENT

2.0L (VIN 1), 2.2L, 2.8L and 3.1L Engines

1. The oil seal can be replaced with the front cover either on or off the engine.

2. Although not absolutely necessary, removal of the right front inner fender splash shield will facilitate access to the front cover.

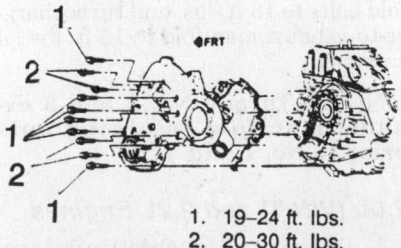

1. 19–24 ft. lbs.
2. 20–30 ft. lbs.

Front cover removal—2.8L and 3.1L engines

3. If the cover is on the engine, remove the crankshaft pulley and hub first.

4. Pry out the seal using a suitable tool, being careful not to distort the seal mating surfaces.

5. Install the new seal so the lip side, is towards the engine.

6. Press it into place with a seal driver.

7. Install the hub and pulley, if removed.

Timing Chain and Sprockets

REMOVAL & INSTALLATION

2.0L (VIN 1) and 2.2L Engines

1. Disconnect the negative battery cable. Remove the front cover.

2. Place the No. 1 piston at **TDC** of the compression stroke so the marks on the camshaft and crankshaft sprockets are in alignment.

3. Loosen the timing chain tensioner nut as far as possible, without actually removing it.

4. Remove the camshaft sprocket bolts and remove the sprocket and chain together. If the sprocket does not slide from the camshaft easily, a light blow with a soft tool at the lower edge of the sprocket will loosen it.

5. Use a gear puller J–2288–8–20 or equivalent, and remove the crankshaft sprocket.

To install:

6. Press the new crankshaft sprocket onto the crankshaft.

7. Install the timing chain over the camshaft sprocket and around the crankshaft sprocket. Make sure the marks on the 2 sprockets are in alignment. Lubricate the thrust surface with Molykote® or equivalent.

8. Align the dowel in the camshaft with the dowel hole in the sprocket and install the sprocket onto the camshaft. Use the mounting bolts to draw the sprocket onto the camshaft and tighten them to 27–33 ft. lbs.

9. Lubricate the timing chain with clean engine oil. Tighten the chain tensioner.

10. Installation of the remaining components is in the reverse order of the removal procedure.

2.8L and 3.1L Engines

1. Disconnect the negative battery cable.

2. Remove the front cover.

3. Position the No. 1 piston at **TDC** with the marks on the crankshaft and camshaft sprockets aligned.

4. Remove the camshaft sprocket bolts.

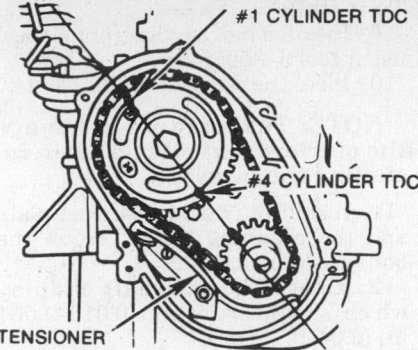

Timing mark alignment—2.0L (VIN 1) and 2.2L engines

5. Remove the camshaft sprocket and chain from the front of the engine.

NOTE: If the sprocket does not move freely from the camshaft, a light blow using a plastic tool on the lower edge of the sprocket should dislodge it.

6. Installation is the reverse of removal. Draw the camshaft sprocket onto the camshaft using the mounting bolts. Lubricate the timing chain with engine oil prior to installation.

Timing Belt Front Cover

REMOVAL & INSTALLATION

2.0L (VIN K and M) Engine

1. Disconnect the negative battery cable.

2. Remove the tensioner and bolt.

3. Remove the serpentine belt.

4. Unsnap the upper and lower cover. Remove the cover.

5. To install reverse the removal procedures. Torque the serpentine belt tensioner to 40 ft. lbs. and the cover retaining bolts to 89 inch lbs.

OIL SEAL REPLACEMENT

2.0L (VIN K and M) Engine

1. Remove the crankshaft sprocket.

2. Remove the crankshaft key and rear thrust washer.

3. Using a suitable prybar, pry out the front oil seal.

4. Place the protective sleeve of special tool set J–33083, seal installer or equivalent, onto the crankshaft.

5. Lubricate the lip of the new seal. Using special tool J–33083, install the seal.

6. Remove the protective sleeve.

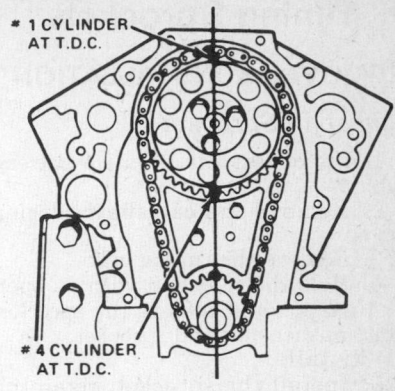

Timing mark alignment—2.8L and 3.1L engines

7. Install the rear thrust washer and key on the crankshaft.

8. Install the crankshaft sprocket.

Timing Belt and Tensioner

REMOVAL & INSTALLATION

2.0L (VIN K and M) Engine

1. Disconnect the negative battery cable.

2. Remove the serpentine belt and timing belt cover.

3. Loosen the water pump bolts and release tension with tool J–33039 or equivalent.

4. Raise and support the vehicle safely.

5. Remove the crankshaft pulley.

6. Lower the vehicle and remove the timing belt.

To install:

7. Turn the crankshaft and the camshaft gears clockwise to align the timing marks on the gears with the timing marks on the rear cover.

8. Install the timing belt, making sure the portion between the camshaft gear and crankcase gear is in tension.

9. Using tool J–33039 or equivalent, turn the water pump eccentric clockwise until the tensioner contacts the high torque stop. Tighten the water pump screws slightly.

10. Turn the engine by the crankshaft gear bolt 720 degrees to fully seat the belt into the gear teeth.

11. Turn the water pump eccentric counterclockwise until the hole in the tensioner arm is aligned with the hole in the base.

12. Torque the water pump screws to 18 ft. lbs. while checking that the tensioner holes remain as adjusted in the prior step.

13. Install the crankshaft pulley, timing belt cover and the serpentine drive belt.

Timing Sprockets

REMOVAL & INSTALLATION

Camshaft Sprocket

1. Disconnect the negative battery cable.
2. Remove the camshaft carrier cover.
3. Remove the timing belt.
4. Hold the camshaft with an open end wrench and remove the sprocket bolt, washer and and sprocket.

To install:

5. Install the sprocket, retaining bolt and washer with the mark on the sprocket lined up with the mark on the rear timing belt cover and torque to 34 ft. lbs. The remainder of the installation is the reverse of removal.

Crankshaft Sprocket

1. Disconnect the negative battery cable.
2. Remove the timing belt.
3. Remove the crankshaft pulley.
4. Remove the bolt and retaining washer and remove the sprocket.

To install:

5. Install the sprocket over the key on the end of the crankshaft.
6. Install the thrust washer and attaching bolt and torque to 114 ft. lbs.
7. Install the crankshaft pulley and timing belt.

Camshaft Carrier

REMOVAL & INSTALLATION

2.0L (VIN K and M) Engine

NOTE: Whenever the camshaft carrier bolts are loosened, it is necessary to remove the cylinder head and replace the cylinder head gasket.

1. Disconnect the negative battery cable. Disconnect the crankcase ventilation hose from the camshaft carrier.
2. Mark and remove the distributor.
3. Remove the camshaft sprocket.
4. Loosen the camshaft carrier and cylinder head attaching bolts a little at a time in sequence.

NOTE: Camshaft carrier and cylinder head bolts should be loosened in sequence and only when the engine is cold.

5. Remove the camshaft carrier.
6. Remove the camshaft thrust plate from the rear of the camshaft carrier.
7. Slide the camshaft rearward and remove it from the carrier.
8. Remove the carrier front oil seal.

To install:

9. Install a new carrier front oil seal using tool J-33085.
10. Place the camshaft in the carrier.

NOTE: Take care not to damage the carrier front oil seal when installing the camshaft.

11. Install the camshaft thrust plate and the retaining bolts. Torque the bolts to 70 inch lbs.
12. Check the camshaft endplay which should be within 0.016–0.064 in. (0.04–0.16mm).
13. Clean the sealing surfaces on cylinder head and carrier. Apply a continuous 3mm bead of RTV sealer.
14. Install the camshaft carrier on the cylinder head.
15. Install the camshaft carrier and cylinder head attaching bolts.
16. Torque the bolts a little at a time, in the proper sequence, at cylinder head, to 18 ft. lbs. Turn each bolt 60 degrees clockwise, in the proper sequence, for 3 times until a 180 degrees rotation is obtained or equivalent, to ½ turn.
17. Install the camshaft sprocket.
18. Install the distributor.
19. Connect the positive crankcase ventilation hose to the camshaft carrier.

NOTE: After remainder of installation is completed, start engine and let it run until the thermostat opens. Torque all cylinder head bolts an additional 30–50 degrees in the proper sequence.

Camshaft

REMOVAL & INSTALLATION

2.0L (VIN 1) and 2.2L Engines

1. Remove the engine assembly.
2. Remove the intake manifold.
3. Remove the cylinder head cover, pivot the rocker arms to the sides and remove the pushrods, keeping them in order. Remove the valve lifters, keeping them in order.
4. Remove the front cover.
5. Remove the distributor.
6. Remove the fuel pump and its pushrod.
7. Remove the timing chain and sprocket.
8. Carefully pull the camshaft from the block, being sure the camshaft lobes do not contact the bearings.

To install:

9. Lubricate the camshaft journals with clean engine oil. Lubricate the lobes with Molykote® or equivalent. Install the camshaft into the engine, being extremely careful not to contact the bearings with the cam lobes.

10. Install the timing chain and sprocket. Install the fuel pump and pushrod. Install the timing cover. Install the distributor.
11. Install the valve lifters. If a new camshaft has been installed, new lifters should be used to ensure durability of the cam lobes.
12. Install the pushrods and rocker arms and the intake manifold.
13. Install the engine assembly.
14. Install the cylinder head cover.

2.0L (VIN K and M) Engine

1. Disconnect the negative battery cable. Remove the camshaft carrier cover.
2. Hold the valves in place with compressed air, using an air adapter J-22794 or equivalent, in the spark plug hole. Compress the valve springs with a special tool J-33302-25 and remove rocker arms. Keep rocker arms in order for reassembly.
3. Remove the timing belt front cover.
4. Remove the timing belt.
5. Remove the camshaft sprocket.
6. Mark and remove the distributor.
7. Remove the camshaft thrust plate from rear of camshaft carrier.
8. Slide the camshaft rearward and remove it from the carrier.

To install:

9. Install a new camshaft carrier front oil seal using tool J-33085 or equivalent.
10. Place the camshaft in the carrier.

NOTE: Take care not to damage the carrier front oil seal when installing the camshaft.

11. Install the camshaft thrust plate retaining bolts. Torque bolts to 70 inch lbs.
12. Check the camshaft endplay, which should be within 0.016–0.064 in.
13. Install the distributor.
14. Install the camshaft sprocket.
15. Install the timing belt.
16. Install the timing belt front cover.
17. Using an air adapter J-22794 or equivalent, in the spark plug hole to hold the valve closed and install valve train compressing fixture J-33302. Compress valve springs and replace rocker arms.
18. Install the camshaft carrier cover.

2.8L and 3.1L Engines

1. Disconnect the negative battery cable. Remove the engine assembly from the vehicle.
2. Remove the intake manifold.
3. Remove the rocker arm covers. Remove the rocker arm nuts, balls, rocker arms and pushrods.

NOTE: Always keep valve train parts in order for correct installation.

4. Remove the upper front cover bolts. Remove the lower cover bolts and the front cover.

5. Remove the camshaft sprocket bolts, camshaft sprocket and timing chain.

6. Remove the camshaft by carefully sliding it out the front of the engine. Measure the camshaft bearing journals using a micrometer and replace the camshaft if the journals exceed 0.0009 in. (0.025mm) out of round.

7. Installation is the reverse of removal. When installing a new camshaft, lubricate the camshaft lobes with GM Engine Oil Supplement (E.O.S.) or equivalent.

Piston and Connecting Rod

POSITIONING

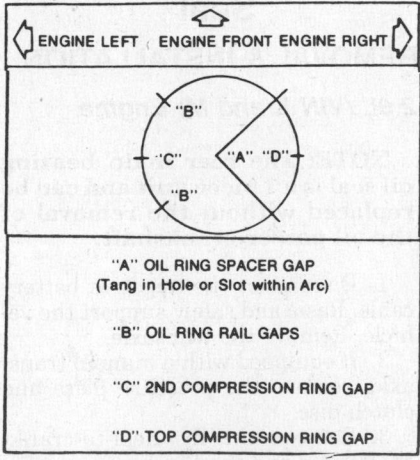

ENGINE LEFT | ENGINE FRONT ENGINE RIGHT

"A" OIL RING SPACER GAP
(Tang in Hole or Slot within Arc)

"B" OIL RING RAIL GAPS

"C" 2ND COMPRESSION RING GAP

"D" TOP COMPRESSION RING GAP

ENGINE LUBRICATION

Oil Pan

REMOVAL & INSTALLATION

2.0L (VIN 1) and 2.2L Engines

1. Disconnect the negative battery cable.

2. Raise and safely support the vehicle. Drain the crankcase.

3. Remove the air conditioning brace, if equipped.

4. Remove the exhaust shield and disconnect the exhaust pipe at the manifold.

5. Remove the starter motor and position it out of the way.

6. Remove the flywheel cover. Remove the oil pan retaining bolts and remove the oil pan.

To install:

NOTE: Prior to oil pan installation, check the sealing surfaces on the pan, cylinder block and front cover are clean and free of oil. If installing the old oil pan, be sure all old RTV has been removed.

7. Apply a ⅛ in. bead of RTV sealant to the oil pan sealing surface. Use a new oil pan rear seal and install the pan in place. Tighten the bolts to 9–13 ft. lbs.

8. Install the flywheel cover and the starter.

9. Connect the exhaust pipe at the manifold.

10. Install the exhaust shield and install the air conditioning brace.

11. Connect the negative battery cable and run the vehicle to normal operating temperature. Refill and check for leaks.

2.0L (VIN K and M) Engine

1. Disconnect the negative battery cable.

2. Raise and safely support the vehicle.

3. Remove the right front wheel assembly.

4. Remove the front splash shield.

5. Drain the crankcase.

6. Remove the exhaust pipe from the manifold, on turbocharged vehicles, remove exhaust pipe from wastegate.

7. Remove the flywheel cover and oil pan scraper. Remove the oil pan retaining bolts and remove the oil pan.

8. To install reverse removal procedures. Use a new gasket and apply a bead of RTV sealant to the oil pan before installation. Torque the oil pan bolts to 4 ft. lbs. Refill and check for leaks.

2.8L and 3.1L Engine

1987–88

1. Disconnect the negative battery cable.

2. Raise and support the vehicle safely.

3. Drain the engine oil.

4. Remove the flywheel shield or clutch housing cover and remove the starter.

5. Remove the oil pan bolts and remove the oil pan.

To install:

6. Clean the gasket mating surfaces.

7. Install a new gasket on the oil pan. Apply silicon sealer to the portion of the pan that contacts the rear of the block.

8. Install the oil pan, nuts and retaining bolts.

9. Install the flywheel shield or clutch housing cover and install the starter.

10. Lower the vehicle, fill the crankcase and connect the battery.

1989–91

1. Disconnect the negative battery cable.

2. Remove the serpentine belt and the tensioner.

3. Support the engine with tool J–28467 or equivalent.

4. Raise and safely support the vehicle. Drain the engine oil.

5. Remove the starter shield and the flywheel cover. Remove the starter.

6. Remove the engine to frame mount retaining nuts.

7. Lower the vehicle.

8. Support the engine using tool J–28467–A or equivalent, then raise and support the vehicle safely.

9. Remove the right tire and wheel assembly. Remove the right inner fender splash shield.

10. Remove the oil pan retaining bolts and nuts and remove the oil pan.

To install:

11. Clean the gasket mating surfaces.

12. Install a new gasket on the oil pan. Apply silicon sealer to the portion of the pan that contacts the rear of the block.

13. Install the oil pan retaining nuts. Tighten the nuts to 89 inch lbs.

14. Install the oil pan retaining bolts. Tighten the rear bolts to 18 inch lbs. and the remaining bolts to 89 inch lbs.

15. Install the right inner fender splash shield.

16. Lower the vehicle and remove the engine support tool.

17. Raise and support the vehicle safely.

18. Install the engine to frame mounting nuts.

19. Install the starter and splash shield. Install the flywheel shield.

20. Lower the vehicle and fill the crankcase with oil, install the belt tensioner and belt and connect the negative battery cable. Run the engine to normal operating temperature and check for leaks.

Oil Pump

REMOVAL & INSTALLATION

2.0L (VIN K and M) Engine

1. Disconnect the negative battery

cable. Remove the crankshaft sprocket.

2. Remove the timing belt rear cover.

3. Disconnect the connector at oil pressure switch.

4. Raise and safely support the vehicle. Drain the engine oil and remove the oil pan.

5. Remove the oil filter.

6. Unbolt and remove the oil pick-up tube.

7. Unbolt and remove the oil pump.

8. Installation is the reverse of removal. Use new gaskets in all instances. Torque the oil pump bolts to 5 ft. lbs. Torque the the oil pick-up tube bolts to 5 ft. lbs. and the oil pan bolts to 4 ft. lbs.

2.0L (VIN 1) and 2.2L Engines

1. Disconnect the negative battery cable.

2. Raise and safely support the vehicle. Drain the engine oil and remove the engine oil pan.

3. Remove the pump attaching bolts and carefully lower the pump.

4. Install in reverse order. To ensure immediate oil pressure on start-up, the oil pump gear cavity should be packed with petroleum jelly. Installation torque is 26–35 ft. lbs. on the oil pump mounting bolts.

2.8L and 3.1L Engines

1. Disconnect the negative battery cable.

2. Raise and safely support the vehicle. Drain the engine oil and remove the oil pan.

3. Remove the rear main bearing cap.

4. Remove the oil pump and extension shaft.

5. Installation is the reverse of the removal procedure. Tighten the rear bearing cap bolt to 30 ft. lbs.

CHECKING

2.0L (VIN 1), 2.2L, 2.8L and 3.1L Engines

1. Drain the oil from the pump and remove the pump cover.

2. Measure the pump gear lash. It should be 0.0037–0.0077 in.

3. Measure the pump gear pocket. It should be as follows:

   a. On pumps with aluminum body the depth should be 1.195–1.198 in. and the diameter should be 1.503–1.506 in.

   b. On pumps with cast iron body the depth should be 1.202–1.205 in. and the diameter should be 1.504–1.506 in.

4. Measure the gear side clearance. It should be 0.003–0.004 in.

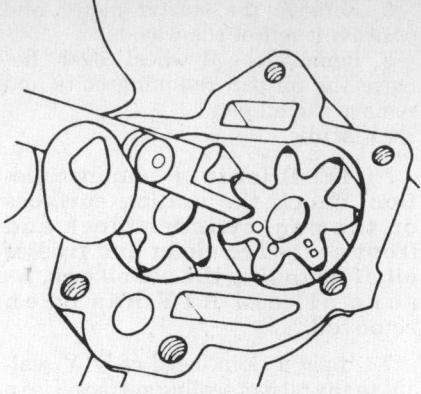

Measuring oil pump gear lash

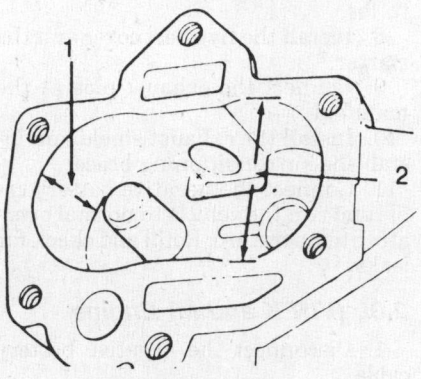

1. Depth of pocket
2. Diameter of pocket

Measuring oil pump gear pocket

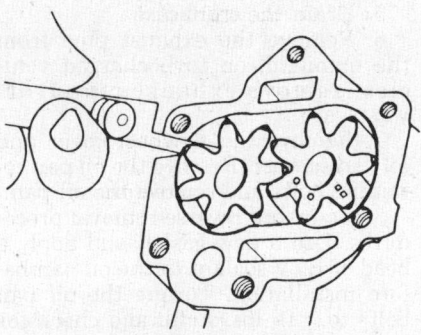

Measuring oil pump gear side clearance

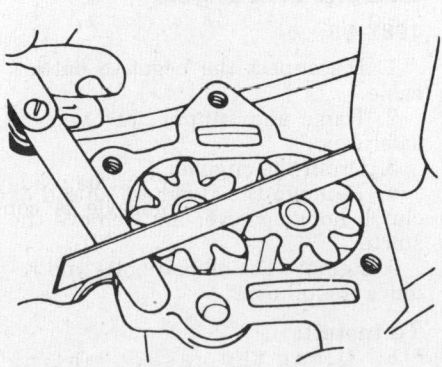

Measuring oil pump end clearance

5. Measure the gear end clearance. It should be as follows:

   a. On pumps with aluminum body the clearance should be 0.0016–0.0067 in.

   b. On pumps with cast iron body the clearance should be 0.002–0.006 in.

6. Lubriacte all internal parts with engine oil during reassembly and install the pump gears.

7. Prime the engine oil galleries by removing the engine oil pump drive unit and rotate the oil pump using a drill motor and appropriate socket and extension.

8. Install the cover and gasket and torque the pump cover bolts to 89 inch lbs.

NOTE: Use only original equipment gaskets. The gasket thickness is critical to proper functioning of the pump.

Rear Main Bearing Oil Seal

REMOVAL & INSTALLATION

2.0L (VIN K and M) Engine

NOTE: The rear main bearing oil seal is a 1 piece unit and can be replaced without the removal of the oil pan or crankshaft.

1. Disconnect the negative battery cable. Rasie and safely support the vehicle. Remove the transaxle.

2. If equipped with a manual transaxle, remove the pressure plate and clutch disc.

3. Remove the flywheel-to-crankshaft bolts and the flywheel.

4. Using a medium pry bar, pry out the old seal; Be careful not to scratch the crankshaft surface.

5. Clean the block and crankshaft-to-seal mating surfaces.

6. Using the seal installation tool no. J-36227 or equivalent, install the new rear seal into the seal retainer. Lubricate the outside of the seal to aid installation and press the seal in evenly with the tool.

7. To complete the assembly, reverse the removal procedures. Use new bolts and torque flywheel to specifications.

2.0L (VIN 1) and 2.2L Engines

1. Disconnect the negative battery cable. Raise and safely support the vehicle.

2. Remove the transaxle assembly.

3. Remove the flywheel.

4. Remove the seal from the dust lip.

5. Clean the cylinder block and crankshaft sealing surface.

6. Inspect the crankshaft for damage. Coat the seal and engine mating surface with engine oil.

7. Install the new seal using seal installation tool J–34686 or equivalent. For remainder of installation, reverse the removal procedure.

2.8L and 3.1L Engines

NOTE: The rear main bearing oil seal is a 1 piece unit and can be replaced without the removal of the oil pan or crankshaft.

1. Disconnect the negative battery cable. Raise and safely support the vehicle.

2. Remove the transaxle assembly.

3. Remove the flywheel.

4. Remove the seal from the dust lip.

NOTE: Care must be exercised during removal so as not to damage the crankshaft outside diameter area.

5. Clean the cylinder block and crankshaft sealing surface.

6. Inspect the crankshaft for nicks, burrs, scratches, etc.

7. Coat the seal and the engine mating surface with engine oil.

8. Install the new seal, using seal installation tool J–34686 or equivalent.

9. To complete installation, reverse remaining removal procedure.

MANUAL TRANSAXLE

For further information on transmissions/transaxles, please refer to "Chilton's Guide to Transmission Repair".

Transaxle Assembly

REMOVAL & INSTALLATION

1. Disconnect the negative battery cable.

2. Install an engine holding bar so one end is supported on the cowl tray over the wiper motor and the other end rests on the radiator support. Use padding and be careful not to damage the paint or body work with the bar. Attach a lifting hook to the engine lift ring and to the bar and raise the engine enough to take the pressure off the motor mounts.

NOTE: If a lifting bar and hook is not available, a chain hoist can be used, however, during the procedure the vehicle must be raised, at which time the chain hoist must be adjusted to keep tension on the engine/transaxle assembly.

3. Remove the heater hose clamp at the transaxle mount bracket. Disconnect the electrical connector and remove the horn assembly.

4. Remove the transaxle mount attaching bolts. Discard the bolts attaching the mount to the side frame; new bolts must be used at installation.

5. Disconnect the clutch master cylinder pushrod from the clutch pedal and disconnect the clutch slave cylinder from the transaxle support bracket and move it aside.

6. Remove the transaxle mount bracket attaching bolts and nuts.

7. Disconnect the ground cables at the transaxle mounting stud.

8. Remove the 4 upper transaxle-to-engine mounting bolts.

9. Raise the vehicle and support it on stands. Remove the left front wheel.

10. Remove the left front inner splash shield. Remove the transaxle strut and bracket.

11. Remove the clutch housing cover bolts.

12. Disconnect the speedometer cable at the transaxle.

13. Disconnect the stabilizer bar at the left suspension support and control arm.

14. Disconnect the ball joint from the steering knuckle.

15. Remove the left suspension support attaching bolts and remove the support and control arm as an assembly.

16. Install boot protectors and disengage the halfshafts at the transaxle. Remove the left side shaft from the transaxle.

17. Position a jack under the transaxle case, remove the lower 2 transaxle-to-engine mounting bolts and remove the transaxle by sliding it towards the driver's side, away from the engine. Carefully lower the jack, guiding the right shaft out the transaxle.

To install:

18. Raise the transaxle into position and guide the right halfshaft into its bore as the transaxle is being raised. The right halfshaft can not be readily installed after the transaxle is connected to the engine.

19. Installation of the remaining components is in the reverse order of removal with the following notes:

a. Tighten the transaxle-to-engine bolts to 55 ft.lbs. on 1987–88 vehicles equipped with a Muncie transaxle, 60 ft. lbs on 1987–88 ve-

hicles equipped with an Isuzu transaxle and 85 ft. lbs on all 1989–91 vehicles.

b. Tighten the suspension support-to-body attaching bolts to 75 ft. lbs. and the clutch housing cover bolts to 10 ft. lbs.

c. Using new bolts, install and tighten the transaxle mount-to-side frame to 40 ft. lbs.

d. When installing the bolts attaching the mount-to-transaxle bracket, check the alignment bolt at the engine mount. If excessive effort is required to remove the alignment bolt, realign the powertrain components and tighten the bolts to 40 ft. lbs. and remove the alignment bolt.

LINKAGE ADJUSTMENT

Shift Cable

1987 WITH MUNCIE TRANSAXLE

1. Disconnect the negative battery terminal from the battery.

2. Shift the transaxle into 1st gear.

3. Loosen shift cable attaching nuts **E** at transaxle lever **D** and **F**.

4. Remove the console trim plate and slide the shifter boot up the shifter handle. Remove the console.

5. With the shift lever in 1st gear position, pulled to left and held against stop, insert a yoke clip to hold the lever hard against the reverse lockout stop. Install a $5/32$ in. or No. 22 drill bit into the alignment hole at the side of shifter assembly.

6. Remove lash from the transaxle by rotating lever **D** in direction of arrow while tightening the nut **E**.

7. Tighten the nut **E** on the lever **F**.

8. Remove the drill bit and yoke clip at the shifter assembly.

9. Install the console, shifter boot and trim plate.

10. Connect the battery cable and road test the vehicle, check for a good neutral gate feel during shifting.

CLUTCH

Clutch Assembly

REMOVAL & INSTALLATION

———— CAUTION ————

The clutch plate contains asbestos, which has been determined to be a cancer causing agent. Never clean the clutch surfaces with compressed air. Avoid inhaling any dust from any clutch surface.

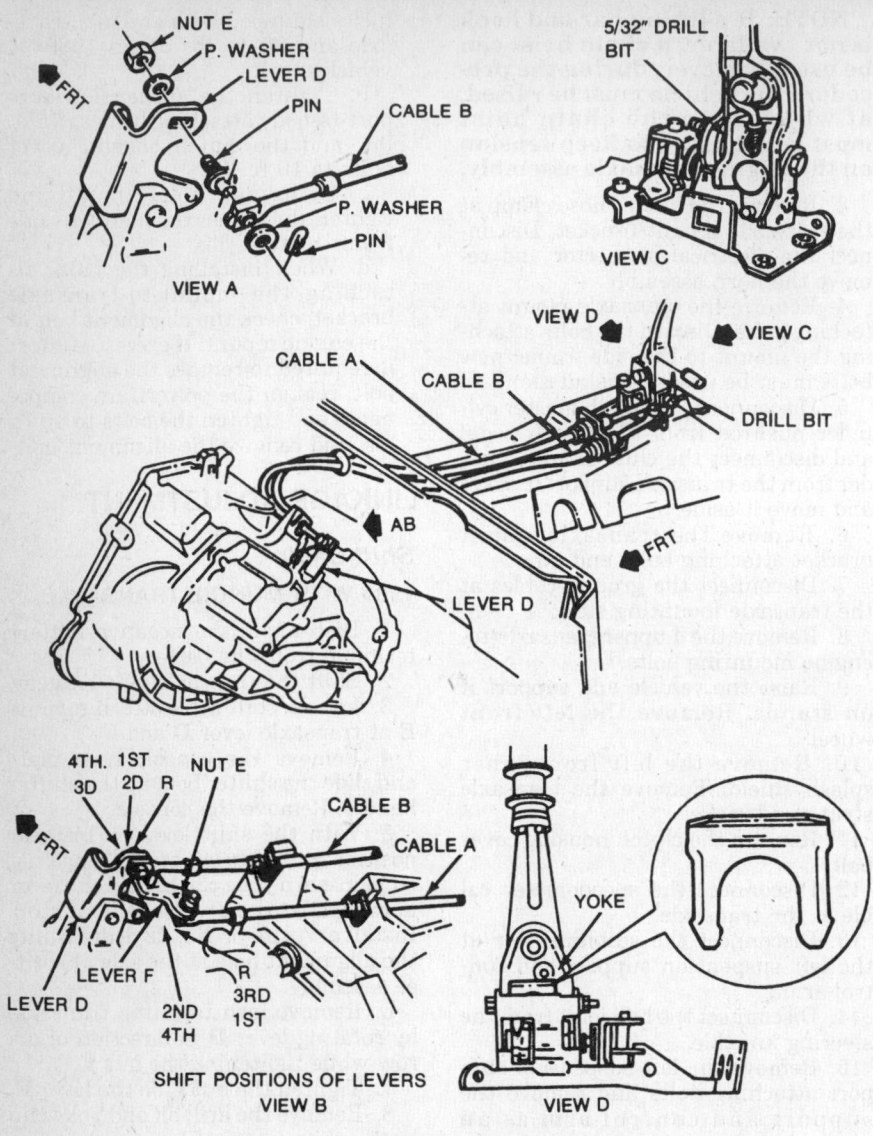

Shift cable adjustment—1987 with Muncie transaxle

1. Disconnect the negative battery cable. Raise and safely support the vehicle. Remove the transaxle.

2. Mark the pressure plate assembly and the flywheel so they can be assembled in the same position to maintain balance.

3. Loosen the attaching bolts 1 turn at a time until spring tension is relieved.

4. Support the pressure plate and remove the bolts. Remove the pressure plate and the clutch disc.

To install:

5. Inspect the flywheel, pressure plate, clutch disc, throwout bearing and the clutch fork for wear.

6. Clean the flywheel mating surfaces. Position the clutch disc and pressure plate into the installed position and support with a dummy shaft or clutch aligning tool.

NOTE: **Clutch plate must be installed correctly. Clutch plate is marked INSTALL FLYWHEEL SIDE. Always replace clutch and pressure plate as a set.**

7. Install the pressure plate-to-flywheel bolts. Tighten in a criss-cross pattern.

8. Lubricate the outside grooves and the inside recess of the release bearing with high temperature grease. Wipe off any excess. Install the release bearing.

9. Install the transaxle.

PEDAL HEIGHT/FREE-PLAY ADJUSTMENT

These vehicles use an hydraulic clutch system which provides automatic clutch adjustment. No adjustment of the clutch linkage or pedal height is required.

Clutch Master/Slave Cylinder

REMOVAL & INSTALLATION

NOTE: **The clutch hydraulic system is serviced as a complete unit. Individual components of the system are not available separately.**

1. Disconnect the negative battery terminal from the battery.

2. Remove the hush panel from the under the dash.

NOTE: **If equipped with the 2.8L or 3.1L engine, remove the air cleaner, mass air flow sensor and air intake duct as an assembly. Disconnect electrical lead at the washer bottle and remove washer bottle from vehicle.**

3. Disconnect the master cylinder pushrod from the clutch pedal.

4. Remove the master cylinder-to-cowl brace nuts and remove master cylinder.

5. Remove the slave cylinder retaining nuts at the transaxle and remove slave cylinder. Remove the hydraulic system as a unit from the vehicle.

6. Installation is the reverse of the removal procedure. Bleed the hydraulic system.

NOTE: **Do not remove the plastic pushrod retainer from the slave cylinder. The strap will break on the first clutch pedal application.**

Hydraulic Clutch System Bleeding

1. Clean dirt and grease from the cap to ensure no foreign substances enter the system.

2. Fill reservoir to the top with approved brake fluid only.

NOTE: **Brake fluid must be certified to DOT 3 specification.**

3. Fully loosen the bleed screw which is in the slave cylinder body.

4. Fluid will now begin to move from the master cylinder, down the tube, to the slave cylinder. The reservoir must be kept full at all times.

5. When the slave cylinder is full, a steady stream of fluid will come from the slave outlet. At this point, tighten bleed screw.

6. Start the engine, push the clutch pedal to the floor and select reverse

gear. There should be no grating of gears. If there is the system still contains air.

AUTOMATIC TRANSAXLE

For further information on transmissions/transaxles, please refer to "Chilton's Guide to Transmission Repair".

Transaxle Assembly

NOTE: By September 1, 1991, Hydra-matic will have changed the name designation of the THM 125C automatic transaxle. The new name designation for this transaxle will be Hydra-matic 3T40. Transaxles built between 1989 and 1990 will serve as transitional years in which a dual system, made up of the old designation and the new designation will be in effect.

REMOVAL & INSTALLATION

1. Disconnect the negative terminal from the battery. Remove the air cleaner, bracket, Mass Air Flow (MAF) sensor and air tube as an assembly.
2. Disconnect the exhaust crossover from the right side manifold and remove the left side exhaust manifold, then, raise and support the manifold/crossover assembly.
3. Disconnect the TV cable from the throttle lever and the transaxle.
4. Remove the vent hose and the shift cable from the transaxle.
5. Remove the fluid level indicator and the filler tube.
6. Using the engine support fixture tool J–28467 or equivalent and the adapter tool J–35953 or equivalent, install them on the engine.
7. Remove the wiring harness-to-transaxle nut.
8. Label and disconnect the wires for the speed sensor, TCC connector and the neutral safety/back up light switch.
9. Remove the upper transaxle-to-engine bolts.
10. Remove the transaxle-to-mount through bolt, the transaxle mount bracket and the mount.
11. Raise and safely support the vehicle.
12. Remove the front wheel assemblies.
13. Disconnect the shift cable bracket from the transaxle.

14. Remove the left side splash shield.
15. Using a modified halfshaft seal protector tool J–34754 or equivalent, install one on each halfshaft to protect the seal from damage and the joint from possible failure.
16. Using care not to damage the halfshaft boots, disconnect the halfshafts from the transaxle.
17. Remove the torsional and lateral strut from the transaxle. Remove the left side stabilizer link pin bolt.
18. Remove the left frame support bolts and move it out of the way.
19. Disconnect the speedometer wire from the transaxle.
20. Remove the transaxle converter cover and matchmark the converter to the flywheel for assembly.
21. Disconnect and plug the transaxle cooler pipes.
22. Remove the transaxle-to-engine support.
23. Using a transmission jack, position and secure it to the transaxle and remove the remaining transaxle-to-engine bolts.
24. Make sure the torque converter does not fall out and remove the transaxle from the vehicle.

NOTE: The transaxle cooler and lines should be flushed any time the transaxle is removed for overhaul or to replace the pump, case or converter.

To install:
25. Put a small amount of grease on the pilot hub of the converter and make sure the converter is properly engaged with the pump.
26. Raise the transaxle to the engine while guiding the right-side halfshaft into the transaxle.
27. Install the lower transaxle mounting bolts, tighten to 55 ft. lbs. and remove the jack.
28. Align the converter with the

marks made previously on the flywheel and install the bolts hand tight.
29. Torque the converter bolts to 46 ft. lbs.; retorque the first bolt after the others.
30. Install the starter assembly. Install the left side halfshaft.
31. Install the converter cover, oil cooler lines and cover. Install the subframe assembly. Install the lower engine mount retaining bolts and the transaxle mount nuts.
32. Install the right and left ball joints. Install the power steering rack, heat shield and cooler lines to the frame.
33. Install the right and left inner fender splash shields. Install the tire assemblies.
34. Lower the vehicle. Connect all electrical leads. Install the upper transaxle mount bolts, tighten to 55 ft. lbs.
35. Attach the crossover pipe to the exhaust manifold. Connect the EGR tube to the crossover.
36. Connect the TV cable and the shift cable. Install the air cleaner and inlet tube.
37. Remove the engine support tool. Connect the negative battery cable.

SHIFT CONTROL CABLE ADJUSTMENT

1. Place the shift lever in the **N**.

NOTE: Neutral can be found by rotating the transaxle selector shaft counterclockwise from **P** through **R** to **N**.

2. Loosely attach the cable to the transaxle shift lever with a nut. Assemble the cable to the cable bracket and to shift lever. Tighten the cable to transaxle shift lever nut.

NOTE: The lever must be held out of **P** when torquing the nut.

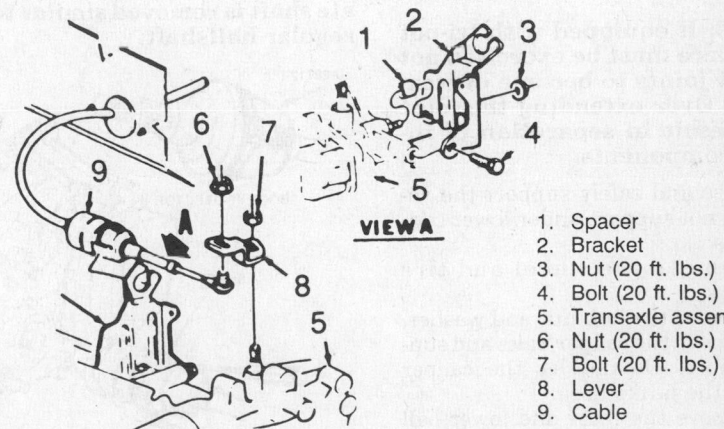

1. Spacer
2. Bracket
3. Nut (20 ft. lbs.)
4. Bolt (20 ft. lbs.)
5. Transaxle assembly
6. Nut (20 ft. lbs.)
7. Bolt (20 ft. lbs.)
8. Lever
9. Cable

Engine compartment shift control cable

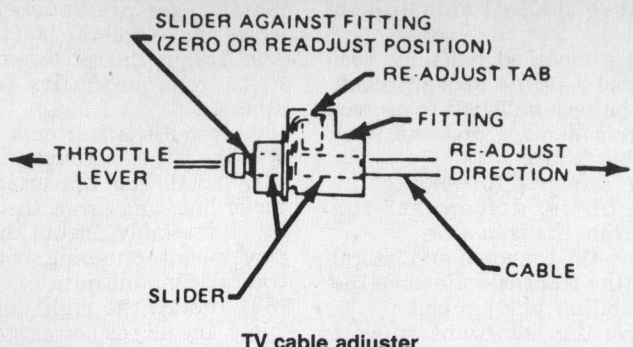

SLIDER AGAINST FITTING
(ZERO OR READJUST POSITION)

RE-ADJUST TAB

FITTING

THROTTLE
LEVER

RE-ADJUST
DIRECTION

SLIDER

CABLE

TV cable adjuster

THROTTLE VALVE (TV) CABLE ADJUSTMENT

Setting of the TV cable must be done by rotating the throttle lever at the carburetor or throttle body. Do not use the accelerator pedal to rotate the throttle lever.

1. With the engine off, depress and hold the reset tab at the engine end of the TV cable.
2. Move the slider until it stops against the fitting.
3. Release the rest tab.
4. Rotate the throttle lever to its full travel.
5. The slider must move (racthet) toward the lever when the lever is rotated to its full travel position.
6. Recheck after the engine is hot and road test the vehicle.

DRIVE AXLE

Halfshaft

REMOVAL & INSTALLATION

NOTE: If equipped with tri-pot joints, care must be exercised not to allow joints to become overextended. Over extending the joint could result in separation of internal components.

1. Raise and safely support the vehicle. Do not support under lower control arms.
2. Remove the wheel and tire assemblies.
3. Remove the hub nut and washer.
4. Remove the caliper bolts and support caliper. Do not let the caliper hang by the brake hose.
5. Remove the rotor and lower ball joint nut.
6. Remove the stabilizer bolt from lower control arm.

NOTE: Install the halfshaft seal boot protectors J–34754 or equivalent, on the outer drive seal.

7. Install J–28733 or equivalent and press the halfshaft in and away from the hub. The halfshaft should only be pressed in until the press fit between the halfshaft and hub is loose.
8. Separate and remove the lower ball joint from the steering knuckle.
9. Install J–28468 or equivalent and slide hammer assembly. Remove the halfshaft.

To install:

10. To install the halfshaft, start the splines of the halfshaft into the transaxle and push halfshaft inward until it snaps into place.
11. Verify that the halfshaft is seated into the transaxle by grasping on the housing and pulling outboard.
12. Torque the new axle shaft nut to 74 ft. lbs. Lower the vehicle and apply a final torque to the axle shaft nut of 191 ft. lbs.
13. The remainder of the installation is the reverse of the removal procedure.

NOTE: If equipped with the 2.8L or 3.1L engine and a manual transaxle, an intermediate shaft assembly is used. The intermediate shaft is removed similar to the regular halfshaft.

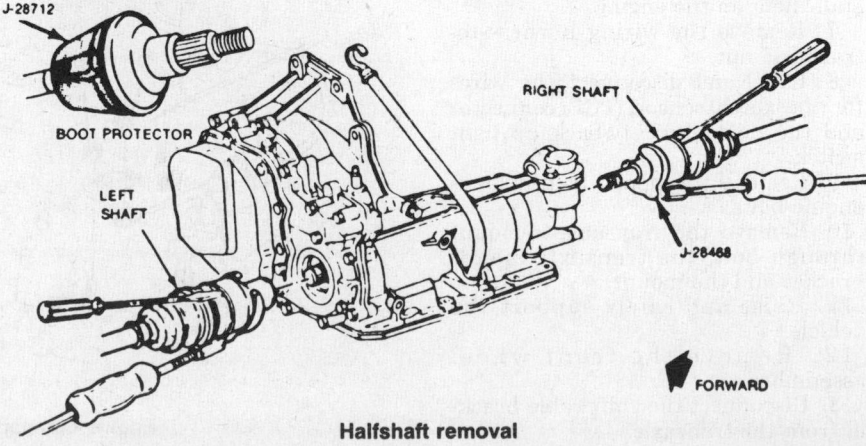

J-28712

BOOT PROTECTOR

LEFT SHAFT

RIGHT SHAFT

J-28468

FORWARD

Halfshaft removal

CV-Boot

REMOVAL & INSTALLATION

Outer

1. Remove the halfshaft assembly.
2. Remove the steel deflector ring by using brass drift to tap it off. If the rubber ring is used, slide it off.
3. Cut the seal retaining clamps and lift the boot up to gain access to retaining ring.
4. Using snapring pliers J–8059 or equivalent, spread the retaining ring inside the outer CV-joint and remove joint from shaft.
5. Slide the boot off shaft.

To install:

6. Clean the splines of the shaft and the CV-joint with solvent and repack the joint. Install a new retaining ring inside the joint.

NOTE: When repacking CV-joint, make sure to add grease to axle boot.

7. Install the inner boot clamp, boot, outer boot clamp on shaft.
8. Push the joint assembly onto the shaft until the ring is seated on the shaft.
9. Slide the boot and 2 clamps onto the joint and install the clamps on both the inner and outer part of the boot. Install deflector ring.
10. Install the halfshaft assembly.

Inner

1. Remove the halfshaft assembly.
2. Cut the seal retaining clamps and lift the boot up to gain access to retaining ring for spider assembly.
3. Using snapring pliers J–8059 or equivalent, remove the retaining ring from shaft and remove the spider assembly. Slide the old boot off axle shaft.

To install:

4. Clean the splines of the shaft and the CV-joint with solvent and repack the joint.

NOTE: When repacking CV-joint, make sure to add grease to axle boot.

5. Install the inner boot clamp, boot, outer boot clamp on shaft.

6. Push the tri-pot assembly onto the shaft until the retaining ring is seated on the shaft.

7. Slide the boot and 2 clamps onto the joint and install the clamps on both the inner and outer part of the boot.

8. Install the halfshaft assembly.

NOTE: Be sure the spacer ring is seated in groove on axle at reassembly.

Front Wheel Hub and Bearings

REMOVAL & INSTALLATION

1. Remove the wheel cover, loosen the hub nut, and raise and support the vehicle safely. Remove the front wheel.

2. Install the boot cover protector on 4 cylinder engine with automatic transaxle.

3. Remove the hub nut.

4. Remove the brake caliper and rotor.

NOTE: Do not allow the brake caliper to hang by the brake hose.

5. Remove the 3 hub and bearing attaching bolts.

6. Remove splash shield.

7. Install special tool J-28733 or equivalent, and press the hub and bearing assembly off the halfshaft.

8. Disconnect the stabilizer link bolt at the lower control arm.

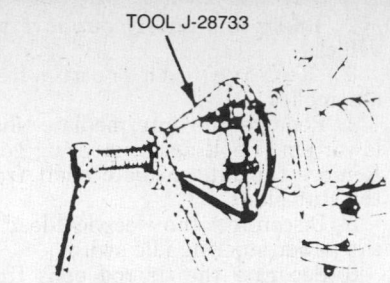

TOOL J-28733

Removal of the hub and bearing assembly

9. Separate the ball joint from steering knuckle.

10. Remove the halfshaft from knuckle and support out of the way.

11. Remove the inner knuckle seal using brass drift pin or equivalent.

NOTE: To remove the steering knuckle at this point, remove both strut to knuckle mounting bolts. Before removing the steering knuckle from the strut, be sure to scribe alignment marks between them, so the installation can be easily performed.

To install:

12. To install, use new O-rings, new bearing seals, new cotter pins, new hub nut and reverse the removal procedures.

13. Torque the steering knuckle-to-strut bolts to 129 ft. lbs.

14. Torque ball joint nut to 42 ft. lbs. Torque new hub and bearing nut to 74 ft. lbs.

15. Torque the 3 hub retaining bolts to 70 ft. lbs.

16. Lower vehicle and apply a final torque to the hub and bearing nut to 191 ft. lbs. for 1987 or 185 ft. lbs. for 1988–91.

STEERING

Steering Wheel

REMOVAL & INSTALLATION

Standard Steering Wheel

1. Disconnect the negative battery cable.

2. Pull the pad from the wheel. The horn lead is attached to the pad at one end; the other end of the pad has a wire with a spade connector. The horn lead is disconnected by pushing and turning; the spade connector is simply unplugged.

3. Remove the retainer under the pad, if equipped.

4. Remove the steering shaft nut.

5. There should be alignment marks already present on the wheel and shaft. If not, matchmark the parts.

6. Remove the wheel with a puller.

To install:

7. Install the wheel on the shaft, aligning the matchmarks. Install the shaft nut and tighten to 30 ft. lbs.

8. Install the retainer.

9. Plug in the spade connector, push and turn the horn lead to connect. Install the pad.

10. Connect the negative battery cable.

Sport Steering Wheel

1. Disconnect the negative battery cable.

2. Pry the center cap from the wheel.

3. Remove the retainer, if equipped.

4. Remove the shaft nut.

5. If the wheel and shaft do not have factory alignment marks, matchmark the parts before removal of the wheel.

6. Install a puller and remove the wheel. A horn spring, eyelet and insulator are underneath.

To install:

7. Install the spring, eyelet and insulator into the tower in the column.

8. Align the matchmarks and install the wheel onto the shaft. Install the retaining nut and tighten to 30 ft. lbs.

9. Install the retainer. Install the center cap. Connect the negative battery cable.

Steering Column

REMOVAL & INSTALLATION

NOTE: Once the steering column is removed from the vehicle, the column is extremely suscepti-

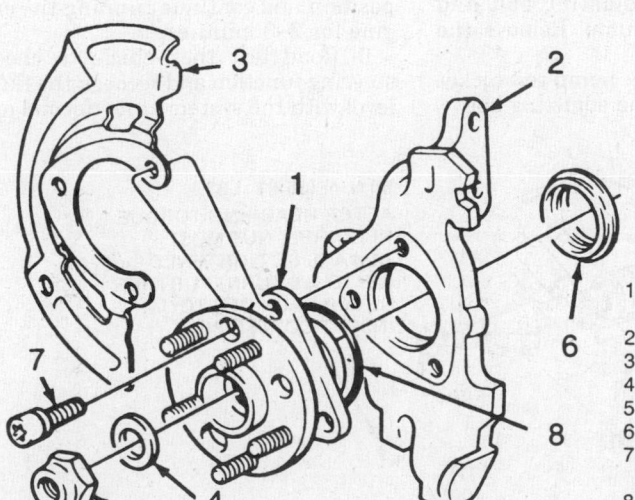

1. Hub and bearing assembly
2. Steering knuckle
3. Shield
4. Washer
5. Hub nut
6. Seal
7. Hub and bearing retaining bolt
8. O-ring

Exploded view of the hub and bearing attachment to the steering knuckle

ble to damage. **Dropping the column assembly on its end could collapse the steering shaft or loosen the plastic injections which maintain column rigidity. If it is necessary to remove the steering wheel, use a standard wheel puller. Under no condition should the end of the shaft be hammered upon, as hammering could loosen or break the plastic injection which maintains column rigidity.**

1. Disconnect the negative battery cable.

2. If column repairs are to be made, remove the steering wheel.

3. Remove the hush panels, as necessary, to gain access to the steering column retaining bolts.

4. Remove the nuts and bolts attaching the flexible coupling to the bottom of the steering column. Remove the safety strap and bolt, if equipped.

5. Remove the steering column trim shrouds and column covers.

6. Disconnect all wiring harness connectors. Remove the dust boot mounting screws and column mounting bracket bolts.

7. Remove the shift cable at the actuator and housing holder.

8. Lower the column to clear the mounting bracket and carefully remove from the vehicle.

9. Install in the reverse order of removal.

NOTE: Some vehicles equipped with tilt steering columns may experience a squeaking noise when turning the steering wheel in a tilted position. This can be caused by insufficient grease in the tilting mechanism.

Power Steering Rack

REMOVAL & INSTALLATION

1. Disconnect the negative battery cable. Remove the air cleaner.

2. Raise and safely support the vehicle.

3. Remove both front wheel assemblies.

4. Remove the intermediate shaft lower pinch bolt at the steering gear. Remove the intermediate shaft from the stub shaft.

5. Disconnect the electrical lead at the power steering idle switch.

6. Separate the tie rod ends from the knuckle assembly. Remove the rear sub-frame mounting bolts and lower the rear of the sub-frame approximately 4 in.

7. Remove the steering rack heat shield. Disconnect the pressure lines at the steering gear.

8. Remove the rack and pinion mounting bolts, remove the rack and pinion through the left wheel opening.

To install:

9. Install the rack and pinion through the left wheel opening. Tighten the mounting bolts to 59 ft. lbs. Connect the pressure lines, tighten the fittings to 20 ft. lbs.

10. Install the rack heat shield, tighten the retaining bolts to 53 inch lbs. Attach the tie rod ends to the steering knuckle.

11. Connect the electrical lead to the power steering idle switch. Attach the intermediate shaft to the stub shaft, tighten the pinch bolt to 35 ft. lbs.

12. Install both wheel assemblies. Lower the vehicle.

13. Install the air cleaner. Connect the negative battery cable. Fill and bleed the power steering system.

Power Steering Pump

REMOVAL & INSTALLATION

1. Disconnect the negative battery cable.

2. Loosen the adjusting bolt and pivot bolt on the pump. Remove the pump drive belt.

3. Remove the 3 pump-to-bracket bolts and remove the adjusting bolt.

4. Remove the high pressure fitting from the pump.

5. Disconnect the reservoir-to-pump hose from the pump.

6. Remove the pump.

7. Installation is in the reverse order of removal. Adjust the belt tension and bleed the system.

BELT ADJUSTMENT

1. Loosen the adjustment nut and bolt in the slotted bracket. Slightly loosen the pivot bolt.

2. Pull the component outward to increase tension. Push inward to reduce tension. Tighten the adjusting nut, bolt and the pivot bolt.

3. Recheck the drive belt tension which is 135 lbs. on a new belt, 75 lbs. on a used belt and readjust, if necessary.

NOTE: On a serpentine belt the correct tension is indicated on the indicator mark of the belt tensioner. If the indicator mark is not within specification, replace the belt or tensioner.

SYSTEM BLEEDING

1. Raise the front of the vehicle and support safely.

2. With the wheels turned all the way to the left, add power steering fluid to the **COLD** mark on the fluid level indicator.

3. Start the engine and check the fluid level at fast idle. Add fluid, if necessary, to bring the level up to the **COLD** mark.

4. Bleed air from the system by turning the wheels from side-to-side without hitting the stops. Keep the fluid level just above the internal pump casting or at the **COLD** mark.

5. Return the wheels to the center position and continue running the engine for 2–3 minutes.

6. Road test the vehicle to check steering function and recheck the fluid level with the system at its normal op-

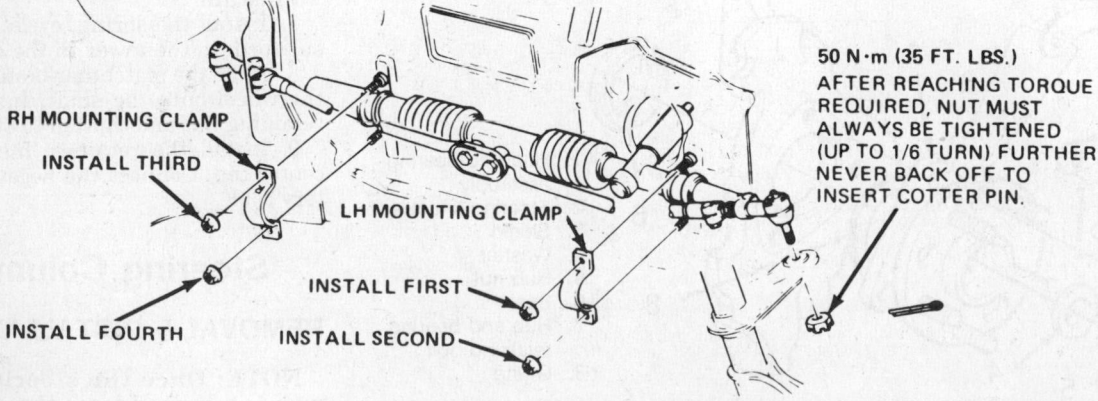

RH MOUNTING CLAMP
INSTALL THIRD
INSTALL FOURTH
LH MOUNTING CLAMP
INSTALL FIRST
INSTALL SECOND

50 N·m (35 FT. LBS.)
AFTER REACHING TORQUE REQUIRED, NUT MUST ALWAYS BE TIGHTENED (UP TO 1/6 TURN) FURTHER. NEVER BACK OFF TO INSERT COTTER PIN.

Manual rack and pinion unit mounting

erating temperature. Fluid should be at the **HOT** mark.

Tie Rod Ends

REMOVAL & INSTALLATION

1. Loosen both pinch bolts at the outer tie rod.
2. Remove the tie rod end from the strut assembly using a suitable removal tool.
3. Unscrew the outer tie rod end from the tie rod adjuster, counting the number of turns required before they are disconnected.
4. Install the new tie rod end, screwing it on the same number of turns as counted in Step 3.
5. When the tie rod end is installed, the tie rod adjuster must be centered between the tie rod and the tie rod end, with an equal number of threads exposed on both sides of the adjuster nut. Tighten the pinch bolts to 20 ft. lbs.
6. Install the tie rod end to the strut assembly and tighten to 50 ft. lbs. If the cotter pin cannot be installed, tighten the nut up to 1/16 in. further. Never back off the nut to align the holes for the cotter pin.
7. Check front end alignment.

BRAKES

For all brake system repair and service procedures not detailed below, please refer to "Brakes" in the Unit Repair section.

Master Cylinder

REMOVAL & INSTALLATION

1. Disconnect the electrical connector from the master cylinder.
2. Place a container under the master cylinder to catch the brake fluid. Disconnect the brake tubes from the master cylinder; use a flare nut wrench if one is available. Plug the ends of the tubes.

NOTE: Brake fluid eats paint. Wipe up any spilled fluid immediately and flush the area with clear water.

3. Remove the 2 nuts attaching the master cylinder to the booster or firewall.
To install:
5. To install, attach the master cylinder to the booster with the nuts. Torque to 22–30 ft. lbs.

6. Remove the tape from the lines and connect to the master cylinder. Torque to 10–15 ft. lbs. Connect the electrical lead.
7. Bleed the brakes.

NOTE: When installing a master cylinder that mounts on an angle, attempts to bleed the system, with the cylinder installed, can allow air to enter the system. To remove air, it is necessary to raise the rear of the vehicle until the master cylinder bore is level.

Proportioning Valve

REMOVAL & INSTALLATION

There is a front and a rear proportioning valve located at the lower left side of the master cylinder.
1. Disconnect the brake lines from the valves. Disconnect the valves from the master cylinder and remove the O-rings.
2. Replace the old O-rings and proportioning valves with new ones and reinstall into the master cylinder.
3. Torque the proportioning valves to 18–30 ft. lbs.

Power Brake Booster

REMOVAL & INSTALLATION

1. Remove the master cylinder from the booster. It is not necessary to disconnect the lines from the master cylinder. Just move the cylinder aside.
2. Disconnect the vacuum booster pushrod from the brake pedal inside the vehicle. It is retained by a bolt. A spring washer is under the bolt head and a flat washer goes on the other side of the pushrod eye, next to the pedal arm.
3. Remove the 4 attaching nuts from inside the vehicle. Remove the booster.
4. Install the booster on the firewall. Tighten the mounting nuts to 22–33 ft. lbs.
5. Connect the pushrod to the brake pedal.
6. Install the master cylinder. Mounting torque is 22–33 ft. lbs.

Brake Caliper

REMOVAL & INSTALLATION

1. Remove 2/3 of the brake fluid from the master cylinder.
2. Raise and safely support the vehicle.
3. Remove the wheel and tire and reinstall 2 nuts to retain the rotor.
4. Position a 12 inch adjustable pli-

ers over the inboard brake shoe tab and inboard caliper housing to bottom the piston in the caliper bore. This provides clearance between the linings and rotor.
5. Remove the bolt attaching the inlet fitting, only if the caliper is to be removed from the vehicle for replacement or overhaul. Plug the fittings. If only shoe and linings are being replaced, proceed to next step.
6. Remove the boots, mounting bolts and sleeve assemblies.
7. Remove the caliper from the rotor and mounting bracket.
8. If only the shoe and linings are being replaced, suspend the caliper with a wire hook from the strut.

To install:
9. Liberally fill both cavities in the housing between the bushings with silicone grease.
10. Install the caliper over the rotor in the mounting bracket.
11. Install the mounting bolt and sleeve assemblies and tighten to 38 ft. lbs.
12. Install the inlet fitting, if removed, and tighten to 33 ft. lbs.
13. Remove the wheel nuts securing the rotor to the hub.
14. Install the wheel and tire, lower the vehicle and fill the master cylinder.
15. Bleed the system if the caliper inlet fitting was removed and recheck fluid level.

Disc Brake Pads

REMOVAL & INSTALLATION

1. Raise and safely support the vehicle.
2. Remove the wheel and tire assemblies.
3. Remove the caliper, as outlined.
4. Pivot the caliper off of the rotor and suspend with a wire hook from the strut.
5. Remove the brake pads.
6. Remove the bushings from the mounting bolt holes.

To install:
7. Lubricate the bushings with silicone grease and install the bushings into the mounting bolt holes.
8. Install the inboard shoe into the caliper and snap the retaining spring into position. The shoe must lay flat against the piston. If it does not, use a large pair of pliers to compress the piston.
9. Install the outboard shoe with the wear sensor at the leading edge of the shoe.
10. Install the caliper onto the rotor. Tighten the mounting bolts to 38 ft. lbs.

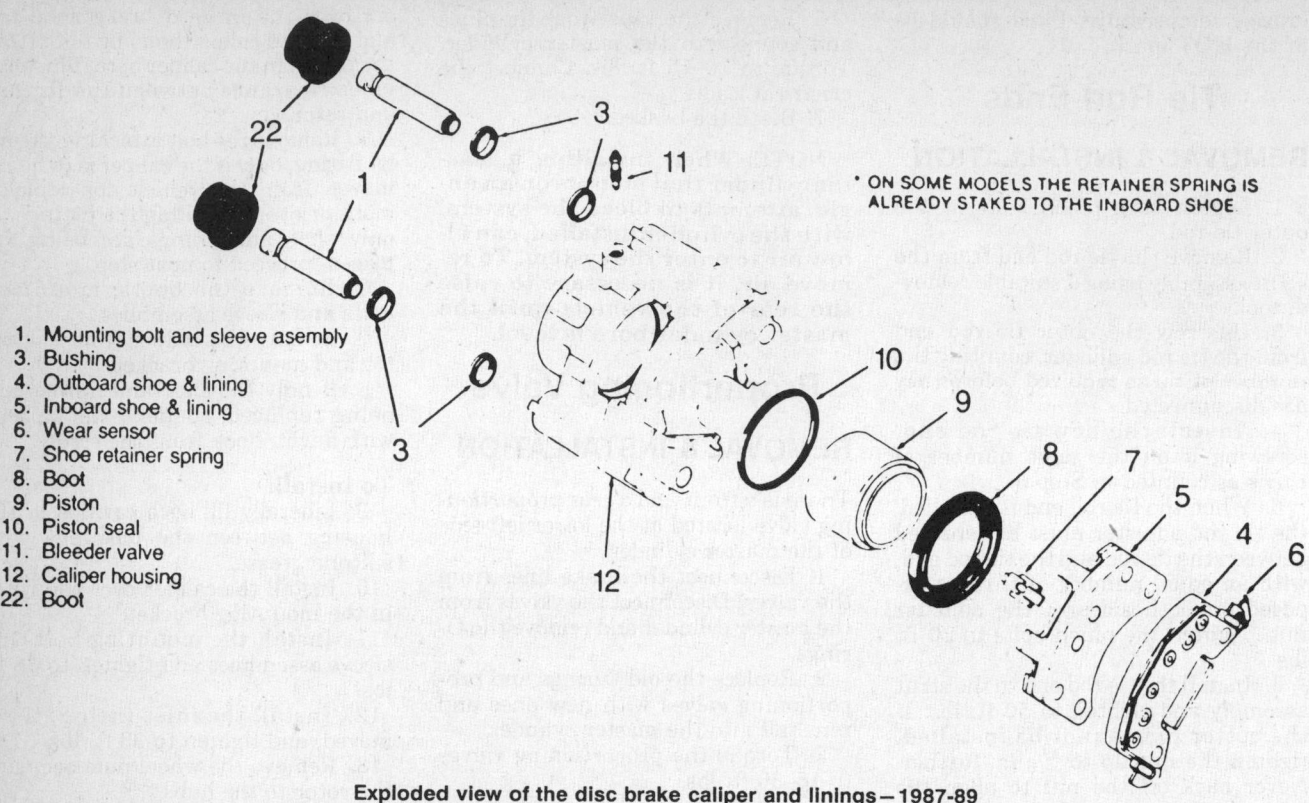

1. Mounting bolt and sleeve asembly
3. Bushing
4. Outboard shoe & lining
5. Inboard shoe & lining
6. Wear sensor
7. Shoe retainer spring
8. Boot
9. Piston
10. Piston seal
11. Bleeder valve
12. Caliper housing
22. Boot

* ON SOME MODELS THE RETAINER SPRING IS ALREADY STAKED TO THE INBOARD SHOE

Exploded view of the disc brake caliper and linings—1987-89

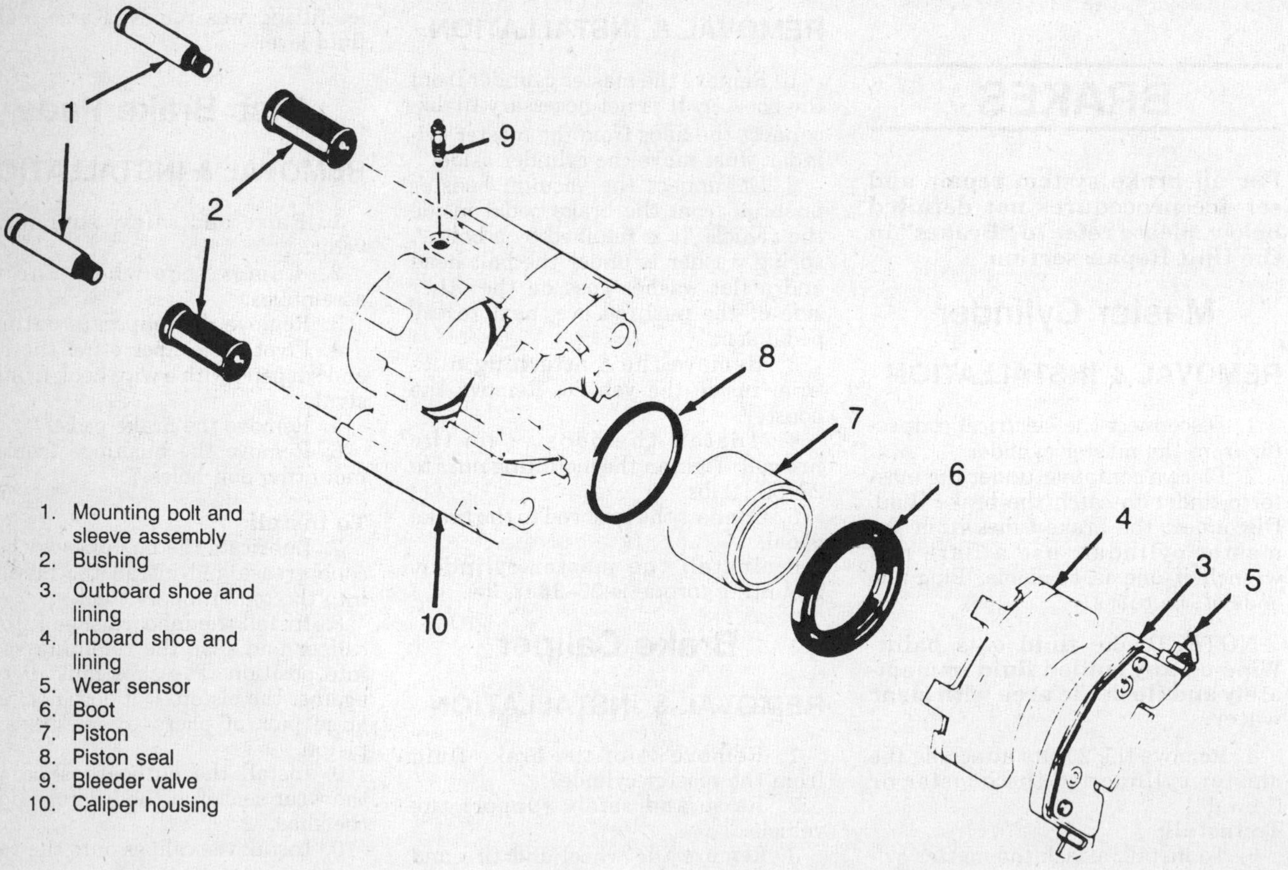

1. Mounting bolt and sleeve assembly
2. Bushing
3. Outboard shoe and lining
4. Inboard shoe and lining
5. Wear sensor
6. Boot
7. Piston
8. Piston seal
9. Bleeder valve
10. Caliper housing

Exploded view of the disc brake caliper and linings—1990-91

11. Apply the brake 3 times with approximately 175 lbs. of force, this will seat the linings.
12. Clinch the outboard shoe retaining tabs using a small pry bar to bend the tabs.
13. The outboard shoe should be locked in a fixed position.
14. Install the tire and wheel assemblies and lower the vehicle.

Brake Rotor

REMOVAL & INSTALLATION

1. Raise and safely support the vehicle.
2. Remove the wheel and tire assemblies.
3. Remove the caliper, as outlined.
4. Pivot the caliper off the rotor and suspend with a wire hook from the strut.
5. Remove the rotor.
To install:
6. Reposition the rotor and install the caliper onto the rotor. Tighten the mounting bolts to 38 ft. lbs.
7. Install the tire and wheel assemblies and lower the vehicle.

Brake Drums

REMOVAL & INSTALLATION

1. Raise and safely support the vehicle.

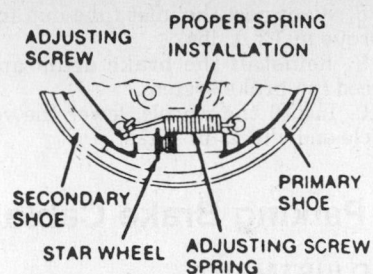

Proper spring installation is with the spring over the adjuster and not the star wheel.

2. Remove the wheel and tire assemblies.
3. Mark the relationship of the drum to the axle flange.
4. Remove the brake drum. If the drum is hard to remove, check to make sure the parking brake is off and the brake adjuster is not turned all the way out.
5. Installation is the reverse of removal.

Brake Shoes

REMOVAL & INSTALLATION

1. Raise and safely support the vehicle.
2. Remove the wheel and tire assemblies.

3. Remove the brake drum, if the drum is hard to remove, check to make sure the parking brake is off and the brake adjuster is not turned all the way out.
4. Remove the return springs, using brake spring pliers.
5. Remove the hold-down springs and pins. Remove the lever pivot.
6. Remove the actuator link while lifting up on the actuator lever.
7. Remove the actuator lever and lever return spring.
8. Remove the parking brake strut and strut spring.
9. Remove the brake shoes, after removing the parking brake cable from the shoe.
10. Remove the adjusting screw assembly and spring. Remove the retaining ring, pin and parking brake lever from the secondary shoe.
To install:
11. Install the parking brake lever on the secondary shoe with the pin and retaining ring.
12. Install the adjusting screw and spring.
13. Install the brake shoe assemblies after installing the parking brake cable on the shoe.
14. Install the parking brake strut and strut spring by spreading the shoes apart.
15. Install the actuator lever and lever return spring.
16. Install the hold-down pins, lever pivot and springs. Install the actuator

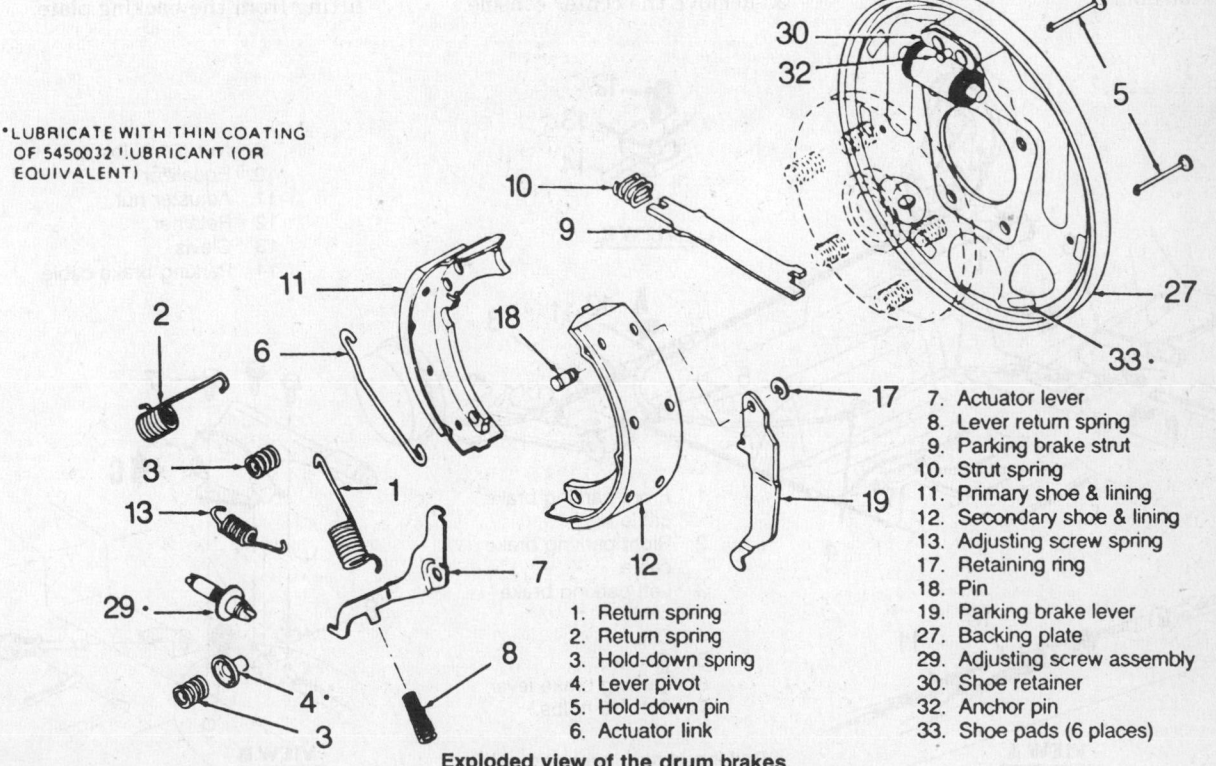

*LUBRICATE WITH THIN COATING OF 5450032 LUBRICANT (OR EQUIVALENT)

1. Return spring
2. Return spring
3. Hold-down spring
4. Lever pivot
5. Hold-down pin
6. Actuator link
7. Actuator lever
8. Lever return spring
9. Parking brake strut
10. Strut spring
11. Primary shoe & lining
12. Secondary shoe & lining
13. Adjusting screw spring
17. Retaining ring
18. Pin
19. Parking brake lever
27. Backing plate
29. Adjusting screw assembly
30. Shoe retainer
32. Anchor pin
33. Shoe pads (6 places)

Exploded view of the drum brakes

link on the anchor pin.

17. Install the actuator link into the actuator lever while holding up on the lever.

18. Install the shoe return springs. Install the brake drum. Install the wheel and tire assemblies.

19. Lower the vehicle and apply the brakes repeatedly. Bleed and adjust the brakes, as required.

Wheel Cylinder

REMOVAL & INSTALLATION

1. Raise the rear of the vehicle and support it safely.

2. Remove the rear wheel and brake drum assembly.

3. Disconnect the inlet tube nut and line from the wheel cylinder.

4. Remove the wheel cylinder retainer using 2 awls or pins ⅛ in. diameter or less.

   a. Insert the awls or pins into the access slots between the wheel cylinder pilot and the retainer locking tabs.

   b. Bend both tabs away simultaneously.

5. Remove the wheel cylinder.

To install:

6. Position the wheel cylinder and hold it in place using a wooden block placed between the the wheel cylinder and the axle flange.

7. Install a new wheel cylinder retainer over the wheel cylinder abutment using a 1⅛ inch 12 point socket and extension.

8. Reconnect the inlet tube nut and torque to 12 ft. lbs.

9. Reinstall the brake drum and bleed the brake system.

10. Install the wheels, lower the vehicle and check for leaks.

Parking Brake Cable

ADJUSTMENT

1. Raise and support the vehicle with both rear wheels off the ground.

2. Pull the parking brake lever exactly 2 ratchet clicks.

NOTE: To prevent damage to the threaded adjusting rod, thoroughly clean and lubricate the threads before turning the adjusting nut.

3. Loosen the equalizer locknut and tighten the adjusting nut until the left rear wheel can just be turned backward using 2 hands but is locked in forward rotation.

4. Tighten the locknut.

5. Release the parking brake. Rotate the rear wheels, there should be no drag.

6. Lower the vehicle.

REMOVAL & INSTALLATION

Front

1. Place the gear selector in **N** and apply the parking brake.

2. Remove the center console.

3. Disconnect the parking brake cable from the lever.

4. Remove the cable retaining nut and the bracket securing the front cable to the floor panel.

5. Raise the vehicle and loosen the equalizer nut.

6. Loosen the catalytic converter shield and remove the parking brake cable from the body.

7. Disconnect the cable from the equalizer and remove the cable from the guide and the underbody clips.

8. Reverse the removal procedure to install and adjust the cable.

Rear

1. Raise and support the rear of the vehicle.

2. Back off the equalizer nut until the cable tension is eliminated.

3. Remove the wheel assembly and brake drums.

4. Insert a small prybar or equivalent, between the brake shoe and the top part of the brake adjuster bracket. Push the bracket to the front and release the top brake adjuster rod.

5. Remove the rear hold-down spring. Remove the actuator lever and the lever return spring.

6. Remove the adjuster screw spring.

7. Remove the top rear brake shoe return spring.

8. Unhook the parking brake cable from the parking brake lever.

9. Depress the conduit fitting retaining tangs and remove the conduit fitting from the backing plate.

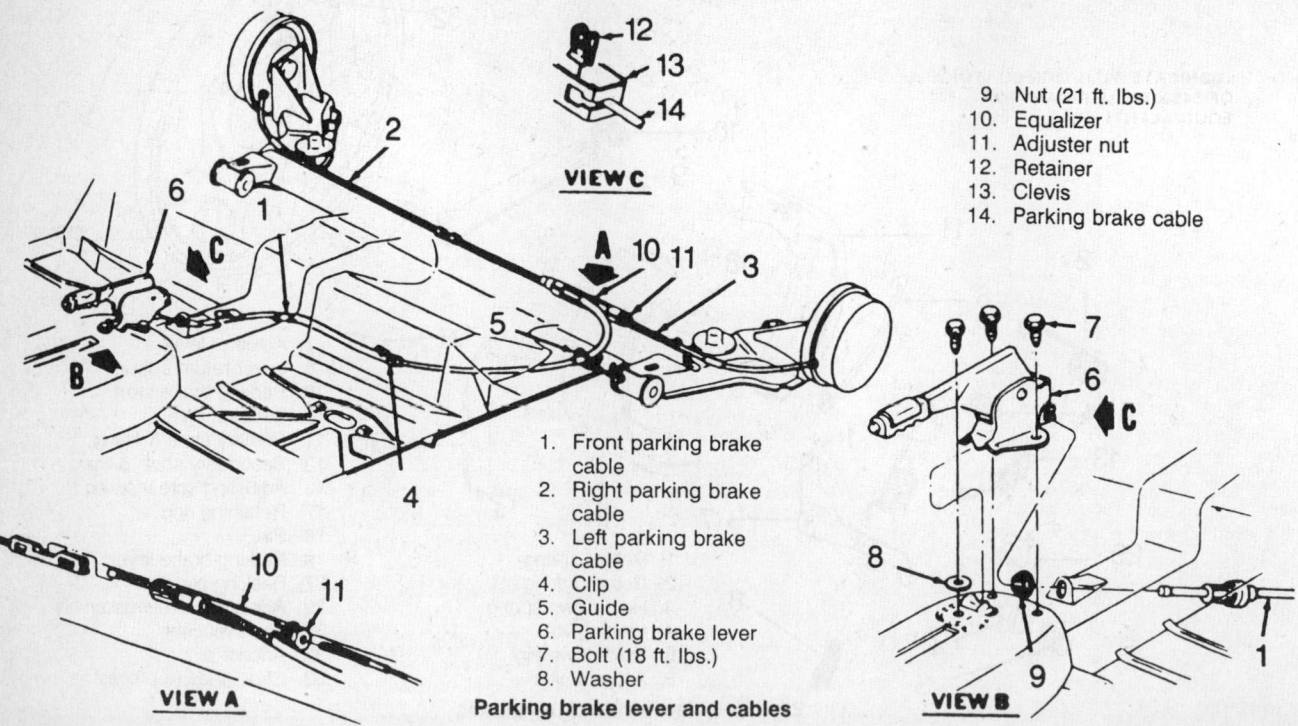

9. Nut (21 ft. lbs.)
10. Equalizer
11. Adjuster nut
12. Retainer
13. Clevis
14. Parking brake cable

VIEW C

VIEW A

1. Front parking brake cable
2. Right parking brake cable
3. Left parking brake cable
4. Clip
5. Guide
6. Parking brake lever
7. Bolt (18 ft. lbs.)
8. Washer

Parking brake lever and cables

VIEW B

10. Remove the cable end button from the connector.

11. Depress the conduit fitting retaining tangs and remove the conduit fitting from the axle bracket.

12. Reverse the procedure to install and adjust the cable.

Brake System Bleeding

The brake system must be bled when any brake line is disconnected or there is air in the system.

NOTE: Never bleed a wheel cylinder when a drum is removed.

1. Clean the master cylinder of excess dirt and remove the cylinder cover and the diaphragm.

2. Fill the master cylinder to the proper level. Check the fluid level periodically during the bleeding process and replenish it, as necessary. Do not allow the master cylinder fall below ½ full.

3. If the master cylinder is suspected or known to have air in the bore, bleed it before any wheel cylinder or caliper as follows:

   a. Disconnect the forward brake line connection at the master cylinder.

   b. Allow brake fluid to fill the master cylinder bore until it begins to flow from the forward line connector port.

   c. Connect the forward brake line to the master cylinder and tighten.

   d. Have a helper depress the brake pedal slowly, one at a time, and hold. Loosen the forward brake line connection at the master cylinder to purge the air from the bore. Tighten the connection and have a helper release the brake pedal slowly. Wait 15 seconds and repeat the sequence. Repeat the sequence including the 15 second wait until all air is removed from the bore.

   e. After all air is removed at the forward connection, repeat the above procedure for the rear connection at the master cylinder.

4. Bleed the individual wheel cylinders or calipers only after all air is removed from the master cylinder.

   a. Attach the proper size box end wrench over the bleeder valve.

   b. Attach a length of vinyl hose to the bleeder screw of the brake to be bled. Insert the other end of the hose into a clear jar half full of clean brake fluid, so the end of the hose is beneath the level of fluid. The correct sequence for bleeding is to work from the brake farthest from the master cylinder to the one closest; right rear, left rear, right front, left front.

5. Have an assistant depress and release the brake pedal one time and hold. Loosen the bleeder valve to purge the air from the cylinder. Tighten the bleeder screw and slowly release the pedal and wait 15 seconds. Repeat the sequence including the 15 second wait until all air is removed.

NOTE: Make sure an assistant presses the brake pedal to the floor slowly. Rapid pumping of the brake pedal pushes the master cylinder secondary piston down the bore in a way that makes it difficult to bleed the rear side of the system.

6. Repeat this procedure at each of the brakes. Remember to check the master cylinder level occasionally. Use only fresh fluid to refill the master cylinder, not the stuff bled from the system.

7. When the bleeding process is complete, refill the master cylinder, install its cover and diaphragm and discard the fluid bled from the brake system.

FRONT SUSPENSION

MacPherson Strut

REMOVAL & INSTALLATION

NOTE: Before removing front suspension components, their positions should be marked so they may be assembled correctly.

1. Remove the 3 strut-to-body nuts.
2. Raise and safely support the vehicle.
3. Lower the vehicle slightly so the weight rests on jackstands at the frame and not on the control arms.
4. Remove the front wheel and tire assemblies. Remove the tie rod from the strut assembly using tool J–24319 or equivalent.
5. Some vehicles may use a silicone (gray) boot on the inboard axle joint. Use the boot protector tool J–33162 or equivalent, on these boots. All other boots are made from a thermoplastic material (black) and do not require the use of a boot seal protector.
6. Disconnect the brake line bracket from the strut assembly.
7. Remove the strut-to-steering knuckle bolts.

NOTE: Support steering knuckle to prevent tension from being applied to brake hose.

8. Remove the strut assembly from the vehicle. Care should be taken to avoid chipping or cracking the spring coating when handling the front suspension coil spring assembly.
9. To install, reverse the removal procedures. Align the strut-to-steering knuckle bolts and tighten (lightly). Torque the strut-to-body nuts to 18 ft. lbs. and the strut-to-steering knuckle bolts to 133 ft. lbs. Check and/or adjust the front end alignment.

Lower Ball Joint

INSPECTION

1. Raise and safely support the vehicle allowing the suspension to hang free.
2. Grasp the wheel at the top and bottom, shake it in an "in-and-out" motion. Check for any horizontal movement of the steering knuckle relative to the lower control arm. Replace the ball joint if such movement is noted.
3. If the ball stud is disconnected from the steering knuckle and any looseness is detected or if the ball stud can be twisted in its socket using finger pressure, replace the ball joint.

REMOVAL & INSTALLATION

NOTE: This procedure requires the use of a special tool. The MacPherson strut suspension design does not use an upper ball joint.

1. Raise and support the vehicle safely. Remove the wheel assembly.
2. Use a ⅛ in. drill bit to drill a hole through the center of each of the 3 ball joint rivets.
3. Use a ½ in. drill bit to drill completely through the rivet.
4. Use a hammer and punch to remove the rivets. Drive them out from the bottom.
5. Use the special tool J–29330 or a ball joint removal tool, to separate the ball joint from the steering knuckle.
6. Disconnect the stabilizer bar from the lower control arm. Remove the ball joint.

To install:
7. Install the new ball joint into the control arm with the 3 bolts supplied with the replacement joint.
8. Installation of the remaining components is in the reverse order of removal. Use a new cotter pin when installing the castellated nut on the ball joint.
9. Check the toe setting and adjust, as necessary.

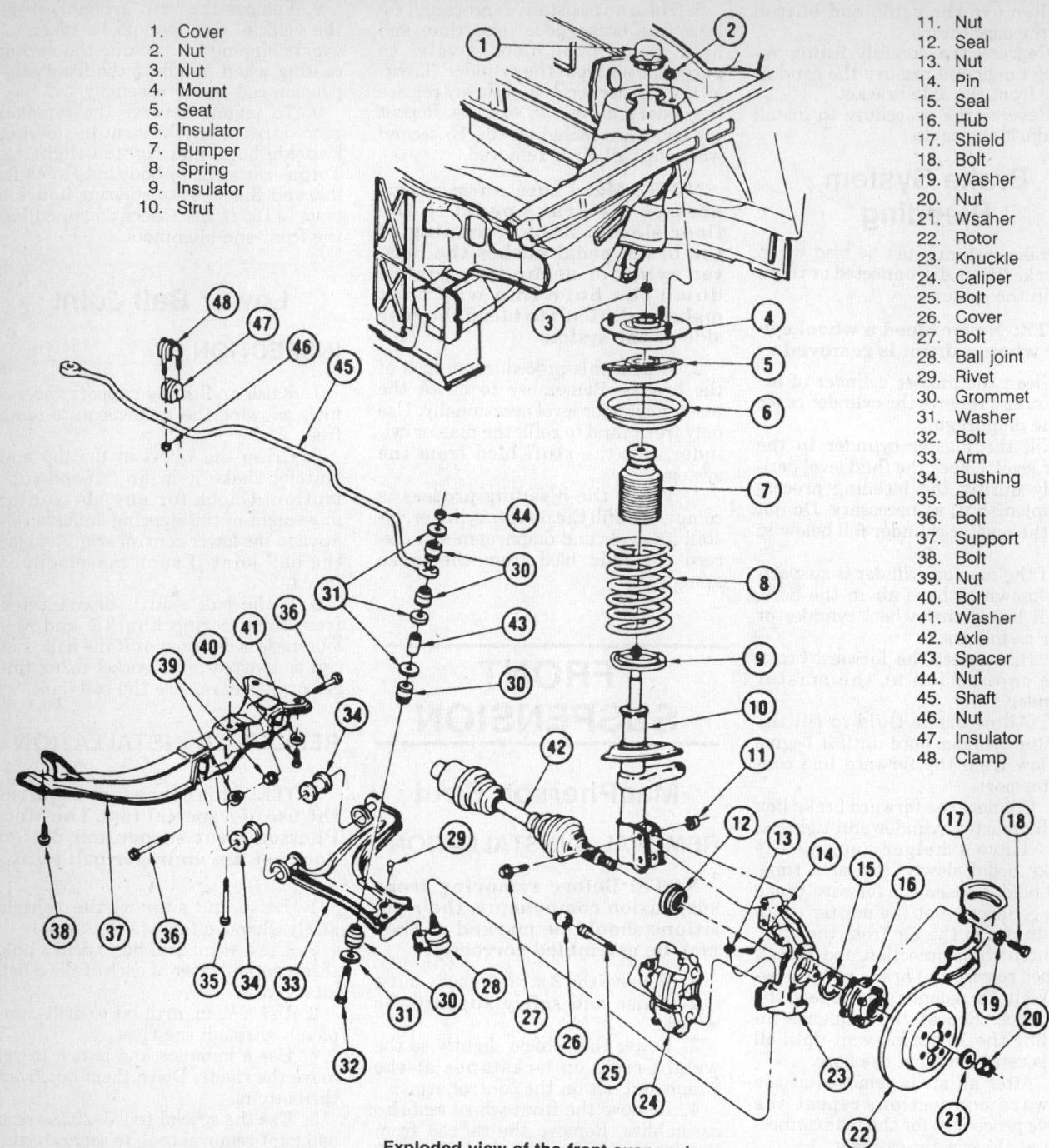

1. Cover
2. Nut
3. Nut
4. Mount
5. Seat
6. Insulator
7. Bumper
8. Spring
9. Insulator
10. Strut

11. Nut
12. Seal
13. Nut
14. Pin
15. Seal
16. Hub
17. Shield
18. Bolt
19. Washer
20. Nut
21. Wsaher
22. Rotor
23. Knuckle
24. Caliper
25. Bolt
26. Cover
27. Bolt
28. Ball joint
29. Rivet
30. Grommet
31. Washer
32. Bolt
33. Arm
34. Bushing
35. Bolt
36. Bolt
37. Support
38. Bolt
39. Nut
40. Bolt
41. Washer
42. Axle
43. Spacer
44. Nut
45. Shaft
46. Nut
47. Insulator
48. Clamp

Exploded view of the front suspension

Lower Control Arms

REMOVAL & INSTALLATION

1. Raise and support the vehicle safely. Remove the wheel assembly.
2. Disconnect the stabilizer bar from the control arm and/or support.
3. Separate the ball joint from the steering knuckle.
4. Remove the 2 control arm-to-support bolts and remove the control arm.

5. If control arm support bar removal is necessary, unscrew the 6 mounting bolts and remove the support.
6. Installation is in the reverse order of removal. Tighten the control arm support rail bolts, in sequence. Check the toe and adjust, as necessary.

Stabilizer Bar
REMOVAL & INSTALLATION

1. Raise and support the vehicle

safely so the front suspension hang free.
2. Remove the left front wheel and tire.
3. Disconnect the stabilizer from the control arms.
4. Disconnect the stabilizer from the support assemblies.
5. Loosen the front bolts and remove the rear and center bolts from the support assemblies to lower them enough to remove the stabilizer shaft.
6. Remove the stabilizer shaft with grommets and insulators.

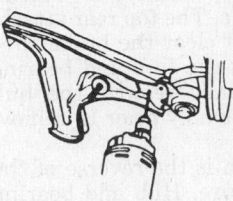

USING 1/8" DRILL, DRILL A PILOT HOLE COMPLETELY THROUGH THE RIVET.

DRILL PILOT HOLE

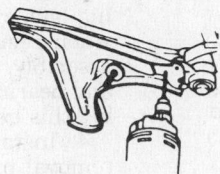

USING A 1/2" OR 13mm DRILL, DRILL COMPLETELY THROUGH THE RIVET. REMOVE BALL JOINT. DO NOT USE EXCESSIVE FORCE TO REMOVE BALL JOINT.

DRILL FINAL HOLE

PLACE J 29330 INTO POSITION AS SHOWN. LOOSEN NUT AND BACK OFF UNTIL . . .

J 29330

KNUCKLE

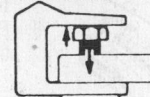

. . . THE NUT CONTACTS THE TOOL. CONTINUE BACKING OFF THE NUT UNTIL THE NUT FORCES THE BALL STUD OUT OF THE KNUCKLE.

SEPARATING BALL JOINT FROM KNUCKLE USING J 29330

7. Installation is the reverse of removal.

Front Wheel Hub and Bearing

For the front wheel hub and bearing procedure, refer to the Drive Axle in this section.

REAR SUSPENSION

Shock Absorbers

REMOVAL & INSTALLATION

1. Open the hatch or trunk lid, remove the trim cover, if present, and remove the upper shock absorber nut.

2. Raise and support the vehicle safely to a convenient working height. It is not necessary to remove the weight of the vehicle from the shock absorbers, however, the vehicle can be left on the ground, if preferred.

3. Remove the lower attaching bolt and remove the shock.

4. If new shock absorbers are being installed, repeatedly compress them while inverted and extend them in

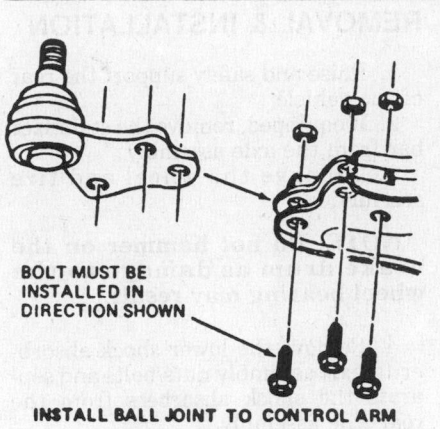

BOLT MUST BE INSTALLED IN DIRECTION SHOWN

INSTALL BALL JOINT TO CONTROL ARM

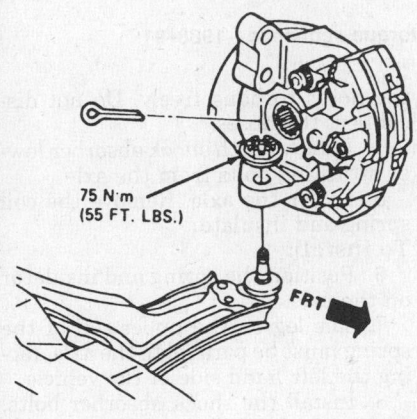

75 N·m (55 FT. LBS.)

FRT

Ball joint removal and installation details

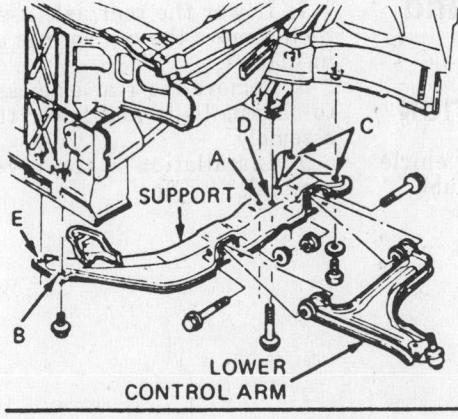

D   C
A
SUPPORT
E
B
LOWER CONTROL ARM

1. LOOSELY INSTALL CENTER BOLT INTO HOLE (A).
2. LOOSELY INSTALL TIE BAR BOLT INTO OUTBOARD HOLE (B).
3. INSTALL BOTH REAR BOLTS INTO HOLES (C) TORQUE REAR BOLTS.
4. INSTALL BOLT INTO CENTER HOLE (D), THEN TORQUE.
5. TORQUE BOLT IN HOLE (A).
6. INSTALL BOLT INTO FRONT HOLE (E), THEN TORQUE.
7. TORQUE BOLT IN HOLE (B).

TORQUE ALL BOLTS TO . . . . . . .80 N·m (59 FT. LBS.)

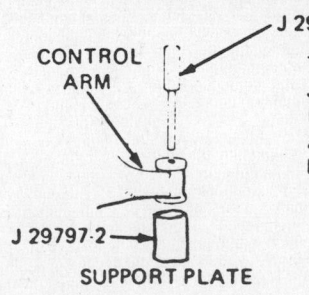

J 29792-1
CONTROL ARM

TO REMOVE, INSERT J 29792-1 INTO BUSHING, SUPPORT CONTROL ARM ON J 29792-2, AND PRESS AS SHOWN.

J 29797-2
SUPPORT PLATE

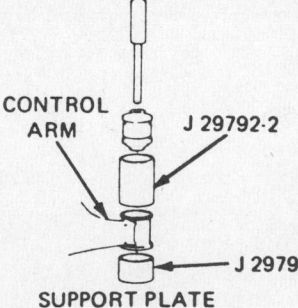

CONTROL ARM
J 29792-2

TO INSTALL, SUPPORT CONTROL ARM ON J 29792-3, PLACE BUSHING INTO J 29792-2, AND PRESS BUSING INTO CONTROL ARM USING J 29792-1. LUBRICATE BUSHING.

J 29792-3
SUPPORT PLATE

Lower control arm installation torque sequence—1987

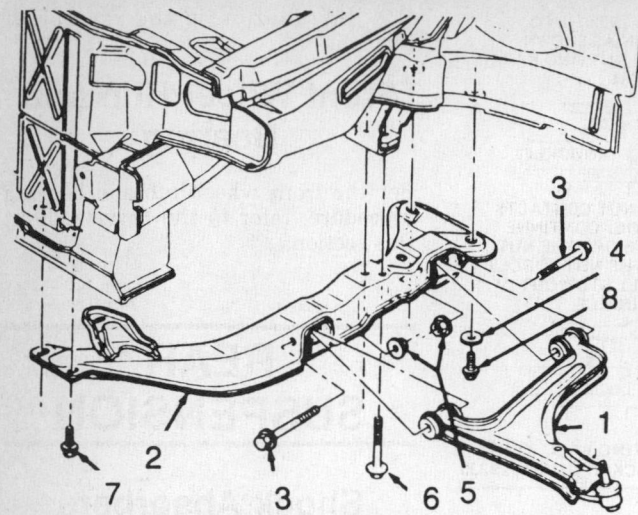

1. Control arm
2. Suspension support
3. Bolt (61 ft. lbs.)
4. Washer
5. Nut
6. Bolt (66 ft. lbs.) tighten first
7. Bolt (65 ft. lbs.) tighten second
8. Bolt (65 ft. lbs.) tighten third

Lower control arm installation torque sequence—1988–91

their normal upright position. This will purge them of air.

5. Install the shocks in the reverse order of removal. Tighten the lower mount nut and bolt to 35 ft. lbs. and the upper to 21 ft. lbs.

Coil Springs

REMOVAL & INSTALLATION

────── CAUTION ──────

The coil springs are under a considerable amount of tension. Be very careful when removing or installing them; they can exert enough force to cause very serious injuries.

1. Raise and support the vehicle safely, use a jack under the axle to support it.
2. Support the axle so it can be raised and lowered.
3. Remove the brake hose attaching brackets both right and left, allowing the hoses to hang freely. Do not disconnect the hoses.
4. Remove both shock absorber lower attaching bolts from the axle.
5. Lower the axle. Remove the coil spring and insulator.
To install:
6. Position the spring and insulator on the axle.
7. The leg on the upper coil of the spring must be parallel to the axle, facing the left hand side of the vehicle.
8. Install the shock absorber bolts. Tighten to 35 ft. lbs.
9. Install the brake line brackets. Tighten to 8 ft. lbs.

Rear Wheel Hub and Bearings

REMOVAL & INSTALLATION

1. Raise and support the vehicle safely. Remove the wheel assembly.

2. Remove the brake drum.

NOTE: Do not hammer on the brake drum to remove; damage to the bearing will result.

3. Remove the 4 hub and bearing retaining bolts and remove the assembly from the axle. The top rear attaching bolt will not clear the brake shoe when removing the hub and bearing assembly. Partially remove the hub and bearing assembly prior to removing this bolt.
4. Installation is the reverse of the removal procedure. Hub and bearing bolt torque is 37 ft. lbs.

Rear Axle Assembly

REMOVAL & INSTALLATION

1. Raise and safely support the rear of the vehicle.
2. If equipped, remove the stabilizer bar from the axle assembly.
3. Remove the wheel and tire assemblies.

NOTE: Do not hammer on the brake drum as damage to the wheel bearing may result.

4. Remove the lower shock absorber-to-axle assembly nuts/bolts and separate the shock absorbers from the rear axle assembly.
5. Disconnect the parking brake cable from the rear axle assembly.
6. Disconnect the brake lines from the rear axle assembly.
7. Lower the rear axle assembly, then remove the coil springs and the insulators.
8. Remove the rear axle assembly-to-chassis bolts and lower the axle assembly.
9. Installation is the reverse of removal.

GM "N" Body

Front Wheel Drive

Buick—Skylark, Somerset
Oldsmobile—Calais
Pontiac—Grand Am

SPECIFICATIONS

VEHICLE IDENTIFICATION CHART

It is important for servicing and ordering parts to be certain of the vehicle and engine identification. The VIN (vehicle identification number) is a 17 digit number visible through the windshield on the driver's side of the dash and contains the vehicle and engine identification codes. The tenth digit indicates model year, and the eighth digit indicates engine code. It can be interpreted as follows:

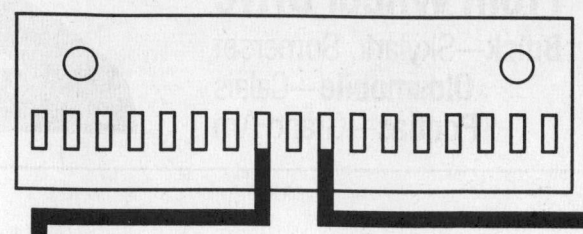

Engine Code							Model Year	
Code	Cu. In.	Liters	Cyl.	Fuel Sys.	Eng. Mfg.		Code	Year
M	122	2.0	4	Turbo	Pontiac		H	1987
A	138	2.3	4	MPFI	Oldsmobile		J	1988
D	138	2.3	4	MPFI	Oldsmobile		K	1989
U	151	2.5	4	TBI	Pontiac		L	1990
L	181	3.0	6	MPFI	Buick		M	1991
N	204	3.3	6	MPFI	Buick			

TBI Throttle Body Injection
MPFI Multi-port Fuel Injection

ENGINE IDENTIFICATION

Year	Model	Engine Displacement cu. in. (liter)	Engine Series Identification (VIN)	No. of Cylinders	Engine Type
1987	Grand Am	122 (2.0)	M	4	OHC
	Grand Am	151 (2.5)	U	4	OHV
	Grand Am	181 (3.0)	L	6	OHV
	Calais	138 (2.3)	D	4	DOHC
	Calais	151 (2.5)	U	4	OHV
	Calais	183 (3.0)	L	6	OHV
	Somerset	151 (2.5)	U	4	OHV
	Somerset	181 (3.0)	L	6	OHV
	Skylark	151 (2.5)	U	4	OHV
	Skylark	181 (3.0)	L	6	OHV
1988	Grand Am	122 (2.0)	M	4	OHC
	Grand Am	138 (2.3)	D	4	DOHC
	Grand Am	151 (2.5)	U	4	OHV
	Calais	138 (2.3)	D	4	DOHC
	Calais	151 (2.5)	U	4	OHV
	Calais	183 (3.0)	L	6	OHV
	Skylark	138 (2.3)	D	4	DOHC
	Skylark	151 (2.5)	U	4	OHV
	Skylark	181 (3.0)	L	6	OHV

ENGINE IDENTIFICATION

Year	Model	Engine Displacement cu. in. (liter)	Engine Series Identification (VIN)	No. of Cylinders	Engine Type
1989	Grand Am	122 (2.0)	M	4	OHC
	Grand Am	138 (2.3)	D	4	DOHC
	Grand Am	138 (2.3)	A	4	DOHC
	Grand Am	151 (2.5)	U	4	OHV
	Calais	138 (2.3)	D	4	DOHC
	Calais	138 (2.3)	A	4	DOHC
	Calais	151 (2.5)	U	4	OHV
	Calais	204 (3.3)	N	6	OHV
	Skylark	138 (2.3)	D	4	DOHC
	Skylark	151 (2.5)	U	4	OHV
	Skylark	204 (3.3)	N	6	OHV
1990-91	Grand Am	138 (2.3)	D	4	DOHC
	Grand Am	138 (2.3)	A	4	DOHC
	Grand Am	151 (2.5)	U	4	OHV
	Calais	138 (2.3)	D	4	DOHC
	Calais	138 (2.3)	A	4	DOHC
	Calais	151 (2.5)	U	4	OHV
	Calais	204 (3.3)	N	6	OHV
	Skylark	138 (2.3)	D	4	DOHC
	Skylark	151 (2.5)	U	4	OHV
	Skylark	204 (3.3)	N	6	OHV

GENERAL ENGINE SPECIFICATIONS

Year	VIN	No. Cylinder Displacement cu. in. (liter)	Fuel System Type	Net Horsepower @ rpm	Net Torque @ rpm (ft. lbs.)	Bore × Stroke (in.)	Compression Ratio	Oil Pressure @ rpm
1987	M	4-122 (2.0)	Turbo	167 @ 4500	175 @ 4000	3.40 × 3.40	8.0:1	NA
	D	4-138 (2.3)	MPFI	150 @ 4500	150 @ 2400	3.62 × 3.35	9.5:1	30 @ 2000
	U	4-151 (2.5)	TBI	92 @ 4400	132 @ 2800	4.00 × 3.00	9.0:1	37 @ 2000
	L	6-181 (3.0)	MPFI	125 @ 4900	150 @ 2400	3.80 × 2.70	9.0:1	37 @ 2400
1988	M	4-122 (2.0)	Turbo	167 @ 4500	175 @ 4000	3.40 × 3.40	8.0:1	NA
	D	4-138 (2.3)	MPFI	150 @ 5200	160 @ 4000	3.62 × 3.35	9.5:1	30 @ 2000
	U	4-151 (2.5)	TBI	98 @ 4300	135 @ 3200	4.00 × 3.00	9.0:1	37 @ 2000
	L	6-181 (3.0)	MPFI	125 @ 4900	150 @ 2400	3.80 × 2.70	9.0:1	37 @ 2400
1989	M	4-122 (2.0)	Turbo	167 @ 4500	175 @ 4000	3.40 × 3.40	8.0:1	NA
	A	4-138 (2.3)	MPFI	180 @ 6200	160 @ 5200	3.62 × 3.35	10.0:1	30 @ 2000
	D	4-138 (2.3)	MPFI	160 @ 6200	155 @ 5200	3.62 × 3.35	9.5:1	30 @ 2000
	U	4-151 (2.5)	TBI	110 @ 5200	135 @ 3200	4.00 × 3.00	9.0:1	37 @ 2000
	N	6-204 (3.3)	MPFI	160 @ 5200	185 @ 3200	3.70 × 3.16	9.0:1	45 @ 2000

GENERAL ENGINE SPECIFICATIONS

Year	VIN	No. Cylinder Displacement cu. in. (liter)	Fuel System Type	Net Horsepower @ rpm	Net Torque @ rpm (ft. lbs.)	Bore × Stroke (in.)	Compression Ratio	Oil Pressure @ rpm
1990-91	A	4-138 (2.3)	MPFI	180 @ 6200	160 @ 5200	3.62 × 3.35	10.0:1	30 @ 2000
	D	4-138 (2.3)	MPFI	160 @ 6200	155 @ 5200	3.62 × 3.35	9.5:1	30 @ 2000
	U	4-151 (2.5)	TBI	110 @ 5200	135 @ 3200	4.00 × 3.00	9.0:1	37 @ 2000
	N	6-204 (3.3)	MPFI	160 @ 5200	185 @ 3200	3.70 × 3.16	9.0:1	45 @ 2000

TBI Throttle Body Injection
MPFI Multi-port Fuel Injection

TUNE-UP SPECIFICATIONS

Year	VIN	No. Cylinder Displacement cu. in. (liter)	Spark Plugs Type	Spark Plugs Gap (in.)	Ignition Timing (deg.) MT	Ignition Timing (deg.) AT	Compression Pressure (psi) ②	Fuel Pump (psi)	Idle Speed (rpm) MT	Idle Speed (rpm) AT	Valve Clearance In.	Valve Clearance Ex.
1987	M	4-122 (2.0)	R42XLS	0.035	①	①	100	35–38	①	①	Hyd.	Hyd.
	D	4-138 (2.3)	FR3LS	0.035	①	①	100	34–44	①	①	Hyd.	Hyd.
	U	4-151 (2.5)	R43TS6	0.060	①	①	100	9–13	①	①	Hyd.	Hyd.
	L	6-181 (3.0)	R44LTS	0.040	—	①	100	34–44	①	①	Hyd.	Hyd.
1988	M	4-122 (2.0)	R42XLS	0.035	①	①	100	35–38	①	①	Hyd.	Hyd.
	D	4-138 (2.3)	FR3LS	0.035	①	①	100	34–44	①	①	Hyd.	Hyd.
	U	4-151 (2.5)	R43TS6	0.060	①	①	100	9–13	①	①	Hyd.	Hyd.
	L	6-181 (3.0)	R44LTS	0.045	—	①	100	34–44	—	①	Hyd.	Hyd.
1989	M	4-122 (2.0)	R42XLS	0.035	①	①	100	35–38	①	①	Hyd.	Hyd.
	A	4-138 (2.3)	FR3LS	0.035	①	①	100	34–44	①	①	Hyd.	Hyd.
	D	4-138 (2.3)	FR3LS	0.035	①	①	100	34–44	①	①	Hyd.	Hyd.
	U	4-151 (2.5)	R43TS6	0.060	①	①	100	9–13	①	①	Hyd.	Hyd.
	N	6-204 (3.3)	R44LTS6	0.045	—	①	100	41–47	—	①	Hyd.	Hyd.
1990	A	4-138 (2.3)	FR3LS	0.035	①	①	100	34–44	①	①	Hyd.	Hyd.
	D	4-138 (2.3)	FR3LS	0.035	①	①	100	34–44	①	①	Hyd.	Hyd.
	U	4-151 (2.5)	R43TS6	0.060	①	①	100	9–13	①	①	Hyd.	Hyd.
	N	6-204 (3.3)	R44LTS6	0.045	—	①	100	41–47	—	①	Hyd.	Hyd.
1991		SEE UNDERHOOD SPECIFICATIONS STICKER										

NOTE: The Underhood Specifications sticker often reflects tune-up specification changes made in production. Sticker figures must be used if they disagree with those in this chart.
① See Underhood Specifications sticker
② Minimum; the lowest reading cylinder should not have less than 70% of the pressure of the highest.

NOTE: To avoid confusion, always replace spark plug wires one at a time.

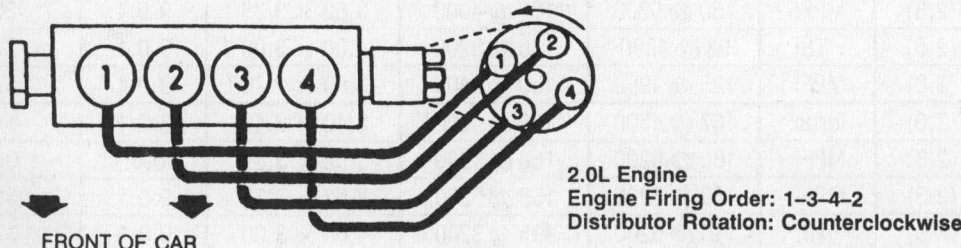

FRONT OF CAR

2.0L Engine
Engine Firing Order: 1–3–4–2
Distributor Rotation: Counterclockwise

FIRING ORDERS

NOTE: To avoid confusion, always replace spark plug wires one at a time.

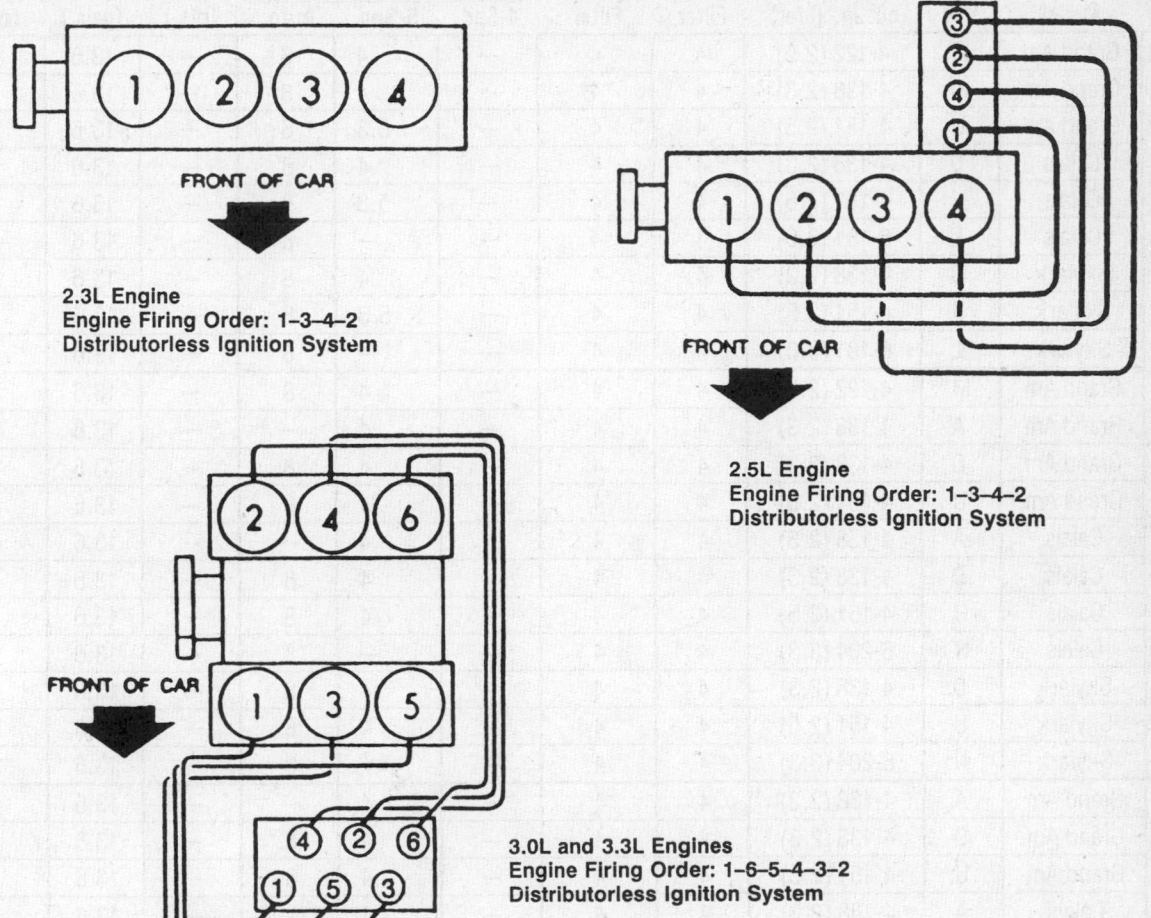

2.3L Engine
Engine Firing Order: 1–3–4–2
Distributorless Ignition System

2.5L Engine
Engine Firing Order: 1–3–4–2
Distributorless Ignition System

3.0L and 3.3L Engines
Engine Firing Order: 1–6–5–4–3–2
Distributorless Ignition System

CAPACITIES

Year	Model	VIN	No. Cylinder Displacement cu. in. (liter)	Engine Crankcase (qts.) with Filter ①	Engine Crankcase (qts.) without Filter	Transmission (pts.) 4-Spd	Transmission (pts.) 5-Spd	Transmission (pts.) Auto. ③	Drive Axle (pts.)	Fuel Tank (gals.)	Cooling System (qts.)
1987	Grand Am	M	4-122 (2.0)	4	4	—	4	8	—	13.6	8
	Grand Am	U	4-151 (2.5)	3	3	—	5.3	8	—	13.6	8
	Grand Am	L	6-181 (3.0)	4	4	—	—	8	—	13.6	10
	Calais	D	4-138 (2.3)	4	4	—	4	8	—	13.6	8
	Calais	U	4-151 (2.5)	②	②	—	5.3	8	—	13.6	8
	Calais	L	6-183 (3.0)	4	4	—	—	8	—	13.6	10
	Somerset	U	4-151 (2.5)	②	②	—	5.3	8	—	13.6	8
	Somerset	L	6-181 (3.0)	4	4	—	—	8	—	13.6	10
	Skylark	U	4-151 (2.5)	②	②	—	5.3	8	—	13.6	8
	Skylark	L	6-181 (3.0)	4	4	—	—	8	—	13.6	10

CAPACITIES

Year	Model	VIN	No. Cylinder Displacement cu. in. (liter)	Engine Crankcase (qts.) with Filter ①	Engine Crankcase (qts.) without Filter	Transmission (pts.) 4-Spd	Transmission (pts.) 5-Spd	Transmission (pts.) Auto. ③	Drive Axle (pts.)	Fuel Tank (gals.)	Cooling System (qts.)
1988	Grand Am	M	4-122 (2.0)	4	4	—	4	8	—	13.6	8
	Grand Am	D	4-138 (2.3)	4	4	—	4	8	—	13.6	8
	Grand Am	U	4-151 (2.5)	4	4	—	5.3	8	—	13.6	8
	Calais	D	4-138 (2.3)	4	4	—	4	8	—	13.6	8
	Calais	U	4-151 (2.5)	4	4	—	5.3	8	—	13.6	8
	Calais	L	6-181 (3.0)	4	4	—	—	8	—	13.6	10
	Skylark	D	4-138 (2.3)	4	4	—	4	8	—	13.6	8
	Skylark	U	4-151 (2.5)	4	4	—	5.3	8	—	13.6	8
	Skylark	L	6-181 (3.0)	4	4	—	—	8	—	13.6	10
1989	Grand Am	M	4-122 (2.0)	4	4	—	4	8	—	13.6	8
	Grand Am	A	4-138 (2.3)	4	4	—	4	—	—	13.6	8
	Grand Am	D	4-138 (2.3)	4	4	—	4	8	—	13.6	8
	Grand Am	U	4-151 (2.5)	4	4	—	4	8	—	13.6	8
	Calais	A	4-138 (2.3)	4	4	—	4	—	—	13.6	8
	Calais	D	4-138 (2.3)	4	4	—	4	8	—	13.6	8
	Calais	U	4-151 (2.5)	4	4	—	4	8	—	13.6	8
	Calais	N	6-204 (3.3)	4	4	—	—	8	—	13.6	10
	Skylark	D	4-138 (2.3)	4	4	—	4	8	—	13.6	8
	Skylark	U	4-151 (2.5)	4	4	—	4	8	—	13.6	8
	Skylark	N	6-204 (3.3)	4	4	—	—	8	—	13.6	10
1990-91	Grand Am	A	4-138 (2.3)	4	4	—	4	—	—	13.6	8
	Grand Am	D	4-138 (2.3)	4	4	—	4	8	—	13.6	8
	Grand Am	U	4-151 (2.5)	4	4	—	4	8	—	13.6	8
	Calais	A	4-138 (2.3)	4	4	—	4	—	—	13.6	8
	Calais	D	4-138 (2.3)	4	4	—	4	8	—	13.6	8
	Calais	U	4-151 (2.5)	4	4	—	4	8	—	13.6	8
	Calais	N	6-204 (3.3)	4	4	—	—	8	—	13.6	10
	Skylark	D	4-138 (2.3)	4	4	—	4	8	—	13.6	8
	Skylark	U	4-151 (2.5)	4	4	—	4	8	—	13.6	8
	Skylark	N	6-204 (3.3)	4	4	—	—	8	—	13.6	10

① When changing the oil filter, additional oil may be needed to fill the crankcase.
② With automatic transaxle: 3 qts
With manual transaxle: 4 qts
③ Drain and refill capacity shown. Dry capacity is 12 pts.

CAMSHAFT SPECIFICATIONS

All measurements given in inches.

Year	VIN	No. Cylinder Displacement cu. in. (liter)	Journal Diameter 1	Journal Diameter 2	Journal Diameter 3	Journal Diameter 4	Journal Diameter 5	Lobe Lift In.	Lobe Lift Ex.	Bearing Clearance	Camshaft End Play
1987	M	4-122 (2.0)	1.6714–1.6720	1.6812–1.6816	1.6911–1.6917	1.7009–1.7015	1.7108–1.7114	0.2409	NA	0.0008–	0.0016–0.0064
	D	4-138 (2.3)	1.3751–1.3760	1.3751–1.3760	1.3751–1.3760	1.3751–1.3760	1.3751–1.3760	0.3400	0.3500	0.0019–0.0043	0.0060–0.0014

CAMSHAFT SPECIFICATIONS

All measurements given in inches.

Year	VIN	No. Cylinder Displacement cu. in. (liter)	Journal Diameter 1	2	3	4	5	Lobe Lift In.	Ex.	Bearing Clearance	Camshaft End Play
1987	U	4-151 (2.5)	1.8690	1.8690	1.8690	1.8690	1.8690	0.3980	0.3980	0.0007–0.0027	0.0015–0.0050
	L	6-181 (3.0)	1.7850–1.7860	1.7850–1.7860	1.7850–1.7860	1.7850–1.7860	—	0.3580	0.3840	0.0005–0.0025	NA
1988	M	4-122 (2.0)	1.6714–1.6720	1.6812–1.6816	1.6911–1.6917	1.7009–1.7015	1.7108–1.7114	0.2409	NA	0.0008	0.0016–0.0064
	D	4-138 (2.3)	1.3751–1.3760	1.3751–1.3760	1.3751–1.3760	1.3751–1.3760	1.3751–1.3760	0.3400	0.3500	0.0019–0.0043	0.0060–0.0014
	U	4-151 (2.5)	1.8690	1.8690	1.8690	1.8690	1.8690	0.3980	0.3980	0.0007–0.0027	0.0015–0.0050
	L	6-181 (3.0)	1.7850–1.7860	1.7850–1.7860	1.7850–1.7860	1.7850–1.7860	—	0.3580	0.3840	0.0005–0.0025	NA
1989	M	4-122 (2.0)	1.6706–1.6712	1.6812–1.6818	1.6911–1.6917	1.7009–1.7015	1.7100–1.7106	0.2625	0.2625	0.0011–0.0035	0.0016–0.0064
	D	4-138 (2.3)	1.3751–1.3760	1.3751–1.3760	1.3751–1.3760	1.3751–1.3760	1.3751–1.3760	0.3400	0.3500	0.0019–0.0043	0.0060–0.0014
	A	4-138 (2.3)	1.3751–1.3760	1.3751–1.3760	1.3751–1.3760	1.3751–1.3760	1.3751–1.3760	0.4100	0.4100	0.0019–0.0043	0.0060–0.0014–
	U	4-151 (2.5)	1.8690	1.8690	1.8690	1.8690	1.8690	0.2480	0.2480	0.0007–0.0027	0.0014–0.0050
	N	6-204 (3.3)	1.7850–1.7860	1.7850–1.7860	1.7850–1.7860	1.7850–1.7860	—	0.2500	0.2550	0.0005–0.0035	NA
1990–91	D	4-138 (2.3)	1.3751–1.3760	1.3751–1.3760	1.3751–1.3760	1.3751–1.3760	1.3751–1.3760	0.3400	0.3500	0.0019–0.0043	0.0060–0.0014
	A	4-138 (2.3)	1.3751–1.3760	1.3751–1.3760	1.3751–1.3760	1.3751–1.3760	1.3751–1.3760	0.4100	0.4100	0.0019–0.0043	0.0060–0.0014–
	U	4-151 (2.5)	1.8690	1.8690	1.8690	1.8690	1.8690	0.2480	0.2480	0.0007–0.0027	0.0014–0.0050
	N	6-204 (3.3)	1.7850–1.7860	1.7850–1.7860	1.7850–1.7860	1.7850–1.7860	—	0.2500	0.2550	0.0005–0.0035	NA

CRANKSHAFT AND CONNECTING ROD SPECIFICATIONS

All measurements are given in inches.

Year	VIN	No. Cylinder Displacement cu. in. (liter)	Crankshaft Main Brg. Journal Dia.	Main Brg. Oil Clearance	Shaft End-play	Thrust on No.	Connecting Rod Journal Diameter	Oil Clearance	Side Clearance
1987	M	4-122 (2.0)	①	0.0006–0.0016	0.0030–0.0120.	3	1.9278–1.9286	0.0007–0.0024	0.0027–0.0095
	D	4-138 (2.3)	2.0470–2.0474	0.0005–0.0020	0.0034–0.0095	3	1.8887–1.8897	0.0005–0.0025	0.0059–0.0177
	U	4-151 (2.5)	2.3000	0.0005–0.0022	0.0035–0.0085	5	2.0000	0.0005–0.0026	0.0060–0.0220
	L	6-181 (3.0)	2.4995	0.0003–0.0018	0.0030–0.0110	2	2.2487–2.2495	0.0005–0.0026	0.0030–0.0150

CRANKSHAFT AND CONNECTING ROD SPECIFICATIONS

All measurements are given in inches.

Year	VIN	No. Cylinder Displacement cu. in. (liter)	Crankshaft				Connecting Rod		
			Main Brg. Journal Dia.	Main Brg. Oil Clearance	Shaft End-play	Thrust on No.	Journal Diameter	Oil Clearance	Side Clearance
1988	M	4-122 (2.0)	①	0.0006–0.0016	0.0030–0.0120	3	1.9278–1.9286	0.0007–0.0024	0.0027–0.0095
	D	4-138 (2.3)	2.0470–2.0474	0.0005–0.0020	0.0034–0.0095	3	1.8887–1.8897	0.0005–0.0025	0.0059–0.0177
	U	4-151 (2.5)	2.3000	0.0005–0.0022	0.0035–0.0085	5	2.0000	0.0005–0.0026	0.0060–0.0220
	L	6-181 (3.0)	2.4988–2.4998	0.0003–0.0018	0.0030–0.0110	2	2.2487–2.2495	0.0003–0.0028	0.0030–0.0150
1989	M	4-122 (2.0)	2.2828–2.2833	0.0006–0.0016	0.0028–0.0118	3	1.9279–1.9287	0.0007–0.0025	0.0028–0.0095
	A	4-138 (2.3)	2.0470–2.0480	0.0005–0.0023	0.0034–0.0095	3	1.8887–1.8897	0.0005–0.0020	0.0059–0.0177
	D	4-138 (2.3)	2.0470–2.0480	0.0005–0.0023	0.0034–0.0095	3	1.8887–1.8897	0.0005–0.0020	0.0059–0.0177
	U	4-151 (2.5)	2.3000	0.0005–0.0020	0.0006–0.0110	5	2.0000	0.0005–0.0030	0.0060–0.0240
	N	6-204 (3.3)	2.4988–2.4998	0.0003–0.0018	0.0030–0.0110	2	2.2487–2.2499	0.0003–0.0026	0.0030–0.0150
1990–91	A	4-138 (2.3)	2.0470–2.0480	0.0005–0.0023	0.0034–0.0095	3	1.8887–1.8897	0.0005–0.0020	0.0059–0.0177
	D	4-138 (2.3)	2.0470–2.0480	0.0005–0.0023	0.0034–0.0095	3	1.8887–1.8897	0.0005–0.0020	0.0059–0.0177
	U	4-151 (2.5)	2.3000	0.0005–0.0020	0.0006–0.0110	5	2.0000	0.0005–0.0030	0.0060–0.0240
	N	6-204 (3.3)	2.4988–2.4998	0.0003–0.0018	0.0030–0.0110	2	2.2487–2.2499	0.0003–0.0026	0.0030–0.0150

① Brown: 2.2830–2.2833
Green: 2.2827–2.2830

VALVE SPECIFICATIONS

Year	VIN	No. Cylinder Displacement cu. in. (liter)	Seat Angle (deg.)	Face Angle (deg.)	Spring Test Pressure (lbs.)	Spring Installed Height (in.)	Stem-to-Guide Clearance (in.)		Stem Diameter (in.)	
							Intake	Exhaust	Intake	Exhaust
1987	M	4-122 (2.0)	45	46	NA	NA	0.0006–0.0020	0.0010–0.0024	NA	NA
	D	4-138 (2.3)	45	①	64–70	1.42–1.44	0.0009–0.0027	0.0015–0.0032	0.2744–0.2751	0.2739–0.2739
	U	4-151 (2.5)	46	45	75	1.44	0.0010–0.0026	0.0013–0.0041	0.3130–0.3140	0.3120–0.3130
	L	6-181 (3.0)	45	45	90	1.73	0.0015–0.0035	0.0015–0.0032	0.3401–0.3412	0.3405–0.3412

VALVE SPECIFICATIONS

Year	VIN	No. Cylinder Displacement cu. in. (liter)	Seat Angle (deg.)	Face Angle (deg.)	Spring Test Pressure (lbs.)	Spring Installed Height (in.)	Stem-to-Guide Clearance (in.)		Stem Diameter (in.)	
							Intake	Exhaust	Intake	Exhaust
1988	M	4-122 (2.0)	45	46	NA	NA	0.0006–0.0020	0.0010–0.0024	0.2744–0.2751	0.2739–0.2754
	D	4-138 (2.3)	45	①	64–70	1.42–1.44	0.0009–0.0027	0.0015–0.0032	0.2744–0.2751	0.2739–0.2754
	U	4-151 (2.5)	46	45	71–78	1.44	0.0010–0.0026	0.0013–0.0041	0.3130–0.3140	0.3120–0.3130
	L	6-181 (3.0)	46	45	90	1.73	0.0015–0.0035	0.0015–0.0032	0.3401–0.3412	0.3405–0.3412
1989	M	4-122 (2.0)	45	46	74–82	NA	0.0006–0.0017	0.0010–0.0024	0.2755–0.2760	0.2747–0.2753
	A	4-138 (2.3)	45	①	71–79	1.42–1.44	0.0009–0.0027	0.0015–0.0032	0.2744–0.2751	0.2740–0.2747
	D	4-138 (2.3)	45	①	64–70	1.42–1.44	0.0009–0.0027	0.0015–0.0032	0.2744–0.2751	0.2740–0.2747
	U	4-151 (2.5)	46	45	75	1.68	0.0010–0.0026	0.0013–0.0041	0.3130–0.3140	0.3120–0.3130
	N	6-204 (3.3)	45	45	76–84	1.69–1.75	0.0015–0.0035	0.0015–0.0032	0.3401–0.3412	0.3405–0.3412
1990–91	A	4-138 (2.3)	45	①	71–79	1.42–1.44	0.0009–0.0027	0.0015–0.0032	0.2744–0.2751	0.2740–0.2747
	D	4-138 (2.3)	45	①	64–70	1.42–1.44	0.0009–0.0027	0.0015–0.0032	0.2744–0.2751	0.2740–0.2747
	U	4-151 (2.5)	46	45	75	1.68	0.0010–0.0026	0.0013–0.0041	0.3130–0.3140	0.3120–0.3130
	N	6-204 (3.3)	45	45	76–84	1.69–1.75	0.0015–0.0035	0.0015–0.0032	0.3401–0.3412	0.3405–0.3412

① Intake: 44°
Exhaust: 44.5°

PISTON AND RING SPECIFICATIONS

All measurements are given in inches.

Year	VIN	No. Cylinder Displacement cu. in. (liter)	Piston Clearance	Ring Gap			Ring Side Clearance		
				Top Compression	Bottom Compression	Oil Control	Top Compression	Bottom Compression	Oil Control
1987	M	4-122 (2.0)	0.0012–0.0020	0.012–0.020	0.012–0.020	0.016–0.055	0.002–0.003	0.001–0.003	NA
	D	4-138 (2.3)	0.0007–0.0020	0.016–0.025	0.016–0.025	0.016–0.055	0.002–0.004	0.0016–0.0031	NA
	U	4-151 (2.5)	0.0014–0.0022	0.010–0.020	0.010–0.020	0.020–0.060	0.002–0.003	0.001–0.003	0.015–0.055
	L	6-181 (3.0)	0.0008–0.0020	0.010–0.020	0.010–0.020	0.015–0.055	0.003–0.005	0.003–0.005	0.0005–0.0065

PISTON AND RING SPECIFICATIONS

All measurements are given in inches.

Year	VIN	No. Cylinder Displacement cu. in. (liter)	Piston Clearance	Ring Gap			Ring Side Clearance		
				Top Compression	Bottom Compression	Oil Control	Top Compression	Bottom Compression	Oil Control
1988	M	4-122 (2.0)	0.0012–0.0020	0.012–0.020	0.012–0.020	0.016–0.055	0.002–0.003	0.001–0.003	NA
	D	4-138 (2.3)	0.0007–0.0020	0.016–0.025	0.016–0.025	0.016–0.055	0.002–0.004	0.0016–0.0031	NA
	U	4-151 (2.5)	0.0014–0.0022	0.010–0.020	0.010–0.020	0.020–0.060	0.002–0.003	0.001–0.003	0.015–0.055
	L	6-181 (3.0)	0.0010–0.0045	0.010–0.020	0.010–0.022	0.015–0.055	0.001–0.003	0.001–0.003	0.0005–0.0065
1989	M	4-122 (2.0)	0.0012–0.0020	0.010–0.020	0.012–0.020	0.016–0.055	0.002–0.004	0.002–0.003	NA
	A	4-138 (2.3)	0.0007–0.0020	0.014–0.024	0.016–0.026	0.016–0.055	0.002–0.004	0.002–0.003	NA
	D	4-138 (2.3)	0.0007–0.0020	0.014–0.024	0.016–0.026	0.016–0.055	0.002–0.004	0.002–0.003	NA
	U	4-151 (2.5)	0.0014–0.0022	0.010–0.020	0.010–0.020	0.020–0.060	0.002–0.003	0.001–0.003	0.015–0.055
	N	6-204 (3.3)	0.0004–0.0022	0.010–0.025	0.010–0.025	0.010–0.040	0.001–0.003	0.001–0.003	0.001–0.008
1990-91	A	4-138 (2.3)	0.0007–0.0020	0.014–0.024	0.016–0.026	0.016–0.055	0.002–0.004	0.002–0.003	NA
	D	4-138 (2.3)	0.0007–0.0020	0.014–0.024	0.016–0.026	0.016–0.055	0.002–0.004	0.002–0.003	NA
	U	4-151 (2.5)	0.0014–0.0022	0.010–0.020	0.010–0.020	0.020–0.060	0.002–0.003	0.001–0.003	0.015–0.055
	N	6-204 (3.3)	0.0004–0.0022	0.010–0.025	0.010–0.025	0.010–0.040	0.001–0.003	0.001–0.003	0.001–0.008

TORQUE SPECIFICATIONS
All readings in ft. lbs.

Year	VIN	No. Cylinder Displacement cu. in. (liter)	Cylinder Head Bolts	Main Bearing Bolts	Rod Bearing Bolts	Crankshaft Pulley Bolts	Flywheel Bolts	Manifold Intake	Manifold Exhaust	Spark Plugs
1987	M	4-122 (2.0)	①	44 ②	26 ②	20	48 ③	16	16	15
	D	4-138 (2.3)	④	15 ⑤	15 ⑥	74 ⑤	22 ②	18	27	17
	U	4-151 (2.5)	⑧	70	32	162	⑨	25	⑩	15
	L	6-181 (3.0)	⑪	100	45	200	60	32	37	20
1988	M	4-122 (2.0)	①	44 ②	26 ②	20	48 ③	16	16	15
	D	4-138 (2.3)	④	15 ⑤	15 ⑥	74 ⑤	22 ②	18	27	17
	U	4-151 (2.5)	⑫	70	32	162	⑨	25	⑩	15
	L	6-181 (3.0)	⑪	100	45	219	60	32	37	20
1989	M	4-122 (2.0)	①	44 ②	26 ②	20	63 ②	18	10	15
	A	4-138 (2.3)	④	15 ⑤	18 ⑬	74 ⑤	22 ②	18	27	17
	D	4-138 (2.3)	④	15 ⑤	18 ⑬	74 ⑤	22 ②	18	27	17
	U	4-151 (2.5)	⑫	65	29	162	⑨	25	⑩	15
	N	6-204 (3.3)	⑭	90	20 ②	219	61	7	30	20
1990–91	A	4-138 (2.3)	⑮	15 ⑤	18 ⑬	74 ⑤	22 ②	18	⑦	17
	D	4-138 (2.3)	⑮	15 ⑤	18 ⑬	74 ⑤	22 ②	18	⑦	17
	U	4-151 (2.5)	⑫	65	29	162	⑨	25	⑩	15
	N	6-204 (3.3)	⑭	90	20 ②	219	61	7	30	20

① Step 1: 18 ft. lbs.
  Step 2: 3 rounds of 60° turns in sequence
  Step 3: An additional 30–50° turn after engine warm up
② Plus an additional 40–50° turn
③ Plus an additional 30° turn
④ Short bolts: 26 ft. lbs. plus an additional 80° turn
  Long bolts: 26 ft. lbs. plus an additional 90° turn
⑤ Plus an additional 90° turn
⑥ Plus an additional 75° turn
⑦ Nuts: 27 ft. lbs.
  Studs: 106 inch lbs.
⑧ Step 1: 18 ft. lbs.
  Step 2: 22 ft. lbs., except front bolt/stud
  Step 3: Front bolt/stud to 29 ft. lbs.
  Step 4: An additional 120° turn, except front bolt/stud
  Step 5: Turn front bolt/stud an additional 90°.
⑨ Manual transaxle: 69 ft. lbs.
  Automatic transaxle: 55 ft. lbs.
⑩ Outer bolts: 30 ft. lbs.
  Inner bolts: 37 ft. lbs.
⑪ Step 1: 25 ft. lbs.
  Step 2: 2 rounds of 90° turns in sequence, not to exceed 60 ft. lbs.
⑫ Step 1: 18 ft. lbs.
  Step 2: 26 ft. lbs., except front bolt/stud
  Step 3: Front bolt/stud to 18 ft. lbs.
  Step 4: An additional 90° turn
⑬ Plus an additional 80° turn
⑭ Step 1: 35 ft. lbs.
  Step 2: An additional 130° turn
  Step 3: An additional 30° turn on center 4 bolts
⑮ Short bolts: 26 ft. lbs. plus an additional 100° turn
  Long bolts: 26 ft. lbs. plus an additional 110° turn

BRAKE SPECIFICATIONS

All measurements in inches unless noted

Year	Model	Lug Nut Torque (ft. lbs.)	Master Cylinder Bore	Brake Disc Minimum Thickness	Brake Disc Maximum Runout	Standard Brake Drum Diameter	Minimum Lining Thickness Front	Minimum Lining Thickness Rear
1987	All	80 [1]	[2]	0.830	0.004	7.879	0.06	0.06
1988	All	80 [1]	[2]	0.830	0.004	7.879	0.06	0.06
1989	All	80 [1]	0.874	0.830	0.004	7.879	0.06	0.06
1990–91	All	80 [1]	0.874	0.830	0.004	7.879	0.06	0.06

[1] Aluminum wheels—100 ft. lbs.
[2] 0.874 in. or 0.937 in.

WHEEL ALIGNMENT

Year	Model		Caster Range (deg.)	Caster Preferred Setting (deg.)	Camber Range (deg.)	Camber Preferred Setting (deg.)	Toe-in (in.)	Steering Axis Inclination (deg.)
1987	Calais		$11/16$P–$2 11/16$P	$1 11/16$P	$7/32$P–$1 13/32$P	$13/16$P	0 [1]	$13 1/2$
	Grand Am		$11/16$P–$2 11/16$P	$1 11/16$P	$7/32$P–$1 13/32$P	$13/16$P	0 [1]	$13 1/2$
	Skylark		$23/32$P–$2 23/32$P	$1 23/32$P	$1/4$P–$1 7/16$P	$27/32$P	0	$13 1/2$
	Somerset		$23/32$P–$2 23/32$P	$1 23/32$P	$1/4$P–$1 7/16$P	$27/32$P	0	$13 1/2$
1988	Calais		$11/16$P–$2 11/16$P	$1 11/16$P	$7/32$P–$1 13/32$P	$13/16$P	0	$13 1/2$
	Grand Am		$11/16$P–$2 11/16$P	$1 11/16$P	$7/32$P–$1 13/32$P	$13/16$P	0	$13 1/2$
	Skylark		$11/16$P–$2 11/16$P	$1 11/16$P	$7/32$P–$1 13/32$P	$13/16$P	0	$13 1/2$
1989	Calais	front	$11/16$P–$2 11/16$P	$1 11/16$P	$1/8$P–$1 1/2$P [2]	$13/16$P [3]	0	$13 1/2$
		rear	—	—	$3/4$N–$1/4$P	$1/4$N	$1/4$	—
	Grand Am	front	$11/16$P–$2 11/16$P	$1 11/16$P	$1/8$P–$1 1/2$P [2]	$13/16$P [3]	0	$13 1/2$
		rear	—	—	$3/4$N–$1/4$P	$1/4$N	$1/4$	—
	Skylark	front	$11/16$P–$2 11/16$P	$1 11/16$P	$1/8$P–$1 1/2$P	$13/16$P	0	$13 1/2$
		rear	—	—	$3/4$N–$1/4$P	$1/4$N	$1/4$	—
1990–91	Calais	front	$11/16$P–$2 11/16$P	$1 11/16$P	$1/8$P–$1 1/2$P [2]	$13/16$P [3]	0	$13 1/2$
		rear	—	—	$3/4$N–$1/4$P	$1/4$N	$1/4$	—
	Grand Am	front	$11/16$P–$2 11/16$P	$1 11/16$P	$1/8$P–$1 1/2$P [2]	$13/16$P [3]	0	$13 1/2$
		rear	—	—	$3/4$N–$1/4$P	$1/4$N	$1/4$	—
	Skylark	front	$11/16$P–$2 11/16$P	$1 11/16$P	$1/8$P–$1 1/2$P [2]	$13/16$P [3]	0	$13 1/2$
		rear	—	—	$3/4$N–$1/4$P	$1/4$N	$1/4$	—

[1] with P215-60R14 tires: $1/16$ out
[2] with 16 in. wheels: $11/16$N–$11/16$P
[3] with 16 in. wheels: 0

ENGINE ELECTRICAL

NOTE: Disconnecting the negative battery cable on some vehicles may interfere with the functions of the on board computer systems and may require the computer to undergo a relearning process, once the negative battery cable is reconnected.

Distributor

REMOVAL

2.0L Engine

1. Disconnect the negative battery cable.
2. Disconnect the coil and Electronic Spark Timing (EST) connectors.
3. Remove the coil wire. Unscrew the distributor cap hold-down screws and lift off the distributor cap with all ignition wires still connected.
4. Matchmark the rotor to the distributor housing and the distributor housing to the cam carrier.

NOTE: Do not crank the engine during this procedure. If the engine is cranked, the rotor's matchmark must be disregarded.

5. Remove the hold-down nuts.
6. Remove the distributor from the engine.

INSTALLATION

Timing Not Disturbed

1. Install a new distributor housing O-ring.
2. Install the distributor in the cam carrier so the rotor is aligned with the matchmark on the housing and the housing is aligned with the matchmark on the cam carrier. Make sure the distributor is fully seated and the distributor tang drive is fully engaged.
3. Install the hold-down nuts.
4. Install the distributor cap and screw the retaining screws into place. Install the coil wire.
5. Connect the coil and EST connectors.
6. Connect the negative battery cable.
7. Adjust the ignition timing and tighten the hold-down nuts.

Timing Disturbed

1. Install a new distributor housing O-ring.
2. Position the engine so the No. 1 piston is at TDC of the compression stroke and the mark on the vibration damper is aligned with **0** on the timing indicator.
3. Install the distributor in the cam carrier so the rotor is aligned with the matchmark on the housing and the housing is aligned with the matchmark on the cam carrier. Make sure the distributor is fully seated and the distributor tang drive is fully engaged.
4. Install the hold-down nuts.
5. Install the distributor cap and screw the retaining screws into place. Install the coil wire.
6. Connect the coil and EST connectors.
7. Connect the negative battery cable.
8. Adjust the ignition timing and tighten the hold-down nuts.

Distributorless Ignition

REMOVAL & INSTALLATION

2.3L ENGINE

INTEGRATED DIRECT IGNITION (IDI) COIL AND MODULE ASSEMBLY

1. Disconnect the negative battery cable.
2. Disconnect 11-pin IDI harness connector.
3. Remove the bolts that fasten the assembly to the camshaft housing.
4. Remove the IDI assembly. If the boots adhere to the spark plugs, remove them by twisting and pulling up on the retainers.
To install:
5. Install the boots and retainers to the housing if they were separated during removal.
6. Align the spark plug boots with the plugs and place the assembly on the camshaft housing.
7. Install the mounting bolts and torque to 19 ft. lbs. (26 Nm).
8. Connect the harness connector.
9. Connect the negative battery cable and check for proper operation.

IGNITION COILS

1. Disconnect the negative battery cable.
2. Remove the IDI assembly.
3. Remove the housing to cover screws and remove the cover.
4. Disconnect the coil harness connectors.
5. Remove the coil(s), contact(s) and seal(s) from the cover.
To install:
6. Install the coil(s) to the cover and connect the connectors.
7. Install new seal(s) to the housing.

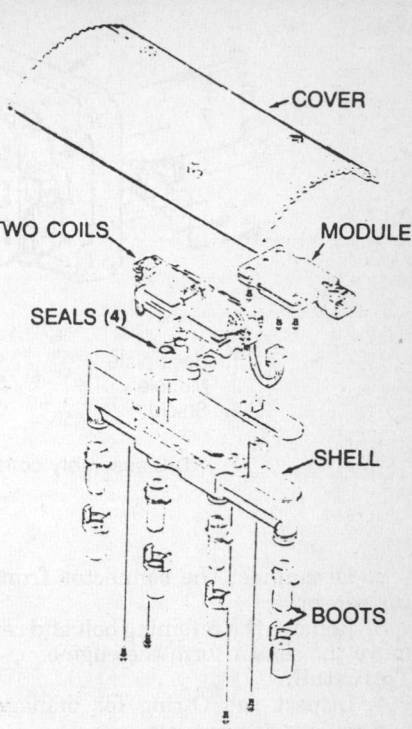

Integrated Direct Ignition (IDI) system components—2.3L engine

Using petroleum jelly to retain, install the contact(s) to the housing.
8. Assemble the cover to the housing, install the screws and torque to 35 inch lbs.
9. Install the IDI assembly.
10. Connect the negative battery cable and check for proper operation.

IGNITION MODULE

1. Disconnect the negative battery cable.
2. Remove the IDI assembly.
3. Remove the housing to cover screws and remove the cover.
4. Disconnect the coil harness connector from the ignition module.
5. Remove the screws that fasten the module to the cover and remove the module from the cover. Do not wipe the heat-protective grease away from the module if it is being reused.
To install:
6. If a new module is used, spread the grease included with the package on the metal face of the module and on the module's seat on the cover.
7. Install the module to the cover and connect the harness connector.
8. Assemble the cover to the housing, install the screws and torque to 35 inch lbs.
9. Install the IDI assembly.
10. Connect the negative battery cable and check for proper operation.

CRANKSHAFT SENSOR

1. Disconnect the negative battery cable.

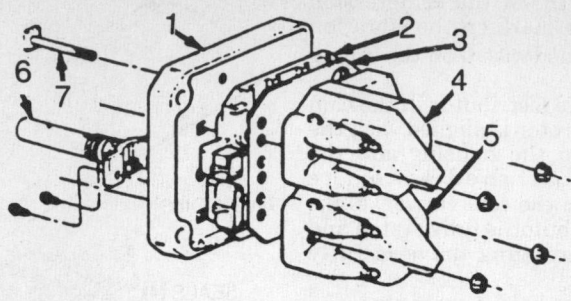

1. Base plate
2. Module
3. Shield
4. 2/3 coil
5. 1/4 coil
6. Crankshaft sensor

DIS assembly components—2.5L engine

2. Disconnect the connector from the sensor.

3. Remove the retaining bolt and remove the sensor form the engine.

To install:

4. Inspect the O-ring for damage and replace, if necessary.

5. Lubricate the O-ring with oil and install the sensor to its bore in the engine.

6. Install the retaining bolt and torque to 88 inch lbs. (10 Nm)

7. Connect the connector.

8. Connect the negative battery cable and check the sensor for proper operation.

2.5L Engine

DISTRIBUTORLESS IGNITION SYSTEM (DIS) ASSEMBLY

1. Disconnect the negative battery cable.

2. Disconnect the connectors from the DIS assembly, located at the rear of the engine.

3. Label and remove the spark plug wires from the assembly.

4. Remove the 3 mounting bolts and remove the assembly from the engine.

To install:

5. Inspect the O-ring for damage and replace, if necessary.

6. Lubricate the O-ring with oil and install the assembly to the engine.

7. Install the retaining bolts and torque to 20 ft. lbs. (27 Nm).

8. Connect the connectors.

9. Connect the negative battery cable and check for proper operation.

CRANKSHAFT SENSOR

1. Disconnect the negative battery cable.

2. Remove the DIS assembly from the engine.

3. Remove the 2 screws that fasten the sensor to the DIS assembly and remove the sensor.

To install:

4. Inspect the O-ring for damage and replace, if necessary.

5. Install the sensor to the DIS assembly and torque the screws to 20 inch lbs.

6. Lubricate the O-ring with oil and install the assembly to the engine.

7. Install the retaining bolts and torque to 20 ft. lbs. (27 Nm).

8. Connect the negative battery cable and check for the sensor proper operation.

IGNITION COILS

1. Disconnect the negative battery cable.

2. Remove the DIS assembly.

3. Remove the coils retaining nuts and remove the coil(s) from the assembly.

4. The installation is the reverse of the removal procedure.

5. Connect the negative battery cable and check the proper operation.

IGNITION MODULE

1. Disconnect the negative battery cable.

2. Remove the DIS assembly.

3. Remove the coils retaining nuts and remove the coils from the assembly.

4. Remove the module from the assembly plate.

5. The installation is the reverse of the removal procedure.

6. Connect the negative battery cable and check the proper operation.

3.0L and 3.3L Engines

C³I COILS AND MODULE

ASSEMBLY

1. Disconnect the negative battery cable.

2. Disconnect the 14-way connector from the module.

3. Label and remove the spark plug wires from the assembly.

4. Remove the fasteners securing the assembly to its mounting bracket and remove the assembly.

To install:

5. Install the assembly to the bracket and install the fasteners.

6. Connect the spark plug wires and the harness conncctor.

7. Connect the negative battery cable and check the for proper operation.

IGNITION COILS

1. Disconnect the negative battery cable.

2. Disconnect the spark plug wires.

3. Remove the screws and remove the coil(s) or coil pack from the ignition module. Disconnect the coil to module connector, if equipped.

To install:

4. Connect the harness connector.

5. Install the coil(s) or coil pack to the ignition module and install the retaining screws.

6. Connect the spark plug wires.

7. Connect the negative battery cable and for proper operation.

CRANKSHAFT SENSOR

1. Disconnect the negative battery cable.

2. Disconnect the serpentine belt from the harmonic balancer.

3. Raise the vehicle and support safely.

4. Remove the right front wheel and splash shield.

5. Remove the harmonic balancer.

6. Disconnect the sensor electrical connector.

7. Remove the sensor and pedestal from the engine and remove the sensor from the pedestal.

To install:

8. Loosely install the sensor to the pedestal.

9. Attach the assembly to the special aligning tool, slide the tool over the crankshaft and torque the pedestal to engine screws to 22 ft. lbs. (30 Nm).

10. Install the harmonic balancer to the crankshaft and torque the retaining bolt to 219 ft. lbs. (300 Nm).

11. If possible, adjust the sensor so the gap between it and the interrupter ring is 0.030 in.

12. Tighten the pinch bolt to 33 inch lbs.

13. Connect the connector.

14. Install the splash shield and wheel.

15. Lower the vehicle and install the belt.

16. Connect the negative battery cable and check the sensor for proper operation.

Ignition Timing

ADJUSTMENT

NOTE: Distributorless ignition systems do not give provisions for setting ignition timing; only the timing on the 2.0L engine can be set. Follow all instructions on the Vehicle Emissions Control Information (VECI) label if they are not consistent with these procedures.

1987 Vehicles

1. Start the engine, set the parking brake and run the engine until at normal operating temperature. Keep all lights and accessories off.
2. Connect the red lead of a tachometer to the terminal of the coil labeled **TACH** and connect the black lead to a good ground.
3. If a magnetic timing unit is available, insert the probe into the receptacle near the timing scale.
4. If a magnetic timing unit is not available, connect a conventional power timing light to the No. 1 cylinder spark plug wire.
5. Aim the timing light at the timing scale or read the magnetic timing unit.
6. Loosen the distributor hold-down nuts so the distributor can be rotated.
7. Turn the distributor in the proper direction until the specified timing according to the VECI label is reached. Tighten the hold-down nuts and recheck the timing.

1988–89 Vehicles

1. Start the engine, set the parking brake and run the engine until at normal operating temperature. Keep all lights and accessories off.
2. Connect the red lead of a tachometer to the terminal of the coil labeled **TACH** and connect the black lead to a good ground.
3. If a magnetic timing unit is available, insert the probe into the receptacle near the timing scale.
4. If a magnetic timing unit is not available, connect a conventional power timing light to the No. 1 cylinder spark plug wire.
5. With parking brake safely set, place automatic transaxle in **D** or leave manual transaxle in neutral.
6. Ground the ALDL connector under the dash by installing a jumper wire between the **A** and **B** terminals. The check engine light should begin flashing.
7. Aim the timing light at the timing scale or read the magnetic timing unit. Record the reading.

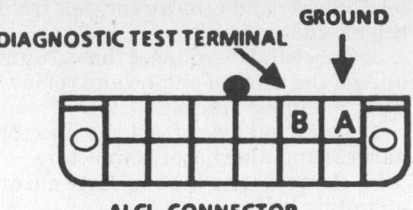

ALCL CONNECTOR

Grounding the ALDL connector

8. Repeat Steps 3–6 using the No. 4 spark plug wire. Record the reading.
9. Use the average of the 2 readings to derive an average timing value.
10. Loosen the distributor hold-down nuts so the distributor can be rotated.
11. Using the average timing value, turn the distributor in the proper direction until the specified timing according to the VECI label is reached.
12. Tighten the hold-down nuts and recheck the timing values.
13. Remove the jumper wire from the ALDL connector. To clear the ECM memory, disconnect the ECM harness from the positive battery pigtail for 10 seconds with the key in the OFF position.

Alternator

For further information on the charging system, please refer to "Charging and Starting" in the Unit Repair section.

PRECAUTIONS

Several precautions must be observed with alternator equipped vehicles to avoid damage to the unit.

- If the battery is removed for any reason, make sure it is reconnected with the correct polarity. Reversing the battery connections may result in damage to the one-way rectifiers.
- When utilizing a booster battery as a starting aid, always connect the positive to positive terminals and the negative terminal from the booster battery to a good engine ground on the vehicle being started.
- Never use a fast charger as a booster to start vehicles.
- Disconnect the battery cables when charging the battery with a fast charger.
- Never attempt to polarize the alternator.
- Do not use test lamps of more than 12 volts when checking diode continuity.
- Do not short across or ground any of the alternator terminals.
- The polarity of the battery, alternator and regulator must be matched

and considered before making any electrical connections within the system.
- Never separate the alternator on an open circuit. Make sure all connections within the circuit are clean and tight.
- Disconnect the battery ground terminal when performing any service on electrical components.
- Disconnect the battery if arc welding is to be done on the vehicle.

BELT TENSION ADJUSTMENT

V-Belt

1. Disconnect the negative battery cable.
2. Loosen the alternator mounting bolts.
3. Using a standard belt tension gauge, install it to the center of the longest span of the drive belt.
4. Use a medium prybar or the adjustment lug on the alternator housing to move the alternator. When the drive belt tension is 90–100 lbs. for a used belt or 165–175 lbs. for a new belt, tighten the alternator mounting bolts.

Serpentine Belt

A single serpentine belt is used to drive engine-mounted accessories. Drive belt tension is maintained by a spring loaded tensioner. The drive belt tensioner can control belt tension over a broad range belt lengths, however, there are limits to the tensioner's ability to compensate.

1. Disconnect the negative battery cable.

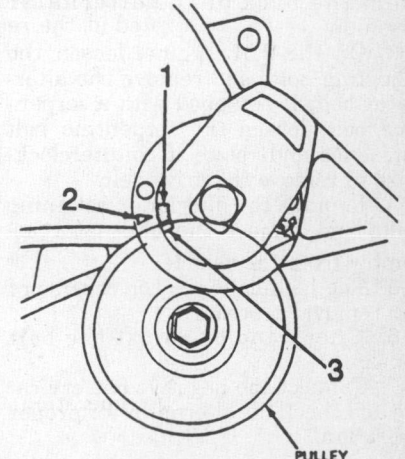

1. Minimum tension range
2. Pointer
3. Maximum tension range

Serpentine belt tensioner operating range

2. Inspect tensioner markings to see if the belt is within operating lengths. Replace the belt if the belt is excessively worn or is outside of the tensioner's operating range.

3. Run the engine until operating temperature is reached. Be sure all accessories are off. Turn the engine off and read the belt tension using a belt tension gauge tool placed halfway between the alternator and the air conditioning compressor. If the vehicle is not equipped with air conditioning, read the tension between the power steering pump and crankshaft pulley. Remove the tool.

4. Run the engine for 15 seconds and turn it off. Using a box-end wrench, apply clockwise force to tighten to the tensioner pulley bolt. Release the force and immediately take a tension reading without disturbing belt tensioner position.

5. Using the same wrench, apply a counterclockwise force to the tensioner pulley bolt and raise the pulley to its fully raised position. Slowly lower the pulley to engage the belt. Take a tension reading without disturbing the belt tensioner position.

6. Average the 3 readings. If their average is lower than specifications, replace the tensioner:
   2.0L and 2.3L engines—50 lbs.
   3.0L engine—79 lbs.
   3.3L engine—67 lbs.

REMOVAL & INSTALLATION

Except 2.3L Engine

1. Disconnect the negative battery cable.
2. Label and disconnect the wiring from the back of the alternator assembly.
3. On the 2.5L engine, loosen the adjusting bolts and remove the alternator belt. If equipped with a serpentine belt, loosen the serpentine belt tensioner and rotate it counterclockwise to remove the drive belt.
4. Remove the alternator retaining bolts and remove the alternator assembly from the vehicle.
5. The installation is the reverse of the removal procedure.
6. Check and/or adjust the belt tension.
7. Connect the negative battery cable and check the alternator for proper operation.

2.3L Engine

1. Disconnect the negative battery cable.
2. Using a 13mm wrench that is at least 24 in. long, loosen the tensioner pulley bolt, rotate the tensioner coun-

terclockwise and remove the belt from the alternator pully.

3. Label and disconnect the vacuum lines at the front of engine and remove their retaining bracket.
4. Label and disconnect the injector harness and alternator connectors.
5. Remove the 2 rear alternator mounting bolts.
6. Remove the front alternator bolt and engine harness clip.

NOTE: Care must be taken during removal and installation not to damage the air conditioning hoses.

7. Remove the alternator by manipulating it between the engine lifting eyelet and the air conditioning hoses.

To install:

8. Position the alternator on the engine.
9. Install the front mounting bolt loosely and install the clip.
10. Install the 2 rear mounting bolts and torque to 37 ft. lbs. (50 Nm).
11. Torque the front mounting bolt to 20 ft. lbs. (26 Nm).
12. Connect the injector harness and alternator connectors.
13. Connect the vacuum lines and install the bracket.
14. Install the belt.
15. Connect the negative battery cable and check the alternator for proper operation.

Starter

For further information on the charging system, please refer to "Charging and Starting" in the Unit Repair section.

REMOVAL & INSTALLATION

Except 2.3L Engine

1. Disconnect the negative battery cable.
2. Raise the vehicle and support safely. Disconnect the electrical wiring from the starter.
3. Remove the dust cover bolts and pull the dust cover back to gain access to the front starter bolt and remove the front starter bolt.
4. Remove the rear support bracket.
5. Pull the rear dust cover back to gain access to the rear starter bolt and remove the rear bolt.

NOTE: Take note of shims' location during removal so they may be installed in their original locations.

6. Push the dust cover back into place and remove the starter from the vehicle.

7. The installation is the reverse of the removal procedure.
8. Torque the starter bolts to 30–35 ft. lbs.

2.3L Engine Except HO

1. Disconnect the negative battery cable.
2. Remove the air cleaner to throttle body duct.
3. Label and disconnect the TPS, IAC and MAP sensor connectors.
4. Remove vacuum harness assembly from intake and position aside.
5. Remove cooling fan shroud retaining bolts and remove the shroud.
6. Remove upper radiator support.
7. Disconnect the connector from the cooling fan and remove the fan assembly. Do not damage the lock tang on the TPS with the fan bracket.
8. Remove the starter mounting bolts.
9. Tilt the rear of starter towards the radiator, pull the starter out and rotate solenoid towards the radiator to gain access to the electrical connections.

NOTE: If present, do not to damage the crank sensor mounted directly to the rear of the starter.

10. Disconnect the connectors from the solenoid.
11. Move the starter toward the driver's side of the vehicle and remove.

To install:

12. Lower the starter and connect the solenoid connectors.
13. Rotate the starter into installation position, properly install any shims that were removed and install the mounting bolts. Torque to 74 ft. lbs. (100 Nm).
14. Install the fan, support and shroud.
15. Install the vacuum harness assembly and connect the TPS, IAC and MAP sensor connectors.
16. Install the air cleaner to throttle body duct.
17. Connect the negative battery cable and check the starter for proper operation.

2.3L HO Engine

1. Disconnect the negative battery cable.
2. Remove the cooling fan assembly.
3. Remove the oil filter, if necessary.
4. Remove the intake manifold brace.
5. Remove the mounting bolts; some engines may have 3 starter mounting bolts. Pull the starter out of the hole and move toward the front of the vehicle.

6. Disconnect the wiring from the solenoid.

7. Remove the starter by lifting it between the intake manifold and the radiator.

To install:

8. Lower the starter between the intake manifold and the radiator and connect the wiring to the solenoid.

9. Rotate the starter into installation position and install the mounting bolts. Torque to 74 ft. lbs. (100 Nm).

10. Install the intake manifold brace and oil filter.

11. Install the cooling fan assembly.

12. Connect the negative battery cable and check the starter for proper operation.

CHASSIS ELECTRICAL

Heater Blower Motor

REMOVAL & INSTALLATION

1. Disconnect negative battery cable.

2. Remove the serpentine belt and/or the power steering pressure hose, as required.

3. Disconnect the connector to the blower motor and remove the cooling tube.

4. Remove the retaining screws and remove the blower from the case.

5. If necessary, remove the fan from the blower motor.

6. The installation is the reverse of the removal procedure.

7. Connect the negative battery cable and check the blower motor for proper operation.

Windshield Wiper Motor

REMOVAL & INSTALLATION

1. Disconnect the negative battery cable.

2. Remove the wiper arm assembly(s) and cowl cover, if necessary.

3. Remove the wiper arm drive link from the crank arm.

4. Disconnect the connectors from the motor.

5. Remove the wiper motor retaining bolts.

6. Remove the wiper motor and crank arm by guiding the assembly through the access hole in the upper shroud panel.

7. The installation is the reverse of the removal procedure.

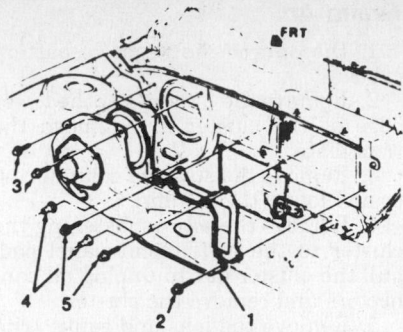

1. Blower assembly
2. Install first
E. Install second
4. Nut
5. Bolt

Removing blower motor assembly

8. Connect the negative battery cable and check the wiper motor for proper operation.

Windshield Wiper Switch

REMOVAL & INSTALLATION

Except 1990–91 Skylark

1. Disconnect the negative battery cable.

2. Remove the cluster trim, instrument panel trim or wiper switch trim screws, as required.

3. Remove the wiper switch retaining screws.

4. Pull the switch out, unplug the connectors and remove the switch assembly.

5. The installation is the reverse of the removal procedure.

6. Connect the negative battery cable and check the wipers and washers for proper operation.

1990–91 Skylark

1. Disconnect the negative battery cable.

2. Remove the lower instrument panel sound insulator, trim pad and steering column trim collar.

3. Straighten the steering wheel so the tires are pointing straight ahead.

4. Remove the steering wheel.

5. Remove the plastic wire protector from under the steering column.

6. Disconnect the turn signal switch, wiper switch and cruise control connectors, if equipped.

7. To disassemble the top of the column:

a. Remove the shaft lock cover.

b. If equipped with telescope steering, remove the first set of spacers, bumper, second set of spacers, and carrier snaping retainer.

c. Depress the lockplate with the proper depressing tool and remove the retaining ring from its groove.

d. Remove the tool, retaining ring, lockplate, cancelling cam and spring.

8. Pull the turn signal lever straight out of the wiper switch.

9. Remove the 3 screws and remove the turn signal switch and actuator lever.

10. Remove the ignition key lamp.

11. Place the key in the **RUN** position and use a thin suitable tool to remove the buzzer switch.

12. Remove the key lock cylinder retaining screw and remove the lock cylinder.

13. Remove the 3 housing cover

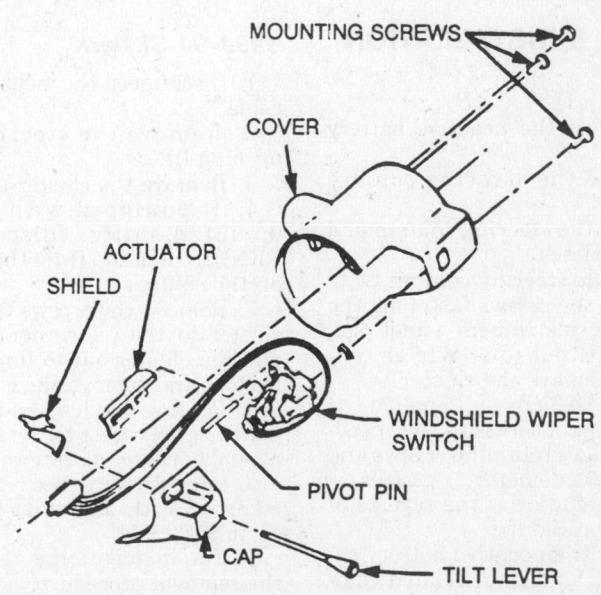

Column mounted windshield wiper switch—1990–91 Skylark

screws and remove the housing cover assembly.

14. Remove the wiper switch pivot pin and remove the switch.

To install:

15. Run the wiring through the opening and down the steering column, position the switch and install the wiper switch pivot pin.

16. Install the housing cover assembly, making sure the dimmer switch actuator is properly aligned.

17. Install the key lock cylinder and place in the **RUN** position. Install the buzzer switch and key lamp.

18. Install the turn signal switch and lever.

19. To assemble the top end of the column:

   a. Install the spring, cancelling cam, lockplate and retaining ring on the steering shaft.

   b. Depress the plate with the depressing tool and install the ring securely in the groove. Remove the tool slowly.

   c. If equipped with telescope steering, install the carrier snapring retainer, lower set of spacers, bumper and upper set of spacers.

   d. Install the shaft lock cover.

20. Connect the turn signal switch, wiper switch and cruise control connectors. Install the wire protector.

21. Install and steering wheel.

22. Install the steering column trim collar, lower instrument panel trim pad and sound insulator.

23. Connect the negative battery cable and check the key lock cylinder, wiper and washer, cruise control, turn signal switch and dimmer switch for proper operation.

Instrument Cluster

REMOVAL & INSTALLATION

Calais

1. Disconnect the negative battery cable.

2. Remove the steering column collar.

3. Remove the steering column and cluster trim plates.

4. Lower the steering column.

5. Remove the screws fastening the cluster to the instrument panel pad, pull the cluster out to unplug all connectors and remove the cluster.

6. Remove the lens and applique, if necessary, to gain access to the speedometer or gauges retaining screws and remove the speedometer or gauges.

7. The installation is the reverse of the removal procedure.

8. Connect the negative battery cable and check all cluster-related components for proper operation.

Grand Am

1. Disconnect the negative battery cable.

2. Remove the 3 screws at the lower edge of the cluster and remove the trim plate.

3. Remove the steering column cover and lower the column.

4. Remove the screws fastening the cluster to the instrument panel pad, pull the cluster out to unplug all connectors and remove the cluster.

5. Remove the lens and gauge trim plate to gain access to the speedometer assembly or gauges retaining screws and remove the speedometer or gauges. If the vehicle is equipped with digital dash, replace it as an assembly.

6. The installation is the reverse of the removal procedure.

7. Connect the negative battery cable and check all cluster-related components for proper operation.

1987–89 Somerset and Skylark

1. Disconnect the negative battery cable.

2. Remove the cluster trim plate, headlight and wiper switch trim plates and the switches.

3. Remove the screws fastening the cluster to the instrument panel pad, pull the cluster out to unplug all connectors and remove the cluster.

4. Remove the lens and gauge trim plate to gain access to the speedometer assembly retaining screws and remove the speedometer or gauges. If the vehicle is equipped with digital gauges, replace them as an assembly.

5. The installation is the reverse of the removal procedure.

6. Connect the negative battery cable and check all cluster-related components for proper operation.

1990–91 Skylark

1. Disconnect the negative battery cable.

2. Remove the steering column opening filler.

3. Remove the cluster trim plate.

4. If equipped with a column-mounted shifter, disconnect the PRNDL cable clip from the shift collar on the column.

5. Remove the screws fastening the cluster to the instrument panel pad, pull the cluster out to unplug all connectors and remove the cluster.

6. Remove the lens and gauge trim plate to gain access to the speedometer assembly retaining screws and remove the speedometer or gauges. If equipped with digital dash, replace it as an assembly.

7. The installation is the reverse of the removal procedure.

8. Connect the negative battery cable and check all cluster-related components for proper operation.

Radio

REMOVAL & INSTALLATION

Console Mounted

NOTE: **If equipped with a compact disc player, removal and installation procedures are the same as for the radio.**

1. Disconnect the negative battery cable.

2. Remove the console bezel.

3. Remove the screws that attach the radio to the console.

4. Pull the radio out, disconnect the connectors, ground cable and antenna and remove the radio.

5. The installation is the reverse of the removal procedure.

6. Connect the negative battery cable and check the radio for proper operation.

Dash Mounted

1987 CALAIS

1. Disconnect the negative battery cable.

2. Open the ashtray and remove the insert.

3. Depress the locking tangs on both sides of the ashtray and remove the lower assembly.

4. Remove the upper ashtray assembly with trim plate.

5. Remove the screws that attach the radio to the instrument panel.

6. Pull the radio out, disconnect the connectors, ground cable and antenna and remove the radio.

7. The installation is the reverse of the removal procedure.

8. Connect the negative battery cable and check the radio for proper operation.

1990–91 SKYLARK

1. Disconnect the negative battery cable.

2. Remove the instrument panel extension bezel.

3. Remove the radio bracket.

4. Remove the screws that attach the radio to the instrument panel.

5. Pull the radio out, disconnect the connectors, ground cable and antenna and remove the radio.

6. The installation is the reverse of the removal procedure.

7. Connect the negative battery cable and check the radio for proper operation.

Headlight Switch

REMOVAL & INSTALLATION

1. Disconnect the negative battery cable.
2. Remove the cluster trim, instrument panel trim or headlight switch trim screws, as required.
3. Remove the headlight switch retaining screws.
4. Pull the switch out, unplug the connectors and remove the switch assembly.
5. The installation is the reverse of the removal procedure.
6. Connect the negative battery cable and check the headlight switch for proper operation.

Dimmer Switch

REMOVAL & INSTALLATION

1. Disconnect the negative battery cable.
2. Remove the lower steering column cover.
3. Unplug the switch, located on the lower portion of the steering column.
4. Hold the actuating rod against its upper seat, remove the screw and nut that attaches the switch to the column and remove the switch.
5. The installation is the reverse of the removal procedure. To adjust the switch:
   a. Depress the switch slightly and insert a $3/32$ in. drill.
   b. Force the switch up to remove the lash.
   c. Tighten the screw and nut.
6. Connect the negative battery cable and check the switch for proper operation.

Turn Signal Switch

REMOVAL & INSTALLATION

1. Disconnect the negative battery cable.
2. Remove the lower instrument panel sound insulator, trim pad and steering column trim collar.
3. Straighten the steering wheel so the tires are pointing straight ahead.
4. Remove the steering wheel.
5. Remove the plastic wire protector from under the steering column.
6. Disconnect the turn signal switch connector at the bottom of the column.
7. To disassemble the top of the column:
   a. Remove the shaft lock cover.
   b. If equipped with telescope steering, remove the first set of spacers, bumper, second set of spacers, and carrier snapring retainer.

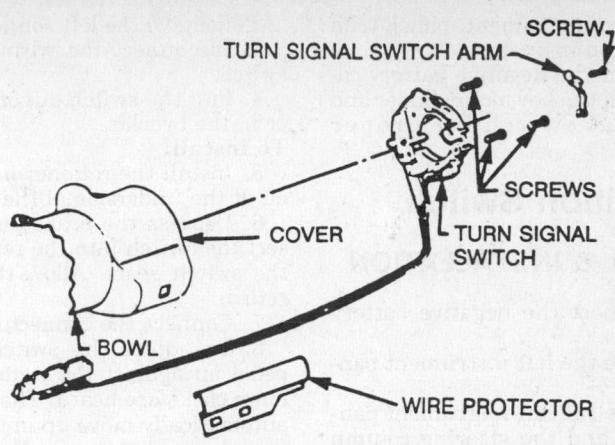

Removing the turn signal switch

   c. Depress the lockplate with the proper depressing tool and remove the retaining ring from its groove.
   d. Remove the tool, ring, lockplate, cancelling cam and spring.
8. Remove the 3 screws, the turn signal switch and actuator lever.

To install:

9. Install the turn signal switch and lever.
10. To assemble the top end of the column:
    a. Install the spring, cancelling cam, lockplate and retaining ring on the steering shaft.
    b. Depress the plate with the depressing tool and install the ring securely in the groove. Remove the tool slowly.
    c. If equipped with telescope steering, install the carrier snapring retainer, lower set of spacers, bumper and upper set of spacers.
    d. Install the shaft lock cover.
11. Connect the turn signal switch connector and install the wire protector.
12. Install the steering wheel.
13. Install the steering column trim collar, lower instrument panel trim pad and sound insulator.
14. Connect the negative battery cable and check the turn signal switch for proper operation.

Ignition Lock Cylinder

REMOVAL & INSTALLATION

1. Disconnect the negative battery cable.
2. Remove the lower instrument panel sound insulator, trim pad and steering column trim collar.
3. Straighten the steering wheel so the tires are pointing straight ahead.
4. Remove the steering wheel.

5. Remove the plastic wire protector from under the steering column.
6. Disconnect the turn signal switch.
7. To disassemble the top of the column:
   a. Remove the shaft lock cover.
   b. If equipped with telescope steering, remove the first set of spacers, bumper, second set of spacers, and carrier snapring retainer.
   c. Depress the lock plate with the proper depressing tool and remove the retaining ring from its groove.
   d. Remove the tool, retaining ring, lockplate, cancelling cam and spring.
8. Remove the 3 screws and pull the turn signal switch out from its mount as far as possible.
9. Place the key in the **RUN** position and use a thin suitable tool to remove the buzzer switch.
10. Remove the key lock cylinder retaining screw and remove the lock cylinder.

To install:

11. Install the key lock cylinder and place in the **RUN** position. Install the buzzer switch and key lamp.
12. Install the turn signal switch and lever.
13. To assemble the top end of the column:
    a. Install the spring, cancelling cam, lock plate and retaining ring on the steering shaft.
    b. Depress the plate with the depressing tool and install the ring securely in the groove. Remove the tool slowly.
    c. If equipped with telescope steering, install the carrier snapring retainer, lower set of spacers, bumper and upper set of spacers.
    d. Install the shaft lock cover.
14. Connect the turn signal switch connector. Install the wire protector.
15. Install the steering wheel.
16. Install the steering column trim

collar, lower instrument panel trim pad and sound insulator.

17. Connect the negative battery cable and check the key lock cylinder and turn signal switch for proper operation.

Ignition Switch

REMOVAL & INSTALLATION

1. Disconnect the negative battery cable.

2. Remove the left instrument panel insulator.

3. Remove the left instrument panel trim pad and the steering column trim collar.

4. Remove the steering column upper support bracket bolts and remove the support bracket.

5. Lower the steering column and support it safely.

6. Disconnect the wiring from the ignition switch.

7. Remove the screws that fasten the ignition switch to the steering column and remove the ignition switch assembly from the steering column.

To install:

8. Before installing, place the slider in the proper position (switch viewed with the terminals pointing up), according to the steering column and accessories:

   a. Standard column with key release—extreme left detent.

   b. Standard column with PARK/LOCK—1 detent from extreme left.

   c. All other standard columns—2 detents from extreme left.

   d. Tilt column with key release—extreme right detent.

   e. Tilt column with PARK/LOCK—1 detent from extreme right.

   f. All other tilt columns—2 detents from extreme right.

9. Install the activating rod into the switch and install the switch to the column. Do not use oversized screws as they could impair the collapsibility of the column.

10. Connect the wiring to the ignition switch. Adjust the switch, as required.

11. Install the steering column.

12. Install the steering column trim collar, instrument panel trim pad and insulator.

13. Connect the negative battery cable and check the ignition switch for proper operation.

Stoplight Switch

REMOVAL & INSTALLATION

1. Disconnect the negative battery cable.

2. Remove the left sound insulator.

3. Disconnect the wiring from the switch.

4. Pull the switch out of the retainer in the bracket.

To install:

5. Install the retainer in the bracket, at the underside of the bracket.

6. Depress the brake pedal and insert the switch into the retainer until the switch seats. Allow the pedal to return.

7. Connect the connector.

8. To adjust the switch, pull the pedal up against the switch until no more clicks are heard. The switch will automatically move up in the retainer providing adjustment. Repeat a few times to ensure that the switch is properly adjusted.

9. Connect the negative battery cable and check the switch for proper operation.

Clutch Switch

REMOVAL & INSTALLATION

Cruise Control Release Switch

1. Disconnect the negative battery cable.

2. Remove the left sound insulator.

3. Disconnect the wiring from the switch.

4. Pull the switch out of the retainer in the bracket.

To install:

5. Install the retainer in the bracket, from the underside of the bracket.

6. Depress the clutch pedal and insert the switch into the retainer until the switch seats. Allow the pedal to return.

7. Connect the connector.

8. To adjust the switch, pull the pedal up against the switch until no more clicks are heard. The switch will automatically move up in the retainer providing adjustment. Repeat a few times to ensure that the switch is properly adjusted.

9. Connect the negative battery cable and check the switch for proper operation.

Neutral Start Switch

1. Disconnect the negative battery cable.

2. Remove the left sound insulator and disconnect the wiring from the switch.

3. Remove the retaining nuts.

4. Remove the switch.

5. The installation is the reverse of the removal procedure.

6. Connect the negative battery cable and check the switch for proper operation.

Neutral Safety Switch

ADJUSTMENT

1. Place the shifter in the **N** detent.

2. The switch is located on the shift shaft on the top of the automatic transaxle. Loosen the switch attaching bolts.

3. Rotate the switch on the shifter assembly to align the service adjustment hole with the carrier tang hole.

4. Insert a $^3/_{32}$ in. maximum diameter gauge pin into the hole to a depth of $^5/_8$ in.

5. Tighten the mounting bolts and remove the pin.

REMOVAL & INSTALLATION

1. Disconnect the negative battery cable. Place the shifter in the **N** detent.

2. Disconnect the shifter linkage.

3. Disconnect the switch.

4. Remove the mounting bolts and remove the switch from the transaxle.

To install:

5. If not already done, place the shifter shaft in the **N** detent.

6. Align the flats of the shift shaft with those of the switch.

7. If replacing the switch, tighten the installation bolts and remove the pre-installed alignment pin.

8. If reusing the old switch, install the mounting bolts loosely and adjust the switch.

9. Connect the negative battery cable and check the switch for proper operation. The reverse lights should come on when the transaxle is shifted into **R**. If the engine can be started in any gear except **P** or **N**, readjust the switch.

Fuses, Circuit Breakers and Relays

LOCATION

Fuses and Circuit Breakers

The fuse block, which contains the fuses and also the circuit breakers for power accessories, is located on the lower left side of the instrument panel, behind an access door.

Various Relays

Horn Relay—located in the convenience center near the fuse block on all vehicles except Grand Am. On Grand Am, it is taped to the wiring harness near the fuse block.

Power Antenna Relay—located on the right side of the instrument panel, below the speaker.

Rear Window Defogger Relay—located on the right side of the instru-

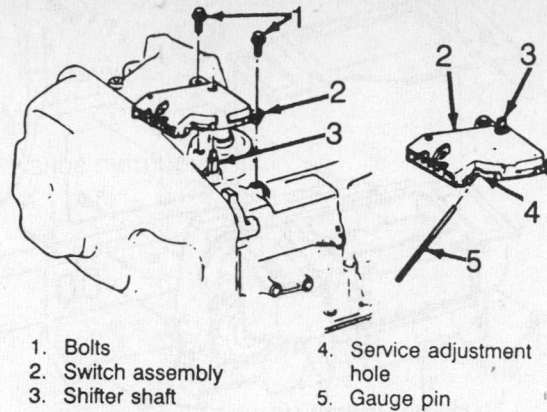

1. Bolts
2. Switch assembly
3. Shifter shaft
4. Service adjustment hole
5. Gauge pin

Neutral safety switch mounted on the transaxle

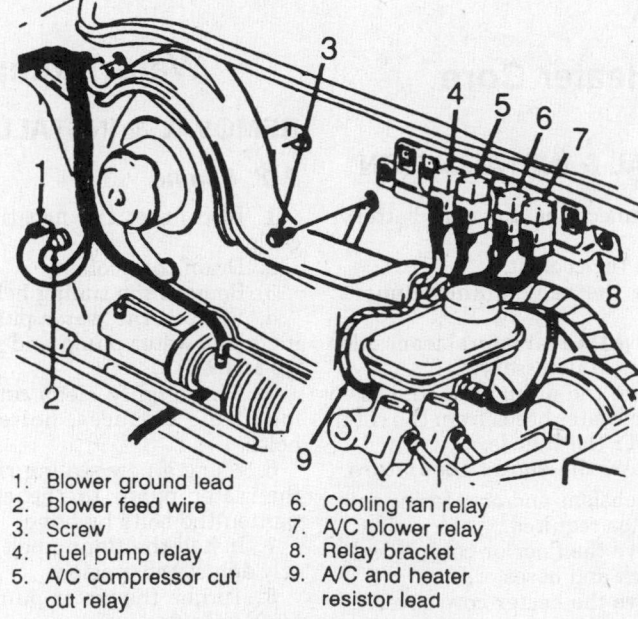

1. Blower ground lead
2. Blower feed wire
3. Screw
4. Fuel pump relay
5. A/C compressor cut out relay
6. Cooling fan relay
7. A/C blower relay
8. Relay bracket
9. A/C and heater resistor lead

Firewall mounted relay identification

ment panel on all vehicles except Grand Am. On Grand Am, it is located near the fuse panel.

Fuel Pump Relay—located in the engine compartment on the relay bracket on the firewall. This relay is closest to the blower.

A/C Compressor Cut Out Relay—located in the engine compartment on the relay bracket on the firewall. This relay is next to the fuel pump relay.

Cooling Fan Relay—located in the engine compartment on the relay bracket on the firewall. This relay is next to the blower speed relay.

Blower Speed Relay—located in the engine compartment on the relay bracket on the firewall. This relay is closest to the master cylinder.

Ignition Key, Seat Belt, Light and Turn Signal Warning Alarm—

located in the convenience center near the fuse block in all vehicles except Grand Am. On Grand Am, it is mounted to a bracket above the glove box.

Cruise Control Module—mounted to a bracket on the left side of the instrument panel.

Instrument Panel Lamp Dimmer Module—located on the lower left tie bar on all vehicles except Grand Am. On Grand Am, it is either mounted to a bracket to the right of the glove box or on the right side of the console front extension bracket.

Flashers

LOCATION

Turn Signal

The turn signal flasher is clipped to

the insrument panel near the fuse block.

Hazard

On all vehicles except Grand Am, the hazard flasher is in the convenience center, located near the fuse block. On Grand Am, the hazard flasher is clipped to the console front extension bracket.

Computer

LOCATION

The ECM is located on the right side of the instrument panel, near the glove box.

Cruise Control

ADJUSTMENT

1. Make sure the throttle lever is in the idle position with the engine off.
2. Pull the servo assembly end of the cable toward the servo without moving the throttle lever.
3. If 1 of the 6 holes in the servo assembly tab aligns with the cable pin, connect the pin to the tab and install the retainer with the tang over the stud.
4. If the pin does not align with a hole, install it to the next hole closest to the throttle lever and install the retainer.
5. Make sure the cable is not stretched in such a way that the throttle lever has been moved of its idle position.

ENGINE COOLING

Radiator

REMOVAL & INSTALLATION

1. Disconnect the negative battery cable.
2. Drain the coolant. Disconnect the the engine strut brace at the radiator, loosen the engine side bolt and swing aside, if equipped.
3. Matchmark and remove the hood latch from the radiator support.
4. Remove the upper hose and coolant reserve tank hose from the radiator.
5. Disconnect the forward light harness connector and fan connector. Remove the electric cooling fan.

6. Raise the vehicle and support safely. Remove the lower hose from the radiator.

7. Disconnect the automatic transaxle cooler hoses, if equipped, and plug them. Lower the vehicle.

8. Remove the radiator to condenser bolts, if equipped with air conditioning. Also remove the refrigerant line clamp bolt.

9. Remove the mounting bolts and clamps and carefully lift the radiator out of the engine compartment.

To install:

10. Lower the radiator into position.

11. Install the mounting clamps and bolts, including those associated with air conditioning parts.

12. Connect the automatic transaxle cooler lines, if equipped.

13. Raise the vehicle and support safely. Connect the lower hose. Lower the vehicle.

14. Install the electric cooling fan and connect the connectors.

15. Connect the upper hose and coolant reserve tank hose.

16. Install the hood latch and strut brace.

17. Fill the system with coolant.

18. Connect the negative battery cable, run the vehicle until the thermostat opens, fill the radiator and recovery tank completely and check the automatic transaxle fluid level.

19. Once the vehicle has cooled, recheck the coolant level.

Electric Cooling Fan
—— CAUTION ——

Make sure the key is in the OFF position when working the electric cooling fan. If not, the fan could turn ON at any time, causing serious personal injury.

TESTING

1. Unplug the fan connector.

2. Using a jumper wire, connect the female terminal of the fan connector to the negative battery terminal.

3. The fan should come ON when the male terminal is connected to the positive battery terminal.

4. If not, the fan is defective and should be replaced.

REMOVAL & INSTALLATION

1. Disconnect the negative battery cable.

2. Unplug the connector.

3. Remove the mounting screws.

4. Remove the fan assembly from the vehicle.

5. The installation is the reverse of the removal procedure.

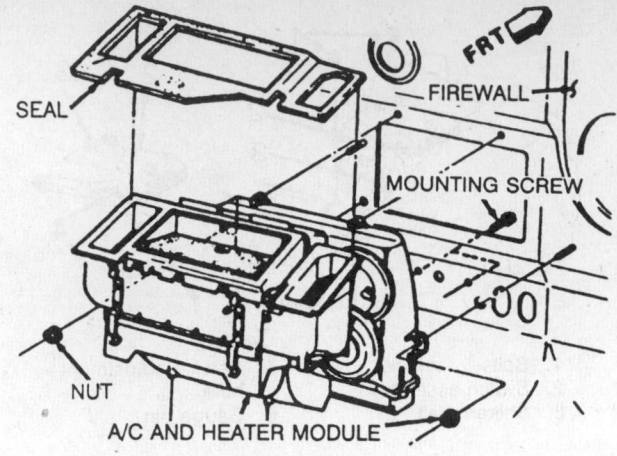
Removing the heater case

Heater Core
REMOVAL & INSTALLATION

1. Disconnect the negative battery cable.

2. Drain the coolant.

3. Raise the vehicle and support safely.

4. Remove the rear lateral transaxle strut mount, if necessary.

5. Remove the drain tube and disconnect the heater hoses from the core tubes. Lower the vehicle.

6. Remove the sound insulators, console extensions and/or steering column filler, as required.

7. Remove the floor or console outlet ductwork and hoses.

8. Remove the heater core cover.

9. Remove the heater core mounting clamps and remove the heater core.

To install:

10. Install the heater core and clamps.

11. Install the heater core cover.

12. Install the outlet hoses and ducts.

13. Install the sound insulators, console extensions and/or steering column filler.

14. Raise the vehicle and support safely. Install the drain tube and connect the heater hoses to the core tubes.

15. Install the rear lateral transaxle strut mount, if removed. Lower the vehicle.

16. Fill the system with coolant.

17. Connect the negative battery cable, run the vehicle until the thermostat opens, fill the radiator and recovery tank completely.

18. Once the vehicle has cooled, recheck the coolant level.

Water Pump
REMOVAL & INSTALLATION
2.0L Engine

1. Disconnect the negative battery cable.

2. Drain the coolant.

3. Remove the timing belt.

4. Remove the water pump retaining bolts, water pump and seal ring.

To install:

5. Thoroughly clean and dry the mounting surfaces, bolts and bolt holes.

6. Using a new sealing ring, install the water pump to the engine and tighten the bolts by hand.

7. Install the timing belt and properly adjust the tension.

8. Torque the water pump bolts to 18 ft. lbs. (24 Nm).

9. Install the timing belt cover and related parts.

10. Fill the system with coolant.

11. Connect the negative battery cable, run the vehicle until the thermostat opens, fill the radiator and recovery tank completely.

12. Once the vehicle has cooled, recheck the coolant level.

2.3L Engine

1. Disconnect the negative battery cable and oxygen sensor connector.

2. Drain the coolant. Remove the heater hose from the thermostat housing for more complete coolant drain.

3. Remove upper and lower exhaust manifold heat shields.

4. Remove the bolt that attaches the exhaust manifold brace to the manifold.

5. Break loose the manifold to exhaust pipe spring loaded bolts using a 13mm box wrench.

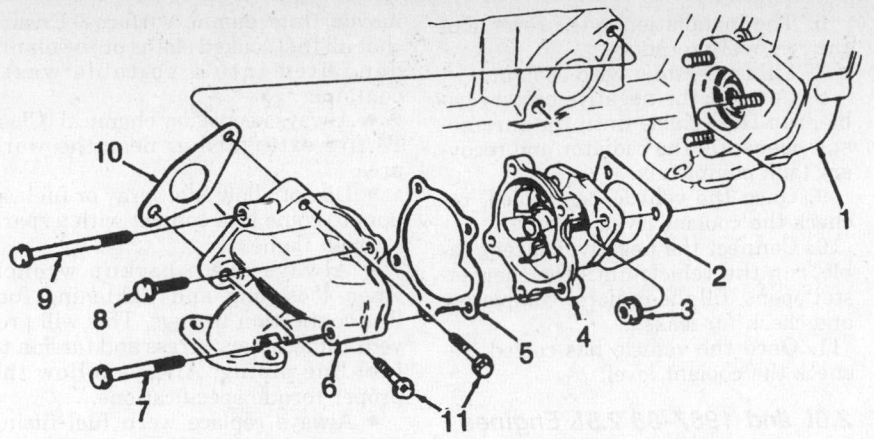

1. Timing chain housing
2. Water pump to timing chain housing gasket
3. Nut
4. water pump
5. Water pump body cover gasket
6. Water pump cover
7. Bolt
8. Bolt
9. Bolt
10. Water pump gasket cover to block gasket
11. water pump cover bolts

Water pump assembly—2.3L engine

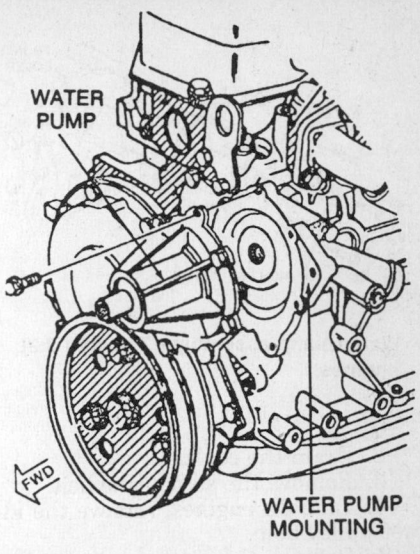

Water pump assembly—2.5L engine

6. Raise the vehicle and support safely.

NOTE: It is necessary to relieve the spring pressure from 1 bolt prior to removing the second bolt. If the spring pressure is not relieved, it will cause the exhaust pipe to twist and bind up the bolt as it is removed.

7. Remove the manifold to exhaust pipe bolts from the exhaust pipe flange as follows:

   a. Unscrew either bolt clockwise 4 turns.

   b. Remove the other bolt.

   c. Remove the first bolt.

8. Pull down and back on the exhaust pipe to disengage it from the exhaust manifold bolts.

9. Remove the radiator outlet pipe from the oil pan and transaxle. If equipped with a manual transaxle, remove the exhaust manifold brace. Leave the lower radiator hose attached and pull down on the outlet pipe to remove it from the water pump.

10. Lower the vehicle.

11. Remove the exhaust manifold, seals and gaskets.

12. Remove the water pump mounting bolts and nuts.

NOTE: On early engines, it may be necessary to loosen and reposition the rear engine mount and bracket for clearance.

13. Remove the water pump and cover assembly and separate the 2 pieces.
To install:
14. Thoroughly clean and dry all mounting surfaces, bolts and bolt holes. Using a new gasket, install the water pump to the cover and tighten the bolts finger tight.

15. Lubricate the splines of the water pump with clean grease and install the assembly to the engine using new gaskets. Install the mounting bolts and nuts finger tight.

16. Lubricate the radiator outlet pipe O-ring with antifreeze and install to the water pump with the bolts finger tight.

17. With all gaps closed, torque the bolts, in the following sequence, to the proper values:

   a. Pump assembly to chain housing nuts—19 ft. lbs. (26 Nm)

   b. Pump cover to pump assembly—106 inch lbs. (12 Nm)

   c. Cover to block, bottom bolt first—19 ft. lbs. (26 Nm)

   d. Radiator outlet pipe assembly to pump cover—125 inch lbs. (14 Nm)

18. Install the exhaust manifold.

19. Raise the vehicle and support safely.

20. Install the exhaust pipe flange bolts evenly and gradually to avoid binding.

21. Connect the radiator outlet pipe to the transaxle and oil pan. Install the exhaust manifold brace, if removed. Lower the vehicle.

22. Install the bolt that attaches the exhaust manifold brace to the manifold.

23. Install the heat shields.

24. Connect the oxygen sensor connector.

25. Fill the radiator with coolant until it comes out the heater hose outlet at the thermostat housing. Then connect the heater hose.

26. Connect the negative battery cable, run the vehicle until the thermostat opens, fill the radiator and recovery tank completely.

27. Once the vehicle has cooled, recheck the coolant level.

2.5L Engine

1. Disconnect the negative battery cable.

2. Drain the coolant.

3. Remove the drive belts, alternator and air conditioning compressor, as required.

4. Remove the water pump mounting bolts and remove the water pump from the vehicle.
To install:
5. Transfer the water pump pulley to the new pump using the proper pulley removal and installation tools.

6. Thoroughly clean and dry the mounting surfaces, bolts and bolt holes. Place a 1/8 in. bead of RTV sealant on the pump's sealing surface.

7. Install the pump to the engine and coat the bolt threads with sealant as they are installed. Torque the bolts to 25 ft. lbs. (34 Nm).

8. Install the alternator and/or air conditioning compressor. Install and adjust the drive belts.

9. Fill the system with coolant.

10. Connect the negative battery cable, run the vehicle until the thermostat opens, fill the radiator and recovery tank completely.

11. Once the vehicle has cooled, recheck the coolant level.

3.0L and 3.3L Engines

1. Disconnect the negative battery cable.

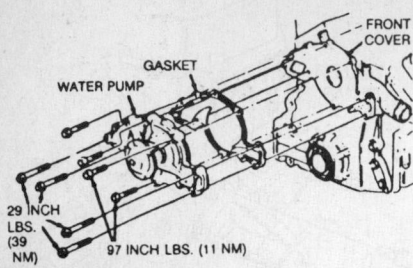

Water pump assembly—3.0L and 3.3L engines

2. Drain the coolant.
3. Remove the serpentine belt.
4. On 3.3L engines, remove the idler pulley bolt.
5. Remove the water pump pulley bolts and remove the pulley. On 3.0L engines, the long bolt is removed through the access hole in the body side rail.
6. Remove the water pump mounting bolts and remove the pump.
To install:
7. Thoroughly clean and dry the mounting surfaces, bolts and bolt holes.
8. Using a new gasket, install the water pump to the engine and torque pump to front cover bolts to 97 inch lbs. (11 Nm) and the pump to block bolts to 29 ft. lbs. (39 Nm).
9. Install the water pump pulley and torque the bolts to 115 inch lbs. (13 Nm).
10. On 3.3L engines, install the idler pulley bolt.
11. Install the serpentine belt.
12. Fill the system with coolant.
13. Connect the negative battery cable, run the vehicle until the thermostat opens, fill the radiator and recovery tank completely.
14. Once the vehicle has cooled, recheck the coolant level.

Thermostat

REMOVAL & INSTALLATION

Except 2.0L and 1987–88 2.5L Engines

1. Disconnect the negative battery cable. Drain the coolant down to thermostat level or below.
2. Remove the air cleaner assembly, as required. Disconnect the coolant sensor on 2.3L engine.
3. Disconnect the hose(s) and remove the thermostat housing.
4. Remove the thermostat and discard the gasket.
5. Clean the housing mating surfaces and use a new gasket.

6. The installation is the reverse of the removal procedure.
7. Fill the system with coolant.
8. Connect the negative battery cable, run the vehicle until the thermostat opens, fill the radiator and recovery tank completely.
9. Once the vehicle has cooled, recheck the coolant level.
10. Connect the negative battery cable, run the vehicle until the thermostat opens, fill the radiator completely and check for leaks.
11. Once the vehicle has cooled, recheck the coolant level.

2.0L and 1987–88 2.5L Engines

1. Disconnect the negative battery cable.
2. Remove the thermostat housing cap.
3. Remove the thermostat and discard the gasket.
4. Clean the housing mating surfaces and use a new gasket.
5. The installation is the reverse of the removal procedure.

FUEL SYSTEM

Fuel System Service Precautions

Safety is the most important factor when performing not only fuel system maintenance but any type of maintenance. Failure to conduct maintenance and repairs in a safe manner may result in serious personal injury or death. Maintenance and testing of the vehicle's fuel system components can be accomplished safely and effectively by adhering to the following rules and guidelines.
• To avoid the possibility of fire and personal injury, always disconnect the negative battery cable unless the repair or test procedure requires that battery voltage be applied.
• Always relieve the fuel system pressure prior to disconnecting any fuel system component (injector, fuel rail, pressure regulator, etc.), fitting or fuel line connection. Exercise extreme caution whenever relieving fuel system pressure to avoid exposing skin, face and eyes to fuel spray. Please be advised that fuel under pressure may penetrate the skin or any part of the body that it contacts.
• Always place a shop towel or cloth around the fitting or connection prior to loosening to absorb any excess fuel due to spillage. Ensure that all fuel spillage (should it occur) is quickly re-

moved from engine surfaces. Ensure that all fuel soaked cloths or towels are deposited into a suitable waste container.
• Always keep a dry chemical (Class B) fire extinguisher near the work area.
• Do not allow fuel spray or fuel vapors to come into contact with a spark or open flame.
• Always use a backup wrench when loosening and tightening fuel line connection fittings. This will prevent unnecessary stress and torsion to fuel line piping. Always follow the proper torque specifications.
• Always replace worn fuel fitting O-rings with new. Do not substitute fuel hose or equivalent where fuel pipe is installed.

RELIEVING FUEL SYSTEM PRESSURE

2.5L and 1987–88 2.0L, 2.3L and 3.0L Engines

1. Loosen the fuel filler cap.
2. Remove the fuse marked fuel pump from the fuse block or disconnect the harness connector at the tank.
3. Start the engine and run at idle until it stalls.
4. Crank the engine for an additional 3 seconds to make sure all of the fuel pressure is exhausted from the fuel lines.
5. Turn the ignition switch off, disconnect the negative battery cable and reinstall the fuel pump fuse or connect the connector at the tank.
6. Tighten the filler cap.

1989–91 2.0L, 2.3L and 3.3L Engines

1. Disconnect the negative battery cable.
2. Loosen the fuel filler cap.
3. Install gauge J-34730-1 to the fuel pressure connection on the fuel pressure regulator assembly. Wrap a shop towel around the connection to avoid any fuel spray.
4. Install the bleed hose into an approved container and open the valve to bleed the fuel pressure.
5. Drain any residual fuel in the gauge into the container.
6. Tighten the filler cap.

Fuel Filter

The fuel filter is located near the rear of the vehicle, forward of the fuel tank.

REMOVAL & INSTALLATION

1. Relieve the fuel system pressure.

2. Raise the vehicle and support safely.

3. Using a backup wrench, remove the fuel line fittings from the fuel filter.

4. Remove the fuel filter mounting screws and remove the filter from the vehicle.

5. The installation is the reverse of the removal procedure. Replace the O-rings. Torque the fuel line to filter connectors to 22 ft. lbs.

Electric Fuel Pump

PRESSURE TESTING

1. Relieve the fuel system pressure.
2. Connect an appropriate fuel pressure gauge to the pressure connection on the fuel pressure regulator assembly, if equipped. If there is no valve, install in-line to the pressure line.
3. Wrap a clean shop towel around the fitting to catch any fuel leakage.
4. Turn the ignition on and read the pressure on the gauge.
5. If not within specifications, inspect the system for clogs, collapsed hoses, kinks or a faulty pump. The fuel pressure can be measured at different points in the system to locate the problem area.
6. Relieve the fuel system pressure and disconnect the gauge.

REMOVAL & INSTALLATION

1. Relieve the fuel system pressure.
2. Raise the vehicle and support safely.
3. Using the proper approved equipment, drain the fuel tank.
4. Disconnect all wiring and hoses from the tank.
5. Place a transmission jack under the center of the tank and apply slight pressure. Remove the tank straps.
6. Remove the fuel tank from the vehicle.
7. Using a hammer and a brass drift, turn the lock ring counterclockwise to release the pump/sending unit assembly.
8. Disassemble the unit to separate the pump itself from the assembly.
To install:
9. Push the fuel pump onto the attaching hose and install the filter on the end of the pump.
10. Install a new tank seal O-ring to the pump.
11. Install the pump into the tank and install the lock ring with a hammer and brass punch turning the ring clockwise.
12. Install the fuel tank.
13. Connect the negative battery cable, start the engine and check for leaks.

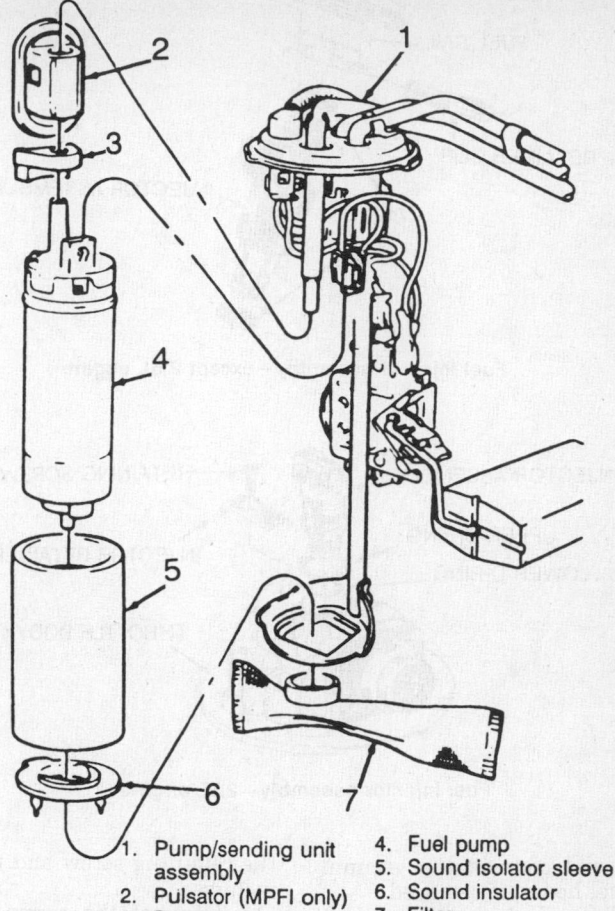

1. Pump/sending unit assembly	4. Fuel pump
2. Pulsator (MPFI only)	5. Sound isolator sleeve
3. Bumper	6. Sound insulator
	7. Filter

Typical fuel pump/sending unit assembly

Fuel Injection

IDLE SPEED ADJUSTMENT

The idle speed is controlled by the ECM, which receives data from various sensors and switches within the fuel injection system. Adjustments are preset at the factory.

Fuel Injector

REMOVAL & INSTALLATION

Except 2.5L Engine

NOTE: Injector removal does not necessitate complete fuel rail removal on 2.0L and 2.3L engines. Use only exact replacements according to the part number inscribed on the injector; some injectors may look identical but each is specifically calibrated for its application.

1. Relieve the fuel system pressure.
2. On 2.0L and 2.3L engines, remove the crankcase ventilation oil/air separator and the fuel pipe clamp bolt.
3. Disconnect the vacuum hose from the pressure regulator.
4. Disconnect the fuel pressure and return hoses, if removing the fuel rail from the vehicle.
5. Remove the fuel rail attaching bolts and separate the fuel rail assembly from the cylinder head.
6. Disconnect the connector(s) from the injector(s).
7. Remove the injector retainer clip and remove the injector from the fuel rail assembly.
To install:
8. Lubricate the new injector O-rings with clean engine oil and install to the injector.
9. Install a new retainer clip to the injector so the opening of the clip faces the injector's terminals.
10. Install the injector assembly to the fuel rail with the terminals facing outward. Make sure the injector is pushed in far enough to fully engage the retainer clip with the machined slots on the rail socket.
11. Install the fuel rail assembly to

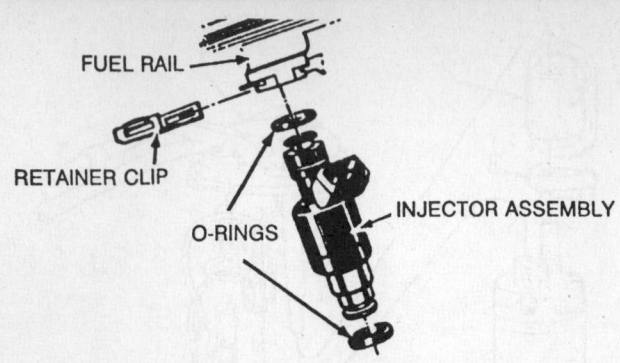

Fuel injector assembly—except 2.5L engine

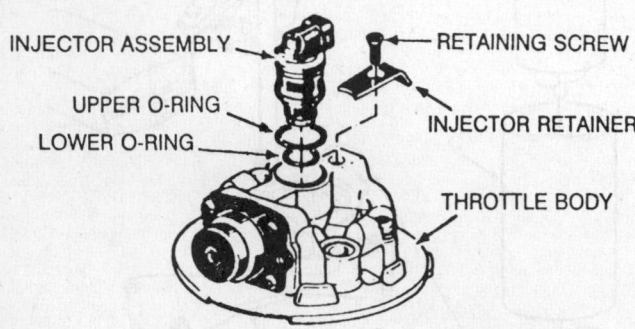

Fuel injector assembly—2.5L engine

the engine and connect the vacuum hose and fuel hoses, if removed.

12. Install the fuel pipe clamp bolt and the crankcase ventilation oil/air separator, if removed.

13. Connect the negative battery cable, start the engine and check for fuel leaks.

2.5L Engine

1. Relieve the fuel system pressure.
2. Disconnect the negative battery cable.
3. Remove the air cleaner.
4. Disconnect the electrical connector from the fuel injector.
5. Remove the injector retainer screw and the retainer.
6. Position a small prybar and a fulcrum on the side of the injector opposite the terminals. Carefully lift the injector out of its cavity in the throttle body.
7. Remove the O-rings from the injector.

To install:

8. Lubricate the O-rings with clean engine oil. Place the upper O-ring in its groove and the lower one flush against the filter.
9. Push the fuel injector straight into the throttle body cavity so the terminals facing the wire grommet cut out.
10. Install the retainer, apply thread locking compound on the threads of

the retaining screw and torque to 27 inch lbs.

11. Connect the connector and install the air cleaner.

12. Connect the negative battery cable, start the engine and check for fuel leaks.

EMISSION CONTROLS

Please refer to "Emission Control" in the Unit Repair section for system maintenance procedures. Due to the complex nature of modern electronic engine control systems, comprehensive diagnosis and testing procedures fall outside the confines of this repair manual. For complete information on diagnosis, testing and repair procedures concerning all modern engine and emission control systems, please refer to "Chilton's Guide to Electronic Engine Controls".

ENGINE MECHANICAL

NOTE: Disconnecting the negative battery cable on some vehicles may interfere with the functions of the on board computer systems and may require the computer to undergo a relearning process, once the negative battery cable is reconnected.

Engine Assembly

REMOVAL & INSTALLATION

2.0L and 2.5L Engines

1. Relieve the fuel system pressure.
2. Disconnect both battery cables and ground straps.
3. Drain the cooling system and remove the cooling fan.
4. Remove the air cleaner assembly.
5. Disconnect the ECM connections and feed harness through the bulkhead. Lay the harness across the engine.
6. Label and disconnect the engine wiring harness and all engine-related connectors and lay across the engine.
7. Label and disconnect the radiator hoses and vacuum lines. Disconnect and plug the fuel lines.
8. On 2.5L engine, remove the air conditioning compressor from the engine and lay it aside, without disconnecting the refrigerant lines. Remove the transaxle struts.
9. If equipped with power steering, remove the power steering pump from its mount and lay it aside. Remove the power steering pump bracket from the engine.
10. If equipped with a manual transaxle, disconnect the clutch and transaxle linkage. Remove the throttle cable from the throttle body.
11. If equipped with an automatic transaxle, disconnect the transaxle cooler lines, shifter linkage, downshift cable and throttle cable from the throttle body.
12. Raise the vehice and support safely.
13. Disconnect all wiring from the transaxle.
14. On 2.0L engine, properly discharge the air conditioning system and remove the compressor. Remove the transaxle strut(s).
15. Disconnect the exhaust pipe from the exhaust manifold and hangers.
16. Disconnect the heater hoses from the heater core tubes and plug them.
17. Remove the front wheels. Re-

move the calipers and wire them up aside. Remove the brake rotors.

18. Matchmark and remove the knuckle-to-strut bolts.

19. Remove the body-to-cradle bolts at the lower control arms. Loosen the remaining body-to-cradle bolts. Remove a bolt at each cradle side, leaving 1 bolt per corner.

20. Using the proper equipment, support the vehicle under the radiator frame support.

21. Position a jack to the rear of the body pan with a 4 × 4 in. × 6 ft. timber spanning the vehicle.

22. Raise the vehicle enough to remove the support equipment.

23. Position a dolly under the engine/transaxle assembly with 3 blocks of wood for additional support.

24. Lower the vehicle slightly, allowing the engine/transaxle assembly to rest on the dolly.

25. Remove all engine and transaxle mount bolts and brackets. Remove the remaining cradle-to-body bolts.

26. Raise the vehicle, leaving engine and transaxle assembly with the suspension on the dolly.

27. Separate the engine and transaxle.

To install:

28. Assemble the engine and transaxle assembly and position on the dolly.

29. Raise the vehicle and support safely. Roll the assembly to the installation position and lower the vehicle over the assembly.

30. Install all engine, transaxle and suspension mounting bolts. Torque all cradle mounting bolts to 65 ft. lbs. (88 Nm). Connect the wiring to the transaxle.

31. Install the knuckle-to-strut bolts and assemble the brakes.

32. Connect the exhaust pipe to the exhaust manifold and hangers.

33. Connect the heater hoses to the heater core tubes.

34. On 2.0L engines, install the air conditioning compressor.

35. Install the wheels and lower the vehicle.

36. On 2.5L engines, install the air conditioning compressor.

37. Install the power steering pump and related parts.

38. If equipped with a manual transaxle, connect the clutch and transaxle linkage. Connect the throttle cable to the throttle body.

39. If equipped with an automatic transaxle, connect the transaxle cooler lines, shifter linkage, downshift cable and throttle cable to the throttle body.

40. Connect the radiator hoses, vacuum lines and fuel lines.

41. Connect the engine wiring harness and all engine-related connectors.

Feed the ECM connections through the bulkhead and connect.

42. Install the air cleaner assembly.

43. Fill all fluids to their proper levels.

44. Connect the battery cables, start the engine and set the timing, if necessary. Check for leaks.

2.3L Engine

1. Relieve the fuel system pressure.

2. Disconnect both battery cables and ground straps from the front engine mount bracket and the transaxle.

3. Drain the cooling system and remove the cooling fan.

4. Remove the air cleaner duct.

5. Disconnect the heater and radiator hoses from the thermostat housing.

6. Properly discharge the air conditioning system and disconnect the hoses from the compressor.

7. Remove the upper radiator support.

8. Disconnect the 2 vacuum hoses from the front of the engine.

9. Label and disconnect all electrical connectors from engine- and transaxle-mounted devices.

10. Unplug the wires at the starter solenoid.

11. Disconnect the power brake vacuum hose from the throttle body.

12. Disconnect the throttle cable and remove the bracket.

13. Remove the power steering pump bracket and lay the pump aside with the lines attached.

14. Disconnect and plug the fuel lines.

15. If equipped with a manual transaxle, disconnect the shifter cables and the clutch actuator cylinder.

16. If equipped with an automatic transaxle, disconnect the shift and TV cables.

17. Disconnect the transaxle and engine oil cooler pipes, if equipped.

18. Remove the exhaust manifold and heat shield.

19. Remove the lower radiator hose and front engine mount.

20. Install engine support fixture J–28467–A.

21. Raise the vehice and support safely.

22. Remove the wheels, right side splash shield and radiator air deflector.

23. Separate the ball joints from the steering knuckles.

24. Using the proper equipment, support the suspension supports, crossmember and stabilizer shaft. Remove the retaining bolts and remove as an assemby.

25. Disconnect the heater hose from the radiator outlet pipe.

26. Remove the halfshafts from the transaxle.

27. Remove the nut from the transaxle mount through bolt.

28. Remove the nut from the rear engine mount through bolt.

29. Remove the rear engine mount body bracket.

30. Position a suitable support fixture below the engine/transaxle assembly and lower the vehicle so the weight of the engine/transaxle assembly is on the support fixture.

31. Remove the transaxle mount through bolt.

32. Mark the threads on fixture J–28467–A so the setting can be duplicated when installing the engine/transaxle assembly. Remove the fixture.

33. Move the engine/transaxle assembly rearward and slowly raise the vehicle from the engine/transaxle assembly.

NOTE: Many of the bell housing bolts are of different lengths; note their locations before removing. It is imperative that these bolts go back in their original locations when assembling the engine and transaxle, or engine damage could result.

34. Separate the engine from the transaxle.

To install:

35. Assemble the engine and transaxle. If equipped with an automatic transaxle, thoroughly clean and dry the torque converter bolts and bolt holes, apply thread locking compound to the threads and torque the bolts to 46 ft. lbs. (63 Nm). If equipped with a manual transaxle, torque the clutch cover bolts to 22 ft. lbs. (30 Nm).

36. Raise the vehicle and support safely. Position the engine/transaxle assembly and lower the vehicle over the assembly until the transaxle mount is indexed, then install the bolt.

37. Install the engine support fixture and adjust to previously indexed setting. Raise the vehicle off of the support fixture.

38. Install the rear mount to body bracket and torque the bolts to 55 ft. lbs. (75 Nm).

39. Install the rear mount nut and torque to 55 ft. lbs. (75 Nm).

40. Install the transaxle mount through bolt and torque the nut to 55 ft. lbs. (75 Nm). Tighten so equal gaps are maintained.

41. Install the halfshafts.

42. Connect the heater hose to the the radiator outlet pipe.

43. Install the suspension supports, crossmember and stabilizer shaft assembly. Tighten the center bolts first, then front, then rear, to a torque of 65 ft. lbs. (90 Nm).

44. Install the ball joints and torque the nuts to a maximum torque of 50 ft. lbs. (68 Nm).

45. Install the radiator air deflector and splash shield.

46. Install the wheels and lower the vehicle.

47. Install the front engine mount nut and torque to 41 ft. lbs. (56 Nm). Remove the engine support fixture. Connect the lower radiator hose.

48. Install the exhaust manifold and heat shield.

49. Connect the transaxle and engine oil cooler pipes, if equipped.

50. If equipped with a manual transaxle, connect the shifter cables and the clutch actuator cylinder.

51. If equipped with an automatic transaxle, connect the shift and TV cables.

52. Connect the fuel lines.

53. Install the power steering pump and related parts.

54. Connect the throttle cable and install the bracket.

55. Connect the power brake vacuum hose to the throttle body.

56. Connect the starter wires.

57. Connect all electrical connectors and cables to the proper engine- or transaxle-mounted devices.

58. Connect the 2 vacuum hoses at the front of the engine.

59. Install the upper radiator support.

60. Using new seals, connect the air conditioning hoses to the compressor.

61. Connect the heater and radiator hoses at the thermostat housing.

62. Install the air cleaner duct.

63. Fill all fluids to their proper levels.

64. Connect the battery cables, start the engine and check for leaks.

3.0L and 3.3L Engine

1. Disconnect the negative battery cable. Relieve the fuel pressure.

2. Matchmark the hinge-to-hood position and remove the hood.

3. Drain the cooling system. Disconnect and label all electrical connectors from the engine, alternator and fuel injection system, vacuum hoses, and engine ground straps. Remove the alternator.

4. Remove the coolant hoses from the radiator and engine. Remove the radiator and cooling fan assembly.

5. Remove the air intake duct. Disconnect the fuel lines from the fuel rail. Disconnect the throttle, TV and cruise control cables from the throttle body.

6. Raise the vehicle and support safely. Drain the engine oil. Disconnect the exhaust pipe from the exhaust manifold.

7. Remove the air conditioning

compressor mounting bolts, and position it aside.

8. Disconnect the heater hoses.

9. Remove the transaxle inspection cover, matchmark the converter to the flexplate and remove the torque converter bolts.

10. Remove the rear engine mount bolts.

11. Remove the lower bell housing bolts. Disconnect and label the starter motor wiring and remove the starter motor from the engine.

12. Lower the vehicle. Remove the power steering pump mounting bolts and set the pump aside.

13. Support the transaxle with a floor jack or equivalent. Attach an engine lifting device to the engine.

14. Remove the upper bell housing bolts.

15. Remove the front engine mount bolts.

16. Lift and remove the engine from the vehicle. If the master cylinder is preventing removal, remove it and plug the brake lines.

To install:

17. Lower the engine into the engine compartment. Align the engine mounts and install the bolts. Torque the bolts to their proper values:

Front engine mount bracket to block – 66 ft. lbs. (90 Nm)

Front engine mount to underbody – 54 ft. lbs. (73 Nm)

Front engine mount to engine bracket – 15 ft. lbs. (20 Nm)

Rear engine mount to bracket – 18 ft. lbs. (24 Nm)

Rear engine mount bracket to underbody – 41 ft. lbs. (56 Nm)

Rear engine mount to engine bracket – 40 ft. lbs. (54 Nm)

18. Install the upper transaxle-to-engine mounting bolts and torque to 55 ft. lbs. 75 Nm). Remove the engine lifting fixture from the engine.

19. Raise the vehicle and support safely.

20. Align the converter marks, install the torque converter bolts and torque to 46 ft. lbs. (63 Nm). Install the transaxle inspection cover.

21. Connect the exhaust pipe to the exhaust manifold. Install the starter motor and connect the wiring.

22. Install the air conditioning compressor. Connect the heater hoses.

23. Lower the vehicle. Install the power steering pump.

24. Install the alternator and belt.

25. Connect all vacuum hoses and electrical connectors to the engine.

26. Connect the fuel lines and all cables to the throttle body. Install the air intake duct.

27. Install the radiator and fan assembly. Connect the fan motor wiring.

Connect the radiator hoses and refill the cooling system.

28. Fill all fluids to their proper levels.

29. Connect the battery cables, start the engine and check for leaks.

Engine Mounts

REMOVAL & INSTALLATION

1. Disconnect the negative battery cable.

2. Matchmark the engine mount to its mounting location.

3. Raise the vehicle and support safely, if necessary. Using the proper equipment, support the weight of the engine.

4. Remove all bolts and nuts that attach the mount to the engine, transaxle or body and remove the mount assembly from the vehicle.

5. Remove the through bolt and separate the insulator from the bracket, as required.

6. The installation is the reverse of the removal procedure. Make sure the matchmarks are aligned before tightening bolts.

Cylinder Head

REMOVAL & INSTALLATION

2.0L Engine

NOTE: Cylinder head gasket replacement is necessary if camshaft carrier/cylinder head bolts are loosened. The head bolts should only be loosened when the engine is cold and should never be reused.

1. Relieve the fuel system pressure. Disconnect the negative battery cable.

2. Drain the coolant. Remove the induction tube.

3. Remove the alternator and bracket.

4. Remove the ignition coil.

5. Matchmark the rotor to the distributor housing and the distributor housing to the cam carrier. Remove the distributor and spark plug wires.

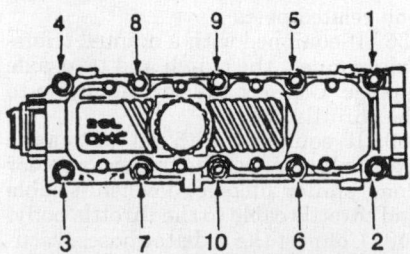

Camshaft carrier/cylinder head bolt torque sequence—2.0L engine

6. Disconnect all cables from the throttle body.

7. Disconnect and tag all electrical connections from the throttle body and intake manifold.

8. Disconnect all vacuum lines and heater hoses.

9. Disconnect and plug the fuel lines.

10. Remove the breather from the camshaft carrier.

11. Remove the upper radiator support.

12. Disconnect the exhaust manifold from the turbocharger and disconnect the oxygen sensor.

13. Label and disconnect wiring at engine harness and thermostat housing.

14. Remove the timing belt.

15. Remove the camshaft carrier/cylinder head bolts in the reverse order of the installation sequence.

16. Remove camshaft carrier, rocker arms and valve lifters.

17. Remove cylinder head and manifolds as an assembly. Remove the head gasket.

To install:

18. Thoroughly clean and dry the mating surfaces and bolt holes. Apply a continuous bead of RTV sealant to the sealing surface of camshaft carrier.

19. Install a new head gasket and position the head on the engine block. Tighten the new head bolts in sequence as follows:

Step 1—Torque to 18 ft. lbs. (25 Nm)

Step 2—Using a torque angle meter, tighten an additional 60°

Step 3—Tighten another additional 60°

Step 4—Tighten a third additional 60°

20. Install the rear cover and timing belt.

21. Connect all wiring to the engine harness and thermostat housing.

22. Install the exhaust manifold to turbo connection and connect the oxygen sensor.

23. Install the upper radiator support.

24. Install the breather on the camshaft carrier.

25. Connect all vacuum and fuel lines.

26. Connect the heater hoses.

27. Connect all electrical connectors to the throttle body and intake manifold.

28. Connect all cables to the throttle body.

29. Install the distributor and spark plug wires, aligning the matchmarks.

30. Install the ignition coil.

31. Install the alternator and bracket.

32. Fill all fluids to their proper levels.

33. Connect the battery cable, start the engine and check for leaks.

34. Tighten all head bolts another additional 30–50°, in sequence, after full engine warm up.

2.3L Engine

1. Relieve the fuel system pressure. Disconnect the negative battery cable and drain cooling system.

2. Disconnect heater inlet and throttle body heater hoses from water outlet. Disconnect the upper radiator hose from the water outlet.

3. Remove the exhaust manifold.

4. Remove the intake and exhaust camshaft housings.

5. Remove the oil cap and dipstick. Pull oil fill tube upward to unseat from block.

6. Label and disconnect the injector harness electrical connector.

7. Disconnect the throttle body air intake duct. Disconnect the cables and bracket and position aside.

8. Remove the throttle body from the intake manifold.

9. Matchmark and disconnect the vacuum hose from intake manifold.

10. Remove intake manifold bracket to block bolt.

11. Disconnect the coolant sensor connectors.

12. Remove the cylinder head bolts in reverse order of the installation sequence.

13. Remove the cylinder head and gasket. Inspect the oil flow check valve for freedom of movement.

To install:

14. Thoroughly clean and dry all bolts, bolt holes and mating surfaces. Inspect the head bolts for any damage and replace, if necessary.

15. Install the cylinder head gasket to the cylinder block and carefully position the cylinder head in place.

16. Coat the head bolt threads with clean engine oil and allow the oil to drain off before installing. Torque the cylinder head bolts in sequence as follows:

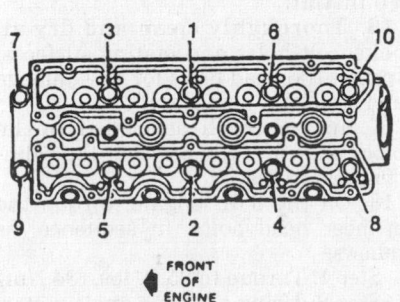

Cylinder head bolt torque sequence— 2.3L engine

Step 1—Torque all head bolts to 26 ft. lbs. (35 Nm)

Step 2—Using a torque angle meter, tighten the short bolts an additional 80° and the long bolts an additional 90°

17. Install the intake manifold bracket.

18. Connect the MAP sensor vacuum hose to the intake manifold.

19. Install the throttle body to the intake manifold.

20. Connect the throttle body air intake duct. Install the throttle cable and bracket.

21. Connect the injector harness electrical connector.

22. Connect the 2 coolant sensor connections.

23. Install the oil cap and dipstick. Install the oil fill tube into the block.

24. Install the exhaust and intake camshaft housings.

25. Install the exhaust manifold.

26. Connect the heater inlet and throttle body heater hoses to the water outlet. Connect the upper radiator hose to the water outlet.

27. Fill all fluids to their proper levels.

28. Connect the battery cable, start the engine and check for leaks.

2.5L Engine

1. Relieve the fuel system pressure.

2. Disconnect the negative battery cable.

3. Drain the coolant and remove the oil dipstick tube.

4. Remove the air cleaner assembly.

5. Raise the vehicle and support safely. Disconnect the exhaust pipe from the manifold.

6. Lower the vehicle.

7. Label and disconnect the electrical wiring and throttle linkage from the throttle body assembly.

8. Disconnect the heater hose from the intake manifold.

9. Remove the ignition coil. Label and disconnect the electrical wiring connectors from the intake manifold and the cylinder head. Remove the alternator.

10. If equipped with a top-mounted air conditioning compressor, remove the compressor and lay it aside.

11. If equipped with power steering, remove the upper bracket from the power steering pump.

12. Remove the radiator hoses from the engine.

13. Remove the valve cover. Label and remove the rocker arms and pushrods.

14. Remove the cylinder head bolts in reverse order of the installation sequence and remove the cylinder head.

To install:

15. Thoroughly clean and dry all bolts, bolt holes and mating surfaces.

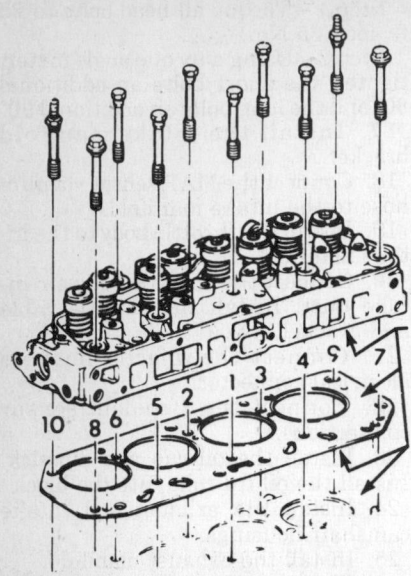

2.5L cylinder head bolt torque sequence

Inspect the head bolts for any damage and replace if necessary.

16. Install the head gasket to the block and carefully position the cylinder head in place.

17. On 1987 vehicles, torque the cylinder head bolts in sequence as follows:

Step 1: Apply sealing compound to the threads of the bolt/studs. Torque all bolts to 18 ft. lbs. (25 Nm)

Step 2, except front bolt/stud: Torque to 22 ft. lbs. (30 Nm)

Step 3: Torque front bolt/stud to 29 ft. lbs. (40 Nm)

Step 4, except front bolt/stud: Using a torque angle meter, tighten an additional 120°

Step 5: Tighten front bolt/stud an additional 90°

18. On 1988–91 vehicles, torque the cylinder head bolts in sequence as follows:

Step 1: Torque all bolts to 18 ft. lbs. (25 Nm)

Step 2, except front bolt/stud: Torque to 26 ft. lbs. (35 Nm)

Step 3: Torque front bolt/stud to 18 ft. lbs. (25 Nm)

Step 4: Using a torque angle meter, tighten all bolts an additional 90°

19. Install the pushrods and rocker arms in their original positions. Install the valve cover with a new gasket.

20. Install the radiator hoses. Install the power steering pump and upper bracket.

21. Install the air conditioning compressor, if removed.

22. Install the ignition coil and connect the electrical wiring connectors to the intake manifold and the cylinder head.

23. Install the alternator.

24. Install the heater hose to the intake manifold.

25. Connect the electrical wiring and throttle linkage to the throttle body assembly.

26. Raise the vehicle and support safely.

27. Install the exhaust pipe to the manifold.

28. Install the air cleaner assembly.

29. Adjust all belt tensions and fill all fluids to their proper levels.

30. Connect the battery cable, start the engine and check for leaks.

3.0L and 3.3L Engines

1. Relieve the fuel system pressure.

2. Disconnect the negative battery cable and drain the coolant.

3. Remove the mass air flow sensor and the air intake duct.

4. Remove C^3I ignition module and wiring.

5. Remove the serpentine drive belt, the alternator and bracket.

6. Label and remove all necessary vacuum lines and electrical connections.

7. Remove the fuel lines, the fuel rail and the spark plug wires.

8. Remove the heater/radiator hoses from the throttle body and intake manifold. Remove the cooling fan and the radiator.

9. Remove the intake manifold.

10. Remove the valve covers. Label and remove the rocker arms, pedestals and pushrods.

11. Remove the left side exhaust manifold.

12. Remove the power steering pump. Remove the dipstick and dipstick tube.

13. Remove the left side head bolts in reverse order of the installation sequence and lift the left cylinder head from the engine.

14. Raise the vehicle and support safely. Remove the right exhaust manifold-to-engine bolts.

15. Remove the right cylinder head-to-engine bolts in reverse of the installation sequence and lift the right cylinder head from the engine.

To install:

16. Thoroughly clean and dry all bolts, bolt holes and mating surfaces. Inspect the head bolts for any damage and replace if necessary.

17. Install the head gasket to the block and carefully position the cylinder head in place.

18. On the 3.0L engine, torque the cylinder head bolts, in sequence, as follows:

Step 1: Torque to 25 ft. lbs. (34 Nm)

Step 2: Using a torque angle meter, tighten an additional 90°

Step 3: Tighten another additional

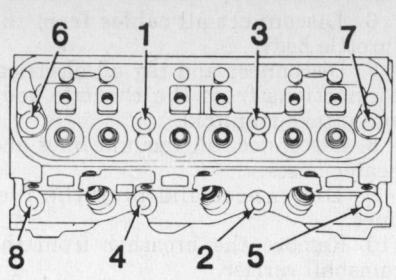

3.0L cylinder head bolt torque sequence and angle—tightening procedure

90°, to a maximum of 60 ft. lbs. (81 Nm)

19. On the 3.3L engine, torque the cylinder head bolts, in sequence, as follows:

Step 1: Torque to 35 ft. lbs. (47 Nm)

Step 2: Using a torque angle meter, tighten an additional 130°

Step 3: Tighten the 4 center bolts an additional 30°

20. Install the intake manifold. Raise the vehicle and support safely. Install the exhaust manifold. Lower the vehicle.

21. Install the power steering pump. Install the dipstick and dipstick tube.

22. Install new valve cover gaskets and install the valve covers.

23. Install the rocker arms, pedestals and bolts. Tighten pedestal bolts to 43 ft. lbs. (58 Nm) for the 3.0L engine and 28 ft. lbs. (38 Nm) for the 3.3L engine.

24. Install the intake manifold assembly.

25. Install the heater and radiator hoses to the throttle body and intake manifold.

26. Install the cooling fan and the radiator.

27. Install the fuel lines, the fuel rail and the spark plug wires.

28. Install all vacuum lines and electrical connections.

29. Install the serpentine drive belt, the alternator and bracket.

30. Install the C^3I ignition module and wiring.

31. Install the mass air flow sensor and the air intake duct.

32. Fill all fluids to their proper levels.

33. Connect the battery cable, start the engine and check for leaks.

Valve Lifters

REMOVAL & INSTALLATION

2.0L Engine

1. Disconnect the negative battery cable. Remove the camshaft carrier cover.

2. Hold the valves in place with

compressed air, using an air adapter in the spark plug hole.

3. Compress the valve springs using a suitable valve spring compressor.

4. Remove rocker arms; keep them in order for reassembly.

5. Remove the lifters.

6. The installation is the reverse of the removal procedure. Soak the lifters in clean engine oil proir to installation.

7. Connect the negative battery cable and check the lifters for proper operation.

2.3L Engine

1. Disconnect the negative battery cable.

2. Remove the camshafts.

3. Remove the lifters from their bores.

4. The installation is the reverse of the removal procedure. Soak the lifters in clean engine oil prior to installation.

5. Connect the negative battery cable and check the lifters for proper operation.

2.5L Engine

1. Relieve the fuel system pressure.

2. Disconnect the negative battery cable.

3. Remove the valve cover and intake manifold.

5. Remove the side pushrod cover.

6. Loosen the rocker arms in pairs and rotate them in order to clear the pushrods.

7. Remove the pushrods, retainer and guide from each cylinder.

8. Remove the valve lifters.

9. The installation is the reverse of the removal procedure. Soak the lifters in clean engine oil prior to installation.

10. Connect the negative battery cable and check the lifters for proper operation.

3.0L and 3.3L Engines

1. Relieve the fuel system pressure.

2. Disconnect the negative battery terminal from the battery.

3. Disconnect and remove the fuel rail and the throttle body from the intake manifold.

4. Drain the cooling system.

5. Remove valve covers and the intake manifold.

6. Remove the rocker arms, pedestals and pushrods. Keep these components in order for accurate installation.

7. Remove the valve lifters.

8. The installation is the reverse of the removal procedure. Soak the lifters in clean engine oil prior to installation.

9. Connect the negative battery cable and check the lifters for proper operation.

Rocker Arms

REMOVAL & INSTALLATION

2.0L Engine

1. Disconnect the negative battery cable. Remove the camshaft carrier cover.

2. Hold the valves in place with compressed air, using an air adapter in the spark plug hole.

3. Compress the valve springs using a suitable valve spring compressor.

4. Remove rocker arms. Keep them in order if they are being reused.

5. The installation is the reverse of the removal procedure.

6. Connect the negative battery cable and check for proper operation.

2.5L Engine

1. Relieve the fuel system pressure.

2. Disconnect the negative battery cable.

3. Remove the valve cover and intake manifold.

4. Remove the rocker arm bolts and remove the rocker arms.

5. The installation is the reverse of the removal procedure. Torque the retaining bolts to 20 ft. lbs. (27 Nm).

6. Connect the negative battery cable and check for proper operation.

3.0L Engine

FRONT HEAD

1. Relieve the fuel system pressure.

2. Disconnect the negative battery cable.

3. Disconnect all electrical components and vacuum hoses which prevent access to the valve cover bolts.

4. Remove the valve cover.

5. Remove the rocker arm pedestal-to-cylinder head bolts, the rocker arm and pedestal assembly.

6. The installation is the reverse of the removal procedure. Torque the rocker arm pedestal bolts to 45 ft. lbs. (60 Nm).

7. Connect the negative battery cable and check for proper operation.

REAR HEAD

1. Relieve the fuel system pressure.

2. Disconnect the negative battery terminal.

3. Remove the C^3I ignition coil module. Disconnect the spark plug wires, electrical connectors, EGR solenoid wiring and vacuum hoses.

4. Remove the serpentine belt, alternator wiring and the rear alternator bracket-to-engine bolt. Rotate the alternator toward the front of the vehicle.

5. Remove the power steering pump from the belt tensioner and remove the tensioner assembly.

6. Remove the engine lift bracket and the rear alternator brace.

7. Drain the radiator below heater hose level. Remove the throttle body heater hoses.

8. Remove the valve cover.

9. Remove the rocker arm pedestal-to-cylinder head bolts. Remove the rocker arm and pedestal assembly.

10. The installation is the reverse of the removal procedure. Torque the rocker arm pedestal bolts to 45 ft. lbs. (60 Nm).

11. Refill the cooling system. Connect the battery cable and check for proper operation.

3.3L Engine

FRONT HEAD

1. Relieve the fuel system pressure.

2. Disconnect the negative battery cable.

3. Disconnect all electrical components and vacuum hoses which prevent access to the valve cover bolts.

4. Remove the serpentine drive belt.

5. Remove the alternator brace bolt and remove the alternator belt.

6. Remove the spark plug wire harness.

7. Remove the valve cover.

8. Remove the rocker arm pedestal-to-cylinder head bolts, the rocker arm and pedestal assembly.

9. The installation is the reverse of the removal procedure. Torque the rocker arm pedestal bolts to 28 ft. lbs. (38 Nm).

10. Connect the negative battery cable and check for proper operation.

REAR HEAD

1. Relieve the fuel system pressure.

2. Disconnect the negative battery terminal.

3. Remove the serpentine drive belt.

4. Loosen the power steering pump bolts and slide the pump forward.

5. Remove the power steering braces.

6. Remove the spark plug wires from the spark plugs.

7. Remove the valve cover.

8. Remove the rocker arm pedestal-to-cylinder head bolts. Remove the rocker arm and pedestal assembly.

9. The installation is the reverse of the removal procedure. Torque the rocker arm pedestal bolts to 28 ft. lbs. (38 Nm).

10. Refill the cooling system. Connect the battery cable and check for proper operation.

Intake Manifold

REMOVAL & INSTALLATION

2.0L Engine

1. Relieve the fuel system pressure. Disconnect the negative battery cable.
2. Remove induction tube and hoses.
3. Label and disconnect the wiring to throttle body, fuel injectors, MAP sensor and wastegate.
4. Disconnect the PCV and vacuum hoses on the throttle body.
5. Disconnect the throttle and cruise control cables, if equipped.
6. Remove the fuel return line from the throttle cable support bracket.
7. Disconnect the wiring to the ignition coil.
8. Remove the vacuum hoses from the rear of the manifold.
9. Remove the transaxle fill tube bracket.
10. Remove the manifold support bracket.
11. Remove the heater tube support bracket on the lower side of the manifold.
12. Disconnect the wires from the injectors.
13. Drain and remove the coolant recovery tank.
14. Remove the serpentine drive belt.
15. Remove the rear bolt from alternator bracket, the power steering adjusting bracket and front alternator adjusting bracket.
16. Remove the alternator.
17. Disconnect the fuel lines to fuel rail and regulator outlet.
18. Remove the retaining nuts and washers and remove the intake manifold.

To install:
19. Thoroughly clean and dry the mating surfaces. Install new gaskets and place the intake manifold in position.
20. Torque the intake manifold retaining nuts to 18 ft. lbs. (24 Nm), starting from the middle and working outward.
21. Connect the fuel return line to the regulator outlet.
22. Install the power steering pump bracket and alternator and power steering pump adjusting brackets.
23. Install the alternator and belt.
24. Install the coolant recovery tank.
25. Connect the injector wiring.
26. Install the heater tube support, manifold support and transaxle fill tube brackets.
27. Connect the vacuum hoses at the rear of the bracket.
28. Install the ignition coil with its bracket.
29. Install the fuel supply line to the throttle cable support bracket.
30. Connect the cables, hoses and connectors to the throttle body.
31. Connect the wiring to the wastegate and MAP sensor.
32. Install the induction tube and hoses.
33. Fill all fluids to their proper levels.
34. Connect the negative battery cable and check for leaks.

2.3L Engine

1. Disconnect the negative battery cable.
2. Remove the coolant fan shroud, vacuum hose and electrical connector from the MAP sensor.
3. Disconnect the throttle body to air cleaner duct.
4. Remove the throttle cable bracket.
5. Remove the power brake vacuum hose, including the retaining bracket to power steering bracket and position it aside.
6. Remove the throttle body from the intake manifold with electrical harness, coolant hoses, vacuum hoses and throttle cable attached. Position these components aside.
7. Remove the oil/air separator bolts and hoses. Leave the hoses attached to the separator, disconnect from the oil fill, chain housing and the intake manifold. Remove as an assembly.
8. Remove the oil fill cap and oil level indicator stick.
9. Pull the oil tube fill upward to unseat from block and remove.
10. Disconnect the injector harness connector.
11. Remove the fill tube, rotating as necessary to gain clearance for the oil/air separator nipple between the intake tubes and fuel rail electrical harness.
12. Remove the intake manifold support bracket bolts and nut. Remove the intake manifold retaining nuts and bolts.
13. Remove the intake manifold.

To install:
14. Thoroughly clean and dry the mating surfaces. Install new gaskets and place the intake manifold in position.
15. Tighten the intake manifold bolts/nuts, in sequence, to 18 ft. lbs. (25 Nm). Tighten intake manifold brace and retainers hand tight. Tighten to specifications in the following order:

    a. Nut to stud bolt – 18 ft. lbs. (25 Nm).

    b. Bolt to intake manifold – 40 ft. lbs. (55 Nm).

    c. Bolt to cylinder block – 40 ft. lbs. (55 Nm).

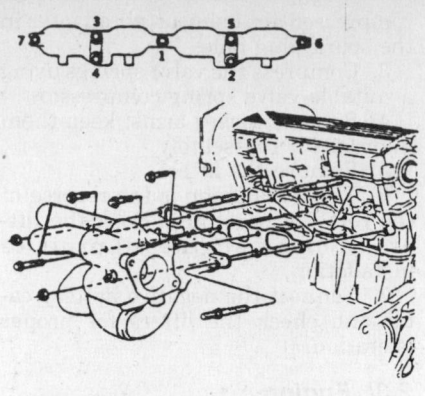

Intake manifold bolt torque sequence – 2.3L engine

16. Lubricate a new oil fill tube ring seal with engine oil and install tube between No. 1 and 2 intake tubes. Rotate as necessary to gain clearance for oil/air separator nipple on fill tube.
17. Locate the oil fill tube in its cylinder block opening. Align the fill tube so it is approximately in its installed position. Press straight down to seat fill tube and seal into cylinder block.
18. Lubricate the hoses and install the oil/air separator assembly. Install the throttle body to intake manifold using a new gasket.
19. Install the power brake vacuum hose and the retaining bracket to power steering bracket.
20. Install the throttle cable bracket.
21. Connect the throttle body to air cleaner duct.
22. Install the coolant fan shroud, vacuum hose and electrical connector to the MAP sensor.
23. Fill all fluids to their proper levels.
24. Connect the negative battery cable and check for leaks.

2.5L Engine

1. Relieve the system fuel pressure. Disconnect the negative battery cable.
2. Drain the coolant. Remove the air cleaner, PCV valve and hose.
3. Disconnect and plug the vacuum lines and fuel lines. Disconnect the wiring and linkages from the throttle body.
4. Disconnect the throttle linkage and bell crank; position the assembly aside for clearance.
5. Disconnect the heater hoses. If equipped with power steering, disconnect and remove the upper power steering pump bracket.
6. Remove the ignition coil.
7. Remove the intake manifold mounting bolts and remove the intake manifold.
8. The installation is the reverse of the removal procedure. Torque the intake manifold mounting bolts, in sequence, to 25 ft. lbs. (34 Nm).

3.0L and 3.3L Engines

1. Relieve the fuel system pressure.
2. Disconnect the negative battery cable.
3. On 3.0L engine, disconnect the mass air flow sensor. Remove the air intake duct.
4. Remove the serpentine drive belt, alternator and bracket.
5. Remove the C³I ignition module and bracket.
6. Label and remove all the necessary vacuum and electrical wiring connectors.
7. Remove the throttle, cruise control and TV cables from the throttle body assembly.
8. Drain the coolant. Disconnect the heater hoses from the throttle body.
9. Remove the upper radiator hose from the intake manifold.
10. Remove the fuel lines, the fuel rail and the fuel injectors. Remove the spark plug wires.
11. Remove the intake manifold mounting bolts and remove the intake manifold.

To install:
12. Thoroughly clean and dry all mating surfaces. On 3.0L engine, apply sealer to steel gaskets. On 3.3L engine, apply sealer to the 4 head-to-block corners.
13. On 3.0L engine, torque the intake manifold bolts in sequence to 32 ft. lbs. (44 Nm). Apply thread lock compund to the threads and torque to 88 inch lbs. (10 Nm) for 3.3L engine.
14. Install the fuel injectors, rail and lines. Install the spark plug wires.
15. Connect the heater hoses to the throttle body.
16. Install the upper radiator hose to the intake manifold.
17. Connect the throttle, cruise control and TV cables to the throttle body assembly.
18. Connect all remaining vacuum and electrical wiring connectors.
19. Install the C³I ignition module and bracket.
20. Install the alternator, bracket and serpentine drive belt.
21. Connect the mass air flow sensor, if equipped. Install the air intake duct.
22. Fill all fluids to their proper levels.
23. Connect the negative battery cable and check for leaks.

Exhaust Manifold

REMOVAL & INSTALLATION

2.0L Engine

1. Disconnect the negative battery cable.
2. Raise vehicle and support safely.
3. Drain the engine coolant.

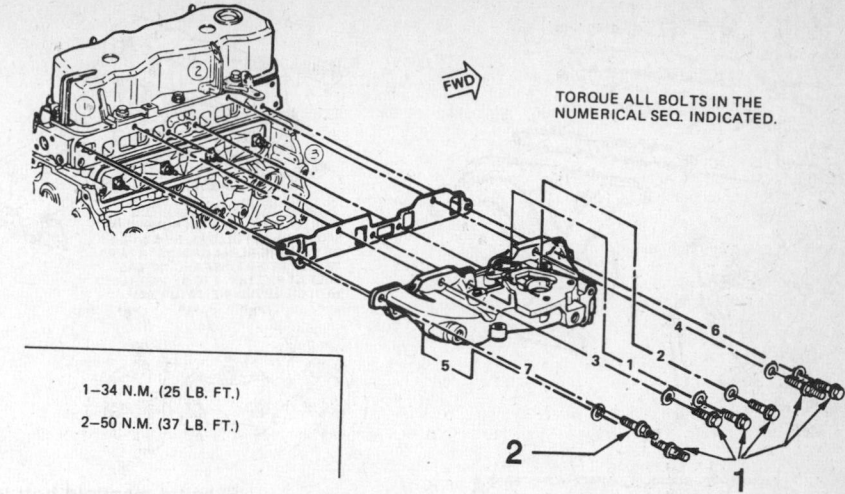

TORQUE ALL BOLTS IN THE NUMERICAL SEQ. INDICATED.

1—34 N.M. (25 LB. FT.)
2—50 N.M. (37 LB. FT.)

Intake manifold bolt torque sequence—2.5L engine

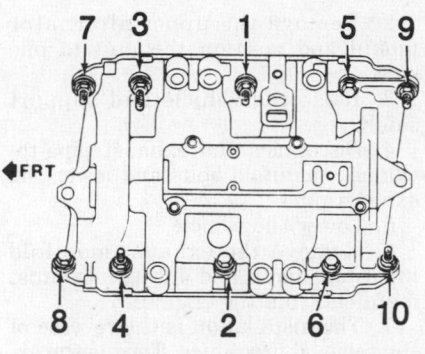

Intake manifold bolt torque sequence—3.0L engine

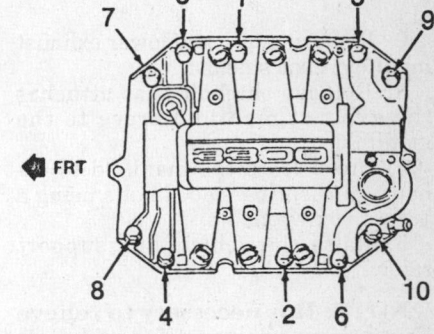

Intake manifold bolt torque sequence—3.3L engine

4. Remove the fan retaining screws.
5. Disconnect the exhaust pipe.
6. Remove the air conditioning compressor rear support bracket.
7. Remove turbocharger support bracket to engine.
8. Disconnect and plug the oil drain pipe at turbocharger.
9. Disconnect water return pipe at turbocharger.
10. Lower vehicle and remove coolant recovery pipe.
11. Remove the air induction tube, coolant fan, oxygen sensor.
12. Disconnect the oil and water feed pipes.
13. Remove air intake duct and vacuum hose at actuator.
14. Remove the exhaust manifold retaining nuts and remove turbocharger and manifold as an assembly.
15. Remove turbocharger from exhaust manifold.

To install:
16. Assemble the turbocharger and exhaust manifold.
17. Clean the exhaust manifold and cylinder head mating surfaces.
18. Install a new gasket and install the manifold/turbocharger assembly

to the engine. Torque the Nos. 2 and 3 manifold runner nuts first, then Nos. 1 and 4, to 18 ft. lbs. (24 Nm).
19. Connect the oil and water feed and return lines.
20. Connect the oxygen sensor.
21. Install the air intake duct and connect the vacuum hose to the actuator.
22. Install the cooling fan.
23. Install the induction tube and coolant recovery tube.
24. Raise the vehicle and support safely.
25. Install the rear turbocharger support bolt.
26. Install the compressor support bracket.
27. Install the oil drain hose.
28. Connect the exhaust pipe.
29. Connect the negative battery cable and check the turbocharger for proper operation and the assembly for leaks.

2.3L Engine

1. Disconnect the negative battery cable and oxygen sensor connector.

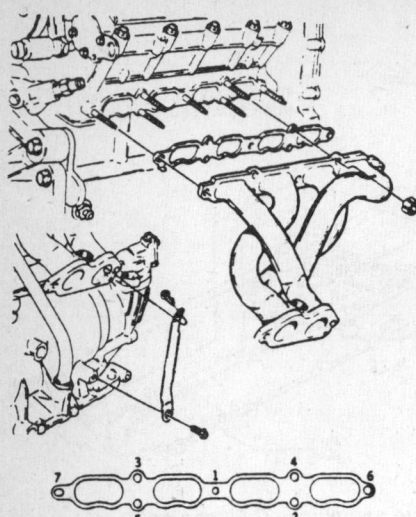

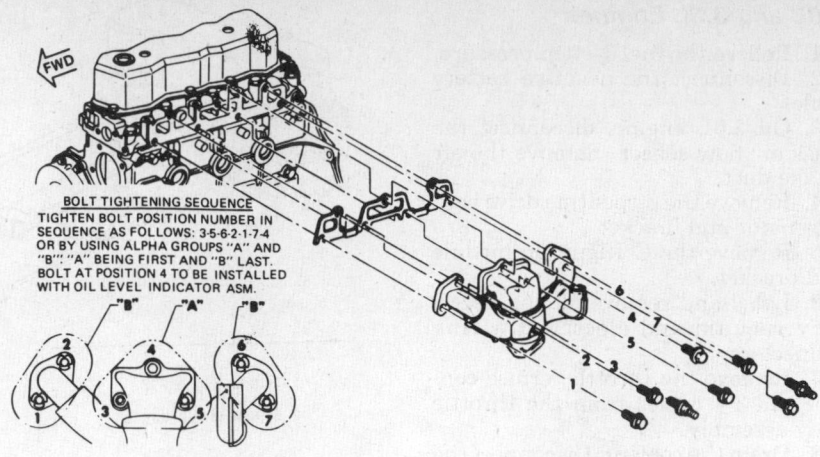

Exhaust manifold bolt torque sequence—2.5L engine

Exhaust manifold bolt torque sequence—2.3L engine

2. Remove upper and lower exhaust manifold heat shields.

3. Remove the bolt that attaches the exhaust manifold brace to the manifold.

4. Break loose the manifold to exhaust pipe spring loaded bolts using a 13mm box wrench.

5. Raise the vehicle and support safely.

NOTE: It is necessary to relieve the spring pressure from 1 bolt prior to removing the second bolt. If the spring pressure is not relieved it will cause the exhaust pipe to twist and bind up the bolt as it is removed.

6. Remove the manifold to exhaust pipe bolts from the exhaust pipe flange as follows:

    a. Unscrew either bolt clockwise 4 turns.

    b. Remove the other bolt.

    c. Remove the first bolt.

7. Pull down and back on the exhaust pipe to disengage it from the exhaust manifold bolts.

8. Lower the vehicle.

9. Remove the exhaust manifold mounting bolts and remove the manifold.

10. The installation is the reverse of the removal procedure. Torque the mounting bolts, in sequence, to 27 ft. lbs. (37 Nm). Install the exhaust pipe flange bolts evenly and gradually to avoid binding.

11. Connect the negative battery cable and check for leaks.

2.5L Engine

1. Disconnect the negative battery cable and oxygen sensor connector. Remove the air cleaner assembly.

2. Remove the upper alternator mount and position the unit to one side.

3. Raise the vehicle and support safely.

4. Disconnect the exhaust pipe-to-exhaust manifold bolts and lower the exhaust pipe.

5. Lower the vehicle.

6. Remove the exhaust manifold mounting bolts and lift the exhaust manifold from the engine.

7. The installation is the reverse of the removal procedure. Torque the exhaust manifold bolts, in sequence, to 32 ft. lbs. (43 Nm).

8. Connect the negative battery cable and check for leaks.

3.0L and 3.3L Engines

FRONT MANIFOLD

1. Disconnect the negative battery cable.

2. Disconnect air cleaner mounting bolts.

3. Remove the bolts attaching the exhaust crossover pipe to the manifold.

4. Disconnect the spark plug wires.

5. Remove the cooling fan.

6. Remove the mounting bolts and remove the manifold.

NOTE: The oil dipstick tube may have to be removed to provide access to the manifold bolts.

7. The installation is the reverse of the removal procedure. Torque the mounting bolts to 37 ft. lbs. (50 Nm) for 3.0L engine and 30 ft. lbs. (41 Nm) for 3.3L engine.

8. Connect the negative battery cable and check for leaks.

REAR MANIFOLD

1. Disconnect the negative battery cable.

2. Remove the 2 bolts attaching exhaust pipe to manifold.

3. Disconnect oxygen sensor wire.

4. Disconnect and tag spark plug wires.

5. Remove 2 nuts retaining crossover pipe to manifold.

6. Remove serpentine belt.

7. Remove power steering pump.

8. Remove heater hose from tube, heat shield and C^3I bracket nuts.

9. Remove the bolts attaching manifold to cylinder head.

10. The installation is the reverse of the removal procedure. Torque the mounting bolts to 37 ft. lbs. (50 Nm) for 3.0L engine and 30 ft. lbs. (41 Nm) for 3.3L engine.

11. Connect the negative battery cable and check for leaks.

Turbocharger Unit

REMOVAL & INSTALLATION

1. Disconnect the negative battery cable.

2. Raise vehicle and support safely.

3. Drain the engine coolant.

4. Remove the fan retaining screws.

5. Disconnect the exhaust pipe.

6. Remove the air conditioning compressor rear support bracket.

7. Remove turbocharger support bracket to engine.

8. Disconnect and plug the oil drain pipe at turbocharger.

9. Disconnect water return pipe at turbocharger.

10. Lower vehicle and remove coolant recovery pipe.

11. Remove the air induction tube, coolant fan, oxygen sensor.

12. Disconnect the oil and water feed pipes.

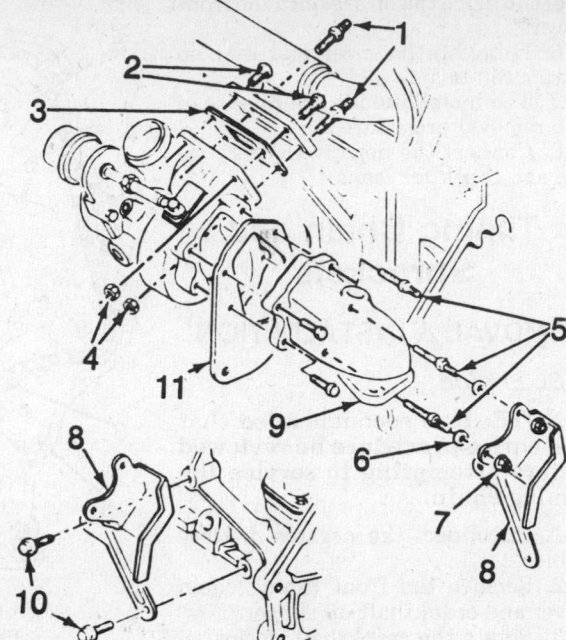

1. Stud
2. Bolt
3. Gasket
4. Nut
5. Stud
6. Washer
7. Nut
8. Support bracket
9. Exhaust outlet elbow
10. Bolt
11. Adapter plate

Turbocharger assembly and related parts

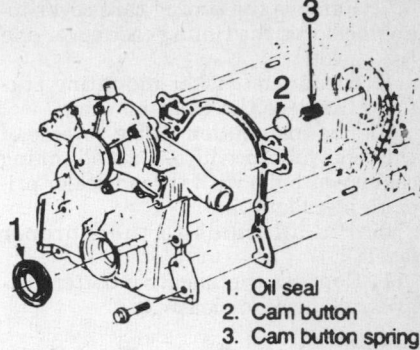

1. Oil seal
2. Cam button
3. Cam button spring

Timing chain front cover—3.0L and 3.3L engines

13. Remove air intake duct and vacuum hose at actuator.
14. Remove the exhaust manifold retaining nuts and remove turbocharger and manifold as an assembly.
15. Remove turbocharger from exhaust manifold.
To install:
16. Assemble the turbocharger and exhaust manifold.
17. Clean the exhaust manifold and cylinder head mating surfaces.
18. Install a new gasket and install the manifold/turbocharger assembly to the engine. Torque the Nos. 2 and 3 manifold runner nuts first, then Nos. 1 and 4, to 18 ft. lbs. (24 Nm).
19. Connect the oil and water feed and return lines.
20. Connect the oxygen sensor.
21. Install the air intake duct and connect the vacuum hose to the actuator.
22. Install the cooling fan.
23. Install the induction tube and coolant recovery tube.
24. Raise the vehicle and support safely.
25. Install the rear turbocharger support bolt.
26. Install the compressor support bracket.
27. Install the oil drain hose.
28. Connect the exhaust pipe.
29. Connect the negative battery cable and check the turbocharger for proper operation and the assembly for leaks.

Timing Chain Front Cover

REMOVAL & INSTALLATION

2.3L Engine

1. Disconnect the negative battery cable. Remove the coolant recovery reservoir.
2. Remove the serpentine drive belt using a 13mm wrench that is at least 24 in. long.
3. Remove upper cover fasteners.
4. Raise the vehicle and support safely.
5. Remove the right front wheel assembly and lower splash shield.
6. Remove the crankshaft balancer assembly.

NOTE: Do not install an automatic transaxle-equipped engine balancer on a manual-transaxle equipped engine or vice-versa.

7. Remove lower cover fasteners and lower the vehicle.
8. Remove the front cover.
9. The installation is the reverse of the removal procedure. Torque the balancer retaining bolt to 74 ft. lbs. (100 Nm).

1990–91 2.5L Engine

1. Disconnect the negative battery cable.

2. Remove the belts. Remove the power steering pump mounting bolts and position it aside.
3. Raise the vehicle and support safely. Remove the inner fender splash shield.
4. Remove the harmonic balancer.
5. Remove the timing case cover-to-engine bolts and the timing case cover.
To install:
6. Thoroughly clean and dry all mating surfaces. Use RTV sealant to seal all mating surfaces.
7. A centering tool fits over the crankshaft seal and is used to correctly position the timing case cover during installation. Install the cover and partially tighten the 2 opposing timing case cover screws.
8. Tighten the remaining cover screws and remove the centering tool from the timing case cover. Final torque of all screws should be 89 inch lbs. (10 Nm).
9. Install the harmonic balancer and torque the bolt to 162 ft. lbs. (220 Nm). Install the belts and the power steering pump.
10. Install the splash shield.
11. Connect the negative battery cable and check for leaks.

3.0L and 3.3L Engines

1. Disconnect the negative battery cable.
2. Drain the coolant and the engine oil. Remove the oil filter.
3. Loosen the water pump pulley bolts, but do not remove them. Remove the serpentine drive belt and the pulley. Remove the water pump-to-engine bolts and the water pump.
4. Raise the vehicle and support safely. Remove the right front wheel assembly and the right inner fender splash shield.
5. Remove the crankshaft harmonic balancer and the crankshaft sensor.
6. Remove the radiator and heater hoses.

7. Remove the timing case cover-to-engine bolts, the timing case cover and the gasket.

8. Clean the gasket mounting surfaces. Replace the front oil seal.

● 9. The installation is the reverse of the removal procedure. Coat all timing case cover bolts with thread sealer prior to installation.

10. Fill all fluids to their proper levels.

11. Connect the negative battery cable and check for leaks.

Timing Gear Front Cover

REMOVAL & INSTALLATION

1987–89 2.5L Engine

1. Disconnect the negative battery cable.

2. Remove the belts.

3. Raise the vehicle and support safely. Remove the inner fender splash shield.

4. Remove the harmonic balancer.

5. Remove the cover-to-engine bolts and the timing cover.

To install:

6. Thoroughly clean and dry all mating surfaces. Use RTV sealant to seal all mating surfaces.

7. A centering tool fits over the crankshaft seal and is used to correctly position the timing case cover during installation. Install the cover and partially tighten the 2 opposing timing case cover screws.

8. Tighten the remaining cover screws and remove the centering tool from the timing case cover. Final torque of all screws should be 89 inch lbs. (10 Nm).

9. Install the harmonic balancer and torque the bolt to 162 ft. lbs. (220 Nm). Install the belts and the power steering pump.

10. Install the splash shield.

11. Connect the negative battery cable and check for leaks.

Front Cover Oil Seal

REPLACEMENT

1. Disconnect the negative battery cable.

2. Remove the front cover.

3. Using a small prybar, pry out the old oil seal.

NOTE: Use care to avoid damage to seal bore or seal contact surfaces.

4. Thoroughly clean and dry the oil seal mounting surface.

5. Use the appropriate installation

tool and drive the oil seal into the front cover.

6. Lubricate balancer and seal lip with clean engine oil.

7. The installation is the reverse of the removal procedure.

8. Connect the negative battery cable and check for leaks.

Timing Chain and Sprockets

REMOVAL & INSTALLATION

2.3L Engine

NOTE: It is recommended that the entire procedure be reviewed before attempting to service the timing chain.

1. Disconnect the negative battery cable.

2. Remove the front timing chain cover and crankshaft oil slinger.

3. Rotate the crankshaft clockwise, as viewed from front of engine (normal rotation) until the camshaft sprocket's timing dowel pin holes align with the holes in the timing chain housing. The mark on the crankshaft sprocket should align with the mark on the cylinder block. The crankshaft sprocket keyway should point upwards and align with the centerline of the cylinder bores. This is the normal timed position.

4. Remove the 3 timing chain guides.

5. Raise the vehicle and support safely.

6. Gently pry off timing chain tensioner spring retainer and remove spring.

NOTE: Two styles of tensioner are used. Early production engines will have a spring post and late production ones will not. Both styles are identical in operation and are interchangeable.

7. Remove the timing chain tensioner shoe retainer.

8. Make sure all the slack in the timing chain is above the tensioner assembly; remove the chain tensioner shoe. The timing chain must be disengaged from the wear grooves in the tensioner shoe in order to remove the shoe. Slide a prybar under the timing chain while pulling shoe outward.

9. If difficulty is encountered removing chain tensioner shoe, proceed as follows:

a. Lower the vehicle.

b. Hold the intake camshaft sprocket with a holding tool and remove the sprocket bolt and washer.

c. Remove the washer from the bolt and re-thread the bolt back into

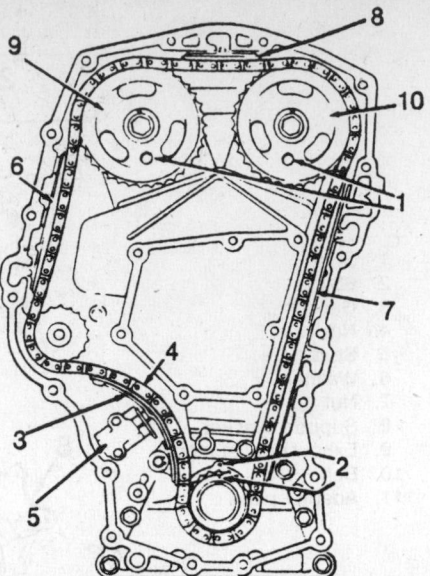

1. Camshaft timing marks
2. Crankshaft timing mark
3. Tensioner shoe assembly
4. Timing chain
5. Tensioner
6. R/H guide
7. L/H guide
8. Upper guide
9. Exhaust camshaft sprocket
10. Intake camshaft sprocket

Timing chain properly installed—2.3L engine

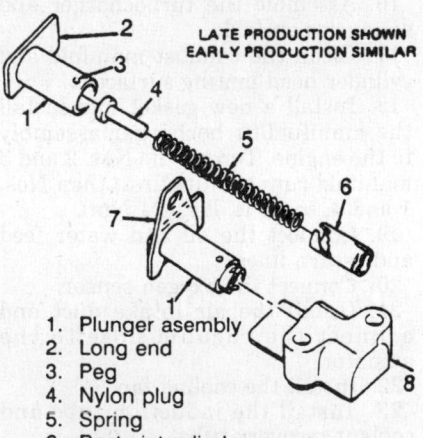

LATE PRODUCTION SHOWN
EARLY PRODUCTION SIMILAR

1. Plunger asembly
2. Long end
3. Peg
4. Nylon plug
5. Spring
6. Restraint cylinder
7. J–36589 anti-release devise
8. Tensioner body

Exploded view of the timing chain tensioner—2.3L engine. Versions may differ slightly with year.

the camshaft by hand, the bolt provides a surface to push against.

d. Remove intake camshaft

sprocket using a 3-jaw puller in the 3 relief holes in the sprocket. Do not attempt to pry the sprocket off the camshaft or damage to the sprocket or chain housing could occur.

10. Remove the tensioner assembly retaining bolts and the tensioner.

—————— CAUTION ——————

The tensioner piston is spring loaded and could fly out causing personal injury.

11. Remove the chain housing to block stud, which is actually the timing chain tensioner shoe pivot.

12. Remove the timing chain.

To install:

13. Tighten intake camshaft sprocket retaining bolt and washer, while holding the sprocket with tool J–36013, if removed.

14. Install the special tool through holes in camshaft sprockets into holes in timing chain housing. This positions the camshafts for correct timing.

15. If the camshafts are out of position and must be rotated more than ⅛ turn in order to install the alignment dowel pins:

a. The crankshaft must be rotated 90 degrees clockwise off of TDC in order to give the valves adequate clearance to open.

b. Once the camshafts are in position and the dowels installed, rotate the crankshaft counterclockwise back to TDC. Do not rotate the crankshaft clockwise to TDC or valve and piston damage could occur.

16. Install the timing chain over the exhaust camshaft sprocket, around the idler sprocket and around the crankshaft sprocket.

17. Remove the alignment dowel pin from the intake camshaft. Using a dowel pin remover tool, rotate the intake camshaft sprocket counterclockwise enough to slide the timing chain over the intake camshaft sprocket. Release the camshaft sprocket wrench. The length of chain between the 2 camshaft sprockets will tighten. If properly timed, the intake camshaft alignment dowel pin should slide in easily. If the dowel pin does not fully index, the camshafts are not timed correctly and the procedure must be repeated.

18. Leave the alignment dowel pins installed.

19. With slack removed from chain between intake camshaft sprocket and crankshaft sprocket, the timing marks on the crankshaft and the cylinder block should be aligned. If marks are not aligned, move the chain 1 tooth forward or rearward, remove slack and recheck marks.

20. Tighten the chain housing to block stud. The stud is installed under

the timing chain. Tighten to 19 ft. lbs. (26 Nm).

21. Reload timing chain tensioner assembly to its 0 position as follows:

a. Assemble restraint cylinder, spring and nylon plug into plunger. Index slot in restraint cylinder with peg in plunger. While rotating the restraint cylinder clockwise, push the restraint cylinder into the plunger until it bottoms. Keep rotating the restraint cylinder clockwise but allow the spring to push it out of the plunger. The pin in the plunger will lock the restraint in the loaded position.

b. Install tool J–36589 or equivalent, onto plunger assembly.

c. Install plunger assembly into tensioner body with the long end toward the crankshaft when installed.

22. Install the tensioner assembly to the chain housing. Recheck plunger assembly installation. It is correctly installed when the long end is toward the crankshaft.

23. Install and tighten timing chain tensioner bolts and tighten to 10 ft. lbs. (14 Nm).

24. Install the tensioner shoe and tensioner shoe retainer. Remove special tool J–36589 and squeeze plunger assembly into the tensioner body to unload the plunger assembly.

25. Lower vehicle and remove the alignment dowel pins. Rotate crankshaft clockwise 2 full rotations. Align crankshaft timing mark with mark on cylinder block and reinstall alignment dowel pins. Alignment dowel pins will slide in easily if engine is timed correctly.

NOTE: If the engine is not correctly timed, severe engine damage could occur.

26. Install 3 timing chain guides and crankshaft oil slinger.

27. Install the timing chain front cover.

28. Connect the negative battery cable and check for leaks.

3.0L, 3.3L and 1990–91 2.5L Engines

1. Disconnect the negative battery cable.

2. Drain the cooling system. Disconnect the cooling hose from the water pump.

3. Raise the vehicle and support safely.

4. Remove the inner fender splash shield.

5. Remove the serpentine drive belt.

6. Remove the crankshaft pulley bolt and slide the pulley from the crankshaft.

7. Remove the front cover.

8. Rotate the crankshaft to align

the timing marks on the sprockets. Remove the chain dampener assembly.

9. Remove the camshaft sprocket-to-camshaft bolt(s), remove the camshaft sprocket and chain and thrust bearing.

10. Remove the crankshaft gear by sliding it forward.

11. Clean the gasket mounting surfaces. Inspect the timing chain and the sprockets for damage and/or wear and replace damaged parts.

To install:

12. Position the crankshaft so the No. 1 piston is at TDC of its compression stroke. Install the thrust bearing on 2.5L engine.

13. Temporarily install the gear on the camshaft and position the camshaft so the timing mark on the gear is pointing straight down.

14. Assemble the timing chain to the gears so the timing marks are aligned, mark-to-mark.

15. Install the camshaft sprocket retaining bolt(s).

16. Install the camshaft thrust bearing, if not already done.

17. Install the timing chain dampener.

18. Install the front cover and all related parts.

19. Connect the negative battery cable and check for leaks.

Timing Gears

REMOVAL & INSTALLATION

1987–89 2.5L Engine

NOTE: If the camshaft gear is to be replaced, the engine must be removed from the vehicle. The crankshaft gear may be replaced with the engine in the vehicle.

1. Disconnect the negative battery terminal from the battery.

2. Raise the vehicle and support safely.

3. Remove the inner fender splash shield.

4. Remove the accessory drive belts.

4. Remove the crankshaft pulley-to-crankshaft pulley bolt and slide the pulley from the crankshaft.

5. If replacing the camshaft gear, perform the following procedures:

a. Remove the engine from the vehicle and secure it onto a suitable holding fixture.

b. Remove the camshaft from the engine.

c. Using an arbor press, press the camshaft gear from the camshaft.

d. To install the camshaft gear onto the camshaft, press the gear onto the shaft until a thrust clearance of 0.0015–0.0050 in. exists.

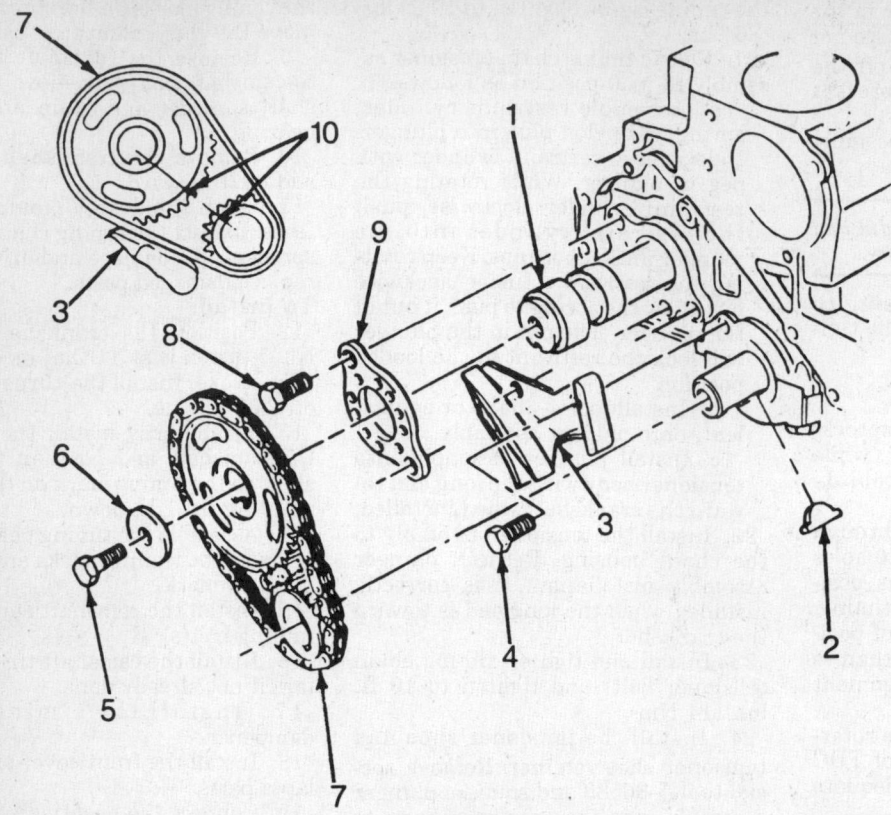

1. Camshaft
2. Key
3. Tensioner
4. Bolt
5. Bolt
6. Washer
7. Timing chain and gears
8. Bolt
9. Thrust bearing
10. Timing marks

Timing chain and timing mark alignment—1990–91 2.5L engine

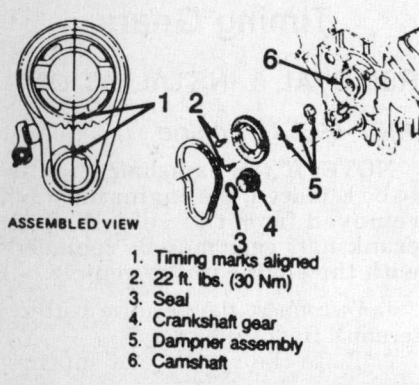

ASSEMBLED VIEW

1. Timing marks aligned
2. 22 ft. lbs. (30 Nm)
3. Seal
4. Crankshaft gear
5. Dampner assembly
6. Camshaft

Timing chain and timing mark alignment—3.0L and 3.3L engines

Aligning the timing marks—1987–89 2.5L engine

Timing Belt Front Cover

REMOVAL & INSTALLATION

2.0L Engine

1. Disconnect negative battery cable.
2. Remove tensioner and bolt.
3. Remove serpentine belt.
4. Unsnap upper and lower cover.
5. The installation is the reverse of the removal procedure.

OIL SEAL REPLACEMENT

1. Disconnect the negative battery cable.

6. If removing the crankshaft gear, perform the following procedures:
   a. Remove the front cover-to-engine bolts.
   b. Remove the retaining bolt and slide the crankshaft gear forward off the crankshaft.
7. Clean the gasket mounting surfaces. Inspect the parts for damage and/or wear and replace damaged parts.
8. The installation is the reverse of the removal procedure. Make sure the timing marks are aligned mark-to-mark when installing.

2. Remove the timing belt sprockets and the inner cover. Remove the crankshaft key and thrust washer.
3. Using a small prybar, pry out the old oil seal.

NOTE: Use care to avoid damage to seal bore and crankshaft.

4. Thoroughly clean and dry the oil seal mounting surface.
5. Use the appropriate installation tool and drive the oil seal into the front cover.
6. The installation is the reverse of the removal procedure.
7. Connect the negative battery cable and check for leaks.

Timing Belt and Tensioner

ADJUSTMENT

2.0L Engine

1987–88

1. Disconnect the negative battery cable. Remove the timing belt cover.
2. Adjust the timing belt using tool J–26486–A gauge and J–33039 to adjust the water pump. With the gauge installed, increase the tension to with-

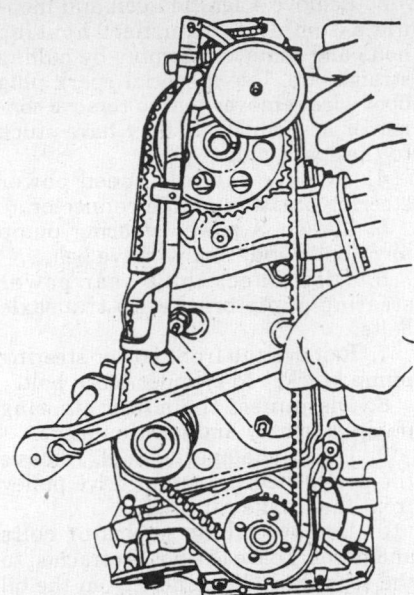

Adjusting the timing belt tension—2.0L engine

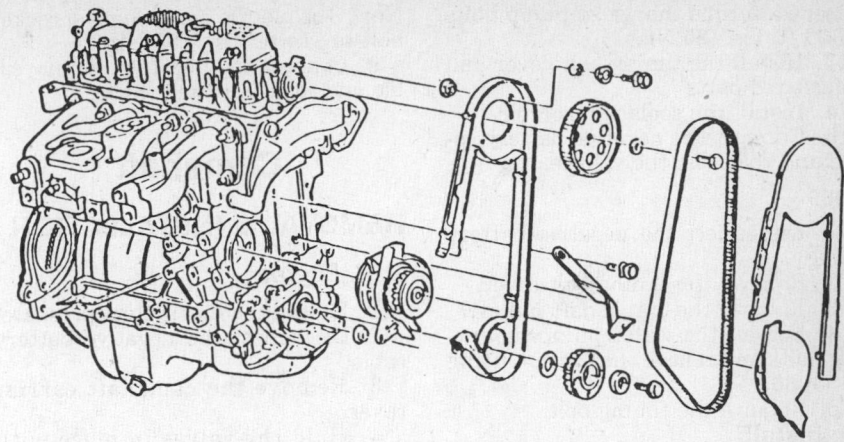

Timing belt and related parts—1987–88 2.0L engine

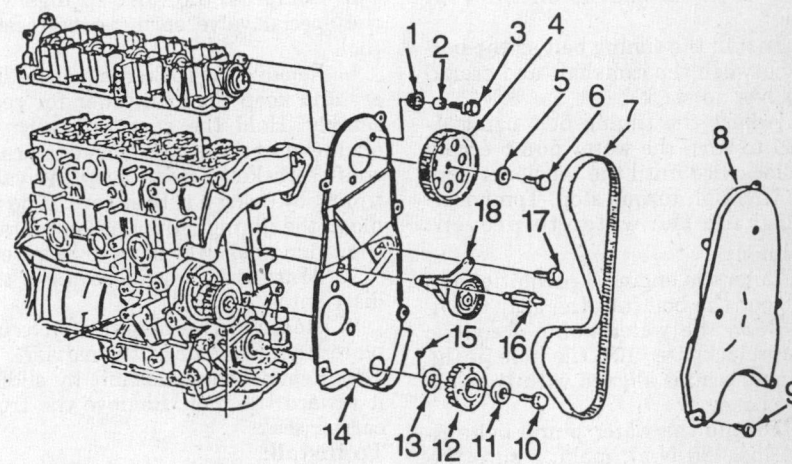

1. Grommet	7. Timing belt	13. Washer
2. Sleeve	8. Front cover	14. Rear cover
3. Bolt	9. Bolt	15. Key
4. Camshaft sprocket	10. Bolt	16. Stud
5. Washer	11. Washer	17. Bolt
6. Bolt	12. Crankshaft sprocket	18. Tensioner

Timing belt and related parts—1989 2.0L engine

in the band on the gauge will ensure an initial over-tensioning.

3. Crank the engine without starting it about 10 revolutions; a tension loss may occur.

4. Recheck the tension with the gauge. If a tension increase is needed, remove the gauge and adjust the water pump. Repeat until the tension is within specification.

NOTE: Do not increase tension with the gauge installed or the resulting tension will be inaccurate.

5. After the proper tension has been reached, torque the water pump bolts to 19 ft. lbs. (25 Nm).

6. Install the timing belt cover and all related parts.

7. Connect the negative battery cable and road test the vehicle.

1989

1. Disconnect the negative battery cable. Remove the timing belt cover.

2. Make sure the portion of the belt between the camshaft and cranksahft has no slack.

3. Adjust the timing belt using J–33039 to turn the water pump eccentric clockwise until the tensioner contacts the high torque stop. Temporarily tighten the water to prevent movement.

4. Turn the engine 2 revolutions.

5. Turn the water pump eccentric counterclockwise until the hole in the tensioner arm is aligned with the hole in the base.

6. Torque the water pump bolts to 19 ft. lbs. (25 Nm), making sure the tensioner hole remains aligned.

7. Install the timing belt cover and all related parts.

8. Connect the negative battery cable and road test the vehicle.

REMOVAL & INSTALLATION

2.0L Engine

1987–88

1. Disconnect the negative battery cable.

2. Remove the timing belt cover.

3. Remove the crankshaft pulley.

4. Remove the coolant reservoir.

5. Loosen the water pump mounting bolts and remove the timing belt.

To install:

6. Position the camshaft so the mark on its sprocket aligns with the mark on the rear timing belt cover.

7. Position the crankshaft so the

mark on the pulley aligns with 10°BTDC on the timing scale.

8. Install the timing belt.

9. Adjust the timing belt using tool J–26486–A gauge and J–33039 to adjust the water pump. Increase the tension—with the gauge installed—to within the band on the gauge will ensure an initial over-tensioning.

10. Crank the engine without starting it about 10 revolutions; a substantial tension loss should occur.

11. Recheck the tension with the gauge. If a tension increase is needed, remove the gauge and adjust the water pump. Repeat until the tension is within specification.

NOTE: Do not increase tension with the gauge installed or the resulting tension will be inaccurate.

12. After the proper tension has been

reached, torque the water pump bolts to 19 ft. lbs. (25 Nm).

13. Install the timing belt cover and all related parts.

14. Install the coolant reservoir.

15. Connect the negative battery cable and road test the vehicle.

1989

1. Disconnect the negative battery cable.

2. Remove the timing belt cover.

3. Remove the crankshaft pulley.

4. Loosen the water pump mounting bolts and relieve the tension using J-33039.

5. Remove the timing belt.

To install:

6. Position the camshaft and crankshaft so the marks on their sprockets aligns with the marks on the rear cover.

7. Install the timing belt so the portion between the camshaft and crankshaft has no slack.

8. Adjust the timing belt using J-33039 to turn the water pump eccentric clockwise until the tensioner contacts the high torque stop. Temporarily tighten the water to prevent movement.

9. Turn the engine 2 revolutions to fully seat the belt into the gear teeth.

10. Turn the water pump eccentric counterclockwise until the hole in the tensioner arm is aligned with the hole in the base.

11. Torque the water pump bolts to 19 ft. lbs. (25 Nm), making sure the tensioner hole remains aligned as in Step 10.

12. Install the timing belt cover and all related parts.

13. Install the crankshaft pulley.

14. Install the timing belt cover and all related parts.

15. Connect the negative battery cable and road test the vehicle.

Timing Sprockets

REMOVAL & INSTALLATION

1. Disconnect the negative battery cable.

2. If removing the camshaft sprocket, remove the camshaft carrier cover.

3. Remove the timing belt cover.

4. Position the engine so the timing marks are aligned for belt installation.

5. Remove the timing belt.

6. If removing the camshaft sprocket, hold the camshaft with an open-end wrench.

7. Remove the camshaft or crankshaft sprocket retaining bolt, washer and the sprocket.

8. The installation is the reverse of the removal procedure. Torque the camshaft sprocket bolt to 34 ft. lbs. (45

Nm). Torque the crankshaft sprocket bolt to 114 ft. lbs. (155 Nm).

9. Connect the negative battery cable and road test the vehicle.

Camshaft

REMOVAL & INSTALLATION

2.0L Engine

1. Relieve the fuel system pressure.

2. Disconnect the negative battery cable.

3. Remove the camshaft carrier cover.

4. Hold the valves in place with compressed air, using air adapters in the spark plug holes.

5. Compress the valve springs with the special valve spring compressing tool.

6. Remove the rocker arms and lifters and keep them in order for reassembly. Hold the camshaft with an open-end wrench and remove the camshaft sprocket. Try to keep the valve timing by using a rubber cord, if possible. If the timing cannot be kept intact, the timing belt will have to be reset.

7. Matchmark and remove the distributor.

8. Remove the camshaft thrust plate from the rear of the carrier.

9. Remove the camshaft by sliding it toward the rear. Remove the front carrier seal.

To install:

10. Install a new carrier seal.

11. Thoroughly lubricate the camshaft and journals with clean oil and install the camshaft.

12. Install the rear thrust plate and torque the bolts to 70 inch lbs. (8 Nm).

13. Install camshaft sprocket, timing belt and cover.

14. Install the distributor.

15. Hold the valves in place with compressed air as in Step 4, compress the valve springs and install the lifters and rocker arms.

16. Apply sealer to the camshaft carrier cover and install.

17. Connect the negative battery cable and road test the vehicle.

2.3L Engine

INTAKE CAMSHAFT

NOTE: Any time the camshaft housing to cylinder head bolts are loosened or removed, the camshaft housing to cylinder head gasket must be replaced.

1. Relieve the fuel system pressure. Disconnect the negative battery cable.

2. Label and disconnect the ignition coil and module assembly electrical connections.

3. Remove 4 ignition coil and module assembly to camshaft housing bolts and remove assembly by pulling straight up. Use a special spark plug boot wire remover tool to remove connector assemblies, if they have stuck to the spark plugs.

4. Remove the idle speed power steering pressure switch connector.

5. Loosen 3 power steering pump pivot bolts and remove drive belt.

6. Disconnect the 2 rear power steering pump bracket to transaxle bolts.

7. Remove the front power steering pump bracket to cylinder block bolt.

8. Disconnect the power steering pump assembly and position aside.

9. Using the special tool, remove the power steering pump drive pulley from the intake camshaft.

10. Remove oil/air separator bolts and hoses. Leave the hoses attached to the separator, disconnect from the oil fill, chain housing and intake manifold. Remove as an assembly.

11. Remove vacuum line from fuel pressure regulator and disconnect the fuel injector harness connector.

12. Disconnect fuel line retaining clamp from bracket on top of intake camshaft housing.

13. Remove fuel rail to camshaft housing retaining bolts.

14. Remove the fuel rail from the cylinder head. Cover injector openings in cylinder head and cover injector nozzles. Leave fuel lines attached and position fuel rail aside.

15. Disconnect the timing chain and housing but do not remove from the engine.

16. Remove intake camshaft housing cover to camshaft housing retaining bolts.

17. Remove the intake camshaft housing to cylinder head retaining bolts. Use the reverse of the tightening sequence when loosening camshaft housing to cylinder head retaining bolts. Leave 2 bolts loosely in place to hold the camshaft housing while separating camshaft cover from housing.

18. Push the cover off the housing by threading 4 of the housing to head retaining bolts into the tapped holes in the cam housing cover. Tighten the bolts in evenly so the cover does not bind on the dowel pins.

19. Remove the 2 loosely installed camshaft housing to head bolts and remove the cover. Discard the gaskets.

20. Note the position of the chain sprocket dowel pin for reassembly. Remove the camshaft carefully; do not damage the camshaft oil seal.

21. Remove intake camshaft oil seal from camshaft and discard seal. This seal must be replaced any time the housing and cover are separated.

22. Remove the camshaft carrier

from the cylinder head and remove the gasket.

To install:

23. Thoroughly clean the mating surfaces of the camshaft carrier and the cylinder head, bolts and bolt holes. Install a new gasket and place the housing on the head. Install 1 bolt loosely to hold in place.

24. Install the lifters into their bores. If the camshaft is being replaced, the lifters must also be replaced. Lubricate camshaft lobes, journals and lifters with camshaft and lifter prelube. The camshaft lobes and journals must be adequately lubricated or engine damage could occur upon start up.

25. Install the camshaft in the same position as when removed. The timing chain sprocket dowel pin should be straight up and align with the centerline of the lifter bores.

26. Install new camshaft housing to camshaft housing cover seals into cover; do not use sealer. Make sure the correct color seal is placed in each groove. Install the cover to the housing.

27. Apply thread locking compound to the camshaft housing and cover retaining bolt threads.

28. Install bolts and torque to 11 ft. lbs. Rotate the bolts, except the 2 rear bolts that hold the fuel pipe to the camshaft housing, an additional 75 degrees, in sequence. Rotate the excepted bolts an additional 25 degrees.

29. Install timing chain housing and timing chain.

30. Uncover fuel injectors and install new fuel injector ring seals lubricated with oil. Install the fuel rail.

31. Install the fuel line retaining clamp and retainer to bracket on top of the intake camshaft housing.

32. Connect the vacuum line to the fuel pressure regulator.

33. Connect the fuel injectors harness connector.

34. Install the oil/air separator assembly.

35. Lubricate the inner sealing surface of the intake camshaft seal with oil and install the seal to the housing.

36. Install the power steering pump pulley onto the intake camshaft.

37. Install the power steering pump assembly and drive belt.

38. Connect the idle speed power steering pressure switch connector.

39. Clean any loose lubricant that is present on the ignition coil and module assembly to camshaft housing bolts. Apply Loctite® 592 or equivalent, onto the ignition coil and module assembly to camshaft housing bolts. Install the bolts and torque to 13 ft. lbs. (18 Nm).

40. Connect the electrical connectors to ignition coil and module assembly.

41. Connect the negative battery cable and road test the vehicle. Check for leaks.

EXHAUST CAMSHAFT

NOTE: Any time the camshaft housing to cylinder head bolts are loosened or removed the camshaft housing to cylinder head gasket must be replaced.

1. Relieve the fuel system pressure. Disconnect the negative battery cable.

2. Label and disconnect the ignition coil and module assembly electrical connections.

3. Remove 4 ignition coil and module assembly to camshaft housing bolts and remove assembly by pulling straight up. Use a special tool to remove connector assemblies if they have stuck to the spark plugs.

4. Remove the idle speed power steering pressure switch connector.

5. Remove the transaxle fluid level indicator tube assembly from exhaust camshaft cover and position aside.

6. Remove exhaust camshaft cover and gasket.

7. Disconnect the timing chain and housing but do not remove from the engine.

8. Remove exhaust camshaft housing to cylinder head bolts. Use the reverse of the tightening procedure when loosening camshaft housing while separating camshaft cover from housing.

9. Push the cover off the housing by threading 4 of the housing to head re-taining bolts into the tapped holes in the camshaft cover. Tighten the bolts in evenly so the cover does not bind on the dowel pins.

10. Remove the 2 loosely installed camshaft housing to cylinder head bolts and remove cover, discard gaskets.

11. Loosely reinstall 1 camshaft housing to cylinder head bolt to retain the housing during camshaft and lifter removal.

12. Note the position of the chain sprocket dowel pin for reassembly. Remove camshaft being careful not to damage the camshaft or journals.

13. Remove the camshaft carrier from the cylinder head and remove the gasket.

To install:

14. Thoroughly clean the mating surfaces of the camshaft carrier and the cylinder head, bolts and bolt holes. Install a new gasket and place the housing on the head. Install 1 bolt loosely to hold in place.

15. Install the lifters into their bores. If the camshaft is being replaced, the lifters must also be replaced. Lubricate camshaft lobes, journals and lifters with camshaft and lifter prelube. The camshaft lobes and journals must be adequately lubricated or engine damage could occur upon start up.

16. Install camshaft in same position as when removed. The timing chain sprocket dowel pin should be straight up and align with the centerline of the lifter bores.

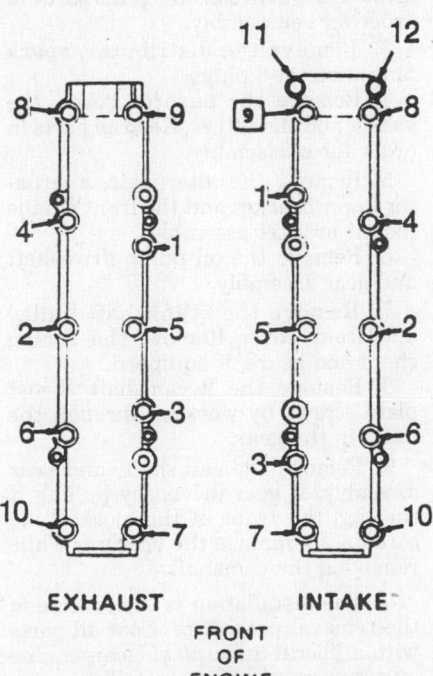

EXHAUST   INTAKE

FRONT
OF
ENGINE

Camshaft housing bolt torque sequence 2.3L engine

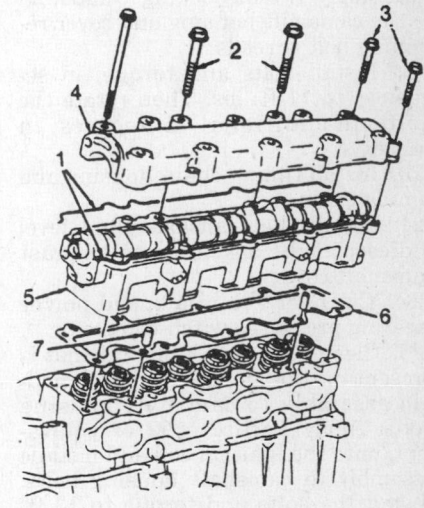

1. Housing cover seals
2. Cylinder head bolts
3. Housing cover bolts
4. Camshaft cover
5. Intake camshaft housing
6. Cylinder head gasket
7. Dowel pins

Camshaft housing assembly components 2.3L engine

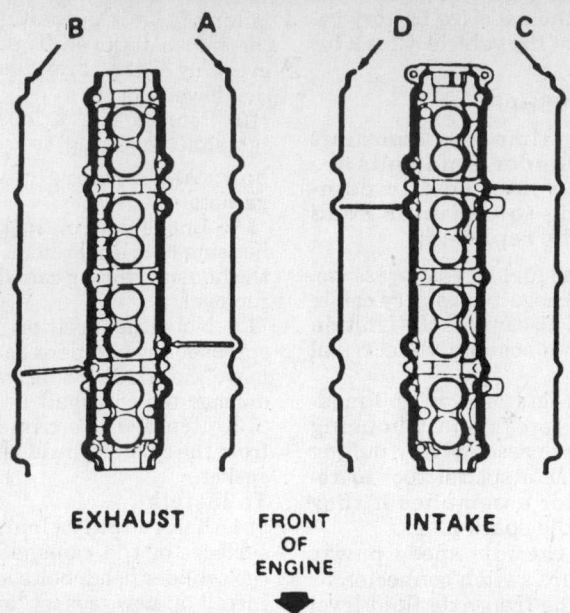

EXHAUST   FRONT OF ENGINE   INTAKE

A. Seal—inner (exhaust—red)
B. Seal—outer (exhaust—red)
C. Seal—outer (intake—blue)
D. Seal—inner (intake—blue)

Camshaft housing cover seal identification—2.3L engine

17. Install new camshaft housing to camshaft housing cover seals into cover; do not use sealer. Make sure the correct color seal is placed in each groove. Install the cover to the housing.

18. Apply thread locking compound to the camshaft housing and cover retaining bolt threads.

19. Install bolts and torque, in sequence, to 11 ft. lbs. Then rotate the bolts an additional 75 degrees, in sequence.

20. Install timing chain housing and timing chain.

21. Install the transaxle fluid level indicator tube assembly to exhaust camshaft cover.

22. Connect the idle speed power steering pressure switch connector.

23. Clean any loose lubricant that is present on the ignition coil and module assembly to camshaft housing bolts. Apply Loctite® 592 or equivalent, onto the ignition coil and module assembly to camshaft housing bolts. Install the bolts and torque to 13 ft. lbs. (18 Nm).

24. Connect the electrical connectors to ignition coil and module assembly.

25. Connect the negative battery cable and road test the vehicle. Check for leaks.

2.5L Engine

1. Disconnect the negative battery cable. Relieve the fuel system pressure

before disconnecting any fuel lines. Remove the engine from the vehicle and secure to a suitable holding fixture.

2. Remove the valve cover, rocker arms and pushrods. Keep all parts in order for reassembly.

3. Remove the distributor, spark plug wires and plugs.

4. Remove the pushrod cover, the gasket and the lifters. Keep all parts in order for reassembly.

5. Remove the alternator, alternator lower bracket and the front engine mount bracket assembly.

6. Remove the oil pump driveshaft and gear assembly.

7. Remove the crankshaft pulley and front cover Remove the timing chain and gears, if equipped.

8. Remove the 2 camshaft thrust plate screws by working through the holes in the gear.

9. Remove the camshaft, and gear assembly, if gear driven by pulling it through the front of the block. Take care not to damage the bearings while removing the camshaft.

10. The installation is the reverse of the removal procedure. Coat all parts with a liberal amount of clean engine oil supplement before installing.

11. Fill all fluids to their proper levels.

12. Connect the negative battery cable and check for leaks.

3.0L and 3.3L Engines

1. Disconnect the negative battery cable. Relieve the fuel system pressure before disconnecting any fuel lines. Remove the engine from the vehicle and secure to a suitable holding fixture.

2. Remove the intake manifold.

3. Remove the valve covers, rocker arm assemblies, pushrods and lifters. Keep all parts in order for reassembly.

4. Remove the crankshaft balancer from the crankshaft.

5. Remove the front cover.

6. Rotate the crankshaft to align the timing marks on the timing sprockets. Remove the camshaft sprocket and the timing chain.

7. Remove the camshaft retainer bolts and slide the camshaft forward out of the engine. Take care not to damage the bearings while removing the camshaft.

8. The installation is the reverse of the removal procedure. Coat all parts with a liberal amount of clean engine oil supplement before installing.

9. Fill all fluids to their proper levels.

10. Connect the negative battery cable and check for leaks.

Crankshaft Force Balancer

REMOVAL & INSTALLATION

2.5L Engine

1. Disconnect the negative battery cable.

2. Raise the vehicle and support safely.

3. Remove the oil pan.

4. Remove the balancer retaining bolts and remove the balancer assembly from the engine.

To install:

5. Turn the crankshaft to TDC, No. 1 cylinder on compression stroke TDC (crank counterweights at BDC).

6. Measure the distance from the engine block to the first cut of the double notch on the reluctor ring. This dimension should be $1^{11}/_{16}$ in. (42.8mm).

7. Mount the balancer with the counterweights parallel, at BDC and pointing away from the crankshaft. When installing the assembly, the end of the housing not equipped with dowel pins must remain in contact with the block or gear engagement could be lost.

8. Install the retaining bolts and tighten as follows:

Short bolts—9 ft. lbs. (12 Nm) plus 75 degree turn

Long bolts—9 ft. lbs. (12 Nm) plus 90 degree turn

9. Install the oil pan and retaining bolts.
10. Fill all fluids to their proper levels.
11. Connect the negative battery cable and check for leaks.

Piston and Connecting Rod

Positioning

NOTCH TOWARD FRONT OF ENGINE

Piston and connecting rod assembly—2.0L and 2.5L engines

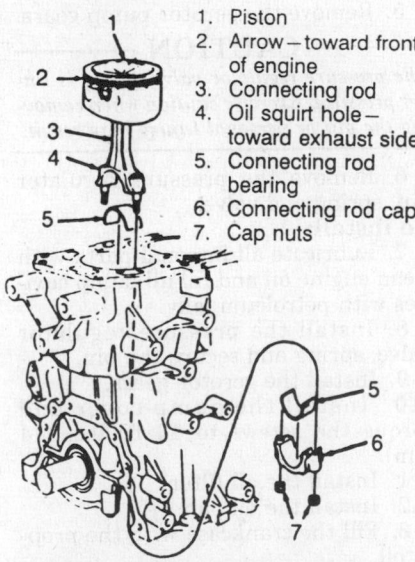

1. Piston
2. Arrow—toward front of engine
3. Connecting rod
4. Oil squirt hole—toward exhaust side
5. Connecting rod bearing
6. Connecting rod cap
7. Cap nuts

Piston and connecting rod assembly—2.3L engine

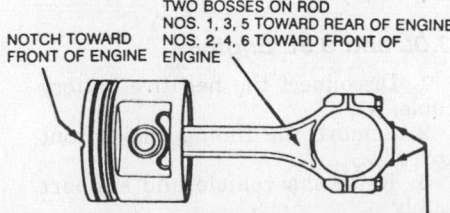

NOTCH TOWARD FRONT OF ENGINE

TWO BOSSES ON ROD
NOS. 1, 3, 5 TOWARD REAR OF ENGINE
NOS. 2, 4, 6 TOWARD FRONT OF ENGINE

CHAMFERED CORNERS ON ROD CAP
NOS. 1, 3, 5 TOWARD FRONT OF ENGINE
NOS. 2, 4, 6 TOWARD REAR OF ENGINE

Piston and connecting rod assembly—3.0L engine

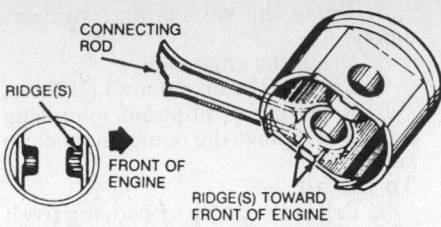

CONNECTING ROD
RIDGE(S)
FRONT OF ENGINE
CONNECTING ROD
RIDGE(S) TOWARD FRONT OF ENGINE

Piston and connecting rod assembly—3.3L engine

ENGINE LUBRICATION

Oil Pan

REMOVAL & INSTALLATION

2.0L Engine

1. Disconnect the negative battery cable.
2. Raise the vehicle and support safely. Remove the right front wheel assembly and the splash shield.
3. Drain the engine oil.
4. Remove the exhaust pipe from the turbocharger.
5. Remove the flywheel inspection cover.
6. Remove the oil pan retaining bolts and remove the oil pan, scraper and gasket.
7. The installation is the reverse of the removal procedure. Use a new gasket and apply sealant at the 4 engine block seams. Use thread locking compound on the bolt threads and torque to 4 ft. lbs. (6 Nm), starting from the middle and working outward.
8. Fill the crankcase with the proper oil.
9. Connect the negative battery cable and check for leaks.

2.3L Engine

1. Disconnect the negative battery cable. Raise the vehicle and support safely.
2. Remove the flywheel inspection cover.
3. Remove the splash shield-to-suspension support bolt. Remove the exhaust manifold brace, if equipped.
4. Remove the radiator outlet pipe-to-oil pan bolt.
5. Remove the transaxle-to-oil pan nut and stud using a 7mm socket.
6. Gently pry the spacer out from between oil pan and transaxle.
7. Remove the oil pan bolts. Rotate the crankshaft, if necessary, and remove the oil pan and gasket from the engine.

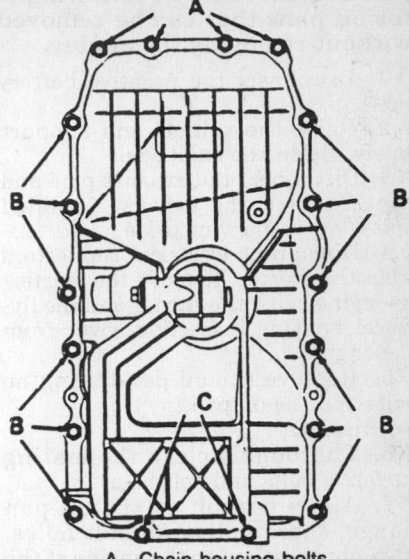

A. Chain housing bolts
B. Block bolts
C. Carrier seal bolts

Oil pan mounting bolts—2.3L engine

8. Inspect the silicone strips across the top of the aluminum carrier at the oil pan-cylinder block-seal housing 3-way joint. If damaged, these strips must be repaired with silicone sealer. Use only enough sealer to restore the strips to their original dimension; too much sealer could cause leakage.
To install:
9. Thoroughly clean and dry the mating surfaces, bolts and bolt holes. Install the oil pan with a new gasket; do not uses sealer on the gasket. Loosely install the pan bolts.
10. Place the spacer in its approximate installed position but allow clearance to tighten the pan bolt above it.
11. Torque the pan to block bolts to 17 ft. lbs. (24 Nm) and the remaining bolts to 106 inch lbs. (12 Nm).
12. Install the spacer and stud.
13. Install the oil pan transaxle nut and bolt.
14. Install the slash shield to suspension support.
15. Install the radiator outlet pipe bolt.
16. Install the exhaust manifold brace, if removed.
17. Install the flywhel inspection cover.
18. Fill the crankcase with the proper oil.
19. Connect the negative battery cable and check for leaks.

2.5L Engine

NOTE: On 1987 vehicles, it may be necessary to remove the engine, when equipped with a manual transaxle, before the oil pan can be removed. The following is for oil pans that can be removed without removing the engine.

1. Disconnect the negative battery cable.
2. Raise the vehicle and support safely. Drain the engine oil.
3. Disconnect the exhaust pipe and hangers from the exhaust manifold and allow it to swing aside.
4. Disconnect electrical connectors from the starter. Remove the starter-to-engine bolts, the starter and the flywheel housing inspection cover from the engine.
5. Remove the oil pan-to-engine bolts and the oil pan.

To install:

6. Thoroughly clean the mating surfaces, bolts and bolt holes.
7. Apply sealant to the oil pan flange, surrounding all bolt holes. Also, apply sealant to the engine at the front and rear seams.
8. Install the oil pan and torque the bolts to 20 ft. lbs. (27 Nm) for 1987–88 vehicles and 89 inch lbs. (10 Nm) for 1989–91 vehicles.
9. Install the flywheel housing cover and exhaust pipe.
10. Fill the crankcase with the proper oil.
11. Connect the negative battery cable and check for leaks.

3.0L and 3.3L Engines

1. Disconnect the negative battery cable.
2. Raise the vehicle and support safely.
3. Drain the engine oil and remove the oil filter.
4. Remove the flywheel cover and the starter.
5. Remove the oil pan, tensioner spring and formed rubber gasket.
6. The installation is the reverse of the removal procedure. Torque the oil pan-to-engine bolts to 88 inch lbs. for the 3.0L engine and 124 inch lbs. for the 3.3L engine.
7. Fill the crankcase with the proper oil.
8. Connect the negative battery cable and check for leaks.

Oil Pump

REMOVAL & INSTALLATION

2.0L Engine

1. Disconnect negative battery cable.
2. Remove the timing belt and crankshaft sprocket.
3. Remove the rear timing belt cover.
4. Disconnect oil pressure sending unit connector.

5. Raise the vehicle and support safely.
6. Drain the engine oil.
7. Remove the oil pan and oil filter.
8. Remove the oil pump mounting bolts and remove the pump and pickup tube.

To install:

9. Prime the pump by pouring fresh oil into the pump intake and turning the driveshaft until oil comes out the pressure port. Repeat a few times until no air bubbles are present.
10. The installation is the reverse of the removal procedure. Use a new gasket and seal and torque the oil pump bolts to 5 ft. lbs. (7 Nm). Use a new ring for the pickup tube.
11. Fill the crankcase with the proper oil.
12. Connect the negative battery cable, check the oil pressure and check for leaks.

2.3L Engine

1. Disconnect the negative battery cable.
2. Raise the vehicle and support safely.
3. Drain the engine oil and remove the oil pan.
4. Remove the oil pump retaining bolts and nut.

1. Oil pump assembly
2. Gear cover
3. Bolts
4. Screen
5. Bolts

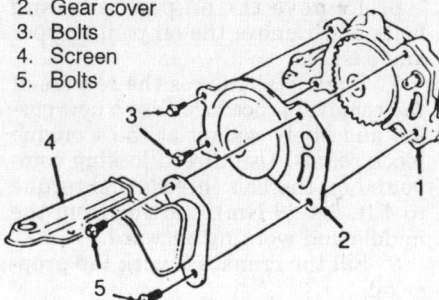

Oil pump assembly—1989–91 2.3L engine

5. Remove the oil pump assembly, shims if equipped, and screen.

To install:

6. With the oil pump assembly off the engine, remove 3 retaining bolts and separate the driven gear cover and screen assembly from the oil pump.
7. Install the oil pump on the block using the original shims, if equipped. Tighten the bolts to 33 ft. lbs. (45 Nm).
8. Mount a dial indicator assembly to measure backlash between oil pump to drive gear.
9. Record oil pump drive to driven gear backlash. Proper backlash is 0.010–0.018 in. When measuring, do not allow the crankshaft to move.
10. If equipped with shims, remove

shims to decrease clearance and add shims to increase clearance. If no shims were present, replace the assembly if proper backlash cannot be obtained.
11. When the proper clearance is reached, rotate crankshaft ½ turn and recheck clearance.
12. Remove oil pump from block, fill the cavity with petroleum jelly and reinstall driven gear cover and screen assembly to pump. Tighten the bolts to 106 inch lbs. (13 Nm).
13. Reinstall the pump assembly to the block. Torque oil pump-to-block bolts 33 ft. lbs. (45 Nm).
14. Install the oil pan.
15. Fill the crankcase with the proper oil.
16. Connect the negative battery cable, check the oil pressure and check for leaks.

2.5L Engine

1. Disconnect the negative battery cable.
2. Drain the engine oil and remove the oil pan.
3. Remove the oil filter.
4. Remove the oil pump cover assembly.
5. Remove the gerotor pump gears.

— CAUTION —

The pressure regulator valve spring is under pressure. Exercise caution when removing the pin or personal injury may result.

6. Remove the pressure regulator pin, spring and valve.

To install:

7. Lubricate all internal parts with clean engine oil and fill all pump cavities with petroleum jelly.
8. Install the pressure regulator valve, spring and secure the pin.
9. Install the gerotor gears.
10. Install the pump cover and torque the screws to 10 ft. lbs. (14 Nm).
11. Install the oil filter.
12. Install the oil pan.
13. Fill the crankcase with the proper oil.
14. Connect the negative battery cable, check the oil pressure and check for leaks.

3.0L and 3.3L Engines

1. Disconnect the negative battery cable.
2. Remove the timing chain front cover.
3. Raise the vehicle and support safely.
4. Drain the engine oil. Lower the vehicle.
5. Remove the oil filter adapter, the pressure regulator valve and the valve spring.

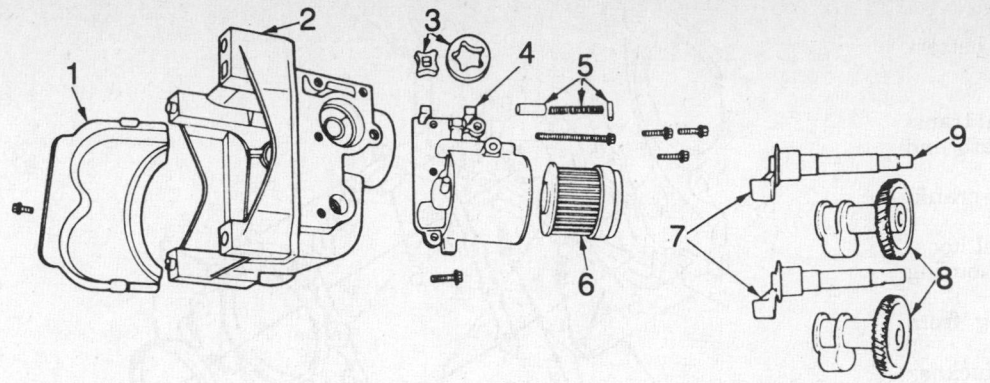

1. Splash guard
2. Balance counterweight assembly
3. Gerotor oil pump assembly
4. Oil pump cover
5. Pressure regulator valve
6. Oil filter
7. Counterweighted balance shaft
8. Balance shaft gear
9. Gerotor oil pump drive

Oil pump assembly and related parts—2.5L engine

6. Remove the oil pump cover-to-oil pump screws and remove the cover.

7. Remove the oil pump gears.

To install:

8. Lubricate the oil pump gears with clean engine oil.

9. Pack the pump cavity with petroleum jelly.

10. Install the oil pump cover screws using a new gasket and torque to 97 inch lbs. (11 Nm).

11. Install the pressure regulator spring and valve.

12. Install the oil filter adaptor using a new gasket. Torque the oil filter adapter-to-engine bolts to 30 ft. lbs. (41 Nm) for the 3.0L engine and 24 ft. lbs. (33 Nm) for the 3.3L engine.

13. Install the timing chain front cover to the engine.

14. Fill the crankcase with clean engine oil.

15. Connect the negative battery cable, check the oil pressure and check for leaks.

CHECKING

2.0L Engine

1. Inspect all components carefully for physical damage of any type and replace worn parts.

2. Check the gear pocket depth. The specification is 0.395–0.397 in. (10.03–10.08mm).

3. Check the gear pocket diameter. The specification is 3.230–3.235 in. (82.02–82.15mm).

4. Check the diameter of the gears. The specifications are 0.014–0.018 in. (0.35–0.45mm) for the drive gear and 0.004–0.007 in. (0.11–0.19mm) for the idler gear.

5. Check the side clearance. The specifications are 2.317–2.319 in. (58.85–58.90mm) for the drive gear and 3.225–3.227 in. (81.91–81.96mm) for the idler gear.

6. Check the end clearance below the pump housing. The specification is 0.001–0.004 in. (0.03–0.10mm).

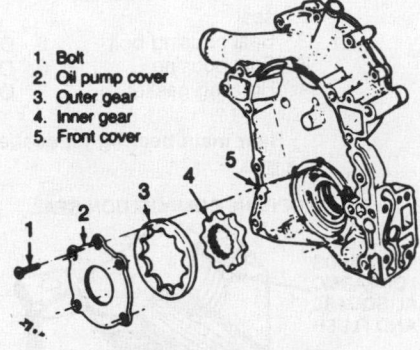

1. Bolt
2. Oil pump cover
3. Outer gear
4. Inner gear
5. Front cover

V6 oil pump assembly

2.3L Engine

1. Inspect all components carefully for physical damage of any type and replace worn parts.

2. Check the gerotor cavity depth. The specification for 1987–88 is 0.689–0.691 in. (17.50–17.55mm) The specification for 1989–91 is 0.674–0.676 in. (17.11–17.16mm).

3. Check the gerotor cavity diameter. The specification for 1987–88 is 2.010–2.012 in. (51.054–51.104mm) The specification for 1989–91 is 2.127–2.129 in. (53.95–54.00mm).

4. Check the inner gerotor tip clearance. The maximum clearance is 0.006 in. (15mm).

5. Check the outer gerotor diameter clearance. The specification is 0.010–0.014 in. (0.254–0.354mm).

2.5L Engine

1. Inspect all components carefully for physical damage of any type and replace worn parts.

2. Check the gerotor cavity depth. The specification for 1987–88 is 0.995–0.998 in. (25.27–25.35mm) The specification for 1989–91 is 0.514–0.516 in. (13.05–13.10mm).

3. Check the gear lash. The specification is 0.009–0.015 in. (0.23–0.38mm).

4. Check the clearance of both gears. The maximum clearance is 0.004 in. (0./10mm).

3.0L and 3.3L Engines

1. Inspect all components carefully for physical damage of any type and replace worn parts.

2. Check the gear pocket depth. The specification is 0.461–0.463 in. (11.71–11.75mm).

3. Check the gear pocket diameter. The specification is 3.508–3.512 in. (89.10–89.20mm).

4. Check the inner gear tip clearance. The maximum clearance is 0.006 in. (0.152mm).

5. Check the outer gear diameter clearance. The specification is 0.008–0.015 in. (0.025–0.089mm).

Rear Main Bearing Oil Seal

REMOVAL & INSTALLATION

2.0L and 2.5L Engines

1. Disconnect the negative battery cable.

2. Remove the transaxle.

3. If equipped with a manual transaxle, remove the pressure plate and clutch disc.

4. Remove the flywheel-to-crankshaft bolts and the flywheel.

5. Using a medium prybar, pry out the old seal; be careful not to scratch the crankshaft surface.

6. Clean the block and crankshaft-to-seal mating surfaces.

7. Using the appropriate seal installation tool, install the new rear seal into the block. Lubricate the outside of the seal to aid installation and press the seal in evenly with the tool.

8. The installation is the reverse of the removal procedure.

9. Connect the negative battery cable and check for leaks.

2.3L Engine

1. Disconnect the negative battery cable.
2. Remove the transaxle.
3. If equipped with a manual transaxle, remove the pressure plate and clutch disc.
4. Remove the flywheel-to-crankshaft bolts and the flywheel.
5. Remove the oil pan-to-seal housing bolts and the block-to-seal housing bolts.
6. Remove the seal housing from the engine.
7. Place 2 blocks of equal thicknes on a flat surface and position the seal housing on the 2 blocks. Remove the seal from the housing.
8. The installation is the reverse of the removal procedure. Use new gaskets when installing.
9. Connect the negative battery cable and for leaks.

3.0L and 3.3L Engines

NOTE: If replacing the entire 2-piece seal, the engine must be removed in order to remove the crankshaft. Use the following if only replacing the lower half of the seal.

1. Disconnect the negative battery cable. Raise the vehicle and support safely.
2. Drain the oil and remove the oil pan.
3. Remove the rear main bearing cap-to-engine bolts and the bearing cap from the engine.
4. Remove the old seal from the bearing cap.

To install:
5. Using a seal packing tool, insert it against one end of the seal in the cylinder block. Pack the old seal into the groove until it is packed tightly. Rrepeat the procedure on the other end of the seal.
6. Measure the amount the seal was driven up and add approximately $\frac{1}{16}$ in. Cut this length from the old seal removed from the lower bearing cap, repeat for the other side.

NOTE: When cutting the seal into short lengths, use a double edged blade and the lower bearing cap as a holding fixture.

7. Using a seal packer guide, install it onto the cylinder block.
8. Using the packing tool, work the short pieces into the guide tool and pack into the cylinder block until the tool hits the built-in stop.

NOTE: It may help to use oil on the short seal pieces when packing into the block.

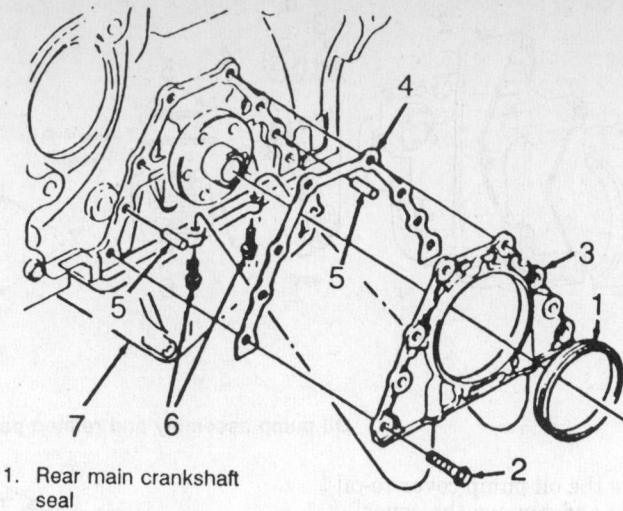

1. Rear main crankshaft seal
2. Seal housing bolt
3. Seal housing
4. Housing gasket
5. Dowel
6. Oil pan bolt
7. Oil pan

Rear main bearing oil seal and housing—2.3L engine

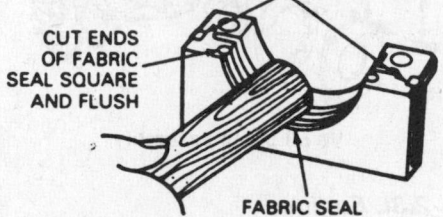

NEOPRENE COMPOSITION SEAL

CUT ENDS OF FABRIC SEAL SQUARE AND FLUSH

FABRIC SEAL

Installing rear main bearing cap oil seal on V6

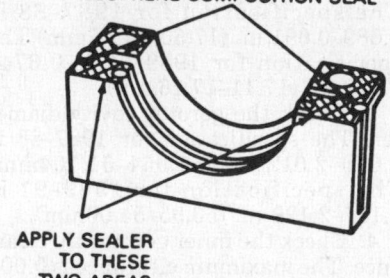

NEOPRENE COMPOSITION SEAL

APPLY SEALER TO THESE TWO AREAS

Applying sealer to bearing cap on V6

9. Repeat Steps 7 and 8 for the other side.
10. Remove the guide tool.
11. Install a new rope seal into the lower bearing cap.
12. Install the lower main bearing cap and torque the main bearing cap bolts to 100 ft. lbs. (135 Nm) for 3.0L engine and 90 ft. lbs. (122 Nm) for 3.3L engine.
13. Install the oil pan.
14. Fill the crankcase with the proper engine oil.

15. Connect the negative battery cable and check for leaks.

MANUAL TRANSAXLE

For further information on transmissions/transaxles, please refer to "Chilton's Guide to Transmission Repair".

Transaxle Assembly

REMOVAL & INSTALLATION

1. Disconnect the negative battery cable from the battery and transaxle. Remove air ducts and tubes, etc. to gain access to transaxle mounting bolts.
2. Remove the power steering pump and brackets and position aside, if necessary.
3. Attach an engine support fixture to the engine lift ring and raise the engine enough to take the pressure off the engine mounts.

NOTE: If a lifting bar is not available, a chain hoist can be used. However, during the removal procedure the vehicle must be raised and the chain hoist adjusted to keep tension on the engine/transaxle assembly.

4. Remove the left side steering column opening filler from inside the vehicle.

5. Disconnect the clutch master cylinder pushrod from the clutch pedal.

6. Disconnect the clutch slave cylinder from the transaxle support bracket and move it aside.

7. Remove the transaxle mount-to-transaxle bolts. Discard the bolts attaching the mount to the side frame. New bolts must be used upon installation.

8. Remove the transaxle mount bracket attaching bolts and nuts. Remove the upper transaxle to engine bolts.

9. Remove the transaxle vent tube and disconnect the reverse light switch.

10. Disconnect the shift cables and retaining clips from the transaxle.

11. Raise the vehicle and support safely.

12. Remove the left front wheel assembly.

13. Remove the left front inner splash shield. Drain the transaxle oil.

14. Remove the transaxle strut and bracket, if equipped.

15. Remove the flywheel housing cover bolts.

16. Disconnect the speedometer cable or sensor from the transaxle.

17. If equipped with a 2.3L engine, remove the radiator outlet pipe support bolt from transaxle.

18. Disconnect the stabilizer bar from the left suspension support and control arm.

19. Disconnect the ball joint-to-steering knuckle nut and separate the ball joint from the steering knuckle.

20. Remove the left suspension support attaching bolts, the support and control arm as an assembly.

21. Use boot protectors and disengage the halfshafts from the transaxle. Remove the left halfshaft from the transaxle.

22. Remove engine mount components and remaining transaxle mount bolts, as required.

23. Position a transmission jack under and secure to the transaxle case. Remove the remaining transaxle-to-engine mounting bolts.

24. Remove the transaxle by sliding it toward the driver's side, away from the engine. Carefully lower the jack, guiding the right or intermediate shaft out of the transaxle. Lower the engine to aid the operation, if necessary.

To install:

25. Install the transaxle into position. As the transaxle is being installed, guide the right halfshaft into place. Lower the engine to its installation position.

26. Connect the negative battery cable to the transaxle case.

27. Install engine mount components and remaining transaxle mount bolts. Install the flywheel cover(s).

28. Remove the support jack when the transaxle is securely mounted.

29. Install the left halfshaft.

30. Install the left suspension support.

31. Install the engine mount crossmember nuts, if removed.

32. Connect the stabilizer bar to the left suspension support and control arm.

33. Install the radiator outlet pipe support bolt, if equipped.

34. Connect the speedometer cable or sensor.

35. Install the transaxle bracket and strut, if equipped.

36. Install the splash shield and wheel. Lower the vehicle.

37. Connect the shift cables and install the retaining clips.

38. Install the transaxle vent tube and connect the reverse light switch connector.

39. Install the upper transaxle to engine bolts. Install the transaxle mount bracket attaching bolts and nuts.

40. Install the new transaxle mount-to-transaxle bolts.

41. Connect the clutch slave cylinder to the support bracket.

42. Connect the clutch master cylinder pushrod to the clutch pedal.

43. Install the steering column opening filler panel.

44. Remove the engine support tool.

45. Install the power steering pump and brackets, if they were removed.

46. Install air ducts, etc. that were removed.

47. Fill the transaxle with the proper fluid.

48. Connect the negative battery cable and check the transaxle for proper operation.

CABLE ADJUSTMENT

1987 Vehicles

1. Disconnect the negative battery cable.

2. Shift the transaxle into 3rd gear.

3. Remove the lock pin, located on the top of the transaxle and reinstall the tapered end down; this will lock the transaxle in 3rd gear.

4. Loosen the shift cable nuts at the transaxle levers.

5. Remove the trim plate from the console and slide the shifter boot up the shifter handle and remove the console.

6. Install a $\frac{5}{32}$ in. or No. 22 drill bit into the alignment hole at the side of the shifter assembly.

7. Install a $\frac{3}{16}$ in. drill bit into the select lever hole and the slot in the shifter plate.

8. Tighten the nuts at the levers and remove the drill bits from the

alignment holes. Remove the lockpin and reinstall with the tapered end up.

9. Road test the vehicle and check for proper shifting. When shifting, there should be a good neutral gate feel.

CLUTCH

Clutch Assembly

REMOVAL & INSTALLATION

1. Disconnect the negative battery cable. Remove the transaxle.

2. Matchmark the clutch/pressure plate cover and flywheel, if reinstalling old parts. Insert a suitable clutch plate alignment tool into the clutch disc hub.

3. Loosen the flywheel to pressure plate bolts gradually and evenly to avoid warpage.

4. Remove the pressure plate/clutch assembly from the flywheel.

5. Sand the flywheel or replace it, if scored, cracked or heat damaged.

6. Sparingly apply anti-sieze compound to the input shaft and clutch disc splines. Install a new release bearing.

To install:

7. Using a suitable clutch disc alignment tool, tighten the pressure plate bolts to center the disc.

8. Torque the pressure plate/clutch assembly mounting bolts to the flywheel gradually and evenly to 20–25 ft. lbs. (27–34 Nm).

9. Install the transaxle.

10. Connect the negative battery cable and check the clutch and reverse lights for proper operation.

Clutch Master and Slave Cylinders

REMOVAL & INSTALLATION

1. Disconnect the negative battery cable.

2. Remove the steering column opening filler from inside the vehicle.

3. Disconnect the clutch master cylinder pushrod from the clutch pedal.

4. Remove the clutch master cylinder retaining nuts at the front of the dash and disconnect the remote fluid reservoir, if equipped.

5. Remove the actuator cylinder retaining nuts at the transaxle.

6. Remove the hydraulic actuating system as an assembly.

To install:

7. Bleed the system, if necessary.

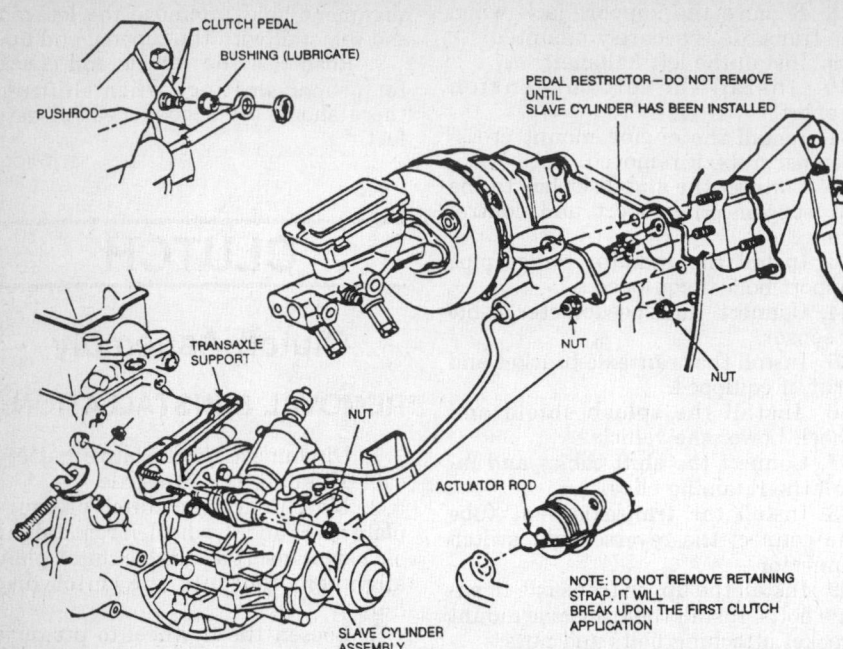

Typical layout of the hydraulic clutch actuating system

8. Install the actuator cylinder to the transaxle, aligning the pushrod into the pocket on the lever. Tighten the retaining nuts evenly to prevent damage.

NOTE: New actuators are packaged with plastic straps to retain the pushrod. Do not break the strap off; it will break upon the first clutch application.

9. Install the master cylinder. Tighten the retaining nuts evenly to prevent damage. Connect the remote fluid reservoir, if equipped. If equipped with a bleed screw and bleeding is necessary, bleed the system.

10. Remove the pushrod restrictor from the master cylinder pushrod. Lubricate the bushing on the clutch pedal. Connect the pushrod to the pedal and install the retaining clip. Make sure the cruise control switch is operating properly.

NOTE: When adjusting the cruise control switch, do not use a force of more than 20 lbs. to pull the pedal up, or damage to the master cylinder pushrod retaining ring could result.

11. Install the steering column opening filler from inside the vehicle.

12. Push the clutch pedal down a few times. This will break the plastic straps on the actuator.

13. Connect the negative battery cable and check for proper operation.

ADJUSTMENT

The hydraulic system used provides automatic clutch adjustment, therefore no adjustment to any portion of the system is required.

Hydraulic Clutch System Bleeding

With Bleed Screw

1. Make sure the reservoir is full of DOT 3 fluid and is kept topped off throuout this procedure.

2. Loosen the bleed screw, located on the actuator cylinder body next to the inlet connection.

3. When a steady stream of fluid comes out the bleeder, tighten it to 17 inch lbs.

4. Refill the fluid reservoir.

5. To check the system, start the engine and wait 10 seconds.

6. Depress the clutch pedal and shift into Reverse. If there is any gear clash, air may still be present.

Without Bleed Screw

1. Remove the actuator cylinder from the transaxle.

2. Loosen the master cylinder retaining nuts to the ends of the studs.

3. Remove the reservoir cap and diaphragm.

4. Depress the actuator cylinder pushrod about ¾ in. into its bore and hold the position.

5. Install the reservoir diaphragm and cap while holding the actuator pushrod.

6. Release the pushrod when the diaphragm and cap are properly installed.

7. With the actuator lower than the master cylinder, hold the actuator vertically with the pushrod end facing the ground.

8. Press the actuator pushrod into its bore with ½ in. strokes. Check the reservoir for bubbles. Continue until no bubbles enter the reservoir.

9. Install the master cylinder and actuator.

10. Refill the fluid reservoir.

11. To check the system, start the engine and wait 10 seconds.

12. Depress the clutch pedal and shift into reverse. If there is any gear clash, air may still be present.

AUTOMATIC TRANSAXLE

For further information on transmissions/transaxles, please refer to "Chilton's Guide to Transmission Repair".

Transaxle Assembly

REMOVAL & INSTALLATION

1. Disconnect the negative battery cable. If necessary, drain the coolant and disconnect the heater core hoses.

2. Remove the air cleaner assembly. If equipped with a 3.0L or 3.3L engine, remove the mass air flow sensor and air intake duct.

3. Disconnect the throttle valve cable from the throttle lever and the transaxle.

4. If equipped with a 2.3L engine, remove the power steering pump and bracket and position it aside.

5. Remove the transaxle dipstick and tube.

6. Install an engine support tool. Insert a ¼ × 2 in. bolt in the hole at the front right motor mount to maintain driveline alignment.

7. Remove the wiring harness-to-transaxle nut. Disconnect the wiring connectors from the speed sensor, TCC connector, neutral safety switch and reverse light switch.

8. Disconnect the shift linkage from the transaxle.

9. Remove the upper 2 transaxle-to-engine bolts and the upper left transaxle mount along with the bracket assembly.

10. Remove the rubber hose from the transaxle vent pipe. Remove the remaining upper engine-to-transaxle bolts.

11. Raise the vehicle and support safely. Remove both front wheels.

12. If equipped with a 2.3L engine, remove both lower ball joints and stabilizer shafts links.

13. Drain the transaxle fluid.

14. Remove the shift linkage bracket from the transaxle.

15. Install a halfshaft boot seal protector on the inner seals.

NOTE: Some vehicles may use a gray silicone boot on the inboard axle joint. Use boot protector tool on these boots. All other boots are made from a black thermo plastic material and do not require the use of a boot seal protector.

16. Remove both ball joint-to-control arm nuts and separate the ball joints from the control arms.

17. Remove both halfshafts and support them with a cord or wire.

18. Remove the transaxle mounting strut.

19. Remove the left stabilizer bar link pin bolt, left frame bushing clamp nuts and left frame support assembly.

20. Remove the torque converter cover. Matchmark the flexplate and torque converter for installation purposes. Remove the torque converter-to-flexplate bolts.

21. Disconnect and plug the transaxle oil cooler lines.

22. Remove the transaxle-to-engine support bracket and install the transaxle removal jack.

23. Remove the remaining transaxle-to-engine retaining bolts and the transaxle from the vehicle.

To install:

24. Securely mount the transxle on the jack.

25. Apply a small amount of grease on the torque converter hub and seat in the oil pump.

26. Position the transaxle in the vehicle and install the lower engine to transaxle bolts.

27. Install the transaxle to engine support bracket. Once the transaxle is securely held in place, remove the jack. Connect the cooler lines.

28. Install the torque converter bolts and torque to specification.

29. Install the torque converter cover.

30. Install the left frame support assembly.

31. Install the left stabilizer shaft frame busing nuts and link pin bolt.

32. Install the transaxle mounting strut.

33. Install the halfshafts. Install the ball joints.

34. Install the shift linkage bracket to the transaxle.

35. Install the wheels and lower the vehicle.

36. Install the upper transaxle to engine bolts.

37. Install the left side transaxle mount.

38. Connect the shift linkage to the transaxle.

39. Connect the wiring connectors to their switches on the transaxle.

40. Remove the 1/4 × 2 in. bolt that was placed in the hole at the front right motor mount to maintain driveline alignment. Remove an engine support tool.

41. Replace the O-ring, lubricate it and install the dipstick tube and dipstick.

42. Install the TV cable and rubber vent tube.

43. Install the air cleaner assembly and air tubes.

44. Connect the heater hoses, if disconnected.

45. Fill all fluids to their proper levels. Adjust cables as required.

46. Connect the negative battery cable and check the transaxle for proper operation and leaks.

TV Cable Adjustment

Except 2.3L Engine

1. Disconnect the negative battery cable.

2. Depress and hold down the adjustment tap at the TV cable adjuster.

3. Release the throttle lever by hand to its full travel position. On the 2.5L engine press the accelerator pedal to the full travel position.

4. The slider must move toward the lever when the lever is rotated to the full travel position or when the accelerator pedal is pressed to the full travel position on the 2.5L engine.

5. Inspect the cable for freedom of movement. The cable may appear to function properly with the engine stopped and cold. Recheck the cable after the engine is warm.

6. Road test the vehicle and check for proper shifting.

2.3L Engine

1. Disconnect the negative battery cable.

2. Rotate the TV cable adjuster body at the transaxle 90 degrees and pull the cable conduit out until the slider mechanism contacts the stop.

3. Rotate the adjuster body back to the original position.

4. Using a torque wrench, rotate the TV cable adjuster until 75 inch lbs. (8.5 Nm) is reached.

5. Road test the vehicle and check for proper shifting.

SHIFT CABLE ADJUSTMENT

1. Place the selector in the N detent.

2. Raise the locking tab on the cable adjuster.

3. Place the shift control assembly on the transaxle in the neutral position.

4. Push the lockiing tab back into position.

DRIVE AXLE

Halfshaft

REMOVAL & INSTALLATION

NOTE: On vehicles equipped with tri-pot joints, care must be exercised not to allow joints to become overextended. Overextending the joint could result in separation of internal components.

1987–88 Vehicles

1. Disconnect the negative battery cable.

2. Raise the vehicle and support it safely the under body lift points. Do not support under lower control arms. Remove wheel assemblies.

3. Remove the shaft nut and washer.

4. Remove caliper bolts and support caliper. Do not let the caliper hang by its brake hose.

5. Remove the rotor and ball joint nut.

6. Remove the stabilizer bolt from lower control arm.

7. Remove the ball joint retaining nut and separate the control arm from the steering knuckle.

8. Pry the halfshaft from the transaxle or intermediate shaft.

9. Install a halfshaft pressing tool and press halfshaft in and away from hub. The halfshaft should only be pressed in until the press fit between the halfshaft and hub is loose.

10. To remove the intermediate shaft:

    a. Remove the detonation sensor.

    b. Remove the power steering pump brace.

    c. Remove the intermediate shaft bracket bolts and remove the assembly.

To install:

11. Install the intermediate shaft, if removed. Torque the bracket bolts to 35 ft. lbs. (47 Nm).

12. Install the halfshaft seal boot protectors on all tri-pot inner joints with silicone boots.

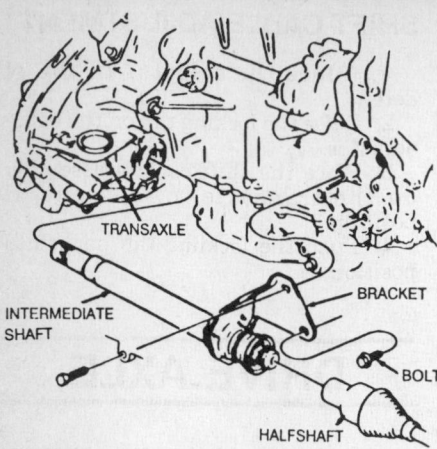

Intermediate shaft assembly—1989–91 vehicles

13. Start splines of halfshaft into transaxle and push halfshaft until it snaps into place.

14. Start the splines by inserting halfshaft into the hub assembly.

15. Install lower ball joint into steering knuckle and install the retaining nut. Install a new cotter pin.

16. Install the rotor and caliper.

17. Install washer and hub nut and torque to 191 ft. lbs. (260 Nm).

18. Install stabilizer bar bushing assembly to lower control arm and torque to 13 ft. lbs. (18 Nm).

19. Remove halfshaft seal boot protector, if used.

20. Install the wheels.

21. Connect the negative battery cable and check for proper operation.

1989–91 Vehicles

1. Disconnect the negative battery cable.

2. Raise the vehicle and support safely.

3. Remove the wheels.

4. Install the halfshaft seal protector on the outer joint.

5. Remove the shaft nut and washer.

6. Remove the ball joint retaining nut and separate the control arm from the steering knuckle. Remove the stabilizer shaft, if necessary.

7. Pull out on lower knuckle area. Using a plastic or rubber mallet, strike the end of the halfshaft to disengage it from the hub and bearing assembly.

8. Separate the halfshaft from the hub and bearing assembly and move the strut assembly rearward.

9. Remove the inner joint from the transaxle or intermediate shaft using the slide hammer tool.

10. To remove the intermediate shaft, remove the rear engine mount through bolt. Then remove the intermediate shaft bracket bolts and remove the assembly.

To install:

11. Install the seal protector to the transxle. Install the intermediate shaft, if removed. Torque the bracket bolts to 35 ft. lbs. (47 Nm).

12. Drive the halfshaft into the transaxle or intermediate shaft by placing a suitable tool into the groove on the joint housing and tapping until seated. Be careful not to damage the axle seal or spring. Verify that the axle is seated by grasping the inner joint housing and pulling outboard.

13. Install the axle to the hub and bearing assembly.

14. Install the washer and nut and torque to 185 ft. lbs. (260 Nm).

15. Install the ball joint to the steering knuckle. Install the stabilizer shaft, if removed.

16. Remove the seal protectors.

17. Install the wheels.

18. Connect the negative battery cable and check for proper operation.

CV-Boot

REMOVAL & INSTALLATION

1. Disconnect the negative battery cable. Raise the vehicle and support safely. Remove the halfshaft assembly.

2. Remove the steel deflector ring by using brass drift to tap it off. If rubber ring is used, slide it off.

3. Cut the seal's retaining clamps and lift the boot up to gain access to retaining ring.

4. Remove the snapring and remove the joint from the shaft.

5. Slide the boot off shaft.

To install:

6. Clean the splines of the shaft and the CV-joint.

7. Install the clamp and boot onto the shaft. Fill the boot with amount of grease specified in the package.

8. Install the joint to the shaft and install a new retaining ring.

9. Crimp the outer clamp securely in the groove.

10. Install the steel deflector ring or rubber ring.

11. Install the halfshaft assembly.

12. Connect the negative battery cable and check for proper operation.

Front Wheel Hub, Knuckle and Bearing

REMOVAL & INSTALLATION

1. Raise the vehicle and support safely.

2. Remove the front wheel assemblies.

3. Install a halfshaft boot seal protector tool on the outer CV-joints and

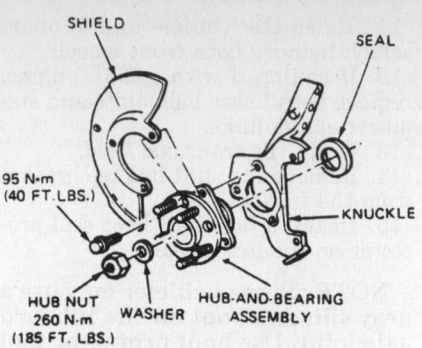

Front hub and bearing assembly, knuckle and related parts

a halfshafte boot seal protector tool on the inner tri-pot joints.

4. Insert a long punch through the caliper and into a rotor vent to keep it from turning.

5. Clean the shaft threads and lubricate them with a thread lubricant.

6. Remove the hub nut and washer.

7. Remove the caliper-to-steering knuckle bolts and support the caliper on a wire aside.

8. Remove the rotor.

9. Remove the halfshaft from the hub and bearing assembly.

10. Remove the 3 hub bolts, the shield and the hub and bearing assembly. Remove the bearing seal from the knuckle.

11. To remove the steering knuckle, perform the following procedures:

   a. At the ball joint-to-steering knuckle and the tie-rod-to-steering knuckle intersections, remove the cotter pins and nuts.

   b. Using a ball joint removal tool, separate the ball joint and the tie-rod end from the steering knuckle.

   c. Matchmark the strut to the knuckle. While supporting the steering knuckle, remove the steering knuckle-to-strut bolts and the steering knuckle from the vehicle.

To install:

12. Install the steering knuckle and all retaining bolts. Torque the bolts to their proper torques:

   a. Align the matchmarks and torque the steering knuckle-to-strut bolts to 140 ft. lbs. (190 Nm).

   b. Torque the ball joint-to-steering knuckle nut to 55–65 ft. lbs. (75–88 Nm) and install a new cotter pin.

   c. Torque the tie-rod-to-steering knuckle nut to 35 ft. lbs. (47 Nm) and install a new cotter pin.

13. Install a new seal to the knuckle.

14. If reinstalling the original assembly, replace the O-ring. Install the hub and bearing assembly, shield and bolts. Torque the bolts to 70 ft. lbs. (95 Nm).

15. Install the halfshaft and brake parts.

16. Install the wheels.

17. Perform a front end alignment, as required.

STEERING

Steering Wheel

REMOVAL & INSTALLATION

1. Disconnect the negative battery cable.

2. Remove the 2 screws that retain the steering pad.

3. Disconnect the horn lead and remove the horn pad.

4. Remove the retainer, nut and dampener, if equipped.

5. Matchmark the steering wheel to the shaft and remove the steering wheel from the vehicle.

6. The installation is the reverse of the removal procedure. Torque the retaining nut to 30 ft. lbs. (41 Nm).

Steering Column

REMOVAL & INSTALLATION

1. Disconnect the negative battery cable.

2. If column repairs are to be made, remove the steering wheel.

3. Remove the steering column-to-intermediate shaft coupling pinch bolt. Remove the safety strap and bolt, if equipped.

4. Remove the steering column trim shrouds and column covers.

5. Disconnect all wiring harness connectors. Remove the dust boot mounting screws and steering column-to-dash bracket bolts.

6. Lower the column to clear the mounting bracket and carefully remove from the vehicle.

7. The installation is the reverse of the removal procedure. Torque the steering mounting nuts to 20 ft. lbs. (27 Nm) and the intermediate shaft coupling pinch bolt to 29 ft. lbs. (39 Nm).

8. Connect the negative battery cable and check all column mounted switches, accessories and the vehicle's steering mechanism for proper operation.

Power Rack and Pinion Steering Gear

ADJUSTMENT

Rack Bearing Preload

1. Center the steering wheel. Raise the vehicle and support safely.

2. Loosen the locknut and turn the adjuster plug clockwise until it bottoms in the housing. Then back off about 1/8 turn and tighten the locknut while holding the position of the adjuster plug.

3. Check the steering for ability to return to center after the adjustment has been completed.

REMOVAL & INSTALLATION

1. Disconnect the negative battery cable. Remove the left side sound insulator.

2. Disconnect the upper pinch bolt on the steering coupling assembly.

3. Disconnect the clamp nuts.

4. Raise the vehicle and support safely. Remove both front wheel assemblies.

5. Remove the clamp nut and the fluid line retainer.

6. Remove the tie rod end-to-steering knuckle cotter pin and castle nut. Using a puller tool, disconnect the tie rod ends from the steering knuckles.

7. Lower the vehicle.

8. Disconnect and plug the fluid lines from the power steering rack.

9. Remove the mounting clamps. Move the steering rack forward and remove the lower pinch bolt on the coupling assembly.

10. Disconnect the coupling from the steering rack.

11. Remove the rack and pinion assembly with the dash seal through the left wheel opening.

To install:

12. If the studs were removed with the mounting clamps, reinstall the studs into the cowl. If the stud is being reused, use Loctite® to secure the threads.

13. Slide the rack and pinion assembly through the left side wheel housing opening and secure the dash seal.

14. Move the assembly forward and install the coupling.

15. Install the lower pinch bolt and torque to 29 ft. lbs. (40 Nm).

16. Connect the fluid lines.

17. Install the clamp nuts. Tighten the left side clamp first, then tighten the right side. Raise the vehicle and support safely.

18. Connect the tie rod ends to the steering knuckle, torque the nut to 35 ft. lbs. (47 Nm) and install a new cotter pin. Install the wheels.

19. Install the line retainer and lower the vehicle.

20. Install the upper pinch bolt on the coupling assembly. Torque to 29 ft. lbs. (40 Nm).

21. Install the sound insulator.

22. Fill the power steering pump with fluid and bleed the system.

23. Connect the negative battery cable and check the rack for proper operation and leaks.

24. Perform a front end alignment, as required.

Power Steering Pump

REMOVAL & INSTALLATION

2.3L Engine

1. Disconnect the negative battery cable.

2. Disconnect the pressure and return lines from the pump.

3. Remove the rear bracket to pump bolts.

4. Remove the drive belt and position aside.

5. Remove the rear bracket to transaxle bolts.

6. Remove the front bracket to engine bolt.

7. Remove the pump and bracket as an assembly.

8. Transfer pulley and bracket, as necessary.

9. The installation is the reverse of the removal procedure.

10. Fill the power steering pump with fluid and bleed the system.

11. Connect the negative battery cable and check the pump for proper operation and leaks.

2.5L Engine

1. Disconnect the negative battery cable.

2. Remove the drive belt.

3. Disconnect and plug the pressure tubes from the power steering pump.

4. Remove the front adjustment bracket-to-rear adjustment bracket bolt.

5. Remove the front adjustment bracket-to-engine bolt and spacer.

6. Remove the pump with the front adjustment bracket.

7. If installing a new pump, transfer the pulley and front adjustment bracket to the new pump.

8. The installation is the reverse of the removal procedure.

9. Adjust the drive belt tension.

10. Fill the power steering pump with fluid and bleed the system.

11. Connect the negative battery cable and check the pump for proper operation and leaks.

2.0L, 3.0L and 3.3L Engines

1. Disconnect the negative battery cable.

2. Remove the serpentine drive belt.

3. Remove the power steering pump-to-engine bolts.

4. Pull the pump forward and disconnect the pressure tubes.

5. Remove the pump and transfer the pulley, as necessary.

6. The installation is the reverse of the removal procedure.

7. Adjust the drive belt tension.

8. Fill the power steering pump with fluid and bleed the system.

9. Connect the negative battery cable and check the pump for proper operation and leaks.

BELT ADJUSTMENT

NOTE: Serpentine belt driven power steering pumps do not require adjustment. If the belt is stretched beyond usable limits, replace it.

1. Place the appropriate gauge on the belt and measure the tension. The specifications are:

2.3L engine, new and used belt—110 lbs.

2.5L and 3.0L engine, used belt—100 lbs; new belt—180 lbs.

2. If the tension is not at specifications, loosen the mounting bolts and move the pump or turn the adjustment stud.

3. Tighten the mounting bolts while holding the adjusted position of the pump.

4. Run the engine for 2 minutes and recheck the tension.

SYSTEM BLEEDING

1. Raise the vehicle so the wheels are off the ground. Turn the wheels all the way to the left. Add power steering fluid to the **COLD** or **FULL COLD** mark on the fluid level indicator.

2. Start the engine and check the fluid level at fast idle. Add fluid, if necessary to bring the level up to the mark.

3. Bleed air from the system by turning the wheels from side-to-side without hitting the stops. Keep the fluid level at the **COLD** or **FULL COLD** mark. Fluid with air in it has a tan appearance.

4. Return the wheels to the center position and continue running the engine for 2–3 minutes.

5. Lower the vehicle and road test to check steering function and recheck the fluid level with the system at its normal operating temperature. Fluid should be at the **HOT** mark when finished.

Tie Rod Ends

REMOVAL & INSTALLATION

Inner Tie Rod

1. Disconnect the negative battery cable. Remove the rack and pinion gear from the vehicle.

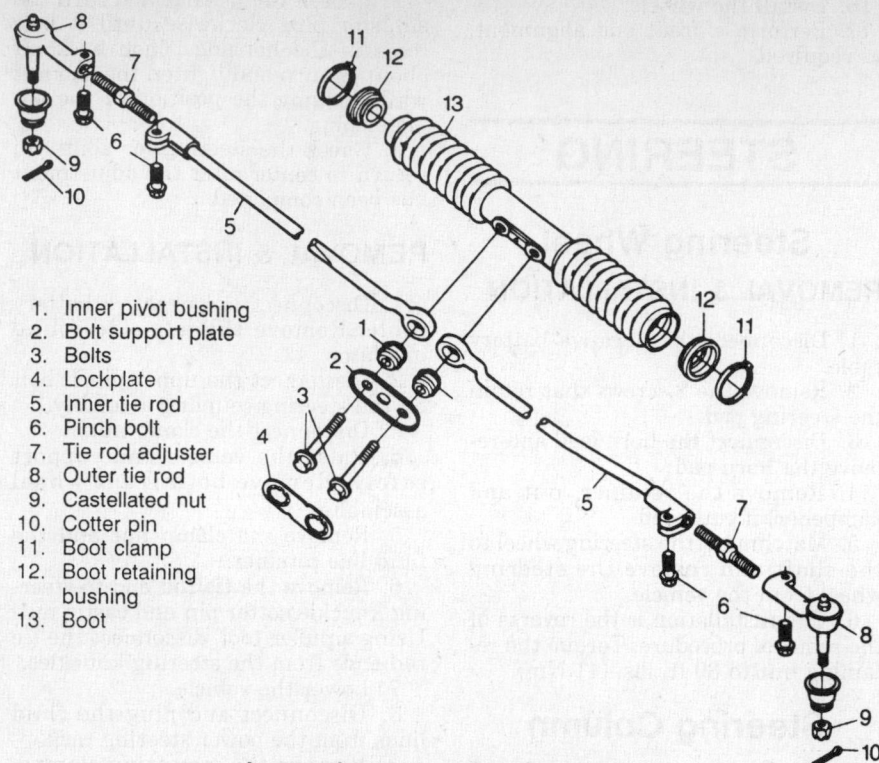

1. Inner pivot bushing
2. Bolt support plate
3. Bolts
4. Lockplate
5. Inner tie rod
6. Pinch bolt
7. Tie rod adjuster
8. Outer tie rod
9. Castellated nut
10. Cotter pin
11. Boot clamp
12. Boot retaining bushing
13. Boot

Inner and outer tie rod end assemblies

2. Remove the lock plate from the inner tie rod bolts.

3. If removing both tie rods, remove both bolts, the bolt support plate and 1 of the tie rod assemblies. Reinstall the removed tie rod's bolt to keep inner parts of the rack aligned. Remove the remaining tie rod.

4. If only removing 1 tie rod, slide the assembly out from between the support plate and the center housing cover washer.

To install:

5. Install the center housing cover washer fitted into the rack and pinion boot.

6. Install the inner tie rod bolts through the holes in the bolt support plate, inner pivot bushing, center housing cover washer, rack housing and into the threaded holes.

7. Torque the bolts to 65 ft. lbs. (90 Nm).

8. Install a new lock plate with its notches over the bolt flats.

9. Install the rack and pinion gear.

10. Fill the power steering pump with fluid and bleed the system.

11. Connect the negative battery cable and check the rack for proper operation and leaks.

Outer Tie Rod

1. Disconnect the negative battery cable.

2. Remove the cotter pin and the

nut from the tie rod ball stud at the steering knuckle.

3. Loosen the pinch bolts.

4. Using the proper tools, separate the tie rod taper from the steering knuckle.

5. Remove the tie rod from the adjuster.

6. The installation is the reverse of the removal procedure.

7. Perform a front end alignment.

BRAKES

For all brake system repair and service procedures not detailed below, please refer to "Brakes" in the Unit Repair section.

Master Cylinder

REMOVAL & INSTALLATION

Except Anti-Lock Brakes

1. Disconnect the negative battery cable. Unplug the fluid level sensor connector.

2. Disconnect and plug the brake lines from the master cylinder.

3. Remove the nuts attaching the master cylinder to the power booster.

4. Remove the master cylinder from the mounting studs.

5. Remove the retaining roll pins and remove the fluid reservoir from the cylinder, if necessary.

To install:

6. Replace the reservoir O-rings and bench bleed the master cylinder.

7. Install to the booster and install the nuts.

8. Install the brake lines to the master cylinder.

9. Fill the reservoir with brake fluid.

10. Connect the negative battery cable and check the brakes for proper operation.

Proportioning Valves

REMOVAL & INSTALLATION

1. Disconnect the negative battery cable.

2. Remove the retaining roll pins and remove the fluid reservoir from the cylinder, if necessary.

3. Remove the proportioner valve cap assemblies.

4. Remove the O-rings.

5. Remove the springs.

6. Carefully remove the proportioner valve pistons.

7. Remove the seals from the pistons.

To install:

8. Thoroughly clean and dry all parts.

9. Lubricate the new piston seals with the silicone grease included in the repair kit or brake assembly fluid. Install to the pistons with the seal lips facing upward toward the cap assembly.

10. Lubricate the stem of the pistons and install to their bores.

11. Install the springs.

12. Lubricate and install the new O-rings in their grooves in the cap assemblies.

13. Install the caps to the master cylinder and torque to 20 ft. lbs. (27 Nm).

14. Install the reservoir, if replaced.

15. Fill the reservoir with brake fluid.

16. Connect the negative battery cable and check the brakes for proper operation.

Power Brake Booster

REMOVAL & INSTALLATION

1. Disconnect the negative battery cable.

2. Disconnect the vacuum hose(s) from the booster.

3. Remove the master cylinder.

4. From inside of the vehicle, remove the booster pushrod from the brake pedal.

5. Remove the nuts that attach the booster to the dash panel and remove it from the vehicle.

6. Transfer the necessary parts to the new booster.

7. The installation is the reverse of the removal procedure.

8. Connect the negative battery cable and check the brakes for proper operation.

Brake Caliper

REMOVAL & INSTALLATION

1. Raise the vehicle and support safely.

2. Remove the tire and wheel assembly.

3. Bottom the piston in its bore for clearance.

4. Remove the bolt that attaches the brake hose from the caliper.

5. Remove the caliper mounting bolt and sleeve assemblies.

6. Lift the caliper off of the rotor.

To install:

7. Install the brake hose to the caliper using new copper washers.

8. Position the caliper over the rotor so the caliper engages the adaptor correctly. Lubricate and install the sleeves and bolts. Torque to 38 ft. lbs. (51 Nm).

9. Install the tire and wheel assembly.

10. Fill the master cylinder and bleed the brakes.

Disc Brake Pads

REMOVAL & INSTALLATION

1. Remove some of the fluid from the master cylinder. Raise the vehicle and support safely.

2. Remove the tire and wheel assembly.

3. Bottom the piston in its bore for clearance.

4. Remove the caliper mounting bolt and sleeve assemblies.

5. Lift the caliper off of the rotor.

6. Remove the pads from the caliper.

To install:

7. Use a large C-clamp to compress the piston back into the caliper bore.

8. Install the pads and anti-rattle clip to the caliper. Adjust the bent-over tabs for a tight fit.

9. Position the caliper over the rotor so the caliper engages the adaptor correctly. Lubricate and install the sleeves and bolts. Torque to 38 ft. lbs. (51 Nm).

10. Install the tire and wheel assembly.

11. Fill the master cylinder and check the brakes for proper operation.

Brake Rotor

REMOVAL & INSTALLATION

1. Raise the vehicle and support safely. Remove the tire and wheel assembly.

2. Remove the caliper and brake pads.

3. Remove the rotor from the hub.

4. The installation is the reverse of the removal procedure.

Brake Drums

REMOVAL & INSTALLATION

1. Raise the vehicle and support safely.

2. Remove the wheel and tire assembly.

3. Remove the drum. If the drum is difficult to remove, remove the plug from the rear of the backing plate and push the self-adjuster lever away from the star wheel. Rotate the star wheel to retract the shoes.

4. The installation is the reverse of the removal procedure.

5. Adjust the brakes as required.

Brake Shoes

NOTE: If unsure of spring positioning, finish one side before starting the other and use the untouched side as a guide.

REMOVAL & INSTALLATION

1. Remove the wheels and drums. Remove the primary and secondary shoe return springs from the anchor pin but leave them installed in the shoes.

2. Lift on the adjuster lever and remove the adjuster cable. Remove the actuating lever link and pawl return spring.

3. Remove the hold-down pin return springs and cups. Remove the parking brake strut and spring. Remove the actuating lever and pawl.

4. Remove the shoes, held together by the lower spring, while separating the parking brake actuating lever from the shoe with a twisting motion.

5. Lift the wheel cylinder dust boots and inspect for fluid leakage.

6. Thoroughly clean and dry the backing plate.

To install:

7. Remove, clean and dry all parts still on the old shoes. Lubricate the star wheel shaft threads and transfer all the parts to the new shoes in their proper locations.

8. To prepare the backing plate, lubricate the bosses, anchor pin and parking brake actuating lever pivot surface lightly with the brake-compatible lubricant.

9. Spread the shoes apart, engage the parking brake actuating lever and position them on the backing plate so the wheel cylinder pins engage properly and the anchor pin holds the shoes up.

10. Install the parking brake strut and the hold-down pin assemblies. Install the actuating lever with the hold-down pin assembly.

11. Install the anchor plate. Lubricate the sliding surface of the adjuster cable plate and install the adjuster cable.

12. Install the shoe return spring opposite the cable, then the remaining spring. Install the actuating lever link, the shoe return springs and assemble the pawl and return spring.

13. Adjust the star wheel.

14. Remove any grease from the linings and install the drum.

15. Complete the brake adjustment with the wheels installed and adjust the parking brake cable.

Wheel Cylinder

REMOVAL & INSTALLATION

1. Raise the vehicle and support safely.

2. Remove the wheel, drum and brake shoes.

3. Remove and plug the brake line from the wheel cylinder.

4. Remove the wheel cylinder bolts and remove the cylinder from the backing plate.

To install:

5. Apply a very thin coating of silicone sealer to the cylinder mounting surface, install the cylinder to the backing plate and install the retaining bolts.

6. Connect the brake line to the wheel cylinder.

7. Install all brake parts that were removed.

8. Install the tire and wheel assembly.

9. Bleed the brakes.

Parking Brake Cable

ADJUSTMENT

1. Adjust the rear brake shoes.

2. Depress the parking brake pedal exactly 3 ratchet clicks.

3. Raise the vehicle and support safely.

4. Check that the equalizer nut groove is liberally lubricated with

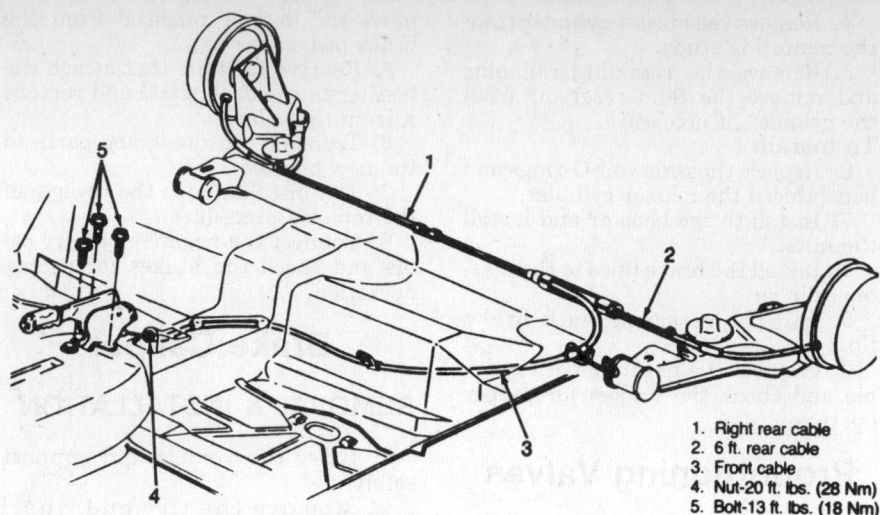

1. Right rear cable
2. 6 ft. rear cable
3. Front cable
4. Nut-20 ft. lbs. (28 Nm)
5. Bolt-13 ft. lbs. (18 Nm)

Parking brake cable routing

chassis lube. Tighten the adjusting nut until the right rear wheel can just be turned to the rear with both hands but is locked when forward rotation is attempted.

5. With the mechanism totally disengaged, both rear wheels should turn freely in either direction with no brake drag. Do not adjust the parking brake so tightly as to cause brake drag.

REMOVAL & INSTALLATION

Front Cable

1. Disconnect the negative battery cable. Raise the vehicle and support safely.

2. Loosen or remove the equalizer nut. Lower the vehicle.

3. Remove the console.

4. Disconnect the parking brake cable from the lever.

5. Remove the nut that secures the front cable to the floor pan.

6. Loosen the catalytic converter shield and the parking brake cable from the body.

7. Remove the cable from the equalizer, guide and underbody clips.

8. The installation is the reverse of the removal procedure.

9. Adjust the cable.

10. Connect the negative battery cable and check the parking brakes for proper operation.

Rear Cables

1. Disconnect the negative battery cable. Raise the vehicle and support safely.

2. Loosen or remove the equalizer nut.

3. Remove the wheel(s) and drum(s).

4. Insert a suitable tool between the

brake shoe and the top part of the brake adjuster bracket. Push the bracket to the front and release the top adjuster bracket rod.

5. Remove the hold-down spring, actuator lever and lever return spring.

6. Remove the adjuster spring.

7. Remove the top rear brake shoe return spring.

8. Disconnect the parking brake cable from the actuating lever.

9. Pull the cable through the backing plate while depressing the retaining tangs.

10. On the right side, remove the cable end button from the connector.

11. Remove the conduit fitting from the axle bracket while depressing the retaining tangs.

To install:

12. Install the conduit fitting into the axle bracket, securing the retaining tangs.

13. Install the cable end button to the connector, if working on the right side.

14. Click the cable assembly into the backing plate.

15. Connect the cable to the actuating lever.

16. Assemble the rear brake components.

17. Install the drum(s) and wheel(s).

18. Adjust the rear brakes and parking brake cable.

19. Connect the negative battery cable and check the parking brakes for proper operation.

Brake System Bleeding

Except Anti-Lock Brakes

NOTE: If using a pressure bleeder, follow the instructions furnished with the unit and choose the correct adaptor for the application. Do not substitute an adapter that "almost fits" as it will not work and could be dangerous.

MASTER CYLINDER

If the master cylinder is off the vehicle it can be bench bled.

1. Connect 2 short pieces of brake line to the outlet fittings, bend them until the free end is below the fluid level in the master cylinder reservoirs.

2. Fill the reservoir with fresh brake fluid. Pump the piston slowly until no more air bubbles appear in the reservoirs.

3. Disconnect the 2 short lines, refill the master cylinder and securely install the cylinder caps.

4. If the master cylinder is on the vehicle, it can still be bled, using a flare nut wrench.

5. Open the brake lines slightly with the flare nut wrench while pressure is applied to the brake pedal by a helper inside the vehicle.

6. Be sure to tighten the line before the brake pedal is released.

7. Repeat the process with both lines until no air bubbles come out.

CALIPERS AND WHEEL CYLINDERS

1. Fill the master cylinder with fresh brake fluid. Check the level often during the procedure.

2. Starting with the right rear wheel, remove the protective cap from the bleeder, if equipped, and place where it will not be lost. Clean the bleed screw.

── **CAUTION** ──
When bleeding the brakes, keep face away from the brake area. Spewing fluid may cause facial and/or visual damage. Do not allow brake fluid to spill on the car's finish; it will remove the paint.

3. If the system is empty, the most effecient way to get fluid down to the wheel is to loosen the bleeder about ½–¾ turn, place a finger firmly over the bleeder and have a helper pump the brakes slowly until fluid comes out the bleeder. Once fluid is at the bleeder, close it before the pedal is released inside the vehicle.

NOTE: If the pedal is pumped rapidly, the fluid will churn and create small air bubbles, which are almost impossible to remove from the system. These air bubbles will eventually congregate and a spongy pedal will result.

4. Once fluid has been pumped to the caliper or wheel cylinder, open the bleed screw again, have the helper

press the brake pedal to the floor, lock the bleeder and have the helper slowly release the pedal. Wait 15 seconds and repeat the procedure (including the 15 second wait) until no more air comes out of the bleeder upon application of the brake pedal. Remember to close the bleeder before the pedal is released inside the vehicle each time the bleeder is opened. If not, air will be induced into the system.

5. If a helper is not available, connect a small hose to the bleeder, place the end in a container of brake fluid and proceed to pump the pedal from inside the vehicle until no more air comes out the bleeder. The hose will prevent air from entering the system.

6. Repeat the procedure on remaining wheel cylinders in order:
   a. left front
   b. left rear
   c. right front

7. Hydraulic brake systems must be totally flushed if the fluid becomes contaminated with water, dirt or other corrosive chemicals. To flush, bleed the entire system until all fluid has been replaced with the correct type of new fluid.

8. Install the bleeder cap(s), if equipped, on the bleeder to keep dirt out. Always road test the vehicle after brake work of any kind is done.

Anti-Lock Brake System Service

PRECAUTION

Failure to observe the following precautions may result in system damage.

● Before performing electric arc welding on the vehicle, disconnect the Electronic Brake Control Module (EBCM) and the hydraulic modulator connectors.

● When performing painting work on the vehicle, do not expose the Electronic Brake Control Module (EBCM) to temperatures in excess of 185°F (85°C) for longer than 2 hrs. The system may be exposed to temperatures up to 200°F (95°C) for less than 15 min.

● Never disconnect or connect the Electronic Brake Control Module (EBCM) or hydraulic modulator connectors with the ignition switch ON.

● Never disassemble any component of the Anti-Lock Brake System (ABS) which is designated non-servicable; the component must be replaced as an assembly.

● When filling the master cylinder, always use Delco Supreme 11 brake fluid or equivalent, which meets DOT-3 specifications; petroleum base fluid will destroy the rubber parts.

FRONT SUSPENSION

MacPherson Strut

REMOVAL & INSTALLATION

1. Remove the 3 mounting nuts from the shock tower under the hood.

2. Raise the vehicle and support safely. Remove the wheel.

3. The control arms must not be supporting the vehicle's weight.

NOTE: Do not allow the tri-pot joints from becoming overextended or they can get separated and damaged.

1. Strut assembly
2. Steering knuckle
3. Bolts
4. Nuts
5. Suspension support
6. Cover
7. Mounting nut

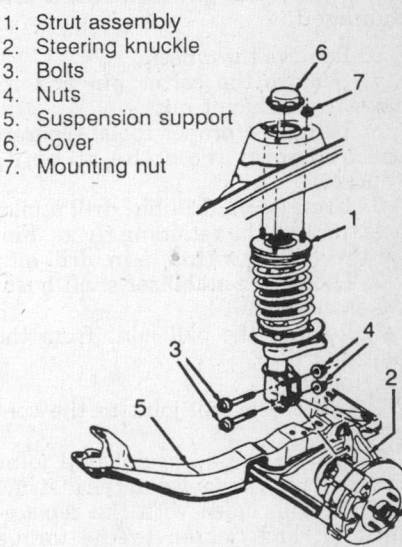

MacPherson strut assembly

4. Matchmark the lower strut mount to the knuckle and remove the strut to knuckle bolts and nuts.

5. While the strut is off of the vehicle, the lower mounting hole may be elongated for alignment purposes. Paint any exposed metal afterward to prevent rusting.

6. The installation is the reverse of the removal procedure. Torque the upper mounting nuts to 18 ft. lbs. (24 Nm). Do not tighten the lower mounting bolts until the front end alignment has been completed.

7. Perform a front end alignment. Torque the strut to knuckle nuts to 133 ft. lbs. (180 Nm).

Lower Ball Joints
INSPECTION

1. Raise the vehicle safely so the front suspension hangs free.

2. Grasp the tire at the top and bottom and move with an in-and-out motion.

3. If any horizontal movement is detected from the knuckle, relative to the control arm, replace the ball joint.

4. Shake the wheel and feel for movement of the stud end or castellated nut at the knuckle boss.

5. Check the nut for loose torque. A loose nut may indicate a bent stude or expanded hole in the knuckle.

6. Replace all parts found to be worn or damaged.

REMOVAL & INSTALLATION

1. Raise the vehicle and support safely.

2. The control arms must not be supporting the vehicle's weight.

NOTE: Do not allow the tri-pot joints from becoming overextended or they can get separated and damaged.

3. Remove the wheel.

4. Remove the cotter pin and remove the ball joint nut.

5. Using the proper tools, separate the ball joint from the steering knuckle.

6. Use a ⅛ in. drill bit, drill a pilot hole through the retaining rivets. Finish the drilling with a ½ in. drill bit.

7. Loosen the stabilizer shaft bushing assembly nut.

8. Remove the ball joint from the control arm.

To install:

9. Install the ball joint to the control arm.

10. Install the 3 special ball joint bolts and nuts as shown in the instruction sheet included with the replacement kit and tighten to the torque specified.

11. Install the ball stud to the steerng knuckle. Install the nut and torque to 40–50 ft. lbs. (55–65 Nm). Install a new cotter pin.

12. Install the stabilizer shaft nut.

13. Install the wheel.

14. Perform a front end alignment and road test the vehicle.

Lower Control Arms

REMOVAL & INSTALLATION

1. Raise the vehicle and support safely. Remove the tire and wheel assembly.

2. Remove the stabilizer shaft.

NOTE: Do not allow the tri-pot joints from becoming overextended or they can get separated and damaged.

3. Remove the ball joint stud retaining nut.

4. Pry the lower control arm from the steering knuckle.

5. Remove the control arm to suspension support bolts and nuts.

6. Remove the control arm from the vehicle.

7. Transfer reusable parts to the new control arm.

8. The installation is the reverse of the removal procedure.

9. Lower the vehicle so the full weight of the vehicle is on the ground.

10. Torque the nuts to 61 ft. lbs. (83 Nm).

11. Perform a front end alignment.

Stabilizer Shaft

REMOVAL & INSTALLATION

1. Raise the vehicle and support safely.

2. Remove the front sway bar brackets and retainers.

3. Remove the sway bar support brackets and bushings from the lower control arm. Remove the sway bar from the vehicle.

4. The installation is the reverse of the removal procedure. Lubricate the sway bar bushings liberally with grease before assembling.

REAR SUSPENSION

Shock Absorbers

REMOVAL & INSTALLATION

1. Disconnect the negative battery cable.

2. Open the deck lid and remove the trim cover.

3. Remove the upper shock attaching nut. Remove 1 shock at a time if removing both.

4. Raise the vehicle and support safely.

5. Remove the lower mounting bolt.

6. Remove the shock from the vehicle.

7. The installation is the reverse of the removal procedure.

Coil Springs

REMOVAL & INSTALLATION

1. Raise the vehicle and support safely.

2. Using the proper equipment, support the weight of the rear axle. Disconnect the brake lines from the rear axle.

3. Remove the bolts that attach the shock to the lower mounting bracket.

4. Lower the axle and remove the coil spring from the vehicle.

5. The installation is the reverse of the removal procedure.

Rear Wheel Bearings

REMOVAL & INSTALLATION

1. Raise the vehicle and support safely.

2. Remove the wheel assembly.

3. Remove the brake drum.

4. Remove the 4 hub/bearing assembly-to-rear axle assembly nuts/bolts and the hub/bearing assembly from the axle.

NOTE: The top rear attaching bolt will not clear the brake shoe when removing the hub and bearing assembly. Partially remove the hub prior to removing this bolt.

5. The installation is the reverse of the removal procedure. Torque the hub/bearing assembly-to-rear axle assembly nuts/bolts to 39 ft. lbs. (53 Nm).

ADJUSTMENT

The rear wheel bearing assembly is non-adjustable and is serviced by replacement only.

Rear Axle Assembly

REMOVAL & INSTALLATION

1. Raise the vehicle safely under the control arms.

2. If equipped, remove the stabilizer bar from the axle assembly.

3. Remove the wheel assemblies.

4. Remove the lower shock absorber-to-axle assembly nuts/bolts and separate the shock absorbers from the rear axle assembly.

5. Disconnect the parking brake cable from the rear axle assembly.

6. Disconnect the brake lines from the rear axle assembly; be sure the assembly is not suspended by the brake lines.

7. Lower the rear axle assembly and remove the coil spring. Transfer all reusable parts to the new assembly.

8. The installation is the reverse of the removal procedure.

9. Torque the rear axle assembly-to-body nuts and bolts to 67 ft. lbs. (91 Nm).

GM "W" Body
Front Wheel Drive

Buick—Regal **Chevrolet**—Lumina
Oldsmobile—Cutlass Supreme
Pontiac—Grand Prix

SPECIFICATIONS

VEHICLE IDENTIFICATION CHART

It is important for servicing and ordering parts to be certain of the vehicle and engine identification. The VIN (vehicle identification number) is a 17 digit number visible through the windshield on the driver's side of the dash and contains the vehicle and engine identification codes. The tenth digit indicates model year and the eighth digit indicates engine code. It can be interpreted as follows:

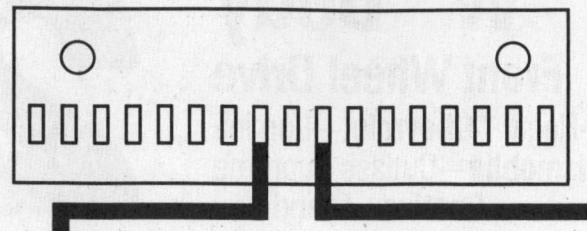

Engine Code						Model Year	
Code	Cu. In.	Liters	Cyl.	Fuel Sys.	Eng. Mfg.	Code	Year
A	138	2.3	L4	MFI	Oldsmobile	J	1988
D	138	2.3	L4	MFI	Oldsmobile	K	1989
R	151	2.5	L4	TBI	Pontiac	L	1990
W	173	2.8	V6	MFI	Chevrolet	M	1991
T	192	3.1	V6	MFI	Chevrolet		
V	231	3.1	V6	MFI	Buick		
L	231	3.8	V6	MFI	Buick		

ENGINE IDENTIFICATION

Year	Model	Engine Displacement cu. in. (liter)	Engine Series Identification (VIN)	No. of Cylinders	Engine Type
1988	Grand Prix	173 (2.8)	W	6	OHV
	Supreme	173 (2.8)	W	6	OHV
	Regal	173 (2.8)	W	6	OHV
1989	Grand Prix	173 (2.8)	W	6	OHV
	Grand Prix	192 (3.1)	T	6	OHV
	Supreme	173 (2.8)	W	6	OHV
	Supreme	192 (3.1)	T	6	OHV
	Regal	173 (2.8)	W	6	OHV
	Regal	192 (3.1)	T	6	OHV
	Lumina	151 (2.5)	R	4	OHV
	Lumina	192 (3.1)	T	6	OHV
1990	Grand Prix	138 (2.3)	D	4	
	Grand Prix	192 (3.1)	T	6	OHV
	Grand Prix	192 (3.1)	V	6	OHV-Turbo
	Supreme	138 (2.3)	A	4	DOHC
	Supreme	138 (2.3)	D	4	DOHC
	Supreme	192 (3.1)	T	6	OHV
	Regal	192 (3.1)	T	6	OHV
	Regal	231 (3.8)	L	6	OHV
	Lumina	151 (2.5)	R	4	OHV
	Lumina	192 (3.1)	T	6	OHV

ENGINE IDENTIFICATION

Year	Model	Engine Displacement cu. in. (liter)	Engine Series Identification (VIN)	No. of Cylinders	Engine Type
1991	Grand Prix	138 (2.3)	D	4	DOHC
	Grand Prix	138 (2.3)	A	4	DOHC
	Grand Prix	192 (3.1)	T	6	OHV
	Supreme	138 (2.3)	D	4	DOHC
	Supreme	192 (3.1)	T	6	OHV
	Regal	192 (3.1)	T	6	OHV
	Regal	231 (3.8)	L	6	OHV
	Lumina	151 (2.5)	R	4	OHV
	Lumina	192 (3.1)	T	6	OHV

OHV—Overhead valve
DOHC—Double overhead cam

GENERAL ENGINE SPECIFICATIONS

Year	VIN	No. Cylinder Displacement cu. in. (liter)	Fuel System Type	Net Horsepower @ rpm	Net Torque @ rpm (ft. lbs.)	Bore × Stroke (in.)	Compression Ratio	Oil Pressure @ rpm
1988	W	6-173 (2.8)	MFI	125 @ 4500	160 @ 3600	3.500 × 2.990	8.9:1	15 @ 1100
1989	R	4-151 (2.5)	TBI	98 @ 4500	134 @ 2800	4.000 × 3.000	8.3:1	26 @ 800
	W	6-173 (2.8)	MFI	125 @ 4500	160 @ 3600	3.500 × 2.990	8.9:1	15 @ 1100
	T	6-192 (3.1)	MFI	140 @ 4500	185 @ 3600	3.500 × 3.310	8.8:1	15 @ 1100
1990	A	4-138 (2.3) ①	MFI	180 @ 6200	160 @ 5200	3.620 × 3.350	10.0:1	30 @ 2000
	D	4-138 (2.3)	MFI	160 @ 6200	155 @ 5200	3.620 × 3.350	9.5:1	30 @ 2000
	R	4-151 (2.5)	TBI	98 @ 4500	134 @ 2800	4.000 × 3.000	8.3:1	35 @ 2000
	T	6-192 (3.1)	MFI	140 @ 4400	185 @ 3200	3.500 × 3.310	8.8:1	15 @ 1100
	V	6-192 (3.1)	MFI ②	205 @ 4800	220 @ 3000	3.500 × 3.310	8.9:1	15 @ 1100
	L	6-231 (3.8)	MFI	165 @ 4800	210 @ 2000	3.800 × 3.400	8.5:1	60 @ 1850
1991	A	4-138 (2.3) ①	MFI	180 @ 6200	160 @ 5200	3.620 × 3.350	10.0:1	30 @ 2000
	D	4-138 (2.3)	MFI	160 @ 6200	155 @ 5200	3.620 × 3.350	9.5:1	30 @ 2000
	R	4-151 (2.5)	TBI	98 @ 4500	134 @ 2800	4.000 × 3.000	8.3:1	35 @ 2000
	T	6-192 (3.1)	MFI	140 @ 4400	180 @ 3600	3.500 × 3.310	8.8:1	15 @ 1100
	L	6-231 (3.8)	MFI	170 @ 4800	220 @ 3200	3.800 × 3.400	8.5:1	60 @ 1850

① High output (H.O.)
② Turbocharged

GASOLINE ENGINE TUNE-UP SPECIFICATIONS

Year	VIN	No. Cylinder Displacement cu. in. (liter)	Spark Plugs Type	Spark Plugs Gap (in.)	Ignition Timing (deg.) MT	Ignition Timing (deg.) AT	Compression Pressure (psi)	Fuel Pump (psi)	Idle Speed (rpm) MT	Idle Speed (rpm) AT	Valve Clearance In.	Valve Clearance Ex.
1988	W	6-173 (2.8)	R43LTSE	0.045	①	①	②	40–47	①	①	Hyd.	Hyd.
1989	R	4-151 (2.5)	R43CTS6	0.060	①	①	②	26–32	①	①	Hyd.	Hyd.
	W	6-173 (2.8)	R43LTSE	0.045	①	①	②	40–47	①	①	Hyd.	Hyd.
	T	6-192 (3.1)	R43LTSE	0.045	①	①	②	40–47	①	①	Hyd.	Hyd.

GASOLINE ENGINE TUNE-UP SPECIFICATIONS

Year	VIN	No. Cylinder Displacement cu. in. (liter)	Spark Plugs Type	Spark Plugs Gap (in.)	Ignition Timing (deg.) MT	Ignition Timing (deg.) AT	Compression Pressure (psi)	Fuel Pump (psi)	Idle Speed (rpm) MT	Idle Speed (rpm) AT	Valve Clearance In.	Valve Clearance Ex.
1990	A	4-138 (2.3)	FR3LS	0.035	①	①	②	40.5–47	①	①	Hyd.	Hyd.
	D	4-138 (2.3)	FR3LS	0.035	①	①	②	40.5–47	①	①	Hyd.	Hyd.
	R	4-151 (2.5)	R43CTS6	0.060	①	①	②	26–32	①	①	Hyd.	Hyd.
	T	6-192 (3.1)	R43LTSE	0.045	①	①	②	40.5–47	①	①	Hyd.	Hyd.
	V	6-192 (3.1)	R42LTS	0.045	①	①	②	40.5–47	①	①	Hyd.	Hyd.
	L	6-231 (3.8)	R44LTS6	0.060	①	①	②	40–47	①	①	Hyd.	Hyd.
1991			SEE UNDERHOOD SPECIFICATION STICKER									

① Ignition timing and idle speed are controlled by the Electronic Control Module. No adjustment is necessary

② Look for uniformity between cylinders rather than pressure. Lowest reading not less than 70% of the highest. No reading less than 100 psi

FIRING ORDERS

NOTE: To avoid confusion, always replace spark plug wires one at a time.

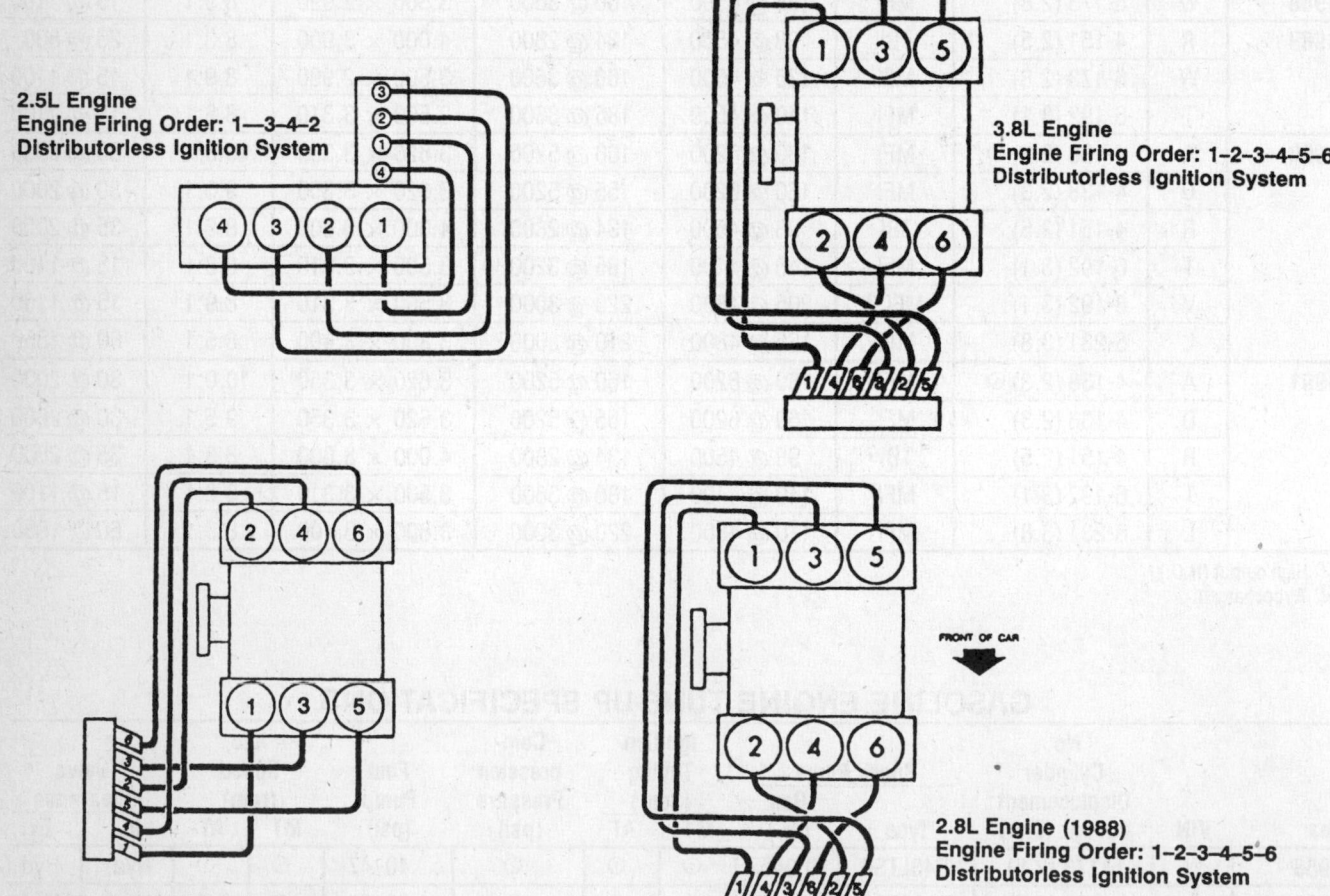

2.5L Engine
Engine Firing Order: 1—3—4—2
Distributorless Ignition System

3.8L Engine
Engine Firing Order: 1—2—3—4—5—6
Distributorless Ignition System

2.8L (1989) and 3.1L Engines
Engine Firing Order: 1—2—3—4—5—6
Distributorless Ignition System

2.8L Engine (1988)
Engine Firing Order: 1—2—3—4—5—6
Distributorless Ignition System

CAPACITIES

Year	Model	VIN	No. Cylinder Displacement cu. in. (liter)	Engine Crankcase with Filter ④	Engine Crankcase without Filter	Transmission (pts.) 4-Spd	Transmission (pts.) 5-Spd	Transmission (pts.) Auto.	Drive Axle (pts.)	Fuel Tank (gal.)	Cooling System (qts.)
1988	Grand Prix	W	6-173 (2.8)	4.0	3.8	—	5	16.0 ①	—	16.0	②
	Cutlass Supreme	W	6-173 (2.8)	4.0	3.8	—	5	16.0 ①	—	16.0	②
	Regal	W	6-173 (2.8)	4.0	3.8	—	—	16.0 ①	—	16.0	②
1989	Grand Prix	W	6-173 (2.8)	4.0	3.8	—	5	12.0 ③	—	16.0	12.6
	Grand Prix	T	6-192 (3.1)	4.0	3.8	—	5	12.0 ③	—	16.0	12.6
	Cutlass Supreme	W	6-173 (2.8)	4.0	3.8	—	5	12.0 ③	—	16.0	12.6
	Cutlass Supreme	T	6-192 (3.1)	4.0	3.8	—	5	12.0 ③	—	16.0	12.6
	Regal	W	6-173 (2.8)	4.0	3.8	—	—	12.0 ③	—	16.0	12.6
	Regal	T	6-192 (3.1)	4.0	3.8	—	—	12.0 ③	—	16.0	12.6
	Lumina	R	4-151 (2.5)	4.0	3.8	—	—	12.0 ③	—	16.0	12.6
	Lumina	T	6-192 (3.1)	4.0	3.8	—	—	12.0 ③	—	16.0	12.6
1990–91	Grand Prix	A	4-138 (2.3)	4.0	4.0	—	4.2	⑤	—	16.5	8.9
	Grand Prix	D	4-138 (2.3)	4.0	4.0	—	4.2	⑤	—	16.5	9.2
	Grand Prix	T	6-192 (3.1)	4.0	4.0	—	4.2	⑤	—	16.5	12.5
	Grand Prix	V	6-192 (3.1)	4.0	4.0	—	4.2	⑤	—	16.5	13.2
	Cutlass Supreme	A	4-138 (2.3)	4.0	4.0	—	4.4	⑤	—	16.5	8.9
	Cutlass Supreme	D	4-138 (2.3)	4.0	4.0	—	4.4	⑤	—	16.5	9.2
	Cutlass Supreme	T	6-192 (3.1)	4.0	4.0	—	4.4	⑤	—	16.5	12.5
	Regal	T	6-192 (3.1)	4.0	4.0	—	—	⑤	—	16.5	12.5
	Regal	L	6-231 (3.8)	4.0	4.0	—	—	⑤	—	16.5	11.1
	Lumina	R	4-151 (2.5)	4.0	4.0	—	—	⑤	—	16.0	9.4
	Lumina	T	6-192 (3.1)	4.0	4.0	—	—	⑤	—	16.0	12.6

① Drain and refill only.
  Complete overhaul—22 pts.
② Without air conditioning—12.3 qts.
  With air conditioning—12.6 qts.
③ Drain and refill only.
  Complete overhaul—16 pts.
④ Add fluid as necessary to bring to appropriate level.
⑤ Hydra-matic 3T40: drain and refill only—14 pts., complete overhaul—18 pts.
  Hydra-matic 4T60: drain and refill only—12 pts., complete overhaul—16 pts.

CAMSHAFT SPECIFICATIONS

All measurements given in inches.

Year	VIN	No. Cylinder Displacement cu. in. (liter)	Journal Diameter					Lobe Lift		Bearing Clearance	Camshaft End Play
			1	2	3	4	5	In.	Ex.		
1988	W	6-173 (2.8)	1.867–1.881	1.867–1.881	1.867–1.881	1.867–1.881	—	0.262	0.273	0.001–0.004	—
1989	R	4-151 (2.5)	1.869	1.869	1.869	1.869	—	0.248	0.248	0.001–0.003	0.0014–0.0050
	W	6-173 (2.8)	1.867–1.881	1.867–1.881	1.867–1.881	1.867–1.881	—	0.262	0.273	0.001–0.004	—
	T	6-192 (3.1)	1.867–1.881	1.867–1.881	1.867–1.881	1.867–1.881	—	0.262	0.273	0.001–0.004	—
1990-91	A	4-138 (2.3)	1.5728–1.5720	1.3751–1.3760	1.3751–1.3760	1.3751–1.3760	1.3751–1.3760	0.410	0.410	0.0019–0.0043	0.0009–0.0088
	D	4-138 (2.3)	1.5728–1.5720	1.3751–1.3760	1.3751–1.3760	1.3751–1.3760	1.3751–1.3760	0.375	0.375	0.0019–0.0043	0.0009–0.0088
	R	4-151 (2.5)	1.869	1.869	1.869	1.869	—	0.248	0.248	0.0007–0.0027	0.0014–0.0050
	T	6-192 (3.1)	1.8677–1.8815	1.8677–1.8815	1.8677–1.8815	1.8677–1.8815	—	0.2626	0.2732	0.001–0.004	—
	V	6-192 (3.1)	1.8677–1.8815	1.8677–1.8815	1.8677–1.8815	1.8677–1.8815	—	0.2626	0.2732	0.001 0.004	—
	L	6-231 (3.8)	1.785–1.786	1.785–1.786	1.785–1.786	1.785–1.786	—	0.250	0.255	0.0005–0.0035	

CRANKSHAFT AND CONNECTING ROD SPECIFICATIONS

All measurements are given in inches.

Year	VIN	No. Cylinder Displacement cu. in. (liter)	Crankshaft				Connecting Rod		
			Main Brg. Journal Dia.	Main Brg. Oil Clearance	Shaft End-play	Thrust on No.	Journal Diameter	Oil Clearance	Side Clearance
1988	W	6-173 (2.8)	2.6473–2.6483	0.0016–0.0032	0.0024–0.0083	3	1.9994–1.9983	0.0013–0.0026	0.0060–0.0170
1989	R	4-151 (2.5)	2.3000	0.0005–0.0220	0.0005–0.0180	5	2.0000	0.0005–0.0030	0.0060–0.0240
	W	6-173 (2.8)	2.6473–2.6483	0.0012–0.0027	0.0024–0.0083	3	1.9994–1.9983	0.0014–0.0036	0.0140–0.0270
	T	6-192 (3.1)	2.6473–2.6483	0.0024–0.0027	0.0012–0.0083	3	1.9994–1.9983	0.0014–0.0036	0.0140–0.0270
1990-91	A	4-138 (2.3)	2.0470–1.0480	0.0005–0.0023	0.0034–0.0095	3	1.8887–1.8897	0.0005–0.0020	0.0054–0.0177
	D	4-138 (2.3)	2.0470–2.0480	0.0005–0.0023	0.0034–0.0095	3	1.8887–1.8897	0.0005–0.0020	0.0054–0.0177
	R	4-151 (2.5)	2.300	0.0005–0.0220	0.0005–0.0180	5	2.0000	0.0005–0.0003	0.0060–0.0240
	T	6-192 (3.1)	2.6473–2.6483	0.0012–0.0030	0.0024–0.0083	3	1.9983–1.9994	0.0016–0.0034	0.0140–0.0270
	V	6-192 (3.1)	2.6473–2.6483	0.0012–0.0030	0.0024–0.0083	3	1.9983–1.9994	0.0011–0.0034	0.0140–0.0270
	L	6-231 (3.8)	2.4988–2.4998	0.0018–0.0030	0.0030–0.0110	3	2.2487–2.2499	0.0003–0.0026	0.0030–0.0150

VALVE SPECIFICATIONS

Year	VIN	No. Cylinder Displacement cu. in. (liter)	Seat Angle (deg.)	Face Angle (deg.)	Spring Test Pressure (lbs.)	Spring Installed Height (in.)	Stem-to-Guide Clearance (in.)		Stem Diameter (in.)	
							Intake	Exhaust	Intake	Exhaust
1988	W	6-173 (2.8)	46	45	90 @ 1.70 ①	1.70	0.0010–0.0027	0.0010–0.0027	NA	NA
1989	R	4-151 (2.5)	46	45	75 @ 1.68 ①	1.68	0.0010–0.0026	0.0013–0.0041	NA	NA
	W	6-173 (2.8)	46	45	90 @ 1.70 ①	1.57	0.0010–0.0027	0.0010–0.0027	NA	NA
	T	6-192 (3.1)	46	45	90 @ 1.70 ①	1.57	0.0010–0.0027	0.0010–0.0027	NA	NA
1990–91	A	4-138 (2.3)	45	②	76 @ 1.43 ①	NA	0.0010–0.0027	0.0015–0.0032	NA	NA
	D	4-138 (2.3)	45	②	76 @ 1.43 ①	NA	0.0010–0.0027	0.0015–0.0032	NA	NA
	R	4-151 (2.5)	45	46	75 @ 1.68	1.68	0.0010–0.0026	0.0013–0.0041	NA	NA
	V	6-192 (3.1)	46	45	90 @ 1.70 ①	1.57	0.0010–0.0027	0.0010–0.0027	NA	NA
	T	6-192 (3.1)	46	45	90 @ 1.70 ①	1.57	0.0010–0.0027	0.0010–0.0027	NA	NA
	L	6-231 (3.8)	46	45	80 @ 1.75 ①	1.70	0.0015–0.0035	0.0015–0.0032	NA	NA

① Valve closed
② Intake—44 degrees
　Exhaust—44.5 degrees

PISTON AND RING SPECIFICATIONS

All measurements are given in inches.

Year	VIN	No. Cylinder Displacement cu. in. (liter)	Piston Clearance	Ring Gap			Ring Side Clearance		
				Top Compression	Bottom Compression	Oil Control	Top Compression	Bottom Compression	Oil Control
1988	W	6-173 (2.8)	0.0020–0.0030	0.016–0.020	0.010–0.020	0.020–0.055	0.001–0.003	0.001–0.003	0.008
1989	R	4-151 (2.5)	0.0020–0.0022	0.010–0.020	0.010–0.020	0.020–0.060	0.002–0.003	0.001–0.003	0.015–0.055
	W	6-173 (2.8)	0.0009–0.0022	0.001–0.020	0.001–0.020	0.001–0.003	0.002–0.003	0.002–0.003	0.008
	T	6-192 (3.1)	0.0009–0.0022	0.001–0.020	0.001–0.020	0.001–0.003	0.002–0.003	0.002–0.003	0.008
1990–91	A	4-138 (2.3)	0.0007–0.0020	0.013–0.023	0.015–0.025	0.015–0.055	0.002–0.004	0.0015–0.0031	0.0195–0.026
	D	4-138 (2.3)	0.0007–0.0020	0.013–0.023	0.015–0.025	0.015–0.055	0.002–0.003	0.0015–0.0031	0.0195–0.206
	R	4-151 (2.5)	0.0014–0.0022	0.010–0.020	0.010–0.020	0.020–0.060	0.002–0.003	0.001–0.003	0.015–0.055
	V	6-192 (3.1)	0.0093–0.0022	0.010–0.020	0.020–0.028	0.010–0.030	0.002–0.003	0.002–0.003	0.008
	T	6-192 (3.1)	0.0043–0.0022	0.010–0.020	0.020–0.028	0.010–0.030	0.002–0.003	0.002–0.003	0.008
	L	6-231 (3.8)	0.0004–0.0022	0.010–0.205	0.010–0.025	0.015–0.055	0.001–0.003	0.001–0.003	0.001–0.008

TORQUE SPECIFICATIONS
All readings in ft. lbs.

Year	VIN	No. Cylinder Displacement cu. in. (liter)	Cylinder Head Bolts	Main Bearing Bolts	Rod Bearing Bolts	Crankshaft Pulley Bolts	Flywheel Bolts	Manifold		Spark Plugs
								Intake	Exhaust	
1988	W	6-173 (2.8)	①	72	40	77	46	4	19	18
1989	R	4-151 (2.5)	②	65	29	162	55	25	④	18
	W	6-173 (2.8)	①	70	37	76	46	③	18	18
	T	6-192 (3.1)	①	70	37	76	46	③	18	18
1990-91	A	4-138 (2.3)	⑤	⑥	⑦	⑧	⑨	18	27	17
	D	4-138 (2.3)	⑤	⑥	⑦	⑧	⑨	18	27	17
	R	4-151 (2.5)	②	65	29	162	55	25	④	18
	V	6-192 (3.1)	①	73	39	76	44	③	18	18
	T	6-192 (3.1)	①	73	39	76	44	③	18	18
	L	6-231 (3.8)	⑩	⑪	⑫	⑬	⑭	⑮	41	20

① Torque in 2 steps:
1st step—33 ft. lbs.
2nd step—Turn an additional 90 degrees (¼) turn
② Torque in 3 steps:
1st step—18 ft. lbs.
2nd step—Bolts "A" through "J" except "I" to 26 ft. lbs. Tighten bolt "I" to 18 ft. lbs.
3rd step—Turn an additional 90 degrees (¼) turn
③ Torque in 2 steps:
1st step—15 ft. lbs.
2nd step—24 ft. lbs.
④ Torque inner bolts to 37 ft. lbs. and outer bolts to 26 ft. lbs.
⑤ Torque in 2 steps:
1st step—Torque all bolts in sequence to 26 ft. lbs.
2nd step—Torque in sequence bolts number 7 and 9 an additional 100 degrees and the remaining bolts 110 degrees
⑥ 15 ft. lbs. plus an additional 90 degree turn
⑦ 18 ft. lbs. plus an additional 80 degree turn
⑧ 74 ft. lbs. plus an additional 90 degree turn
⑨ 22 ft. lbs. plus an additional 45 degree turn
⑩ Torque in 3 steps:
1st step—Tighten all bolts in sequence to 35 ft. lbs.
2nd step—Tighten all bolts in sequence an additional 130 degrees
3rd step—Tighten the center 4 bolts an additional 30 degrees
⑪ 26 ft. lbs. plus an additional 45 degree turn
⑫ 20 ft. lbs. plus an additional 50 degree turn
⑬ 105 ft. lbs. plus an additional 56 degree turn
⑭ 89 inch lbs. plus an additional 90 degree turn
⑮ Intake manifold to cylinder head (lower)— 89 inch lbs.

BRAKE SPECIFICATIONS

All measurements in inches unless noted.

Year	Model	Lug Nut Torque (ft. lbs.)	Master Cylinder Bore	Brake Disc		Standard Brake Drum Diameter	Minimum Lining Thickness	
				Minimum Thickness	Maximum Runout		Front	Rear
1988	Cutlass Supreme	100	0.945	0.972 ①	0.003	—	0.030	0.030
	Grand Prix	100	0.945	0.972 ①	0.003	—	0.030	0.030
	Regal	100	0.945	0.972 ①	0.003	—	0.030	0.030
1989	Cutlass Supreme	100	0.945	0.972 ①	0.004	—	0.030	0.030
	Grand Prix	100	0.945	0.972 ①	0.004	—	0.030	0.030
	Regal	100	0.945	0.972 ①	0.004	—	0.030	0.030
	Lumina	100	0.945	0.972 ①	0.004	—	0.030	0.030
1990–91	Cutlass Supreme	100	0.945	0.972 ①	0.004	—	0.030	0.030
	Grand Prix	100	0.945	0.972 ①	0.004	—	0.030	0.030
	Regal	100	0.945	0.972 ①	0.004	—	0.030	0.030
	Lumina	100	0.945	0.972 ①	0.004	—	0.030	0.030

① Rear rotor discard thickness 0.429

WHEEL ALIGNMENT

Year	Model	Caster		Camber		Toe-in (in.)	Steering Axis Inclination (deg.)
		Range (deg.)	Preferred Setting (deg.)	Range (deg.)	Preferred Setting (deg.)		
1988	Cutlass Supreme	$1^{1}/_{2}$P–$2^{1}/_{2}$P	2P	$^{3}/_{16}$P–$1^{3}/_{16}$P	$^{11}/_{16}$P	$^{3}/_{32}$N–$^{3}/_{32}$P	NA
	Grand Prix	$1^{1}/_{2}$P–$2^{1}/_{2}$P	2P	$^{3}/_{16}$P–$1^{3}/_{16}$P	$^{11}/_{16}$P	$^{3}/_{32}$N–$^{3}/_{32}$P	NA
	Regal	$1^{1}/_{2}$P–$2^{1}/_{2}$P	2P	$^{3}/_{16}$P–$1^{3}/_{16}$P	$^{11}/_{16}$P	$^{3}/_{32}$N–$^{3}/_{32}$P	NA
1989	Cutlass Supreme	$1^{5}/_{16}$P–$2^{5}/_{16}$P	$1^{13}/_{16}$P	$^{3}/_{16}$P–$1^{3}/_{16}$P	$^{11}/_{16}$P	$^{3}/_{32}$N–$^{3}/_{32}$P	NA
	Grand Prix	$1^{5}/_{16}$P–$2^{5}/_{16}$P	$1^{13}/_{16}$P	$^{3}/_{16}$P–$1^{3}/_{16}$P	$^{11}/_{16}$P	$^{3}/_{32}$N–$^{3}/_{32}$P	NA
	Regal	$1^{1}/_{2}$P–$2^{1}/_{2}$P	2P	$^{3}/_{16}$P–$1^{3}/_{16}$P	$^{11}/_{16}$P	$^{3}/_{32}$N–$^{3}/_{32}$P	NA
	Lumina	$1^{1}/_{2}$P–$2^{1}/_{2}$P	2P	$^{3}/_{16}$P–$1^{3}/_{8}$P	$^{11}/_{16}$P	$^{3}/_{32}$N–$^{3}/_{32}$P	NA
1990–91	Cutlass Supreme	$1^{1}/_{2}$P–$2^{1}/_{2}$P	2P	$^{3}/_{16}$P–$1^{3}/_{16}$P	$^{11}/_{16}$P	$^{3}/_{32}$N–$^{3}/_{32}$P	NA
	Grand Prix	$1^{5}/_{16}$P–$2^{5}/_{16}$P	$1^{13}/_{16}$P	$^{3}/_{16}$P–$1^{3}/_{16}$P	$^{11}/_{16}$P	$^{3}/_{32}$N–$^{3}/_{32}$P	NA
	Regal	$1^{1}/_{2}$P–$2^{1}/_{2}$P	2P	$^{3}/_{16}$P–$1^{3}/_{16}$P	$^{11}/_{16}$P	$^{3}/_{32}$N–$^{3}/_{32}$P	NA
	Lumina	$1^{1}/_{2}$P–$2^{1}/_{2}$P	2P	$^{3}/_{16}$P–$1^{3}/_{8}$P	$^{11}/_{16}$P	$^{3}/_{32}$N–$^{3}/_{32}$P	NA

NA—Not adjustable

ENGINE ELECTRICAL

NOTE: Disconnecting the negative battery cable on some vehicles may interfere with the functions of the on board computer systems and may require the computer to undergo a relearning process, once the negative battery cable is reconnected.

Distributorless Ignition

REMOVAL & INSTALLATION

Ignition Coil

2.3L ENGINE

1. Disconnect the negative battery cable.
2. Disconnect the 11 pin (IDI) harness connector at the ignition cover.
3. Remove the 4 ignition cover assembly-to-cylinder head bolts.
4. Remove the ignition assembly from the vehicle.
5. Remove the 4 coil housing-to-cover screws.

NOTE: Be careful not to damage the module terminals when pulling the coil assemblies from the module. Pull slowly and carefully away from the ignition assembly.

6. Disconnect the coil harness connectors.
7. Remove the coils, contacts and seals from the cover.

NOTE: If the spark plug boots stick, use a spark plug connector removing tool J–36011 or equivalent, to remove with a twisting motion.

To install:

8. Install the coils-to-cover.
9. Connect the coil harness.
10. Using new seals, install the seals into the housing.
11. Install the contacts-to-housing. use petroleum jelly to retain the contact in place.
005922stall the housing cover, retaining screws and torque to 35 inch lbs. (4 Nm).
13.
Install the spark plug boots and retainers-to-ignition cover.
14.
Install the ignition assembly-to-cylinder heads. Carefully align the boots to the spark plug terminals.
15.
Apply thread locking compound to the bolts. Install the 4 retaining bolts and torque to 19 ft. lbs. (26 Nm).
16.
Connect the 11 pin connector and negative battery cable.

2.5L ENGINE

1. Disconnect the negative battery cable.

2. Rotate the engine as follows:
a. Block the wheels and put the transaxle in neutral.
b. Position the coolant reservoir out of the way, but do not disconnect the hoses.
c. Remove the torque strut-to-engine bracket nut and bolt.
d. Using a suitable pry bar at the torque strut bracket, rotate the engine and transaxle assembly forward.
e. Align the slave hole in the torque strut with the engine bracket hole.
f. Retain the engine in this position using the torque strut-to-engine bracket bolt.
3. Label each spark plug wire for proper installation.
4. Remove the spark plug and module electrical connectors from the ignition coils.
5. Remove the 2 coil-to-module attaching screws.

NOTE: Be careful not to damage the module terminals when pulling the coil assemblies from the module. Pull slowly and carefully away from the engine.

6. Gently pull the coil assemblies from the module.
7. There are 2 coils that can be replaced separately.

To install:

8. Position the coil on the base plate (module) and tighten the retaining screws to 45 inch lbs. (5 Nm).
9. Install the spark plug and module electrical connectors. Reconnect the negative battery cable.
10. Rotate the engine to the original position as follows:
a. Pull the prybar forward to release the engine weight and remove the bolt from the torque strut slave hole and engine bracket.
b. Allow the engine and transaxle to rotate back to its original position.
c. Remove the pry bar.
d. Install the torque strut-to-engine bracket bolt and nut and torque to 37 ft. lbs. (51 Nm).
e. Reposition the coolant reservoir.

2.8L AND 3.1L ENGINES

1. Remove the air cleaner assembly.
2. Disconnect the negative battery cable.
3. Rotate the engine as follows:
a. Put the transaxle in neutral.
b. Remove the strut-to-engine bracket bolts and swing the strut aside.
c. Replace the passenger side torque strut-to-engine bracket bolt in the engine bracket.
d. Remove the coolant reservoir

1. Ignition coil and module assembly
2. Bolts
3. Cover
4. Spark plug

Ignition coil and module assembly—2.3L engine

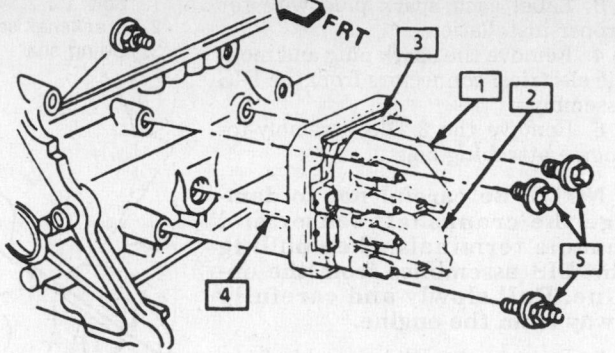

1. No. 2-3 ignition coil
2. No. 1-4 ignition coil
3. Ignition module
4. Crankshaft sensor
5. Bolt (20 ft. lbs.)

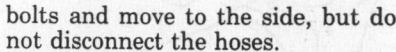

Ignition coils, module and sensor—2.5L engine

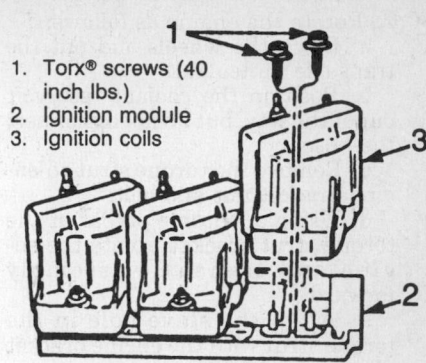

1. Torx® screws (40 inch lbs.)
2. Ignition module
3. Ignition coils

Ignition coil mounting—3.8L engine

bolts and move to the side, but do not disconnect the hoses.

e. Place a prybar in the bracket so that it contacts the bracket and the bolt.

f. Rotate the engine by pulling forward on the prybar.

g. Align the slave hole in the driver side torque strut-to-engine bracket hole.

h. Retain the engine in this position using the torque strut-to-engine bracket bolt.

4. Label each spark plug wire for proper installation.

5. Remove the spark plug and module electrical connectors from the ignition coils.

6. Remove the 2 coil-to-module attaching screws.

NOTE: Be careful not to damage the module terminals when pulling the coil assemblies from the module. Pull slowly and carefully away from the engine.

7. Gently pull the coil assemblies from the module.

8. There are 3 coils that can be replaced separately.

To install:

9. Position the coil on the base plate (module) and tighten the retaining screws to 45 inch lbs. (5 Nm).

10. Install the spark plug and module electrical connectors. Reconnect the negative (–) battery cable.

11. Rotate the engine to the original position as follows:

a. Pull the prybar forward to release the engine weight and remove the bolt from the torque strut slave hole and engine bracket.

b. Allow the engine and transaxle to rotate back to its original position.

c. Remove the prybar.

d. Install the torque strut-to-engine bracket bolt and nut and torque to 37 ft. lbs. (51 Nm).

e. Reposition the coolant reservoir.

3.8L ENGINE

1. Disconnect the negative battery cable.

2. Disconnect and label the spark plug wires.

3. Remove the 2 screws and remove the coil assembly.

To install:

4. Reposition the coil assembly and install the 2 retaining screws.

5. Install the spark plug wires and connect the negative battery cable.

Ignition Module

2.3L ENGINE

1. Disconnect the negative battery cable.

2. Remove the electrical harness, 4 retaining bolts and ignition cover assembly from the vehicle.

3. Remove the 4 housing screws, coil housing and coil harness connectors.

4. Remove the 3 module-to-housing cover screws and module.

To install:

5. If replacing the module or a coil, the new unit should come with a package of silicone grease with it, if not, purchase a tube at your local parts distributor. Spread the grease on the metal face of the module and on the cover where the module seats. The grease must be used for module cooling.

6. Install the module-to-cover, module screws and torque to 35 inch lbs. (4 Nm).

7. Install the coil harness-to-module and housing cover screws. Torque the screws to 35 inch lbs. (4 Nm).

8. Install the spark plug boots and retainers.

9. Install the ignition system-to-cylinder head while carefully aligning the spark plug boots with the terminals.

10. Apply thread locking compound to the bolts. Install the 4 retaining bolts and torque to 19 ft. lbs. (26 Nm).

11. Connect the 11 pin connector and negative battery cable.

2.5L ENGINE

1. Disconnect the negative battery cable.

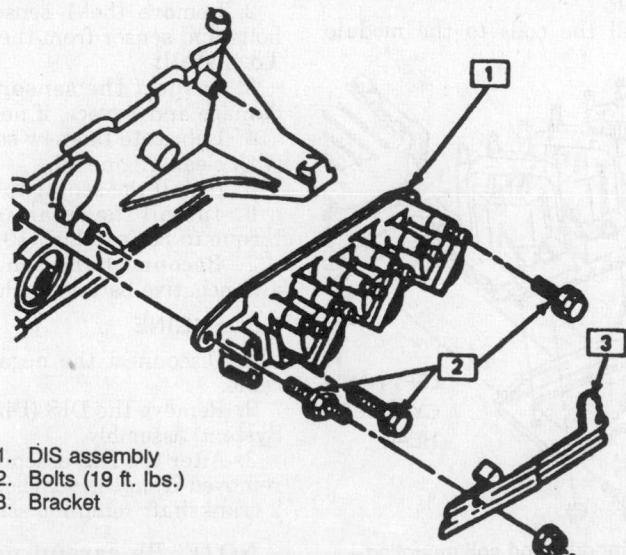

1. DIS assembly
2. Bolts (19 ft. lbs.)
3. Bracket

Coil and module assembly mounting—2.8L and 3.1L engines

2. Rotate the engine as follows:

a. Block the wheels and put the transaxle in neutral.

b. Position the coolant reservoir out of the way, but do not disconnect the hoses.

c. Remove the torque strut-to-engine bracket nut and bolt.

d. Using a suitable prybar at the torque strut bracket, rotate the engine and transaxle assembly forward.

e. Align the slave hole in the torque strut with the engine bracket hole.

f. Retain the engine in this position using the torque strut-to-engine bracket bolt.

3. Label each spark plug wire for proper installation.

4. Remove the spark plug and module electrical connectors from the DIS assembly.

5. Remove the 3 DIS assembly-to-engine attaching bolts.

NOTE: Be careful not to damage the crankshaft sensor and module terminals when pulling the DIS assemblies from the engine. Pull slowly and carefully away from the engine.

7. Remove the DIS assembly from the engine. Remove the DIS assembly from the bracket.

8. Remove the coils from the DIS assembly.

To install:

9. Install the module to the bracket.

10. Install the coil assemblies to the module and torque the screws to 45 inch lbs. (5 Nm).

11. Install the DIS assembly and attaching bolts to the engine and torque to 20 ft. lbs. (27 Nm).

12. Reconnect the spark plugs and module electrical connectors to their original positions as removed.

13. Rotate the engine to its original position as follows:

a. Pull the prybar forward to release the engine weight and remove the bolt from the torque strut slave hole and engine bracket.

b. Allow the engine and transaxle to rotate back to its original position.

c. Remove the prybar.

d. Install the torque strut-to-engine bracket bolt and nut and torque to 37 ft. lbs. (51 Nm).

e. Reposition the coolant reservoir.

2.8L AND 3.1L ENGINES

1. Remove the air cleaner assembly

2. Disconnect the negative battery cable.

3. Raise the vehicle and support safely.

3. Label each spark plug wire for proper installation.

4. Remove the spark plug and module electrical connectors from the DIS assembly.

5. Remove the 3 DIS assembly-to-engine attaching bolts.

6. Remove the 3 DIS assembly-to-engine attaching bolts.

NOTE: Be careful not to damage the crankshaft sensor and module terminals when pulling the DIS assemblies from the engine. Pull slowly and carefully away from the engine.

7. Remove the DIS assembly from the engine. Remove the DIS assembly from the bracket.

8. Remove the coils from the DIS assembly.

To install:

9. Install the module to the bracket.

10. Install the coil assemblies to the module and torque the screws to 45 inch lbs. (5 Nm).

11. Install the DIS assembly and attaching bolts to the engine and torque to 20 ft. lbs. (27 Nm).

12. Reconnect the spark plugs and module electrical connectors to their original positions as removed.

13. Install the air cleaner and reconnect the negative (–) battery cable.

3.8L ENGINE

1. Disconnect the negative battery cable.

2. Disconnect the 14-way connector at the ignition module.

3. Disconnect and label the spark plug wires.

4. Remove the 6 screws securing the coil assemblies to the ignition module and disconnect the coils from the module.

5. Remove the 3 nuts and washers securing the ignition module assembly to the bracket and remove the module.

To install:

6. Install the coils to the module

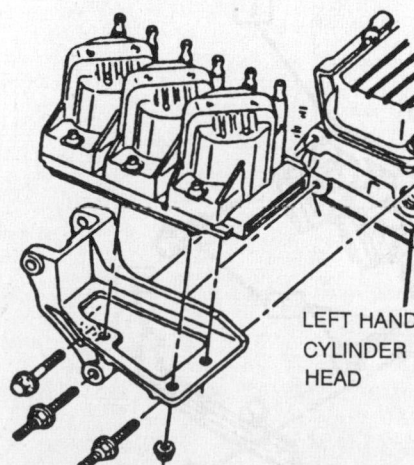

Ignition module and coil mounting— 3.8L engine

LEFT HAND CYLINDER HEAD

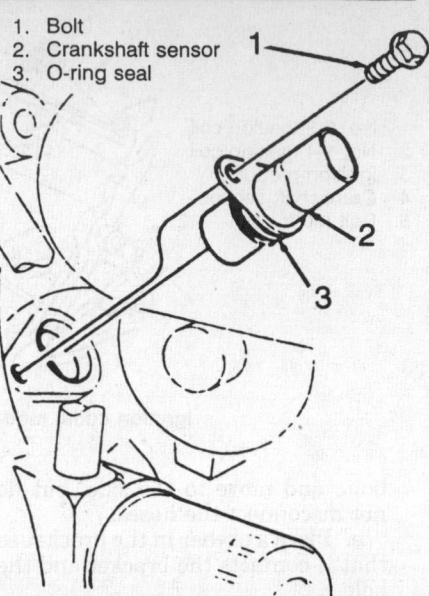

1. Bolt
2. Crankshaft sensor
3. O-ring seal

Crankshaft sensor installation— 2.3L engine

and tighten the 6 retaining screws to 40 inch lbs.

7. Install the 3 nuts and washers securing the ignition module assembly to the bracket and tighten to 70 inch lbs.

8. Connect the spark plug wires.

9. Connect the 14-way connector to the ignition module.

Crankshaft Sensor

The reluctor is an integral part of the crankshaft and the crankshaft sensor is mounted in a fixed position, timing adjustment is NOT possible.

2.3L ENGINE

1. Disconnect the negative battery cable and sensor harness connector above the oil filter.

2. Remove the 1 sensor retaining bolts and sensor from the engine.

To install:

3. Inspect the sensor O-ring for damage and replace, if necessary.

4. Lubricate the new sensor O-ring with clean engine oil.

5. Install the sensor-to-engine.

6. Install the retaining bolt and torque to 88 inch lbs. (10 Nm).

7. Reconnect the sensor harness and negative battery cable.

2.5L ENGINE

1. Disconnect the negative battery cable.

2. Remove the DIS (Direct Ignition System) assembly.

3. After the DIS assembly has been removed from the vehicle, remove the 2 crankshaft retaining screws.

NOTE: Be careful not to damage the crankshaft and module

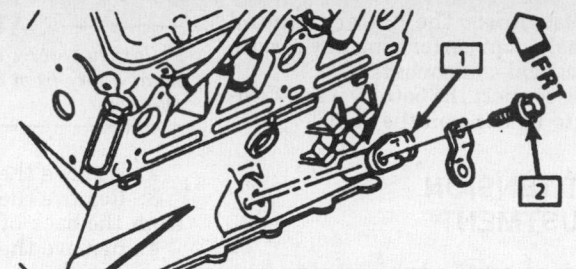

1. Crankshaft sensor
2. Bolt (71 inch lbs.)

Crankshaft sensor Installation—2.8L and 3.1L engines

terminals when pulling the coil assemblies from the engine. Pull slowly and carefully away from the engine.

4. Remove the crankshaft sensor from the DIS assembly.

To install:

5. Inspect the sensor O-ring for wear, leakage or cracks. Replace if necessary.

6. Lubricate the new O-ring seal with engine oil before installing.

7. Install the crankshaft sensor onto the DIS assembly and torque the 2 attaching screws to 20 inch lbs. (2.3 Nm).

NOTE: Use extreme care when installing the crankshaft sensor on the DIS assembly so the sensor terminals are not damaged.

8. Position the coil pack assembly onto the engine. Be careful to position the crankshaft sensor properly into the engine. Torque the 3 coil-to-engine attaching bolts to 9 ft. lbs. (12.2 Nm).

9. Refer to the "Ignition Coil" removal and installation procedures in this section for engine rotating procedures that can be very helpful.

10. Reconnect the spark plug wires and module electrical connectors in their original positions. Reconnect the negative battery cable.

2.8L AND 3.1L ENGINES

1. Disconnect the negative battery cable.

2. Remove the sensor electrical connector.

3. Remove the sensor attaching bolts and sensor from the engine.

To install:

4. Inspect the sensor O-ring for wear, cracks or leakage. Replace if necessary.

5. Lubricate the new O-ring seal with engine oil before installing.

6. Install the sensor and attaching bolt, torque the bolt to 88 inch lbs. (10 Nm).

7. Reconnect the sensor electrical connector and negative battery cable.

3.8L ENGINE

1. Disconnect the negative battery

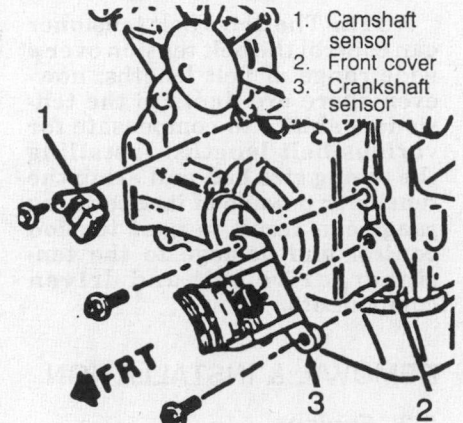

1. Camshaft sensor
2. Front cover
3. Crankshaft sensor

Camshaft and Crankshaft sensor installation—3.8L engine

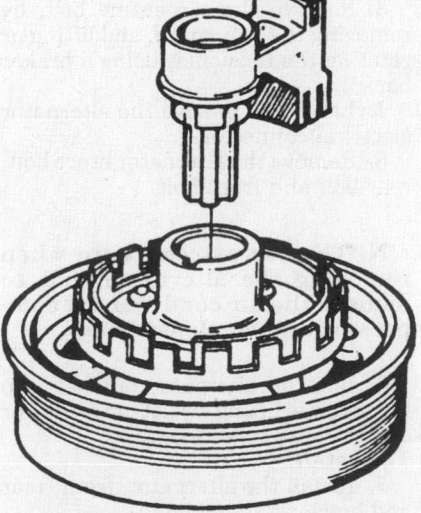

Crankshaft sensor tool to harmonic balancer—3.8L engine

cable and remove the serpentine belt assembly.

2. Raise and support the vehicle safely.

3. Remove the right front wheel assembly.

4. Remove the right inner fender access cover.

5. Remove the crankshaft harmonic balancer retaining bolt and remove the

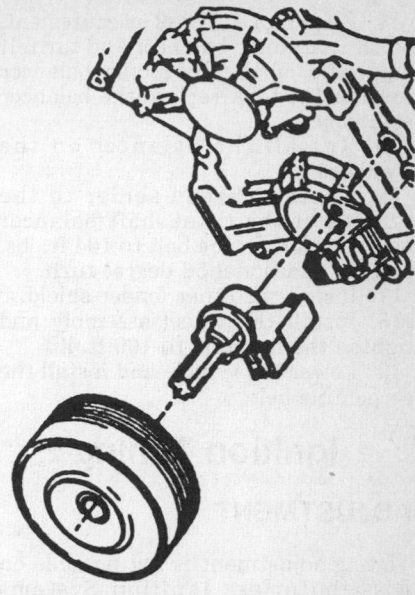

Crankshaft sensor tool to crankshaft—3.8L engine

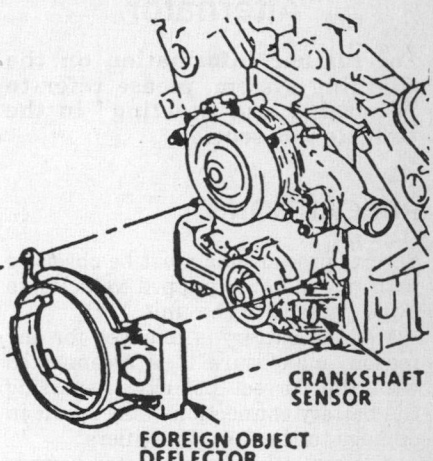

CRANKSHAFT SENSOR

FOREIGN OBJECT DEFLECTOR

Foreign object deflector—3.8L engine

balancer, using tool J–38197 or equivalent.

6. Remove the foreign object deflector.

7. Disconnect the sensor electrical connector.

8. Remove the sensor and pedestal from the block face and remove the sensor from the pedestal.

To install:

9. Loosely install the crankshaft sensor on the pedestal.

10. Position the sensor with the pedestal attached on tool J–37089 or equivalent, and position tool on the crankshaft.

11. Install the bolts to hold the pedestal to the block face and tighten to 14–28 ft. lbs.

12. Torque the pedestal pinch bolt to 36–40 inch lbs.

13. Remove the special tool and install the foreign object deflector.

14. Place tool J–37089 or equivalent, on the harmonic balancer and turn. If any vane of the harmonic balancer touches the tool, replace the balancer assembly.

15. Install the balancer on the crankshaft.

16. Install thread sealer to the threads of the crankshaft balancer bolt and tighten the bolt to 104 ft. lbs. plus an additional 56 degree turn.

17. Install the inner fender shield.

18. Install the wheel assembly and tighten the lug nuts to 100 ft. lbs.

19. Lower the vehicle and install the serpentine belt.

Ignition Timing

ADJUSTMENT

Timing adjustment is not possible on Distributorless Ignition Systems (DIS).

Alternator

For further information on the charging system, please refer to "Charging and Starting" in the Unit Repair section.

PRECAUTIONS

Several precautions must be observed with alternator equipped vehicles to avoid damage to the unit.

• If the battery is removed for any reason, make sure it is reconnected with the correct polarity. Reversing the battery connections may result in damage to the 1-way rectifiers.

• When utilizing a booster battery as a starting aid, always connect the positive to positive terminals and the negative terminal from the booster battery to a good engine ground on the vehicle being started.

• Never use a fast charger as a booster to start vehicles.

• Disconnect the battery cables when charging the battery with a fast charger.

• Never attempt to polarize the alternator.

• Do not use test lamps of more than 12 volts when checking diode continuity.

• Do not short across or ground any of the alternator terminals.

• The polarity of the battery, alternator and regulator must be matched and considered before making any electrical connections within the system.

• Never separate the alternator on an open circuit. Make sure all connections within the circuit are clean and tight.

• Disconnect the battery ground terminal when performing any service on electrical components.

• Disconnect the battery if arc welding is to be done on the vehicle.

BELT TENSION ADJUSTMENT

A single serpentine belt is used to drive all engine mounted components. Drive belt tension is maintained by a spring loaded tensioner.

NOTE: The drive belt tensioner can control the belt tension over a wide range of belt lengths; however, there are limits to the tensioners ability to compensate for various belt lengths. Installing the wrong size belt and using the tensioner outside of its operating range can result in poor tension control and damage to the tensioner, drive belt and driven components.

REMOVAL & INSTALLATION

2.3L Engine

1. Disconnect the negative battery cable.
2. Remove the electrical center fuse block shield.
3. Remove the serpentine belt, by removing the belt guard, and lifting or rotating the tensioner, using a braker bar.
4. Label and remove the alternator electrical connectors.
5. Remove the alternator brace bolt, rear bolt and front bolt.

NOTE: Use extreme care when removing the alternator, not to damage the air conditioning compressor and condensor hose.

6. Lift the alternator out between the engine lifting eyelet and the air conditioning compressor.
To install:
7. Install the alternator, front, rear and brace retaining bolts.
8. Torque the long bolt to 40 ft. lbs. (54 Nm), the short bolt to 19 ft. lbs. (26 Nm) and the brace bolt to 18 ft. lbs. (25 Nm).
9. Connect the alternator electrical connectors, serpentine belt and fuse block shield.
10. Connect the negative battery cable and check for proper operation.

2.5L Engine

1. Disconnect the negative battery cable.

CAUTION
Failure to observe this step may cause personal injury from a hot battery lead at the alternator.

2. Remove the serpentine belt.
3. Remove the electrical connectors from the back of the alternator.
4. Remove the rear (first), front attaching bolts and heat shield.
5. Remove the alternator assembly carefully making sure all wires are disconnected.
To install:
6. Position the alternator into the mounting bracket.
7. Install the front and rear mounting bolts but do not tighten.
8. Install the heat shield with the rear mounting bolts.
9. Install the electrical connectors and tighten the battery cable nut.
10. Torque the mounting bolts to 18 ft. lbs. (25 Nm).
11. Install the serpentine belt.
12. Reconnect the negative battery cable.

2.8L and 3.1L Engines

1. Disconnect the negative battery cable.

CAUTION
Failure to observe this step may cause personal injury from hot battery lead at the alternator.

1. Remove the air cleaner assembly.
2. Remove the serpentine belt.
3. Remove the electrical connectors from the back of the alternator.
4. Remove the rear (first), front attaching bolts and heat shield.
5. Remove the alternator assembly carefully making sure all wires are disconnected.
To install:
6. Position the alternator into the mounting bracket.
7. Install the front and rear mounting bolts but do not tighten.
8. Install the heat shield with the rear mounting bolts.
9. Install the electrical connectors and tighten the battery cable nut.
10. Torque the mounting bolts as follows:
   a. Long bolt to 35 ft. lbs. (47 Nm)
   b. Short bolt to 18 ft. lbs. (25 Nm)
   c. Bracket bolt to 18 ft. lbs. (25 Nm)
11. Install the serpentine belt.
12. Install the air cleaner and negative battery cable.

3.8L Engine

1. Disconnect the negative battery cable.

Failure to observe this step may cause personal injury from hot battery lead at the alternator.

2. Remove the serpentine belt.
3. Remove the electrical connectors from the back of the alternator.
3. Remove the nut and the positive battery connector from the **BAT** terminal.
4. Remove the alternator mounting bolts and remove the alternator from the vehicle.
To install:
5. Installation is the reverse of removal. Tighten all mounting bolts to 20 ft. lbs. and in the following sequence:
   a. Alternator attaching bolt to the direct fire mounting bracket/ rear brace.
   b. Alternator attaching bolt to the power steering and tensioner pulley bracket.
   c. Alternator brace bolt to engine.

NOTE: Make sure that tightening bolts does not bind alternator.

Voltage Regulator

For further information on the charging system, please refer to "Charging and Starting" in the Unit Repair section.

Starter

For further information on the charging system, please refer to "Charging and Starting" in the Unit Repair section.

REMOVAL & INSTALLATION

2.3L Engine

1. Disconnect the negative battery cable.
2. Remove the air cleaner and inlet hose from the throttle body.
3. Remove and plug the coolant reservoir hose at the radiator filler neck.
4. Remove the coolant reservoir.
5. Remove the intake manifold brace bolts.
6. Place a drain pan under the oil filter and remove the filter.
7. Remove the starter retaining bolts, lower the starter onto the frame member and disconnect the starter electrical connectors.
To install:
8. Position the starter into the vehicle, connect the electrical connectors and torque the retaining bolts to 32 ft. lbs. (43 Nm).
9. Install a new oil filter and add engine oil, as needed.

10. Install the intake manifold brace, coolant reservoir and hoses.
11. Add coolant, if needed.
12. Install the air cleaner and inlet hose.
13. Connect the negative battery cable and check for proper operation.

2.5L Engine

1. Disconnect the negative battery cable.

CAUTION

Failure to observe this step may cause personal injury from hot battery lead at the starter motor.

2. Raise and support the vehicle safely.
3. Remove the flywheel inspection cover bolts and cover.
4. Remove the stud from the starter support bracket.
5. Remove the 2 starter mounting bolts and shim, if equipped.
6. Remove the starter motor. Be careful not to damage the starter wires by letting the starter hang down.
7. While holding the starter motor, disconnect the starter electrical connectors from the starter solenoid.
8. Remove the starter from the rear bracket.
To install:
9. Install the support bracket to the starter.
10. Install the starter adjustment shims, if so equipped.
11. Position the starter to the engine mounting flange and torque the bolts to 32 ft. lbs. (43 Nm).
12. Install the bracket-to-engine and torque the stud to 18 ft. lbs. (25 Nm).
13. Install the inspection cover.
14. Lower the vehicle and connect the starter electrical wires. Reconnect the negative battery cable.

2.8L and 3.1L Engines

1. Remove the air cleaner.
2. Disconnect the negative battery cable.

CAUTION

Failure to observe this step may cause personal injury from hot battery lead at the starter motor.

3. Raise the vehicle and support it safely.
4. If equipped with an engine oil cooler, remove the engine oil, oil filter and position the hose next to the starter motor to the side.
5. Remove the nut from the brace at the air conditioning compressor, nut from the brace at the engine and the brace.
6. Remove the flywheel inspection cover.
7. Remove the starter bolts and

shims, if equipped. Do not let the starter hang from the starter wires.
8. Remove the starter wires from the solenoid and remove the starter.
To install:
9. While supporting the starter, connect the starter wires at the solenoid.
10. Install the starter motor-to-engine mount with the shims, if equipped, and the mounting bolts. Torque the bolts to 32 ft. lbs. (43 Nm).
11. If equipped with an engine oil cooler, reposition the hose next to the starter motor, install the oil filter and refill the engine with the proper amount of engine oil.
12. Install the flywheel inspection cover and tighten the bolts.
13. Install the starter support brace to the air conditioning compressor and torque the nut to 23 ft. lbs. (31 Nm).
14. Lower the vehicle, reconnect the negative battery cable and install the air cleaner assembly.

3.8L Engine

1. Disconnect the negative battery cable.

CAUTION

Failure to observe this step may cause personal injury from hot battery lead at the starter motor.

2. If necessary, remove the right side cooling fan.
3. Remove the serpentine drive belt.
4. Disconnect the air conditioning compressor upper support brace and lay the compressor in the fan opening.
5. Raise and support the vehicle safely.
6. Disconnect the engine oil cooler lines at the flex connector.
7. Remove the flywheel inspection cover.
8. Remove the starter motor retaining bolts and remove the starter motor and shims, if used.
9. Disconnect the starter motor wiring and remove the starter from the vehicle.
To install:
10. Position the starter motor and shims, if used, to the engine and tighten the mounting bolts to 32 ft. lbs.
11. Connect the electrical connectors to the starter terminals and tighten the battery nut to 80 inch lbs. and the S terminal nut to 35 inch lbs.
12. Install the flywheel inspection cover.
13. Connect the engine oil cooler lines at the flex connector.
14. Lower the vehicle and install the air conditioner compressor.
15. Install the serpentine drive belt, cooling fan and negative battery cable.

CHASSIS ELECTRICAL

Heater Blower Motor

REMOVAL & INSTALLATION

1. Disconnect the negative terminal from the battery.
2. Disconnect the electrical connections from the blower motor and resistor.
3. Remove the plastic water shield from the right side of the cowl.
4. Remove the blower motor-to-chassis screws and the blower motor.
5. Remove the cage retaining nut and the cage (old style).

NOTE: Some of the new style blower cages are plastic welded to the motor shaft. Use a hot knife to cut a slot in the cage shaft sleeve in 3 places. Cut through the plastic material from the dome to the end of the shaft until the cage splits from the shaft.

To install:
6. Install the cage on the new blower motor with the opening facing away from the motor.
7. Install the blower motor and screws. Install the sound insulator and connect the electrical leads to the motor and resistor.
8. Install the water shield to the cowl. Connect the negative battery cable.

Windshield Wiper Motor

REMOVAL & INSTALLATION

1. Disconnect the negative battery cable.
2. Remove the washer hose, cap and retaining nut from each wiper arm. Remove the wiper arms from the vehicle.
3. Remove the screws retaining the cowl cover. Lower the hood partially and remove the cowl cover. Remove the air inlet panel.
4. Disconnect the wiring harness connectors at the wiper motor and the washer hose at the firewall.
5. Remove the 3 screws from the bellcrank housing and lower the wiper linkage.
6. Remove the wiper module assembly from the vehicle. To remove the wiper motor from the module assembly, remove the 3 screw retaining the motor and remove the motor.

To install:
7. Attach the motor to the module assembly and install the module assembly in the vehicle.
8. Attach the bellcrank to module assembly and install the cowl cover, air inlet panel.
9. Attach the electrical connectors to the motor and attach the washer hose to the firewall. Install the wiper arms, nuts and caps. Torque the nuts to 25 ft. lbs. (34 Nm). Attach the washer hoses to the wiper arms.
10. Connect the negative battery cable.

Windshield Wiper Switch

REMOVAL & INSTALLATION

The windshield wiper switch is mounted on the right side of the instrument cluster, on the Grand Prix. On 1988 Cutlass Supreme, Regal and 1990-91 Lumina, it is located on the left side of the instrument cluster in combination with the headlight switch. On 1989–91 Cutlass Supreme and Regal, the switch is located on the combination switch.

Except 1989–91 Cutlass Supreme and Regal

1. Disconnect the negative battery cable.
2. Remove the screw retaining the switch panel to the instrument panel.
3. Remove the switch from the instrument panel by pulling the bottom out and releasing the top retaining clips.
4. Disconnect the electrical connector from the switch and remove it from the vehicle.
5. To install the switch, connect the electrical leads and push the switch into position.
6. Install the retaining screw. Connect the negative battery cable.

1989–91 Cutlass Supreme and Regal

1. Disconnect the negative battery cable.
2. Remove the steering wheel horn pad, wheel retaining nut and steering wheel.
3. Remove the turn signal cancelling cam assembly.
4. Remove the hazard knob and position the turn signal lever so that the housing cover screw can be removed through the opening in the switch. Remove the housing cover.
5. Remove the wire protector from the opening in the instrument panel bracket and separate the wires.

6. Disconnect the pivot and pulse switch connector. Remove the pivot switch connector and pivot switch.
7. Remove the turn signal screws, signal connector and seventeen way secondary lock from the turn signal connector.
8. Remove the buzzer switch connectors from the turn signal connector using a terminal remover tool J–35689–A. Remove the turn signal switch from the column.

To install:
9. Install the turn signal switch assembly and wire protector.
10. Install the switch retaining screws and torque to 35 inch lbs. (4 Nm).
11. Connect the buzzer switch wires to the turn signal connector, light green into location 9 and the tan/black wire into location 10.
12. Install the 17 way secondary lock.
13. Install the pivot and pulse switch assembly.
14. Install the wiring protector around the instrument panel opening, covering all wires.
15. Install the steering column housing cover and torque the screws to 35 inch lbs. (4 Nm).
16. Install the hazard knob and lubricate the bottom side of the cancelling cam with lithium grease.
17. Install the steering wheel and torque the shaft nut to 30 ft. lbs. (41 Nm).
18. Connect the negative battery cable and check steering column operations.

Instrument Cluster

REMOVAL & INSTALLATION

Cutlass Supreme

1. Disconnect the negative battery cable.
2. Remove the 5 screws retaining the cluster trim plate. Pull the bottom of the trim plate out and remove it from the vehicle.
3. Remove the screws retaining the instrument cluster and remove the cluster from the instrument panel. Disconnect the electrical connectors.
To install:
4. Install the cluster to the instrument panel. Connect the electrical leads.
5. Install the cluster trim panel. Connect the negative battery cable.

Grand Prix, Regal and Lumina

1. Disconnect the negative battery cable.
2. Remove the instrument panel pad from the vehicle.

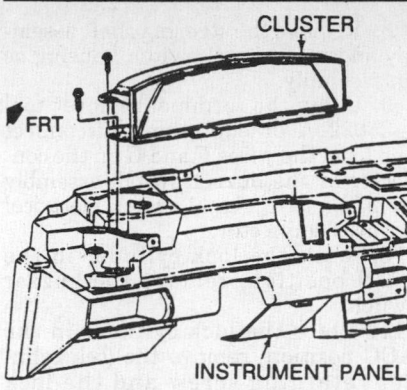

Instrument cluster removal — Grand Prix

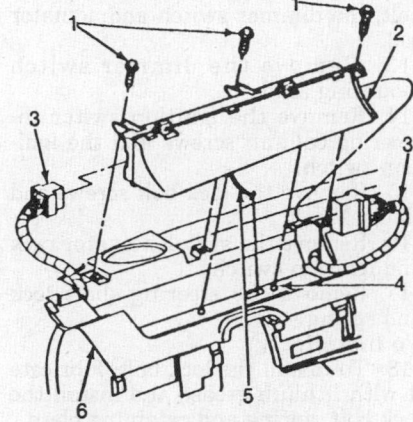

1. Screws   4. Locating tab
2. Cluster   5. PRNDL cable
3. Connector   6. Instrument panel carrier

Instrument cluster removal

3. Remove the cluster trim plate and the 4 screws retaining the instrument cluster. Pull the cluster forward, disconnect the electrical connectors, **PRNDL** cable and remove the cluster from the vehicle.
To install:
4. Install the cluster to the instrument panel. Connect the electrical leads and **PRNDL** cable.
5. Install the upper panel pad.
6. Install the cluster trim panel.
7. Connect the negative battery cable.

Speedometer

The speedometer and gauges are serviced as a unit. Removal of the instrument cluster is necessary in order to gain access to the circuit board that controls the gauges. An electronic speed sensor, mounted on the in the transaxle case tail shaft section, is used instead of a speedometer cable.

Radio

REMOVAL & INSTALLATION

1. Disconnect the negative battery cable.

2. Remove the right side sound insulator panel.
3. Remove the courtesy lamp and connector.
4. Remove the 2 receiver retaining bolts, disconnect the electrical harness and remove the receiver.

To install:

NOTE: When installing the receiver assembly, do not pinch the wires or a short circuit to ground may happen and damage the radio.

5. Connect the electrical harness, antenna cable and tighten the receiver retaining bolts.
6. Install the courtesy lamp and bolt.
7. Install the right side sound insulator panel and connect the negative battery cable.

Headlight Switch

REMOVAL & INSTALLATION

Cutlass Supreme, Regal and Lumina

1. Disconnect the negative battery cable.
2. Remove the 4 instrument cluster trim plate retaining screws and plate. Remove the air outlet trim plate.
3. Remove the 2 screws retaining the switch and remove the switch from the instrument panel.
4. Disconnect the electrical connector from the switch and remove the switch.
5. To install the switch, connect the electrical connector and install the switch in the instrument panel.
6. Install the air outlet and cluster trim plates.
7. Connect the negative battery cable.

Grand Prix

1. Disconnect the negative battery cable.
2. Remove the screw retaining the headlight switch to the instrument panel.
3. Pull the top of the switch out to release the lower retaining clips and remove it from the instrument panel.
4. Disconnect the electrical connector and remove the switch from the vehicle.
5. To install the switch, connect the electrical connector and install the switch in the instrument panel.
6. Connect the negative battery cable.

Dimmer Switch

REMOVAL & INSTALLATION

1. Disconnect the negative battery cable.
2. Place the gear shift in **P** and the lock cylinder in the **OFF-LOCK** position.
3. Remove the steering column.
4. Remove the turn signal, dimmer and pulse switch electrical connectors.
5. Remove the bowl shield.
6. Remove the switch components in order of dimmer switch nut, upper mounting stud, lower mounting stud and switch from the switch actuator rod.

To install:
7. Place the switch slider in the far left position and move back 1 detent to the right of the **OFF-LOCK** position.
8. Insert a $^3/_{32}$ in. drill bit into the adjustment hole on the switch slider during installation.
9. Install the switch and rod.
10. Install the switch jacket and bowl with the lower mounting stud. Tighten the stud to 36 inch lbs. (4 Nm).
11. Remove the adjustment tool.
12. Install the dimmer switch actuator rod with the tab first, through the hole in the instrument panel bracket and into the switch rod cap.
13. Install the dimmer switch and adjust using a $^3/_{32}$ in. drill bit into the hole in the top. Remove all excess lash. Do not tighten at this time.
14. After adjustment has been made, tighten the dimmer switch nut and mounting stud to 36 inch lbs. (4 Nm). Remove the adjusting tool.
15. Install the column jacket, bowl and shield.
16. Connect the turn signal, pulse and dimmer switch electrical connectors.
17. Connect the negative battery cable.

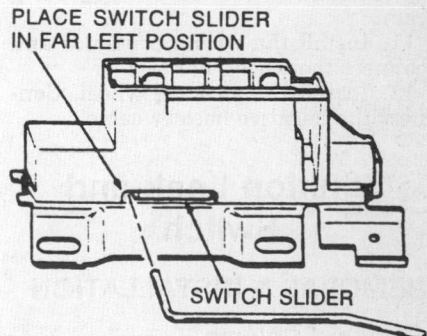

PLACE SWITCH SLIDER IN FAR LEFT POSITION

SWITCH SLIDER

Ignition switch installation position

Turn Signal Switch

REMOVAL & INSTALLATION

NOTE: Tool J-35689-A or equivalent, is required to remove the terminals from the connector on the turn signal switch.

1. Disconnect the negative battery cable. Remove the steering wheel.
2. Pull the turn signal canceling cam assembly from the steering shaft.
3. Remove the hazard warning knob-to-steering column screw and the knob.

NOTE: Before removing the turn signal assembly, position the turn signal lever so the turn signal assembly to steering column screws can all be removed.

4. Remove the column housing cover-to-column housing bowl screw and the cover.

NOTE: If equipped with cruise control, disconnect the cruise control electrical connector.

5. Remove the turn signal lever-to-pivot assembly screw and the lever; 1 screw is in the front and the other screw is in the rear.
6. Remove the wiring protector from the opening in the instrument panel bracket and separate from the wires.
7. Using the terminal remover tool J-35689-A or equivalent, disconnect and label the wires **F** and **G** on the connector at the buzzer switch assembly from the turn signal switch electrical harness connector.
8. Remove the turn signal switch-to-steering column screws and the switch.

To install:

9. Install the turn signal switch to the steering column, torque the turn signal switch-to-steering column screws to 35 inch lbs. (4 Nm).
10. Install the electrical connectors and install the turn signal lever to the pivot assembly. Install the hazard flasher knob. Install the canceling cam.
11. Install the wiring protector and connect the wiring harness.
12. Install the steering wheel. Connect the negative battery cable.

Ignition Lock and Switch

REMOVAL & INSTALLATION

Standard Column

1. Disconnect the negative terminal

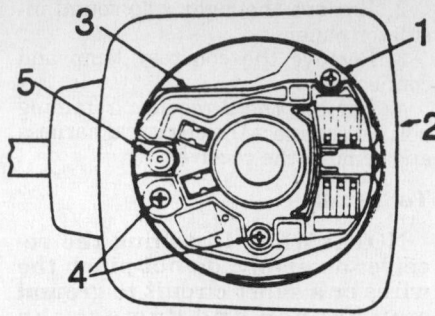

1. Screw
2. Housing cover
3. Turn signal switch
4. Screw
5. Self tapping screw

Turn signal switch mounting

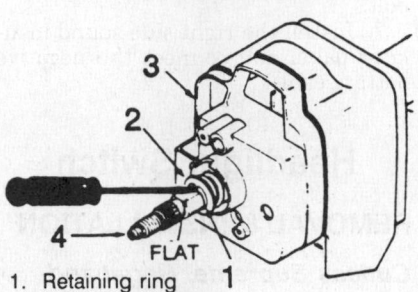

1. Retaining ring
2. Thrust washer
3. Turn signal switch housing
4. Steering shaft assembly

Removing the turn signal switch housing

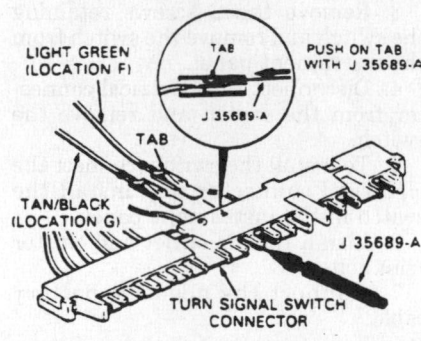

Removing the turn signal switch connector

from the battery. Remove the left side lower trim panel.

2. Remove the steering column-to-support screws and lower the steering column.
3. Disconnect the dimmer switch and turn signal switch connectors.
4. Remove the wiring harness-to-firewall nuts.
5. Remove the steering column-to-steering gear bolt and the steering column from the vehicle.
6. Remove the combination switch.
7. Place the lock cylinder in the **RUN** position.

8. Remove the steering shaft assembly and turn signal switch housing as an assembly.
9. Using the terminal remover tool J-35689-A or equivalent, disconnect and label the wires **F** and **G** on the connector at the buzzer switch assembly from the turn signal switch electrical harness connector.
10. With the lock cylinder in the **RUN** position, remove the buzzer switch.
11. Place the lock cylinder in the **ACC** position, remove the lock cylinder retaining screw and the lock cylinder.
12. Remove the dimmer switch nut/bolt, the dimmer switch and actuator rod.
13. Remove the dimmer switch mounting stud.
14. Remove the ignition switch-to-steering column screws and the ignition switch.
15. Remove the lock bolt screws and the lock bolt.
16. Remove the switch actuator rack and ignition switch.
17. Remove the steering shaft lock and spring.

To install:

18. To install the lock bolt, lubricate it with lithium grease and install the lock bolt, spring and retaining plate.
19. Lubricate the teeth on the switch actuator rack, install the rack and the ignition switch through the opening in the steering bolt until it rests on the retaining plate.
20. Install the steering column lock cylinder set by holding the barrel of the lock cylinder, inserting the key and turning the key to the **ACC** position.
21. Install the lock set in the steering column while holding the rack against the lock plate.
22. Install the lock retaining screw. Insert the key in the lock cylinder and turn the lock cylinder to the **START** position and the rack will extend.

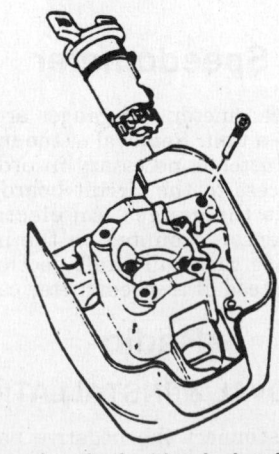

Removing the ignition lock cylinder

23. Center the slotted holes on the ignition switch mounting plate and install the ignition switch mounting screw and nut.

24. Install the dimmer switch and actuator rod into the center slot on the switch mounting plate.

25. Install the buzzer switch and turn the lock cylinder to the **RUN** position. Push the switch in until it is bottomed out with the plastic tab that covers the lock retaining screw.

26. Install the steering shaft and turn signal housing as an assembly.

27. Install the turn signal switch. Install the steering wheel to the column, torque the steering shaft nut to 30 ft. lbs. (41 Nm).

28. Install the steering column in the vehicle. Connect all electrical leads. Install the lower trim panels.

29. Connect the negative battery cable.

Tilt Column

1. Disconnect the negative terminal from the battery. Tilt the column up as far as it will go and remove the left side lower trim panel.

2. Remove the steering column-to-support screws and lower the steering column.

3. Disconnect the dimmer switch and turn signal switch connectors.

4. Remove the wiring harness-to-firewall nuts and steering column.

5. Remove the steering column-to-steering gear bolt and the steering column from the vehicle.

6. Remove the combination switch.

7. Using a flat type pry blade, position it in the square opening of the spring retainer, push downward (to the left) to release the spring retainer. Remove the wheel tilt spring.

8. Remove the spring retainer, the tilt spring and the tilt spring guide.

9. Remove the shoe pin retaining cap. Using the pivot pin removal tool J–21854–01 or equivalent, remove the 2 pivot pins.

10. Place the lock cylinder in the **RUN** position.

11. Pull the shoe release lever and release the steering column housing.

12. Remove the column housing, the steering shaft assembly and turn signal switch housing as an assembly.

13. Using the terminal remover tool J–35689–A or equivalent, disconnect and label the wires **F** and **G** on the connector at the buzzer switch assembly from the turn signal switch electrical harness connector.

14. Place the lock cylinder in the **RUN** position and remove the buzzer switch.

15. Place the lock cylinder in the **ACC** position. Remove the lock cylinder retaining screw and the lock cylinder.

16. Remove the dimmer switch nut/bolt, the dimmer switch and actuator rod.

17. Remove the dimmer switch mounting stud.

18. Remove the ignition switch-to-steering column screws and the ignition switch.

19. Remove the lock bolt screws and the lock bolt.

20. Remove the switch actuator rack and ignition switch.

21. Remove the steering shaft lock and spring.

To install:

22. Torque the steering lock screw to 27 inch lbs. (2.7 Nm), the dimmer switch stud to 35 inch lbs. (4 Nm), the turn signal switch housing screws to 88 inch lbs. (9.8 Nm), the turn signal switch screws to 35 inch lbs. (4 Nm) and the steering wheel locknut to 30 ft. lbs. (41 Nm).

23. To install the lock bolt, lubricate it with lithium grease and install the lock bolt, spring and retaining plate.

24. Lubricate the teeth on the switch actuator rack. Install the rack and the ignition switch through the opening in the steering bolt until it rests on the retaining plate.

25. Install the steering column lock cylinder set by holding the barrel of the lock cylinder, insert the key and turn the key to the **ACC** position.

26. Install the lock set in the steering column while holding the rack against the lock plate.

27. Install the lock retaining screw. Insert the key in the lock cylinder. Turn the lock cylinder to the **START** position and the rack will extend.

28. Center the slotted holes on the ignition switch mounting plate. Install the ignition switch mounting screw and nut.

29. Install the dimmer switch and actuator rod into the center slot on the switch mounting plate.

30. Install the buzzer switch and turn the lock cylinder to the **RUN** position. Push the switch in until it is bottomed out with the plastic tab that covers the lock retaining screw.

31. Install the steering shaft and turn signal housing as an assembly.

32. Install the turn signal switch. Install the steering wheel. Install the column support screws and the lower trim panels.

33. Connect the negative battery cable.

Stoplight Switch

ADJUSTMENT

1. Disconnect the negative battery cable.

2. Remove the left side sound insulator panel.

3. Depress the brake pedal as far as possible and hold.

4. Using a stiff wire with a hooked end, gently pull on the switch set lever and listen for an audible click. If there is NO click, release the brake pedal and repeat the steps. Also, if a click is not heard, the switch may be defective. Connect the negative battery cable.

REMOVAL & INSTALLATION

1. Disconnect the negative battery cable.

2. Remove the 3 fasteners from the left side insulator panel.

3. Slide the steering shaft protective cover towards the cowl.

4. Remove the vacuum hose at the cruise control cut off switch, if so equipped.

5. Remove the stoplamp switch-to-steering column bracket retaining pin.

6. Disconnect the electrical connector.

7. Push the switch arm to the left and towards the cowl to disconnect switch-to-pedal arm. Release the snap clip and remove the switch.

To install:

8. Install the switch and push up until it is seated into the top snap clip.

9. Install the electrical connectors.

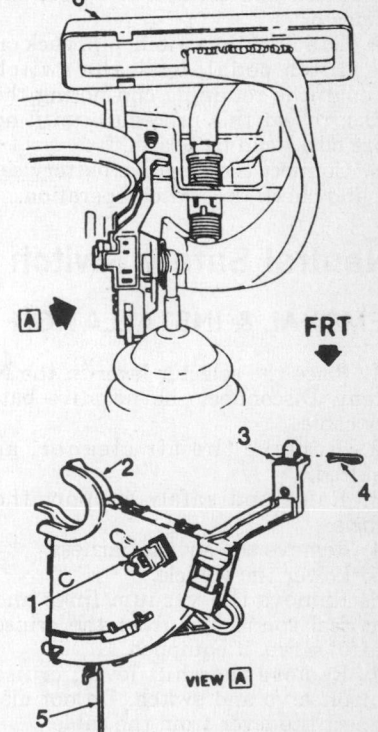

FRT

VIEW Ⓐ

1. Cruise control connector
2. Switch assembly
3. Wave washer
4. Retainer clip
5. Wire hook
6. Brake pedal

Stoplight switch mounting and removal

10. Connect the switch to the pedal.
11. Install the switch-to-steering column retaining pin.
12. Install the vacuum hose if equipped with cruise control.
13. Install the steering shaft protective sleeve.
14. Adjust the stoplight switch.
15. Install the left sound insulator, connect the negative battery cable and check switch operation.

Clutch Switch

ADJUSTMENT

1. Pull back on the clutch pedal and push the switch through the retaining clip noting the clicks.
2. Repeat this procedure until no more clicks can be heard.

REMOVAL & INSTALLATION

1. Disconnect the negative terminal from the battery.
2. Remove the lower left trim panel. Locate the switch on the clutch pedal support.
3. Disconnect the electrical connector from the switch and remove the switch by twisting it out of the tubular retaining clip.
4. Using a new retaining clip, install the switch and connect the electrical connector.
5. To adjust the switch, pull back on the clutch pedal, push the switch through the retaining clip noting the clicks; repeat this procedure until no more clicks can be heard.
6. Connect the negative battery cable and check the switch operation.

Neutral Safety Switch

REMOVAL & INSTALLATION

1. Place the selector lever in the **N** detent. Disconnect the negative battery cable.
2. Remove the air cleaner, as required.
3. Raise and safely support the vehicle.
4. Remove the switch harness.
5. Lower the vehicle.
6. Remove the vacuum lines and electrical connectors from the cruise control servo, if equipped.
7. Remove the shift lever, cruise control servo and switch. Do not disconnect the lever from the cable.
To install:
8. Align the notch on the inner sleeve of the switch with the notch on the switch body.
9. Install the switch and tighten the bolts to 18 ft. lbs. (24 Nm).

10. Install the shift lever and tighten the nut to 15 ft. lbs. (20 Nm).
11. Raise and safely support the vehicle, connect the switch harness and lower the vehicle.
12. Install the cruise control servo, vacuum lines and electrical connectors, if equipped.
13. Install the air cleaner, as required and connect the negative battery cable.

Fuses, Circuit Breakers and Relays

LOCATION

Fusible Links

Fusible links are sections of wire, with special insulation, designed to melt under electrical overload. Replacements are simply spliced into the wire. The wires are located at the starter solenoid terminal and the right side electrical center in the engine compartment.

Circuit Breakers

A circuit breaker is an electrical switch which breaks the circuit during an electrical overload. The circuit breaker will remain open until the short or overload condition in the circuit is corrected. Circuit breakers are located in the fuse panel and component center located behind the instrument panel.

Fuse Panel

The fuse panel is located on the left side of the instrument panel in Regal, Cutlass Supreme and Lumina. It is located on the right side of the instrument panel in the Grand Prix. In order to gain access to the fuse panel, it may be necessary to first remove the lower trim panel.

Various Relays

The coolant fan, air conditioner compressor, are located in the engine compartment mounted to the right side of the firewall on the relay bracket. The high and low blower relays are located in the component center located behind the instrument panel on the left side. The power door lock relay is located on the left side behind the instrument panel.

Flashers

LOCATION

Hazard Flasher

The hazard flasher is located in the component center behind the instrument panel.

Turn Signal

The turn signal flasher is located behind the lower left side of the instrument panel on the steering column support.

Computer

LOCATION

The Electronic Control Module (ECM) is located on the right front wheel well at the front of the strut tower.

Cruise Control
ADJUSTMENT

1. With the servo cable installed on the brackets, place the cable over the stud on the servo lever so the stud engages the slot in the cable end.
2. Connect the cable to the throttle lever and release the lever.
3. Pull the servo end of the cable towards the servo as far as possible without moving the throttle.
4. Attach the cable to the servo in the closest alignment holes without moving the throttle.

NOTE: Do not stretch the cable to attach it to the servo. This will not allow the engine to return to idle.

5. Check the system operation and repeat the adjustment as necessary.

ENGINE COOLING

Radiator

REMOVAL & INSTALLATION

1. Disconnect the negative battery cable.
2. Remove the air cleaner, mounting stud and duct.
3. Drain the engine coolant from the radiator.
4. Remove the coolant recovery bottle.
5. Remove the engine strut brace bolts from the upper tie bar and rotate the struts and brace rearward.

NOTE: To prevent shearing of the rubber bushing, loosen the bolts on the engine strut before swinging the struts.

6. Remove the air intake resonator mounting nut, upper radiator mounting panel bolts and clamps.

7. Disconnect the cooling fan electrical connectors.

8. Remove the upper radiator mounting panel with the fans attached.

9. Remove the upper and lower radiator hoses.

10. Remove the automatic transaxle cooler lines from the radiator.

11. Remove the radiator.

To install:

NOTE: **If a new radiator is being used, transfer all necessary fittings from the old radiator to the new one.**

12. Position the radiator into the lower insulator pads

13. Install the automatic transaxle cooler lines to radiator.

14. Install the upper and lower radiator hoses and tighten the clamps.

15. Install the upper radiator mounting panel with the fans attached and connect the fan wires.

16. Install the mounting panel bolts and clamps. Torque the bolts to 89 inch lbs. (10 Nm).

17. Install the coolant recovery bottle.

18. Swing the engine strut to the proper position and tighten the bolts.

19. Refill the engine with the specified amount of engine coolant.

20. Install the air cleaner and negative battery cable. Start the engine and check for coolant leaks.

Electric Cooling Fan

TESTING

The electric cooling fans are controlled by the electronic control module. The coolant temperature sensor in the engine sends a signal to the ECM when the engine coolant temperature reaches 223°F (205°C). The ECM grounds the cooling fan relay which turns the fan ON. The cooling fan will also turn ON if the air conditioner pressure switch detects a pressure more than 200 psi and the vehicle speed is less than 70 mph (113 Km/h). If the cooling fan is turned ON by the ECM for any reason, the fan will cycle for no less than 30 seconds.

REMOVAL & INSTALLATION

1. Disconnect the negative battery cable.

2. Disconnect the electrical wiring harness from the cooling fan frame.

3. Remove the fan assembly from the radiator support.

4. Install the fan assembly to the radiator support. Torque the fan assembly-to-radiator support bolts to 7 ft. lbs. (9.5 Nm).

5. Attach the wiring harness and connect the negative battery cable.

Cooling Fan Relay

The cooling fan relay is located in the right side electrical center on the inner fender. The heavy duty relay goes into the far left socket and the standard duty relay goes in the center socket.

Heater Core

REMOVAL & INSTALLATION

1. Disconnect the negative battery cable.

2. Drain the cooling system.

3. Remove the upper firewall weatherstrip. Remove the upper cowl.

4. Remove the heater hoses from the core.

5. Inside the vehicle, remove the sound insulator panel. Remove the rear seat duct adapter.

6. Remove the heater duct. Remove the heater core cover and remove the heater core.

To install:

7. Install the heater core and cover. Install the rear seat duct adapter.

8. Install the sound insulator.

9. Attach the heater hoses to the core. Install the upper cowl and the weatherstrip.

10. Fill the cooling system and check for leaks. Connect the negative battery cable.

Water Pump

REMOVAL & INSTALLATION

2.3L Engine

1. Disconnect the negative battery cable.

2. Disconnect the upper engine torque strut and rotate the engine rearward.

3. Disconnect and remove the oxygen sensor, if needed.

4. Remove the exhaust heat shield and EGR valve, if so equipped.

5. Remove the exhaust pipe from manifold.

6. Remove the exhaust manifold.

7. Partially drain the engine coolant.

8. Remove the coolant return hose and lower coolant pipe from the pump.

9. Remove the pump retaining bolts and pump.

To install:

10. Clean the gasket mating surfaces.

11. Install the pump, retaining bolts and torque to 19 ft. lbs. (26 Nm).

12. Install the lower coolant pipe and torque to 124 inch lbs. (14 Nm).

13. Install the coolant return hose.

14. Install the exhaust manifold, oxygen sensor, EGR valve and heat shield.

15. Return the engine to its proper position and install the torque strut.

16. Refill the engine with coolant, connect the negative battery cable, start the engine and check for coolant leaks.

2.5L Engine

1. Disconnect the negative battery cable.

2. Remove the alternator.

3. Remove the convenience center heat shield.

4. Drain about a gallon of engine coolant from the radiator. Enough to be below the water pump level.

5. Remove the 4 water pump-to-engine attaching bolts.

6. Remove the water pump and gasket.

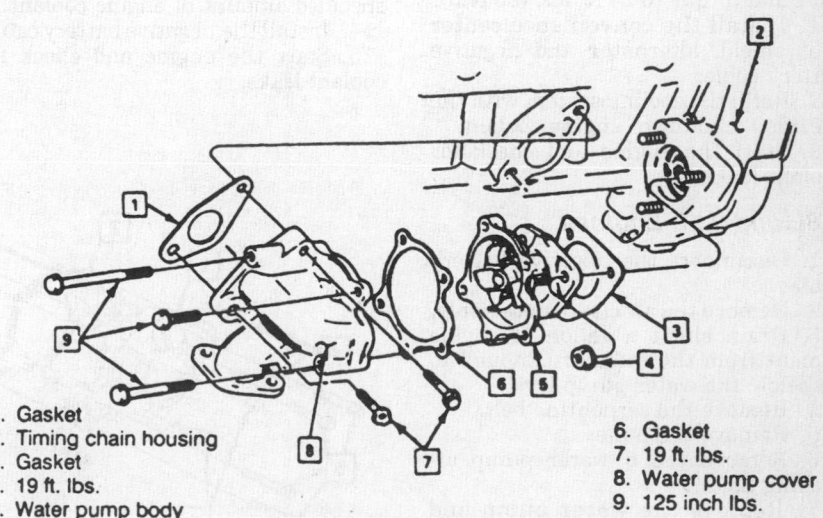

1. Gasket
2. Timing chain housing
3. Gasket
4. 19 ft. lbs.
5. Water pump body
6. Gasket
7. 19 ft. lbs.
8. Water pump cover
9. 125 inch lbs.

Water pump mounting—2.3L engine

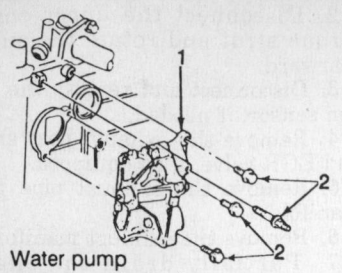

1. Water pump
2. 24 ft. lbs. (33 Nm)

Water pump mounting—2.5L engine

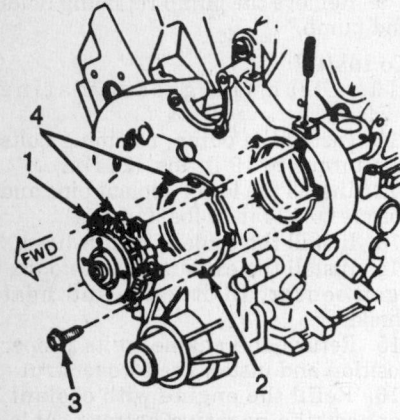

1. Water pump
2. Gasket
3. Mounting bolts
4. Pump locator—must be vertical

Water pump mounting—2.8L and 3.1 engines

7. Remove the pulley from the old pump, if a new pump is being installed.

To install:

8. Clean the water pump mating surfaces.

9. Install the pump and pulley assembly onto the engine with a new gasket.

10. Install the water pump attaching bolts and torque to 24 ft. lbs. (33 Nm).

11. Install the convenience center heat shield, alternator and negative battery cable.

12. Refill the cooling system with the specified amount of engine coolant.

13. Start the engine and check for coolant leaks.

2.8L and 3.1L Engines

1. Disconnect the negative battery cable.

2. Remove the air cleaner assembly.

3. Drain about a gallon of engine coolant from the radiator. Enough to be below the water pump level.

4. Remove the serpentine belt.

5. Remove the pulley.

6. Remove the 5 water pump attaching bolts.

7. Remove the water pump and gasket.

To install:

8. Clean the water pump mounting surfaces.

9. Install the water pump with a new gasket.

10. Install the attaching bolts and torque to 89 inch lbs. (10 Nm).

11. Install the pulley and serpentine belt.

12. Refill the cooling system with the specified amount of engine coolant.

13. Install the air cleaner and negative battery cable.

14. Start the engine and check for coolant leaks.

3.8L Engine

1. Disconnect the negative battery cable.

2. Drain the engine coolant from the radiator.

3. Disconnect the coolant recovery reservoir.

4. Remove the serpentine belt.

NOTE: If more access is needed, remove the inner fender electrical cover.

5. Remove the pulley.

6. Remove the 8 water pump attaching bolts.

7. Remove the water pump and gasket.

To install:

8. Clean the water pump mounting surfaces.

9. Install the water pump with a new gasket.

10. Install the attaching bolts and torque the long bolts to 22 ft. lbs. (30 Nm) and the short bolts to 13 ft. lbs. (18 Nm).

11. Install the pulley and serpentine belt. Tighten the pulley to 115 inch lbs.

12. Reconnect the coolant recovery reservoir.

13. Refill the cooling system with the specified amount of engine coolant.

14. Install the negative battery cable.

15. Start the engine and check for coolant leaks.

Thermostat

REMOVAL & INSTALLATION

2.3L Engine

1. Remove the air cleaner assembly and partially drain the engine coolant into a drain pan.

2. Remove the radiator and heater hoses from the coolant outlet.

3. Remove the electrical connectors from the coolant outlet.

4. Remove the pipe and retaining bolts from the outlet.

5. Remove the outlet and thermostat.

To install:

6. Clean the gasket mating surfaces.

7. Using a new gasket and RTV sealant, install the thermostat and outlet.

8. Torque the bolts to 19 ft. lbs. (26 Nm).

9. Install the pipe, electrical connectors and hoses to the coolant outlet.

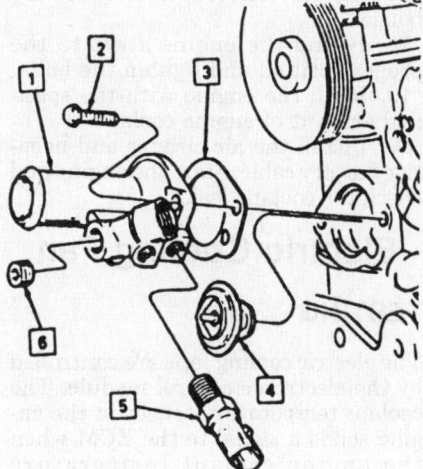

1. Water outlet
2. 19 ft. lbs.
3. Gasket
4. Thermostat
5. Coolant sensor
6. Plug

Thermostat assembly—2.3L engine

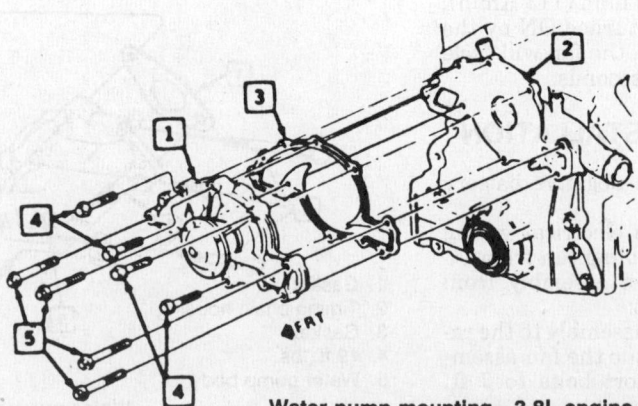

1. Coolant pump
2. Front cover
3. Gasket
4. 13 ft. lbs.
5. 22 ft. lbs.

Water pump mounting—3.8L engine

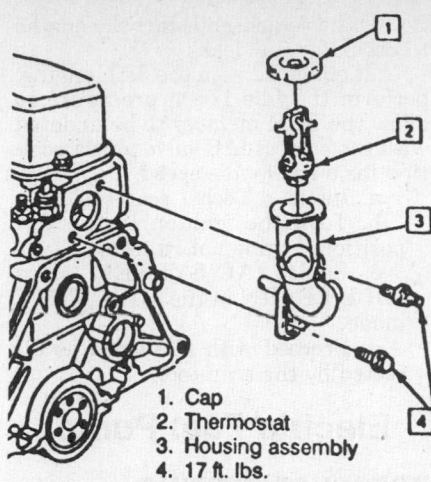

1. Cap
2. Thermostat
3. Housing assembly
4. 17 ft. lbs.

Thermostat assembly—2.5L engine

10. Refill the radiator with the specified amount of engine coolant, connect the negative battery cable and install the air cleaner.

11. Start the engine and check for leaks.

2.5L Engine

1. Drain about a ½ gallon of engine coolant from the radiator.

2. Remove the thermostat housing cap.

3. Remove the thermostat by using the wire handle to lift it out of the housing.

To install:

4. Insert the thermostat and seal into the housing.

5. Install the thermostat housing cap and refill the engine with the proper amount of engine coolant.

2.8L and 3.1L Engines

1. Drain about a ½ gallon of engine coolant from the radiator.

2. Remove the radiator hose from the water outlet.

3. Remove the water outlet attaching bolts and water outlet.

4. Remove the thermostat.

5. Clean the manifold water inlet and water outlet mating surfaces.

To install:

6. Position the thermostat into the intake manifold.

7. Apply a 0.125 inch (3mm) bead of RTV sealer to the thermostat housing.

8. Install the water outlet to the intake manifold. Torque the attaching bolts to 17 ft. lbs. (23 Nm).

9. Install the radiator hose to the water outlet housing.

10. Refill the engine with the specified engine coolant. Start the engine and check for coolant leaks.

3.8L Engine

1. Drain about a ½ gallon of engine coolant from the radiator.

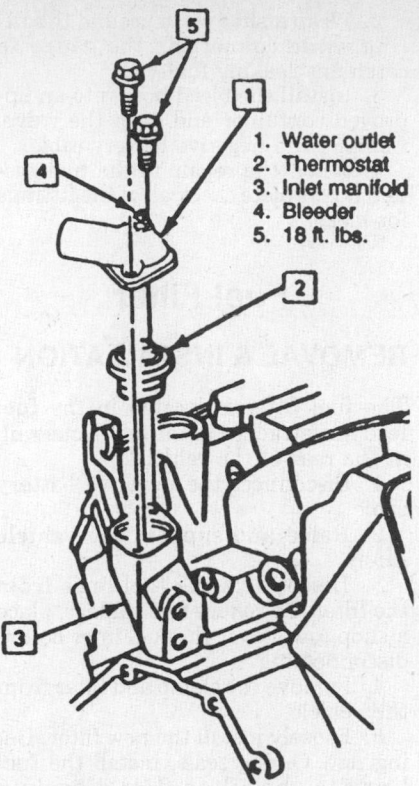

1. Water outlet
2. Thermostat
3. Inlet manifold
4. Bleeder
5. 18 ft. lbs.

Thermostat assembly—2.8L and 3.1L engines

2. Remove the radiator hose from the water outlet.

3. Disconnect the electrical connections from the throttle body assembly.

4. Remove the water outlet attaching bolts and water outlet.

5. Remove the thermostat.

6. Clean the manifold water inlet and water outlet mating surfaces.

To install:

7. Position the thermostat into the intake manifold with a new gasket.

8. Install the water outlet to the intake manifold with RTV sealer. Torque the attaching bolts to 20 ft. lbs. (27 Nm).

9. Install the radiator hose to the water outlet housing.

10. Connect the electrical connections to the throttle body assembly.

11. Refill the engine with the specified engine coolant. Connect the negative battery cable, start the engine and check for coolant leaks.

FUEL SYSTEM

Fuel System Service Precautions

Safety is the most important factor when performing not only fuel system maintenance but any type of maintenance. Failure to conduct maintenance and repairs in a safe manner may result in serious personal injury or death. Maintenance and testing of the vehicle's fuel system components can be accomplished safely and effectively by adhering to the following rules and guidelines.

• To avoid the possibility of fire and personal injury, always disconnect the negative battery cable unless the repair or test procedure requires that battery voltage be applied.

• Always relieve the fuel system pressure prior to disconnecting any fuel system component (injector, fuel rail, pressure regulator, etc.), fitting or fuel line connection. Exercise extreme caution whenever relieving fuel system pressure to avoid exposing skin, face and eyes to fuel spray. Please be advised that fuel under pressure may penetrate the skin or any part of the body that it contacts.

• Always place a shop towel or cloth around the fitting or connection prior to loosening to absorb any excess fuel due to spillage. Ensure that all fuel spillage (should it occur) is quickly removed from engine surfaces. Ensure that all fuel soaked cloths or towels are deposited into a suitable waste container.

• Always keep a dry chemical (Class

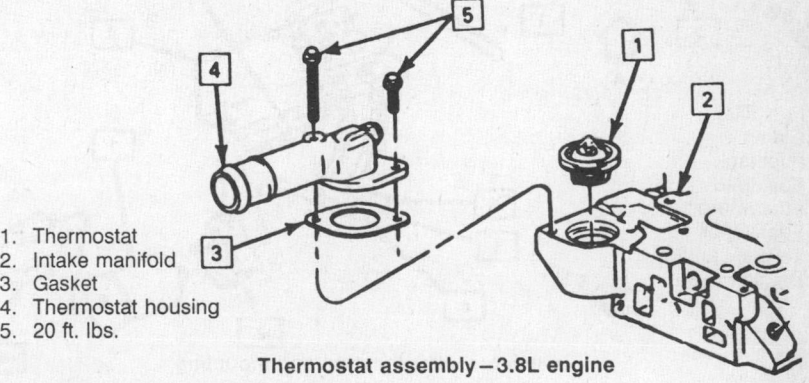

1. Thermostat
2. Intake manifold
3. Gasket
4. Thermostat housing
5. 20 ft. lbs.

Thermostat assembly—3.8L engine

B) fire extinguisher near the work area.

• Do not allow fuel spray or fuel vapors to come into contact with a spark or open flame.

• Always use a backup wrench when loosening and tightening fuel line connection fittings. This will prevent unnecessary stress and torsion to fuel line piping. Always follow the proper torque specifications.

• Always replace worn fuel fitting O-rings with new. Do not substitute fuel hose or equivalent where fuel pipe is installed.

RELIEVING FUEL SYSTEM PRESSURE

2.5L Engine

1. Remove the fuel filler cap.
2. Remove the fuel pump fuse from the fuse block located in the passenger compartment.
3. Start the engine and run until the engine stops due to the lack of fuel.
4. Crank the engine for 3 seconds to ensure all pressure is relieved.
5. Make sure the negative battery cable is disconnected.

Except 2.5L Engine

1. Connect fuel pressure gauge J–34730–1 or equivalent, to the fuel pressure connection.

2. Wrap a shop cloth around the fitting while connecting the gauge to catch any leaking fuel.
3. Install the bleed hose into an approved container and open the valve. Connect the negative battery cable.
4. When the repair to the fuel system is complete check all of the fittings for leaks.

Fuel Filter

REMOVAL & INSTALLATION

The fuel filter is located in the fuel feed line attached to the left frame rail, at the rear of the vehicle.

1. Disconnect the negative battery cable.
2. Raise and support the vehicle safely.
3. Disconnect the fuel lines from the filter. To reduce fuel spillage, place a shop towel over the fuel lines before disconnecting.
4. Remove the clamp and filter from the vehicle.
5. Loosely install the new filter. Using new O-ring seals, install the fuel lines to the filter. Use a backup wrench to prevent the filter from turning and O-ring damage. Torque the fittings to 22 ft. lbs. (30 Nm).
6. Secure the filter to the vehicle. Reconnect the negative battery cable.

Lower the vehicle and start the engine to check for fuel leaks.

7. If equipped with the 3.1L engine, perform the Idle Learn procedure to allow the ECM memory to be updated with the correct IAC valve pintle position for a stable idle speed.

a. Install a Tech 1 scan tool.
b. Turn the ignition to the ON position, engine not running.
c. Select **IAC SYSTEM**, then **IDLE LEARN** in the **MISC TEST** mode.
d. Proceed with idle learn as directed by the scan tool.

Electric Fuel Pump

PRESSURE TESTING

2.5L Engine

1. With the ignition **OFF**, release the fuel pressure and check for fuel in the tank.
2. Connect a fuel pressure gauge J-29658-B or equivalent, to the service fitting. Jump the fuel pump test terminal to 12 volts using a fused jumper wire.
3. With the key in the ON position and engine NOT running, the pressure should be 26-32 psi (179-220 kPa).
4. Listen to the pump running in the tank. If the pump is running, check for obstructed fuel filter, lines or pressure regulator.

Except 2.5L Engine

1. Release the fuel system pressure. Wrap a shop towel around fuel pressure connector on the fuel rail to absorb any leakage that may occur when installing gauge.
2. Connect a fuel pressure gauge J-34730–1 or equivalent, to the service fitting.
3. With the ignition switch **ON** and engine NOT running, the fuel pump pressure should be 40-47 psi (280-325 kPa) and hold steady when the engine is turned OFF.

REMOVAL & INSTALLATION

The fuel pump is an integral part of the fuel level sensor assembly, located in the fuel tank.

1. Disconnect the negative battery cable.
2. Drain all fuel from the fuel tank.
3. Raise and safely support the vehicle. Support the fuel tank and remove the retaining straps.
4. Lower the fuel tank slightly and disconnect the fuel lines, hoses and the sending unit electrical connectors.
5. Remove the tank from the vehicle.

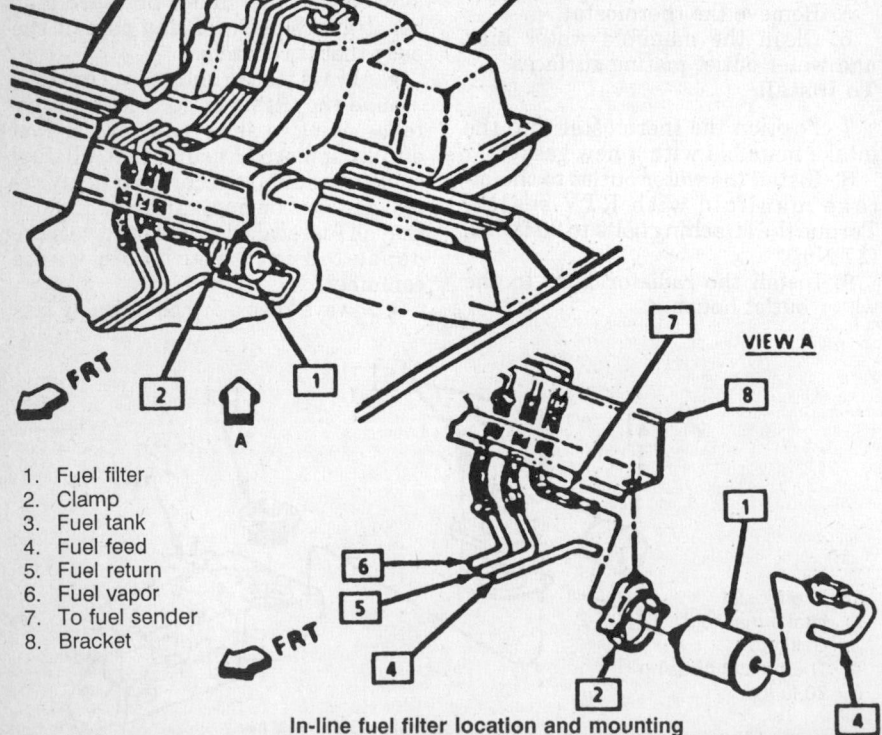

1. Fuel filter
2. Clamp
3. Fuel tank
4. Fuel feed
5. Fuel return
6. Fuel vapor
7. To fuel sender
8. Bracket

In-line fuel filter location and mounting

6. Remove the sending unit retaining cam using tool J–24187 or equivalent, and remove the sending unit assembly from the tank.

7. Use a new O-ring and install the sending unit assembly into the tank.

8. Raise the tank into position and attach all fuel lines, hoses and electrical connectors to the tank.

9. Install the retaining straps. Tighten the tank retaining strap bolts to 26 ft. lbs. (34 Nm).

10. Lower the vehicle and refill the tank. Connect the negative battery cable.

Fuel Injection

IDLE SPEED ADJUSTMENT

Idle speed and mixture are controlled by the ECM. No adjustments are possible.

Fuel Injector

REMOVAL & INSTALLATION

2.5L Engine

1. Disconnect the negative battery cable and release fuel pressure.

2. Remove the air intake duct and disconnect the electrical connector to the fuel injector.

3. Remove the injector screw and retainer.

4. Using a fulcrum, place a suitable prybar under the ridge opposite the connector end and carefully pry the injector out of the cavity.

5. Remove the upper and lower O-rings from the injector and cavity.

6. Inspect the injector and fuel lines for dirt and contamination. If excess contamination is present, the fuel system will have to be flushed.

NOTE: Make sure the replacement injector is an identical part. The injectors from other model 700 systems may fit but are calibrated for different flow rates. Check the part on the side of the throttle body.

To install:

7. Lubricate the new upper and lower O-rings with automatic transmission fluid and place them on the injector. Make sure the upper O-ring is in the groove and the lower one is flush against the filter.

8. Install the injector into the cavity by pushing straight into the fuel injector cavity.

9. Install the injector retainer and coat the screw with thread locking compound. Tighten the attaching screw to 27 inch lbs. (3.0 Nm).

10. Connect the injector electrical connector and negative battery cable.

2.3L, 2.8L and 3.1L Engines

1. Relieve the pressure in the fuel system.

2. Disconnect the negative terminal from the battery. Remove the air inlet tube.

3. Label and disconnect the vacuum lines from the plenum.

4. Remove the EGR valve from the plenum.

5. Remove the 2 throttle body-to-plenum bolts and the throttle body.

6. Remove the throttle cable bracket bolts.

7. Remove the ignition wire shield.

8. Remove the plenum-to-intake manifold mounting bolts and the plenum.

9. Remove the fuel line bracket bolt and disconnect the fuel lines from the fuel rail. Wrap a rag around the lines to collect the excess fuel. Dispose of the rag properly.

10. Remove and discard the fuel line O-rings.

11. Disconnect the electrical connectors from the fuel injectors.

12. Remove the fuel rail assembly with the injectors.

13. Remove the fuel injector-to-fuel rail retaining clip, the fuel injectors and O-rings.

To install:

14. Lubricate the new fuel injector O-rings and install the fuel rail assembly. Torque the fuel rail-to-intake manifold bolts to 19 ft. lbs. (26 Nm).

15. Connect the fuel lines to the fuel rail. Attach the electrical connectors to the injectors.

16. Install the plenum to manifold bolts and tighten and the plenum bolts to 16 ft. lbs. (22 Nm).

17. Install the throttle body to the plenum. Install the EGR valve. Reconnect all vacuum and electrical leads. Install the air inlet tube.

18. Connect the negative battery cable.

3.8L Engine

1. Properly relieve the fuel system pressure. Remove the air cleaner assembly. Disconnect the negative battery cable.

2. Label and disconnect the fuel injector electrical connectors.

3. Remove the fuel rail retaining bolts. Disconnect the electrical connections and the fuel supply line.

4. Remove the fuel rail.

5. Separate the injector from the fuel rail.

6. To install, use new O-rings and reverse the removal procedures. Start the engine and check for leaks.

EMISSION CONTROLS

Please refer to "Emission Control" in the Unit Repair section for system maintenance procedures. Due to the complex nature of modern electronic engine con-

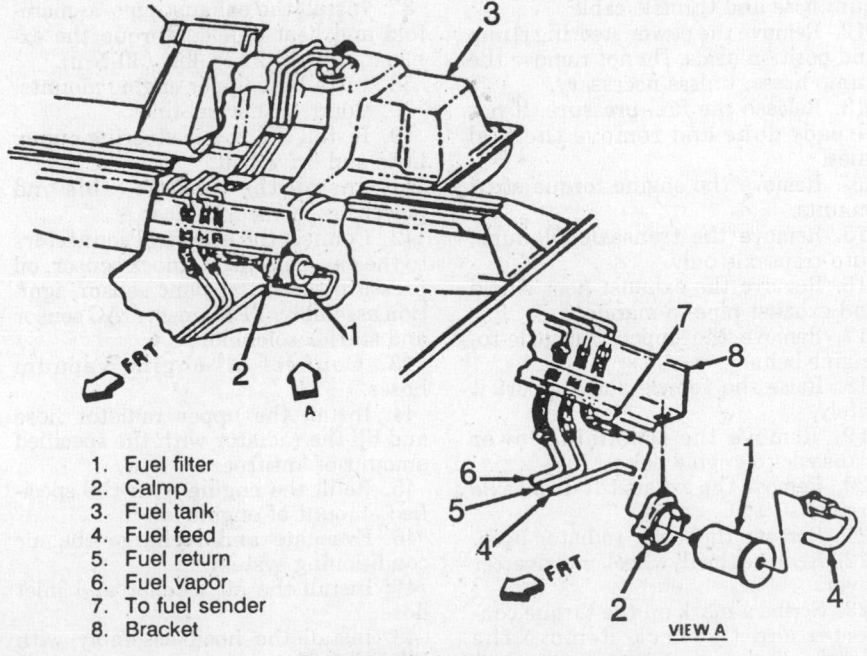

1. Fuel filter
2. Calmp
3. Fuel tank
4. Fuel feed
5. Fuel return
6. Fuel vapor
7. To fuel sender
8. Bracket

VIEW A

Fuel injector removal—2.5L engine

trol systems, comprehensive diagnosis and testing procedures fall outside the confines of this repair manual. For complete information on diagnosis, testing and repair procedures concerning all modern engine and emission control systems, please refer to "Chilton's Guide to Electronic Engine Controls".

Emission Warning Lamps

RESETTING

When the ECM finds a problem, the "Check Engine/Service Engine Soon" light will turn **ON** and a trouble code will be recorded in the ECM memory. If the problem is intermittent, the "Check Engine/Service Engine Soon" light turn **OFF** after 10 seconds, when the fault goes away. However, the trouble code will stay in the ECM memory until the battery voltage to the ECM is removed. Removing the battery voltage for 10 seconds will clear all stored trouble codes. This is done by disconnecting the ECM harness from the positive battery pigtail for 10 seconds with the ignition **OFF** or by disconnecting the ECM fuse, designated ECM or ECM/BAT, from the fuse holder.

NOTE: To prevent ECM damage, the ignition switch must be OFF when disconnecting or reconnecting power to ECM (for example battery cable, ECM pigtail, ECM fuse, jumper cables, etc.).

Whenever the battery is disconnected, on 1990–91 vehicles equipped with the 3.1L engine, an Idle Learn procedure can be performed to allow the ECM memory to be updated with the correct IAC valve pintle position for a stable idle speed.

a. Install a Tech 1 scan tool.
b. Turn the ignition to the **ON** position, engine not running.
c. Select **IAC SYSTEM**, then **IDLE LEARN** in the **MISC TEST** mode.
d. Proceed with idle learn as directed by the scan tool.

ENGINE MECHANICAL

NOTE: Disconnecting the negative battery cable on some vehi-cles may interfere with the functions of the on board computer systems and may require the computer to undergo a relearning process, once the negative battery cable is reconnected.

Engine Assembly

REMOVAL & INSTALLATION

2.3L Engine

1. Disconnect the negative battery cable.
2. Release the fuel system pressure.
3. Mark the hood hinges and remove the hood with an assistant. Drain the engine coolant into a suitable drain pan.
4. Remove the heater hoses at the heater core and thermostat housing.
5. Remove the radiator upper hose.
6. Remove the air cleaner and inlet hose from the vehicle.
7. If equipped with air conditioning, discharge the system.
8. Remove the air conditioning compressor and condenser hose at the compressor, if equipped.
9. Disconnect and label engine the vacuum lines.
10. Disconnect and label the electrical connectors from the alternator, air conditioning compressor, fuel injection harness, starter solenoid, engine ground strap, ignition assembly, coolant sensor, oil pressure sensor, knock sensor, oxygen sensor, Idle Air Control (IAC) valve and Throttle Position Sensor (TPS). The last 2 sensors are located at the throttle body.
11. Disconnect the power brake vacuum hose and throttle cable.
12. Remove the power steering pump and position aside. Do not remove the pump hoses, unless necessary.
13. Release the fuel pressure, if not already done and remove the fuel lines.
14. Remove the engine torque strut mounts.
15. Remove the transaxle fill tube, auto transaxle only.
16. Remove the exhaust heat shield and exhaust pipe-to-manifold.
17. Remove the upper transaxle-to-engine bolts.
18. Raise the vehicle and support it safely.
19. Remove the remaining lower transaxle-to-engine bolts.
20. Remove the exhaust-to-transaxle bracket.
21. Remove the lower radiator hose.
22. Remove the flywheel or converter cover.
23. Scribe a mark on the torque converter and flywheel. Remove the torque converter nuts.

24. Remove the transaxle-to-engine bracket.
25. Lower the vehicle.
26. Install the engine lifting fixture and remove the engine. Place the engine on a suitable workstand.

To install:

NOTE: Make sure all the engine mounting bolts are in their correct location to prevent transaxle and engine damage.

27. Install the engine to a lifting fixture and position the engine in the vehicle. With an assistant, align the engine-to-transaxle.
28. Raise the vehicle and support it safely.
29. Install the transaxle-to-engine bracket and bolts. Torque the engine-to-transaxle bolts to:
a. Positions No. 2, 3, 4, 5, 6 — 71 ft. lbs. (96 Nm).
b. Positions No. 7, 8 — 41 ft. lbs. (56 Nm).
30. Apply thread locking compound and install the torque converter-to-flywheel bolts. Torque the bolts to 46 ft. lbs. (63 Nm). Install the flywheel cover.
31. At the right side of the vehicle, install the engine mount bolt.
32. Install the lower radiator hose and engine ground wires.
33. Install the air conditioning compressor and condensor hose. Connect the compressor and alternator electrical harnesses.
34. Install the heater hoses at the heater core and throttle body.
35. Install the exhaust-to-transaxle bracket.
36. Lower the vehicle.
37. Install the exhaust pipe-to-manifold and heat shield. Torque the exhaust bolts to 22 ft. lbs. (30 Nm).
38. Install the upper engine mounts.
39. Connect the fuel lines.
40. Install the power steering pump, lines and drive belt.
41. Install the throttle cable and power brake vacuum hose.
42. Connect the electrical connectors to the oxygen sensor, knock sensor, oil pressure sensor, coolant sensor, ignition assembly, TPS sensor, IAC sensor and starter solenoid.
43. Connect all engine vacuum hoses.
44. Install the upper radiator hose and fill the radiator with the specified amount of antifreeze.
45. Refill the engine with the specified amount of engine oil.
46. Evacuate and recharge the air conditioning system.
47. Install the air cleaner and inlet hose.
48. Install the hood assembly with the help of an assistant.

49. Recheck all procedures for completion of repair.
50. Recheck all fluid levels.
51. Connect the negative battery cable. Start the engine and check for fluid leaks.

2.5L Engine

1. Disconnect the negative battery cable.
2. Place a suitable drain pan under the radiator drain valve and drain the engine coolant.
3. Remove the air cleaner assembly.
4. Mark the hood hinges with a scribe and remove the hood assembly.
5. Mark and remove all engine wiring. Place all the wire assemblies out of the way.
6. Remove the vacuum, heater and radiator hoses.
7. Remove the air conditioning compressor from the engine and place to the side with a piece of rope or wire. Do not disconnect the hoses from the compressor.
8. Remove the alternator and bracket.
9. Remove the engine torque strut.
10. Remove the throttle and transaxle linkage.
11. Remove the transaxle-to-engine bolts except the 2 upper bolts.
12. Raise the vehicle and support it safely.
13. Remove the engine mount-to-frame bolts.
13. Remove the exhaust pipe from the manifold.
14. Remove the torque converter-to-flywheel bolts.
15. Remove the starter motor.
16. Remove the power steering pump and attach to the inner fender with a piece of rope or wire. Do not disconnect the hoses.
17. Release fuel pressure and remove the fuel lines at the throttle body assembly.
18. Remove the rear engine support bracket.
19. Support the transaxle assembly with a transaxle holding fixture.
20. Disconnect the transaxle from the engine and support with a jack.
21. Attach an suitable engine lifting device.
22. Remove the engine assembly. Use care not to get under the engine assembly in case of lift failure.
23. Place the engine on a suitable work stand.
To install:
24. Place the engine assembly onto a suitable lifting device.
25. With an assistant, install the engine into the vehicle.
26. Position the engine into the engine mounts and engage the transaxle with the engine.

27. Remove the engine lifting device.
28. Install the torque converter bolts and engine-to-transaxle mounting bolts. Torque the torque converter bolts to 55 ft. lbs. (75 Nm).
29. Remove the transaxle holding fixture.
30. Install the rear support bracket bolts.
31. Install the engine mount nuts and torque to 32 ft. lbs. (43 Nm).
32. Install the rear transaxle mount bracket bolts and torque to 35 ft. lbs. (47 Nm).
33. Install the fuel lines to the throttle body assembly.
34. Install the power steering pump.
35. Install the starter motor assembly.
36. Install the flywheel cover plate.
37. Install the exhaust pipe-to-manifold.
38. Install the engine torque strut.
39. Install the alternator and bracket.
40. Install the air conditioning compressor.
41. Install the heater, radiator and vacuum hoses.
42. Install the throttle and transaxle linkages.
43. Install and reconnect all engine wiring harnesses.
44. Install the hood assembly to its original position with an assistant.
45. Refill the cooling system with engine coolant.
46. Reconnect the negative battery cable.
47. Install the air cleaner assembly.
48. Inspect for proper fluid levels.
49. Recheck every procedure for proper reinstallation.
50. Start the vehicle and check for any fluid leaks.

2.8L and 3.1L Engines
ENGINE REMOVED FROM BOTTOM

1. Remove the air cleaner assembly.
2. Disconnect the negative battery cable.
3. Drain the engine coolant into a suitable drain pan.
4. Remove the battery remote jump start terminal from the body but leave the cables attached.
5. Disconnect the cooling fan electrical connectors.
6. Remove the transaxle cooler lines at the radiator and the fluid level indicator.
7. Remove the upper and lower radiator hoses.
8. Remove the heater inlet and outlet hoses.
9. Release the fuel pressure.
10. Remove the serpentine belt from the engine.
11. Remove the shift cable linkage and cable from the mounting bracket.

12. Remove the accelerator and cruise control from the throttle linkage, if equipped.
13. Remove the air conditioning pressure switch wire connector.
14. Remove the vacuum check valve from the power brake booster.
15. Remove the canister purge vacuum line at the engine.
16. Remove the torque struts from the engine.
17. Remove all electrical connectors at the right side cowl.
18. Remove the upper bolts securing the wiring harness plastic bracket-to-body side rail.
19. Remove the ECM and fuse block and set on top of the engine.
20. Remove the strut-to-body mounting nuts.
21. Remove the vacuum hose from the vacuum reservoir.
22. Raise the vehicle and support it safely.
23. Remove the front wheel and tire assemblies.
24. Remove the right side splash shield.
25. Remove the oil filter.
26. Remove the air conditioning compressor and hang from the body with the hoses still connected. Do not disconnect the refrigerant hoses.
27. Remove the exhaust crossover pipe from the manifold.
28. Remove the steering gear pinch bolt.
29. Remove the brake hose from the strut.
30. Remove the brake calipers.
31. Lower the vehicle far enough to place the engine/transaxle table under the frame.
32. Remove the frame bolts.
33. Lower the table with the engine/transaxle attached.
34. Raise the vehicle and remove the engine/transaxle from the vehicle.
35. Seperate the engine from the transaxle and place the engine on a suitable work stand.
To install:
36. Attach the transaxle and engine together and tighten. Slowly lower the body onto the drivetrain.
37. Install the strut bolts to the shock towers.
38. Install the frame bolts.
39. Remove the engine/transaxle table from under the vehicle.
40. Install the brake calipers.
42. Install the brake hose at the strut.
43. Install the steering pinch bolt.
44. Install the exhaust crossover pipe-to-manifold.
45. Install the air conditioning compressor.
46. Install the oil filter and right side splash shield.
47. Install the tire and wheel assem-

blies and torque the lug nuts to 100 ft. lbs. (136 Nm).

48. Install the wiring harness bracket to body side rail.

49. Lower the vehicle.

50. Install the vacuum hose at the vacuum reservoir.

51. Install the ECM and the fuse block.

52. Install the remaining bolts securing the wiring harness bracket to the body side rail.

53. Install the torque struts at engine.

54. Reconnect the canister purge vacuum line and vacuum check valve at the power brake booster.

55. Reconnect the air conditioning pressure switch electrical connector.

56. Reconnect the accelerator and cruise control cables to the mounting bracket.

57. Install the serpentine belt.

58. Install the heater inlet and outlet hoses.

59. Install the radiator upper and lower hoses.

60. Install the transaxle fluid indicator and cooler lines at the radiator.

61. Reconnect the cooling fan electrical connectors.

62. Install the battery remote jump start terminal to body.

63. Refill all necessary fluids, engine oil, coolant, transaxle fluid.

64. Install the battery cables.

65. Install the air cleaner assembly.

66. Recheck all procedures for proper reinstallation.

67. Start the engine and check for any fluid leaks.

2.8L and 3.1L Engines

ENGINE REMOVED FROM TOP

1. Remove the air cleaner and duct assembly.

2. Disconnect the negative battery cable.

3. Mark the hood hinges to ensure proper reinstallation. With an assistant, remove the hood assembly.

4. Mark and remove all necessary engine wiring and place the harnesses out of the way.

5. Remove the throttle, TV and cruise control cables, if equipped, from the throttle body assembly.

6. Release the fuel pressure and remove the fuel lines at the throttle body.

7. Remove the AIR pump and serpentine belt.

8. Position a suitable drain pan under the radiator drain valve and drain the engine coolant.

9. Remove the upper and lower radiator hoses.

10. Remove the air conditioning compressor mounting bolts at the front mounting bracket.

11. Remove the power steering pump and move to the side. Attach to the body with a piece of wire or rope. Do not disconnect the pump hoses.

12. Remove the heater hoses from the engine and move out of the way.

13. Remove the brake booster vacuum hose.

14. Remove the EGR hose from the exhaust manifold.

15. Raise the vehicle and support it safely.

16. Remove the air conditioning compressor from the engine and attach to the body with a piece of rope or wire. Do not disconnect the refrigerant hoses.

17. Remove the flywheel cover, starter motor and torque converter bolts.

18. Remove the transaxle bracket and front engine mount nuts.

19. Remove the exhaust pipe at the crossover pipe.

20. Lower the vehicle.

21. Remove the torque struts and coolant recovery bottle.

22. Remove the left crossover pipe-to-manifold clamp.

23. Pull the engine forward and support with a piece of rope.

24. Disconnect the bulkhead electrical connector.

25. Remove the right crossover pipe-to-manifold clamp.

26. Remove the engine support and allow the engine to move to the normal position.

27. Support the transaxle with a suitable floor jack or equivalent.

28. Remove the remaining transaxle-to-engine bolts.

29. Attach an engine lifting device and remove the engine from the vehicle. Check for connected wires and hoses as the engine is coming out of the body.

30. Place the engine on a suitable work stand.

To install:

31. With an assistant, install a lifting device onto the engine and position into the vehicle.

32. Remove the lifting device.

33. Install the transaxle-to-engine bolts.

34. Remove the transaxle support.

35. Pull the engine assembly forward and support with a piece of rope.

36. Reconnect the right crossover pipe-to-manifold clamp.

37. Reconnect the bulkhead electrical connector.

38. Remove the engine support and allow the engine to roll to the normal position.

39. Install the left crossover pipe-to-manifold clamp.

40. Install the coolant recovery bottle and torque struts.

41. Raise the vehicle and support it safely.

42. Install the crossover-to-exhaust pipe.

43. Install the front engine mount retaining nuts and torque to 32 ft. lbs. (43 Nm).

44. Install the transaxle bracket, torque converter bolts and starter motor.

45. Install the flywheel cover.

46. Install the air conditioning compressor-to-engine.

47. Lower the vehicle.

48. Install the EGR valve to exhaust manifold.

49. Reconnect the brake booster vacuum supply, heater hoses and power steering pump.

50. Install the air conditioning compressor front mounting bracket bolts.

51. Install the radiator hoses, serpentine and AIR pump belts.

52. Reconnect the fuel lines to the throttle body assembly.

53. Install the throttle, TV and cruise control linkage to the throttle body.

54. Reconnect all necessary engine electrical wiring.

55. Install the hood assembly with an assistant.

56. Reconnect the battery cables.

57. Install the air cleaner and duct assembly.

58. Recheck all procedures for proper reinstallation and correct if necessary.

59. Refill the engine with engine oil, coolant and transaxle fluid, if needed.

60. Inspect vehicle for fluid leaks before and after starting the engine.

61. Road test the vehicle and recheck for fluid leaks.

3.8L Engine

1. Disconnect the negative battery cable.

2. Remove the air cleaner assembly.

3. Release the fuel system pressure.

4. disconnect the fuel lines from the rail and mounting brackets.

5. Drain the engine coolant and remove the recovery bottle.

6. Remove the inner fender electrical cover and the fuel injector sight cover.

7. Disconnect the throttle cables from the throttle body and mounting bracket.

8. Remove the rear heat shield from the crossover pipe.

9. Remove the throttle cable mounting bracket and vacuum line as an assembly.

10. Disconnect the exhaust crossover from the manifolds.

11. Disconnect the engine torque strut bolt and strut from the engine.

12. Remove the right side engine cooling fan.

13. Disconnect the vacuum line to the transaxle module.

14. Remove the serpentine belt.
15. Remove the power steering pump and alternator assemblies.
16. Tag and disconnect all electrical connections from the engine.
17. Disconnect the upper and lower radiator, and heater hoses from the engine.
18. Remove the transaxle to engine bolts and ground wire harness.
19. Raise and support the vehicle safely.
20. Remove the right front wheel and inner splash shield.
21. Remove the flywheel cover, scribe a mark on the torque converter and flywheel and remove the flywheel to torque converter bolts.
22. Disconnect the wire harness clamps from the frame near the radiator.
23. Remove the air conditioner compressor from the bracket and lay aside and secure to the frame.
24. Disconnect the wires and remove the starter motor assembly.
25. Safely support the transaxle and remove the transaxle to engine bolt, through the wheel well, using a long extension.
26. Attach a lifting device and remove the engine mount to frame nuts.
27. Drain the engine oil and remove the oil filter.
28. Disconnect the oil cooler pipes from the hose connections.
29. Disconnect the exhaust pipe from the manifold.
30. Lower the vehicle and remove the engine assembly from the vehicle.

To install:
31. With an assistant, install a lifting device onto the engine and position into the vehicle.
32. Support the transaxle, install the transaxle-to-engine bolts and ground wire harness and torque to 46 ft. lbs.
33. Install the heater and upper and lower radiator hoses to the engine.
34. Install all electrical connections to the engine.
35. Install the alternator, power steering pump and serpentine belt.
36. Install the vacuum line to the transaxle module.
37. Install the engine torque strut and bolt and torque to 41 ft. lbs.
38. Install the exhaust crossover pipe.
39. Install the throttle cable mounting bracket and vacuum lines.
40. Install the heat shield to the crossover pipe and the throttle cables to the throttle body and mounting bracket.
41. Install the inner fender electrical cover and the coolant recovery bottle.
42. Install the fuel hoses to the fuel rail and mounting brackets.
43. Raise and support the vehicle safely.

44. Connect the front exhaust pipe to the manifold.
45. Install the oil filter and oil cooler pipes.
46. Install the engine mount nuts to the frame and torque to 32 ft. lbs.
47. Install the transaxle to engine bolt through the wheel well and torque to 46 ft. lbs.
48. Install the starter motor assembly and connect the electrical connectors.
49. Install the air conditioner compressor to the bracket.
50. Install the wire harness clamps to the frame near the radiator.
51. Align the scribe marks, install the torque converter to flywheel bolts and torque to 46 ft. lbs.
52. Install the flywheel cover and the inner fender splash shield.
53. Install the right front wheel assembly and lower the vehicle.
54. Refill the cooling system and bleed the power steering system.
55. Install the right side cooling fan.
56. Install the fuel injector sight shield and the air cleaner assembly.
57. Connect the negative battery cable and install the hood.

Engine Mounts

REMOVAL & INSTALLATION

2.5L Engine

1. Disconnect the negative battery cable.
2. Raise and safely support the vehicle.
3. Remove the engine-to-chassis nuts.
4. Disconnect the engine torque struts.
5. Install an engine support fixture J–28467–A or equivalent.
6. Remove the upper mount-to-engine bracket nuts and remove the mount.

To install:
7. Install the mount and mount-to-engine bracket. Tighten the nuts to 32 ft. lbs. (43 Nm).
8. Install and tighten the torque strut nuts to 32 ft. lbs. (43 Nm).
9. Lower the vehicle and remove the engine support fixture.

2.3L, 2.8L and 3.1L Engines

1. Disconnect the negative battery cable. Raise and safely support the vehicle.
2. Remove the engine mount retaining nuts from below the cradle mounting bracket.
3. Raise the engine slightly to provide clearance and remove the engine mount- to-bracket nuts.
4. Remove the engine mount.

To install:
5. Install the mount in position and tighten the mount-to-bracket nuts to 32 ft. lbs. Lower the engine into position.
6. Install the mounting bracket-to-cradle nuts and tighten to 63 ft. lbs.
7. Lower the vehicle and connect the negative battery cable.

3.8L Engine

1. Disconnect the negative battery cable. Raise and safely support the vehicle.
2. Remove the mount retaining nuts from below the frame mounting bracket.
3. Raise the engine slightly to provide clearance and remove the engine mount- to-bracket nuts using engine support and lifting fixtures J–28467–A, J–28467–90 and J–35953 or equivalent.
4. Remove the engine mount nuts and the mounts.

To install:
5. Install the mount and mount to engine bracket and remove the engine support and lifting fixtures.
6. Install the engine mount to frame nuts and torque to 32 ft. lbs., the engine mount to frame nuts to 32 ft. lbs. and the engine bracket to engine bolts to 70 ft. lbs.
7. Connect the negative battery cable.

Cylinder Head

REMOVAL & INSTALLATION

2.3L Engine

1. Disconnect the negative battery cable.
2. Drain the cooling system.
3. Remove the heater inlet and throttle body heater hoses from the water inlet.
4. Remove the exhaust manifold.
5. Remove the intake and exhaust camshaft housing.
6. Remove the oil fill cap, tube and retainer. Pull the tube up and out of the block.
7. Disconnect and move the fuel injector harness.
8. Release the fuel system pressure.
9. Remove the throttle body and air inlet tube with the hoses and cables still connected. Position the assembly out of the way.
10. Remove the power brake booster hose and throttle cable bracket.
11. Remove the MAP sensor vacuum hose and all electrical connectors from the intake manifold and cylinder head.
12. Remove the radiator inlet hose and coolant sensor connectors.
13. In the reveres order of installa-

tion, remove the cylinder head-to-block retaining bolts.

14. Gently tap the outer edges of the cylinder head with a rubber hammer to dislodge the head gasket. Do not pry a screwdriver between the 2 surfaces.

15. Remove the cylinder head and intake manifold as an assembly.

To install:

16. Clean all gasket mating surfaces with a plastic scraper and solvent. Remove all dirt from the bolts with a wire brush.

17. Clean and inspect the oil flow check valve but do not remove the valve.

18. Check the cylinder head mating surface for flatness using a straight edge and a feeler gauge. Resurface the head if the warpage exceeds 0.010 inch (0.25mm).

19. Check to see if the dowel pins are installed properly, replace, if necessary.

NOTE: To avoid damage, install new spark plugs after the cylinder head has been installed on the engine. In the mean time, plug the holes to prevent dirt from entering the combustion chamber during reinstallation.

20. Do not use any sealing compounds on the new cylinder head gasket. Match the new gasket with the old one to ensure a perfect match.

21. Install the cylinder head and camshaft housing covers.

22. Torque all bolts to 26 ft. lbs. (35 Nm) plus an additional 100 degrees for bolts No. 7 and 9. Torque an additional 110 degrees for all bolts except No. 7 and 9.

23. Install the throttle body heater hoses, upper radiator hose and intake manifold bracket.

24. Install cylinder head and intake manifold electrical connectors and vacuum hoses.

25. Install the throttle body-to-intake manifold with a new gasket. Install the throttle cable, MAP sensor vacuum hose and air cleaner duct.

26. Lubricate the new oil fill tube O-ring and install the fill tube. Make sure the tube is fully seated in the block.

27. Install and torque the exhaust manifold.

28. Fill the radiator with the specified amount of engine coolant.

29. Recheck all procedures to ensure completion of repair.

30. Connect the negative battery cable, start the engine and check for fluid leaks.

2.5L Engine

1. Disconnect the negative battery cable.

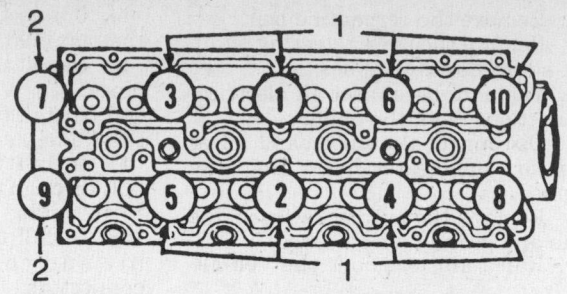

1. 26 ft. lbs (35 Nm) plus 110 degrees
2. 26 ft. lbs (35 Nm) plus 100 degrees

FRONT OF ENGINE

Cylinder head bolt tightening sequence—2.3L engine

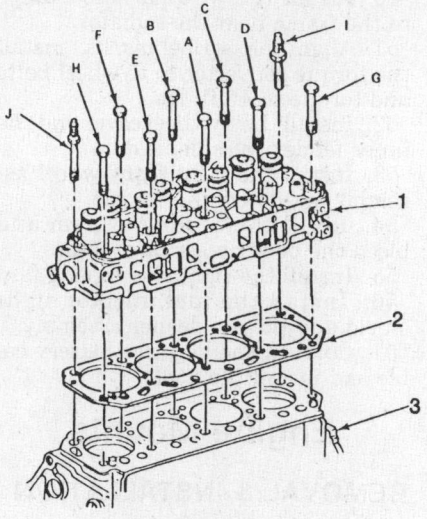

1. Cylinder head
2. Gasket
3. Cylinder block
4. NOTE: Tighten all bolts in proper sequence to 18 ft. lbs. (25 Nm). Tighten bolts A–J (except I) again to 26 ft. lbs. (35 Nm) and bolt I to 18 ft. lbs. (25 Nm). Tighten all the bolts in proper sequence an additional ¼ turn or 90° degrees.

Cylinder head bolt tightening sequence —2.5L engine

2. Drain the cooling system.

3. Raise and safely support the vehicle.

4. Remove the exhaust pipe and oxygen sensor.

5. Lower the vehicle.

6. Remove the oil level indicator tube and auxiliary ground cable.

7. Remove the air cleaner assembly.

8. Disconnect the EFI electrical connections and vacuum hoses.

9. Release the fuel pressure. Remove the wiring connectors, throttle linkage and fuel lines.

10. Remove the heater hose from the intake manifold.

11. Remove the wiring connectors from the manifold and cylinder head.

12. Remove the vacuum hoses, serpentine belt and alternator bracket.

13. Remove the radiator hoses.

14. Remove the rocker arm cover.

15. Loosen the rocker arm nuts and move the rocker arms to the side enough to remove the pushrods.

16. Mark each pushrod and remove from the engine.

NOTE: Mark each valve component to ensure that they are replaced in the same location as removed.

17. Remove the cylinder head bolts.

18. Tap the sides of the cylinder head with a plastic hammer to dislodge the gasket. Remove the cylinder head with the intake and exhaust manifold still attached.

19. If the cylinder head has to be serviced or replaced, remove the intake manifold, exhaust manifold and remaining hardware.

To install:

20. Before installing, clean the gasket surfaces of the head and block.

21. Check the cylinder head for warpage using a straight edge.

22. Match up the old head gasket with the new one to ensure the holes are exact. Install a new gasket over the dowel pins in the cylinder block.

23. Install the cylinder head in place over the dowel pins.

24. Coat the cylinder head bolt threads with sealing compound and install finger tight.

25. Torque the cylinder head bolts, in sequence, in 3 steps.

   a. Torque all bolts to 18 ft. lbs.

   b. Torque bolts "A" through "J" except "I" to 26 ft. lbs. Torque bolt "I" to 18 ft. lbs.

   c. Turn all bolts an additional 90 degree (¼).

26. Install the pushrods, rocker arms and nuts (or bolts) in the same location as removed. Tighten the nuts (or bolts) to 24 ft. lbs. (32 Nm).

27. Install the rocker arm cover.

28. Install the radiator hoses, alternator bracket and serpentine belt.

29. Connect all intake manifold and cylinder head wiring.

30. Install the vacuum hoses and heater hose at manifold.

31. Install the wiring, throttle linkage and fuel lines to the throttle body assembly.

32. Install the oil level indicator tube-to-exhaust manifold.

33. Install the air cleaner assembly and refill the cooling system.

34. Raise and safely support the vehicle.

35. Install the exhaust pipe and oxygen sensor.

36. Lower the vehicle and connect the negative battery cable.

37. Start the engine and check for leaks.

2.8L and 3.1L Engines

LEFT SIDE

1. Disconnect the negative battery cable. Drain the cooling system. Remove the rocker cover.

2. Remove the intake manifold-to-cylinder head bolts and the intake manifold. Disconnect the exhaust crossover from the right exhaust manifold.

3. Disconnect the oil level indicator tube bracket.

4. Loosen the rocker arms nuts, turn the rocker arms and remove the pushrods.

NOTE: Be sure to keep the parts in order for installation purposes.

5. Remove the cylinder head-to-engine bolts; start with the outer bolts and work toward the center. Remove the cylinder head with the exhaust manifold as an assembly.

To install:

6. Clean the gasket mounting surfaces. Inspect the surfaces of the cylinder head, block and intake manifold for damage and/or warpage. Clean the threaded holes in the block and the cylinder head bolt threads.

7. Use new gaskets, align the new cylinder head gasket over the dowels on the block with the note **THIS SIDE UP** facing the cylinder head.

8. Install the cylinder head and exhaust manifold crossover assembly on the engine.

9. Using GM sealant 1052080 or equivalent, coat the cylinder head bolts and install the bolts hand tight.

10. Using the correct sequence, torque the bolts to 33 ft. lbs. (45 Nm). After all bolts are torqued to 33 ft. lbs. (45 Nm), rotate the torque wrench another 90 degrees or ¼ turn. This will apply the correct torque to the bolts.

11. Install the pushrods in the same order that they were removed. Torque the rocker arm nuts to 14–20 ft. lbs. (19–27 Nm).

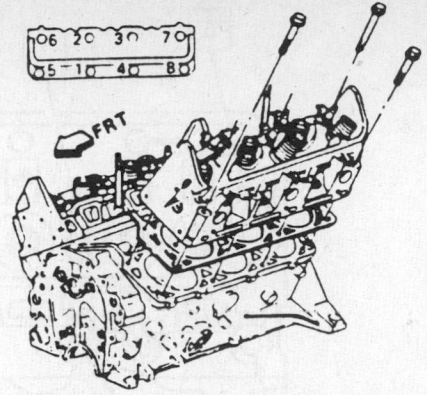

Cylinder head bolt tightening sequence— 2.8L and 3.1L engines

12. Install the intake manifold using a new gasket and following the correct sequence, torque the bolts to the correct specification.

13. Install the oil level indicator tube and install the rocker cover. Install the air inlet tube.

14. Connect the negative battery cable. Refill the cooling system. Start the engine and check for leaks.

RIGHT SIDE

1. Disconnect the negative battery cable. Drain the cooling system.

2. Raise and safely support the vehicle. Remove the exhaust manifold-to-exhaust pipe bolts and separate the pipe from the manifold.

3. Lower the vehicle. Remove the exhaust manifold-to-cylinder head bolts and the manifold.

4. Remove the rocker arm cover. Remove the intake manifold-to-cylinder head bolts and the intake manifold.

5. Loosen the rocker arms nuts, turn the rocker arms and remove the pushrods.

NOTE: Be sure to keep the components in order for reassembly purposes.

6. Remove the cylinder head-to-engine bolts, starting with the outer bolts and working toward the center and the cylinder head.

To install:

7. Clean the gasket mounting surfaces. Inspect the parts for damage and/or warpage.

8. Clean the engine block's threaded holes and the cylinder head bolt threads.

9. To install, use new gaskets and reverse the removal procedures. Using GM sealant 1052080 or equivalent, coat the cylinder head bolts and install the bolts hand tight.

10. Place the cylinder head gasket on the engine block dowels with the note **THIS SIDE UP** facing the cylinder head.

11. Using the torquing sequence, torque the bolts to 33 ft. lbs. (45 Nm). After all bolts are torqued to 33 ft. lbs. (45 Nm), rotate the torque wrench another 90 degrees or ¼ turn. This will apply the correct torque to the bolts.

12. Install the pushrods in the same order as they were removed. Torque the rocker arm nuts to 14–20 ft. lbs. (19–27 Nm).

13. Follow the torquing sequence, use a new gasket and install the intake manifold.

14. Install the oil level indicator tube and install the rocker cover. Install the air inlet tube.

15. Refill the cooling system. Start the engine, allow it to reach normal operating temperatures and check for leaks.

3.8L Engine

LEFT SIDE (FRONT)

1. Disconnect the negative battery cable and remove the air cleaner assembly.

2. Drain the cooling system and remove the intake manifold.

3. Remove the valve covers and remove the rocker arm assemblies.

4. Disconnect the torque strut from the bracket, at the head.

5. Disconnect the vacuum line from the transaxle.

6. Remove the left exhaust manifold.

7. Disconnect the spark plug wires and remove the spark plugs.

8. Remove the alternator front mount bracket and ignition module with bracket.

9. Remove the cylinder head bolts and remove the cylinder head.

10. Clean all gasket mating surfaces and the cylinder head bolt holes in the block.

To install:

11. Place the cylinder head gasket on the engine block dowels with the note **THIS SIDE UP** facing the cylinder head and the arrow facing the front of the engine.

12. Install the cylinder head bolts and tighten as follows:

   a. Tighten the cylinder head bolts, in sequence, to 35 ft. lbs.

   b. Rotate each bolt 130 degrees, in sequence.

   c. Rotate the center 4 bolts an additional 30 degrees, in sequence.

13. Install the rocker arm assemblies and valve covers.

14. Install the intake and exhaust manifolds.

15. Install the alternator front mount bracket and ignition module with bracket and torque the bolts to 37 ft. lbs.

16. Install the spark plugs and wires.

17. Install the torque strut to the

bracket, at the head and torque to 41 ft. lbs.

18. Fill the cooling system, connect the negative battery cable and install the air cleaner assembly.

RIGHT SIDE (REAR)

1. Disconnect the negative battery cable and remove the air cleaner assembly.

2. Drain the cooling system and disconnect the exhaust crossover pipe.

3. Remove the intake manifold.

4. Raise and support the vehicle safely.

5. Disconnect the front exhaust pipe from the manifold.

6. Remove the valve covers.

7. Remove the belt tensioner pulley.

8. Disconnect the heater hose from the engine.

9. Remove the power steering pump mounting bracket and lay the pump to 1 side.

10. Remove the spark plug wires and remove the spark plugs.

11. Disconnect the exhaust manifold and leave in place.

12. Disconnect the electrical connection from the oxygen sensor.

13. Remove the rocker arm assemblies.

14. Remove the cylinder head bolts and remove the cylinder head.

15. Clean all gasket mating surfaces and the cylinder head bolt holes in the block.

To install:

16. Place the cylinder head gasket on the engine block dowels with the note **THIS SIDE UP** facing the cylinder head and the arrow facing the front of the engine.

17. Install the cylinder head bolts and tighten as follows:

　a. Tighten the cylinder head bolts, in sequence, to 35 ft. lbs.

　b. Rotate each bolt 130 degrees, in sequence.

　c. Rotate the center 4 bolts an additional 30 degrees, in sequence.

18. Connect the electrical connection to the oxygen sensor.

19. Install the exhaust manifold and intake manifold.

20. Install the rocker arm assemblies.

21. Install the valve cover.

22. Install the spark plugs and wires.

23. install the power steering pump bracket and torque the bolts to 37 ft. lbs.

24. Install the belt tensioner pulley.

25. Install the heater hose to the engine.

26. Install the exhaust crossover pipe.

27. Raise and support the vehicle safely.

28. Install the front exhaust pipe to the manifold and lower the vehicle.

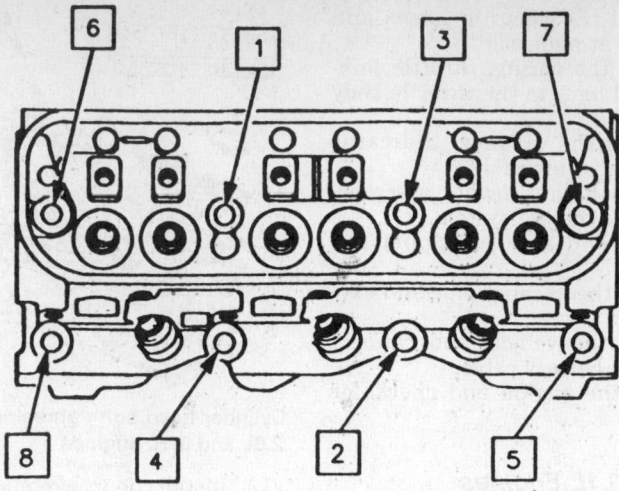

Cylinder head bolt tightening sequence—3.8L engine

29. Fill the cooling system, connect the negative battery cable and install the air cleaner assembly.

Valve Lifters

REMOVAL & INSTALLATION

2.5L Engine

1. Disconnect the negative battery cable.

2. Remove the rocker arm cover.

3. Remove the intake manifold.

4. Remove the pushrod cover.

5. Loosen the rocker arms and move to the side.

6. Mark and remove the pushrods, retainer and lifter guides.

7. Mark and remove the lifters.

NOTE: Mark each valve component location for reassembly.

8. Lubricate all bearing surfaces and lifters with engine oil and install the lifters.

9. Install the lifter guides, retainers and pushrods.

10. Position the rocker arms over the pushrods and tighten the rocker arm nuts to 24 ft. lbs. (32 Nm) with the lifter at the base circle of the camshaft.

11. Install the pushrod cover, intake manifold and rocker arm cover.

12. Connect the negative battery cable.

2.8L and 3.1L Engines

1. Disconnect the negative terminal from the battery.

2. Drain the cooling system.

3. Remove the rocker arm covers and intake manifold.

4. Loosen the rocker arms nuts enough to move the rocker arms to 1 side and remove the pushrods.

5. Remove the lifters from the engine.

6. Using Molykote® or equivalent, coat the base of the new lifters and install them into the engine.

7. Position the pushrods and the rocker arms correctly into their original positions. Torque the rocker arm nuts to 18 ft. lbs. (25 Nm).

8. Install the intake manifold and tighten the intake manifold-to-cylinder head bolts to specification.

9. Install the rocker cover. Connect the negative battery cable.

10. Fill the cooling system.

3.8L Engine

1. Disconnect the negative terminal from the battery.

2. Drain the cooling system.

3. Remove the rocker arm covers and intake manifold.

4. Remove the rocker arm assemblies.

5. Remove the guide retainer bolts and retainer.

6. Remove the valve lifter guides and and valve lifters.

To install:

7. Prelube (dip) the valve lifters with oil before installation.

8. Install the lifter guides, guide retainer and bolts and torque to 27 ft. lbs.

9. Install the rocker arm assemblies, intake manifold and valve covers.

10. Fill the cooling system and connect the negative battery cable.

Valve Lash

ADJUSTMENT

All engines use hydraulic valve lifters. No adjustment is necessary.

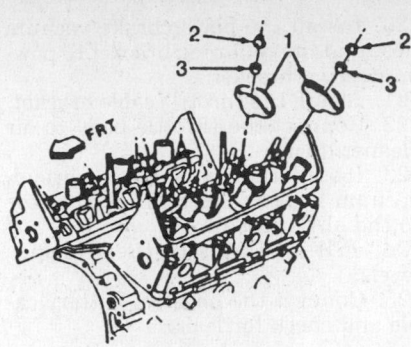

1. Rocker arm
2. 14–20 ft. lbs.
3. Ball

Rocker arm installation—2.8L and 3.1L engines

Rocker Arms

REMOVAL & INSTALLATION

2.5L Engine

1. Disconnect the negative battery cable.
2. Remove the rocker arm cover.
3. Remove the rocker arm bolt and ball.
4. Remove the rocker arm and guide.

NOTE: Mark all valve components so they are reinstalled in their original location.

5. If removed, install the pushrod through the cylinder head and into the lifter seat.
6. Install the guide, rocker arm, ball and bolt. Tighten the rocker arm bolts to 24 ft. lbs. (32 Nm).
7. Install the rocker arm cover.

2.8L and 3.1L Engines

LEFT SIDE

1. Disconnect the negative battery cable. Disconnect the bracket tube from the rocker cover.
2. Remove the spark plug wire cover. Drain the cooling system and remove the heater hose from the filler neck.
3. Remove the rocker arm cover-to-cylinder head bolts and the rocker cover.

NOTE: If the rocker arm cover will not lift off the cylinder head easily, strike the end with the palm of the hand or a rubber mallet.

4. Remove the rocker arm nuts and remove the rocker arms, keep the components in order for installation purposes.

5. Clean the gasket mounting surfaces.
6. To install, use new rocker cover gaskets apply a bead of sealant, GM 1052917 or equivalent, to the rocker cover and install it.
7. Install the spark plug wire cover and attach the heater hose to the filler neck. Fill the cooling system.
8. Torque the rocker arm nuts to 14–20 ft. lbs. (19–27 Nm).

RIGHT SIDE

1. Disconnect the negative battery cable. Disconnect the brake booster vacuum line from the bracket.
2. Disconnect the cable bracket from the plenum.
3. Disconnect the vacuum line bracket from the cable bracket.
4. Disconnect the lines from the alternator brace stud.
5. Remove the rear alternator brace and the serpentine drive belt.
6. Remove the alternator and support it out of the way.
7. Remove the PCV valve.
8. Loosen the alternator bracket.
9. Disconnect the spark plug wires from the spark plugs. Remove the rocker cover-to-cylinder head bolts and the rocker cover.

NOTE: If the rocker arm cover will not lift off the cylinder head easily, strike the end with the palm of the hand or a rubber mallet.

10. Remove the rocker arm nuts and the rocker arms; be sure to keep the

components in order for installation purposes.

To install:

11. Clean the gasket mounting surfaces.
12. To install, use new rocker cover gaskets apply a bead of sealant, GM 1052917 or equivalent, to the rocker cover and install it.
13. Install the spark plug wire cover and attach the heater hose to the filler neck. Fill the cooling system.
14. Tighten the rocker arm nuts to 14–20 ft. lbs. (19–27 Nm).

3.8L Engine

1. Disconnect the negative battery cable.
2. Remove the valve cover.
3. Remove the rocker arm pedestal retaining bolts and remove the pedestal and rocker arm assembly.
4. Remove the pushrods.

NOTE: Intake and exhaust pushrods are the same length. Store components in order so they can reassembled in the same location.

To install:

5. Install the pushrods and make sure they seat in the lifter.
6. Apply a thread lock compound to the bolt threads before reasssembly.
7. Install the pedestal and rocker arm assemblies and tighten the retaining bolts to 28 ft. lbs.
8. Install the valve covers and connect the negative battery cable.

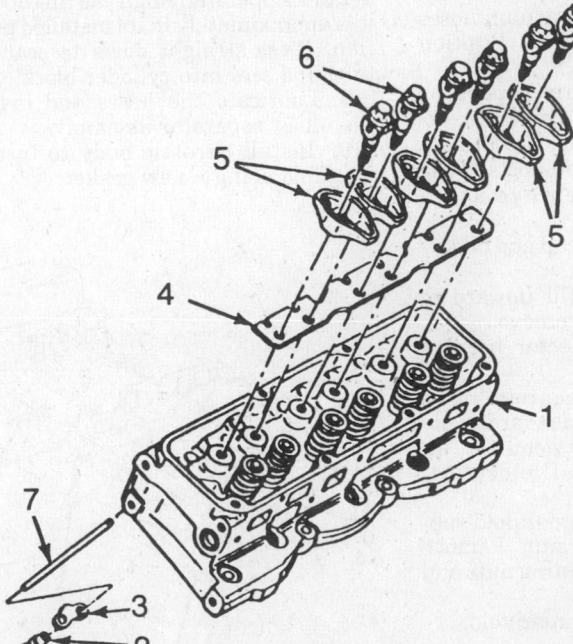

1. Cylinder head
2. Hydraulic valve lifter
3. Lifter guide
4. Valve lifter push rod guide
5. Rocker arms
6. 28 ft. lbs.
7. Pushrod

Rocker arm installation—3.8L engine

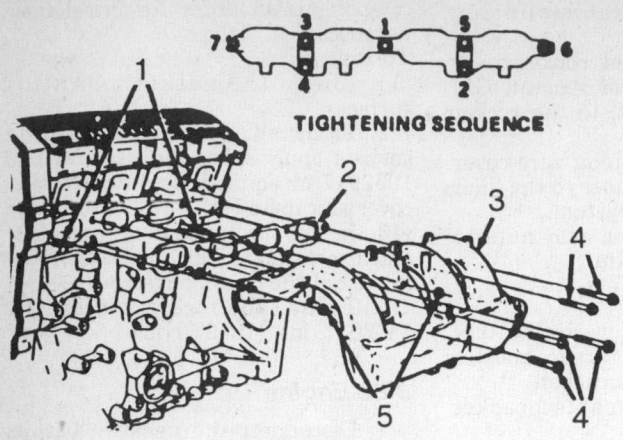

TIGHTENING SEQUENCE

1. Stud
2. Intake manifold gasket
3. Intake manifold
4. Bolt
5. Nut

Intake manifold installation—2.3L engine

Intake Manifold

REMOVAL & INSTALLATION

2.3L Engine

1. Disconnect the negative battery cable.

2. Remove the coolant fan shroud, vacuum hose and electrical connector from the MAP sensor.

3. Disconnect the throttle body to air cleaner duct.

4. Remove the throttle cable bracket.

5. Remove the power brake vacuum hose, including the retaining bracket to power steering bracket and position it to the side.

6. Remove the throttle body from the intake manifold with electrical harness, coolant hoses, vacuum hoses and throttle cable attached. Position these components aside.

7. Remove the oil/air separator bolts and hoses. Leave the hoses attached to the separator, disconnect from the oil fill, chain housing and the intake manifold. Remove as an assembly.

8. Remove the oil fill cap and oil level indicator stick.

9. Pull the oil tube fill upward to unseat from block and remove.

10. Disconnect the injector harness connector.

11. Remove the fill tube, rotating as necessary to gain clearance for the oil/air separator nipple between the intake tubes and fuel rail electrical harness.

12. Remove the intake manifold support bracket bolts and nut. Remove the intake manifold retaining nuts and bolts.

13. Remove the intake manifold.
To install:
14. Thoroughly clean and dry the mating surfaces. Install new gaskets

and place the intake manifold in position.

15. Tighten the intake manifold bolts/nuts, in sequence, to 18 ft. lbs. (25 Nm). Tighten intake manifold brace and retainers hand tight. Tighten to specifications in the following order:

    a. Nut to stud bolt—18 ft. lbs. (25 Nm).

    b. Bolt to intake manifold—40 ft. lbs. (55 Nm).

    c. Bolt to cylinder block—40 ft. lbs. (55 Nm).

16. Lubricate a new oil fill tube ring seal with engine oil and install tube between No. 1 and 2 intake tubes. Rotate as necessary to gain clearance for oil/air separator nipple on fill tube.

17. Locate the oil fill tube in its cylinder block opening. Align the fill tube so it is approximately in its installed position. Press straight down to seat fill tube and seal into cylinder block.

18. Lubricate the hoses and install the oil/air separator assembly.

19. Install throttle body to intake manifold using a new gasket.

20. Install the power brake vacuum hose and the retaining bracket to power steering bracket.

21. Install the throttle cable bracket.

22. Connect the throttle body to air cleaner duct.

23. Install the coolant fan shroud, vacuum hose and electrical connector to the MAP sensor.

24. Fill all fluids to their proper levels.

25. Connect the negative battery cable and check for leaks.

2.5L Engine

1. Disconnect the negative battery cable.

2. Remove the air cleaner assembly.

3. Remove the PCV valve and hose at the throttle body assembly.

4. Drain the engine coolant at the radiator.

5. Release the fuel pressure and remove the fuel lines from the throttle body.

6. Remove the vacuum lines and brake booster hose from the throttle body.

7. Remove all linkage and wiring from the TBI assembly.

8. Rotate the engine forward.

9. Remove the heater hose.

10. Remove the seven intake manifold retaining bolts and the manifold.
To install:
11. Clean all gasket surfaces on the cylinder head and intake manifold.

12. Install the intake manifold with a new gasket.

13. Install all the retaining bolts and washers hand tight.

14. Tighten the bolts, in proper sequence, to 25 ft.lbs. (34 Nm).

15. Rotate the engine to the original position.

16. Install all heater hoses, vacuum hoses, throttle linkages and wiring.

17. Install the fuel lines.

18. Refill the engine coolant.

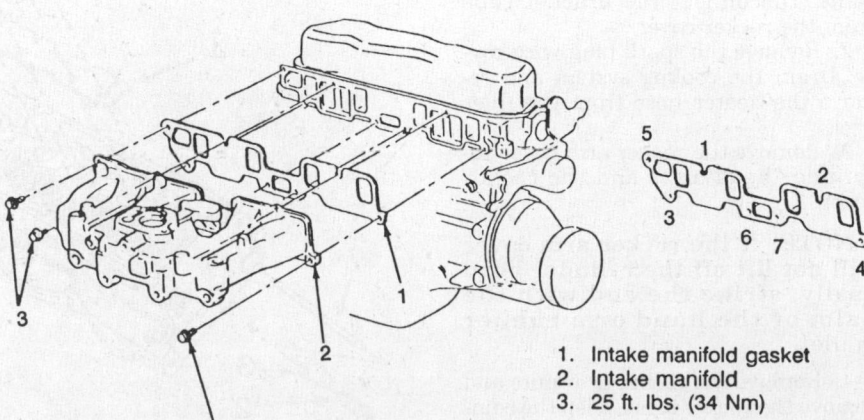

1. Intake manifold gasket
2. Intake manifold
3. 25 ft. lbs. (34 Nm)

Intake manifold installation and torque sequence—2.5L engine

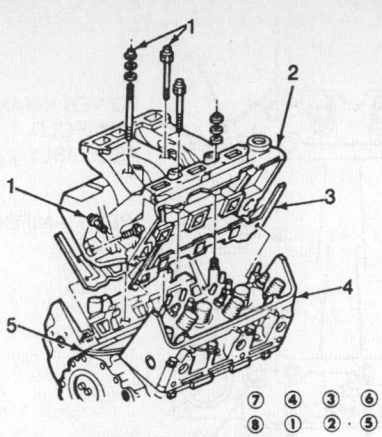

1. Torque in the proper sequence to 15 ft. lbs. (20 Nm), then retorque to 24 ft. lbs. (33 Nm)
2. Intake gasket
3. Gasket
4. Cylinder head
5. Sealer

Intake manifold installation—2.8L and 3.1L engines

FRONT ⑦ ④ ③ ⑥
       ⑧ ① ② ⑤

Intake manifold torque sequence— 2.8L and 3.1 engines

19. Install the PCV valve and hose to the TBI assembly.
20. Install the air cleaner assembly and connect the negative battery cable. Check for leaks.

2.8L A and 3.1L Engines

1. Disconnect the negative battery cable. Drain the cooling system.
2. Disconnect the TV and accelerator cables from the plenum.
3. Remove the throttle body-to-plenum bolts and the throttle body. Remove the EGR valve.
4. Remove the plenum-to-intake manifold bolts and the plenum. Disconnect and plug the fuel lines and return pipes at the fuel rail.
5. Remove the serpentine drive belt. Remove the power steering pump-to-bracket bolts and support the pump out of the way; Do not disconnect the pressure hoses.
6. Remove the alternator-to-bracket bolts and support the alternator out of the way.
7. Loosen the alternator bracket. From the throttle body, disconnect the idle air vacuum hose.
8. Label and disconnect the electrical connectors from the fuel injectors. Remove the fuel rail.

9. Remove the breather tube. Disconnect the runners.
10. Remove both rocker arm cover-to-cylinder head bolts and the covers. Remove the radiator hose from the thermostat housing.
11. Label and disconnect the electrical connectors from the coolant temperature sensor and oil pressure sending unit. Remove the coolant sensor.
12. Remove the bypass hose from the filler neck and cylinder head.
13. Remove the intake manifold-to-cylinder head bolts and the manifold.
14. Loosen the rocker arm nuts, turn them 90 degrees and remove the pushrods; be sure to keep the components in order for installation purposes.
15. Clean all of the gasket mounting surfaces.

To install:

16. Place a bead of RTV sealer or equivalent on each ridge where the intake manifold and block meet. Install the intake manifold gasket in place on the block.
17. Install the pushrods and reposition the rocker arms, tighten the rocker arm nuts to 18 ft. lbs. (25 Nm).
18. Mount the intake manifold on the engine and tighten the bolts to 23 ft. lbs. (29 Nm).
19. Connect the heater inlet pipe to the manifold. Install and connect the coolant sensor.
20. Attach the radiator hoses. Connect the wire at the oil sending switch.
21. Install the rocker covers, tighten the retaining bolts to 90 inch lbs. (10 Nm).
22. Install the runners, breather tube, fuel rail and connect the wires at the fuel injectors.
23. Install the alternator bracket and the alternator. Install the power steering pump.
24. Connect the fuel lines to the fuel rail. Install the EGR valve.
25. Install the plenum and mount the throttle body to the plenum.
26. Connect the accelerator cable and the TV cable.
27. Fill the cooling system. Connect the negative battery cable.
28. Run the engine until it reaches normal operating temperature and check for coolant and oil leaks.

3.8L Engine

1. Relieve the fuel system pressure.
2. Disconnect the negative battery cable. Place a clean drain pan under the radiator, open the drain cock and drain the cooling system.
3. Remove the air cleaner assembly and the fuel injector sight shield.
4. Disconnect the cables from the throttle body and mount bracket.
5. Remove the coolant recovery reservoir.

6. Remove the inner fender electrical cover on the right side.
7. Remove the right rear crossover pipe heat shield.
8. Disconnect the fuel lines from the fuel rail and from the cable bracket.
9. Remove the alternator and brace.
10. Remove the throttle body cable mounting bracket with the vacuum lines and disconnect the vacuum lines.
11. Tag and disconnect the electrical connections at the throttle body and both banks of fuel injectors.
12. Disconnect the vacuum hoses from the canister purge solenoid valve and transaxle module and intake connection.
13. Disconnect the power steering pump and move forward.
14. Disconnect the spark plug wires and lay aside.
15. Disconnect the coolant bypass hose from the intake manifold.
16. Disconnect the solenoid valve mounting bracket and power steering support brace from the intake manifold.
17. Disconnect the heater pipes from the intake and front cover.
18. Disconnect the alternator support brace from the intake.
19. Disconnect the upper radiator hose from the housing.
20. Remove the thermostat housing and thermostat from the intake.
21. Disconnect the electrical connector from the temperature sensor and sensor switch.
22. Remove the intake manifold bolts and manifold as an assembly.

To install:

23. Clean the mating surfaces and install the intake manifold gaskets and seals. Apply sealer to the ends of the of the intake manifold seals.
24. Install the intake manifold and apply thread lock compound to the bolt threads and torque the bolts to 88 inch lbs., twice in sequence.
25. Connect the electrical connector to the temperature sensor and sensor switch.
26. Install the thermostat housing and thermostat with a new gasket.
27. Connect the alternator support brace to the intake.
28. Connect the solenoid valve mounting bracket and power steering support brace to the intake manifold.
29. Connect the heater pipes to the intake and front cover.
30. Connect the coolant bypass hose to the intake manifold.
31. Install the power steering pump support bracket and torque to 37 ft. lbs.
32. Install the spark plug wires on both sides.
33. Install the belt tensioner pulley and tighten to 33 ft. lbs.

34. Install the power steering pump.
35. Connect the vacuum hoses to the canister purge solenoid valve and transaxle module and intake connection.
36. Connect the electrical connections at the throttle body and both banks of fuel injectors.
37. Install the alternator and brace.
38. Connect the throttle body cable mounting bracket with the vacuum lines.
39. Install the right rear crossover pipe heat shield.
40. Install the cables to the throttle body.
41. Connect the fuel lines to the fuel rail and mount bracket.
42. Install the inner fender electrical cover on the right side.
43. Install the coolant recovery reservoir and upper radiator hose. Fill the cooling system.
44. Install the air cleaner assembly and the fuel injector sight shield.
45. Connect the negative battery cable.

Exhaust Manifold

REMOVAL & INSTALLATION

2.3L Engine

1. Disconnect the negative battery

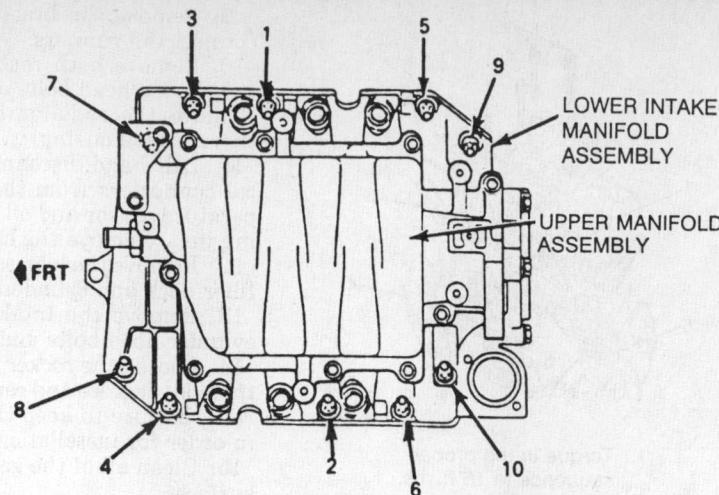

Intake manifold torque sequence—3.8L engine

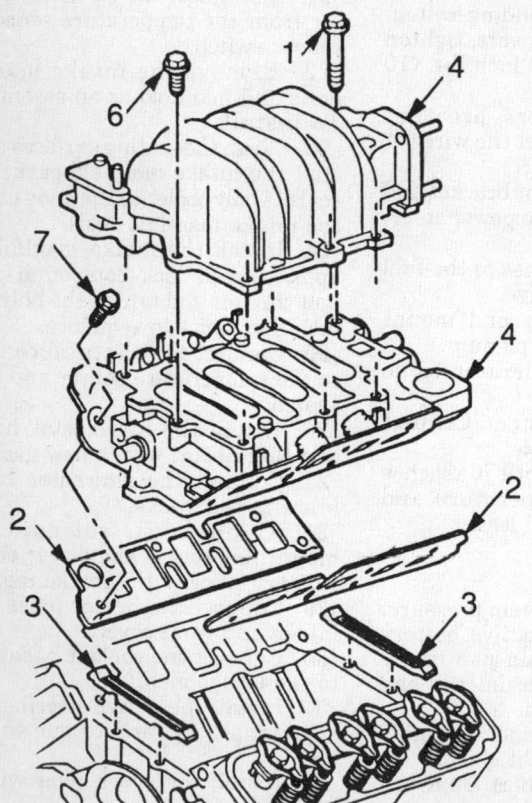

1. 19 ft. lbs.
2. Intake manifold gasket
3. Intake manifold seal
4. Lower intake manifold
5. Upper intake manifold
6. 19 ft. lbs.
7. 88 inch lbs.

Intake manifold installation—3.8L engine

cable and oxygen sensor connector.
2. Remove upper and lower exhaust manifold heat shields.
3. Remove the bolt that attaches the exhaust manifold brace to the manifold.
4. Break loose the manifold to exhaust pipe spring loaded bolts using a 13mm box wrench.
5. Raise the vehicle and support safely.

NOTE: It is necessary to relieve the spring pressure from 1 bolt prior to removing the second bolt. If the spring pressure is not relieved it will cause the exhaust pipe to twist and bind up the bolt as it is removed.

6. Remove the manifold to exhaust pipe bolts from the exhaust pipe flange as follows:
   a. Unscrew either bolt clockwise 4 turns.
   b. Remove the other bolt.
   c. Remove the first bolt.
7. Pull down and back on the exhaust pipe to disengage it from the exhaust manifold bolts.
8. Lower the vehicle.
9. Remove the exhaust manifold mounting bolts and remove the manifold.
10. The installation is the reverse of the removal procedure. Torque the mounting bolts in sequence to 27 ft. lbs. (37 Nm). Install the exhuast pipe flange bolts evenly and gradually to avoid binding.
11. Connect the negative battery cable and check for leaks.

2.5L Engine

1. Disconnect the negative battery cable.
2. Remove the torque strut bolts at the radiator panel and cylinder head.
3. Remove the oxygen sensor and the oil level indicator tube.
4. Raise and safely support the vehicle.
5. Remove the exhaust pipe from the manifold and lower the vehicle.
6. Bend rocking tabs away from the bolts and remove the retaining bolts and washers.
7. Remove the exhaust manifold and gasket.

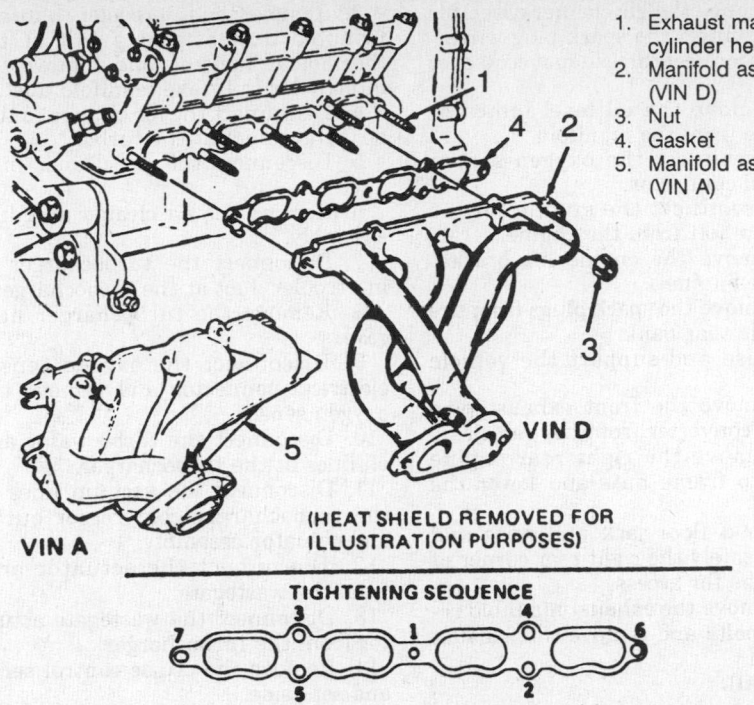

1. Exhaust manifold to cylinder head stud
2. Manifold assembly (VIN D)
3. Nut
4. Gasket
5. Manifold assembly (VIN A)

VIN D

VIN A

(HEAT SHIELD REMOVED FOR ILLUSTRATION PURPOSES)

TIGHTENING SEQUENCE

Exhaust manifold installation and torque sequence—2.3L engine

To install:

8. Clean the sealing surfaces of the cylinder head and manifold.

9. Lubricate the bolt threads with anti-seize compound and install the exhaust manifold with a new gasket.

10. Tighten the bolts in sequence.

11. Bend the locking tabs against the bolts.

12. Raise and support the vehicle safely.

13. Install the exhaust pipe to the manifold and lower the vehicle.

14. Install the oil level indicator tube, oxygen sensor and torque rod bracket at the cylinder head and radiator support.

15. Connect the negative battery cable.

2.8L and 3.1L Engines

LEFT SIDE

1. Disconnect the negative battery cable.

2. Remove the coolant recovery bottle.

3. Relieve the accessory drive belt tension and remove the belt.

4. Remove the air conditioner com-

pressor mounting bolts and support the compressor aside.

5. Remove the right side engine torque strut. Remove the bolts retaining the air conditioner compressor and torque strut mounting bracket, remove the bracket.

6. Remove the heat shield and crossover pipe at the manifold.

7. Remove the exhaust manifold mounting bolts and remove the manifold.

To install:

8. Clean the gasket mounting surfaces.

9. Install the exhaust manifold to the engine, loosely install the mounting bolts.

10. Install the exhaust crossover pipe. Tighten the exhaust manifold bolts to 18 ft. lbs. (25 Nm)

11. Attach the heat shield. Install the air conditioner and torque strut mounting bracket.

12. Install the torque strut. Mount the air conditioner compressor and install the accessory drive belt.

13. Install the coolant recovery bottle and connect the negative battery cable.

RIGHT SIDE

1. Disconnect the negative battery cable.

2. Raise and safely support the vehicle.

1. Gasket
2. Exhaust manifold
3. Lock
4. 26 ft. lbs. (35 Nm)
5. 26 ft. lbs. (35 Nm)
6. 37 ft. lbs. (50 Nm)
7. 37 ft. lbs. (50 Nm)

8. NOTE: When installing the lock tabs on the exhaust manifold, one tab must be bent against a flat of the hex to prevent rotation.

BOLT TIGHTENING SEQUENCE
TIGHTEN BOLT POSITION NUMBER IN SEQUENCE AS FOLLOWS: 3-5-6-2-1-7-4 OR BY USING ALPHA GROUPS "A" AND "B", "A" BEING FIRST AND "B" LAST. OR SIMULTANEOUS GANG DRIVE.

VIEW A

VIEW B

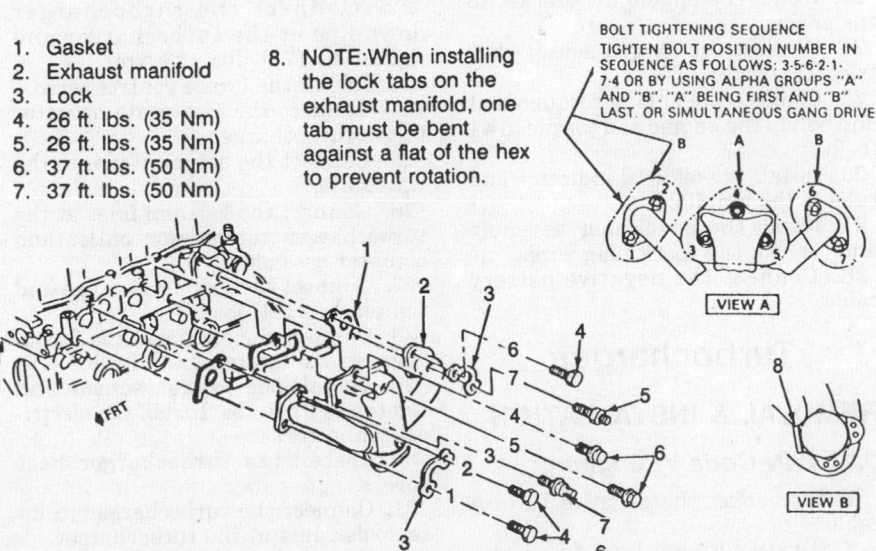

Exhaust manifold installation and torque sequence—2.5L engine

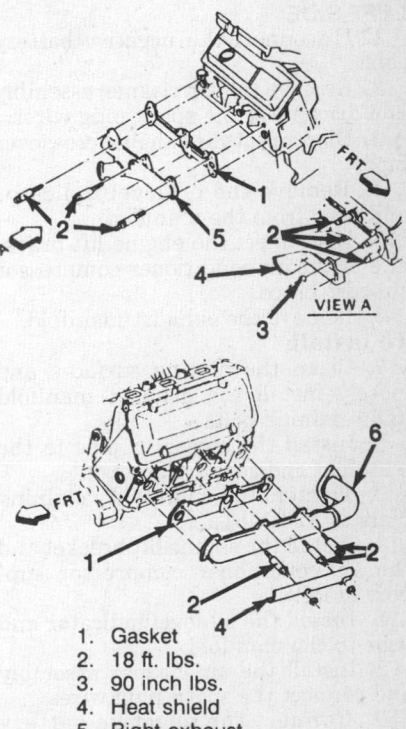

VIEW A

FRT

1. Gasket
2. 18 ft. lbs.
3. 90 inch lbs.
4. Heat shield
5. Right exhaust manifold
6. Left exhaust manifold

Exhaust manifold installation—2.8L and 3.1L engines

3. Remove the exhaust pipe at the crossover. Lower the vehicle.

4. Remove the coolant recovery bottle and remove the engine torque struts.

5. Pull the engine forward and support it.

6. Remove the air cleaner, breather, mass air flow sensor and heat shield.

7. Remove the crossover at the manifold. Disconnect the accelerator and TV cables.

8. Remove the manifold mounting bolts and remove the manifold. Clean the manifold mounting surfaces.

To install:

9. Install the exhaust manifold, loosely install the mounting bolts.

10. Attach the crossover at the manifold. Tighten the manifold mounting bolts to 18 ft. lbs. (25 Nm).

11. Connect the accelerator and TV cables.

12. Attach the air cleaner, breather and mass air flow sensor.

13. Remove the engine support and allow the engine to roll back into position.

14. Install the coolant recovery bottle and the engine torque struts.

15. Raise and safely support the vehicle. Install the exhaust pipe to the crossover.

16. Lower the vehicle. Connect the negative battery cable.

3.8L Engine

LEFT SIDE

1. Disconnect the negative battery cable.

2. Remove the air cleaner assembly and disconnect the spark plug wires.

3. Disconnect the exhaust crossover pipe.

4. Remove the oil level indicator and tube from the manifold.

5. Disconnect the engine lift bracket and the air conditioner compressor support brace.

6. Remove the exhaust manifold.

To install:

7. Clean the mating surfaces and loosely install the exhaust manifold and retaining bolts.

8. Install the crossover pipe to the manifold and support bracket.

9. Tighten the manifold retaining bolts to 41 ft. lbs.

10. Install the engine lift bracket and the air conditioner compressor support brace.

11. Install the oil level indicator and tube to the manifold.

12. Install the air cleaner assembly and connect the spark plug wires.

13. Connect the negative battery cable.

RIGHT SIDE

1. Disconnect the negative battery cable.

2. Remove the air cleaner assembly and disconnect the spark plug wires.

3. Disconnect the exhaust crossover pipe.

4. Remove the oil level indicator and tube from the manifold.

5. Disconnect the oxygen sensor electrical connector.

6. Disconnect the engine torque strut and bolt from the engine.

7. Remove the engine lift bracket from the engine.

8. Remove the spark plugs from the right side rear bank.

9. Raise and support the vehicle safely.

10. Remove the front exhaust pipe and the converter from the vehicle.

11. Remove the right rear engine mount to frame nuts and lower the engine.

12. Use a floor jack and raise and support safely the right rear corner of the engine for access.

13. Remove the exhaust manifold retaining bolts and remove the exhaust manifold.

To install:

14. Clean the mating surfaces and loosely install the exhaust manifold and retaining bolts.

15. Install the crossover pipe to the manifold and support bracket.

16. Tighten the manifold retaining bolts to 41 ft. lbs.

17. Lower the engine and remove the floor jack.

18. Raise and support the vehicle safely.

19. Install the front exhaust pipe and the converter.

20. Install the right rear engine mount to frame nuts and lower the engine.

21. Tighten the crossover bolts.

22. Install the spark plugs to the right side rear bank.

23. Install the engine lift bracket to the engine.

24. Connect the oxygen sensor electrical connector.

25. Connect the engine torque strut and bolt to the engine and torque to 41 ft. lbs.

26. Install the oil level indicator and tube to the manifold.

27. Install the air cleaner assembly and connect the spark plug wires.

28. Connect the negative battery cable.

Turbocharger

REMOVAL & INSTALLATION

3.1L (VIN Code V) Engine

1. Disconnect the negative battery cable.

2. Drain the coolant from the radiator.

3. Remove the intercooler to intake manifold duct attaching bolt at the thermostat housing and remove the intercooler to intake manifold duct.

4. Disconnect the air cleaner to turbocharger duct at the turbo.

5. Disconnect the air cleaner inlet duct.

6. Remove the air cleaner and duct assembly.

7. Disconnect the turbocharger to intercooler duct at the turbocharger.

8. Remove the turbocharger heat covers.

9. Disconnect the oxygen sensor electrical connector and remove the oxygen sensor.

10. Disconnect the turbo water and oil lines at the turbocharger.

11. Disconnect the vacuum lines at the turbocharger compressor outlet and actuator assembly.

12. Disconnect the actuator arm from the wastegate.

13. Disconnect the wastegate actuator from the turbocharger.

14. Remove the cruise control servo and set aside.

15. Disconnect the turbocharger downpipe at the turbocharger.

16. Disconnect the the water supply clamp and rubber hose.

17. Disconnect the turbocharger drain hose at the drain pipe.

18. Remove the turbocharger to exhaust crossover attaching bolts and remove the turbocharger from the engine.

To install:

19. Install the turbocharger to the engine compartment and tighten the turbocharger to exhaust crossover bolts to 17 ft. lbs. (23 Nm).

20. Connect the turbocharger drain hose at the drain pipe.

21. Connect the the water supply clamp and rubber hose.

22. Connect the turbocharger downpipe at the turbocharger and tighten to 17 ft. lbs. (23 Nm).

23. Install the cruise control servo.

24. Connect the wastegate actuator to the turbocharger.

25. Connect the actuator arm to the wastegate.

26. Connect the vacuum lines at the turbocharger compressor outlet and actuator assembly.

27. Connect the turbo water line and tighten to 21 ft. lbs.

28. Connect the oil line at the turbocharger and tighten to 15 ft. lbs.

29. Install the oxygen sensor and tighten to 31 ft. lbs. Install the electrical connector.

30. Install the turbocharger heat covers.

31. Connect the turbocharger to intercooler duct at the turbocharger.

32. Install the air cleaner and duct assembly.

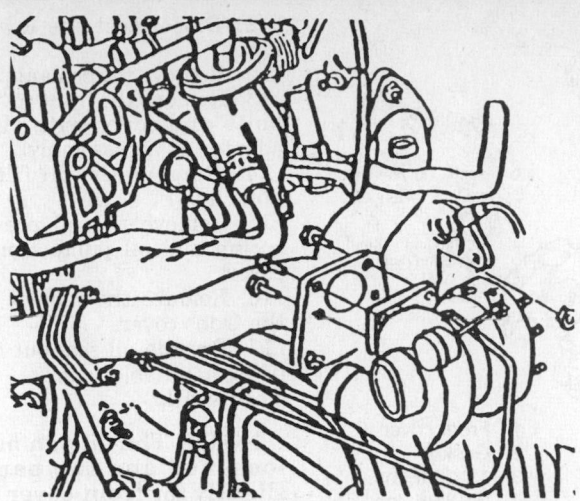

Turbocharger Installation—3.1L engine

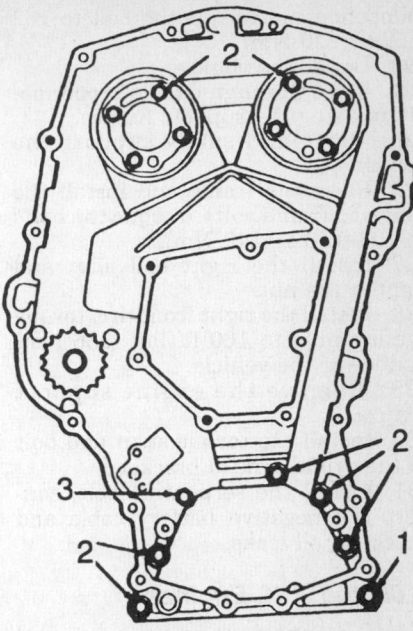

1. Stud end bolt (chain housing to block)
2. Bolt (chain housing to block and cam housing)
3. Stud (timing chain tensioner shoe pivot)

Timing chain cover installation—2.3L engine

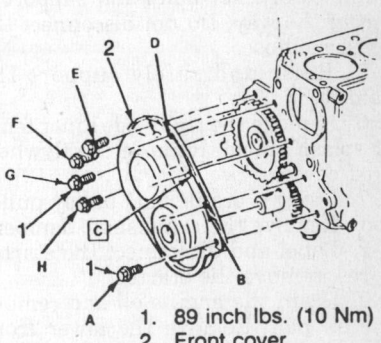

1. 89 inch lbs. (10 Nm)
2. Front cover

Timing case cover assembly—2.5L engine

33. Install the air cleaner to turbocharger duct at the turbo.

34. Install the intercooler to intake manifold duct attaching bolt at the thermostat housing and tighten to 17 ft. lbs. (23 Nm).

35. Fill the radiator with coolant.

36. Connect the negative battery cable.

NOTE: Prime the turbocharger with oil before running the engine. Crank the engine with the fuel pump fuse removed until normal operating oil pressure is achieved.

37. Perform the idle learn procedure to allow the ECM memory to be updated with the correct IAC valve pintle position and provide for a stable idle speed.

   a. Install a Tech 1 scan tool.

   b. Turn the ignition to the ON position, engine not running.

   c. Select IAC SYSTEM, then IDLE LEARN in the MISC TEST mode.

   d. Proceed with idle learn as directed by the scan tool.

Timing Chain/Gear Front Cover

REMOVAL & INSTALLATION

2.3L Engine

1. Disconnect the negative battery cable. Remove the coolant recovery reservoir.

2. Remove the serpentine drive belt using a 13mm wrench that is at least 24 in. long.

3. Remove upper cover fasteners.

4. Raise the vehicle and support safely.

5. Remove the right front wheel assembly and lower splash shield.

6. Remove the crankshaft balancer assembly.

7. Remove lower cover fasteners and lower the vehicle.

8. Remove the front cover.

9. The installation is the reverse of the removal procedure. Torque the balancer retaining bolt to 74 ft. lbs. (100 Nm) plus an additional 90 degree turn.

2.5L Engine

1. Disconnect the negative battery cable.

2. Remove the torque strut bolt at the cylinder head bracket and move the strut out of the way.

3. Remove the serpentine belt.

4. Install the engine support fixture tool J–28467–A and J–36462.

5. Raise and safely support the vehicle.

6. Remove the right front tire assembly.

7. Disconnect the right lower ball joint from the knuckle.

8. Remove the 2 right frame attaching bolts.

9. Loosen the 2 left frame attaching bolts but do not remove.

10. Lower the vehicle.

11. Lower the engine on the right side. Raise and safely support the vehicle.

12. Remove the engine vibration dampener using a dampener puller.

13. Remove the timing cover retaining bolts and cover.

To install:

14. Clean all gasket mating surfaces with solvent and a gasket scraper.

15. Apply a ⅜ in. wide by ³⁄₁₆ in. thick bead of RTV sealer to the joint at the oil pan and timing cover.

16. Apply a ¼ in. wide by ⅛ in. thick bead of RTV sealer to the timing cover at the block mating surface.

17. Install a new timing cover oil seal using a timing cover seal installer tool J–34995 or equivalent.

18. Install the cover onto the block and install the retaining bolts loosely.

19. Install the timing cover seal installer tool J–34995 to align the timing cover.

20. Tighten the opposing bolts to hold the cover in place.

21. Torque the bolts in sequence and to the proper specification. Remove the timing cover oil seal installer tool.

22. Install the crankshaft vibration

dampener and torque the bolt to 162 ft. lbs. (220 Nm).

23. Lower the vehicle.

24. Raise the engine to its proper position using the support fixture.

25. Raise and safely support the vehicle.

26. Raise the frame and install the removed frame bolts. Torque the bolts to 103 ft. lbs. (140 Nm).

27. Install the right ball joint and tighten the nut.

28. Install the right front tire, torque the lug nuts to 100 ft. lbs. (136 Nm) and lower the vehicle.

29. Remove the engine support fixture.

30. Install the torque strut and bolt to the cylinder head bracket.

31. Install the serpentine belt, connect the negative battery cable and check for oil leaks.

2.8L and 3.1L Engines

1. Disconnect the negative terminal from the battery. Drain the cooling system.

2. Remove the serpentine belt and the belt tensioner.

3. Remove the alternator-to-bracket bolts and remove the alternator, with the wires attached, support it out of the way.

4. Remove the power steering pump-to-bracket bolts and support it out of the way. Do not disconnect the pressure hoses.

5. Raise and safely support the vehicle.

6. Remove the right side inner fender splash shield. Remove the flywheel dust cover.

7. Using a crankshaft pulley puller tool. Remove the crankshaft damper.

8. Label and disconnect the starter wires, remove the starter.

9. Drain the engine oil and remove the oil pan. Remove the lower front cover bolts.

10. Lower the vehicle. Disconnect the radiator hose from the water pump.

11. Disconnect the heater coolant hose from the cooling system filler pipe.

12. Remove the bypass and overflow hoses.

13. Remove the water pump pulley. Disconnect the canister purge hose.

14. Remove the spark plug wire shield from the water pump.

15. Remove the upper front cover-to-engine bolts and remove the front cover.

16. Clean front cover mounting surfaces.

To install:

17. Apply a thin bead of silicone sealant on the front cover mating surface and using a new gasket, install the

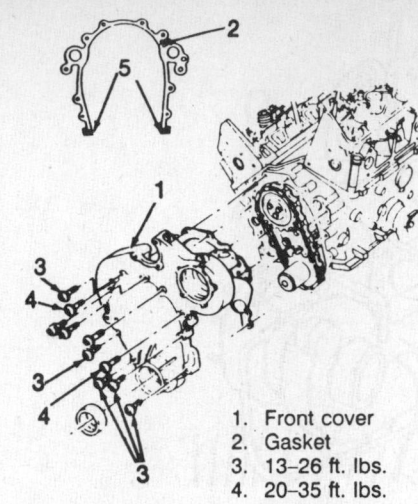

1. Front cover
2. Gasket
3. 13–26 ft. lbs.
4. 20–35 ft. lbs.
5. Apply sealer

Timing case cover assembly—2.8L and 3.1L engines

front cover on the engine with the top bolts to hold it in place.

18. Raise and safely support the vehicle.

19. Install the oil pan. Install the lower front cover bolts, tighten all of the front cover bolts to 26–35 ft. lbs. (35–48 Nm).

20. Install the serpentine belt and idler pulley. Install the damper on the engine using tool J–29113 or equivalent. Install the starter.

21. Install the inner fender splash shield. Lower the vehicle.

22. Attach the radiator hose too the water pump and attach the heater hoses.

23. Install the power steering pump and the alternator.

24. Attach the spark plug wire shield. Fill the cooling system.

25. Connect the negative battery cable. Check for coolant and oil leaks.

3.8L Engine

1. Disconnect the negative battery cable.

2. Remove the crankshaft balancer.

3. Remove the crankshaft sensor cover.

4. Disconnect the electrical connections at the camshaft, crankshaft and oil pressure sensors.

5. Raise and support the vehicle safely.

6. Drain the engine oil and remove the oil pan to front cover bolts.

7. Remove the oil filter and disconnect the oil cooler pipes from the oil filter adapter housing.

8. Lower the vehicle and drain the cooling system.

9. Remove the alternator and brace.

10. Disconnect the heater hoses and pipe and the bypass hose from the cover.

11. Disconnect the lower radiator hose.

12. Remove the coolant pump pulley.

13. Remove the front cover attaching bolts and cover with the oil filter adapter as an assembly.

14. Remove the oil filter adapter housing.

15. Remove the oil pressure valve, spring and oil pump from the front cover.

16. Remove the coolant pump from the front cover.

17. Pry the oil seal out of the cover using a suitable tool.

To install:

NOTE: The oil pan bolts can be loosened and the pan dropped slightly for front cover clearance. If the oil pan gasket is excessively swollen, the oil pan must be removed and the gasket replaced.

18. Clean the mating surfaces of the front cover and cylinder block with a degreaser.

19. Install the oil filter and adapter housing with the oil pressure valve and spring to the cover. Tighten the bolts to 24 ft. lbs.

20. Install the oil pump assembly to the cover.

21. Use a new gasket, apply sealer to the bolt threads and install the coolant pump to the front cover.

22. Lubricate a new front cover oil seal with clean engine oil and install it to the front cover, using tool J–35354 or equivalent. Use the crankshaft balancer bolt with the tool and tighten the bolt until the seal is seated in the cover. Remove the tool.

23. Install the front cover to the engine and install the upper cover bolts. Tighten the upper cover bolts to 124 inch lbs. (14 Nm).

24. Install the crankshaft sensor and adjust, using tool J–37089 or equivalant.

25. Install the sensor cover and electrical connections.

26. Install the crankshaft balancer.

27. Install the oil cooler lines and the oil filter.

28. Lower the vehicle and install the coolant pump pulley.

29. Install the lower radiator hose, bypass hose and heater hoses.

30. Install the alternator and brace.

31. Add engine coolant, oil and connect the negative battery cable.

Front Cover Oil Seal

REPLACEMENT

1. Disconnect the negative terminal from the battery. Remove the serpentine belt.

2. Raise and safely support the ve-

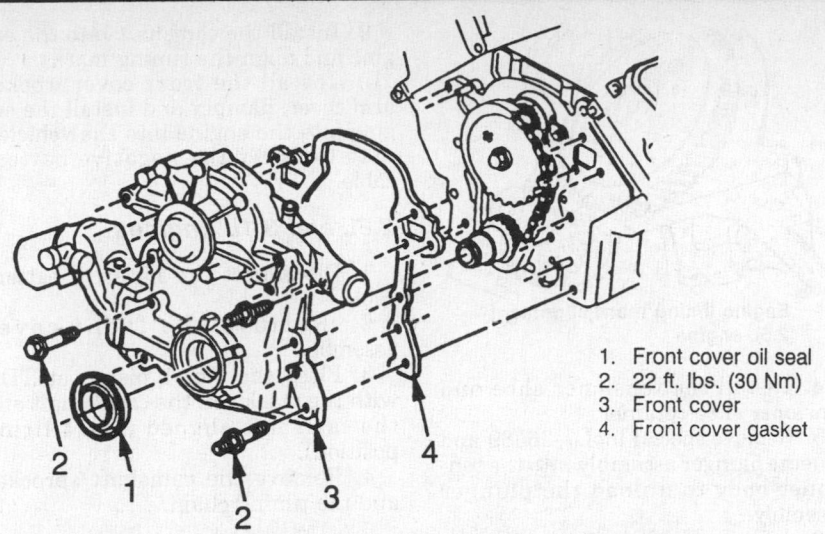

1. Front cover oil seal
2. 22 ft. lbs. (30 Nm)
3. Front cover
4. Front cover gasket

Timing chain cover installation—3.8L engine

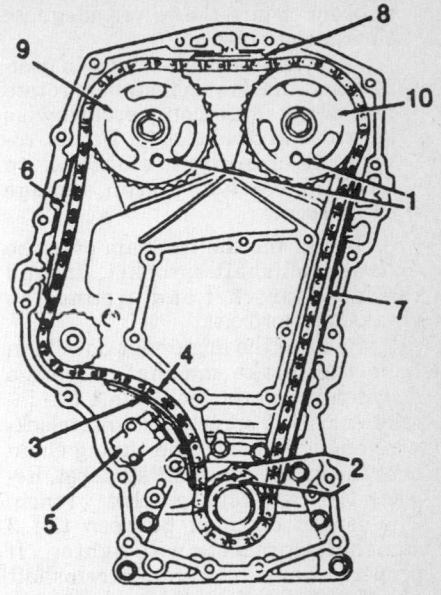

1. Camshaft timing marks	6. R/H guide
2. Crankshaft timing mark	7. L/H guide
3. Tensioner shoe assembly	8. Upper guide
4. Timing chain	9. Exhaust camshaft sprocket
5. Tensioner	10. Intake camshaft sprocket

Timing chain installation—2.3L engine

hicle. Remove the right side inner fender splash shield.

3. Remove the damper retaining bolt.

4. Using a crankshaft pulley puller tool, press the damper pulley from the crankshaft.

5. Using a small prybar, pry out the seal in the front cover.

NOTE: Use care not to damage the seal seat or the crankshaft while removing or installing the seal. Inspect the crankshaft seal surface for signs of wear.

6. Coat the new seal with oil. Using a seal installer tool, drive the new seal in the cover with the lip facing towards the engine.

7. Using a crankshaft pulley installer tool, press the crankshaft pulley onto the crankshaft. Torque the damper bolt to 67–85 ft. lbs. (90–115 Nm) for the 2.8L and 3.1L engine or 162 ft. lbs. (220 Nm) for the 2.5L engine or 105 ft. lbs. plus an additional 56 degree turn for the 3.8L engine or 74 ft. lbs. plus an additional 90 degree turn for the 2.3L engine.

8. Install the inner fender splash shield. Lower the vehicle.

9. Install the serpentine belt. Connect the negative battery cable. Run the engine to normal operating temperature and check for leaks.

Timing Chain and Sprockets

REMOVAL & INSTALLATION

2.3L Engine

NOTE: It is recommended that the entire procedure be reviewed before attempting to service the timing chain.

1. Disconnect the negative battery cable.

2. Remove the front timing chain cover and crankshaft oil slinger.

3. Rotate the crankshaft clockwise, as viewed from front of engine (normal rotation) until the camshaft sprocket's timing dowel pin holes line up with the holes in the timing chain housing. The mark on the crankshaft sprocket should line up with the mark on the cylinder block. The crankshaft sprocket keyway should point upwards and line up with the centerline of the cylinder bores. This is the normal timed position.

4. Remove the 3 timing chain guides.

5. Raise the vehicle and support safely.

6. Gently pry off timing chain tensioner spring retainer and remove spring.

NOTE: Two styles of tensioner are used. Early production engines will have a spring post and late production ones will not. Both styles are identical in operation and are interchangeable.

7. Remove the timing chain tensioner shoe retainer.

8. Make sure all the slack in the timing chain is above the tensioner assembly; remove the chain tensioner shoe. The timing chain must be disengaged from the wear grooves in the tensioner shoe in order to remove the shoe. Slide a prybar under the timing chain while pulling shoe outward.

9. If difficulty is encountered removing chain tensioner shoe, proceed as follows:

a. Lower the vehicle.

b. Hold the intake camshaft sprocket with a holding tool and remove the sprocket bolt and washer.

c. Remove the washer from the bolt and rethread the bolt back into the camshaft by hand, the bolt provides a surface to push against.

d. Remove intake camshaft sprocket using a 3-jaw puller in the 3 relief holes in the sprocket. Do not attempt to pry the sprocket off the camshaft or damage to the sprocket or chain housing could occur.

10. Remove the tensioner assembly retaining bolts and the tensioner.

——— **CAUTION** ———

The tensioner piston is spring loaded and could fly out causing personal injury.

11. Remove the chain housing to block stud (timing chain tensioner shoe pivot).

12. Remove the timing chain.

To install:

13. Tighten intake camshaft sprocket retaining bolt and washer, while holding the sprocket with tool J-36013 if removed.

14. Install the special tool through holes in camshaft sprockets into holes in timing chain housing. This positions the camshafts for correct timing.

15. If the camshafts are out of position and must be rotated more than ⅛ turn in order to install the alignment dowel pins:

a. The crankshaft must be rotated 90 degrees clockwise off of TDC in order to give the valves adequate clearance to open.

b. Once the camshafts are in position and the dowels installed, rotate the crankshaft counterclockwise back to top dead center. Do not rotate the crankshaft clockwise to TDC, or valve or piston damage could occur.

16. Install the timing chain over the exhaust camshaft sprocket, around the idler sprocket and around the crankshaft sprocket.

17. Remove the alignment dowel pin from the intake camshaft. Using a dowel pin remover tool, rotate the intake camshaft sprocket counterclockwise enough to slide the timing chain over the intake camshaft sprocket. Release the camshaft sprocket wrench. The length of chain between the 2 camshaft sprockets will tighten. If properly timed, the intake camshaft alignment dowel pin should slide in easily. If the dowel pin does not fully index, the camshafts are not timed correctly and the procedure must be repeated.

18. Leave the alignment dowel pins installed.

19. With slack removed from chain between intake camshaft sprocket and crankshaft sprocket, the timing marks on the crankshaft and the cylinder block should be aligned. If marks are not aligned, move the chain 1 tooth forward or rearward, remove slack and recheck marks.

20. Tighten the chain housing to block stud (timing chain tensioner shoe pivot). the stud is installed under the timing chain. Tighten to 19 ft. lbs. (26 Nm).

21. Reload timing chain tensioner assembly to its **0** position as follows:

a. Assemble restraint cylinder, spring and nylon plug into plunger. Index slot in restraint cylinder with peg in plunger. While rotating the restraint cylinder clockwise, push the restraint cylinder into the plunger until it bottoms. Keep rotating the restraint cylinder clockwise but allow the spring to push it out of the plunger. The pin in the plunger will lock the restraint in the loaded position.

b. Install tool J–36589 or equivalent, onto plunger assembly.

c. Install plunger assembly into tensioner body with the long end toward the crankshaft when installed.

22. Install the tensioner assembly to the chain housing. Recheck plunger assembly installation. It is correctly installed when the long end is toward the crankshaft.

23. Install and tighten timing chain tensioner bolts and tighten to 10 ft. lbs. (14 Nm).

Engine timing mark alignment—2.5L engine

24. Install the tensioner shoe and tensioner shoe retainer.

25. Remove special tool J–36589 and squeeze plunger assembly into the tensioner body to unload the plunger assembly.

26. Lower vehicle and remove the alignment dowel pins. Rotate crankshaft clockwise 2 full rotations. Align crankshaft timing mark with mark on cylinder block and reinstall alignment dowel pins. Alignment dowel pins will slide in easily if engine is timed correctly.

NOTE: If the engine is not correctly timed, severe engine damage could occur.

27. Install the 3 timing chain guides and crankshaft oil slinger.

28. Install the timing chain front cover.

29. Connect the negative battery cable and check for leaks.

2.5L Engine

TIMING GEARS

1. Disconnect the negative battery cable.

2. Remove the engine from the vehicle.

3. Remove the damper, front cover and camshaft. Align the timing marks on the crank and cam gears.

4. To remove the camshaft gear, use a arbor press and adapter. Position the thrust plate to avoid damage to the woodruff key as the gear is removed.

5. Remove the crankshaft gear with a suitable prybar.

6. Support the camshaft in the arbor press using the press adapter. Position the spacer ring, thrust plate and woodruff key over the end of the shaft and press the gear onto the camshaft.

7. Measure the end clearance with a feeler gauge between the cam journal and thrust plate. The measurement should be between 0.0015–0.0050 in. If the measurement is less than 0.0015 in., replace the spacer ring. If the measurement is more than 0.0050 in., replace the thrust plate.

8. Apply assembly lube GM 1052367 or equivalent, to the cam journals and lobes.

9. Install the camshaft into the engine and align the timing marks.

10. Install the front cover, rocker arm cover, damper and install the engine into the engine into the vehicle.

11. Connect the negative battery cable.

2.8L and 3.1L Engines

1. Disconnect the negative battery cable.

2. Remove the front cover assembly.

3. Place the No. 1 piston at TDC with the marks on the crankshaft and the camshaft aligned (No. 4 firing position).

4. Remove the camshaft sprocket and the timing chain.

NOTE: If the camshaft sprocket does not come off easily, a light blow on the lower edge of the sprocket with a rubber mallet should loosen the sprocket.

5. Remove the crankshaft sprocket with a suitable prybar.

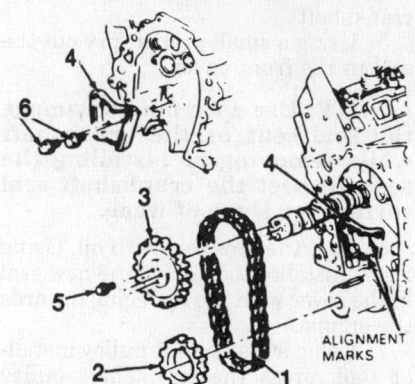

1. Timing chain	4. Damper
2. Crank sprocket	5. 15–20 ft. lbs.
3. Camshaft sprocket	6. 13–18 ft. lbs.

Timing chain and sprockets—2.8L and 3.1L engines

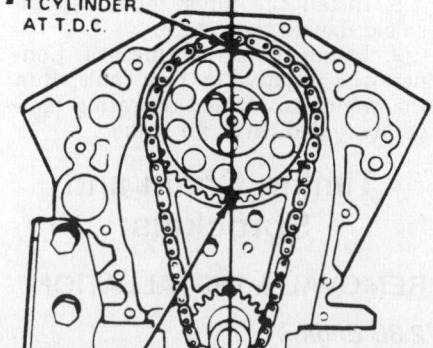

Engine timing mark alignment—2.8L and 3.1L engines

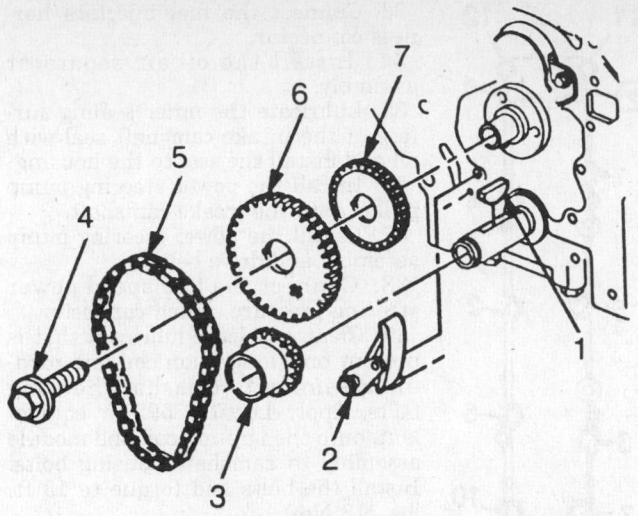

1. Key
2. Damper assembly
3. Crankshaft sprocket
4. 52 ft. lbs. (70 Nm) plus 110 degrees
5. Timing chain
6. Camshaft sprocket
7. Balance shaft drive gear

Timing chain and sprocket installation—3.8L engine

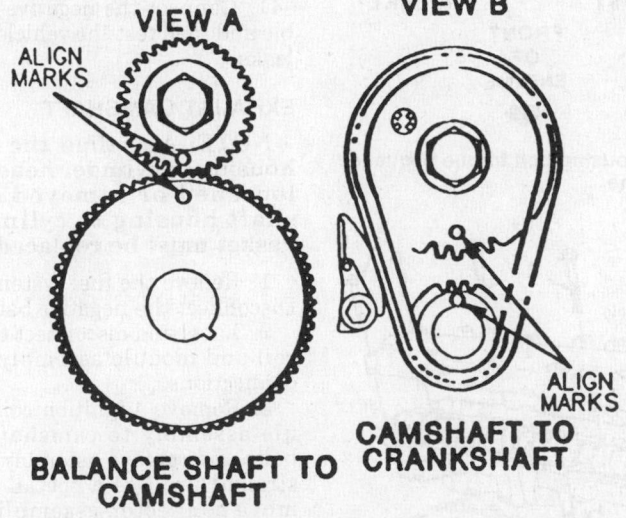

VIEW A

ALIGN MARKS

BALANCE SHAFT TO CAMSHAFT

VIEW B

ALIGN MARKS

CAMSHAFT TO CRANKSHAFT

Timing balancer shaft and camshaft marks—3.8L engines

6. Install the crankshaft sprocket. Apply a coat of Molykote® or equivalent, to the sprocket thrust surface.

7. Hold the camshaft sprocket with the chain hanging down and align the marks on the camshaft and crankshaft sprockets.

8. Align the dowel in the camshaft with the dowel hole in the camshaft sprocket. Install the camshaft sprocket and chain, use the camshaft sprocket bolts to draw the sprocket on to the camshaft. Tighten the sprocket bolts to 18 ft. lbs. (25 Nm).

9. Lubricate the timing chain with engine oil. Install the front cover assembly.

3.8L Engine

1. Disconnect the negative battery cable.

2. Remove the front cover assembly.

3. Align the timing marks on the sprockets and remove the timing chain damper.

4. Remove the camshaft sprocket bolts, camshaft sprocket and chain.

5. Remove the crankshaft sprocket by applying a light blow on the lower edge of the sprocket with a plastic mallet.

To install:

6. If the pistons have been moved in the engine, do the following:

a. Turn the crankshaft so the No. 1 piston is at Top Dead Center (TDC).

b. Turn the camshaft so, with the sprocket temporarily installed, the timing mark is straight down.

7. Assemble the timing chain on the sprockets with the timing marks facing each other.

8. Install the timing chain and sprockets and tighten the camshaft

sprocket bolts to 52 ft. lbs. plus an additional 110 degree turn.

9. Install the timing chain damper and tighten the bolt to 14 ft. lbs.

10. Rotate the engine 2 revolutions and make sure the marks are aligned correctly.

11. Install the front cover assembly.

12. Connect the negative battery cable.

Camshaft

REMOVAL & INSTALLATION

2.3L Engine

INTAKE CAMSHAFT

NOTE: Any time the camshaft housing to cylinder head bolts are loosened or removed, the camshaft housing to cylinder head gasket must be replaced.

1. Relieve the fuel system pressure. Disconnect the negative battery cable.

2. Label and disconnect the ignition coil and module assembly electrical connections.

3. Remove 4 ignition coil and module assembly to camshaft housing bolts and remove assembly by pulling straight up. Use a special spark plug boot wire remover tool to remove connector assemblies if they have stuck to the spark plugs.

4. Remove the idle speed power steering pressure switch connector.

5. Loosen 3 power steering pump pivot bolts and remove drive belt.

6. Disconnect the 2 rear power steering pump bracket to transaxle bolts.

7. Remove the front power steering pump bracket to cylinder block bolt.

8. Disconnect the power steering pump assembly and position to the side.

9. Using the special tool, remove the power steering pump drive pulley from the intake camshaft.

10. Remove oil/air separator bolts and hoses. Leave the hoses attached to the separator, disconnect from the oil fill, chain housing and intake manifold. Remove as an assembly.

11. Remove vacuum line from fuel pressure regulator and disconnect the fuel injector harness connector.

12. Disconnect fuel line retaining clamp from bracket on top of intake camshaft housing.

13. Remove fuel rail to camshaft housing retaining bolts.

14. Remove the fuel rail from the cylinder head. Cover injector openings in cylinder head and cover injector nozzles. Leave fuel lines attached and position fuel rail aside.

15. Disconnect the timing chain and

housing but do not remove from the engine.

16. Remove intake camshaft housing cover to camshaft housing retaining bolts.

17. Remove the intake camshaft housing to cylinder head retaining bolts. Use the reverse of the tightening sequence when loosening camshaft housing to cylinder head retaining bolts. Leave 2 bolts loosely in place to hold the camshaft housing while separating camshaft cover from housing.

18. Push the cover off the housing by threading 4 of the housing to head retaining bolts into the tapped holes in the cam housing cover. Tighten the bolts in evenly so the cover does not bind on the dowel pins.

19. Remove the 2 loosely installed camshaft housing to head bolts and remove the cover. Discard the gaskets.

20. Note the position of the chain sprocket dowel pin for reassembly. Remove the camshaft carefully; do not damage the camshaft oil seal.

21. Remove intake camshaft oil seal from camshaft and discard seal. This seal must be replaced any time the housing and cover are separated.

22. Remove the camshaft carrier from the cylinder head and remove the gasket.

To install:

23. Thoroughly clean the mating surfaces of the camshaft carrier and the cylinder head, bolts and bolt holes. Install a new gasket and place the housing on the head. Install 1 bolt loosely to hold in place.

24. Install the lifters into their bores. If the camshaft is being replaced, the lifters must also be replaced. Lubricate camshaft lobes, journals and lifters with camshaft and lifter prelube. The camshaft lobes and journals must be adequately lubricated or engine damage could occur upon start up.

25. Install the camshaft in the same position as when removed. The timing chain sprocket dowel pin should be straight up and line up with the centerline of the lifter bores.

26. Install new camshaft housing to camshaft housing cover seals into cover; do not use sealer. Make sure the correct color seal is placed in each groove. Install the cover to the housing.

27. Apply thread locking compound to the camshaft housing and cover retaining bolt threads.

28. Install bolts and torque to 11 ft. lbs. Rotate the bolts (except the 2 rear bolts that hold fuel pipe to camshaft housing) an additional 75 degrees in sequence. Rotate the excepted bolts an additional 25 degrees.

29. Install timing chain housing and timing chain.

30. Uncover fuel injectors and install

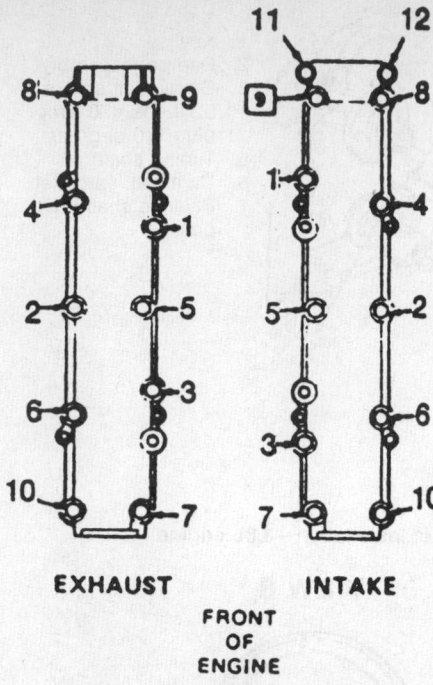

Camshaft housing bolt torque sequence —2.3L engine

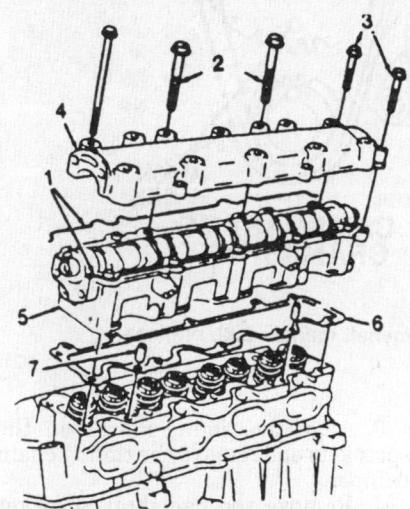

1. Housing cover seals
2. Cylinder head bolts
3. Housing cover bolts
4. Camshaft cover
5. Intake camshaft housing
6. Cylinder head gasket
7. Dowel pins

Camshaft housing assembly— 2.3L engine

new fuel injector ring seals lubricated with oil. Install the fuel rail.

31. Install the fuel line retaining clamp and retainer to bracket on top of the intake camshaft housing.

32. Connect the vacuum line to the fuel pressure regulator.

33. Connect the fuel injectors harness connector.

34. Install the oil/air separator assembly.

35. Lubricate the inner sealing surface of the intake camshaft seal with oil and install the seal to the housing.

36. Install the power steering pump pulley onto the intake camshaft.

37. Install the power steering pump assembly and drive belt.

38. Connect the idle speed power steering pressure switch connector.

39. Clean any loose lubricant that is present on the ignition coil and module assembly to camshaft housing bolts. Apply Loctite® 592 or equivalent, onto the ignition coil and module assembly to camshaft housing bolts. Install the bolts and torque to 13 ft. lbs. (18 Nm).

40. Connect the electrical connectors to ignition coil and module assembly.

41. Connect the negative battery cable and road test the vehicle. Check for leaks.

EXHAUST CAMSHAFT

NOTE: Any time the camshaft housing to cylinder head bolts are loosened or removed the camshaft housing to cylinder head gasket must be replaced.

1. Relieve the fuel system pressure. Disconnect the negative battery cable.

2. Label and disconnect the ignition coil and module assembly electrical connections.

3. Remove 4 ignition coil and module assembly to camshaft housing bolts and remove assembly by pulling straight up. Use a special tool to remove connector assemblies if they have stuck to the spark plugs.

4. Remove the idle speed power steering pressure switch connector.

5. Remove the transaxle fluid level indicator tube assembly from exhaust camshaft cover and position aside.

6. Remove exhaust camshaft cover and gasket.

7. Disconnect the timing chain and housing but do not remove from the engine.

8. Remove exhaust camshaft housing to cylinder head bolts. Use the reverse of the tightening procedure when loosening camshaft housing while separating camshaft cover from housing.

9. Push the cover off the housing by threading 4 of the housing to head retaining bolts into the tapped holes in the camshaft cover. Tighten the bolts evenly so the cover does not bind on the dowel pins.

10. Remove the 2 loosely installed camshaft housing to cylinder head bolts and remove cover, discard gaskets.

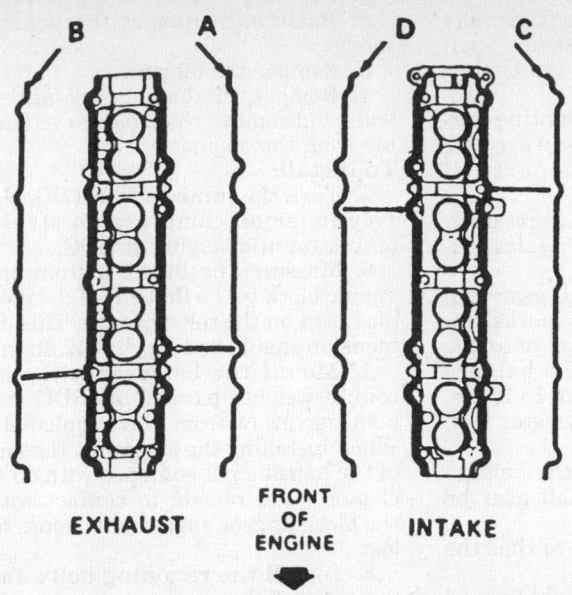

A. Seal – inner (exhaust – red)
B. Seal – outer (exhaust – red)
C. Seal – outer (intake – blue)
D. Seal – inner (intake – blue)

EXHAUST   FRONT OF ENGINE   INTAKE

Camshaft cover assembly – 2.3L engine

11. Loosely install 1 camshaft housing to cylinder head bolt to retain the housing during camshaft and lifter removal.

12. Note the position of the chain sprocket dowel pin for reassembly. Remove camshaft being careful not to damage the camshaft or journals.

13. Remove the camshaft carrier from the cylinder head and remove the gasket.

To install:

14. Thoroughly clean the mating surfaces of the camshaft carrier and the cylinder head, bolts and bolt holes. Install a new gasket and place the housing on the head. Install 1 bolt loosely to hold in place.

15. Install the lifters into their bores. If the camshaft is being replaced, the lifters must also be replaced. Lubricate camshaft lobes, journals and lifters with camshaft and lifter prelube. The camshaft lobes and journals must be adequately lubricated or engine damage could occur upon start up.

16. Install camshaft in same position as when removed. The timing chain sprocket dowel pin should be straight up and align with the centerline of the lifter bores.

17. Install new camshaft housing to camshaft housing cover seals into cover; do not use sealer. Make sure the correct color seal is placed in each groove. Install the cover to the housing.

18. Apply thread locking compound to the camshaft housing and cover retaining bolt threads.

19. Install bolts and torque in sequence to 11 ft. lbs. Then rotate the bolts an additional 75 degrees, in sequence.

20. Install timing chain housing and timing chain.

21. Install the transaxle fluid level indicator tube assembly to exhaust camshaft cover.

22. Connect the idle speed power steering pressure switch connector.

23. Clean any loose lubricant that is present on the ignition coil and module assembly to camshaft housing bolts. Apply Loctite® 592 or equivalent, onto the ignition coil and module assembly to camshaft housing bolts. Install the bolts and torque to 13 ft. lbs. (18 Nm).

24. Connect the electrical connectors to ignition coil and module assembly.

25. Connect the negative battery cable and road test the vehicle. Check for leaks.

2.5L Engine

NOTE: For the removal of the camshaft, the engine assembly must be removed from the vehicle.

1. Disconnect the negative battery cable.
2. Remove the engine assembly from the vehicle.
3. Remove the rocker arm cover and pushrods.
4. Remove the pushrod cover and valve lifters.
5. Remove the serpentine belt, crankshaft pulleys and vibration dampener.
6. Remove the front cover.
7. Remove the camshaft thrust plate screws.

NOTE: The camshaft journals are the same diameter. Care must be taken when removing the camshaft to avoid damage to the cam bearings.

8. Carefully slide the camshaft and gear through the front of the block.
9. To remove the camshaft gear, use a arbor press and adapter.
10. Old and new camshafts should be cleaned with solvent and compressed air before being installed.

To install:

11. Install the camshaft gear onto the camshaft with an arbor press.
12. Measure the end clearance with a feeler gauge between the cam journal and thrust plate. The measurement should be between 0.0015–0.0050 in. If the measurement is less than 0.0015 in., replace the spacer ring. If the measurement is more than 0.0050 in., replace the thrust plate.

NOTE: Always apply assembly lube, GM Engine Oil Supplement (E.O.S) or equivalent, to the cam journals and lobes. If this procedures is not done, cam damage may result.

13. Carefully install the camshaft into the engine block by rotating and pushing forward until seated.
14. Install the thrust plate screws and torque to 89 inch lbs. (10 Nm).
15. Install the front cover, vibration dampener and serpentine belt.
16. Install the valve lifter and pushrod cover.
17. Install the pushrods and rocker arm cover.
18. Install the engine into the vehicle.
19. Refill all necessary fluids.
20. Start the engine and check for leaks.

2.8L, 3.1L and 3.8L Engines

NOTE: For the removal of the camshaft the engine assembly must be removed from the vehicle.

1. Remove the engine assembly from the vehicle.
2. Remove the rocker covers and remove the valve lifters.
3. Remove the front cover assembly, timing chain and sprockets.
4. Remove the camshaft by sliding it from the block.

To install:

5. Coat the camshaft journals with engine oil. Coat the camshaft lobes with GM Engine Oil Supplement (E.O.S) or equivalent.
6. Slide the camshaft into the block.
7. Install the timing chain and sprockets, making sure to align the timing marks.
8. Install the front cover assembly. Install the valve lifters.

9. Install the engine assembly into the vehicle. Run the engine and check for leaks.

Balance Shaft

REMOVAL & INSTALLATION

3.8L Engine

1. Disconnect the negative battery cable. Remove the engine and secure it to a workstand.
2. Remove the flywheel-to-crankshaft bolts and the flywheel.
3. Remove the timing chain cover-to-engine bolts and the cover.
4. Remove the camshaft sprocket-to-camshaft gear bolts, the sprocket, the timing chain and the gear.
5. To remove the balance shaft, perform the following procedures:
  a. Remove the balance shaft gear-to-shaft bolt and the gear.
  b. Remove the balance shaft retainer-to-engine bolts and the retainer.
  c. Using the slide hammer tool, pull the balance shaft from the front of the engine.

To install:
6. If replacing the rear balance shaft bearing, perform the following procedures:
  a. Drive the rear plug from the engine.
  b. Using the camshaft remover/installer tool, press the rear bearing from the rear of the engine.
  c. Dip the new bearing in clean engine oil.
  d. Using the balance shaft rear bearing installer tool, press the new rear bearing into the rear of the engine.
  e. Install the rear cup plug.

7. Using the balance shaft installer tool, screw it into the balance shaft and install the shaft into the engine; remove the installer tool.
8. Clean the gasket mounting surfaces. Inspect the parts for wear and/or damage; replace the parts, if necessary.
9. Install the balance shaft retainer. Torque the balance shaft retainer-to-engine bolts to 27 ft. lbs.
10. Align the balance shaft gear with the camshaft gear timing marks. Install the balance shaft gear onto the balance shaft. Torque the balance gear-to-balance shaft bolt to 15 ft. lbs, then using a torque angle meter tool, rotate another 35 degrees.
11. Align the marks on the balance shaft gear and the camshaft gear by turning the balance shaft.
12. Turn the crankshaft so that the No. 1 piston is at TDC.
13. Install the timing chain and sprocket.
14. Replace the balance shaft front bearing retainer and bolts. Tighten the bolts to 26 ft. lbs.
15. Install the front timing cover and the lifter guide retainer.
16. Install the intake manifold and flywheel assembly. Tighten the flywheel bolts to 89 inch lbs., plus an additional 90 degree turn.
17. Install the engine assembly and connect the negative battery cable. Start the engine and check for leaks.

Crankshaft Force Balancer

REMOVAL & INSTALLATION

2.5L Engine

1. Disconnect the negative battery cable.

2. Raise and support the vehicle safely.
3. Remove the oil pan.
4. Remove the balancer retaining bolts and remove the balancer assembly from the engine.

To install:
5. Turn the crankshaft to TDC, No. 1 cylinder on compression stroke (crank counterweights at BDC).
6. Measure the distance from the engine block to the first cut of the double notch on the reluctor ring. This dimension should be $1\frac{11}{16}$ in. (42.8mm).
7. Mount the balancer with the counterweights parallel, at BDC and pointing away from the crankshaft. When installing the assembly, the end of the housing not equipped with dowel pins must remain in contact with the block or gear engagement could be lost.
8. Install the retaining bolts and tighten as follows:
  Short bolts — 9 ft. lbs. (12 Nm) plus 75 degree turn
  Long bolts — 9 ft. lbs. (12 Nm) plus 90 degree turn
9. Install the oil pan and retaining bolts.
10. Fill all fluids to their proper levels.
11. Connect the negative battery cable and check for leaks.

Piston and Connecting Rod
POSITIONING

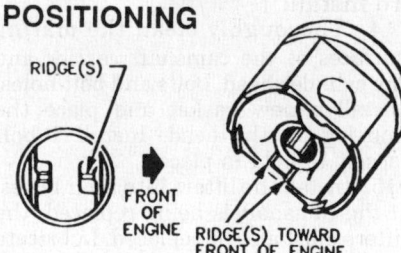

Piston positioning — 3.8L engine

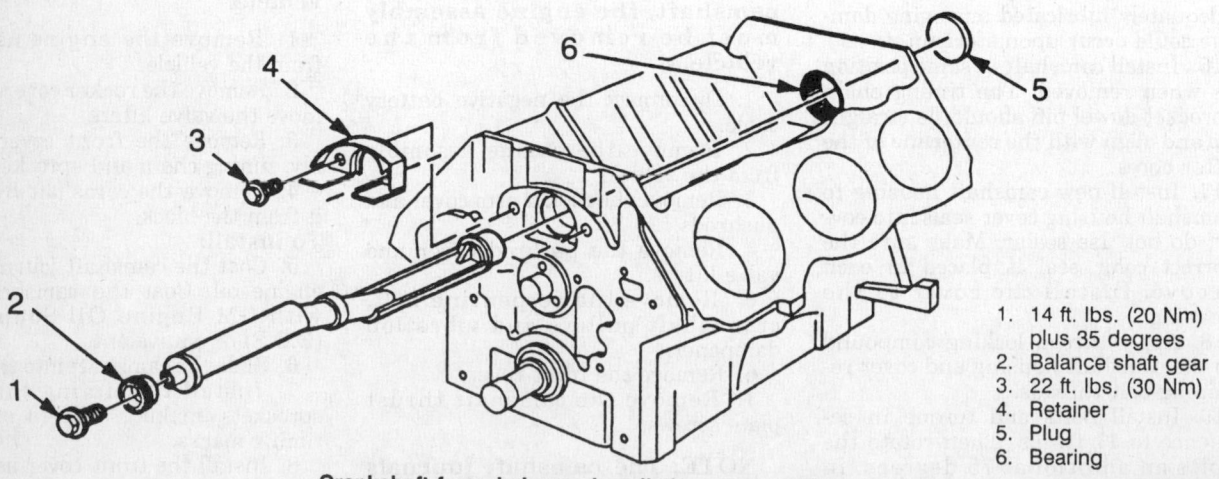

1. 14 ft. lbs. (20 Nm) plus 35 degrees
2. Balance shaft gear
3. 22 ft. lbs. (30 Nm)
4. Retainer
5. Plug
6. Bearing

Crankshaft force balancer installation — 2.5L engine

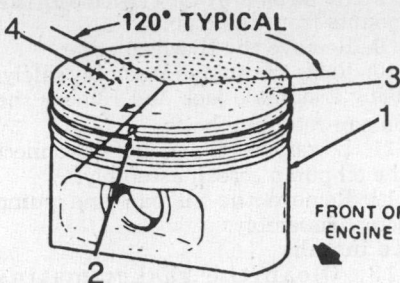

1. Piston
2. Upper compression ring gap
3. Lower compression ring gap
4. Oil ring assembly gap

Piston ring end gap positioning— 2.3L engine

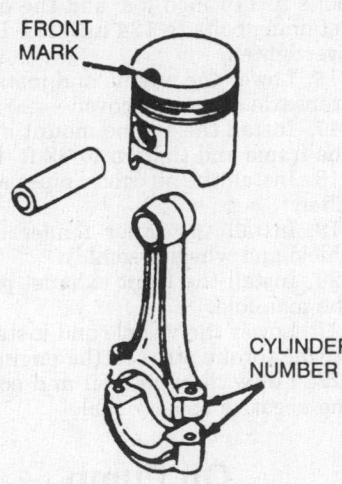

Piston positioning—2.3L, 2.5L, 2.8L and 3.1L engines

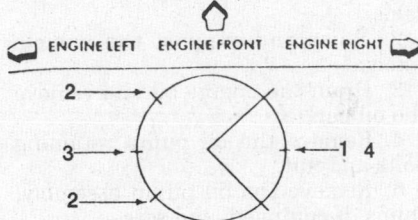

1. Oil ring spacer gap (tang in hole or slot with arc)
2. Oil ring rail gaps
3. 2nd compression ring gap
4. Top compression ring gap

Piston ring end gap positioning—2.5L, 2.8L, 3.1L and 3.8L engines

ENGINE LUBRICATION

Oil Pan

REMOVAL & INSTALLATION

2.3L Engine

1. Disconnect the negative battery cable.
2. Raise and support the vehicle safely.
3. Remove the flywheel inspection cover.
4. Remove the splash shield-to-suspension support bolt. Remove the exhaust manifold brace, if equipped.
5. Remove the radiator outlet pipe-to-oil pan bolt.
6. Remove the transaxle-to-oil pan nut and stud using a 7mm socket.
7. Gently pry the spacer out from between oil pan and transaxle.
8. Remove the oil pan bolts. Rotate the crankshaft if necessary and remove the oil pan and gasket from the engine.
9. Inspect the silicone strips across the top of the aluminum carrier at the oil pan-cylinder block-seal housing 3-way joint. If damaged, these strips must be repaired with silicone sealer. Use only enough sealer to restore the strips to their original dimension; too much sealer could cause leakage.

To install:

10. Thoroughly clean and dry the mating surfaces, bolts and bolt holes. Install the oil pan with a new gasket; do not uses sealer on the gasket. Loosely install the pan bolts.
11. Place the spacer in its approximate installed position but allow clearance to tighten the pan bolt above it.
12. Torque the pan to block bolts to 17 ft. lbs. (24 Nm) and the remaining bolts to 106 inch lbs. (12 Nm).
13. Install the spacer and stud.
14. Install the oil pan transaxle nut and bolt.
15. Install the slash shield to suspension support.
16. Install the radiator outlet pipe bolt.
17. Install the exhaust manifold brace, if removed.
18. Install the flywheel inspection cover.
19. Fill the crankcase with the proper oil.
20. Connect the negative battery cable and check for leaks.

2.5L Engine

1. Disconnect the negative battery cable.

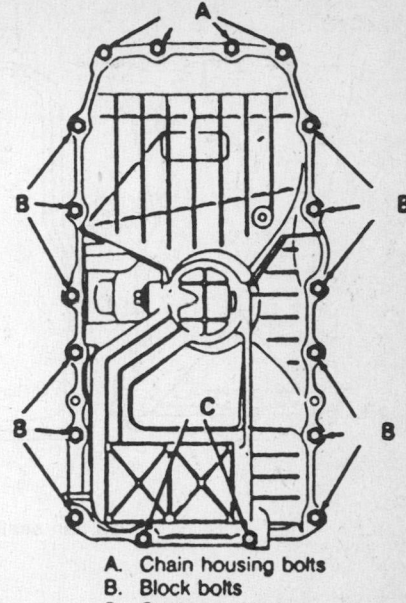

A. Chain housing bolts
B. Block bolts
C. Carrier seal bolts

Oil pan installation—2.3L engine

2. Remove the coolant recovery bottle, engine torque strut, air cleaner and the air inlet.
3. Remove the serpentine belt, loosen and move the air conditioning compressor from the bracket.
4. Remove the oil level indicator and fill tube.
5. Support the engine using an engine support tool J–28467–A and J–36462.
6. Raise and safely support the vehicle, drain the engine oil and remove the oil filter.
7. Remove the starter motor, flywheel cover and turn the front wheels to full right.
8. Remove the engine wiring harness retainers under the oil pan on the right and left sides.
9. Remove the right engine splash shield, front engine mount bracket bolts and nuts.
10. Remove the transaxle mount nuts.
11. Using the engine support fixture tool J–28467–A and J–36462, raise the engine about 2 inches.
12. Remove the front engine mount, bracket and loosen the frame bolts.
13. Remove the oil pan retaining bolts and oil pan.

To install:

14. Clean all gasket surfaces and apply RTV sealer to the oil pan and engine surfaces.
15. Install the oil pan and retaining bolts and tighten to 89 inch lbs. (10 Nm).
16. Install the frame bolts and tighten to 103 ft. lbs. (140 Nm).
17. Install the engine mount, brack-

27 GM "W" BODY

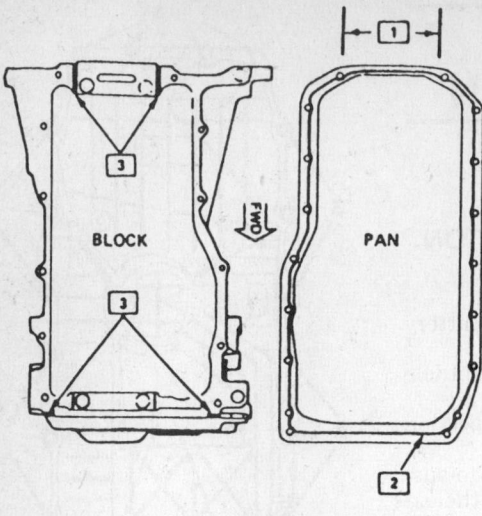

Apply RTV Sealant as specified:
1. 3/8" wide x 3/16" thick
2. 3/16" wide x 1/8" thick
3. 1/8" bead in areas shown

Oil pan sealer locations—2.5L engine

et, lower the engine into position and install the transaxle mount nuts.

18. Install the engine mount nuts and bracket bolts.

19. Install the engine splash shield, wiring harness to the oil pan, flywheel cover and the starter motor.

20. Lower the vehicle and remove the engine support fixtures.

21. Install the oil level indicator and tube assembly.

22. Reinstall the air conditioning compressor to its original location and serpentine belt.

23. Install the air inlet, air cleaner, torque strut and coolant recovery bottle.

24. Connect the negative battery cable and fill the engine with oil.

2.8L and 3.1L Engines

1. Disconnect the negative battery cable.

2. Remove the serpentine belt and the tensioner.

3. Support the engine with tool J–28467 or equivalent.

4. Raise and safely support the vehicle. Drain the engine oil.

5. Remove the right tire and wheel assembly. Remove the right inner fender splash shield.

6. Remove the steering gear pinch bolt. Remove the transaxle mount retaining bolts.

7. Remove the engine-to-cradle mounting nuts. Remove the front engine collar bracket from the block.

8. Remove the starter shield and the flywheel cover. Remove the starter.

9. Loosen, but do not remove the rear engine cradle bolts.

10. Remove the front cradle bolts. Remove the oil pan retaining bolts and nuts. Remove the oil pan.

To install:

11. Clean the gasket mating surfaces.

12. Install a new gasket on the oil pan. Apply silicon sealer to the portion of the pan that contacts the rear of the block.

13. Install the oil pan, nuts and retaining bolts. Tighten to 13–18 ft. lbs. (18–25 Nm).

14. Install the front cradle bolts and tighten the rear cradle bolts. Install the starter and splash shield. Install the flywheel shield.

15. Attach the collar bracket to the block, install the engine-to-cradle nuts. Install the transaxle mount nuts.

16. Install the steering pinch bolt. Install the right inner fender splash shield and tire assembly. Lower the vehicle.

17. Remove the engine support tool. Install the serpentine belt and tensioner.

18. Fill the crankcase to the correct level. Connect the negative battery cable. Run the engine to normal operating temperature and check for leaks.

3.8L Engine

1. Disconnect the negative battery cable.

2. Disconnect the engine torque strut from the engine.

3. Raise and support the vehicle safely.

4. Disconnect the front exhaust pipe from the manifold.

5. Remove the right front wheel and the inner fender splash shield.

6. Drain the engine oil and remove the oil filter.

7. Disconnect the oil cooler pipes and allow to hang loose for access.

8. Remove both front engine mounts from the frame.

9. Remove the flywheel cover.

10. Raise the engine assembly safely, using a suitable jack and remove the oil pan retaining bolts.

11. Lower the oil pan and disconnect the oil pump screen assembly.

12. Remove the oil pan and pump screen assembly.

To install:

13. Clean the gasket mating surfaces.

14. Use a new oil pan gasket and install the oil pan and screen assembly to the engine.

NOTE: If the rear main bearing cap is being installed, then RTV sealant must be placed on the oil pan gasket tabs that insert into the gasket groove of the outer surface on the rear main bearing cap.

15. Tighten the screen assembly bolts to 115 inch lbs. and the oil pan retaining bolts to 124 inch lbs. Do not overtighten.

16. Lower the engine and install the transaxle converter cover.

17. Install the engine mount nuts to the frame and tighten to 32 ft. lbs.

18. Install the oil cooler pipes and oil filter.

19. Install the inner fender splash shield and wheel assembly.

20. Install the front exhaust pipe to the manifold.

21. Lower the vehicle and install the engine torque strut to the engine.

22. Fill with engine oil and connect the negative battery cable.

Oil Pump

REMOVAL & INSTALLATION

2.3L Engine

1. Disconnect the negative battery cable.

2. Raise and support the vehicle safely.

3. Drain the engine oil and remove the oil pan.

4. Remove the oil pump retaining bolts and nut.

5. Remove the oil pump assembly, shims, if equipped, and screen.

To install:

6. With oil pump assembly off engine, remove 3 retaining bolts and separate the driven gear cover and screen assembly from the oil pump.

7. Install the oil pump on the block using the original shims, if equipped. Tighten the bolts to 33 ft. lbs. (45 Nm).

8. Mount a dial indicator assembly to measure backlash between oil pump to drive gear.

9. Record oil pump drive to driven

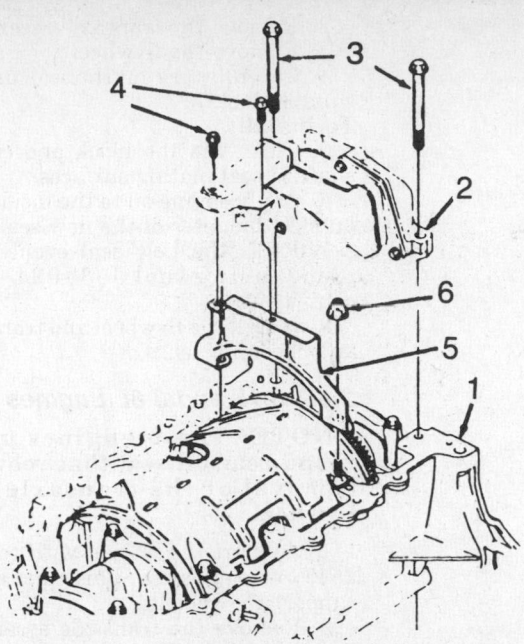

1. Cylinder block
2. Oil pump assembly
3. Oil pump to block bolt
4. Oil pump screen to brace bolt
5. Oil pump to block brace
6. Oil pump brace to block nut

Oil pump installation—2.3L engine

gear backlash. Proper backlash is 0.010–0.018. When measuring, do not allow the crankshaft to move.

10. If equipped with shims, remove shims to decrease clearance and add shims to increase clearance. If no shims were present, replace the assembly if proper backlash cannot be obtained.

11. When the proper clearance is reached, rotate crankshaft ½ turn and recheck clearance.

12. Remove oil pump from block, fill the cavity with petroleum jelly and reinstall driven gear cover and screen assembly to pump. Tighten the bolts to 106 inch lbs. (13 Nm).

13. Reinstall the pump assembly to the block. Torque oil pump-to-block bolts 33 ft.lbs. (45 Nm).

14. Install the oil pan.

15. Fill the crankcase with the proper oil.

16. Connect the negative battery cable, check the oil pressure and check for leaks.

2.5L, 2.8L and 3.1L Engines

NOTE: On the 2.5L engine, the force balancer assembly does not have to be removed to service the oil pump or pressure regulator assemblies.

1. Disconnect the negative battery cable.

2. Raise and safely support the vehicle.

3. Drain the engine oil.

4. Remove the oil pan.

5. Remove the oil pump retaining bolts and remove the oil pump and pump driveshaft.

To install:

6. Install the oil pump and pump driveshaft. Tighten the oil pump mounting bolts to 30 ft. lbs. (41 Nm) for the 2.8L and 3.1L engines and to 89 inch lbs. (10 Nm) for the 2.5L engine.

7. Install the oil pan. Lower the vehicle.

8. Fill the crankcase to the correct level with oil. Run the vehicle and check for leaks.

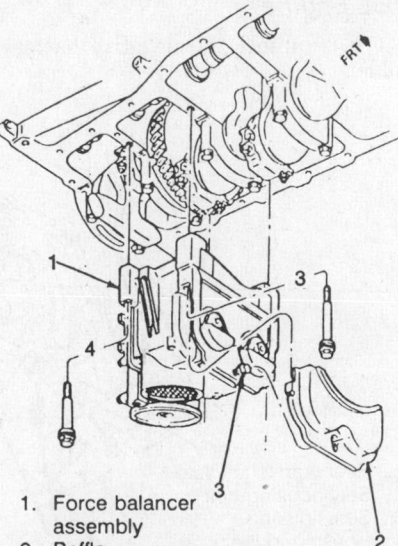

1. Force balancer assembly
2. Baffle
3. 89 inch lbs. (10 Nm)
4. Numbers show bolt position

Oil pump/force balancer assembly— 2.5L engine

3.8L Engine

1. Disconnect the negative battery cable.

2. Raise and safely support the vehicle.

3. Drain the engine oil.

4. Remove the front cover assembly.

5. Remove the oil filter adapter, pressure regulator valve and spring.

6. Remove the oil pump cover attaching screws and remove the cover.

7. Remove the oil pump gears.

To install:

8. Lubricate the gears with petroleum jelly and install the gears into the housing.

9. Pack the gear cavity with petroleum jelly after the gears have been installed in the housing.

10. Install the oil pump cover and screws and tighten to 97 inch lbs.

11. Install the oil filter adapter with new gasket, pressure regulator valve and spring.

12. Install the front cover assembly.

13. Fill with clean engine oil and test oil pressure.

NOTE: Running the engine without measurable oil pressure will cause extensive damage.

CHECKING

2.3L Engine

1. Inspect all components carefully for physical damage of any type and replace worn parts.

2. Check the gerotor cavity depth. The specification is 0.674–0.676 in. (17.11–17.16mm).

3. Check the gerotor cavity diameter. The specification is 2.127–2.129 in. (53.95–54.00mm).

4. Check the inner gerotor tip clearance. The maximum clearance is 0.006 in. (15mm).

5. Check the outer gerotor diameter clearance. The specification is 0.010–0.014 in. (0.254–0.354mm).

2.5L Engine

1. Inspect all components carefully for physical damage of any type and replace worn parts.

2. Check the gerotor cavity depth. The specification for 1987–88 is 0.995–0.998 in. (25.27–25.35mm) The specification for 1989–91 is 0.514–0.516 in. (13.05–13.10mm).

3. Check the gear lash. The specification is 0.009–0.015 in. (0.23–0.38mm).

4. Check the clearance of both gears. The maximum clearance is 0.004 in. (0.10mm).

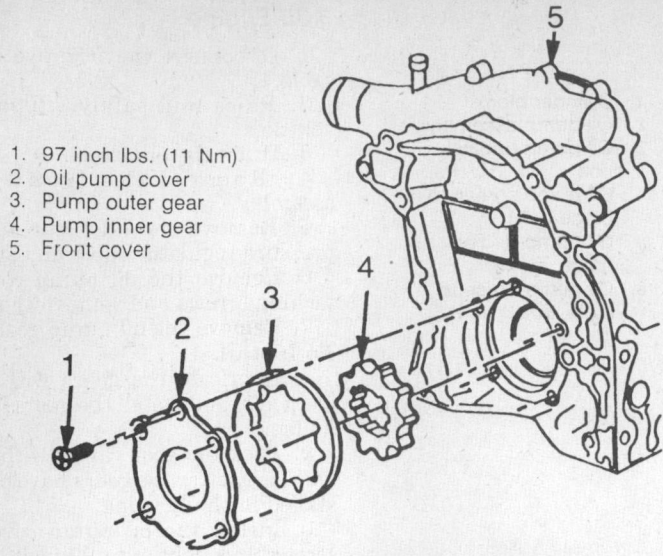

1. 97 inch lbs. (11 Nm)
2. Oil pump cover
3. Pump outer gear
4. Pump inner gear
5. Front cover

Oil pump and housing—3.8L engine

2.8L and 3.1L Engines

1. Inspect all components carefully for physical damage of any type and replace worn parts.
2. Check the gear pocket depth. The specification is 1.195–1.198 in. (30.36–30.44mm).
3. Check the gear pocket diameter. The specification is 1.503–1.506 in. (38.18–38.25mm).
4. Check the gear length. The measurement is 1.199–1.200 in. (30.45–30.48mm).
5. Check the outer gear diameter clearance. The specification is 1.498–1.500 in. (38.05–38.10mm).
6. The pressure regulator valve-to-bore-clearance should be 0.0015–0.0035 in. (0.038mm–0.089mm).

3.8L Engine

1. Inspect all components carefully for physical damage of any type and replace worn parts.
2. The inner tip clearance should be 0.006 in.
3. The outer gear diameter clearance should be 0.008–0.015 in.
4. The gear end clearance or the drop in the housing should be 0.001–0.0035 in.
5. The pressure regulator valve-to-bore clearance should be 0.0015–0.003 in.

Rear Main Bearing Oil Seal

REMOVAL & INSTALLATION

2.3L Engine

1. Disconnect the negative battery cable.

2. Remove the transaxle.
3. Remove the flywheel-to-crankshaft bolts and the flywheel.
4. Remove the oil pan-to-seal housing bolts and the block-to-seal housing bolts.
5. Remove the seal housing from the engine.
6. Place 2 blocks of equal thickness on a flat surface and position the seal housing on the 2 blocks. Remove the seal from the housing.
7. The installation is the reverse of the removal procedure. Use new gaskets when installing.
8. Connect the negative battery cable and for leaks.

2.5L Engine

1. Disconnect the negative battery cable.

1. Rear crankshaft seal
2. Seal housing bolt
3. Seal housing
4. Housing to block gasket
5. Dowel pin
6. Oil pan to seal housing bolt
7. Oil pan

2. Remove the transaxle assembly.
3. Remove the flywheel.
4. Carefully pry out the seal, using a suitable tool.
To install:
5. Clean the the block and crankshaft to seal mating surfaces.
6. Apply engine oil to the inside and outside diameter of the new seal.
7. Press the new seal evenly into place, using tool J–34924–A or equivalent.
8. Install the flywheel and transaxle and check for leaks.

2.8L, 3.1L and 3.8L Engines

NOTE: These engines use a round rear oil seal that requires removal of the transaxle and flywheel.

1. Support the engine with tool J–28467 or equivalent. Raise and safely support the vehicle.
2. Remove the transaxle assembly. Remove the flywheel.
3. Using a small prybar or equivalent, insert it through the dust lip at an angle and pry the old seal from the block.
4. Inspect the seal bore and the crankshaft end for any damage.
5. Coat the inside lip of the seal with engine oil and install it on the seal installation tool J–34686 or equivalent.
6. Align the dowel pin of the tool with the dowel pin of the crankshaft. Install the tool on the crankshaft and turn the wing nut until the tool and seal are fully seated on the crankshaft.
7. Loosen the wing nut and remove the tool. Check the seal to make sure it is properly seated.
8. Install the flywheel and the transaxle.

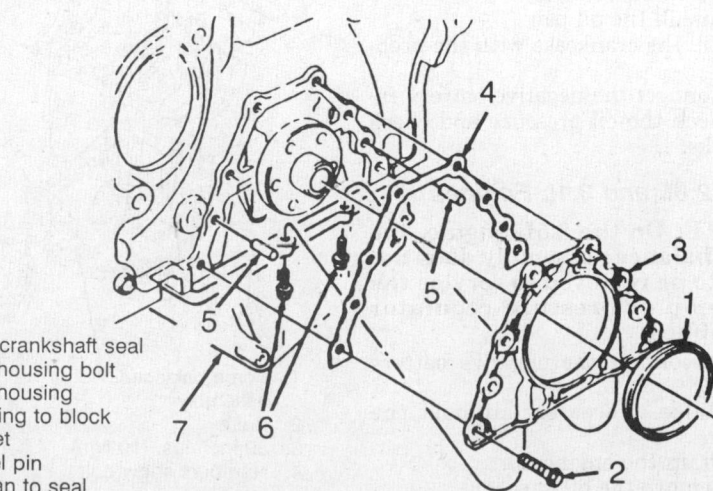

Rear crankshaft seal installation—2.3L engine

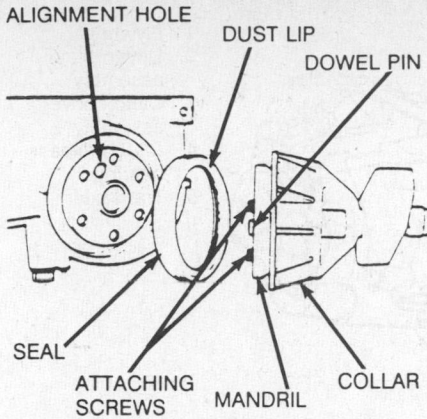

ALIGNMENT HOLE
DUST LIP
DOWEL PIN
SEAL
ATTACHING SCREWS
MANDRIL
COLLAR

Rear main seal replacement—2.8L, 3.1L and 3.8L engines

9. Remove the engine support tool. Run the engine and check for leaks.

MANUAL TRANSAXLE

For further information on transmissions/transaxles, please refer to "Chilton's Guide to Transmission Repair".

Transaxle Assembly

REMOVAL & INSTALLATION

NOTE: **Before performing any maintenance that requires the removal of the slave cylinder, transaxle or clutch housing, the clutch master cylinder pushrod must first be disconnected from the clutch pedal. Failure to disconnect the pushrod will result in permanent damage to the slave cylinder if the clutch pedal is depressed with the slave cylinder disconnected.**

1. Disconnect the negative battery cable.
2. Install the engine support tool J–28467 or equivalent.
3. Remove the air cleaner housing and intake tube. Disconnect the clutch slave cylinder from the transaxle.
4. Disconnect the electrical connection at the speed sensor assembly. Disconnect the clutch and shift cables from the transaxle.
5. Remove the exhaust crossover pipe at the left manifold and remove the EGR tube from the crossover.
6. Loosen the crossover-to-right exhaust manifold clamp and move the

crossover pipe to gain access to the transaxle bolts (V6 engine).
7. Remove the 2 upper transaxle mounting bolts and remove the 2 upper mounting studs. Leave 1 bottom bolt and stud attached.
8. Disconnect the electrical connection at the backup light switch. Raise and safely support the vehicle.
9. Drain the transaxle fluid. Remove the clutch housing cover. Remove both front tire assemblies.
10. Remove the inner fender splash shields from both side of the vehicle. Disconnect the power steering lines from the frame.
11. Remove the rack and pinion heat shield and remove the rack and pinion from the frame.
12. Disconnect the right and left ball joints. Remove the upper transaxle mount retaining bolts. Remove the lower engine mount retaining nuts.
13. Remove the sub-frame retaining bolts and remove the sub-frame from the vehicle. Remove the starter and support it aside.
14. Remove the right and left halfshafts from the transaxle. Support the halfshafts to the frame with wire to prevent damage to the CV-joints. Support the transaxle and remove the remaining bolt and stud. Remove the transaxle from the vehicle.
To install:
15. Align the transaxle with the engine and install. Install the lower transaxle-to-engine mounting bolt and stud, tightening to 55 ft. lbs. (75 Nm).
16. Install the starter assembly. Install the left and right halfshaft.
17. Install the sub-frame and retaining bolts. Install the lower engine mount retaining nuts.
18. Install the upper transaxle retaining bolts, tightening to 55 ft. lbs. (75 Nm). Install the right and left ball joints to the steering knuckles.
19. Install the rack and pinion, heat shield and lines to the frame. Install the right and left inner fender splash shields.
20. Install the clutch housing cover, tighten the screws to 115 inch lbs. (13 Nm). Lower the vehicle.
21. Attach the crossover pipe to the manifolds and attach the EGR pipe to the crossover.
22. Attach the shift and clutch cables to the transaxle. Connect all of the electrical connectors. Install the air cleaner housing and tube. Remove the engine support tool.
23. Fill the transaxle with fluid. Connect the negative battery cable.

Linkage Adjustment

The shift control and cables are preset at the factory and require no adjustments.

CLUTCH

Clutch Assembly

REMOVAL & INSTALLATION

NOTE: **Before any service that requires removal of the slave cylinder, the master cylinder pushrod must be disconnected from the clutch pedal and the connection in the hydraulic lines must be separated using tool J–36221 or equivalent. If not disconnected, permanent damage to the slave cylinder will occur if the clutch pedal is depressed while the system is not resisted by clutch loads.**

1. Disconnect the negative terminal from the battery.
2. From inside the vehicle, remove the sound insulator panel.
3. Disconnect the clutch master cylinder pushrod from the clutch pedal and disconnect the quick connect fitting in the hydraulic line. Remove the actuator from the transaxle housing.
4. Remove the transaxle.
5. With the transaxle removed, matchmark the pressure plate and flywheel assembly to insure proper balance during reassembly.
6. Loosen the pressure plate-to-flywheel bolts, a turn at a time, until the spring pressure is removed.
7. Support the pressure plate and remove the bolts.
8. Remove the pressure plate and disc assembly; be sure to note the flywheel side of the clutch disc.
To install:
9. Clean and inspect the clutch assembly, flywheel, release bearing, clutch fork and pivot shaft for signs of wear. Replace any necessary parts.
10. Position the clutch disc and pressure plate in the appropriate position, support the assembly with alignment tool No. J–29074, J–35822 or equivalent.

NOTE: **Make sure the clutch disc is facing the same direction it was removed. If the same pressure plate is being reused, align the marks made during removal and install, install the pressure plate retaining bolts and tighten them gradually and evenly.**

11. Remove the alignment tool and torque the pressure plate-to-flywheel bolts to 15 ft. lbs. (21 Nm). Lightly lubricate the clutch fork ends. Fill the recess ends of the release bearing with grease. Lubricate the input shaft with a light coat of grease.

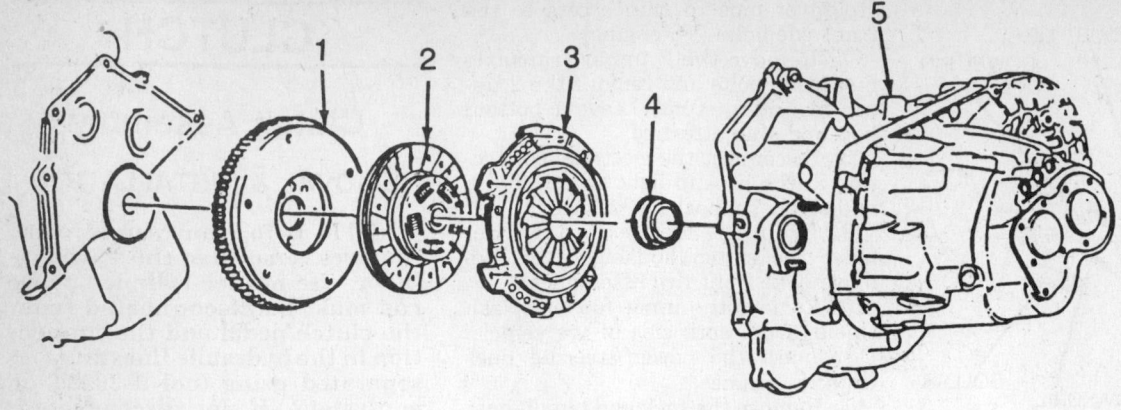

1. Flywheel
2. Driven plate assembly
3. Clutch cover assembly
4. Clutch release bearing
5. Transaxle

Exploded view of the clutch assembly

12. Install the transaxle assembly. Install the clutch master cylinder pushrod and install the sound insulator panel.

NOTE: The clutch lever must not be moved towards the flywheel until the transaxle is bolted to the engine. Damage to the transaxle, release bearing and clutch fork could occur if this is not followed.

13. Connect the negative battery cable. Bleed the clutch system and check the clutch operation.

Clutch Master Cylinder, Actuator and Reservoir

REMOVAL & INSTALLATION

NOTE: The factory hydraulic system is serviced as a single assembly. Replacement hydraulic assemblies are pre-filled with fluid and do not require bleeding. Individual components of the system are not available separately. Check with an aftermarket part supplier to see if individual components can be purchased separately.

1. Disconnect the negative battery cable.
2. Remove the sound insulator inside the vehicle and disconnect the master cylinder pushrod at the clutch pedal.
3. Remove the left upper secondary cowl panel.
4. Remove the 2 master cylinder reservoir-to-strut tower retaining nuts.
5. Remove the anti-rotation screw located next to the master cylinder flange at the pedal support plate.

6. Using wrench flats on the front end of the master cylinder body, twist the cylinder counterclockwise to release the twist lock attachment-to-plate. Do not torque on the hose connection on top of the cylinder body, damage may occur.
7. Remove the 2 actuator-to-transaxle retaining nuts and actuator assembly.
8. Pull the master cylinder with the pushrod attached forward out of the pedal plate. Lift the reservoir off the strut tower studs and remove the 3 components as a complete assembly.

To install:

9. Install the master cylinder into the opening in the pedal plate and rotate 45 degrees by applying torque on the wrench flats only.
10. Install the anti-rotation screw.
11. Install the fluid reservoir-to-strut tower and torque the retaining nuts to 36 inch lbs. (4 Nm).
12. Install a new pushrod bushing and lubricate before installation.
13. Install the master cylinder pushrod-to-clutch pedal.
14. Install the clutch actuator-to-transaxle.
15. Press the clutch pedal down several times to ensure proper operation.
16. Install the left upper secondary cowl panel, sound insulator and connect the negative battery cable.

AUTOMATIC TRANSAXLE

For further information on transmissions/transaxles, please refer to "Chilton's Guide to Transmission Repair".

Transaxle Assembly

NOTE: By September 1, 1991, Hydra-matic will have changed the name designations of the THM 125C and THM 440-R4 automatic transaxle. The new name designation for these transaxles will be Hydra-matic 3T40 and 4T60. Transaxles built between 1989–1990 will serve as transitional years in which a dual system, made up of the old designation and the new designation will be in effect.

REMOVAL & INSTALLATION

1. Disconnect the negative battery cable. Remove the air cleaner, bracket, Mass Air Flow (MAF) sensor and air tube as an assembly.
2. Disconnect the exhaust crossover from the right side manifold and remove the left side exhaust manifold, then, raise and support the manifold/crossover assembly on V6 engines.
3. Disconnect the TV cable from the throttle lever and the transaxle.
4. Remove the vent hose and the shift cable from the transaxle.
5. Remove the fluid level indicator and the filler tube.
6. Using a engine support fixture tool J–28467 or equivalent and the adapter tool J–35953 or equivalent, install them on the engine.
7. Remove the wiring harness-to-transaxle nut.
8. Label and disconnect the wires for the speed sensor, TCC connector and the neutral safety/backup light switch.
9. Remove the upper transaxle-to-engine bolts.
10. Remove the transaxle-to-mount through bolt, the transaxle mount bracket and the mount.

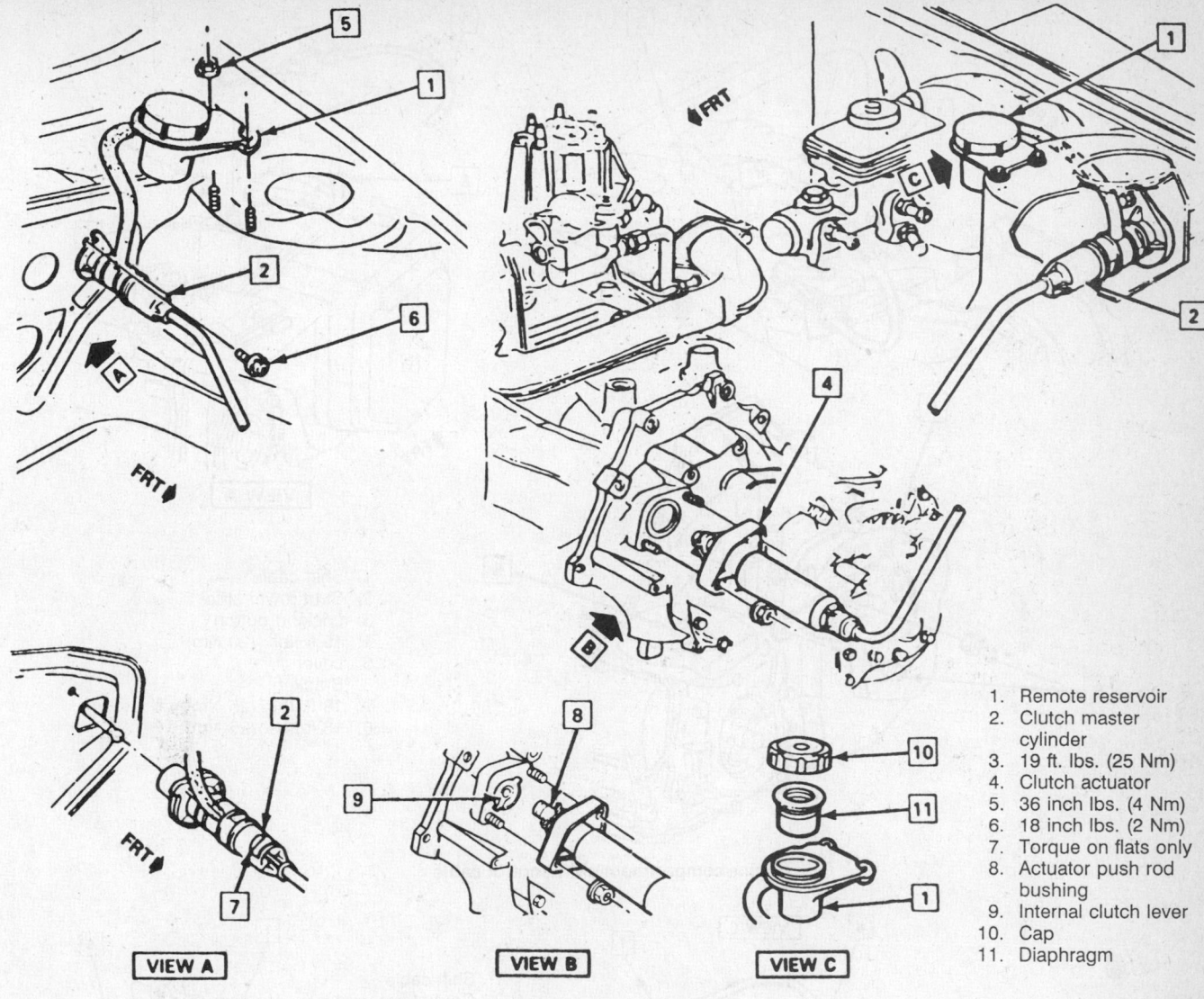

1. Remote reservoir
2. Clutch master cylinder
3. 19 ft. lbs. (25 Nm)
4. Clutch actuator
5. 36 inch lbs. (4 Nm)
6. 18 inch lbs. (2 Nm)
7. Torque on flats only
8. Actuator push rod bushing
9. Internal clutch lever
10. Cap
11. Diaphragm

VIEW A   VIEW B   VIEW C

Clutch hydraulic system

11. Raise and safely support the vehicle.

12. Remove the front wheel assemblies.

13. Disconnect the shift cable bracket from the transaxle.

14. Remove the left side splash shield.

15. Using a modified halfshaft seal protector tool J–34754 or equivalent, install 1 on each halfshaft to protect the seal from damage and the joint from possible failure. Support the halfshafts to the body to prevent CV-joint damage.

16. Using care not to damage the halfshaft boots, disconnect the halfshafts from the transaxle.

17. Remove the torsional and lateral strut from the transaxle. Remove the left side stabilizer link pin bolt.

18. Remove the left frame support bolts and move it out of the way.

19. Disconnect the speedometer wire from the transaxle.

20. Remove the transaxle converter cover and matchmark the converter to the flywheel for assembly.

21. Disconnect and plug the transaxle cooler pipes.

22. Remove the transaxle-to-engine support.

23. Using a transmission jack, position and secure it to the transaxle and remove the remaining transaxle-to-engine bolts.

24. Make sure that the torque converter does not fall out and remove the transaxle from the vehicle.

NOTE: The transaxle cooler and lines should be flushed any time the transaxle is removed for overhaul, or to replace the pump, case or converter.

To install:

25. Put a small amount of grease on the pilot hub of the converter and make sure that the converter is properly engaged with the pump.

26. Raise the transaxle to the engine while guiding the right side halfshaft into the transaxle.

27. Install the lower transaxle mounting bolts, tighten to 55 ft. lbs. (75 Nm) and remove the jack.

28. Align the converter with the marks made previously on the flywheel and install the bolts hand tight.

29. Torque the converter bolts to 46 ft. lbs. (61 Nm). Retorque the first bolt after the others.

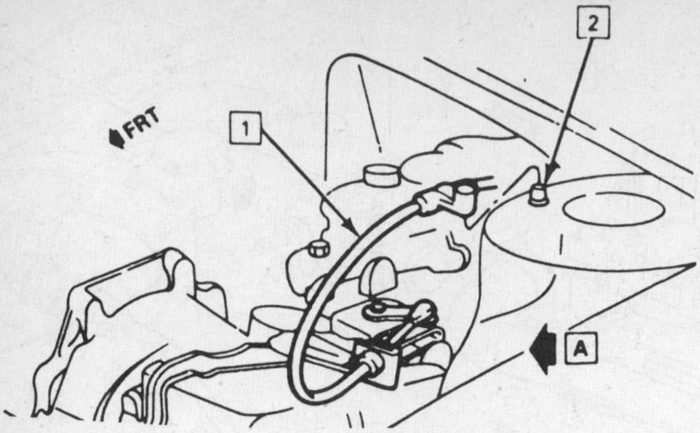

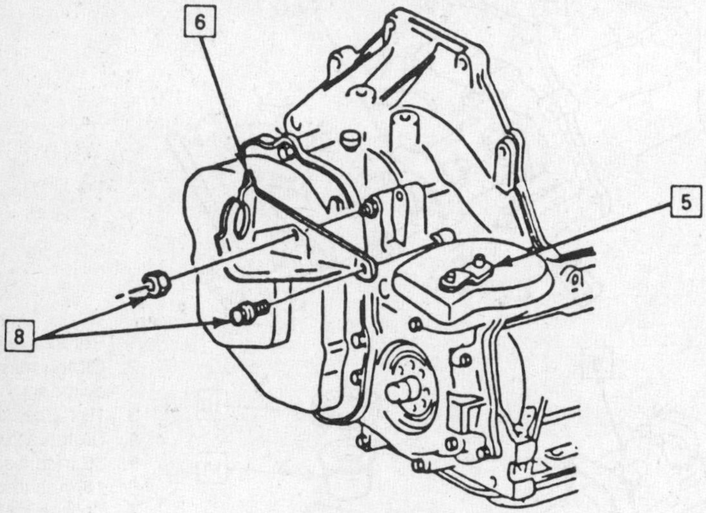

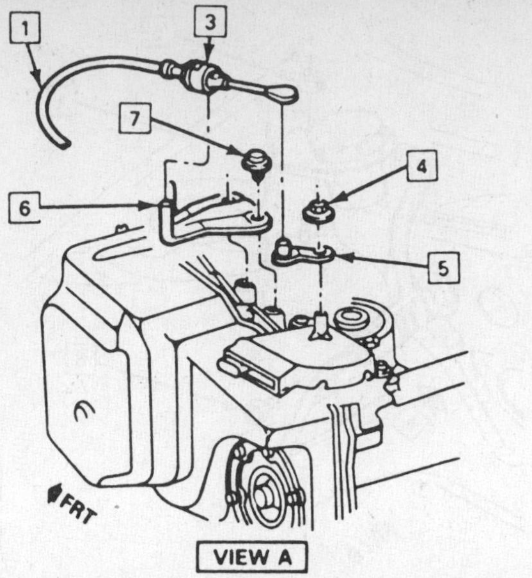

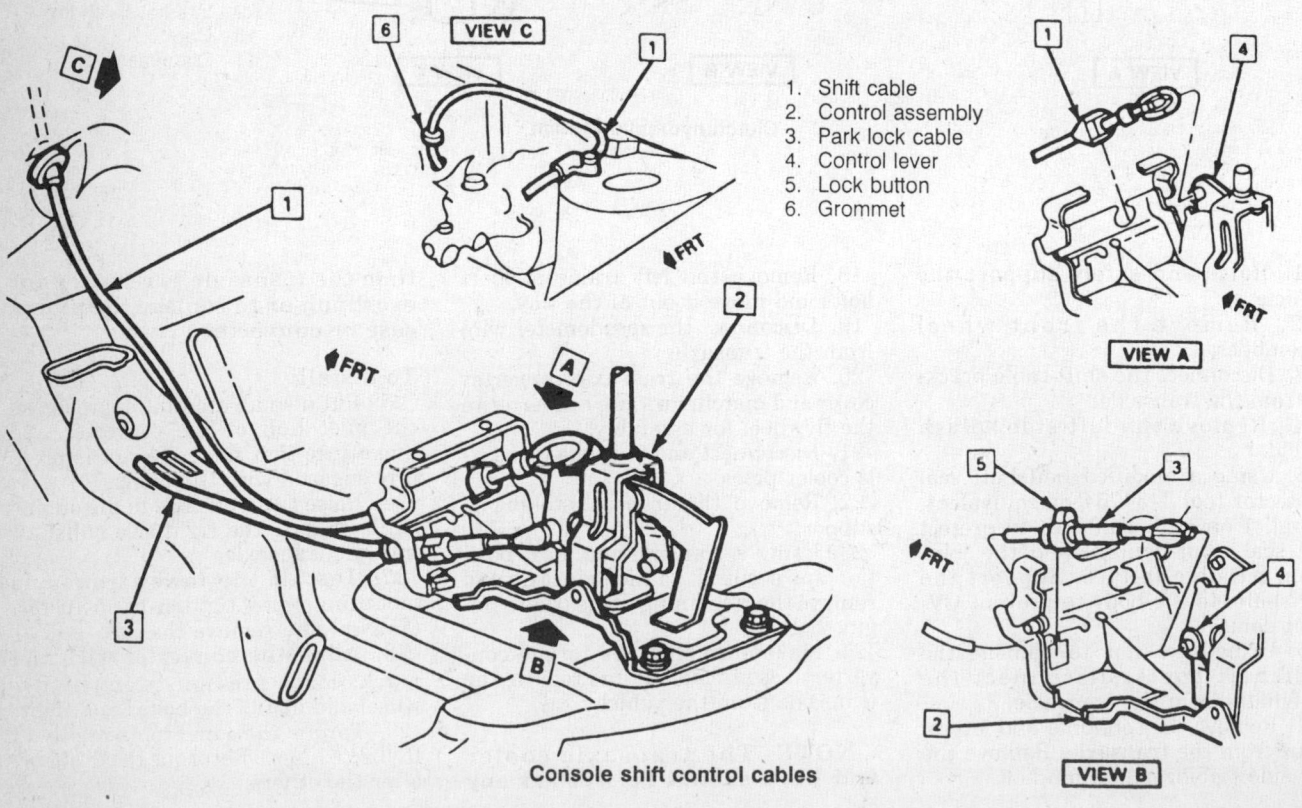

1. Shift cable
2. Strut tower stud
3. Locking button
4. 15 ft. lbs. (20 Nm)
5. Lever
6. Bracket
7. 18 ft. lbs. (25 Nm)
8. 18 ft. lbs. (25 Nm)

Engine compartment shift control cable

1. Shift cable
2. Control assembly
3. Park lock cable
4. Control lever
5. Lock button
6. Grommet

Console shift control cables

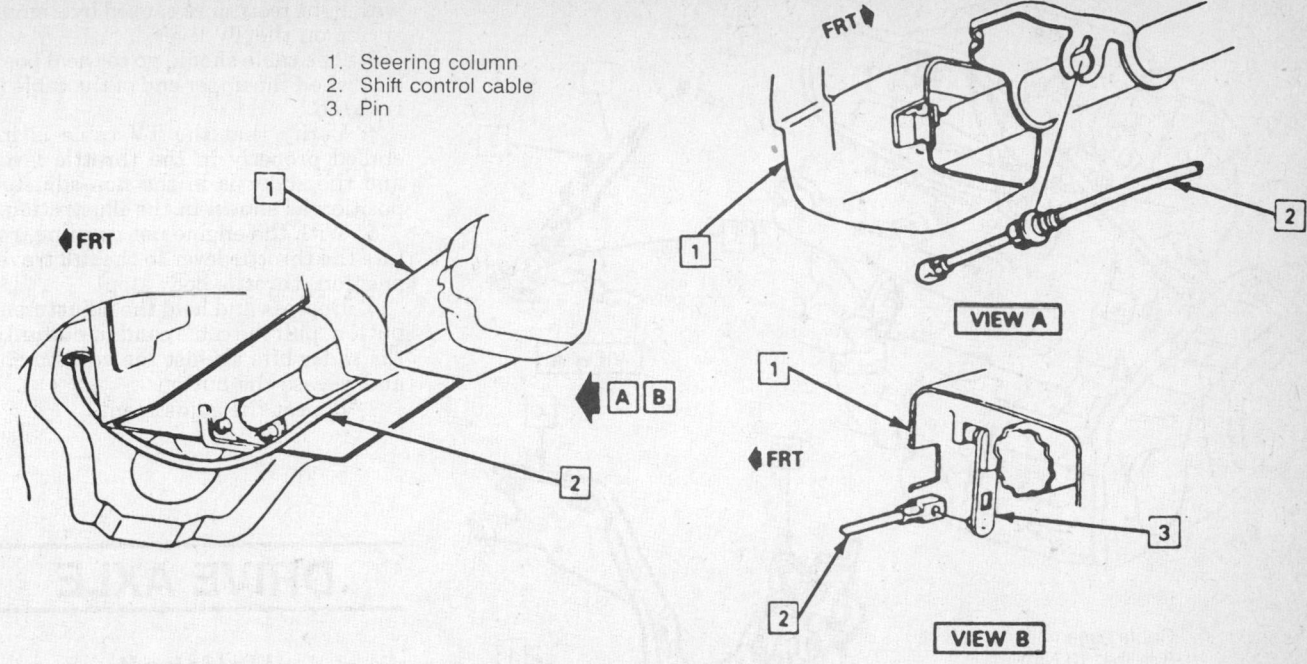

1. Steering column
2. Shift control cable
3. Pin

VIEW A

VIEW B

Column shift control cables

30. Install the starter assembly. Install the left side halfshaft.

31. Install the converter cover, oil cooler lines and cover. Install the subframe assembly. Install the lower engine mount retaining bolts and the transaxle mount nuts.

32. Install the right and left ball joints. Install the power steering rack, heat shield and cooler lines to the frame.

33. Install the right and left inner fender splash shields. Install the tire assemblies.

34. Lower the vehicle. Connect all electrical leads. Install the upper transaxle mount bolts, tighten to 55 ft. lbs. (75 Nm).

35. Attach the crossover pipe to the exhaust manifold. Connect the EGR tube to the crossover.

36. Connect the TV cable and the shift cable. Install the air cleaner and inlet tube.

37. Remove the engine support tool. Connect the negative battery cable.

ADJUSTMENT

Control Cable

1. Disconnect the negative battery cable.

2. Lift up the locking button at the transaxle and cable bracket.

3. Place the transaxle shift lever in the **N** position. This position can be found by rotating the selector shaft/shift lever clockwise from **P** through **R** to **N**.

4. Place the shift control inside the vehicle to the **N** position.

5. Push down the locking button at the cable bracket and connect the negative battery cable.

Park/Lock Control Cable

1. Disconnect the negative battery cable.

2. With the shift lever in the **P** position and the key in the **LOCK** position, make sure that the shifter cannot be moved to another position. The key should be removable from the column.

3. With the key in the **RUN** position and the shifter in the **N** position,

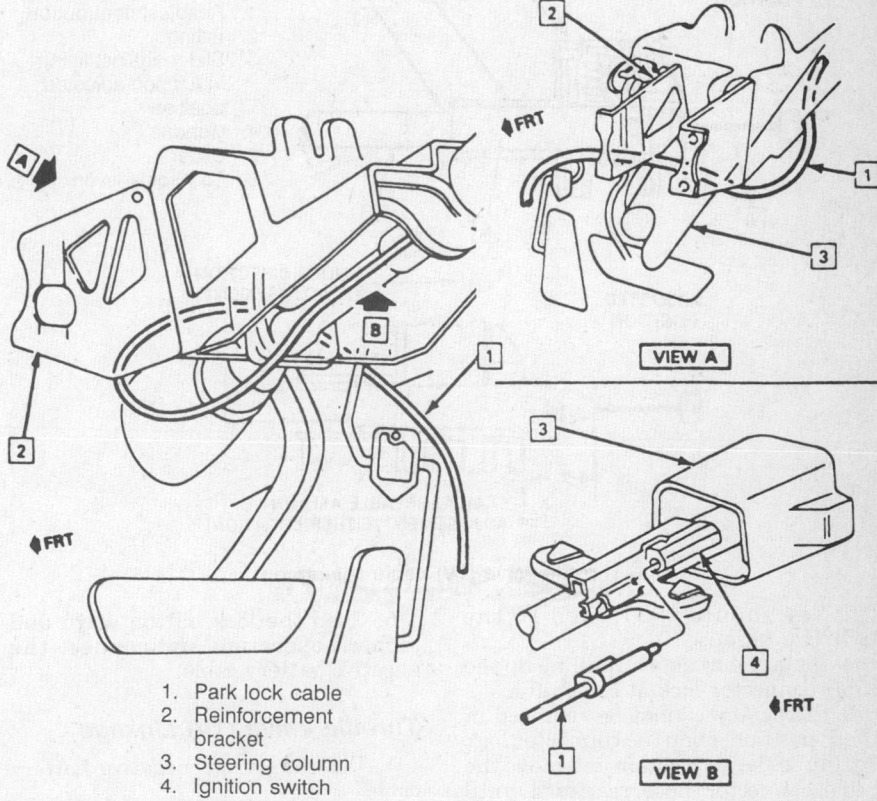

1. Park lock cable
2. Reinforcement bracket
3. Steering column
4. Ignition switch

VIEW A

VIEW B

Park/Lock control cable at column

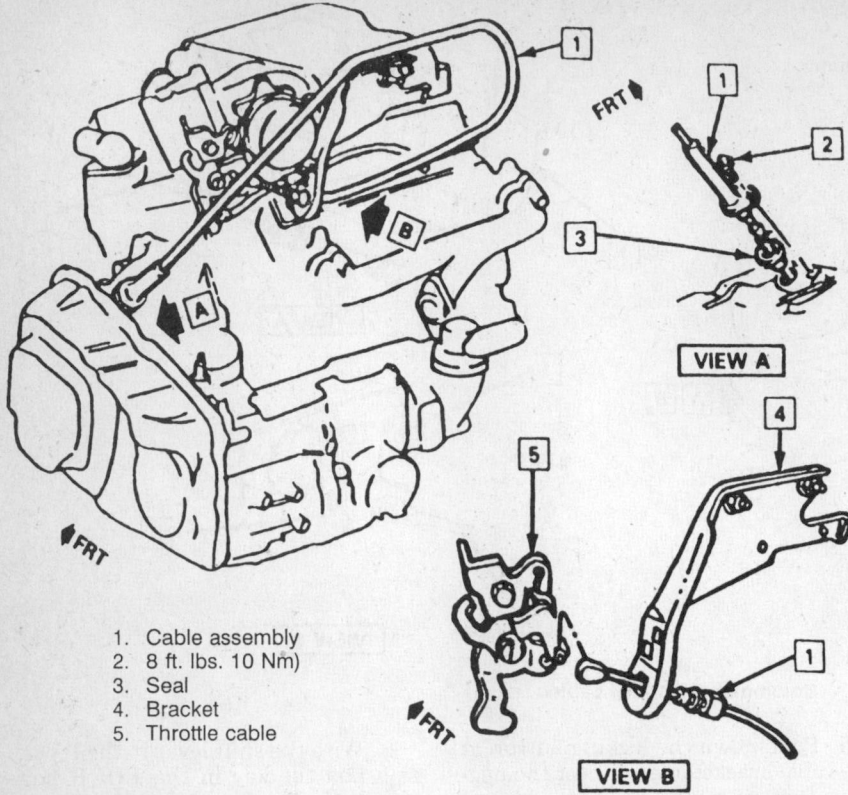

1. Cable assembly
2. 8 ft. lbs. 10 Nm)
3. Seal
4. Bracket
5. Throttle cable

Throttle valve (TV) cable routing

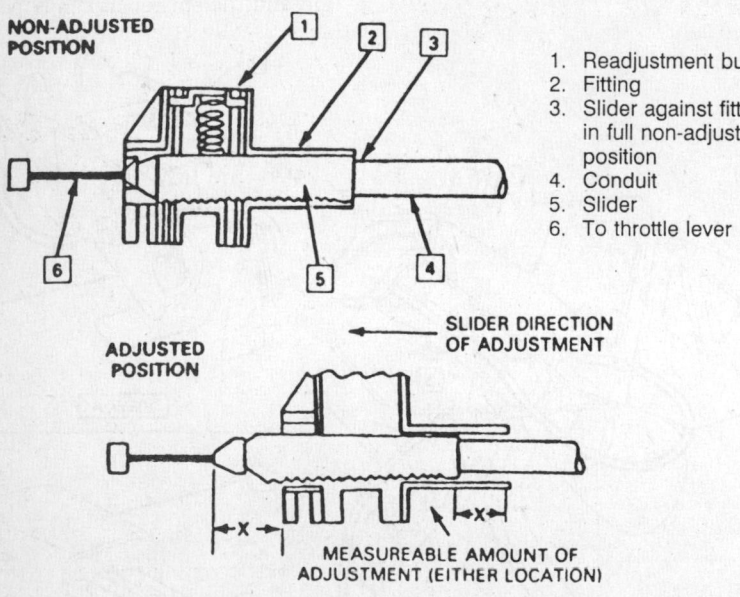

1. Readjustment button
2. Fitting
3. Slider against fitting in full non-adjusted position
4. Conduit
5. Slider
6. To throttle lever

Throttle valve (TV) cable adjustment

the key should NOT turn to the **LOCK** position.

4. Adjust the cable by pulling up the cable connector lock at the shifter.

5. If the key cannot be removed in the **P** position, snap the connector lock button to the up position and move the cable connector nose rearward until the key can be removed from the ignition.

6. Snap the lock button down and recheck operation and connect the negative battery cable.

Throttle Valve (TV) Linkage

1. Disconnect the negative battery cable.

2. Pull on the upper end of the TV cable. It should travel a short distance with light resistance caused by a small spring on the TV lever.

3. The cable should go to the 0 position when the upper end of the cable is released.

4. Verify that the TV cable is installed properly in the throttle lever and the slider is in the non-adjusted position as shown in the illustration.

5. With the engine not running, rotate the throttle lever to the full travel position (throttle body stop).

6. Depress and hold the adjustment button, pull the cable conduit out until the slider hits against the adjustment and release the button.

7. Repeat the adjustment.

DRIVE AXLE

Halfshaft

REMOVAL & INSTALLATION

If equipped with an automatic transaxle, the left halfshaft uses a female spline which installs over a stub shaft protruding from the transaxle. The right halfshaft uses a male and interlocks with the transaxle gears using barrel type snaprings.

If equipped with a manual transaxle, the left halfshaft uses a male spline locking into the gear assembly. The right halfshaft axle uses a female spline that installs into the intermediate axle shaft.

1. With the weight of the vehicle on the tires, loosen the hub nut.

2. Raise and safely support the vehicle.

3. Remove the hub nut.

4. Install boot protectors on the boots.

5. Remove the brake caliper with the line attached and safely support it out of the way; do not allow the caliper to hang from the line.

6. Remove the brake rotor and caliper mounting bracket.

7. Remove the strut-to-steering knuckle bolts. Pull the steering knuckle out of the strut bracket.

8. Using a halfshaft removal tool J–33008 or equivalent and the extention tool J–29794 or equivalent, remove the halfshafts from the transaxle and support them safely.

9. Using a spindle remover tool J–28733 or equivalent, remove the halfshaft from the hub and bearing.

To install:

10. Loosely place the halfshaft on the transaxle and in the hub and bearing.

11. Properly position the steering

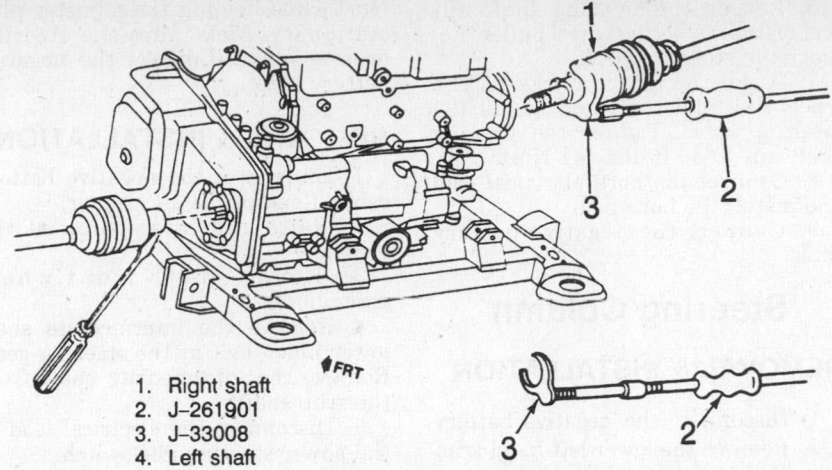

1. Right shaft
2. J-261901
3. J-33008
4. Left shaft

Halfshaft removal and installation

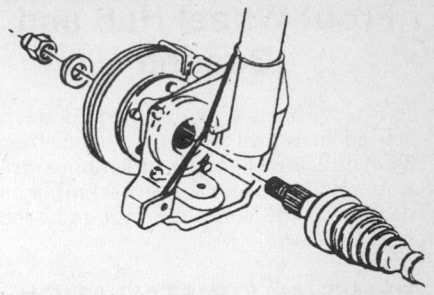

Removing the halfshaft from the hub/knuckle assembly

knuckle to the strut bracket and install the bolt. Torque the bolts to 133 ft. lbs. (178 Nm).

12. Install the brake rotor, caliper bracket and caliper. Place a holding device in the rotor to prevent it from turning.

13. Install the hub nut and washer. Torque the nut to 71 ft. lbs. (95 Nm).

14. Seat the halfshafts into the transaxle.

15. Verify that the shafts are seated by grasping the CV-joint and pulling outwards. Do not grasp the shaft. If the snapring is seated, the halfshaft will remain in place.

16. Remove the boot protectors and lower the vehicle.

17. When the vehicle is lowered with the weight on the wheels, final torque the hub nut to 184 ft. lbs. (250 Nm).

CV-Boot

REMOVAL & INSTALLATION

Inner

1. Remove the halfshaft.
2. Remove the CV-joint housing-to-transaxle bolts.
3. Cut the seal retaining clamps and remove the old boot from the shaft.
4. Using a pair of snapring pliers, remove the retaining ring from the shaft and remove the spider assembly.
5. Using solvent, clean the splines of the shaft and repack the joint.
6. Install the inner boot clamp first and the new boot second.
7. Push the CV-joint assembly onto the shaft until the retaining ring is seated on the shaft.
8. Slide the boot onto the joint. Install both the inner and outer clamps.
9. To complete the installation, reverse the removal procedures.

Outer

1. Remove the halfshaft from the vehicle.
2. Cut off the boot retaining clamps and discard them. Remove the old boot.
3. If equipped with a deflector ring, use a brass drift and carefully tap it off.
4. Using a pair of snapring pliers, spread the retaining ring inside the outer CV-joint and tap the joint off the halfshaft.
5. Using solvent, clean the splines of the halfshaft and the CV-joint and repack the joint. Install a new retaining ring inside the joint.
6. Install the inner boot clamp first, the new boot second.
7. Push the joint assembly onto the halfshaft until the ring is seated on the shaft.
8. Slide the boot onto the joint and install the clamps on both the inner and outer part of the boot.
9. To complete the installation, reverse the removal procedures.

Intermediate Shaft

REMOVAL & INSTALLATION

Manual Transaxle

NOTE: Use care when removing the halfshaft. Tri-pot joints can be damaged if the halfshaft is over-extended. It is important to handle the halfshaft in a manner to prevent overextending.

1. Disconnect the negative battery cable.
2. Raise and support the vehicle safely.
3. Remove the right wheel and tire.
4. Position a drain pan under the transaxle.

5. Remove the right halfshaft assembly.

6. Remove the housing-to-bracket bolts, bracket and housing-to-transaxle bolts.

7. Carefully disengage the intermediate shaft from the transaxle and remove the shaft.

To install:

8. Install the intermediate shaft into position and lock the shaft into the transaxle.

9. Install the housing-to-transaxle bolts and torque to 18 ft. lbs. (25 Nm).

10. Install the bracket-to-engine block bolts and torque to 37 ft. lbs. (50 Nm).

11. Install the housing-to-bracket bolts and torque to 37 ft. lbs. (50 Nm).

12. Coat the splines of the intermediate shaft with chassis grease and install the right halfshaft.

13. Install the front wheels and torque the lug nuts to 100 ft. lbs. (136 Nm).

14. Lower the vehicle and refill the transaxle to the proper level.

15. Connect the negative battery cable and recheck all procedures to ensure complete repair.

Intermediate Shaft Bearing

REMOVAL & INSTALLATION

1. Remove the intermediate shaft from the vehicle.

2. Remove the seal, snapring and washer from the housing.

3. Press the spacer and bearing from the housing using a driver handle and bearing remover tools J-8592 and J-8810 or their equivalents.

To install:

4. Press the bearing into the housing support, using a press and a bearing installer J-36379 or equivalent.

5. Install the spacer, washer and snapring.

6. Install the seal into the housing using a seal installer tool J-23771 or equivalent.

7. Install the intermediate shaft into the vehicle.

Front Wheel Hub and Bearing

The vehicles are equipped with sealed hub and bearing assemblies. The hub and bearing assemblies are non-serviceable. If the assembly is damaged, the complete unit must be replaced.

REMOVAL & INSTALLATION

1. Disconnect the negative battery cable.
2. Loosen the drive axle shaft nut and washer 1 turn.
3. Raise the vehicle and support it safely.
4. Remove the rear wheel, caliper, bracket and rotor.
5. Remove the halfshaft nut and washer.
6. Loosen the 4 hub/bearing-to-knuckle attaching bolts.
7. Using tool J–28733–A or equivalent, push the halfshaft splines back out of the hub/bearing.
8. Remove the ABS sensor, if equipped, and position out of the way.
9. Protect the halfshaft boots, remove the hub/bearing assembly attaching bolts and remove the hub/bearing assembly.
To install:
10. Install the hub/bearing assembly onto the knuckle. Install the 4 attaching bolts and torque to 52 ft. lbs. (70 Nm).
11. Install the ABS sensor, if equipped.
12. Install the rotor, caliper and bracket.
13. Install the rear wheel and torque the lug nut to 100 ft. lbs. (135 Nm).
14. Lower the vehicle and torque the hub nut to 184 ft. lbs. (250 Nm).

STEERING

Steering Wheel

REMOVAL & INSTALLATION

1. Disconnect the negative battery cable.
2. Push down and turn the horn pad and remove retainer.
3. Disconnect the horn electrical lead from the canceling cam tower.
4. Turn the ignition switch to the ON position.
5. Scribe an alignment mark on the steering wheel hub in line with the slash mark on the steering shaft.

6. Loosen the steering shaft nut and install a steering wheel puller. Remove the steering wheel.
7. Align the matchmarks on the wheel hub and shaft and install the steering wheel. Tighten the steering shaft nut to 30 ft. lbs. (41 Nm).
8. Connect the horn electrical lead and install the horn pad.
9. Connect the negative battery cable.

Steering Column

REMOVAL & INSTALLATION

1. Disconnect the negative battery
2. Remove the lower left hand trim panel below the steering column.
3. Push the top of the intermediate shaft seal down for access to the intermediate shaft seal coupling.
4. Remove the intermediate shaft coupling pinch bolt.
5. Disconnect the shift indicator cable end and casing from the column.

NOTE: If the vehicle is equipped with park lock, disconnect the park lock cable from the column.

6. Disconnect the shift cable from the ball stud on the shift lever.
7. Remove the lower column bolts first and then remove the upper bolts. Lower the column to the seat.
8. Disconnect the electrical connectors and remove the column from the vehicle.
To install:
9. Install the column into the vehicle and loosely install the column bolts. Install the intermediate shaft pinch bolt and tighten it to 35 ft. lbs. (48 Nm).
10. Connect the electrical connector and all the shift cables. Connect the park lock cable, if equipped.
11. Tighten the steering column mounting bolts to 18 ft. lbs. (25 Nm).
12. Reposition the intermediate shaft seal and install the trim panel.
13. Connect the negative battery cable.

Power Rack

ADJUSTMENT

1. Disconnect the negative battery cable.
2. Loosen the adjuster plug locknut and turn clockwise until it bottoms in the housing, then back off 50–70 degrees (1 flat).
3. Raise and safely support the vehicle. Center the steering wheel.
4. Tighten the locknut to the adjuster plug. Tighten to 50 ft. lbs. (70

Nm) while holding the adjuster plug stationary. Make sure the steering does not bind. Connect the negative battery cable.

REMOVAL & INSTALLATION

1. Disconnect the negative battery cable. Remove the air cleaner.
2. Raise and safely support the vehicle.
3. Remove both front wheel assemblies.
4. Remove the intermediate shaft lower pinch bolt at the steering gear. Remove the intermediate shaft from the stub shaft.
5. Disconnect the electrical lead at the power steering idle switch.
6. Separate the tie rod ends from the knuckle assembly. Remove the rear sub-frame mounting bolts and lower the rear of the sub-frame approximately 4 in.
7. Remove the steering rack heat shield. Disconnect the pressure lines at the steering rack.
8. Remove the steering rack mounting bolts, remove the rack and pinion through the left wheel opening.
To install:
9. Install the rack and pinion through the left wheel opening. Tighten the mounting bolts to 59 ft. lbs. (81 Nm). Connect the pressure lines, tighten the fittings to 20 ft. lbs. (27 Nm).
10. Install the rack heat shield, tighten the retaining bolts to 53 inch lbs. (6 Nm). Attach the tie rod ends to the steering knuckle.
11. Connect the electrical lead to the power steering idle switch. Attach the intermediate shaft to the stub shaft, tighten the pinch bolt to 35 ft. lbs. (48 Nm).
12. Install both wheel assemblies, tighten lug nuts to 100 ft. lbs. (136 Nm) and lower the vehicle.
13. Install the air cleaner. Connect the negative battery cable. Fill and bleed the power steering system.

Power Steering Pump

REMOVAL & INSTALLATION

2.3L Engine

1. Disconnect the negative battery cable.
2. Remove the air cleaner assembly.
3. Disconnect the left side torque strut from the engine.
4. Separate the throttle cable bracket from the engine torque strut bracket and set aside. Do not remove cables.
5. Remove the engine torque strut bracket.
6. Disconnect the hydraulic pump lines.

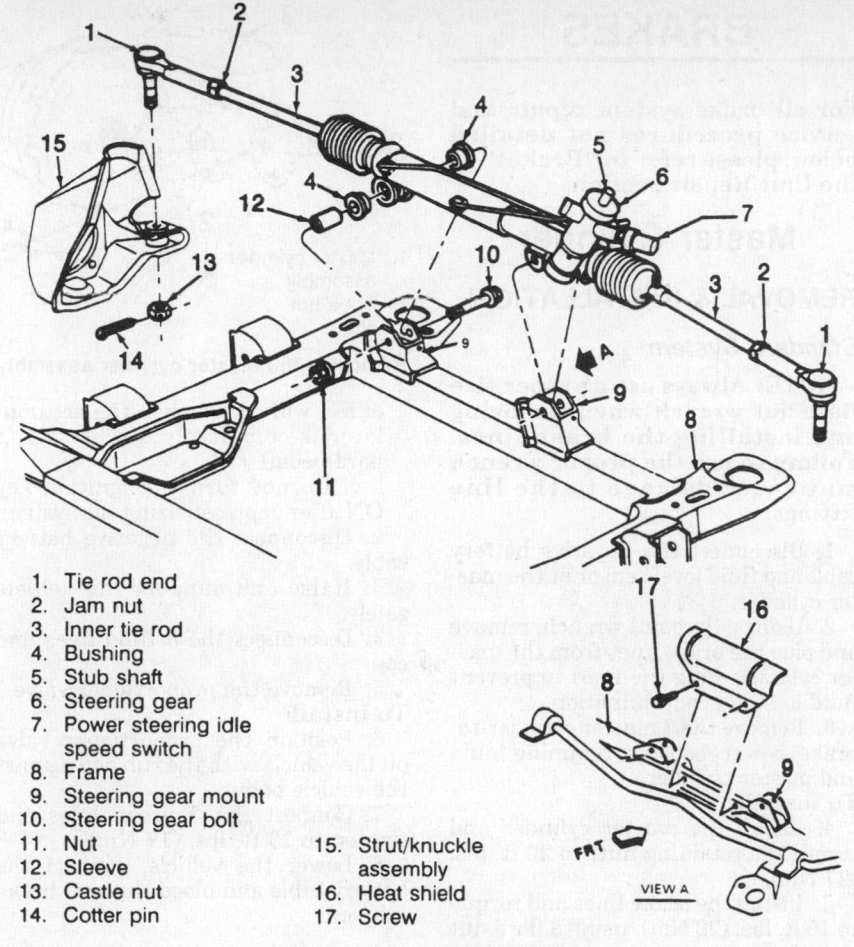

1. Tie rod end
2. Jam nut
3. Inner tie rod
4. Bushing
5. Stub shaft
6. Steering gear
7. Power steering idle
   speed switch
8. Frame
9. Steering gear mount
10. Steering gear bolt
11. Nut
12. Sleeve
13. Castle nut
14. Cotter pin
15. Strut/knuckle
    assembly
16. Heat shield
17. Screw

VIEW A
FRT

Power rack assembly mounting

7. Remove the rear bracket to pump bolts.
8. Remove the drive belt and lay aside.
9. Remove the rear bracket to transaxle bolts.
10. Remove the front bracket to engine bolt and remove the pump with bracket.
11. Transfer the pulley and bracket, as necessary.
To install:
12. Install the pump, pulley and bracket.
13. Install the front bracket to engine bolt.
14. Install the rear bracket to transaxle bolts.
15. Install the rear bracket to pump bolts.
16. Install the drive belt.
17. Connect the hydraulic pump lines.
18. Install the engine torque strut bracket.
19. Install the throttle cable bracket to the engine torque strut bracket.
20. Connect the left side torque strut to the engine.

21. Install the air cleaner assembly.
22. Fill with fluid and bleed the air from the system.
23. Connect the negative battery cable and check for leaks.

2.5L Engine

1. Disconnect the negative battery cable.
2. Raise and safely support the vehicle.
3. Remove the pressure and return hoses from the pump and drain the fluid.
4. Lower the vehicle, remove the ECM heat shield and serpentine belt.
5. Remove the pump mounting bolts and pump.
6. Install the pump and tighten the bolts to 20 ft. lbs. (27 Nm).
7. Install the serpentine belt, ECM heat shield. Raise and safely support the vehicle.
8. Install the inlet and outlet hoses and lower the vehicle.
9. Refill the pump with power steering fluid and bleed the system. Connect the negative battery cable.

2.8L, 3.1L and 3.8L Engines

1. Disconnect the negative terminal from the battery.
2. Remove the pressure and return hoses from the pump and drain the system into a suitable container.
3. Cap the fittings at the pump.
4. Remove the serpentine belt.
5. Locate the pump attaching bolts through the pulley and remove the bolts.
6. Remove the pump assembly.
To install:
7. Install the pump and torque the mounting bolts to 18 ft. lbs. (25 Nm) for the 2.8L and 3.1L engines or 20 ft. lbs. (27 Nm), in sequence, top bolt first, bottom bolt second, for the 3.8L engine.
8. Reconnect the hoses to the pump and install the serpentine belt.
9. Refill the power steering pump reservoir and bleed the system. Connect the negative battery cable.

BELT ADJUSTMENT

Belt tension is maintained by the tensioner and is not adjustable.

SYSTEM BLEEDING

NOTE: Automatic transmission fluid is not compatible with the seals and hoses of the power steering system. Under no circumstances should automatic transmission be used in place of power steering fluid in this system.

1. With the engine turned off, turn the wheels all the way to the left.
2. Fill the reservoir with power steering fluid until the level is at the cold mark on the reservoir.
3. Start and run the engine at fast idle for 15 seconds. Turn the engine off.
4. Recheck the fluid level and fill it to the cold mark.
5. Start the engine and bleed the system by turning the wheels in both directions slowly to the stops.
6. Stop the engine and check the fluid. Fluid that still has air in it will be a light tan color.
7. Repeat this procedure until all of the air is removed from the system.

Tie Rod Ends

REMOVAL & INSTALLATION

Outer

1. Disconnect the negative battery cable.
2. Remove the cotter pin and hex

slotted nut from the outer tie rod assembly.

3. Loosen the jam nut and remove the tie rod from the steering knuckle using a steering linkage removing tool J-35917 or equivalent.

4. Holding the inner tie rod stationary, count the amount of turns to remove the outer tie rod.

To install:

5. Lubricate the inner rod threads with anti-seize compound and install the outer tie rod the same amount of turns that it took to remove.

6. Install the outer tie rod-to-knuckle and install the slotted nut. Torque the nut to 35 ft. lbs. (50 Nm) and to 45 ft. lbs. (60 Nm) maximum to align the cotter pin slot. Do not back off to align the cotter pin.

7. Install a new cotter pin and bend over. Torque the jam nut to 50 ft. lbs. (70 Nm) and connect the negative battery cable.

Inner

1. Disconnect the negative battery cable.

2. Remove the rack and pinion assembly from the vehicle.

3. Remove the outer tie rod end.

4. Remove the jam nut, boot clamps and boot. Use side cutters to cut the boot clamps.

5. Remove the shock dampener from the inner tie rod and slide back on the rack.

NOTE: Do not let the rack slide out of the rack housing while the tie rods are moved.

6. Place suitable wrenches on the flats of the rack and inner tie rod assemblies.

7. Rotate the housing counterclockwise until the inner rod separates from the rack.

To install:

8. Install the inner tie rod end onto the rack and torque to 70 ft. lbs. (95 Nm) with suitable wrenches.

9. Support the rack assembly in a vise.

10. Stake both sides of the inner tie rod housing to the flats on the rack.

11. Slide the shock dampener over the housing until it engages.

12. Install the boot and new boot clamps. Do not tighten the clamps at this time.

13. Apply grease to the inner tie rod, housing and boot.

14. Aign the breather tube with the boot, making sure it is not twisted.

15. Crimp the boot clamps with a keystone clamp pliers tool J-22610 or equivalent.

16. Install the jam nut and outer tie rod end.

17. Install the rack and pinion assembly into the vehicle.

BRAKES

For all brake system repair and service procedures not detailed below, please refer to "Brakes" in the Unit Repair section.

Master Cylinder

REMOVAL & INSTALLATION

Standard System

NOTE: Always use a proper size flare nut wrench when removing and installing the brake lines. Failure to use the proper wrench may cause damage to the line fittings.

1. Disconnect the negative battery cable and fluid level sensor at the master cylinder.

2. Using a flare nut wrench, remove and plug the brake lines from the master cylinder. Plug the lines to prevent fluid loss and contamination.

3. Remove the 2 master cylinder-to-brake power booster retaining nuts and master cylinder.

To install:

4. Install the master cylinder and torque the retaining nuts to 20 ft. lbs. (27 Nm).

5. Install the brake lines and torque to 15 ft. lbs. (20 Nm), using a flare nut wrench.

6. Connect the fluid level sensor electrical wire.

7. Fill the master cylinder to the proper level with new brake fluid meeting DOT 3 specifications.

8. Bleed the system.

9. Connect the negative battery cable and recheck the fluid level.

10. Do not move the vehicle until a firm brake pedal is felt.

Proportioning Valve

REMOVAL & INSTALLATION

Standard System

The proportioning valves are an integral part of the master cylinder assembly.

Anti-Lock Brake System

There is a remote proportioning valve located in the rear of the vehicle. The valve is not serviceable and must be replaced as a complete unit.

1. Depressurize the ABS brake system as follows:

a. With the ignition key **OFF**, firmly apply and release the brake pedal a minumum of 40 times.

b. A noticeable change in the ped-

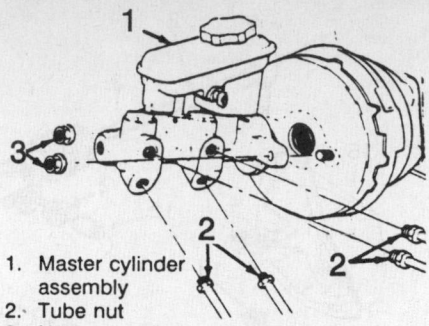

1. Master cylinder assembly
2. Tube nut
3. Nut

Removing the master cylinder assembly

al feel will occur when the accumulator is completely discharged (a hard pedal).

c. Do not turn the ignition key **ON** after depressurizing the system.

2. Disconnect the negative battery cable.

3. Raise and support the vehicle safely.

4. Disconnect the 3 fluid lines and cap.

5. Remove the proportioner valve.

To install:

6. Position the proportioner valve on the vehicle with the rub pad against the vehicle body.

7. Connect the 3 brake lines and tighten to 13 ft. lbs. (17 Nm).

8. Lower the vehicle, connect the battery cable and bleed the rear brake calipers.

Power Brake Booster

REMOVAL & INSTALLATION

1. Disconnect the negative battery cable.

2. From inside the engine compartment, remove the secondary dash panels. The panels around the booster assembly.

3. Remove the booster grommet bolt and grommet

4. Remove the master cylinder from the power booster.

5. Scribe a mark on the front and rear booster covers in case the 2 covers get separated during removal.

NOTE: When disconnecting the pushrod from the brake pedal, the brake pedal must be kept stationary or damage to the brake switch may result.

6. Disconnect the brake pushrod from the brake pedal.

7. Unlock the booster from the front of the dash as follows.

a. Install a booster holding tool J-22805-01 to the master cylinder mounting studs.

b. Torque the stud nuts to 28 ft. lbs. (38 Nm).

c. Use a suitable prybar to pry the locking tab on the booster out of the locking notch on the mounting flange.

d. At the same time, turn the booster counterclockwise with a large wrench on the booster holding tool.

e. Do not attempt to remove the booster until the pushrod has been disconnected from the brake pedal.

To install:

8. Lubricate the inside and outside diameters of the grommet and front housing seal with silicone grease before installation.

9. Install the booster by turning the booster holding tool clockwise until the locking flanges are engaged. Make sure the locking tab is fully seated to prevent rotation of the booster.

10. Install the booster pushrod to the brake pedal.

11. Install the master cylinder, booster grommet and secondary dash panel.

12. Connect the negative battery cable and bleed the system if the fluid pipes were disconnected from the master cylinder.

Brake Caliper

REMOVAL & INSTALLATION

Front

1. Remove ⅔ of the brake fluid from the brake reservoir using a syringe or equivalent.

2. Raise and support the vehicle safely.

3. Mark the relationship of the wheel-to-hub and bearing assembly.

4. Remove the tire and wheel. Install 2 lug nuts to retain the rotor.

5. If the caliper is going to be removed, disconnect and plug the brake hose.

6. Remove the caliper mounting bolts and pull the caliper from the mounting bracket and rotor. Support the caliper with wire if not removing.

To install:

7. Inspect the bolt boots and support bushings for cuts or damage, replace if necessary.

8. Install the caliper over the rotor into the mounting bracket. Make sure the bolt boots are in place.

9. Lubricate the entire shaft of the mounting bolts and cavities with silicone grease.

10. Install the mounting bolts and torque to 79 ft. lbs. (107 Nm).

11. Install the brake hose, using new copper washers and torque to 32 ft. lbs. (44 Nm).

12. Remove the 2 wheel lugs, install the wheels and torque the lug nuts to 100 ft. lbs. (136 Nm).

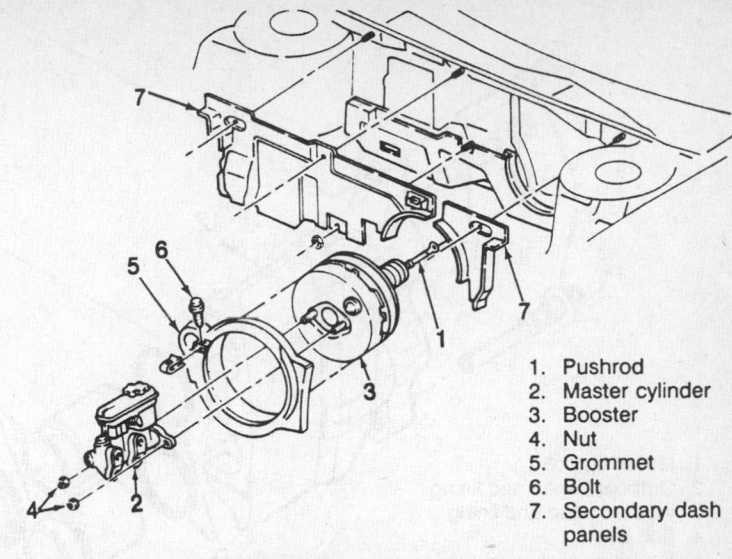

Removing the power brake booster

1. Pushrod
2. Master cylinder
3. Booster
4. Nut
5. Grommet
6. Bolt
7. Secondary dash panels

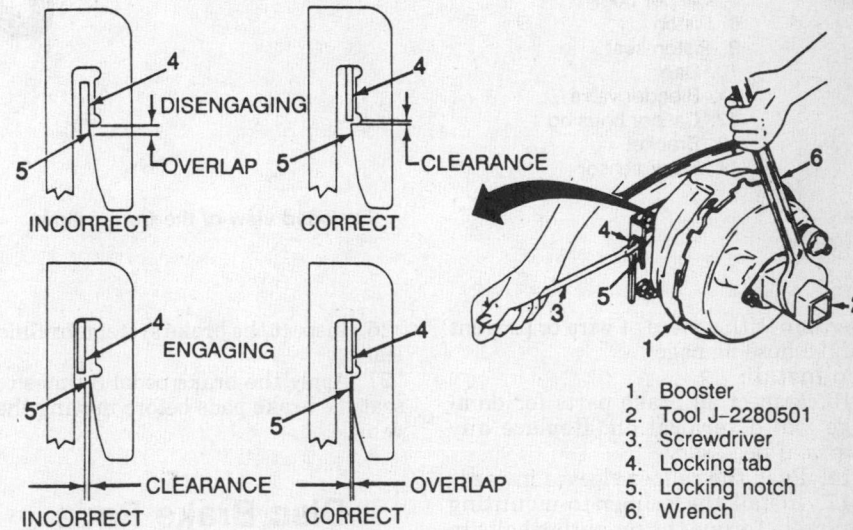

Unlocking the brake booster from the mounting flange

1. Booster
2. Tool J–2280501
3. Screwdriver
4. Locking tab
5. Locking notch
6. Wrench

13. Lower the vehicle.

14. Fill the master cylinder and bleed the calipers.

15. Check for hydraulic leaks. Pump the brake pedal a few times before moving the vehicle.

Rear

1. Remove ⅔ of the brake fluid from the reservoir with a syringe.

2. Raise and support the vehicle safely.

3. Remove the rear wheel assembly and install 2 lug nuts to retain the rotor.

4. Remove the brake shield assembly.

5. Loosen the tension on the parking brake cable at the equalizer.

6. Remove the parking cable and return spring from the lever.

7. Hold the cable lever and remove the lock nut, lever and seal.

8. Push the piston into the caliper bore using 2 adjustable pliers over the inboard pad tabs.

NOTE: Do not allow pliers to contact the actuator screw. Protect the piston so the contact surface does not get damaged.

9. Reinstall the lever seal with the sealing bead against the caliper housing, lever and locknut.

10. Remove and plug the brake hose inlet fitting only if the caliper is going to be removed from the vehicle.

11. Remove the bolt and bracket to gain access to the upper mounting bolt.

12. Remove the caliper mounting bolts, caliper and hang from the sus-

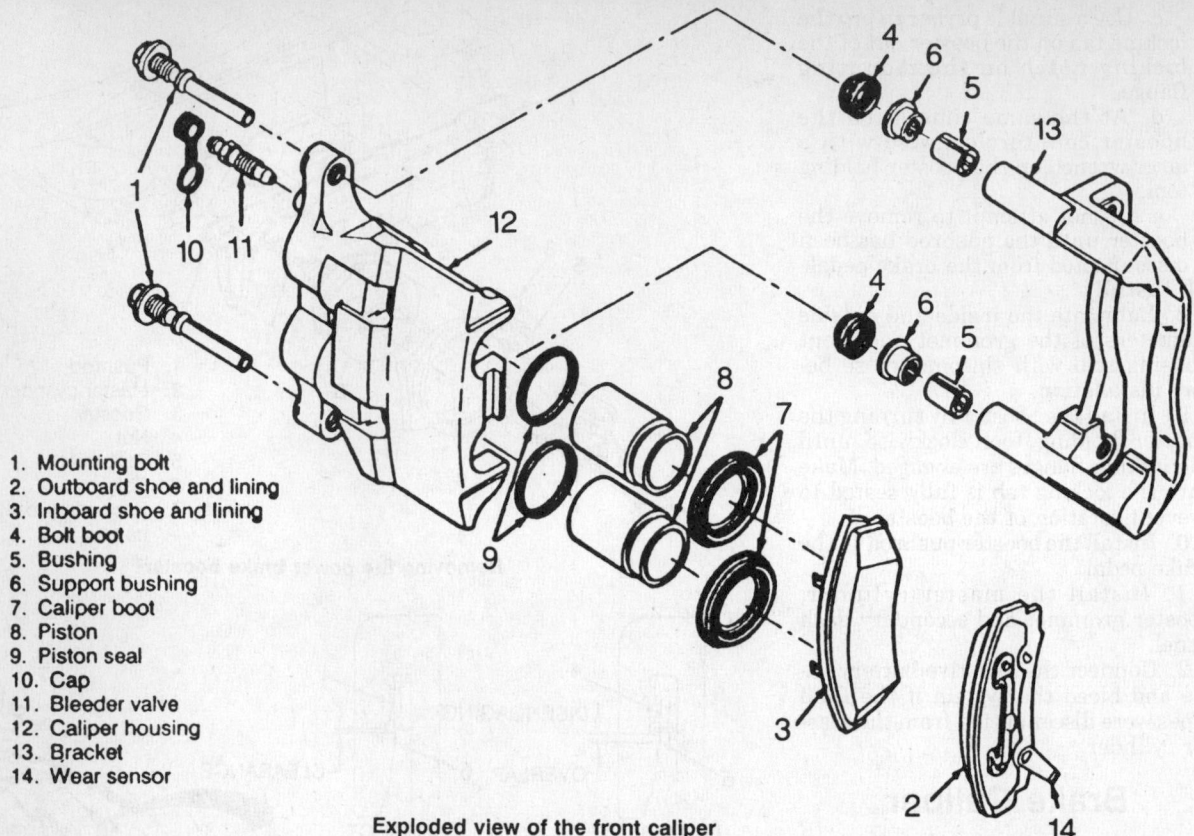

1. Mounting bolt
2. Outboard shoe and lining
3. Inboard shoe and lining
4. Bolt boot
5. Bushing
6. Support bushing
7. Caliper boot
8. Piston
9. Piston seal
10. Cap
11. Bleeder valve
12. Caliper housing
13. Bracket
14. Wear sensor

Exploded view of the front caliper

pension with a piece of wire to prevent brake hose damage.

To install:

13. Inspect all brake parts for damage and deterioration. Replace any parts, if necessary.

14. Push the caliper sleeves inward.

15. Install the caliper-to-mounting bracket. Torque the mounting bolts to 92 ft. lbs. (125 Nm).

16. Install the bracket and bolt after the mounting bolts have been torqued.

17. Install the brake hose inlet with new copper washers, if removed. Torque the hose bolt to 32 ft. lbs. (44 Nm).

18. Remove the locknut, lever and seal. Lubricate the lever seal and lever shaft.

19. Install the seal and lever with the lever facing down.

20. Hold the lever back against the stop and torque the lock nut to 35 ft. lbs. (47 Nm).

21. Install the return spring and parking brake cable and adjust.

22. Install the brake shield and rear wheel assembly. Torque the lug nuts to 100 ft. lbs. (136 Nm).

23. Lower the vehicle.

24. Fill the brake reservoir with DOT 3 brake fluid.

25. Bleed the caliper if removed from the vehicle.

26. Inspect the brake system for fluid leaks.

27. Apply the brake pedal 3 times to seat the brake pads before moving the vehicle.

Disc Brake Pads

REMOVAL & INSTALLATION

Front

1. Disconnect the negative battery cable.

2. Raise and support the vehicle safely.

3. Remove the wheel and tire assembly.

4. Remove the 2 caliper mounting bolts, caliper and hang from the suspension with a piece of wire. Do not hang by the brake hose.

5. Using a suitable prybar, lift up the outboard pad retaining spring so that it will clear the center lug.

6. Remove the inboard pad by unsnapping the pad from the pistons.

To install:

7. Remove about ⅔ of the fluid from the brake reservoir with a syringe or equivalent.

8. Install the inboard pad-to-caliper pistons. Bottom the pistons in the cali-

per bore using a C-clamp and the inboard brake pad.

9. Make sure both inboard pad tangs are inside the piston cavity.

10. Install the outboard pad by snapping the pad retainer spring over the housing center lug and into the housing slot.

11. Make sure both pads remain free of grease or oil. The wear sensor should be at the trailing edge of the pad during rotation.

10. Install the caliper assembly, wheels assembly and lower the vehicle.

11. Fill the master cylinder to the **FULL** mark and apply the brake pedal 3 times to seat the pads. Connect the negative battery cable.

Rear

1. Raise and support the vehicle safely.

2. Remove the rear wheels assemblies.

3. Remove the rear caliper and hang by the suspension with a piece of wire to prevent brake hose damage.

4. Using a suitable prybar, disengage the buttons on the outboard pad from the holes in the caliper housing.

5. Press in on the edge of the inboard pad and tilt outward to release the pad from the pad retainer.

6. Remove the 2 way check valve

1. Nut
2. Lever
3. Return spring
4. Bolt
5. Bracket
6. Lever seal
8. Outboard pad
9. Inboard pad
10. Pad retainer
11. Bolt boot
12. Sleeve
13. Caliper boot
14. 2-way check valve

15. Piston assembly
16. Retainer
17. Piston locator
18. Piston seal
19. Actuator screw
20. Balance spring and retainer
21. Thrust washer
22. Shaft seal
23. Cap
24. Bleeder valve
25. Caliper housing
26. Wear sensor
27. Mounting bolt

Exploded view of the rear caliper

from the end of the caliper piston using a small prybar.

To install:

NOTE: Do not allow pliers to contact the actuator screw. Protect the piston so the contact surface does not get damaged.

7. Bottom the piston into the caliper bore by positioning a twelve inch adjustable pliers over the caliper housing and piston surface.

8. Lubricate a new 2 way check valve and install it into the end of the piston.

9. Install the inboard brake pad. Engage the pad edge in the retainer tabs closest to the caliper bridge. Press down and snap the tabs at the open side of the caliper. The wear sensor should be at the leading edge of the pad during wheel rotation. The back of the pad must lay flat against the piston. The button on the back of the pad must engage the D-shaped notch in the piston.

NOTE: If the piston will not align or retract into the bore. Turn the piston clockwise using a piston turning tool J-7624 or equivalent.

10. Install the outboard brake pad. Snap the pad retainer spring into the slots in the caliper housing. The back of the pad must lay flat against the caliper.

11. Install the caliper onto the mounting bracket.

12. Apply force at least 3 times to the brake pedal to seat the brake pads before moving the vehicle.

13. Install the rear wheels and torque the lug nuts to 100 ft. lbs. (136 Nm).

14. Lower the vehicle and check for fluid leaks.

Brake Rotor

REMOVAL & INSTALLATION

1. Raise and support the vehicle safely.

2. Remove the wheel and tire assembly.

3. Remove the brake caliper and support with a wire to the body.

4. Remove the rotor assembly.

To install:

5. Install the brake rotor over the hub assembly.

6. Install the brake caliper.

7. Install the wheel and tire assembly. Torque the lug nuts to 100 ft. lbs. (136 Nm).

8. Lower the vehicle and pump the brake pedal before moving.

Parking Brake Cable

ADJUSTMENT

1. Apply the parking brake pedal 3 times with heavy force.

2. Do not apply the main brake pedal during this step. Fully apply and release the parking brake 3 times.

3. Raise and support the vehicle safely.

4. Make sure the parking brake is fully released.

5. Remove the rear wheel assemblies and install 2 lug nuts to retain the rotors.

6. The parking brake levers at the calipers should be against the lever stop on the caliper housing. If not

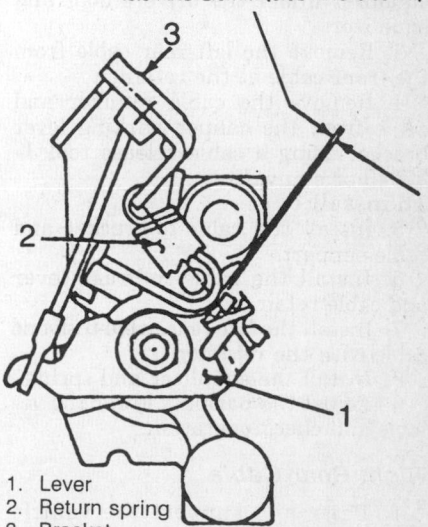

CLEARANCE MUST BE BETWEEN
.0.5 AND 2.0mm (0.02 AND 0.08 IN.)

1. Lever
2. Return spring
3. Bracket

Parking brake adjustment

against the stops, check the cables for binding.

7. Tighten the parking brake cable at the adjuster until either the right or left lever reaches the correct dimensions shown.

8. Operate the parking brake several times to check adjustments. A firm pedal should be present.

9. Remove the 2 wheel lugs, install the rear wheels and lower the vehicle.

REMOVAL & INSTALLATION

Front Cable

1. Raise and support the vehicle safely.

2. Loosen the equalizer under the drivers side door.

3. Remove the front cable from the left rear cable at the retainer.

4. Remove the nut at the underbody bracket.

5. Remove the clip from underbody.

6. Lower the vehicle.

7. Remove the cable from the parking brake lever assembly using a brake cable release tool J–37043 or equivalent.

To install:

8. Install the cable to the parking brake lever assembly.

9. Raise and support the vehicle safely.

10. Install the clip-to-underbody and the nut at the underbody bracket.

11. Install the front cable-to-left rear cable at the retainer.

12. Adjust the cable, lower the vehicle and check operation.

Left Rear Cable

1. Raise and support the vehicle safely.

2. Remove the spring from the equalizer under the drivers door and equalizer.

3. Remove the left rear cable from the front cable at the retainer.

4. Remove the cable retainer and cable from the caliper parking lever bracket using a cable release tool J–37043 or equivalent.

To install:

5. Install the cable-to-bracket and cable support.

6. Install the cable-to-brake lever and cable retainer.

7. Install the left rear cable-to-front cable with the retainer.

8. Install the equalizer and spring.

9. Adjust the parking, lower the vehicle and check operation.

Right Rear Cable

1. Raise and support the vehicle safely.

2. Remove the spring from the

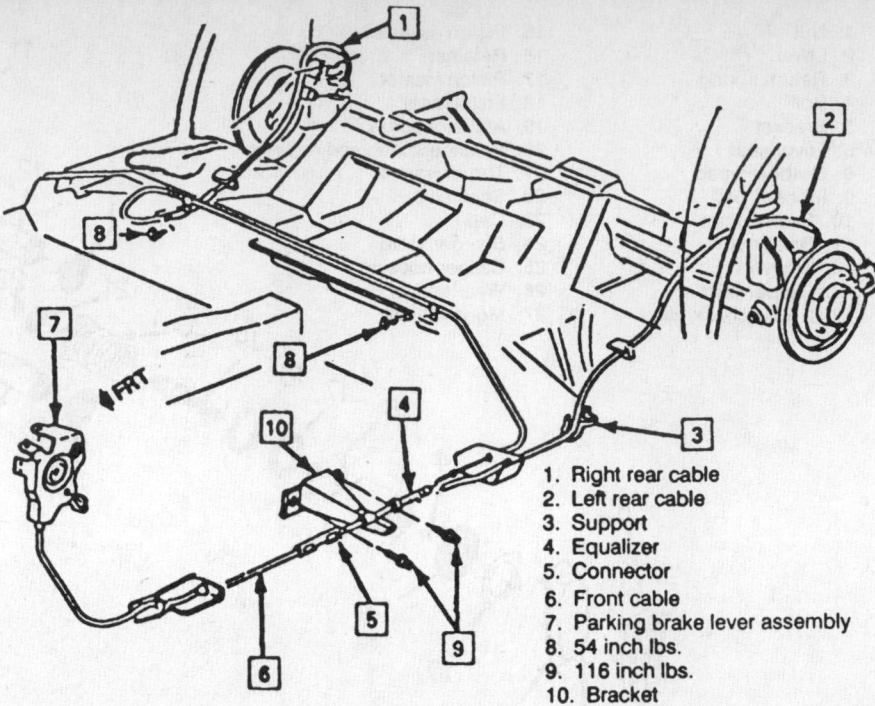

1. Right rear cable
2. Left rear cable
3. Support
4. Equalizer
5. Connector
6. Front cable
7. Parking brake lever assembly
8. 54 inch lbs.
9. 116 inch lbs.
10. Bracket

Parking brake cable routing

equalizer under the drivers door and equalizer.

3. Remove the cable from the underbody bracket using a cable release tool J–37043 or equivalent.

4. Remove the bolts from the clips above the fuel tank.

5. Remove the cable retainer and cable from the caliper parking lever bracket using a cable release tool J–37043 or equivalent.

To install:

6. Position the cable above the fuel tank.

7. Install the cable-to-bracket and cable support.

8. Install the cable-to-brake lever and cable retainer.

9. Install the clips above the fuel tank.

10. Install the cable-to-underbody brackets.

11. Install the equalizer and spring.

12. Adjust the parking brake, lower the vehicle and check operation.

Brake System Bleeding

The brake system must be bled after the hydraulic system has been serviced. Air enters the system when components are removed and this air has to be removed to prevent poor system performance.

The time required to bleed the sys-

tem can be reduced by removing as much air as possible before installing the master cylinder onto the vehicle. This is called bench bleeding the master cylinder. Place the master cylinder in a vise or holding fixture, run tubing from the fluid pipe fittings to the reservoir, fill the cylinder with DOT 3 brake fluid and pump the brake pushrod until most of the air is removed from the master cylinder. Install the master cylinder onto the vehicle and bleed all 4 wheels.

Standard System

1. Fill the master cylinder reservoir with brake fluid and keep the reservoir at least half full during the bleeding operation.

2. If the master cylinder has air in the bore, it must be removed before bleeding the calipers. Bleed the master cylinder as follows:

a. Disconnect the forward brake pipe at the master cylinder.

b. Fill the reservoir until fluid begins to flow from the forward pipe connector port.

c. Reconnect the forward brake pipe and tighten.

d. Depress the brake pedal slowly 1 time and hold. Loosen the forward brake pipe and purge the air from the bore. Tighten the brake pipe, wait 15 seconds and repeat until all air is removed.

e. When the air is removed from the forward brake pipe, repeat the same procedures for the rear brake pipe.

3. Bleed the calipers in the following order, (right front, right rear, left rear, left front).

4. Install a box end wrench over the bleeder valve and connect a clear tube onto the valve. Place the other end of the tube into a container of new brake fluid. The end of the tube must be submerged in brake fluid.

5. Depress the brake pedal slowly 1 time and hold. Loosen the bleeder valve to purge the air from the caliper. Close the valve and release the pedal. Repeat the procedure until all air is removed from the brake fluid.

6. Do not pump the brake pedal rapidly, this causes the air to brake up and make bleeding difficult.

7. After the calipers have been bled, check the brake pedal for spongeness and the **BRAKE** warning lamp for low fluid level.

8. Repeat the bleeding operation if a spongy pedal is felt and fill the reservoir to the **MAX** line.

Anti-Lock Brake System (ABS)

—————— CAUTION ——————

Use only clean DOT 3 brake fluid from a sealed container in the anti-lock brake system. Any other type of fluid may cause severe damage to the internal components causing brake failure and personal injury.

1. Make sure the vehicle ignition is **OFF**.

2. Disconnect the negative battery cable.

3. Depressurize the ABS system as follows.

  a. With the ignition key **OFF**, firmly apply and release the brake pedal a minimum of 40 times.

  b. A noticeable change in the pedal feel will occur when the accumulator is completely discharged (a hard pedal).

  c. Do not turn the ignition key **ON** after depressurizing the system unless instructed to do so.

4. Clean and remove the reservoir cap.

5. Fill the reservoir with DOT 3 brake fluid.

6. Raise the vehicle and support the vehicle safely.

7. Bleed the right front wheel by attaching a clean hose to the bleeder valve and submerge the other end into a container of partially filled brake fluid.

8. Open the valve and slowly depress the brake pedal.

9. Tap lightly on the brake caliper with a rubber mallet to dislodge the air bubbles.

10. Close the valve and release the brake pedal. Repeat until all air is removed.

11. Repeat steps 7–10 on the left front wheel.

12. Connect the negative battery cable and turn the ignition key to the **RUN** position without starting the vehicle. Allow the pump to run to pressurize the accumulator.

13. Bleed the right rear brake by installing a bleeder hose and container, open the valve, with the ignition **ON** slowly depress the pedal part way until the fluid begins to flow from the bleeder valve and allow the fluid to flow for 15 seconds.

14. Close the valve and release the brake pedal.

15. Fill the reservoir with fluid to 1 inch below the FULL mark.

16. Repeat steps 13–16 for the left rear wheel.

17. Lower the vehicle and bleed the Powermaster III isolation valves (at the master cylinder) as follows.

  a. Attach a clear hose and container to the Powermaster III inboard bleeder valves.

  b. With the ignition in the **ON** position, apply the pedal, slowly open the valve and allow fluid to flow until no air bubbles are seen.

  c. Close the valve and repeat the steps to the outboard bleeder valve until no air bubbles are present.

18. Bleed the accumulator as follows.

  a. Turn the ignition key to the **OFF** position, depressurize the system and wait 2 minutes to allow the air to settle.

  b. Remove the reservoir cover and check the fluid level. Add if necessary.

  c. Install the reservoir cap.

  d. Turn the ignition key to the **RUN** position but do not start the engine.

  e. When the pump has stopped, depress the brake pedal and repeat the **OFF/RUN** procedures 10 times to cycle the solenoids.

19. Apply the brake pedal and note the pedal feel and travel.

20. If the pedal feels firm and smooth without excessive travel, the system is properly bled. Connect the negative battery cable.

Anti-Lock Brake System Service

PRECAUTIONS

Failure to observe the following precautions may result in system damage.

• The brake system uses a hydraulic accumulator which when fully charged, contains brake fluid at high pressure. Before disconnecting any hydraulic lines, hoses or fittings, be sure that the accumulator is fully depressurized.

• Never disassemble any component of the Anti-Lock Brake System (ABS) which is designated non-servicable; the component must be replaced as an assembly.

• Replace all components included in repair kits used to service the system.

• When filling the master cylinder, always use Delco Supreme 11 brake fluid or equivalent, which meets DOT-3 specifications; petroleum base fluid will destroy the rubber parts.

• Avoid spilling brake fluid on the vehicles painted surfaces, wiring, cables or electrical connectors. Brake fluid will damage paint and electrical connections.

RELIEVING ANTI-LOCK BRAKE SYSTEM PRESSURE

—————— CAUTION ——————

Failure to fully depressurize the system before performing service operations could result in personal injury from a high pressure spray of brake fluid.

1. With the ignition key **OFF**, firmly apply and release the brake pedal a minimum of 40 times.

2. A noticeable change in the pedal feel will occur when the accumulator is completely discharged (a hard pedal).

3. Do not turn the ignition key **ON** after depressurizing the system.

Powermaster III Unit

REMOVAL & INSTALLATION

1. Depressurize the ABS brake system as follows:

  a. With the ignition key **OFF**, firmly apply and release the brake pedal a minimum of 40 times.

  b. A noticeable change in the pedal feel will occur when the accumulator is completely discharged (a hard pedal).

  c. Do not turn the ignition key **ON** after depressurizing the system.

2. Disconnect the negative battery cable.

3. Disconnect the 3 Powermaster III electrical connectors and move out of the way.

4. Remove and plug the 3 metal brake lines using flare nut wrenches. Plug the lines to prevent fluid loss and contamination.

5. Remove the hair pin clip from inside the vehicle at the brake pedal.

6. Remove the 2 ABS unit-to-cowl retaining nuts.

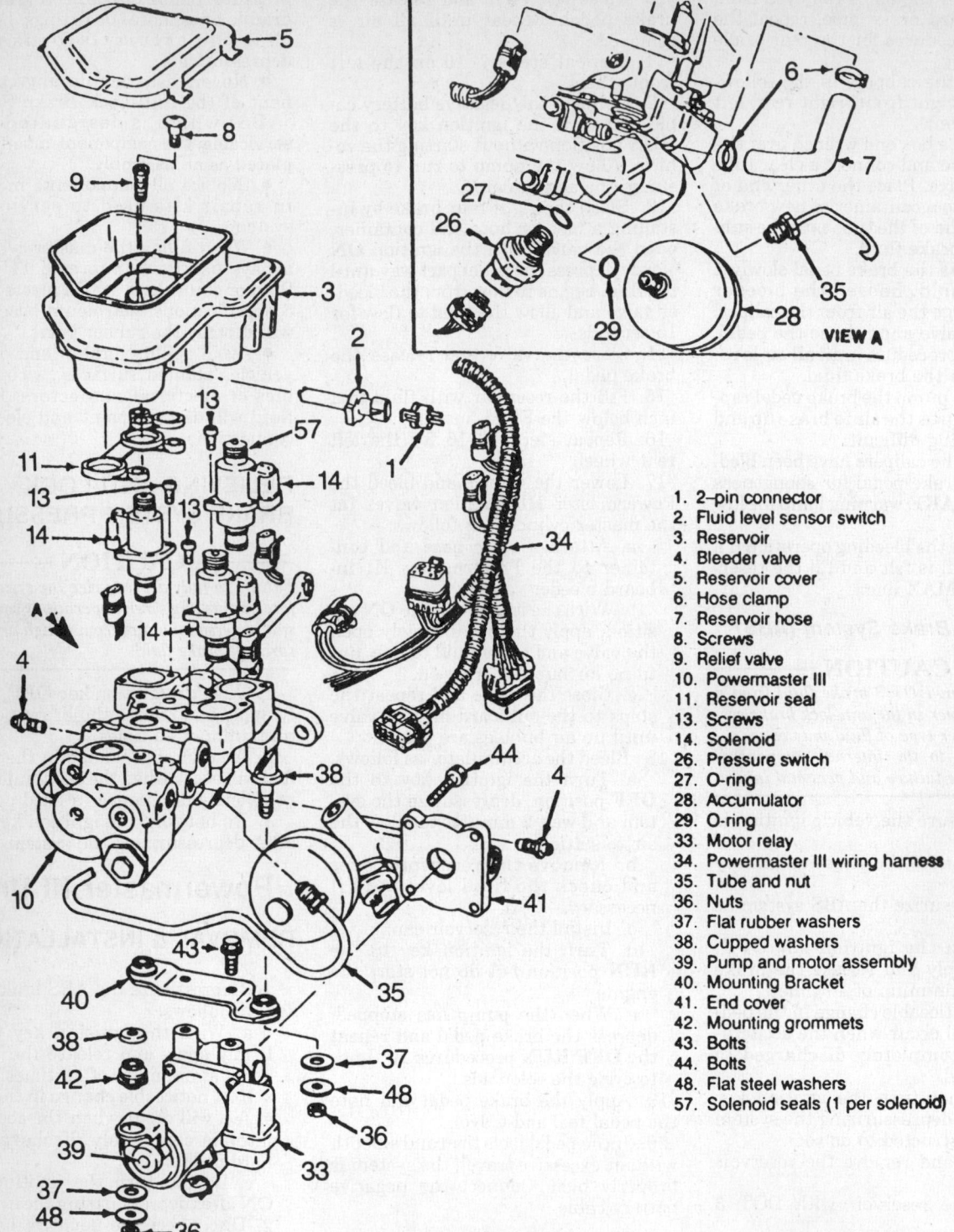

1. 2–pin connector
2. Fluid level sensor switch
3. Reservoir
4. Bleeder valve
5. Reservoir cover
6. Hose clamp
7. Reservoir hose
8. Screws
9. Relief valve
10. Powermaster III
11. Reservoir seal
13. Screws
14. Solenoid
26. Pressure switch
27. O-ring
28. Accumulator
29. O-ring
33. Motor relay
34. Powermaster III wiring harness
35. Tube and nut
36. Nuts
37. Flat rubber washers
38. Cupped washers
39. Pump and motor assembly
40. Mounting Bracket
41. End cover
42. Mounting grommets
43. Bolts
44. Bolts
48. Flat steel washers
57. Solenoid seals (1 per solenoid)

Exploded view of the Powermaster III unit

7. Remove the ABS unit. Make sure none of the electrical connectors are still connected.
To install:
8. Lightly lubricate the entire outer surface of the pushrod with silicone grease.

9. Position the ABS unit into the vehicle. Loosely install the retaining nuts and pushrod.
10. Install the pushrod hair pin clip and torque the 2 retaining nuts to 15–25 ft. lbs. (20–34 Nm).
11. Install the 3 brake pipes using

flare nut wrenches. Torque the pipes to 11 ft. lbs. (20 Nm).
12. Install the ABS unit electrical connectors.
13. Adjust the stoplamp switch.
14. Bleed the ABS system. Reconnect the negative battery cable.

Accumulator

The accumulator is a nitrogen charged pressure vessel which holds the brake fluid under high pressure. The accumulator can not be repaired and must be replaced as an assembly.

REMOVAL & INSTALLATION

1988–89

1. Disconnect the negative battery cable.
2. Depressure the ABS system as follows.

   a. With the ignition key **OFF**, firmly apply and release the brake pedal a minumum of 40 times.

   b. A noticeable change in the pedal feel will occur when the accumulator is completely discharged (a hard pedal).

   c. Do not turn the ignition key **ON** after depressurizing the system unless instructed to do so.
3. Remove the accumulator by turning the hex nut on the end of the accumulator with a 17mm socket. The unit can be removed by sliding out from beneath the ABS unit, towards the left front wheel well.
4. Remove the O-ring seal from the accumulator.
To install:
5. Lightly lubricate the new O-ring seal and install it on the accumulator.
6. Install the accumulator and torque the unit to 23–36 ft. lbs. (31–35 Nm).
7. Bleed the system.

1990–91

1. Disconnect the negative battery cable.
2. Depressure the ABS system as follows.

   a. With the ignition key **OFF**, firmly apply and release the brake pedal a minimum of 40 times.

   b. A noticeable change in the pedal feel will occur when the accumulator is completely discharged (a hard pedal).

   c. Do not turn the ignition key **ON** after depressurizing the system unless instructed to do so.
3. Remove the air cleaner duct and stud, if used.
4. Disconnect the 30 amp pump motor fusible element **K** from the ABS power center.
5. Remove the accumulator by turning the hex nut on the end of the accumulator with a 17mm socket. The unit can be removed by sliding out from beneath the ABS unit, towards the left front wheel well.
6. Remove the O-ring seal from the accumulator.

To install:
7. Lightly lubricate the new O-ring seal and install it on the accumulator.
8. Install the accumulator and torque the unit to 24 ft. lbs. (33 Nm).
9. Install the air cleaner duct and stud, if used.
10. Bleed the system.

Sensor

REMOVAL & INSTALLATION

Front

1. Raise and support the vehicle safely and disconnect the negative battery cable.
2. Disconnect the wiring harness connector from the sensor.
3. Remove the 2 front wheel speed sensor bolts, the 1 connector bracket bolt and remove the speed sensor.
To install:
4. Position the speed sensor and install the 2 front wheel speed sensor bolts and tighten to 59 ft. lbs. Install the 1 bracket bolt and tighten to 89 inch lbs.
5. Inspect the air gap. Proper air gap should be between 0.19–0.68 in. (0.48 − 1.73 mm). If the air gap is not correct, look for damaged or misaligned components that would effect air gap.
6. Install the sensor connector to the wiring harness. Install the Connector Position Assurance (CPA) locking pin.
7. Route the wire to avoid contact with suspension components.
8. Lower the vehicle.

Rear

The rear wheel speed sensors and rings are an integral part of the hub and bearing assemblies. Should a speed sensor or ring require replacement, the entire hub and bearing assembly must be replaced.

Brake Controller

REMOVAL & INSTALLATION

1. Disconnect the negative battery cable.
2. Turn the ignition switch **OFF**.
3. Slide the passenger seat forward.
4. Tip the passenger seat forward, if applicable.
5. Remove the bolts securing the case cover and side the the brake controller out of the case.
6. Disconnect the wiring connectors from the controller.
To install:
7. Connect the wiring connectors to the controller. Install the connector locking pins.
8. Install the controller into the case, install the cover and tighten the bolts.
9. Return the passenger seat to the correct position and connect the negative battery cable.

FRONT SUSPENSION

MacPherson Strut/ Knuckle

REMOVAL & INSTALLATION

——————— **CAUTION** ———————

Do not remove the strut cartridge nut without compressing the coil spring first. This procedure must be followed because it keeps the coil spring compressed. Use care to support the strut assembly adequately because the coil spring is under heavy load, if released too quickly personal injury could result. Never remove the center strut nuts unless the spring is compressed with a MacPherson strut spring compressor tool J-26584 or equivalent. The vehicle weight can be used when the strut assembly is still in the vehicle and only the strut cartridge is going to be replaced.

1. Disconnect the negative battery cable.
2. Loosen the cover plate bolts.
3. Loosen the wheel nuts. Raise and safely support the vehicle.
4. Remove the wheel assembly. Remove the brake caliper and bracket assembly, hang the caliper aside. Do not hang the caliper by the brake lines.
5. Remove the brake rotor. Remove the hub and bearing attaching bolts.
6. Remove the halfshaft. Remove the tie rod attaching nut. Using tool J–35917 or equivalent, separate the tie rod from the steering knuckle.
7. Remove the lower ball joint attaching nut and separate the lower ball from the lower control arm.
8. Remove the hub and bearing attaching bolts and hub assembly.
9. Remove the cover plate bolts and remove the strut from the vehicle.
To install:
10. Install the strut mount cover plate, tighten the nuts after lowering the vehicle. Install the lower ball joint and torque to 81 inch lbs. (10 Nm), plus an additional 120 degrees (2 flats) turn until the cotter pin hole is lined up.
11. Install the tie rod and torque to 40 ft. lbs. (54 Nm) to line up the cotter pin hole.

12. Install the halfshaft and install the hub and bearing-to-knuckle attaching bolts, tighten to 52 ft. lbs. (70 Nm).

13. Install the brake rotor and caliper assembly.

14. Install the wheel assembly, tighten the wheel lug nuts to 100 ft. lbs. (136 Nm).

15. Lower the vehicle, tighten the strut cover bolts to 17 ft. lbs. (24 Nm) and tighten the wheel nuts.

16. Connect the negative battery cable.

Strut Cartridge

REMOVAL & INSTALLATION

The front MacPherson strut assembly does not have to be removed from the vehicle to remove the strut cartridge.

────── CAUTION ──────

Do not remove the strut cartrige nut without compressing the coil spring first. This procedure must be followed because it keeps the coil spring compressed. Use care to support the strut assembly adequately because the coil spring is under heavy load, if released too quickly personal injury could result. Never remove the center strut nuts unless the spring is compressed with a MacPherson strut spring compressor tool J-26584 or equivalent.

NOTE: The vehicle weight can be used when the strut assembly is still in the vehicle and only the strut cartridge is going to be replaced. Do not service the the strut cartridge unless the weight of the vehicle is on the suspension. The weight of the vehicle keeps the spring compressed.

1. Disconnect the negative battery cable.

2. Scribe the strut mount cover plate-to-body to ensure proper camber adjustment.

3. Remove the 3 strut mount plate retaining nuts and cover.

4. Remove the strut shaft nut using a No. 50 Torx® bit.

5. Remove the strut mount bushing by prying with a suitable prybar.

6. Remove the jounce bumper retainer using a jounce bumper spanner wrench tool J-35670 or equivalent. Remove the jounce bumper by attaching the strut extension rod tool J-35668 or equivalent. Compress the shaft down into the cartridge. Remove the extension rod and pull out the jounce bumper.

7. Remove the strut cartridge closure nut by attaching the strut extension rod and re-extending the shaft. Remove the extension rod and un-

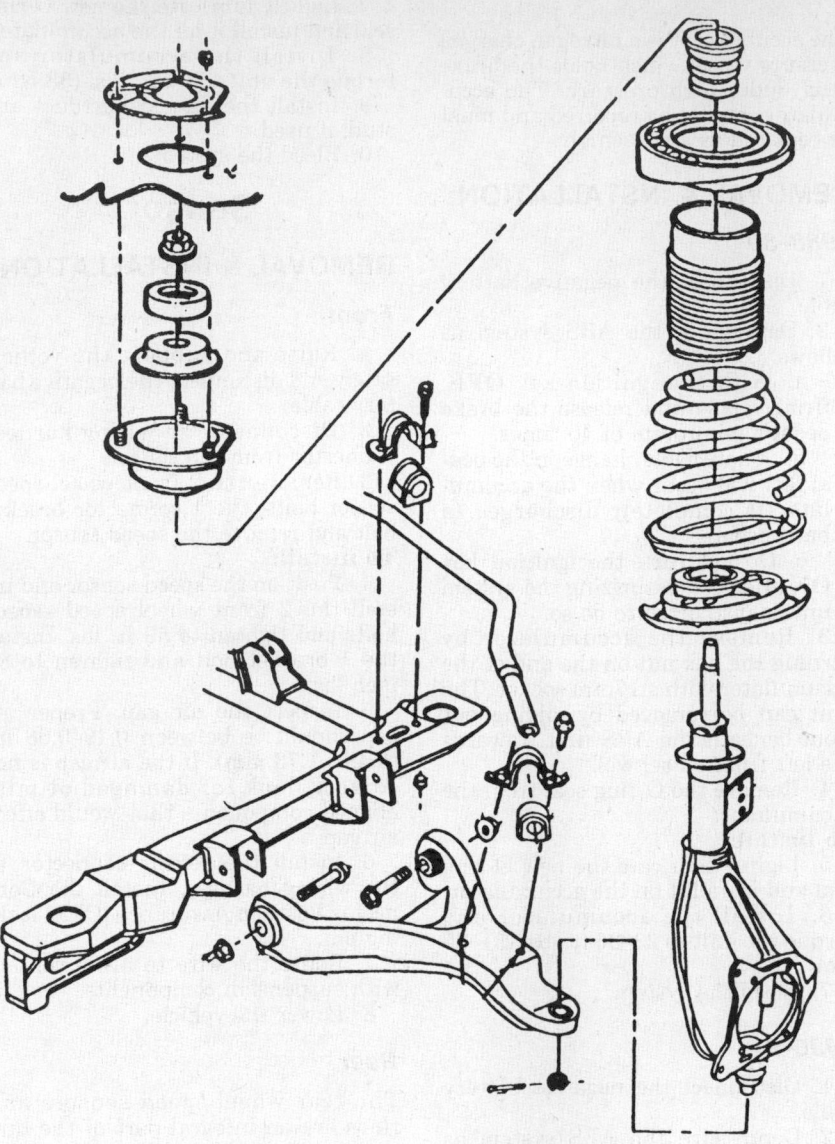

Exploded view of the front suspension

screw the closure nut using a strut cap nut wrench J-35671 or equivalent.

8. Remove the strut cartridge and oil from the strut tube using a suction device.

To install:

9. Install the self contained replacement cartridge using the strut cap nut wrench J-35671 or equivalent. The cartridge does not need oil added unless specified. If oil is not supplied with the cartridge, add the specified amount of hydraulic jack oil.

10. Install the jounce bumper and retainer.

11. Install the strut mount bushing. Use a soap solution to lubricate the bushing during installation.

12. Install the strut shaft nut and torque to 72 ft. lbs. (98 Nm).

13. Align the scribed marks from the strut cover-to-body. Install the strut cover plate and nuts. Torque the nuts to 17 ft. lbs. (24 Nm).

14. Connect the negative battery cable and check for proper suspension operation.

Coil Springs

REMOVAL & INSTALLATION

1. Remove the MacPherson strut assembly.

2. Mount the strut assembly in a strut compressing tool J-34013-A and J-34013-88 or equivalent. Compress the spring using the forcing screw. Release the spring tension enough to re-

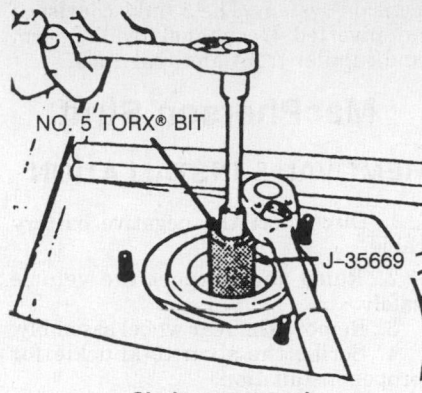

Shaft nut removal

NO. 5 TORX® BIT

J–35669

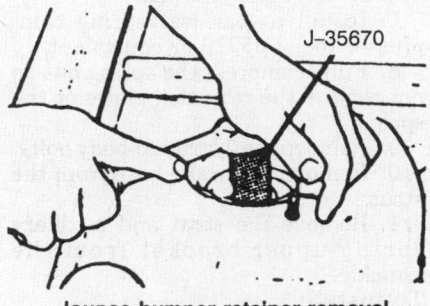

Jounce bumper retainer removal

J–35670

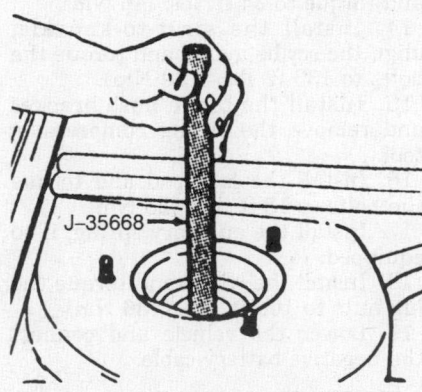

Compressing the shaft down into the cartridge

J–35668

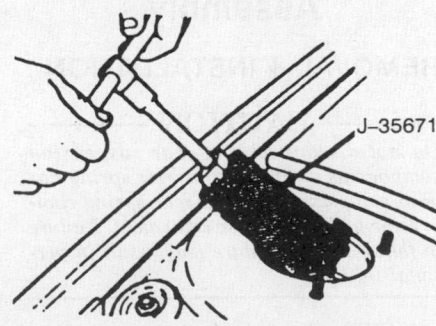

Srut closure nut removal

J–35671

move the spring insulator.

3. Using a Torx® bit and a strut shaft nut remover tool J-35669 or equivalent, remove the strut shaft nut. Make sure there is no spring tension on the shaft.

4. Release all spring tension and remove the spring and insulator. Remove any component needed to perform repair.

To install:

5. Inspect all components for wear and damage.

6. Install the spring seat and bearing.

7. Install the lower spring insulator. The lower spring coil end must be visible between the step and the first retention tab of the insulator.

8. Install the spring, dust shield and jounce bumper.

9. Install the upper spring insulator. The upper spring coil end must be between the step and location mark on the insulator.

10. Install the jounce bumper retainer-to-strut mount using a jounce bumper spanner tool J-35670 or equivalent.

11. Align the strut cartridge shaft with a strut extension rod tool J-35668 or equivalent.

12. Install the strut mount and the upper strut mount bushing.

13. Compress the strut assembly us-

ing the strut spring compressor tool J-34013-A and J-34013-88 or equivalent.

14. Install the shaft nut using the strut rod installer and Torx® bit. Torque the shaft nut to 72 ft. lbs. (98 Nm).

15. Install the MacPherson strut assembly.

Lower Ball Joint

INSPECTION

1. Raise and safely support the vehicle, allowing the front suspension to hang freely.

2. Grasp and shake the wheel at the top and bottom to feel if there is any in and out movement.

3. Replace the ball joint if any movement is detected.

4. When the ball joint is disconnected from the knuckle, check for any looseness or if the ball joint can be twisted freely in the socket by hand.

REMOVAL & INSTALLATION

1. Raise and safely support the vehicle.

2. Remove the wheel assembly.

3. Remove the ball joint heat shield retaining nuts and remove the heat shield.

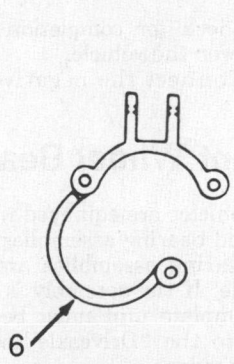

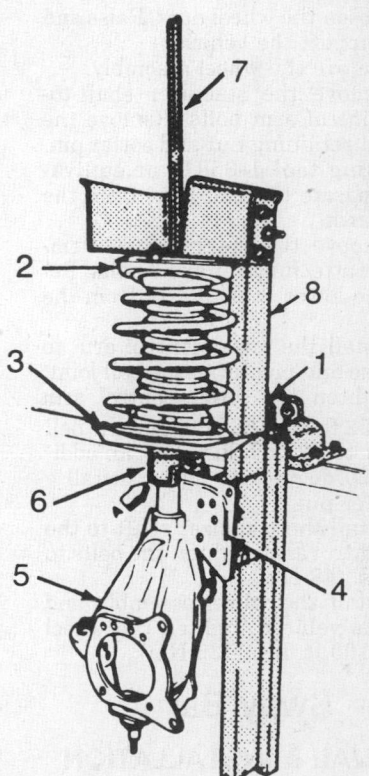

1. Compressor forcing screw
2. Upper strut mount
3. Lower seat and bearing
4. Spring plate
5. Strut/knuckle assembly
6. J-34013-88
7. J-35668
8. J-34013A

MacPherson strut spring compressor

4. Remove the ball joint cotter pin and nut.

5. Loosen, but do not remove, the stabilizer bar bushing bolts.

6. Using tool J–35917 or equivalent, remove the ball joint from the lower control arm.

7. Using an ⅛ in. drill bit, make a pilot hole in each of the rivets retaining the ball joint to the lower control arm. Using a ½ in. drill bit, drill out and remove the ball joint.

To install:

8. Install the ball joint to the lower control arm, install the retaining nut hand tight.

9. Install the ball joint to the steering knuckle. Install the 4 ball joint retaining nuts and bolts, supplied with the replacement joint.

10. Tighten the stabilizer bushing bar bushing bolts to 35 ft. lbs. (48 Nm). Tighten the ball joint retaining nut to 89 inch lbs. (10 Nm) and an additional 120 degrees (2 flats). Install a new cotter pin.

NOTE: Do not at any time loosen the ball joint nut to align it when installing the cotter pin.

11. Install the ball joint heat shield and tighten the retaining bolts to 5 ft. lbs. (7 Nm).

Lower Control Arms

REMOVAL & INSTALLATION

1. Loosen the wheel nuts. Raise and safely support the vehicle.

2. Remove the wheel assembly.

3. Remove the stabilizer shaft-to-lower control arm bolts. Remove the ball joint retaining nut and cotter pin.

4. Using tool J–35917 or equivalent, Separate the ball joint from the control arm.

5. Remove the lower control arm-to-frame attaching nuts and bolts. Remove the lower control arm from the vehicle.

6. Install the lower control arm to the frame and pivot it to the ball joint.

7. Tighten the lower control arm bolts to 52 ft. lbs. (69 Nm) and the ball joint nut to 89 inch lbs., plus an additional 120 degrees (2 flats). Install a new cotter pin.

8. Install the stabilizer shaft to the lower control arm, tighten the bolts to 35 ft. lbs. (48 Nm).

9. Install the wheel assembly and lower the vehicle. Tighten the wheel nuts to 100 ft. lbs. (136 Nm).

Sway Bar

REMOVAL & INSTALLATION

1. Disconnect the negative battery cable.

2. Raise and support the vehicle safely.

3. Remove the front wheel.

4. Move the steering shaft dust seal for access to the pinch bolt.

5. Remove the pinch bolt from the lower intermediate steering shaft.

6. Loosen all the stabilizer insulator clamp attaching nuts and bolts.

7. Place a jackstand under the center of the rear frame crossmember.

8. Loosen the 2 front frame-to-body bolts (4 turns only).

9. Remove the 2 rear frame-to-body bolts and lower the rear of the frame just enough to gain access to remove the stabilizer shaft.

10. Remove the insulators and clamps from the frame and control arms. Pull the stabilizer shaft rearward, swing down and remove from the left side of the vehicle.

To install:

11. Install the stabilizer shaft through the left side of the vehicle.

12. Coat the new insulators with rubber lubricant.

13. Loosely install the clamps-to-control arms and clamps-to-frame.

14. Raise the frame into position while guiding the steering gear into place.

15. Install new frame-to-body bolts and torque to 103 ft. lbs. (140 Nm).

16. Remove the frame jackstand.

17. Torque the stabilizer clamps-to-frame and control arms to 35 ft. lbs. (47 Nm).

18. Install the steering gear pinch bolt and dust seal.

19. Install the front wheels and torque the lug nuts to 100 ft. lbs. (136 Nm).

20. Check for completion of repair and lower the vehicle.

21. Connect the negative battery cable.

Front Wheel Bearings

The vehicles are equipped with sealed hub and bearing assemblies. The hub and bearing assemblies are non-serviceable. If the assembly is damaged, the complete unit must be replaced. Refer to the "Driveaxle" section for the procedure.

REAR SUSPENSION

The rear suspension features a lightweight composite fiberglass mono-leaf transverse spring. Each wheel is mounted to a tri-link independent suspension system. The 3 links consist of an inverted U channel trailing arm and tubular front and rear rods.

MacPherson Strut

REMOVAL & INSTALLATION

1. Disconnect the negative battery cable.

2. Raise and support the vehicle safely.

3. Remove the rear wheel assembly.

4. Scribe the strut-to-knuckle for proper installation.

5. Remove the auxiliary spring, if so equipped.

6. Remove the jack pad.

7. Install a rear leaf spring compressor tool J–35778 or equivalent.

8. Fully compress the spring but do not remove the retention plates or the spring.

9. Remove the 2 strut-to-body bolts.

10. Remove the brake hose from the strut.

11. Remove the strut and auxiliary spring upper bracket from the knuckle.

To install:

12. Position the strut to the body and knuckle bracket.

13. Install the strut-to-body bolts and torque to 34 ft. lbs. (46 Nm).

14. Install the strut-to-knuckle, align the scribe marks and torque the bolts to 133 ft. lbs. (180 Nm).

15. Install the brake hose bracket and remove the spring compressing tool.

16. Install the jack pad and torque the bolts to 18 ft. lbs. (25 Nm).

17. Install the auxiliary spring, if so equipped.

18. Install the wheel and torque the lug nuts to 100 ft. lbs. (136 Nm).

19. Lower the vehicle and connect the negative battery cable.

NOTE: The rear strut assembly is not serviceable. The assembly is replaced as a complete unit.

Transverse Spring Assembly

REMOVAL & INSTALLATION

——— **CAUTION** ———

Do not disconnect any rear suspension components until the transverse spring has been compressed using a rear spring compressor tool J–35778 or equivalent. Failure to follow this procedure may result in personal injury.

NOTE: Do not use any corrosive cleaning agents, silicone lubri-

cants, engine degreasers, solvents, etc. on or near the fiberglass rear transverse spring. These materials may cause extensive spring damage.

1. Disconnect the negative battery cable.

2. Raise the vehicle and support it safely.

3. Remove the jack pad in the middle of the spring.

4. Remove the spring retention plates and the right trailing arm at the knuckle.

5. Separate the rear leaf spring compressor tool J-35778 or equivalent, from the center shank and hang the center shank of the tool at the spring center.

NOTE: Attach the center shank of the compressor from the front side of the vehicle only.

6. Install the compressor body to the center shank and spring. Important, always center the spring on the rollers of the spring compressor.

7. Fully compress the spring using the spring compressor tool J-35778 or equivalent.

8. Slide the spring to the left side. It may be necessary to pry the spring to the left using a prybar against the right knuckle. When prying, do not damage any components.

9. Relax the spring to provide removal clearance from the right side and remove the spring.

To install:

10. Using the spring compressor tool, compress the spring and install it through the left knuckle. Slide towards the left side as far as possible and raise the right side of the spring as far as possible.

11. Compress the spring fully and install it into right knuckle.

NOTE: The rear spring retention plates are designed with tabs on 1 end. The tabs must be aligned with the support assembly to prevent damage to the fuel tank.

12. Center the spring to align the holes for the spring retention plate bolts.

13. Install the spring retention plates and bolts. Do not tighten at this time.

14. Position the trailing arm and install the bolt. Torque the bolt to 192 ft. lbs. (260 Nm).

15. Remove the spring compressor tool J-35778.

16. Torque the spring retention plate bolts to 15 ft. lbs. (20 Nm).

17. Install the jack pads and torque the bolts to 18 ft. lbs. (25 Nm).

18. Install the wheels and torque the lug nuts to 100 ft. lbs. (136 Nm).

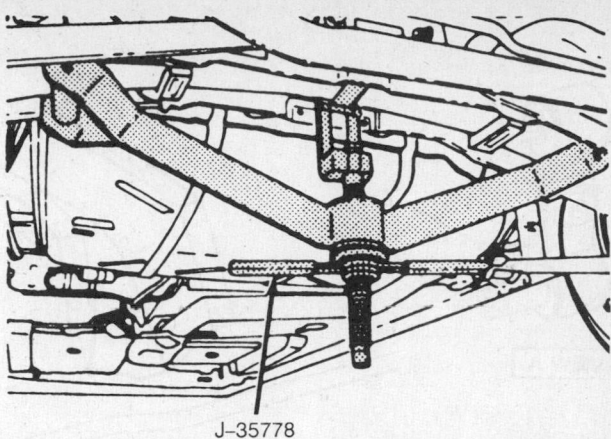

J-35778

Transverse spring compressed

19. Lower the vehicle and connect the negative battery cable.

Knuckle

REMOVAL & INSTALLATION

1. Disconnect the negative battery cable.

2. Raise and support the vehicle safely.

3. Remove the rear wheels and scribe the strut-to-knuckle.

4. Remove the jack pad and install the rear leaf spring compressor tool J-35778 or equivalent.

5. Fully compress the spring but do not remove the spring or retention plates.

6. Remove the auxiliary spring, if so equipped. If not equipped, remove the rod -to-knuckle bolt.

7. Remove the front rod-to-knuckle.

8. Remove the brake hose bracket, caliper and rotor. Do not leave the caliper hang by the brake hose.

9. Remove the hub and bearing assembly, trailing arm and the strut/upper auxiliary spring bracket from the knuckle. Remove the knuckle.

To install:

10. Install the knuckle and position it to the strut/upper auxiliary spring bracket. Hand start the bolts, but do not tighten.

11. Install the front rod and trailing arm-to-knuckle. Hand tighten the bolts.

12. Torque the trailing arm bolt and nut to 192 ft. lbs. (260 Nm).

13. Install the hub/bearing assembly and torque the bolts to 52 ft. lbs. (70 Nm).

14. Install the rotor and caliper.

15. Align the scribe marks to ensure proper alignment. Torque the strut-to-knuckle attaching bolts to 133 ft. lbs. (180 Nm).

16. Remove the rear leaf spring compressor.

17. Install the jack pad, auxiliary spring, if equipped, and rod-to-knuckle bolt. Apply thread locking compound to the knuckle bolts.

18. Torque the rod-to-knuckle bolts to 66 ft. lbs. (90 Nm), plus 120 degrees.

19. Install the rear wheels and torque the lug nuts to 100 ft. lbs. (136 Nm).

20. Check for completion of repair, lower the vehicle and connect the negative battery cable.

Tri-Link Suspension Assembly

REMOVAL & INSTALLATION

Trailing Arm

1. Raise and support the vehicle safely.

2. Remove the trailing arm-to-knuckle nut and bolt.

3. Remove the trailing arm-to-body nut, bolt and arm.

To install:

4. Install the trailing arm, bolts and nuts.

5. Torque the arm-to-knuckle bolt to 192 ft. lbs. (260 Nm) and the arm-to-body bolt to 48 ft. lbs. (65 Nm).

6. Lower the vehicle and recheck all repair procedures.

Rear Rod

1. Raise and support the vehicle safely.

2. Remove the rear wheels.

3. Remove the auxiliary spring, if so equipped. If not equipped, remove the rod-to-knuckle bolt.

4. Remove the lower auxiliary spring bracket at the rod, if so equipped.

5. Scribe the toe adjusting cam, remove the rod-to-crossmember bolt and rod.

To install:

6. Install the rod, push the bolt

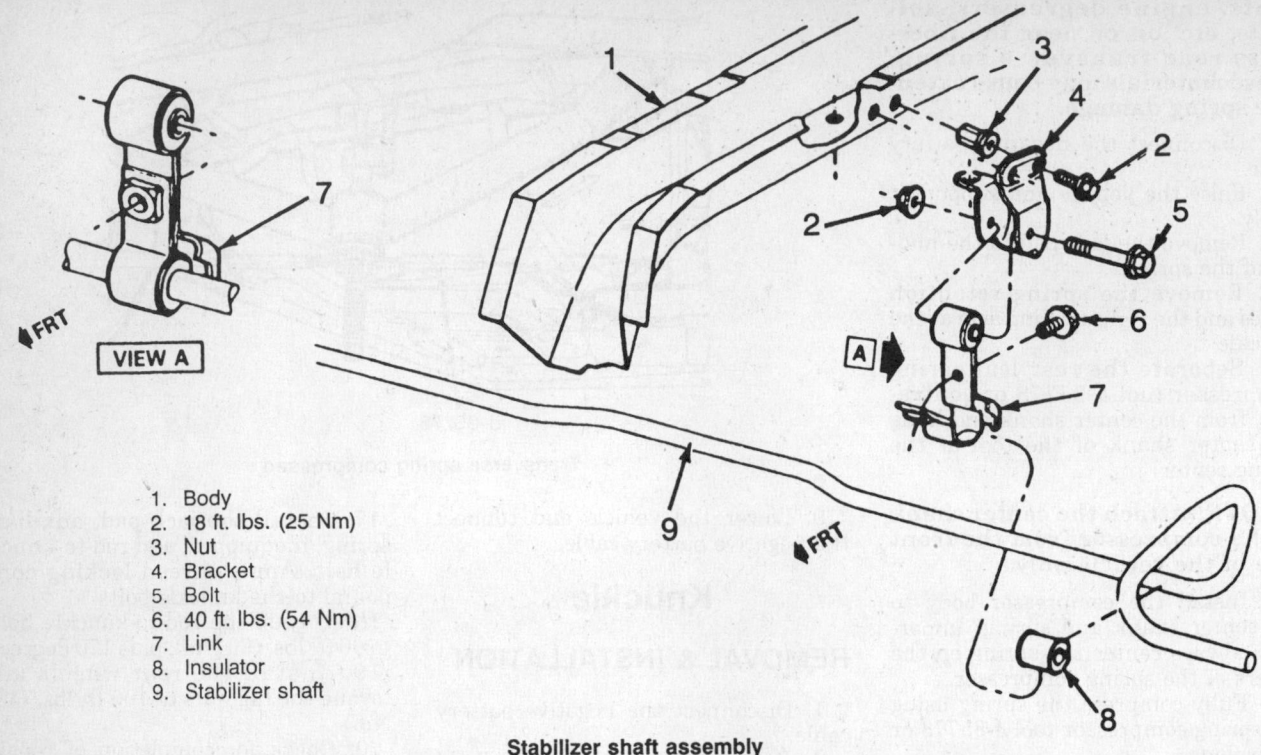

1. Body
2. 18 ft. lbs. (25 Nm)
3. Nut
4. Bracket
5. Bolt
6. 40 ft. lbs. (54 Nm)
7. Link
8. Insulator
9. Stabilizer shaft

Stabilizer shaft assembly

through the rod bushing and install the adjusting cam in its original location. Do not tighten at this time.

7. Install the lower auxiliary spring bracket-to-rod, if equipped. Torque the nut to 133 ft. lbs. (180 Nm).

8. Install the rod-to-knuckle with thread locking compound. Do not tighten.

9. Install the rear wheels and lower the vehicle.

10. Torque the rod-to-crossmember bolt to 66 ft. lbs. (90 Nm), plus 120 degrees.

11. Adjust the rear toe.

Front Rod

1. Raise and support the vehicle safely.

2. Remove the rear wheels.

3. Remove the rod-to-knuckle bolt and exhaust pipe heat shield.

4. Lower and support the fuel tank just enough for access to the bolt at the frame.

5. Remove the rod-to-frame bolt and rod.

To install:

6. Install the rod, bolt and nut. Do not tighten at this time.

7. Apply thread locking compound to the rod-to-knuckle bolt.

8. Torque the rod-to-frame and rod-to-knuckle bolts to 66 ft. lbs. (90 Nm), plus 120 dregrees.

9. Reposition the fuel tank.

10. Install the exhaust pipe heat shield, rear wheels and lower the vehicle.

Stabilizer Shaft

REMOVAL & INSTALLATION

1. Disconnect the negative battery cable.

2. Raise and support the vehicle safely.

3. Remove the right and left stabilizer shaft link bolts and open the brackets to remove the insulators.

4. Remove the right and left strut-to-knuckle-to-stabilizer shaft nuts. Do not remove the strut-to-knuckle bolts.

5. Remove the stabilizer shaft by prying the shaft on 1 side for clearance at the strut.

To install:

6. Install the stabilizer shaft by prying the shaft on 1 side for clearance at the strut.

7. Install the insulator brackets-to-stabilizer shaft-to-knuckle bolts. Do NOT tighten at this time.

8. Install the right and left stabilizer shaft link bolts.

9. Torque the link bolts to 40 ft. lbs. (54 Nm) and the knuckle bolts to 133 ft. lbs. (180 Nm).

10. Check for completion of repair, connect the negative battery cable and lower the vehicle.

Rear Wheel Bearings

These cars are equipped with sealed hub and bearing assemblies. The hub and bearing assemblies are non-serviceable. If the assembly is damaged, the complete unit must be replaced.

REMOVAL & INSTALLATION

1. Disconnect the negative battery cable.

2. Raise and support the vehicle safely.

3. Remove the rear wheel, caliper, bracket and rotor.

4. Loosen the 4 hub/bearing-to-knuckle attaching bolts.

5. Remove the hub/bearing assembly.

To install:

6. Install the hub/bearing assembly onto the knuckle. Install the 4 attaching bolts and torque to 52 ft. lbs. (70 Nm).

7. Install the rotor, caliper and bracket.

8. Install the rear wheel and torque the lug nut to 100 ft. lbs. (135 Nm).

9. Lower the vehicle and connect the negative battery cable.

Unit Repair Sections

28 General Maintenance

Introduction

Routine maintenance is probably the most important part of automobile care and the easiest to neglect. A regular program aimed at monitoring essential systems ensures that all components are in good and safe working order, and can prevent small problems from developing into major headaches. Routine maintenance also pays off big dividends in keeping major repair costs at a minimum and extending the life of the car.

The vehicle owner's manual includes a maintenance schedule indicating service intervals in numbers of months or thousands of miles. This schedule should always be followed. We have provided in this section a guide to service intervals based on an averaging of manufacturer's recommendations. In most cases the suggested interval offered here will be close to that given by the manufacturer of your car, but the manufacturer's schedule should always take precedence.

We have divided the maintenance work to be done into three categories: Under Hood, Under Car, and Exterior. The checks in each section require only a few minutes of attention every few weeks and the services to be performed can be easily accomplished in a morning. The most important part of any maintenance program is regularity. The few minutes or occasional morning spent on these seemingly trivial tasks will forestall or eliminate major problems later.

Under Hood Maintenance

AUTOMATIC TRANSMISSION, AUTOMATIC TRANSAXLE

The fluid level in the automatic transmission or transaxle should be checked every three months or 6000 miles. All automatic transmissions have a dipstick for fluid level checks.

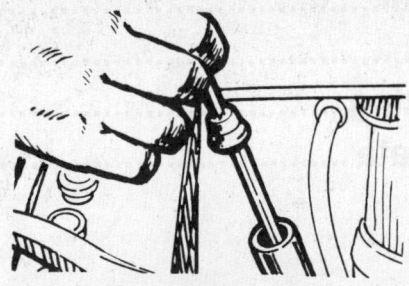

Check the automatic transmission fluid level with the dipstick provided

1. Drive the car until it is at normal operating temperature. The level should not be checked immediately after the car has been driven for a long time at high speed, or in city traffic in hot weather; in those cases, the transmission should be given a half hour to cool down.
2. Stop the car, apply the parking brake, then shift slowly through all gear positions, ending in Park. Leave the engine running.

3. Remove the dipstick, wipe it clean, then reinsert it, pushing it fully home.
4. Pull the dipstick again and, holding it horizontally, read the fluid level.
5. Cautiously feel the end of the dipstick to determine the temperature. Most dipsticks are marked with both cool and hot levels. If the fluid is not up to the correct level, more will have to be added.

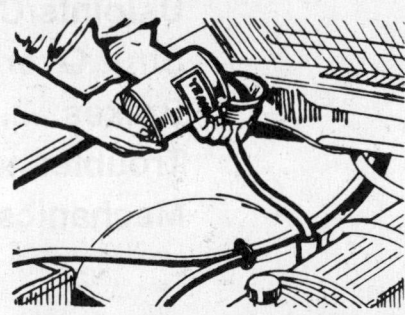

Fill the automatic transmission through the dipstick tube

NOTE: On General Motors Citation, Omega, Phoenix, Skylark, Cavalier, Cimarron, J2000, Celebrity, Cierra and 6000 models, the "Cold" level marks (dimples) are above the "Hot" level area.

6. Fluid is added through the dipstick tube. You will probably need the aid of a spout or a long-necked funnel. Be sure that whatever you pour through is perfectly clean and dry. Fluid recommendations can be found in the owner's manual or the Auto-

matic Transmission Unit Repair Section in this book. Add fluid slowly and in small amounts, checking the level frequently between additions. Do not overfill, which will cause foaming, fluid loss, slippage, and possible transmission damage.

BATTERY

Fluid Level (Except "Maintenance Free" Batteries)

Check the battery electrolyte level at least once a month, or more often in hot weather or during periods of extended car operation. The level can be checked through the case on translucent polypropylene batteries; the cell caps must be removed on other models. The electrolyte level in each cell should be kept filled to the split ring inside, or the line marked on the outside of the case.

If the level is low add only distilled water or colorless, odorless drinking water through the opening until the level is correct. Each cell is completely separate from the others, so each must be checked and filled individually.

If water is added in freezing weather, the car should be driven several miles to allow the water to mix with the electrolyte. Otherwise, the battery could freeze.

Specific Gravity (Except "Maintenance Free" Batteries)

At least once a year, check the specific gravity of the battery. It should be between 1.20 and 1.26 at room temperature. See the "Charging and Starting Systems" Section in this book for details.

Cables and Clamps

Once a year, the battery terminals and the cable clamps should be cleaned. Loosen the clamps and remove the cables, negative cable first. On batteries with posts on top, the use of a puller specially made for the purpose is recommended. These are inexpensive, and available in auto parts stores. Side terminal battery cables are secured with a bolt.

Clean the cable clamps and the battery terminal with a wire brush, until all corrosion, grease, etc. is removed and the metal is shiny. It is especially important to clean the inside of the clamp thoroughly, since a small deposit of foreign material or oxidation there will prevent a sound electrical connection and inhibit either starting or charging. Special tools are available for cleaning these parts, one type for conventional batteries and another type for side terminal batteries.

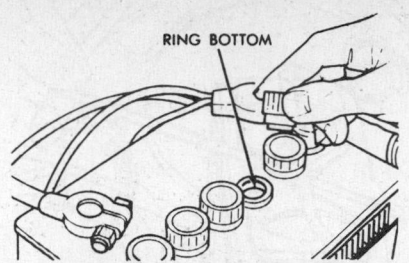

Fill the battery cell to the bottom of the split ring

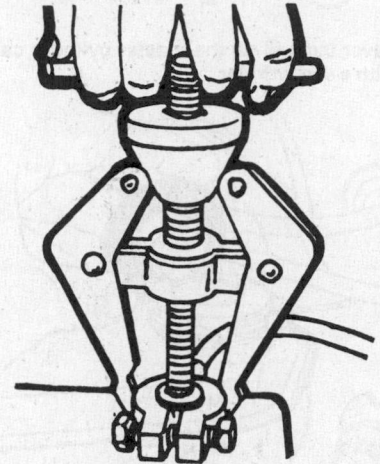

Use a puller to remove the clamp on post-type batteries

Clean the clamp with a wire brush

Before installing the cables, loosen the battery hold-down clamp or strap, remove the battery and check the battery tray. Clear it of any debris, and check it for soundness. Rust should be wire brushed away, and the metal given a coat of anti-rust paint. Replace the battery and tighten the hold-down clamp or strap securely, but be careful not to overtighten, which will crack the battery case.

After the clamps and terminals are clean, reinstall the cables, negative cable last; do not hammer on the clamps to install. Tighten the clamps securely, but do not distort them. Give

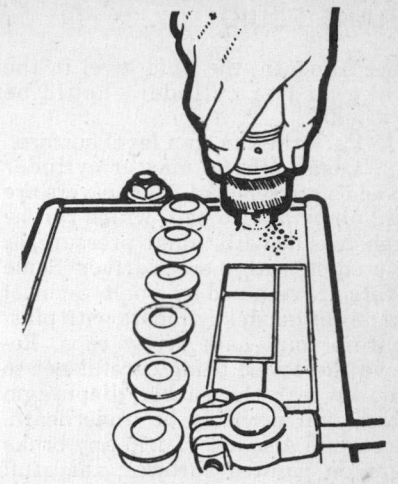

The posts are easily cleaned with a wire brush, or the battery post tool shown

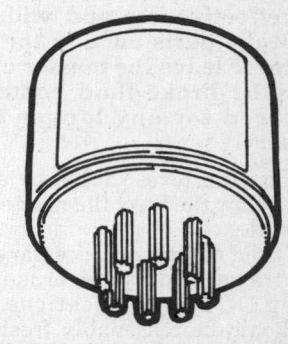

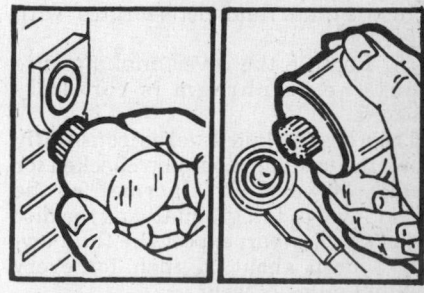

A special tool is required to clean the terminals and clamps on side terminal batteries

the clamps and terminals a thin external coat of grease after installation, to retard corrosion.

Check the cables at the same time that the terminals are cleaned. If the cable insulation is cracked or broken, or if the ends are frayed, the cable should be replaced with a new cable of the same length and gauge.

CAUTION
Keep flame or sparks away from the battery; it gives off explosive hydrogen gas. Battery electrolyte contains sulphuric acid. If you should splash any on your skin or in your eyes, flush the affected area with plenty of clear water; if it lands in your eyes, get medical help immediately.

BRAKE FLUID

Once a month, the fluid level in the brake master cylinder should be checked.

1. Park the car on a level surface.
2. Clean off the master cylinder cover before removal. Most covers are held on by a wire bail, which can be pushed aside with thumb pressure, or levered off with a screwdriver. Some covers are retained by a bolt. Some of the newer master cylinders with plastic reservoirs have screw caps. Remove the cover, being careful not to drop or tear the rubber diaphragm which will probably be underneath. Be careful also not to drip any brake fluid on painted surfaces; the stuff eats paint.

NOTE: Brake fluid absorbs moisture from the air, which reduces effectiveness and will corrode brake parts once in the system. Never leave the master cylinder or the brake fluid container uncovered for any longer than necessary.

3. The fluid level should be about ¼ inch below the lip of the master cylinder well.
4. If fluid addition is necessary, use only extra heavy duty disc brake fluid meeting DOT 3 specifications. The fluid should be reasonably fresh, because brake fluid deteriorates with age.
5. Replace the cover, making sure that the diaphragm is correctly seated.

If the brake fluid level is constantly low, the system should be checked for leaks. However, it is normal for the fluid level to fall gradually as the disc brake pads wear; expect the fluid level to drop about ⅛ inch for every 10,000 miles of wear.

BELT TENSION ADJUSTMENT

Every six months or 12,000 miles, check the water pump, alternator, power steering pump, air pump, and air conditioning compressor drive belts for proper tension. Also look for signs of wear, fraying, separation, glazing and so on, and replace the belts as required.

Belt tension should be checked with a gauge made for the purpose. If a gauge is not available, tension can be checked with moderate thumb pressure applied to the belt at its longest span midway between pulleys. If the belt has a free span less than twelve inches, it should deflect approximately ⅛–¼ inch. If the span is longer

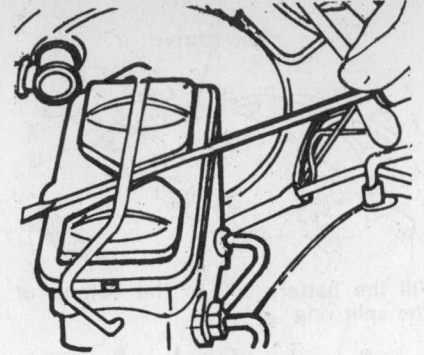

Lever the ball off the master cylinder cap with a screwdriver

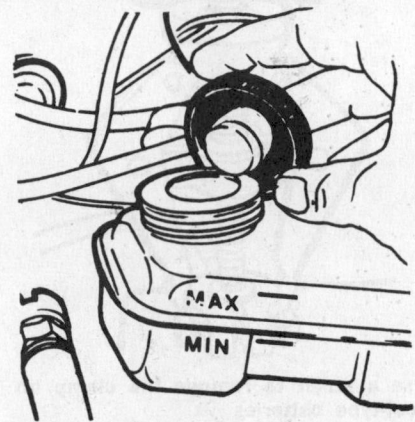

Screw caps are used on some master cylinders

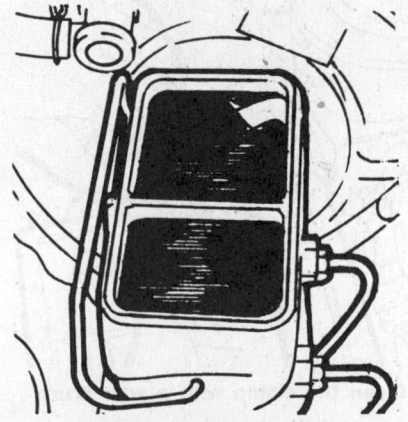

Proper brake fluid level

than twelve inches, deflection can range between ⅛–⅜ inches.

NOTE: On cars except American Motors models which use a one-piece "serpentine" belt to drive all accessories, belt tension is automatically adjusted. On cars which have two "serpentine" belts, or one "serpentine" belt as well as conventional V-belts, and on all American Motors models with the "serpentine" belt, belt

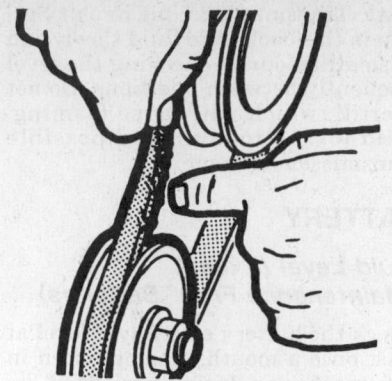

Check the belts for wear

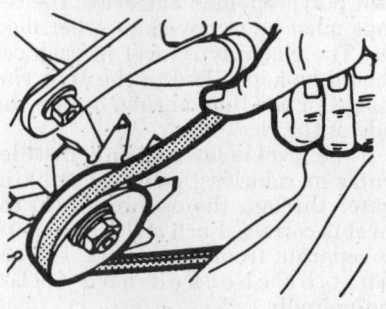

Check the belt tension at the middle of the longest span between pulleys

tensions usually must be checked and adjusted. Belt tension is higher on "serpentine" belts and cannot be tested with thumb pressure. Some Ford models (Thunderbird/XR-7 with AOD transmission) require special tools for adjustment. American Motors "serpentine" belts are adjusted at the alternator.

To adjust or replace belts:

1. Loosen the driven accessory's pivot and mounting bolts. Some air conditioning compressor belts are tensioned by an idler pulley; in this case, loosen the idler pulley and use a ½ in. drive ratchet in the square hole provided to lever the idler pulley up or down.
2. Move the accessory toward or away from the engine until the tension is correct. You can use a wooden hammer handle or broomstick as a lever, but do not use anything metallic.
3. Tighten the bolts and recheck the tension. If new belts have been installed, run the engine for a few minutes, then recheck and readjust as necessary.

NOTE: If the driven component has two drive belts, the belts should be replaced in pairs to maintain proper tension.

It is better to have belts too loose

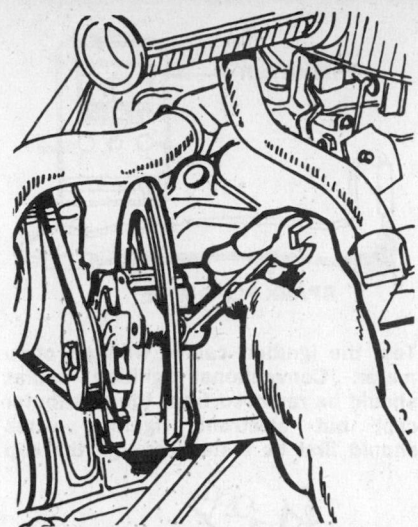

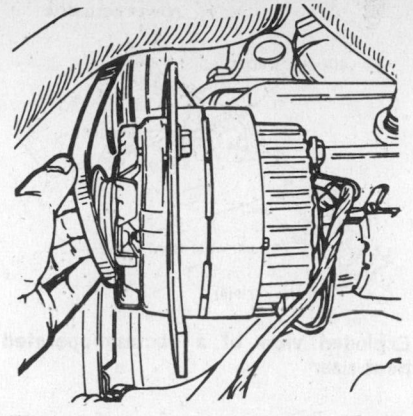

Slip the replacement belt over the pulley

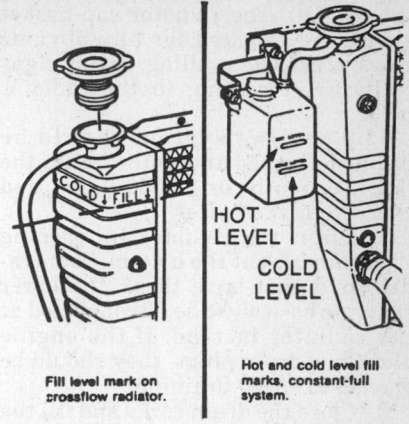

Fill level mark on crossflow radiator.

Hot and cold level fill marks, constant-full system.

Proper coolant level is about one inch below the radiator neck, or between the lines on the recovery tank

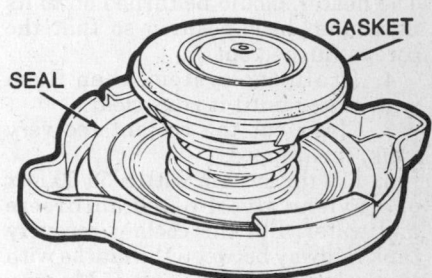

Check the radiator cap gasket and sealing surface

To either adjust or remove a belt, loosen the driven component's adjusting bolt

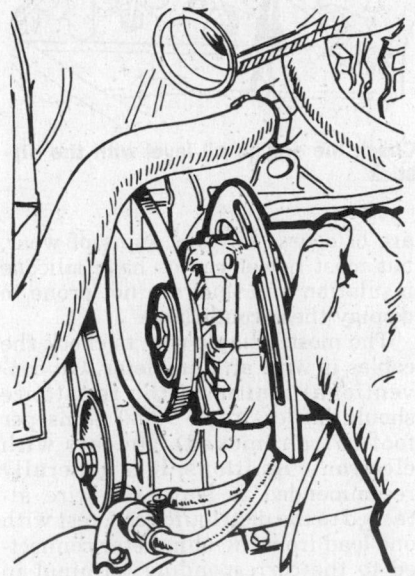

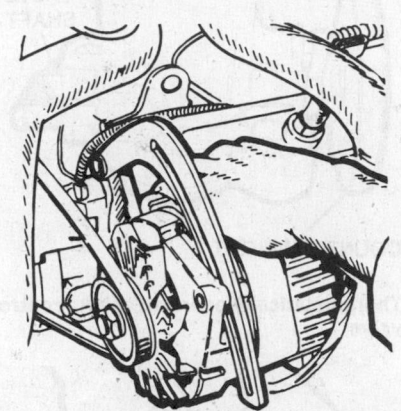

Pull outwards on the component to tension the belt, then tighten the bolts; recheck the belt tension after tightening

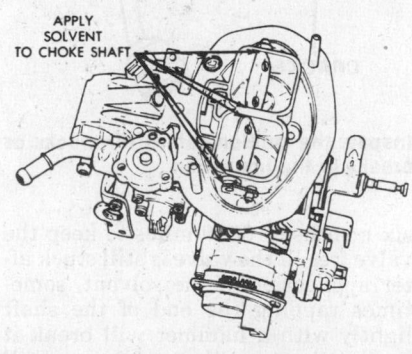

Use a spray solvent on the choke shaft, but do not apply any lubricants

Push the component toward the engine to remove the belt

than too tight, because overtight belts will lead to bearing failure, particularly in the water pump and alternator. However, loose belts place an extremely high impact load on the driven component due to the whipping action of the belt.

CARBURETOR AND CHOKE LINKAGE

Every 12 months or 6000 miles, examine the carburetor linkage and choke plate for free movement. The choke plate action can generally be freed, if necessary, with the application of a solvent made for the purpose to the ends of the choke shaft. This solvent

will also clean grease and dirt from the throttle linkage.

COOLING SYSTEM

Once a month, the engine coolant level should be checked. On cars without a coolant recovery system, this should only be done when the engine is cold.

Remove the radiator cap, the coolant level should be about one inch below the radiator filler neck.

--- **CAUTION** ---

To avoid injury when working with a hot engine, cover the radiator cap with a thick cloth. Wear a heavy glove to protect your hand. Turn the radiator cap slowly to the first stop, and allow all the pressure to vent (indicated when the hissing noise stops). When the pressure has been released, remove the cap the rest of the way.

On cars with a coolant recovery tank, coolant should be visible within the tank; as long as the coolant is between the markings on the tank, the level is correct.

If coolant is needed, a 50/50 mix of ethylene glycol-based antifreeze and water should always be used, both winter and summer. This is imperative on cars with air conditioning; without the antifreeze, the heater core could freeze when the air conditioning is used. Add coolant to the radiator if the car does not have a coolant recovery system. Add coolant to the recovery tank on cars so equipped.

The radiator hoses and clamps and the radiator cap should be checked at the same time as the coolant level. Hoses which are brittle, cracked, or swollen should be replaced. Clamps should be checked for tightness (screwdriver tight only; do not allow the clamp to cut into the hose or crush the fitting). The radiator cap gasket should be checked for any obvious tears, cracks or swelling, or any signs of incorrect seating in the radiator neck.

The cooling system should be drained, flushed and refilled after the first 24 months or 24,000 miles, and every year thereafter.

1. Drain the radiator by opening the drain cock at the bottom. Some radiators do not have these; the lower radiator hose must be disconnected at the radiator instead. If the engine block has drain plugs, they should be opened to speed draining.

2. Close the drain cocks and fill the system with clear water. A cooling system flushing additive can be used, if desired.

3. Run the engine until it is hot. The heater should be turned on to its maximum heat position so that the core is flushed out.

4. Drain the system, then flush with water until it runs clear.

5. Clean out the coolant recovery tank, if equipped.

6. Fill the system with a 50/50 mix of ethylene glycol-based antifreeze and water. Fill the coolant recovery tank midway between the marks with this mixture also (except G.M. cars, which should be filled to the "Full Cold" mark).

7. Run the engine until it is hot, then let it cool and top up the radiator or coolant recovery tank as necessary with the anti-freeze/water mixture.

HEAT RISER

The heat riser is a thermostatically or vacuum operated valve in the exhaust manifold. (Not all cars have one.) It closes when the engine is warming up, to direct hot exhaust gases to the intake manifold, in order to preheat the incoming fuel/air mixture. If it sticks open, the result will be frequent stalling during warmup, especially in cold and damp weather. If it sticks shut, the result will be a rough idle after the engine is warm.

NOTE: Some 1981 and later GM engines are equipped with an electrically heated ceramic grid mounted below the carburetor which takes the place of a heat riser.

The heat riser should move freely. It can be checked easily when the engine is cold by giving the counterweight on the valve shaft a twirl, or pulling the vacuum rod to open and shut the valve. If the valve is sticking or binding, a quick shot of solvent made for the purpose will free it up. This solvent should be applied every

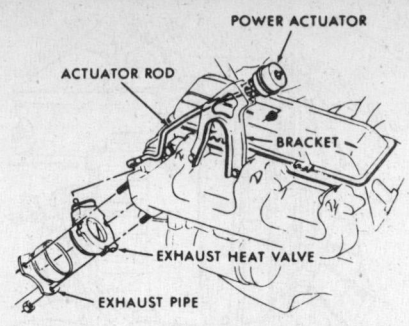

Exploded view of a vacuum-operated heat riser

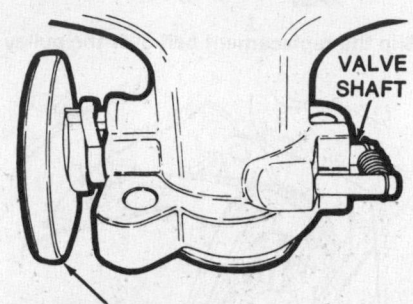

Thermostatically-operated heat control valve

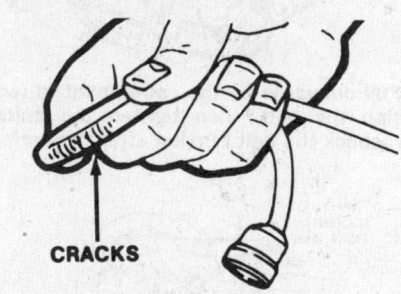

Inspect the ignition cables for cracks or breaks in the insulation

six months or 6000 miles to keep the valve free. If the valve is still stuck after application of the solvent, sometimes rapping the end of the shaft lightly with a hammer will break it loose. Otherwise, the components will have to be removed for further repairs.

IGNITION WIRES

The ignition system receives regular attention in the form of a tune-up, and thus is not covered here. But one of the most commonly overlooked components is the ignition cable, or spark plug wire.

Although they rarely show any visible signs of deterioration, the ignition cables should be checked at every tune-up, and replaced every 50,000 miles. Cracking and embrittlement

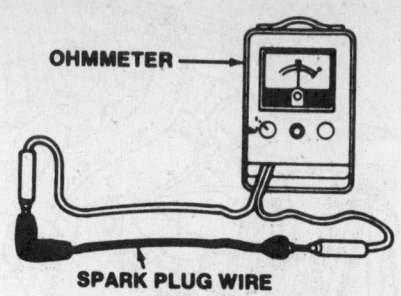

Test the ignition cables with an ohmmeter. Conventional ignition cables should be removed from the distributor cap, but electronic ignition wires should first be tested through the cap

Check the engine oil level with the dipstick

are of course obvious signs of wear, but most newer cables have silicone insulation and thus are not prone to display these conditions.

The most reliable way to check the cables is with an ohmmeter. On conventional ignitions, the resistance should be less than 7,000 ohms per foot (wire removed). On cars with electronic ignitions, it is generally recommended to leave the wire attached to the distributor cap, test with one lead from the ohmmeter connected to the corresponding terminal in the distributor cap, the other lead touched to the disconnected end of the cable at the spark plug. Then, if resistance seems close to the limit, remove the wire from the cap and retest. In general, the spark plug wires on electronic ignitions should be replaced if the total resistance is over 36,000 ohms. (50,000 ohms on Ford and Chrysler products).

Always replace the cables with new ones of the same type. Replace the wires one at a time, working from the longest to the shortest.

OIL LEVEL

The engine oil should be checked on a regular basis, ideally at each fuel stop, or once a week. It is best to check when the engine is at operating temperature, but checking the level immediately after shutting off the engine will give a false reading, because all of the oil will not yet have drained back into the crankcase. The car should be parked on a level surface to obtain an accurate reading.

1. Remove the oil dipstick. Wipe it clean, then replace it, seating it firmly.

2. Remove the dipstick again and hold it horizontally to prevent the oil from running. The level should be between the "Add" and "Full" marks on the dipstick. The dipstick may be marked "Add" and "Safe", or may have lines scribed on it; in any case, the oil level should be above the lower marking.

3. If the oil is below the lower mark, enough oil should be added to the engine to raise the level to the upper mark. The markings are usually spaced so that one-half to one quart of oil will raise the level from the "Add" mark to the "Full" mark. Oil is added through the capped opening in the valve cover. Only oils labeled SE or SF should be used; select a viscosity that will be compatible with the temperatures expected until the next drain interval.

NOTE: The diesel engines used in GM cars require the use of SF/CC or SF/CD type oils only. Do not use oil which is rated for SE or SF use only, or which is rated for CD use. Do not use the oil if the rating CD appears anywhere on the can, either alone or in combination with ratings other than SF, such as SE/CD. The use of CD type oil will void the manufacturer's warranty, and may cause expensive engine damage and leakage.

4. Replace the dipstick, then check the level again after any additions of oil. Be careful not to overfill, which will lead to leakage and seal damage.

POWER STEERING

The power steering fluid level is checked with a dipstick inserted into the pump reservoir. The dipstick may be attached to the reservoir cap, or inserted into a tube on the pump body. The level should be checked at every oil change. On all cars except Ford products, the level can be checked with the fluid either warm or cold; on Fords, the engine must be at operating temperature.

1. On Ford products, with the engine hot and idling, turn the steering wheel back and forth to the full right and full left stops several times, then center the wheels and shut off the engine.

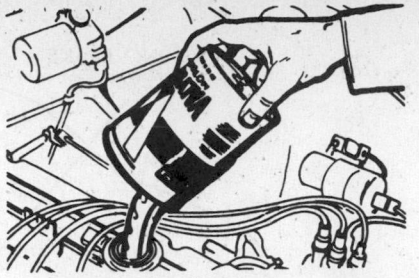

Add oil through the valve cover

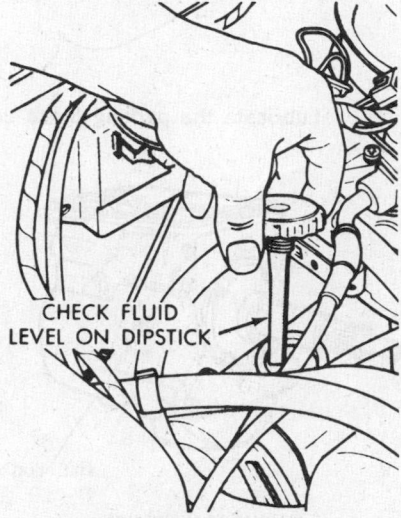

CHECK FLUID LEVEL ON DIPSTICK

The power steering level is checked with the dipstick installed in the reservoir

2. On all cars, with the engine off, pull or unscrew the dipstick and check the level. If the engine is warm, the level should be between the "Hot" and "Cold" marks on the dipstick; on Fords, the level should be between the "Cold Full" and "Hot Full" marks. If the engine is cold, the fluid should be between the "Add" and "Cold" marks; this does not apply to Ford products.

3. If the level is low, add power steering fluid until correct. Be careful not to overfill, which will cause fluid loss and seal damage.

WINDSHIELD WASHER FLUID

Check the fluid level in the windshield washer tank at every oil level check. The fluid can be mixed in a 50% solution with water, if desired, as long as temperatures remain above freezing. Below freezing, the fluid should be used full strength. Never add engine coolant antifreeze to the washer fluid, because it will damage the car's paint.

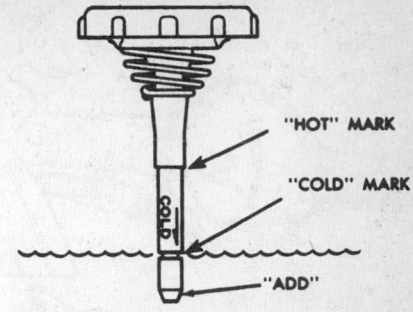

"HOT" MARK
"COLD" MARK
"ADD"

Power steering dipstick markings, typical of all types except Ford

Under Car

AXLE

The fluid level in the drive axle should be checked every 12 months or 12,000 miles. On the front wheel drive Omni, Horizon, Aries, Reliant LeBaron and Dodge 400 with automatic transmission, the drive axle lubricant is separate from the automatic fluid and must be checked separately. The level can be checked through the fill plug in the drive axle housing.

On the American Motors Eagle, SX/4 and Kammback, both drive axles should be checked. Both assemblies have fill plugs for this purpose.

1. With the car parked on a level surface, remove the filler plug. The plug can be found either in the rear cover of the differential, or on the front of the pinion housing.

2. If lubricant dribbles out when the plug is removed, the level is correct. Otherwise, stick in your finger (watch out for sharp threads); the fluid should be even with or just a little below the filler hole.

3. If lubricant is needed, use SAE 80W-90 GL-5 gear oil (SAE 80W GL-5 in very cold climates) to fill standard axles. Limited slip axles require a special lubricant, available in auto parts stores. The Omni, Horizon, Aries, Reliant Dodge 400 and LeBaron drive axles should be filled with DEXRON II ATF fluid.

4. When the level is correct, install the plug and tighten until snug. Do not overtighten.

Drive axles should be drained and refilled according to the manufacturer's maintenance schedule, usually found in the owner's manual. If the unit is used in severe driving conditions (trailer towing, etc.) the lubricant should be changed more often. Some later model drive axles do not require regular draining and refilling. Refer to the owner's manual for information on this subject. The axle may be drained by removing the drain

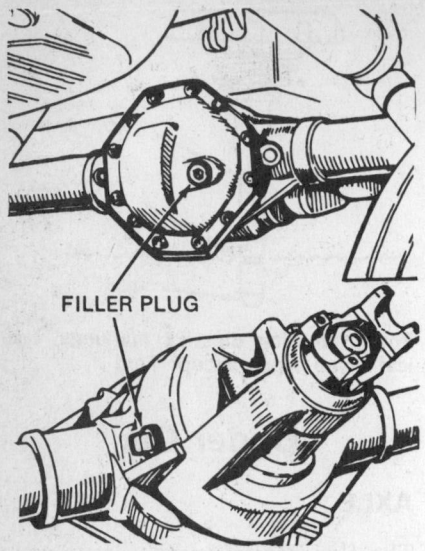

FILLER PLUG

Rear axle filler plug locations

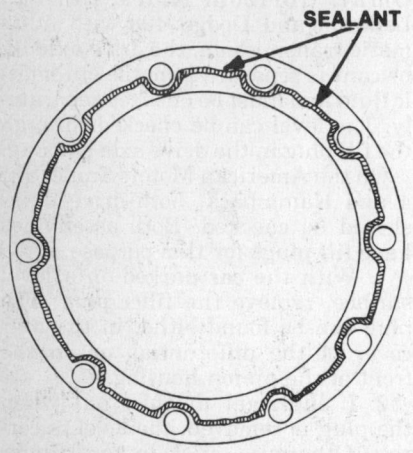

SEALANT

Apply a bead of silicone sealer to the rear cover if no gasket is used

plug at the bottom of the axle housing, if present. Otherwise the rear cover (if equipped) must be removed or a suction gun used through the filler hole. Always use silicone sealer or a gasket when re-installing the rear cover. Run sealer around the insides of the bolt holes. Tighten the bolts a few turns at a time in a crisscross pattern.

EXHAUST SYSTEM

The exhaust system should be checked twice a year for general soundness. Inspect the pipes for holes, broken welds, leaking seams, or loose connections. Leaks at connections can sometimes be successfully repaired with the use of a commercial exhaust pipe sealer, but holes or breaks warrant replacement of the part. The exhaust pipe hangers and straps should be examined for any breaks or cracks;

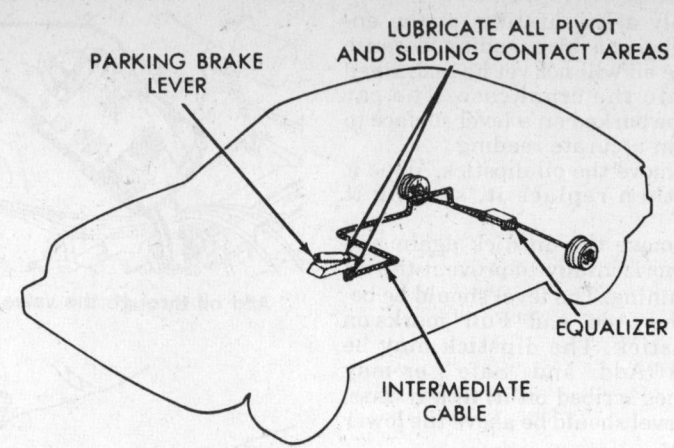

PARKING BRAKE LEVER

LUBRICATE ALL PIVOT AND SLIDING CONTACT AREAS

EQUALIZER

INTERMEDIATE CABLE

Lubricate the parking brake cable with white waterproof grease

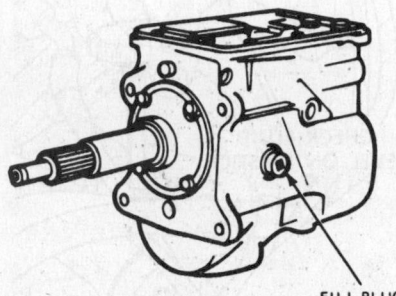

FILL PLUG

MANUAL TRANSMISSION
FILL TO BOTTOM OF FILLER HOLE WITH VEHICLE ON LEVEL GROUND.

Typical manual transmission filler plug location

replace these as necessary. Some slight cracking of rubber hangers is normal, but deep cracks or cuts are cause for replacement.

CAUTION

Check the exhaust system only when it is cold. The temperature on an exhaust system using a catalytic converter can reach 1000°F after only a short period of engine operation.

MANUAL TRANSMISSION OR MANUAL TRANSAXLE

The fluid level in the manual transmission (or transaxle on front wheel drive cars) should be checked twice a year, or every 6000 miles.

1. Park the car on a level surface. The transmission should be cool to the touch.

2. Remove the filler plug from the side of the transmission or transaxle. If lubricant trickles out as the plug is removed, the fluid level is correct. If not, stick in your finger (watch out for

sharp threads); the lubricant should be right up to the edge of the filler hole.

3. If lubricant is needed, use SAE 80W-90 GL-5 gear lubricant (SAE 80W GL-5 in extremely cold climates) in manual transmission.

Front wheel drive transaxles use different lubricants. The Omni and Horizon with the A412 transaxle (starter on the radiator side of the engine) require GL-4 hypoid gear lubricant; the same SAE viscosities apply (80W-90 or 80W; 75W in temperatures below -30°F). GL-5 classification lubricants are specifically not recommended. Omnis and Horizons with the A460 transaxle (starter on the firewall side of the engine), and all Aries, Reliant LeBaron and Dodge 400 models use DEXRON II automatic transmission fluid.

The front wheel drive Citation, Omega, Phoenix, Skylark Cavalier, J2000, Cimarron, Celebrity, Cierra and 6000 require DEXRON II automatic transmission fluid. The use of a manual transmission lubricant is specifically not recommended.

The Ford Escort, EXP, and Mercury Lynx and LN-7 use Ford Type F automatic transmission fluid. The use of a manual transmission lubricant is specifically not recommended.

4. When the level is correct, install the filler plug and tighten until snug.

PARKING BRAKE LINKAGE

The parking brake cable assembly should be inspected twice a year for fraying, kinks, and binding. A smooth white waterproof lubricant should be applied at the same time to all pivot points and areas in sliding contact.

SUSPENSION LUBRICATION

Depending on the year of manufacture, there may be as many as twelve grease fittings on the suspension parts, or as few as two. Typical locations for grease nipples are on the ball joints, control arm pivot points, steering linkage, and the tie-rod ends.

Lubricate these fittings with a small hand operated grease gun filled with EP chassis lubricant. Pump grease into the fitting slowly, until it begins to ooze out around the joint, or until the grease begins to expand the rubber boot around the fitting. Be extremely careful not to rupture any seals or boots, as this will lead to lubricant loss and contamination of the parts involved.

Occasionally, the grease nipples may become clogged with dirt or hardened grease. If so, unscrew them with a wrench of the proper size and clean them out with solvent. When reinstalled, they may be covered with plastic caps made for the purpose, or a piece of aluminum foil.

The chassis and suspension parts should be lubricated once a year, or every 7500 miles, whichever comes first.

TRANSFER CASE

If you have a four-wheel drive AMC car, you should check the transfer case lubricant level every 5000 miles.

1. Park the car on a level surface.
2. Check the build date tag on the rear of the transfer case.
3. If the transfer case was built after March 1980, the fill plug will be at location "A" in the illustration. Remove the fill plug. The lubricant should be right up to the edge of the filler hole. Check and correct as necessary.
4. If the transfer case was built before March, 1980, the filler plug may be in any one of the four locations shown in the illustration. Check to see which one you have, then remove the filler plug. Use a length of wire to measure the distance from the bottom edge of the fill hole to the lubricant. The correct distance depends on the location of the hole:
   • "A" 0.56 inch
   • "B" 1.13 inch
   • "C" 1.20 inch
   • "D" 0.56 inch
5. The correct fluid to use is 10W-30 SE or SF motor oil. Capacity is 4.0 pints, regardless of when the transfer case was built. Some early owner's manuals may have listed the capacity as 3.0 pints, but this is incorrect; revised publications call for a capacity of 4.0 pints.

The transfer case should be drained and refilled every 15,000 miles. The drain plug is located at the lower edge of the rear face of the case. Installation torque for the plugs is 18 ft. lbs. The case is made from aluminum, so this figure should not be exceeded.

Exterior

DRAIN HOLES AND UNDERBODY

Most cars have drain holes spaced along the lower edge of the rocker panels and doors. These holes should be cleared of any debris or rust twice a year. A small screwdriver can be used to open plugged drain holes.

Every spring, the underbody should be flushed with clear water to remove deposits of mud, road salt, and debris. It is advisable to loosen any packed-in sediment before flushing to assure a more thorough cleaning.

HINGES AND LOCKS

Once a year, the door, hood, and trunk hinges, and all locks should be lubricated to ensure smooth operation. The hinge points should be lightly oiled. Lock cylinders may be easily lubricated with a shot of silicone spray directed into the keyhole. Silicone lubricant also works well on the door latch mechanisms, and keeps the door, trunk, and window weather seals pliable when applied in a light film.

TIRES

Tires should be checked weekly for proper air pressure. A chart, located either in the glove compartment or on the driver's or passenger's door, gives the recommended inflation pressures. Maximum fuel economy and tire life will result if the pressure is maintained at the highest figure given on the chart.

Pressures should be checked before driving since pressure can increase as much as six pounds per square inch (psi) due to heat buildup. It is a good idea to have your own accurate pressure gauge, because not all gauges on service station air pumps can be trusted. When checking pressures, do not neglect the spare tire. Note that some spare tires require pressures considerably higher than those used in the other tires.

While you are about the task of checking air pressure, inspect the tire treads for cuts, bruises and other damage. Check the air valves to be sure that they are tight. Replace any missing valve caps.

Check the tires for uneven wear that might indicate the need for front end alignment or tire rotation. Tires

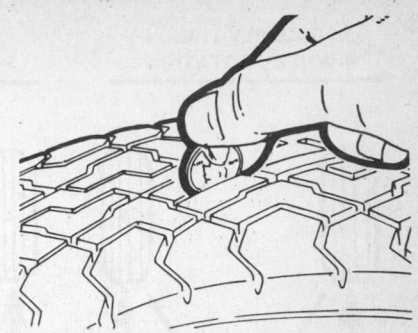

Tire tread depth can be checked with a penny. If the top of Lincoln's head is visible, the tires are due for replacement

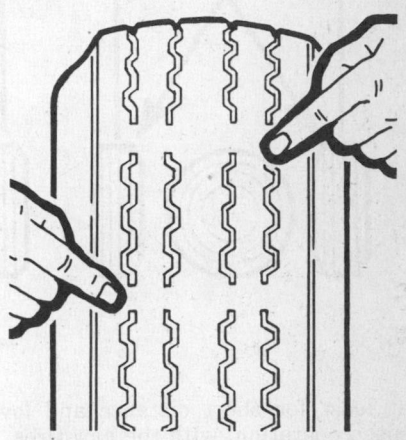

Tread wear indicators will appear as a band across the tire when the tread has worn out.

should be replaced when a tread wear indicator appears as a solid band across the tread.

When buying new tires, give some thought to the following points, especially if you are considering a switch to larger tires or a different profile series:

1. All four tires must be of the same construction type. This rule cannot be violated. Radial, bias, and bias-belted tires must not be mixed.
2. The wheels should be the correct width for the tire. Tire dealers have charts of tire and rim compatibility. A mismatch will cause sloppy handling and rapid tire wear. The tread width should match the rim width (inside bead to inside bead) within an inch. For radial tires, the rim width should be 80% or less of the tire (not tread) width.
3. The height (mounted diameter) of the new tires can change speedometer accuracy, engine speed at a given road speed, fuel mileage, acceleration, and ground clearance. Tire manufacturers furnish full measurement specifications.
4. The spare tire should be usable,

BIAS PLY TIRE 4-WHEEL ROTATION	BIAS PLY TIRE 5-WHEEL ROTATION	RADIAL PLY TIRES 4-WHEEL ROTATION	RADIAL PLY TIRES 5-WHEEL ROTATION

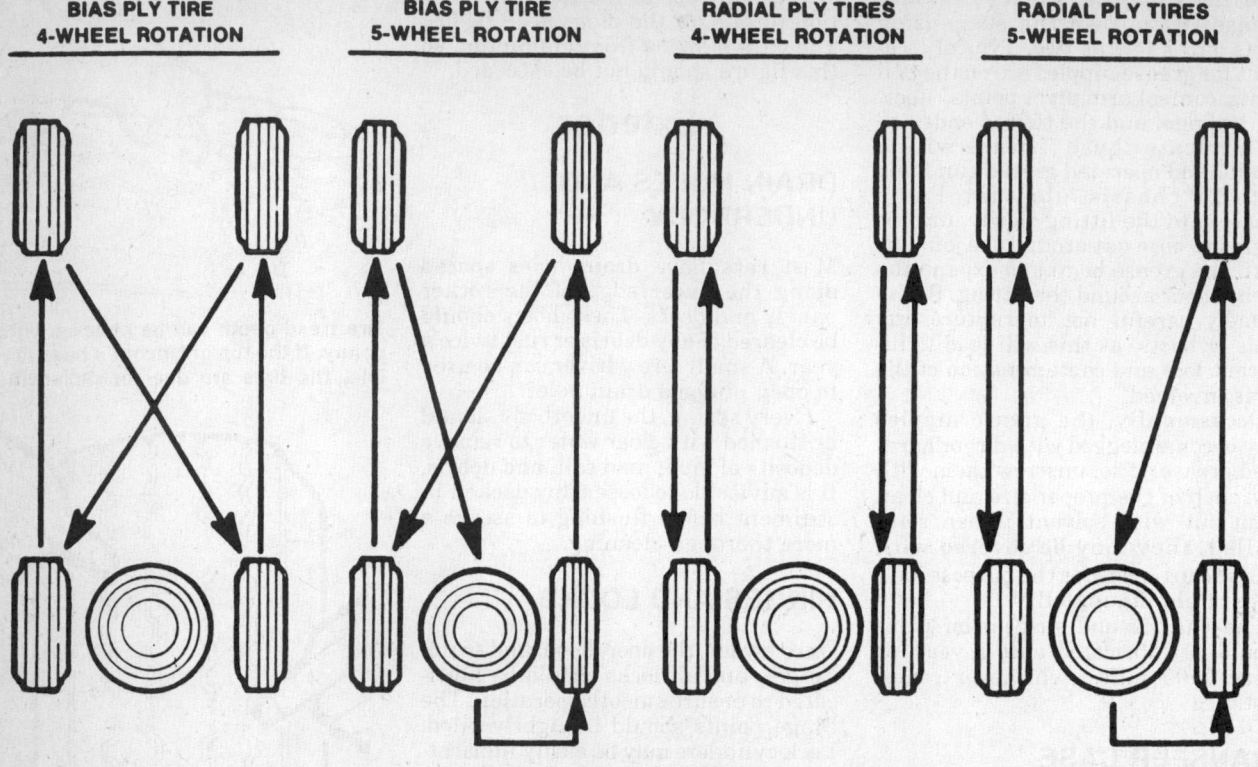

Tire rotation diagrams

at least for short distance and low speed operation, with the new tires.

5. There shouldn't be any body interference when loaded, on bumps, or in turns.

Tire Rotation

Tire rotation is recommended every 6000 miles or so, to obtain maximum tire wear. The pattern you use depends on whether or not your car has a usable spare. Radial tires should not be cross-switched (from one side of the car to the other); they last longer if their direction of rotation is not changed. Snow tires sometimes have directional arrows molded into the side of the carcass; the arrow shows the direction of rotation. They will wear very rapidly if the rotation is reversed. Studded tires will lose their studs if their rotational direction is reversed.

NOTE: Mark the wheel position or direction of rotation on radial tires or studded snow tires before removing them.

Storage

Store the tires at the proper inflation pressure if they are mounted on wheels. Keep them in a cool dry place, laid on their sides. If the tires are stored in the garage or basement, do not let them stand on a concrete floor; set them on strips of wood.

WINDSHIELD WIPERS AND WASHERS

For maximum effectiveness and longest element life, the windshield and wiper blades should be kept clean. Dirt, tree sap, road tar and so on will cause streaking, smearing and blade deterioration if left on the glass. It is advisable to wash the windshield carefully with a commercial glass cleaner at least once a month. Wipe off the rubber blades with the wet rag afterwards.

For access to the blades on wiper systems which park below the hood line, turn the ignition key to "On" and run the wipers to the center of the windshield. Shut the wipers off with the ignition key, not the wiper switch. Do not attempt to move the wipers by hand; damage to the motor and drive mechanism will result.

If the blades are found to be cracked, broken or torn, they should be replaced immediately. Replacement intervals will vary with usage, although ozone deterioration usually limits blade life to about one year. If the wiper pattern is smeared or streaked, or if the blade chatters across the glass, the elements should be replaced. It is easiest and most sensible to replace the elements in pairs.

There are basically three different types of refills, which differ in their

method of replacement. One type has two release buttons, approximately one-third of the way up from the ends of the blade frame. Pushing the buttons down releases a lock and allows the rubber filler to be removed from the frame. The new filler slides back into the frame and locks in place.

The second type of refill has two metal tabs which are unlocked by squeezing them together. The rubber filler can then be withdrawn from the frame jaws. A new refill is installed by inserting the refill into the front frame jaws and sliding it rearward to engage the remaining frame jaws. There are usually four jaws; be certain when installing that the refill is engaged in all of them. At the end of its travel, the tabs will lock into place on the front jaws of the wiper blade frame.

The third type is a refill made from polycarbonate. The refill has a simple locking device at one end which flexes downward out of the groove into which the jaws of the holder fit, allowing easy release. By sliding the new refill through all the jaws and pushing through the slight resistance when it reaches the end of its travel, the refill will lock into position.

Regardless of the type of refill used, make sure that all of the frame jaws are engaged as the refill is pushed into place and locked. The metal blade holder and frame will scratch the glass if allowed to touch it.

TRICO

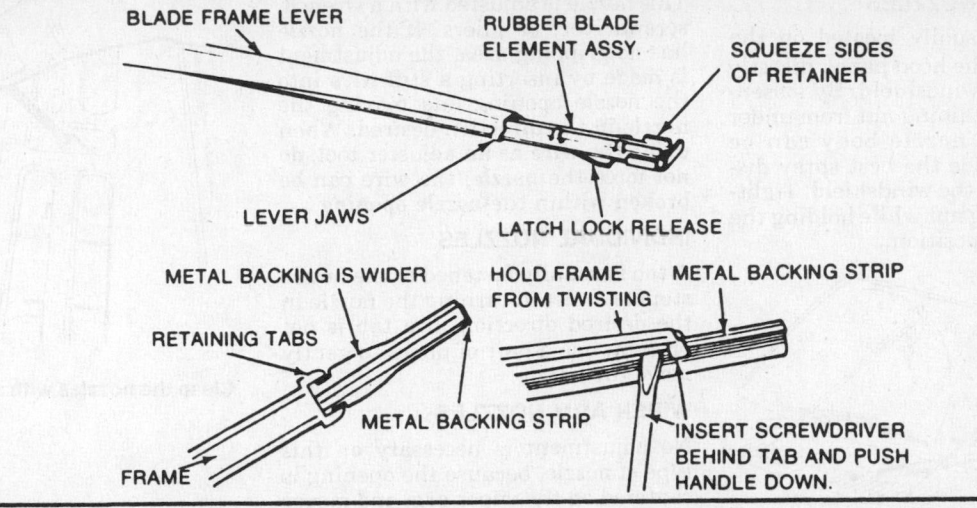

BLADE FRAME LEVER

RUBBER BLADE ELEMENT ASSY.

SQUEEZE SIDES OF RETAINER

LEVER JAWS

LATCH LOCK RELEASE

METAL BACKING IS WIDER

HOLD FRAME FROM TWISTING

METAL BACKING STRIP

RETAINING TABS

METAL BACKING STRIP

FRAME

INSERT SCREWDRIVER BEHIND TAB AND PUSH HANDLE DOWN.

ANCO

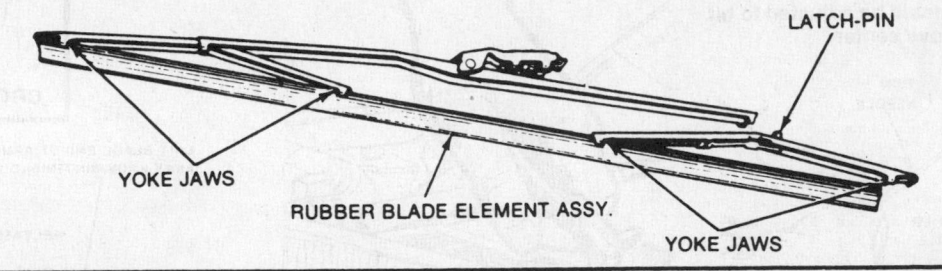

LATCH-PIN

YOKE JAWS

RUBBER BLADE ELEMENT ASSY.

YOKE JAWS

POLYCARBONATE

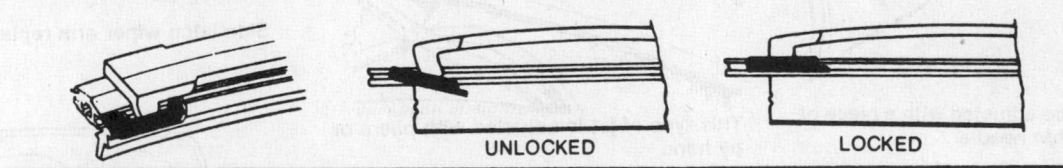

UNLOCKED

LOCKED

TRIDON

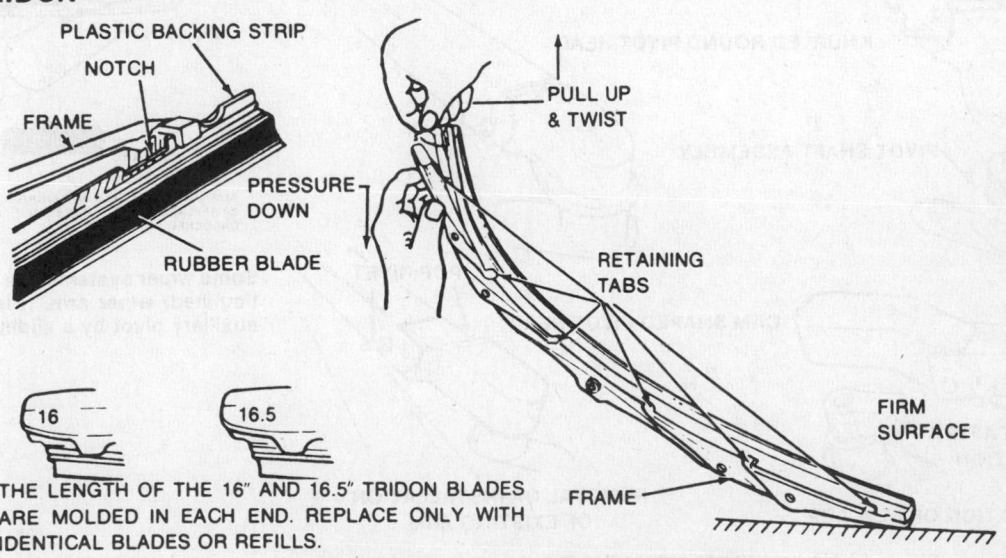

PLASTIC BACKING STRIP

NOTCH

FRAME

PULL UP & TWIST

PRESSURE DOWN

RETAINING TABS

RUBBER BLADE

FIRM SURFACE

16

16.5

FRAME

THE LENGTH OF THE 16" AND 16.5" TRIDON BLADES ARE MOLDED IN EACH END. REPLACE ONLY WITH IDENTICAL BLADES OR REFILLS.

Windshield wiper blade replacement methods

Washer Nozzle Adjustment

CENTERED SINGLE POST — NON-ADJUSTABLE NOZZLES

This type is usually located on the rear center of the hood panel, directly in front of the windshield. By loosening the body retaining nut from under the hood, the nozzle body can be turned to provide the best spray discharge to cover the windshield. Tighten the retaining nut while holding the nozzle body in position.

CENTERED SINGLE POST — ADJUSTABLE NOZZLES

This nozzle is adjusted with a wrench, screwdriver, or pliers. If the nozzle has no gripping area, the adjustment is made by inserting a stiff wire into the nozzle opening and moving the nozzle in the direction desired. When using the wire as an adjuster tool, do not force the nozzle; the wire can be broken within the nozzle opening.

INDIVIDUAL NOZZLES

A tab is usually fastened to the nozzle stem to assist in turning the nozzle in the desired direction. If a tab is not present, use a pair of pliers to gently move the nozzle.

WIPER ARM NOZZLES

No adjustment is necessary on this type of nozzle, because the opening is centered on the wiper arm and moves along with the arm.

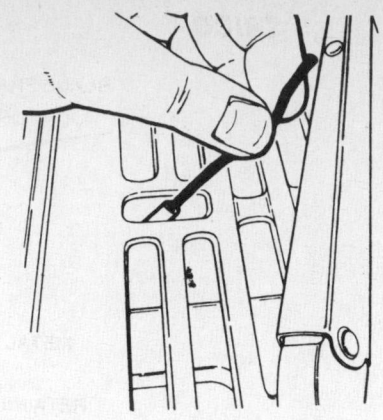

Clean the nozzles with a piece of fine wire

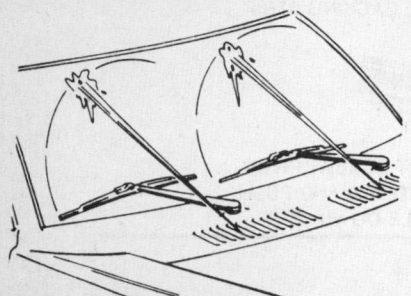

Washer nozzles should be adjusted to hit the windshield above center

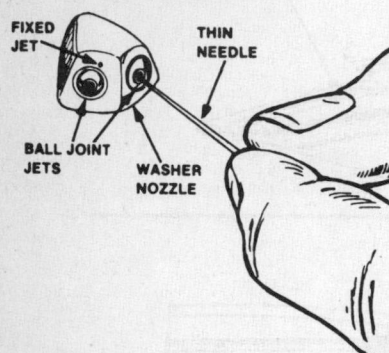

FIXED JET
THIN NEEDLE
BALL JOINT JETS
WASHER NOZZLE

Some jets can be adjusted with a piece of fine wire or a thin needle

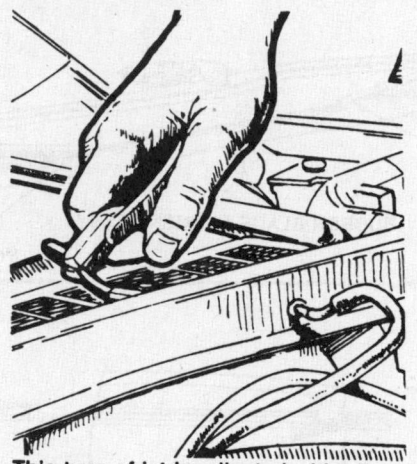

This type of jet is adjusted with pliers or by hand

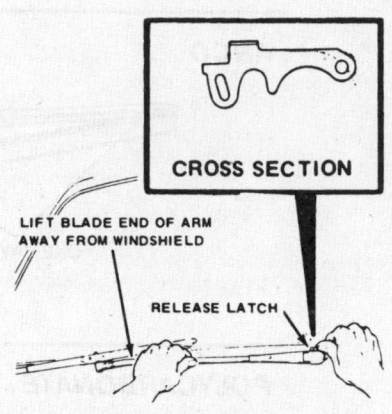

CROSS SECTION
LIFT BLADE END OF ARM AWAY FROM WINDSHIELD
RELEASE LATCH

Side latch wiper arm replacement

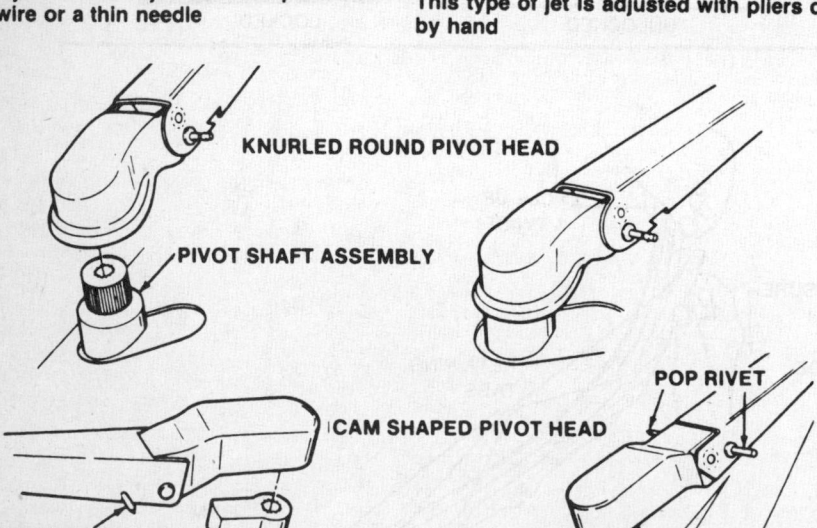

KNURLED ROUND PIVOT HEAD
PIVOT SHAFT ASSEMBLY
CAM SHAPED PIVOT HEAD
POP RIVET
REMOVE PIN AFTER INSTALLATION
INSTALLATION OF NEW ARM
REMOVAL OR INSTALLATION OF EXISTING ARM

Pin and hole type wiper arm replacement

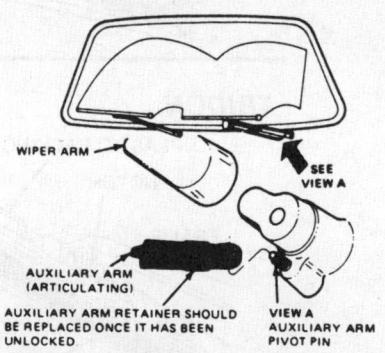

WIPER ARM
SEE VIEW A
AUXILIARY ARM (ARTICULATING)
AUXILIARY ARM RETAINER SHOULD BE REPLACED ONCE IT HAS BEEN UNLOCKED
VIEW A AUXILIARY ARM PIVOT PIN

Some wiper systems use an auxiliary (articulated) wiper arm. It is secured to an auxiliary pivot by a sliding lock.

Tools and Equipment

In addition to the normal assortment of screwdrivers and pliers, automotive service work requires an investment in wrenches, sockets and the handles needed to drive them, and various measuring tools such as torque wrenches and feeler gauges.

The best approach to gathering the required equipment is to proceed slowly, buying high-quality tools as they are needed. An initial investment should be made in a set of quality wrenches, ranging in size from $\frac{1}{4}$ inch to one inch, if your car has standard bolts, or from 5mm to 19mm if your car has metric fasteners. High quality forged wrenches are available in three styles; open end, box end, and combination open/box end. The combination tools are generally the most desirable as a starter set; the wrenches shown in the illustration are of the combination type.

NOTE: Many later model American cars use both metric and standard nuts and bolts.

The other set of tools inevitably required is a ratchet handle and socket set. This set should have the same size range as your wrench set. The ratchet, extension, and flex drives fro the sockets are available in many sizes; it is advisable to choose a $\frac{3}{8}$ inch drive set initially. One break in the inch/metric sizing war is that metric-sized sockets sold in the U.S. have inch-sized drive ($\frac{1}{4}$, $\frac{3}{8}$, $\frac{1}{2}$, etc.). Sockets are available in six and twelve point versions; six point types are generally cheaper and are a good choice for a first set.

The choice of a drive handle for the sockets should be made with some care. If this is your first set, take the plunge and invest in a flexhead ratchet; it will get into many places otherwise accessible only through a long chain of universal joints, extensions and adapters. An alternative is a flex handle; such a tool is shown in the illustration, below the ratchet handle. In addition to the range of sockets mentioned, a rubber-lined spark plug socket should be purchased. Spark plugs have either a $\frac{13}{16}$ or a $\frac{5}{8}$ inch hex; get the correct socket for the plugs in your car.

The most important thing to consider when purchasing hand tools is quality. Don't be misled by the low cost of "bargain" tools. Forged wrenches, tempered screwdriver blades, and fine tooth ratchets are a much better investment than their less expensive counterparts. The skinned knuckles and frustration inflicted by poor quality tools make any job an unhappy core. Another consideration is that quality tools sold by reputable firms come with an on-the-spot replacement guarantee; if the tool breaks, you get a new one, no questions asked.

The tools needed for basic maintenance jobs, in addition to those just mentioned, include:

1. Jackstands, for support;
2. Oil filter wrench;
3. Oil filler spout or funnel;
4. Grease gun;
5. Battery hydrometer;
6. Battery post and clamp cleaner;
7. Container for draining oil;
8. Many rags for the inevitable spills.

In addition to these items there are several others which are not absolutely necessary, but handy to have around. These include a transmission funnel and filler tube, a drop (trouble) light on a long cord, an adjustable wrench (crescent wrench), and slip joint pliers.

A more extensive list of tools, suitable for tune-up work, can be drawn up easily. While the tools involved are slightly more sophisticated, they need not be outrageously expensive. For example, there are several inexpensive tach/dwell meters on the market that are every bit as good for the average mechanic as a $100.00 professional model. The key to these purchases is to make them with an eye towards adaptability and wide range. Using the tach/dwell meter example again, if the model you buy runs up to at least 1,500 rpm on the tachometer scale, the dwell meter works on 4, 6, or 8 cylinder engines, and the tachometer unit is adaptable to both conventional and electronic ignitions, it will serve for a long time on a variety of automobiles. A basic list of tune-up tools could include:

1. A tach/dwell meter;
2. Spark plug gauge and gapping tool;
3. Feeler blades;
4. Timing light.

In this list, the choice of a timing light should be made carefully. A light which works on the DC current supplied by the car battery is the best choice; it should have a xenon tube for brightness. If your car has electronic ignition, the light should have an inductive pick-up (the timing light illustrated has one of these), and since nearly all cars will have electronic ignition in the future, this feature is a reasonable one to look for.

In addition to these basic tools, there are several other tools and gauges you may find useful. These include:

1. A compression gauge. The screw-in type is slower to use, but eliminates the possibility of a faulty reading due to escaping pressure.
2. A manifold vacuum gauge.
3. A test light.
4. An induction meter. This is used

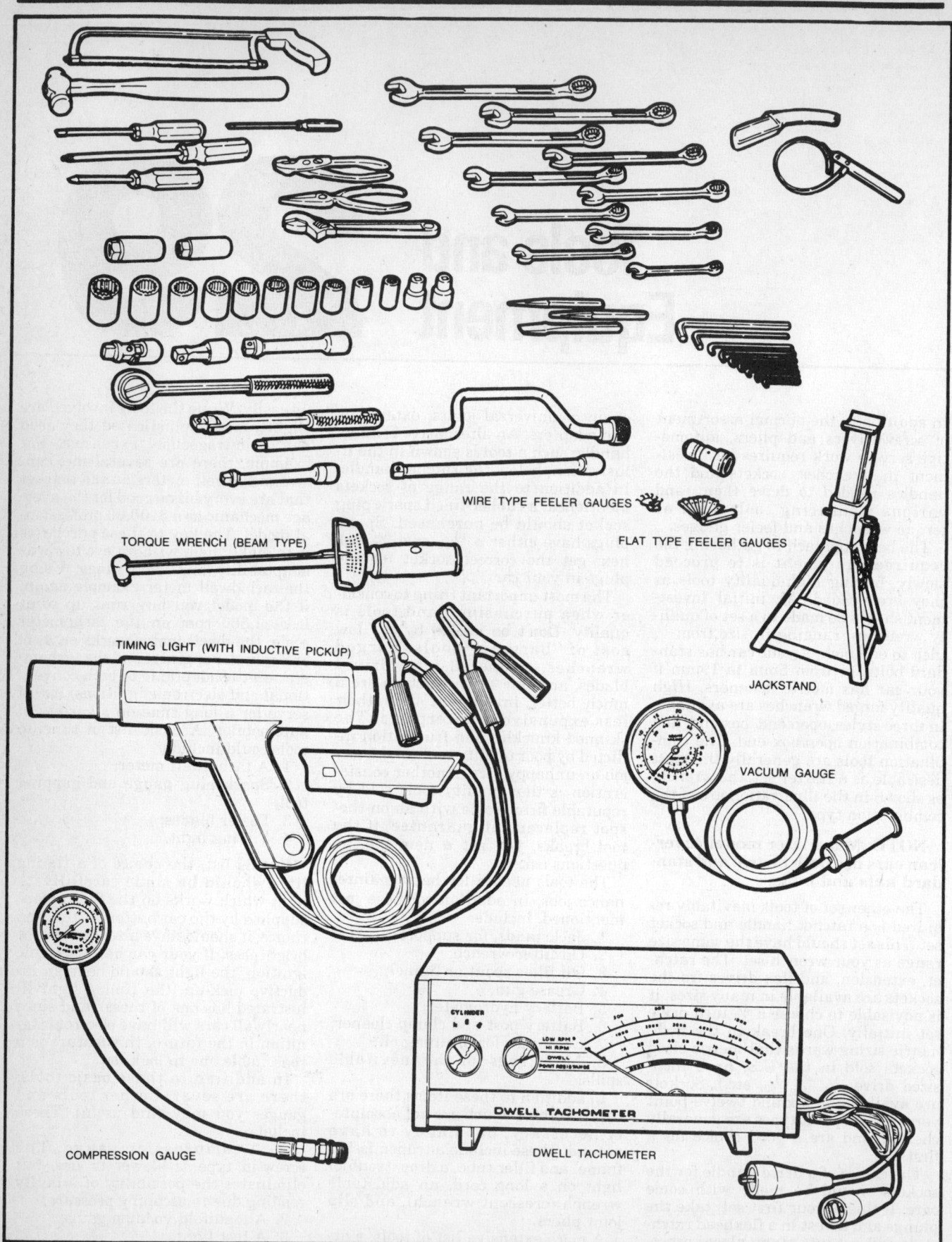

WIRE TYPE FEELER GAUGES

FLAT TYPE FEELER GAUGES

TORQUE WRENCH (BEAM TYPE)

JACKSTAND

TIMING LIGHT (WITH INDUCTIVE PICKUP)

VACUUM GAUGE

COMPRESSION GAUGE

CYLINDER

LOW RPM
HI RPM

DWELL
POINT RESISTANCE

DWELL TACHOMETER

DWELL TACHOMETER

A basic tool collection will handle almost any automotive repair work

to determine whether or not there is current flowing in a wire, and thus is extremely helpful in electrical troubleshooting.

Finally, you will probably find a torque wrench necessary for all but in the most basic of work. The beam type models are perfectly adequate, although the newer click (break-away) type are more precise. Whichever type you choose, plan on having it recalibrated every once in a while.

Special Tools

Several procedures in this manual refer to special tools needed to make repairs or adjustments. These tools can be purchased from the following companies:

AMC, GM
Special Tool Division
Kent-Moore Corp.
29784 Little Mack
Roseville, MI 48066

Ford
Owatonna Tool Co.
Owatonna, MN 55060

Chrysler
Miller Special Tools
A Division of Utica Tool Co.
32615 Park Lane
Garden City, MI 48135

SPECIAL TEST EQUIPMENT

A variety of diagnostic tools are available to help troubleshoot and repair computerized engine and emission control systems. The most sophisticated of these devices are the console-type engine analyzers that usually occupy a garage service bay, but there are several types of aftermarket electronic testers available that will allow quick circuit tests of the engine control system by plugging directly into a special test connector located in the engine compartment or under the dashboard. Several tool and equipment manufacturers offer simple, hand-held testers that measure various circuit voltage levels on command to check all system components for proper operation. Although these testers usually cost about $300–500, consider that the average computer-controlled carburetor can cost twice as much and the money saved by not replacing perfectly good sensors in an attempt to correct a problem could justify the purchase price of a special diagnostic tester.

These testers can allow quick and easy test measurements while the en-

Aftermarket hand-held testers can make diagnosing computer-controlled systems easier

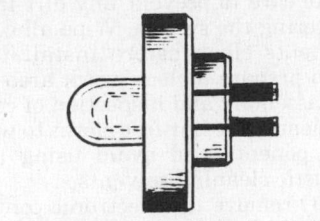

Throttle body fuel injector tester

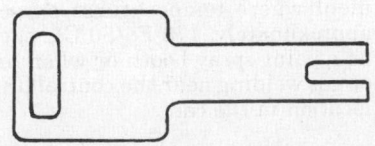

Special key for activating GM on-board diagnosis system. Insert the prongs into the diagnostic test terminals located under the dash

gine is operating or while the car is being driven. In addition, the on-board computer memory can be read to access any stored trouble codes; in effect allowing the computer to tell you where it hurts and aid trouble diagnosis by pinpointing exactly which circuit or component is malfunctioning. In the same manner, repairs can be tested to make sure the problem has been corrected. The biggest advantage these special testers have is their relatively easy hookups that minimize or eliminate the chances of making the wrong connections and getting false voltage readings or damaging the on-board computer.

NOTE: It should be remembered that these testers check voltage levels in circuits; they don't detect mechanical problems or failed components if the circuit voltage falls within the preprogrammed limits stored in the tester PROM unit. Also, most of the

hand-held testes are designed to work only on one or two systems made by a specific manufacturer.

A variety of aftermarket testers are available to help diagnose different computerized engine control systems. Owatonna Tool Company (OTC), for example, markets a device called the OTC Monitor 2000 which plugs directly into the assembly line diagnostic link (ALDL). When the correct manufacturer cartridge is plugged into the unit, the OTC tester makes diagnosis a simple matter of pressing the correct buttons. An adapter is supplied with the tester to allow connection to all types of ALDL links, regardless of the number of pin terminals used.

Servicing Your Car Safely

It is virtually impossible to anticipate all of the hazards involved with automotive maintenance and service, but care and common sense will prevent most accidents. The rules of safety for mechanics range from "don't smoke around gasoline," to "use the proper tool for the job." The trick to avoiding injuries is to develop safe work habits and take every possible precaution.

Any computer-based electronic engine control system is extremely sensitive to electrical voltages and cannot tolerate careless or haphazard testing or service procedures. An inexperienced individual can literally do major damage looking for a minor problem by using the wrong kind of test equipment or connecting test leads or connectors with the ignition switch ON. When selecting test equipment, make sure the manufacturers instructions state that the tester is compatible with whatever type of electronic control system is being serviced. Read all instructions carefully and double check all test points before installing probes or making any connections.

Aftermarket electronic testers are available from a variety of sources, as well as from the manufacturer, but care should be taken that the test equipment being used is designed to diagnose a particular system accurately without damaging the control unit (ECU) or components being tested.

DO'S

• DO keep a fire extinguisher and first aid kit within easy reach.
• DO wear safety glasses or goggles when cutting, drilling, grinding or prying, even if you have 20-20 vi-

sion. If you wear glasses for the sake of vision, they should be made of hardened glass that can serve also as safety glasses, or wear safety goggles over your regular glasses.

• DO shield your eyes whenever you work around the battery. Batteries contain sulphuric acid. In case of contact with the eyes or skin, flush the area with water or a mixture of water and baking soda and get medical attention immediately.

• DO remove the battery cables before charging the battery. Never use a high-output charger on an installed battery or attempt to use any type of "hot shot" (24 volt) starting aid.

• DO use safety stands for any undercar service. Jacks are for raising vehicles; safety stands are for making sure the vehicle stays raised until you want it to come down. Whenever the car is raised, block the wheels remaining on the ground and set the parking brake.

• DO use adequate ventilation when working with any chemicals or hazardous materials. Follow the manufacturer's directions for usage. Brake fluid, anti-freeze, solvents, paints, etc. are all deadly poisons if taken internally. Seal the containers tightly after use and store them safely, out of the reach of children.

• DO use caution when working on clutches or brakes. The asbestos used in the friction material will cause lung cancer if inhaled. Wipe the component with a damp rag to remove dust, and dispose of the rag after use.

• DO disconnect the negative battery cable when working on the electrical system. The secondary ignition system can contain up to 40,000 volts.

• DO properly maintain your tools. Loose hammerheads, mushroomed punches and chisels, frayed or poorly grounded electrical cords, excessively worn screwdrivers, spread open-end wrenches, cracked sockets, slipping ratchets, or faulty droplight sockets can cause accidents.

• DO use the proper size and type of tool for the job being done.

• DO when possible, pull on a wrench handle rather than push on it, and adjust your stance to prevent a fall.

• DO be sure that adjustable

wrenches are tightly closed on the nut or bolt and pulled so that the face is on the side of the fixed jaw.

• DO select a wrench or socket that fits the nut or bolt. The wrench or socket should sit straight, not cocked.

• DO strike squarely with a hammer; avoid glancing blows.

• DO set the parking brake and block the drive wheels if the work requires the engine running.

• DO depressurize the fuel system before attempting to disconnect any fuel lines. Although only fuel injection vehicles use a pressurized fuel system, it's a good idea to exercise caution whenever disconnecting any fuel line or hose during service procedures. Take precautions to avoid a fire hazard.

• DO use clean rags and tools when working on an open fuel system and take care to prevent any dirt from entering the system. Wipe all components clean before installation and prepare a clean work area for disassembly and inspection of components. Use lint-free cloths to wipe components and avoid using any caustic cleaning solvents.

• DO remove the electronic control unit (on-board computer) if the vehicle is to be placed in an environment where temperatures exceed approximately 176°F (80°C), such as a paint spray booth or when arc or gas welding near the control unit location in the car.

DON'TS

• DON'T run an engine in a garage or anywhere else without proper ventilation—EVER! Carbon monoxide is poisonous; it takes a long time to leave the human body and you can build up a deadly supply of it in your system by simply breathing in a little every day. You may not realize you are slowly poisoning yourself. Always use power vents, windows, fans or open the garage doors.

• DON'T work around moving parts while wearing a necktie or other loose clothing. Short sleeves are much safer than long, loose sleeves; hard-toed shoes with neoprene soles protect your toes and give a better grip on slippery surfaces. Jewelry such as watches, rings, fancy belt buckles, beads or body adornment

of any kind is not safe working around a car. Long hair should be hidden under a hat or cap.

• DON'T use pockets for toolboxes. A fall or bump can drive a screwdriver deep into your body. Even a wiping cloth hanging from the back pocket can wrap around a spinning shaft or fan.

• DON'T smoke when working around gasoline, cleaning solvent or other flammable material.

• DON'T use gasoline to wash your hands; there are excellent soaps available. Gasoline may contain lead, and lead can enter the body through a cut, accumulating in the body until you are very ill. Gasoline also removes all the natural oils from the skin so that bone dry hands will suck up oil and grease.

• DON'T service the air conditioning system unless you are equipped with the necessary tools and training. The refrigerant, R-12, is extremely cold when compressed, and when released into the air will instantly freeze any surface it contacts, including your eyes. Although the refrigerant is normally non-toxic, R-12 becomes a deadly poisonous gas in the presence of an open flame. One good whiff of the vapors from burning refrigerant can be fatal.

• DON'T install or remove battery cables with the key ON or the engine running. Jumper cables should be connected with the key OFF to avoid power surges that can damage electronic control units. Engines equipped with computer controlled systems should avoid both giving and getting jump starts due to the possibility of serious damage to components from arcing in the engine compartment when connections are made with the ignition ON.

• DON'T remove or attach wiring harness connectors with the ignition switch ON, especially to the electronic control unit.

• DON'T drop any components during service procedures and never apply 12 volts directly to any component (like a fuel injector) unless instructed specifically to do so. Some component electrical windings are designed to safely handle only 4 or 5 volts and can be destroyed in seconds if 12 volts are applied directly to the connector.

Air Conditioning Service 30

AIR CONDITIONING SYSTEMS

Automotive air conditioning systems are basic in design and operation, but many different components are used by the vehicle manufacturers to operate and control the systems to their specifications.

Basic System

The basic air conditioning system utilizes the compressor, condenser, evaporator, receiver-drier, expansion valve and a thermostatic or ambient type switch to control evaporator freeze-up. The controls are manually operated and the unit is basic in design. This system is usually installed as an add-on or after-market unit. A sight glass may be used in the system.

GENERAL SERVICING PROCEDURES

The most important aspect of air conditioning service is the maintenance of a pure and adequate charge of refrigerant in the system. A refrigeration system cannot function properly if a significant percentage of the charge is lost. Leaks are common be-

cause the severe vibration encountered in an automobile can easily cause a sufficient cracking or loosening of the air conditioning fittings; as a result, the extreme operating pressures of the system force refrigerant out.

The problem can be understood by considering what happens to the system as it is operated with a continuous leak. Because the expansion valve regulates the flow of refrigerant to the

evaporator, the level of refrigerant there is fairly constant. The receiver-drier stores any excess of refrigerant, and so a loss will first appear there as a reduction in the level of liquid. As this level nears the bottom of the vessel, some refrigerant vapor bubbles will begin to appear in the stream of liquid supplied to the expansion valve. This vapor decreases the capacity of the expansion valve very little as the valve opens to compensate for

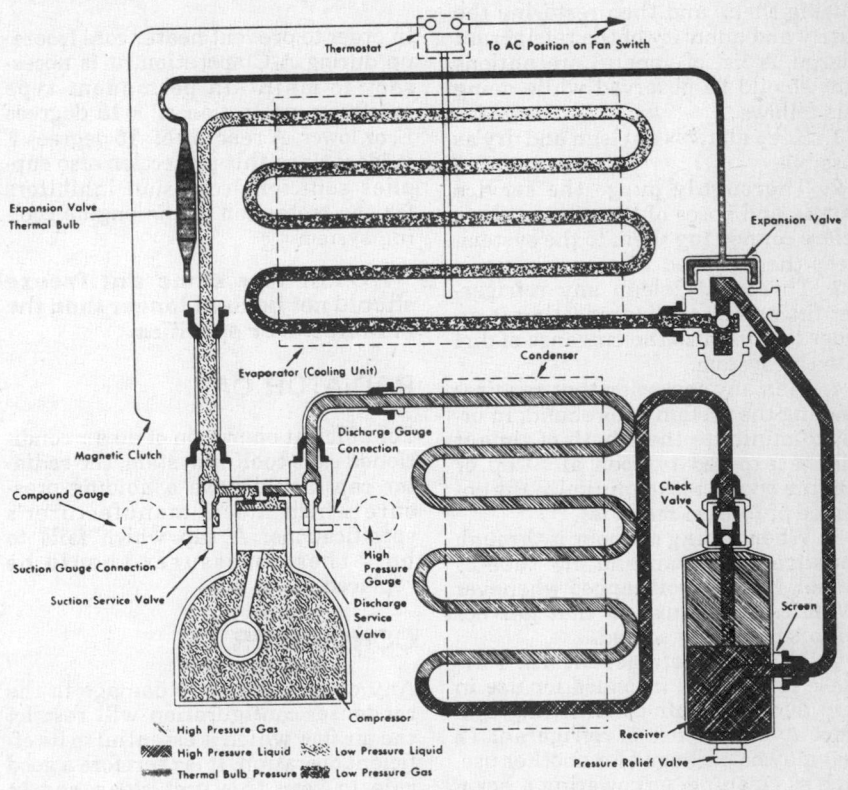

Basic air conditioning system

30-1

its presence. As the quantity of liquid in the condenser decreases, the operating pressure will drop there and throughout the high side of the system. As the R-12 continues to be expelled, the pressure available to force the liquid through the expansion valve will continue to decrease, and, eventually, the valve's orifice will prove to be too much of a restriction for adequate flow even with the needle fully withdrawn.

At this point, low side pressure will start to drop, and severe reduction in cooling capacity, marked by freeze-up of the evaporator coil, will result. Eventually, the operating pressure of the evaporator will be lower than the pressure of the atmosphere surrounding it, and air will be drawn into the system wherever there are leaks in the low side.

Because all atmospheric air contains at least some moisture, water will enter the system and mix with the R-12 and the oil. Trace amounts of moisture will cause sludging of the oil, and corrosion of the system. Saturation and clogging of the filter-drier, and freezing of the expansion valve orifice will eventually result. As air fills the system to a greater and greater extent, it will interfere more and more with the normal flows of refrigerant and heat.

From this description, it should be obvious that much of the repairman's time will be spent detecting leaks, repairing them, and then restoring the purity and quantity of the refrigerant charge. A list of general precautions that should be observed while doing this follows:

1. Keep all tools as clean and dry as possible.

2. Thoroughly purge the service gauges and hoses of air and moisture before connecting them to the system. Keep them capped when not in use.

3. Thoroughly clean any refrigerant fitting before disconnecting it, in order to minimize the entrance of dirt into the system.

4. Plan any operation that requires opening the system beforehand, in order to minimize the length of time it will be exposed to open air. Cap or seal the open ends to minimize the entrance of foreign material.

5. When adding oil, pour it through an extremely clean and dry tube or funnel. Keep the oil capped whenever possible. Do not use oil that has not been kept tightly sealed.

6. Use only refrigerant 12. Purchase refrigerant intended for use in only automatic air conditioning systems. Avoid the use of refrigerant 12 that may be packaged for another use, such as cleaning, or powering a horn, as it is impure.

7. Completely evacuate any system that has been opened to replace a component, or that has leaked sufficiently to draw in moisture and air. This requires evacuating air and moisture with a good vacuum pump for at least one hour.

If a system has been open for a considerable length of time it may be advisable to evacuate the system for up to 12 hours (overnight).

8. Use a wrench on both halves of a fitting that is to be disconnected, so as to avoid placing torque on any of the refrigerant lines.

9. When overhauling a compressor, pour some of the oil into a clean glass and inspect it. If there is evidence of dirt or metal particles, or both, flush all refrigerant components with clean refrigerant before evacuating and recharging the system. In addition, if metal particles are present, the compressor should be replaced.

10. Schrader valves may leak only when under full operating pressure. Therefore, if leakage is suspected but cannot be located, operate the system with a full charge of refrigerant and look for leaks from all Schrader valves. Replace any faulty valves.

Additional Preventive Maintenance Checks

ANTIFREEZE

In order to prevent heater core freeze-up during A/C operation, it is necessary to maintain permanent type antifreeze protection of +15 degrees F, or lower. A reading of -15 degrees F is ideal since this protection also supplies sufficient corrosion inhibitors for the protection of the engine cooling system.

NOTE: The same antifreeze should not be used longer than the manufacturer specifies.

RADIATOR CAP

For efficient operation of an air conditioned car's cooling system, the radiator cap should have a holding pressure which meets manufacturer's specifications. A cap which fails to hold these pressures should be replaced.

CONDENSER

Any obstruction of or damage to the condenser configuration will restrict the air flow which is essential to its efficient operation. It is therefore a good rule to keep this unit clean and in proper physical shape.

NOTE: Bug screens are regarded as obstructions.

CONDENSATION DRAIN TUBE

This single molded drain tube expels the condensation, which accumulates on the bottom of the evaporator housing, into the engine compartment. If this tube is obstructed, the air conditioning performance can be restricted and condensation buildup can spill over onto the vehicle's floor.

Safety Precautions

Because of the importance of the necessary safety precautions that must be exercised when working with air conditioning systems and R-12 refrigerant, a recap of the safety precautions are outlined.

1. Avoid contact with a charged refrigeration system, even when working on another part of the air conditioning system or vehicle. If a heavy tool comes into contact with a section of copper tubing or a heat exchanger, it can easily cause the relatively soft material to rupture.

2. When it is necessary to apply force to a fitting which contains refrigerant, as when checking that all system couplings are securely tightened, use a wrench on both parts of the fitting involved, if possible. This will avoid putting torque on refrigerant tubing. (It is advisable, when possible, to use tube or line wrenches when tightening these flare nut fittings.)

3. Do not attempt to discharge the system by merely loosening a fitting, or removing the service valve caps and cracking these valves. Precise control is possible only when using the service gauges. Place a rag under the open end of the center charging hose while discharging the system to catch any drops of liquid that might escape. Wear protective gloves when connecting or disconnecting service gauge hoses.

4. Discharge the system only in a well ventilated area, as high concentrations of the gas can exclude oxygen and act as an anaesthetic. When leak testing or soldering, this is particularly important, as toxic gas is formed when R-12 contacts any flame.

5. Never start a system without first verifying that both service valves are back-seated, if equipped, and that all fittings throughout the system are snugly connected.

6. Avoid applying heat to any refrigerant line or storage vessel. Charging may be aided by using wa-

ter heated to less than 125° to warm the refrigerant container. Never allow a refrigerant storage container to sit out in the sun, or near any other source of heat, such as a radiator.

7. Always wear goggles when working on a system to protect the eyes. If refrigerant contacts the eyes, it is advisable in all cases to see a physician as soon as possible.

8. Frostbite from liquid refrigerant should be treated by first gradually warming the area with cool water, and then gently applying petroleum jelly. A physician should be consulted.

9. Always keep refrigerant drum fittings capped when not in use. Avoid sudden shock to the drum, which might occur from dropping it, or from banging a heavy tool against it. Never carry a drum in the passenger compartment of a car.

10. Always completely discharge the system before painting the vehicle (if the paint is to be baked on), or before welding anywhere near refrigerant lines.

AIR CONDITIONING TOOLS AND GAUGES

Test Gauges

Most of the service work performed in air conditioning requires the use of a set of two gauges, one for the high (head) pressure side of the system, the other for the low (suction) side.

The low side gauge records both pressure and vacuum. Vacuum readings are calibrated from 0 to 30 inches and the pressure graduations read from 0 to no less than 60 psi.

The high side gauge measures pressure from 0 to at least 600 psi. Both gauges are threaded into a manifold that contains two hand shut-off valves. Proper manipulation of these valves and the use of the attached test hoses allow the user to perform the following services:

1. Test high and low side pressures.
2. Remove air, moisture, and contaminated refrigerant.
3. Purge the system (of refrigerant).
4. Charge the system (with refrigerant).

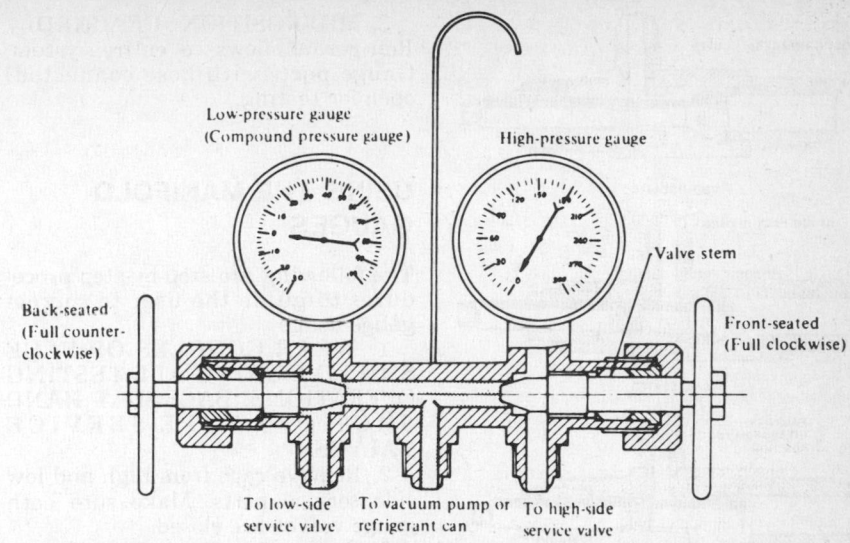

Typical manifold gauge set

NOTE: Chrysler Corp. requires the use of a third gauge on those units that have an evaporator pressure regulator (EPR) valve mounted on the suction side of the compressor.

The manifold valves are designed so they have no direct effect on gauge readings, but serve only to provide for, or cut off, flow of refrigerant through the manifold. During all testing and hook-up operations, the valves are kept in a closed position to avoid disturbing the refrigeration system. The valves are opened only to purge the system of refrigerant or to charge it.

When purging the system, the center hose is uncapped at the lower end, and both valves are cracked open slightly. This allows refrigerant pressure to force the entire contents of the system out through the center hose. During charging, the valve on the high side of the manifold is closed, and the valve on the low side is cracked open. Under these conditions, the low pressure in the evaporator will draw refrigerant from the relatively warm refrigerant storage container into the system.

Service Valves

For the user to diagnose an air conditioning system he or she must gain "entrance" to the system in order to observe the pressures. There are two types of terminals for this purpose, the hand shut off type and the familiar Schrader valve.

The Schrader valve is similar to a tire valve stem and the process of connecting the test hoses is the same as threading a hand pump outlet hose to a bicycle tire. As the test hose is threaded to the service port the valve

core is depressed, allowing the refrigerant to enter the test hose outlet. Removal of the test hose automatically closes the system.

Extreme caution must be observed when removing test hoses from the Schrader valves as some refrigerant will normally escape, usually under high pressure. (Observe safety precautions.)

Some systems have hand shut-off valves (the stem can be rotated with a special ratcheting box wrench) that can be positioned in the following three ways:

1. FRONT SEATED – Rotated to full clockwise position.
    a. Refrigerant will not flow to

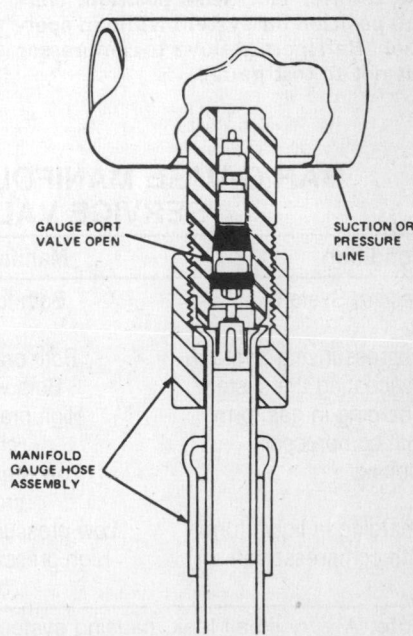

Manifold gauge hose connected to a Schraeder type service port

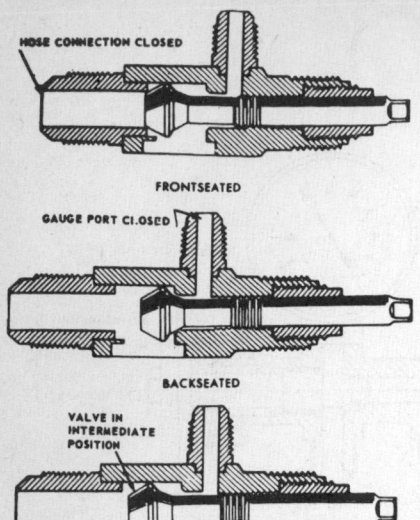

HOSE CONNECTION CLOSED

FRONTSEATED

GAUGE PORT CLOSED

BACKSEATED

VALVE IN INTERMEDIATE POSITION

MID-POSITION (CRACKED)

Manual service valve positions

compressor, but will reach test gauge port. COMPRESSOR WILL BE DAMAGED IF SYSTEM IS TURNED ON IN THIS POSITION.

b. The compressor is now isolated and ready for service. However, care must be exercised when removing service valves from the compressor as a residue of refrigerant may still be present within the compressor. Therefore, remove service valves slowly observing all safety precautions.

2. BACK SEATED — Rotated to full counter clockwise position. Normal position for system while in operation. Refrigerant flows to compressor but not to test gauge.

3. MID-POSITION (CRACKED) — Refrigerant flows to entire system. Gauge port (with hose connected) open for testing.

USING THE MANIFOLD GAUGES

The following are step-by-step procedures to guide the user to correct gauge usage.

1. WEAR GOGGLES OR FACE SHIELD DURING ALL TESTING OPERATIONS. BACKSEAT HAND SHUT-OFF TYPE SERVICE VALVES.

2. Remove caps from high and low side service ports. Make sure both gauge valves are closed.

3. Connect low side test hose to service valve that leads to the evaporator (located between the evaporator outlet and the compressor).

4. Attach high side test hose to service valve that leads to the condenser.

5. Mid-position hand shutoff type service valves.

6. Start engine and allow for warm-up. All testing and charging of the system should be done after engine and system have reached normal operation temperatures (except when using certain charging stations).

7. Adjust air conditioner controls to maximum cold.

8. Observe gauge readings.

When the gauges are not being used it is a good idea to:

a. Keep both hand valves in the closed position.

b. Attach both ends of the high and low service hoses to the manifold, if extra outlets are present on the manifold, or plug them if not.

Also, keep the center charging hose attached to an empty refrigerant can. This extra precaution will reduce the possibility of moisture entering the gauges. If air and moisture have gotten into the gauges, purge the hoses by supplying refrigerant under pressure to the center hose with both gauge valves open and all openings unplugged.

DISCHARGING, EVACUATING AND CHARGING

Discharging the System

CAUTION

Perform operation in a well-ventilated area.

When it is necessary to remove (purge) the refrigerant pressurized in the system, follow this procedure:

1. Operate air conditioner for at least 10 minutes.

2. Attach gauges, shut off engine and air conditioner.

3. Place a container or rag at the outlet of the center charging hose on the gauge. The refrigerant will be discharged there and this precaution will avoid its uncontrolled exposure.

4. Open low side hand valve on gauge slightly.

5. Open high side hand valve slightly.

NOTE: Too rapid a purging process will be identified by the appearance of an oily foam. If this occurs, close the hand valves a little more until this condition stops.

6. Close both hand valves on the gauge set when the pressures read 0 and all the refrigerant has left the system.

Evacuating the System

Before charging any system it is necessary to purge the refrigerant and draw out the trapped moisture with a suitable vacuum pump. Failure to do so will result in ineffective charging and possible damage to the system.

Use this hook-up for the proper evacuation procedure:

1. Connect both service gauge hoses to the high and low service outlets.

BAR GAUGE MANIFOLD AND COMPRESSOR SERVICE VALVE SETTINGS

Condition	Manifold Valves	Compressor Valves
Testing System	Both fully closed	Both cracked off backseat
Depressurizing System	Both cracked open	Both at mid position
Evacuating the system	Both wide open	Both at mid position
Charging in gas form with compressor running	High pressure valve closed	High pressure valve cracked off backseat
	Low pressure valve cracked	Low pressure valve at mid position
Charging in liquid form with compressor off	Low pressure valve closed	Both valves mid positioned
	High pressure valve wide open	

Note: A very small leak, causing system discharge about every two weeks, can be caused by a leaky Schrader type service valve. Check these valves with extra care when testing for a small leak.

2. Open high and low side hand valves on gauge manifold.

3. Open both service valves a slight amount (from back seated position), allow refrigerant to discharge from system.

4. Install center charging hose of gauge set to vacuum pump.

5. Operate vacuum pump for at least one hour. (If the system has been subjected to open conditions for a prolonged period of time it may be necessary to "pump the system down" overnight. Refer to "System Sweep" procedure.)

NOTE: If low pressure gauge does not show at least 28" hg. within 5 minutes, check the system for a leak or loose gauge connectors.

6. Close hand valves on gauge manifold.

7. Shut off pump.

8. Observe low pressure gauge to determine if vacuum is holding. A vacuum drop may indicate a leak.

System Sweep

An efficient vacuum pump can remove all the air contained in a contaminated air conditioning system very quickly, because of its vapor state. Moisture, however, is far more difficult to remove because the vacuum must force the liquid to evaporate before it will be able to remove it from the system. If a system has become severely contaminated, as, for example, it might become after all the charge was lost in conjunction with vehicle

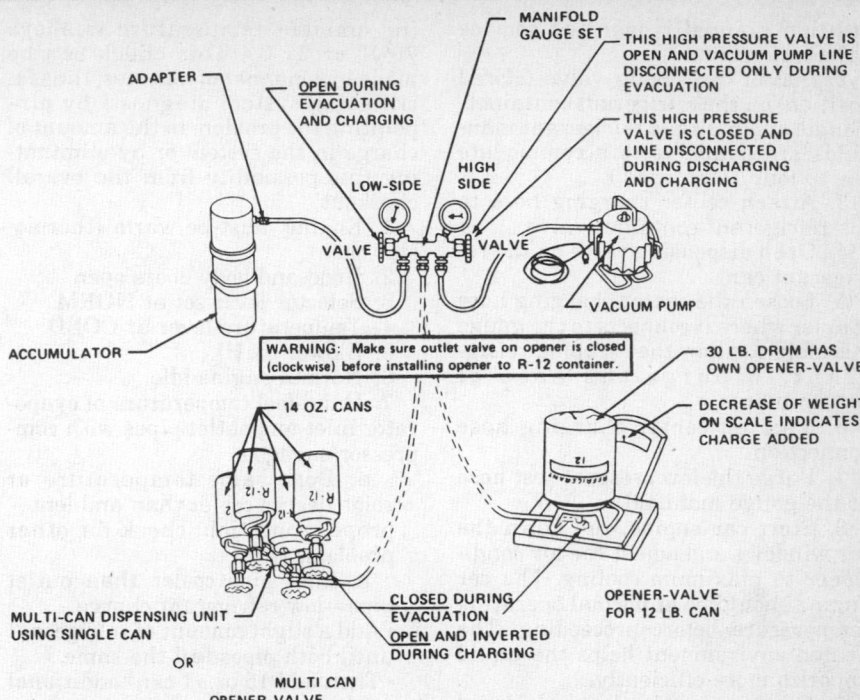

WARNING: Make sure outlet valve on opener is closed (clockwise) before installing opener to R-12 container.

Typical gauge connections for discharge, evacuation and charging the system

accident damage, moisture removal is extremely time consuming. A vacuum pump could remove all of the moisture only if it were operated for 12 hours or more.

Under these conditions, sweeping the system with refrigerant will speed the process of moisture removal considerably. To sweep, follow the following procedure:

1. Connect vacuum pump to

gauges, operate it until vacuum ceases to increase, then continue operation for ten more minutes.

2. Charge system with 50% of its rated refrigerant capacity.

3. Operate system at fast idle for ten minutes.

4. Discharge the system.

5. Repeat twice the process of charging to 50% capacity, running the system for ten minutes, and discharging it, for a total of three sweeps.

6. Replace drier.

7. Pump system down as in Step 1.

8. Charge system.

Charging the System

─── CAUTION ───
Never attempt to charge the system by opening the high pressure gauge control while the compressor is operating. The compressor accumulating pressure can burst the refrigerant container, causing sever personal injuries.

BASIC SYSTEM

In this procedure the refrigerant enters the suction side of the system as a vapor while the compressor is running. Before proceeding, the system should be in a partial vacuum after adequate evacuation. Both hand valves on the gauge manifold should be closed.

1. Attach both test hoses to their respective service valve ports. Mid-

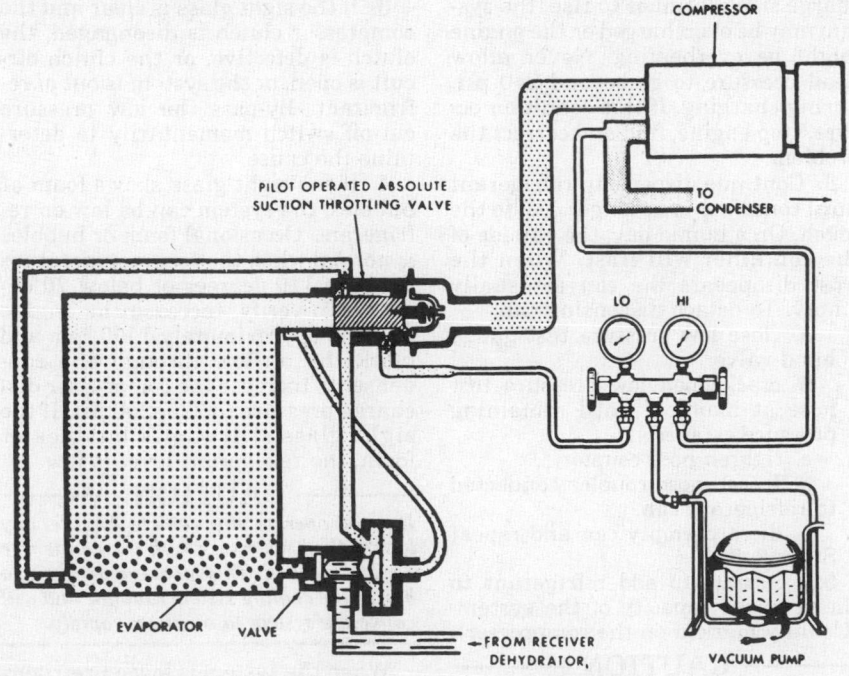

Schematic for evacuating the system

position manually operated service valves, if present.

2. Install dispensing valve (closed position) on the refrigerant container. (Single and multiple refrigerant manifolds are available to accommodate one to four 15 oz. cans.)

3. Attach center charging hose to the refrigerant container valve.

4. Open dispensing valve on the refrigerant can.

5. Loosen the center charging hose coupler where it connects to the gauge manifold to allow the escaping refrigerant to purge the hose of contaminants.

6. Tighten center charging hose connection.

7. Purge the low pressure test hose at the gauge manifold.

8. Start car engine, roll down the car windows and adjust the air conditioner to maximum cooling. The car engine should be at normal operating temperature before proceeding. The heated environment helps the liquid vaporize more efficiently.

9. Crack open the low side hand valve on the manifold. Manipulate the valve so that the refrigerant that enters the system does not cause the low side pressure to exceed 40 psi. Too sudden a surge may permit the entrance of unwanted liquid to the compressor. Since liquids cannot be compressed, the compressor will suffer damage if compelled to attempt it. If the suction side of the system remains in a vacuum the system is blocked. Locate and correct the condition before proceeding any further.

NOTE: Placing the refrigerant can in a container of warm water (no hotter than 125°F) will speed the charging process. Slight agitation of the can is helpful too, but be careful not to turn the can upside down.

Some manufacturers allow for a partial charging of the A/C system in the form of a liquid (can inverted and compressor off) by opening the high side gauge valve only, and putting the high side compressor service valve in the middle position (if so equipped). The remainder of the refrigerant is then added in the form of a gas in the normal manner, through the suction side only.

SYSTEMS WITHOUT SIGHT GLASS, EXCEPT CCOT SYSTEM

The following procedure can be used to quickly determine whether or not an air conditioning system has the proper charge of refrigerant (provid-

ing ambient temperature is above 70°F, or 21°C). This check can be made in a manner of minutes, thus facilitating system diagnosis by pinpointing the problem to the amount of charge in the system or by eliminating this possibility from the overall checkout.

1. Engine must be warm (thermostat open).
2. Hood and body doors open.
3. Selector lever set at NORM.
4. Temperature lever at COLD.
5. Blower on HI.
6. Normal engine idle.
7. Hand-feel temperature of evaporator inlet and outlet pipes with compressor engaged.

   a. Both same temperature or some degree cooler than ambient — proper condition: check for other problems.

   b. Inlet pipe cooler than outlet pipe — low refrigerant charge.
   • Add a slight amount of refrigerant until both pipes feel the same.
   • Then add 15 oz. (1 can) additional refrigerant.

   c. Inlet pipe has frost accumulation — outlet pipe warmer: proceed as in Step b above.

If during the charging process the head pressure exceeds 200 psi, place an electric fan in front of the car and direct the turbulent air to the condenser. If no fan is available, repeatedly pour cool water over the top of the condenser. These cooling actions may be necessary on an extremely warm day to help dissipate the heat emitted by the engine during idle.

If this fails and pressure on the discharge side continues to rise, the system may be overcharged or the engine might be overheating. Never allow head pressure to go beyond 240 psi. during charging. If this condition occurs, stop engine, find and correct the problem.

8. Continue dispensing refrigerant until container is no longer cool to the touch. On a humid day, the outside of the container will frost. When the frost disappears the can is usually empty. To detach dispensing can:

   a. close low pressure test gauge hand valve.

   b. crack open low pressure test hose at manifold until remaining pressure escapes.

   c. tighten hose coupler.

   d. loosen hose coupler connected to refrigerant can.

   e. discard empty can and repeat Steps 2–8.

9. Continue to add refrigerant to the required capacity of the system. (Usually marked on the compressor).

CAUTION
DO NOT OVERCHARGE. This condition

is usually indicated by an abnormally high side pressure reading and a noisy compressor resulting in ineffective cooling and damage to the system.

SYSTEMS WITH A SIGHT GLASS

The air conditioning systems that use a sight glass as a means to check the refrigerant level, should be carefully checked to avoid under or over charging. The gauge set should be attached to the system for verification of pressures.

To check the system with the sight glass, clean the glass and start the vehicle engine. Operate the air conditioning controls on maximum for approximately five minutes to stabilize the system. The room temperature should be above 70 degrees. Check the sight glass for one of the following conditions:

1. If the sight glass is clear, the compressor clutch is engaged, the compressor discharge line is warm and the compressor inlet line is cool, the system has a full charge of refrigerant.

2. If the sight glass is clear, the compressor clutch is engaged and there is no significant temperature difference between the compressor inlet and discharge lines, the system is empty or nearly empty. By having the gauge set attached to the system a measurement can be taken. If the gauge reads less than 25 psi, the low pressure cutoff protection switch has failed.

3. If the sight glass is clear and the compressor clutch is disengaged, the clutch is defective, or the clutch circuit is open, or the system is out of refrigerant. By-pass the low pressure cut-off switch momentarily to determine the cause.

4. If the sight glass shows foam or bubbles, the system can be low on refrigerant. Occasional foam or bubbles is normal when the room temperature is above 110 degrees or below 70 degrees. To verify, increase the engine speed to approximately 1500 rpm and block the airflow through the condenser to increase the compressor discharge pressure to 225–250 psi. If the sight glass still shows bubbles or foam, the refrigerant level is low.

CAUTION
Do not operate the vehicle engine any longer than necessary with the condenser airflow blocked. This blocking action also blocks the cooling system radiator and will cause the system to overheat rapidly.

When the system is low on refrigerant, a leak is present or the system was not properly charged. Use a leak detector and locate the problem area and repair. If no leakage is found, charge the system to its capacity. (Refer to the refrigerant capacity chart at the end of this section).

CAUTION

It is not advisable to add refrigerant to a system utilizing the suction throttling valve and a sight glass, because the amount of refrigerant required to remove the foam or bubbles will result in an overcharge and potentially damaged system components.

CCOT SYSTEM

When charging the CCOT system, attach only the low pressure line to the low pressure gauge port, located on the accumulator. Do not attach the high pressure line to any service port or allow it to remain attached to the vacuum pump after evacuation. Be sure both the high and the low pressure control valves are closed on the gauge set. To complete the charging of the system, follow the outline supplied.

1. Start the engine and allow to run at idle, with the cooling system at normal operating temperature.
2. Attach the center gauge hose to a single or multi-can dispenser.
3. With the multi-can dispenser inverted, allow one pound or the contents of one or two 14 oz. cans to enter the system through the low pressure side by opening the gauge low pressure control valve.
4. Close the low pressure gauge control valve and turn the A/C system on to engage the compressor. Place the blower motor in its high mode.
5. Open the low pressure gauge control valve and draw the remaining charge into the system. Refer to the capacity chart at the end of this section for the individual vehicle or system capacity.
6. Close the low pressure gauge control valve and the refrigerant source valve, on the multi-can dispenser. Remove the low pressure hose from the accumulator quickly to avoid

Amount of refrigerant / Check item	Almost no refrigerant	Insufficient	Suitable	Too much refrigerant
Temperature of high pressure and low pressure lines.	Almost no difference between high pressure and low pressure side temperature.	High pressure side is warm and low pressure side is fairly cold.	High pressure side is hot and low pressure side is cold.	High pressure side is abnormally hot.
State in sight glass.	Bubbles flow continuously. Bubbles will disappear and something like mist will flow when refrigerant is nearly gone.	The bubbles are seen at intervals of 1 - 2 seconds.	Almost transparent. Bubbles may appear when engine speed is raised and lowered. No clear difference exists between these two conditions.	No bubbles can be seen.
Pressure of system.	High pressure side is abnormally low.	Both pressure on high and low pressure sides are slightly low.	Both pressures on high and low pressure sides are normal.	Both pressures on high and low pressure sides are abnormally high.
Repair.	Stop compressor immediately and conduct an overall check.	Check for gas leakage, repair as required, replenish and charge system.		Discharge refrigerant from service valve of low pressure side.

Using a sight glass to determine the relative refrigerant charge

loss of refrigerant through the Schrader valve.

7. Install the protective cap on the gauge port and check the system for leakage.
8. Test the system for proper operation.

Leak Testing the System

There are several methods of detecting leaks in an air conditioning system; among them, the two most popular are (1) halide leak-detection or the "open flame method," and (2) electronic leak-detection.

The halide leak detection is a torch like device which produces a yellow-green color when refrigerant is introduced into the flame at the burner. A purple or violet color indicates the presence of large amounts of refrigerant at the burner.

An electronic leak detector is a small portable electronic device with an extended probe. With the unit activated the probe is passed along those components of the system which contain refrigerant. If a leak is detected, the unit will sound an alarm signal or activate a display signal depending on the manufacturer's design. It is advisable to follow the manufacturer's instructions as the design and function of the detection may vary significantly.

CAUTION

Caution should be taken to operate either type of detector in well ventilated areas, so as to reduce the chance of personal injury, which may result from coming in contact with poisonous gases produced when R-12 is exposed to flame or electric spark.

REFRIGERANT FLUSHING INFORMATION CHART

Refrigerant	Vaporizes °C(°F)①	Approximate Closed Container Pressure① kPa (psi)②					Adaptability
		15.57°C (60°F)	21.13°C (70°F)	26.69°C (80°F)	32.25°C (90°F)	37.81°C (100°F)	
R-12	−29.80 (−21.6)	393 (57)	483 (70)	579 (84)	689 (100)	807 (117)	Self Propelling
F-114	3.56 (38.4)	55.16 (8)	89.63 (13)	131 (19)	172 (25)	221 (32)	
F-11③	23.74 (74.7)	27 (8 in Hg)	10 (3 in Hg)	7 (1)	34 (5)	62 (9)	
F-113	47.59 (117.6)	74 (22 in Hg)	64 (19 in Hg)	54 (16 in Hg)	44 (13 in Hg)	27 (8 in Hg)	Pump Required

①At sea level atmospheric pressure.
②kPa (psi) unless otherwise noted.
③F-11 is also available in pressurized containers. This makes it suitable for usage when special flushing equipment is not available. However, it is more toxic than R-12 and F-114.

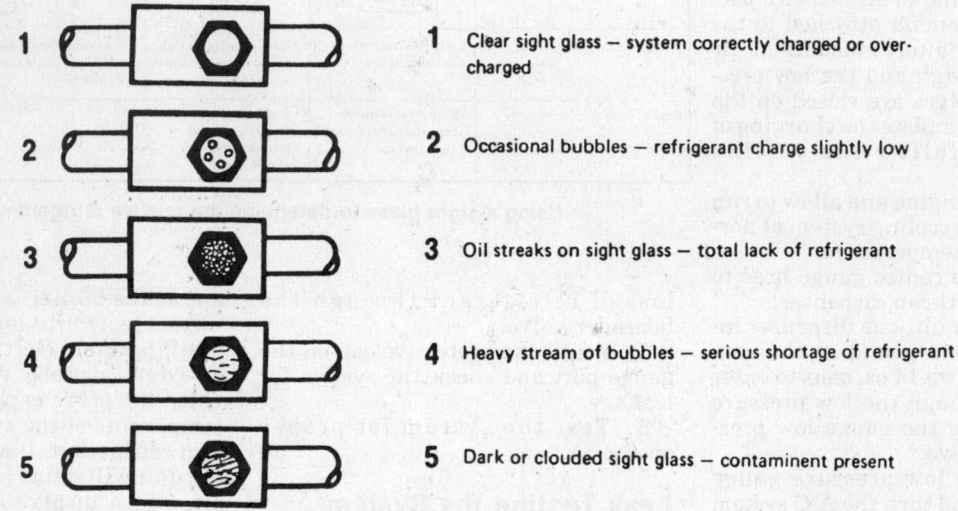

1 Clear sight glass — system correctly charged or over-charged

2 Occasional bubbles — refrigerant charge slightly low

3 Oil streaks on sight glass — total lack of refrigerant

4 Heavy stream of bubbles — serious shortage of refrigerant

5 Dark or clouded sight glass — contaminent present

Sight glass examination of refrigerant flow

Charging and Starting

31

SOLENOID AND NEUTRAL SAFETY SWITCH

IDENTIFICATION

Solenoids

WITHOUT RELAYS

This type of starter solenoid is always mounted on the starter. It makes electrical contact for the starter, it pulls the starter and the drive clutch into mesh with the flywheel. The Chrysler reduction gear starter has this solenoid embodied in the starter housing, however an internal relay is integral to the brush plate. The ignition by-pass terminal is usually marked **R** or **IGN**, if it is used.

WITH SEPARATE RELAYS

The solenoid is always mounted on the starter. In addition to making contact for the starter, it also pulls the starter drive clutch gear into mesh with the flywheel. A single control terminal is used on the solenoid. The relay is usually found mounted to the inner fender panel or on the firewall.

WITH BUILT-IN RELAYS

These units are mounted on the starter and are connected, through linkage, to the starter clutch. The relay portion is built into the solenoid assembly.

Neutral Safety Switches

The purpose of the neutral safety switch is to prevent the starter from cranking the engine except when the transmission is in the **NEUTRAL** or the **PARK** positions. On some vehi-

cles, the neutral safety switch is located on the transmission; it serves to ground the solenoid or magnetic switch, whichever is used. On other vehicles, the neutral safety switch is located either at the bottom of the steering column (where it contacts the shift mechanism), on the steering column, underneath the dash or on the shift linkage (console).

Some manual transmission models have a clutch linkage safety switch to prevent starter operation unless the clutch pedal is depressed. On most cars, the neutral safety switch and the back-up light switch are combined into a single switch mechanism.

TROUBLESHOOTING NEUTRAL SAFETY SWITCHES—QUICK TEST

If the starter fails to function and the neutral safety switch is to be checked, a jumper can be placed across its terminals. If the starter then functions, the safety switch is defective. In the case of the neutral safety switches having 1 wire, the wire must be grounded for testing purposes. If the starter works with the wire grounded, the switch is defective.

NEUTRAL SAFETY SWITCH BACK-UP LIGHT SWITCH

When the neutral safety switch is built in combination with the back-up light switch, the easiest way to tell which terminals are for the back-up lights is to place a jumper on and across each pair of wires. The pair of wires which light the back-up lamps should be ignored when testing the neutral safety switch. Once the back-up light wires have been located, jump the other pair of wires to test the neutral safety switch. If the starter functions only when the jumper is placed across these

2 wires, the neutral safety switch is defective or requires adjustment.

STARTER MOTORS

Chrysler Reduction Gear Starter Motor

DISASSEMBLY & ASSEMBLY

1. Support the assembly in a vise equipped with soft jaws; do not clamp. Care must be used not to distort or damage the die cast aluminum housing.
2. Remove the housing bolts and remove the end housing.
3. Carefully pull the armature up and out of the gear housing, remove the starter frame and the field assembly. Remove the steel and the fiber thrust washers.

NOTE: On V8 engines the starting motors have the wire of the shunt field coil soldered to the brush terminal. The 6 cylinder engines have the 4 coils in series and do not have a wire soldered to the brush terminal. One pair of brushes is connected to this terminal, while the other pair is attached to the series field coils by means of a terminal screw. Carefully pull the frame and the field assembly up enough to expose the terminal screw and the solder connection of the shunt field at the brush terminal. Place 2 wooden blocks between the starter

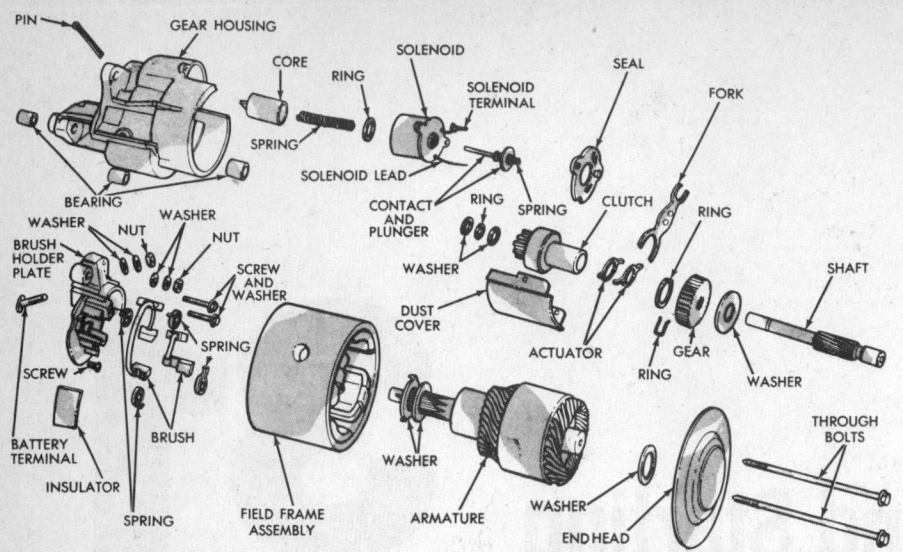

Rear wheel drive reduction gear motor—Chrysler Corp.

about $\frac{1}{16}$ in. side movement to insure proper pinion gear engagement.

Bosch and Mitsubishi Starter

DISASSEMBLY & ASSEMBLY

1. Position the assembly in the proper holding fixture. Disconnect the field coil wire from the solenoid terminal.

2. Remove the solenoid mounting screws (and the solenoid Bosch automatic transmission) and work the solenoid (plunger Bosch automatic transmission) off the shift fork.

3. On Nippondenso units remove the bearing cover, armature shaft lock, washer, spring and seal.

4. On Bosch units remove the screws holding down the end shield bearing cap and remove the cap and washers.

5. Remove the through bolts and the commutator end frame cover. Remove the brushes and the brush plate. Slide the field frame off over the armature.

6. Take out the shift lever pivot bolt. Take off the rubber gasket and metal plate.

7. For the Bosch (automatic transmission) and all Nippondenso units remove the armature assembly and shift lever from the drive end housing. For the Bosch (manual transmission) press the stop collar off the snapring, remove the snapring, remove the clutch assembly and remove the drive end housing from the armature.

8. For all except the Bosch (manual transmission), press the stop collar off the snapring and remove the snapring, stop collar and clutch.

9. Brushes that are worn more than one half the length of new brushes, or are oil soaked should be replaced. New brushes are $\frac{11}{16}$ in. long.

Assembly:

10. Do not immerse the starter clutch unit in cleaning solvent. Solvent will wash the lubricant from the clutch.

11. Place the drive unit on the armature shaft and while holding the armature rotate the pinion. The drive pinion should rotate smoothly in 1 direction only. The pinion may not rotate easily but as long as it rotates smoothly it is in good condition. If the clutch unit does not function properly or if the pinion is worn, chipped or burred replace the unit.

frame and gear housing to facilitate removal of the terminal screw and unsoldering of the shunt field wire at the brush terminal.

4. Support the brush terminal with a finger behind the terminal and remove the screw.

5. On the V8 engine starters, unsolder the shunt field coil lead from the brush terminal and the housing.

6. The brush holder plate with the terminal, the contact and the brushes is serviced as an assembly.

7. Clean the old sealant from around the plate and the housing, remove the brush holder attaching screw.

8. On the shunt type, unsolder the solenoid winding from the brush terminal, remove the $\frac{11}{32}$ in. nut, the washer and the insulator from solenoid terminal.

9. Remove the brush holder plate with the brushes as an assembly.

10. Remove gear housing ground screw and remove the solenoid assembly from the well. Remove the nut, the washer and the seal from starter (battery) terminal, remove the terminal from the plate.

11. Remove the solenoid contact and plunger from the solenoid. Remove the coil sleeve. Remove the solenoid return spring, coil retaining washer, retainer and the dust cover from the gear housing.

12. Release the snapring which locates the driven gear pinion shaft and remove the front retaining ring. Push the pinion shaft rearward, remove the snapring, thrust washers, clutch and the pinion. Remove the shift fork nylon actuators.

13. Remove the driven gear and the friction washer. Pull the shifting fork forward and remove the moving core.

14. Remove the fork retainer pin and the shifting fork assembly. The gear housing with bushings is serviced as an assembly.

Assembly:

15. Any brushes that are worn more than ½ the length of new brushes or are oil soaked, should be replaced.

16. When resoldering the shunt field and the solenoid lead, make a strong low resistance connection using a high temperature solder and a resin flux. Do not use acid or acid core solder. Do not break the shunt field wire units when removing and installing the brushes.

17. Do not immerse the starter clutch unit in a cleaning solvent. The outside of the clutch and the pinion must be cleaned with a cloth so as not to wash the lubricant from the inside of the clutch.

18. Rotate the pinion, the pinion gear should rotate smoothly and in 1 direction only. If the starter clutch unit does not function properly or if the pinion is worn, chipped or burred, replace the starter clutch unit.

19. Inspect the commutator and the brush contact surface when the starter is assembled, for flat spots, out of roundness or excessive wear.

20. Reface the commutator (if necessary), by removing only a sufficient amount of metal to provide a smooth, even surface.

21. Using light pressure, clean the grooves of the face of the commutator with a pointed tool. Do not remove any metal or widen the grooves.

22. Assembly is the reverse of the disassembly procedure. After lubricating the plates with a small amount of SAE 10 engine oil, they should have

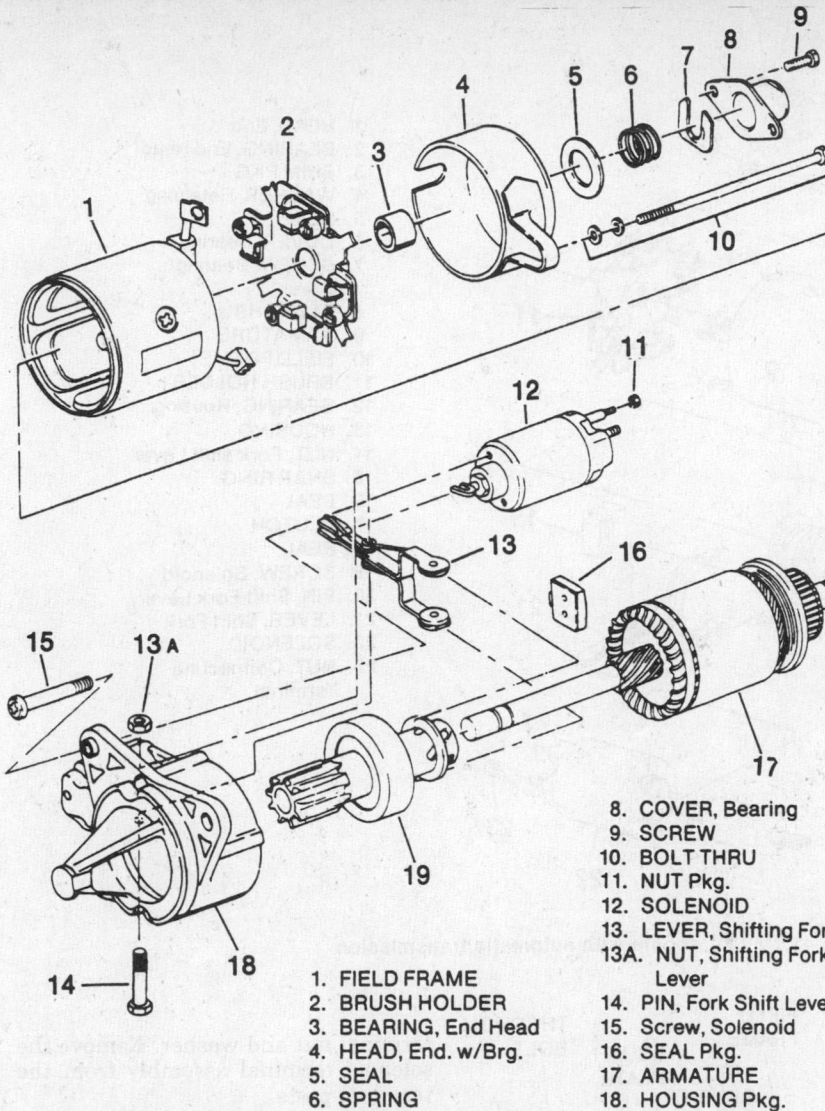

8. COVER, Bearing
9. SCREW
10. BOLT THRU
11. NUT Pkg.
12. SOLENOID
13. LEVER, Shifting Fork
13A. NUT, Shifting Fork Lever
14. PIN, Fork Shift Lever
15. Screw, Solenoid
16. SEAL Pkg.
17. ARMATURE
18. HOUSING Pkg.
19. CLUTCH Pkg.

1. FIELD FRAME
2. BRUSH HOLDER
3. BEARING, End Head
4. HEAD, End. w/Brg.
5. SEAL
6. SPRING
7. PLATE

Exploded view of the Nippondenso starter—1.7L with manual transaxle

12. Assembly is the reverse of the disassembly procedure. Lubricate the armature shaft and splines with SAE 10 or 30 W oil.

13. On all except the Bosch (manual transmission) install the clutch, stop collar, lock ring and shaft fork on the armature. On the Bosch (manual transmission) install the drive end housing on the armature. Install the clutch, stop collar and snapring on the armature.

14. On all except the Bosch (manual transmission) install the armature assembly and shift fork in the drive end housing. On Bosch units install the shim and armature shaft lock. Check the endplay it should be 0.002–0.021 in.

1987–90 Nippondenso Starter

DISASSEMBLY & ASSEMBLY

1. Position the assembly in a suitable holding fixture. Remove the rubber boot from the field coil terminal. Remove the nut from the field coil terminal stud. Remove the field coil terminal from the stud.

2. Remove the through bolts. Remove the splash shield. Remove the end shield screws from the brush plate. Remove the starter end shield.

3. Slide the brushes from their holders. Pry the retaining springs back for access and remove the brush plate.

4. Slide the armature out of the starter housing. Remove the starter housing from the gear housing. Remove the solenoid terminal cover.

5. Remove the solenoid terminal nut and washer. Remove the battery

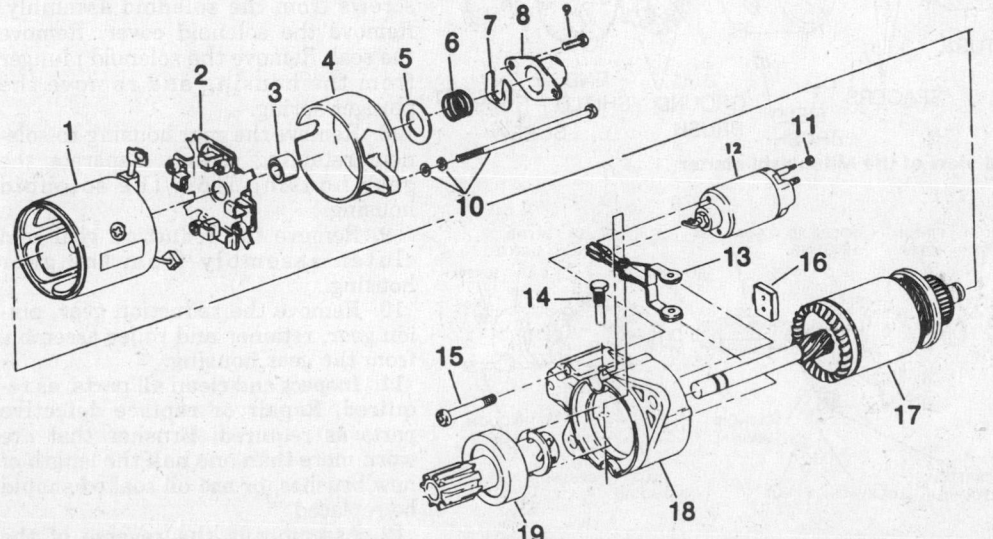

1. FIELD FRAME
2. BRUSH HOLDER
3. BEARING, End Head
4. HEAD, End w/Brg.
5. SEAL
6. SPRING
7. PLATE
8. COVER, Bearing
9. SCREW
10. BOLT THRU
11. NUT Pkg.
12. SOLENOID
13. LEVER, Shift Fork
14. PIN, Fork Shift Lever
15. SCREW, Solenoid
16. SEAL Pkg.
17. ARMATURE Pkg.
18. HOUSING Pkg.
19. CLUTCH Pkg.

Exploded view of the Nippondenso starter—except 1.7L with manual transaxle

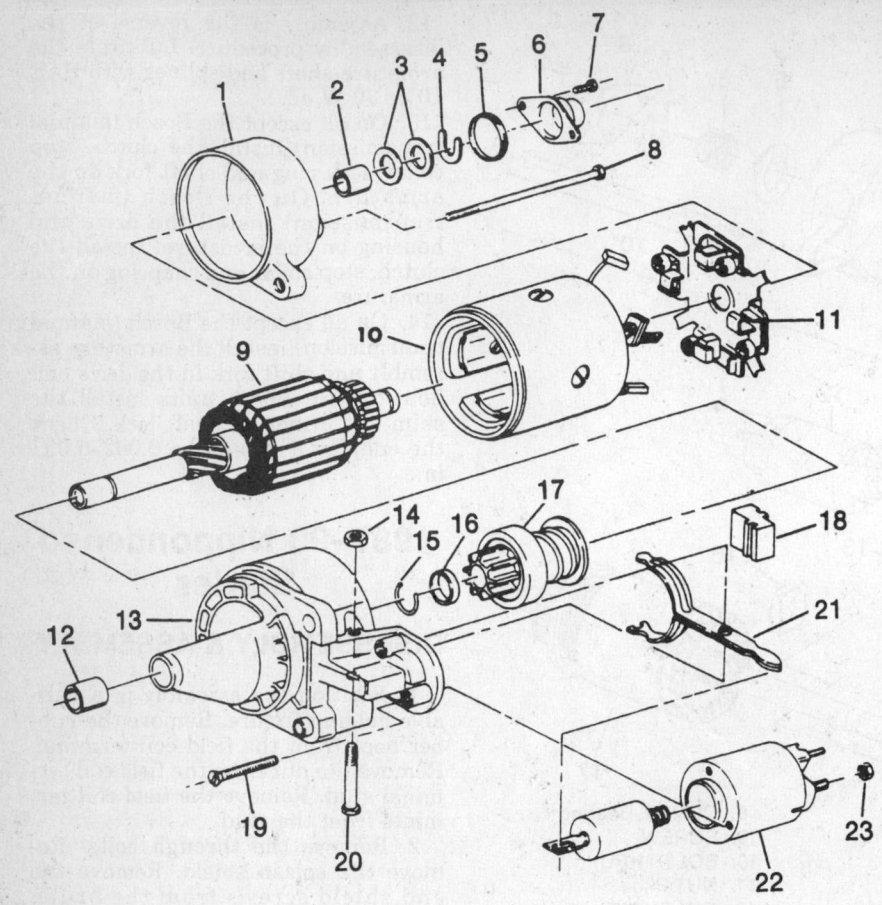

1. HEAD, End
2. BEARING, End Head
3. SHIM PKG.
4. WASHER, Retaining
5. SEAL
6. COVER, Bearing
7. SCREW, Bearing Cover
8. BOLT THRU
9. ARMATURE
10. FIELD FRAME
11. BRUSH HOLDER
12. BEARING, Housing
13. HOUSING
14. NUT, Fork shift Lever
15. SNAP RING
16. SEAL
17. CLUTCH
18. SEAL
19. SCREW, Solenoid
20. PIN, Shift Fork Lever
21. LEVER, Shift Fork
22. SOLENOID
23. NUT, Connecting Terminal

Bosch starter – 1.7L 2.2L engine with automatic transmission

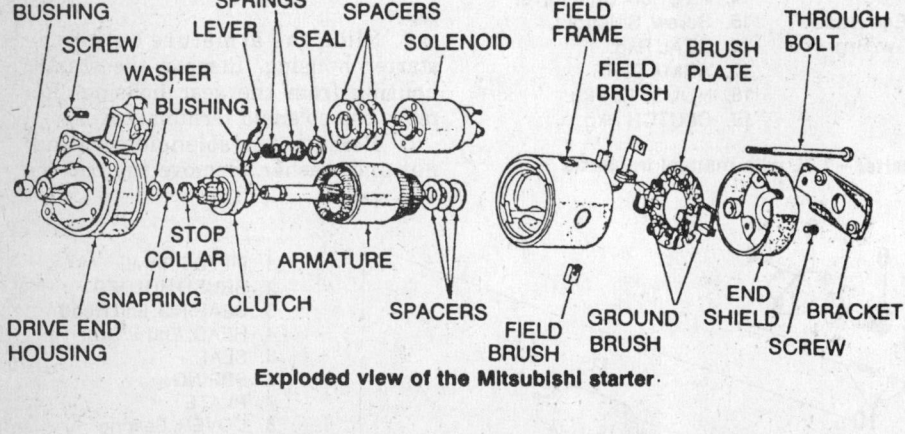

Exploded view of the Mitsubishi starter

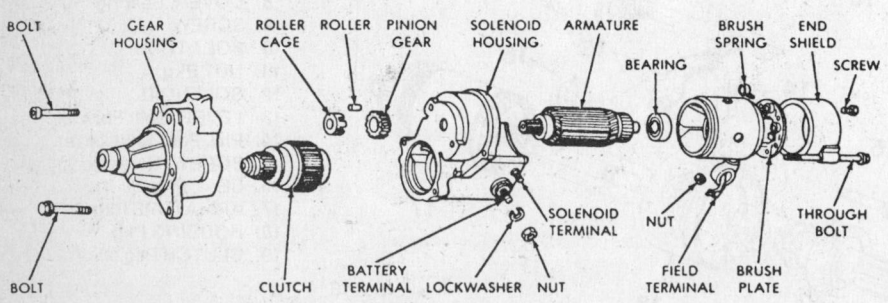

Exploded view of the Nippondenso starter – 1987-90 Chrysler

terminal nut and washer. Remove the solenoid terminal assembly from the terminal posts.

6. Remove the solenoid terminal from the insulator. Remove the battery terminal from the insulator.

7. Remove the solenoid cover screws from the solenoid assembly. Remove the solenoid cover. Remove the seal. Remove the solenoid plunger from the housing and remove the plunger spring.

8. Remove the gear housing-to-solenoid retaining screws. Separate the gear housing from the solenoid housing.

9. Remove the reduction gear and clutch assembly from the gear housing.

10. Remove the reduction gear, pinion gear, retainer and roller assembly from the gear housing.

11. Inspect and clean all parts, as required. Repair or replace defective parts as required. Brushes that are worn more than one half the length of new brushes, or are oil soaked should be replaced.

12. Assembly is the reverse of the disassembly procedure.

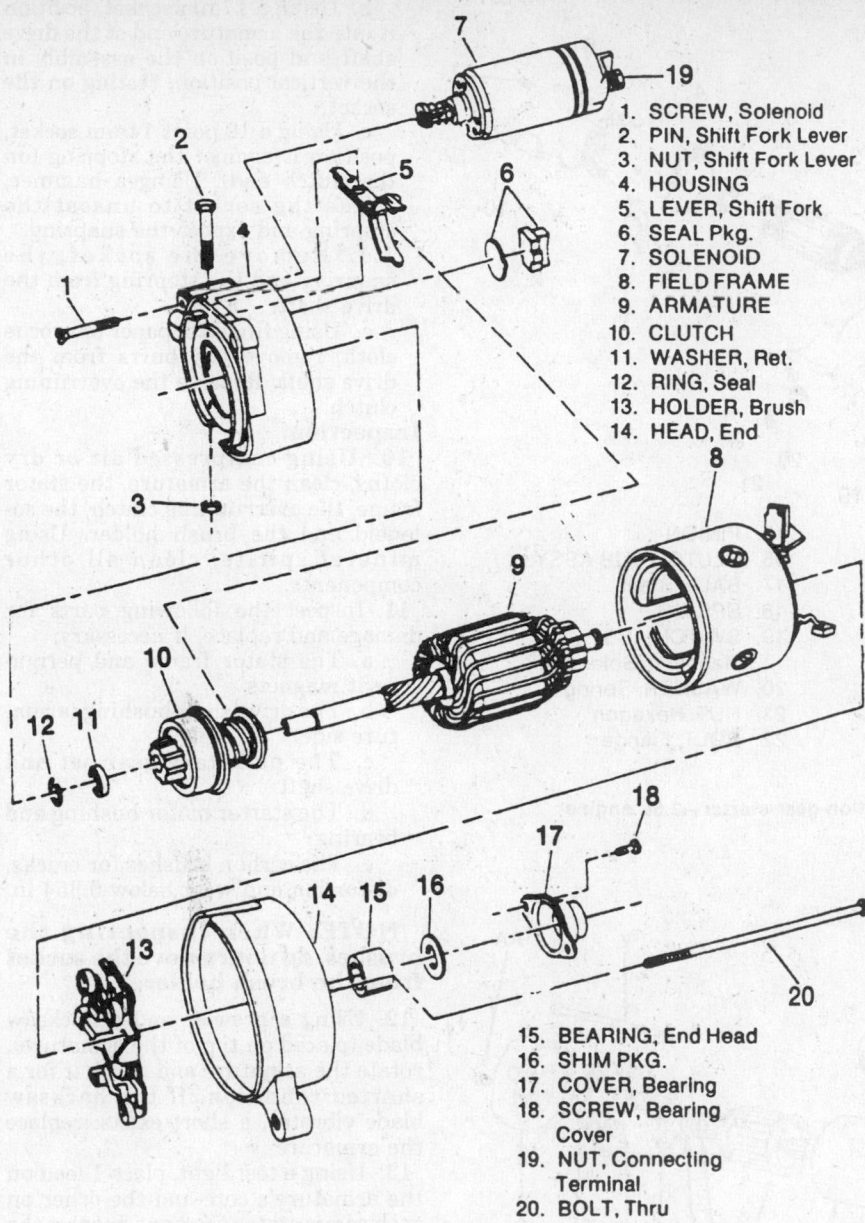

1. SCREW, Solenoid
2. PIN, Shift Fork Lever
3. NUT, Shift Fork Lever
4. HOUSING
5. LEVER, Shift Fork
6. SEAL Pkg.
7. SOLENOID
8. FIELD FRAME
9. ARMATURE
10. CLUTCH
11. WASHER, Ret.
12. RING, Seal
13. HOLDER, Brush
14. HEAD, End

15. BEARING, End Head
16. SHIM PKG.
17. COVER, Bearing
18. SCREW, Bearing Cover
19. NUT, Connecting Terminal
20. BOLT, Thru

Bosh starter—1.7L engine with manual transmission

age insulation. Wipe these parts with a cloth only.

9. Do not immerse drive unit in cleaning solvent. The drive clutch is pre-lubricated at the factory and solvent will wash lubrication from clutch.

10. The drive unit may be cleaned with a brush moistened with cleaning solvent and wiped dry with a cloth. Brushes that are worn more than ½ the length of new brush, or are oil soaked, should be replaced.

11. Field brushes are serviced as part of the field and frame assembly. Ground brushes and all springs come as part of the brush plate assembly.

12. The assembly is the reverse of the disassembly procedure.

Mitsubishi Reduction Gear Starter

DISASSEMBLY & ASSEMBLY

3.0L Eagle Premier
2.0L Chrysler Laser

NOTE: Do not place the stator frame in a vise or strike it with a hammer for damage to the permanent magnets could occur.

1. Disconnect the coil wire from the solenoid.
2. Remove the solenoid-to-front end frame screws and the solenoid.
3. Loosen (do not remove) the commutator shield-to-brush holder screws.
4. Remove the through bolts, the rubber retainer (under solenoid) and the coin washer.

NOTE: When removing the output shaft assembly, do not loose the armature shaft ball.

5. Remove the stator frame, the commutator shield and output shaft assembly as a unit. Separate the clutch fork from the output shaft assembly.
6. From the stator frame, pull the output shaft assembly forward, then, push the armature and commutator shield to the rearward.
7. Remove the commutator shield-to-brush holder plate screws and the shield; do not remove the brush holder assembly.
8. Using a 22mm socket, slide it up against the commutator, slide the brush holder assembly onto the socket and position the socket/brush holder assembly aside.
9. To disassemble the output shaft assembly, perform the following procedures:
   a. Remove the rubber packing ring and the gears.

Nippondenso/ Mitsubishi Reduction Starter

DISASSEMBLY & ASSEMBLY

1. Position the assembly in a suitable holding fixture. Disconnect the wire terminal from the field coil stud and move the rubber shield away from the wire end.
2. Remove the through bolts from the end frame. Remove the screws from the end of the frame cap. Remove the upper left solenoid screw and remove the wire retainer.
3. Remove the end shield. Remove

the field frame brushes from the brush plate.
4. Remove the brush plate and slide the armature out of the field frame and remove the field frame.
5. Remove the screws from the gear housing and remove the gear housing from the solenoid.
6. Remove the clutch rollers and retainer. Remove the pinion and clutch. Remove the solenoid steel ball and spring.
7. Remove the solenoid cover screws, remove the solenoid cover and remove the solenoid plunger.
8. Do not immerse parts in cleaning solvent. Immersing the field frame, coil assembly and armature will dam-

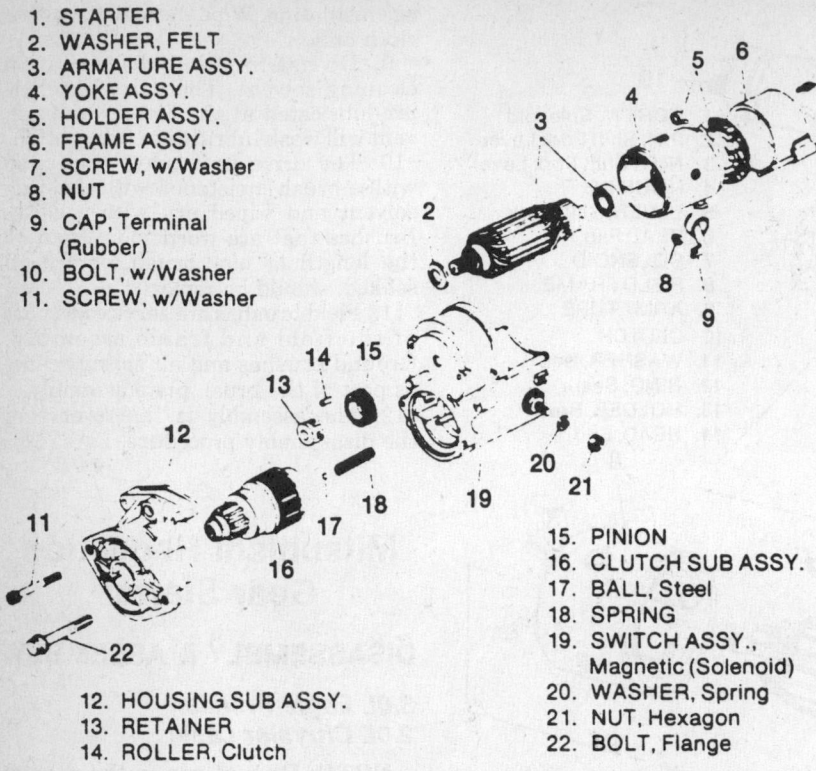

1. STARTER
2. WASHER, FELT
3. ARMATURE ASSY.
4. YOKE ASSY.
5. HOLDER ASSY.
6. FRAME ASSY.
7. SCREW, w/Washer
8. NUT
9. CAP, Terminal (Rubber)
10. BOLT, w/Washer
11. SCREW, w/Washer

12. HOUSING SUB ASSY.
13. RETAINER
14. ROLLER, Clutch

15. PINION
16. CLUTCH SUB ASSY.
17. BALL, Steel
18. SPRING
19. SWITCH ASSY., Magnetic (Solenoid)
20. WASHER, Spring
21. NUT, Hexagon
22. BOLT, Flange

Nippondenso and Mitsubishi reduction gear starter—2.6L engine

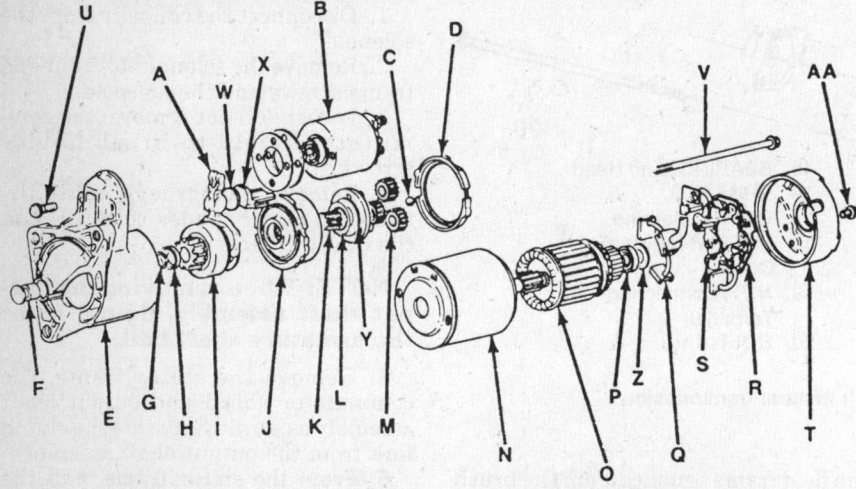

A. Clutch fork
B. Solenoid
C. Armature shaft ball
D. Rubber packing ring
E. Front end housing
F. Drive shaft bushing
G. Snapring
H. Stopring
I. Clutch gear assembly
J. Internal gear assembly
K. Driveshaft
L. Washer
M. Planetary gear set

N. Frame with magnetics
O. Armature
P. Bearing
Q. Brushes
R. Holder assembly brush
S. Spring brush set
T. End cover
U. Screw
V. Through bolts
W. Coin washer
X. Rubber retainer
Y. Z Washer
Z. Wave washer
AA. Screw

Exploded view of the Mitsubishi starter—AMC Eagle Premier 3.0L and Chrysler Laser 2.0L

b. Using a 17mm socket, position it into the armature end of the drive shaft and position the assembly in the vertical position, resting on the socket.

c. Using a 12 point 14mm socket, position it against the stopring (on the clutch end). Using a hammer, strike the socket to unseat the stopring and expose the snapring.

d. Remove the socket, the snapring and the stopring from the drive shaft.

e. Using fine sandpaper or crocus cloth, remove any burrs from the drive shaft. Remove the overrunning clutch.

Inspection:

10. Using compressed air or dry cloths, clean the armature, the stator frame, the overrunning clutch, the solenoid and the brush holder. Using mineral spirits, clean all other components.

11. Inspect the following parts for damage and replace, if necessary:

a. The stator frame and permanent magnets

b. The drive shaft bushing (armature side)

c. The planetary gear set and drive shaft

d. The starter motor bushing and bearing

e. The carbon brushes for cracks, distortion and wear below 0.354 in.

NOTE: When inspecting the brushes, do not remove the socket from the brush holder.

12. Using a growler and a hacksaw blade (placed on top of the armature), rotate the armature and check it for a shorted condition. If the hacksaw blade vibrates, a short exists; replace the armature.

13. Using a test light, place 1 lead on the armature's core and the other on each commutator segment, inspect the armature for a grounded condition. If a ground exists, the test light will turn **ON**; replace the armature.

14. Using a test light, place the leads on the adjacent commutator segments. If the test light turns **ON** between any 2 segments, the armature is shorted and must be replaced.

15. Inspect the commutator out-of-round, if it is more than 0.001 in., reface it on a lathe.

Assembly:

16. Using motor oil, lubricate the drive shaft and the overrunning clutch bushing. Using Lubriplate®, lubricate the overrunning clutch spiral cut splines.

17. Install the overrunning clutch on the drive shaft/planetary gear assembly, followed by the stopring and the snapring; sure to seat the snapring in

the shaft groove and crimp the it with a pair of pliers.

18. Using a battery terminal puller, attach it to the drive shaft tip and press the stopring over the snapring.

NOTE: When install the stopring, be careful not to scratch the drive shaft.

19. Install the clutch fork, with the assembled planetary gear set, lubricated with lithium grease, into the front end housing; make sure the locating lugs are properly seated in the front end housing.

20. Install the coin washer and the rubber fork retainer.

21. Install the rubber backing ring by placing the largest rubber lug at the top.

22. Install the brush holder onto the armature's commutator; make sure the brushes and brush holders are seated in the holder. Inspect the flex washer and install the commutator shield onto the armature. Install the brush holder screws but do not tighten them.

23. Install the armature assembly into the stator frame and seat the wire grommet into the frame.

24. Be sure the armature spline gear is seated in the planetary gear seat with the armature shaft ball in place. Seat the armature shaft in the shaft bushing bore; rotate the stator frame to align the tabs on the drive housing frame.

25. Install the through bolts and torque to 28 inch lbs. Torque the brush holder screws to 18 inch lbs.

26. To complete the assembly, reverse the disassembly procedures.

Bosch Starter

DISASSEMBLY & ASSEMBLY

CHRYSLER 2.5L ENGINE

1. Position the assembly in a suit-able holding fixture. Remove the field terminal nut. Remove the field terminal. Remove the field washer.

2. Remove the solenoid mounting screws. Work the solenoid off of the shift fork and remove the solenoid from the starter.

3. Remove the starter end shield bushing cap screws. Remove the starter end shield bushing cap. Remove the end shield bushing and C-washer.

4. Remove the starter end shield bushing washer. Remove the starter end shield bushing seal.

5. Remove the starter through bolts. Remove the starter end shield. Remove the brush plate.

6. Slide the field frame off of the starter and over the armature. Remove the armature assembly from the drive end housing.

7. Remove the rubber seal from the drive end housing. Remove the starter drive gear train.

8. Remove the dust plate. Press the stop collar off the snapring using the proper tool. Loosen the snapring using a snapring pliers.

9. Remove the output shaft snapring. Remove the clutch stop ring collar. Remove the clutch assembly from the starter.

10. Remove the clutch shift lever bushing. Remove the clutch shift lever. Position a suitable tool and remove the C-clip retainer.

11. Remove the retaining washer. Remove the sun and the planetary gears from the annulus gear,

12. Assembly is the reverse of the disassembly procedure. Replace all defective components as required.

Hitachi Gear Reduction Starter

DISASSEMBLY & ASSEMBLY

1. Position the assembly in a suit-able holding fixture. Disconnect the wire lead at the solenoid. Remove the solenoid-to-starter bolts and the solenoid from the shift lever.

2. Remove the torsion spring from the solenoid. Remove the starter through bolts and the rear cover.

3. Remove the brushes from the brush holder. Remove the frame, the armature and the brush holder as a unit, from the gear case.

4. Carefully remove the brushes and the commutator, do not allow them to contact the adjacent parts.

5. Remove the brush holder and pull the armature assembly from the frame. Remove the bearing retainer and the pinion from the gear case. Remove the retaining clip and disassemble the pinion assembly. Inspect the component parts, replace any that are damaged or worn.

6. To assemble, apply lubricant to the pinion assembly and reverse the removal procedures. After the armature has been installed, raise the end of the brush springs and install the brushes. Install the brush holder by aligning it with the frame.

Ford Positive Engagement Starter

DISASSEMBLY & ASSEMBLY

1. Remove the starter from the vehicle. Position the unit in a soft jawed vise.

2. Remove the cover screw, the cover, through bolts, starter drive end housing and the starter drive plunger lever return spring.

3. Remove the pivot pin from the starter gear plunger lever, the lever and the armature. Remove the stopring retainer and the thrust washer from the armature shaft.

4. Remove the stopring from the groove in the armature shaft and discard it. Remove the starter drive gear

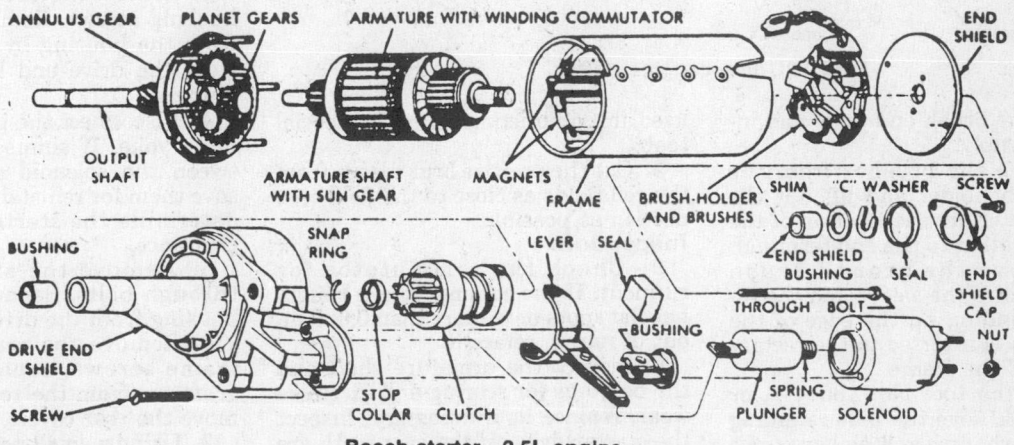

Bosch starter—2.5L engine

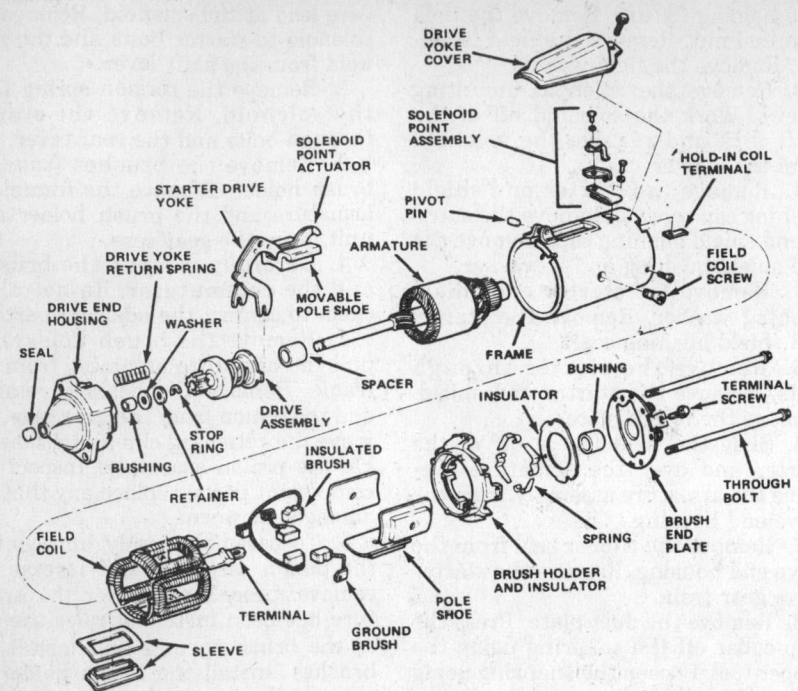

Exploded view of the Ford positive engagement starter motor—AMC similar

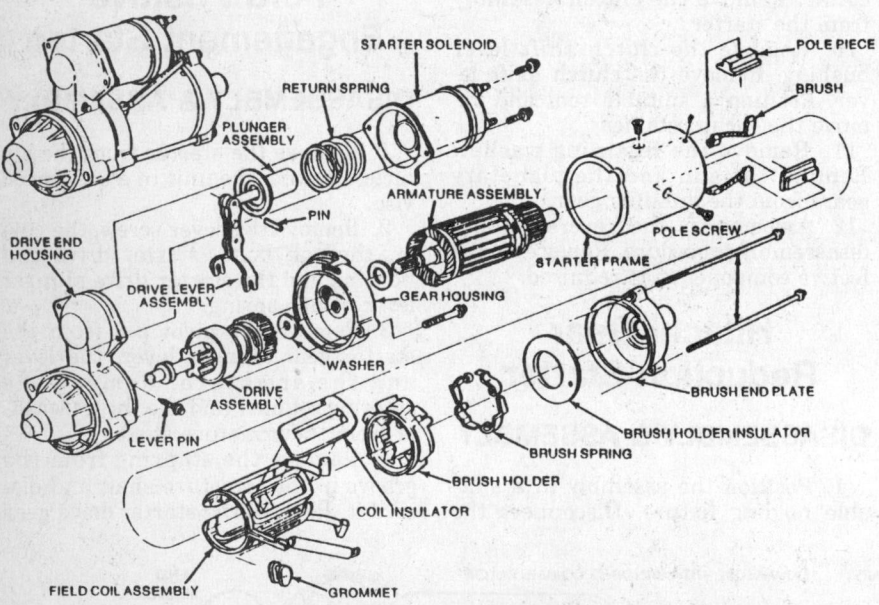

Ford 2.2L diesel engine starter

assembly, the brush end plate and insulator assembly.

5. Remove the brushes from the plastic brush holder and lift out the brush holder. Note the location of the holder in relation to the end terminal.

6. Remove the ground brush screws. Remove the sleeve and the retainer by bending up the edge of the sleeve which is inserted in the rectangular hole of the frame.

7. Using the tool No. 10044–A or equivalent, remove the pole retaining screws. An arbor press may have to be

used in conjunction with the special tool.

8. Cut the positive brush leads from the coil fields as close to the field connection as possible.

Inspection:

9. Check the commutator for runnout. If the commutator is rough, has flat spots or is more than 0.005 in. out of round, reface it.

10. Inspect the armature shaft and the bearings for scoring and excessive wear; replace it, if necessary. Inspect the starter drive; if the gear teeth are

pitted, broken or excessively worn, replace the starter drive.

Assembly:

11. Lubricate the necessary parts and reverse the disassembly procedures.

12. Solder the field coil-to-starter switch terminal posts. Check for continuity and grounds in the assembled coils.

13. Position the ground brushes-to-starter frame and rivet securely.

14. Install the starter motor drive gear assembly onto the armature shaft. Install a new stopring, a new stopring retainer and thrust washer.

15. Install the armature.

16. Position the drive gear plunger lever to the frame and starter drive assembly. Fill the end housing bearing bore a ¼ full or grease. Position the drive end housing onto the frame and make sure the return spring engages the lever tang. Install the pivot pin.

17. Install the brush holder, the brushes and the brush springs; make sure the brushes are positioned properly to avoid grounding.

18. Install the brush end plate; be sure the end plate insulator is positioned correctly on the end plate.

19. Install the through bolts and torque to 55–80 inch lbs. (6–9 Nm).

20. Install the starter drive plunger ever cover and tighten the screw.

21. Check the starter no-load current draw; it should be 80 amps.

Ford Direct Drive Starter

DISASSEMBLY & ASSEMBLY

Ford Festiva and Tracer 1.8L Chrysler Laser and Eagle Summit

1. Position the starter in a soft jawed vice.

2. Remove the field strap-to-solenoid nut and the field strap.

3. Remove the solenoid-to-drive end housing screws. Remove the solenoid from the housing by guiding it away from the drive end housing and the plunger.

4. Disconnect the plunger from the drive yoke. If shims are present between the solenoid and the starter, save them for reinstallation; the shims determine the starter pinion depth clearance.

5. Remove the starter housing through bolts. Separate the starter housing from the drive end housing.

6. Remove the rear cover-to-field frame screws, separate the strap grommet from the rear cover and remove the rear cover.

7. Using a small pry bar, lift the re-

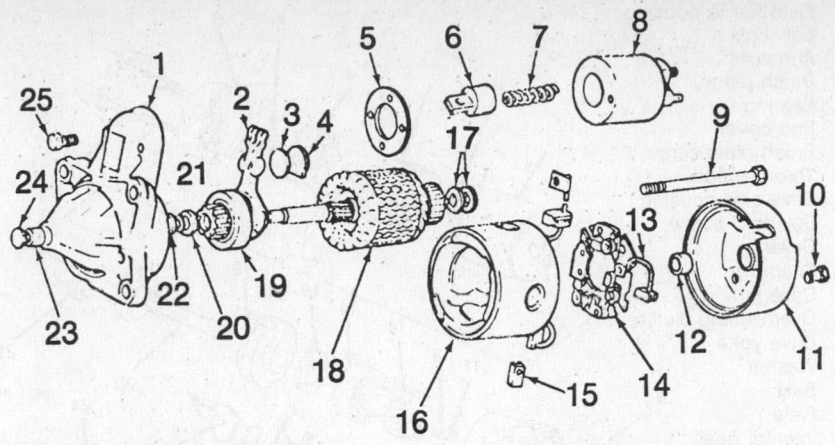

1. Drive end housing
2. Drive yoke
3. Cover plate seal
4. Cover plate
5. Gasket
6. Plunger
7. Plunger spring
8. Solenoid housing
9. Through bolt
10. Cover screw
11. End cover
12. End cover bushing
13. Negative brush
14. Brush plate
15. Positive brush
16. Field frame housing
17. Armature washers
18. Armature
19. Drive pinion
20. Collar
21. Snapring
22. Drive washer
23. Drive end housing bushing
24. Drive end housing plug
25. Solenoid screw

Exploded view of the Ford direct drive starter—Ford Festiva, Ford Tracer and Chrysler Laser (1989–90) 1.8L and Eagle Summit

taining springs and remove the brushes from their channels.

NOTE: Before removing the brush plate, remove the brushes from the plate; this will prevent possible damage to the brushes.

8. Note the position of the yoke and separate it from the drive pinion. Remove the armature and the drive pinion from the drive housing.

9. From the drive housing, remove the yoke, seal and washer.

NOTE: When removing the drive pinion, do not clamp it in a vise, for damage to the internal parts may occur.

10. Using a deep socket or equivalent, drive the armature collar towards the armature to expose the snapring. Remove the snapring from the armature's groove and slide the drive pinion from the armature.

Inspection:

11. Using an ohmmeter, check the each commutator-to-armature core for grounds; there should be no movement of the ohmmeter indicator. If the ohmmeter indicates a ground, replace the armature.

12. Inspect the commutator burn spots, scored surface and/or dirt. Using a set of V-blocks and a dial indica-

tor, check the commutator runout. If the runout is greater than 0.002 in., refinish the commutator or replace the armature.

13. Using a micrometer, check the commutator's outer diameter; if it is less than 1.220 in., replace the armature.

NOTE: Never use emery cloth to clean the commutator face.

14. Inspect the depth of the insulating material between the commutator segments; it should be greater than 0.008 in. If necessary to undercut the insulating material, use a broken hacksaw blade and scrap the material to a depth of 0.020–0.031 in.

15. If the armature core shows signs of scuffing, the bushings are probably worn and need replacement.

16. Inspect the field coil for corrosion, insulation burnt/bare spots and/or deterioration; if necessary, replace the field coil housing assembly.

17. Using an ohmmeter, check the field strap connector-to-brushes for continuity; if there is no continuity, replace the field coil housing assembly.

18. Using an ohmmeter, check for continuity between the field strap connector and the field coil housing; if there is continuity, replace the field coil housing assembly. When performing this test, be certain the brushes

and wires are not touching the housing.

19. Measure the brush lengths for wear, if they are near or beyond 0.453 in., replace the brushes.

20. To inspect the drive pinion, perform the following procedures:

a. Inspect the drive pinion teeth for excessive wear or milling. If either condition exists, the drive pinion and flywheel (manual) or flexplate (automatic) must be replaced.

b. To check the one-way clutch, try to turn the drive pinion in both directions; it should turn freely one-way and lock up the other way.

Assembly:

21. Lubricate the armature splines with Lubriplate® 777 or equivalent. Install the drive pinion and the locking collar on the armature. Install the snapring and pull the collar over the snapring to secure it.

22. Using Lubriplate® 777 or equivalent, lubricate the shift fork and install it into the drive end housing. Engage the armature assembly into the drive end housing and couple the shift fork with the drive pinion.

23. Position the drive end housing into a soft jawed vise (nose down) and install the plug and seal into the housing recess.

24. Lower the field coil housing over the armature and seat it onto the drive end housing; position the housing so the field strap is on the solenoid side.

25. Install the washers onto the armature. Load the brushes into the brush plate holders. With the brushes pull all the way back in the holders, position the brush springs on the brush sides.

26. Install the brush plate over the commutator. Push the brushes toward the commutator until the springs snap onto the brush ends. Make sure the brush wires do not contact any metal parts.

27. Seat the field strap grommet and the rear cover. Install the through bolts and torque them to 55–75 ft. lbs. Install the solenoid and shims (if equipped).

28. To check the pinion depth, perform the following procedures:

a. If the field strap was connected to the solenoid terminal, disconnect it.

b. Using a 12V battery, attach the negative (−) terminal to the solenoid's M-terminal and the positive (+) terminal to the solenoid's S-terminal; this will energize the solenoid.

NOTE: When energizing the solenoid, do not engage it for more than 20 seconds. Between each engagement, allow it to cool for at least 3 minutes.

c. Using a feeler gauge and the solenoid energized, check the drive pinion-to-collar gap; it should be 0.020–0.080 in. If necessary, add or subtract shims between the solenoid and drive end housing until the desired depth is achieved.

Ford Probe Starter

DISASSEMBLY & ASSEMBLY

1. Secure the starter in a soft jawed vise.

2. Remove the field wire from the solenoid's M-terminal. Remove the solenoid-to-starter screws and pull the solenoid from the starter; if there are any shims, save them for reinstallation purposes.

3. Disconnect the plunger and spring from the drive yoke.

4. Matchmark the end cover-to-field frame housing position. Remove the brush plate screws, the starter housing through bolts, the end cover, washer and brush holder assembly.

5. Remove the armature and the field frame housing; be careful not to lose the gear assembly ball.

6. Remove the internal gear gasket, the 3 planetary gears, the solenoid cover plate and seal and pull the gear assembly from the drive end housing.

7. Remove the gear assembly ball. Note the direction of the drive yoke faces and remove it from the gear assembly.

8. Using a deep socket, drive the collar from the snapring. From the driveshaft, remove the snapring. the collar, the drive pinion the internal gear and washer.

9. Using a small prybar, remove the brushes from the brush plate.

Inspection:

10. To inspect the armature, perform the following procedures:

    a. Using digital volt-ohmmeter, check for continuity between the commutator's segments and core; if there is continuity, replace the armature. Check for continuity between the commutator's segments and the shaft; it there is continuity, replace the armature.

    b. Using a set of V-blocks and a dial micrometer, measure the commutator's runout; if the runout is more than 0.002 in. (0.05mm), lightly turn the commutator on a lathe. If the commutator's runout is excessive, replace the armature.

    c. Using a micrometer, check the commutator's outer diameter; if it is less than 1.13 in. (28.8mm), replace the armature.

    d. Using crocus cloth, clean the commutator's face of burnt spots and/or scoring; do not use emery cloth.

1. Field frame housing
2. Ball
3. Armature
4. Brush plate
5. Bearing
6. End cover
7. Brush plate screw
8. Through bolt
9. Drive end housing
10. Solenoid screw
11. Collar
12. Snapring
13. Drive pinion
14. Overrunning clutch
15. Drive yoke
16. Washer
17. Seal
18. Plate
19. Internal gear
20. Driveshaft
21. Planetary gear
22. Plunger
23. Spring
24. Solenoid

Exploded view of the starter—Ford Probe

    e. If the depth between the commutator segments is less than 0.008 in. (0.2mm), use a broken hacksaw blade to undercut the insulating material to 0.020–0.031 in. (0.5–0.8mm).

11. Inspect the armature bearing for looseness, binding or abnormal noise; if necessary, replace it.

12. Inspect the drive pinion and flywheel ring gear for wear, milling and/or chipping; if necessary, replace the drive pinion and/or ring gear.

13. Inspect the internal and planetary gears for wear and/or damage; replace the gears if, necessary.

14. Inspect the brushes for wear by measuring the amount of useable brush remaining; the new brush is 0.69 in. (17.5mm) and the wear limit is 0.39 in. (10.0mm). Check the brushes for free movement in the brush holder; if necessary, clean the brush channels.

Assembly:

15. Using Lubriplate® 777 or equivalent, lubricate the necessary parts.

16. Onto the armature, install the washer, the internal gear, the drive pinion and collar.

17. Install the snapring into the driveshaft groove and press the collar over the snapring.

18. Install the drive yoke onto the gear assembly; be sure the drive yoke faces the correct direction.

19. Install the gasket onto the internal gear. Slide the gear assembly into the drive end housing. Install the solenoid cover plate seal and cover plate.

20. Install the planetary gears and ball. Align the matchmarks and install the field frame housing onto the drive end housing.

21. Position the brushes into the brush holder and secure the brushes by positioning the brush springs on the side of the brushes.

22. Position the brush holder over the armature's commutator and adjust the brush springs so they press the brushes onto the commutator.

23. Slide the armature/brush holder assembly into the field frame housing and align the matchmarks. Install the through bolts and the brush holder screws.

24. Connect the plunger and spring into the drive yoke. Install the solenoid onto the drive end housing; be sure to replace any shims that were removed.

25. Using a 12V battery, connect the negative (−) lead to the starter frame and the positive (+) lead to the solenoid's S-terminal; the solenoid should kick out the pinion.

NOTE: Do not engage the solenoid for more than 20 seconds at a time and allow 3 minutes for the solenoid to cool before attempting to energize it again.

26. With the solenoid activated, use a feeler gauge, measure the gap between the pinion and the collar; the gap should be 0.02–0.08 in. (0.5–2.0mm). If the gap is outside the measurement range, add or subtract shims until it is within specifications.

27. Install the field strap to the M-terminal on the solenoid and torque the nut to 90–110 inch lbs. (10–12 Nm).

Delco 5MT, 10MT and 27MT Starters

DISASSEMBLY & ASSEMBLY

NOTE: In 1989, the identification for the 5MT starter was converted to the SD200 and SD250 starters.

1. Remove the starter from the vehicle. Position the unit in a soft jawed vise.
2. Remove the field coil connector screw and the solenoid-to-starter screws. Rotate the solenoid 90 degrees and remove it along with the plunger return spring.
3. Remove the starter through bolts, the commutator end frame and washer.
4. Remove the field frame assembly from the drive gear housing.
5. If equipped, remove the center bearing screws. Remove the drive gear housing from the armature shaft.
6. To remove the overrunning clutch from the armature shaft, perform the following procedures:
   a. Remove the washer or collar from the armature shaft.
   b. Using a ⅝ in. deep socket, slide it over the shaft and against the retainer. Using the socket as a driving tool, tap it with a hammer to move the retainer of the snapring.
   c. Remove the snapring from the groove in the shaft; if the snapring is distorted, replace it.
   d. Remove the retainer and the clutch assembly from the armature shaft.
7. If required, the shaft lever and the plunger can be disassembled by removing the roll pin.
8. To replace the starter brushes, remove the brush holder pivot pin which positions the insulated and the ground brushes. Remove the brush spring.
9. On 5MT starters, to replace the brushes remove the screw from the brush holder and separate the brushes from the holder.

Inspection:

10. Inspect armature commutator, shaft and bushings, overrunning clutch pinion, brushes and springs for discoloration, damage or wear; replace the damaged parts.
11. Check fit of armature shaft in bushing in drive housing. The shaft should fit snugly in the bushing; if it is worn, replace it.
12. Inspect armature commutator. If commutator is rough, it should be refinished on a lathe. Do not undercut or turn to less than 1.650 in. O.D. Inspect

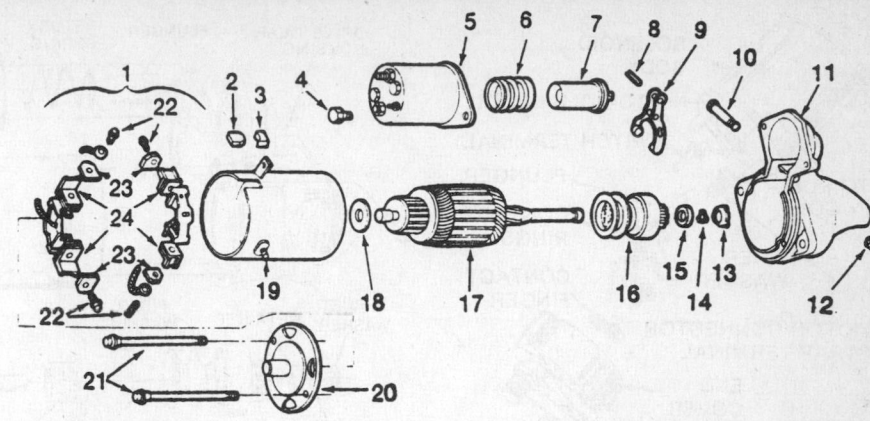

1 Brush and holder set	13 Thrust collar
2 Grommet	14 Pinion stop retainer ring
3 Grommet	15 Pinion stop collar
4 Screw	16 Clutch and drive assembly
5 Solenoid	17 Armature
6 Plunger return spring	18 Washer
7 Plunger	19 Frame and field assembly
8 Plunger pin	20 Commutator end frame
9 Shift fork	21 Through bolts
10 Shift fork shaft	22 Screw
11 Drive end housing	23 Brush
12 Shift fork shaft retaining ring	24 Brush holder

Exploded view of the Delco-Remy 5 MT starter, typical

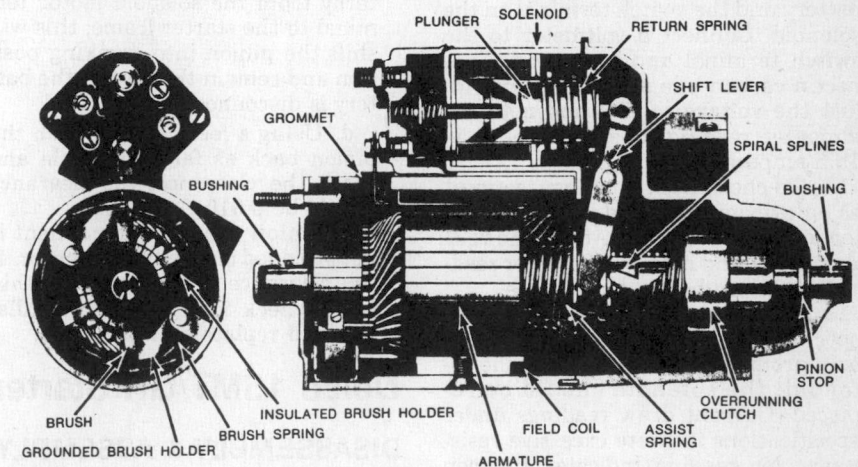

Typical Delco-Remy starter motor, using an assist spring—light duty Chevrolet illustrated

the points where the armature conductors join the commutator bars to make sure they have a good connection. A burned commutator bar is usually evidence of a poor connection.

13. Using a growler and holding hacksaw blade over armature core while armature is rotated, inspect the armature for short circuits. If saw blade vibrates, armature is shorted.
14. Using a test lamp place a lead on the shunt coil terminal and connect the other lead to a ground brush. The test should be made using both ground brushes to insure continuity through the brushes and leads. If the lamp fails to light, the field coil is open and will require replacement.
15. Using a test lamp place a lead on the series coil terminal and the other on the insulated brush. If the lamp fails to light the series coil is open and will require repair or replacement. The test should be made from each insulated brush to check brush and lead continuity.
16. If equipped with a shunt coil separate the series and shunt coil strap terminals during the test. Do not allow the strap terminals to touch case or other ground. Using a test lamp place a lead on the grounded brush holder and the other lead on either insulated brush. If the lamp lights a grounded series coil is indicated and must be repaired or replaced.

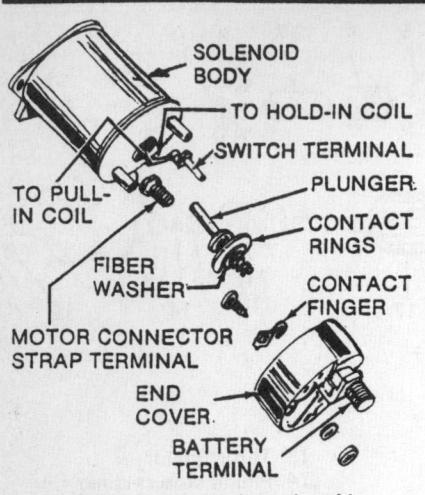

Delco-Remy starter solenoid

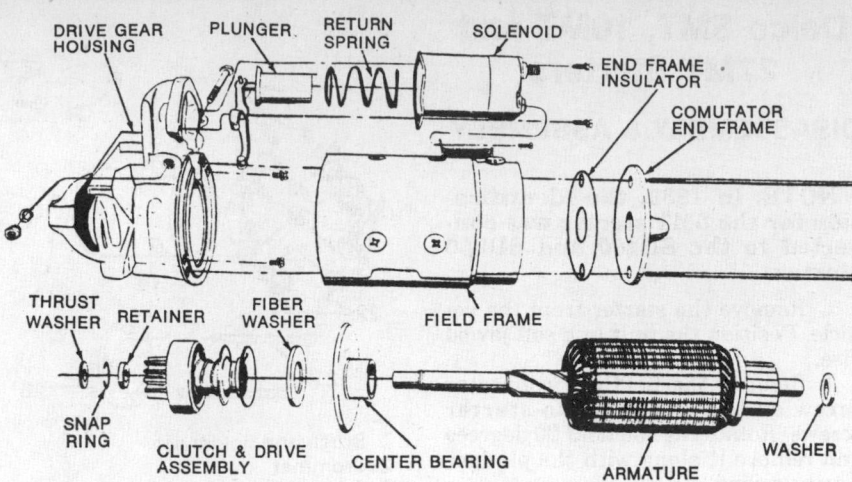

Exploded view of the GM 27 MT starter

NOTE: If the solenoid has not been removed from the starter, the connector strap terminals must be removed before making the following tests. Complete the tests as fast as possible in order to prevent overheating the solenoid.

17. To check the starter winding, connect an ammeter in series with 12V battery and the switch terminal on the solenoid. Connect a voltmeter to the switch terminal and to ground. Connect a carbon pile across battery. Adjust the voltage to 10V and note the ammeter reading; it should be 14.5–16.5 amperes.

18. To check both windings, connect as for previous test and ground the solenoid motor terminal. Adjust the voltage to 10V and note the ammeter reading; it should be 41–47 amperes.

19. Current draw readings over specifications indicate shorted turns on a ground in the windings of the solenoid; the solenoid should be replaced. Current draw readings under specifications indicate excessive resistance. No reading indicates an open circuit. Check the connections and replace the solenoid (if necessary). Current readings will decrease as the windings heat up.

Assembly:

20. To assemble, reverse the disassembly procedures. Be sure to replace or repair all defective components as required.

NOTE: When the starter has been disassembled or the solenoid replaced, it is necessary to check the pinion clearance. Pinion clearance must be checked in order to prevent the buttons on the shift lever yoke from rubbing on the clutch collar during engine cranking.

21. To check the pinion clearance, perform the following procedures:

a. Disconnect the motor field coil connector from the solenoid motor terminal and insulate the terminal.

b. Connect the positive 12V battery lead to the solenoid switch terminal and the negative lead to the starter frame.

c. Touch a jumper lead momentarily from the solenoid motor terminal to the starter frame; this will shift the pinion into cranking position and remain there until the battery is disconnected.

d. Using a feeler gauge, push the pinion back as far as possible and check the clearance; the clearance should be 0.010–0.140 in.

e. Pinion clearance adjustment is not provided on the starter motor. If the clearance does not fall within limits check for improper installation and replace all worn parts.

Delco 15MT/GR Starter

DISASSEMBLY & ASSEMBLY

1. Remove the starter from the vehicle. Position the unit in a soft jawed vise.

2. Remove the field coil screw, the field frame through bolts and separate the field frame assembly from the drive gear assembly. Separate the armature and the commutator end frame from the field frame.

3. Remove the solenoid screws and the solenoid from the drive housing.

4. Remove the retaining ring, shift lever shaft and housing through bolts. Separate the drive assembly, drive housing and gear assembly.

5. To remove the overrunning clutch from the armature shaft, perform the following procedures:

a. Remove the washer or collar from the armature shaft.

b. Using a ⅝ in. deep socket, slide it over the shaft and against the retainer. Use the socket as a driving tool, tap the socket with a hammer to move the retainer off of the snapring.

c. Remove the snapring from the groove in the shaft; if the snapring is distorted, replace it.

d. Remove the retainer and the clutch assembly from the armature shaft.

6. To replace the starter brushes, remove the brush holder pivot pin which positions the insulated and the ground brushes. Remove the brush spring.

7. Inspect armature commutator, shaft and bushings, overrunning clutch pinion, brushes and springs for discoloration, damage or wear; replace the damaged parts (if necessary). Check the armature shaft fit in drive housing bushing; the shaft should fit snugly in the bushing. If the bushing is worn, it should be replaced.

Inspection:

8. Inspect armature commutator. If commutator is rough, it should be refinished on a lathe; do not undercut or turn to less than 1.650 in. O.D. Inspect the points where the armature conductors join the commutator bars to make sure they have a good connection. A burned commutator is usually evidence of a poor connection.

9. Using a growler and holding hacksaw blade over armature core while armature is rotated, check the armature for short circuits; if the saw blade vibrates, the armature is shorted.

10. Using a test lamp, place a lead on the shunt coil terminal and the other lead to a ground brush. The test should be made from both ground brushes to insure continuity through both brushes and leads. If the lamp fails to light, the field coil is open and will require replacement.

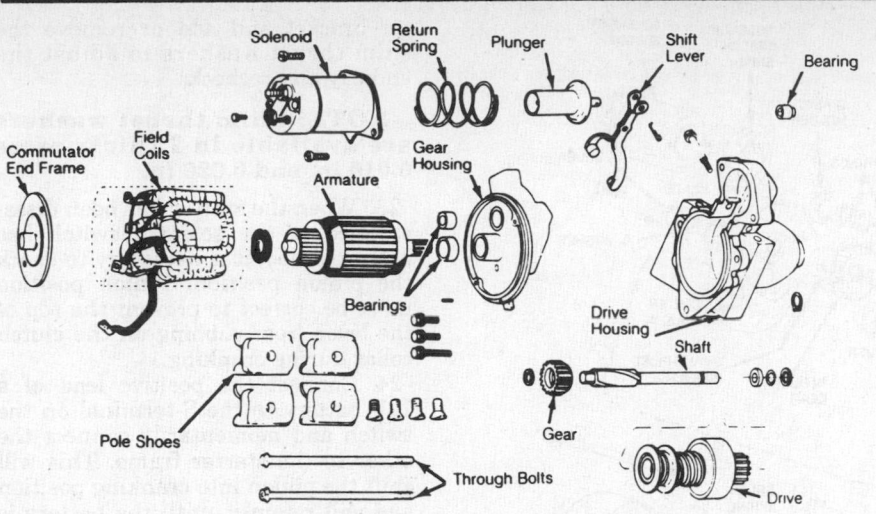

Exploded view of the GM 15MT/GR starter

11. Using a test lamp, place a lead on the series coil terminal and the other lead on the insulated brush. If the lamp fails to light, the series coil is open and will require repair or replacement. The test should be made from each insulated brush to check brush and lead continuity.

12. If equipped with a shunt coil, separate the series and shunt coil strap terminals during this test; do not allow the strap terminals to touch the case or other ground. Using a test lamp, place a lead on the grounded brush holder and the other lead on either insulated brush. If the lamp lights, a grounded series coil is indicated and must be repaired or replaced.

NOTE: If the solenoid has not been removed from the starter, the connector strap terminals must be removed before making the following tests. Complete the tests as fast as possible in order to prevent overheating the solenoid.

13. To check the starter winding, connect an ammeter in series with a 12V battery, the switch terminal and to ground. Connect a carbon pile across the battery. Adjust the voltage to 10V and note the ammeter reading; it should be 14.5–16.5 amperes.

14. To check both windings, connect as for previous test. Ground the solenoid motor terminal, adjust the voltage to 10V and note the ammeter reading; it should be 41–47 amperes.

15. Current draw readings above specifications indicate shorted turns or a ground in the windings of the solenoid; the solenoid should be replaced. Current draw readings under specifications indicate excessive resistance. No reading indicates an open circuit. Check the connections and replace solenoid (if necessary). Current readings will decrease as windings heat up.

Assembly:

16. The roller bearing in the drive housing and the roller bearings in the gear housing must be replaced (if they are dry); do not lubricate or reuse the bearings.

17. To replace the gear housing bearing, use a tube or solid cylinder that just fits inside the housing to push bearing toward the armature side. In the opposite direction, use the tube or cylinder to press bearing flush with housing.

18. To replace the gear housing drive shaft bearing, use a tube or collar that just fits inside the housing and press bearing out; press against the open end of bearing. To install a new bearing, press against the closed end, using a thin wall tube or collar that fits in space between bearing and housing. Do not press against the flat end of the bearing; this will bend the thin metal of the bearing. As required, replace the drive housing bearing.

19. To assemble, reverse the disassembly procedures. Be sure to replace or repair all defective components as required.

NOTE: When the starter has been disassembled or the solenoid replaced, it is necessary to check the pinion clearance. The pinion clearance must be checked in order to prevent the buttons on the shift lever yoke from rubbing on the clutch collar during engine cranking.

20. To check the pinion clearance, perform the following procedures:

    a. Disconnect the motor field coil connector from the solenoid motor terminal and insulate the terminal.

    b. Connect the positive (+) 12V battery lead to the solenoid switch terminal and the other to the starter frame.

    c. Touch a jumper lead momentarily from the solenoid motor terminal to the starter frame; this will shift the pinion into cranking position and retain it until the battery is disconnected.

    d. Using a feeler gauge, push the pinion back as far as possible, to take up any movement, and check the clearance; the clearance should be 0.010–0.140 in.

    e. Means for adjusting pinion clearance is not provided on the starter motor. If the clearance does not fall within limits, check for improper installation and replace worn parts.

Delco 15MT/GR Aluminum Starter

DISASSEMBLY & ASSEMBLY

1. Remove the starter from the vehicle. Position the unit in a soft jawed vise.

2. Remove the field connector nut, the solenoid switch screws and the solenoid.

3. If equipped with shims between the solenoid and the drive end housing, retain these for installation purposes.

4. Remove the starter through bolts and the brush holder bolts. Remove the commutator end frame from the armature and bearing assembly. Remove the field frame assembly and the armature from the center housing.

5. Pry back each brush spring so that each brush can be backed away from the armature about ¼ in. Release the spring to hold the brushes in the backed out position, then remove the armature from the field frame and brush holder.

6. Remove the shaft cover-to-center housing screws and the shaft cover. Remove the C-shaped washer and plate. Remove the center housing bolts, the center housing shim and thrust washers.

7. Remove the reduction gear, the spring holder and the lever springs.

8. To remove the drive pinion, perform the following procedures:

    a. Using a ⅝ in. socket, slide it over the shaft against the stopper.

    b. Using the socket as a driving tool, tap it with a hammer to move the stopper off the ring.

    c. Remove the stopper and the drive pinion.

9. Remove the pinion shaft and the lever assembly. Note the direction of the lever and the lever holders.

Inspection:

10. Clean all parts in the proper cleaning solution. Inspect all parts for

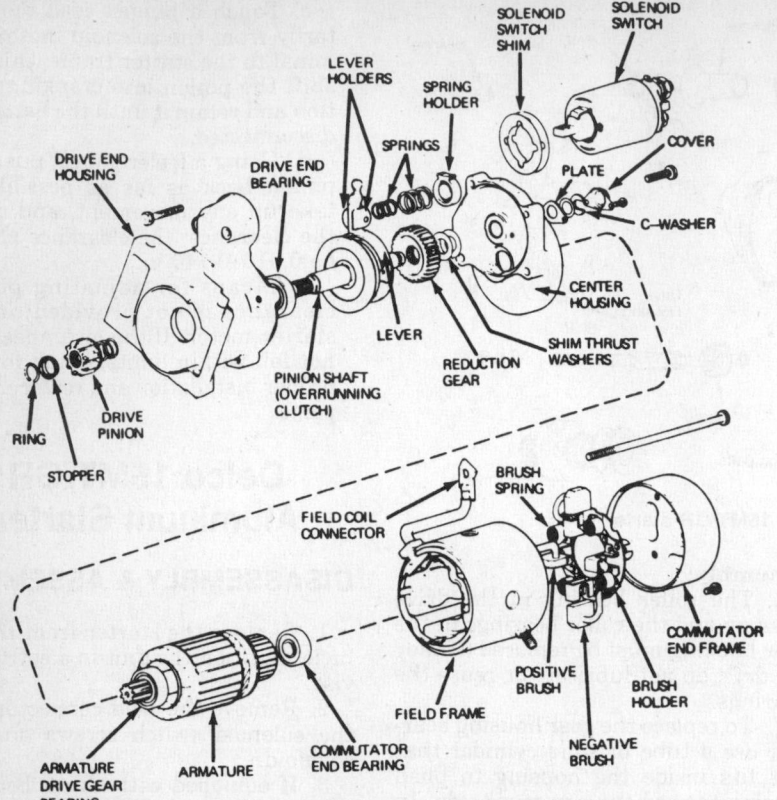

Exploded view of the GM ALU/GR diesel starter

wear and damage; replace or repair defective components as required. Inspect all bearings for wear, roughness or dryness; replace damaged bearings with new ones.

11. Inspect the armature commutator. If the commutator is rough, it should be refinished on a lathe; do not turn the commutator to less than 1.480 in. outside diameter.

12. With the brush holder assembly still attached to the field frame, test the field coils for open. Using a test lamp, place a test lead on the field coil connector and the other test lead on the positive (+) brush.

13. The test light should turn **ON**. If the test light fails to light, the field coil is open; the field coil must be replaced. Repeat the test on the other positive brush.

14. To test the field coil for ground, place a test light lead on the field coil connector and the other lead on the field frame; the test light should stay **OFF**. If the test light turns **ON**, the field coils are grounded to the field frame assembly; the field frame must be replaced.

Assembly:

15. To replace the brushes, remove the positive brushes from the brush holder, the brush holder and the negative brush assembly from the field frame.

16. Cut the old brush leads off of

their mountings as close to brush connection point as possible. Solder the new brushes as required. Careful installation of the positive side is necessary to prevent grounding of the brush connection point having no insulation.

17. Reinstall the positive and negative brushes in the brush holder assembly and position the assembly in the starter housing.

18. In order to replace the drive end bearing, it will be necessary to press the bearing out of the drive end housing using a press. Replace the armature commutator end bearing and the armature drive end bearing.

19. To assemble, reverse the disassembly procedures. Be sure to check all parts for wear and damage; repair or replace defective parts.

20. If either the drive end housing, pinion shaft, reduction gear, shim washers or center housing were replaced, it will be necessary to check the endplay for the pinion shaft. Install the plate and C-shaped washer onto the end of the pinion shaft.

21. With the drive end housing mounted in a soft jawed vise, measure the endplay. Insert feeler gauge between C-washer and cover plate, pry the pinion shaft in the axial direction to check the endplay; it should be 0.004–0.020 in.

22. If the endplay is not correct, remove the plate, C-shaped washer, cen-

ter bracket and add or remove the shim thrust washers to adjust the endplay and recheck.

NOTE: Shim thrust washers are available in 2 thicknesses 0.010 in. and 0.020 in.

23. When the starter has been disassembled or the solenoid switch has been replaced, it is necessary to check the pinion position. Pinion position must be correct to prevent the top of the lever from rubbing on the clutch collar during cranking.

24. Connect the positive lead of a 12V battery to the S-terminal on the switch and momentarily connect the other to the starter frame. This will shift the pinion into cranking position and will retain it until the battery is disconnected. Do not leave engaged more than 30 seconds at a time.

25. Using a dial indicator (with pinion engaged), push the pinion shaft back by hand and measure the amount of pinion shaft movement; the clearance should be 0.020–0.080 in.

26. If the amount does not fall within limits, adjust it by adding or removing the shims which are located between the switch and the front bracket; adding shims decreases the amount of the movement. Solenoid switch shims are available in 2 thicknesses 0.020 in. and 0.010 in.

Ducellier and Paris-Rhone Starter

DISASSEMBLY & ASSEMBLY

Medallion

1. Support the starter in a soft jawed vise.

2. Remove the rear mounting bracket-to-starter nuts, the bracket and the plastic cap.

3. Disconnect the field wire from the solenoid.

4. Remove the solenoid-to-starter nuts and the solenoid.

5. From the end cover, remove the nuts, the through bolts and the end cover.

6. Using a pin punch at the drive end housing, drive the yoke axle pin from the housing.

7. At the positive brushes, move the brush spring clips to the side of the brushes and pull the brushes away from the armature. Carefully pull the field housing from the drive end housing.

8. Remove the pinion yoke and armature from the drive end housing.

9. Using a deep socket which fits over the armature shaft, tap the stop collar (driving it toward the armature) to expose the snapring. Remove the

snapring from the groove and slide it from the shaft.

NOTE: When removing the snapring, be careful not to bend or distort it.

10. Remove the stop collar, the drive pinion and the support plate.

11. Using compressed air or a brush, clean the drive pinion, the drive end frame, the armature, the field coils and the starter frame; all other parts can be cleaned in solvent.

12. Inspect the condition of the starter parts, perform the following procedures:

a. Check for broken wires or badly soldered connections.

b. Replace any bushings which are scored or badly worn.

c. If the armature's commutator more than 0.005 in. out of round, reface it on a lathe.

NOTE: NEVER use emery cloth to clean a commutator.

d. The drive pinion should be free of excessive wear or damage.

e. If the brushes are cracked, broken, distorted or worn to less than 0.314 in., replace them.

f. Using a growler and a hacksaw blade (placed on top of the armature), rotate the armature and check it for a shorted condition. If the hacksaw blade vibrates, a short exists; replace the armature.

g. Using a test light, place 1 lead on the armature's core and the other on each commutator segment, inspect the armature for a grounded condition. If a ground exists, the test light will turn **ON**; replace the armature.

h. Using a test light, check for continuity between the positive brushes; if no continuity exists, replace the winding. Repeat this test for the negative windings.

i. Using a test light, place 1 lead on the coil housing and the other on each coil lead, make sure there is NO continuity; if continuity exists, replace the winding(s).

Assembly:
13. Lubricate the necessary parts and place the support plate onto the armature, followed by the drive pinion and the stop collar. Carefully slide the snapring into the armature groove. Slide the stop collar over the snapring until it locks.

14. Position the armature and pinion yoke into the drive end housing. Install the pinion yoke axle pin.

15. Install the coil housing over the armature and onto the drive end housing. Position the brush holder onto the coil housing. Install the brushes and secure the brush springs.

A. End housing bushing
B. End housing
C. Yoke axle
D. Pinion yoke and solenoid shaft
E. Solenoid spring
F. Spacer
G. Pad

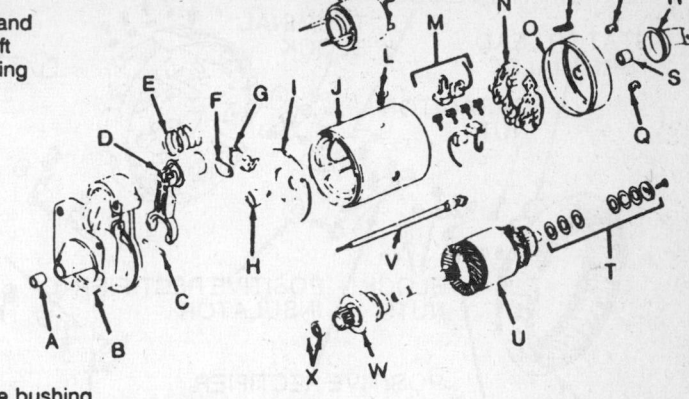

H. Support plate bushing
I. Support plate
J. Armature/field winding housing
K. Solenoid
L. Pole shoe screw
M. Brush and spring assembly

N. Brush holder
O. End cover
P. Grommet
Q. Support bracket nut
R. Cap
S. Brush holder bushing

T. Armature brake assembly
U. Armature
V. Through bolts
W. Drive pinion
X. Collar and snapring

Exploded view of the Ducellier and Paris-Rhone starter — Medallion

16. Install the solenoid to the drive end housing. Position the field wire grommet to the coil housing and connect field wire to the solenoid.

17. Install the end cover to the coil housing and the install the through bolts/nuts. Install the armature brake assembly, the plastic cover and the mounting bracket.

ALTERNATORS

Chrysler 60, 78, 114 and 117 Amp with External Regulator

The 60 and 78 amp alternators are equipped with 6 built-in silicon rectifiers, while the 114 and 117 amp alternators are equipped with 12 built-in silicon rectifiers.

DISASSEMBLY & ASSEMBLY

To prevent damage to the brush assemblies (114 and 117 amp), they should be removed before proceeding with the disassembly of the alternator. The brushes are mounted in a plastic holder that positions the brushes vertically against the slip-rings.

1. Remove the retaining screw, flat washer, nylon washer and field terminal and carefully lift the plastic holder containing the spring and brush assembly from the end housing.

2. The ground brush (60 amp) is positioned horizontally against the slipring and is retained in the holder that is integral with the end housing. Remove the retaining screw and lift the clip, spring and brush assembly from the end housing. The stator is laminated so don't burr the stator or end housings.

3. Remove the through bolts and pry between the stator and drive end housing with a suitable tool. Carefully separate the drive end housing, pulley and rotor assembly from the stator and rectifier housing assembly.

4. The pulley is an interference fit on the rotor shaft. Remove with a puller and special adapters.

5. Remove the nuts and washers and, while supporting the end frame, tap the rotor shaft with a plastic hammer and separate the rotor and end housing.

6. The drive end ball bearing is an interference fit with the rotor shaft. Remove the bearing with puller and adapters.

NOTE: Further dismantling of the rotor is not advisable, as the remainder of the rotor assembly is not serviced separately.

7. Remove the DC output terminal nuts and washers and remove the terminal screw. Remove the inside capacitor (on units so equipped).

8. Remove the insulator.

NOTE: Positive rectifiers are pressed into the heat sink and negative rectifiers in the end housing. When removing the rec-

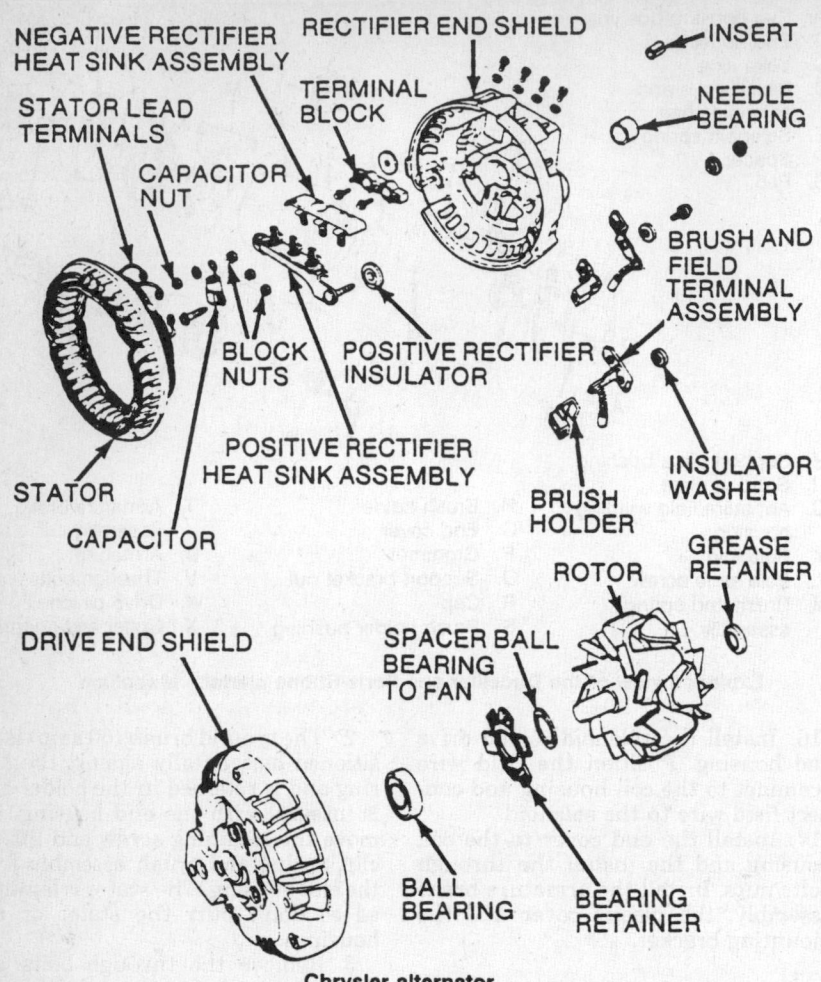

NEGATIVE RECTIFIER HEAT SINK ASSEMBLY
RECTIFIER END SHIELD
INSERT
STATOR LEAD TERMINALS
TERMINAL BLOCK
NEEDLE BEARING
CAPACITOR NUT
BRUSH AND FIELD TERMINAL ASSEMBLY
BLOCK NUTS
POSITIVE RECTIFIER INSULATOR
POSITIVE RECTIFIER HEAT SINK ASSEMBLY
INSULATOR WASHER
STATOR
BRUSH HOLDER
CAPACITOR
ROTOR
GREASE RETAINER
DRIVE END SHIELD
SPACER BALL BEARING TO FAN
BALL BEARING
BEARING RETAINER

Chrysler alternator

tifiers it is necessary to support the end housing and the heat sink in order to prevent damage to the castings. Another caution is in order relative to the diode rectifiers. Don't subject them to unnecessary jolting. Heavy vibration or shock may ruin them. Cut rectifier wire at point of crimp. Support rectifier housing. The factory tool is cut away and slotted to fit over the wires and around the bosses in the housing. Be sure that the bore of the tool completely surrounds the rectifier, then press the rectifier out of the housing. The roller bearing in the rectifier end frame is a press fit. To protect the end housing, it is necessary to support the housing with a tool when pressing out the bearing.

Assembly:

9. Support the heat sink or rectifier end housing on circular plate.
10. Check rectifier identification to be sure the correct rectifier is being used. The part numbers are stamped on the case of the rectifier. They are also marked red for positive and black for negative.

11. Start the new rectifier into the casting and press it in squarely. Do not start rectifier with a hammer or it will be ruined.
12. Crimp the new rectifier wire to the wires disconnected at removal or solder using a heat sink with rosin core solder.
13. Support the end housing on tool so that the notch in the support tool will clear the raised section of the heat sink, press the bearing into position with tool SP-3381, or equivalent. New bearings are prelubricated, additional lubrication is not required.
14. Insert the drive end bearing in the drive end housing and install the bearing plate, washers and nuts to hold the bearing in place.
15. Position the bearing and drive end housing on the rotor shaft and, while supporting the base of the rotor shaft, press the bearing and housing in position on the rotor shaft with an arbor press and arbor tool. Be careful that there is no cocking of the bearing at installation; or damage will result. Press the bearing on the rotor shaft until the bearing contacts the shoulder on the rotor shaft.

16. Install pulley on rotor shaft. Shaft of rotor must be supported so that all pressing force is on the pulley hub and rotor shaft. Do not exceed 6800 lbs. pressure. Pulley hub should just contact bearing inner race.
17. Some alternators will be found to have the capacitor mounted internally. Be sure the heat sink insulator is in place.
18. Install the output terminal screw with the capacitor attached through the heat sink and end housing.
19. Install insulating washers, lockwashers and locknuts.
20. Make sure the heat sink and insulator are in place and tighten the locknut.
21. Position the stator on the rectifier end housing. Be sure that all of the rectifier connectors and phase leads are free of interference with the rotor fan blades and that the capacitor (internally mounted) lead has clearance.
22. Position the rotor assembly in the rectifier end housing. Align the through bolt holes in the stator with both end housings.
23. Enter stator shaft in the rectifier end housing bearing, compress stator and both end housings manually and install through bolts, washers and nuts.
24. Install the insulated brush and terminal attaching screw.
25. Install the ground screw and attaching screw.
26. Rotate pulley slowly to be sure the rotor fan blades do not hit the rectifier and stator connectors.

Chrysler 60 and 78 amp Alternator with Voltage Regulator in Engine Electronics

DISASSEMBLY & ASSEMBLY

The alternators are equipped with 6 built in silicon rectifiers, that convert AC current into DC current.

1. Remove the retaining screw, flat washer, nylon washer and field terminal and carefully lift the plastic holder containing the spring and brush assembly from the end housing.
2. The ground brush (60 amp) is positioned horizontally against the slipring and is retained in the holder that is integral with the end housing. Remove the retaining screw and lift the clip, spring and brush assembly from the end housing. The stator is laminated so don't burr the stator or end housings.
3. Remove the through bolts and pry between the stator and drive end housing with a suitable tool. Carefully

separate the drive end housing, pulley and rotor assembly from the stator and rectifier housing assembly.

4. The pulley is an interference fit on the rotor shaft. Remove with a puller and special adapters.

5. Remove the nuts and washers and, while supporting the end frame, tap the rotor shaft with a plastic hammer and separate the rotor and end housing.

6. The drive end ball bearing is an interference fit with the rotor shaft. Remove the bearing with puller and adapters.

NOTE: Further dismantling of the rotor is not advisable, as the remainder of the rotor assembly is not serviced separately.

7. Remove the DC output terminal nuts and washers and remove terminal screw and inside capacitor (on units so equipped).

8. Remove the insulator.

NOTE: Positive rectifiers are pressed into the heat sink and negative rectifiers in the end housing. When removing the rectifiers it is necessary to support the end housing and the heat sink in order to prevent damage to the castings. Another caution is in order relative to the diode rectifiers. Don't subject them to unnecessary jolting. Heavy vibration or shock may ruin them. Cut rectifier wire at point of crimp. Support rectifier housing. The factory tool is cut away and slotted to fit over the wires and around the bosses in the housing. Be sure that the bore of the tool completely surrounds the rectifier, then press the rectifier out of the housing. The roller bearing in the rectifier end frame is a press fit. To protect the end housing, it is necessary to support the housing with a tool when pressing out the bearing.

Assembly:

9. Support the heat sink or rectifier end housing on circular plate.

10. Check rectifier identification to be sure the correct rectifier is being used. The part numbers are stamped on the case of the rectifier. They are also marked red for positive and black for negative.

11. Start the new rectifier into the casting and press it in squarely. Do not start rectifier with a hammer or it will be ruined.

12. Crimp the new rectifier wire to the wires disconnected at removal or solder using a heat sink with rosin core solder.

13. Support the end housing on tool so that the notch in the support tool will clear the raised section of the heat sink, press the bearing into position with tool SP-3381, or equivalent. New bearings are prelubricated, additional lubrication is not required.

14. Insert the drive end bearing in the drive end housing and install the bearing plate, washers and nuts to hold the bearing in place.

15. Position the bearing and drive end housing on the rotor shaft and, while supporting the base of the rotor shaft, press the bearing and housing in position on the rotor shaft with an arbor press and arbor tool. Be careful that there is no cocking of the bearing at installation; or damage will result. Press the bearing on the rotor shaft until the bearing contacts the shoulder on the rotor shaft.

16. Install pulley on rotor shaft. Shaft of rotor must be supported so that all pressing force is on the pulley hub and rotor shaft. Do not exceed 6800 lbs. pressure. Pulley hub should just contact bearing inner race.

17. Some alternators will be found to have the capacitor mounted internally. Be sure the heat sink insulator is in place.

18. Install the output terminal screw with the capacitor attached through the heat sink and end housing.

19. Install insulating washers, lockwashers and locknuts.

20. Make sure the heat sink and insulator are in place and tighten the locknut.

21. Position the stator on the rectifier end housing. Be sure that all of the rectifier connectors and phase leads are free of interference with the rotor fan blades and that the capacitor (internally mounted) lead has clearance.

22. Position the rotor assembly in the rectifier end housing. Align the through bolt holes in the stator with both end housings.

23. Enter stator shaft in the rectifier end housing bearing, compress stator and both end housings manually and install through bolts, washers and nuts.

24. Install the insulated brush and terminal attaching screw.

25. Install the ground screw and attaching screw.

26. Rotate pulley slowly to be sure the rotor fan blades do not hit the rectifier and stator connectors.

Chrysler 40/90 and 50/120 Amp Alternator with External Regulator

The 40/90 alternator is used as standard equipment. When the vehicle is equipped with for lamps or a police/taxi package, the 50/120 alternator is used.

DISASSEMBLY & ASSEMBLY

1. Remove the rectifier dust cover nut and separate the cover from the alternator.

2. Remove the brush holder bolts and separate it from the alternator.

3. Remove the stator lead, the rectifier and capacitor bolts. Separate the rectifier and insulator from the alternator.

4. If disassembling a 50/120 alternator rectifier, perform the following procedures:

   a. Remove the connecting strap from between the rectifiers.

   b. Remove the buss bar and insulator screws.

   c. Separate the insulators from the rectifier.

5. From the shield end, remove the through bolts.

6. From the drive end shield, separate the stator and rectifier end shield.

7. Separate the stator from the rectifier end shield.

8. Remove the drive pulley nut, the washer, the pulley and the fan.

9. Press the rotor shaft from the drive end shield.

NOTE: If the bearing is defective, replace the drive end shield as an assembly.

10. If necessary to remove the rectifi-

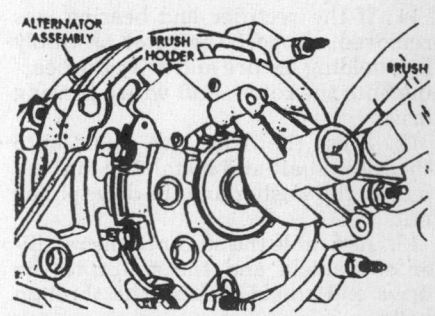

Removing the brush assembly—Chrysler 40/90 alternator

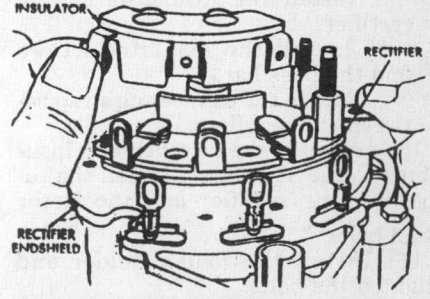

Removing and installing the rectifier assembly—Chrysler 40/90 alternator

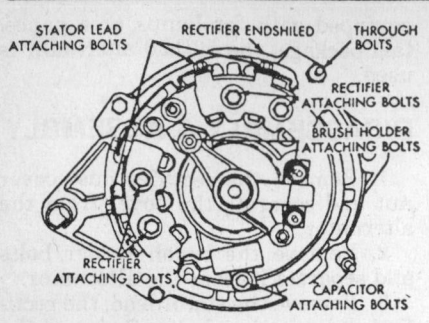

View of the rectifier end shield assembly bolts—Chrysler 90 and 120 amp alternator

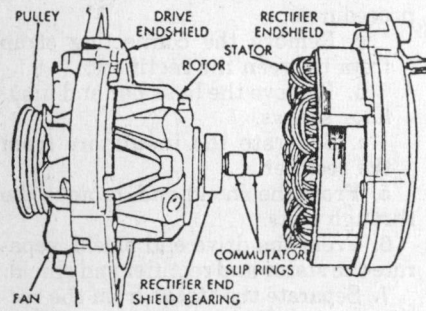

View of the stator and drive end shield assemblies—Chrysler 90 and 120 amp alternator

er end bearing from the rotor assembly, use a bearing puller to press the bearing from the rotor shaft.

Assembly:

11. If the rectifier end bearing was removed, support the rotor assembly in a holding fixture and drive the bearing onto the rotor shaft with a bearing driver.

12. Press the drive end shield onto the rotor shaft and install the fan, the pulley, the washer and the drive pulley nut.

13. Assemble the stator to the rectifier end shield and the stator to the drive end shield. Install the through bolts.

14. If assembling a 50/120 alternator rectifier, perform the following procedures:

   a. Install the insulators on the rectifier.

   b. Install the insulator screws and the buss bar.

   c. Attach the connecting strap between the rectifiers.

15. Assemble the rectifier and insulator to the alternator. Install the capacitor, the rectifier and the stator lead bolts.

16. Install the brush holder and tighten the bolts.

17. Install the rectifier dust cover and nut.

Chrysler 40/90 and 50/120 Amp Alternator with Voltage Regulator in Engine Electronics

The 40/90 has 6 built-in silicon rectifiers, while the 50/120 has 12 built-in silicon rectifiers. The voltage regulator is built into the power and logic modules.

1. Remove the dust cover mounting nut. Remove the dust cover.

2. Remove the brush holder assembly mounting screws. Remove the brush holder assembly.

3. Remove the stator to rectifier mounting screws. Remove the stator-to-rectifier assembly mounting screws. Remove the rectifier insulator. Remove the capacitor mounting screw. Remove the rectifier assembly.

4. Remove the through bolts. Carefully pry between the stator and the drive end shield, using a suitable tool and separate the end shields. The stator is laminated, do not burr the stator or the end shield.

5. Position the drive end of the alternator over the bosses of the holding fixture. Do not position the rotor plastic termination plate over the fixture boss or damage to the assembly will result.

6. Bolt the drive end of the assembly to shield fixture. Loosen the pulley mounting nut. Remove the pulley mounting nut. Remove the pulley washer.

7. Remove the poly-vee pulley. Remove the fan. Remove the front bearing spacer. Press the rotor assembly out of the drive end shield.

8. Remove the inner bearing spacer. Position the alternator bearing puller tool under the rear rotor bearing. Tighten the right puller bolt a ½ turn. Tighten the left puller bolt a ½ turn. Continue tightening the tool a ½ turn on each bolt until the rear rotor bearing is free. Remove the rear rotor bearing assembly from the rotor.

9. Position the rotor assembly in the holding fixture. Position the rear rotor bearing onto the rotor shaft.

10. Drive the rear rotor bearing onto the rotor until it bottoms. The rear rotor position is critical and must be installed using special tools C–4885 and C–4894.

11. Remove the front bearing retaining screws. Press the front bearing out of the drive end shield.

12. Carefully remove the stator from the rectifier end shield.

Assembly:

13. Be sure to repair or replace defective components as required.

14. To the front of the rotor, install the inner bearing spacer and press the drive end shield onto the rotor.

NOTE: The front drive end shield bearing must be replaced anytime the rotor or drive end shield is removed, for the front bearing is a press fit and may be damaged upon removal.

15. Position the drive end shield into a holding fixture so the fixture bosses do not contact the rotor plastic termination plate and tighten the holding bolt.

16. At the front of the drive end shield, install the pulley spacer (flat side up), the fan, the pulley, the washer and the pulley nut. Torque the pulley nut to 80–105 ft. lbs. (108–125 Nm).

17. Remove the drive end shield and rotor assembly from the holding fixture.

18. To assemble the rear end housing for the 40/90, perform the following procedures:

   a. Apply joint compound to the rectifier end shield surface, under the rectifier mounting position.

   b. Position the rectifier assembly to the rectifier drive end housing.

   c. Install the rectifier insulator, the insulator mounting screws and torque the screws to 36–46 inch lbs. (4–6 Nm).

   d. Install the capacitor terminal over the rectifier assembly battery terminal stud and torque the mounting screw to 36–48 inch lbs. (4–6 Nm).

   e. Install the alternator battery terminal nut and torque to 30–50 inch lbs. (3–6 Nm).

   f. Install the stator-to-rectifier screws and torque to 12–18 inch lbs. (1–2 Nm).

   g. Slide the brushes into their cavity. Install the brush holder assembly and torque the screws to 12–18 inch lbs. (1–2 Nm).

   h. Install the dust cover and torque the nut to 12–18 inch lbs. (1–2 Nm).

19. To assemble the rear end housing for the 50/120, perform the following procedures:

   a. Apply joint compound to the rectifier end shield surface, under the rectifier mounting position.

   b. Position the rectifier assemblies No. 1 and No. 2 to the rectifier drive end housing.

   c. Install the rectifier insulators, the insulator mounting screws and torque to 36–46 inch lbs. (4–6 Nm).

   d. Install the capacitor terminal over the rectifier assembly No. 2 battery terminal stud and torque the mounting screw to 36–48 inch lbs. (4–6 Nm).

e. Install the alternator battery terminal nut and torque to 30–50 inch lbs. (3–6 Nm).

f. Position a jumper strap between the rectifier assemblies No. 1 and No. 2.; torque the nut to 36–48 inch lbs. (4–6 Nm) and the screw to 15–35 inch lbs. (2–4 Nm).

g. Position the 3 buss bars to the rectifier assemblies and torque the screws to 12–18 inch lbs. (1–2 Nm).

h. Slide the brushes into their cavity, Install the brush holder assembly and torque the screws to 12–18 inch lbs. (1–2 Nm).

i. Install the dust cover and torque the nut to 12–18 inch lbs. (1–2 Nm).

20. Assemble the rear end housing to the drive end shield and rotor assemlby. Install the through bolts and torque to 48–72 inch lbs. (5–8 Nm).

21. Install the rear bearing oil seal.

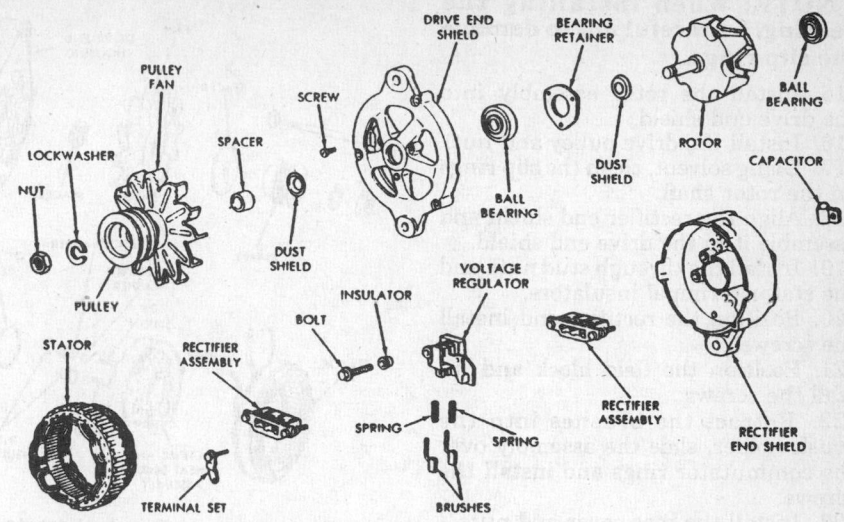

Mitsubishi alternator

Mitsubshi Alternator with Internal Regulator

DISASSEMBLY & ASSEMBLY

1. Place the alternator in a vise or similar holding fixture, mark the body components and remove the through bolts.

2. Pry between the stator and the drive end shield and carefully separate the drive end plate, the pulley and the rotor assembly from the stator and rectifier end shield assembly.

3. Carefully clamp the rotor and remove the pulley nut from the end of the shaft. Remove the pulley, the pulley fan, the pulley fan spacer and the alternator drive end shield from the rotor shaft.

4. The front bearing can be removed from the front drive housing by the removal of the dust seals, front and rear, the bearing retainer screws, the retainer, exposing the bearing so that it can be tapped from the drive housing.

5. To remove the stator assembly. The 6 stator leads must be unsoldered from the rectifiers, as per the manufacturer's recommendation.

6. Remove the rectifiers from the stator end shield housing.

7. Remove the brush holder and regulator retaining screw.

8. Remove the battery terminal retaining nut and remove the capacitor from the terminal.

9. Remove the regulator and rectifier assembly. Unsolder 1 rectifier-to-regulator assembly and remove the other rectifier assembly by sliding the battery stud out of the regulator.

10. Inspect the rotor bearing surface

for scores and make the necessary off vehicle test on the electrical components.

11. The assembly of the alternator is the reverse of the removal procedure. Certain steps must be performed as the alternator is assembled.

12. Install the seals in the front and in the rear of the front bearing with the angled lip away from the bearing.

13. Push the brushes into the brush holder and insert a wire to hold them in the raised position. Install the rotor and remove the holding wire.

Nippondenso 75, 90 and 120 Amp Alternators

The alternators appear to be the same, except, the 75 amp alternator is equipped with 3 sets of diodes and the 90 amp and 120 amp alternators are equipped with 4 sets.

DISASSEMBLY & ASSEMBLY

1. Remove the B+ insulator nut and insulator. Remove the rear cover nuts and cover.

2. Remove the brush holder screws and the brush holder.

3. Remove the field block screws and the block.

4. Remove the rectifier and stator terminal screws and the rectifier.

5. Remove the stator terminal rubber insulators and the end shield through stud nuts.

6. With the drive pulley facing downward, tap rectifier end shield upward and separate the 2 end shields.

7. Remove the drive pulley nut and the drive pulley.

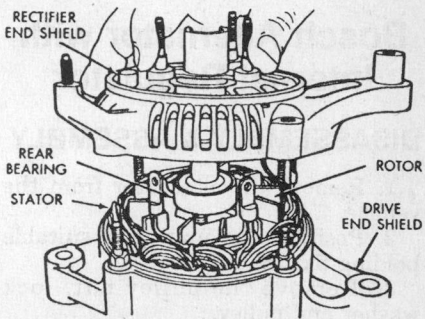

Separating the end shields— Nippondenso 75, 90 and 120 amp alternators

NOTE: Do not handle the slip rings of the rotor with the bare hands for oil or grease may restrict contact.

8. Pull the rotor assembly from the drive end shield.

9. Using a wheel puller, press the rectifier end shield bearing from the rotor shaft.

NOTE: When removing the bearing, be careful not to damage the slip rings.

10. From the drive end shield, remove the bearing retainer screws and the retainer.

11. Using a socket and a light hammer, place the drive end shield on a work surface and tap the bearing from the shield.

Assembly:

12. Using a socket, slightly smaller than the bearing, tap the bearing into the drive end shield.

13. Install the bearing retainer in the drive end shield.

14. Using a shop press, press the rectifier end shield bearing onto the rotor shaft.

NOTE: When installing the bearing, be careful not to damage the slip rings.

15. Install the rotor assembly into the drive end shield.
16. Install the drive pulley and nut.
17. Using solvent, clean the slip rings on the rotor shaft.
18. Align the rectifier end shield and assemble it to the drive end shield.
19. Install the through stud nuts and the stator terminal insulators.
20. Position the rectifier and install the screws.
21. Position the field block and install the screws.
22. Retract the brushes into the brush holder, slide the assembly over the commutator rings and install the screws.
23. Install the rear cover and nuts.
24. Align the B+ insulator guide boss into the rear cover hole and install the nut.

Bosch Alternator with Internal Regulator

DISASSEMBLY & ASSEMBLY

1. Remove the alternator from the vehicle.
2. Position the unit in a suitable holding fixture.
3. Remove the pulley nut, lock washer and pulley.
4. Remove the fan spacer and the pulley fan from the alternator shaft.
5. Remove the Woodruff key from the rotor shaft.
6. From the rear of the alternator disconnect the capacitor terminal and remove the capacitor mounting screw. Remove the capacitor from the alternator.
7. Remove the voltage regulator and brush holder mounting screw. Remove the holder.
8. Remove the D+ stud nut, lock washer, stud washer and stud insulators.
9. Remove the battery (B+) stud nut, lock washer, stud flat washer and the stud insulator.
10. Remove the alternator through bolts.
11. Pry between the stator and the drive end shield with a suitable tool. Carefully separate the drive end shield, pulley and rotor assembly away from the stator and rectifier end shield assembly.
12. Press the rotor out of the drive end shield and remove the spacer. Remove the alternator pulley fan spacer.
13. Remove the alternator drive end bearing screws. Remove the drive end shield bearing retainer.
14. Press out the drive end shield

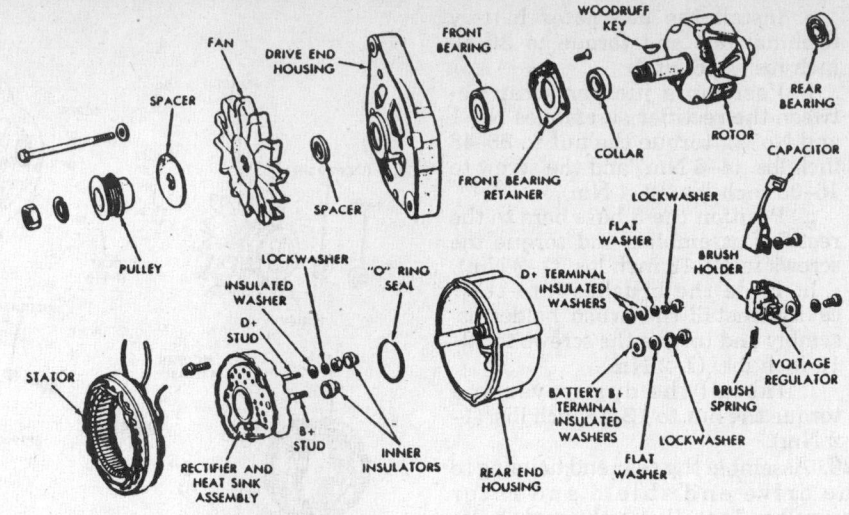

Bosch alternator with internal regulator

bearing. Remove the front drive bearing from the front drive end shield.
15. To test the positive and negative rectifiers use tool C–3929–A or equivalent.

NOTE: Do not break the plastic cases of the rectifiers. These cases are for protection against corrosion. Be sure to always touch the test probe to the metal pin of the nearest rectifier.

16. Position the rear end shield and the stator assembly on an insulated surface. Connect the test lead clip to the alternator battery output terminal.
17. Plug in tool C–3829–A or equivalent. Touch the metal pin of each of the positive rectifiers with the test probe.
18. Readings for satisfactory rectifiers will be 1¾ amperes or more. Readings should be approximately the same and the meter needle must move in same direction for all 3 rectifiers.
19. When some rectifiers are good and one is shorted, the reading taken at good rectifiers will be low and reading taken at shorted rectifiers will be 0. Disconnect stator lead-to-rectifiers reading 0 and retest. Reading of good rectifiers will now be within satisfactory range.
20. When 1 rectifier is open it will read approximately 1 ampere and good rectifiers will read within satisfactory range.
21. To test the negative rectifiers connect the test clip of tool C–3829–A to the rectifier end housing.
22. Touch the metal pin of each of the negative rectifiers with the test probe.
23. Test specifications are the same and test results will be approximately the same as for positive case rectifiers,

except meter will read on opposite side of scale.

NOTE: If a negative rectifier shows shorted, remove the stator from rectifier assembly and retest. It is possible that a stator winding could be grounded to the stator laminations or the rectifier end shield, which would indicate a shorted negative rectifier.

24. Unsolder the stator-to-rectifier leads. Mark the stator coil frame to aid in reinstallation of the stator. Remove the stator from the rectifier end shield assembly.
25. Remove the rectifier assembly mounting screws. Remove the rectifier assembly.
26. Remove the inner battery (B+) stud insulator.
27. Remove the D+ stud insulator, stud nut, stud flatwasher and stud insulating washer.
28. Remove the rear bearing oil and dust seal. Check the rotor bearing surface for scoring.
29. Using puller C–4068 or equivalent, remove the rear rotor bearing.
30. Check outside circumference of slip-ring for dirt and roughness. Clean or polish with fine sandpaper, as required. A badly roughened slip-ring or a worn down slip-ring should be replaced.
31. To check for an open rotor field coil, connect an ohmmeter to slip-rings. Ohmmeter readings should be between 1.5–2 ohms on rotor coils at room temperature ambient conditions. Resistance between 2.5–3.0 ohms would result from alternator rotors that have been operated on vehicle at higher engine compartment temperatures. Reading above 3.5 ohms would indicate high resistance rotor coils and further testing or replacement may be required.

32. To check for a shorted field coil, connect an ohmmeter to the slip-rings. If reading is below 1.5 ohms, field coil is shorted.

33. To check for a grounded rotor field coil; connect an ohmmeter from each slip-ring to the rotor shaft.

NOTE: Ohmmeter should be set for infinite reading when probes are apart and 0 when probes are shorted. The ohmmeter should read infinite. If reading is 0 or higher, rotor is grounded.

34. Check for continuity between leads of stator coil. Press test probe firmly to each of 3 phase (stator) lead terminals 1 at a time. If there is no continuity, the stator coil is defective. Replace the stator assembly.

35. To test the stator for ground, check for continuity between the stator coil leads and the stator coil frame. If there is no continuity the stator is grounded and must be replaced.

36. To test the inner and outer brush circuit, use an ohmmeter and touch 1 test probe to the inner brush and the other test probe to the brush terminal. If continuity does not exist replace the brush assembly. Repeat the same procedure for the outer brush.

37. To assemble the alternator reverse the disassembly procedure.

38. Be sure to check all parts for wear. Replace defective components as required.

39. Push the brushes into the brush holder and insert a wire to hold them in the raised position. Install the rotor and remove the holding wire.

Bosch 65 Amp Alternator with External Regulator

DISASSEMBLY & ASSEMBLY

1. Remove the alternator from the vehicle. Mount the unit in a suitable holding fixture.
2. Hold the alternator pulley and remove the pulley retaining nut.
3. Remove the pulley lockwasher, pulley fan spacer and pulley from the alternator assembly.
4. Remove the Woodruff key from the rotor shaft.
5. From the rear of the alternator remove the brush holder retaining screws. Remove the brush holder.
6. To test the inner and outer brush circuits, use an ohmmeter and touch 1 test probe to the inner brush and the other test probe to the brush terminal. If continuity does not exist replace the brush assembly. Repeat the same test for the outer brush circuit.

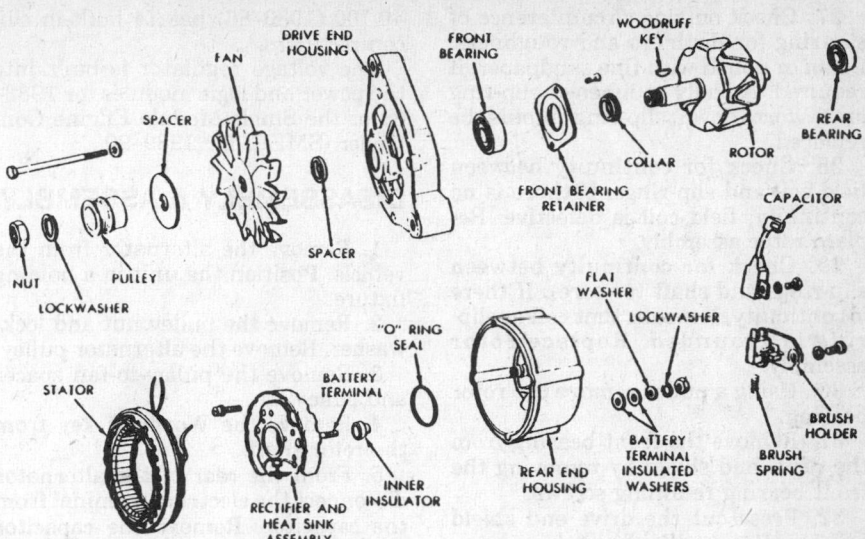

Bosch alternator with external regulator

7. Disconnect the capacitor electrical connection and remove the capacitor retaining screw. Remove the capacitor from its mounting on the alternator.
8. Remove the ground stud nut and stud washer.
9. Remove the alternator through bolts that retain the unit together.
10. Using the proper tool, separate the stator and the drive end shield.
11. To test the positive and negative rectifiers use tool C–3929–A or equivalent.

NOTE: Do not break the plastic cases of the rectifiers. These cases are for protection against corrosion. Be sure to always touch the test probe to the metal pin of the nearest rectifier.

12. Position the rear end shield and the stator assembly on an insulated surface. Connect the test lead clip to the alternator battery output terminal.
13. Plug in tool C–3829–A or equivalent. Touch the metal pin of each of the positive rectifiers with the test probe.
14. Reading for satisfactory rectifiers will be 1¾ amperes or more. Reading should be approximately the same and meter needle must move in the same direction for all 3 rectifiers.
15. When some rectifiers are good and 1 is shorted, the reading taken at good rectifiers will be low and the reading at shorted rectifiers will be 0. Disconnect stator lead-to-rectifiers reading 0 and retest. Reading of good rectifiers will now be within satisfactory range.
16. When a rectifier is open, it will read approximately 1 ampere and good rectifiers will read within satisfactory range.

17. To test the negative rectifiers, connect the test clip of tool C–3829–A to the rectifier end housing.
18. Touch the metal pin of each of the negative rectifiers with the test probe.
19. Test specifications are the same and test results will be approximately same as for positive case rectifiers except that the meter will read on opposite side of scale.

NOTE: If a negative rectifier shows a shorted condition, remove stator from rectifier assembly and retest. It is possible that a stator winding could be grounded to stator laminations or to an rectifier end shield which would indicate a shorted negative rectifier.

20. Remove the battery (B+) stud nut, stud lockwasher, stud flatwasher and stud insulator.
21. Remove the rectifier assembly retaining screws. Remove the stator assembly along with the rectifier unit. Unsolder the stator to rectifier leads.
22. Check for continuity between stator coil leads. Press test probe firmly to each of 3 phase (stator) lead terminals separately. If there is no continuity, stator coil is defective. Replace stator assembly.
23. To test stator for ground, check for continuity between stator coil leads and stator coil frame. If there is continuity stator is grounded. Replace stator assembly.
24. Remove the rear bearing oil and dust seal. Check the rotor bearing surface for wear and scoring. Replace as required.
25. Remove the inner battery (B+) stud insulator.
26. Press the rotor out of the drive end shield and remove the spacer.

27. Check outside circumference of slip-ring for dirtiness and roughness. Clean or polish with fine sandpaper, if required. A badly roughened slip-ring or a worn down slip-ring should be replaced.

28. Check for continuity between field coil and slip-rings. If there is no continuity, field coil is defective. Replace rotor assembly.

29. Check for continuity between slip-rings and shaft (or core). If there is continuity, it means that coil or slip-ring is grounded. Replace rotor assembly.

30. Using a puller remove the rotor bearing.

31. Remove the front bearing from the drive end shield by removing the front bearing retaining screws.

32. Press out the drive end shield bearing. Remove the front drive bearing from the front drive end shield.

Assembly:

33. Be sure to check all parts for wear and replace the defective components as required.

34. Install the rear rotor bearing oil and dust seal.

35. Install the inner alternator battery terminal insulator.

36. Solder the stator leads to the rectifier assembly; be sure to use needle nose pliers as a heat sink.

37. Position the stator and rectifier assembly. the rectifier mounting screws, both terminal insulators, the insulator washer, the insulator lockwasher and the insulator nut.

38. Position and press the front bearing into the drive end shield. Install the bearing retainer.

39. Position the drive end shield and spacer over the rotor. Press the drive end shield onto the rotor.

40. Install the rectifier end shield over the drive end shield. Install the through bolts and tighten.

41. Install the capacitor and terminal plug onto the alternator assembly.

42. Push the brushes into the brush holder and install the brush holder onto the alternator assembly.

43. Install the Woodruff key into the shaft and the fan over the shaft.

44. Install the drive pulley-to-fan spacer, the pulley, the lockwasher and the nut over the shaft. Secure the pulley and tighten the nut.

Bosch 35/75, 40/90, 90 RS and 40/100 Amp Alternators

The alternators are alike, except, the 35/75 has 6 built-in silicon rectifiers, the 40/90 has 12 (1983–87) or 8 (1988–90) built-in silicon rectifiers and the 40/100 (1983–86) has 14 built-in silicon rectifiers.

The voltage regulator is built into the power and logic modules for 1983–88 or the Single Module Engine Controller (SMEC) for 1989–90.

DISASSEMBLY & ASSEMBLY

1. Remove the alternator from the vehicle. Position the unit in a holding fixture.

2. Remove the pulley nut and lockwasher. Remove the alternator pulley.

3. Remove the pulley-to-fan spacer and pulley fan.

4. Remove the Woodruff key from the rotor shaft.

5. From the rear of the alternator disconnect the electrical terminal from the capacitor. Remove the capacitor retaining screw and the capacitor.

6. Remove the brush holder retaining screw and remove the brush holder from its mounting on the rear of the alternator.

7. Remove the alternator through bolts. Using a suitable tool pry between the stator and the drive end shield and carefully separate the assembly.

8. Press the rotor out of the drive end shield and remove the spacer. Remove the pulley fan spacer.

9. Remove the front alternator drive end bearing screws.

10. Remove the drive end shield bearing retainer and press out the drive end shield bearing.

11. Remove the front drive bearing from the front of the drive end shield.

12. To test the positive and negative rectifiers use tool C–3929–A or equivalent.

NOTE: Do not break the plastic cases of the rectifiers. These cases are for protection against corrosion. Be sure to always touch the test probe to the metal pin of the nearest rectifier.

13. Position the rear end shield and the stator assembly on an insulated surface. Connect the test lead clip to the alternator battery output terminal.

14. Plug in tool C–3829–A or equivalent. Touch the metal pin of each of the positive rectifiers with the test probe.

15. Reading for satisfactory rectifiers will be 1¾ amperes or more. Reading should be approximately the same and meter needle must move in same direction for all 3 rectifiers.

16. When some rectifiers are good and 1 is shorted the reading taken at good rectifiers will be low and the reading at shorted rectifiers will be 0. Disconnect stator lead-to-rectifiers reading 0 and retest. Reading of good rectifiers will now be within satisfactory range.

17. When a rectifier is open it will read approximately 1 ampere and the good rectifiers will read within the satisfactory range.

18. Touch the metal pin of each of the negative rectifiers with the test probe.

19. Test specifications are the same and the test results will be approximately the same as for positive case rectifiers except that the meter will read on opposite side of scale.

NOTE: If a negative rectifier shows shorted remove stator from the rectifier assembly and retest. It is possible that a stator winding could be grounded to stator laminations or rectifiers end shield which would indicate a shorted negative rectifier.

20. Unsolder the stator-to-rectifier leads. Mark the stator coil frame, to aid in reinstallation of the stator. Remove the stator from the rectifier end shield assembly.

21. Remove the rectifier assembly mounting screws. Remove the rectifier assembly.

22. Remove the inner battery (B+) stud insulator.

23. Remove the D+ stud insulator, stud nut, stud flatwasher and stud insulating washer.

24. Remove the rear bearing oil and dust seals. Check the rotor bearing surface for scoring.

25. Using puller C–4068 or equivalent, remove the rear rotor bearing.

26. Check the outside circumference of slip-ring for dirt and roughness. Clean or polish with fine sandpaper, if required. A badly roughened slip-ring or a worn down slip-ring should be replaced.

27. To check for an open rotor field coil, connect an ohmmeter to the slip-rings. Ohmmeter reading should be 1.5–2 ohms on rotor coils at room ambient conditions. Resistance of 2.5–3.0 ohms would result from alternator rotors that have been operated on vehicles at higher engine compartment temperatures. Readings above 3.5 ohms would indicate high resistance rotor coils and further testing or replacement may be required.

28. To check for a shorted field coil connect an ohmmeter to the slip-rings. If reading is below 1.5 ohms, the field coil is shorted.

29. To check for a grounded rotor field coil connect an ohmmeter from each slip-ring to the rotor shaft.

NOTE: Ohmmeter should be set for infinite reading when probes are apart and 0 when probes are shorted. The ohmmeter should read infinite. If reading is 0 or higher, rotor is grounded.

30. Check for continuity between leads of stator coil. Press test probe firmly to each of 3 phase (stator) lead terminals 1 at a time. If there is no continuity, stator coil is defective. Replace stator assembly.

31. To test the stator for ground check for continuity between the stator coil leads and the stator coil frame. If there is no continuity the stator is grounded and must be replaced.

32. To test the inner and outer brush circuit, use an ohmmeter and touch 1 test probe to the inner brush and the other test probe to the brush terminal. If continuity does not exist replace the brush assembly. Repeat the same procedure for the outer brush.

Assembly:

33. Be sure to check all parts for wear and replace the defective components as required.

34. Install the rear rotor bearing oil and dust seal.

35. Install the inner alternator battery B+ terminal insulator.

36. Position the rectifier assembly. Install the rectifier mounting screws, the insulator, the insulator washer, the insulator lockwasher and the insulator nut.

37. Position the stator assembly into the rectifier end shield. Align the scribe marks on the stator and the rectifier end shield.

38. Solder the stator leads to the rectifier assembly; be sure to use needle nose pliers as a heat sink.

39. Position and press the front bearing into the drive end shield. Install the bearing retainer and the pulley fan spacer onto the drive end shield.

40. Position the drive end shield and spacer over the rotor. Using a socket wrench, press the drive end shield onto the rotor.

41. Install the rectifier end shield and stator assembly into the drive end shield and rotor assembly. Install the through bolts and tighten.

42. Push the brushes into the brush holder and install the brush holder onto the alternator assembly.

43. Install the capacitor and terminal plug onto the alternator assembly.

44. Install the Woodruff key into the shaft and the fan over the shaft.

45. Install the drive pulley-to-fan spacer, the pulley, the lockwasher and the nut over the shaft. Secure the pulley and tighten the nut.

Delcotron SI Alternators

DISASSEMBLY & ASSEMBLY

1. Remove the alternator from the vehicle. Position the assembly in a suitable holding fixture.

2. Make scribe marks on the alternator case and frames to aid in reassembly.

3. Remove the through bolts. Separate the drive end frame assembly from the rectifier end frame assembly.

4. Remove the rectifier attaching nuts and the regulator attaching screws from the end frame assembly.

5. Separate the stator, diode trio and voltage regulator from the end frame assembly.

Inspection:

6. On the 10SI alternator, check the stator for open circuits using an ohmmeter. If high readings are obtained replace the stator.

7. Check the stator for grounds using an ohmmeter. If readings are low replace the stator.

8. Using an ohmmeter check the rotor for grounds. The ohmmeter reading should be very high if not replace the rotor.

9. Using an ohmmeter, check the rotor for opens. If the ohmmeter reading is not 2.4–3.5 ohms replace the rotor.

10. To check the diode trio connect the ohmmeter to the diode trio and reverse the lead connections. The ohmmeter should read high and low if not replace the diode trio. Repeat the same test between the single connector and each of the other connectors.

11. Check rectifier bridge with ohmmeter connected from grounded heat sink-to-flat metal on terminal. Reverse the leads. If both readings are the same replace rectifier bridge.

12. Repeat test between the grounded heat sink and the other flat metal clips.

13. Repeat test between the insulated heat sink and flat metal clips.

14. Clean or replace the alternator brushes as required. Position the brushes in the brush holder and retain them in place using the brush retainer wire or equivalent.

15. To remove the rotor and drive end bearing, remove the shaft nut, washer and pulley, fan and collar. Push the rotor from the housing.

16. Remove the retainer plate from inside the drive end frame. Push the bearing out. Clean or replace parts as required.

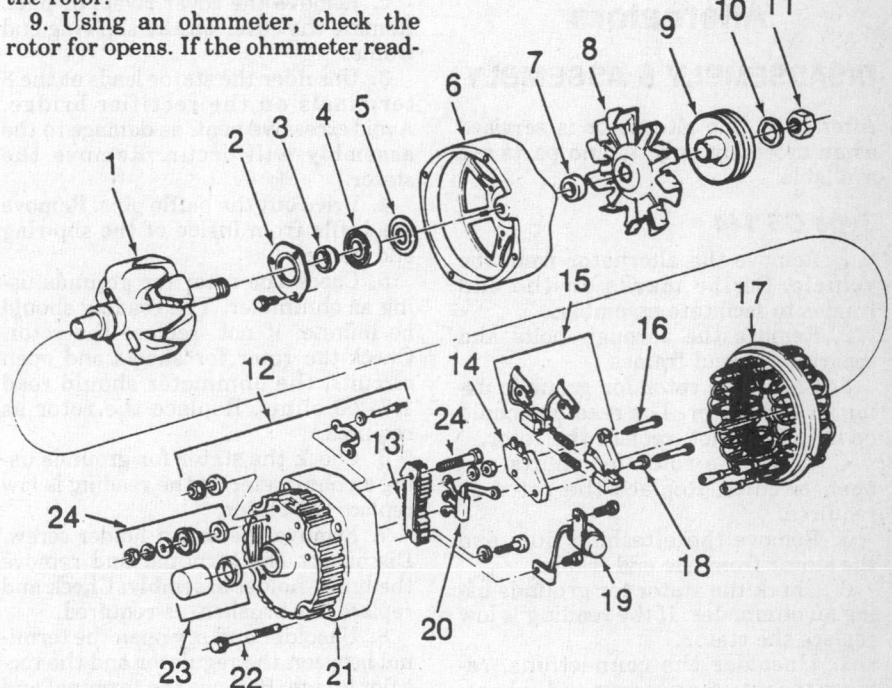

1 Rotor	9 Pulley	17 Stator
2 Front bearing retainer	10 Lockwasher	18 Insulating washer
3 Inner collar	11 Pulley nut	19 Capacitor
4 Bearing	12 Terminal assembly	20 Diode trio
5 Washer	13 Rectifier bridge	21 Rear housing
6 Front housing	14 Regulator	22 Through bolt
7 Outer collar	15 Brush assembly	23 Bearing and seal assembly
8 Fan	16 Screw	24 Terminal assembly

Delcotron 10-SI alternator—exploded view

Assembly:

17. Press against the outer bearing race to push the bearing in. On early production alternators it will be necessary to fill the bearing cavity with lubricant. Late production alternators use a sealed bearing and lubricant is not required for assembly.

18. Press rotor into the end frame. Assemble the collar, fan, pulley, washer and nut. Torque the shaft nut to 40–60 ft. lbs.

19. Push slip-ring end bearing out from the outside toward inside of end frame.

20. On 10SI and 15SI, place flat plate over new bearing and press from outside toward inside until bearing is flush with the end frame.

21. On 15SI alternators use the thin wall tube in the space between the grease cup and the housing to push the bearing in flush with the housing.

22. Assemble the brush holder, regulator, resistor, diode trio, rectifier bridge and stator to slip-ring end frame.

23. Assemble end frames together with through bolts. Remove the brush retainer wire.

Delcotron CS Alternators

DISASSEMBLY & ASSEMBLY

After 1987, the alternator is serviced as an assembly only, for no parts are available.

Type CS 144

1. Remove the alternator from the vehicle. Scribe marks on the end frames to facilitate assembly.

2. Remove the through bolts and separate the end frames.

3. Check the rotor for grounds using an ohmmeter. The reading should be infinite, if not, replace the rotor.

4. Check the rotor for shorts and open circuits. Replace the rotor as required.

5. Remove the attaching nuts and the stator from the end frame.

6. Check the stator for grounds using an ohmmeter. If the reading is low replace the stator.

7. Unsolder the connections, remove the retaining screws and connector from the end frame. Separate the regulator and the brush holder from the end frame.

8. Check the rectifier bridge using an ohmmeter. Replace as required. Check the heat sink, using an ohmmeter. Replace as required. Clean the brushes. Replace them as required.

9. To remove the rotor and drive end bearing, hold the rotor using a hex

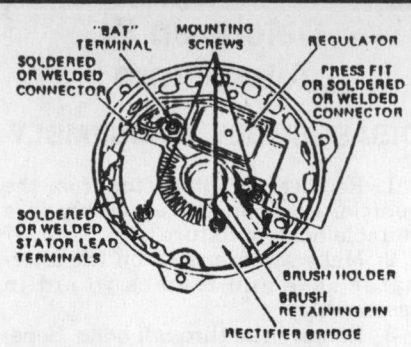

GM Delcotron alternator component location

wrench in the shaft end while removing the nut. Push the rotor from the housing. Remove the plate and push the bearing out.

10. Assembly is the reverse of the disassembly procedure. Repair or replace defective components as required.

Type CS 130

1. Remove the alternator from the vehicle. Scribe marks on the end frames to facilitate assembly. Remove the through bolts and separate the end frames.

2. Remove the cover rivets or pins. Remove the cover on the slip-ring end frame.

3. Unsolder the stator leads at the 3 terminals on the rectifier bridge. Avoid excessive heat, as damage to the assembly will occur. Remove the stator.

4. Drive out the baffle pins. Remove the baffle from inside of the slip-ring end frame.

5. Check the rotor for grounds using an ohmmeter. The reading should be infinite, if not, replace the rotor. Check the rotor for shorts and open circuits, the ohmmeter should read 1.7–2.3 ohms. Replace the rotor as required.

6. Check the stator for grounds using an ohmmeter. If the reading is low replace the stator.

7. Remove the brush holder screw. Disconnect the terminal and remove the brush holder assembly. Check and replace the brushes, as required.

8. Unsolder and pry open the terminal between the regulator and the rectifier bridge. Remove the terminal and the retaining screws. Remove the regulator and the rectifier bridge from the end frame.

9. To check the rectifier bridge, connect the proper (analog reading) ohmmeter, using the low scale, to 1 terminal and the heat sink, record the reading. Reverse the test leads and record the reading. If both readings are the same replace the rectifier bridge.

Check the other diodes in the same manner.

10. To remove the rotor and drive end bearing, hold the rotor using a hex wrench in the shaft end while removing the nut. Push the rotor from the housing. Remove the plate and push the bearing out.

11. Assembly is the reverse of the disassembly procedure. Repair or replace defective components as required.

Delcotron Alternator with Rear Vacuum Pump

DISASSEMBLY & ASSEMBLY

1. Remove the alternator from the vehicle. Position the unit in a suitable holding fixture.

2. Remove the vacuum pump retaining bolts. Remove the vacuum pump from the rear of the alternator while holding the center plate.

3. Remove the brush cover retaining bolts and brushes. Wrap the pump drive shaft spline with tape in order to protect the rear seal from damage.

4. Inspect the vacuum pump for wear and damage, replace defective components as required. Measure the length of the vanes, replace if not within specification (0.511–0.531 in.) Measure the inside diameter of the housing and replace if not within specification (2.440–2.441 in.).

5. Examine the check valve for damage. Apply light pressure to the valve and make sure the valve operates properly. Replace as required.

6. Check the inner face of the rear cover on the vacuum pump for oil leakage. Check the inner face of the oil seal for wear and damage. Replace the oil seal in the rear end housing of the vacuum pump as required.

7. Remove the alternator through bolts which hold the unit together. Matchmark the assembly to aid in reassembly. Separate the front end housing from the stator and rear end housing.

8. Remove the pulley nut, fan and front end housing from the rotor.

9. Remove the front bearing retainer screws. Remove the front bearing retainer and the bearing from the front end housing.

10. Remove the bolt and nuts retaining the stator, diodes and brush holder to the rear end housing. Note the position of the insulating washers for reassembly.

11. Separate the rear end housing from the stator and diode assembly.

12. Remove the diodes from the stator by melting the solder from the ter-

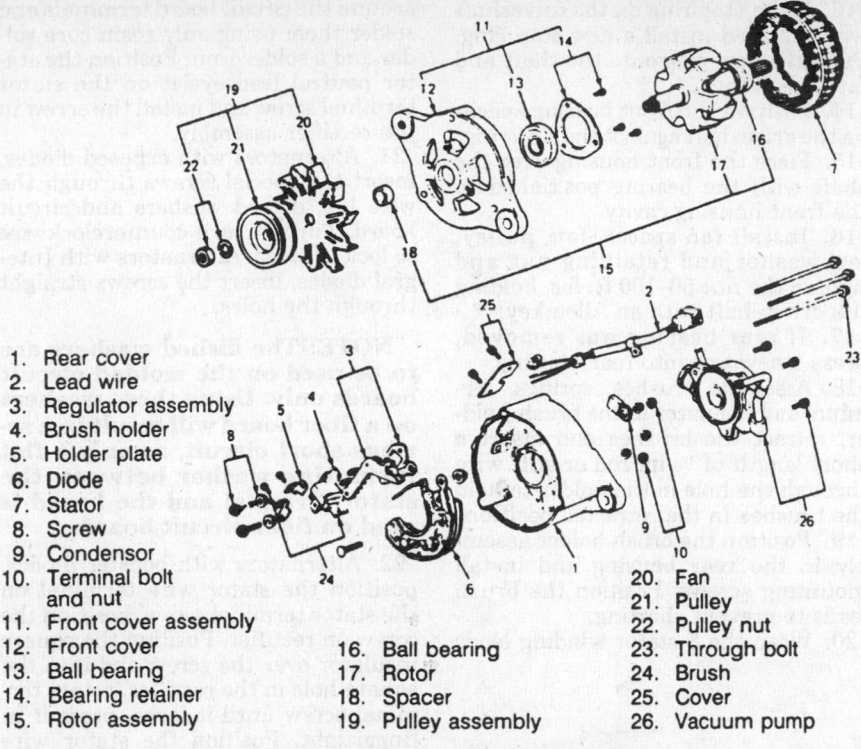

1. Rear cover
2. Lead wire
3. Regulator assembly
4. Brush holder
5. Holder plate
6. Diode
7. Stator
8. Screw
9. Condensor
10. Terminal bolt
    and nut
11. Front cover assembly
12. Front cover
13. Ball bearing
14. Bearing retainer
15. Rotor assembly

16. Ball bearing
17. Rotor
18. Spacer
19. Pulley assembly
20. Fan
21. Pulley
22. Pulley nut
23. Through bolt
24. Brush
25. Cover
26. Vacuum pump

Delcotron alternator with vacuum pump

minals. Be sure to protect the diodes while melting the solder.

13. Remove the solder from the voltage regulator holder plate terminal. Remove the voltage regulator.

Inspection:

14. Check the slip-ring surfaces of the rotor for wear and damage, repair or replace as required.

15. Measure the outside diameter of the rotor slip-rings. If ring diameter is not 1.18–1.24 in., replace the rotor.

16. Connect the ohmmeter test leads to each slip-ring. Resistance should be 4.2 ohms at 68°F. If continuity does not exist the coil is open and the rotor must be replaced.

17. Connect the ohmmeter to either slip-ring and the rotor core. If continuity exists the coil is grounded and the rotor must be replaced.

18. Check the front and rear rotor bearings for wear and damage. Replace defective parts as required.

19. Check for continuity across the stator coils. If continuity does not exist in any 1 stator coil replace the stator assembly.

20. Check for continuity across any of the stator coils and the stator core. If continuity exists, 1 of the stator coils is grounded and the stator must be replaced.

21. Coil resistance should be 0.05 ohms at 68°F and should be measured from the coil lead to terminal N.

22. Inspect the alternator brush assembly for wear and damage. Replace defective components as required.

23. Check for continuity of positive diodes between each stator coil terminal and the battery terminal of rectifier assembly. Reverse the ohmmeter leads and recheck for continuity.

24. If continuity exists in both polarity directions or does not exist in both directions diode is defective and must be replaced.

25. Check for continuity of negative diodes between each stator lead and E-terminal or rectifier assembly. Reverse ohmmeter leads and recheck for continuity. Continuity should exist in 1 direction only.

26. Assemble a test circuit using the following components: One 10 ohm 3 watt resistor (R_1) one 0–300 ohm 3 watt variable resistor (R_2), two 12 volt batteries (BAT_1 and BAT_2) and one 0–30 volt DC voltmeter.

27. Adjust variable resistor (R_2) until voltage at V_4 reads the same as voltage at V_3 (this should be all the way to 1 end of travel or 0 ohms).

28. Connect the test circuit to the integrated circuit regulator terminals. Measure voltage at V_1 and V_2. Voltage should measure 10–13 volts at V_1 and 0–2 volts at V_2.

29. Disconnect terminal S from circuit and measure voltage at V_3. Voltage at V_3 should be 20–26 volts. Reconnect terminal S.

30. Measure voltage at V_4 while increasing resistance at R_2 from 0 ohms. V_4 voltmeter reading should increase from 2 volts to 10–13 volts. Stop in-

creasing R_2 when voltage reaches 10–13 volts.

31. If increase at V_4 is interrupted at any point up to 10–13 volts, while increasing resistance at R_2, regulator is defective.

32. Measure voltage at V_4 with R_2 at same setting as previous step that produced 10–13 volt reading at V_2. If V_4 not within 14–14.6 volts, regulator is defective.

33. Disconnect wire at terminal S. Connect it to terminal B. Repeat Step 30. If V_2 does not vary or V_4 is not within 14.5–16.6 volts, regulator is defective.

Assembly:

34. To assemble the alternator reverse the disassembly procedure. Be sure to check all parts for wear and damage. Replace defective components as required.

35. Insert the brushes into the brush holder and insert a wire to retain them in place. Install the rotor and remove the retaining wire.

Ford Alternator with External Regulator

DISASSEMBLY & ASSEMBLY

Rear Terminal

1. Mark both end housings with a scribe mark for assembly.
2. Remove the through bolts.
3. Separate the front housing and rotor from the stator and rear housing.
4. Remove the nuts from the rectifier-to-rear housing mounting studs and remove rear housing.
5. Remove the brush holder mounting screws and the holder, brushes, springs, insulator and terminal.
6. If replacement is necessary press the bearing from the rear end housing while supporting the housing on the inner boss.
7. If rectifiers are to be replaced carefully unsolder the leads from the terminals. Use only a 100 watt soldering iron. Leave the soldering iron in contact with the diode terminals only long enough to remove the wires. Use a heat sink in order to protect the diodes.
8. There are various types of rectifier assembly circuit boards installed in production. One type has the circuit board spaced away from the diode plates and the diodes are exposed. Another type consists of a single circuit board with integral diodes; and still another has integral diodes with an additional booster diode plate containing 2 diodes.
9. This last type is used only on the 8 diode (61 amp) alternator. To disas-

semble use the following procedures. Exposed diodes, remove the screws from the rectifier by rotating bolt heads ¼ turn clockwise to unlock and remove. Integral diodes, press out the stator terminal screw, making sure not to twist it while doing this. Do not remove the grounded screw. Booster diodes, press out the stator terminal screw about ¼ in., remove the nut from the end of the screw and lift screw from circuit board. Be sure not to twist it as it comes out.

10. Remove the drive pulley and fan. On alternator pulleys with threaded holes in the outer end of the pulley use a standard puller for removal.

11. Remove the screws that hold the front bearing retainer and remove the front housing. If the bearing is to be replaced press it from the housing.

Assembly:

12. Press the front bearing into the front housing boss by putting pressure on outer race only. Install bearing retainer.

13. If the stop ring on the driveshaft was damaged install a new stop ring. Push the new ring onto the shaft and into the groove.

14. Position the front bearing spacer on the driveshaft against the stop ring.

15. Place the front housing over the shaft with the bearing positioned in the front housing cavity.

16. Install fan spacer, fan, pulley, lockwasher and retaining nut and tighten the nut 60–100 ft. lbs. holding the drive shaft with an Allen key.

17. If rear bearing was removed, press a new one into rear housing.

18. Assemble brushes, springs, terminal and insulator in the brush holder, retract the brushes and insert a short length of ⅛ in. rod or stiff wire through the hole in the holder to hold the brushes in the retracted position.

19. Position the brush holder assembly in the rear housing and install mounting screws. Position the brush leads to prevent shorting.

20. Wrap the 3 stator winding leads

around the circuit board terminals and solder them using only rosin core solder and a solder iron. Position the stator neutral lead eyelet on the stator terminal screw and install the screw in the rectifier assembly.

21. Alternators with exposed diodes, insert the special screws through the wire lug, dished washers and circuit board. Turn ¼ turn counterclockwise to lock in place. Alternators with Integral diodes, insert the screws straight through the holes.

NOTE: The dished washers are to be used on the molded circuit boards only. Using these washers on a fiber board will result in a serious short circuit, as only a flat insulating washer between the stator terminal and the board is used on fiber circuit boards.

22. Alternators with booster diodes, position the stator wire terminal on the stator terminal screw, position the screw on rectifier. Position the square insulator over the screw and into the square hole in the rectifier, rotate terminal screw until it locks, press it in fingertight. Position the stator wire and press the terminal screw into the rectifier and insulator with a vise.

23. Place the radio noise suppression condenser on the rectifier terminals. With molded circuit board and install the STA and BAT terminal insulators. With fiber circuit board place the square stator terminal insulator in the square hole in the rectifier assembly. Position the BAT terminal insulator.

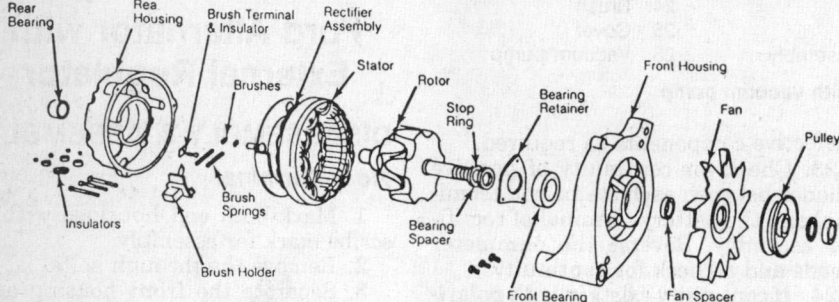

Exploded view of the Ford rear terminal alternator with an external voltage regulator

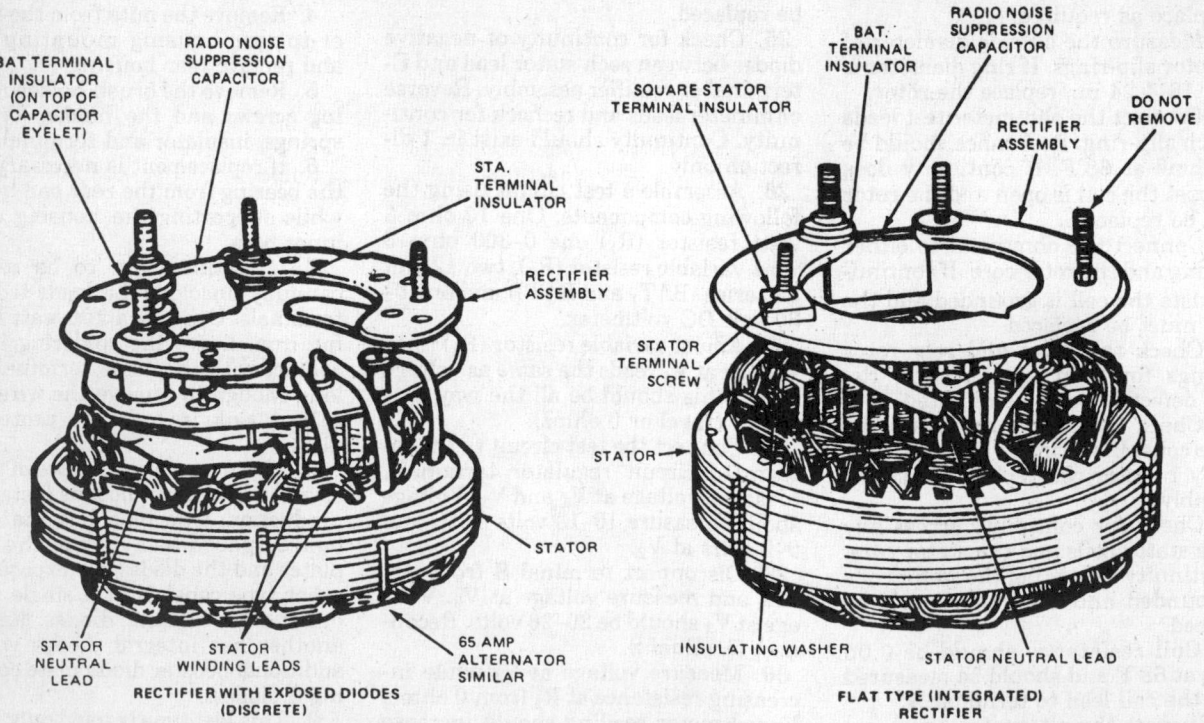

Exploded view of the Ford alternator with an external regulator—typical stator and rectifier assemblies

24. Position the stator and rectifier assembly in the rear housing, making sure all terminal insulators are seated properly in the recesses. Position the STA, BAT and FLD insulators on terminal bolts and install the nuts.

25. Clean the rear bearing surface of the rotor shaft with a rag and then position rear housing and stator assembly over rotor. Align matchmarks made during disassembly and install the through bolts. Remove brush retracting wire and place a dab of silicone sealer over the hole.

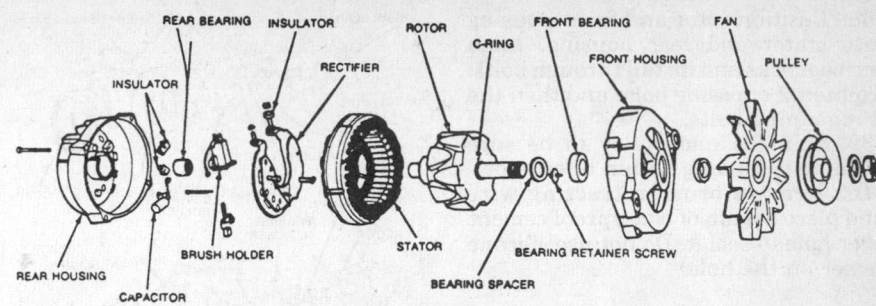

Exploded view of the Ford side terminal alternator

Side Terminal Alternators

NOTE: When disassembling the side terminal alternator the brush holder would be removed after the rectifier is removed. During the assembly the brush holder would be installed in the reverse order.

1. Mark both end housings and stator with a scribe mark for assembly.

2. Remove through bolts and separate front housing and rotor from rear housing and stator. Slots are provided in front housing to aid in disassembly. Do not separate rear housing from stator at this time.

3. Remove drive pulley nut. Remove the lockwasher, pulley, fan and fan spacer from rotor shaft.

4. Pull rotor and shaft from front housing and remove spacer from rotor shaft.

5. Remove the bearing-to-front housing screws. If bearing is damaged or has lost lubricant, remove bearing from housing. To remove bearing, support housing close to bearing boss and press bearing from housing.

6. Unsolder and disengage 3 stator leads from the rectifier. Work quickly to prevent overheating the rectifier.

7. Lift stator from rear housing.

8. Unsolder and disengage the brush holder lead from rectifier. Work quickly to prevent overheating rectifier.

9. Remove screw attaching capacitor lead-to-rectifier.

10. Remove the rectifier-to-rear housing screws.

11. Remove the terminal nuts and insulator from outside housing. Remove rectifier from the housing.

12. Remove the brush holder-to-housing screws. Remove brushes and holder.

13. Remove any sealing compound from rear housing and brush holder.

14. Remove capacitor-to-rear housing screw and capacitor.

15. If bearing replacement is necessary, support rear housing close to the bearing boss and press the bearing out of housing.

Inspection:

16. Wipe rotor, stator and bearings with a clean cloth. Do not clean these parts with solvent.

17. Rotate front bearing on drive end of rotor shaft. Check for any scraping noise, looseness or roughness. Look for excessive lubricant leakage. If any of these conditions exist, replace bearing.

18. Inspect rotor shaft rear bearing surface for roughness or severe chatter marks. Replace rotor assembly if shaft is not smooth.

19. Place rear bearing on slip-ring end of rotor shaft and rotate bearing. Make the same check for noise, looseness, or roughness as was made for the front bearing. Inspect rollers and cage for damage. Replace bearing if these conditions exist, or if lubricant is lost or contaminated.

20. Check pulley and fan for excessive looseness on rotor shaft. Replace any pulley that is loose or bent out of shape.

21. Check both the front and rear housings for cracks, particularly in the webbed areas and at the mounting ear. Replace damaged or cracked housing.

22. Check all wire leads on both stator and rotor assemblies for loose or broken soldered connections and for burned insulation. Resolder poor connections. Replace parts that show signs of burned insulation.

23. Check slip-rings for nicks and surface roughness. Nicks and scratches may be removed by turning down slip-rings. Do not go beyond minimum diameter of 1.22 in. If rings are badly damaged, replace rotor assembly.

24. Replace brushes if they are worn shorter than ¼ in.

Assembly:

25. If front housing bearing is being replaced, press new bearing in housing. Apply pressure on bearing outer race only. Install the bearing retaining screws and tighten to 25–40 inch lbs.

26. Place inner spacer on rotor shaft and insert rotor shaft into front housing and bearing.

27. Install fan spacer, fan, pulley, lockwasher and nut on rotor shaft. Use the proper tool to tighten pulley nut.

28. If rear bearing is being replaced, press a new bearing in from inside housing until rear bearing face is flush with boss outer surface.

29. Position brush terminal on brush holder. Install springs and brushes in brush holder and insert a piece of stiff wire to hold brushes in place.

30. Brushes and springs are serviced as part of brush holder assembly. Position brush holder in rear housing and install attaching screws. Brush retaining wire must stick out enough to be grabbed and pulled from housing assembly.

31. Waterproof glue sealer may have to be pushed out of pin hole in housing. Push brush holder toward brush holder attaching screws. Reseal crack between brush holder and brush cavity in rear housing with Caulking Cord or equivalent body sealer. Do not use silicone base sealer for this application.

32. Position capacitor to rear housing and install attaching screw. Place 2 rectifier insulators on bosses inside housing.

33. Place insulator on BAT (large) terminal of rectifier and position rectifier in rear housing. Place outside insulator on BAT terminal and install the nuts on BAT and GRD terminals fingertight. Install, but do not tighten, rectifier attaching screws.

34. Tighten the BAT terminal nuts to 35–50 inch lbs. and GRD terminal nuts to 25–35 inch lbs. on outside of rear housing. Tighten the rectifier attaching screws to 40–50 inch lbs.

35. Position capacitor lead-to-rectifier and install attaching screw.

36. Press brush holder lead on rectifier pin and solder securely. Work quickly to prevent overheating of rectifier.

37. Position stator in rear housing and align scribe marks. Press 3 stator leads on rectifier pins and solder securely using rosin core electrical solder. Work quickly to prevent overheating rectifier.

38. Position rotor and front housing into stator and rear housing. Align scribe marks and install through bolts. Tighten 2 opposing bolts and then the 2 remaining bolts.

39. Spin fan and pulley to be sure nothing is binding within alternator.

40. Remove brush retracting wire and place a daub of waterproof cement over hole to seal it. Do not use silicone sealer on the hole.

BRUSH REPLACEMENT

1. Remove the brush holder and cover assembly from the rear housing.

2. Remove the terminal bolts from the brush holder and cover assembly. Remove the brush assemblies.

3. Position the new brush terminals on the terminal bolts and assemble the terminals, bolts, brush holder washers and nuts. The insulating washer mounts under the FLD terminal nut. The entire brush and cover assembly is also available for service.

4. Depress the brush springs in the brush holder cavities and insert the brushes on top of the springs. Hold the brushes in position by inserting a stiff wire in the brush holder.

5. Install the brush holder and cover assembly into the rear housing. Remove the brush retracting wire and put a dab of silicone cement over the hole.

Ford Alternator with Internal Regulator

DISASSEMBLY & ASSEMBLY

1. Remove the alternator from the vehicle. Position the unit in a suitable holding fixture.

2. Remove the voltage regulator and the brush holder from the rear of the alternator assembly.

3. Remove the brush holder-to-voltage regulator screws and separate the components.

4. Matchmark the alternator end housings and stator frame to aid in assembly.

5. Remove the alternator through bolts. Separate the front housing and the rotor assembly from the stator and the rear housing.

6. Unsolder the 3 stator leads from the rectifier assembly. Be careful that the rectifiers are not in contact with the solder iron as overheating them will cause damage.

7. Remove the rectifier assembly from the rear of the alternator housing. Press the rear alternator housing bearing from the rear housing.

8. From the front housing of the al-

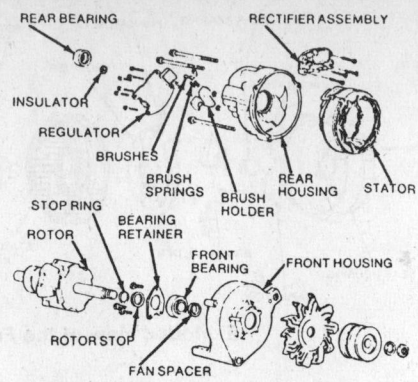

REAR BEARING / RECTIFIER ASSEMBLY
INSULATOR
REGULATOR
BRUSHES
BRUSH SPRINGS / BRUSH HOLDER / REAR HOUSING / STATOR
STOP RING
ROTOR / BEARING RETAINER
FRONT BEARING / FRONT HOUSING
ROTOR STOP
FAN SPACER

Exploded view of the Ford alternator with an internal voltage regulator

ternator remove the drive pulley nut from the rotor shaft.

9. Remove the lockwasher, drive pulley, fan and fan spacer from the rotor shaft.

10. Remove the rotor from the front housing. Remove the front bearing spacer from the rotor shaft. Do not remove the rotor stop ring unless it must be replaced.

11. Remove the front housing bearing retainer and bearing.

12. Assembly of the alternator is the reverse of the disassembly procedure. Be sure to clean and check all parts for wear and defects. Repair or replace defective components as required.

Ford Internal Fan Alternator with Internal Regulator

DISASSEMBLY & ASSEMBLY

1989–90

FESTIVA, PROBE AND TRACER

1. Remove the alternator housing screws.

2. Using a 200W soldering iron, heat the rear bearing area of the rear housing; the heat will expand the rear housing to allow the rear bearing to be removed from the housing.

3. Using a small pry bar, separate the rear housing and stator assembly from the front housing; be careful not to lose the stopper spring which fits around the circumference of the rear bearing.

4. Place the rotor in a soft-jawed vise with the jaws around the outside of the rotor. Remove the pulley retaining nut, the pulley, both front seals and the spacer.

5. Separate the rotor from the front housing.

6. If necessary to remove the front bearing, perform the following procedures:

a. Remove the front bearing retainer plate-to-housing screws and the plate.

b. Using a shop press and the socket, press the bearing from the front housing.

7. To disassemble the rear housing, perform the following procedures:

a. Remove the nut and insulator from the B-terminal.

b. Remove the rectifier-to-housing screw and the brush holder/regulator assembly-to-housing screws.

c. Using a small pry bar, separate the stator from the rear housing.

d. Remove the stator assembly, with the rectifier and brush holder/regulator assembly attached.

e. From the brush holder, remove both plastic shields.

f. Using a soldering iron, unsolder the stator-to-rectifier leads; work quickly to avoid overheating the diodes.

Assembly:

8. To assemble the rear housing, perform the following procedures:

a. Using a soldering iron and rosin core solder, solder the stator leads to the rectifier assembly; work quickly to avoid overheating the diodes.

b. Install both plastic shields to the brush holder/regulator assembly.

c. Install the stator assembly, with the rectifier and brush holder attached, to the rear housing. Position the stator into the housing so one of the shallow lamination ridges aligns with the case bolt holes.

d. Install the rectifier and brush holder screws.

e. Install the B-terminal insulator and nut. Torque the nut to 1.0–4.6 ft. lbs. (4.2 Nm).

9. Using a straight, stiff wire, depress the brushes and insert the wire through the rear housing, to hold the brushes for assembly purposes.

10. If the front bearing was removed, use a shop press and a socket to press the bearing into the front housing. Install the bearing retainer plate.

11. Position the rotor in a soft-jawed vise, with the clamp around the outside of the rotor. Install the spacer the inner shield, the front housing, the outer shield, the pulley, the lockwasher and the nut. Torque the nut to 36–65 ft. lbs. (49–88 Nm).

12. Using a 200W soldering iron, heat the bearing area of the rear housing; be sure to heat the housing to 122–144°F (50–60°C). Install the front housing assembly to the rear housing assembly by indexing the larger mounting brackets.

13. Install the case bolts and tighten

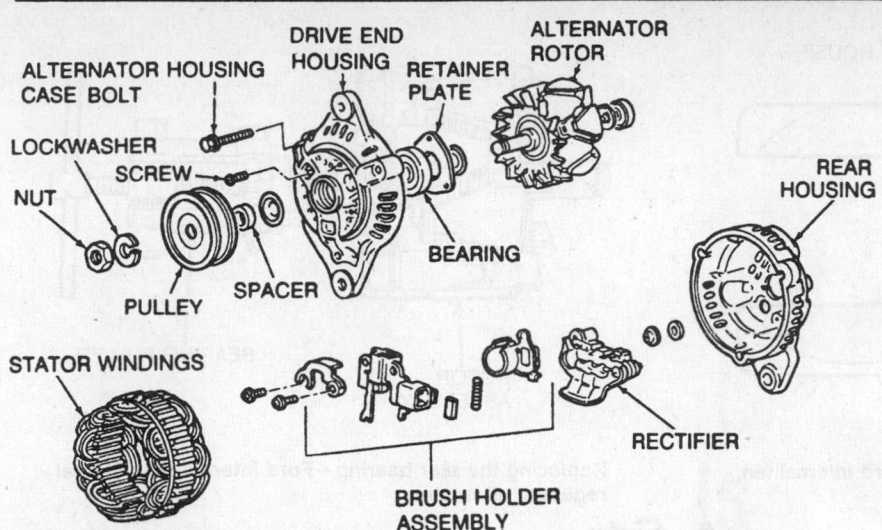

Exploded view of the internal fan alternator with an internal voltage regulator—
Festiva, Probe and Tracer

gradually to draw the halves together uniformly.

14. Remove the wire used to retain the brushes.

15. Rotate the alternator to be sure there is no drag and the rotor spins freely; if resistance or drag is present, disassemble the alternator and determine the cause.

COUGAR, SABLE, TAURUS AND THUNDERBIRD

1. Remove the alternator housing screws.

2. Using a 200W soldering iron, heat the rear bearing area of the rear housing; the heat will expand the rear housing to allow the rear bearing to be removed from the housing.

3. Using a small pry bar, separate the rear housing and stator assembly from the front housing; be careful not to lose the stopper spring which fits around the circumference of the rear bearing.

4. Place the rotor in a soft-jawed vise with the jaws around the outside of the rotor. Remove the pulley retaining nut and the pulley.

5. Separate the rotor from the front housing.

6. If necessary to remove the front bearing, perform the following procedures:

   a. Remove the front bearing retainer plate-to-housing screws and the plate.

   b. Using a shop press and the socket, press the bearing from the front housing.

7. To disassemble the rear housing, perform the following procedures:

   a. Remove the nut and insulator from the B-terminal.

   b. Remove the rectifier-to-housing screws and the brush holder/regulator assembly-to-housing screw.

   c. Using a small pry bar, separate the stator from the rear housing.

   d. Remove the stator assembly, with the rectifier and brush holder/regulator assembly attached.

   e. From the brush holder, remove both plastic shields.

   f. Using a soldering iron, unsolder the stator-to-rectifier leads; work quickly to avoid overheating the diodes.

Assembly:

8. To assemble the rear housing, perform the following procedures:

   a. Using a soldering iron and rosin core solder, solder the stator leads to the rectifier assembly; work quickly to avoid overheating the diodes.

   b. Install both plastic shields to the brush holder/regulator assembly.

   c. Install the stator assembly, with the rectifier and brush holder attached, to the rear housing. Position the stator into the housing so one of the shallow lamination ridges aligns with the case bolt holes.

   d. Install the rectifier and brush holder screws.

   e. Install the B-terminal insulator and nut. Torque the nut to 1.0–4.6 ft. lbs. (4.2 Nm).

9. Using a straight, stiff wire, depress the brushes and insert the wire through the rear housing, to hold the brushes for assembly purposes.

10. If the front bearing was removed, use a shop press and a socket to press the bearing into the front housing. Install the bearing retainer plate.

11. Position the rotor in a soft-jawed vise, with the clamp around the outside of the rotor. Install the spacer the inner shield, the front housing, the outer shield, the pulley, the lockwasher and the nut. Torque the nut to 36–65 ft. lbs. (49–88 Nm).

12. Using a 200W soldering iron, heat the bearing area of the rear housing; be sure to heat the housing to 122–144°F (50–60°C). Install the front housing assembly to the rear housing assembly by indexing the larger mounting brackets.

13. Install the case bolts and tighten gradually to draw the halves together uniformly.

14. Remove the wire used to retain the brushes.

15. Rotate the alternator to be sure there is no drag and the rotor spins freely; if resistance or drag is present, disassemble the cause.

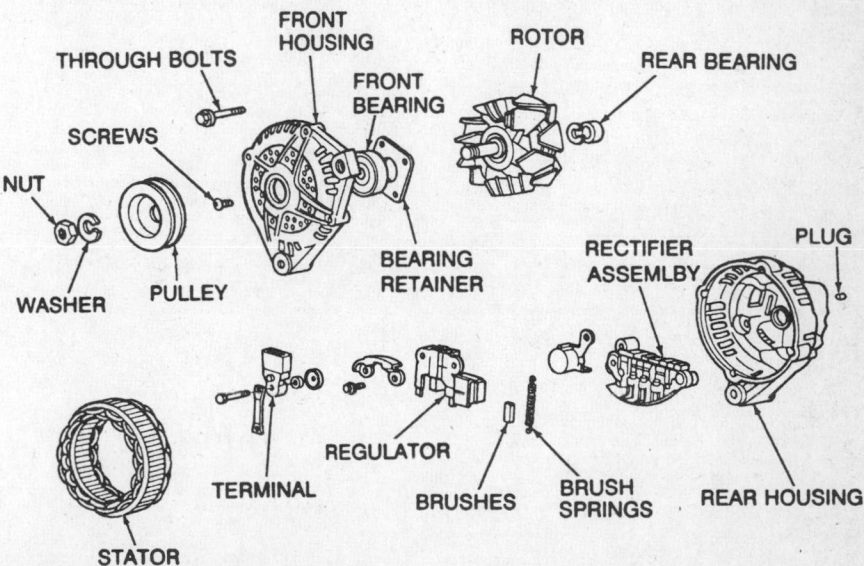

Exploded view of the internal fan alternator with an internal voltage regulator—
Cougar, Sable, Taurus and Thunderbird

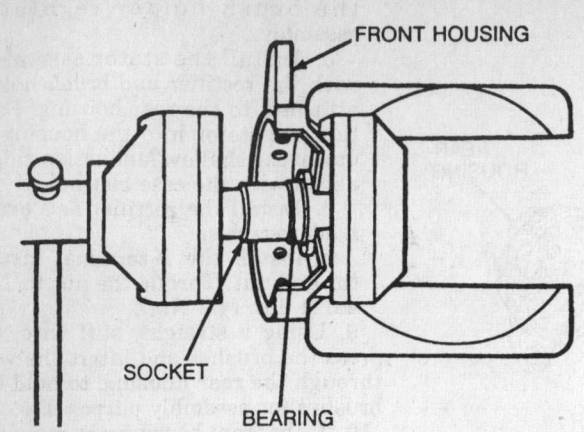

Replacing the front housing bearing—Ford internal fan, internal regulator alternator

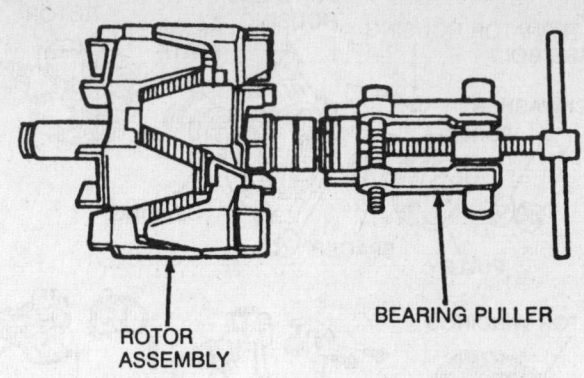

Replacing the rear bearing—Ford internal fan, internal regulator alternator

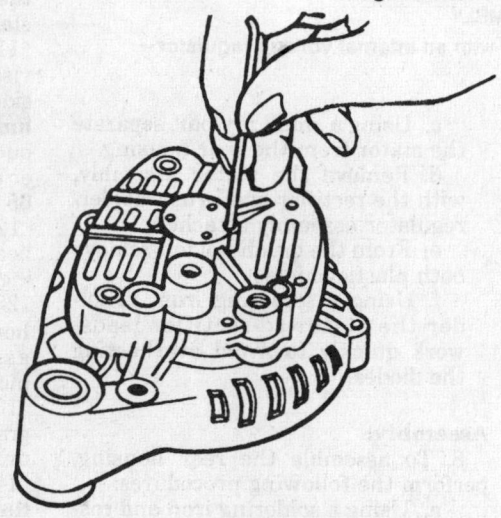

Inserting a wire to hold the brushes during assembly—Ford internal fan, internal regulator alternator

Carburetor Service 32

CARBURETOR APPLICATION CHART AND INDEX

Car Manufacturer	Year	Carburetor Manufacturer	Carburetor Model	Page Numbers	
				Adjustments	Specifications
Chrysler Corp.	1987–89	Holley	2280, 6280	32–4	32–9
	1987–88	Holley	5220	32–10	32–11
	1987–88	Holley	6520	32–10	32–12
	1987–88	Rochester	Quadrajet	32–12	32–20
Ford Motor Co.	1987–90	Motorcraft	7200VV	32–2	32–3
	1987	Holley	1949	32–4	32–7
	1987–89	Aisan (Festiva)	NA	32–23	—
General Motors	1987	Holley	5210C	32–9	32–11
	1987–90	Rochester	Angle Degree to Decimal Conversion		
	1987	Rochester	2SE, E2SE	32–12	32–15
	1987	Rochester	M2ME, E2ME	32–15	32–17
	1987–90	Rochester	Quadrajet	32–17	32–20

NOTE: New model carburetor part numbers and specifications are not released by the manufacturers until well after the press date for this manual. These will be included in the next edition. New model carburetor part numbers are obtained from the most current factory sources, however, carburetors which are new or redesigned by the manufacturer during the production year and designated with new part numbers may not appear.
NA Not available

FORD MOTORCRAFT CARBURETORS

Model 7200 VV

Since the design of the 7200 VV (variable venturi) carburetor differs considerably from the other carburetors in the Ford lineup, an explanation in the theory and operation is presented here.

In exterior appearance, the variable venturi carburetor is similar to conventional carburetors and like a conventional carburetor, it uses a normal float and fuel bowl system. However, the similarity ends there. In place of a normal choke plate and fixed area venturis, the 7200 VV carburetor has a pair of small oblong castings in the top of the upper carburetor body where the choke plate would normally be located. These castings slide back and forth across the top of the carburetor in response to air/fuel demands. Their movement is controlled by a spring-loaded diaphragm valve regulated by a vacuum signal taken below the venturis in the throttle bores. As the throttle is opened, the strength of the vacuum signal increases, opening the venturis and allowing more air to enter the carburetor.

Fuel is admitted into the venturi area by means of tapered metering rods that fit into the main jets. These rods are attached to the venturis and the venturis open or close in response to air demand. The fuel needed to maintain the proper mixture increases or decreases as the metering rods slide in the jets. In comparison to a conventional carburetor with fixed venturis and a variable air supply, this system provides much more precise control of the fuel/air supply during all modes of operation. Because of the variable venturi principle, there are fewer fuel metering systems and fuel passages. The only auxiliary fuel metering systems required are an idle trim, accelerator pump (similar to a conventional carburetor), starting enrichment and cold running enrichment.

NOTE: Adjustment, assembly and disassembly of this carburetor require special tools for some of the operations. Do not attempt any operations on this carburetor without first obtaining special tools needed for that particular operation. Special tools needed for the following adjustments are identified in the procedure.

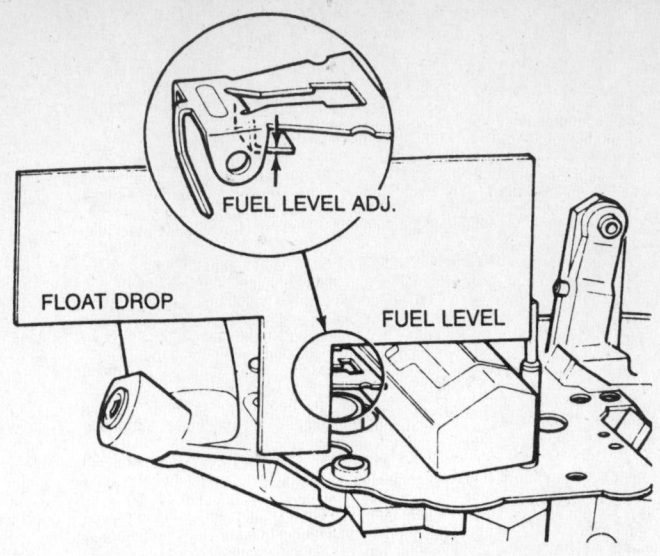

7200 VV float level adjustment

FLOAT LEVEL

Adjustment

1. Remove and invert the upper part of the carburetor, with the gasket in place.

2. Measure the vertical distance between the carburetor body, outside the gasket and the bottom of the float.

3. To adjust, bend the float operating lever that contacts the needle valve. Make sure that the float remains parallel to the gasket surface.

FLOAT DROP

Adjustment

1. Remove and hold the upper part of the carburetor upright.

2. Measure the vertical distance between the carburetor body, outside the gasket and the bottom of the float.

3. Adjust by bending the stop tab on the float lever that contacts the hinge pin.

FAST IDLE SPEED

Adjustment

1. With the engine warmed and idling, place the fast idle lever on the step of the fast idle cam specified on the engine compartment sticker or in the specifications chart. Disconnect and plug the EGR vacuum line.

2. Make sure the high speed cam positioner lever is disengaged.

3. Turn the fast idle speed screw to adjust to the specified speed.

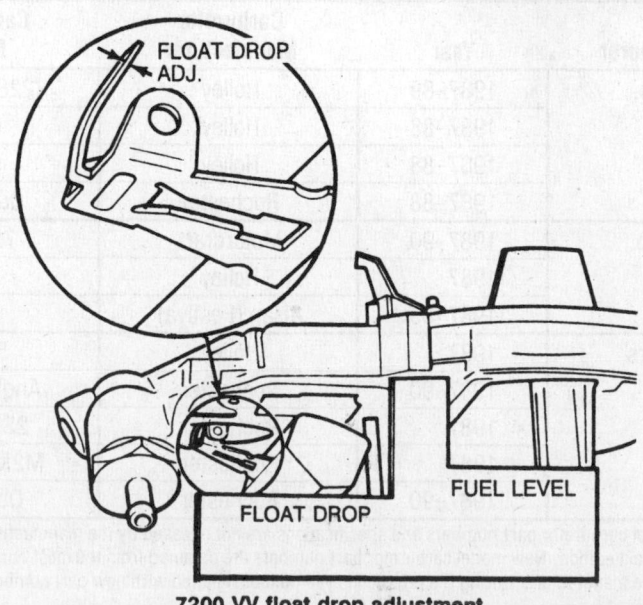

7200 VV float drop adjustment

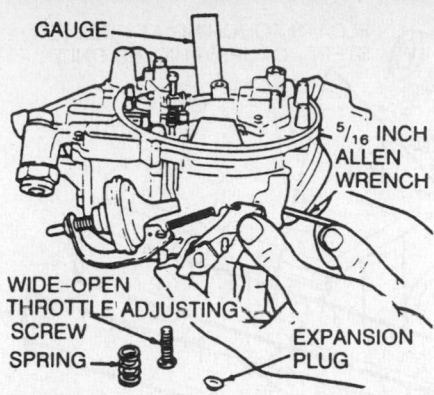

7200–Wide open throttle limiter adjustment

FAST IDLE CAM

Adjustment

Use of a stator cap special tool T77L–9848–A or equivalent, is required for this procedure. It fits over the choke thermostatic lever when the choke cap is removed.

1. Remove the choke coil cap. The top rivets will have to be drilled out; the bottom rivet will have to be driven out from the rear. New rivets must be used upon installation.

2. Place the fast idle lever in the corner of the specified step of the fast idle cam, the highest step is first, with the high speed cam positioner retracted.

3. If the adjustment is being made with the carburetor removed, hold the throttle lightly closed with a rubber band.

4. Turn the stator cap tool clockwise until the lever contacts the fast idle cam adjusting screw.

5. Turn the fast idle cam adjusting screw until the index mark on the cap lines up with the specified mark on the casting.

6. Remove the stator cap tool. Install the choke coil cap and set to the specified housing mark.

COLD ENRICHMENT METERING ROD

Adjustment

A dial indicator and a stator cap tool T77L–9848–A or equivalent, are required for this adjustment.

1. Remove the choke coil cap.

2. Attach a weight to the choke coil mechanism to seat the cold enrichment rod.

3. Install and zero a dial indicator with the tip on top of the enrichment rod. Raise and release the weight to verify zero on the dial indicator.

4. With the stator cap at the index position, the dial indicator should read the specified dimension on the specification tag. If needed, turn the adjusting nut to correct.

5. Install the choke cap at the correct setting.

VENTURI VALVE LIMITER

Adjustment

1. Remove the carburetor. Take off the venturi valve cover and the 2 rollers.

2. Use a center punch to loosen the expansion plug at the rear of the carburetor main body on the throttle side and remove the expansion plug.

3. Use an Allen wrench to remove the venturi valve wide open stop screw.

4. Hold the throttle wide open.

5. Apply a light closing pressure on the venturi valve and check the gap between the valve and the air horn wall. To adjust, move the venturi valve to the wide open position and insert an Allen wrench into the stop screw hole. Turn clockwise to increase the gap. Remove the wrench and check the gap again.

6. Replace the wide open stop screw and turn it clockwise until it contacts the valve.

7. Push the venturi valve wide open and check the gap. Turn the stop screw to bring the gap to specifications.

8. Reassemble the carburetor with a new expansion plug.

CONTROL VACUUM REGULATOR (CVR)

Adjustment

The cold enrichment metering rod adjustment must be checked and set before making this adjustment.

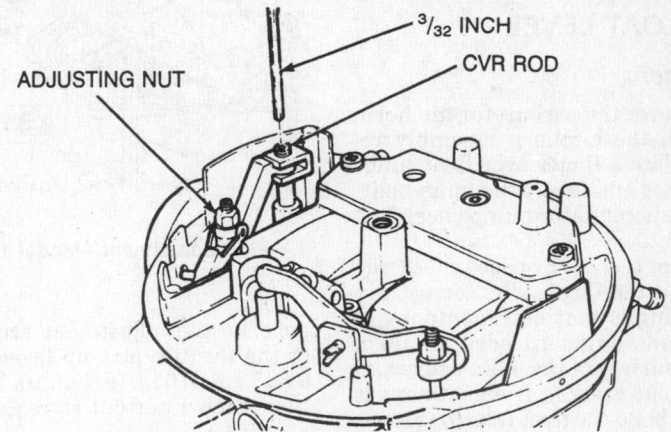

7200 VV control vacuum regulator adjustment

MOTORCRAFT MODEL 7200 VV SPECIFICATIONS

Year	Model	Float Level (in.)	Float Drop (in.)	Fast Idle Cam Setting/Step	Cold Enrichment Metering Rod (in.)	Control Vacuum (in. H₂O)	Venturi Valve Limiter (in.)	Choke Cap Setting (notches)
1987	E2AE-AJA	1.010–1.070	1.430–1.490	0.360/2nd step	③	②	①	Index
	E2AE-APA	1.010–1.070	1.430–1.490	0.360/2nd step	③	②	①	Index
1988	E7AE-AA	1.010–1.070	1.430–1.490	0.360/2nd step	③	②	①	Index
	E8AE-AA	1.010–1.070	1.430–1.490	0.360/2nd step	③	②	①	Index
1989–90	ALL	1.010–1.070	1.430–1.490	0.360/2nd step	③	②	①	Index

① Maximum opening: 0.99/1.01
Wide open on throttle: 0.39/.41
② See text
③ Maximum opening: 0.99/1.01
Wide open on throttle: 0.74/.76

1. After adjusting the cold enrichment metering rod, leave the dial indicator in place but remove the stator cap. Do not re-zero the dial indicator.

2. Press down on the CVR rod until it bottoms on its seat. Measure this amount of travel with the dial indicator.

3. If the adjustment is incorrect, hold the ⅜ in. CVR adjusting nut with a box wrench to prevent it from turning. Use a 3/32 in. Allen wrench to turn the CVR rod; turning counter-clockwise will increase the travel and vice versa.

HOLLEY CARBURETORS

Model 1949

This carburetor is a single venturi booster type carburetors, which uses 13 basic systems. This carburetor is used on the 2.3L High Swirl Combustion (HSC) engine, in the 1987 Tempo and Topaz and is also used in Canada.

DRY FLOAT LEVEL

Adjustment

1. Remove the carburetor air horn.
2. With the air horn assembly removed, place a finger over float hinge pin retainer and invert the main body. Catch the accelerator pump check ball and weight.
3. Using a straight-edge, check the position of the floats. The correct dry float setting is that both pontoons at the extreme outboard edge by flush with the surface of the main body casting (without gasket). If adjustment is required, bend the float tabs to raise or lower the float level.
4. Once adjustment is correct, turn main body right side up and check the float alignment. The float should move freely throughout its range without contacting the fuel bowl walls. If the float pontoons are misaligned, straighten them by bending the float arms. Recheck the float level adjustment.
5. During assembly, insert the check ball first and then the weight.

AUXILIARY MAIN JET/ PULLOVER VALVE

Adjustment

The length of the auxiliary main jet/ pullover valve adjustment screw which protrudes through the back side (side

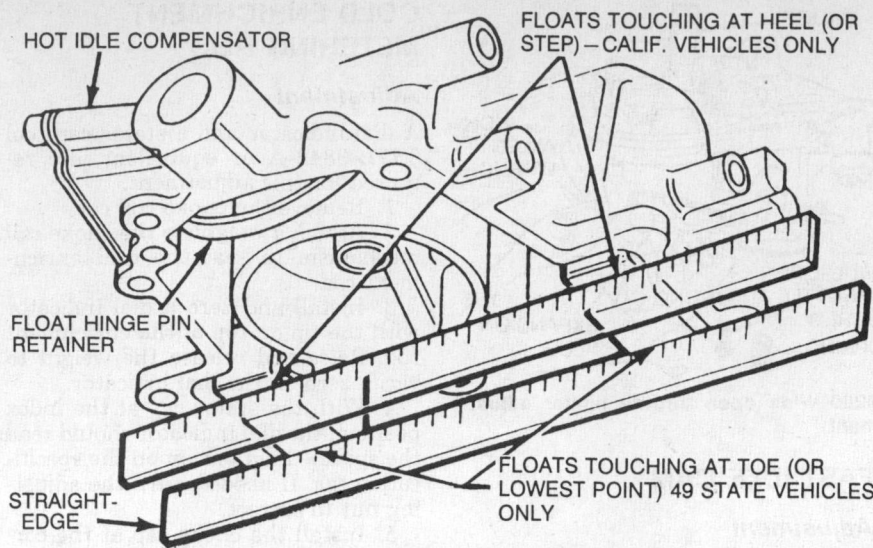

Float alignment—Model 1949

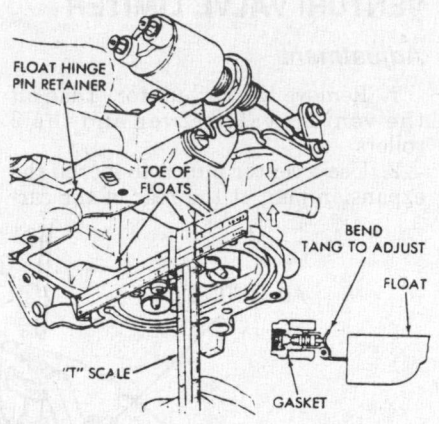

Float adjustment—Model 1949

opposite the adjustment screw head) of the throttle pick-up lever must be 0.345 ± 0.010 in. (8.76mm). To adjust, turn screw in or out as required.

MECHANICAL FUEL BOWL VENT (LEVER CLEARANCE)

Adjustment

OFF VEHICLE

1. Secure the choke plate in the wide-open position.
2. Set the throttle at the TSP **OFF** position.
3. Turn the TSP **OFF** idle adjustment screw counterclockwise until the throttle plate is closed in the throttle bore.
4. Fuel bowl vent clearance: Dimension A should be within 0.120 ± 0.010 in. (3.05mm).
5. If the adjustment is out of specification, bend the bowl vent actuator lever at the adjustment point to obtain the required clearance.

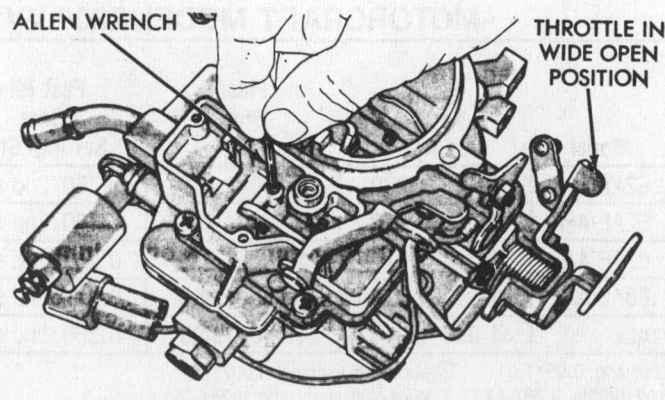

Mechanical power valve adjustment—Model 1949

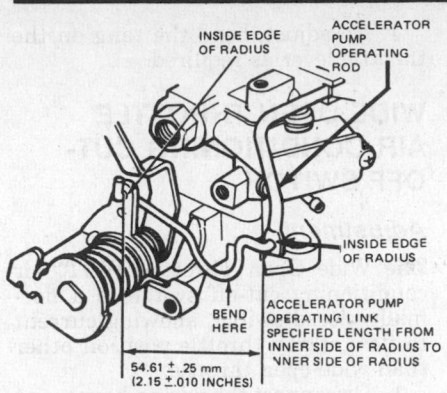

Auxiliary main jet/pullover valve (timing adjustment) — Model 1949

NOTE: Do not bend the fuel bowl vent arm and/or adjacent portion of the actuator lever. TSP OFF rpm must be set after the carburetor installation.

ON VEHICLE

NOTE: This adjustment must be performed after the curb idle speed has been set to the specification.

1. Secure the choke plate in the wide open position.
2. Turn the ignition key **ON** to activate the TSP, engine not running. Open the throttle so that the TSP plunger extends.
3. Verify that the throttle is in the idle set position (contacting the TSP plunger). Measure the clearance of the fuel bowl vent arm to the bowl vent actuating lever.
4. Fuel bowl vent clearance: Dimension A should be within 0.020–0.040 in.

NOTE: There is a difference in the on vehicle and off vehicle specification.

5. If the dimension is out of specification, bend the bowl vent actuator lever at the adjustment point to obtain the required clearance.

NOTE: Do not bend the fuel bowl vent arm and/or adjacent portion of the actuating lever.

ACCELERATOR PUMP STROKE

Adjustment

1. Check the length of the accelerator pump operating link from its inside edge at the accelerator pump operating rod to its inside edge at the throttle lever hole. The dimension should be 2.150 ±0.010 in. (54.61 ±.25mm).
2. Adjust to the proper length by bending the loop in the operating link.

CHOKE PLATE PULLDOWN

Adjustment

This adjustment is preset at the factory and protected by a tamper resistant plug.

FAST IDLE CAM INDEX

Adjustment

1. With the engine cool, position the fast idle screw on the high step of the fast idle cam.
2. Activate the pulldown motor by applying an external vacuum source of 15–20 in. Hg.
3. Apply light pressure to the upper edge of the choke plate in the closing direction to remove clearance between the pulldown motor clevis and the modulator stem.
4. Open the throttle slightly and allow the fast idle cam to drop.
5. Close the throttle and measure the clearance between the top edge of the fast idle rpm adjusting screw and the shoulder of the fast idle cam highest step; Dimension A is the fast idle cam index shown in the illustration.

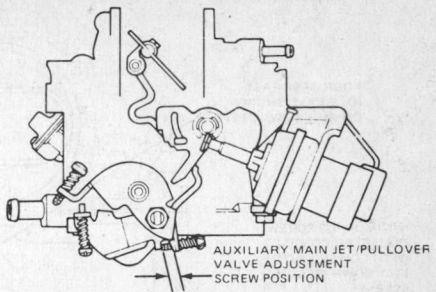

Accelerator pump stroke adjustment — Model 1949

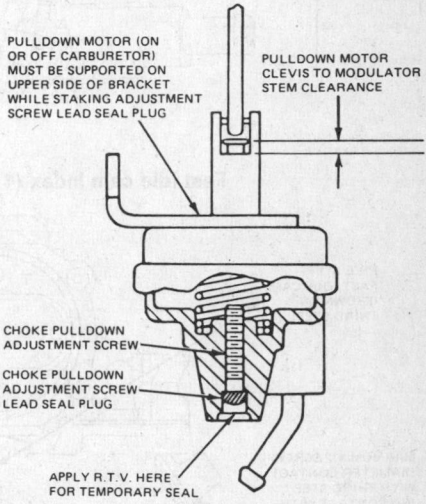

Choke pulldown adjustment — Model 1949

6. Remove the light closing pressure from the upper edge of the choke plate.
7. Open the throttle to the wide open position and return slowly.
8. The fast idle adjustment screw must contact the lower end of the fast idle cam kickdown step by at least half of its diameter on carburetors with 4 step cams, or must contact the third step by at least half of its diameter without contacting the second or fourth steps on carburetors with 5 step cams.
9. If Steps 5 and 8 are okay, the fast idle cam index is within specification. If adjustment is necessary, bend the fast idle cam link at the loop to obtain 0.020–0.030 in. at Dimension A.

DECHOKE

Adjustment

1. With the engine off and cool, hold the throttle in the wide open position.
2. Use a drill of the specified size and measure the clearance between the upper edge of the choke plate and the air horn wall.
3. With slight pressure against the choke shaft, a slight drag should be felt when the gauge is withdrawn.

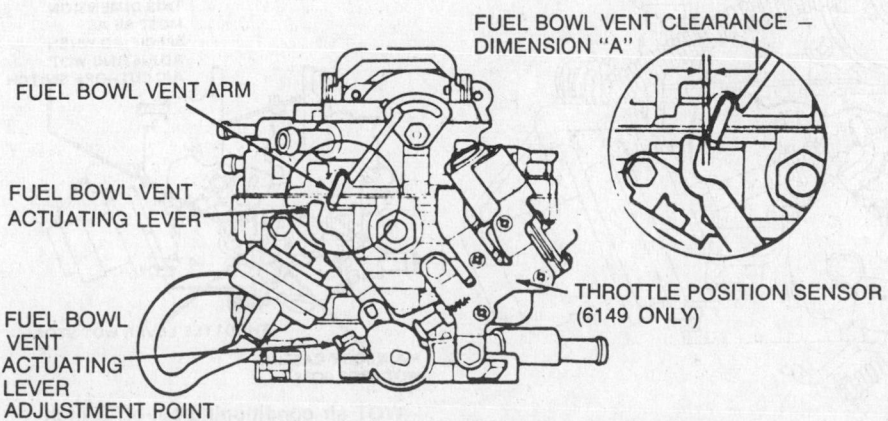

Mechanical fuel pump vent adjustment — Model 1949

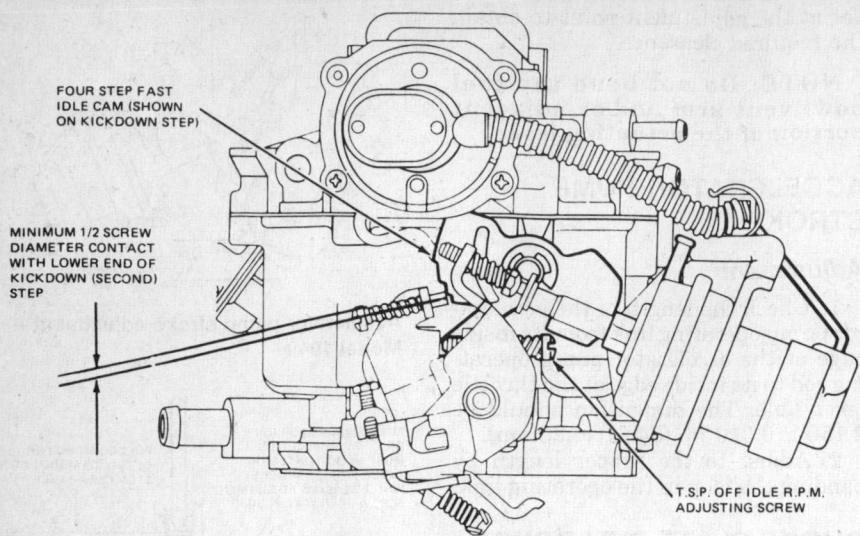

MINIMUM 1/2 SCREW DIAMETER CONTACT WITH LOWER END OF KICKDOWN (SECOND) STEP

FOUR STEP FAST IDLE CAM (SHOWN ON KICKDOWN STEP)

T.S.P. OFF IDLE R.P.M. ADJUSTING SCREW

Fast idle cam index (4 step idle cams) – Model 1949

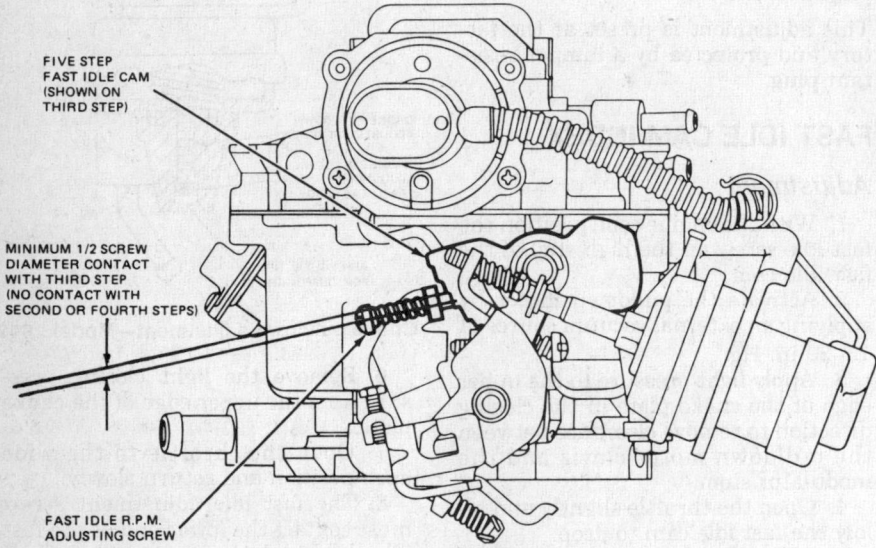

FIVE STEP FAST IDLE CAM (SHOWN ON THIRD STEP)

MINIMUM 1/2 SCREW DIAMETER CONTACT WITH THIRD STEP (NO CONTACT WITH SECOND OR FOURTH STEPS)

FAST IDLE R.P.M. ADJUSTING SCREW

Fast idle cam index (5 step idle cam) – Model 1949

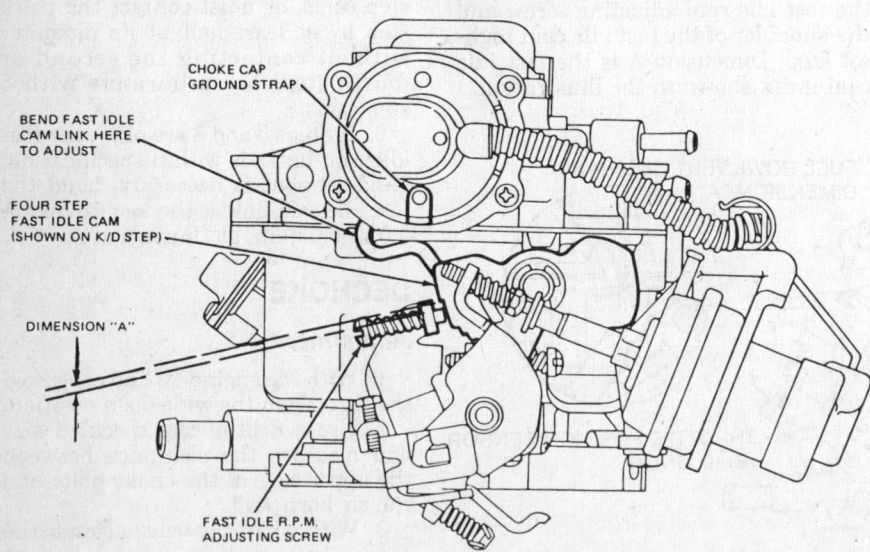

CHOKE CAP GROUND STRAP

BEND FAST IDLE CAM LINK HERE TO ADJUST

FOUR STEP FAST IDLE CAM (SHOWN ON K/D STEP)

DIMENSION "A"

FAST IDLE R.P.M. ADJUSTING SCREW

Fast idle cam index adjustment – Model 1949

4. To adjust, bend the tang on the throttle lever as required.

WIDE OPEN THROTTLE AIR CONDITIONING CUT-OFF SWITCH

Adjustment

The Wide Open Throttle (WOT) air conditioning cut-off switch is a normally closed switch, allowing current to flow at any throttle position other than wide-open throttle.

1. Disconnect the wiring harness at the switch connector.

2. Connect a 12 volt DC power supply and test lamp. With the throttle at curb idle, TSP off idle or fast idle position, the test light must be on. If the test lamp does not light, replace the switch assembly.

3. Rotate the throttle to the wide-open position. The test lamp must go off, indicating an open circuit.

4. If the lamp remains on, insert a 0.165 in. drill or gauge between the throttle lever WOT stop and the WOT stop boss on the carburetor main body casting. Hold the throttle open as far as possible against the gauge. Loosen the switch mounting screws sufficiently to allow the switch to pivot. Rotate the switch assembly so the test lamp just goes out with the throttle held in

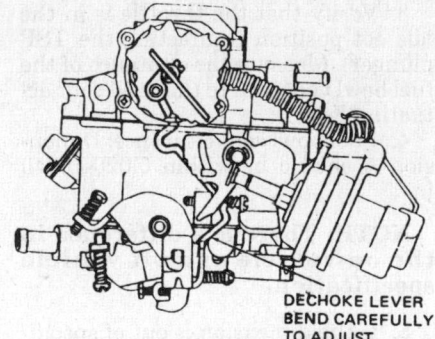

DECHOKE LEVER BEND CAREFULLY TO ADJUST

Dechoke adjustment – Model 1949

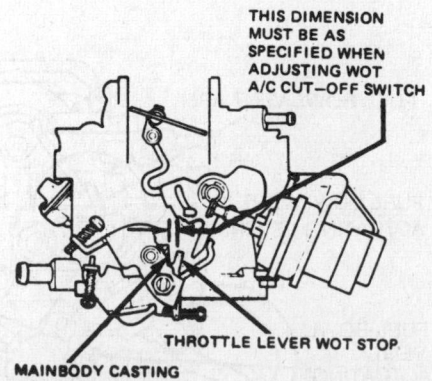

THIS DIMENSION MUST BE AS SPECIFIED WHEN ADJUSTING WOT A/C CUT-OFF SWITCH

THROTTLE LEVER WOT STOP

MAINBODY CASTING WOT STOP BOSS

WOT air conditioning cut-off switch clearance adjustment – Model 1949

HOLLEY MODEL 1949
Ford Motor Co.

Year	Carb. Iden.	Dry Float Level (in.)	Pump Hole No. Setting	Choke Plate Pulldown (in.)	Fast Idle Cam Linkage (in.)	Dechoke (in.)	Choke Setting
1987	E43E-ADA	①	2	0.080–0.120	0.020–0.030	0.180–0.220	2 Rich
	E43E-AEA	①	2	0.080–0.120	0.020–0.030	0.180–0.220	2 Rich
	E73E-AV ②	①	2	0.090–0.120	0.020–0.030	0.180–0.220	1 Rich
	E73E-BB ②	①	2	0.090–0.120	0.020–0.030	0.180–0.220	1 Rich

① Both float pontoons at outboard edge flush with surface of main body casting (without gasket)
② Canada only

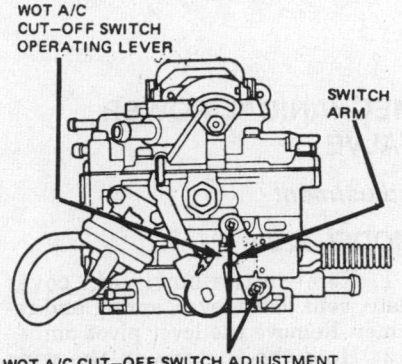

WOT A/C cut-off switch adjustment screws—Model 1949

the above referenced position. If the lamp does not go **OFF** within the allowable adjustment rotation, replace the switch. If the lamp goes out, tighten the switch bracket-to-carburetor screws to 45 inch lbs. (5 Nm) and remove drill or gauge and repeat Step 3.

Model 2280 and 6280

FLOAT LEVEL

Adjustment

1. Remove the carburetor air horn.
2. Invert the carburetor body taking care to catch the pump intake

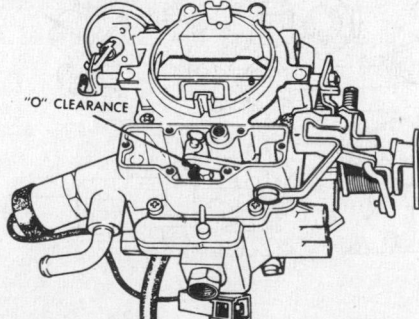

Accelerator pump stroke adjustment—model 6280

check ball so that only the weight of the floats is forcing the needle against the seat. Hold a finger against the hinge pin retainer to fully seat the float in the float pin cradle.

3. Lay a straight edge across the float bowl. The toe of each float should be as per specifications from the straight edge. If necessary, bend the float tang to adjust.

ACCELERATOR PUMP STROKE

Measurement

MODEL 2280

1. Remove the bowl vent cover plate and vent valve lever spring. Take care to avoid loosening the vent valve retainer.

2. Make sure that the accelerator pump connector rod is in the inner hole of the pump operating lever and the throttle is at curb idle.

3. Place a straight edge on the bowl vent cover surface of the air horn, over the accelerator pump lever.

4. The lever surface should be flush with the air horn. If not, adjust it by bending the pump connector rod at the 90 degree bend.

NOTE: If this adjustment is changed, both the bowl vent and the mechanical power valve adjustments must be reset.

MODEL 6280

1. Remove the bowl vent cover plate and gasket.
2. With all pump links and levers installed, adjust the accelerator pump

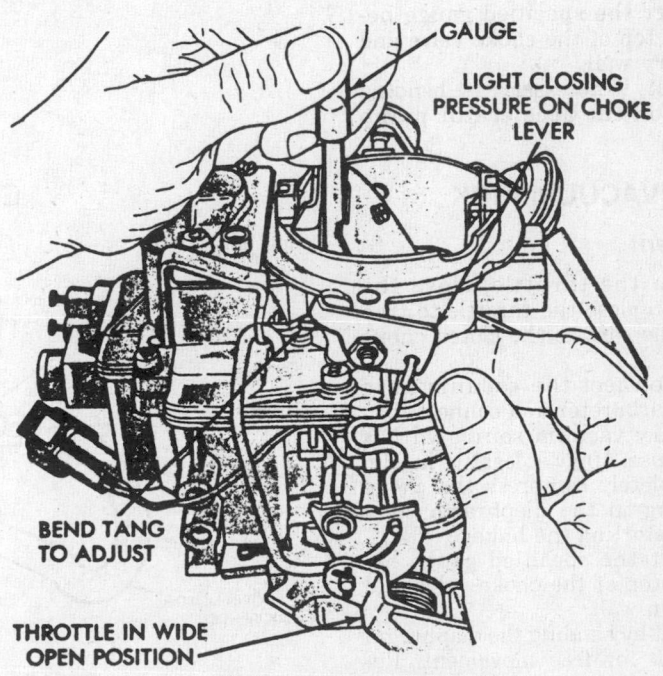

Choke unloader adjustment

32 CARBURETOR SERVICE

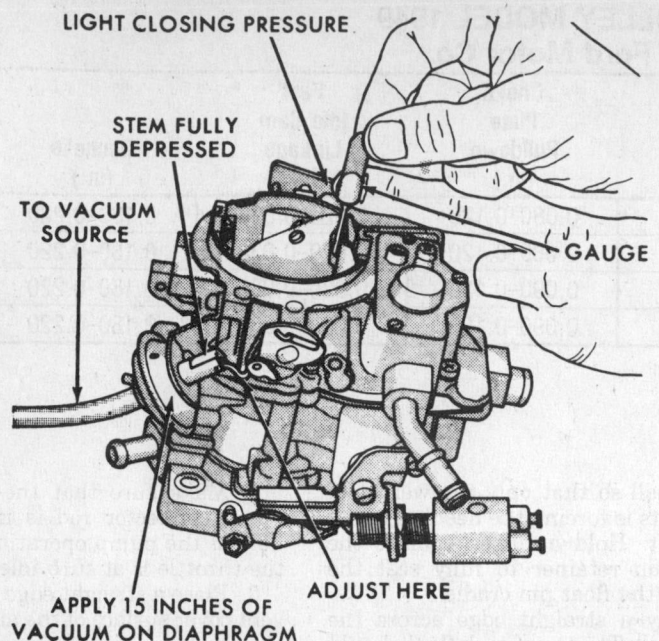

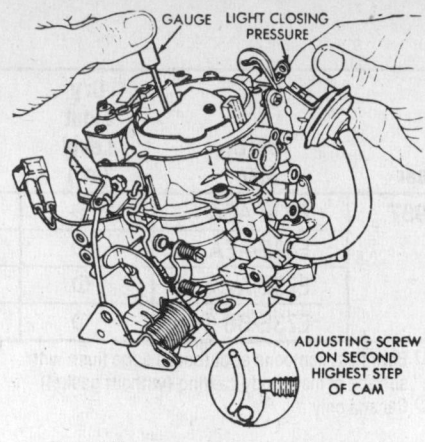

Fast idle cam position adjustment

Choke vacuum kick adjustment

cap nut for zero clearance between the pump lever and the cap nut. Check that the wide open throttle can be reached without binding.

3. Install the gasket and the bowl vent cover plate.

CHOKE UNLOADER

Adjustment

1. Hold the throttle valves in the wide open position.

2. Lightly press a finger against the control lever to move the choke valve toward the closed position.

3. Insert the specified gauge between the top of the choke valve and the air horn wall.

4. Adjust, if necessary, by bending the tang on the accelerator pump lever.

CHOKE VACUUM KICK

Adjustment

1. Open the throttle, close the choke, then close the throttle to trap the fast idle cam at the closed choke position.

2. Disconnect the vacuum hose from the carburetor and connect it to an auxiliary vacuum source with a length of hose. Apply at least 15 in. Hg.

3. Completely compress the choke lever spring in the diaphragm stem without distorting the linkage.

4. Insert the specified gauge between the top of the choke valve and the air horn wall.

5. Adjust by bending the diaphragm link. Check for free movement. Replace the vacuum hose.

FAST IDLE CAM POSITION

Adjustment

1. Position the adjusting screw on the second highest step of the fast idle cam.

2. Move the choke towards the closed position with light finger pressure.

3. Insert the specified gauge between the choke valve and the air horn wall.

4. Adjust by opening or closing the U-bend in the fast idle connector link.

MECHANICAL POWER VALVE

Adjustment

MODEL 2280

1. Remove the bowl vent cover plate, vent valve lever, spring and retainer. Remove the lever pivot pin.

2. Hold the throttle in the wide open position.

3. Using a $5/64$ in. Allen wrench, press the mechanical power valve adjustment screw down and release it to determine if clearance exists. Turn the screw clockwise until clear is zero.

4. Adjust by turning the screw a turn counterclockwise.

5. Install all parts.

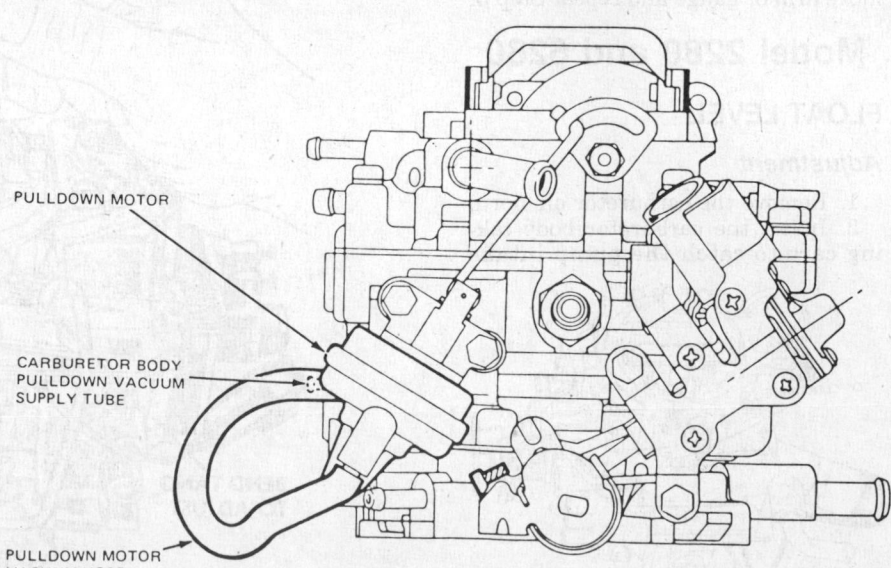

Fast idle adjustment—measure the choke clearance

HOLLEY MODEL 2280/6280
Chrysler Corporation

Year	Carb. Part No.	Float Level (in.)	Accelerator Pump Adjustment (in.)	Fast Idle (rpm)	Choke Unloader Clearance (in.)	Vacuum Kick (in.)	Fast Idle Cam Position (in.)	Choke
1987	R-40276A	9/32	0.180	①	0.280	0.130	0.060	Fixed
	R-40245A	9/32	0.050	①	0.200	0.140	0.052	Fixed
1988	R-40276A	9/32	0.180	①	0.280	0.130	0.060	Fixed
	R-40354A	9/32	0.050	①	0.200	0.140	0.052	Fixed
1989	R-40354A	9/32	0.180	①	0.280	0.130	0.060	Fixed

① Refer to underhood sticker

Model 5210-C

The Holley 5210–C is a progressive 2 barrel carburetor with an automatic choke system which is activated by a water heated thermostatic coil. An electrically heated choke is used on most later models. It also has an exhaust gas recirculation system with the valve located in the intake manifold. It is used on 1987 Chevettes (Canada).

FLOAT LEVEL

Adjustment

1. With the carburetor air horn inverted and the float tang resting lightly on the inlet needle, insert the specified gauge between the air horn and the float.

2. Bend the float tang if an adjustment is needed.

FAST IDLE CAM

Adjustment

1. Place the fast idle screw on the second step of the fast idle cam and against the shoulder of the high step.

2. Place the specified drill or gauge on the down side of the choke plate.

3. To adjust, bend the choke lever tang.

CHOKE PLATE PULLDOWN (VACUUM BREAK)

Adjustment

1. Attach a hand vacuum pump to the vacuum break diaphragm; apply vacuum and seat the diaphragm.

2. Push the fast idle cam lever down to close the choke plate.

3. Take any slack out of the linkage in the open choke position.

② BEND TANG TO ADJUST

① WITH AIR HORN INVERTED INSERT SPECIFIED PLUG GAUGE BETWEEN FLOAT AND AIR HORN

5210-C Float level adjustment

② BEND TANG IF ADJUSTMENT REQUIRED

① WITH AIR HORN REMOVED DISTANCE FROM BOTTOM OF AIR HORN TO TOP OF FLOAT SHOULD BE 1" ±1/8"

5210-C Float drop adjustment

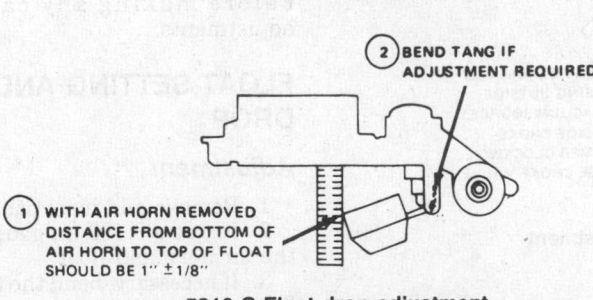

② INSERT SPECIFIED GAUGE BETWEEN LOWER EDGE OF CHOKE VALVE & INSIDE AIR HORN WALL NOTE: HOLD GAUGE VERTICAL

③ BEND TANG IF ADJUSTMENT IS REQUIRED.

① SET FAST IDLE CAM SO THAT SCREW IS HELD AGAINST SECOND HIGH STEP OF CAM

5210-C Fast idle cam adjustment

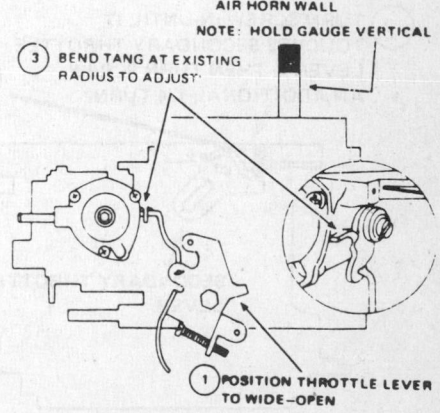

② INSERT SPECIFIED GAUGE BETWEEN LOWER EDGE OF CHOKE VALVE & INSIDE AIR HORN WALL

NOTE: HOLD GAUGE VERTICAL

③ BEND TANG AT EXISTING RADIUS TO ADJUST

① POSITION THROTTLE LEVER TO WIDE–OPEN

5210-C Choke unloader adjustment

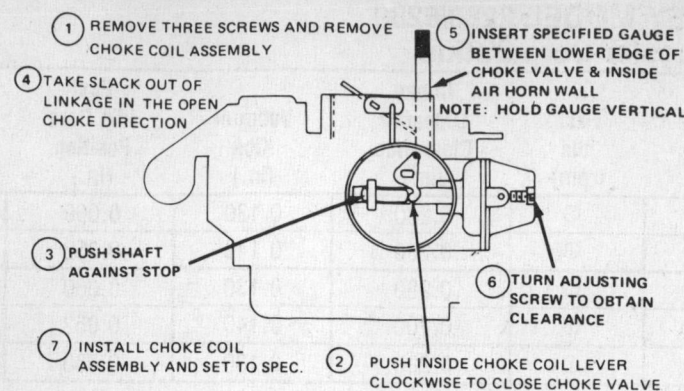

5210-C Vacuum break (choke plate pulldown) adjustment

① REMOVE THREE SCREWS AND REMOVE CHOKE COIL ASSEMBLY
④ TAKE SLACK OUT OF LINKAGE IN THE OPEN CHOKE DIRECTION
③ PUSH SHAFT AGAINST STOP
⑦ INSTALL CHOKE COIL ASSEMBLY AND SET TO SPEC.
⑤ INSERT SPECIFIED GAUGE BETWEEN LOWER EDGE OF CHOKE VALVE & INSIDE AIR HORN WALL NOTE: HOLD GAUGE VERTICAL
⑥ TURN ADJUSTING SCREW TO OBTAIN CLEARANCE
② PUSH INSIDE CHOKE COIL LEVER CLOCKWISE TO CLOSE CHOKE VALVE

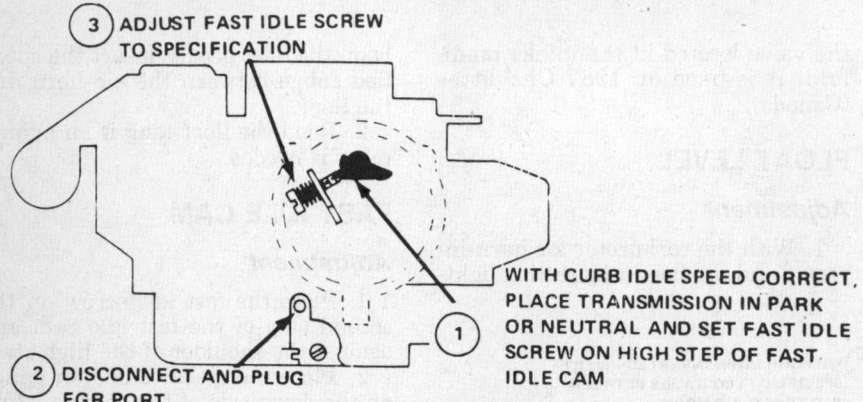

5210-C Fast idle speed adjustment

③ ADJUST FAST IDLE SCREW TO SPECIFICATION
① WITH CURB IDLE SPEED CORRECT, PLACE TRANSMISSION IN PARK OR NEUTRAL AND SET FAST IDLE SCREW ON HIGH STEP OF FAST IDLE CAM
② DISCONNECT AND PLUG EGR PORT

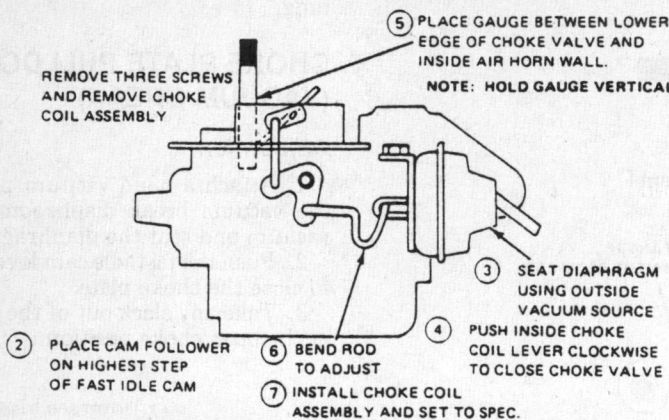

5210-C Secondary vacuum break adjustment

REMOVE THREE SCREWS AND REMOVE CHOKE COIL ASSEMBLY
⑤ PLACE GAUGE BETWEEN LOWER EDGE OF CHOKE VALVE AND INSIDE AIR HORN WALL. NOTE: HOLD GAUGE VERTICAL
③ SEAT DIAPHRAGM USING OUTSIDE VACUUM SOURCE
④ PUSH INSIDE CHOKE COIL LEVER CLOCKWISE TO CLOSE CHOKE VALVE
② PLACE CAM FOLLOWER ON HIGHEST STEP OF FAST IDLE CAM
⑥ BEND ROD TO ADJUST
⑦ INSTALL CHOKE COIL ASSEMBLY AND SET TO SPEC.

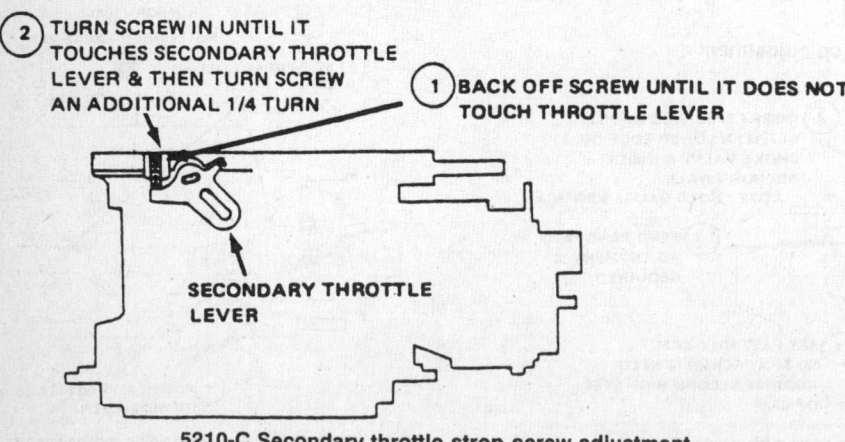

5210-C Secondary throttle strop screw adjustment

② TURN SCREW IN UNTIL IT TOUCHES SECONDARY THROTTLE LEVER & THEN TURN SCREW AN ADDITIONAL 1/4 TURN
① BACK OFF SCREW UNTIL IT DOES NOT TOUCH THROTTLE LEVER
SECONDARY THROTTLE LEVER

4. Insert the specified gauge between the lower edge of the choke plate and the air horn wall.

5. If the clearance is incorrect, turn the vacuum break adjusting screw, located in the break housing, to adjust.

CHOKE UNLOADER

Adjustment

1. Position the throttle lever at the wide open position.

2. Insert a gauge of the size specified in the chart between the lower edge of the choke valve and the air horn wall.

3. Bend the unloader tang for adjustment.

FAST IDLE SPEED

Adjustment

1. The engine must be at normal operating temperature with the air cleaner off.

2. With the engine running, position the fast idle screw on the high step of the cam. Plug the EGR port on the carburetor.

3. Adjust the speed by turning the fast idle screw.

Model 5220 and 6520

Both carburetors are staged dual venturi carburetors. The model 6520 has the electronic feedback system while the model 5220 is of the conventional design. On the 6520, always check the condition of hoses and related wiring before making any carburetor adjustments.

FLOAT SETTING AND FLOAT DROP

Adjustment

1. Remove and invert the air horn.

2. Insert a 0.480 in. gauge between the air horn and float.

3. If necessary, bend the tang on the float arm to adjust.

4. Turn the air horn right side up and allow the float to hang freely. Measure the float drop from the bottom of the air horn to the bottom of the float. It should be exactly 1⅞ in. Correct by bending the float tang.

VACUUM KICK

Adjustment

1. Open the throttle, close the choke, then close the throttle to trap the fast idle system at the closed choke position.

2. Disconnect the vacuum hose to

HOLLEY MODEL 5210-C
Chevrolet Chevette

Year	Carb. Part No. ① ②	Float Level (Dry) (in.)	Fast Idle Cam (in.)	Secondary Vacuum Break (in.)	Fast Idle Setting (rpm)	Choke Unloader (in.)	Choke Setting
1987 Canada	14076393	0.50	0.100	③	④	0.325	Fixed
	14076394	0.50	0.090	③	④	0.275	Fixed

① Located on tag attached to the carburetor, or on the casting or choke plate
② GM Identification numbers are used in place of the Holley numbers
③ Hot: 0.250 Cold: 0.100
④ See underhood sticker

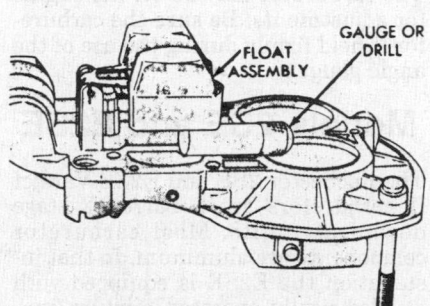

Float setting adjustment

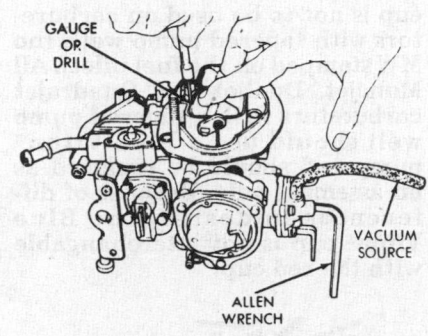

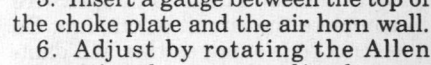

Vacuum kick adjustment

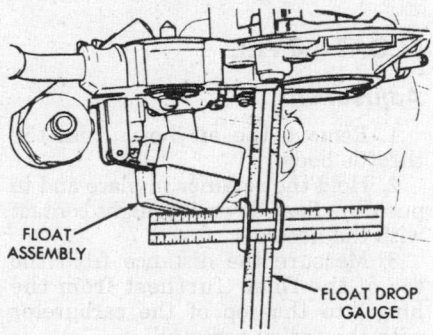

Float drop measurement

the carburetor and connect it to an auxiliary vacuum source.

3. Apply at least 15 in. Hg vacuum to the unit.

4. Apply sufficient force to close the choke valve without distorting the linkage.

5. Insert a gauge between the top of the choke plate and the air horn wall.

6. Adjust by rotating the Allen screw in the center diaphragm housing.

7. Replace the vacuum hose.

FAST IDLE SPEED
Adjustment

1. Remove the air cleaner, disconnect and plug the EGR linebut do not disconnect the spark control computer vacuum line. Turn the air conditioning off.

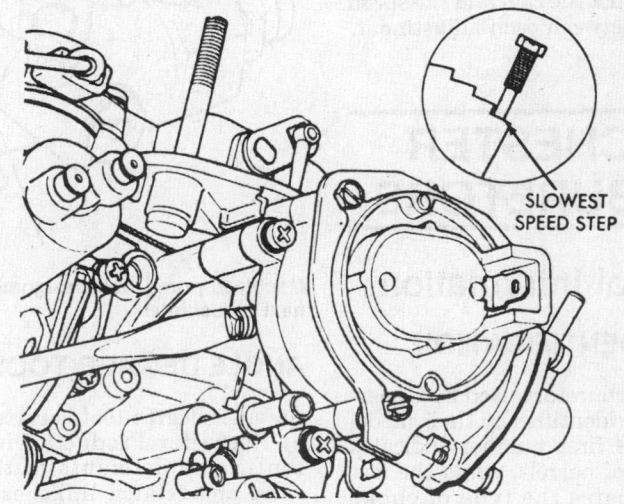

Fast idle speed adjustment

HOLLEY MODEL 5220
Chrysler Corporation

Year	Carb. Part No.	Accelerator Pump Hole No.	Dry Float Level (in.)	Vacuum Kick (in.)	Fast Idle RPM (w/fan)	Throttle Stop Speed RPM	Choke
1987	R-40060-2	—	0.480	0.055	①	—	Fixed
	R-40233	—	0.480	0.095	①	—	Fixed
	R-40234	—	0.480	0.095	①	—	Fixed
	R-40240	—	0.480	0.095	①	—	Fixed

① See underhood sticker

HOLLEY MODEL 6520
Chrysler Corporation

Year	Carb. Part No.	Accelerator Pump Hole No.	Dry Float Level (in.)	Float Drop (in.)	Vacuum Kick (in.)	Fast Idle RPM
1987	R-40295A	—	0.480	1.875	0.075	①
	R-40296A	—	0.480	1.875	0.075	①

① Refer to underhood sticker

2. Disconnect the radiator fan electrical connector and use a jumper wire to complete the circuit at the fan. Do not short to ground, as this will damage the system.

3. With the parking brake set and the transmission in **N**, engine still off, open the throttle and place the fast idle screw on the slowest step of the cam.

4. Start the engine and check the idle speed. If it continues to rise slowly, the idle stop switch is not grounded properly.

5. Adjust the fast idle with the screw, moving the screw off the cam each time to adjust. Allow the screw to fall back against the cam and the speed to stabilize between each adjustment.

ROCHESTER CARBURETORS

General Information

MODEL IDENTIFICATION

Rochester carburetors used by General Motors are identified by their model number. The first number indicates the number of barrels, while the last letters indicates the type of choke used. These are V for the manifold mounted choke coil, C for the choke coil mounted on the carburetor and E for electric choke, also mounted on the carburetor. Model numbers ending in A indicate an altitude-compensating carburetor.

NOTE: Due to the presence of ethyl alcohol in some gasolines, the black rubber pump cup swells causing driveability complaints. In order to correct this problem, all Varajet, Dualjet and Quadrajet carburetors with a MW designation (machined pump well) stamped on the carburetor next to the fuel inlet should use a Red Viton® pump cup when rebuilding

the carburetor. The Red Viton® cup is not to be used on carburetors with tapered pump wells (no MW stamped on the fuel inlet). All Monojet, Dualjet and Quadrajet carburetors with a tapered pump well should use a Blue Viton® pump and should be replaced as an assembly only. Because of differences in design, the Blue Viton® cup is not interchangable with the red cup.

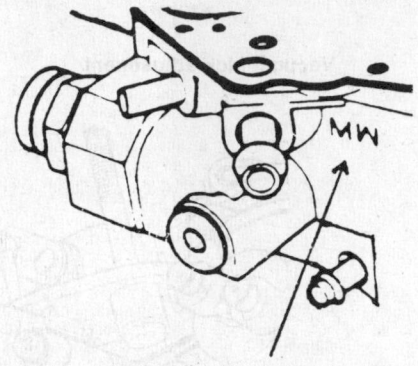

Machined pump well designation shown next to fuel inlet

ANGLE DEGREE TOOL

An angle degree tool is recommended by Rochester Products Division, to confirm adjustments to the choke valve and related linkages on their model 2 and 4 barrel carburetors, in place of the plug type gauges. Decimal and degree conversion charts are provided for use by technicians who have access to an angle gauge and not plug gauges. It must be remembered that the relationship between the decimal and the angle readings are not exact, due to manufacturers tolerances.

To use the angle gauge, rotate the degree scale until zero (0) is opposite the pointer. With the choke valve completely closed, place the gauge magnet squarely on top of the choke valve and rotate the bubble until it is centered. Make the necessary adjustments to have the choke valve at the specified degree angle opening as read from the degree angle tool.

The carburetor may be off the engine for adjustments. Be sure the carburetor is held firmly during the use of the angle gauge.

Models 2SE and E2SE

The Rochester 2SE and E2SE Varajet II carburetors are 2 barrel, 2 stage downdraft units. Most carburetor components are aluminum. In that installation the E2SE is equipped with an electrically operated mixture control solenoid, controlled by the electronic control module.

FLOAT LEVEL

Adjustment

1. Remove the air horn from the throttle body.

2. Hold the retainer in place and to push the float down into light contact with the needle.

3. Measure the distance from the toe of the float (furthest from the hinge) to the top of the carburetor with the gasket removed.

4. To adjust, remove the float and gently bend the arm to specification. After adjustment, check the float alignment in the chamber.

NOTE: Some carburetors have a float stabilizer spring. If used, remove the spring with float. Use care when removing.

ACCELERATOR PUMP

Adjustment

No accelerator pump adjustment is required.

FAST IDLE

Adjustment

1. Set the ignition timing and curb idle speed and disconnect and plug hoses as directed on the emission control decal.

2. Place the fast idle screw on the second step of the cam.

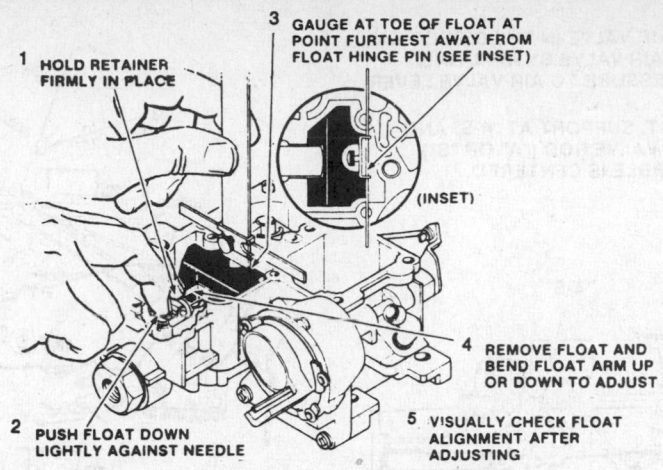

1 HOLD RETAINER FIRMLY IN PLACE

3 GAUGE AT TOE OF FLOAT AT POINT FURTHEST AWAY FROM FLOAT HINGE PIN (SEE INSET)

(INSET)

4 REMOVE FLOAT AND BEND FLOAT ARM UP OR DOWN TO ADJUST

2 PUSH FLOAT DOWN LIGHTLY AGAINST NEEDLE

5 VISUALLY CHECK FLOAT ALIGNMENT AFTER ADJUSTING

2SE, E2SE float adjustment

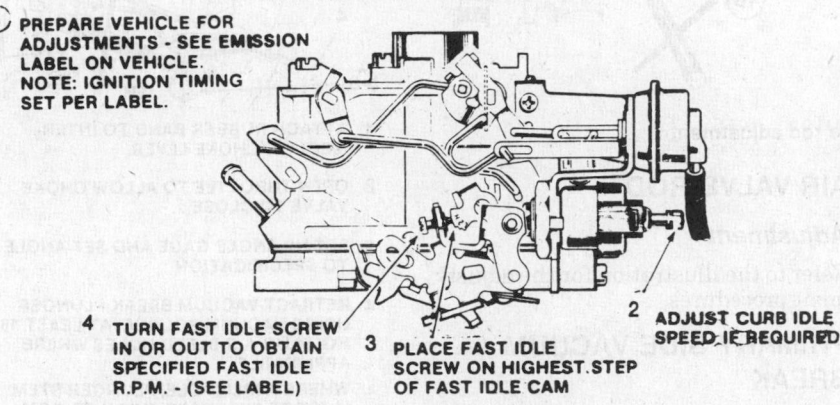

1 PREPARE VEHICLE FOR ADJUSTMENTS - SEE EMISSION LABEL ON VEHICLE. NOTE: IGNITION TIMING SET PER LABEL.

4 TURN FAST IDLE SCREW IN OR OUT TO OBTAIN SPECIFIED FAST IDLE R.P.M. - (SEE LABEL)

3 PLACE FAST IDLE SCREW ON HIGHEST STEP OF FAST IDLE CAM

2 ADJUST CURB IDLE SPEED IF REQUIRED

2SE, E2SE fast idle adjustment

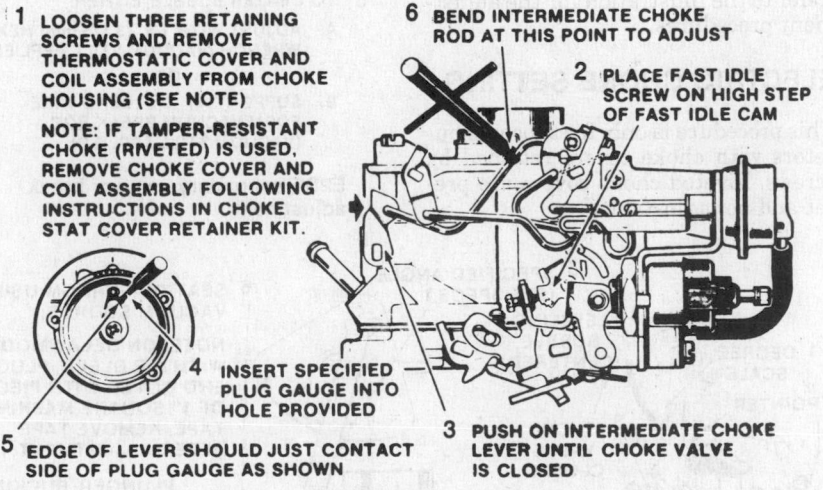

1 LOOSEN THREE RETAINING SCREWS AND REMOVE THERMOSTATIC COVER AND COIL ASSEMBLY FROM CHOKE HOUSING (SEE NOTE)

NOTE: IF TAMPER-RESISTANT CHOKE (RIVETED) IS USED, REMOVE CHOKE COVER AND COIL ASSEMBLY FOLLOWING INSTRUCTIONS IN CHOKE STAT COVER RETAINER KIT.

6 BEND INTERMEDIATE CHOKE ROD AT THIS POINT TO ADJUST

2 PLACE FAST IDLE SCREW ON HIGH STEP OF FAST IDLE CAM

4 INSERT SPECIFIED PLUG GAUGE INTO HOLE PROVIDED

5 EDGE OF LEVER SHOULD JUST CONTACT SIDE OF PLUG GAUGE AS SHOWN

3 PUSH ON INTERMEDIATE CHOKE LEVER UNTIL CHOKE VALVE IS CLOSED

2SE, E2SE choke coil lever adjustment

3. Start the engine and adjust the engine speed to specification with the fast idle screw.

NOTE: On carburetors using a clip to retain the pump rod in the pump lever, no pump adjustment is required. On models using the clipless pump rod, the pump rod adjustment should not be changed from the original factory setting unless gauging shows it to be out of specification. The pump lever is made from heavy duty, hardened steel making bending difficult. Do not remove the pump lever for bending unless absolutely necessary.

CHOKE COIL LEVER

Adjustment

1. Remove the retaining screws and remove the choke cover and coil. On carburetors with a riveted choke cover, drill out the rivets and remove the cover and choke coil.

NOTE: A choke cover retainer kit is required for reassembly.

2. Place the fast idle screw on the high step of the cam.
3. Close the choke by pushing in on the intermediate choke lever. On FWD, the intermediate choke lever is behind the choke vacuum diaphragm.
4. Insert a drill or gauge of the specified size into the hole in the choke housing. The choke lever in the housing should be up against the side of the gauge.
5. If the lever does not just touch the gauge, bend the intermediate choke rod to adjust.

FAST IDLE CAM (CHOKE ROD)

Adjustment

Refer to the illustration for the adjustment procedures.

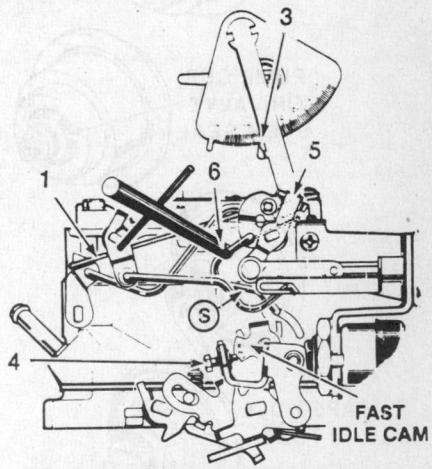

FAST IDLE CAM

1 ATTACH RUBBER BAND TO INTERMEDIATE CHOKE LEVER.
2 OPEN THROTTLE TO ALLOW CHOKE VALVE TO CLOSE.
3 SET UP ANGLE GAGE AND SET ANGLE TO SPECIFICATIONS.
4 PLACE FAST IDLE SCREW ON SECOND STEP OF CAM AGAINST RISE OF HIGH STEP.
5 PUSH ON CHOKE SHAFT LEVER TO OPEN CHOKE VALVE AND TO MAKE CONTACT WITH BLACK CLOSING TANG.
6 SUPPORT AT "S" AND ADJUST BY BENDING FAST IDLE CAM ROD UNTIL BUBBLE IS CENTERED.

Choke link—fast idle cam adjustment

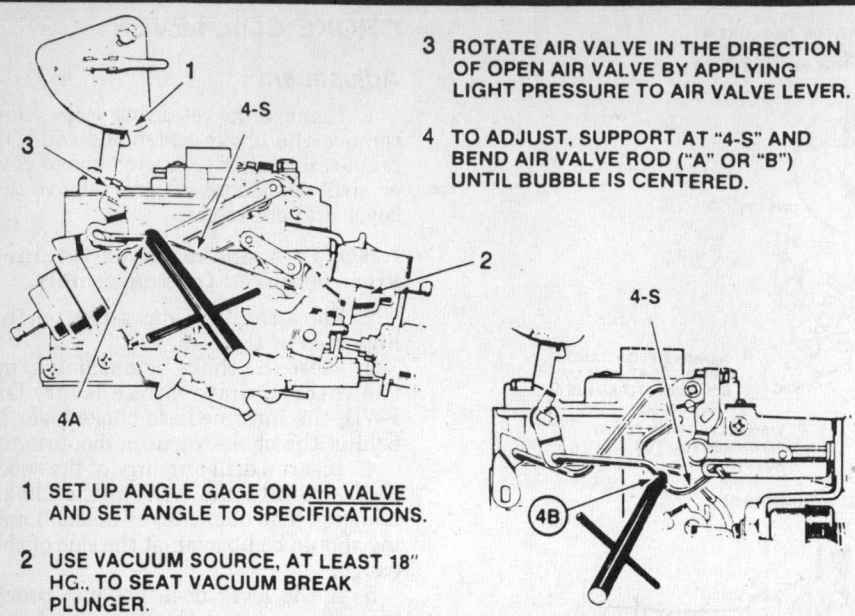

3 ROTATE AIR VALVE IN THE DIRECTION OF OPEN AIR VALVE BY APPLYING LIGHT PRESSURE TO AIR VALVE LEVER.

4 TO ADJUST, SUPPORT AT "4-S" AND BEND AIR VALVE ROD ("A" OR "B") UNTIL BUBBLE IS CENTERED.

1 SET UP ANGLE GAGE ON AIR VALVE AND SET ANGLE TO SPECIFICATIONS.

2 USE VACUUM SOURCE, AT LEAST 18" HG., TO SEAT VACUUM BREAK PLUNGER.

E2SE air valve rod adjustment

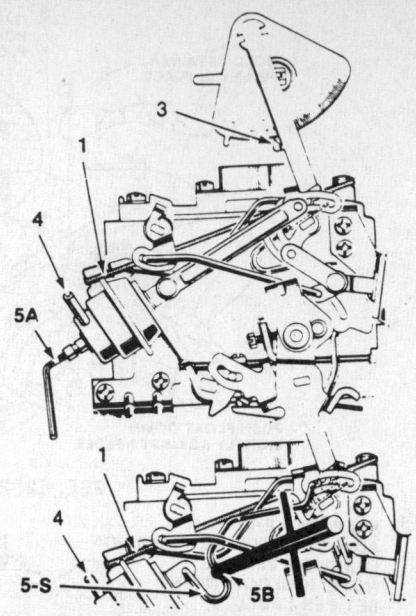

1 ATTACH RUBBER BAND TO INTER- MEDIATE CHOKE LEVER.

2 OPEN THROTTLE TO ALLOW CHOKE VALVE TO CLOSE.

3 SET UP ANGLE GAGE AND SET ANGLE TO SPECIFICATION.

4 RETRACT VACUUM BREAK PLUNGER USING VACUUM SOURCE, AT LEAST 18' HG. PLUG AIR BLEED HOLES WHERE APPLICABLE.

WHERE APPLICABLE, PLUNGER STEM MUST BE EXTENDED FULLY TO COM- PRESS PLUNGER BUCKING SPRING.

5 TO CENTER BUBBLE, EITHER:

A. ADJUST WITH 1/8" (3.175 mm) HEX WRENCH (VACUUM STILL APPLIED) -OR

B. SUPPORT AT "5-S", BEND WIRE- FORM VACUUM BREAK ROD (VACUUM STILL APPLIED)

E2SE secondary vacuum break adjustment

PLUGGING AIR BLEED HOLES

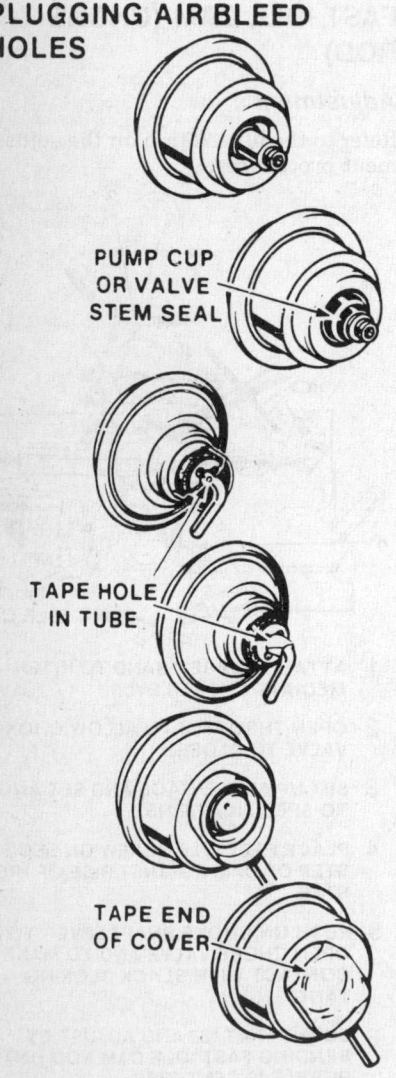

PUMP CUP OR VALVE STEM SEAL

TAPE HOLE IN TUBE

TAPE END OF COVER

Vacuum break information—E2SE

AIR VALVE ROD

Adjustment

Refer to the illustration for the adjust- ment procedures.

PRIMARY SIDE VACUUM BREAK

Adjustment

Refer to the illustration for the adjust- ment procedures.

ELECTRIC CHOKE SETTING

This procedure is only for those carbu- retors with choke covers retained by screws. Riveted choke covers are pre- set and nonadjustable.

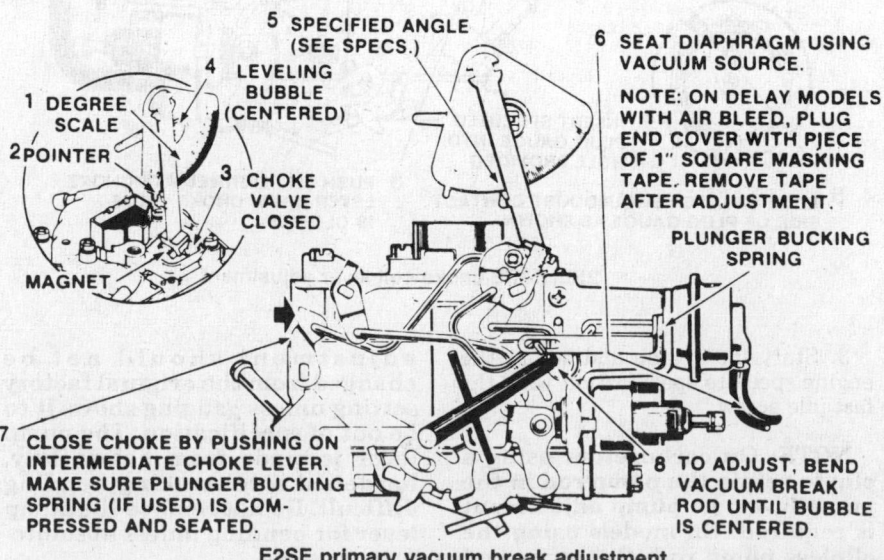

5 SPECIFIED ANGLE (SEE SPECS.)

4 LEVELING BUBBLE (CENTERED)

1 DEGREE SCALE

2 POINTER

3 CHOKE VALVE CLOSED

MAGNET

6 SEAT DIAPHRAGM USING VACUUM SOURCE.

NOTE: ON DELAY MODELS WITH AIR BLEED, PLUG END COVER WITH PIECE OF 1" SQUARE MASKING TAPE. REMOVE TAPE AFTER ADJUSTMENT.

PLUNGER BUCKING SPRING

7 CLOSE CHOKE BY PUSHING ON INTERMEDIATE CHOKE LEVER. MAKE SURE PLUNGER BUCKING SPRING (IF USED) IS COM- PRESSED AND SEATED.

8 TO ADJUST, BEND VACUUM BREAK ROD UNTIL BUBBLE IS CENTERED.

E2SE primary vacuum break adjustment

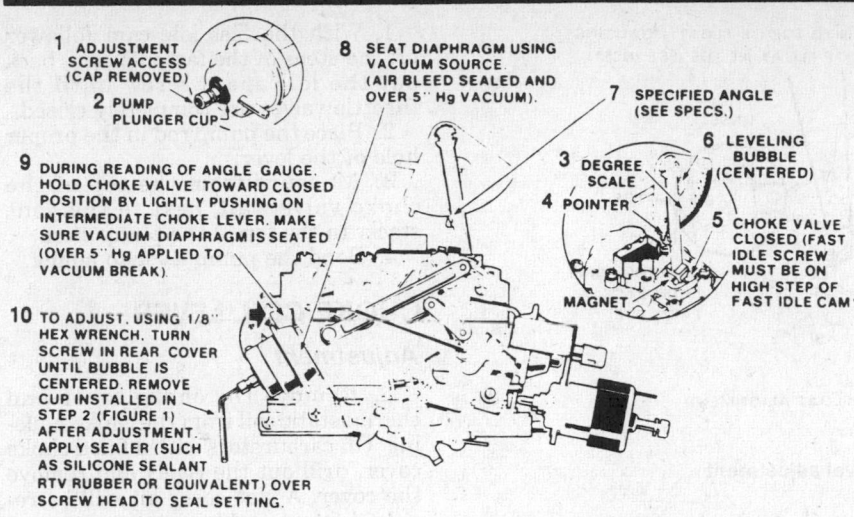

1. ADJUSTMENT SCREW ACCESS (CAP REMOVED)
2. PUMP PLUNGER CUP
9. DURING READING OF ANGLE GAUGE. HOLD CHOKE VALVE TOWARD CLOSED POSITION BY LIGHTLY PUSHING ON INTERMEDIATE CHOKE LEVER. MAKE SURE VACUUM DIAPHRAGM IS SEATED (OVER 5" Hg APPLIED TO VACUUM BREAK).
10. TO ADJUST, USING 1/8" HEX WRENCH, TURN SCREW IN REAR COVER UNTIL BUBBLE IS CENTERED. REMOVE CUP INSTALLED IN STEP 2 (FIGURE 1) AFTER ADJUSTMENT. APPLY SEALER (SUCH AS SILICONE SEALANT RTV RUBBER OR EQUIVALENT) OVER SCREW HEAD TO SEAL SETTING.
8. SEAT DIAPHRAGM USING VACUUM SOURCE (AIR BLEED SEALED AND OVER 5" Hg VACUUM).
7. SPECIFIED ANGLE (SEE SPECS.)
6. LEVELING BUBBLE (CENTERED)
3. DEGREE SCALE
4. POINTER
5. CHOKE VALVE CLOSED (FAST IDLE SCREW MUST BE ON HIGH STEP OF FAST IDLE CAM)
MAGNET

E2SE secondary vacuum break adjustment GM A series

1. Loosen the retaining screws.
2. Place the fast idle screw on the high step of the cam.
3. Rotate the choke cover to align the cover mark with the specified housing mark.

NOTE: The specification INDEX which appears in the specification table refers to the center mark between 1 NOTCH LEAN and 1 NOTCH RICH.

SECONDARY VACUUM BREAK

Adjustment

Refer to the illustration for the adjustment procedures.

CHOKE UNLOADER

Adjustment

Refer to the illustration for the adjustment procedures.

Models M2ME and E2ME

The Rochester Dualjet E2ME Model 210 is a variation of the M2ME, modified for use with the Electronic Fuel Control System. An electrically operated mixture control solenoid is mounted in the float bowl. Mixture is thus controlled by the Electronic Control Module, in response to signals from the oxygen sensor mounted in the exhaust system upstream of the catalytic converter.

FLOAT LEVEL

Adjustment

The E2ME procedure is the same except for the method that the float arm is adjusted. For the E2ME only, if the float level is too high, hold the retainer firmly in place and push down on the center of the float to adjust.

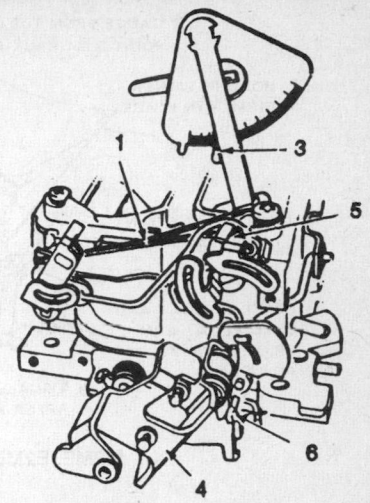

1. ATTACH RUBBER BAND TO INTERMEDIATE CHOKE LEVER.
2. OPEN THROTTLE TO ALLOW CHOKE VALVE TO CLOSE.
3. SET UP ANGLE GAGE AND SET ANGLE TO SPECIFICATIONS.
4. HOLD THROTTLE LEVER IN WIDE OPEN POSITION.
5. PUSH ON CHOKE SHAFT LEVER TO OPEN CHOKE VALVE AND TO MAKE CONTACT WITH BLACK CLOSING TANG.
6. ADJUST BY BENDING TANG UNTIL BUBBLE IS CENTERED.

E2SE choke unloader adjustment

1. If float level is low on the E2ME, lift out the metering rods.
2. Remove the solenoid connector screws.
3. Turn the lean mixture solenoid screw in clockwise, counting the exact number of turns until the screw is lightly bottomed in the bowl.
4. Turn the screw out counterclockwise and remove it.
5. Lift out the solenoid and connector.

2SE, E2SE CARBURETOR SPECIFICATIONS
General Motors—Canada

Year	Carburetor Identification	Float Level (in.)	Pump Rod (in.)	Fast Idle (rpm)	Choke Coil Lever (in.)	Fast Idle Cam (deg./in.)	Air Valve Rod (in.)	Primary Vacuum Break (deg./in.)	Choke Setting (notches)	Secondary Vacuum Break (deg./in.)	Choke Unloader (deg./in.)	Secondary Lockout (in.)
1987	17084312	5/16	Fixed	①	0.085	—	1	18/0.096	Fixed	20/0.110	35/0.220	—
	17084314	5/16	Fixed	①	0.085	—	1	16/0.083	Fixed	20/0.110	30/0.179	—
	17085482	3/8	Fixed	①	0.085	—	1	28/0.164	Fixed	32/0.195	45/0.304	—
	17085483	3/8	Fixed	①	0.085	—	1	28/0.164	Fixed	32/0.195	45/0.304	—
	17085484	3/8	Fixed	①	0.085	—	1	28/0.164	Fixed	32/0.195	45/0.304	—
	17085485	3/8	Fixed	①	0.085	—	1	28/0.164	Fixed	32/0.195	45/0.304	—

① See underhood decal

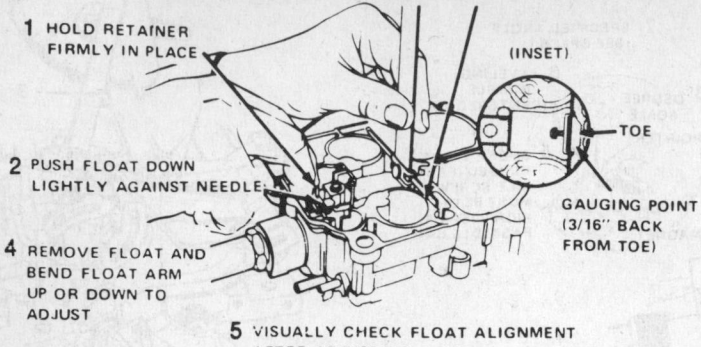

3 GAUGE FROM TOP OF CASTING TO TOP OF FLOAT – GAUGING
POINT 3/16" BACK FROM END OF FLOAT AT TOE (SEE INSET)

1 HOLD RETAINER
FIRMLY IN PLACE

(INSET)

TOE

2 PUSH FLOAT DOWN
LIGHTLY AGAINST NEEDLE

GAUGING POINT
(3/16" BACK
FROM TOE)

4 REMOVE FLOAT AND
BEND FLOAT ARM
UP OR DOWN TO
ADJUST

5 VISUALLY CHECK FLOAT ALIGNMENT
AFTER ADJUSTING

M2ME, E2ME float level adjustment

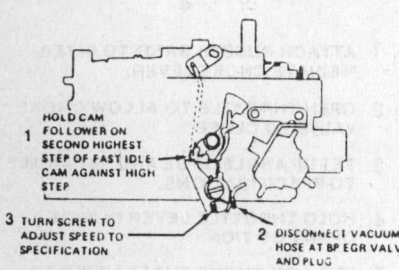

1 HOLD CAM
FOLLOWER ON
SECOND HIGHEST
STEP OF FAST IDLE
CAM AGAINST HIGH
STEP

3 TURN SCREW TO
ADJUST SPEED TO
SPECIFICATION

2 DISCONNECT VACUUM
HOSE AT BP EGR VALVE
AND PLUG

**M2ME, E2ME fast idle speed
adjustment—Typical**

6. Remove the float and bend the arm up to adjust.

7. Install the parts, installing the mixture solenoid screw in until it is lightly bottomed, then turning it out the exact number of turns counted earlier.

FAST IDLE SPEED

Adjustment

1. Place the fast idle lever on the high step of the fast idle cam.

2. Turn the fast idle screw out until the throttle valves are closed.

3. Turn the screw in to contact the lever, then turn it in the number of turns listed in the specifications. Check this preliminary setting against the sticker figure.

FAST IDLE CAM (CHOKE ROD)

Adjustment

1. Adjust the fast idle speed.

2. Place the cam follower lever on the second step of the fast idle cam, holding it firmly against the rise of the high step.

3. Close the choke valve by pushing upward on the choke coil lever inside the choke housing, or by pushing up on the vacuum break lever tang.

4. Gauge between the upper edge of the choke valve and the inside of the air horn wall.

5. Bend the tang on the fast idle cam to adjust.

ACCELERATOR PUMP

Adjustment

This adjustment is not required on E2ME carburetors used in conjunction with the computer controlled systems.

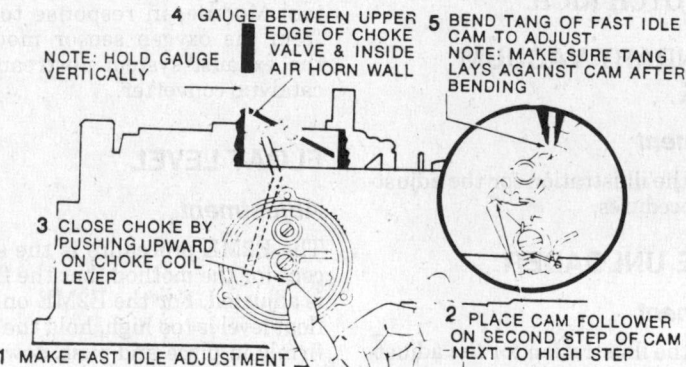

4 GAUGE BETWEEN UPPER
EDGE OF CHOKE
VALVE & INSIDE
AIR HORN WALL

NOTE: HOLD GAUGE
VERTICALLY

5 BEND TANG OF FAST IDLE
CAM TO ADJUST
NOTE: MAKE SURE TANG
LAYS AGAINST CAM AFTER
BENDING

3 CLOSE CHOKE BY
PUSHING UPWARD
ON CHOKE COIL
LEVER

1 MAKE FAST IDLE ADJUSTMENT

2 PLACE CAM FOLLOWER
ON SECOND STEP OF CAM
NEXT TO HIGH STEP

M2ME, E2ME fast idle cam adjustment—Typical

1. With the fast idle cam follower off the steps of the fast idle cam, back out the idle speed screw until the throttle valves are completely closed.

2. Place the pump rod in the proper hole of the lever.

3. Measure from the top of the choke valve wall, next to the vent stack, to the top of the pump stem.

4. Bend the pump lever to adjust.

CHOKE COIL LEVER

Adjustment

1. Remove the choke cover and thermostatic coil from the choke housing. On carburetors with a fixed choke cover, drill out the rivets and remove the cover. A stat cover kit will be required for assembly.

2. Push up on the coil tang (counterclockwise) until the choke valve is closed. The top of the choke rod should be at the bottom of the slot in the choke valve lever. Place the fast idle cam follower on the high step of the cam.

3. Insert a 0.120 in. plug gauge in the hole in the choke housing.

4. The lower edge of the choke coil lever should just contact the side of the plug gauge.

5. Bend the choke rod to adjust.

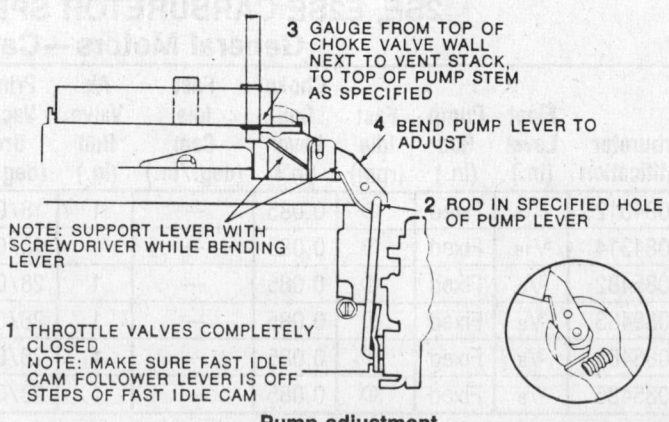

3 GAUGE FROM TOP OF
CHOKE VALVE WALL
NEXT TO VENT STACK,
TO TOP OF PUMP STEM
AS SPECIFIED

4 BEND PUMP LEVER TO
ADJUST

2 ROD IN SPECIFIED HOLE
OF PUMP LEVER

NOTE: SUPPORT LEVER WITH
SCREWDRIVER WHILE BENDING
LEVER

1 THROTTLE VALVES COMPLETELY
CLOSED
NOTE: MAKE SURE FAST IDLE
CAM FOLLOWER LEVER IS OFF
STEPS OF FAST IDLE CAM

Pump adjustment

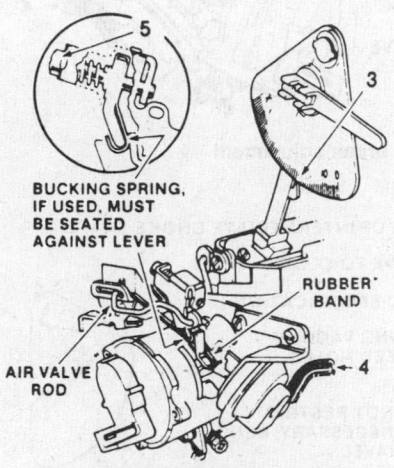

5 BEND CHOKE ROD AT THIS POINT TO ADJUST (SEE INSERT)

CHOKE VALVE CLOSED

2 PUSH UP ON THERMOSTATIC COIL TANG (COUNTERCLOCKWISE) UNTIL CHOKE VALVE IS CLOSED

4 LOWER EDGE OF LEVER SHOULD JUST CONTACT SIDE OF PLUG GAUGE

1 LOOSEN THREE RETAINING SCREWS AND REMOVE THE THERMOSTATIC COVER AND COIL ASSEMBLY FROM CHOKE HOUSING

3 INSERT SPECIFIED PLUG GAUGE

M2ME, E2ME choke coil lever adjustment—Typical

FRONT/REAR VACUUM BRAKE

Adjustment

A choke valve measuring gauge J–26701 or equivalent, is used to measure angle (degrees instead of inches).

CHOKE UNLOADER

Adjustment

1. With the choke valve completely closed, hold the throttle valves wide open.
2. Measure between the upper edge of the choke valve and air horn wall.
3. Bend the tang on the fast idle lever to obtain the proper measurement.

BUCKING SPRING, IF USED, MUST BE SEATED AGAINST LEVER

RUBBER BAND

AIR VALVE ROD

1 ATTACH RUBBER BAND TO GREEN TANG OF INTERMEDIATE CHOKE SHAFT

2 OPEN THROTTLE TO ALLOW CHOKE VALVE TO CLOSE

3 SET UP ANGLE GAGE AND SET TO SPECIFICATION

4 RETRACT VACUUM BREAK PLUNGER USING VACUUM SOURCE, AT LEAST 18" HG. PLUG AIR BLEED HOLES WHERE APPLICABLE ON QUADRAJETS, AIR VALVE ROD MUST NOT RESTRICT PLUNGER FROM RETRACTING FULLY. IF NECESSARY, BEND ROD (SEE ARROW) TO PERMIT FULL PLUNGER TRAVEL. FINAL ROD CLEARANCE MUST BE SET AFTER VACUUM BREAK SETTING HAS BEEN MADE.

5 WITH AT LEAST 18" HG STILL APPLIED, ADJUST SCREW TO CENTER BUBBLE

E2ME front vacuum break adjustment

Quadrajet

The Rochester Quadrajet carburetor is a 2 stage, 4-barrel downdraft carburetor. It has been built in many variations designated as 4MC, M4MC, M4MCA, M4ME, M4MEA, E4MC and E4ME.

The first M in the identification indicates that the carburetor is of a modified primary metering (open loop) design, while the first E indicates electronically controlled. The C has an integral hot air choke, while the E has an electric choke.

The primary side of the carburetor is equipped with 2 primary bores and a triple venturi with plain tube nozzles. During off idle and part throttle operation, the fuel is metered through tapered metering rods operating in specially designed jets positioned by a manifold vacuum responsive piston.

The secondary side of the carburetor contains 2 secondary bores. An air valve is used on the secondary side for metering control and supplements the primary bore. The secondary air valve operates tapered metering rods which regulate the fuel in constant proportion to the air being supplied.

FAST IDLE SPEED

Adjustment

1. Position the fast idle lever on the high step of the fast idle cam.

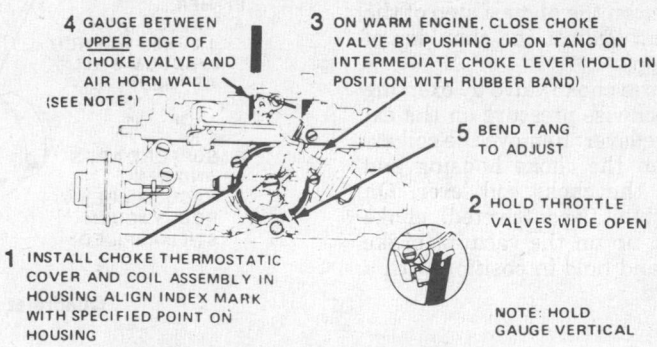

4 GAUGE BETWEEN UPPER EDGE OF CHOKE VALVE AND AIR HORN WALL (SEE NOTE*)

3 ON WARM ENGINE, CLOSE CHOKE VALVE BY PUSHING UP ON TANG ON INTERMEDIATE CHOKE LEVER (HOLD IN POSITION WITH RUBBER BAND)

5 BEND TANG TO ADJUST

2 HOLD THROTTLE VALVES WIDE OPEN

1 INSTALL CHOKE THERMOSTATIC COVER AND COIL ASSEMBLY IN HOUSING ALIGN INDEX MARK WITH SPECIFIED POINT ON HOUSING

NOTE: HOLD GAUGE VERTICAL

M2ME, E2ME unloader adjustment—typical

M2ME, E2ME CARBURETOR SPECIFICATIONS
General Motors

Year	Carburetor Identification	Float Level (in.)	Choke Rod (in.)	Choke Unloader (deg./in.)	Vacuum Break Lean or Front (deg./in.)	Vacuum Break Rich or Rear (deg./in.)	Pump Rod (in.)	Choke Coil Lever (in.)	Automatic Choke (notches)
1987	17086190	10/32	0.096	35/0.195	28/0.164	24/0.136	①	0.120	Fixed
	17087170	9/32	0.139	0.243	17/0.090	19/0.103	9/32 ①	0.120	Fixed

① Not Adjustable
② Canada only

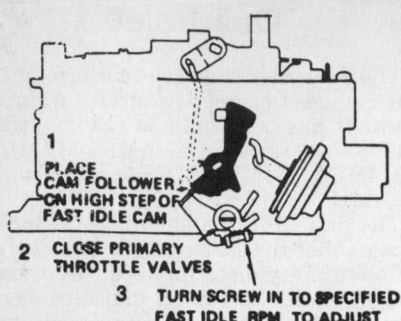

1 PLACE CAM FOLLOWER ON HIGH STEP OF FAST IDLE CAM

2 CLOSE PRIMARY THROTTLE VALVES

3 TURN SCREW IN TO SPECIFIED FAST IDLE RPM TO ADJUST

Quadrajet fast idle adjustment

2. Be sure that the choke is wide open and the engine warm. Plug the EGR vacuum hose. Disconnect the vacuum hose to the front vacuum break unit, if there are 2.

3. Make a preliminary adjustment by turning the fast idle screw out until the throttle valves are closed, then turning it in the specified number of turns after it contacts the lever.

4. Use the fast idle screw to adjust the fast idle to the speed and under the conditions, specified on the engine compartment sticker or in the specifications chart.

FAST IDLE CAM CHOKE ROD

Adjustment

1. Adjust the fast idle and place the cam follower on the highest step of the fast idle cam against the shoulder of the high step.

2. Close the choke valve by exerting counter-clockwise pressure on the external choke lever. Remove the coil assembly from the choke housing and push upon the choke coil lever. On models with a fixed (riveted) choke cover, push up on the vacuum brake lever tang and hold in position with a rubber band.

1 ATTACH RUBBER BAND TO GREEN TANG OF INTERMEDIATE CHOKE SHAFT

2 OPEN THROTTLE TO ALLOW CHOKE VALVE TO CLOSE

3 SET UP ANGLE GAGE AND SET TO SPECIFICATION

4 RETRACT VACUUM BREAK PLUNGER USING VACUUM SOURCE. AT LEAST 18" HG. PLUG AIR BLEED HOLES WHERE APPLICABLE

ON QUADRAJETS, AIR VALVE ROD MUST NOT RESTRICT PLUNGER FROM RETRACTING FULLY. IF NECESSARY, BEND ROD (SEE ARROW) TO PERMIT FULL PLUNGER TRAVEL. FINAL ROD CLEARANCE MUST BE SET AFTER VACUUM BREAK SETTING HAS BEEN MADE.

5 WITH AT LEAST 18" HG STILL APPLIED, ADJUST SCREW TO CENTER BUBBLE

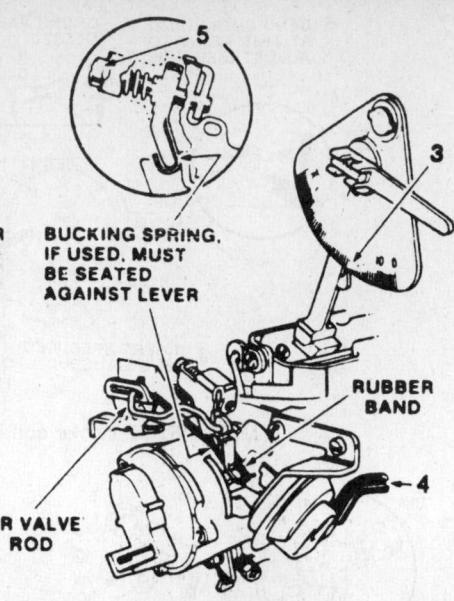

BUCKING SPRING, IF USED, MUST BE SEATED AGAINST LEVER

RUBBER BAND

AIR VALVE ROD

Quadrajet front vacuum break adjustment

1 ATTACH RUBBER BAND TO GREEN TANG OF INTERMEDIATE CHOKE SHAFT.

2 OPEN THROTTLE TO ALLOW CHOKE VALVE TO CLOSE.

3 SET UP ANGLE GAGE AND SET ANGLE TO SPECIFICATION.

RETRACT VACUUM BREAK PLUNGER. USING VACUUM SOURCE. AT LEAST 18" HG. PLUG AIR BLEED HOLES WHERE APPLICABLE.

4A ON QUADRAJETS. AIR VALVE ROD MUST NOT RESTRICT PLUNGER FROM RETRACTING FULLY. IF NECESSARY, BEND ROD HERE TO PERMIT FULL PLUNGER TRAVEL. WHERE APPLICABLE. PLUNGER STEM MUST BE EXTENDED FULLY TO COMPRESS PLUNGER BUCKING SPRING.

5 TO CENTER BUBBLE. EITHER:
A. ADJUST WITH 1/8" HEX WRENCH (VACUUM STILL APPLIED)

-OR-

B. SUPPORT AT "S" AND BEND VACUUM BREAK ROD (VACUUM STILL APPLIED)

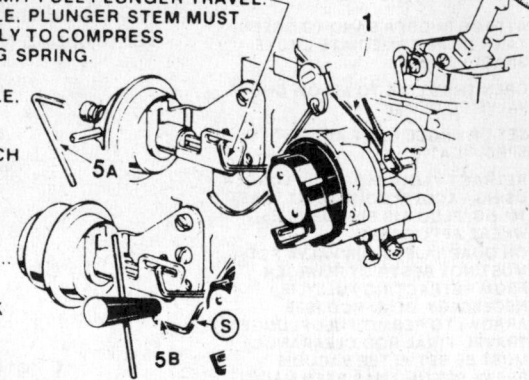

Quadrajet rear vacuum break adjustment—typical

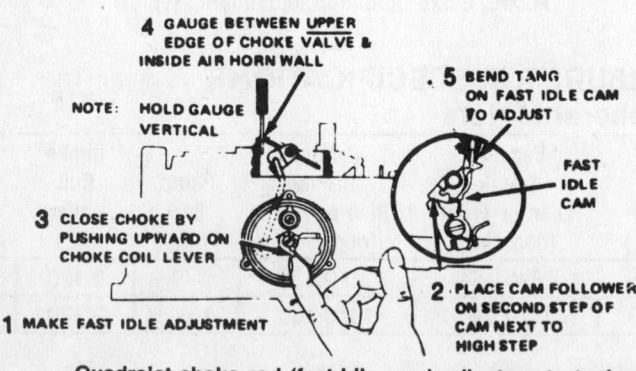

4 GAUGE BETWEEN UPPER EDGE OF CHOKE VALVE & INSIDE AIR HORN WALL

NOTE: HOLD GAUGE VERTICAL

3 CLOSE CHOKE BY PUSHING UPWARD ON CHOKE COIL LEVER

1 MAKE FAST IDLE ADJUSTMENT

5 BEND TANG ON FAST IDLE CAM TO ADJUST

FAST IDLE CAM

2 PLACE CAM FOLLOWER ON SECOND STEP OF CAM NEXT TO HIGH STEP

Quadrajet choke rod (fast idle cam) adjustment—typical

3. Insert a gauge of the proper size between the upper edge of the choke valve and the inside air horn wall.

4. To adjust the valve, bend the tang on the fast idle cam. Be sure that the tang rests against the cam after bending.

PRIMARY (FRONT) VACUUM BREAK

Adjustment

A choke valve measuring gauge J-26701 or equivalent, is used to measure angle (degrees instead of inches).

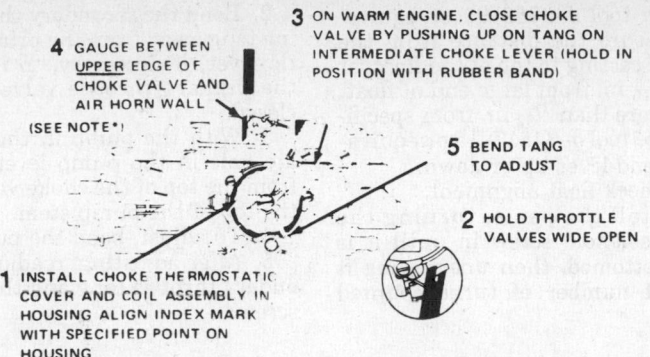

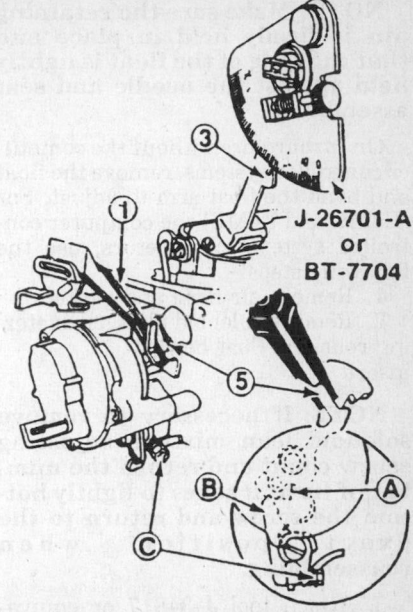

4 GAUGE BETWEEN UPPER EDGE OF CHOKE VALVE AND AIR HORN WALL (SEE NOTE*)

3 ON WARM ENGINE, CLOSE CHOKE VALVE BY PUSHING UP ON TANG ON INTERMEDIATE CHOKE LEVER (HOLD IN POSITION WITH RUBBER BAND)

5 BEND TANG TO ADJUST

2 HOLD THROTTLE VALVES WIDE OPEN

1 INSTALL CHOKE THERMOSTATIC COVER AND COIL ASSEMBLY IN HOUSING ALIGN INDEX MARK WITH SPECIFIED POINT ON HOUSING

Quadrajet unloader adjustment—typical

J-26701-A or BT-7704

① Attach rubber band to Vacuum Break Lever of Intermediate Choke Shaft.

② Open Throttle to allow Choke Valve to close.

③ Set up Angle Gage and set to specification.

④ Place Fast Idle Cam Ⓐ on second step against Cam Follower Lever Ⓑ, with Lever contacting rise of High Step. If Lever does not contact Cam, turn Fast Idle Adjusting Screw Ⓒ in additional turn(s).

⑤ Adjust, if bubble is not recentered, by bending Fast Idle Cam Kick Lever with pliers.

Feedback Quadrajet—Fast idle cam adjustment

SECONDARY (REAR) VACUUM BRAKE

Adjustment

A choke valve measuring gauge J-26701 or equivalent, is used to measure the angle (degrees instead of inches).

CHOKE LINK

Adjustment

Refer to the illustration for E4MC fast idle cam adjustment.

CHOKE UNLOADER

Adjustment

1. Push up on the vacuum break lever to close the choke valve and fully open the throttle valves.
2. Measure the distance from the upper edge of the choke valve to the air horn wall.
3. To adjust, bend the tang on the fast idle lever.

CHOKE COIL LEVER

Adjustment

MC AND ME CARBURETORS

1. Remove the choke cover and thermostatic coil from the choke hous-ing. On models with a fixed (riveted) choke cover, the rivets must be drilled out. A choke stat kit is necessary for assembly. Place the fast idle cam follower on the high step.
2. Push up on the coil tang (counter-clockwise) until the choke valve is closed. The top of the choke rod should be at the bottom of the slot in the choke valve lever.
3. Insert a 0.120 in. drill bit in the hole in the choke housing.
4. The lower edge of the choke coil lever should just contact the side of the plug gauge.
5. Bend the choke rod at the top angle to adjust.

SECONDARY CLOSING

Adjustment

This adjustment assures proper closing of the secondary throttle plates.

1. Set the slow idle as per instructions in the appropriate car section. Make sure that the fast idle cam follower is not resting on the fast idle cam and the choke valve is wide open.
2. There should be 0.020 in. clearance between the secondary throttle actuating rod and the front of the slot on the secondary throttle lever with the closing tang on the throttle lever resting against the actuating lever.
3. Bend the secondary closing tang

on the primary throttle actuating rod or lever to adjust.

SECONDARY OPENING

Adjustment

1. Open the primary throttle valves until the actuating link contacts the upper tang on the secondary lever.
2. With the 2 point linkage, the bottom of the link should be in the center of the secondary lever slot.
3. With the 3 point linkage, there should be 0.070 in. clearance between the link and the middle tang.
4. Bend the upper tang on the secondary lever to adjust as necessary.

FLOAT LEVEL

Adjustment

With the air horn assembly removed, measure the distance from the air horn gasket surface (gasket removed) to the top of the float at the toe ($\frac{9}{16}$ in. back from the toe).

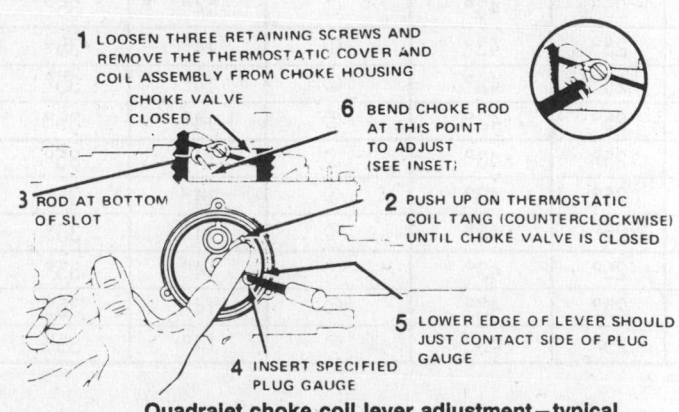

1 LOOSEN THREE RETAINING SCREWS AND REMOVE THE THERMOSTATIC COVER AND COIL ASSEMBLY FROM CHOKE HOUSING

CHOKE VALVE CLOSED

6 BEND CHOKE ROD AT THIS POINT TO ADJUST (SEE INSET)

3 ROD AT BOTTOM OF SLOT

2 PUSH UP ON THERMOSTATIC COIL TANG (COUNTERCLOCKWISE) UNTIL CHOKE VALVE IS CLOSED

5 LOWER EDGE OF LEVER SHOULD JUST CONTACT SIDE OF PLUG GAUGE

4 INSERT SPECIFIED PLUG GAUGE

Quadrajet choke coil lever adjustment—typical

NOTE: Make sure the retaining pin is firmly held in place and that the tang of the float is lightly held against the needle and seat assembly.

On carburetors without the computer controlled systems, remove the float and bend the float arm to adjust. For (E4MC and E4ME) the computer controlled systems carburetors, use the following steps:

1. Remove air horn and gasket.
2. Remove solenoid plunger, metering rods and float bowl insert.

NOTE: If necessary to remove solenoid lean mixture adjusting screw count and record the number of turns it takes to lightly bottom the screw and return to the exact position when reassembling.

3. Attach tool J–34817 or equivalent to float bowl.
4. Place tool J–34817–3 or equivalent in base with contact pin resting on outer edge of float lever.

5. With tool J–9789–90 or equivalent, measure the distance from the top of the casting to top of the float, at a point $3/16$ in. from large end of float.
6. If more than $2/32$ in. from specification, use tool J–34817–15 or equivalent to bend lever up or down.
7. Recheck float alignment.
8. Install the parts, turning the mixture solenoid screw in until it is lightly bottomed, then unscrewing it the exact number of turns counted earlier.

ACCELERATOR PUMP

Adjustment

The accelerator pump is not adjustable on computer controlled carburetors (E4MC and E4ME).

1. Close the primary throttle valves by backing out the slow idle screw and making sure that the fast idle cam follower is off the steps of the fast idle cam.

2. Bend the secondary throttle closing tang away from the primary throttle lever, if necessary, to insure that the primary throttle valves are fully closed.
3. With the pump in the appropriate hole in the pump lever, measure from the top of the choke valve wall to the top of the pump stem.
4. To adjust, bend the pump lever.
5. After adjusting, readjust the secondary throttle tang and the slow idle screw.

AIR VALVE SPRING

Adjustment

To adjust the air valve spring windup, loosen the Allen head lockscrew and turn the adjusting screw counterclockwise to remove all spring tension. With the air valve closed, turn the adjusting screw clockwise the specified number of turns after the torsion spring contacts the pin on the shaft. Hold the adjusting screw in this position and tighten the lockscrew.

QUADRAJET CARBURETOR SPECIFICATIONS
Chrysler Products

Year	Carburetor Identification	Float Level (in.)	Air Valve Spring (turn)	Pump Rod (in.)	Primary Vacuum Break (in./deg.)	Secondary Vacuum Break (in./deg.)	Secondary Opening (in.)	Choke Rod (in./deg.)	Choke Unloader (in./deg.)	Fast Idle Speed (rpm)
1987	17085433	$14/32$	$7/8$	—	0.140/25	—	—	0.120/20	0.179/30	①
1988	17085433	$14/32$	$7/8$	—	0.140/25	—	—	0.120/20	0.179/30	①
1989	17085433	$14/32$	$7/8$	—	0.140/25	—	—	0.120/20	0.180/30	①

① Refer to the underhood sticker

QUADRAJET CARBURETOR SPECIFICATIONS
Cadillac

Year	Carburetor Identification	Float Level (in.)	Air Valve Spring (turn)	Pump Rod (in.)	Primary Vacuum Break (deg.)	Secondary Vacuum Break (deg.)	Secondary Opening (in.)	Choke Rod (in./deg.)	Choke Unloader (in./deg.)	Fast Idle Speed (rpm)
1987	17086008	$11/32$	$1/2$	Fixed	25°	43°	①	14°	35°	②
	17086009	$14/32$	$1/2$	Fixed	25°	43°	①	14°	35°	②
1988	17086008	$11/32$	$1/2$	Fixed	25°	43°	①	14°	35°	②
	17086009	$14/32$	$1/2$	Fixed	25°	43°	①	14°	35°	②
	17088115	$11/32$	$1/2$	Fixed	25°	43°	①	14°	35°	②
1989	17086008	$11/32$	$1/2$	Fixed	25°	43°	①	14°	35°	②
	17086009	$14/32$	$1/2$	Fixed	25°	43°	①	14°	35°	②
	17088115	$11/32$	$1/2$	Fixed	25°	43°	①	14°	35°	②
1990	17086008	$11/32$	$1/2$	Fixed	25°	43°	①	14°	35°	②
	17086009	$14/32$	$1/2$	Fixed	25°	43°	①	14°	35°	②
	17088115	$11/32$	$1/2$	Fixed	25°	43°	①	14°	35°	②

① No measurement necessary on two point linkage
② See underhood decal

QUADRAJET CARBURETOR SPECIFICATIONS
Buick

Year	Carburetor Identification	Float Level (in.)	Air Valve Spring (turn)	Pump Rod (in.)	Primary Vacuum Break (deg.)	Secondary Vacuum Break (deg.)	Secondary Opening (in.)	Choke Rod (deg.)	Choke Unloader (deg.)	Fast Idle Speed (rpm)
1987	17086008	11/32	1/2	Fixed	25°	43°	①	14°	35°	②
1988	17086008	11/32	1/2	Fixed	25°	43°	①	14°	35°	②
	17088115	11/32	1/2	Fixed	25°	43°	①	14°	35°	②
1989	17088115	11/32	1/2	Fixed	25°	43°	①	14°	35°	②
1990	17088115	11/32	1/2	Fixed	25°	43°	①	14°	35°	②

① No measurement necessary on two point linkage
② See underhood decal

QUADRAJET CARBURETOR SPECIFICATIONS
Chevrolet

Year	Carburetor Identification	Float Level (in.)	Air Valve Spring (turn)	Pump Rod (in.)	Primary Vacuum (deg./in.)	Secondary Vacuum (deg./in.)	Secondary Opening (in.)	Choke Rod (deg./in.)	Choke Unloader (deg./in.)	Fast Idle Speed (rpm)
1987	17086008	11/32	7/8	Fixed	0.157/27	—	①	14°	0.243/35°	②
	17087129	11/32	7/8	Fixed	0.157/27	—	①	20°	0.243/38°	②
	17087130	11/32	7/8	Fixed	0.157/27	—	①	20°	0.243/38°	②
	17087132	11/32	7/8	Fixed	0.157/27	—	①	20°	0.243/38°	②
1988	17087306	11/32	7/8	Fixed	27°	—	①	20°	32°	②
	17087129	11/32	7/8	Fixed	27°	—	①	20°	32°	②
	17087132	11/32	7/8	Fixed	27°	—	①	20°	32°	②
1989	17088115	11/32	1/2	Fixed	25°	43°	①	14°	35°	②
1990	17088115	11/32	1/2	Fixed	25°	43°	①	14°	35°	②

① No measurement necessary on two point linkage
② See underhood decal

QUADRAJET CARBURETOR SPECIFICATIONS
Oldsmobile

Year	Carburetor Identification	Float Level (in.)	Air Valve Spring (turn)	Pump Rod (in.)	Primary Vacuum Break (in./deg.)	Secondary Vacuum Break (in./deg.)	Secondary Opening (in.)	Choke Rod (in./deg.)	Choke Unloader (in./deg.)	Fast Idle Speed (rpm)
1987	17086008	11/32	1/2	Fixed	0.142/25	0.287/43	①	0.171/14°	0.220/35°	②
	17086009	14/32	1/2	Fixed	0.142/25	0.287/43	①	0.171/14°	0.220/35°	②
1988	17086008	11/32	1/2	Fixed	25°	43°	①	14°	35°	②
	17088115	11/32	1/2	Fixed	25°	43°	①	14°	35°	②
1989	17088115	11/32	1/2	Fixed	25°	43°	①	14°	35°	②
1990	17088115	11/32	1/2	Fixed	25°	43°	①	14°	35°	②

① No measurement necessary on two point linkage
② See underhood decal

QUADRAJET CARBURETOR SPECIFICATIONS
Pontiac

Year	Carburetor Identification	Float Level (in.)	Air Valve Spring (turn)	Pump Rod (in.)	Primary Vacuum Break (in./deg.)	Secondary Vacuum Break (in./deg.)	Secondary Opening (in.)	Choke Rod (in./deg.)	Choke Unloader (in./deg.)	Fast Idle Speed (rpm)
1987	17087130	11/32	7/8	Fixed	0.157/27	—	①	0.110	0.243/38	②
	17087131	11/32	7/8	Fixed	0.157/27	—	①	0.110	0.243/38	②
	17087133	11/32	7/8	Fixed	0.157/27	—	①	0.110	0.243/38	②
	17086008	11/32	1/2	Fixed	0.142/25	0.287/43	①	0.071	0.220/35	②
1988	17086008	11/32	1/2	Fixed	25°	43°	—	14°	35°	②
	17088115	11/32	1/2	Fixed	25°	43°	—	14°	35°	②
1989	17088115	11/32	1/2	Fixed	25°	43°	①	14°	35°	②

① No measurement necessary on two point linkage; see text
② See underhood decal

QUADRAJET CARBURETOR SPECIFICATIONS
All Canadian Models

Year	Carburetor Identification	Float Level (in.)	Air Valve Spring (turn)	Pump Rod (in.)	Primary Vacuum Break (deg./in.)	Secondary Vacuum Break (deg./in.)	Secondary Opening (deg./in.)	Choke Rod (deg./in.)	Choke Unloader (deg./in.)	Fast Idle Speed (rpm)
1987	17087117	1/2	7/8	9/32	23/0.129	—	①	0.077	26/0.149	②
	17087118	1/2	7/8	9/32	23/0.129	—	①	0.077	26/0.149	②
	17087119	1/2	7/8	9/32	23/0.129	—	①	0.077	26/0.149	②
	17087120	1/2	7/8	9/32	23/0.129	—	①	0.077	26/0.149	②
	17087123	1/2	7/8	9/32	23/0.129	—	①	0.077	26/0.149	②
	17087124	1/2	7/8	9/32	23/0.129	—	①	0.077	26/0.149	②
	17087125	1/2	7/8	9/32	25/0.142	—	①	0.077	26/0.149	②
	17087126	1/2	7/8	9/32	25/0.142	—	①	0.077	26/0.149	②
	17087207	13/32	1/2	9/32	21/0.117	—	①	0.077	28/0.164	②
	17087211	13/32	1/2	9/32	21/0.117	—	①	0.077	28/0.164	②
1988	17086008	11/32	1/2	Fixed	25/0.142	43°	①	14°	35°	②
	17088115	11/32	1/2	Fixed	25/0.142	43°	①	14°	35°	②
	17087211	11/32	1/2	9/32	21/0.117	—	①	14°	28/0.164	②
1989	17086008	11/32	1/2	Fixed	25/0.142	43°	①	14°	35°	②
	17088115	11/32	1/2	Fixed	25/0.142	43°	①	14°	35°	②
	17087211	11/32	1/2	9/32	21/0.117	—	①	14°	28/0.164	②
1990	17086008	11/32	1/2	Fixed	25/0.142	43°	①	14°	35°	②
	17088115	11/32	1/2	Fixed	25/0.142	43°	①	14°	35°	②
	17087211	11/32	1/2	9/32	21/0.117	—	①	14°	28/0.164	②

① No measurement necessary on two point linkage
② See underhood decal

AISAN CARBURETORS

Festiva 2 Barrel

The Festiva uses a 2 barrel electronically controlled feedback carburetor made by Aisan. To set the idle mixture on this vehicle requires the use of an exhaust gas analyzer. Before condemning this carburetor, make certain fuel pressure is correct. All ignition and electronic controls and must also be functioning properly. If removing the base plate note the location of the hollow attaching screw, the hole provides vacuum to the power valve. The following adjustments can be made with the carburetor on the vehicle except the throttle plate adjustments.

FLOAT LEVEL

Adjustment

1. Hold air horn upright with float hanging free.
2. Measure the distance from the gasket to the bottom edge of the float. Float drop should be 1.850–1.929 in. (47–49mm).
3. Bend tap on hinge if not within specifications.
4. Invert the air horn to adjust float level.
5. Measure the distance from the gasket to the top edge of the float. Float level should be 0.327–0.366 in. (8.3–9.3mm).

CHOKE BREAKER

Adjustment

1. Set choke plate to fully closed position.
2. Disconnect vacuum hose at the pulldown and apply 16 in. Hg of vacuum.
3. Hold choke plate closed as far as possible without forcing it.
4. Set fast idle cam on fourth step, if ambient temperature is below 86°F or third step if above 86°F.
5. Check choke gap with $^5/_{16}$ drill. Adjust by bending breaker adjuster tab.

CHOKE UNLOADER

Adjustment

1. Hold the choke plate closed as far

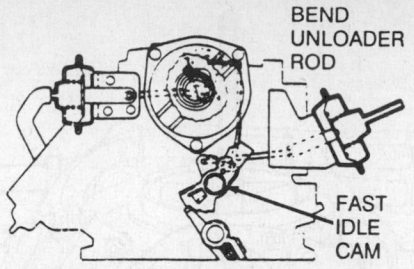

Festiva choke unloader adjustment

as possible without forcing it.
2. Distance between choke plate and air horn should be 0.059–0.076 in. (drill size $^1/_{16}$) while holding throttle wide open.
3. Adjust clearance by bending rod.

CHOKE PLATE CLEARANCE

Adjustment

1. Set fast idle on third step of cam.
2. Distance between choke plate and air horn should be 0.024–0.037 in. (drill size $^1/_{32}$).
3. Adjust clearance by bending the tap.

SECONDARY THROTTLE PLATE

Adjustment

1. With carburetor assembly removed from engine, slowly open throttle while watching the secondary plate.
2. When the secondary plate just starts to open the clearance to the throttle wall should be 0.0372 in. (⅜ drill size).
3. Adjust clearance by bending tap at secondary shaft.

THROTTLE OPENING

Adjustment

1. With carburetor assembly removed from engine, position idle cam against the third step.
2. The distance between the throttle and venturi wall should be 0.009–0.014 in. (0.25–0.36mm).
3. Adjust to specifications using the fast idle cam screw.

IDLE MIXTURE

Adjustment

NOTE: To perform the idle mixture adjustment an emission analyzer must be used to identify CO concentration.

1. Run engine to reach normal temperature.
2. Insert probe into the secondary air hose and plug hose to prevent leaking past the probe lead.
3. Adjust mixture screw until analyzer shows CO concentration of 1.5–2.5 percent.

CURB IDLE

Adjustment

1. Run engine to reach normal temperature, place transaxle in N and set parking brake.
2. Adjust idle to 700–760 rpm using idle adjusting screw.

FAST IDLE BREAKER

Adjustment

1. Run engine to reach normal temperature.
2. Set fast idle cam on 2nd step.
3. Turn fast idle cam breaker adjusting screw to obtain an engine speed of 1650–2150 rpm.

FAST IDLE ADJUSTMENT

Adjustment

1. Disconnect and plug vacuum hose at the fast idle cam servo.
2. Set fast idle cam on 2nd step.
3. Adjust engine speed to 1650–2150 rpm using fast idle screw.

ELECTRICAL LOAD IDLE-UP

Adjustment

1. Run engine to reach normal temperature.
2. Disconnect brown electrical connector at electrical vacuum solenoid.
3. Increase engine speed to 2000 rpm and let return to idle.
4. Adjust servo nut to obtain at idle of 750–850 rpm.

AIR CONDITIONING IDLE-UP

Adjustment

1. Run engine to reach normal temperature.
2. Disconnect orange electrical connector at air conditioning vacuum solenoid.
3. Increase engine speed to 2000 rpm and let return to idle.
4. Adjust A/C idle-up screw to obtain 1200–1300 rpm.

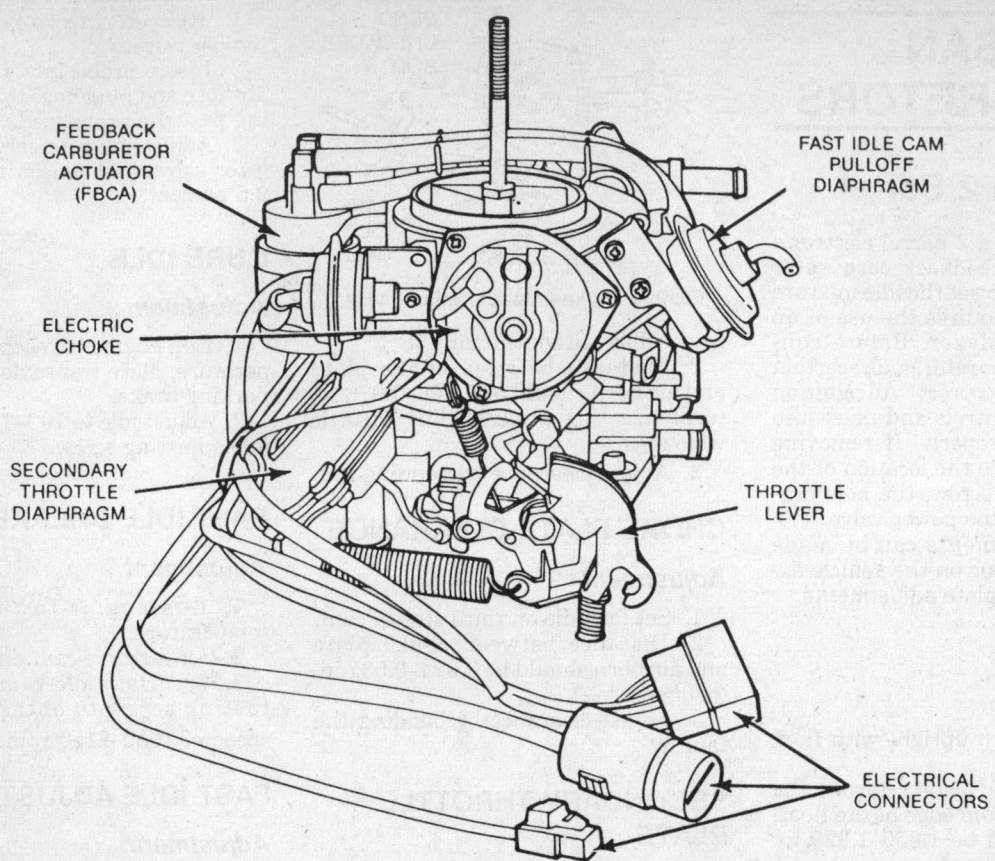

FEEDBACK
CARBURETOR
ACTUATOR
(FBCA)

FAST IDLE CAM
PULLOFF
DIAPHRAGM

ELECTRIC
CHOKE

SECONDARY
THROTTLE
DIAPHRAGM

THROTTLE
LEVER

ELECTRICAL
CONNECTORS

Festiva feedback carburetor assembly

Turbocharging

Theory

The internal combustion engine can be thought of as an air pump. The action of the pistons moving down or up in their cylinders when the intake or exhaust valves are open alternately draws air and fuel into the engine or expels burnt gases into the atmosphere. The amount of air and fuel pulled into the engine (known as an engine's volumetric efficiency) is governed by the drawing efficiency of the piston as it descends in its cylinder, and by the scavenging effect of the exiting exhaust gases, which act to pull additional air/fuel mixture in through the open intake valves during valve overlap periods. The more air and fuel each cylinder pulls in, the more power the engine will produce.

Theoretically, a normally aspirated engine should be able to draw in an amount of air and fuel equal to its displacement (e.g. a 350 cu in. engine should draw in 350 cu in. of air and fuel). In practice, however, only about 80% of the displacement capacity is drawn through because of flow restrictions, the slight pressure drop through the carburetor, and the inability of the exhaust stroke to drive out all of the burnt gases.

There are several ways to increase an engine's drawing power (volumetric efficiency). These include increasing valve overlap, increasing engine bore and/or stroke, supercharging the engine, or (the most popular approach) turbocharging.

In effect, the turbocharger is an air pump which crams more air/fuel mixture into the cylinders than they could possibly draw in by themselves.

In doing so, the turbocharger increases the engine's volumetric efficiency past its normal 80%, which proportionately increases engine horsepower and torque output.

Perhaps the most advantageous aspect of the turbocharger is that it does not require usable engine horsepower to operate. By comparison, say a car is climbing a steep hill and the driver decides to turn on the air conditioner. The moment the air conditioner is turned on, a power drain on the engine can usually be felt. That's because some of the power that was being used to drive the car up the hill is now being used to turn the air conditioner compressor. A turbocharger, on the other hand, does not drain power from the engine to operate because it uses the free energy of the exhaust gases as they are blown out of the en-

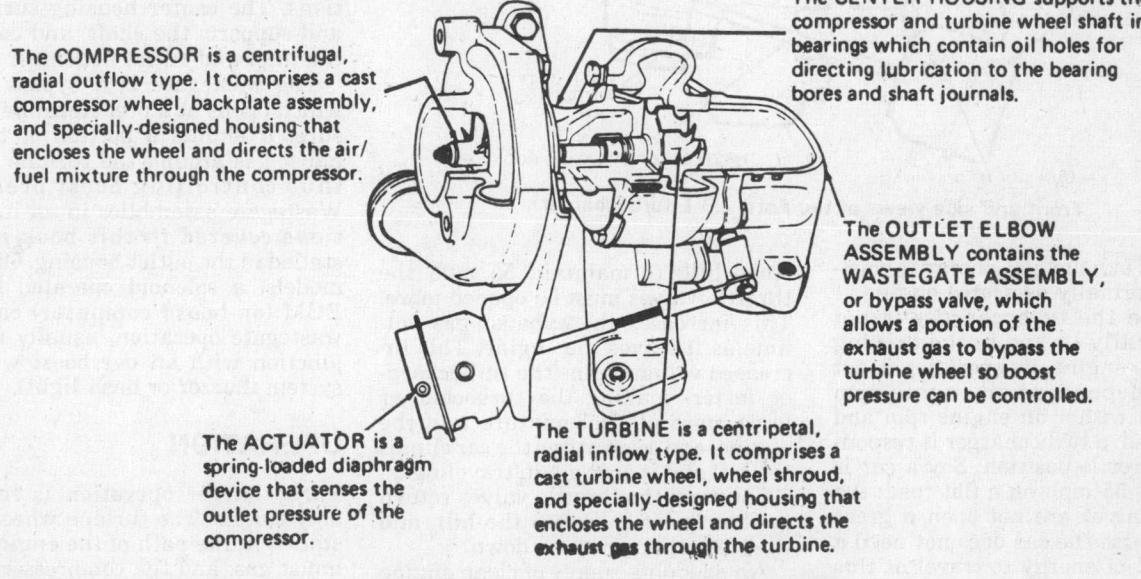

The COMPRESSOR is a centrifugal, radial outflow type. It comprises a cast compressor wheel, backplate assembly, and specially-designed housing that encloses the wheel and directs the air/fuel mixture through the compressor.

The CENTER HOUSING supports the compressor and turbine wheel shaft in bearings which contain oil holes for directing lubrication to the bearing bores and shaft journals.

The OUTLET ELBOW ASSEMBLY contains the WASTEGATE ASSEMBLY, or bypass valve, which allows a portion of the exhaust gas to bypass the turbine wheel so boost pressure can be controlled.

The ACTUATOR is a spring-loaded diaphragm device that senses the outlet pressure of the compressor.

The TURBINE is a centripetal, radial inflow type. It comprises a cast turbine wheel, wheel shroud, and specially-designed housing that encloses the wheel and directs the exhaust gas through the turbine.

Turbocharger components, typical of all models

33 TURBOCHARGING

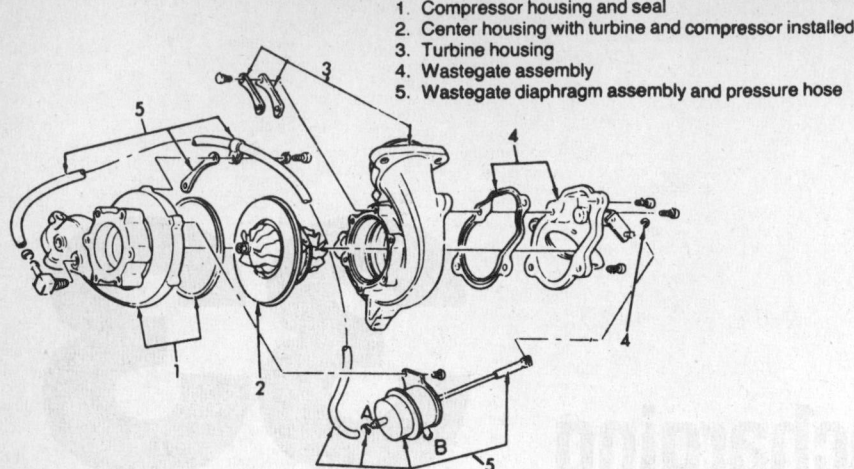

1. Compressor housing and seal
2. Center housing with turbine and compressor installed
3. Turbine housing
4. Wastegate assembly
5. Wastegate diaphragm assembly and pressure hose

Typical GM 3.8L (231 cu in.) engine turbocharger. "A" is pressure side of wastegate diaphragm, "B" is vacuum side

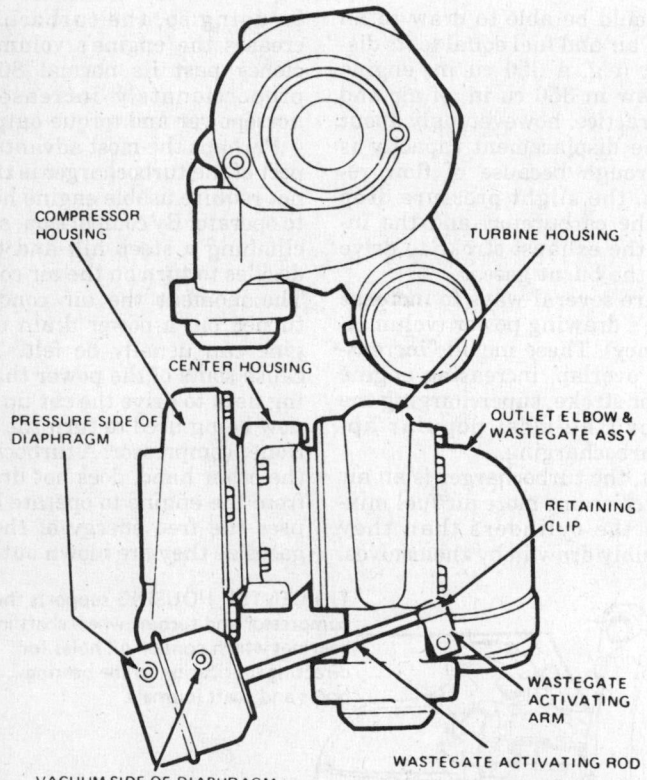

COMPRESSOR HOUSING

TURBINE HOUSING

CENTER HOUSING

PRESSURE SIDE OF DIAPHRAGM

OUTLET ELBOW & WASTEGATE ASSY

RETAINING CLIP

WASTEGATE ACTIVATING ARM

WASTEGATE ACTIVATING ROD

VACUUM SIDE OF DIAPHRAGM

Front and side views of the Ford 2.3 L turbocharger

gine. This exhaust gas energy is wasted on a normally aspirated engine.

Because the turbocharger is not mechanically linked to the driving part of the engine, its operation is not directly dependent on engine rpm alone, but rather on engine rpm and engine load: a turbocharger is responsive to throttle position. Say a car is driving at 55 mph on a flat road: the throttle valves are not open a great deal, because the car does not need a great deal of energy to travel at this speed. Soon the car starts to climb a

steep hill: to maintain 55 mph the throttle valves must be opened more. This increases the exhaust gas volume as it leaves the engine. This increased volume spins the turbocharger faster, making the turbocharger force more air/fuel mixture into the engine, and so on. After the car climbs the hill and is once again traveling on a flat road, the throttle valves return to their position before the hill, and the turbocharger slows down.

An adequate supply of clean engine oil is essential for cooling and lubrica-

tion and to maintain the turbocharger bearing assembly. The turbocharger wheels routinely operate at 130,000–140,000 rpm during boost and any interruption in the oil supply to the bearing assembly can result in major turbocharger damage. Contamination of the engine oil can also cause serious damage. Any time a basic engine bearing (main, connecting rod or camshaft) is replaced due to damage, the oil and oil filter must be changed and the turbocharger flushed with clean engine oil to remove any contamination. In addition, any time the turbocharger is removed for service or as part of another procedure, the oil and oil filter should be changed. When first starting the engine after removing the turbocharger, fill the turbocharger oil passage with clean engine oil and crank the engine a few times to allow oil pressure to build up. It's also a good idea to allow the engine to idle for one minute before shutting it off, especially when running at freeway speeds for long periods of time, to prevent the possibility of turbocharger bearing damage due to sudden oil starvation.

COMPONENTS

The turbocharger unit consists of two vaned wheels (compressor and turbine) connected by a common axle (shaft), and a housing which can be sub-divided into three sections: inlet (or compressor), center, and outlet (or turbine). The inlet housing surrounds the compressor wheel, and connects to the air intake and the intake manifold. The outlet housing surrounds the turbine wheel, and connects to the exhaust system; it also houses the wastegate assembly in many installations. The center housing surrounds and supports the shaft, and connects the inlet and outlet housings.

The wastegate is a bypass valve, which opens at a predetermined pressure. It shunts a portion of the exhaust gas around the turbine wheel, thus controlling boost pressure. Wastegate assemblies in all installations covered in this book are installed in the outlet housing. On some models, a solenoid operated by the ECM (on-board computer) controls wastegate operation, usually in conjunction with an overboost warning system (buzzer or dash light).

OPERATION

Turbocharger operation is remarkably simple. The turbine wheel is installed in the path of the engine's exhaust gas, and the compressor wheel is installed in the intake path. Exhaust gas is directed through the turbine housing, causing the turbine wheel to spin. This spinning motion is transferred by the connecting shaft to the compressor wheel. As the compressor wheel spins, it packs the intake charge into a dense mass, which is fed into the engine. Combustion converts the charge into exhaust. The exhaust charge is directed through the turbine housing, where it spins the turbine wheel, and then out through the turbine housing discharge into the exhaust system.

Thus, turbocharger operation is self-perpetuating. However, unchecked turbocharger operation will increase compressor pressure (called boost pressure) beyond the design limits of the engine, and will seriously damage internal engine components. Boost pressure is controlled by the wastegate. When boost pressure rises to a predetermined value, the wastegate opens, bypassing exhaust flow around the turbine.

Greater volumetric efficiency is a benefit of the turbocharging process, but increased cylinder pressure is a drawback, because it raises the engine's octane requirement. The two are inseparable, so a method must be devised to compensate for the increased octane requirement to avoid detonation (spark knock). Water injection, alcohol injection, low boost pressures, charge intercoolers, ignition spark retardation, and alcohol fuels have all been used to control detonation, with varying degrees of success.

Ford controls detonation by limiting boost and by spark retardation. Wastegate operation begins at five psi, and enough exhaust gas is routed around the turbine to limit boost to a maximum of six psi. The electronic ignition system has been modified in the turbocharged engine to include two spark retardation points. When boost pressure reaches approximately one-half to one psi, a switch in the intake manifold sends a signal to the ignition module, which retards ignition timing six degrees. A second manifold switch sends its signal when boost reaches four psi, resulting in an additional six degrees of retard.

The General Motors system of detonation control is slightly different. Boost is limited to a maximum of approximately six psi. In addition, a detonation sensor is installed in the engine block (V6) or intake manifold (V8). Vibrations caused by detonation are transmitted to the sensor, which sends a signal to the Electronic Spark Control (ESC) module. The module processes this signal, and sends a command signal to the HEI distribu-

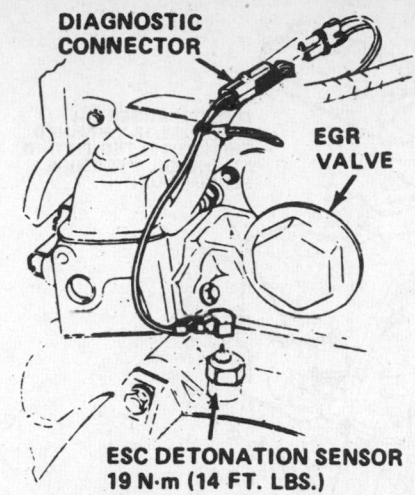

Buick 231 V6 (3.8 L) detonation sensor installation

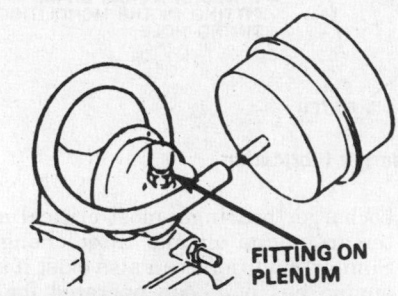

New type GM wastegate diaphragm uses plenum vacuum only

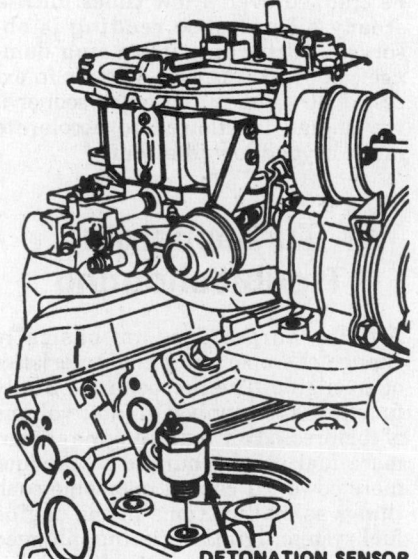

Pontiac turbocharged V8 detonation sensor location

tor to retard timing. Timing retard ranges up to 22° on V6s, or 15° on V8s.

LUBRICATION

The turbocharger shaft spins in bearings lubricated by engine oil. Turbine

speeds routinely reach 120,000–140,000 rpm, making an adequate and well-filtered oil supply critical for proper operation. Any interruption or contamination of the oil supply will result in engine damage as well. Ford cautions that accelerating the engine to top rpm immediately after starting can result in engine and turbocharger damage (due to the lack of oil pressure). Immediately shutting down the engine after it has been operated at high rpm for an extended period can also result in turbocharger damage, since oil pressure will be shut off, but the turbine will continue to spin for a few moments. Shutting the throttle abruptly when the engine is at high speed can also cause extensive damage, but for a different reason: sudden closed throttle operation causes the mixture to become very lean, resulting in detonation, high engine temperature, and consequent damage.

General Motors recommends the following procedure before starting the engine when changing the oil and filter, or performing any operation which results in oil drainage or loss:

1. Disconnect the ignition switch connector (pink wire) from the HEI distributor module.

2. Crank the engine several times until the oil light goes out. Do not crank the engine for more than thirty seconds at a time to avoid starter damage.

3. Reconnect the pink wire. Start the engine.

Turbocharger Maintenance

Proper maintenance is important, particularly regarding air and oil filtration, to maximize the service life and performance of the turbocharger. Experience has shown that the main cause of turbocharger failure is due to oil lag, restriction or lack of oil flow and dirt in the oil. The second principle cause of failure is foreign objects entering the compressor and/or turbine wheels.

AIR INTAKE SYSTEM

Dust or sand entering the turbocharger compressor housing from a leaky air inlet system can seriously erode the compressor wheel blades and will result in deterioration of turbocharger and engine performance. The wearing away of the blades, if uneven, can induce shaft motion which will pound out the turbocharger shaft bearings. Ingestion of sand or dust will also cause excessive wear on engine parts, such as pistons, rings, valves, etc.

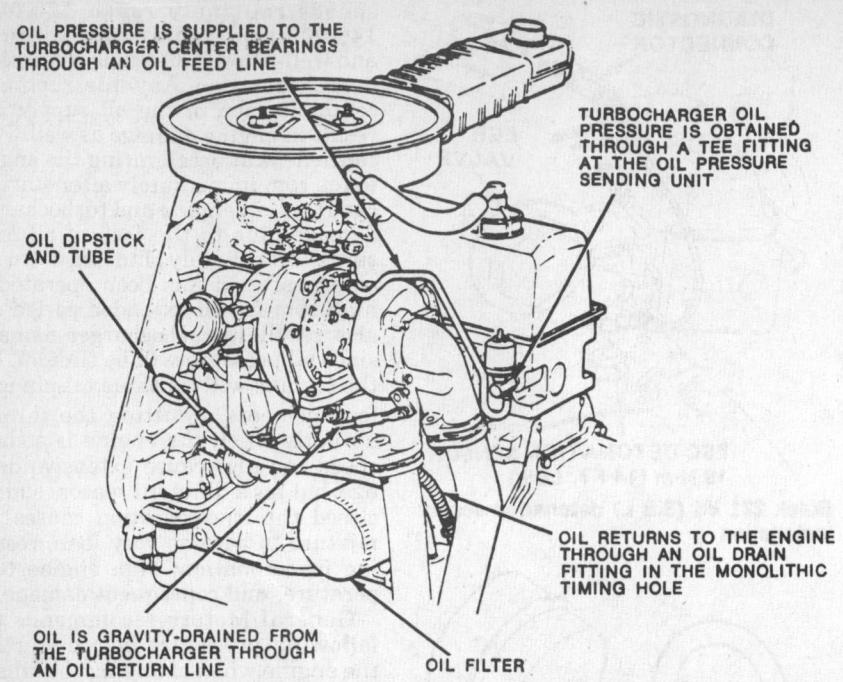

OIL PRESSURE IS SUPPLIED TO THE TURBOCHARGER CENTER BEARINGS THROUGH AN OIL FEED LINE

TURBOCHARGER OIL PRESSURE IS OBTAINED THROUGH A TEE FITTING AT THE OIL PRESSURE SENDING UNIT

OIL DIPSTICK AND TUBE

OIL RETURNS TO THE ENGINE THROUGH AN OIL DRAIN FITTING IN THE MONOLITHIC TIMING HOLE

OIL IS GRAVITY-DRAINED FROM THE TURBOCHARGER THROUGH AN OIL RETURN LINE

OIL FILTER

Ford 2.3 L turbocharger lubrication

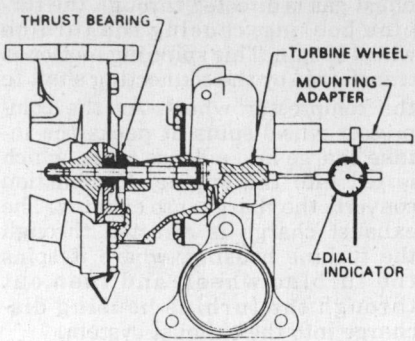

THRUST BEARING

TURBINE WHEEL

MOUNTING ADAPTER

DIAL INDICATOR

Thrust bearing clearance measurement

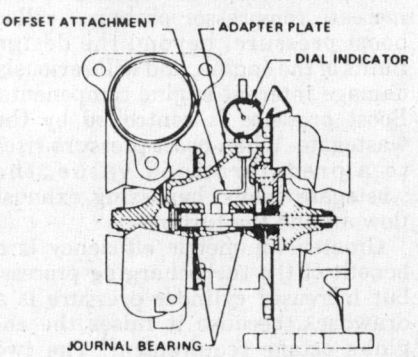

OFFSET ATTACHMENT

ADAPTER PLATE

DIAL INDICATOR

JOURNAL BEARING

Journal bearing clearance measurement

Plugged or restricted air cleaner systems (due to neglected air filter changes) will reduce air pressure and volume at the compressor air inlet and cause the turbocharger to lose performance. The restricted air cleaner and the resultant air pressure drop between cleaner and turbocharger can, during engine idle periods, cause oil pullover at the compressor end of the turbocharger and result in an oil leak at the seal.

LUBRICATION SYSTEM

Dirt or foreign material, when introduced into the turbocharger bearing system by the lube oil, causes wear on the center housing bearing bore surfaces. Contaminents act as abrasives and will eventually cause the shaft hub and either or both wheels to rub on the housings, causing the rotating assembly to turn slower. Engine power loss, excessive smoke, excessive noise and appearance of oil at either or both ends of the turbocharger could be noted. Contaminated and dirty oil problems can be eliminated by regular oil and filter changes.

A turbocharger should never be operated under engine load conditions with less than 30 psi oil pressure. The turbocharger is much more sensitive to a limited oil supply than an engine, due to the high rotational speed of the shaft and relatively small area of the bearing surfaces. Oil pressure and flow lag during engine starting can have a detrimental effect on the tur-

bocharger bearings, most critical after an engine oil and filter change. Similar conditions can also exist if an engine has not been operated for a long period of time, since engine lube systems tend to bleed down. Before allowing the engine to start, it should be cranked over a few times until a steady oil pressure reading is observed. Turbocharger bearing damage can occur if the oil delay is in excess of 30 seconds and much sooner if the engine is allowed to accelerate much beyond low idle rpm.

Turbocharger Troubleshooting

A turbocharger does not basically change the operating characteristics of an engine. The turbocharger's only function is to supply a greater volume of compressed air to the engine so that more fuel can be burned to produce more power. It cannot overcome such things as malfunctions in the engine fuel system, ignition timing, plugged air cleaner elements, etc. If a turbocharged engine system has malfunctioned and the turbocharger has been inspected and determined to be functioning normally, proceed with troubleshooting as though the engine were naturally aspirated (non-turbocharged). Simply replacing a good turbocharger with another will not correct engine deficiencies. Always inspect and asses turbocharger condi-

tion before removing it from the engine as follows:

1. Remove the inlet and exhaust ducts from the turbocharger.

2. Inspect both turbocharger wheels for blade damage caused by foreign material entering the turbocharger. The wheels can be visually checked by simply looking through the compressor housing inlet opening while holding the the throttle blade open. A light is necessary when examining the turbine wheel blade tips since they are positioned inside the turbine housing. Look between the turbine wheel blades from the exhaust outlet end of the turbine housing.

3. Inspect the outer blade tip edges on both wheels adjacent to their respective housing bores and check for wheel rub.

4. Rotate the shaft wheel assembly by hand and feel for drag or binding conditions. Push the shaft to one side, rotate it and feel for rub. It should turn smoothly.

5. Lift both ends of the shaft up and down at the same time and feel for excessive journal bearing clearance. If clearance is normal, very little shaft movement will be detected. Actual shaft end play can be measured with a dial indicator without removing the turbocharger from the engine.

6. If the shaft assembly rotates

freely and no wheel damage, binding or rub has been noted, it can be assumed that the turbocharger is not in need of service.

—————— CAUTION ——————

Operation of the turbocharger without all normally installed inlet ducts and filters connected can result in personal injury and equipment damage from foreign objects entering the turbocharger.

TESTING WASTEGATE OPERATION

As noted before, the wastegate is a safety valve for the engine. If the wastegate sticks shut, boost pressure will build until the air/fuel mixture charge becomes too powerful for the mechanical components (pistons, bearings, etc.) and causes engine damage.

If the wastegate sticks open, little or no boost will be received from the turbocharger, which translates into mediocre engine performance. The simplest wastegate test is to remove the pressure hose at the wastegate diaphragm unit, connect a pressure pump (such as the type used for cooling system testing) and apply pressure. At the specified opening pressure (7 psi for Ford, 8.5–9.5 for GM), the link between the wastegate and its diaphragm unit will just move (about .015 in). The movement is not great, but it should be easy to see.

If the wastegate does not move, try to operate the linkage by hand. It should move under moderate hand pressure. If it moves, the problem is probably in the diaphragm unit (broken diaphragm). To test the diaphragm, remove the vacuum hose from the diaphragm, hook up a manual vacuum pump and apply 25 in. Hg of vacuum to the diaphragm unit. If the vacuum drops below 18 in. Hg within one minute, replace the diaphragm unit.

NOTE: Some 1981 and later GM turbos have a new type of diaphragm which opens the wastegate during idle and part throttle, when there's no boost, to reduce engine backpressure and improve fuel economy. To test this type of unit, apply about 20 in. Hg of vacuum to the diaphragm unit: the wastegate link should move slightly. This unit operates solely with plenum vacuum and can be identified by the absence of a boost pressure signal line on the diaphragm unit.

TESTING OPERATION OF GM DETONATION SENSOR

Connect a tachometer and timing light to the engine, run the engine at 1800–2500 rpm and tap on the intake manifold next to the detonation sensor.

NOTE: Be careful to keep all wires, clothing and tools away from moving engine parts.

Rap continuously, quickly and moderately hard. This should trigger the detonation sensor. When it triggers, engine speed should drop at least 200 rpm and timing should retard at least 4°, probably more.

TURBOCHARGER TROUBLESHOOTING

Problem	Cause	How To Check	Solution
No boost	Gasket leak, hole in exhaust system	Temporarily block tailpipe with engine running. Any exhaust leaks in the system will be heard.	Repair leaks (usually at gasket surfaces)
	Dirty air filter	Remove air filter and check	Replace or clean filter
	Blocked air intake	Visually inspect for blockage	Clear intake
	Worn valves or rings	Compression test engine	Repair
	Throttle valves not opening completely	Manually operate throttle linkage, check valve movement	Adjust linkage, repair carburetor
	Exhaust blockage	Check catalytic converter for melted and blocked catalyst, check muffler and exhaust pipes for debris	Replace catalytic converter, repair exhaust system
	Wastegate stuck open	Test wastegate operation	Repair or replace wastegate assembly
Fuel odor under boost	Leak at compressor or intake manifold	Look for fuel stains at fittings	Tighten fittings or replace gaskets
Ignition miss at high speed, under load	Spark plug gap too large	Remove spark plugs, measure gap	Reduce gap
	Faulty coil	Test Coil	Replace
Ignition miss (often)	Excessive resistance in ignition cables	Check cable resistance (see Tune-Up Unit Repair section)	Replace cables as necessary
Oil leaks into turbine	Blocked oil return hose	Remove hose and check for blockage or crimps	Repair or replace hose

TURBOCHARGER TROUBLESHOOTING

Problem	Cause	How To Check	Solution
Detonation	Fuel octane rating too low	Check octane rating of fuel used against that recommended by manufacturer (consult owner's manual)	Switch to higher octane unleaded fuel
	Faulty sensor	Check G.M. as instructed here; have Ford system checked by qualified technician	Replace as necessary
	Faulty ignition retard unit	Refer to qualified technician	Repair or replace as necessary
	Engine overheating	Check coolant level, debris clogged radiator, no coolant circulation, blocked thermostat	Repair or replace as necessary
Poor idle	Air leak between compressor and carburetor	Listen at joints for hissing sound while the engine idles	Repair

Emission Controls 34

GENERAL INFORMATION

The earth's atmosphere, at or near sea level, consists of approximately 78% nitrogen, 21% oxygen and 1% other gases. If it were possible to remain in this state, 100% clean air would result. However, many varied causes allow other gases and particulates to mix with clean air, causing the air to become unclean or polluted. Some of these pollutants are visible while others are invisible, with each having the capability of causing distress to the eyes, ears, throat, skin and respiratory system. These pollutants can also cause damage to the environment and to the many man made objects that are exposed to the elements. To better understand the causes of air pollution, pollutants can be categorized into 3 separate types, natural, industrial and automotive.

Natural Polution

This type of pollution has been present on earth before man appeared and is still a factor to be considered when discussing air pollution, although it causes only a small percentage of the present overall pollution problem existing in our country. It is the direct result of decaying organic matter, windborn smoke and particulates from such natural events as forest fires, volcanic ash, sand and dust which can spread over a large area of the countryside.

Industrial Polution

This type of pollution is caused primarily by industrial processes which are the burning of coal, oil and natural gas. The by-product of which in turn produces smoke and fumes. This type of polution occurs most severely during still, damp and cool weather. Working with Federal, State and Local mandated rules, regulations and by carefully monitoring the emissions, industries have greatly reduced the amount of pollutant emitted from their industrial sources.

Automotive Polution

This type of air pollution is the automotive emissions. The emissions from the internal combustion engine were not an appreciable problem years ago because of the small number of registered vehicles and the nation's small highway system. However, during the early 1950's, the trend of the American people was to move from the cities to the surrounding suburbs. This caused an immediate problem in the transportation area because the majority of the suburbs were not afforded mass transit conveniences. This lack of transportation created an attractive market for the automobile, which re-sulted in a dramatic increase in the number of vehicles produced and sold, along with a marked increase in highway construction between the cities and the suburbs. Multi-car families emerged with much emphasis placed on the individual vehicle per family member. As the increase in vehicle ownership and usage occurred, so did the pollutant levels in and around the cities. It was noted that a fog and smoke type haze was being formed and at times, remained in suspension over the cities and did not quickly dissipate. At first this smog, was thought to result from industrial pollution, but it was determined that the automobile emission was largely to blame.

CATEGORIZING VEHICLE EMISSIONS AND CONTROLS

To recognize the sources and methods used to control vehicle emission, 3 major categories have been established. They are crankcase emissions and controls, fuel evaporative emissions and controls and exhaust emissions and controls.

Regardless of the manufacturer, or

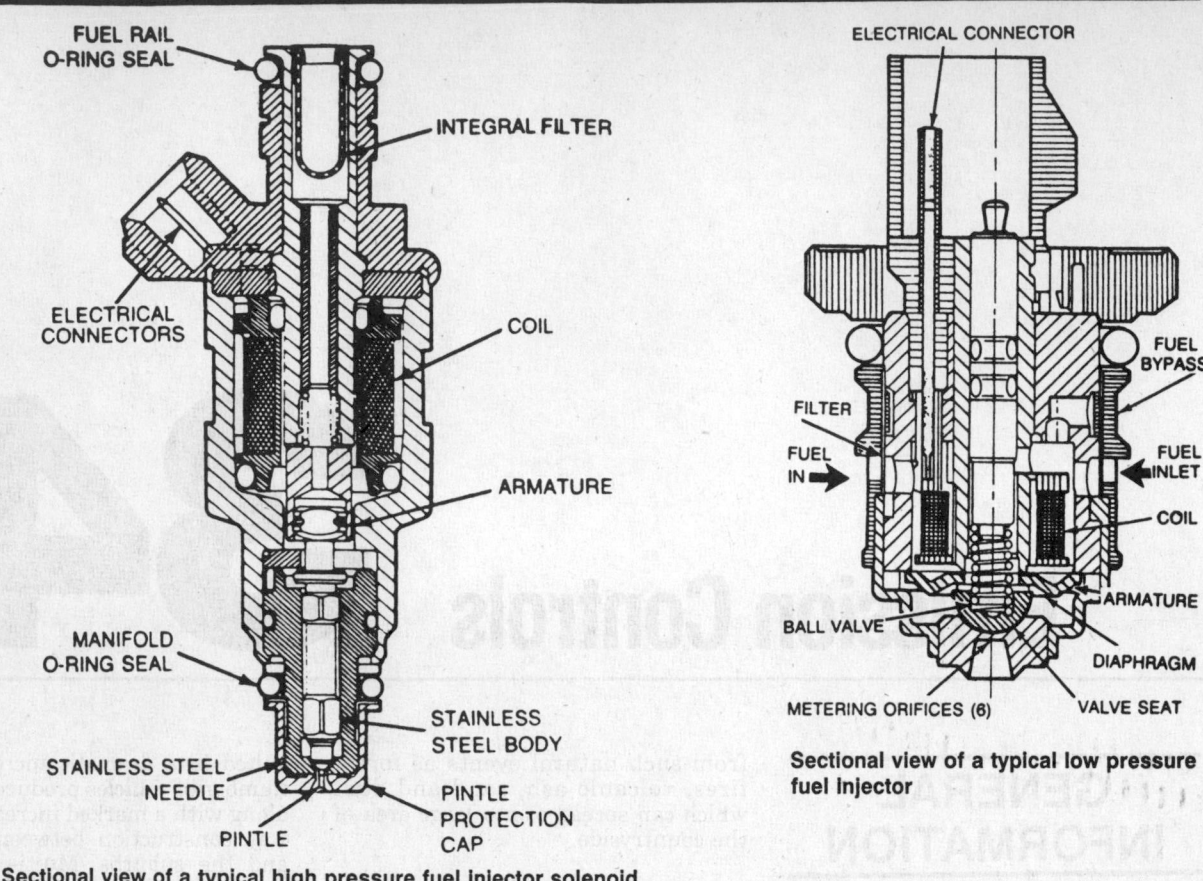

FUEL RAIL
O-RING SEAL

INTEGRAL FILTER

ELECTRICAL
CONNECTORS

COIL

ARMATURE

MANIFOLD
O-RING SEAL

STAINLESS STEEL
NEEDLE

PINTLE

STAINLESS
STEEL BODY

PINTLE
PROTECTION
CAP

Sectional view of a typical high pressure fuel injector solenoid

ELECTRICAL CONNECTOR

FUEL
BYPASS

FILTER

FUEL
IN

FUEL
INLET

COIL

ARMATURE

BALL VALVE

DIAPHRAGM

METERING ORIFICES (6)

VALVE SEAT

Sectional view of a typical low pressure
fuel injector

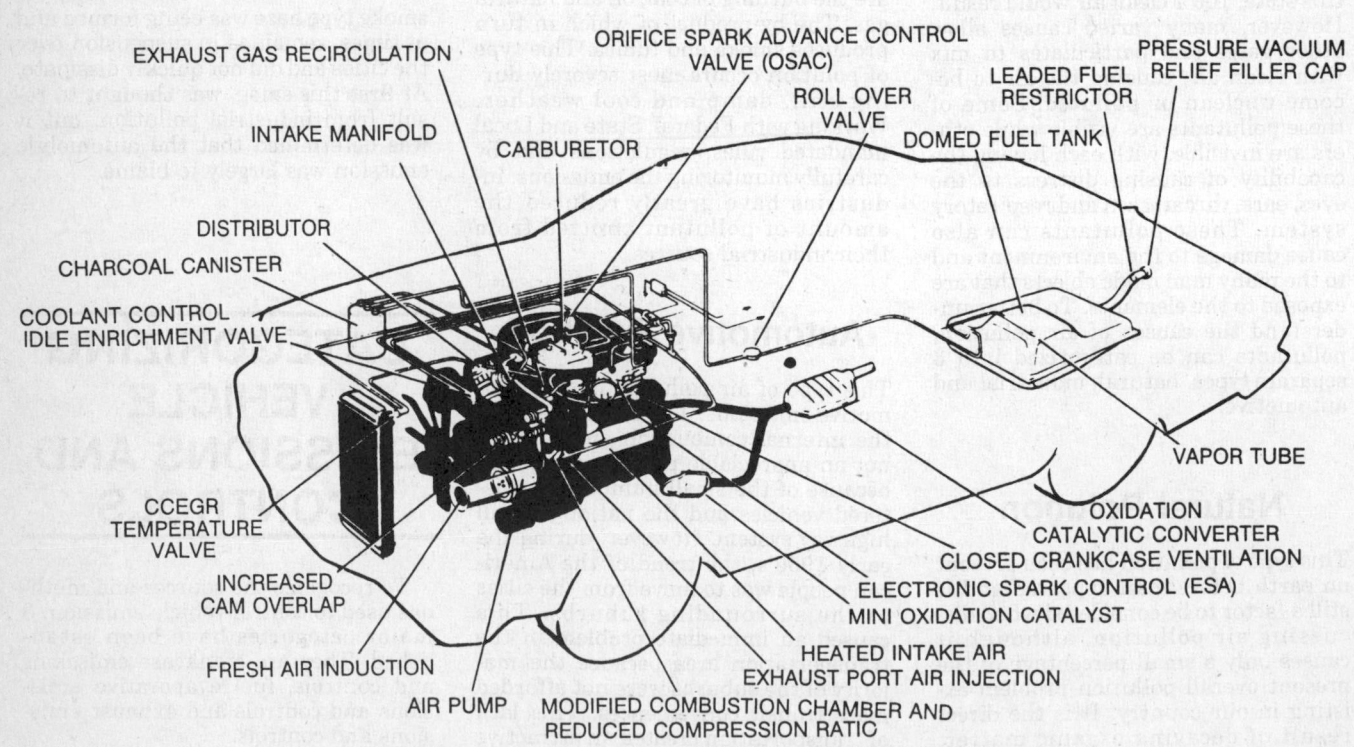

EXHAUST GAS RECIRCULATION

INTAKE MANIFOLD

DISTRIBUTOR

CHARCOAL CANISTER

COOLANT CONTROL
IDLE ENRICHMENT VALVE

CCEGR
TEMPERATURE
VALVE

INCREASED
CAM OVERLAP

FRESH AIR INDUCTION

AIR PUMP

CARBURETOR

ORIFICE SPARK ADVANCE CONTROL
VALVE (OSAC)

ROLL OVER
VALVE

DOMED FUEL TANK

LEADED FUEL
RESTRICTOR

PRESSURE VACUUM
RELIEF FILLER CAP

VAPOR TUBE

OXIDATION
CATALYTIC CONVERTER

CLOSED CRANKCASE VENTILATION

ELECTRONIC SPARK CONTROL (ESA)

MINI OXIDATION CATALYST

HEATED INTAKE AIR

EXHAUST PORT AIR INJECTION

MODIFIED COMBUSTION CHAMBER AND
REDUCED COMPRESSION RATIO

Typical emission control system component schematic—carbureted vehicles

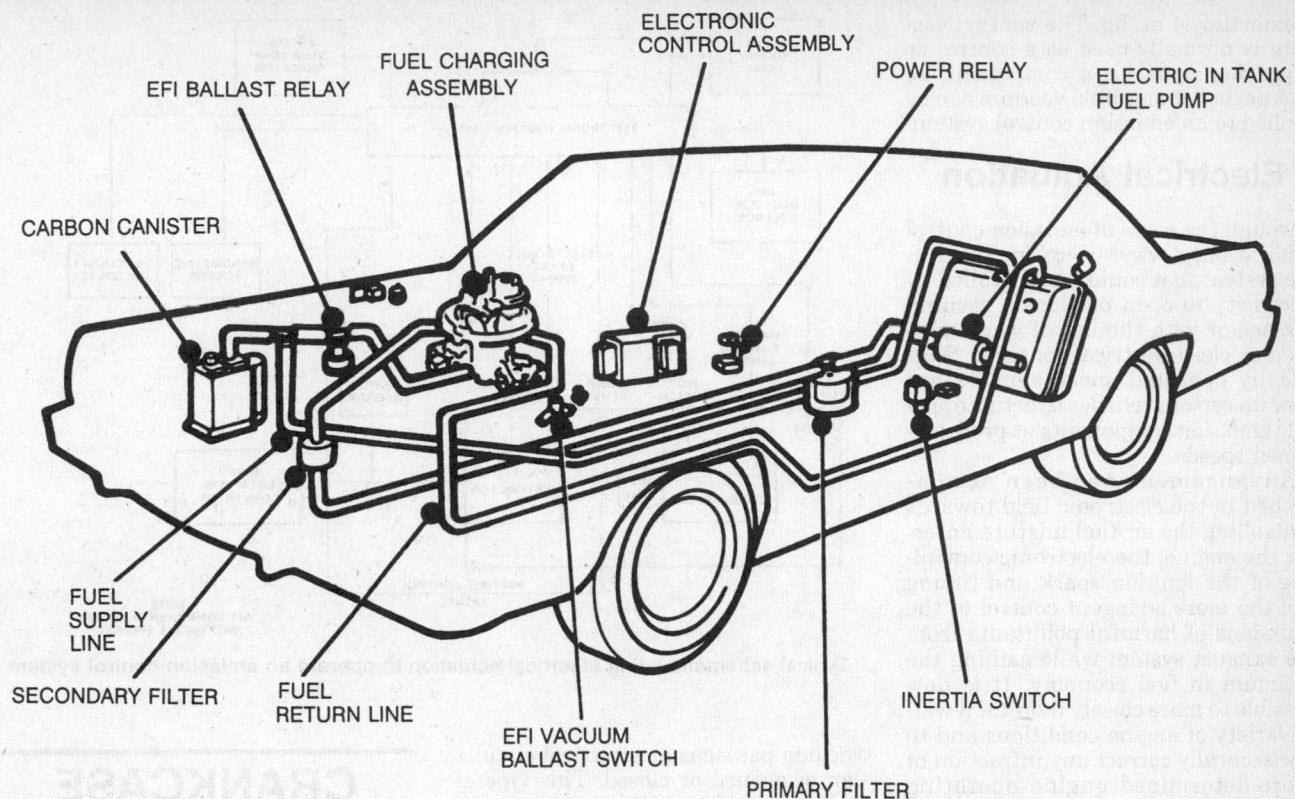

EFI BALLAST RELAY

FUEL CHARGING ASSEMBLY

ELECTRONIC CONTROL ASSEMBLY

POWER RELAY

ELECTRIC IN TANK FUEL PUMP

CARBON CANISTER

FUEL SUPPLY LINE

SECONDARY FILTER

FUEL RETURN LINE

EFI VACUUM BALLAST SWITCH

PRIMARY FILTER

INERTIA SWITCH

Typical emission control system component schematic—fuel injected vehicle

type of emission control device that is used, a means of actuation must be applied to the device in order for it to operate at a specific time or temperature during either the vehicle operation modes or during the combustion process. The actuating methods commonly used are vacuum, electrical, temperature and mechanical.

Vacuum Sources

The most common method of component actuation is by engine vacuum and has been used since the conception of emission controls. Three major sources of vacuum are obtained from the engine are manifold vacuum, ported vacuum and venturi vacuum. However, with the increased use of smaller engines, the demand for engine vacuum could not be totally supplied by the engine. Vacuum pumps were added to the engine and assisted in supplying the necessary required vacuum needs.

MANIFOLD VACUUM

The engine could be considered a large vacuum pump by having a constant negative pressure developed within the intake manifold as the engine is operated. The tap for this type vacuum is taken from the below the throttle plates or directly from the intake man-

ifold. This source of vacuum will vary in strength between 17–22 in. hg. at idle, to approximately 0 in. hg. at wide open throttle. With the engine in a deceleration mode, the manifold vacuum will be at its highest, which is above idle specifications. Manifold vacuum, normally in conjunction with a vacuum reservoir or amplifier to insure an adequate vacuum volume, is used to actuate the emission control components rapidly.

PORTED VACUUM

The ported vacuum tap is located directly above the throttle plates. When the throttle plates are closed, no ported vacuum signal is present, but as the throttle plates are opened, the vacuum tap is exposed and senses the vacuum below the throttle plates. The ported vacuum signal will vary from 0 in. hg. to approximately 14 in. hg., depending upon the throttle plate opening and the manner in which the port and tap are designed. It should be remembered that ported vacuum is not present at times when the throttle plates are closed or at wide open throttle. Ported vacuum is used in both control and actuation of various systems and components, depending upon the operational needs of the component.

VENTURI VACUUM

Such as the name implies, the venture vacuum tape is located in the venturi chamber of the carburetor throat and is depending upon the velocity of air flowing through the venturi chamber. An example would be as the throttle plates are opened and the velocity of the air flow increases, so would the venturi vacuum signal. The venturi vacuum varies from 0 in. hg. to ap-

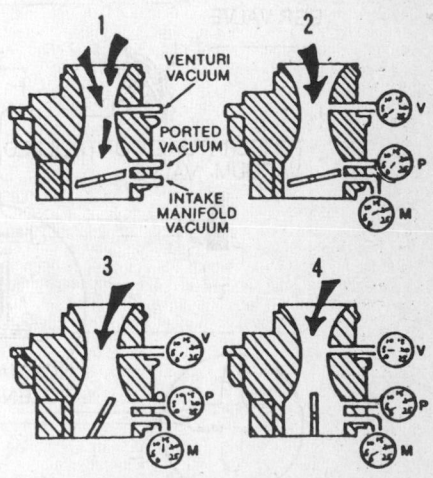

1 - SOURCES OF DIFFERENT VACUUMS
2 - IDLE
3 - OFF IDLE
4 - WIDE OPEN THROTTLE (WOT)

Engine vacuum sources

proximately 4 in. hg. The venturi vacuum is normally used as a control or triggering signal to a component, so that ported or manifold vacuum can be applied to an emission control system.

Electrical Actuation

Through the years of emission control application, devices were installed in the system that could be controlled by electricity to open or close a vacuum passage or with the use of vacuum to open or close electrical contacts. Electrically operated speed sensors are used on certain vehicles to actuate specific emission components at predetermined speeds.

Advancement has been accomplished in the electronic field towards controlling the air/fuel mixture entering the engine, the electronic controlling of the ignition spark and timing and the more stringent control of the emissions of harmful pollutants from the exhaust system while gaining the optimum in fuel economy. It is now possible to more closely monitor a wider variety of engine conditions and to electronically correct any infraction of a pre-determined engine operating mode, through the vehicle computer. Most computer systems are programmed to store and release malfunctioning or system defects information by electronically probing its many circuits.

Temperature Actuation

Various temperature switches are used on the engine to sense coolant temperature change and to react at specific temperature points so that

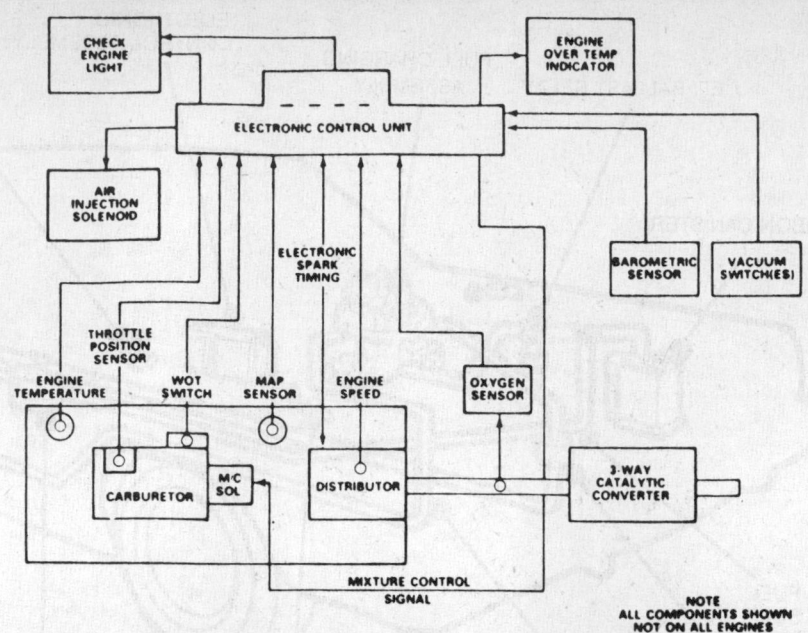

Typical schematic using electrical actuation to operate an emission control system

vacuum passages or electrical circuits can be opened or closed. This type of switch can control numerous vacuum or electrical circuits from a single supply source.

Mechanical Actuation

Mechanical switches are used to control the opening or closing of vacuum passages or the operation of electrical switches through the use of linkages, transmission shift rails or through manual operation.

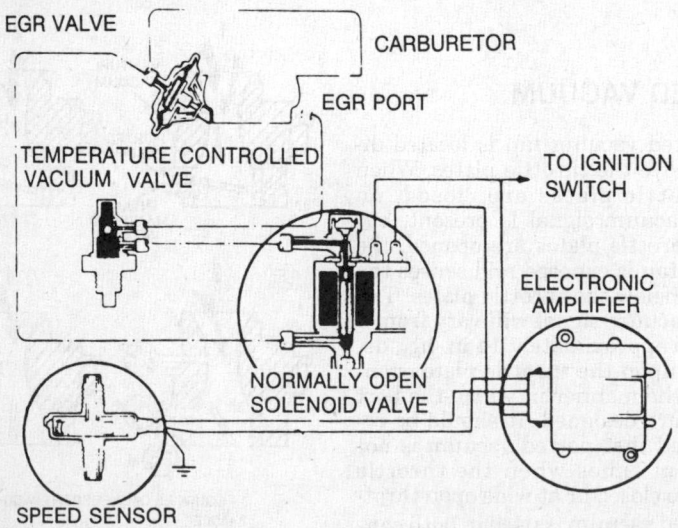

Typical schematic using temperature, electronics and manual actuation to operate an emission control system

CRANKCASE EMISSION CONTROL SYSTEM

System Description

Crankcase emissions are responsible for approximately 20% of all harmful automotive pollutants before any emission controls were installed on the vehicles. Crankcase emissions are the result of compression gasses being forced past the piston rings on both the compression and power strokes, resulting in an accumulation of gases, known as blowby gases, in the engine crankcase. These blowby gases become mixed with vapors from the agitated lubricating oil and must be relieved from the crankcase area to prevent internal engine pressures from building up.

Prior to the early 60's a road draft tube was used to ventilate the crankcase, which allowed the pollutants to be emitted into the atmosphere. With the installation of a regulating valve and necessary plumbing, the road draft tube was eliminated and the gases routed to the air intake area, to be drawn into the engine to be reburned with the air/fuel mixture. At first, engine vacuum was used as the controlling factor to draw the crankcase gases into the engine, but was found that the vacuum source varied at the wrong times. Different systems were experimented with, some with flow control valves while others merely direct the gases to the air cleaner assembly. Other systems had open breather caps to allow fresh air to enter the system while others had sealed breather caps with the fresh air supply being tapped from the air cleaner snorkel.

By 1968, all vehicles manufactured in the United States were equipped with a closed crankcase ventilation system, which did not allow any of the blowby gases and oil vapors to escape into the atmosphere. It is a closed sys-

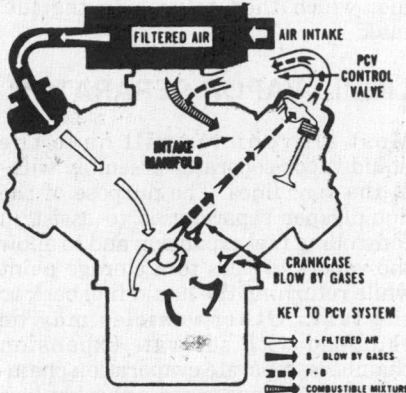

Typical closed crankcase ventilation control system

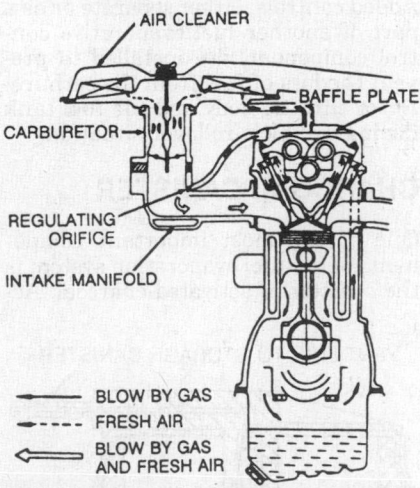

Positive crankcase ventilation system using a regulating orifice rather that a PCV valve

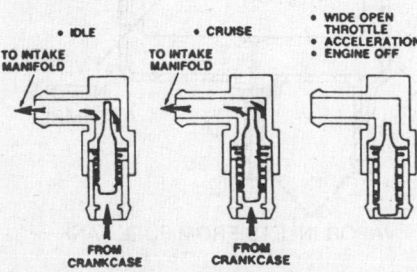

PCV valve operation

tem which utilizes a flow regulating valve called the positive crankcase ventilation valve, PCV valve, or may use a restrictor orifice in place of the PCV valve.

System Operation

The PCV valve is constructed and calibrated to perform the task of metering the gases from the crankcase as required and is matched to engine operation in the following manner. When the engine is idling, only a small amount of air and fuel is needed for combustion, resulting in a small amount of blowby gases being produced because the compression and power strokes are not occuring as frequently as at higher speeds. The PCV valve reacts to this lack of blowby gases and tends to restrict the flow into the induction system. As the engine speed increases, the compressions and power strokes occur more often, along with the addition of more fuel and air needed for combustion. This results in the formation of more blowby gases and the need to purge the crankcase of them. The PCV valve reacts to this increase in blowby gases by allowing more of the gases to be drawn into the air/fuel mixture. The PCV valve is constructed and calibrated in such a manner as to prevent engine backfires from entering the crankcase to avoid detonation of the accumulated blowby gases.

In the closed crankcase ventilation system, the fresh air intake that is located in the air cleaner or snorkel, has a dual role. Not only is it a source of fresh air for the crankcase ventilation system, but it doubles as an overload release of blowby gases into the system air stream should the PCV valve fail to control the build up of blowby gases. This happens rather than allowing the excess gases to escape into the atmosphere. With the use of this closed system the hydrocarbon (HC) emissions produced in the crankcase are prevented from entering the atmosphere.

FUEL EVAPORATIVE SYSTEM

System Description

Fuel evaporation vapors are found to account for approximately 20% of the total automotive emission problem

and is more severe as the temperature increases. The sources of the hydrocarbon vapor emissions were the fuel tank and carburetor bowl, both which were vented into the atmosphere. Another problem was the overfilling of the fuel tank, which under changes of temperatures or by having the vehicle parked on an incline, would spill gasoline from the tank. A means of trapping the vapor emission and preventing gasoline leakage was a major undertaking.

One of the early systems used, was the engine crankcase to store the fuel vapors when the engine was not running. When the engine was started, the vapors were purged from the crankcase by the positive crankcase ventilation system. Certain drawbacks were noted in this system, some of which were the dilution of engine lubricating oils with gasoline, an over rich air/fuel mixture during the purge cycle and the danger of gasoline vapor detonation within the crankcase during engine start up.

To prevent fuel loss from the tank due to expansion, an expansion dome has been manufactured into the top of the fuel tank and the fill pipes have been redesigned to prevent filling the fuel tank above a desired level. Certain vehicles use added plumbing to increase the area volume needed, should the fuel expand. This added plumbing is normally part of the vapor control system with necessary valves to control both vapors and liquids included. After much experimenting and testing, a general system was designed that could control both vapor and liquid emissions by sealing the fuel system from the atmosphere. Although each vehicle manufacturer has designed their own vapor control system, similar components are used, resulting in systems that are basically the same in the manner or vapor collection and storage. However, the manner in which the vapors are purged may vary greatly.

System Components

SEALED FUEL TANK CAP

The first step in sealing the fuel system was to replace the vented fuel tank filler cap with a sealed cap. The venting of the fuel tank is accomplished through another component of the system which controls the vapor emission by storage. To prevent damage to the tank should excessive internal or external pressure exist due to this closed system, a pressure/vacuum relief valve is incorporated in the sealing cap. A tank pressure of $\frac{1}{2}$–1 psi.

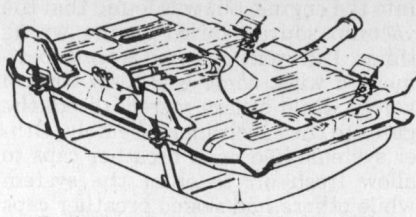

Typical emission related fuel tank

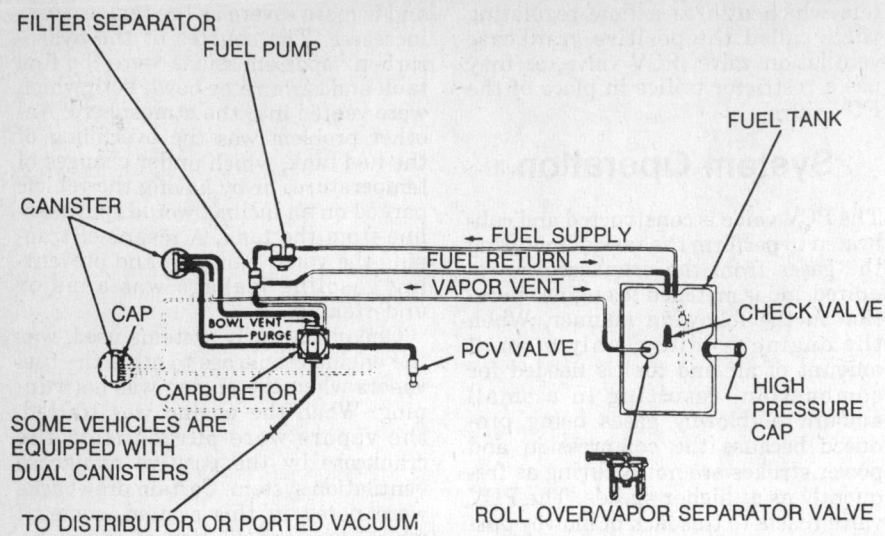

Typical evaporative control system schematic

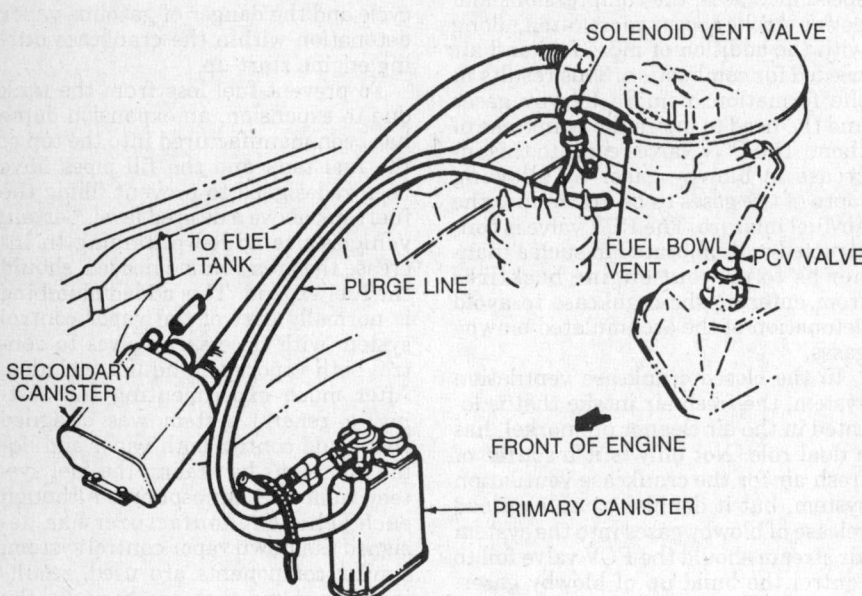

Typical box type evaporative control system schematic

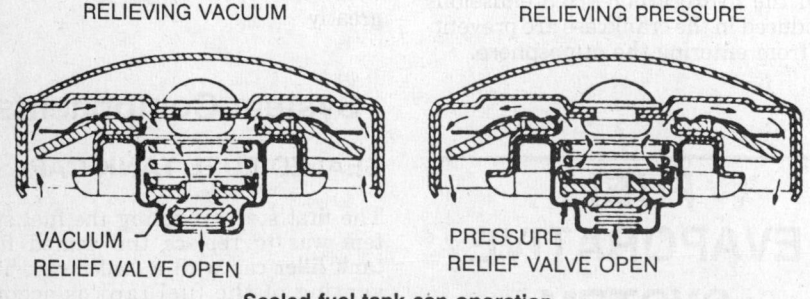

Sealed fuel tank cap operation

can exist in the tank and is controlled by the relief valve.

FUEL TANK

The fuel tank has been redesigned to provide approximately 10% of the total tank volume for expansion space, should the fuel expand due to temperature changes. An overfill protector is provided by the filler neck to assure the expansion space is maintained during the tank filling. The tank vapor venting is controlled by having a vent tap at or near the expansion chamber dome. A foam type filter or a vapor separator is used to allow the vapors to pass, but prevents the passage of liquid, which then returns to the fuel tank.

LIQUID/VAPOR SEPARATOR

Most all vehicles will have the liquid/vapor separator assembly within the vent lines. The purpose of the liquid/vapor separator is to assist in controlling fuel expansion and to allow the vapors to pass to a storage point while returning the liquid fuel back to the tank. Other vehicles may be equipped with separate expansion chambers, separate evaporation chambers and with one or more check valves in the lines. These components are usually located near the fuel tank. Added controls, either separate or as a part of another fuel evaporative control component, are installed to prevent the loss of fuel from the carburetor or throttle body and the fuel tank during a vehicle rollover situation.

CHARCOAL CANISTER

One of the most important components of the fuel evaporation system is the canister of activated charcoal. Ac-

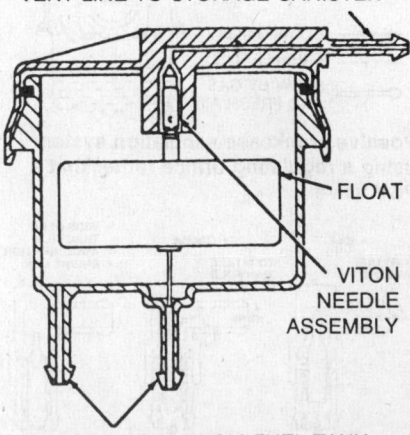

Typical liquid check valve assembly

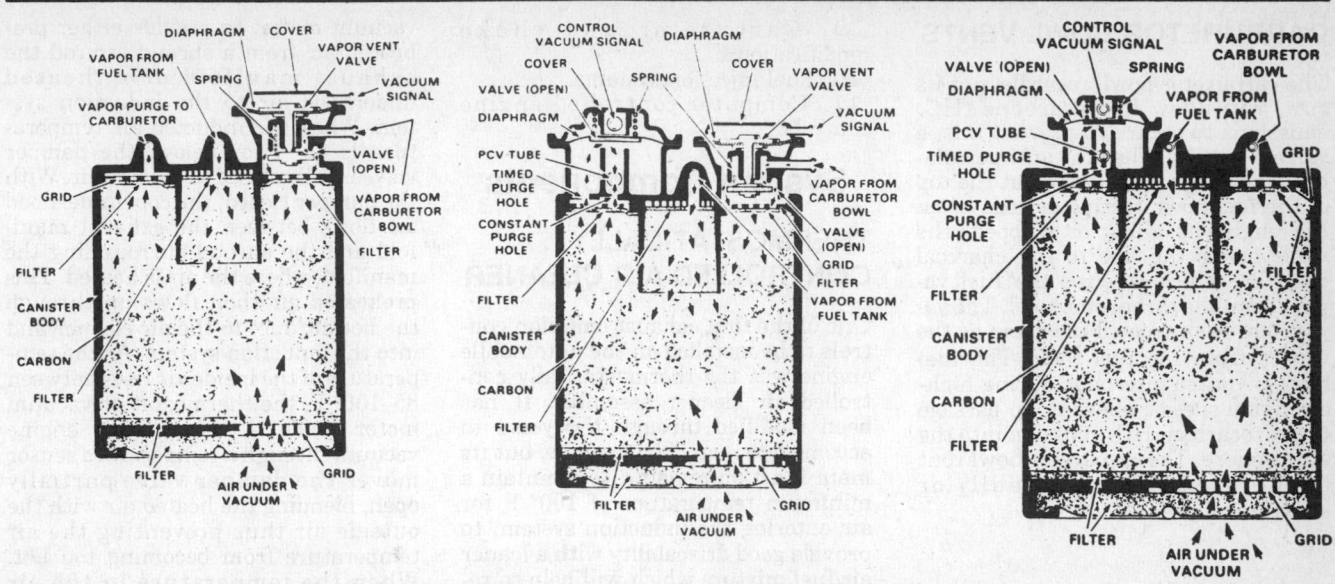

Typical vapor canisters used in the evaporative emission control system

tivated charcoal has the capabilities to absorb and store fuel vapors. The charcoal can be purged with fresh air and cleaned of its vapors, resulting in its reuse many times. When the vehicle is not running, the fuel vapors are routed to the canister where they are absorbed and stored by the activated charcoal. When the engine is started, either engine vacuum or the air flow through the air cleaner, draws the vapors from the charcoal by allowing a metered amount of air to pass over and through the charcoal and then routed into the engine's induction system.

Three different types of purge methods are used to cleanse the vapors from the canister. The first method is the variable purge which draws the va-

por laden air into the air cleaner from the canister. The variable air flow through the canister is dependent upon the air flow through the air cleaner and into the engine. The second method is called the demand purge system which connects the canister to the fuel metering system. As the throttle is opened, the engine vacuum draws the cleansing air through the canister and into the engine air flow. This type of system only operates when the throttle plates are open, therefore preventing the vapors from entering the fuel sytem metering device when the engine is idling. The third system is a combination of a constant and demand purge. One purge line is routed to the PCV line which

provides a continual purge, but by having a restriction in the passage, the flow rate is controlled. Another passage is routed to the fuel metering device. However, as the throttle plates are opened, the engine vacuum acts upon the restriction in the PCV line, opening the restriction and allowing more vapors and air to flow through the PCV system and into the intake air/fuel flow.

With the increased use of fuel injection and electronics, the vapors are purged from the canister at specific engine rpm and temperatures, so as not to upset the controlled air/fuel mixture and cause increased emissions from the combustion chambers.

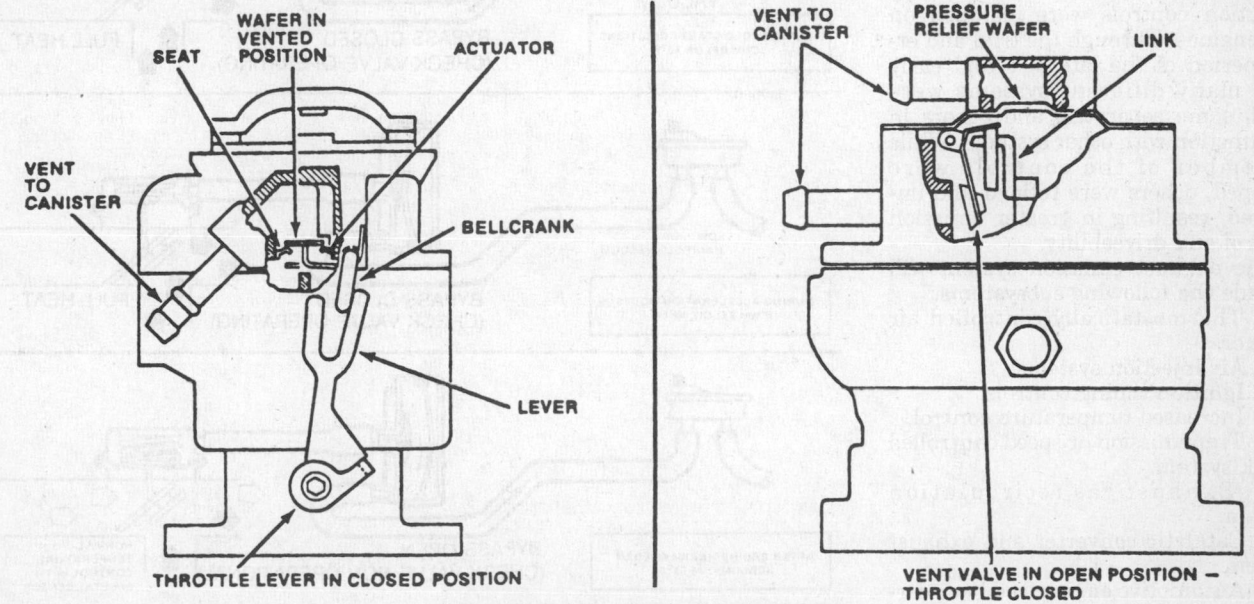

Typical carburetor bowl vent assemblies

CARBURETOR BOWL VENTS

The carburetor bowl, regardless of its size, will allow hydrocarbons (HC) emissions to occur. To prevent this, a valve normally called the anti-percolation valve, has been located at the top of the fuel bowl. During periods when the engine is idling or stopped, the valve opens the line to the charcoal canister, which receives the fuel vapors from the carburetor bowl. The vapors are then treated the same as the vapors from the fuel tank. The fuel bowl is vented internally during higher engine speeds, allowing no passage of hydrocarbon (HC) emission into the atmosphere. The carburetor bowl vent is operated either manually or electronically.

EXHAUST EMISSION CONTROL SYSTEM

System Description

The exhaust emission control system encompasses the automotive engine from the entrance of air into the engine's induction system until the exhaust byproduct of the combustion process emerges from the tail pipe. The engine exhaust was found to be responsible for approximately 60% of all automobile emissions before any pollution controls were installed on the engines. Through the trial and error period of the late 60's and early 70's many different systems were used, some separately and others in conjunction with other systems. While a number of the controls were dropped, others were refined and improved, resulting in greater emission control and driveability.

The exhaust emission system will include the following subsystems.

1. Thermostatically controlled air cleaner.
2. Air injection systems.
3. Ignition timing controls.
4. Increased temperature control.
5. Transmission or speed controlled spark system.
6. Exhaust gas recirculation system.
7. Catalytic converter and exhaust system.
8. Automotive engine feed back carburetor systems.
9. Carburetor and choke modifications.
10. Fuel injection systems.
11. Computer controlled engine controls.

System Components

THERMOSTATICALLY CONTROLLED AIR CLEANER

One of the first exhaust emission controls to be installed on the automobile engine was the thermostatically controlled air cleaner assembly. It has been modified through the years to accomodate many applications, but its main function remains, to maintain a minimum temperature of 100° F for air entering the induction system, to provide good driveability with a leaner air/fuel mixture which will help to reduce the exhaust emission of hydrocarbons (HC) and carbon monoxide (CO).

A damper valve, located in the snorkel or nozzle of the air cleaner housing, is operated by a thermostat or a vacuum motor, to provide either preheated air from a shroud around the exhaust manifold or unheated underhood air to the induction system. When the inducted air temperature is 85° F or below, the damper valve is fully closed to outside air. With the damper closed, the cool underhood air flows between the exhaust manifold and the shroud surrounding the manifold, where the air is heated. This preheated air then flows up through the hot air duct to the air cleaner and into the induction system. As the temperature of the inside air rises between 85–100° F, the thermostat or vacuum motor which is controlled by engine vacuum through a temperature sensor moves the damper valve partially open, blending the heated air with the outside air thus preventing the air temperature from becoming too hot. When the temperature in the air cleaner rises above 130° F, the thermostat or temperature sensor controlled vacuum motor opens the damper valve, assisted by a damper door spring, to outside air.

Regardless of the name given to this

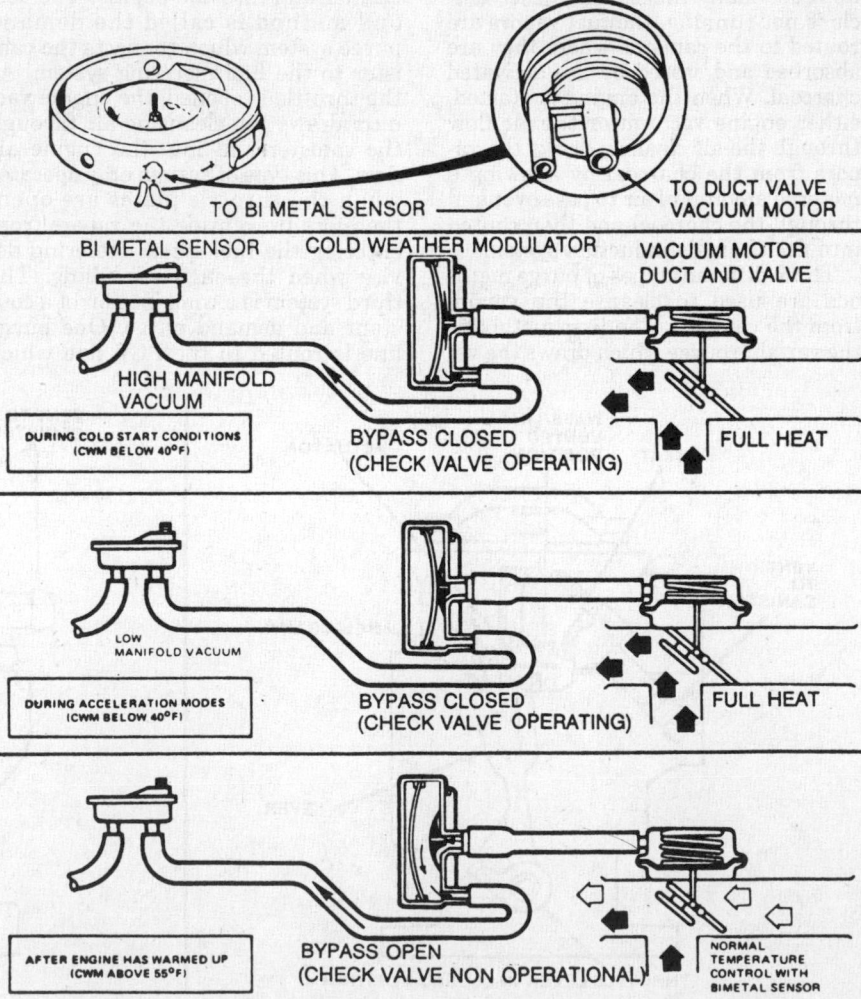

Operating sequences of the vacuum sensor operated air control valve

system by the vehicle manufacturer, its basic function and operation has remained the same throughout its application years. It is extremely important in the control of engine warm-up emissions, vehicle driveability and prevention of fuel icing, that all components of the thermostatically controlled air cleaner assembly be connected and operating.

AIR INJECTION SYSTEM

One of the major problems of the internal combustion engine is the fact that complete burning of the air/fuel mixture does not occur within the combustion chambers. This unburned mixture is swept from the combustion chamber along with the burned exhaust gases and emitted through the exhaust system and into the atmosphere. To prevent excessive emission of the unburned and burned gases containing large portions of hydrocarbons (HC) and carbon monoxide (C0), a means was devised to further burn the gases as they were forced from the cylinders by injecting fresh, oxygen laden air into the heated exhaust gas stream.

The addition of oxygen to the exhaust manifold and the exhaust pipes reducs the amount of unburned gases in the emitted exhaust. This after burner type system remains in use on many engine families. The vehicle manufacturers have modified, added and reduced the control components of the original system through the years, but the basic system to inject fresh air into the heated exhaust stream, still remains.

Two different systems are used on present day engines, one system using a belt driven air pump and the other system using the positive and negative exhaust system pressure pulsation to draw in fresh air.

Air Pump System

The major components of the air pump systems are.

1. Air pump which supplies filtered low pressure air to the system, normally 2–5 psi.

2. Diverter valve which diverts air pump output air to the atmosphere during deceleration to prevent backfire. A pressure relief valve is incorporated to protect the system.

3. Check valve which prevents hot exhaust gases from entering the system.

4. Air manifold which distributes the fresh air to each exhaust port of other area of the exhaust system.

5. Air nozzle which injects the air into the exhaust system.

6. Manifold vacuum signal line which senses manifold vacuum to acti-

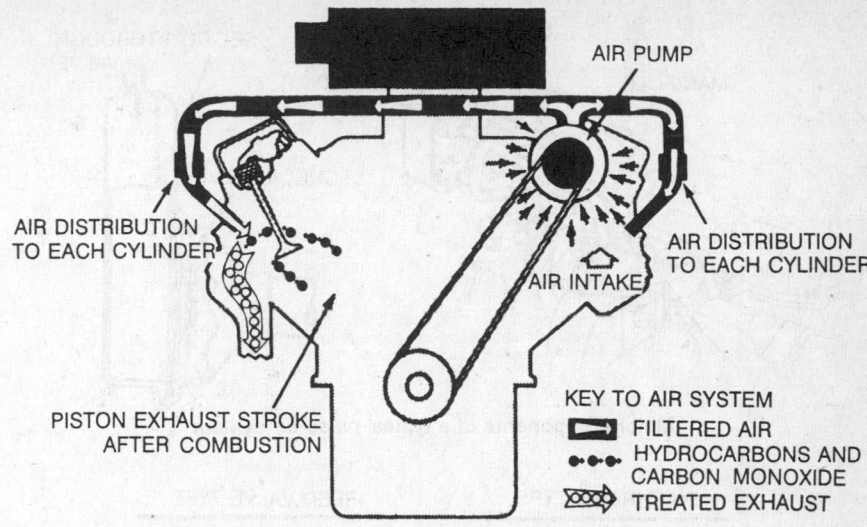

Typical air injection system flow schematic

KEY TO AIR SYSTEM
- FILTERED AIR
- HYDROCARBONS AND CARBON MONOXIDE
- TREATED EXHAUST

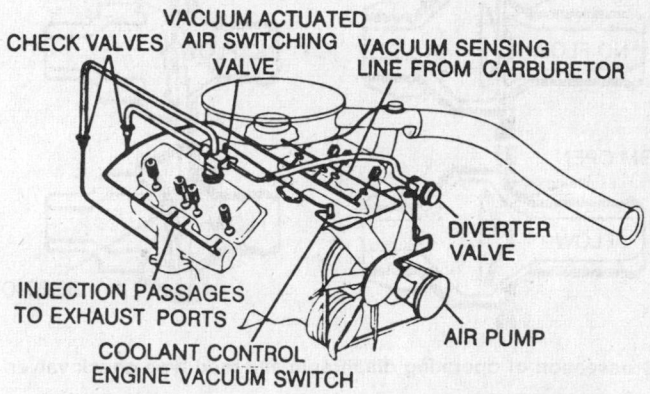

Major components of a typical air injection system

vate the diverter valve.

During the engine's normal operating condition, the air pump is supplying fresh air to the diverter valve which passes the air on to the air nozzles for injection into the exhaust stream. As the air is mixed with the hot exhaust gases, further combustion takes place in the exhaust system. During periods of deceleration, high manifold vacuum and a rich mixture is present in the combustion chambers. If fresh air was to be injected into the exhaust system during this condition, backfiring would occur. The diverter valve senses the high intake manifold vacuum and vents the fresh air from the air pump to the atmosphere. A switch valve is used by some manufacturers to redirect the fresh air from the exhaust valve port area to another location down stream in the exhaust system when the engine has warmed up to normal operating temperature, in order to avoid increasing the oxides of nitrogen (NOx) emissions while relying upon the heat of the exhaust to further the burning of the hydrocar-

bons (HC) at the exhaust valve ports. Since the addition of the three-way catalytic converters and oxygen sensors to the exhaust system, the air injection system has been modified and electronically controlled to critically monitor the entrance of fresh air into the exhaust stream during different engine operational modes and at different locations.

Pulse Air Injection System

The pulse air injection system does not use an air pump, but relies on the positive high pressure and negative low pressure pulses of the exhaust flow from the engine to operate one or more one-way check valves, which allows filtered fresh air to enter the exhaust stream at periods of negative low pressure and to prevent the leakage of exhaust gases back through the inlet air tubing. The fresh air induction through the one-way valve is normally accomplished at idle or slightly above.

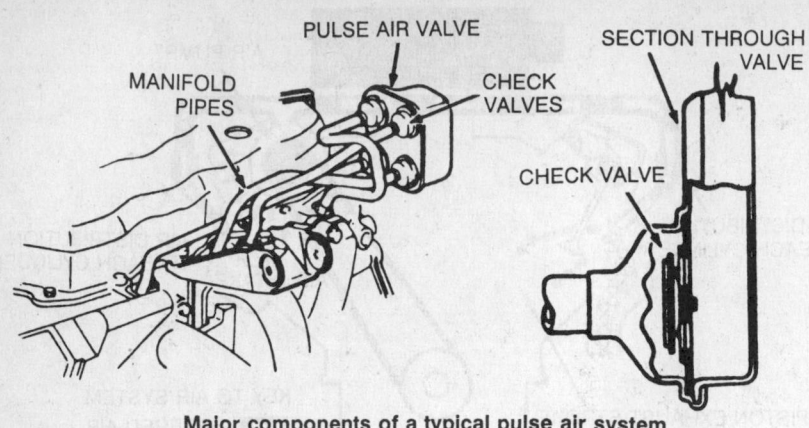

Major components of a typical pulse air system

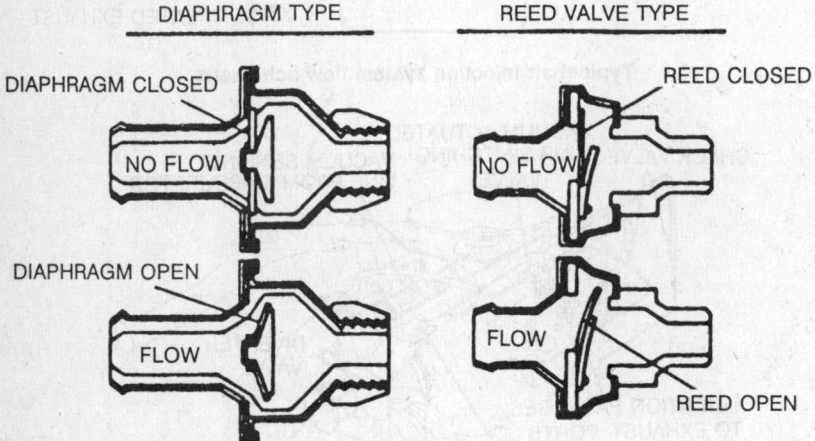

DIAPHRAGM TYPE

REED VALVE TYPE

Crossection of operating diaphragm and reed type check valves

IGNITION TIMING CONTROLS

The purpose of the timing or spark controls is to fire the air/fuel mixture in the combustion chamber at a specific time in order to derive the most power from the mixture, while burning it as completely as possible to rid it of excess hydrocarbons (HC) and still maintain a combustion chamber temperature that prevents excess formations of nitrogen oxides (NOx).

Electronic Ignition

To increase the ignition system's durability to over 50,000 miles of engine operation and to eliminate adjustment or replacement of the contact point sets, and electronically controlled ignition system was introduced as standard equipment on American made automobiles, beginning with the 1975 model year.

The distributor primary circuit was changed from a breaker plate and cam assembly in the distributor, to a magnetic signal generating system which detects the distributor shaft position

and sends electrical pulses to an electronic control module, which takes the place of the mechanically operated point set, in the off-on switch of the primary current to the ignition coil. The armature and pick-up assembly has no effect on the dwell period which

is controlled by the control module. Therefore, dwell never needs to be adjusted. With a dwell that remains constant, we do not need to continually read just the ignition timing to compensate for mechanical wear in the ignition system.

With the use of the electronics in the controlling of the distributor operations, on-board vehicle computers were added to control the many operations of the electronic components, such as the fuel delivery and spark timing for optimum engine performance. Many electronic sensors have been added to the systems to inform the computer(s) that adjustments may be necessary to maintain the vehicle's electronic performance. An example of the quickness of the computer to regulate and direct changes to the electronic components, is that changes are continually being made by an electronic component between 10–50 times per second to maintain the engine in its optimum performance.

Ignition Coil

The ignition coil is the component of the ignition system that must produce voltage of enough intensity and strength to cross a predetermined spark plug gap to ignite the air/fuel mixture in the combustion chamber, under any and all engine operation conditions. To achieve this responsibility, the ignition coil must increase the primary voltage form an average of 12 volts to a secondary voltage, through induction, as high as 30,000 volts.

Distribution of Spark

To route the secondary voltage to the spark plugs, heavily insulate wiring, distributor caps and rotors are used. With the use of electronic ignition sys-

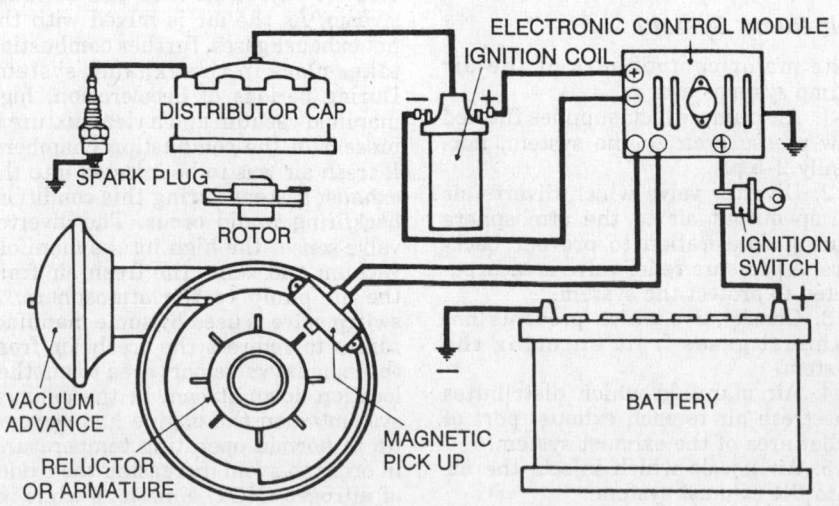

Typical electronic ignition system electrical schematic

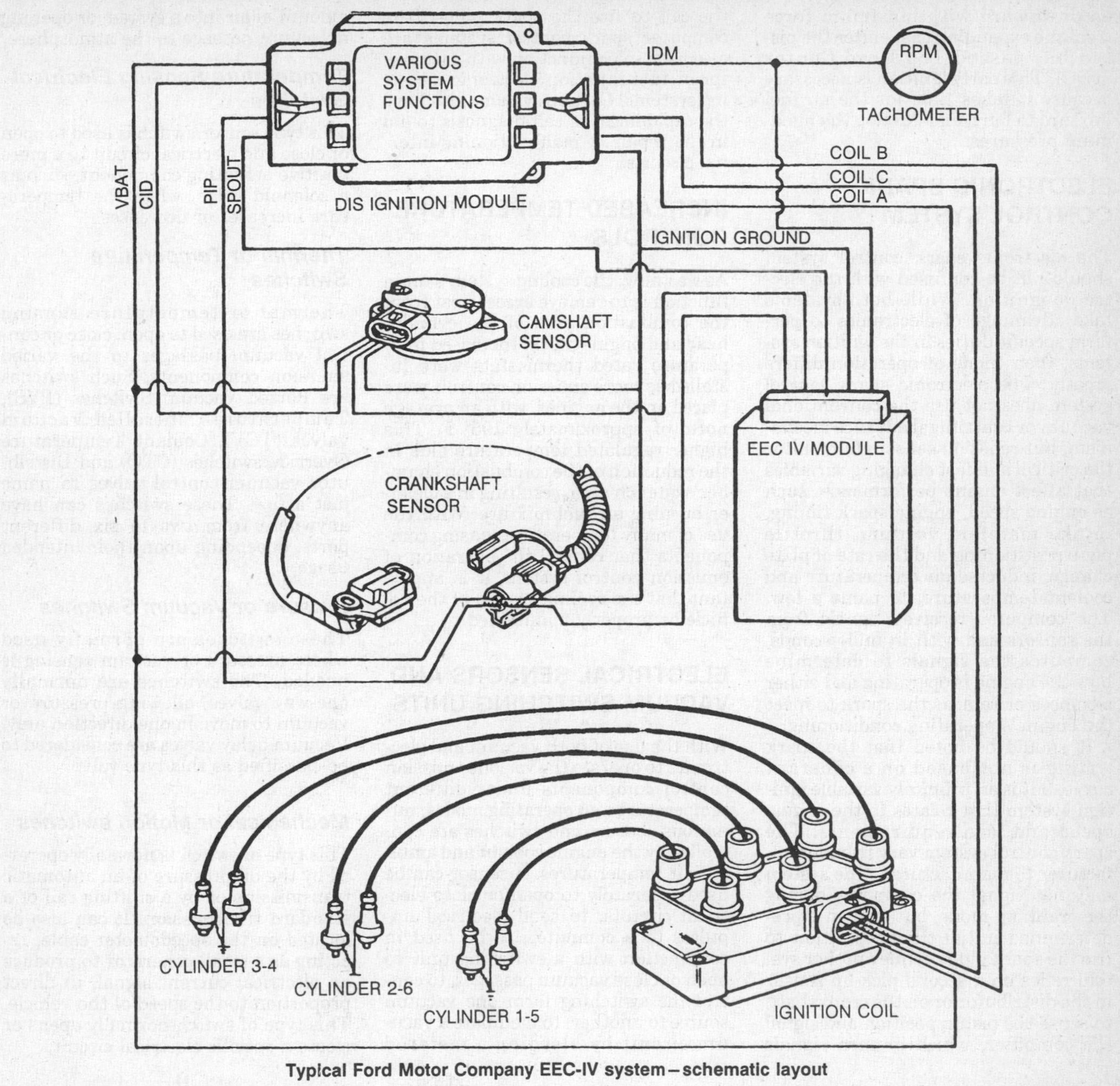

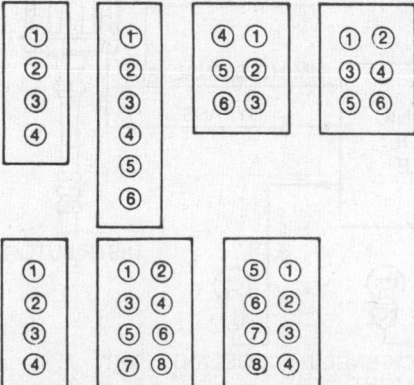

VARIOUS
SYSTEM
FUNCTIONS

IDM

RPM

TACHOMETER

COIL B
COIL C
COIL A

VBAT
CID
PIP
SPOUT

DIS IGNITION MODULE

IGNITION GROUND

CAMSHAFT
SENSOR

EEC IV MODULE

CRANKSHAFT
SENSOR

CYLINDER 3-4

CYLINDER 2-6

CYLINDER 1-5

IGNITION COIL

Typical Ford Motor Company EEC-IV system—schematic layout

tems and its increase in the secondary voltage output, the insulating capacity of the secondary ignition system had to be increased to prevent leakage or crossfiring of the increased voltage, on its way to the spark plugs. It is most important that correct replacement secondary ignition parts be used to avoid causing engine misfires through the loss of secondary current due to the use of inferior replacement parts.

Firing Sequence

To have the ignition system ignite the air/fuel mixture in the proper cylinder at the right time, a firing order sequence must be established by the engine manufacturer, in proper time

Typical engine cylinder numbering configurations

with the pistons and the valve movement. In order to conduct tests or repairs to the system, the repair person must know the firing order sequence, the cylinder numbering order, the rotation of the distributor rotor and the location of the corresponding electrical terminals on the distributor cap, connected by the secondary cables to their respective spark plugs, which are screwed into the cylinder's combustion chamber, beginning with the No. 1 cylinder.

Spark Timing

The air/fuel mixture must be ignited before the piston reaches Top Dead Center (TDC) to have the piston driven downward with maximum force from the expanding gases after the piston has passed Top Dead Center (TDC). This early ignition is necessary because it takes time for the air/fuel mixture to burn and develop the maximum pressures.

ELECTRONIC SPARK CONTROL SYSTEM

The electronic spark control system should not be confused with the electronic ignition. While both systems take advantage of electronics to perform specific duties in the ignition systems, their mode of operation differs greatly. The electronic spark control system does not use the conventional vacuum or centrifugal advance mechanism, but relies on sensors to monitor the critical and fast changing variables that affect engine performance, such as engine speed, engine spark timing, intake manifold vacuum, throttle plate positioning and the rate of plate change, inducted air temperature and coolant temperature, to name a few. The computer receives signals from the sensors and with in mill-seconds, computes the signals to determine how the engine is operating and either advances or retards the spark to meet the engine's operating conditioning.

It should be noted that the spark timing is not based on a constant curve, but is an infinitely variable ignition system that relates to the engine speed and load requirements. The spark control system vary from manufacturer to manufacturer. One system may not signal the computer during the cranking mode, but rely on a predetermined initial timing position to fire the spark plugs, while another system relies on a second pick-up sensor in the distributor or on the crankshaft, to sense the piston position and signal the computer, which in turn signals

the coil to fire the spark plugs. The computer spark control systems are also used in conjunction with carburetor or fuel injection electronic metering systems. Certain systems also have the capabilities of self-diagnosis to aid in the repair of malfunctioning internal circuits.

INCREASED TEMPERATURE CONTROLS

As we know, the cooling system's main function is to remove excess heat from the combustion area of the cylinder head and engine block. Increased temperature rated thermostats were installed as more emission controls were placed on the engines, with an average norm of approximately 195° F. This higher regulated temperature aids in the reduction of the combustion chamber's quench area, resulting in a cleaner burning air/fuel mixture. With the use of many temperature sensing components that control the operation of emission control system, it is important that the cooling system of the vehicle be properly maintained.

ELECTRICAL SENSORS AND VACUUM SWITCHING UNITS

With the use of both vacuum and electronics to operate the various emission control components under different temperature and operating modes, numerous sensors and switches are controlled by the engine coolant and ambient air temperatures. A sensor can be used separately to open or close electrical circuits, to send electrical impulses to a computer, to be used in conjunction with a switching unit to open or close vacuum passages, to control the switching form one vacuum source to another, to modulate a vacuum circuit by bleeding a metered

amount of air into a system or opening a vacuum passage to the atmosphere.

Temperature Sensing Electrical Switches

This type sensor/switch is used to open or close and electrical circuit to a more positive actuating component, such as a solenoid valve, when the temperature increases or decreases.

Thermal or Temperature Switches

Thermal or temperature sensing switches are used to open, close or control vacuum passages to the varied emission components. Such switches are Ported Vacuum Switches (PVS), Temperature Controlled Vacuum valves (TCV), Coolant Temperature Override switches (CTO) and Distributor vacuum control valves to name just a few. These switches can have anywhere from two to six different ports, depending upon their intended usage.

Presure or Vacuum Switches

These switches are normally used where pressure or vacuum sensing is needed. The switches are normally one-way valves, allowing pressure or vacuum to move in one direction only. Vacuum delay valves are considered to be classified as this type valve.

Mechanical or Motion switches

This type of switch is normally operated by the oil pressure of an automatic transmission or by a shifting rail of a standard transmission. It can also be located on the speedometer cable, reacting as a small generator to produce an electrical current signal, in direct proportion to the speed of the vehicle. This type of switch normally opens or closes a specific electrical circuit.

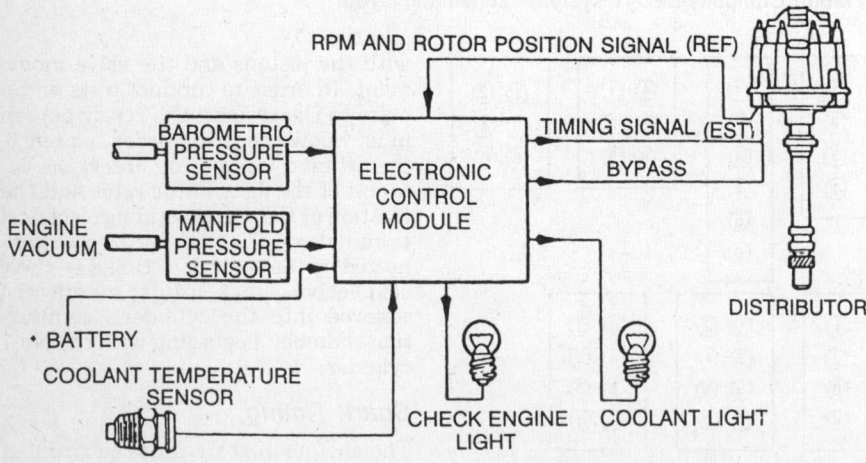

Typical first generation electronic spark timing control system

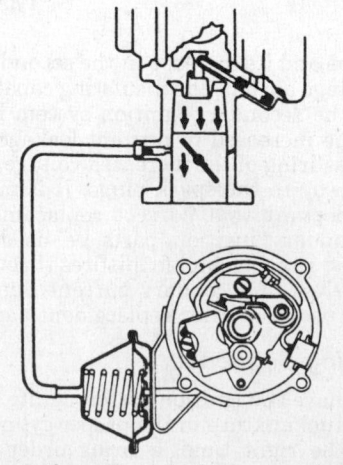

Crossection of a typical vacuum advance mechanism

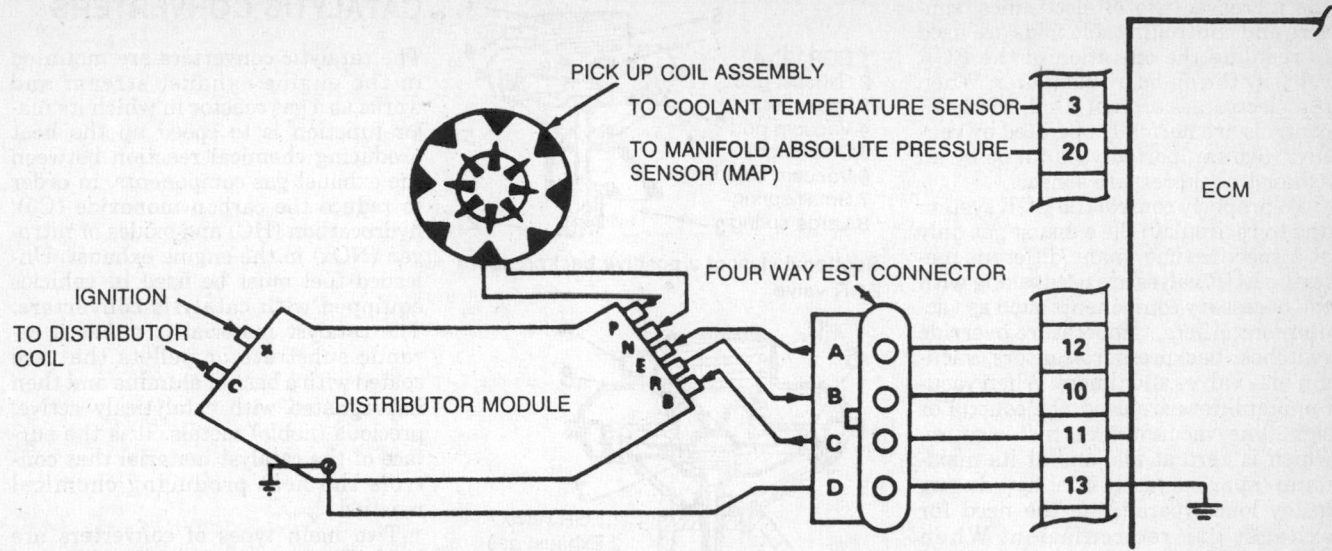

Typical usage of vacuum and temperature sensors to control EST

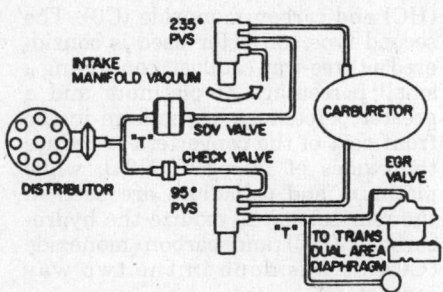

Typical temperature sensing valves used to control vacuum actuated components

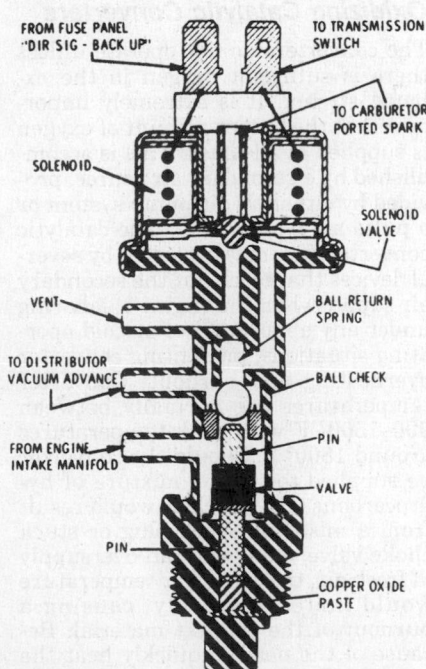

Crossection of a typical vacuum control valve for distributor vacuum advance operation

EXHAUST GAS RECIRCULATION SYSTEM (EGR)

In their attempt to reduce hydrocarbons (HC) emission, the manufacturers increased the combustion chamber temperatures to more thoroughly burn the air/fuel mixture. With the increase in temperature and pressure, another pollutant was created, oxides of nitrogen (N0x).

At temperatures below 2500° F, nitrogen remains an inert gas, but with combustion temperatures reaching as high as 4500° F, the nitrogen combines with the oxygen in the air/fuel mixture, resulting in the formation of oxides of nitrogen (NOx) a harmful pollutant. Through experimentation, it was found that a portion of the exhaust gases could be redirected into the combustion chamber, along with the inducted air/fuel mixture, resulting in the temperature of the burning process being lowered, causing a reduction in the emission of the oxides of nitrogen (NOx). The amount of the recirculated exhaust gases has to be carefully controlled. If too much exhaust gas is supplied at the wrong time, the engine may stall and be very rough at idle. If not enough exhaust gas is recirculated, the oxides of nitrogen (NOx) will not be reduced.

EGR Valves

Varied types of EGR valves are used with different control components, so that the proper amount of recirculated gas is directed into the air/fuel mixture at a specific time. The EGR valves are vacuum operated, either by intake manifold of by ported vacuum. With

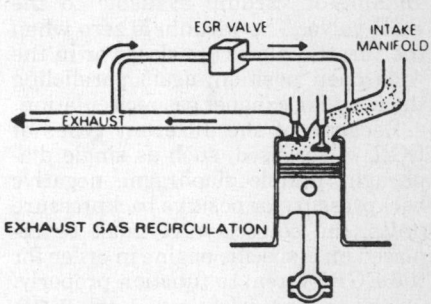

Typical EGR system schematic

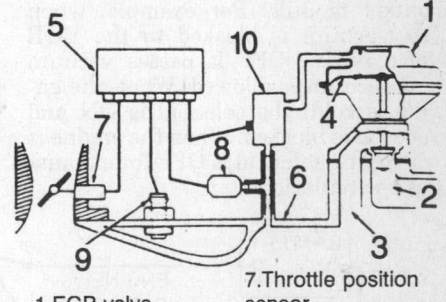

1. EGR valve
2. Exhaust gas
3. Intake air
4. Diaphragm
5. Electronic control module
6. Manifold vacuum
7. Throttle position sensor
8. Manifold pressure sensor
9. coolant temperature sensor
10. EGR control solenoid

Typical operation of a vacuum solenoid controlled EGR valve

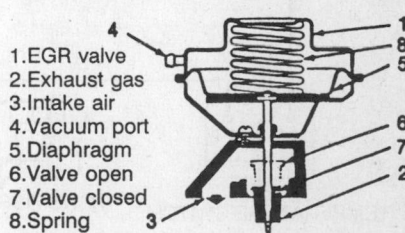

1. EGR valve
2. Exhaust gas
3. Intake air
4. Vacuum port
5. Diaphragm
6. Valve open
7. Valve closed
8. Spring

Sectional view of a ported EGR valve

the increased use of electronics, sensors and controlling solenoids are used to regulate the operation of the EGR valve by the on-board computer. When the electronics are not used, the EGR controls are normally operated by venturi vacuum, ported vacuum or by an exhaust backpressure sensor.

To properly control the EGR system and to recirculate the exhaust gas only at a specific time, many different metering EGR valves are used, along with the necessary components such as vacuum amplifiers, temperature override switches, backpressure sensors, vacuum bias valves and timers. When vacuum amplifiers are used, the control or signalling vacuum is venturi vacuum, which is zero at idle and at its maximum (approximately 4 in. hg.) during heavy loads, paralleling the need for exhaust gas recirculation. When ported vacuum is used, the position of the throttle plate regulates the amount of vacuum available to the EGR valve. The vacuum is zero when the throttle plates are closed or in the wide open position, again paralleling the need for exhaust gas recirculation.

Because of the different types of EGR valves used, such as single diaphragm, double diaphragm, negative backpressure or positive backpressure units, the correct valve must be replaced on a specific engine in order for the EGR system to function properly. Some new models control the EGR valve by a signal from the electronic control module. For example, when ON vacuum is blocked to the EGR valve. When OFF it passes vacuum and vacuum is allowed. When the engine is cold, the solenoid is ON and vacuum is blocked. When the engine is warm, the solenoid is OFF for exhaust gas recirculation.

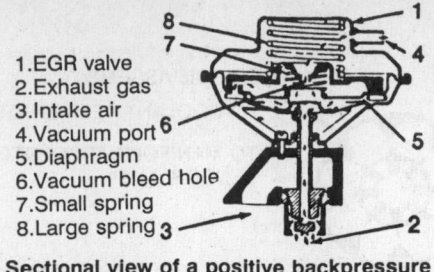

1. EGR valve
2. Exhaust gas
3. Intake air
4. Vacuum port
5. Diaphragm
6. Vacuum bleed hole
7. Small spring
8. Large spring

Sectional view of a positive backpressure EGR valve

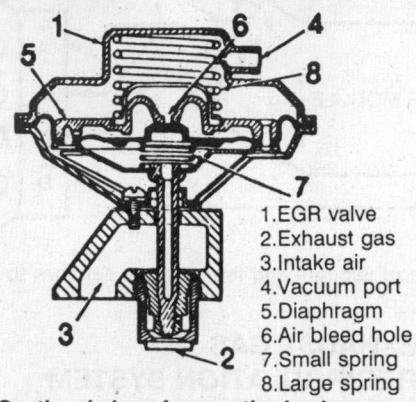

1. EGR valve
2. Exhaust gas
3. Intake air
4. Vacuum port
5. Diaphragm
6. Air bleed hole
7. Small spring
8. Large spring

Sectional vies of a negative backpressure EGR valve

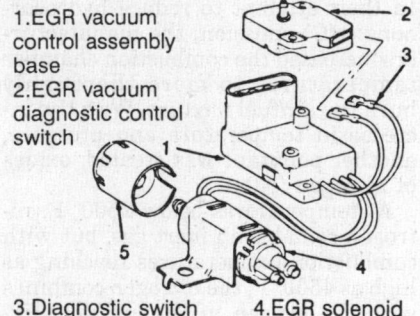

1. EGR vacuum control assembly base
2. EGR vacuum diagnostic control switch
3. Diagnostic switch connectors
4. EGR solenoid
5. Filter

Typical General Motors EGR control solenoid

CATALYTIC CONVERTERS

The catalytic converters are mounted in the engine exhaust stream and works as a gas reactor in which its major function is to speed up the heat producing chemical reaction between the exhaust gas components, in order to reduce the carbon monoxide (CO), hydrocarbon (HC) and oxides of nitrogen (NOx) in the engine exhaust. Unleaded fuel must be used in vehicles equipped with catalytic converters. The catalyst material is either a ceramic substrate or pellets that are coated with a base of alumina and then impregnated with catalyticaly active, precious (noble) metals. It is the surface of the catalyst material that controls the heat producing chemical reaction.

Two main types of converters are used. The first type contains, platinum and palladium to effectively catalyze the oxidation of the hydrocarbons (HC) and carbon monoxide (CO). The second type converter used is considered a three-way catalyst, containing a small percentage of platinum and a greater percentage of rhodium in the front part of the converters to reduce the oxides of nitrogen (NOx), while platinum and palladium are used in the rear section to oxidize the hydrocarbons (HC) and carbon monoxide (CO), as was done in the two way converters.

Oxidizing Catalytic Converters

The converters do not operate unless there is sufficient oxygen in the exhaust stream. It is extremely important that the proper amount of oxygen is supplied at all times. This is accomplished by a secondary air source, provided by either an air pump system or a pulse air type system. The catalytic converter system is protected by several devices that block out the secondary air supply when the engine is laboring under any abnormal hot or cold operating situations, preventing converter overheating and burnout. Converter temperatures are normally between 900–1500° F with peak temperatures around 1800° F. Should the converter be supplied too rich a mixture of hydrocarbons (HC), such as would result from a misfiring spark plug or stuck choke valve, along with an oversupply of fresh air, the converter temperature would increase sharply, causing a burnout of the catalyst material. Because of the need to quickly heat the converters units, smaller or mini converters are placed in the exhaust stream before the main converter to preheat the exhaust gas.

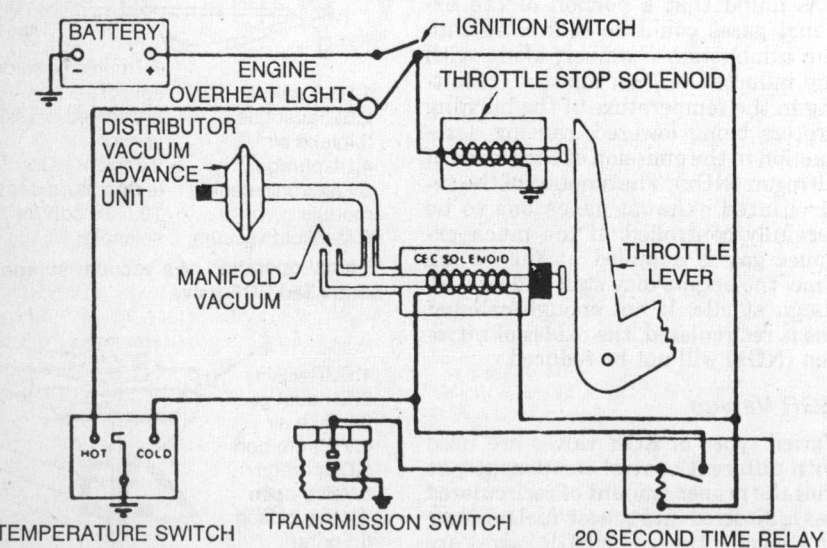

EGR system using various types of emission sensing and actuating controls

Three-way Catalytic Converters

The three-way catalytic converters use a combination of catalyst which produce two different chemical reactions, oxidation and reduction. By adding fresh air to the unburned hydrocarbons (HC) and carbon monoxide (C0) within the converter, the oxidizing of combustion process takes place. Just the reverse process is required to lower the oxides of nitrogen (N0x) emissions. The oxides of nitrogen (N0x) already contains excessive oxygen and the process of separating the excess oxygen from the nitrogen is called a reducing reaction. This reducing or re-

verter to operate properly, the engine's air/fuel ratio must be held within a tight range, called a Stoichiometric range. This is accomplished with the use of the latest computer controlled electronic engine components. Different control components are used by the vehicle manufacturers to prevent converter damage and/or burnout.

THERMAL REACTOR SYSTEM

The thermal reactor is installed in place of the exhaust manifold. It is

FUEL INJECTION SYSTEMS

A number of different fuel injection systems are used on today's vehicles to improve the emissions, miles per gallon and the driveability demands on the automobile. The injection systems range from a metering of the inducted air velocity to the use of computer or microprocessor units to operate the systems, allowing the proper amount of fuel to mix with the inducted air. Sensors are used to signal the control unit that changes in air/fuel mixture is needed as the driving mode changes. The fuel injectors can be located near the intake valve ports on some systems and this system is know as Multiport Fuel Injection. The fuel is injected into the ports from injector groups of two, three or four injectors. A sequential type of fuel injection is also used, known as SFI and is based on the firing order of the engine. The throttle body injection system, known as TBI, uses an injector unit(s), mounted in the throttle body to inject fuel as needed into the intake manifold. An electronic control module is used, in conjunction with sensors to control the system.

Engine Condition

A definate relationship exists between emission controls and engine tune-up. An engine that is out of tune after many miles of operation, can result in failure of the emission controls to properly perform their jobs. Malfunctioning emission controls can cause poor engine performance, so we can understand that proper engine operation is dependent upon thorough testing and servicing of all components related to both performance and emission controls. Because the engine is responsible for approximately 80% of the emissions and its condition reflects on its operational capacities, a knowledge of its basic operation is necessary when attempting to service it. We know that compression, ignition and fuel distribution are the basic needs of the engine in order to start and run. However, how these three basic needs are coordinated through the action of the crankshaft, camshaft, cylinder components and distributor must be understood, in order for the engine to operate under all speeds and loads. If a malfunctioning cylinder or other internal problems are suspected, a compression test, a cylinder balance test or other mechanical tests should be done to determine the engine's internal condition, prior to any attempted tune-up on the engine.

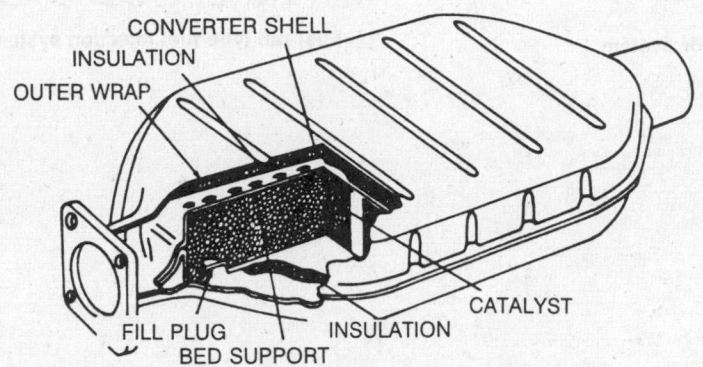

CONVERTER SHELL
INSULATION
OUTER WRAP
FILL PLUG
BED SUPPORT
INSULATION
CATALYST

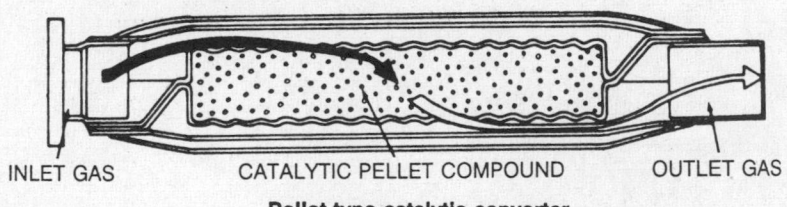

INLET GAS   CATALYTIC PELLET COMPOUND   OUTLET GAS

Pellet type catalytic converter

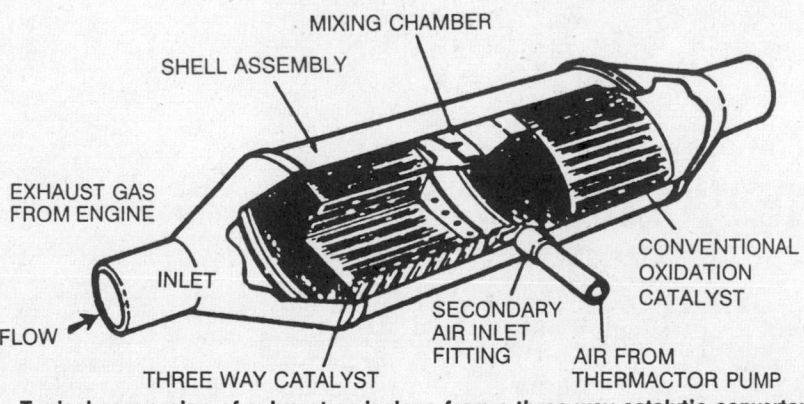

MIXING CHAMBER
SHELL ASSEMBLY
EXHAUST GAS FROM ENGINE
INLET
FLOW
THREE WAY CATALYST
SECONDARY AIR INLET FITTING
AIR FROM THERMACTOR PUMP
CONVENTIONAL OXIDATION CATALYST

Typical conversion of exhaust emissions from a three way catalytic converter

duction process is done in the front section of the converter while the oxidizing process is accomplished in the section. A fresh air connector is located on the center of the converter shell, to add fresh air from the air systems as required. To enable the three-way con-

much heavier and heat resistant. Its purpose is to collect the exhaust gases in a common area, to keep their temperature higher for a longer period of time, thus allowing further oxidation or burning of the exhaust gas and secondary air mix burned emissions.

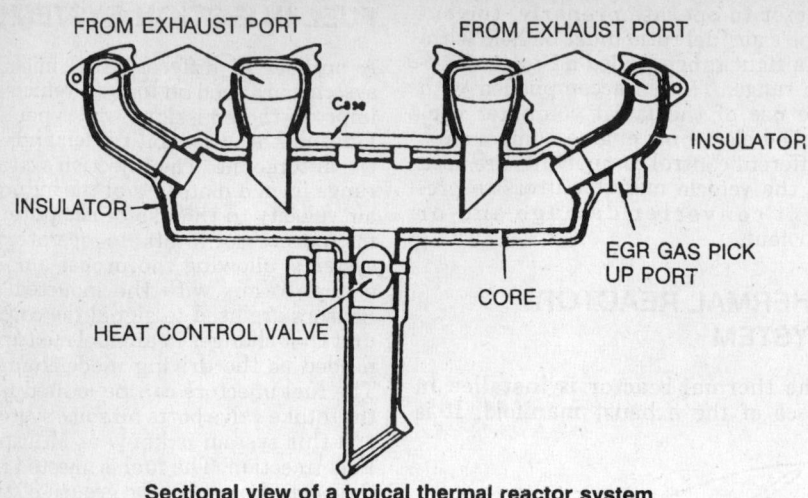

Sectional view of a typical thermal reactor system

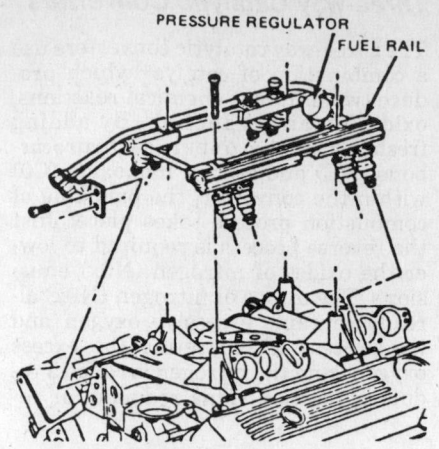

Fuel rail type fuel injection system

Electronic Engine Controls 35

ENGINE ELECTRONICS

In the ladder part of the 1960's, Robert Bosch introduce the first true electronically controlled engine with an on-board computer. Today, almost every car produced has some kind of electronic control. The once mechanically controlled engine functions are all but extinct.

The first system, Bosch D-Jetronic, is comprised of electrically energized fuel injectors in which the injection time is controlled by an electronic control unit (ECU). The early system delivered a basic quantity of fuel and varied from this point depending upon engine load, engine speed and engine temperature.

Since the early days of ECU, the controls have become more complex, with a much greater amount of computer memory and even the ability to learn.

In this section the topics will include different types of electronically controlled fuel induction, spark control, the sensors and switches that provide the ECU with information, other non-engine related controls that the ECU might supply and some ECU self-diagnostics.

The most common fuel induction system with an ECU is electronic fuel injection. In this system fuel can be delivered many different ways. One of which is the single point injection (SPI) were one or two injectors are mounted on a throttle body assembly. Fuel is delivered constantly through the injector(s), but in varying quanti-

ties. The SPI system very much resembles a carbureted system. SPI is more commonly known as throttle body injection (TBI). Another fuel injection system is multi-point injection (MPI). This system supplies one injector for each cylinder, usually positioned in the intake manifold, just above the intake valve. In MPI, fuel can be injected in two ways. One is to energize a group of injectors, thus atomizing fuel in the intake manifold and storing it for a short time until the intake valve opens. The second way is to sequentially energize each cylinder's injector as the intake valve is opened. This injection is the more efficient, effective and more complex system.

Another fuel induction system utilizing an ECU is the feedback carburetor (FBC). A conventional carburetor is still used but it has a more precise air/fuel mixture control which is achieved through an integral mixture control solenoid. The solenoid is energized on and off by the ECU to maintain mixture demand. The ECU calculates air/fuel mixture demand changes by the data it receives through remote sensors. The most important sensor (and makes the system possible) is an oxygen (O_2) sensor (which will be discussed later in this section). The ECU monitors the exhaust gases for rich/lean conditions by way of the O_2 sensor and, in turn, controls the air/fuel mixture by increasing or decreasing the duty cycles (on and off) to the mixture control solenoid for an optimum 14.7:1 air/fuel ratio.

ECU Self-Diagnostics

The ECU can detect a malfuction or

abnornality in the sensors or in the ECU itself and display a warning light on the instrument panel when it does. When this occurs, the ECU stores a trouble code for future system diagnosis. If the problem is sever enough to where it inhibits closed loop operation, the ECU will assume a backup system. This fail-safe circuit is pre-programmed into the ECU for minimal driveability operation so the vehicle can be driven to a nearby service facility. The trouble codes are usually a two digit numbers identified by the number of diagnostic LED or check engine light flashes. The trouble codes assist the service technician in isolating a faulty circuit or component within the system.

Electronic Data Sensors

The engine control system consists of various data sensors. Although data sensor names and applications vary from system to system, the most common input sensors/switches are:

- oxygen (O_2) sensor
- coolant temperature sensor
- manifold air pressure (MAP) sensor
- vehicle speed sensor (VSS)
- throttle position sensor (TPS)
- engine speed reference or distributor reference (rpm)
- air flow sensor
- air intake temperature sensor
- crankshaft sensor
- detonation (knock) sensor
- throttle body temperature sensor
- throttle idle switch
- transmission or drive switch
- a/c compressor clutch switch

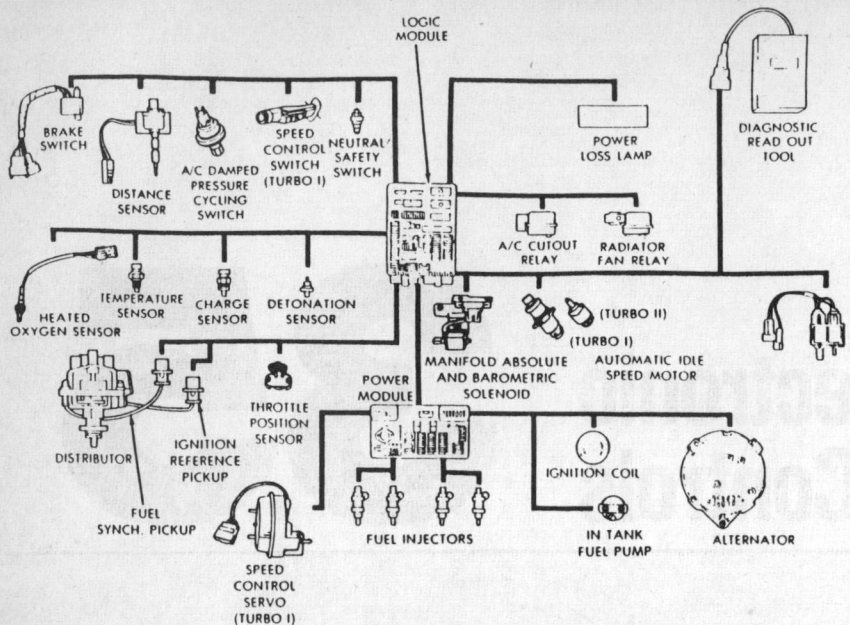

Electronic engine control components

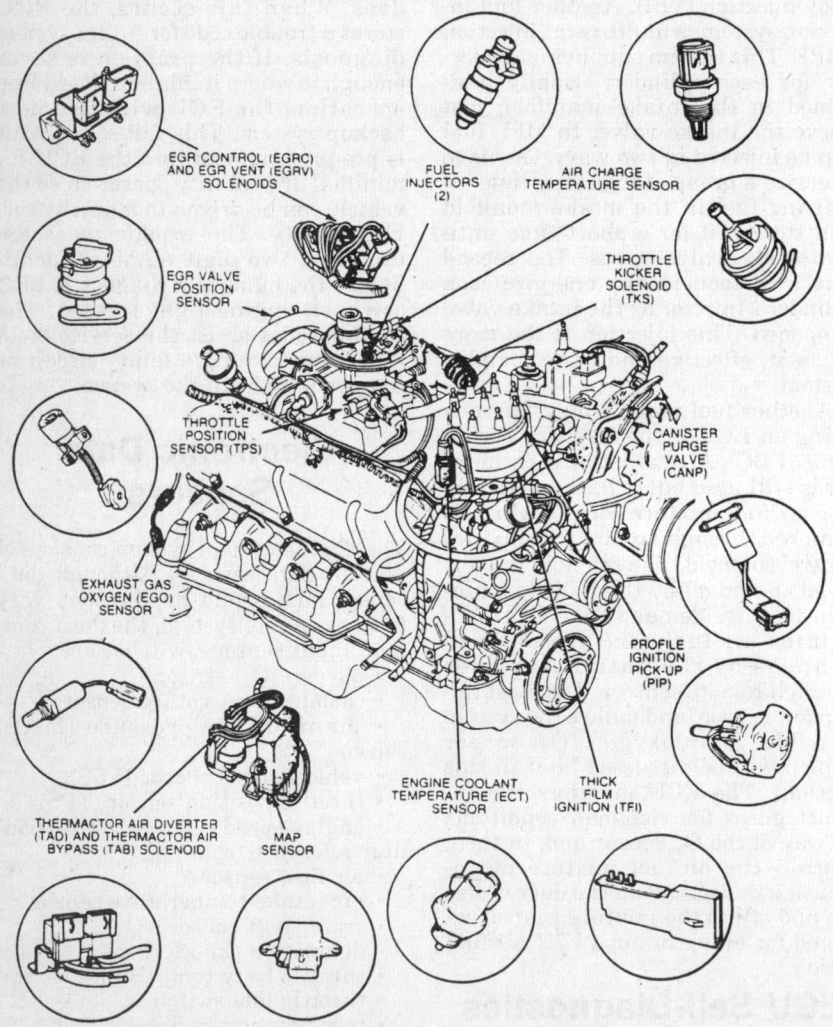

Electronic engine control component locations

- power steering pump switch
- altitude or barometric pressure sensor
- wide open throttle switch

Electronically Controlled Devices

Some of the output devices that the ECU may control vary from system to system, but the most common output or ECU controlled devices are:

- fuel injector(s)
- air/fuel mixture solenoid
- fuel pump relay
- a/c compressor clutch relay
- idle air control (IAC) valve
- idle speed control (ISC) motor
- ignition spark/timing
- canister purge solenoid
- torque converter clutch solenoid (automatic transmission)
- air management system (air induction)
- idle-up or throttle kicker solenoid
- alternator field control (charging system)
- turbocharger boost wastegate
- cooling fan relay

Component Description

THROTTLE BODY

The throttle body, in most fuel injected systems, is usually an alumunum housing that consists of one or two throttle blades which are attached to a throttle shaft. The housing has a throttle position sensor (TPS) sensor, idle air control motor and, in some cases, throttle body temperature sensor. On SPI systems, the housing also has an injector(s) and (in some cases) a fuel pressure regulator. The throttle body throttle blade controls the amount of air that enters the engine as well as the amount of vacuum.

ELECTRONIC CONTROL UNIT (ECU)

The ECU monitors and controls all engine control functions. The ECU consists of input and output devices, a central processing unit, a power supply and various memory banks. The input and output devices of the ECU convert electrical signals received by the data sensors and switches to the digital signal that are used by the central processing unit. The central processing unit receives digital signals that are used to perform all mathematical computations and logic

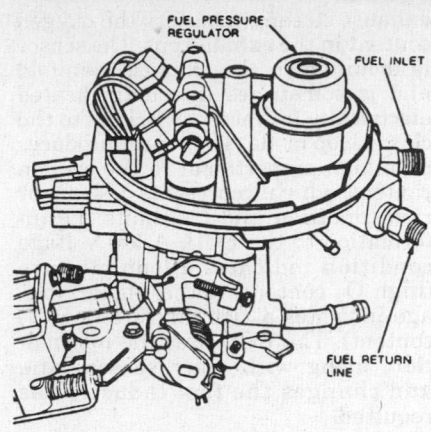

Throttle body – TBI

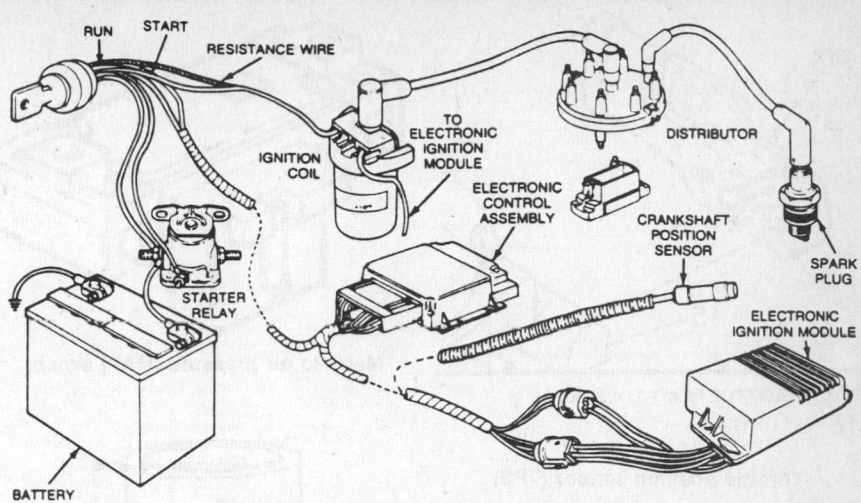

Electronic ignition system using ECU

functions necessary to deliver proper air/fuel mixture. The central processing unit is also responsible for calculating spark timing information. The main source of power that allows the ECU to function is generated from the battery of the vehicle and transported through the ignition system. The memory bank of the ECU is programmed with exact information that is used by the ECU during the open loop mode. This data is also used when a sensor of other component fails, allowing the vehicle to be driven to a repair facility.

CALIBRATION ASSSEMBLY OR PROM (PROGRAMMABLE READ ONLY MEMORY)

Some vehicle manufactures use one ECU for several different model vehicles. This interchangeable ECU is possible through the use of a calibration assembly or prom. Information about the vehicle's engine, transmission, body and drive axle ratio are programmed and permanently stored into the assembly. If the battery supply should become disconnected from the ECU, the data stored into the assembly is not lost.

ELECTRONIC SPARK CONTROL (ESC)

The vehicles equipped with an ESC have the ability to change the ignition timing under any and all operating conditions. Data from various remote sensors (coolant temperature, throttle position, rpm, etc.) is transmitted to the ESC. The ESC computes the information and triggers the ignition spark at precisely the right instant. Some ESC systems (ie.,turbocharged engines) use a detonation (knock) sensor which senses pre-ignition and

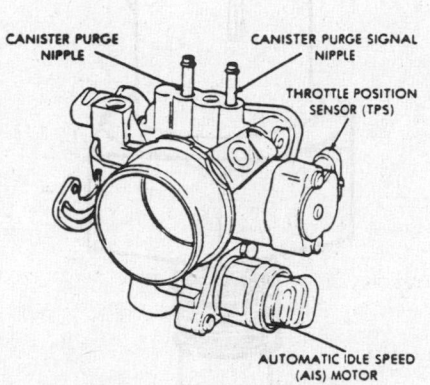

Throttle body – MFI

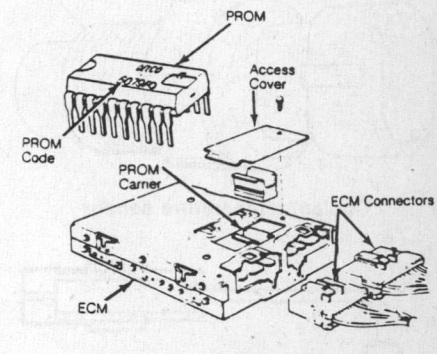

Electronic control unit prom

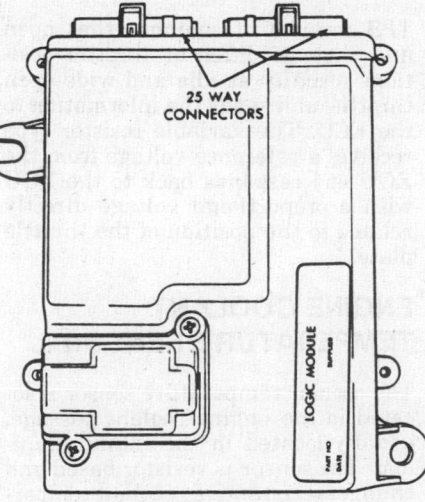

Electronic control unit

transmits the information to the ESC. The ESC modifies spark advance and boost pressure in order to eliminate knock.

MASS AIR FLOW SENSOR

The mass air flow (MAF) sensor is

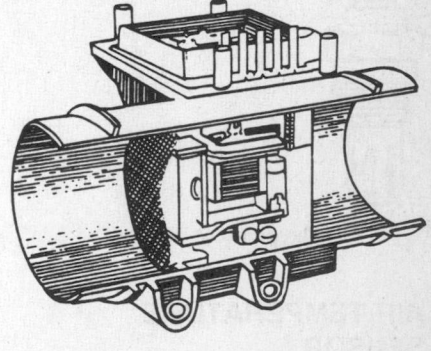

Mass air flow (MAF) sensor

only incorporated in some Multi-point fuel injection systems. The MAF sensor is a very complex device which measures the air mass of the engine intake. Because the air mass is always changing with temperature, humidity and altitude, the fuel delivery rate must be adjusted to compensate for these changes so that a precise fuel mixture can be maintained.

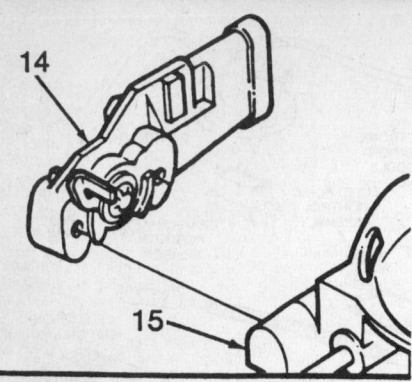

14 THROTTLE POSITION SENSOR
15 TBI UNIT

Throttle position sensor (TPS)

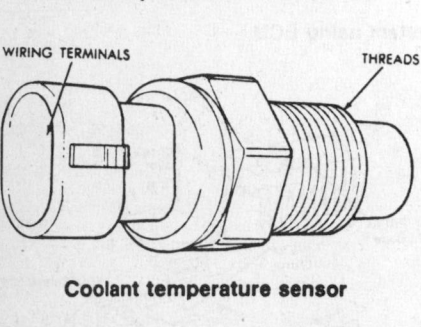

WIRING TERMINALS   THREADS

Coolant temperature sensor

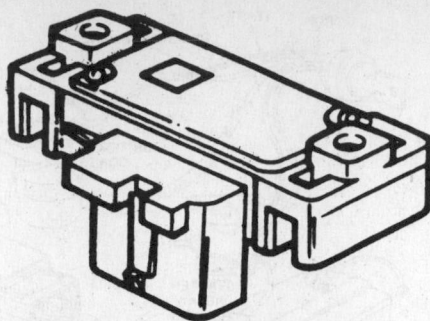

Manifold air pressure (MAP) sensor

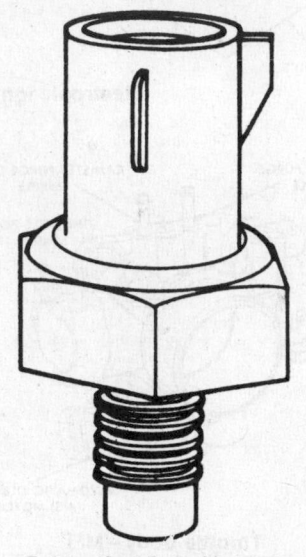

Detonation (knock) sensor

Oxygen (O₂) sensor

AIR TEMPERATURE SENSOR

The air temperature sensor is located in the air stream of the air flow meter. The sensor supplies incoming air temperature information to the ECU. The ECU uses this data, along with other data, to regulate fuel injection rate.

THROTTLE POSITION SENSOR (TPS)

The TPS can be either a switch (or a combination of switches) or a variable resistor which is much more accurate in throttle position. The switch type

TPS consists of switches that open and close at different throttle positions (usually at idle and wide open throttle) and sends the information to the ECU. The variable resistor type receives a reference voltage from the ECU and responds back to the ECU with a proportional voltage directly related to the position of the throttle plate.

ENGINE COOLANT TEMPERATURE SENSOR

The coolant temperature sensor is located in the engine coolant passage, usually located in the intake manifold. The sensor is resistor based and changes resistance as coolant temperature changes. The sensor uses a reference voltage and the output voltage is sent to the ECU. The ECU calculates engine warm up and provides an optimum fuel enrichment when the engine is cold.

OXYGEN (O₂) SENSOR

The O₂ sensor, which is placed in the

exhaust stream, monitors the oxygen content in the exhaust gas. The sensor is mounted in the exhaust manifold and is sometimes internally heated electrically for faster switching to the closed loop mode. The sensor produces a voltage proportional to the oxygen content which represents a lean or rich condition and transmits the information to the ECU. A low voltage condition indicates a lean mixture (high O₂ content) and a higher voltage indicates a rich mixture (low O₂ content). The ECU uses the information, along with other sensor data, and changes the fuel induction as required.

CYLINDER HEAD TEMPERATURE SENSOR

The cylinder head temperature sensor monitors the temperature of the cylinder head and transmits the information to the ECU. The sensor is located in the cylinder head and is a temperature sensitive resistive unit known as a thermistor.

VEHICLE SPEED SENSOR (VSS)

The VSS provides vehicle speed data to the ECU in the form of pulse signals. There are many different types of VSS, some using a reed switch installed in the speed meter unit and others using a optical type. In the optical type a light emitting diode (LED) is used to transmit light and photo diode receives the light. A shutter device, which is usually in-line with the speedometer cable, allows the LED light to reach the photo diode in vehicle speed related pulses. The reed switch type relies on a reed switch that opens and closes by way of a rotating magnet. The magnet rotates proportionally with the vehicle speed.

MANIFOLD AIR PRESSURE (MAP) SENSOR

The MAP sensor is a device that monitors manifold absolute pressure. The sensor is mounted remotely and senses vacuum through a connecting hose. The MAP sensor has a reference voltage from the ECU and transmits remaining voltage to the ECU to calculate engine load. The ECU uses this data along with other data to determine fuel demands.

DETONATION (KNOCK) SENSOR

The detonation sensor generates a

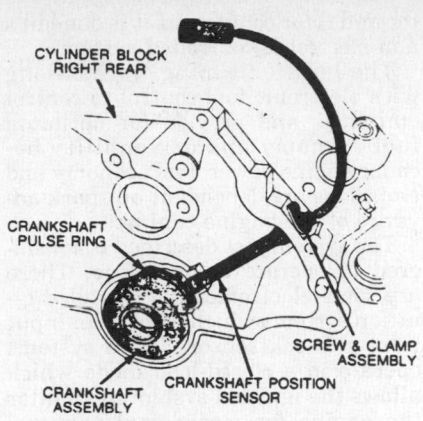

Crankshaft position sensor

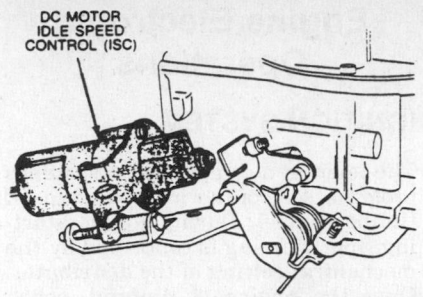

Idle speed control (ISC) motor

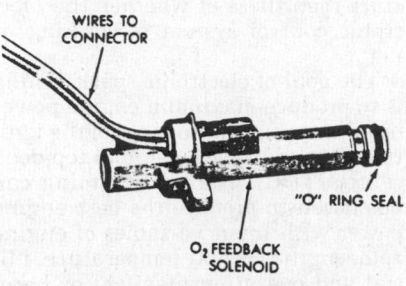

Air/fuel mixture solenoid

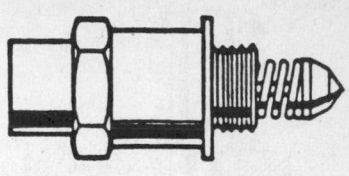

DUAL TAPER VALVE

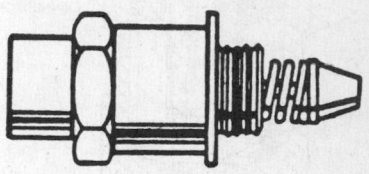

BLUNT PINTLE

Idle air control (IAC) valves

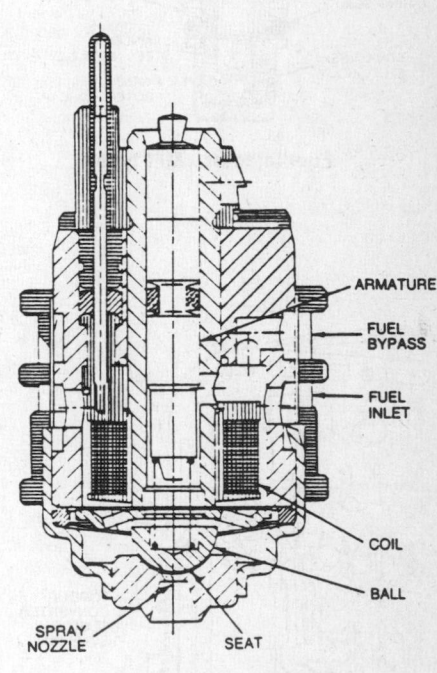

Fuel Injector—TBI type

signal when pre-ignition (knock) occurs in one or more combustion chambers. The sensor is made of a material that is sensitive to oscillation that the engine knock produces and sends signals to the ECU. The ECU, in turn, delays the ignition signal which retards the ignition timing and continues to do this until the engine knock ceases.

CRANKSHAFT (REFERENCE MARK) SENSOR

The crankshaft sensor may be located at either the rear of the engine, at the flywheel or at the front of the engine, near the crankshaft pulley. The sensor detects crankshaft position in relation to top dead center and transmits the signals to ECU.

IDLE SPEED CONTROL (ISC) MOTOR

The ISC is sometimes included on a feedback carburetor system and mounted to the side of the carburetor. The motor driven ISC would maintain a steady idle by way of the ECU. When an added load is put on the engine (air conditioning or when vehicle is in drive) the ECU could increase the idle via the ISC by extending a plunger which would open the throttle valve.

AIR/FUEL MIXTURE SOLENOID

The air/fuel mixture solenoid on feedback carburetor operates in conjunction with the fixed metering jets and/or the manually adjustable idle speed mixture screw. The ECU energizes and de-energizes the solenoid in the closed loop mode. The solenoid usually controls a fixed air bleed and/or fuel discharge port.

IDLE AIR CONTROL (IAC)

The IAC in a fuel injection system controls the air flow around the throttle plate by extending and retracting a bypass valve in the bypass port. The ECU controls the valve by sending voltage pulses called counts or steps to increase or decrease the bypass air flow, thus increasing and decreasing the idle speed.

FUEL INJECTOR

Throttle Body Type

The fuel injector is an electric solenoid controlled by the ECU. The ECU controls the injector by varying voltage pulse widths. When electrical current is supplied to the injector a spring loaded ball is lifted from its seat. This allows fuel to flow through spray orifices and deflects off the sharp edge of the injector nozzle. This action causes the fuel to form a 45° cone shaped spray pattern before entering the air stream in the throttle body.

Multiport Type

The fuel injector is an electric solenoid controlled by the ECU. The ECU controls the injector by varying voltage pulse widths. When electrical current is supplied to the injector, the armature and pintle move a short distance against a spring, opening a small orifice. Fuel is supplied to the inlet of the injector by the fuel pump, then passes through the injector,

around the pintle and out the orifice. Since the fuel is under high pressure, a fine spray is developed in the shape of a hollow cone. The injector, through this spraying action, atomizes the fuel and distributes it into the air entering the combustion chamber.

TORQUE CONVERTER CLUTCH (TCC) SOLENOID

The TCC solenoid is used on some automatic transmission, which allows for better fuel economy. When certain engine and vehicle speeds have been met, the ECU energizes the solenoid. This allows transmission fluid to flow into passages in the torque converter,

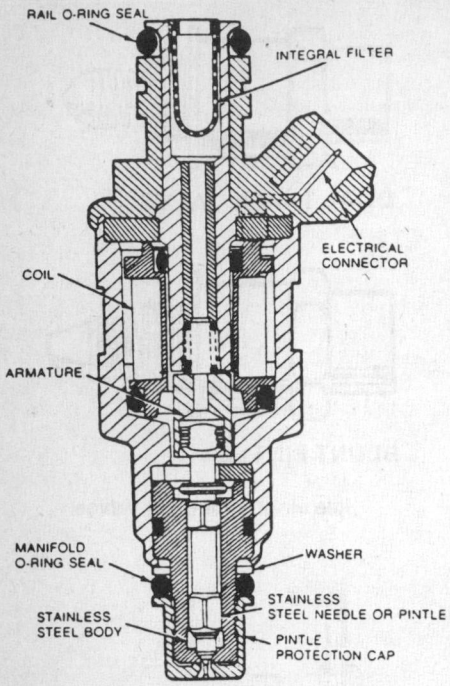

Fuel Injector—MFI type

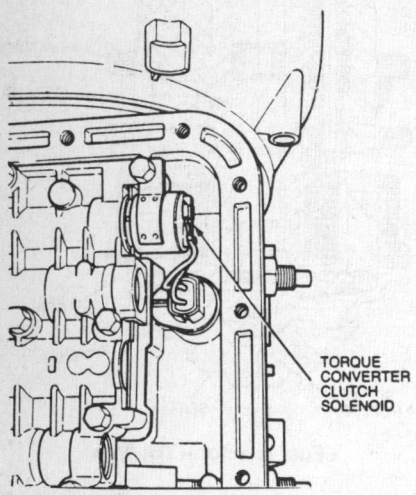

Torque converter clutch (TCC) solenoid

which causes the converter to lock up. This lockup is similar to a direct connection made possible in a manual transmission.

FUEL PUMP RELAY

The fuel is supplied under pressure, usually by an electric fuel pump. The ECU controls the fuel pump relay, which controls the fuel pump operation. When the ignition is switch ON, the fuel pump relay is energized and the fuel pump is activated. The pump primes the fuel system with fuel to a pre-determined pressure.

Engine Electronic Operations

IGNITION SYSTEM

The logic in a computerized system's program selects the method of spark timing control. During engine starting, spark timing is controlled by the mechanical setting of the distributor. Once the engine is running, spark timing is turned over to the ECU. This scheme ensures that the car will start regardless of whether the electronic control system is working or not.

The goal of electronic spark timing is to produce maximum engine power by adjustment the advance of the ignition firing in relationship to top dead center (TDC). The spark timing can be chosen to produce the best engine power with input variables of engine rpm, engine coolant temperature, initial and operating manifold or barometric pressure.

The total spark advance is determined by computing the information received from the various engine sensors which affect spark timing. The processor will then adjust the timing according to information that has been calibrated in it. The processor has programmed into it specific information on:

Warm-Up Spark Advance – this is used when the engine is cold, since a greater amount of advance is required while the engine warms up.

Special Spark Advance – to improve fuel economy during steady driving conditions.

Spark Advance Due to Barometric Pressure – this is used when barometric pressure exceeds a preset calibrated amount.

All of this information is then added together and the initial mechanical advance (if equipped) is subtracted to determine the final spark advance.

The processor receives a timing pulse from a sensor which indicates crankshaft position for top dead center and engines rpm. The processor makes a decision based upon this information and the information that was calibrated into it. at that time, the computer sends a pulse to the ignition actuator circuit which opens the ignition coil primary circuit to generate a secondary voltage pulse to fire the spark plugs. In some cases, the circuitry to open the primary of the coil may be in the computerized controller. The spark selection is performed mechanically by the distribu-

tor and rotor contacts as it is done in a non-electronic controlled system.

The ignition timing works along with electronic fuel control to control emissions and provide for optimum fuel economy and driveability because engine power, fuel economy and emissions are dependent on spark advance of the engine timing.

The system just described is considered to operate in open-loop. There are some electronically controlled ignition systems which receive an input from a knock sensor. These systems operate in a closed-loop mode which allows the ignition system to monitor the engine for mechanical changes, such as engine knock.

Engine knock is a condition where the air/fuel mixture in the cylinder does not burn normally. the pressure rise during this burning is so rapid compared to normal combustion that it is accompanied by an audible "knock".

Through some low level knock is acceptable, it is important to avoid excessive knock. To control engine knock, a knock sensor is installed in the engine or intake manifold. This helps to detect excessive engine knock.

The knock sensor is a tuned accelerometer and produces an output voltage depending on the amount of engine vibration occurring in a certain frequency band. When the processor receives a signal from the knock sensor, it retards the spark advance until the knocking stops and then starts increasing it again. This cycle is repeated as long as engine knock occurs.

FUEL CONTROL

In order for the processor to control fuel, it requires a sensor or sensors to monitor the state of the engine, and one or more actuators to do the actual controlling. The sensors measure: exhaust gas oxygen, manifold or barometric absolute pressure, engine rpm and speed, inlet air and coolant temperatures. Actuators are energized to control the air/fuel ratio.

The primary purpose of this control system is to maintain air/fuel ratio at or near 14.7:1 ratio. This is accomplished in two modes (during normal engine operation) open and closed loop. The electronic fuel control system can operate in closed loop only when certain conditions are satisfied. Open loop mode is employed whenever these conditions are not satisfied. However, for either mode, the exhaust emissions will satisfy federal requirements if the average air/fuel ratio is held within the tolerance limits.

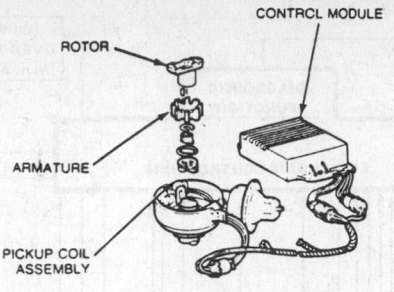

Electronic spark timing system

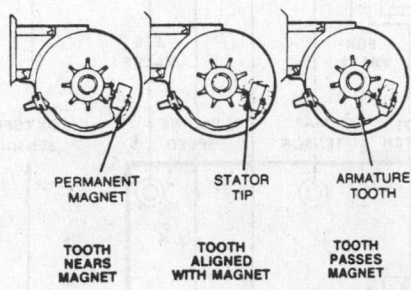

Solid state ignition system

Distributor pick-up coil and armature assembly

In addition to open and closed loop control modes, a practical fuel control system has other operating modes depending on engine conditions. These handle such conditions as starting, rapid acceleration or heavy load, sudden deceleration, idling, etc.

An automotive engine has various operating modes as the operating conditions change. Preprogrammed into the processor, control logic determines the operating mode from the engine conditions that exist. From these engine conditions, the system determines which operating modes are to be performed.

There are seven different engine operating modes which affect fuel control: engine crank, engine warmup, open loop, closed loop control, hard acceleration, deceleration and idle. The program for mode control logic determines the engine operating mode by reading various sensors.

When the ignition switch is initially switched on, the mode control logic automatically selects an engine-start control scheme which provides the low air/fuel ratio required for starting the engine. Once the engine rpm rises above the cranking value, the controller identifies the engine-started mode and passes control to the program for the engine warm-up mode. This operating mode keeps the air/fuel ratio low to prevent engine stall during cool weather until engine coolant temperature rises above a preset value.

When the coolant temperature rises, the mode control logic directs the system to operate in the open loop control mode until a certain time has elapsed and the exhaust gas sensor warms up enough to provide accurate readings. This condition is detected by monitoring the exhaust gas sensor's output for voltage readings above a certain minimum air/fuel mixture voltage set point. when the sensor has indicated a rich mixture a certain number of times (depending on calibration), and after the engine has been in open loop for a specific time, the control mode logic selects the closed loop mode for the system.

The engine remains in the closed loop mode until either the exhaust gas sensor cools and fails to switch (from rich to lean) for a certain length of time, or a hard acceleration or deceleration occurs. If the sensor cools, the control mode logic selects the open loop mode again.

During hard acceleration of heavy engine loads, the control mode logic chooses a scheme which provides a rich air/fuel mixture for the duration of the acceleration or heavy load. This scheme provides maximum power, but poor emissions control and poor fuel economy. After the need for enrichment has passed, control is returned to either open or closed loop depending on the control mode logic selection conditions that exist at that time.

During periods of deceleration, the air/fuel ratio is increased to reduce emissions of HC and CO due to unburned fuel. When idle conditions are present, control mode logic passes system control to the idle speed control mode. In this mode, the engine speed is controlled to reduce engine roughness and stalling which might occur because the idle load has changed due to air conditioner compressor operation, alternator operation, or gearshift positioning from PARK or NEUTRAL to DRIVE.

Engine Crank

While the engine is being cranked, the fuel control system must provide an intake air/fuel ratio anywhere from 2:1 to 12:1, depending on engine temperature. Low temperatures affect the carburetor's ability to atomize or mix the incoming air and fuel. At low temperature, the fuel tends to form into large droplets. The larger fuel droplets tend to increase the apparent air/fuel ratio because the amount of usable fuel in the air is reduced, therefore, the system must provide a decreased air/fuel ratio to provide the engine with a more combustible air/fuel mixture. The engine temperature is read by the processor through an analog to digital converter from a temperature sensor in the engine water coolant passage. The processor's calibration determines what the proper air/fuel ratio must be at that temperature. The air/fuel is determined and controlled as in the open loop mode.

Engine Warm-up

While the engine is warming up, an enriched air/fuel ratio is still needed to keep it running smoothly, but the required air/fuel ratio changes as the temperature increases. Therefore, the fuel control system will stay in the open loop mode, but the air/fuel ratio commands continue to be altered due to the temperature changes. The emphasis in this control mode is on rapid and smooth engine warm-up. Fuel economy and emission control are still a secondary concern. The controller determines the warm-up time period based on the coolant temperature when the warm-up mode was selected. Naturally, an initially cold engine requires a longer warm-up time than a warm engine. The time allowed by the controller timer is chosen according to the calibration of the processor.

OPEN LOOP CONTROL

Open loop fuel control is used when the engine has not reached a preset operating condition. This condition is sensed by various sensors located in and around the engine, and include engine coolant temperature, air charge temperature, engine time on, etc. After all these preset conditions are met, the system will go into closed loop. During certain operating conditions, such as a wide open throttle condition the system will go back into open loop.

CLOSED LOOP CONTROL

Closed loop fuel control is selected when the engine is warm and the exhaust gas oxygen sensor exceeds its minimum operating temperature. The intake air/fuel ratio is controlled in a closed loop by measuring the ex-

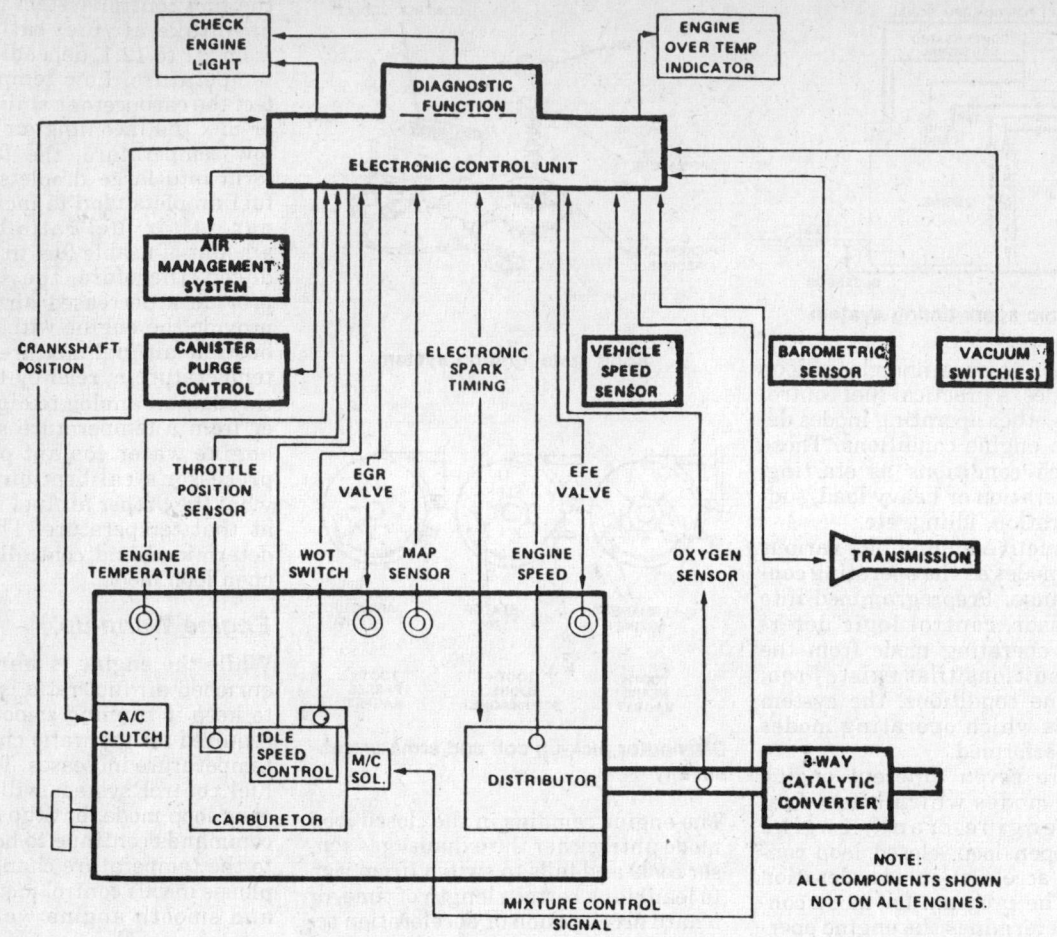

Typical electronic feedback carburetor system

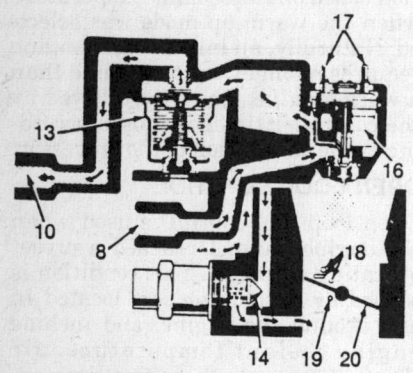

8 FUEL SUPPLY
10 FUEL RETURN
13 PRESSURE REGULATOR (PART OF FUEL METER COVER)
14 IDLE AIR CONTROL (IAC) VALVE (SHOWN OPEN)
16 FUEL INJECTOR
17 FUEL INJECTOR TERMINALS
18 PORTED VACUUM SOURCES*
19 MANIFOLD VACUUM SOURCE*
20 THROTTLE VALVE

*May Be Different on some Models.

Throttle body injection air and fuel flow

haust gas at the exhaust manifold and altering the input fuel flow rate or the air entering the main metering systems (depending on the type of fuel system used).

ACCELERATION ENRICHMENT (OPEN LOOP)

During periods of heavy engine load, such as wide open acceleration, fuel control is adjusted to provide an enriched ratio to maximize engine power while neglecting fuel economy and emission.

The computer detects this condition by reading the throttle position sensor voltage or the MAP sensor. Low intake manifold vacuum or throttle position corresponds to heavy engine loads. The fuel control system controller responds by increasing the amount of fuel to enter the intake manifold or to decrease the amount of air n the main metering system. This enrichment allows the engine to operate with a power greater than that allowed when emissions and fuel economy are controlled within specifications.

DECELERATION AND IDLE SPEED CONTROL (OPEN LOOP)

During periods of light engine load and high rpm, such as during closed throttle deceleration, coasting or engine idle, the engine requires a very lean air/fuel ratio to reduce excess emissions of HC and CO. Deceleration is indicated by a sudden increase in manifold vacuum and throttle position, indicating a closed throttle. When these conditions are detected by the processor, it computes a change in the amount of fuel required or amount of air entering the main or idle speed passages (depending on type of fuel system used). On certain engine engine applications which electronic fuel injection, the fuel may even be turned completely off during closed throttle deceleration.

Idle speed control is used to prevent engine stall during idle. The goal is to allow the engine to idle at as low an rpm as possible, yet keep the engine from running rough and stalling when power takeoff accessories such as air conditioning compressors are turned on.

Engine Rebuilding

This section describes, in detail, the procedures involved in rebuilding a typical engine. The procedures are basically identical to those used in rebuilding engines of nearly all design and configurations.

The section is divided into two parts. The first, Cylinder Head Reconditioning, assumes that the cylinder head is removed from the engine, all manifolds are removed, and the cylinder head is on a workbench. The camshaft should be removed from overhead cam cylinder heads. The second section, Cylinder Block Reconditioning, covers the block, pistons, connecting rods and crankshaft. It is assumed that the engine is mounted on a work stand, and the cylinder head and all accessories are removed.

Procedures are identified as follows:

Unmarked—Basic procedures that must be performed in order to successfully complete the rebuilding process.

Starred (*)—Procedures that should be performed to ensure maximum performance and engine life.

Double starred (**)—Procedures that may be performed to increase engine performance and reliability.

In many cases, a choice of methods is also provided. Methods are identified in the same manner as procedures. The choice of method for a procedure is at the discretion of the user.

The tools required for the basic rebuilding procedure should, with minor exceptions, be those included in a mechanic's tool kit. An accurate torque wrench, and a dial indicator (reading in thousandths) mounted on a universal base should be available. Special tools, where required, all are readily available from the major tool suppliers. The services of a competent automotive machine shop must also be readily available.

When assembling the engine, any parts that will be in frictional contact must be prelubricated, to provide protection on initial start-up. Any product specifically formulated for this purpose may be used. NOTE: *Do not use engine oil.* Where semi-permanent (locked but removable) installation of bolts or nuts is desired, threads should be cleaned and coated with Loctite® or a similar product (non-hardening).

Aluminum has become increasingly popular for use in engines, due to its low weight and excellent heat transfer characteristics. The following precautions must be observed when handling aluminum engine parts:

—Never hot-tank aluminum parts.

—Remove all aluminum parts (identification tags, etc.) from engine parts before hot-tanking (otherwise they will be removed during the process).

—Always coat threads lightly with engine oil or anti-seize compounds before installation, to prevent seizure.

—Never over-torque bolts or spark plugs in aluminum threads. Should stripping occur, threads can be restored using any of a number of thread repair kits available (see next section).

Magnaflux and Zyglo are inspection techniques used to locate material flaws, such as stress cracks. Magnafluxing coats the part with fine magnetic particles, and subjects the part to a magnetic field. Cracks cause breaks in the magnetic field, which are outlined by the particles. Since Magnaflux is a magnetic process, it is applicable only to ferrous materials. The Zyglo process coats the material with a fluorescent dye penetrant, and then subjects it to blacklight inspection, under which cracks glow brightly. Parts made of any material may be tested using Zyglo. While Magnaflux and Zyglo are excellent for general inspection, and locating hidden defects, specific checks of suspected cracks may be made at lower cost and more readily using spot check dye. The dye is sprayed onto the suspected area, wiped off, and the area is then sprayed with a developer. Cracks then will show up brightly. Spot check dyes will only indicate surface cracks; therefore, structural cracks below the surface may escape detection. When questionable, the part should be tested using Magnaflux or Zyglo.

REPAIRING DAMAGED THREADS

Several methods of repairing damaged threads are available. Heli-Coil® (shown here), Keenserts® and Microdot® are among the most widely used. All involve basically the same principle—drilling out stripped threads, tapping the hole and installing a prewound insert— making welding, plugging and oversize fasteners unnecessary.

Two types of thread repair inserts are usually supplied—a standard type for most Inch Coarse, Inch Fine, Metric Coarse and Metric Fine thread sizes and a spark plug type to fit most spark plug port sizes. Consult the individual manufacturer's catalog to determine exact applications. Typical thread repair kits will contain a selection of prewound threaded inserts, a tap (corresponding to the outside diameter threads of the insert) and an installation tool. Most manufacturers also supply blister-packed thread repair inserts separately and a master kit with a variety of taps and inserts plus installation tools.

Before effecting a repair to a threaded hole, remove any snapped, broken or damaged bolts or studs. Penetrating oil can be used to free frozen threads; the offending item can be removed with locking pliers or with a screw or stud extractor. After the hole is clear, the thread can be repaired as follows.

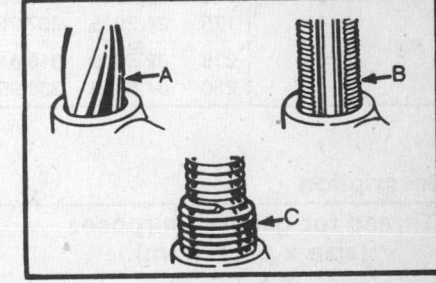

A. Drill out the damaged threads with the specified drill. Drill completely through the hole or to the bottom of a blind hole.

B. With the tap supplied tap the hole to receive the threaded insert. Keep the tap well oiled and back it out frequently to avoid clogging the threads.

C. Screw the threaded insert onto the installation tool until the tang engages the slot. Screw the insert into the tapped hole until it is ¼–½ turn below the top surface. After installation, break the tang off with a hammer and punch.

STANDARD TORQUE SPECIFICATIONS AND CAPSCREW MARKINGS

Newton-Meter has been designated as the world standard for measuring torque and will gradually replace the foot-pound and kilogram-meter torque measuring standard. Torquing tools are still being manufactured with foot-pounds and kilogram-meter scales, along with the new Newton-Meter standard. To assist the repairman, foot-pounds, kilogram-meter and Newton-Meter are listed in the following charts, and should be followed as applicable.

U.S. BOLTS

SAE Grade Number	1 or 2			5			6 or 7			8		
Capscrew Head Markings Manufacturer's marks may vary. Three-line markings on heads below indicate SAE Grade 5. 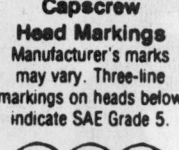	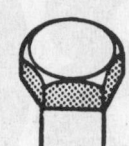											
Usage	Used Frequently			Used Frequently			Used at Times			Used at Times		
Quality of Material	Indeterminate			Minimum Commercial			Medium Commercial			Best Commercial		
Capacity Body Size	Torque			Torque			Torque			Torque		
(inches)–(thread)	Ft-Lb	kgm	Nm	Ft-Lb	kgm	Nm	Ft-Lb	kgm	Nm	Ft-Lb	kgm	Nm
1/4–20	5	0.6915	6.7791	8	1.1064	10.8465	10	1.3630	13.5582	12	1.6596	16.2698
–28	6	0.8298	8.1349	10	1.3830	13.5582				14	1.9362	18.9815
5/16–18	11	1.5213	14.9140	17	2.3511	23.0489	19	2.6277	25.7605	24	3.3192	32.5396
–24	13	1.7979	17.6256	19	2.6277	25.7605				27	3.7341	36.6071
3/8–16	18	2.4894	24.4047	31	4.2873	42.0304	34	4.7022	46.0978	44	6.0852	59.6560
–24	20	2.7660	27.1164	35	4.8405	47.4536				49	6.7767	66.4351
7/16–14	28	3.8132	37.9629	49	6.7767	66.4351	55	7.6065	74.5700	70	9.6810	94.9073
–20	30	4.1490	40.6745	55	7.6065	74.5700				78	10.7874	105.7538
1/2–13	39	5.3937	52.8769	75	10.3725	101.6863	85	11.7555	115.2445	105	14.5215	142.3609
–20	41	5.6703	55.5885	85	11.7555	115.2445				120	16.5860	162.6960
9/16–12	51	7.0533	69.1467	110	15.2130	149.1380	120	16.5960	162.6960	155	21.4365	210.1490
–18	55	7.6065	74.5700	120	16.5960	162.6960				170	23.5110	230.4860
5/8–11	83	11.4789	112.5329	150	20.7450	203.3700	167	23.0961	226.4186	210	29.0430	284.7180
–18	95	13.1385	128.8027	170	23.5110	230.4860				240	33.1920	325.3920
3/4–10	105	14.5215	142.3609	270	37.3410	366.0660	280	38.7240	379.6240	375	51.8625	508.4250
–16	115	15.9045	155.9170	295	40.7985	399.9610				420	58.0860	568.4360
7/8–9	160	22.1280	216.9280	395	54.6285	535.5410	440	60.8520	596.5520	605	83.6715	820.2590
–14	175	24.2025	237.2650	435	60.1605	589.7730				675	93.3525	915.1650
1–8	236	32.5005	318.6130	590	81.5970	799.9220	660	91.2780	894.8280	910	125.8530	1233.7780
–14	250	34.5750	338.9500	660	91.2780	849.8280				990	136.9170	1342.2420

METRIC BOLTS

Description Thread for general purposes (size x pitch (mm))	Torque ft-lbs. (Nm) Head Mark 4		Head Mark 7	
6 x 1.0	2.2 to 2.9	(3.0 to 3.9)	3.6 to 5.8	(4.9 to 7.8)
8 x 1.25	5.8 to 8.7	(7.9 to 12)	9.4 to 14	(13 to 19)
10 x 1.25	12 to 17	(16 to 23)	20 to 29	(27 to 39)
12 x 1.25	21 to 32	(29 to 43)	35 to 53	(47 to 72)
14 x 1.5	35 to 52	(48 to 70)	57 to 85	(77 to 110)
16 x 1.5	51 to 77	(67 to 100)	90 to 120	(130 to 160)
18 x 1.5	74 to 110	(100 to 150)	130 to 170	(180 to 230)
20 x 1.5	110 to 140	(150 to 190)	190 to 240	(160 to 320)
22 x 1.5	150 to 190	(200 to 260)	250 to 320	(340 to 430)
24 x 1.5	190 to 240	(260 to 320)	310 to 410	(420 to 550)

CAUTION: Bolts threaded into aluminum require much less torque

NOTE: This engine rebuilding section is a guide to accepted rebuilding procedures. Typical examples of standard rebuilding procedures are illustrated.

CYLINDER HEAD RECONDITIONING

Procedure	Method
Identify the valves:	Invert the cylinder head, and number the valve faces front to rear, using a permanent felt-tip marker.
Remove the rocker arms (OHV engines only):	Remove the rocker arms with shaft(s) or balls and nuts. Wire the sets of rockers, balls and nuts together, and identify according to the corresponding valve.
Remove the camshaft (OHC engines only):	See the engine service procedures earlier in this book for details concerning specific engines.
Remove the valves and springs:	Using an appropriate valve spring compressor (depending on the configuration of the cylinder head), compress the valve springs. Lift out the keepers with needlenose pliers, release the compressor, and remove the valve, spring, and spring retainer.
Remove glow plugs and fuel injectors (Diesel engines only):	Label and remove all fuel injectors and glow plugs from the head. Glow plugs unscrew. See the appropriate car section for injector removal. Inspect glow plugs for bulges, cracks or signs of melting. Clean injector tips with a steel brush, then inspect for evidence of melting.
**Remove pre-combustion chamber inserts (Diesel engines only): 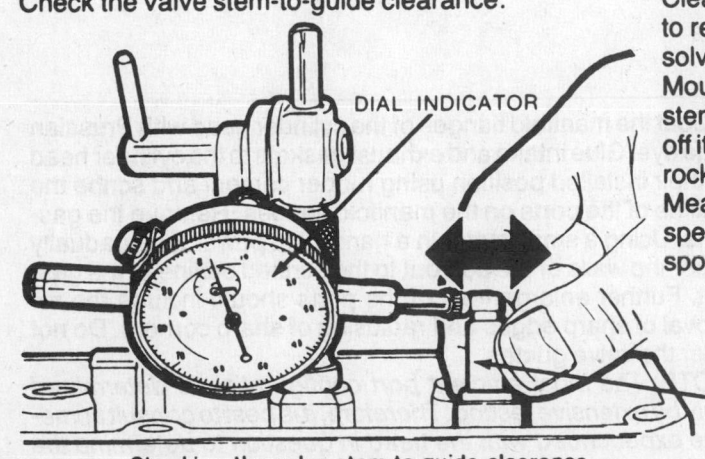	**Remove the pre-combustion chambers using a hammer and a thin, blunt brass drift, inserted through the injector hole (or glow plug hole, whichever is more convenient). If chamber is to be reused, carefully remove all carbon from it. NOTE: *Remove chamber only if being replaced, if a glow plug tip has broken off and must be removed, or if chamber is obviously damaged or loose.*

Removing pre-combustion chamber with a drift (© G.M. Corp.)

Check the valve stem-to-guide clearance:	Clean the valve stem with lacquer thinner or a similar solvent to remove all gum and varnish. Clean the valve guides using solvent and an expanding wire-type valve guide cleaner. Mount a dial indicator so that the stem is at 90° to the valve stem, as close to the valve guide as possible. Move the valve off its seat, and measure the valve guide-to-stem clearance by rocking the stem back and forth to actuate the dial indicator. Measure the valve stems using a micrometer, and compare to specifications, to determine whether stem or guide wear is responsible for excessive clearance.

DIAL INDICATOR

VALVE STEM

Checking the valve stem-to-guide clearance

CYLINDER HEAD RECONDITIONING

Procedure	Method
De-carbon the cylinder head and valves:	Chip carbon away from the valve heads, combustion chambers, and ports, using a chisel made of hardwood. Remove the remaining deposits with a stiff wire brush. NOTE: *Ensure that the deposits are actually removed, rather than burnished.*

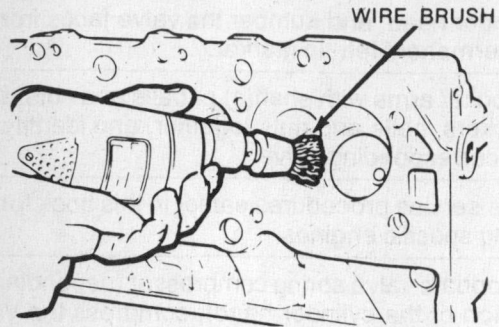

Removing carbon from the cylinder head

Procedure	Method
Hot-tank the cylinder head (cast iron heads only): CAUTION: *Do not hot-tank aluminum parts.*	Have the cylinder head hot-tanked to remove grease, corrosion, and scale from the water passages. NOTE: *In the case of overhead cam cylinder heads, consult the operator to determine whether the camshaft bearings will be damaged by the caustic solution.*
Degrease the remaining cylinder head parts:	Using solvent (i.e., Gunk), clean the rockers, rocker shaft(s) (where applicable), rocker balls and nuts, springs, spring retainers, and keepers. Do not remove the protective coating from the springs.
Check the cylinder head for warpage:	Place a straight-edge across the gasket surface of the cylinder head. Using feeler gauges, determine the clearance at the center of the straight-edge. Measure across both diagonals, along the longitudinal centerline, and across the cylinder head at several points. If warpage exceeds .003′ in a 6′ span, or .006′ over the total length, the cylinder head must be resurfaced. NOTE: *If warpage exceeds the manufacturer's maximum tolerance for material removal, the cylinder head must be replaced.* When milling the cylinder heads of V-type engines, the intake manifold mounting position is altered, and must be corrected by milling the manifold flange a proportionate amount.

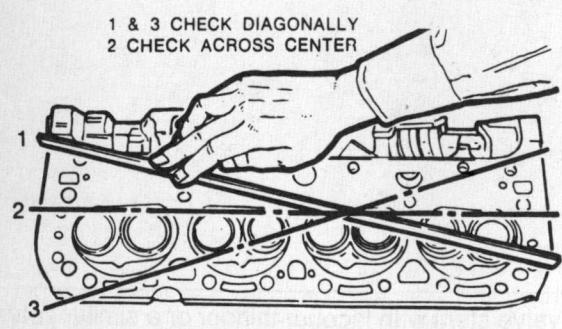

1 & 3 CHECK DIAGONALLY
2 CHECK ACROSS CENTER

Checking cylinder head for warpage

Procedure	Method
**Porting and gasket matching:	**Coat the manifold flanges of the cylinder head with Prussian blue dye. Glue intake and exhaust gaskets to the cylinder head in their installed position using rubber cement and scribe the outline of the ports on the manifold flanges. Remove the gaskets. Using a small cutter in a hand-held power tool gradually taper the walls of the port out to the scribed outline of the gasket. Further enlargement of the ports should include the removal of sharp edges and radiusing of sharp corners. Do not alter the valve guides. NOTE: *The most efficient port configuration is determined only by extensive testing. Therefore, it is best to consult someone experienced with the head in question to determine the optimum alterations.*

CYLINDER HEAD RECONDITIONING

Procedure	Method

*Knurling the valve guides:

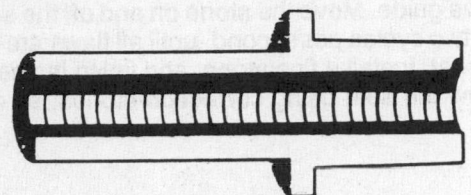

Cut-away view of a knurled valve guide

*Valve guides which are not excessively worn or distorted may, in some cases, be knurled rather than replaced. Knurling is a process in which metal is displaced and raised, thereby reducing clearance. Knurling also provides excellent oil control. The possibility of knurling rather than replacing valve guides should be discussed with a machinist.

Replacing the valve guides:
NOTE: *Valve guides should only be replaced if damaged or if an oversize valve stem is not available.*

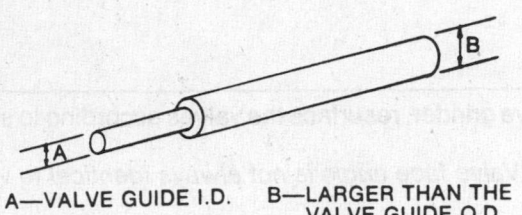

A—VALVE GUIDE I.D.   B—LARGER THAN THE VALVE GUIDE O.D.
Valve guide removal tool

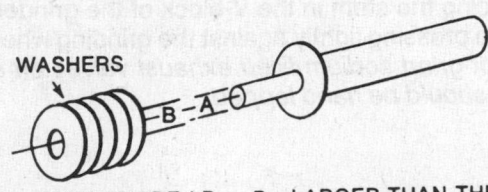

WASHERS

A—VALVE GUIDE I.D.   B—LARGER THAN THE VALVE GUIDE O.D.

Valve guide installation tool (with washers used for installation)

Depending on the type of cylinder head, valve guides may be pressed, hammered, or shrunk in. In cases where the guides are shrunk into the head, replacement should be left to an equipped machine shop. In other cases, the guides are replaced as follows: Press or tap the valve guides out of the head using a stepped drift (see illustration). Determine the height above the boss that the guide must extend, and obtain a stack of washers, their I.D. similar to the guide's O.D., of that height. Place the stack of washers on the guide, and insert the guide into the boss.
NOTE: *Valve guides are often tapered or beveled for installation.*
Using the stepped installation tool (see illustration), press or tap the guides into position. Ream the guides according to the size of the valve stem.

Replacing valve seat inserts:

Replacement of valve seat inserts which are worn beyond resurfacing or broken, if feasible, must be done by a machine shop.

Resurfacing the valve seats using reamers:

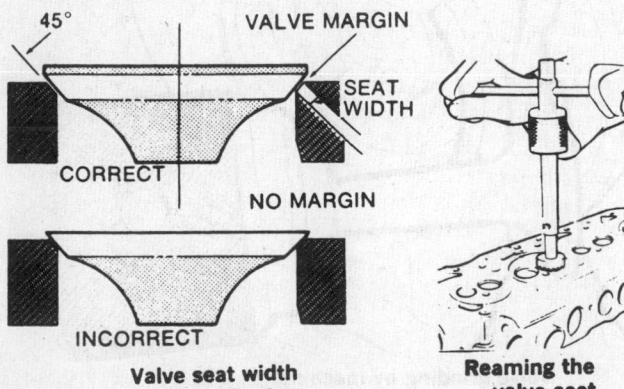

45°

VALVE MARGIN

SEAT WIDTH

CORRECT

NO MARGIN

INCORRECT

Valve seat width and centering

Reaming the valve seat

Select a reamer of the correct seat angle, slightly larger than the diameter of the valve seat, and assemble it with a pilot of the correct size. Install the pilot into the valve guide, and using steady pressure, turn the reamer clockwise.
CAUTION: *Do not turn the reamer counterclockwise.*
Remove only as much material as necessary to clean the seat. Check the concentricity of the seat (see below). If the dye method is not used, coat the valve face with Prussian blue dye, install and rotate it on the valve seat. Using the dye marked area as a centering guide, center and narrow the valve seat to specifications with correction cutters.
NOTE: *When no specifications are available, minimum seat width for exhaust valves should be 5/64", intake valves 1/16".*
After making correction cuts, check the position of the valve seat on the valve face using Prussian blue dye.
NOTE: *Do not cut induction hardened seats; they must be ground.*

CYLINDER HEAD RECONDITIONING

Procedure	Method

*Resurfacing the valve seats using a grinder:

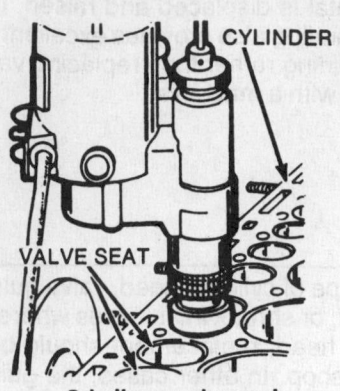

CYLINDER

VALVE SEAT

Grinding a valve seat

*Select a pilot of the correct size, and a coarse stone of the correct seat angle. Lubricate the pilot if necessary, and install the tool in the valve guide. Move the stone on and off the seat at approximately two cycles per second, until all flaws are removed from the seat. Install a fine stone, and finish the seat. Center and narrow the seat using correction stones, as described above.

Resurfacing (grinding) the valve face:

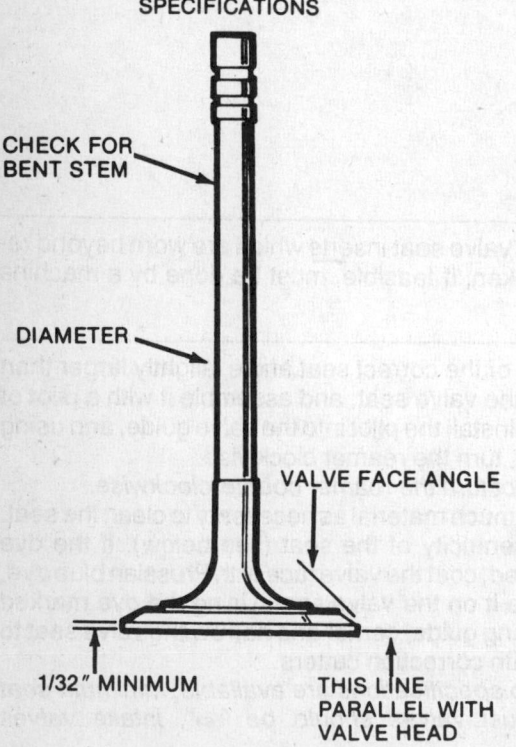

FOR DIMENSIONS,
REFER TO
SPECIFICATIONS

CHECK FOR
BENT STEM

DIAMETER

VALVE FACE ANGLE

1/32" MINIMUM

THIS LINE
PARALLEL WITH
VALVE HEAD

Critical valve dimensions

Using a valve grinder, resurface the valves according to specifications.
CAUTION: *Valve face angle is not always identical to valve seat angle.*
A minimum margin of 1/32" should remain after grinding the valve. The valve stem top should also be squared and resurfaced, by placing the stem in the V-block of the grinder, and turning it while pressing lightly against the grinding wheel.
NOTE: *Do not grind sodium filled exhaust valves on a machine. These should be hand lapped.*

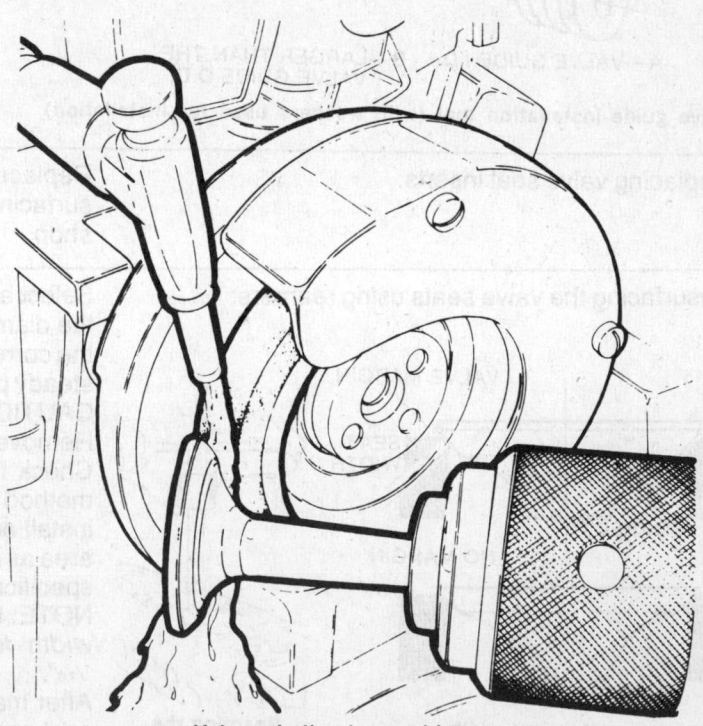

Valve grinding by machine

CYLINDER HEAD RECONDITIONING

Procedure	Method

Checking the valve seat concentricity:

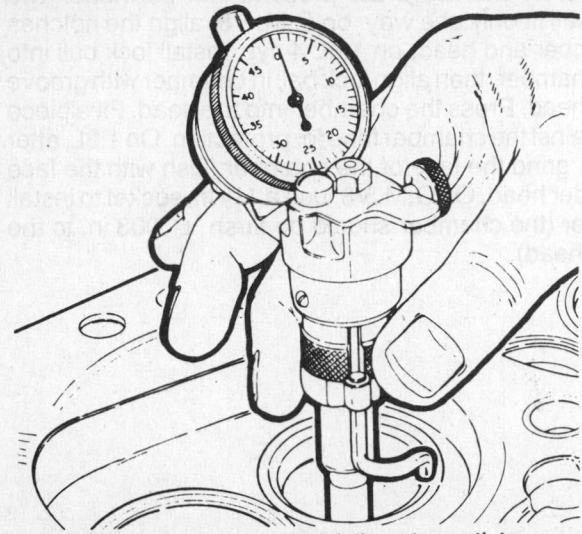

Checking valve seat concentricity using a dial gauge

Coat the valve face with Prussian blue dye, install the valve, and rotate it on the valve seat. If the entire seat becomes coated, and the valve is known to be concentric, the seat is concentric.
*Install the dial gauge pilot into the guide, and rest the arm on the valve seat. Zero the gauge, and rotate the arm around the seat. Run-out should not exceed .002″.

---

*Lapping the valves:
NOTE: *Valve lapping is done to ensure efficient sealing of resurfaced valves and seats.*

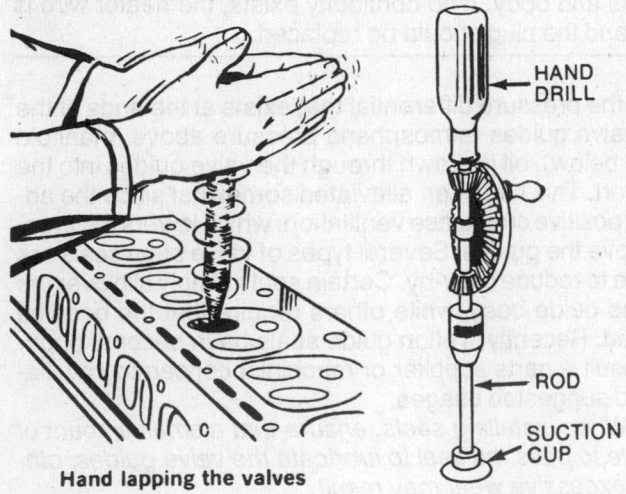

Home made mechanical valve lapping tool

Hand lapping the valves

*Invert the cylinder head, lightly lubricate the valve stems, and install the valves in the head as numbered. Coat valve seats with fine grinding compound, and attach the lapping tool suction cup to a valve head.
NOTE: *Moisten the suction cup.*
Rotate the tool between the palms, changing position and lifting the tool often to prevent grooving. Lap the valve until a smooth, polished seat is evident. Remove the valve and tool, and rinse away all traces of grinding compound.
**Fasten a suction cup to a piece of drill rod, and mount the rod in a hand drill. Proceed as above, using the hand drill as a lapping tool.
CAUTION: *Due to the higher speeds involved when using the hand drill, care must be exercised to avoid grooving the seat.* Lift the tool and change direction of rotation often.

Check the valve springs:

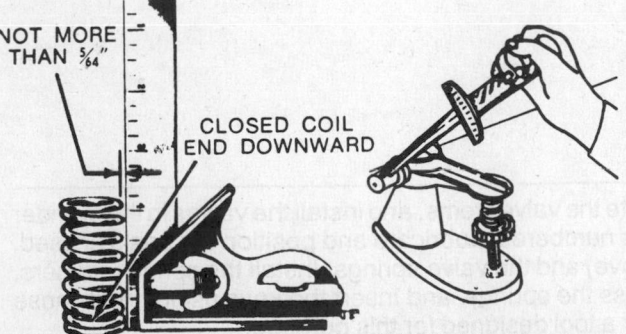

Checking valve spring free length and squareness

Measuring valve spring test pressure

Place the spring on a flat surface next to a square. Measure the height of the spring, and rotate it against the edge of the square to measure distortion. If spring height varies (by comparison) by more than 1/16″ or if distortion exceeds 1/16″, replace the spring.
**In addition to evaluating the spring as above, test the spring pressure at the installed and compressed (installed height minus valve lift) height using a valve spring tester. Springs used on small displacement engines (up to 3 liters) should be ∓ 1 lb. of all other springs in either position. A tolerance of ∓ 5 lbs. is permissible on larger engines.

CYLINDER HEAD RECONDITIONING

Procedure	Method

Install pre-combustion chambers (Diesel engines only)

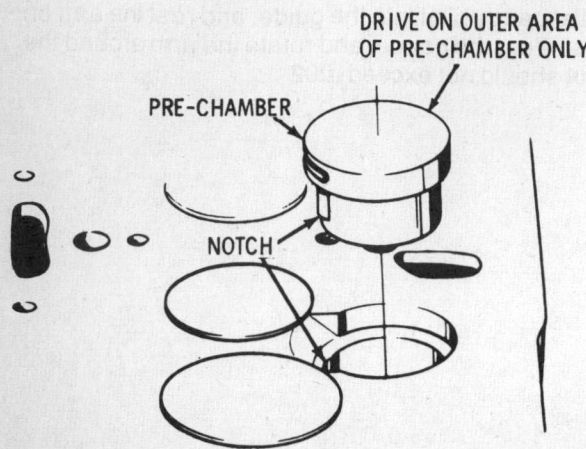

DRIVE ON OUTER AREA OF PRE-CHAMBER ONLY

PRE-CHAMBER

NOTCH

Align the notches to install the pre-combustion chamber
(© G.M. Corp.)

Pre-combustion chambers are press-fit into the head. The chambers will fit only one way: on G.M. V8, align the notches in the chamber and head; on 1.8L 4 cyl., install lock ball into groove in chamber, then align lock ball in chamber with groove in cylinder head. Press the chamber into the head. Fit a piece of metal against the chamber face for protection. On 1.8L, after installation, grind the face of the chamber flush with the face of the cylinder head. On G.M. V8, use a 1¼ in. socket to install the chamber (the chamber should be flush ± .003 in. to the face of the head).

Install fuel injectors and glow plugs (Diesel engines)

Before installing glow plugs, check for continuity across plug terminals and body. If no continuity exists, the heater wire is broken and the plug should be replaced.

---

*Install valve stem seals:

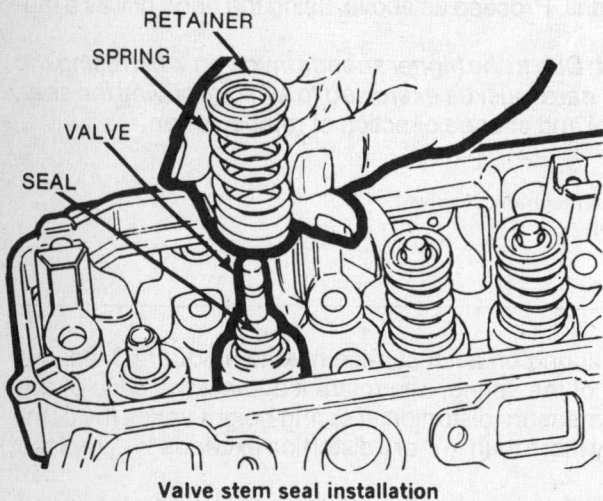

RETAINER

SPRING

VALVE

SEAL

Valve stem seal installation

*Due to the pressure differential that exists at the ends of the intake valve guides (atmospheric pressure above, manifold vacuum below), oil is drawn through the valve guides into the intake port. This has been alleviated somewhat since the addition of positive crankcase ventilation, which lowers the pressure above the guides. Several types of valve stem seals are available to reduce blow-by. Certain seals simply slip over the stem and guide boss, while others require that the boss be machined. Recently, Teflon guide seals have become popular. Consult a parts supplier or machinist concerning availability and suggested usages.

NOTE: *When installing seals, ensure that a small amount of oil is able to pass the seal to lubricate the valve guides; otherwise, excessive wear may result.*

Install the valves:

Lubricate the valve stems, and install the valves in the cylinder head as numbered. Lubricate and position the seals (if used, see above) and the valve springs. Install the spring retainers, compress the springs, and insert the keys using needlenose pliers or a tool designed for this purpose.

NOTE: *Retain the keys with wheel bearing grease during installation.*

CYLINDER HEAD RECONDITIONING

Procedure	Method

Check valve spring installed height:

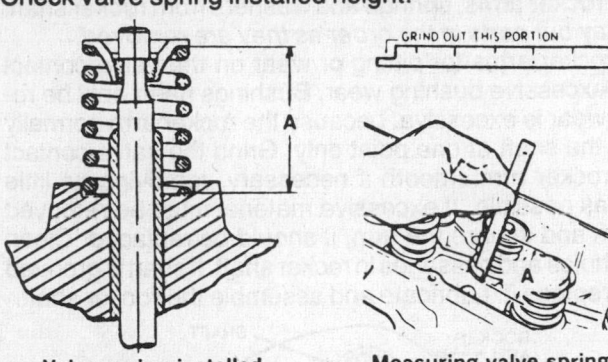

Valve spring installed
height dimension

Measuring valve spring
installed height

Measure the distance between the spring pad and the lower edge of the spring retainer, and compare to specifications. If the installed height is incorrect, add shim washers between the spring pad and the spring.
CAUTION: *Use only washers designed for this purpose.*

Install the camshaft (OHC engines only) and check end play:

See the engine service procedures earlier in this book for details concerning specific engines.

Inspect the rocker arms, balls, studs, and nuts (OHV engines only):

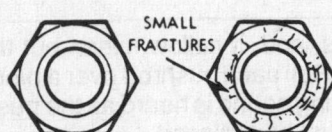

Stress cracks in the rocker nuts

Visually inspect the rocker arms, balls, studs, and nuts for cracks, galling, burning, scoring or wear. If all parts are intact, liberally lubricate the rocker arms and balls, and install them on the cylinder head. If wear is noted on a rocker arm at the point of valve contact, grind it smooth and square, removing as little material as possible. Replace the rocker arm if excessively worn. If a rocker stud shows signs of wear, it must be replaced (see below). If a rocker nut shows stress cracks, replace it. If an exhaust ball is galled or burned, substitute the intake ball from the same cylinder (if it is intact), and install a new intake ball.
NOTE: *Avoid using new rocker balls on exhaust valves.*

Replacing rocker studs (OHV engines only):

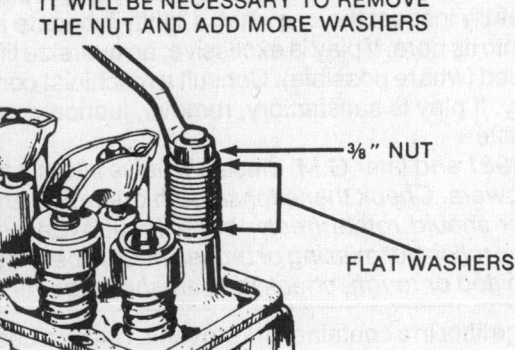

AS STUB BEGINS TO PULL UP,
IT WILL BE NECESSARY TO REMOVE
THE NUT AND ADD MORE WASHERS

3/8" NUT

FLAT WASHERS

Extracting a pressed-in rocker stud

In order to remove a threaded stud, lock two nuts on the stud, and unscrew the stud using the lower nut. Coat the lower threads of the new stud with Loctite®, and install.
Two alternative methods are available for replacing pressed in studs. Remove the damaged stud using a stack of washers and a nut (see illustration). In the first, the boss is reamed .005–.006" oversize, and an oversize stud pressed in. Control the stud extension over the boss using washers, in the same manner as valve guides. Before installing the stud, coat it with white lead and grease. To retain the stud more positively drill a hole through the stud and boss, and install a roll pin. In the second method, the boss is tapped, and a threaded stud installed. Retain the stud using Loctite® Stud and Bearing Mount.

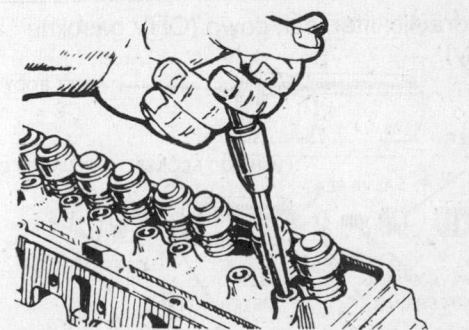

Reaming the stud bore for oversize rocker studs

CYLINDER HEAD RECONDITIONING

Procedure	Method

Inspect the rocker shaft(s) and rocker arms (OHV engines only):

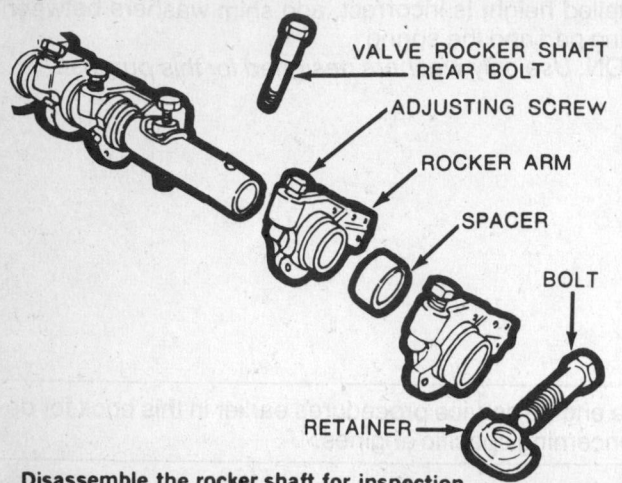

- VALVE ROCKER SHAFT REAR BOLT
- ADJUSTING SCREW
- ROCKER ARM
- SPACER
- BOLT
- RETAINER

Disassemble the rocker shaft for inspection

Remove rocker arms, springs and washers from rocker shaft. NOTE: *Lay out parts in the order as they are removed.*
Inspect rocker arms for pitting or wear on the valve contact point, or excessive bushing wear. Bushings need only be replaced if wear is excessive, because the rocker arm normally contacts the shaft at one point only. Grind the valve contact point of rocker arm smooth if necessary, removing as little material as possible. If excessive material must be removed to smooth and square the arm, it should be replaced. Clean out all oil holes and passages in rocker shaft. If shaft is grooved or worn, replace it. Lubricate and assemble the rocker shaft.

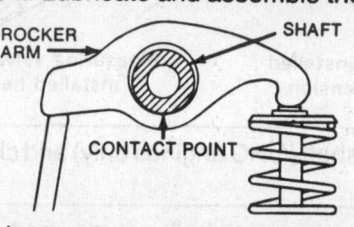

- ROCKER ARM
- SHAFT
- CONTACT POINT

Rocker arm-to-rocker shaft contact area

Inspect the camshaft bushings and the camshaft (OHC engines):

See next section.

Inspect the pushrods (OHV engines only):

Remove the pushrods, and, if hollow, clean out the oil passages using fine wire. Roll each pushrod over a piece of clean glass. If a distinct clicking sound is heard as the pushrod rolls, the rod is bent, and must be replaced.

*The length of all pushrods must be equal. Measure the length of the pushrods, compare to specifications, and replace as necessary.

Inspect the valve lifters (OHV engines only):

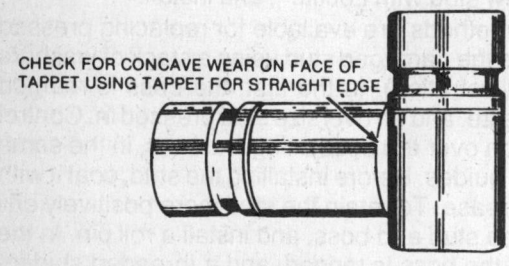

CHECK FOR CONCAVE WEAR ON FACE OF TAPPET USING TAPPET FOR STRAIGHT EDGE

Checking the lifter face

Remove lifters from their bores, and remove gum and varnish, using solvent. Clean walls of lifter bores. Check lifters for concave wear as illustrated. If face is worn concave, replace lifter, and carefully inspect the camshaft. Lightly lubricate lifter and insert it into its bore. If play is excessive, an oversize lifter must be installed (where possible). Consult a machinist concerning feasibility. If play is satisfactory, remove, lubricate, and reinstall the lifter.
NOTE: *1981 and later G.M. diesel V8 valve lifters have roller cam followers. Check these for smooth operation and wear. The roller should rotate freely, but without excessive play. Check the rollers for missing or broken needle bearings. If the roller is pitted or rough, check the camshaft lobe for wear.*

*Testing hydraulic lifter leak down (OHV gasoline engines only):

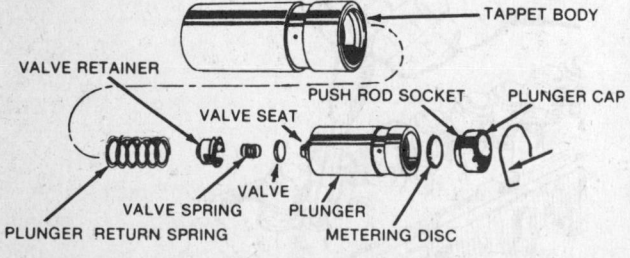

- TAPPET BODY
- VALVE RETAINER
- PUSH ROD SOCKET
- PLUNGER CAP
- VALVE SEAT
- VALVE
- PLUNGER
- METERING DISC
- VALVE SPRING
- PLUNGER RETURN SPRING

Typical exploded view of hydraulic valve lifter

Submerge lifter in a container of kerosene. Chuck a used pushrod or its equivalent into a drill press. Position container of kerosene so pushrod acts on the lifter plunger. Pump lifter with the drill press, until resistance increases. Pump several more times to bleed any air out of lifter. Apply very firm, constant pressure to the lifter, and observe rate at which fluid bleeds out of lifter. If the fluid bleeds very quickly (less than 15 seconds), lifter is defective. If the time exceeds 60 seconds, lifter is sticking. In either case, recondition or replace lifter. If lifter is operating properly (leak down time 15–60 seconds), lubricate and install it.

CYLINDER HEAD RECONDITIONING

Procedure	Method
Bleed the hydraulic lifters (diesel engines only):	After the cylinder heads are installed on G.M. V8 diesels, the valve lifters must be bled down before the crankshaft is turned. Failure to bleed down the lifters will cause damage to the valve train. See diesel engine rocker arm replacement procedure in Oldsmobile 88, 98, etc. car section for procedures. NOTE: *When installing new lifters, prime by working the lifter plunger while submerged in clean kerosene or diesel fuel.*

CYLINDER BLOCK RECONDITIONING

Procedure	Method
Checking the main bearing clearance: 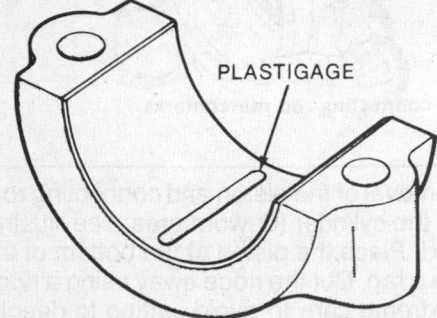 **Plastigage® installed on the lower bearing shell** 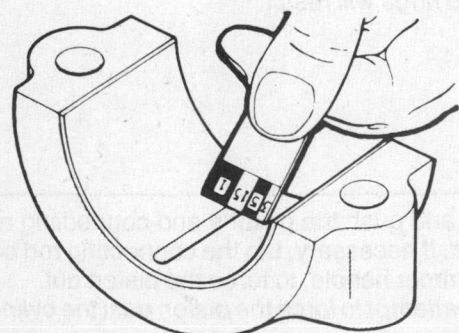 **Measuring Plastigage® to determine bearing clearance**	Invert engine, and remove cap from the bearing to be checked. Using a clean, dry rag, thoroughly clean all oil from crankshaft journal and bearing insert. NOTE: *Plastigage is soluble in oil; therefore, oil on the journal or bearing could result in erroneous readings.* Place a piece of Plastigage along the full length of journal, reinstall cap, and torque to specifications. Remove bearing cap, and determine bearing clearance by comparing width of Plastigage to the scale on Plastigage envelope. Journal taper is determined by comparing width of the Plastigage strip near its ends. Rotate crankshaft 90° and retest, to determine journal eccentricity. NOTE: *Do not rotate crankshaft with Plastigage installed.* If bearing insert and journal appear intact, and are within tolerances, no further main bearing service is required. If bearing or journal appear defective, cause of failure should be determined before replacement. *Remove crankshaft from block (see below). Measure the main bearing journals at each end twice (90° apart) using a micrometer, to determine diameter, journal taper and eccentricity. If journals are within tolerances, reinstall bearing caps at their specified torque. Using a telescope gauge and micrometer, measure bearing I.D. parallel to piston axis and at 30° on each side of piston axis. Subtract journal O.D. from bearing I.D. to determine oil clearance. If crankshaft journals appear defective, or do no meet tolerances, there is no need to measure bearings; for the crankshaft will require grinding and/or undersize bearings will be required. If bearing appears defective, cause for failure should be determined prior to replacement.
Checking the connecting rod bearing clearance:	Connecting rod bearing clearance is checked in the same manner as main bearing clearance, using Plastigage. Before removing the crankshaft, connecting rod side clearance also should be measured and recorded. *Checking connecting rod bearing clearance, using a micrometer, is identical to checking main bearing clearance. If no other service is required, the piston and rod assemblies need not be removed.

CYLINDER BLOCK RECONDITIONING

Procedure	Method

Removing the crankshaft:

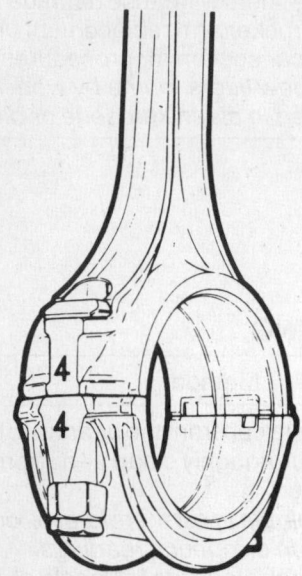

Connecting rod matched to cylinder with a number stamp

Using a punch, mark the corresponding main bearing caps and saddles according to position (i.e., one punch on the front main cap and saddle, two on the second, three on the third, etc.). Using number stamps, identify the corresponding connecting rods and caps, according to cylinder (if no numbers are present). Remove the main and connecting rod caps, and place sleeves of plastic tubing over the connecting rod bolts, to protect the journals as the crankshaft is removed. Lift the crankshaft out of the block.

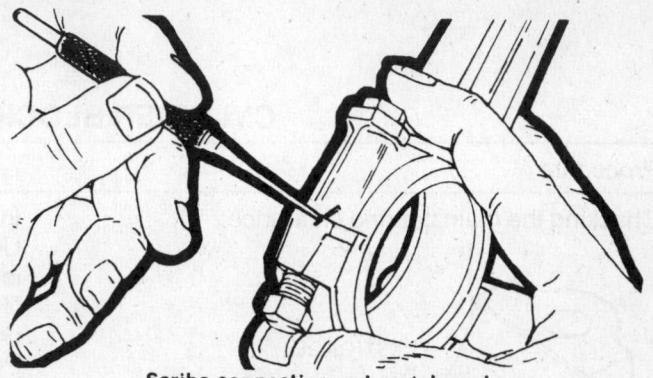

Scribe connecting rod matchmarks

Remove the ridge from the top of the cylinder:

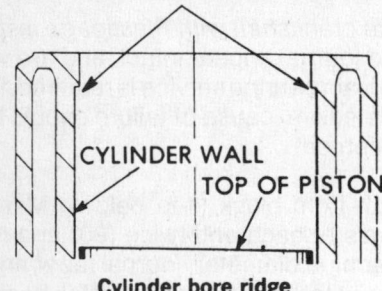

RIDGE CAUSED BY CYLINDER WEAR

CYLINDER WALL
TOP OF PISTON

Cylinder bore ridge

In order to facilitate removal of the piston and connecting rod, the ridge at the top of the cylinder (unworn area; see illustration) must be removed. Place the piston at the bottom of the bore, and cover it with a rag. Cut the ridge away using a ridge reamer, exercising extreme care to avoid cutting to deeply. Remove the rag, and remove cuttings that remain on the piston.
CAUTION: *If the ridge is not removed, and new rings are installed, damage to rings will result.*

Removing the piston and connecting rod:

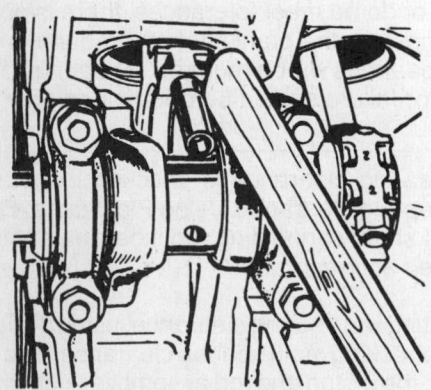

Removing the piston

Invert the engine, and push the pistons and connecting rods out of the cylinders. If necessary, tap the connecting rod boss with a wooden hammer handle, to force the piston out.
CAUTION: *Do not attempt to force the piston past the cylinder ridge* (see above).

CYLINDER BLOCK RECONDITIONING

Procedure	Method
Service the crankshaft:	Ensure that all oil holes and passages in the crankshaft are open and free of sludge. If necessary, have the crankshaft ground to the largest possible undersize. **Have the crankshaft Magnafluxed, to locate stress cracks. Consult a machinist concerning additional service procedures, such as surface hardening (e.g., nitriding, Tuftriding) to improve wear characteristics, cross drilling and chamfering the oil holes to improve lubrication, and balancing.
Removing freeze plugs:	Drill a small hole in the middle of the freeze plugs. Thread a large sheet metal screw into the hole and remove the plug with a slide hammer.
Remove the oil gallery plugs:	Threaded plugs should be removed using an appropriate (usually square) wrench. To remove soft, pressed in plugs, drill a hole in the plug, and thread in a sheet metal screw. Pull the plug out by the screw using pliers.
Hot-tank the block: NOTE: *Do not hot-tank aluminum parts.*	Have the block hot-tanked to remove grease, corrosion, and scale from the water jackets. NOTE: *Consult the operator to determine whether the camshaft bearings will be damaged during the hot-tank process.*

Check the block for cracks:	Visually inspect the block for cracks or chips. The most common locations are as follows:
	    Adjacent to freeze plugs.
	    Between the cylinders and water jackets.
	    Adjacent to the main bearing saddles.
	    At the extreme bottom of the cylinders.
	Check only suspected cracks using spot check dye (see introduction). If a crack is located, consult a machinist concerning possible repairs.
	
	**Magnaflux the block to locate hidden cracks. If cracks are located, consult a machinist about feasibility of repair.

Install the oil gallery plugs and freeze plugs:	Coat freeze plugs with sealer and tap into position using a piece of pipe, slightly smaller than the plug, as a driver. To ensure retention, stake the edges of the plugs. Coat threaded oil gallery plugs with sealer and install. Drive replacement soft plugs into block using a large drift as a driver. *Rather than reinstalling lead plugs, drill and tap the holes, and install threaded plugs.
*Check the deck height:	*The deck height is the distance from the crankshaft centerline to the block deck. To measure, invert the engine, and install the crankshaft, retaining it with the center main cap. Measure the distance from the crankshaft journal to the block deck, parallel to the cylinder centerline. Measure the diameter of the end (front and rear) main journals, parallel to the centerline of the cylinders, divide the diameter in half, and subtract it from the previous measurement. The results of the front and rear measurements should be identical. If the difference exceeds .005″, the deck height should be corrected. NOTE: *Block deck height and warpage should be corrected at the same time.*

CYLINDER BLOCK RECONDITIONING

Procedure	Method

Check the block deck for warpage:

Using a straightedge and feeler gauges, check the block deck for warpage in the same manner that the cylinder head is checked (see Cylinder Head Reconditioning). If warpage exceeds specifications, have the deck resurfaced.
NOTE: *In certain cases a specification for total material removal (Cylinder head and block deck) is provided. This specification must not be exceeded.*

Check the bore diameter and surface:

Visually inspect the cylinder bores for roughness, scoring, or scuffing. If evident, the cylinder bore must be bored or honed oversize to eliminate imperfections, and the smallest possible oversize piston used. The new pistons should be given to the machinist with the block, so that the cylinders can be bored or honed exactly to the piston size (plus clearance). If no flaws are evident, measure the bore diameter using a telescope gauge and micrometer, or dial guage, parallel and perpendicular to the engine centerline, at the top (below the ridge) and bottom of the bore. Subtract the bottom measurements from the top to determine taper, and the parallel to the centerline measurements from the perpendicular measurements to determine eccentricity. If the measurements are not within specifications, the cylinder must be bored or honed, and an oversize piston installed. If the measurements are within specifications the cylinder may be used as is, with only finish honing (see below).
NOTE: *Prior to boring, check the block deck warpage, height and bearing alignment.*
CAUTION: *The 4 cyl. 140 G.M. engine cylinder walls are impregnated with silicone. Boring or honing can be done only by a shop with the proper equipment.*

Measuring the cylinder bore with a dial gauge

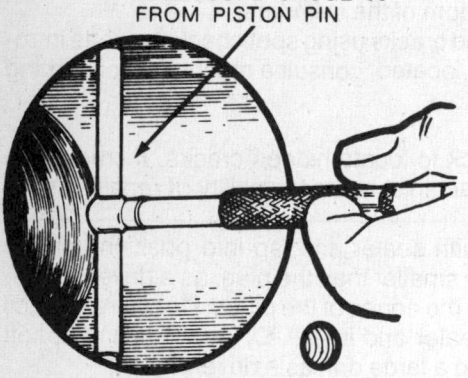

TELESCOPE GAUGE 90° FROM PISTON PIN

Measuring cylinder bore with a telescope gauge

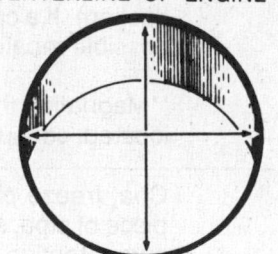

←— CENTERLINE OF ENGINE —→

A—AT RIGHT ANGLE TO CENTERLINE OF ENGINE
B—PARALLEL TO CENTERLINE OF ENGINE
Cylinder bore measuring points

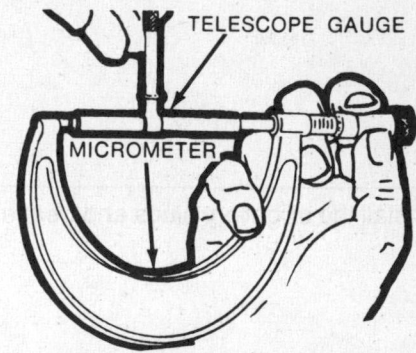

TELESCOPE GAUGE

MICROMETER

Determining cylinder bore by measuring telescope gauge with a micrometer

Check the cylinder block bearing alignment:

Remove the upper bearing inserts. Place a straightedge in the bearing saddles along the centerline of the crankshaft. If clearance exists between the straightedge and the center saddle, the block must be alignbored.

Checking main bearing saddle alignment

CYLINDER BLOCK RECONDITIONING

Procedure	Method

Clean and inspect the pistons and connecting rods:

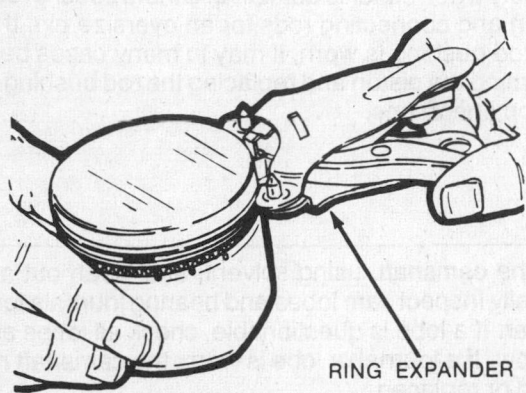

RING EXPANDER

Removing the piston rings

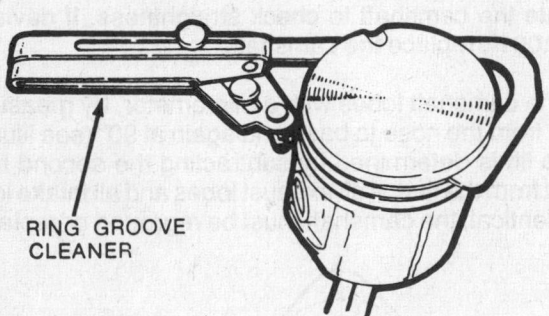

RING GROOVE CLEANER

Cleaning the piston ring grooves

Using a ring expander, remove the rings from the piston. Remove the retaining rings (if so equipped) and remove piston pin.
NOTE: *If the piston pin must be pressed out, determine the proper method and use the proper tools; otherwise the piston will distort.*
Clean the ring grooves using an appropriate tool, exercising care to avoid cutting too deeply. Thoroughly clean all carbon and varnish from the piston with solvent.
CAUTION: *Do not use a wire brush or caustic solvent on pistons.*
Inspect the pistons for scuffing, scoring, cracks, pitting, or excessive ring groove wear. If wear is evident, the piston must be replaced. Check the connecting rod length by measuring the rod from the inside of the large end to the inside of the small end using calipers (see illustration). All connecting rods should be equal length. Replace any rod that differs from the others in the engine.

*Have the connecting rod alignment checked in an alignment fixture by a machinist. Replace any twisted or bent rods.

*Magnaflux the connecting rods to locate stress cracks. If cracks are found, replace the connecting rod.

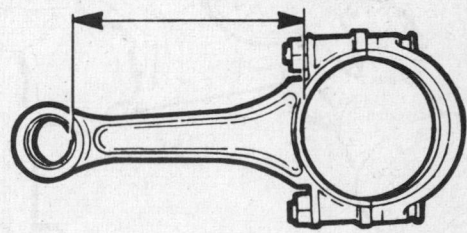

Check the connecting rod length (arrow)

Fit the pistons to the cylinders:

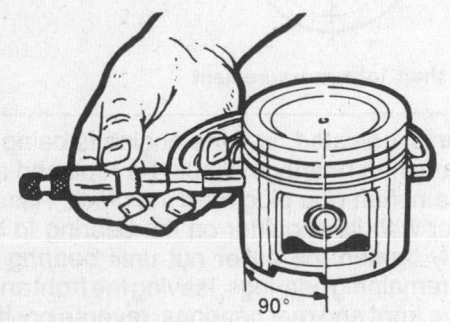

90°

Measuring the piston prior to fitting

Using a telescope gauge and micrometer, or a dial gauge, measure the cylinder bore diameter perpendicular to the piston pin, 2½° below the deck. Measure the piston perpendicular to its pin on the skirt. The difference between the two measurements is the piston clearance. If the clearance is within specifications or slightly below (after boring or honing), finish honing is all that is required. If the clearance is excessive, try to obtain a slightly larger piston to bring clearance within specifications. Where this is not possible, obtain the first oversize piston, and hone (or if necessary, bore) the cylinder to size.

Assemble the pistons and connecting rods:

Inspect piston pin, connecting rod small end bushing, and piston bore for galling, scoring, or excessive wear. If evident, replace defective part(s). Measure the I.D. of the piston boss and connecting rod small end, and the O.D. of the piston pin. If within specifications, assemble piston pin and rod.
CAUTION: *If piston pin must be pressed in, determine the proper method and use the proper tools; otherwise the piston will distort.*

CYLINDER BLOCK RECONDITIONING

Procedure	Method

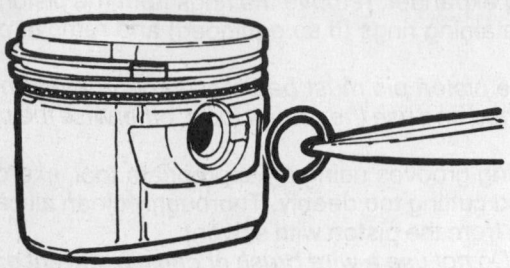

Installing piston pin lock rings

Install the lock rings; ensure that they seat properly. If the parts are not within specifications, determine the service method for the type of engine. In some cases, piston and pin are serviced as an assembly when either is defective. Others specify reaming the piston and connecting rods for an oversize pin. If the connecting rod bushing is worn, it may in many cases be replaced. Reaming the piston and replacing the rod bushing are machine shop operations.

Clean and inspect the camshaft:

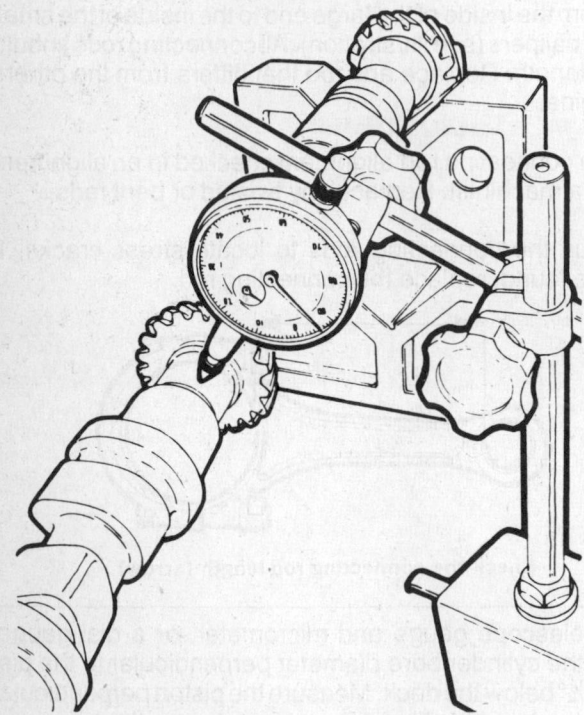

Checking the camshaft for straightness

Degrease the camshaft, using solvent, and clean out all oil holes. Visually inspect cam lobes and bearing journals for excessive wear. If a lobe is questionable, check all lobes as indicated below. If a journal or lobe is worn, the camshaft must be reground or replaced.

NOTE: *If a journal is worn, there is a good chance that the bushings are worn.*

If lobes and journals appear intact, place the front and rear journals in V-blocks, and rest a dial indicator on the center journal. Rotate the camshaft to check straightness. If deviation exceeds .001°, replace the camshaft.

*Check the camshaft lobes with a micrometer, by measuring the lobes from the nose to base and again at 90° (see illustration). The lift is determined by subtracting the second measurement from the first. If all exhaust lobes and all intake lobes are not identical, the camshaft must be reground or replaced.

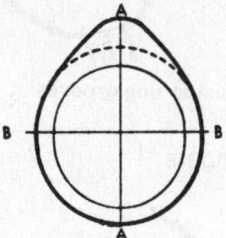

Camshaft lobe measurement

Replace the camshaft bearings (OHV engines only):

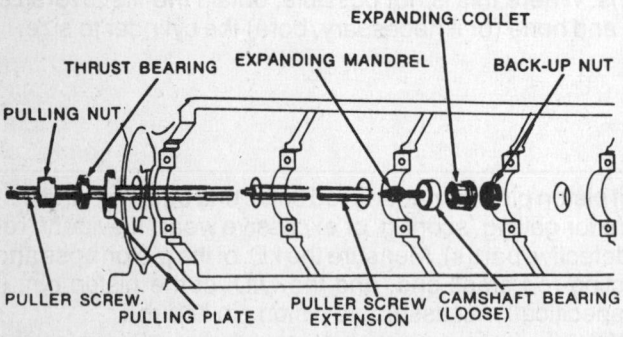

Camshaft removal and installation tool (typical)

If excessive wear is indicated, or if the engine is being completely rebuilt, camshaft bearings should be replaced as follows: Drive the camshaft rear plug from the block. Assemble the removal puller with its shoulder on the bearing to be removed. Gradually tighten the puller nut until bearing is removed. Remove remaining bearings, leaving the front and rear for last. To remove front and rear bearings, reverse position of the tool, so as to pull the bearings in toward the center of the block. Leave the tool in this position, pilot the new front and rear bearings on the installer, and pull them into position: Return the tool to its original position and pull remaining bearings into postion.

NOTE: *Ensure that oil holes align when installing bearings.*

Replace camshaft rear plug, and stake it into position to aid retention.

CYLINDER BLOCK RECONDITIONING

Procedure	Method

Finish hone the cylinders:

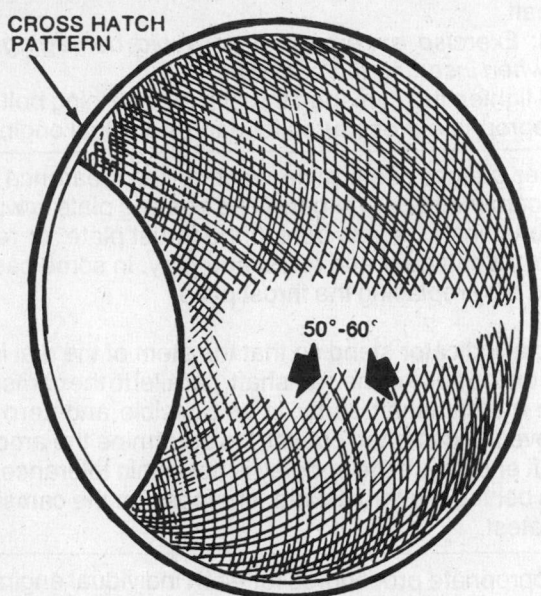

CROSS HATCH PATTERN

50°-60°

Chuck a flexible drive hone into a power drill, and insert it into the cylinder. Start the hone, and move it up and down the cylinder at a rate which will produce approximately a 60° cross-hatch pattern (see illustration).

NOTE: *Do not extend the hone below the cylinder bore.*

After developing the pattern, remove the hone and recheck piston fit. Wash the cylinders with a detergent and water solution to remove abrasive dust, dry, and wipe several times with a rag soaked in engine oil.

Check piston ring end-gap:

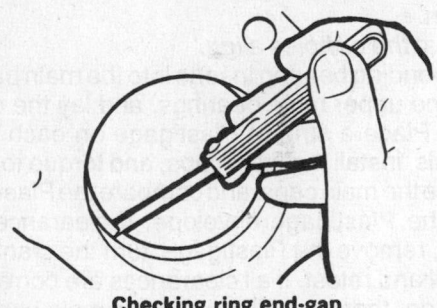

Checking ring end-gap

Compress the piston rings to be used in a cylinder, one at a time, into that cylinder, and press them approximately 1″ below the deck with an inverted piston. Using feeler gauges, measure the ring end-gap, and compare to specifications. Pull the ring out of the cylinder and file the ends with a fine file to obtain proper clearance.

CAUTION: *If inadequate ring end-gap is utilized, ring breakage will result.*

Install the piston rings:

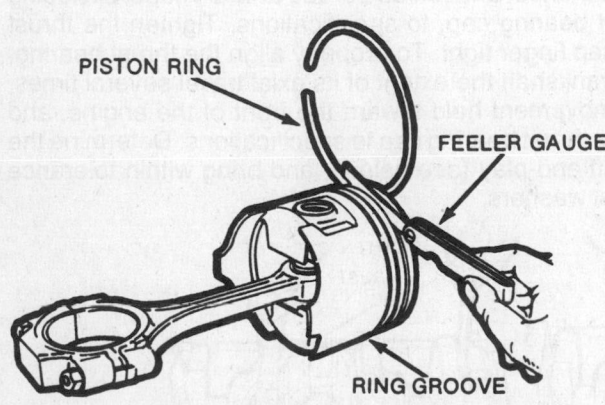

PISTON RING

FEELER GAUGE

RING GROOVE

Checking ring side clearance

Inspect the ring grooves in the piston for excessive wear or taper. If necessary, recut the groove(s) for use with an over-width ring or a standard ring and spacer. If the groove is worn uniformly, overwidth rings, or standard rings and spacers may be installed without recutting. Roll the outside of the ring around the groove to check for burrs or deposits. If any are found, remove with a fine file. Hold the ring in the groove, and measure side clearance. If necessary, correct as indicated above.

NOTE: *Always install any additional spacers above the piston ring.*

The ring groove must be deep enough to allow the ring to seat below the lands (see illustration). In many cases, a "go-no-go" depth gauge will be provided with the piston rings. Shallow grooves may be corrected by recutting, while deep grooves require some type of filler or expander behind the piston. Consult the piston ring supplier concerning the suggested method. Install the rings on the piston, lowest ring first, using a ring expander.

NOTE: *Position the ring markings as specified by the manufacturer (see car section).*

CYLINDER BLOCK RECONDITIONING

Procedure	Method

Install the camshaft (OHV engines only):

Liberally lubricate the camshaft lobes and journals, and install the camshaft.
CAUTION: *Exercise extreme care to avoid damaging the bearings when inserting the camshaft.*
Install and tighten the camshaft thrust plate retaining bolts. See the appropriate procedures for each individual engine.

Check camshaft end-play (OHV engines only):

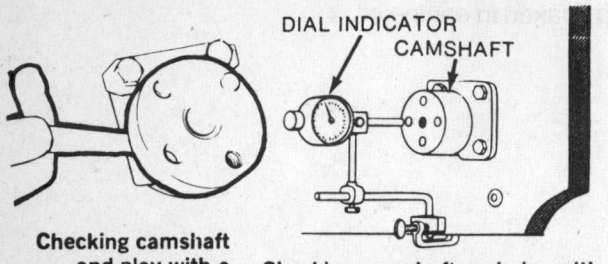

Checking camshaft end-play with a feeler gauge

Checking camshaft end-play with a dial indicator

Using feeler gauges, determine whether the clearance between the camshaft boss (or gear) and backing plate is within specifications. Install shims behind the thrust plate, or reposition the camshaft gear and retest end-play. In some cases, adjustment is by replacing the thrust plate.

*Mount a dial indicator stand so that the stem of the dial indicator rests on the nose of the camshaft, parallel to the camshaft axis. Push the camshaft as far in as possible and zero the gauge. Move the camshaft outward to determine the amount of camshaft endplay. If the endplay is not within tolerance, install shims behind the thrust plate, or reposition the camshaft gear and retest.

Install the rear main seal (where applicable):

See the appropriate procedures for each individual engine.

Install the crankshaft:

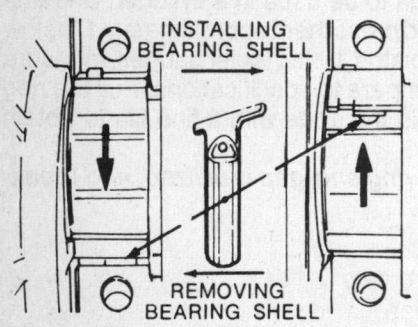

Removal and installation of upper bearing insert using a roll-out pin

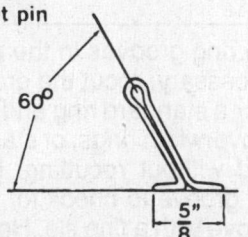

Home-made bearing roll-out pin

Thoroughly clean the main bearing saddles and caps. Place the upper halves of the bearing inserts on the saddles and press into position.
NOTE: *Ensure that the oil holes align.*
Press the corresponding bearing inserts into the main bearing caps. Lubricate the upper main bearings, and lay the crankshaft in position. Place a strip of Plastigage on each of the crankshaft journals, install the main caps, and torque to specifications. Remove the main caps, and compare the Plastigage to the scale on the Plastigage envelope. If clearances are within tolerances, remove the Plastigage, turn the crankshaft 90°, wipe off all oil and retest. If all clearances are correct, remove all Plastigage, thoroughly lubricate the main caps and bearing journals, and install the main caps. If clearances are not within tolerance, the upper bearing inserts may be removed, without removing the crankshaft, using a bearing roll out pin (see illustration). Roll in a bearing that will provide proper clearance, and retest. Torque all main caps, excluding the thrust bearing cap, to specifications. Tighten the thrust bearing cap finger tight. To properly align the thrust bearing, pry the crankshaft the extent of its axial travel several times, the last movement held toward the front of the engine, and torque the thrust bearing cap to specifications. Determine the crankshaft end-play (see below), and bring within tolerance with thrust washers.

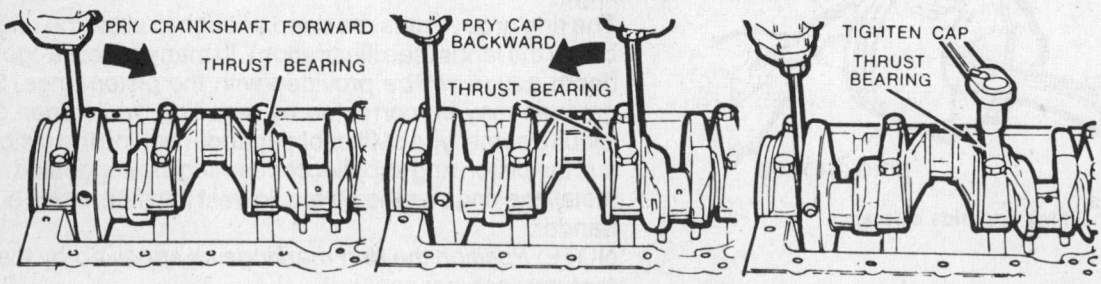

Aligning the thrust bearing

CYLINDER BLOCK RECONDITIONING

Procedure	Method

Measure crankshaft end-play:

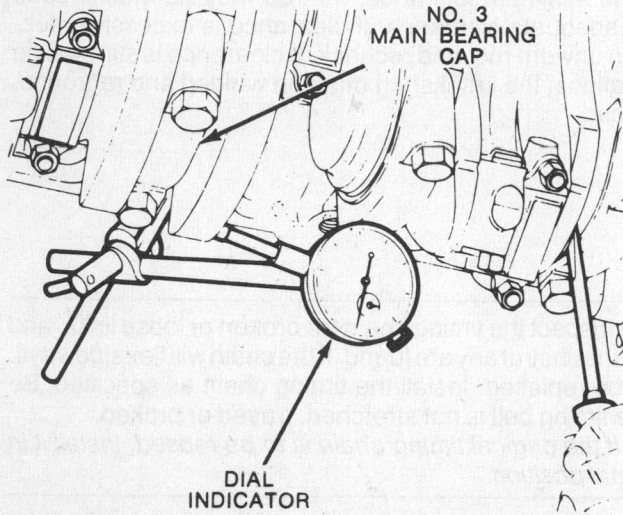

Checking crankshaft end-play with a dial indicator

Mount a dial indicator stand on the front of the block, with the dial indicator stem resting on the nose of the crankshaft, parallel to the crankshaft axis. Pry the crankshaft the extent of its travel rearward, and zero the indicator. Pry the crankshaft forward and record crankshaft end-play.

NOTE: *Crankshaft end-play also may be measured at the thrust bearing, using feeler gauges* (see illustration).

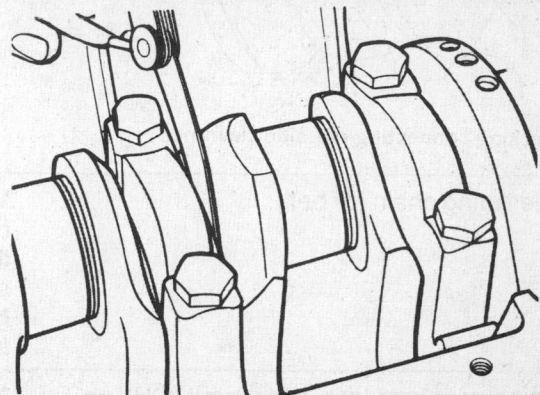

Checking crankshaft end-play with a feeler gauge

Install the pistons:

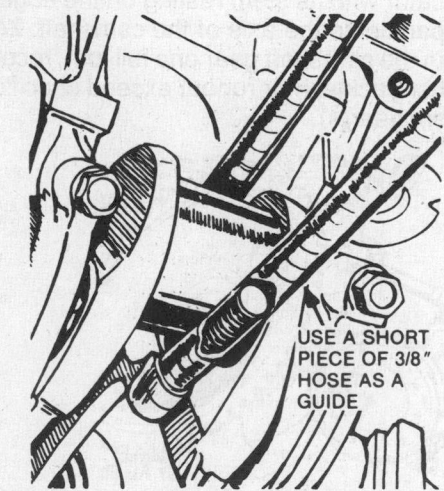

Tubing used to protect crankshaft journals and cylinder walls during piston installation

Press the upper connecting rod bearing halves into the connecting rods, and the lower halves into the connecting rod caps. Position the piston ring gaps according to specifications (see car section), and lubricate the pistons. Install a ring compressor on a piston, and press two long (8″) pieces of plastic tubing over the rod bolts. Using the tubes as a guide, press the pistons into the bores and onto the crankshaft with a wooden hammer handle. After seating the rod on the crankshaft journal, remove the tubes and install the cap finger tight. Install the remaining pistons in the same manner. Invert the engine and check the bearing clearance at two points (90° apart) on each journal with Plastigage.

NOTE: *Do not turn the crankshaft with Plastigage installed.* If clearance is within tolerances, remove *all* Plastigage, thoroughly lubricate the journals, and torque the rod caps to specifications. If clearance is not within specifications, install different thickness bearing inserts and recheck.

CAUTION: *Never shim or file the connecting rods or caps.* Always install plastic tube sleeves over the rod bolts when the caps are not installed, to protect the crankshaft journals.

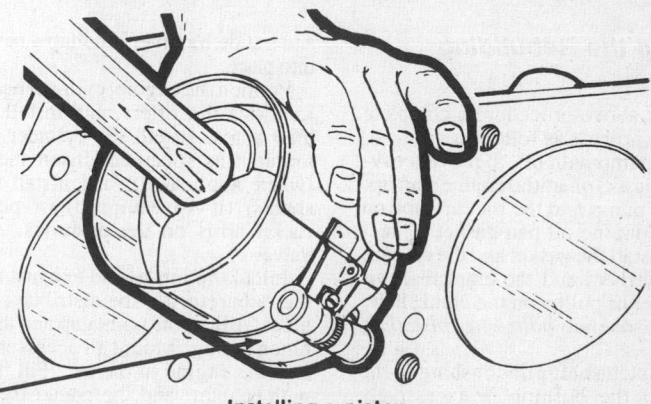

Installing a piston

CYLINDER BLOCK RECONDITIONING

Procedure	Method
Check connecting rod side clearance: 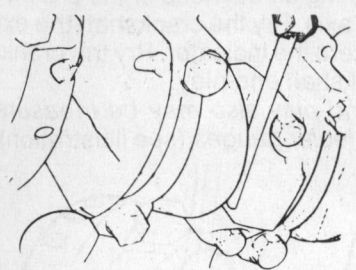 Checking connecting rod side clearance	Determine the clearance between the sides of the connecting rods and the crankshaft, using feeler gauges. If clearance is below the minimum tolerance, the rod may be machined to provide adequate clearance. If clearance is excessive, substitute an unworn rod, and recheck. If clearance is still outside specifications, the crankshaft must be welded and reground, or replaced.
Inspect the timing chain (or belt):	Visually inspect the timing chain for broken or loose links, and replace the chain if any are found. If the chain will flex sideways, it must be replaced. Install the timing chain as specified. Be sure the timing belt is not stretched, frayed or broken. NOTE: *If the original timing chain is to be reused, install it in its original position.*
Check timing gear backlash and runout (OHV engines): 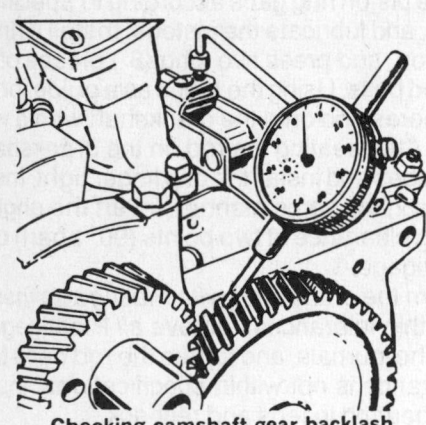 Checking camshaft gear backlash	Mount a dial indicator with its stem resting on a tooth of the camshaft gear (as illustrated). Rotate the gear until all slack is removed, and zero the indicator. Rotate the gear in the opposite direction until slack is removed, and record gear backlash. Mount the indicator with its stem resting on the edge of the camshaft gear, parallel to the axis of the camshaft. Zero the indicator, and turn the camshaft gear one full turn, recording the runout. If either backlash or runout exceed specifications, replace the worn gear(s). 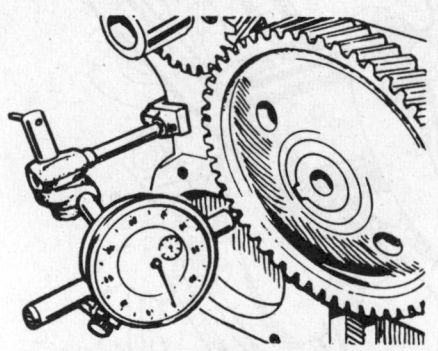 Checking camshaft gear runout

Completing the Rebuilding Process

Following the above procedures, complete the rebuilding process as follows:

Fill the oil pump with oil, to prevent cavitating (sucking air) on initial engine start up. Install the oil pump and the pickup tube on the engine. Coat the oil pan gasket as necessary, and install the gasket and the oil pan. Mount the flywheel and the crankshaft vibration damper or pulley on the crankshaft. NOTE: *Always use new bolts when installing the flywheel.*

Inspect the clutch shaft pilot bushing in the crankshaft. If the bushing is excessively worn, remove it with an expanding puller and a slide hammer, and tap a new bushing into place.

Position the engine, cylinder head side up. Lubricate the lifters, and install them into their bores. Install the cylinder head, and torque it as specified. Insert the pushrods (where applicable), and install the rocker shaft(s) (if so equipped) or position the rocker arms on the pushrods. Adjust the valves.

Install the intake and exhaust manifolds, the carburetor(s), the distributor and spark plugs. Adjust the point gap and the static ignition timing. Mount all accessories and install the engine in the car. Fill the radiator with coolant, and the crankcase with high quality engine oil.

Break-in Procedure

Start the engine, and allow it to run at low speed for a few minutes, while checking for leaks. Stop the engine, check the oil level, and fill as necessary. Restart the engine, and fill the cooling system to capacity. Check the point dwell angle and adjust the ignition timing and the valves. Run the engine at low to medium speed (800–2500 rpm) for approximately ½ hour, and retorque the cylinder head bolts. Road test the car, and check again for leaks.

Follow the manufacturer's recommended engine break-in procedure and maintenance schedule for new engines.

U-Joint, CV-Joint Overhaul 37

UNIVERSAL JOINTS

U-Joint is mechanic's jargon for universal joint. U-Joints should not be confused with U-bolts, which are U-shaped bolts used to connect U-joints to the differential pinion flange.

Universal joints provide flexibility between the driveshaft and axle housing to accommodate changes in the angle between them. Changes of length are accommodated by the sliding splined yoke between the driveshaft and transmission. The engine and transmission are mounted rigidly on the car frame. The angles between the transmission, driveshaft and axle change constantly as the car responds to various road conditions.

To give flexibility and still transmit power as smoothly as possible, several types of universal joints are used. The most common type of universal joint is the cross and yoke type. Yokes are used on the ends of the driveshaft with the yoke arms opposite each other. Another yoke is used opposite the driveshaft and when placed together, both yokes engage a center member, or cross, with four arms spaced 90° apart. The U-joint cross is alternately referred to as a spider, and the arms are called trunnions. A bearing cup (or cap) is used on each arm of the cross to accommodate movement as the driveshaft rotates. The bearings used are needle bearings.

A conventional universal joint will cause the driveshaft to speed up and slow down through each revolution and cause a corresponding change in the velocity of drive shaft. This change in speed causes natural vibrations to occur through the driveline, necessitating a third type of universal joint: The constant velocity joint. A rolling ball moves in a curved groove, located between two yoke-and-cross universal joints, connected to each other by a coupling yoke. The result is a uniform motion as the driveshaft rotates, avoiding the fluctuations in driveshaft speed. This type of joint is found in cars with sharp driveline angles, or where the extra measure of isolation is desirable.

Cross And Yoke U-Joint

OVERHAUL

There are two types of cross and yoke U-joints. One type retains the cross within the yoke with C-shaped snap rings. This type is found on all American Motors, Chrysler, and Ford Cars. GM cars generally use the second type of joint, which is held together by injection molded plastic retainer rings. The second type cannot be reassembled with the same parts, once disassembled. However, repair kits are available.

Snapring Type

1. Remove the driveshaft. For the correct procedure, see the car section for the model you are working on.

2. If the front yoke is to be disassembled, matchmark the driveshaft and sliding splined yoke (transmission yoke) so that driveline balance is preserved upon reassembly. Remove the snap rings which retain the bearing caps.

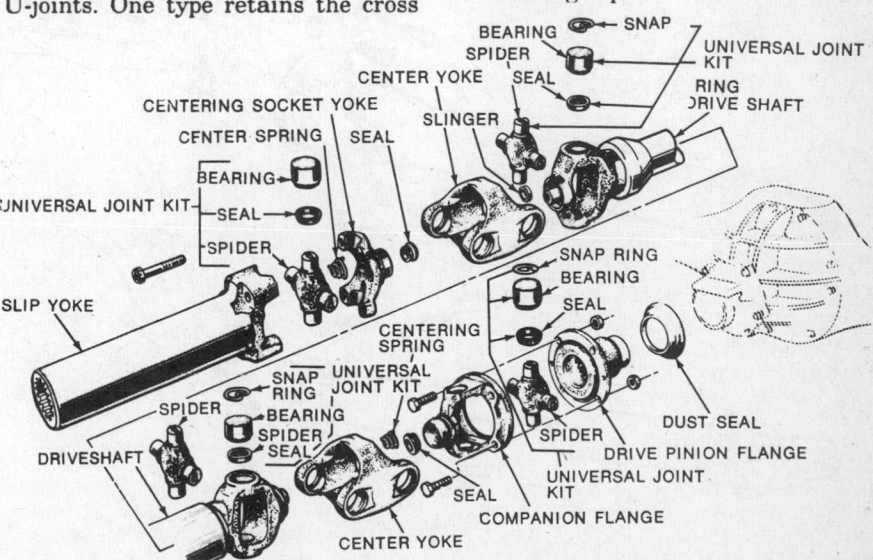

Typical driveshaft with cardan type U–joints

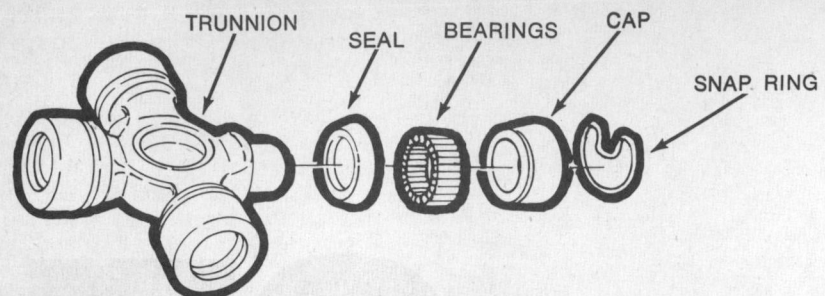

TRUNNION SEAL BEARINGS CAP SNAP RING

Snap ring type universal joint

3. Select two sockets, one small enough to pass through the yoke holes for the bearing caps, the other large enough to receive the bearing cap.

4. Using a vise or a press, position the small and large sockets on either side of the U-joint. Press in on the smaller socket so that it presses the opposite bearing cap out of the yoke and into the larger socket. If the cap does not come all the way out, grasp it with a pair of pliers and work it out.

5. Reverse the position of the sockets so that the smaller socket presses on the cross. Press the other bearing cap out of the yoke.

6. Repeat the procedure on the other bearings.

7. To install, grease the bearing caps and needles throughly if they are not pregreased. Start a new bearing cap into one side of the yoke. Position the cross in the yoke.

8. Select two sockets small enough to pass through the yoke holes. Put the sockets against the cross and the cap, and press the bearing cap $\frac{1}{4}$ inch below the surface of the yoke. If there is a sudden increase in the force needed to press the cap into place, or if the cross starts to bind, the bearings are

cocked, They must be removed and re-started in the yoke. Failure to do so will greatly reduce the life of the bearing.

9. Install a new snap ring.

10. Start a new bearing into the opposite side. Place a socket on it and press in until the opposite bearing contacts the snap ring.

11. Install a new snap ring. It may be necessary to grind the facing surface of the snap ring slightly to permit easier installation.

12. Install the other bearings in the same manner.

13. Check the joint for free movement. If binding exists, smack the yoke ears with a brass or plastic faced hammer to seat the bearing needles. Do not strike the bearings, and support the shaft firmly. Do not install the driveshaft until free movement exists at all joints.

Plastic Retainer Type

Remove and install the bearing caps

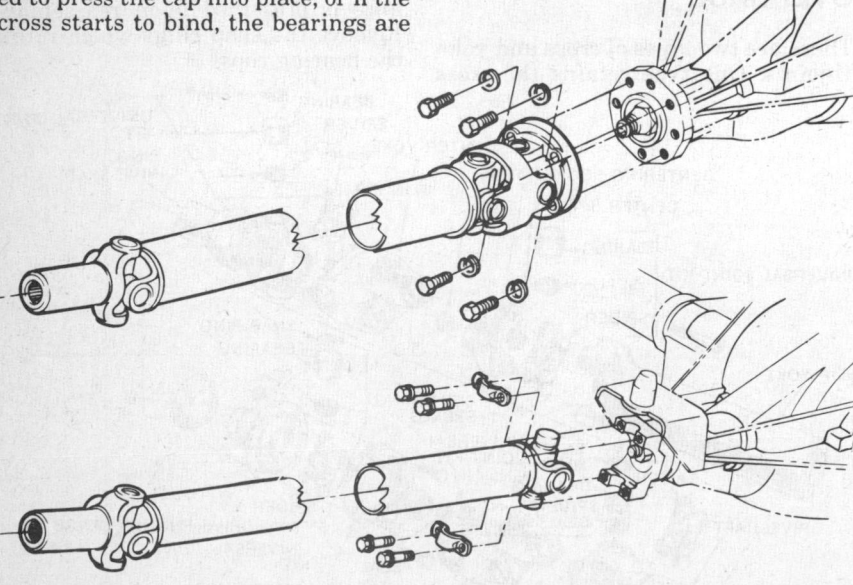

The driveshaft may be retained to the differential pinion by a flange (top) or by U-bolts or straps (bottom)

and trunnion (cross) as described for the snap-ring type universal joints. On an original universal joint, however, the bearing caps will be secured in the yokes with injected plastic. The plastic will shear when the bearing caps are pressed. Service snap-rings are installed in the groove on the inside (of yoke) of the installed caps.

NOTE: The plastic which retains the bearing will be sheared when the bearing cup is pressed out. Be sure to remove the remains of the plastic retainer from the ears of the yoke. It is easier to remove the remains if a small pin or punch is first driven through the injection holes in the yoke. Failure to remove all of the plastic remains may prevent the bearing cups from being pressed into place and the bearing retainers from being properly seated.

BEARING FOR SNAP RING RETAINER

NYLON RETAINER

SNAP RING

BEARING FOR NYLON RETAINER

GROOVE FOR SNAP RING

U-joint locking methods

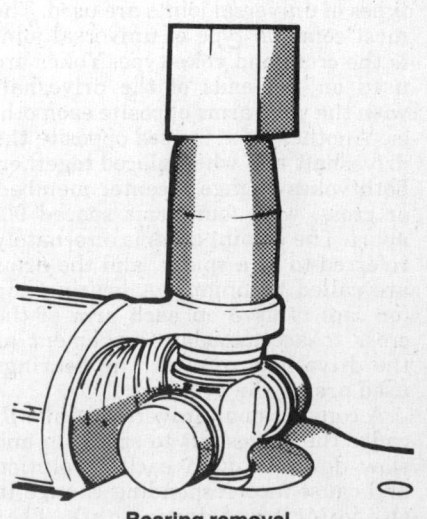

Bearing removal

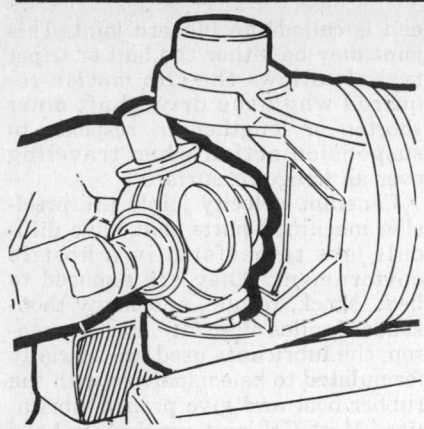

Press a bearing cap into the yoke, then install the cross

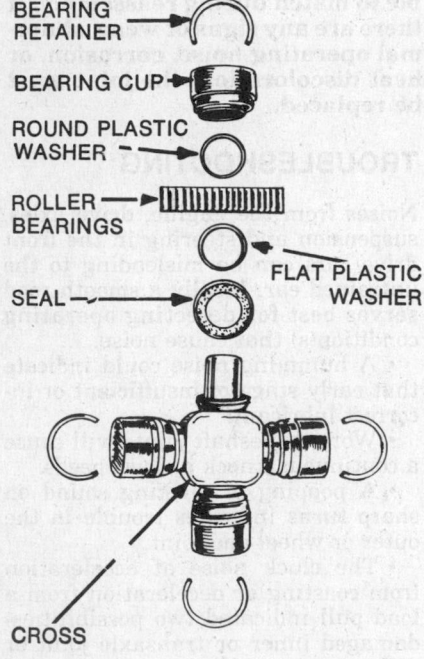

BEARING RETAINER

BEARING CUP

ROUND PLASTIC WASHER

ROLLER BEARINGS

SEAL

FLAT PLASTIC WASHER

CROSS

Plastic retainer U-joint repair kit components

Cardan Type U-Joint

OVERHAUL

Ford and Chrysler products with Cardan type U-joints use snap rings to retain the bearing cups in the yokes. Most GM cars have plastic retainers. Be sure to obtain the correct rebuilding kit.

1. Use a punch to mark the coupling yoke and the adjoining yokes before disassembly, to ensure proper reassembly and driveline balance.

2. It is easiest to remove the bearings from the coupling yoke first. Follow the order indicated in the illustration.

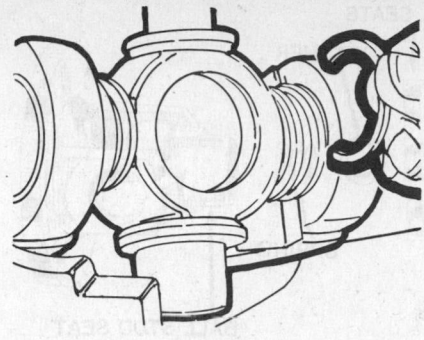

Service snap rings are installed inside the yoke

3. Support the driveshaft horizontally on a press stand, or on the workbench if a vise is being used.

4. If snap rings are used to retain the bearing cups, remove them. Place the rear ear of the coupling yoke over a socket large enough to receive the cup. Place a smaller socket, or a cross press made for the purpose, over the opposite cup. Press the bearing cup out of the coupling yoke ear. If the cup is not completely removed, insert a spacer and complete the operation, or grasp the cup with a pair of slip joint pliers and work it out. If the cups are retained by plastic, this will shear the retainers. Remove any bits of plastic.

5. Rotate the driveshaft and repeat the operation on the opposite cup.

6. Disengage the trunnions of the spider, still attached to the flanged yoke, from the coupling yoke, and pull the flanged yoke and spider from the center ball on the ball support tube yoke.

NOTE: The joint between the shaft and coupling yoke can be serviced without disassembly of the joint between the coupling yoke and flanged yoke.

7. Pry the seal from the ball cavity, remove the washers, spring and three seats. Examine the ball stud seat and the ball stud for scores or wear. Worn parts can be replaced with a kit. Clean the ball seat cavity and fill it with grease. Install the spring, washer, ball seats, and spacer (washer) over the ball.

8. To assemble, insert one bearing cup part way into one ear of the ball support tube yoke and turn this cup to the bottom.

9. Insert the spider (cross) into the tube so that the trunnion (arm) seats freely in the cup.

10. Install the opposite cup part way, making sure that both cups are straight.

11. Press the cups into position, making sure that both cups squarely engage the spider. Back off if there is a sudden increase in resistance, indicating that a cup is cocked or a needle bearing is out of place.

12. As soon as one bearing retainer groove clears the yoke, stop and install the retainer (plastic retainer models). On models with snap rings, press the cups into place, then install the snap rings over the cups.

13. If difficulty is encountered installing the plastic retainers or the snap rings, smack the yoke sharply with a hammer to spring the ears slightly.

14. Install one bearing cup part way into the ear of the coupling yoke, Make sure that the alignment marks are matched, then engaged the coupling yoke over the spider and press

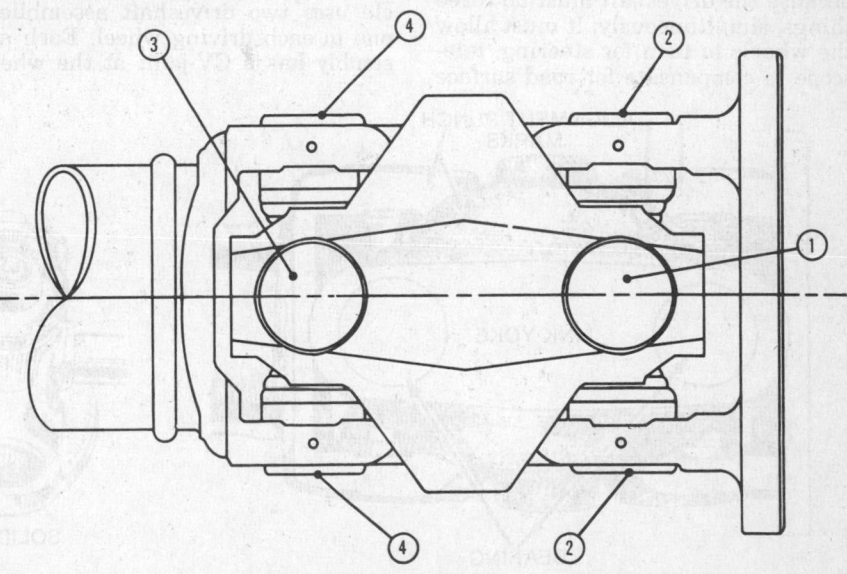

Cardan joint disassembly sequence

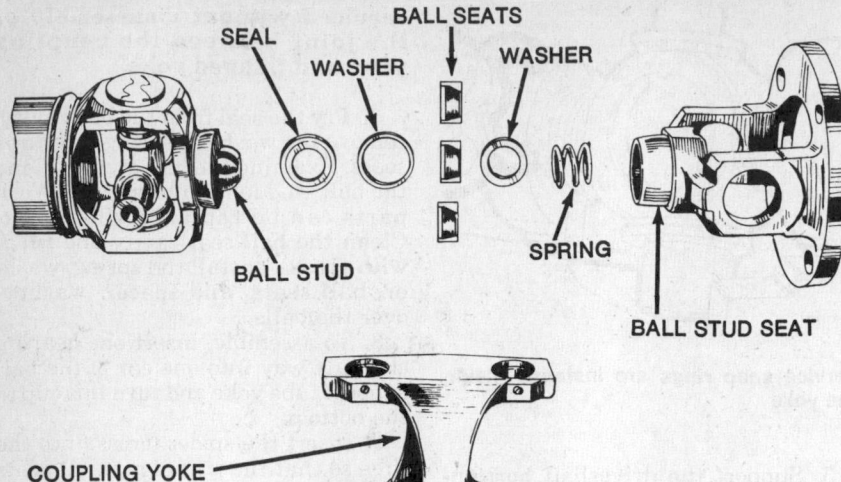

Cardan type joint

in the cups, installing the retainers or snap rings as before.

15. Install the cups and spider into the flanged yoke as with the previous yoke.

NOTE: The flange yoke should snap over center to the right or left and up or down by the pressure of the ball seat spring.

CONSTANT VELOCITY JOINTS

Front wheel drive vehicles present several unique problems to engineers because the driveshaft must do three things, simultaneously. It must allow the wheels to turn for steering, telescope to compensate for road surface vibrations, and it must transmit torque continuously without vibration.

To compensate for these three factors a two-joint driveshaft allows the front wheels to perform these functions. This driveshaft mates disc type straight groove ball joint design with the bell type Rzeppa CV universal joint.

The Rzeppa joint on the outboard end of each driveshaft provides steering ability by allowing drive wheels to steer up to 43° while transmitting all available torque to the wheels. The inboard joint allows telescoping (up to 1½ in.) through the rolling actions of balls in straight grooves and operates at angles up to 20°. The combined action of these two ball type U-joints eliminates vibration.

The typical front wheel drive vehicle uses two driveshaft assemblies-one to each driving wheel. Each assembly has a CV-joint at the wheel

end is called the inboard joint. This joint may be either the ball or tripot type. It allows the slip motion required when the driveshaft must shorten or lengthen in response to suspension action when traveling over an irregular surface.

Constant velocity joints are precision machined parts that have difficult jobs to perform in a hostile enviornment. They are exposed to heat, shock, torque, and many thousands of miles of service. For this reason, the lubricants used are specially formulated to be compatible with the rubber boot and give proper lubrication. Most CV-joint repair kits have this special lubricant included.

NOTE: Wear patterns in a used ball or tripot CV-joint are impossible to match during reassembly. If there are any signs of wear, abnormal operating noise, corrosion, or heat discoloration, the joint must be replaced.

TROUBLESHOOTING

Noises from the engine, drive axles, suspension and steering in the front drive cars can be misleading to the untrained ear. Ideally a smooth road serves best for detecting operating condition(s) that cause noise.

• A humming noise could indicate that early stage of insufficient or incorrect lubricant.

• Worn driveshaft joints will cause a continuous knock at low speeds.

• A popping or clicking sound on sharp turns indicates trouble in the outer or wheel end joint.

• The cluck noise at acceleration from coasting or deceleration from a load pull indicated two possibilities-damaged inner or transaxle joint or differential problem(s).

• An inner joint will create a vibra-

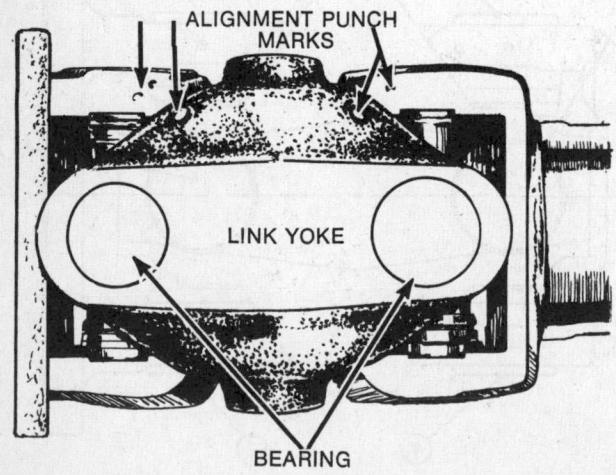

Match marks for double cardan joint

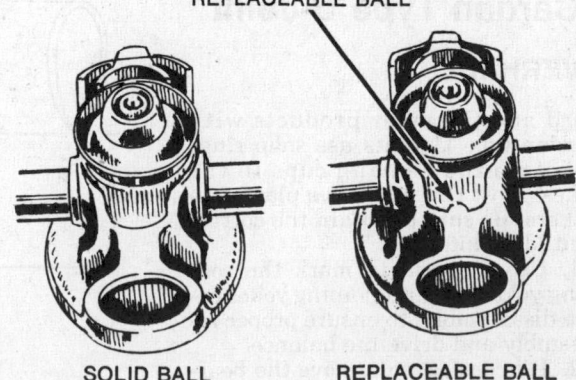

Solid and replaceable U-Joint balls

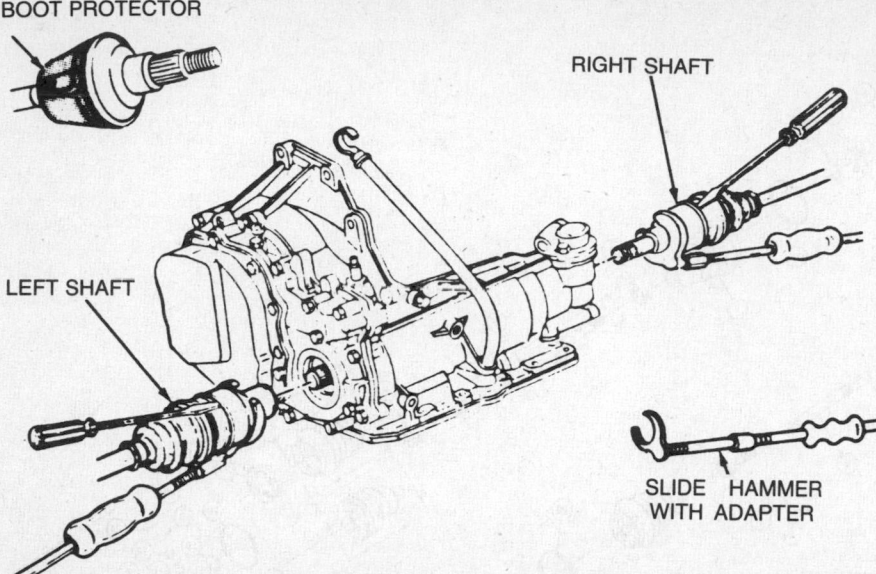

BOOT PROTECTOR
RIGHT SHAFT
LEFT SHAFT
SLIDE HAMMER
WITH ADAPTER

Removing axle shafts on GM models

tion during acceleration due to plunging action hanging up and releasing repeatedly. Probable cause would be foreign particles or lack of lubrication, or improper assembly.

• Remember that tires, suspension, engine, and exhaust system are all up front to add their noises.

• Make a check with front wheels elevated off ground. Spin the wheels by hand to determine if wheel bearing could be noisy or if out of round tires are causing vibration. Many wheel bearings are prelubed and sealed at the factory.

CAUTION

Personal injury can occur from spinning wheels by engine power. Spinning a wheel at excess speed may cause damage to CV-joints that could be operating at angles too steep when wheels are allowed to hang. Overspeeding might also cause damage to tires and the differential.

SHAFT REMOVAL

1. Remove the hub nut and discard it.
2. Drain the lubricant from the transaxle. Remove the differential cover (Chrysler only).
3. The speedometer pinion gear assembly must be removed before the right driveshaft can be removed (automatic transaxles only).
4. Rotate the driveshaft to view the circlip.
5. Compress the circlip tangs with needle nose pliers as you pry into the side gear. This compresses the circlip in position for shaft removal later. Keep an awl between the differential pinion shaft and the end face of the shaft to prevent circlip reentry to the groove.

NOTE: This applies to Chrysler cars only.

6. Remove the ball joint clamp bolt. Drop the lower arm too allow clearance. This will permit the front wheel to swing free.
7. Pull the outer splined shaft from the wheel hub away. Do not pull on the shaft. Grasp the joint housing.
8. Remove the inner joint by pulling outward on the inner joint housing. Do not pull the shaft.

NOTE: Do not allow the assembly to hang at either end. This can jam the CV-joint and cause vibration during operation. If necessary, support the shaft at either end by rope or wire.

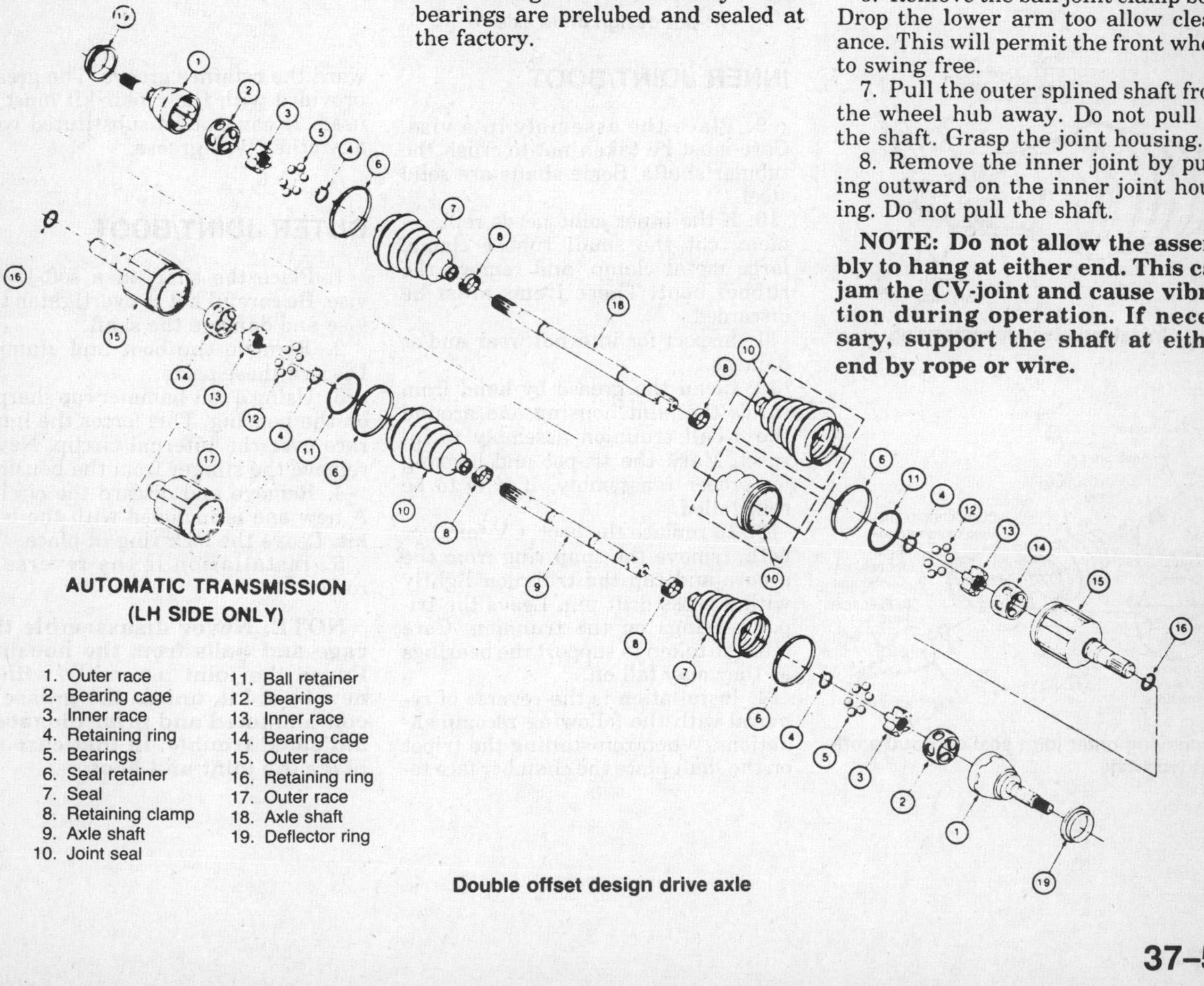

AUTOMATIC TRANSMISSION
(LH SIDE ONLY)
1. Outer race
2. Bearing cage
3. Inner race
4. Retaining ring
5. Bearings
6. Seal retainer
7. Seal
8. Retaining clamp
9. Axle shaft
10. Joint seal
11. Ball retainer
12. Bearings
13. Inner race
14. Bearing cage
15. Outer race
16. Retaining ring
17. Outer race
18. Axle shaft
19. Deflector ring

Double offset design drive axle

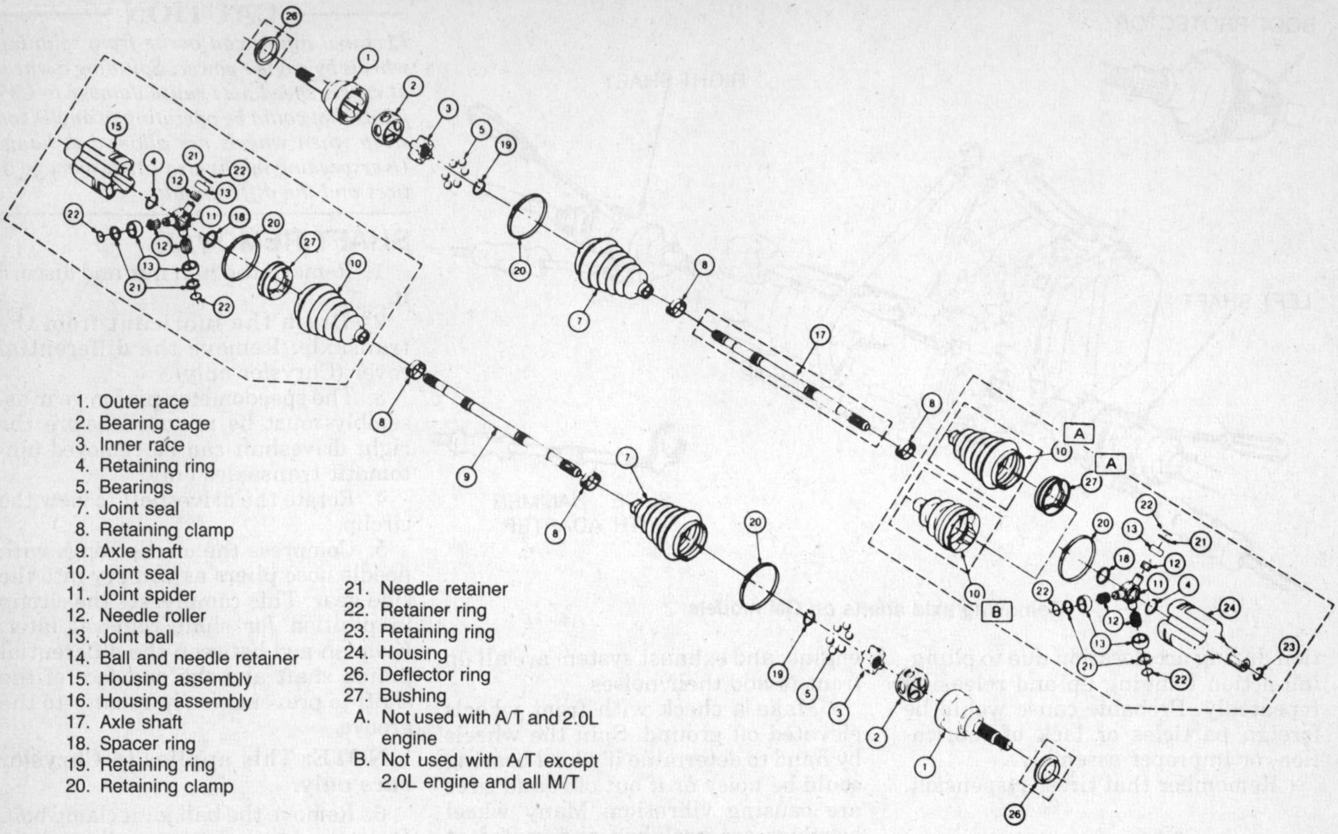

1. Outer race
2. Bearing cage
3. Inner race
4. Retaining ring
5. Bearings
7. Joint seal
8. Retaining clamp
9. Axle shaft
10. Joint seal
11. Joint spider
12. Needle roller
13. Joint ball
14. Ball and needle retainer
15. Housing assembly
16. Housing assembly
17. Axle shaft
18. Spacer ring
19. Retaining ring
20. Retaining clamp

21. Needle retainer
22. Retainer ring
23. Retaining ring
24. Housing
26. Deflector ring
27. Bushing
A. Not used with A/T and 2.0L engine
B. Not used with A/T except 2.0L engine and all M/T

Tri-pot design drive axle

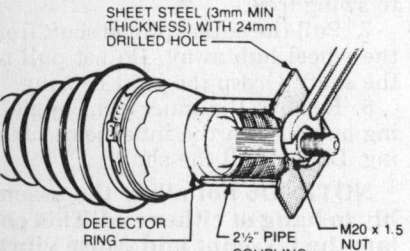

Installing steel deflector ring

SHEET STEEL (3mm MIN THICKNESS) WITH 24mm DRILLED HOLE

DEFLECTOR RING

2½" PIPE COUPLING

M20 x 1.5 NUT

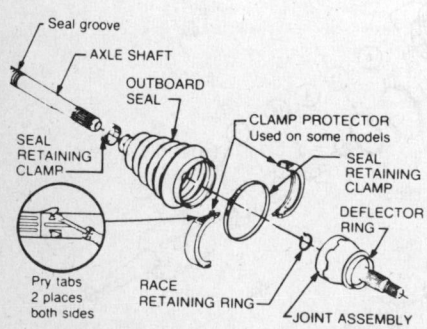

Removing outer joint seal on double off-set type axle

Seal groove
AXLE SHAFT
OUTBOARD SEAL
SEAL RETAINING CLAMP
CLAMP PROTECTOR Used on some models
SEAL RETAINING CLAMP
DEFLECTOR RING
Pry tabs 2 places both sides
RACE RETAINING RING
JOINT ASSEMBLY

INNER JOINT/BOOT

9. Place the assembly in a vise. Care must be taken not to crush the tubular shafts. Some shafts are solid steel.

10. If the inner joint needs replacement, cut the small rubber clamp, large metal clamp, and remove the rubber boot. These items must be discarded.

11. Inspect for internal wear and/or damage.

12. Clean the grease by hand from inside the joint housing and around the 3 ball trunnion assembly to inspect. Mark the tri-pot and housing for proper reassembly, If it is to be reinstalled.

13. To replace the boot, CV-joint, or both, remove the snap ring from the groove and tap the trunnion lightly with a brass drift pin. Leave the tripot bearings on the trunnion. Care must be taken to support the bearings as they may fall off.

14. Installation is the reverse of removal with the following recommendations. When reinstalling the tripot on the shaft place the chamber face to-ward the retainer groove. The grease provided with the repair kit must be used. It can not be substituted with any other type grease.

OUTER JOINT/BOOT

1. Place the shaft in a soft-jawed vise. Be careful not to overtighten the vise and damage the shaft.

2. Remove the boot and clamps. Discard these parts.

3. Using a soft hammer rap sharply on the housing. This forces the inner race over the internal circlip. Never remove the slinger from the housing.

4. Remove and discard the circlip. A new one is included with the boot kit. Leave the lock ring in place.

5. Installation is the reverse of removal.

NOTE: Never disassemble the cage and balls from the housing. Reuse the joint assembly with a new boot kit, unless the grease is contaminated and prior diagnosis indicated trouble. In that case replace the joint and boot.

Strut Overhaul **38**

STRUT SERVICE AND REPAIR

MacPherson struts are appearing on the front (and rear) wheels of more and more cars. The strut design takes up less room in the engine compartment, compared to a conventional upper and lower arm with shock absorber arrangement. The trend toward smaller, lighter and more efficient packaging mandates the use of a strut suspension to permit more room for engine accessories and front wheel drive components.

Strut Suspension Design

In a conventional front suspension, the wheel is attached to a spindle, which is in turn, connected to upper and lower control arms through upper and lower ball joints. A coil spring between the control arms (sometimes on top of the upper arm) supports the weight of the vehicle and a shock absorber controls rebound and dampens oscillations.

In a strut type suspension, the strut performs a shock dampening function, like a shock absorber, but unlike a conventional shock absorber, the strut is a structural part of the vehicle's suspension.

The strut assembly usually contains a spring seat to retain the coil spring that supports the vehicle's weight. The shock absorber is built into the body of the strut housing. The strut is normally attached at the bottom to the lower control arm and at the top to the car body. The upper mount usually features a bearing that permits the

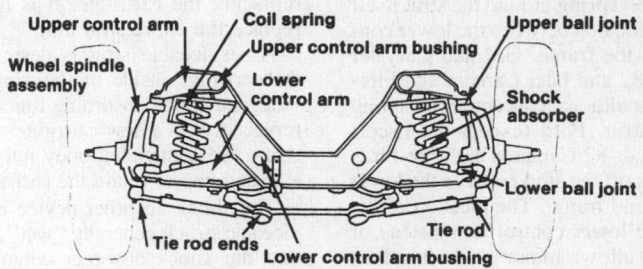

Conventional upper and lower arm suspension

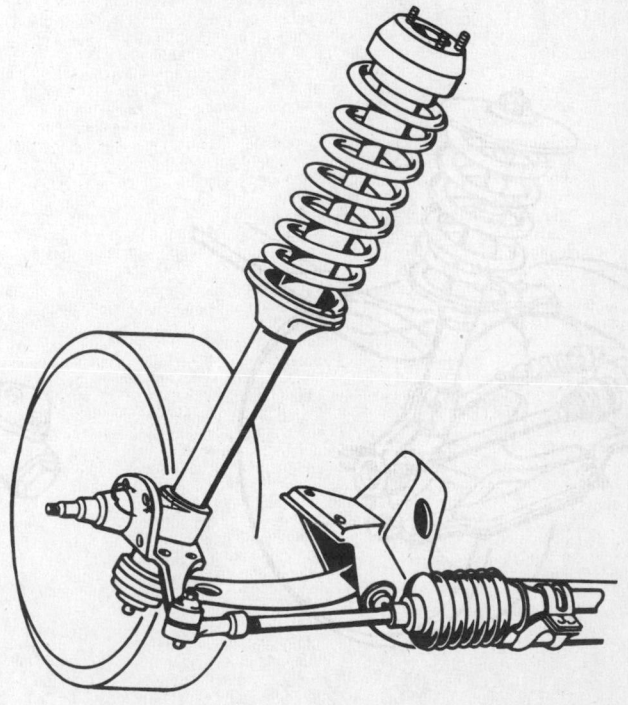

Strut with concentric coil spring (rear wheel drive)

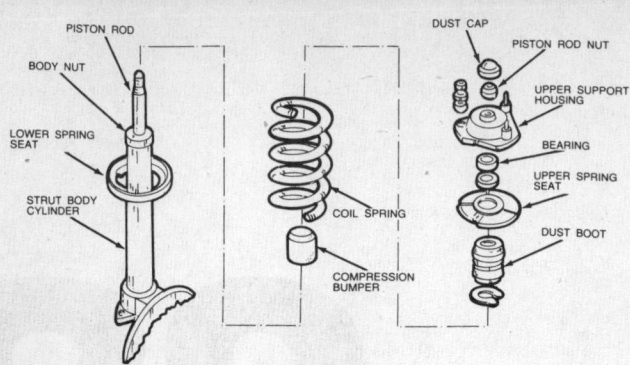

Exploded view of a typical strut

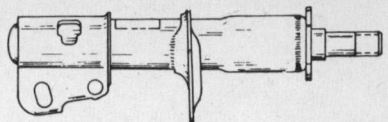

A sealed strut has no body nut and is serviceable by replacement

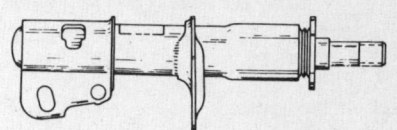

Serviceable struts have a removeable body nut to allow replacement of the strut cartridge

coil spring to rotate as the wheels turn for smoother steering. The entire design eliminates the need for the upper control arm, upper ball joint and many of the conventional suspension bushings. The lower ball joint is no longer a load carrying unit, because it is isolated from the weight of the vehicle.

Domestic struts have taken 2 forms—a concentric coil spring around the strut itself and a spring located between the lower control arm and the frame. GM and Chrysler (except for '82 and later Camaro and Firebird) use the traditional concentric coil spring around the strut. Ford (except the Escort and Lynx) and '82 Camaros and Fire-birds use the spring off the strut between the lower control arm and frame. The location of the spring on the lower control arm instead of on the strut, allows minor road vibrations to be absorbed through the chassis rather than be fed back to the driver through the steering system.

Serviceability

Struts fall into 2 broad categories—serviceable and sealed units. A sealed strut is designed so that the top closure of the strut assembly is permanently sealed. There is no access to the shock absorber cartridge inside the strut housing and no means of replacing the cartridge. It is necessary to replace the entire strut unit.

A serviceable strut is designed so that the cartridge inside the housing, that provides the shock absorbing function, can be replaced with a new cartridge. Serviceable struts use a threaded body nut in place of a sealed cap to retain the cartridge.

The shock absorber device inside a serviceable strut is generally "wet". This means that the shock absorber contains oil that contacts and lubricates the inner wall of the strut body. The oil is sealed inside the strut by the body nut, O-ring and piston rod seal.

Servicing a "wet" strut with the equivalent components involves a thorough cleaning of the inside of the strut body, absolute cleanliness and great care in reassembly.

Cartridge inserts were developed to simplify servicing "wet" struts. The insert is a factory sealed replacement for the strut shock absorber. The replacement cartridge is simply substituted for the original shock absorber cartridge and retained with the body nut, avoiding the near laboratory-like conditions required to service a "wet" strut with "wet" service components.

Most OEM domestic struts are serviced by replacement of the entire unit. There is no strut cartridge to replace. Exceptions to this general rule are the struts used on GM front wheel drive J-cars and A-cars, which feature an internally threaded housing, accessible by removing the OEM cap from the housing. Once the old cartridge is removed, a new cartridge can be threaded

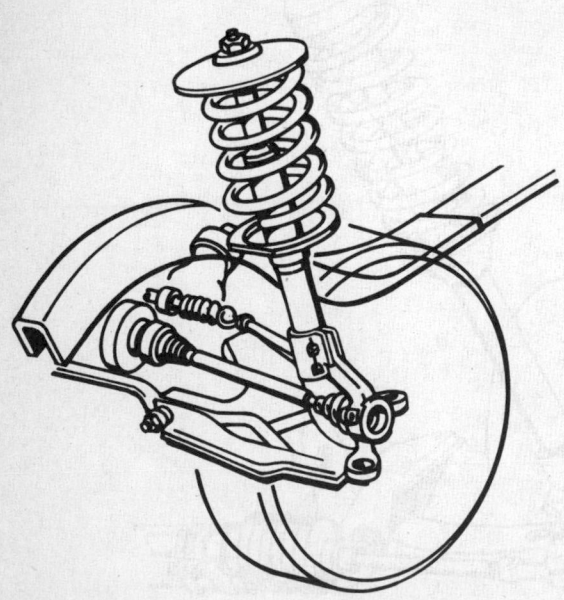

Strut with concentric coil spring (front wheel drive)

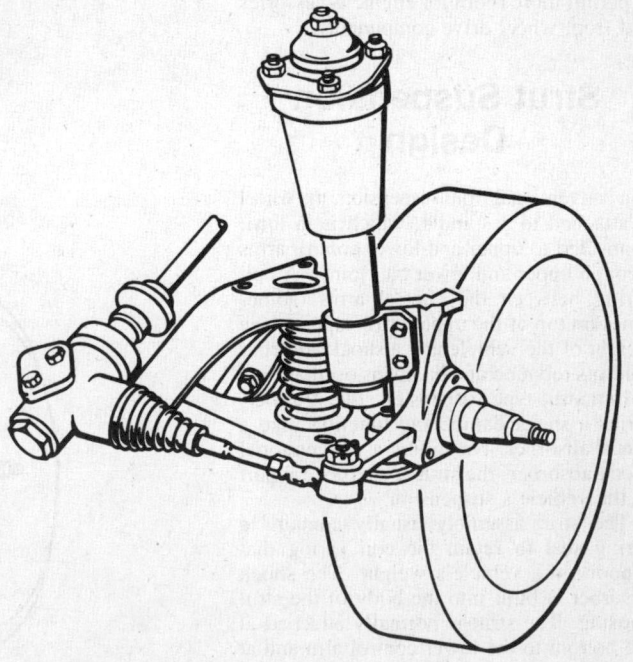

Modified MacPherson strut design with coil spring on the lower arm

into the housing.

Sealed, OEM units can also be serviced by replacement with an aftermarket unit, that will permit future servicing by cartridge replacement.

WHEEL ALIGNMENT

It is not always necessary to re-align the wheels after struts are serviced. If care is taken matchmarking affected components and in reassembling, alignment may be unaffected. However, if wheels were not in proper alignment prior to service, or if the entire strut assembly was replaced, a wheel alignment check should be made. Generally, only camber is adjustable, and then only within a narrow range.

Do not attempt to bend components to correct wheel alignment.

Since the majority of OEM struts are serviced by replacement, most manufacturers recommend wheel alignment following strut replacement.

Tools

Without the right tools, a strut job will take longer than necessary and can be dangerous.

A normal selection of hand tools such as open end and box wrenches, sockets, pliers, screwdrivers and hammers are necessary to work on struts. Extensions and universal joints will help reach tight spots. Be sure to have both metric and inch-sized wrenches on hand. Two big time-savers are "crowsfeet" and ratcheting box wrenches in assorted sizes. Torx fasteners are also showing up more and more in chassis fasteners.

In addition to the normal handtools, some sort of spanner is necessary to remove the body nut on serviceable struts. Sometimes a pipe wrench can be used successfully.

Strut and cartridge replacement requires a spring compressor.

Makeshift tools for compressing coil springs—threaded rod, chains, wire or other methods—should never be used. The coil spring is under tremendous compression and can fly off causing personal injury and damage to equipment. Use only a good quality spring compressor such as described below.

Economy, or manual, spring compressors are the least expensive but more time consuming to use. Angle hooks grasp the spring coils and must be compressed with a wrench. For those who service struts infrequently, this is probably the wisest investment for purchase.

Other manual spring compressors (jaws type) are faster to operate, have a more positive gripping action and can be used on or off the car. These types are probably not cost effective for the do-it-yourselfer, but can be rented from auto supply stores for single-time use.

For volume work, compressors that are pneumatically or hydraulically operated are

MAINTAINING WHEEL ALIGNMENT

The location and method of adjusting wheel alignment determines the components that must be match-marked to maintain wheel alignment. There are 4 basic methods of adjusting wheel alignment. Almost all cars use one of these or a slight variation.

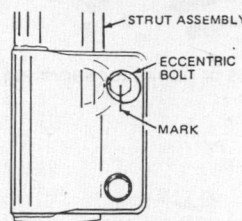

Mark the eccentric (camber adjusting bolt) relative to the clevis mounting bracket.

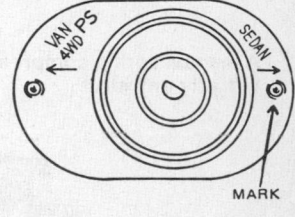

Mark the mounting stud that faces the front of the vehicle. This type of bracket is reversible for varying applications.

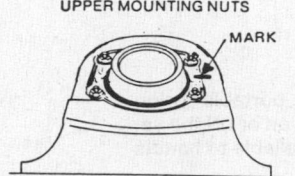

Mark the upper support housing relative to the inner fender before removing the strut from the upper mount.

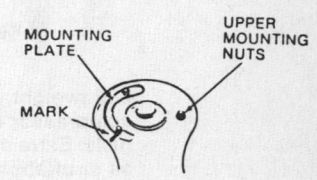

Mark the location of the mounting plate relative to the location on the inner fender.

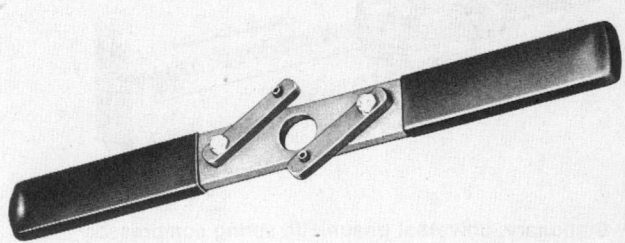

A simple spanner wrench designed for use with body nuts equipped with recessed lugs. A pipe wrench is a frequent substitute

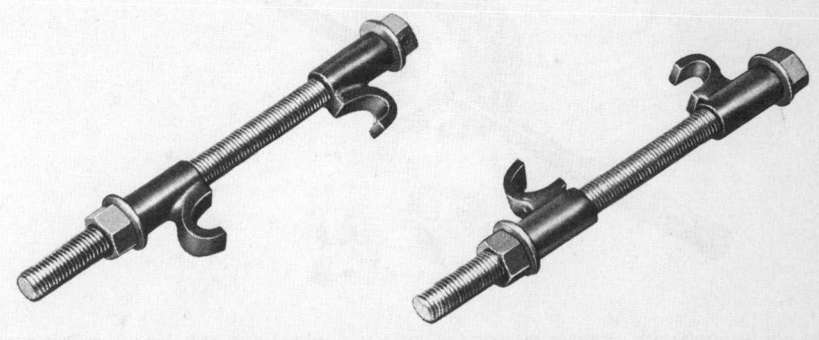

An economical manual spring compressor

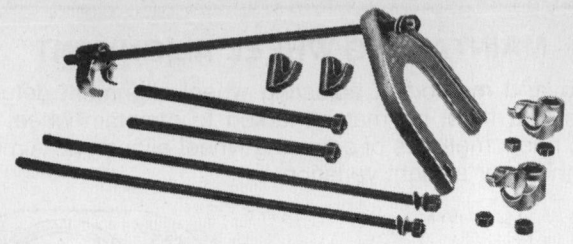

A manual spring compressor with plates or hooks for servicing virtually any strut

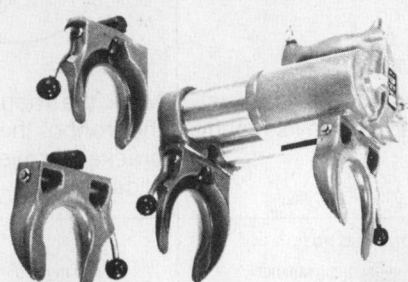

Lightweight, air operated, portable spring compressor can be used on or off the vehicle. Extra shoes are available to handle all strut applications

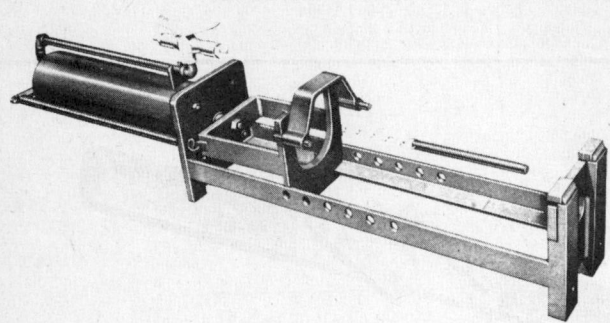

Stationary, universal pneumatic spring compressor

Spanner wrench with adaptor inserts for various applications of body nuts. This type of spanner can be used with a torque wrench for retorqueing the body nut

best. Air operated compressors are suitable for all types of struts (through use of adaptors), are lightweight and can be used on or off the vehicle. Bench mounted hydraulically operated units are probably the safest, but are also the most expensive and require that the strut be removed from the vehicle, which means separating brake lines and other connections which can be time consuming.

There are also universal kits that fit all struts in either the manual or air operated types.

Regardless of what type of spring compressor you're using, GM front wheel drive A-, J-, and X-cars as well as Chrysler Corp. Omni, Horizon and K-cars, require the use of a special spring compressor with self-leveling plates to grasp the spring seats as the spring is compressed. Likewise, the portable, pneumatic units have extra wide shoe sets suitable for these cars. The shoes are also epoxy coated to avoid scratching the coated springs on these models.

GM front wheel drive A-, J- and X-cars also make use of a camber assist tool, that makes camber adjustment a one man job.

A tube cutter is necessary on GM J-cars to cut the welded top from the strut housing for cartridge replacement.

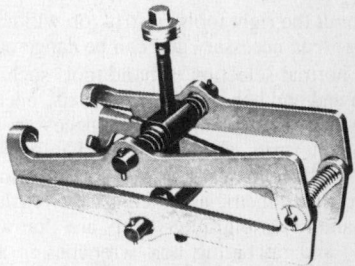

"Jaws" type spring compressor

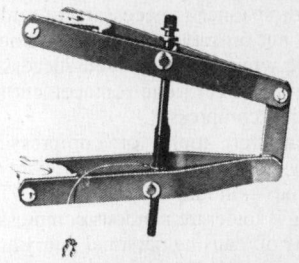

Spring compressor for GM and Chrysler product applications

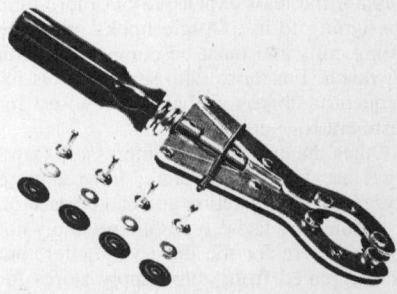

A tube cutter allows opening of the GM J-car struts for cartridge replacement

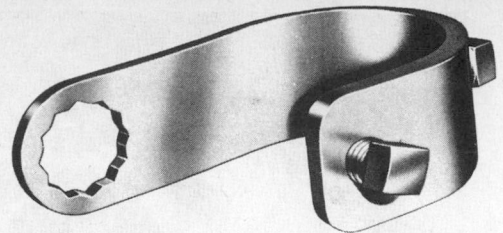

A camber assist tool makes GM cars a one-man job

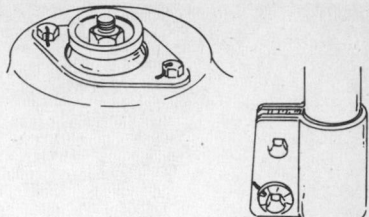

Mark the position of the attachments that control wheel alignment. See Maintaining Wheel Alignment earlier in this section

Repair Tips

1. Make sure you have all the tools you'll need. NEVER IMPROVISE A SPRING COMPRESSOR.

2. Normally both front struts should be repaired or replaced at the same time.

3. The easiest way to work on most struts is to remove the entire unit from the vehicle, unless you have access to an air operated spring compressor. Some struts, however, can, and should, be repaired while installed on the vehicle.

4. Always read the instructions packaged with any replacement parts. In particular, note whether the body nut is supplied new or re-used.

5. Mark the position(s) of any bearing plate nuts or cam bolts to assure proper alignment after installation.

6. Be sure to protect the rubber boot on the drive axle of front wheel drive cars.

7. If necessary to remove the brake caliper, do not let the caliper hang by the brake hose. Suspend the caliper from a wire hook or rope.

8. Be careful in clamping a strut in a vise. Special fixtures are available to hold struts in a vise, but are not necessary if care is used to be sure the housing is not crushed or dented. A block of soft wood on either side of the housing will prevent most damage.

9. Use a spring compressor to relieve tension from the spring. Be sure to clean and lubricate the screw threads, particularly on hand operated (manual) spring compressors.

Some springs have a special coating that should not be scuffed.

10. If you are replacing the strut cartridge, clean the inside of the strut housing and the body nut threads before replacing the oil and installing a new cartridge.

11. Be sure to use OEM quality fasteners any time a fastener is replaced.

STRUT OVERHAUL (OFF-CAR)

Following is a typical overhaul procedure of a serviceable MacPherson strut, after having removed the strut from the vehicle. The vehicle should be firmly supported. If it is necessary, to separate the brake line from the strut for strut removal, the brakes will have to be bled after reinstallation. See the manufacturer's car section for specific MacPherson strut removal and installation procedures.

Photos Courtesy Gabriel Div., Maremont Corp.

Step 1. Examine the strut assembly for damage, dented strut body, spring seat, broken or missing strut mounting parts. Any of these will require replacement of the complete assembly. Also inspect other suspension components for wear or damage

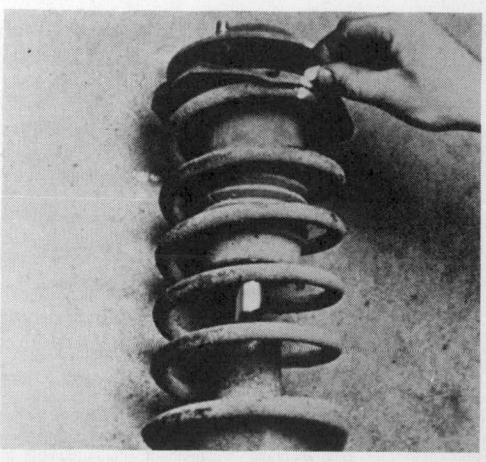

Step 2. Matchmark the upper end of the coil spring and bearing plate to avoid confusion during reassembly

Step 3. To make servicing easier, clamp the strut in a strut vise. The strut vise is designed to clamp the strut tight without damage to strut cylinder. It is very handy for strut work and can be used in your shop vise or mounted to any bench

Step 4. Before using the manual spring compressor, lubricate both sides of the thrust washers and the threads with a light coat of grease

Step 5. Install the compressor hooks on opposite sides of the coil spring with the hooks attached to the upper-most and lower-most spring coils. To avoid possible slippage, use tape or small hose clamps on either side of the compressor hooks

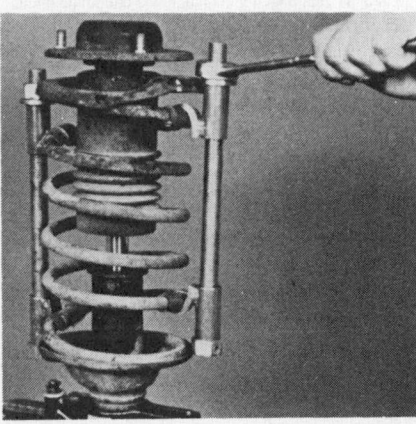

Step 6. Alternately tighten the bolts a few turns at a time until all tension is removed from the spring seat

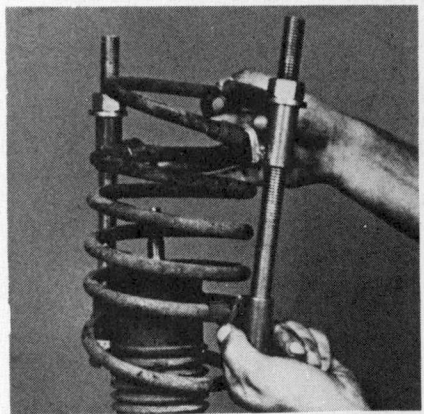

Step 7. Remove the piston rod nut and disassemble the upper mounting parts, keeping them in order for reassembly. Remove the coil spring. There is no need to remove the compressor from the coil spring

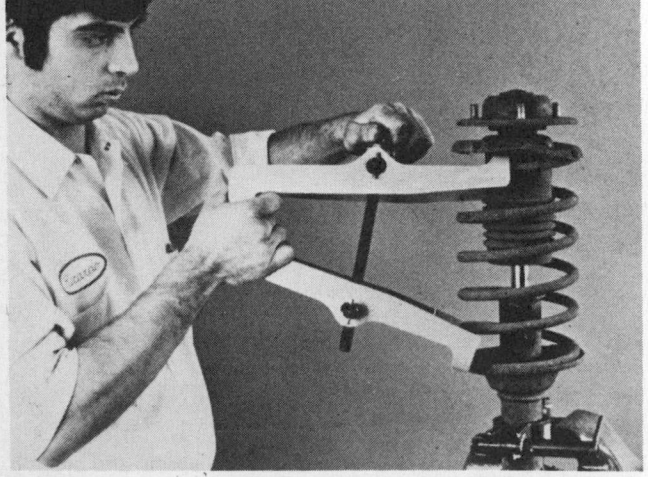

Step 8. An alternative to the manual compressor is the "jaws" type. Turn the load screw to open or close the compressor until the maximum number of spring coils can be engaged

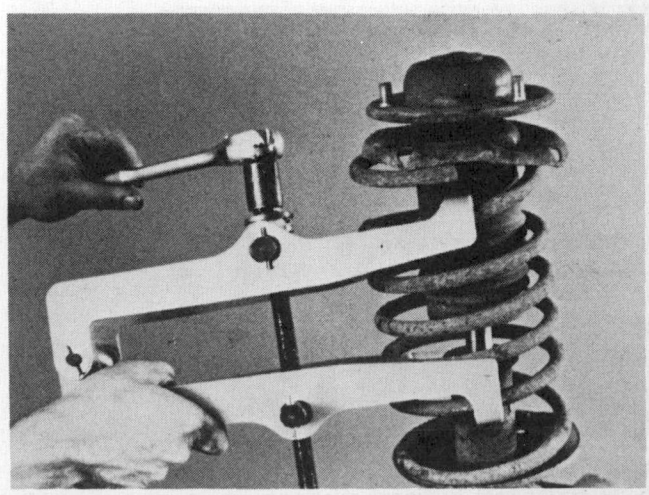

Step 9. Tighten the load screw until the coil spring is loose from the spring seats. There is no need to compress the spring any further

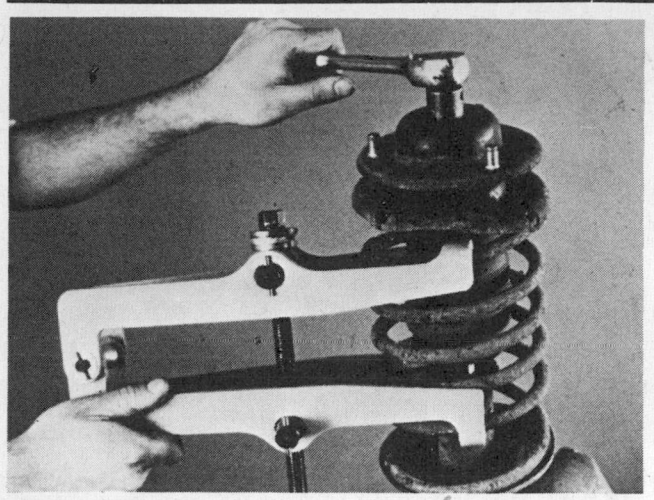

Step 10. Remove the piston rod nut and disassemble the upper mounting parts

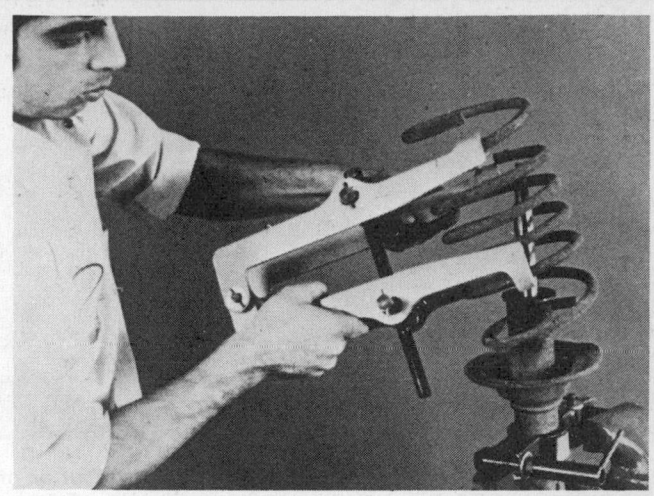

Step 11. Like the manual compressor, there is no need to remove the compressor from the coil spring. Remove the coil spring and compressor

Step 12. Keep the upper mounting parts in order of their removal. They'll be re-assembled in reverse order

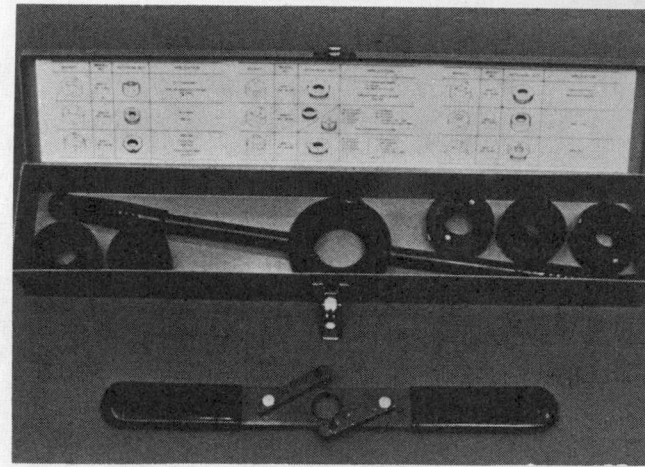

Step 13. A spanner wrench is necessary to remove body nuts, although a pipe wrench will do the job

Step 14. Use the spanner wrench or pipe wrench to loosen the body nut

Step 15. Remove the body nut and discard if a new body nut came with the replacement cartridge. If not, save the body nut

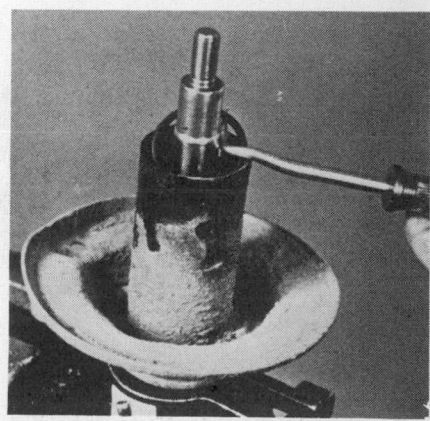

Step 16. Use a scribe or suitable tool to remove the O-ring from the top of the housing

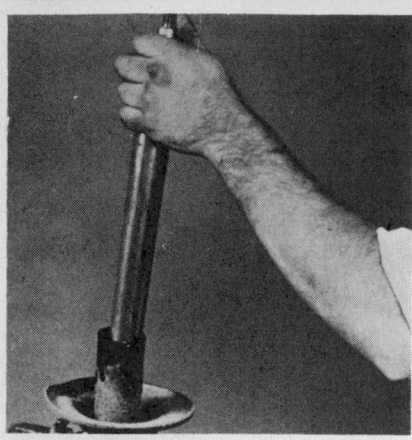

Step 17. Grasp the piston rod and pull cartridge out of the housing. Remove it slowly to avoid splashing oil. Be sure all pieces come out of the housing

Step 18. Pour all of the strut fluid into a suitable container, clean the inside of the strut cylinder, and inspect the cylinder for dents and to insure that all loose parts have been removed from inside of strut body

Step 19. Refill the cylinder with one ounce (a shot glass) of the original oil or fresh oil. The oil helps dissipate internal cartridge heat during operation and results in a cooler running, longer lasting unit. Do not put too much oil in—otherwise the oil may leak at the body nut after it expands when heated

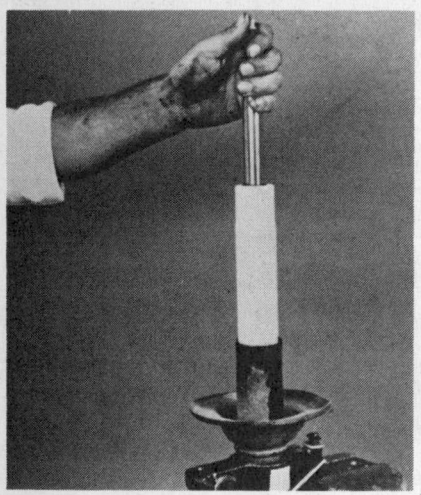

Step 20. Insert the new replacement cartridge into the strut body

Step 21. Push the piston rod *all* the way down, to avoid damage to the piston rod if the spaner wrench slips, and start the body nut by hand. Be sure it is not cross-threaded

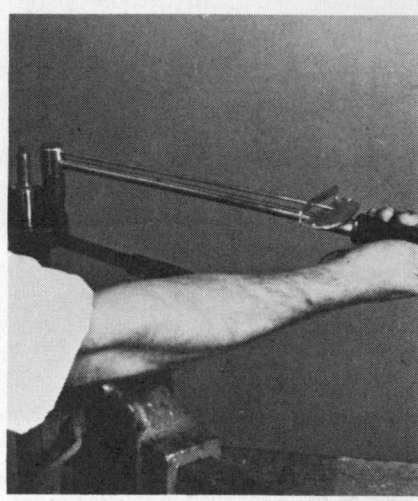

Step 22. Tighten the body nut securely

Step 23. Inspect the loose parts prior to re-assembly. Note the chalk mark location for proper seating of the upper spring seat

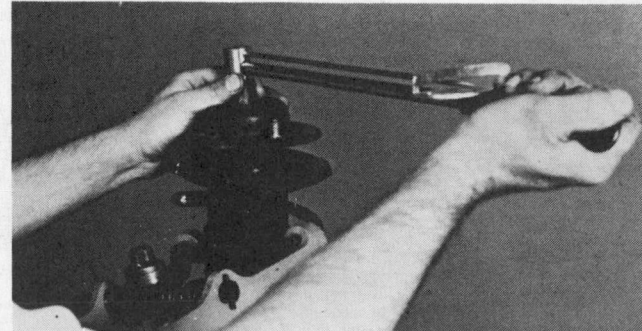

Step 24. Re-assemble the coil spring and upper mounting parts in reverse order. Tighten the piston rod nut and remove the spring compressor. Install the dust cap. Install the strut in the vehicle. See the car section for details

STRUT OVERHAUL

Most domestic car OEM MacPherson struts are sealed units and not repairable. The exceptions are GM front wheel drive A- and J-cars, which use replaceable cartridges. All other cars must use aftermarket struts to be serviceable at a future date. The following procedures cover disassembly of the strut, installation of a serviceable strut, reassembly and cartridge replacement on GM front wheel drive A- and J-models. Consult the applicable manufacturer's car section for removal and installation procedures.

Photos Courtesy Gabriel Div., Maremont Corp.

Step 1. Most domestic cars are serviced initially by replacing the entire strut rather than by using a replacement cartridge. This is necessary because the original equipment struts are sealed shut and cannot be serviced with a replacement cartridge. After-market struts are designed with serviceable threaded body nuts which means they can be serviced in the future by installing a replacement cartridge, using normal cartridge service methods, rather than by replacing the entire strut

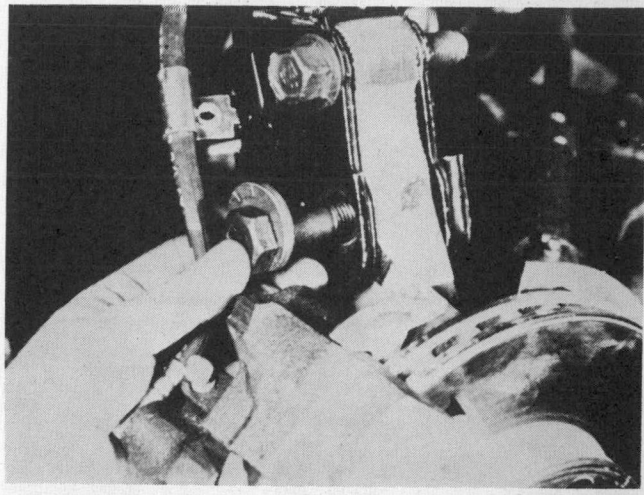

Step 2. An X-car is shown, but the lower mount on the Citation is typical of many vehicles. They all have two bolt clevis mounts and the position of the strut determines the camber adjustment. This means that if you are replacing a sealed strut, front end alignment is necessary because the original alignment is eliminated when you change the strut. If the car has a serviceable strut, you can retain the alignment by marking the position of the mounting bolt relative to the strut. GM has made a running change on the lower mount of their X-Car. The earlier type had an eccentric bolt for camber adjustment. Camber on the latest type is adjusted by pushing or pulling on the wheel with the bolts loosened slightly, but the eccentric can be installed on later cars

Step 3. A special type spring compressor is required for the GM cars and Chrysler K and L cars. A compressor should be used that does not damage the protective coating on the coil spring. Virtually any compressor can be used on other car lines/models

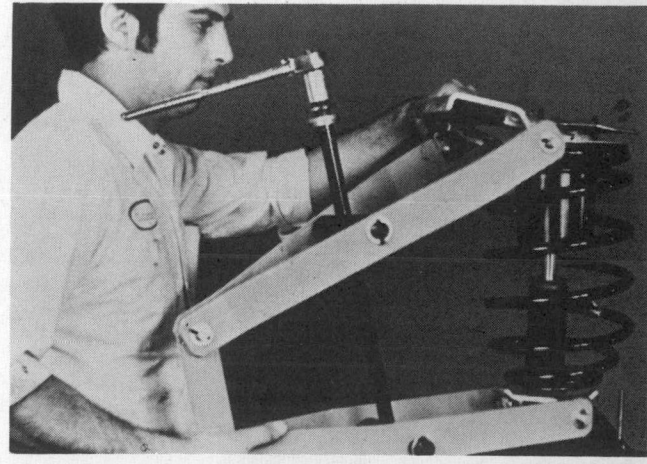

Step 4. Secure the strut in the strut vise; turn the load screw counter-clockwise until the lower plate can be fitted under the lower spring seat and the upper plate can be fitted between the upper spring seat and support housing

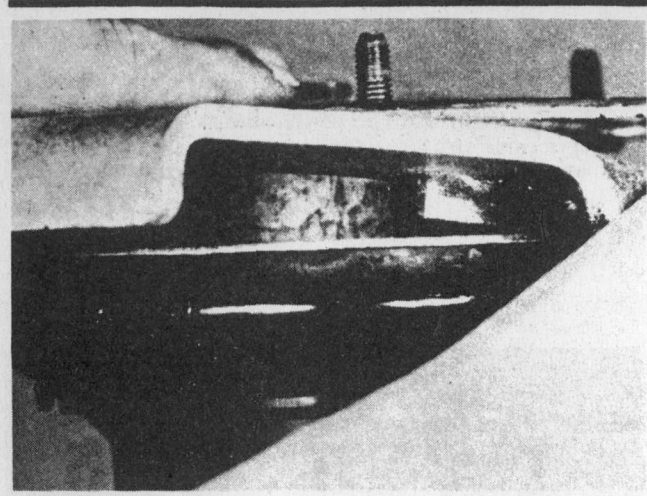

Step 5. Make sure that the crescent shaped bars on the upper compression plate are located inside the upper spring seat

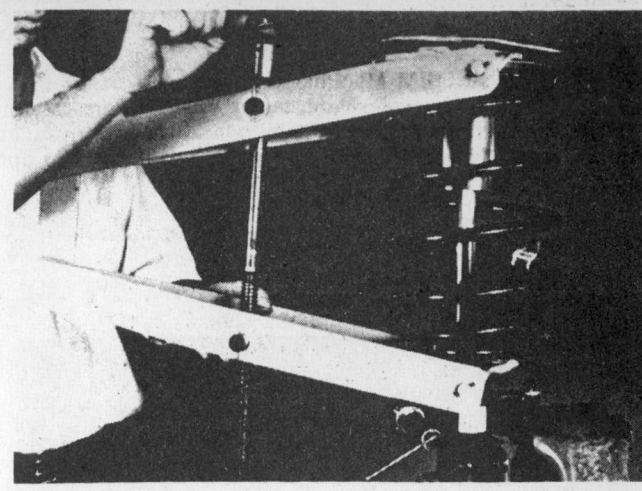

Step 6. Turn the load screw clockwise enough to tighten the compression plates on the spring seats. Stop and make sure that the coil spring will not arch, and that the pivot points are aligned with the center-line of the coil spring

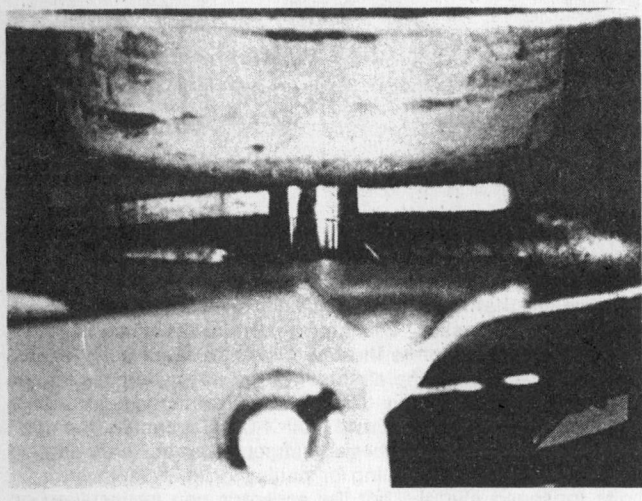

Step 7. Continue to tighten the load screw until the upper support housing can be pulled up to expose about ½ inch of piston rod. This assures that the spring load has been removed from upper spring seat

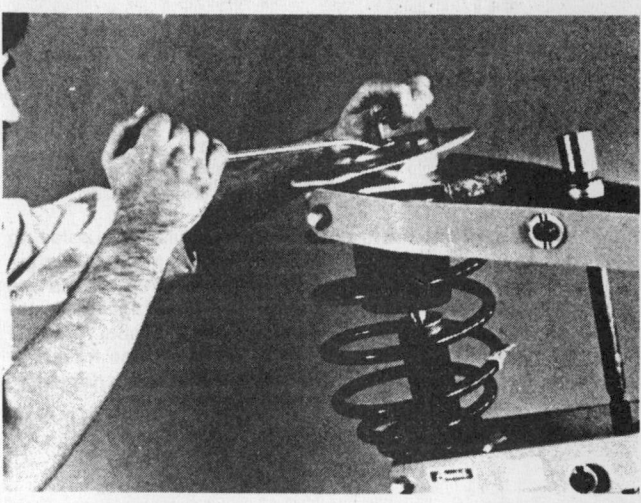

Step 8. Remove the piston rod nut with the aid of a wrench to keep the piston rod from turning and remove upper support housing

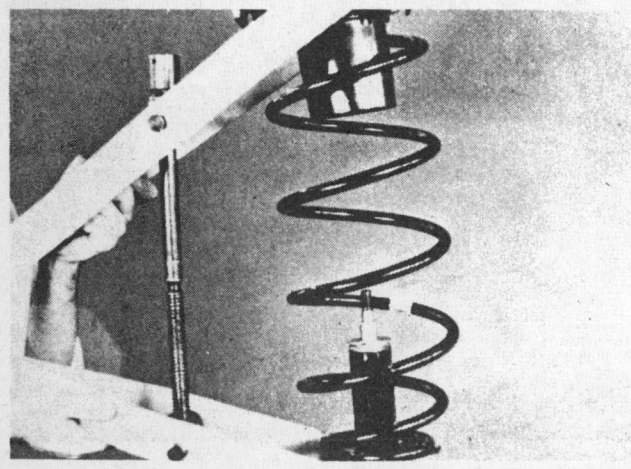

Step 9. Turn the load screw counter-clockwise until the spring tension is completely relieved. Remove the compressor, coil spring and upper support housing from the strut.

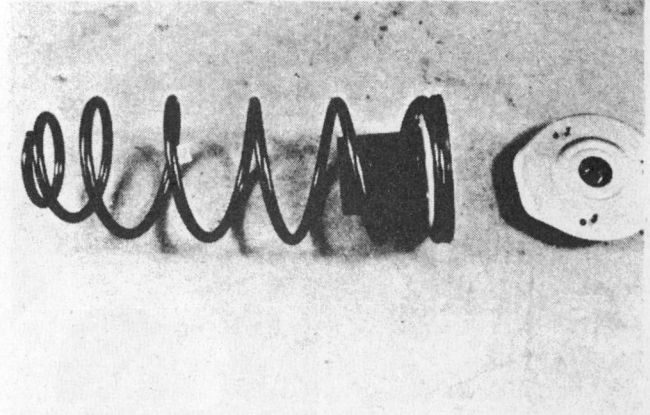

Step 10 Assemble the upper mounting parts in order of their removal. They'll be re–assembled in reverse order

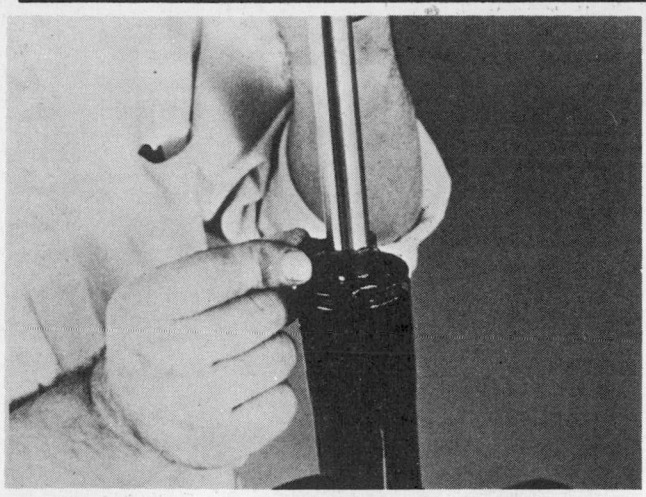

Step 11. Place the new strut in the vise and extend piston rod fully and install clip (spring type clothes pin will do) as shown. This keeps the piston rod extended while assembling the spring and upper mounting parts.

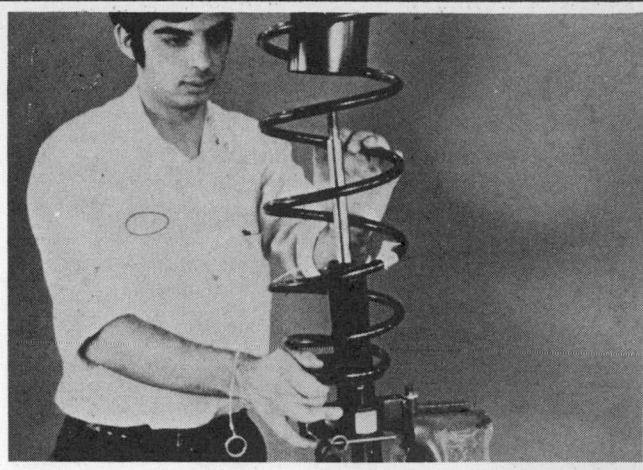

Step 12. Install the coil spring and upper spring seat on the new strut

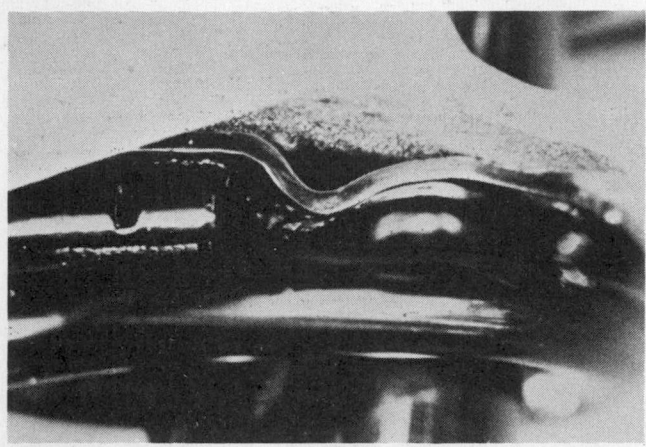

Step 13. Make sure that the spring helix is aligned with the lower spring seat

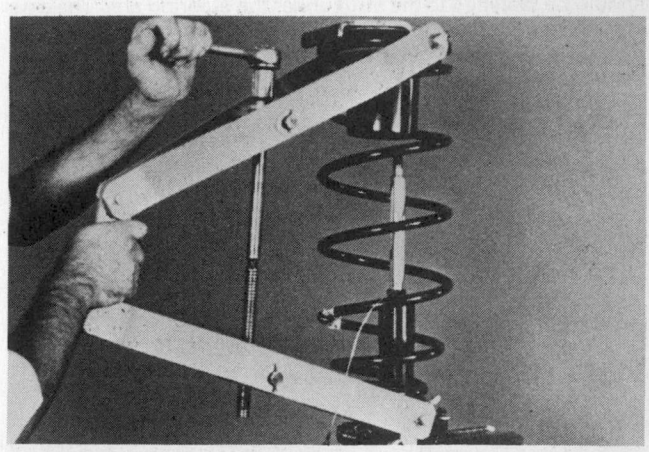

Step 14. Locate upper and lower compression plates on spring seat

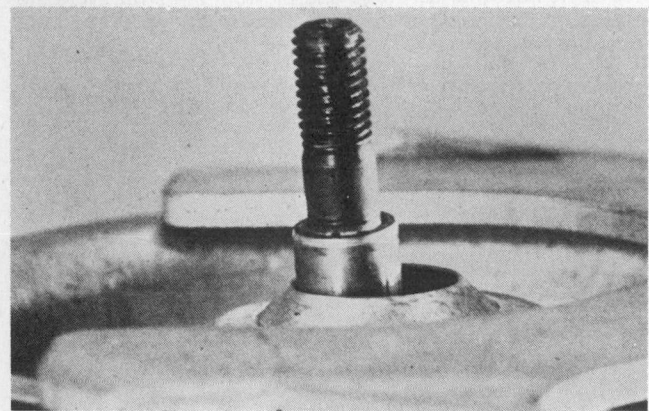

Step 15. Make sure that the crescent shaped bars on the upper compression plate are located on the upper spring seat as shown. Turn the load screw clockwise enough to tighten the compression plates on the upper and lower spring seats. Stop. Again, to assure that the coil spring will not arch, make sure that the pivot points are aligned with the centerline of the coil spring. Then continue turning the load screw clockwise until about 1½ inches of piston rod is showing above the upper spring seat

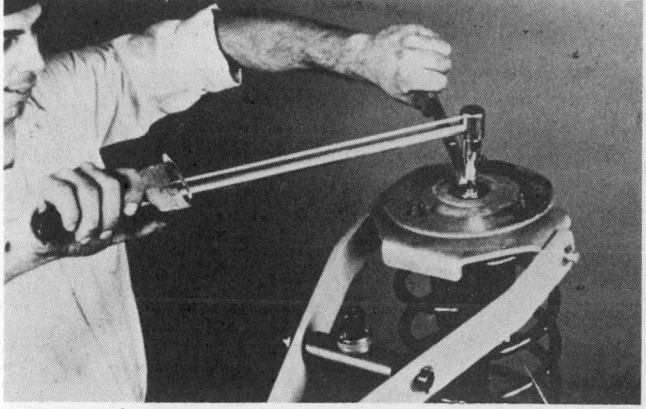

Step 16. Install upper support housing on piston rod. Tighten the piston rod nut and remove the compressor from the strut and the strut from the vise. Install the strut. See the car section for details

GM J- AND A-CARS ONLY

Step 1. Place the strut assembly in a vise, and compress the coil spring. Remove the piston rod, upper support housing, spring seat and coil spring. If the universal pneumatic spring compressor is used, an adaptor provided with the compressor should be fastened to the strut under the steering arm. The ears of the adaptor should be aligned with steering arm. The adaptor provides a square seating surface for the strut while it is being compressed

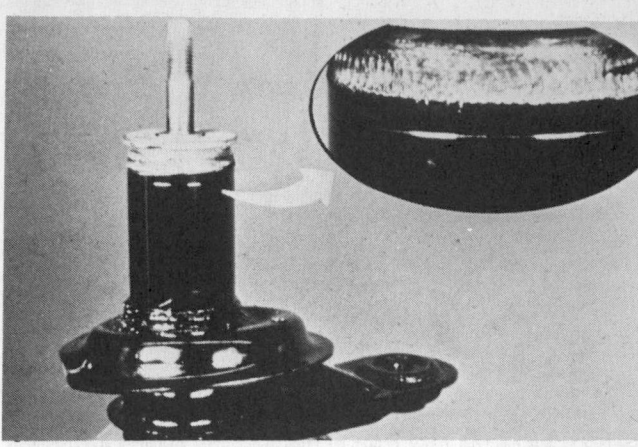

Step 2. J and A–car struts have a welded upper closure, but the strut is designed so the damping mechanism can be replaced with a cartridge insert. Just below the spin weld there is a cut-line scribed in the strut body

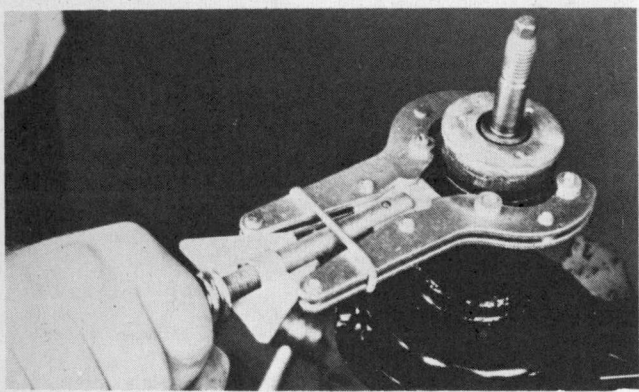

Step 3. Using a pipe cutter, cut open the strut body at the scribed line. (Note: *It is important that the cut be made on the cut-line*)

Step 4. Remove the cartridge and oil from the strut. Note the threads on the inside of the strut. Deburr the top of the strut body if necessary

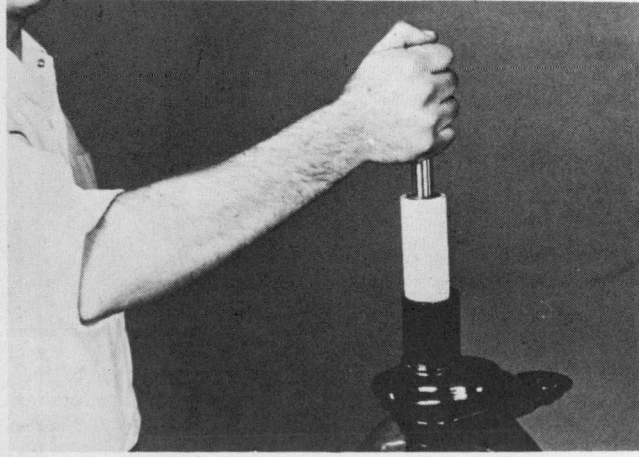

Step 5. Pour about one ounce of oil into the strut body and insert the replacement cartridge. Push the piston rod down and start the body nut by hand. Tighten the nut securely

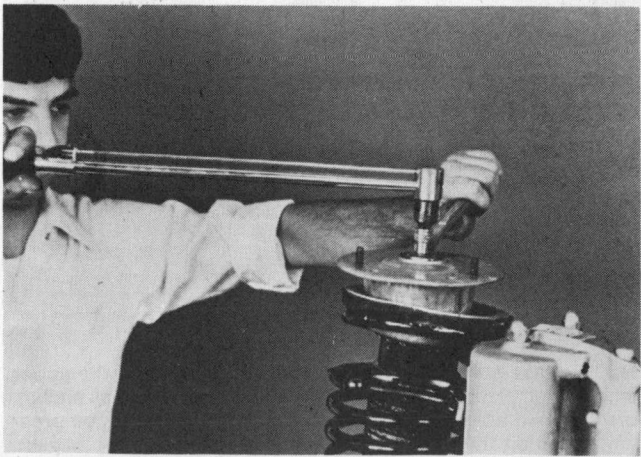

Step 6. Assemble spring, upper spring seat, and upper support housing on the strut, and tighten the new piston rod nut. The renewed strut is now ready to install on the vehicle. Release the spring tension

— MACPHERSON STRUT PROBLEM DIAGNOSIS —

Problems with MacPherson struts generally fall into 3 main categories: suspension, tire wear and steering. In general, the symptoms encountered are not significantly different from those encountered on conventional suspensions.

Suspension

Sag

Vehicle "sag" is a visible tilt of the car from one side to the other or one end to the other while parked on a level surface.

Weak or damaged strut springs could cause this condition and should be repaired immediately.

Sag will also cause steering and tire wear problems to be more pronounced and vehicle instability on rough roads. Front wheel alignment will not solve the problem.

Weak strut springs increase vehicle sag. See "Tire Cupping"

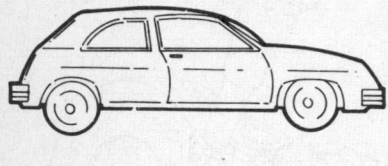

Cartridge Leaks

Strut cartridge leaks (not seepage) indicate the need for cartridge or strut replacement. Be sure the leakage is coming from the strut, and not from elsewhere on the vehicle.

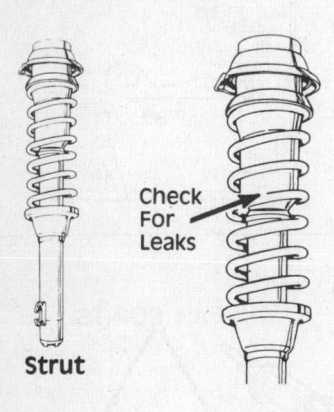

Strut

Abnormal Tire Wear

Wear on One Side

One sided tire wear indicates incorrect camber. Check the causes in the accompanying illustration and be sure the wheel alignment is correct.

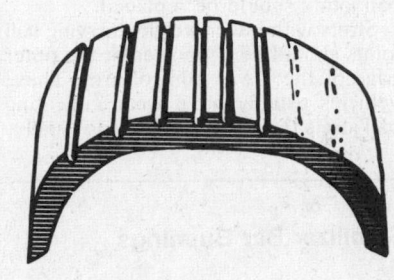

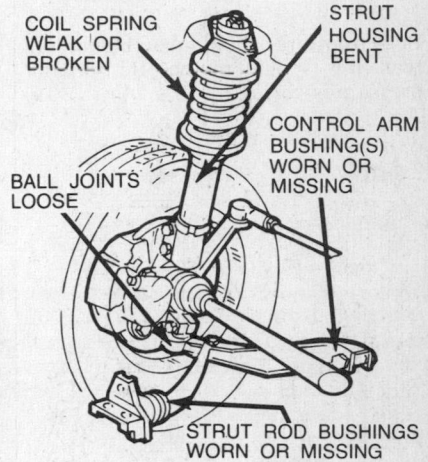

COIL SPRING WEAK OR BROKEN — STRUT HOUSING BENT — CONTROL ARM BUSHING(S) WORN OR MISSING — BALL JOINTS LOOSE — STRUT ROD BUSHINGS WORN OR MISSING

Tire "Cupping"

Cupped tires indicate any or all of the following problems.

1. A weak strut cartridge can be verified by bouncing each corner of the car vigorously and letting go. The car should not bounce more than once, if the shock absorber cartridges are good.

2. Weak strut springs allow sag to increase with only a slight amount of downward pressure. A visual inspection will reveal any broken springs or shiny spots.

3. Check for loose or worn wheel bearings with the weight of the car off of the wheel.

4. Check the wheel balance.

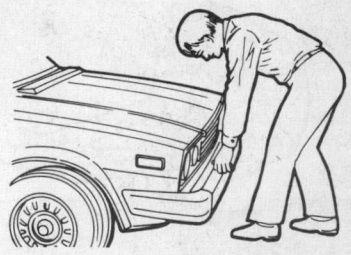

Tread Edge Wear

Wear along tread edges (feathering) indicates a suspension or steering system problem.

1. Strut rod bushings are worn or missing.

2. Tie rod end wear can be determined by grabbing the tie rod end firmly and forcing it up, down or sideways to check for lost motion.

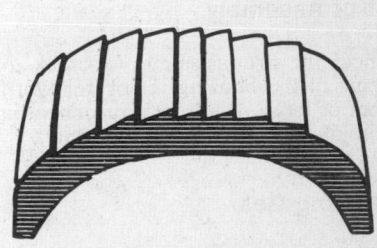

MACPHERSON STRUT PROBLEM DIAGNOSIS

Problems with MacPherson struts generally fall into 3 main categories: suspension, tire wear and steering. In general, the symptoms encountered are not significantly different from those encountered on conventional suspensions.

Steering

Tires

Both front tires should match and both rear tires should match. Be sure air pressure is correct.

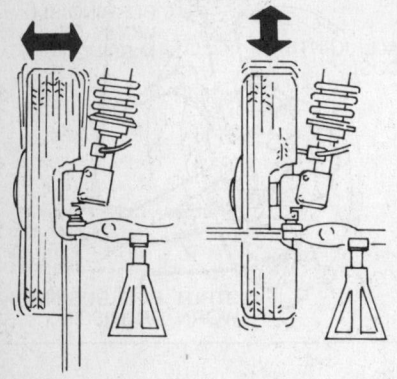

Ball Joints

Support the car under the frame or crossmember so that the jack does not interfere with the control arm. Rock the tire in and out and up and down. Excessive movement means that both ball joints should be replaced.

Struts with lower weight-carrying ball joints should be supported at the outer edge of the lower control arm. These vehicles usually have wear indicating ball joints that can be checked visually.

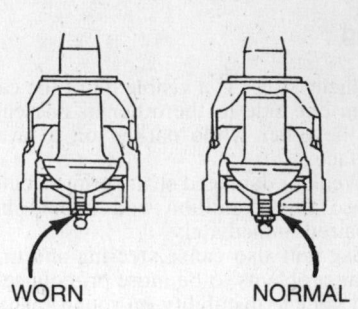

WORN   NORMAL

Strut Rod Bushings

Grasp the strut rod and shake it. Any noticeable play indicates excessive wear and need for parts replacement.

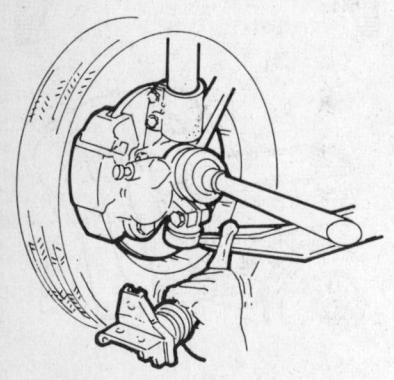

Stabilizer Bar Bushings

Check for worn bushings or lost motion with the vehicle level and the weight evenly distributed on all wheels.

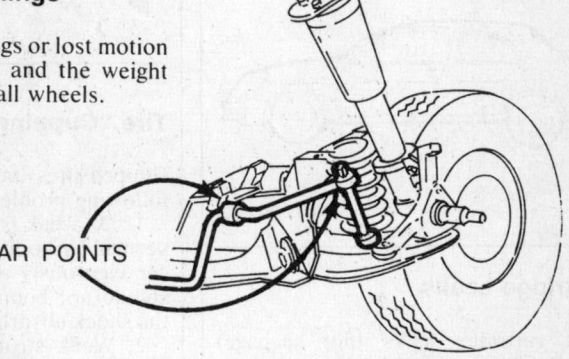

WEAR POINTS

Control Arm Bushings

Support the car under the frame or body and remove the weight from the wheel and control arm. Check for free-play in the bushings at the pivot point, using a pry bar.

NOTE: Some control arm bushings are serviceable only by replacing the entire arm.

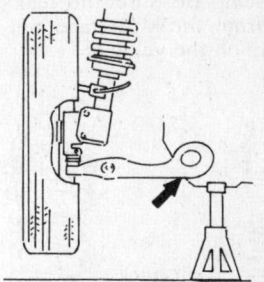

Strut Assembly

Check the strut assembly for cracks or dents in the housing. Look for worn, bent or loose piston rods or dents that will inhibit piston rod movement.

Steering Gear

Check for worn steering gear or loose or worn mounting bolts and bushings.

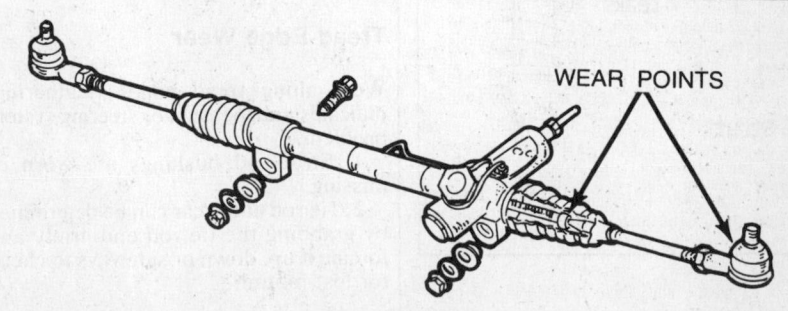

WEAR POINTS

Brakes  39

Hydraulic Brake Component Service

BASIC OPERATING PRINCIPLES

The hydraulic brake system transports the power required to force the frictional surfaces of the braking system together from the pedal to the individual brake units at each wheel. A hydraulic system is used for 2 reasons. First, fluid under pressure can be carried to all parts of an automobile by small hoses (some of which are flexible) without taking up a significant amount of room or posing routing problems. Second, a great mechanical advantage can be given to the brake pedal end of the system and the foot pressure required to actuate the brakes can be reduced by making the surface area of the master cylinder pistons smaller than that of any of the pistons in the wheel cylinders or calipers.

The master cylinder consists of a double reservoir and piston assembly as well as other springs, fittings, etc. Double (dual) master cylinders are designed to separate the wheels from the others into a pair of hydraulic systems. The standard approach has been have separate circuits for the front and rear wheels. Newer models may have a diagonally split system; i.e. a front wheel and the opposite side rear wheel are in a separate circuit from the other front and rear wheel.

Steel lines carry the brake fluid to a point on the vehicles frame near each wheel. A flexible hose usually carries the fluid to the disc caliper or wheel cylinder. The flexible line allows for suspension and steering movement.

The rear wheel cylinders contain 2 pistons, 1 at either end, which push outward in opposite directions. Most brake calipers contain a single piston, however in some cases they may contain more.

All pistons employ some type of seal, usually made of rubber, to minimize fluid leakage. A rubber dust boot seals the outer end of the cylinder against dust and dirt. The boot fits around the outer end of the piston on disc brake calipers and around the brake actuating rod on the wheel cylinders.

The hydraulic system operates as follows: When at rest, the entire system, from the piston(s) in the master cylinder to those in the wheel cylinders or calipers, is full of brake fluid. Upon application of the brake pedal, fluid trapped in front of the master cylinder piston(s) is forced through the lines to the wheel cylinders and calipers. Here, it forces the pistons outward, in the case of drum brakes and inward toward the disc, in the case of disc brakes. The motion of the pistons is opposed by return springs mounted outside the cylinders in drum brakes and by internal springs or spring seals, in disc brakes.

Upon release of the brake pedal, a spring located inside the master cylinder immediately returns the master cylinder pistons to the normal position. The pistons contain check valves and the master cylinder has compensating ports drilled in it. These are uncovered as the pistons reach their normal position. The piston check valves allow fluid to flow toward the wheel cylinders or calipers as the pistons withdraw. Then, as the rubber boot/seal or return springs force the brake pads or shoes into the released position, the excess fluid returns to the reservoir through the compensating ports.

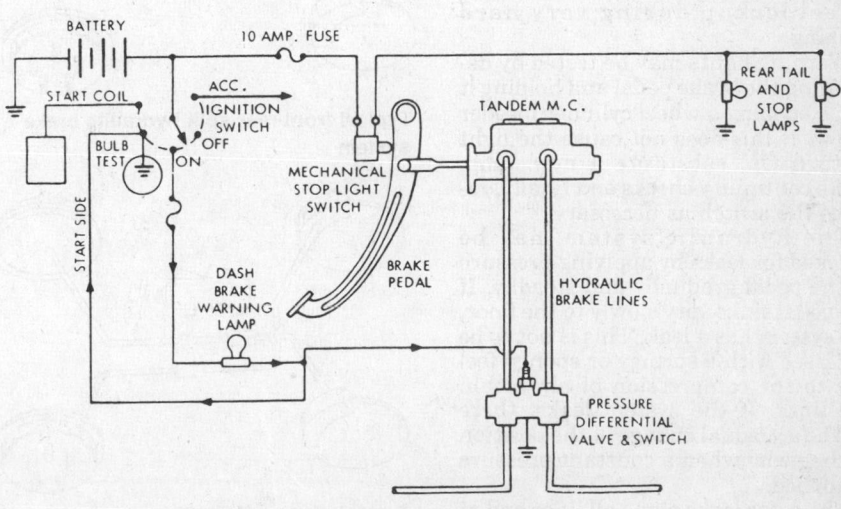

Typical dual brake system

The dual master cylinder has 2 pistons, located 1 behind the other. The primary piston is actuated directly by mechanical linkage from the brake pedal. The secondary piston is actuated by fluid trapped between the 2 pistons. If a leak develops in front of the secondary piston, it moves forward until it bottoms against the front of the master cylinder. The fluid trapped between the pistons will operate opposite sides of the split system. If the other side of the system develops a leak, the primary piston will move forward until direct contact with the secondary piston takes place and it will force the secondary piston to actuate the other side of the split system. In either case the brake pedal drops closer to the floor board and less braking power is available.

The brake system uses a switch to warn the driver when only half of the brake system is operational. This switch is usually located in a valve body which is mounted on the firewall or the frame below the master cylinder. A hydraulic piston receives pressure from both circuits, each circuit's pressure being applied to opposite end of the piston. When the pressures are in balance, the piston remains stationary. When a circuit has a leak, however, the greater pressure in that circuit during brake application will push the piston to 1 side, closing the switch and activating the brake warning light.

In disc brake systems, this valve body contains a metering valve and, in some cases, a proportioning valve or valves. The metering valve keeps pressure from traveling to the disc brakes on the front wheels until the brake shoes on the rear wheels have contacted the drums, ensuring that the front brakes will never be used alone. The proportioning valve controls the pressure to the rear brakes to avoid rear wheel lockup during very hard braking.

Warning lights may be tested by depressing the brake pedal and holding it while opening a wheel cylinder bleeder screw. If this does not cause the light to turn On, substitute a new lamp, make continuity checks and finally, replace the switch as necessary.

The hydraulic system may be checked for leaks by applying pressure to the pedal gradually and steadily. If the pedal sinks very slowly to the floor, the system has a leak. This is not to be confused with a springy or spongy feel due to the compression of air within the lines. If the system leaks, there will be a gradual change in the position of the pedal when a constant pressure is applied.

Check for leaks along all lines and at wheel cylinders or calipers. If no exter-nal leaks are apparent, the problem is inside the master cylinder.

DISC BRAKES

Disc brake systems utilize a disc (rotor) with brake pads positioned on either side of it. Braking effect is achieved in a manner similar to the way you would squeeze a spinning phonograph record between your fingers. The disc (rotor) is a casting which may be equipped with cooling fins between the 2 braking surfaces. The fins (if equipped) enable air to circulate between the braking surfaces making them less sensitive to heat buildup and more resistant to fade. Dirt and water do not affect braking action since contaminants are thrown off by the centrifugal action of the rotor or scraped off by the pads. Also, the equal clamping action of the brake pads tends to ensure uniform, straightline stops. Disc brakes are inherently self-adjusting.

DRUM BRAKES (REAR)

Drum brakes employ 2 brake shoes mounted on a stationary backing plate. These shoes are positioned inside a circular drum which rotates with the wheel assembly. The shoes are held in place by springs, this allows them to slide toward the drums (when they are applied) while keeping the linings and drums in alignment. The shoes are actuated by a wheel cylinder

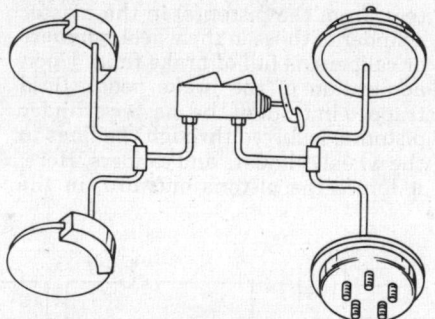

Typical front/rear split hydraulic brake system

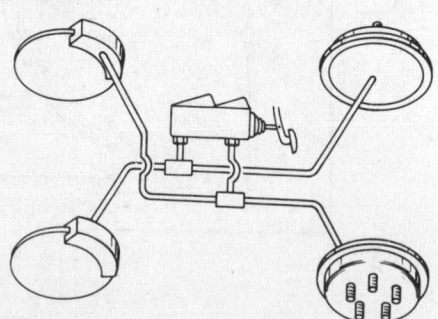

Typical diagonally split hydraulic brake system

which is mounted at the top of the backing plate. When the brakes are applied, hydraulic pressure forces the wheel cylinder's actuating links outward. Since these links bear directly against the top of the brake shoes, the tops of the shoes are then forced against the inner side of the drum. This action forces the bottoms of the 2 shoes to contact the brake drum by rotating the entire assembly slightly (known as servo action). When pressure within the wheel cylinder is relaxed, return springs pull the shoes back away from the drum.

Rear drum brakes are (in most cases) designed to self-adjust themselves during application. Motion causes both shoes to rotate very slightly with the drum, rocking an adjusting lever, thereby causing rotation of the adjusting screw or lever.

POWER BRAKE SYSTEM

Power brakes operate just as standard brake systems except in the actuation of the master cylinder pistons. A vacuum diaphragm is located on the front of the master cylinder and assists the driver in applying the brakes, reducing both the effort and travel he must put into moving the brake pedal.

The vacuum diaphragm housing is connected to the intake manifold by a vacuum hose. A check valve is placed at the point where the hose enters the diaphragm housing, so that during periods of low manifold vacuum brake assist vacuum will not be lost.

Depressing the brake pedal closes off the vacuum source and allows atmospheric pressure to enter on 1 side of the diaphragm. This causes the master cylinder pistons to move and apply the brakes. When the brake pedal is released, vacuum is applied to both sides of the diaphragm and the return springs return the diaphragm and the master cylinder pistons to the released position. If the vacuum fails, the brake pedal rod will butt against the end of the master cylinder actuating rod and direct mechanical application will occur as the pedal is depressed.

MASTER CYLINDERS

───── CAUTION ─────

The master cylinder unit is a highly calibrated unit specifically designed for the vehicle it is on. Although cylinders may look alike there are many differences in calibration. If replacement is necessary, make sure the replacement unit is the correct cylinder for the vehicle.

NOTE: Some GM vehicles are equipped with "Quick Take-Up"

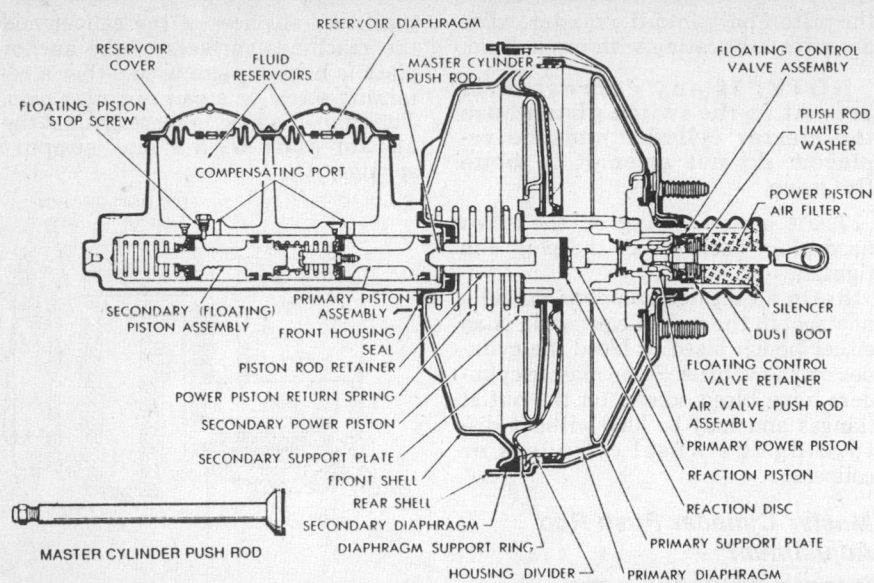

RESERVOIR COVER
RESERVOIR DIAPHRAGM
FLUID RESERVOIRS
RESERVOIR COVER
MASTER CYLINDER PUSH ROD
FLOATING CONTROL VALVE ASSEMBLY
FLOATING PISTON STOP SCREW
COMPENSATING PORT
PUSH ROD LIMITER WASHER
POWER PISTON AIR FILTER
SECONDARY (FLOATING) PISTON ASSEMBLY
FRONT HOUSING SEAL
PISTON ROD RETAINER
POWER PISTON RETURN SPRING
SECONDARY POWER PISTON
SECONDARY SUPPORT PLATE
FRONT SHELL
REAR SHELL
SECONDARY DIAPHRAGM
DIAPHRAGM SUPPORT RING
HOUSING DIVIDER
SILENCER
DUST BOOT
FLOATING CONTROL VALVE RETAINER
AIR VALVE PUSH ROD ASSEMBLY
PRIMARY POWER PISTON
REACTION PISTON
REACTION DISC
PRIMARY SUPPORT PLATE
PRIMARY DIAPHRAGM

MASTER CYLINDER PUSH ROD

Typical dual master cylinder

master cylinders which provide a large volume of fluid to the brakes at low pressure when the brake pedal is initially applied. This large volume of fluid is needed because self retracting piston seals are used on the caliper pistons. The piston seals pull the pistons into the calipers after the brakes are released, thereby preventing the brake pads from causing a drag on the rotors.

The "Quick Take-Up" master cylinder has a hydraulically operated brake warning light switch incorporated in the master cylinder body. The piston is accessible by removing the large plug at the front of the master cylinder body. Only remove the plug when overhauling the cylinder, as brake fluid will escape.

Overhaul procedures on these master cylinders are basically the same as those on conventional master cylinders.

Servicing Master Cylinders

NOTE: Plastic reservoirs need to be removed only for the following reasons: Reservoir is damaged or the rubber grommet(s) between the reservoir and bore is leaking. Removal of stop pin from Chrysler style plastic reservoir master cylinder to allow removal of pistons. Pin is located underneath front reservoir nipple. Service "Quick Take-up" valve on GM quick take-up master cylin-

ders. The reservoir should be removed by first clamping the cylinder flange in a vice. Next remove the reservoir for the Chrysler style. Grasp the reservoir base on the end and pull away from the body. GM reservoirs must be removed by prying between the reservoir and casting with a pry bar. Grommets can be reused if they are in good condition. Whether or not the reservoir is removed, it and the cover or caps should be thoroughly cleaned.

1. Remove the cylinder from the vehicle and drain the brake fluid.
2. Mount the cylinder in a vise so that the outlets are up and remove the rubber boot seal from the hub.
3. Remove the stop pin or screw from the bottom of the front reservoir, if present.
4. Remove the snapring from the front of the bore and the primary piston assembly.
5. Remove the secondary piston assembly using compressed air or a piece of wire.
6. Clean the metal parts in brake fluid and discard the rubber parts.
7. Inspect the bore for damage or wear, then check the pistons for damage and proper clearance in the bore.

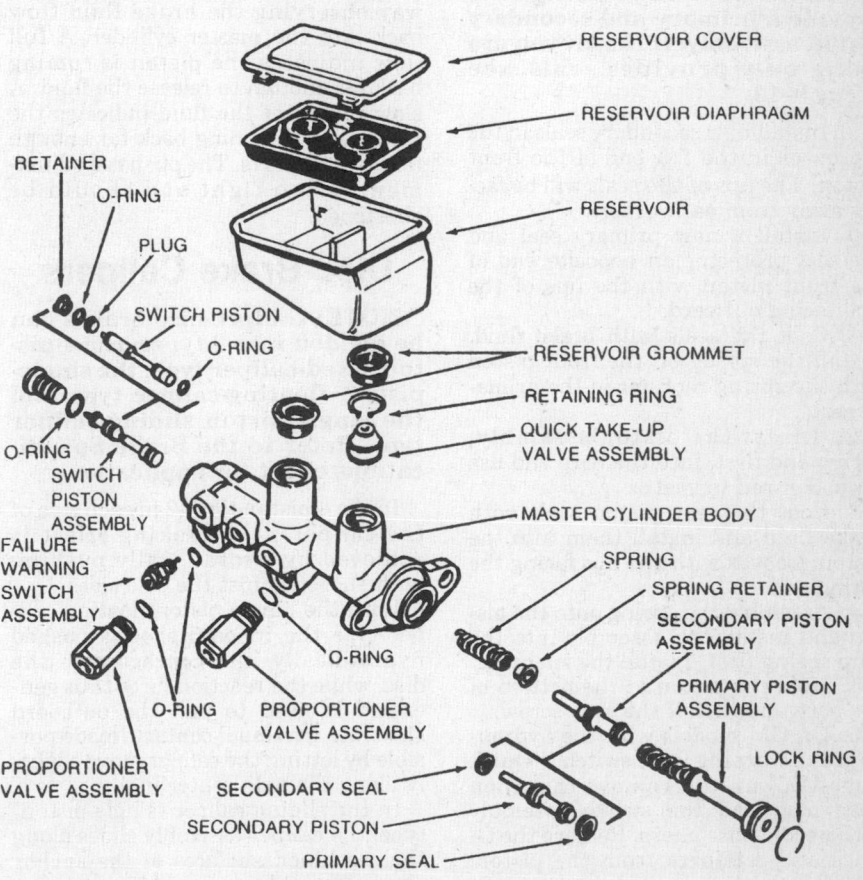

RESERVOIR COVER
RESERVOIR DIAPHRAGM
RESERVOIR
RETAINER
O-RING
PLUG
SWITCH PISTON
O-RING
RESERVOIR GROMMET
RETAINING RING
QUICK TAKE-UP VALVE ASSEMBLY
O-RING
SWITCH PISTON ASSEMBLY
FAILURE WARNING SWITCH ASSEMBLY
MASTER CYLINDER BODY
SPRING
SPRING RETAINER
SECONDARY PISTON ASSEMBLY
PRIMARY PISTON ASSEMBLY
O-RING
PROPORTIONER VALVE ASSEMBLY
PROPORTIONER VALVE ASSEMBLY
O-RING
SECONDARY SEAL
SECONDARY PISTON
PRIMARY SEAL
LOCK RING

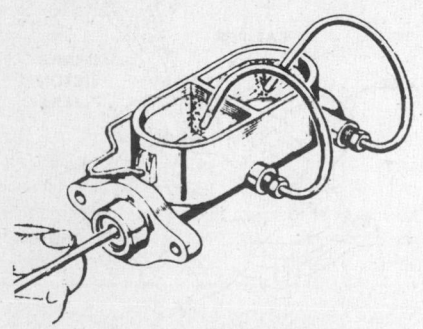

Pre-bleeding master cylinder

GM "Quick Take Up" master cylinder

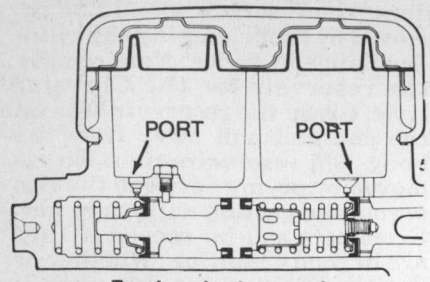

Feed and return ports

— CAUTION —

Aluminum cylinder bores cannot be honed. The cylinder must be replaced if the bore is pitted or scored.

8. If the bore is only slightly scored or pitted it may be honed. Always use hones that are in good condition and completely clean the cylinder with brake fluid when the honing is completed. If any sign of wear or corrosion is apparent on "Quick Take-Up" master cylinder bores, the master cylinder must be replaced; it cannot be honed. If any evidence of contamination exists in the master cylinder the entire hydraulic system should be flushed and refilled with clean brake fluid. Blow out the passages with compressed air.

NOTE: Most rebuilding kits provide a primary and secondary piston assembly. If the kit you are using only provides seals, see Steps 9–13.

9. Install new secondary seals in the 2 grooves in the flat end of the front piston. The lips of the seals will be facing away from each other.
10. Install a new primary seal and the seal protector on opposite end of the front piston with the lips of the seal facing outward.
11. Coat the seals with brake fluid. Install the spring on the front piston with the spring retainer in the primary seal.
12. Insert the piston assembly, spring end first, into the bore and use a wooden rod to seat it.
13. Coat the rear piston seals with brake fluid and install them into the piston grooves with the lips facing the spring end.
14. Assemble the spring onto the piston and install the assembly into the bore spring first. Install the snapring.
15. Hold the piston at the bottom of the bore and install the stop screw.
16. On GM models with the hydraulic brake warning light switch ("Quick Take-Up" units), remove the Allen head plug and the switch assembly with needle nose pliers. Remove the O-rings and retainers from the piston. Install new O-rings and retainers, fit

the piston back into the master cylinder after lubricating with brake fluid.

NOTE: If any corrosion is present in the switch piston bore the master cylinder must be replaced; do not attempt to hone the bore.

17. Fit a new O-ring on the Allen head plug, then install the plug and tighten.
18. On all master cylinders, install a new seal in the hub (if equipped), then either bench bleed or bleed the cylinder on the vehicle. Some master cylinders have bleed screws on the outlet flanges and may be bled without disturbing the wheel cylinders or calipers.

Master Cylinder Push Rod Adjustment

MODELS EQUIPPED WITH ADJUSTABLE PUSH ROD

After assembly of the master cylinder to the power section, the piston cup in the hydraulic cylinder should just clear the compensating port hole when the brake pedal is full released. If the push rod is too long, it will hold the piston over the port. A push rod that is too short, will give too much loose travel (excessive pedal play). Apply the brakes and release the pedal all the way observing the brake fluid flow back into the master cylinder. A full flow indicates the piston is coming back far enough to release the fluid. A slow return of the fluid indicates the piston is not coming back far enough to clear the ports. The push rod adjustment is too tight and should be shortened.

Disc Brake Calipers

NOTE: Caliper disc brakes can be divided into 3 types: the 4-piston, fixed-caliper type; the single-piston, floating-caliper type and the single-piston sliding-caliper type. Refer to the Brake Specifications chart for applications.

In the 4 piston type (2 in each side of the caliper), the braking effect is achieved by hydraulically pushing both shoes against the disc sides.

With the single piston floating-caliper type the inboard shoe is pushed hydraulically into contact with the disc, while the reaction force thus generated is used to pull the outboard shoe into frictional contact (made possible by letting the caliper move slightly along the axle centerline).

In the sliding caliper (single piston) type, the caliper assembly slides along the machined surfaces of the anchor plate. A steel key located between the

machined surfaces of the caliper and the machines surfaces of the anchor plate is held in place with either a retaining screw or a pair of cotter pins. The caliper is held in place against the anchor plate with 1 or 2 support springs.

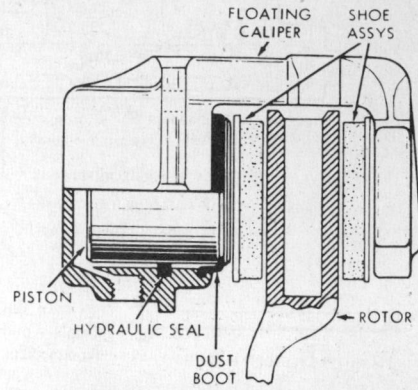

Floating caliper disc brake

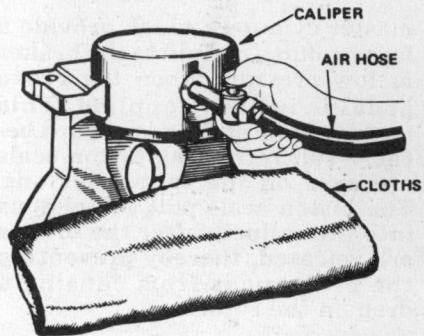

Removing piston pneumatically

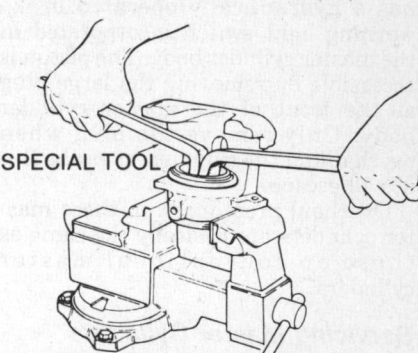

Removing hollow end piston

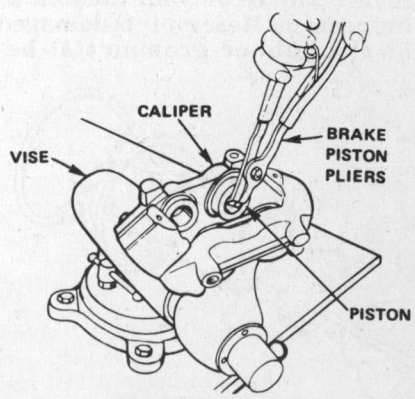

Removing pistons

SERVICING THE CALIPER ASSEMBLY

NOTE: The following is a general caliper service procedure. Before proceeding, check under the individual disc brake section for your vehicle (Delco Moraine, Bendix, etc.) for any special servicing procedures.

1. Raise and support the front of the vehicle on jackstands, then remove the front wheels.
2. Working on a side at a time only, disconnect the hydraulic inlet line from the caliper and plug the end. Remove the caliper mounting bolts or pins and the shims (if used), then slide the caliper off the disc.
3. Remove the disc pads from the caliper or mounting adapter. If the old ones are to be reused, make them so that they can be reinstalled in their original positions.
4. Open the caliper bleed screw and drain the fluid. Clean the outside of the caliper and mount it in a vise with padded jaws.

─── **CAUTION** ───

When cleaning any brake components, use only brake fluid or denatured (Isopropyl) alcohol. Never use a mineral-based solvent, such as gasoline or paint thinner, since it will swell and quickly deteriorate the rubber parts. Alcohol must NOT be allowed to remain in any component that will hold brake fluid, this would lower the boiling point of the brake fluid.

5. Remove the bridge bolts (fixed type), separate the caliper halves and remove the 2 O-ring seals from the transfer holes.
6. Pry the lip on (each) piston dust boot from its groove, then remove the piston assemblies and spring(s) from the bore(s). If necessary, air pressure may be used to force the pistons out of the bore(s), using care to prevent the piston from popping out of control.
7. Remove the boot(s) and seal(s) from the piston(s), then clean the piston(s) in brake fluid. Blow out the caliper passages with an air hose.
8. Inspect the cylinder bore(s) for scoring, pitting or corrosion. Corrosion is a pitted or rough condition not to be confused with staining. Light rough spots may be removed by rotating crocus cloth, using finger pressure, in the bores. DO NOT polish with an in and out motion or use any other abrasive.
9. If the piston(s) are pitted, scored or worn, they must be replaced. A corroded or deeply scored caliper should also be replaced.
10. Check the clearance of the piston(s) in the bores using a feeler gauge. Clearance should be 0.002–0.006 in. If there is excessive clearance the caliper must be replaced.
11. Replace all rubber parts and lubricate with brake fluid. Install the seals (or square cut rings) and boots in the grooves in each piston. The seal should be installed in the groove closest to the closed end of the piston with the seal lips facing the closed end. The lip on the boot should be facing the seal.
12. Lubricate the piston and bore with brake fluid. Position the piston return spring (if equipped), large coil first, in the piston bore.
13. Install the piston in the bore, taking great care to avoid damaging the seal lip as it passes the edge of the cylinder bore.
14. Compress the lip on the dust boot into the groove in the caliper. Be sure the boot is full seated in the groove, as poor sealing will allow contaminants to ruin the bore.
15. On fixed calipers: Position the O-rings in the cavities around the caliper transfer holes and fit the caliper halves together. Install the bridge bolts (lubricated with brake fluid) and be sure to torque to specification.
16. Install the disc pads in the caliper or adapter and remount the caliper on the hub. Connect the brake line to the caliper and bleed the brakes. Replace the wheels. Recheck the brake fluid level, check the brake pedal travel and road test the vehicle.

OVERHAUL TIPS

Field reports indicate that 2 factors determine whether to replace or rebuild calipers: Can the piston or pistons be removed? Will the bleed screw break off when removal is attempted? (Rebuilders will not accept a caliper with a broken bleed screw.) Since there is no way to predict how a bleed screw will react, follow this procedure to attempt removal.

1. Insert a drill shank into the bleed screw hole (snug fit).
2. Tap the screw on all sides.
3. Using a 6-point wrench, apply pressure gently while working the drill up and down slightly.
4. If the drill starts to bind, the screw is beginning to collapse and cannot be removed intact.
5. Heating the caliper is another successful, but time consuming, bleed screw removal technique. Remove the caliper from the vehicle. Heat the caliper. Shrink the bleed screw by applying dry ice and attempt to remove.

DISC BRAKE BLEEDER SCREW REPLACEMENT

1. Using the existing hole in bleed screw for a pilot, drill a ¼ in. hole completely through existing bleeder.
2. Increase the hole size to 7/16 in.
3. Tap the hole using a ¼ in. (18-national pipe thread) ½ in. deep (full thread).
4. Install the bleeder repair kit.

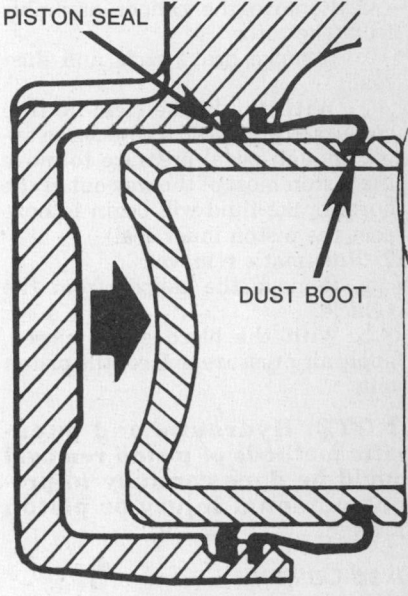

Brake applied

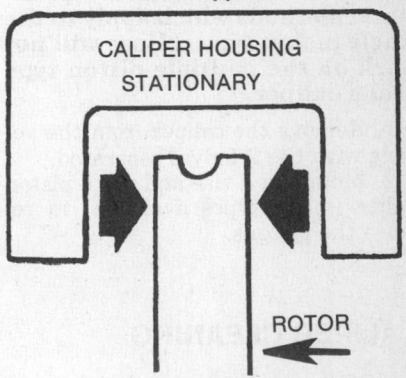

Fixed caliper type

Replacing disc brake bleeder screw

5. Test for leaks and full brake pedal pressure.

FROZEN PISTONS

Sliding or Floating Caliper

1. Hydraulic removal:
   a. Remove the caliper assembly from the rotor.
   b. Remove brake pads and dust seal.
   c. With the brake flexible line connected and bleed screw closed apply enough pedal pressure to move the piston most of the way out of the bore (brake fluid will begin to ooze past the piston inner seal).
2. Pneumatic removal:
   a. Remove the caliper from the vehicle.
   b. With the bleed screw closed, apply air pressure to force the piston out.

NOTE: Hydraulic and pneumatic methods of piston removal should be done carefully to prevent personal injury or piston damage.

Fixed Caliper

NOTE: The hydraulic or pneumatic methods which apply to the single piston type caliper will not work on the multiple piston type brake caliper.

1. Remove the caliper from the vehicle with the 2 halves separated.
2. Mount in a vise and use a piston puller (many types available) to remove the pistons.

CALIPER CLEANING

NOTE: Castings may be cleaned with any type cleaning fluid after all the rubber seals have been removed.

It is important that all traces of cleaning fluid be completely removed from the caliper casting. Rubber components are compatible with alcohol and/or brake fluid. Use a lint free wiping cloth to clean the caliper and parts. Black stains on the pistons or walls, caused by the seals, will not do harm; however, extreme cleanliness is essential. Blow out the passages with compressed air. A fine grade of crocus cloth may be used to correct minor imperfections in the cylinder bore. Slide crocus cloth with finger pressure in a circular rather than a lengthwise motion. DO NOT use any form of abrasive on a plated piston. Discard a piston which is pitted or has signs of plating wear.

REBUILDING CALIPERS

NOTE: If a fine stone honing of a caliper bore is necessary it should be done with skill and caution. Some vehicles can develop 800 psi hydraulic pressure on severe application so the honing must never exceed 0.003 in. Also

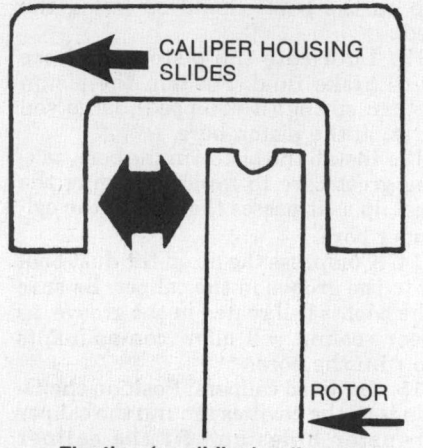

Floating (or sliding) caliper type

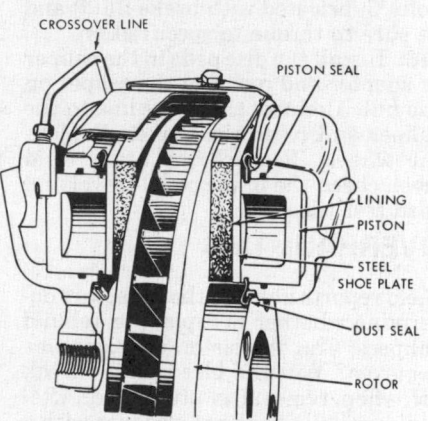

Fixed caliper disc brake

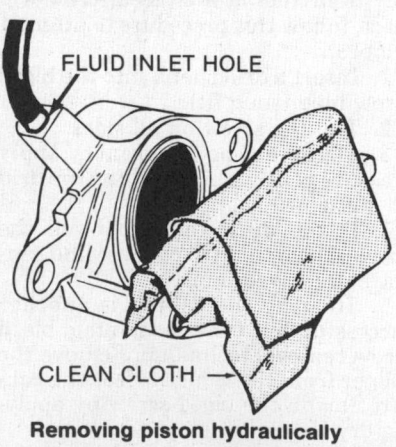

Removing piston hydraulically

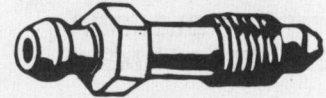

Bleed screw

the dust seal groove must be free of rust or nicks so that a perfect mating surface is possible on the piston and casting.

Installing Stroking Type Seals and Boots

Stretch the boot and seal over the piston and seat them. The seal lip on the Bendix and Delco styles, faces toward hydraulic pressure; boot lips face toward the brake shoe. Locate the return spring (if used) in the cylinder and carefully start the piston into the cylinder to avoid nicking the seal. Alignment tools are available for inserting the lip cup seals. Fully depress the piston into the bore in order to fasten the boot lip to the caliper housing. On the Delco types, use a wooden drift or a special seating tool to seat the boot ring in the caliper counterbore. It must be flush or below the caliper machined surface.

Installing Fixed Position (Rectangular Ring) Seals and Boots

Insert a rectangular ring seal into bore and at any location, push the ring into the seal groove. From this area, with a finger, gently work around the bore until the ring is seated in this channel. Be sure the ring does not twist or roll in the groove. When the boot lip is retained inside the cylinder bore, insert the boot in the same manner. Then work the inside of the boot over the pressure end of the piston, stretching the boot with a small plastic tool and pressing the piston through the seal, straight in, until it bottoms. The inside of the boot should slide on the piston and come to rest in the boot groove. If the boot lip is retained outside of the cylinder bore, first stretch boot over the piston and seat it in its groove, then press the piston through the seal. Fully depress the piston to 50–100 lbs. in order to fasten the boot lip in place. On the Delco-Moraine types, use a wooden drift or a special seating tool to seat the metal boot ring in the caliper counterbore below the face of the caliper.

Installing Fixed-Caliper Bridge Bolts

If the caliper contains internal fluid crossover passages, be sure to install new O-ring seals at the joints. Mate the caliper halves and install high tensile strength bridge bolts. Never replace the bridge bolts with ordinary standard hardware bolts.

Wheel Cylinders

Wheel cylinders contain a pair of op-

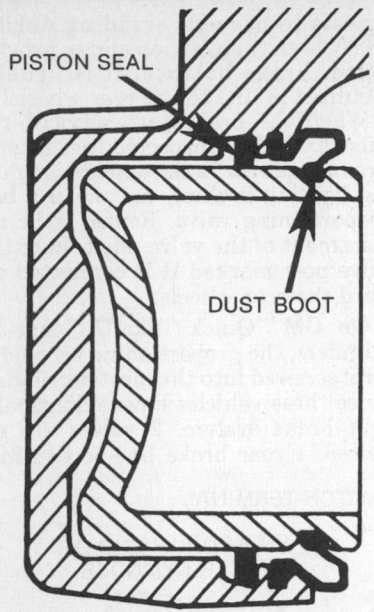

Brake released

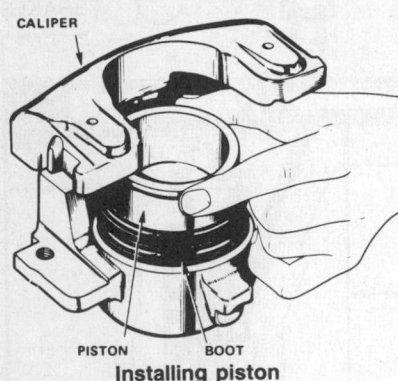

Installing piston

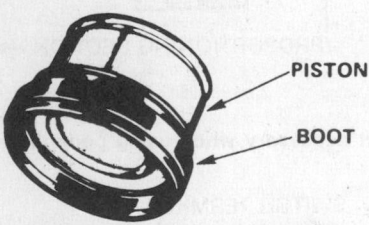

Assembling boot on piston

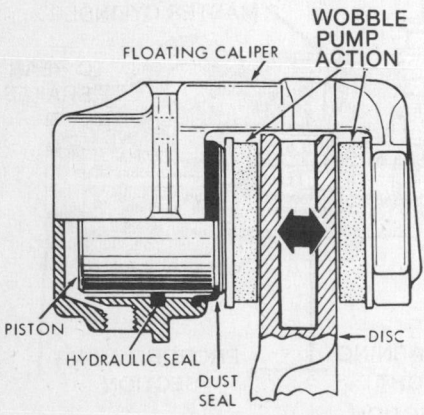

Wobble pump action

posed pistons fitted with rubber cups, compression spring and sometimes expander washers to keep the cups tight against the pistons.

SERVICING

1. Raise and support the vehicle on jackstands. Remove the wheel and drum assemblies from the side to be serviced.

2. Remove the brake shoes, then clean the backing plate and the wheel cylinder. Rebuilding can be done on the vehicle, depending on the design of the brake backing plate. If the backing plate is recessed to the point that it is impossible to get a hone into the cylinder, the cylinder has to be removed.

3. To remove the cylinder; disconnect the brake line from the rear of the cylinder, remove the mounting bolts or retainers and the cylinders.

NOTE: On some models, the wheel cylinder is contained by a retaining ring. In order to remove the rear wheel cylinders, remove the wheel cylinder retainer. Insert 2 pin punches or equivalent tools into the access slots and bend both tabs at the same time thereby releasing the cylinder. Use a new retainer when reinstalling the wheel cylinder. The new retainer can be driven on using a $1\frac{1}{8}$ in. socket with an extension bar.

4. Remove the rubber boots (dust covers) from the ends of the cylinder. Remove the pistons, the piston cups (expanders, if equipped) and the spring from the inside of the cylinder. Remove the bleeder screw and make sure it is not clogged.

5. Discard all of the parts that the rebuilding kit will replace.

6. Examine the inside of the cylinder. If it is severely rusted, pitted or scratched install a new or rebuilt cylinder.

7. If the condition of the cylinder in-

dicates that it can be rebuilt, hone the bore. Light honing will provide a new surface on the inside of the cylinder which promotes better cup sealing.

8. Wash out the cylinder with brake

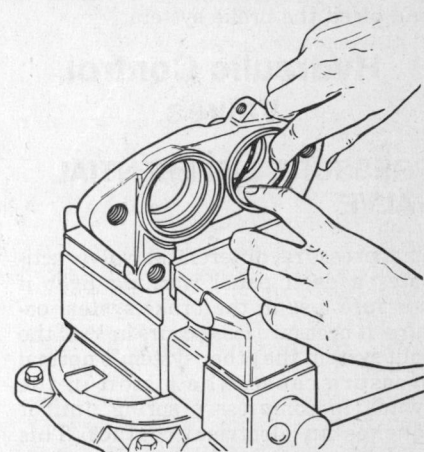

Installing fixed position rectangular ring seal (seal lip toward pressure side)

Wheel cylinder components

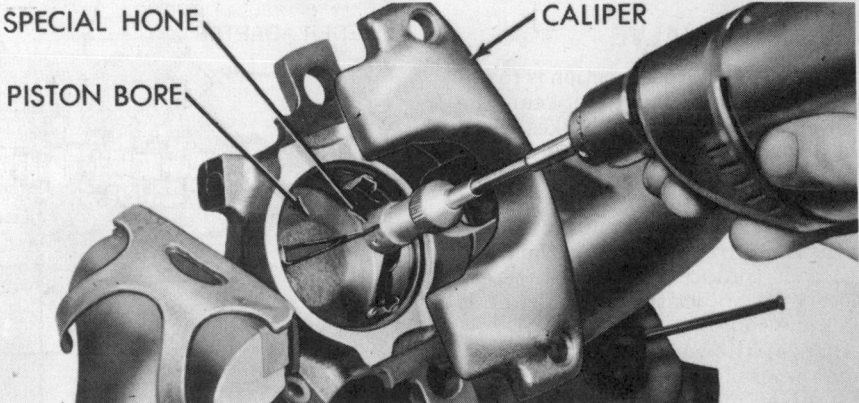

Honing cylinder bore

fluid after honing. Reassemble the cylinder using the new parts provided in the kit. When assembling the cylinder dip all parts in brake fluid.

9. Install the cylinder on the vehicle. Reinstall the brakes, drum/wheel and bleed the brake system.

Hydraulic Control Valves

PRESSURE DIFFERENTIAL VALVE

The pressure differential valve activates a dash panel warning light if pressure loss in the brake system occurs. If pressure loss occurs in ½ of the split system the other system's normal pressure causes the piston in the switch to compress a spring until it touches an electrical contact. This turns the warning lamp on the dash panel to light, thus warning the driver of possible brake failure.

On some vehicles, the spring balance piston automatically resets as the brake pedal is released warning the driver only upon brake application. On other vehicles, the light remains on until manually cancelled.

Valves may be located separately, as part of a combination valve, or incorporated into the master cylinder.

Resetting Valves

On some vehicles, the valve piston(s) remain off center after failure until necessary repairs are made. The valve will automatically reset itself (after repairs) when pressure is equal on both sides of the system.

If the light does not go out, bleed the brake system that is opposite the failed system. If front brakes failed, bleed the rear brakes, this should force the light control piston toward center.

If this fails, remove the terminal switch. If brake fluid is present in the electrical area, the seals are gone, replace the complete valve assembly.

METERING VALVE

The metering valve's function is to improve braking balance between the front disc and rear drum brakes, especially during light brake application.

The metering valve prevents the application of the front disc brakes until the rear brakes overcome the return spring pressure. Thus, when the front disc pads contact the rotor, the rear shoes will contact the brake drum at the same time.

Inspect the metering valve each time the brakes are serviced. A slight amount of moisture inside the boot does not indicate a defective valve,

however, fluid leakage indicates a damaged or worn valve. If fluid leakage is present the valve must be replaced.

The metering valve can be checked very simply. With the vehicle stopped, gently apply the brakes. At about 1 in. of travel a very small change in pedal effort (like a small bump) will be felt if the valve is operating properly. Metering valves are not serviceable and must be replaced (if defective).

PROPORTIONING VALVE

The proportioning (pressure control) valve is used, on some vehicles, to reduce the hydraulic pressure to the rear wheels to prevent skidding during heavy brake application and to provide better brake balance. It is usually mounted in line to the rear wheels.

When the brakes are serviced the valve should be inspected for leakage. Premature rear brake application during lighting braking can mean a bad proportioning valve. Repair is by replacement of the valve. Make sure the valve port marked **R** is connected toward the rear wheels.

On GM "Quick Take-Up" master cylinders, the proportioning valve(s) is (are) screwed into the master cylinder. Since these vehicles have a diagonally split brake system, 2 valves are required. 1 rear brake line screws into

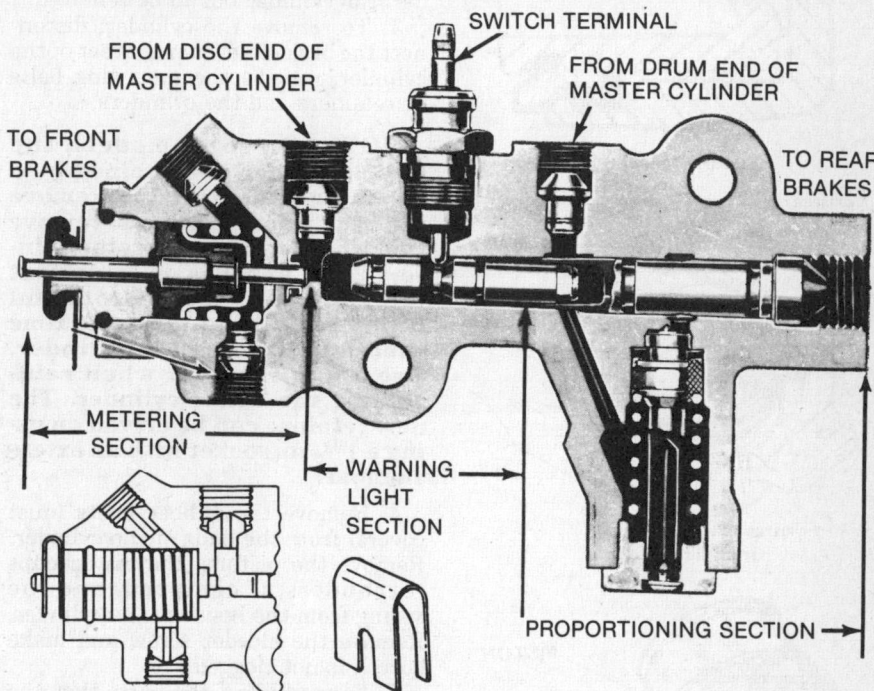

Hold valve out .060 in pressure bleed only-not necessary when using pedal bleed method

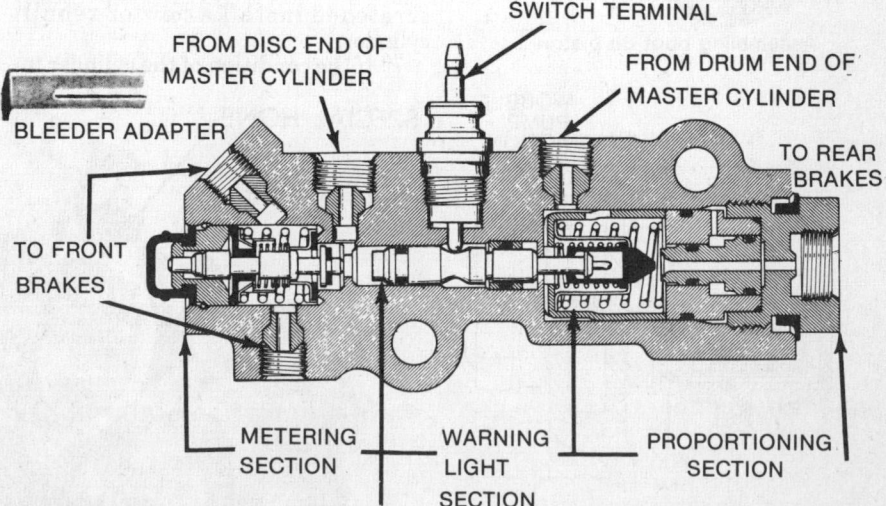

Push valve in when pressure bleeding-not necessary when using pedal bleed method

each valve. The early type valves (GM front wheel drive) were steel and silver colored, an occasional "clunking" noise was encountered on some early models, but does not affect brake efficiency. Replacement valves are now made of aluminum. Never mix an aluminum valve with a steel valve, always use 2 aluminum valves.

COMBINATION VALVE

The combination valve may perform 2 or 3 functions. They are: metering, proportioning and brake failure warning.

Variations of the two-way combination valve are: proportioning and brake failure warning or metering and brake failure warning.

A three-way combination valve directs the brake fluid to the appropriate wheel, performs necessary valving and contains a brake failure warning.

The combination valve is usually mounted under the hood close to the master cylinder, where the brake lines can easily be connected and routed to the front or rear wheels.

The combination valve is non-serviceable and must be replaced if malfunctioning.

Brake Bleeding

The hydraulic brake system must be free of air to operate properly. Air can enter the system when hydraulic parts are disconnected for servicing or replacement, or when the fluid level in the master cylinder reservoirs is very low. Air in the system will give the brake pedal a spongy feeling upon application.

The quickest and easiest of the 2 ways for system bleeding is the pressure method but special equipment is needed to externally pressurize the hydraulic system. The other, more commonly used method of brake bleeding is done manually.

BLEEDING SEQUENCE

Bleeding may be required at only 1 or 2 wheels or at the master cylinder, depending upon what point the system was opened to air. If after bleeding the cylinder caliper that was rebuilt or replaced and the pedal still has a spongy feeling upon application, it will be necessary to bleed the entire system. Bleed the system in the following order:

1. **Master cylinder**: If the cylinder is not equipped with bleeder screws, open the brake line(s) to the wheels slightly while pressure is applied to the brake pedal. Be sure to tighten the line before the brake pedal is released. The procedure for bench bleeding the master cylinder is in the following section.

2. **Power Brake Booster**: If the unit is equipped with bleeder screws, it should be bled after the master cylinder. The vehicle's engine should be off and the brake pedal applied several times to exhaust any vacuum in the booster. If the unit is equipped with 2 bleeder screws, always bleed the higher bleeder screw first.

3. **Combination Valve**: If equipped with a bleeder screw.

4. **Front/Back Split Systems**: Start with the wheel farthest away from the master cylinder, usually the right-rear wheel. Bleed the other rear wheel then the right-front and left-front.

NOTE: If you are unsuccessful in bleeding the front wheels, it may be necessary to deactivate the metering valve. This is accomplished by either pushing in, or pulling out a button or stem on the valve. The valve may be held by hand, with a special tool or taped, it should remain deactivated while the front brakes are bled.

5. **Diagonally Split System**: Start with the right-rear then the left-front. The left-rear then the right-front.

6. **Rear Disc Brakes**: If the vehicle is equipped with rear disc brakes and the calipers have 2 bleeder screws, bleed the inner first then the outer.

NOTE: DO NOT allow brake fluid to spill on the vehicles finish, it will remove the paint. Flush the area with water.

MANUAL BLEEDING

1. Clean the bleed screw at each wheel.

2. Start with the wheel farthest from the master cylinder (right-rear).

3. Attach a small rubber hose to the bleed screw and place the end in a clear container of brake fluid.

4. Fill the master cylinder with brake fluid. (Check often during bleeding). Have an assistant slowly pump up the brake pedal and hold pressure.

5. Open the bleed screw about one-quarter turn, press the brake pedal to the floor, close the bleed screw and slowly release the pedal. Continue until no more air bubbles are forced from the cylinder on application of the brake pedal.

6. Repeat procedure on remaining wheel cylinders and calipers, still working from cylinder/caliper farthest from the master cylinder.

NOTE: Master cylinders equipped with bleed screws may be bled independently. When bleeding the Bendix-type dual master cylinder it is necessary to solidly cap 1 reservoir section while bleeding the other to prevent pressure loss through the cap vent hole.

---------- **CAUTION** ----------

The bleeder valve at the wheel cylinder must be closed at the end of each stroke and before the brake pedal is released, to insure that no air can enter the system. It is also important that the brake pedal be returned to the full up position so the piston in the master cylinder moves back enough to clear the bypass outlets.

PRESSURE BLEEDING DISC BRAKES

Pressure bleeding disc brakes will close the metering valve and the front brakes will not bleed. For this reason it is necessary to manually hold the metering valve open during pressure bleeding. Never use a block or clamp to hold the valve open and never force the valve stem beyond its normal position.

Of the 2 different types of valves used, the most common type requires the valve stem to be held in while bleeding the brakes, while the second type requires the valve stem to be held out (0.060 in. minimum travel). Determine the type of visual inspection.

---------- **CAUTION** ----------

Special adapters are required when pressure bleeding cylinders with plastic reservoirs. Pressure bleeding equipment should be diaphragm type; placing a diaphragm between the pressurized air supply and the brake fluid. This prevents moisture and other contaminants from entering the hydraulic system.

NOTE: Front disc/rear drum equipped vehicles use a metering valve which closes off pressure to the front brakes under certain conditions. These systems contain manual release actuators, which must be engaged to pressure bleed the front brakes.

1. Connect the tank hydraulic hose and adapter to the master cylinder.

2. Close the hydraulic valve on the bleeder equipment.

3. Apply air pressure to the bleeder equipment following the equipment manufacturer's recommendations for correct air pressure.

4. Open the valve to bleed air out of the pressure hose to the master cylinder. Never bleed this system using the secondary piston stopscrew on the bottom of many master cylinders.

5. Open the hydraulic valve and bleed each wheel cylinder or caliper.

Bleed the rear brake system first when bleeding both front and rear systems.

FLUSHING HYDRAULIC BRAKE SYSTEMS

Hydraulic brake systems must be totally flushed if the fluid becomes contaminated with water, dirt or other corrosive chemicals. To flush, simply bleed the entire system until all of the fluid has been replaced with the correct type of new fluid.

BENCH BLEEDING MASTER CYLINDER

Bench bleeding the master cylinder before installing it on the vehicle reduces the possibility of getting air into the lines.

1. Connect 2 short pieces of brake line to the outlet fittings, bend them until the free end is below the fluid level in the master cylinder reservoirs.

2. Fill the reservoirs with fresh brake fluid. Pump the piston until no more air bubbles appear in the reservoir(s).

3. Disconnect the 2 short lines, refill the master cylinder and securely install the cylinder cap(s).

4. Install the master cylinder on the vehicle. Attach the lines but do not completely tighten them. Force any air that might have been trapped in the connection by slowly depressing the brake pedal. Tighten the lines before releasing the brake pedal.

GM QUICK TAKE-UP SYSTEM BLEEDING

Bleed the master cylinder as follows: disconnect the left-front brake line from the master cylinder. Fill the cylinder with fluid until it flows from the opened port. Connect the line and tighten the fitting. Apply the brake pedal slowly 1 time and keep it applied. Loosen the same brake line fitting to allow any air to escape. Retighten the fitting and release the brake pedal slowly. Wait 15 seconds and repeat the procedure until all of the air is expelled. Bleed the right-front connection in the same manner. Bleed the cylinders and calipers after you are sure all the air is out of the master cylinder.

── **CAUTION** ──

Rapid pumping will move the secondary piston down the bore and make it difficult to bleed the system. Always apply slow pedal pressure.

Power Brakes

VACUUM OPERATED BOOSTER

Power brakes operate just as standard brake systems except in the actuation of the master cylinder pistons. A vacuum diaphragm is located on the front of the master cylinder to assist in applying the brakes, reducing both the effort and travel needed to move the brake pedal.

The vacuum diaphragm housing is connected to the intake manifold by a vacuum hose. A check valve is placed at the point where the hose enters the diaphragm housing, so that during periods of low manifold vacuum brake assist vacuum will not be lost.

Depressing the brake pedal closes off the vacuum source and allows atmospheric pressure to enter on 1 side of the diaphragm. This causes the master cylinder pistons to move and apply the brakes. When the brake pedal is released, vacuum is applied to both sides of the diaphragm, the return springs return the diaphragm and master cylinder pistons to the released position. If the vacuum fails, the brake pedal rod will butt against the end of the master cylinder actuating rod and direct mechanical application will occur as the pedal is depressed.

The hydraulic and mechanical problems that apply to conventional brake systems also apply to power brakes should be checked if the tests and chart below do not reveal the problem. Tests for a system vacuum leak as described below:

1. Operate the engine at idle with the transmission in Neutral without touching the brake pedal for at least 1 minute.

2. Turn **OFF** the engine and wait 1 minute.

3. Test for the presence of assist vacuum by depressing the brake pedal and releasing it several times. Light application will produce less and less pedal travel, if vacuum was present. If there is no vacuum, air is leaking into the system somewhere.

4. Test the system operation as follows:

   a. Pump the brake pedal (with engine off) until the supply vacuum is entirely gone.

   b. Put light, steady pressure on the pedal. Start the engine and operate it at idle with the transmission in neutral.

   c. If the system is operating, the brake pedal should fall toward the floor when constant pressure is maintained on the pedal.

NOTE: Power brake systems may be tested for hydraulic leaks just as ordinary systems are tested, except that the engine should be idling with the transmission in neutral throughout the test.

POWER BRAKE BOOSTER TROUBLESHOOTING

NOTE: The following items are in addition to those listed in the "General Troubleshooting" section. Check those items first.

Hard Pedal

1. Faulty vacuum check valve
2. Vacuum hose kinked, collapsed, plugged leaky or improperly connected
3. Internal leak in unit
4. Damaged vacuum cylinder
5. Damaged valve plunger
6. Broken or faulty springs
7. Broken plunger stem

Grabbing Brakes

1. Damaged vacuum cylinder
2. Faulty vacuum check valve
3. Vacuum hose leaky or improperly connected
4. Broken plunger stem

Pedal Goes to Floor

Generally, when this problem occurs, it is not caused by the power brake booster. In rare cases, a broken plunger stem may be at fault.

OVERHAUL

Most power brake boosters are serviced by replacement only. In many cases, repair parts are not available. A good many special tools are required for rebuilding these units. For these reasons, it would be most practical to replace a failed booster with a new or remanufactured unit.

Hydro-Boost
Hydro-Boost II

Hydro-Boost differs from conventional power brake systems, in that it operates from the power steering pump fluid pressure rather than intake manifold vacuum.

The Hydro-Boost unit contains a spool valve with an open center which controls the strength of pump pressure when braking occurs. A lever assembly controls the valve's position. A boost piston provides the force necessary to operate the conventional master cylinder on the front of the booster.

A reserve of at least 2 assisted brake applications is supplied by an accumulator which is spring loaded on earlier and pneumatic on later models. The accumulator is an integral part of the Hydro-Boost II unit. The brakes can be applied manually if the reserve system is depleted.

All system checks, tests and troubleshooting procedure are the same for the 2 systems.

HYDRO-BOOST SYSTEM CHECKS

1. A defective Hydro-Boost cannot cause any of the following conditions: Noisy brakes, fading pedal or pulling brakes. If any of these occur, check elsewhere in the brake system.

2. Check the fluid level in the master cylinder. It should be within ¼ in. of the top; if not, add only DOT-3 or DOT-4 brake fluid until the correct level is reached.

3. Check the fluid level in the power steering pump. The engines should be at normal running temperature and stopped. The level should register on the pump dipstick. Add power steering fluid to bring the reservoir level up to the correct level. Low fluid level will result in both poor steering and stopping ability.

─────── CAUTION ───────
The brake hydraulic system uses brake fluid only, while the power steering and Hydro-Boost systems use power steering fluid only. Don't mix the two.

4. Check the power steering pump belt tension and inspect all of the power steering/Hydro-Boost hoses for kinks or leaks.

5. Check and adjust the engine idle speed, as necessary.

6. Check the power steering pump fluid for bubbles. If air bubbles are present in the fluid, bleed the system. Fill the power steering pump reservoir to specifications with the engine at normal operating temperature. With the engine running, rotate the steering wheel through its normal travel 3–4 times, without holding the wheel against the stops. Check the fluid level again.

7. If the problem still exists, go on to the Hydro-Boost test sections and troubleshooting chart.

HYDRO-BOOST TESTS

Functional Test

1. Check the brake system for leaks or low fluid level. Correct as necessary.

2. Place the transmission in Neutral and stop the engine. Apply the brakes 4–5 times to empty the accumulator.

3. Keep the pedal depressed with moderate (25–40 lbs.) pressure and start the engine.

4. The brake pedal should fall slightly and then push back up against your foot. If no movement is felt, the Hydro-Boost system is not working.

Accumulator Leak Test

1. Run the engine at normal idle. Turn the steering wheel against either stop; hold it there for no longer than 5 seconds. Center the steering wheel and stop the engine.

2. Keep applying the brakes until a "hard" pedal is obtained. There should be a minimum of 2 power (1 on Hydro-Boost II) assisted brake applications when pedal pressure of 20–25 lbs. is applied.

3. Start the engine and allow it to idle. Rotate the steering wheel against the stop. Listen for a light "hissing" sound; this is the accumulator being charged. Center the steering wheel and stop the engine.

4. Wait 1 hour and apply the brakes without starting the engine. As in Step 2, there should be at least 2 (1 on Hydro-Boost II) stops with power assist. If not, the accumulator is defective and must be replaced.

Hydro-Boost System Bleeding

NOTE: The system should be bled whenever the booster is removed and installed.

1. Fill the power steering pump until the fluid level is at the base of the pump reservoir neck. Disconnect the battery lead from the distributor.

NOTE: On diesel engines remove the electrical lead to the fuel solenoid terminal on the injection pump before cranking the engine.

2. Raise the front of the vehicle, turn the wheels all the way to the left and crank the engine for a few seconds.

3. Check the steering pump fluid level. If necessary, add fluid to the **ADD** mark on the dipstick.

4. Lower the vehicle, connect the battery lead and start the engine. Check the fluid level and add fluid to the **ADD** mark if necessary. With the engine running, turn the wheels from side-to-side to bleed air from the system. Make sure that the fluid level stays above the internal pump casting.

5. The Hydro-Boost system should now be fully bled. If the fluid is foaming after bleeding, stop the engine, let the system set for 1 hour. Add fluid to the **ADD** mark if necessary, then with the engine running, turn the wheels from side-to-side to bleed air from the system. Repeat this step if necessary.

6. The preceding procedures should be effective in removing excess air from the system, however, sometimes air may still remain trapped. When this happens the booster may make a "gulping" noise when the brake is applied. Lightly pumping the brake pedal

with the engine running should cause this noise to disappear. After the noise stops, check the pump fluid level and add as necessary.

HYDRO-BOOST TROUBLESHOOTING

High Pedal and Steering Effort (Idle)

1. Loose/broken power steering pump belt
2. Low power steering fluid level
3. Leaking hoses or fittings
4. Low idle speed
5. Hose restriction
6. Defective power steering pump

High Pedal Effort (Idle)

1. Binding pedal/linkage
2. Fluid contamination
3. Defective Hydro-Boost unit

Poor Pedal Return

1. Binding pedal linkage
2. Restricted booster return line
3. Internal return system restriction

Pedal Chatter/Pulsation

1. Power steering/pump drivebelt slipping
2. Low power steering fluid level
3. Defective power steering pump
4. Defective Hydro-Boost unit

Brakes Oversensitive

1. Binding pedal/linkage
2. Defective Hydro-Boost unit

Noise

1. Low power steering fluid level
2. Air in the power steering fluid
3. Loose power steering pump drivebelt
4. Hose restrictions

OVERHAUL

Ford Motor Company services the Hydro-Boost unit with a replacement new or rebuilt unit only. No provisions are made for overhaul of the unit. GM Hydro-Boost units may be overhauled by qualified mechanics.

─────── CAUTION ───────
DO NOT attempt to interchange the parts between the Hydro-Boost units of different makes of vehicles, because of pressure differentials and differences of the tolerances of the internal parts. Pressure could exceed the normal accumulator release pressure of 1400 psi and injury or damage could result.

DISC BRAKES

Disc Brake Rotors

RUNOUT

Manufacturers differ widely on permissible runout but too much can sometimes be felt as a pulsation at the brake pedal. A wobble pump effect is created when a rotor is not perfectly smooth and the pad hits the high spots forcing fluid back into the master cylinder. This alternating pressure causes a pulsating feeling which can be felt at the pedal when the brakes are applied.

To check the actual runout of the rotor, perform the following procedures:

1. Tighten the wheel spindle nut to a snug bearing adjustment, end-play removed.

2. Fasten a dial indicator on the suspension at a convenient place so that the indicator stylus contacts the rotor face approximately 1 in. from its outer edge.

3. Set the dial at zero. Check the total indicator reading while turning the rotor 1 full revolution. If the rotor is warped beyond the runout specification, it is likely that it can be successfully remachined.

Lateral Runout: A wobbly movement of the rotor from side-to-side as it rotates. Excessive lateral runout causes the rotor faces to knock back the disc pads and can result in chatter, excessive pedal travel, pumping or fighting pedal and vibration during the braking action.

Parallelism (lack of): Refers to the amount of variation in the thickness of the rotor. Excessive variation can cause pedal vibration or fight, front end vibrations and possible "grab" during the braking action; a condition comparable to an "out-of-round brake drum." Check parallelism with a micrometer. "Mike" the thickness at 8 or more equally spaced points, equally distant from the outer edge of the rotor, preferably at midpoints of the braking surface. Parallelism then is the amount of variation between maximum and minimum measurements.

Surface or Micro-inch finish, flatness, smoothness: Different from parallelism, these terms refer to the degree of perfection of the flat surface on each side of the rotor; that is, the minute hills, valleys and swirls inherent in machining the surface. In a visual inspection, the remachined surface should have a find ground polish with, at most, only a faint trace of non-directional swirls.

SERVICING THE DISC ROTOR

Disc Replacement

1. Raise and support the vehicle on jackstands, then remove the wheel/tire assembly.

2. Remove the caliper. Secure the caliper out of the way suspended by wire, DO NOT allow the caliper to hang by the brake hose.

3. Remove the wheel bearing nut from the spindle and the outer wheel bearing from the hub.

4. Remove the hub and disc assembly from the spindle.

5. To install, reverse the removal procedures.

NOTE: The disc is removable from the hub on the Eldorado, Toronado and Corvette (rear only). To separate the rear disc and hub on a (1982-87) Corvette the 3 hub-to-disc attaching rivets must be drilled out. This can be done with the hub and rotor mounted on the vehicle. It is not necessary to install new rivets when the disc is installed.

DRUM BRAKES

———— CAUTION ————

The asbestos dust thrown off from the brake linings or disc pads may be dangerous to your health if inhaled. Never use compressed air or your own breath to blow the dust from the brake assembly. Use an aerosol brake cleaner, damp rag or a vacuum cleaner with an approved asbestos filter. Dispose of the rag or cleaner bag properly. Do not move a vehicle until a firm brake pedal is obtained.

Brake Drums

BRAKE DRUM TYPES

The FULL-CAST drum has a cast iron web (back) of $3/16$–$1/4$ in. thickness (passenger vehicle sizes) whereas the COMPOSITE drum has a steel web approximately $1/8$ in. thick. These 2 types of drums, with few exceptions are not interchangeable.

BRAKE DRUM DEPTH

Rest a straight edge across the drum diameter on the open side. The actual drum depth then is the measurement at a right angle from the straight edge to that part of the web which mates against the hub mounting flange.

ALUMINUM DRUMS

When replaced by other types, aluminum drums must be replaced in pairs.

METALLIC BRAKES

Drums designed for use with standard brake linings should not be used with metallic brakes.

REMOVING TIGHT DRUMS

Difficulty removing a brake drum can be caused by shoes which are expanded beyond the drum's inner diameter or shoes which have cut into and ridged the drum. In either case back off the adjuster to obtain sufficient clearance for removal.

BRAKE DRUM INSPECTION

The condition of the brake drum surface is just as important as the surface to the brake lining. All drum surfaces should be clean, smooth, free from hard spots, heat checks, score marks and foreign matter embedded in the drum surface. They should not be out of round, bell-mouthed or barrel shaped. It is recommended that all drums be first checked with a drum micrometer to see if they are within oversize limits. If the drum is within safe limits, even though the surface appears smooth, it should be turned not only to assure a true drum surface but also to remove any possible contamination in the surface from previous brake linings, road dusts, etc. Too much metal removed from a drum is unsafe and may result in:

1. Brake fade due to the thin drum being unable to absorb the heat generated.

2. Poor and erratic brake due to distortion of drums.

3. Noise due to possible vibration caused by thin drums.

4. A cracked or broken drum on a severe or very hard brake application.

NOTE: Brake drum run-out should not exceed 0.005 in. Drums turned to more than 0.060 in. oversize are unsafe and should be replaced with new drums, except for some heavy ribbed drums which have an 0.080 in. limit. It is recommended that the diameters of the left and right drums on every axle be within 0.010 in. of each other. In order to avoid erratic brake action when replacing drums, it is always good to replace the drums on both wheels at the same time. If the drums are true, smooth up any slight scores by polishing with fine emery cloth. If deep scores or grooves are present, which cannot be removed by this method, then the drum must be turned.

Troubleshooting and Diagnosis

ENGINE

Gasoline Engine Troubleshooting

See applicable Car or Unit Repair section for specific service procedures

INDEX TO PROBLEMS

Problem Symptom	Begin at Specific Diagnosis, Number
Engine Won't Start	
Starter doesn't turn	1.1, 2.1
Starter turns, engine doesn't	2.1
Starter turns engine very slowly	1.1, 2.4
Starter turns engine normally	3.1, 4.1
Starter turns engine very quickly	6.1
Engine fires intermittently	4.1
Engine fires consistently	5.1, 6.1
Engine Runs Poorly	
Hard starting	3.1, 4.1, 5.1, 8.1
Rough idle	4.1, 5.1, 8.1
Stalling	3.1, 4.1, 5.1, 8.1
Engine dies at high speeds	4.1, 5.1
Hesitation (on acceleration from standing stop)	5.1, 8.1
Poor pickup	4.1, 5.1, 8.1
Lack of power	3.1, 4.1, 5.1, 8.1
Backfire through the carburetor	4.1, 8.1, 9.1
Backfire through the exhaust	4.1, 8.1, 9.1
Blue exhaust gases	6.1, 7.1
Black exhaust gases	5.1
Running on (after the ignition is shut off)	3.1, 8.1
Susceptible to moisture	4.1
Engine misfires under load	4.1, 7.1, 8.4, 9.1
Engine misfires at speed	4.1, 8.4
Engine misfires at idle	3.1, 4.1, 5.1, 7.1, 8.4

SAMPLE SECTION

Test and Procedure	Results and Indications	Proceed to
4.1 Check for spark: Hold each spark plug wire approximately ¼″ from ground with gloves or a heavy, dry rag. Crank the engine and observe the spark.	If no spark is evident	4.2
	If spark is good in some cases	4.3
	If spark is good in all cases	4.6

SPECIFIC DIAGNOSIS

This section is arranged so that following each test, instructions are given to proceed to another, until a problem is diagnosed.

SECTION 1—BATTERY

Test and Procedure	Results and Indications	Proceed to
1.1 Inspect the battery visually for case condition (corrosion, cracks) and water level.	If case is cracked, replace battery.	1.4
	If the case is intact, remove corrosion with a solution of baking soda and water. (CAUTION: Do not get the solution into the battery). Fill with water.	1.2

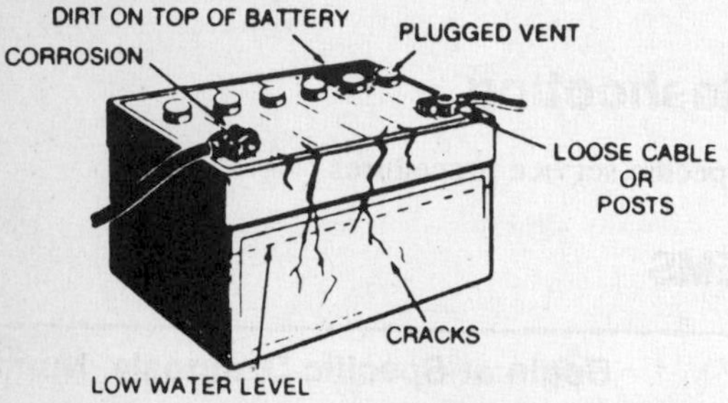

DIRT ON TOP OF BATTERY
CORROSION
PLUGGED VENT
LOOSE CABLE OR POSTS
CRACKS
LOW WATER LEVEL

Inspect the battery case

Test and Procedure	Results and Indications	Proceed to
1.2 Check the battery cable connections: Insert a screwdriver between the battery post and the cable clamp. Turn the headlights on high beam, and observe them as the screwdriver is gently twisted to ensure good metal to metal contact.	If the lights brighten, remove and clean the clamp and post; coat the post with petroleum jelly, install and tighten the clamp.	1.4
	If no improvement is noted	1.3

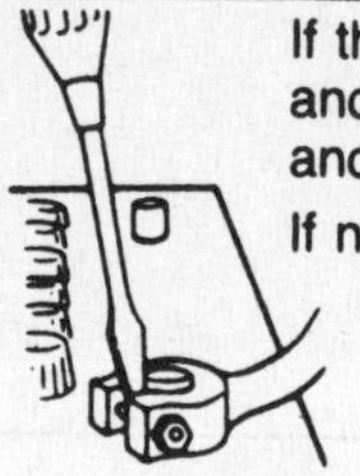

TESTING BATTERY CABLE CONNECTIONS USING A SCREWDRIVER

Test and Procedure	Results and Indications	Proceed to
1.3 Test the state of charge of the battery using an individual cell tester or hydrometer.	If indicated, charge the battery. **NOTE: If no obvious reason exists for the low state of charge (i.e., battery age, prolonged storage), proceed to:**	1.4

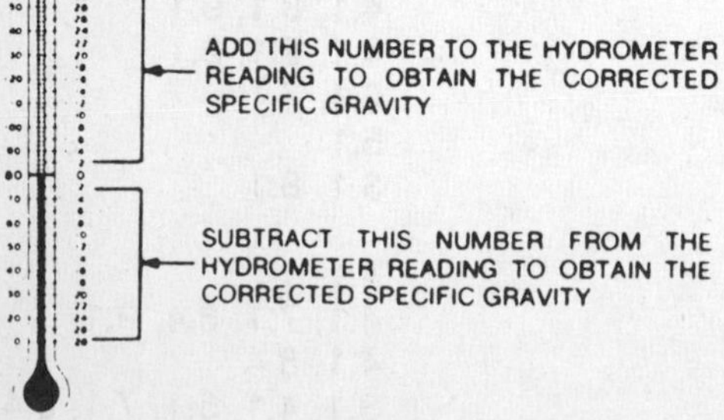

°F

ADD THIS NUMBER TO THE HYDROMETER READING TO OBTAIN THE CORRECTED SPECIFIC GRAVITY

SUBTRACT THIS NUMBER FROM THE HYDROMETER READING TO OBTAIN THE CORRECTED SPECIFIC GRAVITY

Specific Gravity (@ 80° F.)

Minimum	Battery Charge
1.260	100% Charged
1.230	75% Charged
1.200	50% Charged
1.170	25% Charged
1.140	Very Little Power Left
1.110	Completely Discharged

The effects of temperature on battery specific gravity (left) and amount of battery charge in relation to specific gravity (right)

Test and Procedure	Results and Indications	Proceed To
1.4 Visually inspect battery cables for cracking, bad connection to ground, or bad connection to starter.	If necessary, tighten connections or replace the cables.	2.1

SECTION 2—STARTING SYSTEM

Test and Procedure	Results and Indications	Proceed to
Note: Tests in Group 2 are performed with coil high tension lead disconnected to prevent accidental starting.		
2.1 Test the starter motor and solenoid: Connect a jumper from the battery post of the solenoid (or relay) to the starter post of the solenoid (or relay).	If starter turns the engine normally	2.2
	If the starter buzzes, or turns the engine very slowly	2.4
	If no response, replace the solenoid (or relay).	3.1
	If the starter turns, but the engine doesn't, ensure that the flywheel ring gear is intact. If the gear is undamaged, replace the starter drive.	3.1
2.2 Determine whether ignition override switches are functioning properly (clutch start switch, neutral safety switch), by connecting a jumper across the switch(es), and turning the ignition switch to "start".	If starter operates, adjust or replace switch.	3.1
	If the starter doesn't operate	2.3
2.3 Check the ignition switch "start" position: Connect a 12V test lamp or voltmeter between the starter post of the solenoid (or relay) and ground. Turn the ignition switch to the "start" position, and jiggle the key.	If the lamp doesn't light or the meter needle doesn't move when the switch is turned, check the ignition switch for loose connections, cracked insulation, or broken wires. Repair or replace as necessary.	3.1
	If the lamp flickers or needle moves when the key is jiggled, replace the ignition switch.	3.3

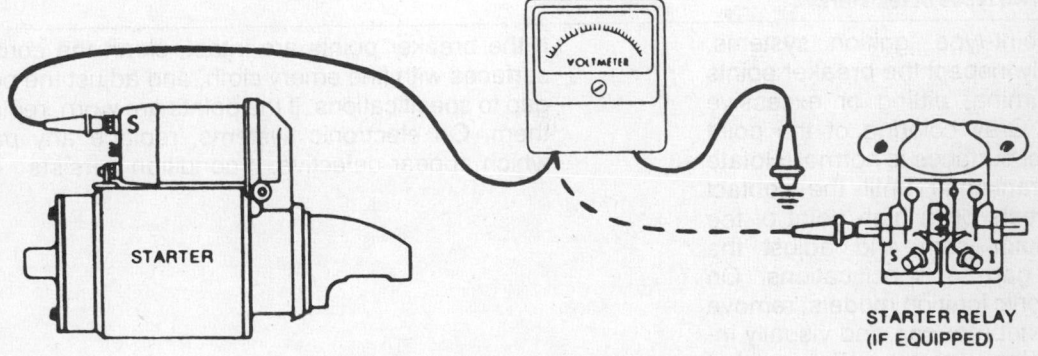

Checking the ignition switch "start" position

2.4 Remove and bench test the starter, according to specifications in the car section.	If the starter does not meet specifications, repair or replace as needed	3.1
	If the starter is operating properly	2.5

Test and Procedure	Results and Indications	Proceed To
2.5 Determine whether the engine can turn freely: Remove the spark plugs, and check for water in the cylinders. Check for water on the dipstick, or oil in the radiator. Attempt to turn the engine using an 18″ flex drive and socket on the crankshaft pulley nut or bolt.	If the engine will turn freely only with the spark plugs out, and hydrostatic lock (water in the cylinders) is ruled out, check valve timing.	9.2
	If engine will not turn freely, and it is known that the clutch and transmission are free, the engine must be disassembled for further evaluation.	See Car Section

SECTION 3—PRIMARY ELECTRICAL SYSTEM

Test and Procedure	Results and Indications	Proceed to
3.1 Check the ignition switch "on" position: Connect a jumper wire between the distributor side of the coil and ground, and a 12V test lamp between the switch side of the coil and ground. Remove the high tension lead from the coil. Turn the ignition switch on and jiggle the key.	If the lamp lights	3.2
	If the lamp flickers when the key is jiggled, replace the ignition switch.	3.3
	If the lamp doesn't light, check for loose or open connections. If none are found, remove the ignition switch and check for continuity. If the switch is faulty, replace it.	3.3

Checking the ignition switch "on" position

3.2 Check the ballast resistor or resistance wire for an open circuit, using an ohmmeter.  Two types of resistors	Replace the resistor or resistance wire if the resistance is zero. **NOTE: Some ignition systems have no ballast resistor.**	3.3
3.3 On point-type ignition systems, visually inspect the breaker points for burning, pitting or excessive wear. Gray coloring of the point contact surfaces is normal. Rotate the crankshaft until the contact heel rests on a high point of the distributor cam and adjust the point gap to specifications. On electronic ignition models, remove the distributor cap and visually inspect the armature. Ensure that the armature pin is in place, and that the armature is on tight and rotates when the engine is cranked. Make sure there are no cracks, chips or rounded edges on the armature.	If the breaker points are intact, clean the contact surfaces with fine emery cloth, and adjust the point gap to specifications. If the points are worn, replace them. On electronic systems, replace any parts which appear defective. If condition persists	3.4

Test and Procedure	Results and Indications	Proceed To
3.4 On point-type ignition systems, connect a dwell-meter between the distributor primary lead and ground. Crank the engine and observe the point dwell angle. On electronic ignition systems, conduct a stator (magnetic pickup assembly) test. See Electronic Ignition Unit Repair Section.	On point-type systems, adjust the dwell angle if necessary. **NOTE: Increasing the point gap decreases the dwell angle and vice-versa.**	**3.6**
	If the dwell meter shows little or no reading	**3.5**
	On electronic ignition systems, if the stator is bad, replace the stator. If the stator is good, proceed to the other tests in The Electronic Ignition Unit Repair Section.	

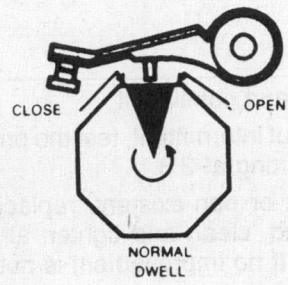 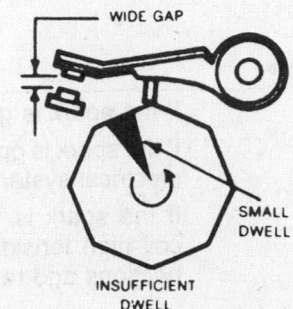 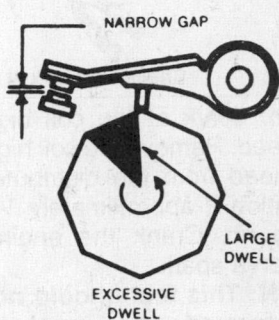

Dwell is a function of point gap

3.5 On the point-type ignition systems, check the condenser for short: connect an ohmeter across the condenser body and the pigtail lead.	If any reading other than infinite is noted, replace the condenser	**3.6**

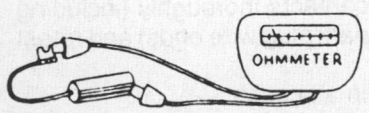

Checking the condenser for short

3.6 Test the coil primary resistance: On point-type ignition systems, connect an ohmmeter across the coil primary terminals, and read the resistance on the low scale. Note whether an external ballast resistor or resistance wire is used. On electronic ignition systems, test the coil primary resistance.	Point-type ignition coils utilizing ballast resistors or resistance wires should have approximately 1.0 ohms resistance. Coils with internal resistors should have approximately 4.0 ohms resistance. If values far from the above are noted, replace the coil.	**4.1**

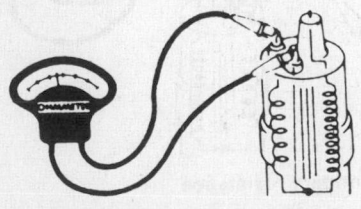

Checking the coil primary resistance

SECTION 4—SECONDARY ELECTRICAL SYSTEM

Test and Procedure	Results and Indications	Proceed to
4.1 Check for spark: Hold each spark plug wire approximately ¼" from ground with gloves or heavy, dry rag. Crank the engine, and observe the spark.	If no spark is evident	4.2
	If spark is good in some cylinders	4.3
	If spark is good in all cylinders	4.6

Check for spark at the plugs

Test and Procedure	Results and Indications	Proceed to
4.2 Check for spark at the coil high tension lead: Remove the coil high tension lead from the distributor and position it approximately ¼" from ground. Crank the engine and observe spark. **CAUTION: This test should not be performed on engines equipped with electronic ignition.**	If the spark is good and consistent	4.3
	If the spark is good but intermittent, test the primary electrical system starting at 3.3.	3.3
	If the spark is weak or non-existent, replace the coil high tension lead, clean and tighten all connections and retest. If no improvement is noted	4.4

Test and Procedure	Results and Indications	Proceed to
4.3 Visually inspect the distributor cap and rotor for burned or corroded contacts, cracks, carbon tracks, or moisture. Also check the fit of the rotor on the distributor shaft (where applicable).	If moisture is present, dry thoroughly, and retest per 4.1.	4.1
	If burned or excessively corroded contacts, cracks, or carbon tracks are noted, replace the defective part(s) and retest per 4.1.	4.1
	If the rotor and cap appear intact, or are only slightly corroded, clean the contacts thoroughly (including the cap towers and spark plug wire ends) and retest per 4.1.	
	If the spark is good in all cases	4.6
	If the spark is poor in all cases	4.5

CORRODED OR LOOSE WIRE

HIGH RESISTANCE CARBON

EXCESSIVE WEAR OF BUTTON

ROTOR TIP BURNED AWAY

Inspect the distributor cap and rotor

Test and Procedure	Results and Indications
4.4 Check the coil secondary resistance: On point-type systems connect an ohmmeter across the distributor side of the coil and the coil tower. Read the resistance on the high scale of the ohmmeter. On electronic ignition systems, see The Electronic Ignition Unit Repair Section for specific tests.	The resistance of a satisfactory coil should be between 4,000 and 10,000 ohms. If resistance is considerably higher (i.e., 40,000 ohms) replace the coil and retest per 4.1. **NOTE: This does not apply to high performance coils.**

Testing the coil secondary resistance

Spark Plug Analysis

Normal

APPEARANCE

This plug is typical of one operating normally. The insulator nose varies from a light tan to grayish color with slight electrode wear. The presence of slight deposits is normal on used plugs and will have no adverse effect on engine performance. The spark plug heat range is correct for the engine and the engine is running normally.

CAUSE

Properly running engine

RECOMMENDATION

Before reinstalling this plug, the electrodes should be cleaned and filed square. Set the gap to specifications. If the plug has been in service for more than 10–12,000 miles, the entire set should probably be replaced with a fresh set of the same heat range.

Incorrect Heat Range

APPEARANCE

The effects of high temperature on a spark plug are indicated by clean white, often blistered insulator. This can also be accompanied by excessive wear of the electrode, and the absence of deposits.

CAUSE

Check for the correct spark plug heat range. A plug which is too hot for the engine can result in overheating. A car operated mostly at high speeds may require a colder plug. Also check ignition timing, cooling system level, fuel mixture and leaking intake manifold.

RECOMMENDATION

If all ignition and engine adjustments are known to be correct, and no other malfunction exists, install spark plugs one heat range colder.

Oil Deposits

APPEARANCE

The firing end of the plug is covered with a wet, oily coating.

CAUSE

The problem is poor oil control. On high mileage engines, oil is leaking past the rings or valve guides into the combustion chamber. A common cause is also a plugged PCV valve, and a ruptured fuel pump diaphragm can also cause this condition. Oil fouled plugs such as these are often found in new or recently overhauled engines, before normal oil control is achieved, and can be cleaned and reinstalled.

RECOMMENDATION

A hotter spark plug may temporarily relieve the problem, but the engine is probably in need of engine work.

Carbon Deposits

APPEARANCE

Carbon fouling is easily identified by the presence of dry, soft, black, sooty deposits.

CAUSE

Changing the heat range can often lead to carbon fouling, as can prolonged slow, stop-and-start driving. If the heat range is correct, carbon fouling can be attributed to a rich fuel mixture, sticking choke, clogged air cleaner, worn breaker points, retarded timing or low compression. If only one or two plugs are carbon fouled, check for corroded or cracked wires on the affected plugs. Also look for cracks in the distributor cap between the towers of affected cylinders.

RECOMMENDATION

After the problem is corrected, these plugs can be cleaned and reinstalled if not worn severely.

Ash Deposits

APPEARANCE

Ash deposits are characterized by light brown or white colored deposits crusted on the side or center electrodes. In some cases it may give the plug a rusty appearance.

CAUSE

Ash deposits are normally derived from oil or fuel additives burned during normal combustion. Normally they are harmless, though excessive amounts can cause misfiring. If deposits are excessive in short mileage, the valve guides may be worn. Reddish or rusty deposits are caused by manganese, an anti-knock compound replacing lead in unleaded gas. No engine malfunction is indicated.

RECOMMENDATION

Ash-fouled plugs can be cleaned, gapped and reinstalled.

Splash Deposits

APPEARANCE

Splash deposits occur in varying degrees as spotty deposits on the insulator.

CAUSE

These usually occur after a long delayed tune-up. By-products of combustion have accumulated on pistons and valves because of a delayed tune-up. Following tune-up or during hard acceleration, the deposits loosen and are thrown against the hot surface of the plug. If the deposits accumulate sufficiently, misfiring can occur.

RECOMMENDATION

These plugs can be cleaned, gapped and reinstalled.

High Speed Glazing

APPEARANCE

Glazing appears as shiny coating on the plug, either yellow or tan in color.

CAUSE

During hard, fast acceleration, plug temperatures rise suddenly. Deposits from normal combustion have no chance to fluff-off; instead, they melt on the insulator forming an electrically conductive coating which causes misfiring.

RECOMMENDATION

Glazed plugs are not easily cleaned. They should be replaced with a fresh set of plugs of the correct heat range. If the condition recurs, using plugs with a heat range one step colder may cure the problem.

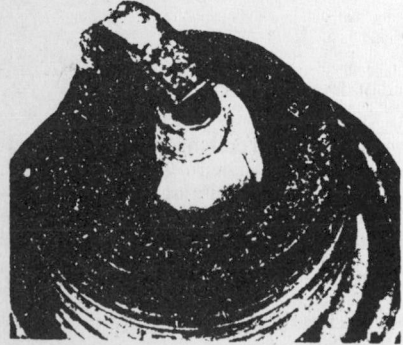

Detonation

APPEARANCE

Detonation is usually characterized by a broken plug insulator.

CAUSE

A portion of the fuel charge will begin to burn spontaneously, from the increased heat following ignition. The explosion that results applies extreme pressure to engine components, frequently damaging spark plugs and pistons.

Detonation can result by over-advanced ignition timing, inferior gasoline (low octane) lean air fuel mixture, poor carburetion, engine lugging or an increase in compression ratio due to combustion chamber deposits or engine modification.

RECOMMENDATION

Replace the plugs after correcting the problem.

Test and Procedure	Results and Indications	Proceed To

4.5 Visually inspect the spark plug wires for cracking or brittleness. Ensure that no two wires are positioned so as to cause induction firing (adjacent and parallel). Remove each wire, one by one, and check resistance with an ohmmeter.

Replace any cracked or brittle wires. If any of the wires are defective, replace the entire set. Replace any wires with excessive resistance (over 8000 Ω per foot for suppression wire), and separate any wires that might cause induction firing.

4.6

Misfiring can be the result of spark plug leads to adjacent, consecutively firing cylinders running parallel and too close together

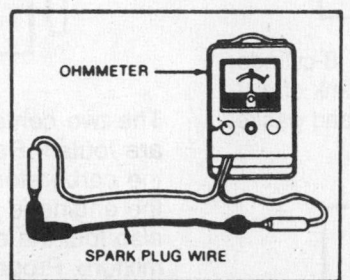

On point-type ignition systems, check the spark plug wires as shown. On electronic ignitions, do not remove the wire from the distributor cap terminal; instead, test through the cap

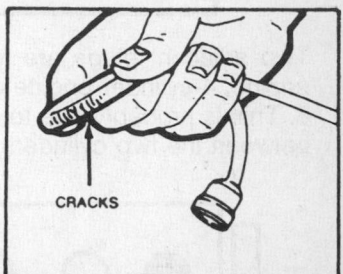

Spark plugs wires can be checked visually by bending them in a loop over your finger. This will reveal any cracks, burned or broken insulation. Any wire with cracked insulation should be replaced

4.6 Remove the spark plugs, noting the cylinders from which they were removed, and evaluate according to the chart in this section.

See chart.

See Chart

4.7 Reinstall the spark plugs.
NOTE: Modern electronic ignition systems generate extremely high voltages and high heats. The spark plug boots can soften and actually fuse to the ceramic insulator of the spark plugs after long exposures to high temperature and voltage. If this happens, the boot (and possibly the wire) must be replaced.

To help alleviate this condition, many manufacturers are recommending new silicone compounds to slow the deterioration. The compounds are generally nonconductive, protective lubricants that will not dry out, harden, or melt away. They form a weather-tight seal between rubber or plastic and metal and are found in several typical locations: Inside the insulating boots of spark plug wires, inside primary ignition circuit cable connectors, on distributor and rotor cap electrodes, and under the GM HEI control module.

4.8

Application Point	Silicone Compound
GENERAL MOTORS: Under HEI module	Supplied with new module, or use GE-642 or DC-340
FORD MOTOR COMPANY: Inside spark plug boots, on end of cable when installing new boot, and on rotor and cap electrodes	Ford part number D7AZ-19A331-A or use GE-627 or DC-111
CHRYSLER CORPORATION: ¼" deep within spark control computer connector cavity coating rotor electrode	Use Mopar part number 2932524 or NLGI Grade 2 EP (not a silicone) supplied with new rotor, or use GE-628 or DC-111
AMERICAN MOTORS (Prestolite system): Distributor primary connector—coat male terminal, fill female ¼ full	AMC part number 8127445 or GE-623

GE: General Electric
DC: Dow Corning

Test and Procedure	Results and Indications	Proceed To

4.8 Examine the location of all the plugs.

The following diagrams illustrate some of the conditions that the location of plugs will reveal.

4.9

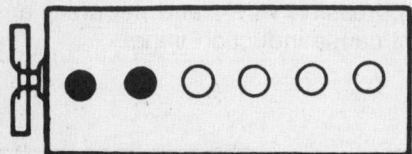

Two adjacent plugs are fouled in a 6-cylinder engine, 4-cylinder engine or either bank of a V-8. This is probably due to a blown head gasket between the two cylinders.

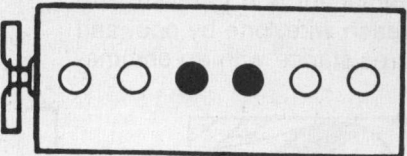

The two center plugs in a 6-cylinder engine are fouled. Raw fuel may be "boiled" out of the carburetor into the intake manifold after the engine is shut-off. Stop-start driving can also foul the center plugs, due to overly rich mixture. Proper float level, a new float needle and seat or use of an insulating spacer may help this problem.

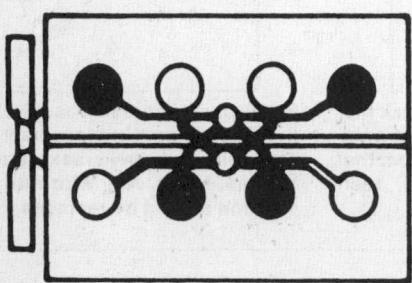

An unbalanced carburetor is indicated. Following the fuel flow on this particular design shows that the cylinders fed by the right-hand barrel are fouled from overly rich mixture, while the cylinders fed by the left-hand barrel are normal.

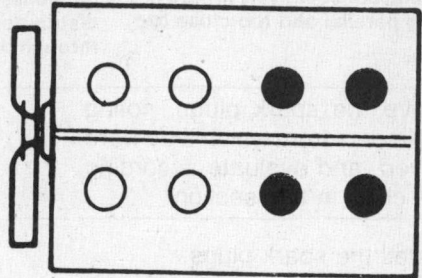

If the four rear plugs are overheated, a cooling system problem is suggested. A thorough cleaning of the cooling system may restore coolant circulation and cure the problem.

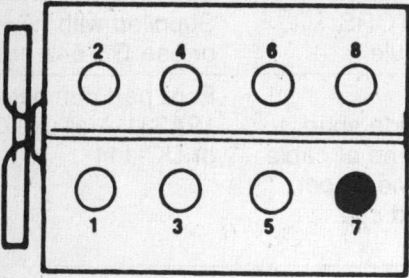

Finding one plug overheated may indicate an intake manifold leak near the affected cylinder. If the overheated plug is the second of two adjacent, consecutively firing plugs, it could be the result of ignition cross-firing. Separating the leads to these two plugs will eliminate cross-fire.

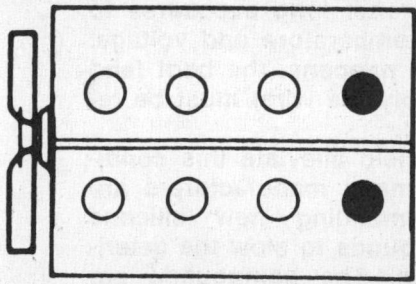

Occasionally, the two rear plugs in large, lightly used V-8's will become oil fouled. High oil consumption and smoky exhaust may also be noticed. It is probably due to plugged oil drain holes in the rear of the cylinder head, causing oil to be sucked in around the valve stems. This usually occurs in the rear cylinders first, because the engine slants that way.

Test and Procedure	Results and Indications	Proceed To
4.9 Determine the static ignition timing. Using the crankshaft pulley timing marks as a guide, locate top dead center on the compression stroke of the number one cylinder.	The rotor should be pointing toward the No. 1 tower in the distributor cap, and, on electronic ignitions, the armature spoke for that cylinder should be lined up with the stator.	4.10
4.10 Check coil polarity: Connect a voltmeter negative lead to the coil high tension lead, and the positive lead to ground. **NOTE: Reverse the hook-up for positive ground systems.** Crank the engine momentarily. **Checking coil polarity**	If the voltmeter reads up-scale, the polarity is correct.	5.1
	If the voltmeter reads down-scale, reverse the coil polarity (switch the primary leads).	5.1

SECTION 5—FUEL SYSTEM

Test and Procedure	Results and Indications	Proceed to
5.1 Determine that the air filter is functioning efficiently: Hold paper elements up to a strong light, and attempt to see light through the filter.	Clean permanent air filters in solvent (or manufacturer's recommendation), and allow to dry. Replace paper elements through which light cannot be seen.	5.2
5.2 Determine whether a flooding condition exists: Flooding is identified by a strong gasoline odor, and excessive gasoline present in the throttle bore(s) of the carburetor. **If the engine floods repeatedly, check the choke butterfly flap**	If flooding is not evident	5.3
	If flooding is evident, permit the gasoline to dry for a few moments and restart.	
	If flooding doesn't recur	5.7
	If flooding is persistent	5.5
5.3 Check that fuel is reaching the carburetor: Detach the fuel line at the carburetor inlet. Hold the end of the line in a cup (not styrofoam), and crank the engine. **Check the fuel pump by disconnecting the output line (fuel pump-to-carburetor) at the carburetor and operating the starter briefly**	If fuel flows smoothly	5.7
	If fuel doesn't flow	5.4
	If fuel flows erratically.	
	NOTE: Make sure that there is fuel in the tank	

Test and Procedure	Results and Indications	Proceed To
5.4 Test the fuel pump: Disconnect all fuel lines from the fuel pump. Hold a finger over the input fitting, crank the engine (with electric pump, turn the ignition or pump on); and feel for suction.	If suction is evident, blow out the fuel line to the tank with low pressure compressed air until bubbling is heard from the fuel filler neck. Also blow out the carburetor fuel line (both ends disconnected).	5.7
	If no suction is evident, replace or repair the fuel pump. **NOTE: Repeated oil fouling of the spark plugs, or a no-start condition, could be the result of a ruptured vacuum booster pump diaphragm, through which oil or gasoline is being drawn into the intake manifold (where applicable).**	5.7
5.5 Occasionally, small specks of dirt will clog the small jets and orifices in the carburetor. With the engine cold, hold a flat piece of wood or similar material over the carburetor, where possible, and crank the engine.	If the engine starts, but runs roughly the engine is probably not run enough.	
	If the engine won't start.	5.9
5.6 Check the needle and seat: Tap the carburetor in the area of the needle and seat.	If flooding stops, a gasoline additive (e.g., Gumout) will often cure the problem.	5.7
	If flooding continues, check the fuel pump for excessive pressure at the carburetor (according to specifications). If the pressure is normal, the needle and seat must be removed and checked, and/or the float level adjusted.	5.7
5.7 Test the accelerator pump by looking into the throttle bores while operating the throttle.	If the accelerator pump appears to be operating normally	5.8
	If the accelerator pump is not operating, the pump must be reconditioned. Where possible, service the pump with the carburetor(s) installed on the engine. If necessary, remove the carburetor. Prior to removal	5.8

Check for gas at the carburetor by looking down the carburetor throat while someone moves the accelerator

Test and Procedure	Results and Indications	Proceed To
5.8 Determine whether the carburetor main fuel system is functioning: Spray a commercial starting fluid into the carburetor while attempting to start the engine.	If the engine starts, runs for a few seconds, and dies	5.9
	If the engine doesn't start	6.1
5.9 Uncommon fuel system malfunctions: See below:	If the problem is solved	6.1
	If the problem remains, remove and recondition the carburetor.	

Condition	Indication	Test	Prevailing Weather Conditions	Remedy
Vapor lock	Engine will not re-start shortly after running.	Cool the components of the fuel system until the engine starts. Vapor lock can be cured faster by draping a wet cloth over a mechanical fuel pump.	Hot to very hot	Ensure that the exhaust manifold heat control valve is operating. Check with the vehicle manufacturer for the recommended solution to vapor lock on the model in question.
Carburetor icing	Engine will not idle, stalls at low speeds.	Visually inspect the throttle plate area of the throttle bores for frost.	High humidity, 32–40° F.	Ensure that the exhaust manifold heat control valve is operating, and that the intake manifold heat riser is not blocked.
Water in the fuel	Engine sputters and stalls; may not start.	Pump a small amount of fuel into a glass jar. Allow to stand, and inspect for droplets of a layer of water.	High humidity, extreme temperature changes.	For droplets, use one or two cans of commercial gas line anti-freeze. For a layer of water, the tank must be drained, and the fuel lines blown out with compressed air.

SECTION 6—ENGINE COMPRESSION

Test and Procedure	Results and Indications	Proceed to
6.1 Test engine compression: Remove all spark plugs. Block the throttle wide open. Insert a compression gauge into a spark plug port, crank the engine to obtain the maximum reading, and record.	If compression is within limits on all cylinders	7.1
	If gauge reading is extremely low on all cylinders	6.2
	If gauge reading is low on one or two cylinders: (If gauge readings are identical and low on two or more adjacent cylinders, the head gasket must be replaced.)	6.2

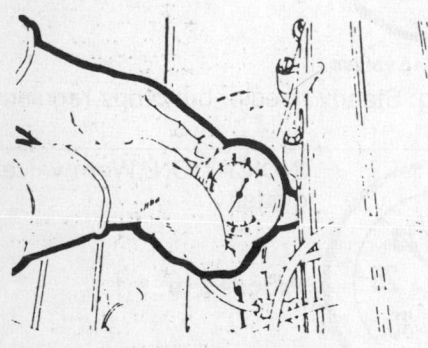

Checking compression

6.2 Test engine compression (wet): Squirt approximately 30 cc. of engine oil into each cylinder, and re-test per 6.1.	If the readings improve, worn or cracked rings or broken pistons are indicated:	See Car Section
	If the readings do not improve, burned or excessively carboned valves or a jumped timing chain are indicated. **NOTE: A jumped timing chain is often indicated by difficult cranking.**	7.1

SECTION 7—ENGINE VACUUM

Test and Procedure	Results and Indications	Proceed to
7.1 Attach a vacuum gauge to the intake manifold beyond the throttle plate. Start the engine, and observe the action of the needle over the range of engine speeds.	See below.	**See below**

Normal engine

Gauge reading: Steady, from 17–22 in./Hg.

INDICATION: Normal engine in good condition

Proceed to: 8.1

Sticking valves

Gauge reading: Intermittent fluctuation at idle

INDICATION: Sticking valves or ignition miss

Proceed to: 9.1, 8.3

Incorrect valve timing

Gauge reading: Low (10–15 in./Hg) but steady

INDICATION: Late ignition or valve timing, low compression, stuck throttle valve, leaking carburetor or manifold gasket

Proceed to: 6.1

Carburetor requires adjustment

Gauge reading: Drifting needle

INDICATION: Improper carburetor adjustment or minor intake leak.

Proceed to: 7.2

Blown head gasket

Gauge reading: Needle fluctuates as engine speed increases

INDICATION: Ignition miss, blown cylinder head gasket, leaking valve or weak valve spring

Proceed to: 8.3, 6.1

Burnt or leaking valves

Gauge reading: Steady needle, but drops regularly

INDICATION: Burnt valve or faulty valve clearance: Needle will fall when defective valve operates

Proceed to: 9.1

Clogged exhaust system

Gauge reading: Gradual drop in reading at idle

INDICATION: Choked muffler, excessive back pressure in system

Proceed to: 10.1

Worn valve guides

Gauge reading: Needle vibrates excessively at idle, but steadies as engine speed increases

INDICATION: Worn valve guides

Proceed to: 9.1

White pointer = steady gauge hand

Black pointer = fluctuating gauge hand

Test and Procedure	Results and Indications	Proceed To
7.2 Attach a vacuum gauge per 7.1, and test for an intake manifold leak. Squirt a small amount of oil around the intake manifold gaskets, carburetor gaskets, plugs and fittings. Observe the action of the vacuum gauge.	If the reading improves, replace the indicated gasket, or seal the indicated fitting or plug:	**8.1**
	If the reading remains low:	**7.3**
7.3 Test all vacuum hoses and accessories for leaks as described in 7.2. Also check the carburetor body (dashpots, automatic choke mechanism, throttle shafts) for leaks in the same manner.	If the reading improves, service or replace the offending part(s):	**8.1**
	If the reading remains low:	**6.1**

SECTION 8—SECONDARY ELECTRICAL SYSTEM

Test and Procedure	Results and Indications	Proceed to
8.1 Remove the distributor cap and check to make sure that the rotor turns when the engine is cranked. Visually inspect the distributor components.	Clean, tighten or replace any components which appear defective.	**8.2**
8.2 Connect a timing light (per manufacturer's recommendation) and check the dynamic ignition timing. Disconnect and plug the vacuum hose(s) to the distributor if specified, start the engine, and observe the timing marks at the specified engine speed.	If the timing is not correct, adjust to specifications by rotating the distributor in the engine: (Advance timing by rotating distributor opposite normal direction of rotor rotation, retard timing by rotating distributor in same direction as rotor rotation.)	**8.3**
8.3 Check the operation of the distributor advance mechanism(s): To test the mechanical advance, disconnect the vacuum lines from the distributor advance unit and observe the timing marks with a timing light as the engine speed is increased from idle. If the mark moves smoothly, without hesitation, it may be assumed that the mechanical advance is functioning properly. To test vacuum advance and or retard systems, alternately crimp and release the vacuum line, and observe the timing mark for movement. If movement is noted, the system is operating.	If the systems are functioning	**8.4**
	If the systems are not functioning, remove the distributor, and test on a distributor tester.	**8.4**
8.4 Locate an ignition miss: With the engine running, remove each spark plug wire, one at a time, until one is found that doesn't cause the engine to roughen and slow down. **CAUTION: Do not pull on the wire to remove the boot from the plug. Be sure your hand is insulated from the wire.**	When the missing cylinder is identified	**4.1**

SECTION 9—VALVE TRAIN

Test and Procedure	Results and Indications	Proceed to
9.1 Evaluate the valve train: Remove the valve cover, and ensure that the valves are adjusted to specifications. A mechanic's stethoscope may be used to aid in the diagnosis of the valve train. By pushing the probe on or near push rods or rockers, valve noise often can be isolated. A timing light also may be used to diagnose valve problems. Connect the light according to manufacturer's recommendations, and start the engine. Vary the firing moment of the light by increasing the engine speed (and therefore the ignition advance), and moving the trigger from cylinder to cylinder. Observe the movement of each valve.	Sticking valves or erratic valve train motion can be observed with the timing light. The cylinder head must be disassembled for repairs.	**See Car Section**
9.2 Check the valve timing: Locate top dead center of the No. 1 piston, and install a degree wheel or tape on the crankshaft pulley or damper with zero corresponding to an index mark on the engine. Rotate the crankshaft in its direction of rotation, and observe the opening of the No. 1 cylinder intake valve. The opening should correspond with the correct mark on the degree wheel according to specifications.	If the timing is not correct, the timing cover must be removed for further investigation.	**See Car Section**

SECTION 10—EXHAUST SYSTEM

Test and Procedure	Results and Indications	Proceed to
10.1 Determine whether the exhaust manifold heat control valve is operating: Operate the valve by hand to determine whether it is free to move. If the valve is free, run the engine to operating temperature and observe the action of the valve, to ensure that it is opening.	If the valve sticks, spray it with a suitable solvent, open and close the valve to free it, and retest. If the valve functions properly If the valve does not free, or does not operate, replace the valve.	**10.2** **10.2**
10.2 Ensure that there are no exhaust restrictions: Visually inspect the exhaust system for kinks, dents, or crushing. Also note that gases are flowing freely from the tailpipe at all engine speeds, indicating no restriction in the muffler or resonator.	Replace any damaged portion of the system.	**11.1**

SECTION 11—COOLING SYSTEM

Test and Procedure	Results and Indications	Proceed to
11.1 Visually inspect the fan belt for glazing, cracks, and fraying, and replace if necessary. Tighten the belt so that the longest span has approximately ½″ play at its midpoint under thumb pressure (see Maintenance Section).	Replace or tighten the fan belt as necessary. **Checking belt tension**	**11.2**
11.2 Check the fluid level of the cooling system.	If full or slightly low, fill as necessary.	**11.5**
	If extremely low	**11.3**
11.3 Visually inspect the external portions of the cooling system (radiator, radiator hoses, thermostat elbow, water pump seals, heater hoses, etc.) for leaks. If none are found, pressurize the cooling system to 14–15 psi.	If cooling system holds the pressure	**11.5**
	If cooling system loses pressure rapidly, reinspect external parts of the system for leaks under pressure. If none are found, check dipstick for coolant in crankcase. If no coolant is present, but pressure loss continues	**11.4**
	If coolant is evident in crankcase, remove cylinder head(s), and check gasket(s). If gaskets are intact, block and cylinder head(s) should be checked for cracks or holes.	
	If the gasket(s) is blown, replace, and purge the crankcase of coolant.	**12.6**
	NOTE: Occasionally, due to atmospheric and driving conditions, condensation of water can occur in the crankcase. This causes the oil to appear milky white. To remedy, run the engine until hot, and change the oil and oil filter.	
11.4 Check for combustion leaks into the cooling system: Pressurize the cooling system as above. Start the engine, and observe the pressure gauge. If the needle fluctuates, remove each spark plug wire, one at a time, noting which cylinder(s) reduce or eliminate the fluctuation.	Cylinders which reduce or eliminate the fluctuation, when the spark plug wire is removed, are leaking into the cooling system. Replace the head gasket on the affected cylinder bank(s). **Pressurizing the cooling system**	**See Car Section**

Test and Procedure	Results and Indications	Proceed To
11.5 Check the radiator pressure cap: Attach a radiator pressure tester to the radiator cap (wet the seal prior to installation). Quickly pump up the pressure, noting the point at which the cap releases.	If the cap releases within ±1 psi of the specified rating, it is operating properly.	**11.6**
	If the cap releases at more than ±1 psi of the specified rating, it should be replaced.	**11.6**

Checking radiator pressure cap

Test and Procedure	Results and Indications	Proceed To
11.6 Test the thermostat: Start the engine cold, remove the radiator cap, and insert a thermometer into the radiator. Allow the engine to idle. After a short while, there will be a sudden, rapid increase in coolant temperature. The temperature at which this sharp rise stops is the thermostat opening temperature.	If the thermostat opens at or about the specified temperature	**11.7**
	If the temperature doesn't increase (If the temperature increases slowly and gradually, replace the thermostat.)	**11.7**
11.7 Check the water pump: Remove the thermostat elbow and the thermostat, disconnect the coil high tension lead (to prevent starting), and crank the engine momentarily.	If coolant flows, replace the thermostat and retest per 11.6.	**11.6**
	If coolant doesn't flow, reverse flush the cooling system to alleviate any blockage that might exist. If system is not blocked, and coolant will not flow, replace the water pump.	**See Car Section**

SECTION 12—LUBRICATION

Test and Procedure	Results and Indications	Proceed to
12.1 Check the oil pressure gauge or warning light: If the gauge shows low pressure, or the light is on for no obvious reason, remove the oil pressure sender. Install an accurate oil pressure gauge and run the engine momentarily.	If oil pressure builds normally, run engine for a few moments to determine that it is functioning normally, and replace the sender.	—
	If the pressure remains low	12.2
	If the pressure surges	12.3
	If the oil pressure is zero	12.3
12.2 Visually inspect the oil: If the oil is watery or very thin, milky, or foamy, replace the oil and oil filter.	If the oil is normal	12.3
	If after replacing oil the pressure remains low	12.3
	If after replacing oil the pressure becomes normal	—
12.3 Inspect the oil pressure relief valve and spring, to ensure that it is not sticking or stuck. Remove and thoroughly clean the valve, spring, and the valve body.	If the oil pressure improves	—
	If no improvement is noted	12.4
12.4 Check to ensure that the oil pump is not cavitating (sucking air instead of oil): See that the crankcase is neither over nor underfull, and that the pickup in the sump is in the proper position and free from sludge.	Fill or drain the crankcase to the proper capacity, and clean the pickup screen in solvent if necessary. If no improvement is noted	12.5
12.5 Inspect the oil pump drive and the oil pump:	If the pump drive or the oil pump appear to be defective, service as necessary and retest per 12.1.	12.1
	If the pump drive and pump appear to be operating normally, the engine should be disassembled to determine where blockage exists.	
12.6 Purge the engine of ethylene glycol coolant: Competely drain the crankcase and the oil filter. Obtain a commercial butyl cellosolve base solvent, designated for this purpose, and follow the instructions precisely. Following this, install a new oil filter and refill the crankcase with the proper weight oil. The next oil and filter change should follow shortly thereafter (1000 miles).		

How To Read Tire Wear

The way your tires wear is a good indicator of other parts of the suspension. Abnormal wear patterns are often caused by the need for simple tire maintenance, or for front end alignment.

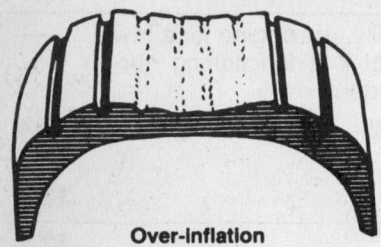

Over-inflation

Excessive wear at the center of the tread indicates that the air pressure in the tire is consistently too high. The tire is riding on the center of the tread and wearing it prematurely. Occasionally, this wear pattern can result from outrageously wide tires on narrow rims. The cure for this is to replace either the tires or the wheels.

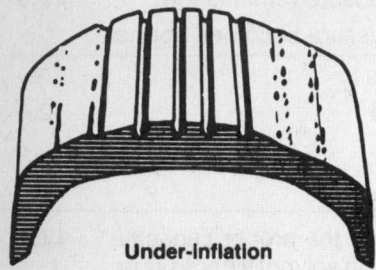

Under-inflation

This type of wear usually results from consistent under-inflation. When a tire is under-inflated, there is too much contact with the road by the outer treads, which wear prematurely. When this type of wear occurs, and the tire pressure is known to be consistently correct, a bent or worn steering component or the need for wheel alignment could be indicated.

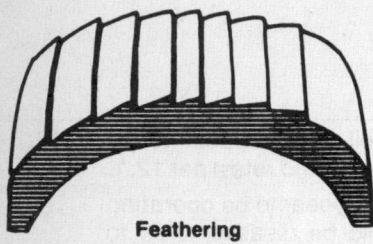

Feathering

Feathering is a condition when the edge of each tread rib develops a slightly rounded edge on one side and a sharp edge on the other. By running your hand over the tire, you can usually feel the sharper edges before you'll be able to see them. The most common causes of feathering are incorrect toe-in setting or deteriorated bushings in the front suspension.

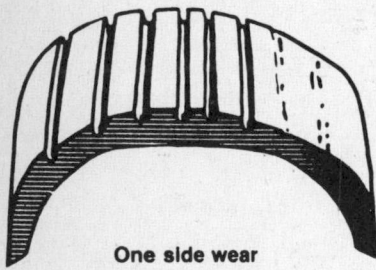

One side wear

When an inner or outer rib wears faster than the rest of the tire, the need for wheel alignment is indicated. There is excessive camber in the front suspension, causing the wheel to lean too much putting excessive load on one side of the tire. Misalignment could also be due to sagging springs, worn ball joints, or worn control arm bushings. Be sure the vehicle is loaded the way it's normally driven when you have the wheels aligned.

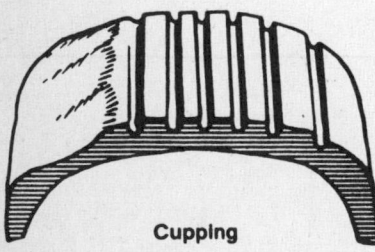

Cupping

Cups or scalloped dips appearing around the edge of the tread almost always indicate worn (sometimes bent) suspension parts. Adjustment of wheel alignment alone will seldom cure the problem. Any worn component that connects the wheel to the suspension can cause this type of wear. Occasionally, wheels that are out of balance will wear like this, but wheel imbalance usually shows up as bald spots between the outside edges and center of the tread.

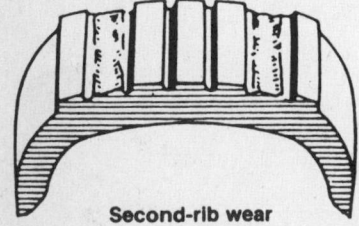

Second-rib wear

Second-rib wear is usually found only in radial tires, and appears where the steel belts end in relation to the tread. It can be kept to a minimum by paying careful attention to tire pressure and frequently rotating the tires. This is often considered normal wear but excessive amounts indicate that the tires are too wide for the wheels.

Mechanics Data 41

SI METRIC TABLES

The following tables are given in SI (International System) metric units. SI units replace both customary (English) and the older gavimetric units. The use of SI units as a new worldwide standard was set by the International Committee of Weights and Measures in 1960. SI has since been adopted by most countries as their national standard.

These tables are general conversion tables which will allow you to convert customary units, which appear in the text, into SI units.

The following are a list of SI units and the customary units, used in this book, which they replace:

To measure:	Use SI units:	Which replace (customary units):
mass	kilograms (kg)	pounds (lbs)
temperature	Celsius (°C)	Fahrenheit (°F)
length	millimeters (mm)	inches (in.)
force	newtons (N)	pounds force (lbs)
capacities	liters (l)	pints/quarts/gallons (pts/qts/gals)
torque	newton-meters (N·m)	foot pounds (ft lbs)
pressure	kilopascals (kPa)	pounds per square inch (psi)
volume	cubic centimeters (cm³)	cubic inches (cu in.)
power	kilowatts (kW)	horsepower (hp)

If you have had any prior experience with the metric system, you may have noticed units in this chart which are not familiar to you. This is because, in some cases, SI units differ from the older gravimetric units which they replace. For example, newtons (N) replace kilograms (kg) as a force unit, kilopascals (kPa) replace atmos-pheres or bars as a unit of pressure, and, although the units are the same, the name Celsius replaces centigrade for temperature measurement.

If you are not using the SI tables, have a look at them anyway; you will be seeing a lot more of them in the future.

41-1

ENGLISH TO METRIC CONVERSION: MASS (WEIGHT)

Current mass measurement is expressed in pounds and ounces (lbs. & ozs.). The metric unit of mass (or weight) is the kilogram (kg). Even although this table does not show conversion of masses (weights) larger than 15 lbs, it is easy to calculate larger units by following the data immediately below.

To convert ounces (oz.) to grams (g): multiply th number of ozs. by 28
To convert grams (g) to ounces (oz.): multiply the number of grams by .035

To convert pounds (lbs.) to kilograms (kg): multiply the number of lbs. by .45
To convert kilograms (kg) to pounds (lbs.): multiply the number of kilograms by 2.2

lbs	kg	lbs	kg	oz	kg	oz	kg
0.1	0.04	0.9	0.41	0.1	0.003	0.9	0.024
0.2	0.09	1	0.4	0.2	0.005	1	0.03
0.3	0.14	2	0.9	0.3	0.008	2	0.06
0.4	0.18	3	1.4	0.4	0.011	3	0.08
0.5	0.23	4	1.8	0.5	0.014	4	0.11
0.6	0.27	5	2.3	0.6	0.017	5	0.14
0.7	0.32	10	4.5	0.7	0.020	10	0.28
0.8	0.36	15	6.8	0.8	0.023	15	0.42

ENGLISH TO METRIC CONVERSION: TEMPERATURE

To convert Fahrenheit (°F) to Celsius (°C): take number of °F and subtract 32; multiply result by 5; divide result by 9

To convert Celsius (°C) to Fahrenheit (°F): take number of °C and multiply by 9; divide result by 5; add 32 to total

Fahrenheit (F)		Celsius (C)		Fahrenheit (F)		Celsius (C)		Fahrenheit (F)		Celsius (C)	
°F	°C	°C	°F	°F	°C	°C	°F	°F	°C	°C	°F
−40	−40	−38	−36.4	80	26.7	18	64.4	215	101.7	80	176
−35	−37.2	−36	−32.8	85	29.4	20	68	220	104.4	85	185
−30	−34.4	−34	−29.2	90	32.2	22	71.6	225	107.2	90	194
−25	−31.7	−32	−25.6	95	35.0	24	75.2	230	110.0	95	202
−20	−28.9	−30	−22	100	37.8	26	78.8	235	112.8	100	212
−15	−26.1	−28	−18.4	105	40.6	28	82.4	240	115.6	105	221
−10	−23.3	−26	−14.8	110	43.3	30	86	245	118.3	110	230
−5	−20.6	−24	−11.2	115	46.1	32	89.6	250	121.1	115	239
0	−17.8	−22	−7.6	120	48.9	34	93.2	255	123.9	120	248
1	−17.2	−20	−4	125	51.7	36	96.8	260	126.6	125	257
2	−16.7	−18	−0.4	130	54.4	38	100.4	265	129.4	130	266
3	−16.1	−16	3.2	135	57.2	40	104	270	132.2	135	275
4	−15.6	−14	6.8	140	60.0	42	107.6	275	135.0	140	284
5	−15.0	−12	10.4	145	62.8	44	112.2	280	137.8	145	293
10	−12.2	−10	14	150	65.6	46	114.8	285	140.6	150	302
15	−9.4	−8	17.6	155	68.3	48	118.4	290	143.3	155	311
20	−6.7	−6	21.2	160	71.1	50	122	295	146.1	160	320
25	−3.9	−4	24.8	165	73.9	52	125.6	300	148.9	165	329
30	−1.1	−2	28.4	170	76.7	54	129.2	305	151.7	170	338
35	1.7	0	32	175	79.4	56	132.8	310	154.4	175	347
40	4.4	2	35.6	180	82.2	58	136.4	315	157.2	180	356
45	7.2	4	39.2	185	85.0	60	140	320	160.0	185	365
50	10.0	6	42.8	190	87.8	62	143.6	325	162.8	190	374
55	12.8	8	46.4	195	90.6	64	147.2	330	165.6	195	383
60	15.6	10	50	200	93.3	66	150.8	335	168.3	200	392
65	18.3	12	53.6	205	96.1	68	154.4	340	171.1	205	401
70	21.1	14	57.2	210	98.9	70	158	345	173.9	210	410
75	23.9	16	60.8	212	100.0	75	167	350	176.7	215	414

ENGLISH TO METRIC CONVERSION: LENGTH

To convert inches (ins.) to millimeters (mm): multiply number of inches by 25.4

To convert millimeters (mm) to inches (ins.): multiply number of millimeters by .04

Inches	Decimals	Milli-meters	Inches to millimeters inches	mm	Inches	Decimals	Milli-meters	Inches to millimeters inches	mm
1/64	0.051625	0.3969	0.0001	0.00254	33/64	0.515625	13.0969	0.6	15.24
1/32	0.03125	0.7937	0.0002	0.00508	17/32	0.53125	13.4937	0.7	17.78
3/64	0.046875	1.1906	0.0003	0.00762	35/64	0.546875	13.8906	0.8	20.32
1/16	0.0625	1.5875	0.0004	0.01016	9/16	0.5625	14.2875	0.9	22.86
5/64	0.078125	1.9844	0.0005	0.01270	37/64	0.578125	14.6844	1	25.4
3/32	0.09375	2.3812	0.0006	0.01524	19/32	0.59375	15.0812	2	50.8
7/64	0.109375	2.7781	0.0007	0.01778	39/64	0.609375	15.4781	3	76.2
1/8	0.125	3.1750	0.0008	0.02032	5/8	0.625	15.8750	4	101.6
9/64	0.140625	3.5719	0.0009	0.02286	41/64	0.640625	16.2719	5	127.0
5/32	0.15625	3.9687	0.001	0.0254	21/32	0.65625	16.6687	6	152.4
11/64	0.171875	4.3656	0.002	0.0508	43/64	0.671875	17.0656	7	177.8
3/16	0.1875	4.7625	0.003	0.0762	11/16	0.6875	17.4625	8	203.2
13/64	0.203125	5.1594	0.004	0.1016	45/64	0.703125	17.8594	9	228.6
7/32	0.21875	5.5562	0.005	0.1270	23/32	0.71875	18.2562	10	254.0
15/64	0.234375	5.9531	0.006	0.1524	47/64	0.734375	18.6531	11	279.4
1/4	0.25	6.3500	0.007	0.1778	3/4	0.75	19.0500	12	304.8
17/64	0.265625	6.7469	0.008	0.2032	49/64	0.765625	19.4469	13	330.2
9/32	0.28125	7.1437	0.009	0.2286	25/32	0.78125	19.8437	14	355.6
19/64	0.296875	7.5406	0.01	0.254	51/64	0.796875	20.2406	15	381.0
5/16	0.3125	7.9375	0.02	0.508	13/16	0.8125	20.6375	16	406.4
21/64	0.328125	8.3344	0.03	0.762	53/64	0.828125	21.0344	17	431.8
11/32	0.34375	8.7312	0.04	1.016	27/32	0.84375	21.4312	18	457.2
23/64	0.359375	9.1281	0.05	1.270	55/64	0.859375	21.8281	19	482.6
3/8	0.375	9.5250	0.06	1.524	7/8	0.875	22.2250	20	508.0
25/64	0.390625	9.9219	0.07	1.778	57/64	0.890625	22.6219	21	533.4
13/32	0.40625	10.3187	0.08	2.032	29/32	0.90625	23.0187	22	558.8
27/64	0.421875	10.7156	0.09	2.286	59/64	0.921875	23.4156	23	584.2
7/16	0.4375	11.1125	0.1	2.54	15/16	0.9375	23.8125	24	609.6
29/64	0.453125	11.5094	0.2	5.08	61/64	0.953125	24.2094	25	635.0
15/32	0.46875	11.9062	0.3	7.62	31/32	0.96875	24.6062	26	660.4
31/64	0.484375	12.3031	0.4	10.16	63/64	0.984375	25.0031	27	690.6
1/2	0.5	12.7000	0.5	12.70					

ENGLISH TO METRIC CONVERSION: TORQUE

To convert foot-pounds (ft. lbs.) to Newton-meters: multiply the number of ft. lbs. by 1.3

To convert inch-pounds (in. lbs.) to Newton-meters: multiply the number of in. lbs. by .11

in lbs	N·m	in lbs	N·m	in lbs	N·m	in lbs	N·m	in lbs	N·m
0.1	0.01	1	0.11	10	1.13	19	2.15	28	3.16
0.2	0.02	2	0.23	11	1.24	20	2.26	29	3.28
0.3	0.03	3	0.34	12	1.36	21	2.37	30	3.39
0.4	0.04	4	0.45	13	1.47	22	2.49	31	3.50
0.5	0.06	5	0.56	14	1.58	23	2.60	32	3.62
0.6	0.07	6	0.68	15	1.70	24	2.71	33	3.73
0.7	0.08	7	0.78	16	1.81	25	2.82	34	3.84
0.8	0.09	8	0.90	17	1.92	26	2.94	35	3.95
0.9	0.10	9	1.02	18	2.03	27	3.05	36	4.0/

ENGLISH TO METRIC CONVERSION: TORQUE

Torque is now expressed as either foot-pounds (ft./lbs.) or inch-pounds (in./lbs.). The metric measurement unit for torque is the Newton-meter (Nm). This unit—the Nm—will be used for all SI metric torque references, both the present ft./lbs. and in./lbs.

ft lbs	N-m	ft lbs	N-m	ft lbs	N-m	ft lbs	N-m
0.1	0.1	33	44.7	74	100.3	115	155.9
0.2	0.3	34	46.1	75	101.7	116	157.3
0.3	0.4	35	47.4	76	103.0	117	158.6
0.4	0.5	36	48.8	77	104.4	118	160.0
0.5	0.7	37	50.7	78	105.8	119	161.3
0.6	0.8	38	51.5	79	107.1	120	162.7
0.7	1.0	39	52.9	80	108.5	121	164.0
0.8	1.1	40	54.2	81	109.8	122	165.4
0.9	1.2	41	55.6	82	111.2	123	166.8
1	1.3	42	56.9	83	112.5	124	168.1
2	2.7	43	58.3	84	113.9	125	169.5
3	4.1	44	59.7	85	115.2	126	170.8
4	5.4	45	61.0	86	116.6	127	172.2
5	6.8	46	62.4	87	118.0	128	173.5
6	8.1	47	63.7	88	119.3	129	174.9
7	9.5	48	65.1	89	120.7	130	176.2
8	10.8	49	66.4	90	122.0	131	177.6
9	12.2	50	67.8	91	123.4	132	179.0
10	13.6	51	69.2	92	124.7	133	180.3
11	14.9	52	70.5	93	126.1	134	181.7
12	16.3	53	71.9	94	127.4	135	183.0
13	17.6	54	73.2	95	128.8	136	184.4
14	18.9	55	74.6	96	130.2	137	185.7
15	20.3	56	75.9	97	131.5	138	187.1
16	21.7	57	77.3	98	132.9	139	188.5
17	23.0	58	78.6	99	134.2	140	189.8
18	24.4	59	80.0	100	135.6	141	191.2
19	25.8	60	81.4	101	136.9	142	192.5
20	27.1	61	82.7	102	138.3	143	193.9
21	28.5	62	84.1	103	139.6	144	195.2
22	29.8	63	85.4	104	141.0	145	196.6
23	31.2	64	86.8	105	142.4	146	198.0
24	32.5	65	88.1	106	143.7	147	199.3
25	33.9	66	89.5	107	145.1	148	200.7
26	35.2	67	90.8	108	146.4	149	202.0
27	36.6	68	92.2	109	147.8	150	203.4
28	38.0	69	93.6	110	149.1	151	204.7
29	39.3	70	94.9	111	150.5	152	206.1
30	40.7	71	96.3	112	151.8	153	207.4
31	42.0	72	97.6	113	153.2	154	208.8
32	43.4	73	99.0	114	154.6	155	210.2